KU-026-423

Cambridge Advanced Learner's Dictionary

CAMBRIDGE
UNIVERSITY PRESS

PUBLISHED BY THE PRESS SYNDICATE OF THE UNIVERSITY OF CAMBRIDGE
The Pitt Building, Trumpington Street, Cambridge, United Kingdom

CAMBRIDGE UNIVERSITY PRESS
The Edinburgh Building, Cambridge CB2 2RU, UK
40 West 20th Street, New York, NY 10011–4211, USA
477 Williamstown Road, Port Melbourne, VIC 3207, Australia
Ruiz de Alarcón 13, 28014 Madrid, Spain
Dock House, The Waterfront, Cape Town 8001, South Africa

http://www.cambridge.org

© Cambridge University Press 2003

This book is in copyright. Subject to statutory exception
and to the provisions of relevant collective licensing agreements,
no reproduction of any part may take place without
the written permission of Cambridge University Press.

Defined words which we have reason to believe constitute
trademarks have been labelled as such. However, neither the
presence nor absence of such labels should be regarded as
affecting the legal status of any trademarks.

First published 1995 as *Cambridge International Dictionary of English*

This edition first published 2003 as *Cambridge Advanced Learner's Dictionary*

Printed in Italy at Legoprint S.p.A.

Typeface Nimrod, Frutiger®

A catalogue record for this book is available from the British Library

Library of Congress Cataloguing in Publication data applied for

ISBN 0 521 82422 2 hardback
ISBN 0 521 53105 5 paperback
ISBN 0 521 82423 0 hardback + CD-ROM
ISBN 0 521 53106 3 paperback + CD-ROM
ISBN 3 12 5179947 Klett paperback edition
ISBN 3 12 5179939 Klett hardback + CD-ROM edition

ABBREVIATION	a shortened form of a word
APPROVING	praising someone or something
AUS	Australian English
CHILD'S WORD	used by children
DATED	used in the recent past and often still used by older people
DISAPPROVING	used to express dislike or disagreement with someone or something
FEMALE	
FIGURATIVE	used to express not the basic meaning of a word, but an imaginative one
FORMAL	used in serious or official language or when trying to impress other people
HUMOROUS	used when you are trying to be funny
INFORMAL	used in ordinary speech (and writing) and not suitable for formal situations
IRISH ENGLISH	
LEGAL	specialized language used in legal documents and in law courts
LITERARY	formal and descriptive language used in literature
MALE	
NORTHERN ENGLISH	used in the North of England
NOT STANDARD	commonly used but not following the rules of grammar
OFFENSIVE	very rude and likely to offend people
OLD USE	used a long time ago in other centuries
POLITE WORD / PHRASE	a polite way of referring to something that has other ruder names
SAYING	a common phrase or sentence that gives advice, an opinion, etc.
SCOTTISH ENGLISH	
SLANG	extremely informal language, used mainly by a particular group, especially young people
SPECIALIZED	used only by people in a particular subject such as doctors or scientists
TRADEMARK	the official name of a product
UK	British English
US	American English

LIBRARY
LAUDER COLLEGE

Lauder College

T37452

Contents

Editorial Team

Managing Editors
Kate Woodford
Guy Jackson

Senior Commissioning Editor
Patrick Gillard

Electronic Development Manager
Andrew Harley

Senior Systems Developer
Dominic Glennon

Editors
Jane Bottomley
Diane Cranz
Lucy Hollingworth
Ginny Klein
Mairi MacDonald
Kerry Maxwell
Clea McEnery
Julie Moore
Glennis Pye
Daryl Tayar

Bob Clevenger
Lucy Hollingworth
Ginny Klein
Kerry Maxwell
Clea McEnery
Julie Moore
Glennis Pye
Daryl Tayar

Study Pages
Mairi Macdonald

Editorial assistance
Rebecca Haynes
Anthony Howe
Tess Kaunhoven
Michael McKend
Deborah Sanders

Jane Setter
Michael Stevens

Design and Production
Sam Dumiak
Clive Rumble

Typesetting
Morton Typesetting,
Scarborough

Design and Illustrations
Oxford Designers &
Illustrators

CD-ROM Project Manager
Diane Cranz

Pronunciation Editor
Laura Watkinson

Proofreaders
Jane Bottomley
Pat Bulhosen

Cambridge International Corpus

Corpus Controller
Ann Fiddes

Corpus
Marie Allan
Jean Hudson
Diane Nicholls
Michael Stevens

Systems Developers
Richard Eradus
Bob Fairchild

Editorial Team for the First Edition published as the *Cambridge International Dictionary of English*

Editor-in-Chief
Paul Procter

Editors
Susan Allen-Mills

Ann Fiddes
Paul Heacock
Guy Jackson
Susan Jellis
Ann Kennedy

Daryl Tayar
Martin Tolley
Sally Webber
Susannah Wintersgill
Kate Woodford

Introduction

It seems a very long time since I first heard about the death of printed dictionaries. I was assured, very confidently, in the early 1980s, that everything would be electronic by the new century. Nobody would bother to flick through 1600 pages when they could just hit the 'enter' key.

Well we are now well into the new century and people seem just as keen to buy the printed book. You may well have bought a version of this *Cambridge Advanced Learner's Dictionary* with a CD-ROM attached, but the medium which you are currently using to read these words is the same medium that was used in the first Cambridge University Press book in 1584 – paper and ink. So why has the printed dictionary survived so well?

Maybe people see their dictionary as a friend. Perhaps a bond is created in all the hours that a learner spends together with a dictionary. Perhaps some of the character of the book rubs off on the reader. And what kind of character would they find in the *Cambridge Advanced Learner's Dictionary?*

Friendly, that would be one part of the character. We have made the page as friendly and easy to read as possible, with coloured printing to make the words easier to find, and with a special clear way of showing idioms and phrasal verbs. We have also included an 'Idiom Finder' at the back of the dictionary so that you can find idioms even if you don't know which part of the dictionary to look in.

'Helpful' would also be part of the character. You will find 'Common Learner Error' notes spread throughout the dictionary, to make sure that you don't make the mistakes that many learners make. The notes are based on the Cambridge Learner Corpus, which is a 15-million word collection of learners' English based on what students have written in the Cambridge exams from Cambridge ESOL. This corpus means that we can really see what learners' English is like – and find ways to make it even better.

'Well-informed' is certainly part of the character. You will find thousands of up-to-date words as you look through the dictionary, including many that have only just come into the language. We can make sure that these important new words are included because we have the huge Cambridge International Corpus to help us. This has over 500 million words from British English and American English, from spoken English and written English, and from many specialized types of English, such as Law and Computers and Science.

If you find that the character of the *Cambridge Advanced Learner's Dictionary* is one that appeals to you, then I should point out that you are actually making friends with a large group of talented people who created this book and its predecessor, the *Cambridge International Dictionary of English*. All of them have an excellent 'feel for language' and a clear understanding of what learners need to know. The corpus resources can give us information, but only good lexicographers can put it into a book that you can make friends with. I hope you enjoy getting to know them.

Patrick Gillard
January 2003

How to use the dictionary

How do I find the word or phrase I want?

Look for a single word as a coloured **headword** at the beginning of an entry. Entries are generally arranged alphabetically.

Words are sometimes grouped together at an entry when they are used as different parts of speech or because they are very closely related and similar in form and meaning.

Look for a **compound word** (two or more words used together as a single word) at its alphabetical place in the list of entries.

A word may be followed by a GUIDEWORD (a word or short phrase in capital letters). This means that the word has two or more main meanings and that there is at least one other entry for that word. The different GUIDEWORDS help you to find the sense of the word that you need.

chemical /'kem.ɪ.kᵊl/ *noun* [C] any basic substance which is used in or produced by a reaction involving changes to atoms or molecules: *The government has pledged to reduce the amount of chemicals used in food production.* ○ *Each year, factories release millions of tonnes of **toxic** (= poisonous) chemicals into the atmosphere.*

chemical /'kem.ɪ.kᵊl/ *adj* relating to chemicals: *The chemical **industry** produces such things as petrochemicals, drugs, paint and rubber.* **chemically** /'kem.ɪ.kli/ *adv*: *The fund provides money to clean up chemically polluted industrial sites.*

chemical engi'neering *noun* [U] the design and operation of machinery used in industrial chemical processes

chemical e'quation *noun* [C] a symbolic representation of the changes which happen in a chemical reaction

chemical 'formula *noun* [C] the representation of a substance using the symbols of its elements: H_2O *is the chemical formula for water.*

chemical re'action *noun* [C] a process in which the atomic or MOLECULAR structure of a substance is changed

chemical 'warfare *noun* [U] the use of poisonous gases and other harmful chemicals against enemy forces

chemical 'weapon *noun* [C] a substance, such as a poisonous gas rather than an explosive, which can be used to kill or injure people

chemise /ʃə'miːz/ *noun* [C] a loose piece of clothing for women, which covers the top part of the body, and which is worn under other clothes

chemist SCIENCE /'kem.ɪst/ *noun* [C] a person who studies chemistry, or a scientist who works with chemicals or studies their reactions

chemist MEDICINE *UK* /'kem.ɪst/ *noun* [C] **1** (*US* **druggist**, *ALSO* **pharmacist**) a person whose job is to prepare and sell medicines in a shop **2** (*UK ALSO* **chemist's**, *US* **drugstore**, *ALSO* **pharmacy**) a shop where you can buy medicines, make-up and products used for washing yourself ⊃See usage note at **pharmacy**.

If there is a variant or less common form of a word it is shown in brackets soon after the main headword.

'combat ,trousers *plural noun* (*ALSO* **combats**) loose trousers made of strong material with large pockets on the outside of the legs: *British Army camouflage-pattern combat trousers*

If the word you are looking for is grouped in an entry that is distant from its alphabetical position, a reference will often tell you where to find it.

complex 'word *noun* [C] SPECIALIZED a word consisting of a main part and one or more other parts

compliance /kəm'plaɪ.ənts/ *noun* [U] ⊃See **comply**.

compliant /kəm'plaɪ.ənt/ *adj* ⊃See **comply**.

Sometimes the second word of a headword is shown in brackets. This shows that the meaning is the same whether or not you use the first word or both words together.

combine ('harvester) *noun* [C] a large farming machine which cuts the plant, separates the seed from the stem and cleans the grain as it moves across a field

Some words in the alphabetical list include 'the' before the coloured headword, to show that they are always used in this form.

the 'contrary OPPOSITE *noun* [S] the opposite: *I was worried that it might be too difficult for me but I found the contrary.*

● **on the contrary** used to show that you think or feel the opposite of what has just been stated: *"Didn't you find the film exciting?" "On the contrary, I nearly fell asleep half way through it!"*

Look for fixed phrases and idioms listed on separate lines following the • symbol. If an idiom is not listed under the word you expect, the 'Idiom Finder' at the end of the dictionary (on page 1491) will help you to find it.

red [COLOUR] /red/ *adj* **redder, reddest 1** of the colour of fresh blood: *red lipstick* ○ *The dress was bright red.* **2** describes hair which is an orange-brown colour **3 go/turn (bright) red** If you go/turn red, your face becomes red because you are angry or embarrassed: *Look, you've embarrassed him – he's gone bright red!* **4** If your eyes are red, the white part of your eyes and the skin around your eyes is red, because of crying, tiredness, too much alcohol, etc.
• be like a red rag to a bull *MAINLY UK* to be certain to produce an angry or violent reaction: *Don't tell him you're a vegetarian – it's like a red rag to a bull.*

How do I find the meaning of a word or phrase?

You will find a definition following the part of speech for the word. The definitions only use words from the Defining Vocabulary (a limited list of fairly common and basic words that students are very likely to understand).

Any word in the definition which is harder to understand is shown in SMALL CAPITALS. If you don't understand the word, you can look for the meaning of that word at its own entry, although sometimes we give a brief explanation to help you.

When a word has more than one meaning, the GUIDEWORDS help you to find the right one quickly.

ˌcream ˈcracker *noun* [C] *UK* a hard biscuit which is not sweet and is often eaten with cheese
creamer /ˈkriː.məʳ/ [US] /-mɚ/ *noun* **1** [U] a powder which is added to hot drinks instead of milk or cream: *I've run out of milk – would you like some creamer instead?* **2** [C] *US* a small container for serving cream in
ˌcream of ˈtartar *noun* [U] a white powder used in baking
ˌcream ˈsoda *noun* [C or U] *US* (a) fizzy drink flavoured with VANILLA
ˌcream ˈtea *noun* [C] *MAINLY UK* a light meal of SCONES (= small bread-like cakes) with jam and cream
crease [FOLD] /kriːs/ *noun* [C] a line on cloth or paper where it has been folded or crushed: *He ironed a crease down the front of each trouser leg.*
crease /kriːs/ *verb* [I or T] If cloth, paper, etc. creases, or if you crease it, it gets a line in it where it has been folded or crushed: *The seatbelt has creased my blouse.* ○ *It's a nice dress, but it creases very easily.*
creased /kriːst/ *adj* with a crease: *creased trousers*
crease [CRICKET] /kriːs/ *noun* [S] *UK SPECIALIZED* a line marked on the ground where the player stands to hit the ball in cricket

GUIDEWORDS show you when a word has more than one main meaning. Other smaller differences in meaning are shown by separate numbered definitions within one entry.

crime /kraɪm/ *noun* **1** [U] illegal activities: *a life of crime* ○ *rising crime* ○ *crime prevention* ○ ***petty*** (= unimportant) *crime/**serious** crime* **2** [C] an illegal act: *He has admitted **committing** several crimes, including two murders.* ○ *The defendant is **accused of/charged with** a range of crimes, from theft to murder.* ○ *A knife was found at **the scene of the** crime* (= the place where the crime happened). ○ *Bombing civilians is a crime **against humanity*** (= a cruel crime against many people). **3** [S] an immoral or very foolish act or situation: *To have hundreds of homeless people sleeping in the streets of a rich city like London is **a** crime .* ○ ***It** would be **a** crime* (= a waste) ***to** spend such a beautiful day indoors.*
• Crime doesn't pay. *SAYING* said to emphasize that you believe criminals are always punished for their crimes

We show you when a word has a special meaning when it is used in a particular pattern or combination of words, or in a fixed phrase.

Some fixed phrases and combinations of words have a special meaning that is not clear from the meanings of the separate words. These are listed with their meanings usually at the entry for the first important word of that phrase or idiom.

If you are not sure where to find a particular phrase, or whether a particular combination of words has a special meaning, look in the 'Idiom Finder' on page 1491.

credit [PRAISE] /ˈkred.ɪt/ *noun* [U] **1** praise, approval or honour: *She got no credit for solving the problem.* ○ *Her boss **took** credit **for** it/**took** (all) **the** credit instead.* ○ ***To** her (great) credit, she admitted she was wrong.* ○ *I **gave** him credit **for*** (= thought that he would have) *better judgment than he showed.* **2 be a credit to *sb/sth*** to do something that makes a person, group or organization feel proud or receive praise: *She is a credit to her family.*
do your family/parents/teacher, etc. credit to cause someone who has been or is responsible for you to receive praise by your good behaviour or successful actions: *She does her teachers credit.*
• all credit to *sb* used to show that you think a person deserves a lot of praise for something that they have done: *All credit to her, she did it all herself.*
• credit where credit's due an expression which means that you should praise someone who deserves it, although you might dislike some things about them: *I don't especially like the woman but, credit where credit's due, she's very efficient.*

In addition to the definitions there are many pictures to help you to understand what a word means. If there is a picture, a reference like this will tell you where to look.

'crew ,cut *noun* [C] a hairstyle in which the hair is cut very short ➔See picture **Hairstyles and Hats** on page **Centre 8**

How do I use this word or phrase?

The examples printed in *italics* in the entry for a word or phrase show you how that word or phrase is commonly used in written and spoken English. They can help you to use a word naturally and to check that you have found the right word.

Sometimes a word shown in an example is shown in **bold**. This tells you that it is a **collocation** (a word that is very commonly used with the word you have looked up).

Labels in small italics show you the part of speech of a word. Labels in square brackets give you extra grammatical information about the word. See the list of Grammar codes and labels at the front of the dictionary.

crop PLANT /krɒp/ ⓤ /krɑːp/ *noun* **1** [C] (the total amount gathered of) a plant such as a grain, fruit or vegetable grown in large amounts: *The main crops grown for export are coffee and rice.* ○ *a **bumper** (= very good) potato crop* **2** [C usually sing] *INFORMAL* a group of people or things with something in common, that exist at a particular time: *The judges will select the best from this year's crop **of** first novels.*
crop /krɒp/ ⓤ /krɑːp/ *verb* -pp- **1** [I usually + adv or prep] If a plant crops, it produces fruit, flowers, etc: *The carrots have cropped* (= grown) *well this year.* **2** [T usually passive] to grow crops on land: *The land is intensively-cropped.*

When grammar information is given *before any numbered definitions*, that grammar pattern is true for all uses of the word.

When grammar information is given *before an individual definition*, that grammar pattern is true only for that meaning of the word.

When grammar information is given *before an example*, that grammar pattern is true only for the particular use of the word shown in the example.

crumb /krʌm/ *noun* [C] **1** a very small piece of bread, cake or biscuit ➔See also **breadcrumbs**. **2** a small amount of something: *a crumb of hope/comfort*
crumble BREAK /'krʌm.bl̩/ *verb* **1** [I or T] to break, or cause something to break, into small pieces: *She nervously crumbled the bread between her fingers.* ○ *The cliffs on which the houses are built are starting to crumble.* **2** [I] to weaken in strength and influence: *Support for the government is crumbling.*

Plurals, verb forms, comparatives and superlatives are shown if they are irregular.

curriculum /kə'rɪk.jʊ.ləm/ *noun* [C] *plural* **curricula** or **curriculums** the group of subjects studied in a school, college, etc: *the school curriculum* ➔See also **the national curriculum**. Compare **syllabus**. **curricular** /kə'rɪk.jʊ.lə/ ⓤ /-lə/ *adj* SPECIALIZED
curriculum vitae /kə,rɪk.jʊ.ləm'viː.taɪ/ *noun* [C] *plural* **curriculum vitaes** or **curricula vitae** *FORMAL* a CV

How do I pronounce this word?

British and American pronunciations of a word are shown after the headword. These are written using the International Phonetic Alphabet (IPA). See inside the back cover of the dictionary for full information about the phonetic symbols.

At entries for compound words, stress marks show you which part(s) of the compound you should stress when you say it. The pronunciation for each word in a compound is shown at the entry for that word.

curry FOOD /'kʌr.i/ ⓤ /'kɝː-/ *noun* [C or U] a dish, originally from India, consisting of meat or vegetables cooked in a spicy sauce: *a hot* (= very spicy) *curry* ○ *a mild* (= slightly spicy) *curry* ○ *vegetable/chicken/lamb curry*
curry OBTAIN /'kʌr.i/ ⓤ /'kɝː-/ *verb* DISAPPROVING **curry favour** to praise someone, especially someone in authority, in a way that is not sincere, in order to obtain some advantage for yourself: *He's always trying to curry favour **with** the boss.*
,curry 'paste *noun* [C or U] a soft mixture of spices and oil, used to flavour CURRIES
'curry ,powder *noun* [U] a dry mixture of spices used to flavour CURRIES

What else should I know about this word or phrase?

Labels in SMALL CAPITALS give important information about how and where a particular word or phrase is used. When a label is placed inside a numbered sense, it is true only for that particular sense.

diddle CHEAT /'dɪd.l̩/ *verb* [T] *INFORMAL* to obtain money from someone in a way which is not honest: *He diddled me! He said that there were six in a bag, but there were only five.* ○ *I checked the bill and realized the restaurant had diddled me **out of** £5.*
diddly /'dɪd.l̩.i/ *noun* [U] (ALSO **diddly-squat**) *US INFORMAL* anything: *He hasn't done diddly all day.* ○ *There's no point in asking Ellen – she doesn't know diddly.*
diddums! /'dɪd.əmz/ *exclamation* UK HUMOROUS something you say to show that you feel no sympathy for someone who is behaving like a child: *He called you a bad name, did he? Ah, diddums!*

If the word you have looked up is only used in British English, and a different word is used in American English, the variant word is shown.

Di,rectory En'quiries *UK group noun* [U] (*US* **Directory Assistance**) a service which you can telephone in order to find out someone's telephone number

If the word has a different spelling in American or British English, the variant spelling is shown.

discolour *UK*, *US* **discolor** /dɪ'skʌl.əʳ/ [US] /-ɚ/ *verb* [I or T] to (cause something to) change from the original colour and therefore to look unpleasant: *The coal fire had discoloured the paintwork.* **discoloration** /dɪ,skʌl.ə'reɪ.ʃᵊn/ *noun* [C or U]

Notes warn you about any special difficulties or common learner errors associated with a word.

discreet /dɪ'skriːt/ *adj* careful not to cause embarrassment or attract too much attention, especially by keeping something secret: *The family made discreet enquiries about his background.* ○ *They are very good assistants, very discreet – they wouldn't go shouting to the press about anything they discovered while working for you.* * NOTE: Do not confuse with **discrete**. **discreetly** /dɪ'skriːt.li/ *adv*

COMMON LEARNER ERROR

discuss

Discuss is not followed by a preposition.

We discussed the plans for the wedding.

~~*We discussed about the plans for the wedding.*~~

You can, however, **discuss something with someone**.

Can I discuss this report with you?

Should I know any other words that relate to this one?

Cross-references help you learn more vocabulary connected with a word. They often refer to words with a similar or contrasting meaning.

If you have the CD of this dictionary, you can look up related words at every entry using the 'SMART thesaurus' feature.

empathy /'em.pə.θi/ *noun* [U] the ability to share someone else's feelings or experiences by imagining what it would be like to be in their situation ➲Compare **sympathy** UNDERSTANDING. **empathetic** /,em.pə'θet.ɪk/ [US] /-'θeţ-/ *adj*

empathize, *UK USUALLY* **-ise** /'em.pə.θaɪz/ *verb* [I] to be able to understand how someone else feels: *It's very easy to empathize* ***with*** *the characters in her books.* ➲Compare **sympathize** at **sympathy** UNDERSTANDING.

emperor /'em.pᵊr.əʳ/ [US] /-pɚ.ɚ/ *noun* [C] a male ruler of an empire ➲See also **empress**.

empire [COUNTRIES] /'em.paɪəʳ/ [US] /-paɪr/ *noun* [C] a group of countries ruled by a single person, government or country: *the Holy Roman Empire* ➲See also **imperial** EMPIRE.

Some cross-references direct you to other words belonging to a particular group of related things.

EMU /,iː.em'juː/ *noun* [U] *ABBREVIATION FOR* European Monetary Union: the process within the European Union which is intended to result in a united economic system ➲Compare **ECU; EMS**.

A **bold** word at the end of a definition shows a more common synonym (word that has the same meaning) for the word you have looked up.

epicure /'ep.ɪ.kjʊəʳ/ [US] /-kjʊr/ *noun* [C] (*ALSO* **epicurean**) *FORMAL* a person who enjoys food and drink of a high quality; a **gourmet**

In a definition, we explain the meaning of an important related word that is not in the Defining Vocabulary, when you need it to understand the meaning.

epidural /,ep.ɪ'djʊə.rəl/ [US] /-'dʊr.ᵊl/ *noun* [C] when an ANAESTHETIC (= substance which stops you feeling pain) is put into the nerves in a person's lower back with a special needle: *They gave my wife an epidural when she was giving birth.*

A note tells you when the opposite of a word is formed with **in-** rather than **un-**.

equity /'ek.wɪ.ti/ [US] /-ţi/ *noun* [U] **1** *FORMAL* when everyone is treated fairly and equally: *a society based on equity and social justice* * NOTE: The opposite of equity is **inequity**.

Numbers that are used as words

You will sometimes find these numbers used like ordinary words in English, especially in newspapers or on the Internet. This page tells you what they mean and how they are pronounced.

0800 number /ˌəʊ.eɪtˈhʌn.drədˌnʌm.bəʳ/ *noun* [C] in the UK, a free telephone number that begins with 0800, provided by companies or other organizations offering advice or information

0898 number /ˌəʊ.eɪtˈnaɪn.eɪtˌnʌm.bəʳ/ *noun* [C] in the UK, an expensive telephone number that begins with 0898 that is provided by companies offering services such as CHAT LINES

12A /ˌtwelvˈeɪ/ in the UK, a symbol that marks a film that cannot be legally watched alone by children who are under twelve years old

15 /ˌfɪfˈtiːn/ in the UK, a symbol used to mark a film that cannot be legally watched by children who are under fifteen years old

18 /ˌeɪˈtiːn/ in the UK, a symbol used to mark a film that cannot be legally watched by children who are under eighteen years old

180 /ˌwʌnˈeɪ.t̬i/ *noun* [C usually sing] *US INFORMAL* a sudden change from a particular opinion, decision or plan to an opposite one: *Jack's **done** a 180 and agreed to come on the trip.*

2:1 /ˌtuːˈwʌn/ *noun* [C] (*ALSO* **upper second**) a degree qualification from a British university that is below a first and above a 2:2

2:2 /ˌtuːˈtuː/ *noun* [C] (*ALSO* **lower second**) a degree qualification from a British university that is below a 2:1 and above a third

20/20 vision /ˌtwen.tiˌtwen.tiˈvɪʒ.ənn/ *noun* [S] the ability to see perfectly, without needing to wear glasses or CONTACT LENSES: *You're so lucky to **have** 20/20 vision, Dom.*

.22 /ˌpɔɪnt.tuːˈtuː/ *noun* [C] a type of gun that fires small bullets, used especially for hunting small animals

24/7 /ˌtwen.ti.fɔːˈsev.ən/ [US] /-t̬i.fɔːʳ-/ *adv, adj INFORMAL* twenty four hours a day, seven days a week: all the time: *We're open for business 24/7.* ○ *We offer 24/7 internet access.*

24-hour clock /twen.tiˌfɔː.raʊəˈklɒk/ *noun* [S] the system of using 24 numbers instead of 12 to refer the hours in the day

3-D /ˌθriːˈdiː/ in a 3-D film or picture, the objects look real and solid instead of looking like a normal flat picture: *a 3-D effect* ○ *These computer games rely on 3-D graphics.* ○ *The picture looks great because it's **in** 3-D*

3G /ˌθriːˈdʒiː/ *adj* describes technology that is new and improved, especially MOBILE PHONES on which you can use the Internet, watch television, etc. 3G is short for 'third generation': *They invested heavily in 3G mobile phone networks.* ○ *Learn how to create 3G websites.*

.45 /ˌfɔː.tiˈfaɪv/ [US] /ˌfɔːr.t̬i-/ *noun* [C] a large type of PISTOL (= small gun)

4WD *noun* [C or U] *WRITTEN ABBREVIATION FOR* **four-wheel drive**: a vehicle that has power supplied by the engine to all four wheels so that it can travel easily over difficult ground

4x4 /ˌfɔː.baɪˈfɔːʳ/ [US] /ˌfɔːr.baɪˈfɔːr/ *noun* [C or U] *ABBREVIATION FOR* **four-wheel drive**: a vehicle that has power supplied by the engine to all four wheels so that it can travel easily over difficult ground

$64,000 question /ˌsɪk.sti.fɔːrˌθaʊ.zəndˈdɑː.lɚkwes.tʃən/ *noun* [C usually sing] (*ALSO* **million dollar question**) an important or difficult question, on which a lot depends: *The $64, 000 dollar question is, can we repeat last year's success?*

800 number /ˌeɪtˈhʌn.drədˌnʌm.bəʳ/ [US] /-bɚ/ *noun* [C] in the US, a free telephone number that begins with 800, provided by companies or other organizations offering advice or information

900 number /ˌnaɪnˈhʌn.drədˌnʌm.bəʳ/ [US] /-bɚ/ *noun* [C] in the US, an expensive telephone number that begins with 900, provided by companies offering services such as CHAT LINES

911 /ˌnaɪn.wʌnˈwʌn/ the telephone number used in the US to call the emergency services

9/11 /ˌnaɪn.ɪˈlev.ən/ *MAINLY US* September the eleventh, written in US style: the date of the attacks on the World Trade Center and the Pentagon in the US in 2001: *Since 9/11 there has been more co-operation between Russia and America.*

999 /ˌnaɪn.naɪnˈnaɪn/ the telephone number used in Britain to call the emergency services: *a hoax 999 call* ○ *There's been an accident – dial 999 and ask for an ambulance.*

A

A [LETTER] (*plural* **A's**), **a** (*plural* **a's**) /eɪ/ *noun* [C] the 1st letter of the English alphabet
• **from A to B** from one place to another: *Using this software a driver can now work out the quickest route from A to B.*
• **from A to Z** including everything: *This book tells the story of her life from A to Z.*

A [MUSIC] /eɪ/ *noun* [C or U] *plural* **A's** or **As** a note in Western music: *This concerto is in the key of A major.*

A [MARK] /eɪ/ *noun* [C or U] *plural* **A's** or **As** a mark in an exam or for a piece of work that shows that your work is considered excellent: *Sophie* ***got*** *(an) A for English.* ○ *She got* ***straight*** *As* (= All her marks were As) *in her end-of-year exams.* ○ *US Jim is a* ***straight*** *A student* (= All his marks are A).

A [ELECTRICITY] *ABBREVIATION FOR* **amp** ELECTRICITY

a [NOT PARTICULAR] *WEAK* /ə/, *STRONG* /eɪ/ *determiner* (*ALSO* **an**) **1** used before a noun to refer to a single thing or person that has not been mentioned before, especially when you are not referring to a particular thing or person, or you do not expect listeners or readers to know which particular thing or person you are referring to: *I've bought a car.* ○ *She's got a boyfriend.* ○ *There was a sudden loud noise.* ○ *What a shame that you couldn't go to the party.* ○ *I heard a child crying.* ○ *Is he a friend* ***of*** *yours* (= one of your friends)*?* **2** used to state what type of thing or person something or someone is: *She wants to be a doctor when she grows up.* ○ *This is a very mild cheese.* ○ *Experts think the painting may be a Picasso* (= by Picasso). **3** used to mean any or every thing or person of the type you are referring to: *Can you ride a bike?* ○ *A cheetah can run faster than a lion.* ○ *A teacher needs to have a lot of patience.* **4** used before some uncountable nouns when you want to limit their meaning in some way, such as when describing them more completely or referring to one example of them: *I only have a limited knowledge of Spanish.* ○ *He has a great love of music.* ○ *There was a fierceness in her voice.* **5** used before some nouns of action when referring to one example of the action: *Take a look at this, Jez.* ○ *I'm just going to have a wash.* ○ *There was a knocking at the door.* **6** used when referring to a unit or container of something, especially something you eat or drink: *I'd love a coffee.* ○ *All I had for lunch was a yogurt.* **7** used before the first but not the second of two nouns that are referred to as one unit: *a cup and saucer* ○ *a knife and fork* **8** used in front of a person's name when referring to someone who you do not know: *There's a Ms Evans to see you.* **9** used in front of a person's family name when they are a member of that family: *Is that a Wilson over there?* **10** used before the name of a day or month to refer to one example of it: *My birthday is on a Friday this year.* ○ *It's been a very wet June.* **11** used before some words that express a number or amount: *a few days* ○ *a bit of wool* ○ *a lot of money*

COMMON LEARNER ERROR

a or an?

a is used before consonants or before vowels which are pronounced as consonants.

a dog
a university

an is used before vowels.

an old building
~~*a old building*~~

a [ONE] *WEAK* /ə/, *STRONG* /eɪ/ *determiner* (*ALSO* **an**) **1** one: *a hundred* ○ *a thousand* ○ *a dozen* ○ *There were three men and a woman.* **2** used between a fraction and a unit of measurement: *half a mile* ○ *a quarter of a kilo* ○ *three-quarters of an hour* ○ *six-tenths of a second* **3** used when saying how often something happens in a certain period: *Take one tablet three times a day.* ○ *I swim once a week.* **4** used when saying how much someone earns or how much something costs in a certain period: *She earns $100 000 a year.* ○ *My plumber charges £20 an hour.* ○ *I pay £5 a week for my parking permit.*

A4 /ˌeɪˈfɔː/ [US] /-ˈfɔːr/ *noun* [U], *adj* paper that is a standard European size of 21 centimetres by 29.7 centimetres: *a sheet of A4* ○ *A4 paper*

AA [DEGREE] /ˌeɪˈeɪ/ *noun* [C] *ABBREVIATION FOR* Associate in Arts: a degree given by an American college to someone after they have completed a two-year course, or a person who has this degree

AA [ALCOHOL] /ˌeɪˈeɪ/ *group noun* [S] *ABBREVIATION FOR* Alcoholics Anonymous: an organization for people who drink too much alcohol and want to cure themselves of this habit: *an AA meeting*

the ˌAˈA [CARS] *group noun* [S] *ABBREVIATION FOR* the Automobile Association: a British organization which gives help and information to drivers who are members of it

AAA /ˌeɪ.eɪˈeɪ/ *group noun* [S] *ABBREVIATION FOR* American Automobile Association: an American organization which gives help and information to drivers who are members of it

aah /ˈɑː/ *exclamation ANOTHER SPELLING OF* **ah**

aardvark /ˈɑːd.vɑːk/ [US] /ˈɑːrd.vɑːrk/ *noun* [C] an African mammal with a long nose and large ears which lives underground and eats insects

AB /ˌeɪˈbiː/ *noun* [C] *US FOR* **BA**

aback /əˈbæk/ *adv* **be taken aback** to be very shocked or surprised: *I was rather taken aback* ***by*** *her honesty.*

abacus /ˈæb.ə.kəs/ *noun* [C] a square or rectangular frame holding an arrangement of small balls on metal rods or wires, which is used for counting, adding and subtracting

abandon [LEAVE] /əˈbæn.dən/ *verb* [T] to leave a place, thing or person forever: *We had to abandon the car.* ○ *By the time the rebel troops arrived, the village had already been abandoned.* ○ *As a baby he'd been abandoned by his mother.* ○ *We were sinking fast, and the captain gave the order to abandon* ***ship***. **abandoned** /əˈbæn.dənd/ *adj*: *An abandoned baby was found in a box on the hospital steps.* **abandonment** /əˈbæn.dən.mənt/ *noun* [U] *The abandonment of the island followed nuclear tests in the area.*

abandon [STOP] /əˈbæn.dən/ *verb* [T] to stop doing an activity before you have finished it: *The match was abandoned at half-time because of the poor weather conditions.* ○ *They had to abandon their attempt to climb the mountain.* ○ *The party has now abandoned its policy of unilateral disarmament.* **abandonment** /əˈbæn.dən.mənt/ *noun* [U]
▲ **abandon** ***yourself*** **to** ***sth*** *phrasal verb* [R] to allow yourself to be controlled completely by a feeling or way of living: *He abandoned himself to his emotions.*

abandon /əˈbæn.dən/ *noun LITERARY* **with (gay/wild) abandon** in a completely uncontrolled way: *We danced with wild abandon.*

abase ***yourself*** /əˈbeɪs/ *verb* [R] *FORMAL* to make yourself seem to be less important or not to deserve respect **abasement** /əˈbeɪ.smənt/ *noun* [U] *The pilgrims knelt in* ***self****-abasement.*

abashed /əˈbæʃt/ *adj* [after v] embarrassed: *He said nothing but looked abashed.*

abate /əˈbeɪt/ *verb* [I] *FORMAL* to become less strong: *The storm/wind/rain has started to abate.* ○ *The fighting in the area shows no sign of abating.* ➲See also **unabated**. **abatement** /əˈbeɪt.mənt/ *noun* [U]

abattoir *MAINLY UK* /ˈæb.ə.twɑːʳ/ [US] /-twɑːr/ *noun* [C] (*MAINLY US* **slaughterhouse**) a place where animals are killed for their meat

abbess /ˈæb.es/ *noun* [C] a woman who is in charge of a CONVENT

abbey /ˈæb.i/ *noun* [C] a building where monks or nuns live or used to live. Some abbeys are now used as churches: *Westminster Abbey*

abbot /ˈæb.ət/ *noun* [C] a man who is in charge of a MONASTERY

abbreviate /əˈbriː.vi.eɪt/ *verb* [T usually passive] to make a word or phrase shorter by using only the first letters of

[A]

each word: *'Daniel' is often abbreviated* ***to*** *'Dan'.* ○ *'Chief Executive Officer' is abbreviated* ***as*** *'CEO'.* **abbreviated** /ə'briː.vi.eɪ.tɪd/ [US] /-t̬ɪd/ *adj*: *'Di' is the abbreviated* ***form*** *of 'Diane'.* **abbreviation** /əˌbriː.vi'eɪ.ʃən/ *noun* [C] *'ITV' is the abbreviation* ***for*** *'Independent Television'.*

ABC [ALPHABET] /ˌeɪ.biː'siː/ *noun* [S] (*US USUALLY* **ABCs**) *INFORMAL* **1** the alphabet: *He's learning his ABC at school.* **2** basic information about a subject: *What I need is a book that contains* ***the*** *ABC* ***of*** *carpentry.*

ABC [US TV] /ˌeɪ.biː'siː/ *group noun* [S] *ABBREVIATION FOR* American Broadcasting Company: an organization that broadcasts on television in the US

the ˌAB'C [AUSTRALIAN TV] *group noun* [S] *ABBREVIATION FOR* the Australian Broadcasting Corporation: an organization that broadcasts on radio and television in Australia and is paid for by the government

abdicate [GIVE UP] /'æb.dɪ.keɪt/ *verb* [I or T] If a king or queen abdicates, they make a formal statement that they no longer want to be king or queen: *King Edward VIII abdicated (the British throne) in 1936 so that he could marry Mrs Simpson, a divorced woman.* **abdication** /ˌæb.dɪ'keɪ.ʃən/ *noun* [C or U]

abdicate [NOT DO] /'æb.dɪ.keɪt/ *verb FORMAL DISAPPROVING* **abdicate responsibility** to stop controlling or managing something that you are in charge of: *She was accused of abdicating all responsibility for the project.* **abdication** /ˌæb.dɪ'keɪ.ʃən/ *noun* [U] *FORMAL The council denied that their decision represented any abdication* ***of*** *responsibility.*

abdomen /'æb.də.mən/ *noun* [C] *SPECIALIZED* the lower part of a person's or animal's body, which contains the stomach, bowels and other organs, or the end of an insect's body **abdominal** /æb'dɒm.ɪ.nəl/ [US] /-'dɑː.mə-/ *adj*: *abdominal pains*

abdominals /æb'dɒm.ɪ.nəlz/ [US] /-'dɑː.mə-/ *plural noun* (*INFORMAL* **abs**) muscles in the abdomen

abduct /æb'dʌkt/ *verb* [T] to force someone to go somewhere with you, often using threats or violence: *The company director was abducted* ***from*** *his car by terrorists.* **abduction** /æb'dʌk.ʃən/ *noun* [C or U] *There has been a series of abductions* ***of*** *young children* ***from*** *schools in the area.* ○ *He was charged with abduction.* **abductor** /æb'dʌk.tə^r/ [US] /-tɚ/ *noun* [C] *She was tortured by her abductors.*

aberrant /ə'ber.ənt/ *adj FORMAL* different from what is typical or usual, especially in an unacceptable way: *aberrant behaviour/sexuality*

aberration /ˌæb.ə'reɪ.ʃən/ *noun* [C or U] *FORMAL* a temporary change from the typical or usual way of behaving: ***In a moment of*** *aberration, she agreed to go with him.* ○ *I'm sorry I'm late – I had a* ***mental*** *aberration and forgot we had a meeting today.*

abet /ə'bet/ *verb* [T] **-tt-** to help or encourage someone to do something wrong or illegal: *His accountant had* ***aided and*** *abetted him in the fraud.* **abettor** /ə'bet.ə^r/ [US] /-'bet̬.ɚ/ *noun* [C]

abeyance /ə'beɪ.ənts/ *noun* [U] *FORMAL* a state of not happening or being used at present: *Hostilities between the two groups have been* ***in*** *abeyance since last June.* ○ *The project is being* ***held in*** *abeyance until agreement is reached on funding it.*

abhor /ə'bɔː^r/ [US] /æb'hɔːr/ *verb* [T not continuous] **-rr-** *FORMAL* to hate a way of behaving or thinking, often because you think it is immoral: *I abhor all forms of racism.*

abhorrent /ə'bɒr.ənt/ [US] /æb'hɔːr-/ *adj FORMAL* morally very bad: *an abhorrent crime* ○ *Racism of any kind is abhorrent* ***to*** *me.* **abhorrence** /ə'bɒr.ənts/ [US] /æb'hɔːr-/ *noun* [S or U] *She looked at him* ***in/with*** *abhorrence.* ○ *She has* ***an*** *abhorrence* ***of*** *change.*

abide /ə'baɪd/ *verb* [I usually + adv or prep] *OLD USE* to live or stay somewhere: *He abided in the wilderness for forty days.*

• **can't abide** ***sb/sth*** If you can't abide someone or something, you dislike them very much: *I can't abide her.* ○ *He couldn't abide laziness.*

▲ **abide by** ***sth*** *phrasal verb* to accept or obey an agreement, decision or rule: *Competitors must abide by the judge's decision.*

abiding /ə'baɪ.dɪŋ/ *adj* [before n] describes a feeling or memory that you have for a long time: *My abiding* ***memory*** *is of him watering his plants in the garden on sunny afternoons.*

ability [POWER] /ə'bɪl.ɪ.ti/ [US] /-ə.t̬i/ *noun* [C or U] the physical or mental power or skill needed to do something: *There's no doubting her ability.* ○ [+ to infinitive] *She* ***had the*** *ability* ***to*** *explain things clearly and concisely.* ○ *She's a woman of considerable abilities.* ○ *I have children in my class of very* ***mixed*** *abilities* (= different levels of skill or intelligence). ○ *a mixed ability class* ➲See also **able** CAN DO; **able** SKILFUL.

-ability [QUALITY] /-ə.bɪl.ɪ.ti/ [US] /-ə.t̬i/ *suffix* (*ALSO* **-ibility**) used to form nouns from adjectives ending in '-able' or '-ible', to mean the quality of being the stated adjective: *suitability* ○ *stability*

abject [EXTREME] /'æb.dʒekt/ *adj FORMAL* **abject misery/poverty/terror, etc.** when someone is extremely unhappy, poor, frightened, etc: *They live in abject poverty.* ○ *This policy has turned out to be an abject failure.*

abject [WITHOUT RESPECT] /'æb.dʒekt/ *adj FORMAL* showing no pride or respect for yourself: *an abject apology* ○ *He is almost abject in his respect for his boss.* **abjectly** /'æb.dʒekt.li/ *adv*

abjure /əb'dʒʊə^r/ [US] /-dʒʊr/ *verb* [T] *VERY FORMAL* to state publicly that you no longer agree with a belief or way of behaving: *He abjured his religion/his life of dissipation.*

ablaze [BURNING] /ə'bleɪz/ *adj* [after v] **1** burning very strongly: *The house was ablaze, and the flames and smoke could be seen for miles around.* **2** brightly lit or brightly coloured: *The ballroom was ablaze* ***with*** *lights.* ○ *The field was ablaze* ***with*** *poppies and wild flowers.*

ablaze [EMOTION] /ə'bleɪz/ *adj* [after v] full of energy, interest or emotion: *Her eyes were ablaze* ***with*** *excitement.*

able [CAN DO] /'eɪ.bl̩/ *adj* **be able to do** ***sth*** to have the necessary physical strength, mental power, skill, time, money or opportunity to do something: *Will she be able to cope with the work?* ○ *He's never been able to admit to his mistakes.* ○ *I'm sorry that I wasn't able to phone you yesterday.* ○ *It's so wonderful being able to see the sea from my window.* ➲See also **ability**.

USAGE

be able to

be able to is used instead of **can** when future tenses, perfect tenses, etc. are used.

I can't find your book.
I haven't been able to find your book.

able [SKILFUL] /'eɪ.bl̩/ *adj* clever or good at what you do: *an able child/student/secretary* ○ *This problem is now being looked at by some of the ablest minds/scientists in the country.* ➲See also **ability**.

ably /'eɪ.bli/ *adv*: *He performs his duties very ably* (= skilfully).

-able [CAN BE] /-ə.bl̩/ *suffix* (*ALSO* **-ible**) added to verbs to form adjectives which mean able to receive the action of the stated verb: *breakable* ○ *washable* ○ *moveable*

-able [WORTH BEING] /-ə.bl̩/ *suffix* (*ALSO* **-ible**) added to verbs to form adjectives which mean worth receiving the action of the stated verb: *an admirable person* ○ *an acceptable answer*

able-bodied /ˌeɪ.bl̩'bɒd.id/ [US] /-'bɑː.did/ *adj* describes someone who is healthy and has no illness, injury or condition that makes it difficult to do the things that other people do: *All able-bodied young men were forced to join the army.* **the ˌable-'bodied** *plural noun*: *It is hard for the able-bodied to understand the difficulties that disabled people encounter in their daily lives.*

ablution /ə'bluː.ʃən/ *noun* [U] *FORMAL* the act of washing yourself: *Ablution is part of some religious ceremonies.* **ablutions** /ə'bluː.ʃənz/ *plural noun HUMOROUS I must just* ***perform my*** *ablutions* (= wash myself)!

abnormal /æb'nɔː.məl/ [US] /-'nɔːr-/ *adj* different from what is usual or average, especially in a way that is bad: *abnormal behaviour/weather/conditions* ○ *Tests revealed some abnormal skin cells.*

abnormality /ˌæb.nɔːˈmæl.ə.ti/ [US] /-nɔːrˈmæl.ə.t̬i/ *noun* [C or U] something abnormal, usually in the body: *genetic/congenital abnormalities* ○ *An increasing number of tests are available for detecting* ***foetal*** *abnormalities.* ○ *The X-rays showed some slight abnormality.* **abnormally** /æbˈnɔː.məl.i/ [US] /-ˈnɔːr-/ *adv*: *The success rate was abnormally high.*

Abo /ˈæb.əʊ/ [US] /-oʊ/ *noun* [C] *plural* **Abos** *AUS* an **Aborigine**. This word is generally considered offensive.

aboard /əˈbɔːd/ [US] /-ˈbɔːrd/ *adv, prep* used when talking about getting onto a ship, aircraft, bus or train: *The flight attendant welcomed us aboard.* ○ *Welcome aboard flight BA345 to Tokyo.* ○ *The train's about to leave. All aboard!* ○ *We spent two months* ***aboard ship*** (= on the ship).

abode /əˈbəʊd/ [US] /-ˈboʊd/ *noun* [C usually sing] the place where someone lives: *FORMAL The defendant is* ***of no fixed*** *abode* (= has no permanent home). ○ *HUMOROUS Welcome to my* ***humble*** *abode!*

abolish /əˈbɒl.ɪʃ/ [US] /-ˈbɑː.lɪʃ/ *verb* [T] to end an activity or custom officially: *I think bullfighting should be abolished.* ○ *National Service was abolished in Britain in 1962.* **abolition** /ˌæb.əˈlɪʃ.ən/ *noun* [U] *William Wilberforce campaigned for the abolition of slavery.*
abolitionist /ˌæb.əˈlɪʃ.ən.ɪst/ *noun* [C] a person who supports the abolition of something

abominable /əˈbɒm.ɪ.nə.bl̩/ [US] /-ˈbɑː.mɪ-/ *adj* very bad or unpleasant: *The prisoners are forced to live in abominable conditions.* ○ *The weather's been abominable all week.* **abominably** /əˈbɒm.ɪ.nə.bli/ [US] /-ˈbɑː.mɪ-/ *adv*: *He behaved abominably towards her.*

aˌbominable ˈsnowman *noun* [C] a **yeti**

abomination /əˌbɒm.ɪˈneɪ.ʃən/ [US] /-ˌbɑː.mɪ-/ *noun* [C] *FORMAL* something that disgusts you: *Foxhunting is an abomination.*
abominate /əˈbɒm.ɪ.neɪt/ [US] /-ˈbɑː.mɪ-/ *verb* [T not continuous] *FORMAL* to hate something very much: *He abominates cruelty of all kinds.*

aboriginal /ˌæb.əˈrɪdʒ.ɪ.nəl/ *adj* describes a person or living thing that has existed in a country or continent since the earliest time known to people: *aboriginal forests* ○ *aboriginal inhabitants*

Aborigine /ˌæb.əˈrɪdʒ.ən.i/ *noun* [C] a member of the race of dark-skinned people who were the first people to live in Australia **Aboriginal** /ˌæb.əˈrɪdʒ.ɪ.nəl/ *adj*: *Aboriginal art/traditions*
Aboriginal /æb.əˈrɪdʒ.ɪ.nəl/ *noun* [C] an Aborigine

abort [STOP] /əˈbɔːt/ [US] /-ˈbɔrt/ *verb* [T] to cause something to stop or fail before it begins or before it is complete: *The plan/flight had to be aborted at the last minute.*
abortion /əˈbɔː.ʃən/ [US] /-ˈbɔːr-/ *noun* [C] *SLANG* a failure: *This project is a complete abortion.*
abortive /əˈbɔː.tɪv/ [US] /-ˈbɔːr.t̬ɪv/ *adj FORMAL* describes an attempt or plan that you have to give up because it has failed: *He made two abortive attempts on the French throne.*

abort [END PREGNANCY] /əˈbɔːt/ [US] /-ˈbɔːrt/ *verb* **1** [T] to stop the development of a baby that has not been born, usually by having a medical operation: *Do you think it's wrong to use aborted* ***foetuses*** *for medical research?* **2** [I] another word for **miscarry**, see at **miscarriage**
abortion /əˈbɔː.ʃən/ [US] /-ˈbɔːr-/ *noun* [C or U] the intentional ending of a pregnancy, usually by a medical operation: *She decided to* ***have/get*** *an abortion.* ○ *Abortion is restricted in some American states.* ➲Compare **miscarriage**; **stillbirth**.
abortionist /əˈbɔː.ʃən.ɪst/ [US] /-ˈbɔːr-/ *noun* [C] a person who performs abortions to end unwanted pregnancies, often illegally and for money

abound /əˈbaʊnd/ *verb* [I] to exist in large numbers: *Theories abound about how the earth began.*
▲ **abound in/with** ***sth*** *phrasal verb* If something abounds in/with other things, it has a lot of them: *The coast here abounds with rare plants.*

about [CONNECTED WITH] /əˈbaʊt/ *prep* on the subject of; connected with: *What's that book about?* ○ *a film about the Spanish Civil War* ○ *We were talking/laughing about Sophie.* ○ *He's always* ***(going) on*** *about what a great job he's got.* ○ *I'm worried about David.* ○ *I really don't know what all the fuss is about.* ○ *I wish you'd* ***do something*** *about* (= take action to solve the problem of) *your bedroom – it's a real mess.* ○ *UK INFORMAL Could you make me a coffee too* ***while*** *you're about* ***it*** (= while you are making one for yourself)*?* ○ *What didn't you like about the play?* ○ ***There's something*** *about* (= in the character of) *her attitude that worries me.* ○ ***There's something*** *special about him* (= in his character). ○ *"Is that your car?" "Yes,* ***what*** *about it* (= why are you asking me)*?"*
* This is sometimes said in an angry or threatening way.
• **How/What about?** used when suggesting or offering something to someone: *How about a trip to the zoo this afternoon?* ○ *"Coffee, Sarah?" "No, thanks." "What about you, Kate?"*

about [APPROXIMATELY] /əˈbaʊt/ *adv* a little more or less than the stated number or amount; approximately: *about six feet tall* ○ *about two months ago* ○ *"What time are you leaving work today?" "About five."* ○ *We're about* (= almost) *ready to leave.* ○ *Well, I think* ***that's*** *about* ***it*** *for now* (= we have almost finished what we are doing for the present).

about [IN THIS PLACE] *UK* /əˈbaʊt/ *adv, prep, adj* [after v] (*US* **around**) positioned or moving in or near a place, often without a clear direction, purpose or order: *She always leaves her clothes lying about on the floor.* ○ *They heard someone moving about outside.* ○ *I've been running about all morning trying to find you.* ○ *UK FORMAL Do you have such a thing as a pen about* ***you/your person*** (= Have you got a pen)*?* ○ *Is John about* (= somewhere near)*?* ○ *There's a lot of flu about* (= many people have it) *at the moment.*

about [INTENDING] /əˈbaʊt/ *adj* **be about to do** ***sth*** to be going to do something very soon: *I was about to leave when Mark arrived.* ○ *She looked as if she was about to cry.*

about-turn *UK* /əˌbaʊtˈtɜːn/ [US] /-ˈtɝːn/ *noun* [C] (*US* **about-face**) **1** a change of direction: *I'd only gone a little way down the street when I remembered I hadn't locked the door, so I* ***made/did*** *a quick about-turn and ran back to the house.* **2** a complete change of opinion or behaviour: *This is the Government's second about-turn* ***on*** *the issue.*

above [HIGHER POSITION] /əˈbʌv/ *adv, prep* in or to a higher position than something else: *There's a mirror above the washbasin.* ○ *He waved the letter excitedly above his head.* ○ *She's rented a room above a shop.* ○ *Her name comes above mine on the list.* ○ *The helicopter was hovering above the building.*

above [MORE] /əˈbʌv/ *adv, prep* **1** more than an amount or level: *It says on the box it's for children aged three and above.* ○ *Rates of pay are above* ***average****.* ○ *Temperatures rarely rise above zero in winter.* ○ *She values her job above her family.* ○ *They value their freedom above* ***(and beyond) all else****.* **2 above all** most importantly: *Above all, I'd like to thank my family.*

above [RANK] /əˈbʌv/ *adv, prep* in a more important or advanced position than someone else: *Sally's a grade above me.*

above [TOO IMPORTANT] /əˈbʌv/ *adv, prep* too good or important for something: *No one is above suspicion in this matter.* ○ *He's not above* ***lying*** (= he sometimes lies) *to protect himself.*

above [ON PAGE] /əˈbʌv/ *adv, adj* When used in a piece of writing, above means higher on the page, or on a previous page: *Please send the articles to the address given above.*
the aˈbove *plural noun* all the people or things listed earlier: ***All of*** *the above should be invited to the conference.*

aˌbove ˈboard *adj* [after v] describes a plan or business agreement that is honest and not trying to deceive anyone: *The deal was completely* ***open and*** *above board.*

above-mentioned /əˌbʌvˈmen.tʃənd/ *adj FORMAL* refers to things or people in a document or book that have been mentioned earlier: *All of the above-mentioned films won Oscars for best director.* ➲Compare **undermentioned**.

abracadabra /ˌæb.rə.kəˈdæb.rə/ *exclamation* said by someone who is performing a magic trick, in order to

[A]

help them perform it successfully

abrade /əˈbreɪd/ *verb* [T] *SPECIALIZED* to remove part of the surface of something by rubbing

abrasion /əˈbreɪ.ʒən/ *noun SPECIALIZED* **1** [U] the process of rubbing away the surface of something: *There seems to have been some abrasion of the surface.* **2** [C] a place where the surface of something, such as skin, has been rubbed away: *She had a small abrasion on her knee.*

abrasive [CLEANING SUBSTANCE] /əˈbreɪ.sɪv/ *noun* [C] a substance used for rubbing away the surface of something, usually to clean it or make it shiny: *You'll need a strong abrasive for cleaning this sink.* **abrasive** /əˈbreɪ.sɪv/ *adj*: *an abrasive cleaner/powder/liquid*

abrasive [UNPLEASANT] /əˈbreɪ.sɪv/ *adj* rude and unfriendly: *She has a rather abrasive* ***manner***. **abrasively** /əˈbreɪ.sɪv.li/ *adv* **abrasiveness** /əˈbreɪ.sɪv.nəs/ *noun* [U]

abreast /əˈbrest/ *adv* **1** describes two or more people who are next to each other and moving in the same direction: *We were running/cycling* ***two*** *abreast.* ○ *The motorcyclist came abreast* ***of*** *her car and shouted abuse at her.* **2 keep abreast of *sth*** to stay informed about the most recent facts about a subject or situation: *I try to keep abreast of any developments.*

abridge /əˈbrɪdʒd/ *verb* [T] to make a book, play or piece of writing shorter by removing details and unimportant information: *The book was abridged for children.* **abridged** /əˈbrɪdʒd/ *adj*: *I've only read the abridged* ***edition/version*** *of her novel.* **abridgment, abridgement** /əˈbrɪdʒ.mənt/ *noun* [C or U]

abroad [FOREIGN PLACE] /əˈbrɔːd/ *adj* [after v], *adv* in or to a foreign country or countries: *He's currently abroad on business.* ○ *We always* ***go*** *abroad in the summer.*

abroad [OUT] /əˈbrɔːd/ *adj* [after v] **1** *LITERARY OR OLD USE* outside; not at home: *Not a soul was abroad that morning.* **2** *FORMAL* describes ideas, feelings and opinions that are shared by many people: *There's a rumour abroad that she intends to leave the company.*

abrogate /ˈæb.rəʊ.geɪt/ [US] /-rə-/ *verb* [T] *FORMAL* to end a law, agreement or custom formally: *The treaty was abrogated in 1929.* **abrogation** /ˌæb.rəʊˈgeɪ.ʃən/ [US] /-rə-/ *noun* [S or U]

abrupt [SUDDEN] /əˈbrʌpt/ *adj* describes something that is sudden and unexpected, and often unpleasant: *an abrupt change/movement* ○ *Our conversation came to an abrupt end when George burst into the room.* ○ *The road ended in an abrupt* (= sudden and very steep) *slope down to the sea.* **abruptly** /əˈbrʌpt.li/ *adv*: *The talks ended abruptly when one of the delegations walked out in protest.* **abruptness** /əˈbrʌpt.nəs/ *noun* [U]

abrupt [UNFRIENDLY] /əˈbrʌpt/ *adj* using too few words when talking, in a way that seems rude and unfriendly: *an abrupt manner/reply* ○ *He is sometimes very abrupt* ***with*** *clients.* **abruptly** /əˈbrʌpt.li/ *adv* **abruptness** /əˈbrʌpt.nəs/ *noun* [U]

ABS /ˌeɪ.biːˈes/ *noun* [U] *ABBREVIATION FOR* anti-lock braking system: a brake fitted to some road vehicles that prevents SKIDDING (= uncontrolled sliding) by reducing the effects of sudden braking

abs /æbz/ *plural noun INFORMAL* ABDOMINAL muscles: *exercises to tone/build up your abs*

abscess /ˈæb.ses/ *noun* [C] a painful swollen area on or in the body, which contains pus (= thick, yellow liquid): *She had an abscess* ***on*** *her gum.*

abscond [ESCAPE] /æbˈskɒnd/ [US] /-ˈskɑːnd/ *verb* [I] to go away suddenly and secretly in order to escape from somewhere: *Two prisoners absconded last night.* ○ *She absconded* ***from*** *boarding school* ***with*** *her boyfriend.* **absconder** /æbˈskɒn.dər/ [US] /-ˈskɑːn.dɚ/ *noun* [C] *A 14 year-old absconder from a children's home in Bristol was found alive and well in London this morning.*

abscond [STEAL] /æbˈskɒnd/ [US] /-ˈskɑːnd/ *verb* [I] to go away suddenly and secretly because you have stolen something, usually money: *They absconded* ***with*** *£10 000 of the company's money.*

abseil *UK* /ˈæb.seɪl/ *verb* [I] (*US* **rappel**) to go down a very steep slope by holding on to a rope which is fastened to the top of the slope: *She abseiled* ***down*** *the rock face.* **abseil** *UK* /ˈæb.seɪl/ *noun* [C] (*US* **rappel**)

absence [NOT PRESENT] /ˈæb.sənts/ *noun* [C or U] when someone is not where they are usually expected to be: *A new manager was appointed* ***during/in*** *her absence.* ○ *She has had repeated absences* ***from*** *work this year.*

• **Absence makes the heart grow fonder.** *SAYING* This means that we feel more affection for people we love when they are not with us.

absent /ˈæb.sənt/ *adj* not in the place where you are expected to be, especially at school or work: *John has been absent* ***from*** *school/work for three days now.* ○ *We drank a toast to absent* ***friends***.

absent *yourself* /æbˈsent/ *verb* [R] *FORMAL* to not go to a place where you are expected to be, especially a school or place of work: *You cannot choose to absent yourself (****from*** *work/school) on a whim.*

absentee /ˌæb.sənˈtiː/ *noun* [C] someone who is not at school or work when they should be: *There are several absentees in the school this week, because a lot of people have got flu.* **absenteeism** /ˌæb.sənˈtiː.ɪ.zəm/ *noun* [U] *The high rate of absenteeism is costing the company a lot of money.*

absence [NOT EXISTING] /ˈæb.sənts/ *noun* [U] when something does not exist: *He drew attention to the absence* ***of*** *concrete evidence against the defendant.* ○ ***In the*** *absence* ***of*** (= because there were not) *more suitable candidates, we decided to offer the job to Mr Conway.*

absent /ˈæb.sənt/ *adj* not present: *Any sign of remorse was completely absent* ***from*** *her face.*

absent /ˈæb.sənt/ *adj* describes a person or the expression on their face when they are not paying attention to what is happening near them, and are thinking about other things **absently** /ˈæb.sənt.li/ *adv*

ˌabsentee ˈballot *US noun* [C] (*AUS* **absentee vote**) a piece of paper which voters who are unable to be present at an election can vote on and send in by post

ˌabsentee ˈlandlord *noun* [C] a person who rents out a house, apartment or farm to someone, but rarely or never visits it

absent-minded /ˌæb.səntˈmaɪn.dɪd/ *adj* describes someone who tends to forget things or does not pay attention to what is happening near them because they are thinking about other things **absent-mindedly** /ˌæb.səntˈmaɪn.dɪd.li/ *adv*: *She absent-mindedly left her umbrella on the bus.* **absent-mindedness** /ˌæb.səntˈmaɪn.dɪd.nəs/ *noun* [U]

absinthe, absinth /ˈæb.sæ̃θ/ /-sɪntθ/ [US] /-ˈ-/ *noun* [U] a strong alcoholic drink which is green and has a bitter taste

absolute [VERY GREAT] /ˌæb.səˈluːt/ /ˈ---/ *adj* **1** very great or to the largest degree possible: *a man of absolute integrity/discretion* ○ *I have absolute faith in her judgment.* ○ *There was no absolute proof of fraud.* **2** [before n] used when expressing a strong opinion: *He's an absolute idiot!* ○ *That's absolute rubbish!*

absolutely /ˌæb.səˈluːt.li/ /ˈ--ˌ--/ *adv* **1** completely: *I believed/trusted him absolutely.* ○ *You must be absolutely silent or the birds won't appear.* ○ *We've achieved absolutely nothing today.* **2** used for adding force to a strong adjective which is not usually used with 'very', or to a verb expressing strong emotion: *It's absolutely impossible to work with all this noise.* ○ *The food was absolutely disgusting/delicious.* ○ *I absolutely loathe/adore jazz.* **3** used as a way of strongly saying 'yes': *"It was an excellent film, though." "Absolutely!"* **4 absolutely not** used as a way of strongly saying 'no': *"Are you too tired to continue?" "Absolutely not!"*

absolute [NOT CHANGING] /ˌæb.səˈluːt/ /ˈ---/ *adj* [before n] not dependent on anything else; true, right, or the same in all situations: *an absolute law/principle/doctrine* ○ *Do you think there's such a thing as absolute truth/beauty?* ○ *Her contribution was better than most, but* ***in*** *absolute* ***terms*** (= without comparing it with anything else) *it was still rather poor.*

absolute [POWERFUL] /ˌæb.səˈluːt/ /ˈ---/ *adj* describes a ruler who has unlimited power: *an absolute monarch*

absolutism /ˈæb.sə.luː.tɪ.zəm/ [US] /-t̬ɪ-/ *noun* [U] a political system in which a single ruler, group or political party has complete power over a country

ˌabsolute maˈjority *noun* [C] in an election, when someone has the support of more than half of the voters

ˌabsolute ˈzero *noun* [U] the lowest temperature possible, which is -273.15°C

absolve /əbˈzɒlv/ ⓤ /-ˈzɑːlv/ *verb* [T] FORMAL (especially in religion or law) to free someone from guilt, blame or responsibility for something: *The report absolved her from/of all blame for the accident.* ○ *The priest absolved him (of all his sins).*

absolution /ˌæb.səˈluː.ʃən/ *noun* [U] FORMAL official forgiveness, especially in the Christian religion, for something bad that someone has done or thought: *She was granted/given absolution.*

absorb /əbˈzɔːb/ ⓤ /-ˈzɔːrb/ *verb* [T] **1** to take something in, especially gradually: *Plants absorb carbon dioxide.* ○ *In cold climates, houses need to have walls that will absorb heat.* ○ *Towels absorb moisture.* ○ *The drug is quickly absorbed into the bloodstream.* ○ *Our countryside is increasingly being absorbed by/into the large cities.* ⊃See also **self-absorbed**. **2** to understand facts or ideas completely and remember them: *It's hard to absorb so much information.* **3** to reduce the effect of a physical force, shock or change: *The barrier absorbed the main impact of the crash.* **4** If someone's work, or a book, film, etc. absorbs them, or they are absorbed in it, their attention is given completely to it: *Simon was so absorbed in his book, he didn't even notice me come in.*

absorbent /əbˈzɔː.bənt/ ⓤ /-ˈzɔːr-/ *adj* able to take liquid in through the surface and to hold it: *absorbent paper*

absorbency /əbˈzɔː.bənt.si/ ⓤ /-ˈzɔːr-/ *noun* [U] the ability to absorb liquid

absorption /əbˈzɔːp.ʃən/ ⓤ /-ˈzɔːrp-/ *noun* [U] *Some poisonous gases can enter the body by absorption through the skin.* ○ *Her absorption in her work (= giving all of her attention to it) is so great that she thinks about nothing else.* ⊃See also **self-absorbed**.

absorbing /əbˈzɔː.bɪŋ/ ⓤ /-ˈzɔːr-/ *adj* describes something that is very interesting and keeps your attention: *I read her last novel and found it very absorbing.*

abstain NOT DO /æbˈsteɪn/ *verb* [I] to not do something, especially something enjoyable that you think might be bad: *He took a vow to abstain from alcohol/smoking/sex.*

abstainer /æbˈsteɪ.nər/ ⓤ /-nɚ/ *noun* [C] **abstention** /æbˈsten.ʃən/ *noun* [U] FORMAL *Abstention from alcohol is essential while you are taking this medication.* **abstinence** /ˈæb.stɪ.nənts/ *noun* [U] *The best way to avoid pregnancy is total abstinence from sex.*

abstain NOT VOTE /æbˈsteɪn/ *verb* [I] to decide not to use your vote: *63 members voted in favour, 39 opposed and 5 abstained.* **abstainer** /æbˈsteɪ.nər/ ⓤ /-nɚ/ *noun* [C] **abstention** /æbˈsten.ʃən/ *noun* [C or U] *There were high levels of abstention (from voting) in the last elections.* ○ *There were ten votes in favour, six against, and three abstentions.*

abstemious /æbˈstiː.mi.əs/ *adj* FORMAL not doing things which give you pleasure, especially not eating good food or drinking alcohol

abstract GENERAL /ˈæb.strækt/ *adj* **1** existing as an idea, feeling or quality, not as a material object: *Truth and beauty are abstract concepts.* **2** describes an argument or discussion that is general and not based on particular examples: *This debate is becoming too abstract – let's have some hard facts!*

the ˈabstract *noun* [S] general ideas: *I have difficulty dealing with the abstract – let's discuss particular cases.* ○ *So far we've only discussed the question in the abstract (= without referring to any real examples).*

abstraction /æbˈstræk.ʃən/ *noun* [C] FORMAL *She's always talking in abstractions (= in a general way, without real examples).*

abstract ART /ˈæb.strækt/ *adj* describes a type of painting, drawing or sculpture which tries to represent the real or imagined qualities of objects or people by using shapes, lines and colour, and does not try to show their outer appearance as it would be seen in a photograph: *abstract art* ○ *an abstract painter*

abstract /ˈæb.strækt/ *noun* [C] a painting which represents the qualities of something, not its outer appearance

abstract SHORT DOCUMENT /ˈæb.strækt/ *noun* [C] a shortened form of a speech, article, book, etc., giving only the most important facts or arguments: *There is a section at the end of the magazine which includes abstracts of recent articles/books.*

abstracted /æbˈstræk.tɪd/ *adj* FORMAL not giving attention to what is happening around you because you are thinking about something else: *He gave her an abstracted glance, then returned to his book.* **abstractedly** /æbˈstræk.tɪd.li/ *adv*

ˌabstract ˈnoun *noun* [C] a noun which refers to a thing which does not exist as a material object: *'Happiness', 'honesty' and 'liberty' are abstract nouns.* ⊃Compare **concrete noun**.

abstruse /æbˈstruːs/ *adj* FORMAL difficult to understand: *an abstruse philosophical essay*

absurd /əbˈsɜːd/ ⓤ /-ˈsɝːd/ *adj* ridiculous or unreasonable; foolish in an amusing way: *What an absurd thing to say!* ○ *Don't be so absurd! Of course I want you to come.* ○ *It's an absurd situation – neither of them will talk to the other.* ○ *Do I look absurd in this hat?*

the absurd things that happen that are ridiculous or unreasonable: *The whole situation borders on the absurd.* ○ *She has a keen sense of the absurd.*

absurdly /əbˈsɜːd.li/ ⓤ /-ˈsɝːd-/ *adv*: *You're behaving absurdly.* ○ *It was absurdly (= unreasonably) expensive.*

absurdity /əbˈzɜː.dɪ.ti/ /-ˈsɜː-/ ⓤ /-ˈzɝː.də.t̬i/ *noun* [C or U] *Standing there naked, I was suddenly struck by the absurdity of the situation.* ○ *There are all sorts of absurdities (= things that are ridiculous) in the proposal.*

ABTA /ˈæb.tə/ *group noun* [S] ABBREVIATION FOR Association of British Travel Agents: a British organization which protects travellers and people on holiday if a company that arranges travel fails to do something or stops trading

abundant /əˈbʌn.dənt/ *adj* FORMAL more than enough: *an abundant supply of food* ○ *There is abundant evidence that cars have a harmful effect on the environment.* ○ *Cheap consumer goods are abundant (= exist in large amounts) in this part of the world.* **abundance** /əˈbʌn.dənts/ *noun* [S or U] *There was an abundance of wine at the wedding.* ○ *We had wine in abundance.*

abundantly /əˈbʌn.dənt.li/ *adv*: FORMAL *The plant grows abundantly in woodland.* ○ *You've made your feelings abundantly clear (= very clear).*

abuse BEHAVIOUR /əˈbjuːz/ *verb* [T] to use or treat someone or something wrongly or badly, especially in a way that is to your own advantage: *She is continually abusing her position/authority by getting other people to do things for her.* ○ *I never expected that he would abuse the trust I placed in him.* ○ *Several of the children had been sexually/physically/emotionally abused.*

abuse /əˈbjuːs/ *noun* [C or U] when someone uses or treats someone or something wrongly or badly, especially in a way that is to their own advantage: *an abuse (= wrong use) of privilege/power/someone's kindness* ○ *sexual/physical/mental abuse (= bad treatment)* ○ *She claimed to have been a victim of child abuse (= the treatment of children in a bad, esp. sexual, way).* ○ *Drug and alcohol abuse (= Using these substances in a bad way) contributed to his early death.*

abuser /əˈbjuː.zər/ ⓤ /-zɚ/ *noun* [C] someone who abuses someone or something: *a child abuser* ○ *a drug/solvent abuser*

abuse SPEECH /əˈbjuːz/ *verb* [T] to speak to someone rudely or cruelly: *The crowd started abusing him after he failed to save a goal.*

abuse /əˈbjuːs/ *noun* [U] rude and offensive words said to another person: *He had apparently experienced a lot of verbal abuse from his co-workers.* ○ *He hurled (a stream/torrent of) abuse at her (= He said a lot of rude and offensive things to her).* ○ *'Idiot!' is a mild term of abuse (= an insulting expression).*

abusive /əˈbjuː.sɪv/ *adj* using rude and offensive words: *an abusive letter/telephone call* ○ *He was apparently abusive to the flight attendants because they refused to serve him alcohol.*

abut /əˈbʌt/ *verb* [T no passive; I + prep] -tt- FORMAL If a building or area of land abuts on something, it is next to it or touches it on one side: *Mexico abuts **(on)** some of the richest parts of the United States.* ○ *Their house abutted **(onto)** the police station.*

abuzz /ə'bʌz/ *adj* [after v] filled with noise and activity: *When we arrived, the party was in full swing and the room was abuzz.* ○ *The air was abuzz **with** military helicopters, airlifting injured people and equipment.*

abysmal /ə'bɪz.məl/ *adj* very bad: *abysmal working conditions* ○ *The food was abysmal.* ○ *The standard of the students' work is abysmal.* **abysmally** /ə'bɪz.məl.i/ *adv*: *an abysmally poor book*

abyss /ə'bɪs/ *noun* [C usually sing] **1** *LITERARY* a very deep hole which seems to have no bottom **2** a difficult situation that brings trouble or destruction: *The country is **sinking/plunging into** an abyss **of** violence and lawlessness.* ○ *She found herself **on the edge of** an abyss.*

AC [ELECTRICITY] /ˌeɪ'siː/ *noun* [U] *ABBREVIATION FOR* alternating current: electrical current which regularly changes the direction in which it flows ➲Compare **DC** ELECTRICITY.

AC [AIR] /ˌeɪ'siː/ *noun* [C or U] *US ABBREVIATION FOR* **air conditioner** or **air conditioning**

acacia /ə'keɪ.ʃə/ *noun* [C or U] a tree from warm parts of the world which has small leaves and yellow or white flowers

academic [STUDYING] /ˌæk.ə'dem.ɪk/ *adj* **1** relating to schools, colleges and universities, or connected with studying and thinking, not with practical skills: *academic subjects/qualifications/books* ○ *an academic institution* ○ *the academic year* (= the time, usually from September to June, during which students go to school or college) ○ *academic standards* **2** describes someone who is clever and enjoys studying: *I was never a particularly academic child.* **academically** /ˌæk.ə'dem.ɪ.kli/ *adv*: *She's always done well academically.* ○ *It may be that a child is bright, but not academically inclined.*

academe /'æk.ə.diːm/ *noun* [U] *FORMAL* the part of society, especially universities, that is connected with study and thinking

academia /ˌæk.ə'diː.mi.ə/ *noun* [U] the part of society, especially universities, that is connected with studying and thinking, or the activity or job of studying: *A graduate of law and economics from Moscow State University, he had spent his life **in** academia.*

academic /ˌæk.ə'dem.ɪk/ *noun* [C] (*US ALSO* **academician**) someone who teaches at a college, or who studies as part of their job

academic [THEORETICAL] /ˌæk.ə'dem.ɪk/ *adj*: theoretical and not related to practical effects in real life: *a purely academic argument/question*

academy /ə'kæd.ə.mi/ *noun* [C] an organization intended to protect and develop an art, science, language, etc., or a school which teaches a particular subject or trains people for a particular job: *a military/police academy* ○ *the Royal Academy of Dramatic Art*

academician /əˌkæd.ə'mɪʃ.ən/ *noun* [C] a member of an academy: *In 1823 he became professor and academician at Munich.*

AˌcademyA'ward *noun* [C] (*ALSO* **Oscar**) one of a set of American prizes given each year to the best film, the best actor or actress in any film and to other people involved in the production of films

a cappella /ˌæ.kə'pel.ə/ [US] /ˌɑː-/ *adj* [before n], *adv* *SPECIALIZED* sung by a group of people without the help of any musical instruments

accede /ək'siːd/ *verb*

PHRASAL VERBS WITH **accede** ▼

▲ **accede to *sth*** [AGREE] *phrasal verb FORMAL* to agree to do what people have asked you to do: *He graciously acceded to our request.* ○ *It is doubtful whether the government will ever accede to the nationalists' demands for independence.*

▲ **accede to *sth*** [BECOME] *phrasal verb FORMAL* **accede to the throne/accede to power** to become king or queen, or to take a position of power: *The diaries were written in 1837 when Queen Victoria acceded to the throne.*

accession /ək'seʃ.ən/ *noun* [U] *1926 was the year of Emperor Hirohito's accession **to the throne**.*

accelerate [MOVE FASTER] /ək'sel.ə.reɪt/ [US] /'-ɚ.eɪt/ *verb* [I] **1** When a vehicle or its driver accelerates, the speed of the vehicle increases: *I accelerated to overtake the bus.* ➲Compare **decelerate**. **2** If a person or object accelerates, it goes faster.

acceleration /əkˌsel.ə'reɪ.ʃən/ *noun* [U] when something goes faster, or its ability to do this: *An older car will have poor acceleration.* ○ *High winds significantly hampered the plane's acceleration.*

accelerator /ək'sel.ə.reɪ.təʳ/ [US] /-ɚ.eɪ.t̬ɚ/ *noun* [C] **1** the PEDAL (= part that you push with your foot) in a vehicle that makes it go faster ➲See picture **Car** on page Centre 12 **2** *SPECIALIZED* in physics, a machine which makes PARTICLES (= small pieces of matter) move very fast

accelerate [HAPPEN FASTER] /ək'sel.ə.reɪt/ [US] /-ɚ.eɪt/ *verb* [I or T] to happen or make something happen sooner or faster: *Inflation is likely to accelerate this year, adding further upward pressure on interest rates.* ○ *They use special chemicals to accelerate the growth of crops.*

acceleration /əkˌsel.ə'reɪ.ʃən/ *noun* [S or U] *The acceleration **in** the decline of manufacturing industry is being blamed on the high value of sterling.*

accent [PRONUNCIATION] /'æk.sənt/ *noun* [C] the way in which people in a particular area, country or social group pronounce words: *He's got a strong French/Scottish accent.* ○ *She's French but she **speaks with** an impeccable English accent.* ○ *He speaks with a **broad/heavy/strong/thick** Yorkshire accent.* ○ *I thought I could detect a slight West Country accent.* **accented** /-tɪd/ [US] /-t̬ɪd/ *adj*: *He spoke in **heavily** accented English.*

accent [MARK] /'æk.sənt/ *noun* [C] a mark written or printed over a letter to show you how to pronounce it: *a grave accent* ○ *There's an acute accent **on** the 'e' of 'café'.*

accent [EMPHASIS] /'æk.sənt/ *noun* [C] *SPECIALIZED* a special emphasis given to a particular syllable in a word, word in a sentence, or note in a set of musical notes: *The accent falls **on** the final syllable.*

• **the accent is on *sth*** great importance is given to a particular thing or quality: *This season the accent is definitely on long, flowing romantic clothes.*

accent /ək'sent/ *verb* [T] to emphasize: *In any advertising campaign, you must accent the areas where your product is better than the competition.* ○ *SPECIALIZED Accent the first note of every bar.*

accentuate /ək'sen.tju.eɪt/ *verb* [T] to emphasize a particular feature of something or to make something more noticeable: *Her dress was tightly belted, accentuating the slimness of her waist.* ○ *The new policy only serves to accentuate the inadequacy of provision for the homeless.* **accentuation** /əkˌsen.tju'eɪ.ʃən/ *noun* [U]

accept [TAKE] /ək'sept/ *verb* **1** [T] to agree to take something: *Do you accept credit cards?* ○ *She was in London to accept an award for her latest novel.* ○ *I offered her an apology, but she wouldn't accept it.* ○ *I accept full responsibility for the failure of the plan.* ○ *The new telephones will accept coins of any denomination.* **2** [I or T] to say 'yes' to an offer or invitation: *We've offered her the job, but I don't know whether she'll accept it.* ○ *I've just accepted an invitation to the opening-night party.* ○ *I've been invited to their wedding but I haven't decided whether to accept.*

acceptable /ək'sep.tə.bl̩/ *adj*: *"Will a £50 donation be enough?" "Yes, that would be quite acceptable (= enough)."*

acceptability /əkˌsep.tə'bɪl.ɪ.ti/ [US] /-ə.t̬i/ *noun* [U]

acceptance /ək'sep.tənts/ *noun* [C or U]

COMMON LEARNER ERROR

accept or agree?

When you **accept** an invitation, job, or offer, you say yes to something which is offered. **Accept** is never followed by another verb.

They offered me the job and I've accepted it.

~~*They offered me the job and I've accepted to take it.*~~

When you **agree** to do something, you say that you will do something which someone asks you to do.

They offered me the job and I agreed to take it.

accept [APPROVE] /ək'sept/ *verb* [T] to consider something or someone as satisfactory: *The manuscript was accepted* *for publication last week.* ○ *She was accepted **as** a full member of the society.* ○ *His fellow workers refused to accept him* (= to include him as one of their group).

acceptable /əkˈsept.ə.bl/ *adj* satisfactory and able to be agreed to or approved of: *Clearly we need to come to an arrangement that is acceptable **to** both parties.* ○ *So what is an acceptable level of radiation?* ○ *This kind of attitude is simply not acceptable.*

acceptance /əkˈsep.tᵊnts/ *noun* [C or U] *I've had acceptances from three universities* (= Three universities have agreed to take me as a student). ○ *The idea rapidly **gained** acceptance* (= became approved of) *in political circles.*

accepted /əkˈsep.tɪd/ *adj*: *'Speed bump' now seems to be the generally accepted term* (= the word that most people use) *for those ridges in the road that slow traffic down.*

accept [BELIEVE] /əkˈsept/ *verb* [T] to believe that something is true: *The police refused to accept her version of the story.* ○ *He still hasn't accepted the situation* (= realized that he cannot change it). ○ [+ that] *I can't accept **that** there's nothing we can do.*

access /ˈæk.ses/ *noun* [U] the method or possibility of approaching a place or person, or the right to use or look at something: *The only access **to** the village is by boat.* ○ *The main access **to*** (= entrance to) *the building is at the side.* ○ *The tax inspector **had/gained** complete access **to** the company files.* ○ *The system has been designed to **give** the user quick and easy access **to** the required information.* ○ *The children's father was **refused** access **to** them at any time* (= refused official permission to see them).

access /ˈæk.ses/ *verb* [T] to open a computer FILE (= a collection of information stored on a computer) in order to look at or change information in it

accessible /əkˈses.ə.bl/ *adj* **1** able to be reached or easily obtained: *The resort is easily accessible by road, rail and air.* ○ *The problem with some of these drugs is that they are so very accessible.* **2** easy to understand: *Lea Anderson is a choreographer who believes in making dance accessible.* ○ *Covent Garden has made some attempt to make opera accessible **to** a wider public.*

accessibility /əkˌses.əˈbɪl.ɪ.ti/ [US] /-ə.t̬i/ *noun* [U] *Two new roads are being built to increase accessibility **to** the town centre.* ○ *The accessibility of her plays* (= the fact that they can be understood) *means that she is able to reach a wide audience.*

ˈaccess ˌcourse *noun* [C] *UK* a set of classes which people take so they can obtain a qualification which can be used to get into university or college: *She didn't have any formal qualifications but took an access course to get into university.*

accession /əkˈseʃ.ᵊn/ *noun* [U] ➲See at **accede to** BECOME.

accessory [EXTRA] /əkˈses.ᵊr.i/ [US] /-ɚ-/ *noun* [C usually pl] something added to a machine or to clothing, which has a useful or decorative purpose: *She wore a green wool suit with **matching** accessories* (= shoes, hat, bag, etc.). ○ *Sunglasses are much more than a **fashion** accessory.* ○ *Accessories for the top-of-the-range car include leather upholstery, a CD player, electric windows and a sunroof.*

accessorize, *UK USUALLY* **-ise** /əkˈses.ᵊr.aɪz/ [US] /-ɚ.aɪz/ *verb* [T] *MAINLY US* to add an accessory or accessories to something: *She was wearing a little black dress, accessorized simply with a silver necklace.*

accessory [CRIMINAL] /əkˈses.ᵊr.i/ [US] /-ɚ-/ *noun* [C] someone who helps another person to commit a crime but does not take part in it: *an accessory **to** murder*

• **accessory after the fact** *LEGAL* someone who helps someone after they have committed a crime, for example by hiding them from the police

• **accessory before the fact** *LEGAL* someone who helps in the preparation of a crime

ˈaccess proˌvider *noun* [C] (*ALSO* **ISP**) a company that provides access to the Internet, allows you to use email, and gives you space on the Internet to display documents: *the UK's largest **internet** access provider*

ˈaccess ˌroad *noun* [C] (*ALSO* **access route**) **1** a road leading from or to a particular place **2** *UK* a road leading to a motorway

ˈaccess ˌtime *noun* [C usually sing] *SPECIALIZED* the time it takes a computer to find information

accident /ˈæk.sɪ.dᵊnt/ *noun* [C] **1** something which happens unexpectedly and unintentionally, and which often damages something or injures someone: *Josh **had** an accident and spilled water all over his work.* ○ *She was injured in a car/road accident* (= when one car hit another). ○ *I didn't mean to knock him over - it was an accident.* **2 by accident** without intending to, or without being intended: *I deleted the file by accident.* ○ *I found her letter by accident as I was looking through my files.*

• **an accident waiting to happen** a very dangerous situation in which an accident is very likely

• **have an accident** to urinate or excrete unexpectedly and unintentionally: *Even a six-year-old can have an accident at night sometimes.*

• **more by accident than design** because of luck and not because of skill or organization: *The play was a success more by accident than design.*

• **Accidents will happen.** *SAYING* said after an accident in order to make it seem less bad

accidental /ˌæk.sɪˈden.tᵊl/ [US] /-t̬ᵊl/ *adj* happening by chance: *Reports suggest that 11 soldiers were killed by accidental fire from their own side.* ○ *The site was located after the accidental discovery of bones in a field.*

accidentally /ˌæk.sɪˈden.tᵊl.i/ [US] /-t̬ᵊl-/ *adv*: *I accidentally knocked a glass over.*

• **accidentally on purpose** If you do something accidentally on purpose, you do it intentionally but pretend it happened by chance: *I've never liked these glasses of Peter's. I might drop them one day – accidentally on purpose.*

ˌaccidental ˈdeath *noun* [C] *LEGAL* a VERDICT (= opinion stated at the end of a trial) that is given when a death was the result of an accident and not of murder or SUICIDE

accident-prone /ˈæk.sɪ.dᵊntˌprəʊn/ [US] /-ˌproʊn/ *adj* describes someone who often has accidents, usually because they are very awkward or clumsy

acclaim /əˈkleɪm/ *noun* [U] public approval and praise: *Despite the **critical** acclaim, the novel did not sell well.* ○ *Hamlet was played by Romania's leading actor, Ion Caramitrou, **to** rapturous acclaim.*

acclaim /əˈkleɪm/ *verb* [T often passive] to give public approval and praise: *She was universally/widely/publicly acclaimed **for** her contribution to the discovery.* ○ *She is being acclaimed* (= publicly recognized) ***as** the greatest dancer of her generation.* **acclaimed** /əˈkleɪmd/ *adj*: *an acclaimed artist/writer/poet* ○ *a highly acclaimed novel/film* ○ *'Dinner Party', based on the **critically** acclaimed novel by Bill Davies, was made into a film last year.*

acclamation /ˌæk.ləˈmeɪ.ʃᵊn/ *noun* [U] *FORMAL His speech was greeted with (shouts of) acclamation* (= loud expressions of approval).

acclimatize, *UK USUALLY* **-ise** /əˈklaɪ.mə.taɪz/ [US] /-t̬aɪz/ *verb* [I or T] (*US ALSO* **acclimate**) to (cause to) change to suit different conditions of life, weather, etc: *More time will be needed for the troops and equipment to become acclimatized **to** desert conditions.* ○ *We found it impossible to acclimatize ourselves **to** the new working conditions.* ○ *The defending champion is Grant Turner of England, who has acclimatized **to** the 90°F sunshine by spending the past month in Florida.* ○ *"Why is it that it rains all the time in England?" "Don't worry – you'll soon acclimatize."* **acclimatization**, *UK USUALLY* **-isation** /əˌklaɪ.mə.taɪˈzeɪ.ʃᵊn/ [US] /-t̬ɪ-/ *noun* [U]

accolade /ˈæk.ə.leɪd/ *noun* [C] *FORMAL* praise and approval: *This is his centennial year and he's been granted the **ultimate** accolade – his face on a set of three postage stamps.* ○ *Her approval was the **highest** accolade he could have received.*

accommodate [FIND A PLACE FOR] /əˈkɒm.ə.deɪt/ [US] /-ˈkɑː.mə-/ *verb* [T] to provide with a place to live or to be stored in: *New students may be accommodated **in** halls of residence.* ○ *FORMAL There wasn't enough space to accommodate the files.*

accommodation /əˌkɒm.əˈdeɪ.ʃᵊn/ [US] /-ˌkɑː.mə-/ *noun* [U] *MAINLY UK* a place to live, work, stay, etc. in: *There's a shortage of cheap accommodation* (= places to live). ○ *We* *have first and second class accommodation (= seats) on this flight.*

accommodations /əˌkɒm.əˈdeɪ.ʃ°nz/ ⓤⓈ /-ˌkɑː.mə-/ *plural noun us* a place to stay when you are travelling, especially a hotel room: *Sweepstakes winners will enjoy a week-long stay in luxury accommodations in Las Vegas.*

accommodate ⃞SUIT⃞ /əˈkɒm.ə.deɪt/ ⓤⓈ /-ˈkɑː.mə-/ *verb* [T] to give what is needed to someone: *The new policies fail to accommodate the disabled.* ○ *We always try to accommodate (= help) our clients with financial assistance if necessary.*

ac'commodate yourself *verb* [R] to change yourself or your behaviour to suit another person or new conditions: *Some find it hard to accommodate themselves to the new working conditions.*

accommodating /əˈkɒm.ə.deɪ.tɪŋ/ ⓤⓈ /-ˈkɑː.mə.deɪ.tɪŋ/ *adj* describes a person who is eager or willing to help other people, for example by changing their plans: *I'm sure she'll help you – she's always very accommodating.*

accompaniment /əˈkʌm.p°n.ɪ.mənt/ *noun* [C] something that you eat or drink with something else: *A dry champagne makes the ideal accompaniment for/to this dish.*

accompany ⃞GO WITH⃞ /əˈkʌm.pə.ni/ *verb* [T] **1** to go with someone or to be provided or exist at the same time as something: *The course books are accompanied by four cassettes.* ○ *Depression is almost always accompanied by insomnia.* ○ *The salmon was accompanied by (= served with) a fresh green salad.* **2** *SLIGHTLY FORMAL* to show someone how to get to somewhere: *Would you like me to accompany you to your room?* **3** *FORMAL* to go with someone to a social event or to an entertainment: *"May I accompany you to the ball?" he asked her.* ○ *I have two tickets for the theatre on Saturday evening – would you care to accompany me?*

accompanying /əˈkʌm.pə.ni.ɪŋ/ *adj* appearing or going with someone or something else: *Front-page stories broke the news of the princess leaving, and accompanying photographs showed her getting on the plane.* ○ *Children under 17 require an accompanying parent or guardian to see this film.*

accompany ⃞MUSIC⃞ /əˈkʌm.pə.ni/ *verb* [T] to sing or play an instrument with another musician or singer: *Miss Jessop accompanied Mr Bentley on the piano.*

accompaniment /əˈkʌm.p°n.ɪ.mənt/ *noun* [C or U] a song with piano accompaniment ○ *HUMOROUS We worked to the accompaniment of (= while hearing the sound of) Mr French's drill.* **accompanist** /əˈkʌm.pə.nɪst/ *noun* [C] *The singer's accompanist on the piano was Charles Harman.*

accomplice /əˈkʌm.plɪs/ ⓤⓈ /-ˈkɑːm-/ *noun* [C] a person who helps someone else to commit a crime or to do something morally wrong

accomplish /əˈkʌm.plɪʃ/ ⓤⓈ /-ˈkɑːm-/ *verb* [T] to finish something successfully or to achieve something: *The students accomplished the task in less than ten minutes.* ○ *She accomplished such a lot during her visit.* ○ *I feel as if I've accomplished nothing since I left my job.*

accomplishment /əˈkʌm.plɪʃ.mənt/ ⓤⓈ /-ˈkɑːm-/ *noun* **1** [C] something that is successful, or that is achieved after a lot of work or effort: *Getting the two leaders to sign a peace treaty was his greatest accomplishment.* ⇨See also **accomplishment** at **accomplished**. **2** [U] the completion of something: *We celebrated the successful accomplishment of our task.*

accomplished /əˈkʌm.plɪʃt/ ⓤⓈ /-ˈkɑːm-/ *adj* skilled: *She's a very accomplished pianist/painter/horsewoman.* ○ *He was accomplished in all the arts.*

accomplishment /əˈkʌm.plɪʃ.mənt/ ⓤⓈ /-ˈkɑːm-/ *noun* [C] a skill: *Cordon-bleu cookery is just one of her many accomplishments.* ⇨See also **accomplishment** at **accomplish**.

accord ⃞AGREEMENT⃞ /əˈkɔːd/ ⓤⓈ /-ˈkɔːrd/ *noun* [C or U] (a formal) agreement: *On 31 May the two leaders signed a peace accord.* ○ *Before 1987, the accord between the Labour government and the unions was a simple affair.* ○ *The project is completely in accord with government policy.*

● **of your own accord** If you do something of your own accord, you do it without being asked to do it: *She came*

of her own accord. No one asked her to come.

● **with one accord** *FORMAL* If people do something with one accord, they do it together and in complete agreement: *With one accord, the delegates walked out of the conference.*

accordance /əˈkɔː.d°nts/ ⓤⓈ /-ˈkɔːr-/ *noun FORMAL* **in accordance with a rule/law/wish/etc.** following or obeying a rule/law/wish/etc: *In accordance with her wishes, she was buried in France.*

accordingly /əˈkɔː.dɪŋ.li/ ⓤⓈ /-ˈkɔːr-/ *adv FORMAL* in a way that is suitable or right for the situation: *When we receive your instructions we shall act accordingly.* ○ *She's an expert in her field, and is paid accordingly.*

accord ⃞GIVE⃞ /əˈkɔːd/ ⓤⓈ /-ˈkɔːrd/ *verb* [T] *FORMAL* to treat someone specially, usually by showing respect: [+ two objects] *The massed crowds of supporters accorded him a hero's welcome.* ○ *Certainly in our society teachers don't enjoy the respect that is accorded to doctors and lawyers.*

▲ **accord with sth** *phrasal verb FORMAL* to be the same as something, or to agree with something: *His version of events does not accord with witnesses' statements.*

ac'cording ˌto ⃞AS STATED BY⃞ *prep* as stated by: *According to Sarah they're not getting on very well at the moment.* ○ *According to our records you owe us $130.*

ac'cording ˌto ⃞FOLLOWING⃞ *prep* in a way that agrees with: *Students are all put in different groups according to their ability.*

● **according to plan** Something that happens according to plan, happens in the way it was intended to: *Did it all go according to plan?*

accordion /əˈkɔː.di.ən/ ⓤⓈ /-ˈkɔːr-/ *noun* [C] a box-shaped musical instrument, held in the hands, consisting of a folded central part with a keyboard at each end, which is played by pushing the two ends towards each other

accost /əˈkɒst/ ⓤⓈ /-ˈkɑːst/ *verb* [T often passive] *FORMAL* to approach or stop and speak to someone in a threatening way: *I'm usually accosted by beggars and drunks as I walk to the station.*

account ⃞BANK⃞ /əˈkaʊnt/ (*ALSO* **bank account**) an arrangement with a bank to keep your money there and to allow you to take it out when you need to: *I've opened an account with a building society.* ○ *I paid the money into my account this morning.* ○ *(UK) She paid the cheque into/(US) She deposited the check in her account.* ○ *I need to draw some money out of my account.*

● **turn/use sth to good account** *UK FORMAL* to use your skills and abilities to produce good results: *I think we'd all agree that you turned your negotiating skills to very good account in this afternoon's meeting.*

account ⃞SHOP⃞ /əˈkaʊnt/ *noun* [C] **1** an agreement with a shop or company that allows you to buy things and pay for them later: *Could you put it on/charge it to my account (= can I pay for it later), please?* ○ *Do you have an account at this store/with us, madam?* ○ *Could you please pay/settle your account in full (= give us all the money you owe us).* **2** a customer who does business with a company: *If the advertising agency loses the United Beer account, it will make a big dent in their profits.*

account ⃞REPORT⃞ /əˈkaʊnt/ *noun* [C] a written or spoken description of an event: *She gave a thrilling account of her life in the jungle.* ○ *He kept a detailed account of the suspect's movements.* ○ *Several eyewitnesses' accounts differed considerably from the official version of events.*

● **by/from all accounts** as said by most people: *By all accounts, San Francisco is a city that's easy to fall in love with.*

● **be brought/called to account** *MAINLY UK* to be forced to explain something you did wrong, and usually to be punished: *We must ensure that the people responsible for the violence are brought to account.*

● **by your own account** Something that is true by your own account is what you claim to be true: *By his own account, he's quite wealthy.*

account ⃞REASON⃞ /əˈkaʊnt/ *noun FORMAL* **on account of sth** because of something: *He doesn't drink alcohol on account of his health.*

● **on your account** If something is said to be on someone's or something's account, it is because of that person or thing: *I'm not very hungry so please don't cook on my account* (= don't cook just for me). ○ *They were tired, but not any less enthusiastic on that account.*

• **on no account** If something must on no account/not on any account be done, it must not be done at any time or for any reason: *Employees must on no account make personal telephone calls from the office.* ○ *These records must not on any account be changed.*

• **take into account/take account of** to consider or remember when judging a situation: *I hope my teacher will take into account the fact that I was ill just before the exams when she marks my paper.* ○ *A good architect takes into account the building's surroundings.* ○ *Britain's tax system takes no account of children.* ○ *I think you have to take into account* ***that*** *he's a good deal younger than the rest of us.*

account [JUDGE] /ə'kaʊnt/ *verb* [T + obj + n or adj] *FORMAL* to think of someone or something in the stated way; judge: *She was accounted a genius by all who knew her work.*

account [IMPORTANCE] /ə'kaʊnt/ *noun FORMAL* **be of no/little account** to not be important: *It's of no account to me whether he comes or not.* ○ *His opinion is of little account to me.*

PHRASAL VERBS WITH **account**

▲ **account (to** ***sb*****) for** ***sth*** [EXPLAIN] *phrasal verb* to explain the reason for something or the cause of something: *Can you account for your absence last Friday?* ○ *She was unable to account for over $5 000* (= she could not explain where the money was). ○ *He has to account to his manager for* (= tell his manager about and explain) *all his movements.*

• **There's no accounting for taste.** *SAYING* said when it is difficult to explain why different people like different things, especially things which you do not like: *"I love working at weekends." "Well, there's no accounting for taste, is there!"*

▲ **account for** ***sth*** [BE] *phrasal verb* to form the total of something: *Students account for the vast majority of our customers.*

accountable /ə'kaʊn.tə.bl̩/ Ⓤⓢ /-t̬ə-/ *adj* Someone who is accountable is completely responsible for what they do and must be able to give a satisfactory reason for it: *She is accountable only* ***to*** *the managing director.* ○ *The recent tax reforms have made government more accountable* ***for*** *its spending.* ○ *Politicians should be accountable* ***to*** *the public who elected them.* **accountability** /ə,kaʊn.tə'bɪl.ɪ.ti/ Ⓤⓢ /-t̬ə'bɪl.ə.t̬i/ *noun* [U] *There were furious demands for greater police accountability* (= for the police to be made to explain their actions to the public).

accountant /ə'kaʊn.tᵊnt/ Ⓤⓢ /-t̬ᵊnt/ *noun* [C] someone who keeps or examines the records of money received, paid and owed by a company or person: *a firm of accountants* **accountancy** *UK* /ə'kaʊn.tᵊnt.si/ Ⓤⓢ /-t̬ᵊnt-/ *noun* [U] (*US* **accounting**) the job of being an accountant: *He works in accountancy.* ○ *an accountancy firm*

accounting /ə'kaʊn.tɪŋ/ Ⓤⓢ /-t̬ɪŋ/ *noun* [U] **1** the skill or activity of keeping records of the money a person or organization earns and spends **2** *US* (*UK* **accountancy**) the job of being an accountant

accounts /ə'kaʊnts/ *plural noun* an official record of all the money a person or company has spent and received: *I* ***keep*** *my own accounts.*

accoutrements, *US ALSO* **accouterments** /ə'kuː.trə.mənts/ Ⓤⓢ /ə'kuː.t̬ɚ.mənts/ *plural noun FORMAL* the equipment needed for a particular activity or way of life

accredit /ə'kred.ɪt/ *verb* [T] to officially recognize, accept or approve of someone or something: *The agency was not accredited by the Philippine Consulate to offer contracts to Filipinos abroad.* **accredited** /ə'kred.ɪ.tɪd/ Ⓤⓢ /-t̬ɪd/ *adj* officially recognized or approved: *an accredited drama school* ○ *accredited war correspondents* **accreditation** /ə,kred.ɪ'teɪ.ʃᵊn/ Ⓤⓢ /-'teɪ-/ *noun* [U] *The college received/was given full accreditation in 1965.*

accretion /ə'kriː.ʃᵊn/ *noun* [C or U] *FORMAL* gradual increase or growth by the addition of new layers or parts: *The fund was increased by the accretion of new shareholders.* ○ *The room hadn't been cleaned for years and showed several accretions of dirt and dust.*

accrue /ə'kruː/ *verb* [I] *FORMAL* to increase in number or amount over a period of time: *Interest will accrue* ***on*** *the account at a rate of 7%.* ○ *Little benefit will accrue* ***to*** *London* (= London will receive little benefit) *from the new road scheme.*

accumulate /ə'kjuː.mjʊ.leɪt/ *verb* **1** [T] to collect a large number of things over a long period of time: *As people accumulate more wealth, they tend to spend a greater proportion of their incomes.* ○ *The company said the debt was accumulated during its acquisition of nine individual businesses.* ○ *We've accumulated so much rubbish over the years.* **2** [I] to gradually increase in number or amount: *A thick layer of dust had accumulated in the room.* ○ *If you don't sort out the papers on your desk on a regular basis they just keep on accumulating.* **accumulation** /ə,kjuː.mjʊ'leɪ.ʃᵊn/ *noun* [C or U] *Despite this accumulation of evidence, the Government persisted in doing nothing.* ○ *Accumulations of sand can be formed by the action of waves on coastal beaches.*

accumulator *UK* /ə'kjuː.mjʊ.leɪ.təʳ/ Ⓤⓢ /-t̬ɚ/ *noun* [C] (*US* **storage battery**) a battery that collects and stores electricity

accurate /'æk.jʊ.rət/ *adj* correct, exact and without any mistakes: *an accurate machine* ○ *an accurate description* ○ *The figures they have used are just not accurate.* ○ *Her novel is an accurate reflection of life in post-war Spain.* ○ *We hope to become more accurate* ***in*** *predicting earthquakes.* * NOTE: The opposite is **inaccurate**. **accurately** /'æk.jʊ.rət.li/ *adv*: *The plans should be drawn as accurately as possible, showing all the measurements.* **accuracy** /'æk.jʊ.rə.si/ *noun* [U] *We can predict changes with* ***a*** *surprising* ***degree of*** *accuracy.*

accursed /ə'kɜː.sɪd/ /-'kɜːst/ Ⓤⓢ /-'kɝːst/ *adj* [before n] *OLD USE* very annoying: *I can't get around like I used to – it's this accursed rheumatism!*

accusative /ə'kjuː.zə.tɪv/ Ⓤⓢ /-t̬ɪv/ *noun* [U] the form of a noun, pronoun or adjective which is used in some languages to show that the word is the DIRECT OBJECT of a verb **accusative** /ə'kjuː.zə.tɪv/ Ⓤⓢ /-t̬ɪv/ *adj*: *the accusative plural*

accuse /ə'kjuːz/ *verb* [T] to say that someone has done something morally wrong, illegal or unkind: *"It wasn't my fault." "Don't worry, I'm not accusing you."* ○ *He's been accused* ***of*** *robbery/murder.* ○ *Are you accusing me* ***of*** *lying?* ○ *The surgeon was accused* ***of*** *negligence.*

• **stand accused of** ***sth*** *FORMAL* If you stand accused of doing something wrong, people say that you have done it: *The government stands accused of eroding freedom of speech.*

accusation /,æk.jʊ'zeɪ.ʃᵊn/ *noun* [C or U] a statement saying that someone has done something morally wrong, illegal or unkind, or the fact of accusing someone: *You can't just make* ***wild*** *accusations like that!* ○ *He glared at me* ***with an air of*** *accusation.* ○ [+ **that**] *What do you say to the accusation* ***that*** *you are unfriendly and unhelpful?* **accusatory** /ə'kjuː.zə.tri/ /,æk.jʊ'zeɪ.tᵊr.i/ Ⓤⓢ /-tɔː.ri/ *adj FORMAL* suggesting that you think someone has done something bad: *When he spoke his tone was accusatory.* ○ *She gave me an accusatory look.* **the ac'cused** *noun* [C + sing or pl v] *LEGAL* the person who is on trial in a court, or the people on trial in a court: *The accused protested her innocence.* ○ *The accused were all found guilty.* **accuser** /ə'kjuː.zəʳ/ Ⓤⓢ /-zɚ/ *noun* [C] **accusing** /ə'kjuː.zɪŋ/ *adj*: *an accusing glance/look* **accusingly** /ə'kjuː.zɪŋ.li/ *adv*: *"Has this dog been fed today?" she asked accusingly.*

accustom /ə'kʌs.təm/ *verb*

▲ **accustom** ***yourself*** **to** ***sth*** *phrasal verb* [R] to make yourself familiar with new conditions: *It'll take time for me to accustom myself to the changes.*

accustomed /ə'kʌs.təmd/ *adj* **1** familiar with something: *She quickly became accustomed* ***to*** *his messy ways.* ○ *I'm not accustomed* ***to*** *being treated like this.* **2** *FORMAL* usual: *She performed the task with her accustomed ease.*

A

ace [PLAYING CARD] /eɪs/ *noun* [C] one of the four playing cards with a single mark or spot, which have the highest or lowest value in many card games: *the ace of hearts/clubs/spades/diamonds*
• **come within an ace of *sth*** *UK* to almost achieve something: *She came within an ace of winning the match.*
• **an ace up *your* sleeve** (*US ALSO* **an ace in the hole**) secret knowledge or a secret skill which will give you an advantage
• **have/hold all the aces** to be in a strong position when you are competing with someone else because you have all the advantages: *In a situation like this, it's the big companies who hold all the aces.*

ace [SKILLED PERSON] /eɪs/ *noun* [C] *INFORMAL* a person who is very skilled at something: *a tennis/flying ace*
ace /eɪs/ *adj OLD-FASHIONED SLANG* excellent: *He's an ace footballer.* ○ *That's an ace bike you've got there.*
ace /eɪs/ *verb* [T] *US INFORMAL* to do very well in an exam: *I was up all night studying, but it was worth it – I aced my chemistry final.*

ace [TENNIS] /eɪs/ *noun* [C] in tennis, a SERVE (= a hit of the ball which starts play) which is so strong and fast that the other player cannot return the ball: *That's the third ace that Violente has* ***served*** *this match.*

acerbic /əˈsɜː.bɪk/ [US] /-ˈsɝː-/ *adj FORMAL* describes something that is spoken or written in a way that is direct, clever and cruel: *The letters show the acerbic* ***wit*** *for which Parker was both admired and feared.* **acerbity** /əˈsɜː.bə.ti/ [US] /-ˈsɝː.bə.t̬i/ *noun* [U]

acetaminophen /əˌsiː.təˈmɪn.ə.fen/ [US] /-t̬ə-/ *noun* [C or U] *plural* **acetaminophens** or **acetaminophen** *US FOR* **paracetamol**

acetate /ˈæs.ɪ.teɪt/ *noun* [U] a chemical substance made from ACETIC ACID, or a smooth artificial cloth made from this

acetic acid /əˌsiː.tɪkˈæs.ɪd/ [US] /-t̬ɪk-/ *noun* [U] a colourless acid with a strong smell which is contained in vinegar

acetone /ˈæs.ɪ.təʊn/ [US] /-t̬oʊn/ *noun* [U] a strong-smelling colourless liquid which is used in the production of various chemicals and is sometimes added to paint to make it more liquid

acetylene /əˈset.ə.liːn/ [US] /-ˈset̬-/ *noun* [U] a colourless gas which burns with a very hot bright flame, used in cutting and joining metal

ache /eɪk/ *noun* [C] **1** a continuous pain which is unpleasant but not strong: *As you get older, you have all sorts of aches* ***and pains.*** ○ *I've got a* ***dull*** (= slight) *ache* ***in*** *my lower back.* **2** used in combinations with parts of the body to mean a continuous pain in the stated part: *earache/headache/toothache/backache* ○ *I've had a stomach ache all morning.* **ache** /eɪk/ *verb* [I] *My head/tooth/back aches.* ○ *I ache/I'm aching* ***all over.*** ○ *I've got one or two aching muscles after yesterday's run.*
achy /ˈeɪ.ki/ *adj: INFORMAL I've been feeling tired and achy* (= full of pains) *all morning.*
▲ **ache for *sth*** *phrasal verb LITERARY* to want something very much: *He was lonely and aching for love.*

achieve /əˈtʃiːv/ *verb* [T] to succeed in finishing something or reaching an aim, especially after a lot of work or effort: *The government's training policy, he claimed, was achieving its* ***objectives.*** ○ *She finally achieved her* ***ambition*** *to visit South America.* ○ *I've been working all day, but I feel as if I've achieved nothing.* ➲See also **underachieve.**
achievable /əˈtʃiː.və.bl̩/ *adj* describes a task, etc. that is possible to achieve: *Before you set your targets, make sure that they are achievable.*
achiever /əˈtʃiː.vəʳ/ [US] /-vɚ/ *noun* **1 high/low achiever** a person who achieves more/less than the average: *Not enough attention is given to the low achievers in the class.* **2 under achiever** someone who is less successful than they should be at school or at work
achievement /əˈtʃiːv.mənt/ *noun* [C or U] something very good and difficult that you have succeeded in doing: *Whichever way you look at it, an Olympic silver medal is a remarkable achievement for one so young.* ○ *The Tale of Genji has been described as the greatest achievement of Japanese literature.* ○ *It gives you a* ***sense of*** *achievement if you actually make it to the end of a very long book.*

Achilles heel /əˌkɪl.iːzˈhɪəl/ *noun* [C usually sing] a small fault or weakness in a person or system that can result in its failure: *A misbehaving minister is regarded as a government's Achilles heel and is expected to resign.*

Achilles tendon /əˌkɪl.iːzˈten.dən/ *noun* [C] a small muscular cord just above the heel, connecting the heel bone to the muscles in the lower part of the leg ➲See picture **The Body** on page Centre 5

achingly /ˈeɪ.kɪŋ.li/ *adv LITERARY* extremely: *Sung by the world's greatest tenor, this aria is achingly beautiful.*

achoo /əˈtʃuː/ *exclamation* **atishoo**

acid [LIQUID SUBSTANCE] /ˈæs.ɪd/ *noun* [C or U] any of various usually liquid substances which can react chemically with and sometimes dissolve other materials: *acetic/hydrochloric/lactic acid* ○ *Vinegar is an acid.*
acid /ˈæs.ɪd/ *adj* **1** containing acid, or having similar qualities to an acid: *an acid taste/smell* ○ *acid soil* **2** describes a remark or way of speaking that is cruel or criticizes something in an unkind way: *her acid wit* ○ *When she spoke her tone was acid.* **acidify** /əˈsɪd.ɪ.faɪ/ *verb* [I or T] **acidity** /əˈsɪd.ɪ.ti/ [US] /-ə.t̬i/ *noun* [U] *High acidity levels in the water mean that the fish are not so large.*
acidly /ˈæs.ɪd.li/ *adv*: *"I suppose you expect me to thank you for coming," he said acidly* (= unpleasantly).

acid [DRUG] /ˈæs.ɪd/ *noun* [U] *SLANG FOR* **LSD** (= an illegal drug which makes people see things that do not exist)

ˌacid ˈjazz *noun* [U] a style of popular dance music which is a mix of FUNK, SOUL and jazz

acidophilus /ˌæ.s.ɪˈdɒf.ɪ.ləs/ [US] /ˌæ.s.ɪˈdɑː.fᵊ.ləs/ *noun* [U] *SPECIALIZED* a type of BACTERIUM (= a very small organism) used to make YOGURT or as a medicine to help people digest food if they have a stomach illness

ˌacid ˈrain *noun* [U] rain which contains large amounts of harmful chemicals as a result of burning substances such as coal and oil

the ˈacid ˌtest *noun* [S] the true test of the value of something: *It looks good, but will people buy it? That's the acid test.*

acknowledge /əkˈnɒl.ɪdʒ/ [US] /-ˈnɑː.lɪdʒ/ *verb* [T] to accept, admit or recognize something, or the truth or existence of something: [+ v-ing] *She acknowledged having been at fault.* ○ [+ that] *She acknowledged* ***that*** *she had been at fault.* ○ *You must acknowledge the truth of her argument.* ○ *Historians generally acknowledge her* ***as*** *a genius in her field.* ○ [+ obj + to infinitive] *She is usually acknowledged* ***to*** *be one of our best artists.* ○ *They refused to acknowledge* (= to recognize officially) *the new government.* ○ *Please acknowledge* ***receipt of*** (= say that you have received) *this letter.* ○ *He didn't even acknowledge my* ***presence*** (= show that he had seen me). ○ *The government won't even acknowledge the existence of the problem.*
acknowledgment, acknowledgement /əkˈnɒl.ɪdʒ.mənt/ [US] /-ˈnɑː.lɪdʒ-/ *noun* [C or U] *We sent her a copy of the book* ***in*** *acknowledgment* ***of*** *her part in its creation.* ○ *I applied for four jobs, but I've only had one acknowledgment* (= letter saying that my letter has been received) *so far.*
acknowledgments, acknowledgements /əkˈnɒl.ɪdʒ.mənts/ [US] /-ˈnɑː.lɪdʒ-/ *plural noun* a short text at the beginning or end of a book where the writer names people or other works that have helped in writing the book

the acme /ðiˈæk.mi/ *noun* [S] *LITERARY* the highest point of perfection or achievement: *To act on this world-famous stage is surely the acme* ***of*** *any actor's career.*

acne /ˈæk.ni/ *noun* [U] a skin disease common in young people, in which small red spots appear on the face and neck: *Acne is the curse of adolescence.*

acolyte /ˈæk.ᵊl.aɪt/ *noun* [C] *FORMAL OR SPECIALIZED* any follower or helper, or someone who helps a priest in some religious ceremonies

acorn /ˈeɪ.kɔːn/ [US] /-kɔːrn/ *noun* [C] an oval nut that grows on an OAK tree and has a cup-like outer part

acoustic /əˈkuː.stɪk/ *adj* **1** relating to sound or hearing: *The microphone converts acoustic waves to electrical signals for transmission.* **2** describes a musical instru-

ment that is not made louder by electrical equipment: *an acoustic guitar*
acoustic /əˈkuː.stɪk/ *noun* [C usually pl] the way in which the structural characteristics of a building or room affect the qualities of musical or spoken sound: *The concert was recorded in a French church that is famous for its acoustics.* **acoustically** /əˈkuː.stɪ.kli/ *adv*
acoustics /əˈkuː.stɪks/ *noun* [U] *SPECIALIZED* the scientific study of sound

acquaint /əˈkweɪnt/ *verb*
▲ **acquaint *sb* with *sth*** *phrasal verb FORMAL* to make someone or yourself aware of something: [R] *Take time to acquaint yourself with the rules.* ○ *The Broadcasting Museum also offers Saturday workshops to acquaint children with the world of radio.*

acquaintance /əˈkweɪn.tᵊnts/ *noun* **1** [C] a person that you have met but do not know well: *a business acquaintance* **2** [U] *FORMAL* used in some expressions about knowing or meeting people: *It was at the Taylors' party that I first **made his** acquaintance* (= first met him). ○ *I wasn't sure about Darryl when I first met her, but **on further** acquaintance* (= knowing her a little more) *I rather like her.* **3** [U] *FORMAL* knowledge of a subject: *Sadly, my acquaintance **with** Spanish literature is rather limited.*
• **have a passing/slight/nodding acquaintance with *sth*** *FORMAL* to have very little knowledge or experience of a subject: *I'm afraid I have only a nodding acquaintance with his works.*
acquaintanceship /əˈkweɪn.tᵊnt.ʃɪp/ *noun* [C or U] *FORMAL* *Ours was a strictly professional acquaintanceship* (= relationship).

acquainted /əˈkweɪn.tɪd/ [US] /-t̬ɪd/ *adj* [after v] *FORMAL* knowing or being familiar with a person: *"Do you know Daphne?" "No, I'm afraid we're not acquainted."* ○ *I am not personally acquainted **with** the gentleman in question.*
acquainted /əˈkweɪn.tɪd/ [US] /-t̬ɪd/ *adj FORMAL* **be acquainted with *sth*** to know or be familiar with something, because you have studied it or have experienced it before: *Police said the thieves were obviously well acquainted with the alarm system at the department store.*

acquiesce /ˌæk.wiˈes/ *verb* [I] *FORMAL* to accept or agree to something, often unwillingly: *Reluctantly, he acquiesced **to/in** the plans.*
acquiescent /ˌæk.wiˈes.ᵊnt/ *adj*: *FORMAL* *She has a very acquiescent nature* (= agrees to everything without complaining). **acquiescence** /ˌæk.wiˈes.ᵊnts/ *noun* [U] *I was surprised by her acquiescence **to/in** the scheme.*

acquire /əˈkwaɪəʳ/ [US] /-ˈkwaɪɚ/ *verb* [T] to obtain something: *He acquired the firm in 1978.* ○ *I was wearing a **newly/recently** acquired jacket.* ○ *I **seem to** have acquired* (= obtained although I don't know how) *two copies of this book.* ○ *During this period he acquired **a reputation** for being a womanizer.*
• **an acquired taste** something that you dislike at first, but that you start to like after you have tried it a few times: *Olives are an acquired taste.*
acquirer /əˈkwaɪ.rəʳ/ [US] /-rɚ/ *noun* [C] *MAINLY US* a company that buys other companies, usually to sell them for a profit: *A business with so much growth is sure to generate interest among potential acquirers.*
acquisition /ˌæk.wɪˈzɪʃ.ᵊn/ *noun* [C or U] *The museum has been heavily criticized over its acquisition **of** the four-million-dollar sculpture.* ○ *I like your earrings – are they **a recent** acquisition* (= did you get them recently)*?*
acquisitive /əˈkwɪz.ɪ.tɪv/ [US] /-ə.t̬ɪv/ *adj FORMAL MAINLY DISAPPROVING* eager to possess and collect things: *We live in an acquisitive society which views success primarily in terms of material possessions.*

acquit [DECIDE NOT GUILTY] /əˈkwɪt/ *verb* [T often passive] **-tt-** to decide officially in a court of law that someone is not guilty of a particular crime: *She was acquitted **of** all the charges against her.* ○ *Five months ago he was acquitted on a shoplifting charge.* ➲Compare **convict**. **acquittal** /əˈkwɪt.ᵊl/ [US] /-ˈkwɪt̬-/ *noun* [C or U] *The first trial ended in a hung jury, the second in acquittal.* ○ *Of the three cases that went to trial, two ended in acquittals.*

acˈquit yourself [PERFORM] *verb* [R] *FORMAL* to do better than expected in a difficult situation: *I thought that he acquitted himself admirably in today's meeting.*

acre /ˈeɪ.kəʳ/ [US] /-kɚ/ *noun* [C] a unit for measuring area, equal to 4047 square metres or 4840 square yards: *He's got 400 acres of land in Wales.*
acreage /ˈeɪ.kᵊr.ɪdʒ/ [US] /-kɚ-/ *noun* [U] *What acreage is her estate* (= How big is it, measured in acres)*?*

acrid /ˈæk.rɪd/ *adj* describes a smell or taste that is strong and bitter and causes a burning feeling in the throat: *Clouds of acrid **smoke** issued from the building.*

acrimonious /ˌæk.rɪˈməʊ.ni.əs/ [US] /-ˈmoʊ-/ *adj FORMAL* full of anger, arguments and bad feeling: *an acrimonious dispute* ○ *Their marriage ended eight years ago in an acrimonious **divorce**.* **acrimoniously** /ˌæk.rɪˈməʊ.ni.ə.sli/ [US] /-ˈmoʊ-/ *adv*: *In 1967, he separated acrimoniously from his wife.* **acrimony** /ˈæk.rɪ.mə.ni/ *noun* [U] *The acrimony of the dispute has shocked a lot of people.*

acrobat /ˈæk.rə.bæt/ *noun* [C] a person who entertains people by doing difficult and skilful physical things, such as walking along a high wire
acrobatic /ˌæk.rəˈbæt.ɪk/ [US] /-ˈbæt̬-/ *adj*: *an acrobatic* (= skilled and graceful) *leap into the air* ○ *an acrobatic young dancer* **acrobatics** /ˌæk.rəˈbæt.ɪks/ [US] /-ˈbæt̬-/ *noun* [U] *He had spent the last ten years in a Peking Opera school, studying martial arts and acrobatics.*

acronym /ˈæk.rəʊ.nɪm/ [US] /-rə-/ *noun* [C] an abbreviation consisting of the first letters of each word in the name of something, pronounced as a word: *AIDS is an acronym for 'Acquired Immune Deficiency Syndrome'.*

across /əˈkrɒs/ [US] /-ˈkrɑːs/ *adv, prep* from one side to the other of something with clear limits, such as an area of land, a road or river: *She walked across the field/road.* ○ *They're building a new bridge across the river.*
across /əˈkrɒs/ [US] /-ˈkrɑːs/ *prep* **1** on the opposite side of: *The library is just across the road.* **2** in every part of a particular place or country: *Voting took place peacefully across most of the country.*
• **across country** travelling in a direction where roads or public transport do not go, or where main roads or railways do not go: *Getting a train across country from Cambridge to Chester can be difficult.*
• **across the board** happening or having an effect on people at every level and in every area: *The improvement has been across the board, with all divisions either increasing profits or reducing losses.* ○ *The initiative has across-the-board support.*

acrostic /əˈkrɒs.tɪk/ [US] /-ˈkrɑː.stɪk/ *noun* [C] *SPECIALIZED* a text, usually a poem, in which particular letters, such as the first letters of each line, spell a word or phrase

acrylic /əˈkrɪl.ɪk/ *adj* made of a substance or cloth produced by chemical processes from a type of acid: *an acrylic scarf/sweater* ○ *acrylic paint*
acrylic /əˈkrɪl.ɪk/ *noun* **1** [U] a type of cloth or plastic produced by chemical processes **2** [C usually pl] a type of paint

act [DO SOMETHING] /ækt/ *verb* [I] to do something for a particular purpose, or to behave in the stated way: [+ to infinitive] *Engineers acted quickly **to** repair the damaged pipes.* ○ *She acted without thinking.* ○ *The anaesthetic acted* (= had an effect) *quickly.* ○ *Who is acting **for/on behalf of*** (= who is representing) *the defendant?* ○ *He acted **as if** he'd never met me before.* ○ *Don't be so silly – you're acting **like** a child!* ○ *He never acts **on** other people's advice* (= does what other people suggest). ○ *Acting **on impulse*** (= without thinking first) *can get you into a lot of trouble.* **act** /ækt/ *noun* [C] *an act **of** aggression/bravery/madness/terrorism* ○ *a kind/thoughtless/selfish act* ○ *The **sexual** act itself meant little to her.* ○ *The simple act of telling someone about a problem can help.* ○ *Primitive people regarded storms as an act **of God**.*
acting /ˈæk.tɪŋ/ *adj* **acting chairman/manager, etc.** someone who does a job for a short time while the person who usually does that job is not there: *He'll be the acting director until they can appoint a permanent one.* ➲See also **acting** at **act** PERFORM.

act [PERFORM] /ækt/ *verb* [I or T] to play a part; to perform in a film, play, etc: *Ellis Pike was chosen to act the **part** of*

[A]

the lawyer in the film. ○ *Have you ever acted* ***in*** *a play before?*

• **act the fool/martyr, etc.** to behave in a particular, usually bad, way: *Why are you always acting the fool?*

act /ækt/ *noun* **1** [S] behaviour which hides your real feelings or intentions: *Was she really upset or was that just an act?* **2** [C] a person or group that performs a short piece in a show, or the piece that they perform: *a comedy/juggling/trapeze act* ○ *Our next act is a very talented young musician.* **3** [C] a part of a play or opera: *Shakespeare's plays were written in five acts.* ○ *The hero does not enter until the second act/Act Two.*

• **do a disappearing/vanishing act** to go away, usually because you do not want to do something or meet someone: *Tim always does a vanishing act when my mother comes to stay.*

• **get/muscle in on the act** *INFORMAL* to take advantage of something that someone else started: *We did all the hard work of setting up the company, and now everyone wants to get in on the act.*

• **get** ***your*** **act together** *INFORMAL* to start to organize yourself so that you do things in an effective way: *She's so disorganized – I wish she'd get her act together.*

• **be a hard/tough act to follow** *INFORMAL* to be so good it is not likely that anyone or anything that comes after will be as good: *His presidency was very successful – it'll be a hard act to follow.*

• **put on an act** *INFORMAL* to behave or speak in a false or artificial way: *He's just putting on an act for the boss's benefit.*

acting /ˈæk.tɪŋ/ *noun* [U] the job of performing in films or plays: *He wants to get into acting.* ➲See also **acting** at **act** DO SOMETHING.

actor /ˈæk.təʳ/ [US] /-tɚ/ *noun* [C] (*FEMALE ALSO* **actress**) someone who pretends to be someone else while performing in a film, theatrical performance, or television or radio programme: *"Who's your favourite actor?" "Robert de Niro."* ○ *She's the highest-paid actress in Hollywood.*

act [LAW] /ækt/ *noun* [C] *LEGAL* a law or formal decision made by a parliament or other group of elected lawmakers: *an act of parliament* ○ *the Betting and Gaming Act* ○ *Almost two hundred suspects were detained in Britain last year* ***under*** *the Prevention of Terrorism Act.* ○ *The state legislature* ***passed*** *an act banning the sale of automatic weapons.*

PHRASAL VERBS WITH **act** ▼

▲ **act as** ***sth*** [JOB] *phrasal verb* to do a particular job, especially one that you do not normally do: *He was asked to act as an advisor on the project.*

▲ **act as** ***sth*** [EFFECT] *phrasal verb* to have a particular effect: *Some people say that capital punishment acts as a deterrent.*

▲ **act** ***sth*** **out** [PERFORM] *phrasal verb* [M] to perform the actions and say the words of a situation or story: *The children acted out their favourite poem.*

▲ **act** ***sth*** **out** [EXPRESS] *phrasal verb* [M] to express your thoughts, emotions or ideas in your actions: *Children's negative feelings often get acted out in bad behaviour.*

▲ **act up** [BEHAVE BADLY] *phrasal verb* If a person, especially a child, acts up, they behave badly: *Sophie got bored and started acting up.*

▲ **act up** [NOT PERFORM] *phrasal verb INFORMAL* If a machine or part of the body acts up, it does not perform as well as it should: *My car always acts up in cold weather.* ○ *Her shoulder was acting up* (= hurting because of injury).

action [DOING SOMETHING] /ˈæk.ʃᵊn/ *noun* [U] the process of doing something, especially when dealing with a problem or difficulty: *This problem calls for* ***swift/prompt*** *action from the government.* ○ [+ to infinitive] *Action* ***to*** *prevent the spread of the disease is high on the government's agenda.* ○ *We must* ***take*** *action* (= do something) *to deal with the problem before it spreads to other areas.* ○ *So what's the* ***plan of*** *action* (= What are we going to do)? ○ *The complaints system* ***swings into*** *action* (= starts to work) *as soon as a claim is made.* ○ *The committee was* ***spurred into*** *action* (= encouraged to do something) *by the threat of government cuts.*

• **be out of action** If a machine or vehicle is out of action, it is not working or cannot be used: *I'm afraid the TV's out of action.*

• **out of action** If an athlete is out of action, they are injured or ill and cannot compete: *Jackson's torn ligaments will keep him out of action for the rest of the season.*

action [SOMETHING DONE] /ˈæk.ʃᵊn/ *noun* [C] **1** something that you do: *She has to accept the consequences of her actions.* ○ *I asked him to explain his actions.* **2** a physical movement: *I'll say the words and you can mime the actions.* ○ *It only needs a small wrist action* (= movement of the wrist) *to start the process.*

• **Actions speak louder than words.** *SAYING* said to emphasize that what you do is more important and shows your intentions and feelings more clearly than what you say

action [ACTIVITY] /ˈæk.ʃᵊn/ *noun* [U] things which are happening, especially exciting or important things: *I like films with a lot of action.* ○ *In her last novel, the action* (= the main events) *moves between Greece and southern Spain.*

• **a man of action** a man who prefers to do things rather than think about and discuss them

• **a piece/slice of the action** *INFORMAL* involvement in something successful that someone else has started: *Now research has proved that the drug is effective everyone wants a slice of the action.*

• **where the action is** at the place where something important or interesting is happening: *A journalist has to be where the action is.*

action [WAR] /ˈæk.ʃᵊn/ *noun* [U] fighting in a war: *Her younger son was* ***killed in*** *action.* ○ *He was reported* ***missing in*** *action.* ○ *He* ***saw*** *action* (= fought as a soldier) *in the trenches.*

action [MOVEMENT] /ˈæk.ʃᵊn/ *noun* [C or U] the way something moves or works: *We studied the action of the digestive system.* ○ *The car has a very smooth braking action.*

action [EFFECT] /ˈæk.ʃᵊn/ *noun* [S] the effect something has on another thing: *They recorded the action of the drug* ***on*** *the nervous system.*

action [LEGAL PROCESS] /ˈæk.ʃᵊn/ *noun* [C or U] a legal process that is decided in a court of law: *a libel action* ○ *She* ***brought*** *an action* ***(for*** *negligence)* ***against*** *the hospital.* ○ *A* ***criminal*** *action was* ***brought against*** *him.* ○ *The book was halted in South Africa by a threat of* ***legal*** *action.*

actionable /ˈæk.ʃᵊn.ə.bl̩/ *adj SPECIALIZED* If something is actionable, it gives someone a good reason for making an accusation in a law court: *She denies that her company has been involved in any actionable activity.*

action [DEAL WITH] /ˈæk.ʃᵊn/ *verb* [T usually passive] to do something to deal with a particular problem or matter: *I'll just run through the minutes of the last meeting, raising those points which still have to be actioned.*

action-packed /ˌæk.ʃᵊnˈpækt/ *adj* full of exciting events: *an action-packed thriller/weekend/finale*

ˌaction ˈreplay *UK noun* [C] (*US* **instant replay**) a repeat of an important moment from a sports event shown on television, often more slowly to show the action in detail: *They showed an action replay of the goal.*

ˈaction ˌstations *plural noun UK INFORMAL* **1** when you are as ready as possible to perform a task you have been preparing for: *The whole school was* ***at*** *action stations for the inspectors' visit.* **2 action stations!** used to tell people to get ready immediately to do the particular jobs which they have been given to do: *Right, everyone – action stations! We're starting the show in 3 minutes.*

activate /ˈæk.tɪ.veɪt/ [US] /-t̬ɪ-/ *verb* [T] **1** to cause something to start: *The alarm is activated by the lightest pressure.* **2** *SPECIALIZED* to make a chemical reaction happen more quickly, especially by heating **activation** /ˌæk.tɪˈveɪ.ʃᵊn/ [US] /-t̬ɪ-/ *noun* [U]

active [BUSY/INVOLVED] /ˈæk.tɪv/ *adj* **1** busy with or ready to perform a particular activity: *physically and mentally active* ○ *You've got to try to* ***keep*** *active as you grow older.* ○ *Enemy forces remain active in the mountainous areas around the city.* ○ *She's very active* ***in*** (= involved in) *local politics.* ○ *Both of his parents were very* ***politically*** *active.* ○ *It is important to educate children before they become* ***sexually*** *active.* ○ *He takes a more active* ***role*** *in the team nowadays.* ○ *She's an active* ***member*** *of her trade union* (= not only belongs to it, but does work to help it). **2** describes a volcano that might ERUPT (= throw out hot liquid rock or other matter) at any time

actively /ˈæk.tɪv.li/ *adv*: *He's very actively* ***involved*** *in* (= does a lot of work for) *the local Labour Party.* ○ *It's nice having a man who actively* ***encourages*** *me to spend money.* ○ *I've been actively looking for a job* (= trying hard to find one) *for six months.*

active [GRAMMAR] /ˈæk.tɪv/ *adj* An active verb or sentence is one in which the subject is the person or thing which performs the stated action: *'Catrin told me' is an active sentence, and 'I was told by Catrin' is passive.* ➲Compare **the passive** GRAMMAR.

activism /ˈæk.tɪ.vɪ.zᵊm/ *noun* [U] the use of direct and noticeable action to achieve a result, usually a political or social one: *black/student activism* ○ *The levels of trade union and* ***political*** *activism in this country have greatly declined in the past fifteen years.*

activist /ˈæk.tɪ.vɪst/ *noun* [C] a person who believes strongly in political or social change and works hard to try and make this happen: *He's been a trade union/party activist for many years.* ○ *a gay activist*

activity [MOVEMENT] /ækˈtɪv.ɪ.ti/ [US] /-ə.t̬i/ *noun* [U] when a lot of things are happening or people are moving around: *There was a lot of activity in preparation for the Queen's visit.* ○ *Ministers are concerned by the low level of* ***economic*** *activity.* ○ *There was a sudden* ***flurry of*** *activity when the director walked in.*

activity [WORK] /ækˈtɪv.ɪ.ti/ [US] /-ə.t̬i/ *noun* [C or U] the work of a group or organization to achieve an aim: *He was found guilty of* ***terrorist*** *activity.* ○ *criminal activities*

activity [ENJOYMENT] /ækˈtɪv.ɪ.ti/ [US] /-ə.t̬i/ *noun* [C usually pl] something that is done for enjoyment, especially an organized event: *His spare-time activities include cooking, tennis and windsurfing.* ○ *We offer our guests a wide range of outdoor/sporting activities.*

actor *noun* [C] (*ALSO* **actress**) ➲See at **act** PERFORM.

actual /ˈæk.tʃu.əl/ /-tju-/ /-tʃʊl/ *adj* [before n] real; existing in fact: *We had estimated about 300 visitors, but the actual number was much higher.* ○ *The exams are in July, but the actual results* (= the results themselves) *don't appear until September.*

• **in actual fact** really: *I thought she was Portuguese, but in actual fact she's Brazilian.*

actuality /ˌæk.tʃuˈæl.ə.ti/ /-tju-/ [US] /-ə.t̬i/ *noun* [C usually pl] *FORMAL* a fact: *He's out of touch with the actualities of life in Africa.*

• **in actuality** *FORMAL* really: *In actuality, there were few job losses last year.*

COMMON LEARNER ERROR

actual or current ?

Use **actual** when you mean 'real'.

His friends call him Jo-Jo, but his actual name is John.

Use **current** to talk about things which are happening or which exist now.

She started her current job two years ago.
the current economic situation
~~*the actual economic situation*~~

actually [IN FACT] /ˈæk.tʃu.ə.li/ /-tju-/ /-tʃʊ.li/ *adv* in fact or really: *I didn't actually see her – I just heard her voice.* ○ *So what actually happened?*

actually [SURPRISE] /ˈæk.tʃu.ə.li/ /-tju-/ /-tʃʊ.li/ *adv* used in sentences in which there is information that is in some way surprising or the opposite of what most people would expect: *I didn't like him at first, but in the end I actually got quite fond of him.* ○ *I'm one of the few people who doesn't actually like champagne.* ○ *HUMOROUS Don't tell me he actually paid for you! You are honoured!*

actually [OPPOSITE] /ˈæk.tʃu.ə.li/ /-tju-/ /-tʃʊ.li/ *adv* used as a way of making a sentence slightly more polite, for example when you are expressing an opposing opinion, correcting what someone else has said or refusing an offer: *"Alexander looks like he'd be good at sports." "Actually, he's not."* ○ *Actually, Gavin, it was Tuesday of last week, not Wednesday.* ○ *"Do you mind if I smoke?" "Well, actually, I'd rather you didn't."*

actuary /ˈæk.tju.ə.ri/ [US] /-er.i/ *noun* [C] a person who calculates the probability of accidents, such as fire, flood or loss of property, and informs insurance companies how much they should charge their customers

actuate /ˈæk.tʃu.eɪt/ /-tju-/ *verb* [T] *SPECIALIZED OR FORMAL* to make a machine work or be the reason a person acts in a certain way: *A detonator is any device containing an explosive that is actuated by heat, percussion, friction, or electricity.* ○ *He was actuated almost entirely by altruism.*

acuity /əˈkjuː.ə.ti/ [US] /-ə.t̬i/ *noun* [U] *FORMAL* the ability to hear, see or think accurately and clearly: *Tiredness also affects visual acuity.* ○ *He was a man of great political acuity.*

.ac.uk /ˌækˈʌk/ *INTERNET ABBREVIATION FOR* the last part of an Internet address that belongs to a British university or college

acumen /ˈæk.jʊ.mən/ *noun* [U] *FORMAL* skill in making correct decisions and judgments in a particular subject, such as business or politics: *She has considerable* ***business/financial*** *acumen.*

acupuncture /ˈæk.jʊ.pʌŋk.tʃəʳ/ [US] /-tʃɚ/ *noun* [U] a treatment for pain and illness in which thin needles are positioned just under the surface of the skin at special nerve centres around the body: *Acupuncture originated in China.*

acute [EXTREME] /əˈkjuːt/ *adj* **1** If a bad situation is acute, it causes severe problems or damage: *She felt acute embarrassment/anxiety/concern at his behaviour.* ○ *The problem of poverty is particularly acute in rural areas.* **2** An acute pain or illness is one that quickly becomes very severe: *acute abdominal pains* ○ *an acute* ***attack*** *of appendicitis*

acutely /əˈkjuːt.li/ *adv* completely or extremely: *Management is acutely* ***aware*** *of the resentment that their decision may cause.* ○ *Another scandal would be acutely* ***embarrassing*** *for the government.* **acuteness** /əˈkjuːt.nəs/ *noun* [U]

acute [ACCURATE/CLEVER] /əˈkjuːt/ *adj* (of the senses, intelligence, etc.) very good, accurate and able to notice very small differences: *acute eyesight/hearing* ○ *an acute sense of smell* ○ *a woman of acute intelligence/judgement*
acutely /əˈkjuːt.li/ *adv* **acuteness** /əˈkjuːt.nəs/ *noun* [U]

acute [ANGLE] /əˈkjuːt/ *adj* describes an angle that is less than 90 degrees ➲Compare **obtuse** ANGLE.

aˌcute (ˈaccent) *noun* [C] a sign which is written above a letter in some languages, showing you how to pronounce the letter: *There's an acute accent on the e in blé which is the French word for corn.*

ad /æd/ *noun* [C] *INFORMAL FOR* **advertisement**, see at **advertise**: *I often prefer the ads on TV to the actual programmes.*

AD, *US USUALLY* **A.D.** /ˌeɪˈdiː/ *adv ABBREVIATION FOR* Anno Domini: used in the Christian CALENDAR when referring to a year after Jesus Christ was born: *in 1215 AD/AD 1215* ○ *during the seventh century AD* ➲Compare **BC**.

adage /ˈæd.ɪdʒ/ *noun* [C] a wise saying; PROVERB: *He remembered the* ***old*** *adage 'Look before you leap'.*

ˈad ˌagency *noun* [C] a company that produces advertisements

Adam /ˈæd.əm/ *noun* a character in the Bible who was the first man made by God

adamant /ˈæd.ə.mənt/ *adj* impossible to persuade, or unwilling to change an opinion or decision: [+ **that**] *I've told her she should stay at home and rest but she's adamant* ***that*** *she's coming.* **adamantly** /ˈæd.ə.mənt.li/ *adv*: *The mayor is adamantly opposed to any tax increase.*

Adam's apple /ˌæd.əmzˈæp.l̩/ *noun* [C] the part of your throat that sticks out and tends to move up and down when you speak or swallow

adapt [CHANGE] /əˈdæpt/ *verb* [T] to change something to suit different conditions or uses: *Many software companies have adapted popular programs* ***to*** *the new operating system.* ○ *The recipe here is a pork roast* adapted *from Caroline O'Neill's book 'Louisiana Kitchen'.* ○ [+ **to** infinitive] *We had to adapt our plans **to** fit Jack's timetable.* ○ *The play had been adapted **for** (=* changed to make it suitable for) *children.* ○ *Davies is busy adapting Brinkworth's latest novel **for** television.*

adapted /ə'dæp.tɪd/ *adj: Both trees are **well** adapted **to** London's dry climate and dirty air.*

adaptable /ə'dæp.tə.bļ/ *adj* able or willing to change in order to suit different conditions: *The survivors in this life seem to be those who are adaptable **to** change.*

adaptability /ə,dæp.tə'bɪl.ɪ.ti/ ⓤ /-ə.t̬i/ *noun* [U] *Adaptability is a necessary quality in an ever-changing work environment.*

adaptation /,æd.əp'teɪ.ʃ⁰n/ *noun* [C or U] *Evolution occurs as a result of adaptation (=* the process of changing) *to new environments.* ○ *Last year she starred in the film adaptation of Bill Cronshaw's best-selling novel.*

adaptive /ə'dæp.tɪv/ *adj* SPECIALIZED possessing an ability to change to suit different conditions

adapt BECOME FAMILIAR /ə'dæpt/ *verb* [I] to become familiar with a new situation: *The good thing about children is that they adapt very easily **to** new environments.* ○ *It took me a while to adapt **to** the new job.*

adapter DEVICE, **adaptor** /ə'dæp.tə'/ ⓤ /-t̬ɚ/ *noun* [C] **1** MAINLY UK a type of **plug** ELECTRICAL DEVICE which makes it possible to connect two or more pieces of equipment to the same electrical supply **2** a device which is used to connect two pieces of equipment

adapter WRITER, **adaptor** /ə'dæp.tə'/ ⓤ /-t̬ɚ/ *noun* [C] a person who makes slight changes to a book, play or other piece of text so that it can be performed

ADC /,eɪ.diː'siː/ *noun* [C] ABBREVIATION FOR **aide-de-camp**

add /æd/ *verb* [I or T] to put something with something else to increase the number or amount or to improve the whole: *If you add (=* calculate the total of) *three and four you get seven.* ○ *Beat the butter and sugar together and slowly add the eggs.* ○ *She's added a Picasso to her collection.* ○ *Her colleagues' laughter only added **to** (=* increased) *her embarrassment.* ○ [+ **that**] *She was sad, she said, but added (=* said also) *that she felt she had made the right decision.* ○ [+ speech] *"Oh, and thank you for all your help!" he added as he was leaving.* ○ *It's $45 – $50 if you add **in** (=* include) *the cost of postage.* ○ *Don't forget to add **on** your travelling expenses/add your expenses **on**.*

● **to add insult to injury** said when you feel that someone has made a bad situation worse by doing something else to upset you: *They told me I was too old for the job, and then to add insult to injury, they refused to pay my expenses!*

added /'æd.ɪd/ *adj* extra: *He had the added disadvantage of being the only man present.* ○ *She lost her job last week, and now added **to that** she's pregnant again.*

addition /ə'dɪʃ.⁰n/ *noun* [C or U] *Twice a week the children are tested in basic mathematical skills such as addition (=* calculating the total of different numbers put together) *and subtraction.* ○ *Most working environments are improved by **the** addition **of** (=* adding) *a few plants and pictures.* ○ *A secretary would be **a welcome/useful** addition **to** our staff.* ○ **In** addition **to** his flat in London, he has a villa in Italy and a castle in Scotland. ○ HUMOROUS *I hear you're expecting a small addition **to** the family (=* you are going to have a baby)*!*

additional /ə'dɪʃ.⁰n.⁰l/ *adj* extra: *additional costs/problems* ○ *There will be an extra charge for any additional passengers.*

additionally /ə'dɪʃ.⁰n.⁰l.i/ *adv: Additionally (=* also)*, we request a deposit of $200 in advance.*

PHRASAL VERBS WITH **add** ▼

▲ **add (sth) up** *phrasal verb* [M] to calculate the total of two or more numbers: *If you add those four figures up, it comes to over £500.* ○ *She added the bill up.* ○ *I'm not very good at adding up!*

● **not add up** INFORMAL If a situation does not add up, there is no reasonable or likely explanation for it: *Why would she disappear the day before her holiday? It just doesn't add up.*

▲ **add up to** *sth* AMOUNT *phrasal verb* to become a particular amount: *The various building programmes add up to several thousand new homes.* ○ *We thought*

we'd bought lots of food, but it didn't add up to much when we'd spread it out on the table.

▲ **add up to** *sth* RESULT *phrasal verb* to have a particular result or effect: *It all added up to a lot of hard work for all of us.* ○ *Their proposals do not add up to any real help for the poor.*

ADD /,eɪ.diː'diː/ *US ABBREVIATION FOR* Attention Deficit Disorder: a condition in which someone, especially a child, is often in a state of activity or excitement and unable direct their attention towards what they are doing

addendum /ə'den.dəm/ *noun* [C] *plural* **addenda** SPECIALIZED something that has been added to a book, speech or document

adder /'æd.ə'/ ⓤ /-ɚ/ *noun* [C] a type of poisonous snake

addict /'æd.ɪkt/ *noun* [C] a person who cannot stop doing or using something, especially something harmful: *a drug/heroin addict* ○ *a gambling addict* ○ HUMOROUS *I'm a chocolate/shopping addict.*

addicted /ə'dɪk.tɪd/ *adj: By the age of 14 he was addicted **to** heroin.* ○ *I'm addicted **to** (=* I very often eat/drink) *chocolate/lattes.* ○ *I know that if I start watching a soap opera I immediately become **hopelessly** addicted.* addiction /ə'dɪk.ʃ⁰n/ *noun* [C or U] *drug addiction* ○ *his addiction to alcohol*

addictive /ə'dɪk.tɪv/ *adj* **1** An addictive drug is one which you cannot stop taking once you have started: *Tobacco is **highly** addictive.* **2** describes an activity or food that you cannot stop doing or eating once you have started: *The problem with video games is that they're addictive.* ○ *These nuts are addictive – I can't stop eating them.* **3** **addictive personality** a set of characteristics which mean that you very quickly become addicted to drugs, food, alcohol, etc: *He's got an addictive personality.*

additive /'æd.ɪ.tɪv/ ⓤ /-ə.t̬ɪv/ *noun* [C] a substance which is added to food in order to improve its taste or appearance or to preserve it: *food additives* ○ *This margarine is **full of** additives – just look at the label!*

addle /'æd.ļ/ *verb* [T] MAINLY HUMOROUS to make someone feel confused and unable to think clearly: *I think my brain's been addled by the heat!*

addled /'æd.ļd/ *adj*: MAINLY HUMOROUS *I'm afraid my sun-addled (=* confused) *brain couldn't make any sense of the instructions.*

add-on /'æd.ɒn/ ⓤ /-ɑːn/ *noun* [C] **1** a piece of equipment which can be connected to a computer to give it an extra use: *A modem is a useful add-on.* **2** an extra part which is added, especially to an officially organized plan, system, agreement, etc: *Legal expenses cover is often sold as an add-on **to** household insurance policies.*

address HOME DETAILS /ə'dres/ ⓤ /'æd.res/ *noun* [C] **1** the number of the house and name of the road and town where a person lives or works and where letters can be sent: *her business/home address* ○ *a change of address* ○ *I'll just look her phone number up in my address **book**.* **2** SPECIALIZED the place where a piece of information is stored in a computer's memory

address /ə'dres/ *verb* [T] to write a name or address on an envelope or parcel: *The parcel was wrongly addressed.* ○ *So why did you open a letter that was addressed **to** me?*

addressee /,æd.res'iː/ *noun* [C] a person whose name or address is written on a letter or parcel

address SPEAK TO /ə'dres/ *verb* [T] FORMAL to speak or write to someone: *He addressed a few introductory remarks to the audience.* ○ *He likes to be addressed **as** 'Sir' or 'Mr Partridge'.*

address /ə'dres/ ⓤ /'æd.res/ *noun* [C] a formal speech: *She gave an address **to** the Royal Academy.*

address DEAL WITH /ə'dres/ *verb* [T] to give attention to or deal with a matter or problem: *The **issue** of funding has yet to be addressed.*

adduce /ə'djuːs/ ⓤ /-'duːs/ *verb* [T often passive] FORMAL to give reasons why you think something is true: *None of the evidence adduced in court was conclusive.*

adenoids /'æd.ə'n.ɔɪdz/ *plural noun* the soft mass of flesh between the back of the nose and the throat, which sometimes makes breathing difficult **adenoidal** /ˌæd.ᵊn'ɔɪ.dᵊl/ *adj*

adept /ə'dept/ *adj* having a natural ability to do something that needs skill: *She's very adept* ***at dealing*** *with the media.* ○ *Tamsin Palmer gave an impressive and technically adept performance on the piano.* **adeptly** /ə'dept.li/ *adv*

adequate /'æd.ə.kwət/ *adj* enough or satisfactory for a particular purpose: *Have we got adequate food for twenty guests?* ○ *I didn't have adequate time to prepare.* ○ *It's not by any means a brilliant salary but it's adequate* ***for*** *our needs.* ○ *The council's provision for the elderly is* ***barely*** *adequate* (= is not enough). ○ **[+ to infinitive]** *Will future oil supplies be adequate* ***to*** *meet world needs?* ✻ NOTE: The opposite is **inadequate**. **adequately** /'æd.ə.kwət.li/ *adv*: *While some patients can be adequately cared for at home, others are best served by care in a hospital.* **adequacy** /'æd.ə.kwə.si/ *noun* **[U]** *The adequacy of public health care has been brought into question.*

ADHD /ˌeɪ.diː.eɪtʃ'diː/ *noun* **[U]** *MAINLY UK ABBREVIATION FOR* **attention deficit hyperactivity disorder**

adhere /əd'hɪəʳ/ [US] /-'hɪr/ *verb* **[I]** *FORMAL* to stick firmly: *A smooth, dry surface helps the tiles adhere* ***to*** *the wall.*
adherent /əd'hɪə.rənt/ [US] /-'hɪr.ᵊnt/ *adj FORMAL* sticky: *an adherent surface*
adhesion /əd'hiː.ʒən/ *noun* **[U]** the ability to stick: *At this stage a resin is used with a high level of adhesion.*
▲ **adhere to** ***sth*** *phrasal verb FORMAL* to continue to obey a rule or maintain a belief: *She adhered to her principles/ideals throughout her life.* ○ *They failed to adhere to the terms of the agreement/treaty.* ○ *The translator has obviously adhered very* ***strictly*** *to the original text.*
adherence /əd'hɪə.rənts/ [US] /-'hɪr.ᵊnts/ *noun* **[U]** *He was noted for his strict adherence* ***to*** *the rules.*
adherent /əd'hɪə.rənt/ [US] /-'hɪr.ᵊnt/ *noun* **[C]** *FORMAL* a person who strongly supports a particular person, principle or set of ideas: *She has long been an adherent of the Communist Party.*

adhesive /əd'hiː.sɪv/ *noun* **[C or U]** glue: *You'll need a/some strong adhesive to mend that chair.*
adhesive /əd'hiː.sɪv/ *adj* sticky: *adhesive tape/paper*

ad hoc /ˌæd'hɒk/ [US] /-'hɑːk/ *adj* **[before n]** made or happening only for a particular purpose or need, not planned in advance: *an ad hoc committee/meeting* ○ *We deal with problems* ***on an*** *ad hoc* ***basis*** (= as they happen).

adieu /ə'djuː/ /-'djʊ/ [US] /-'duː/ *exclamation LITERARY OR OLD USE* goodbye: *She* ***bade*** (= said to) *him adieu and left.*

ad infinitum /ˌæd.ɪn.fɪ'naɪ.təm/ [US] /-t̬əm/ *adv* forever, without ending: *"Why was she such a lousy boss?" "Oh, because she was unreasonable, disrespectful, rude, inconsiderate – I could go on ad infinitum."*

adios /ˌæd.i'ɒs/ [US] /-'oʊs/ *exclamation MAINLY US INFORMAL* goodbye

adipose /'æd.ɪ.pəʊs/ /-pəʊz/ [US] /-ə.poʊs/ *adj* **[before n]** *SPECIALIZED* of animal fat: *adipose* ***tissue*** (= fat)

adj *noun ABBREVIATION FOR* **adjective**

adjacent /ə'dʒeɪ.sᵊnt/ *adj FORMAL* very near, next to, or touching: *They work in adjacent buildings.* ○ *They lived in a house adjacent* ***to*** *the railway.*

adjective /'ædʒ.ek.tɪv/ *noun* **[C]** a word that describes a noun or pronoun: *'Big', 'boring', 'purple', 'quick' and 'obvious' are all adjectives.* **adjectival** /ˌædʒ.ek'taɪ.vᵊl/ *adj*: *an adjectival phrase* **adjectivally** /ˌædʒ.ek'taɪ.vᵊl.i/ *adv*: *In 'kitchen table', the noun 'kitchen' is used adjectivally.*

adjoin /ə'dʒɔɪn/ *verb* **[I or T]** *FORMAL* to be very near, next to, or touching: *The stables adjoin the west wing of the house.* ○ *It's at this point that these three neighbourhoods adjoin.*
adjoining /ə'dʒɔɪ.nɪŋ/ *adj*: **[before n]** *We asked for adjoining rooms* (= rooms next to each other).

adjourn /ə'dʒɜːn/ [US] /-'dʒɝːn/ *verb* **[I or T]** *FORMAL* to have a pause or rest during a formal meeting or trial: *The meeting was adjourned* ***until*** *Tuesday.* ○ *Shall we adjourn* ***for*** *lunch?* **adjournment** /ə'dʒɜːn.mənt/ [US] /-'dʒɝːn-/ *noun* **[C or U]** *The defence attorney requested an adjournment.* ○ *The court's adjournment means that a decision will not be reached until December at the earliest.*
▲ **adjourn to** ***somewhere*** *phrasal verb HUMOROUS* to finish doing something and go somewhere, usually for a drink and some food: *Shall we adjourn to the sitting room for coffee?*

adjudge /ə'dʒʌdʒ/ *verb* **[T often passive]** *FORMAL* to announce a decision or consider something, especially officially: **[+ to infinitive]** *Half an hour into the game Paterson was adjudged* ***to*** *have fouled Jackson and was sent off.* ○ **[+ n or adj]** *In October 1990, Mirchandani was adjudged bankrupt.* ○ *Fairbanks was adjudged the winner, a decision which has outraged a good few members of the boxing fraternity.*

adjudicate /ə'dʒuː.dɪ.keɪt/ *verb* **[I or T]** to act as judge in a competition or argument, or to make a formal decision about something: *He was asked to adjudicate* ***on*** *the dispute.* ○ *He was called in to adjudicate a local land dispute.* ○ **[+ two objects]** *The game was adjudicated a win for Black.*
adjudication /əˌdʒuː.dɪ'keɪ.ʃᵊn/ *noun* **[C or U]** *The legality of the transaction is still* ***under*** *adjudication* (= being decided) *in the courts.* ○ *His adjudication was later found to be faulty.* **adjudicator** /ə'dʒuː.dɪ.keɪ.təʳ/ [US] /-t̬ɚ/ *noun* **[C]** *She acted as adjudicator in the dispute.*

adjunct /'ædʒ.ʌŋkt/ *noun* **[C]** *FORMAL* something added or connected to a larger or more important thing: *I hoped I would find the computer course a useful adjunct* ***to*** *my other studies.* ○ *In grammar, an adjunct is an adverb or adverbial phrase that gives extra information in a sentence.*

adjure /ə'dʒʊəʳ/ [US] /-'dʒʊr/ *verb* **[T + to infinitive]** *FORMAL* to ask or order someone to do something: *The judge adjured him* ***to*** *answer truthfully.*

adjust [CHANGE] /ə'dʒʌst.mənt/ *verb* **[T]** **1** to change something slightly, especially to make it more correct, effective, or suitable: *If the chair is too high you can adjust it to suit you.* ○ *As a teacher you have to adjust your methods to suit the needs of slower children.* **2** to arrange your clothing to make yourself look tidy: *She adjusted her skirt, took a deep breath and walked into the room.*
adjustable /ə'dʒʌs.tə.bl̩/ *adj* able to be changed to suit particular needs: *The height of the steering wheel is adjustable.* ○ *Is the strap on this helmet adjustable?*
adjustment /ə'dʒʌst.mənt/ *noun* **[C or U]** a small change: *She made a few* ***minor*** *adjustments* ***to*** *the focus of her camera.*

adjust [BECOME FAMILIAR] /ə'dʒʌst.mənt/ *verb* **[I]** to become more familiar with a new situation: *I can't adjust* ***to*** *liv*-***ing*** *on my own.* ○ *Her eyes slowly adjusted* ***to*** *the dark.* ○ *The lifestyle is so very different – it takes a while to adjust.*
adjustment /ə'dʒʌst.mənt/ *noun* **[C or U]** the ability to become more familiar with a new situation: *He has so far failed to make the adjustment* ***from*** *school* ***to*** *work.*

adjutant /'ædʒ.ʊ.tᵊnt/ *noun* **[C]** a military officer who does office work and who is responsible for rules and punishment among the lower ranks

ˌ**ad 'lib** *adj* **[before n]**, *adv* said without any preparation or thought in advance: *I'd forgotten the notes for my speech so I had to* ***do*** *it ad lib.* ○ *ad-lib comments*
ad-lib /ˌæd'lɪb/ *verb* **[I or T]** to speak in public without having planned what to say: *She ad-libbed her way through the entire speech.*

adman /'æd.mæn/ *noun* **[C]** a man who works in advertising

administer [MANAGE] /əd'mɪn.ɪ.stəʳ/ [US] /-stɚ/ *verb* **[T often passive]** to control the operation or arrangement of something; to manage or govern: *The country was administered by the British until very recently.* ○ *The economy has been badly administered by the present government.*
administration /ədˌmɪn.ɪ'streɪ.ʃᵊn/ *noun* **1** **[U]** (*INFORMAL* **admin**) the arrangements and tasks needed to control the operation of a plan or organization: *Teachers complain that more of their time is taken up with administration than with teaching.* ○ *She has little experience in administration* (= in organizing a business, etc.). **2** **[C]** a period of government in the United States: *the Bush administration/the last Republican administration*
administrative /əd'mɪn.ɪ.strə.tɪv/ [US] /-t̬ɪv/ *adj* relating to the arrangements and work which is needed to con-

trol the operation of a plan or organization: *administrative work* ○ *an administrative problem* ○ *Your responsibilities will be mainly administrative.* **administratively** /əd'mɪn.ɪs.trə.tɪv.li/ ⓤ /-t̬ɪv-/ *adv* **administrator** /əd'mɪn.ɪ.streɪ.tə^r/ ⓤ /-t̬ɚ/ *noun* [C] *From 1969 to 1971, he was administrator of the Illinois state drug abuse program.* ○ *She works as a school administrator.*

administer GIVE /əd'mɪn.ɪ.stə^r/ ⓤ /-stɚ/ *verb* [T] FORMAL **1** to cause someone to receive something: *to administer medicine/punishment/relief* ○ *Tests will be administered to schoolchildren at seven, twelve and sixteen years.* ○ FIGURATIVE *The latest opinion polls have administered a severe blow to the party.* **2 administer an oath to sb** to be present while someone says an OATH (= formal promise) officially

admiral /'æd.mɪ.rəl/ *noun* [C] an officer of very high rank in the navy: *Admiral Nelson*

the Admiralty /ðɪ'æd.mɪ.rəl.ti/ ⓤ /-t̬i/ *noun* [S] in the past, in Britain, the government department in charge of the navy

admire /əd'maɪə^r/ ⓤ /-'maɪr/ *verb* [T] to respect and approve of someone or their behaviour, or to find someone or something attractive and pleasant to look at: *I admired him for his determination.* ○ *I really admire people who can work in such difficult conditions.* ○ *We stood for a few moments, admiring the view.* ○ *I was just admiring your jacket, Delia.*

admirable /'æd.mɪ.rə.bl̩/ *adj* deserving respect or approval: *I think you showed admirable tact/restraint/self-control in your answer.* ○ *The police did an admirable job in keeping the fans calm.*

admirably /'æd.mɪ.rə.bli/ *adv*: *I think she coped admirably* (= very well) *with a very difficult situation.*

admiration /ˌæd.mɪ'reɪ.ʃ^ən/ *noun* [U] when you admire someone or something: *My admiration for that woman grows daily.* ○ *She gazed in admiration at his broad, muscular shoulders.*

admirer /əd'maɪə.rə^r/ ⓤ /-'maɪr.ɚ/ *noun* [C] someone who finds someone else sexually attractive, or someone who admires someone or something: *She's got plenty of admirers.* ○ *She's got a secret admirer who keeps sending her gifts.* ○ *The policy has few admirers* (= few people like it).

admiring /əd'maɪə.rɪŋ/ ⓤ /-'maɪr.ɪŋ/ *adj* showing admiration: *Annette was getting lots of admiring looks/glances in her new red dress.* ○ *She was surrounded by a group of admiring photographers.*

admiringly /əd'maɪə.rɪŋ.li/ ⓤ /-'maɪr.ɪŋ-/ *adv*: *The women sitting opposite us were gazing admiringly* (= with admiration) *at baby Joe.*

admissible /əd'mɪs.ɪ.bl̩/ *adj* FORMAL considered satisfactory and acceptable in a law court: *The judge ruled that new evidence was admissible.* ✳ NOTE: The opposite is **inadmissible**. **admissibility** /əd,mɪs.ə'bɪl.ɪ.ti/ ⓤ /-ə.t̬i/ *noun* [U]

admit ACCEPT /əd'mɪt/ *verb* [I or T] -tt- to agree that something is true, especially unwillingly: *He admitted his guilt/mistake.* ○ [+ (that)] *She admitted (that) she had made a mistake.* ○ [+ v-ing] *She admitted making a mistake.* ○ *At first he denied stealing the money but he later admitted (to) it.* ○ *I wasn't entirely honest with him, I admit, but I didn't actually tell him any lies.* ○ [+ to infinitive] *The new law was generally admitted to be difficult to enforce.*
● **admit defeat** to accept that you have failed and give up: *After several attempts to untie the knot, I admitted defeat and cut through it with a knife.*

admission /əd'mɪʃ.^ən/ *noun* [C or U] when you agree that something is true, especially unwillingly: *Her silence was taken as an admission of guilt/defeat.* ○ [+ that] *I felt he would see my giving up now as an admission that I was wrong.* ○ *By/On his own admission* (= as he has said) *he has achieved little since he took over the company.*

admittedly /əd'mɪt.ɪd.li/ ⓤ /-'mɪt̬-/ *adv* used when you are agreeing that something is true, especially unwillingly: *Admittedly, I could have tried harder but I still don't think all this criticism is fair.*

admit ALLOW IN /əd'mɪt/ *verb* [T] -tt- **1** to allow someone to enter a place: *Each ticket admits one member and one*

guest. ○ *Men will not be admitted to the restaurant without a tie.* ○ LITERARY *A gap between the curtains admitted the faint glimmer of a street lamp.* **2** to allow a person or country to join an organization: *Spain was admitted to the European Community in 1986.* **3** to allow someone to enter a hospital because they need medical care: *She was admitted to hospital* (US *to the hospital*) *suffering from shock.*

admission /əd'mɪʃ.^ən/ *noun* [C or U] when someone is given permission to enter a place, or the money that you pay to enter a place: *Admission to the exhibition will be by invitation only.* ○ *How much do they charge for admission.* ○ *The admission charge/fee is £2.* ○ *There's a notice outside the building which says 'No admission before 12 noon'.*

admissions /əd'mɪʃ.^ənz/ *plural noun* the people allowed into a college, hospital, or other place, or the process of allowing people in: *Half of all hospital admissions are emergencies, and these are treated straightaway.*

admittance /əd'mɪt.^ənts/ ⓤ /-'mɪt̬-/ *noun* [U] FORMAL permission to enter a place: *The sign read 'Private – no admittance'.* ○ *The enquiry centred on how the assassin had gained admittance to* (= succeeded in entering) *the building.*

▲ **admit of** *sth phrasal verb* FORMAL to allow something or make it possible: *The present schedule does not admit of modification* (= it cannot be changed). ○ *The latest events admit of several interpretations.*

admixture /əd'mɪks.tʃə^r/ ⓤ /-tʃɚ/ *noun* [C usually sing] SPECIALIZED something that is added to something else: *Platinum combines with phosphorus and arsenic and is seldom found without an admixture of related metals.*

admonish /əd'mɒn.ɪʃ/ ⓤ /-'mɑː.nɪʃ/ *verb* [T] to tell someone that they have done something wrong: *His mother admonished him for eating too quickly.* **2** [T + to infinitive] to advise someone to do something: *Her teacher admonished her to work harder for her exams.*

admonition /ˌæd.mə'nɪʃ.^ən/ *noun* [C] (ALSO **admonishment**) FORMAL a piece of advice that is also a warning to someone about their behaviour: *The most common parental admonition must surely be "Don't stay out late".* **admonitory** /əd'mɒn.ɪ.t^ər.i/ ⓤ /-'mɑː.nə.tɔːr.i/ *adj*: *an admonitory remark*

ad nauseam /ˌæd'nɔː.zi.æm/ ⓤ /-'nɑː-/ *adv* If someone discusses something ad nauseam, they talk about it so much that it becomes very boring: *He talks ad nauseam about how clever his children are.*

ado /ə'duː/ *noun* **without further/more ado** without wasting more time: *And so, without further ado, let me introduce tonight's speaker.*

adobe /ə'dəʊ.bi/ ⓤ /-'doʊ-/ *noun* [U] a mixture of earth and straw made into bricks and dried in the sun, used to build houses in some parts of the world: *an adobe house*

adolescent /ˌæd.ə'les.^ənt/ *noun* [C] a young person who is developing into an adult

adolescent /ˌæd.ə'les.^ənt/ *adj* **1** being or relating to an adolescent: *an adolescent boy* ○ *adolescent concerns/traumas/problems* **2** describes an adult or an adult's behaviour that is silly and childish: *adolescent humour/behaviour*

adolescence /ˌæd.ə'les.^ənts/ *noun* [U] the period of time in a person's life when they are developing into an adult: *a troubled adolescence* ○ *yet another novel about the joys and sorrows of adolescence*

Adonis /ə'dəʊ.nɪs/ ⓤ /-'dɑː.nɪs/ *noun* [C] a very beautiful or sexually attractive young man: *She walked in on the arm of some blond Adonis.*

adopt TAKE CHILD /ə'dɒpt/ ⓤ /-'dɑːpt/ *verb* [I or T] to take another person's child into your own family and legally raise him or her as your own child: *They've adopted a baby girl.* ○ *She had the child adopted* (= She gave her baby to someone else to raise). ○ *They have no children of their own, but they're hoping to adopt.* ➔Compare **foster** TAKE CARE OF. **adopted** /ə'dɒp.tɪd/ ⓤ /-'dɑːp-/ *adj*: *They've got two adopted children and one of their own.*

adoption /ə'dɒp.ʃ^ən/ ⓤ /-'dɑːp-/ *noun* [C or U] *She was homeless and had to put her child up for adoption* (= asked for the child to be taken by another adult or family as their own). ○ *The last ten years have seen a* dramatic fall in the number of adoptions.

adoptive /əˈdɒp.tɪv/ ⓤ /-ˈdɑːp-/ *adj* [before n] An adoptive parent is one who has adopted a child.

adopt START /əˈdɒpt/ ⓤ /-ˈdɑːpt/ *verb* [T] to accept or start to use something new: *I think it's time to adopt a different strategy in my dealings with him.* ○ *The new tax would force companies to adopt energy-saving measures.* ○ *He's adopted a remarkably light-hearted attitude towards the situation.* **adoption** /əˈdɒp.ʃⁿn/ ⓤ /-ˈdɑːp-/ *noun* [U] *Several suggestions have been offered for adoption by the panel.*

adopt CHOOSE /əˈdɒpt/ ⓤ /-ˈdɑːpt/ *verb* [T] to choose or claim as your own: *Dr Kennedy has been adopted **as** the party's candidate for South Cambridge.* ○ *Roz has adopted one or two funny mannerisms since she's been away.*

adopted /əˈdɒp.tɪd/ ⓤ /-ˈdɑːp-/ *adj* [before n] *Spain is my adopted country* (= not the country where I was born, but the one where I have chosen to live). **adoption** /əˈdɒp.ʃⁿn/ ⓤ /-ˈdɑːp-/ *noun* [U] *England was Conrad's **country of** adoption.*

adore LOVE /əˈdɔːʳ/ ⓤ /-ˈdɔːr/ *verb* [T not continuous] to love someone very much, especially in an admiring or respectful way, or to like something very much: *She has one son and she adores him.* ○ *I **absolutely** adore chocolate.* ○ [+ v-ing] *Don't you just adore lying in a hot bath?*

adorable /əˈdɔː.rə.bl̩/ ⓤ /-ˈdɔːr.ə-/ *adj* describes a person or animal that makes you feel great affection because they are so attractive and often small: *She has the most adorable two-year-old girl.* ○ *an adorable puppy* **adoration** /ˌæd.əˈreɪ.ʃⁿn/ *noun* [U] very strong love for someone: *her complete adoration of her brother* **adoring** /əˈdɔː.rɪŋ/ *adj* showing very strong love for someone: *I refuse to play the part of the adoring wife.*

adore WORSHIP /əˈdɔːʳ/ ⓤ /-ˈdɔːr/ *verb* [T not continuous] FORMAL to worship: *Let us adore God for all his works.* **adoration** /ˌæd.əˈreɪ.ʃⁿn/ ⓤ /-ˈɚ-/ *noun* [U] *The painting depicts the three wise men kneeling in adoration of the baby Jesus.*

adorn /əˈdɔːn/ ⓤ /-ˈdɔːrn/ *verb* [T] LITERARY to add something decorative to a person or thing: *The bride's hair was adorned **with** pearls and white flowers.* **adornment** /əˈdɔːn.mənt/ ⓤ /-ˈdɔːrn-/ *noun* [C or U] LITERARY something decorative, or the act of decorating something or someone

adrenalin, adrenaline /əˈdren.ⁿl.ɪn/ *noun* [U] a hormone produced by the body when you are frightened, angry or excited, which makes the heart beat faster and prepares the body to react to danger: *These arguments always **get** my adrenalin **going*** (= make me excited or angry).

adrift /əˈdrɪft/ *adj* [after v] **1** If a boat is adrift, it is moving on the water but is not controlled by anyone because of a problem: *He spent three days adrift on his yacht.* **2** If a person is adrift, they do not have a clear purpose in life and do not know what they want to do: *Da Silva plays a bright, lonely student from New York, adrift in small-town Arizona.* **3** INFORMAL **go/come adrift** to become loose: *The hem of my skirt's come adrift again.* **4** INFORMAL **go adrift** If plans go adrift they fail or do not produce the correct results: *Something seems to have gone adrift in our calculations.*

adroit /əˈdrɔɪt/ *adj* very skilful and quick in the way you think or move: *an adroit reaction/answer/movement of the hand* ○ *She became adroit **at** deal**ing** with difficult questions.* **adroitly** /əˈdrɔɪt.li/ *adv*: *She adroitly avoided the question.* ○ *He adroitly slipped the money into his pocket.* **adroitness** /əˈdrɔɪt.nəs/ *noun* [U]

ADSL /ˌeɪ.diːˈes.ⁿel/ *noun* [U] SPECIALIZED ABBREVIATION FOR asymmetric digital subscriber line: a system for providing a very fast Internet connection that allows you to use a telephone at the same time

adulation /ˌæd.jʊˈleɪ.ʃⁿn/ *noun* [U] very great admiration or praise for someone, especially when it is more than is deserved: *Minelli is a born performer – she loves the excitement and she loves the adulation.* **adulatory** /ˌæd.jʊˈleɪ.tʰr.i/ ⓤ /ˈædʒ.ⁿl.ə.tɔːr.i/ *adj*: FORMAL *I found myself irritated by the adulatory* (= showing too much admiration) *tone of her biography.*

adult /ˈæd.ʌlt/ /əˈdʌlt/ *noun* [C] a person or animal that has grown to full size and strength: *An adult under British law is someone over 18 years old.* ○ *Adults pay an admission charge but children get in free.*

adult /ˈæd.ʌlt/ /əˈdʌlt/ *adj* **1** grown to full size and strength: *an adult male/elephant* ○ *She spent most of her adult **life** in prison.* **2** typical of or suitable for adults: *Let's try to be adult about this.* **3** Adult films, magazines and books show naked people and sexual acts and are not for children.

adulthood /ˈæd.ʌlt.hʊd/ /əˈdʌlt-/ *noun* [U] the part of someone's life when they are an adult: *People in Britain legally **reach** adulthood at 18.* ○ *Responsibility, I suppose, is what defines adulthood.*

,adult eduˈcation *noun* [U] classes, which usually take place in the evening, for people who have finished their school education

adulterate /əˈdʌl.tə.reɪt/ ⓤ /-tʲə.reɪt/ *verb* [T usually passive] to make food or drink weaker or to lower its quality, by adding something else: *There were complaints that the beer had been adulterated **with** water.* **adulterated** /əˈdʌl.tə.reɪ.tɪd/ ⓤ /-tʲɪd/ *adj*: *adulterated drugs/food* **adulteration** /əˌdʌl.təˈreɪ.ʃⁿn/ *noun* [U]

adulterer /əˈdʌl.tə.rəʳ/ ⓤ /-tʲɚ.ɚ/ *noun* [C] OLD USE a married man who has sex with a woman who is not his wife, or a man who has sex with another man's wife: *Her husband was a compulsive adulterer.*

adulteress /əˈdʌl.tə.rəs/ ⓤ /-tʲɚ.əs/ *noun* [C] a female adulterer

adultery /əˈdʌl.tʰr.i/ ⓤ /-tʲɚ.i/ *noun* [U] sex between a married man or woman and someone who is not their wife or husband: *Many people in public life have **committed** adultery.* **adulterous** /əˈdʌl.tʰr.əs/ ⓤ /-tʲɚ-/ *adj*: *He had an adulterous relationship with his wife's best friend.*

adumbrate /ˈæd.əm.breɪt/ *verb* [T] FORMAL to give only the main facts and not the details about something, especially something that will happen in the future: *The project's objectives were adumbrated in the report.* **adumbration** /ˌæd.əmˈbreɪ.ʃⁿn/ *noun* [U]

adv *noun* ABBREVIATION FOR **adverb**

advance FORWARD /ədˈvɑːnts/ ⓤ /-ˈvænts/ *verb* [I or T] to go or move something forward, or to develop or improve something: *The fire advanced steadily through the forest.* ○ *The troops advanced **on** the city* (= approached it, ready to attack). ○ *We have advanced greatly in our knowledge of the universe.* ○ *Her study has considerably advanced* (= helped) *the **cause** of equal rights.* ○ [+ two objects] *Could you advance me £50* (= pay it to me before the regular time) *until Tuesday?* ○ *He's just trying to advance* (= improve) *his own career.*

advancing /ədˈvɑːnt.sɪŋ/ ⓤ /-ˈvænt-/ *adj*: *He only recently stopped working, due to his advancing **years*** (= because he is becoming old).

advance /ədˈvɑːnts/ ⓤ /-ˈvænts/ *noun* **1** [C or U] the forward movement of something, or an improvement or development in something: *Nothing could stop the advance **of** the flood waters.* ○ *Recent advances **in** medical science mean that this illness can now be cured.* ○ *She asked for a £300 advance **on** her salary* (= money paid before the regular time). **2** [C usually pl] an attempt to start a romantic relationship with someone: *She rejected his unwelcome advances.*

● **in advance** before a particular time, or before doing a particular thing: *If you're going to come, please let me know in advance.*

● **in advance of** *sth/sb* FORMAL before something or someone: *She arrived in advance of everyone else.*

advance /ədˈvɑːnts/ ⓤ /-ˈvænts/ *adj* [before n] happening, done or ready before an event: *advance payment/booking* ○ *We got no advance **warning/notice** of the changes.*

advanced /ədˈvɑːntst/ ⓤ /-ˈvæntst/ *adj* **1** highly developed: *This is the most advanced type of engine available.* **2** at a higher, more difficult level: *an advanced English course* **3** US **advanced class/course** a school class which is doing work of a higher standard than is usual for students at that stage in their education

advancement /ədˈvɑːnt.smənt/ ⓤ /-ˈvænt-/ *noun* [U] *All she was interested in was the advancement* (= improve-

A

ment, development) *of her own career.*

advance [SUGGEST] /əd'vɑːnts/ [US] /-'vænts/ *verb* [T] *FORMAL* to suggest an idea or theory: *the theory advanced in this article*

ad,vance di'rective *noun* [C] a **living will**

advantage /əd'vɑːn.tɪdʒ/ [US] /-'væn.t̬ɪdʒ/ *noun* **1** [C or U] a condition giving a greater chance of success: *The advantage **of** booking tickets in advance is that you get better seats.* ○ *Despite the twin advantages **of** wealth and beauty, she did not have a happy life.* ○ [+ to infinitive] *It would be **to** your advantage* (= It would improve the situation for you) ***to** agree to his demands.* ○ *For a goalkeeper, **it's** a great advantage **to** have big hands.* ○ *His height and reach **give** him a big advantage **over*** (= make him better than) *other boxers.* ○ *UK FORMAL "Do you know how old I am?" "I'm afraid you **have the** advantage **of** me there* (= you know the answer but I do not)*."* **2** [U] the word used in tennis when a player has won the point after DEUCE: *Advantage Miss Williams!* **3 take advantage of *sth/sth*** to use the good things in a situation: *I thought I'd take advantage of the sports facilities while I'm here.* **4** *DISAPPROVING* **take advantage of *sb/sth*** to treat someone badly in order to get something good from them: *I think she takes advantage of his good nature.* ○ *I know she's offered to babysit any time but I don't want her to think we're taking advantage of her.*
advantageous /,æd.væn'teɪ.dʒəs/ *adj* giving benefits or helping to make you more successful: *advantageous interest rates* ○ *The lower tax rate is particularly advantageous **to** poorer families.* **advantageously** /,æd.væn'teɪ.dʒə.sli/ *adv*

advent [START] /'æd.vent/ /-vənt/ *noun* [S] the arrival of an event, invention or person: *Life in Britain was transformed by **the** advent **of** the steam engine.*

Advent [CHRISTMAS] /'æd.vent/ /-vənt/ *noun* [U] the period of four weeks before Christmas

'Advent ,calendar *noun* [C] a decorative piece of card, often hung on the wall, which has a small door-like opening for each of the days of the month before Christmas. Children open one of these doors each day, finding a picture under it.

adventist /'æd.ven.tɪst/ /-vən-/ *noun* [C] ➲See **Seventh-Day Adventist**.

adventitious /,æd.vən'tɪʃ.əs/ /-ven-/ *adj FORMAL* not expected or planned: *an adventitious event/situation* **adventitiously** /,æd.vən'tɪʃ.ə.sli/ /-ven-/ *adv*

adventure /əd'ven.tʃər/ [US] /-tʃɚ/ *noun* [C or U] an unusual, exciting and possibly dangerous activity such as a journey or experience, or the excitement produced by such an activity: *She **had** some exciting adventures in Egypt.* ○ *We got lost on the Metro – it was **quite an** adventure.* ○ *Sam won't come – he's got no **sense of** adventure* (= he does not enjoy dangerous or exciting situations).
adventurer /əd'ven.tʃə.rər/ [US] /-tʃɚ.ɚ/ *noun* [C] **1** someone who enjoys and looks for dangerous and exciting experiences: *He was something of an adventurer, living most of his life abroad.* **2** *DISAPPROVING* a person who takes risks, acts dishonestly or uses his or her sexual attractiveness to become rich or powerful: *He was portrayed in the press as a gold-digger and adventurer.*
adventurous /əd'ven.tʃər.əs/ [US] /-tʃɚ.əs/ *adj* willing to try new or difficult things, or exciting and often dangerous: *I'm trying to be more adventurous with my cooking.* ○ *She led an adventurous life.* ○ *He's not very adventurous sexually.* **adventurously** /əd'ven.tʃər.ə.sli/ [US] /-tʃɚ-/ *adv*

ad'venture ,playground *noun* [C] a public open space where children can play and climb on structures, usually made of wood, ropes and old tyres

adverb /'æd.vɜːb/ [US] /-vɝːb/ *noun* [C] a word which describes or gives more information about a verb, adjective, adverb or phrase: *In the phrase 'she smiled cheerfully', the word 'cheerfully' is an adverb.* ○ *In the phrase 'the house was spotlessly clean', the word 'spotlessly' is an adverb.* **adverbial** /əd'vɜː.bi.əl/ [US] /-'vɝː-/ *adj*: *an adverbial phrase*

adversary /'æd.və.sər.i/ [US] /'æd.vɚ.ser-/ *noun* [C] *FORMAL* an enemy: *He saw her as his main adversary within the company.*
adversarial /,æd.və'seə.ri.əl/ [US] /-vɚ'ser.i-/ *adj FORMAL* involving opposition or disagreement: *In the old days of two-party adversarial politics, voting was easy.*

adverse /'æd.vɜːs/ /-'-/ [US] /æd'vɝːs/ *adj* [before n] having a negative or harmful effect on something: *The match has been cancelled due to adverse **weather conditions**.* ○ *They received a lot of adverse **publicity/criticism** about the changes.* ○ *So far the drug is thought not to have any adverse **effects**.*
adversely /'æd.vɜː.sli/ /-'--/ [US] /æd'vɝː-/ *adv*: *A lot of companies have been adversely* (= in a harmful way) ***affected** by the recession.*

adversity /əd'vɜː.sə.ti/ [US] /-'vɝː.sə.t̬i/ *noun* [C or U] a difficult or unlucky situation or event: *She was always cheerful **in** adversity.* ○ *The road to happiness is paved with adversities.*

advert /'æd.vɜːt/ [US] /-vɝːt/ *noun* [C] *UK* **advertisement**, see at **advertise**: *an advert **for** the local radio station*

advertise /'æd.və.taɪz/ [US] /-vɚ-/ *verb* [I or T] to make something known generally or in public, especially in order to sell it: *We advertised our car* (= published a description of it together with the price we wanted for it) *in the local newspaper.* ○ *He advertises his services on the company notice board.* ○ *I'm going to advertise **for*** (= put a notice in the newspaper, local shop, etc., asking for) *someone to clean my house.* ○ *There's no harm in applying for other jobs, but if I were you, I wouldn't advertise **the fact*** (= make it generally known) *at work.*
advertisement /əd'vɜː.tɪ.smənt/ [US] /'æd.vɝː.taɪz.mənt/ *noun* [C] **1** (*INFORMAL* **ad**, *UK ALSO INFORMAL* **advert**) a picture, short film, song, etc. which tries to persuade people to buy a product or service: *a television/newspaper advertisement **for** a new car* ○ *She scanned the job/property advertisements in the paper.* **2 be an advertisement for *sth*** If you are an advertisement for something, you show its good effects: *I'm afraid I'm not a very good advertisement for the diet since I've actually put on weight!* **advertiser** /'æd.və.taɪ.zər/ [US] /-vɚ.taɪ.zɚ/ *noun* [C] *Whilst claiming to promote positive images of women, advertisers are in fact doing the very opposite.*
advertising /'æd.və.taɪ.zɪŋ/ [US] /-vɚ-/ *noun* [U] the business of trying to persuade people to buy products or services: *Fiona works **in** advertising.* ○ *the advertising industry*

advertorial /,æd.və'tɔː.ri.əl/ [US] /-'tɔːr.i-/ *noun* [C] an advertisement in a newspaper or magazine that is designed to look like an article by the writers of the magazine

advice /əd'vaɪs/ *noun* [U] an opinion which someone offers you about what you should do or how you should act in a particular situation: *Steven **gave** me some good advice.* ○ *I think I'll **take** your advice* (= do what you suggest) *and get the green dress.* ○ *Can I give you **a piece of** advice?* ○ *I need some advice **on** which computer to buy.* ○ [+ to infinitive] *My advice is **to** go by train.* ○ *We went to Paris **on** Sarah's advice.* * NOTE: Do not confuse with the verb, **advise**.
advise /əd'vaɪz/ *verb* **1** [I or T] to give someone advice: [+ to infinitive] *I think I'd advise him **to** leave the company.* ○ *His doctor advised him **against** smoking.* ○ *I'd strongly advise **against** making a sudden decision.* ○ [+ that] *They're advising **that** children be kept out of the sun altogether.* ○ [+ v-ing] *I'd advise waiting until tomorrow.* ○ [+ question word] *She advised us **when** to come.* ○ *She advises the President* (= gives information and suggests types of action) ***on** African policy.* ○ *You **would be well-advised to*** (= It would be wise for you to) *have the appropriate vaccinations before you go abroad.* * NOTE: Do not confuse with the noun, **advice**. **2** [T] *FORMAL* to give someone official information about something: *They were advised **of** their rights.* ○ [+ that] *Our solicitors have advised **that** the costs could be enormous.*
advisable /əd'vaɪ.zə.bl/ *adj* [after v] If something is advisable, it will avoid problems if you do it: [+ to infinitive] *It's advisable **to** book seats at least a week in advance.* ○ *A certain amount of caution is advisable at this point.*
advisability /əd,vaɪ.zə'bɪl.ɪ.ti/ [US] /-ə.t̬i/ *noun* [U] *They dis-*

cussed the advisability of building so near to the airport. **adviser** /əd'vaɪ.zəʳ/ [US] /-zɚ/ *noun* [C] (*ALSO* **advisor**) someone whose job is to give advice about a subject: *She is the party's main economic adviser.* ○ *a financial advisor* **advisory** /əd'vaɪ.zᵊr.i/ [US] /-zɚ-/ *adj*: *She is employed by the president in an advisory capacity* (= giving advice). **advisory** /əd'vaɪ.zᵊr.i/ *noun* [C usually pl] *US* an official announcement that contains advice, information or a warning: *weather/travel advisories* ○ *Television companies sometimes broadcast advisories before violent movies.*

COMMON LEARNER ERROR

advice

Remember that this word is not countable.

She gave me lots of advice.
~~*She gave me lots of advices.*~~

If you want to use **advice** in a countable way, say **a piece of advice**.

He gave me a good piece of advice.
~~*He gave me a good advice.*~~

COMMON LEARNER ERROR

advice or advise?

Be careful not to confuse the noun **advice** with the verb **advise**.

I advise you to see a lawyer.
~~*I advice you to see a lawyer.*~~

advisedly /əd'vaɪ.zɪd.li/ *adv FORMAL* If you say you are using a word advisedly, you mean you are choosing it after thinking about it very carefully: *This action is barbaric – and I use the word advisedly.*

advisement /əd'vaɪz.mənt/ *noun* [U] *US* the process or activity of advising someone about something: *a counseling and advisement center* ○ *Contact Dr. Gray about academic advisement.* ○ *student/graduate/career advisement*
• **take *sth* under advisement** *US* to consider something such as advice or information carefully: *Thank you for your input, Mr. Walters – I'll take what you've said under advisement.*

advocate [SUPPORT] /'æd.və.keɪt/ *verb* [T] to publicly support or suggest an idea, development or way of doing something: [+ v-ing] *She advocates* ***taking*** *a more long-term view.* ○ *He advocates the return of capital punishment.* **advocate** /'æd.və.kət/ *noun* [C] *He's a strong advocate* ***of*** *state ownership of the railways.* **advocacy** /'æd.və.kə.si/ *noun* [U] *She is renowned for her advocacy* ***of*** *human rights.*

advocate [LAWYER] /'æd.və.kət/ *noun* [C] a lawyer who defends someone in a court of law

adze, *US USUALLY* **adz** /ædz/ *noun* [C] a tool like an axe with the blade at an angle of approximately 90° to the handle, which is used for cutting and shaping wood

aegis /'iː.dʒɪs/ *noun FORMAL* **under the aegis of** *sb/sth* with the protection or support of someone or something, especially an organization: *The project was set up under the aegis of the university.*

aeon /'iː.ɒn/ [US] /-ɑːn/ *noun* [C] *MAINLY UK FOR* **eon**

aerate /eə'reɪt/ [US] /er'eɪt/ *verb* [T] **1** to add a gas to liquid, especially a drink: *aerated water* **2** to allow air to act on something: *Earthworms help to aerate the soil.* ○ *aerated soil* **aeration** /eə'reɪ.ʃᵊn/ [US] /er'eɪ-/ *noun* [U]

aerial [RADIO] /'eə.ri.əl/ [US] /'er.i-/ *noun* [C] (*US ALSO* **antenna**) a structure made of metal rods or wires which receives or sends out radio or television signals ➲See picture **Car** on page Centre 12

aerial [AIR] /'eə.ri.əl/ [US] /'er.i-/ *adj* in or from the air, especially from an aircraft: *Meanwhile, the massive aerial* ***bombardment/bombing*** *of military targets continued unabated.* ○ *aerial* ***photography***

aerie /'ɪə.ri/ [US] /'ɪr.i/ *noun* [C] *MAINLY US FOR* **eyrie**

aero- /eə.rəʊ-/ [US] /er.oʊ-/ *prefix* of the air or of air travel: *aerodynamics* ○ *aeronautics*

aerobatics /ˌeə.rəʊ'bæt.ɪks/ [US] /ˌer.oʊ'bæṭ-/ *plural noun* skilful changes of position of an aircraft, such as flying upside down or in a circle: *The crowd was entertained with a display of aerobatics.* **aerobatic** /ˌeə.rəʊ'bæt.ɪk/ [US] /ˌer.oʊ'bæṭ-/ *adj*: *an aerobatic display*

aerobics /eə'rəʊ.bɪks/ [US] /er'oʊ-/ *noun* [U] energetic physical exercises, often performed with a group of people to music, which make the heart, lungs and muscles stronger and increase the amount of oxygen in the blood: *She* ***does*** *aerobics.* ○ *I go to aerobics* (= to a class where we are taught such exercises) *once a week.* ○ *an aerobics instructor/teacher* **aerobic** /eə'rəʊ.bɪk/ [US] /er'oʊ-/ *adj*: *aerobic* ***exercise***

aerodrome /'eə.rə.drəʊm/ [US] /'er.ə.droʊm/ *noun* [C] *UK OLD-FASHIONED FOR* **airfield**

aerodynamics /ˌeə.rəʊ.daɪ'næm.ɪks/ [US] /ˌer.oʊ-/ *noun* [U] the science which studies the movement of gases and the way solid bodies, such as aircraft, move through them **aerodynamic** /ˌeə.rəʊ.daɪ'næm.ɪk/ [US] /ˌer.oʊ-/ *adj*: *aerodynamic principles* ○ *an aerodynamic design/car* **aerodynamically** /ˌeə.rəʊ.daɪ'næm.ɪ.kli/ [US] /ˌer.oʊ-/ *adv*: *aerodynamically designed/efficient*

aerogramme, *US ALSO* **aerogram** /'eə.rəʊ.græm/ [US] /'er.ə-/ *noun* [C] an **airletter**

aeronautics /ˌeə.rə'nɔː.tɪks/ [US] /ˌer.ə'nɑː.ṭɪks/ *noun* [U] the technology and science of designing, building and operating aircraft **aeronautic** /ˌeə.rə'nɔː.tɪk/ [US] /ˌer.ə'nɑː.ṭɪk/ *adj*: *aeronautic design/engineering* **aeronautical** /ˌeə.rə'nɔː.tɪ.kᵊl/ [US] /ˌer.ə'nɑː.ṭɪ-/ *adj*

aeroplane /'eə.rə.pleɪn/ [US] /'er-/ *noun* [C] (*US* **airplane**) *UK* a vehicle designed for air travel, which has wings and one or more engines: *She has her own private aeroplane.* ➲See picture **Planes, Ships and Boats** on page Centre 14

aerosol /'eə.rəʊ.sɒl/ [US] /'er.ə.sɑːl/ *noun* [C] a metal container in which liquids are kept under pressure and forced out in a spray

aerospace /'eə.rəʊ.speɪs/ [US] /'er.oʊ-/ *adj* [before n] producing or operating aircraft or spacecraft: *the aerospace industry* ○ *an aerospace company*

aesthetic, *US ALSO* **esthetic** /es'θet.ɪk/ [US] /-'θeṭ-/ *adj* **1** relating to the enjoyment or study of beauty: *The new building has little aesthetic value/appeal.* **2** describes an object or a work of art that shows great beauty: *furniture which is both aesthetic and functional*

aesthetics, *US ALSO* **esthetics** /es'θet.ɪks/ [US] /-'θeṭ-/ *noun* [U] the formal study of art, especially in relation to the idea of beauty **aesthetically**, *US ALSO* **esthetically** /es'θet.ɪ.kli/ [US] /-'θeṭ-/ *adv*: *I like objects to be both functional and aesthetically* ***pleasing***.

aesthete, *US ALSO* **esthete** /'iːs.θiːt/ *noun* [C] a person who understands and enjoys beauty: *The ugliness of the city would make an aesthete like you shudder.*

AFAIK, **afaik** *INTERNET ABBREVIATION FOR* as far as I know: used when you believe that something is true, but you are not completely certain

afar /ə'fɑːʳ/ [US] /-'fɑːr/ *adv* from or at a great distance: *People came* ***from*** *afar to see the show.* ○ *HUMOROUS I've never actually spoken to him – I've just admired him* ***from*** *afar.*

affable /'æf.ə.bl̩/ *adj* friendly and easy to talk to: *He struck me as an affable sort of a man.* ○ *She was quite affable at the meeting.* **affably** /'æf.ə.bli/ *adv*: *He greeted us affably.* **affability** /ˌæf.ə'bɪl.ɪ.ti/ [US] /-ə.ṭi/ *noun* [U] *FORMAL*

affair [MATTER] /ə'feəʳ/ [US] /-'fer/ *noun* [C] **1** a situation or subject that is being dealt with or considered; a matter: *She organizes her* ***financial*** *affairs very efficiently.* ○ *He's always* ***meddling in*** (= trying to influence) *other people's affairs.* ○ *What I do in my spare time is my affair* (= only involves me). **2** a matter or situation which causes strong public feeling, usually of moral disapproval: *The arms-dealing affair has severely damaged the reputation of the government.* ○ *The President's* ***handling*** *of the affair has been criticised.*

affair [RELATIONSHIP] /ə'feəʳ/ [US] /-'fer/ *noun* [C] a sexual relationship, especially a secret one: *She's* ***having*** *an affair with a married man.* ○ *The book doesn't make any mention of his* ***love*** *affairs.* ○ *an extramarital affair*

affair [EVENT] /ə'feəʳ/ [US] /-'fer/ *noun* [C] an event: *The party turned out to be a quiet affair.*

A

affair [THING] /ə'feəʳ/ [US] /-'fer/ *noun* [C] *OLD-FASHIONED* an object of the type stated: *She wore a long black velvet affair.*

af,fairs of 'state *plural noun* important government matters

affect [INFLUENCE] /ə'fekt/ *verb* [T] to have an influence on someone or something, or to cause them to change: *Both buildings were badly affected by the fire.* ○ *The divorce affected every aspect of her life.* ○ *It's a disease which affects mainly older people.* ○ *I was deeply affected by the film* (= It caused strong feelings in me).
affecting /ə'fek.tɪŋ/ *adj FORMAL* causing a strong emotion, especially sadness: *It was an affecting sight.*

COMMON LEARNER ERROR

affect or effect?

Do not confuse the verb **affect** with the noun **effect**, which means the result of a particular influence.

Global warming is one of the most serious effects of pollution.

Do not confuse the verb **affect** with the verb **effect**, which is formal and means to make something happen.

The management wish to effect a change in company procedure.

affect [PRETEND] /ə'fekt/ *verb* [T] **1** *FORMAL* to pretend to feel or think something: *To all his problems she affected indifference.* **2** *FORMAL MAINLY DISAPPROVING* to start to wear or do something in order to make people admire or respect you: *At university he affected an upper-class accent.* ○ *He's recently affected a hat and cane.*
affected /ə'fek.tɪd/ *adj DISAPPROVING* artificial and not sincere: *an affected manner/style of writing* ○ *I found her very affected.* **affectedly** /ə'fek.tɪd.li/ *adv*: *She laughed affectedly.*
affectation /ˌæf.ek'teɪ.ʃᵊn/ *noun* [C or U] *DISAPPROVING* behaviour or speech that is not sincere: *She has so many little affectations.* ○ *His manner reeks of affectation.* ○ *"It doesn't concern me," he said with* ***an*** *affectation* ***of*** (= pretending) *nonchalance.*

affection /ə'fek.ʃᵊn/ *noun* [C or U] a feeling of liking for a person or place: *He* ***had*** *a* ***deep*** *affection for his aunt.* ○ *She* ***felt*** *no affection* ***for*** *the child.*
affections /ə'fek.ʃᵊnz/ *plural noun* feelings of liking or love: *The former president still holds a place in the nation's affections.* ○ *Sula seems to have transferred her affections from Jon to his brother.*
• **win *sb's* affections** to succeed in persuading someone to love you
affectionate /ə'fek.ʃᵊn.ət/ *adj* showing feelings of liking or love: *an affectionate kiss* ○ *He's an affectionate little boy.* **affectionately** /ə'fek.ʃᵊn.ət.li/ *adv*: *She smiled affectionately at him.*

affidavit /ˌæf.ə'deɪ.vɪt/ *noun* [C] a written statement which someone makes after they have sworn officially to tell the truth, and which might be used as proof in a court of law

affiliate /ə'fɪl.i.eɪt/ *verb* [T] to cause a group to become part of or form a close relationship with another, usually larger, group or organization: *a college affiliated* ***to*** *the University of London* ○ *The school is affiliated* ***with*** *a national association of driving schools.*
affiliate /ə'fɪl.i.ət/ *noun* [C] *Our college is an affiliate* ***of*** (= is connected with or controlled by) *the university.*
affiliation /əˌfɪl.i'eɪ.ʃᵊn/ *noun* [C or U] a connection with a political party or religion, or with a larger organization: *The group has affiliations* ***with*** *several organizations abroad.* ○ *Their lack of affiliation* ***to*** *any particular bank allows them to give objective financial advice.* ○ *political affiliations*

affili'ation ˌorder *noun* [C] *UK LEGAL* a legal order in which a man who is not married to the mother of his child must pay money to the mother to support his child

affinity /ə'fɪn.ɪ.ti/ [US] /-ə.t̬i/ *noun* **1** [S] an attraction or sympathy for someone or something, especially because of shared characteristics: *She seems to have a natural affinity* ***for/with*** *water.* **2** [C or U] a close similarity between two things: *There are several close affinities* ***between*** *the two paintings.*

af'finity ˌcard *noun* [C] a credit card that earns a small amount of money for a charity each time something is bought with it

affirm /ə'fɜːm/ [US] /-'fɝːm/ *verb* [T] *FORMAL* **1** to state something as true: [+ (*that*)] *The suspect affirmed* ***(that)*** *he had been at home all evening.* ○ *She affirmed her intention to apply for the post.* **2** to publicly state your support for an opinion or idea: *The government has affirmed its commitment to equal rights.* **affirmation** /ˌæf.ə'meɪ.ʃᵊn/ [US] /-ɚ-/ *noun* [C or U] *We welcome the government's affirmation of its intention to act.*

affirmative /ə'fɜː.mə.tɪv/ [US] /-'fɝː.mə.t̬ɪv/ *adj* relating to a statement that shows agreement or says 'yes': *an affirmative answer/response* * NOTE: The opposite is **negative**.
affirmative /ə'fɜː.mə.tɪv/ [US] /-'fɝː.mə.t̬ɪv/ *noun* [C or U] a word or statement that shows agreement or says 'yes': *She asked the question expecting an affirmative.* ○ *He replied* ***in the*** *affirmative* (= He said yes). ○ *MAINLY US "Were you in New York on March 3rd?" "Affirmative* (= Yes)." **affirmatively** /ə'fɜː.mə.tɪv.li/ [US] /-'fɝː.mə.t̬ɪv-/ *adv*: *She answered affirmatively.*

af,firmative 'action *noun* [U] If a government or an organization takes affirmative action, it gives preference to women, black people, or other groups which are often treated unfairly, when it is choosing people for a job.

affix [FIX] /ə'fɪks/ *verb* [T] *FORMAL* to fix one thing to another: *She affixed a stamp* ***to*** *the envelope.*

affix [WORD PART] /'æf.ɪks/ *noun* [C] a letter or group of letters which are added to the beginning or end of a word to make a new word: *The affixes un- and -less are often used to make negative words, such as 'unhappy' and 'careless'.*

afflict /ə'flɪkt/ *verb* [T] If a problem or illness afflicts a person or thing, they suffer from it: *It is an illness which afflicts women more than men.* ○ *a country afflicted by civil war*
affliction /ə'flɪk.ʃᵊn/ *noun* [C or U] *FORMAL* something that makes you suffer: *Malnutrition is one of the common afflictions of the poor.*

affluent /'æf.lu.ənt/ *adj* having a lot of money or owning a lot of things; rich: *affluent nations/neighbourhoods*
affluence /'æf.lu.ənts/ *noun* [U] *What we are seeing increasingly is a society of private affluence and public squalor.*

afford [BE ABLE] /ə'fɔːd/ [US] /-'fɔːrd/ *verb* **can afford** to be able to buy or do something because you have enough money or time: *I don't know how he can afford a new car on his salary.* ○ *Few people are able to afford cars like that.* ○ *She couldn't afford the time off work to see him.* ○ [+ **to** infinitive] *I can't afford* ***to*** *buy a house.*
• **cannot afford** (*FORMAL* **can ill afford**) If you cannot afford to do something, you must not do it because it would cause serious problems for you: *We can't afford to make any mistakes at this stage in the project.* ○ *He can ill afford to fail any of his exams.*
affordable /ə'fɔː.də.bl̩/ [US] /-'fɔːr-/ *adj* not expensive: *nice clothes at affordable prices*

COMMON LEARNER ERROR

afford to do something

When **afford** is followed by a verb, it is always in the **to** + **infinitive** form.

We can't afford to go on holiday this year.
~~*We can't afford going on holiday this year.*~~

afford [GIVE] /ə'fɔːd/ [US] /-'fɔːrd/ *verb* [T] *FORMAL* to allow someone to have something pleasant or necessary: *The hut afforded little protection from the elements.* ○ [+ two objects] *Her seat afforded her an uninterrupted view of the stage.*

afforest /ə'fɒr.ɪst/ [US] /-'fɔːr.əst/ *verb* [T] to plant trees on an area of land in order to make a forest **afforestation** /æfˌɒr.ɪ'steɪ.ʃᵊn/ [US] /əˌfɔːr.ə-/ *noun* [U]

affray /ə'freɪ/ *noun* [C] *LEGAL* a fight in a public place: *Wallace was* ***charged with*** *causing an affray at a Southampton nightclub.*

affront /əˈfrʌnt/ noun [C] a remark or action intended to insult or offend someone: *He regarded the comments as an affront* ***to*** *his dignity.* **affront** /əˈfrʌnt/ verb [T usually passive] FORMAL *I was most affronted* ***by*** *his comments.* ○ *an affronted look/glance*

afghan hound /ˌæf.ɡænˈhaʊnd/ noun [C] a tall thin dog with long smooth hair and a pointed nose

aficionado /əˌfɪʃ.i.əˈnɑː.dəʊ/ ⓤ /-doʊ/ noun [C] plural **aficionados** FORMAL someone who is very interested in and enthusiastic about a particular subject: *a club for model railway aficionados* ○ *an aficionado* ***of*** *French films*

afield /əˈfiːld/ adv **far/further afield** a long distance away: *We export our products to countries as far afield as Japan and Canada.* ○ *Our students come from Europe, Asia and even further afield.*

AFK, **afk** INTERNET ABBREVIATION FOR away from keyboard: used when you stop taking part in a discussion in a CHAT ROOM for a short time

aflame /əˈfleɪm/ adj LITERARY **1** [after v] burning: *The whole village was aflame.* **2** [after v] red or golden, as if burning: *It was autumn and the trees were aflame* ***with*** *colour.* ○ *Her cheeks were aflame* ***with*** *embarrassment/ anger.* **3** very excited: *Aflame* ***with*** *desire, he took her in his arms.*

afloat /əˈfləʊt/ ⓤ /-ˈfloʊt/ adj [after v] **1** floating on water: *She spent seven days afloat on a raft.* ○ *He managed to* ***keep/stay*** *afloat by holding on to the side of the boat.* **2** having enough money to pay what you owe: *Many small businesses are struggling to* ***stay/keep*** *afloat.*

aflutter /əˈflʌt.əʳ/ ⓤ /-ˈflʌt̬.ɚ/ adj [after v] HUMOROUS excited and nervous: *I'm* ***all*** *aflutter about meeting him after so long.* ○ *Paul had walked into the room and set my* ***heart*** *aflutter.*

afoot /əˈfʊt/ adj [after v] happening or being planned or prepared: *There are* ***plans*** *afoot to launch a new radio station.*

afore /əˈfɔːʳ/ ⓤ /-ˈfɔːr/ adv, prep, conjunction OLD USE **before** EARLIER

aforementioned /əˈfɔː.men.tʃ⁅ⁿd/ ⓤ /-ˈfɔːr-/ adj [before n] (ALSO **aforesaid**) FORMAL mentioned earlier: *The aforementioned Mr Parkes then entered the cinema.*

the aforementioned /ði.əˈfɔː.men.tʃ⁅ⁿd/ ⓤ /-ˈfɔːr-/ noun (ALSO **the aforesaid**) the person or people mentioned earlier: *The aforementioned was/were seen waiting outside the building.*

afoul /əˈfaʊl/ adv **run/fall afoul of sth/sb** to experience problems, punishment or harm because you disobey a rule or disagree with a powerful organization, group or person: *He was fifteen when he first ran afoul of* ***the law.*** ○ *At one point Seeger fell afoul of the US government for his antiwar actions.*

afraid FEAR /əˈfreɪd/ adj [after v] feeling fear, or feeling anxiety about the possible results of a particular situation: *He was/felt suddenly afraid.* ○ *I've always been afraid* ***of*** *flying/heights/spiders.* ○ *She was afraid* ***for*** *her children* (= feared that they might be hurt). ○ [+ to infinitive] *Don't be afraid* ***to*** *say what you think.* ○ [+ (that)] *She was afraid* ***(that)*** *he might be upset if she told him.*

afraid SORRY /əˈfreɪd/ adj **I'm afraid...** used to politely introduce bad news or disagreement: *This is your room – it's rather small, I'm afraid.* ○ *I don't agree at all, I'm afraid.* ○ *I'm afraid you've completely misunderstood my question.* ○ [+ (that)] *I'm afraid* ***(that)*** *we can't come this evening after all.* ○ *"Was she impressed with our work?" "I'm afraid not* (= No).*"* ○ *"Does this mean I've got to leave?" "I'm afraid so* (= Yes).*"*

A-frame /ˈeɪ.freɪm/ noun [C] US a simple house shaped like an A, with two of its four walls sloping inward and meeting at the top to act as a roof **A-frame** /ˈeɪ.freɪm/ adj: [before n] *an A-frame chalet*

afresh /əˈfreʃ/ adv If you do something afresh, you deal with it again in a new way: *She tore up the letter and* ***started*** *afresh.* ○ *We agreed to* ***look*** *afresh at her original proposal.*

Africa /ˈæf.rɪ.kə/ noun [U] the continent that is to the south of the Mediterranean Sea, to the east of the Atlantic Ocean and to the west of the Indian Ocean

African /ˈæf.rɪ.kən/ adj relating or belonging to Africa: *African history/music*

African /ˈæf.rɪ.kən/ noun [C] someone from Africa

African ˈviolet noun [C] a small plant with purple, pink or white flowers which is grown in a container in a house

Afrikaans /ˌæf.rɪˈkɑːns/ ⓤ /ˌɑː.frɪˈ-/ noun [U] a language which is related to Dutch and is spoken in South Africa

Afrikaner /ˌæf.rɪˈkɑː.nəʳ/ ⓤ /ˌɑː.frɪˈkɑː.nɚ/ noun [C] a South African person whose family were originally Dutch and whose first language is Afrikaans

Afro HAIR /ˈæf.rəʊ/ /-roʊ/ noun [C] plural **Afros** a way of arranging the hair so that it is very thick, curly and has a rounded shape, especially like that of some black people

Afro- CONTINENT /ˈæf.rəʊ-/ ⓤ /ˈæf.roʊ-/ prefix of or connected with Africa: *Afro-Caribbean culture* ○ *Afro-American literature*

aft /ɑːft/ ⓤ /æft/ adj, adv SPECIALIZED in or towards the back part of a boat

after /ˈɑːf.təʳ/ ⓤ /ˈæf.tɚ/ prep **1** following in time, place or order: *Shall we go for a walk after breakfast?* ○ *Some people believe in* ***life*** *after death.* ○ *Her name came after mine on the list.* ○ *There's a good film on the day after tomorrow.* ○ *She waited until* ***well*** *after midnight.* ○ US *It's a quarter after four.* ○ *She just keeps on working,* ***day*** *after* ***day***, ***week*** *after* ***week*** (= continuously). ○ *We've had* ***meeting*** *after* ***meeting*** (= many meetings) *to discuss this point.* ○ *Jessie seemed very small after* (= in comparison with) *Michael's children.* ○ *After* (= Despite) *everything I've done for you, is this the way you treat me?* ○ *After* (= Because of) *what she did to me, I'll never trust her again.* ○ *The children have to learn to tidy up after themselves* (= after they have made things untidy). ○ *She slammed the door after* (= behind) *her.* ○ *We ran after* (= followed) *him, but he escaped.* ○ *Could you lock up after you* (= when you leave), *please?* **2** typical of or similar to the style of: *a painting after Titian* ○ *a concerto after Mozart*

• **be after sb/sth** INFORMAL to be looking for someone or something or trying to find or get them: *The police are after him.* ○ *I'm after a tie to go with this shirt.* ○ *I'm sure she's after my husband.* ○ *He's after* (= wants for himself) *Jane's job.*

• **after all 1** despite earlier problems or doubts: *The rain has stopped, so the game will go ahead after all.* **2** used to add information that shows that what you have just said is true: *I do like her – after all, she is my sister.*

• **after you 1** used to politely say that someone can go in front of you or serve themselves with food before you: *"Can I pour you some coffee?" "Oh no, after you."* **2** UK INFORMAL used to ask another person to give you something which they are using when they have finished using it: *After you* ***with*** *the newspaper, Jack.*

after /ˈɑːf.təʳ/ ⓤ /ˈæf.tɚ/ conjunction at a time which is later than another event: *Three months after they moved out, the house was still empty.* ○ *Soon/shortly after we joined the motorway, the car started to make a strange noise.* ○ *I went to the post office* ***straight/immediately*** *after I left you.*

after /ˈɑːf.təʳ/ ⓤ /ˈæf.tɚ/ adv later than someone or something else: *Hilary got here at midday and Nicholas arrived* ***soon*** *after.* ○ *I can't go next week – how about the week after* (= the following week)? ○ NOT STANDARD *She got back at 4.30 and went to see Emilie after* (= after she got back). **after-** /ɑːf.tə-/ ⓤ /æf.tɚ-/ prefix an after-dinner speech ○ *an after-hours club* ○ *after-sales service*

afterbirth /ˈɑːf.tə.bɜːθ/ ⓤ /ˈæf.tɚ.bɝːθ/ noun [U] the material, including the PLACENTA, which is pushed out of a woman's or female animal's body soon after she has given birth

aftercare /ˈɑːf.tə.keəʳ/ ⓤ /ˈæf.tɚ.ker/ noun [U] the care of people after they have left a hospital or prison

ˈafter efˌfects plural noun unpleasant effects that follow an event or accident, sometimes continuing for a long time or happening some time after it

afterglow /ˈɑːf.tə.ɡləʊ/ ⓤ /ˈæf.tɚ.ɡloʊ/ noun [C usually sing or U] a pleasant feeling produced after an experience, event, feeling, etc: *The team were* ***basking in the*** *afterglow* ***of*** *winning the cup.*

afterlife /ˈɑːf.tə.laɪf/ ⓤ /ˈæf.tɚ-/ noun [S] the life, for example in heaven, which some people believe begins

A

after death: *They'll be reunited **in the** afterlife.*

aftermath /ˈɑːf.tə.mæθ/ /-mɑːθ/ [US] /ˈæf.tɚ-/ *noun* [S] the period which follows an unpleasant event or accident, and the effects which it causes: *Many more people died **in the** aftermath **of** the explosion.*

afternoon /ˌɑːf.təˈnuːn/ [US] /ˌæf.tɚ-/ *noun* [C or U] the period which starts at about twelve o'clock or after the meal in the middle of the day and ends at about six o'clock or when the sun goes down: *It was a sunny afternoon.* ○ *She works three afternoons a week at the library.* ○ *It was on a Saturday afternoon.* ○ *My baby usually sleeps **in the** afternoons.* ○ *Let's go to the park **this** afternoon.* ○ *I spoke to her **yesterday** afternoon.* ○ *I'll meet you **tomorrow** afternoon at about 3.30.* ○ *She's coming round **on** Wednesday afternoon.* ○ *He's been in a bad mood **all** afternoon.* ○ *She likes to have an afternoon nap.* ○ *We got an early-/mid-/late-afternoon flight.*

afternoons /ˌɑːf.təˈnuːnz/ [US] /ˌæf.tɚ-/ *adv US* every afternoon or on many afternoons: *He works afternoons.*

COMMON LEARNER ERROR

afternoon

If you talk about what happens during the afternoon, use the preposition 'in'.

In the afternoon I phoned my girlfriend.
~~*At the afternoon I phoned my girlfriend.*~~

If you say a day of the week before 'afternoon', use the preposition 'on'.

I'm going to the dentist on Tuesday afternoon.
~~*I'm going to the dentist in Tuesday afternoon.*~~

ˌafternoon ˈtea *noun* [C or U] *MAINLY UK* a small meal eaten in the late afternoon, usually including cake and a cup of tea

afters /ˈɑːf.təz/ [US] /ˈæf.tɚz/ *noun* [U] *UK INFORMAL* sweet food eaten at the end of a meal; dessert: *What's **for** afters, Dad?*

aftershave (lotion) /ˈɑːf.tə.ʃeɪvˌləʊ.ʃᵊn/ [US] /ˈæf.tɚ.ʃeɪvˌloʊ-/ *noun* [U] a liquid with a pleasant smell which a man puts on his face after SHAVING

aftershock /ˈɑːf.tə.ʃɒk/ [US] /ˈæf.tɚ.ʃɑːk/ *noun* [C] a sudden movement of the Earth's surface which often follows an earthquake and which is less violent than the first main movement: *The initial earthquake was followed by **a series of** aftershocks.*

aftertaste /ˈɑːf.tə.teɪst/ [US] /ˈæf.tɚ-/ *noun* [C usually sing] the taste that a particular food or other substance leaves in your mouth when you have swallowed it: *The medicine left an unpleasant aftertaste.*

afterthought /ˈɑːf.tə.θɔːt/ [US] /ˈæf.tɚ.θɑːt/ *noun* [C usually sing] an idea, thought or plan which was not originally intended but is thought of at a later time: *She only asked me to her party **as an** afterthought.* ○ *The pillars seem to have been **added** to the entrance **as an** afterthought.*

afterwards /ˈɑːf.tə.wədz/ [US] /ˈæf.tɚ.wɚdz/ *adv* (*US ALSO* **afterward**) after the time mentioned; later: *We had tea, and afterwards we sat in the garden for a while.* ○ *They separated, and **soon/shortly** afterwards Jane left the country.*

Aga (cooker) /ˈɑː.gəˌkʊk.əʳ/ [US] /-ɚ/ *noun* [C] *UK TRADEMARK* a large iron cooker which keeps its heat

again [ONE MORE TIME] /əˈgen/ /-ˈgeɪn/ [US] /-ˈgen/ *adv* **1** one more time: *Could you spell your name again, please?* ○ *If he does it again I'll have to tell him.* ○ *Deborah's late again.* ○ *Throw it away and **start** again.* **2** back to the original place or condition: *We went to Edinburgh and **back** again all in one day.* ○ *Get some rest and you'll soon be well again.*

• **once again** If something happens once again, it has already happened several times before: *You are reminded once again of the author's love of the sea.*

• **Never again!** said after an unpleasant experience to show that you do not intend to do it again: *He drove me back home last night. Never again!*

• **yet again** If something happens yet again, it has already happened many times before: *I'm afraid it's been delayed yet again.*

• **again and again** repeatedly: *I've told you again and again not to do that.*

• **all over again** If you do something all over again, you start again from the beginning: *It's already taken me two hours – I don't want to have to do it all over again.*

• **then again** (*ALSO* **there again**) used when you have had a new thought that is different or opposite to what you have just said: *I like to travel but, then again, I'm very fond of my home.*

again [IN ADDITION] /əˈgen/ /-ˈgeɪn/ [US] /-ˈgen/ *adv* in addition to the amount we know about or have mentioned already: *They are paid half **as much** again as we are.*

against [IN OPPOSITION] /əˈgentst/ /-ˈgeɪntst/ [US] /-ˈgentst/ *prep* **1** in opposition to: *She spoke against the decision to close the college.* ○ *Fifty people voted against the new proposal.* ○ *I'm very much against the idea that it is the woman's job to bring up the child.* ○ *Germany are playing against Brazil in the cup final tonight.* ○ *She's always rebelled against authority.* ○ *She sold the house even though it was against his wishes.* ○ *They called a demonstration to protest against proposed job cuts.* ○ *Are you **for or** against my proposal?* ○ *Sanctions against the country should be lifted.* ○ *Stricter controls will help in the fight against inflation.* ○ *Criminal charges will be brought against the driver.* ○ *They decided not to take legal action against him.* ○ *They were **up** against a powerful pressure group.* ○ *We **came up** against a lot of problems in the course of building our extension.* ○ *The **chances/odds** against you winning such a competition are enormous.* ○ *It's against **the law*** (= illegal) *to leave children under a certain age alone in the house.* ○ *It's against my **beliefs/principles** to be nice to someone I dislike just because they're in a senior position.* ○ *Against **all probability*** (= although it was extremely unlikely) *we found ourselves in the same hotel.* ○ *I wouldn't dare say anything against him* (= criticize him) *to his mother!* **2** in the opposite direction to: *The last part of the course was hard because I was running against the wind.* ○ *Commuting is not so bad when you are travelling against the traffic.*

• **have *sth* against *sb*** If you have something against someone, you dislike them for a reason: *I've **nothing** against him – I just don't have much in common with him.*

• **against *your* better judgment** If something is against your better judgment, you think it would be wiser not to do it: *Against my better judgment, I gave him the job.*

• **be/come up against a brick wall** to be unable to make more progress with a plan or discussion because someone is stopping you

• **be up against it** *INFORMAL* to be having or likely to have serious problems or difficulties: *With seven members of the team missing, Hull are going to be up against it.* ○ *Many families are up against it, unable to afford even basic items.*

• **count/go/work against** If something counts/goes/works against you, it gives you a disadvantage: *Lack of experience will generally count against you in an interview.*

• **against time/the clock** If you do something against time/the clock, you do it as fast as possible and try to finish it before a certain time: *It was a real race against time to get all the costumes sewn for the play.*

against [TOUCHING] /əˈgentst/ /-ˈgeɪntst/ [US] /-ˈgentst/ *prep* next to and touching or being supported by (something): *Why don't we put the bed against the wall?* ○ *He loved the feel of her soft hair against his skin.* ○ *The rain beat against her face as she struggled through the wind.* ○ *The police officer had him up against the wall, both arms behind his back.* ○ *She leant against the door.*

against [PROTECTION] /əˈgentst/ /-ˈgeɪntst/ [US] /-ˈgentst/ *prep* as a protection or defence from the bad effects of: *We've insured the car against fire, theft and accident.* ○ *The police have to arm themselves against attack.*

against [BACKGROUND] /əˈgentst/ /-ˈgeɪntst/ [US] /-ˈgentst/ *prep* with the background of or compared to: *Paintings look best against a simple white wall.*

• **as against** compared to: *He earns $80 000 a year, as against my $40 000.*

agape /ə'geɪp/ *adj* with the mouth open, especially showing surprise or shock: *We watched, our mouths agape in excitement.*

Aga saga /'ɑ:.gə,sɑ:.gə/ *noun* [C] *UK HUMOROUS* a novel about the lives of people who have a good standard of living and live in the English countryside

agate /'æg.ət/ *noun* [C or U] a hard stone with strips of colour, used in jewellery

age TIME SPENT ALIVE /eɪdʒ/ *noun* [C or U] the period of time someone has been alive or something has existed: *Do you know the age of that building?* ○ *What age* (= How old) *is your brother?* ○ *I'd guess she's about my age* (= she is about as old as I am). ○ *She was 74 years of age when she wrote her first novel.* ○ *He left home at the age of 16.* ○ *I was married with four children at your age.* ○ *She's starting to show/look her age* (= to look as old as she is). ○ *I'm really beginning to feel my age* (= feel old). ○ *His girlfriend's twice his age* (= twice as old as he is) ⊃See also **ages**.

● **Act your age!** said to someone to tell them to stop behaving like someone who is much younger

● **come of age 1** to reach the age when you are legally recognized as an adult and become old enough to vote **2** If something has come of age, it has reached its full successful development.

● **the age of consent** the age at which someone is considered by the law to be old enough to agree to have sex with someone

● **under age** legally too young to do something: *He was prosecuted for having sex with a girl who was under age.* ○ *under age drinking*

aged /eɪdʒd/ *adj* [before n] of the age of: *They've got one daughter, Isabel, aged 3.*

age PROCESS /eɪdʒ/ *noun* [U] the process of getting older: *Her back was bent with age.* ○ *This cheese/wine improves with age.* ○ *Her temper hasn't improved with age!*

age /eɪdʒ/ *verb* [I or T] *UK* **ageing** or *US* **aging**, **aged**, **aged** *She's aged* (= She looks older) *since the last time we met.* ○ *The brandy is aged* (= left to develop) *in oak for ten years.*

aged /'eɪ.dʒɪd/ *adj* old: *She has two rather aged aunts.*

the 'aged *plural noun* old people when considered as a group: *The hospital was built to meet the needs of the aged.* **ageing**, *US USUALLY* **aging** /'eɪ.dʒɪŋ/ *adj:* *an ageing Hollywood actor* ○ *the ageing process* ○ *aging computers/machinery*

age PERIOD /eɪdʒ/ *noun* [C] a particular period in time: *the Victorian age* ○ *the modern age* ○ *the nuclear age*

age LONG TIME /eɪdʒ/ *noun* [C] a long time: *It's been an age since we last spoke.*

-age ACTION /-ɪdʒ/ *suffix* used to form nouns which refer to the action or result of something: *blockage* ○ *shrinkage* ○ *wastage* ○ *All breakages must be paid for.*

-age STATE /-ɪdʒ/ *suffix* used to form nouns which refer to a state or condition: *bondage* ○ *marriage* ○ *shortage*

-age PLACE /-ɪdʒ/ *suffix* used to form nouns which are names of places: *orphanage* ○ *vicarage*

'age ,group *noun* [C] (*ALSO* **age range,** *ALSO* **age bracket**) people of a similar age, considered as a group: *51% of enquiries were from those in the 25 to 40 age group.*

ageism, *US USUALLY* **agism** /'eɪ.dʒɪ.zᵊm/ *noun* [U] treating people unfairly because of their age **ageist**, *US USUALLY* **agist** /'eɪ.dʒɪst/ *adj: an ageist remark/job advertisement*

ageless /'eɪdʒ.ləs/ *adj* describes someone or something that never looks older: *She is beautiful and, at forty-three, somehow ageless.*

'age ,limit *noun* [C] the age at which a person is allowed or not allowed to do something: *the upper age limit* ○ *The lower age limit for buying cigarettes in the UK is 16.*

agenda /ə'dʒen.də/ *noun* [C] **1** a list of matters to be discussed at a meeting: *There were several important items on the agenda.* ○ *The question of security is high on the agenda for this afternoon's meeting.* **2** a list of aims or possible future achievements: *Women's rights have been put back on the agenda* (= are being discussed publicly again). ○ *The subject of safety must be placed high on/at the top of the agenda* (= must be discussed because it is

very important). ○ *Education was placed firmly on the political agenda in the Prime Minister's week-end speech.*

● **set the agenda** to decide what subjects other people should discuss and deal with

agent REPRESENTATIVE /'eɪ.dʒᵊnt/ *noun* [C] **1** a person who acts for or represents another: *Please contact our agent in Spain for further information.* **2** a person who represents an actor, artist or writer **3** someone who works secretly for the government or other organization: *a secret/foreign agent*

agency /'eɪ.dʒᵊnt.si/ *noun* [C] **1** a business which represents one group of people when dealing with another group: *an advertising/employment/estate/travel agency* ⊃See also **agency** at **agent** CAUSE. **2** a government organization: *an overseas-aid agency* ○ *the Central Intelligence Agency*

agent CAUSE /'eɪ.dʒᵊnt/ *noun* [C] a person or thing that produces a particular effect or change: *a powerful cleaning agent* ○ *a raising agent for cakes* ○ *a clotting agent* ○ *LITERARY He was the agent of their destruction.*

agency /'eɪ.dʒᵊnt.si/ *noun FORMAL* **through the agency of sb** because of the actions of someone: *She was freed from prison through the agency of her doctor.* ⊃See also **agency** at **agent** REPRESENTATIVE.

agent provocateur /,æʒ.ɑ̃ː.prə,vɒk.ə'tɜːʳ/ US /,ɑːʒ.ɑ̃ː.-prou,vɑː.kə'tɜː/ *noun* [C] *plural* **agents provocateurs** a person who intentionally encourages people working against a government to do something illegal so that they can be caught

age-old /'eɪdʒ.ᵊould/ US /-'ould-/ *adj* [before n] *LITERARY* very old: *an age-old story of love and betrayal*

ages /'eɪ.dʒɪz/ *plural noun MAINLY UK INFORMAL* a very long time: *It takes ages to cook.* ○ *I've been waiting for ages.* ○ *It's been ages since I've seen her.*

agglomeration /ə,glɒm.ə'reɪ.ʃᵊn/ US /-,glɑː.mə-/ *noun* [C] (*ALSO* **agglomerate**) *FORMAL* a large group of many different things gathered together: *an agglomeration of various ethnic and religious groupings*

aggrandizement, *UK USUALLY* **-isement** /ə-'græn.dɪz.mənt/ *noun* [U] *FORMAL DISAPPROVING* increase in power, importance or wealth: *He gives a lot of money to charity, but personal aggrandizement/self-aggrandizement is his motive.*

aggravate MAKE WORSE /'æg.rə.veɪt/ *verb* [T] **1** to make a bad situation worse: *Attempts to restrict parking in the city centre have further aggravated the problem of traffic congestion.* **2** to make a disease worse: *The treatment only aggravated the condition.*

aggravate ANNOY /'æg.rə.veɪt/ *verb* [T] *INFORMAL* to annoy someone: *Stop aggravating me, will you!*

aggravating /'æg.rə.veɪ.tɪŋ/ US /-tɪŋ/ *adj INFORMAL* annoying: *I find him really aggravating.*

aggravation /,æg.rə'veɪ.ʃᵊn/ *noun* [U] (*UK ALSO* **aggro**) *INFORMAL* trouble or difficulty: *I've been getting a lot of aggravation at work recently.* ○ *I'd complain to the manager but it's not worth the aggro.*

,aggravated as'sault *noun* [U] *LEGAL* a serious, violent attack on someone

,aggravated 'burglary *noun* [U] *UK LEGAL* a crime that involves using a weapon or committing another crime while illegally entering a person's house

aggregate /'æg.rɪ.gət/ *noun* [C or U] something formed by adding together several amounts or things; a total: *They purchased an aggregate of 3000 shares in the company.* ○ *Snowflakes are loose aggregates of ice crystals.* ○ *Arsenal lost the second game, but got through to the final on aggregate* (= adding together all their goals).

aggregate /'æg.rɪ.gət/ *adj* [before n] total: *The seven companies have an aggregate turnover of £5.2 million.*

aggregate /'æg.rɪ.geɪt/ *verb* [T] to combine into a single group or total **aggregation** /,æg.rɪ'geɪ.ʃᵊn/ *noun* [U]

aggression /ə'greʃ.ᵊn/ *noun* [U] **1** spoken or physical behaviour which is threatening or involves harm to someone or something: *Some types of dog are bred for aggression.* ○ *an act of aggression* **2** forceful playing in sport that is intended to win points

A

aggressive /əˈgres.ɪv/ *adj* **1** behaving in an angry and violent way towards another person: *Men tend to be more aggressive than women.* ○ *If I criticize him, he gets aggressive and starts shouting.* **2** determined to win or succeed and using forceful action to achieve victory or success: *an aggressive election campaign* ○ *aggressive marketing tactics* ○ *Both players both won their first-round matches in aggressive style.*
aggressively /əˈgres.ɪv.li/ *adv*: *Small children often behave aggressively.* ○ *The company is aggressively* (= with determination) *pursuing new business opportunities.* ○ *They played more aggressively* (= forcefully) *in the second half.*
aggressor /əˈgres.əʳ/ [US] /-ɚ/ *noun* [C] a person or country that starts an argument, fight or war by attacking first

aggrieved /əˈgriːvd/ *adj* unhappy and angry because of unfair treatment: *He felt aggrieved* ***at*** *not being chosen for the team.* ○ *One aggrieved customer complained that he still hadn't received the book he had ordered several weeks ago.*

aggro /ˈæg.rəʊ/ [US] /-roʊ/ *noun* [U] **1** *UK SLANG* violent or threatening behaviour, especially between groups of young people: *There was some aggro between rival football fans at the station.* **2** *UK INFORMAL* trouble or difficulty: *Why are you being so uncooperative? I don't need this aggro.*

aghast /əˈgɑːst/ [US] /-ˈgæst/ *adj* [after v] suddenly filled with strong feelings of shock and anxiety: *He looked at her aghast.*

agile [PHYSICALLY QUICK] /ˈædʒ.aɪl/ [US] /-ᵊl/ *adj* able to move your body quickly and easily: *Monkeys are very agile climbers.* ○ *You need to have agile fingers to do this kind of work.* **agility** /əˈdʒɪl.ɪ.ti/ [US] /-ə.t̬i/ *noun* [U] *He's got the agility of a mountain goat.*

agile [MENTALLY QUICK] /ˈædʒ.aɪl/ [US] /-ᵊl/ *adj* able to think quickly and clearly: *For a man of 80, he has a remarkably agile* ***mind***. **agility** /əˈdʒɪl.ɪ.ti/ [US] /-ə.t̬i/ *noun* [U] *This job requires considerable* ***mental*** *agility.*

agin /əˈgɪn/ *prep NORTHERN ENGLISH* against: *The whole world seemed agin him.*

aging /ˈeɪ.dʒɪŋ/ *MAINLY US present participle of* **age** PROCESS

agism /ˈeɪ.dʒɪ.zᵊm/ *noun* [U] *MAINLY US FOR* **ageism**

agitate [ARGUE] /ˈædʒ.ɪ.teɪt/ *verb* [I] to argue energetically, especially in public, in order to achieve a particular type of change: *The unions continue to agitate* ***for*** *higher pay.* ○ *As a young man, he had agitated* ***against*** *the Vietnam war.* **agitation** /ˌædʒ.ɪˈteɪ.ʃᵊn/ *noun* [U] *The anti-war agitation is beginning to worry the government.*
agitator /ˈædʒ.ɪ.teɪ.təʳ/ [US] /-t̬ɚ/ *noun* [C] *It is thought that the strike was the work of undercover political agitators.*

agitate [MAKE ANXIOUS] /ˈædʒ.ɪ.teɪt/ *verb* [T] to make someone feel anxious and not calm: *I didn't want to agitate her by telling her.* **agitated** /ˈædʒ.ɪ.teɪ.tɪd/ [US] /-t̬ɪd/ *adj*: *She became very agitated when her son failed to return home.*
agitation /ˌædʒ.ɪˈteɪ.ʃᵊn/ *noun* [U] anxiety: *He arrived home in a* ***state of*** *agitation.*

agitate [SHAKE] /ˈædʒ.ɪ.teɪt/ *verb* [T] *SPECIALIZED* to shake a liquid: *Pour the powder into the solution and agitate it until the powder has dissolved.*

agitprop /ˈædʒ.ɪt.prɒp/ [US] /-prɑːp/ *noun* [U] (the spreading of) strongly political ideas or arguments expressed especially through plays, art, books, etc.

aglow /əˈgləʊ/ [US] /-ˈgloʊ/ *adj* [after v] *LITERARY* bright; shining with light and colour: *a city at night, aglow* ***with*** *lights* ○ *His face was* ***all*** *aglow* ***with*** *excitement.*

AGM /ˌeɪ.dʒiːˈem/ *noun* [C] *UK ABBREVIATION FOR* **annual general meeting**

agnostic /ægˈnɒs.tɪk/ [US] /-ˈnɑː.stɪk/ *noun* [C] someone who does not know, or believes that it is impossible to know, whether a god exists: *Although he was raised a Catholic, he was an agnostic for most of his adult life.* ➲Compare **atheist**.
agnostic /ægˈnɒs.tɪk/ [US] /-ˈnɑː.stɪk/ *adj* having the beliefs of an agnostic **agnosticism** /ægˈnɒs.tɪ.sɪ.zᵊm/ [US] /-ˈnɑː.stə-/ *noun* [U]

ago /əˈgəʊ/ [US] /-ˈgoʊ/ *adv* back in the past; back in time from the present: *He left the house over an hour ago.* ○ *The dinosaurs died out 65 million years ago.* ○ ***Long*** *ago/****A long time*** *ago, there lived a girl called Cinderella.*

agog /əˈgɒg/ [US] /-ˈgɑːg/ *adj* [after v] excited; eager (to know or see more): *We waited agog for news.*

agonize /ˈæg.ə.naɪz/ *verb*
▲ **agonize over/about** ***sth***, *UK USUALLY* **-ise** *phrasal verb* If you agonize over/about something, you spend time anxiously trying to make a decision about it: *She agonized for days about whether she should take the job.*

agony /ˈæg.ə.ni/ *noun* [C or U] extreme physical or mental pain or suffering: *She lay there screaming* ***in*** *agony.* ○ *I was* ***in*** *an agony* ***of*** *suspense.* ○ *We've both* ***suffered*** *agonies* ***of*** *guilt over what happened.*
agonized, *UK USUALLY* **-ised** /ˈæg.ə.naɪzd/ *adj* showing or feeling extreme physical or mental pain: *We heard an agonized cry.* ○ *She gave him an agonized look.*
agonizing, *UK USUALLY* **-ising** /ˈæg.ə.naɪ.zɪŋ/ *adj* **1** causing extreme physical or mental pain: *an agonizing death* **2** causing extreme anxiety: *She went through an agonizing few weeks waiting for the test results.* ○ *We are faced with an agonizing choice/decision/dilemma.* **agonizingly**, *UK USUALLY* **-isingly** /ˈæg.ə.naɪ.zɪŋ.li/ *adv*

ˈagony ˌaunt *UK noun* [C usually sing] a person, usually a woman, who publicly gives advice to people with personal problems, especially in a regular magazine or newspaper article

ˈagony ˌcolumn *UK noun* [C usually sing] the part of a magazine or newspaper where letters from readers about their personal problems are printed, together with advice about how to deal with them: *She wrote in to an agony column.*

agoraphobia /ˌæg.rəˈfəʊ.bi.ə/ [US] /-ˈfoʊ-/ *noun* [U] *SPECIALIZED* fear of open spaces, going outside, or distance from a place of safety ➲Compare **claustrophobia**.
agoraphobic /ˌæg.rəˈfəʊ.bɪk/ [US] /-ˈfoʊ-/ *noun* [C] a person who suffers from agoraphobia **agoraphobic** /ˌæg.rəˈfəʊ.bɪk/ [US] /-ˈfoʊ-/ *adj*

agrarian /əˈgreə.ri.ən/ [US] /-ˈgrer.i-/ *adj SPECIALIZED* **1** related to the land, especially farms, and its ownership: *This is prime agrarian land.* **2** describes a place or country that is dependent on farming rather than industry: *This part of the country is mainly agrarian.*

agree /əˈgriː/ *verb* **1** [I or T] to have the same opinion, or to accept a suggestion or idea: *Ann and I never seem to agree.* ○ *I agree* ***with*** *you on this issue.* ○ *My father and I don't agree* ***about/on*** *very much.* ○ [+ that] *I agree* ***that*** *he should be invited.* ○ [+ question word] *Experts seem unable to agree* ***whether*** *the drug is safe or not.* ○ [+ speech] *"You're absolutely right," agreed Jake.* ○ *I suggested that we should meet, and they agreed* (= said yes). ○ [+ to infinitive] *The bank has agreed* (= is willing) ***to*** *lend me £5000.* ➲See Note **accept or agree?** at **accept** TAKE. **2** [T] *UK* to accept something: *We finally agreed a deal.* **3** [I] If two or more statements, ideas, sets of numbers, etc. agree, they are the same or very similar: *We've got five accounts of what happened and none of them agree.* **4** [I] *SPECIALIZED* When two words agree, or one word agrees with another word, they have the same grammatical form. For example, the words may both be singular or plural, masculine or feminine, etc.
• **agree to differ** If two people agree to differ, they accept that they have different opinions about something and stop trying to persuade each other that they are right.
• **couldn't agree more/less** If you say you couldn't agree more/less, you mean you completely agree/disagree.
agreed /əˈgriːd/ *adj* **1** accepted: *We have to stick to the agreed price.* ○ *"So we'll meet at 5.30, shall we?" "Agreed* (= yes)*."* **2 be agreed** If two or more people are agreed, they have the same opinion: *Are we all agreed* ***(on*** *that)?* ○ [+ that] *The members are agreed* ***that*** *the proposal should be rejected.*

PHRASAL VERBS WITH **agree** ▼

▲ **agree to** ***sth*** *phrasal verb* to agree something: *Both sides in the conflict have agreed to the terms of the peace treaty.*
▲ **agree with** ***sth*** [THINK] *phrasal verb* [usually in negatives] to think that something is morally acceptable: *I don't agree with hunting.*

▲ **agree with** *sb* AFFECT *phrasal verb* If a situation or new conditions agree with you, they make you feel healthy and happy: *You look well – the mountain air must agree with you.*

● **not agree with** *sb* If a type of food or drink does not agree with you, it makes you feel slightly ill: *Those onions I ate didn't agree with me.*

agreeable PLEASANT /ə'griː.ə.bļ/ *adj FORMAL* pleasant; pleasing: *We spent a most agreeable evening by the river.*

agreeable AGREEING /ə'griː.ə.bļ/ *adj* **1** able to be accepted by everyone: *The talks are aimed at finding a* **mutually** *agreeable solution.* ○ *We must find a compromise that is agreeable* **to** *both sides of the party.* **2** *FORMAL* willing to do or accept something: *If Bridget is agreeable* **to** *the proposal, we'll start the project in June.*

agreeably /ə'griː.ə.bli/ *adv* with enjoyment or pleasure: *We were agreeably* **surprised** *by the price.*

agreement /ə'griː.mənt/ *noun* [C or U] **1** when people have the same opinion, or when they approve of or accept something: *The whole family was* **in** *agreement* **with** *her* **about/on** *what they should do.* ○ *If the three parties cannot* **reach** *agreement now, there will be a civil war.* ○ *I don't think you'll ever get Tony's agreement* **to** *these proposals.* ○ [+ that] *There's widespread agreement* **that** *the law should be changed.* **2** a decision or arrangement, often formal and written, between two or more groups or people: *The dispute was settled by an agreement that satisfied both sides.* ○ *The government has* **entered into/signed** *an international arms-control agreement.* ○ *They have* **broken (the terms of)** *the agreement* **on** *human rights.* ○ *Finally the two sides have* **reached** *an agreement.* ○ *In the sentence 'Kate was brushing her hair', 'Kate' and 'her' are* **in** *agreement* (= they are correctly expressed according to the rules of grammar).

agribusiness /'æg.rɪ.bɪz.nɪs/ *noun* [U] *SPECIALIZED* the various businesses that are connected with producing, preparing and selling farm products

agriculture /'æg.rɪ.kʌl.tʃəʳ/ US /-tʃɚ/ *noun* [U] farming: *Agriculture is still largely based on traditional methods in some countries.* ○ *The area depends on agriculture for most of its income.* ○ *Seventy percent of the country's population practises subsistence agriculture.* ⊃Compare **horticulture**.

agricultural /ˌæg.rɪ'kʌl.tʃᵊr.ᵊl/ US /-tʃɚ.ᵊl/ *adj*: *The world's supply of agricultural land is shrinking fast.* ○ *She's studying agricultural science.* ○ *The country's economy is mainly agricultural* (= based on farming) *and depends on crops like coffee.*

agrochemical /ˌæg.rəʊ'kem.ɪ.kᵊl/ US /-roʊ-/ *noun* [C] a chemical that is used in farming to help grow crops or kill insects

aground /ə'graʊnd/ *adj* [after v], *adv* If a boat or ship is aground, it is unable to move because it is touching ground or in a place where this very little water: *The ship is currently aground off the Brittany coast.* ○ *The oil tanker* **ran/went** *aground on a mud bank in thick fog.*

ah /ɑː/ *exclamation* (*ALSO* **aah**) used to express understanding, pleasure, pain, surprise or the fact that you have noticed something: *Ah, I see.* ○ *Why has the train stopped? Ah, now we're off again.* ○ *Ah, Jessica, how wonderful to see you!* ○ *Ah, what a lovely baby!*

aha /ɑː'hɑː/ *exclamation* used when you suddenly understand or find something: *Aha, now I see what you mean!* ○ *Aha, that's where I put my keys!*

ahead IN FRONT /ə'hed/ *adv* **1** in front: *The road ahead is very busy.* ○ *Turn left at the traffic lights, and you'll see the hospital* **straight** *ahead.* ○ *Rick walked on ahead of us.* ○ *You* **go on** *ahead of* (= before) *me, and I'll meet you there.* **2** having more points than someone else in a competition or competitive situation: *Apparently, the latest opinion polls put the Democrats 15% ahead* **of** *the Republicans.* ○ *Barcelona was ahead after ten minutes.* **3** making more progress than someone else: *Sophie is* **way** (= far) *ahead of the other children in her class.*

ahead IN THE FUTURE /ə'hed/ *adv* in or into the future; before: *She has a difficult time ahead* **of** *her.* ○ *He couldn't bear to think of the lonely year ahead.*

ahem /ə'hem/ *exclamation MAINLY HUMOROUS* used to describe the little cough that someone gives to express

slight embarrassment, amusement, doubt or disapproval, or to attract attention

ahold /ə'həʊld/ US /-'hoʊld/ US **1** get ahold of *sth* to obtain something: *Drugs are too easy to get ahold of.* **2** get ahold of *sb* to find or communicate with someone: *I'd like to get ahold of Debbie and talk to her about this.* **3** grab/take, etc. ahold of *sth/sb* to take hold of something or someone: *I grabbed ahold of his legs and held on so he could not get away.* **4** get/grab, etc. ahold of *sb/sth* to get power or control over someone or something: *Once the drugs get ahold of you, it just changes you completely.*

-aholic, **-oholic** /-ə.hɒl.ɪk/ US /-hɑː.lɪk/ *suffix* unable to stop doing or taking something: *a workaholic* ○ *an alcoholic* ○ *a chocoholic*

ahoy /ə'hɔɪ/ *exclamation* **1** a shout used, especially by people in boats, to attract attention: *Ahoy there!* **2** used, especially on a boat, when you see something, usually something which is in the distance: *Land ahoy!* ○ *Ship ahoy!*

AI /ˌeɪ'aɪ/ *noun* [U] *ABBREVIATION FOR* **artificial intelligence** or **artificial insemination**

aid /eɪd/ *noun* **1** [U] help or support: *He gets about* **with** *the aid* **of** *a walking stick.* ○ *She* **went to the** *aid* **of** *a man trapped in his car.* ○ *A woman in the street saw that he was in trouble and* **came to** *his aid.* **2** [C] a piece of equipment that helps you to do something: *teaching aids, such as books and videos* ○ *A thesaurus is a useful aid to writing.* **3** [U] help in the form of food, money, medical supplies or weapons that is given by a richer country to a poorer country: *The Vatican has agreed to donate $80 000 in* **humanitarian/emergency** *aid to countries affected by the war.* ○ *About a fifth of the country's income is in the form of* **foreign/overseas** *aid.*

● **in aid of** *sb/sth UK* in order to collect money for a group of people who need it: *a concert in aid of famine relief*

● **What's** *sth* **in aid of?** *UK INFORMAL* said when you want to know the reason for something: *What's all this shouting in aid of?*

aid /eɪd/ *verb* [T] to help: *Huge projects designed to aid poorer countries can sometimes do more harm than good.* ○ *His excuse for drinking brandy is that it's said to aid digestion.*

● **aid and abet** *sb LEGAL OR HUMOROUS* to help someone do something illegal or wrong: *Three tax inspectors were accused of aiding and abetting the men charged with fraud.*

aide /eɪd/ *noun* [C] a person whose job is to help someone important, such as a member of a government or a military officer of high rank: *a senior government aide* ○ *an aide* **to** *the Prime Minister*

aide-de-camp (*plural* **aides-de-camp**) /ˌeɪd.də'kɑː/ US /-'kæmp/ *noun* [C] (*ABBREVIATION* **ADC**) a military or naval officer who helps an officer of higher rank: *He became Napoleon's aide-de-camp in 1804.*

aide-mémoire /ˌeɪd.mem'wɑːʳ/ US /-'wɑːr/ *noun* [C] *FORMAL* something, usually written, that helps you to remember something

AIDS, **Aids** /eɪdz/ *noun* [U] *ABBREVIATION FOR* Acquired Immune Deficiency Syndrome: a serious disease caused by a virus which destroys the body's natural protection from infection, and which usually causes death: *In Britain, AIDS tests are now performed on all people who offer to become blood donors.* ○ *Don had* **full-blown** *AIDS for over a year before he died.* ⊃Compare **HIV**.

ail CAUSE DIFFICULTY /eɪl/ *verb* [T] *FORMAL* to cause difficulty and problems for: *The government seems to have no understanding of* **what** *ails the country.*

ailing /'eɪ.lɪŋ/ *adj* experiencing difficulty and problems: *the country's ailing economy* ○ *Ted asked me if I could help him fix his ailing car.*

ail BE/MAKE ILL /eɪl/ *verb* [I or T] *OLD USE* to be ill, or to cause to be ill: *She had been ailing for years before she died.* ○ **What's** *ailing you? Is it your leg again?* **ailing** /'eɪ.lɪŋ/ *adj*: *He's visiting his ailing father.*

aileron /'eɪ.lə.rɒn/ *noun* [C] *SPECIALIZED* a part along the back edge of an aircraft's wing which can be moved to help the aircraft turn or to keep it level

A

ailment /ˈeɪl.mənt/ *noun* [C] an illness: *Treat **minor** ailments yourself.*

aim POINT /eɪm/ *verb* [I or T] to point or direct a weapon towards someone or something that you want to hit: *Aim (the arrow) a little above the target.* ○ *Aim **at** the yellow circle.* ○ *There are hundreds of nuclear missiles aimed **at** the main cities.* ○ *She aimed (= directed) a kick **at** my shins.* ○ *Let's aim **for** (= go in the direction of) Coventry first, and then we'll have a look at the map.*

aim /eɪm/ *noun* [U] the act of pointing a weapon towards something: *He fired six shots at the target, but his aim was terrible, and he missed all of them.* ○ *She raised her gun, **took** aim and fired.*

aim INTEND /eɪm/ *verb* [I] to intend: [+ *to* infinitive] *I aim **to** be a millionaire by the time I'm 35.* ○ *We are aiming **for** (= planning to achieve) a 50% share of the German market.*

aim /eɪm/ *noun* [C] a result that your plans or actions are intended to achieve: *My **main** aim **in** life is to be a good husband and father.* ○ *Our **short-term** aim is to deal with our current financial difficulties, but our **long-term** aim is to improve the company's profitability.* ○ *The leaflet has been produced **with the** aim **of** increas**ing** public awareness of the disease.*

aimless /ˈeɪm.ləs/ *adj MAINLY DISAPPROVING* without any clear intentions, purpose or direction: *She said that her life seemed aimless after her children left home.* **aimlessly** /ˈeɪm.lə.sli/ *adv*: *While she waited, she walked aimlessly around the car park.* **aimlessness** /ˈeɪm.lə.snəs/ *noun* [U]

PHRASAL VERBS WITH **aim** ▼

▲ **aim at** *sth* INTEND *phrasal verb* to plan, hope or intend to achieve something: *The talks are aiming at a compromise.* ○ [+ *v-ing*] *The government's campaign is aimed at influenc**ing** public opinion.*

▲ **aim** *sth* **at** *sb* DIRECT *phrasal verb* [usually passive] If information is aimed at a particular person or group of people, it is made known in a way that influences them or makes them interested in something: *These advertisements are specifically aimed at young people.*

ain't /eɪnt/ *verb NOT STANDARD* am not, is not, are not, has not, or have not: *He ain't going.* ○ *"Can I have a fag?" "I ain't got none left."*

• **If it ain't broke, don't fix it.** *INFORMAL SAYING* said when you recognize that something is in a satisfactory state, and there is no reason to try to change it

air GAS /eə^r/ ⓊⓈ /er/ *noun* [U] the mixture of gases which surrounds the earth and which we breathe: *I went outside to get some **fresh** air.* ○ *You should put some air in your tyres – they look flat to me.* ⊃See also **airy** LIGHT; **airy** NOT SERIOUS; **airy** DELICATE.

• **be walking/floating on air** to be very happy and excited because something very pleasant has happened to you: *Ever since she met Mark, she's been walking on air.*

airless /ˈeə.ləs/ ⓊⓈ /ˈer-/ *adj DISAPPROVING* describes a place where it is difficult to breathe or the air is not fresh: *an airless office* ○ *My hotel room was small, airless and uncomfortable.*

the air AREA *noun* [S] the space above the ground, especially high above the ground: *The air was filled with the scent of roses.* ○ *Throw your gun down and put your hands in the air.* ○ *The police fired **into** the air to clear the demonstrators from the streets.*

• **in the air** If something is in the air, you feel that it is happening or about to happen: *Love/Change/Spring is in the air.*

• **up in the air** If a matter is up in the air, it is uncertain, often because other matters have to be decided first: *The whole future of the project is still up in the air.*

air AIRCRAFT /eə^r/ ⓊⓈ /er/ *noun* [U] travel in an aircraft: *I don't travel much **by** air.* ○ *an air crash/disaster* ○ *air travel*

air BROADCAST /eə^r/ ⓊⓈ /er/ *verb* [I or T] US to broadcast something on radio or television: *The game will be aired **live on** CBS at 7.00 tonight.* ○ *The interview with the President will air tomorrow morning.*

air /eə^r/ ⓊⓈ /er/ *noun* **be on/off (the) air** If a programme or a person is on/off (the) air, they are/are not broadcasting on radio or television: *The radio station is on air from 6.00 a.m.* ○ *As soon as the war started, any broadcasts with a military theme were **taken** off the air.*

air MANNER /eə^r/ ⓊⓈ /er/ *noun* [S] manner or appearance: *She has **an** air **of** confidence about her.*

• **airs and graces** false ways of behaving that are intended to make other people feel that you are important and belong to a high social class

• **put on airs (and graces)** (*ALSO* **give** *yourself* **airs (and graces)**) *DISAPPROVING* to behave as if you are more important than you really are

air DRY /eə^r/ ⓊⓈ /er/ *verb* [I or T] to become dry and/or fresh, or to cause to become dry and/or fresh: *My mother always airs the sheets before she makes the beds.* ○ *Leave the windows open to let the room air a bit.* **airing** /ˈeə.rɪŋ/ ⓊⓈ /ˈer.ɪŋ/ *noun* [S] *The room was damp and smelly so we opened all the windows and **gave** it a good airing* (= made the air fresh and dry).

air MAKE KNOWN /eə^r/ ⓊⓈ /er/ *verb* [T] to make opinions or complaints known to other people: *Putting a complaint in the suggestions box is one way of airing your **grievances**.* ○ *He'll air his **views** on the war whether people want to listen or not.* **airing** /ˈeə.rɪŋ/ ⓊⓈ /ˈer.ɪŋ/ *noun* [S] *The arguments for and against the proposals have been **given** a good airing* (= have been discussed in public).

air TUNE /eə^r/ ⓊⓈ /er/ *noun* [C] a simple tune: *Bach's Air on a G String*

ˈair ˌambulance *noun* [C] a plane or HELICOPTER equipped for flying ill or injured people to hospital

airbag /ˈeə.bæg/ ⓊⓈ /ˈer-/ *noun* [C] a bag in a vehicle that automatically fills with air if the vehicle is involved in an accident, in order to protect the driver or a passenger from injury: *In the event of a collision, the airbag stops the driver of the car from hitting his or her chest on the steering wheel.*

airbase /ˈeə.beɪs/ ⓊⓈ /ˈer-/ *noun* [C] a military airport, where military aircraft are kept and can land and take off

airbed UK /ˈeə.bed/ ⓊⓈ /ˈer-/ *noun* [C] (*US* **air mattress**) a large rectangular rubber or plastic bag which you fill with air so that you can lie on it in water or use it as a bed

airborne /ˈeə.bɔːn/ ⓊⓈ /ˈer.bɔːrn/ *adj* in the air, or carried by air or wind or by an aircraft; flying: *The airborne radioactive particles have covered a huge area of Russia.* ○ *Airborne troops were dropped by parachute behind enemy lines.* ○ *The old plane had great difficulty **getting** airborne* (= rising into the air).

ˈair ˌbrake *noun* [C] a BRAKE operated by air pressure which is used on large vehicles such as buses and trains

airbrick /ˈeə.brɪk/ ⓊⓈ /ˈer-/ *noun* [C] UK a special type of brick that has small holes in it which allow air to go through a wall

airbridge /ˈeə.brɪdʒ/ ⓊⓈ /ˈer-/ *noun* [C] UK a covered passage by which passengers can go from an airport building to an aircraft

airbrush /ˈeə.brʌʃ/ ⓊⓈ /ˈer-/ *noun* [C] a machine that scatters paint using air pressure, which is used for painting or for delicate improvement work on photographs **airbrush** /ˈeə.brʌʃ/ ⓊⓈ /ˈer-/ *verb* [T] *It's so obvious in the photo that her wrinkles have been airbrushed **out** (= removed from the photograph by putting paint over them with an airbrush).*

air-conditioned /ˈeə.kənˌdɪʃ.ᵊnd/ ⓊⓈ /ˈer-/ *adj* describes a building, room or vehicle in which the air is kept cool: *an air-conditioned office*

ˈair conˌditioner *noun* [C] a machine which keeps the air in a building cool

---

COMMON LEARNER ERROR

air conditioning

The correct form of the noun is 'air conditioning', not 'air condition'.

All rooms have television, phone and air conditioning.

~~All rooms have television, phone and air condition.~~

ˌair conˈditioning *noun* [U] the system used for keeping the air in a building or vehicle cool: *I wish my car had air conditioning.*

air-cooled /ˈeə.kuːld/ [US] /ˈer-/ *adj* If an engine is air-cooled, it is kept cool by a flow of air. ➲Compare **water-cooled**.

aircraft /ˈeə.krɑːft/ [US] /ˈer.kræft/ *noun* [C] *plural* **aircraft** any vehicle, with or without an engine, which can fly, such as a plane or helicopter: *military aircraft* ➲See picture **Planes, Ships and Boats** on page Centre 14

ˈaircraft ˌcarrier *noun* [C] a large ship that carries military aircraft and has a long, flat surface where they take off and land

aircrew /ˈeə.kruː/ [US] /ˈer-/ *group noun* [C] all the people, including the pilot, who work on an aircraft to fly it or to take care of the passengers

ˈair ˌdrop *noun* [C] the act of delivering supplies or equipment by dropping them from aircraft: *UN planes have made air drops to 300 flood-hit villages.* **ˈair ˌdrop** *verb* [T]

airfare /ˈeə.feə/ [US] /ˈer.fer/ *noun* [C] the price of a journey by aircraft: *Transatlantic airfares are going up.*

airfield /ˈeə.fiːld/ [US] /ˈer-/ *noun* [C] (*UK OLD-FASHIONED* **aerodrome**) a level area where aircraft can take off and land, which has fewer buildings and services than an airport and is used by fewer passengers

ˈair ˌforce *noun* [C usually sing] the part of a country's military forces which uses aircraft and fights in the air: *the United States Air Force*

ˌAir Force ˈOne *noun* the plane that the US president uses for official journeys

air freshener /ˈeəˌfreʃ.ᵊn.əʳ/ [US] /ˈerˌfreʃ.ᵊn.ɚ/ *noun* [C or U] a substance or device which makes a room or vehicle smell pleasant: *We need some more air freshener for the bathroom.*

airgun /ˈeə.gʌn/ [US] /ˈer-/ *noun* [C] a gun which uses air pressure to fire a PELLET (= small metal ball)

airhead /ˈeə.hed/ [US] /ˈer-/ *noun* [C] *SLANG* a stupid person: *She's such an airhead.*

ˈair hostˌess *noun* [C] *UK OLD-FASHIONED* a woman who serves passengers on an aircraft

ˈairing ˌcupboard *noun* [C] *UK* a heated cupboard where clothes, sheets, etc. that have been washed and are almost dry are put so that they can become completely dry

air-kiss /ˈeə.kɪs/ [US] /ˈer-/ *verb* [I or T] to perform an action similar to kissing someone without touching them with your lips, especially in an insincere way **ˈair ˌkiss** *noun* [C]

airletter /ˈeəˌlet.əʳ/ [US] /ˈerˌlet̬.ɚ/ *noun* [C] (*ALSO* **aerogramme**) a letter which is sent by aircraft, usually consisting of a single very thin sheet of paper which is folded and then stuck at the edges to form its own envelope

airlift /ˈeə.lɪft/ [US] /ˈer-/ *noun* [C] an operation organized to move supplies or people, by aircraft, to or from a place that is difficult to reach because of war, flooding, etc. **airlift** /ˈeə.lɪft/ [US] /ˈer-/ *verb* [T] *Over 10000 refugees were airlifted* ***out of*** *the region.*

airline /ˈeə.laɪn/ [US] /ˈer-/ *noun* [C] a business that operates regular services for carrying passengers and/or goods by aircraft: *What airline did you fly?*

airliner /ˈeəˌlaɪ.nəʳ/ [US] /ˈerˌlaɪ.nɚ/ *noun* [C] a large passenger aircraft

airlock [ROOM] /ˈeə.lɒk/ [US] /ˈer.lɑːk/ *noun* [C] a room between two areas that have different air PRESSURE (= the force produced by the air on an area), which allows you to go from one area to the other, without changing these pressures: *Airlocks are commonly found on submarines and manned spacecraft.*

airlock [BUBBLE] /ˈeə.lɒk/ [US] /ˈer.lɑːk/ *noun* [C] a bubble in a pipe that prevents liquid from flowing along it

airmail /ˈeə.meɪl/ [US] /ˈer-/ *noun* [U] a system of sending letters and parcels by aircraft: *If you send it* ***(by)*** *airmail, it'll be very expensive.*

airman /ˈeə.mən/ [US] /ˈer-/ *noun* [C] a low-ranking member of the British or US air force

ˈair ˌmattress *noun* [C] *US FOR* **airbed** or **Lilo**

ˈAir ˌMile *noun* [C] *TRADEMARK* a point worth one mile of a plane journey that is given free when you buy products or services from particular companies

airplane /ˈeə.pleɪn/ [US] /ˈer-/ *noun* [C] *US FOR* **aeroplane** ➲See picture **Planes, Ships and Boats** on page Centre 14

airplay /ˈeə.pleɪ/ [US] /ˈer-/ *noun* [U] (the amount of) broadcasting time that someone or something, such as a piece of recorded music, has on the radio: *Unless a song* ***gets*** *lots of airplay, it won't sell in the shops.* ➲Compare **airtime**.

ˈair ˌpocket *noun* [C] an area in the sky where the air is flowing differently from the way it is in the surrounding parts, which sometimes causes aircraft to go up or down suddenly

airport /ˈeə.pɔːt/ [US] /ˈer.pɔːrt/ *noun* [C] a place where aircraft regularly take off and land, with buildings for passengers to wait in: *an international airport* ○ *a military airport* ○ *Gatwick Airport* ○ *an airport terminal/runway*

ˈair ˌpower *noun* [U] the force of a country's military aircraft and the ability of these aircraft to be used for attacking and defending the country

ˈair ˌrage *noun* [U] when a passenger suddenly becomes angry and violent on an aircraft during a flight: *an increase in air rage incidents*

ˈair ˌraid *noun* [C] an attack by enemy aircraft, usually dropping bombs: *an air raid* ***shelter/siren***

air-rifle /ˈeə.raɪ.fl/ [US] /ˈer-/ *noun* [C] a gun with a long barrel which is fired from the shoulder, and which uses air pressure to fire a PELLET (= small metal ball) ➲See also **airgun**.

air-sea rescue /ˌeə.siːˈres.kjuː/ [US] /ˌer-/ *noun* [C] the act of using aircraft, including helicopters, and boats to try to save people in danger at sea

airship *MAINLY UK* /ˈeə.ʃɪp/ [US] /ˈer-/ *noun* [C] (*MAINLY US* **blimp**) a large aircraft without wings, used especially in the past and consisting of a large bag filled with gas which is lighter than air and powered by engines. Passengers were carried in an enclosed structure hanging below.

airshow /ˈeə.ʃəʊ/ [US] /ˈer.ʃoʊ/ *noun* [C] a public show of flying skills and special aircraft, often performed at an AIRBASE (= military airport) specially opened to visitors

airsick /ˈeə.sɪk/ [US] /ˈer-/ *adj* having the feeling that you will vomit because of the movement of an aircraft you are travelling in **airsickness** /ˈeəˌsɪk.nəs/ [US] /ˈer-/ *noun* [U]

airspace /ˈeə.speɪs/ [US] /ˈer-/ *noun* [U] the air or sky above a country, which is considered to belong to that country: *The government claimed that the plane had illegally entered its airspace.*

airspeed /ˈeə.spiːd/ [US] /ˈer-/ *noun* [U] the speed of an aircraft, measured against the speed of the air through which it is moving

airstream /ˈeə.striːm/ [US] /ˈer-/ *noun* [C] a current of air: *a strong south-westerly airstream* ○ *Migrating birds make use of airstreams to assist them on their long journey south.*

airstrike /ˈeə.straɪk/ [US] /ˈer-/ *noun* [C] an attack by military aircraft on a city, enemy soldiers, or their supplies, either by bombing or by firing guns

airstrip /ˈeə.strɪp/ [US] /ˈer-/ *noun* [C] (*ALSO* **landing strip**) a long, flat piece of land from which trees, rocks, etc. have been removed so that aircraft can take off and land: *We landed at a tiny airstrip in the middle of the jungle.*

ˈair ˌterminal *noun* [C] a building in an airport or in a place near an airport where aircraft passengers gather before their flight leaves or from which they leave after their flight has arrived

airtight /ˈeə.taɪt/ [US] /ˈer-/ *adj* completely closed so that no air can get in or out: *Biscuits will stay crisp if you keep them in an airtight container.*

airtime /ˈeə.taɪm/ [US] /ˈer-/ *noun* [U] (the amount of) broadcasting time that someone or something has on television or radio: *The smaller political parties are campaigning to be allowed free airtime before general elections.* ➲Compare **airplay**.

A

air-to-air /ˌeə.tə'eəʳ/ ⓤ /ˌer.tə'er/ *adj* [before n] involving a weapon which is fired from an aircraft at another aircraft: *an air-to-air missile*

air-to-ground /ˌeə.tə'ɡraʊnd/ ⓤ /ˌer.tə-/ *adj* [before n] (ALSO **air-to-surface**) involving a weapon which is fired from an aircraft at a place on the ground: *an air-to-ground attack*

ˌair traffic con'trol *noun* [U], *group noun* the activity of managing aircraft from the ground as they take off, fly and land, or the people who do this: *Air traffic control at Heathrow have given us clearance to land in 20 minutes.* **ˌair traffic con'troller** *noun* [C]

airwaves /'eə.weɪvz/ ⓤ /'er-/ *plural noun* the radio waves used for broadcasting radio and television programmes, or more generally, radio or television broadcasting time: *The new series of Batman will be **on the** airwaves at 6 pm every Tuesday.*

airway /'eə.weɪ/ ⓤ /'er-/ *noun* [C] SPECIALIZED the passage through the mouth and throat that carries air to the lungs

airworthy /'eəˌwɜː.ði/ ⓤ /'erˌwɝː-/ *adj* describes an aircraft which is in safe working condition and safe to fly **airworthiness** /'eəˌwɜː.ðɪ.nəs/ ⓤ /'erˌwɝː-/ *noun* [U]

airy ⌈LIGHT⌉ /'eə.ri/ ⓤ /'er.i/ *adj* APPROVING with a lot of light and space: *The new offices are light and airy.* **airiness** /'eə.rɪ.nəs/ ⓤ /'er.ɪ-/ *noun* [U]

airy ⌈DELICATE⌉ /'eə.ri/ ⓤ /'er.i/ *adj* delicate, as if full of air: *a light, airy fabric*

airy ⌈NOT SERIOUS⌉ /'eə.ri/ ⓤ /'er.i/ *adj* showing a lack of worry or serious thought: *"I don't care – you choose," he said, with an airy wave of the hand.* **airily** /'eə.rɪ.li/ ⓤ /'er-/ *adv*: *"He can do what he likes – it doesn't bother me," she said airily.*

airy-fairy /ˌeə.ri'feə.ri/ ⓤ /ˌer.i'fer.i/ *adj* UK INFORMAL not practical or based on reality: *She's talking about selling her house and buying an old castle in Ireland. It all sounds a bit airy-fairy to me.*

aisle /aɪl/ *noun* [C] **1** a long narrow space between rows of seats in an aircraft, cinema or church: *Would you like an aisle seat or would you prefer to be by the window?* **2** a long narrow space between the rows of shelves in a large shop: *You'll find the shampoo and the soap in the fourth aisle along from the entrance.*
● **go/walk down the aisle** INFORMAL to get married

aitch /eɪtʃ/ *noun* [C] the letter 'h' written as a word
● **drop *your* aitches** UK to not pronounce the 'h' at the beginning of words

ajar /ə'dʒɑːʳ/ ⓤ /-'dʒɑːr/ *adj* [after v] describes a door that is slightly open: *We **left** the door ajar so that we could hear what they were saying.*

aka /ˌeɪ.keɪ'eɪ/ ABBREVIATION FOR also known as: used when someone has another name: *James Brown, aka the 'Godfather of Soul'*

akimbo /ə'kɪm.bəʊ/ ⓤ /-boʊ/ *adj* [after n] If a person's arms are akimbo, they are bent at the ELBOWS (= the middle part of the arm where it bends) and they have their hands on their hips: *He stood, **arms** akimbo, refusing to move.*

akin /ə'kɪn/ *adj* [after v] similar; having some of the same qualities: *They speak a language akin to French.*

-al /-əl/ *suffix* used to add the meaning 'connected with' to adjectives, or 'the action of' to nouns: *medical* (= connected with medicine) ○ *approval* (= the act of approving)

à la /'æl.æ/ *prep* in the style of: *She has her hair blonde and curly, à la Marilyn Monroe.*

alabaster /ˌæl.ə'bæs.təʳ/ ⓤ /'æl.ə.bæs.tɚ/ *noun* [U] an almost transparent white stone, often used for making decorative objects

à la carte /ˌæl.ə'kɑːt/ ⓤ /-'kɑːrt/ *adj* [before n], *adv* If you eat à la carte, you choose each dish from a separate list instead of eating a fixed combination of dishes at a fixed price: *You get more choice if you eat à la carte/from the à la carte menu.* ⊃Compare **table d'hôte**.

alack /ə'læk/ HUMOROUS **alas and alack** an expression of sadness

alacrity /ə'læk.rə.ti/ ⓤ /-ţi/ *noun* [U] FORMAL speed and eagerness: *She accepted the money with alacrity.*

Aladdin's cave /əˌlæd.ɪnz'keɪv/ *noun* [S] UK a store of very many interesting or unusual objects: *His shop, a veritable Aladdin's cave of antiques, is for sale.*

à la mode ⌈MODERN⌉ /ˌæl.ə'məʊd/ ⓤ /-'moʊd/ *adj* [after v], *adv* OLD-FASHIONED in the most modern style or fashion

à la mode ⌈FOOD⌉ /ˌæl.ə'məʊd/ ⓤ /-'moʊd/ *adj* [after n] US served with ice cream: *apple pie à la mode*

alarm ⌈ANXIETY⌉ /ə'lɑːm/ ⓤ /-lɑːrm/ *noun* [U] sudden anxiety and fear, especially that something dangerous or unpleasant might happen: *I didn't tell her that he was late because I didn't want to **cause** her any alarm.* ○ *Villagers have reacted with alarm to news of a proposed new road.*
alarm /ə'lɑːm/ ⓤ /-lɑːrm/ *verb* [T] *I didn't want to alarm him by telling him that she was ill.* **alarmed** /ə'lɑːmd/ ⓤ /-lɑːrmd/ *adj*: *I was a bit alarmed **at/by** how much weight she'd lost.* ○ [+ to infinitive] *I was alarmed **to** hear that she was coming.* ○ [+ that] *I'm rather alarmed **that** we haven't heard anything.*

alarming /ə'lɑː.mɪŋ/ ⓤ /-'lɑːr-/ *adj* causing anxiety or fear: *alarming news* ○ *There has been an alarming rise in the rate of inflation.* **alarmingly** /ə'lɑː.mɪŋ.li/ ⓤ /-lɑːr-/ *adv*: *Alarmingly, the hole in the ozone layer has doubled in size this year.*

alarmist /ə'lɑː.mɪst/ ⓤ /-'lɑːr-/ *adj* DISAPPROVING intentionally showing only the bad and dangerous things in a situation, and so worrying people: *The government has dismissed newspaper reports of 200 dead as being alarmist.* **alarmist** /ə'lɑː.mɪst/ ⓤ /-lɑːr-/ *noun* [C]

alarm ⌈WARNING⌉ /ə'lɑːm/ ⓤ /-lɑːrm/ *noun* [C] **1** a warning of danger, typically a loud noise or flashing light: *If there's any trouble, **raise/sound the** alarm by pulling the emergency cord.* ○ *The first two bomb alerts were **false** alarms, but the third was for real.* **2** a device which makes a loud noise to warn of danger: *a burglar/car/fire/smoke alarm* **3** If an electronic device such as a watch or computer has an alarm, it can be set to make a noise at a particular time.
● **raise the alarm** to make people aware of the danger of something: *A local doctor was the first to raise the alarm about this latest virus.*
● **ring/sound alarm bells** If something rings/sounds alarm bells, it makes you start to worry because it is a sign that there may be a problem: *The name rang alarm bells in her mind.*

alarmed /ə'lɑːmd/ ⓤ /-lɑːrmd/ *adj* An alarmed vehicle has an alarm in it which, when active, will make a loud noise if anyone enters or touches the vehicle: *Warning: this building is alarmed.*

a'larm ˌcall *noun* [C] a telephone call to wake you up at a particular time, for example in a hotel

a'larm (ˌclock) *noun* [C] a clock that you can set to wake you up at a particular time with a loud noise: *I've **set the** alarm for 7.30.* ○ *The alarm **went off** at 7.30.*

alas /ə'læs/ *adv* OLD-FASHIONED OR FORMAL used to express sadness or regret: *I love football but, alas, I have no talent as a player.* ○ *"Will you be able to come tomorrow?" "Alas, no."*
● **alas and alack** HUMOROUS an expression of sadness

albatross ⌈BIRD⌉ /'æl.bə.trɒs/ ⓤ /-trɑːs/ *noun* [C] a large white bird with long strong wings that lives near the sea, found especially in the areas of the Pacific and South Atlantic oceans

albatross ⌈PROBLEM⌉ /'æl.bə.trɒs/ ⓤ /-trɑːs/ *noun* [S] something or someone you want to be free from because they are causing you problems: *Her own supporters see her as an albatross who could lose them the election.*

albeit /ɔːl'biː.ɪt/ ⓤ /ɑːl-/ *conjunction* FORMAL although: *The evening was very pleasant, albeit a little quiet.* ○ *He tried, albeit without success.*

albino /æl'biː.nəʊ/ ⓤ /-'baɪ.noʊ/ *noun* [C] *plural* **albinos** a person or animal with white skin and hair and pink eyes **albino** /æl'biː.nəʊ/ ⓤ /-'baɪ.noʊ/ *adj*

album ⌈MUSIC⌉ /'æl.bəm/ *noun* [C] a CD or record, etc. that has several pieces of music on it: *Have you heard their new album?*

album ⌈BOOK⌉ /'æl.bəm/ *noun* [C] a book with plain pages, typically used for collecting together and protecting stamps or photographs: *a stamp/photograph album* ○ *We've put the best wedding photos into an album.*

albumen /ˈæl.bjʊ.mən/ [US] /ælˈbjuː-/ *noun* [U] SPECIALIZED the clear part inside an egg which is white when cooked

alchemy /ˈæl.kə.mi/ *noun* [U] **1** a type of chemistry, especially from about 1100 to 1500, which dealt with trying to find a way to change ordinary metals into gold and with trying to find a medicine which would cure any disease **2** a process that is so effective that it seems like magic: *She manages,* ***by*** *some extraordinary alchemy, to turn the most ordinary of ingredients into the most delicious of dishes.* **alchemist** /ˈæl.kə.mɪst/ *noun* [C]

alcohol /ˈæl.kə.hɒl/ [US] /-hɑːl/ *noun* [U] a colourless liquid which can make you drunk, and which is also used as a SOLVENT (= a substance that dissolves another) and in fuel and medicines: *Most wines contain between 10% and 15% alcohol.* ○ *I could smell the alcohol on his breath.* ○ *an alcohol-**free** lager*

alcoholic /ˌæl.kəˈhɒl.ɪk/ [US] /-ˈhɑː.lɪk/ *adj* containing alcohol: *Could I have something non-alcoholic, like orange juice, please?*

alcoholic /ˌæl.kəˈhɒl.ɪk/ [US] /-ˈhɑː.lɪk/ *noun* [C] (SLANG **alky, alkie**) a person who is unable to give up the habit of drinking alcohol very frequently and in large amounts

alcoholism /ˈæl.kə.hɒl.ɪ.zəm/ [US] /-hɑː.lɪ-/ *noun* [U] the condition of being an alcoholic: *Alcoholism cost me my job, my health and finally my family.*

alcopop /ˈæl.kəʊ.pɒp/ [US] /ˈæl.koʊ.pɑːp/ *noun* [C] a sweet fizzy alcoholic drink that tastes as if it does not contain alcohol

alcove /ˈæl.kəʊv/ [US] /-koʊv/ *noun* [C] a small space in a room, formed by one part of a wall being further back than the parts on each side: *We've put some bookshelves in the alcove.*

al dente /ælˈden.teɪ/ *adj* APPROVING describes a cooked vegetable or pasta that is still firm when bitten

alderman /ˈɔːl.də.mən/ [US] /ˈɑːl.dɚ-/ *noun* [C] **1** in Britain, in the past, a member of a local government chosen by the other members **2** in the US, Australia and Canada, an elected member of a city government

ale /eɪl/ *noun* [C or U] any of various types of beer, typically one that is dark and bitter: *brown ale*

alert /əˈlɜːt/ [US] /-ˈlɝːt/ *adj* quick to see, understand and act in a particular situation: *I'm not feeling very alert today – not enough sleep last night!* ○ *A couple of alert readers wrote in to the paper pointing out the mistake.* ○ *Parents should be alert **to** sudden changes in children's behaviour.*

alert /əˈlɜːt/ [US] /-ˈlɝːt/ *noun* [C or U] a warning to people to be prepared to deal with something dangerous: *a **bomb** alert* ○ *The army was **put on (full)** alert as the peace talks began to fail.* ○ *The public were warned to be **on the** alert **for*** (= watching carefully for) *suspicious packages.*

alert /əˈlɜːt/ [US] /-ˈlɝːt/ *verb* [T] to warn someone of a possibly dangerous situation: *An anonymous letter alerted police **to** the possibility of a terrorist attack at the airport.* **alertness** /əˈlɜːt.nəs/ [US] /-ˈlɝːt-/ *noun* [U]

ˈA ˌlevel *noun* [C or U] (FORMAL **advanced level**) a qualification obtained by a public examination taken in British schools by children aged 17 or 18: *You usually need three A levels to get into university.* ○ *I failed my History A level.* ○ *Have you got an A level **in** maths?* ○ *This problem should be easy enough for someone who's done physics **at** A level.* ➲Compare **GCSE**.

alfalfa /ˌælˈfæl.fə/ *noun* [U] a plant grown as food for especially farm animals, or used in salads before it is completely developed

alfresco /ˌælˈfres.kəʊ/ [US] /-koʊ/ *adj, adv* (especially of food and eating) outside: *an alfresco lunch on the patio* ○ *Most summer evenings we eat alfresco.*

algae /ˈæl.giː/ *plural noun* very simple, usually small plants that grow in or near water and do not have ordinary leaves or roots

algebra /ˈæl.dʒə.brə/ *noun* [U] a part of mathematics in which signs and letters represent numbers **algebraic** /ˌæl.dʒəˈbreɪ.ɪk/ *adj*

algorithm /ˈæl.gə.rɪ.ðəm/ *noun* [C] SPECIALIZED a set of mathematical instructions that must be followed in a fixed order, and that, especially if given to a computer, will help to calculate an answer to a mathematical problem

alias /ˈeɪ.li.əs/ *prep* used when giving the name that a person is generally known by, after giving their real name: *Grace Kelly, alias Princess Grace of Monaco*

alias /ˈeɪ.li.əs/ *noun* [C] a false name, especially one used by a criminal: *He travels **under*** (= using) *an alias.*

alibi /ˈæl.ɪ.baɪ/ *noun* [C] **1** proof that someone who is thought to have committed a crime could not have done it, especially the fact or claim that they were in another place at the time it happened: *He has a **cast-iron*** (= very strong) *alibi – he was in hospital the week of the murder.* **2** an excuse for something bad or for a failure: *After eight years in power, the government can no longer use the previous government's policy as an alibi **for** its own failure.*

alien /ˈeɪ.li.ən/ *adj* **1** coming from a different country, race, or group; foreign: *an alien culture* **2** strange and not familiar: *When I first went to New York, it all felt very alien **to** me.* **3** [before n] relating to creatures from another planet: *an alien spacecraft*

alien /ˈeɪ.li.ən/ *noun* [C] **1** LEGAL a foreigner, usually someone who lives in a country of which they are not a legal CITIZEN: *When war broke out the government rounded up thousands of aliens and put them in temporary camps.* **2** a creature from a different world

alienate [LOSE SUPPORT] /ˈeɪ.li.ə.neɪt/ *verb* [T] to cause someone or a group of people to stop supporting and agreeing with you: *All these changes to the newspaper have alienated most of its traditional readers.* **alienation** /ˌeɪ.li.əˈneɪ.ʃən/ *noun* [U] *This short-sighted alienation of their own supporters may lose them the election.*

alienate [NOT WELCOME] /ˈeɪ.li.ə.neɪt/ *verb* [T] to make someone feel that they are different and do not belong to a group: *Disagreements can alienate teenagers **from** their families.*

alienation /ˌeɪ.li.əˈneɪ.ʃən/ *noun* [U] the feeling that you have no connection with the people around you: *Depressed people frequently feel a sense of alienation **from** those around them.*

alight [BURNING] /əˈlaɪt/ *adj* [after v] **1** burning; on fire: *I had to use a bit of petrol to **get** the fire alight.* ○ *The rioters overturned several cars and **set** them alight.* ○ *He was smoking in bed and his blankets **caught** alight.* ○ *The sky was alight **with*** (= brightly lit up by) *hundreds of fireworks.* **2** LITERARY showing excitement and happiness: *Her eyes were alight **with** mischief.*

alight [GET OUT] /əˈlaɪt/ *verb* [I] **alighted** or OLD-FASHIONED **alit, alighted** or OLD-FASHIONED **alit** FORMAL to get out of a vehicle, especially a train or bus: *The suspect alighted **from** the train at Euston and proceeded to Heathrow.*

alight [TO LAND] /əˈlaɪt/ *verb* [I + adv or prep] **alighted** or OLD-FASHIONED **alit, alighted** or OLD-FASHIONED **alit** **1** FORMAL to land on something: *A butterfly alighted gently **on** the flower.* **2** LITERARY to find or unexpectedly see something: *As she glanced round the room her eyes alighted **upon** a small child.* ○ *I spent an hour in the bookshop before alighting **on** the perfect present.*

align /əˈlaɪn/ *verb* [T] to put two or more things into a straight line: *When you've aligned the notch on the gun **with** the target, fire!* ○ *Align the ruler **and** the middle of the paper and then cut it straight.* **alignment** /əˈlaɪn.mənt/ *noun* [U] *The problem is happening because the wheels are **out of** alignment **with** each other.*

▲ **align *yourself* with *sb/sth*** *phrasal verb* [R] If you align yourself with an organization or person, you agree with and support their aims: *The party is under pressure to align itself more closely with industry.* ○ *The major unions are aligned with the government on this issue.*

alignment /əˈlaɪn.mənt/ *noun* [C] an agreement between a group of countries, political parties or people who want to work together because of shared interests or aims: *New alignments are being formed within the business community.*

alike /əˈlaɪk/ *adj* [after v] similar; like each other: *The children all **look** very alike.*

alike /əˈlaɪk/ *adv* **1** in a similar way: *The twins even dress alike.* ○ *My father treated us all alike.* **2** used after referring to two groups of people or things to show that both groups are included: *Friends and family alike were devastated by the news of her death.*

alimentary canal /ˌæl.ɪˌmen.tᵊr.i.kəˈnæl/ ⓤ /-tˢ-/ *noun* [C] the tube-like passage from the mouth, through the stomach to the anus, through which food travels during digestion

alimony /ˈæl.ɪ.mə.ni/ ⓤ /-moʊ-/ *noun* [U] a regular amount of money that a court of law orders a person, usually a man, to pay to their partner after a DIVORCE (= marriage that has legally ended)

alive /əˈlaɪv/ *adj* **1** [after v] living; having life; not dead: *He must be ninety if he's still alive.* ○ *Doctors kept him alive on a life-support machine.* ○ *She's alive and well and living in New Zealand.* **2** If something is alive, it continues to exist: *Relatives of the missing sailors are struggling to keep their hopes alive.*
• **come alive 1** If a place comes alive, it becomes filled with activity: *The city centre really comes alive at the weekend.* **2** If you make something come alive, you make it seem real and interesting: *She's a writer who really knows how to make her characters come alive.*
• **alive to sth** UK If you are alive to something, you are thinking about it or aware of it: *I ski for the excitement, but I'm also always alive to the risks.*
• **alive with** If something is alive with something else, it is so covered with or full of them that it appears to be living and moving: *The pond was alive with frogs.*
• **be alive and well/kicking 1** to continue to live or exist and be full of energy: *She said she'd seen him last week and he was alive and kicking.* **2** to continue to be popular or successful: *Despite rumours to the contrary, feminism is alive and well.* ○ *Traditional jazz is still alive and kicking in New Orleans.*

alkali /ˈæl.kᵊl.aɪ/ *noun* [C or U] *plural* **alkalis** or **alkalies** SPECIALIZED a substance which has the opposite effect or chemical behaviour to an acid **alkaline** /ˈæl.kᵊl.aɪn/ *adj*: *Some plants will not grow in very alkaline soils.*

alky, **alkie** /ˈæl.ki/ *noun* [C] SLANG an **alcoholic**, see at **alcohol**

all EVERY ONE /ɔːl/ ⓤ /ɑːl/ *determiner, predeterminer, pronoun* every one (of), or the complete amount or number (of), or the whole (of): *All animals have to eat in order to live.* ○ *She's got four children, all under the age of five.* ○ *The cast all lined up on stage to take their bow.* ○ *Have you drunk all (of) the milk?* ○ *Have you drunk it all?* ○ *All the eggs got broken.* ○ *Now the money's all mine!* ○ *All my friends agree.* ○ *I've been trying all day/week to contact you.* ○ *She had £2000 under the bed and the thieves took it all.* ○ *I had to use all my powers of persuasion to get her to agree.* ○ *Remember all that trouble we had with the police last year?* ○ *So long as he's happy – that's all that matters* (= the most important thing). ○ *All* (= The only thing) *I need is a roof over my head and a decent meal.* ○ *The judge cleared the court of all but* (= everyone except) *herself and the witness.* ○ *Why do you get so angry with me all the time* (= very often)? ○ *It's very kind of you to come all the way to meet me.*
• **all in all** considering all the different parts of the situation together: *All in all, I think you've done very well.*
• **all of sth** used to emphasize the amount or number of something, usually when something is small in a disappointing or unusual way: *In the last two years the book has sold all of 200 copies.*
• **all the ... you** have the only and small amount or number of something you have: *Her parents died when she was a baby, so I was all the family she ever had.*
• **be all (that) you can do** INFORMAL If it is all (that) you can do to do something, you are trying very hard to do it and it is difficult: *This is so boring, it's all I can do to stay awake.*
• **That's all I/you/we need!** used when something bad has happened to make a situation that is already difficult worse: *And now it's raining – that's all I need!*
• **All good things (must) come to an end.** SAYING said when you accept that even enjoyable experiences cannot last forever

COMMON LEARNER ERROR

all + a period of time
You do not type 'the' when you use **all** + a period of time.
all day/morning/week/year/summer
~~all the day/morning/week/year/summer~~

all COMPLETELY /ɔːl/ ⓤ /ɑːl/ *adv* **1** completely: *The cake was all eaten last night.* ○ *The downstairs rooms were painted all in greens and blues.* ○ *The baby got food all over her dress.* ○ *Don't let her get you all upset.* ○ *She's been all over town looking for you.* ○ *I've been hearing all about your weekend!* ○ *We had a difficult time but it's all over now.* ○ *The Princess lived all alone/by herself in the middle of the forest.* **2** used after a number to mean that both teams or players in a game have equal points: *The score at half-time was still four all.*
• **all round** UK (US **all around**) **1** in every way: *It was a ghastly business all round.* ○ *It's been a good day all around.* **2** for everyone: *I'm paying, so it's drinks all round.*
• **all but** almost: *The game was all but over by the time we arrived.*
• **be all go** UK If a situation or place is all go, it is extremely busy: *It was all go in town today.*
• **all in** If you say that you are all in, you mean that you are very tired and unable to do anything more.
• **go all out** to put all your energy or enthusiasm into what you are doing: *The team went all out for a win.*
• **be sb all over** INFORMAL to be the typical behaviour of a particular person: *She's always talking – that's Claire all over.*
• **all the** All the is used before comparative adjectives and adverbs to mean 'even' or 'much': *She felt all the better for the drink.* ○ *I've lost ten kilos in weight and I feel all the fitter for it.*
• **be not all there** INFORMAL to be slightly stupid or strange

all- /ɔːl-/ ⓤ /ɑːl-/ *prefix* **1** used in front of many nouns to form adjectives meaning 'every', 'every type of' or 'the whole of' that particular thing: *an all-night bar* (= a bar that is open for the whole night) **2** used in front of many adjectives and present participles to mean 'everything' or 'everyone': *an all-inclusive price* ○ *all-conquering armies* **3** used in front of many nouns and adjectives to mean 'completely': *all-cotton socks* (= socks that are made completely of cotton) ○ *When cooking the sauce, don't forget that all-important* (= most or very important) *ingredient, fresh basil.* ○ *Do you believe in an all-powerful god* (= one with unlimited power)?

Allah /ˈæl.ə/ *noun* the name of God for Muslims

all-American TYPICALLY AMERICAN /ˌɔːl.əˈmer.ɪ.kᵊn/ ⓤ /ˌɑːl-/ *adj* [before n] considered to be typical of the United States, and respected and approved of by Americans: *He was the perfect image of a clean-cut, all-American boy.*

all-American WHOLE COUNTRY /ˌɔːl.əˈmer.ɪ.kᵊn/ ⓤ /ˌɑːl-/ *adj* [before n] involving people or things from everywhere in the United States: *an all-American beauty contest/business consortium*

all-American SPORT /ˌɔːl.əˈmer.ɪ.kᵊn/ ⓤ /ˌɑːl-/ *adj* [before n] US describes an AMATEUR sports person from the United States who is considered to be one of the best in their sport: *an all-American football player* **all-American** /ˌɔːl.əˈmer.ɪ.kᵊn/ ⓤ /ˌɑːl-/ *noun* [C] *The team was led by an all-American from Yale.*

allay /əˈleɪ/ *verb* [T] FORMAL to make someone feel less worried or frightened: *The government is desperately trying to allay public fears/concern about the spread of the disease.*

the all-clear /ˌɔːlˈklɪəʳ/ ⓤ /ˌɑːlˈklɪr/ *noun* [S] a signal that tells you that a dangerous or difficult situation has ended: *The police gave us the all-clear and we drove on.*

all-comers /ˈɔːlˌkʌm.əz/ ⓤ /ˈɑːlˌkʌm.ɚz/ *plural noun* any people who want to take part in a particular competition or activity

allegation /ˌæl.əˈgeɪ.ʃᵊn/ *noun* [C] FORMAL a statement which has not been proven to be true which says that someone has done something wrong or illegal: *Several of her patients have made allegations of professional mis-*

[A]

conduct ***about/against*** *her.* ○ [+ **that**] *Allegations* ***that*** *Mr Dwight was receiving money from known criminals have caused a scandal.*

allege /əˈledʒ/ *verb* [T] *FORMAL* to state that someone has done something illegal or wrong without giving proof: [+ (**that**)] *The two men allege* ***(that)*** *the police forced them to make false confessions.* ○ [+ **to infinitive**] *Mr Smythe is alleged* ***to*** *have been at the centre of an international drugs ring.* ○ [+ **that**] ***It*** *was alleged* ***that*** *Johnson had struck Mr Rahim on the head.*

alleged /əˈledʒd/ *adj*: *FORMAL It took 15 years for the alleged criminals* (= people thought to be criminals) *to prove their innocence.* **allegedly** /əˈledʒ.ɪd.li/ *adv*: *That's where he allegedly killed his wife.*

allegiance /əˈliː.dʒᵊnts/ *noun* [C or U] *FORMAL* loyalty and support for a ruler, country, group or belief: *Soldiers must* ***swear*** *allegiance* ***to*** *the Crown/the King.* ○ *In many American schools, the students* ***pledge*** *allegiance* ***(to the flag)*** *at the beginning of the school day.* ○ *As an Englishman who'd lived for a long time in France, he felt a certain conflict of allegiances when the two countries played soccer.*

allegory /ˈæl.ə.gə.ri/ [US] /-gɔːr.i/ *noun* [C or U] a story, play, poem, picture or other work in which the characters and events represent particular qualities or ideas, related to morality, religion or politics: *The play can be read as allegory.* ○ *Saint Augustine's 'City of God' is an allegory* ***of*** *the triumph of Good over Evil.* **allegorical** /ˌæl.əˈgɒr.ɪ.kᵊl/ [US] /-ˈgɔːr-/ *adj* **allegorically** /ˌæl.ɪˈgɒr.ɪ.kli/ [US] /-ˈgɔːr-/ *adv*

allegro /əˈleg.rəʊ/ [US] /-roʊ/ *noun* [C] *plural* **allegros** *SPECIALIZED* a piece of classical music that is played in a fast and energetic way **allegro** /əˈleg.rəʊ/ [US] /-roʊ/ *adj, adv*: *the allegro movement* ○ *Sing the second verse allegro.*

alleluia /ˌæl.ɪˈluː.jə/ *exclamation, noun* [C] **hallelujah**

Allen key /ˈæl.ənˌkiː/ *noun* [C] (*ALSO* **Allen wrench**) *TRADEMARK* an L-shaped metal tool with six sides that is used to turn a screw with a six-sided hole in the top

allergen /ˈæl.ə.dʒən/ [US] /-ɚ-/ *noun* [C] *SPECIALIZED* a substance which can cause an ALLERGY (= condition of the body reacting badly to something), but which is harmless to most people

allergy /ˈæl.ə.dʒi/ [US] /-ɚ-/ *noun* [C] a condition that makes a person become ill or develop skin or breathing problems because they have eaten certain foods or come in contact with certain substances: *an allergy* ***to*** *wheat* ○ *a wheat allergy*

allergic /əˈlɜː.dʒɪk/ [US] /-lɝː-/ *adj* **1** [after v] having an allergy: *I'm allergic* ***to*** *cats.* **2** [before n] caused by an allergy: *an allergic* ***reaction*** **3** *HUMOROUS* having a strong dislike of something: *My dad's allergic* ***to*** *pop music.*

alleviate /əˈliː.vi.eɪt/ *verb* [T] *FORMAL* to make something bad such as pain or problems less severe: *The drugs did nothing to alleviate her pain/suffering.* **alleviation** /əˌliː.viˈeɪ.ʃᵊn/ *noun* [U] *the alleviation of poverty*

alley /ˈæl.i/ *noun* [C] (*ALSO* **alleyway**) a narrow road or path between buildings, or a path in a park or garden, especially bordered by trees or bushes

• **up/down** ***your*** **alley** *US* to be the type of thing that you are interested in or that you enjoy doing: *Kate loves dancing, so salsa lessons would be* ***right*** *up her alley.*

alliance /əˈlaɪ.ᵊnts/ *noun* ➲See at **ally**.

allied /ˈæl.aɪd/ /əˈlaɪd/ *adj* **1** [before n] connected by a political or military agreement: *an allied offensive* ○ *allied bombers/forces* **2** *FORMAL* similar or related in some way: *Computer science and allied subjects are not taught here.* **3** combined: *It takes a lot of enthusiasm, allied* ***with/to*** *a love of children to make a good teacher.*

the ˈAllies *plural noun* the countries, including the US, the UK, the USSR and France, that fought against THE AXIS in World War Two

Allied /ˈæl.aɪd/ *adj* [before n] relating to the Allies: *Allied forces* ○ *the Allied landings in Normandy*

alligator /ˈæl.ɪ.geɪ.təʳ/ [US] /-t̬ɚ/ *noun* [C] (*US INFORMAL* **gator**) a large hard-skinned reptile that lives in and near rivers and lakes in the hot, wet parts of America and China. It has a long nose that is slightly wider and shorter than that of a CROCODILE.

all-important /ˌɔːl.ɪmˈpɔː.tənt/ *adj* extremely important: *It was Johansson who scored the all-important goal shortly before half-time.*

all-inclusive /ˌɔːl.ɪnˈkluː.sɪv/ [US] /ˌɑːl-/ *adj* including everything: *a seven-night all-inclusive package* ○ *an all-inclusive resort*

all-in-one /ˌɔːl.ɪnˈwʌn/ [US] /ˌɑːl-/ *adj UK* doing the work of two or more usually separate parts: *an all-in-one cleaner and polish*

all-in-one /ˌɔːl.ɪnˈwʌn/ [US] /ˌɑːl-/ *noun* [C] *UK* a piece of clothing that covers the whole body rather than being divided into a separate top and bottom part

all-in wrestling /ˌɔːl.ɪnˈres.lɪŋ/ [US] /ˌɑːl-/ *noun* [U] a type of WRESTLING (= sport in which people fight) in which there are few or no limits

alliteration /əˌlɪt.əˈreɪ.ʃᵊn/ [US] /əˌlɪt̬-/ *noun* [U] the use, especially in poetry, of the same sound or sounds, especially CONSONANTS, at the beginning of several words that are close together: *'Round the rugged rocks the ragged rascal ran' uses alliteration.* ➲Compare **assonance**.

all-nighter /ˌɔːlˈnaɪ.təʳ/ [US] /ˌɑːlˈnaɪ.t̬ɚ/ *noun* [C] **1** *INFORMAL* an event that lasts all night **2** *US INFORMAL* a time when you spend all night studying, especially for an exam: *I* ***pulled*** *an all-nighter last night.*

allocate /ˈæl.ə.keɪt/ *verb* [T] to give something to someone as their share of a total amount, for them to use in a particular way: *The government is allocating £10 million* ***for*** *health education.* ○ [+ **two objects**] *As project leader, you will have to allocate people jobs/allocate jobs* ***to*** *people.* ○ *It is not the job of the investigating committee to allocate blame* ***for*** *the disaster/to allocate blame* ***to*** *individuals.* **allocation** /ˌæl.əˈkeɪ.ʃᵊn/ *noun* [U] *the allocation of resources/funds/time*

allot /əˈlɒt/ [US] /-ˈlɑːt/ *verb* [T] **-tt-** to give a share of something available for a particular purpose: [+ **two objects**] *They allotted everyone a separate desk.* ○ *They allotted a separate desk* ***to*** *everyone.* ○ *The ministry of culture will be allotted about $6 million less this year.* ○ *Three hours have been allotted* ***to/for*** *this task.*

allotted /əˈlɒt.ɪd/ [US] /-ˈlɑː.t̬ɪd/ *adj*: *Did you finish your essay in the allotted* ***time*** (= the time available)*?* **allotment** /əˈlɒt.mənt/ [US] /-ˈlɑːt-/ *noun* [C or U] *The allotment of the company's shares to its employees is still to be decided.* ○ *We have used up this year's allotment of funds.*

allotment /əˈlɒt.mənt/ [US] /-ˈlɑːt-/ *noun* [C] *UK* a small piece of ground in or just outside a town that a person rents for growing vegetables, fruits or flowers

all-out /ˈɔːl.aʊt/ [US] /ɑːl-/ *adj* [before n] complete and with as much effort as possible: *We made an all-out* ***effort*** *to get the project finished on time.*

allow [PERMIT] /əˈlaʊ/ *verb* [T] to make it possible for someone to do something, or to not prevent something from happening; permit: [+ **to infinitive**] *Do you think Dad will allow you* ***to*** *go to Jamie's party?* ○ *You're not allowed* ***to*** *talk during the exam.* ○ *Her proposals* ***would*** *allow* (= make it possible for) *more people* ***to*** *stay in full-time education.* ○ *The loophole has allowed hundreds of drink-drivers* ***to*** *avoid prosecution.* ○ *The government has* ***refused to*** *allow foreign journalists into the area for several weeks.* ○ *Prisoners have been moved to allow the demolition of part of the prison.* ○ *Pets aren't allowed in this hotel.* ○ [+ **v-ing**] *Smok****ing*** *is not allowed in this restaurant.* ○ [+ **two objects**] *He didn't allow us enough time to finish the test.* ○ *Red Cross officials were allowed* ***access*** *to the prison for the first time a few days ago.* ○ *UK The referee decided to allow* (= officially accept) *the goal.* ○ [**R + object**] *At the weekend I allow myself* (= I permit myself the special pleasure of having) *a box of chocolates.* ○ *How much time do you allow yourself* (= make available to yourself) *to get ready in the morning?*

• **allow me** *OLD-FASHIONED* a polite expression used when offering to help in some way: *You can't carry all those bags yourself – please, allow me.*

allowable /əˈlaʊ.ə.bl̩/ *adj*: *A certain level of error is allowable* (= permitted to happen). ○ *UK Taxpayers should claim as many allowable expenses* (= expenses on which no taxes are paid) *as possible against their taxed income.*

A

allowance /ə'laʊ.ᵊnts/ *noun* [C] **1** money that you are given regularly, especially to pay for a particular thing: *The perks of the job include a company pension scheme and a generous **travel** allowance.* ○ *I couldn't have managed at college if I hadn't had an allowance from my parents.* **2** an amount of something that you are allowed: *The **baggage/luggage** allowance for most flights is 20 kilos.* **3** *MAINLY US FOR* **pocket money** CHILD'S MONEY

COMMON LEARNER ERROR

allow or **let**?

Allow and **let** have similar meanings. **Allow** is used in more formal or official situations, especially when talking about rules and laws. It is used in the verb pattern – **allow** + **object** + **to infinitive**.

The new legislation allows companies to charge for this service.
We can't allow this situation to continue.

Let is used in more informal and spoken situations and is used in the verb pattern – **let** + **object** + **infinitive without to**.

Dad won't let her drive his car.
She let her hair grow longer.
~~*Dad won't let her to drive his car.*~~

allow [ADMIT] /ə'laʊ/ *verb* [+ *that*] *FORMAL* to admit or agree that something is true: *She allowed **that** she might have been too suspicious.*

PHRASAL VERBS WITH **allow** ▼

▲ **allow for *sth*** *phrasal verb* to take something into consideration when you are planning something: *We allowed for living expenses of £20 a day.* ○ [+ **v-ing**] *You should allow for the plane **being** delayed.* ○ *We have to allow for the **possibility** that we might not finish on schedule.*
allowance /ə'laʊ.ᵊnts/ *noun* **make allowance for** to prepare for the possibility of: *We should make allowance for bad weather and have plenty of umbrellas available.*
• **make allowances for** To make allowances for someone or their characteristics is to take their characteristics into consideration and not judge them too severely: *You should make allowances for him – he's been quite ill recently.* ○ *"This is a poor piece of work." "Yes, but you should make allowances for the fact that she's only seven."*
▲ **allow of *sth*** *phrasal verb FORMAL* If a rule or situation allows of something, it permits it: *This rule allows of no exceptions.* ○ *The evidence allows of only one interpretation – he was murdered by his wife.*

alloy [METAL] /'æl.ɔɪ/ *noun* [C] a metal that is made by mixing two or more metals, or a metal and another substance: *Brass is an alloy **of** copper and zinc.*

alloy [SPOIL] /ə'lɔɪ/ *verb* [T] *LITERARY* to spoil or reduce in value: *My pleasure in receiving the letter was somewhat alloyed by its contents.*

ˌall 'right [SATISFACTORY], **alright** *adj* [after v], *adv* (in a way that is) satisfactory or reasonably good: *"What did you think of the film?" "It was all right. Nothing special."* ○ *Are you managing all right in your new job?* ○ *I wouldn't say she's rich, but she's **doing** all right* (= being reasonably successful). ○ *Is **everything** all right, madam?*

ˌall 'right [GOOD], **alright** *adj* [after v] *INFORMAL* very good: *You can work at home? That's all right, isn't it?*

ˌall 'right [GREETING], **alright** *exclamation UK INFORMAL* used to greet someone at the same time as asking whether they are well: *"All right, John?" "Not bad thanks, and you?"*

ˌall 'right [APPROVAL], **alright** *exclamation SLANG* said with the main emphasis on 'right', expressing approval of what has been said or done: *"Did you hear I hit that creep who'd been pestering me?" "All right!"*

ˌall 'right [SAFE], **alright** *adj* [after v], *adv* safe, well or not harmed: *She was very ill for a while but she's all right now.* ○ *Are you sure you'll be all right on your own?* ○ *Did you get home all right* (= safely) *last night?*

ˌall 'right [AGREED], **alright** *adv*, used to show that something is agreed, understood or acceptable: *All right, I'll lend you the money.* ○ *All right, that's enough noise!* ○ *Tell me if you start to feel sick, all right?* ○ *"Are you sure you won't come for a drink with us?" "All right then. If you insist."* ○ *All right, so I made a mistake* (= I accept that I was wrong). ○ *I'd rather not go to Tricia's party if that's all right **with** you.* ○ *Would it be all right **if** I came?* ○ [+ **to infinitive**] *Chris wants to know if **it'll** be all right **to** come over to see us this evening.* ○ *She seems to think that **it's perfectly** all right **to** break the law.*
• **It's all right** (*ALSO* **That's all right**) an answer to someone who has just thanked you for something or just said they are sorry for something they have done: *"Thank you for the flowers." "It's all right* (= There's no need to thank me). *I thought they might cheer you up."* ○ *"I'm sorry I broke the vase." "Oh, that's all right* (= it's not important). *It wasn't very expensive."*

ˌall 'right [CERTAINLY], **alright** *adv INFORMAL* certainly or without any doubt: *"Are you sure it was Gillian with him?" "Oh, it was her all right."*

all-round /ˌɔːl'raʊnd/ [US] /ˌɑːl-/ *adj* [before n] (*US* **all-around**) describes a person who has a good variety of skills and abilities: *She's a fantastic all-round sportswoman.*

all-rounder /ˌɔːl'raʊn.dəʳ/ [US] /ˌɑːl'raʊn.dɚ/ *noun* [C] *UK* a person who has a good variety of skills and abilities

allspice /'ɔːl.spaɪs/ [US] /'ɑːl-/ *noun* [U] a powder made from a small fruit grown in hot countries, which is used as a spice in cooking

all-star /'ɔːl.stɑːʳ/ [US] /'ɑːl.stɑːr/ *adj* [before n] having or including famous actors or players: *His latest film featured an all-star **cast**.* ○ *an all-star baseball team*

all-time /'ɔːl.taɪm/ [US] /'ɑːl-/ *adj* [before n] An all-time high, low, best, etc. is the highest, lowest, best, etc. level that has ever been: *After three years of drought, the water in the lake had reached an all-time low.*

allude /ə'luːd/ *verb*
▲ **allude to *sb/sth*** *phrasal verb FORMAL* to mention someone or something in an indirect way: *She mentioned some trouble that she'd had at home and I guessed she was alluding to her son.*

allure /ə'ljʊəʳ/ /-'lʊəʳ/ [US] /-'lʊr/ *noun* [U] attraction, charm or excitement: *the allure **of** working in television* ○ ***sexual** allure* **alluringly** /ə'ljʊə.rɪŋ.li/ /-'lʊə.rɪŋ.li/ [US] /-'lʊr.ɪŋ-/ *adv*

alluring /ə'ljʊə.rɪŋ/ /-'lʊə-/ [US] /-'lʊr.ɪŋ/ *adj* attractive or exciting: *I didn't find the prospect of a house with no electricity very alluring.* ○ *She was wearing a most alluring dress at Sam's dinner party.*

allusion /ə'luː.ʒᵊn/ *noun* [C] something that is said or written that intentionally makes you think of a particular thing or person: *The film is full of allusions **to** Hitchcock.* ○ *Her novels are packed with **literary** allusions.*
allusive /ə'luː.sɪv/ *adj FORMAL* containing a lot of allusions: *Her music is witty, ironic and allusive.* **allusiveness** /ə'luː.sɪv.nəs/ *noun* [U]

alluvial /ə'luː.vi.əl/ *adj SPECIALIZED* consisting of earth and sand that has been left by rivers, floods, etc: *an alluvial plain* ○ *Some alluvial **deposits** are a rich source of diamonds.*

ally /'æl.aɪ/ *noun* [C] **1** a country that has agreed officially to give help and support to another one, especially during a war: *North Korea is one of China's **staunchest** allies.* ○ *During World War One, Turkey and Germany were allies/Turkey was an ally of Germany.* **2** someone who helps and supports someone else: *He is generally considered to be the Prime Minister's **closest** political ally.*
alliance /ə'laɪ.ᵊnts/ *noun* [C] **1** a group of countries, political parties or people who have agreed to work together because of shared interests or aims: *a **military** alliance* ○ *NATO is sometimes called the Atlantic Alliance.* **2** an agreement to work with someone else to try to achieve the same thing: *The three smaller parties have **forged/formed** an alliance **against** the government.* ○ *Some of us feel that the union is **in alliance with** management against us.*

ally /ə'laɪ/ *verb*
▲ **ally *yourself* to/with *sb*** *phrasal verb* [R] to join someone and support them: *He allied himself with the left of the party.*

alma mater /ˌæl.məˈmɑː.təʳ/ /-ˈmeɪ.təʳ/ US /-ˈmɑː.ţəʳ/ *noun* **1** (*ALSO* **Alma Mater**) *FORMAL* **your alma mater** the school, college or university where you studied **2** [S] *US* the official song of a school, college or university

almanac, **almanack** /ˈɔːl.mə.næk/ /ˈæl-/ *noun* [C] a book published every year that contains facts and information such as important days, times of the sun rising and going down or changes in the moon

almighty GOD /ɔːlˈmaɪ.ti/ US /-ţi/ *adj* (of God) having the power to do everything: *Almighty God*
• **God/Christ almighty!** *INFORMAL* an expression of anger or surprise. Some people consider this offensive.
the Al'mighty *noun* [S] God: *We must pray to the Almighty for forgiveness.*

almighty BIG /ɔːlˈmaɪ.ti/ US /-ţi/ *adj* [before n] *INFORMAL* very big, loud or serious: *All of a sudden we heard an almighty crash from the kitchen.* ○ *There was an almighty* **row** *when I asked them to leave.*

almond /ˈɑː.mənd/ US /ˈɑːl-/ *noun* [C] an edible oval nut with a hard shell, or the tree that it grows on: *ground/ toasted almonds*

ˌalmond ˈpaste *noun* [U] *UK* **marzipan**

almost /ˈɔːl.məʊst/ US /ˈɑːl.moʊst/ *adv* nearly: *She's almost thirty.* ○ *It was almost six o'clock when he left.* ○ *I almost wish I hadn't invited him.* ○ *It'll cost almost as much to repair it as it would to buy a new one.* ○ *Almost* **all** *the passengers on the ferry were French.* ○ *They'll almost* **certainly** *forget to do it.* ○ *The town was almost entirely destroyed during the war.* ○ *We were bitten by mosquitoes almost* **every** *night.* ○ *The boat sank almost* **immediately** *after it had struck the rock.* ○ *Most artists find it almost* **impossible** *to make a living from art alone.*

alms /ɑːmz/ *plural noun OLD USE* clothing, food or money that is given to poor people: *In the past, people thought it was their religious duty to* **give** *alms to the poor.*

almshouse /ˈɑːmz.haʊs/ *noun* [C] a private house built in the past where old or poor people could live without having to pay rent

aloe /ˈæl.əʊ/ US /-oʊ/ *noun* [C] an evergreen plant with thick pointed leaves

aloe vera /ˌæl.əʊˈvɪə.rə/ US /-oʊˈvɪr.ə/ *noun* [C or U] a type of plant with thick pointed leaves which is used to heal damaged skin found in the leaves

aloft /əˈlɒft/ US /-ˈlɑːft/ *adv FORMAL* in the air or in a higher position: *We* **held** *our glasses aloft.*

alone WITHOUT PEOPLE /əˈləʊn/ US /-ˈloʊn/ *adj* [after v], *adv* without other people: *He likes being alone in the house.* ○ *She decided to climb the mountain alone.* ○ *Do you like living alone?* ○ *At last, we're alone together* (= there are just the two of us here). ○ *The Swedes are* **not** *alone* **in** *finding their language under pressure from the spread of English.* ○ *I don't like the man and I'm* **not** *alone* **in that** (= other people agree).

COMMON LEARNER ERROR

alone or **lonely**?

Alone means that no other person is with you.

I prefer working alone – I hate crowded offices.

Do not confuse with **lonely**, which means feeling sad because you are alone.

She's been feeling very lonely since her husband died.

~~I prefer working lonely.~~

---

alone ONLY /əˈləʊn/ US /-ˈloʊn/ *adj* [after n] only or without any others: *She alone must decide what to do* (= no one else can do it for her). ○ *These facts alone* (= even if nothing else is considered) *show that he's not to be trusted.* ○ *He won't get the job through charm alone* (= he will need something else). ○ *The airfare alone would use up all my money, never mind the hotel bills.* ○ *Price alone is not a reliable indicator of quality.*

along DIRECTION /əˈlɒŋ/ US /-ˈlɑːŋ/ *prep* from one part of a road, river, etc. to another: *a romantic walk along the beach/river*
• **along the** **way** during the time that something is happening or that you are doing something: *I've been in*

this job for thirty years, and I've picked up a good deal of expertise along the way.

along NEXT TO /əˈlɒŋ/ US /-ˈlɑːŋ/ *prep* in a line next to something long: *a row of houses along the river* ○ *Cars were parked all along the road.*

along PARTICULAR PLACE /əˈlɒŋ/ US /-ˈlɑːŋ/ *prep* at a particular place on a road, river, etc: *Somewhere along this road there's a garage.*

along FORWARD /əˈlɒŋ/ US /-ˈlɑːŋ/ *adv* moving forward: *We were just walking along, chatting.*
• **all along** from the very beginning: *Do you think he's been cheating us all along?*

along WITH YOU /əˈlɒŋ/ US /-ˈlɑːŋ/ *adv* with you: *Why don't you* **take** *him along* **with** *you when you go?* ○ *I'll* **bring** *some food along and we can have a picnic.*
• **come/go/be along for the ride** *INFORMAL* to join in an activity without playing an important part in it: *My husband is speaking at the dinner and I'm* **just** *going along for the ride.*
• **along with** *sb/sth* in addition to someone or something else: *California, along with Florida and Hawaii, is among the most popular US tourist destinations.*

alongside /əˌlɒŋˈsaɪd/ US /əˈlɑːŋ.saɪd/ *prep, adv* beside, or together with: *A car pulled up alongside (ours).* ○ *The new pill will be used alongside existing medicines.* ○ *Most of the staff refused to* **work** *alongside the new team.* ○ *Britain* **fought** *alongside France, Turkey and Sardinia during the Crimean War.*

aloof /əˈluːf/ *adj* **1** describes an unfriendly person who refuses to take part in things: *She seemed rather aloof when in fact she was just shy.* **2** not interested or involved, usually because you do not approve of what is happening: *Whatever is happening in the office, she always* **remains** *aloof.* ○ *She kept herself aloof* **from** *her husband's business.* **aloofness** /əˈluːf.nəs/ *noun* [U]

alopecia /ˌæl.əʊˈpiː.ʃə/ US /ˌæl.oʊˈpiː.ʃə/ *noun* [U] *SPECIALIZED* loss of hair, especially from the head, which either happens naturally or is caused by disease

aloud /əˈlaʊd/ *adv* in a voice loud enough to be heard; not silently or quietly: *He* **read** *her letter aloud to the rest of the family.* ○ *People are starting to* **wonder** *aloud* (= question publicly) *whether the economic reforms have gone too far.*

alpaca /ælˈpæk.ə/ *noun* [U] a type of wool used for making luxury clothes

alpha, α /ˈæl.fə/ *noun* [C] the first letter of the Greek alphabet ➔Compare **beta**; **gamma**.

alphabet /ˈæl.fə.bet/ *noun* [C] a set of letters arranged in a fixed order which is used for writing a language: *the Cyrillic alphabet* **alphabetical** /ˌæl.fəˈbet.ɪ.kᵊl/ US /-ˈbeţ-/ *adj* (*ALSO* **alphabetic**) *an alphabetical list* ○ *The names are published* **in** *alphabetical order.* **alphabetically** /ˌæl.fəˈbet.ɪ.kli/ US /-ˈbeţ-/ *adv*: *I've* **arranged** *the pictures of the animals alphabetically from aardvark to zebra.*

ˌalpha ˈmale *noun* [C usually sing] *SPECIALIZED* the most successful and powerful male in any group

alpine /ˈæl.paɪn/ *adj* relating to the **ALPS** (= the highest mountains in Europe) or other mountainous areas: *Our window looked out on a beautiful alpine scene.* ○ *Alpine ski resorts*

ˈalpine (ˌplant) *noun* [C] a plant that grows naturally in high mountain areas where trees are unable to grow

already /ɔːlˈred.i/ US /ɑːl-/ /ˈ---/ *adv* **1** before the present time: *I asked him to come to the exhibition but he'd already seen it.* ○ *The concert had already begun by the time we arrived.* ○ *I've already told him.* ○ *As I have already mentioned, I doubt that we will be able to raise all the money we need.* **2** earlier than the time expected: *Are you buying Christmas cards already? It's only September!* ○ *I've only eaten one course and I'm already full.*

alright /ɔːlˈraɪt/ US /ɑːl-/ *adj, adv, exclamation* **all right**

Alsatian /ælˈseɪ.ʃᵊn/ *noun* [C] (*ALSO* **German shepherd**) a large brown and black dog, often used for guarding buildings and in police work

also /ˈɔːl.səʊ/ US /ˈɑːl.soʊ/ *adv* in addition: *She's a photographer and also writes books.* ○ *I'm cold, and I'm also hungry and tired.*

A

also-ran /ˈɔːl.səʊ.ræn/ [US] /ˈɑːl.soʊ-/ *noun* [C] someone in a competition who is unlikely to do well or who has failed

altar /ˈɔːl.təʳ/ /ˈɒl-/ [US] /-t̬ɚ/ *noun* [C] a type of table used in ceremonies in a Christian church or in other religious buildings

alter [CHANGE] /ˈɒl.təʳ/ [US] /ˈɑːl.t̬ɚ/ *verb* **1** [I or T] to change something, usually slightly, or to cause the characteristics of something to change: *We've had to alter some of our plans.* ○ *Although long-distance phone calls are going up, the charge for local calls will not alter.* ○ *Giving up our car has radically altered our lifestyle.* **2** [T] to change the size of clothes so that they fit better: *I took the coat back to the shop to have it altered.* **alteration** /ˌɒl.təˈreɪ.ʃᵊn/ [US] /ˌɑːl.t̬ə-/ *noun* [C or U] *Several police officers are being questioned about the alteration of the documents.* ○ *The house needed extensive alterations when we moved in.* ○ *Some alterations **to** our original plans might be necessary.*

alter [REMOVE ORGANS] /ˈɒl.təʳ/ [US] /ˈɑːl.t̬ɚ/ *verb* [T] *US POLITE WORD FOR* **castrate** or **spay**

altercation /ˌɒl.təˈkeɪ.ʃᵊn/ [US] /ˌɑːl.t̬ɚ-/ *noun* [C] *FORMAL* a loud argument or disagreement: *According to witnesses, the altercation **between** the two men started inside the restaurant.*

ˌalter ˈego *noun* [C] *plural* **alter egos** the side of someone's personality which is not usually seen by other people: *Clark Kent is Superman's alter ego.*

alternate /ˈɒl.tə.neɪt/ [US] /ˈɑːl.t̬ɚ-/ *verb* **1** [I usually + adv or prep] to happen or exist one after the other repeatedly: *She alternated **between** cheerfulness and deep despair.* **2** [T usually + adv or prep] to make something happen or exist one after the other repeatedly: *He alternated working in the office **with** long tours overseas.*

alternate /ɒlˈtɜː.nət/ [US] /ɑːlˈtɝː-/ *adj* [before n] **1** with first one thing, then another thing, and then the first thing again: *a dessert with alternate layers of chocolate and cream* **2** If something happens on alternate days, it happens every second day: *Private cars are banned from the city on alternate days.* **3** *US* (*UK* **alternative**) An alternate plan or method is one that you can use if you do not want to use another one. **alternating** /ˈɒl.tə.neɪ.tɪŋ/ [US] /ˈɑːl.t̬ɚ.neɪ.t̬ɪŋ/ *adj*: *alternating moods of anger and sadness* **alternately** /ɒlˈtɜː.nət.li/ [US] /ɑːlˈtɝː-/ *adv*: *The film is alternately depressing and amusing.*

alternative /ɒlˈtɜː.nə.tɪv/ [US] /ɑːlˈtɝː.nə.t̬ɪv/ *noun* [C] something that is different from something else, especially from what is usual, and offering the possibility of choice: *an alternative **to** coffee* ○ *There must be an alternative **to** people sleeping on the streets.* ○ *I'm afraid I have **no** alternative **but to** ask you to leave* (= that is what I have to do).

alternative /ɒlˈtɜː.nə.tɪv/ [US] /ɑːlˈtɝː.nə.t̬ɪv/ *adj* **1** (*US ALSO* **alternate**) An alternative plan or method is one that you can use if you do not want to use another one. *The opposition parties have so far failed to set out an alternative strategy.* ○ *An alternative venue for the concert is being sought.* **2** describes things that are considered to be unusual and which tend to have a small but enthusiastic group of people who support them: *alternative comedy*

alternatively /ɒlˈtɜː.nə.tɪv.li/ [US] /ɑːlˈtɝː.nə.t̬ɪv-/ *adv* used to suggest another possibility: *We could go to the Indian restaurant, **or** alternatively, we could try that new Italian place.*

alˌternative ˈenergy *noun* [U] energy from moving water, wind, the sun and gas from animal waste: *alternative energy **sources***

alˌternative ˈlifestyle *noun* [C usually sing] a way of living that is unusual, especially when you choose not to have the type of home and job that is considered normal in modern society: *to pursue/seek an alternative lifestyle* ○ *Living the vegan alternative lifestyle that we do, my friends and I are a little overwhelmed by the commercialism of Christmas.*

alˌternative ˈmedicine *noun* [U] a wide range of treatments for medical conditions that people use instead of or with western medicine: *Alternative medicine includes treatments such as acupuncture, homeopathy and hypnotherapy.*

alternator /ˈɒl.tə.neɪ.təʳ/ [US] /ˈɑːl.tɚ.neɪ.t̬ɚ/ *noun* [C] *SPECIALIZED* a device which produces AC electricity

although /ɔːlˈðəʊ/ [US] /ɑːlˈðoʊ/ *conjunction* **1** despite the fact that: *She walked home by herself, although she knew that it was dangerous.* ○ *He decided to go, although I begged him not to.* **2** but: *He's rather shy, although he's not as bad as he used to be.* ○ *She'll be coming tonight, although I don't know exactly when.*

altimeter /ˈæl.tɪ.miː.təʳ/ [US] /ælˈtɪm.ə.t̬ɚ/ *noun* [C] a device used in an aircraft to measure how high it is from the ground

altitude /ˈæl.tɪ.tjuːd/ [US] /-t̬ə.tuːd/ *noun* [C] height above sea level: *We are currently flying **at** an altitude of 15 000 metres.* ○ *Mountain climbers use oxygen when they reach **higher** altitudes.*

alto /ˈæl.təʊ/ [US] /-toʊ/ *noun* [C] *plural* **altos** (a woman with) a low adult female singing voice or (a boy with) the lowest boys' singing voice: *She began by singing soprano, then changed to alto.*

alto /ˈæl.təʊ/ [US] /-toʊ/ *adj* describes a musical instrument which is of a size between SOPRANO and TENOR: *an alto saxophone/flute*

altogether /ˌɔːl.təˈgeð.əʳ/ [US] /ˌɑːl.təˈgeð.ɚ/ *adv* completely or in total: *That'll be £52.50 altogether, please.* ○ *The government ought to abolish the tax altogether.* ○ *She wrote less and less often, and eventually she stopped altogether.* ○ *It's all right working with him, but living with him would be a different matter altogether.* ○ *I'm not altogether sure I want that* (= I have doubts about it). ○ *He's bad-tempered, selfish and altogether* (= including everything) *an unpleasant man.* ○ *I think Graham will agree, but convincing Mary will be altogether more* (= much more) *difficult.*
• **be in the altogether** *OLD-FASHIONED* to be naked

altruism /ˈæl.tru.ɪ.zᵊm/ *noun* [U] willingness to do things which benefit other people, even if it results in disadvantage for yourself: *She's not known for her altruism.* **altruist** /ˈæl.tru.ɪst/ *noun* [C] **altruistic** /ˌæl.truˈɪs.tɪk/ *adj*: *I doubt whether her **motives** for donating the money are altruistic – she's probably looking for publicity.* **altruistically** /ˌæl.truˈɪs.tɪ.kli/ *adv*

aluminium *UK* /ˌæl.jʊˈmɪn.i.əm/ *noun* [U] (*US* **aluminum**) a light metallic element which is silver in colour and used especially for making cooking equipment and aircraft parts: *an aluminium saucepan* ○ *Cover the fish with aluminium **foil** and cook over a low heat for 4 to 5 minutes.* ○ *We take all our aluminium **cans** for recycling.*

aluminum /əˈluː.mɪ.nəm/ *noun* [U] *US FOR* **aluminium**

alumna /əˈlʌm.nə/ *noun* [C] *plural* **alumnae** *MAINLY US* a female alumnus

alumnus /əˈlʌm.nəs/ *noun* [C] *plural* **alumni** *MAINLY US* someone who has left a school, college or university after completing their studies there: *the alumni of St MacNissi's College* ○ *Several **famous** alumni have agreed to help raise money for the school's restoration fund.*

always /ˈɔːl.weɪz/ [US] /ˈɑːl-/ *adv* **1** every time, all the time or forever: *It's always cold in this room.* ○ *I've always liked him.* ○ *I'll always remember you.* ○ [+ v-ing] *DISAPPROVING* *You're always complaining.* ○ *I always thought I'd have children eventually.* ○ *She always spells my name wrong.* **2** used with 'can' or 'could' to suggest another possibility: *If you miss this train you can always catch the next one.*

Alzheimer's (disease) /ˈælts.haɪ.məz.dɪˌziːz/ [US] /-mɚz-/ *noun* [U] a disease of the brain that affects especially old people, which results in the gradual loss of memory, speech, movement and the ability to think clearly: *an Alzheimer's patient*

am [BE] *STRONG* /æm/, *WEAK* /əm/ *I form of* **be**: *Am I included?*

a.m. [MORNING], **am** /ˌeɪˈem/ *adv* used when referring to a time between twelve o'clock at night and twelve o'clock in the middle of the day: *The first election results are expected around 1 a.m.* ➲Compare **p.m.** TIME.

AM [RADIO] /ˌeɪˈem/ *noun* [U] *ABBREVIATION FOR* amplitude modulation: a type of radio broadcasting in which the strength of the signal changes, producing sound of a lower quality than FM: *You're listening to Radio Gold, broadcasting 24 hours a day on 909 AM.*

AM [POLITICIAN] /ˌeɪˈem/ *noun* [C] *UK ABBREVIATION FOR* Assembly Member: a person who has been elected to the Welsh Assembly

amalgam [METALS] /əˈmæl.ɡəm/ *noun* [U] *SPECIALIZED* a mixture of metals, especially one used by dentists to repair teeth: *an amalgam filling*

amalgam [MIXTURE] /əˈmæl.ɡəm/ *noun* [S] a combination of parts that create a complete whole: *The show was a wonderful amalgam **of** dance, music and drama.* ○ *Nearly every new parent feels an amalgam **of** joy and terror.*

amalgamate /əˈmæl.ɡə.meɪt/ *verb* [I or T] to join or unite to form a larger organization or group, or to make separate organizations do this: *The electricians' union is planning to amalgamate **with** the technicians' union.* ○ *The different offices will be amalgamated **as/into** employment advice centres.* **amalgamation** /əˌmæl.ɡəˈmeɪ.ʃən/ *noun* [C or U] *The association was **formed by** the amalgamation of several regional environmental organizations.* ○ *The company began as an amalgamation of small family firms.*

amanuensis /əˌmæn.juˈen*t*.sɪs/ *noun* [C] *plural* **amanuenses** *FORMAL* a person whose job is to write down what another person says or to copy what another person has written

amass /əˈmæs/ *verb* [T] to get a large amount of something, especially money or information, by collecting it over a long period: *She has amassed a huge **fortune** from her novels.* ○ *Some of his colleagues envy the enormous **wealth** that he has amassed.*

amateur /ˈæm.ə.təʳ/ [US] /-t̬ɚ/ *adj* **1** taking part in an activity for pleasure, not as a job: *an amateur astronomer/boxer/historian* ○ *He was an amateur singer until the age of 40, when he turned professional.* ➲Compare **professional** at **profession**. **2** relating to an activity, especially a sport, where the people taking part do not receive money: *amateur athletics*

amateur /ˈæm.ə.təʳ/ [US] /-t̬ɚ/ *noun* [C] **1** a person who takes part in an activity for pleasure, not as a job: *This tennis tournament is open to both amateurs and professionals.* ➲Compare **professional** at **profession**. **2** *DISAPPROVING* someone who lacks skill in what they do: *I won't be giving them any more work – they're a bunch of amateurs.*

amateurish /ˈæm.ə.tə.rɪʃ/ [US] /ˌæm.əˈtɝː.ɪʃ/ *adj* *DISAPPROVING* lacking skill, or showing a lack of skill: *Their website looks amateurish.* **amateurishly** /ˈæm.ə.tə.rɪʃ.li/ [US] /ˌæm.əˈtɝː.ɪʃ-/ *adv* **amateurishness** /ˈæm.ə.tə.rɪʃ.nəs/ [US] /ˌæm.əˈtɝː.ɪʃ-/ *noun* [U]

amateur dramatics /ˌæm.ə.tə.drəˈmæt.ɪks/ [US] /-t̬ɚ.drəˈmæt̬-/ *plural noun* theatrical performances in which the people involved are not paid but take part for their own enjoyment

amatory /ˈæm.ə.tᵊr.i/ [US] /-tɔːr-/ *adj* *FORMAL* relating to sexual love: *amatory adventures*

amaze /əˈmeɪz/ *verb* [T] to cause someone to be extremely surprised: [+ question word] *I was amazed **by how** well he looked.* ○ *You've done all your homework in an hour? You amaze me.* ○ [+ that] ***It** amazes me **that** she's got the energy for all those parties.* ○ [+ to infinitive] ***It** amazes me **to** think that Anna is now in charge of the company.* ○ ***It** amazes me **how** you can put up with living in such a dirty house.* ○ ***It never ceases to** amaze me **how** he can talk for so long without ever saying anything interesting.*

amazed /əˈmeɪzd/ *adj* extremely surprised: *She was amazed **at** how calm she felt after the accident.* ○ *I was **absolutely** amazed when I heard he'd been promoted.* ○ [+ to infinitive] *Mr Graham was amazed **to** find 46 ancient gold coins inside the pot.* ○ *I was amazed **to hear** that Chris had won first prize.* ○ *We were amazed **to discover** that we'd been at school together.* ○ [+ (that)] *I'm amazed **(that)** she didn't complain.*

amazement /əˈmeɪz.mənt/ *noun* [U] extreme surprise: *She stared **in** amazement.* ○ ***To my** amazement, he ate the whole lot.*

amazing /əˈmeɪ.zɪŋ/ *adj* extremely surprising: *This stain remover really works – it's amazing!* ○ *The new theatre is going to cost an amazing* (= very large) ***amount** of money.* ○ *APPROVING This wine is really amazing* (= very good). ○ ***It's** amazing **to** think that the managing director is only 23.* ○ ***It's** amazing **that** no one else has applied for the job.* ○ *The amazing **thing** is that it was kept secret for so long.* ○ *What an amazing **coincidence**!*

amazingly /əˈmeɪ.zɪŋ.li/ *adv*: *The food was amazingly **good**.* ○ *Amazingly **enough*** (= Very surprisingly), *no one else has applied for the job.*

amazon /ˈæm.ə.zᵊn/ [US] /-zɑːn/ *noun* [C] *HUMOROUS* a tall strong or forceful woman **amazonian** /ˌæm.əˈzəʊ.ni.ən/ [US] /-ˈzoʊ-/ *adj*

Amazonian /ˌæm.əˈzəʊ.ni.ən/ [US] /-ˈzoʊ-/ *adj* relating to the area around the Amazon river in South America: *the Amazonian **rain forest***

ambassador /æmˈbæs.ə.dəʳ/ [US] /-dɚ/ *noun* [C] an important official who lives in a foreign country to represent his or her own country there, and who is officially accepted in this position by that country: *Britain's ambassador **in** Moscow has refused to comment.* ○ *She's a former ambassador **to** the United States.* ○ *Late last night, the French ambassador was summoned to the Foreign Office to discuss the crisis.*

ambassadorial /æmˌbæs.əˈdɔː.ri.əl/ [US] /-ˈdɔːr.i-/ *adj*: *He achieved ambassadorial rank* (= the rank of ambassador) *in 1958.*

amber /ˈæm.bəʳ/ [US] /-bɚ/ *noun* [U] **1** a hard transparent yellowish-brown substance which was formed in ancient times from the liquid of trees and is used in jewellery: *He has a collection of prehistoric insects **preserved in** amber.* ○ *an amber necklace* **2** *UK* (*US ALSO* **yellow**) the yellowish-orange traffic light which shows between the green and the red to warn drivers that the lights are about to change: *The lights turned to amber.* ○ *an amber **light***

ambidextrous /ˌæm.bɪˈdek.strəs/ *adj* able to use both hands equally well

ambience, **ambiance** /ˈæm.bi.ᵊn*t*s/ [US] /ˌɑːm.biˈɑːn*t*s/ *noun* [S] *LITERARY* the character of a place or the quality it seems to have: *Despite being a busy city, Dublin has the ambience **of** a country town.*

ambient /ˈæm.bi.ᵊnt/ *adj* [before n] *SPECIALIZED* (especially of environmental conditions) existing in the surrounding area: *ambient conditions/lighting/noise/temperature*

ˌambient ˈmusic *noun* [U] a type of music which has no tune or beat but which is intended to relax people or create a particular mood

ambiguous /æmˈbɪɡ.ju.əs/ *adj* having or expressing more than one possible meaning, sometimes intentionally: *His reply to my question was somewhat ambiguous.* ○ *The wording of the agreement is ambiguous.* ○ *The government has been ambiguous on this issue.* **ambiguously** /æmˈbɪɡ.ju.ə.sli/ *adv*: *Some questions were badly or ambiguously worded.*

ambiguity /ˌæm.bɪˈɡjuː.ɪ.ti/ [US] /-ə.t̬i/ *noun* [C or U] *We wish to remove any ambiguity* (= confusion) *concerning our demands.* ○ *There are some ambiguities in the legislation.*

ambit /ˈæm.bɪt/ *noun* [U] *FORMAL* the range or limits of influence of something: *They believe that all the outstanding issues should **fall within the** ambit **of** the talks.*

ambition /æmˈbɪʃ.ᵊn/ *noun* [C or U] a strong desire for success, achievement, power or wealth: *She's got a lot of ambition.* ○ [+ to infinitive] *His ambition is ultimately **to** run his own business.* ○ *He has already **achieved** his main ambition in life – to become wealthy.* ○ *political ambitions* ○ *She doubts whether she'll ever be able to **fulfil** her ambition.* ○ *I've always had a **burning*** (= very great) *ambition to be a film director.* ○ *After his heart attack, he abandoned his ambition **to become** Prime Minister.*

ambitious /æmˈbɪʃ.əs/ *adj* **1** having a great desire to be successful, powerful or wealthy: *an ambitious **young** lawyer* ○ *He's very ambitious **for** his children* (= He's anxious that they should be successful). **2** If a plan or idea is ambitious, it needs a great amount of skill and effort to be successful or be achieved: *She has some ambitious expansion **plans** for her business.* ○ *The government has announced an ambitious programme to modernize the railway network.* ○ *The original comple-*

tion date was over-ambitious, so we have had to delay the opening by six months. ambitiously /æm'bɪʃ.ə.sli/ *adv*

ambivalent /æm'bɪv.ə.lənt/ *adj* having two opposing feelings at the same time, or being uncertain about how you feel: *I felt very ambivalent **about** leaving home.* ○ *He has fairly ambivalent **feelings** towards his father.* ○ *an ambivalent **attitude** to exercise* ambivalence /æm-'bɪv.ə.lənts/ *noun* [U] *her ambivalence **towards** men* ambivalently /æm'bɪv.ə.lənt.li/ *adv*

amble /ˈæm.bḷ/ *verb* [I usually + adv or prep] to walk in a slow and relaxed way: *He was ambling **along** the beach.* ○ *She ambled **down** the street, stopping occasionally to look in the shop windows.*
amble /ˈæm.bḷ/ *noun* [S] a slow, relaxed walk: *There's nothing I enjoy more than a leisurely amble across the moor.*

ambrosia /æmˈbrəʊ.zi.ə/ /-ʒə/ ⓤ /-ˈbroʊ.ʒə/ *noun* [U] LITERARY the food eaten by Greek and Roman gods, or a very pleasant food which could be compared with this: *The chocolate mousse she makes is sheer ambrosia* (= tastes extremely good).

ambulance /ˈæm.bjʊ.lənts/ *noun* [C] a special vehicle used to take ill or injured people to hospital: *I **called** an ambulance.* ○ *We were woken in the night by the wail of ambulance sirens.* ○ *an ambulance **driver*** ○ *An ambulance **crew** was called to his home, but he was dead by the time they arrived.*

ambulance ˌchaser *noun* [C] INFORMAL DISAPPROVING a lawyer or reporter who obtains work by taking advantage of someone else's bad luck or accident without considering their feelings: *An ambulance chaser contacted her the day she was injured and persuaded her to sue the city council for negligence.* ambulance-chasing /ˈæm.bjʊ.lənts ˌtʃeɪ.sɪŋ/ *adj* [before n] INFORMAL

ambulanceman /ˈæm.bjʊ.lənts.mən/ *noun* [C] UK a man whose job is to drive an AMBULANCE and to help or give treatment to the people carried in it
ambulancewoman /ˈæm.bjʊ.lənts,wʊm.ən/ *noun* [C] UK a female ambulanceman

ambulatory /ˌæm.bjəˈleɪ.tᵊr.i/ ⓤ /ˈæm.bjə.lə.tɔːr-/ *adj* SPECIALIZED relating to or describing people being treated for an injury or illness who are able to walk, and who, when treated in a hospital, are usually not staying for the night in a bed: *an ambulatory surgery and radiology centre* ○ *We will be opening two new ambulatory **care** facilities for private patients in May.*

ambush /ˈæm.bʊʃ/ *verb* [T] to suddenly attack a person or a group of people after hiding and waiting for them: *Five soldiers died after their bus was ambushed on a country road.* ○ *He was ambushed **by gunmen** on his way to work.*
ambush /ˈæm.bʊʃ/ *noun* [C or U] **1** an occasion when a person or group of people are ambushed: *Several passers-by were killed **in** the ambush.* ○ *Fear of ambush prevents the police from going to high-risk areas.* **2** lie/wait in ambush If someone lies in/waits in ambush, they hide and wait for someone in order to attack them.

ameba /əˈmiː.bə/ *noun* [C] *plural* **amebas** or **amebae** MAINLY US FOR **amoeba**
amebic /əˈmiː.bɪk/ *adj* MAINLY US FOR **amoebic**

ameliorate /əˈmiː.ljə.reɪt/ *verb* [T] FORMAL to make a bad or unpleasant situation better: *Foreign aid is badly needed to ameliorate the effects of the drought.* amelioration /ə,miː.li.əˈreɪ.ʃᵊn/ *noun* [U]

COMMON LEARNER ERROR

ameliorate

The word **ameliorate** is formal and quite rare in English. You should only use it if you are sure that you need a formal word. If you are not sure, then use the word **improve** which is not formal.

Travel can improve your understanding of other cultures.
~~Travel can ameliorate your understanding of other cultures.~~

---

amen /ˌɑːˈmen/ /ˌeɪ-/ *exclamation* FORMAL said or sung at the end of a prayer or sometimes a religious song to express agreement with what has been said
● **amen to that** said to show that you agree strongly with something that someone has just said: *"Thank goodness*

we didn't go." "Amen to that!"

amenable /əˈmiː.nə.bḷ/ *adj* willing to accept or be influenced by a suggestion: *She might be more amenable **to** the idea if you explained how much money it would save.* ○ *Do you think the new manager will **prove** more amenable **to** our proposals?*

amend /əˈmend/ *verb* [T] to change the words of a text, typically a law or a legal document: *MPs were urged to amend the law to prevent another oil tanker disaster.* ○ *In line 20, 'men' should be amended* (= changed) *to 'people'.* ○ *Until the constitution is amended, the power to appoint ministers will remain with the president.*
amendment /əˈmend.mənt/ *noun* **1** [C or U] a change made to the words of a text: *I insisted that the book did not need amendment.* ○ *I've made a few last-minute amendments **to** the article.* ○ *Presidential power was reduced by a **constitutional** amendment in 1991.* **2** [C] a change to a law that is not yet in operation and is still being discussed: *An amendment to the **bill** was agreed without a vote.*

amends /əˈmendz/ *plural noun* **make amends** to do something good to show that you are sorry about something you have done: *She tried to make amends **by** inviting him out to dinner.* ○ *I wanted to make amends **for** the worry I've caused you.*

amenity /əˈmiː.nɪ.ti/ ⓤ /əˈmen.ə.t̬i/ *noun* [C usually pl] **1** something, such as a swimming pool or shopping centre, that is intended to make life more pleasant or comfortable for the people in a town, hotel or other place: *The council has some spare cash which it proposes to spend on **public** amenities.* **2 basic amenities** things considered to be necessary to live comfortably such as hot water: *The 200-year-old jail is overcrowded, understaffed and **lacking in** basic amenities.*

America /əˈmer.ɪ.kə/ *noun* [U] **1** the US **2** North or South America
American /əˈmer.ɪ.kən/ *adj* **1** of or relating to the US: *They drive a big American car.* **2** of or relating to North or South America
● **as American as apple pie** typical of the way of life in the US: *Leather jackets are as American as apple pie and Harley-Davidsons.*
American /əˈmer.ɪ.kən/ *noun* [C] someone from the US: *He said he was proud to be an American.* **Americanize**, UK USUALLY **-ise** /əˈmer.ɪ.kᵊn.aɪz/ *verb* [T] *Linda Chan was born in Hong Kong but grew up in New York and quickly became Americanized.* ○ DISAPPROVING *Many European cities have been Americanized with burger bars and diners.* **Americanization** /ə,mer.ɪ.kᵊn.aɪˈzeɪ.ʃᵊn/ *noun* [U] (UK USUALLY **-isation**)
Americanism /əˈmer.ɪ.kə.nɪ.zᵊm/ *noun* [C] a word or expression which originated in the United States but is used by people in other countries, especially those where English is spoken

the A,merican ˈDream *noun* [S] the belief that everyone in the US has the chance to be successful, rich and happy if they work hard

A,merican ˈfootball UK *noun* [U] (US **football**) a game for two teams of eleven players in which an oval ball is moved along the field by running with it or throwing it ⊃See picture **Sports** on page Centre 10

A,merican ˈIndian *noun* [C] a **Native American**

Aˈmerican ,plan *noun* US FOR **full board**

Amerindian /ˌæm.əˈrɪn.di.ən/ *noun* [C], *adj* **American Indian**

amethyst /ˈæm.ə.θɪst/ *noun* [C or U] a transparent purple stone used for making jewellery
amethyst /ˈæm.ə.θɪst/ *adj* purple

amiable /ˈeɪ.mi.ə.bḷ/ *adj* describes a person or their behaviour that is pleasant and friendly: *He seemed an amiable young man.* ○ *So amiable was the mood of the meeting that a decision was soon reached.* amiably /ˈeɪ.mi.ə.bli/ *adv*: *They were chatting quite amiably on the phone last night so I assumed everything was okay.* amiability /ˌeɪ.mi.əˈbɪl.ɪ.ti/ ⓤ /-ə.t̬i/ *noun* [U] *I hate all that false amiability that goes on at parties.*

amicable /ˈæm.ɪ.kə.bḷ/ *adj* **1** relating to behaviour between people that is pleasant and friendly often despite a difficult situation: *His manner was perfectly*

A

amicable but I felt uncomfortable. **2** relating to an agreement or decision that is achieved without arguments or unpleasantness: *Few people have amicable divorces.* ○ *Eventually we reached an amicable settlement.* **amicably** /ˈæm.ɪ.kə.bli/ *adv*: *I hope we can settle this amicably.*

amid /əˈmɪd/ *prep* (*ALSO* **amidst**) *FORMAL* in the middle of or surrounded by; among: *On the floor, amid mounds of books, were two small envelopes.* ○ *The new perfume was launched amidst a fanfare of publicity.*

amidships /əˈmɪd.ʃɪps/ *adv* in the middle part of a ship

amino acid /əˌmiː.nəʊˈæs.ɪd/ [US] /-noʊ-/ *noun* [C] a chemical substance found in plants and animals

amiss /əˈmɪs/ *adj* [after v] wrong; not suitable or as expected: *I could see by the look on their faces that* ***something was*** *amiss.*

• **not go amiss** *INFORMAL* If something might/would not go amiss, it would be useful and might help to improve a situation: *A word of apology might not go amiss.* ○ *A sense of proportion would not come amiss in all of this.*

• **take *sth* amiss** to be offended by something that someone has said to you: *I was worried that he might take my remark amiss.*

amity /ˈæm.ɪ.ti/ [US] /-ə.t̬i/ *noun* [U] *FORMAL* friendship; a good relationship: *The two groups had lived* ***in*** *perfect amity for many years before the recent troubles.*

ammeter /ˈæm.iː.təʳ/ [US] /-t̬ɚ/ *noun* [C] a device for measuring the strength of an electric current in units called AMPS

ammonia /əˈməʊ.ni.ə/ [US] /-ˈmoʊ-/ *noun* [U] a gas with a strong unpleasant smell used in making explosives, FERTILIZERS (= substances which help plants grow) and some cleaning products **ammonium** /əˈməʊ.ni.əm/ [US] /-ˈmoʊ-/ *noun* [U] *SPECIALIZED* *ammonium chloride* ○ *ammonium nitrate*

ammunition /ˌæm.jʊˈnɪʃ.ᵊn/ *noun* [U] **1** (*INFORMAL* **ammo**) objects that can be shot from a weapon such as bullets or bombs: *a good supply of ammunition* ○ *a shortage of ammunition* **2** facts that can be used to support an argument: *His bad behaviour* ***provided plenty of*** *ammunition for his opponents.*

amnesia /æmˈniː.zi.ə/ /-ʒə/ *noun* [U] loss of the ability to remember: *In his later life he suffered periods of amnesia.*

amnesty /ˈæm.nɪ.sti/ *noun* **1** [C or U] a decision by a government that allows political prisoners to be free: *Most political prisoners were freed under the terms of the amnesty.* **2** [C usually sing] a fixed period of time during which people are not punished for committing a particular crime: *People who hand in illegal weapons will not be prosecuted during the amnesty.* ○ *The government refused to declare an amnesty* ***for*** *people who had not paid the disputed tax.*

ˌAmnesty Interˈnational *group noun* [S] an international organization which works to persuade governments to release people who are in prison for their beliefs and to stop the use of TORTURE and punishment by death

amniocentesis /ˌæm.ni.əʊ.senˈtiː.sɪs/ [US] /-oʊ-/ *noun* [C or U] *plural* **amniocenteses** a medical test in which a needle is used to remove a small amount of the liquid that surrounds a baby in the mother's womb in order to examine the baby's condition

amoeba (*plural* **amoebae** or **amoebas**), *MAINLY US* **ameba** (*plural* **amebas** or **amebae**) /əˈmiː.bə/ *noun* [C] a very small simple organism consisting of only one cell **amoebic**, *MAINLY US* **amebic** /əˈmiː.bɪk/ *adj*

aˌmoebic ˈdysentery *noun* [U] an illness of the bowels caused by an amoeba

amok, **amuck** /əˈmɒk/ [US] /-ˈmʌk/ *adv* **run amok** to be out of control and act in a wild or dangerous manner: *The army ran amok after one of its senior officers was killed.* ○ *The two dogs ran amok in a school playground.*

among /əˈmʌŋ/ *prep* (*ALSO* **amongst**) **1** in the middle of or surrounded by other things: *I saw a few familiar faces among the crowd.* ○ *Rescue teams searched among the wreckage for survivors.* **2** happening as part of a group of people or things: *a decision that has caused a lot of anger among women* ○ *Relax, you're amongst friends.* ○ *Talk about it among yourselves* (= Talk to each other about it without me) *for a while.* ○ *She has worked as an estate agent among* ***other things*** (= as well as other things).

amoral /ˌeɪˈmɒr.əl/ [US] /ˌeɪˈmɔːr-/ *adj* without moral principles: *Humans, he argues, are amoral and what guides them is not any sense of morality but an instinct for survival.* ➲Compare **immoral**; **moral**. **amorality** /ˌeɪ.mɒrˈæl.ɪ.ti/ [US] /-mɔːrˈæl.ə.t̬i/ *noun* [U] *The glorious thing about Almodovar's films is their unashamed amorality.*

amorous /ˈæm.ə.rəs/ [US] /-ɚ.əs/ *adj* of or expressing sexual desire: *The film centres around the amorous* ***adventures/exploits*** *of its handsome hero.* ○ *Amanda had rejected his amorous advances.*

amorphous /əˈmɔː.fəs/ [US] /-ˈmɔːr-/ /eɪ-/ *adj* having no fixed form or shape: *an amorphous* ***mass*** *of jelly*

amortize, *UK USUALLY* **-ise** /əˈmɔː.taɪz/ [US] /æmˈɔːr-/ *verb* [T] *FORMAL* to reduce a debt by paying small regular amounts: *The value of the machinery is amortized over its estimated useful life.* **amortizable**, *UK USUALLY* **-isable** /əˈmɔː.taɪ.zə.bl̩/ [US] /ˌæm.ɔːr-/ *adj* **amortization**, *UK USUALLY* **-isation** /əˌmɔː.tɪˈzeɪ.ʃᵊn/ [US] /æmˌɔːr.t̬ə-/ *noun* [U]

amount /əˈmaʊnt/ *noun* [C] a collection or mass especially of something which cannot be counted: *They didn't deliver the right amount* ***of*** *sand.* ○ *Small amounts* ***of*** *land were used for keeping animals.* ○ *He paid regular amounts* ***of*** *money to a charity.* ○ *I didn't expect the bill to come to this amount* (= of money). ○ *The new tax caused a huge amount* ***of*** *public anger.* ○ *I had* ***a certain*** *amount* ***of*** (= some) *difficulty finding the house.* ○ *You wouldn't believe* ***the*** *amount* ***of*** *trouble* (= what a lot of trouble) *I've had with this car.*

• **any amount of** a very large amount of: *We had any amount of people applying for the job.*

USAGE

amount of or **number of?**

Amount of is used with uncountable nouns.

I should reduce the amount of coffee I drink.
Did you use the right amount of flour?

Number of is used with countable nouns.

We don't know the number of people involved yet.
They received a large number of complaints.

amount /əˈmaʊnt/ *verb*

PHRASAL VERBS WITH **amount** ▼

▲ **amount to *sth*** [ADD UP TO] *phrasal verb* [not continuous] to become a particular amount: *The annual cost of income support to unmarried mothers amounted to £700 million in that year.*

▲ **amount to *sth*** [BE] *phrasal verb* [not continuous] to be the same as something, or to have the same effect as something: *His behaviour amounted to serious professional misconduct.* ○ *He gave what amounted to an apology on behalf of his company.*

amour propre /ˌæ.mʊəˈprɒ.prə/ [US] /ˌɑː.mʊrˈproʊ.prə/ *noun* [U] *LITERARY* a belief and confidence in your own ability and value

amp [ELECTRICITY] /æmp/ *noun* [C] (*FORMAL* **ampere**) the standard unit of measurement for the strength of an electrical current: *a thirty-amp fuse*

amperage /ˈæm.pə.rɪdʒ/ [US] /-prɪdʒ/ *noun* [U] the strength of electrical current needed to make a piece of electric equipment work

amp [SOUND] /æmp/ *noun* [C] *INFORMAL* an **amplifier**, see at **amplify**

ampersand /ˈæm.pə.sænd/ [US] /-pɚ-/ *noun* [C] the sign (&) used for 'and'

amphetamine /æmˈfet.ə.miːn/ /-mɪn/ [US] /-fet̬-/ *noun* [C or U] any of several types of drug used as a STIMULANT (= a substance which makes the mind or body more active): *Floyd was banned from racing after a drug test revealed traces of amphetamine in his urine.*

A

amphibian /æm'fɪb.i.ən/ *noun* [C] an animal, such as a frog, which lives both on land and in water but must lay its eggs in water

amphibious /æm'fɪb.i.əs/ *adj* **1** of or relating to a type of animal which lives both on land and in water: *amphibious animals* **2** relating to vehicles which operate both on land or in water: *amphibious vehicles/aircraft* ○ *an amphibious landing/attack* (= from the sea onto the land)

amphitheatre *MAINLY UK, US USUALLY* **amphitheater** /'æmp.fɪ,θɪə.təʳ/ [US] /-fə,θiː.ə.t̬ɚ/ *noun* [C] a circular or oval area of ground around which rows of seats are arranged on a steep slope, for watching plays, sports, etc. outside

amphora /'æm.fᵊr.ə/ [US] /-fɚ.ə/ *noun* [C] *plural* **amphorae** or **amphoras** a long narrow clay container, wider at the top than at the base, which has two handles and was used in ancient times especially for storing oil or wine

ample /'æm.pl̩/ *adj* **1** more than enough: *You'll have ample* ***opportunity*** *to ask questions after the talk.* ○ *There's ample* ***evidence*** *that the lawyer knew exactly what she was doing.* ○ *They had ample warning of the factory closure.* **2** *HUMOROUS* If the shape of someone's body or part of their body is ample, it is large: *her ample* ***bosom*** ○ *His ample* ***girth*** (= His big stomach) *was clear evidence of his passion for food.*

amply /'æm.pli/ *adv*: *They face a hard task, as yesterday's discussions amply* (= clearly) *demonstrated.*

amplify /'æm.plɪ.faɪ/ *verb* [T] **1** to make something louder: *amplified music/guitar* **2** *FORMAL* to increase the size or effect of something: *A funeral can amplify the feelings of regret and loss for the relatives.*

amplification /,æm.plɪ.fɪ'keɪ.ʃᵊn/ *noun* [U] **1** Amplification makes music or other sounds louder: *electronic amplification* **2** *FORMAL* added detail: *The horror lies in the violence itself, which needs no amplification.*

amplifier /'æm.plɪ.faɪ.əʳ/ [US] /-ɚ/ *noun* [C] (*INFORMAL* **amp**) an electrical device which makes sounds louder

amplitude [LARGE AMOUNT] /'æm.plɪ.tjuːd/ [US] /-tuːd/ *noun* [U] *FORMAL* a large amount or wide range: *The sheer amplitude of the novel invites comparisons with Tolstoy and George Eliot.*

amplitude [CURVE] /'æm.plɪ.tjuːd/ [US] /-tuːd/ *noun* [C usually sing] *SPECIALIZED* the distance between the top and the base of a curve

ampoule, *US ALSO* **ampule** /'æm.puːl/ *noun* [C] a small, usually glass, container for a single measured amount of medicine, especially for an injection

amputate /'æm.pjʊ.teɪt/ *verb* [I or T] to cut off a part of the body: *They had to amputate his foot to free him from the wreckage.* ○ *In these cases there is no choice but to amputate.* **amputation** /,æm.pjʊ'teɪ.ʃᵊn/ *noun* [C or U] *Amputation of the limb is really a last resort.* ○ *Most amputations in this region are the result of accidents with land mines.*

amputee /,æm.pjʊ'tiː/ *noun* [C] a person who has had an arm or leg cut off

amuck /ə'mʌk/ *adv* **amok**

amulet /'æm.jʊ.lət/ [US] /-jə-/ *noun* [C] an object worn because it is believed to protect against evil, disease or unhappiness

amuse /ə'mjuːz/ *verb* [I or T] to entertain someone, especially by humorous speech or action or by making someone laugh or smile, or to keep someone happy, especially for a short time: *I've brought with me an article from yesterday's paper that I thought might amuse you.* ○ [+ obj + to infinitive] *I think* ***it*** *amuses him* ***to*** *see people make fools of themselves.* ○ [R] *We amused ourselves by watching the passers-by.* ○ *I bought a magazine to amuse myself while I was on the train.* ○ *Apparently these stories are meant to amuse.*

amused /ə'mjuːzd/ *adj* showing that you think something is funny: *an amused smile* ○ *She was very amused* ***by/at*** *your comments.*

• **be not amused** to be annoyed: *I told Helena about what had happened and she was not amused.*

• **keep *sb* amused** to keep someone interested and help them to have an enjoyable time: *Toddlers don't need expensive toys and games to keep them amused.*

amusement /ə'mjuːz.mənt/ *noun* **1** [U] the feeling of being entertained or made to laugh: *She looked at him* ***with*** *amusement.* ○ *I looked on* ***in*** *amusement as they started to argue.* ○ *Carl came last in the race,* ***(much) to*** *my amusement.* ○ *I play the piano just* ***for*** *my* ***own*** *amusement* (= to entertain myself not other people). **2** [C] an activity that you can take part in for entertainment: *There was a range of* ***fairground*** *amusements, including rides, stalls and competitions.*

amusing /ə'mjuː.zɪŋ/ *adj* entertaining: *an amusing story/person/situation* **amusingly** /ə'mjuː.zɪŋ.li/ *adv*: *On the subject of childbirth she is amusingly frank.*

a'musement ar,cade *noun* [C] a place in which you can pay to play games on machines

a'musement ,park *noun* [C] a **funfair** or **theme park**

amyl nitrite /,æ.mɪl'naɪ.traɪt/ *noun* [U] (*ALSO* **amyl nitrate**) a drug which can be used for increasing pleasure during sex and was originally used for treating ANGINA

an [NOT PARTICULAR] *WEAK* /ən/, *STRONG* /æn/ *determiner* used instead of 'a' when the following word begins with a vowel sound: *an easy question* ○ *an interesting story* ○ *an orange* ○ *an honour* ⮊See Note **a or an?** at **a** NOT PARTICULAR.

-an [BELONG TO] /-ᵊn/ *suffix* (*ALSO* **-ean, -ian**) connected with or belonging to the stated place, group or type: *an American* ○ *a Canadian* ○ *a Korean* ○ *a Christian* ○ *Russian literature* ○ *Italian opera*

anabolic steroid /,æn.ə.bɒl.ɪk'ster.ɔɪd/ [US] /-bɑː.lɪk-'stɪr.ɔɪd/ *noun* [C] a hormone that causes muscle and bone growth. Anabolic steroids are sometimes used illegally by athletes competing in sports competitions: *The gold-medal winning weightlifter was disqualified after testing positive for anabolic steroids.*

anachronism /ə'næk.rə.nɪ.zᵊm/ *noun* [C] a person, thing or idea which exists out of its time in history, especially one which happened or existed later than the period being shown, discussed, etc: *For some people, marriage is an anachronism from the days when women needed to be protected.*

anachronistic /ə,næk.rə'nɪs.tɪk/ *adj*: *He described the law as anachronistic* (= more suitable for an earlier time) *and ridiculous.* **anachronistically** /ə,næk.rə-'nɪs.tɪ.kli/ *adv*

anaconda /,æn.ə'kɒn.də/ [US] /-'kɑːn-/ *noun* [C] a large South American snake which curls around a live animal and crushes it to kill it for food

anaemia, *MAINLY US* **anemia** /ə'niː.mi.ə/ *noun* [U] a medical condition in which there are not enough red blood cells in the blood: *The main symptoms of anaemia are tiredness and pallor.*

anaemic /ə'niː.mɪk/ *adj* **1** (*MAINLY US* **anemic**) suffering from anaemia: *Lack of iron in your diet can make you anaemic.* **2** lacking energy and effort: *Both actors gave fairly anaemic performances.*

anaerobic /,æn.ə'rəʊ.bɪk/ [US] /-er'oʊ-/ *adj* not needing or without oxygen: *Some bacteria can only live in anaerobic* ***conditions.***

anaesthesia, *MAINLY US* **anesthesia** /,æn.əs'θiː.zi.ə/ /-ʒə/ *noun* [U] **1** a state in which someone does not feel pain, usually because of drugs they have been given **2** *SPECIALIZED* the inability to feel heat, cold, pain, touch, etc.

anaesthetic, *MAINLY US* **anesthetic** /,æn.əs'θet.ɪk/ [US] /-'θet̬-/ *noun* [C or U] a substance that makes you unable to feel pain: *The operation is performed* ***under*** *anaesthetic.* ○ *The procedure is carried out under* ***local*** *anaesthetic* (= a substance that makes you unable to feel pain in part of your body). ○ *I've never had* ***general*** *anaesthetic* (= a substance that makes you unconscious so you do not feel pain).

anaesthetist, *MAINLY US* **anesthetist** /ə'niːs.θə.tɪst/ [US] /-t̬ɪst/ *noun* [C] a doctor who gives anaesthetic to people in hospital **anaesthetize**, *UK USUALLY* **-ise**, *MAINLY US* **anesthetize** /ə'niːs.θə.taɪz/ [US] /-t̬aɪz/ *verb* [T]

anagram /'æn.ə.græm/ *noun* [C] a word or phrase made by using the letters of another word or phrase in a different order: *'Neat' is an anagram* ***of*** *'a net'.*

[A]

anal [BODY PART] /ˈeɪ.nəl/ *adj* relating to the opening at the end of the INTESTINES through which solid excrement leaves the body: *the anal passage/sphincter* ○ *anal sex* **anally** /ˈeɪ.nə.li/ *adv*

anal [MENTAL STATE] /ˈeɪ.nəl/ *adj INFORMAL* **anally retentive**: *his anal fondness for filing*

analgesic /ˌæn.əlˈdʒiː.zɪk/ *noun* [C] a type of drug which stops you from feeling pain: *This cream contains a mild analgesic to soothe stings and bites.* **analgesic** /ˌæn.əlˈdʒiː.zɪk/ *adj*: *analgesic properties*

ˌanally reˈtentive *adj* (*ALSO* **anal retentive**) *INFORMAL* describes someone who is too worried about being organized and tidy: *Don't you think Adrian's a bit anally retentive? Look how obsessively orderly everything is in his garage.*

analogue [SIMILAR], *US ALSO* **analog** /ˈæn.ə.lɒg/ Ⓤⓢ /-lɑːg/ *noun* [C] *FORMAL* something which is similar to or can be used instead of something else: *He has been studying the European analogues **of** the British Parliament.*

analogue [WATCH], *US ALSO* **analog** /ˈæn.ə.lɒg/ Ⓤⓢ /-lɑːg/ *adj* **analogue clock/watch** a clock/watch which has HANDS (= narrow pointers) that show what time it is

analogue [SOUND], *US ALSO* **analog** /ˈæn.ə.lɒg/ Ⓤⓢ /-lɑːg/ *adj* describes a recording which is made by changing the sound waves into electrical signals of the same type ➲Compare **digital**.

analogy /əˈnæl.ə.dʒi/ *noun* [C or U] a comparison between things which have similar features, often used to help explain a principle or idea: *He **drew** an analogy **between** the brain and a vast computer.* ○ *It is sometimes easier to illustrate an abstract concept **by** analogy **with*** (= by comparing it with) *something concrete.* **analogous** /əˈnæl.ə.gəs/ *adj*: *The experience of mystic trance is in a sense analogous **to** sleep or drunkenness.*

analyse *UK*, *US* **analyze** /ˈæn.əl.aɪz/ *verb* [T] to study or examine something in detail, in order to discover more about it: *Researchers analysed the purchases of 6300 households.* ○ *Water samples taken from streams were analysed **for** contamination by chemicals.*

analysis /əˈnæl.ə.sɪs/ *noun* [C or U] *plural* **analyses** when you analyse something: *Chemical analysis revealed a high content of copper.* ○ *I was interested in Clare's analysis **of*** (= examination of and judgment about) *the situation.*

• **in the last/final analysis** something you say when you are talking about what is most important or true in a situation: *In the final analysis, the only people who will benefit are property owners.*

analyst /ˈæn.ə.lɪst/ *noun* [C] someone whose job is to study or examine something in detail: *a financial/food/political/systems analyst*

analytical /ˌæn.əˈlɪt.ɪ.kəl/ Ⓤⓢ /-ˈlɪt̬-/ *adj* (*FORMAL* **analytic**) examining or tending to examine things very carefully: *He has a very analytical **mind**.* ○ *Some students have a more analytical approach to learning.* **analytically** /ˌæn.əˈlɪt.ɪ.kli/ Ⓤⓢ /-ˈlɪt̬-/ *adv*

anarchism /ˈæn.ə.kɪ.zəm/ Ⓤⓢ /-ɚ-/ *noun* [U] the political belief that there should be little or no formal or official organization to society but that people should work freely together

anarchist /ˈæn.ə.kɪst/ Ⓤⓢ /-ɚ-/ *noun* [C] **1** a person who believes in anarchism: *He was a poet, an anarchist and a vegan.* ○ *an anarchist group/slogan/bookshop* **2** *DISAPPROVING* someone who wishes to destroy the existing government and laws: *anarchist tendencies/demonstrations* **anarchistic** /ˌæn.əˈkɪs.tɪk/ Ⓤⓢ /-ɚ-/ *adj*

anarchy /ˈæn.ə.ki/ Ⓤⓢ /-ɚ-/ *noun* [U] lack of organization and control, especially in society because of an absence or failure of government: *What we are witnessing is the country's slow slide into anarchy.* ○ *The country has been in **a state of** anarchy since the inconclusive election.* ○ *If the pay deal isn't settled amicably there'll be anarchy in the factories.* **anarchic** /əˈnɑː.kɪk/ Ⓤⓢ /-ˈnɑːr-/ *adj*: *Milligan's anarchic humour has always had the power to offend as well as entertain.*

anathema /əˈnæθ.ə.mə/ *noun* [C usually sing; U] something which is greatly disliked or disapproved of: *Credit controls are anathema **to** the government.* ○ *For older employees, the new system is an anathema.*

anatomy /əˈnæt.ə.mi/ Ⓤⓢ /-ˈnæt̬-/ *noun* **1** [U] the scientific study of the body and how its parts are arranged: *An understanding of human anatomy is important to a dancer.* ○ *He later became professor of anatomy at Kiel.* **2** [C or U] the structure of an animal or plant: *the female anatomy* ○ *the anatomy of a leaf* **3** [C] *HUMOROUS* a person's body: *On which part of her anatomy is she tattooed?* **4** [C] *FORMAL* a detailed examination of a subject: *The whole play reads like an anatomy **of** evil.* **anatomical** /ˌæn.əˈtɒm.ɪ.kəl/ Ⓤⓢ /-ˈtɑː.mɪ-/ *adj*: *anatomical drawings*

-ance /-ənts/ *suffix* **-ence**

ancestor /ˈæn.ses.təʳ/ Ⓤⓢ /-tɚ/ *noun* [C] a person, plant, animal or object that is related to one existing at a later point in time: *There were portraits of his ancestors on the walls of the room.* ○ *This wooden instrument is the ancestor of the modern metal flute.* ➲Compare **descendant**. **ancestral** /ænˈses.trəl/ *adj* [before n] *an ancestral home* ○ *ancestral rights* **ancestry** /ˈæn.ses.tri/ *noun* [C or U] *He was proud of his Native American ancestry.* ○ *His wife was **of** royal ancestry.* ○ *The family has **traced** its ancestry **back to** the Norman invaders.*

anchor [WEIGHT] /ˈæŋ.kəʳ/ Ⓤⓢ /-kɚ/ *noun* [C] **1** a heavy metal object, usually shaped like a cross with curved arms, on a strong rope or chain, which is dropped from a boat into the water to prevent the boat from moving away: *We **dropped** anchor* (= lowered the anchor into the water) *and stopped.* ○ *It was time to **weigh** anchor* (= pull up the anchor and sail away). ➲See picture **Planes, Ships and Boats** on page Centre 14 **2** someone or something that gives support when needed: *She was my anchor when things were difficult for me.* ○ *This treaty has been called the anchor* (= strongest part) *of their foreign policy.*

anchor /ˈæŋ.kəʳ/ Ⓤⓢ /-kɚ/ *verb* **1** [I or T] to lower an anchor into the water in order to stop a boat from moving away **2** [T] to make something or someone stay in one position by fastening them firmly: *We anchored ourselves **to** the rocks with a rope.*

anchorage /ˈæŋ.kər.ɪdʒ/ Ⓤⓢ /-kɚ-/ *noun* [C or U] *The bay is well-known as a safe anchorage* (= place to anchor). ○ *The anchorage **point*** (= fixing point) *for the seat belt is not adjustable.*

anchor [BROADCASTER] /ˈæŋ.kəʳ/ Ⓤⓢ /-kɚ/ *noun* [C] *MAINLY US* an anchorman or anchorwoman

anchorite /ˈæŋ.kər.aɪt/ Ⓤⓢ /-kɚ-/ *noun* [C] someone who lives alone away from other people for religious reasons; a **hermit**

anchorman /ˈæŋ.kə.mæn/ Ⓤⓢ /-kɚ-/ *noun* [C] *MAINLY US* a man who is the main news reader on a television or radio news programme: *The late-night current affairs programme has a new anchorman.*

anchor /ˈæŋ.kəʳ/ Ⓤⓢ /-kɚ/ *verb* [T] *MAINLY US* *She will anchor* (= introduce) *the new morning news show.*

anchorwoman /ˈæŋ.kəˌwʊm.ən/ Ⓤⓢ /-kɚ-/ *noun* [C] *MAINLY US* a female anchorman

anchovy /ˈæn.tʃə.vi/ /ænˈtʃəʊ-/ Ⓤⓢ /ˈæn.tʃoʊ-/ *noun* [C or U] *plural* **anchovies** a small fish with a strong salty taste: *Decorate the top of the pizza with anchovies/strips of anchovy*

ancien régime /ɒntˌsjæn.reɪˈʒiːm/ Ⓤⓢ /ˌɑːnt.si.æn-/ *noun* [U] *FORMAL* an old system, particularly a political or social one, which has been replaced by a more modern system

ancient /ˈeɪn.tʃənt/ *adj* **1** of or from a long time ago, having lasted for a very long time: *ancient civilizations/rights/laws* ○ *ancient monuments/ruins/woodlands* ○ *the ancient kingdoms of Mexico* ○ *People have lived in this valley since ancient **times**.* ○ *History, ancient **and modern**, has taught these people an intense distrust of their neighbours.* **2** *INFORMAL* very old: *He's got an ancient computer.* **3** describes the period in European history from the earliest known societies to the end of the Roman empire: *the ancient Egyptians/Greeks/Romans* ○ *The ancient Britons inhabited these parts of England before the Roman invasion.*

A

COMMON LEARNER ERROR

ancient

Ancient cannot be used to refer to something or someone that existed in the recent past but not now. Use **former** or **ex** for this meaning.

A party was organized for former students of the school.
~~A party was organized for ancient students of the school.~~
my ex-girlfriend
~~my ancient girlfriend~~

Be careful not to confuse **ancient** with **old**. Ancient means thousands or hundreds of years old.

a medical centre for old/elderly people
~~a medical centre for ancient people~~

---

ancillary /æn'sɪl.²r.i/ ⓤ /'æn.sə.ler.i/ *adj* providing support or help; additional; extra: *ancillary staff/workers* ○ *an ancillary role* ○ *Campaigning to change government policy is ancillary to the charity's direct relief work.*

-ancy /-²nt.si/ *suffix* **-ency**

and ALSO *STRONG* /ænd/, *WEAK* /ənd, ən/ *conjunction* used to join two words, phrases, parts of sentences or related statements together; also or in addition to: *Ann and Jim* ○ *boys and girls* ○ *knives and forks* ○ *We were wet and tired.* ○ *We kissed and hugged each other.* ○ *Tidy up your room. And don't forget to make your bed!*
● **and all 1** and everything else: *She bought the whole lot – house, farm, horses and all.* **2** *UK SLANG* too: *I'd like some and all.*
● **and all that** *INFORMAL* and everything related to the subject mentioned: *She likes grammar and all that.*
● **and/or** used to mean that either one of two things or both of them is possible: *Many pupils have extra classes in the evenings and/or at weekends.*
● **and so on** (*ALSO* **and so forth**) together with other similar things: *schools, colleges and so on*

and THEN *STRONG* /ænd/, *WEAK* /ənd, ən/ *conjunction* **1** used to join two parts of a sentence, one part happening after the other part: *I got dressed and had my breakfast.* **2** as a result: *Bring the flowers into a warm room and they'll soon open.* ○ *Stand over there and then you'll be able to see it better.* **3** with certain verbs, 'and' can mean 'in order to': *I asked him to* **go** *and find my glasses.* ○ *Come and see* (= in order to see) *me tomorrow.* ○ **Wait and see** (= wait in order to see) *what happens.* ○ *INFORMAL* **Try and get** (= Try to get) *some tickets for tonight's performance.*

and VERY *STRONG* /ænd/, *WEAK* /ənd, ən/ *conjunction* If 'and' is used to join two words which are the same, it makes their meaning stronger: *She spends hours and hours* (= a very long time) *on the telephone.* ○ *The sound grew louder and louder* (= very loud). ○ *We laughed and laughed* (= laughed a lot).

and DESPITE *STRONG* /ænd/, *WEAK* /ənd, ən/ *conjunction* used to express surprise: *You're a vegetarian and you eat fish?*

andante /æn'dæn.ti/ /-teɪ/ ⓤ /ɑːn'dɑːn.teɪ/ /æn'dæn.ti/ *noun* [C usually sing] *SPECIALIZED* a piece of classical music that should be played quite slowly: *Handel's Violin Andante in A minor* **andante** /æn'dæn.teɪ/ ⓤ /ɑːn'dɑːn.teɪ/ *adj, adv* the andante movement ○ *The second movement of the symphony should be played andante.*

androgynous /æn'drɒdʒ.ɪ.nəs/ ⓤ /-'drɑː.dʒɪ-/ *adj* **1** not clearly male or female: *With her lean frame and cropped hair, Lennox had a fashionably androgynous look.* **2** *SPECIALIZED* having both male and female features **androgyny** /æn'drɒdʒ.ə.ni/ ⓤ /-'drɑː.dʒə-/ *noun* [U] One or two of the earlier photos reveal an intriguing androgyny not normally associated with the actress.

android /'æn.drɔɪd/ *noun* [C] a ROBOT (= computer-controlled machine) which is made to look like a human

anecdote /'æn.ɪk.dəʊt/ ⓤ /-doʊt/ *noun* [C] a short often amusing story, especially about something someone has done: *He told one or two amusing anecdotes about his years as a policeman.*

anecdotal /ˌæn.ɪk'dəʊ.t²l/ ⓤ /-'doʊ.t²l/ *adj* describes information that is not based on facts or careful study: *anecdotal* **evidence**

anemia /ə'niː.mi.ə/ *noun* [U] *MAINLY US FOR* **anaemia**

anemone /ə'nem.ə.ni/ *noun* [C] any of several types of small plant, wild or grown in gardens, with red, blue or white flowers

anesthesia /ˌæn.əs'θiː.zi.ə/ /-ʒə/ *noun* [U] *MAINLY US FOR* **anaesthesia**

anesthetic /ˌæn.əs'θet.ɪk/ ⓤ /-'θet̬-/ *noun* [C] *MAINLY US FOR* **anaesthetic**

anesthesiologist /ˌæn.əs.θiː.zi'ɒl.ə.dʒɪst/ ⓤ /ˌæn.əs.θiː.-zi'ɑː.lə.dʒɪst/ *noun* [C] *US SPECIALIZED* **anesthetist**

anesthetist /ə'niːs.θə.tɪst/ ⓤ /-t̬ɪst/ *noun* [C] *US FOR* **anaesthetist**, see at **anaesthesia**

anew /ə'njuː/ ⓤ /-'nuː/ *adv* *FORMAL* again or one more time, especially in a different way: *The film tells anew the story of his rise to fame and power.*

angel /'eɪn.dʒ²l/ *noun* **1** [C] a good spiritual creature in stories or some religions, usually represented as a human with wings: *According to the Bible, an angel told Mary that she would have God's son Jesus.* **2** [C] someone who is very good, helpful or kind: *Be an angel and help me with this.* **3** [as form of address] used when speaking to someone you like very much and know very well: *What's the matter, angel?* **4** [C] a person in the theatre who provides money for a show to be planned
● **be no angel** to sometimes behave badly: *He's no angel but he can't be blamed for everything that has happened.*
● **be on the side of the angels** *UK* to be doing something good or kind: *He was, in this matter at least, firmly on the side of the angels.*

angelic /æn'dʒel.ɪk/ *adj* very beautiful and very good: *an angelic voice/face/smile* **angelically** /æn'dʒel.ɪ.kli/ *adv*

angelica /æn'dʒel.ɪ.kə/ *noun* [U] the green stem of a plant, preserved with sugar and used for decorating cakes and other sweet food, or the plant itself: *strips of angelica*

the Angelus /ði'æn.dʒ²l.əs/ *noun* [S] **1** prayers said in the morning, in the middle of the day and in the evening in the Roman Catholic church **2** the ringing of bells to show that it is time for these prayers

anger /'æŋ.gə²/ ⓤ /-gɚ/ *noun* [U] a strong feeling which makes you want to hurt someone or be unpleasant because of something unfair or hurtful that has happened: *I think he feels a lot of anger* **towards** *his father who treated him very badly as a child.* ○ *There is a danger that anger* **at** *the new law may turn into anti-government feeling.* ○ *The people showed no surprise or anger* **at** *their treatment.* ○ *He found it hard to contain* (= control) *his anger.*

anger /'æŋ.gə²/ ⓤ /-gɚ/ *verb* [T] to make someone angry: *The remark angered him.* ○ *It always angers me to see so much waste.*

angina (pectoris) /æn.dʒaɪ.nə'pek.tə.rɪs/ ⓤ /-tɚ-/ *noun* [U] a disease which repeatedly causes sudden strong pains in the chest because blood containing oxygen is prevented from reaching the heart muscle by blocked ARTERIES

angioplasty /'æn.dʒi.əʊˌplæs.ti/ ⓤ /-oʊ-/ *noun* [C or U] *SPECIALIZED* a medical operation to remove a blockage from an artery in a person who has ANGINA

angle SPACE /'æŋ.gl/ *noun* [C] **1** the space between two lines or surfaces at the point at which they touch each other, measured in degrees: *The interior angles of a square are* **right** *angles or angles of 90 degrees.* ○ *The boat settled into the mud* **at** *a 35 degree angle/an angle of 35 degrees.* ○ *The picture was hanging* **at an** *angle.* ○ *He wore his hat* **at a jaunty** *angle* (= not straight or vertical). ➔See also **angular**. **2** the corner of a building, table or anything with straight sides

angle /'æŋ.gl/ *verb* [T] *The stage had been steeply angled* (= was sloping very noticeably).

angled /'æŋ.gld/ *adj*: *His angled shot* (= from the side, not from straight in front) *beat the goalkeeper from 20 yards.*

angle POSITION /'æŋ.gl/ *noun* [C] a position from which something is viewed: *The tower is visible* **from** *every angle/all angles.* ○ *I realised I was looking at it* **from** *the wrong angle.*

angle WAY OF THINKING /'æŋ.gl/ *noun* [C] a way of considering, judging or dealing with something: *Try looking at*

the problem ***from*** *another angle/****from*** *my angle.* ○ *The press was looking for a* ***new/fresh*** *angle* ***on*** *the situation.*
angle /ˈæŋ.gl̩d/ *verb* [T] to direct information at a particular group of people: *The magazine is angled* ***at*** *the 20-35 year-old women's market.*
▲ **angle for *sth*** *phrasal verb* MAINLY DISAPPROVING If someone is angling for something, they are trying to get something without asking for it directly: *He's clearly angling for a job/an invitation.*

angler /ˈæŋ.gləʳ/ [US] /-glɚ/ *noun* [C] ➲See at **angling**

Anglican /ˈæŋ.glɪ.kən/ *adj* relating to the Church of England, or an international Church connected with it: *Desmond Tutu became the most famous Anglican archbishop in South Africa.* ○ *Outside England, the Anglican Church is often referred to as the Episcopal(ian) Church.* ○ *an Anglican priest*
Anglican /ˈæŋ.glɪ.kən/ *noun* [C] a member of the Anglican church: *He's an Anglican.* **Anglicanism** /ˈæŋ.glɪ.kə.nɪ.zᵊm/ *noun* [U]

anglicism /ˈæŋ.glɪ.sɪ.zᵊm/ *noun* [C] an English word or phrase that is used in another language: *'Le weekend' is an anglicism used by the French.*

anglicize, UK USUALLY **-ise** /ˈæŋ.glɪ.saɪz/ *verb* [T] to make or become English in sound, appearance or character: *She married Norwegian immigrant Niels Larsen who later anglicized his name.*

angling /ˈæŋ.glɪŋ/ *noun* [U] the sport of trying to catch fish with a rod, LINE (= plastic thread) and hook
angler /ˈæŋ.gləʳ/ [US] /-glɚ/ *noun* [C] a person whose hobby is catching fish

Anglo- /æŋ.gləʊ-/ [US] /æŋ.gloʊ-/ *prefix* of or connected with Britain or England

Anglo-American /ˌæŋ.gləʊ.əˈmer.ɪ.kᵊn/ [US] /ˌæŋ.gloʊ-/ *adj* describes something involving the UK and US: *an Anglo-American agreement*

Anglo-Catholic /ˌæŋ.gləʊˈkæθ.ᵊl.ɪk/ [US] /ˌæŋ.gloʊ-/ *adj* refers to the group in the ANGLICAN (= Church of England) church whose religious practice is similar to that of the Roman Catholic church

Anglo-Indian /ˌæŋ.gləʊˈɪn.di.ən/ [US] /ˌæŋ.gloʊ-/ *noun* [C] **1** a person with British and Indian parents or grandparents **2** OLD-FASHIONED an English person born or living in India **Anglo-Indian** /ˌæŋ.gləʊˈɪn.di.ən/ [US] /ˌæŋ.gloʊ-/ *adj*

anglophile /ˈæŋ.gləʊ.faɪl/ [US] /-glə-/ *noun* [C] a person who is not British but is interested in, likes or supports Britain and its people and customs

anglophone /ˈæŋ.gləʊ.fəʊn/ [US] /-glə.foʊn/ *noun* [C] SPECIALIZED a person who speaks English, especially in countries where other languages are also spoken
anglophone /ˈæŋ.gləʊ.fəʊn/ [US] /-glə.foʊn/ *adj*: *The anglophone countries of Africa include Kenya and Zimbabwe.*

Anglo-Saxon /ˌæŋ.gləʊˈsæk.sᵊn/ [US] /ˌæŋ.gloʊ-/ *adj* **1** describes the people who lived in England from about 600 AD and their language and customs **2** describes modern societies which are based on or influenced by English customs **Anglo-Saxon** /ˌæŋ.gləʊˈsæk.sᵊn/ [US] /ˌæŋ.gloʊ-/ *noun* [C] ➲See also **WASP** PERSON.

angora /æŋˈgɔː.rə/ [US] /-ˈgɔːr.ə/ *noun* [U] the wool, fibre or material made from the long soft hair of a type of rabbit or goat: *an angora sweater*

angostura (bitters) /ˌæŋ.gə.stjʊə.rəˈbɪt.əz/ [US] /-gə.stʊr.əˈbɪt̬.ɚz/ *plural noun* a bitter liquid which can be used to flavour alcoholic drinks

angry /ˈæŋ.gri/ *adj* **1** having a strong feeling against someone who has behaved badly, making you want to shout at them or hurt them: *He's really angry* ***at/with*** *me for upsetting Sophie.* ○ *I don't understand what he's angry* ***about.*** ○ [+ that] *They feel angry* ***that*** *their complaints were ignored.* ○ *I* ***got*** *really angry* ***with*** *her.* ○ *It made me really angry.* **2** LITERARY describes a stormy sea or sky **3** If an infected area of the body is angry, it is red and painful: *On her leg was an angry sore.* **angrily** /ˈæŋ.grɪ.li/ *adv*: *"Don't do that!" she shouted angrily.* ○ *Demonstrators protested angrily following the jury's verdict.* ○ *The Prime Minister* ***reacted*** *angrily to claims that he had lied to the House of Commons.*

angst /æŋkst/ [US] /ɑːŋkst/ *noun* [U] strong anxiety and unhappiness, especially about personal problems: *All my children went through a period of late-adolescent angst.*

anguish /ˈæŋ.gwɪʃ/ *noun* [U] extreme unhappiness caused by physical or mental suffering: *His anguish* ***at*** *the outcome of the court case was very clear.* ○ ***In*** *her anguish she forgot to leave a message.* **anguished** /ˈæŋ.gwɪʃt/ *adj*: *an anguished cry*

angular /ˈæŋ.gjʊ.ləʳ/ [US] /-lɚ/ *adj* having a clear shape with sharp points: *Her features were too angular, her face a little too long for beauty.* **angularity** /ˌæŋ.gjʊˈlær.ɪ.ti/ [US] /-ˈler.ə.t̬i/ *noun* [U]

animal [CREATURE] /ˈæn.ɪ.məl/ *noun* [C] **1** something that lives and moves but is not a human, bird, fish or insect: *wild/domestic animals* ○ *Both children are real animal* ***lovers.*** ○ *Surveys show that animal* ***welfare*** *has recently become a major concern for many schoolchildren.* ○ *animal-****rights*** *activists* ➲See picture **Animals and Birds** on page Centre 4 **2** anything that lives and moves, including people, birds, etc: *Humans, insects, reptiles, birds and mammals are all animals.*
animal *adj* **1** made or obtained from, an animal or animals: *animal products* ○ *animal fat/skins* **2** relating to, or taking the form of, an animal or animals rather than a plant or human being: *the animal kingdom* ○ *The island was devoid of all animal life* (= There were no animals on the island).

animal [BAD PERSON] /ˈæn.ɪ.məl/ *noun* [C] INFORMAL an unpleasant, cruel person or someone who behaves badly: *He's a real animal when he's had too much to drink.*

animal [TYPE] /ˈæn.ɪ.məl/ *noun* [C] used to describe what type of person or thing someone or something is: *At heart she is a political animal.* ○ *She is that* ***rare*** *animal* (= she is very unusual), *a brilliant scientist who can communicate her ideas to ordinary people.* ○ *Feminism in France and England are rather different animals* (= are different).

animal [PHYSICAL] /ˈæn.ɪ.məl/ *adj* [before n] relating to physical desires or needs, and not spiritual or mental ones: *As an actor Russell Crowe has a sort of animal* ***magnetism.*** ○ *She knew that Dave wasn't the right man for her but she couldn't deny the animal* ***attraction*** *between them.*

ˌanimal ˈhusbandry *noun* [U] SPECIALIZED the farming of animals to produce foods such as meat, eggs and milk

the ˈanimal ˌkingdom *noun* [S] the group of all living creatures that are animals

animate [ALIVE] /ˈæn.ɪ.mət/ *adj* living; having life

animate [ACTIVE] /ˈæn.ɪ.meɪt/ *verb* [T] to make someone seem more happy or active: *A sparkle in his eyes animated his face whenever he smiled.*
animated /ˈæn.ɪ.meɪ.tɪd/ [US] /-t̬ɪd/ *adj* full of interest and energy: *There was an extremely animated discussion on the subject.* ○ *They must have been having an interesting conversation – they both looked very animated.*
animatedly /ˈæn.ɪ.meɪ.tɪd.li/ [US] /-t̬ɪd-/ *adv*
animation /ˌæn.ɪˈmeɪ.ʃᵊn/ *noun* [U] enthusiasm and energy: *She spoke with great animation about her latest discoveries.*

animated /ˈæn.ɪ.meɪ.tɪd/ [US] /-t̬ɪd/ *adj* describes films, drawings, PUPPETS or models that are photographed and shown in a way that makes them move and appear to be alive
animation /ˌæn.ɪˈmeɪ.ʃᵊn/ *noun* [C or U] moving pictures: *Encyclopedias on CD-ROM include sound, illustrations and simple animations.* ○ *Thanks to* ***computer*** *animation, it is now possible to make cartoon films much more quickly than in the past.* **animator** /ˈæn.ɪ.meɪ.təʳ/ [US] /-t̬ɚ/ *noun* [C] *Walt Disney is the most famous animator of feature-length films.*

animatronics /ˌæn.ɪ.məˈtrɒn.ɪks/ /-ˈtrɑː.nɪks/ *noun* [U] SPECIALIZED the use of machines controlled by computers to make PUPPETS and models move in a natural way in films and other types of entertainment **animatronic** /ˌæn.ɪ.məˈtrɒn.ɪk/ [US] /-ˈtrɑː.nɪk/ *adj*: *The most popular exhibit in the museum was a giant animatronic dinosaur.*

animism /ˈæn.ɪ.mɪ.zᵊm/ *noun* [U] SPECIALIZED the belief that all natural things, such as plants, animals, rocks,

A

thunder and earthquakes, have SPIRITS (= beings that cannot be seen) and can influence human events **animist** /ˈæn.ɪ.mɪst/ *noun* [C], *adj*

animosity /ˌæn.ɪˈmɒs.ɪ.ti/ [US] /-ˈmɑː.sə.t̬i/ *noun* [C or U] strong dislike, opposition or anger: *Of course we're competitive but there's no personal animosity* ***between*** *us.* ○ *In spite of his injuries, he* ***bears no*** *animosity* ***towards*** *his attackers.* ○ *The European Community helped France and Germany forget the old animosities* ***between*** *them.*

anise /ˈæn.ɪs/ /ænˈiːs/ *noun* [U] a Mediterranean plant with small yellowish white flowers and seeds that taste of LIQUORICE, used for flavouring food and drink

aniseed /ˈæn.ɪ.siːd/ *noun* [U] the seeds of the anise plant, used to flavour sweet food and LIQUEURS: *aniseed balls*

ankle /ˈæŋ.kl̩/ *noun* [C] the joint which connects the foot to the leg, or the thin part of the leg just above the foot: *I fell over and* ***sprained/twisted*** *my ankle.* ➲See picture **The Body** on page Centre 5

ˈankle ˌboot *noun* [C] short boots which cover only the foot and ankle

ˈankle ˌsock *noun* [C] (*US ALSO* **anklet**) a short sock which covers only the foot and ankle

anklet [JEWELLERY] /ˈæŋ.klət/ *noun* [C] a chain or ring worn as jewellery around the ankle

anklet [SOCK] /ˈæŋ.klət/ *noun* [C] *US FOR* **ankle sock**

annals /ˈæn.əlz/ *plural noun FORMAL* historical records of the activities of a country or organization, or history in general: *The signing of the Treaty of Rome was the greatest event in the annals* ***of*** *European integration.* ○ *Quite whether he will* ***go down in*** *the annals* ***of*** *American history* (= be considered) *as a great leader remains to be seen.*

anneal /əˈniːl/ *verb* [T] *SPECIALIZED* to make metal or glass soft by heating and then cooling it slowly

annex /ænˈeks/ *verb* [T] to take possession of an area of land or a country, usually by force or without permission: *Britain annexed this small island west of Scotland in 1955.* **annexation** /ˌæn.ekˈseɪ.ʃən/ *noun* [C or U]

annexe *UK, US* **annex** /ˈæn.ɪks/ *noun* [C] an extra building added to a larger building: *Delicate and valuable books are kept in an air-conditioned annexe* ***to*** *the main library.*

annihilate /əˈnaɪ.ɪ.leɪt/ *verb* [T] **1** to destroy completely so that nothing is left: *a city annihilated by an atomic bomb* **2** *INFORMAL* to defeat completely: *He was annihilated in the finals of the competition.*
annihilation /əˌnaɪ.ɪˈleɪ.ʃən/ *noun* [U] *During the Cold War the threat of nuclear annihilation was always on people's minds.* ○ *INFORMAL The opposition party's candidate suffered annihilation* (= complete defeat) *at the polls.*

anniversary /ˌæn.ɪˈvɜː.sər.i/ [US] /-ˈvɝː.sɚ-/ *noun* [C] the day on which an important event happened in a previous year: *We always celebrate our* ***wedding*** *anniversary with dinner in an expensive restaurant.* ○ *Tomorrow is the thirtieth anniversary* ***of*** *the revolution.*

annotate /ˈæn.əʊ.teɪt/ [US] /-ə-/ *verb* [T] *FORMAL* to add a brief explanation or opinion to a text or drawing: *Annotated editions of Shakespeare's plays help readers to understand old words.* **annotation** /ˌæn.əʊˈteɪ.ʃən/ [US] /-ə-/ *noun* [C or U] *The annotation of literary texts makes them more accessible.* ○ *The revised edition of the book includes many useful annotations.*

announce /əˈnaʊnts/ *verb* [T] **1** to state or make known, especially publicly: *They announced the death of their mother in the local paper.* ○ *She announced the winner of the competition* ***to*** *an excited audience.* ○ [+ that] *The Prime Minister has announced* ***that*** *public spending will be increased next year.* **2** to show that something is going to happen: *The first few leaves in the gutter announced the beginning of autumn.*
announcement /əˈnaʊnt.smənt/ *noun* [C or U] something that someone says officially, giving information about something, or when someone announces something: *The President* ***made*** *an unexpected announcement this morning.*
announcer /əˈnaʊnt.səʳ/ [US] /-sɚ/ *noun* [C] someone who introduces programmes or reads the news on the television or radio: *a radio/TV announcer*

annoy /əˈnɔɪ/ *verb* [T] to make someone angry: *Tim really annoyed me in the meeting this morning.* ○ *I'm sorry – is my cough annoying you?* ○ [+ that] ***It*** *annoys me* ***that*** *she just expects us to help.* ○ ***It*** *really annoys me when people expect me to tip as well as pay a service charge in a restaurant.*
annoyance /əˈnɔɪ.ənts/ *noun* [C or U] *I can understand your annoyance – I'd be furious if she ever treated me like that.* ○ ***(Much) to*** *our annoyance,* (= We were very annoyed that) *we couldn't see anything from the back row of the theatre.* ○ *One of the greatest annoyances* (= things that caused us to be annoyed) *was being bitten by mosquitoes every night.*
annoyed /əˈnɔɪd/ *adj* angry: *I was so annoyed* ***with*** *him for turning up late.* ○ *He was annoyed* ***at*** *the way she tried to take over the whole meeting.* ○ *My parents were rather annoyed* ***(that)*** *I hadn't told them about the accident.* ○ *She was annoyed* ***to*** *discover that her husband had taken her car keys.*
annoying /əˈnɔɪ.ɪŋ/ *adj* making you feel annoyed: *It's really annoying when a train is late and there's no explanation.* ○ *He's got a really annoying laugh.* ➲See Note **embarrassing** or **annoying?** at **embarrassing**.
annoyingly /əˈnɔɪ.ɪŋ.li/ *adv*: *Rather annoyingly, I'd just bought the hardback when the paperback edition came out.*

annual [EVERY YEAR] /ˈæn.ju.əl/ /-jʊl/ *adj* [before n] happening once every year, or relating to a period of one year: *an annual event/visit/holiday* ○ *annual income/salary/profit* ○ *Companies publish annual* ***reports*** *to inform the public about the previous year's activities.*
annually /ˈæn.ju.ə.li/ /-jʊ.li/ *adv*: *Your starting salary is £13 000 per annum and will be reviewed annually* (= once every year).
annualized, *UK USUALLY* **-ised** /ˈæn.ju.ə.laɪzd/ /-jʊ.laɪzd/ *adj SPECIALIZED Exports fell at an annualized rate* (= the rate calculated over a year) *of 12.3%, while imports rose at a 7.5% pace.*

annual [BOOK] /ˈæn.ju.əl/ /-jʊl/ *noun* [C] **1** a book or magazine published once a year, especially for children, with the same title and style but different contents **2** *US FOR* **yearbook**: *a high school annual*

annual [PLANT] /ˈæn.ju.əl/ /-jʊl/ *noun* [C] a plant which grows, produces seeds, and dies within one year ➲Compare **biennial**; **perennial** PLANT.

ˌannual ˌgeneral ˈmeeting *UK noun* [C] (*ABBREVIATION* **AGM**, *US* **annual meeting**) a meeting that happens once every year in which a company or other organization discusses the past year's activities and elects new officers

annuity /əˈnjuː.ə.ti/ [US] /-t̬i/ *noun* [C] a fixed amount of money paid to someone every year, usually until their death, or the insurance agreement or investment which provides the money that is paid: *annuity policy/income* ○ *She receives a small annuity.*

annul /əˈnʌl/ *verb* [T] **-ll-** *LEGAL* to officially announce that something such as a law, agreement, or marriage no longer exists: *His second marriage was annulled because he never divorced his first wife.*
annulment /əˈnʌl.mənt/ *noun* [C or U] *Judges only* ***grant*** *marriage annulments in exceptional circumstances.* ○ *The discovery of the election fraud has led to the annulment of 50 000 votes.*

annum /ˈæn.əm/ *noun* ➲See **per annum**.

annus mirabilis /ˌæn.əs.mɪˈrɑː.bɪ.lɪs/ *noun* [C] *plural* **anni mirabiles** *FORMAL* a year of extremely good events: *1969 was the annus mirabilis in which man first landed on the moon.*

anode /ˈæn.əʊd/ [US] /-oʊd/ *noun* [C] *SPECIALIZED* the positive part of an electrical CELL at which electrons leave a system ➲Compare **cathode**.

anodize, *UK USUALLY* **-ise** /ˈæn.əʊ.daɪz/ [US] /-oʊ-/ *verb* [T] *SPECIALIZED* to cover a metal with a layer of OXIDE (= a chemical combination of oxygen and one other element) by using an electric current

anodyne /ˈæn.əʊ.daɪn/ [US] /-oʊ-/ *adj FORMAL MAINLY DISAPPROVING* intended to avoid causing offence or disagreement, especially by not expressing strong feelings or opinions: *This is daytime television at its most anodyne.*

○ *Somehow this avoids being just another silly pop song with anodyne lyrics about love and happiness.*

anoint [CHOOSE] /ə'nɔɪnt/ *verb* [T] *FORMAL* to choose someone to do a particular job, usually by a person in authority: [+ obj + as + n] *It remains to be seen whom the chairman will anoint* ***as*** *his successor.*

anointed /ə'nɔɪn.tɪd/ [US] /-t̬ɪd/ *adj FORMAL He's generally believed to be the anointed* ***heir/successor*** *to* (= the one who will be chosen for) *the presidency.* **anointment** /ə'nɔɪnt.mənt/ *noun* [U]

anoint [CEREMONY] /ə'nɔɪnt/ *verb* [T] **1** to make someone holy in a religious ceremony by putting holy water or oil on them **2** to make someone king or queen, especially as part of a religious ceremony: [+ obj + n] *In 751 Pepin was anointed king.* **anointment** /ə'nɔɪnt.mənt/ *noun* [U] **anointed** /ə'nɔɪn.tɪd/ [US] /-t̬ɪd/ *adj*

anomaly /ə'nɒm.ə.li/ [US] /-'nɑː.mə-/ *noun* [C or U] *FORMAL* a person or thing that is different from what is usual, or not in agreement with something else and therefore not satisfactory: *Statistical anomalies can make it difficult to compare economic data from one year to the next.* ○ *The anomaly of the social security system is that you sometimes have more money without a job.* **anomalous** /ə'nɒm.ə.ləs/ [US] /-'nɑː.mə-/ *adj: In a multicultural society is it not anomalous to have a blasphemy law which only protects one religious faith?* **anomalously** /ə'nɒm.ə.lə.sli/ [US] /-'nɑː.mə-/ *adv*

anomie /'æ.nɒ.mi/ *noun* [U] *FORMAL* a lack of moral or social principles in a person or in society

anon [SOON] /ə'nɒn/ [US] /-'nɑːn/ *adv OLD USE OR HUMOROUS* soon or in the near future: *See you anon.*

Anon. [WITHOUT NAME] /ə'nɒn/ [US] /-'nɑːn/ (*ALSO* **anon.**) *WRITTEN ABBREVIATION FOR* **anonymous** (= a writer whose name is not known), usually written at the end of a piece of writing

anonymous /ə'nɒn.ɪ.məs/ [US] /-'nɑː.nə-/ *adj* **1** made or done by someone whose name is not known or not made public: *The money was donated by an anonymous* ***benefactor.*** ○ *Police said an anonymous* ***caller*** *warned that a bomb was about to go off.* ○ *An attempt to implant an embryo using an egg from an anonymous woman* ***donor*** *was unsuccessful.* ○ *He received an anonymous* ***letter*** *threatening to disclose details of his affair if he didn't pay the money.* ○ *For reasons of personal safety, the informant wishes to* ***remain*** *anonymous.* **2** having no unusual or interesting features: *He has a rather anonymous face.* **anonymously** /ə'nɒn.ɪ.mə.sli/ [US] /-'nɑː.nə-/ *adv: The donation was made anonymously.*

anonymity /ˌæn.ɒn'ɪm.ɪ.ti/ [US] /-ə'nɪm.ə.t̬i/ *noun* [U] when someone's name is not given or known: *The police have reassured witnesses who may be afraid to come forward that they will be guaranteed anonymity.*

anopheles /ə'nɒf.ɪ.liːz/ [US] /-'nɑː.fə-/ *noun* [C] *plural* **anopheles** *SPECIALIZED* a type of MOSQUITO (= small flying insect), especially one which spreads MALARIA to humans

anorak [COAT] *MAINLY UK* /'æn.ə.ræk/ *noun* [C] (*US USUALLY* **parka**) a short, waterproof coat that protects the wearer against cold, wet and windy weather, usually with a part for covering the head ⊃See picture **Clothes** on page Centre 6

anorak [PERSON] /'æn.ᵊr.æk/ *noun* [C] *UK DISAPPROVING* a boring person who is too interested in the unimportant details of a hobby and finds it difficult to meet and spend time with other people: *There are enough facts and figures in this book to keep even the most obsessive anorak fascinated for hours.*

anorexia (nervosa) /æn.əˌrek.si.ə.nə'vəʊ.sə/ *noun* [U] a serious illness often resulting in dangerous weight loss, in which a person, especially a girl or woman, does not eat, or eats too little, because they fear becoming fat: *Reports of anorexia and other eating disorders are on the increase, with 6000 new cases in the UK every year.* ⊃Compare **bulimia**. **anorexic** /ˌæn.ə'rek.sɪk/ *adj, noun* [C] (*ALSO* **anorectic**) *She looks anorexic to me.* ○ *Anorexics tend to be obsessional and perfectionist.*

another [ADDITIONAL] /ə'nʌð.əʳ/ [US] /-ɚ/ *determiner, pronoun* one more person or thing or an additional amount: *I'm going to have another piece of cake.* ○ *"Would you get me a bar of chocolate from the kitchen?" "Another one?!"* ○ *We can fit another person in my car.* ○ *Danny's had* ***yet*** *another car accident.* ○ ***For*** *another £30* (= For £30 more) *you can buy the model with remote control.* ○ *Just think,* ***in*** *another three months* (= three months from now) *it'll be summer again.*

• **one ... after another** a lot of things, one after the other: *I'm not surprised he's feeling ill – he was eating one ice-cream after another!*

• **A.N. Other** *UK* used at the end of a list of people to refer to someone whose name is not yet known: *The conference will be attended by Ian Taylor, Joe Sellars and A.N. Other.*

COMMON LEARNER ERROR

another or other?

Another means 'one other' and is used with a noun in the singular. Make sure that you write it as one word, not two words.

Would you like another cup of coffee?
~~*Would you like other cup of coffee?*~~
~~*Would you like an other cup of coffee?*~~

Other is used with a noun in the plural and means different things or people from the ones you are talking about.

She had other ambitions.
~~*She had another ambitions.*~~

another [DIFFERENT] /ə'nʌð.əʳ/ [US] /-ɚ/ *determiner, pronoun* a different person or thing: *She's finished with that boyfriend and found herself another* ***(one).*** ○ *Do you want to exchange this toaster for another* ***(one)*** *or do you want your money back?*

• **be another matter/thing 1** to be a different situation which is likely to be judged differently: *Cars are useful, but their impact on the environment is another matter altogether.* **2** to be very different and likely to involve more problems or difficulties: *Feeling guilty for the homeless is one thing, finding cheap secure accommodation for them is quite another (thing).*

• **be another story** to be something that you do not want to say more about at this particular time: *When we finally got home, we found that we'd been burgled – but that's another story.*

• **one another** each other: *They gave one another presents when they met at the airport.*

• **one way or another** in some way that is not known yet: *We'll get out of this mess one way or another.*

Ansaphone, **Ansafone** /'ɑːnt.sə.fəʊn/ [US] /'ænt.sə.foʊn/ *noun* [C] *TRADEMARK* an **answerphone**

answer [REACTION] /'ɑːnt.səʳ/ [US] /'ænt.sɚ/ *noun* [C] a reaction to a question, letter, telephone call, etc: *The Minister promised to give a written answer* ***to*** *the MP's detailed question.* ○ *We've written to him asking him if he's free on that date but we haven't had an answer yet.* ○ *I've just rung him but there was no answer.* ○ *I didn't realise we had to write each answer on a new sheet of paper.* ○ *I got eight correct answers and two wrong ones in last week's exam.* ○ ***In*** *answer* ***to*** *your letter of May 30th, I am writing to accept your offer of £3575 in compensation.*

• ***sb's*** **answer to** ***sb/sth*** If something or someone is the answer to another thing or person, they are considered to be similar or as good: *Channel 4 is independent television's answer to BBC2.* ○ *She's Lithuania's answer to Madonna.*

answer /'ɑːnt.səʳ/ [US] /'ænt.sɚ/ *verb* [I or T] to say, write or do something as a reaction to a question, letter, telephone call etc: *I can't answer (you) without more detailed information.* ○ *You haven't answered my* ***question.*** ○ *I wrote asking whether he'd be coming to the party but he hasn't answered yet.* ○ [+ speech] *"I'd love to have dinner with you, but I won't be able to get there before nine o'clock," she answered.* ○ [+ that] *She answered* ***that*** *she wouldn't be able to come before nine o'clock.* ○ *Someone's at the door – would you answer it please?* ○ *I phoned last night but nobody answered.* ○ *FORMAL Does anyone here answer* ***to the name of*** (= Is anyone here called) *Wallis?*

answer [SOLUTION] /'ɑːnt.səʳ/ [US] /'ænt.sɚ/ *noun* [C] a solution to a problem: *It's a difficult situation and I don't* *know what the answer is.* ○ *There's no **easy** answer **to** the problem.*

answer [MATCH] /ˈɑːnt.sə^r/ US /ˈænt.sɚ/ *verb* [I or T] (*ALSO* **answer to**) to match a description: *A woman who answers to the suspect's description was seen in the area on the night of the crime.*

answer [BE SUITABLE FOR] /ˈɑːnt.sə^r/ US /ˈænt.sɚ/ *verb* [T] to be suitable for and satisfy someone's needs: *He showed me some software that answered my requirements exactly.* ○ *I've got a bit of furniture round the back that I think might answer your needs.*

PHRASAL VERBS WITH **answer**   ▼

▲ **answer** *(sb)* **back** [REPLY RUDELY] *phrasal verb* to speak rudely when answering someone in authority: *Don't you dare answer me back, young lady!*

▲ **answer back** [REACT] *phrasal verb* to react to criticism by arguing or explaining: *The company criticized in the documentary was given the opportunity to answer back.*

▲ **answer for** *sth* [BE RESPONSIBLE] *phrasal verb* to be responsible for something bad, or to be punished for something: *I expect parents to answer for their children's behaviour.* ○ *"Why do you think there's so much violence nowadays?" "Well, violence on television has **a lot to** answer for* (= is the cause of much of it)*."*

▲ **answer for** *sb/sth* [TRUST] *phrasal verb* If you say that you can answer for someone or for a quality that they have, you mean that you know from experience that they can be trusted, or that they have that quality: *I can certainly answer for her professionalism, and wholeheartedly recommend her to any employer.*

▲ **answer to** *sb phrasal verb* to take orders from, obey and explain your actions to someone: *The great thing about working for yourself is that you don't have to answer to anyone.*

answerable /ˈɑːnt.s^ər.ə.bl̩/ US /ˈænt.sɚ-/ *adj* **1 be answerable for** *sth* to be responsible for something that happens: *Soldiers who obey orders to commit atrocities should be answerable for their crimes.* **2 be answerable to** *sb* If you are answerable to someone, you have to explain your actions to them because they have the main control and responsibility: *Any European central bank should be directly answerable to the European Parliament.*

ˈanswering ma,chine *noun* [C] *MAINLY US FOR* **answerphone**

ˈanswering ,service *noun* [C usually sing] a company that receives and answers telephone calls for its customers

answerphone *MAINLY UK* /ˈɑːnt.sə.fəʊn/ US /ˈænt.sɚ.foʊn/ *noun* [C] (*MAINLY US* **answering machine**) a device connected to a telephone which answers calls automatically and records messages from callers: *She wasn't in so I **left a message** on her answerphone.* ○ *I rang several times last week, but I kept **getting** his answerphone.*

ant [INSECT] /ænt/ *noun* [C] a very small insect which lives under the ground in large and highly organized social groups ➔See also **anthill**.

● **have ants in** *your* **pants** *OLD-FASHIONED HUMOROUS* to not be able to keep still because you are very excited or worried about something

-ant [PERFORM] /-ənt/ *suffix* (*ALSO* **-ent**) (a person or thing) performing or causing the stated action: *assistant* ○ *participant* ○ *disinfectant* ○ *an expectant look* ○ *a defiant child*

antacid /ˌænˈtæs.ɪd/ *noun* [C or U] a substance used to reduce or prevent acid collecting in the body, particularly in the stomach

antagonism /ænˈtæg.ə.nɪ.z^əm/ *noun* [C or U] hate, extreme unfriendliness or active opposition: *There's a history of antagonism **between** the two teams.* ○ *the antagonism **towards** neighbouring states* ○ *the historic antagonisms **between** the countries of western Europe*

antagonist /ænˈtæg.ə.nɪst/ *noun* [C] *FORMAL* a person who is strongly opposed to something or someone: *The antagonists in this dispute are quite unwilling to compromise.* ➔Compare **protagonist** *SUPPORTER*.

antagonistic /ænˌtæg.əˈnɪs.tɪk/ *adj* actively opposing or showing unfriendliness and opposition to something or someone: *He's extremely antagonistic **towards** all critics.*

antagonize, *UK USUALLY* **-ise** /ænˈtæg.ə.naɪz/ *verb* [T] to make someone feel opposition or dislike towards you: *It's a very delicate situation and I've no wish to antagonize him.*

the An'tarctic *noun* [S] the very cold area around the South Pole which includes Antarctica and the surrounding seas: *The protection of the Antarctic from commercial exploitation is an important goal of environmentalists.* **Antarctic** /ænˈtɑːk.tɪk/ US /-ˈtɑːrk-/ *adj*: *the Antarctic Ocean/Circle/Zone* ○ *an Antarctic explorer/expedition*

ante [RISK] /ˈæn.ti/ US /-t̬i/ *noun* [C] an amount of money that each person must risk in order to be part of a game that involves *GAMBLING*: *a $30 ante*

● **up the ante** If you up the ante, you increase your demands or the risks in a situation in order to achieve a better result: *The government has upped the ante by refusing to negotiate until a ceasefire has been agreed.*

ante /ˈæn.ti/ US /-t̬i/ *verb*

▲ **ante up** *(sth) phrasal verb US INFORMAL* to give money, often unwillingly: *At least 200 people have been persuaded to ante up big money for the charity event.*

ante- [BEFORE] /æn.ti-/ US /-t̬i-/ *prefix* before or in front of: *antedate* ○ *antenatal* ○ *anteroom* ➔Compare **pre-** and **post-**.

anteater /ˈænt.iː.tə^r/ US /-t̬ɚ/ *noun* [C] a mammal which eats *ANTS* or *TERMITES* and has no teeth, a long nose and tongue

antebellum /ˌæn.tɪˈbel.əm/ *adj* [before n] *MAINLY US* relating to the time before a war, especially the American Civil War: *Many homes and churches of the antebellum South can still be visited today.*

antecedent /ˌæn.tɪˈsiː.d^ənt/ *noun* [C] **1** *FORMAL* someone or something existing or happening before, especially as the cause or origin of something existing or happening later: *Charles Babbage's mechanical calculating engines were the antecedents of the modern computer.* ○ *Many people feel a great curiosity to find out about their antecedents.* **2** *SPECIALIZED* a word or phrase which a pronoun refers back to: *In the sentence 'He picked a book off the shelf and handed it to Sally, 'book' is the antecedent of 'it'.* **antecedent** /ˌæn.tɪˈsiː.d^ənt/ *adj FORMAL* previous: *When the college was established in 1546, it inherited a hall from each of three antecedent institutions.*

antechamber /ˈæn.ti.tʃeɪm.bə^r/ US /-t̬i.tʃeɪm.bɚ/ *noun* [C] an **anteroom**

antedate /ˌæn.tiˈdeɪt/ US /ˈæn.t̬i.deɪt/ *verb* [T] *FORMAL FOR* **predate**

antediluvian /ˌæn.ti.dɪˈluː.vi.ən/ US /-t̬i-/ *adj MAINLY HUMOROUS* extremely old-fashioned: *My mother has some hopelessly antediluvian ideas about the role of women.*

antelope /ˈæn.tɪ.ləʊp/ US /-t̬^əl.oʊp/ *noun* [C] *plural* **antelope** or **antelopes** a deer-like mammal with horns and long thin legs which allow it to run very fast: *a **herd of** antelope*

antenatal *UK* /ˌæn.tiˈneɪ.t^əl/ US /-ˈneɪ.t̬^əl/ *adj* [before n] (*US* **prenatal**) happening or existing before birth: *antenatal care/classes* ○ *the antenatal clinic* ➔Compare **postnatal**. **antenatally** /ˌæn.tiˈneɪ.t^əl.i/ US /-t̬^əl-/ *adv*: *Some foetal abnormalities can now be detected antenatally.*

antenna [ORGAN] /ænˈten.ə/ *noun* [C] *plural* **antennae** either of a pair of long thin hair-like organs which are found on the heads of insects and *CRUSTACEANS* (= animals with hard outer shells) and which are used to feel with

antenna [SKILL] /ænˈten.ə/ *noun* [C usually pl] *plural* **antennae** or **antennas** the natural ability to notice things and understand their importance: *Her finely-tuned political antennae helped her to sense problems that less-experienced politicians might not detect.*

antenna [PART OF RADIO] /ænˈten.ə/ *noun* [C] *plural* **antennas** *MAINLY US FOR* **aerial** *RADIO* ➔See picture **Car** on page Centre 12

anterior /ænˈtɪə.ri.ə^r/ US /-ˈtɪr.i.ɚ/ *adj* [before n] *SPECIALIZED* positioned at or towards the front: *Specimens for examination were taken from the anterior side of the left ventricle from each heart.* ➔Compare **posterior**.

anteroom /'æn.ti.rʊm/ /-ruːm/ [US] /-t̬i-/ *noun* [C] (*ALSO* **antechamber**) *FORMAL* a small room, especially a waiting room, which leads into a larger, more important room: *The ministers waited for their meeting in the Cabinet anteroom.*

anthem /'ænt.θəm/ *noun* [C] **1** a song which has special importance for a particular group of people, an organization or a country, often sung on a special occasion: *The* ***national*** *anthems of the teams are played at the beginning of a big international football match.* ○ *John Lennon's "Imagine" has become the anthem of peace-lovers all over the world.* **2** a short religious song sung by a choir with organ music

anthemic /æn'θem.ɪk/ *adj FORMAL* describes music that has qualities that are suitable for an anthem, such as a strong tune and seriousness

anther /'ænt.θəʳ/ [US] /-θɚ/ *noun* [C] the part of a flower that contains POLLEN

anthill /'ænt.hɪl/ *noun* [C] a pile of earth created by ANTS when they are making their nests underground

anthology /æn'θɒl.ə.dʒi/ [US] /-'θɑː.lə-/ *noun* [C] a collection of artistic works which have a similar form or subject, often those considered to be the best: *an anthology of modern quotations/American verse* ○ *This Bob Dylan anthology includes some rare recordings of his best songs.* ➲Compare **omnibus** SEVERAL PARTS. **anthologist** /æn'θɒl.ə.dʒɪst/ [US] /-'θɑː.lə-/ *noun* [C]

anthracite /'ænt.θrə.saɪt/ *noun* [U] (*ALSO* **hard coal**) a very hard type of coal which burns slowly and produces a lot of heat with very little smoke and a small flame

anthrax /'æn.θræks/ *noun* [U] a disease which causes fever, swelling and often death in animals, especially sheep and cattle, and can be passed on to humans

anthropo- /ænt.θrəʊ.pəʊ-/ [US] /-θrə.pə-/ *prefix* (*ALSO* **anthrop-**) relating to human beings: *anthropomorphism*

anthropocentric /ˌænt.θrəʊ.pəʊ'sen.trɪk/ [US] /-θrə.pə-/ *adj FORMAL* considering human beings and their existence as the most important and central fact in the universe **anthropocentrism** /ˌænt.θrəʊ.pəʊ'sen.trɪ.zᵊm/ [US] /-θrə.pə-/ *noun* [U]

anthropoid /'ænt.θrəʊ.pɔɪd/ [US] /-θrə-/ *adj* [before n] like a human being or an ape: *Gorillas, chimpanzees and gibbons are all anthropoid apes, having long arms, no tails and highly developed brains.* **anthropoid** /'ænt.θrəʊ.pɔɪd/ [US] /-θrə-/ *noun* [C] *Monkeys, apes and humans are all anthropoids.*

anthropology /ˌænt.θrə'pɒl.ə.dʒi/ [US] /-'pɑː.lə-/ *noun* [U] the study of the human race, its culture and society and its physical development **anthropological** /ˌænt.θrə.pə'lɒdʒ.ɪ.kᵊl/ [US] /-'lɑː.dʒɪ-/ *adj*: *anthropological research/fieldwork* ○ *the Anthropological Library/Department* **anthropologically** /ˌænt.θrə.pə'lɒdʒ.ɪ.kli/ [US] /-'lɑː.dʒɪ-/ *adv*

anthropologist /ˌænt.θrə'pɒl.ə.dʒɪst/ [US] /-'pɑː.lə-/ *noun* [C] someone who scientifically studies human beings, their customs, beliefs and relationships

anthropomorphism /ˌænt.θrə.pəʊ'mɔː.fɪ.zᵊm/ [US] /-pə'mɔːr-/ *noun* [U] the showing or treating of animals, gods and objects as if they are human in appearance, character or behaviour: *The books 'Alice in Wonderland', 'Peter Rabbit' and 'Winnie-the-Pooh' are classic examples of anthropomorphism.* **anthropomorphic** /ˌænt.θrə.pəʊ'mɔː.fɪk/ [US] /-pə'mɔːr-/ *adj*

anti- /æn.ti-/ [US] /-t̬i-/ [US] /-taɪ-/ *prefix* opposed to or against; opposite of or preventing ➲Compare **pro-**.

anti /'æn.ti/ [US] /-t̬i/ *adj, prep, noun* [C] *plural* **antis** *INFORMAL We've received a lot of anti letters about* (= letters opposing) *that newspaper article.* ○ *Just because I won't join you, it doesn't mean that I'm anti* (= against) *you.* ○ *So what do you think about smoking in public places – are you (a) pro or (an) anti?* (= do you support or oppose it)*?*

anti-abortion /ˌæn.ti.ə'bɔː.ʃᵊn/ [US] /-t̬i.ə'bɔːr-/ *adj* supporting the belief that ABORTION (= the intentional ending of pregnancy) is morally wrong: *anti-abortion activists/groups*

anti-ageing /ˌæn.ti'eɪ.dʒɪŋ/ [US] /-t̬i-/ *adj* [before n] describes substances that are intended to prevent or limit the process of becoming old: *anti-ageing creams*

anti-aircraft /ˌæn.ti'eə.krɑːft/ [US] /-t̬i'er.kræft/ *adj* describes weapons equipment or activities that are intended to destroy or defend against enemy aircraft: *an anti-aircraft missile/gun/weapon* ○ *anti-aircraft defences/fire*

antibacterial /ˌæn.ti.bæk'tɪə.ri.əl/ [US] /-t̬i.bæk'tɪr.i-/ *adj* intended to kill or reduce the harmful effects of bacteria especially when used on the skin: *an antibacterial facial wash*

antibiotic /ˌæn.ti.baɪ'ɒt.ɪk/ [US] /-t̬i.baɪ'ɑː.t̬ɪk/ *noun* [C or U] a medicine or chemical that can destroy harmful bacteria in the body or limit their growth: *I'm* ***taking*** *antibiotics for a throat infection.* ○ *a one-month* ***course of*** *antibiotics* ○ *Some types of antibiotic are used to promote growth in farm animals.* ○ *He's* ***on*** *antibiotics for an ear infection.*

antibody /'æn.tiˌbɒd.i/ [US] /-t̬iˌbɑː.di/ *noun* [C] a protein produced in the blood which fights diseases by attacking and killing harmful bacteria: *Antibodies found in breast milk protect newborn babies against infection.* ➲See also **antigen**.

anti-choice /ˌæn.ti'tʃɔɪs/ [US] /-t̬i-/ *adj DISAPPROVING* opposing the idea that a pregnant woman should have the freedom to choose an abortion: *the anti-choice lobby*

Antichrist /'æn.ti.kraɪst/ [US] /-t̬i-/ *noun* [C] originally the main enemy of Jesus Christ who was expected to rule the world until Jesus Christ's Second Coming, now any enemy of Jesus Christ or the Christian religion:

anticipate /æn'tɪs.ɪ.peɪt/ *verb* [T] to imagine or expect that something will happen, sometimes taking action in preparation for it happening: *We don't anticipate any trouble.* ○ *We had one or two difficulties along the way that we didn't anticipate.* ○ *Are you anticipating a lot of people at the party tonight?* ○ [+ v-ing] *They anticipate having several applicants for the job.* ○ [+ that] *They anticipate* ***that*** *they will have several applicants for the job* ○ *It's always best to anticipate a problem before it arises.* ○ [+ question word] *At this stage we can't really anticipate* ***what*** *will happen.* ○ *The anticipated inflation figure is lower than last month's.* ○ *The army anticipated* (= took action in preparation for) *the explosion by evacuating the town.*

anticipation /ænˌtɪs.ɪ'peɪ.ʃᵊn/ *noun* [U] **1** a feeling of excitement about something that is going to happen in the near future: *As with most pleasures, it's not so much the experience itself as the anticipation that is enjoyable.* ○ *The postponement of the film's sequel has held cinemagoers* ***in eager*** *anticipation for several months.* **2 in anticipation (of)** in preparation for something happening: *She's even decorated the spare room in anticipation of your visit.*

anti-clerical /ˌæn.ti'kler.ɪ.kᵊl/ [US] /-t̬i-/ *adj* opposed to organized religion having influence in politics and public life: *an anti-clerical law/constitution* **anti-clericalism** /ˌæn.ti'kler.ɪ.kᵊl.ɪ.zᵊm/ [US] /-t̬i-/ *noun* [U]

anticlimax /ˌæn.ti'klaɪ.mæks/ [US] /-t̬i-/ *noun* [C or U] an event or experience which causes disappointment because it is less exciting than was expected or because it happens immediately after a much more interesting or exciting event: *When you really look forward to something it's often an anticlimax when it actually happens.* ○ *Coming home after a trip somewhere is always* ***a bit of an*** *anticlimax.* ○ *Even when you win a match there's often a sense of anticlimax – you always feel you could have played better.* **anticlimactic** /ˌæn.ti.klaɪ'mæk.tɪk/ [US] /-t̬ɪk/ *adj*: *There was so much publicity and hype beforehand, that the performance itself was a touch anticlimactic.*

anti-clockwise *UK* /ˌæn.ti'klɒk.waɪz/ [US] /-t̬i'klɑːk-/ *adj, adv* (*US* **counterclockwise**) in the opposite direction to the movement of the hand of a clock or watch: *"How do I get the top off this bottle?" "Push it down and twist it anticlockwise."*

anticoagulant /ˌæn.ti.kəʊ'æg.jʊ.lənt/ [US] /-t̬i.koʊ-/ *noun* [C] a drug which prevents or slows down the process of blood forming a CLOT (= a solid lump) **anticoagulant** /ˌæn.ti.kəʊ'æg.jʊ.lənt/ [US] /-t̬i.koʊ-/ *adj*: *an anticoagulant drug*

A

anti-consumerist /ˌæn.ti.kən'sjuː.mər.ɪst/ [US] /-t̬i.kən'suː.mɚ.ɪst/ *adj* opposed to the idea that people should be able to buy an unlimited amount of goods, and to the effect that such freedom has on the physical and social conditions in which people live: *Craig doesn't have a car as a part of his anti-consumerist stance.*

antics /'æn.tɪks/ [US] /-t̬ɪks/ *plural noun* amusing, silly or strange behaviour: *But the rock-star whose stage antics used to include smashing guitars is older and wiser now.* ○ *The crowds were once again entertained by the number one tennis player's antics on and off the court.*

anticyclone /ˌæn.ti'saɪ.kləʊn/ [US] /-t̬i'saɪ.kloʊn/ *noun* [C] an area of high ATMOSPHERIC pressure which causes calm weather: *Anticyclones cause cloudless blue skies and high temperatures in summer.*

anti-depressant /ˌæn.ti.dɪ'pres.ᵊnt/ [US] /-t̬i-/ *noun* [C] a drug used to reduce feelings of sadness and anxiety: *She's been* ***on*** *anti-depressants ever since her husband died.* ○ *anti-depressant drugs*

antidote /'æn.ti.dəʊt/ [US] /-t̬i.doʊt/ *noun* [C] **1** a chemical, especially a drug, which limits the effects of a poison: *Sales of nerve gas antidotes increased dramatically before the war.* **2** a way of preventing or acting against something bad: *Regular exercise is the best antidote* ***to*** *tiredness and depression.*

anti-federalist /ˌæn.ti'fed.ᵊr.ᵊl.ɪst/ [US] /-t̬i'fed.ɚ-/ *adj* (*US* **anti-federal**) opposed to the establishment of a system of government in which power is divided between a single central government and several regional ones: *The Foreign Secretary assured anti-federalist MPs that he would not agree to anything which limited British sovereignty.* **anti-federalist** /ˌæn.ti'fed.ᵊr.ᵊl.ɪst/ [US] /-t̬i-'fed.ɚ-/ *noun* [C] *Many voters are staunch anti-federalists, opposed to the concept of regional government.*

antifreeze /'æn.ti.friːz/ [US] /-t̬i-/ *noun* [U] a liquid which is added to water in order to lower the temperature at which it freezes, used especially in car RADIATORS (= cooling systems) in very cold weather

antigen /'æn.tɪ.dʒᵊn/ /-dʒen/ [US] /-t̬i-/ *noun* [C] *SPECIALIZED* a substance that causes the production of ANTIBODIES in the body

anti-hero /'æn.tiˌhɪə.rəʊ/ [US] /-t̬iˌhir.oʊ/ *noun* [C usually sing] the central character in a play, book or film who does not possess traditionally HEROIC qualities, such as bravery, and is admired instead for what society generally considers to be a weakness of their character: *He plays the classic anti-hero who drops out of society to join a world of impoverished artists and writers.*

antihistamine /ˌæn.ti'hɪs.tə.mɪn/ /-miːn/ [US] /-t̬i-/ *noun* [C or U] a type of drug which is used to treat medical conditions caused by an extreme reaction to particular substances: *Antihistamine is often used to treat hay fever and insect bites.*

anti-inflammatory /ˌæn.ti.ɪn'flæm.ə.tri/ [US] /-t̬i.ɪn-ˌflæm.ə.tɔːr.i/ *adj* describes a drug that is used to reduce pain and swelling: *anti-inflammatory drugs for arthritis* **anti-inflammatory** /ˌæn.ti.ɪn'flæm.ə.tri/ [US] /-t̬i.ɪn-ˌflæm.ə.tɔːr.i/ *noun* [C] *Aspirin is an anti-inflammatory.*

antiknock /ˌæn.ti'nɒk/ [US] /ˌæn.t̬i'nɑːk/ *noun* [U] a chemical which is added to the fuel of a car engine in order to make the fuel burn more effectively **anti-knocking** /ˌæn.ti'nɒk.ɪŋ/ [US] /-'nɑː.kɪŋ/ *adj* [before n]

anti-life /ˌən.ti'laɪf/ [US] /-t̬i-/ *adj* *DISAPPROVING* supporting the idea that a pregnant woman should have the freedom to choose an abortion: *the anti-life lobby*

anti-lock /ˌæn.ti'lɒk/ [US] /-t̬i'lɑːk/ *adj* [before n] describes a type of brake which prevents the uncontrolled sliding of a vehicle by reducing the effects of sudden braking

antilogarithm /ˌæn.ti'lɒg.ə.rɪ.ðᵊm/ [US] /-'lɑː.gɚ.ɪ-/ *noun* [C] (*INFORMAL* **antilog**) the number to which a LOGARITHM belongs

antimacassar /ˌæn.ti.mə'kæs.əʳ/ [US] /-t̬i.mə'kæs.ɚ/ *noun* [C] a cloth, used mainly in the past, for putting over the back of a chair in order to keep it clean or to decorate it

antimony /'æn.tɪ.mə.ni/ /æn'tɪm.ə-/ [US] /'æn.t̬ə.moʊ-/ *noun* [U] a metallic and poisonous element which is hard but easily broken and has a silvery white appearance. It is used to strengthen and harden other metals and to make SEMICONDUCTORS for computers.

anti-noise /'æn.ti.nɔɪz/ [US] /-t̬i-/ *noun* [U] sound which is produced in such a way that it matches exactly and removes the effect of loud and possibly harmful noises, such as those produced by large engines in factories

anti-nuclear /ˌæn.ti'njuː.klɪəʳ/ [US] /-t̬i'nuː.klɪr/ *adj* opposed to the production and use of nuclear weapons, or to the production of electricity from nuclear power: *the anti-nuclear lobby/movement* ○ *Most environmentalists are vehemently anti-nuclear.*

anti-oxidant /ˌæn.ti'ɒk.sɪ.dᵊnt/ [US] /-t̬i-/ *noun* [C] a substance which slows down the rate at which something decays because of OXIDIZATION (= combining with oxygen)

antipasto /ˌæn.ti'pæs.təʊ/ [US] /-t̬i'pɑː.stoʊ/ *noun* [C] *plural* **antipastos** or **antipasti** something eaten at the beginning of an Italian meal, typically a small plate of sliced preserved meat, sliced sausage or vegetables

antipathy /æn'tɪp.ə.θi/ *noun* [C or U] (an example of) strong dislike, opposition or anger: *Despite the deep antipathies* ***between*** *them, the two sides have managed to negotiate an agreement.* ○ *Declarations of racial antipathy* ***against*** *ethnic minorities will not be tolerated.* ○ *He is a private man with a deep antipathy* ***to/towards*** *the press.* **antipathetic** /ˌæn.ti.pə'θet.ɪk/ [US] /-t̬i.pə'θet̬-/ *adj* *FORMAL* *antipathetic attitudes towards smokers*

anti-personnel /ˌæn.ti.pɜː.sᵊn'el/ [US] /-t̬i.pɝː-/ *adj* [before n] describes weapons intended to kill or injure people rather than damage weapons or buildings: *anti-personnel mines*

antiperspirant /ˌæn.tɪ'pɜː.spər.ənt/ [US] /-t̬ɪ'pɝː.rspər.ənt/ *noun* [C or U] a substance which is put on the skin, especially under the arms, in order to prevent or reduce sweating **antiperspirant** /ˌæn.tɪ'pɜː.spər.ənt/ [US] /-t̬ɪ-'pɝː.rspər.ənt/ *adj*: *an antiperspirant deodorant*

the Antipodes /ðiː.æn'tɪp.ə.diːz/ *plural noun* *MAINLY HUMOROUS* a way of referring to Australia and New Zealand by people living in the northern HEMISPHERE (= half of the earth): *I rather fancy the Antipodes for a holiday this summer.* **Antipodean** /ænˌtɪp.ə'diː.ən/ *noun* [C], *adj*: *an Antipodean accent* ○ *Of course for Antipodeans it's now winter.*

antiquarian /ˌæn.tɪ'kweə.ri.ən/ [US] /-t̬ɪ'kwer.i-/ *adj* connected with the trade, collection or study of old and valuable or rare objects: *an antiquarian bookshop/bookseller*

antiquarian /ˌæn.tɪ'kweə.ri.ən/ [US] /-t̬ɪ'kwer.i-/ *noun* [C] a person who studies or collects objects or artistic works from the distant past **antiquarianism** /ˌæn.tɪ-'kweə.ri.ə.nɪ.zᵊm/ [US] /-t̬ɪ'kwer.i-/ *noun* [U]

antiquary /'æn.tɪ.kwə.ri/ [US] /-t̬ə.kwer.i/ *noun* [C] *OLD USE FOR* **antiquarian**

antiquated /'æn.tɪ.kweɪ.tɪd/ [US] /-t̬ə.kweɪ.t̬ɪd/ *adj* old-fashioned or unsuitable for modern society: *It will take many years to modernise these antiquated industries.* ○ *Compared with modern satellite dishes, ordinary TV aerials look positively antiquated.* ○ *antiquated ideas/attitudes/values* ○ *antiquated laws/machinery/technology*

antique /æn'tiːk/ *noun* [C] something made in an earlier period and collected and valued because it is beautiful, rare, old or of high quality: *You can't give away Granny's old bookcase – it's a valuable antique.* ○ *My mother* ***collects*** *antiques.* **antique** /æn'tiːk/ *adj*: *an antique* ***dealer*** ○ *antique shops/markets/fairs/auctions* ○ *antique silver/jewellery/lace/furniture*

antiquity /æn'tɪk.wɪ.ti/ [US] /-wə.t̬i/ *noun* **1** [U] the distant past, especially before the sixth century: *Cannabis has been used for medicinal purposes since antiquity.* ○ *Before creating this sculpture, she studied all the masterpieces of* ***classical*** *antiquity.* **2** [C] something of great age: *Under Greek law, all antiquities that are discovered in Greece belong to the government.*

anti-racist /ˌæn.ti'reɪ.sɪst/ [US] /-t̬i-/ *adj* opposed to the unfair treatment of people who belong to other racial groups: *anti-racist legislation* **anti-racist** /ˌæn.ti'reɪ.sɪst/ [US] /-t̬i-/ *noun* [C]

antirrhinum /ˌæn.tɪ'raɪ.nəm/ [US] /-t̬ɪ-/ *noun* [C] *FORMAL FOR* **snapdragon**

anti-Semitism /ˌæn.ti'sem.ɪt.ɪ.zᵊm/ [US] /-t̬i-/ *noun* [U] the strong dislike or cruel and unfair treatment of Jewish

A

people: *Nazi anti-Semitism forced him to emigrate to the USA.* **anti-Semite** /ˌæn.tiˈse.maɪt/ [US] /-t̬i-/ *noun* [C] *He was a virulent anti-Semite.* **anti-Semitic** /ˌæn.ti.sɪˈmɪ.tɪk/ [US] /-t̬i.sə-/ *adj*: *anti-Semitic propaganda* ○ *anti-Semitic remarks*

antiseptic /ˌæn.tɪˈsep.tɪk/ [US] /-t̬ɪ-/ *noun* [C or U] a chemical used for preventing infection in an injury, especially by killing bacteria: *Antiseptic is used to sterilize the skin before giving an injection.* ○ *Many of the ingredients for antiseptics come from the rainforests.*
antiseptic /ˌæn.tiˈsep.tɪk/ [US] /-t̬ɪk/ *adj* **1** completely free from infection: *In the 1870s and 1880s, doctors began to follow the principles of antiseptic surgery.* **2** DISAPPROVING too clean and lacking imagination and character: *There's an air of antiseptic cleanliness about the new town centre, with its covered shopping mall and perfect flower displays.*

anti-social /ˌæn.tiˈsəʊ.ʃəl.i/ [US] /-t̬iˈsoʊ-/ *adj* **1** harmful to society: *anti-social* ***behaviour*** ○ *Increasingly, smoking is regarded as an anti-social habit.* **2** tending to avoid spending time with other people: *I hope they won't think I'm anti-social if I don't join them in the bar.* **anti-socially** *adv*

anti-spam /ˌæn.tiˈspæm/ [US] /-t̬i-/ *adj* [before n] produced and used to prevent people sending and receiving unwanted emails, especially advertisements: *anti-spam legislation/policies/resources/tools*

antistatic /ˌæn.tiˈstæt.ɪk/ [US] /-t̬iˈstæt̬-/ *adj* relating to devices or methods for preventing damage when electricity collects on the surface of objects

anti-tank /ˌæn.tiˈtæŋk/ [US] /-t̬i-/ *adj* [before n] describes weapons which destroy or damage enemy TANKS (= large military fighting vehicles): *anti-tank missiles/rockets*

anti-terrorist /ˌæn.tiˈter.ə.rɪst/ [US] /-t̬iˈter.ɚ.ɪst/ *adj* Anti-terrorist laws or activities are intended to prevent or reduce TERRORISM (= violent acts for political purposes): *Several governments have adopted tough new anti-terrorist legislation in the wake of the attacks.*

antithesis /ænˈtɪθ.ə.sɪs/ *noun* [C] *plural* **antitheses** the exact opposite: *She is slim and shy – the very antithesis* ***of*** *her sister.* ○ *He is the exact antithesis of what I find attractive in men.* ○ *Thanks to the collapse of communism the political antithesis* ***between*** *Left and Right is less important.* **antithetical** /ˌæn.tɪˈθet.ɪ.kəl/ [US] /-t̬ɪˈθet̬-/ *adj* (ALSO **antithetic**) FORMAL *antithetical views*

antitrust /ˌæn.tiˈtrʌst/ [US] /-t̬i-/ *adj* US SPECIALIZED antitrust laws prevent companies from unfairly controlling prices

anti-viral /ˌæn.tiˈvaɪ.rəl/ [US] /-t̬i-/ *adj* describes a drug or treatment that is used to cure an infection or disease caused by a virus: *an anti-viral agent/drug* **anti-viral** /ˌæn.tiˈvaɪ.rəl/ [US] /-t̬i-/ *noun* [C]

anti-virus /ˌæn.tiˈvaɪə.rəs/ [US] /-t̬iˈvaɪ-/ *adj* [before n] produced and used to protect the main memory of a computer against infection by a virus: *anti-virus* ***software/programs*** ○ *an anti-virus company/product/package* ↄCompare **virus** SMALL ORGANISM.

antler /ˈænt.ləʳ/ [US] /-lɚ/ *noun* [C] a horn with branch-like parts which grows on the head of a usually male deer: *a pair of antlers*

antonym /ˈæn.tə.nɪm/ [US] /-t̬ən.ɪm/ *noun* [C] SPECIALIZED a word which means the opposite of another word: *Two antonyms of 'light' are 'dark' and 'heavy'.* ↄCompare **synonym**. **antonymous** /ænˈtɒn.ɪ.məs/ [US] /-ˈtɑː.nɪ-/ *adj*: *'Long' and 'short' are antonymous (words).*

antsy /ˈænt.si/ *adj* US SLANG very nervous, anxious or unpleasantly excited: *It was a long drive and the children started to* ***get*** *antsy.* ○ *I always get antsy* ***about*** *meeting my husband's boss.*

anus /ˈeɪ.nəs/ *noun* [C] the opening at the end of the ALIMENTARY CANAL through which solid waste leaves the body **anal** /ˈeɪ.nəs/ *adj* **anally** /ˈeɪ.nəl.i/ *adv*

anvil [EQUIPMENT] /ˈæn.vɪl/ *noun* [C] a heavy block of iron on which heated pieces of metal are shaped by hammering

anvil [BONE] /ˈæn.vɪl/ *noun* [C] SPECIALIZED one of the small bones of the ear

anxiety [WORRY] /æŋˈzaɪ.ə.ti/ [US] /-t̬i/ *noun* **1** [U] an uncomfortable feeling of nervousness or worry about something that is happening or might happen in the future: *Children normally feel a lot of anxiety* ***about*** *their first day at school.* ○ *That explains his anxiety* ***over*** *his health.* ○ *Her son is a source of considerable anxiety.* **2** [C] something that causes a feeling of fear and worry: *job anxieties*
anxious /ˈæŋk.ʃəs/ *adj* worried and nervous: *My mother always gets a bit anxious if we don't arrive when we say we will.* ○ *I saw my sister's anxious face at the window.* ○ *The drought has made farmers anxious* ***about*** *the harvest.* **anxiously** /ˈæŋk.ʃə.sli/ *adv*: *We* ***waited*** *anxiously by the phone.*

anxiety [EAGERNESS] /æŋˈzaɪ.ə.ti/ [US] /-t̬i/ *noun* [U + to infinitive] eagerness to do something: *Peter's leaving at the end of this week – hence his anxiety* ***to*** *get his work finished.*
anxious /ˈæŋk.ʃəs/ *adj*: *Developing countries which are anxious* ***for*** *hard currency can rarely afford to protect the environment.* ○ [+ to infinitive] *I'm anxious* ***to*** *get home to open my presents.* ○ [+ that] *I'm anxious* ***that*** *we get there on time because I don't think there'll be many seats left.*
anxiously /ˈæŋk.ʃə.sli/ *adv*: *Tomorrow the children will receive their anxiously* ***awaited*** *presents.*

anxiety [MEDICAL CONDITION] /æŋˈzaɪ.ə.ti/ [US] /-t̬i/ *noun* [U] a medical condition characterized by continual feelings of fear and worry: *He has helped patients suffering from anxiety, depression, and eating disorders.* ○ *an anxiety disorder/attack*

any [SOME] /ˈen.i/ *determiner, pronoun* some, or even the smallest amount or number of: *Is there any of that lemon cake left?* ○ *There was hardly any food left by the time we got there.* ○ *"Is there some butter I could use?" "No, there's some margarine but there isn't any butter."* ○ *"Is there any* ***more*** *soup?" "No, I'm afraid there isn't any left."* ○ *I haven't seen any of his films.* ○ *I don't expect we'll have any* ***more*** *trouble from him.* ○ *I go to church for weddings but not for any* ***other*** *reason.* ○ *Are you sure there isn't any way of solving this problem?* ↄSee also **any more** at **more**. See Note **some or any?** at **some** UNKNOWN AMOUNT.

any [NOT IMPORTANT WHICH] /ˈen.i/ *determiner, pronoun* one of or each of a particular type of person or thing when it is not important which: *Any food would be better than nothing at all.* ○ *"Which of these cakes may I eat?" "Any."* ○ *The offer was that you could have any three items of clothing you liked for £30.* ○ INFORMAL *On Sundays I just wear any* ***old*** *thing* (= anything) *that I happen to find lying around.* ○ *Any of you should be able to answer this question.* ○ *Any idiot with a basic knowledge of French should be able to book a hotel room in Paris.* ○ *Any advice* (= Whatever advice) *that you can give me would be greatly appreciated.* ○ *Any* ***minute/day/time now*** (= Very soon) *there's going to be a massive quarrel between those two.* ○ *There were a lot of computers at the exhibition, any (one) of which would have suited me perfectly.*

any [AT ALL] /ˈen.i/ *adv* at all or in the least: *Can't you run any faster?* ○ *Those trousers don't look any different from the others.* ○ *Are you feeling any better after your illness?* ○ *Houses in this area used to be a real bargain, but they're not cheap any* ***more*** (= now). ○ *This radio is****n't*** *any* ***good*** (= it's useless) *– I'll have to buy another.* ○ *I used to walk to work every day, but* ***not*** *any* ***longer*** (= not now). ○ US INFORMAL *I tried talking him out of it, but that didn't help any – he still left home.*

anybody /ˈen.iˌbɒd.i/ [US] /-ˌbɑː.di/ *pronoun* **anyone**

anyhow [ANYWAY] /ˈen.i.haʊ/ *adv* **anyway**

anyhow [WITHOUT CARE] /ˈen.i.haʊ/ *adv* (INFORMAL **any old how**) without care or interest; in an untidy way: *He looked a complete mess – dressed anyhow with hair sticking up on end.*

anymore /ˌen.iˈmɔːʳ/ [US] /-ˈmɔːr/ *adv* US FOR **any more**, see at **more**

anyone /ˈen.i.wʌn/ *pronoun* (ALSO **anybody**) **1** used in questions and negatives to mean 'a person or people': *I haven't spoken to anyone all day.* ○ *I haven't told anyone.* ○ *Was there anyone you knew at the meeting?* ○ *Has anyone seen my glasses anywhere?* ↄSee Note **some or any?** at **some** UNKNOWN AMOUNT. **2** any person or any people: *Anyone can go – you don't have to be invited.* ○ *Anyone could dress well with all that money.*

A

• **anyone who is/was anyone** all the most famous and important people: *In those days anyone who was anyone dined in this exclusive little restaurant.*

anyplace /ˈen.i.pleɪs/ *adv* US FOR **anywhere**: *Oh just put it anyplace – it doesn't matter where.*

anyroad /ˈen.i.rəʊd/ [US] /-roʊd/ *adv* UK NORTHERN ENGLISH FOR **anyway**

anything /ˈen.i.θɪŋ/ *pronoun* any event, act or object whatever, or (especially in questions or negatives) something: *If he eats anything with wheat in it he's very sick.* ○ *Let me know if anything happens won't you.* ○ *Is there anything I can do to help?* ○ *I didn't know anything about computers till I started this job.* ○ *Did you notice anything strange about him?* ○ *I was looking for a birthday present for my mother but I didn't find anything suitable.* ○ *Spending Christmas with him and his brother – I can't imagine anything worse!* ○ *Was there anything* ***else*** *you wanted to say or is that it?* ○ *Have you got anything less expensive?* ○ *She could be anything* (= any age) ***between*** *30* ***and*** *40.* ○ *"What did you do at the weekend?" "I don't think we did anything much."* ➲See Note **some or any?** at **some** UNKNOWN AMOUNT.

• **anything but** If you say that someone or something is anything but a particular quality, you mean that the person or thing is the opposite of that particular quality: *She's meant to be really nice but she was anything but nice when I met her.*

• **as ... as anything** MAINLY UK INFORMAL used to add emphasis to an adjective or adverb: *He's as fat as anything* (= very fat).

• **for anything (in the world)** INFORMAL If you say that you would not do a particular thing for anything (in the world) it means that you certainly would not do it: *I wouldn't have missed your party for anything.*

anytime /ˈen.i.taɪm/ *adv* at a time which is not or does not need to be decided or agreed: *Call round to see me anytime.* ○ US *We don't expect the economic situation to change anytime* ***soon***.

anyway /ˈen.i.weɪ/ *adv* (ALSO **anyhow**) **1** whatever else is happening; not considering other things: *Of course I don't mind taking you home – I'm going that way anyway.* ○ *"I thought you said everyone had left." "Well, some of them have anyway."* ○ *Her parents were opposed to her giving up her course, but she did it anyway.* **2** used in conversation to emphasize what is being said: *I don't have time to go and anyway it's too expensive.* ○ *What was he doing with so much of the company's money in his personal account anyway?* **3** In conversation, anyway is also used to change the subject, return to an earlier subject or get to the most interesting point: *Anyway, as I said, I'll be away next week.* ○ *Anyway, in the end I didn't wear your jacket.*

anyways /ˈen.i.weɪz/ *adv* US INFORMAL FOR **anyway**

anywhere /ˈen.i.weəʳ/ [US] /-wer/ *adv* (US ALSO **anyplace**) in, to or at any place or (especially in questions or negatives) some place: *I can't find my keys anywhere.* ○ *You won't find a prettier village anywhere in England.* ○ *Did you go anywhere interesting this summer?* ○ *Go anywhere in the world and you'll find some sort of hamburger restaurant.* ○ *Is there anywhere in particular you wanted to go to eat tonight?* ○ *I was wondering if there was anywhere I could go to get this mended.* ○ *There are quite a few words that they use in that part of the country that you don't hear anywhere* ***else***. ○ *As a teacher you could expect to be paid anywhere* (= any amount) ***between*** *£7* ***and*** *£15 per hour.* ○ *He charges anywhere* ***from*** *$20* ***to*** *$50 for a haircut and blow-dry.* ○ *Is there anywhere to eat around here?* ○ *They live in some tiny little village* ***miles from*** *anywhere* (= a very long way from any main towns or villages). ➲See Note **some or any?** at **some** UNKNOWN AMOUNT.

• **anywhere near** INFORMAL close in time, quality, distance or amount: *Are we anywhere near finishing yet or is there still some way to go?*

• **not anywhere near** very much less: *He isn't anywhere near* ***as*** *popular as he used to be.*

• **not anywhere to be found** impossible to see or find: *We searched the house, but it wasn't anywhere to be found.*

• **not get/go anywhere** INFORMAL If you are not getting/going anywhere, you are not improving or advancing a particular situation: *I've been sorting out my study all day, but it's such a mess I don't feel I'm getting anywhere.*

AOB /ˌeɪ.əʊˈbiː/ [US] /-oʊ-/ UK WRITTEN ABBREVIATION FOR any other business: used at the end of the list of subjects to be discussed at a meeting

A-OK /ˌeɪ.əʊˈkeɪ/ [US] /-oʊ-/ *adj* [after v] US INFORMAL completely right or acceptable: *The doctor says I'm A-OK now, that there's absolutely nothing wrong with me.*

aorta /eɪˈɔː.tə/ [US] /-ˈɔːr.t̬ə/ *noun* [C] the main artery which takes blood to the other parts of the body **aortic** /eɪˈɔː.tɪk/ [US] /-ˈɔːr.t̬ɪk/ *adj*: *the aortic valve*

apace /əˈpeɪs/ *adv* LITERARY OR OLD USE quickly: *The project is coming on apace* (= advancing quickly).

apart [SEPARATE] /əˈpɑːt/ [US] /-ˈpɑːrt/ *adv* **1** separated by a distance or, less commonly, by time: *Stand with your feet wide apart.* ○ *How far apart should the speakers be?* ○ *We were asked to stand in two lines three metres apart.* ○ *The two lines of children moved slowly apart.* ○ *The garage, large enough for two cars, is set apart* ***from*** (= not joined to) *the house.* ○ *I forget the exact age difference between Mark and his brother – they're two or three years apart.* **2** into smaller pieces: *My jacket is so old it's* ***falling*** *apart.* ○ *I* ***took*** *the motor apart* (= separated it into pieces) *to see how it worked.*

apart /əˈpɑːt/ [US] /-ˈpɑːrt/ *adj* [after v] living or staying in a different place from the person that you are married to or have a close relationship with: *When you're apart you rely so heavily on the phone.*

apart [EXCEPT] /əˈpɑːt/ [US] /-ˈpɑːrt/ *adv* **apart from** except for or not considering: *He works until nine o'clock every evening, and that's* ***quite*** *apart from the work he does over the weekend.* ○ *Apart from the salary/Salary apart, it's not a bad job.* ○ *Apart from you and me/You and me apart, I don't think there was anyone there under thirty.*

apartheid /əˈpɑː.taɪt/ /-teɪt/ [US] /-ˈpɑːr.t̬aɪt/ *noun* [U] (in the past in South Africa) a political system in which people of different races are separated: *the long-awaited dismantling* (= end) *of apartheid*

apartment MAINLY US /əˈpɑːt.mənt/ [US] /-ˈpɑːrt-/ *noun* [C] (UK USUALLY **flat**) a set of rooms for living in, especially on one floor of a building: *I'll give you the keys to my apartment.* ○ *They have six holiday/luxury apartments for sale.*

aˈpartment ˌbuilding/ˌblock US *noun* [C] (UK **block of flats**) a large building that is divided into apartments

apartments /əˈpɑːt.mənts/ [US] /-ˈpɑːrt-/ *plural noun* a set of large rooms with expensive furniture and decoration in, for example, a public building or castle: *The Royal Apartments are open to the public.*

apathetic /ˌæp.əˈθet.ɪk/ [US] /-ˈθet̬-/ *adj* lacking interest or energy; unwilling to take action especially over a matter of importance: *Young people today are so apathetic* ***about*** *politics.* ○ *Don't be so apathetic – how are you going to get a job if you don't even write a letter?*

apathy /ˈæp.ə.θi/ *noun* [U] when someone lacks interest or energy and is unwilling to take action especially over a matter of importance: ***widespread*** *apathy among students* ○ *voter apathy*

ape [ANIMAL] /eɪp/ *noun* [C] an animal like a large monkey which has no tail and uses its arms to swing through trees: *Chimpanzees and gorillas are both apes.*

• **go ape** (OFFENSIVE **go ape-shit**) INFORMAL to become extremely angry: *She went ape because I was half an hour late.*

ape [COPY] /eɪp/ *verb* [T] DISAPPROVING to copy something or someone badly and unsuccessfully: *He called the new building unoriginal and said that it merely aped the classical traditions.*

aperitif /əˌper.ɪˈtiːf/ *noun* [C] an alcoholic drink, especially one which is drunk before a meal: *Would you like an aperitif before dinner?*

aperture /ˈæp.ə.tʃəʳ/ [US] /-ɚ.tʃɚ/ *noun* [C] a small and often narrow opening, especially one that allows light into a camera

apex [TOP] /ˈeɪ.peks/ *noun* [C] *plural* **apexes** or **apices** SPECIALIZED the highest point or top of a shape or object: *the apex of a triangle/pyramid* ○ FIGURATIVE *He reached* ***the apex of*** (= the most successful part of) *his career during that period.* **apical** /ˈeɪ.pɪ.kəl/ *adj*

APEX [TRAVEL] /ˈeɪ.peks/ *noun* [U], *adj* [before n] *ABBREVIATION FOR* Advance Purchase Excursion: a system of cheap travel tickets which must be bought a particular number of days before travelling: *an APEX **fare***

aphid /ˈeɪ.fɪd/ *noun* [C] any of various small insects, such as the GREENFLY, which suck the juices of plants for food

aphorism /ˈæf.ə.rɪ.zᵊm/ [US] /-ɚ.ɪ-/ *noun* [C] a short clever saying which is intended to express a general truth: *Oscar Wilde was famous for such aphorisms as 'Experience is the name everyone gives to their mistakes'.*

aphrodisiac /ˌæf.rəˈdɪz.i.æk/ [US] /-ˈdiː.ʒæk/ *noun* [C] something, usually a drug or food, which is believed to cause sexual desire in people: *Are oysters really an aphrodisiac?* ○ *They say that power is an aphrodisiac.* **aphrodisiac** /ˌæf.rəˈdɪz.i.æk/ [US] /-ˈdiː.ʒæk/ *adj*: *the aphrodisiac properties of champagne*

apiary /ˈeɪ.pi.ə.ri/ [US] /-er.i/ *noun* [C] a place where people keep bees, especially a collection of HIVES (= containers in which bees live) kept to provide honey

apical /ˈeɪ.pɪ.kᵊl/ *adj* ➲See at **apex** TOP.

apices /ˈeɪ.pɪ.siːz/ *plural of* **apex** TOP.

apiece /əˈpiːs/ *adv* each: *In good condition, dolls from this period sell for £500 apiece.*

aplenty /əˈplen.ti/ [US] /-t̬i/ *adj* [after n] *OLD USE* available in large amounts: *If that's not enough, there are shows, films and amusements aplenty.*

aplomb /əˈplɒm/ [US] /-ˈplɑːm/ *noun* [U] confidence and style: *Rosalind conducted the meeting **with** characteristic aplomb/**with** her usual aplomb.*

apocalypse /əˈpɒk.ə.lɪps/ [US] /-ˈpɑː.kə-/ *noun* [S or U] **1** a very serious event resulting in great destruction and change: *The book offers a vision of the future in which there is a great nuclear apocalypse.* **2 the Apocalypse** in the Bible, the total destruction and end of the world **apocalyptic** /əˌpɒk.əˈlɪp.tɪk/ [US] /-ˌpɑː.kə-/ *adj*: *apocalyptic visions of a nuclear confrontation* ○ *apocalyptic warnings about our destruction of the environment*

apocryphal /əˈpɒk.rɪ.fᵊl/ [US] /-ˈpɑː.krɪ-/ *adj FORMAL* describes a story that is probably not true although often told and believed by some people to have happened: *an apocryphal **story*** ○ *It's a good story but I dare say it's apocryphal.*

apogee /ˈæp.ə.dʒiː/ *noun* [S] *FORMAL* the most successful, popular or powerful point: *At their apogee, the novels of Spillane claimed worldwide sales of over 180 million.*

apolitical /ˌeɪ.pəˈlɪt.ɪ.kᵊl/ [US] /-ˈlɪt̬-/ *adj* not interested in or connected with politics, or not connected to any political party: *The organization insists that it is apolitical and does not identify with any one particular party.*

apologetic /əˌpɒl.əˈdʒet.ɪk/ [US] /-ˌpɑː.ləˈdʒet̬.ɪk/ *adj* expressing regret about having caused someone inconvenience or unhappiness: *She was so apologetic **about** forgetting my birthday it was almost embarrassing.* ○ *I hope he was suitably apologetic **for** breaking your glasses.* **apologetically** /əˌpɒl.əˈdʒet.ɪ.kli/ [US] /-ˌpɑː.ləˈdʒet̬-/ *adv*: *She offered us her burnt cakes and smiled apologetically.*

apologist /əˈpɒl.ə.dʒɪst/ [US] /-ˈpɑː.lə-/ *noun* [C] *FORMAL* a person who supports a particular belief or political system, especially an unpopular one, and speaks or writes in defence of it: *communism and its apologists* ○ *There are few apologists **for** the old system.*

apology /əˈpɒl.ə.dʒi/ [US] /-ˈpɑː.lə-/ *noun* [C] (*ALSO* **apologia**) *FORMAL* a formal explanation or defence of a belief or system, especially one that is unpopular ➲See also **apology** at **apologize**.

apologize, *UK USUALLY* **-ise** /əˈpɒl.ə.dʒaɪz/ [US] /-ˈpɑː.lə-/ *verb* [I] to tell someone that you are sorry for having done something that has caused them inconvenience or unhappiness: *I must apologize **to** Isobel for my lateness.* ○ *Trains may be subject to delay on the northern line – we apologize **for** any inconvenience caused.* ○ *She apologized **profusely for** having to leave at 3.30 p.m.*

apology /əˈpɒl.ə.dʒi/ [US] /-ˈpɑː.lə-/ *noun* [C or U] an act of saying sorry: *I have an apology to **make** to you – I'm afraid I opened your letter by mistake.* ○ *He's demanding a **full** apology **from** the newspaper for making untrue allegations about his personal life.* ○ *"Was he at all sorry for what he'd done?" "Oh he was **full of** apologies* (= extremely sorry)*."* ○ *She complained to the company about its awful service and they sent her a **written** apology.* ○ *I **owe** you an apology – I'm afraid I forgot to send Amanda that report.* ○ *a letter of apology* ➲See also **apology** at **apologist**.

(*your*) aˈpologies *plural noun FORMAL* a message politely informing someone that you cannot be present at their meeting or party: *The vice-chair has **sent** his apologies – he's abroad at present.* ○ *Apologies were received from Phil Baker and Malcolm Johnson.*

• **be an apology for *sth*** *UK INFORMAL* to be an extremely bad example of something: *You're not coming out because you're tired? That's an apology for an excuse!*

• **make *your* apologies (for *sth*)** *FORMAL* to say that you are sorry for something: *I made my apologies and left.*

apoplectic /ˌæp.əˈplek.tɪk/ *adj* extremely and noticeably angry, or in a state of violent excitement, usually caused by great anger: *He was apoplectic **with** rage/fury.* **apoplexy** /ˈæp.ə.plek.si/ *noun* [U] *In a **fit of** apoplexy* (= great anger), *he thumped the table with both hands.*

apostasy /əˈpɒs.tə.si/ [US] /-ˈpɑː.stə-/ *noun* [U] *FORMAL* the act of giving up your religious or political beliefs and leaving a religion or a political party: *In those days apostasy was punishable by death.* **apostate** /əˈpɒs.teɪt/ [US] /-ˈpɑː.steɪt/ *noun* [C] *FORMAL* a person who has given up their religion or left a political party

apostle /əˈpɒs.l̩/ [US] /-ˈpɑː.sl̩/ *noun* [C] **1** any of the twelve original followers of Jesus Christ **2** *FORMAL* someone who strongly supports a particular belief or political movement: *an apostle **of** world peace/liberty* **apostolic** /ˌæp.əˈstɒl.ɪk/ [US] /-ˈstɑː.lɪk/ *adj FORMAL*

apostrophe /əˈpɒs.trə.fi/ [US] /-ˈpɑː.strə-/ *noun* [C] **1** the ' punctuation mark that shows when a letter or a number has been omitted, or is used before or after *s* to show possession: *I'm* (= I am) ○ *they're* (= they are) ○ *'65* (= 1965) ○ *Helen's laugh* ○ *Charles' cooking* ○ *a baby's hand* ○ *babies' hands* **2** used before *s* to show the plural of a number or a letter: *the 1920's* ○ *I always forget there are four s's in possession.*

apothecary /əˈpɒθ.ə.kᵊr.i/ [US] /-ˈpɑː.θə-/ *noun* [C] a person who in the past made and sold medicines

apotheosis /əˌpɒθ.iˈəʊ.sɪs/ [US] /-ˌpɑː.θiˈoʊ-/ *noun* [C usually sing] *plural* **apotheoses** *FORMAL* **1** the best or most extreme example of something: *Most people agree that her acting career **achieved** its apotheosis in this film.* ○ *Bad taste in clothes **reached** its apotheosis in the 1970s.* **2 the apotheosis of *sb*** the act of making someone into a god: *One of the large paintings showed the Apotheosis of the Emperor Trajan.*

appal (-ll-), *US USUALLY* **appall** /əˈpɔːl/ [US] /-ˈpɑːl/ *verb* [T] to make someone have strong feelings of shock or of disapproval: *I was appalled **at/by** the lack of staff in the hospital.* ○ *The state of the kitchen appalled her.* **appalled** /əˈpɔːld/ [US] /-ˈpɑːld/ *adj*: *an appalled silence/fascination* **appalling** /əˈpɔː.lɪŋ/ [US] /-ˈpɑː-/ *adj* **1** shocking and very bad: *appalling injuries* ○ *Prisoners were kept in the most appalling conditions.* **2** very bad: *appalling weather* ○ *The journey home was appalling.* **appallingly** /əˈpɔː.lɪŋ.li/ [US] /-ˈpɑː-/ *adv*: *The number of casualties was appallingly high in both wars.* ○ *The whole play was appallingly* (= very badly) *acted.*

apparatus [EQUIPMENT] /ˌæp.əˈreɪ.təs/ [US] /-ˈræt̬.əs/ *noun* [C or U] *plural* **apparatus** or **apparatuses** a set of equipment or tools or sometimes a machine which is used for a particular purpose: *a piece of apparatus* ○ *The divers checked their breathing apparatus.*

apparatus [ORGANIZATION] /ˌæp.əˈreɪ.təs/ [US] /-ˈræt̬.əs/ *noun* [C usually sing] *plural* **apparatus** or **apparatuses** an organization or system, especially a political one: *The whole apparatus of communism was already falling apart.*

apparel /əˈpær.ᵊl/ *noun* [U] **1** *MAINLY US* clothes of a particular type when they are being sold in a shop: *sports apparel* **2** *OLD USE OR FORMAL* clothes

apparent /əˈpær.ᵊnt/ [US] /-ˈper-/ *adj* **1** able to be seen or understood: *Her unhappiness was apparent **to** everyone.* ○ [+ that] *It was becoming increasingly apparent **that** he* *could no longer look after himself.* ○ *I was on the metro this morning when* ***for no*** *apparent* ***reason*** *the man opposite suddenly screamed.* **2** [before n] seeming to exist or be true: *There are one or two apparent discrepancies between the two reports.* ○ *She has this apparent innocence which, I suspect, she uses to her advantage.*

apparently /ə'pær.ᵊnt.li/ [US] /-'per-/ *adv* **1** used to say you have read or been told something although you are not certain it is true: *Apparently it's going to rain today.* ○ *Apparently he's had enough of England and is going back to Australia.* **2** used when the real situation is different from what you thought it was: *You know I told you Alice's party was on the 13th, well I saw her last night and apparently it's on the 14th.* ○ *She looks about 10 but apparently she's 14.* ○ *I thought they were married but apparently* ***not*** (= they are not married). **3** used to say that something seems to be true, although it is not certain: *An eighty-year-old woman was badly hurt in what the police describe as an apparently motiveless attack* (= an attack with no obvious purpose).

apparition /ˌæp.ə'rɪʃ.ᵊn/ *noun* [C] the spirit of a dead person appearing in a form which can be seen

appeal [ATTRACT] /ə'piːl/ *verb* [I not continuous] to interest or attract someone: *I've haven't been skiing – it's never really appealed.* ○ *It's a programme designed to appeal mainly* ***to*** *16 to 25 year-olds.* ○ *I think what appeals* ***to*** *me about his painting is the colours he uses.*

appeal /ə'piːl/ *noun* [U] the quality in someone or something that makes them attractive or interesting: ***sex*** *appeal* ○ *Spielberg films have a* ***wide*** *appeal.* ○ *Parties on river-boats have* ***lost*** *their appeal since one sank last year killing thirty-three people.*

appealing /ə'piː.lɪŋ/ *adj* **1** attractive or interesting: *The idea of not having to get up early every morning is rather appealing* ***(to*** *me).* ○ *He had a nice smile and an appealing personality.* ✻ NOTE: The opposite is **unappealing**. **2** describes someone's expression or way of speaking when it makes you want to help or protect them: *a little dog with appealing big brown eyes* **appealingly** /ə'piː.lɪŋ.li/ *adv*

appeal [ARGUE] /ə'piːl/ *verb* [I] **1** to formally request that especially a legal or official decision is changed: *The parents appealed* ***against*** *the school's decision not to admit the child.* ○ *The footballer appealed* ***to*** *the referee* ***for*** *a free kick.* **2** LEGAL to request a higher law court to consider again a decision made by a lower court, especially in order to reduce or prevent a punishment: *The teenager has been given leave* (= allowed) *by the High Court to appeal* ***against*** *her two-year sentence.* ○ *They're appealing* ***to*** *the High Court to reduce the sentence to a fine.*

appeal /ə'piːl/ *noun* [C or U] a request especially to a court of law to change a previous decision: *The case went to the* ***court of*** *appeal/the appeal* ***court****.* ○ *He won his appeal and the sentence was halved.* ○ *She has* ***lodged*** (= made) *an appeal* ***against*** *the severity of the fine.*

appeal [REQUEST] /ə'piːl/ *verb* [I] to make a serious or formal request, especially to the public, for money or help: *They're appealing* ***for*** *clothes and blankets to send to the devastated region.* ○ *The police are appealing* ***to*** *the public* ***for*** *any information about the missing girl.* ○ *I tried to appeal* ***to*** (= ask for support based on) *his sense of loyalty, stressing how good the company had been to him.* ○ [+ to infinitive] *Church leaders have appealed* ***to*** *the government* ***to*** *halt the war.*

appeal /ə'piːl/ *noun* [C] when a lot of people are asked to give money, information or help: *They're* ***launching*** (= starting) *an appeal to raise money for famine victims.* ○ [+ to infinitive] *The police have issued an appeal* ***to*** *the public* ***to*** *stay away from the centre of town at the weekend.*

appear [BE PRESENT] /ə'pɪəʳ/ [US] /-'pɪr/ *verb* [I] **1** to become noticeable or to be present: *He suddenly appeared in the doorway.* ○ *We'd been in the house a month when dark stains started appearing on the wall.* ○ *His name appears in the film credits for lighting.* ○ *If she hasn't appeared* (= arrived) *by ten o'clock I'm going without her.* ○ *The film, currently in the States, will be appearing on our screens* (= we will be able to see it) *later this year.* ○ *I've noticed that smaller cars are starting to appear* (= be produced or sold) *again.* **2** If you appear in court, you are there officially because you are involved in a trial: *Both women will be appearing* ***before*** *magistrates later this week.*

appearance /ə'pɪə.rənts/ [US] /-'pɪr.ᵊnts/ *noun* [C] an occasion when someone appears in public: *It was his first appearance on television/television appearance* ***as*** *president.* ○ *She will be making a* ***public*** *appearance, signing copies of her latest novel.* ○ *This was the defendant's third* ***court*** *appearance for the same offence.*

● **put in an appearance** to be present somewhere for a short time: *I didn't really want to go to the party but I thought I'd better put in an appearance.*

appear [SEEM] /ə'pɪəʳ/ [US] /-'pɪr/ *verb* [L or I; not continuous] to seem: *You've got to appear* ***(to be)*** *calm in an interview even if you're terrified underneath.* ○ *To people who don't know him he probably appears* ***(to be)*** *rather unfriendly.* ○ *Things aren't always* ***what they*** *appear* ***to be.*** ○ [+ to infinitive] *She appears* ***to*** *actually like the man, which I find incredible.* ○ ***There*** *appears* ***to*** *be some mistake.* ○ [+ (that)] ***It*** *appears* ***(that)*** *she left the party alone.* ○ ***It*** *appears to me* ***(that)*** (= I think that) *we need to make some changes.* ○ FORMAL ***It would*** *appear* ***(that)*** (= It seems that) *nobody on board the aircraft actually had a licence to fly it.* ○ [+ adv or prep] ***It*** *appears* ***as if/as though*** *I was wrong.* ○ *Everything was not* ***as*** *it appeared – secret deals had been done.* ○ *I know* ***how*** *it must appear, but it's not really as bad as it looks.* ○ *"Has he left?" "****It*** *appears* ***not/so.****"* ○ [after *so*] *"I think we're late." "****So it*** *appears."*

appearance /ə'pɪə.rənts/ [US] /-'pɪr.ᵊnts/ *noun* [C or U] the way a person or thing looks to other people: *a middle-aged man* ***of*** *smart appearance* ○ *You can* ***alter/change*** *the whole appearance* ***of*** *a room just by lighting it in a certain way.* ○ *There was nothing unusual about/in her physical appearance.* ○ *The large car outside the house gave the appearance* ***of*** *wealth* (= suggested wealthy people lived there). ○ *Appearances can be deceptive.*

● **to/from all appearances** judging from what can be seen: *To all appearances their marriage is fine, but I think she gives him a bad time in private.*

appear [PERFORM] /ə'pɪəʳ/ [US] /-'pɪr/ *verb* [I usually + adv or prep] to perform publicly in a play, film or dance: *Dave Gilmore is currently appearing* ***as*** *Widow Twanky in the Arts Theatre's production of "Puss in Boots".* ○ *She appears briefly in the new Bond film.* **appearance** /ə'pɪə.rənts/ [US] /-'pɪr.ᵊnts/ *noun* [C] *He made his first* ***stage/TV*** *appearance at the age of six.*

▲ **appear for** ***sb*** *phrasal verb* If a lawyer appears for someone, he or she acts for the person: *Ms Hawley was appearing for the defence.*

appease /ə'piːz/ *verb* [T] FORMAL DISAPPROVING to prevent further disagreement in arguments or war by giving to the other side an advantage that they have demanded: *She claimed that the government had only changed the law in order to appease their critics.* **appeasement** /ə'piːz.mənt/ *noun* [U] *Appeasement of dictators, said the president, led to wide scale bloodshed.*

appellation /ˌæp.ə'leɪ.ʃᵊn/ *noun* [C] FORMAL a name or title: *Mussolini was known by the more familiar appellation 'Il Duce'.*

append /ə'pend/ *verb* [T] FORMAL to add something to the end of a piece of writing: *The author appends a short footnote* ***to*** *the text explaining the point.*

appendage /ə'pen.dɪdʒ/ *noun* [C] FORMAL **1** something which exists as a smaller and less important part of something larger: *The committee is a* ***mere*** *appendage* ***of*** *the council and has no power of its own.* ○ *The organism has small leaf-like appendages.* **2** an arm, leg or other body part: *He had a tattoo on every visible appendage.*

appendix [BODY PART] /ə'pen.dɪks/ *noun* [C] *plural* **appendixes** a small tube-shaped part which is joined to the intestines on the right side of the body and has no use in humans: *She* ***had*** *her appendix* ***out*** (= medically removed) *last summer.*

appendectomy /ˌæp.en'dek.tə.mi/ /-ᵊn-/ *noun* [C] SPECIALIZED a medical operation to remove the appendix

appendicitis /əˌpen.dɪ'saɪ.tɪs/ [US] /-t̬ɪs/ *noun* [U] an illness in which the appendix is infected and painful and usually needs to be removed in an operation

appendix [BOOK PART] /ə'pen.dɪks/ *noun* [C] *plural* **appendixes** or **appendices** a separate part at the end of a book or magazine which gives additional information: *There's an appendix at the end of the book with a list of dates.*

appertain /ˌæp.ə'teɪn/ [US] /-ɚ-/ *verb*
▲ **appertain to** ***sth*** *phrasal verb* FORMAL to be connected to or belong to: *She enjoyed the privileges appertaining to the office of chairman.*

appetite [FOOD] /'æp.ɪ.taɪt/ *noun* [C or U] a desire for food: *All that walking has **given** me an appetite.* ○ *I won't have any chocolate, thanks. It will **spoil*** (= reduce) *my appetite.* ○ *I haven't **got much of** an appetite* (= I am not hungry). ○ *The children all **have healthy/good** appetites* (= they eat a lot). ○ *Both viruses cause fever and **loss of** appetite.*
appetizing, UK USUALLY **-ising** /'æp.ɪ.taɪ.zɪŋ/ *adj* describes food or smells that make you want to eat: *appetizing smells from the kitchen*

appetite [DESIRE] /'æp.ɪ.taɪt/ *noun* [C] a strong desire or need: *her appetite **for** adventure* ○ *his **insatiable** sexual appetite* ○ *I've read an excerpt of the book on the Web and it's **whetted** my appetite* (= increased my interest in it).

appetizer /'æp.ɪ.taɪ.zəʳ/ [US] /-zɚ/ *noun* [C] (UK USUALLY **-iser**) **1** a small amount of food eaten before a meal: *At 6:30, everyone gathered for drinks and appetizers in the lounge.* **2** MAINLY US the first part of a meal: *The average cost of a full three-course meal – appetizer, main course and dessert – including tip and a modest wine is about $25.*

applaud [CLAP] /ə'plɔːd/ [US] /-'plɑːd/ *verb* [I or T] to show enjoyment or approval of something such as a performance or speech by clapping the hands repeatedly to make a noise: *You should have heard the audience applaud – the noise was fantastic.* ○ *She was applauded for a full five minutes after her speech.*
applause /ə'plɔːz/ [US] /-'plɑːz/ *noun* [U] *His speech **met with*** (= received) *loud applause.* ○ *So let's have a **round of** applause, please, **for*** (= please applaud) *a very lovely and talented young lady who is going to sing for us.*

applaud [PRAISE] /ə'plɔːd/ [US] /-'plɑːd/ *verb* [T] FORMAL to say that you admire and agree with a person's action or decision: *We applaud the family's decision to remain silent over the issue.*

apple /'æp.l̩/ *noun* [C or U] a round fruit with a firm white flesh and a green, red or yellow skin: *to peel an apple* ○ *apple **pie/sauce*** ○ *an apple **tree*** ➲See picture **Fruit** on page Centre 1
• **be in apple-pie order** UK OLD-FASHIONED to be perfectly arranged and tidy: *Their house is always in apple-pie order.*
• **apple of** ***sb's*** **eye** OLD-FASHIONED the person who someone loves most and is very proud of: *His youngest daughter was the apple of his eye.*
• **An apple a day keeps the doctor away.** SAYING This means that eating an apple each day can help to keep you healthy.

applejack /'æp.l̩.dʒæk/ *noun* [U] MAINLY US a type of brandy made from apples

ˈ**apple** ˌ**juice** *noun* [U] juice from crushed apples, used for a drink or to make vinegar

applet /'æp.lət/ *noun* [C] SPECIALIZED a small computer program that is automatically copied onto a computer when you look at a document that needs this program to make it work: *The user confirms their order and downloads an applet which asks them for their personal and payment details.*

appliance /ə'plaɪ.ənts/ *noun* [C] a device, machine or piece of equipment, especially an electrical one that is used in the house such as a cooker or washing machine: *electric/domestic/household appliances*

applicable /ə'plɪk.ə.bl̩/ *adj* ➲See at **apply** RELATE TO

appliqué /'æp.lɪ.keɪ/ *noun* [U] decorative work in which one piece of cloth is sewn or fixed onto another, or the activity of decorating cloth in this way **appliqué** /'æp.lɪ.keɪ/ *verb* [T]

apply [REQUEST] /ə'plaɪ/ *verb* [I] to request something, usually officially, especially by writing or sending in a form: *By the time I saw the job advertised it was already too late to apply.* ○ *Please apply in writing **to** the address below.* ○ *We've applied **to** a charitable organization **for** a grant for the project.* ○ [+ to infinitive] *Tim's applied **to** join the police.*
application /ˌæp.lɪ'keɪ.ʃən/ *noun* [C or U] an official request for something, usually in writing: *a **letter of** application* ○ *Free information will be sent out **on** application **to*** (= if you ask) *the central office.* ○ *I've sent off applications **for** four different jobs.* ○ *Have you filled in the application **form** for your passport yet?* ○ [+ to infinitive] *South Africa has submitted an application **to** host the World Cup.*
applicant /'æp.lɪ.kənt/ *noun* [C] a person who formally requests something, especially a job, or a place at college or university: *How many applicants did you have **for** the job?*

apply [RELATE TO] /ə'plaɪ/ *verb* [I] (especially of rules or laws) to have a connection or be important: *That bit of the form is for UK citizens – it doesn't apply **to** you.* ○ *Those were old regulations – they don't apply any more.*
applicable /ə'plɪk.ə.bl̩/ *adj* affecting or relating to a person or thing: *This part of the law is only applicable **to** companies employing more than five people.* ○ *The new qualifications are applicable **to** all European countries.*
application /ˌæp.lɪ'keɪ.ʃən/ *noun* [C or U] *The new laws have (a) particular application **to** the self-employed.*

apply [PUT ON] /ə'plaɪ/ *verb* [T] to spread or rub a substance such as cream or paint on a surface: *Apply the suntan cream liberally **to** exposed areas every three hours and after swimming.* ○ *The paint should be applied thinly and evenly.*
application /ˌæp.lɪ'keɪ.ʃən/ *noun* [C or U] when you spread or rub a substance such as cream or paint on a surface, or a layer of cream or paint: *Leave the paint to dry between applications.* ○ *Regular application of the cream should reduce swelling within 24 hours.*
applicator /'æp.lɪ.keɪ.təʳ/ [US] /-t̬ɚ/ *noun* [C] a device used to put something on or into a particular place: *Please use the sponge applicator provided.*

apply [USE] /ə'plaɪ/ *verb* [T] to make use of something or use it for a practical purpose: *He wants a job in which he can apply his foreign languages.* ○ *The court heard how the driver had failed to apply his brakes in time.* ○ *If you apply pressure to a cut it's meant to stop the bleeding.*
applied /ə'plaɪd/ *adj* [before n] relating to a subject of study, especially a science, that has a practical use: ***pure and** applied mathematics/science*
application /ˌæp.lɪ'keɪ.ʃən/ *noun* **1** [C or U] a way in which something can be used for a particular purpose: *The design has many applications.* ○ *the application of this research in the treatment of cancer* **2** [U] the determination to work hard over a period of time in order to succeed at something: *Joshua clearly has ability in this subject but lacks application.* **3** [C] a computer program that is designed for a particular purpose: *spreadsheet applications*

apˈ**ply** ***yourself*** [WORK HARD] *verb* [R] If you apply yourself to something, you work hard at it, directing your abilities and efforts in a determined way so that you succeed: *You can solve any problem if you apply yourself.*

appoint /ə'pɔɪnt/ *verb* [T] to choose someone officially for a job or responsibility: *We've appointed three new teachers this year.* ○ *He's just been appointed **(as)** director of the publishing division.* ○ [+ to infinitive] *A commission has just been appointed **to** investigate fraud claims.* **appointed** /ə'pɔɪn.tɪd/ [US] /-t̬ɪd/ *adj*: *I'd like to introduce our newly appointed members of staff.* ➲See also **appointed**; **self-appointed**.
appointee /əˌpɔɪn'tiː/ *noun* [C] someone who has been chosen officially for a job or responsibility: *a government appointee* ○ *The new appointee will be working closely with both departments.*
appointment /ə'pɔɪnt.mənt/ *noun* [C or U] *his appointment **as** senior lecturer* ○ *We would like to announce **the** appointment **of** Julia Lewis **as** head of sales.* ○ *Our department expects to **make** five new appointments* (= appoint five new people) *this year alone.* ➲See also **appointment**.

• **by appointment** in the UK, used by businesses to show that their goods and services are sold to the Queen, and that they are of good quality: *Carter's Ltd, confectioners by appointment to the Queen*

appointed /əˈpɔɪn.tɪd/ ⓤ /-t̬ɪd/ *adj FORMAL* If buildings or rooms are appointed in a particular way, they have furniture and equipment of the stated standard: *It says in the ad that the bathroom is spacious and well-appointed.* ⊃See also **appointed** at **appoint**; **well-appointed**.

appointment /əˈpɔɪnt.mənt/ *noun* [C] **1** a formal arrangement to meet or visit someone at a particular time and place: *I'd like to make an appointment with Doctor Evans, please.* ○ *She had to cancel her dental appointment.* ○ [+ to infinitive] *I've got an appointment to see Ms Edwards at two o'clock/a two o'clock appointment with Ms Edwards.* ○ *If he didn't have a secretary to remind him, he wouldn't keep (= remember to be present at) any of his appointments.* ○ *That's the second appointment he's missed (= not been present at).* ⊃See also **appointment** at **appoint**. **2 by appointment** at a previously arranged time: *House for sale, two bedrooms. Viewing by appointment only.*

appoint /əˈpɔɪnt/ *verb* [T often passive] *FORMAL* A date has been appointed (= arranged) *for the election.* ○ *Ten minutes before the appointed time (= the arranged time), he sat nervously outside her office.*

apportion /əˈpɔː.ʃ ən/ ⓤ /-ˈpɔːr-/ *verb* [T] *FORMAL* to give or share out, especially blame or money among several people or things: *When we know how much is profit, then we can apportion the money among/between us.* ○ *The investigation into the air crash would inevitably apportion blame to certain members of the crew.*

apposite /ˈæp.ə.zɪt/ /-zaɪt/ *adj FORMAL* suitable and right for the occasion: *an apposite phrase/quotation/remark* ○ *The film starts in a graveyard, an apposite image for the decaying society which is the theme of the film.*

appraise /əˈpreɪz/ *verb* [T] **1** to examine someone or something in order to judge their qualities, success or needs: *At the end of each teaching practice, trainee teachers are asked to appraise their own performance.* ○ *In co-operation with other professionals, social workers will appraise the individual's needs.* ○ *He coolly appraised the situation, deciding which person would be most likely to succeed.* **2** *US FOR* **value** *MONEY: The ring was appraised at $40,000.*

appraisal /əˈpreɪ.z əl/ *noun* [C or U] **1** when you examine someone or something in order to judge their qualities, success or needs: *The newspaper gave an editorial appraisal of the government's achievements of the past year.* **2 (job/performance) appraisal** when an employee meets with their manager or employer to discuss their progress, aims and needs at work: *Many companies operate regular job appraisals, often on an annual basis.*

appraisee /ə.preɪˈziː/ *noun* [C] a person who is being appraised

appraiser /əˈpreɪ.z əʳ/ ⓤ /-z ɚ/ *noun* [C] a person who appraises someone or something

appreciable /əˈpriː.ʃə.bl̩/ *adj* If an amount or change is appreciable, it is large or noticeable enough to have an important effect: *There has been an appreciable drop in the number of unemployed since the new government came to power.* **appreciably** /əˈpriː.ʃə.bli/ *adv: Her health has improved appreciably since she changed her treatment.*

appreciate VALUE /əˈpriː.ʃi.eɪt/ *verb* [T] **1** to recognize or understand that something is valuable, important or as described: *There's no point buying him expensive wines – he doesn't appreciate them.* ○ *We appreciate the need for immediate action.* ○ [+ that] *I appreciate that it's a difficult decision for you to make.* ○ [+ question word] *I don't think you appreciate how much time I spent preparing this meal.* **2 I/We appreciate...** used when you are thanking someone or showing that you are grateful: *We really appreciate all the help you gave us last weekend.* ○ [+ v-ing] *I appreciate your making the effort to come.* **3 would appreciate** used when you are politely requesting something: *I would appreciate it if you could let me know (= Please let me know) in advance whether or not you will be coming.*

appreciation /ə.priː.ʃiˈeɪ.ʃ ən/ *noun* [U] when you recognize or understand that something is valuable, important or as described: *Max has no appreciation of the finer things in life.* ○ *The crowd cheered in appreciation.* ○ *Children rarely show any appreciation of/for what their parents do for them.* ○ *These flowers are a token of my appreciation of/for all your help.*

appreciative /əˈpriː.ʃə.tɪv/ ⓤ /-t̬ɪv/ *adj* showing that you understand how good something is, or are grateful for something: *It's nice to have an appreciative audience.* ○ *I'm very appreciative of all the support you've given me.* **appreciatively** /əˈpriː.ʃə.tɪv.li/ ⓤ /-t̬ɪv-/ *adv: She smiled appreciatively at him.*

appreciate INCREASE /əˈpriː.ʃi.eɪt/ *verb* [I] to increase in value: *The value of our house has appreciated by 50% in the last two years.* ○ *Our house has appreciated (in value) by 50% in the last two years.* ✱ NOTE: The opposite is **depreciate**.

appreciation /ə.priː.ʃiˈeɪ.ʃ ən/ *noun* [U] *There has been little appreciation (= increase) in the value of property recently.*

apprehend CATCH /ˌæp.rɪˈhend/ *verb* [T] *FORMAL* to catch and arrest someone who has not obeyed the law: *The police have finally apprehended the killer.* **apprehension** /ˌæp.rɪˈhen.ʃ ən/ *noun* [U] *Both the army and the police were involved in the apprehension of the terrorists.*

apprehend UNDERSTAND /ˌæp.rɪˈhend/ *verb* [T] *FORMAL* to understand something **apprehension** /ˌæp.rɪˈhen.ʃ ən/ *noun* [U]

apprehension /ˌæp.rɪˈhen.ʃ ən/ *noun* [U] anxiety about the future or a fear that something unpleasant is going to happen: *It's normal to feel a little apprehension before starting a new job.* ○ *There is some apprehension in the office about who the new director will be.*

apprehensive /ˌæp.rɪˈhent.sɪv/ *adj* feeling anxious about something that you are going to do: *I'm a bit apprehensive about tomorrow's meeting.* ○ *I've invited a lot of people to the party, but I'm a bit apprehensive that no one will come.* **apprehensively** /ˌæp.rɪˈhent.sɪv.li/ *adv: They looked at each other apprehensively.*

apprentice /əˈpren.tɪs/ ⓤ /-t̬ɪs/ *noun* [C] someone who has agreed to work for a skilled person for a particular period of time and often for low payment, in order to learn that person's skills: *Most of the work was done by apprentices.* ○ *an apprentice carpenter*

apprentice /əˈpren.tɪs/ ⓤ /-t̬ɪs/ *verb* [T usually passive] *OLD USE* to make someone an apprentice: *Michelangelo was apprenticed to Ghirlandaio in Florence for three years.*

apprenticeship /əˈpren.tɪs.ʃɪp/ ⓤ /-t̬ɪs-/ *noun* [C or U] a period of time working as an apprentice

apprise /əˈpraɪz/ *verb* [T] *FORMAL* to inform: *The President has been apprised of the situation.*

approach COME NEAR /əˈprəʊtʃ/ ⓤ /-ˈproʊtʃ/ *verb* [I or T] to come near or nearer to something or someone in space, time, quality or amount: *We could just see the train approaching in the distance.* ○ *If you look out of the window on the left of the bus, you'll see that we're now approaching the Tower of London.* ○ *I see it's approaching lunchtime, so let's take a break.* ○ *In my opinion, no other composers even begin to approach (= come near in quality to) Mozart.* ○ *The total amount raised so far is approaching (= almost) $1000.* ○ *He's very active for a man approaching 80 (= who is almost 80 years old).*

approach /əˈprəʊtʃ/ ⓤ /-ˈproʊtʃ/ *noun* [C or U] *The siren signalled the approach of an ambulance (= that it was getting nearer).* ○ *Many kinds of birds fly south at the approach of winter (= as winter gets nearer).* ○ *Please fasten your seat belts, the plane is now making its final approach (in)to (= is coming near to and preparing to land at) Heathrow.* ○ *We got stuck in a traffic jam on the approach road.*

• **the closest/nearest approach to sth** *MAINLY UK* the most similar thing to something else that is mentioned: *That's the nearest approach to an apology you're going to get from Paula.*

approachable /əˈprəʊ.tʃə.bl̩/ ⓤ /-ˈproʊ-/ *adj* If a place is approachable, you can reach it or get near to it: *It's one of the few lakeside villages approachable by car.*

COMMON LEARNER ERROR

approach

The verb **approach** is not normally followed by a preposition.

He approached the door.

He approached to the door.

---

approach COMMUNICATE /əˈprəʊtʃ/ ⓤ /-ˈproʊtʃ/ *verb* [T] to speak, write or visit someone in order to do something such as make a request or business agreement: *We've just approached the bank **for/about** a loan.* ○ *She's been approached by a modelling agency.*

approach /əˈprəʊtʃ/ ⓤ /-ˈproʊtʃ/ *noun* [C] an act of communicating with another person or group in order to ask for something: *The hospital is **making approaches to** local businesses* (= asking them to help) *in their bid to raise money.* ○ *I hear that Everton have **made an approach to*** (= an attempt to make a business arrangement with) *Arsenal to buy one of their players.*

approachable /əˈprəʊ.tʃə.bļ/ ⓤ /-ˈproʊ-/ *adj* friendly and easy to talk to: *Graham's always very approachable – why don't you talk the problem over with him?* ✳ NOTE: The opposite is **unapproachable**.

approach DEAL WITH /əˈprəʊtʃ/ ⓤ /-ˈproʊtʃ/ *verb* [T] to deal with something: *I'm not sure how to approach the problem.*

approach /əˈprəʊtʃ/ ⓤ /-ˈproʊtʃ/ *noun* [C] a way of considering something: *Since our research so far has not produced any answers to this problem, we need to **adopt** a different **approach to** it.* ○ *I've just read an interesting book which has a new **approach to** Shakespeare.* ○ *Michael is always very logical **in** his approach.*

approbation /ˌæp.rəʊˈbeɪ.ʃ^ən/ *noun* [U] *FORMAL* approval or agreement, often given by an official group; praise: *The council has finally indicated its approbation of the plans.*

appropriate SUITABLE /əˈprəʊ.pri.ət/ ⓤ /-ˈproʊ-/ *adj* suitable or right for a particular situation or occasion: *appropriate footwear for the country* ○ *Is this film appropriate **for** small children?* ○ *I didn't think his comments were very appropriate at the time.* ○ *Is this an appropriate occasion to discuss finance?* ○ *Please complete the appropriate parts of this form* (= the parts that are right or necessary for your particular situation) *and return it as soon as possible.* ✳ NOTE: The opposite is **inappropriate**. **appropriately** /əˈprəʊ.pri.ət.li/ ⓤ /-ˈproʊ-/ *adv*: *She didn't think we were appropriately dressed for a wedding.* **appropriateness** /əˈprəʊ.pri.ət.nəs/ ⓤ /-ˈproʊ-/ *noun* [U]

appropriate TAKE /əˈprəʊ.pri.eɪt/ ⓤ /-ˈproʊ-/ *verb* [T] *FORMAL* to take something for your own use, usually without permission: *He lost his job when he was found to have appropriated some of the company's money.* **appropriation** /əˌprəʊ.priˈeɪ.ʃ^ən/ ⓤ /-ˌproʊ-/ *noun* [U]

appropriate KEEP MONEY /əˈprəʊ.pri.eɪt/ ⓤ /-ˈproʊ-/ *verb* [T] *FORMAL* to keep a sum of money to use for a particular purpose: *The government have appropriated millions of pounds **for** the project.* **appropriation** /əˌprəʊ.priˈeɪ.ʃ^ən/ ⓤ /-ˌproʊ-/ *noun* [C] *SPECIALIZED* a sum of money to be used for a particular purpose: *The committee approved an appropriation of £10 000.* **appropriations** /əˌprəʊ.priˈeɪ.ʃ^ənz/ ⓤ /-ˌproʊ-/ *plural noun*: *The foundation was promised a 7% increase to bring its appropriations to $2.07 billion.*

approve GOOD OPINION /əˈpruːv/ *verb* [I] to have a positive opinion of someone or something: *She doesn't approve **of** my friends.* ○ *He doesn't approve **of** smok**ing**.* ○ *I thoroughly approve **of** what the government is doing.* ✳ NOTE: The opposite is **disapprove**.

approval /əˈpruː.v^əl/ *noun* [U] when you have a positive opinion of someone or something: *He showed his approval by smiling broadly.* ○ *Alan is someone who always needs the approval of other people.* ○ *Sam always tried hard to **win** his father's approval.* ○ *FORMAL Does the wine **meet with your** approval* (= Do you like the wine)?

● **on approval** If you buy something on approval, you can return it without payment if it is not satisfactory.

approving /əˈpruː.vɪŋ/ *adj* showing that you have a positive opinion about something or someone: *She gave him an approving smile.* **approvingly** /əˈpruː.vɪŋ.li/ *adv*: *She smiled at him approvingly.*

COMMON LEARNER ERROR

approve

If you are using **approve** to say that you think something is good, then you cannot say that you 'approve something'. You have to say that you 'approve **of** something'.

He doesn't approve his brother's behaviour.

He doesn't approve of his brother's behaviour.

---

approve PERMIT /əˈpruːv/ *verb* [T] to accept, permit or officially agree to something: *We had to wait months for the council to approve our plans to extend the house.* ○ *The court approved the sale of the property.*

approval /əˈpruː.v^əl/ *noun* [U] official permission: *The project has now **received** approval from the government.* ○ *The teacher gave the student **a nod of** approval.*

approved /əˈpruːvd/ *adj* describes something that is generally or officially accepted as being correct or satisfactory: *What's the approved way of dealing with this?* ○ *This school only offers approved language courses.*

ap,proved 'school *noun* [C] *UK OLD-FASHIONED FOR* **young offenders' institution** (= a prison for young people)

approx /əˈprɒks/ ⓤ /-ˈprɑːks/ *adv ABBREVIATION FOR* **approximately**

approximate /əˈprɒk.sɪ.mət/ ⓤ /-ˈprɑːk-/ *adj* not completely accurate but close: *The train's approximate time of arrival is 10.30.* ○ *The approximate cost will be about $600.* ○ *Can you give me an approximate idea of the numbers involved?*

approximate /əˈprɒk.sɪ.meɪt/ ⓤ /-ˈprɑːk-/ *verb* [I + adv or prep; T] *FORMAL* to be almost the same as: *The newspaper reports of the discussion only **roughly** approximated **to*** (= were not exactly the same as) *what was actually said.* ○ *Student numbers this year are expected to approximate 5000* (= to be about 5000).

approximately /əˈprɒk.sɪ.mət.li/ ⓤ /-ˈprɑːk-/ *adv* close to a particular number or time although not exactly that number or time: *The job will take approximately three weeks, and cost approximately £1000.*

approximation /əˌprɒk.sɪˈmeɪ.ʃ^ən/ ⓤ /-ˌprɑːk-/ *noun* [C] *FORMAL* a guess of a number that is not exact but that is close: *Could you give me a **rough** approximation **of** how many people will be coming?* ○ *What he said bore no approximation **to** the truth* (= was not at all like the truth).

appurtenance /əˈpɜː.tɪ.nənts/ ⓤ /-ˈpɝː.ţɪ-/ *noun* [C usually pl] *FORMAL* a possession or piece of property that is considered to be a typical feature of a particular way of living: *Books and CDs are among the appurtenances **of** student life.*

APR /ˌeɪ.piːˈɑːr/ ⓤ /-ˈɑːr/ *noun* [S] *ABBREVIATION FOR* Annual Percentage Rate: the rate at which someone who borrows money is charged, calculated over a period of twelve months: *The interest rate on my credit card is currently 25.5% APR.*

après-ski /ˌæp.reɪˈskiː/ *noun* [U] social activities which take place in the evening at hotels and restaurants in places where people go to ski: *après-ski entertainment*

apricot FRUIT /ˈeɪ.prɪ.kɒt/ ⓤ /-kɑːt/ *noun* [C] a small round soft fruit with a pale orange furry skin ⊃See picture **Fruit** on page Centre 1

apricot COLOUR /ˈeɪ.prɪ.kɒt/ ⓤ /-kɑːt/ *noun* [U] pale orange

April /ˈeɪ.prəl/ *noun* [C or U] (*WRITTEN ABBREVIATION* **Apr**) the fourth month of the year, after March and before May: *20(th) April/April 20(th)* ○ *The meeting is **on** the fourth of April/April the fourth/(MAINLY US) April fourth* ○ *I did a course in London **last** April/I'm doing a course in London **next** April.* ○ *We came back **in** April.* ○ *This has been one of the driest Aprils for years.*

April 'fool *noun* **1** [C usually sing] a trick played on someone on April Fools' Day, or the person who is tricked **2** *UK* (*US* **April fools!**) said on April Fools' Day

when you have tricked someone

April Fool's Day /ˌeɪ.prəlˈfuːlz.deɪ/ (*UK ALSO* **All Fools' Day**) 1 April, a day when people play tricks on people, then say (*UK*) 'April fool!' (*US*) 'April fools!'

a priori /ˌeɪ.praɪˈɔː.raɪ/ /-priːˈɔː.ri/ /-ˈɔːr.aɪ/ *adj* [before n], *adv FORMAL* relating to an argument that suggests the probable effects of a known cause, or using general principles to suggest likely effects: *"It's freezing outside, you must be cold" is an example of a priori reasoning.*

apron CLOTHING /ˈeɪ.prən/ *noun* [C] a piece of clothing that you wear over the front of other clothes to keep the clothes clean while you are doing something dirty, such as cooking or cleaning in the house

apron AIRPORT /ˈeɪ.prən/ *noun* [C] the part of an airport in which aircraft are turned around or loaded

apron THEATRE /ˈeɪ.prən/ *noun* [C] (*ALSO* **apron stage**) part of a stage in a theatre that is in front of the curtain

apropos RELATED /ˌæp.rəˈpəʊ/ /-ˈpoʊ/ *adv, prep FORMAL* used to introduce something which is related to or connected with something that has just been said: *I had a letter from Sally yesterday – apropos (of) which, did you send her that article?* ○ *Apropos what you said yesterday, I think you made the right decision.*

apropos SUITABLE /ˌæp.rəˈpəʊ/ /-ˈpoʊ/ *adj* [after v] *FORMAL* suitable in a particular situation or at a particular time: *clothes which are apropos to the occasion*

apse /æps/ *noun* [C] *SPECIALIZED* the rounded or many-sided end of especially the east end of a church

apt SUITABLE /æpt/ *adj* suitable or right for a particular situation: *an apt comment/description* **aptly** /ˈæpt.li/ *adv*: *We spent a week at the aptly named Grand View Hotel.* **aptness** /ˈæpt.nəs/ *noun* [U] *FORMAL*

apt LIKELY /æpt/ *adj* **be apt to do** *sth*/**be apt to be** *sth* to be likely to do something or to often do something: *The kitchen roof is apt to* (= be likely to) *leak when it rains.* ○ *She's in her eighties now and apt to be a bit forgetful.*

apt CLEVER /æpt/ *adj FORMAL* having a natural ability or skill; clever: *We have some particularly apt students in the class this year.* **aptness** /ˈæpt.nəs/ *noun* [U] *OLD-FASHIONED FORMAL an aptness for/at drawing*

aptitude /ˈæp.tɪ.tjuːd/ /-tuːd/ *noun* [C or U] a natural ability or skill: *My son has no/little aptitude for sport.* ○ *We will take your personal aptitudes and abilities into account.*

aptitude ˌtest *noun* [C] a test to find out whether someone has a natural ability for a particular type of work: *I had to take an aptitude test before I began training as a nurse.*

aqua /ˈæk.wə/ *noun* [U] **1** *UK SPECIALIZED* water, when it is used in make-up and beauty products **2** *US* a greenish-blue colour

aqua-aerobics /ˌæk.wə.eəˈrəʊ.bɪks/ /-erˈoʊ-/ *noun* [U] (*ALSO* **aquaerobics**) exercises performed to music in a swimming pool, usually in an organized group: *an aqua-aerobics class*

Aqua-Lung /ˈæk.wə.lʌŋ/ *noun* [C] *TRADEMARK* a container of air which someone carries on their back while swimming under the water, which has a tube taking air to their mouth or nose to allow them to breathe

aquamarine STONE /ˌæk.wə.məˈriːn/ *noun* [C or U] a greenish-blue stone used in jewellery

aquamarine COLOUR /ˌæk.wə.məˈriːn/ *noun* [U] greenish blue

aquaplane *UK* /ˈæk.wə.pleɪn/ *verb* [I] (*US* **hydroplane**) If a motor vehicle aquaplanes, it slides out of control on a wet road.

aquarium /əˈkweə.ri.əm/ /-ˈkwer.i-/ *noun* [C] *plural* **aquariums** or **aquaria 1** a glass container in which fish and other water animals can be kept **2** a building, usually open to the public, which holds many aquariums

Aquarius /əˈkweə.ri.əs/ /-ˈkwer.i-/ *noun* [C or U] the eleventh sign of the zodiac, relating to the period 21 January to 19 February, or a person born during this period **Aquarian** /əˈkweə.ri.ən/ /-ˈkwer.i-/ *noun* [C], *adj*

aquatic /əˈkwæt.ɪk/ /-ˈkwæt̬-/ *adj* living or growing in, happening in, or connected with water: *aquatic plants* ○ *aquatic sports* **aquatically** /əˈkwæt.ɪ.kli/ /-ˈkwæt̬-/ *adv*

aquatint /ˈæk.wə.tɪnt/ *noun* [C] a picture produced by cutting it into a copper sheet with acid and then printing it: *an aquatint by Picasso*

aqueduct /ˈæk.wɪ.dʌkt/ *noun* [C] a structure for carrying water across land, especially one that looks like a high bridge with many arches, which carries pipes or a canal across a valley

aqueous /ˈeɪ.kwi.əs/ *adj SPECIALIZED* like or containing water: *an aqueous solution*

aquiline /ˈæk.wɪ.laɪn/ *adj LITERARY* of or like an eagle: *an aquiline nose* (= a nose curved like an eagle's beak) ○ *aquiline features* (= a face with this type of nose)

Arab /ˈær.əb/ /ˈer-/ *noun* [C] a person from the Middle East or North Africa who speaks Arabic as a first language **Arab** /ˈær.əb/ /ˈer-/ *adj*: *The Arab countries include Iraq, Saudi Arabia, Syria and Egypt.* **Arabian** /əˈreɪ.bi.ən/ *adj*: *the Arabian peninsula*

Arabic /ˈær.ə.bɪk/ /ˈer-/ *noun* [U] the language of the people of the Middle East and North Africa: *There are many regional types of Arabic.* **Arabic** /ˈær.ə.bɪk/ /ˈer-/ *adj*

arabesque POSITION /ˌær.əˈbesk/ /ˌer-/ *noun* [C] a position in ballet dancing in which the dancer stands on one leg with the other leg held out straight behind

arabesque ART /ˌær.əˈbesk/ /ˌer-/ *noun* [C or U] a type of decoration based on flowers, leaves and branches which are often twisted together, found especially in Islamic art

Arabic ˈnumeral *noun* [C usually pl] a symbol used for writing a number in many parts of the world: *1 and 2 are Arabic numerals, I and II are Roman numerals.* ⊃Compare **Roman numeral**.

arable /ˈær.ə.bl̩/ /ˈer-/ *adj* describes farming and farm land that is used for, or is suitable for, growing crops: *arable farming/farmers/farms/land*

arachnid /əˈræk.nɪd/ *noun* [C] *SPECIALIZED* any of a group of small animals, similar to insects but with four pairs of legs, which include spiders, SCORPIONS, TICKS and MITES

arachnophobia /əˌræk.nəˌfəʊ.bi.ə/ /-ˌfoʊ-/ *noun* [U] *SPECIALIZED* a very strong fear of spiders

arbiter /ˈɑː.bɪ.tər/ /ˈɑːr.bɪ.tɚ/ *noun* [C] someone who makes a judgment or solves an argument or decides what will be done: *the arbiters of fashion/taste* ○ *The government will be the final arbiter in the dispute over the new road.*

arbitrage /ˌɑː.bɪˈtrɑːʒ/ /ˈɑːr.bɪ.trɑːʒ/ *noun* [U] *SPECIALIZED* the method on the STOCK EXCHANGE of buying something in one place and selling it in another place at the same time, in order to make a profit from the difference in price in the two places

arbitrageur /ˌɑː.bɪ.trɑːˈʒɜːʳ/ /ˈɑːr.bɪ.trɑː.ʒɚ/ *noun* [C] *SPECIALIZED* a person who makes money from arbitrage

arbitrary CHANCE /ˈɑː.bɪ.trə.ri/ /ˈɑːr.bə.trer-/ *adj* based on chance rather than being planned or based on reason: *arbitrary decision-making* ○ *What guided your choice of destination or was it arbitrary?* **arbitrarily** /ˌɑː.bɪˈtreə.rɪ.li/ /ˌɑːr.bɪˈtrer.ɪ-/ *adv*: *We made the decision to go to Italy quite arbitrarily.* **arbitrariness** /ˈɑː.bɪ.trə.rɪ.nəs/ /ˈɑːr.bɪ.trer.ɪ-/ *noun* [U]

arbitrary UNFAIR /ˈɑː.bɪ.trə.ri/ /ˈɑːr.bə.trer-/ *adj DISAPPROVING* using unlimited personal power without considering other people's wishes: *an arbitrary ruler* ○ *The company has been the subject of an arbitrary take-over.*

arbitrate /ˈɑː.bɪ.treɪt/ /ˈɑːr-/ *verb* [I or T] to make a judgment in an argument, usually because asked to do so by those involved: *I've been asked to arbitrate between the opposing sides.* ○ *An outside adviser has been brought in to arbitrate the dispute between the management and the union.*

arbitration /ˌɑː.bɪˈtreɪ.ʃᵊn/ /ˌɑːr-/ *noun* [U] *Both sides in the dispute have agreed to go to arbitration* (= to have the disagreement solved by an outside person who has been chosen by both sides).

arbitrator /ˈɑː.bɪ.treɪ.təʳ/ /ˈɑːr.bɪ.treɪ.t̬ɚ/ *noun* [C] a person who has been officially chosen to make a decision between two people or groups who do not agree

arboreal /ɑːˈbɔː.ri.əl/ /ɑːrˈbɔːr.i-/ *adj SPECIALIZED* of or living in trees: *arboreal animals* ○ *Many people believe that humans evolved from arboreal ancestors.*

A

arbour *UK, US* **arbor** /ˈɑː.bəʳ/ ⓤ /ˈɑːr.bɚ/ *noun* [C] a sheltered place in a garden formed by trees and bushes which are grown to partly enclose it: *a rose arbour*

arc ⎡CURVE⎤ /ɑːk/ ⓤ /ɑːrk/ *noun* [C] the shape of part of a circle, or other curved line: *The ball rose **in** a high arc and fell behind the boundary line.*

arc /ɑːk/ ⓤ /ɑːrk/ *verb* [I] to move in the shape of an arc: *The rocket arced gracefully into the sky.*

arc ⎡ELECTRICAL FLOW⎤ /ɑːk/ ⓤ /ɑːrk/ *noun* [C] a powerful flow of electricity which goes across a space between two points

arc /ɑːk/ ⓤ /ɑːrk/ *verb* [I usually + adv or prep] to make an electric arc

arcade /ɑːˈkeɪd/ ⓤ /ɑːr-/ *noun* [C] a covered area or passage in which there are shops, or a covered passage joined to a building on one side and with columns and arches along the other side: *a shopping arcade*

Arcadia /ɑːˈkeɪ.di.ə/ ⓤ /ɑːr-/ *noun* [S] *LITERARY* a representation of life in the countryside believed to be perfect **Arcadian** /ɑːˈkeɪ.di.ən/ ⓤ /ɑːr-/ *adj*

arcane /ɑːˈkeɪn/ ⓤ /ɑːr-/ *adj FORMAL* mysterious and known only by a few people: *He was the only person who understood all the arcane details of the agreement.* ○ *This argument may seem arcane to those not closely involved in the world of finance.*

arch ⎡CURVED STRUCTURE⎤ /ɑːtʃ/ ⓤ /ɑːrtʃ/ *noun* [C] **1** a structure consisting of a curved top on two supports, which holds the weight of something above it: *In many churches the side aisles are separated from the central aisle by a row of arches.* ○ *Passing through the arch, you enter an open courtyard.* ➷See also **archway**. **2** something that has the shape of this structure, often used for decoration **3** the raised curve on the bottom of your foot: *She's got very high arches.* ➷See picture **The Body** on page Centre 5

arch /ɑːtʃ/ ⓤ /ɑːrtʃ/ *verb* [I or T] to make the shape of an arch: *Trees arch **over** the river.* ○ *Her eyebrows arched in contempt.* ○ *She watched the cat arch its **back**.*

arched /ɑːtʃt/ ⓤ /ɑːrtʃt/ *adj*: *The entrance to the cathedral is through an arched door* (= a door with a curved structure surrounding it).

arch ⎡NOT SERIOUS⎤ /ɑːtʃ/ ⓤ /ɑːrtʃ/ *adj* describes behaviour that is not serious and suggests you are behaving this way intentionally for the effect that it will have: *an arch tone of voice* **archly** /ˈɑːtʃ.li/ ⓤ /ˈɑːrtʃ-/ *adv*: *She smiled archly at him.* ○ *"I fail to understand what you're suggesting," said Clare archly.*

arch- ⎡MAIN⎤ /ɑːtʃ-/ ⓤ /ɑːrtʃ-/ *prefix* most important: *an archbishop* ○ *an archduke*

arch- ⎡EXTREME⎤ /ɑːtʃ-/ ⓤ /ɑːrtʃ-/ *prefix* greater or especially worse than others of the same type: *an arch-criminal* ○ *his arch-enemy* ○ *He's always been an arch-opponent of the scheme.*

archaeology, *US ALSO* **archeology** /ˌɑː.kiˈɒl.ə.dʒi/ ⓤ /ˌɑːr.kiˈɑː.lə-/ *noun* [U] the study of the buildings, graves, tools and other objects which belonged to people who lived in the past, in order to learn about their culture and society **archaeological**, *US ALSO* **archeological** /ˌɑː.ki.əˈlɒdʒ.ɪ.kəl/ ⓤ /ˌɑːr.ki.əˈlɑː.dʒɪ-/ *adj*: *an archaeological dig/excavation* ○ *an area/site of archaeological interest* **archaeologically**, *US ALSO* **archeologically** /ˌɑː.ki.əˈlɒdʒ.ɪ.kli/ ⓤ /ˌɑːr.ki.əˈlɑː.dʒɪ-/ *adv*

archaeologist, *MAINLY US* **archeologist** /ˌɑː.kiˈɒl.ə.dʒɪst/ ⓤ /ˌɑːr.kiˈɑː.lə-/ *noun* someone who studies the buildings, graves, tools and other objects of people who lived in the past

archaic /ɑːˈkeɪ.ɪk/ ⓤ /ɑːr-/ *adj* of or belonging to the distant past; from an ancient period in history: *an archaic system of government* ○ *an archaic law/rule/language* **archaically** /ɑːˈkeɪ.ɪ.kli/ ⓤ /ɑːr-/ *adv*

archaism /ɑːˈkeɪ.ɪ.zᵊm/ ⓤ /ɑːr-/ *noun* [C] *SPECIALIZED* a word or expression that is not generally used any more

archangel /ˈɑːkˌeɪn.dʒᵊl/ ⓤ /ˈɑːrk-/ /ˈ-,--/ *noun* [C] an ANGEL of high rank: *the Archangel Gabriel*

archbishop /ˌɑːtʃˈbɪʃ.əp/ ⓤ /ˌɑːrtʃ-/ /ˈ-,--/ *noun* [C] a bishop of the highest rank who is in charge of churches and other bishops in a particular large area: *The Arch-*

bishop of Canterbury holds the highest position in the Church of England.

archbishopric /ˌɑːtʃˈbɪʃ.ə.prɪk/ ⓤ /ˌɑːrtʃ-/ *noun* [C] **1** the period of time during which a person serves as an archbishop **2** the area of which an archbishop is in charge

archdeacon /ˌɑːtʃˈdiː.kən/ ⓤ /ˌɑːrtʃ-/ /ˈ-,--/ *noun* [C] in the ANGLICAN (= Church of England) church, a priest next in rank below a bishop

archdiocese /ˌɑːtʃˈdaɪə.sɪs/ ⓤ /ˌɑːrtʃ-/ *noun* [C] the area of which an ARCHBISHOP in some Christian churches is in charge

archduke /ˌɑːtʃˈdjuːk/ ⓤ /ˌɑːrtʃˈduːk/ *noun* [C] a man of the highest rank, especially in the past in the Austrian royal family: *The assassination of the Archduke Ferdinand started off the first World War.*

arch-enemy /ˌɑːtʃˈen.ɪ.mi/ ⓤ /ˌɑːrtʃ-/ *noun* [C] an especially bad enemy

archeology /ˌɑː.kiˈɒl.ə.dʒi/ ⓤ /ˌɑːr.kiˈɑː.lə-/ *noun* [U] *MAINLY US FOR* **archaeology**

archer /ˈɑː.tʃəʳ/ ⓤ /ˈɑːr.tʃɚ/ *noun* [C] a person who shoots arrows from a bow for sport or, in the past, as a weapon **archery** /ˈɑː.tʃə.ri/ ⓤ /ˈɑːr.tʃɚ.i/ *noun* [U] the art or sport of shooting arrows ➷See picture **Sports** on page Centre 10

archetype /ˈɑː.kɪ.taɪp/ ⓤ /ˈɑːr-/ *noun* [C] a typical example of something; the original model of something from which others are copied: *The United States is **the** archetype **of** a federal society.* **archetypal** /ˌɑː.kɪˈtaɪ.pᵊl/ ⓤ /ˌɑːr-/ /ˈ-,--/ *adj* (*ALSO* **archetypical**) *an archetypal English gentleman* **archetypically** /ˌɑː.kɪˈtɪp.ɪ.kli/ ⓤ /ˌɑːr-/ *adv*

archipelago /ˌɑː.kɪˈpel.ə.gəʊ/ ⓤ /ˌɑːr.kɪˈpel.ə.goʊ/ *noun* [C] *plural* **archipelagos** or **archipelagoes** a group of small islands or an area of sea in which there are many small islands: *the Hawaiian archipelago*

architect /ˈɑː.kɪ.tekt/ ⓤ /ˈɑːr-/ *noun* [C] **1** a person whose job is to design new buildings and make certain that they are built correctly **2** a person responsible for completing a particular plan or aim: *Bevan was the architect of the British National Health Service.*

architecture /ˈɑː.kɪ.tek.tʃəʳ/ ⓤ /ˈɑːr.kɪ.tek.tʃɚ/ *noun* [U] **1** the art and science of designing and making buildings: *to study architecture* **2** the style in which buildings are made: *Roman architecture* **architectural** /ˌɑː.kɪˈtek.tʃᵊr.ᵊl/ ⓤ /ˌɑːr.kɪˈtek.tʃɚ-/ *adj*: *architectural drawings/plans* ○ *a building of architectural interest* **architecturally** /ˌɑː.kɪˈtek.tʃᵊr.ᵊl.i/ ⓤ /ˌɑːr.kɪˈtek.tʃɚ-/ *adv*

archive /ˈɑː.kaɪv/ ⓤ /ˈɑːr-/ *noun* [C] **1** (*ALSO* **archives**) a collection of historical records relating to a place, organization or family: *archive film/footage/material* ○ *These old photographs should go in the family archives.* **2** (*ALSO* **archives**) a place where historical records are kept: *I've been studying village records in the local archive.* **3** a computer FILE used to store electronic information or documents that you no longer need to use regularly

archive /ˈɑː.kaɪv/ ⓤ /ˈɑːr-/ *verb* [T] **1** to store historical records or documents in an archive **2** in computing, to store electronic information that you no longer need to use regularly: *This software helps firms archive and retrieve emails.* **archival** /ˈɑː.kaɪ.vᵊl/ ⓤ /ɑːr-/ *adj*

archivist /ˈɑː.kɪ.vɪst/ ⓤ /ˈɑːr-/ *noun* [C] a person whose job is to take care of archives

archly /ɑːtʃ.li/ ⓤ /ɑːrtʃ-/ *adv* ➷See at **arch** NOT SERIOUS

archway /ˈɑːtʃ.weɪ/ ⓤ /ˈɑːrtʃ-/ *noun* [C] an entrance or passage formed by an arch

ˈarc ˌlamp *noun* [C] (*ALSO* **arc light**) a device which gives light produced by an electric arc

the ˈArctic *noun* [S] the most northern part of the world, which is very cold: *Polar bears live in the Arctic.* **Arctic** /ˈɑːk.tɪk/ ⓤ /ˈɑːrk-/ *adj*: *No trees grow in the Arctic regions.* ○ *FIGURATIVE The North of England has been experiencing Arctic* (= very cold) *conditions these past few days.*

the ˌArctic ˈCircle *noun* [S] an imaginary line around the Earth at approximately 70° North

ˈarc ˌwelding *noun* [U] the joining together of pieces of metal using an electric arc

ardent /ˈɑː.dᵊnt/ [US] /ˈɑːr-/ *adj* **[before n]** showing strong feelings: *an ardent supporter of Manchester United* ○ *an ardent feminist* **ardently** /ˈɑː.dᵊnt.li/ [US] /ˈɑːr-/ *adv*

ardour *UK*, *US* **ardor** /ˈɑː.dəʳ/ [US] /ˈɑːr.dɚ/ *noun* **[U]** great enthusiasm or love: *His ardour* ***for*** *her cooled after only a few weeks.*

arduous /ˈɑː.dju.əs/ [US] /ˈɑːr.dʒu-/ *adj* difficult, tiring and needing a lot of effort: *an arduous climb/task/journey* **arduously** /ˈɑː.dju.ə.sli/ [US] /ˈɑːr.dʒu-/ *adv* **arduousness** /ˈɑː.dju.ə.snəs/ [US] /ˈɑːr.dʒu-/ *noun* **[U]**

are *STRONG* /ɑːʳ/ [US] /ɑːr/, *WEAK* /əʳ/ [US] /ɚ/ *we/you/they form of* **be**: *Are you hungry?* ○ *They're* (= They are) *very late.*

area [PLACE] /ˈeə.ri.ə/ [US] /ˈer.i-/ *noun* **[C]** a particular part of a place, piece of land or country: *All areas* ***of*** *the country will have some rain tonight.* ○ *The area* ***of*** *New York to the south of Houston Street is known as Soho.* ○ *Houses in* ***the*** *London area* (= in and around London) *are very expensive.* ○ *He's an area manager* (= is responsible for business in a particular part of the country or world) *for a computer company.* ○ *This is a very poor area* (= part of the town, country or world). ○ *Dogs are not allowed in the children's play area.*
• **in the area/region of** approximately: *The repair work will cost in the area of £200.*

area [MEASURE] /ˈeə.ri.ə/ [US] /ˈer.i-/ *noun* **[C or U]** the size of a flat surface calculated by multiplying its length by its width: *the area of a rectangle* ○ *Meadow Farm is 50 square kilometres* ***in*** *area.*

area [SUBJECT] /ˈeə.ri.ə/ [US] /ˈer.i-/ *noun* **[C]** a subject or activity, or a part of it: *Marketing is Paul's area.* ○ *Software is not really my area of expertise.*

ˈarea ˌcode *noun* **[C]** a **dialling code**

arena /əˈriː.nə/ *noun* **[C]** **1** a large flat enclosed area used for sports or entertainment: *an Olympic/a sports arena* **2** an activity that involves argument and discussion: *After 30 years in the political arena, our local member of parliament is retiring next year.*

aren't /ɑːnt/ [US] /ɑːrnt/ *short form of* **1** are not: *The boys aren't going to the party.* **2** am not, used in questions: *I'm late again, aren't I?*

argon /ˈɑː.gɒn/ [US] /ˈɑːr.gɑːn/ *noun* **[U]** a gas which is found in the air and is sometimes used to make electric lights

argot /ˈɑː.gəʊ/ [US] /ˈɑːr.goʊ/ *noun* **[C or U]** words and expressions which are used by small groups of people and which are not easily understood by other people: *thieves' argot*

arguable /ˈɑːg.ju.ə.bl̩/ [US] /ˈɑːrg-/ *adj* If something is arguable, there could be some disagreement about it: *It is arguable which way is quicker.*
• **It is arguable that...** it is possibly true that: *It is arguable that the government has failed in this respect.*
arguably /ˈɑːg.ju.ə.bli/ [US] /ˈɑːrg-/ *adv* possibly: *He is arguably the world's best football player.* ○ *Arguably, the drug should not have been made available before it had been thoroughly tested.*

argue [DISAGREE] /ˈɑːg.juː/ [US] /ˈɑːrg-/ *verb* **[I]** to speak angrily to someone, telling them that you disagree with them: *The children are always arguing.* ○ *Kids, will you stop arguing* ***with*** *each other?* ○ *They were arguing* ***over/about*** *which film to go and see.*

argue [REASON] /ˈɑːg.juː/ [US] /ˈɑːrg-/ *verb* **[I or T]** to give the reasons for your opinion, idea, belief, etc: *The minister argued* ***for/in favour of/against*** *making cuts in military spending.* ○ **[+ that]** *The minister argued* ***that*** *cuts in military spending were needed.* ○ *You can argue the* ***case*** *either way.* ➲See also **well-argued**.
• **argue the toss** *UK INFORMAL DISAPPROVING* to disagree with a decision or statement: *It doesn't matter what you say, he'll always argue the toss!*

argue [SHOW] /ˈɑːg.juː/ [US] /ˈɑːrg-/ *verb* **[T]** to show that something is true or exists: *The evidence argues a change in policy.*

argument [DISAGREEMENT] /ˈɑːg.jʊ.mənt/ [US] /ˈɑːrg-/ *noun* **[C or U]** a disagreement, or the process of disagreeing: *The children* ***had*** *an argument* ***about/over*** *what game to play.* ○ *He* ***got into an*** *argument* ***with*** *Jeff in the pub last night.* ○ *A decision was finally made after some* ***heated*** *argument.*

argumentative /ˌɑːg.jʊˈmen.tə.tɪv/ [US] /ˌɑːrg.jʊˈmen.t̬ə.t̬ɪv/ *adj DISAPPROVING* often arguing or wanting to argue: *Don't be so argumentative.* **argumentatively** /ˌɑːg.jʊˈmen.tə.tɪv.li/ [US] /ˌɑːrg.jʊˈmen.t̬ə.t̬ɪv-/ *adv*

argument [REASON] /ˈɑːg.jʊ.mənt/ [US] /ˈɑːrg-/ *noun* **[C or U]** a reason or reasons why you support or oppose an idea or suggestion, or the process of explaining them: *Now that we've heard all the arguments* ***for*** *and* ***against*** *the proposal, shall we vote on it?* ○ **[+ that]** *Her husband was not convinced by her argument* ***that*** *they needed a bigger house.* ○ *I don't think that's a very* ***strong/convincing/powerful*** *argument.* ○ *The central argument* (= main point) ***of*** *the book is that some of the plays were not written by Shakespeare.* ○ *They were engaged in argument for hours.*

argy-bargy, **argie-bargie** /ˌɑː.dʒiˈbɑː.dʒi/ [US] /ˌɑːr.dʒiˈbɑːr-/ *noun* **[U]** *UK INFORMAL* loud argument or disagreement which is not usually serious: *Did you hear all that argy-bargy last night?*

aria /ˈɑː.ri.ə/ [US] /ˈɑːr.i-/ *noun* **[C]** a song sung by one person in an opera

-arian /-eə.ri.ən/ [US] /-er.i-/ *suffix* (a person who has) a connection with or belief in the stated subject: *a librarian* (= person who works in a library) ○ *a vegetarian* (= a person who does not eat meat) ○ *humanitarian aid* (= help for injured, ill or hungry people)

arid /ˈær.ɪd/ [US] /ˈer-/ *adj* **1** very dry and without enough rain for plants: *The desert is so arid that nothing can grow there.* **2** *FORMAL* unsuccessful: *After several arid years, the company has started to become successful.* **3** *FORMAL* not interesting and lacking in imagination: *I found his writing extremely arid.*

Aries /ˈeə.riːz/ [US] /ˈer.iːz/ *noun* **[C or U]** the first sign of the zodiac, relating to the period 21 March to 20 April, represented by a RAM, or a person born during this period

aright /əˈraɪt/ *adv OLD USE OR LITERARY* correctly: *Did I* ***hear/understand*** *you aright?*

arise [HAPPEN] /əˈraɪz/ *verb* **[I]** **arose, arisen** *FORMAL* to happen: *Should the* ***opportunity*** *arise, I'd love to go to China.* ○ *Could you work on Saturday, should the* ***need*** *arise* (= if it were to be necessary)? ○ *Are there any* ***matters arising from*** (= caused by) *the last meeting?*

arise [GET UP] /əˈraɪz/ *verb* **[I]** **arose, arisen** *LITERARY* to get out of bed: *We arose early on Christmas morning.*

the aristocracy /ðiˌær.ɪˈstɒk.rə.si/ [US] /-ˌer.ɪˈstɑː.krə-/ *group noun* **[C]** a class of people who hold high social rank: *members of the aristocracy*
aristocrat /ˈær.ɪ.stə.kræt/ [US] /ˈer-/ *noun* **[C]** *Many aristocrats* (= members of the aristocracy) *were killed in the French Revolution.* **aristocratic** /ˌær.ɪ.stəˈkræt.ɪk/ [US] /ˌer.ɪ.stəˈkræt̬-/ *adj*: *an aristocratic family*

arithmetic /əˈrɪθ.mə.tɪk/ [US] /-t̬ɪk/ *noun* **[U]** **1** the part of mathematics that involves the adding and multiplying, etc. of numbers: *I've never been very good at arithmetic.* ○ *an arithmetic test* **2** calculations involving adding and multiplying, etc. numbers: *I did some quick* ***mental*** *arithmetic and decided it was going to cost too much.* ○ *I can't work out which of these packets of washing powder is cheaper – could you* ***do the*** *arithmetic for me?*
arithmetical /ˌær.ɪθˈmet.ɪ.kᵊl/ [US] /ˌer.ɪθˈmet̬-/ *adj* (*ALSO* **arithmetic**) *arithmetical problems* **arithmetically** /ˌær.ɪθˈmet.ɪ.kli/ [US] /ˌer.ɪθˈmet̬-/ *adv*

arithˌmetical/arithˌmetic proˈgression *noun* **[C]** a SEQUENCE (= ordered series of numbers) in which the numbers increase or decrease by the same amount, such as 3, 6, 9..., or 9, 6, 3

the ark /ðiˈɑːk/ [US] /-ˈɑːrk/ *noun* **[S]** (*ALSO* **Noah's ark**) (in the Bible) a large wooden ship built by Noah in order to save his family and a male and female of every type of animal when the world was covered by a flood
• **be/come out of the ark** *UK* to be very old-fashioned: *Her hat was straight out of the ark.*
• **went out with the ark** If an object or method went out with the ark, it has not been used for a long time.
• **the Ark of the Covenant** (in the Bible) a wooden box which contained the writings of Jewish law, and which

represented to the people of Israel the presence of God leading them

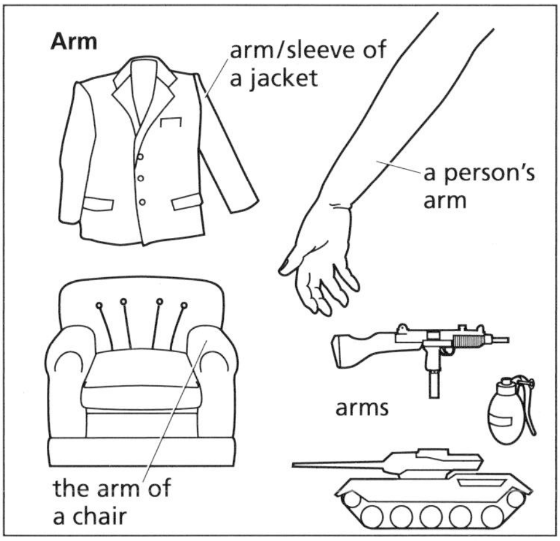

arm [BODY PART] /ɑːm/ [US] /ɑːrm/ *noun* [C] **1** either of the two long parts of the upper body which are fixed to the shoulders and have the hands at the end: *My arms ache from carrying this bag.* ○ *She* ***put/threw*** *her arms* ***round*** *me, and gave me a hug.* ○ *He* ***took/held*** *her* ***in*** *his arms* (= held her closely). ○ *Bill arrived at the party with his new girlfriend* ***on*** *his arm* (= her hand resting on his arm). ➲See picture **The Body** on page Centre 5 **2** The arm of a piece of clothing or furniture is a part of it that you put your arm in or on: *the arm of a jacket* ○ *the arm of a chair* **3** An arm of land or water is a long, thin part of it that is joined to a larger area. **4** An arm of an organization is a part of it that is responsible for a particular activity or place: *The British company is one arm of a large multinational.*

• **ˌarm in ˈarm** with your arm gently supporting or being supported by someone else's arm: *We walked arm in arm along the river bank.*

• **keep *sb* at arm's length** to not allow someone to become too friendly with you: *I always had the feeling she was keeping me at arm's length.*

• **an arm and a leg** *INFORMAL* a lot of money: *These shoes* ***cost*** *me an arm and a leg.*

arm [PROVIDE WEAPONS] /ɑːm/ [US] /ɑːrm/ *verb* **1** [I or T] to provide yourself or others with a weapon or weapons: *Nobody knows who is arming the terrorists.* ○ [R] *I armed myself* ***with*** *a baseball bat and went to investigate the noise.* ○ *They are currently arming for war.* ✻ NOTE: The opposite is **disarm**. **2** [T] to provide yourself or others with equipment or knowledge in order to complete a particular task: [R] *She armed herself* ***for*** *the interview by finding out all she could about the company in advance.* ○ *I went to the meeting armed* ***with*** *the relevant facts and figures.*

armed /ɑːmd/ [US] /ɑːrmd/ *adj* using or carrying weapons: *an armed robbery* ○ *armed conflict* ○ *These men are armed* ***and dangerous****, and should not be approached.* ✻ NOTE: The opposite is **unarmed**.

arms /ɑːmz/ [US] /ɑːrmz/ *plural noun* weapons and equipment used to kill and injure people: *They have been charged with supplying arms to the guerillas.* ○ *An arms* ***cache*** *was discovered in South Wales.* ○ *The minister has called on the terrorists to* ***lay down*** *their arms* (= stop fighting). ○ *They are willing to* ***take up*** *arms* (= prepare to fight) *(****against*** *the government) if they have to.*

• **under arms** provided with weapons and willing to fight: *The rebels now have thousands of people under arms.*

• **be up in arms** *INFORMAL* to be very angry: *They're up in arms* ***about/over*** *the new management scheme.*

armada /ɑːˈmɑː.də/ [US] /ɑːr-/ *noun* [C] a large group of war ships: *The Spanish Armada was sent by the king of Spain to invade England in 1588.*

armadillo /ˌɑː.məˈdɪl.əʊ/ [US] /ˌɑːr.məˈdɪl.oʊ/ *noun* [C] *plural* **armadillos** a small animal whose body is covered in hard strips that allow it to curl into a ball when attacked: *Armadillos range from South America to the southern part of the US.*

Armageddon /ˌɑː.məˈged.ᵊn/ [US] /ˌɑːr-/ *noun* [S or U] a final war between good and evil at the end of the world, as described in the Bible, or, more generally, any event of great destruction: *an environmental Armageddon*

armaments /ˈɑː.mə.mənts/ [US] /ˈɑːr-/ *plural noun* weapons or military equipment: *the country's armaments programme*

armament /ˈɑː.mə.mənts/ [US] /ˈɑːr-/ *noun* [U] the process of increasing the number and strength of a country's weapons: *As the country prepares for war, more and more money is being spent on armament.*

armband /ˈɑːm.bænd/ [US] /ˈɑːrm-/ *noun* **1** [C] a piece of material that a person wears around the arm as a sign of something, for example an official position: *All the stewards at the racetrack were wearing armbands.* ○ *black armbands for a funeral* **2** [C usually pl] *UK* (*US* **waterwings**) a hollow ring-shaped piece of plastic filled with air, which children who cannot swim wear on their arms in water to help them float

ˈarm ˌcandy *noun* [U] *US INFORMAL* a very attractive person who goes to social events with someone and pretends to be their romantic partner

armchair [CHAIR] /ˈɑːm.tʃeəʳ/ [US] /ˈɑːrm.tʃer/ *noun* [C] a comfortable chair with sides that support your arms: *She sat in an armchair by the fire, reading a newspaper.*

armchair [NO EXPERIENCE] /ˈɑːm.tʃeəʳ/ [US] /ˈɑːrm.tʃer/ *adj* [before n] describes a person who knows, or claims to know, a lot about a subject without having direct experience of it: *an armchair critic/gardener/traveller*

-armed /-ɑːmd/ [US] /-ɑːrmd/ *suffix* having the stated number or type of arms: *a one-armed person*

the ˌarmed ˈforces *plural noun* a country's military forces, usually an army, navy and air force

armful /ˈɑːm.fʊl/ [US] /ˈɑːrm-/ *noun* [C] the amount that a person can carry in one or both arms: *She struggled along with an armful* ***of*** *clothes.*

armhole /ˈɑːm.həʊl/ [US] /ˈɑːrm.hoʊl/ *noun* [C] an opening in a shirt, coat, etc. through which you put your arm

armistice /ˈɑː.mɪ.stɪs/ [US] /ˈɑːr-/ *noun* [S] an agreement between two countries or groups at war to stop fighting for a particular time, especially to talk about possible peace: *A two-week armistice has been* ***declared*** *between the rival factions.*

armour *UK, US* **armor** /ˈɑː.məʳ/ [US] /ˈɑːr.mɚ/ *noun* [U] **1** strong protective covering, especially for the body: *Police put on* ***body*** *armour before confronting the rioters.* ○ *In the past, knights used to wear* ***(suits of)*** *armour* (= protective covering made of metal) *in battle.* ○ *These grenades are able to pierce the armour of tanks.* **2** military vehicles that are covered in strong metal to protect them from attack: *The troops were backed by tanks, artillery and other heavy armour.*

armoured *UK, US* **armored** /ˈɑː.məd/ [US] /ˈɑːr.mɚd/ *adj* protected by a strong covering, or using military vehicles protected by strong covering: *an armoured tank* ○ *armoured troops* ○ *an armoured division* (= military group)

armourer *UK, US* **armorer** /ˈɑː.mə.rəʳ/ [US] /ˈɑːr.mɚ.ɚ/ *noun* [C] a person who makes, repairs and supplies weapons

armoury *UK, US* **armory** /ˈɑː.mə.ri/ [US] /ˈɑːr.mɚ.i/ *noun* [C] **1** all the weapons and military equipment that a country possesses: *The two countries signed an agreement to reduce their nuclear armouries.* **2** a place where weapons and other military equipment is stored: *Fighter planes have successfully bombed the enemy's main armoury.* **3** items or qualities that can be used to good effect in a particular situation: *The only weapon left in his armoury was indifference.*

ˌarmoured personˈnel ˌcarrier *noun* [C] a special vehicle covered with strong metal which is used for carrying soldiers

armour-plated /ˌɑː.məˈpleɪ.tɪd/ [US] /ˌɑːr.mɚ-/ *adj* describes something that has been covered with special protective metal

armpit /ˈɑːm.pɪt/ ⓤ /ˈɑːrm-/ *noun* [C] the hollow place under your arm where your arm joins your body: *sweaty/hairy armpits* ⊃See picture **The Body** on page Centre 5

• be the armpit of *sth* HUMOROUS to be an extremely unpleasant, often dirty, place: *the armpit of the North*

armrest /ˈɑːm.rest/ ⓤ /ˈɑːrm-/ *noun* [C] (*ALSO* **arm**) the part of a chair that supports the arm

arms /ɑːmz/ ⓤ /ɑːrmz/ *plural noun* ⊃See at **arm** PROVIDE WEAPONS

ˈarms conˌtrol *noun* [U] the limitation of the number of weapons a country is allowed to possess, usually in agreement with another country

ˈarms ˌrace *noun* [S] the situation in which two or more countries try to have more and stronger weapons than each other

arm-twisting /ˈɑːm.twɪs.tɪŋ/ ⓤ /ˈɑːrm-/ *noun* [U] the use of persuasion or threats which make it very difficult for someone to refuse to do something: *The vote was won only as the result of much arm-twisting by the government.*

ˈarm ˌwrestling *noun* [U] a game played by two people who place the ELBOWS (= the middle part of the arm where it bends) of their right arms on a table, hold hands and then try to push the other person's hand down onto the table

army /ˈɑː.mi/ ⓤ /ˈɑːr-/ *noun* **1** [C] a military force that has the training and equipment to fight on land: *Both the armies suffered heavy losses in the battle.* ○ *The minister is believed to have been killed by the rebel army.* **2** [C usually sing] a large group of people who share similar aims or beliefs: *She brought an army of supporters with her.*

army /ˈɑː.mi/ ⓤ /ˈɑːr-/ *group noun* **the army** a particular country's fighting force: *When did you join the army?* ○ *He has decided on a career in the British Army.* ○ *The army was/were called out to enforce the curfew.*

army-navy store /ˌɑː.miˈneɪ.viˌstɔːʳ/ ⓤ /ˌɑːr.miˈneɪ.viˌstɔːr/ *noun* [C] US FOR **army surplus store**

ˌarmy ˈsurplus *noun* [U] clothes and equipment that are not needed by the army, and are made available for sale to the public

ˌarmy ˈsurplus ˌstore *noun* [C] (*US USUALLY* **army-navy store**, *AUS ALSO* **army disposals store**) a shop where army surplus is sold

aroma /əˈrəʊ.mə/ ⓤ /-ˈroʊ-/ *noun* [C] a strong pleasant smell, usually from food or drink: *the aroma of freshly baked bread* ○ *a wine with a light fruity aroma*

aromatic /ˌær.əʊˈmæt.ɪk/ ⓤ /ˌer.əˈmæt̬-/ *adj* having a pleasant smell: *aromatic herbs*

aromatherapy /əˌrəʊ.məˈθer.ə.pi/ ⓤ /-ˌroʊ-/ *noun* [U] the treatment of anxiety or minor medical conditions by rubbing pleasant-smelling natural oils into the skin or breathing in their smell: *aromatherapy massage* ○ *aromatherapy oils* **aromatherapist** /əˌrəʊ.məˈθer.ə.pɪst/ ⓤ /-ˌroʊ-/ *noun* [C] *a trained aromatherapist* **aromatherapeutic** /əˌrəʊ.mə.θe.rəˈpjuː.tɪk/ ⓤ /ə-ˌroʊ.mə.θe.rəˈpjuː.tɪk/ *adj*

arose /əˈrəʊz/ ⓤ /-ˈroʊz/ *past simple of* **arise**

around IN THIS DIRECTION /əˈraʊnd/ *prep, adv* (MAINLY UK **round**) in a position or direction surrounding, or in a direction going along the edge of or from one part to another (of): *We sat around the table.* ○ *He put his arm around her.* ○ *A crowd had gathered around the scene of the accident.* ○ *She had a woollen scarf around her neck.* ○ *The moon goes around the Earth.* ○ *I walked around the side of the building.* ○ *As the bus left, she turned around* (= so that she was facing in the opposite direction) *and waved goodbye to us.* ○ *He put the wheel on the* **right/wrong way** around (= facing the right/wrong way). ○ *The children were dancing around* (= from one part to another of) *the room.* ○ *I spent a year travelling around* (= from one part to another of) *Africa and the Middle East.* ○ *The museum's collection includes works of art from all around* (= all the different parts of) *the world.* ○ *She passed a plate of biscuits around* (= from one person to another). ○ *This virus has been going around* (= from one person to another).

around APPROXIMATELY /əˈraʊnd/ *adv* about; approximately: *around six feet tall* ○ *around two months ago* ○ *around four o'clock* ○ *She earns around forty thousand a year.*

around IN THIS PLACE /əˈraʊnd/ *adv, prep* positioned or moving in or near a place, often without a clear direction, purpose or order: *He always leaves his clothes lying around (on the floor).* ○ *She went into town and spent two hours just walking around.* ○ *Let's take the children to the park so they can run around for a bit.* ○ *I used to live around* (= near) *here.* ○ *She's never around* (= near here) *when you need her.* ○ *Will you be around* (= here or somewhere near)? *next week?* ○ *There's a lot of flu around* (= a lot of people have it) *at the moment.* ○ *Mobile phones* **have been** around (= existed) *for quite a while.*

arouse /əˈraʊz/ *verb* [T] **1** to cause someone to have a particular feeling: *It's a subject which has aroused a lot of interest.* ○ *Our* **suspicions** *were first aroused when we heard a muffled scream.* ⊃See also **rouse**. **2** to cause someone to feel sexual excitement

aroused /əˈraʊzd/ *adj* sexually excited

arousal /əˈraʊ.zᵊl/ *noun* [U] *a state of* **(sexual)** *arousal* (= being sexually excited)

arpeggio /ɑːˈpedʒ.i.əʊ/ ⓤ /ɑːrˈpedʒ.i.oʊ/ *noun* [C] *plural* **arpeggios** the notes of a musical CHORD played quickly one after the other instead of together

arr. ARRIVE WRITTEN ABBREVIATION FOR **arrives** or **arrival**: used in TIMETABLES to show the time at which a bus, train or aircraft reaches a place: *Flight 226: dep. 10.25, arr. 13.45.*

arr. ARRANGE *adj* WRITTEN ABBREVIATION FOR **arranged**: describes a piece of music that has been changed so that it can be played by a different instrument

arraign /əˈreɪn/ *verb* [T] LEGAL to formally accuse someone in a court of law of a particular crime and ask them to state whether they are guilty or not: *He was arraigned on charges of aiding and abetting terrorists.* **arraignment** /əˈreɪn.mənt/ *noun* [C or U]

arrange PLAN /əˈreɪndʒ/ *verb* [I or T] to plan or prepare for; to organize: *I'm trying to arrange my work so that I can have a couple of days off next week.* ○ *The meeting has been arranged for Wednesday.* ○ [+ to infinitive] *They arranged to have dinner the following month.* ○ *I've already arranged with him to meet at the cinema.* ○ *She's arranged for her son to have swimming lessons.* ○ [+ that] *I'd deliberately arranged that they should arrive at the same time.* ○ [+ question word] *We haven't yet arranged when to meet.*

arrangement /əˈreɪndʒ.mənt/ *noun* **1** [C usually pl] a plan for how something will happen: *They'd made all the arrangements for the party.* ○ [+ to infinitive] *Arrangements were made to move the prisoners to another jail.* ○ *What are your current child-care arrangements?* **2** [C or U] an agreement between two people or groups about how something happens or will happen: [+ that] *We had an arrangement that he would clean the house and I would cook.* ○ *I'm sure we can* **come to** *an arrangement* (= reach an agreement). ○ *You can only withdraw money from this account by* **(prior)** *arrangement* (= after making plans to do so) **with** *the bank.*

COMMON LEARNER ERROR

arrange or arrange for?

Don't forget to use 'for' when you say that you are **arranging for** someone to do something or for something to happen.

I will arrange for all the new trainees to visit the factory next week.
~~I will arrange all the new trainees to visit the factory next week.~~
We have arranged for the talk to be held on Wednesday.
~~We have arranged the talk to be held on Wednesday.~~

arrange PUT IN POSITION /əˈreɪndʒ/ *verb* [T] to put something in a particular order: *She arranged her birthday cards along the shelf.* ○ *Who arranged these flowers so beautifully?* ○ *His books are* **neatly** *arranged in alphabetical order.*

arrangement /əˈreɪndʒ.mənt/ *noun* [C] *There was a striking arrangement of dried flowers* (= a group of them which had been put in a particular order) *on the table.*

arranger /ə'reɪn.dʒəʳ/ [US] /-dʒɚ/ *noun* **[C]** *a flower arranger*

arrange [MUSIC] /ə'reɪndʒ/ *verb* **[T]** to change a piece of music so that it can be played in a different way, for example by a particular instrument: *Beethoven's fifth symphony has been arranged* ***for*** *the piano.*

arrangement /ə'reɪndʒ.mənt/ *noun* **[C]** a piece of music that has been changed so that it can be played in a different way, especially by a different instrument: *This new arrangement of the piece is for saxophone and piano.*

arranger /ə'reɪn.dʒəʳ/ [US] /-dʒɚ/ *noun* **[C]** *The famous jazz musician, Duke Ellington, was a composer, arranger and pianist.*

ar,ranged 'marriage *noun* **[C]** a marriage in which the parents choose who their son or daughter will marry

arrant /'ær.ᵊnt/ [US] /'er-/ *adj* **[before n]** *OLD-FASHIONED* total: *He dismissed the rumours as 'arrant nonsense'.*

array /ə'reɪ/ *noun* **[C usually sing]** a large group of things or people, especially one which is attractive or causes admiration and often one which has been positioned in a particular way: *There was a splendid array* ***of*** *food on the table.* ○ *They sat before an array* ***of*** *microphones and cameras.*

array /ə'reɪ/ *verb* **[T usually passive] 1** to arrange a group of things in a particular way: *A large number of magazines were arrayed on the stand.* ○ *Arrayed* (= Standing in a group) *before him were 40 schoolchildren in purple and green.* **2** to arrange a group of soldiers in a position for fighting

arrayed /ə'reɪd/ *adj* **[after v]** *FORMAL* dressed in a particular, especially splendid way: *She was arrayed* ***in*** *purple velvet.*

arrears /ə'rɪəz/ [US] /-'rɪrz/ *plural noun* money that is owed and should already have been paid: *rent arrears*

• **in arrears 1** owing money that should have been paid in the past: *My account is badly in arrears.* ○ *They are in arrears* ***on/with*** *their mortgage payments.* **2** If someone is paid in arrears, they are paid at the end of the period of time during which the money was earned: *I'm paid a week in arrears.*

arrest [CATCH] /ə'rest/ *verb* **[T]** If the police arrest someone, they take them away to ask them about a crime which they might have committed: *He was arrested when customs officers found drugs in his bag.* ○ *The police arrested her* ***for*** *drinking and driving.* **arrest** /ə'rest/ *noun* **[C or U]** *Two arrests were made, but the men were later released without charge.* ○ *She was stopped outside the shop and placed/put* ***under*** *arrest.*

arrest [STOP] /ə'rest/ *verb* **[T]** *FORMAL* to stop or interrupt the development of something: *The treatment has so far done little to arrest the spread of the cancer.*

arrest [ATTRACT NOTICE] /ə'rest/ *verb* **[T]** *FORMAL* to attract or catch someone's attention: *A photo of a small boy arrested my* ***attention****.*

arresting /ə'res.tɪŋ/ *adj* very attractive in a way that attracts a lot of attention: *an arresting looking woman*

arrive /ə'raɪv/ *verb* **[I]** to reach a place, especially at the end of a journey: *What time will your train arrive?* ○ *It was dark by the time we arrived* ***at*** *the station.* ○ *We arrived* ***in*** *Prague later that day.* ○ *I arrived back to find that my room had been burgled.* ○ *What time does the mail usually arrive* (= is it delivered)*?* ○ *I ordered some CDs over a month ago, but they still haven't arrived* (= I have not received them). ○ *The leaves starting to turn brown is a sign that autumn has arrived* (= begun). ○ *Their baby Olivia arrived* (= was born) *on the date she was expected.*

• **to have arrived** to have achieved success and often fame: *He felt he had truly arrived when he first got his part in a Broadway play.*

arrival /ə'raɪ.vᵊl/ *noun* **1 [C or U]** when someone or something arrives somewhere: *Hundreds gathered to await the boxer's arrival* ***at*** *the airport.* ○ ***On*** *arrival* ***at*** *the police station, they were taken to an interview room.* ○ *We regret the late arrival* ***of*** *Flight 237.* ○ *New arrivals* (= people who have just come to a place) *were being housed in refugee camps.* ○ *Sue and Michael are delighted to announce the arrival* (= birth) ***of*** *Emily, born on August 21.* ○ *The arrival* (= introduction) *of satellite television changed the face of broadcasting.* **2 [C]** *INFORMAL* a baby which has recently been born: *Their* ***new*** *arrival was keeping them busy.*

COMMON LEARNER ERROR

arrive

You **arrive at** a building or a part of a building.

We arrived at the theatre just as the play was starting.
I arrived at the front entrance to find the door locked.

You **arrive in** a town, city or country.

When do you arrive in London?

You **arrive home/here/there/etc.** without a preposition.

We arrived home yesterday.

▲ **arrive at** ***sth*** *phrasal verb* to reach an agreement about something: *We all argued about it for hours and eventually arrived at a decision.*

arriviste /,ær.iː'viːst/ *noun* **[C]** *DISAPPROVING* a person who wants to move into a higher class in society

arrogant /'ær.ə.gᵊnt/ [US] /'er-/ *adj* unpleasantly proud and behaving as if you are more important than, or know more than, other people: *I found him arrogant and rude.* **arrogantly** /'ær.ə.gᵊnt.li/ [US] /'er-/ *adv*: *The authorities had behaved arrogantly, she said.* **arrogance** /'ær.ə.gᵊnts/ [US] /'er-/ *noun* **[U]** *He has a self-confidence that is sometimes seen as arrogance.*

arrogate /'ær.əʊ.geɪt/ [US] /'er.ə-/ *verb* **[T]** *FORMAL* to take something without having the right to do so: *They arrogate* ***to*** *themselves the power to punish people.*

arrow /'ær.əʊ/ [US] /'er.oʊ/ *noun* **[C] 1** a weapon that is like a long thin stick with a sharp point at one end and often feathers at the other, shot from a bow: *Robin Hood asked to be buried where his arrow landed.* ➲Compare **dart** WEAPON. ➲See picture **Sports** on page Centre 10 **2** a sign consisting of a straight line with an upside down V shape at one end of it, which points in a particular direction, and is used to show where something is: *I followed the arrows to the car park.*

arrowhead /'ær.əʊ.hed/ [US] /'er.oʊ-/ *noun* **[C]** the sharp point at the end of an arrow

arrowroot /'ær.əʊ.ruːt/ [US] /'er.oʊ-/ *noun* **[U]** a starch in the form of powder, which is made from a West Indian plant and is used in cooking, especially to thicken sauces

arse *UK* /ɑːs/ [US] /ɑːrs/ *noun* **[C]** (*US* **ass**) *OFFENSIVE* the part of your body that you sit on: *She's got a huge arse.*

• **My arse!** *OFFENSIVE* said when you do not believe what someone has just said: *"She says she's got food poisoning." "Food poisoning, my arse! She just drank too much last night."*

• **not know** ***your*** **arse from** ***your*** **elbow** *OFFENSIVE* to be stupid and unable to understand very simple things

• **Move/shift** ***your*** **arse!** *OFFENSIVE* used to rudely tell someone to hurry up or to get out of your way

• **get off** ***your*** **arse** (*ALSO* **get** ***your*** **arse in gear**) *OFFENSIVE* to force yourself to start doing something or to make yourself hurry: *Tell him to get off his arse and do some work for once.* ○ *If she doesn't get her arse in gear she's going to be late.*

• **go arse over tit/tip** *UK* (*US* **go ass over (tea)kettle**) *OFFENSIVE* to lose your balance suddenly and fall over: *I fell off my bike and went arse over tit.*

arse /ɑːs/ [US] /ɑːrs/ *verb*

▲ **arse about/around** *phrasal verb UK OFFENSIVE* to act in a silly way or waste time: *I wish he'd stop arsing around and actually do some work.*

arsed /ɑːst/ [US] /ɑːrst/ *adj UK INFORMAL* **not be arsed** If you cannot be arsed **to** do something, you do not want to make the effort to do it: **[+ *to* infinitive]** *I can't be arsed* ***to*** *go shopping this afternoon.*

arsehole [UNPLEASANT PERSON] *UK* /'ɑːs.həʊl/ [US] /'ɑːrs.hoʊl/ *noun* **[C]** (*US* **asshole**) *OFFENSIVE* an unpleasant or stupid person: *Some arsehole had parked so I couldn't get out.*

arsehole [BODY PART] *UK* /'ɑːs.həʊl/ [US] /'ɑːrs.hoʊl/ *noun* **[C]** (*US* **asshole**) *OFFENSIVE* the **anus**

arse-licker UK /ˈɑːs.lɪk.əʳ/ US /ˈɑːrs.lɪk.ɚ/ noun [C] (US **ass-licker**) OFFENSIVE a person who tries to get an advantage from other people by being extremely pleasant to them in a way which is not sincere

arsenal /ˈɑː.sⁿn.ºl/ US /ˈɑːr-/ noun [C] **1** a building where weapons and military equipment are stored: *The army planned to attack enemy arsenals.* **2** a collection of weapons: *The country has agreed to reduce its nuclear arsenal.*

arsenic /ˈɑː.sⁿn.ɪk/ US /ˈɑːr-/ noun [U] a very poisonous element, often used to kill rats and able to kill people

arson /ˈɑː.sⁿn/ US /ˈɑːr-/ noun [U] the crime of intentionally starting a fire in order to damage or destroy something, especially a building: *A cinema was burnt out in north London last night. Police suspect arson.* **arsonist** /ˈɑː.sⁿn.ɪst/ US /ˈɑːr-/ noun [C] *Police are blaming arsonists for the spate of fires in the Greenfields housing estate.*

art /ɑːt/ US /ɑːrt/ noun **1** [U] the making of objects, images, music, etc. that are beautiful or that express feelings: *Can television and pop music really be considered art?* ○ *I enjoyed the ballet, but it wasn't really great art.* **2** [U] the activity of painting, drawing and making sculpture: *Art and English were my best subjects at school.* ○ *an art teacher* **3** [U] paintings, drawings and sculptures: *The gallery has an excellent collection of modern art.* ○ *an exhibition of Native American art* ○ *Peggy Guggenheim was one of the twentieth century's great art collectors.* ○ *The Frick is an art **gallery** in New York.* **4** [C] an activity through which people express particular ideas: *Drama is an art that is traditionally performed in a theatre.* ○ *Do you regard film as entertainment or as an art?* ○ *She is doing a course in the performing arts.* **5** [C] a skill or special ability: *the art of conversation* ○ *Getting him to go out is **quite** an art* (= needs special skill).

artist /ˈɑː.tɪst/ US /ˈɑːr.tɪst/ noun [C] **1** someone who paints, draws or makes sculptures: *Monet is one of my favourite artists.* ●Compare **artiste**. **2** someone who creates things with great skill and imagination: *He described her as one of the greatest film artists of the 20th century.*

artistic /ɑːˈtɪs.tɪk/ US /ɑːr-/ adj **1** [before n] relating to art: *the artistic director of the theatre* ○ *artistic endeavours* ○ *a work of artistic merit* **2** able to create or enjoy art: *His friends are all artistic – they're painters, musicians and writers.* **3** skilfully and attractively made: *That's a very artistic flower arrangement you have there.* **artistically** /ɑːˈtɪs.tɪ.kli/ US /ɑːr-/ adv

artistry /ˈɑː.tɪ.stri/ US /ˈɑːr.tɪ-/ noun [U] great skill in creating or performing something, such as in writing, music, sport, etc: *You have to admire the artistry of her novels.*

the arts plural noun the making or showing or performance of painting, acting, dancing and music: *More government money is needed for the arts.* ○ *public interest in the arts* ●See also **arts**.

arty /ˈɑː.ti/ US /ˈɑːr.ti/ adj INFORMAL USUALLY DISAPPROVING being or wishing to seem very interested in everything connected with art and artists: *She hangs out with a lot of arty types.*

art deco /ˌɑːtˈdek.əʊ/ US /ˌɑːrtˈdeɪ.koʊ/ noun [U] a style of decoration that was especially popular in the 1930s and uses simple shapes and lines and strong colours

artefact MAINLY UK /ˈɑː.tɪ.fækt/ US /ˈɑːr.tɪ-/ noun [C] (MAINLY US **artifact**) an object that is made by a person, such as a tool or a decoration, especially one that is of historical interest: *The museum's collection includes artefacts dating back to prehistoric times.*

artery BLOOD /ˈɑː.t°r.i/ US /ˈɑːr.tɚ-/ noun [C] one of the thick tubes that carry blood from the heart to other parts of the body: *Hardening of the coronary arteries can lead to a heart attack.* **arterial** /ɑːˈtɪə.ri.°l/ US /ɑːrˈtɪr.i-/ adj: *the arterial walls*

artery ROAD/RAILWAY /ˈɑː.t°r.i/ US /ˈɑːr.tɚ-/ noun [C] an important road or railway line: *the main arteries leading into London* **arterial** /ɑːˈtɪə.ri/ US /ɑːrˈtɪr.i-/ adj: *arterial roads*

artesian well /ɑːˌtiː.zi.ºnˈwel/ US /ɑːrˌtiː.ʒ°n-/ noun [C] a hole in the ground from which water is forced to the surface by natural pressure

artful /ˈɑːt.f°l/ US /ˈɑːrt-/ adj clever and skilful, especially in getting what you want: *He has shown himself to be an artful politician.* ○ *The prime minister dealt with the interviewer's questions in a very artful way.* **artfully** /ˈɑːt.f°l.i/ US /ˈɑːrt-/ adv: *His clothes were artfully arranged to look stylishly casual.* **artfulness** /ˈɑːt.f°l.nəs/ US /ˈɑːrt-/ noun [U]

art-house /ˈɑːt.haʊs/ US /ˈɑːrt-/ adj (ALSO **arthouse**) used to describe films/movies from other countries or the type of films/movies that small film companies make: *an arthouse cinema* (= a cinema that shows mainly this type of film) **ˈart ˌhouse** noun [C]

arthritis /ɑːˈθraɪ.tɪs/ US /ɑːr-/ noun [U] a serious condition in which a person's joints become painful, swollen and stiff: *In later life she was crippled with arthritis.* **arthritic** /ɑːˈθrɪt.ɪk/ US /ɑːrˈθrɪt̬-/ adj: *Her hands were swollen and arthritic.* ○ *arthritic joints*

arthritic /ɑːˈθrɪt.ɪk/ US /ɑːrˈθrɪt̬-/ noun [C] a person who suffers from arthritis: *Many arthritics find it difficult to climb stairs.*

artichoke /ˈɑː.tɪ.tʃəʊk/ US /ˈɑːr.tɪ.tʃoʊk/ noun [C] a **globe artichoke** or **Jerusalem artichoke**

article NEWSPAPER /ˈɑː.tɪ.kl/ US /ˈɑːr.tɪ-/ noun [C] a piece of writing on a particular subject in a newspaper or magazine: *There was an interesting article **on** vegetarianism in the paper yesterday.*

article OBJECT /ˈɑː.tɪ.kl/ US /ˈɑːr.tɪ-/ noun [C] a particular thing, especially one which is one of several things of a similar type or in the same place: *Guests are advised not to leave any articles of value in their hotel rooms.* ○ *An article **of clothing** was found near the river.* ○ *articles of furniture*

article GRAMMAR /ˈɑː.tɪ.kl/ US /ˈɑːr.tɪ-/ noun [C] any of the English words 'a', 'an' and 'the' or words in other languages that do the same job as these ●See **definite article** and **indefinite article**.

article LAW /ˈɑː.tɪ.kl/ US /ˈɑːr.tɪ-/ noun [C] a separate part in a written document such as a legal agreement: *East and West Germany united under article 23 of the Bonn constitution.*

● **be doing/in articles** UK to be working in a law office while training to be a lawyer

articled /ˈɑː.tɪ.kld/ US /ˈɑːr.tɪ-/ adj UK training to become a lawyer: *She is articled **to** a big law firm* (= she is working there as part of her training) *in the City of London.* ○ *an articled **clerk***

article of 'faith noun [C] something that you believe in very strongly: *Socialism was an article of faith with his parents.*

articulate CLEAR /ɑːˈtɪk.jʊ.lət/ US /ɑːr-/ adj able to express thoughts and feelings easily and clearly, or showing this quality: *an intelligent and highly articulate young woman* ○ *She gave a witty, entertaining and articulate speech.* **articulately** /ɑːˈtɪk.jʊ.lət.li/ US /ɑːr-/ adv **articulateness** /ɑːˈtɪk.jʊ.lət.nəs/ US /ɑːr-/ noun [U] (ALSO **articulacy**)

articulate SAY /ɑːˈtɪk.jʊ.leɪt/ US /ɑːr-/ verb [T] FORMAL **1** to express in words: *I found myself unable to articulate my feelings.* ○ *Many people are opposed to the new law, but have had no opportunity to articulate their opposition.* **2** to pronounce: *When children first learn to talk, there are some sounds that they find difficult to articulate.* **articulation** /ɑːˌtɪk.jʊˈleɪ.ʃ°n/ US /ɑːr-/ noun [U] *A good singer needs to have good articulation* (= a clear way of pronouncing words).

articulated /ɑːˈtɪk.jʊ.leɪ.tɪd/ US /ɑːrˈtɪk.jʊ.leɪ.tɪd/ adj describes a vehicle that consists of two or more parts which bend where they are joined, in order to help the vehicle turn corners: *an articulated vehicle* ○ UK *An articulated **lorry** has overturned on the south-bound carriageway, shedding its load.*

artifact /ˈɑː.tɪ.fækt/ US /ˈɑːr.tɪ-/ noun [C] an **artefact**

artifice /ˈɑː.tɪ.fɪs/ US /ˈɑːr.tɪ-/ noun [C or U] FORMAL (the use of) a clever trick or something intended to deceive: *Amazingly for Hollywood, she seems almost entirely without artifice.*

artificial /ˌɑː.tɪˈfɪʃ.°l/ US /ˌɑːr.tɪ-/ adj **1** made by people, often as a copy of something natural: *clothes made of artificial fibres* ○ *an artificial heart* ○ *an artificial lake*

○ *artificial fur/sweeteners/flowers* **2** DISAPPROVING not sincere: *Their cheerfulness seemed rather strained and artificial.*

artificially /ˌɑː.tɪˈfɪʃ.ᵊl.i/ ⓤ /ˌɑːr.ṭɪ-/ *adv:* *Most mushrooms sold in supermarkets have been grown artificially* (= not in natural conditions) *in manure.* **artificiality** /ˌɑː.tɪˌfɪʃ.iˈæl.ɪ.ti/ ⓤ /ˌɑːr.ṭɪˌfɪʃ.iˈæl.ə.ṭi/ *noun* [U]

artificial insemi'nation *noun* [U] (ABBREVIATION **AI**) the process of putting sperm into a female using methods which do not involve sexual activity between a male and female

artificial in'telligence *noun* [U] (ABBREVIATION **AI**) the study of how to produce machines that have some of the qualities that the human mind has, such as the ability to understand language, recognize pictures, solve problems and learn

artificial respi'ration *noun* [U] the act of forcing air in and out of the lungs of a person who has stopped breathing, especially by blowing into their mouth and pressing their chest to help them start breathing again: *Rescuers pulled the child from the river, and she was* **given** *artificial respiration.*

artillery /ɑːˈtɪl.ᵊr.i/ ⓤ /ɑːrˈtɪl.ɚ-/ *noun* [U] very large guns that are moved on wheels or metal tracks, or the part of the army which uses these: *Naval gunfire and ground-based artillery are generally less accurate than many aircraft-borne weapons.*

artisan /ˈɑː.tɪ.zæn/ ⓤ /ˈɑːr.ṭɪ-/ *noun* [C] a person who does skilled work with his or her hands

artist /ˈɑː.tɪst/ ⓤ /ˈɑːr.tɪst/ *noun* [C] ⊃See at **art**. **artistic** /ɑːˈtɪs.tɪk/ ⓤ /ɑːr-/ *adj* **artistically** /ɑːˈtɪs.tɪ.kli/ ⓤ /ɑːr-/ *adv* **artistry** /ˈɑː.tɪ.stri/ ⓤ /ˈɑːr.ṭɪ-/ *noun* [U]

artiste /ɑːˈtiːst/ ⓤ /ɑːr-/ *noun* [C] a skilled entertainer especially a dancer, singer or actor: *a popular 19th century music-hall artiste* ○ *circus artistes*

artless /ˈɑːt.ləs/ ⓤ /ˈɑːrt-/ *adj* simple and honest; not wanting to deceive: *"Why did you take the money?" she asked the child. "Because I wanted it,"* came the artless reply. **artlessly** /ˈɑːt.lə.sli/ ⓤ /ˈɑːrt-/ *adv* **artlessness** /ˈɑːt.lə.snəs/ ⓤ /ˈɑːrt-/ *noun* [U]

art nouveau /ˌɑː.nuːˈvəʊ/ ⓤ /ˌɑːrt.nuːˈvoʊ/ *noun* [U] a style of art and decoration that uses curling lines and plant and flower shapes

arts /ɑːts/ ⓤ /ɑːrts/ *plural noun* subjects, such as history, languages and philosophy, that are not scientific subjects: *At school I was quite good at arts, but hopeless at science.* ○ *Children should be given a well-balanced education in both the arts and the sciences.* ○ *arts graduates/degrees* ⊃See also **arts**.

arts and 'crafts *plural noun* the skills of making objects, such as decorations, furniture and POTTERY (= objects made from clay), by hand

artwork /ˈɑːt.wɜːk/ ⓤ /ˈɑːrt.wɝːk/ *noun* [U] the pieces of art, such as drawings and photographs, that are used in books, newspapers and magazines: *All the artwork in the book has been done by the author.*

arty /ˈɑː.ti/ ⓤ /ˈɑːr.ṭi/ *adj* ⊃See at **art**.

arty-crafty UK /ˌɑː.tiˈkrɑːf.ti/ ⓤ /ˌɑːr.ṭiˈkræf-/ *adj* (US **artsy-craftsy**) INFORMAL interested or involved in making decorative objects: *an arty-crafty market/gift-shop*

arty-farty UK /ˌɑː.tiˈfɑː.ti/ ⓤ /ˌɑːr.ṭiˈfɑːr.ṭi/ *adj* (US **artsy-fartsy**) INFORMAL DISAPPROVING describes someone who is too concerned with trying to impress other people with their artistic knowledge and ability: *Phil and his arty-farty friends*

arugula US /əˈruː.gə.lə/ *noun* [U] (UK **rocket**) a plant whose long green leaves are used in salads

Aryan /ˈeə.ri.ən/ ⓤ /ˈer.i.ən/ *adj* relating to white people from northern Europe, especially those with pale hair and blue eyes, who were believed by the NAZIS to be better than members of all other races

as COMPARISON WEAK /əz/, STRONG /æz/ *adv* used in comparisons to refer to the degree of something: *She'll soon be as tall as her mother.* ○ *I can't run as fast as you.* ○ *skin as soft as a baby's* ○ *It's not as good as it used to be.*

as FOR THIS PURPOSE WEAK /əz/, STRONG /æz/ *prep* used to describe the purpose or quality of someone or some-

thing: *She works as a waitress.* ○ *It could be used as evidence against him.* ○ *The news came as quite a shock to us.* ○ *I meant it as a joke.*

as BECAUSE WEAK /əz/, STRONG /æz/ *conjunction* because: *As it was getting late, I decided to book into a hotel.* ○ *You can go first as you're the oldest.*

as WHILE WEAK /əz/, STRONG /æz/ *conjunction* while; during the time that: *I saw him as I was coming into the building.* ○ *He gets more attractive as he gets older.*

as ALTHOUGH WEAK /əz/, STRONG /æz/ *conjunction* although: *Angry as he was, he couldn't help smiling.*

as LIKE WEAK /əz/, STRONG /æz/ *conjunction* in the same way: *He got divorced,* **(just)** *as his parents had done years before.* ○ *This year, as in previous years, tickets sold very quickly.* ○ *As* **with** *his earlier movies, the special effects in his latest film are brilliant.* ○ *As* **is** *often the case with children, Amy was completely better by the time the doctor arrived.* ○ *As I was just saying, I think the proposal needs further consideration.* ○ *Knowing him as I do, I can't believe he would do such a thing.*

● **as for** *sb/sth* used to talk about how another person or thing is affected by something: *As for Louise, well, who cares what she thinks.*

● **as of/from** starting from a particular time or date: *As of next month, all the airline's fares will be going up.*

● **as if/though** used to describe how a situation seems to be: *She looked as if she'd had some bad news.* ○ *I felt as though I'd been lying in the sun for hours.* ○ *They stared at me as if I was crazy.*

● **As if!** INFORMAL said to show that you do not believe something is possible: *"Did you get a pay rise?" "As if!"*

● **as is** in the state that something is in at the present time: *Will you wait till it's finished or take it home as is?*

● **as it is** already: *I'm not buying the children anything else today – I've spent far too much money as it is.*

● **as you wish/like** FORMAL used to agree to a request, especially when you do not approve: *"I think we should leave now." "Very well. As you wish."*

● **as to/for** changing the subject to: *As to where we'll get the money from, we'll talk about that later.*

● **as to** FORMAL about: *He was uncertain as to which road to take.* ○ *There's no decision as to when the work might start.*

● **as and when** UK (US **if and when**) at the time that something happens: *We don't own a car – we just rent one as and when we need it.*

● **as it were** sometimes said after a figurative or unusual expression: *If he still refuses we could always apply a little pressure, as it were.*

asap, ASAP /ˌeɪ.es.eɪˈpiː/ ABBREVIATION FOR as soon as possible: *Please reply asap.*

asbestos /æsˈbes.tɒs/ ⓤ /-tɑːs/ *noun* [U] a soft greyish-white material that does not burn, and which was used, especially in the past, in buildings, clothing, etc. as a protection against fire, and as a form of INSULATION (= way of stopping heat from escaping)

asbestosis /ˌæs.besˈtəʊ.sɪs/ ⓤ /-ˈtoʊ-/ *noun* [U] a serious medical condition caused by breathing asbestos fibres into the lungs

ascend HEIGHT /əˈsend/ *verb* [I or T] FORMAL to move up or climb something: *They slowly ascended the steep path up the mountain.* ○ *The divers have begun to ascend* **to** *the surface of the water.* ○ *There's a long flight of steps ascending* (= leading up) **to** *the cathedral doors.*

ascent /əˈsent/ *noun* [C usually sing] *She made her first successful ascent* (= climb) *of Everest last year.* ○ *We struggled up the slippery ascent* (= slope).

ascend IMPORTANCE /əˈsend/ *verb* [I] FORMAL to rise to a position of higher rank: *He eventually ascended* **to** *the position of chief executive.*

● **ascend the throne** FORMAL to become queen or king

ascent /əˈsent/ *noun* [S] FORMAL when someone starts to become successful: *His ascent* **to** *power was rapid and unexpected.*

ascendancy, ascendency /əˈsen.dᵊnt.si/ *noun* [U] FORMAL a position of power, strength or success: *They are in danger of losing their political ascendancy* (= controlling power). ○ *Supporters of the proposal are currently* **in the**

*ascendancy (**over** its opponents)* (= are more powerful than them).

ascendant /ə'sen.dᵊnt/ *noun FORMAL* **in the ascendant** increasingly successful or powerful: *He's very much in the ascendant in Hollywood.*

ascending /ə'sen.dɪŋ/ *adj* increasing in size or value: *I shall list my objections to the plan in ascending **order** of importance.*

Ascension Day /ə'sen.ʃ(ə)n,deɪ/ *noun* [C or U] the sixth Thursday after EASTER SUNDAY, when Christians celebrate Christ's journey from Earth to Heaven

ascertain /,æs.ə'teɪn/ [US] /-ɚ-/ *verb* [T] *FORMAL* to discover; to make certain: *The police have so far been unable to ascertain the cause of the explosion.* ○ [+ *that*] *I ascertained **that** no one could overhear us before I told Otto the news.* ○ [+ question word] *Have you ascertained **whether** she's coming or not?*

ascetic /ə'set.ɪk/ [US] /-'seṭ-/ *adj* avoiding physical pleasures and living a simple life, often for religious reasons: *They live a very ascetic life.* **ascetic** /ə'set.ɪk/ [US] /-'seṭ-/ *noun* [C] *He lived as an ascetic.* **ascetically** /ə'set.ɪ.kli/ [US] /-'seṭ-/ *adv* **asceticism** /ə'set.ɪ.sɪ.zᵊm/ [US] /-'seṭ-/ *noun* [U]

ASCII /'æs.ki/ *noun* [U] *ABBREVIATION FOR* American Standard Code for Information Interchange: a way of storing numbers, letters or symbols for exchanging information between computer systems: *a document in ASCII format*

ascorbic acid /ə,skɔː.bɪk'æs.ɪd/ [US] /-,skɔːr-/ *noun* [U] *SPECIALIZED* **vitamin C**

ascot *US* /'æs.kət/ [US] /-kɑːt/ *noun* [C] (*UK* **cravat**) a wide straight piece of material worn like a tie in the open neck of a shirt

ascribe /ə'skraɪb/ *verb*

PHRASAL VERBS WITH **ascribe** ▼

▲ **ascribe *sth* to *sth*** [CAUSE] *phrasal verb FORMAL* to believe or say that something is caused by something else: *To what do you ascribe your phenomenal success?*

▲ **ascribe *sth* to *sb*** [CREATION] *phrasal verb FORMAL* to believe that something was said, written or created by a particular person: *After years of research, scholars have finally ascribed this anonymous play to Christopher Marlowe.*

▲ **ascribe *sth* to *sb/sth*** [QUALITY] *phrasal verb FORMAL* to believe that someone or something has a particular quality: *People like to ascribe human feelings to animals.*

ASEAN /ə'ziː.ᵊn/ *group noun* [S] *ABBREVIATION FOR* Association of South East Asian Nations: an economic organization that also makes decisions about social and political matters of the member countries

aseptic /,eɪ'sep.tɪk/ *adj* medically clean or without infection: *an aseptic wound/dressing/bandage*

asexual /,eɪ'sek.sju.ᵊl/ *adj* **1** without sex or sexual organs: *asexual reproduction* **2** lacking interest in sexual relationships: *I must say I've always found him rather asexual.* **asexually** /,eɪ'sek.sju.ᵊl.i/ *adv* **asexuality** /,eɪ.sek.sju'æl.ɪ.ti/ [US] /-ə.ṭi/ *noun* [U]

ash [POWDER] /æʃ/ *noun* [U] the soft grey or black powder that is left after a substance, especially tobacco, coal or wood, has burnt: *cigarette ash*

ashes /'æʃ.ɪz/ *plural noun* what is left of something after it has been destroyed by fire, especially what is left of a human body after it has been burnt: *Her ashes were **scattered** at sea.* ○ *Allied bombing left Dresden in ashes in 1945.*

ash [TREE] /æʃ/ *noun* **1** [C] a forest tree which has a smooth grey bark, small greenish flowers and seeds shaped like wings **2** [U] the wood from an ash

ASH [ORGANIZATION] /æʃ/ *group noun* [S] *ABBREVIATION FOR* Action on Smoking and Health: an organization in Australia, the UK, and the US that discourages the sale and use of tobacco products

ashamed /ə'ʃeɪmd/ *adj* [after v] feeling guilty or embarrassed about something you have done or a quality in your character: *You've got nothing to be ashamed **of**.* ○ *She ought to be thoroughly ashamed **of herself** – talking to her mother like that!* ○ [+ to infinitive] *He was ashamed **to** admit to his mistake.* ○ [+ *that*] *I was ashamed **that** I'd made so little effort.* ○ *I'm ashamed **to** be seen with you when you behave so badly!* ○ *I **felt** so ashamed of myself for making such a fuss.* ○ *How could you treat her like that? I'm so ashamed **of** you* (= embarrassed to be connected with you)*!*

,ash 'blonde *adj* describes hair which is very pale yellow, almost white **,ash 'blonde** *noun* [C] *She's an ash blonde.*

ashcan /'æʃ.kæn/ *noun* [C] *US OLD-FASHIONED FOR* **dustbin**

ashen /'æʃ.ᵊn/ *adj* lacking colour, or pale grey in colour: *Julie walked in, ashen-**faced** with shock.* ○ *She was thin and her face was ashen.*

ashore /ə'ʃɔːʳ/ [US] /-'ʃɔːr/ *adv* towards or onto land from an area of water: *We swam ashore.* ○ *A few pieces of wood had washed ashore.* ○ *Strong winds blew the ship ashore.*

ashtray /'æʃ.treɪ/ *noun* [C] a small dish or container, sometimes decorative, in which people can leave cigarette ash and cigarette ends

,Ash 'Wednesday *noun* [C or U] the first day of LENT in the Christian religion

Asia /'eɪ.ʒə/ *noun* [U] the continent that is to the east of Europe, the west of the Pacific Ocean and the north of the Indian Ocean

Asian /'eɪ.ʒᵊn/ *noun* [C] **1** someone who comes from the continent of Asia, or a member of a race originally from Asia **2** in the US, Canada, Australia and New Zealand, someone from China, Japan or countries near them **3** in the UK, someone from India, Pakistan or countries near them

Asian /'eɪ.ʒᵊn/ *adj* of or related to Asia

Asiatic /,eɪ.zi'æt.ɪk/ [US] /-'æṭ-/ *adj SPECIALIZED* relating to Asia, especially when considering its physical position, or its plants and animals, rather than social or cultural matters: *Anatolia is the Asiatic region of Turkey* (= the part of Turkey which is in Asia rather than Europe).

aside [TO ONE SIDE] /ə'saɪd/ *adv* **1** on or to one side: ***Stand** aside, please, and let these people pass.* ○ *He **pulled** the curtain aside.* ○ *I gave her a plate of food but she pushed it aside.* ○ *I've forgotten my cheque book, so could you **put** this book aside* (= keep this book) *for me and I'll come back later on.* ○ *She **took** me aside* (= took me away from the people) *to tell me the news.* **2 put/set *sth* aside** If you put/set aside money, you save it for a particular purpose: *Every week I put aside a few pounds for a new TV.* **3 leave/put *sth* aside** If you leave or put a problem or request aside, you ignore it until you are able to solve it: *Let's leave that matter aside for now and talk about the more urgent problem facing us.*

• **aside from** except for: *Money continues to be a problem but aside from that we're all well.* ○ *I hardly watch any television, aside from news and current affairs.*

aside [REMARK] /ə'saɪd/ *noun* [C] **1** a remark that someone makes in a quiet voice because they do not want everyone to hear it: *a whispered aside* **2** a remark or story in a speech or text which is not part of the main subject: *The informative asides about rural life make this wine guide rather special.*

asinine /'æs.ɪ.naɪn/ *adj FORMAL* extremely stupid: *an asinine comment*

ask [QUESTION] /ɑːsk/ [US] /æsk/ *verb* [I or T] to put a question to someone, or to request an answer from someone: [+ two objects] *She asked me a question.* ○ *Can I ask you a favour?/(FORMAL) Can I ask a favour **of** you?* ○ *She asked a question **about** Welsh history.* ○ *She asked me **about** Welsh history.* ○ *She asked **about** Welsh history.* ○ [+ question word] *I've no idea what time the train leaves. Ask the guard **whether** he knows.* ○ *I asked the guard the time of the train's departure.* ○ *I asked **when** the train would leave.* ○ [+ speech] *"What time does the train leave?" I asked.* ○ *If you need any help, please don't hesitate to ask.* ○ *You should ask (your accountant) **for** some financial advice.* ○ [+ to infinitive] *You should ask your accountant **to** give you some financial advice.* ○ *I asked **to** see my accountant.* ○ *I'd like to ask your **advice/opinion** on a financial matter.* ○ *You have to ask **permission** to leave.* ○ [+ *that*] *FORMAL The solicitor asked **that** her client (should) be allowed to make a telephone call.* ○ *FORMAL*

*We ask **that** any faulty goods (should) be returned in their original packaging.*
- **don't ask me** INFORMAL said when you do not know the answer to a question: *Don't ask me where you've left your glasses!*
- **if you ask me** said when giving your opinion on something: *If you ask me, people should go on a training course before they become parents.*
- **you may well ask** (ALSO **well may you ask**) HUMOROUS it would be very interesting to know: *How could Jonathan afford to buy a new suit? You may well ask.*
- **be asking for it/trouble** to be behaving stupidly in a way that is likely to cause problems for you: *Drinking alcohol before driving is really asking for trouble.* ○ *I'm not surprised she lost her job – she was really asking for it.*
- **be sb's for the asking** If something is someone's for the asking, they only have to ask for it and it will be given to them: *With three years' experience behind her, the promotion was Kate's for the asking.*

COMMON LEARNER ERROR

ask for

Remember to use the preposition 'for' when you **ask for** something or **ask** someone **for** something.

Please do not hesitate to ask me for more details, if you need them.
~~Please do not hesitate to ask me more details, if you need them.~~

ask EXPECT /ɑːsk/ US /æsk/ *verb* [T] to expect or demand something: *Greg's asking* (= expecting to be paid) *£250 000 for his house.* ○ *He asks too much of me – I can't always be there to help him.* ○ *It's asking a lot when your boss wants you to work weekends as well as evenings.*

ask INVITE /ɑːsk/ US /æsk/ *verb* [T] to request or invite someone to go somewhere with you or to come to your home: UK *I've asked David to the party.* ○ [+ to infinitive] US *I've asked David to come to the party.* ○ *"Are you going to Muriel's party?" "No, I haven't been asked."* ○ *Ian's asked us over for dinner next Friday.* ○ UK *Ian's asked us round to/for dinner next Friday.* ○ [+ to infinitive] *In fact they've asked us to stay for the whole weekend.*

PHRASAL VERBS WITH **ask** ▼

▲ **ask after sb** UK *phrasal verb* (US **ask about**, SCOTTISH ENGLISH **ask for**) to ask for information about someone, especially about their health: *Tell your father I was asking after him.*
▲ **ask around** *phrasal verb* to ask a lot of different people in order to get information or help: *Our babysitter's just moved away, so we're asking around for a replacement.*
▲ **ask for sb** SPEAK TO *phrasal verb* to say that you would like to see or speak to someone: *A young man was here asking for you this morning.*
▲ **ask for sth** PRAISE *phrasal verb* If you say you couldn't ask for someone or something better, you mean that that person or thing is the best of their kind: *She's great to work for – I really couldn't ask for a better boss.*
▲ **ask sb in** *phrasal verb* [M] to invite someone to come into a building or room, especially your home: *I'd ask you in for a coffee but I have to get up early for work in the morning.*
▲ **ask sb out** *phrasal verb* [M] to invite someone to come with you to a place such as the cinema or a restaurant, especially as a way of starting a romantic relationship: *She's asked Steve out to the cinema this evening.* ○ *You should ask her out sometime.*

askance /ə'skɑːnts/ US /-'skænts/ *adv* **look askance** to look at or think about someone or something with doubt, disapproval or a lack of trust: *They looked askance at our scruffy old clothes.*

askew /ə'skjuː/ *adj* [after v], *adv* not straight or level: *Isn't that picture slightly askew?* ○ *My hat was askew so I adjusted it in the mirror.*

asking price *noun* [S] the amount of money someone wants when they sell something, especially a building or a piece of land: *The asking price for the flat was £89 500.*

a/s/l? INTERNET ABBREVIATION FOR age, sex and location: used when you are talking to someone in a CHAT ROOM and you want to ask how old they are, if they are male or female, and where they live: *"a/s/l?" "20/f/London* (= I am 20, I am female and I live in London)*"*

asleep /ə'sliːp/ *adj* [after v] **1** sleeping or not awake: *I fell asleep* (= I started to sleep) *as soon as my head hit the pillow.* ○ *I'm surprised to see you awake – ten minutes ago you were fast/sound* (= completely) *asleep.* ○ *I've only just got up and I'm still half asleep* (= not completely awake). **2** If your arm or leg is asleep, it cannot feel anything because it has been in the same position for so long that the blood supply has been cut off.

A/S level *noun* [C] a British examination of a standard between GCSE and A LEVEL which allows more subjects to be studied than is possible at A level because less information needs to be learnt for it: *I'm doing* (= studying) *5 A/S levels.* ○ *A/S-level French*

asp /æsp/ *noun* [C] a small poisonous snake found especially in North Africa which was a symbol of royalty in ancient Egypt

asparagus /ə'spær.ə.gəs/ US /-'sper-/ *noun* [U] a plant with pale green juicy stems that are cooked and eaten as a vegetable: *asparagus spears* ➔See picture **Vegetables** on page Centre 2

aspartame /'æs.pə.teɪm/ US /-pɚ-/ *noun* [U] (TRADEMARK **NutraSweet**) a very sweet substance which contains very little energy and is used instead of sugar to sweeten drinks and foods

aspect FEATURE /'æs.pekt/ *noun* [C] one part of a situation, problem, subject, etc: *Which aspects of the job do you most enjoy?* ○ *His illness affects almost every aspect of his life.* ○ *That's the most worrying aspect of the situation.* ○ *Lighting is a vitally important aspect of film-making.* ○ *Have you thought about the problem from every aspect?*

aspect DIRECTION /'æs.pekt/ *noun* [C] the direction in which a building, window, room or sloping field faces, or the view which can be seen because of this direction: *The dining room has a southern aspect which allows us to make the most of the sun.*

aspect APPEARANCE /'æs.pekt/ *noun* [S] FORMAL the appearance or visual effect of a place, or the expression on a person's face: *The glasses and the beard lend him a rather scholarly aspect.*

COMMON LEARNER ERROR

aspect

Do not use **aspect** to describe what someone looks like. It always sounds formal when it is used with this meaning, and it is easy to make a mistake. You should use the word **appearance** instead.

The author describes Caroline's physical appearance in great detail.
~~The author describes Caroline's physical aspect in great detail.~~

aspect GRAMMAR /'æs.pekt/ *noun* [C or U] SPECIALIZED the form of a verb which shows how the meaning of a verb is considered in relation to time, typically expressing whether an action is complete, habitual or continuous

asperity /ə'sper.ɪ.ti/ US /-ə.t̬i/ *noun* [U] FORMAL the quality of being severe in the way that you speak and behave: *the asperity of her manner*

aspersions /ə'spɜː.ʒ°nz/ US /-'spɝː-/ /-ʃ°nz/ *plural noun* FORMAL **cast aspersions on** ➔See at **cast** DOUBT.

asphalt /'æs.fɔːlt/ US /-fɑːlt/ *noun* [U] a black sticky substance mixed with small stones or sand, which forms a strong surface when it hardens

asphalt /'æs.fɔːlt/ US /-fɑːlt/ *verb* [T] to cover something, typically a roof or road, with asphalt: *an asphalted road/pitch/court*

asphyxiate /əs'fɪk.si.eɪt/ *verb* [T often passive] FORMAL to cause someone to be unable to breathe, usually resulting in death: *The murder inquiry found that the children had been asphyxiated.* **asphyxiation** /əs,fɪk.si'eɪ.ʃ°n/ *noun* [U]

aspic /'æs.pɪk/ *noun* [U] a transparent jelly made from animal bones which is used in cold savoury foods

aspidistra /ˌæs.pɪ'dɪs.trə/ *noun* [C] a large evergreen plant, usually grown inside, which has purple flowers shaped like bells and long strong leaves

aspirant /'æs.pɪ.rˀnt/ /ə'spaɪ-/ ⓤ /'æs.pɚ.ˀnt/ *noun* [C] FOR-MAL someone who very much wants to achieve something: *an aspirant to the throne*

aspirate /'æs.pɪ.rət/ ⓤ /-pɚ.ət/ *noun* [C] SPECIALIZED the sound represented in English by the letter 'h', in words such as 'house'

aspirate /'æs.pɪ.reɪt/ *verb* **1** [T] to pronounce a word with the sound 'h' **2** [I or T] US SPECIALIZED to breathe in, or to breathe a substance into your lungs by accident **aspiration** /ˌæs.pɪ'reɪ.ʃˀn/ ⓤ /-pɚ'eɪ-/ *noun* [U]

aspiration /ˌæs.pɪ'reɪ.ʃˀn/ ⓤ /-pɚ'eɪ-/ *noun* [C usually pl; U] something that you hope to achieve: *I've never had any political aspirations.* ○ *It's a story about the lives and aspirations of poor Irish immigrants.*

aspirational /ˌæs.pɪ'reɪ.ʃˀn.ˀl/ ⓤ /-pɚ'eɪ-/ *adj* UK showing that you want to have more money and a higher social position than you now have: *Trendy trainers and designer labels have become aspirational status symbols, especially among the young.*

aspire /ə'spaɪəʳ/ ⓤ /-'spaɪr/ *verb*
▲ **aspire to** *sth phrasal verb* to have a strong desire or hope to do or have something: *Few people who aspire to fame ever achieve it.* ○ [+ to infinitive] *As a child, he aspired to be a great writer.*

aspirin /'æs.pɪ.rɪn/ *noun* [C or U] *plural* **aspirin** or **aspirins** a common drug which reduces pain, especially headaches, fever and swelling: *I always take a couple of aspirins when I feel a cold starting.* ○ *Aspirin should not be given to young children.*

aspiring /ə'spaɪə.rɪŋ/ ⓤ /-'spaɪr.ɪŋ/ *adj* **an aspiring actor/politician/writer, etc.** someone who is trying to become a successful actor, politician, writer, etc.

ass ANIMAL /æs/ *noun* [C] OLD USE a **donkey**

ass STUPID PERSON /æs/ *noun* [C] INFORMAL a stupid person: *a pompous ass*
● **make an ass of yourself** INFORMAL to behave stupidly and look ridiculous: *Simon always makes a complete ass of himself when he's had too much to drink.*
● **The law is an ass.** UK SAYING said about a law that is so stupid that it should be changed or REPEALED

ass BOTTOM /æs/ *noun* **1** [C] MAINLY US OFFENSIVE ARSE (= the part of the body that you sit on) **2** [U] US OFFENSIVE used by men to refer to sexual activity, or to women considered only as sex objects: *I've never seen so much gorgeous ass.* **3** MAINLY US OFFENSIVE **your ass** yourself: *Get your ass in my office now!*
● **bore the ass off sb** MAINLY US OFFENSIVE to bore someone a lot: *Jamie? He bores the ass off me!*
● **talk sb's ass off** MAINLY US OFFENSIVE to talk to someone too much
● **work sb's ass off** MAINLY US OFFENSIVE to make someone work very hard: *They work your ass off but they pay you well.*
● **work your ass off** MAINLY US OFFENSIVE to work very hard: *I worked my ass off for that man.*
● **be up sb's ass** MAINLY US OFFENSIVE to be driving too close to the car in front of you: *I had a sports car up my ass for the first fifty miles.*
● **be on sb's ass** MAINLY US OFFENSIVE to annoy someone by refusing to leave them alone: *The police have been on my ass ever since I got out of jail.*
● **Shove/stick sth up your ass!** MAINLY US OFFENSIVE used to tell someone angrily that you do not want or need something that they are offering you or telling you to do: *If she asks me to work over the weekend I'll tell her to shove it up her ass!*

assail /ə'seɪl/ *verb* FORMAL **1** [T] to attack someone violently or criticize someone strongly: *The victim had been assailed with repeated blows to the head and body.* ○ *He was assailed with insults and abuse as he left the court.* **2** [T often passive] to cause someone to experience a lot of unpleasant things: *to be assailed by doubts/fears/problems*

assailant /ə'seɪ.lənt/ *noun* [C] FORMAL a person who attacks another person: *Can you describe your assailant?*

assassin /ə'sæs.ɪn/ *noun* [C] someone who kills a famous or important person usually for political reasons or in exchange for money: *John Lennon's assassin was Mark*

Chapman. ○ *She hired an assassin to eliminate her rival.*

assassinate /ə'sæs.ɪ.neɪt/ *verb* [T] to kill someone famous or important: *a plot to assassinate the Queen* **assassination** /əˌsæs.ɪ'neɪ.ʃˀn/ *noun* [C or U] *an assassination attempt* ○ *the assassination of the opposition leader*

assault /ə'sɒlt/ ⓤ /-'sɑːlt/ *noun* **1** [C or U] a violent attack: *He was charged with sexual assault.* ○ UK *The number of indecent assaults has increased alarmingly over the past year.* ○ *an assault on a police officer* ○ *They launched an assault on the capital yesterday.* **2** [C] a determined or serious attempt to do something difficult: *Women's groups have demanded a nationwide assault on sexism in the workplace.* ○ *She died heroically during an assault on the world's second-highest mountain.*

assault /ə'sɒlt/ ⓤ /-'sɑːlt/ *verb* [T] to attack someone violently: *A woman and a man have been convicted of assaulting a police officer following last month's demonstration.* ○ *He had attempted to sexually assault the woman but was scared off when she shouted for help.*

asˌsault and ˈbattery *noun* [U] LEGAL a threat to attack someone followed by a violent physical act

asˈsault ˌcourse UK *noun* [C] (US **obstacle course**) an area of land on which soldiers have to run between and climb over or cross various objects which are designed to test their strength and physical condition: FIGURATIVE *Meetings with tax inspectors are often bureaucratic assault courses.*

assay /ə'seɪ/ /æs'eɪ/ *verb* [T] SPECIALIZED to perform an examination on a chemical in order to test its purity **assay** /ə'seɪ/ /æs'eɪ/ *noun* [C]

assemblage /ə'sem.blɪdʒ/ *noun* **1** [C] FORMAL a collection of things or a group of people or animals: *A varied assemblage of birds was probing the mud for food.* **2** [U] the process of joining or putting things together

assembly GATHERING /ə'sem.bli/ *noun* **1** [C] a group of people, especially one gathered together regularly for a particular purpose, such as government, or more generally, the process of gathering together, or the state of being together: *the United Nations General Assembly* ○ *She has been tipped as a future member of the Welsh Assembly.* **2** US **Assembly** one of the two parts of the government that makes laws in many US States: *the New York Assembly* ○ *The Senate and the Assembly put aside political differences to pass the aid package.* **3** [C or U] a gathering in a school of several classes for a group activity such as singing, a theatrical performance or a film: *All pupils are expected to attend school assembly.* ○ *There's a religious assembly every morning.*

assemble /ə'sem.bl̩/ *verb* [I or T] to come together in a single place or bring parts together in a single group: *We assembled in the meeting room after lunch.* ○ *to assemble data* ○ *At the staff meeting, the manager told the assembled company (= everyone there) that no one would lose their job.*

assemblyman /ə'sem.bli.mæn/ /-mən/ *noun* [C] US a man who belongs to a part of the official law-making body in many US states

assemblywoman /ə'sem.bli.ˌwʊm.ən/ *noun* [C] US a female assemblyman

assembly JOINING /ə'sem.bli/ *noun* **1** [U] the process of putting together the parts of a machine or structure **2** [C] SPECIALIZED the structure produced by this process: *The frame needs to be strong enough to support the engine assembly (= structure).*

assemble /ə'sem.bl̩/ *verb* [T] to make something by joining separate parts: *furniture that is easy to assemble*

asˈsembly ˌline *noun* [C usually sing] a line of machines and workers in a factory which a product moves along while it is being built or produced. Each machine or worker performs a particular job, which must be completed before the product moves to the next position in the line: *assembly-line workers*

assent /ə'sent/ *noun* [U] FORMAL official agreement to or approval of an idea, plan or request: *Once the directors have given their assent to the proposal we can begin.* ○ *She nodded her assent to the proposal.* ○ UK *Before an Act of Parliament can become law, it needs to receive*

***Royal** Assent* (= an official signature) *from the monarch.* ➲Compare **dissent**.

assent /ə'sent/ *verb* [I] FORMAL *Have they assented **to** (=* agreed to) *the terms of the contract?*

assert /ə'sɜːt/ [US] /-'sɝːt/ *verb* [T] **1** FORMAL to say that something is certainly true: [+ **that**] *He asserts **that** she stole money from him.* **2** to do something to show that you have power: *Throughout the Cold War, the Allies asserted their **right** to move freely between the two Berlins.* ○ *She very rarely asserts her **authority** over the children.*

as'sert *yourself* *verb* [R] to behave in a way which expresses your confidence, importance or power and earns you respect from others: *I really must assert myself more in meetings.*

assertion /ə'sɜː.ʃᵊn/ [US] /-'sɝː-/ *noun* [C + **that**] a statement that you strongly believe is true: *I certainly don't agree with his assertion **that** men are better drivers than women.*

assertive /ə'sɜː.tɪv/ [US] /-'sɝː.t̬ɪv/ *adj* describes someone who behaves confidently and is not frightened to say what they want or believe: *If you really want the promotion, you'll have to be more assertive.* **assertively** /ə'sɜː.tɪv.li/ [US] /-'sɝː.t̬ɪv-/ *adv*: *Prince Charles condemned the assertively modernist style of architecture.* **assertiveness** /ə'sɜː.tɪv.nəs/ [US] /-'sɝː.t̬ɪv-/ *noun* [U]

as'sertiveness ˌtraining *noun* [U] a way of teaching people how to communicate confidently and obtain what they want without annoying others

assess /ə'ses/ *verb* [T] to judge or decide the amount, value, quality or importance of something: *The insurers will need to assess the flood damage.* ○ *They assessed the cost of the flood damage **at** £1500.* ○ *Examinations are not the only means of assessing a student's ability.* ○ *It's too early to assess the long-term consequences of the collapse of the Soviet Union.* ○ [+ **question word**] *We need to assess **whether** the project is worth doing.* **assessment** /ə'ses.mənt/ *noun* [C or U] *Both their assessments of production costs were hopelessly inaccurate.* **assessor** /ə'ses.əʳ/ [US] /-ɚ/ *noun* [C] *The assessor stated that the fire damage was not as severe as the hotel's owner had claimed.*

assessable income /əˌses.ə.bḷ'ɪn.kʌm/ *noun* [U] UK SPECIALIZED the amount of money which is considered when calculating tax payments

asset /'æs.et/ /-ɪt/ *noun* **1** [C] a useful or valuable quality, skill or person: *He'll be a great asset **to** the team.* ○ *Her eyes are her **best** asset* (= most attractive feature). ○ *Knowledge of languages is a real asset in this sort of work.* **2** [C usually pl] something valuable belonging to a person or organization which can be used for the payment of debts: *A company's assets can consist of cash, investments, buildings, machinery, specialist knowledge or copyright material such as music or computer software.* ○ ***liquid** assets* (= money, or things which can easily be changed into money) ➲Compare **liabilities** at **liable** RESPONSIBLE.

asset-stripping /'æs.etˌstrɪ.pɪŋ/ /-ɪt-/ *noun* [U] DISAPPROVING when a company buys an unsuccessful company cheaply and sells its ASSETS (= buildings, equipment, or land) separately at a profit **asset-stripper** /'æs.et.strɪp.əʳ/ /-ɪt-/ [US] /-ɚ/ *noun* [C]

asshole /'æs.həʊl/ [US] /-hoʊl/ *noun* [C] MAINLY US **arsehole**

assiduous /ə'sɪd.ju.əs/ *adj* FORMAL showing hard work, care and attention to detail: *assiduous research/efforts* ○ *an assiduous student* ○ *The Government has been assiduous **in** the fight against inflation.* **assiduously** /ə'sɪd.ju.ə.sli/ *adv*: *Before apartheid ended, I assiduously avoided buying South African products.* **assiduousness** /ə'sɪd.ju.ə.snəs/ *noun* [U]

assign [CHOOSE] /ə'saɪn/ *verb* **1** [T often passive] to give a particular job or piece of work to someone: [+ **two objects**] *UN troops were assigned the task of rebuilding the hospital.* ○ [+ **to infinitive**] *The case has been assigned **to** our most senior officer.* **2** [T] If you assign a time for a job or activity, you decide it will be done during that time: *Have you assigned a day **for** the interviews yet?* **3** [T] If you assign a characteristic to something, you state that it possesses it. **4** [T] to decide a reason for something: *Detectives have been unable to assign a motive **for** the murder.* ○ *The report assigned the **blame** for the accident **to** inadequate safety regulations.* **assignment** /ə'saɪn.mənt/ *noun* [U] *assignment **of** the various tasks* ➲See also **assignment**; **assignment** at **assign** SEND.

assign [SEND] /ə'saɪn/ *verb* [T] to send someone somewhere to do a job: *She was assigned **to** the newspaper's Berlin office.* **assignment** /ə'saɪn.mənt/ *noun* [C or U] *a foreign/diplomatic assignment* ○ *Both journalists were killed by terrorists whilst **on** assignment* (= doing jobs) *in Colombia.* ➲See also **assignment**; **assignment** at **assign** CHOOSE.

assign [COMPUTING] /ə'saɪn/ *verb* [T] SPECIALIZED to put a value in a particular position in the memory of a computer

assign [GIVE LEGALLY] /ə'saɪn/ *verb* [T] LEGAL to give property, money or rights using a legal process: *Her property was assigned **to** her grandchildren.*

▲ **assign *sb* to *sth*** *phrasal verb* [often passive] to choose someone to do a particular job: *Which police officer has been assigned to this case?*

assignation /ˌæs.ɪg'neɪ.ʃᵊn/ *noun* [C] FORMAL a meeting, especially a secret or forbidden one between lovers

assignment /ə'saɪn.mənt/ *noun* [C] a piece of work given to someone, typically as part of their studies or job: *a freelance/photo assignment* ○ *I have a lot of reading assignments to complete before the end of term.* ➲See also **assignment** at **assign** CHOOSE; **assignment** at **assign** SEND.

assimilate /ə'sɪm.ɪ.leɪt/ *verb* [I or T] to take in, fit into, or become similar (to): *The European Union should remain flexible enough to assimilate more countries quickly.* ○ *You shouldn't expect immigrants to assimilate **into** an alien culture immediately.* ○ *It's hard to assimilate* (= learn and understand) *so much information.* ○ *In this form vitamins can be easily assimilated by the body.* **assimilation** /əˌsɪm.ɪ'leɪ.ʃᵊn/ *noun* [U] *The assimilation of ethnic Germans in the US was accelerated by the two world wars.*

assist /ə'sɪst/ *verb* [I or T] FORMAL to help: *The army arrived to assist **in** the search.* ○ *You will be expected to assist the editor **with** the selection of illustrations for the book.*

• **assist the police with/in their inquiries** UK If someone is assisting the police with their inquiries it usually means they have been taken to the police station for official questioning about a crime.

assistance /ə'sɪs.tᵊnts/ *noun* [U] help: *The company needs more **financial** assistance from the Government.* ○ *A £1 billion investment would be **of** considerable assistance to the railways.* ○ *Can I be **of any** assistance, madam* (= Can I help)*?* ○ *Teachers can't **give** pupils any assistance in exams.*

• **come to *sb's* assistance** to help someone

assistant /ə'sɪs.tᵊnt/ *noun* [C] **1** someone who helps someone else to do a job: *an administrative/office assistant* ○ *an assistant editor/manager* **2** UK someone who works in a shop, selling goods to customers and giving advice about the goods sold in the shop: *a **sales/shop** assistant*

assizes /ə'saɪ.zɪz/ *plural noun* (in Wales and England until 1971) one or more of the meetings of the most important court in each county which were usually held four times a year by a travelling judge

assn *noun* [C] ABBREVIATION FOR **association**

assoc ABBREVIATION FOR **association** or **associate**

associate [CONNECT] /ə'səʊ.si.eɪt/ [US] /-'soʊ-/ *verb* [T] to connect someone or something in your mind with someone or something else: *Most people associate this brand **with** good quality.*

associate [FRIEND] /ə'səʊ.si.ət/ [US] /-'soʊ-/ *noun* [C] someone who is closely connected to another person as a companion, friend or business partner: *A close associate of the author denied reports that she had cancer.* ○ *a business associate*

associate [LOWER RANK] /ə'səʊ.si.ət/ [US] /-'soʊ-/ *adj* [before n] used in the title of a person whose rank is slightly lower or less complete than the full official position described: *an associate member of an organization* ○ *associate director/producer*

A

PHRASAL VERBS WITH **associate** ▼

▲ **associate** *sth* **with** *sth* phrasal verb If problems or dangers are associated with a particular thing or action, they are caused by it: *The cancer risks associated with smoking have been well documented.*

▲ **associate with** *sb* phrasal verb to spend time with a group of people, especially people who are disapproved of: *I don't want my children associating with drug-addicts and alcoholics.*

associated /ə'səʊ.si.eɪ.tɪd/ ⓤ /-'soʊ.si.eɪ.t̬ɪd/ adj connected: *She was prepared to take on the job, with all its associated risks.*

as,sociate pro'fessor noun [C] US a high-ranking teacher in a college or university who has a lower rank than a PROFESSOR

associate's degree /ə,səʊ.si.eɪts.dɪ'griː/ ⓤ /-'soʊ-/ noun [C] US the qualification given to a student by a JUNIOR COLLEGE after successfully completing two years of study

associate /ə'səʊ.si.ət/ ⓤ /-'soʊ/ noun [C] US someone who holds an associate's degree: *an associate of arts*

association GROUP /ə,səʊ.si'eɪ.ʃ°n/ ⓤ /-,soʊ-/ group noun [C] a group of people who are united in a single organization for a particular purpose: *The Football Association ○ The British Medical Association is/are campaigning for a complete ban on tobacco advertising.*

association INVOLVEMENT /ə,səʊ.si'eɪ.ʃ°n/ ⓤ /-,soʊ-/ noun **1** [U] when you are involved in or connected to someone or something: *her association **with** the university ○ This event was organized in association **with** the Sports Council.* **2** [C or U] a feeling or thought that relates to someone or something: *The south of France has positive associations for me as I used to holiday there as a child.*

as,sociation 'football noun [U] UK FORMAL soccer

assonance /'æs.°n.°nts/ noun [U] SPECIALIZED the similarity in sound between two syllables that are close together, created either by the same CONSONANTS and different vowels (e.g. 'hit' and 'heart') or by the same vowels but different consonants (e.g. 'back' and 'hat') ⊃Compare **alliteration**.

assorted /ə'sɔː.tɪd/ ⓤ /-'sɔːr.t̬ɪd/ adj consisting of various types mixed together: *a case of assorted wines*

assortment /ə'sɔːt.mənt/ ⓤ /-'sɔːrt-/ noun [C usually sing] a group of different types of something: *an assortment **of** vegetables ○ An unlikely assortment **of** rock stars and politicians attended the charity concert.*

asst adj ABBREVIATION FOR **assistant**

assuage /ə'sweɪdʒ/ verb [T] FORMAL to make unpleasant feelings less strong: *The government has tried to assuage the public's fears.*

assume ACCEPT /ə'sjuːm/ ⓤ /-'suːm/ verb [T] to accept something to be true without question or proof: [+ (that)] *I assumed (that) you knew each other because you went to the same school. ○ Let's assume (that) they're coming and make plans on that basis. ○* [+ to infinitive] *We can't assume the suspects to be guilty simply because they've decided to remain silent. ○ We mustn't assume the suspects' guilt.*

as'suming (that) conjunction accepting as true without question or proof: *Even assuming that smokers do see the health warnings, I doubt they'll take any notice.*

assumption /ə'sʌmp.ʃ°n/ noun [C] something that you accept as true without question or proof: *People tend to **make** assumptions **about** you when you have a disability. ○ These calculations are **based on** the assumption that prices will continue to rise.*

assume PRETEND /ə'sjuːm/ ⓤ /-'suːm/ verb [T] to pretend to have a different name or be someone you are not, or to express a feeling falsely: *Moving to a different town, he assumed a false name. ○ During the investigation, two detectives assumed the identities of antiques dealers. ○ He assumed a look of indifference but I knew how he felt.*

assume TAKE CONTROL /ə'sjuːm/ ⓤ /-'suːm/ verb [T] to take or claim responsibility or control, sometimes without the right to do so, or to begin to possess a characteristic: *The new President assumes office at midnight tonight. ○ The terrorists assumed control of the plane and forced* it to land in the desert. ○ *The issue has assumed considerable political proportions* (= has become a big political problem). **assumption** /ə'sʌmp.ʃ°n/ noun [U] *The revolutionaries' assumption of power took the army by surprise.*

assure SAY WITH CERTAINTY /ə'ʃɔːʳ/ ⓤ /-'ʃɜːʳ/ verb [T] to tell someone confidently that something is true, especially so that they do not worry: *The unions assured the new owners of the workers' loyalty to the company. ○* [+ speech] *"Don't worry, your car will be ready tomorrow," the mechanic assured him. ○* [+ (that)] *She assured him (that) the car would be ready the next day. ○ The Prime Minister assured the electorate (that) taxes would not be increased after the election. ○ You can rest assured* (= feel confident) *that I shall be there as promised.*

assurance /ə'ʃɔː.rənts/ ⓤ /-'ʃɜː.ⁿts/ noun **1** [C] a promise: [+ (that)] *She gave me her assurance (that) she would post the cheque immediately. ○ Despite the Government's repeated assurances **to the contrary**, taxation has risen over the past decade.* **2** [U] confidence: *He spoke with calm assurance.*

assured /ə'ʃɔːd/ ⓤ /-'ʃɜːd/ adj (ALSO **self-assured**) showing skill and confidence: *an assured performance*

assuredly /ə'ʃɔː.rɪd.li/ ⓤ /-'ʃɜː.ɪd-/ adv: *After a disappointing first set, Hewitt played assuredly* (= confidently) *and went on to win the match.*

assure MAKE CERTAIN /ə'ʃɔːʳ/ ⓤ /-'ʃɜːʳ/ verb [T] to cause something to be certain: *The play's popularity has been assured by the critics' rave reviews.* **assured** /ə'ʃɔːd/ ⓤ /-'ʃɜːd/ adj: *Now that the finance has been secured, the production of the film is assured.*

assuredly /ə'ʃɔː.rɪd.li/ ⓤ /-'ʃɜː.ɪd-/ adv: *These problems might not be solved by money alone, but they will assuredly* (= certainly) *not be solved without it.*

assure PROTECT /ə'ʃɔːʳ/ ⓤ /-'ʃɜːʳ/ verb [T] UK (of an organization) to promise to pay a sum of money to a person or their family if they become ill, get injured, or die, in return for small regular payments

assurance /ə'ʃɔː.rənts/ ⓤ /-'ʃɜː.ⁿts/ noun [U] UK a type of insurance against events which will certainly happen, such as death, not ones which may happen, such as illness, fire or having your property stolen

asterisk /'æs.t°r.ɪsk/ ⓤ /-tə-/ noun [C] the symbol (*) which is used to refer readers to a note at the bottom of a page of text, or to show that a letter is missing from a word: *Sometimes taboo words are written with asterisks to avoid causing offence.*

asterisk /'æs.t°r.ɪsk/ ⓤ /-tə-/ verb [T] to write an asterisk next to something: *I have asterisked the books that are essential reading for the course.*

astern /ə'stɜːn/ ⓤ /-'stɜːn/ adv behind a ship, or going backwards when in a ship

asteroid /'æs.t°r.ɔɪd/ ⓤ /-tə.rɔɪd/ noun [C] one of many rocky objects, varying in width from over 900 kilometres to less than one kilometre, which circle the sun

asthma /'æs.mə/ ⓤ /'æz.mə/ noun [U] a medical condition which makes breathing difficult by causing the air passages to become narrow or blocked: *an asthma sufferer ○ an asthma **attack*** **asthmatic** /æs'mæt.ɪk/ ⓤ /æz'mæt̬-/ adj, noun [C] *an asthmatic attack ○ She's been (an) asthmatic since her childhood.*

astigmatism /ə'stɪg.mə.tɪ.z°m/ noun [U] a fault in the LENS of the eye which reduces the quality of sight, especially a fault which stops the eye from FOCUSSING **astigmatic** /,æs.tɪg'mæt.ɪk/ ⓤ /-'mæt̬-/ adj

astonish /ə'stɒn.ɪʃ/ ⓤ /-'stɑː.nɪʃ/ verb [T] to surprise someone very much: *I was astonished **by** how much she'd grown. ○ What astonished me was that he didn't seem to mind.* **astonished** /ə'stɒn.ɪʃt/ ⓤ /-'stɑː.nɪʃt/ adj [+ to infinitive] *I was astonished **to** see Miriam there. ○ They looked astonished when I announced I was pregnant. ○ The doctors were astonished **at** the speed of her recovery.*

astonishing /ə'stɒn.ɪ.ʃɪŋ/ ⓤ /-'stɑː.nɪ-/ adj very surprising: *Her first novel enjoyed an astonishing success. ○* [+ infinitive] *It's astonishing to think that only a few years ago Communism dominated eastern Europe.* **astonishingly** /ə'stɒn.ɪ.ʃɪŋ.li/ ⓤ /-'stɑː.nɪ-/ adv: *Astonishingly, I've never visited King's College Chapel in all the years I've lived*

[A]

here. ○ *She did astonishingly well in her exams.*

astonishment /əˈstɒn.ɪʃ.mənt/ [US] /-ˈstɑː.nɪʃ-/ *noun* [U] very great surprise: ***To the** astonishment **of** her colleagues, she resigned.* ○ *She gasped **in** astonishment.*

astound /əˈstaʊnd/ *verb* [T] to surprise or shock someone very much: *The news astounded me.*

astounded /əˈstaʊn.dɪd/ *adj* very surprised or shocked: [+ *to* infinitive] *I was astounded **to** hear that Tim had left.*

astounding /əˈstaʊn.dɪŋ/ *adj* very surprising or shocking: *an astounding fact/decision/revelation* ○ *an astounding* (= very great) *victory/achievement/success*

astoundingly /əˈstaʊn.dɪŋ.li/ *adv*

astrakhan /ˈæs.trə.kæn/ *noun* [U] (a type of cloth which looks like) the skin of very young sheep from Astrakhan in southern Russia which is covered in usually grey or black wool that is tightly curled and looks like fur

astral [STARS] /ˈæs.trəl/ *adj* relating to the stars or outer space

astral [UNKNOWN FORCES] /ˈæs.trəl/ *adj* [before n] relating to unknown forces; SUPERNATURAL

astray /əˈstreɪ/ *adv* away from the correct path or correct way of doing something: *The letter must have **gone** astray in the post.* ○ *I was **led** astray by an out-of-date map.* ○ *Her parents worried that she might be **led** astray* (= encouraged to behave badly) *by her unsuitable friends.*

astride /əˈstraɪd/ *prep* with a leg on each side of something: *She sat proudly astride her new motorbike.* ○ FIGURATIVE *The town lies astride* (= on either side of) *the River Havel.*

astride /əˈstraɪd/ *adv* with legs wide apart: *He stood there, legs astride.*

astringent [SEVERE] /əˈstrɪn.dʒᵊnt/ *adj* describes remarks which are clever but very critical or unkind: *astringent criticism* ○ *her astringent wit* **astringently** /əˈstrɪn.dʒᵊnt.li/ *adv* **astringency** /əˈstrɪn.dʒᵊnt.si/ *noun* [U]

astringent [MEDICINE] /əˈstrɪn.dʒᵊnt/ *noun* [C or U] a drug or cream that causes the skin or other tissue to tighten so that the flow of blood or other liquids stops: *You can use (an) astringent to make your skin less oily.* **astringent** /əˈstrɪn.dʒᵊnt/ *adj*

astro- /æs.trəʊ-/ [US] /-troʊ-/ *prefix* relating to space, the planets, stars or other objects in space, or to a structure in the shape of a star: *astrology* ○ *astronaut*

astrology /əˈstrɒl.ə.dʒi/ [US] /-ˈstrɑː.lə-/ *noun* [U] the study of the movements and positions of the sun, moon, planets and stars, and the skill of describing the expected effect that these are believed to have on the character and behaviour of humans **astrologer** /əˈstrɒl.ə.dʒəʳ/ [US] /-ˈstrɑː.lə.dʒɚ/ *noun* [C] **astrological** /ˌæs.trəˈlɒdʒ.ɪ.kᵊl/ [US] /-ˈlɑː.dʒɪ-/ *adj*: *an astrological chart/forecast*

astronaut /ˈæs.trə.nɔːt/ [US] /-nɑːt/ *noun* [C] a person who has been trained for travelling in spacecraft

astronautics /ˌæs.trəʊˈnɔː.tɪks/ [US] /-trəˈnɑː.t̬ɪks/ *noun* [U] the technology and science of travelling in space

astronomical [LARGE] /ˌæs.trəˈnɒm.ɪ.kᵊl/ [US] /-ˈnɑː.mɪ-/ *adj* (ALSO **astronomic**) describes an amount which is extremely large: *an astronomical rent/bill/price/fee* **astronomically** /ˌæs.trəˈnɒm.ɪ.kli/ [US] /-ˈnɑː.mɪ-/ *adv*: *Oil prices have risen astronomically* (= by a lot) *since the early 70s.*

astronomical [SCIENTIFIC] /ˌæs.trəˈnɒm.ɪ.kᵊl/ [US] /-ˈnɑː.mɪ-/ *adj* [before n] connected with astronomy: *the Royal Astronomical Society* ○ *astronomical observations/instruments*

astronomy /əˈstrɒn.ə.mi/ [US] /-ˈstrɑː.nə-/ *noun* [U] the scientific study of the universe and of objects which exist naturally in space, such as the moon, the sun, planets and stars **astronomer** /əˈstrɒn.ə.məʳ/ [US] /-ˈstrɑː.nə.mɚ/ *noun* [C]

astrophysics /ˌæs.trəʊˈfɪz.ɪks/ [US] /-troʊ-/ *noun* [U] the type of astronomy which uses physical laws and ideas to explain the behaviour of the stars and other objects in space **astrophysical** /ˌæs.trəʊˈfɪz.ɪ.kᵊl/ [US] /-troʊ-/ *adj* **astrophysicist** /ˌæs.trəʊˈfɪz.ɪ.sɪst/ [US] /-troʊ-/ *noun* [C]

Astroturf /ˈæs.trəʊ.tɜːf/ [US] /-troʊ.tɝːf/ *noun* [U] TRADEMARK a type of artificial grass surface, used especially for sports grounds

astute /əˈstjuːt/ [US] /-ˈstuːt/ *adj* clever and quick to see how to take advantage of a situation: *an astute investor/businesswoman* ○ *his astute handling of the situation* ○ *an astute observer of human behaviour* **astutely** /əˈstjuːt.li/ [US] /-ˈstuːt-/ *adv* **astuteness** /əˈstjuːt.nəs/ [US] /-ˈstuːt-/ *noun* [U]

asunder /əˈsʌn.dəʳ/ [US] /-dɚ/ *adv* LITERARY into forcefully separated pieces; apart: *Their lives were **torn** asunder by the tragedy.*

asylum [PROTECTION] /əˈsaɪ.ləm/ *noun* [U] protection or safety, especially that given by a government to foreigners who have been forced to leave their own countries for political reasons: *to **seek/apply for political** asylum*

asylum [HOSPITAL] /əˈsaɪ.ləm/ *noun* [C] OLD USE a hospital for people with mental illnesses: *a lunatic asylum*

asylum-seeker /əˈsaɪ.ləmˌsiː.kəʳ/ [US] /-kɚ/ *noun* [C] someone who leaves their own country for their safety, often for political reasons or because of war, and who travels to another country hoping that the government will protect them and allow them to live there: *genuine/bogus asylum-seekers* ○ *A record number of asylum-seekers arrived in the UK last month.*

asymmetric /ˌeɪ.sɪˈmet.rɪk/ *adj* (ALSO **asymmetrical**) with two halves, sides or parts which are not exactly the same in shape and size; without SYMMETRY: *Lisette came back from holiday in New York with a trendy asymmetric haircut.* **asymmetrically** /ˌeɪ.sɪˈmet.rɪ.kli/ *adv* **asymmetry** /eɪˈsɪm.ə.tri/ *noun* [C or U]

ˌasymmetric ˈbars UK *plural noun* (US **uneven bars**) two horizontal bars of different height which are used in an event in women's GYMNASTICS, or the event itself

at [PLACE] WEAK /ət/, STRONG /æt/ *prep* used to show an exact position or particular place: *We'll meet you at the entrance.* ○ *That bit at the beginning of the film was brilliant.* ○ *She's sitting at the table in the corner.* ○ *She was standing at the top of the stairs.* ○ *The dog came and lay down at* (= next to) *my feet.* ○ *There's someone at the door* (= someone is outside the door and wants to come in). ○ *We spent the afternoon at a football match.* ○ *I'll give you my number at work/home/the office.* ○ *I enjoyed my three years at university.* ○ *I rang her but she was at lunch* (= away from here, eating her lunch). ➲See Note **in or at?** at **in** INSIDE.

at [TIME] WEAK /ət/, STRONG /æt/ *prep* used to show an exact or a particular time: *There's a meeting at 2.30 this afternoon.* ○ *Are you free at lunchtime?* ○ *In theory, women can still have children at the age of 50.* ○ *The bells ring at regular intervals through the day.* ○ *At no **time/point** did the company do anything illegal.* ○ *I'm busy at **the moment** – can you call back later?* ○ *It's a shame I wasn't here to meet you – I was in London at **the time*** (= then).

at [DIRECTION] WEAK /ət/, STRONG /æt/ *prep* towards; in the direction of: *She smiled at me.* ○ *They waved at us as we drove by.* ○ *She aimed at the target.* ○ *"Look at me! Look at me!" called the little girl.* ○ *He's always shouting at the children.*

at [CAUSE] WEAK /ət/, STRONG /æt/ *prep* used to show the cause of something, especially a feeling: *We were surprised at the news.* ○ *I was quite excited at the prospect.* ○ *Why does no one ever laugh at my jokes?*

at [CONDITION] WEAK /ət/, STRONG /æt/ *prep* used to show a state, condition or continuous activity: *a country at war* ○ *children at play*

at [JUDGMENT] WEAK /ət/, STRONG /æt/ *prep* used to show the activity in which someone's ability is being judged: *I was never very good at sports.* ○ *He's very good at getting on with people.* ○ *She's hopeless at organizing things.*

at [AMOUNT] WEAK /ət/, STRONG /æt/ *prep* **1** used to show a price, temperature, rate, speed, etc: *I'm not going to buy those shoes at $150!* ○ *Inflation is running at 5%.* ○ *He was driving at 120 mph when the police spotted him.* **2** the @ symbol, used in financial records to show the price, rate, etc. of a particular item or of each of a number of items on a list

at [INTERNET] /æt/ *noun* [U] the @ symbol that joins the name of a person or a department in an organization to a DOMAIN NAME to make an email address: *You can email cide@cambridge.org to find out more about this dic-*

tionary. ○ "What's your email address?" "It's cide at cambridge dot org."

at 'all adv (used to make negatives and questions stronger) in any way or of any type: He's had no food at all. ○ I haven't been at all well recently. ○ I'm afraid I've got **nothing** at all to say. ○ Is there any uncertainty at all about the way she died? ○ Why bother getting up at all when you don't have a job to go to?

atavistic /ˌæt.əˈvɪs.tɪk/ ⑩ /ˌæt̬-/ adj FORMAL (of behaviour) happening because of a very old natural and basic habit from the distant past, not because of a conscious decision or present need or usefulness: an atavistic fear of the dark **atavism** /ˈæt.ə.vɪ.zᵊm/ ⑩ /ˈæt̬-/ noun [U]

ate /et/ ⑩ /eɪt/ past simple of **eat**

atelier /ˌæt.elˈi.eɪ/ noun [C] LITERARY a room or building in which an artist works

atheist /ˈeɪ.θi.ɪst/ noun [C] someone who believes that God or gods do not exist ◒Compare **agnostic**. **atheist** /ˈeɪ.θi.ɪst/ adj (ALSO **atheistic**) **atheism** /ˈeɪ.θi.ɪ.zᵊm/ noun [U]

athlete /ˈæθ.liːt/ noun [C] a person who is very good at sports or physical exercise, especially one who competes in organized events: He became a **professional** athlete at the age of 16. ○ She has the build of an athlete.

athletic /æθˈlet.ɪk/ ⑩ /-ˈleṭ-/ adj **1** strong, healthy and good at sports: She looks very athletic. **2** [before n] relating to athletes or the sport of athletics: This college has a long tradition of athletic excellence.

athleticism /æθˈlet.ɪ.sɪ.zᵊm/ ⑩ /-ˈleṭ-/ noun [U] The team's superb athleticism (= skill in running, jumping, throwing, etc.) compensated for their lack of international experience.

athletics UK /æθˈlet.ɪks/ ⑩ /-ˈleṭ-/ noun [U] (US **track and field**) the general name for a particular group of competitive sports, including running, jumping and throwing: an athletics team/club/meeting ◒See picture **Sports** on page Centre 10

athlete's foot /ˌæθ.liːtsˈfʊt/ noun [U] a disease in which the skin between the toes cracks and feels sore

ath,letic sup'porter noun [C] US FORMAL FOR **jock-strap**

-ation /-eɪ.ʃᵊn/ suffix **-ion** ACTION

atishoo UK /əˈtɪʃ.uː/ exclamation (ALSO **achoo**) used, especially in writing, to represent the sound of a sneeze

-ative /-ə.tɪv/ ⑩ /-ə.t̬ɪv/ suffix (ALSO **-ive**) added to verbs to form adjectives meaning showing the ability to perform the activity represented by the verb

atlas /ˈæt.ləs/ noun [C] a book containing maps: a road atlas ○ an atlas of the world

ATM /ˌeɪ.tiːˈem/ noun [C] ABBREVIATION FOR automated teller machine: a machine, usually in a wall outside a bank, from which you can take money out of your bank account using a special card

atmosphere AIR /ˈæt.məs.sfɪəʳ/ ⑩ /-sfɪr/ **1 the atmosphere** the mixture of gases around the Earth: These factories are releasing toxic gases into the atmosphere. **2** [S] the air that you breathe in a place: The atmosphere in the room was so stuffy I could hardly breathe. **3** [C] the mixture of gases that surrounds some planets, such as the Earth; the air

atmospheric /ˌæt.məsˈfer.ɪk/ adj [before n] relating to the air or to the atmosphere: Plants are the main source of atmospheric oxygen. ○ If atmospheric **conditions** are right, it may be possible to see this group of stars tonight.

atmospherics /ˌæt.məsˈfer.ɪks/ plural noun SPECIALIZED unusual conditions in the atmosphere, such as those caused by lightning, or the continuous short, sharp noises produced by a radio during these conditions

COMMON LEARNER ERROR

atmosphere (spelling)

Many learners forget the final 'e' of this word. One way to remember the correct spelling is that the second part of the word is 'sphere'.

Meteors usually burn up in the Earth's atmosphere.

atmosphere CHARACTER /ˈæt.məs.fɪəʳ/ ⑩ /-fɪr/ noun **1** [S] the character or feeling or mood of a place or situation:

There's a very relaxed atmosphere in our office. ○ There has been **an** atmosphere **of** gloom in the factory since it was announced that it would be closing. **2** [U] APPROVING a feeling that a place has of being pleasant and interesting or exciting: You want a restaurant that serves good food but has a bit of atmosphere too. ○ He put on some soft music and turned the lights down in order to give the room a bit more atmosphere.

atmospheric /ˌæt.məsˈfer.ɪk/ adj APPROVING creating a special feeling, such as mystery or romance: atmospheric lighting/music

atoll /ˈæt.ɒl/ ⑩ /-ɑːl/ noun [C] a ring-shaped island formed of CORAL (= rock-like natural substance) which surrounds a LAGOON (= area of sea water): the Bikini atoll

atom /ˈæt.əm/ ⑩ /ˈæt̬-/ noun [C] the smallest unit of any chemical element, consisting of a positive nucleus surrounded by negative electrons. Atoms can combine to form a molecule: A molecule of carbon dioxide (CO_2) has one carbon atom and two oxygen atoms. ○ FIGURATIVE He hasn't an atom **of** sense (= He has no sense), that boy.

atomic /əˈtɒm.ɪk/ ⑩ /-ˈtɑː.mɪk/ adj **1** relating to atoms: atomic structure/nuclei ◒See also **nuclear**. **2** using the energy that is created when an atom is divided: atomic **energy/power** ○ atomic scientists **atomically** /əˈtɒm.ɪ.kli/ ⑩ /-ˈtɑː.mɪ-/ adv

atom ,bomb noun [C] (ALSO **atomic bomb**) SLIGHTLY OLD-FASHIONED an extremely powerful bomb that uses the explosive power that results from splitting the atom

atomizer UK USUALLY **-iser** /ˈæt.ə.maɪ.zəʳ/ ⑩ /ˈæt̬.ə.maɪ.zɚ/ noun [C] a device that changes a liquid into small drops by forcing it out through a very small hole: Atomizers are used for putting on perfume.

atonal /ˌeɪˈtəʊ.nᵊl/ ⑩ /-ˈtoʊ-/ adj SPECIALIZED not written in any particular musical KEY (= set of notes)

atone /əˈtəʊn/ ⑩ /-ˈtoʊn/ verb

▲ **atone for** sth phrasal verb FORMAL to do something that shows that you are sorry for something bad that you did: The country's leader has expressed a wish to atone for his actions in the past.

atonement /əˈtəʊn.mənt/ ⑩ /-ˈtoʊn-/ noun [U] He said that young hooligans should do community service as atonement **for** their crimes.

atop /əˈtɒp/ ⑩ /-ˈtɑːp/ prep MAINLY US on or at the top of: She sat atop a two-metre high wall.

atrium /ˈeɪ.tri.əm/ noun [C] plural **atriums** a very large room, often with glass walls or roof, especially in the middle of a large shop or office building

atrocious VERY BAD /əˈtrəʊ.ʃəs/ ⑩ /-ˈtroʊ-/ adj of very bad quality: an atrocious film/piece of acting ○ The weather has been atrocious all week. ○ Conditions in the prison were atrocious. **atrociously** /əˈtrəʊ.ʃə.sli/ ⑩ /-ˈtroʊ-/ adv: The children have been behaving atrociously.

atrocious CRUEL /əˈtrəʊ.ʃəs/ ⑩ /-ˈtroʊ-/ adj violent and shocking: an atrocious crime **atrociously** /əˈtrəʊ.ʃə.li/ ⑩ /-ˈtroʊ-/ adv

atrocity /əˈtrɒs.ɪ.ti/ ⑩ /-ˈtrɑː.sɪ.t̬i/ noun [C or U] when someone does something extremely violent and shocking: They're on trial for **committing** atrocities **against** the civilian population. ○ These people are guilty of acts of great atrocity (= cruelty).

atrophy /ˈæt.rə.fi/ verb [I] (of a part of the body) to be reduced in size and therefore strength, or, more generally, to become weaker: After several months in a hospital bed, my leg muscles had atrophied. ○ In the 1980s, their political power gradually atrophied (= became weaker). **atrophy** /ˈæt.rə.fi/ noun [U]

attach CONNECT /əˈtætʃ/ verb [T] to fasten, join or connect; to place or fix in position: I attached a photo **to** my application form. ○ Use this cable to attach the printer **to** the computer. ○ In Britain, packets of cigarettes come with a government health warning attached **to** them (= on them). ○ SLIGHTLY FORMAL I attach (= am sending, usually with a letter) a copy of our latest report. ◒Compare **detach**. See also **attached**.

attachment /əˈtætʃ.mənt/ noun [C] an extra piece of equipment that can be added to a machine: This food processor has a special attachment for grinding coffee.

attach TAKE GOODS /əˈtætʃ/ verb [T] UK LEGAL to officially take someone's money or the things that they own, or to

A

arrest them, usually because they have failed to pay money that they owe

attachment /əˈtætʃ.mənt/ *noun* [C or U] *UK LEGAL* the act of arresting a person for failing to obey the order of a court, or of officially taking their property because they have failed to pay money that they owe

attach COMPUTING /əˈtætʃ/ *verb* [T] to join a FILE (= a collection of electronic information), such as a document, picture or computer program, to an email **attachment** /əˈtætʃ.mənt/ *noun* [C] *I'll email my report to you* **as an** *attachment.* ○ *I wasn't able to* **open** *that attachment.*

PHRASAL VERBS WITH **attach** ▼

▲ **attach** *sth* **to** *sth* QUALITY *phrasal verb SLIGHTLY FORMAL* To attach a particular quality to something is to consider it to have that quality: *I don't attach any importance/significance to these rumours.* ○ *She attaches great value to being financially independent.*

▲ **attach to** *sb/sth phrasal verb MAINLY UK FORMAL* If you say that a particular quality attaches to someone or something, you mean that they have that quality: *Don't worry – it was an accident and no blame attaches to either of you.* ○ [+ v-ing] *Great honour attaches to win**ning** this award.*

▲ **attach** *yourself* **to** *sb/sth* JOIN *phrasal verb* [R] If you attach yourself to a person or group, you join them, usually for a limited period of time: *Being on his own, he attached himself to a noisy group at the bar.*

attaché /əˈtæʃ.eɪ/ ⓤ /ˌæt̬.əˈʃeɪ/ *noun* [C] a person who works in an EMBASSY and has a particular area of responsibility in which they have specialist knowledge: *a naval/military/press/cultural attaché*

at'taché ˌcase *noun* [C] a hard-sided rectangular case, used especially for carrying business documents; a type of **briefcase**

attached /əˈtætʃt/ *adj* **be attached to** *sb/sth* to like someone or something very much: *The children are very attached to their grandparents.* ○ *I'm very attached to my old guitar.* ⊃See also **attach**.

attachment /əˈtætʃ.mənt/ *noun* [C or U] a feeling of love or strong connection to someone or something: *At university I* **formed** *a strong attachment* **to** *one of my tutors.* ○ *She is unlikely to give up her lifelong attachment* **to** *feminist ideas.* ⊃See also **attachment** at **attach**.

attack /əˈtæk/ *verb* **1** [I or T] to try to hurt or defeat using violence: *He was attacked and seriously injured by a gang of youths.* ○ *Army forces have been attacking the town since dawn.* ○ *Most wild animals won't attack unless they are provoked.* ⊃Compare **defend**. **2** [T] to criticize someone strongly: *She wrote an article attacking the judges and their conduct of the trial.* ○ *The report attacks the idea of exams for 7- and 8-year-olds.* **3** [T] If something, such as a disease or a chemical, attacks something, it damages it: *AIDS attacks the body's immune system.* ○ *My rose bushes are being attacked by greenfly.* **4** [I or T] If players in a team attack, they move forward to try to score points, goals, etc. **5** [T] to deal with something quickly and in an efficient way: *We have to attack these problems now and find some solutions.* ○ *The children rushed in and eagerly attacked the food* (= quickly started to eat it).

attack /əˈtæk/ *noun* **1** [C or U] a violent act intended to hurt or damage someone or something: *a racist attack* ○ *Enemy forces have* **made** *an attack* **on** *the city.* ○ *These bomb blasts suggest that the terrorists are* **(going) on the** *attack* (= trying to defeat or hurt other people) *again.* ○ *The town was once again* **under** *attack* (= being attacked). **2** [C or U] when you say something to strongly criticize someone or something: *a scathing attack on the president* ○ *The government has* **come under** *attack* **from all sides** *for cutting education spending.* **3** [C] a sudden and short period of illness: *an attack of asthma/ flu/malaria* ○ *FIGURATIVE an attack of the giggles* **4** [C or U] the part of a team in some sports which tries to score points: *The team has a strong attack, but its defence is weak.* ○ *The team is strong (UK)* **in**/(US) **on** *attack but useless in defence.* **5** [U] when you play a sport in a determined way and try hard to score points: *The team needs to put some more attack into its game.*

attacker /əˈtæk.əʳ/ ⓤ /-ɚ/ *noun* [C] a person who uses violence to hurt someone: *The police think she must have known her attacker.*

attain /əˈteɪn/ *verb* [T] *FORMAL* to reach or succeed in getting something; to achieve: *He has attained the highest grade in his music exams.* ○ *We need to identify the best ways of attaining our* **objectives/goals.** ○ *India attained independence in 1947, after decades of struggle.*

attainable /əˈteɪ.nə.bl̩/ *adj FORMAL* possible to achieve: *We must ensure that we do not set ourselves goals that are not attainable.*

attainment /əˈteɪn.mənt/ *noun* **1** [U] *FORMAL* when you achieve something: *the attainment of a goal* ○ *attainment* **targets 2** [C usually pl] *UK FORMAL* Someone's attainments are the things they have done and the skills they have learned.

attempt /əˈtempt/ *verb* [T] to try to do something, especially something difficult: [+ **to** infinitive] *He attempted* **to** *escape through a window.* ○ *He attempted a joke, but no one laughed.* ○ *There's no point in even attempting an explanation – he'll never listen.* **attempted** /əˈtemp.tɪd/ *adj* [before n] *LEGAL* A man is being questioned in relation to the attempted **murder/robbery** last night.

attempt /əˈtempt/ *noun* [C] when you try to do something, especially something difficult: [+ **to** infinitive] *She* **made** *a few half-hearted attempts* **to** *join in their conversation.* ○ *He* **made no** *attempt to be sociable.* ○ *This is my second attempt* **at** *the exam.* ○ *None of our attempts* **at** *contacting Dr James was successful.* ○ *They closed the road* **in an** *attempt* (= to try to) *to reduce traffic in the city.*

● **an attempt on** *sb's* **life** an act of trying to kill someone: *This is the third attempt on the President's life this year.*

attend BE PRESENT /əˈtend/ *verb SLIGHTLY FORMAL* **1** [I or T] to go to an event, place, etc: *Over two hundred people attended the funeral.* ○ *The meeting is on the fifth and we're hoping everyone will attend.* ⊃See also **attend** at **attention** NOTICE; **well-attended**. **2** [T] to go officially and usually regularly to a place: *Which school do your children attend?* ○ *I attended the classes/seminars/lectures for a month or two.*

attendance /əˈten.dᵊnts/ *noun* [C or U] *Attendance at* (= Going to) *lectures is compulsory.* ○ *Attendances at church are falling* (= Fewer people are regularly going there).

COMMON LEARNER ERROR

attend or **wait/expect**?

Attend cannot be used to talk about being in a place when you know that someone or something will come there soon. For this meaning you should use **wait for** or **expect**.

Her mother was waiting for her outside in the car.

~~Her mother was attending her outside in the car.~~

'We're expecting a delivery at three o'clock, ' she said.

~~'We're attending a delivery at three o'clock, ' she said.~~

---

attend PROVIDE HELP /əˈtend/ *verb* [T] to provide a service to someone, especially as part of your job; to care for or deal with someone or something: *The Princess was attended by her ladies-in-waiting.* ⊃See also **attend** at **attention** NOTICE.

attendance /əˈten.dᵊnts/ *noun* [U] *He never goes out without his security men* **in** *attendance* (= with him and taking care of him).

attendant /əˈten.dᵊnt/ *noun* [C] **1** someone whose job is to be in a place and help visitors or customers: *a cloakroom/museum attendant* **2** someone whose job is to travel or live with an important person and help them: *The Prince was followed by his attendants.*

attention /əˈten.tʃᵊn/ *noun* [U] special care or treatment: *The paintwork will* **need** *a little attention.* ○ *If symptoms persist seek* **medical** *attention* (= visit a doctor). ⊃See also **attention** NOTICE; **attention** WAY OF STANDING.

attentive /əˈten.tɪv/ ⓤ /-t̬ɪv/ *adj* If someone is attentive, they are very helpful and take care of you: *He was very attentive to her when she was ill.* ○ *A good teacher is always attentive* **to** *their students'* **needs.** **attentively** /əˈten.tɪv.li/ ⓤ /-t̬ɪv-/ *adv* **attentiveness** /əˈten.tɪv.nəs/ ⓤ /-t̬ɪv-/ *noun* [U]

A

attend [RESULT FROM] /ə'tend/ *verb* [T] *FORMAL* to happen as a result of, and at the same time as: *the publicity that attends a career in television* ➲See also **attend** at **attention** NOTICE.
attendant /ə'ten.dənt/ *adj FORMAL There are too many risks attendant* **on** (= resulting from) *such a large investment of money.*
▲ **attend to** ***sb/sth*** *phrasal verb* to deal with something or help someone: *Doctors tried to attend to the worst injured soldiers first.* ○ *I always have so many things to attend to when I come into the office after a trip abroad.*

attention [NOTICE] /ə'ten.tʃən/ *noun* [U] notice, thought or consideration: *Ladies and gentlemen, could I* ***have your*** *attention, please?* ○ *They're organizing a campaign to* ***draw*** *people's attention* ***to*** *the environmentally harmful effects of using their cars.* ○ *He likes being* ***the centre of*** *attention* (= having a lot of people notice him) ○ *I knocked on the window to* ***get/attract/catch*** *her attention* (= make her notice me). ○ *After an hour, my attention started to* ***wander*** (= I stopped taking notice). ○ *Don't* ***pay*** *any attention* ***to*** (= take any notice of) *Nina – she doesn't know what she's talking about.* ○ *If you don't* ***pay*** *attention* (= listen carefully) *now, you'll get it all wrong later.* ○ *Wait a moment and I'll* ***give*** *you my* ***full/undivided*** *attention* (= I'll listen to and think about only you). ○ *Many countries are starting to* ***turn*** *their attention* ***to*** (= to consider) *new forms of energy.* ➲See also **attention** at **attend** PROVIDE HELP.
attentions /ə'tent.ʃənz/ *plural noun: Many countries are starting to* ***turn*** *their attentions* (= attention) **to** *new forms of energy.*
attend /ə'tend/ *verb* [I] *FORMAL* to give attention to what someone is saying: *I'm afraid I wasn't attending* ***to*** *what was being said.* ➲See also **attend** BE PRESENT, PROVIDE HELP, RESULT FROM.
attentive /ə'ten.tɪv/ [US] /-t̬ɪv/ *adj* listening carefully: *an attentive audience* **attentively** /ə'ten.tɪv.li/ [US] /-t̬ɪv-/ *adv: The children sat* ***listening*** *attentively to the story.*

attention [WAY OF STANDING] /ə'ten.tʃən/ *noun* [U] (especially in the armed forces) a way of standing, with the feet together, arms by your sides, head up and shoulders back and not moving: *soldiers standing* ***at/to*** *attention*

at,tention ,deficit hyperac'tivity dis,order *noun* [U] (*ABBREVIATION* **ADHD**) *UK* a condition in which someone, especially a child, is often in a state of activity or excitement and unable to direct their attention towards what they are doing ✱ NOTE: This condition is usually called **attention deficit disorder** in the US.

at'tention ,span *noun* [C] the length of time that you can keep your thoughts and interest fixed on something: *Young children have quite short attention spans.*

attenuate /ə'ten.ju.eɪt/ *verb* [T] *FORMAL* to make something smaller, thinner or weaker: *Radiation from the sun is attenuated by the Earth's atmosphere.* **attenuated** /ə'ten.ju.eɪ.tɪd/ [US] /-t̬ɪd/ *adj* **attenuation** /ə,ten.ju'eɪ.ʃən/ *noun* [U]

attest /ə'test/ *verb* [I or T] *FORMAL* to show something or to say or prove that something is true: *Thousands of people came out onto the streets to attest their support for the democratic opposition party.* ○ *The number of old German cars still on the road attests* ***(to)*** *the excellence of their manufacture.* ○ *As his career attests, he is a cricketer of world-class standard.* ○ *SPECIALIZED The will needs to be attested* (= officially marked to show that the signature of the person who made the will is correct) *by three witnesses.*
attestation /,æt.es'teɪ.ʃən/ [US] /,æt̬-/ *noun* [C] *SPECIALIZED* a formal statement which you make and officially say is true

attic /'æt.ɪk/ [US] /'æt̬-/ *noun* [C] the space or room at the top of a building, under the roof, often used for storing things: *I've got boxes of old clothes in the attic, which I really should throw out.* ○ *an attic bedroom at the top of the house*

attire /ə'taɪər/ [US] /-'taɪr/ *noun* [U] *FORMAL* clothes, especially of a particular or formal type: *I hardly think jeans are appropriate attire for a wedding.* **attired** /ə'taɪəd/ [US] /-'taɪrd/ *adj* [after v] *She was attired from head to foot in black.*

attitude [OPINION] /'æt.ɪ.tjuːd/ [US] /'æt̬.ɪ.tuːd/ *noun* **1** [C or U] a feeling or opinion about something or someone, or a way of behaving that is caused by this: *It's often very difficult to change people's attitudes.* ○ [+ that] *She* ***takes*** *the attitude* ***that*** *children should be allowed to learn at their own pace.* ○ *He has a very bad attitude* ***to/towards*** *work.* ○ *He seems to have undergone a change* ***in/of*** *attitude recently, and has become much more co-operative.* ○ *I don't like your attitude* (= the way you are behaving). ○ *That boy has a real attitude* ***problem*** (= behaves in a way that makes it difficult for other people to have a relationship with him or work with him). **2** [U] If you say that someone has attitude, you mean that they are confident and independent, often in a rude or unpleasant way.

attitude [POSITION] /'æt.ɪ.tjuːd/ [US] /'æt̬.ɪ.tuːd/ *noun* [C] *LITERARY* a position of the body: *She lay sprawled across the sofa, in an attitude* ***of*** *complete abandon.*
● **strike an attitude** *FORMAL* to hold your body in a way which suggests a particular quality or feeling: *He struck an attitude* ***of*** *offended dignity and marched out of the room.*

attorney /ə'tɜː.ni/ [US] /-'tɝː-/ *noun* [C] *US FOR* lawyer: *a defense attorney* ○ *an attorney for the plaintiff* ○ *a civil/criminal attorney* ➲See Note **lawyer, solicitor, barrister and attorney** at **lawyer**.

At,torney 'General *noun* [C] *plural* **Attorneys General** or **Attorney Generals** the top legal officer in some countries, who advises the leader of the government

attract /ə'trækt/ *verb* **1** [T] (of people, things, places, etc.) to pull or draw someone or something towards them, by the qualities they have, especially positive and admirable ones: *These flowers are brightly coloured in order to attract butterflies.* ○ *The circus is attracting huge* ***crowds/audiences.*** ○ *Magnets attract iron filings.* ○ *The government is trying to attract industry* ***to*** *the area* (= to persuade people to place their industry there). ○ *Her ideas have attracted a lot of* ***attention/criticism*** *in the scientific community.* **2** [T usually passive] If you are attracted by or to someone, you like them, often finding them sexually desirable: *I'm not physically/sexually attracted to him.*
attraction /ə'træk.ʃən/ *noun* **1** [C or U] something which makes people want to go to a place or do a particular thing: *Life in London has so many attractions – nightclubs, good restaurants and so on.* ○ ***tourist*** *attractions* ○ *The opportunity to travel is one of the* ***main*** *attractions of this job.* ○ *Skiing* ***holds*** *no attraction* ***for*** *me.* **2** [U] when you like someone, especially sexually, because of the way they look or behave: *She felt an immediate physical attraction* ***to*** *him.*
attractive /ə'træk.tɪv/ [US] /-t̬ɪv/ *adj* very pleasing in appearance or sound, or causing interest or pleasure: *a very attractive young woman* ○ *I* ***find*** *him very attractive* (= He attracts me sexually). ○ *attractive countryside* ○ *an attractive colour scheme* ○ *Spending 12 hours on a plane isn't a very attractive* (= pleasant) *prospect.* ○ *an attractive offer* (= an offer with benefits for me) ○ *We need to make the club attractive* ***to*** (= interesting to) *a wider range of people.* **attractively** /ə'træk.tɪv.li/ [US] /-t̬ɪv-/ *adv: She always dresses very attractively.* ○ *Their house is attractively decorated.* **attractiveness** /ə'træk.tɪv.nəs/ [US] /-t̬ɪv-/ *noun* [U] *her attractiveness to men* ○ *High mortgage rates have decreased the attractiveness of house-owning.*

attribute /'æt.rɪ.bjuːt/ *noun* [C] a quality or characteristic that someone or something has: *Organizational ability is an essential attribute for a good manager.*
attribute /ə'trɪb.juːt/ /-juːt/ *verb*

PHRASAL VERBS WITH **attribute** ▼

▲ **attribute** ***sth*** **to** ***sb*** [QUALITY] *phrasal verb* to think that someone or something has a particular quality or feature: *I wouldn't dream of attributing such a lack of judgment to you.*
▲ **attribute** ***sth*** **to** ***sb/sth*** [RESULT] *phrasal verb* to say or think that something is the result or work of something or someone else: *The doctors have attributed the cause of the illness to an unknown virus.* ○ *To what do you*

attribute this delay? ○ *Most experts have attributed the drawing to Michelangelo.*
attributable /əˈtrɪb.jʊ.tə.bl̩/ [US] /-t̬ə-/ *adj* [after v] caused by: *Do you think that these higher-than-average temperatures are attributable **to** global warming?* **attribution** /ˌæt.rɪˈbjuː.ʃᵊn/ *noun* [U] *The usual attribution **of** the work **to** Leonardo is now disputed by several experts.*

attributive /əˈtrɪb.jʊ.tɪv/ [US] /-t̬ɪv/ *adj* SPECIALIZED (of the position or use of an adjective, noun or phrase) before a noun: *In 'a sudden movement', 'sudden' is an adjective in the attributive position.* ○ *In 'the television aerial', 'television' is a noun used in an attributive way.* **attributively** /əˈtrɪb.jʊ.tɪv.li/ [US] /-t̬ɪv-/ *adv*

attrition /əˈtrɪʃ.ᵊn/ *noun* [U] **1** SLIGHTLY FORMAL the gradual weakening and destroying of something, especially the strength or confidence of an enemy by repeatedly attacking it: *Terrorist groups and the government have been engaged in a costly **war of** attrition since 1968.* **2** US FOR **natural wastage**

attuned to /əˈtjuːnd/ [US] /-ˈtuːnd/ *adj* [after v] **1** able to understand, or being very familiar with: *A good nurse has to be attuned to the needs of his or her patients.* **2** If your ears are attuned to a particular sound, they are able to recognize it very easily: *A mother's ears are attuned to even the slightest variation in her baby's breathing.*

atypical /ˌeɪˈtɪp.ɪ.kᵊl/ *adj* not typical; different from all the others of its type: *The sociable behaviour of lions is considered atypical **of** the cat family.*

aubergine UK /ˈəʊ.bə.ʒiːn/ [US] /ˈoʊ.bɚ-/ *noun* [C] (US **eggplant**) an oval purple vegetable which is white inside and which is usually eaten cooked ➲See picture **Vegetables** on page Centre 2

auburn /ˈɔː.bən/ [US] /ˈɑː.bɚn/ *adj* (of hair) reddish brown: *auburn-haired*

auction /ˈɔːk.ʃᵊn/ [US] /ˈɑːk-/ *noun* [C or U] a usually public sale of goods or property, where people make higher and higher BIDS (= offers of money) for each item, until the item is sold to the person who will pay most: *a furniture auction* ○ *They're **holding** an auction **of** jewellery on Thursday.* ○ *The painting will be sold **at**/(UK ALSO) **by** auction next week.* ○ *The house and its contents are being **put up for** auction.*
auction /ˈɔːk.ʃᵊn/ [US] /ˈɑːk-/ *verb* [T] *The stamps will be auctioned* (= sold by public auction) *tomorrow.* ○ *The family is auctioning **(off)** its art collection.*
auctioneer /ˌɔːk.ʃəˈnɪəʳ/ [US] /ˌɑːk.ʃəˈnɪr/ *noun* [C] a person in charge of an auction who calls out the prices that people offer

audacious /ɔːˈdeɪ.ʃəs/ [US] /ɑː-/ *adj* showing a willingness to take risks or offend people: *He described the plan as ambitious and audacious.* ○ *an audacious remark/suggestion* **audaciously** /ɔːˈdeɪ.ʃə.sli/ [US] /ɑː-/ *adv* **audaciousness** /ɔːˈdeɪ.ʃə.snəs/ [US] /ɑː-/ *noun* [U]
audacity /ɔːˈdæs.ɪ.ti/ [US] /ɑːˈdæs.ɪ.t̬i/ *noun* [U] [+ **to** infinitive] *It took a lot of audacity* (= bravery) ***to** stand up and criticize the chairman.* ○ DISAPPROVING *He **had the** audacity* (= rudeness) **to** *blame me for his mistake.*

audible /ˈɔː.dɪ.bl̩/ [US] /ˈɑː-/ *adj* able to be heard: *The lecturer spoke so quietly that he was scarcely audible at the back of the hall.* ○ *She gave an audible sigh of relief.* **audibly** /ˈɔː.dɪ.bli/ [US] /ˈɑː-/ *adv*

audience [GROUP OF PEOPLE] /ˈɔː.di.ənts/ [US] /ˈɑː-/ *group noun* [C] the group of people gathered in one place to watch or listen to a play, film, someone speaking, etc., or the (number of) people watching or listening to a particular television or radio programme, or reading a particular book: *She lectures to audiences all over the world.* ○ *The secret to public speaking is to get the audience on your side.* ○ *The audience was/were clearly delighted with the performance.* ○ *The magic show had a lot of audience **participation**, with people shouting things to the performers and going up on stage.* ○ *The television company has **lost** a large part of its audience* (= the group of people who watch its programmes) *since it changed its programming.* ○ *Her latest book should appeal to a large audience* (= many people will want to read it).

audience [FORMAL MEETING] /ˈɔː.di.ənts/ [US] /ˈɑː-/ *noun* [C] a formal meeting that you have with an important person: *She had a private audience **with** the king.*

audio /ˈɔː.di.əʊ/ [US] /ˈɑː.di.oʊ/ *adj* connected with sound and the recording and broadcasting of sound: *an audio cassette* ○ *audio tape* ○ *an audio signal*

audio-visual /ˌɔː.di.əʊˈvɪʒ.u.əl/ [US] /ˌɑː.di.oʊ-/ *adj* [before n] (ABBREVIATION **AV**) describes something that involves seeing or hearing: *audio-visual equipment/aids/software*

audit [FINANCE] /ˈɔː.dɪt/ [US] /ˈɑː-/ *verb* [T] SPECIALIZED to make an official examination of the ACCOUNTS of a business **audit** /ˈɔː.dɪt/ [US] /ˈɑː-/ *noun* [C] *The company has an audit at the end of each financial year.* **auditor** /ˈɔː.dɪt.əʳ/ [US] /ˈɑː.dɪ.t̬ɚ/ *noun* [C] *The external auditors come in once a year.*

audit [EDUCATION] /ˈɔː.dɪt/ [US] /ˈɑː-/ *verb* [T] US to go to a class or educational course for pleasure or interest, without being tested or receiving a qualification at the end: *As a senior citizen, he is allowed to audit university classes.*

audition /ɔːˈdɪʃ.ᵊn/ [US] /ɑː-/ *noun* [C] a short performance that an actor, musician, dancer, etc. gives in order to show their ability and suitability for a particular play, film, show, etc: *His audition went well and he's fairly hopeful about getting the part.* ○ *The director is **holding** auditions next week **for** the major parts.*
audition /ɔːˈdɪʃ.ᵊn/ [US] /ɑː-/ *verb* [I or T] to give a short performance in order to show your suitability for a role in a film, play, show, etc, or to make someone do this: *I'm auditioning **for** the part of Lady Macbeth.* ○ *We're auditioning local rock bands **for** the music festival.*

auditorium /ˌɔː.dɪˈtɔː.ri.əm/ [US] /ˌɑː.dɪ.tɔːr.i-/ *noun* [C] *plural* **auditoriums** or **auditoria 1** the part of a theatre, or similar building, where the people who are watching and listening sit: *No smoking in the auditorium.* **2** MAINLY US a large public building such as a theatre

auditory /ˈɔː.dɪ.tri/ [US] /ˈɑː-/ *adj* SPECIALIZED of or about hearing: *It's an artificial device which stimulates the auditory areas of the brain.*

au fait /ˌəʊˈfeɪ/ [US] /ˌoʊ-/ *adj* **be au fait with *sth*** to be familiar with or informed about something: *Are you au fait with the rules of the game?*

auger /ˈɔː.gəʳ/ [US] /ˈɑː.gɚ/ *noun* [C] a tool consisting of a twisted rod of metal fixed to a handle, used for making large holes in wood or in the ground

augment /ɔːgˈment/ [US] /ɑːg-/ *verb* [T] FORMAL to increase the size or value of something by adding something to it: *He would have to find work to augment his income.* **augmentation** /ˌɔːg.menˈteɪ.ʃᵊn/ [US] /ˌɑːg-/ *noun* [C or U]

au gratin /ˌəʊˈgræt.æ̃/ *adj* [after n] cooked with a covering of cheese or small pieces of bread mixed with butter: *potatoes au gratin*

augur /ˈɔː.gəʳ/ [US] /ˈɑː.gɚ/ *verb* [I + adv or prep; T] FORMAL to be a sign of especially good or bad things in the future: *The company's sales figures for the first six months augur **well** for the rest of the year.* ○ *Do you think that this recent ministerial announcement augurs* (= is a sign of) *a shift in government policy?*
augury /ˈɔːg.jʊ.ri/ [US] /ˈɑːg.jɚ.i/ *noun* [C] FORMAL a sign of what might happen in the future: *These sales figures are a good augury **for** another profitable year.*

August [MONTH] /ˈɔː.gəst/ [US] /ˈɑː-/ *noun* [C or U] (WRITTEN ABBREVIATION **Aug**) the eighth month of the year, after July and before September: *13(th) August/August 13(th)* ○ *We're going to Australia **on** the first of August/August the first/*(MAINLY US) *August first.* ○ *We've got friends coming at the end of August.* ○ *They got married **last** August/are getting married **next** August.* ○ *Cairo **during/in** August is unbearably hot and crowded.* ○ *It was one of the hottest Augusts on record.*

august [IMPORTANT] /ɔːˈgʌst/ [US] /ɑː-/ *adj* FORMAL having great importance and especially of the highest social class: *the society's august patron, the Duke of Norfolk*

aunt /ɑːnt/ [US] /ænt/ *noun* [C] (ALSO **auntie**, ALSO **aunty**) the sister of someone's father or mother, or the wife of someone's uncle: *I have an aunt in Australia.* ○ *Auntie Camille*

au pair /ˌəʊˈpeəʳ *noun* [C] a foreign person, usually a young woman, who lives with a family in order to learn their language and who looks after the children or cleans the house in return for meals, a room and a small payment

aura /'ɔː.rə/ [US] /'ɔːr.ə/ *noun* [C] **1** a feeling or character that a person or place seems to have: *The woods **have** an aura **of** mystery.* ○ *There's an aura **of** sadness **about** him.* **2** a type of light that some people say they can see around people and animals

aural /'ɔː.rəl/ [US] /'ɔːr.əl/ *adj* relating to hearing: *aural teaching aids, such as tapes*

aureole /'ɔː.ri.əʊl/ [US] /'ɔːr.i.oʊl/ *noun* [C] LITERARY a bright circle of light, especially around the head; a **halo**

the aurora australis /ə,rɔː.rə.ɒs'treɪ.lɪs/ [US] /-,rɔːr.ə.ɔː-'streɪ-/ *noun* [S] (ALSO **the Southern Lights**) a pattern of differently coloured lights that are sometimes seen in the night sky in the most southern parts of the world ⮊Compare **the aurora borealis**.

the aurora borealis /ə,rɔː.rə.bɒr.i'ɑː.lɪs/ [US] /-,rɔːr.ə.bɔːr.i'æl.ɪs/ *noun* [S] (ALSO **the Northern Lights**) a pattern of differently coloured lights that are sometimes seen in the night sky in the most northern parts of the world ⮊Compare **the aurora australis**.

auspices /'ɔː.spɪ.sɪz/ [US] /'ɑː-/ *plural noun* FORMAL **under the auspices of *sb/sth*** with the protection or support of someone or something, especially an organization: *Financial aid is being provided to the country under the auspices of the International Monetary Fund.*

auspicious /ɔː'spɪʃ.əs/ [US] /ɑː-/ *adj* FORMAL suggesting a positive and successful future: *They won their first match of the season 5-1 which was an auspicious **start/beginning**.* ○ *Our first meeting was not auspicious – we had a huge argument.* **auspiciously** /ɔː'spɪʃ.ə.sli/ [US] /ɑː-/ *adv*

Aussie /'ɒz.i/ [US] /'ɑː.zi/ *adj, noun* [C] INFORMAL Australian, or an Australian person

austere /ɔː'stɪəʳ/ [US] /ɑː'stɪr/ *adj* without comfort; plain and without decoration; severe: *an austere childhood during the war* ○ *The courtroom was a large dark chamber, an austere place.* ○ *He was a tall, austere, forbidding figure.* **austerely** /ɔː'stɪə.li/ [US] /ɑː'stɪr-/ *adv*: *Her dress was simple and austerely elegant.*

austerity /ɔː'ster. ɪ.ti/ [US] /'ɑː.ster.ɪ.t̬i/ *noun* [C or U] *The wartime austerity* (= lack of luxuries and comfort) *of my early years prepared me for later hardships.* ○ *The austerities of life in a small rural community were not what I was used to.*

Australasia /,ɒs.trə'leɪ.ʒə/ [US] /ɑː.strə-/ *noun* [U] the continent and islands that are to the east of the Indian Ocean, the west of the Pacific Ocean and the south of Asia

Australasian /,ɒs.trə'leɪ.ʒən/ [US] /,ɑː.strə-/ *adj* of or from Australasia (= the area of the world consisting of Australia and New Zealand and the islands near them)

Australasian /,ɒs.trə'leɪ.ʒən/ [US] /,ɑː.strə-/ *noun* [C] a person from Australasia

Australian /ɒs'treɪ.li.ən/ [US] /ɑː'streɪ-/ *noun* [C] a person from Australia

Australian /ɒs'treɪ.li.ən/ [US] /ɑː'streɪ-/ *adj* from, belonging to, or relating to Australia: *Australian wine/weather/politics*

authentic /ɔː'θen.tɪk/ [US] /ɑː'θen.t̬ɪk/ *adj* If something is authentic, it is real, true, or what people say it is: *an authentic 1920s dress* ○ *authentic Italian food* ○ *He was there and saw what happened, so his is the only authentic account.*

authenticate /ɔː'θen.tɪ.keɪt/ [US] /ɑː'θen.t̬ɪ-/ *verb* [T] to prove that something is real, true, or what people say it is: *They used carbon dating tests to authenticate the claim that the skeleton was 2 million years old.* **authentication** /ɔː,θen.tɪ'keɪ.ʃən/ [US] /ɑː,θen.t̬ɪ-/ *noun* [U]

authenticity /,ɔː.θen'tɪs.ɪ.ti/ [US] /,ɑː.θen'tɪs.ə.t̬i/ *noun* [U] the quality of being real or true: *The poems are supposed to be by Sappho, but they are actually of doubtful authenticity.* ○ *The authenticity of her story is beyond doubt.*

author /'ɔː.θəʳ/ [US] /'ɑː.θɚ/ *noun* [C] **1** the writer of a book, article, play, etc: *He is the author **of** two books on French history.* **2** FORMAL a person who begins or creates something: *She's the author **of** the company's recent success/**of** all our troubles.*

author /'ɔː.θəʳ/ [US] /'ɑː.θɚ/ *verb* [T] **1** FORMAL to write a book, article, etc: *He has authored more than 30 books.* **2** MAINLY US to create something: *The deal is being authored by a Greek diplomat.*

authoring /'ɔː.θə.rɪŋ/ [US] /'ɑː.θɚ.ɪŋ/ *noun* [U] the design and creation of computer programs and websites: *authoring tools/software* ○ *web authoring*

authorial /ɔː'θɔː.ri.əl/ [US] /ɑː'θɔːr.i-/ *adj* [before n] FORMAL relating to the author of a book

authorship /'ɔː.θə.ʃɪp/ [US] /'ɑː.θɚ-/ *noun* [U] *The article is of unknown authorship* (= It is not known who wrote it). ○ *She is being attacked for her authorship **of*** (= being the person who wrote) *the policy document.*

authoritarian /,ɔː.θɒr.ɪ'teə.ri.ən/ [US] /ə,θɔːr.ɪ'ter.i-/ *adj* DISAPPROVING demanding total obedience and refusing to allow people freedom to act as they wish: *an authoritarian regime/government/ruler* ○ *His manner is extremely authoritarian.* **authoritarian** /,ɔː.θɒr.ɪ'teə.ri.ən/ [US] /ə,θɔːr.ɪ'ter.i-/ *noun* [C] *My father was a real authoritarian so we were brought up very strictly.* **authoritarianism** /ɔː,θɒr.ɪ'teə.ri.ə.nɪ.zəm/ [US] /ə,θɔːr.ɪ'ter-/ *noun* [U]

authoritative /ɔː'θɒr.ɪ.tə.tɪv/ [US] /ə'θɔːr.ɪ.t̬ə.t̬ɪv/ *adj* **1** seeming to have an ability to control: *She has an authoritative **manner** that at times is almost arrogant.* **2** containing complete and accurate information, and therefore respected: *The book is an authoritative account of World War Two.* **authoritatively** /ɔː'θɒr.ɪ.tə.tɪv.li/ [US] /ə'θɔːr.ɪ.t̬ə.t̬ɪv-/ *adv*

authority /ɔː'θɒr.ɪ.ti/ [US] /ə'θɔːr.ɪ.t̬i/ *noun* **1** [U] the moral or legal right or ability to control: *The United Nations has **used/exerted/exercised** its authority **to** restore peace in the area.* ○ *We need to get the support of someone **in** authority* (= an important or high-ranking person). ○ *They've been acting illegally and without authority* (= permission) *from the council.* ○ [+ to infinitive] *I'll give my lawyers authority* (= permission) ***to** act on my behalf.* ○ *He's got no authority **over*** (= ability to control) *his students.* ○ *She spoke **with** authority* (= as if she was in control or had special knowledge). **2** [C] a group of people with official responsibility for a particular area of activity: *the health authority* ○ *the local housing authority* **3** [C] an expert on a subject: *She's a world authority **on** 19th-century Irish history.*

• **have something on good authority** to be able to believe a piece of information because you trust the person who told you it: *I have it on good authority **that** she's getting married.*

the au'thorities *plural noun* the group of people with official responsibility for a particular area: *I'm going to report these holes in the road to the authorities.*

authorize, UK USUALLY **-ise** /'ɔː.θər.aɪz/ [US] /'ɑː.θɚ-/ *verb* [T] to give official permission for something to happen, or to give someone official permission to do something: *Who authorized this expenditure?* ○ [+ to infinitive] *I authorized my bank **to** pay her £3000.*

authorized, UK **-ised** /'ɔː.θər.aɪzd/ [US] /'ɑː.θɚ-/ *adj*: *This is a restricted area, open to authorized* (= permitted) *personnel only.* **authorization**, UK USUALLY **-isation** /,ɔː.θər.aɪ'zeɪ.ʃən/ [US] /,ɑː.θɚ-/ *noun* [C or U] *This information cannot be disclosed without authorization **from** a minister.* ○ [+ to infinitive] *The authorization **to** sell the shares arrived too late.*

autism /'ɔː.tɪ.zəm/ [US] /'ɑː.t̬ɪ-/ *noun* [U] a failure to develop social abilities, language and other communication skills to the usual level: *Autism is four times more common in boys than in girls.* **autistic** /ɔː'tɪs.tɪk/ [US] /ɑː-/ *adj*: *One child in 5 000 is autistic.*

auto [CARS] /'ɔː.təʊ/ [US] /'ɑː.t̬oʊ/ *adj* [before n] relating to cars: *auto insurance/mechanics/engineers* ○ *the auto industry/market/business*

auto /'ɔː.təʊ/ [US] /'ɑː.t̬oʊ/ *noun* [C] *plural* **autos** US OLD-FASHIONED a car

auto- [INDEPENDENT] /ɔː.təʊ-/ [US] /ɑː.t̬oʊ-/ *prefix* of or by yourself, or operating independently and without needing help: *an autofocus camera* ○ *an auto-immune disease*

autobahn /'ɔː.təʊ.bɑːn/ /'aʊ-/ [US] /'ɑː.t̬oʊ-/ *noun* [C] a motorway in German-speaking countries

autobiography /,ɔː.təʊ.baɪ'ɒg.rə.fi/ [US] /,ɑː.t̬ə.baɪ'ɑː.grə-/ *noun* [C or U] a book about a person's life, written by that person, or the area of literature relating to such books: *The TV series 'An Angel at my Table' was based on the autobiographies of the New Zealand author Janet Frame.* ◦ *His life story is recounted in two fascinating volumes of autobiography.* ⊃Compare **biography**. **autobiographer** /ˌɔː.təʊ.baɪˈɒg.rə.fəʳ/ /ˌɑː.tə.baɪˈɑː.grə.fɚ/ *noun* [C] *Biographers tend to be more accurate and objective than autobiographers.* **autobiographical** /ˌɔː.təʊˌbaɪ.əʊˈgræf.ɪ.kᵊl/ /ˌɑː.tə.baɪ.ə-/ *adj:* *an autobiographical story/novel/poem*

autocracy /ɔːˈtɒk.rə.si/ /ɑːˈtɑː.krə-/ *noun* **1** [U] government by a single person or small group that has unlimited power or authority, or the power or authority of such a person or group **2** [C] a country or society which has this form of government

autocrat /ˈɔː.tə.kræt/ /ˈɑː.tə-/ *noun* [C] a ruler with unlimited power, or someone who demands total obedience from other people

autocratic /ˌɔː.təˈkræt.ɪk/ /ˌɑː.tə̬ˈkræt-/ *adj* like an autocrat: *an autocratic ruler/regime* ◦ *an autocratic style of government/leadership/management* ◦ *The President resigned after 30 years of autocratic rule.* **autocratically** /ˌɔː.təˈkræt.ɪ.kli/ /ˌɑː.tə̬ˈkræt-/ *adv*

autocross /ˈɔː.təʊ.krɒs/ /ˈɑː.təʊ.krɑːs/ *noun* [U] *UK* the sport of racing cars around a rough grass track

Autocue *UK TRADEMARK* /ˈɔː.təʊ.kjuː/ /ˈɑː.təʊ-/ *noun* [C or U] (*US TRADEMARK* **TelePrompter**) an electronic device which makes it possible for broadcasters to read text while looking directly at the television camera

autoeroticism /ˌɔː.təʊ.ɪˈrɒt.ɪ.sɪ.zᵊm/ /ˌɑː.təʊ.ɪˈrɑː.t̬ɪ-/ *noun* [U] the use of your own body and imagination to obtain sexual pleasure **autoerotic** /ˌɔː.təʊ.ɪˈrɒt.ɪk/ /ˌɑː.təʊ.ɪˈrɑː.t̬ɪk/ *adj*

autograph /ˈɔː.tə.grɑːf/ /ˈɑː.tə.græf/ *noun* [C] a signature of a famous person: *Did you get his autograph?* **autograph** /ˈɔː.tə.grɑːf/ /ˈɑː.tə.græf/ *verb* [T] to write your signature on something for someone else to keep: *I got her to autograph my T-shirt.* ◦ *She gave me an autographed photograph of herself.*

auto-immune /ˌɔː.təʊ.ɪˈmjuːn/ /ˌɑː.təʊ-/ *adj* [before n] *SPECIALIZED* relating to a condition in which someone's ANTIBODIES attack substances that are naturally found in the body: *One type of diabetes is an auto-immune disease/disorder that may be triggered by a virus.*

Automat /ˈɔː.təʊ.mæt/ /ˈɑː.tə-/ *noun* [C] *US TRADEMARK* a restaurant where food is obtained from enclosed boxes whose doors open when money is put in

automate /ˈɔː.tə.meɪt/ /ˈɑː.tə-/ *verb* [T] to make a process in a factory or office operate by machines or computers, in order to reduce the amount of work done by humans and the time taken to do the work: *Massive investment is needed to automate the production process.* **automated** /ˈɔː.tə.meɪ.tɪd/ /ˈɑː.tə.meɪ.t̬ɪd/ *adj: a fully automated system* **automation** /ˌɔː.təˈmeɪ.ʃᵊn/ *noun* [U] *office/factory automation*

automated ˈteller maˌchine *noun* [C] (*ABBREVIATION* **ATM**) **cash machine**

automatic [INDEPENDENT] /ˌɔː.təˈmæt.ɪk/ /ˌɑː.tə̬ˈmæt-/ *adj* An automatic machine or device is able to operate independently of human control: *automatic doors* ◦ *an automatic rifle* ◦ *automatic focus on a camera* **automatically** /ˌɔː.təˈmæt.ɪ.kli/ /ˌɑː.tə̬ˈmæt-/ *adv: The camera adjusts the lens aperture and shutter speed automatically.*

automatic [NOT CONSCIOUS] /ˌɔː.təˈmæt.ɪk/ /ˌɑː.tə̬ˈmæt-/ *adj* done without thinking about it: *Over time, driving just becomes automatic.* ◦ *My automatic response was to pull my hand away.*

automatic [CERTAIN] /ˌɔː.təˈmæt.ɪk/ /ˌɑː.tə̬ˈmæt-/ *adj* certain to happen as part of the normal process or system: *Citizenship is automatic for children born in this country.* ◦ *You get an automatic promotion after two years.* **automatically** /ˌɔː.təˈmæt.ɪ.kli/ /ˌɑː.tə̬ˈmæt-/ *adv: Employees who steal are dismissed automatically.*

automatic [VEHICLE] /ˌɔː.təˈmæt.ɪk/ /ˌɑː.tə̬ˈmæt-/ *noun* [C] a vehicle in which you do not have to change the gears: *Kate drives an automatic.*

automatic ˈpilot *noun* [C or U] **auto-pilot**

automatic transˈmission *noun* [U] a system that allows a vehicle to change gear without being controlled

by the driver ⊃Compare **manual transmission**.

automaton /ɔːˈtɒm.ə.tᵊn/ /ɑːˈtɑː.mə.t̬ᵊn/ *noun* [C] *plural* **automatons** or **automata** a machine which operates on its own without the need for human control, or a person who acts like a machine, without thinking or feeling: *I do the same route to work every day, like some sort of automaton.*

automobile /ˈɔː.tə.məʊ.biːl/ /ˈɑː.t̬ə.moʊ-/ *noun* [C] *US* car: *the automobile industry*

automotive /ˌɔː.təˈməʊ.tɪv/ /ˌɑː.t̬əˈmoʊ.t̬ɪv/ *adj* [before n] relating to road vehicles: *the automotive industry* ◦ *automotive manufacturing/engineers*

autonomy /ɔːˈtɒn.ə.mi/ /ɑːˈtɑː.nə-/ *noun* [U] the right of a group of people to govern itself, or to organize its own activities: *Demonstrators demanded immediate autonomy **for** their region.* ◦ *The universities are anxious to preserve their autonomy **from** central government.* **autonomous** /ɔːˈtɒn.ə.məs/ /ɑːˈtɑː.nə-/ *adj* independent and having the power to make your own decisions: *an autonomous region/province/republic/council*

auto-pilot, autopilot /ˈɔː.təʊˌpaɪ.lət/ /ˈɑː.t̬oʊ-/ *noun* [C or U] a device which keeps aircraft, spacecraft and ships moving in a particular direction without human involvement: *The plane was **on** autopilot when it crashed.*

● **on autopilot** doing something without thinking about it or without making an effort: *I worked the last hour of my shift on autopilot.*

autopsy /ˈɔː.tɒp.si/ /ˈɑː.tɑːp-/ *noun* [C or U] the cutting open and examination of a dead body in order to discover the cause of death: *They **carried out/performed** an autopsy.* ◦ *The body arrived for autopsy at the Dallas hospital.*

autosuggestion /ˌɔː.təʊ.sə'dʒes.tʃᵊn/ /ˌɑː.t̬oʊ-/ *noun* [U] the influencing of your physical or mental state by thoughts and ideas which come from yourself rather than from other people: *Autosuggestion is the power of mind over matter – if you convince yourself that you are cured, you will be.* **autosuggestive** /ˌɔː.təʊ.səˈdʒes.tɪv/ /ˌɑː.t̬oʊ-/ *adj: Autosuggestive techniques can help in the treatment of diseases which cannot be cured by conventional medicine.*

autumn /ˈɔː.təm/ /ˈɑː.t̬m̩/ *noun* [C or U] (*US ALSO* **fall**) the season of the year between summer and winter, lasting from September to November north of the equator and from March to May south of the equator, when fruits and crops become ripe and are gathered, and leaves fall: *We like to travel **in the** autumn when there are fewer tourists.* ◦ *We always clear out the garage **in** early autumn.* ◦ *Last autumn we went to Germany.* ◦ *autumn colours/leaves*

● **autumn years** *LITERARY* Someone's autumn years are the later years of their life, especially after they have stopped working.

autumnal /ɔːˈtʌm.nᵊl/ /ɑː-/ *adj* typical of autumn: *autumnal colours/sunshine/days*

auxiliary /ɔːgˈzɪl.i.ᵊr.i/ /ɑːgˈzɪl.i.er-/ *adj* giving help or support, especially to a more important person or thing: *auxiliary staff/nurses*

auxiliary /ɔːgˈzɪl.i.ᵊr.i/ /ɑːgˈzɪl.i.er-/ *noun* **1** [C] a person whose job is to give help or support to other workers: *semi-skilled auxiliaries* **2** [C usually pl] a soldier of one country who fights for another country

auxiliary ˈnurse *UK noun* [C] (*US* **nurse's aide,** *AUS* **nursing aid**) someone whose job is helping nurses to take care of people

auxiliary (ˈverb) *noun* [C] a verb that gives grammatical information, for example about tense, which is not given by the main verb of a sentence: *The first verb in each of the following sentences is an auxiliary – I would love a drink, When did you arrive?, She has finished her book.*

AV /ˌeɪˈviː/ *adj* [before n] *ABBREVIATION FOR* **audio-visual:** *Our teacher sent us to the AV room for an overhead projector.*

avail /əˈveɪl/ *noun* [U] use, purpose, advantage, or profit: *We tried to persuade her not to resign, but **to no** avail* (= did not succeed). ◦ *My attempts to improve the situation were **of little/no** avail.*

avail /əˈveɪl/ *verb* [T] OLD USE *Our efforts availed us **nothing*** (= did not help).
▲ avail *yourself* of *sth phrasal verb* [R] FORMAL to use something to your advantage or benefit: *Employees should avail themselves of the opportunity to buy cheap shares in the company.*

available /əˈveɪ.lə.bļ/ *adj* able to be obtained, used, or reached: *Is this dress available in a larger size?* ○ *Our autumn catalogue is now available **from** our usual stockists.* ○ *There's no money available **for** an office party this year.* ○ *It is vital that food is **made** available **to** the famine areas.* ○ [+ to infinitive] *I'm afraid I'm not available to help with the show on the 19th.* ○ *Every available officer will be assigned to the investigation.* ○ *Do you have any double rooms available this weekend?* **availability** /əˌveɪ.ləˈbɪl.ɪ.ti/ US /-ə.t̬i/ *noun* [U] *The ready availability of guns has contributed to the escalating violence.* ○ *Abortion rates are high because the availability of contraceptives is limited.*

avalanche /ˈæv.ə.lɑːntʃ/ US /-æntʃ/ *noun* [C] **1** a large amount of ice, snow and rock falling quickly down the side of a mountain **2** the sudden arrival of too many things: *We were swamped by an avalanche **of** letters/phone calls/complaints*

the ˌavantˈgarde *group noun* [S] (the work of) the painters, writers, musicians and other artists whose ideas, styles and methods are highly original or modern in comparison to the period in which they live: *New York is the international capital of the musical avantgarde.* **avant-garde** /ˌæv.ɑ̃ːˈgɑːd/ US /-ˈgɑːrd/ *adj: avant-garde art/cinema/painting* ○ *It was one of the first avant-garde works to appeal to a wide audience.*

avarice /ˈæv.ə.rɪs/ US /-ɚ-/ *noun* [U] FORMAL an extremely strong desire to obtain or keep wealth; GREED: *Her business empire brought her wealth **beyond the dreams of** avarice* (= an extremely large amount of money). **avaricious** /ˌæv.əˈrɪʃ.əs/ *adj* **avariciously** /ˌæv.əˈrɪʃ.ə.sli/ *adv*

avatar /ˈæv.ə.tɑːr/ US /-tɑːr/ *noun* [C] in computing, an image which represents you in ONLINE games, CHAT ROOMS, etc. and which you can move around the screen using the mouse or keys: *By typing in simple commands you could pick up objects and talk to other avatars, with your words displayed in a cartoon bubble above your head.*

Ave *noun* [U] WRITTEN ABBREVIATION FOR **avenue** ROAD: *13 Victoria Ave*

avenge /əˈvendʒ/ *verb* [T] FORMAL to do harm to or punish the person responsible for something bad done to you or your family or friends in order to achieve a fair situation: *He swore he would avenge his brother's death.* ○ *She determined to avenge her**self on** the killer.* ○ *At the end of the film, the murderer is killed by his victim's avenging girlfriend.* **avenger** /əˈven.dʒər/ US /-dʒɚ/ *noun* [C] *Russell Crowe stars as a grief-stricken avenger on the trail of his family's killers.*

avenue ROAD /ˈæv.ə.njuː/ US /-nuː/ *noun* [C] **1** a wide road, with trees or tall buildings on both sides, or a wide countryside path or road with trees on both sides: *Fremont Avenue* **2** UK a road of this type which leads to a large house

avenue POSSIBILITY /ˈæv.ə.njuː/ US /-nuː/ *noun* [C] a method or way of doing something; a possibility: *We should **explore/pursue** every avenue in the search for an answer to this problem.* ○ *Only two avenues are **open** to us – either we accept his offer or we give up the fight completely.*

aver /əˈvɜːr/ US /-ˈvɜːː/ *verb* [T] -rr- FORMAL to state the truth of something strongly: *The lawyer averred her client's innocence.* ○ [+ speech] *"He's guilty, I tell you," she averred.* ○ [+ that] *She averred **that** he was guilty.*

average AMOUNT /ˈæv.ə.rɪdʒ/ US /-ɚ-/ *noun* [C or U] the result obtained by adding two or more amounts together and dividing the total by the number of amounts: *The average of the three numbers 7, 12 and 20 is 13, because the total of 7, 12 and 20 is 39, and 39 divided by 3 is 13.* ○ *Prices have risen by an average **of** 4% over the past year.* ○ *My income's rather variable, but I earn £73 a day **on** average.*

average /ˈæv.ə.rɪdʒ/ US /-ɚ-/ *adj* [before n] an average number is obtained by adding two or more amounts together and dividing the total by the number of amounts: *average earnings/income/rainfall* ○ *The average age of the US soldiers who fought in the Vietnam War was 19.*

average /ˈæv.ə.rɪdʒ/ US /-ɚ-/ *verb* [T] to reach a particular amount as an average: *Enquiries to our office average 1000 calls a month.* ○ *Many doctors average* (= work an average of) *70 hours a week.* ○ *Trainee accountants average* (= earn an average of) *£12 000 per year.*

average USUAL STANDARD /ˈæv.ə.rɪdʒ/ US /-ɚ-/ *noun* [S or U] a standard or level which is considered to be typical or usual: *The audience figures were lower than average for this sort of film.* ○ *In western Europe, a 7- to 8-hour working day is about **the** average* (= typical). ○ *On average, people who don't smoke are healthier than people who do.* ○ *The quality of candidates was **(well) below/above** average.* ○ *I expect to spend **an** average **of** $15 to $20 on a meal in a restaurant.*

average /ˈæv.ə.rɪdʒ/ US /-ɚ-/ *adj* typical and usual: *The average person in the street is a lot better off than they were forty years ago.* ○ *a student of average ability* ○ *The food was fairly average* (= not excellent, although not bad). **averagely** /ˈæv.ə.rɪdʒ.li/ US /-ɚ-/ *adv*: *He's an averagely attractive man.*

PHRASAL VERBS WITH **average** ▼

▲ average *sth* out CALCULATE *phrasal verb* [M] to calculate the average of a set of numbers or amounts: *If I average out what I earn a month, it's about one and a half thousand pounds.*

▲ average out EQUAL *phrasal verb* to be or become equal in amount or number: *The highs and lows of life tend to average out in the end.*

▲ average out at *sth phrasal verb* to have a particular number or amount as the average: *My annual holiday varies, but it averages out at five weeks a year.*

averse /əˈvɜːs/ US /-ˈvɜːːs/ *adj* [after v] strongly disliking or opposed to: *Few MPs are averse **to** the attention of the media.* ○ *I'm **not** averse **to*** (= I like) *the occasional glass of champagne myself.*

aversion /əˈvɜː.ʃən/ US /-ˈvɜːː.ʒən/ *noun* [C usually sing] (a person or thing which causes) a feeling of strong dislike or a lack of willingness to do something: *I felt an instant aversion **to** his parents.* ○ *She has a deep aversion **to** getting up in the morning.* ○ *Greed is my **pet** aversion* (= the thing I dislike most of all).

aˈversion ˌtherapy *noun* [U] a method of treating habits or types of behaviour that are not desirable, by causing the patient to connect them with unpleasant feelings: *Despite what many people think, aversion therapy is no longer used by professional psychologists in this country.*

avert PREVENT /əˈvɜːt/ US /-ˈvɜːːt/ *verb* [T] to prevent something bad from happening; avoid: *to avert a crisis/conflict/strike/famine* ○ *to avert disaster/economic collapse*

avert TURN /əˈvɜːt/ US /-ˈvɜːːt/ *verb* [T] to turn away your eyes or thoughts: *I averted my gaze/eyes while he dressed.* ○ *We tried to avert our thoughts **from** our massive financial problems.*

aviary /ˈeɪ.vi.ə.ri/ US /-er.i/ *noun* [C] a large cage or enclosure in which birds are kept as pets

aviation /ˌeɪ.viˈeɪ.ʃən/ *noun* [U] the activity of flying aircraft, or of designing, producing and maintaining them: *the British Civil Aviation Authority* ○ *the US Federal Aviation Administration* ○ *aviation fuel* **aviator** /ˈeɪ.vi.eɪ.tər/ US /-t̬ɚ/ *noun* [C] OLD-FASHIONED *Amy Johnson was a pioneering aviator who made record-breaking flights to Australia and South Africa in the 1930s.*

avid /ˈæv.ɪd/ *adj* extremely eager or interested: *an avid football fan* ○ *an avid supporter of the arts* ○ *He took an avid interest in the project.* ○ FORMAL *She hadn't seen him for six months and was avid for news.* **avidly** /ˈæv.ɪd.li/ *adv*: *She reads avidly.* ○ *We avidly awaited news of him.* **avidity** /əˈvɪd.ɪ.ti/ US /-ə.t̬i/ *noun* [U] FORMAL

A

avionics /ˌeɪ.viˈɒn.ɪks/ ⓤ /-ˈɑː.nɪks/ *noun* [U] the science and technology of the electronic devices used in AERO-NAUTICS and ASTRONAUTICS: *Avionics forms an important part of the defence industry.*
  avionics /ˌeɪ.viˈɒn.ɪks/ ⓤ /-ˈɑː.nɪks/ *plural noun* the electronic devices of an aircraft or spacecraft: *The sophisticated avionics enable the helicopter to operate at night.* **avionic** /ˌeɪ.viˈɒn.ɪk/ ⓤ /-ˈɑː.nɪk/ *adj: Aircraft today use complex avionic systems.*

avocado (*plural* avocados) /ˌæv.əˈkɑː.dəʊ/ ⓤ /-doʊ/ *noun* [C] (*UK ALSO* **avocado pear**) a tropical fruit with thick green or purple skin and oily green edible flesh which has a large round seed at the centre ⊃See picture **Fruit** on page Centre 1

avoid /əˈvɔɪd/ *verb* [T] to stay away from someone or something, or prevent something from happening or not allow yourself to do something: *I try to avoid supermarkets on Saturdays – they're always so busy.* ○ [+ v-ing] *I try to avoid going shopping on Saturdays.* ○ *The report studiously avoided any mention of the controversial plan.* ○ *The plane* **narrowly** *avoided disaster when one of the engines cut out on take-off.* ○ *I left the pub to avoid a fight* (= prevent a fight from happening). ○ *Unnecessary paperwork should be avoided* (= prevented) **at all costs.** ○ *I'm* **anxious to** *avoid the motorway at rush hour.* ○ *Do you think Tim's avoiding me? I haven't seen him all day.*
  ● **avoid** *sth* **like the plague** to be determined to avoid something completely: *I'm not a fan of parties – in fact I avoid them like the plague.*
  avoidable /əˈvɔɪ.də.bl̩/ *adj* possible to avoid: *A number of illnesses are entirely avoidable.* ○ *In spite of these latest threats, war may still be avoidable.* **avoidance** /əˈvɔɪ.dᵊnts/ *noun* [U] *The avoidance of injury is critical to a professional athlete.*

COMMON LEARNER ERROR

avoid doing something

When **avoid** is followed by a verb, the verb is always in the **-ing** form.

I avoided seeing him for several days.
~~I avoided to see him for several days.~~

avow /əˈvaʊ/ *verb* [T] FORMAL to state or admit something: [+ that] *He avowed that he regretted what he had done.* ○ *It is a society in which homosexuality is rarely avowed.*
  avowed /əˈvaʊd/ *adj* [before n] FORMAL stated: *The Government's avowed intent/purpose/aim is to reduce tax.* ○ *An avowed traditionalist, he is against reform of any kind.* **avowedly** /əˈvaʊ.ɪd.li/ *adv: an avowedly feminist author* **avowal** /əˈvaʊ.əl/ *noun* [C or U] *They were imprisoned for their avowal of anti-government beliefs.* ○ [+ to infinitive] *Her public avowals* **to** *reduce crime have yet to be put into effect.*

avuncular /əˈvʌŋ.kjʊ.ləʳ/ ⓤ /-lɚ/ *adj* FORMAL friendly, caring or helpful, like the expected behaviour of an uncle: *an avuncular, quietly-spoken man* ○ *His avuncular image belies his steely determination.*

await /əˈweɪt/ *verb* [T] FORMAL to wait for, or be waiting for something: *He's anxiously awaiting his test results.* ○ *A marvellous reception awaited me on my first day at work.* ○ *The* **long/eagerly** *awaited sequel is now available on video.*

awake /əˈweɪk/ *adj* [after v] **1** not sleeping: *"Is Oliver awake yet?" "Yes, he's* **wide** (= completely) *awake and running around his bedroom."* ○ *I find it so difficult to* **stay** *awake during history lessons.* ○ *I drink a lot of coffee to* **keep** *me awake.* ○ *She used to* **lie** *awake at night worrying about how to pay the bills.* **2** MAINLY UK **be awake to** *sth* If you are awake to something, you are aware of it: *Businesses need to be awake to the advantages of European integration.*
  awake /əˈweɪk/ *verb* [I or T] awoke or US ALSO **awaked**, **awoken 1** LITERARY to stop sleeping or to make someone stop sleeping: *I awoke at seven o'clock.* ○ *She awoke me at seven.* **2** to become aware of something or to make someone become aware of something: *The chance meeting awoke the old passion between them.* ○ *Young people need to awake* **to** *the risks involved in casual sex.*

awaken /əˈweɪ.kᵊn/ *verb* [I or T] LITERARY to stop sleeping or to make someone stop sleeping: *They were awakened by the sound of gunfire.* ○ *I awakened at dawn to find him beside me.*

PHRASAL VERBS WITH **awaken** ▼

  ▲ **awaken (sth) in** *sb phrasal verb* LITERARY If a desire, interest or emotion awakens or is awakened in you, you become aware of it for the first time: *My holiday in Paris awakened a passion for French food in me.*
  ▲ **awaken** *sb* **to** *sth phrasal verb* LITERARY If you awaken someone to something, you make them aware of it or make them remember it: *I awakened him to his responsibilities for his children.*

awakening /əˈweɪ.kᵊn.ɪŋ/ *noun* [S] when you start to be aware of something or feel something: *a religious awakening* ○ *the awakening of public concern about the environment* ○ *He's in for a* **rude** *awakening* (= will be shocked) *when he starts work!*

award /əˈwɔːd/ ⓤ /-ˈwɔːrd/ *verb* [T] to give money or a prize following an official decision: *He was awarded first prize in the essay competition.* ○ *The jury awarded libel damages of £100 000.* ○ [+ two objects] *The university awarded her a $500 travel grant.* **award** /əˈwɔːd/ ⓤ /-ˈwɔːrd/ *noun* [C] *They have authorized awards of £900* **to** *each of the victims.* ○ *the Academy Award for Best Director*

a'ward-ˌwinning *adj* [before n] having won a prize or prizes for being of high quality or very skilled: *an award-winning author/TV series/design.*

aware /əˈweəʳ/ ⓤ /-ˈwer/ *adj* [after v] **1** knowing that something exists, or having knowledge or experience of a particular thing: [+ that] *I wasn't even aware that he was ill.* ○ *Were you aware* **of** *the risks at the time?* ○ *She was* **well** (= very) *aware that he was married.* ○ *"Has Claude paid the phone bill?" "Not* **as far as I'm** *aware."* (= I don't think so) ○ *I suddenly became aware* **of** (= started to notice) *him looking at me.* **2** having special interest in or experience of something and so being well informed of what is happening in that subject at the present time: *to be ecologically/politically aware* ○ *sexually aware* **awareness** /əˈweə.nəs/ ⓤ /-ˈwer-/ *noun* [U] *Public awareness* **of** *the problem will make politicians take it seriously.* ○ *Environmental awareness has increased dramatically over the past decade.*

awash /əˈwɒʃ/ ⓤ /-ˈwɑːʃ/ *adj* [after v] **1** covered with a liquid, especially water: *By the time I discovered the problem, the floor was awash.* **2** having an amount of something which is very large or larger than necessary or desirable: *The city is awash* **with** *drugs.*

away SOMEWHERE ELSE /əˈweɪ/ *adv* somewhere else, or to or in a different place, position or situation: *Ms Watson is away on holiday until the end of the week.* ○ *Keep/Stay away* **from** *him.* ○ *Just go away and leave me alone!* ○ *The recent flood has swept away the footbridge.* ○ *I've given away all my old clothes to charity.* ○ *UK Would you like your burger to eat in or take away?*
  away /əˈweɪ/ *adj* An away match or game is played at an opposing team's sports ground: *We lost the away game but won both the home games.*

away DISTANT /əˈweɪ/ *adv* at a distance (of or from here): *How* **far** *away is the station?* ○ *The office is a half-hour drive away.* ○ *We live 5 km away* **from** *each other.* ○ *Life's so much quieter away* **from** *the city.* ○ INFORMAL *Oh, it's* **miles** *away* (= a long distance from here).

away IN THE FUTURE /əˈweɪ/ *adv* in the future; from now: *My English exam's only a week away and I haven't even started to prepare.*

away INTO PLACE /əˈweɪ/ *adv* in or into the usual or a suitable especially enclosed place: *Would you put the ice-cream away in the freezer?* ○ *My grandparents had £800 hidden away in an old shoe box.*

away GRADUALLY /əˈweɪ/ *adv* gradually until mostly or completely gone: *All the snow had melted away.* ○ *The music faded away as the procession moved slowly up the street.* ○ *We used to while away* (= spend time at) *the weekends at my aunt's cottage in the country.* ○ *We danced the night away* (= until the night was over).

away CONTINUOUSLY /əˈweɪ/ *adv* continuously or repeatedly, or in a busy way: *I was still writing away when the exam finished.* ○ *Chris has been working away in the garden all day.* ○ *We were chatting away at the*

A

back and didn't hear what he said.

awe /ɔː/ ⓤ /ɑː/ *noun* [U] a feeling of great respect sometimes mixed with fear or surprise: *I've always held musicians in awe. ○ As children we were rather in awe of our grandfather. ○ You can't help but stand in awe of (= respect greatly and fear slightly) powerful people.* **awe** /ɔː/ ⓤ /ɑː/ *verb* [T] *UK* aweing *or US* awing *I was awed but not frightened by the huge gorilla. ○ Her paintings have awed and amazed the public for half a century. ○ The audience was awed into silence by her stunning performance.* **awed** /ɔːd/ ⓤ /ɑːd/ *adj: We stood there in awed silence. ○ "How does she manage to run so fast at her age?" he asked in awed tones.*

awe-inspiring /'ɔː.ɪnˌspaɪə.rɪŋ/ ⓤ /'ɑː.ɪnˌspaɪr.ɪŋ/ *adj* causing you to feel great respect or admiration: *Niagara Falls really is an awe-inspiring sight. ○ Her knowledge of computers is quite awe-inspiring.*

awesome /'ɔː.səm/ ⓤ /'ɑː-/ *adj* **1** causing feelings of great admiration, respect or fear: *An awesome challenge/task lies ahead of them. ○ awesome scenery* **2** *US INFORMAL* extremely good: *You look totally awesome in that dress.*

awestruck /'ɔː.strʌk/ ⓤ /'ɑː-/ *adj* (*ALSO* **awestricken**) filled with feelings of admiration or respect: *an awestruck admirer/fan/visitor/tourist ○ I could tell she was impressed from the awestruck expression on her face.*

awful BAD /'ɔː.fᵊl/ ⓤ /'ɑː-/ *adj* extremely bad or unpleasant: *He suffered awful injuries in the crash. ○ We had awful weather. ○ She's got an awful boss. ○ What an awful thing to say! ○ Would life be so awful without a car? ○ The food was awful. ○ She'd been ill and she looked awful.* **awfully** /'ɔː.fᵊl.i/ ⓤ /'ɑː-/ *adv: England played awfully throughout the game.* **awfulness** /'ɔː.fᵊl.nəs/ ⓤ /'ɑː-/ *noun* [U] *You can't appreciate the true/sheer awfulness of war until you've actually experienced it.*

awful VERY GREAT /'ɔː.fᵊl/ ⓤ /'ɑː-/ *adj* [before n] very great: *I don't know an awful lot (= very much) about art, but I'm learning. ○ Fortunately it won't make an awful lot of difference if I don't pass the test. ○ It was an awful risk to take.*

awfully /'ɔː.fᵊl.i/ ⓤ /'ɑː-/ *adv* (*US INFORMAL ALSO* **awful**) very or extremely, when used before an adjective or adverb: *It's an awfully long time since we last saw each other. ○ I'm awfully sorry, but we've forgotten to reserve you a table.*

awhile /ə'waɪl/ *adv LITERARY* for a short time: *Stay awhile and rest. ○ I read awhile, then slept.*

awkward DIFFICULT /'ɔː.kwəd/ ⓤ /'ɑː.kwɚd/ *adj* difficult to use, do, or deal with: *It's an awkward corner to drive round, so take it slowly. ○ Some of the questions were rather awkward. ○ It was an awkward ascent, but we reached the top eventually. ○* [+ to infinitive] *My car's quite awkward to drive. ○ He's an awkward customer (= a difficult person to deal with).* **awkwardly** /'ɔː.kwəd.li/ ⓤ /'ɑː.kwɚd-/ *adv: The car was parked awkwardly across the pavement.*

awkward ANXIOUS /'ɔː.kwəd/ ⓤ /'ɑː.kwɚd/ *adj* **1** causing inconvenience, anxiety or embarrassment: *an awkward position/situation ○ There followed an awkward silence while we all tried to think of something to say. ○ They'd chosen an awkward time to call as I'd just got into the bath. ○ The police asked some awkward questions about where the money had come from.* **2** embarrassed or nervous: *I always feel awkward when I'm with Chris – he's so difficult to talk to. ○ He seemed a little awkward when I first met him.* **awkwardly** /'ɔː.kwəd.li/ ⓤ /'ɑː.kwɚd-/ *adv: He shifted awkwardly from one foot to the other. ○ The publication of the economic statistics was awkwardly timed for the Government.* **awkwardness** /'ɔː.kwəd.nəs/ ⓤ /'ɑː.kwɚd-/ *noun* [U] *In spite of the divorce there was no awkwardness between them – in fact they seemed very much at ease.*

awkward NOT HELPFUL /'ɔː.kwəd/ ⓤ /'ɑː.kwɚd/ *adj MAINLY UK* intentionally not helpful; UNCOOPERATIVE: *Just stop being so awkward and help me push the car, will you!* **awkwardly** /'ɔː.kwəd.li/ ⓤ /'ɑː.kwɚd-/ *adv*

awkward MOVEMENT /'ɔː.kwəd/ ⓤ /'ɑː.kwɚd/ *adj* moving in a way that is not attractive: *His movements were slow and awkward.* **awkwardly** /'ɔː.kwəd.li/ ⓤ /'ɑː.kwɚd-/

adv: She fell awkwardly when she was skiing and twisted her ankle. ○ He walked awkwardly across the room, aware that they were watching.

awning /'ɔː.nɪŋ/ ⓤ /'ɑː-/ *noun* [C] (*US ALSO* **sunshade**, *AUS ALSO* **sunblind**) a cloth or plastic cover attached to a building or structure and supported by a frame which is used to protect someone or something from the sun or rain: *The gaily striped awnings of the little shops and market stalls made an attractive scene.*

awoke /ə'wəʊk/ ⓤ /-'woʊk/ *past simple of* **awake**

awoken /ə'wəʊ.kᵊn/ ⓤ /-'woʊ-/ *past participle of* **awake**

AWOL /'eɪ.wɒl/ ⓤ /-wɑːl/ *adj* [after v] *ABBREVIATION FOR* absent without leave: describes a member of the armed forces who is away without permission: *The pilot is serving 22 days detention for going AWOL.*

● **go AWOL** *INFORMAL* If something has gone AWOL, it is not in its usual place or has been stolen: *Two computers have gone AWOL from the office.*

awry /ə'raɪ/ *adj*, *adv* **1** not in the intended way: *Anything that goes awry (= goes wrong) in the office is blamed on Pete. ○ The strike has sent the plans for investment seriously awry.* **2** in the wrong position: *She rushed in, her face red and sweaty and her hat awry.*

aw-shucks /ɔː'ʃʌks/ *adj* [before n] *US* showing a shy or a modest character or way of behaving: *He shrugged and gave us one of his aw-shucks smiles.*

aw shucks *exclamation US HUMOROUS OR OLD-FASHIONED* used to show that you feel embarrassed or shy ⊃See also **shucks**.

axe TOOL, *US ALSO* **ax** /æks/ *noun* [C] a tool used for cutting wood and which consists of a heavy iron or steel blade at the end of a long wooden handle: *Julian used an axe to chop down the old apple tree.*

● **have an axe to grind** to have a strong opinion about something, which you often try to persuade other people is correct: *Environmentalists have no political axe to grind – they just want to save the planet.*

axe REDUCE, *US ALSO* **ax** /æks/ *verb* [T] to reduce services, jobs, payments greatly or completely without warning or in a single action: *Because of the recession the company is to axe 350 jobs. ○ The TV series will be axed owing to a decline in popularity.*

the axe, *US ALSO* **the ax** *noun* [S] *UK* when someone loses their job: *Over 500 staff are facing the axe at the Nottingham factory.*

● **get the axe** *UK* When a service or plan gets the axe, it is stopped or prevented from happening: *Religious programmes will be the first to get the axe if she's put in charge of the station.*

axes /'æk.siːz/ *plural of* **axis**

axiom /'æk.si.əm/ *noun* [C] **1** *FORMAL* a statement or principle which is generally accepted to be true, but is not necessarily so: *It is a widely held axiom that governments should not negotiate with terrorists.* **2** *SPECIALIZED* a formal statement or principle in mathematics, science, etc., from which other statements can be obtained: *Euclid's axioms form the foundation of his system of geometry.*

axiomatic /ˌæk.si.ə'mæt.ɪk/ ⓤ /-'mæt̬-/ *adj FORMAL* obviously true and therefore not needing to be proved: *It is an axiomatic fact that governments rise and fall on the state of the economy. ○ It seems axiomatic that everyone would benefit from a better scientific education.* **axiomatically** /ˌæk.si.ə'mæt.ɪ.kli/ ⓤ /-'mæt̬-/ *adv*

axis /'æk.sɪs/ *noun* [C] *plural* **axes 1** a real or imaginary straight line which goes through the centre of a spinning object, or a line which divides a SYMMETRICAL shape into two equal halves, or a line used on a GRAPH used to show the position of a point: *The Earth revolves about the axis which joins the North and South Poles. ○ The diameter of a circle is also an axis. ○ Plot distance on the vertical Y-axis against time on the horizontal X-axis.* **2** an agreement between governments or politicians to work together to achieve a particular aim: *the Franco-German axis*

the 'Axis *noun* the countries, including Germany, Italy and Japan, that fought against THE ALLIES in World War Two: *the Axis powers/nations*

axle /'æk.sl̩/ *noun* [C] a bar connected to the centre of a circular object such as a wheel which allows or causes it to turn, especially one connecting two wheels of a vehicle

ayatollah /ˌaɪ.ə'tɒl.ə/ [US] /-'toʊ.lə/ *noun* [C] a high-ranking religious leader of SHIITE Muslims in Iran

aye /aɪ/ *adv* *MAINLY UK* another word for 'yes': *"Would you prefer not to work?" "Oh aye, I'd stop tomorrow if I could."* ○ *All those who support this proposal say "Aye".*

aye *noun* [C] a vote or voter in support of a suggestion, idea, law, etc: ***The ayes have it*** (= The people who voted 'yes' have won).

AZT /ˌeɪ.zed'tiː/ [US] /-ziː-/ *noun* [U] a drug used in the treatment of AIDS (= a serious disease which destroys the body's natural protection from infection)

azure /'æʒ.əʳ/ /'æz.jʊəʳ/ [US] /-ɚ/ *adj, noun* [U] (having) the bright blue colour of the sky on a sunny day: *The once azure skies of Athens have been ruined by atmospheric pollution.*

B

B [LETTER] (*plural* **B's** or **Bs**), **b** (*plural* **b's** or **bs**) /biː/ *noun* [C] the 2nd letter of the English alphabet

B [MUSIC] /biː/ *noun* [C or U] *plural* **B's** or **Bs** a note in Western music: *Bach's Mass in B minor*

B [MARK] /biː/ *noun* [C or U] *plural* **B's** or **Bs** a mark in an exam or for a piece of work that shows that your work is good but not excellent: *I was a bit disappointed just to be given a B, as I was hoping for an A.* ○ *I* ***got*** *B for physics last term.*

b [NUMBER] *noun* (*UK* **bn**) *US WRITTEN ABBREVIATION FOR* **billion**

b. *adj ABBREVIATION FOR* **born** BEGIN TO EXIST: *John Winston Lennon (b. 9 October 1940, Liverpool, d. 8 December 1980, New York).*

B2B /ˌbiː.təˈbiː/ [US] /-t̬ə-/ *ABBREVIATION FOR* business-to-business: describing or involving business arrangements or trade between different businesses, rather than between businesses and the general public: *a B2B* ***exchange/company*** ○ *Mr Pirouz is confident about the potential for B2B* ***e-commerce****.*

B2C /ˌbiː.təˈsiː/ [US] /-t̬ə-/ *ABBREVIATION FOR* business-to-consumer: describing or involving the sale of goods or services directly to individual customers for their own use, rather than to businesses: *B2C* ***companies/e-commerce*** ○ *We would not rule out the possibility of re-entering the B2C market if conditions change.*

BA /ˌbiːˈeɪ/ *noun* [C] (*US ALSO* **AB**) *ABBREVIATION FOR* Bachelor of Arts: a first college degree in the ARTS or SOCIAL SCIENCES, or someone who has this degree: *Farida* ***has*** *a BA* ***in*** *history from the University of Sussex.*

baa /bɑː/ [US] /bæ/ *noun* [C] the sound that a sheep or lamb makes **baa** /bɑː/ [US] /bæ/ *verb* [I] **baaing, baaed, baaed**

babble [TALK] /ˈbæb.l̩/ *verb* [I or T] to talk or say something in a quick, confused, excited or foolish way: *The children babbled excitedly among themselves.* ○ *She was babbling something* ***about*** *her ring being stolen.* **babble** /ˈbæb.l̩/ *noun* [U] *I could hear the babble* (= low continuous sound) ***of*** *voices in the next room.*

babble [WATER NOISE] /ˈbæb.l̩/ *verb* [I] *LITERARY* (of a stream) to make the low, continuous noise of water flowing over stones: *They rested a while by a babbling* ***brook****.*

babe /beɪb/ *noun* [C] **1** *LITERARY* a small baby: *a newborn babe* **2** *INFORMAL* an affectionate way of addressing a wife, husband, lover, etc: *It's up to you, babe. I'll do whatever you say.* **3** *INFORMAL* a sexually attractive young person: *He's a* ***total*** *babe.*

ˌbabe in ˈarms *noun* [C] *MAINLY UK* a very young baby

babel /ˈbeɪ.bəl/ *noun* [S] *FORMAL* a state of confusion caused by many people talking at the same time or using different languages: *a babel* ***of*** *voices.*

baboon /bəˈbuːn/ *noun* [C] a type of large monkey found in Africa and Asia, which has a long pointed face like a dog and large teeth

baby /ˈbeɪ.bi/ *noun* [C] **1** a very young child, especially one that has not yet begun to walk or talk: *a newborn baby* ○ *a six-week-old baby* ○ *a baby boy* ○ *baby clothes* ○ *baby food* ○ *Sandra* ***had*** *a baby* (= gave birth to it) *on May 29th.* ○ *Owen is the baby* (= the youngest person) *of the family.* **2** a very young animal: *a baby elephant/monkey* **3 baby carrot/sweetcorn, etc.** a type of vegetable that is specially grown to stay small **4** *DISAPPROVING* an adult or especially an older child who is crying or behaving childishly: *It didn't hurt that much – don't be such a baby!* **5** *MAINLY US* an affectionate way of addressing a wife, husband or lover: *Oh baby, I love you.* **6** *INFORMAL* Someone's baby is something that they have a special interest in and responsibility for: *I don't know much about the project – it's Philip's baby.* **baby** /ˈbeɪ.bi/ *verb* [T] *INFORMAL* to treat an older child as if he or she is a much younger child: *The boys were now ten and twelve and didn't want their mother to baby them.*

babyish /ˈbeɪ.bi.ɪʃ/ *adj DISAPPROVING* only suitable for a baby: *The older children found the toys too babyish.* **babyhood** /ˈbeɪ.bɪ.hʊd/ *noun* [U] the period of time when you are a baby

ˈbaby ˌboom *noun* [C usually sing] a large increase in the number of babies born among a particular group of people during a particular time: *There was a baby boom in Britain and the US after World War II.*

baby boomer /ˈbeɪ.biˌbuː.m.əʳ/ [US] /-ɚ/ *noun* [C] (*US INFORMAL* **boomer**) a person who was born during a baby boom, especially the one that happened in Britain and the US between approximately 1945 and 1965

ˈbaby ˌcarriage *noun* [C] (*ALSO* **baby buggy**) *US FOR* **pram**

ˈBabyˌgro *noun* [C] *UK TRADEMARK* a piece of clothing for a baby which covers the whole body

ˈbaby ˌmilk *noun* [U] artificial milk which can be given to babies instead of milk from their mother

babysit (**babysitting, babysat, babysat**) /ˈbeɪ.bi.sɪt/ *verb* [I or T] (*US ALSO* **sit**) to take care of someone's baby or child while that person is out, usually by going to their home: *I babysit* ***for*** *Jane on Tuesday evenings while she goes to her yoga class.* **babysitter** /ˈbeɪ.biˌsɪt.əʳ/ [US] /-ˌsɪt̬.ɚ/ *noun* [C] (*MAINLY US* **sitter**) *I promised the babysitter that we'd be home by midnight.* **babysitting** /ˈbeɪ.biˌsɪt.ɪŋ/ [US] /-ˌsɪt̬.ɪŋ/ *noun* [U] *He earns a bit of extra pocket money by babysitting.*

ˈbaby ˌtalk *noun* [U] the words that a very young child uses, or the words used by adults when they talk to babies

ˈbaby ˌtooth *noun* [C] (*ALSO* **milk tooth**) one of the teeth of young children and some other young mammals that fall out and are replaced by permanent teeth

bacchanalian /ˌbæk.əˈneɪ.li.ən/ *adj LITERARY* (especially of a party) involving a lot of drinking of alcohol, uncontrolled behaviour and possibly sexual activity: *a bacchanalian orgy*

baccy /ˈbæk.i/ *noun* [U] *UK SLANG FOR* **tobacco**

bachelor /ˈbætʃ.əl.əʳ/ [US] /-ɚ/ *noun* [C] a man who has never married: *He remained a bachelor until he was well into his 40s.* ○ *Simon is a* ***confirmed*** *bachelor* (= He is unlikely ever to want to get married).

ˈbachelor ˌparty *noun* [C] *US* a party for a man who is going to get married, to which only his male friends are invited ➲See also **stag night/party**.

bachelor's degree /ˌbætʃ.əl.əz.dɪˈgriː/ [US] /-ɚ/ *noun* [C] a first degree at college or university

bacillus /bəˈsɪl.əs/ *noun* [C] *plural* **bacilli** a BACTERIUM (= an extremely small organism) which is shaped like a rod. There are various types of bacillus, some of which can cause disease.

back [RETURN] /bæk/ *adv* **1** in, into or towards a previous place or condition, or an earlier time: *When you take the scissors, remember to put them back.* ○ *He left a note saying 'Gone out. Back soon'.* ○ *She went to America for two years, but now she's back* (= has returned). ○ *He looked back* (= looked behind him) *and saw they were following him.* ○ *Looking at her old photographs* ***brought*** *back* (= made her remember) *a lot of memories.* ○ *I was woken by a thunderstorm, and I couldn't* ***get*** *back* ***to*** *sleep* (= could not return to sleep). ○ *The last time we saw Lowell was back* (= at an earlier time) *in January.* ○ *This tradition dates back to* (= to the earlier time of) *the 16th century.* **2** in return: *If he hits me, I'll hit him back.* ○ *You're not just going to let her say those things about you without fighting back, are you?* **3** in reply: *I'm busy at the moment – can I call you back?* ○ *I wrote to Donna several months ago, but she hasn't written back yet.*

• **back to square one** If you are back to square one, you have to start working on a plan from the beginning because your previous attempt failed completely: *If this doesn't work we're back to square one.*

back [FURTHER AWAY] /bæk/ *adv* further away in distance: *If we push the table back against the wall, we'll have more room.* ○ *"Keep back!" he shouted, "Don't come any closer!"* ○ *He sat back on the sofa.* ○ *She threw back her head and laughed uproariously.* ○ *The house is set back* ***from*** *the road.*

B

• **back and forth** moving first in one direction and then in the opposite one: *She swayed gently back and forth to the music.*

back /bæk/ *verb* [I or T; + adv or prep] to (cause to) move backwards: *Ann gave up driving when she backed the car into the garage door.* ○ *Please could you back your car up a few feet so that I can get mine out of the drive?*

back FURTHEST PART /bæk/ *noun* [C] **1** the inside or outside part of an object, vehicle, building, etc. that is furthest from the front: *He jotted her name down on the back of an envelope.* ○ *I found my tennis racket at the back of the cupboard.* ○ *We sat at the back of the bus.* ○ *Our seats were right at the back of the theatre.* ○ *"Where's Ted?" "He's* (UK) *out/round the back/* (US) *out back* (= in the area behind the house)*."* ○ *There is a beautiful garden at the back of/* (US ALSO) *in back of* (= behind) *the house.* ○ *If there's no reply at the front door, come round the back* (= to the part of the house that is furthest from the front). ○ *He put his jacket on the back of his chair* (= the part of the chair which you put your back against when you sit on it). **2 the back of your hand** the side of your hand that has hair growing on it

• **back to front** UK (US **backwards**) with the back part of something where the front should be: *You've put your jumper on back to front.*

• **the back of beyond** UK INFORMAL a place far away from any big town: *They live in some village in the back of beyond.*

• **at/in the back of your mind** If something is at/in the back of your mind, you intend to do it, but are not actively thinking about it: *It's been at the back of my mind to call José for several days now, but I haven't got round to it yet.*

back /bæk/ *adj* [before n] at or near the back of something: *She left the house by the back door.* ○ *The back seat of the car folds down.*

• **take a back seat** to choose not to be in a position of responsibility in an organization or activity

• **on the back burner** If something is on the back burner, it is temporarily not being dealt with or considered, especially because it is not urgent or important: *We've all had to put our plans on the back burner for a while.*

back /bæk/ *verb* [T] *The material is backed with a heavy lining* (= has another material put onto the back of it to make it stronger or protect it).

backing /'bæk.ɪŋ/ *noun* [C or U] *It's strong cloth – it might be useful as (a) backing* (= something put on the back of something else in order to make it stronger or protect it).

back SUPPORT /bæk/ *verb* [T] to give support to someone or something with money or words: *The management has refused to back our proposals.* ○ *The horse I backed* (= risked money on so that I could win more money if it won a race) *came in last.* ○ *Will you back me up* (= say that I am telling the truth) *if I say that I never saw him?*

• **back the wrong horse** to make the wrong decision and support a person or action that is later unsuccessful: *In all his years as a book publisher, he rarely backed the wrong horse.*

backing /'bæk.ɪŋ/ *noun* [U] **1** support, especially money, that someone gives a person or plan: *If I go ahead with the plan, can I count on your backing?* **2** music or singing which is played or performed to support a song or tune, especially a popular one: *a backing track* ○ *She sang as part of an all-women backing* (US USUALLY *backup) group.*

backer /'bæk.ə*ʳ*/ (US) /-ɚ/ *noun* [C] someone who gives financial support to something: *We need financial backers for the project.* **-backed** /-bækt/ *suffix* government-backed contracts ○ US-backed intervention

back BODY PART /bæk/ *noun* [C] the part of your body that is opposite to the front, from your shoulders to your bottom: *I've got a bad back.* ○ *Sleeping on a bed that is too soft can be bad for your back.* ○ *He lay on his back, staring at the ceiling.* ○ *I turned my back* (= turned round so that I could not see) *while she dressed.* ○ *She put her back out* (= caused a serious injury to her back) *lifting a box.* ⊃See picture **The Body** on page Centre 5

• **behind sb's back** If you do something behind someone's back, you do it without them knowing, in a way which

is unfair: *I dread to think what they say about me behind my back.*

• **be on sb's back** INFORMAL to criticize someone several times in an annoying way: *She's on my back again about those sales figures – I just haven't had a moment to do them.*

• **get off my back!** INFORMAL used to tell someone to stop criticizing you: *Why don't you get off my back! I'm doing my best.*

• **on the back of sth** soon after an earlier success, and as a result of it: *The advertising agency secured the contract on the back of their previous successful campaigns.*

• **on the back of sb/sth** by using or taking advantage of someone or something else: *They have carried on their business operations by riding on the back of established firms.*

• **have your back to/against the wall** to have very serious problems which limit the ways in which you can act: *He owes money to everyone – he's really got his back to the wall now.*

• **put/get sb's back up** INFORMAL to annoy someone: *Just ignore him – he's only trying to put your back up.*

back SPORT /bæk/ *noun* [C] (in some sports, such as football or hockey) one of the players in a team who try to stop players from the other team from scoring goals, rather than trying to score goals themselves ⊃Compare **forward** SPORT.

PHRASAL VERBS WITH **back**   ▼

▲ **back away** MOVE *phrasal verb* to move backwards away from something or someone, usually because you are frightened: *She saw that he had a gun and backed away.*

▲ **back away** NOT SUPPORT *phrasal verb* to show that you do not support a plan or idea any more and do not want to be involved with it: *The government has backed away from plans to increase taxes.*

▲ **back down** *phrasal verb* to admit that you were wrong or that you have been defeated: *Eventually, Roberto backed down and apologized.* ○ *Local residents have forced the local council to back down from/on its plans to build a nightclub in their street.*

▲ **back off** STOP *phrasal verb* INFORMAL to stop being involved in a situation, usually in order to allow other people to deal with it themselves: *She started to criticize me, then she suddenly backed off.* ○ *Just back off and let us do this on our own, will you?*

▲ **back off** MOVE *phrasal verb* to move backwards away from someone, usually because you are frightened: *I saw the knife and backed off.*

▲ **back onto sth** *phrasal verb* If a building backs onto something, its back faces that thing: *The house backs onto a narrow alley.*

▲ **back out** *phrasal verb* to decide not to do something that you had said you would do: *You agreed to come. You can't back out now!* ○ *They backed out of the deal the day before they were due to sign the contract.*

▲ **back sb up** SUPPORT *phrasal verb* [M] **1** to support or help someone: *My family backed me up throughout the court case.* **2** to say that someone is telling the truth: *Honestly, that's exactly what happened – Claire will back me up.*

▲ **back sth up** PROVE *phrasal verb* [M often passive] to prove something is true: *His claims are backed up by recent research.*

▲ **back sth up** COMPUTERS *phrasal verb* [M] to make an extra copy of computer information: *Make sure you back up your files* ⊃See also **backup**.

▲ **back (sth) up** DRIVE *phrasal verb* [M] to drive backwards

▲ **back up** TRAFFIC *phrasal verb* If the traffic backs up, the vehicles have to wait in a long line because there are too many of them: *The traffic is starting to back up on the M25.*

backed up /ˌbækt'ʌp/ *adj* [after v] *The traffic is backed up for six miles on the road to the coast.*

backache /'bæk.eɪk/ *noun* [C or U] a pain in your back: *Gardening gives me such backache.*

backbench /ˌbæk'bentʃ/ *noun* [C usually pl] (the seats used by) members of the British Parliament who do not have official positions in the government or in an opposition political party: *The Prime Minister expects strong support from the Labour backbenches.* ○ *a backbench revolt* ⊃Compare **frontbench**. **backbencher** /ˌbæk'ben.tʃər/ US /-tʃɚ/ *noun* [C] *The advantage of being a backbencher is that you can speak your mind.* ⊃Compare **frontbencher** at **frontbench**.

backbiting /'bæk.baɪ.tɪŋ/ US /-tɪŋ/ *noun* [U] unpleasant and unkind words that are said about someone who is not there: *A lot of backbiting goes on in our office.*

backbone BONES /'bæk.bəʊn/ US /-boʊn/ *noun* [C] **1** the spine: *She stood with her backbone rigid.* ⊃See picture **The Body** on page Centre 5 **2 the backbone of sth** the most important part of something, providing support for everything else: *Farming and cattle-raising are the backbone of the country's economy.*

backbone STRENGTH /'bæk.bəʊn/ US /-boʊn/ *noun* [U] bravery and strength of character: [+ *to* infinitive] *Will he **have** the backbone to tell them what he thinks?*

backbreaking /'bæk.breɪ.kɪŋ/ *adj* needing a lot of hard physical effort and very tiring: *Digging the garden was backbreaking **work**.*

backchat /'bæk.tʃæt/ *noun* [U] (US USUALLY **back talk**) rude remarks made when answering someone in authority: *That's enough backchat! You do as you're told.*

backcomb UK /'bæk.kəʊm/ US /-koʊm/ *verb* [T] (US **tease**) to hold your hair away from your head and comb it towards your head, in order to make it look thicker

'back ˌcopy *noun* [C] (ALSO **back issue/number**) a newspaper or magazine of an earlier date than the one now on sale

backdate /ˌbæk'deɪt/ /'--/ *verb* [T] to make something, especially a pay increase, effective from an earlier time: *They got a pay rise in March which was backdated **to** January.* ⊃Compare **predate**; **postdate**.

ˌback 'door *adj* [before n] DISAPPROVING relating to something that is indirect, secretive or dishonest: *The Prime Minister's proposal was immediately dismissed as a back door tax increase.*

backdrop /'bæk.drɒp/ US /-drɑːp/ *noun* **1** [C] (MAINLY UK **backcloth**) a large piece of cloth with buildings, countryside, etc. painted on it that is hung at the back of a stage during a performance **2** [S] the view behind something: *The mountains form a dramatic backdrop to the little village.* **3** [S] the general situation in which particular events happen: *Their love affair began **against** a backdrop of war.*

backfire HAVE RESULT /ˌbæk'faɪər/ US /-'faɪr/ *verb* [I] (of a plan) to have the opposite result from the one you intended: *Her plans to make him jealous backfired **on** her when he went off with her best friend.*

backfire MAKE NOISE /'bæk.faɪər/ US /-faɪr/ *verb* [I] (of an engine) to make a loud noise as a result of fuel burning too early: *I was woken by the sound of a truck backfiring.*

backgammon /'bæk.gæm.ən/ *noun* [U] a game for two people in which you throw dice and move circular pieces around a special board with narrow triangular shaped patterns on it

background THINGS BEHIND /'bæk.graʊnd/ *noun* **1** [S] the things that can be seen or heard behind other things that are closer or louder: *The little figure that you can just see **in the** background **of** the photograph is me.* ○ *If you listen carefully to this piece of music, you can hear a flute **in the** background.* ○ *We couldn't hear what they were saying on the tape – there was too much background noise.* ⊃Compare **the foreground**. **2** [C] the things that can be seen behind the main things or people in a picture: *The artist himself did not paint the backgrounds **to** his pictures – they were done by his pupils.* ○ *He has photographed her **against** lots of different backgrounds.* ○ *They were filmed **against** a background **of** dark fir trees.* ○ *The book's cover has white lettering **on** a blue background.* **3** [S or U] the conditions that existed before a particular event happened, and which help to explain why it happened: *These decisions have had to be taken **against** a background of high unemployment.* ○ *Can you give me some background **on** (= information about the*

conditions that existed before) *the situation?*

background /'bæk.graʊnd/ *adj* [before n] describes something that is done before, and in preparation for, something else: *Students are expected to do some background reading before the course starts.* ○ *The book provides background **information** on the history of the region.*

the 'background *noun* [S] If someone or something is in the background, they are not the main point of attention: *Her worries about her job have **faded into** the background since she learnt about her father's illness.*

background EXPERIENCE /'bæk.graʊnd/ *noun* [C] your family and your experience of education, living conditions, wealth, etc: *The school has pupils **from** many different ethnic/cultural/religious backgrounds.* ○ *They **come from** a privileged/wealthy background.* ○ *a background **in** publishing*

backhand /'bæk.hænd/ *noun* [C] (in sports such as tennis) a hit in which the arm is brought across the body with the back of the hand facing the same direction as the hit itself, or the player's ability to perform this hit: *What a wonderful backhand return!* ○ *Henin has one of the finest backhands in the game.* ○ *Serve to his backhand.* ⊃Compare **forehand**.

backhanded /ˌbæk'hæn.dɪd/ *adj* (of something said) seeming pleasant but possibly critical or unkind in reality: *a backhanded **compliment***

backhander /ˌbæk'hæn.dər/ US /-dɚ/ *noun* [C] INFORMAL FOR **bribe**

backlash /'bæk.læʃ/ *noun* [C] a strong feeling among a group of people in reaction to a tendency or recent events in society or politics: *the sixties backlash **against** bourgeois materialism* ○ *the backlash **against** feminism*

backless /'bæk.ləs/ *adj* (of a dress) not covering most of your back

backlist /'bæk.lɪst/ *noun* [C] (a list of) all the books a particular PUBLISHER (= an organization that publishes text or music) has produced in the past which are still available: *a publisher's backlist*

backlit /'bæk.lɪt/ *adj* lit up from behind, especially in order to create a special effect: *His trophies were proudly displayed in a backlit cabinet.*

backlog /'bæk.lɒg/ US /-lɑːg/ *noun* [C usually sing] a large amount of things that you should have done before and must do now: *I've got a huge backlog **of** work to do.*

backpack /'bæk.pæk/ *noun* [C] a **rucksack**

backpack /'bæk.pæk/ *verb* [I] to travel or camp while carrying your clothes and other things that you need in a backpack: *We backpacked around Thailand.*

backpacker /'bæk.pæk.ər/ US /-ɚ/ *noun* [C] a person who travels with a backpack **backpacking** /'bæk.pæk.ɪŋ/ *noun* [U] to go backpacking ○ *a backpacking trip/holiday*

ˌback 'passage *noun* [C] UK POLITE PHRASE FOR **rectum**

backpedal /'bæk.ped.əl/ /-'--/ *verb* [I] -ll- OR US USUALLY -l- **1** to pedal backwards on a bicycle: *Some types of bike have brakes which you operate by backpedalling.* **2** to change an opinion that you had expressed before, or do something different from what you had said you would do: *As soon as I said I thought she was wrong, she started backpedalling.* ○ *He said he'd help, but now he's starting to backpedal **(on** his promise).*

ˌback 'road *noun* [C] a small road which does not have much traffic on it

backroom /'bæk.ruːm/ /'--/ /-rʊm/ *noun* [C] a room in which work or other activities are done out of public view or secretly: *backroom staff* ○ *backroom negotiations*

ˈbackroom ˌboys *plural noun* people in an organization whose work is not seen by the public

ˈback ˌsaw *noun* [C] US FOR **tenon saw**

back-seat driver /ˌbæk.siːt'draɪ.vər/ US /-vɚ/ *noun* [C] a passenger in a car who keeps giving advice to the driver that the driver has not asked for: FIGURATIVE *It is expected that the former prime minister will be a backseat driver (= have a controlling influence on what happens) in the new government.*

backside /'bæk.saɪd/ *noun* [C] INFORMAL the part of the body that you sit on; your bottom: *After cycling for the whole day, my backside was very sore.*

• **a boot/kick up** *the/your* **backside** SLANG when you are told forcefully to start doing something more quickly or actively: *She's so lazy – she needs a good boot up the backside.*

• **get off** *your* **backside** SLANG to stop being lazy: *Get off your backside and do some work!*

• **sit (around) on** *your* **backside** SLANG DISAPPROVING to do nothing: *I do all the work, while all you do is sit around on your backside all day.*

backslapping /ˈbækˌslæp.ɪŋ/ *noun* [U] a noisy expression of happiness and positive feelings, usually showing admiration for a shared success: *There was a party after the ceremony where much drinking and backslapping went on.*

backslide /ˈbæk.slaɪd/ *verb* [I] **backslid, backslid** to go back to doing something bad when you have been doing something good, especially to stop working hard or to fail to do something that you had agreed to do: *My diet was going well but I'm afraid I've been backsliding a bit recently.*

back-stabber /ˈbækˌstæb.əʳ/ ⑩ /-ɚ/ *noun* [C] someone who says harmful things about you when you are not there to defend yourself or your reputation ⊃See also **stab** *sb* **in the back** at **stab**.

backstage /ˈbæk.steɪdʒ/ /-ˈ-/ *adj, adv* **1** in the area behind the stage in a theatre, especially the rooms in which actors change their clothes or where equipment is kept: *We went backstage after the show to meet the actors.* ○ *backstage workers* **2** If something happens backstage, it is not generally known about: *The organizers say it's a fair contest but who knows what goes on backstage?*

backstop PLAYER /ˈbæk.stɒp/ ⑩ /-stɑːp/ *noun* [C] **1** (in ROUNDERS) a player who stands directly behind the player from the opposing team who is trying to hit the ball, and attempts to catch the ball after it has been thrown if the person does not hit it **2** US INFORMAL FOR **catcher** ⊃See at **catch** TAKE HOLD.

backstop FENCE /ˈbæk.stɒp/ ⑩ /-stɑːp/ *noun* [C] (in baseball) a high fence behind the player hitting the ball, which prevents balls from leaving the playing area if they are not hit or caught

back streets *plural noun* the older and poorer areas of a town or city: *She grew up in the back streets of Bolton.*

back-street abortion UK *noun* [C] (US **back-alley abortion**) an illegal and usually dangerous operation to end a pregnancy done by someone who is not medically qualified

backstroke /ˈbæk.strəʊk/ ⑩ /-stroʊk/ *noun* [S or U] a way of swimming in which you lie on your back and move one arm and then the other straight behind you so that they pass the sides of your head, while kicking with your legs: *Can you do backstroke?*

back talk *noun* [U] US FOR **backchat**

back-to-back CLOSE TOGETHER /ˌbæk.təˈbæk/ *adj* [before n], *adv* close together and facing in opposite directions: UK *back-to-back terraced houses* ○ *The office was full of computers, and we had to sit back-to-back in long rows.*

back-to-back CONTINUOUS /ˌbæk.təˈbæk/ *adj* [before n], *adv* happening one after another, without interruption: *Coming up after the break, three Rolling Stones classics back-to-back.* ○ *Schumacher is celebrating back-to-back victories in the French and British Grand Prix.*

backtrack /ˈbæk.træk/ *verb* [I] **1** to go back along a path you have just followed: *We went the wrong way and had to backtrack till we got to the right turning.* **2** to say that you did not mean something you said earlier or say that you have changed your opinion: [+ speech] *"All right," he backtracked, "It's possible that I was mistaken."* ○ *The officers were forced to backtrack on their statements.* ○ *She refused to backtrack from her criticisms of the proposal.*

backup /ˈbæk.ʌp/ *noun* **1** [C or U] (ALSO **back-up**) (someone or something that provides) support or help, or something that you have arranged in case your main plans, equipment, etc. go wrong: *We're going to need some professional backup for this project.* ○ *The party is going to be outdoors, so we'll need to organize somewhere as a*

backup in case it rains. ○ *Remember, your colleagues are your backup* **system** *when things go wrong.* **2** [C] a copy of information that is held on computer, which is stored separately from the computer: *Before we leave work each day, we* **make** *a backup* **of** *all the records we have entered into the computer that day.* ○ *The department's backup* **disks** *are all stored in a different building.* **3** [C] US a player who plays when the person who usually plays is not available: *He's a backup for the Dallas Cowboys.*

backup software *noun* [U] computer programs which automatically create copies of the information on a computer system so that it can be stored separately and used to replace the original information if it is damaged or lost

backward /ˈbæk.wəd/ ⑩ /-wɚd/ *adj* not advanced: *When he was a child, his teachers thought he was backward* (= unable to learn as much as most children). ○ *People still think of it as a backward country/region/area* (= one without industry or modern machines). ⊃See also **backward** at **backwards**.

• **be backward in coming forward** to be shy and not tending to express desires or opinions: *I'm sure Matt will tell you what he thinks of the idea – he's not usually backward in coming forward.*

backwardness /ˈbæk.wəd.nəs/ ⑩ /-wɚd-/ *noun* [U] *They were accused of backwardness* (= very old-fashioned ways) *because they had no washing machine.*

backward-looking /ˈbæk.wədˌlʊk.ɪŋ/ ⑩ /-wɚd-/ *adj* DISAPPROVING opposed to change or new ideas: *The business is rapidly losing money because of their backward-looking ideas.*

backwards /ˈbæk.wədz/ ⑩ /-wɚdz/ *adv* **1** (US ALSO **backward**) towards the direction which is opposite to the one in which you are facing or opposite to the usual direction: *I walked backwards towards the door.* ○ *He took a step backwards to allow her to pass.* ○ *He began counting backwards: "Ten, nine, eight ..."* ⊃Compare **forwards**. **2** returning to older and less effective ways: *The breakdown in negotiations will be seen as a step backwards.*

• **backwards and forwards** first in one direction and then in the opposite one: *Paul paced anxiously backwards and forwards.*

• **bend/lean over backwards** to try very hard to do something: *I've been bending over backwards trying to help you and this is all the thanks I get!*

backward /ˈbæk.wəd/ ⑩ /-wɚd/ *adj*: *She left without a backward* (= directed behind her) *glance.* ○ *He did a brilliant backward* (= directed towards his back) *somersault.*

backwash /ˈbæk.wɒʃ/ ⑩ /-wɑːʃ/ *noun* **1** [U] the backward movement of waves, or the backward movement of water caused by something, such as a boat, passing through it: *The water-skier was caught in the backwash from a passing motorboat.* **2** [S] an indirect effect: *The economic and political backwash of the war is still being felt.*

backwater /ˈbæk.wɔː.təʳ/ ⑩ /-wɑː.t̬ɚ/ *noun* [C] **1** a part of a river where the water does not flow: *We tied the boat up in a quiet backwater overnight.* **2** DISAPPROVING a place which is not influenced by new ideas or events that happen in other places, and which does not change: *He grew up in a rural backwater.* ⊃Compare **jerkwater**.

the backwoods /ðəˈbæk.wʊdz/ *plural noun* a place in the countryside which is a long way from any town and in which not many people live: *They spent their childhood in the backwoods.*

backyard /ˌbækˈjɑːd/ ⑩ /-ˈjɑːrd/ *noun* [C] **1** UK a small enclosed space at the back of a house, usually with a hard surface: *The house was a small backyard, surrounded by a high brick wall.* **2** US a space at the back of a house, usually enclosed by a fence, and covered with grass

• **in** *your* **backyard** INFORMAL in the area where you live, or in the area of interest or activity which you are involved in or responsible for: *How would you feel about them building a nuclear power station in your backyard?* ○ *We should take a look at what is happening in our* **own** *backyard before criticizing what is taking place in other countries.*

B

bacon /ˈbeɪ.kᵊn/ *noun* [U] (thin slices of) meat from the back or sides of a pig which is often eaten fried: *a bacon sandwich* ○ *a slice/rasher of bacon* ○ *bacon and eggs*

bacteria /bækˈtɪə.ri.ə/ [US] /-ˈtɪr.i-/ *plural of* **bacterium**

bacterial /bækˈtɪə.ri.ᵊl/ [US] /-ˈtɪr.i-/ *adj* caused by, made from, or relating to BACTERIA (= very small organisms): *a bacterial infection* ○ *bacterial contamination/growth*

bacteriology /bækˌtɪə.riˈɒl.ə.dʒi/ [US] /-ˌtɪr.iˈɑː.lə-/ *noun* [U] the scientific study of bacteria and other very small living things, especially those which cause disease **bacteriological** /bækˌtɪə.ri.əˈlɒdʒ.ɪ.kᵊl/ [US] /-ˌtɪr.i.əˈlɑː.-dʒɪ-/ *adj* **bacteriologist** /bækˌtɪə.riˈɒl.ə.dʒɪst/ [US] /-ˌtɪr.i-ˈɑː.lə-/ *noun* [C]

bacterium /bækˈtɪə.ri.əm/ [US] /-ˈtɪr.i-/ *noun* [C usually pl] *plural* **bacteria** a type of very small organism that lives in air, earth, water, plants and animals, often one which causes a disease: *an illness caused by bacteria in drinking water* ○ *The bacterium 'Streptococcus pneumoniae' causes about a third of some 3,000 annual meningitis cases.*

bad [UNPLEASANT] /bæd/ *adj* **worse, worst** unpleasant; causing difficulties or harm: *Our holiday was spoiled by bad **weather**.* ○ *We've just had some very bad **news**.* ○ *I had a very bad **night*** (= did not sleep well) *last night.* ○ *Watch out – he's **in a** bad **mood/temper*** (= being unpleasant to everyone). ○ *She's just a bad **loser*** (= She is unpleasant when she loses). ○ *The company has been getting a lot of bad **publicity**/getting a bad **press*** (= harmful things have been written or said about it) *recently.* ○ *The queues were so bad* (= unpleasantly long) *that I didn't bother waiting.* ○ *The company's financial situation is **looking** rather bad* (= likely to be difficult) *at the moment.* ○ *The damage caused by the storm was **nothing like as/nowhere near as** bad* (= not as serious) **as** *we'd feared it might be.* ○ *Breathing in other people's cigarette smoke is bad **for** you* (= has a harmful effect on your health). ○ *This is rather a bad* (= not convenient or suitable) *time for me to talk. Can I call you back later?*

• **feel bad** to feel ashamed and sorry: *Knowing that I hurt her makes me feel really bad.* ○ *I feel bad **about** letting them down.*

• **not (too) bad** *INFORMAL* quite good or satisfactory: *"How are things?" "Not too bad, thanks."*

• **not bad** *INFORMAL* very good: *He was best in his age group – not bad, eh?*

• **give *sth* up as a bad job** to stop doing something because you do not feel it is worth continuing: *After three attempts to mend it, I gave it up as a bad job.*

• **go from bad to worse** If a situation goes from bad to worse, it was difficult and unpleasant, and is becoming even more so: *Things have gone from bad to worse.*

• **have got it bad** *INFORMAL* to be very much in love

• **be in a bad way** *UK* to be ill, unhappy, or in a bad state: *She was thin and tired-looking and generally in a bad way.* ○ *After 17 years of Conservative government, the country was in a bad way.*

bad /bæd/ *adv US INFORMAL FOR* badly (= very much): *He needs the money real bad.* ○ *My arm hurts so bad.*

badly /ˈbæd.li/ *adv* **worse, worst 1** in a severe and harmful way: *She was badly affected by the events in her childhood.* ○ *Fortunately, none of the passengers were badly **hurt/injured** in the crash.* ○ *I thought he was **treated** very badly.* **2** very much: *He needs the money really badly.* ○ *They are badly **in need of** help.*

bad [LOW QUALITY] /bæd/ *adj* **worse, worst** low quality; not acceptable: *The plumber made rather a bad job of the repairs.* ○ *Are the company's current difficulties a result of bad* (= harmful) ***luck** or bad* (= of low quality) *judgment?* ○ *He has some very bad **habits**.* ○ *In some parts of the world, it is considered bad **manners** to pick up food or cutlery with the left hand.* ○ *He was sent home from school for bad **behaviour**.* ○ *That remark was in (rather) bad **taste**, wasn't it?* ○ *I'm very bad **at** cooking* (= cannot do it very well). **badly** /ˈbæd.li/ *adv* **worse, worst** *The event was very badly organized.* ○ *I thought he behaved very badly.* ○ *Their children are extremely badly-**behaved**.*

bad [EVIL] /bæd/ *adj* **worse, worst** (of people or actions) evil or morally unacceptable: *There are a lot of bad people in the world.* ○ *He's got his faults but he's not a bad person.*

badness /ˈbæd.nəs/ *noun* [U] *There is goodness and badness in everyone.*

bad [PAINFUL] /bæd/ *adj* **worse, worst** causing or experiencing pain: *She can't walk up all those steps, not with her bad leg!* ○ *a bad cough*

bad [DECAYED] /bæd/ *adj* harmful to eat because of being decayed: *We'd better eat this chicken before it **goes** bad.*

ˌbad ˈblood *noun* [U] feelings of hate between people because of arguments in the past: *There has been bad blood **between** the two families for years.*

ˌbad ˈbreath *noun* [U] breath that smells unpleasant

ˌbad ˈdebt *noun* [C] a debt that is not likely to be paid: *The bank expects to lose £703 million of last year's profits as a result of bad debts.*

baddie /ˈbæd.i/ *noun* [C] (*ALSO* **baddy**) *MAINLY UK INFORMAL* a bad person in a film, book, etc: *In the old cowboy films, the baddies always get beaten in the end.*

bade /bæd/ *past simple of* **bid** TELL

ˌbad ˈfaith *noun* [U] dishonest or unacceptable behaviour: *They **acted in** bad faith by selling her a car that they knew to be faulty.*

ˌbad ˈfeeling *noun* [U] **bad blood**

badge /bædʒ/ *noun* [C] a small piece of metal, plastic, cloth, etc., with words or a picture on it, that is pinned or sewn to your clothing, often to show your support for a political organization or belief, or your rank, or membership of a group, etc: *Everyone at the conference wore a badge with their name on.*

• **be a badge of *sth*** to be something which shows that you have achieved a particular thing: *For Tony, owning a big car was a badge of **success**.*

badger [ANIMAL] /ˈbædʒ.əʳ/ [US] /-ɚ/ *noun* [C] an animal with greyish brown fur, a black and white head and a pointed face, which lives underground and comes out to feed at night

badger [ASK] /ˈbædʒ.əʳ/ [US] /-ɚ/ *verb* [T] to persuade someone by telling them repeatedly to do something, or to question someone repeatedly: *Stop badgering me – I'll do it when I'm ready.* ○ [+ into v-ing] *She's been badgering me **into** doing some exercise.* ○ [+ to infinitive] *Every time we go into a shop, the kids badger me **to** buy them sweets.*

ˌbad ˈhair ˌday *noun* [C] *INFORMAL* a day when you feel that you look unattractive and everything seems to go wrong: *I'm **having** a bad hair day.*

badinage /ˈbæd.ɪ.nɑːʒ/ *noun* [U] *LITERARY* conversation or remarks that are joking and not serious; BANTER

badlands /ˈbæd.lændz/ *plural noun* a dry area without plants and with large rocks that the weather has worn into strange shapes, especially the area like this in Dakota and Nebraska in the US

ˌbad ˈlanguage *noun* [U] words that are considered offensive by most people: *There's far too much bad language on television.*

ˌbad ˈlot *noun* [C usually sing] *UK INFORMAL* a bad and unpleasant person: *He's not a bad lot – just a bit wild.*

badly-off /ˌbæd.liˈɒf/ [US] /-ˈɑːf/ *adj* having little money and few of the things you need to live: *They're not badly-off but they don't have much money to spare.*

badminton /ˈbæd.mɪn.tᵊn/ *noun* [U] a sport in which two or four people hit a SHUTTLECOCK (= a light object with feathers) over a high net

badmouth /ˈbæd.maʊθ/ /-maʊð/ *verb* [T] *INFORMAL* to criticize (someone or something) in a very unpleasant manner: *Stop badmouthing him all the time.*

bad-tempered /ˌbædˈtemp.əd/ [US] /-ɚd/ *adj* describes a person who becomes angry and annoyed easily: *She's very bad-tempered in the mornings!*

baffle /ˈbæf.l̩/ *verb* [T] to cause someone to be completely unable to understand or explain something: *She was **completely** baffled **by** his strange behaviour.* **bafflement** /ˈbæf.l̩.mənt/ *noun* [U] **baffling** /ˈbæf.lɪŋ/ *adj*: *I found what he was saying completely baffling.*

bag [CONTAINER] /bæg/ *noun* [C] a soft container made out of paper or thin plastic, or a stronger container made of leather, plastic or other material, usually with a handle, in which you carry personal things or clothes and other items that you need for travelling: *a paper/plastic bag* ○ *a shopping bag* (= a bag in which shopping is carried)

○ *a bag of apples/nuts* ○ *Don't eat that whole bag of* (= the amount the bag contains) *sweets at once.* ○ *I hadn't even packed my bags* (= put the things I own in cases/bags).

• **bags of** *sth* MAINLY UK INFORMAL a lot of something: *Come and stay with us – we've got bags of room.* ○ *Don't panic, there's bags of time yet.*

• **bags under** *your* **eyes** dark, loose or swollen skin under your eyes because of tiredness or old age

• **be in the bag** INFORMAL If something is in the bag, you are certain to get it or to achieve it: *Once we'd scored the third goal, the match was pretty much in the bag.*

• **be** *your* **bag** OLD-FASHIONED SLANG to be something that you are interested in: *Tennis isn't really my bag, I'm afraid.*

bag /bæg/ *verb* [T] **-gg-** to put something in a bag: *Shall I bag (up) those tomatoes for you?*

bagful /ˈbæg.fʊl/ *noun* [C] the amount that a bag contains: *a bagful of shoes/socks/shirts*

bag OBTAIN /bæg/ *verb* [T] **-gg-** INFORMAL to get something before other people have a chance to take it: [+ two objects] *Bag us some decent seats/Bag some decent seats for us if you get there first, won't you?* ⊃See also **bags.**

bag KILL /bæg/ *verb* [T] **-gg-** to hunt and kill an animal or bird

bag WOMAN /bæg/ *noun* [C] SLANG a rude and insulting name for a woman, especially an older one: *Silly old bag!*

bag CRITICIZE /bæg/ *verb* [T] **-gg-** AUS INFORMAL to criticize or laugh at someone or something in an unkind way: *Stop bagging her (out) – she's doing her best.*

bagatelle SMALL AMOUNT /ˌbæg.əˈtel/ *noun* [C usually sing] LITERARY something, especially a sum of money, that is small and unimportant: *A thousand pounds is a mere bagatelle to him.*

bagatelle GAME /ˌbæg.əˈtel/ *noun* [C] a game in which small balls are hit, usually by a small rod on a spring which the player pulls, towards numbered holes on a board with a rounded end

bagel /ˈbeɪ.gəl/ *noun* [C] a small soft chewy roll of bread in the shape of a ring: *an onion bagel*

bag-for-'life *noun* [C] UK a strong plastic shopping bag that you buy cheaply from a supermarket and use many times, usually one that the supermarket replaces when it is broken and then RECYCLES

baggage BAGS /ˈbæg.ɪdʒ/ *noun* [U] all the cases and bags that you take with you when you travel; LUGGAGE: *How many pieces of baggage do you have?* ○ *We had to pay extra for our excess baggage* (= our bags and cases which weighed more than was allowed).

baggage FEELINGS /ˈbæg.ɪdʒ/ *noun* [U] the beliefs and feelings that you have which influence how you think and behave: *We all carry a lot of emotional baggage around with us.*

baggage al,lowance *noun* [C usually sing] the weight or number of cases and bags that you are allowed to take onto an aircraft without paying extra

baggage ,car *noun* [C] US FOR **luggage van**

baggage ,handler *noun* [C] a person who takes passengers' bags and cases, and puts them onto an aircraft or removes them from an aircraft

baggage ,room *noun* [C usually sing] US FOR **left-luggage office**

baggy /ˈbæg.i/ *adj* (of clothes) hanging loosely because of being too big or having been stretched: *baggy trousers* ○ *My T-shirt went all baggy in the wash.*

bag /bæg/ *verb* [I] **-gg-** *I hate these trousers – they bag (out)* (= hang loosely) *at the back.*

bags /bægz/ *plural noun* UK OLD-FASHIONED trousers with a wide and loose style: *Oxford bags*

bag ,lady *noun* [C] a woman who has no home and carries everything that she owns around with her in plastic bags

bag of 'bones *noun* [S] INFORMAL someone who is extremely thin: *The child was just a bag of bones when we found her.*

bagpipes /ˈbæg.paɪps/ *plural noun* (ALSO **pipes**) a type of musical instrument, played especially in Scotland and Ireland, from which you produce sound by blowing air into a leather bag and forcing it out through pipes **bagpipe** /ˈbæg.paɪp/ *adj* [before n] *bagpipe music*

bags /bægz/ *verb* [T] (ALSO **bagsy**) UK CHILD'S WORD to have the right to have or do something because you say you want it first: *Bags I sit in the front seat!* (= I said I wanted to do it first, so I should do it, not you.) ⊃See also **bag** OBTAIN.

baguette /bægˈet/ *noun* [C] (UK ALSO **French stick**) a long thin white loaf of bread, of a type which originally came from France: *a ham and cheese baguette*

bah /bɑː/ *exclamation* OLD USE an expression of annoyance or disapproval

baht /bɑːt/ *noun* [C] the standard unit of money used in Thailand

bail MONEY /beɪl/ *noun* [U] a sum of money which a person who has been accused of a crime pays to a law court so that they can be released until their trial. The payment is a way of making certain that the person will return to court for trial: *He was released/remanded on bail (of $100 000).* ○ *Because of a previous conviction, the judge refused to grant bail* (= allow the accused person to be released). ○ *Her parents have agreed to put up/stand/*(US) *post* (= pay) *bail for her.*

bail /beɪl/ *verb* [T] *She was yesterday bailed* (= released having paid a sum of money) *for three weeks on drink-driving offences.* ○ [+ to infinitive] *He was bailed to appear at the Magistrates' Court next month.*

bail REMOVE WATER /beɪl/, UK ALSO **bale** /beɪl/ *verb* [I] to remove water from a boat using a container: *The boat's sinking! Start bailing quickly!*

PHRASAL VERBS WITH **bail**   ▼

▲ **bail out** JUMP, UK ALSO **bale out** *phrasal verb* to jump out of an aircraft with a parachute because the aircraft is going to have an accident: *The plane's engine failed and the pilot was forced to bail out.*

▲ **bail out** STOP, UK ALSO **bale out** *phrasal verb* MAINLY US to stop doing or being involved with something: *The actor has bailed out of the film after only three weeks' shooting.*

▲ **bail** *sth* **out** REMOVE WATER, UK ALSO **bale** *sth* **out** *phrasal verb* [M] to remove water from the bottom of a boat

▲ **bail** *sb/sth* **out** HELP, UK ALSO **bale** *sb* **out** *phrasal verb* [M] to help a person or organization that is in difficulty, usually by giving or lending them money: *She keeps running up huge debts and asking friends to bail her out.*

bailout /ˈbeɪl.aʊt/ *noun* [C usually sing] MAINLY US *Three years of huge losses forced the bank to seek a government bailout.* ○ *The Clinton administration last winter assembled the $50 billion emergency bailout package to ease a financial crisis in Mexico.*

▲ **bail** *sb* **out** PAY *phrasal verb* [M] to pay money to a court so that someone can be released from prison until their trial

bailiff BRITISH OFFICIAL /ˈbeɪ.lɪf/ *noun* [C] (in Britain) an official who takes away someone's POSSESSIONS (= the things that someone owns) when they owe money: *They didn't pay their rent, so the landlord called/sent in the bailiffs.*

bailiff US OFFICIAL /ˈbeɪ.lɪf/ *noun* [C] (in the US) an official who is responsible for prisoners who are appearing in court

bailiff LAND /ˈbeɪ.lɪf/ *noun* [C] (in Britain) a person whose job is to take care of someone else's land or property

bails /beɪlz/ *plural noun* the two small pieces of wood on top of the STUMPS in a game of cricket, which can be knocked off with the ball to make the player who is batting out

bairn /beən/, US /bern/ *noun* [C] SCOTTISH ENGLISH OR NORTHERN ENGLISH a child

bait FOOD /beɪt/ *noun* **1** [U] a small amount of food on a hook or in a special device used to attract and catch a fish or animal: *They were digging up worms to use for bait.* ○ *We put down some poisoned bait to kill the rats.* **2** [C or U] something that is said or offered to people in order to make them react in a particular way: *Free holidays were offered as (a) bait to customers.* ○ *I told my sister I'd lend her my new shirt if she let me borrow her* *jacket, but she didn't* ***take*** *the bait.*

bait /beɪt/ *verb* [T] to put food on a hook or in a special device to attract and catch a fish or animal: *Have you got any stale cheese that I can bait the mousetrap* ***with****?*

bait [MAKE ANGRY] /beɪt/ *verb* [T] to intentionally make a person angry by saying or doing things to annoy them: *Ignore him – he's just baiting you.* ○ *I suspect he was just baiting me.*

bait [DOG] /beɪt/ *verb* [T] to make dogs attack an animal for cruel entertainment: *In the past,* ***bear****-baiting was a common form of entertainment in Britain.*

baize /beɪz/ *noun* [U] thick, usually green, woollen material used to cover the special tables on which snooker, billiards and card games are played

BAK, bak *INTERNET ABBREVIATION FOR* back at the keyboard: used when you return to a discussion in a CHAT ROOM after you have left it for a short time

bake /beɪk/ *verb* **1** [I or T] to cook inside a cooker, without using added liquid or fat: *I made the icing while the cake was baking.* ○ *a baked potato* ○ *freshly baked bread* ○ *Bake* ***at*** *180°C for about 20 minutes.* ○ *Bake* ***for*** *5-7 minutes in a preheated oven.* ○ *a baking dish/tin/tray* **2** [I or T] to make something such as earth or clay hard by heating it, usually in order to make bricks **3** [I] *INFORMAL* to be or become very hot: ***It's*** *baking outside.* ○ *You'll bake in that fleece jacket!*

ˌbaked ˈbeans *plural noun* beans that have been cooked in tomato sauce, sugar and spices, and are usually sold in TINS (= cylindrical metal containers)

ˌbaked poˈtato *noun* [C] (*UK ALSO* **jacket potato**) a potato baked whole without the skin being removed

Bakelite /ˈbeɪ.kə.laɪt/ *noun* [U] *TRADEMARK* a type of hard plastic used especially in the past: *a 1940s Bakelite radio*

baker /ˈbeɪ.kəʳ/ [US] /-kɚ/ *noun* [C] **1** a person whose job is to make bread and cakes for sale, or to sell bread and cakes **2** (*UK ALSO* **baker's**) a shop where bread and cakes are sold and sometimes made

baker's dozen /ˌbeɪ.kəzˈdʌz.ən/ [US] /-kɚz-/ *noun* [S] *OLD-FASHIONED* 13

bakery /ˈbeɪ.kər.i/ [US] /-kɚ.i/ *noun* [C] a place where bread and cakes are made and sometimes sold

ˈbaking ˌpowder *noun* [U] a mixture of powders used to make cakes rise and become light when they are baked

ˈbaking ˌsheet *noun* [C] a flat metal dish used to cook things in an oven

ˈbaking ˌsoda *noun* [U] **1** a mixture of powders used to make cakes rise and become light when they are baked **2** *MAINLY US FOR* **bicarbonate of soda**

balaclava /ˌbæl.əˈklɑː.və/ *noun* [C] a closely fitting woollen covering for the head and neck ➲See picture **Hairstyles and Hats** on page Centre 8

balalaika /ˌbæl.əˈlaɪ.kə/ *noun* [C] a type of musical instrument with a three-sided body and three strings, played especially in Russia

balance [EQUALITY] /ˈbæl.ənts/ *noun* **1** [S or U] a state where things are of equal weight or force; **equilibrium**: *The toddler wobbled and* ***lost*** *his balance* (= started to fall sideways). ○ *She had to hold onto the railings to* ***keep*** *her balance* (= to stop herself from falling). ○ *New tax measures are designed to* ***redress*** *the balance* (= make the situation more equal) *between rich and poor.* ○ *We must* ***strike a*** *balance* ***between*** *reckless spending* ***and*** *penny-pinching* (= try to have something between these two things). **2** [U] The balance on a piece of electronic equipment for playing music is the particular mixture of different sounds, or the device which controls this.

• **on balance** after thinking about all the different facts or opinions: *I would say that, on balance, it hasn't been a bad year.*

balance /ˈbæl.ənts/ *verb* **1** [I or T] to be in a position where you will stand without falling to either side, or to put something in this position: *The flamingoes balanced gracefully* ***on*** *one leg.* ○ *She balanced a huge pot effortlessly* ***on*** *her head and walked down to the river.* **2** [T] to give several things equal amounts of importance, time or money so that a situation is successful: *I struggle to balance work and family commitments.* **3** [T] to arrange a system that relates to money so that the amount of money spent is not more than the amount received: *Stringent measures were introduced so that the government could balance its* ***budget/the economy****.*

• **balance the books** to make certain that the amount of money spent is not more than the amount of money received: *If the business loses any more money, we won't be able to balance the books this year.*

balanced /ˈbæl.əntst/ *adj*: *The news programme prided itself on its balanced reporting* (= one that considered all sides). ○ *The committee is* ***evenly*** *balanced, with six members from each party.* ➲See also **well-balanced**.

balance [WEIGHING DEVICE] /ˈbæl.ənts/ *noun* [C] a device used for weighing things. It consists of two dishes hanging on a bar which shows when the contents of both dishes weigh the same.

• **in the balance** If a situation is in the balance it has reached a stage where it will soon be decided one way or another: *The game* ***hung*** *in the balance until the last minute when an exciting point decided it.*

balance [AMOUNT] /ˈbæl.ənts/ *noun* [C usually sing] the amount of money you have in a bank account, or the amount of something that you have left after you have spent or used up the rest: *Once we know how much money we'll need, let's spend the balance* (= the amount left). ○ *The company's success is reflected in its healthy* ***bank*** *balance.*

PHRASAL VERBS WITH **balance** ▼

▲ **balance *sth* against *sth*** *phrasal verb* to compare the advantages and disadvantages of something: *The ecological effects of the factory need to be balanced against the employment it generates.*

▲ **balance *(sth)* out/up** *phrasal verb* [M] to be equal in amount or value, or to make things equal in amount or value: *We'd better ask a few men to the party to balance up the numbers.* ○ *I spend a lot one month and not so much the next and in the end it balances out.*

ˌbalanced ˈdiet *noun* [C] a combination of the correct types and amounts of food: *If you have a balanced diet, you are getting all the vitamins you need.*

ˌbalance of ˈpayments *noun* [S] (*ALSO* **balance of trade**) the difference between the money that a country receives from EXPORTS and the money that it spends on IMPORTS

ˌbalance of ˈpower *noun* [S] a position in which both or all of the groups or people involved, usually in a political situation, have equal power: *Both countries have a vested interest in* ***maintaining*** *the balance of power.*

• **hold the balance of power** to be able to support one or other opposing sides in a competition, and therefore decide who will win: *When the election is over, this will be the party holding the balance of power.*

ˈbalance ˌsheet *noun* [C] a statement that shows the value of a company's ASSETS (= items of positive value) and its debts

ˈbalancing ˌact *noun* [C usually sing] a situation in which a person tries to give care and attention to two or more activities at the same time: *I found myself having to do a balancing act* ***between*** *work and family.*

balcony /ˈbæl.kə.ni/ *noun* [C] **1** an area with a wall or bars around it that is joined to the outside wall of a building on an upper level: *We had drinks on the hotel balcony.* **2** an area of seats at an upper level in a theatre: *Our seats are in row F of the balcony.*

bald [WITHOUT HAIR] /bɔːld/ [US] /bɑːld/ *adj* with little or no hair on the head: *At twenty he was already* ***going*** *bald.*

• **as bald as a coot** *UK* (*US* **as bald as a cue ball**) *HUMOROUS* completely bald: *When he took off his hat, we saw that he was as bald as a coot!*

balding /ˈbɔːl.dɪŋ/ [US] /ˈbɑːl-/ *adj*: *Eammon was plump and balding* (= becoming bald) *but somehow very attractive to women.*

baldy, baldie /ˈbɔːl.di/ [US] /ˈbɑːl-/ *noun* [C] *HUMOROUS* an unkind name for someone who has lost or is losing the hair on their head: *"Hey, baldy!"* **baldness** /ˈbɔːld.nəs/ [US] /ˈbɑːld-/ *noun* [U]

bald [PLAIN] /bɔːld/ [US] /bɑːld/ *adj* basic and with no unnecessary words; not detailed: *There was just this bald* *statement of resignation – no explanation or anything.* **baldly** /ˈbɔːld.li/ [US] /ˈbɑːld-/ *adv*: *To put it baldly, I can't afford to take the risk.* **baldness** /ˈbɔːld.nəs/ [US] /ˈbɑːld-/ *noun* [U] *The baldness of her question shocked him.*

ˌbald ˈeagle *noun* [C] a large North American eagle with a white head

balderdash /ˈbɔːl.də.dæʃ/ [US] /ˈbɑːl.dɚ-/ *noun* [U], *exclamation* OLD-FASHIONED nonsense; something that is stupid or not true: *"Balderdash!" he spluttered indignantly.*

ˈbald ˌpatch UK *noun* [C] (US **bald spot**) an area of a person's head that has no hair: *He tries to hide his bald patch by brushing his hair across it.*

ˌbald ˈtyre *noun* [C] a tyre that has worn away to become very smooth and is therefore dangerous

bale [LARGE AMOUNT] /beɪl/ *noun* [C] a large amount of something such as hay, paper, wool or cloth that has been tied tightly together

bale /beɪl/ *verb* [I or T] *We were baling* ***(up)*** (= tying up) *the hay all day.*

bale [REMOVE WATER] /beɪl/ *verb* MAINLY UK to **bail** REMOVE WATER

▲ **bale out** *phrasal verb* UK FOR **bail out**

baleful /ˈbeɪl.fəl/ *adj* LITERARY full of evil intentions; threatening: *He gave me a baleful look.* ○ *his baleful influence* **balefully** /ˈbeɪl.fəl.i/ *adv*: *She glared balefully at me.*

balk [BE UNWILLING], **baulk** /bɔːk/ [US] /bɑːlk/ *verb* [I] to be unwilling to do something or to allow something to happen: *I balked* ***at*** *the prospect of spending four hours on a train with him.*

balk [WOOD] /bɔːk/ [US] /bɑːlk/ *noun* [C] (ALSO **baulk**) a rough thick piece of wood

the ˈBalkans *plural noun* a region in southeast Europe between the Mediterranean Sea and the Black Sea

ball [ROUND OBJECT] /bɔːl/ [US] /bɑːl/ *noun* [C] **1** any object in the shape of a sphere, especially one used as a toy by children or in various sports such as tennis and football: *a beach/golf/tennis ball* ○ *Just try to concentrate on* ***hitting*** *the ball.* ○ *The kitten* ***curled*** *itself* ***into a*** *ball* (= the shape of a ball). **2** a long piece of thread that has been rolled into a ball: *a ball of string/wool* **3** The ball of your foot or thumb is the rounded part where the toes join the foot and the thumb joins the hand.

• **be on the ball** to be quick to understand and react to things: *I didn't sleep well last night and I'm not really on the ball today.*

• **start/set/get the ball rolling** to do something which starts an activity, or to start doing something in order to encourage other people to do the same: *I decided to set the ball rolling and got up to dance.*

• **the ball is in *sb's* court** If the ball is in someone's court, they have to do something before any progress can be made in a situation: *It's up to you what to do – the ball is in your court now.*

• **a whole new ball game** a completely different situation, often one which is difficult or which you know little about: *We'd done a lot of climbing in Scotland but the Himalayas were a whole new ball game.*

ball [DANCE] /bɔːl/ [US] /bɑːl/ *noun* [C] a large formal occasion where people dance: *Did you go to the Summer Ball last year?*

• **have a ball** INFORMAL to enjoy yourself very much: *"So how was the party last night?" "Oh, it was brilliant, – we had a ball!"*

ballad /ˈbæl.əd/ *noun* [C] a song or poem that tells a story, or (in popular music) a slow love song

ball-and-socket /ˌbɔːl.ənˈsɒk.ɪt/ [US] /ˌbɑːl.ənˈsɑː.kɪt/ *adj* [before n] SPECIALIZED relating to a joint consisting of a round end and a hollow socket that fit together and move easily: *The hip joint is a ball-and-socket joint.*

ballast /ˈbæl.əst/ *noun* [U] heavy matter such as sand or stone that is used at the bottom of a ship or a BALLOON to make it heavier, or the small stones on which railways and roads are made

ˌball ˈbearing *noun* [C] a small metal ball or several of these arranged in a ring to make particular parts of a machine move more easily

ˈball ˌboy/ˌgirl *noun* [C] a boy/girl who picks up balls during a tennis competition and gives them back to the players

ballcock /ˈbɔːl.kɒk/ [US] /ˈbɑːl.kɑːk/ *noun* [C] a device in a water TANK that consists of a floating ball fixed to a rod which controls the level of water

ballerina /ˌbæl.əˈriː.nə/ *noun* [C] a female ballet dancer

ballet /ˈbæl.eɪ/ [US] /-ˈ-/ *noun* [C or U] (a theatrical work with) a type of dancing where carefully organized movements tell a story or express an idea: *a ballet* ***dancer*** ○ *By the age of fifteen he had already composed his first ballet* (= music for a ballet). **balletic** /bəˈlet.ɪk/ [US] /-ˈlet̬-/ *adj*: *balletic movements*

ˈballet ˌshoe *noun* [C] a type of flat soft shoe worn by ballet dancers

ˈball ˌgame *noun* [C] US a baseball match

ballgown /ˈbɔːl.gaʊn/ [US] /ˈbɑːl-/ *noun* [C] a formal dress that is often made from an expensive material and usually has a long skirt

ballistic /bəˈlɪs.tɪk/ *adj* INFORMAL **go ballistic** to become extremely angry: *If your dad finds out you've been skipping school, he'll go ballistic.*

balˌlistic ˈmissile *noun* [C] a missile which is powered to direct it on its flight, but which continues and falls towards its target without power

ballistics /bəˈlɪs.tɪks/ *noun* [U] the study of objects that are shot or thrown through the air, such as a bullet from a gun

balloon /bəˈluːn/ *noun* [C] **1** a small, very thin rubber bag that you blow air into or fill with a light gas until it is round in shape, used for decoration at parties or as a children's toy: *We tied balloons and streamers to the ceiling ready for the party.* **2** (ALSO **hot-air balloon**) a very large balloon that is filled with hot air or gas and can carry people in a BASKET (= container made of straw) hanging under it: *People first flew in a balloon in 1783.* **3** a **speech bubble**

• **the balloon goes up** If the balloon goes up, a situation suddenly becomes very serious or unpleasant: *The balloon went up last Friday when the scandal became public.*

balloonist /bəˈluː.nɪst/ *noun* [C] a person who takes part in the sport of travelling by balloon: *He's a keen balloonist.*

balloon /bəˈluːn/ *verb* [I] **1** to get bigger and rounder: *I ballooned when I became pregnant with my second baby.* **2** to quickly increase in size, weight or importance: *The rumours soon ballooned* ***into*** *a full-grown scandal.*

ballot /ˈbæl.ət/ *noun* [C] a system or occasion of secret voting: *Representatives were elected* ***by*** *ballot.* ○ *They decided to* ***hold a*** *ballot* (= organize a ballot).

• **put *sth* to the ballot** to vote secretly on a particular matter: *OK, this seems to be an area of disagreement, so let's put it to the ballot.*

ballot /ˈbæl.ət/ *verb* [T] *The union decided to ballot its members on the issue* (= find out their views by organizing a secret vote).

ˈballot (ˌpaper) *noun* [C] a piece of paper on which you write your vote

ballot-rigging /ˈbæl.ətˌrɪg.ɪŋ/ *noun* [U] getting the election result you want by an illegal method: *Rumours of ballot-rigging discouraged many from voting.*

ballpark /ˈbɔːl.pɑːk/ [US] /ˈbɑːl.pɑːrk/ *noun* [C] US a large structure enclosing a field on which ball games, especially baseball games, are played

ˈballpark ˌfigure *noun* [C] MAINLY US a number which is a guess, but which you believe is near the correct number: *We'll have to go away and cost this carefully, but as a ballpark figure I'd say that it'll be about two million dollars.*

ballpoint /ˈbɔːl.pɔɪnt/ [US] /ˈbɑːl-/ *noun* [C] (ALSO **ballpoint pen**) a pen with a small metal ball at the end that puts ink on the paper: *We aren't allowed to write* ***in*** *ballpoint at school.*

ballroom /ˈbɔːl.rʊm/ /-ruːm/ [US] /ˈbɑːl-/ *noun* [C] a large room that is used for dancing

ˌballroom ˈdancing *noun* [U] a type of dancing where a man and a woman dance together using steps and

B

movements to special music, such as the WALTZ or TANGO

balls /bɔːlz/ ⓤ /bɑːlz/ *plural noun* OFFENSIVE **1** testicles: *She fought off her attacker by kicking him in the balls.* **2** complete nonsense or stupidity: *What he said was a load of balls.* ○ *"All men are pigs." "Balls* (= I completely disagree)*!"* **3** bravery and confidence: *You have to admit it – the woman's got balls!*
• **have sb by the balls** OFFENSIVE to have someone in a situation where you have complete power over them
ballsy /'bɔːl.zi/ ⓤ /'bɑːl-/ *adj* US OFFENSIVE *She's one ballsy* (= brave and determined) *lady!*

balls /bɔːlz/ ⓤ /bɑːlz/ *verb*
▲ **balls** (**sth**) **up** *phrasal verb* [M] UK OFFENSIVE to spoil something by making a mistake or doing something stupid: *Trust me to balls up the interview!*
balls-up /'bɔːlz.ʌp/ ⓤ /'bɑːlz-/ *noun* [C usually sing] OFFENSIVE *The whole trip was a complete balls-up.*

bally /'bæl.i/ *adj, adv* OLD-FASHIONED SLANG used to express anger or annoyance with something or someone: *a bally stupid idea* ○ *I bally well hope he finds the money he owes me.*

ballyhoo /ˌbæl.ɪ'huː/ ⓤ /'---/ *noun* [U] OLD-FASHIONED SLANG a lot of noise and activity, often with no real purpose: *I can't see what all this ballyhoo is about.*

balm /bɑːm/ *noun* [C or U] **1** an oil that is obtained from particular tropical trees and used especially to treat injuries or reduce pain: *a new skin balm* **2** something that gives comfort: *Her gentle words were a balm to me.*

balmy /'bɑː.mi/ *adj* (of weather) pleasantly warm: *a balmy summer evening*

baloney NONSENSE /bə'ləʊ.ni/ ⓤ /-'loʊ-/ *noun* [U] INFORMAL nonsense: *That's a load of baloney if you ask me.*

baloney SAUSAGE /bə'ləʊ.ni/ ⓤ /-'loʊ-/ *noun* [C or U] US a smoked sausage, sliced and eaten cold

balsam /'bɒl.sᵊm/ ⓤ /'bɑːl-/ *noun* [C or U] a pleasant-smelling substance used as the base for medical or beauty treatments: *a balsam shampoo*

balsamic vinegar /bɒlˌsæm.ɪk'vɪn.ɪ.gəʳ/ ⓤ /-gɚ/ *noun* [U] a type of sweet dark Italian vinegar made from grapes in a traditional way

balsa (wood) /'bɒl.sə,wʊd/ ⓤ /'bɑːl-/ *noun* [U] very light wood which is soft and easily cut, sometimes used in making model aircraft

balti /'bɒl.ti/ ⓤ /'boʊ-/ *noun* [C or U] spicy food from Pakistan that is cooked and served in a metal dish and eaten with bread

balustrade /ˌbæl.ə'streɪd/ /'---/ *noun* [C] a RAILING or wall to prevent people from falling over the edge of stairs, a BALCONY, etc.

bamboo /bæm'buː/ *noun* [U] a tall tropical grass with hard hollow stems, or the stems of this plant: *Use bamboo canes to support tomato plants.*

bamboozle /bæm'buː.zl̩/ *verb* [T] INFORMAL to trick or deceive someone, often by confusing them: *She was bamboozled into telling them her credit card number.*

ban /bæn/ *verb* [T usually passive] -nn- to forbid, especially officially: *The film was banned* (= the government prevented it from being shown) *in several countries.* ○ [+ from + v-ing] *She was banned from driving for two years.*
ban /bæn/ *noun* [C] *There should be a ban on talking loudly in cinemas* (= an order preventing this).

banal /bə'nɑːl/ *adj* boring, ordinary and not original: *He just sat there making banal remarks all evening.* ○ *banal pop songs* **banality** /bə'næl.ə.ti/ ⓤ /-t̬i/ *noun* [C or U] FORMAL

banana /bə'nɑː.nə/ ⓤ /-'næn.ə/ *noun* [C or U] a long curved fruit with a yellow skin and soft, sweet white flesh inside: *a bunch of bananas* ○ *banana milkshake* ⊃See picture **Fruit** on page Centre 1

ba,nana re'public *noun* [C] DISAPPROVING a small country, especially in South and Central America, that is poor and often badly and immorally ruled

bananas /bə'nɑː.nəz/ ⓤ /-'næn.əz/ *adj* [after v] INFORMAL very silly: *You're going out in this weather? You must be bananas!* ○ *She'll go bananas when you tell her the news* (= she will be extremely angry).

ba'nana ˌskin *noun* [C] UK INFORMAL a sudden unexpected situation that makes a person appear foolish

or causes them difficulty: *The new tax has proved to be a banana skin for the government.*

ba,nana 'split *noun* [C] a sweet dish made of a banana cut in half with ice cream and cream on top

bancassurance /'bæŋ.kə.ʃʊə.rents/ ⓤ /'bæŋ.kə.ʃʊ.rents/ *noun* [U] UK SPECIALIZED a business activity in which banks sell services and products usually sold by insurance companies

band MUSICIANS /bænd/ *group noun* [C] **1** a group of musicians who play modern music together: *a jazz/rock band* ○ *The Beatles are probably the most famous band in the world.* **2 boy/girl band** a group of fashionable young men or women who perform popular songs together and dance as a group: *He made his name in the nineties boyband Boyzone, before going on to a highly successful solo career.*

band STRIP /bænd/ *noun* [C] a thin flat piece of cloth, elastic, metal or other material put around something to fasten or strengthen it, or a long narrow piece of colour, light, etc. that is different from what surrounds it: *a wrist band* ○ *a red silk band* ○ *A narrow band of grass separated the greenhouse from the vegetable garden.*

band RANGE /bænd/ *noun* [C] a particular range of values, numbers, etc: *The scheme is devised for young people in the 15 – 20 age band.*

band GROUP /bænd/ *noun* [C] a group of people who share the same interests or beliefs, or who have joined together for a special purpose: *The former president still has a small band of supporters.*

band /bænd/ *verb*
▲ **band together** *phrasal verb* to join together as a group in order to be able to do something better: *We decided to band together and organize a protest.*

bandage /'bæn.dɪdʒ/ *noun* [C or U] (US ALSO **gauze**) a long narrow piece of cloth which is tied around an injury or a part of someone's body that has been hurt **bandage** /'bæn.dɪdʒ/ *verb* [T] *You ought to bandage* (**up**) *that cut.* ○ *the dog's bandaged paw*

Band-Aid /'bænd.eɪd/ *noun* [C] TRADEMARK a small piece of sticky cloth or plastic that you use to cover and protect a cut in the skin

,band-aid so'lution *noun* [C] MAINLY US a temporary solution that does not deal with the cause of a problem: *Tax credits given to students are merely a band-aid solution to the rising cost of getting an education.*

bandanna, bandana /bæn'dæn.ə/ *noun* [C] a brightly coloured piece of cloth that is worn around the neck or head

,B and 'B *noun* [C] ABBREVIATION FOR **bed and breakfast**

bandicoot /'bæn.dɪ.kuːt/ *noun* [C] a type of MARSUPIAL (= small animal which lives in a bag on its mother's body after birth) which lives in Australia

bandit /'bæn.dɪt/ *noun* [C] an armed thief, especially one belonging to a group that attack people travelling through the countryside

bandleader /'bænd,liː.dəʳ/ ⓤ /-dɚ/ *noun* [C] OLD-FASHIONED a person who leads a large group of especially jazz musicians while they play, and who often plays an instrument at the same time: *Glenn Miller was one of the most famous bandleaders of the 1930s.*

bandmaster /'bænd,mɑː.stəʳ/ ⓤ /-,mæs.tɚ/ *noun* [C] a person who leads the music of a military BAND or a BRASS BAND

bandsman /'bændz.mən/ *noun* [C] a person who plays a musical instrument in a military BAND or a BRASS BAND

bandstand /'bænd.stænd/ *noun* [C] a covered place where musical groups can play outside

bandwagon /'bænd,wæg.ᵊn/ *noun* [C usually sing] an activity, group, movement, etc. that has become successful or fashionable and so attracts many new people: *a bandwagon effect*
• **jump/climb/get on the bandwagon** to become involved in an activity which is successful so that you can get the advantages of it yourself: *The success of the product led many firms to try to jump on the bandwagon.*

bandwidth /'bænd.wɪtθ/ *noun* [C usually sing] **1** the amount of information that can be sent between computers, through a telephone wire, etc: *The system* *will handle not only telephone calls and data messages but other signals that need **high** bandwidth, for instance those that encode TV pictures.* ○ *high bandwidth **services/applications*** **2** the range of FREQUENCIES used to send information over a distance using telephone wires **3** in radio, the width of a particular WAVEBAND

bandy /'bæn.di/ *adj* (of legs) bending out at the knees: *I couldn't help laughing at his bandy legs.*

bandy /'bæn.di/ *verb*

▲ **ˌbandy *sth* a'bout/a'round** *phrasal verb* **[M]** to mention something often, without careful consideration or attention: *Large figures were bandied about, but no money was ever paid.*

• **bandy words** *OLD-FASHIONED* to argue: *I haven't come here to bandy words **with** you.*

bane /beɪn/ *noun* **the bane of *sth*** a cause of continual trouble or unhappiness: *Keeping noise levels low is the bane of airport administration.* ○ *That cat is the bane of my life!*

bang [NOISE] /bæŋ/ *verb* **[I or T]** to (cause something to) make a sudden very loud noise or noises: *She banged her fist angrily on the table.* ○ *Outside a door was banging in the wind.* ○ *He could hear someone banging **at** the door.* ○ *I could hear her in the kitchen banging **about*** (= doing things noisily). ➲See **bang/beat the drum** at **drum** INSTRUMENT.

bang /bæŋ/ *noun* **[C]** a sudden very loud noise: *The window slammed shut with a loud bang.*

• **go with a bang** *UK* (*US* **go over with a bang**) *INFORMAL* If a party or event goes with a bang, it is very exciting and successful.

• **more bang for your buck(s)** *INFORMAL* the best result for the smallest effort

bang /bæŋ/ *exclamation*: *"Bang! Bang! You're dead!" said the child, pointing a plastic gun at me.* ○ *The balloon **went** bang* (= made a sudden loud noise) *when it landed on the bush.*

• **bang goes *sth*** *INFORMAL* said when you have just lost the opportunity to do something: *He says I have to work late tonight – so bang goes my trip to the cinema.*

bang [HIT] /bæŋ/ *verb* **[T]** to hit a part of the body accidentally against something: *I banged my head **against/on** the shelf as I stood up.*

bang /bæŋ/ *noun* **[C]** *I think she must have got a bang* (= hit) ***on** the head.*

bang [SEX] /bæŋ/ *verb* **[I]** *OFFENSIVE* to have sex

bang [EXACTLY] /bæŋ/ *adv INFORMAL* exactly or directly: *The car came to a halt bang **in the middle of** the road.* ○ *I live bang **opposite** the cinema.* ○ *I turned the corner and walked **slap** bang **into** him.* ○ *software that is bang* (= completely) ***up-to-date***

• **be bang on** *INFORMAL* to be exactly right: *What was your answer? 76? That's absolutely bang on!*

PHRASAL VERBS WITH **bang** ▼

▲ **bang on** *phrasal verb INFORMAL DISAPPROVING* to talk about something for a long time, especially in a way that is boring to other people: *My parents are always banging on **about** how much better life was 20 years ago.*
* NOTE: This is usually used in the continuous form.

▲ **bang *sb* up** *phrasal verb* **[M]** *SLANG* to lock someone up, especially in prison: *She's terrified of him and won't make a statement until we've got him banged up in the cells.*

banger [CAR] /'bæŋ.əʳ/ [US] /-ɚ/ *noun* **[C]** *UK* a very old car in bad condition

banger [FIREWORK] /'bæŋ.əʳ/ [US] /-ɚ/ *noun* **[C]** *UK* a small noisy firework

banger [FOOD] /'bæŋ.əʳ/ [US] /-ɚ/ *noun* **[C]** *UK INFORMAL FOR* **sausage**: *bangers **and mash*** (= potatoes)

bangle /'bæŋ.gl̩/ *noun* **[C]** a ring of stiff plastic, metal, etc. worn around the wrist or arm as jewellery

bangs /bæŋz/ *plural noun US FOR* **fringe** HAIR ➲See picture **Hairstyles and Hats** on page Centre 8

banish /'bæn.ɪʃ/ *verb* **[T]** **1** to send someone away, especially from their country, and forbid them to come back: *He was banished **to** an uninhabited island for a year.* ○ *They were banished* (= sent out) ***from** the library for making a noise.* **2** to get rid of something completely: *You must try to banish all thoughts of revenge **from** your mind.* **banishment** /'bæn.ɪʃ.mənt/ *noun* **[U]**

banister /'bæn.ɪ.stəʳ/ [US] /-stɚ/ *noun* **[C]** (*ALSO* **banisters**) the row of poles at the side of stairs and the wooden or metal bar on top of them

banjo /'bæn.dʒəʊ/ [US] /-dʒoʊ/ *noun* **[C]** *plural* **banjos** or **banjoes** a stringed musical instrument with a long neck and a hollow circular body

bank [ORGANIZATION] /bæŋk/ *noun* **[C]** **1** an organization where people and businesses can invest or borrow money, change it to foreign money, etc., or a building where these services are offered: *High street banks have been accused of exploiting small firms.* ○ *I need to go to the bank at lunch time.* ○ *I had to take out a bank **loan** to start my own business.* **2** A bank of something, such as blood or human organs for medical use, is a place which stores these things for later use: *a blood bank* ○ *a sperm bank* **3** In GAMBLING, the bank is money that belongs to the owner and can be won by the players.

bank /bæŋk/ *verb* **[I or T]** *I used to bank **with** Lloyd's* (= keep my money there).

bankable /'bæŋ.kə.bl̩/ *adj* likely to make money: *She is currently Hollywood's most bankable actress* (= Her films make large profits).

bankability /bæŋ.kə'bɪl.ɪ.ti/ [US] /-ə.t̬i/ *noun* **[C]** an ability to make money: *His bankability as a pop star decreased as he got older.*

banker /'bæŋ.kəʳ/ [US] /-kɚ/ *noun* **[C]** **1** someone with an important position in a bank: *She was a successful banker by the time she was forty.* **2** the person in gambling games who is responsible for looking after the money

banking /'bæŋ.kɪŋ/ *noun* **[U]** the business of operating a bank: *The intricacies of international banking remained a mystery to him.*

bank [RAISED GROUND] /bæŋk/ *noun* **[C]** sloping raised land, especially along the sides of a river: *By the time we reached the opposite bank, the boat was sinking fast.* ○ *These flowers generally grow on sloping **river** banks and near streams.*

COMMON LEARNER ERROR

bank

Do not use **bank** if you mean a long seat for people to sit on (for example, in a park). The correct word for this kind of seat is **bench**.

The old man sat down on the bench to rest for a while.
~~*The old man sat down on the bank to rest for a while.*~~

bank [MASS] /bæŋk/ *noun* **[C]** a pile or mass of earth, clouds, etc: *A dark bank **of** cloud loomed on the horizon.*

bank /bæŋk/ *verb* **[I or T]** *The snow had banked **up*** (= formed into a mass) *in the corner of the garden.* ○ *We banked **up** the fire* (= put more coal on it) *to keep it burning all night.*

bank [MACHINES] /bæŋk/ *noun* **[C]** a row of similar things, especially machines or parts of machines: *a bank of switches*

bank [TURN] /bæŋk/ *verb* **[I]** (of an aircraft) to fly with one wing higher than the other when turning: *We felt the plane bank steeply as it changed direction.*

▲ **bank on *sb/sth*** *phrasal verb* to expect something or depend on something happening: *Can I bank on your support?* ○ **[+ v-ing]** *I wouldn't bank on him be**ing** there.* ○ *"Do you think she'll come?" "I wouldn't bank on **it**".* ○ *I'd banked on gett**ing** a pay rise this year.*

'bank acˌcount *noun* **[C]** an arrangement with a bank where the customer puts in and removes money and the bank keeps a record of it

'bank ˌbalance *noun* **[C]** the amount of money in a bank account: *I'd like to check my bank balance, please.*

'bank ˌcharges *plural noun* sums of money paid by a customer for a bank's services: *You'll pay some hefty bank charges if you go overdrawn without permission.*

banker's card /'bæŋ.kəz.kɑːd/ [US] /-kɚz.kɑːrd/ *noun* **[C]** a **cheque guarantee card**

banker's order /ˌbæŋ.kəz'ɔː.dəʳ/ [US] /-kɚz'ɔːr.dɚ/ *noun* **[C]** a **standing order**

ˌbank ˈholiday *noun* [C] *UK* an official holiday when banks and most businesses are closed for a day

ˈbank ˌmanager *noun* [C] the person in charge of a local bank: *I got an angry letter from my bank manager the other day.*

banknote /ˈbæŋk.nəʊt/ [US] /-noʊt/ *noun* [C] a piece of printed paper that has a particular value as money: *a £20 banknote* ○ *Hidden in the suitcase were wads of banknotes.*

the Bank of England /ˌbæŋk.əvˈɪŋ.glənd/ *noun* [S] the CENTRAL BANK of the United Kingdom

ˈbank ˌrate *noun* [C] the amount of interest that a bank charges, especially the lowest amount that it is allowed to charge, when it lends money

bankroll /ˈbæŋk.rəʊl/ [US] /-roʊl/ *verb* [T] *INFORMAL* to support a person or activity financially: *a joint program bankrolled by the U.S. space agency*

bankrupt /ˈbæŋ.krʌpt/ *adj* **1** *LEGAL* unable to pay what you owe, and having control of your financial matters given, by a court of law, to a person who sells your property to pay your debts: *He **went** bankrupt after only a year in business.* ○ *The recession has led to many small businesses **going** bankrupt.* **2** *INFORMAL* having no money: *I shall go bankrupt if you children keep on asking for more pocket money!* **3** *DISAPPROVING* lacking in a particular quality: *He believes that modern society is **morally** bankrupt.*

bankrupt /ˈbæŋ.krʌpt/ *verb* [T] *LEGAL They feared that the loss would bankrupt them* (= cause them to become bankrupt).

bankrupt /ˈbæŋ.krʌpt/ *noun* [C] *LEGAL He was **declared** a bankrupt* (= stopped by a court of law from managing his own financial matters) *in 1991.* **bankruptcy** /ˈbæŋ.krəpt.si/ *noun* [C or U] *The company was forced into bankruptcy.* ○ *The toll of bankruptcies was rising daily.*

ˈbank ˌstatement *noun* [C] a printed record of the money put into and removed from a bank account

banner /ˈbæn.əʳ/ [US] /-ɚ/ *noun* [C] **1** a long piece of cloth, often stretched between two poles, with a sign written on it, usually carried by people taking part in a march: *The demonstrators walked along the street, waving banners and shouting angrily.* **2** an idea, principle or belief that is strongly supported by someone: *They won the election **under** the banner **of** lower taxes.*

ˈbanner (ˌad) *noun* [C] (*ALSO* **banner advertisement**) an advertisement that appears across the top of a WEB PAGE

ˌbanner ˈheadline *noun* [C] a large title of a story in a newspaper that stretches across the top of the front page

banns /bænz/ *plural noun* a public announcement, made in a church, that two people are going to get married: *The banns were **published** in their local parish church.*

banquet /ˈbæŋ.kwɪt/ *noun* [C] a large formal meal for many people, often followed by speeches in honour of someone: *Medieval banquets are held in the castle once a month.* **banqueting** /ˈbæŋ.kwɪ.tɪŋ/ [US] /-t̬ɪŋ/ *noun* [U] *The dinner is to be held in the banqueting hall/suite.*

banshee /ˈbæn.ʃiː/ *noun* [C] a female spirit in traditional Irish stories whose crying sound tells you that someone in your family is going to die

bantam /ˈbæn.təm/ [US] /-t̬əm/ *noun* [C] a small breed of chicken

bantamweight /ˈbæn.təm.weɪt/ [US] /-t̬əm-/ *noun* [C] a boxer weighing between 51 and 53.5 kilograms

banter /ˈbæn.təʳ/ [US] /-t̬ɚ/ *noun* [U] conversation which is amusing and not serious: *He considered himself a master of witty banter.*

banter /ˈbæn.təʳ/ [US] /-t̬ɚ/ *verb* [I] to talk to someone in a friendly and amusing way: *He stood around bantering **with** his colleagues.* **bantering** /ˈbæn.tᵊr.ɪŋ/ [US] /-t̬ɚ-/ *adj: I grew weary of his bantering style of conversation.*

banyan /ˈbæn.jæn/ *noun* [C] an Indian fruit tree with branches that grow down into the ground to form additional trunks

bap /bæp/ *noun* [C] *UK* a round soft form of bread which is usually smaller than a loaf: *a soft white bap*

baptism /ˈbæp.tɪ.zᵊm/ *noun* [C or U] a Christian ceremony in which a person has water poured on their head, or is covered briefly in water, in order to show that they have become a member of the Christian Church: *infant baptism*

• **a baptism of/by fire** a very difficult first experience of something: *I was given a million-dollar project to manage in my first month – it was a real baptism of fire.*

baptize, *UK USUALLY* **-ise** /bæpˈtaɪz/ *verb* [T] [+ obj + n] *Were you baptized a Catholic?* ➲See also **christen**.

Baptist /ˈbæp.tɪst/ *noun* [C] a member of a Christian group that believes that baptism should not happen until a person is old enough to ask for it and to understand its meaning

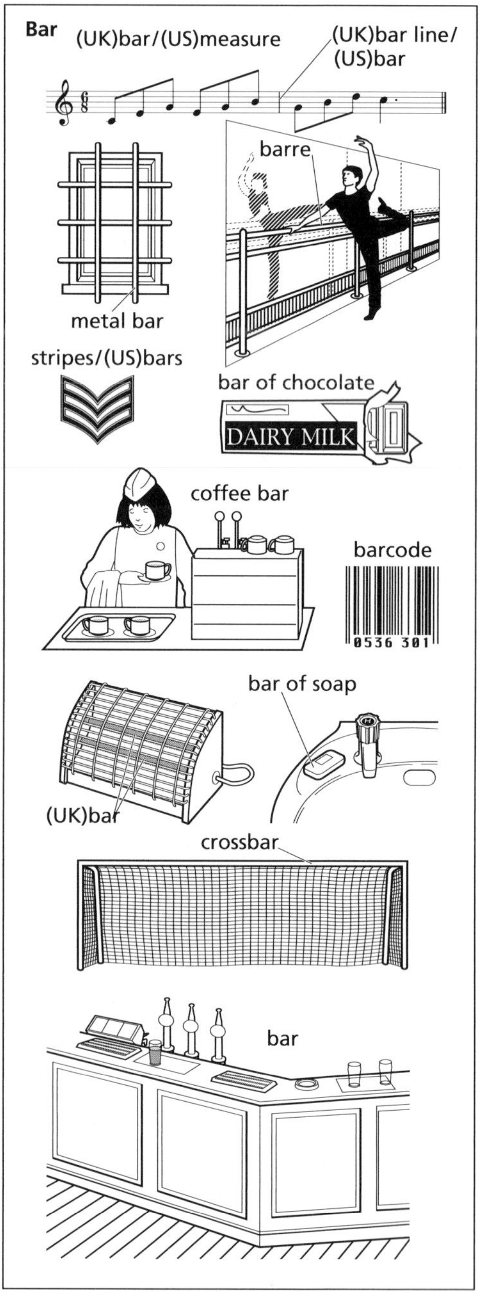

bar [PIECE OF MATERIAL] /bɑːʳ/ [US] /bɑːr/ *noun* [C] **1** a straight stick made of metal: *The gorilla rattled the bars of its*

cage. **2** a substance that has been made into a solid, rectangular shape: *a bar of soap* ○ *a chocolate bar* **3** The bar of an electric heater is a long thin wire in the shape of a spring which is wrapped tightly around a tube. When electricity passes through it, it produces heat and red light. **4** *US FOR* **stripe** MATERIAL

● **behind bars** in prison: *He's spent most of his life behind bars.*

bar /bɑːʳ/ ⓤ /bɑːr/ *verb* [T] **-rr-** *We barred* (= put bars across) *the door to stop anyone getting into the room.*

barred /bɑːd/ ⓤ /bɑːrd/ *adj*: *They arrived at the house to find the door locked and barred* (= with a bar of wood or metal across the front of it).

bar DRINKING PLACE /bɑːʳ/ ⓤ /bɑːr/ *noun* [C] a place where especially alcoholic drinks are sold and drunk, or the area in such a place where the person serving the drinks stands: *They noticed him going into the hotel bar.* ○ *There weren't any free tables, so I sat at the bar.* ○ *Why don't you ask the guy behind the bar* (= serving drinks there)?

bar MUSIC /bɑːʳ/ ⓤ /bɑːr/ *noun* [C] (*US ALSO* **measure**) one of the small equal parts into which a piece of music is divided, containing a fixed number of beats: *Waltzes have three beats in/to the bar* (= in each bar).

bar PREVENT /bɑːʳ/ ⓤ /bɑːr/ *verb* [T] **-rr-** to prevent something or someone from doing something or going somewhere, or to forbid something: *The centre of the town was barred to/(US USUALLY) barred off to football supporters.* ○ *The incident led to him being barred from the country/barred from playing for England.* ○ *I tried to push past her but she barred my way/path* (= stood in front of me and prevented me from getting past).

bar /bɑːʳ/ ⓤ /bɑːr/ *noun* [C] *A lack of formal education is no bar to becoming rich* (= does not make it impossible to become rich).

bar EXCEPT /bɑːʳ/ ⓤ /bɑːr/ *prep SLIGHTLY FORMAL* except: *Everyone is leaving the village, bar the very old and ill.* ○ *They're the best songwriters of this century, bar none* (= no one else is better).

● **(all) over bar the shouting** *UK* If an activity is all over bar the shouting, the result of it is known, but it has not been officially completed or stated, so people can still claim that a different result is possible: *With practically all the results declared, the Nationalist Party has 68% of the vote, so it's all over bar the shouting.*

barring /bɑːrɪŋ/ ⓤ /bɑːr.ɪŋ/ *prep*: *We should arrive at ten o'clock, barring any* (= if there are no) *unexpected delays.*

the Bar LAWYERS *group noun* [S] **1** *UK* lawyers who are allowed to argue a case in a higher court **2** *US* all lawyers thought of as a group

● **be called to the Bar** *UK* to qualify as a lawyer who can argue a case in a higher court

● **be admitted to the Bar** *US* to qualify as a lawyer

barb /bɑːb/ ⓤ /bɑːrb/ *noun* [C] **1** the sharp part which points backwards from a fish hook or arrow, making it hard to remove it from something **2** a remark that is clever but cruel and hurtful: *I tried to ignore their barbs about my new jacket.*

barbed /bɑːbd/ ⓤ /bɑːrbd/ *adj* **1** having a sharp point which curves backwards **2** critical and unkind: *She made some rather barbed comments about my lifestyle.*

barbarian /bɑːˈbeə.ri.ən/ ⓤ /bɑːrˈber.i-/ *noun* [C] **1** a member of a group of people from a very different country or culture that is considered to be less socially advanced and more violent than your own: *The walled city was attacked by barbarian hordes.* **2** *DISAPPROVING* a person with little education who has no interest in art and culture: *How can you call those barbarians your friends?*

barbaric /bɑːˈbær.ɪk/ ⓤ /bɑːr-/ *adj* extremely cruel and unpleasant: *She found the idea of killing animals for pleasure barbaric.* ○ *barbaric acts of violence*

barbarism /ˈbɑː.bə.rɪ.zᵊm/ ⓤ /ˈbɑːr.bə.rɪ-/ *noun* [U] extremely cruel and unpleasant behaviour: *He witnessed some appalling acts of barbarism during the war.*

barbarity /bɑːˈbær.ə.ti/ ⓤ /bɑːrˈbær.ə.ti/ *noun* [C or U] *This barbarity* (= extreme cruelty) *must cease!* ○ *The dictatorship has been responsible for countless*

barbarities (= extremely cruel acts).

barbarous /ˈbɑː.bᵊr.əs/ ⓤ /ˈbɑːr.bɚ-/ *adj FORMAL* describes behaviour that is extremely social or unpleasant, or fails to reach acceptable social standards: *His murder was an outrageous and barbarous act.* ○ *How can they forgive such barbarous behaviour?*

barbecue /ˈbɑː.bɪ.kjuː/ ⓤ /ˈbɑːr-/ *noun* [C] (*UK INFORMAL* **barbie**, *WRITTEN ABBREVIATION* **BBQ**) a metal frame on which meat, fish or vegetables are cooked outside over a fire, or a meal prepared using such a frame which is eaten outside, often during a party **barbecue** /ˈbɑː.bɪ.kjuː/ ⓤ /ˈbɑːr-/ *verb* [T] *Their traditional sausages are delicious grilled or barbecued.*

barbecue ˈsauce *noun* [C or U] a spicy sauce which is used to flavour food cooked on a barbecue

barbed ˈwire *noun* [U] a type of strong wire with sharp points on it, used to prevent people or animals from entering or leaving a place, especially a field: *a barbed wire fence*

barber /ˈbɑː.bəʳ/ ⓤ /ˈbɑːr.bɚ/ *noun* [C] a man whose job is cutting men's hair

barber's (*plural* **barbers**) /ˈbɑː.bəz/ ⓤ /ˈbɑːr.bɚz/ *noun* [C] (*US ALSO* **barbershop**) a shop where a barber works

barbershop /ˈbɑː.bə.ʃɒp/ ⓤ /ˈbɑːr.bɚ.ʃɑːp/ *noun* [U] a type of singing in which four, usually male, voices in close combination perform popular romantic songs, especially from the 1920s and 1930s: *a barbershop quartet*

barber's pole /ˈbɑː.bəz.pəʊl/ ⓤ /ˈbɑːr.bɚz.poʊl/ *noun* [C] a pole with red and white strips that traditionally is put on the front of a barber's shop

barbiturate /bɑːˈbɪt.jʊ.rət/ ⓤ /bɑːr-/ *noun* [C] a strong drug that makes people calm or helps them to sleep: *He died from an overdose of alcohol and barbiturates.*

Barbour /ˈbɑː.bəʳ/ ⓤ /ˈbɑːr.bɚ/ *noun* [C] *UK TRADEMARK* a type of green waterproof coat

ˈbar ˌchart/ˌgraph *noun* [C] a mathematical picture in which different amounts are represented by thin vertical or horizontal rectangles which have the same width but vary in height or length

ˈbar ˌcode *noun* [C] a small rectangular pattern of thick and thin black lines of magnetic ink printed on an item, or on its container, etc. so that its details can be read by and recorded on a computer system: *A hand-held scanner is used to read bar codes.*

bard /bɑːd/ ⓤ /bɑːrd/ *noun* [C] **1** *LITERARY* a poet **2** the **Bard** William Shakespeare

bare /beəʳ/ ⓤ /ber/ *adj* without any clothes or not covered by anything: *Don't walk around outside in your bare feet.* ○ *There's no carpet in the room, just bare floorboards.* ○ *The cupboard/room was completely bare.* (= there was nothing in it.) ○ *I just packed the bare essentials* (= the most basic things). ○ *There isn't much time, so I'll just give you the bare facts/details* (= I'll only give you the most important information). ○ *She eats only the bare minimum* (= the least possible) *to stay alive.* ⇨See also **barefoot**.

● **with your bare hands** without using any type of tool or weapon: *He wrestled the lion to the ground with his bare hands.*

bare /beəʳ/ ⓤ /ber/ *verb* [T] *The men bared their heads* (= took their hats off as a sign of respect) *as they entered the church.* ○ *He became nervous when the dog growled and bared its teeth at him* (= showed its teeth to him).

● **bare your heart/soul** to tell someone your secret thoughts and feelings: *We don't know each other that well. I certainly wouldn't bare my soul to her.*

bareback /ˈbeə.bæk/ ⓤ /ˈber-/ *adj, adv* without a saddle on the back of a horse that is being ridden: *a bareback rider* ○ *Is it difficult riding bareback?*

the ˌbare ˈbones *plural noun* the most important facts about something, which provide a structure to which more detail might be added later: *the bare bones of the story* ○ *I don't need all the details – just give me the bare bones.*

barefaced /ˈbeə.feɪst/ ⓤ /ˈber-/ *adj DISAPPROVING* not trying to hide your bad behaviour: *That's a barefaced lie!*

barefoot /ˈbeə.fʊt/ ⓤ /ˈber-/ *adj, adv* not wearing any shoes or socks: *We took off our shoes and socks and*

B

walked barefoot along the beach.

bareheaded /ˌbeəˈhed.ɪd/ ⓤⓈ /ˈber-/ *adj, adv* without any covering on your head

bare in'finitive *noun* [C] SPECIALIZED in grammar, the infinitive form of a verb without the word 'to': *In the sentence 'Let her go, she's done nothing wrong!', the bare infinitive is the word 'go'.*

barely /ˈbeə.li/ ⓤⓈ /ˈber-/ *adv* by the smallest amount; almost not: *They have barely enough (= no more than what is needed) to pay the rent this month.* ○ *She was barely (= only just) fifteen when she won her first championship.*

barf /bɑːf/ ⓤⓈ /bɑːrf/ *verb* [I] SLANG to vomit: *He got drunk and barfed all over the carpet.* **barf** /bɑːf/ ⓤⓈ /bɑːrf/ *noun* [U]

barf ,bag *noun* [C] MAINLY US SLANG a waterproof paper bag provided for each passenger on an aircraft in case they need to vomit

bargain AGREEMENT /ˈbɑː.gɪn/ ⓤⓈ /ˈbɑːr-/ *noun* [C] an agreement between two people or groups in which each promises to do something in exchange for something else: *"I'll tidy the kitchen if you clean the car." "OK, it's a bargain."* ○ *The management and employees eventually struck/made a bargain (= reached an agreement).*
• **into the bargain** (US ALSO **in the bargain**) in addition to other facts previously mentioned: *He's intelligent, witty, a loving husband, and an excellent cook into the bargain.*
bargain /ˈbɑː.gɪn/ ⓤⓈ /ˈbɑːr-/ *verb* [I or T] Unions bargain **with** employers for better rates of pay each year. ○ *I realized that by trying to gain security I had bargained away my freedom (= exchanged it for something of less value).*

bargain LOW PRICE /ˈbɑː.gɪn/ ⓤⓈ /ˈbɑːr-/ *noun* [C] something on sale at a lower price than its true value: *This coat was half-price – a real bargain.* ○ *The airline regularly offers last-minute bookings at bargain prices.* ○ *The sales had started and the bargain hunters (= people looking for things at a low price) were out in force.*
▲ **bargain for/on** *sth phrasal verb* to expect or be prepared for something: *We hadn't bargained on such a long wait.* ○ *The strength of the opposition was rather more than she'd bargained for.*

bargain 'basement *noun* [C usually sing] an underground room in a shop where items are sold at reduced prices: *Jonathan manages to buy all his clothes at bargain-basement prices (= very cheaply).*

bargaining ,chip *noun* [C] (UK **bargaining counter**) something which someone else wants that you are willing to lose in order to reach an agreement: *Missiles were used as a bargaining chip in negotiations for economic aid.*

bargaining ,power *noun* [C or U] the ability of a person or group to get what they want: *Rising unemployment has diminished the bargaining power of people with jobs.*

barge HURRY /bɑːdʒ/ ⓤⓈ /bɑːrdʒ/ *verb* [I or T; usually + adv or prep] to hurry somewhere or through a place in a rude and forceful way: *They barged through the crowds.* ○ *When the doors opened she barged her way to the front of the queue.* ○ *The man barged (= pushed) into her and ran on without stopping.*

barge BOAT /bɑːdʒ/ ⓤⓈ /bɑːrdʒ/ *noun* [C] a long boat with a flat bottom, used for carrying heavy loads on rivers or canals

---

PHRASAL VERBS WITH **barge** ▼

▲ **barge in/barge into** *sth* ENTER *phrasal verb* INFORMAL to walk into a room quickly, without being invited: *I wish he'd knock instead of just barging in.*
▲ **barge in** INTERRUPT *phrasal verb* INFORMAL to interrupt rudely: *Sorry to barge in, but I couldn't help overhearing what you were saying.*

---

baritone /ˈbær.ɪ.təʊn/ ⓤⓈ /-toʊn/ *noun* [C] a man with a singing voice that is lower than a TENOR but not as low as a BASS, or a musical instrument with this range

barium meal UK /ˌbeə.ri.əmˈmiːl/ ⓤⓈ /ˌber.i-/ *noun* (US **barium sulphate**) a chemical that is swallowed by a person just before an X-ray is taken of their stomach

and bowels, so that these organs can be seen clearly

bark DOG /bɑːk/ ⓤⓈ /bɑːrk/ *noun* [C] the loud, rough noise that a dog and some other animals make
• *sb's* **bark is worse than** *their* **bite** If someone's bark is worse than their bite, they are not as unpleasant as they seem, and their actions are not as bad as their threats: *Don't let her frighten you, her bark is worse than her bite.*
bark /bɑːk/ ⓤⓈ /bɑːrk/ *verb* **1** [I] (of a dog) to make a loud rough noise: *They heard a dog barking outside.* **2** [T] to shout at someone in a forceful manner: *The sergeant barked (out) a succession of orders to the new recruits.*
• **be barking up the wrong tree** INFORMAL to be wrong about the reason for something or the way to achieve something: *She thinks it'll solve the problem, but I reckon she's barking up the wrong tree.*

bark TREE /bɑːk/ ⓤⓈ /bɑːrk/ *noun* [U] the hard outer covering of a tree

barkeeper /ˈbɑːˌkiː.pəʳ/ ⓤⓈ /ˈbɑːrˌkiː.pɚ/ *noun* [C] (ALSO **barkeep**) US a person who serves drinks in a bar, or the owner or manager of a bar: *She spent the summer working as a barkeeper at the resort.*

barker /ˈbɑː.kəʳ/ ⓤⓈ /ˈbɑːr.kɚ/ *noun* [C] OLD-FASHIONED a person who advertises an activity at a public event by calling out to people who are walking past: *a fairground/circus barker*

barking ('mad) *adj* [after v] UK OLD-FASHIONED INFORMAL crazy or extremely foolish: *She must have been barking mad to lend him so much money.*

barley /ˈbɑː.li/ ⓤⓈ /ˈbɑːr-/ *noun* [U] a tall grass-like plant with long straight hairs growing from the head of each stem, or the grain obtained from this plant which is used for food and for making beer and whisky

barley ,sugar *noun* [C or U] a hard sweet made from boiled sugar

barley ,water *noun* [U] **1** UK a drink made from barley and fruit juice **2** US a drink made from barley and water boiled together for the purpose of making an ill person feel better

bar ,line UK *noun* [C] (US **bar**) a vertical line that divides one bar from another in a written piece of music

barmaid /ˈbɑː.meɪd/ ⓤⓈ /ˈbɑːr-/ *noun* [C] UK a woman who makes and serves drinks in a bar

barman /ˈbɑː.mən/ ⓤⓈ /ˈbɑːr-/ *noun* [C] MAINLY UK a man who serves drinks in a bar

bar mitzvah /ˌbɑːˈmɪts.və/ ⓤⓈ /ˌbɑːr-/ *noun* [C usually sing] a Jewish ceremony held to celebrate a boy reaching the age of 13, in which he is given the religious responsibilities and duties of an adult man

barmy /ˈbɑː.mi/ ⓤⓈ /ˈbɑːr-/ *adj* MAINLY UK INFORMAL behaving strangely, or very silly: *Not another one of her barmy ideas!*

barn /bɑːn/ ⓤⓈ /bɑːrn/ *noun* [C] a large building on a farm in which hay and grain are kept

barnacle /ˈbɑː.nə.kl̩/ ⓤⓈ /ˈbɑːr-/ *noun* [C] a small sea creature with a shell that sticks very tightly and in large numbers to rocks and the bottom of boats

barn ,dance *noun* [C] an informal dance in which people do traditional dancing in rows and circles, changing partners regularly

barney /ˈbɑː.ni/ ⓤⓈ /ˈbɑːr-/ *noun* [C] MAINLY UK INFORMAL a loud argument

barnstorm /ˈbɑːn.stɔːm/ ⓤⓈ /ˈbɑːrn.stɔːrm/ *verb* [I or T] MAINLY US **1** to travel to a lot of small towns and make political speeches to try to obtain people's votes or support: *He plans to barnstorm across the state to generate public support.* **2** In the past, to barnstorm was to travel to a lot of small towns and perform flying tricks in aircraft.

barnstorming /ˈbɑːn.stɔː.mɪŋ/ ⓤⓈ /ˈbɑːrn.stɔːr.mɪŋ/ *adj* exciting and energetic: *It was a barnstorming performance.*

barnyard /ˈbɑːn.jɑːd/ ⓤⓈ /ˈbɑːrn.jɑːrd/ *noun* [C] MAINLY US FOR **farmyard**

barometer /bəˈrɒm.ɪ.təʳ/ ⓤⓈ /-ˈrɑː.mɪ.t̬ɚ/ *noun* [C] **1** a device that measures air pressure and shows when the weather is likely to change **2** something that can show how a particular situation is developing, or how people's opinions on a particular matter are changing:

This survey is considered to be a reliable barometer ***of*** *public opinion.*

baron /ˈbær.ᵊn/ *noun* [C] **1** (the title of) a British man who has the lowest rank in the highest social class **2** an extremely powerful person in a particular area of business: *media/press barons* ○ *a drug baron*

baroness /ˈbær.ᵊn.es/ /ˌ--ˈ-/ *noun* [C] a British woman who has the lowest rank in the highest social class, or who is the wife of a baron

baronial /bəˈrəʊ.ni.əl/ [US] /-ˈroʊ-/ *adj*: *baronial* (= great) *splendour*

barony /ˈbær.ᵊn.i/ *noun* [C] the rank of a baron, or the land owned by a baron

baronet /ˈbær.ᵊn.et/ /ˌ--ˈ-/ *noun* [C] a man who has the lowest title of honour that can be given in Britain, below a BARON but above a knight, and given from father to son

baronetcy /ˈbær.ᵊn.et.si/ *noun* [C] *Robert's grandfather was given the baronetcy* (= rank of baronet) *after the war.*

baroque /bəˈrɒk/ [US] /-ˈrɑːk/ *adj* relating to the heavily decorated style in buildings, art and music that was popular in Europe in the 17th century and the early part of the 18th century: *baroque architecture/painters*

barrack /ˈbær.ək/ *verb* [T] *UK* to shout loudly in order to interrupt someone that you disagree with: *Every time the minister got up to speak he was barracked mercilessly.*

barracking /ˈbær.ə.kɪŋ/ *noun* [U] *UK She could not make herself heard above the constant barracking* (= shouting).

▲ **barrack for *sb*** *phrasal verb AUS* to shout encouragement to the players in a football team

barracks /ˈbær.əks/ *group noun* [C] *plural* **barracks** a building or group of buildings where soldiers live: *The barracks was/were surrounded by a high wall.*

barracuda /ˌbær.əˈkuː.də/ *noun* [C] **1** a large tropical sea fish with sharp teeth, that eats other fish and can attack people **2** *US DISAPPROVING* a person who does business in a selfish way: *In the world of high finance, you have to keep an eye on the barracudas.*

barrage [ATTACK] /ˈbær.ɑːʒ/ [US] /bəˈrɑːʒ/ *noun* [C usually sing] **1** continuous firing of large guns to protect soldiers advancing on an enemy: *an artillery barrage* **2 a barrage of *sth*** a great number of complaints, criticisms or questions suddenly directed at someone: *The TV station has received a barrage of complaints about the amount of violence in the series.* ○ *He faced a barrage of questions over his handling of the problem.*

barrage [STRUCTURE] /ˈbær.ɑːʒ/ [US] /bəˈrɑːʒ/ *noun* [C] a structure that is built across a river to provide water for farming, to produce electricity, or to enable boats to travel more easily: *The proposed tidal barrage would generate enough electricity to supply between 60 000 and 80 000 homes.*

ˈbarrage balˌloon *noun* [C] a large BALLOON, especially one of a group that is tied to the ground with steel ropes in order to stop enemy aircraft which are flying low

barre /bɑːʳ/ [US] /bɑːr/ *noun* [C] a horizontal bar fixed at a convenient height for dancers to hold on to, in order to help them balance while exercising

barrel [CONTAINER] /ˈbær.ᵊl/ *noun* [C] **1** a large container, made of wood, metal or plastic, with a flat top and bottom and curved sides that make it fatter in the middle: *They drank a whole barrel of beer* (= the contents of a barrel) *at the party.* **2** In the oil industry, a barrel of oil is equal to 159 litres.

• **be a barrel of laughs/fun** *INFORMAL* to be amusing or enjoyable: *"He's a bit serious isn't he?" "Yeah,* ***not exactly*** *a barrel of laughs."*

• **have *sb* over a barrel** *INFORMAL* to put someone in a very difficult situation in which they have no choice about what they do: *She knows I need the work so she's got me over a barrel in terms of what she pays me.*

barrel [GUN PART] /ˈbær.ᵊl/ *noun* [C] the long part of a gun that is shaped like a tube

ˈbarrel ˌorgan *noun* [C] a large musical instrument that plays music when you turn a handle on the side. In the past, barrel organs were played outside to entertain people, often with a monkey sitting on top.

ˈbarrel ˌroll *noun* [C] a movement of an aircraft in which it turns over and then back up again

barren /ˈbær.ᵊn/ *adj* **1** unable to produce plants or fruit: *We drove through a barren, rocky* ***landscape.*** ➲Compare **fertile** LAND. **2** *LITERARY* unable to have babies ➲Compare **fertile** REPRODUCTION. **3** not productive: *She became very depressed during the barren years when she was unable to paint.* ➲Compare **fertile** IMAGINATIVE. **barrenness** /ˈbær.ᵊn.nəs/ *noun* [U]

barrette /bəˈret/ *noun* [C] *US FOR* **hair slide** ➲See picture **Hairstyles and Hats** on page Centre 8

barricade /ˈbær.ɪ.keɪd/ /--ˈ-/ *noun* [C] a line or pile of objects put together, especially quickly, to stop people from going where they want to go: *Inmates* ***erected*** *a barricade between themselves and prison officers.*

barricade /ˈbær.ɪ.keɪd/ /--ˈ-/ *verb* [T] *Barricade the doors!* ○ [R + adv or prep] *Terrified villagers have barricaded them****selves into*** *their houses.*

barrier /ˈbær.i.əʳ/ [US] /-ɚ/ *noun* [C] **1** a long pole, fence, wall or natural feature, such as a mountain or sea, that stops people from going somewhere: *Barriers have been erected all along the route the Pope will take.* ○ *Passengers are requested to show their tickets at the barrier* (= the gate in some railway stations through which you must go to get a train). ○ *The mountains acted as a natural barrier* ***to*** *the spread of the disease.* **2** anything that prevents people from being together or understanding each other: *Despite the* ***language*** *barrier* (= not speaking the same language), *they soon became good friends.* ○ *Shyness is one of the biggest barriers* ***to making*** *friends* (= something that makes this difficult).

ˈbarrier ˌcream *noun* [C] *UK* a cream that stops dirt or chemicals from getting through to the skin

barring /ˈbɑː.rɪŋ/ [US] /ˈbɑːr.ɪŋ/ *prep* ➲See at **bar** EXCEPT

barrio /ˈbær.i.əʊ/ [US] /ˈbɑːr.i.oʊ/ *noun* [C] in the US, a part of a city where poor, mainly Spanish-speaking people live

barrister /ˈbær.ɪ.stəʳ/ [US] /-stɚ/ *noun* [C] a type of lawyer in Britain, Australia and some other countries who is qualified to give specialist legal advice and can argue a case in both higher and lower law courts ➲See Note **lawyer, solicitor, barrister and attorney** at **solicitor**.

barrow /ˈbær.əʊ/ [US] /-oʊ/ *noun* [C] **1** a **wheelbarrow 2** *UK* a vehicle moved by a person from which especially fruit and vegetables are sold at the side of a road

ˈbarrow ˌboy *noun* [C] *UK* in the past, a man or boy who sold fruit and vegetables from a barrow

ˈbar ˌstool *noun* [C] a tall seat with no support for the back or arms, for sitting on while drinking or eating at a bar

bartender *MAINLY US* /ˈbɑːˌten.dəʳ/ [US] /ˈbɑːrˌten.dɚ/ *noun* [C] (*UK ALSO MALE* **barman**) someone who makes and serves drinks in a bar

barter /ˈbɑː.təʳ/ [US] /ˈbɑːr.t̬ɚ/ *verb* [I or T] to exchange goods for other things rather than for money: *He bartered his stamp collection* ***for*** *her comics.* ○ *We spent a whole hour bartering* ***with*** *stallholders for souvenirs.* **barter** /ˈbɑː.təʳ/ [US] /ˈbɑːr.t̬ɚ/ *noun* [U] *The currency has lost so much of its value that barter has become the preferred way of doing business.*

basalt /ˈbæs.ɒlt/ [US] /-ɑːlt/ *noun* [U] a type of black rock that comes from a volcano

base [BOTTOM] /beɪs/ *noun* [C] **1** the bottom part of an object, on which it rests, or the lowest part of something: *a crystal glass with a heavy base* ○ *At the base of the cliff was a rocky beach.* ○ *This cream provides an excellent base for your make-up* (= a good bottom layer on which other layers can be put). **2** the activity or people from which someone or something gets most of their support, money, etc: *A strong economy depends on a healthy* ***manufacturing*** *base.* ○ *We're aiming to expand our* ***customer*** *base.*

base [MAIN PLACE] /beɪs/ *noun* [C] **1** the main place where a person lives and works, or a place that a company does business from, or a place where there are military buildings and weapons and where members of the armed forces live: *I spend a lot of time in Brussels, but London is still my base.* ○ *Nice is an excellent base* ***for*** (= place to stay when) *exploring the French Riviera.* ○ *an*

B

old naval/military base **2** one of the four positions on a square that a player must reach to score a point in the game of baseball

base /beɪs/ *verb* [T usually + adv or prep] *Where is your firm based?* ○ *He was based in* (= He lived in or was at a military establishment in) *Birmingham during the war.*
-based /-beɪst/ *suffix a Manchester-based company* ○ *community-based programs*

base MAIN PART /beɪs/ *noun* [C usually sing] the main part of something: *a cocktail with a whisky base*
-based /-beɪst/ *suffix This is a cream-based sauce* (= Cream is the main thing in it).

base NOT HONOURABLE /beɪs/ *adj LITERARY* not honourable and lacking in morals: *I accused him of having base motives.* **basely** /ˈbeɪ.sli/ *adv* **baseness** /ˈbeɪs.nəs/ *noun* [U]

base MATHEMATICS /beɪs/ *noun* [C usually sing] *SPECIALIZED* the number on which a counting system is built: *A binary number is a number written* **in** *base 2, using the two numbers 0 and 1.*

base CHEMISTRY /beɪs/ *noun* [C] *SPECIALIZED* a chemical that dissolves in water and combines with an acid to create a SALT
▲ **base** *sth* **on** *sth phrasal verb* If you base something on facts or ideas, you use those facts or ideas to develop it: *The film is based on a short story by Thomas Mann.*

baseball /ˈbeɪs.bɔːl/ US /-bɑːl/ *noun* [C or U] (the ball used in) a game played especially in North America by two teams of nine players, in which a player hits a ball with a bat and tries to run around four BASES on a large field before the other team returns the ball: *Jake never* **played** *baseball like the other kids.* ○ *He had a baseball and a couple of bats in his sports bag.* ⊃See picture **Sports** on page Centre 10

baseball ˌcap *noun* [C] a tightly fitting hat, originally worn by baseball players, with a long flat piece at the front to protect the eyes from the sun ⊃See picture **Hairstyles and Hats** on page Centre 8

baseball ˌjacket *noun* [C] a jacket made of a shiny material which fits tightly round the waist and fastens with a zip

baseboard /ˈbeɪs.bɔːd/ US /-bɔːrd/ *noun* [C or U] *US FOR* **skirting board**

base ˌcamp *noun* [C usually sing] a place where food and general supplies are kept, especially for people climbing a mountain

base ˌform *noun* [C] *SPECIALIZED* in grammar, the simplest form of a verb, without a special ending: *The base form of 'calling' is 'call'.*

baseless /ˈbeɪs.ləs/ *adj FORMAL* not based on facts: *baseless accusations/allegations/rumours* ○ *She assured me that my fears were baseless.*

baseline /ˈbeɪs.laɪn/ *noun* [C usually sing] **1** a line on a sports field such as the one in tennis, which marks the end of the playing area, or the one in baseball which marks the path along which players run: *She delivered a final serve from the baseline to win the match.* **2** an imaginary line used as a starting point for making comparisons: *a baseline assessment*

basement /ˈbeɪs.mənt/ *noun* [C] a part of a building consisting of rooms that are partly or completely below the level of the ground: *Our kitchenware department is in the basement.* ○ *a basement flat/apartment*

base ˌmetal *noun* [C] *SPECIALIZED* a common metal such as lead, TIN or copper which is not a precious metal and which reacts easily with other chemicals

base ˌrate *noun* [C] *UK SPECIALIZED* a RATE (= level of payment) decided by the government or the Bank of England which banks use when deciding how much to charge for lending money: *Your mortgage interest payments are two percent below the base rate.*

bases /ˈbeɪ.siːz/ *plural of* **base** /ˈbeɪ.sɪz/ *or plural of* **basis** /ˈbeɪ.sɪz/

bash HIT /bæʃ/ *verb* [I or T] *INFORMAL* to hit hard: *He bashed his arm* **against** *a shelf.* ○ *I could hear her bashing* **away on** *a typewriter* (= hitting the keys loudly).
bash /bæʃ/ *noun* [C usually sing] *INFORMAL* a hit: *a bash* **on** *the head*

-basher /-bæʃ.əʳ/ US /-ɚ/ *suffix SLANG DISAPPROVING* **gay/queer-basher** someone who hates homosexuals and attacks them violently
-bashing /-bæʃ.ɪŋ/ *suffix SLANG DISAPPROVING* **gay/queer-bashing** violence directed at homosexuals

bash CRITICIZE /bæʃ/ *verb* [T] to criticize someone severely: *He kept bashing local government officials.*
-basher /-bæʃ.əʳ/ US /-ɚ/ *suffix DISAPPROVING* **union-basher** someone who strongly criticizes TRADE UNIONS and tries to limit their power
-bashing /-bæʃ.ɪŋ/ *suffix DISAPPROVING* **union-bashing** strong criticism of TRADE UNIONS

bash PARTY /bæʃ/ *noun* [C] *INFORMAL* a party: *He had a big bash for his 18th birthday.*

bash ATTEMPT /bæʃ/ *noun UK INFORMAL* **have a bash** to try to do something you have not done before: *I've never been skiing before, but I'm prepared to have a bash* (*at it*).
▲ **bash on** *phrasal verb UK INFORMAL* to continue doing something that is difficult, boring or takes a long time: *Oh well, that's enough chatting. I suppose I'd better bash on* **with** *this essay.* ⊃See also **carry on** *CONTINUE*.

bashful /ˈbæʃ.fʰl/ *adj* tending to feel uncomfortable with other people and be embarrassed easily; shy: *She gave a bashful* (= embarrassed) *smile as he complimented her on her work.* **bashfully** /ˈbæʃ.fʰl.i/ *adv* **bashfulness** /ˈbæʃ.fʰl.nəs/ *noun* [U]

basic /ˈbeɪ.sɪk/ *adj* providing the base or starting point from which something can develop; simple and not complicated: *I really need to get some basic financial advice.* ○ *He only has a basic command of English* (= He only knows the most important and simple words and expressions). ○ *The basic* (= most important) *problem is that they don't talk to each other enough.* ○ *It's the most basic model* (= it only has the most simple features). ○ *The crisis has led to price rises in basic foodstuffs, such as meat, cheese and sugar.*
basics /ˈbeɪ.sɪks/ *plural noun* the simplest and most important facts, ideas or things connected with something: *I really must learn the the basics of first aid.* ○ *The college can't even afford basics such as books and paper.*
● **back to basics** If you get back to basics, you start to give your attention to the simplest and most important matters after ignoring them for a while: *This is all part of a new back-to-basics campaign to raise standards.*

basically /ˈbeɪ.sɪ.kli/ *adv* used when referring to the main or most important characteristic or feature of something: *Basically,* (= The most important thing is that) *they want a lot more information about the project before they'll put any more into it.* ○ *"So what's the difference between these two TVs?" "Well, they're basically* **the same**, but the more expensive one comes with a remote control." ○ *The car's basically sound* (= in good condition), *but the paintwork needs a bit of attention.* ○ *The village has remained basically unchanged for over 300 years.*

BASIC /ˈbeɪ.sɪk/ *noun* [U] a common language for programming computers which uses instructions that are similar to English

ˌbasic ˈsalary *noun* [C] what a person earns before other sums of money, such as payments for working extra hours, are added

basil /ˈbæz.ʰl/ US /ˈbeɪ.zʰl/ *noun* [U] a herb with a sweet smell which is used to add flavour in cookery

basilica /bəˈsɪl.ɪ.kə/ /-ˈzɪl-/ *noun* [C] a public building in ancient Rome which was round at one end and had two rows of columns supporting the roof, or a church with a similar design

basin /ˈbeɪ.sʰn/ *noun* [C] **1** *MAINLY UK* an open round container shaped like a bowl with sloping sides, used for holding food or liquid: *a pudding basin* **2** *MAINLY UK* the amount of something that a basin can hold: *a basin of water* **3** *MAINLY US* a **washbasin**: *I've cleaned the basin and scrubbed the bath.* **4** *MAINLY UK* the area of land from which streams run into a river, lake or sea **5** *MAINLY UK* a sheltered area of deep water where boats are kept

basis /ˈbeɪ.sɪs/ *noun* [C] *plural* **bases 1** the most important facts, ideas, etc. from which something is developed:

*This document will **form** the basis **for** our discussion.* ○ *Their proposals have no proven scientific basis.* ○ *Decisions were often made **on the basis of*** (= using) *incorrect information.* **2** a way or method of doing something: *Most of our staff work for us **on a voluntary** basis* (= They work without being paid).

bask /bɑːsk/ [US] /bæsk/ *verb* **[I usually + adv or prep]** to lie or sit enjoying the warmth especially of the sun: *We could see seals on the rocks, basking **in** the sun.*

▲ **bask in *sth*** *phrasal verb* to take pleasure from something that makes you feel good: *He basked in his moment of glory, holding the trophy up to the crowd.*

basket /ˈbɑː.skɪt/ [US] /ˈbæs.kɪt/ *noun* **[C] 1** a light container, often with a handle, which is made of thin bendable strips of wood or plastic woven together and is used for carrying or storing things: *a shopping/picnic basket* ○ *a wicker basket* ○ *a laundry/clothes basket* ○ *We picked lots of strawberries, but we'd eaten half the basket* (= the contents of the basket) *by the time we got home.* **2** In the game of basketball, a basket is an open net hanging from a metal ring through which the players try to throw the ball to score points for their team, or the successful throwing of the ball through the ring. **3** a group of related things: *the value of the pound against a basket **of** world currencies*

basketful /ˈbɑː.skɪt.fʊl/ [US] /ˈbæs.kɪt-/ *noun* **[C]** the amount of something that a basket can hold: *a basketful of apples*

basketwork /ˈbɑː.skɪt.wɜːk/ [US] /ˈbæs.kɪt.wɝːk/ *noun* **[U]** (*ALSO* **basketry**) the making of baskets and other objects by weaving together thin bendable strips of wood

COMMON LEARNER ERROR

basket or **basketball?**

In some languages **basketball** and **volleyball** are referred to as just **basket** and **volley**, but in English a **basket** is the round net itself and a **volley** is a method of hitting the ball. For the names of the sports you have to use **basketball** and **volleyball**.

I love basketball.
~~*I love basket.*~~

basketball /ˈbɑː.skɪt.bɔːl/ [US] /ˈbæs.kɪt.bɑːl/ *noun* **[C or U]** (a ball used in) a game played by two teams of five men or six women who score points by throwing a large ball through an open net hanging from a metal ring ➲See picture **Sports** on page Centre 10

ˈ**basket ˌcase** [PERSON] *noun* **[C]** *INFORMAL* someone who is extremely nervous or anxious and is therefore unable to organize their life: *By the end of the course I was a complete basket case*

ˈ**basket ˌcase** [COUNTRY/COMPANY] *noun* **[C]** a country or company that is very unsuccessful financially: *Twenty years ago the country was an **economic** basket case.*

basque [CLOTHING] /bæsk/ /bɑːsk/ [US] /bæsk/ *noun* **[C]** tight-fitting underwear for women which covers the top part of the body and provides support for the breasts

Basque [RACE] /bæsk/ /bɑːsk/ [US] /bæsk/ *adj* connected with a race living in the area around the Pyrenees in Spain and France, or connected with the language of this race: *the Basque provinces*

Basque /bæsk/ /bɑːsk/ [US] /bæsk/ *noun* **[C or U]** the language of the Basque area, or a person from the Basque area

bas-relief /ˌbæs.rɪˈliːf/ *noun* **[C or U]** a type of art in which shapes are cut from the surrounding stone so that they stand out slightly against a flat background, or a work of art done in this way

bass [MUSICAL RANGE] /beɪs/ *noun plural* **basses 1 [C or U]** the lowest range of musical notes, or a man with a singing voice in this range: *He **sings** bass.* ○ *Italy's leading bass* **2 [U]** the set of low musical sounds on a radio, music system, etc., or the button that controls them: *Turn down the bass.* **3 [C]** a **double bass**

bass /beɪs/ *adj* **[before n]** playing, singing or producing the lowest range of musical notes: *a bass drum/guitar/trombone*

bassist /ˈbeɪ.sɪst/ *noun* **[C]** someone who plays either the BASS GUITAR or the DOUBLE BASS.

bass [FISH] /bæs/ *noun* **[C]** *plural* **bass** a type of fish found in rivers or the sea

ˈ**bass ˌclef** *noun* **[C usually sing]** a sign on a STAVE (= the five lines on which music is written) which shows that the notes are below MIDDLE C (= the C near the middle of a piano keyboard)

ˌ**bass ˈdrum** *noun* **[C]** a large drum that produces a low sound

basset (hound) /ˈbæs.ɪtˌhaʊnd/ *noun* **[C]** a type of dog with smooth hair, a long body, short legs and long ears

ˌ**bass (guiˈtar)** *noun* **[C]** a four-string electric guitar that plays very low notes: *He plays (the) bass guitar.*

bassinet /bæs.ɪˈnet/ *noun* **[C]** *US FOR* **carrycot**

bassoon /bəˈsuːn/ *noun* **[C]** a musical instrument that is played by blowing into a long wooden tube while pressing metal keys

bastard [UNPLEASANT] /ˈbɑː.stəd/ [US] /ˈbæs.tɚd/ *noun* **[C]** *OFFENSIVE* an unpleasant person: *He was a bastard **to** his wife.* ○ *You lied to me, **you** bastard!* ○ *HUMOROUS You won again? You **lucky** bastard* (= I don't think you deserve it)*!* ○ *This crossword's a bastard* (= very difficult).

bastard [CHILD] /ˈbɑː.stəd/ [US] /ˈbæs.tɚd/ *noun* **[C]** *OLD USE* a person born to parents who are not married to each other; an ILLEGITIMATE child: *He was born in 1798, the bastard son of a country squire and his mistress.*

bastardize, *UK USUALLY* **-ise** /ˈbɑː.stə.daɪz/ [US] /ˈbæs.tɚ-/ *verb* **[T]** to change something in a way which makes it fail to represent the values and qualities that it is intended to represent **bastardized**, *UK USUALLY* **-ised** /ˈbɑː.stə.daɪzd/ [US] /ˈbæs.tɚ-/ *adj*: *a bastardized **form** of the word/language*

baste [POUR] /beɪst/ *verb* **[T]** to pour hot fat and liquid over meat while it is cooking: *Baste the turkey at regular intervals.*

baste [SEW] /beɪst/ *verb* **[T]** *MAINLY US FOR* **tack** SEW: *Baste the seams.*

bastion /ˈbæs.ti.ən/ *noun* **[C] 1** something which maintains or defends especially a belief or a way of life that is disappearing or threatened: *British public schools are regarded as one of the **last** bastions **of** upper-class privilege.* **2** a part of the wall of a castle that sticks out from it in order to protect it

bat [STICK] /bæt/ *noun* **[C]** a specially shaped piece of wood used for hitting the ball in many games: *a baseball/cricket/rounders/table tennis bat* ➲See also **batsman**.

● **do *sth* off *your* own bat** *UK INFORMAL* to do something without anyone else telling you or asking you to do it: *I didn't ask her to buy them a present – she did it off her own bat.*

● **off the bat** *US* immediately: *You can't expect to be accepted in a new town **right/straight** off the bat.*

bat /bæt/ *verb* **[I or T] -tt-** to try to hit a ball with a bat: *He batted the ball high into the air.* ○ *Jones will be the first to bat.*

batter /ˈbæt.əʳ/ [US] /ˈbæt̬.ɚ/ *noun* **[C]** (*ALSO* **hitter**) the person in baseball or ROUNDERS whose turn it is to hit the ball, or a person who is good at this activity ➲See picture **Sports** on page Centre 10

bat [ANIMAL] /bæt/ *noun* **[C]** a small animal like a mouse with wings that flies at night

● **have bats in the belfry** *OLD-FASHIONED DISAPPROVING* to be silly and foolish with confused behaviour ➲See also **batty**.

bat [EYE] /bæt/ *verb* **[T] -tt-** (especially of women) to open and close your eyes quickly several times, especially to attract attention or admiration: *She smiled and batted her **eyelashes** at him.*

● **not bat an eyelid** to show no sign of surprise or worry when something unexpected happens: *She told him she'd spent all her savings but he didn't bat an eyelid.*

batch /bætʃ/ *noun* **[C]** a group of things or people dealt with at the same time or considered similar in type: *The cook brought in a fresh batch **of** homemade cakes.* ○ *We looked at the job applications **in** two batches.*

ˌ**batch ˈprocessing** *noun* **[U]** *SPECIALIZED* the processing of several jobs by a computer, one after the other

bated /ˈbeɪ.tɪd/ [US] /-t̬ɪd/ *adj* **with bated breath** in an anxious or excited way: *I waited for the results with bated breath.*

bath /bɑːθ/ ⓤ /bæθ/ *noun* **1** [C] *UK* (*US* **bathtub**) a long plastic, metal or CERAMIC container which is filled with water so that a person can sit or lie in it to wash their whole body **2** [C usually sing] the activity of washing yourself or someone else in a bath: *MAINLY UK Susannah* **has** *a long hot bath every evening.* ○ *MAINLY US I* **took** *a bath this morning.* ○ *bath oil* **3** [C] *US* used to refer to a bathroom when describing a home: *a four-bedroom two-bath house* **4** [C] *UK* a health treatment: *mud/thermal baths* **5** [C] *UK* any container holding liquid: *a bird bath*
• **run a bath** *UK* (*US* **fill the tub**) to fill a bath with water for washing: *I'll run you a bath while you take off those wet clothes.*

bath *UK* /bɑːθ/ ⓤ /bæθ/ *verb* [I or T] (*MAINLY US* **bathe**) to wash in a bath or to wash someone in a bath: *OLD-FASHIONED She baths every morning.* ○ *I usually bath the kids in the evening.*

'**bath ,cubes** *plural noun* (*ALSO* **bath salts**) small hard pieces that you put in bath water to make it smell pleasant or to make the water dissolve soap more easily

bathe SWIM /beɪð/ *verb* [I] to swim, especially in the sea, a river or a lake: *Children suffering from the illness had bathed* **in** *sea water contaminated by sewage.* **bathe** /beɪð/ *noun* [S] *UK FORMAL*
bather /'beɪ.ðə'/ ⓤ /-ðɚ/ *noun* [C] a person who is swimming in the sea, river, etc.
bathing /'beɪ.ðɪŋ/ *noun* [U] the activity of going for a swim: *At midnight they all decided to* **go** *bathing.*

bathe COVER /beɪð/ *verb* [T] **1** to cover with a liquid, especially in order to make part of the body feel better: *I bathed my feet* **in** *salt water.* **2** to cover with something that causes a pleasant feeling or appearance: *In the afternoon the sun bathes the city* **in** *shades of pink and gold.* **3** *US FOR* **bath** (= to wash)

'**bathing ,costume** *noun* [C] *UK OLD-FASHIONED* a piece of clothing that you wear for swimming

'**bathing ,suit** *noun* [C] a piece of clothing that you wear for swimming

'**bathing ,trunks** *plural noun UK OLD-FASHIONED* **swimming trunks**

'**bath ,mat** *noun* [C] a cover that you stand on after getting out of a bath or shower to stop the floor from getting wet, or a piece of rubber which is put inside the bath or shower to prevent you sliding and falling

bathos /'beɪ.θɒs/ ⓤ /-θɑːs/ *noun* [U] *LITERARY* a sudden, especially not intended, change from a beautiful or important subject to a silly or very ordinary one ⊃Compare **pathos**.

'**bath ,rack** *noun* [C] a set of metal bars or an open plastic container which is put across a bath and used to hold washing equipment such as soap

bathrobe /'bɑː.rəʊb/ ⓤ /'bæθ.roʊb/ *noun* [C] **1** a loose-fitting piece of clothing like a coat worn before or after a bath **2** a **dressing gown**

bathroom /'bɑː.θrʊm/ ⓤ /-ruːm/ ⓤ /'bæθ-/ *noun* [C] **1** a room with a bath and/or shower and often a toilet: *an ensuite bathroom* (= a bathroom joined to a bedroom) **2** *US* a toilet: *Where's the bathroom* (= toilet)?
• **go to the bathroom** *US* to use the toilet: *Wait a moment, – I just need to go to the bathroom.*

'**bathroom ,suite** *noun* [C] the set of fixed objects in a bathroom which includes a bath and/or shower, a toilet and a sink

baths /bɑːðz/ ⓤ /bæðz/ *group noun* [C] *plural* **baths 1** *UK OLD-FASHIONED* **swimming baths 2** a public place where people went in the past to have a hot bath

bathtime /'bɑː.θtaɪm/ ⓤ /'bæθ-/ *noun* [C or U] the time at which a child has a bath, or the activity of having a bath: *Let's start to put the toys away – it's nearly bath-time.*

'**bath ,towel** *noun* [C] a large towel with which you dry yourself after a bath or shower

bathtub /'bɑː.θtʌb/ ⓤ /'bæθ-/ *noun* [C] (*ALSO* **tub**) *US FOR* **bath**

batik /bæt'iːk/ *noun* [U] a method of printing patterns on cloth, in which wax is put on the cloth before it is put in the DYE (= substance for changing the colour of cloth), or the cloth itself

batman /'bæt.mən/ *noun* [C] the personal servant of an officer especially in the British armed forces

bat mitzvah /,bæt'mɪts.və/ *noun* [C usually sing] a Jewish ceremony held to celebrate a girl reaching the age of 13, in which she is given the religious responsibilities and duties of an adult woman

baton MUSIC /'bæt.ɒn/ ⓤ /'bæt.ᵊn/ *noun* [C] a stick used by a CONDUCTOR (= person who controls the performance of a group of musicians) to show the speed of the music

baton SPORT /'bæt.ɒn/ ⓤ /'bæt.ᵊn/ *noun* [C] a stick that is passed from one runner to another in a RELAY RACE

baton MARCHING /'bæt.ɒn/ ⓤ /'bæt.ᵊn/ *noun* [C] a hollow metal stick that a MAJORETTE or DRUM MAJOR spins and throws while marching

baton WEAPON /'bæt.ɒn/ ⓤ /'bæt.ᵊn/ *noun* [C] (*UK ALSO* **truncheon**, *US ALSO* **nightstick**) a thick heavy stick used as a weapon by police officers

'**baton ,charge** *noun* [C] *UK* when a large group of police run forward in an attacking movement carrying their batons

batsman /'bæt.smən/ *noun* [C] in cricket, a person whose turn it is to hit the ball or a person who regularly does this activity: *a former England batsman*

battalion /bə'tæl.i.ən/ *noun* [C] a military unit consisting of three or more COMPANIES

batten /'bæt.ᵊn/ ⓤ /'bæt-/ *noun* [C] a long piece of wood, often fixed to something to strengthen it
batten /'bæt.ᵊn/ ⓤ /'bæt-/ *verb* [T] *The boxes were securely battened* (= fastened with pieces of wood) *before the journey.*
• **batten down the hatches 1** to fasten the entrances to the lower part of a ship using wooden boards **2** to pre-pare for a difficult situation: *When you're coming down with flu all you can do is batten down the hatches and wait for it to pass.*
▲ **batten on** *sb phrasal verb LITERARY* to live well by using someone else's money: *He's spent these last five years battening on a rich aunt of his.*

batter HIT /'bæt.ə'/ ⓤ /'bæt.ɚ/ *verb* [T; I + adv or prep] to hit and behave violently towards a person, especially a woman or child, repeatedly over a long period of time, or to hit something with force many times: *He was battered* **to death** *with a rifle-butt.* ○ *He was battering* **(at/on)** *the door with his fists and howling.* ○ *The waves battered* **against** *the rocks at the bottom of the cliff.* ○ *The burglars had battered* **down** *the door of the house* (= hit it so hard that it broke and fell down). ⊃See also **batter** at **bat** STICK.
battered /'bæt.əd/ ⓤ /'bæt.ɚd/ *adj* **1** hurt by being repeatedly hit: *She set up a sanctuary for battered* **wives**. **2** damaged, especially by being used a lot: *battered furniture/toys*
battering /'bæt.ᵊr.ɪŋ/ ⓤ /'bæt.ɚ.ɪŋ/ *noun* [C or U] an act of hitting someone: *baby/wife battering* ○ *FIGURATIVE Once again, our team had* **taken** *a battering* (= had been defeated heavily). **battery** /'bæt.ᵊr.i/ ⓤ /'bæt.ɚ.i/ *noun* ASSAULT AND BATTERY

batter FOOD /'bæt.ə'/ ⓤ /'bæt.ɚ/ *noun* [U] a mixture of flour, eggs and milk, used to make pancakes or to cover food before frying it: *fish* **in** *batter* **battered** /'bæt.əd/ ⓤ /'bæt.ɚd/ *adj*: *battered cod*

'**battering ,ram** *noun* [C] a long heavy pole which was used by armies in the past to break down especially castle doors, and which is now used by police and fire officers to break down house doors

battery ELECTRICAL DEVICE /'bæt.ᵊr.i/ ⓤ /'bæt.ɚ.i/ *noun* [C] a device that produces electricity to provide power for radios, cars, etc: *a rechargeable battery* ○ *a battery-operated hair dryer* ○ *This alarm clock takes two medium-sized batteries.* ○ *I think the battery is* **dead/gone**/(*UK especially of a car battery*) **flat** (= has lost its power).

battery LARGE NUMBER /'bæt.ᵊr.i/ ⓤ /'bæt.ɚ.i/ *noun* **1** a **battery of** *sth* a number of things of a similar type: *In the kitchen an impressive battery of stainless steel utensils hangs on the wall.* **2** [C] a number of large guns and similar weapons operating together in the same place: *The shore battery opened fire.* **3** *UK* [C] a system of producing a large number of eggs cheaply by keeping a lot of chickens in rows of small cages: *battery **farming*** ○ *battery **hens***

battle /ˈbæt.l̩/ (US) /ˈbæt̬-/ *noun* [C] **1** a fight between armed forces: *the Battle of the Somme* ○ *Her only brother was killed **in** battle* (= while fighting). **2** an argument between two groups or against a situation that a group wants to change: *The aid agency continues the battle **against** ignorance and superstition.* ○ *The battle **for** women's rights still goes on.*

• **do battle** to fight or argue in a serious way: *No agreement was reached and both sides prepared to do battle.*

• **battle of wits** when two people or two groups use their intelligence and ability to think quickly to try to defeat each other

battle /ˈbæt.l̩/ (US) /ˈbæt̬-/ *verb* [I] **1** to fight: *Twenty years ago this summer, police battled **with** residents in this inner city area for three days.* ○ *For years the two nations battled **over** territory.* **2** to try hard to achieve something in a difficult situation: *He had to battle **against** prejudice to get a job.* ○ *The parents battled **for** the right to be involved in the decision-making.* ○ *We battled **with** the elements **to** get the roof fixed.*

battleaxe [WEAPON] *UK, US* **battle-ax** /ˈbæt.l̩.æks/ (US) /ˈbæt̬-/ *noun* [C] a large axe used as a weapon in the past

battleaxe [WOMAN] *UK, US* **battle-ax** /ˈbæt.l̩.æks/ (US) /ˈbæt̬-/ *noun* [C] a fierce and unpleasant older woman with strong opinions: *Our headmistress was a real **old** battleaxe.*

ˈbattle ˌcry *noun* [C] **1** a shout given by soldiers as they run towards the enemy **2** a phrase used by people supporting a particular cause: *'Reclaim the night' was the battle cry of women fighting for the right to walk safely at night.*

battledress /ˈbæt.l̩.dres/ (US) /ˈbæt̬-/ *noun* [U] uniform worn by soldiers and other military groups especially when they go to fight

battlefield /ˈbæt.l̩.fiːld/ (US) /ˈbæt̬-/ *noun* [C] **1** a place where a BATTLE is being fought or has been fought in the past: *They carried the wounded from the battlefield.* ○ *a Civil War battlefield* **2** a subject on which people strongly disagree: *The issue has become a political battlefield in recent years.*

battleground /ˈbæt.l̩.graʊnd/ (US) /ˈbæt̬-/ *noun* [C] a **battlefield**

battlements /ˈbæt.l̩.mənts/ (US) /ˈbæt̬-/ *plural noun* a wall around the top of a castle, with regular spaces in it through which the people inside the castle can shoot

battleship /ˈbæt.l̩.ʃɪp/ (US) /ˈbæt̬-/ *noun* [C] a very large military ship with big guns

batty /ˈbæt.i/ (US) /ˈbæt̬-/ *adj INFORMAL DISAPPROVING* silly and foolish with confused behaviour: *my batty old aunt*

bauble /ˈbɔː.bl̩/ (US) /ˈbɑː-/ *noun* [C] **1** a piece of bright but cheap jewellery **2** a ball-shaped Christmas decoration for hanging on a tree

baulk /bɔːk/ (US) /bɑːlk/ *verb* [I], *noun* [C] **balk**

bauxite /ˈbɔːk.saɪt/ (US) /ˈbɑːk-/ *noun* [U] a type of rock from which ALUMINIUM is produced

bawdy /ˈbɔː.di/ (US) /ˈbɑː-/ *adj* containing humorous remarks about sex: *bawdy humour/songs* **bawdily** /ˈbɔː.dɪ.li/ (US) /ˈbɑː-/ *adv* **bawdiness** /ˈbɔː.dɪ.nəs/ (US) /ˈbɑː-/ *noun* [U]

bawl /bɔːl/ (US) /bɑːl/ *verb* [I or T] to shout in a very loud rough voice, or to cry loudly: *She bawled **at** me to sit down.* ○ *The two girls were now bawling* (= crying loudly) *in unison.*

▲ **bawl *sb* out** *phrasal verb* [M] *US INFORMAL* to tell someone angrily that something they have done is wrong: *He's always bawling out people in meetings.*

bay [COAST] /beɪ/ *noun* [C] a part of the coast where the land curves in so that the sea is surrounded by land on three sides: *We sailed into a beautiful, secluded bay.* ○ *Dublin Bay* ○ *the Bay **of** Naples*

• **hold/keep *sth/sb* at bay** to prevent someone or something unpleasant from harming you: *Exercise can help keep fat at bay.*

• **at bay** If an animal is at bay, it is about to be caught or attacked.

bay [SPACE] /beɪ/ *noun* [C] a partly enclosed or marked space: *Visitors must park their cars in the marked bays.* ➲See also **sickbay**.

bay [CALL] /beɪ/ *verb* [I] (of dogs and wolves) to make a low and long deep cry repeatedly

• **bay for blood** *DISAPPROVING* If a group of people are baying for blood, they want someone to be hurt or punished: *By now the crowd was baying for blood.*

bay [TREE] /beɪ/ *noun* [C] (*ALSO* **bay tree**) a small evergreen tree which has leaves that are used to add flavour to cooking

bay [HORSE] /beɪ/ *noun* [C] a reddish brown horse

ˈbay ˌleaf *noun* [C] a leaf from a BAY tree, often dried and used in cooking to add flavour

bayonet /ˈbeɪ.ə.nət/ *noun* [C] a long sharp blade fixed on to a rifle **bayonet** /ˈbeɪ.ə.nət/ *verb* [T] **-t-** or **-tt-** *He viciously bayoneted the straw dummy.*

bayou /ˈbaɪ.uː/ *noun* [C] (in the southern US) an area of slowly moving water away from the main river

ˌbay ˈwindow *noun* [C] a window that sticks out from the outer wall of a house and usually has three sides

bazaar /bəˈzɑːʳ/ (US) /-ˈzɑːr/ *noun* [C] **1** an area of small shops and people selling things, especially in the Middle East and India, or any group of small shops or people selling goods of the same type **2** an event where people sell things to raise money, especially for an organization which helps other people: *a Christmas bazaar*

bazooka /bəˈzuː.kə/ *noun* [C] a long tube-shaped gun, fired from the shoulder, which is used to fire missiles at especially military vehicles

the BBC /ðəˌbiː.biːˈsiː/ *noun* [S] (*UK INFORMAL* **the Beeb**) *ABBREVIATION FOR* the British Broadcasting Corporation: a British organization that broadcasts on television, radio and the Internet ➲Compare **ITV**.

BBC English /ˌbiː.biː.siːˈɪŋ.glɪʃ/ *noun* [U] the standard way in which middle-class speakers of southern British English pronounce words

BBQ *ABBREVIATION FOR* **barbecue**

BC, *US USUALLY* **B.C.** /ˌbiːˈsiː/ *adv ABBREVIATION FOR* Before Christ: used in the Christian CALENDAR when referring to a year before Jesus Christ was born: *The Battle of Actium took place in 31 BC.* ➲Compare **AD**.

BCNU, **bcnu** *INTERNET ABBREVIATION FOR* be seeing you: a way of saying goodbye at the end of an e-mail or when leaving a discussion in a CHAT ROOM

USAGE

Forms of the verb **to be**.

This is a table of all the usual forms of the irregular verb **to be**. Short forms are given in brackets.

present tense	past tense
I am (I'm)	*I was*
you are (your're)	*you were*
he/she/it is (he's/she's/it's)	*he/she/it was*
we are (we're)	*we were*
you are (you're)	*you were*
they are (they're)	*they were*

past participle

been	*She has been ill.*

present participle

being	*He's being silly.*

short negative forms

aren't *isn't* *wasn't* *weren't*

Aren't you hot in that coat?

be [DESCRIPTION] *STRONG* /biː/, *WEAK* /bi, bɪ/ *verb* **being, was were, been 1** [L] used to say something about a person, thing or state, to show a permanent or temporary quality, state, job, etc: *He is rich.* ○ *It's cold today.* ○ *I'm Andy.* ○ *That's all for now.* ○ *What do you want to be* (=

B

What job do you want to do) *when you grow up?* ○ *These books are* (= cost) *50p each.* ○ *Being afraid of the dark, she always slept with the light on.* ○ *Never having been ill himself, he wasn't a sympathetic listener.* ○ *Be quiet!* ○ *Do be quiet!* ○ [+ v-ing] *The problem is deciding what to do.* ○ [+ **to** infinitive] *The hardest part will be **to** find a replacement.* ○ [+ that] *The general feeling is **that** she should be asked to leave.* ○ ***It's** not **that** I don't like her – **it's** just **that** we rarely agree on anything!* ➲See **be that as it may** at **may** POSSIBILITY. **2** [I usually + adv or prep] used to show the position of a person or thing in space or time: *The food was already on the table.* ○ *Is anyone there?* ○ *The meeting is now* (= will happen) *next Tuesday.* ○ ***There's** a hair in my soup.* **3** [L] used to show what something is made of: *Is this plate pure gold?*

be [CONTINUE] *STRONG* /biː/, *WEAK* /bi, bɪ/ *auxiliary verb* [+ v-ing] **being, was were, been** used with the present participle of other verbs to describe actions that are or were still continuing: *I'm still eat**ing**.* ○ *She's study**ing** to be a lawyer.* ○ *The audience clearly wasn't enjoy**ing** the show.* ○ *You're always complain**ing**.* ○ *I'll be com**ing** back* (= I plan to come back) *on Tuesday.*

be [PASSIVE] *STRONG* /biː/, *WEAK* /bi, bɪ/ *auxiliary verb* [+ past participle] **being, was were, been** used with the past participle of other verbs to form the passive: *I'd like to go but I haven't been ask**ed**.* ○ *Troublemakers are encourag**ed** to leave.* ○ *A body has been discover**ed** by the police.*

be [ALLOW] *STRONG* /biː/, *WEAK* /bi, bɪ/ *verb* [+ **to** infinitive] **being, was were, been** used to say that someone should or must do something: *You're **to** sit in the corner and keep quiet.* ○ *Their mother said they were **not to*** (= not allowed to) *play near the river.* ○ *There's no money left – what are we **to** do?*

be [FUTURE] *STRONG* /biː/, *WEAK* /bi, bɪ/ *verb* [+ **to** infinitive] **being, was were, been 1** *FORMAL* used to show that something will happen in the future: *We are **to*** (= We are going to) *visit Australia in the spring.* ○ *She was **never to** see* (= She never saw) *her brother again.* **2** used in CONDITIONAL sentences to say what might happen: *If I were **to** refuse they'd be very annoyed.* ○ *FORMAL Were I **to** refuse they'd be very annoyed.*

be [CAN] *STRONG* /biː/, *WEAK* /bi, bɪ/ *verb* [+ **to** infinitive] **being, was were, been** used to say what can happen: *The exhibition of modern prints is currently **to** be seen at the City Gallery.*

be [EXIST] *STRONG* /biː/, *WEAK* /bi, bɪ/ *verb* [I] **being, was were, been** to exist or live: *FORMAL Such terrible suffering should never be.* ○ *OLD USE OR LITERARY By the time the letter reached them their sister had ceased to be* (= died).

▲ **be in for *sth*** *phrasal verb* to be going to experience something unpleasant very soon: *The weather forecast says we're in for heavy rain this evening.* ○ *You'll be in for **it*** (= She will be very angry) *if you don't do what she tells you.*

beach /biːtʃ/ *noun* [C] an area of sand or small stones beside the sea or another area of water such as a lake: *We spent the day **on** the beach.* ○ *a beach café* ○ *a beach towel*

beach /biːtʃ/ *verb* [T] *The boat had been beached* (= been pulled or forced out of the water) *near the rocks.*

beached /biːtʃt/ *adj* [before n] describes a whale or DOLPHIN that has swum onto a beach and cannot return to the water

ˈ**beach** ˌ**ball** *noun* [C] a large, light brightly coloured ball filled with air that people play with especially on the beach

ˈ**beach** ˌ**buggy** *noun* [C] a small car with large wheels and open sides that is designed to drive on areas covered in sand

ˈ**beach** ˌ**bum** *noun* [C] *INFORMAL* someone who spends most of their time enjoying themselves on the beach

beachcomber /ˈbiːtʃˌkəʊ.məʳ/ [US] /-ˌkoʊ.mɚ/ *noun* [C] a person who walks along beaches looking for objects of value or interest

beachfront /ˈbiːtʃ.frʌnt/ *noun* [C] *US* a strip of land along a beach: *a house on the beachfront* ○ *a beachfront property*

beachhead /ˈbiːtʃ.hed/ *noun* [C] an area of land beside the sea or a river that an attacking army has taken control of and from where it can advance into enemy country: *The troops quickly **established** a beachhead and were preparing to advance.* ➲Compare **bridgehead**.

ˈ**beach re**ˌ**sort** *noun* [C] a place where people can go for holidays which has a beach and beach activities as its main attraction

beachwear /ˈbiːtʃ.weəʳ/ [US] /-wer/ *noun* [U] clothes that you wear on a beach

beacon /ˈbiː.kᵊn/ *noun* [C] a light or fire on the top of a hill that acts as a warning or signal: *As part of the centenary celebrations a chain of beacons was **lit** across the region.* ○ *FIGURATIVE She was a beacon **of** hope in troubled times.*

bead /biːd/ *noun* [C] **1** a small coloured often round piece of plastic, wood, glass, etc. with a hole through it. It is usually put on a string with a lot of others to make jewellery: *She wore a necklace of brightly coloured wooden beads.* **2** a very small amount of liquid: *Beads **of** sweat stood out on his forehead.* **beaded** /ˈbiː.dɪd/ *adj*: *She wore an elaborately beaded twenties-style dress.* ○ *After an hour of aerobics your face will be beaded **with** sweat.*

beading /ˈbiː.dɪŋ/ *noun* [C or U] a long thin piece of wood stuck to the edge of, or used to decorate, wooden furniture, picture frames, etc.

beady /ˈbiː.di/ *adj DISAPPROVING* (of eyes) small and bright, especially like a bird's eyes: *His beady little eyes were fixed on the money I held out.* ○ *She's always got her beady eyes on what I'm doing* (= She watches me closely).

beagle /ˈbiː.gl̩/ *noun* [C] a dog with short hair, a black, brown and white coat, short legs and long ears: *Snoopy is the world's most famous beagle.*

beak [BIRD'S MOUTH] /biːk/ *noun* [C] the hard pointed part of a bird's mouth: *Birds use their beaks to pick up food.* ○ *INFORMAL He'd be quite handsome if it wasn't for that great beak* (= large nose) *of his.* ➲See picture **Animals and Birds** on page Centre 4

beak [JUDGE] /biːk/ *noun* [C] *UK OLD-FASHIONED SLANG* a judge

beaker /ˈbiː.kəʳ/ [US] /-kɚ/ *noun* [C] a cup, usually with no handles, used for drinking, or a glass or plastic container used in chemistry: *She gave the children beakers **of** juice.*

be-all /ˌbiː.ɔːl.ənᵈˈend.ɔːl/ [US] /-ɑːl.ənᵈˈend.ɑːl/ *noun* **the be-all and end-all** the most important thing: *We all agreed that winning was not the be-all and end-all.* ○ *It was the period when everyone saw men in space as the be-all and end-all **of** space exploration.*

beam [LIGHT] /biːm/ *noun* [C] **1** a line of light that shines from a bright object: *We could just pick out the path in the weak beam of the (UK USUALLY) torch/(US) flashlight.* ○ *The rabbit stopped, mesmerized by the beam **of** the car's headlights.* ➲See also **moonbeam**; **sunbeam**. **2** a line of RADIATION or PARTICLES flowing in one direction: *a **laser** beam* ○ *an **electron** beam*

beam /biːm/ *verb* [I or T] to send out a beam of light, or an electrical or radio signal, etc: *The midday sun beamed* (= shone brightly) ***down on** the boat as it drifted along.* ○ *The concert was beamed* (= broadcast) *by satellite all over the world.*

beam [WOOD] /biːm/ *noun* [C] **1** a long thick piece of wood, metal or concrete, especially used to support weight in a building or other structure: *The sitting room had exposed **wooden** beams and a large fireplace.* **2 the beam** in the sport of women's GYMNASTICS, a wooden bar on which the competitors balance and perform movements

beam [SMILE] /biːm/ *verb* [I] to smile with obvious pleasure: *She beamed **with** delight/pleasure at his remarks.* ○ *The child beamed **at** his teacher as he received the award.* ○ [+ speech] *"I'm so pleased to see you," he beamed* (= said as he smiled).

beaming /ˈbiː.mɪŋ/ *adj*: *She gave a beaming* (= wide and happy) ***smile**.*

bean /biːn/ *noun* [C] a seed, or the pod containing seeds, of various climbing plants, eaten as a vegetable: *green beans* ○ *French beans* ○ *baked beans* ○ *Coffee beans are*

the bean-like seeds of the coffee tree.
• **not have a bean** *INFORMAL* to have no money

beanbag [SEAT] /ˈbiːn.bæɡ/ *noun* [C] (*ALSO* **beanbag chair**) a soft seat consisting of a large cloth bag filled with dried beans or something similar

beanbag [TOY] /ˈbiːn.bæɡ/ a small bag filled with dried beans which is used as a children's toy

ˈbean ˌcounter *noun* [C] *US INFORMAL DISAPPROVING* an ACCOUNTANT (= person who works in finance), especially one who works for a large company and does not like to allow employees to spend money: *It looked like the project was going to be approved, but the bean counters said it wasn't cost-effective.*

ˈbean ˌcurd *noun* [U] **tofu**

ˈbean ˌfeast *noun* [C usually sing] *UK OLD-FASHIONED, INFORMAL* a party or social occasion

beanie /ˈbiː.ni/ *noun* [C] **1** a small hat which fits closely to the head: *a beanie hat/cap* **2** *AUS FOR* **bobble hat**

beano /ˈbiː.nəʊ/ [US] /-noʊ/ *noun* [C] *plural* **beanos** *OLD-FASHIONED INFORMAL* a party

beanpole /ˈbiːn.pəʊl/ [US] /-poʊl/ *noun* [C] *INFORMAL HUMOROUS* a very tall thin person

ˈbean ˌsprout *noun* [C] beans that have just started to grow and are eaten as vegetables ➲See picture **Vegetables** on page Centre 2

bear [ANIMAL] /beəʳ/ [US] /ber/ *noun* [C] a large, strong wild mammal with a thick furry coat that lives especially in colder parts of Europe, Asia and North America: *a brown/black bear* ○ *a bear cub* (= young bear) ➲See also **grizzly (bear)**; **polar bear**; **teddy (bear)**.
• **be like a bear with a sore head** (*US ALSO* **like a (real) bear**) *INFORMAL* to be in a bad mood which causes you to treat other people badly and complain a lot: *You're like a bear with a sore head this morning. What's wrong with you?*
bearish /ˈbeə.rɪʃ/ [US] /ˈber.ɪʃ/ *adj* looking or behaving like a bear ➲See also **bearish** at **bear** FINANCE.

bear [CARRY] /beəʳ/ [US] /ber/ *verb* [T] **bore, borne** or *US ALSO* **born** *SLIGHTLY FORMAL* to carry and move something to a place: *At Christmas the family descend on the house bearing* ***gifts***. ○ *Countless waiters bore trays of drinks into the room.* ○ *The sound of the ice-cream van was borne into the office on the wind.*
bearer /ˈbeə.rəʳ/ [US] /ˈber.ɚ/ *noun* [C] **1** a person whose job is to carry something, or a person who brings a message: *He was a* ***coffin/pall*** *bearer at his father's funeral.* ○ *I'm sorry to be the bearer* ***of bad news***. **2** *SPECIALIZED* the person who owns an official document or bank note
bearing /ˈbeə.rɪŋ/ [US] /ˈber.ɪŋ/ *noun* [U] *SLIGHTLY FORMAL* someone's way of moving and behaving: *She had a proud, distinguished bearing.* ➲See also **bearing**; **bearing** at **bear** CHANGE DIRECTION, **bear on**.

bear [SUPPORT] /beəʳ/ [US] /ber/ *verb* [T] **bore, borne** or *US ALSO* **born** to hold or support something: *The chair, too fragile to bear her* ***weight***, *collapsed.* **-bearing** /-beə.rɪŋ/ [US] /-ber.ɪŋ/ *suffix a load-bearing wall*

bear [ACCEPT] /beəʳ/ [US] /ber/ *verb* [T] **bore, borne** or *US ALSO* **born** to accept, TOLERATE or ENDURE especially something unpleasant: *The strain must have been enormous but she bore it well.* ○ *Tell me now! I can't bear* ***the suspense***! ○ *It's your decision – you must bear* ***the responsibility*** *if things go wrong.* ○ [+ **to** infinitive] *He couldn't bear* ***to*** *see the dog in pain.* ○ [+ v-*ing*] *I can't bear being bored.*
• **not bear thinking about** to be too unpleasant or frightening to think about: *"What if she'd been travelling any faster?" "It doesn't bear thinking about."*
bearable /ˈbeə.rə.bl̩/ [US] /ˈber.ə-/ *adj* If an unpleasant situation is bearable, you can accept or deal with it: *As far as she was concerned, only the weekends* ***made*** *life bearable.*

bear [KEEP] /beəʳ/ [US] /ber/ *verb* [T] **bore, borne** or *US ALSO* **born** to have or continue to have something: *Their baby bears* ***a strong resemblance/an uncanny likeness to*** *its grandfather.* ○ *The stone plaque bearing his name was smashed to pieces.* ○ *On display were boxing gloves which bore Rocky Marciano's signature.* ○ [+ two objects] *I don't bear them any ill feeling* (= I do not continue to be angry with or dislike them). ○ *Thank you for your advice, I'll bear it* ***in mind*** (= will remember and consider it).
• **bear the scars** to still suffer emotional pain from something unpleasant that happened in the past

bear [PRODUCE] /beəʳ/ [US] /ber/ *verb* [T] **bore, borne** or *US ALSO* **born** to give birth to young, or (of a tree or plant) to give or produce especially fruit or flowers: *She had borne six children by the time she was thirty.* ○ [+ two objects] *When his wife bore him* ***a child*** *he could not hide his delight.* ○ *Most animals bear their young in the spring.* ○ *The pear tree they planted has never borne* ***fruit***.
• **bear fruit** *FORMAL* If something someone does bears fruit, it produces successful results: *Eventually her efforts bore fruit and she got the job she wanted.*
• **bear testimony/witness** *FORMAL* **1** to say you know from your own experience that something happened or is true: *She bore witness* ***to*** *his patience and diligence.* **2** If something bears testimony to a fact, it proves that it is true: *The iron bridge bears testimony* ***to*** *the skills developed in that era.*
• **bear false witness** *OLD USE* to lie

bear [CHANGE DIRECTION] /beəʳ/ [US] /ber/ *verb* [I usually + adv or prep] **bore, borne** or *US ALSO* **born** to change direction slightly so that you are going in a particular direction: *The path followed the coastline for several miles, then bore inland.* ○ *After you go past the church keep bearing* ***left/right***.
bearing /ˈbeə.rɪŋ/ [US] /ˈber.ɪŋ/ *noun* [C] *SPECIALIZED* an exact position, measured CLOCKWISE (= to the right) from north. Bearings are given as three numbers: *Nottingham is 70 km from Birmingham* ***on a*** *bearing* ***of*** *045 degrees.* ○ *The yachtsman* ***took*** *a bearing* ***on*** (= found his position by using) *the lighthouse.* ➲See also **bearing**; **bearing** at **bear** CARRY, **bear on**.
bearings /ˈbeə.rɪŋz/ [US] /ˈber.ɪŋz/ *plural noun*: *The road system was so complicated that we had to stop to* ***get/find*** *our bearings* (= discover our exact position) *several times.* ○ *They* ***lost*** *their bearings* (= did not know where they were) *in the dark.*
• **get/find your bearings** to succeed in becoming familiar with a new situation: *It takes a while to get your bearings when you start a new job.*

bear [FINANCE] /beəʳ/ [US] /ber/ *noun* [C] *SPECIALIZED* a person who sells shares when prices are expected to fall in order to make a profit by buying them back again at a lower price ➲Compare **bull** FINANCE.
bearish /ˈbeə.rɪʃ/ [US] /ˈber.ɪʃ/ *adj SPECIALIZED* expecting a fall in prices: *The overall oil price outlook is expected to remain bearish.* ➲See also **bearish** at **bear** ANIMAL.

PHRASAL VERBS WITH **bear** ▼

▲ **bear down on** ***sb/sth*** *phrasal verb* to move in a threatening way towards someone or something: *I looked up to see the car bearing down on me, out of control.*

▲ **bear on** ***sth*** *phrasal verb SLIGHTLY FORMAL* to be connected or related to; to influence: *I don't see how that information bears on this case.*
bearing /ˈbeə.rɪŋ/ [US] /ˈber.ɪŋ/ *noun* **have a bearing on** ***sth*** to have an influence on something or a relationship to something: *What you decide now could have a considerable bearing on your future.* ➲See also **bearing**; **bearing** at **bear** CARRY, **bear** CHANGE DIRECTION.

▲ **bear** ***sb/sth*** **out** *phrasal verb* [M] to support the truth of something: *His version of events just isn't borne out by the facts.* ○ *If you tell them what happened I will bear you out (on it).*

▲ **bear up** *phrasal verb* to deal with a very sad or difficult situation in a brave and determined way: *"How has she been since the funeral?" "Oh, she's bearing up."*
∗ NOTE: This is usually used in the continuous form.

▲ **bear with** ***sb*** *phrasal verb* to be patient and wait while someone does something: *If you'll just bear with me* ***for a moment***, *I'll find you a copy of the drawings.*

beard [HAIR] /bɪəd/ [US] /bɪrd/ *noun* [C] **1** the hair that some men allow to grow on the lower part of their face: *a flowing white beard* ○ *He's* ***growing*** *a beard.* ○ *He* ***shaved off*** *his beard but kept his moustache.* **2** the long hair that grows under a goat's mouth
bearded /ˈbɪə.dɪd/ [US] /ˈbɪr.dɪd/ *adj* with a beard: *A thin, bearded man sat opposite me on the train.* **beardless** /ˈbɪəd.ləs/ [US] /ˈbɪrd-/ *adj*

B

beard [VISIT] /bɪəd/ [US] /bɪrd/ *verb* [T] *LITERARY* to face, meet or deal with an unpleasant or frightening person in a brave or determined way: *With a nervous swallow he bearded the formidable-looking librarian behind the desk.*
• **beard the lion (in *his/her* den)** to visit an important person in the place where they work, in order to tell or ask them something unpleasant

ˈbear ˌhug *noun* [C] the action of putting your arms around someone very tightly and quite roughly

bearing /ˈbeə.rɪŋ/ [US] /ˈber.ɪŋ/ *noun* [C] a part of a machine which supports another part that turns round: *a wheel bearing* ○ *a roller bearing* ➲See also **bearing** at **bear** CARRY, **bear** CHANGE DIRECTION, **bear on**.

ˈbear ˌmarket *noun* [C] a time when the price of shares is falling and a lot of people are selling them

bearskin [BEAR] /ˈbeə.skɪn/ [US] /ˈber-/ *noun* [C] the fur-covered skin of a bear, especially when it has been removed from its body: *An old bearskin **rug** lay on the floor.*

bearskin [HAT] /ˈbeə.skɪn/ [US] /ˈber-/ *noun* [C] a tall black fur hat which is worn by particular soldiers, especially on ceremonial occasions

beast /biːst/ *noun* [C] **1** *FORMAL* an animal, especially a large or wild one: *a wild beast* ○ *The room wasn't fit for man or beast.* **2** *OLD-FASHIONED* an unpleasant, annoying or cruel person: *He was a beast to her throughout their marriage.*
• **beast of burden** *LITERARY* an animal such as a donkey or an ox which is used to carry or pull things
beastly /ˈbiːst.li/ *adj* *OLD-FASHIONED* unkind or unpleasant: *Why are you being so beastly **to** me?* ○ *We've had beastly weather all summer.*

beastie [ANIMAL] /ˈbiː.sti/ *noun* [C] *SCOTTISH ENGLISH OR HUMOROUS* an animal: *A lot of beasties live in the forest.* ○ *These otters are particularly vicious beasties, with very sharp teeth.*

beastie [INSECT] /ˈbiː.sti/ *noun* [C] *INFORMAL* an insect: *Keep still, you've got a beastie in your hair.*

beat [HIT] /biːt/ *verb* [I or T; usually + adv or prep] **beat, beaten** or *US ALSO* **beat 1** to hit repeatedly: *They saw him beating his dog with a stick.* ○ *The child had been brutally/savagely beaten.* ○ *She was beaten **to death**.* ○ [+ obj + adj] *He was beaten **senseless**.* ○ *Beat the **drum**.* ○ *The rain was beating **down** incessantly **on** the tin roof.* ○ *To make an omelette you must first beat* (= mix repeatedly using a utensil) *the eggs.* ➲See **bang/beat the drum** at **drum** INSTRUMENT. **2 beat a path through *sth*** to form a path in an area where long grass or bushes grow closely together, by hitting the plants with your hands or an object, or by stepping on them: *We beat a path through the undergrowth.*
• **beat a path to *sb's* door** to be eager to buy or obtain something from someone: *I tried to sell my old bike by advertising it in the local paper, but I didn't have a lot of people beating a path to my door.*
• **beat around the bush** (*UK ALSO* **beat about the bush**) to avoid talking about what is important: *Don't beat around the bush – get to the point!*
• **beat *sb's* brains out** *INFORMAL* to hit someone repeatedly with great force
• **beat *your* breast/chest** to show great sadness or guilt in an obvious or public way: *There's no point in beating your breast about losing the money – you won't get it back.*
• **Beat it!** *SLANG* Go away!
• **beat a retreat** (*ALSO* **beat *your* retreat**) to run away from a dangerous or unpleasant situation: *When we saw the police arriving we beat a **hasty** retreat.*
beaten /ˈbiː.tᵊn/ [US] /-t̬ᵊn/ *adj*: *She was wearing a necklace of beaten gold* (= gold made flat by having been hit repeatedly with a hard object).
• **off the beaten track** (*US ALSO* **off the beaten path**) in a place where few people go, far from any main roads and towns: *The farmhouse we stayed in was completely off the beaten track.*
beater /ˈbiː.təʳ/ [US] /-t̬ɚ/ *noun* [C] **1** a device which is used for repeatedly hitting something, especially in order to clean it, or for mixing especially foods. Beater is often used as a combining form: *an electric beater* ○ *a carpet-beater* ○ *an egg-beater* **2** used as a combining form to mean a person who repeatedly hits people, especially members of their family: *a child-beater* ○ *a wife-beater* **3** a person paid by hunters to force birds and animals into a place where they can be seen and therefore shot **beating** /ˈbiː.tɪŋ/ [US] /-t̬ɪŋ/ *noun* [C] *She **gave** her son a severe beating.*

beat [DEFEAT] /biːt/ *verb* [T] **beat, beaten** or *US ALSO* **beat 1** to defeat or do better than: *Simon always beats me **at** tennis.* ○ *Holland beat Belgium **(by)** 3-1.* ○ *Our team was comfortably/easily/soundly beaten in the first round of the competition.* ○ *The nationalists were **narrowly** beaten in the local election.* ○ *He beat me **fair and square*** (= without cheating). ○ *They were beaten **hands down*** (= completely) *by their opponents.* ○ *She has beaten her own **record** of three minutes ten seconds.* ○ *US He beat **out** all the top competitors in his sport.* ○ [+ v-ing] *INFORMAL Taking the bus sure beats* (= is better than) *walk**ing**.* ○ *SLANG Taking the bus beats **the hell out of*** (= is much better than) *walking all the way there.* ○ *You can't beat* (= there is nothing better than) *a cold beer on a hot afternoon.* ➲See Note **win or beat?** at **win**. **2** To beat something that is going to happen is to take action before the thing happens: *Let's try to beat the traffic problems by leaving early in the morning.* ○ *I always do my shopping early to beat **the rush**.*
• **beat *sb* at *their* own game** to use to your own advantage the methods by which someone else has tried to defeat you
• **beat *sb* to it** to do something before someone else does it: *I was just going to tidy up the kitchen, but you've beaten me to it.*
• **beat the rap** *US* to escape or avoid blame or punishment
• **that beats everything** (*US ALSO* **that beats all**) *SLANG* expressions showing great surprise: *You mean she just left her job without telling anyone she was going? Well, that beats everything!*
• **it beats me** (*ALSO* **what beats me**) *SLANG* said when you do not understand a situation or someone's behaviour: *It beats me how she got the job.* ○ *What beats me is why she stays with him.*
• **If you can't beat 'em, join 'em.** *SAYING* said when you accept that you cannot be as successful as someone else without doing what they do although you do not approve or agree with it
beating /ˈbiː.tɪŋ/ [US] /-t̬ɪŋ/ *noun* [C] a defeat: *We **took** a beating in our last match.*
• **take some beating** If something will take some beating, it is so good that it is hard to improve on it: *Green's new world record will take some beating.*

beat [MOVEMENT] /biːt/ *verb* [I or T] **beat, beaten** or *US ALSO* **beat 1** to (cause to) make a regular movement or sound: *The doctor could feel no pulse beating.* ○ *The hummingbird beats its wings at great speed.* **2 beat time** to make a regular sound or movement to music
beat /biːt/ *noun* [C or U] **1** a regular movement or sound, especially that made by your heart: *I put my head on his chest but I could feel no heart beat.* ○ *My heart missed a beat when she said, "Yes, I'll marry you".* **2** in music, a regular emphasis, or a place in the music where such an emphasis is expected: *The guitar comes in **on** the third beat.* ○ *Make sure you play **on** the beat* (= on the beats). ○ *He tapped his foot to the beat* (= rhythm) *of the music.*

beat [AREA] /biːt/ *noun* [C usually sing] an area for which someone, such as a police officer, has responsibility as part of their job: *Bob has worked as an officer **on** this particular beat for 20 years.*
• **be on/walking the beat** A police officer who is on/walking the beat is on duty, walking around rather than driving in a police car.

beat [TIRED] /biːt/ *adj* [after v] *INFORMAL* extremely tired: *I'm beat – I'm going to bed.* ○ *UK You've been working too hard, you look **dead** beat.* ➲See also **deadbeat** PERSON, **deadbeat** IN DEBT.

PHRASAL VERBS WITH **beat** ▼

▲ **beat *sth/sb* back** *phrasal verb* [M] If you beat back someone or something dangerous, you use force to move them away from you: *Riot police beat back the crowds of demonstrators.*

▲ **beat down** SUN *phrasal verb* If the sun beats down, it shines very strongly and makes the air very hot: *The tropical sun beat down on them mercilessly.*

▲ **beat sb down** MONEY *phrasal verb* [M] INFORMAL to persuade someone to accept a lower amount of money for something: *He wanted £50 for the bike, but I managed to beat him down (to £35).*

▲ **beat sb off** DEFEAT *phrasal verb* [M] to manage to defeat someone who is attacking you: *She beat off her attacker by hitting him with her handbag.* ○ FIGURATIVE *The company managed to beat off the competition and secure the contract.*

▲ **beat off** SEX *phrasal verb* US OFFENSIVE to **masturbate**

▲ **beat sth out** MUSIC *phrasal verb* [M] to make sounds that have a particular rhythm by hitting something such as a drum: *The drummer beat out a steady rhythm while we marched.*

▲ **beat sth out** FIRE *phrasal verb* [M] to make a fire go out by hitting it repeatedly with an object, such as a blanket: *She beat the flames out with her bare hands.*

▲ **beat sb out** DEFEAT *phrasal verb* [M] MAINLY US to defeat someone or do better than them in a competition, sport or business: *They beat out several other rivals for the contract.*

▲ **beat sth out of sb** *phrasal verb* to make someone say things they do not want to by hitting them: *The men claimed that the police had beaten the confession out of them.*

▲ **beat sb up** *phrasal verb* [M] INFORMAL to hurt someone badly by hitting or kicking them again and again: *He claims he was beaten up by the police.*

beatific /ˌbiː.əˈtɪf.ɪk/ *adj* LITERARY expressing happiness and calmness, especially in a holy way: *The angels in the painting have beatific smiles.* **beatifically** /ˌbɪəˈtɪf.ɪ.kli/ *adv*

beatify /biˈæt.ɪ.faɪ/ US /-ˈæt̬-/ *verb* [T] to announce formally in the Roman Catholic church that someone who is dead has lived a holy life, usually as the first stage in making that person a saint **beatification** /biˌæt.ɪ.fɪˈkeɪ.ʃən/ US /-ˌæt̬-/ *noun* [C or U]

beatnik /ˈbiːt.nɪk/ *noun* [C] (especially in the 1950s and 1960s) a young person who did not accept society's customs and principles, and who had long hair and wore untidy clothes

beat-up /ˈbiːt.ʌp/ US /ˈbiːt̬-/ *adj* (ALSO **beaten-up**) INFORMAL (of things) in bad condition: *a beat-up old car*

beau /bəʊ/ US /boʊ/ *noun* [C] *plural* **beaus** or **beaux** OLD-FASHIONED a boyfriend

beaut /bjuːt/ *noun* [C] OLD-FASHIONED INFORMAL something which, or someone who, is very good or noticeable: *Let me have a look at that bruise. Oh, that's a beaut!* **beaut** /bjuːt/ *adj* AUS INFORMAL *That was a beaut dinner, Mike!*

beauteous /ˈbjuː.ti.əs/ US /-t̬i-/ *adj* LITERARY very attractive to look at; beautiful

beautician /bjuːˈtɪʃ.ən/ *noun* [C] a trained person whose job it is to improve the appearance of a customer's face, body and hair, using CREAMS (= smooth thick liquids), make-up and other types of treatment, often in a BEAUTY SALON

beauty /ˈbjuː.ti/ US /-t̬i/ *noun* **1** [C or U] the quality of being pleasing, especially to look at, or someone or something that gives great pleasure, especially by being looked at: *This is an area of outstanding natural beauty.* ○ *The piece of music he played had a haunting beauty.* ○ *beauty products/treatments* ○ *She was a great beauty (= a beautiful woman) when she was young.* ○ *The beauty of this plan (= what makes it good) is that it won't cost too much.* **2** [C] INFORMAL something that is an excellent example of its type: *She showed me her car – it's a beauty.* ○ *Your roses are beauties this year.*

• *your* **beauty sleep** HUMOROUS the sleep that you need in order to feel and look healthy and attractive

• **Beauty is in the eye of the beholder.** SAYING This means that not all people have the same opinions about what is attractive.

• **Beauty is only skin deep.** SAYING said to emphasize that a person's character is more important than how they look

beautiful /ˈbjuː.tɪ.fəl/ US /-t̬ɪ-/ *adj* **1** very attractive: *a beautiful woman* ○ *breathtakingly beautiful scenery* ○ *She was wearing a beautiful dress.* **2** very pleasant: *a beautiful piece of music* ○ *beautiful weather* **3** MAINLY US very kind: *You did a beautiful thing in helping those poor children.*

• **the beautiful game** UK football

• **the beautiful people** fashionable, rich people: *This café is a favourite haunt of the beautiful people.*

beautifully /ˈbjuː.tɪ.fəl.i/ US /-t̬ɪ-/ *adv*: *She dresses beautifully.* ○ *The children behaved beautifully (= very well).* ○ *Their house is beautifully decorated.*

beautify /ˈbjuː.tɪ.faɪ/ US /-t̬ɪ-/ *verb* [T] MAINLY HUMOROUS to improve the appearance of someone or something: [R] *I'm just going to beautify myself – it should only take a few hours.* **beautification** /ˌbjuː.tɪ.fɪˈkeɪ.ʃən/ US /-t̬ɪ-/ *noun* [U]

'beauty ˌcontest/ˌpageant *noun* [C] a competition in which women are judged for their physical attractiveness

'beauty ˌqueen *noun* [C] a woman who wins a BEAUTY CONTEST (= a competiton in which women are judged for their physical attractiveness)

'beauty ˌsalon/ˌparlour *noun* [C] (US ALSO **beauty shop**) a place where your hair, face and body can be given special treatments to improve their appearance

'beauty ˌspot COUNTRYSIDE *noun* [C] a place in the countryside which is particularly attractive

'beauty ˌspot SKIN *noun* [C] a small dark mark on a woman's face that is considered to make her look more attractive

beaux /bəʊz/ US /boʊz/ *plural of* **beau**

beaver /ˈbiː.vər/ US /-və/ *noun* [C] *plural* **beavers** or **beaver** **1** an animal with smooth fur, sharp teeth and a large flat tail, which lives in a DAM (= a wall of sticks and earth) that it builds across a river **2** INFORMAL a person who works very hard: *a busy beaver* ➲See also **eager beaver**.

beaver /ˈbiː.vər/ US /-və/ *verb*

▲ **beaver away** *phrasal verb* INFORMAL to work hard for a long time: *She has been beavering away at that essay for hours.*

bebop /ˈbiː.bɒp/ US /-bɑːp/ *noun* [U] (ALSO **bop**) a type of jazz music

becalmed /bɪˈkɑːmd/ *adj* If a ship with sails is becalmed, it cannot move because of lack of wind.

became /bɪˈkeɪm/ *past simple of* **become**

because /bɪˈkəz/ /-ˈkɒz/ US /-ˈkɑːz/ *conjunction* for the reason that: *"Why did you do it?" "Because Carlos told me to".* ○ *We can't go to Julia's party because we're going away that weekend.* ○ *Just because I'm lending you my dress for tonight doesn't mean you can borrow it whenever you want to.* ○ INFORMAL *Have you been away, because (= the reason I am asking is that) we haven't seen you recently?*

be'cause ˌof *prep* as a result of: *The train was delayed because of bad weather.*

COMMON LEARNER ERROR

because or because of?

Use **because of** if what follows is simply a noun or a noun phrase.

The flight was delayed because of technical problems.

~~The flight was delayed because technical problems.~~

beck /bek/ *noun* [C] UK a small stream

• **at sb's beck and call** always willing and able to do whatever someone asks: *Go and get it yourself! I'm not at your beck and call, you know.*

beckon /ˈbek.ən/ *verb* **1** [I or T] to move your hand or head in a way that tells someone to come nearer: *The customs official beckoned the woman to his counter.* ○ *"Hey you!", she called, beckoning me over with her finger.* ○ *He beckoned to me, as if he wanted to speak to me.* **2** [I] If something beckons, it attracts people: *For many young people, the bright lights of London beckon,* though a lot of them end up sleeping on the streets. **3** [I] If an event or achievement beckons, it is likely to happen: *She's an excellent student, **for** whom a wonderful future beckons.*

become BE /bɪˈkʌm/ *verb* [L] **became, become** to start to be: *I was becoming increasingly suspicious of his motives.* ○ *It was becoming cold, so we lit the fire.* ○ *After giving up smoking, he became fat and irritable.* ○ *Margaret Thatcher became Britain's first woman prime minister in 1979.* ○ *He has just become a father.*

COMMON LEARNER ERROR

become or get?

Be careful not to confuse **become** and **get**.

Of course, we got a lot of support from family and friends.

~~Of course, we became a lot of support from family and friends.~~

become SUIT /bɪˈkʌm/ *verb* [T] **became, become** OLD-FASHIONED to cause to look attractive or to be suitable for: *That colour really becomes you.*

becoming /bɪˈkʌm.ɪŋ/ *adj* OLD-FASHIONED *That's a most becoming (= attractive) dress, my dear.*

▲ **become of sb/sth** *phrasal verb* [not continuous] If you ask what became of someone or something, you want to know where they are and what happened to them: *Whatever became of that parcel you sent?* ○ *And Mickey Adams – I wonder what became of him.*

BEd /biːˈed/ *noun* [C] ABBREVIATION FOR Bachelor of Education: a degree taken by some teachers, or a person who has this degree

bed FURNITURE /bed/ *noun* [C or U] a large rectangular piece of furniture, often with four legs, which is used for sleeping on: *He lived in a room with only two chairs, a bed and a table.* ○ *He likes to have breakfast **in** bed on a Saturday morning.* ○ *She didn't get **out of** bed till lunchtime today.* ○ *I'm exhausted – I'm **going to** bed (= going to get into a bed in order to sleep).* ○ *I always **put the** children **to** bed (= make certain that they get into a bed and are comfortable there ready for going to sleep) at 7.30 p.m.*

• **put sth to bed** INFORMAL to start printing something

• **in bed** having sex: *She found her boyfriend in bed with another woman.*

• **be in bed with** INFORMAL to work with a person or organization, or to be involved with them, in a way which causes other people not to trust you: *The newspaper editor is obviously in bed with the President.*

• **go to bed with sb** INFORMAL to have sex with someone

• **get out of bed (on) the wrong side** (US **get up on the wrong side of the bed**) to be in a bad mood and to be easily annoyed all day

• **make the bed** to make a bed tidy after you have slept in it

• **bed of nails** a difficult situation or way of life

• **You've made your bed and now you must lie in it.** SAYING said to someone who must accept the unpleasant results of something they have done

bed /bed/ *verb* [T] -dd- OLD-FASHIONED to have sex with someone

bed BOTTOM /bed/ *noun* [C] **1** the bottom or something that serves as a base: *Many strange plants and fish live on the sea bed.* ○ *The railway was built on a bed **of** solid rock.* **2 a bed of sth** a pile of one type of food on which other food is arranged as a meal: *roasted vegetables on a bed of rice*

bed AREA OF GROUND /bed/ *noun* [C] a piece of ground used for planting in a garden: *They've got some beautiful **flower** beds in their garden.*

• **bed of roses** an easy and happy existence

PHRASAL VERBS WITH **bed** ▼

▲ **bed down** SLEEP *phrasal verb* to lie down somewhere, usually somewhere different from where you usually sleep, in order to go to sleep: *I bedded down **on** the couch for the night.*

▲ **bed down** WORK WELL *phrasal verb* UK If a new process or organization beds down, it starts to operate well because it has existed for long enough: *It did not take the procedure long to bed down.*

Bed

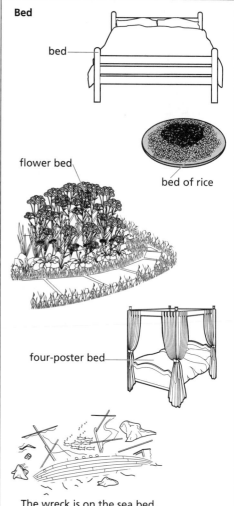

bed

flower bed

bed of rice

four-poster bed

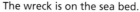

The wreck is on the sea bed.

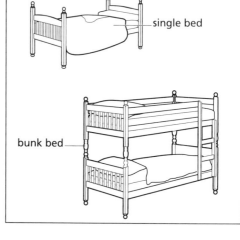

single bed

bunk bed

▲ **bed** *sth* **out** *phrasal verb* [M] to move young or delicate plants from inside and plant them outside: *May is the time to bed out the geraniums.*

,bed and 'board *noun* [U] *UK FOR* **board and lodging**

,bed and 'breakfast *noun* [C or U] (*ABBREVIATION* **B & B, B and B**) a room to sleep in for the night and a morning meal, or a private house or small hotel offering this: *Can you recommend a good bed and breakfast near Brighton?* ○ *There are several bed and breakfast **places** near the station.* ○ *We're staying at a farm that **does** bed and breakfast.*

bedaub /bɪˈdɔːb/ /-ˈdɑːb/ *verb* [T] *FORMAL* to cover very roughly with something sticky or dirty: *The child's face was bedaubed with chocolate.*

bed-bath *UK* /ˈbed.bɑːθ/ /-bæθ/ *noun* [C usually sing] (*US* **sponge bath**) a wash that you give to someone who cannot leave their bed

bedbug /ˈbed.bʌg/ *noun* [C] a very small insect which lives mainly in beds and feeds by sucking people's blood

bedclothes /ˈbed.kləʊðz/ /-kloʊðz/ *plural noun* the sheets and covers which you put on a bed

bedding /ˈbed.ɪŋ/ *noun* [U] the covers on a bed, or the dry grass, etc., that an animal sleeps on

'bedding ,plant *noun* [C] a type of plant which is planted outside in a bed when it is beginning to flower, and dug up when it has finished flowering

bedeck /bɪˈdek/ *verb* [T usually passive] *LITERARY* to decorate or cover: *The hall was bedecked with flowers.*

bedevil /bɪˈdev.ᵊl/ *verb* [T] -ll- or *US USUALLY* -l- to confuse, annoy or cause problems or difficulties for someone or something: *Ever since I started playing tennis, I've been bedevilled by back pains.*

bedfellow /ˈbed.fel.əʊ/ /-oʊ/ *noun* [C] a person connected with another in a particular activity: *The priest and the politician made **strange/odd/unlikely** bedfellows in their campaign for peace.*

bedlam /ˈbed.ləm/ *noun* [U] a noisy lack of order: *It was bedlam at the football ground after the match was suspended.*

'bed ,linen *noun* [U] the sheets and pillow and duvet covers that you put on a bed

Bedouin /ˈbed.u.ɪn/ *noun* [C] *plural* **Bedouin** or **Bedouins** a member of an Arab tribe living in or near the desert

bedpan /ˈbed.pæn/ *noun* [C] a flat dish used as a toilet by people who are too ill to get out of bed

bedpost /ˈbed.pəʊst/ /-poʊst/ *noun* [C] one of the four corner poles that support a bed

● **between you, me and the bedpost** said when you are telling someone a secret: *Between you, me and the bedpost, Jim is thinking about leaving the company.*

bedraggled /bɪˈdræg.l̩d/ *adj* wet, dirty and untidy

bedridden /ˈbed.rɪ.dᵊn/ *adj* having to stay in bed because of illness or injury: *His aunt was 93 and bedridden.*

bedrock /ˈbed.rɒk/ /-rɑːk/ *noun* **1** [U] the hard area of rock in the ground which holds up the loose earth above **2** [S] the main principles on which something is based: *Some people believe that the family is **the** bedrock **of** society.*

bedroom /ˈbed.rʊm/ /-ruːm/ *noun* [C] a room used for sleeping in: *Our home has three bedrooms.*

bedroom /ˈbed.rʊm/ /-ruːm/ *adj* [before n] relating to sexual activity: *My dad was embarrassed by the bedroom scenes in the play.* ○ *He has bedroom **eyes** (= looks as if he is interested in sex).*

-**bedroomed** /-bed.rʊmd/ /-ruːmd/ *suffix* a *two-bedroomed house* (= a house having two bedrooms)

'bedroom com,munity *noun* [C] *US FOR* a **dormitory town**

bedside /ˈbed.saɪd/ *noun* [C usually sing] the area beside a bed: *I like to have a telephone **at** my bedside.*

,bedside 'manner *noun* [S] the way in which a doctor treats people who are ill, especially in relation to kind, friendly and understanding behaviour: *He has a lovely bedside manner.*

'bedside 'table *UK noun* [C] (*US* **nightstand/night table**) a small table which is kept beside a bed

bedsit /ˈbed.sɪt/ *noun* [C] (*ALSO* **bedsitter**, *FORMAL* **bed-sitting room**) *UK* a rented room which has a bed, table, chairs and somewhere to cook in it: *He lives in a tiny student bedsit.*

,bed-'sitting ,room *noun* [C] *UK FORMAL FOR* **bedsit**

bedsore /ˈbed.sɔːʳ/ /-sɔːr/ *noun* [C] a painful wound on the body caused by having to lie in bed for a long time

bedspread /ˈbed.spred/ *noun* [C] a decorative cover put on a bed, on top of sheets and blankets

bedstead /ˈbed.sted/ *noun* [C] the wooden or metal frame of an old-fashioned bed

bedtime /ˈbed.taɪm/ *noun* [U] the time at which you usually get into your bed in order to sleep: *Put your toys away now, it's bedtime.* ○ *Eleven o'clock is past my bedtime.* ○ *I like to have a hot drink at bedtime.* ○ *He reads his children a bedtime **story** every night.*

bed-wetting /ˈbed.wet.ɪŋ/ /-t̬ɪŋ/ *noun* [U] the habit, which is often found among young children, of urinating while sleeping

bee [INSECT] /biː/ *noun* [C] a yellow and black flying insect which makes honey and can sting you: *A **swarm of** bees flew into the garden.* ○ *My arm swelled up where I was **stung** by a bee.* ⊃See also **bumblebee**.

● **be (as) busy as a bee** to be moving about quickly doing many things

● **have a bee in your bonnet** to keep talking about something again and again because you think it is very important: *She never stops talking about dieting – she's got a real bee in her bonnet **about** it.*

● **be the bee's knees** *UK INFORMAL* to be excellent or of an extremely high standard: *Have you tried this ice-cream? It's the bee's knees, it really is.*

bee [GROUP] /biː/ *noun* [C] *US* a group of people who come together in order to take part in a particular activity: *a sewing bee* ○ *a spelling bee*

the Beeb /ðə ˈbiːb/ *noun* [S] *UK INFORMAL FOR* **the BBC**

beech /biːtʃ/ *noun* [C or U] a tree with a smooth grey trunk and small nuts, or the wood from this tree: *a row of beeches* ○ *a chair made of beech* ○ *a beech floor/hedge*

beef [MEAT] /biːf/ *noun* [U] the flesh of cattle which is eaten: *The spaghetti sauce is made with (UK **MINCED**)/(US **GROUND**) beef.* ○ *People in England often have **roast beef and Yorkshire pudding** for lunch on Sundays.* ○ *He is a beef **cattle** farmer.*

beefy /ˈbiː.fi/ *adj INFORMAL* **1** describes someone who looks strong, heavy and powerful: *a beefy footballer* **2** powerful and effective: *I want to buy myself a beefier computer.*

beef [COMPLAIN] /biːf/ *verb* [I] *INFORMAL* to complain: *He was beefing **about** having to do the shopping.*

beef /biːf/ *noun* [C] *INFORMAL* a complaint: *My main beef **about** the job is that I have to work on Saturdays.*

▲ **beef** *sth* **up** *phrasal verb* [M] *INFORMAL* to make something stronger or more important: *We need to find some new players to beef up the team.* ○ *The company has plans to beef up its production.* ○ *Your report on the new car park is fine, but why don't you beef it up a bit **with** some figures?*

beefburger /ˈbiːfˌbɜː.gəʳ/ /-ˌbɝː.gɚ/ *noun* [C] *UK FOR* **hamburger** (= beef pressed into a circle, fried and eaten between two halves of a bread roll)

beefcake /ˈbiːf.keɪk/ *noun* [C or U] *SLANG* an attractive man with big muscles, or men with such bodies as shown in pictures or in shows ⊃Compare **cheesecake** WOMEN.

Beefeater /ˈbiːˌfiː.təʳ/ /-t̬ɚ/ *noun* [C] a guard at the Tower of London who wears a 16th century uniform

,beef to'mato *UK noun* [C] (*US* **beefsteak tomato**) a type of very large tomato

beehive [CONTAINER] /ˈbiː.haɪv/ *noun* [C] a box-like container in which bees are kept so that their honey can be collected

beehive [HAIR] /ˈbiː.haɪv/ *noun* [C] a woman's hairstyle in which the hair is arranged in a pile high on the head

beekeeper /ˈbiːˌkiː.pəʳ/ /-pɚ/ *noun* [C] someone who looks after bees in order to produce honey **beekeeping** /ˈbiːˌkiː.pɪŋ/ *noun* [U]

beeline /ˈbiː.laɪn/ *noun* **make a beeline for** to go directly and quickly towards: *At parties he always makes a beeline for the prettiest woman in the room.*

Beemer /ˈbiː.məʳ/ [US] /-mɚ/ *noun* [C] INFORMAL a motorcycle or car made by BMW

been /biːn/ *past participle of* **1 be 2** used to mean 'visited', 'travelled' or 'arrived': *I've never been* **to** *Kenya, but I hope to visit it next year.* ○ *The postman hasn't been here yet.* ○ *The doctor's just been* (= has arrived and left). **3** used as the past participle of 'go' when the action referred to is finished: *She's been to the hairdresser's* (= and now she has returned).

beep /biːp/ *verb* **1** [I or T] to cause to make a short loud sound: *The taxi-driver beeped (his horn) impatiently* **at** *the cyclist.* ○ *I don't like those watches that keep beeping every hour.* **2** [T] US (UK **bleep**) to call someone, for example a doctor, by sending a signal to a BEEPER which they carry **beep** /biːp/ *noun* [C] *The voice on the answerphone said "Please leave any message after the beep".*
beeper US /ˈbiː.pəʳ/ [US] /-pɚ/ *noun* [C] (UK **bleeper**) PAGER, see at **page** CALL

beer /bɪəʳ/ [US] /bɪr/ *noun* [C or U] an alcoholic drink made from grain: *He asked for a pint of beer.* ○ *This beer is* **brewed** *in Mexico.* ○ *After a hard day's work I enjoy a beer* (= a glass or container of beer) *or two.*
beery /ˈbɪə.ri/ [US] /ˈbɪr.i/ *adj* smelling of beer: *beery breath* ○ *a beery kiss*

ˈ**beer ˌbelly** *noun* [C usually sing] (ALSO **beer gut**) INFORMAL the fat stomach that a man develops when he has drunk a lot of beer for many years

ˈ**beer ˌgarden** *noun* [C] an area of land often belonging to a pub where people can sit outside and have a drink

ˈ**beer ˌmat** *noun* [C] a small piece of cardboard which you put under a glass to protect a table surface

beeswax /ˈbiːz.wæks/ *noun* [U] the fatty substance which bees produce, and which is used for making candles and polish for wood

beet /biːt/ *noun* [C or U] **1** a plant with a thick root, which is often fed to animals or used to make sugar **2** MAINLY US FOR **beetroot** ➲See picture **Vegetables** on page Centre 2

beetle [INSECT] /ˈbiː.tl̩/ [US] /-t̬l̩/ *noun* [C] an insect with a hard shell-like back: *a black beetle* ○ *a death watch beetle* ○ *a dung beetle*

beetle [HURRY] /ˈbiː.tl̩/ [US] /-t̬l̩/ *verb* [I] UK INFORMAL to go somewhere quickly: *Hoping to miss the traffic jams, she beetled* **off** *home at four o'clock.*

beetroot UK /ˈbiː.truːt/ *noun* [C or U] (US USUALLY **beet**) the small round dark red root of a plant, which is eaten cooked as a vegetable, especially cold in salads ➲See picture **Vegetables** on page Centre 2

befall /bɪˈfɔːl/ [US] /-ˈfɑːl/ *verb* [I or T] **befell, befallen** OLD USE If something bad or dangerous befalls you, it happens to you: *Should any harm befall me on my journey, you may open this letter.*

befit /bɪˈfɪt/ *verb* [T] **-tt-** FORMAL to be suitable or right for: *She was buried in the cathedral, as befits someone of her position.* **befitting** /bɪˈfɪt.ɪŋ/ [US] /-ˈfɪt̬-/ *adj*

before [EARLIER] /bɪˈfɔːʳ/ [US] /-ˈfɔːr/ *prep, adv, conjunction* at or during a time earlier than (the thing mentioned): *You should always wash your hands before meals.* ○ *Before leaving he said good-bye to each of them.* ○ *He said he had never seen her before.* ○ *She's always up before* (= earlier than) *dawn.* ○ *Before he could reach the door, she quickly closed it.* ○ *Before we make a decision, does anyone want to say anything else?* ○ *It was an hour before* (= until) *the police arrived.* ○ *She had to give the doorman a tip before* (= in order that) *he would help her with her suitcases.* ○ *I feel as though I've been here before* (= in the past).

before [IN FRONT] /bɪˈfɔːʳ/ [US] /-ˈfɔːr/ *prep* **1** in front of: *The letter K comes before L in the English alphabet.* ○ *Many mothers put their children's needs before their own.* ○ *We have the whole weekend before us – what shall we do?* ○ *He stood up before a whole roomful of people, and asked her to marry him.* **2** To be before someone or a group of people, is to be formally considered or examined by that person or group: *The proposal before the committee is that we try and reduce our spending by 10%.* ○ *The men* **appeared** *before the judge yesterday.* **3** If a place is before another place, you will arrive at it first when you are travelling towards the second place: *The bus stop is just before the school.*

beforehand /bɪˈfɔː.hænd/ [US] /-ˈfɔːr-/ *adv* earlier (than a particular time); in advance: *I knew she was coming that afternoon because she had phoned beforehand to say so.*

befriend /bɪˈfrend/ *verb* [T] to be friendly towards someone: *He was befriended by an old lady.*

befuddled /bɪˈfʌd.l̩d/ *adj* confused: *I'm so tired, my poor befuddled brain can't absorb any more.*

beg /beg/ *verb* **-gg- 1** [I or T] to ask for something urgently and without pride because you want it very much: *They begged* **for** *mercy.* ○ [+ speech] *"Please, please forgive me!" she begged (him).* ○ [+ obj + to infinitive] *He begged her* **to** *stay, but she simply laughed and put her bags in the car.* **2** [I or T] to ask for food or money because you are poor: *There are more and more homeless people begging* **on the streets** *these days.* ○ *She had to beg* **for** *money and food for her children.* **3** [I] If a dog begs, it sits with its front legs in the air as if to ask for something: *They have trained their dog to* **sit up and** *beg.*
• **beg the question** If a statement or situation begs the question, it causes you to ask a particular question: *Spending the summer travelling round India is a great idea, but it does rather beg the question of how we can afford it.* ○ *To discuss the company's future begs the question whether it has a future.*
• **go begging** UK INFORMAL If something is going begging, it is available to be taken because no one else wants it: *If that bottle of wine is going begging, I'll have it.*
• **I beg to differ/disagree** a polite way of saying "I do not agree"
• **beg, borrow or steal** to do whatever is necessary to obtain something: *I'm going to get a dress for the ball, whether I have to beg, borrow or steal one.*
• **I beg your pardon** a polite way of saying "I am sorry" or "Could you repeat what you just said?"
▲ **beg off** *sth phrasal verb* to ask to be allowed not to do something that you are expected to do: *She begged off early* **from** *the party because she was so tired.*

began /bɪˈgæn/ *past simple of* **begin**

beget /bɪˈget/ *verb* [T] **begetting, begot** or MAINLY OLD USE **begat, begotten** or **begot 1** LITERARY OR OLD USE to be the father of: *In the Bible it says that Adam begat Cain and Abel.* **2** to cause: *Poverty begets hunger, and hunger begets crime.*

beggar /ˈbeg.əʳ/ [US] /-ɚ/ *noun* [C] **1** a poor person who lives by asking others for money or food **2** UK INFORMAL a person, especially when you are expressing an opinion about something that they have done, or that has happened to them: *You've won again, you lucky beggar.* ○ *Those children have been running about in my rose garden again, the little beggars* (= annoying people)*!*
• **Beggars can't be choosers.** SAYING said when you recognize that you must accept an offer or a situation because it is the only one available to you: *I would have preferred a house of my own rather than sharing, but beggars can't be choosers, I suppose.*
beggar /ˈbeg.əʳ/ [US] /-ɚ/ *verb* [T] *His cruelty beggared belief/description* (= was impossible to believe/describe).

begin /bɪˈgɪn/ *verb* [I or T] **beginning, began, begun** to start to be, do, etc: *I began the book six months ago, but I can't seem to finish it.* ○ *I have so much to tell you, I don't know where to begin.* ○ *What time does the concert begin?* ○ *The bridge was begun five years ago and the estimated cost has already doubled.* ○ *The film they want to watch begins* **at** *seven.* ○ *If you want to learn to play a musical instrument, it might be a good idea to begin* **on** *something simple.* ○ *The word 'cat' begins* **with** *the letter 'c'.* ○ *The meeting began* **promisingly**, *but then things started to go wrong.* ○ [+ v-ing] *Jane has just begun learn***ing** *to drive.* ○ [+ to infinitive] *After waiting for half an hour she was beginning* **to** *get angry.* ○ [+ speech] *"Well," he began* (= started by saying). *"I don't quite know how to tell you this."*
• **can't (even) begin** If you can't (even) begin to do something, it is very difficult for you to do it: *As a wealthy businessman, he couldn't even begin to imagine real poverty.*

B

• **to begin with** **1** at the beginning of a process, event or situation: *There were six of us to begin with, then two people left.* **2** used to give the first important reason for something: *The hotel was awful! To begin with, our room was far too small. Then we found that the shower didn't work.*

beginner /bɪˈgɪn.əʳ/ [US] /-ɚ/ *noun* [C] *This class is for beginners* (= people who are just starting to do the activity) *only.*

beginning /bɪˈgɪn.ɪŋ/ *noun* [C usually sing; U] *Notes on how to use this dictionary can be found* ***at*** *the beginning* ***of*** *the book.* ○ *She sat down and read the book straight through* ***from*** *beginning* ***to end.*** ○ *I enjoyed my job* ***at/in*** *the beginning* (= when I started it)*, but I'm bored with it now.* ○ *The city had its beginnings* (= origins) *in Roman times.*

• **the beginning of the end** the point where something starts to get gradually worse, until it fails or ends completely: *It was the beginning of the end* ***for*** *their marriage when he started drinking.*

beginner's luck /bɪˌgɪn.əzˈlʌk/ [US] /-ɚz-/ *noun* [U] unexpected success experienced by a person who is just starting a particular activity: *When I won the first contest I entered, he put it down to beginner's luck.*

begone /biˈgɒn/ [US] /-ˈgɑːn/ *exclamation* OLD USE OR LITERARY go away: *"Begone!" he shouted. "And never let me see your face again!"*

begonia /bɪˈgəʊ.ni.ə/ [US] /-ˈgoʊ-/ *noun* [C] a garden plant with brightly coloured flowers

begrudge /bɪˈgrʌdʒ/ *verb* [T] to allow or give unwillingly: [+ two objects] *I don't begrudge him his freedom.* ○ *They begrudged every day they had to stay with their father.* ○ [+ v-ing] *She begrudged pay****ing*** *so much for an ice-cream cone.*

beguile /bɪˈgaɪl/ *verb* [T] LITERARY to charm, attract or interest, sometimes in order to deceive: *He was completely beguiled by her beauty.* ○ *The salesman beguiled him* ***into*** *buying a car he didn't want.*

beguiling /bɪˈgaɪ.lɪŋ/ *adj*: *That's a beguiling* (= interesting) *argument, but I'm not convinced by it.* **beguilingly** /bɪˈgaɪ.lɪŋ.li/ *adv*: *She smiled beguilingly at him.*

begun /bɪˈgʌn/ *past participle of* **begin**

behalf /bɪˈhɑːf/ [US] /-ˈhæf/ *noun* **on behalf of *sb*/on *sb's* behalf** representing; instead of: *On behalf of the entire company, I would like to thank you for all your work.* ○ *Unfortunately, George cannot be with us today so I am pleased to accept this award on his behalf.* ○ *Please don't leave on my behalf* (= because of me).

behave /bɪˈheɪv/ *verb* [I or T] to act in a particular way, or to be good by acting in a way which has society's approval: *She always behaves* ***well/badly*** *when her aunts come to visit.* ○ *Whenever there was a full moon he would start behaving strangely.* ○ [R] *Did the children behave (them****selves****)?*

-behaved /-bɪ.heɪvd/ *suffix* used after a word describing how someone behaves: *well/badly/perfectly-behaved children*

behaviour UK, US **behavior** /bɪˈheɪ.vjəʳ/ [US] /-vjɚ/ *noun* [U] Someone's behaviour is how they behave: *Her behaviour is often appalling.* ○ *He was notorious for his violent and threatening behaviour.*

behavioural UK, US **behavioral** /bɪˈheɪ.vjə.rəl/ [US] /-vjɚ.əl/ *adj* relating to behaviour: *She studied behavioural* ***psychology*** *at college.*

behaviourism UK, US **behaviorism** /bɪˈheɪ.vjə.rɪ.zᵊm/ [US] /-vjɚ.ɪ-/ *noun* [U] SPECIALIZED the theory that the study of the human mind should be based on people's actions and behaviour, and not on what they say that they think or feel **behaviourist** UK, US **behaviorist** /bɪˈheɪ.vjə.rɪst/ [US] /-vjɚ.ɪst/ *adj, noun* [C] *He's written a behaviourist* ***account*** *of the emotions.*

beˈhaviour ˌtherapy *noun* [U] (ALSO **behavioural therapy**) SPECIALIZED in psychology, a form of treatment which tries to change someone's particular unwanted behaviour rather than treating the cause of it

behead /bɪˈhed/ *verb* [T often passive] to cut off someone's head

beheld /bɪˈheld/ *past simple and past participle of* **behold**

behemoth /bɪˈhiː.mɒθ/ [US] /-mɑːθ/ *noun* [C] FORMAL something that is extremely large and often extremely powerful: *a grocery chain behemoth*

behest /bɪˈhest/ FORMAL **at *sb's* behest/at the behest of *sb*** because someone has asked or ordered you to do something: *The budget proposal was adopted at the president's behest.*

behind [BACK] /bɪˈhaɪnd/ *prep, adv* at the back (of): *Look behind you!* ○ *I hung my coat behind the door.* ○ *Alex led, and I followed along behind.* ○ MAINLY UK *As hard as she tried, she always* ***fell*** *behind the other swimmers in the races.* ○ *I was annoyed to discover that I'd* ***left*** *my bag behind* (= in the place I had left). ○ *After the party a few people* ***stayed*** *behind* (= stayed when others had gone) *to help clear up.* ○ *The old woman was behind* ***with*** (= late paying) *the rent.* ○ FIGURATIVE *I knew that behind* (= hidden by) *her smile was sadness.*

behind /bɪˈhaɪnd/ *prep* responsible for or the cause of: *He wondered what was behind his neighbour's sudden friendliness.* ○ *Marie Curie was the woman behind enormous changes in the science of chemistry.*

• **behind the wheel** driving a motor vehicle: *I'm a different person when I'm behind the wheel.*

• **be behind *sb* (all the way)** to support someone (completely) in what they are doing

• **Behind every great/successful man there stands a woman.** SAYING said to emphasize that men's success often depends on the work and support of their wives

behind [BODY PART] /bɪˈhaɪnd/ *noun* [C] INFORMAL the part of the body on which a person sits; BOTTOM: *He tripped and fell on his behind.* ○ *Why don't you* ***get off*** *your behind* (= stand up) *and do something!*

behindhand /bɪˈhaɪnd.hænd/ *adv, adj* UK FORMAL delayed in doing something or slower doing something then expected: *I worked late last night because I was behindhand* ***with*** *my accounts.*

behold /bɪˈhəʊld/ [US] /-ˈhoʊld/ *verb* [T] **beheld, beheld** MAINLY OLD USE to see or look at: *The new bridge is an incredible sight to behold.* **beholder** /bɪˈhəʊl.dəʳ/ [US] /-ˈhoʊl.dɚ/ *noun* [C]

beholden /bɪˈhəʊl.dᵊn/ [US] /-ˈhoʊl-/ *adj* [after v] FORMAL feeling you have a duty to someone because they have done something for you: *She wanted to be independent and beholden* ***to*** *no one.*

behove UK /bɪˈhəʊv/ [US] /-ˈhoʊv/ *verb* (US **behoove**) OLD-FASHIONED FORMAL **it behoves *sb* to** it is right for someone to do something: *It* ***ill*** *behoves you to* (= You should not) *speak so rudely of your parents.*

beige /beɪʒ/ *adj, noun* [U] (of) a pale creamy brown colour

being [PERSON] /ˈbiː.ɪŋ/ *noun* [C or U] a person or thing that exists or the state of existing: *A nuclear war would kill millions of living beings.* ○ *Strange beings from outer space are still a popular subject for sci-fi films.* ○ *We do not know exactly how life first* ***came into*** *being* (= began to exist.)

being [BE] /ˈbiː.ɪŋ/ *present participle of* **be**

bejewelled /bɪˈdʒuː.ᵊld/ *adj* (US USUALLY **bejeweled**) wearing a lot of jewellery or decorated with jewels: *a bejewelled woman* ○ *a bejewelled crown*

belabour /bɪˈleɪ.bəʳ/ [US] /-bɚ/ *verb* [T] **1** UK (US **belabor**) to explain something more than necessary: *There's no need to belabour the* ***point*** *– you don't need to keep reminding me.* **2** UK (US **belabor**) OLD-FASHIONED to hit someone or something hard and repeatedly: *She belaboured him with her walking stick.* **3** UK to criticize someone

belated /bɪˈleɪ.tɪd/ [US] /-t̬ɪd/ *adj* coming later than expected: *a belated apology* ○ *They did make a belated* ***attempt*** *to reduce the noise.* ○ *Belated birthday greetings!*

belatedly /bɪˈleɪ.tɪd.li/ [US] /-t̬ɪd-/ *adv*

belch /beltʃ/ *verb* [I or T] to allow air from the stomach to come out noisily through the mouth: *He belched noisily.* ○ FIGURATIVE *The exhaust pipe belched* ***out*** (= produced) *dense black smoke.* **belch** /beltʃ/ *noun* [C] *The baby let out a loud, satisfied belch.*

beleaguered /bɪˈliː.gəd/ [US] /-gɚd/ *adj* **1** FORMAL troubled by someone or a situation: *The arrival of the fresh medical supplies was a welcome sight for the beleaguered doctors working in the refugee camps.* **2**

surrounded by an army: *The occupants of the beleaguered city had no means of escape.*

belfry /ˈbel.fri/ *noun* [C] the tower of a church where bells are hung

Belgian /ˈbel.dʒᵊn/ *adj* from, belonging to or relating to Belgium

Belgian /ˈbel.dʒᵊn/ *noun* [C] a person from Belgium

belie /bɪˈlaɪ/ *verb* [T] **belying, belied, belied** to show something to be false, or to hide something such as an emotion: *Her calm face belied the terror she was feeling.*

belief /bɪˈliːf/ *noun* [C or S or U] the feeling of certainty that something exists or is true: *All non-violent religious and political beliefs should be respected equally.* ○ [+ **that**] *It is my (firm) belief that nuclear weapons are immoral.* ○ *His belief* ***in*** *God gave him hope during difficult times.* ○ *Recent revelations about corruption have* ***shaken*** *many people's belief* ***in*** (= caused people to have doubts about) *the police.* ○ *The brutality of the murders was* ***beyond*** *belief* (= too difficult to be imagined). ○ *He called at her house* ***in the*** *belief* ***that*** (= confident that) *she would lend him the money.*

believe /bɪˈliːv/ *verb* [T] to think that something is true, correct or real: *Strangely, no one believed us when we told them we'd been visited by a creature from Mars.* ○ [+ **that**] *He believes* ***that*** *all children are born with equal intelligence.* ○ [+ **speech**] *She's arriving tomorrow, I believe.* ○ *"Is she coming alone?" "We believe* ***not/so*** (= We think she is not/is)." ○ [+ **obj** + **to infinitive**] *I believe her* ***to*** *be the finest violinist in the world.* ○ [+ **obj** + **adj**] *All the crew are missing, believed dead.*

• **not believe a word of it** to not believe that something is true: *He told me she was just a friend, but I don't believe a word of it!*

• **believe it or not** (*ALSO* **would you believe it?**) said when telling someone about something that is true, although it seems unlikely: *He's upstairs doing his homework, believe it or not.*

• **not believe *your* eyes/ears** to be so surprised by what you see or hear that you think you are imagining it: *I couldn't believe my ears* ***when*** *she said they were getting divorced.* ○ *She couldn't believe her eyes* ***when*** *she saw him pull out a gun*

• **not believe *your* luck** to be very surprised and very pleased

• **make believe** to pretend or imagine: *Let's make believe* ***(that)*** *we're pirates.* ➲See also **make-believe**.

• **believe *sth* when *you* see it** If you say you will believe something when you see it you mean you think it will not happen: *"Hetty says she'll be here at 7.00." "I'll believe that when I see it."*

believable /bɪˈliː.və.bl̩/ *adj* If something is believable, it seems possible, real or true: *I didn't find any of the characters in the film believable.*

believer /bɪˈliː.vəʳ/ [US] /-vɚ/ *noun* [C] a person who has a religious belief or has confidence in the benefit of something: *She's been a believer since she survived a terrible car accident.* ○ *Harvey's a* ***great*** *believer* ***in*** *health food.* ○ *I'm a great believer* ***in*** *allowing people to make their own mistakes.*

PHRASAL VERBS WITH **believe**

▲ **believe in *sth*** *phrasal verb* **1** to be certain that something exists: *Do you believe in ghosts?* **2** to be confident that something is effective and right: *They don't believe in living together before marriage.* ○ *He believes in saying what he thinks.*

▲ **be'lieve in *sb*** *phrasal verb* to trust someone because you think that they can do something well or that they are a good person: [R] *Gradually, since her divorce, she's beginning to believe in herself again.*

Belisha beacon /bə,liː.ʃəˈbiː.kᵊn/ *noun* [C] in Britain, a post with a flashing orange light on top which shows someone where they can walk across a road

belittle /bɪˈlɪt.l̩/ [US] /-ˈlɪt̬-/ *verb* [T] to make an action or a person seem unimportant: *Though she had spent hours fixing the computer he belittled her efforts.* ○ *Stop belittling yourself – your work is highly valued.*

bell /bel/ *noun* [C] a hollow metal object shaped like a cup which makes a ringing sound when hit by something hard, especially a CLAPPER: *The church bells* ***rang out*** *to welcome in the New Year.* ○ *I stood at the front door and* ***rang*** *the bell several times.* ➲See **(as) clear as a bell** at **clear** ABLE TO BE UNDERSTOOD; **be as sound as a bell** at **sound** GOOD CONDITION.

• **give *sb* a bell** *UK INFORMAL* to telephone someone: *Give me a bell sometime next week, won't you?*

• **warning/alarm bells start to ring/sound** used to describe an occasion when you realize that something is wrong: *When Frank suggested coming to stay for a couple of days, alarm bells rang* ***in my head.***

• **with bells on** *US INFORMAL* To do something or go somewhere with bells on is to do it or go there eagerly: *"Are you coming to Paul's tonight." "Sure, I'll be there – with bells on."*

belladonna /,bel.əˈdɒn.ə/ [US] /-ˈdɑː.nə/ *noun* [U] **deadly nightshade**

bell-bottoms /ˈbel.bɒt.ᵊmz/ [US] /-bɑː.t̬əmz/ *plural noun* trousers that are very wide below the knee

bellboy /ˈbel.bɔɪ/ *noun* [C] (*US ALSO* **bellhop**) a man in a hotel employed to carry cases, open doors, etc.

belle /bel/ *noun* [C] *OLD-FASHIONED* a beautiful and charming woman or one who is beautifully dressed

• **be the belle of the ball** to be the most attractive woman at party or similar event: *She wore a dress of crimson silk to the dinner and was the belle of the ball.*

belles-lettres /,belˈlet.rə/ *plural noun SPECIALIZED* literary works that are beautiful and pleasing in an artistic way, rather than being very serious or full of information

bellicose /ˈbel.ɪ.kəʊs/ [US] /-koʊs/ *adj FORMAL* wishing to fight or start a war: *The general made some bellicose statements about his country's military strength.*

belligerent /bəˈlɪdʒ.ᵊr.ənt/ [US] /-ɚ-/ *adj* **1** *DISAPPROVING* wishing to fight or argue: *a belligerent person* ○ *a belligerent gesture* ○ *Watch out! Lee's in a belligerent mood.* **2** *SPECIALIZED* fighting a war: *The belligerent countries are having difficulties funding the war.*

belligerence /bəˈlɪdʒ.ᵊr.ənts/ [US] /-ɚ-/ *noun* [U] (*ALSO* **belligerency**) *DISAPPROVING I can't stand his belligerence* (= his wish to argue with people all the time).

belligerently /bəˈlɪdʒ.ᵊr.ənt.li/ [US] /-ɚ-/ *adv*

ˈbell ˌjar *noun* [C] a large glass cover shaped like a bell used to cover chemical equipment, especially to prevent any gas produced from escaping

bellow /ˈbel.əʊ/ [US] /-oʊ/ *verb* [I or T] to shout in a loud voice, or (of a cow or large animal) to make a loud, deep sound: [+ **speech**] *"Keep quiet!" the headmaster bellowed across the room.* ○ *We could hear the sergeant bellowing commands to his troops.* **bellow** /ˈbel.əʊ/ [US] /-oʊ/ *noun* [C] *He gave a bellow* ***of*** *rage.*

bellows /ˈbel.əʊz/ [US] /-oʊz/ *plural noun* a tool used to blow air, especially into a fire to make it burn better: *a* ***pair of*** *bellows*

bell-pull /ˈbel.pʊl/ *noun* [C **usually sing**] *UK* a cord or handle that is pulled to ring a bell

bell-push /ˈbel.pʊʃ/ *noun* [C] *UK* a button, usually by the front door of a house, which makes a bell ring inside

bell-ringer /ˈbel̩rɪŋ.əʳ/ [US] /-ɚ/ *noun* [C] a **campanologist** ➲See at **campanology**.

bellwether /ˈbel̩we.ðəʳ/ [US] /-ðɚ/ *noun* [C] *MAINLY US* someone or something which shows how a situation will develop or change: *The report, which is viewed as a bellwether for economic trends, implied that the national economy could be slowing down.*

belly /ˈbel.i/ *noun* [C] **1** *INFORMAL* the stomach or the front part of the body between your chest and your legs: *He fell asleep with a full belly and a happy heart.* ○ *Now six months pregnant, Gina's belly had begun to swell.* **2** the rounded or curved part of an object: *The belly of the aircraft was painted red.*

• **go/turn belly up** *INFORMAL* If a company or plan goes/turns belly up, it fails: *The business went belly up after only six months.*

-bellied /-bel.ɪd/ /-id/ *suffix* having a belly of the type mentioned: *pot-bellied* ○ *big-bellied*

bellyache [PAIN] /ˈbel.i.eɪk/ *noun* [C] *INFORMAL* a pain in the stomach

bellyache [COMPLAIN] /'bel.i.eɪk/ *verb* [I] *INFORMAL* to complain: *I wish you'd stop bellyaching and just get on with the job.* **bellyaching** /'bel.i.eɪk/ *noun* [U]

'belly ˌbutton *noun* [C] *INFORMAL OR CHILD'S WORD* **navel**

'belly ˌdance *noun* [C] a dance originally from the Middle East in which a woman moves her hips and stomach **'belly ˌdancer** *noun* [C]

'belly ˌflop *noun* [C] an awkward jump into water in which a person's stomach hits the water

bellyful /'bel.i.fʊl/ *noun INFORMAL* **have a bellyful of *sb/sth*** to have more than you can deal with of someone or something bad or annoying: *I've had a bellyful of their lies.*

'belly ˌlaugh *noun* [C] a loud, uncontrolled laugh: *I've never heard Robin laugh like that – it was a real belly laugh.*

belong /bɪ'lɒŋ/ [US] /-'lɑːŋ/ *verb* **1** [I + adv or prep] to be in the right or suitable place: *This table belongs **in** the sitting-room.* ○ *Where do these spoons belong?* ○ *These papers belong **with** the others.* **2** [I] to feel happy or comfortable in a situation: *After three years in Cambridge, I finally feel as if I belong here.*

PHRASAL VERBS WITH **belong** ▼

▲ **belong to *sb*** [PROPERTY] *phrasal verb* to be someone's property: *This book belongs to Sarah.* ○ *You shouldn't take what doesn't belong to you.*
belongings /bɪ'lɒŋ.ɪŋz/ [US] /-'lɑːŋ-/ *plural noun* the things that a person owns, especially those which can be carried: *I put a few **personal** belongings in a bag and left the house for the last time.*

▲ **belong to *sth*** [BE A MEMBER] *phrasal verb* to be a member of a group or organization: *They belong to the same chess club.*

beloved /bɪ'lʌv.ɪd/ /-'lʌvd/ *adj SLIGHTLY FORMAL* loved very much: *Her beloved husband died last year.* ○ *She was forced to leave her beloved Paris and return to Lyon.* ○ *Eric was a gifted teacher beloved **by** all those he taught over the years.*
my/her/your, etc. beloved /bɪ'lʌv.ɪd/ *noun* someone that you love and with whom you have a romantic relationship: *He's sending some flowers to his beloved.*

below /bɪ'ləʊ/ [US] /-'loʊ/ *adv, prep* in a lower position (than), under: *From the top of the skyscraper the cars below us looked like insects.* ○ *Do you usually wear your skirts above or below the knee?* ○ *The author's name was printed below the title.* ○ *They have three children below **the age of*** (= younger than) *four.* ○ *The temperature has fallen below zero/freezing* (= cooled to less than zero) *recently.* ○ *Last night it was eight degrees below* (= eight degrees less than zero). ○ *His marks in English have been below* (= less than) ***average*** *for some time now.* ○ *She has three people **working** below her* (= people to whom she gives orders). ○ *For further information on this subject, **see** below* (= lower on the page or later in the book). ○ *The ship's captain went below* (= to the lower, covered part of the ship).
● **below the belt** *INFORMAL* If a remark is below the belt it is particularly hurtful and unfair.

belt [CLOTHING] /belt/ *noun* [C] **1** a strip of leather or material worn around the waist to support clothes or for decoration: *She **fastened** her belt tightly around her waist.* ○ *He had eaten so much that he had to **undo** his belt a couple of notches.* ➲See picture **Clothes** on page Centre 6 **2** a flat strip of material in a machine that moves round continuously to keep another part turning, or to keep objects on it moving round: *a fan belt* ○ *a conveyor belt*
● **belt and braces** *UK INFORMAL* when two or more actions are done to be extra careful about something when only one is really necessary: *I wrote to them and telephoned as well – belt and braces, I admit.*
● **have *sth* under *your* belt** to have learned or succeeded in something which might be a benefit in the future: *Basic computer skills are a good thing to have under your belt.*
belt /belt/ *verb* [T] *I belted my coat* (= tied it with a belt) *tightly.*

belt [AREA] /belt/ *noun* [C usually sing] an area, usually just outside a city, where a particular group of people live, such as the commuter belt and stockbroker belt, or an area that is known for a particular characteristic, such as the cotton belt

belt [MOVE FAST] /belt/ *verb* [I + adv or prep] *UK INFORMAL* (especially of a vehicle) to travel with great speed: *The car was belting **along/down** the road.*

belt [HIT] /belt/ *verb* [T] *INFORMAL* to hit hard, especially with violence: *He belted him **in** the face.* **belt** /belt/ *noun* [C] *a belt **on** the jaw*

PHRASAL VERBS WITH **belt** ▼

▲ **belt *sth* out** *phrasal verb* [M] *INFORMAL* to sing or play a musical instrument very loudly: *The band was belting out all the old favourites.*

▲ **belt up** [BE QUIET] *phrasal verb UK VERY INFORMAL* used to tell someone to stop talking or making a noise: *Just belt up, will you! I'm trying to concentrate.*

▲ **belt up** [FASTEN] *UK INFORMAL phrasal verb* (*US* **buckle up**) to fasten the belt that keeps you in your seat in a car or a plane: *Don't forget, belt up before you drive off.* * NOTE: This is usually used in the imperative form.

beltway /'belt.weɪ/ *noun* [C] *US FOR* **ring road**

belying /bɪ'laɪ.ɪŋ/ *present participle of* **belie**

bemoan /bɪ'məʊn/ [US] /-'moʊn/ *verb* [T] *FORMAL* to complain about or express sadness: *Researchers at universities are always bemoaning their lack of funds.*

bemused /bɪ'mjuːzd/ *adj* slightly confused: *I must admit that I was rather bemused **by** his sudden anger.*

bench /bentʃ/ *noun* [C] a long, usually hard, seat for two or more people, often found in public places, or a long table for working on: *a park bench* (= a seat in a public garden) ○ *a work bench* (= a table for working at)
● **the bench** **1** a seat or area of seats where players sit during a game when they are not playing: *He was injured, and spent the last few weeks of the season **on** the bench.* **2** the judge or MAGISTRATE, or the place where they sit, in a court of law: *Kindly address your remarks to the bench, Mr Smith.*
● **serve/sit/be on the bench** to work as a judge or MAGISTRATE
● **take the bench** *US* **1** to become a judge or MAGISTRATE **2** If a judge takes the bench they begin a formal meeting of a law court.
the 'benches *plural noun* in the British parliament building, the seats used by the members: *There was jeering from the Labour benches.*

benchmark /'bentʃ.mɑːk/ [US] /-mɑːrk/ *noun* [C] a level of quality which can be used as a standard when comparing other things: *Her outstanding performances set a new benchmark for singers throughout the world.* **benchmark** /'bentʃ.mɑːk/ [US] /-mɑːrk/ *adj*: *a benchmark case*
benchmark /'bentʃ.mɑːk/ [US] /-mɑːrk/ *verb* [T] to measure the quality of something by comparing it with something else of an accepted standard: *His reports pointed out that we do not have reliability in the sense of all schools being benchmarked **against** the best.* **benchmarking** /'bentʃˌmɑː.kɪŋ/ [US] /-ˌmɑːr-/ *noun* [U] *rigorous benchmarking of research performance* ○ *The Government is planning to launch a benchmarking scheme to guide consumers.*

'bench ˌtop *noun* [C] *AUS FOR* a **worktop**

bend [CURVE] /bend/ *verb* [I or T] **bent, bent** to (cause to) curve: *I bent **down** and picked up the coins lying on the road.* ○ *Now, bend **forward/over** and touch your toes!* ○ *Make sure you bend your knees when you're picking up heavy objects.* ○ *The road bends to the left after the first set of traffic lights.* ○ *After her fall she complained that she couldn't bend her leg properly.* ➲See also **bent**.
● **bend the law/rules** to change the rules in a way that is considered to be unimportant or not harmful: *Can't you bend the rules a little? I was only a few minutes late.*
● **bend *sb's* ear** *INFORMAL* to talk too much, especially about a problem
● **on bended knee** in a position in which the knee of one leg is touching the floor: *He **went down** on bended knee to ask her to marry him.*

B

bend /bend/ *noun* [C] a curved part of something: *There's a bend in the pipe so you can't see from one end to the other.* ○ *The car came* ***round the*** *bend on the wrong side of the road.,*

• **round the bend** UK INFORMAL To be/go round the bend is to be/become mentally confused or unable to act in a reasonable way: *If I'd stayed there any longer I'd have gone round the bend.*

• **drive/send *sb* round the bend** UK INFORMAL to make someone very bored or very angry: *My mother's been driving me round the bend.* ○ *Staying at home all day was driving her round the bend.*

bendable /'ben.də.bl̩/ *adj* Something which is bendable can be bent: *bendable copper pipe*

bendy /'ben.di/ *adj* UK describes something that has many bends in it or that can be easily bent: *a bendy road* ○ *a bendy toy*

bend [ACCEPT] /bend/ *verb* [I] **bent, bent** to unwillingly accept the opinions or decisions of other people: *The local council was forced to bend* ***to*** *public pressure.*

bender /'ben.dəʳ/ [US] /-dɚ/ *noun* [C] INFORMAL a period during which a large amount of alcoholic liquid is drunk: *They* ***went on a*** *bender for two days after they won the championship.*

the bends *plural noun* a serious medical condition that DIVERS (= swimmers under water) get when they come up to the surface of the sea too quickly

beneath [BELOW] /bɪ'niːθ/ *prep* in or to a lower position than, under: *Jeremy hid the letter beneath a pile of papers.* ○ *We huddled together for warmth beneath the blankets.* ○ *After weeks at sea, it was wonderful to feel firm ground beneath our feet once more.* ○ *Emma was so tired and hungry that her legs were beginning to* ***give way*** *beneath her* (= she was about to fall over). **beneath** /bɪ'niːθ/ *adv*: *She looked out of the window at the children playing beneath.*

beneath [NOT GOOD ENOUGH] *preposition* **be beneath you** If someone thinks an activity is beneath them, they think they should not have to do it because they are too important or too clever: *Office work of any description he felt was beneath him.*

benedictine [ALCOHOL] /ˌben.ɪ'dɪk.tiːn/ *noun* [U] a type of alcoholic drink

Benedictine [RELIGIOUS PERSON] /ˌben.ɪ'dɪk.tiːn/ *noun* [C] a monk or a nun who is a member of a Christian group which follows the rules of St Benedict

benediction /ˌben.ɪ'dɪk.ʃᵊn/ *noun* [C] a prayer asking God for help and protection

benefactor /'ben.ɪ.fæk.təʳ/ [US] /-t̬ɚ/ *noun* [C] (FEMALE ALSO **benefactress**) someone who gives money to help an organization, society or person

beneficent /bɪ'nef.ɪ.sᵊnt/ *adj* FORMAL helping people and doing good acts: *a beneficent aunt*

beneficiary /ˌben.ɪ'fɪʃ.ᵊr.i/ [US] /-i.er.i/ *noun* [C] a person or group who receives money, advantages, etc. as a result of something else: *Her husband was the chief beneficiary* ***of*** *her will.*

benefit /'ben.ɪ.fɪt/ *noun* [C or U] **1** a helpful or good effect, or something intended to help: *The discovery of oil brought many benefits to the town.* ○ *One of the many benefits* ***of*** *foreign travel is learning how to cope with the unexpected.* ○ *He's had* ***the*** *benefit* ***of*** *an expensive education and yet he continues to work as a waiter.* ○ *I didn't* ***get/derive (much)*** *benefit* ***from*** *school.* ○ *With the benefit* ***of hindsight*** (= Helped by the knowledge since learned) *it is easy for us to see where we went wrong.* ○ SLIGHTLY FORMAL *She drinks a lot less now,* ***to the*** *benefit* ***of*** (= resulting in an improvement in) *her health as a whole.* **2** the money given by the government to people who need financial help, for example because they cannot find a job: MAINLY UK *unemployment benefit* ○ *I'm* ***on*** *benefit at the moment.*

• **give *sb* the benefit of the doubt** to believe something good about someone, rather than something bad, when you have the possibility of doing either: *I didn't know whether his story was true or not, but I decided to give him the benefit of the doubt.*

benefit /'ben.ɪ.fɪt/ *verb* [I or T] **-t-** to be helped by something or to help someone: *I feel that I have benefited greatly* ***from*** *her wisdom.* ○ *How can we benefit those who most need our help?*

beneficial /ˌben.ɪ'fɪʃ.ᵊl/ *adj*: *The improvement in sales figures had a beneficial* (= helpful or good) ***effect/influence*** *on the company as a whole.* ○ *A stay in the country will be beneficial* ***to*** *his health.*

'benefit ˌconcert *noun* [C] a musical performance held to raise money for people in need, where the performers usually play for free

'benefits ˌpackage *noun* [C] things such as medical insurance that employees receive in addition to money

benevolent /bɪ'nev.ᵊl.ᵊnt/ *adj* kind and helpful: *He was a benevolent old man, he wouldn't hurt a fly.* **benevolence** /bɪ'nev.ᵊl.ᵊnts/ *noun* [U] **benevolently** /bɪ'nev.ᵊl.ᵊnt.li/ *adv*: *She smiled benevolently at me.*

be'nevolent soˌciety *noun* [C] an organization which gives money to and helps a particular group of people in need: *a benevolent society for sailors' widows*

benighted /bɪ'naɪ.tɪd/ [US] /-t̬ɪd/ *adj* LITERARY without knowledge or morals: *Some of the early explorers thought of the local people as benighted savages who could be exploited.*

benign /bɪ'naɪn/ *adj* **1** pleasant and kind: *a benign old lady* **2** describes a growth that is not likely to cause death: *a benign tumour* ➲Compare **malignant**. **benignly** /bɪ'naɪn.li/ *adv*: *The policeman smiled benignly at the motorist.*

bent [BEND] /bent/ *past simple and past participle of* **bend**

bent [SKILL] /bent/ *noun* [S] a natural skill: *She has* ***a*** *scientific bent/****a*** *bent* ***for*** *science.*

bent [DISHONEST] /bent/ *adj* MAINLY UK SLANG (especially of a person in a position of authority) dishonest: *a bent copper*

bent [HOMOSEXUAL] /bent/ *adj* UK OLD-FASHIONED OFFENSIVE (especially of men) homosexual

ˌbent 'double *adj* describes a person who is standing with their upper body curved forwards and down towards the ground, often as a result of strong emotion or pain: *He was bent double* ***with laughter/pain.***

'bent ˌon *adj* [after v] determined to do or have something: *He was bent on getting married as soon as possible.*

benumbed /bɪ'nʌmd/ *adj* FORMAL unable to feel because of cold, shock, etc: *a face benumbed with cold*

benzene /'ben.ziːn/ *noun* [U] a colourless liquid from which many other chemicals can be made

bequeath /bɪ'kwiːð/ *verb* [T + two objects] FORMAL to arrange to give money or property to others after your death: *Her father bequeathed her the family fortune in his will.* ○ *Picasso bequeathed most of his paintings and sculptures* ***to*** *Spain and France.*

bequest /bɪ'kwest/ *noun* [C] the money or property belonging to someone which they say that, after their death, they wish to be given to other people: *Her will included small bequests* ***to*** *her family, while most of her fortune went to charity.*

berate /bɪ'reɪt/ *verb* [T] FORMAL to criticize or speak in an angry manner to someone: *As he left the meeting, he was berated by angry demonstrators.* ○ *Doctors are often berated* ***for*** *being poor communicators, particularly when they have to give patients bad news.*

bereaved /bɪ'riːvd/ *adj* having a close relative or friend who has recently died: *a bereaved widow* ○ *The bereaved parents wept openly.*

the be'reaved *plural noun*: *It is generally accepted that the bereaved* (= people whose relatives or friends have recently died) *benefit from counselling.*

bereavement /bɪ'riːv.mənt/ *noun* [C or U] the death of a close relative or friend: *She has recently* ***suffered*** *a bereavement.*

bereft /bɪ'reft/ *adj* [after v] FORMAL lacking something or feeling great loss: *Alone now and almost penniless, he was bereft* ***of*** *hope.* ○ *After the last of their children had left home the couple* ***felt*** *utterly bereft.*

beret /'ber.eɪ/ [US] /bə'reɪ/ *noun* [C] a round flat hat made of soft material ➲See picture **Hairstyles and Hats** on page Centre 8

berk, **burk** /bɜːk/ [US] /bɝːk/ *noun* [C] *UK SLANG* a stupid person: *I felt a* ***right*** *berk when I couldn't remember where I'd parked the car.*

berry /ˈber.i/ *noun* [C] a small round fruit on particular plants and trees

berserk /bəˈzɜːk/ [US] /-ˈzɝːk/ *adj* very angry and out of control: *My mother will* ***go*** *berserk* (= be extremely angry) *when she finds out I've ruined her favourite dress.*

berth /bɜːθ/ [US] /bɝːθ/ *noun* [C] a bed in a boat, train, etc., or a place for a ship or boat to stay in a port: *She booked a berth on the train from London to Aberdeen.*

berth /bɜːθ/ [US] /bɝːθ/ *verb* [I or T] *The ship berthed* (= was tied up at the port) ***at*** *Sydney.*

beseech /bɪˈsiːtʃ/ *verb* [T] **beseeched** or **besought**, **beseeched** or **besought** *OLD USE* to ask for something in an anxious way that shows you need it very much; BEG: *Stay a little longer, I beseech you!*

beset /bɪˈset/ *adj* [after v] troubled (by); full (of): *With the amount of traffic nowadays, even a trip across town is beset* ***by/with*** *dangers.*

beside /bɪˈsaɪd/ *prep* **1** at the side of, next to: *Come and sit here beside me.* ○ *Our school was built right beside a river.* **2** compared to another person or thing: *Those books seem rather dull beside this one.*

• **be beside the point** to be in no way connected to the subject that is being discussed: *Let's stick to discussing whether the road should be built at all. The exact cost is beside the point.*

• **be beside *yourself*** If you are beside yourself with a particular feeling or emotion, it is so strong that it makes you almost out of control: *He was beside himself with grief when she died.*

besides /bɪˈsaɪdz/ *adv, prep* in addition to; also: *Do you play any other sports besides football and basketball?* ○ *She won't mind your being late – besides, it's hardly your fault.*

besiege /bɪˈsiːdʒ/ *verb* [T often passive] **1** to surround a place, especially with an army, to prevent people or supplies getting in or out: *The town had been besieged for two months but still resisted the aggressors.* **2** When someone is besieged, a lot of people surround them: *When the pop star tried to leave her hotel she was besieged* ***by*** *waiting journalists and fans.* **3** to make many requests or complaints about something: *After showing the controversial film, the television company was besieged with phone calls and letters from angry viewers.*

besmeared /bɪˈsmɪəd/ [US] /-ˈsmɪrd/ *adj* [after v] *FORMAL* marked with dirt, oil, etc: *His face was besmeared* ***with*** *chocolate.*

besmirch /bɪˈsmɜːtʃ/ [US] /-ˈsmɝːtʃ/ *verb* [T] *LITERARY* to say bad things about someone to influence other people's opinion of them: *His accusations were false, but they served to besmirch her* ***reputation****.*

besotted /bɪˈsɒt.ɪd/ [US] /-ˈsɑː.t̬ɪd/ *adj* completely in love and therefore likely to behave in an unusual way or be foolish: *He was so completely besotted* ***with*** *her that he couldn't see how badly she treated him.*

besought /bɪˈsɔːt/ [US] /-sɑːt/ *past simple and past participle of* **beseech**

bespeak /bɪˈspiːk/ *verb* [T] **bespoke**, **bespoken** *FORMAL* to suggest or show: *His letter bespeaks his willingness to help.*

bespectacled /bɪˈspek.tɪ.kl̩d/ *adj FORMAL* wearing glasses: *a small, bespectacled man in a drab suit*

bespoke *UK FORMAL* /bɪˈspəʊk/ [US] /-ˈspoʊk/ *adj* (*US* **custom-made**) specially made to for a particular person: *a bespoke suit* ○ *bespoke furniture*

beˌspoke ˈtailor *noun* [C] *UK FORMAL* a person who makes or sells clothing that is specially made for the customer

best [SUPERLATIVE OF GOOD] /best/ *adj* of the highest quality, or being the most suitable, pleasing or effective type of thing or person: *This is the best meal I've ever had.* ○ *He's one of our best students.* ○ *Are you sure this is the best way of doing it?* ○ *What's the best* (= shortest or quickest) *way to get to the station?* ○ *Your parents only want what is best* ***for*** *you.* ○ *She was my best* ***friend*** (= the friend for whom I had the most affection). ○ ***It's*** *best* (= It is wise) ***to*** *get to the supermarket early.*

• **the best of a bad bunch/lot** the person or thing of a group that is not as bad as the others, although none of the group is good

• **be on *your* best behaviour** to behave extremely well and be very polite on a particular occasion: *I'd just met his parents for the first time so I was on my best behaviour.*

• **May the best man/person win.** said before a race or competitive activity, meaning that you want the person who is the fastest, strongest or most skilled to win or succeed

• **put *your* best foot forward** to try as hard as you can

• **be the best thing since sliced bread** *INFORMAL* to be an excellent person or thing

• **with the best will in the world** *UK* used to mean 'I would like to if I possibly could', in a situation where you cannot do something: *With the best will in the world, I can't employ him in the shop unless I can trust him.*

best [SUPERLATIVE OF WELL] /best/ *adv* **1** in the most suitable, pleasing or satisfactory way, or to the greatest degree: *Which evening would suit you best for the party?* ○ *The Grand Canyon is best seen at sunset when it seems to change colour.* ○ *He couldn't decide which one he* ***liked*** *best* (= preferred). **2** to the greatest degree when used as the superlative of adjectives beginning with 'good' or 'well': *They were the best-dressed couple at the party.* ○ *He was voted the best-looking* (= most attractive) *actor in Hollywood.*

• **as best *you* can** *MAINLY UK* as well as you can: *It is a difficult passage, but just translate it as best you can.*

• **do as *you* think best** to choose the action that you judge to be most suitable: *"Do you think I should take this job or try for another?" "You should do as you think best."*

• **had best/better** *MAINLY UK* used to suggest an action or to show that it is necessary: *You had best tell her* (= It would be wise if you told her) *that you won't be able to come to her party.* ○ *We'd best be going now* (= We should go now).

best [EXCELLENT] /best/ *noun* [S] the most excellent in a group of things or people: *My tastes are simple – I only like* ***the*** *best.* ○ *He wanted* ***the*** *best for his children – good schools, a nice house and trips abroad.* ○ *I like all of Hitchcock's films, but I think 'Notorious' is* ***the*** *best.* ○ *Chris and I are* ***the*** *best* ***of*** *friends* (= We are very close friends).

• **all the best!** *MAINLY UK INFORMAL* used to say goodbye or to end a letter to someone you know well

• **at best** even when considered in the most positive way: *The food was bland at best, and at worst completely inedible.*

• **at *its* best** at the highest standard achievable: *The documentary was an example of investigative journalism at its best.*

• **be at *your* best** to be as active or intelligent as you can be: *I'm not at my best in the morning.*

• **at the best of times** when everything is going well: *Our car is slow* ***even*** *at the best of times.*

• **best of all** this is the most pleasing thing: *There was wonderful food, good company and, best of all, a jazz band.*

• **best of luck** an expression used to wish someone success before an exam or a difficult activity: *Best of luck* ***with*** *your exams!* ○ *We would like to wish you* ***the*** *(very) best of luck* ***with*** *your move to the States.*

• **the best of both worlds** a situation in which you can enjoy the advantages of two very different things at the same time: *She works in the city and lives in the country, so she* ***gets*** *the best of both worlds.*

• **the best of** In a sport such as tennis, if you play the best of a particular number of games, you play that number of games and the winner is the player who wins the greatest number of those games: *Shall we play the best of five?*

• **do/try *your* best** to make the greatest effort possible: *It doesn't matter if you fail, just do your best.*

• **have had the best of** If you have had the best of something, you have enjoyed the most pleasant part of it, and everything that is left is worse: *I think we've already had the best of the hot weather this summer.*

B

• **make the best of** to make an unsatisfactory situation as pleasant as possible: *We'll have to spend the night here, so we might as well make the best of it.*
• **for the best** If an action is for the best, it is done to improve a situation or produce a good result, although it might seem unpleasant at the time: *Ending a relationship is always hard but in this case it's definitely for the best.*
• **to the best of *your* ability** as well as you can: *Just do the job to the best of your ability.*
• **to the best of *my* knowledge/belief** from what I know and understand from the information that I have: *To the best of my knowledge, the chemicals which were found are not dangerous.*
• **with the best of them** *INFORMAL* as well as anyone: *He can dance with the best of them.*

best [DEFEAT] /best/ *verb* **[T]** *FORMAL* to defeat someone in a fight or competition: *He bested his opponent in just two rounds.*

best-before date /ˌbest.bɪˈfɔːˌdeɪt/ [US] /-ˈfɔːr-/ *noun* **[C]** the day or month before which food or drink should be eaten or drunk

ˌbest ˈbet *noun* **[C usually sing]** *INFORMAL* Your best bet is the action which is most likely to be successful: *If you want to get to the station before 10 o'clock, your best bet would be to take a taxi.*

bestial /ˈbes.ti.əl/ *adj DISAPPROVING* cruel or animal-like: *The soldiers were accused of bestial acts against unarmed civilians.*
bestiality /ˌbes.tiˈæl.ə.ti/ [US] /-t̬i/ *noun* **[U]** *DISAPPROVING the bestiality* (= cruelty) *of war* ➲See also **bestiality**.

bestiality /ˌbes.tiˈæl.ə.ti/ [US] /-t̬i/ *noun* **[U]** sex between a person and an animal ➲See also **bestiality** at **bestial**.

bestiary /ˈbes.ti.ə.ri/ [US] /-er.i/ *noun* **[C]** a book written in the Middle Ages containing descriptions of real and imaginary animals which was intended to teach morals and to entertain

bestir *yourself* /bɪˈstɜːʳ/ [US] /-ˈstɝː/ *verb* **[R]** *FORMAL* to become active after a period of rest: *I'd better bestir myself – there's work to be done.*

ˌbest ˈman *noun* **[S]** a male friend or relative of the BRIDEGROOM who stands with him and helps him during a marriage ceremony

bestow /bɪˈstəʊ/ [US] /-ˈstoʊ/ *verb* **[T often passive]** *FORMAL* to give something as an honour or present: *The Chancellorship of the University was bestowed **upon** her in 1992.* ○ *The George Cross is a decoration that is bestowed **on** British civilians for acts of great bravery.* **bestowal** /bɪˈstəʊ.əl/ [US] /-ˈstoʊ-/ *noun* **[U]** *Her father's blessing represented a bestowal of consent **upon** her forthcoming marriage.*

ˌbest ˈpractice *noun* **[C or U]** a working method, or set of working methods, which is officially accepted as being the best to use in a particular business or industry, usually described formally and in detail: *to develop a model for best practice in medicine/electronic commerce* ○ *a best-practice policy/programme*

bestrew /bɪˈstruː/ *verb* **[T usually passive]** **bestrewed, bestrewn** or **bestrewed** *LITERARY* to lie covering a surface, or to cover a surface with things that are far apart and in no particular arrangement: *During the festival, the city streets are bestrewn **with** flowers.*

bestride /bɪˈstraɪd/ *verb* **[T]** **bestrode, bestridden** *FORMAL* to sit or stand with a leg on either side of an object or animal: *He bestrode the chair as though it were a horse.*

bestseller /ˌbestˈsel.əʳ/ [US] /-ɚ/ *noun* **[C]** a book which is extremely popular and has sold in very large numbers: *J K Rowling's 'Harry Potter' novels are all bestsellers.* ○ *His latest book has gone to number two in the bestseller **list*** (= the list of the most popular books).
best-selling /ˌbestˈsel.ɪŋ/ *adj* **[before n]** *She's a best-selling **author*** (= an author whose books are very popular).

ˌbest ˈwishes *plural noun* a polite way of finishing a letter to a person whom you know quite well

bet /bet/ *verb* **betting, bet, bet 1** **[I or T]** to risk money on the result of an event or a competition, such as a horse race, in the hope of winning more money: *He regularly goes to the races and bets heavily.* ○ *She bet £500 000 **on** the horse which came in second.* ○ **[+ two objects + *that*]** *I bet you $25 **that** I'll get there before you.* **2** **[T]** *INFORMAL* If you say you bet (someone) that something is true or will happen, you mean you are certain that it is true or will happen: **[+ obj + (*that*)]** *I bet you **(that)** she's missed the bus.* ○ **[+ (*that*)]** *I bet **(that)** he won't come.*
• **I bet** (*ALSO* **I'll bet**) *INFORMAL* said to show that you understand why someone has a particular opinion or feels a particular way: *"I'm so annoyed with her." "I'll bet."* ○ *"I was so relieved I didn't have to clean up after the party." "I bet you were."*
• **you bet** *INFORMAL* used to emphasize a statement or to mean 'certainly': *"Are you coming to the party?" "You bet!"*
• **(how much) do you want to bet?** *INFORMAL* said in answer to something that someone has said, meaning that you are certain that they are wrong: *"Surely she won't be late this time." "How much do you want to bet?"*
• **don't bet on it** (*ALSO* **I wouldn't bet on it**) *INFORMAL* used to tell someone that you think something is unlikely to be true or to happen: *"Do you think they'll give me back the money they owe me?" "I wouldn't bet on it."*
• **you can bet your life** (*ALSO* **you can bet your bottom dollar**) used to say that you are completely certain that something is true or will happen: *You can bet your bottom dollar **that** he'll be the next president.*

bet /bet/ *noun* **[C]** **1** an amount of money which you risk on the result of an event or a competition, such as a horse race: *He **placed/put** a bet **on** the grey horse.* **2** *INFORMAL* a guess or opinion: **[+ (*that*)]** *My bet is **(that)** their baby will be a girl.*
• ***do sth* for a bet** (*US USUALLY* ***do sth* on a bet**) to do something dangerous or risky because someone say that they do not think you will: *She jumped in the fountain for a bet.*
• **a fair bet** *UK* something which is likely to happen: *It's a fair bet **(that)** the government will increase taxes in the coming term.*
• **a good bet** something that would be useful, clever or enjoyable to do: *Putting your savings in a high-interest account is a good bet.*
• **your best bet** the best decision or choice: *Your best bet would be to take a bus to the airport.*
• **a safe bet** something that you are certain will happen: *It's a safe bet **(that)** Martin will be the last to arrive.*
betting /ˈbet.ɪŋ/ [US] /ˈbet̬-/ *noun* **[U]** the habit of putting bets on horse races, sports events, etc: *Betting can be as addictive as drinking or smoking.*

beta, β /ˈbiː.tə/ [US] /ˈbeɪ.t̬ə/ *noun* **[C]** the second letter of the Greek alphabet ➲Compare **alpha**; **gamma**.

beta-carotene /ˌbiː.təˈkær.ə.tiːn/ [US] /ˌbeɪ.t̬əˈker-/ *noun* **[U]** a form of CAROTENE which the body is able to change into vitamin A, found especially in green, red and orange vegetables

betel /ˈbiː.tᵊl/ [US] /-t̬ᵊl/ *noun* **[U]** a plant that grows in south east Asia which has leaves and red nuts that act as a drug when chewed

bête noire /betˈnwɑːʳ/ [US] /-ˈnwɑːr/ *noun* **[C]** *plural* **bêtes noires** a person or thing that you particularly dislike or that annoys you: *My particular bête noire is cigarette ends being left in half-empty glasses.*

betide /bɪˈtaɪd/ *verb* **[I or T]** *LITERARY* to happen (to) ➲See **woe betide** at **woe**.

betoken /bɪˈtəʊ.kᵊn/ [US] /-ˈtoʊ-/ *verb* **[T]** *OLD USE* to be a sign of something

betray [NOT LOYAL] /bɪˈtreɪ/ *verb* **[T]** **1** to not be loyal to your country or a person, often by doing something harmful such as helping their enemies: *He was accused of betraying his country during the war.* ○ *She felt betrayed by her mother's lack of support.* ○ *For years they betrayed Britain's secrets **to** Russia.* ○ *FORMAL He promised never to betray her* (= never to leave her for another person). **2** *FORMAL* If someone betrays something such as a promise, they do not do what they said they would: *The government has been accused of betraying its election promises.* ○ *By staying out so late, they have betrayed my trust* (= disappointed me because I had trusted them to not be late). **betrayal** /bɪˈtreɪ.əl/ *noun* **[C or U]** *I felt a sense of betrayal when my friends refused to support me.* ○ *This was the first in a series of betrayals.*

betray [SHOW] /bɪˈtreɪ/ *verb* [T] to show feelings, thoughts or a particular characteristic without intending to: *If he is nervous on stage, he does not betray it.* ○ *Although she often seems quite cold and harsh, her smiling eyes betray her true nature.*

betroth /bɪˈtrəʊð/ [US] /-ˈtroʊð/ *verb* [T] OLD USE to cause someone to promise formally to marry someone: *She was betrothed* ***to*** *her cousin at an early age.* **betrothal** /bɪˈtrəʊ.ðəl/ [US] /-ˈtroʊ-/ *noun* [C] *The play revolves round the betrothal of a duke* ***to*** *a doctor's daughter.*

betrothed /bɪˈtrəʊðd/ [US] /-ˈtroʊðd/ *noun* [S] FORMAL OR OLD USE *He sent a dozen roses to his betrothed* (= the woman whom he had promised to marry).

better [COMPARATIVE OF GOOD] /ˈbet.əʳ/ [US] /ˈbeţ.ɚ/ *adj* **1** of a higher standard, or more suitable, pleasing or effective than other things or people: *He stood near the front to get a better view.* ○ *Relations between the two countries have never been better.* ○ *The film was better* ***than*** *I expected.* ○ *She is much better* ***at*** *tennis than I am.* ○ *It is* ***far*** (= much) *better to save some of your money than to spend it all at once.* ○ *Fresh vegetables are better* ***for*** *you* (= more beneficial to you) *than canned ones.* ○ *The longer you keep this wine,* ***the*** *better it tastes* (= It has a better flavour if you keep it for a long time). ○ *The bed was hard, but it was better* ***than nothing*** (= than not having a bed). **2** If you are or get better after an illness or injury, you are healthy and no longer ill: *I hope you* ***get*** *better soon.*

• **better luck next time** said to tell someone that you hope they will succeed when they try again: *I'm sorry to hear that you failed your driving test. Better luck next time, eh!*

• **be better than sex** INFORMAL to be extremely enjoyable or exciting: *For me, nothing compares with the thrill of surfing - it's better than sex.*

• **get better** to improve: *After the cease-fire, the situation in the capital got better.* ○ *She's getting much better at pronouncing English words.*

• **go one better** to do something which is more advanced or more generous than someone else: *I gave her a card, but my brother went one better and bought her a present.*

• **no better than (a)** ***sth*** If you say that someone is no better than a person who is unpleasant or unkind, you mean that they have behaved in a similar way to this type of person: *People who don't pay their bus fares are no better than common criminals.*

• **Better late than never.** SAYING said when you think that it is better for someone or something to be late than never to arrive or to happen

• **Better safe than sorry.** SAYING said when you think it is best not to take risks even when it seems boring or difficult to be careful

• **Better the devil you know (than the devil you don't).** UK SAYING said when you think it is wiser to deal with someone familiar, although you do not like them, than to deal with someone who you do not know, who might be worse

better [COMPARATIVE OF WELL] /ˈbet.əʳ/ [US] /ˈbeţ.ɚ/ *adv* **1** in a more suitable, pleasing or satisfactory way, or to a greater degree: *The next time he took the test, he was better prepared.* ○ *She did much better* (= was more successful) *in the second half of the match.* ○ *I* ***like*** *this jacket much better than* (= I prefer it to) *the other one.* ○ *She knows her way around the college better* ***than*** *I do.* **2** to a greater degree, when used as the comparative of adjectives beginning with 'good' or 'well': *She is better-looking* (= more attractive) *than her brother.* ○ *He is much better-known for his poetry than his song-writing.*

• **better still** (ALSO **even better**) used to say that a particular choice would be more satisfactory: *Why don't you give her a call or, better still, go and see her?*

• ***sb*** **would do better** UK it would be wiser: *You would do better* ***to*** *bring the plants inside in the winter.*

• ***sb*** **had better** ***do sth*** used to give advice or to make a threat: *You'd better* (= You should) *go home now before the rain starts.* ○ *He'd better pay me back that money he owes me soon,* ***or else***.

better [IMPROVEMENT] /ˈbet.əʳ/ [US] /ˈbeţ.ɚ/ *noun* [U] **1** something that is of a higher standard than others: *He ran the 100 metres in 9.91 seconds, and I have not seen better* (= a faster result) *this year.* **2** behaviour, work or treatment that is more suitable, pleasing or satisfactory: *You shouldn't have been so mean to your mother – she* ***deserves*** *better.* ○ *I didn't think he would go out without telling me – I expected better* ***of*** *him.*

• **so much the better** (ALSO **all the better**) INFORMAL used to say that a particular action or situation would be even more successful: *If you can go there this afternoon, so much the better.*

• **for better or (for) worse** If you do something for better or (for) worse, you accept the bad results of the action as well as the good ones: *Anyway, for better or for worse, I followed her advice.*

• **for the better** If something changes for the better, it improves: *Most people think that things have changed for the better since the new government came to power.*

• **get the better of** ***sb*** **1** to defeat someone in a competition: *He fought fiercely, but his opponent easily got the better of him.* **2** If a feeling gets the better of you, you cannot stop yourself from allowing that feeling to make you do something, despite knowing that what you are doing is wrong: *Her curiosity got the better of her and she opened the door and peeped inside.*

betters /ˈbet.əz/ [US] /ˈbeţ.ɚz/ *plural noun* OLD-FASHIONED people of a higher rank or social position than you: *As children, we were taught not to argue with our* ***elders and*** *betters.*

better [IMPROVE] /ˈbet.əʳ/ [US] /ˈbeţ.ɚ/ *verb* [T] to improve a situation: *The organization was established to better conditions for the disabled.*

ˈ**better** ***yourself*** *verb* [R] to improve your social position, often by getting a better job or education: *He tried to better himself by taking evening classes.*

betterment /ˈbet.ə.mənt/ [US] /ˈbeţ.ɚ-/ *noun* [U] *Several changes have been made for the betterment* (= improvement) *of the sport.*

ˌ**better ˈhalf** *noun* [S] HUMOROUS A person's better half is their husband, wife or usual sexual partner.

ˌ**better ˈnature** *noun* [C usually sing] A person's better nature is the more honourable or moral side of their character.

ˌ**better ˈoff** [MORE MONEY] *adj* **be better off** to have more money than you had in the past or more money than most other people: *Obviously we're better off now we're both working.* ○ *When his parents died, he found himself $100 000 better off* (= he had $100 000 more than he had in the past).

the better-off /ðəˌbet.əˈrɒf/ [US] /-ˌbeţ.ɚˈɑːf/ *plural noun* people who have more money than most others: *The tax on fuel will not have a serious impact on the better-off, but it will greatly affect the poor.*

ˌ**better ˈoff** [BETTER SITUATION] *adj* **be better off** to be in a better situation, if or after something happens: *He'd be better off working for a bigger company.*

ˈ**betting** ˌ**shop** *noun* [C] UK a place where people go to bet on horse races or other sports events

between [SPACE] /bɪˈtwiːn/ *prep, adv* **1** in or into the space which separates two places, people or objects: *The town lies halfway between Rome and Florence.* ○ *Standing between the two adults was a small child.* ○ *She squeezed between the parked cars and ran out into the road.* ○ *A narrow path ran* ***in*** *between the two houses.* **2** If something is between two amounts, it is greater than the first amount but smaller than the second: *She weighs between 55 and 60 kilograms.* ○ *The competition is open to children between six and twelve years of age.* ○ *The room was either extremely cold or hot, never anything* ***in*** *between* (= in the middle).

between [TIME] /bɪˈtwiːn/ *prep, adv* (ALSO **in between**) in the period of time which separates two different times or events: *You shouldn't eat in between meals.* ○ *There is a break of ten minutes between classes.* ○ *The shop is closed for lunch between 12.30 and 1.30.*

• **between times** during the periods between the separate events mentioned: *If you only go to the supermarket once a month, what do you do between times?*

between [AMONG] /bɪˈtwiːn/ *prep* **1** among two or more people or things: *The money was divided equally between several worthy causes.* ○ *We drank two bottles of wine between four of us.* ○ *Trade between the two countries* (=

Their trade with each other) *has increased sharply in the past year.* ○ *There is a great deal of similarity between Caroline and her mother* (= They are very similar). ○ *You'll have to* ***choose*** *between* (= choose either) *a holiday or a new washing machine.* ○ *She was* ***torn*** *between loyalty to her father and love for her husband* (= She could not decide which one to support). **2** A discussion, argument or game between two or more people or groups of people involves both people or groups: *The negotiations between the union and management have broken down.* ○ *There has always been a fierce rivalry between the two clubs.* ○ *Tonight's game is between the New Orleans Saints and the Los Angeles Rams.*

• **between you and me** (*US ALSO* **between us**) an expression used to tell someone that what you are about to say should be kept secret: *Don't tell this to anyone else – it's just between you and me.*

between [CONNECTING] /bɪˈtwiːn/ *prep* **1** connecting two or more places, things or people: *There is a regular train service between Glasgow and Edinburgh.* ○ *The survey shows a link between asthma and air pollution.* **2** from one place to another: *He commutes daily between Leeds and Manchester.*

between [SEPARATING] /bɪˈtwiːn/ *prep* separating two places or things: *The wall between East and West Berlin came down in 1989.* ○ *The report states that the gap between the rich and the poor has increased dramatically over the past decade.*

betwixt /bɪˈtwɪkst/, *OLD USE* **betwixt and between** between two positions, choices or ideas and unable or unwilling to decide between them

bevel /ˈbev.ᵊl/ *noun* **[C] 1** a sloping edge **2** a tool used to make a sloping edge

bevel /ˈbev.ᵊl/ *verb* **[T] -ll-** or *US USUALLY* **-l-** to give something, such as a piece of wood or metal, a sloping edge: *He bevelled the edges of the bookcase.*

bevelled *UK, MAINLY US* **beveled** /ˈbev.ᵊld/ *adj* having a sloping edge or surface: *A picture frame often has bevelled* ***edges****.*

beverage /ˈbev.ᵊr.ɪdʒ/ [US] /-ɚ-/ *noun* **[C]** *FORMAL* a drink of any type: ***Hot*** *beverages include tea, coffee and hot chocolate.* ○ *We do not sell* ***alcoholic*** *beverages.*

bevvy /ˈbev.i/ *noun* **[C]** *UK SLANG* an alcoholic drink: *Are you coming down the pub for a bevvy?*

bevy /ˈbev.i/ *noun* **[C]** a large group of people, especially women or girls, or a large group of similar things: *Victorian postcards often featured bevies* ***of*** *bathing beauties.*

bewail /bɪˈweɪl/ *verb* **[T]** *LITERARY* to express great sadness or disappointment about something: *He bewailed his misfortune and the loss of his most treasured possessions.*

beware /bɪˈweəʳ/ [US] /-ˈwer/ *verb* **1 [I or T]** used to warn someone to be very careful about something or someone: *Beware salespeople who promise offers that seem too good to be true.* ○ *You should beware* ***of*** *undercooked food when staying in hot countries.* ○ *Beware* ***of*** *falling asleep while sunbathing.* * NOTE: **Beware** is only used in the imperative or infinitive form. **2 [I]** used on signs to warn people of something dangerous: *Beware* ***of*** *the dog.* ○ *Beware – poisonous chemicals.*

USAGE

beware

You can only use this verb in the infinitive form or as an order.

Beware of the dog.
Beware of giving your credit card number to register on a website.

bewigged /bɪˈwɪgd/ *adj LITERARY* wearing a covering of artificial hair on the head

bewilder /bɪˈwɪl.dəʳ/ [US] /-dɚ/ *verb* **[T]** to confuse someone: *The instructions completely bewildered me.*

bewildered /bɪˈwɪl.dəd/ [US] /-dɚd/ *adj*: *Arriving in a strange city at night, I felt alone and bewildered.*

bewildering /bɪˈwɪl.dᵊr.ɪŋ/ [US] /-dɚ.ɪŋ/ *adj* **1** confusing and difficult to understand: *He gave me directions to his house, but I found them utterly bewildering.* **2** making you feel confused because you cannot decide what you want: *The college offers a bewildering range of courses.*

bewilderment /bɪˈwɪl.də.mənt/ [US] /-dɚ-/ *noun* **[U]** *a state of bewilderment* ○ *As he walked through the door, she stared at him* ***in*** *utter bewilderment.*

bewitch /bɪˈwɪtʃ/ *verb* **1 [T often passive]** to charm someone greatly so that you have the power to influence them: *He was bewitched by her beauty.* **2 [T]** to put a magic spell on someone or something in order to control them

bewitching /bɪˈwɪtʃ.ɪŋ/ *adj* so beautiful or attractive that you cannot think about anything else: *He was mesmerized by her bewitching green eyes.*

beyond [FURTHER AWAY] /biˈɒnd/ [US] /-ˈɑːnd/ *prep, adv* further away in the distance (than something): *In the distance, beyond the river, was a small town.* ○ *From the top of the hill we could see our house and the woods beyond.*

beyond [OUTSIDE A LIMIT] /biˈɒnd/ [US] /-ˈɑːnd/ *prep, adv* **1** outside or after (a stated limit): *Few people live beyond the age of a hundred.* ○ *We cannot allow the work to continue beyond the end of the year.* ○ *I've got nothing to tell you beyond* (= in addition to) *what I told you earlier.* ○ *The repercussions will be felt throughout the industry and beyond* (= in other areas). ○ *His thoughtlessness is beyond* ***belief*** (= is so great that it is impossible to believe). ○ *LITERARY Her beauty is beyond* ***compare*** (= is so great that nothing can be compared to it). ○ *Tonight's performance has been cancelled due to* ***circumstances*** *beyond* ***our control*** (= events which we are unable to deal with). ○ *She has always lived beyond her* ***means*** (= spent more than she has earned). ○ *He survived the accident, but his car was damaged beyond* ***repair*** (= damaged so badly it could not be repaired). **2** *INFORMAL* If something is beyond you, you are unable to understand it: *I'm afraid physics is completely beyond me.*

• **from beyond the grave** after a person has died

• **beyond a joke** If something is beyond a joke, it has stopped being amusing and is now a serious matter: *I used to think he was funny, but his behaviour has now gone way beyond a joke.*

• **beyond the pale** If someone's behaviour is beyond the pale, it is unacceptable: *Her recent conduct is beyond the pale.*

• **beyond reasonable doubt** *UK* (*US* **beyond a reasonable doubt**) *LEGAL* If a legal case or a person's guilt is proved beyond reasonable doubt, there is enough proof for the person accused of a crime to be judged guilty: *Her guilt was established beyond reasonable doubt.*

• **beyond a shadow of a doubt** If you know or believe something beyond a shadow of a doubt, you are certain that it is true: *He is responsible beyond a shadow of a doubt.*

• **beyond *your* wildest dreams** to a degree or in a way you had never thought possible: *Suddenly she was rich beyond her wildest dreams.* ○ *The scheme succeeded beyond my wildest dreams.*

BF, bf *INTERNET ABBREVIATION FOR* boyfriend

BFPO /ˌbiː.ef.piːˈəʊ/ [US] /-ˈoʊ/ *noun* **[U]** *ABBREVIATION FOR* British Forces Post Office: *BFPO is used as part of an address for letters sent to members of the British armed forces living in other countries.*

<bg> *INTERNET ABBREVIATION FOR* big grin: used to show that you are smiling a lot in an e-mail or when talking to someone in a discussion in a CHAT ROOM

bhaji, bhajee /ˈbɑː.dʒi/ *noun* **[C]** a spicy Indian cake made of vegetables, flour, egg and water, which is fried in oil: *an onion bhaji*

bi- [TWICE] /baɪ-/ *prefix* twice, or once every two: *We meet bi-monthly* (= twice every month or once every two months).

bi- [TWO] /baɪ-/ *prefix* having two: *a biped* (= an animal which walks on two legs) ○ *a biplane* (= an old-fashioned aircraft with two wings)

biannual /baɪˈæn.ju.əl/ *adj* **[before n]** happening twice a year: *The committee has just published its biannual report.* ➲Compare **annual** EVERY YEAR; **biennial**.

bias [PREFERENCE] /ˈbaɪ.əs/ *noun* **1 [C usually sing; U]** a tendency to support or oppose a particular person or thing in an unfair way by allowing personal opinions to influence

B

your judgment: *The government has accused the media of bias.* ○ *Reporters must be impartial and not show political bias.* ○ *There was clear evidence of a strong bias* ***against*** *her.* ○ *There has always been a slight bias* ***in favour of/towards*** *employing arts graduates in the company.* **2** [C usually sing] a preference towards a particular subject or thing: *She showed a scientific bias at an early age.*

bias /ˈbaɪ.əs/ *verb* [T] **-ss-** or *US USUALLY* **-s-** *The judge ruled that the information should be withheld on the grounds that it would bias the jury* ***against*** (= influence them unfairly against) *the accused.*

biased, *UK ALSO* **biassed** /ˈbaɪ.əst/ *adj* showing an unreasonable like or dislike for a person based on personal opinions: *The newspapers gave a very biased report of the meeting.* ○ *I think she's beautiful but then I'm biased since she's my daughter.* * NOTE: The opposite is **unbiased**.

bias [CLOTHING] /ˈbaɪ.əs/ *noun* [U] *SPECIALIZED* a direction at a angle across the threads of woven material: *The dresses in his new winter collection are all cut* ***on the*** *bias* (= in a diagonal direction across the cloth).

biathlon /baɪˈæθ.lən/ Ⓤⓢ /-lɑːn/ *noun* [C] a sports competition which combines skiing and shooting a rifle ➲Compare **decathlon**; **heptathlon**; **pentathlon**.

bib /bɪb/ *noun* [C] a cover made of cloth or plastic which is worn by young children when eating to protect their clothes

• **your best bib and tucker** *UK OLD-FASHIONED* your best clothes which you wear on special occasions

Bible /ˈbaɪ.bl̩/ *noun* [C or S] **1** (*ALSO* **Holy Bible**) (a copy of) the holy book of the Christian religion consisting of the Old and New Testaments, or the holy book of the Jewish religion consisting of the Law, the Prophets and the Writings: *In* ***the*** *Bible it says that Adam and Eve were the first human beings.* ○ *Her parents gave her a bible when she was a young child.* ○ *Bible-****reading*** *classes are held in the church hall every Thursday evening.* **2 bible** a book, magazine, etc. which gives important advice and information about a particular subject: *Vogue magazine quickly became the bible* ***of*** *fashionable women.*

biblical /ˈbɪb.lɪ.kəl/ *adj* in or relating to the Bible: *They named their son Isaac after the biblical character.*

• **but not in the biblical sense** *HUMOROUS* If you say you know someone but not in the biblical sense, you mean you have not had sex with them: *"Did you know her?" "Yes – not in the biblical sense, of course."*

Bible-basher /ˈbaɪ.bl̩ˌbæʃ.əʳ/ ʊʃ /-ɚ/ *noun* [C] (*MAINLY US* **Bible-thumper**) *INFORMAL DISAPPROVING* someone who tries in a forceful or enthusiastic way to persuade other people to believe in the Christian religion and the Bible

Bible-bashing /ˈbaɪ.bl̩ˌbæʃ.ɪŋ/ *adj* [before n] (*MAINLY US* **Bible-thumping**) *She was born in the Bible-thumping Arkansas town of Lonoke.*

the ˈBible ˌBelt *noun* [S] the southern and central regions of the United States where many people have traditional Christian beliefs

bibliography /ˌbɪb.liˈɒg.rə.fi/ Ⓤⓢ /-ˈɑː.grə-/ *noun* [C] a list of the books and articles that have been used by someone when writing a particular book or article: *Other sources of information are found in the bibliography at the end of this article.*

bibliophile /ˈbɪb.li.ə.faɪl/ *noun* [C] *FORMAL* a person who loves or collects books

bicameral /ˌbaɪˈkæm.ər.əl/ Ⓤⓢ /-ɚ.əl/ *adj SPECIALIZED* (of a government group) with two parts, such as the Senate and the House of Representatives in the United States: *a bicameral legislature*

bicarb /ˈbaɪ.kɑːb/ Ⓤⓢ /-kɑːrb/ *noun* [U] *INFORMAL* **bicarbonate of soda**

bicarbonate of soda *MAINLY UK* /baɪˌkɑː.bən.ət.əvˈsəʊ.də/ Ⓤⓢ /-ˌkɑːr.bən.ət.əvˈsoʊ-/ *noun* [U] (*MAINLY US* **baking soda**) a white powder used to make foods rise in baking: *Mix together 250g plain flour and a teaspoon of bicarbonate of soda and then add to the cake mixture.*

bicentenary /ˌbaɪ.senˈten.ər.i/ /-ˈtiː.nər-/ Ⓤⓢ /ˈten.ɚ-/ *noun* [C] (*US* **bicentennial**) the day or year which is 200 years after a particular event, especially an important one; the 200th ANNIVERSARY: *A statue was erected to mark the bicentenary* ***of*** *the composer's birth.* ○ *bicentenary celebrations*

bicentennial /ˌbaɪ.senˈten.i.əl/ /-sən-/ *noun, adj US FOR* **bicentenary**: *bicentennial celebrations*

biceps /ˈbaɪ.seps/ *noun* [C] *plural* **biceps** the large muscle at the front of the upper arm ➲Compare **triceps**.

bicker /ˈbɪk.əʳ/ Ⓤⓢ /-ɚ/ *verb* [I] *DISAPPROVING* to argue about unimportant matters: *Will you two stop bickering!* ○ *They're always bickering* ***with*** *each other* ***about/over*** *their personal problems.* **bickering** /ˈbɪk.ər.ɪŋ/ Ⓤⓢ /ˈ-ɚ-/ *noun* [U] *The council finally elected a leader after several days of bickering.*

bickie *UK* /ˈbɪk.i/ *noun* [C] (*AUS ALSO* **bikkie**) *INFORMAL FOR* **biscuit** FLAT CAKE: *I've bought a packet of choccy* (= chocolate) *bickies for tea.*

bicycle /ˈbaɪ.sɪ.kl̩/ *noun* [C] a two-wheeled vehicle that you sit on and move by turning the two PEDALS (= flat parts you press with your feet): *I go to work* ***by*** *bicycle.* ○ *He* ***got on*** *his bicycle and rode off.* ○ *You should never* ***ride*** *your bicycle without lights at night.*

bid [OFFER] /bɪd/ *verb* **bidding**, **bid**, **bid** **1** [I or T] to offer a particular amount of money for something which is for sale and compete against other people to buy it, especially at a public sale of goods or property: *She knew she couldn't afford it, so she didn't bid.* ○ *The communications group has shown an interest in bidding* ***for*** *the company.* ○ *A foreign collector has bid £500 000* ***for*** *the portrait.* ○ [+ two objects] *What am I bid* ***for*** *this fine vase?* **2** [I] If two or more people bid for a job, they compete with each other to do the work by offering to do it for a particular amount of money: *The department is trying to ensure fairer competition among firms bidding* ***for*** *government contracts.* **3** [T + *to* infinitive] If someone bids to do something, they compete with other people to do it: *Paris is bidding* ***to*** *host the next Olympics.*

bid /bɪd/ *noun* [C] **1** an offer of a particular amount of money for something which is for sale: *I* ***made*** *a bid of $150* ***for*** *the painting.* ○ *She* ***made/put in*** *a bid of £69 000 for the flat, which was accepted.* **2** an offer to do something when you are competing with other people to do it: [+ *to* infinitive] *Sydney* ***made*** *a successful bid* ***to*** *host the Olympic Games.* ○ *I gave the job to the contractors who* ***made/gave*** *the lowest bid* (= who offered to do the work for the lowest amount of money). **3** an attempt to achieve or obtain something: *Her bid* ***for*** *re-election was unsuccessful.* ○ *The company has managed to fight off a hostile* ***takeover*** *bid* (= an attempt by another company to take control of it). ○ *The government has reduced the cost of borrowing in a bid* ***to*** *get the economy moving again.*

bidder /ˈbɪd.əʳ/ Ⓤⓢ /-ɚ/ *noun* [C] *In an auction, goods or property are sold to the* ***highest*** *bidder* (= the person who offers the most money for it).

bidding /ˈbɪd.ɪŋ/ *noun* [U] **1** when people offer to pay a particular amount of money for something: *Most of the bidding was done by telephone.* **2 open the bidding** to make the first offer of money for an object at a public sale of goods

bid [TELL] /bɪd/ *verb* [T] **bidding**, **bid**, or **bade**, **bidden** *OLD-FASHIONED* to give a greeting to someone, or to ask someone to do something: [+ two objects] *They bade her good morning.* ○ *I must now bid you* ***farewell*** (= say goodbye to you). ○ *LITERARY She bade her hopes* ***farewell*** (= She stopped being hopeful). ○ [+ (*to*) infinitive] *He bade* (= asked) *them* ***(to)*** *leave at once.*

bidding /ˈbɪd.ɪŋ/ *noun* [U] *OLD-FASHIONED* ***At*** *my grandmother's bidding* (= request), *I wore my best dress.*

ˈbidding ˌwar *noun* [C usually sing] when two or more companies or people compete against each other in order to buy something: *British distributors are currently involved in a bidding war* ***for*** *the film.* ○ *L'Oreal wins bidding war for Maybelline.*

biddy /ˈbɪd.i/ *noun* [C] *INFORMAL DISAPPROVING* an old woman: *an* ***old*** *biddy*

bide /baɪd/ *verb* **bide** your **time** to wait calmly for a good opportunity to do something: *She was biding her time until she could get her revenge.*

bidet /ˈbiː.deɪ/ Ⓤⓢ /bɪˈdeɪ/ *noun* [C] a small low bath in which a person washes their bottom and sex organs

B

biennial /baɪˈen.i.əl/ *adj* happening once every two years ➲Compare **annual** EVERY YEAR; **biannual**. **biennial** /baɪˈen.i.əl/ *noun* [C] a plant that lives for two years, producing seeds and flowers in its second year ➲Compare **annual** PLANT; **perennial** PLANT.

bier /bɪəʳ/ [US] /bɪr/ *noun* [C] a frame on which a dead body or a coffin is carried before a funeral

biff /bɪf/ *verb* [T] INFORMAL to hit someone, especially with the fist: *I biffed him on the jaw.* **biff** /bɪf/ *noun* [C] *a biff on the nose*

bifocals /ˌbaɪˈfəʊ.kəlz/ [US] /-ˈfoʊ-/ *plural noun* glasses with lenses that are divided into two parts. The upper half is for looking at things far away and the lower half is for reading or for looking at things that are near. **bifocal** /ˌbaɪˈfəʊ.kəl/ [US] /-ˈfoʊ-/ *adj*: *bifocal lenses*

bifurcate /ˈbaɪ.fə.keɪt/ [US] /-fɚ-/ *verb* [I] FORMAL (of roads, rivers, branches) to divide into two parts: *A sample of water was taken from the point where the river bifurcates.*

big [LARGE] /bɪg/ *adj* **bigger**, **biggest** **1** large in size or amount: *He's a big man.* ○ *Could I try these shoes in a bigger size?* ○ *They've got a big house in the country.* ○ *She has blonde hair and big blue eyes.* ○ *She's had a big pay rise.* ○ *I had a* ***great*** *big slice of chocolate cake for tea.* ○ *A thousand people took part in the region's biggest-****ever*** *cycle race.* ○ INFORMAL *You write August with a big* (= capital) *'a'.* ○ INFORMAL *She's always been a big* ***spender*** (= She has always spent a lot of money). ○ INFORMAL *You're not a very big* ***eater****, are you?* (= You do not eat a lot). **2** INFORMAL older or more like an adult: *Her big* (= older) ***sister/brother*** *told her to go away.* ○ *I'm ashamed of you. You're big enough to know better* (= at an age where you should know that your behaviour is not acceptable). **3** [before n] INFORMAL used to add emphasis: *You're a big* (= such a) *bully!* ○ *He fell for her* ***in a*** *big* ***way*** (= was greatly attracted to her).

• **be big on *sth*** INFORMAL to like something very much: *I'm not very big on classical music.*

• **be big of *sb*** INFORMAL DISAPPROVING If an action is big of you, it is kind, good, or helpful. This phrase is usually used humorously or angrily to mean the opposite: *You can spare me an hour next week? That's really big of you!*

• **the bigger the better** how valuable or desirable something is is decided by how big it is: *He likes getting big presents – the bigger the better as far as he's concerned.*

big [IMPORTANT] /bɪg/ *adj* **bigger**, **biggest** **1** important, because of being powerful, influential or having a serious effect: *He had a big decision to make.* ○ *There's a big difference between starting up a business and just talking about it.* ○ *The big story in the news this week is the minister's resignation.* ○ *The four biggest banks are all planning to cut their service charges.* **2** INFORMAL **be big in *somewhere/sth*** to be important or famous in a particular place or type of work: *They're big in Japan, but no one's heard of them here.* **3** INFORMAL If a product or activity is big, it is extremely popular: *Grunge music was very big in the early 1990s.*

• **Big deal!** INFORMAL said when you do not think that what someone has said or done is important or special: *"I ran five miles this morning." "Big deal! I ran ten."*

• **be no big deal** INFORMAL to not be a serious problem: *It just means we'll have to pay a little more – it's no big deal.*

• **big fish/gun/noise** (US **big shot/wheel**) INFORMAL a person who has an important or powerful position in a group or organization: *She's a big gun in city politics.* ○ *He's a big shot in advertising.*

• **have big ideas** INFORMAL to have plans which need great effort, skill and luck to achieve: *She's got big ideas* ***about*** *starting up her own company.*

• **What's the big idea?** INFORMAL used to ask someone why they have done something annoying: *What's the big idea? I was watching that programme!*

• **too big for *your* boots** UK (US **too big for *your* britches**) INFORMAL behaving as if you are more important than you really are: *He's been getting a bit too big for his boots since he got that promotion.*

• **make it big** INFORMAL to become famous or successful

• **The bigger they are, the harder they fall.** SAYING said to emphasize that the more important or powerful a person is, the more difficult it is for them when they lose their power or importance

biggie /ˈbɪg.i/ *noun* [C] INFORMAL something which is very important or successful: *The new Schwarzenegger movie will be the Hollywood biggie this summer.*

▲ **big *sb/sth* up** *phrasal verb* [M] INFORMAL to talk a lot about how excellent someone or something is, sometimes praising them or it more than is deserved

bigamy /ˈbɪg.ə.mi/ *noun* [U] the crime of marrying a person while already legally married to someone else: *In court, he admitted that he had* ***committed*** *bigamy.* ➲Compare **monogamy**; **polygamy**. **bigamist** /ˈbɪg.ə.mɪst/ *noun* [C] *He was accused of being a bigamist.* **bigamous** /ˈbɪg.ə.məs/ *adj*: *a bigamous marriage* **bigamously** /ˈbɪg.ə.mə.sli/ *adv*: *She has been married four times, once bigamously.*

the ˌBig ˈApple *noun* [S] INFORMAL New York City: *She's planning a trip to the Big Apple.*

ˌbig ˈband *noun* [C] a large group of musicians who play jazz and dance music, especially in the past: *Big band* ***music*** *was very popular during the 1930s and 40s.*

the ˌbig ˈbang *noun* [S] the large explosion that many scientists believe created the universe

the ˈbig ˌboys *plural noun* INFORMAL the most important people in an activity or organization, or the most powerful and influential businesses in a particular area: *We're only a small business and don't have the capital to compete with the big boys.*

ˌBig ˈBrother *noun* [S] a government, ruler or person in authority that has complete power and tries to control people's behaviour and thoughts, and limit their freedom

ˌbig ˈbucks *plural noun* US FOR **big money**

ˌbig ˈbusiness [BUSINESS] *noun* [U] powerful and influential businesses and financial organizations when considered as a group: *The party receives most of its financial support from big business.*

ˌbig ˈbusiness [POPULAR] *noun* something which makes a lot of money: *Health clubs are big business these days.*

ˌbig ˈcat *noun* [C] a lion, TIGER or other large, wild animal from the cat family: *Tigers are among the rarest of the big cats.*

the ˌbig ˈday *noun* [S] INFORMAL the day when you get married: *When's the big day, then?*

big dipper /ˌbɪgˈdɪp.əʳ/ [US] /-ɚ/ *noun* [C] UK OLD-FASHIONED a small railway in an amusement park which travels very quickly along a narrow track that slopes and bends suddenly

the Big Dipper /ˌbɪgˈdɪp.əʳ/ [US] /-ɚ/ *noun* [S] US FOR **the Plough**, see at **plough**

Bigfoot /ˈbɪg.fʊt/ *noun* [C] (ALSO **Sasquatch**) a large hairy human-like creature reported to exist in the northwestern United States and western Canada

ˌbig ˈgame *noun* [U] large wild animals that are hunted and shot for sport

ˌbig ˈhair *noun* [U] INFORMAL hair that forms a large shape all around the head: *I had really big hair like Farrah Fawcett's.*

big-headed /ˌbɪgˈhed.ɪd/ *adj* DISAPPROVING thinking that you are more important or more clever than you really are: *She's so big-headed!* ➲Compare **swollen head**. **big-head** /ˈbɪg.hed/ *noun* [C] *He's always boasting. He's such a big-head!* ○ *Stop praising him or he'll* ***get*** *a big head.*

big-hearted /ˌbɪgˈhɑːt.ɪd/ [US] /-ˈhɑːr.t̬ɪd/ *adj* kind and generous

ˌbig ˈhitter *noun* [C] an important and influential person or thing, especially of their particular type: *The big hitters in the cast include Michael Caine and Ewan McGregor.*

ˌbig ˈmoney *noun* [U] INFORMAL a large amount of money: *Tournament organizers need to offer big money to attract the top players.*

ˈbig ˌmouth *noun* [C usually sing] INFORMAL DISAPPROVING If someone is or has a big mouth, they tend to say things which are meant to be kept secret: *He* ***is/has*** *such a big mouth.* ○ *He went and* ***opened*** *his big mouth and told them the whole story.*

ˌbig ˈname *noun* [C] *INFORMAL* a famous or important person: *Are there any big names in the movie?* ○ *She's a big name **in** politics.*

bigot /ˈbɪg.ət/ *noun* [C] *DISAPPROVING* a person who has strong, unreasonable beliefs and who thinks that anyone who does not have the same beliefs is wrong: *a religious bigot* ○ *He was known to be a loud-mouthed, opinionated bigot.* **bigoted** /ˈbɪg.ə.tɪd/ Ⓤⓢ /-t̬ɪd/ *adj*: *She's so bigoted that she refuses to accept anyone who doesn't think like her.* **bigotry** /ˈbɪg.ə.tri/ *noun* [U] *religious/racial bigotry*

the ˌBig ˈSmoke *noun* [S] *INFORMAL* a large city, especially London: *I wouldn't like to live in the Big Smoke.*

the ˈbig ˌtime [SUCCESS] *noun* [S] *INFORMAL* the state of being famous or successful: *She finally **hit** the big time* (= became famous or successful) *with her latest novel.* ○ *You've really **made** the big time now* (= become famous or successful).

ˈbig ˌtime [GREATLY] *adv US INFORMAL* If you do something big time, you do it to a great degree: *"How was the interview?" "Terrible, I messed up big time."* ○ *Chrissy's into disco big time* (= likes disco a lot).

big-time [MOST SUCCESSFUL] /ˈbɪg.taɪm/ *adj* [before n] *US INFORMAL* highest or most successful: *Steve Largent was regarded as Seattle's first big-time football star.*

ˌbig ˈtoe *noun* [C] the largest toe on your foot ➲See picture **The Body** on page Centre 5

ˌbig ˈtop *noun* [C usually sing] the main tent in a CIRCUS

ˌbig ˈwheel *UK noun* [C] (*US* **ferris wheel**) a large vertical wheel in an amusement park with seats which stay horizontal as the wheel turns round

bigwig /ˈbɪg.wɪg/ *noun* [C] *INFORMAL* a person who has an important or powerful position: *We were invited to a lunch with **local** bigwigs.*

ˌbig ˈword *noun* [C] *INFORMAL* a long, difficult word, or a word which expresses a serious or important idea: *He tried to impress his teachers by using big words in all his essays.*

bijou /ˈbiː.ʒuː/ *adj* [before n] *UK* (especially of a building) small but attractive and fashionable: *The harbour front is lined with bijou cafés and bars.* ○ *The estate agent described the flat as a bijou **residence**.*

bike /baɪk/ *noun* [C] **1** a bicycle: *It would be better for the environment if more people used bikes rather than cars.* ○ *My youngest child is learning to **ride** a bike.* **2** *INFORMAL* a motorcycle

• **On yer bike!** *UK SLANG* a rude way of telling someone to go away: *"Can you lend me some money?" "On yer bike, mate!"*

bike /baɪk/ *verb* **1** [I] *INFORMAL* to go somewhere by bicycle: *Should we bike to the park, or walk?* **2** [T] to use a motorcycle to deliver something to someone: *We biked a copy **over** to Greg at the BBC.*

biker *UK AND US* /ˈbaɪ.kəʳ/ Ⓤⓢ /-kɚ/ *noun* [C] (*AUS* **bikie**) *INFORMAL* a member of a GANG (= group) of motorcyclists: *We were overtaken by a crowd of bikers doing over 90 mph.*

ˈbike ˌrack *noun* [C] *US* a **cycle rack**

ˈbike ˌshed *noun* [C] *UK* a small building in which bicycles are stored: *Your bike will be safer if you leave it in the bike shed.*

bikini /bɪˈkiː.ni/ *noun* [C] a two-piece SWIMMING COSTUME for women: *a bikini top* ○ *bikini bottoms/briefs* ○ *One-piece swimming costumes are more fashionable than bikinis this year.* ➲See picture **Clothes** on page Centre 6

bikkie /ˈbɪk.i/ *noun* [C] *AUS INFORMAL FOR* **biscuit** FLAT CAKE

bilabial /ˌbaɪˈleɪ.bi.əl/ *adj SPECIALIZED* (of a sound) made using both lips: *'P' is a bilabial consonant.*

bilateral /ˌbaɪˈlæt.ᵊr.ᵊl/ Ⓤⓢ /-ˈlæt̬.ɚ-/ *adj* involving two groups or countries: *France and Germany have signed a bilateral **agreement** to help prevent drug smuggling.* ➲Compare **multilateral**; **unilateral**. **bilaterally** /ˌbaɪˈlæt.ᵊr.ᵊl.i/ Ⓤⓢ /-ˈlæt̬.ɚ-/ *adv*

bilberry /ˈbɪl.bᵊr.i/ Ⓤⓢ /-ber-/ *noun* [C] the dark blue fruit of a small bush which grows wild in Great Britain and northern Europe, similar to a BLUEBERRY

bile /baɪl/ *noun* [U] **1** a bitter yellow liquid produced by the liver which helps to digest fat: *Meat-eaters must produce extensive bile **acids** in their intestines to properly digest the meat that they eat.* **2** when you feel or show BITTER (= angry and upset) feelings: *His article was full of loathing and bile.*

bilious /ˈbɪl.i.əs/ *adj* **1** relating to an illness caused by too much bile, which can cause vomiting: *She suffered from bilious **attacks**.* **2** If someone is bilious, they are always in a bad mood: *a bilious old man* **3** extremely unpleasant: *His shirt was a bilious shade of green.*

bilge [TALK] /bɪldʒ/ *noun* [U] *OLD-FASHIONED SLANG* worthless talk; nonsense: *Don't talk such bilge!*

bilge [SHIP] /bɪldʒ/ *noun* [C usually pl] the bottom inside part of a ship where dirty water collects: *The bilges had been pumped and the ship was ready to set sail once again.*

ˈbilge ˌwater *noun* [U] the dirty water that collects in the bottom inside part of a ship

bilingual /baɪˈlɪŋ.gwᵊl/ *adj* (of a person) able to use two languages for communication, or (of a thing) using or involving two languages: *She works as a bilingual secretary for an insurance company.* ○ *a bilingual dictionary* ➲Compare **monolingual**; **multilingual**; **trilingual**.

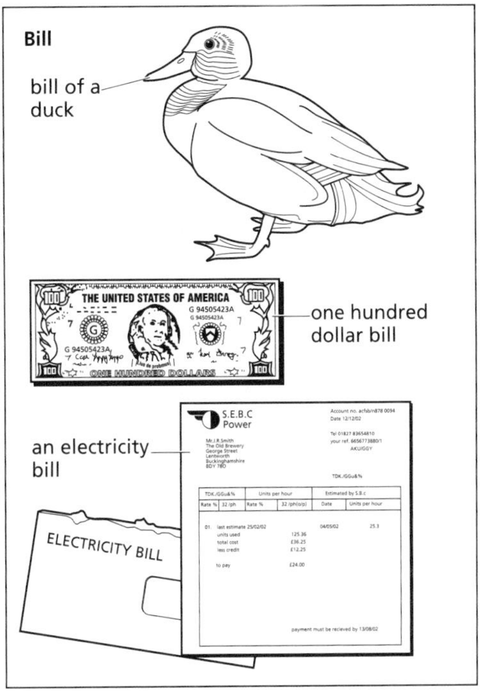
Bill
bill of a duck
THE UNITED STATES OF AMERICA
one hundred dollar bill
S.E.B.C Power
an electricity bill
ELECTRICITY BILL

bill [REQUEST FOR PAYMENT] /bɪl/ *noun* [C or S] a request for payment of money owed, or the piece of paper on which it is written: *an electricity/gas/phone bill* ○ *They sent us a bill **for** the work they had done.* ○ *She **ran up*** (= caused herself to have) *a huge phone bill talking to her boyfriend for hours.* ○ *They asked the waitress for the bill.* ○ *Could we have the bill, please?* ○ *Her mother agreed to **foot*** (= pay) *the bill.*

bill /bɪl/ *verb* [T] to give or send someone a bill asking for money that they owe for a product or service: *Please bill me for any expenses you incur.*

billing /ˈbɪl.ɪŋ/ *noun* [U] *itemized* (= detailed) *billing*

bill [MONEY] *MAINLY US* /bɪl/ *noun* [C] (*UK USUALLY* **note**) a piece of paper money: *a dollar/one-dollar bill* ○ *a ten-dollar bill* ➲See also **billfold**.

bill [LAW] /bɪl/ *noun* [C] a formal statement of a planned new law that is discussed before being voted on: *The bill was **amended*** (= changed). ○ *When a bill is **passed** in parliament it becomes law.* ○ *INFORMAL The bill was **thrown out*** (= did not go past the first stage of discussion and will not become law).

bill NOTICE /bɪl/ *noun* [C] a notice giving information about especially an event or performance
• **be on the bill** to be performing in a show: *There were lots of big names (= famous people) on the bill.*
• **head/top the bill** to be the most important actor in a show
• **fill/fit the bill** to be exactly what is needed in a particular situation: *That box will fill the bill nicely.*
bill /bɪl/ *verb* [T usually passive] to advertise something with a particular description: *The film was billed as a romantic comedy.*
billing /'bɪl.ɪŋ/ *noun* [U] **1** information, especially about a performance: *Unfortunately, the show never lived up to (= was not as good as) its billing.* **2** star/top billing in a show or film, etc. when someone is advertised as the most important actor/actress
▲ **bill sb as sth** *phrasal verb* [usually passive] to describe someone in a particular way in order to advertise them: *The young author was billed as 'the new Beckett'.*

bill BIRD /bɪl/ *noun* [C] the beak of a bird

the (old) 'Bill POLICE *noun* [S] *UK SLANG* the police

billabong /'bɪl.ə.bɒŋ/ ⓤ /-bɑːŋ/ *noun* [C] *AUS* a low area of ground which was part of a river in the past, which only fills up with water when the river floods

billboard /'bɪl.bɔːd/ ⓤ /-bɔːrd/ *noun* [C] *US FOR* **hoarding** ADVERTISEMENT

billet /'bɪl.ɪt/ *noun* [C] a place for especially soldiers to stay in for a short time: *Our billets were about a mile out of town, in a row of farm cottages.* **billet** /'bɪl.ɪt/ *verb* [T] *The soldiers were billeted in the town hall.*

billfold /'bɪl.fəʊld/ ⓤ /-foʊld/ *noun* [C] *US FOR* **wallet** (= a small folding case for carrying money)

billhook /'bɪl.hʊk/ *noun* [C] a tool with a wide blade on top of a long pole used for cutting branches off trees

billiards /'bɪl.i.ədz/ ⓤ /'bɪl.jɚdz/ *noun* [U] a game played by two people on a table covered in green cloth in which a CUE (= a long pole) is used to hit balls against each other and into pockets around the table **billiard** /'bɪl.i.əd/ ⓤ /'bɪl.jɚd/ *adj* [before n] *a billiard table ○ a billiard ball*

billion /'bɪl.jən/ *noun* [C] **1** 1 000 000 000: *Cosmetics is a billion dollar industry.* **2** *UK OLD-FASHIONED* 1 000 000 000 000 ✳ NOTE: This number is now called a **trillion**.
billionaire /ˌbɪl.jə'neəʳ/ ⓤ /-'ner/ *noun* [C] a person whose wealth is at least 1 000 000 000 in their country's money

bill of 'fare *noun* [C usually sing] *OLD-FASHIONED* a MENU (= list of food) in a restaurant

bill of 'rights *noun* [S] a statement of the basic laws which are meant to protect a country's CITIZENS from lack of justice and lack of fairness

billow /'bɪl.əʊ/ ⓤ /-oʊ/ *verb* [I] to spread over a large area, or (especially of items made of cloth) to become filled with air and appear to be larger: *Smoke billowed (out) from the burning building. ○ The sheets/shirts hanging on the line billowed in the breeze. ○ We watched the boats with their billowing sails.* **billow** /'bɪl.əʊ/ ⓤ /-oʊ/ *noun* [C usually pl] *billows of smoke*

billy /'bɪl.i/ *noun* [C] (*ALSO* **billycan**) *UK* a metal container used for cooking outside over a fire

'billy ˌclub *noun* [C] *US FOR* **truncheon**

'billy ˌgoat *noun* [C] a male goat

billy-o /'bɪl.i.əʊ/ ⓤ /-oʊ/ *adv UK OLD-FASHIONED SLANG* **like billy-o** a lot or very quickly, strongly, etc: *We worked like billy-o to get it finished.*

bimbo /'bɪm.bəʊ/ ⓤ /-boʊ/ *noun* [C] *plural* **bimboes** or **bimbos** *SLANG DISAPPROVING* a young woman considered to be attractive but not intelligent: *He went out with a succession of blonde bimbos.*

bimonthly /ˌbaɪ'mʌntθ.li/ *adj, adv* happening or appearing every two months or twice a month: *a bimonthly publication/report ○ The magazine is published bimonthly, with six issues a year.*

bin WASTE /bɪn/ *noun* [C] *UK* **1** a container for waste: *a litter bin ○ a rubbish bin ○ The supermarket has installed recycling bins for old newspapers, bottles and cans. ○ Do you want this or shall I throw it in the bin?*

➔See picture **In the Office** on page Centre 15 **2** a **dustbin**
bin /bɪn/ *verb* [T] **-nn-** *UK Shall I bin these old shoes (= throw them in the bin)?*

bin STORAGE /bɪn/ *noun* [C] a large storage container: *a bread bin*

binary /'baɪ.n³r.i/ ⓤ /-nɚ-/ *adj* consisting of two parts
binary 'number *noun* [C] a number that is expressed using 1 and 0: *Computers operate using binary numbers.*

'bin ˌbag/ˌliner *noun* [C] *UK* a **dustbin bag/liner**

bind TIE /baɪnd/ *verb* **bound, bound 1** [T] to tie tightly or to fasten: *They bound the packages with brightly coloured ribbon. ○ Bind together the two broken ends. ○ The prisoner was bound hand and foot.* **2** [T] to unite people: *The things which bind them together are greater than their differences.* **3** [T] (*ALSO* **bind up**) To bind a part of the body, especially a part which is damaged, is to tie something round it: *He had already bound the child's arm when I arrived.* **4** [T] to sew or stick material along the edges of something such as a jacket, in order to make it stronger or to decorate it **5** [T] to make separate pieces of paper into a book: *There are several different ways to bind a book, for example you can stitch or stick the pages together.* ➔See also **bookbinding**. **6** [I or T] When an egg or water is used especially in cooking to bind something it provides a way of making everything stick together in a solid mass: *The mixture wouldn't bind (together).*
binder /'baɪn.dəʳ/ ⓤ /-dɚ/ *noun* [C] **1** a hard cover in which paper documents or magazines are stored: *a leather/plastic binder* **2** a **bookbinder**
binding /'baɪn.dɪŋ/ *noun* **1** [C or U] the type of cover that a book has **2** [U] a thin strip of material which can be sewn along the edges of clothes or other objects
bound /baʊnd/ *adj*: *We found the girl bound (= tied) and gagged. ○ The book was bound (= covered) in shiny green leather.*
-bound /-baʊnd/ *suffix* **1** A book which is -bound is covered or held together in the stated way: *a leather-bound book ○ a spiral-bound notebook* **2** Clothes or other objects which are -bound have the edges covered in the stated way: *leather-bound cuffs*

bind UNPLEASANT SITUATION /baɪnd/ *noun* [S] *INFORMAL* a difficult situation in which you are prevented from acting as you might like: *Having to visit her every week is a terrible bind. ○ Borrowing money may put you in a real bind.*
▲ **bind sb to sth** *phrasal verb* [usually passive] to force someone to keep a promise: *His sister had been bound to secrecy. ○ We are bound to the original contract.*

bindi /'bɪn.di/ *noun* [C] a small coloured mark or jewel that is worn between the eyebrows, especially by Hindu women to show that they are married: *Many of my single Hindu friends do wear bindis to parties.*

binding /'baɪn.dɪŋ/ *adj* (especially of an agreement) which cannot be legally avoided or stopped: *a binding agreement ○ The contract wasn't legally binding.*

binge /bɪndʒ/ *noun* [C] *INFORMAL* an occasion when an activity is done in an extreme way, especially eating, drinking or spending money: *a drinking/eating/spending binge ○ The annual office binge (= party) is in December. ○ He went on a five day drinking binge.*
binge /bɪndʒ/ *verb* [I] bingeing or binging *INFORMAL* to eat a lot of something: *I tend to binge on chocolate when I'm watching TV.*

'binge ˌeating *noun* [U] eating a lot of food, especially without being able to control yourself

bingo GAME /'bɪŋ.gəʊ/ ⓤ /-goʊ/ *noun* [U] a game in which prizes can be won by matching numbers on a card with those chosen by chance

bingo SURPRISE /'bɪŋ.gəʊ/ ⓤ /-goʊ/ *exclamation INFORMAL* an expression of surprise and, usually, pleasure: *I was just about to borrow some money when bingo! – the cheque arrived.*

binman /'bɪn.mæn/ *noun* [C] *UK* a **dustman**

binoculars /bɪ'nɒk.jʊ.ləz/ ⓤ /-'nɑː.kjʊ.lɚz/ *plural noun* a pair of tubes with glass at either end that you look through to see things far away: *a pair of binoculars*

bio- /baɪ.əʊ-/ ⓤ /-oʊ-/ *prefix* connected with life and living things: *bioethics ○ biodiversity*

biochemical /ˌbaɪ.əʊˈkem.ɪ.kəl/ [US] /-oʊ-/ *adj* connected with the chemistry of living things **biochemically** /baɪ.əʊˈkem.ɪ.kli/ [US] /-oʊˈ-/ *adv*

biochemistry /ˌbaɪ.əʊˈkem.ɪ.stri/ [US] /-oʊ-/ *noun* [U] the scientific study of the chemistry of living things **biochemist** /ˌbaɪ.əʊˈkem.ɪst/ [US] /-oʊ-/ *noun* [C]

biodata /ˈbaɪ.əʊˌdeɪ.tə/ [US] /-oʊˌdeɪ.t̬ə/ *noun* [U] details about someone's life, job and achievements

biodegradable /ˌbaɪ.əʊ.dɪˈgreɪ.dɪ.bl̩/ [US] /-oʊ-/ *adj* able to decay naturally and harmlessly: *Biodegradable packaging helps to limit the amount of harmful chemicals released into the atmosphere.* **biodegrade** /ˌbaɪ.əʊ.dɪˈgreɪd/ [US] /ˌ-oʊ-/ *verb* [I] *Some plastics are designed to biodegrade when their useful life is over.*

biodiversity /ˌbaɪ.əʊ.daɪˈvɜː.sɪ.ti/ [US] /-oʊ.dɪˈvɝː.sə.t̬i/ *noun* [U] the number and variety of plant and animal species that exist in a particular environmental area or in the world generally, or the problem of preserving and protecting this: *a new National Biological Survey to protect species habitat and biodiversity*

bioethics /ˈbaɪ.əʊˌeθ.ɪks/ [US] /-oʊ-/ *noun* [U] the study and consideration of what is right and wrong in biological advances and activities such as GENETIC ENGINEERING and the TRANSPLANTATION of organs: *The uproar led to the establishment of bioethics committees to oversee research.*

biofeedback /ˌbaɪ.əʊˈfiːd.bæk/ [US] /-oʊ-/ *noun* [U] a method by which a person learns to control their heart rate or other physical or mental processes by using information from recordings of those processes

biography /baɪˈɒg.rə.fi/ [US] /-ˈɑː.grə-/ *noun* [C or U] the life story of a person written by someone else: *He wrote a biography **of** Winston Churchill.* ➲Compare **autobiography**; **hagiography**.

biographer /baɪˈɒg.rə.fəʳ/ [US] /-ˈɑː.grə.fɚ/ *noun* [C] *Boswell was Dr Johnson's biographer* (= wrote his life story). **biographical** /ˌbaɪ.əʊˈgræf.ɪ.kəl/ [US] /-oʊ-/ *adj*: *There was a biographical note about the author on the back of the book.*

bioˌlogical ˈclock *noun* [C] your body's natural habit of sleeping, eating, growing, etc. at particular times: *Long-haul flights can seriously disrupt your biological clock.*

• **biological clock is ticking (away)** *INFORMAL* When a woman says her biological clock is ticking (away), she means that she is worried that she is getting too old to have a baby.

bioˌlogical conˈtrol *noun* [U] the use of one plant or animal to control another, especially to prevent disease or damage

biology /baɪˈɒl.ə.dʒi/ [US] /-ˈɑː.lə-/ *noun* [U] the scientific study of the natural processes of living things: *human biology* ○ *marine biology* ○ *molecular biology* ○ *The book deals with the reproductive biology **of** the buffalo.*

biological /ˌbaɪ.əˈlɒdʒ.ɪ.kəl/ [US] /-ˈlɑː.dʒɪ-/ *adj* **1** connected with the natural processes of living things: *the biological sciences* ○ *Eating is a biological **necessity**!* **2** [before n] related by birth: *She decided to search for her biological **mother** after her adoptive parents died.* **3** *UK* describes a substance used for cleaning that uses ENZYMES to remove dirt: *biological washing powder* ➲See also **non-bio**. **4** using living matter, such as bacteria, to seriously harm and kill people and animals, and to damage crops: *biological weapons/warfare* **biologically** /ˌbaɪ.əˈlɒdʒ.ɪ.kli/ [US] /-ˈlɑː.dʒɪ-/ *adv*: *biologically active/stable chemicals*

biologist /baɪˈɒl.ə.dʒɪst/ [US] /-ˈɑː.lə-/ *noun* [C] a scientist who studies biology

bionic /baɪˈɒn.ɪk/ [US] /-ˈɑː.nɪk/ *adj* **1** using artificial materials and methods to produce especially a human activity or movement: *a bionic arm/leg* **2** *HUMOROUS* used to refer to a person who has greater powers of strength, speed etc. than seem to be possible for a human: *a bionic man/woman*

biophysics /ˌbaɪ.əʊˈfɪz.ɪks/ [US] /-oʊ-/ *noun* [U] the science that uses the laws and methods of physics to explain biology

biopic /ˈbaɪ.əʊ.pɪk/ [US] /-oʊ-/ *noun* [C] *INFORMAL* a film about the life of a real person

biopsy /ˈbaɪ.ɒp.si/ [US] /-ɑːp-/ *noun* [C] the removal and examination of tissue from an ill person, in order to discover more about their illness: *a tissue biopsy*

biorhythm /ˈbaɪ.əʊ.rɪ.ðəm/ [US] /-oʊ-/ *noun* [C] a regular pattern of physical processes in an organism: *Some people believe your biorhythms can influence your moods and behaviour.*

biosphere /ˈbaɪ.əʊ.sfɪəʳ/ [US] /-oʊ.sfɪr/ *noun* [U] *SPECIALIZED* the part of the Earth's environment where life exists

biotechnology /ˌbaɪ.əʊ.tekˈnɒl.ə.dʒi/ [US] /-oʊ.tekˈnɑː.lə-/ *noun* [U] (*INFORMAL* **biotech**) the use of living things, especially cells and bacteria, in industrial processes: *a biotech company/firm*

bipartisan /ˌbaɪˈpɑː.tɪ.zæn/ [US] /-ˈpɑːr.t̬ɪ-/ *adj* supported by or consisting of two political parties: *a bipartisan committee*

biped /ˈbaɪ.ped/ *noun* [C] *SPECIALIZED* an animal that walks on two legs ➲Compare **quadruped**.

biplane /ˈbaɪ.pleɪn/ *noun* [C] an old type of aircraft with two sets of wings, one above the other ➲Compare **monoplane**. ➲See picture **Planes, Ships and Boats** on page Centre 14

bipolar disorder /baɪˈpəʊ.lə.dɪˌsɔː.dəʳ/ [US] /-ˈpoʊ.lɚ.dɪˌsɔːr.dɚ/ *noun* [U] *SPECIALIZED* **manic depression**

birch [TREE] /bɜːtʃ/ [US] /bɝːtʃ/ *noun* [C] a tree with a smooth, often white bark and thin branches

the birch [PUNISHMENT] *noun* [S] *UK* an official punishment in the past, which involved hitting a person across the bottom with a stick, or the stick itself **birch** /bɜːtʃ/ [US] /bɝːtʃ/ *verb* [T]

bird [CREATURE] /bɜːd/ [US] /bɝːd/ *noun* [C] a creature with feathers and wings, usually able to fly: *caged/wild birds* ○ *sea birds* ○ *wading birds* ○ *Most birds lay eggs in the spring.* ○ *Penguins and ostriches are **flightless** birds* (= they cannot fly). ○ *We watched a **flock** of birds fly over the field.* ➲See also **dickybird**; **hummingbird**; **songbird**. ➲See picture **Animals and Birds** on page Centre 4

• **the birds and the bees** *HUMOROUS* the basic facts about sex and reproduction: *She's only six, but she already knows about the birds and the bees.*

• **be (strictly) for the birds** *US INFORMAL* to be worthless or ridiculous

• **(as) free as a bird** completely free to do as you want

• **bird's eye view** a view from a very high place which allows you to see a large area: *Climb to the top of the Eiffel Tower if you want a bird's eye view of Paris.*

• **do bird** *UK OLD-FASHIONED SLANG* to spend time in prison

• **A bird in the hand (is worth two in the bush).** *SAYING* said when you recognise that you should not risk losing something you already have by trying to get something you think might be better

birdlike /ˈbɜːd.laɪk/ [US] /ˈbɝːd-/ *adj* looking or behaving similar to a bird: *He was a little birdlike man with a pointed nose and darting eyes.*

bird [PERSON] /bɜːd/ [US] /bɝːd/ *noun* [C] **1** *OLD-FASHIONED* a particular type of person: *He's a rare bird, is Nick.* **2** *UK SLANG* a young woman: *Is that Lee's new bird?* **3** *INFORMAL* **old bird** an older woman: *DISAPPROVING This old bird was lecturing the shop assistant about her manners.* ○ *APPROVING She's a **game** old bird* (= energetic and willing to do risky things).

• **birds of a feather** *SLIGHTLY DISAPPROVING* people who are similar in character: *He'll get on well with Anthony – they're birds of a feather.*

• **Birds of a feather flock together.** *SAYING* said about people who have similar characters or interests, especially ones of which you disapprove, and who tend to spend time with each other

• **The bird has flown.** *UK SAYING* said when the person you are looking for has gone away or escaped

ˈbird ˌbath *noun* [C] a bowl filled with water for birds to drink and BATHE (= cover themselves in water) in

bird-brained /ˈbɜːd.breɪnd/ [US] /ˈbɝːd-/ *adj* *INFORMAL* stupid

birdbrain /ˈbɜːd.breɪn/ [US] /ˈbɝːd-/ *noun* [C usually sing] *MAINLY US INFORMAL* a stupid person

birdcage /ˈbɜːd.keɪdʒ/ [US] /ˈbɝːd-/ *noun* [C] a container in which birds are kept so that people can look at them

ˈbird ˌdog *noun* [C] *US FOR* **gun dog**

'bird ,feeder *noun* [C] a device containing nuts or seeds for wild birds to eat

birdhouse /'bɜːd.haʊs/ ⓤ /'bɝːd-/ *noun* [C] US FOR **nesting box**

birdie [BIRD] /'bɜː.di/ ⓤ /'bɝː-/ *noun* [C] CHILD'S WORD a small bird

birdie [GOLF] /'bɜː.di/ ⓤ /'bɝː-/ *noun* [C] (in golf) getting the ball into the hole in one shot (= hit) less than PAR (= the expected number) for that hole **birdie** /'bɜː.di/ ⓤ /'bɝː-/ *verb* [I or T] *He birdied the fifth and the eighteenth and finished two strokes under par.*

birdie [NET GAME] /'bɜː.di/ ⓤ /'bɝː-/ *noun* [C] US FOR **shuttle-cock**

birdlike /'bɜːd.laɪk/ ⓤ /'bɝːd-/ *adj* ➔See at **bird** CREATURE

,bird of 'paradise *noun* [C] a bird found in New Guinea, of which the male has brightly coloured feathers

,bird of 'passage *noun* [C] **1** UK a bird which MIGRATES (= moves from one area to another when the season changes) **2** a person who stays for only a short period of time in one place, job, etc: *At present the organization has to rely on young, inexperienced graduates who are usually birds of passage.*

,bird of 'prey *noun* [C] *plural* **birds of prey** a bird, such as an eagle or a HAWK, that kills and eats small birds and animals

birdseed /'bɜːd.siːd/ ⓤ /'bɝːd-/ *noun* [U] seeds for feeding birds

birdsong /'bɜːd.sɒŋ/ ⓤ /'bɜːd.sɑːŋ/ *noun* [U] the musical calls of a bird or birds

'bird ,table *noun* [C] a raised structure outside a building on which food for wild birds is put

bird-watching /'bɜːd.wɒtʃ.ɪŋ/ ⓤ /'bɝːd.wɑː.tʃɪŋ/ *noun* [U] the hobby of studying wild birds in their natural surroundings **bird-watcher** /'bɜːd.wɒtʃ.əʳ/ ⓤ /'bɝːd.wɑː.tʃɚ/ *noun* [C]

Birkenstock /'bɜː.kᵊn.stɒk/ ⓤ /'bɝːr.kᵊn.stɑːk/ *noun* [C usually pl] TRADEMARK a type of shoe which is very comfortable and which is often worn by people who care about the Earth and environmental problems

Biro /'baɪ.rəʊ/ ⓤ /-roʊ/ *noun* [C] *plural* **Biros** UK TRADEMARK a type of **ballpoint**

birth /bɜːθ/ ⓤ /bɝːθ/ *noun* **1** [C or U] the time when a baby comes out of its mother's body: *It was a difficult birth.* ○ *He weighed eight pounds at birth.* ○ *More men are present at the births of their children these days.* ○ *The application form will ask for your country/place of birth* (= where you were born). **2** [C] a child which is born: *The percentage of live births* (= children who are born alive and continue to live) *continues to increase.* ○ *Registration of births and deaths became compulsory in 1871.* **3** [U] the position of the family into which you are born, especially its social position: *He had received all the advantages of birth* (= having been born into a family of a high social class) *and an expensive education.* **4 American/Italian, etc. by birth** born in a particular place or having parents with a particular nationality: *Oscar Wilde was Irish by birth.*

● **give birth** When a woman or female animal gives birth, she produces a baby from her body: *She gave birth to twins.* ○ *Our cat gave birth last night.* ○ FIGURATIVE *This extraordinary experience gave birth to* (= gave him the idea for) *his latest novel.*

'birth cer,tificate *noun* [C] a document recording a baby's birth including such information as name, time, place, and parents

'birth con,trol *noun* [U] the various methods or types of equipment that allow people to have sex without having children: *a new type of birth-control pill*

birthday /'bɜːθ.deɪ/ ⓤ /'bɝːθ-/ *noun* [C] the day that is exactly a year or number of years after a person was born: *Happy birthday!* ○ *Are you going to Ellen's birthday party next week?* ○ *It's her 21st birthday.*

● **in *your* birthday suit** HUMOROUS not wearing any clothes

'birth ,defect *noun* [C] a physical or chemical problem with a body part or process which is present at birth

birthmark /'bɜːθ.mɑːk/ ⓤ /'bɝːθ.mɑːrk/ *noun* [C] a brownish or reddish mark which is on a person's skin from when they are born

'birth ,mother *noun* [C] the woman who gave birth to a child, although she may not now be the child's legal mother

'birth ,parent *noun* [C] the woman who gave birth to a child or the man who helped to CONCEIVE a child (= cause a baby to begin to form), although she or he may not now be the child's legal parent

birthplace /'bɜːθ.pleɪs/ ⓤ /'bɝːθ-/ *noun* [C usually sing] the house, town, etc. where a person was born

'birth ,rate *noun* [C usually sing] the number of births which happen during a period of time in a particular place

birthright /'bɜːθ.raɪt/ ⓤ /'bɝːθ-/ *noun* [C usually sing; U] something which you believe you deserve to have because of your family situation or social class, or because you believe it is your right as a human being: *Americans see freedom of expression as their birthright.* ○ *Some men see well-paid, powerful jobs as their birthright.*

biscuit [FLAT CAKE] UK /'bɪs.kɪt/ *noun* [C] (US **cookie**) a small, flat cake that is dry and usually sweet: *chocolate/ginger biscuits* ○ *a packet of biscuits* ○ *We had tea and biscuits at 3.30 p.m.*

● **(really) take the biscuit** UK (US **(really) take the cake**) INFORMAL You say that something or someone (really) takes the biscuit when they have done something that you find particularly annoying or surprising: *And you say she's opening your letters now? Oh, that really takes the biscuit!*

biscuit [BREAD] /'bɪs.kɪt/ *noun* [C] US a type of bread usually baked in small, round pieces: *baking-powder biscuits* ○ *biscuits and gravy*

bisect /baɪ'sekt/ *verb* [T] to divide something into two, usually equal, parts: *The new road will bisect the town.*

bisexual /baɪ'sek.sju.ᵊl/ *noun* [C] a person who is attracted to both men and women ➔Compare **heterosexual**; **homosexual**. **bisexual** /baɪ'sek.sju.ᵊl/ *adj*

bishop /'bɪʃ.əp/ *noun* [C] **1** a priest of high rank who is in charge of the priests of lower rank in a particular area: *the Bishop of Durham* ○ *Bishop Desmond Tutu* **2** (in chess) a piece that moves from corner to corner along squares of the same colour

bishopric /'bɪʃ.ə.prɪk/ *noun* [C] **1** the period of time during which a person serves as a bishop **2** an area of a country for which a bishop is responsible

bison /'baɪ.sᵊn/ *noun* [C] *plural* **bisons** or **bison** a large wild animal, similar to a cow but having a larger head and hairy shoulders, found especially in North America

bisque /biːsk/ /bɪsk/ *noun* [U] a thick creamy soup especially made from SHELLFISH (= sea creatures that live in shells)

bistro /'biː.strəʊ/ ⓤ /-stroʊ/ *noun* [C] *plural* **bistros** a small informal restaurant or bar, especially in France or in a French style

bit [AMOUNT] /bɪt/ *noun* [C] **1** INFORMAL a small piece or amount of something: *Would you like a bit of chocolate?* ○ *The glass smashed into little bits.* ○ *There were bits of paper all over the floor.* ○ *She tries to do a bit of exercise every day.* **2** INFORMAL a bit a short period of time: *I'm just going out for a bit. See you later.* **3** a bit of sth a slight but not serious amount or type of something: *Maria's put on a bit of weight, hasn't she?* ○ *It's a bit of a nuisance.* ○ *He's a bit of a pain.*

● **a bit ...** **1** slightly: *The dress is a bit too big for me.* ○ *That was a bit silly, wasn't it?* ○ *I'm a bit nervous.* ○ *I was hoping there'd be some food - I'm a bit hungry.* ○ *Would you like a bit more cake?* ○ *It's a bit like a Swiss chalet.* **2** UK very: *Blimey, it's a bit cold!* ○ *And she didn't invite him? That was a bit mean!*

● **be a bit much** INFORMAL to be a situation, request or behaviour that is unfair, unreasonable, or more than you can deal with: *I thought being asked to miss my lunch was a bit much.*

● **be a bit of all right** UK SLANG to be an attractive person

● **bit by bit** gradually: *I saved up the money bit by bit.*

- **bit of fluff/stuff/skirt** UK SLANG a sexually attractive woman: *Have you seen his latest bit of skirt?*
- **bit on the side** MAINLY UK HUMOROUS a sexual relationship with someone who is not married to you, or the person with whom you have the relationship: *We've thought for a while that he was having a bit on the side.*
- **not a bit** not in any way: *She wasn't a bit worried about her exams.* ○ *My parents were not a bit happy* (= were very unhappy) *about my choice.* ○ *"Are you getting tired?" "Not a bit."*
- **not a bit of it** UK INFORMAL said when a situation or event is very different from what you expected: *I thought he would be sorry, but not a bit of it.*
- **quite a bit** a lot: *She's got quite a bit of money.*
- **to bits** into small pieces: *The car was blown to bits.* ○ *It just fell to bits in my hands.*

bit [HORSE] /bɪt/ *noun* [C] a piece of metal put in a horse's mouth to allow the person riding it to control its movements
- **get the bit between your teeth** (US ALSO **take the bit between your teeth**) to do what you have decided to do in a forceful and energetic way: *She wasn't keen at first, but she loved it once she got the bit between her teeth.*

bit [COMPUTER] /bɪt/ *noun* [C] SPECIALIZED a unit of information in a computer that must be either 0 or 1: *a 32-bit computer* (= a computer that processes 32 bits of information at a time)

bit [COIN] /bɪt/ *noun* [C] UK OLD USE a small coin: *threepenny/sixpenny bit* ○Compare **two bits**.

bit [TOOL] /bɪt/ *noun* [C] the part of a tool used for cutting or DRILLING (= making holes)

bit [BITE] /bɪt/ *past simple of* **bite**

bitch [ANIMAL] /bɪtʃ/ *noun* [C] a female dog

bitch [COMPLAIN] /bɪtʃ/ *verb* [I] INFORMAL to complain and make unkind remarks about someone or something: *She's always bitching about Tanya.*

bitch /bɪtʃ/ *noun* **1** [S] INFORMAL when you complain or talk unkindly about people: *Most of us enjoy having a (good) bitch from time to time.* **2** [C] OFFENSIVE an unkind or unpleasant woman: *She can be a real bitch.* **3** [S] INFORMAL something which causes difficulties or problems, or which is unpleasant: *I've had a bitch of a week at work.*
- **life's a bitch (and then you die)** INFORMAL said when you find a situation difficult or have had a bad experience

bitchy /bɪtʃ.i/ *adj* INFORMAL often talking unkindly about other people: *She's so bitchy!* ○ *a bitchy remark* **bitchiness** /bɪtʃ.ɪ.nəs/ *noun* [U]

bite /baɪt/ *verb* **bit, bitten 1** [I or T] to use your teeth to cut into something or someone: *He bit into the apple.* ○ *An insect bit me on the arm.* ○ *He bites his fingernails.* **2** [I] to have a bad or unpleasant effect: *Higher mortgage rates are beginning to bite.* **3** [I] When a fish bites, it swallows the food on the hook at the end of a fishing line: *The fish aren't biting today.* **4** [I] to show interest in buying something: *The new service is now available but clients don't seem to be biting.*
- **sb/sth won't bite** HUMOROUS you do not need to be frightened of a particular person or thing: *Just go and ask her – she won't bite.*
- **bite off more than you can chew** INFORMAL to try to do something which is too difficult for you: *Clinton conceded, "We bit off more than we could chew in our original health care reform proposals."*
- **bite the bullet** to force yourself to do something unpleasant or difficult, or to be brave in a difficult situation: *I hate going to the dentist, but I suppose I'll just have to bite the bullet.*
- **bite the dust 1** to fall so that your body hits the ground heavily: *As they came round the bend several riders bit the dust.* **2** to end in failure: *His career bit the dust when he lost his job.*
- **bite the hand that feeds you** to act badly towards the person who is helping or has helped you
- **bite sb's head off** INFORMAL to speak to someone in a quick angry way, for no good reason: *I only asked if I could help – there's no need to bite my head off!*
- **bite your lip** to prevent yourself from showing your reaction to something by speaking or laughing: *I really*

wanted to laugh – I had to bite my lip.
- **bite your tongue** to stop yourself from saying something which you would really like to say: *I wanted to tell him exactly what I thought of him, but I had to bite my tongue.*

bite /baɪt/ *noun* **1** [C] when you bite something: *He took a bite* (= bit a piece) *out of the apple.* ○ *He had two bites* (= bit two pieces) *of apple.* **2** [C] a sore place or injury where an animal or insect has bitten you **3** [S] when a fish bites the hook on the end of a fishing line and is caught **4** [U] If food has bite, it has a sharp or strong taste: *I like mustard with a bit of bite.* **5** [U] a powerful effect: *This satire has (real) bite.*
- **have a bite to eat** (ALSO **have a quick bite**) INFORMAL to eat some food or a small meal
- **another/a second bite of the cherry** another opportunity to do something: *He missed a medal in the 100m, but will get a second bite of the cherry in the 400m.*

PHRASAL VERBS WITH **bite** ▼

▲ **bite sth back** *phrasal verb* [M] UK to stop yourself from saying something or from expressing an emotion: *bite back tears/laughter*

▲ **bite into sth** *phrasal verb* to reduce something valuable: *People are worried about inflation biting into their savings and investments.*

bite-sized /baɪt.saɪzd/ *adj* describes something that is small enough to put in your mouth whole: *Cut the cheese into bite-sized pieces.*

biting [COLD] /baɪ.tɪŋ/ US /-t̬ɪŋ/ *adj* describes weather that is extremely cold, especially when it causes you physical pain: *a biting wind* ○ *biting cold*

biting [CRITICAL] /baɪ.tɪŋ/ US /-t̬ɪŋ/ *adj* DISAPPROVING describes words or people that are critical, usually in a clever but unkind way: *He made some biting remarks about the whole occasion.* ○ *a biting wit*

bitmap /bɪt.mæp/ *noun* [C] a computer image formed from PIXELS which are each stored as a value of one or more BITS (= units of information)

'bit ,part *noun* [C] a small and unimportant part in a film or a play

,bits and 'pieces *plural noun* (UK ALSO **bits and bobs**) INFORMAL small things or jobs of different types

bitter [TASTE] /bɪt.əʳ/ US /bɪt̬.ɚ/ *adj* with an unpleasantly sharp taste: *a bitter flavour/taste/liquid*
- **a bitter pill (to swallow)** something that is very unpleasant but which must be accepted: *Losing the championship to a younger player was a bitter pill to swallow.*
bitterness /bɪt.ə.nəs/ US /bɪt̬.ɚ-/ *noun* [U] an unpleasantly sharp taste

bitter [ANGRY] /bɪt.əʳ/ US /bɪt̬.ɚ/ *adj* **1** describes a person who is angry and unhappy because they cannot forget bad things which happened in the past: *I feel very bitter about my childhood and all that was denied me.* ○ *She'd suffered terribly over the years but it hadn't made her bitter.* **2** describes an experience that causes deep pain or anger: *Failing the final exams was a bitter disappointment for me.* ○ *She learnt through bitter experience that he was not to be trusted.* **3** expressing a lot of hate and anger: *a bitter fight/row* ○ *bitter recriminations* ○ *He gave me a bitter look.*
- **to the bitter end** until something is finished
bitterly /bɪt.ə.li/ US /bɪt̬.ɚ-/ *adv* in a way which shows strong negative emotion such as anger or disappointment: *She wept bitterly at the news.* ○ *He was bitterly disappointed not to get the job.* **bitterness** /bɪt.ə.nəs/ US /bɪt̬.ɚ-/ *noun* [U] *He was full of bitterness after he lost his job.*

bitter [COLD] /bɪt.əʳ/ US /bɪt̬.ɚ/ *adj* describes weather that is extremely cold, especially in a way that causes physical pain: *a bitter wind* ○ *Wrap up warmly – it's bitter outside.*
bitterly /bɪt.ə.li/ US /bɪt̬.ɚ-/ *adv* **bitterly cold** extremely and unpleasantly cold

bitter [BEER] /bɪt.əʳ/ US /bɪt̬.ɚ/ *noun* [U] UK a type of dark brown beer with a bitter taste: *a pint of bitter* ○Compare **mild** BEER.

B

ˌbitter ˈlemon *noun* **[C or U]** a fizzy drink with a slight taste of lemon which is not alcoholic but is sometimes mixed with alcoholic drinks

bittern /ˈbɪt.ən/ [US] /ˈbɪt̬.ɚn/ *noun* **[C]** a type of European water bird which has long legs and is related to the HERON

bitters /ˈbɪt.əz/ [US] /ˈbɪt̬.ɚz/ *noun* **[U]** a strong bitter alcoholic drink made from spices and plant products that is mixed with other alcoholic drinks

bittersweet [EMOTION] /ˌbɪt.əˈswiːt/ [US] /ˌbɪt̬.ɚ-/ /ˈ---/ *adj* containing a mixture of sadness and happiness

bittersweet [TASTE] /ˌbɪt.əˈswiːt/ [US] /ˌbɪt̬.ɚ-/ /ˈ---/ *adj* tasting both bitter and sweet

ˌbittersweet ˈchocolate *noun* **[U]** *US FOR* **dark chocolate**

bitty /ˈbɪt.i/ [US] /ˈbɪt̬-/ *adj UK INFORMAL* made up of a lot of different things that do not fit together well: *I enjoyed the film but I found it quite bitty, jumping from one family's story to another.*

bitumen /ˈbɪtʃ.ʊ.mən/ [US] /bɪˈtuː-/ *noun* **[U]** a black sticky substance such as TAR or ASPHALT, used for making roads and roofs

bivouac /ˈbɪv.u.æk/ *noun* **[C]** **1** a temporary shelter or camp for sleeping in outside, not in the form of a tent: *The children made a bivouac at the bottom of the garden with some poles and an old blanket.* **2 bivouac (tent)** a small light tent just big enough for one or two people to lie in **bivouac** /ˈbɪv.u.æk/ *verb* **[I usually + adv or prep]** **bivouacking, bivouacked, bivouacked** *The soldiers bivouacked in the mountains for two nights.*

biweekly /baɪˈwiːk.li/ *adj, adv* happening or appearing every two weeks or twice a week: *a biweekly meeting/magazine*

bizarre /bɪˈzɑːʳ/ [US] /-ˈzɑːr/ *adj* very strange and unusual: *a bizarre situation* ○ *bizarre behaviour* **bizarrely** /bɪˈzɑː.li/ [US] /-ˈzɑːr-/ *adv* **bizarreness** /bɪˈzɑː.nəs/ [US] /-ˈzɑːr-/ *noun* **[U]**

BL /ˌbiːˈel/ *noun* **[C]** (*ALSO* **LLB**) *US ABBREVIATION FOR* Bachelor of Laws: a degree in law

blab /blæb/ *verb* **[I or T]** **-bb-** *INFORMAL* to talk carelessly or too much, often telling others something you should keep secret: *Someone blabbed* ***to*** *the press.*

blabber /ˈblæb.əʳ/ [US] /-ɚ/ *verb* **[I]** *INFORMAL* to talk a lot, especially in a way people find annoying or embarrassing: *He's always blabbering* ***on about*** *computers.*

blabbermouth /ˈblæb.ə.maʊθ/ [US] /-ɚ-/ *noun* **[C]** *INFORMAL DISAPPROVING* a person who talks carelessly, often telling secrets to other people

black [DARK IN COLOUR] /blæk/ *adj, noun* **[U]** (having) the darkest colour there is, like night without light: *black shoes* ○ *She often dresses* ***in*** *black* (= in black clothes).

• **be in the black** If a bank account is in the black, it contains some money, and if a person or business is in the black, they have money in the bank and are not in debt. ➲Compare **be in the red** at **red** COLOUR.

• **black and blue** with dark marks on your skin caused by being hit or having an accident: *His arm was black and blue.*

• **black and white** describes photography that has no colours except black, white and grey: *The old newsreels were filmed* ***in*** *black and white.* ○ *a black-and-white photo*

• **black-and-white** describes a subject or situation in which it is easy to understand what is right and wrong: *Disarmament isn't a black-and-white issue for me.*

• **be (down) in black and white** to be written down: *I couldn't believe it was true, but there it was, in black and white.*

• **see things in black and white** to have a simple view of what is right and wrong or good and bad

black /blæk/ *verb* **[T]** to put a black substance on something or to make something black: *The commandos blacked their faces.* **blacken** /ˈblæk.ᵊn/ *verb* **[T]** *The folds of the curtains were blackened* ***with*** *dirt.* **blackness** /ˈblæk.nəs/ *noun* **[U]**

black [BAD] /blæk/ *adj* without hope: *The future looked black.*

• **paint a black picture of *sth/sb*** to describe a situation or person as extremely bad

• **not be as black as *you are* painted** not to be as bad as people say you are

black /blæk/ *verb* **[T]** If a trade union blacks goods or people, it refuses to handle or work with them.

blacken /ˈblæk.ᵊn/ *verb* **blacken *sb's* name/image/reputation, etc.** to spoil someone's reputation: *The financial crash blackened the image of investment for many small investors.*

black [PEOPLE] /blæk/ *adj* relating or belonging to people with black or dark brown skin, especially people who live in Africa or whose family originally came from Africa: *black culture* ○ *black Americans*

black /blæk/ *noun* **[C]** *OFFENSIVE* a black person

PHRASAL VERBS WITH **black** ▼

▲ **black *sth* out** [COVER] *phrasal verb* **[M]** to cover a face or a name so that it cannot be seen: *In the TV interview, they blacked out the victim's face.*

▲ **black *sth* out** [NO LIGHT] *phrasal verb* **[M]** to make a place dark, especially by covering or switching off all the lights: *The entire city was blacked out overnight.*

▲ **black out** [UNCONSCIOUS] *phrasal verb* to become unconscious suddenly but for a short period

ˌblack ˈAfrica *noun* **[U]** the part of Africa south of the Sahara Desert

blackball /ˈblæk.bɔːl/ [US] /-bɑːl/ *verb* **[T]** to vote against allowing someone to be a member of an organization or group: *He was initially blackballed because of a dispute he once had with a couple of the committee members.*

ˌblack ˈbelt *noun* **[C]** **1** the symbol of a very high standard in the sport of JUDO or KARATE **2** someone who has recieved a black belt as a symbol of achieving a very high standard in JUDO or KARATE: *He's a black belt at karate.*

blackberry /ˈblæk.bᵊr.i/ [US] /-ber-/ *noun* **[C]** a small dark purple fruit that grows wild in Europe and is usually cooked before being eaten: *blackberry and apple pie*

• **go blackberrying** to gather wild blackberries

blackbird /ˈblæk.bɜːd/ [US] /-bɝːd/ *noun* **[C]** a European bird with black feathers and a bright yellow beak in the male and brown feathers in the female ➲See picture **Animals and Birds** on page Centre 4

blackboard /ˈblæk.bɔːd/ [US] /-bɔːrd/ *noun* **[C]** a dark surface on a wall or frame which a teacher writes on with chalk

ˌblack ˈbox *noun* **[C]** a small machine that records information about an aircraft during its flight, and which is used to discover the cause of an accident

ˌblack ˈcoffee *noun* **[C or U]** coffee without milk or cream

ˌblack ˈcomedy *noun* **[C or U]** a film, play, etc. that looks at the amusing side of things we usually consider very serious, like death and illness

blackcurrant /ˌblækˈkʌr.ᵊnt/ [US] /ˈblæk.kɝː-/ *noun* **[C]** a small round dark purple fruit that grows on a bush and is usually cooked before being eaten: *blackcurrant jam/juice*

the ˌBlack ˈDeath *noun* **[S]** a disease that killed an extremely large number of people in Europe and Asia in the 14th century

ˌblack eˈconomy *noun* **[C usually sing]** business activity and income which people do not record in order to avoid paying tax on it

blacken /ˈblæk.ᵊn/ *verb* **[T]** ➲See at **black** DARK IN COLOUR, **black** BAD

ˌblack ˈeye *noun* **[C]** an eye where the skin around it has gone dark because it has been hit: *He had a fight at school and came home with a black eye.*

black-eyed bean *UK* /ˌblæk.aɪdˈbiːn/ *noun* **[C]** (*US* **black-eyed pea**) a small, pale-coloured, edible bean with a black spot

blackfly /ˈblæk.flaɪ/ *noun* **[C or U]** a small black insect with two wings that feeds on the juices of plants: *Do your broad beans suffer from blackfly* (= are they attacked by blackfly)*?*

blackguard /ˈblæg.ɑːd/ /-əd/ [US] /-ɑːrd/ *noun* **[C]** *OLD-FASHIONED* a person, usually a man, who is not honourable and has no moral principles

blackhead /'blæk.hed/ *noun* [C] a very small dark spot on the skin caused by a blocked PORE (= small hole in the skin's surface)

,**black 'hole** *noun* [C] **1** SPECIALIZED a region in space where GRAVITY is so strong that nothing, not even light, can escape **2** an imaginary place in which things are lost

,**black 'humour** *noun* [U] an amusing way of looking at or treating something that is serious or sad

,**black 'ice** *noun* [U] a dangerous type of ice on roads which is so thin that it cannot be seen by a driver

blackjack CARD GAME /'blæk.dʒæk/ *noun* [U] (ALSO **pontoon**) a type of card game played for money

blackjack WEAPON /'blæk.dʒæk/ *noun* [C] US a short thick metal stick covered in rubber or leather, used to hit people with

blackleg /'blæk.leg/ *noun* [C] UK DISAPPROVING a person who works while others that they work with are on strike; a **scab**

blacklist /'blæk.lɪst/ *noun* [C] a list of people, countries, etc. who are considered by a particular authority or group to be unacceptable and who should be avoided and not trusted
  blacklist /'blæk.lɪst/ *verb* [T often passive] to put someone's name on a blacklist: *They were blacklisted because of their extreme right-wing views.*

,**black 'look** *noun* [C] when your face is full of anger and hate: *She gave me a black look.*

,**black 'magic** *noun* [U] a type of magic that is believed to use evil SPIRITS (= beings which cannot be seen) to do harmful things

blackmail /'blæk.meɪl/ *noun* [U] when you obtain money from people or force them to do something by threatening to make known a secret of theirs or to harm them: *In a position of authority, a weakness for the opposite sex leaves you open to blackmail.* **blackmail** *verb* [T] *They used the photographs to blackmail her into spying for them.* **blackmailer** /'blæk,meɪ.lə^r/ ⑤ /-lɚ/ *noun* [C]

Black Maria /,blæk.mə'raɪə/ *noun* [C] OLD-FASHIONED a police vehicle used to transport prisoners

,**black 'mark** *noun* [C usually sing] INFORMAL when people notice and remember something which you have done wrong or failed to do: *If I'm late for work again, it will be another black mark against me.*

,**black 'market** *noun* [S] illegal trading of goods that are not allowed to be bought and sold, or that there are not enough of for everyone who wants them: *During the war, they bought food on the black market.* ○ *They blamed high taxes for the growth of a black market in cigarettes.* ,**black market'eer** *noun* [C]

,**Black 'Mass** *noun* [C usually sing] a ceremony in which the Devil is worshipped instead of the Christian God

,**black 'mood** *noun* [C] a very unhappy feeling: *She was in one of her black moods today.*

blackness /'blæk.nəs/ *noun* [U] ➾See at **black** DARK IN COLOUR

blackout HIDE /'blæk.aʊt/ *noun* [C] **1** a time when all lights must be hidden by law, or when there is no light or power because of an electricity failure: *war-time blackouts* ○ *Power lines were blown down and we had a blackout of several hours.* **2** the action taken to make certain that information about something is not reported to the public: *a news blackout*

blackout UNCONSCIOUSNESS /'blæk.aʊt/ *noun* [C] a short period of unconsciousness: *He can't drive because he suffers from blackouts.*

,**black 'pepper** *noun* [U] a powder made by crushing whole black PEPPERCORNS, used to give food a hot spicy taste

,**black 'pudding** *noun* [C or U] MAINLY UK a type of sausage made of pig's blood, fat and grain, which is very dark in colour

,**black 'sheep** *noun* [S] a person who has done something bad which brings embarrassment or disrespect to their family: *He's the black sheep of the family.*

blacksmith /'blæk.smɪθ/ *noun* [C] a person who makes and repairs iron tools and HORSESHOES

'**black ,spot** *noun* [C usually sing] UK **1** a place on a road that is considered to be dangerous because several accidents have happened there: *This corner is an accident black spot.* **2** a place where something is particularly bad: *an unemployment black spot*

,**black 'tie** *noun* [U] clothes worn for formal social occasions. For men, this is a black BOW TIE, white shirt and black suit, and for women, a long dress: *Do we need to wear black tie?* ,**black 'tie** *adj*: *a black-tie event* ○ *Tonight's dinner is black tie.*

,**black 'widow** *noun* [C] a very poisonous spider that lives in warm areas

bladder /'blæd.ə^r/ ⑤ /-ɚ/ *noun* [C] a bag-like organ inside the body of a person or animal, where urine is stored before it leaves the body: *to empty your bladder* (= urinate)

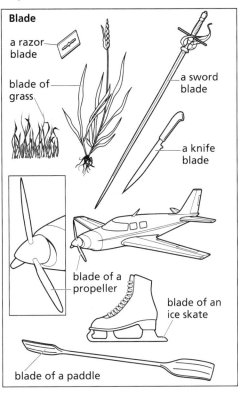

Blade

a razor blade

blade of grass

a sword blade

a knife blade

blade of a propeller

blade of an ice skate

blade of a paddle

blade PART OF KNIFE /bleɪd/ *noun* [C] **1** the flat part on a knife or similar tool or weapon, with a very thin edge used for cutting: *a sword with a steel blade* ○ *a packet of razor blades* **2** a wide flat part on a tool or machine, used to push back water or air: *a propeller blade* ○ *windscreen wiper blades* **3** used in the names of other objects which are flat, thin and sometimes long, like a blade: *a shoulder blade* ○ *a blade of grass*

blah blah (blah) /,blɑː.blɑː'blɑː/ *exclamation*, INFORMAL a phrase used to represent boring speech: *Oh blah blah blah – I've heard it all before!*

Blairite /'bleə.raɪt/ ⑤ /'bler.aɪt/ *noun* [C] a supporter of the British Prime Minister Tony Blair and his political ideas and methods: *Not every new MP is a squeaky-clean Blairite; some are even Old Labour leftists.* **Blairite** /'bleə.raɪt/ ⑤ /'bler.aɪt/ *adj*: *Blairite policies*

blame /bleɪm/ *verb* [T] to say or think that someone or something did something wrong or is responsible for something bad happening: *Don't blame me* (= It is not my fault) *if you miss the bus!* ○ *Hugh blames his mother for his lack of confidence.* ○ *Hugh blames his lack of confidence on his mother.* ○ *You can't really blame Helen for not wanting to get involved.*

B

• **I don't blame *you*** said in order to tell someone that you understand why they are doing something and that you agree with their reason for doing it: *I don't blame him for getting angry – she's behaving dreadfully.*
• **be to blame** to be the reason for something that happens: *The hot weather is partly to blame **for** the water shortage.*
• **A bad workman blames his tools.** *UK SAYING* said when someone has blamed a mistake or failure on the things that they use for their work
blame /bleɪm/ *noun* [U] *Health officials **put** the blame **for** the disease **on*** (= state that the reason for the disease is) *poor housing conditions.* ○ *If anything goes wrong, I'll **take** the blame* (= I will state that it is my fault). ○ *They tried to **pin*** (= put) *the blame **for** the killing **on** an innocent army officer.* ○ *We want to find out what happened, not to **apportion** blame* (= to say someone or something was wrong).
blameless /ˈbleɪm.ləs/ *adj* not responsible for anything bad: *It was mainly my fault, but she wasn't entirely blameless.*
blameworthy /ˈbleɪmˌwɜː.ði/ [US] /-ˌwɝː-/ *adj FORMAL* having done something wrong
blanch [PALE] /blɑːntʃ/ [US] /blæntʃ/ *verb* **1** [I] to turn pale: *While most people would blanch at the prospect of so much work, Daniels seems to enjoy it.* **2** [T] to make a plant pale by covering it up so that the light does not reach it as it grows
blanch [BOIL] /blɑːntʃ/ [US] /blæntʃ/ *verb* [T] to put vegetables or similar foods into boiling water for a few minutes to make them white, remove the skins, get rid of strong flavours, or prepare them for freezing: *blanched almonds*
blancmange /bləˈmɒnʒ/ [US] /-ˈmɑːndʒ/ *noun* [U] a cold sweet food made from milk, sugar and CORNFLOUR
bland /blænd/ *adj USUALLY DISAPPROVING* lacking a strong taste or character or lacking in interest or energy: *I find chicken a little bland.* ○ *Pop music these days is so bland.* **blandly** /ˈblænd.li/ *adv* **blandness** /ˈblænd.nəs/ *noun* [U]
blandishments /ˈblæn.dɪʃ.mənts/ *plural noun FORMAL* pleasant and persuasive words or actions: *She was impervious to his blandishments.*
blank [EMPTY] /blæŋk/ *adj* empty or clear, or containing no information or mark: *a blank sheet of paper* ○ *a blank tape/computer screen* ○ *Sign your name in the blank space at the bottom of the form.*
blank /blæŋk/ *noun* [C] **1** a space in a piece of writing or on a form, left empty for information to be added: *Fill in the blanks in this form.* **2** something not yet marked or finished, such as a key not yet cut into a finished shape
blank [NOT REACTING] /blæŋk/ *adj* showing no understanding or no emotion in your facial expression: *a blank stare/expression* **blankly** /ˈblæŋk.li/ *adv*: *He just **stared** blankly at me.*
blank *verb*

PHRASAL VERBS WITH **blank** ▼

▲ **blank *sth* out** [COVER] *phrasal verb* [M] to intentionally cover over something that is written so that it cannot be read: *Some of the names in the report have been blanked out.*
▲ **blank *sth* out** [FORGET] *phrasal verb* [M] to stop yourself thinking about a memory because it is unpleasant and you would prefer not to remember it: *There may be traumatic incident in your past that you have blanked out.*
ˌblank (ˈcartridge) *noun* [C] a small tube containing explosive but no bullet, used in a gun in order to make a loud noise without causing harm: *The starter's pistol **fires** blanks.*
ˌblank ˈcheque *noun* [C] a cheque that has a person's signature but does not yet have the amount of money written on it
blanket [COVER] /ˈblæŋ.kɪt/ *noun* [C] a flat cover made of wool or similar warm material, usually used on a bed
• **a blanket of *sth*** a thick covering layer of something: *The ground was covered by a thick blanket of snow.*
blanket /ˈblæŋ.kɪt/ *verb* [T often passive] *LITERARY* to cover something completely with a thick layer: *Outside the fields were blanketed **in** fog.*
blanket [UNLIMITED] /ˈblæŋ.kɪt/ *adj* [before n] including or affecting everything, everyone, or all cases, in a large group or area: *a blanket ban* ○ *'Man', as a blanket **term** for both men and women, is now considered sexist.*
ˌblank ˈverse *noun* [U] a type of poetry that does not rhyme, usually with ten syllables in each line
blare /bleəʳ/ [US] /bler/ *verb* [I or T] to make an unpleasantly loud noise: *The loudspeakers blared across the square.* ○ *The radio was blaring **(out)** martial music.* **blare** /bleəʳ/ [US] /bler/ *noun* [S] *the blare of trumpets*
blarney /ˈblɑː.ni/ [US] /ˈblɑːr-/ *noun* [U] a friendly and charming way of talking which makes someone good at persuading people to do things: *Don't listen to any of his blarney!*
blasé /ˌblɑːˈzeɪ/ *adj* bored or not excited, or wishing to seem so: *He flies first class so often, he's become blasé **about** it.*
blaspheme /ˌblæsˈfiːm/ *verb* [I] to use words which show a lack of respect for God or religion, or to swear
blasphemous /ˈblæs.fɪ.məs/ *adj* considered offensive to God or religion: *a blasphemous remark* **blasphemously** /ˈblæs.fɪ.mə.sli/ *adv*
blasphemy /ˈblæs.fə.mi/ *noun* [C or U] something which you say or do that shows you do not respect God or a religion: *to be accused of blasphemy* ○ *FIGURATIVE HUMOROUS Elvis Presley fans think that any criticism of him is blasphemy.*
blast [DESTROY] /blɑːst/ [US] /blæst/ *verb* **1** [I or T] to explode or destroy something or someone with explosives, or to break through or hit something with a similar, very strong force: *A tunnel was to be blasted through the mountains.* ○ *They heard the guns blasting **away** all night.* ○ *FIGURATIVE Their latest record blasted (its way) up the charts* (= moved very quickly because of its popularity). ➲See also **sandblast**. **2** [T] *INFORMAL* to criticise someone or something severely: *The government was blasted by the opposition for failing to reduce inflation.*
blast /blɑːst/ [US] /blæst/ *noun* [C] **1** an explosion: *Three people were injured **in** the blast.* **2** a sudden strong blow of air: *A blast **of** cold air hit him as he opened the window.*
• **a blast from the past** *HUMOROUS* something that you experience which surprises you because it is a very long time since you last experienced it and you had almost forgotten about it
blast [NOISE] /blɑːst/ [US] /blæst/ *verb* [I] to make a very loud and unpleasant noise: *guns/music blasting **(away/out)***
blast /blɑːst/ [US] /blæst/ *noun* [C] a sudden loud noise: *a blast **of** music* ○ *The headteacher blew three blasts **on** a whistle.*
blast [EVENT] /blɑːst/ [US] /blæst/ *noun* [C usually sing] *US INFORMAL* an exciting or enjoyable experience or event, often a party: *You should have come with us last night, we had a real blast!*
▲ **blast off** *phrasal verb* If a rocket blasts off, it leaves the ground to go into space.
blast-off /ˈblɑːst.ɒf/ [US] /ˈblæst.ɑːf/ *noun* [U] the moment when a spacecraft leaves the ground: *Five seconds to blast-off!*
blasted /ˈblɑː.stɪd/ [US] /ˈblæs-/ *adj* [after v] *INFORMAL* drunk: *Patrick got/was absolutely blasted last night.*
ˈblast ˌfurnace *noun* [C] a container in which iron is produced by blowing extremely hot air through a mixture of iron ORE, COKE and LIMESTONE
ˈblast (ˌit) *exclamation OLD-FASHIONED INFORMAL* an expression of anger or annoyance: *Oh blast! I've left my keys at home!*
blasted /ˈblɑː.stɪd/ [US] /ˈblæs-/ *adj* [before n] *OLD-FASHIONED INFORMAL* used in phrases to express anger or annoyance: *I've forgotten my blasted keys!*
blatant /ˈbleɪ.tᵊnt/ *adj* describes something bad that is very obvious or intentional: *a blatant lie* ○ *The whole episode was a blatant attempt to gain publicity.*
blatantly /ˈbleɪ.tᵊnt.li/ *adv*: *It was blatantly **obvious** that she was telling a lie.*
blather /ˈblæð.əʳ/ [US] /-ɚ/ *verb* [I] (*ALSO* **blether**) *INFORMAL* to talk for a long time in a foolish or annoying way: *What on earth are you blathering **on** about?* ○ *Stop*

blethering, woman! **blather** /ˈblæð.əʳ/ [US] /-ɚ/ *noun* **[U]** (*ALSO* **blether**)

blaze [BURN] /bleɪz/ *verb* **[I]** **1** to burn brightly and strongly: *The sun was blazing* ***down*** *that afternoon.* **2** *LITERARY* to be brightly lit or full of colour: *Isaac's eyes suddenly blazed* ***with*** *anger.*

• **blaze a trail** to do something that has never been done before: *Elvis Presley blazed a trail in pop music.*

blaze /bleɪz/ *noun* **[C]** a large strong fire: *Firefighters took two hours to* ***control*** *the blaze.*

• **a blaze of *sth*** something that has a sudden very powerful or noticeable effect: *The garden is a blaze of* ***colour*** *in autumn.* ○ *His book was launched in a blaze of* ***publicity.***

• **what the blazes ... ?** *OLD-FASHIONED INFORMAL* used to give force to something you feel angry about: *What the blazes did he do that for?*

blazing /ˈbleɪ.zɪŋ/ *adj* **1** very bright and hot or powerful: *We quickly grew tired in the blazing* ***sunshine.*** **2** **[before n]** very fierce: *They used to have some blazing* ***rows*** *over money.*

blaze [MARK] /bleɪz/ *noun* **[C]** a white mark on the face of a horse or other animal

blazer /ˈbleɪ.zəʳ/ [US] /-zɚ/ *noun* **[C]** a type of jacket, often with the symbol of a school or organization sewn on the front pocket and worn as part of a uniform: *my new/old* ***school*** *blazer*

blazon /ˈbleɪ.zᵊn/ *verb* **[T]** **emblazon**

bleach /bliːtʃ/ *noun* **[U]** a strong chemical used for cleaning things or removing colour from things

bleach /bliːtʃ/ *verb* **[T]** to remove the colour from something or make it lighter using chemicals: *Gary's had his hair bleached.*

bleachers /ˈbliː.tʃəz/ [US] /-tʃɚz/ *plural noun US* a sloping area of seats at a sports ground which are not covered and are therefore not expensive to sit in

bleak /bliːk/ *adj* **1** If weather or a place is bleak, it is cold, empty and not welcoming or attractive: *The house stands on a bleak, windswept moor.* **2** If a situation is bleak, there is little or no hope for the future: *The economic* ***outlook*** *is bleak.* **bleakness** /ˈbliːk.nəs/ *noun* **[U]**

bleary /ˈblɪə.ri/ [US] /ˈblɪr.i/ *adj* If you have bleary eyes, your eyes are red and watery and you cannot see clearly, because you are tired or have just woken up: *to be bleary-****eyed***

blearily /ˈblɪə.rɪ.li/ [US] /ˈblɪr.ɪ-/ *adv*: *Carl stared blearily* (= in a very tired way) *at the newspaper.*

bleat /bliːt/ *verb* **[I]** **1** When a sheep or goat bleats, it makes a high, shaking sound. **2** *INFORMAL* to complain in an annoying way: *She's always bleating* ***(on)*** *about how badly she's been treated.* **bleat** /bliːt/ *noun* **[C]**

bleed /bliːd/ *verb* **bled, bled** **1** **[I]** to lose blood: *Your arm is bleeding.* ○ *He was bleeding heavily.* **2** **[T]** *OLD USE* to make someone lose blood, as a cure for an illness **3** **[T]** If you bleed a closed system such as a RADIATOR or a brake, you remove air or liquid from it to make it work correctly.

• **bleed *sb* dry** *INFORMAL* to take a lot of money from someone over a period of time: *The West is bleeding poorer countries dry through interest payments on their debts.*

bleeding /ˈbliː.dɪŋ/ *adj* **[before n]**, *UK SLANG* used when you are annoyed with something: *I can't get the bleeding car to start!*

bleeding-edge /ˌbliː.dɪŋˈedʒ/ *adj* **[before n]** relating to or describing systems, devices or ideas that are so modern that they still being developed: *bleeding-edge technology*

ˌbleeding ˈheart *noun* **[C]** *DISAPPROVING* someone who shows too much sympathy for everyone: *I'm sick of bleeding-heart liberal politicians.*

bleep /bliːp/ *noun* **[C]** a short high sound made by a machine, especially if it is repeated: *He wears a wristwatch with an irritating bleep.*

bleep /bliːp/ *verb* **1** **[I]** (of a machine) to make a short high sound: *I heard his alarm clock bleeping this morning.* **2** **[T]** *UK* (*US* **beep**) to call someone, for example a doctor, by sending a signal to a BLEEPER which they carry: *Bleep me if his condition worsens.*

bleeper *UK* /ˈbliː.pəʳ/ [US] /-pɚ/ *noun* **[C]** (*US* **beeper**) a small device that you carry or wear, which moves or makes a noise to tell you that someone wants you to telephone them

blemish /ˈblem.ɪʃ/ *noun* **1** **[C]** a mark on something that spoils its appearance: *freckles, scars and other minor* ***skin*** *blemishes* **2** **[C or U]** a fault in a person's character: *Is any politician's record* ***without*** *blemish on this issue?*

blemish /ˈblem.ɪʃ/ *verb* **[T]** *This latest revelation has seriously blemished* (= spoilt) *the governor's* ***reputation.***

blench /blentʃ/ *verb* **[I]** **1** to move back or away suddenly or react physically because something frightens, disgusts or upsets you: *At the sight of the dead animal, Diana blenched.* **2** *HUMOROUS* to be very unwilling to do something: *My sister blenches* ***at*** *the very thought of changing a baby's nappy.*

blend /blend/ *verb* **[I or T]** to mix or combine together: *Blend the ingredients into a smooth paste.* ○ *The cushions blend well* ***with*** *the colour of the carpet.*

blend /blend/ *noun* **[C]** a mixture of different things or styles: *a rich blend of the finest coffee beans* ○ *Their music is a blend of jazz and African rhythms.*

blended /ˈblen.dɪd/ *adj* describes a drink which contains two or more different types of the same product: *blended whisky*

blender /ˈblen.dəʳ/ [US] /-dɚ/ *noun* **[C]** an electric machine used in the kitchen for breaking down foods or making smooth liquid substances from soft foods and liquids

▲ **blend in/blend into *sth*** *phrasal verb* to look or seem the same as surrounding people or things and therefore not be easily noticeable: *We tried to blend into the crowd.* ○ *They have adopted local customs and tried to blend in with the community.*

bless /bles/ *verb* **[T]** **blessed** or *LITERARY* **blest**, **blessed** or *LITERARY* **blest** to ask for God's help and protection for someone or something, or to call or make someone or something holy

• **be blessed with *sth*** *FORMAL* to be lucky in having a particular thing: *Fortunately we were blessed with fine weather.* ○ *She is blessed with both beauty and brains.*

• **bless my soul!** (*ALSO* **bless me!**, *ALSO* **well I'm blessed!**) *OLD-FASHIONED* an expression of surprise

• **bless you!** something you say to a person who has just sneezed

• **bless you** (*ALSO* **bless your heart**) something you say to tell someone you are grateful to them when they have been kind to you: *"Here, let me help you with your shopping." "Oh, bless you, dear."*

blessed /blest/ /ˈbles.ɪd/ *adj* **1** *FORMAL* holy: *Blessed are the meek for they shall inherit the earth.* **2** *LITERARY* bringing you happiness, luck, or something you need: *blessed peace/rain/silence* ○ *a blessed relief* **3** **[before n]** *INFORMAL* an expression of annoyance: *Take that blessed cat out!*

blessing /ˈbles.ɪŋ/ *noun* **1** **[C or U]** when a priest asks God to take care of a particular person or a group of people: *The mass always ends with a blessing.* ○ *We ask God's blessing* ***on*** *Joan at this difficult time.* **2** **[C]** something which is extremely lucky or makes you happy: *It was a blessing* ***that*** *no one was killed in the accident.*

• ***sb's*** **blessing** approval that someone gives to a plan or action: *The government has* ***given*** *its blessing* ***to*** *a plan to improve the rights of children.* ○ *Eventually they got married with her father's blessing.*

• **a blessing in disguise** something that seems bad or unlucky at first, but results in something good happening later: *Losing that job was a blessing in disguise really, and I ended up in a much more enjoyable career.*

the ˌBlessed ˈVirgin *noun* **[U]** a name for the mother of Christ

blether /ˈbleð.əʳ/ [US] /-ɚ/ *noun, verb* **blather**

blew /bluː/ *past simple of* **blow**

blight /blaɪt/ *noun* **[S]** **1** a disease that damages and kills plants **2** something which spoils or has a very bad effect on something, often for a long time: *His arrival* ***cast a*** *blight* ***on*** *the wedding day.*

blight /blaɪt/ *verb* **[T]** to spoil something: *A broken leg blighted her* ***chances*** *of winning the championship.*

blimey /ˈblaɪ.mi/ *exclamation UK OLD-FASHIONED INFORMAL* an expression of surprise: *Blimey, what a lot of food!*

blimp /blɪmp/ *noun* **[C]** *MAINLY US* an AIRSHIP

blind [SIGHT] /blaɪnd/ *adj* unable to see: *She's been blind since birth.* ○ *He started to* **go** (= become) *blind in his sixties.*
• **(as) blind as a bat** *INFORMAL HUMOROUS* unable to see well: *I'm as blind as a bat without my glasses.*
blind /blaɪnd/ *verb* [T] to make someone unable to see, permanently or for a short time: *She was blinded in an accident at an early age.* ○ *Turning the corner the sun blinded me, so I didn't see the other car.*
• **blind *sb* with science** *UK* to confuse someone by using difficult or technical words to describe something
the blind *plural noun* people who are unable to see: *She trains guide dogs for the blind.*
• **the blind leading the blind** used to describe a situation where a person who knows nothing is getting advice and help from another person who knows almost nothing
blindly /ˈblaɪnd.li/ *adv* not able to see or not noticing what is around you: *The room was completely dark and I fumbled blindly for the door.* **blindness** /ˈblaɪnd.nəs/ *noun* [U]

blind [NOT AWARE] /blaɪnd/ *verb* [T] to make someone unable to notice or understand something: *We mustn't let our prejudices blind us* **to** *the facts of the situation.*
blind /blaɪnd/ *adj* describes an extreme feeling that happens without thought or reason: *blind anger/faith/prejudice* ○ *He was blind* **with** *fury* (= so angry that he could not behave reasonably).
• **be blind to *sth*** to not be aware of something or to refuse to notice something that is obvious to others: *She seems blind to his faults.*
• **not take a blind bit of notice** *UK INFORMAL* to pay no attention: *He didn't take a blind bit of notice* **of** *what I said.*
blindly /ˈblaɪnd.li/ *adv* not thinking about or understanding what you are doing: *They just blindly followed orders.* **blindness** /ˈblaɪnd.nəs/ *noun* [U]

blind [WINDOW] /blaɪnd/ *noun* [C] (*US* **shade**) a cover for a window made of a single piece or strips of cloth, paper or plastic that is pulled up or down by a string: *a roller blind* ○ *a Venetian blind* ➲See picture **In the Office** on page Centre 15

ˌblind ˈalley *noun* [C] a situation or method that is not effective or will not produce results: *This sort of thinking just seems to be* **leading** *us* **up/down** *a blind alley.*

ˌblind ˈdate *noun* [C] **1** when two people who have never met each other go out for a romantic social meeting: *Elaine arranged for me to* **go on** *a blind date with a bloke from her office.* **2** either of the people who meet for a blind date

ˌblind ˈdrunk *adj INFORMAL* extremely drunk

blinder /blaɪn.dəʳ/ Ⓤⓢ /-dɚ/ *noun* [S] *UK INFORMAL* an excellent performance at some activity, especially in sport: *Weir* **played a** *blinder in yesterday's semi-final.*

blindfold /ˈblaɪnd.fəʊld/ Ⓤⓢ /-foʊld/ *noun* [C] a strip of cloth which covers someone's eyes and stops them from seeing
blindfold /ˈblaɪnd.fəʊld/ Ⓤⓢ /-foʊld/ *verb* [T] to cover someone's eyes with a blindfold: *She was blindfolded and taken somewhere in the back of a van.* **blindfold** /ˈblaɪnd.fəʊld/ Ⓤⓢ /-foʊld/ *adv HUMOROUS I've been there so often I could probably drive there blindfold.*

blinding /ˈblaɪn.dɪŋ/ *adj* extremely bright: *There was loud bang and a sudden blinding* **light**.
• **a blinding flash** an idea or answer that suddenly becomes obvious: *The answer came to her* **in** *a blinding flash.*
blindingly /ˈblaɪn.dɪŋ.li/ *adv* extremely: *It's blindingly* **obvious** *that she's not happy at school.*

blind man's buff /ˌblaɪnd.mænzˈbʌf/ *noun* [U] a children's game in which one person has a cloth tied over their eyes and tries to catch the others

blindside [SURPRISE] /ˈblaɪnd.saɪd/ *verb* [T] *US* to surprise someone, usually with harmful results: *The recession blindsided a lot of lawyers who had previously taken for granted their comfortable income.*

ˈblind ˌside [NOT SEEN] *noun* [S] the area behind and slightly to one side of you which you cannot see, for example when you are driving

ˈblind ˌspot *noun* [C usually sing] **1** an area that you are not able to see, especially the part of a road you cannot see when you are driving, behind and slightly to one side of the car: *It can be very dangerous if there's a vehicle* **in your** *blind spot.* **2** a subject that you find very difficult to understand at all, sometimes because you are not willing to try: *I am quite good at English, but I* **have** *a bit of* **a** *blind spot where spelling is concerned.*

bling bling /blɪŋˈblɪŋ/ *adj MAINLY US SLANG* describes jewellery which attracts attention because it is big and expensive, or describes a person who wears this jewellery **bling bling** /blɪŋˈblɪŋ/ *noun* [U]

blink /blɪŋk/ *verb* **1** [I or T] When you blink, you close and then open your eyes quickly once or several times, and when an eye blinks, it does this: **2** [I] *LITERARY* If a light blinks, it flashes on and off.
• **not blink** *INFORMAL* to not show any shock or surprise: *When he was told I was expecting twins, Harry didn't even blink.*
blink /blɪŋk/ *noun* [C usually sing] the act of blinking
• **in the blink of an eye** extremely quickly: *In the blink of an eye, he was gone.*
• **on the blink** *INFORMAL* When a machine is on the blink, it is not working correctly.

blinker /ˈblɪŋ.kəʳ/ Ⓤⓢ /-kɚ/ *noun* [C] *US* a light on the outside of a vehicle which turns on and off quickly to show other people you are going to turn in that direction ➲See picture **Car** on page Centre 12

blinkered /ˈblɪŋ.kəd/ Ⓤⓢ /-kɚd/ *adj* A blinkered person is unable or unwilling to understand other people's beliefs, and blinkered opinions or ways of behaving show an inability or unwillingness to understand other people: *He's very blinkered in his outlook.*

blinkers *UK* /ˈblɪŋ.kəz/ Ⓤⓢ /-kɚz/ *plural noun* (*US* **blinders**) two pieces of leather that are put at the side of a horse's eyes so that it can only see forward

blinking /ˈblɪŋ.kɪŋ/ *adj* [before n] *UK OLD-FASHIONED INFORMAL* an expression of annoyance: *It's a blinking nuisance!*

blip /blɪp/ *noun* [C] **1** a small spot of light, sometimes with a short sharp sound, that appears on a RADAR screen, or a sudden sharp V-shaped bend in a line on a computer screen **2** a temporary change that does not have any special meaning: *Last month's rise in inflation was described by the chancellor as only a blip.*

bliss /blɪs/ *noun* [U] perfect happiness: *Lying on a sunny beach is my idea of* **sheer** *bliss.* ○ *wedded/domestic bliss*
blissful /ˈblɪs.fᵊl/ *adj* extremely or completely happy: *a blissful childhood/holiday* ○ *We spent a blissful year together before things started to go wrong.*
• **in blissful ignorance** not knowing any of the unpleasant facts about something: *All the time his business was failing, he kept his wife and family in blissful ignorance.*
blissfully /ˈblɪs.fᵊl.i/ *adv* in an extremely happy way: *They seemed blissfully* **happy**. ○ *All this time I was blissfully* **unaware** *of the situation.*

bliss /blɪs/ *verb*
▲ **bliss *(sb)* out** *phrasal verb INFORMAL* to become, or to make someone, completely happy and relaxed: *to bliss out* **on** *music/LSD*
blissed out /ˌblɪstˈaʊt/ *adj*: *They sat two by two, blissed out in the sunshine.*

blister /ˈblɪs.təʳ/ Ⓤⓢ /-tɚ/ *noun* [C] **1** a painful red swelling on the skin that contains liquid, caused usually by continuous rubbing, especially on your heel, or by burning: *New shoes always give me blisters.* **2** a hollow rounded swelling that appears on a surface **blister** /ˈblɪs.təʳ/ Ⓤⓢ /-tɚ/ *verb* [I or T] *The sun blistered the paintwork.* ○ *I burnt my shoulders over the weekend and they're starting to blister.* **blistered** /ˈblɪs.təd/ Ⓤⓢ /-tɚd/ *adj*
blistering /ˈblɪs.tᵊr.ɪŋ/ Ⓤⓢ /-tɚ-/ *adj* **1** extremely hot: *We went out in the blistering* **heat**. **2** extremely fast: *The runners set off at a blistering* **pace**. **3** extremely angry and hurtful: *blistering remarks/sarcasm*

blithe /blaɪð/ *adj OLD-FASHIONED* happy and without worry: *She shows a blithe disregard for danger.*
blithely /ˈblaɪð.li/ *adv*: *She blithely agreed to the contract without realising what its consequences would be.*

blithering idiot /ˌblɪð.ᵊr.ɪŋˈɪd.i.ət/ Ⓤⓢ /-ɚ-/ *noun* [C] *OLD-FASHIONED INFORMAL* an extremely stupid person

blitz [ATTACK] /blɪts/ *noun* [C] a fast, violent attack on a town, city, etc. usually with bombs dropped from aircraft

the Blitz *noun* [S] the big attacks on British towns made by German aircraft in 1940-1: *She was killed* ***in/during*** *the Blitz.* **blitz** /blɪts/ *verb* [T]

blitz [ACTIVITY] /blɪts/ *noun* [C] **1** a lot of energetic activity: *The car was launched with a massive* ***media/advertising blitz****, involving newspapers, magazines, television and radio.* **2** *SPECIALIZED* when both players have to make a lot of moves in a very short period at the end of a timed game of chess, before the time allowed is past

• **a blitz on *sth*** *INFORMAL* a great effort to improve something or do something that needs to be done: *We* ***had*** *a blitz on the house at the weekend and cleaned it completely.*

blitzkrieg /ˈblɪts.kriːg/ *noun* [C] a sudden attack involving aircraft and forces on the ground, which is intended to surprise and quickly defeat the enemy

blizzard /ˈblɪz.əd/ Ⓤⓢ /-ɚd/ *noun* [C] **1** a severe snow storm with strong winds: *We once got* ***stuck in*** *a blizzard for six hours.* ○ *In Sussex, blizzard* ***conditions*** *made the main roads almost impassable.* **2** *INFORMAL* a large amount of something which arrives or is produced together in a confusing or badly organized way: *a blizzard* ***of*** *statistics/handouts*

bloated /ˈbləʊ.tɪd/ Ⓤⓢ /ˈbloʊ.t̬ɪd/ *adj* **1** swollen and rounded because of containing too much air, liquid or food: *a bloated stomach* ○ *a bloated* (= uncomfortably full) ***feeling*** **2** *DISAPPROVING* unnecessarily large or wealthy: *a bloated bureaucracy* ○ *a bloated capitalist*

bloat /bləʊt/ Ⓤⓢ /bloʊt/ *verb* [I or T] to swell up, or to make someone or something bloated: *If I eat it, my stomach bloats* ***up****.* **bloating** /ˈbləʊ.tɪŋ/ Ⓤⓢ /ˈbloʊ.t̬ɪŋ/ *noun* [U] *He suffered from indigestion and bloating.*

bloater /ˈbləʊ.təʳ/ Ⓤⓢ /ˈbloʊ.t̬ɚ/ *noun* [C] a HERRING or MACKEREL that has been preserved with salt and lightly smoked

blob /blɒb/ Ⓤⓢ /blɑːb/ *noun* [C] a fat round drop, usually of something sticky or thick: *a blob* ***of*** *glue/paint*

bloc /blɒk/ Ⓤⓢ /blɑːk/ *noun* [C] a group of countries or people that have similar political interests: *The European Union is a powerful* ***trading/trade*** *bloc.* ○ *the former* ***Eastern/Communist*** *bloc countries*

block [LUMP] /blɒk/ Ⓤⓢ /blɑːk/ *noun* [C] a solid straight-sided lump of hard material: *a block of wood/ice*

the block *noun* [S] *OLD USE* a large piece of wood on which criminals had their head cut off: *Anne Boleyn* ***went to*** (= was killed on) *the block.*

• **have/put *your* head on the block** to risk a bad thing happening to you by doing something or helping someone: *I'm not going to put my head on the block* ***for*** *you.*

block [GROUP] /blɒk/ Ⓤⓢ /blɑːk/ *noun* [C] a group of things bought, dealt with, or considered together: *a block of tickets/seats/shares* ○ *Corporate-hospitality firms make block* ***bookings*** (= buy large numbers of seats) *at big sporting events.*

block [BUILDING] /blɒk/ Ⓤⓢ /blɑːk/ *noun* [C] a large, usually tall building divided into separate parts for use as offices or homes by several different organizations or people: *an office block* ○ *UK a tower block* ○ *UK a block of flats*

block [AREA] /blɒk/ Ⓤⓢ /blɑːk/ *noun* [C] **1** *MAINLY US* the distance along a street from where one road crosses it to the place where the next road crosses it, or one part of a street like this, especially in a town or city: *The museum is just six blocks away.* ○ *My friend and I live* ***on the*** *same block.* **2** a square group of buildings or houses with roads on each side: *I took a walk around the block.*

• **round/around the block** on the next street which crosses this street: *He lives just round the block.*

block [PREVENT] /blɒk/ Ⓤⓢ /blɑːk/ *verb* [T] to prevent movement through something, or to prevent something from happening or succeeding: *A fallen tree is blocking the road.* ○ *My view was blocked by a tall man in front of me.* ○ *She was very talented and I felt her parents were blocking her* ***progress****.* ○ *A group of politicians blocked the* ***proposal****.*

block /blɒk/ Ⓤⓢ /blɑːk/ *noun* [C usually sing] *A block* ***in*** (= An object blocking) *the pipe was preventing the water from coming through.*

blockage /ˈblɒk.ɪdʒ/ Ⓤⓢ /ˈblɑː.kɪdʒ/ *noun* [C or U] something that stops something else passing through, or when something does this: *His death was caused by a blockage in one of his arteries.* **blocked** /blɒkt/ Ⓤⓢ /blɑːkt/ *adj*: *The road is blocked – you'll have to go round the other way.* ○ *I've got a sore throat and a blocked* ***(up)*** ***nose****.*

PHRASAL VERBS WITH **block** ▼

▲ **block *sth* in** *phrasal verb* [M] to put a vehicle so close to another vehicle that it cannot drive away: *Another car had parked behind me and blocked me in.*

▲ **block *sth* off** *phrasal verb* [M] to close a road, path or entrance so that people cannot use it: *All the roads out of the town had been blocked off by the police.*

▲ **block *sth* out** [STOP FROM PASSING] *phrasal verb* [M] to stop light or noise from passing through something: *The tree outside the window blocks out the sun.*

▲ **block *sth* out** [STOP FROM THINKING] *phrasal verb* [M] to stop yourself from thinking about an unpleasant memory because it upsets you: *He's trying to block out memories of the accident.*

▲ **block *sth* up** *phrasal verb* [M] to fill a narrow space with something so that nothing can pass through: *In autumn, leaves block the drains up.*

blockade /blɒkˈeɪd/ Ⓤⓢ /blɑːˈkeɪd/ *noun* [C] when a country or place is surrounded by soldiers or ships to stop people or goods from going in or out: *an air and sea blockade* ○ *The Soviet blockade* ***of*** *Berlin was* ***lifted*** *in May 1949.* ○ *There is still some hope that the* ***economic*** *blockade will work and make military intervention unnecessary.* **blockade** /blɒkˈeɪd/ Ⓤⓢ /blɑːˈkeɪd/ *verb* [T] *The Estonian port of Tallinn was blockaded for a time by Soviet warships.*

ˌblock and ˈtackle *noun* [U] a device for raising objects off the ground, consisting of one or more small wheels with a rope or chain going around them, connected to a high part of a building

blockbuster /ˈblɒkˌbʌs.təʳ/ Ⓤⓢ /ˈblɑːkˌbʌs.tɚ/ *noun* [C] *INFORMAL* a book or film that is very successful, especially because of its exciting contents: *a blockbuster movie/novel*

ˌblock ˈcapitals *plural noun* (*ALSO* **block letters**) a style of writing in which each letter of a word is written separately and clearly using the capital letters of the alphabet: *Please print your name and address in block capitals.*

blockhead /ˈblɒk.hed/ Ⓤⓢ /ˈblɑːk-/ *noun* [C] *OLD-FASHIONED INFORMAL* a stupid person

ˌblock of ˈflats *UK noun* [C] (*US* **apartment building**) a large building that is divided into apartments

ˌblock ˈvote *noun* [C] (*ALSO* **card vote**) *UK* a large number of votes that are made in the same way by one person who represents a large group of people

bloke /bləʊk/ Ⓤⓢ /bloʊk/ *noun* [C] *UK INFORMAL* a man, often one who is considered to be ordinary: *Paul's a really good bloke* (= I like him a lot). ○ *He's a funny (sort of) bloke* (= slightly strange).

blokeish, blokish /ˈbləʊ.kɪʃ/ Ⓤⓢ /ˈbloʊ-/ *adj UK INFORMAL* describes a man who behaves in the way people traditionally think ordinary men behave when they are together: *He's too blokeish for me – always talking about football and cars.*

blonde, blond /blɒnd/ Ⓤⓢ /blɑːnd/ *adj* with pale yellow or golden hair: *blonde hair/highlights* ○ *a blonde woman/a blond man*

blonde /blɒnd/ Ⓤⓢ /blɑːnd/ *noun* [C] a woman with pale yellow or golden hair: *Who's the blonde talking to Bob?*

• **Blondes have more fun.** *SAYING* said to express the common belief that men are more attracted to women with BLONDE (= pale yellow or golden) hair and give them more attention

blood [LIQUID] /blʌd/ *noun* [U] the red liquid that is sent around the body by the heart, and carries oxygen and important substances to organs and tissue, and removes waste products: *He* ***lost*** *a lot of blood in the accident.*

B

B

• **give/donate blood** to allow a trained person to take some blood from your body so that it can be stored and is ready to be given to people who have lost a lot of blood during an accident or operation

• **new/fresh blood** people who join an organization and who can provide new ideas and energy: *The company has brought in some new blood in an effort to revive its fortunes.*

• **make *your* blood boil** to make you extremely angry: *The way they have treated those people makes my blood boil.*

• **be after *sb's* blood** INFORMAL to be very angry with someone and threatening to harm them: *You'd better stay out of her way – she's after your blood.*

• **make *your* blood run cold** A sound, sight or thought that makes your blood run cold frightens you very much: *I heard a tapping on the window which made my blood run cold.*

• **blood and guts** INFORMAL extreme violence: *There was a bit too much blood and guts in the film for my liking.*

• **get blood out of/from a stone** to make someone give or tell you something, when it is extremely difficult because of the character or mood of the person or organization you are dealing with: *Persuading Chris to buy a round of drinks is like getting blood out of a stone.*

bloody /'blʌd.i/ *adj* **1** bleeding: *a bloody nose* **2** extremely violent and involving a lot of blood and injuries: *It was a long and bloody battle and many men were killed.* **-blooded** /-blʌd.ɪd/ *suffix*: *warm-blooded*

bloodied /'blʌd.id/ *adj* LITERARY covered in blood

bloodless /'blʌd.ləs/ *adj* **1** describes a military operation involving no deaths: *The rebel soldiers seized power in a bloodless **coup**.* **2** describes a face or skin that is extremely pale: *His face was thin and bloodless.* **3** without emotion

blood [FAMILY] /blʌd/ *noun* [U] family relationship by birth rather than marriage: *They are related **by** blood.* ○ *She has Russian blood* (= one or more of her relatives was Russian).

• **be in the/*your* blood** If an ability or skill is in someone's blood, they have it naturally, usually because it already exists in their family: *His father and grandmother were painters too so it's obviously in the blood.*

• **Blood is thicker than water.** SAYING said to emphasize that you believe that family connections are always more important than other types of relationships

blood [FIRST EXPERIENCE] /blʌd/ *verb* [T] to give someone their first experience of something: *They decided to blood him in the full international team at the age of only 18.*

'blood ˌbank *noun* [C] a cool place where blood is stored before it is used in hospitals

bloodbath /'blʌd.bɑːθ/ [US] /-bæθ/ *noun* [S] an extremely violent event in which a great number of people are killed: *Is there nothing that the outside world can do to **prevent a** bloodbath?*

'blood ˌcount *noun* [C usually sing] the number of red and white blood cells in a person's blood, or a medical test to discover this

blood-curdling /'blʌdˌkɜː.dl̩.ɪŋ/ [US] /-ˌkɝː-/ *adj* causing a feeling of extreme fear: *a blood-curdling story/scream*

'blood ˌdonor *noun* [C] someone who regularly gives some of their blood for ill people who need it

'blood ˌgroup UK FOR **blood type**

bloodhound /'blʌd.haʊnd/ *noun* [C] a large dog that has a very good ability to smell things, and is used for hunting animals or finding people who are lost

bloodletting /'blʌdˌlet.ɪŋ/ [US] /-ˌlet̬-/ *noun* **1** [U] FORMAL killing and violence, especially between enemy groups involved in an argument that has existed for a long time: *ethnic bloodletting* **2** [S or U] when a company reduces the number of people working for it: *EWS carried out further bloodletting by sacking senior employees, but has acquired a new chief executive.* **3** [U] in the past, a medical treatment in which blood was taken from a person who was ill

'blood ˌlust *noun* [U] when people enjoy being violent or watching other people being violent

'blood ˌmoney *noun* [U] **1** DISAPPROVING money paid to the family of a murdered person **2** money paid to someone for killing someone else, or for giving information about a person who has killed someone

'blood ˌpoisoning *noun* [U] **septicaemia** or **toxaemia**

'blood ˌpressure *noun* [U] a measure of the pressure at which the blood flows through the body: *The nurse will **take** your blood pressure in a moment.* ○ *to have/suffer from **high/low** blood pressure*

'blood ˌrelation *noun* [C] (ALSO **blood relative**) someone who is related to you by birth rather than through marriage

bloodshed /'blʌd.ʃed/ *noun* [U] killing and violence: *The army was brought in to try to prevent further bloodshed.*

bloodshot /'blʌd.ʃɒt/ [US] /-ʃɑːt/ *adj* When your eyes are bloodshot, they are red or pink on the white parts.

'blood ˌsport *noun* [C usually pl] any sport that involves animals being killed or hurt to excite the people watching or taking part

bloodstain /'blʌd.steɪn/ *noun* [C] a mark made by blood, often as a result of a violent event

bloodstained /'blʌd.steɪnd/ *adj* marked with blood: *Bloodstained **clothing** was found near the scene.*

bloodstream /'blʌd.striːm/ *noun* [S] the flow of blood around the body: *The drug works more quickly if it is injected directly into the bloodstream.*

'blood ˌtest *noun* [C] a scientific examination of a person's blood to find out whether they have any diseases or lack any important substances

bloodthirsty /'blʌdˌθɜː.sti/ [US] /-ˌθɝː-/ *adj* eager to see or take part in violence and killing: *a bloodthirsty killer/mob*

'blood ˌties *plural noun* the relationships that exist by birth rather than through marriage

'blood transˌfusion *noun* [C] a process in which blood that has been taken from one person is put into another person's body, especially after an accident or during an operation

'blood ˌtype *noun* [C] (UK ALSO **blood group**) one of the groups that human blood is divided into: *a rare/common blood type*

'blood ˌvessel *noun* [C] any of the tubes through which blood flows in the body

• **(almost) burst a blood vessel** HUMOROUS to become very angry about something: *Mum almost burst a blood vessel when I told her what happened.*

bloody [ANGER] /'blʌd.i/ *adj* [before n], *adv* MAINLY UK VERY INFORMAL used to express anger or to emphasize what you are saying in a slightly rude way: *I've had a bloody **awful** week.* ○ *It's a bloody **disgrace** that some war widows don't get a decent pension.* ○ *Don't be a bloody **idiot**!* ○ *This computer's bloody **useless**! It's always going wrong.* ○ *Don't you tell me what to do! I'll do what I bloody **well** like in my own house.*

• **bloody hell** VERY INFORMAL a rude way of expressing great anger or annoyance: *Bloody hell! I've lost my wallet.* ○ *What the bloody hell did you do that for?*

bloody [EMPHASIS] /'blʌd.i/ *adj* [before n], *adv* MAINLY UK VERY INFORMAL used to emphasize an adjective, adverb or noun in a slightly rude way: *Life would be bloody **boring** if nothing ever went wrong.* ○ *Don't be so bloody **stupid**.* ○ *She's done bloody **well** to reach the semi-final.* ○ *You must think I'm a bloody **fool**.* ○ *I had a bloody **good** time last night.* ○ *I'm afraid there's **not a** bloody **thing*** (= nothing) *you can do about it.* ○ *I can't see **a** bloody **thing*** (= anything) *in here.*

bloody mary, **Bloody Mary** /ˌblʌd.i'meə.ri/ [US] /-'mer.i/ *noun* [C] an alcoholic drink made of VODKA and tomato juice

bloody-minded /ˌblʌd.i'maɪn.dɪd/ *adj* INFORMAL describes someone who makes things difficult for others and opposes their views for no good reason: *He's just being bloody-minded* **bloody-mindedness** /ˌblʌd.i'maɪn.dɪd.nəs/ *noun* [U] INFORMAL

bloom /bluːm/ *verb* [I] **1** When a flower blooms, it opens or is open, and when a plant or tree blooms it produces flowers: *These flowers will bloom all through the* *summer.* **2** to grow or develop successfully: *Rimbaud's poetic genius bloomed early.*

bloom /bluːm/ *noun* **1** [C] a flower on a plant **2** [S or U] *LITERARY* health, energy and attractiveness: *He was nineteen, in the* ***full*** *bloom of youth.*

• **be in bloom** to be producing flowers: *The apple trees are in* ***full*** *bloom* (= completely covered in flowers).

• **come into bloom** to start to produce flowers: *The roses are just coming into bloom.*

blooming /ˈbluː.mɪŋ/ *adj* A person who is blooming has a healthy, energetic and attractive appearance: *Jo looked really well, – positively blooming.*

bloomer [MISTAKE] /ˈbluː.məʳ/ [US] /-mɚ/ *noun* [C] *UK OLD-FASHIONED SLANG* a silly or embarrassing mistake which does not have serious results

bloomer [BREAD] /ˈbluː.məʳ/ [US] /-mɚ/ *noun* [C] *UK* a type of large loaf which has diagonal cuts on the top

bloomers /ˈbluː.məz/ [US] /-mɚz/ *plural noun* **1** in the past, large loose-fitting underwear worn below the waist by women **2** in the past, long loose trousers made to fit tightly around the ankles, worn by women under a skirt or for sport

blooming /ˈbluː.mɪŋ/ *adj* [before n], *adv* (*ALSO* **bloomin'**) *MAINLY UK OLD-FASHIONED INFORMAL* used to emphasize a noun, adverb or adjective, or to express annoyance: *It's a blooming disgrace!* ○ *I'm not going to bloomin' well apologise to him!* ➲See also **blooming** at **bloom**.

blooper /ˈbluː.pəʳ/ [US] /-pɚ/ *noun* [C] *US INFORMAL* an amusing mistake made by an actor during the making of a film or television programme and usually removed before the film or programme is shown

blossom /ˈblɒs.ᵊm/ [US] /ˈblɑː.sᵊm/ *verb* [I] **1** When a tree or plant blossoms, it produces flowers before producing edible fruit: *The cherry tree is beginning to blossom.* **2** When people blossom, they become more attractive, successful or confident, and when good feelings or relationships blossom, they develop and become stronger: *She has really blossomed recently.* ○ *She is suddenly blossoming* ***into*** *a very attractive woman.* ○ *Sean and Sarah's friendship blossomed* ***into*** *love.*

blossom /ˈblɒs.ᵊm/ [US] /ˈblɑː.sᵊm/ *noun* [C or U] a small flower, or the small flowers on a tree or plant: *apple/cherry blossom*

• **be in blossom** to be flowering

blot [SPOILED] /blɒt/ [US] /blɑːt/ *noun* [C] a small area of ink made by mistake: *an ink blot*

• **a blot on** ***sb's*** **character** *SLIGHTLY FORMAL* a fault that spoils someone's reputation

• **a blot on the landscape** something such as an ugly building that spoils a pleasant view

blot /blɒt/ [US] /blɑːt/ *verb* [T] **-tt-** to make a blot or blots on something

• **blot** ***your*** **copybook** *UK* to do something that makes other people respect or trust you less: *I really blotted my copybook by missing the meeting.*

blot [DRY] /blɒt/ [US] /blɑːt/ *verb* [T] **-tt-** to dry a wet surface, or writing done in ink, by pressing something soft and absorbent against it: *I signed my name and blotted the paper.* ○ *She put on her lipstick and then carefully blotted her lips* ***with*** *a tissue.*

blotter /ˈblɒt.əʳ/ [US] /ˈblɑː.t̬ɚ/ *noun* [C] a large piece of BLOTTING PAPER with a stiff back which is used to absorb ink, and is often put on the top of a DESK to protect it when writing

PHRASAL VERBS WITH **blot** ▼

▲ **blot** ***sth*** **out** [SUN] *phrasal verb* [M] to hide or block the light from something, especially the sun: *A dark cloud suddenly blotted out the sun.*

▲ **blot** ***sth*** **out** [MEMORY] *phrasal verb* [M] to stop yourself, or to prevent you, thinking about something unpleasant: *Perhaps there are some memories so bad that you have to blot them out.*

blotch /blɒtʃ/ [US] /blɑːtʃ/ *noun* [C usually pl] an irregularly-shaped mark, for example on a person's skin: *Her face was covered in purple blotches.* **blotchy** /ˈblɒtʃ.i/ [US] /ˈblɑː.tʃi/ *adj*: *He'd been crying and his face was all blotchy.*

ˈblotting ˌpaper *noun* [U] thick soft paper for pressing onto a piece of paper you have just written on in ink, in order to dry it

blotto /ˈblɒt.əʊ/ [US] /ˈblɑː.t̬oʊ/ *adj OLD-FASHIONED SLANG* extremely drunk

blouse /blaʊz/ [US] /blaʊs/ *noun* [C] a shirt for a woman or girl: *a white silk blouse*

blow [SEND OUT AIR] /bləʊ/ [US] /bloʊ/ *verb* **blew, blown** **1** [I or T] to move and make currents of air, or to be moved or make something move on a current of air: *The wind was blowing* ***harder*** *every minute.* ○ *The letter blew* ***away*** *and I had to run after it.* ○ *The gale-force wind had blown the fence* ***down***. ○ *I blew the dust* ***off*** *the books.* ○ *I wish you wouldn't blow smoke* ***in*** *my face.* **2** [I or T] to make a sound by forcing air out of your mouth and through an instrument, or to make a sound when someone does this: *Ann blew a few notes on the trumpet.* ○ *He scored the winning goal just before the whistle blew* (= had a stream of air sent through so that it made a sound). **3** [T] to shape glass which has been heated until it is soft into an object by blowing air into it down a tube: *a beautiful blown glass vase*

• **blow** ***your*** **nose** to force air from your lungs and through your nose to clear it

• **blow** ***sb*** **a kiss** (*ALSO* **blow a kiss to/at** ***sb***) to kiss your hand and blow on it in the direction of someone

• **blow the cobwebs away** *UK* to get rid of feelings of tiredness, usually with fresh air or exercise: *We went for a five-mile jog to blow the cobwebs away.*

• **blow the gaff** *UK OLD-FASHIONED* to make known a secret: *He's a good bloke – he wouldn't blow the gaff* ***on*** *us.*

• **blow hot and cold** to sometimes like or be interested in something or someone and sometimes not, so people are confused about how you really feel: *He's been blowing hot and cold* ***about*** *the trip to Holland ever since I first suggested it.*

• **blow** ***your*** **own trumpet/horn** to tell everyone proudly about your achievements

• **blow the whistle on** ***sb/sth*** *INFORMAL* to cause something bad that someone is doing to stop, especially by bringing it to the attention of other people

blow /bləʊ/ [US] /bloʊ/ *noun* [C usually sing] when you blow something, such as your nose or an instrument: *Have a good blow* (= blow your nose well).

blowy /ˈbləʊ.i/ [US] /ˈbloʊ-/ *adj INFORMAL* windy: *a blowy day*

blow [DESTROY] /bləʊ/ [US] /bloʊ/ *verb* **blew, blown** **1** [T] to cause something to be destroyed by a bomb, technical failure, etc: *His car had been blown* ***to*** *pieces.* **2** [I or T] If an electrical FUSE (= short thin piece of wire) blows, or if something electrical blows a fuse, the device it is fitted to stops working because it is receiving too much electricity. **3** [I] *INFORMAL* If a tyre blows, it suddenly gets a hole in it and goes flat. **4** [T] *INFORMAL* to spend a large amount of money, especially on things that are not really necessary: *When I first got paid I blew it all* ***on*** *a night out.*

• **blow** ***sth*** **sky-high** to seriously damage something by making it explode: *The explosion blew the building sky-high.*

• **blow** ***sb's*** **cover** to make known secret information about who someone is or what they are doing

• **blow a fuse/gasket** *OLD-FASHIONED INFORMAL* to become very angry: *When he told her how much it cost, she blew a gasket.*

• **blow** ***sb's*** **brains out** *SLANG* to kill someone by shooting them in the head

• **blow it** (*ALSO* **blow** ***your*** **chance**) *INFORMAL* to fail to take advantage of an opportunity by doing or saying something wrong: *I really I blew it when I turned down that job offer, didn't I?*

• **blow** ***your*** **mind** *INFORMAL* If something blows your mind, you find it very exciting and unusual: *There was one scene in the film that really blew my mind.* ➲See also **mind-blowing**.

• **blow (it)!** *OLD-FASHIONED INFORMAL* an expression of annoyance: *Oh, blow it! I've forgotten to invite Paul to the party.*

• **(well) I'll be blowed!** (*ALSO* **blow me!**) *OLD-FASHIONED INFORMAL* an expression of great surprise: *"Kate's getting*

B

married." "Well, I'll be blowed!"
• **be blowed if ...** OLD-FASHIONED INFORMAL If someone says that they are blowed if they will do something, they are determined not to do it: *I'm blowed if I'm going to pay for his taxi home.*

blow [HIT] /bləʊ/ [US] /bloʊ/ *noun* [C] a hard hit with a hand or a weapon: *a sharp blow* ***to*** *the stomach*
• **come to blows** to have a physical fight or a serious argument with someone: *Demonstrators nearly came to blows* ***with*** *the police during the march.* ○ *Do you think the two countries will come to blows* ***over*** *this?*

blow [BAD EVENT] /bləʊ/ [US] /bloʊ/ *noun* [C] an unexpected event that has a damaging effect on someone or something: *Losing his job was a severe blow* ***to*** *his confidence.* ○ *Her death came as a terrible blow* ***to*** *her parents.*

blow [DRUG] /bləʊ/ [US] /bloʊ/ *noun* [U] **1** SLANG **cannabis** **2** US SLANG **cocaine**

PHRASAL VERBS WITH **blow**

▲ **blow *sb* away** [PLEASE] *phrasal verb* [M] MAINLY US INFORMAL to surprise or please someone very much: *The ending will blow you away.*
▲ **blow *sb/sth* away** [DEFEAT] *phrasal verb* [M] US INFORMAL to defeat someone or something completely, especially in a sports competition: *They blew the other team away in the second half of the game.*
▲ **blow *sb* away** [KILL] *phrasal verb* [M] US INFORMAL to kill a person by shooting them
▲ **blow *sth/sb* off** *phrasal verb* [M] US to treat something or someone as if they are not important: *Just blow off his comments, he's only joking.*
▲ **blow *(sth)* out** [STOP BURNING] *phrasal verb* [M] If a flame blows out or you blow it out, it stops burning when a person or the wind blows on it: *After dinner she blew out the candles.* ○ *The sudden breeze made the candles blow out.*
▲ **blow *sb* out** [NOT MEET SOMEONE] *phrasal verb* [M] INFORMAL to disappoint someone by not meeting them or not doing something that you had arranged to do with them: *She was supposed to go to that party with me, but she blew me out.*
▲ **blow over** [SITUATION] *phrasal verb* When an argument blows over, it becomes gradually less important until it ends and is forgotten: *I thought that after a few days the argument would blow over.*
▲ **blow over** [STORM] *phrasal verb* When a storm blows over, it becomes gradually less strong until it ends: *The storm raged all night but by morning it had blown over.*
▲ **blow *(sb/sth)* up** [DESTROY] *phrasal verb* [M] to destroy something or kill someone with a bomb, or to be destroyed or killed by a bomb: *They threatened to blow up the plane if their demands were not met.* ○ *He drove over a landmine and his jeep blew up.*
▲ **blow *sth* up** [FILL WITH AIR] *phrasal verb* [M] to fill something with air: *Would you help me blow up these balloons?*
▲ **blow *sth* up** [PHOTO] *phrasal verb* [M] to print a photograph or picture in a larger size
▲ **blow up** [STORM] *phrasal verb* When a storm blows up, it begins.
▲ **blow up** [ANGER] *phrasal verb* INFORMAL to suddenly become very angry: *My dad blew up (****at*** *me) when he saw the phone bill.*

blow-by-blow /ˌbləʊ.baɪˈbləʊ/ [US] /ˌbloʊ.baɪˈbloʊ/ *adj* [before n] INFORMAL A blow-by-blow description contains every detail and action of an event: *You'll have to tell me about your night our with Hamish – I want a blow-by-blow* ***account****!*

blow-dry /ˈbləʊ.draɪ/ [US] /ˈbloʊ-/ *verb* [T] to dry your hair using an electric HAIR DRYER **blow-dry** /ˈbləʊ.draɪ/ [US] /ˈbloʊ-/ *noun* [C] *She had a cut and blow-dry.*

the ˈblower *noun* [S] UK OLD-FASHIONED INFORMAL the telephone: *Get* ***on*** *the blower and invite him round.*

blowgun /ˈbləʊ.gʌn/ [US] /ˈbloʊ-/ *noun* [C] US FOR **blowpipe**

blowhard /ˈbləʊ.hɑːd/ [US] /ˈbloʊ.hɑːrd/ *noun* [C] US INFORMAL DISAPPROVING a person who likes to talk about how important they are

blowhole /ˈbləʊ.həʊl/ [US] /ˈbloʊ.hoʊl/ *noun* [C] an opening in the top of the head of a whale, through which it breathes

ˈblow ˌjob *noun* [C usually sing] OFFENSIVE the sexual activity of moving the tongue across or sucking the penis in order to give pleasure

blowlamp /ˈbləʊ.læmp/ [US] /ˈbloʊ-/ *noun* [C] UK a **blowtorch**

blowout [EXPLOSION] /ˈbləʊ.aʊt/ [US] /ˈbloʊ-/ *noun* [C] MAINLY US a sudden bursting of a tyre on a road vehicle while it is moving quickly

blowout [MEAL] /ˈbləʊ.aʊt/ [US] /ˈbloʊ-/ *noun* [C] **1** UK INFORMAL a very large meal **2** US INFORMAL a large party or social occasion

blowpipe UK /ˈbləʊ.paɪp/ [US] /ˈbloʊ-/ *noun* [C] (US **blowgun**) a weapon in the shape of a tube with which arrows are fired by blowing through it

blowsy, blowzy /ˈblaʊ.zi/ *adj* describes a woman who is quite fat and untidy looking, often with badly fitting clothes

blowtorch /ˈbləʊ.tɔːtʃ/ [US] /ˈbloʊ.tɔːrtʃ/ *noun* [C] (UK ALSO **blowlamp**) a tool used to heat metal or remove paint from a surface by producing an extremely hot flame

blowy /ˈbləʊ.i/ [US] /ˈbloʊ-/ *adj* ➲See at **blow** SEND OUT AIR.

blubber [CRY] (-bb-) /ˈblʌb.əʳ/ [US] /-ɚ/ *verb* [I] (UK INFORMAL **blub**) INFORMAL DISAPPROVING to cry in a noisy and childish way: *There he sat, cowering against the wall, blubbering like a child.* ○ *Oh stop blubbing! Your knee can't hurt that much.*

blubber [FAT] /ˈblʌb.əʳ/ [US] /-ɚ/ *noun* [U] **1** the thick layer of fat under the skin of sea mammals such as whales, which keeps them warm **2** INFORMAL too much body fat on a human: *Take some exercise and get rid of some of that blubber!*

bludgeon /ˈblʌdʒ.ᵊn/ *verb* [T] **1** to hit someone hard and repeatedly with a heavy weapon: *The two boys had been mercilessly bludgeoned* ***to death.*** **2** to force someone to do something: *The children bludgeoned their parents* ***into*** *taking them to the zoo.*

blue [COLOUR] /bluː/ *adj* of the colour of the sky without clouds on a bright day, or a darker or lighter variety of this: *a faded blue shirt* ○ *pale blue eyes* ○ *Her hands were blue* ***with cold*** (= slightly blue because of the cold).
blue /bluː/ *noun* [C or U] a blue colour
• **until *you are* blue in the face** If you say or shout something until you are blue in the face, you are wasting your efforts because you will get no results: *You can tell her to tidy her room until you are blue in the face, but she won't do it.*
• **out of the blue** If something happens out of the blue, it is completely unexpected: *One day, out of the blue, she announced that she was leaving.*
• **once in a blue moon** very rarely: *My sister lives in Alaska, so I only see her once in a blue moon.*
• **scream/shout blue murder** INFORMAL to show your annoyance about something, especially by shouting or complaining very loudly: *He'll scream blue murder if he doesn't get his way.*
bluish, blueish /ˈbluː.ɪʃ/ *adj* slightly blue: *bluish-grey*

blue [SEXUAL] /bluː/ *adj* showing or mentioning sexual activity in a way that offends many people: *a blue joke* ○ *a blue movie/film* ○ *His humour is a bit too blue for my tastes.*

blue [SAD] /bluː/ *adj* [after v] INFORMAL feeling or showing sadness: *He's been a bit blue since he failed his exams.*
blues /bluːz/ *noun* [U] a type of slow, sad music, originally from the southern US, in which the singer typically sings about their difficult life or bad luck in love: *Billie Holiday was famous for singing the blues.* ○ *a famous blues singer*
• **have the blues** INFORMAL to feel sad

blue [SPORTS] /bluː/ *noun* [C] UK a person who has played a sport for Oxford University against Cambridge University or for Cambridge University against Oxford University, or the title given to them for this

ˈblue ˌbaby *noun* [C] a baby born with slightly blue skin, usually because it has something wrong with its heart

bluebell /ˈbluː.bel/ *noun* [C] **1** a small European plant that usually grows in woods and has blue flowers shaped like bells ➲See picture **Flowers and Plants** on page Centre 3 **2** *SCOTTISH ENGLISH FOR* **harebell**

blueberry /ˈbluːˌbᵊr.i/ /-ˌber-/ *noun* [C] the dark blue fruit of a bush that is grown in North America, similar to a BILBERRY

bluebird /ˈbluː.bɜːd/ [US] /-bɝːd/ *noun* [C] a small blue singing bird found in North America

blue-blooded /ˌbluːˈblʌd.ɪd/ *adj* describes someone who has been born into a family which belongs to the highest social class

bluebottle /ˈbluːˌbɒt.l̩/ [US] /-ˌbɑː.t̬l̩/ *noun* [C] a big fly with a dark blue shiny body

ˌblue ˈcheese *noun* [U] a cheese with a strong flavour that has thin blue lines of bacteria going through it

blue-chip /ˈbluː.tʃɪp/ *adj* [before n] A blue-chip company or investment is one that can be trusted and is not likely to fail.

blue-collar /ˌbluːˈkɒl.əʳ/ [US] /-ˈkɑː.lɚ/ *adj* [before n] describes people who do physical or unskilled work in a factory rather than office work

blue-eyed boy *UK* /ˌbluː.aɪdˈbɔɪ/ *noun* [C usually sing] (*US* **fair-haired boy**) *INFORMAL DISAPPROVING* a boy or man who is particularly liked and is treated well by someone, especially someone in authority

bluegrass /ˈbluː.grɑːs/ [US] /-græs/ *noun* [U] a type of COUNTRY music from the southern US played on stringed instruments such as guitars, BANJOS and violins

bluejay /ˈbluː.dʒeɪ/ *noun* [C] a small North American bird with a bright blue back, a grey front and feathers that stand up on the top of its head

ˌblue ˈjeans *plural noun US OLD-FASHIONED* JEANS (= trousers made of blue denim)

ˈblue ˌlaw *noun* [C] *US OLD-FASHIONED INFORMAL* a law that limits activities which are considered to be immoral for religious reasons, such as shopping or working on Sundays

blueprint /ˈbluː.prɪnt/ *noun* [C] **1** a photographic copy of an early plan for a building or machine **2** an early plan or design which explains how something might be achieved: *It is unlikely that their blueprint **for** economic reform will be put into action.*

ˌblue ˈribbon *noun* [C] **1** (*UK ALSO* **blue riband**) the highest prize in a competition or event: *He won the men's blue-ribbon **event**, the 100 metres freestyle.* **2** a decoration made of strips of blue cloth which is given to the winner of a competition

bluestocking /ˈbluːˌstɒk.ɪŋ/ [US] /-ˌstɑː.kɪŋ/ *noun* [C] *OLD-FASHIONED* an intelligent and highly educated woman who spends most of her time studying and is therefore not approved of by some men

ˈblue ˌtit *noun* [C] a small European bird with a blue head and wings and a yellow front

bluff [PRETEND] /blʌf/ *verb* [I or T] to deceive someone by making them think either that you are going to do something when you really have no intention of doing it, or that you have knowledge that you do not really have, or that you are someone else: *Is he going to jump or is he only bluffing?* ○ *Tony seems to know a lot about music, but sometimes I think he's only bluffing.* ○ *She bluffed the doorman **into** think**ing** that she was a reporter.*

• **bluff *your* way into/out of *sth*** If you bluff your way into or out of a situation, you get yourself into or out of it by deceiving people: *However did Mina manage to bluff her way into that job?* ○ *He's one of those people who is very good at bluffing their way out of trouble.*

bluff /blʌf/ *noun* [C or U] an attempt to bluff: *When she said she was leaving him, he thought it was **only** a bluff.*

bluff [CLIFF] /blʌf/ *noun* [C] a cliff or very steep bank

bluff [TOO HONEST] /blʌf/ *adj* direct or too honest, often in a way that people find rude: *Despite her bluff **manner**, she's actually a very kind woman.*

bluish /ˈbluː.ɪʃ/ *adj* ➲See at **blue** COLOUR

blunder [MISTAKE] /ˈblʌn.dəʳ/ [US] /-dɚ/ *noun* [C] a big mistake, usually caused by lack of care or thought: *He said that the tax was a major political blunder.* ○ *I **made** a bit of a blunder by getting his name wrong.*

blunder /ˈblʌn.dəʳ/ [US] /-dɚ/ *verb* [I] to make a big mistake, usually because of lack of care or thought: *Police blundered by not releasing more details about the case to focus public interest.* **blundering** /ˈblʌn.dᵊr.ɪŋ/ [US] /-dɚ-/ *adj* [before n] *You blundering idiot! What do you think you're doing?*

blunder [MOVE] /ˈblʌn.dəʳ/ [US] /-dɚ/ *verb* [I usually + adv or prep] to move in a awkward way: *I could hear him blundering **around** in the darkness.* **blunderer** /ˈblʌn.dᵊr.əʳ/ [US] /-dɚ.ɚ/ *noun* [C]

blunderbuss /ˈblʌn.də.bʌs/ [US] /-dɚ-/ *noun* [C] an old-fashioned gun with a wide mouth that shoots a lot of small metal balls

blunt [NOT SHARP] /blʌnt/ *adj* describes a pencil, knife, etc. that is not sharp, and therefore not able to write, cut, etc. well

blunt /blʌnt/ *verb* [T] **1** to make something less sharp **2** to make a feeling less strong: *My recent bad experience has rather blunted my **enthusiasm** for travel.*

blunt [RUDE] /blʌnt/ *adj* saying what you think without trying to be polite or caring about other people's feelings: *I'll be blunt – that last piece of work you did was terrible.* **bluntly** /ˈblʌnt.li/ *adv*: *She told me bluntly that I should lose weight.* ○ ***To put it** bluntly, I can't afford it.* **bluntness** /ˈblʌnt.nəs/ *noun* [U]

blur /blɜːʳ/ [US] /blɝː/ *noun* [S] **1** something that you cannot see clearly: *If I don't wear my glasses, everything is **just a** blur.* **2** something that you cannot remember or understand clearly: *It all happened so long ago that it's **just a** blur to me now.* ○ *The last few days seem to have gone by **in a** blur.*

blur /blɜːʳ/ [US] /blɝː/ *verb* [I or T] -rr- **1** to (make something or someone) become difficult to see clearly: *As she drifted into sleep, the doctor's face began to blur and fade.* **2** to make the difference between two things less clear, or to make it difficult to see the exact truth about something: *This film blurs the **line/distinction/boundary** between reality and fantasy.*

blurred /blɜːd/ [US] /blɝːd/ *adj* **1** difficult to see, understand or separate clearly: *The photograph was very blurred.* ○ *Do you agree that male and female roles are becoming blurred ?* **2** unable to see clearly: *My eyes were blurred **with** tears.* **blurry** /ˈblɜː.ri/ [US] /ˈblɝː.i/ *adj*: *The picture on the TV went blurry.*

blurb /blɜːb/ [US] /blɝːb/ *noun* [C] a short description of a book or film, etc., written by the people who have produced it, and intended to make people want to buy it or see it: *The blurb on the back of the book says that it 'will touch your heart'.*

blurt /blɜːt/ [US] /blɝːt/ *verb*

▲ **blurt *sth* out** *phrasal verb* [M] to say something suddenly and without thinking, usually because you are excited or nervous: *He blurted everything out about the baby, though we'd agreed to keep it a secret for a while.* ○ [+ speech] *She suddenly blurted out, "I can't do it".* ○ [+ that] *Late one evening, Gianni blurted out **that** he loved her.*

blush /blʌʃ/ *verb* [I] to become pink in the face, usually from embarrassment: *I always blush when I speak in public.* ○ *I blush **to think** of what a fool I made of myself.* **blush** /blʌʃ/ *noun* [C] *A blush of shame crept up his face.*

blusher /ˈblʌʃ.əʳ/ [US] /-ɚ/ *noun* [C or U] (*US ALSO* **blush**) (a) powder or cream that is put on the cheeks to make them look pink

bluster /ˈblʌs.təʳ/ [US] /-tɚ/ *verb* [I] to speak in a loud angry or offended way, usually with little effect: [+ speech] *"You had no right to do it, no right at all," he blustered.* **bluster** /ˈblʌs.təʳ/ [US] /-tɚ/ *noun* [U] *I knew that it was all bluster and he wasn't really angry with me.*

blustery /ˈblʌs.tᵊr.i/ [US] /-t̬ɚ-/ *adj* very windy: *a blustery day* ○ *blustery weather*

Blu-Tack /ˈbluː.tæk/ *noun* [U] *TRADEMARK* a soft sticky substance that can be used more than once to temporarily fix light things to a wall or similar surface: *Helga stuck her posters up with Blu-Tack.*

blvd *noun WRITTEN ABBREVIATION FOR* **boulevard**

BM *US* /ˌbiːˈem/ *noun* [C] (*UK* **MB**) *ABBREVIATION FOR* Bachelor of Medicine: a degree in medicine, or a person who has this

B

B-movie /ˈbiːˌmuː.vi/ *noun* [C] a cheaply made film, often of poor quality, which in the past was shown before the main film in a cinema

bmp, BMP *ABBREVIATION FOR* **bitmap**; used at the end of the name of a computer file which stores an image as a bitmap

bn *UK* (*US* **b**) *ABBREVIATION FOR* **billion**

BO /ˌbiːˈəʊ/ [US] /-ˈoʊ/ *noun* [U] *ABBREVIATION FOR* **body odour**

boa /ˈbəʊ.ə/ [US] /ˈboʊ-/ *noun* [C] a long thin item of clothing made of feathers, and worn around the neck, especially by women: *a feather boa*

boa (constrictor) /ˈbəʊə.kənˌstrɪk.təʳ/ [US] /ˈboʊə.kənˌstrɪk.t̬ɚ/ *noun* [C] a large, strong snake, found in South and Central America, that kills animals and birds by wrapping itself around them and crushing them

boar /bɔːʳ/ [US] /bɔːr/ *noun* [C] a male pig kept for breeding on a farm, or a type of wild pig ⊃Compare **hog** ANIMAL; **sow** ANIMAL.

board [WOOD] /bɔːd/ [US] /bɔːrd/ *noun* [C] **1** a thin flat piece of cut wood or other hard material used for a particular purpose: *Cut the vegetables on a (UK)* ***chopping****/(US)* ***cutting*** *board.* ○ *There was a 'For Sale' board outside the house.* ⊃See also **above board**; **breadboard**; **soundboard**. **2** a flat piece of wood or other hard material with a special pattern on it, used for playing games: *a chess board* **3** a **blackboard** or **whiteboard**: *The teacher wrote her name up on* ***the*** *board.* **4** a **noticeboard**: *I stuck the notice (up) on* ***the*** *board.* **5** a **diving board**: *I dived off the top board today, Dad.*

• **go by the board** to be forgotten or omitted: *Does this mean our holiday plans will have to go by the board?*

the boards *plural noun* **1** the wooden fence surrounding the ice surface in ice hockey **2** *OLD-FASHIONED* the stage in a theatre

boarding /ˈbɔː.dɪŋ/ [US] /ˈbɔːr-/ *noun* [U] boards that have been fastened side by side to each other

board [PEOPLE] /bɔːd/ [US] /bɔːrd/ *group noun* [C usually sing] the group of people who are responsible for controlling and organizing a company or organization: *Every decision has to be passed by* ***the*** *board* ***(of directors)****.* ○ *She started in the firm by making the tea and now she's* ***on the*** *board/a board member.* ○ ***The*** *board* ***of governors*** *meet/meets once a month to discuss school policy.*

boards /bɔːdz/ [US] /bɔːrdz/ *plural noun US INFORMAL* an official examination given by some medical and business organizations in the US: *This is my last chance to pass the boards.*

board [STAY] /bɔːd/ [US] /bɔːrd/ *verb* **1** [I] to pay to sleep and eat meals in someone's house: *During his stay in England he boarded* ***with*** *a family in Bath.* **2** [I] to sleep and eat at school during the school TERM: *When you went to school were you a day-student or did you board?* **3** [T] to arrange for a pet animal to be temporarily taken care of at a place other than its home: *He boards the dog* ***out*** *when he goes on business trips.*

board /bɔːd/ [US] /bɔːrd/ *noun* [U] meals provided when you are staying somewhere, usually for money

boarder /ˈbɔː.dəʳ/ [US] /ˈbɔːr.dɚ/ *noun* [C] a student at a school who sleeps and eats there and only goes home during school holidays ⊃Compare **day pupil**.

boarding /ˈbɔː.dɪŋ/ [US] /ˈbɔːr-/ *noun* [U] **1** an arrangement where students sleep and eat meals at their school during the school TERM: *Both their children go to boarding* ***school****.* **2** an arrangement where pet animals are temporarily kept and cared for in a place which is not their home: *The dogs go to boarding* ***kennels*** *while we're away.*

board [GET ON] /bɔːd/ [US] /bɔːrd/ *verb* [I or T] to get onto or allow people to get onto a boat, train or aircraft: *At London airport she boarded a plane to Australia.* ○ *Will passengers waiting to board please go to the ticket counter?*

• **on board 1** on a boat, train or aircraft: *As soon as I was on board, I began to have second thoughts about leaving.* **2** as part of a group or team, especially for a special purpose: *Let's* ***bring*** *Rob on board for the Saudi deal – he's the expert.*

• **take *sth* on board** to understand or accept an idea or a piece of information: *Banks need to take on board the views of their customers.*

▲ **board *sth* up** *phrasal verb* [M] to cover a door or window with wooden boards: *Shopkeepers are boarding up their windows in case rioting breaks out.*

ˌboard and ˈlodging *UK noun* [U] (*US* **room and board**) the meals and room that are provided when someone pays to stay somewhere, for example when working or studying away from home

ˈboard ˌgame *noun* [C] any of many games, for example chess, in which small pieces are moved around on a board with a pattern on it

ˈboarding ˌcard *UK noun* [C] (*US AND ALSO UK* **boarding pass**) a card that a passenger must have to be allowed to enter an aircraft or a ship

ˈboarding ˌhouse *noun* [C] a private house where you can pay to stay and receive meals

boardroom /ˈbɔːd.rʊm/ /-ruːm/ [US] /ˈbɔːrd-/ *noun* [C] a room where the people who control a company or organization meet

ˈboard ˌshorts *plural noun AUS FOR* **bathing trunks**

boardwalk /ˈbɔːd.wɔːk/ [US] /ˈbɔːrd.wɑːk/ *noun* [C] *US* a path made of wooden boards built along a beach

boast [SPEAK PROUDLY] /bəʊst/ [US] /boʊst/ *verb* [I or T] *DISAPPROVING* to speak too proudly or happily about what you have done or what you own: *He didn't talk about his exam results in case people thought he was boasting.* ○ *Parents enjoy boasting* ***about*** *their children's achievements.* ○ [+ that] *They boasted* ***that*** *they had never lost a single game.* **boast** /bəʊst/ [US] /boʊst/ *noun* [C] [+ that] ***It*** *is her proud boast* ***that*** *she has never missed a single episode of the soap opera.*

boastful /ˈbəʊst.fəl/ [US] /ˈboʊst-/ *adj DISAPPROVING* praising yourself and what you have done **boastfully** /ˈbəʊst.fəl.i/ [US] /ˈboʊst-/ *adv* **boastfulness** /ˈbəʊst.fəl.nəs/ [US] /ˈboʊst-/ *noun* [U]

boast [POSSESS] /bəʊst/ [US] /boʊst/ *verb* [T not continuous] to have or possess something to be proud of: *Ireland boasts beautiful beaches, great restaurants and friendly locals.*

boat /bəʊt/ [US] /boʊt/ *noun* [C] **1** a small vehicle for travelling on water: *a rowing/sailing boat* ○ *a fishing boat* ○ *We took turns to* ***row*** *the boat up the river.* ⊃See picture **Planes, Ships and Boats** on page Centre 14 **2** *INFORMAL* a ship: *Are you travelling* ***by*** *boat or by air?* ○ *I'm* ***taking the*** *boat from Dover to Calais.* **boating** /ˈbəʊ.tɪŋ/ [US] /ˈboʊ.t̬ɪŋ/ *noun* [U] *We decided to* ***go*** *boating on the lake.* ○ *a boating accident*

boatload /ˈbəʊt.ləʊd/ [US] /ˈboʊt.loʊd/ *noun* [C] **1** the number of people or the amount of something that can be transported by a boat: *a boatload of refugees/tourists* **2** *INFORMAL* a large amount: *They made boatloads of money from that project.*

boater /ˈbəʊ.təʳ/ [US] /ˈboʊ.t̬ɚ/ *noun* [C] a stiff hat made of straw with a flat top

ˈboat ˌhook *noun* [C] a long pole with an iron hook on the end, used to pull a boat towards you, to push a boat away, etc.

boathouse /ˈbəʊt.haʊs/ [US] /ˈboʊt-/ *noun* [C] a small building beside a river or lake, and in which boats are kept

ˈboat ˌpeople *plural noun* people who have left their country by boat, usually hoping to finding safety in another place

boatswain, bosun /ˈbəʊ.sən/ [US] /ˈboʊ-/ *noun* [C] the officer on a ship who is responsible for looking after the ship's equipment

boatyard /ˈbəʊt.jɑːd/ [US] /ˈboʊt.jɑːrd/ *noun* [C] a place where boats are made, kept or repaired

bob [MOVE] /bɒb/ [US] /bɑːb/ *verb* **-bb- 1** [I] to move up and down quickly and gently especially on the surface of water: *In the harbour, the boats bobbed gently* ***up and down*** *on the water.* **2** [I usually + adv or prep; T] to move quickly in a particular direction: *I dropped the bottle into the sea and watched it bob* ***up*** *to the surface a moment later.* ○ *Suddenly a head bobbed* ***up*** *from behind the hedge.* ○ *She bobbed* ***a curtsy*** (= bent down from the knees briefly at the knees as a sign of respect) ***to*** *the Queen.* **bob** /bɒb/ [US] /bɑːb/ *noun* [C] *She acknowledged me* *with a quick bob **of** her **head**.*

bob HAIRSTYLE /bɒb/ ⓤ /bɑːb/ *noun* [C] *plural* **bobs** a women's hairstyle with the hair cut to neck length all around the head: *I've had/worn my hair **in** a bob for ages.* **bobbed** /bɒbd/ ⓤ /bɑːbd/ *adj*: *short, bobbed hair*

bob MONEY /bɒb/ ⓤ /bɑːb/ *noun* [C] *plural* **bob** UK OLD-FASHIONED INFORMAL a **shilling** (= a British coin used in the past that was worth 5p): *That coat cost me forty bob in 1956.*

Bob /bɒb/ ⓤ /bɑːb/ *noun* UK INFORMAL, OLD-FASHIONED **Bob's your uncle** used to mean that something will happen very quickly and simply: *Just tell them you're a friend of mine and, Bob's your uncle, you'll get the job.*

bobbin /ˈbɒb.ɪn/ ⓤ /ˈbɑː.bɪn/ *noun* [C] a small round or tube-shaped object around which thread is put, often before putting it in a sewing machine

bobble MAINLY UK /ˈbɒb.l̩/ ⓤ /ˈbɑː.bl̩/ *noun* [C] (*US* **pompom**) a small round ball of soft material used as decoration

'bobble ˌhat UK *noun* [C] (*AUS* **beanie**) a woollen hat with a small round woollen ball on top ➔See picture **Hairstyles and Hats** on page Centre 8

bobby /ˈbɒb.i/ ⓤ /ˈbɑː.bi/ *noun* [C] UK OLD-FASHIONED INFORMAL a police officer: *People liked seeing their friendly local/neighbourhood bobby on his beat.*

'bobby ˌpin *noun* [C] US FOR **hairgrip**

bobs /bɒbz/ ⓤ /bɑːbz/ UK INFORMAL **bits and bobs** small things or jobs of different types

bobsleigh UK /ˈbɒb.sleɪ/ ⓤ /ˈbɑːb-/ *noun* [C] (*US* **bobsled**) a small vehicle with long metal blades under it, built for racing down ice-covered tracks

bod PERSON /bɒd/ ⓤ /bɑːd/ *noun* [C] UK INFORMAL OLD-FASHIONED a person: *She's a bit of an odd bod.*

bod BODY /bɒd/ ⓤ /bɑːd/ *noun* [C] US INFORMAL FOR **body** PHYSICAL STRUCTURE: *That guy has a great bod!*

bode /bəʊd/ ⓤ /boʊd/ *verb* [I or T] FORMAL to be a sign of something that will happen in the future, usually something particularly good or bad: *These recently published figures bode **ill**/do not bode **well** for the company's future.* ○ *The hurricane bodes disaster **for** those areas in its path.*

bodge /bɒdʒ/ ⓤ /bɑːdʒ/ *noun* [C], *verb* [T] (ALSO **bodge up**) UK FOR **botch**

bodice /ˈbɒd.ɪs/ ⓤ /ˈbɑː.dɪs/ *noun* [C] **1** the upper part of a woman's dress: *She was wearing a ballgown with a **fitted** bodice.* **2** OLD USE a piece of women's underwear that fits tightly to the body above the waist

bodice-ripper /ˈbɒd.ɪsˌrɪp.ər/ ⓤ /ˈbɑː.dɪsˌrɪp.ɚ/ *noun* [C] HUMOROUS a romantic story, set in the past, in which there is a lot of sex

body PHYSICAL STRUCTURE /ˈbɒd.i/ ⓤ /ˈbɑː.di/ *noun* [C] **1** the whole physical structure that forms a person or animal: *A good diet and plenty of exercise will help you to keep your body healthy.* ○ *She rubbed sun lotion over her entire body.* ➔See picture **The Body** on page Centre 5 **2** the main part of a person's or animal's body, without the head, or without the head, arms and legs: *He had a fat body but rather thin legs and arms.* **3** a dead person: *A body was washed up on the beach last week.* **4** the painted metal shell of a vehicle, such as a car or an aircraft ➔See also **bodywork**. **5** UK (*US* **bodysuit**) a piece of tight-fitting women's clothing that covers the top half of the body, and which fastens between the legs

● **keep body and soul together** to be able to pay for your food, clothing and somewhere to live: *His wages are barely enough to keep body and soul together.*

-bodied /-bɒd.id/ ⓤ /-bɑː.did/ *suffix* having a particular type of body: *a long-bodied doll*

bodily /ˈbɒd.ɪ.li/ ⓤ /ˈbɑː.dɪ-/ *adj* relating to the human body: *bodily fluids* (= blood, SALIVA, etc.) ○ *They didn't cause him any bodily **harm**.* ○ *to lose control of your bodily functions*

bodily /ˈbɒd.ɪ.li/ ⓤ /ˈbɑː.dɪ-/ *adv* If you lift or carry someone bodily, you lift or carry them in your arms: *He carried her bodily up the stairs.*

body GROUP OF PEOPLE /ˈbɒd.i/ ⓤ /ˈbɑː.di/ *group noun* [C] a group of people who have joined together for a particular reason: *a governing body* ○ *an advisory body* ○ *The RSPCA is a respected body working for animal welfare.* ○ *There is a large body **of** people who are unaware of their basic rights.*

body AMOUNT /ˈbɒd.i/ ⓤ /ˈbɑː.di/ *noun* [C] **1** a large amount of something: *There is a growing body **of** evidence to support their claim.* ○ *She collected a huge body of information on the subject.* ○ *A substantial body **of opinion** (= A large group of people with the same opinion) is opposed to any change.* **2** FORMAL A body of water is a large area of water, such as a lake.

the ˈbody MAIN PART *noun* [S] **1** the main part of a book, article, etc: *I thought the most interesting details in the book were not in the body **of** the text, but in the notes at the end.* **2** the main part of a large building: *to enter the body of the cathedral*

body OBJECT /ˈbɒd.i/ ⓤ /ˈbɑː.di/ *noun* [C] SPECIALIZED a separate object or mass: *The distance between the two bodies in space was measured daily.*

body QUALITY /ˈbɒd.i/ ⓤ /ˈbɑː.di/ *noun* [U] a strong or thick quality: *This Bordeaux **has** a flowery bouquet and plenty of body* (= strong flavour). ○ *Conditioner can give your hair more body.* **-bodied** /-bɒd.id/ ⓤ /-bɑː.did/ *suffix a medium-bodied wine*

'body ˌbag *noun* [C] a heavy plastic bag used to transport a dead person, especially a soldier who has been killed in a war

'body ˌblow *noun* [C] **1** something that causes serious problems and disappointment for a person trying to do something: *Having all her research notes stolen was a real body blow for her.* **2** when someone hits the main part of your body

bodybuilding /ˈbɒd.iˌbɪl.dɪŋ/ ⓤ /ˈbɑː.di-/ *noun* [U] special exercises that you do regularly to make your muscles bigger **bodybuilder** /ˈbɒd.iˌbɪl.dər/ ⓤ /ˈbɑː.diˌbɪl.dɚ/ *noun* [C]

'body ˌclock *noun* [C] INFORMAL Your body clock is your body's natural tendency to sleep, eat, etc. at particular times.

bodyguard /ˈbɒd.i.gɑːd/ ⓤ /ˈbɑː.di.gɑːrd/ *noun* [C], *group noun* a person or group of people whose job is to protect someone from attack: *The prince is always accompanied by his bodyguards.*

'body ˌlanguage *noun* [U] the movements or positions by which you unintentionally show other people how you are feeling: *I could tell from her body language that she was very embarrassed.*

'body ˌodour *noun* [U] (ABBREVIATION **BO**) an unpleasant smell on a person's body that is caused by sweat

'body ˌstocking *noun* [C] an item of clothing made of thin material that tightly covers the whole body, except for the head, and which is often worn by dancers

bodysuit /ˈbɒd.i.suːt/ ⓤ /ˈbɑː.di-/ *us noun* (*UK* **body**) a piece of tight-fitting women's clothing that covers the top half of the body and fastens between the legs

bodysurf /ˈbɒd.i.sɜːf/ ⓤ /ˈbɑː.di.sɜːf/ *verb* [I] to SURF (= ride on waves) without a board to lie on, but using your body like a board on the water

bodywarmer UK /ˈbɒd.iˌwɔː.mər/ ⓤ /ˈbɑː.diˌwɔːr.mɚ/ *noun* [C] (*US* **vest**) a short jacket, without sleeves and made of thick cloth, that fits closely to your body

bodywork /ˈbɒd.i.wɜːk/ ⓤ /ˈbɑː.di.wɜːk/ *noun* [U] **1** the painted metal shell that covers a car, aircraft, etc: *My car's bodywork is in terrible condition.* **2** US the process of making or repairing the outer shell of a vehicle

Boer /bɔːr/ ⓤ /bɔːr/ *noun* [C] a white person in South Africa who is related to the Dutch people who went to live there in the 17th century

boffin /ˈbɒf.ɪn/ ⓤ /ˈbɑː.fɪn/ *noun* [C] MAINLY UK INFORMAL a scientist who is considered to know a lot about science and not to be interested in other things: *a technical/computer boffin*

bog WET AREA /bɒg/ ⓤ /bɑːg/ *noun* [C or U] soft, wet earth, or an area of this

boggy /ˈbɒg.i/ ⓤ /ˈbɑː.gi/ *adj* describes ground that is soft and wet

bog TOILET /bɒg/ US /bɑːg/ noun [C] UK SLANG a toilet: *I'm just going to nip to the bog.* ○ *We've run out of bog paper/roll.*

bog /bɒg/ US /bɑːg/ verb

▲ **bog off** phrasal verb SLANG to go away: *Bog off and leave me alone.*

bogey FEAR, **bogie**, **bogy** /ˈbəʊ.gi/ US /ˈboʊ-/ noun [C usually sing] something that causes fear among a lot of people, often without reason: *the bogey of unemployment*

bogey NOSE UK /ˈbəʊ.gi/ US /ˈboʊ-/ noun [C] (US **booger**) SLANG a piece of dried mucus from inside the nose

bogey ,man noun [C] (ALSO **bogy man**, US ALSO **boogey-man**) an imaginary evil person who harms children: *Be good, or the bogey man will come and get you!*

bogged down /ˌbɒgd'daʊn/ US /ˌbɑːgd-/ adj **get bogged down** to become so involved in something difficult or complicated that you cannot do anything else: *Let's not get bogged down with individual complaints.* ○ UK *Try not to get too bogged down in the details.*

boggle /ˈbɒg.l̩/ US /ˈbɑː.gl̩/ verb **1** [I or T] to (cause something or someone to) have difficulty imagining or understanding something: *My mind boggles at the amount of money they spend on food.* ○ *It boggles the imagination, doesn't it?* ➔See also **mind-boggling**. **2** [I] to be very surprised and uncertain about how to deal with something: *He boggled at the suggestion.*

bog 'standard adj UK INFORMAL DISAPPROVING completely ordinary, without anything special added: *My last car was just a bog standard model.*

bogus /ˈbəʊ.gəs/ US /ˈboʊ-/ adj false, not real or not legal: *On investigation, his claim was found to be bogus.* ○ *She produced some bogus documents to support her application.*

bogy /ˈbəʊ.gi/ US /ˈboʊ-/ noun [C] ➔See **bogey** FEAR.

bohemian /bəʊˈhiː.mi.ən/ US /boʊ-/ noun [C] (INFORMAL **boho**) a person who is interested in art, music and/or literature and lives in a very informal manner, ignoring the usually accepted ways of behaving **bohemian** /bəʊˈhiː.mi.ən/ US /boʊ-/ adj (INFORMAL **boho**) *a bohemian lifestyle*

boil HEAT /bɔɪl/ verb **1** [I or T] to reach, or cause something to reach, the temperature at which a liquid starts to turn into a gas: *Liquid nitrogen boils at a very low temperature.* ○ *She scalded herself on some boiling water.* ○ *If you give water to a small baby to drink, you have to boil it first.* **2** [I or T] to heat a container, especially one used for cooking, until the liquid in it starts to turn into a gas: *Could you boil the kettle for me?* ○ *The pan's boiling.* **3** [T] to cook food by putting it in water that is boiling: *I've boiled some potatoes for dinner.* ○ *boiled carrots* ➔See picture **In the Kitchen** on page Centre 16 **4** [T] to wash clothes in a container of very hot water **5** **boil dry** If a container or food boils dry, all the liquid in the container in which the food was cooking turns to gas. **6** [I usually continuous] INFORMAL to be extremely angry: *He was boiling with rage.*

• **can't boil an egg** HUMOROUS Someone who can't boil an egg, is unable to cook even the simplest meal.

boil /bɔɪl/ noun [S] **1** when you wash or cook something in very hot water **2** **the boil** the state of boiling: *Bring the water to the boil, then add the pasta.* ○ *Let the liquid come to the boil and then reduce the heat.*

• **go off the boil** UK to lose interest or become less urgent: *They were really excited about the project, but now they seem to have gone off the boil.*

boiled /bɔɪld/ adj: *boiled eggs/bacon* ○ *a hard-/soft-boiled egg* (= one boiled for a long/short time)

,**boiling** ('**hot**) adj INFORMAL very hot: *I wish I'd worn something cooler – I'm boiling.* ○ *We don't usually have such boiling hot weather.*

boil SWELLING /bɔɪl/ noun [C] a painful red swelling on the skin, that is filled with pus (= thick yellow liquid)

PHRASAL VERBS WITH **boil** ▼

▲ **boil away** phrasal verb When a liquid boils away, it all turns into a gas so that none of it is left in liquid form.

▲ **boil (sth) down** LIQUID phrasal verb [M] to heat a liquid or food so that part of it is turned into gas and its amount is reduced

▲ **boil sth down** INFORMATION phrasal verb [M] to reduce information, usually so that it contains only its most important parts: *He had boiled down a lengthy report to just a few paragraphs.*

▲ **boil down to sth** phrasal verb If a situation or problem boils down to something, that is the main reason for it: *The problem boils down to one thing – lack of money.*

▲ **boil over** PERSON phrasal verb If a difficult situation or negative emotion boils over, it cannot be controlled any more and people start to argue or fight.

▲ **boil over** LIQUID phrasal verb **1** If a liquid that is being heated boils over, it rises up and flows over the edge of the pan: *Take the milk off the heat before it boils over.* **2** If a pan boils over, the liquid in it rises up and flows over the edge: *That saucepan is boiling over.*

▲ **boil up** EMOTION phrasal verb If a bad emotion boils up, it becomes very strong and difficult to control: *Anger suddenly boiled up in him.*

▲ **boil sth up** LIQUID phrasal verb [M] to heat up liquid or food in a pan until it boils: *Could you boil some water up for me?*

boiled 'sweet UK noun [C] (US **hard candy**) a hard, often brightly coloured sweet

boiler /ˈbɔɪ.ləʳ/ US /-lɚ/ noun [C] **1** a device that heats water by burning gas or oil, especially to provide heating and hot water in a house **2** the part of a steam engine where water is heated to provide power

boiler ,suit UK noun [C] (US USUALLY **coveralls**) a suit made in one piece, which is worn for doing dirty work

boiling ,point noun **1** [C] The boiling point of a liquid is the temperature at which it becomes a gas: *The boiling point of water is 100°C.* **2** [U] the point when a situation is about to go out of control and become violent: *The situation in the inner city was reaching/at boiling point, so the police were out in force.* **3** [U] the stage at which someone is about to become very angry

boisterous /ˈbɔɪ.stʰr.əs/ US /-stɚ-/ adj noisy, energetic and rough: *boisterous children* ○ *a boisterous game* **boisterously** /ˈbɔɪ.stʰr.əs.li/ US /-stɚ-/ adv

bold BRAVE /bəʊld/ US /boʊld/ adj brave; not fearing danger: *She was a bold and fearless climber.* ○ *The newspaper made the bold move/took the bold step of publishing the names of the men involved.* **boldly** /ˈbəʊld.li/ US /ˈboʊld-/ adv **boldness** /ˈbəʊld.nəs/ US /ˈboʊld-/ noun [U] *He is famous for the boldness of his business methods.*

bold NOTICEABLE /bəʊld/ US /boʊld/ adj strong in colour or shape, and very noticeable to the eye: *They painted the kitchen in bold colours – crimson, purple and blue.*

• **in bold (type/print)** printed in thick dark letters: ***This sentence is printed in bold.***

bold NOT SHY /bəʊld/ US /boʊld/ adj not shy, especially in a way that shows a lack of respect: *He was a bold and defiant little boy.*

• **(as) bold as brass** with extreme confidence or without the respect or politeness people usually show: *She marched into the shop, as bold as brass, and demanded her money back.*

bolero PIECE OF CLOTHING /bəˈleə.rəʊ/ US /-ˈler.oʊ/ noun [C] plural **boleros** a woman's short jacket that stops just above the waist and has no buttons

bolero DANCE /bəˈleə.rəʊ/ US /-ˈler.oʊ/ noun [C] plural **boleros** a Spanish dance, or the music it is danced to: *Ravel's Bolero*

bollard /ˈbɒl.ɑːd/ US /ˈbɑː.lɚd/ noun [C] **1** a short thick post that boats can be tied to **2** MAINLY UK a post that is put in the middle or at the end of a road to keep vehicles off or out of a particular area

bollocking /ˈbɒl.ə.kɪŋ/ US /ˈbɑː.lə-/ noun [C] UK OFFENSIVE angry words spoken to someone who has done something wrong: *She gave me a right bollocking for being late.*

bollocks BODY PART /ˈbɒl.əks/ US /ˈbɑː.ləks/ plural noun OFFENSIVE FOR **testicles**

bollocks NONSENSE /ˈbɒl.əks/ US /ˈbɑː.ləks/ noun [U] UK OFFENSIVE nonsense: *That's a load of bollocks.* ○ *Bollocks to that* (= that's nonsense)*!*

bologna /bəˈləʊ.ni/ /-njə/ US /-ˈloʊ-/ /-njə/ noun [U] (ALSO **baloney**) US a cooked smoked sausage which is sliced and eaten cold

boloney /bəˈləʊ.ni/ [US] /-ˈloʊ-/ *noun* [U] **baloney**
Bolshevik /ˈbɒl.ʃə.vɪk/ [US] /ˈboʊl-/ *adj, noun* [C] connected with the political system introduced by Lenin in Russia in 1917, or a supporter of that system **Bolshevism** /ˈbɒl.ʃə.vɪ.zᵊm/ [US] /ˈboʊl-/ *noun* [U]
bolshy, bolshie /ˈbɒl.ʃi/ [US] /ˈboʊl-/ *adj* UK INFORMAL describes someone who tends to argue and make difficulties: *He's a bit bolshy these days.*
bolster [SUPPORT] /ˈbəʊl.stəʳ/ [US] /ˈboʊl.stɚ/ *verb* [T] to support or improve something or make it stronger: *More money is needed to bolster the industry.* ○ *She tried to bolster my* ***confidence/morale*** (= encourage me and make me feel stronger) *by telling me that I had a special talent.* ○ *They need to do something to bolster their* ***image***.
bolster [FOR SLEEPING] /ˈbəʊl.stəʳ/ [US] /ˈboʊl.stɚ/ *noun* [C] a long firm cylindrical pillow

Bolt

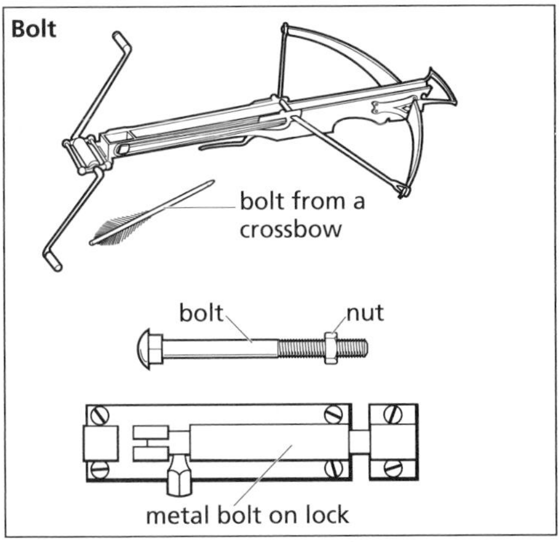

bolt [LOCK] /bəʊlt/ [US] /boʊlt/ *noun* [C] a metal bar on a door or window that slides across to lock it closed: *I closed the window and* ***drew the*** *bolt* (= slid the bolt across).
bolt /bəʊlt/ [US] /boʊlt/ *verb* [I or T] *Have you locked and bolted the door?* ○ *The door bolts on the inside.*
bolt [SCREW] /bəʊlt/ [US] /boʊlt/ *noun* [C] a screw-like metal object without a point which is used with a NUT to fasten things together
bolt /bəʊlt/ [US] /boʊlt/ *verb* [T usually + adv or prep] to fasten something with a bolt: *On a ship the furniture is often bolted* ***to*** *the deck.*
bolt [LIGHTNING] /bəʊlt/ [US] /boʊlt/ *noun* [C] a flash of lightning that looks like a white line against the sky: *The house next to ours was struck by a bolt* ***of lightning***. ➲See also **thunderbolt**.
• **a bolt from/out of the blue** something completely unexpected that surprises you very much: *The news of his marriage was a bolt from the blue.*
bolt [MOVE QUICKLY] /bəʊlt/ [US] /boʊlt/ *verb* [I] to move very fast, especially as a result of being frightened: *Frightened by the car horn, the horse bolted.*
bolt /bəʊlt/ [US] /boʊlt/ *noun* **make a bolt for *somewhere*** to try to escape by running towards something: *The thief tried to make a bolt for the exit.*
bolt [EAT] /bəʊlt/ [US] /boʊlt/ *verb* [T] (ALSO **bolt down**) to eat food very quickly: *Don't bolt your food like that – you'll get indigestion.*
bolt [ROLL] /bəʊlt/ [US] /boʊlt/ *noun* [C] a length or roll of cloth or wallpaper
bolt [WEAPON] /bəʊlt/ [US] /boʊlt/ *noun* [C] a type of short ARROW (= a thin stick-like weapon with a point at one end) shot from a CROSSBOW (= a type of weapon)
▲ **bolt *sth* on** *phrasal verb* to add an extra part or feature: *Other insurers will allow you to bolt on critical illness cover to standard life cover.*
bolt-on /ˈbəʊlt.ɒn/ [US] /ˈboʊlt.ɑːn/ *adj* [before n] added to a main product, service or plan as a smaller, extra part or feature, especially in business: *Mr Bungey said the business would continue to make bolt-on* ***acquisitions***.
bolt-hole /ˈbəʊlt.həʊl/ [US] /ˈboʊlt.hoʊl/ *noun* [C] MAINLY UK a place where you can hide, especially to escape from other people
ˌ**bolt ˈupright** *adv* vertical and very straight: *Suddenly she* ***sat*** *bolt upright as if something had startled her.*
bomb [WEAPON] /bɒm/ [US] /bɑːm/ *noun* [C] a weapon that explodes and is used to kill or hurt people or to damage buildings: *A 100-pound bomb* ***exploded/went off*** *today, injuring three people.* ○ *The terrorists had* ***planted*** *a bomb near the police station.* ○ *During the Second World War, the British* ***dropped*** *a huge number of bombs on Dresden.*
the bomb *noun* [S] one or more ATOM BOMBS: *The US was the first country to have the bomb.*
a bomb *noun* UK INFORMAL a lot of money: *That coat must have cost a bomb.*
• **go like a bomb** to move very quickly: *His new car goes like a bomb.*
• **go (like/down) a bomb** UK INFORMAL to be very successful or popular: *The party's really going a bomb, isn't it?* ○ *Your fruit punch went down a bomb.*
bomb /bɒm/ [US] /bɑːm/ *verb* [T] **1** to drop bombs on something: *Planes bombed the city every night.* **2** to destroy something by exploding a bomb inside it: *This pub was bombed a few years ago.* ○ *The building was completely bombed* ***out*** (= completely destroyed by a bomb).
bombing /ˈbɒm.ɪŋ/ [US] /ˈbɑː.mɪŋ/ *noun* [C or U] *Heavy bombing has gutted the city.* ○ *There was a* ***wave of*** *bombings in London.*
bomber /ˈbɒm.əʳ/ [US] /ˈbɑː.mɚ/ *noun* [C] **1** a person who uses bombs: *Rajiv Gandhi is believed to have been killed by a suicide bomber* (= a person who carries a bomb on their body). **2** an aircraft that drops bombs: *The invasion on land was supported by bombers in the air.*
bomb [FAILURE] /bɒm/ [US] /bɑːm/ *noun* [S] US INFORMAL something which has failed: *The play was a real bomb.*
bomb /bɒm/ [US] /bɑːm/ *verb* [I] US INFORMAL to fail: *Her last book really bombed.*
bomb [GO FAST] /bɒm/ [US] /bɑːm/ *verb* [I + adv or prep] INFORMAL to travel very fast in a vehicle: *He was bombing along on his motorbike.*
bombard /bɒmˈbɑːd/ [US] /bɑːmˈbɑːrd/ *verb* [T] to attack a place with continuous shooting or bombs: *The troops bombarded the city, killing and injuring hundreds.*
bombardment /ˌbɒmˈbɑːd.mənt/ [US] /ˌbɑːmˈbɑːrd-/ *noun* [C or U] *The use of modern weapons has made it more difficult to protect civilians from* ***aerial*** *bombardment.*
▲ **bombard *sb* with *sth*** *phrasal verb* to direct so many things at someone, especially to ask them so many questions, that they find it difficult to deal with them: *The children bombarded her with questions.*
bombardier /bɒm.bəˈdɪəʳ/ [US] /ˌbɑːm.bəˈdɪr/ *noun* [C] **1** a soldier with a low rank in the ARTILLERY of some armies **2** a military person who aims and often releases bombs from an aircraft
bombastic /bɒmˈbæs.tɪk/ [US] /bɑːm-/ *adj* using long and difficult words, usually to make people think you know more than you do: *a bombastic preacher* ○ *a bombastic statement*
bombast /ˈbɒm.bæst/ [US] /ˈbɑːm-/ *noun* [U] language that is intentionally difficult, usually to make something sound more important than it is
ˈ**bomb disˌposal ˌunit** UK *noun* [C] (US **bomb squad**) a group of people whose job is to examine and remove bombs that are found, and to prevent them from exploding
bombed /bɒmd/ [US] /bɑːmd/ *adj* US INFORMAL experiencing the strong effect of alcohol or illegal drugs
ˈ**bomber ˌjacket** *noun* [C] a short jacket that fits tightly at the waist, often made of leather
ˈ**bomb ˌscare** *noun* [C] an event in which people are warned that a bomb has been left somewhere and people are told to leave the area or building
bombshell [NEWS] /ˈbɒm.ʃel/ [US] /ˈbɑːm-/ *noun* [C usually sing] a sudden and often unpleasant piece of news: *My sister* ***dropped*** *a bombshell by announcing she was leaving her job.*

bombshell WOMAN /'bɒm.ʃel/ US /'bɑːm-/ *noun* [C] a very attractive woman: *a **blonde** bombshell*

bombsite /'bɒm.saɪt/ US /'bɑːm-/ *noun* [C] an empty area in a town where all the buildings have been destroyed by a bomb

bona fide, bonafide /ˌbəʊ.nəˈfaɪ.di/ US /ˌboʊ-/ *adj* real, not false: *Make sure you are dealing with a bona fide company.*

bona fides /ˌbəʊ.nəˈfaɪ.diːz/ US /ˌboʊ-/ *plural noun* LEGAL good or sincere intentions

bonanza /bəˈnæn.zə/ *noun* [C] **1** a situation from which large profits are made: *The rise in house prices meant that those who were selling enjoyed a bonanza.* ○ *April was a bonanza month for car sales.* **2** a large amount of something good: *The magazine will hold another fashion bonanza in the spring.*

bond CONNECTION /bɒnd/ US /bɑːnd/ *noun* [C] a close connection joining two or more people: *the bond(s) of friendship/love* ○ *There has been a close bond **between** them ever since she saved him from drowning.* ○ *In societies with strong family bonds (= relationships), people tend to live longer.* **bond** /bɒnd/ US /bɑːnd/ *verb* [I or T] *The aim was to bond the group into a closely-knit team.* ○ *The hospital gives mothers no quiet private time in which to bond **with** their babies.*

bonding /'bɒn.dɪŋ/ US /'bɑːn-/ *noun* [U] the process by which a close emotional relationship is developed: *Much of the bonding between mother and child takes place in those early weeks.*

bond GLUE /bɒnd/ US /bɑːnd/ *verb* [I or T] to stick materials together, especially using glue: *This new adhesive can bond metal **to** glass.* **bond** /bɒnd/ US /bɑːnd/ *noun* [C] *When the glue has set, the bond (= joint) formed is watertight.*

bond DOCUMENT /bɒnd/ US /bɑːnd/ *noun* [C] an official paper given by the government or a company to show that you have lent them money that they will pay back to you at an INTEREST RATE that does not change: *I invested some money in savings bonds.*

bond PROMISE /bɒnd/ US /bɑːnd/ *noun* [C] **1** a written agreement or promise: *They have entered into a solemn bond.* **2** *US LEGAL* a sum of money that is paid to formally promise that someone accused of a crime and being kept in prison will appear for trial if released: *The judge ordered that he post a $10 000 bond pending his appeal.*

bondage SERVANT /'bɒn.dɪdʒ/ US /'bɑːn-/ *noun* [U] LITERARY the state of being another person's slave: *The slaves were kept **in** bondage until their death.*

bondage SEX /'bɒn.dɪdʒ/ US /'bɑːn-/ *noun* [U] the activity of tying parts of a person's body so that they cannot move in order to get or give sexual pleasure: *They were **into** (= They liked) bondage.* ○ *bondage gear*

bonds /bɒndz/ US /bɑːndz/ *plural noun* LITERARY **1** the ropes or chains that hold prisoners and prevent them moving around or escaping: *Loose his bonds and set him free.* **2** something that prevents you from doing what you want: *She longed to escape from the bonds **of** children and housework.*

bone BODY PART /bəʊn/ US /boʊn/ *noun* [C or U] **1** any of the hard parts inside a human or animal that make up its frame: *The child was so thin that you could see her bones.* ○ *human/animal bones* **2** the bone in meat or fish: *There's still a lot of meat left on the bone – shall I slice some off for you?* ○ *I don't like fish because I hate the bones.*

• **a bone of contention** something that two or more people argue about fiercely over a long period of time

• **to the bone** all the way through, or very badly: *I was frozen/chilled to the bone after waiting so long for the bus.*

• **have a bone to pick with *sb*** to want to talk to someone about something annoying they have done: *I've got a bone to pick with you, – you've been using my shaver again.*

• **make no bones about *sth*** not to try to hide your feelings: *He made no bones about his dissatisfaction with the service.*

• **bone dry** completely dry

• **bone idle** *UK* extremely lazy: *He never does any exercise – he's bone idle.*

-boned /-bəʊnd/ US /-boʊnd/ *suffix* having bones of the type mentioned: *She is **big**-boned, but she's not fat.*

bony /'bəʊ.ni/ US /'boʊ-/ *adj* very thin: *long bony fingers*

bone /bəʊn/ US /boʊn/ *verb* [T] to take the bones out of something: *Ask the fishmonger to bone the fish for you.*

boneless /'bəʊn.ləs/ US /'boʊn-/ *adj* (US ALSO **boned**) without a bone: *boneless breast of chicken*

▲ **bone up** *phrasal verb* INFORMAL to learn as much as you can about something for a special reason: *She boned up **on** economics before applying for the job.*

bone SEX /bəʊn/ US /boʊn/ *verb* [I or T] OFFENSIVE to have sex with someone

bone 'china *noun* [U] a delicate and expensive type of CHINA made using animal bone powder

bonehead /'bəʊn.hed/ US /'boʊn-/ *noun* [C] SLANG a stupid person

bone ˌmarrow *noun* [U] **marrow** TISSUE

bone ˌmeal *noun* [U] a substance made from crushed dried bones that is used to improve the earth to make plants grow better

boner PENIS /'bəʊ.nər/ US /'boʊ.nɚ/ *noun* [C] MAINLY US OFFENSIVE an **erection** (= when a man's penis is hard)

boner MISTAKE /'bəʊ.nər/ US /'boʊ.nɚ/ *noun* [C] US INFORMAL a mistake which causes embarrassment to the person who makes it

bonfire /'bɒn.faɪər/ US /'bɑːn.faɪr/ *noun* [C] a large fire that is made outside to burn unwanted things, or for pleasure

bonfire ˌnight *noun* [C or U] *UK* another name for Guy Fawkes Night, the night of November 5 when many people in Britain light bonfires and have fireworks

bong /bɒŋ/ US /bɑːŋ/ *noun* [C] a musical noise made especially by a large clock: *I heard the bong of the grandfather clock.*

bongo (drum) /'bɒŋ.ɡəʊˌdrʌm/ US /'bɑːŋ.ɡoʊ-/ *noun* [C] one of a pair of small drums that are played with the hands

bonhomie /ˌbɒn.əˈmi/ US /ˌbɑː.nəˈmiː/ *noun* [U] FORMAL friendliness and happiness

bonk HIT /bɒŋk/ US /bɑːŋk/ *verb* [T] INFORMAL HUMOROUS to hit someone or something, not very hard: *He bonked me on the head with his newspaper.* **bonk** /bɒŋk/ US /bɑːŋk/ *noun* [C] *a bonk on the head*

bonk HAVE SEX /bɒŋk/ US /bɑːŋk/ *verb* [I or T] UK HUMOROUS SLANG to have sex with someone: *'I bonked the prince,' says sexy Sarah' declared the newspaper headline.*

bonkers /'bɒŋ.kəz/ US /'bɑːŋ.kɚz/ *adj* [after v] INFORMAL HUMOROUS silly or stupid: *She must be bonkers to do that.*

bon mot /ˌbɒn ˈməʊ/ US /ˌbɑːnˈmoʊ/ *noun* [C] *plural* **bons mots** FORMAL a clever remark

bonnet HAT /'bɒn.ɪt/ US /'bɑː.nɪt/ *noun* [C] a type of hat that covers the ears and is tied under the chin, worn by babies or, especially in the past, by women ➲See picture **Hairstyles and Hats** on page Centre 8

bonnet METAL COVER *UK* /'bɒn.ɪt/ US /'bɑː.nɪt/ *noun* [C] (US **hood**) the metal cover over the part of a car where the engine is: *I looked under the bonnet and clouds of smoke poured out.* ➲See picture **Car** on page Centre 12

bonny /'bɒn.i/ US /'bɑː.ni/ *adj* MAINLY SCOTTISH ENGLISH beautiful and healthy: *a bonny baby* ○ *a bonny lass*

bonsai (tree) /'bɒn.saɪˌtriː/ US /ˌbɑːnˈsaɪ-/ *noun* [C] a very small tree that is grown in a small container and is stopped from growing bigger by continually cutting the roots and branches

bonus /'bəʊ.nəs/ US /'boʊ-/ *noun* [C] **1** an extra amount of money that is given to you as a present or reward in addition to the money you were expecting: *a productivity bonus* ○ *a Christmas bonus* ○ *The company used to give discretionary bonus payments.* **2** a pleasant additional thing: *I love the job, and it's an **added** bonus that it's so close to home.*

bon vivant (*plural* **bons vivants**) /ˌbɒn.viːˈvɒnt/ US /ˌbɑːn.viːˈvɑːnt/ *noun* [C] (*UK ALSO* **bon viveur**) a person who enjoys good food and wines and likes going to restaurants and parties

bon voyage /ˌbɒ̃.vɔɪˈɑːʒ/ US /ˌbɑːn.vwaɪ-/ *exclamation* a phrase said to people who are going away, which means

'I hope you have a safe and enjoyable journey'

bony /'bəʊ.ni/ [US] /'boʊ-/ *adj* ⊃See at **bone**.

bonzer /'bɒn.zəʳ/ [US] /'bɑːn.zɚ/ *adj* AUS OLD-FASHIONED INFORMAL very good or pleasant

boo [DISAPPROVAL] /buː/ *verb* [I or T] **booing, booed, booed** to make an expression of strong disapproval or disagreement: *People at the back started booing loudly.* ○ *Her singing was so bad that she was booed* ***off*** *the stage.* **boo** /buː/ *noun* [C] *plural* **boos**

boo [SURPRISE] /buː/ *exclamation* an expression, usually shouted, used to surprise and frighten someone who does not know you are near them: *She jumped out of the cupboard and shouted 'Boo!'.*

boob [MISTAKE] /buːb/ *noun* [C] UK INFORMAL a silly mistake: *Forgetting the President's name was a bit of a boob.* **boob** /buːb/ *verb* [I] to make a silly mistake: *He boobed rather badly* ***by*** *getting her name wrong.*

boob [BREAST] /buːb/ *noun* [C] VERY INFORMAL a woman's breast: *You know her – blonde hair and big boobs.*

'boob ˌjob *noun* INFORMAL **have a boob job** to have an operation to change the shape of the breasts, usually to make them larger: *So do you think she's had a boob job?*

boo-boo /'buː.buː/ *noun* [C] *plural* **boo-boos 1** INFORMAL a mistake: *Oops, I think I* ***made*** *a boo-boo there – I hope she's not too upset.* **2** US CHILD'S WORD a slight injury: *Tess fell down and got a boo-boo on her hand.*

'boob ˌtube [CLOTHING] *noun* [C] INFORMAL a piece of women's clothing that is made of an elastic material and only covers the breasts

'boob ˌtube [TV] *noun* [C] US INFORMAL FOR television

booby /'buː.bi/ *noun* [C] (US ALSO **boob**) OLD-FASHIONED a stupid person

'booby ˌprize *noun* [C] a prize given as a joke to the person who finishes last in a competition

'booby ˌtrap *noun* [C] something dangerous, especially a bomb, that is hidden inside somewhere that looks safe: *The bodyguard was killed while checking the president's car for booby traps.* ○ *a booby-trap bomb* ○ *They put a bucket of water on top of his door as a booby trap.* **booby-trap** /'buː.bi.træp/ *verb* [T] *The police discovered that the car was booby-trapped.*

booger /'buː.gəʳ/ [US] /-gɚ/ *noun* [C] US FOR **bogey** NOSE

boogeyman /'buː.gi.mæn/ *noun* [C] US FOR **bogey man**

boogie /'buː.gi/ *verb* [I] **boogieing, boogied, boogied** INFORMAL to dance to pop music: *We boogied away all night long.* **boogie** /'buː.gi/ *noun* [S] *I like a good boogie.*

boohoo /ˌbuː'huː/ *exclamation* the sound of noisy, childish crying: *"Boohoo!" she wailed "I'm lost."*

book [TEXT] /bʊk/ *noun* **1** [C] a set of pages that have been fastened together inside a cover to be read or written in: *I took a book with me to read on the train.* ○ *She wrote a book* ***on*** *car maintenance.* **2** [C] one of the parts into which a very long book, such as the Bible, is divided: *the book of Job* **3** [C] a number of one type of item fastened together flat inside a cover: *a book* ***of*** *stamps/tickets/matches* **4** [S] when a BOOKMAKER accepts and pays out sums of money which are risked on a particular result: *They've already* ***opened/started*** *a book* ***on*** *the result of the next World Cup.*

• **in *my* book** in my opinion: *She's never lied to me, and in my book that counts for a lot.*

books /bʊks/ *plural noun* the written records of money that a business has spent or received: *At the end of the year, the accountant goes over* (= checks) ***the*** *books.* ○ *Running a school is much more of a business than it used to be, – by law we have to* ***balance*** *our books.*

• **be on the books** to be employed by a company, or (pay to) belong to a organization, society, sports team, etc: *There are 256 people on the books at the cement works.* ○ *The nursery has 30 babies on the books and 13 on the waiting list.*

• **be in *sb's* good/bad books** If you are in someone's good/bad books, they are pleased/not pleased with you: *He's in Melanie's bad books because he arrived 2 hours late.* ○ *I cleaned the bathroom yesterday so I'm in Mum's good books.*

book [ARRANGE] /bʊk/ *verb* [I or T] to arrange to have a seat, room, entertainer, etc. at a particular time in the future: [+ two objects] *I've booked us two tickets to see 'Carmen'/ I've booked two tickets* ***for*** *us to see 'Carmen'.* ○ *She'd booked a table* ***for*** *four at their favourite restaurant.* ○ *Will booked a seat on the evening flight to Edinburgh.* ○ *We were advised to book early if we wanted to get a room.* ○ *They booked a jazz band for their wedding.* ○ *The hotel/restaurant/theatre is* ***fully*** *booked* ***(up)*** (= all the rooms/tables/tickets have been taken). ○ *I'd like to go but I'm afraid I'm booked* ***up*** (= I have arranged to do other things) *until the weekend.* **bookable** /'bʊk.ə.bl̩/ *adj*: *bookable seats* **booking** /'bʊk.ɪŋ/ *noun* [C] *We* ***made*** *the booking three months ago.* ○ *Julian was ill so we had to* ***cancel*** *the booking.* ○ *The show had already taken £4 million in* ***advance*** *bookings.* ○ *I filled in the booking* ***form*** *and sent it off.*

book [MAKE A RECORD] /bʊk/ *verb* [T] If a police officer, REFEREE, etc. books someone, they write down their name in an official record because they have done something wrong: *A player in a football match who is booked twice in a game is sent off the field.* ○ *My grandmother was booked* ***for*** *speeding last week.* **bookable** /'bʊk.ə.bl̩/ *adj*: *a bookable offence*

▲ **book in/book into *somewhere*** *phrasal verb* UK to say that you have arrived and sign an official book when you get to a hotel: *After booking into our hotel, we went straight down to the beach.* ○ *As soon as she arrived in Tokyo, she booked in at her hotel.*

▲ **book *sb* in/book *sb* into *sth*** *phrasal verb* MAINLY UK to arrange for someone to stay at a hotel: *They've booked us into the hotel in the main square.* ○ *I've booked you in at the Savoy.*

bookbinding /'bʊkˌbaɪn.dɪŋ/ *noun* [U] the skill of fastening loose pages together inside a cover to make a book **bookbinder** /'bʊkˌbaɪn.dəʳ/ [US] /-dɚ/ *noun* [C] **bookbinder's** /'bʊkˌbaɪn.dəz/ [US] /-dɚz/ *noun* [C] *plural* **bookbinders** a place where bookbinders work

bookcase /'bʊk.keɪs/ *noun* [C] a piece of furniture with shelves to put books on

'book ˌclub *noun* [C] an organization in which members can buy books more cheaply than in the shops

bookend /'bʊk.end/ *noun* [C] an object used, especially in pairs, to keep a row of books standing vertically

bookie /'bʊk.i/ *noun* [C] INFORMAL FOR **bookmaker**

'booking ˌoffice *noun* [C] UK a place, usually in a theatre, where tickets can be bought before a performance

bookish /'bʊk.ɪʃ/ *adj* MAINLY DISAPPROVING describes someone who enjoys reading books, especially serious books

bookkeeping /'bʊkˌkiː.pɪŋ/ *noun* [U] the job or activity of keeping an exact record of the money that has been spent or received by a business or other organization **bookkeeper** /'bʊkˌkiː.pəʳ/ [US] /-pɚ/ *noun* [C]

booklet /'bʊk.lət/ *noun* [C] a very thin book with a small number of pages and a paper cover, giving information about something

bookmaker /'bʊkˌmeɪ.kəʳ/ [US] /-kɚ/ *noun* [C] (INFORMAL **bookie**) a person who accepts and pays out sums of money risked on a particular result, especially of horse races

the bookmaker's /ðə'bʊkˌmeɪ.kəz/ [US] /-kɚz/ *noun* [C] a place where bookmakers work: *He went down to the bookmaker's in Chesterton Road to place a bet on the race.*

bookmark [PLACE IN BOOK] /'bʊk.mɑːk/ [US] /-mɑːrk/ *noun* [C] (ALSO **bookmarker**) a piece of card, leather or plastic that you put between the pages of a book so that you can find a page again quickly

bookmark [COMPUTING] /'bʊk.mɑːk/ [US] /'bʊk.mɑːrk/ *verb* [T] to make a record of the address of an Internet document on your computer so that you can find it again easily: *Don't forget to bookmark this page.* **bookmark** /'bʊk.mɑːk/ [US] /'bʊk.mɑːrk/ *noun* [C] *Keep this site as a bookmark.*

bookmobile /'bʊkˌmə.biːl/ [US] /-ˌmoʊ-/ *noun* [C] US FOR **mobile library**

bookplate /'bʊk.pleɪt/ *noun* [C] a decorative piece of paper stuck inside the front cover of a book to show who owns it

B

bookseller /ˈbʊkˌsel.əʳ/ [US] /-ɚ/ *noun* [C] a person or company that sells books

bookshelf /ˈbʊk.ʃelf/ *noun* [C] *plural* **bookshelves** a shelf in a BOOKCASE

bookshop *MAINLY UK* /ˈbʊk.ʃɒp/ [US] /-ʃɑːp/ *noun* [C] (*US USUALLY* **bookstore**) a shop where books are sold

bookstall /ˈbʊk.stɔːl/ [US] /-stɑːl/ *noun* [C] *MAINLY UK* a table or a very small shop with an open front where books, magazines, etc. are sold

ˈbook ˌtoken *noun* [C] *UK* a card worth a particular amount of money that is given as a present, and which can only be used to buy a book: *a £10 book token*

bookworm /ˈbʊk.wɜːm/ [US] /-wɝːm/ *noun* [C] *INFORMAL* a person who reads a lot

boom [PERIOD OF GROWTH] /buːm/ *noun* [C or U] a period of sudden economic growth, especially one that results in a lot of money being made: *This year has seen a boom* ***in*** *book sales.* ○ *The insurance business suffered from a vicious cycle of boom* ***and bust.*** ○ *the* ***property*** *boom*

boom /buːm/ *verb* [I] *The leisure industry is booming* (= is very successful).

boom [SOUND] /buːm/ *verb* [I or T] to make a very deep and loud hollow sound: *The cannons boomed* ***(out)*** *in the night.* ○ *He boomed* ***(out)*** *an order to the soldiers.*

boom /buːm/ *noun* [C] a deep and loud hollow sound

booming /ˈbuː.mɪŋ/ *adj*: *a booming voice*

boom [BOAT] /buːm/ *noun* [C] *SPECIALIZED* (on a boat) a long pole that moves and that has a sail fastened to it

boom [FILMING] /buːm/ *noun* [C] a long pole with a MICROPHONE on one end, used in television or film-making, which is held above the actors so that it records their voices but cannot be seen by the viewers

ˈboom ˌbox *noun* [C] *US INFORMAL* a large radio and tape player you can carry with you

boomerang /ˈbuː.mə.ræŋ/ *noun* [C] a curved stick that, when thrown in a particular way, comes back to the person who threw it

boomerang /ˈbuː.mə.ræŋ/ *verb* [I] If a plan boomerangs, it brings a harmful result instead of the intended good one: *Our plan to take over the business could boomerang* ***on*** *us if we're not careful.*

ˈboom ˌtown *noun* [C] a town that experiences sudden economic growth

boon /buːn/ *noun* [C usually sing] something that is very helpful and improves the quality of life: *Guide dogs are a great boon* ***to*** *the partially sighted.*

ˌboon comˈpanion *noun* [C usually sing] *LITERARY* a very close friend

the boondocks /ðəˈbuːn.dɒks/ [US] /-dɑːks/ *plural noun US DISAPPROVING* any area in the country that is quiet, has few people living in it, and is a long way away from a town or city

boondoggle /ˈbuːnˌdɒg.l̩/ [US] /-ˌdɑː.gl̩/ *noun* [C] *US INFORMAL* a useless and expensive piece of work, especially one which is paid for by the public: *The senator called the new highways proposal "...a fraud and a boondoggle that the taxpayer should not tolerate".*

boor /bʊəʳ/ [US] /bʊr/ *noun* [C] a person who is rude and does not consider other people's feelings **boorish** /ˈbʊər.ɪʃ/ [US] /ˈbɔː.rɪʃ/ *adj*: *I found him rather boorish and aggressive.*

boost /buːst/ *verb* [T] to improve or increase something: *The theatre managed to boost its audiences by cutting ticket prices.* ○ *Share prices were boosted by reports of the President's recovery.* ○ *I tried to boost his* ***ego*** (= make him feel more confident) *by praising his cooking.*

boost /buːst/ *noun* [C usually sing] when something is boosted: *The lowering of interest rates will give a much-needed boost* ***to*** *the economy.* ○ *Passing my driving test was such a boost* ***to*** *my* ***confidence.***

booster /ˈbuː.stəʳ/ [US] /-stɚ/ *noun* [C] **1** something which improves or increases something: *a* ***confidence/morale*** *booster.* **2** an engine on a spacecraft that gives extra power for the first part of a flight: *a rocket booster* **3** an additional small amount of a drug given to strengthen the effect of the same drug given some time before, to protect a person from illness: *a polio booster*

ˈbooster ˌseat *noun* [C] (*ALSO* **booster cushion**) *MAINLY UK* a seat for a young child, usually used in a car, that raises him or her to a higher level

boot [SHOE] /buːt/ *noun* [C] a type of shoe that covers the whole foot and the lower part of the leg: *wellington boots* ○ *walking boots* ○ *riding boots* ➲See picture **Clothes** on page Centre 6

• **the boot/shoe is on the other foot** the situation is now the opposite of what it was, especially because someone who was weak now has power

• **to boot** *OLD-FASHIONED* in addition; also: *He's kind, handsome and wealthy to boot.* ✱ NOTE: This is used after the final adjective in a list.

boot [KICK] /buːt/ *verb* [T usually + adv or prep] *INFORMAL* to kick someone or something hard with the foot: *They booted him* ***in*** *the head.*

boot /buːt/ *noun* [C] *INFORMAL* a kick with the foot: *He* ***gave*** *the ball a good boot.*

• **put the boot in** *INFORMAL* **1** to kick someone when they are already on the ground **2** to make a bad situation worse, by being critical or unkind: *After he lost his job, his wife put the boot in by announcing she was leaving him.*

the boot [END] *noun* [S] *INFORMAL* when your job is taken away from you, usually because you have done something wrong or badly: *She* ***got*** *the boot for stealing money from the till.* ○ *Williams has been* ***given*** *the boot* ***from*** *the team.*

boot [CAR] *UK* /buːt/ *noun* [C] (*US* **trunk**) a covered space at the back of a car, for storing things in ➲See picture **Car** on page Centre 12

boot [WHEEL] /buːt/ *noun* [C] (*ALSO* **Denver boot**) *US* a **wheel clamp**

boot [COMPUTER] /buːt/ *verb* [I or T] (*ALSO* **boot up**) *SPECIALIZED* When a computer boots (up), it becomes ready for use by getting the necessary information into its memory, and when you boot (up) a computer, you cause it to do this.

ˈboot ˌcamp *noun* [C] **1** *US* a place for training soldiers **2** a place for young criminals, which is used instead of prison, and is similar to a place where soldiers are trained

ˈboot ˌcut *adj* **bootleg** [TROUSERS]

bootee, *US ALSO* **bootie** /ˈbuː.ti/ [US] /-t̬i/ *noun* [C] a baby's soft boot that is often made of wool

booth /buːð/ [US] /buːθ/ *noun* [C] **1** a small enclosed box-like space that a person can go into: *a* ***telephone*** *booth* ○ *a* ***polling*** *booth* **2** a partly enclosed area, table, or small tent at a fair, exhibition or similar event

bootlace /ˈbuːt.leɪs/ *noun* [C] a long thin cord or strip of leather used to fasten boots

bootleg [ILLEGAL] /ˈbuːt.leg/ *adj* illegally made, copied or sold: *bootleg CDs/liquor*

bootleg /ˈbuːt.leg/ *verb* [I or T] **-gg-** to illegally make, copy or sell something **bootlegger** /ˈbuːtˌleg.əʳ/ [US] /-ɚ/ *noun* [C]

bootleg [TROUSERS] /ˈbuːt.leg/ *adj* (*ALSO* **boot cut**) describes trousers which are slightly wider at the ankle than at the knee: *bootleg jeans* **bootlegs** /ˈbuːt.legz/ *plural noun*: *a pair of bootlegs*

bootstraps /ˈbuːt.stræps/ *plural noun* **pull/haul** yourself **up by** your **bootstraps** to succeed by your own hard work and without any help from anyone else

booty /ˈbuː.ti/ [US] /-t̬i/ *noun* [U] any valuable items or money stolen by an army at war or by thieves

booze /buːz/ *noun* [U] *INFORMAL* alcohol: *The party's at Kate's on Friday night – bring some booze.*

• **on the booze** *UK INFORMAL* drinking a lot of alcohol: *Every Friday night Rick would* ***go*** *out on the booze.*

booze /buːz/ *verb* [I] *INFORMAL* to drink alcohol: *Have you been out boozing again?*

boozy /ˈbuː.zi/ *adj INFORMAL* drinking or containing a lot of alcohol: *a boozy night out*

boozer /ˈbuː.zəʳ/ [US] /-zɚ/ *noun* [C] **1** *INFORMAL* a person who drinks a lot **2** *UK INFORMAL* a pub: *the* ***local*** *boozer*

booze-up /ˈbuːz.ʌp/ *noun* [C] *INFORMAL* a party or similar occasion where people drink a lot of alcohol

bop DANCE /bɒp/ ⓤ /bɑːp/ *verb* [I] **-pp-** INFORMAL to dance to pop music: *They were all bopping to the music.* **bop** /bɒp/ ⓤ /bɑːp/ *noun* [C usually sing] *There are a couple of decent clubs where you can go for a bop.*

boppy /ˈbɒp.i/ ⓤ /ˈbɑː.pi/ *adj* INFORMAL describes music that is good for dancing to

bop HIT /bɒp/ ⓤ /bɑːp/ *verb* [T usually + adv or prep] **-pp-** HUMOROUS to hit someone or something, especially in a playful way: *to bop someone on the head*

bop MUSIC /bɒp/ ⓤ /bɑːp/ *noun* [U] (*ALSO* **bebop**) a type of jazz music first played by small groups in the 1940s

borax /ˈbɔː.ræks/ ⓤ /ˈbɔːr.æks/ *noun* [U] a white powder used to make glass and cleaning products

Bordeaux /bɔːˈdəʊ/ ⓤ /bɔːrˈdoʊ/ *noun* [C or U] *plural* **Bordeaux** (a type of) white and especially red wine from the Bordeaux area of France: *You can't go wrong choosing Bordeaux.* ○ *They've got several nice Bordeaux in stock.*

bordello /bɔːˈdel.əʊ/ ⓤ /bɔːrˈdel.oʊ/ *noun* [C] *plural* **bordellos** LITERARY a **brothel**

border DIVISION /ˈbɔː.dər/ ⓤ /ˈbɔːr.dɚ/ *noun* [C] the line that divides one country from another: *Were you stopped at the border?* ○ *The train crosses the border between France and Spain.* ○ *The two countries have had frequent border disputes.*
border /ˈbɔː.dər/ ⓤ /ˈbɔːr.dɚ/ *verb* [T] *Swaziland borders* (= is next to) *South Africa and Mozambique.* **bordering** /ˈbɔː.dər.ɪŋ/ ⓤ /ˈbɔːr.dɚ-/ *adj: bordering countries/counties*

border EDGE /ˈbɔː.dər/ ⓤ /ˈbɔːr.dɚ/ *noun* [C] **1** a strip that goes around or along the edge of something, often as decoration: *The dress was white with a delicate lace border.* ○ *a picture with a decorative/plain border* **2** a narrow strip of ground around a garden, which is usually planted with flowers: *to weed/plant the borders*
border /ˈbɔː.dər/ ⓤ /ˈbɔːr.dɚ/ *verb* [T usually passive] to form a line around the edge of something: *The fields are bordered by tall trees.*
▲ **border on** *sth phrasal verb* If behaviour or a quality or feeling borders on something more extreme, it is almost that thing: *His suggestion borders on the ridiculous.* ○ *She possesses a self-confidence that borders on arrogance.*

borderline /ˈbɔː.də.laɪn/ ⓤ /ˈbɔːr.dɚ-/ *adj* between two very different conditions, with the possibility of belonging to either one of them: *Only in borderline cases* (= cases where students might succeed or fail) *will pupils have an oral exam.* ○ *She was a borderline candidate.*
borderline /ˈbɔː.də.laɪn/ ⓤ /ˈbɔːr.dɚ-/ *noun* [S] something that separates two different qualities: *The borderline between friendship and intimacy is often hard to define.*

bore FAIL TO INTEREST /bɔːr/ ⓤ /bɔːr/ *verb* [T] to talk or act in a way that makes someone lose interest and become tired: *"Am I boring you?" she asked anxiously.*
bore /bɔːr/ ⓤ /bɔːr/ *noun* **1** [C] DISAPPROVING someone who talks too much about boring subjects: *I had to sit next to Michael at dinner – he's such a bore.* **2** [S] INFORMAL an activity or situation that is annoying or unpleasant: *Ironing is such a bore.* ○ [+ v-ing] *It's an awful bore cooking a meal every night.* ○ [+ to infinitive] *It's such a bore to have to write this out all over again.*
bored /bɔːd/ ⓤ /bɔːrd/ *adj* feeling tired and unhappy because something is not interesting or because you have nothing to do: *It was a cold, wet day and the children were bored.* ○ *He was getting bored with/of doing the same thing every day.*
● **bored stiff** (*ALSO* **bored to death/tears**) INFORMAL extremely unhappy because something is not interesting or because you have nothing to do
boring /ˈbɔː.rɪŋ/ ⓤ /ˈbɔːr.ɪŋ/ *adj* not interesting or exciting: *She finds opera boring.* ○ *It's boring to sit on the plane with nothing to read.* ○ *a boring lecture* ○ *The film was so boring I fell asleep.* **boringly** /ˈbɔː.rɪŋ.li/ ⓤ /ˈbɔːr.-ɪŋ-/ *adv: The film has a boringly predictable ending.*
boredom /ˈbɔː.dəm/ ⓤ /ˈbɔːr-/ *noun* [U] when you are bored: *They started quarrelling out of sheer boredom.*

COMMON LEARNER ERROR

bored or **boring**?

Bored is used to describe the way that someone feels when something is not interesting.

He didn't enjoy the lesson and he was bored.
He didn't enjoy the lesson and he was boring.

Boring is used to describe the uninteresting thing or person that makes you feel **bored**.

The lesson was long and boring.
The lesson was long and bored.

bore MAKE A HOLE /bɔːr/ ⓤ /bɔːr/ *verb* [I or T; usually + adv or prep] to make a hole in something using a tool: *He used a drill to bore a hole in the wall.* ○ *The workmen bored through the rock.*
bore /bɔːr/ ⓤ /bɔːr/ *noun* [C] (*US USUALLY* **gauge**) SPECIALIZED the cylindrical hole along the length of a pipe or tube, or the DIAMETER (= measurement across the widest part) of this hole: *a narrow bore* ○ *a bore of 16 millimetres*
-bore MAINLY UK /-bɔːr/ ⓤ /-bɔːr/ *suffix* (*US USUALLY* **gauge**) used in adjectives to express the width of a circular hole in a cylindrical object, especially the inside of a gun barrel: *a twelve-bore shotgun*

bore BEAR /bɔːr/ ⓤ /bɔːr/ *past simple of* **bear**
▲ **bore into** *sb phrasal verb* If someone's eyes bore into you, they look at you very hard and make you feel nervous.

borehole /ˈbɔː.həʊl/ ⓤ /ˈbɔːr.hoʊl/ *noun* [C] a deep hole made in the ground when looking for oil, gas or water: *We must sink a borehole so that people will have water.* ○ *They obtained information about the rock by drilling boreholes.*

born BEGIN TO EXIST /bɔːn/ ⓤ /bɔːrn/ *adj* **1** **be born** When a person or animal is born, they come out of their mother's body and start to exist: *She was born in 1950.* ○ *We saw a lamb being born.* ○ *Diana was born into an aristocratic family.* ○ *Ann was born and brought up in Ealing.* **2** having started life in a particular way: *The toll of babies born with AIDS is rising.* ○ *Stevie Wonder was born blind.* **3** **be born** If an idea is born, it starts to exist.
● **born of** *sth* SLIGHTLY FORMAL existing as the result of something: *With a courage born of necessity, she seized the gun and ran at him.*
● **born and bred** describes someone who was born and grew up in a particular place, and has the typical character of someone who lives there: *He's a Parisian born and bred.*
● **born with a silver spoon in your mouth** to have a high social position and wealth from birth
● **not be born yesterday** to not be stupid or easy to deceive: *You don't fool me – I wasn't born yesterday.*
● **wish you had never been born** to be extremely unhappy: *When I've finished with you you're going to wish you'd never been born!*
-born /-bɔːn/ ⓤ /-bɔːrn/ *suffix* born in the way, place or order mentioned: *newborn* ○ *Ben Okri is a Nigerian-born poet and novelist.* ○ *the first-born son*

born NATURAL /bɔːn/ ⓤ /bɔːrn/ *adj* having a natural ability or tendency: *a born writer/athlete* ○ [+ to infinitive] *I felt born to look after animals.*

born-again /ˌbɔːn.əˈgen/ ⓤ /ˌbɔːrn.əˈgen/ *adj* **1** describes someone who has decided to accept a particular type of EVANGELICAL Christianity, especially after a deep spiritual experience: *Cliff Richard is a born-again Christian.* **2** [before n] describes someone who is extremely enthusiastic about a new interest or hobby: *She's a born-again health freak.*

borne BEAR /bɔːn/ ⓤ /bɔːrn/ *past participle of* **bear**
-borne MOVED BY /-bɔːn/ ⓤ /-bɔːrn/ *suffix* carried or moved by a particular thing: *airborne* ○ *waterborne*

borough /ˈbʌr.ə/ ⓤ /ˈbɝː.oʊ/ *noun* [C] a town, or a division of a large town

borrow RECEIVE /ˈbɒr.əʊ/ ⓤ /ˈbɑːr.oʊ/ *verb* **1** [T] to get or receive something from someone with the intention of giving it back after a period of time: *Could I borrow your* *bike **from** (NOT STANDARD **off**) you until next week?* ○ *She used to borrow money and not bother to pay it back.* ○ *He borrowed a novel from the library.* ⊃See Note **lend or borrow?** at **lend**. **2** [I or T] to take money from a bank or financial organization and pay it back over a period of time: *Like so many companies at that time, we had to borrow **heavily** to survive.* **3** [T] to take and use a word or idea from another language or piece of work: *English has borrowed many words **from** French.*

• **live on borrowed time 1** to continue living after a point at which you might easily have died: *Since his cancer was diagnosed, he feels as if he's living on borrowed time.* **2** to continue to exist longer than expected: *It is unlikely that serious decisions will be taken by a minority government living on borrowed time.*

borrower /ˈbɒr.əʊ.əʳ/ [US] /ˈbɑːr.oʊ.ɚ/ *noun* [C] a person or organization, etc. that borrows: *Building societies are encouraging new borrowers.* **borrowing** /ˈbɒr.əʊ.ɪŋ/ [US] /ˈbɑːr.oʊ-/ *noun* [C or U] *Public borrowing has increased in recent years.*

borrow [MATHEMATICS] /ˈbɒr.əʊ/ [US] /ˈbɑː.roʊ/ *verb* [T] to put a number into a different column when doing SUBTRACTION

borscht, borsch /bɔːʃt/ [US] /bɔːrʃt/ *noun* [U] a type of soup made from BEETROOT (= a small dark red vegetable)

borstal /ˈbɔː.stəl/ [US] /ˈbɔːr-/ *noun* [C or U] *UK OLD USE* a prison for boys who were too young to be sent to an ordinary prison

bosom /ˈbʊz.əm/ *noun* [C usually sing] **1** a woman's breasts: *a large/ample bosom* **2** *LITERARY* the front of a person's chest, especially when thought of as the centre of human feelings: *She **held** him tightly **to** her bosom.* ○ *A dark jealousy stirred **in** his bosom.*

• **in the bosom of *sth*** *FORMAL* If you are in the bosom of a group of people, especially your family, you are with them and protected and loved by them.

bosomy /ˈbʊz.əm.i/ *adj* describes a woman with large breasts

ˌbosom ˈfriend/ˈbuddy/ˈpal *noun* [C] a friend that you like a lot and have a very close relationship with

boss [MANAGER] /bɒs/ [US] /bɑːs/ *noun* [C] the person who is in charge of an organization and who tells others what to do: *She was the boss of a large international company.* ○ *I started up my own business and now I'm my **own** boss* (= I work for myself and no one tells me what to do). ○ *INFORMAL Who's the boss* (= the person who makes all the important decisions) *in your house?*

boss /bɒs/ [US] /bɑːs/ *verb* [T usually + adv or prep] *INFORMAL DISAPPROVING* to tell someone what to do all the time: *I wish he'd stop bossing me **around/about**.*

bossy /ˈbɒs.i/ [US] /ˈbɑː.si/ *adj DISAPPROVING* describes someone who is always telling people what to do **bossiness** /ˈbɒs.ɪ.nəs/ [US] /ˈbɑː.sɪ-/ *noun* [U]

boss [DECORATION] /bɒs/ [US] /bɑːs/ *noun* [C] a raised rounded decoration, such as on a SHIELD or a ceiling

boss-eyed /ˈbɒs.aɪd/ /ˌ-ˈ-/ [US] /ˈbɑːs-/ *adj UK SLANG* having eyes that look in towards the nose; CROSS-EYED

ˈbossy ˌboots *noun* [S] *CHILD'S WORD* someone who is very bossy

bosun /ˈbəʊ.sən/ [US] /ˈboʊ-/ *noun* [C] a **boatswain**

boˌtanic(al) ˈgarden *noun* [C] (*ALSO* **botanic(al) gardens**) a garden, which is usually open to the public, where a wide range of plants are grown for scientific study and educational purposes

botanist /ˈbɒt.ən.ɪst/ [US] /ˈbɑː.tən-/ *noun* [C] a scientist who studies plants

botany /ˈbɒt.ən.i/ [US] /ˈbɑː.tən-/ *noun* [U] the scientific study of plants **botanical** /bəˈtæn.ɪ.kəl/ *adj* (*ALSO* **botanic**) *a botanical print* ○ *botanical/botanic gardens* ○ *Several new botanical species have been discovered in the last year.*

botch /bɒtʃ/ [US] /bɑːtʃ/ *verb* [T] (*UK ALSO* **bodge**) to spoil something by doing it badly: *We botched **(up)** our first attempt at wallpapering the bathroom.*

botched /bɒtʃt/ [US] /bɑːtʃt/ *adj* (*UK ALSO* **bodged**) *Our landlord redecorated the bedroom, but it was such a botched **job*** (= it was so badly done) *that we decided to redo it.* ○ *Thousands of women are infertile as a result of botched **abortions**.* **botch(-up)** /ˈbɒtʃ.ʌp/ [US] /ˈbɑːtʃ-/ *noun* [C] (*UK ALSO* **bodge(-up)**) *The company made a series of botches before it went bankrupt.* ○ *The concert was very badly organized. In fact, the whole thing was a real botch-up.*

both /bəʊθ/ [US] /boʊθ/ *predeterminer, determiner, pronoun* (referring to) two people or things together: *Both my parents are teachers.* ○ *They have two grown children, both **of whom** live abroad.* ○ *She has written two novels, both **of which** have been made into television series.* ○ *Both Mike and Jim have red hair./Mike and Jim both have red hair.* ○ *I loved them both/I loved both **of** them.* ○ *The problem with both **of these** proposals is that they are hopelessly impractical.* ○ *Are both **of us** invited, or just you?* ○ *Would you like milk or sugar or both?* ○ *Both men **and** women have complained about the advertisement.* ○ *I felt both happy and sad at the same time.* ○ *I think it's important to listen to both **sides** of the argument.* ○ *Improved child-care facilities would benefit both sexes, not just women.* ○ *I failed my driving test because I didn't keep both hands on the steering wheel.*

bother [MAKE AN EFFORT] /ˈbɒð.əʳ/ [US] /ˈbɑː.ðɚ/ *verb* [I or T] to make the effort to do something: [+ to infinitive] *He hasn't even bothered **to** write.* ○ *You could have phoned us but you just didn't bother.* ○ [+ v-ing] *Don't bother mak**ing** the bed – I'll do it later.* ○ [+ v-ing or + to infinitive] *You'd have found it if you'd bothered look**ing/to** look.* ○ *You won't get any credit for doing it, **so why** bother?*

• **can't be bothered** *UK INFORMAL* If you can't be bothered doing/to do something, you are too lazy or tired to do it: *I can't be bothered to iron my clothes.* ○ *Most evenings I can't be bothered cooking.*

bother /ˈbɒð.əʳ/ [US] /ˈbɑː.ðɚ/ *noun* [U] trouble or problems: *I can take you – it's really no bother.* ○ *Some people don't get married because they don't want **the** bother* (= they don't want to make the effort that is necessary). ○ *Please **don't go to any** bother on my account* (= don't make any special effort for me). ○ *It hardly seems **worth** the bother to go all that way just for two nights.* ○ *UK I had **a bit of** bother getting hold of his phone number.*

bother [ANNOY] /ˈbɒð.əʳ/ [US] /ˈbɑː.ðɚ/ *verb* [T] to annoy or cause problems for someone: *Don't bother your father when he's working.* ○ *I'm **sorry to** bother **you**, but could you direct me to the station?* ○ *I didn't want to bother her **with** work matters on her day off.* ○ *The noise was beginning to bother us, so we left.* ○ *She threatened to call the police if he didn't stop bothering her.*

bother /ˈbɒð.əʳ/ [US] /ˈbɑː.ðɚ/ *noun* [S] *UK* an annoying person or an annoying piece of work: *I'm sorry to be a bother, but could I have that number again?*

Bother! /ˈbɒð.əʳ/ [US] /ˈbɑː.ðɚ/ *exclamation UK OLD-FASHIONED* used to express annoyance: *Oh bother! It's raining and I left my umbrella at home.*

bother [WORRY] /ˈbɒð.əʳ/ [US] /ˈbɑː.ðɚ/ *verb* [T] to make someone feel worried or upset: *Does it bother you that he's out so much of the time?* ○ *Living on my own has never bothered me.* ○ *I don't care if he doesn't come – it doesn't bother me.* ○ [+ that] *It bothers me **that** he doesn't seem to notice.*

botheration /ˌbɒð.əˈreɪ.ʃən/ [US] /ˌbɑː.ðə-/ *exclamation UK OLD-FASHIONED* an expression of annoyance: *Oh botheration! I can't find my keys anywhere.*

bothered /ˈbɒð.əd/ [US] /ˈbɑː.ðɚd/ *adj* [after v] **1** If you are bothered about something, it is important to you and you are worried about it: *He's very bothered **about** what people think of him.* ○ *They were an hour late and she didn't seem at all bothered.* ○ *The bright sunshine made him feel **hot and** bothered* (= hot and uncomfortable). **2** *UK INFORMAL* **not bothered** If you are not bothered about something, it is not important to you or does not worry you: *"Tea or coffee?" "Either – I'm not bothered."* ○ *I'm not bothered whether I go or not.*

bothersome /ˈbɒð.ə.səm/ [US] /ˈbɑː.ðɚ-/ *adj OLD-FASHIONED* causing annoyance or trouble: *a bothersome little man* ○ *bothersome noise*

Botox /ˈbəʊ.tɒks/ [US] /ˈboʊ.tɑːks/ *noun* [U] *TRADEMARK* a substance which is injected into the skin of the face in order to make the skin look smooth and young **Botox** /ˈbəʊ.tɒks/ [US] /ˈboʊ.tɑːks/ *verb* [T]

bottle CONTAINER /'bɒt.l/ ⓤ /'bɑː.t̬l/ *noun* [C] **1** a container for liquids, usually made of glass or plastic, with a narrow neck: *a milk bottle* ○ *a wine bottle* ○ *a bottle of beer/whisky* ○ ***Plastic** bottles are lighter than glass ones.* **2** a special container with a rubber top for giving milk and other drinks to a baby: *Give the baby her bottle when she wakes up.* ○ *Most medical experts believe that breast-feeding is better than bottle-**feeding**.*

• **the bottle** *INFORMAL* the habit of regularly drinking a lot of alcohol: *She started to **hit** the bottle* (= drink too much alcohol) *after her divorce.*

bottle /'bɒt.l/ ⓤ /'bɑː.t̬l/ *verb* [T] *The wine is bottled* (= put into bottles) *at the vineyard.* ○ *To bottle fruit you put fresh fruit into special containers.* **bottled** /'bɒt.ld/ ⓤ /'bɑː.t̬ld/ *adj: bottled water* ○ *bottled gas*

bottle BRAVERY /'bɒt.l/ ⓤ /'bɑː.t̬l/ *noun* [U] *UK SLANG APPROVING* bravery or willingness to take risks: *It took **a lot of** bottle to do what she did.*

PHRASAL VERBS WITH **bottle** ▼

▲ **bottle out** *phrasal verb UK SLANG* to suddenly decide not to do something because you feel frightened and lose your confidence: *I was going to enter a belly-dancing contest, but I bottled out at the last minute.*

▲ **bottle** *sth* **up** *phrasal verb* [M] When a person bottles things up, they refuse to talk about things that make them angry or worried.

bottle ,bank *noun* [C] *UK* a large container into which people put empty bottles and other glass objects so that the glass can be used again

bottled 'water *noun* [U] water which has been treated in order to make it very clean or which has come from a special place, and which is sold in bottles

bottle-feed /'bɒt.l.fiːd/ ⓤ /'bɑː.t̬l-/ *verb* [I or T] to feed a baby with milk from a bottle: *She bottle-fed both of her babies.* ⊃Compare **breast-feed**. **bottle-feeding** /'bɒt.l-.fiː.dɪŋ/ ⓤ /'bɑː.t̬l-/ *noun* [U]

bottle 'green *noun* [U] very dark green

bottleneck /'bɒt.l.nek/ ⓤ /'bɑː.t̬l-/ *noun* [C] **1** a place where a road becomes narrow, or a place where there is often a lot of traffic, causing the traffic to slow down or stop: *Roadworks are causing bottlenecks in the city centre.* **2** a problem that delays progress: *Is there any way of getting round this bureaucratic bottleneck?*

bottle ,opener *noun* [C] a device for removing the metal top from a bottle ⊃Compare **corkscrew**.

bottle ,top *noun* [C] (*US ALSO* **bottle cap**) a circular piece of metal used to close a bottle of beer or a fizzy drink

bottom LOWEST PART /'bɒt.əm/ ⓤ /'bɑː.t̬əm/ *noun* [C usually sing] **1** the lowest part of something: *He stood at the bottom **of** the stairs and called up to me.* ○ *Extra information will be found at the bottom of the page.* ○ *The ship had sunk to the bottom of the sea/the sea bottom.* ○ *UK They live at the bottom of our street* (= the other end of the street from us). ○ *UK The apple tree at the bottom* (= end) *of the garden is beginning to blossom.* ○ *At school, Einstein was (at the) bottom of* (= the least successful student in) *his class.* ○ *The manager of the hotel started **at the** bottom* (= in one of the least important jobs) *30 years ago, as a porter.* ○ *The rich usually get richer, while the people **at the** bottom* (= at the lowest position in society) *stay there.* **2 bottoms** the lower part of an item of clothing that consists of two parts: *I've found my bikini bottoms but not my top.* ○ *Have you seen my pyjama/tracksuit bottoms anywhere?*

• **at bottom** *UK FORMAL* in a basic way: *Jealousy is, at bottom, a lack of self-confidence.*

• **be at the bottom of** *sth* to be the real reason for or the cause of something: *The desire for money is at the bottom of much of the world's violence.*

• **the bottom drops/falls out of the market** If the bottom drops out of the market of a product, people stop buying it: *The bottom has fallen out of the fur coat market.*

• **bottoms up!** *INFORMAL HUMOROUS* sometimes said by people in a friendly way just before drinking an alcoholic drink together

• **from the bottom of** *your* **heart** very sincerely: *When I said I loved you, I **meant** it from the bottom of my heart.*

• **get to the bottom of** *sth* to discover the truth about a situation: *I'm not sure what is causing the problem, but I'm determined to get to the bottom of it.*

bottom BODY PART /'bɒt.əm/ ⓤ /'bɑː.t̬əm/ *noun* [C] the part of your body that you sit on: *She slipped and fell on her bottom.* ⊃See picture **The Body** on page Centre 5

bottom /'bɒt.əm/ ⓤ /'bɑː.t̬əm/ *verb*

▲ **bottom out** *phrasal verb* to have reached the lowest point in a continuously changing situation and to be about to improve: *The government claims that the recession is bottoming out.*

bottom 'drawer *UK OLD-FASHIONED noun* [C usually sing] (*US* **hope chest**, *AUS ALSO* **glory box**) clothes, LINENS, etc. that a young woman traditionally collects for use after she is married: *Kate's grandmother has given her a quilt for her bottom drawer.*

bottomless /'bɒt.əm.ləs/ ⓤ /'bɑː.t̬əm-/ *adj* without a limit or end: *The generosity of the local people is bottomless.*

bottomless 'pit *noun* [C usually sing] something that seems to have no limits, or a situation that will never end: *We'll be pouring money into a bottomless pit if we try to keep that factory open.*

bottom 'line MONEY *noun* [S] the final line in the accounts of a company or organization, which states the total profit or loss that has been made: *How will the rise in interest rates affect our bottom line?*

the ,bottom 'line IMPORTANT FACT *noun* [S] the most important fact in a situation: *The bottom line is that we need another ten thousand dollars to complete the project.*

botulism /'bɒt.jʊ.lɪ.zᵊm/ ⓤ /'bɑː.tʃə-/ *noun* [U] a serious type of food poisoning caused by bacteria in badly preserved food

boudoir /'buːd.wɑːʳ/ ⓤ /-wɑːr/ *noun* [C] a luxurious room used in the past by a woman for sleeping, dressing, relaxing and entertaining

bouffant /'buː.fɒŋ/ ⓤ /-fɑːnt/ *adj* describes a hairstyle in which the hair is arranged in a high rounded shape

bougainvillea /ˌbuː.gᵊn'vɪl.i.ə/ *noun* [C or U] a climbing plant, common in hot countries, that has red and purple flowers

bough /baʊ/ *noun* [C] *LITERARY* a large branch of a tree

bought /bɔːt/ ⓤ /bɑːt/ *past simple and past participle of* **buy**

bouillabaisse /ˌbuː.jə'bes/ *noun* [C or U] a thick soup made from fish, vegetables and spices

bouillon /'buː.jɒŋ/ ⓤ /'bʊl.jɑːn/ *noun* [C or U] a thin clear soup made by boiling meat and vegetables in water

bouillon ,cube *noun* [C] *US FOR* **stock cube**

boulder /'bəʊl.dəʳ/ ⓤ /'boʊl.dɚ/ *noun* [C] a very large rock

boules /buːl/ *noun* [U] a game played especially in France, in which metal balls are thrown so that they land as close as possible to a smaller ball

boulevard /'buː.lə.vɑːd/ ⓤ /'bʊl.ə.vɑːrd/ *noun* [C] (*WRITTEN ABBREVIATION* **Blvd**) a wide road in a city, usually with trees on each side or along the centre: *We strolled along the boulevard.*

bounce JUMP /baʊnts/ *verb* **1** [I or T] to (cause to) move up or away after hitting a surface: *The ball bounced **off** the post and into the net.* ○ *She bounced the ball quickly.* ○ *Her bag bounced* (= moved up and down) *against her side as she walked.* ○ *The children had broken the bed by bouncing* (= jumping up and down) *on it.* ○ *He bounced the baby* (= lifted it up and down) *on his knee.* ○ *FIGURATIVE Television pictures from all over the world are bounced **off** satellites* (= are sent to and returned from). **2** [I usually + adv or prep] to move in an energetic and enthusiastic manner: *Tom bounced **in**, smiling broadly.*

bounce /baʊnts/ *noun* [C or U] when something bounces, or the quality that makes something able to bounce: *In tennis you must hit the ball before its second bounce.* ○ *FIGURATIVE This shampoo will give your hair bounce* (= make it look attractively thick) *and shine.*

bouncy /'baʊnt.si/ *adj* **1** able to bounce: *This ball's not very bouncy.* **2** happy and energetic: *He's always bouncy in the morning.*

bounce NOT PAY /baʊnts/ *verb* [I or T] INFORMAL to (cause a cheque to) not be paid or accepted by a bank because of a lack of money in the account: *I had to pay a penalty fee when my cheque bounced.* ○ *To my horror the bank bounced the cheque.*

bounce EMAIL /baʊnts/ *verb* [I or T] If an email that you send bounces or is bounced, it comes back to you because the address is wrong or there is a computer problem.

PHRASAL VERBS WITH **bounce** ▼

▲ **bounce back** *phrasal verb* to start to be successful again after a difficult period, for example after experiencing failure, loss of confidence, illness or unhappiness: *Stock prices bounced back after a steep plunge earlier this week.* ○ *Children often seem to bounce back from illness more quickly than adults do.*

▲ **bounce sb into sth** *phrasal verb* UK to force somebody to do something that they do not want to do, usually relating to politics: [+ v-ing] *The opposition hopes to bounce the Prime Minister into calling an early election.*

▲ **bounce sth off sb** *phrasal verb* If you bounce something off someone, you tell someone about an idea or plan in order to find out what they think of it: *Can I bounce a couple of ideas off you?*

bouncer /'baʊnt.səʳ/ ⓤ /-sɚ/ *noun* [C] someone whose job is to stand outside a bar, party, etc. and either stop people who cause trouble from coming in or force them to leave

bouncing /'baʊnt.sɪŋ/ *adj* [before n] (especially of a baby) healthy and energetic: *We've got two grandchildren – a three-year-old girl and a bouncing baby boy.*

bound BIND /baʊnd/ *past simple and past participle of* **bind** TIE

bound CERTAIN /baʊnd/ *adj* [after v] certain or extremely likely to happen: [+ to infinitive] *You're bound to forget people's names occasionally.* ○ *You're bound to feel nervous about your interview.* ○ *These two young musicians are bound for international success* (= are certain to be successful).

● **be bound and determined** US to be seriously intending to do something: *They are bound and determined to build their own house someday.*

● **I'll be bound** UK OLD-FASHIONED I am certain: *He's in the pub, I'll be bound.*

bound FORCED /baʊnd/ *adj* [after v; + to infinitive] having a moral or legal duty to do something: *The company is bound by a special agreement to involve the union in important decisions.* ○ *She feels (duty) bound to tell him everything.*

bound BORDER /baʊnd/ *verb* [T usually passive] to mark or form the limits of: *The village is bounded on one side by a river.*

boundless /'baʊnd.ləs/ *adj* having no limit: *boundless optimism* ○ *She has boundless energy and enthusiasm.*

bounds /baʊndz/ *plural noun* legal or social limits: *The committee felt that newspaper coverage of the murder went beyond reasonable bounds.* ○ *What you did was beyond/outside the bounds of acceptable behaviour.* ○ *His desire for political power apparently knows no bounds* (= seems to be unlimited).

● **be out of bounds** If an area is out of bounds, people are not allowed to go there.

bound DIRECTION /baʊnd/ *adj* [after v] going to: *She was on a plane bound for Moscow when she became ill.*

-bound /-baʊnd/ *suffix* Northbound traffic (= traffic which is travelling north) *is moving very slowly because of the accident.* ○ US *The line did not close completely, but inbound and outbound trains* (= trains which were arriving and leaving) *had to share one of the two tracks near the station.*

-bound PREVENTING LEAVING /-baʊnd/ *suffix* (causing people to be) unable to leave a place because of an unwanted condition: *During his long illness he was completely housebound* (= he could not leave the house). ○ *She has been wheelchair-bound for several years.* ○ *The airport was completely fogbound* (= covered by fog). ⊃See also **-bound** at **bound** DIRECTION.

bound JUMP /baʊnd/ *verb* [I usually + adv or prep] to move quickly with large jumping movements

bound /baʊnd/ *noun* [C] *With one bound* (= quick large jump) *the dog was over the fence.*

boundary /'baʊn.dºr.i/ /-dri/ ⓤ /-dɚ-/ *noun* [C] **1** a real or imagined line that marks the edge or limit of something: *The Ural mountains mark the boundary between Europe and Asia.* ○ *Residents are opposed to the prison being built within the city boundary.* **2** the limit of a subject or principle: *Electronic publishing is blurring the boundaries between dictionaries and encyclopedias.*

bounden duty /ˌbaʊn.dºn'djuː.ti/ ⓤ /-'duː.ti/ *noun* [U] OLD-FASHIONED OR HUMOROUS something that you feel you must do: *She felt that it was her bounden duty to tell the police about the incident.*

bounder /'baʊn.dəʳ/ ⓤ /-dɚ/ *noun* [C] OLD-FASHIONED a man who behaves badly or immorally, especially in his relationships with women

bound 'up *adj* [after v] closely connected or involved: *The survival of whales is intimately bound up with the health of the ocean.*

bounty REWARD /'baʊn.ti/ ⓤ /-ti/ *noun* [C] a sum of money paid as a reward: *A bounty of $10 000 has been offered for the capture of his murderer.*

bounty KINDNESS /'baʊn.ti/ ⓤ /-ti/ *noun* **1** [U] LITERARY great kindness or willingness to give: *The charity is totally dependent on the Church's bounty.* **2** [C usually sing] a large amount: *a bounty of food*

bountiful /'baʊn.tɪ.fºl/ ⓤ /-tɪ-/ *adj* LITERARY We found a *bountiful* (= large) *supply of coconuts on the island.*

bounty hunter *noun* [C] someone who searches for criminals or hunts animals in exchange for a reward

bouquet FLOWERS /bʊ'keɪ/ /bəʊ-/ ⓤ /boʊ-/ *noun* [C] a group of flowers that have been fastened together and attractively arranged so that they can be given as a present or carried on formal occasions: *a bouquet of flowers* ○ *Chris sent me a lovely bouquet when I was ill.*

bouquet SMELL /bʊ'keɪ/ ⓤ /boʊ-/ *noun* [C or U] SPECIALIZED the characteristic smell of a wine or LIQUEUR: *This wine has a rich, oaky bouquet.*

bourbon /'bɜː.bºn/ ⓤ /'bɝː-/ *noun* [C or U] a type of American whiskey

bourgeois /'bɔːʒ.wɑː/ ⓤ /'bʊrʒ-/ *adj* DISAPPROVING belonging to or typical of the MIDDLE CLASS (= a social group between the rich and the poor), especially in supporting established customs and values, or in having a strong interest in money and possessions: *It's a bit bourgeois, isn't it, joining a golf club?*

the bourgeoisie /ˌðə.bɔːʒ.wɑː'ziː/ ⓤ /-ˌbʊrʒ-/ *group noun* [S] (in Marxism) the part of society, including employers and people who run large companies, which has most of the wealth and takes advantage of ordinary workers: *The new bourgeoisie, which was created by the Industrial Revolution, had money to spend and wanted to travel.*

bout BRIEF PERIOD /baʊt/ *noun* [C] a brief period of illness or involvement in an activity: *She had a bout of flu over Christmas.* ○ *He suffered from periodic bouts of insanity.* ○ *a drinking bout* (= brief period of drinking a lot of alcohol)

bout SPORT /baʊt/ *noun* [C] a boxing or WRESTLING match: *He's a former heavyweight champion and is expected to win the bout easily.*

boutique /buː'tiːk/ *noun* [C] a small shop that sells fashionable clothes, shoes, jewellery, etc.

bovine /'bəʊ.vaɪn/ ⓤ /'boʊ-/ *adj* **1** SPECIALIZED connected with cows: *a bovine virus* ⊃See also **BSE**. **2** slow or stupid in a way that a cow is thought to be: *He had a gentle, rather bovine expression.*

bovver /'bɒv.əʳ/ ⓤ /'bɑː.vɚ/ *noun* [U] UK INFORMAL violent or threatening behaviour

bow BEND /baʊ/ *verb* [I or T] to bend your head or body forward, especially as a way of showing someone respect or expressing thanks to people who have watched you perform: *They bowed to the Queen.* ○ *We bowed our heads in prayer.* ○ *He bowed down* (= very low) *before* (= in front of) *the king and begged for mercy.* ⊃Compare **curtsy**.

Bow

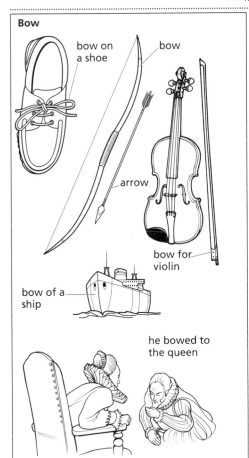

bow on a shoe

bow

arrow

bow for violin

bow of a ship

he bowed to the queen

B

• **bow and scrape** DISAPPROVING to show too much politeness or attention to someone: *It's embarrassing to see staff bowing and scraping to the new director.*

PHRASAL VERBS WITH **bow** ▼

▲ **bow down to sb** *phrasal verb* MAINLY UK to agree to obey someone: *He expects me to bow down to him and do everything he tells me.*

▲ **bow out** *phrasal verb* to leave a job or stop doing an activity, usually after a long time: *She'll be bowing out at the end of the month, after presenting the programme for eight years.*

▲ **bow to sb/sth** *phrasal verb* to do what someone else wants you to do, usually unwillingly: *Eventually the government was forced to bow to public **pressure** and reform the tax.*

bow /baʊ/ *noun* [C] when you bend your head or body forward, especially as a way of showing someone respect or expressing thanks to people who have watched you perform: *The audience applauded enthusiastically, and she came back on stage to **take** another bow.*

bowed /baʊd/ *adj* bent over: *He struggled along the path, bowed **under** the weight of the heavy bags he was carrying.*

bow FRONT PART /baʊ/ *noun* [C] (*ALSO* **bows**) the front part of a ship ⊃Compare **stern** SHIP PART.

• **fire a (warning) shot across sb's bow(s)** SLIGHTLY FORMAL to do something in order to warn someone that you will take strong action if they do not change their behaviour: *Airline staff have fired a warning shot across the company's bows by threatening to strike if higher pay increases are not offered.*

bow WEAPON /bəʊ/ US /boʊ/ *noun* [C] a weapon for shooting arrows, made of a long thin piece of wood bent into a curve by a tightly stretched string: *bow **and arrows*** ⊃See also **crossbow.** ⊃See picture **Sports** on page Centre 10

bowed /bəʊd/ US /boʊd/ *adj* curved: *The table had delicate bowed legs.*

bow MUSIC /bəʊ/ US /boʊ/ *noun* [C] a long thin piece of wood with hair from the tail of a horse stretched along it, which is used to play musical instruments that have strings: *Violins are played with bows.*

bow KNOT /bəʊ/ US /boʊ/ *noun* [C] a knot with two curved parts and two loose ends which is used as a decoration or to tie shoes: *I tied the ribbon around the parcel in a pretty bow.*

bowdlerize, UK ALSO **-ise** /ˈbaʊd.lə.raɪz/ *verb* [T] DISAPPROVING to remove words or parts from a book, play or film that are considered to be unsuitable or offensive: *The version of the play that I saw had been dreadfully bowdlerized.*

bowel /ˈbaʊ.əlz/ *noun* [C usually pl] **1** the long tube that carries solid waste from the stomach out of the body: *He has trouble with his bowels.* ○ *bowel cancer/ cancer of the bowel* **2 move your bowels** (said especially by doctors and nurses) to excrete the solid waste that is contained in the bowels

• **the bowels of sth** the parts of something that are furthest from the outside: *The fire started deep in the bowels of the ship.*

bowel ˌmovement *noun* [C] (*ABBREVIATION* **BM**) POLITE EXPRESSION (used especially by doctors and nurses) the act of emptying the contents of the bowels, or the material that is emptied

bower /ˈbaʊ.əʳ/ US /-ɚ/ *noun* [C] LITERARY a pleasant place under the branches of a tree in a wood or garden

bowl DISH /bəʊl/ US /boʊl/ *noun* [C] **1** a round container that is open at the top and is deep enough to hold fruit, sugar, etc., or the rounded inside part of something: *a soup/cereal/salad/sugar bowl* ○ *a bowl of soup/rice/ porridge* ○ *She eats a bowl (= the contents of a bowl) **of** cereal every morning.* ○ *Sift the flour and baking powder into a **mixing** bowl.* ○ *The **toilet** bowl was cracked and stained, and the walls were covered in mould.* ○ UK *Just put the dirty dishes in the **washing-up** bowl, and I'll do them later.* **2** MAINLY US a large bowl-shaped building or structure which is used for important sports events or musical performances: *the Hollywood Bowl*

• **Life is just a bowl of cherries.** something that you say which means that life is very pleasant. This phrase is often used humorously to mean the opposite.

bowl CRICKET /bəʊl/ US /boʊl/ *verb* [I or T] to throw a ball towards a BATSMAN (= the player who hits the ball) using a vertical circular movement of the arm while running: *Pringle was tired after bowling for an hour.*

bowler /ˈbəʊ.ləʳ/ US /ˈboʊ.lɚ/ *noun* **1 fast/pace bowler** a bowler who bowls the ball fast: *It isn't easy to score runs against pace bowlers.* **2 spin bowler** a bowler who spins the ball so that when it hits the ground it bounces in an unexpected way, making it difficult to hit

bowling /ˈbəʊ.lɪŋ/ US /ˈboʊ-/ *noun* [U] *The England captain **opened the** bowling (= bowled first).*

bowl ROLL /bəʊl/ US /boʊl/ *verb* [I or T] to roll a ball along a smooth grass or artificial surface during a game

bowl /bəʊl/ US /boʊl/ *noun* [C] a large ball used in the game of BOWLS

bowling /ˈbəʊ.lɪŋ/ US /ˈboʊ-/ *noun* [U] (UK ALSO **tenpin bowling**) a game played inside, in which you roll a heavy ball down a track to try to knock down a group of PINS (= tall, thin wooden objects)

bowls /bəʊlz/ US /boʊlz/ *noun* [U] a game played either outside on smooth grass or inside on an artificial surface, in which the players roll a large black or brown ball as close as possible to a smaller white ball: *Bowls is one of the most popular sports in Britain.*

PHRASAL VERBS WITH **bowl** ▼

▲ **bowl down/along sth** *phrasal verb* to go quickly: *They bowled down the street on their new bicycles.*

▲ **bowl *sb* out** *phrasal verb* [M] in the game of cricket, to make someone have to leave the cricket field by hitting the WICKET (= three vertical sticks) behind them with the ball

▲ **bowl *sb* over** [KNOCK DOWN] *phrasal verb* [M usually passive] to knock someone to the ground by running into them: *She was almost bowled over by a huge dog.*

▲ **bowl *sb* over** [PLEASE] *phrasal verb* [M usually passive] to surprise and please someone greatly: *She was bowled over when she heard she'd won the competition.*

bow-legged /ˈbəʊ.leg.ɪd/ [US] /ˈboʊ-/ *adj* A bow-legged person has legs that curve out at the knees.

ˌbowler (ˈhat) *noun* [C] (*US ALSO* **derby**) a man's hat that is black and has a round hard top ➲See picture **Hairstyles and Hats** on page Centre 8

ˈbowling ˌalley *noun* [C] a building in which you can go bowling, or the narrow track along which balls are rolled during a bowling game

ˈbowling ˌball *noun* [C] a large, heavy ball with three holes for your fingers, which is used in the sport of BOWLING

ˈbowling ˌgreen *noun* [C] an area of very short, smooth grass where you can play BOWLS

ˌbow ˈtie *noun* [C] a special type of TIE (= a strip of cloth put around a collar) in the shape of a bow, worn especially by men on formal occasions ➲See picture **Clothes** on page Centre 6

ˌbow ˈwindow *noun* [C] a curved window that sticks out from the wall of a house

bow-wow /ˌbaʊˈwaʊ/ /ˈ--/ *noun* [C], *exclamation CHILD'S WORD* a dog, or the sound that a dog makes: *A cow goes 'moo' and a dog goes 'bow-wow'.*

box [CONTAINER] /bɒks/ [US] /bɑːks/ *noun* [C] **1** a square or rectangular container with stiff sides and sometimes a lid: *a cardboard box* ○ *a cigar box* ○ *a matchbox* **2** a box and its contents, or just the contents of a box: *a box of matches* ○ *He ate a whole box of chocolates.* **3** any square or rectangular space on a form, sports field, road etc., which is separated from the main area by lines: *If you would like more information, mark this box.* **4** a small enclosed space: *a jury/telephone box* ○ *Their new house is just a box* (= very small). **5** a small area with seats which is separate from the other seats in a theatre or at the side of a sports field: *Can you see Prince Charles in the **royal** box?* **6** *UK* (*US* **cup**) a piece of hard plastic worn by men to protect their sex organs when playing sport

box /bɒks/ [US] /bɑːks/ *verb* [T] (*ALSO* **box up**) to put something in a box: *Should I box these shoes up for you, or would you like to wear them now?*

boxy /ˈbɒk.si/ [US] /ˈbɑːk-/ *adj DISAPPROVING* shaped like a box: *The trouble with many small houses is that they tend to be boxy.*

the box [TELEVISION] *noun UK INFORMAL* television: *There's nothing worth watching **on** the box tonight.*

box [SPORT] /bɒks/ [US] /bɑːks/ *verb* [I or T] to fight someone in the sport of BOXING: *He used to box every weekend.* ○ *I've boxed **(against)** some of the best.*

• **box *sb's* ears** (*UK ALSO* **give *sb* a box on the ears**) *OLD-FASHIONED* to hit someone on the ears, usually as a punishment

box [TREE] /bɒks/ [US] /bɑːks/ *noun* [U] a small evergreen tree with small shiny leaves ➲See also **boxwood**.

PHRASAL VERBS WITH **box**

▲ **box *sb/sth* in** [MOVE] *phrasal verb* [M often passive] to move so close to someone or something that they cannot move away: *When I got back to my car, I found it had been boxed in by a lorry.*

▲ **box *sb* in** [NOT ALLOW] *phrasal verb* [M often passive] to prevent someone from doing what they want to do: *She did not want to send her son to a school where he would be boxed in by so many rules and regulations.*

ˌboxed ˈin *adj* [after v] prevented from doing what you want to do: *He feels boxed in at work and wants greater freedom to develop his ideas.*

boxcar /ˈbɒks.kɑːʳ/ [US] /ˈbɑːks.kɑːr/ *noun* [C] *US* a railway carriage with a roof, which is used for carrying goods

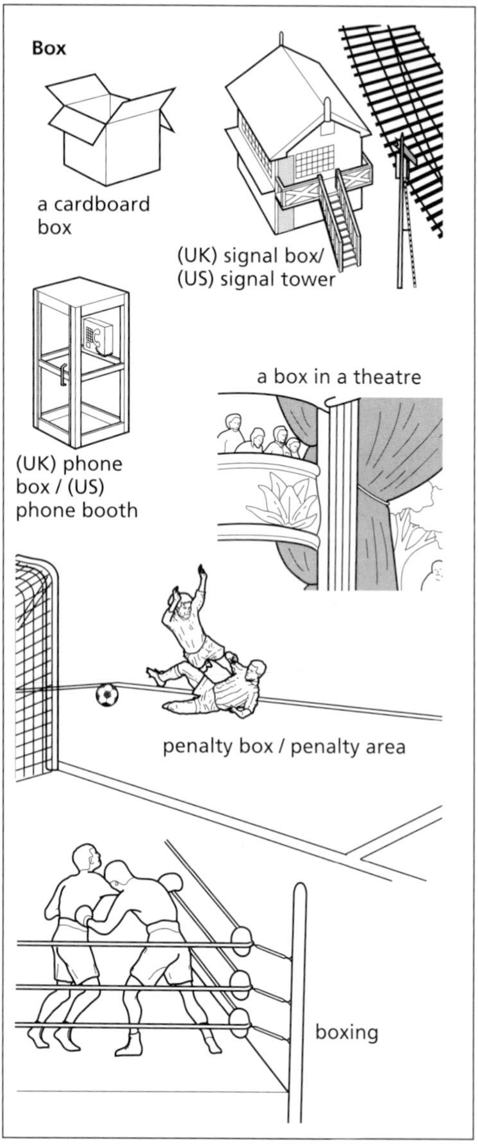
Box
a cardboard box
(UK) signal box/ (US) signal tower
(UK) phone box / (US) phone booth
a box in a theatre
penalty box / penalty area
boxing

boxer [SPORT] /ˈbɒk.səʳ/ [US] /ˈbɑːk.sɚ/ *noun* [C] someone who takes part in the sport of boxing: *He was a **heavyweight** boxer before he became an actor.*

boxer [DOG] /ˈbɒk.səʳ/ [US] /ˈbɑːk.sɚ/ *noun* [C] a dog of medium size with short light brown hair and a short flat nose

ˈboxer ˌshorts *plural noun* (*ALSO* **boxers**) loosely-fitting men's underwear, similar to short trousers ➲See picture **Clothes** on page Centre 6

boxing /ˈbɒk.sɪŋ/ [US] /ˈbɑːk-/ *noun* [U] a sport in which two competitors fight by hitting each other with their hands: *Many doctors believe that boxing is too dangerous and should be banned.* ○ *He's a former world heavyweight boxing champion.* ➲See picture **Sports** on page Centre 10

ˈBoxing ˌDay *noun* [C or U] in Britain, the day after Christmas Day

ˈboxing ˌgloves *plural noun* a pair of large thick hand coverings that are worn for protection when boxing ➲See picture **Sports** on page Centre 10

'**boxing** ,**ring** *noun* [C usually sing] a small enclosed area where boxers compete

'**box** ,**junction** *UK noun* [C] (*US* **box**) a place where two roads cross with a square of yellow lines painted in the centre, which you can drive over only when the road in front is clear

'**box** ,**lunch** *noun* [C] (*ALSO* **bag lunch**) *US FOR* **packed lunch**

'**box** (,**number**) *noun* [C] a number that you can give instead of your address, especially in newspaper advertisements: *Please reply to Box 307, The Times, London.*

'**box** ,**office** *noun* **1** [C] the place in a theatre or cinema where tickets are sold: *The box office opens at ten.* **2** the popularity and financial success of a film or actor: *Her last film was a surprise box-office hit.*

boxroom /'bɒks.ruːm/ /-rʊm/ ⑨ /'baːks-/ *noun* [C] *UK* a small room in a house used for storing large objects such as cases and furniture

'**box** ,**spanner** *UK noun* [C] (*US* **box wrench**) a cylindrical tool with a six-sided end that is used for tightening and loosening nuts and bolts in places that are difficult to reach

'**box** ,**spring** *noun* [C] a spring or set of springs attached to a frame and enclosed in a cloth covering, for supporting a bed

boxwood /'bɒks.wʊd/ ⑨ /'baːks-/ *noun* [U] a hard wood obtained from a BOX tree: *Boxwood is used for making small carved objects and tool handles.*

boy /bɔɪ/ *noun* [C] a male child or, more generally, a male of any age: *a teenage/adolescent boy* ○ *As a young boy, my father used to walk three miles to school.* ○ *You've been a very naughty boy!* ○ *Their little boy* (= Their young son) *is very sick.* ○ *All right, boys and girls, quiet down!*
• **my (dear) boy** *UK OLD-FASHIONED* a friendly way of addressing a man: *Look here, my boy, this simply won't do.*
• **(Oh) boy!** *MAINLY US INFORMAL* an exclamation used to express excitement or to say something emphatically: *Boy, that was good!*
the boys *plural noun INFORMAL* a group of male friends: *He used to like spending Friday nights with the boys.*
• **one of the boys** *INFORMAL* a typical male: *He plays football, drinks a lot of beer and generally acts like one of the boys.*
• **the/our boys** an approving way of speaking about your country's soldiers: *We must not forget our boys serving far from home.*
• **the boys in blue** *INFORMAL* an affectionate name for the police
• **Boys will be boys.** *SAYING* said to emphasize that people should not be surprised when boys or men act in a rough, noisy or selfish way because this is part of the male character

boyhood /'bɔɪ.hʊd/ *noun* [C or U] the period when a person is a boy, and not yet a man, or the state of being a boy: *I had a very happy boyhood.* ○ *The transition from boyhood to manhood can be a confusing period.* ○ *It was his boyhood ambition/dream to become a film director.* ○ *James Bond was a boyhood hero of mine.* ⊃See also **childhood** at **child**; **girlhood** at **girl**.

boyish /'bɔɪ.ɪʃ/ *adj* describes behaviour or characteristics that are like those of a boy: *a boyish grin* ○ *She had her hair cut in a boyish style.* ○ *Even as an old man he retained his boyish charm.* ○ *She found his boyish good looks very attractive.* **boyishly** /'bɔɪ.ɪʃ.li/ *adv*: *He is still boyishly handsome at the age of 45.*

boycott /'bɔɪ.kɒt/ ⑨ /-kaːt/ *verb* [T] to refuse to buy a product or take part in an activity as a way of expressing strong disapproval: *People were urged to boycott the country's products.* ○ *The union called on its members to boycott the meeting.* **boycott** /'bɔɪ.kɒt/ ⑨ /-kaːt/ *noun* [C] *A boycott of/against goods from the EU began in June.*

boyfriend /'bɔɪ.frend/ *noun* [C] a man or boy with whom a person is having a romantic or sexual relationship: *He's not my boyfriend – we're just good friends!* ○ *Cathy's ex-boyfriend was a really nice guy.* ⊃Compare **girl-friend**.

boy-meets-girl /ˌbɔɪ.miːts'gɜːl/ ⑨ /-gɜːrl/ *adj* [before n] relating to a story, book or film whose main subject is romance: *It was the usual boy-meets-girl sort of film.*

,**Boy** '**Scout** *noun* [C] *OLD-FASHIONED OR US FOR* a member of the Scouts

'**boy** ,**toy** *noun* [C] *US INFORMAL* an attractive young man, especially one who has relationships with older, powerful, or successful people ⊃See also **toy boy**.

,**boy** '**wonder** *noun* [C] a young man who has achieved more than what is expected for his age

bozo /'bəʊ.zəʊ/ ⑨ /'boʊ.zoʊ/ *noun* [C] *plural* **bozos** *MAINLY US SLANG* a stupid person: *Some bozo on a motorcycle almost ran me over.*

bra /braː/ *noun* [C] (*FORMAL* **brassiere**) a piece of women's underwear that supports the breasts ⊃See picture **Clothes** on page Centre 6

brace **yourself** PREPARE /breɪs/ *verb* [R] to prepare yourself physically or mentally for something unpleasant: *The passengers were told to brace themselves* (= to press their bodies hard against something or hold them very stiff) *for a crash landing.* ○ *She told me she had some bad news for me and I braced myself for a shock.*

brace SUPPORT /breɪs/ *noun* [C] *plural* **braces** something that connects, fastens, strengthens or supports: *I had to wear a brace* (*US USUALLY* **braces**) *for my crooked teeth when I was a teenager.* ○ *He was recently fitted with a brace for his bad back.*
braces /'breɪ.sɪz/ *plural noun* **1** *UK* (*US* **suspenders**) a pair of narrow straps which stretch from the front of the trousers over your shoulders to the back to hold them up: *a pair of braces* **2** *US* **callipers** LEG SUPPORT
brace /breɪs/ *verb* [T] to support an object in order to stop it from falling down: *The side wall of the old house was braced with a wooden support.*

brace PAIR /breɪs/ *noun* [C] *plural* **brace** two things of the same type, especially two wild birds that have been killed for sport or food: *a brace of pheasants*

bracelet /'breɪ.slət/ *noun* [C] a piece of jewellery which is worn around the wrist or arm: *a gold/silver/diamond bracelet* ○ *a chain bracelet*

bracing /'breɪ.sɪŋ/ *adj* (especially of air or an activity) healthy and fresh: *We enjoyed a bracing walk on the beach.*

bracken /'bræk.ən/ *noun* [U] a large FERN (= a type of plant) that grows thickly in open areas of countryside, especially on hills, and in woods

bracket SYMBOL /'bræk.ɪt/ *noun* [C usually pl] either of two symbols put around a word, phrase or sentence in a piece of writing to show that what is between them should be considered as separate from the main part: *Biographical information is included in brackets.* ○ *UK You should include the date of publication in* **round** *brackets* (*also esp. US and ANZ* **parentheses**) *after the title.* ○ *Grammar patterns in this dictionary are shown in* (*UK*) **square** *brackets/*(*US*) *brackets. For example, a countable noun is marked [C].*
bracket /'bræk.ɪt/ *verb* [T] *I've bracketed* (= put brackets around) *the bits of text that could be omitted.*

bracket GROUP /'bræk.ɪt/ *noun* [C] a set group with fixed upper and lower limits: *They were both surgeons in a high income bracket.* ○ *Most British university students are in the 18 – 22 age bracket.* ○ *Her pay rise brought her into a new tax bracket.*
bracket /'bræk.ɪt/ *verb* [T] If you bracket two or more things or people, you consider them to be similar or connected to each other: *He's often bracketed with the romantic poets of this period although this does not reflect the range of his work.*

bracket SUPPORT /'bræk.ɪt/ *noun* [C] a piece of metal, wood or plastic, usually L-shaped, that is fastened to a wall and used to support something such as a shelf

brackish /'bræk.ɪʃ/ *adj* Brackish water is salty, dirty and unpleasant.

bradawl /'bræd.ɔːl/ ⑨ /-aːl/ *noun* [C] a small sharp tool used for making holes

brag /bræg/ *verb* [I] -**gg**- *INFORMAL DISAPPROVING* to speak too proudly about what you have done or what you own: *She's always bragging about how much money she*

B

earns. ○ [+ that] *They bragged **that** their team had never been beaten.*

braggart /ˈbræg.ət/ [US] /-ɚt/ *noun* [C] *OLD-FASHIONED DISAPPROVING* someone who proudly talks a lot about themselves and their achievements or possessions

brahmin, brahman /ˈbrɑː.mɪn/ *noun* [C] a member of the highest Hindu CASTE (= social group): *Brahmins traditionally become priests in the Hindu religion.*

braid [CLOTH] /breɪd/ *noun* [U] (*ALSO* **braiding**) a thin strip of cloth or twisted threads, which is fixed onto clothes, uniform or other items made of cloth, as decoration: *The captain of the ship wore a peaked cap decorated with **gold** braid* (= twisted gold threads).

braid [HAIR] /breɪd/ *verb* [I or T], *noun* [C] *US FOR* **plait** ➲See picture **Hairstyles and Hats** on page Centre 8

braille, Braille /breɪl/ *noun* [U] a system of printing for blind people, in which each letter is represented as a raised pattern which can be read by touching with the fingers: *The book has been printed in six languages and in braille.*

brain /breɪn/ *noun* **1** [C] the organ inside the head that controls thought, memory, feelings and activity: *Doctors tried desperately to reduce the swelling in her brain.* ○ *The accident left him with permanent brain **damage**.* ○ *His wife died from a brain **tumour**.* **2** [C] used to refer to intelligence: *Marie has an amazing brain* (= is very intelligent). ○ *That can't possibly be the right way to do it – **use** your brain!* **3** [C usually pl] *INFORMAL* a very intelligent person, especially one who has spent a lot of time studying: *We've got the best brains in the land working on this problem.*

• **have *sth* on the brain** *INFORMAL DISAPPROVING* to not be able to stop thinking or talking about one particular thing: *You've got cars on the brain. Can't we talk about something else for a change?*

brain /breɪn/ *verb* [T] *INFORMAL* to hit someone on the head: *I'll brain you if you don't keep quiet.*

-brained /-breɪnd/ *suffix* **1** having a particular type of brain: *These dinosaurs were large-brained and more intelligent than most.* **2** *DISAPPROVING* used in various phrases to describe someone as stupid or badly organized: *bird-brained* ○ *harebrained* ○ *scatterbrained*

brainless /ˈbreɪn.ləs/ *adj INFORMAL* stupid: *What sort of brainless idiot would do that?*

brains /breɪnz/ *plural noun* intelligence: *The poor child inherited his mother's brains and his father's looks.* ○ *He's got brains but he's too lazy to use them* (= He is clever but lazy).

brains /breɪnz/ *noun* **the brains** the cleverest person of a group, especially the person who plans what the group will do: *My little brother's the brains **of** the family.*

brainy /ˈbreɪ.ni/ *adj INFORMAL* clever: *Sarah was beautiful and brainy.*

brainchild /ˈbreɪn.tʃaɪld/ *noun* [S] a clever and original idea, plan or invention: *The project was the brainchild **of** one of the students.*

brain-dead /ˈbreɪn.ded/ *adj* If someone is brain-dead, they have serious and permanent damage to their brain, and need machines in order to stay alive.

ˈbrain ˌdeath *noun* [U] when a person's brain stops working and they need machines in order to stay alive

ˈbrain ˌdrain *noun* [S] when large numbers of educated and highly skilled people leave their own country to live and work in another one where pay and conditions are better: *Britain has suffered a huge brain drain in recent years.*

ˈbrain ˌpower *noun* [U] *INFORMAL* your intelligence or your ability to think: *Solving this problem has taken all my brain power.*

brainstorm [SUGGEST] /ˈbreɪn.stɔːm/ [US] /-stɔːrm/ *verb* [I or T] (of a group of people) to suggest a lot of ideas for a future activity very quickly before considering some of them more carefully: *The team got together to brainstorm (the project).* **brainstorming** /ˈbreɪnˌstɔː.mɪŋ/ [US] /-ˌstɔːr-/ *noun* [U] *We need to do some brainstorming before we get down to detailed planning.* ○ *We're having a brainstorming **session** on Friday.*

brainstorm [MENTAL STATE] /ˈbreɪn.stɔːm/ [US] /-stɔːrm/ *noun* [C] **1** *UK INFORMAL* a sudden state of being unable to think clearly: *I must have **had** a brainstorm – I went shopping and forgot to take any money.* **2** *US FOR* **brainwave**

brainteaser /ˈbreɪnˌtiː.zəʳ/ [US] /-zɚ/ *noun* [C] (*ALSO* **teaser**) a problem for which it is hard to find the answer, especially one which people enjoy trying to solve as a game: *The paper publishes two brainteasers every Saturday.*

ˈbrain ˌtrust *US noun* [C] (*UK* **brains trust**) a group of people who advise a leader: *The candidate's brain trust is gathering this weekend to plan strategy for the primary election.*

brainwash /ˈbreɪn.wɒʃ/ [US] /-wɑːʃ/ *verb* [T] *DISAPPROVING* to make someone believe something by continually telling them that it is true and preventing any other information from reaching them: *The government is trying to brainwash them **into** thinking that war is necessary.* **brainwashing** /ˈbreɪnˌwɒʃ.ɪŋ/ [US] /-ˌwɑːʃ-/ *noun* [U] *Many people thought the religious sect was guilty of brainwashing.*

brainwave [IDEA] *UK* /ˈbreɪn.weɪv/ *noun* [C] (*US* **brainstorm**) *INFORMAL* a sudden clever idea: *I couldn't see how I could get home from the station – then I **had a** brainwave, Eric could meet me.* ➲See also **brain wave**.

ˈbrain ˌwave [PATTERN] *noun* [C] any of several patterns of electrical activity in the brain ➲See also **brainwave**.

braise /breɪz/ *verb* [T] to cook food slowly in a covered dish in a little fat and liquid: *braised celery* ○ *braising steak*

brake /breɪk/ *noun* [C] a device which makes a vehicle go slower or stop, or a PEDAL, bar or handle which makes this device work: *She had no brakes on her bicycle.* ○ *The taxi driver suddenly (UK)**applied**/(US)**put on** his brakes.* ○ *INFORMAL I **slammed on*** (= quickly used) *the brake, but it was too late.* ○ *All our new models have **anti-lock** brakes.*

• **put a brake on** (*ALSO* **put the brakes on**) to slow down or stop an activity: *The government has put a brake on further spending.*

brake /breɪk/ *verb* [I] to make a vehicle go slower or stop, using its brake: *When it's icy, brake **gently**.* ○ *He would zoom up to junctions and brake hard/sharply at the last minute.*

ˈbrake ˌcable *noun* [C] one of the wires on a bicycle which connect the part of the brake that you operate with your hand, to the part that stops the wheel

ˈbrake ˌlight *noun* [C] one of the red lights at the back of a motor vehicle, that light up when the brakes are used

ˈbrake ˌpedal *noun* [C] the bar which you push down with your foot to make a vehicle slow down or stop ➲See picture **Car** on page Centre 12

bramble /ˈbræm.bl̩/ *noun* **1** [C or U] a wild bush with thorns, that produces BLACKBERRIES: *We carefully pushed our way through the low brambles.* **2** [C] *UK* a **blackberry**: *We stopped to pick brambles by the side of the road.* ○ *bramble jam* **3** [C] *US* any wild bush with thorns

bran /bræn/ *noun* [U] the outer covering of grain that is separated when making white flour. Bran is added to other foods because it contains a lot of the FIBRE needed for a healthy body: *wheat/oat bran* ○ *Both these breakfast cereals have added bran.*

branch [TREE PART] /brɑːntʃ/ [US] /bræntʃ/ *noun* [C] one of the parts of a tree that grows out from the main trunk and has leaves, flowers or fruit on it: *bare/leafy/flowering branches* ○ *The fruit on the lower branches was protected from the sun.* ○ *Watch out for **overhanging** branches.*

branch /brɑːntʃ/ [US] /bræntʃ/ *verb* [I] **1** to produce branches: *The top of the tree had been cut off to encourage it to branch **(out)** lower down.* **2** to divide into two: *The road branches at the bottom of the hill.*

branch [PART] /brɑːntʃ/ [US] /bræntʃ/ *noun* [C] **1** a part of something larger: *Immunology is a branch **of** biological science.* ○ *One branch **of** their family* (= One group of relatives) *emigrated to Brazil.* ○ *In the US, the president is part of the executive branch of the government.* **2** one of the offices or groups that form part of a large business organization: *I used to work in the **local** branch **of** a large bank.* ○ *She's a branch **manager**.* ○ *Take the forms into your local branch **office**.*

branch [RIVER] /brɑːntʃ/ [US] /bræntʃ/ *noun* [C] a part of a river or road that leaves the main part: *This branch of the river eventually empties into the Atlantic.*

PHRASAL VERBS WITH **branch**

▲ **branch off** *phrasal verb* If a road or path branches off, it goes in another direction: *We drove down a narrow track that branched off* ***from*** *the main road.*
▲ **branch off *sth*** *phrasal verb* to leave a main road by turning into a smaller road: *We branched off the main route and went through the countryside.*
▲ **branch out** *phrasal verb* to start to do something different from what you usually do, especially in your job: *This designer has recently branched out* ***into*** *children's wear.* ○ *After a couple of years working for other people, she branched out* ***on*** *her* ***own*** (= started her own business).

ˈ**branch ˌline** *noun* [C] a railway that goes from the main railway to small towns and countryside areas

brand [PRODUCT] /brænd/ *noun* [C] **1** a type of product made by a particular company: *This isn't my usual brand* ***of*** *deodorant.* ○ *When I go to a supermarket I usually buy* ***own*** *(*US ***store****/*AUS ***generic****) brands* (= the cheaper products with the shop's own name on them). **2** **brand of *sth*** a particular type of something, or way of doing something: *a team that plays a distinctive brand of football* ○ *Do you like his brand of humour?*
branding /ˈbræn.dɪŋ/ *noun* [U] the act of giving a company a particular design or symbol in order to advertise its products and services: *The successful branding and marketing of the new beer has already boosted sales and increased profits.*

brand [JUDGE] /brænd/ *verb* [T + obj + n or adj] to say that you think someone is as stated: *Because of one minor offence he was branded* ***(as)*** *a common criminal.* ○ *The newspapers have branded the rebel MP disloyal.*

brand [MARK] /brænd/ *verb* [T] to mark an animal such as a cow by burning or freezing its skin to show you own it: *The cattle were rounded up and branded.* **brand** /brænd/ *noun* [C] *The brand was still visible on the animal's hide.*

brand [FLAME] /brænd/ *noun* [C] *LITERARY* a piece of burning wood used to give light

ˈ**branding ˌiron** *noun* [C] a long piece of metal with a special design at one end, used to burn an owner's mark on the skin of animals such as cows and horses

brandish /ˈbræn.dɪʃ/ *verb* [T] to wave something in the air in a threatening or excited way: *She brandished a saucepan* ***at*** *me so I ran out of the kitchen.*

ˈ**brand ˌname** *noun* [C] the name given to a particular product by the company that makes it

ˌ**brand ˈnew** *adj* completely new, especially not yet used: *How can he afford to buy himself a brand new car?* ○ *His coat looked as if it was brand new.*

brandy /ˈbræn.di/ *noun* [C or U] a strong alcoholic drink made from wine and sometimes flavoured with fruits

ˌ**brandy ˈbutter** *noun* [U] a sweet food made of sugar, butter and brandy, and served especially at Christmas in Britain on CHRISTMAS PUDDING and MINCE PIES

ˈ**brandy ˌsnap** *noun* [C] *MAINLY UK* a thin hard biscuit which is rolled into a tube

brash /bræʃ/ *adj DISAPPROVING* (of people) showing too much confidence and too little respect, or (of clothes) too bright and colourful: *a brash young banker* ○ *Don't you think that suit's a bit brash for a funeral?* **brashness** /ˈbræʃ.nəs/ *noun* [U]

brass [METAL] /brɑːs/ [US] /bræs/ *noun* **1** [U] a bright yellow metal made from copper and ZINC: *The door handles were made of brass.* **2** [C] a thin piece of brass on the floor or wall in a church, with a picture or writing cut into it: *The church has several beautiful medieval brasses.*
• **brass monkey weather** *UK INFORMAL* extremely cold weather
• **get down to brass tacks** to start talking about the most important or basic facts of a situation: *Let's get down to brass tacks. Who's paying for all this?*
brassy /ˈbrɑː.si/ [US] /ˈbræs.i/ *adj* like brass in colour, or too bright: *a brassy yellow*

brass [MUSICAL INSTRUMENTS] /brɑːs/ [US] /bræs/ *adj* [before n] (of a musical instrument) made of metal and played by blowing: *The trumpet and trombone are brass instruments.* ○ *He plays in the brass section of the orchestra.* ➲Compare **percussion**; **woodwind**.
the brass *group noun* [S] the group of brass instruments or players in a BAND or orchestra: *The brass seems to me too loud in this recording.*
brassy /ˈbrɑː.si/ [US] /ˈbræs.i/ *adj DISAPPROVING She had a brassy* (= unpleasantly loud) *voice.*

brass [CONFIDENCE] /brɑːs/ [US] /bræs/ *noun* [U] *UK INFORMAL* complete self-confidence and lack of fear: *I don't know how she* ***has the*** *brass* ***to*** *do it.*
brassy /ˈbrɑː.si/ [US] /ˈbræs.i/ *adj DISAPPROVING* describes a woman who speaks and laughs too loudly and who dresses in bright, cheap clothes, often wearing too much make-up: *She was your typical brassy blonde.*

brass [MONEY] /brɑːs/ [US] /bræs/ *noun* [U] *UK OLD-FASHIONED INFORMAL* money

ˌ**brass ˈband** *noun* [C] a band in which most of the musical instruments are made of brass

brassed off /ˌbrɑːstˈɒf/ [US] /ˌbræstˈɑːf/ *adj* [after v] *UK INFORMAL* annoyed and bored: *I'm getting a bit brassed off* ***with*** *his attitude.*

brasserie /ˈbræs.ə.ri/ [US] /ˌbræs.əˈriː/ *noun* [C] a French-style restaurant that serves cheap and simple food

brassiere /ˈbræz.i.eəʳ/ [US] /brəˈzɪr/ *noun* [C] *FORMAL FOR* **bra**

ˌ**brass ˈknuckles** *plural noun US FOR* **knuckle-duster**

brass-rubbing /ˈbrɑːsˌrʌb.ɪŋ/ [US] /ˈbræs-/ *noun* [C or U] the activity of putting a sheet of paper on top of a brass in a church, and rubbing it with a special pencil to make a picture, or a picture that is made in this way

brat /bræt/ *noun* [C] *INFORMAL DISAPPROVING* a child, especially one who behaves badly: *She's behaving like a (UK* ***spoilt****)/(US* ***spoiled****) brat.*

bravado /brəˈvɑː.dəʊ/ [US] /-doʊ/ *noun* [U] a show of bravery, especially when unnecessary and dangerous, to make people admire you: *It was an* ***act of*** *bravado that made him ask his boss to resign.*

brave [WITHOUT FEAR] /breɪv/ *adj* showing no fear of dangerous or difficult things: *a brave soldier* ○ *It was a brave decision to quit her job and start her own business.* ○ *She was very brave* ***to*** *learn to ski at fifty.* ○ *Of the three organizations criticized, only one was brave* ***enough to*** *face the press.* ○ *Richards has made a brave* ***attempt*** *to answer his critics.* ○ *This action will cause problems, despite the bank's brave* ***talk/words*** *about carrying on as if nothing had happened.*
• **put on a brave face** (*ALSO* **put a brave face on it**) to behave as if a problem is not important or does not worry you: *She seems all right but I suspect she's just putting on a brave face.*
brave /breɪv/ *verb* [T] to deal with an unpleasant or difficult situation: *Shall we brave the snow and go for a walk* (= go for a walk although it is snowing)*?* ○ *LITERARY She braved the wrath of her parents by refusing to marry the man they had chosen.* **bravely** /ˈbreɪv.li/ *adv: She faced the consequences bravely.* **bravery** /ˈbreɪ.vᵊr.i/ [US] /-vɚ-/ *noun* [U] *They were awarded medals for their bravery.*

brave [FIGHTER] /breɪv/ *noun* [C] *OLD-FASHIONED* a young Native American WARRIOR (= fighting man). This is usually considered offensive.

ˈ**brave ˌnew** *adj* [before n] used to refer to something new, especially to suggest that there is some doubt that it can be good or successful: *They introduced customers to the brave new* ***world*** *of telephone banking.*

bravo /ˌbrɑːˈvəʊ/ /ˈ--/ [US] /ˈbrɑː.voʊ/ *exclamation* used to express your pleasure when someone, especially a performer, has done something well

bravura /brəˈvjʊə.rə/ [US] /-ˈvjʊr.ə/ *noun* [U] unnecessary actions to make what is being done look more exciting or clever than it is: *He gave a bravura* ***performance****.*

brawl /brɔːl/ [US] /brɑːl/ *noun* [C] a noisy, rough, uncontrolled fight: *a* ***drunken*** *brawl*
brawl /brɔːl/ [US] /brɑːl/ *verb* [I] *The young men had nothing better to do than brawl* (= fight) *in the streets.*

B

brawn [STRENGTH] /brɔːn/ ⓤ /brɑːn/ *noun* [U] physical strength and big muscles: *She said she preferred brawn to brains* (= a man who is physically attractive rather than a clever one). **brawny** /ˈbrɔːni/ ⓤ /ˈbrɑː-/ *adj*: *He was a big brawny man with huge hands.*

brawn [FOOD] /brɔːn/ ⓤ /brɑːn/ *noun* [U] *UK* meat from the head of a pig, cooked and pressed into a block

bray /breɪ/ *verb* [I] to make a loud, unpleasant noise like a donkey: *The mules suddenly started braying.* ○ *She had a loud, braying laugh.*

brazen /ˈbreɪzən/ *adj* obvious, without any attempt to be hidden: *There were instances of brazen cheating in the exams.* ○ *He told me a brazen lie.* **brazenly** /ˈbreɪzən.li/ *adv*

brazen /ˈbreɪzən/ *verb*

▲ **brazen** *sth* **out** *phrasal verb* [M] to act confidently and not admit that a problem exists: *I decided to brazen it out and hoped they wouldn't notice the scratch on the car.*

brazen 'hussy *noun* [C] *HUMOROUS* a woman who wants to attract sexual attention: *"You asked him out? Oh, you brazen hussy, you!"*

brazier /ˈbreɪ.ʒə^r/ ⓤ /-ʒɚ/ *noun* [C] a metal container for burning coal, wood, etc., used outside, to give warmth or to cook on

Brazil nut /brəˈzɪlnʌt/ *noun* [C] a large curved nut, which grows in a hard three-sided shell

BRB, brb *INTERNET ABBREVIATION FOR* be right back: used when you stop taking part in a discussion in a CHAT ROOM for a short time

breach [BROKEN PROMISE/RULE] /briːtʃ/ *noun* [C] an act of breaking a law, promise, agreement or relationship: *They felt that our discussions with other companies constituted a breach of/in our agreement.* ○ *He was sued for breach of contract.* ○ *There have been serious security breaches* (= breaks in our security system).
● **(a) breach of the peace** *LEGAL* (an example of) illegal noisy or violent behaviour in a public place
● **be in breach of** *sth* *FORMAL* to be breaking a particular law or rule: *The cinema was in breach of the Health and Safety Act for having no fire doors.*
breach /briːtʃ/ *verb* [T] *FORMAL* to break a law, promise, agreement or relationship: *They breached the agreement they had made with their employer.*

breach [OPENING] /briːtʃ/ *verb* [T] *FORMAL* to make an opening in a wall or fence, especially in order to attack someone or something behind it: *Their defences were easily breached.*
breach /briːtʃ/ *noun* [C] *FORMAL A cannon ball had made a breach* (= a hole) *in their castle walls.*

bread /bred/ *noun* [U] a food made from flour, water and usually yeast, mixed together and baked: *a slice of bread* ○ *a loaf of bread* ○ *white/brown bread* ○ *UK wholemeal/ (US) whole wheat bread* ○ *sliced bread* ○ *This bread is fresh/stale.* ○ *Do you bake your own bread?*
● **(your) (daily) bread** the money that you need so that you can pay for food, clothes and other ordinary needs: *He earns his daily bread as a tourist guide.*
● **your bread and butter** a job or activity that provides you with the money you need to live: *Gardening is my bread and butter at the moment.*
● **bread-and-butter** Bread-and-butter ideas or problems are the basic things that directly relate to most people: *Health and education are the sort of bread-and-butter issues that people vote on.*
● **bread and circuses** *LITERARY* activities or official plans that are intended to keep people happy and to stop them from noticing or complaining about problems
● **Man cannot live by bread alone.** *SAYING* used to say that people need not just food, but also poetry, art, music, etc. to live happily

bread basket [CONTAINER] *noun* [C] an open container in which bread is put on a table during a meal

bread basket [FARMING] *noun* [S] a large farming area which provides other areas with food: *The Eastern Province is the country's bread basket.*

bread bin *UK noun* [C] (*US* **bread box**) a container in which bread is stored ⊃See picture **In the Kitchen** on page Centre 16

breadboard /ˈbred.bɔːd/ ⓤ /-bɔːrd/ *noun* [C] a wooden board that is used to cut bread on

breadcrumbs /ˈbred.krʌmz/ *plural noun* very small pieces of dried bread, especially used in cooking: *Sprinkle the breadcrumbs over the mixture before baking.*

breaded /ˈbred.ɪd/ *adj* covered in breadcrumbs before being cooked: *breaded chicken breasts*

breadfruit /ˈbred.fruːt/ *noun* [C] *plural* **breadfruit** a large round tropical fruit which looks and feels like bread after it has been baked

bread knife *noun* [C] a long sharp knife that has a row of sharp points along one edge, and is used to cut bread

breadline [GROUP] /ˈbred.laɪn/ *noun* [C] *US* a group of people waiting outside a particular building to be given food: *You'll see breadlines outside many New York churches at lunchtime.*

the 'bread,line [INCOME] *noun* [S] *UK* the level of income someone has when they are extremely poor: *Most students are on/close to/below the breadline.*

breadth /bredθ/ *noun* **1** [C or U] the distance from one side to another: *The length of this box is twice its breadth.* **2** [S] when something includes many different items, features, subjects or qualities: *The breadth of her knowledge is amazing.* ○ *He showed an astonishing breadth of learning for one so young.*

breadwinner /ˈbred.wɪn.ə^r/ ⓤ /-ɚ/ *noun* [C] the member of a family who earns the money that the family needs: *Men are often expected to be the breadwinner in a family.*

break [DAMAGE] /breɪk/ *verb* [I or T] broke, broken to (cause something to) separate suddenly or violently into two or more pieces, or to (cause something to) stop working by being damaged: *The dish fell to the floor and broke.* ○ *Charles is always breaking things.* ○ *She fell and broke her arm* (= broke the bone in her arm). ○ *I dropped the vase and it broke into pieces.* ○ *I think I've broken your cassette player.* ○ *I picked it up and the handle broke off.* ○ *We heard the sound of breaking glass.*
● **break your back** *INFORMAL* to work extremely hard: *He broke his back to get the project done on time.*
● **break the back of** *sth* *UK* to get most or the worst part of a particular task done: *We've broken the back of it now and we should be finished by Friday.*
● **break the bank** *HUMOROUS* to cost too much: *It only costs £2. That's not going to break the bank.*
● **break bread 1** *OLD USE* to eat a meal **2** to take **Holy Communion**
● **break cover** When an animal or person breaks cover, they run out of their hiding place.
● **break down barriers** to improve understanding and communication between people who have different opinions: *The talks were meant to break down barriers between the two groups.*
● **break fresh/new ground** to do or discover something new: *This recovery technique breaks new ground.*
● **break even** to have no profit or loss at the end of especially a business activity: *After paying for our travel costs, we barely* (= only just) *broke even.*
● **break sb's heart 1** to make someone who loves you very sad, usually by telling them you have stopped loving them: *He's broken a lot of girls' hearts.* **2** If an event or situation breaks your heart, it makes you feel very sad: *She really broke her mother's heart when she left home.*
● **break it/the news to sb** to tell someone about something unpleasant which will affect or upset them: *Come on, what happened? Break it to me gently* (= in a kind way). ○ *I didn't want to be the one to break the news to him.*
● **break the ice** *INFORMAL* to make people who have not met before feel more relaxed with each other: *Someone suggested that we play a party game to break the ice.* ⊃See also **ice-breaker**.
● **break the mould** *UK, US* **break the mold** to be new and different: *Their approach to sports teaching broke the mould.*
● **break ranks** to publicly show disagreement or criticism of the group that you belong to: *His medical colleagues advised him not to break ranks by talking about the*

hospital's problems to the newspapers.

• **break wind** to release gas from the bowels through the bottom

break /breɪk/ *noun* [C] where something has separated in an accident: *There's a break in the pipe.*

breakable /'breɪ.kə.bl̩/ *adj* describes something that might easily break: *Have you got anything breakable in your bag?*

breakage /'breɪ.kɪdʒ/ *noun* [C] something that has been broken: *Any breakages must be paid for.*

break USE FORCE /breɪk/ *verb* [I or T; usually + adv or prep] **broke**, **broken** to go somewhere or do something by force: *He threatened to break the door **down** (= enter using force). ○ The horse tried to break **free** from its stable. ○ In the storm the boat broke **loose** from its moorings. ○ The thieves broke the safe **open** and stole the diamonds. ○ The police broke **up** the fight (= ended it forcefully). ○ She broke his grip and ran away.*

• **breaking and entering** illegally forcing your way into a house, especially to steal something

break /breɪk/ *noun* [C] *A group of prisoners **made a break** (= escaped) from the jail some years back.* ⊃See also **breakout**.

-breaker /-breɪ.kər/ US /-kɚ/ *suffix* someone who uses force to go into or open the stated thing: *a house-breaker ○ a safebreaker*

break DIVIDE /breɪk/ *verb* [I or T; + adv or prep] **broke**, **broken** to (cause something to) divide into two or more parts or groups: *These enzymes break **down** food in the stomach (= cause food to separate into smaller pieces). ○ I asked her to break her expenses **down** into food, accommodation, travel and personal costs.*

break INTERRUPT /breɪk/ *verb* [T] **broke**, **broken** to interrupt or to stop something for a brief period: *We usually break for lunch at 12.30. ○ I needed something to break **the monotony** of my typing job. ○ The phone rang, breaking **my concentration**. ○ UK They decided to break their **journey** in Singapore.*

break /breɪk/ *noun* **1** [C] an interruption: *Finally there was a break **in** the rain and we went out.* **2** [C] MAINLY UK the short period of advertisements between television programmes: *I'll make us a cup of tea in the next break.* **3** [C] a short period of rest, when food or drink is sometimes eaten: *a coffee/UK tea break ○ a lunch/dinner break ○ We'll **take** another break at 3.30. ○ They worked through the night without a break. ○ Do you usually **take** a **morning/afternoon** break?* **4** [U] (ALSO **breaktime**) MAINLY UK the regular time in the middle of the morning or afternoon, for school students to talk or play, and sometimes have food or drink: *We were talking about it at break.* **5** [C] a time away from work or your regular activity, or a holiday: *Take a couple of weeks off – you need a break. ○ How long is the Christmas break this year? ○ We decided to have a **short/spring/winter/weekend** break in Paris. ○ I'll read your report **over** (= during) the Easter break. ○ I need a break **from** typing.*

• **give sb a break** to stop criticizing, annoying or behaving in an unpleasant way to someone: *Give her a break – she's only a child and she didn't mean any harm.*

break END /breɪk/ *verb* [I or T] **broke**, **broken** to destroy or end something, or to come to an end: *Eventually someone spoke, breaking the silence. ○ She laughed and that broke the tension. ○ The enemy were unable to break the **code** (= understand it and so make it useless). ○ She broke (= did better than) the **record** for the 5000 metres. ○ Outside workers were brought in in an attempt to break (= end) the **strike**. ○ They tried to break his **will** (= make him lose his control) but he resisted. ○ He thought she would break (= lose her self-control) under the strain.*

break /breɪk/ *noun* [C] when you end a relationship, connection or way of doing something: *Their decision to not call their daughter Jane was a break **with** family **tradition**.*

• **make a break** (ALSO **make the break**) to stop having a close relationship with someone, especially stop living with them, or to change a course of action that you have had for a long time: *You've been in your job for years – it's time you made a break. ○ When a relationship ends, it's often best to make a **clean/complete** break (= suddenly and completely stop seeing each other).*

break DISOBEY /breɪk/ *verb* [T] **broke**, **broken** to fail to keep a law, rule or promise: *He didn't know he was breaking **the law** (= doing something illegal). ○ She broke her **promise/word** to me (= did not do what she promised she would).*

-breaker /-breɪ.kər/ US /-kɚ/ *suffix* a lawbreaker (= a person who breaks the law)

break NOTICE /breɪk/ *verb* [I or T] **broke**, **broken** **1** to come or bring to notice; to (cause to) be known: *When the **scandal** broke (= came to the public's attention), the company director committed suicide. ○ It was the local newspaper which first broke the **story** (= told the public). ○ I don't want to be the one to break **the news** to him (= tell him the bad news).* **2 dawn/day breaks** When DAWN or day breaks, the sun starts to appear in the sky early in the morning: *Dawn broke **over** the city.*

break OPPORTUNITY /breɪk/ *noun* [C] an opportunity for improving a situation, especially one which happens unexpectedly: *Her **big** break came when she was offered a role in a Spielberg film.*

break MOVE /breɪk/ *verb* [I usually + adv or prep] **broke**, **broken** (of waves) to reach and move over the beach, hit a cliff or wall, etc: *A huge wave broke **on/against** the shore/ **over** the boat.*

breaker /'breɪ.kər/ US /-kɚ/ *noun* [C] a wave moving toward the coast: *We swam out beyond the breakers.*

break VOICE /breɪk/ *verb* [I] **broke**, **broken** If someone's voice breaks, it changes from one state to another: *When a boy's voice breaks it begins to sound like a man's. ○ Her voice was breaking **with** emotion as she pleaded for her child's return.*

break SPORT /breɪk/ *verb* **break serve** (in tennis) to win a game in which another player is SERVING (= hitting the ball first): *Sampras broke Ivanisevic's serve in the second set.*

break /breɪk/ *noun* [C] **1** in tennis, a game won by the player who was not serving (= hitting the ball first): *Rafter must get another break **(of serve)** to win.* **2** in snooker and billiards, the number of points that a player gets during one turn at hitting the balls

break /breɪk/ *noun* LITERARY **break of day** when the sun rises in the morning: *We set out **at** break of day.* ⊃See also **daybreak**.

PHRASAL VERBS WITH break ▼

▲ **break away** ESCAPE *phrasal verb* to leave or to escape from someone who is holding you: *He grabbed her, but she managed to break away. ○ FIGURATIVE One or two of the tourists broke away **from** the tour group.*

▲ **break away** NOT AGREE *phrasal verb* to stop being part of a group because you begin to disagree with them: *In the early 1980s some members of the British Labour Party broke away to form the Social Democratic Party.*

▲ **break down** MACHINE *phrasal verb* If a machine or vehicle breaks down, it stops working: *Our car broke down and we had to push it off the road.*

▲ **break down** COMMUNICATION *phrasal verb* If a system, relationship or discussion breaks down, it fails because there is a problem or disagreement.

▲ **break down** CRY *phrasal verb* to be unable to control your feelings and to start to cry: *When we gave her the bad news, she broke down and cried.*

▲ **break sb in** PREPARE *phrasal verb* [M] If you break someone in, you train them to do a new job or activity: *The boss did not believe in breaking his staff in gently.*

▲ **break sth in** SHOES *phrasal verb* [M] to wear new shoes or use new equipment for short periods to make them more comfortable: *My new hiking boots will be great once I've broken them in.*

▲ **break in/break into sth** BUILDING *phrasal verb* to get into a building or car using force, usually to steal something: *The burglars broke in through the kitchen window. ○ My car's been broken into twice this month.*

▲ **break in** INTERRUPT *phrasal verb* to interrupt when someone else is talking: *As she was talking, he suddenly broke in, saying, "That's a lie".*

▲ **break sth in** USE CAREFULLY *phrasal verb* [M] US FOR **run in** USE CAREFULLY

B

▲ **break into *sth*** *phrasal verb* to suddenly begin to do something: *He felt so happy that he broke into* ***song*** (= suddenly began to sing). ○ *She walked quickly, occasionally breaking into a* ***run*** (= starting to run).

▲ **break *sth* off** [SEPARATE] *phrasal verb* [M] to separate a part from a larger piece, or to become separate: *He broke off a piece of chocolate.*

▲ **break *sth* off** [RELATIONSHIP] *phrasal verb* [M] to end a relationship: *They've broken off their engagement.* ○ *The governments have broken off diplomatic relations.*

▲ **break *(sth)* off** [STOP DOING] *phrasal verb* to suddenly stop speaking or doing something: *She broke off in the middle of a sentence.*

▲ **break out** [START] *phrasal verb* If something dangerous or unpleasant breaks out, it suddenly starts: *War broke out* ***in*** *1914.* ○ *Fighting has broken out all over the city.*

• **break out in a rash/spots/sweat** to suddenly have spots or sweat appear on your skin: *She broke out in a rash after eating some strawberries.* ○ *It didn't take much exercise to make him break out in (a) sweat.* ○ *When I heard the noise I broke out in a* ***cold*** *sweat.*

▲ **break out** [ESCAPE] *phrasal verb* to escape from prison: *They broke out* ***of*** *prison and fled the country.*

▲ **break through *sth*** *phrasal verb* to force yourself through something that is holding you back: *Protesters broke through the barriers.*

▲ **break *sth* up** [DIVIDE] *phrasal verb* [M] to divide into many pieces, or to divide something into many pieces: *The company has been broken up and sold off.*

▲ **break *(sth)* up** [END] *phrasal verb* [M] If an occasion when people meet breaks up or someone breaks it up, it ends and people start to leave: *The meeting broke up at ten to three.* ○ *I don't want to break up* ***the party*** *but I really have to go now.*

• **break it up** *INFORMAL* said to stop people fighting: *Break it up, you two!*

▲ **break up** *phrasal verb* If someone who is talking on a MOBILE PHONE (= telephone without a wire) is breaking up, their voice can not fully be heard.

▲ **break up** [STOP CLASSES] *phrasal verb UK* When schools and colleges, or the teachers and students who go to them break up, their classes stop and the holidays start: *We broke up* ***for*** *the holidays in June.*

▲ **break up** [END A RELATIONSHIP] *phrasal verb* If a marriage breaks up or two people in a romantic relationship break up, their marriage or their relationship ends: *Jenny and George have broken up.* ○ *She's just broken up* ***with*** *her boyfriend.*

▲ **break with *sth*** *phrasal verb* to intentionally not continue doing something that is normal, expected or traditional: *We decided to break with* ***tradition*** *and not spend Christmas with our family.* ○ *The country's leadership is determined to break with past practices and to solve urgent economic problems.*

breakaway /'breɪ.kə.weɪ/ *noun* [C] an act of separation from a group, especially because of disagreement: *The sports association accepted the inevitability of a breakaway by the elite clubs.* ○ *The breakaway group formed a new political party.*

break-dancing /'breɪk,dɑːnt.sɪŋ/ [US] /-,dænt-/ *noun* [U] a form of dance with very energetic movements

breakdown [FAILURE] /'breɪk.daʊn/ *noun* [C] a failure to work or be successful: *I had a breakdown* (= my car stopped working) *in the middle of the road.* ○ *Both sides blamed each other for the breakdown* ***of*** *talks.* ➲See also **break down** MACHINE.

breakdown [DIVISION] /'breɪk.daʊn/ *noun* [C or U] a division of something into smaller parts: *We asked for a breakdown* ***of*** *the accident figures* ***into*** *day time and night time.* ○ *The rate of breakdown of muscle protein was assessed.*

breakdown [ILLNESS] /'breɪk.daʊn/ *noun* [C] a **nervous breakdown**

'breakdown ,truck *noun* [C] *UK FOR* **tow truck** ➲See picture **Cars and Trucks** on page Centre 13

breaker's yard /'breɪ.kəz,jɑːd/ [US] /-kɚz,jɑːrd/ *noun* [C] *UK* a place where old cars are taken apart and the parts are sold

breakfast /'brek.fəst/ *noun* [C or U] a meal eaten in the morning as the first meal of the day: *What do you want* ***for*** *breakfast?* ○ *Jane never eats breakfast.* ○ *She arrived shortly after breakfast.* ○ *Breakfast is served in the dining room from 8.30-10.* ○ *I love to eat breakfast* ***in bed*** *on Saturdays.* **breakfast** /'brek.fəst/ *verb* [I] *FORMAL They breakfasted hurriedly* ***on*** *tea and toast.*

,breakfast 'television *noun* [U] television shows consisting of many short sections that people can watch while they are getting up in the morning and eating breakfast

break-in /'breɪk.ɪn/ *noun* [C] an occasion when a building is entered illegally by a criminal or criminals, usually by damaging a window or door, especially in order to steal something

'breaking ,point *noun* [S] the stage at which your control over yourself or a situation is lost: *The situation reached breaking point when his son crashed the family car.* ○ *Her nerves were* ***at*** *breaking point.*

breakneck /'breɪk.nek/ *adj* [before n] carelessly fast and dangerous: *They were cycling along* ***at*** *breakneck* ***speed/at a*** *breakneck* ***pace.***

breakout /'breɪk.aʊt/ *noun* [C] a violent escape, especially by a group, from prison: *There has been a mass breakout* ***from*** *one of Germany's top security jails.*

'break ,point *noun* [C] In tennis if you win a break point, you have broken (= won a game against) the opposing player's SERVE.

breakthrough /'breɪk.θruː/ *noun* [C] an important discovery or event that helps to improve a situation or provide an answer to a problem: *Scientists are hoping for a breakthrough* ***in*** *the search for a cure for cancer.* ○ *A* ***major*** *breakthrough* ***in*** *negotiations has been achieved.*

break-up [DIVISION] /'breɪk.ʌp/ *noun* [S] a gradual division into smaller pieces: *It was feared that the break-up* ***of*** *the oil tanker would result in further pollution.*

break-up [END] /'breɪk.ʌp/ *noun* [C] the coming to an end of a business or personal relationship, caused by the separation of those involved: *Long separations had contributed to their* ***marriage*** *break-up.* ○ *The break-up* ***of*** *the pop group came as no surprise.*

breakwater /'breɪk,wɔː.tər/ [US] /-,wɑː.t̬ɚ/ *noun* [C] a very large wall that is built from the coast out into the sea to protect a beach or harbour from big waves

bream /briːm/ *noun* [C or U] *plural* **bream** or **breams** **1** a type of edible fish found especially in lakes and rivers **2** **sea bream** a fish like a bream that lives in the sea

breast [WOMAN] /brest/ *noun* [C] either of the two soft, rounded parts of a woman's chest that produce milk after she has a baby: *When a woman becomes pregnant her breasts tend to grow larger.* ○ *breast* ***cancer*** ○ *Do you think she's had breast* ***implants?*** **-breasted** /-bres.tɪd/ [US] /-t̬ɪd/ *suffix a big/small-breasted woman*

breast [BIRD] /brest/ *noun* [C or U] **1** the front part of a bird's body: *A robin is easy to identify because of its red breast.* **2** the meat from the front part of the body of a bird or other animal: *I had a cold* ***chicken*** *breast and salad for lunch.* ○ *breast of turkey/lamb/veal*

breast [CHEST] /brest/ *noun* [C] *LITERARY* **1** a person's chest: *The dagger entered his breast.* **2** the centre of a person's feelings: *A feeling of love surged* ***in*** *his breast.*

breast [CLOTHING] /brest/ *noun* [C] the part of a piece of clothing that covers a person's chest: *He put a silk hanky in his breast* ***pocket*** (= a pocket on the top front part of a shirt or coat).

-breasted /-bres.tɪd/ *suffix* **1** **double-breasted** describes a jacket or coat which has two sets of buttons and two wide parts at the front, one of which covers the other when the buttons are fastened **2** **single-breasted** describes a jacket or coat which fastens in the centre with one row of buttons

breastbone /'brest.bəʊn/ [US] /-boʊn/ *noun* [C] the long, flat vertical bone in the centre of your chest ➲See picture **The Body** on page Centre 5

breast-feed /'brest.fiːd/ *verb* [I or T] **breast-fed, breast-fed** When a mother breast-feeds her baby, she feeds it with milk directly from her breasts rather than with artificial or cow's milk from a bottle. **breast-feeding** /ˈbrest,fiː.dɪŋ/ *noun* [U]

breastplate /ˈbrest.pleɪt/ *noun* [C] a piece of ARMOUR (= metal military clothing worn in the past) that protects the chest

breaststroke /ˈbrest.strəʊk/ [US] /-stroʊk/ *noun* [S or U] a way of swimming in which the arms make a circular movement in front of the body while the knees are brought up towards the body and then kicked out and back: *I can only* ***do*** *breaststroke.*

breath /breθ/ *noun* [C or U] the air that goes into and out of your lungs: *Her breath smelled of garlic.* ○ *Without pausing to* ***draw*** *breath* (= breathe) *she told me everything.* ○ *I had to stop running to* ***catch*** *my breath/*(UK ALSO) ***get*** *my breath* ***back*** (= be able to breathe comfortably again). ○ *She was dizzy and* ***short of*** *breath* (= unable to breathe in enough air). ○ *He burst into the room, red-faced and* ***out of*** *breath* (= unable to breathe comfortably because of tiredness or excitement). ○ *How long can you* ***hold your*** *breath* (= stop breathing) *for?* ○ *The doctor told me to* ***take a deep*** *breath* (= breathe in a lot of air).

• **a breath of air** the smallest amount of wind: *There wasn't a breath of air in the room.*

• **a breath of (fresh) air** a short period of time spent outside: *I need a breath of fresh air.*

• **a breath of fresh air** someone or something that is new and different and makes everything seem more exciting: *Angela's so cheerful and lively – she's* ***like*** *a breath of fresh air when she visits.*

• **take *sb's* breath away** be extremely beautiful or surprising: *The beauty of the Taj Mahal took my breath away.*

• **Don't hold *your* breath.** HUMOROUS said in order to tell someone that an event is not likely to happen: *She said she might have finished by this afternoon but don't hold your breath.*

• **in the same breath** If you say two things in the same breath, you say two things that are so different that if one is true, the other must be false: *You say you're bored and frustrated but in the same breath say you're resigned to staying in the same job.*

• **under *your* breath** quietly so that other people can not hear exactly what you are saying: *He muttered something under his breath.*

• **with *your* last/dying breath** LITERARY just before you die: *She asked him with her dying breath to look after her child.*

breathe /briːð/ *verb* **1** [I or T] to move air into and out of the lungs: *It's so airless in here – I can hardly breathe.* ○ *The instructor told us to breathe* ***in*** *deeply and then breathe* ***out*** *slowly.* ○ *I'm sorry if I'm breathing* (= blowing out air containing) *garlic fumes all* ***over*** *you!* ○ [+ speech] *"Here they come," he breathed* (= said very quietly). **2** [I] SPECIALIZED If you allow wine to breathe, you open the bottle for a short time before you drink from it, in order to improve the wine's flavour.

• **breathe (new) life into** to bring new ideas and energy to: *We need some new people to breathe life into this project.*

• **breathe *your* last** LITERARY to die: *Her eyes fluttered open for a moment and then she breathed her last.*

• **breathe down *sb's* neck** DISAPPROVING to stay close to someone, watching everything that they do: *It's awful having a boss who breathes down your neck all the time.*

breathing /ˈbriː.ðɪŋ/ *noun* [U] the act of taking air into your lungs and releasing it: *She lay awake listening to her sister's steady breathing.* ○ *I could hear the sound of* ***heavy*** *breathing as he slowly climbed the stairs.*

breather /ˈbriː.ðəʳ/ [US] /-ðɚ/ *noun* [C] INFORMAL a brief rest: *He'd been working hard and felt he needed (to* ***have/take****) a breather.*

breathless /ˈbreθ.ləs/ *adj* not able to breathe easily: *I was breathless after climbing the stairs.* ○ *That one kiss had left her breathless* ***with*** *excitement.* **breathlessly** /ˈbreθ.ləs.li/ *adv*

breathy /ˈbreθ.i/ *adj*: *Marilyn Monroe was famous for her breathy* (= sexy because the breath can be heard) *voice.*

breathalyse UK, US **breathalyze** /ˈbreθ.ᵊl.aɪz/ *verb* [T] to test a driver's breath to see how much alcohol they have drunk

breathalyser UK, US **breathalyzer** /ˈbreθ.ᵊl.aɪ.zəʳ/ [US] /-zɚ/ *noun* [C] TRADEMARK a device like a small bag with a tube at one end, which the police can ask a driver to blow into to see how much alcohol the driver has drunk

breath freshener /ˈbreθ,freʃ.ᵊn.əʳ/ [US] /-ɚ/ *noun* [C or U] something you eat to make your breath smell pleasant: *People often suck a peppermint as a breath freshener.*

ˈbreathing ˌroom *noun* [U] US **breathing space**

ˈbreathing ˌspace *noun* [C or U] (US ALSO **breathing room**) a period of rest in order to gain strength or give you more time to think about what to do next: *I wanted a little breathing space between jobs.* ○ *The court's decision gave us some breathing space.*

breathtaking /ˈbreθ,teɪ.kɪŋ/ *adj* extremely exciting, beautiful or surprising: *The view from the top of the mountain is breathtaking.* ○ *His performance is described in the paper as 'a breathtaking display of physical agility'.* **breathtakingly** /ˈbreθ,teɪ.kɪŋ.li/ *adv*: *The scenery really was breathtakingly* ***beautiful****.*

ˈbreath ˌtest *noun* [C] a test in which the police ask a driver to blow into a BREATHALYSER (= a bag-like device) to show whether they have drunk too much alcohol to be allowed to drive

breeches /ˈbrɪtʃ.ɪz/ /ˈbriː.tʃɪz/ *plural noun* (US **britches**) trousers that do not cover the whole of the leg: *riding breeches* ○ *a pair of breeches*

breed /briːd/ *verb* **bred, bred 1** [I or T] to keep animals for the purpose of producing young animals in a controlled way, or (of animals) to have sex and reproduce: *Terriers are bred* ***for*** *their fighting instincts.* ○ *The blackbird, like most birds, breeds in the spring.* ○ *His main income comes from breeding cattle.* ➲See also **inbred** ESTABLISHED; **inbred** RELATED; **purebred**; **thoroughbred**; **well-bred**. **2** [T] to cause something to happen, usually something bad: *Favouritism breeds* ***resentment****.*

breed /briːd/ *noun* [C] **1** a particular type of animal or plant: *a breed of dog/cat/horse/sheep/cattle* ○ *What's your favourite breed of dog/dog breed?* **2** INFORMAL a type of person: *Arletty was that* ***rare*** *breed* ***of*** *actress – beautiful, sexy and funny.* ○ *A* ***new*** *breed* ***of*** *film-maker has taken over Hollywood.* ○ *Authentic blues singers are a* ***dying*** *breed* (= becoming rare) *these days.*

breeder /ˈbriː.dəʳ/ [US] /-dɚ/ *noun* [C] someone who breeds animals: *She was one of the country's top sheep breeders.*

breeding /ˈbriː.dɪŋ/ *noun* [U] **1** the keeping of animals or plants in order to breed from them: *The family's business was horse-breeding.* ○ *We used to keep pigs for breeding purposes.* ○ *The penguins' breeding* ***season*** *has begun.* **2** (ALSO **good breeding**) OLD-FASHIONED polite and socially correct behaviour that someone has because they were taught it when they were a child

ˈbreeding ˌground *noun* [C] **1** a place where animals breed and produce their babies: *These animals always return to the same breeding ground.* **2** a place where something develops easily, especially something unpleasant: *Poor housing conditions are breeding grounds* ***for*** *crime.*

breeze [WIND] /briːz/ *noun* [C] a light and pleasant wind: *a warm/cool breeze* ○ *She let the gentle breeze cool her face.*

breezy /ˈbriː.zi/ *adj*: *It was a sunny, breezy day* (= one with quite strong but pleasant winds), *just right for sailing.*

breeze [WALK] /briːz/ *verb* [I usually + adv or prep] to walk somewhere quickly and confidently, without anxiety or embarrassment: *She just breezed* ***in*** *as if she'd only been away a day instead of a year.*

breezy /ˈbriː.zi/ *adj*: *He had the breezy* (= happy and confident) *manner of a salesman.* **breezily** /ˈbriː.zɪ.li/ *adv*

breeze [SOMETHING EASY] /briːz/ *noun* [S] INFORMAL something which is easy to achieve, often unexpectedly: *You won't have any problems with the entrance test – it's an absolute breeze.*

breeze /briːz/ *verb* [I usually + adv or prep] INFORMAL to easily complete or win something: *She breezed* ***through*** *the song as though she'd been singing it for years.* ○ MAINLY US *In 1985 he breezed* ***to*** *victory with 78% of the vote.*

[B]

brethren /ˈbreð.rən/ *plural noun* OLD-FASHIONED (used as a form of address to members of an organization or religious group) brothers

brevity /ˈbrev.ɪ.ti/ [US] /-ə.ţi/ *noun* [U] using only a few words or lasting only a short time: *His essays are models of clarity and brevity.* ○ *Brevity is, in almost everything, a virtue.*

brew /bruː/ *verb* **1** [T] to make beer **2** [I or T] If you brew tea or coffee, you add boiling water to it to make a hot drink, and if it brews, it gradually develops flavour in the container in which it was made: [+ two objects] *He brewed us some coffee./He brewed some coffee* ***for*** *us.* **3** [I] If an unpleasant situation or a storm is brewing, you feel that it is about to happen: *It was too quiet – I felt that trouble was brewing.* ○ *A storm was brewing in the distance.*

brewer /ˈbruː.əʳ/ [US] /-ɚ/ *noun* [C] a person or company that makes beer

brew /bruː/ *noun* **1** [C] a type of beer, especially one made in a particular place or at a particular time **2** [C usually sing] UK INFORMAL a drink of tea or a drink of beer: *Make us a brew, Bren.* **3** [C] a mixture of several things: *They gave her a strange brew to drink.* ○ *War, with its fear, its deprivation, its excitement and violence makes for a very* ***heady*** *brew* (= powerful combination).

brewery /ˈbrʊə.ri/ [US] /ˈbrʊr.i/ *noun* [C] a company that makes beer or a place where beer is made

brewpub /ˈbruː.pʌb/ *noun* [C] US a pub which makes and sells beer

briar, brier /ˈbraɪəʳ/ [US] /braɪr/ *noun* [C or U] a wild rose bush with long stems and sharp thorns

bribe /braɪb/ *verb* [T] to try to make someone do something for you by giving them money, presents or something else that they want: *He bribed immigration officials and entered the country illegally.* ○ [+ to infinitive] *They bribed the waiter* ***to*** *find them a better table.*

bribe /braɪb/ *noun* [C] money or a present that you give to someone so that they will do something for you, usually something dishonest: *He was accused of* ***accepting/taking*** *bribes from wealthy businessmen.* **bribery** /ˈbraɪ.bᵊr.i/ [US] /-bɚ-/ *noun* [U] *The organization was rife with bribery* ***and corruption.***

bric-a-brac /ˈbrɪk.ə.bræk/ *noun* [U] small decorative objects of various types and of no great value: *It's one of those shops that sells antiques and bric-a-brac.*

brick [BUILDING BLOCK] /brɪk/ *noun* [C] a rectangular block of hard material used for building walls and houses: *The chimney was made of bricks.* ○ *We lived in a Victorian terrace of* ***red****-brick houses.* ○ *He was so embarrassed – his face went brick-****red*** (= a dark red). ➲See also **airbrick; redbrick.**

• **bricks and mortar** property in the form of buildings usually when considered as an investment: *I was nearly forty when I finally invested in bricks and mortar.*

• **You can't make bricks without straw.** UK SAYING used to say that you cannot make something without the necessary materials

brick [GOOD PERSON] /brɪk/ *noun* [C usually sing] OLD-FASHIONED OR HUMOROUS a very helpful and kind person who can be trusted: *Thanks for bringing all that food along to the party, Tony,* ***you're a*** *brick!*

brick /brɪk/ *verb*

▲ **brick up** ***sth*** *phrasal verb* [M] to build a wall of bricks around something, or to fill something with bricks: *The doors and windows had been bricked up to prevent squatters from getting in.*

brickbat /ˈbrɪk.bæt/ *noun* [C] a spoken attack; an insult: *The members of parliament hurled brickbats at the minister.*

bricklayer /ˈbrɪkˌleɪ.əʳ/ [US] /-ɚ/ *noun* [C] (UK INFORMAL **brickie**) a person who builds walls or buildings using bricks, especially as a job **bricklaying** /ˈbrɪkˌleɪ.ɪŋ/ *noun* [U] *Bricklaying is a skilled job.*

brickwork /ˈbrɪk.wɜːk/ [US] /-wɝːk/ *noun* [U] the bricks in a wall or walled building

bride /braɪd/ *noun* [C] a woman who is about to get married or has just got married: *He returned from New York with his lovely* ***new*** *bride.* ○ *The bride* ***and groom*** *posed for pictures outside the church.* ○ *As the* ***mother of the*** *bride, I feel obliged to wear something really spectacular.*

bridal /ˈbraɪ.dᵊl/ *adj* [before n] of a woman about to be married, or of a marriage ceremony: *The magazine had a section on bridal wear* (= the clothes that a woman wears at her marriage). ○ *We stayed in the hotel's bridal* ***suite*** (= the rooms for recently married people).

bridegroom /ˈbraɪd.grʊm/ /-gruːm/ *noun* [C] (ALSO **groom**) a man who is about to get married or has just got married: *The bridegroom was late for the ceremony.*

bridesmaid /ˈbraɪdz.meɪd/ *noun* [C] a girl or woman who during the marriage ceremony helps the woman who is getting married

bride-to-be /ˌbraɪd.təˈbiː/ *noun* [C] *plural* **brides-to-be** a woman who is going to be married soon

bridge [LARGE STRUCTURE] /brɪdʒ/ *noun* **1** [C] a structure that is built over a river, road or railway to allow people and vehicles to cross from one side to the other: *We drove* ***across/over*** *the bridge.* ○ *The Brooklyn Bridge spans the East River from Brooklyn to Manhattan.* **2** [C usually sing] something that makes it easier to make a change from one situation to another: *Voluntary work can provide a bridge* ***between*** *staying at home* ***and*** *working full-time.*

bridge /brɪdʒ/ *verb* [T] *The river had been bridged* (= a bridge had been built over it) *at its narrowest point.* ○ *We must bridge* ***the gap*** *between* (= bring together) *labour and management.*

bridge [TEETH] /brɪdʒ/ *noun* [C] (ALSO **bridgework**) a piece of material that contains one or more artificial teeth and is kept in place by being fastened to the natural teeth

bridge [NOSE] /brɪdʒ/ *noun* [C usually sing] the top part of the nose, between the eyes, or (on a pair of glasses) the piece that is supported by the top part of the nose: *The blow caught him right on the bridge of his nose.*

bridge [MUSICAL INSTRUMENT] /brɪdʒ/ *noun* [C] a small piece of wood over which the strings are stretched on a musical instrument such as a guitar or violin

bridge [PART OF A SHIP] /brɪdʒ/ *noun* [C] the raised part of a ship on which the CAPTAIN and other officers stand and from where they control the movement of the ship

bridge [GAME] /brɪdʒ/ *noun* [U] a card game for four players who play in pairs

bridgehead /ˈbrɪdʒ.hed/ *noun* [C] a good position that an army has taken in enemy land, from which it can attack the enemy more effectively: *The advance troops* ***established a*** *bridgehead early in the fighting.* ➲Compare **beachhead.**

ˈbridging ˌloan UK *noun* [C] (US **bridge loan**) an arrangement by which a bank lends a person some money for a short time until that person can get the money from somewhere else, often so that they can buy another house before they sell their own

bridle [CONTROL] /ˈbraɪ.dl̩/ *noun* [C] a set of leather strips that are put around a horse's head to allow its rider to control it

bridle /ˈbraɪ.dl̩/ *verb* [T] *Polly saddled and bridled* (= put a bridle on) *her favourite horse.*

bridle [SHOW ANGER] /ˈbraɪ.dl̩/ *verb* [I] to show sudden annoyance: *She bridled* ***at*** *the suggestion that she had been dishonest.*

ˈbridle ˌpath *noun* [C] (UK ALSO **bridleway**) a track in the countryside that you ride horses on

Brie /briː/ *noun* [U] a soft French cheese

brief [SHORT IN TIME] /briːf/ *adj* **1** lasting only a short time or containing few words: *His acceptance speech was mercifully brief.* ○ *I had a brief look at her report before the meeting.* ○ *It'll only be a brief visit because we really haven't much time.* ○ *After a brief* ***spell/stint*** *in the army, he started working as a teacher.* ○ *The company issued a brief* ***statement*** *about yesterday's accident.* **2** used to express how quickly time goes past: *For a few brief weeks we were very happy.*

brief /briːf/ *noun* **in brief** If something is said in brief, it is said in a very short form, with very few details: *"So you didn't enjoy the party then." "In brief, no."*

briefly /ˈbriː.fli/ *adv*: *We chatted briefly* (= for a short time) *about the weather.* ○ *Briefly* (= Using few words), *the company needs to cut its expenditure.*

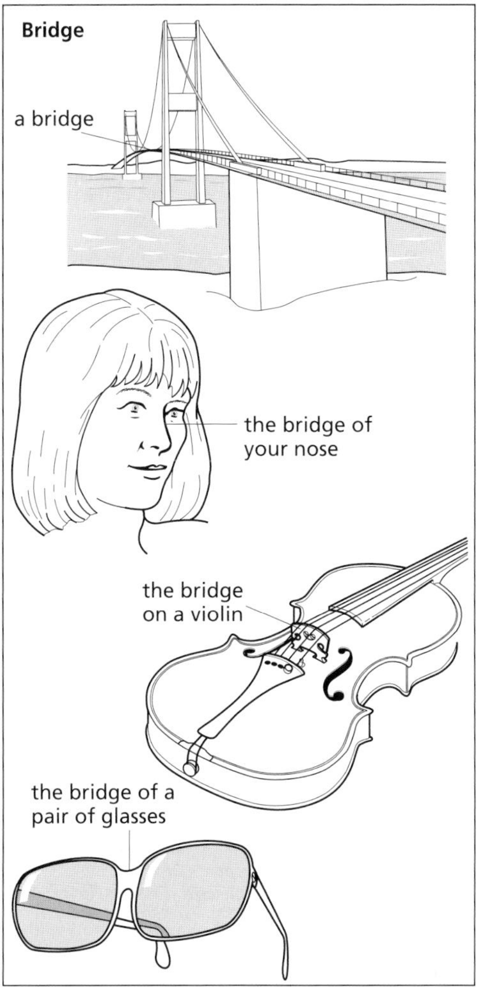
Bridge
a bridge
the bridge of
your nose
the bridge
on a violin
the bridge of a
pair of glasses

brief [SHORT IN LENGTH] /briːf/ *adj* (of clothes) very short: *She was wearing a rather brief skirt, as I recall.*

brief [GIVE INSTRUCTIONS] /briːf/ *verb* **[T]** *FORMAL* to give someone instructions or information about what they should do or say: *We had already been briefed* ***about/on*** *what the job would entail.* ➲Compare **debrief**.

brief /briːf/ *noun* **[C]** **1** *UK* a set of instructions or information: **[+ to infinitive]** *It was my brief* ***to*** *make sure that the facts were set down accurately.* **2** *LEGAL* a document or set of documents containing the details about a court case

briefing /ˈbriː.fɪŋ/ *noun* **[C or U]** information that is given to someone just before they do something, or a meeting where this happens: *They received (a) thorough briefing before they left the country.* ○ *We had to attend a briefing once a month.*

briefcase /ˈbriːf.keɪs/ *noun* **[C]** a rectangular case, used especially for carrying business documents

briefs /briːfs/ *plural noun* a piece of underwear worn by men or women, covering the area between the waist and the tops of the legs: *cotton briefs*

brier /ˈbraɪəʳ/ [US] /braɪr/ *noun* **[C]** a **briar**

brig /brɪg/ *noun* **[C]** *US* a military prison, especially one on a US navy ship

brigade /brɪˈgeɪd/ *noun* **1** **[C]** a large group of soldiers in an army **2** **[C usually sing]** *INFORMAL* a group of people who have something in common, especially an enthusiasm for a particular belief or subject: *Since she gave up smoking she's joined the anti-smoking brigade.*

brigadier /ˌbrɪg.əˈdɪəʳ/ /ˈ---/ [US] /-ˈdɪr/ *noun* **[C]** an officer in the British army whose rank is above a COLONEL and below a MAJOR-GENERAL, and who is in charge of a BRIGADE

brigadier-general /ˌbrɪg.ə.dɪəˈdʒen.ᵊr.ᵊl/ [US] /-dɪr-ˈdʒen.ɚ-/ *noun* **[C]** *US* an officer of the US Army of the same rank as a brigadier

brigand /ˈbrɪg.ᵊnd/ *noun* **[C]** *LITERARY* an armed thief, especially one of a group living in the countryside and stealing from people travelling through the area

bright [LIGHT] /braɪt/ *adj* full of light, shining: *bright sunshine* ○ *The rooms were bright and airy.* ○ *The lights are too bright in here – they're hurting my eyes.* ○ *A bright star was shining in the East.* ○ *When she looked up her eyes were bright* ***with*** *tears.* ○ *In 1983 I moved to London, attracted by the bright* ***lights*** (= the promise of excitement) *of the city.*

brighten /ˈbraɪ.tᵊn/ [US] /-t̬ᵊn/ *verb* **[I or T]** to (cause to) become lighter: *The room was small and dark, without so much as a ray of light to brighten the gloom.* ○ *It was rainy this morning, but* ***it*** *brightened* ***up*** (= the sun started shining) *after lunch.* **brightly** /ˈbraɪt.li/ *adv*: *a brightly lit room* **brightness** /ˈbraɪt.nəs/ *noun* **[U]** *The brightness of the snow made him blink.*

bright [COLOUR] /braɪt/ *adj* strong in colour: *Leslie always wears bright* ***colours****.* ○ *He said hello and I felt my face turn bright red.* ○ *a bright* ***shade*** *of green* **brightly** /ˈbraɪt.li/ *adv*: *brightly coloured flowers*

bright [INTELLIGENT] /braɪt/ *adj* (of a person) clever and quick to learn: *They were bright children, always asking questions.* ○ *She was enthusiastic and full of bright* ***ideas*** (= clever ideas) *and suggestions.*

bright [HAPPY] /braɪt/ *adj* full of hope for success or happiness: *You're very bright* ***and cheerful*** *this morning.* ○ *Things are starting to look brighter* ***for*** *British businesses.* ○ *She's an excellent student with a bright* ***future****.*

• **bright-eyed and bushy-tailed** eager and cheerful: *He always leaps out of bed bright-eyed and bushy-tailed.*

brighten /ˈbraɪ.tᵊn/ [US] /-t̬ᵊn/ *verb* **[I or T]** to (cause to) become happy or hopeful: *Her* ***eyes*** *brightened when she saw him enter the room.* ○ *There are, however, one or two items of good news to brighten the economic picture a bit.* **brightly** /ˈbraɪt.li/ *adv*: *Despite her fear, she spoke brightly to the group.*

brights /braɪts/ *plural noun US INFORMAL* A car's brights are its HEADLIGHTS (= the powerful lights at the front) on full power.

ˌbright ˈspark *noun* **[C]** **1** *UK* a person who is lively and intelligent **2** *HUMOROUS* a stupid person: ***Some*** *bright spark left the door open overnight.*

brill /brɪl/ *adj, exclamation UK INFORMAL FOR* **brilliant** VERY GOOD: *You should buy this CD – it's brill!*

brilliant [CLEVER] /ˈbrɪl.i.ənt/ *adj* extremely clever or highly skilled: *Her mother was a brilliant scientist.* ○ *He gave a brilliant performance.* ○ *The idea was quite brilliant.* ○ *She seemed to have a brilliant career ahead of her* (= was likely to be extremely successful). **brilliantly** /ˈbrɪl.i.ənt.li/ *adv*: *He seems to do everything brilliantly – piano playing, skiing, sailing.* **brilliance** /ˈbrɪl.i.ənts/ *noun* **[U]** *Her first novel showed signs of brilliance.*

brilliant [SHINING] /ˈbrɪl.i.ənt/ *adj* full of light, shining or bright in colour: *The sky was a brilliant, cloudless blue.* ○ *I was dazzled by a brilliant light.* **brilliantly** /ˈbrɪl.i.ənt.li/ *adv* **brilliance** /ˈbrɪl.i.ənts/ *noun* **[U]** *I had never seen diamonds shine with such brilliance before.*

brilliant [VERY GOOD] /ˈbrɪl.i.ənt/ *adj UK INFORMAL* very good: *"Did you like the film?" "I thought it was brilliant."* ○ *She's got a brilliant sense of humour.* ○ *Oh, brilliant! My parcel's arrived.*

brilliantine /ˈbrɪl.i.ən.tiːn/ *noun* **[U]** a type of oil used to make men's hair smooth and shiny

brim [PART OF HAT] /brɪm/ *noun* **[C usually sing]** the bottom part of a hat that sticks out all round ➲Compare **crown** TOP PART. **-brimmed** /-brɪmd/ *suffix She wore a* ***wide****-brimmed hat.*

brim [TOP] /brɪm/ *noun* **[C]** the very top edge of a container: *She poured the cream until it reached the brim.* ○ *He* ***filled*** *the jug* ***to the*** *brim.* ○ *She passed him the mug,* ***filled/full to the*** *brim* ***with*** *hot black coffee.*

[B]

brim /brɪm/ *verb* [I] **-mm-** to become full of something, especially a liquid: *Her eyes brimmed **with tears** when she heard that he was alive.* ○ FIGURATIVE *His recent triumphs have left the tennis ace brimming **(over) with*** (= full of) *confidence and energy.*

brimful /brɪmˈfʊl/ *adj* **brimful of *sth*** full of something good: *Nobody could call this year's Cannes film festival brimful of wonderful surprises.*

brimstone /ˈbrɪm.stəʊn/ [US] /-stoʊn/ *noun* [U] OLD USE the chemical SULPHUR

brine /braɪn/ *noun* [U] water with salt in it, especially when used to preserve food: *tuna/olives **in** brine*

briny /ˈbraɪ.ni/ *adj* describes water that contains a lot of salt

the briny *noun* [S] UK OLD-FASHIONED HUMOROUS the sea: *Do you fancy a dip in the briny?*

bring [TOWARDS PLACE] /brɪŋ/ *verb* [T] **brought, brought** to take or carry someone or something to a place or a person, or in the direction of the person speaking: *"Shall I bring anything **to** the party?" "Oh, just a bottle."* ○ [+ two objects] *Bring me that knife/Bring that knife **to** me.* ○ *Can you help me bring **in*** (= take into the house) *the shopping?* ○ *The police brought several men **in for questioning*** (= took them to the police station because they might have been involved in a crime). ○ *This subject brings me **to*** (= causes me to come to) *the second part of the discussion.* ○ *What brings you* (= Why have you come) ***to** London?* ○ *When they visit us they always bring their dog **with** them.*

• **bring home the bacon** INFORMAL to earn money for a family to live on: *I can't sit around all day – someone's got to bring home the bacon.*

• **bring up the rear** to be at the back of a group which is going somewhere: *You two go ahead – Sam and I'll bring up the rear.*

• **bring *sb* to book** UK to punish someone and make them explain their behaviour

COMMON LEARNER ERROR

bring or **take?**

Bring means moving someone or something towards the speaker or towards the place where you are now.

Did you bring me any food?

I've brought you a birthday present.

Take is used to talk about moving someone or something away from the speaker or the place where you are now.

Don't forget to take your umbrella with you when you leave.

bring [CAUSE] /brɪŋ/ *verb* [T] **brought, brought** to cause, result in or produce a state or condition: [+ two objects] *She's brought us so much happiness over the years.* ○ [+ v-ing] *The explosion brought the whole building crashing to the ground.* ○ *Several trees were brought **down*** (= made to fall) *by the storm.* ○ *The closure of the factory brought poverty **to** the town* (= resulted in it becoming poor). ○ *Bring the water* (UK) ***to the boil***/(US) ***to a boil*** (= make it start boiling). ○ *She suddenly brought the interview **to an end*** (= caused it to end). ○ *Her tragic story brought **tears to** my **eyes*** (= made me cry). ○ *What **will the future** bring for these refugees?*

• **not bring *yourself* to do something** to not be able to force yourself to do something that you think is unpleasant: *I just couldn't bring myself to speak to him about it.*

• **bring *sb* up short** MAINLY UK to make someone suddenly stop doing something or talking, usually because they are surprised: *Her rudeness brought me up short.*

bring [LAW] /brɪŋ/ *verb* [T] **brought, brought** to make or begin as part of an official legal process: *He was arrested for fighting, but police have decided not to bring **charges**.*

PHRASAL VERBS WITH **bring** ▼

▲ **bring *sth* about** *phrasal verb* [M] to cause something to happen: *He brought about his company's collapse by his reckless spending.*

▲ **bring *sb/sth* along** *phrasal verb* MAINLY UK to take someone or something with you: *Can I bring a friend along to the party?*

▲ **bring *sb* around** *phrasal verb* [M] MAINLY US FOR **bring [sb] round**

▲ **bring *sth* back** [RETURN] *phrasal verb* [M] to return from somewhere with something: [+ two objects] *Can you bring me back some milk?*

▲ **bring *sth* back** [REMEMBER] *phrasal verb* [M] to make someone think about something from the past: *The photos brought back some wonderful memories.*

▲ **bring *sth* back** [DO AGAIN] *phrasal verb* [M] to start to do or use something that was done or used in the past: *Few politicians are in favour of bringing back the death penalty.*

▲ **bring *sb* down** [PEOPLE] *phrasal verb* [M] to cause someone in a position of power to lose their job: *This scandal could bring down the government.*

▲ **bring *sth* down** [REDUCE] *phrasal verb* [M] to reduce the level of something: *When are they going to bring down the price of DVD players?*

▲ **bring *sth* forward** *phrasal verb* [M] MAINLY UK to change the date or time of an event so that it happens earlier than planned: *The elections were brought forward by three months.*

▲ **bring *sth* in** [INTRODUCE] *phrasal verb* [M] to introduce something new such as a product or a law: *New safety regulations have been brought in.*

▲ **bring *sth* in** [MONEY] *phrasal verb* [M] to make money: *Their chain of pubs and restaurants brings in millions of pounds a year.*

▲ **bring *sb* in** [JOB] *phrasal verb* [M] to ask someone to do a particular job: *We need to bring in an expert to deal with this problem.*

▲ **bring *sth* off** *phrasal verb* [M] to succeed in doing something difficult: *It was an important event, and she's managed to bring it off brilliantly.*

▲ **bring *sth* on** *phrasal verb* [M] to make something happen, usually something bad: *The loud music brought on another one of his headaches.*

▲ **Bring it on!** *phrasal verb* MAINLY US INFORMAL said to show that you are prepared and willing to compete in a competition or to do something difficult: *England versus Brazil – bring it on!*

▲ **bring *sb* out** [MAKE CONFIDENT] *phrasal verb* [M] UK to make a shy person happier and more confident: *Paulo's very shy – he needs bringing out.*

▲ **bring *sth* out** [PRODUCE] *phrasal verb* [M] to produce something to sell to the public: *They've just brought out a new, smaller phone.*

▲ **bring *sth* out** [MAKE NOTICEABLE] *phrasal verb* [M] to make a particular quality or detail noticeable: *A crisis can bring out the best and the worst in people.* ○ *The seasoning really brings out the flavour of the meat.*

▲ **bring *sb* out in *sth*** *phrasal verb* UK If something brings you out in spots, a RASH, etc., it causes them to appear on your skin: *Seafood always brings me out in huge spots.*

▲ **bring *sb* round** [MAKE CONSCIOUS] *phrasal verb* (US USUALLY **bring *sb* around**) to make someone become conscious again after being unconscious: *I gave him a sniff of smelling salts to bring him round.*

▲ **bring *sb* round** [PERSUADE] *phrasal verb* (US USUALLY **bring *sb* around**) to persuade someone to have the same opinion as you have: *At first they refused but I managed to bring them round (**to** my way of thinking).*

▲ **bring *sb* to** *phrasal verb* to make someone become conscious again after being unconscious: *He lost consciousness after the fall, and they were unable to bring him to.*

▲ **bring *sb/sth* together** *phrasal verb* to cause people to be friendly with each other: *The disaster brought the community together.*

▲ **bring *sb* up** [CARE FOR] *phrasal verb* [M] to care for a child until it is an adult, often giving it particular beliefs: *She was brought up by her grandmother.* ○ *They brought her up **(as/to be)** a Catholic.* ○ [+ to infinitive] *David was brought up **to** respect authority.*

▲ **bring *sth* up** [TALK] *phrasal verb* [M] to start to talk about a particular subject: *She's always bringing up her health problems.*

▲ **bring *sth* up** [VOMIT] *phrasal verb* [M] UK INFORMAL to vomit something: *She was crying so much I thought she'd bring up her breakfast.*

ˌbring and ˈbuy ˌsale *noun* [C] *UK* a sale, usually to collect money for a charity, where people bring things to be sold and buy things brought by other people

brink /brɪŋk/ *noun* [S] **1** the point where a new or different situation is about to begin: *Extreme stress had driven him to **the brink of** a nervous breakdown.* ○ *Scientists are **on the brink of*** (= extremely close to) *a major new discovery.* **2** *LITERARY* the edge of a cliff or other high area: *She was standing right **on the brink of** the gorge.*

brinkmanship /ˈbrɪŋk.mən.ʃɪp/ *noun* [U] the activity, especially in politics, of trying to get what you want by saying that if you do not get it, you will do something dangerous: *The talks have collapsed and both sides have resorted to brinkmanship.*

brioche /ˈbri.ɒʃ/ [US] /-ɑːʃ/ *noun* [C or U] soft, slightly sweet bread made with eggs and butter

briquette, briquet /brɪˈket/ *noun* [C] a small block made from coal dust or PEAT, used as fuel in a fire

brisk /brɪsk/ *adj* quick, energetic and active: *a brisk walk* ○ *He set a brisk **pace** and we struggled to keep up.* ○ *Her tone on the telephone was brisk* (= she spoke quickly and used few words) ***and businesslike***. **briskly** /ˈbrɪsk.li/ *adv*: *She walked briskly into town.* ○ *Beat the eggs whites briskly until soft peaks form.* ○ *"Let's get it over with," he said briskly.* **briskness** /ˈbrɪsk.nəs/ *noun* [U]

brisket /ˈbrɪs.kɪt/ *noun* [U] meat from the chest of a cow

bristle /ˈbrɪs.l̩/ *noun* **1** [C] a short stiff hair, usually one of many: *The old woman had a few grey bristles sprouting from her chin.* **2** [C or U] The bristles of a brush are the stiff hairs or hair-like pieces of plastic which are attached to it: *The best quality men's shaving brushes are made from badger bristle.* ○ *My toothbrush has blue and white plastic bristles.*

bristle /ˈbrɪs.l̩/ *verb* **1** [I] (of hair) to stand up: *The cat's fur bristled and it arched its back.* **2** to react angrily: *She bristled **at** the suggestion that she had in any way neglected the child.*

bristly /ˈbrɪs.li/ *adj*: *He had furry eyebrows and bristly* (= short, sticking up) *hair cropped short.*

▲ **bristle with *sth*** *phrasal verb* to have a large amount of something, or to be full of something: *The helicopter hovered above them bristling with machine guns.*

Brit /brɪt/ *noun* [C] *INFORMAL* a British person: *You could tell by their clothes that they were Brits.*

britches /ˈbrɪtʃ.ɪz/ *plural noun US FOR* **breeches**

British /ˈbrɪt.ɪʃ/ [US] /ˈbrɪt̬-/ *adj* of the United Kingdom of Great Britain and Northern Ireland: *He's got a British passport.*

the British *plural noun* people from Britain

ˌBritish ˈSummer ˌTime *noun* [U] (*ABBREVIATION* **BST**) the time used in the UK from late March to late October, that is one hour later than Greenwich Mean Time

Briton /ˈbrɪt.ən/ [US] /ˈbrɪt̬-/ *noun* [C] a British person: *Six Britons are believed to have been involved in the accident.*

Britpop /ˈbrit.pɒp/ [US] /ˈbrit.pɑːp/ *noun* [U] *INFORMAL* British pop music of the 1990s, influenced by music of the 1960s, especially music by the Beatles

brittle /ˈbrɪt.l̩/ [US] /ˈbrɪt̬-/ *adj* **1** delicate and easily broken: *As you get older your bones become increasingly brittle.* ○ *The pond was covered in a brittle layer of ice.* **2** unkind and unpleasant: *She gave a brittle laugh and turned away.*

bro [BROTHER] /brəʊ/ [US] /broʊ/ *noun* [C] *plural* **bros** *INFORMAL* a brother

bro [FRIEND] /brəʊ/ [US] /broʊ/ *noun* [C] *plural* **bros** *MAINLY US INFORMAL* used mainly by Black Americans as a way of addressing a male friend

broach [BEGIN] /brəʊtʃ/ [US] /broʊtʃ/ *verb* [T] to begin a discussion of something difficult: *At some point we've got to discuss money but I don't know quite how to broach the **subject** with him.*

broach [JEWELLERY] /brəʊtʃ/ [US] /broʊtʃ/ *noun* [C] *US FOR* **brooch**

broad [WIDE] /brɔːd/ [US] /brɑːd/ *adj* **1** very wide: *We walked down a broad avenue lined with trees.* ○ *He flashed a broad **grin** at us.* ○ *My brother is very broad-**shouldered**.* ➲Compare **narrow**. **2** If something is a particular distance broad, it measures this distance from side to side: *This river is over 500 metres broad at its widest point.* ○ *O'Connell Bridge in Dublin is famous for being broader than it is long.*

• **in broad daylight** If a crime is committed in broad daylight, it happens during the day, when it could have been seen and prevented: *Thieves had broken into the car in broad daylight and stolen the stereo.*

• **broad in the beam** *OLD-FASHIONED HUMOROUS* having wide hips and a large bottom

broaden /ˈbrɔː.dən/ [US] /ˈbrɑː-/ *verb* [I or T] to cause something to become wider: *The track broadens and becomes a road at this point.* ○ *They are broadening the bridge to speed up the flow of traffic.* **broadness** /ˈbrɔːd.nəs/ [US] /ˈbrɑːd-/ *noun* [U] *She was struck by the broadness of his back.*

broad [GENERAL] /brɔːd/ [US] /brɑːd/ *adj* including a wide range of things; general: *The politician gave a broad **outline** of his proposals.* ○ *The magazine covers a broad **range** of subjects, from sewing to psychology.*

broaden /ˈbrɔː.dən/ [US] /ˈbrɑː-/ *verb* [T] to increase the range of something: *They've introduced all sorts of new elements to that programme in order to broaden its **appeal**.* ○ *I hoped that going to university might broaden my **horizons*** (= increase the range of my knowledge and experience). **broadly** /ˈbrɔːd.li/ [US] /ˈbrɑːd-/ *adv*: *Broadly **speaking**, don't you think women make better drivers than men?*

broad [STRONG] /brɔːd/ [US] /brɑːd/ *adj* (of an ACCENT (= way of speaking)) strong and noticeable, showing where the person who is speaking comes from: *He spoke with a broad Australian accent.*

broad [INFORMATION] *adj* **broad hint** a HINT (= when you let someone know something indirectly) that is easy to understand

broad [WOMAN] /brɔːd/ [US] /brɑːd/ *noun* [C] *US OFFENSIVE* a woman

broadband /ˈbrɔːd.bænd/ [US] /ˈbrɑːd-/ *noun* [U] a system that enables many messages or large amounts of information to be sent at the same time and very quickly between computers or other electronic devices: *Internet connection via broadband offers many advantages.* ○ *broadband services/networks/technology/transmission*

ˌbroad ˈbean *noun* [C] a large edible pale green bean ➲See picture **Vegetables** on page Centre 2

broadcast /ˈbrɔːd.kɑːst/ [US] /ˈbrɑːd.kæst/ *verb* [I or T] **broadcast** or *US ALSO* **broadcasted**, **broadcast** or *US ALSO* **broadcasted** to send out a programme on television or radio: *Radio Caroline used to broadcast **from** a boat in the North Sea.* ○ *The tennis championship is broadcast live **to** several different countries.* ○ *FIGURATIVE I'm leaving but please don't broadcast* (= tell everyone) *the fact.*

broadcast /ˈbrɔːd.kɑːst/ [US] /ˈbrɑːd.kæst/ *noun* [C] a television or radio programme: *a radio/television broadcast* ○ *We watched a **live** broadcast of the concert.*

broadcaster /ˈbrɔːdˌkɑː.stər/ [US] /ˈbrɑːdˌkæs.tɚ/ *noun* [C] someone whose job is to speak on radio or television programmes: *He was a famous broadcaster in the 1930s.*

broadcasting /ˈbrɔːdˌkɑː.stɪŋ/ [US] /ˈbrɑːdˌkæs.tɪŋ/ *noun* [U] *Huge amounts of money are spent on sports broadcasting.*

▲ **broaden out** *phrasal verb* to become wider: *The river broadens out around the next bend.*

the ˈbroad ˌjump *noun* [S] *US FOR* **the long jump**

broadminded /ˌbrɔːdˈmaɪn.dɪd/ [US] /ˌbrɑːd-/ *adj APPROVING* willing to accept other people's behaviour and beliefs, especially sexual behaviour: *At seventy she was surprisingly broadminded.* ➲Compare **narrow-minded**.

broadmindedness /ˌbrɔːdˈmaɪn.dɪd.nəs/ [US] /ˌbrɑːd-/ *noun* [U] *My parents always prided themselves on their broadmindedness.*

broadsheet /ˈbrɔːd.ʃiːt/ [US] /ˈbrɑːd-/ *noun* [C] *UK* a newspaper that is printed on large paper, or an advertisement printed on a large sheet of paper: *In Britain, the broadsheets are generally believed to be more serious than the tabloids.*

broadside /ˈbrɔːd.saɪd/ [US] /ˈbrɑːd-/ *noun* [C] **1** a strong written or spoken attack (on someone): *The opposition **fired/launched** yet another broadside **at** the prime minister.* **2** *SPECIALIZED* the firing of all the guns on one side of a naval ship at the same time

brocade /brə'keɪd/ *noun* [U] heavy cloth with a raised design often of gold or silver threads: *curtains of rich brocade*

B

broccoli /'brɒk.əl.i/ [US] /'brɑː.kəl-/ *noun* [U] a vegetable with a thick green stem and a tree-like dark green top ➲See picture **Vegetables** on page Centre 2

brochette /brɒʃ'et/ [US] /broʊ'ʃet/ *noun* [C or U] a long thin metal pin which is pushed through small pieces of meat or vegetables to hold them in place while they are cooked, or a dish of food cooked this way: *brochettes of lamb*

brochure /'brəʊ.ʃəʳ/ [US] /broʊ'ʃʊr/ *noun* [C] a type of small magazine that contains pictures and information on a product or a company

brogue /brəʊg/ [US] /broʊg/ *noun* [C usually sing] an Irish or sometimes Scottish way of speaking English: *She spoke in her soft lilting brogue.*

brogues /brəʊgz/ [US] /broʊgz/ *plural noun* strong leather shoes, usually worn by men, often with a pattern in the leather

broil /brɔɪl/ *verb* [T] *US FOR* **grill** COOK

broiling /'brɔɪ.lɪŋ/ *adj US INFORMAL It was already broiling* (= very hot weather) *by breakfast time.*

broiler /'brɔɪ.ləʳ/ [US] /-lɚ/ *noun* [C] a young chicken suitable for ROASTING or GRILLING

'broiler ,pan *noun* [C] *US FOR* **grill pan**

broke [BREAK] /brəʊk/ [US] /broʊk/ *past simple of* **break**

broke [POOR] /brəʊk/ [US] /broʊk/ *adj* [after v] *INFORMAL* without money: *I can't afford to go on holiday this year – I'm* ***(flat)*** *broke.* ○ *INFORMAL Many small businesses* ***went*** *broke* (= lost all their money) *during the recession.*

• **go for broke** *INFORMAL* to risk everything in the hope of having great success

broken [BREAK] /'brəʊ.kən/ [US] /'broʊ-/ *past participle of* **break**

broken [DAMAGED] /'brəʊ.kən/ [US] /'broʊ-/ *adj* **1** damaged, no longer able to work: *He attacked the man with a broken bottle.* ○ *My watch is broken.* ○ *Careful – there's broken* ***glass*** *on the floor.* **2** [before n] suffering emotional pain so great that it changes the way you live, usually as a result of an unpleasant event: *He was* ***a*** *broken* ***man*** *after his wife died.*

broken [INTERRUPTED] /'brəʊ.kən/ [US] /'broʊ-/ *adj* interrupted or not continuous: *He tried to explain what had happened in broken* (= not spoken easily and stopping a lot) *English.*

broken [ENDED] /'brəʊ.kən/ [US] /'broʊ-/ *adj* destroyed or ended: *a broken engagement* ○ *She comes from a broken* ***home*** (= one where the parents have separated).

broken [NOT KEPT] /'brəʊ.kən/ [US] /'broʊ-/ *adj* (of a law, rule or promise) disobeyed or not kept: *a broken promise*

broken-down /,brəʊ.kən'daʊn/ [US] /broʊ-/ *adj* describes something that does not now work: *a broken-down washing machine*

broken-hearted /,brəʊ.kən'hɑː.tɪd/ [US] /,broʊ.kən'hɑːr.t̬ɪd/ *adj* extremely unhappy: *She was broken-hearted when her boyfriend left her.*

broker /'brəʊ.kəʳ/ [US] /'broʊ.kɚ/ *noun* [C] a person who buys and sells foreign money, shares in companies, etc., for other people, or a person who talks to opposing sides, especially governments, making arrangements for them or bringing to an end disagreements: *a commodity/insurance/mortgage broker* ○ *I called my broker for advice about investing in the stock market.* ○ *During the war Wallas became a power broker in governmental circles.*

broker /'brəʊ.kəʳ/ [US] /'broʊ.kɚ/ *verb* [T] to arrange something such as a deal, agreement, etc. between two or more groups or countries: *The foreign ministers have failed in their attempts to broker a ceasefire.*

brolly /'brɒl.i/ [US] /'brɑː.li/ *noun* [C] *UK INFORMAL FOR* **umbrella** DEVICE

bromide /'brəʊ.maɪd/ [US] /'broʊ-/ *noun* **1** [C or U] *OLD-FASHIONED* a drug used to calm people who are very unhappy or worried: *He took a/some bromide to calm his nerves.* **2** [C] *FORMAL* a remark or statement which, although it might be true, is boring and meaningless because it has been said so many times before

bronchial /'brɒŋ.ki.əl/ [US] /'brɑːŋ-/ *adj* of or being the pipes that carry air from the WINDPIPE (= tube in the throat) to the lungs: *bronchial tubes* ○ *He had bronchial* ***pneumonia*** *as a child.*

bronchitis /brɒŋ'kaɪ.tɪs/ [US] /brɑːŋ'kaɪ.t̬ɪs/ *noun* [U] an illness in which the BRONCHIAL tubes become infected and swollen, resulting in coughing and difficulty in breathing

bronco /'brɒŋ.kəʊ/ [US] /'brɑːŋ.koʊ/ *noun* [C] *plural* **broncos** a wild horse of the western US

brontosaurus /,brɒn.tə'sɔː.rəs/ [US] /,brɑːn.t̬ə'sɔːr.əs/ *noun* [C] *plural* **brontosauruses** or **brontosauri** a large DINOSAUR that ate plants and had four legs, a very long neck and tail and a small head

Bronx cheer /,brɒŋks'tʃɪəʳ/ [US] /,brɑːŋks'tʃɪr/ *noun* [C] *US SLANG* a rude sound made by sticking the tongue out and blowing

bronze /brɒnz/ [US] /brɑːnz/ *noun* **1** [U] a brown metal made of copper and TIN: *The church bells are made of bronze.* **2** [U] a dark orange-brown colour, like the metal bronze **3** [C] a statue made of bronze **4** [C] a **bronze (medal)**

bronze /brɒnz/ [US] /brɑːnz/ *adj* being dark orange-brown in colour, like the metal bronze

bronzed /brɒnzd/ [US] /brɑːnzd/ *adj* If someone is bronzed, their skin is attractively brown because they have been in the sun: *Elaine came back from her holiday looking bronzed and beautiful.*

the 'Bronze ,Age *noun* [S] the time in the past when tools and weapons were made of bronze, before iron was discovered ➲Compare **the Iron Age**; **the Stone Age**.

,bronze ('medal) *noun* [C] a small round piece of bronze given to a person who finishes third in a competition: *He* ***got*** *a bronze in the high jump.*

bronzer /'brɒn.zəʳ/ [US] /'brɑːn.zɚ/ *noun* [C or U] a cream or powder that you put on your face and body to make your skin look brown from being in the sun

brooch, *US ALSO* **broach** /brəʊtʃ/ [US] /broʊtʃ/ *noun* [C] a small piece of jewellery with a pin at the back that is fastened to a woman's clothes: *She wore a small silver brooch.*

brood [GROUP] /bruːd/ *noun* [C] **1** a group of young birds all born at the same time: *The blackbird flew back and forth to its brood.* **2** *HUMOROUS* a person's young children: *Ann was at the party with her brood.*

broody /'bruː.di/ *adj* **1** If a HEN (= female chicken) is broody, she is ready to lay eggs and sit on them. **2** *INFORMAL* describes someone, especially a woman, who feels as if they would like to have a baby: *Much to her surprise, Ruth started feeling broody in her late twenties.*

broodiness /'bruː.di.nəs/ *noun* [U] *It always brings on an attack of broodiness when I go and see my sister and her children.*

brood [THINK] /bruːd/ *verb* [I] to think for a long time about things that make you sad, worried or angry: *I wish she wouldn't sit brooding in her room all day.*

brooding /'bruː.dɪŋ/ *adj*: *He stood there in the corner of the room, a dark, brooding* (= worrying) ***presence***.

broody /'bruː.di/ *adj* always thinking unhappy thoughts

'brood ,mare *noun* [C] a female horse kept especially for breeding

brook [STREAM] /brʊk/ *noun* [C] a small stream: *I could hear the sound of a* ***babbling*** *brook.*

brook [NOT ALLOW] /brʊk/ *verb FORMAL* **brook no** ***sth*****/not brook** ***sth*** to not allow or accept something, especially difference of opinion or intention: *She won't brook any criticism of her work.*

broom [BRUSH] /bruːm/ /brʊm/ *noun* [C] a brush with a long handle, used for cleaning the floor

broom [PLANT] /bruːm/ *noun* [U] a bush with small yellow flowers

broomstick /'bruːm.stɪk/ /'brʊm-/ *noun* [C] **1** a broom made of sticks: *In children's books, witches are often shown riding broomsticks.* **2** the long handle of a broom

Bros. /brɒs/ [US] /brɑːs/ *plural noun ABBREVIATION FOR* brothers (when used in a company's name): *He hired a suit from Moss Bros.*

broth /brɒθ/ ⓤ /brɑːθ/ *noun* [U] a thin soup, often with vegetables or rice in it: *chicken/turkey/beef broth*

brothel /ˈbrɒθ.ᵊl/ ⓤ /ˈbrɑː.θᵊl/ *noun* [C] a place where men go and pay to have sex with prostitutes

brother /ˈbrʌð.ər/ ⓤ /-ɚ-/ *noun* [C] **1** a man or boy with the same parents as another person: *Do you have any brothers and sisters?* ○ *I have three brothers and a sister.* ○ *Johnny is my younger/older/big/baby/little brother.* ○ *My brother lives in Washington.* **2** a man who is a member of the same group as you or who shares an interest with you or has a similar way of thinking to you: [as form of address] *"Let us unite, brothers and fight this unjust law!"* **3** used as the title of a man, such as a monk, who belongs to a religious organization: *Brother Michael and Brother John were deep in conversation.* **4** US INFORMAL sometimes used by a black man to address or refer to another black man

• **I am not my brother's keeper.** SAYING used as a way of saying that you are not responsible for what someone else does or for what happens to them

brotherly /ˈbrʌð.ᵊl.i/ ⓤ /-ɚ.li/ *adj* showing the kindness, interest or affection that you would expect a brother to show: *Can I give you some brotherly advice?*

brotherhood /ˈbrʌð.ə.hʊd/ ⓤ /-ɚ-/ *group noun* [C] (the members of) a particular organization or (more generally) friendship and loyalty: *The various groups eventually fused into a single brotherhood.* ○ *The ideal of the brotherhood **of man** (= where everyone loves each other) is still far from reality.*

brother-in-law /ˈbrʌð.ə.rɪn.lɔː/ ⓤ /-ɚ.ɪn.lɑː/ *noun* [C] *plural* **brothers-in-law** the brother of your husband or wife, or the man who is married to your sister, or the man who is married to the sister of your wife or husband

brougham /bruːm/ *noun* [C] a light carriage with four wheels and a roof

brought /brɔːt/ ⓤ /brɑːt/ *past simple and past participle of* **bring**

brouhaha /ˈbruː.hɑː.hɑː/ *noun* [U] OLD-FASHIONED INFORMAL a lot of noise or angry complaining about something: *the brouhaha **over** his latest film*

brow /braʊ/ *noun* **1** [C usually sing] LITERARY the forehead: *She **wrinkled** her brow as she thought.* ○ *He paused at the top of the hill and **mopped** his brow (= rubbed the sweat away).* **2** [S] the top part of a hill or the edge of something high such as a cliff or rock: **the brow of the** hill

browbeat /ˈbraʊ.biːt/ *verb* [T] **browbeat, browbeaten** to try to force someone to do something by threatening them or using strong and unfair persuasion: *Don't be browbeaten **into** working more hours than you want.*

brown /braʊn/ *adj, noun* [C or U] (of) the colour of chocolate or earth: *dark/light brown* ○ *Both my parents have curly brown hair.*

brown /braʊn/ *verb* [I or T] to make food brown by cooking it: *Lightly brown the onion before adding the tomatoes.* ○ *Allow the meat to brown before adding the vegetables.*

• **browned off** UK OLD-FASHIONED annoyed: *I think she gets a bit browned off with him borrowing the car all the time.*

brownish /ˈbraʊ.nɪʃ/ *adj* slightly brown: *She's got brownish-green eyes.*

brown-bag /ˌbraʊnˈbæg/ *verb* [I or T] US to take your own food to eat during the day, usually in a brown paper bag: *The park has become a place where office workers brown-bag **it** and take leisurely strolls.* **brown-bag** *adj* **brown-bag lunch:** *There are as many brown-bag lunches eaten today as lunches in restaurants.*

brown bread *noun* [U] MAINLY UK bread which is light brown in colour, often still containing all the natural features of the grain in it

brownfield /ˈbraʊn.fiːld/ *adj* [before n] UK describes an area of land in a town or city that was previously used for industry and where new buildings can be built: *Planners are committed to developing the city's brownfield **sites** before granting permission to build on the rural outskirts.*

Brownie GIRL /ˈbraʊ.ni/ *noun* [C] (UK ALSO **Brownie Guide**) a girl aged between 7 and 10 years old who is a member

of the international organization for young women called the Guides, or the Girl Scouts in the US: *The girls wanted to join a Brownie **pack** (= group).*

• **earn/get/score brownie points** HUMOROUS to get praise or approval for something you have done: *I thought I could score some brownie points with my mother-in-law by offering to cook dinner.*

brownie CAKE /ˈbraʊ.ni/ *noun* [C] a small square chocolate cake, often with nuts in it

brown paper *noun* [U] a strong type of brown paper which is often used for wrapping items in when they are to be sent through the post

brown rice *noun* [U] rice which still has its outer covering

brownstone /ˈbraʊn.stəʊn/ ⓤ /-stoʊn/ *noun* [C] MAINLY US a house with its front built of a reddish brown stone, especially common in New York City

brown sugar *noun* [U] sugar that has only been partly REFINED

browse LOOK /braʊz/ *verb* [I] to look through a book or magazine without reading everything, or to walk around a shop looking at several items without intending to buy any of them: *I was browsing **through** fashion magazines to find a new hairstyle.* ○ *"Are you looking for anything in particular, madam?" "No, I'm just browsing."* **browse** /braʊz/ *noun* [S] MAINLY UK We went for a browse around an antique shop. ○ *I **had** a browse **through** the books on his desk.*

browse COMPUTING /braʊz/ *verb* [T] to look at information on the Internet: *to browse the World Wide Web*

browser /ˈbraʊ.zər/ ⓤ /ˈbraʊ.zɚ/ *noun* [C] a computer program that enables you to read information on the Internet: *a Web browser*

browse FEED /braʊz/ *verb* [I] (of animals) to feed on grass, leaves, etc. in a relaxed way: *Deer were browsing **(on grass)** under the trees.*

bruise /bruːz/ *noun* [C] an injury or mark where the skin has not been broken but is darker in colour, often as a result of being hit by something: *His arms and back were **covered in** bruises.* ○ *She had a few **cuts and** bruises but nothing serious.* ○ *One or two of the peaches had bruises on them.*

bruise /bruːz/ *verb* [I or T] to develope a bruise or to cause someone or something to have a bruise: *How did you bruise your arm?* ○ *Bananas and other soft fruits bruise easily.*

bruised /bruːzd/ *adj* **1** having bruises: *a bruised shoulder/knee/elbow* ○ *She was **badly** bruised but otherwise unhurt.* **2** emotionally hurt as a result of a bad experience: *Divorce generally leaves both partners feeling rather bruised.*

bruising /ˈbruː.zɪŋ/ *noun* [U] bruises: *The bruising should soon become less painful.*

bruiser /ˈbruː.zər/ ⓤ /-zɚ/ *noun* [C] INFORMAL DISAPPROVING a big, strong, rough man: *He's an ugly bruiser – I wouldn't like to meet him down a dark alley!*

bruising /ˈbruː.zɪŋ/ *adj* A bruising experience is one in which someone defeats you or is very rude to you: *I had a bruising **encounter** with my ex-husband last week.*

bruit /bruːt/ *verb* [T] FORMAL to tell everyone a piece of news: *It's been bruited **abroad/around** that he's going to leave the company.*

brumby /ˈbrʌm.bi/ *noun* [C] AUS a wild horse, especially one that has escaped from a farm

Brummie /ˈbrʌm.i/ *noun* [C] UK INFORMAL a person who comes from the Birmingham area, in central England **Brummie** *adj*: *a Brummie accent*

brunch /brʌntʃ/ *noun* [C] a meal eaten in the late morning; a combination of breakfast and lunch: *We always have brunch together on Sunday.*

brunette /bruːˈnet/ *noun* [C] a white woman or girl with dark hair: *a tall brunette*

brunt /brʌnt/ *noun* **the brunt of** the main force of something unpleasant: *The infantry have **taken/borne** the brunt of the missile attacks.* ○ *Small companies are **feeling the full** brunt of the recession.*

brush TOOL /brʌʃ/ *noun* **1** [C] an object with short pieces of stiff hair, plastic or wire fixed into a usually wooden

B

or plastic base or handle, which is used for cleaning, tidying the hair or painting: *I can't find my brush, but I still have my comb.* ○ *You'll need a stiff brush to scrape off the rust.* ○ *a clothes brush* ○ *a nail brush* ○ *a scrubbing (UK)/scrub (US) brush* ○ *a pastry brush* **2** [C] used as a combining form: *a hairbrush* ○ *a toothbrush* ○ *a paintbrush* **3** [S] *MAINLY UK* an act of cleaning with a brush: *These shoes need **a good** brush.* ○ *Don't forget to **give your hair a** brush before you go out.*

brush /brʌʃ/ *verb* [T] to clean something or make something smooth with a brush: *When did he last brush his **teeth**, she wondered?* ○ *She brushed her **hair** with long, regular strokes.* ○ [+ obj + adj] *My trousers got covered in mud, but luckily I was able to brush them clean.*

brushed /brʌʃt/ *adj: Her nightdress was made of brushed **nylon/cotton*** (= cloth treated to make it soft and furry).

brush [TOUCH] /brʌʃ/ *verb* **1** [I + adv or prep; T] to touch (something) quickly and lightly or carelessly: *Charlotte brushed **against** him* (= touched him quickly and lightly with her arm or body) *as she left the room.* ○ *His lips gently brushed her cheek and he was gone.* **2** [T + adv or prep] to move something somewhere using a brush or your hand: *Jackie brushed the hair out of her eyes.* ○ *He brushed **away** a tear.* ○ *She stood up and brushed the wrinkles from her dress.*

brush /brʌʃ/ *noun* [C usually sing] **1** a brief light touch: *He felt the brush **of** her hand on his.* **2 a brush with sth** when you experience something, or almost experience something, especially something unpleasant: *Jim **had** a brush with death* (= was nearly killed) *on the motorway.* ○ *Was that your first brush with **the law*** (= experience of being in trouble with the police)*?*

brush [BUSHES] /brʌʃ/ *noun* [U] *US* small low bushes or the rough land they grow on, or BRUSHWOOD: *We spotted a jackrabbit hidden in the brush.* ○ *The dry weather has increased the risk of brush **fires**.*

brush [TAIL] /brʌʃ/ *noun* [C] the tail of a fox

PHRASAL VERBS WITH **brush** ▼

▲ **brush *sb/sth* aside** *phrasal verb* [M] to refuse to consider something seriously because you feel that it is not important: *She brushed their objections aside, saying "Leave it to me."*

▲ **brush *sb/sth* off** [CLEAN] *phrasal verb* [M] to remove dust or dirt from someone or something by using your hands or a brush: *He brushed the snow off his coat.*

▲ **brush *sth* off** [NOT ACCEPT] *phrasal verb* [M] to refuse to listen to what someone says, or to refuse to think about something seriously: *He just brushed off all their criticisms.*

▲ **brush past *sb*** *phrasal verb* to walk quickly past someone, usually because you do not want to speak to them: *Ignoring their protests, Newman brushed past waiting journalists.*

▲ **brush up on *sth*** *phrasal verb* to improve your knowledge of something already learned but partly forgotten: *I thought I'd brush up on my French before going to Paris.*

the brush-off /ðə'brʌʃ.ɒf/ [US] /-ɑːf/ *noun INFORMAL* **give someone the brush-off** to refuse to talk or be pleasant to someone: *So she's given you the brush-off, has she?*

brushstroke /'brʌʃ.strəʊk/ [US] /-stroʊk/ *noun* [C usually pl] **1** the way in which something, especially paint, is put on to a surface with a brush: *The artist painted this picture using tiny/vigorous/swirling brushstrokes* (= movements of the brush). **2** the way in which a plan or idea is explained: *She described the project in very **broad** brushstrokes* (= without any details).

brushwood /'brʌʃ.wʊd/ *noun* [U] (*ALSO* **brush**) small branches that have broken off from trees and bushes

brushwork /'brʌʃ.wɜːk/ [US] /-wɝːk/ *noun* [U] the particular style that an artist has of putting paint with a brush onto the painting

brusque /bruːsk/ [US] /brʌsk/ *adj* quick and rude in manner or speech: *His secretary was rather brusque **with** me.* **brusquely** /'bruː.skli/ [US] /'brʌs.kli/ *adv: "I simply haven't got time to deal with the problem today," she said brusquely.* **brusqueness** /'bruːsk.nəs/ [US] /'brʌsk-/ *noun* [U]

brussel sprout /ˌbrʌs.əlz'spraʊt/ *noun* [C] (*ALSO* **brussels sprout,** *UK ALSO* **sprout**) a green vegetable like a very small cabbage that is boiled and eaten ⊃See picture **Vegetables** on page Centre 2

brutal /'bruː.təl/ [US] /-t̬əl/ *adj* **1** cruel, violent and completely without feelings: *a brutal dictator* ○ *He had presided over a brutal regime in which thousands of people had 'disappeared'.* ○ *He was imprisoned in 1945 for the brutal **murder** of a 12-year old girl.* **2** not caring about someone's feelings: *She spoke with brutal **honesty** – I was too old for the job.* **brutally** /'bruː.təl.i/ [US] /-t̬əl-/ *adv: The old man had been brutally attacked/murdered.* ○ *To be brutally **honest/frank**, you look fat in that dress.*

brutality /bruː'tæl.ə.ti/ [US] /-t̬i/ *noun* [C or U] *the brutalities of war* ○ *Seeing so much brutality* (= cruelty) ***towards** prisoners had not hardened them to it.*

brutalize, *UK USUALLY* **-ise** /'bruː.təl.aɪz/ [US] /-t̬əl-/ *verb* [T] to treat someone in a cruel and violent way: *The police in that country routinely brutalize prisoners.*

brute /bruːt/ *noun* [C] **1** *DISAPPROVING* a rough and sometimes violent man: [as form of address] *Take your hands off me, you brute!* ○ *In the end she used brute **force*** (= extreme physical strength) *to push him out.* **2** an animal, especially a large one: *Your dog's an ugly brute, isn't it?* ○ *The oldest elephant was lame, poor brute.*

brutish /'bruː.tɪʃ/ [US] /-t̬ɪʃ/ *adj* rough, unpleasant and often violent: *It has been said that life is often 'nasty, brutish, and short'.*

bruv /brʌv/ *noun* [C usually sing] *UK INFORMAL HUMOROUS* a brother: *So he's a bit of an idiot, but he's still my bruv, ain't he?*

BS /ˌbiː'es/ *noun US INFORMAL ABBREVIATION FOR* **bullshit**

BSc *UK* /ˌbiː.es'siː/ *noun* [C] (*US* **BS**) *ABBREVIATION FOR* Bachelor of Science: a first level university degree in science: *C.G. Smith, BSc* ○ *a BSc **in** geology/chemistry/biology*

BSE /ˌbiː.es'iː/ *noun* [U] *ABBREVIATION FOR* bovine spongiform encephalopathy: a brain disease in cattle which causes the death of the animal

B-side /'biː.saɪd/ *noun* [C] the less important side of a SINGLE (= a record containing one song on each side)

BST /ˌbiː.es'tiː/ *noun* [U] *ABBREVIATION FOR* **British Summer Time**

BTW, btw *INTERNET ABBREVIATION FOR* by the way: used when you are writing something that relates to the subject you are discussing, but is not the main point of the discussion: *I hope you enjoyed your holiday in Paris. BTW, can you recommend a good hotel?*

bub /bʌb/ *noun* [C] *US OLD-FASHIONED INFORMAL* a form of address used to a man, sometimes in a slightly angry way: *That may be what you do at home, but listen, bub, you don't do it here!*

bubble /'bʌb.l̩/ *noun* [C] a ball of air in a liquid, or a delicate hollow sphere floating on top of a liquid or in the air: *As water begins to boil, bubbles rise ever faster to the surface.* ○ *I love champagne – I think it's the bubbles that make it so nice.*

• **the bubble bursts** If the bubble bursts, a very happy, pleasant or successful time suddenly ends: *Three years into her marriage, the bubble burst.*

bubble /'bʌb.l̩/ *verb* [I] to produce bubbles: *We could hear the porridge bubbling **away*** (= bubbling strongly) *in the pot.*

bubbly /'bʌb.li/ *noun* [U] *INFORMAL* **champagne** (= expensive, fizzy white or pink alcoholic drink): *Let's crack open a bottle of bubbly to celebrate.* ⊃See also **bubbly**.

▲ **bubble over** *verb* [I] to be very excited and enthusiastic: *She was bubbling over **with** excitement/enthusiasm.*

ˌbubble and 'squeak *noun* [U] *UK* a food made by mixing together and heating cooked potato and cabbage

'bubble ˌbath *noun* [C or U] a special liquid soap with a pleasant smell, that you put in a bath to make lots of bubbles

'bubble ˌgum *noun* [U] CHEWING GUM that you can blow into the shape of a bubble

bubble-jet /ˈbʌb.l̩.dʒet/ *adj* [before n] *SPECIALIZED* describes a very fast and quiet method of printing, in which the ink is directed electronically onto the paper: *a bubble-jet printer*

ˈbubble ˌwrap *noun* [U] *TRADEMARK* a sheet of plastic bubbles that is used for wrapping items in order to protect them, for example, when they are being posted or delivered somewhere

bubbly /ˈbʌb.li/ *adj INFORMAL* (especially of a woman or girl) attractively full of energy and enthusiasm ➲See also **bubbly** at **bubble**.

bubonic plague /ˌbjuːbɒn.ɪkˈpleɪg/ [US] /-ˈbuː.nɪk-/ *noun* [U] a very infectious disease spread by rats, causing swelling, fever and usually death. In the 14th century it killed half the people living in Europe.

buccaneer /ˌbʌk.əˈnɪəʳ/ [US] /-ˈnɪr/ *noun* [C] a person who attacked and stole from ships at sea, especially in the 17th and 18th centuries; a **pirate**

buck [MONEY] /bʌk/ *noun* [C] *plural* **bucks** *INFORMAL* **1** a dollar: *Can I borrow a couple of bucks?* ○ *He charged me twenty bucks for a new hubcap.* **2** used in a number of expressions about money, usually expressions referring to a lot of money: *He earns **mega**-bucks* (= a lot of money) *working for an American bank.* ○ *So what's the best way to **make a fast** buck* (= earn money easily and quickly)*?*

buck [ANIMAL] /bʌk/ *noun* [C] *plural* **buck** or **bucks** the male of some animals such as deer and rabbits, or (in South Africa) a male or female ANTELOPE ➲Compare **doe**.

buck [RESPONSIBILITY] /bʌk/ *noun MAINLY DISAPPROVING* **pass the buck** to blame someone or make them responsible for a problem that you should deal with: *She's always trying to pass the buck and I'm sick of it!* **buck-passing** /ˈbʌk.pɑː.sɪŋ/ [US] /-pæs.ɪŋ/ *noun* [U]

• **The buck stops here.** *SAYING* said by someone who is responsible for making decisions and who will be blamed if things go wrong

buck [JUMP] /bʌk/ *verb* [I] (of a horse) to jump into the air and kick out with the back legs ➲See also **buck up**.

• **buck the trend** to be noticeably different from the way that a situation is developing generally, especially in connection with financial matters: *This company is the only one to have bucked the trend of a declining industry.*

• **buck the system** to refuse to follow the rules of an organization: *Alex is always looking for ways to buck the system.*

▲ **buck (sb/sth) up** *phrasal verb UK INFORMAL* to become happier or more positive or to make someone happier or more positive: *Oh, buck up for heaven's sake, Anthony! I'm sick of looking at your miserable face.* ○ *She was told that if she didn't buck her **ideas** up* (= start working in a more positive way)*, she'd be out of a job.* ○ *A holiday will buck her up.*

bucket /ˈbʌk.ɪt/ *noun* [C] a container with an open top and a handle, often used for carrying liquids: *Armed with a bucket and a mop, I started washing the floor.* ○ *I took my two-year old nephew down to the beach with his bucket **and spade**.*

• **in buckets** *INFORMAL* in great amounts: *The rain came down in buckets.*

• **weep buckets** *UK* (*US* **cry buckets**) *INFORMAL* to cry a lot: *That was such a sad film – I wept buckets at the end of it.*

• **sweat buckets** *INFORMAL* to sweat a lot: *It was my first interview and I was sweating buckets.*

bucket /ˈbʌk.ɪt/ *verb*

▲ **bucket down** *phrasal verb UK INFORMAL* to rain heavily: *It's absolutely bucketing down.*

bucketload /ˈbʌk.ɪt.ləʊd/ [US] /-loʊd/ *noun* [C usually pl] *UK INFORMAL* a large amount of something: *He has bucketloads **of** charm.*

ˈbucket ˌseat *noun* [C] a rounded seat with high sides for one person, especially in a car

ˈbucket ˌshop *noun* [C] *UK INFORMAL* a travel company that sells aircraft tickets at a low price

buckle [FASTENER] /ˈbʌk.l̩/ *noun* [C] a piece of metal at one end of a belt or strap, used to fasten the two ends together

buckle /ˈbʌk.l̩/ *verb* [I or T] to fasten or be fastened with a buckle **buckled** /ˈbʌk.l̩d/ *adj*: *a tightly buckled belt*

buckle [BEND] /ˈbʌk.l̩/ *verb* [I or T] to bend or become bent, often as a result of force, heat or weakness: *The intense heat from the fire had caused the factory roof to buckle.* ○ *Both **wheels** on the bicycle had been badly buckled.* ○ *I felt faint and my **knees** began to buckle.*

buckle [BE DEFEATED] /ˈbʌk.l̩/ *verb* **buckle under *sth*** to be defeated by a difficult situation: *But these were difficult times and a lesser man would have buckled under the strain.*

▲ **buckle down** *phrasal verb* to start working hard: *He'll have to buckle down (**to** his work) soon if he wants to pass these exams.*

ˌbuck ˈnaked *adj US INFORMAL* completely naked

buck's fizz *UK* /ˌbʌksˈfɪz/ *noun* [C or U] (*US* **mimosa**) an alcoholic drink made from champagne and orange juice

buckshot /ˈbʌk.ʃɒt/ [US] /-ʃɑːt/ *noun* [U] many small balls of metal fired from a SHOTGUN

buckskin /ˈbʌk.skɪn/ *noun* [U] soft, strong leather made from the skin of a deer or a sheep

ˌbuck ˈteeth *plural noun INFORMAL* upper front teeth that stick out **buck-toothed** /ˌbʌkˈtuːθt/ *adj*

buckwheat /ˈbʌk.wiːt/ *noun* [U] small dark grain used for feeding animals and for making flour

bucolic /bjuˈkɒl.ɪk/ [US] /-ˈkɑː.lɪk/ *adj LITERARY* relating to the countryside: *The painting shows a typically bucolic scene with peasants harvesting crops in a field.*

bud [PLANT PART] /bʌd/ *noun* [C] a small part of a plant, that develops into a flower or leaf

• **in bud** covered with buds: *It was springtime and the fruit trees were in bud.*

bud /bʌd/ *verb* [I] **-dd-** to produce buds: *The unusually cold winter has caused many plants to bud late this year.*

bud [MAN] /bʌd/ *noun* [C] *US INFORMAL* **buddy**

Buddha /ˈbʊd.ə/ *noun* **1** [S] the Indian holy man (563-483 BC) on whose life and teachings Buddhism is based **2** [C] an image or statue of Buddha

Buddhism /ˈbʊd.ɪ.zᵊm/ *noun* [U] a religion that originally comes from India, and teaches that personal spiritual improvement will lead to escape from human suffering

Buddhist /ˈbʊd.ɪst/ *noun* [C] someone who believes in Buddhism **Buddhist** /ˈbʊd.ɪst/ *adj*: *a Buddhist temple*

budding /ˈbʌd.ɪŋ/ *adj* beginning to develop or show signs of future success in a particular area: *While still at school she was clearly a budding **genius**.*

buddy /ˈbʌd.i/ *noun* [C] **1** *INFORMAL* a friend: *Bob and I have been great buddies for years.* **2** (*ALSO* **bud**) *US* used to address another man, especially if annoyed: *Drink up and go home, buddy.*

budge /bʌdʒ/ *verb* [I or T] **1** If something will not budge or you cannot budge it, it will not move: *I've tried moving the desk but it won't budge/I can't budge it.* **2** If someone will not budge, or you cannot budge them, they will not change their opinion: *I've tried persuading her, but she **won't** budge.*

▲ **budge up** *phrasal verb UK INFORMAL* said to someone in order to ask them to move so that there is room for you

budget [FINANCIAL PLAN] /ˈbʌdʒ.ɪt/ *noun* **1** [C or U] a plan to show how much money a person or organization will earn and how much they will need or be able to spend: *The firm has **drawn up** a budget for the coming financial year.* ○ *Libraries are finding it increasingly difficult to remain **within** (their) budget.* **2** [C] the amount of money you have available to spend: *an annual budget of £40 million*

ˌthe ˈBudget *noun* [C] the official statement that a government makes about how much it will collect in taxes and spend on public services in the future

budget /ˈbʌdʒ.ɪt/ *verb* [I or T] to plan how much money you will spend on something: *An extra £20 million has been budgeted **for** schools this year.* **budgetary** /ˈbʌdʒ.ɪ.tri/ [US] /-ter.i/ *adj*: *budgetary constraints*

budget [CHEAP] /ˈbʌdʒ.ɪt/ *adj* [before n] very cheap: *a budget holiday/hotel/price*

budgie /ˈbʌdʒ.i/ *noun* [C] (*FORMAL* **budgerigar**) a small, brightly coloured bird, often kept as a pet

buff [COLOUR] /bʌf/ *noun* [U], *adj* (of) a pale yellowish brown colour: *a buff envelope*

B

• **in the buff** *INFORMAL* naked

buff [MAKE SHINE] /bʌf/ *verb* [T] to rub an object made of metal, wood or leather in order to make it shine, using a soft, dry cloth

buff [PERSON] /bʌf/ *noun* [C] *INFORMAL* a person who knows a lot about and is very interested in a particular subject: *a computer/opera/film buff*

buffalo /ˈbʌf.ə.ləʊ/ [US] /-loʊ/ *noun* [C] *plural* **buffaloes** or **buffalo** a large animal of the cattle family, with long curved horns ➲See picture **Animals and Birds** on page Centre 4

buffer [PROTECTION] /ˈbʌf.əʳ/ [US] /-ɚ/ *noun* [C] **1** something or someone that helps protect from harm: *I bought a house as a buffer* ***against*** *inflation.* **2** the protective metal parts at the front and back of a train or at the end of a track, that reduce damage if the train hits something

buffer /ˈbʌf.əʳ/ [US] /-ɚ/ *verb* [T] to provide protection against harm

buffer [MAN] /ˈbʌf.əʳ/ [US] /-ɚ/ *noun* [C] *UK OLD-FASHIONED* a foolish old man: *Silly old buffer!*

ˈbuffer ˌstate *noun* [C] a peaceful country between two larger countries, that reduces the chances of war between them

ˈbuffer ˌzone *noun* [C] an area intended to separate two armies that are fighting

buffet [MEAL] /ˈbʊf.eɪ/ [US] /bəˈfeɪ/ *noun* [C] **1** a meal where people serve themselves from a variety of types of usually cold food: *Are you having a sit-down meal or a buffet at the wedding?* **2** *UK* a restaurant in a station, where food and drinks can be bought and eaten

buffet [HIT] /ˈbʌf.ɪt/ *verb* [T] (of wind, rain, etc.) to hit something repeatedly and with great force: *The little boat was buffeted mercilessly by the waves.*

ˈbuffet ˌcar *noun* [C] *MAINLY UK* a carriage on a train where food and drinks can be bought

buffoon /bəˈfuːn/ *noun* [C] a person who does silly things, usually to make other people laugh: *Doesn't he get tired of* ***playing the*** *buffoon in class?* **buffoonery** /bəˈfuː.nᵊr.i/ [US] /-nɚ-/ *noun* [U]

bug [INSECT] /bʌg/ *noun* [C] a very small insect

bug [ILLNESS] /bʌg/ *noun* [C] *INFORMAL* a bacteria or a virus causing an illness that is usually not serious: *I had a* ***tummy/stomach*** *bug last week.* ○ *There's a bug* ***going around*** (= an illness that many people are getting).

bug [COMPUTER] /bʌg/ *noun* [C] a mistake or problem in a computer program: *A bug caused the company's computer system to crash.*

bug [DEVICE] /bʌg/ *noun* [C] a very small device fixed on to a telephone or hidden in a room, that allows you to listen to what people are saying without them knowing

bug /bʌg/ *verb* [T] **-gg-** *She suspected that her phone had been bugged* (= that a listening device had been hidden inside it).

bug [ANNOY] /bʌg/ *verb* [T] **-gg-** *INFORMAL* to annoy or worry someone: *He's been bugging me all morning.*

bug [ENTHUSIASM] /bʌg/ *noun* [S] *INFORMAL* a very strong enthusiasm for something: *He's* ***been bitten by*** *the sailing bug.*

bugbear /ˈbʌg.beəʳ/ [US] /-ber/ *noun* [C] a particular thing that annoys or upsets you: *Smoking is a particular bugbear* ***of*** *his.*

bug-eyed /bʌgˈaɪd/ *adj* having eyes that stick out

bugger [ANNOYANCE] /ˈbʌg.əʳ/ [US] /-ɚ/ *noun* [C] **1** *UK OFFENSIVE* a silly or annoying person: *Well you shouldn't have drunk so much, should you, you daft bugger!* ○ *The stupid bugger's given me the wrong ticket!* **2** *INFORMAL* used to or about someone that you feel sympathy for: *The* ***poor*** *bugger has nowhere else to sleep.* **3** *US INFORMAL* a person or animal, especially a young one that you feel affection for: *He's a cute little bugger, isn't he?* **4** *UK OFFENSIVE* something that is very difficult or annoying: *This tin is a bugger to open.*

bugger /ˈbʌg.əʳ/ [US] /-ɚ/ *exclamation UK OFFENSIVE* used to express annoyance: *Oh bugger, it's raining!*

• **bugger all** *UK OFFENSIVE* very little or nothing: *You've done bugger all to help.* ○ *"How much do you know about marketing?" "Bugger all."*

• **Bugger it!** *UK OFFENSIVE* used to express great annoyance: *Bugger it! I'm going to miss my train.*

• **Bugger me!** *UK OFFENSIVE* used to express great surprise: *Bugger me! Did you see the speed that motorbike was going?*

bugger [DAMAGE] /ˈbʌg.əʳ/ [US] /-ɚ/ *verb* [T] *UK OFFENSIVE* to break or spoil something: *You've just buggered your chances of promotion!*

buggered /ˈbʌg.əd/ [US] /-ɚd/ *adj UK OFFENSIVE* broken, or very tired: *The television's buggered, but I can't afford to get it mended.* ○ *I walked over twenty miles – I was buggered the next day.*

• **I'm buggered if...** *UK OFFENSIVE* used to show that you definitely will not or cannot do something: *I'm buggered if I'm going to lend him any more money.*

bugger [HAVE SEX] /ˈbʌg.əʳ/ [US] /-ɚ/ *verb* [T] *OFFENSIVE OR LEGAL* to have sex by putting the penis in another person's anus **buggery** /ˈbʌg.ᵊr.i/ [US] /ˈ-ɚ-/ *noun* [U]

PHRASAL VERBS WITH **bugger**

▲ **bugger about** [BE SILLY] *phrasal verb UK OFFENSIVE* to waste time doing silly or unimportant things: *Will you stop buggering about and get in here!*

▲ **bugger *sb* about** [TREAT BADLY] *phrasal verb UK OFFENSIVE* to treat someone badly by wasting their time or causing them problems: *Stop buggering me about and tell me the truth!*

▲ **bugger off** *phrasal verb UK OFFENSIVE* to leave or go away, used especially as a rude way of telling someone to go away: *By the time I got there you two had already buggered off!* ○ *Bugger off, you git!*

▲ **bugger *sth* up** *phrasal verb* [M] *UK OFFENSIVE* to damage something or cause problems by doing something stupid: *Mike's buggered up the video again.*

buggy [BABY CHAIR] /ˈbʌg.i/ *noun* [C] *UK* **pushchair**

buggy [CAR] /ˈbʌg.i/ *noun* [C] a small car, usually with no roof, which is designed for driving on rough ground: *a golf/dune buggy* ➲See picture **Cars and Trucks** on page Centre 13

buggy [CARRIAGE] /ˈbʌg.i/ *noun* [C] *OLD-FASHIONED* a light carriage pulled by one horse

bugle /ˈbjuː.gl̩/ *noun* [C] a musical instrument like a small TRUMPET, used especially in the army

build [MAKE] /bɪld/ *verb* **built, built 1** [I or T] to make something by putting bricks or other materials together: *They're building new houses by the river.* ○ *The birds built their nest in the small fir tree.* ○ *These old houses are built* (= made) ***of*** *stone.* ○ *Contractors have started building on waste land near the town.* **2** [T] to create and develop something over a long period of time: *We want to build a better future for our children.*

• **Rome wasn't built in a day.** *SAYING* said to emphasize that you can not expect to do important things in a short period of time

builder /ˈbɪl.dəʳ/ [US] /-dɚ/ *noun* [C] a person whose job it is to make buildings

build [BODY] /bɪld/ *noun* [C or U] the size and shape of a person's body: *She was of slim build with short, dark hair.*

PHRASAL VERBS WITH **build**

▲ **build around *sth*** *phrasal verb* [usually passive] to base something on an idea or principle: *The independence movement sought to unify the country with a national identity built around a common language.*

▲ **build *sth* in/into *sth*** *phrasal verb* to include something as part of a plan, system or agreement: *When drawing up a contract it is vital to build in safety measures.* ○ *FIGURATIVE Inequalities are often built into* (= cannot be separated from) *society.*

▲ **build on *sth*** *phrasal verb* to use a success or achievement as a base from which to achieve more success: *We must build on our reputation to expand the business.* ○ *A good relationship is built on trust.*

▲ **build *(sb/sth)* up** [INCREASE] *phrasal verb* [M] to increase or become larger or stronger, or to cause someone or something to do this: *Tension is building up* ***between*** *the two communities.* ○ *They gave him soup to build up his*

***strength*/*build him up.* ○ *It took her ten years to build up her publishing business.*

build-up /ˈbɪld.ʌp/ *noun* [C] *The build-up* (= increase) *of troops in the region makes war seem more likely.*

▲ **build *sth/sb* up** [PRAISE] *phrasal verb* [M] to praise something or someone in a way which will influence people's opinions: *For weeks the media has been building up the national basketball team.*

build-up /ˈbɪld.ʌp/ *noun* [C] *The group got a big build-up before their tour, being touted by many as the next Beatles.*

building /ˈbɪl.dɪŋ/ *noun* [C or U] a structure with walls and a roof such as a house or factory, or the business of making these: *The once-empty site was now covered with buildings.* ○ *He started off in the building **trade** before opening his own restaurant.*

ˈbuilding ˌblock *noun* [C] a piece of wood or plastic used by children to build things with

ˈbuilding ˌblocks *plural noun* the basic things that are put together to make something exist: *Science and the arts are the building blocks of a good education.*

ˈbuilding ˌsite *noun* [C] a piece of land on which a house or other building is being built

ˈbuilding soˌciety *UK noun* [C] (*US* **savings and loan association**) a business that lends you money if you want to buy a house, or pays you interest on money you invest there

built-in /ˌbɪltˈɪn/ *adj* If a place or piece of equipment has built-in objects, they are permanently attached and cannot be easily removed: *All the rooms have built-in **cupboards/wardrobes**.*

built-up /ˌbɪltˈʌp/ *adj* A place that is built-up is one where there are a lot of buildings: *a built-up **area***

bulb [PLANT] /bʌlb/ *noun* [C] a round root of some plants from which the plant grows: *tulip bulbs*

bulb [LIGHT] /bʌlb/ *noun* [C] a **light bulb**

bulbous /ˈbʌl.bəs/ *adj* If a part of the body is bulbous, it is fat and round: *He had a huge bulbous nose.*

bulge /bʌldʒ/ *verb* [I] to stick out in a round shape: *Her bags were bulging **with** shopping* ○ *My stomach is bulging with all that I've eaten.*

bulge /bʌldʒ/ *noun* [C] **1** a curved shape sticking out from the surface of something: *I wondered what the bulge in her coat pocket was.* **2** a sudden increase that soon returns to the usual level: *There was a bulge **in** spending in the early part of the year.*

bulging /ˈbʌl.dʒɪŋ/ *adj*: *She dragged her bulging* (= very full) *suitcase up the stairs.*

bulimia /bʊˌlɪm.i.ə.nɜːˈvəʊ.sə/ /-ˈliː.mi-/ [US] /-nɝːˈvoʊ-/ *noun* [U] a mental illness in which someone eats uncontrollably and in large amounts, then vomits to remove the food from their body ⊃Compare **anorexia (nervosa)**. **bulimic** /bʊˈlɪm.ɪk/ /-ˈliː.mɪk/ *noun* [C], *adj*

bulk /bʌlk/ *noun* **1** [C usually sing] something or someone that is very large: *She eased her large bulk out of the chair.* **2** [U] large size or mass: *It was a document of surprising bulk.* **3** **in bulk** in large amounts: *The office buys paper in bulk to keep down costs.* **4** **the bulk of** most of: *In fact, the bulk of the book is taken up with criticizing other works.*

• **bulk buy** to buy in large amounts: *Because we're such a large family we find it cheaper to bulk buy foods we eat a lot of.*

• **bulk large** *LITERARY* to be present and important: *Fears of his death bulked large in her thoughts.*

bulk /bʌlk/ *verb*

▲ **bulk *sth* out** *phrasal verb* [M] to make something bigger or thicker by adding something: *I added some potatoes to the stew to bulk it out.*

bulkhead /ˈbʌlk.hed/ *noun* [C] *SPECIALIZED* a wall which divides the inside of a ship or aircraft

bulky /ˈbʌl.ki/ *adj* too big and taking up too much space: *bulky equipment*

bull [ANIMAL] /bʊl/ *noun* [C] a male cow, or the male of particular animals such as the elephant or the whale: *They did not see the sign by the gate saying 'Beware of the bull'.*

• **bull in a china shop** If someone is like a bull in a china shop, they are very careless in the way that they move or behave: *We told her it was a delicate situation but she went into the meeting like a bull in a china shop.*

• **take the bull by the horns** to do something difficult in a brave and determined way: *Why don't you take the bull by the horns and tell him to leave?*

bull [FINANCE] /bʊl/ *noun* [C] *SPECIALIZED* a person who buys shares in companies hoping the price will rise, so that they can be sold later at a profit ⊃Compare **bear** FINANCE. See also **bullish**.

bull [NONSENSE] /bʊl/ *noun* [U] *INFORMAL* complete nonsense or something that is not true: *Don't **give** me **that** bull **about** not knowing the time.*

ˈbull ˌbar *noun* [C usually pl] a metal frame fixed in front of the front lights of a vehicle to prevent serious damage if the vehicle hits an animal

bulldog /ˈbʊl.dɒg/ [US] /-dɑːg/ *noun* [C] a small dog that can be fierce and has a muscular body, short legs and a large square-shaped face

ˈbulldog ˌclip *UK noun* [C] (*US* **clip**) *TRADEMARK* a metal device used for holding pieces of paper together

bulldozer /ˈbʊlˌdəʊ.zəʳ/ [US] /-ˌdoʊ.zɚ/ *noun* [C] a heavy vehicle with a large blade in front, used for pushing earth and stones along and for flattening areas of ground at the same time

bulldoze /ˈbʊl.dəʊz/ [US] /-doʊz/ *verb* [T] **1** to destroy buildings and flatten an area with a bulldozer: *The township was bulldozed **(flat)** in the 1950s.* **2** to force someone to do something, although they might not want to: *She bulldozed her daughter **into** buying a new dress.*

bull dyke *noun* [C] *OFFENSIVE* a LESBIAN (= woman who is sexually attracted to other women) who is very like a man in appearance and behaviour

bullet /ˈbʊl.ɪt/ *noun* [C] **1** a small, metal object that is fired from a gun: *A bullet had lodged in the boy's leg.* **2** a **bullet (point)**

bulletin /ˈbʊl.ə.tɪn/ [US] /-t̬ɪn/ *noun* [C] a short news programme on television or radio often about something that has just happened, or a short newspaper printed by an organization: *an hourly news bulletin* ○ *The company publishes a fortnightly bulletin for its staff.*

ˈbulletin ˌboard *noun* [C] **1** *US FOR* **noticeboard** **2** a place on a computer system where users can read messages and add their own

ˈbullet (ˌpoint) *noun* [C] a symbol, often a small black circle, used in text to show separate items in a list

bullet-proof /ˈbʊl.ɪt.pruːf/ *adj* Something which is bullet-proof prevents bullets from going through it: *bullet-proof glass* ○ *a bullet-proof vest*

bullfight /ˈbʊl.faɪt/ *noun* [C] a traditional public entertainment, particularly in Spain, in which a person fights and sometimes kills a bull **bullfighter** /ˈbʊlˌfaɪ.təʳ/ [US] /-t̬ɚ/ *noun* [C] **bullfighting** /ˈbʊlˌfaɪ.tɪŋ/ [US] /-t̬ɪŋ/ *noun* [U]

bullfinch /ˈbʊl.fɪntʃ/ *noun* [C] a small European bird with a black head and a pink chest

bullfrog /ˈbʊl.frɒg/ [US] /-frɑːg/ *noun* [C] a large North American frog that makes a loud, deep, rough noise

bullheaded /ˌbʊlˈhed.ɪd/ *adj* *DISAPPROVING* very determined to do what you want to do, especially without considering other people's feelings

bullhorn /ˈbʊl.hɔːn/ [US] /-hɔːrn/ *noun* [C] *US OLD-FASHIONED FOR* **megaphone**

bullion /ˈbʊl.i.ən/ *noun* [U] gold or silver in the form of bars: *gold bullion*

bullish /ˈbʊl.ɪʃ/ *adj* **1** giving your opinions in a powerful and confident way: *She's being very bullish about the firm's future.* **2** describes a financial market in which share prices are rising

ˈbull ˌmarket *noun* [C] a time when the prices of most shares are rising

bullock /ˈbʊl.ək/ *noun* [C] a young male cow that has had its testicles removed

bullpen /ˈbʊl.pen/ *noun* [C] *US* in baseball, a place near the playing area where PITCHERS (= people throwing the ball) can throw the ball to get ready to play in the game

bullring /ˈbʊl.rɪŋ/ *noun* [C] a circular area surrounded by seats, used for BULLFIGHTS

bull's-eye /ˈbʊl.zaɪ/ *noun* [C usually sing] the circular centre of the object aimed at in games such as DARTS, or

B

the shot or throw that hits this: *I was amazed when I got a bull's-eye.*

bullshit /ˈbʊl.ʃɪt/ *exclamation, noun* [U] OFFENSIVE complete nonsense or something that is not true: *Bullshit! He never said that!* ○ *He gave me some excuse but it was **a load of** bullshit.*

bullshit /ˈbʊl.ʃɪt/ *verb* [I or T] **-tt-** OFFENSIVE to try to persuade or impress someone by saying things that are not true: *You're bullshitting me!* ○ *Quit bullshitting, will you!* **bullshitter** /ˈbʊl̩ʃɪt.əʳ/ [US] /-ɚ/ *noun* [C]

ˌbull ˈterrier *noun* [C] a strong-looking type of dog with short hair

bully /ˈbʊl.i/ *verb* [T] to hurt or frighten someone who is smaller or less powerful than you, often forcing them to do something they do not want to do: *Our survey indicates that one in four children is bullied at school.* ○ *Don't let anyone bully you **into** doing something you don't want to do.* **bullying** /ˈbʊl.i.ɪŋ/ *noun* [U] *Bullying is a problem in many schools.*

bully /ˈbʊl.i/ *noun* [C] someone who hurts or frightens someone who is smaller or less powerful than them, often forcing them to do something they do not want to do: *You're just a **big** bully!* ○ *Teachers usually know who the bullies are in a class.*

• **bully for sb** HUMOROUS used to show that you do not think what someone has done or said is very exciting or interesting: *"He's started ironing his own shirts." "Well, bully for him!"*

ˈbully ˌboy *noun* [C] INFORMAL a rough and threatening man, especially one paid by someone to hurt or frighten other people: *bully-boy tactics*

bulrush /ˈbʊl.rʌʃ/ *noun* [C] a plant with tall stems that grows near rivers and lakes

bulwark /ˈbʊl.wək/ [US] /-wɚk/ *noun* [C] something that protects you from dangerous or unpleasant situations: *My savings were to be a bulwark **against** unemployment.*

bum [BODY PART] /bʌm/ *noun* [C] MAINLY UK INFORMAL the part of the body that you sit on; bottom

bum [PERSON] /bʌm/ *noun* [C] US INFORMAL someone who has no home or job and lives by asking other people for money

bum /bʌm/ *verb* [T] **-mm-** SLANG to ask someone for something without intending to pay for it: *Could I bum a cigarette **off** you?*

bum [BAD] /bʌm/ *adj* [before n] SLANG bad in quality or useless: *He gave us bum directions, but we eventually found the place.*

PHRASAL VERBS WITH **bum** ▼

▲ **bum around** [LAZY] *phrasal verb* INFORMAL to spend time being lazy and doing very little: *I wish you'd stop bumming around and start looking for a job.*

▲ **bum around/about** ***(somewhere)*** [TRAVEL] *phrasal verb* INFORMAL to travel around in different places or in a particular area, with no plans, no job and little money: *After college she spent a year bumming around the States.*

bumbag UK /ˈbʌm.bæg/ *noun* [C] (US **fanny pack**) a small bag fixed to a long strap which you fasten around your waist, and which is used for carrying money, keys, etc.

bumble /ˈbʌm.bl̩/ *verb* [I + adv or prep] to speak or move in a confused way

bumbling /ˈbʌm.blɪŋ/ *adj* confused and showing no skill: *I've never seen such bumbling incompetence!*

bumblebee /ˈbʌm.bl̩.biː/ *noun* [C] a large hairy bee

bumf, **bumph** /bʌmpf/ *noun* [U] MAINLY UK INFORMAL printed information, such as an advertisement or official document, that is usually unwanted and not interesting: *I got a load of bumf from my bank in the post today.*

bummer /ˈbʌm.əʳ/ [US] /-ɚ/ *noun* [S] OFFENSIVE something that is very annoying or inconvenient: *"I've left my wallet at home." "What a bummer!"* ○ US *I locked my keys in the car – bummer!*

bump [RAISED AREA] /bʌmp/ *noun* [C] a round, raised area on a surface or on the body: *Her bicycle hit a bump in the road and threw her off.* ○ *Tim had a nasty bump on his head from when he'd fallen over.*

bump /bʌmp/ *verb* [I + adv or prep] to travel, usually in a vehicle, in an uncomfortable way because the surface you are moving over is rough: *We bumped **along** the track in our car holding on to our seats.*

bumpy /ˈbʌm.pi/ *adj* not smooth: *We drove along a narrow, bumpy road.* ○ *It might be a bumpy **flight*** (= an uncomfortable and rough flight) *because there's a lot of air turbulence ahead.*

• **have a bumpy ride** INFORMAL to have a difficult time: *She's had a bumpy ride at work over the last few months.*

bump [HIT] /bʌmp/ *verb* **1** [I + adv or prep] to hit something with force: *She bumped **into** his tray, knocking the food onto his lap.* ➲See picture **Phrasal Verbs** on page Centre 9 **2** [T usually + adv or prep] to hurt part of your body by hitting it against something hard: *I bumped my head **on** the shelf as I stood up.*

bump /bʌmp/ *noun* [C] **1** the sound of something falling to the ground: *We heard a bump from the next room.* **2** an accident involving a car, especially one which is not serious: *A van drove into their car but luckily it was just a bump.*

PHRASAL VERBS WITH **bump** ▼

▲ **bump into *sb*** *phrasal verb* to meet someone you know when you have not planned to meet them: *We bumped into Kate when we were in London last week.*

▲ **bump *sb* off** *phrasal verb* [M] SLANG to murder someone

▲ **bump *sth* up** *phrasal verb* [M] INFORMAL to increase the amount or size of something: *The distributors will probably bump up the **price** of the software when the next version is released.*

bumper [CAR PART] /ˈbʌm.pəʳ/ [US] /-pɚ/ *noun* [C] a horizontal bar along the lower front and lower back part of a motor vehicle to help protect it if there is an accident ➲See picture **Car** on page Centre 12

• **bumper to bumper** when there are so many cars and they are so close that they are almost touching each other: *By eight o'clock the traffic was bumper to bumper.*

bumper [BIG] /ˈbʌm.pəʳ/ [US] /-pɚ/ *adj* [before n] unusually large in amount: *Farmers have reported a bumper **crop** this year.*

ˈbumper ˌcar *noun* [C usually pl] (UK ALSO **dodgem**) a small electric car driven for entertainment in a special enclosed space where the aim is to try to hit other cars

ˈbumper ˌsticker *noun* [C] a sign that you stick on a car, often with a funny message on it ➲See picture **Car** on page Centre 12

bumph /bʌmpf/ *noun* [U] ANOTHER SPELLING OF **bumf**

bumpkin /ˈbʌmp.kɪn/ *noun* [C] (ALSO **country bumpkin**) INFORMAL DISAPPROVING a person from the countryside who is considered to be awkward and stupid

bumptious /ˈbʌmp.ʃəs/ *adj* DISAPPROVING unpleasantly confident: *a bumptious young man* **bumptiousness** /ˈbʌmp.ʃə.snəs/ *noun* [U]

ˌbum ˈsteer *noun* [S] US a piece of bad advice: *He gave us a bum steer about that restaurant – it was terrible!*

bun [FOOD] /bʌn/ *noun* [C] **1** a small, sweet, usually round cake: *a currant bun* **2** MAINLY US a small round loaf of bread, especially one which is cut horizontally and holds a BURGER: *a hamburger bun*

• **have a bun in the oven** OLD-FASHIONED HUMOROUS to be pregnant

bun [HAIRSTYLE] /bʌn/ *noun* [C] a woman's hairstyle where the hair is gathered into a round shape at the back of the head: *She wore her hair **in a** bun.*

bun [BOTTOM] /bʌn/ *noun* [C usually pl] MAINLY US SLANG a BUTTOCK (= one side of a person's bottom)

bunch /bʌntʃ/ *noun* **1** [C] a number of things of the same type fastened or closely grouped together: *a bunch of flowers/grapes/bananas/keys* ○ MAINLY US INFORMAL *The reorganization will give us **a whole** bunch* (= a lot) ***of** problems.* **2** [S] a group of people: *They're a bunch **of** hooligans.* ○ *Your friends are a nice bunch.*

• **the best/pick of the bunch** the best person or thing from a group of similar people or things: *Send in your poems and we'll publish the pick of the bunch.*

bunches /ˈbʌn.tʃɪz/ *plural noun* UK If a girl has her hair in bunches, it is tied together in two parts with one at each side of her head: *As a little girl she wore her hair **in** bunches.*

bunch /bʌntʃ/ *verb*

PHRASAL VERBS WITH **bunch**

▲ **bunch** ***(sth)*** **up/together** [GROUP] *phrasal verb* to move close together to form a tight group: *The monkeys bunched together in their cage.* ○ *We were all bunched up at the back of the room.*

▲ **bunch** ***(sth)*** **up** [MATERIAL] *phrasal verb* [M] If material bunches up, or if someone bunches it up, it moves into tight folds: *Your shirt's all bunched up at the back.*

bundle [TIED OBJECTS] /ˈbʌn.dl̩/ *noun* [C] a number of things that have been fastened or are held together: *a bundle of clothes/newspapers/books* ○ *a bundle **of** sticks*

• **a bundle (of joy)** a baby: *Three days after the birth, Paul and Sandra took their precious bundle of joy home.*

• **a bundle of laughs** *INFORMAL* an amusing fun person or situation: *He's not exactly a bundle of laughs, is he?*

• **a bundle of nerves** *INFORMAL* someone who is extremely nervous and anxious: *Sorry for shouting – I'm a bundle of nerves these days.*

• **go a bundle on** ***sth*** *UK INFORMAL* to like something very much: *I don't go a bundle on his taste in clothes.*

bundle [PUSH] /ˈbʌn.dl̩/ *verb* [I or T; + adv or prep] to push or put someone or something somewhere quickly and roughly: *He bundled his clothes **into** the washing machine.* ○ *She was bundled **into** the back of the car.* ○ *The children were bundled **off** to school early that morning.*

bundle [SELL TOGETHER] /ˈbʌn.dl̩/ *verb* [T] to include an additional computer program or other product with something that you sell: *The system came bundled **with** a word processor, spreadsheet and graphics program.* **bundling** /ˈbʌnd.lɪŋ/ *noun* [U] *the bundling of services/software/products*

PHRASAL VERBS WITH **bundle**

▲ **bundle** ***(sb)*** **up** [DRESS] *phrasal verb* [M] to put warm clothes on yourself or someone else: *The kids were bundled up in coats and scarves.*

▲ **bundle** ***sth*** **up** [TIE] *phrasal verb* [M] to tie a number of things together

bung [CLOSING DEVICE] *MAINLY UK* /bʌŋ/ *noun* [C] (*US USUALLY ALSO* **stopper**) a round piece of rubber, wood, etc. that is used to close the hole in a container

bung [MONEY] /bʌŋ/ *noun* [C] *UK INFORMAL* a payment made to someone to persuade them to do something, usually something dishonest: *Of course both the politicians denied taking bungs.*

bung [PUT] /bʌŋ/ *verb* [T + adv or prep] *MAINLY UK INFORMAL* to put something somewhere in a careless way: *"Where shall I put my coat?" "Oh, bung it anywhere."*

▲ **bung** ***sth*** **up** *phrasal verb* [M] *UK INFORMAL* to cause something to be blocked so that it does not work in the way it should: *The toilet was bunged up with paper.*

bunged-up /ˌbʌŋdˈʌp/ *adj UK INFORMAL* If your nose is bunged-up, you find it difficult to breathe because you have a cold.

bungalow /ˈbʌŋ.gəl.əʊ/ [US] /-oʊ/ *noun* [C] a house that has only one storey: *It was a seaside town filled with small white bungalows.*

bungee (cord) /ˈbʌn.dʒiˌkɔːd/ [US] /-ˌkɔːrd/ *noun* [C] *MAINLY US* a cord that stretches with a hook at each end, which is used to hold things in place, especially on a bicycle or car

bungee jumping, **bungy jumping** /ˈbʌn.dʒiˌdʒʌm.pɪŋ/ *noun* [U] the sport of jumping off a very high bridge or similar structure, with a long elastic rope tied to your legs, so that the rope pulls you back before you hit the ground ⊃See picture **Sports** on page Centre 10

bungle /ˈbʌŋ.gl̩/ *verb* [T] to do something wrong, in a careless or stupid way **bungled** /ˈbʌŋ.gl̩d/ *adj*: *a bungled robbery* **bungler** /ˈbʌŋ.gləʳ/ [US] /-glɚ/ *noun* [C] *He's an incompetent bungler.* **bungling** /ˈbʌŋ.glɪŋ/ *adj*: *What bungling **idiot** wired up the plug like this!*

bunion /ˈbʌn.jən/ *noun* [C] a painful swelling on the first joint of the big toe

bunk [BED] /bʌŋk/ *noun* [C] a narrow bed that is fixed to a wall, especially in a boat or a train

ˈbunk (ˌbed) *noun* [C often pl] one of two beds fixed together, one on top of the other: *The twins sleep in bunk beds.* ○ *Can I sleep in the top bunk?*

bunk [NONSENSE] /bʌŋk/ *noun* [U] (*ALSO* **bunkum**) *OLD-FASHIONED INFORMAL* complete nonsense or something that is not true: *Most economists think his theories are sheer bunk.*

bunk [LEAVE] /bʌŋk/ *noun UK OLD-FASHIONED SLANG* **do a bunk** to leave suddenly and unexpectedly: *They'd done a bunk without paying the rent.*

bunk /bʌŋk/ *verb*

PHRASAL VERBS WITH **bunk**

▲ **bunk down** *phrasal verb INFORMAL* to sleep: *We were able to bunk down in a spare room for the night.*

▲ **bunk off** ***(sth)*** *phrasal verb UK INFORMAL* to stay away from school or work or to leave early, especially without permission: *A lot of people bunk off early on Friday.* ○ *It was a sunny day so they decided to bunk off **school**.*

bunker [SHELTER] /ˈbʌŋ.kəʳ/ [US] /-kɚ/ *noun* [C] a shelter, usually underground, that has strong walls to protect the people inside it from bullets and bombs

bunker [GOLF] /ˈbʌŋ.kəʳ/ [US] /-kɚ/ *noun* [C] (*US ALSO* **sand trap**) in the game of golf, a hollow area of ground filled with sand, that is difficult to hit a ball out of

bunny (rabbit) /ˈbʌn.iˌræb.ɪt/ *noun* [C] *CHILD'S WORD* a rabbit

bunny slope /ˈbʌn.iˌsləʊp/ [US] /-ˌsloʊp/ *noun* [C] *US FOR* **nursery slope**

bunsen burner /ˈbʌn.sənˌbɜː.nəʳ/ [US] /-ˌbɝː.nɚ/ *noun* [C] a small device that burns gas to produce a flame which is used to heat things in scientific work and experiments

bunting /ˈbʌn.tɪŋ/ [US] /-t̬ɪŋ/ *noun* [U] rows of brightly-coloured little flags that are hung across roads or above a stage as decoration for special occasions

buoy /bɔɪ/ [US] /ˈbuː.i/ *noun* [C] a floating object on the top of the sea, which is used for directing ships and warning them of possible danger

buoy /bɔɪ/ [US] /ˈbuː.i/ *verb* **1** [T] to prevent someone or something from sinking: *The very salty water buoyed her **(up)** as she swam.* **2** [T usually passive] to make someone feel happier or more confident about a situation: *She was buoyed **(up)** by the warm reception her audience gave her.* **3** [T usually passive] to support something and make it more successful: *House prices have been buoyed **(up)** in the area by the possibility of a new factory opening.*

buoyancy /ˈbɔɪ.ənt.si/ *noun* [U] **1** the ability to float: *We tested the boat for its buoyancy.* **2** an ability to stay happy despite having difficulties: *He was a man of remarkable buoyancy.*

buoyant /ˈbɔɪ.ənt/ *adj*: *After reading the letter he was in a buoyant* (= happy) ***mood.*** **buoyantly** /ˈbɔɪ.ənt.li/ *adv*

bur /bɜːʳ/ [US] /bɝː/ *noun* [C] *ANOTHER SPELLING OF* **burr** SEED

burble [MAKE SOUND] /ˈbɜː.bl̩/ [US] /ˈbɝː-/ *verb* [I] to make a low continuous bubbling sound, like water moving over stones

burble [TALK] /ˈbɜː.bl̩/ [US] /ˈbɝː-/ *verb* [I or T] to talk about something continuously and in an unclear way: *She was burbling **(on) about** what she'd do if she won the lottery.*

burden /ˈbɜː.dən/ [US] /ˈbɝː-/ *noun* [C] **1** a heavy load that you carry: *The little donkey struggled under its **heavy** burden.* **2** something difficult or unpleasant that you have to deal with or worry about: *the burden of responsibility* ○ *My elderly mother worries that she's **a** burden **to** me.* ○ *Buying a house often places a large financial burden **on** young couples.*

• **burden of proof** *LEGAL* the responsibility for proving something

burden /ˈbɜː.dən/ [US] /ˈbɝː-/ *verb* [T] *I don't want to burden* (= trouble) *you **with** my problems.*

burdensome /ˈbɜː.dən.səm/ [US] /ˈbɝː-/ *adj FORMAL* causing difficulties or work: *a burdensome task*

bureau [ORGANIZATION] /ˈbjʊə.rəʊ/ [US] /ˈbjʊr.oʊ/ *noun* [C] *plural* **bureaux** or *US USUALLY* **bureaus** **1** an organization or a business that collects or provides information: *Her dis-*

appearance was reported to the police department's Missing Persons Bureau. **2** MAINLY US a government organization: *the Federal Bureau of Investigation*

bureau [FURNITURE] /ˈbjʊə.rəʊ/ [US] /ˈbjʊr.oʊ/ *noun* [C] *plural* **bureaux** or US USUALLY **bureaus** **1** UK a piece of furniture with a lid that opens to form a writing surface **2** US FOR **chest of drawers**

bureaucracy /bjʊəˈrɒk.rə.si/ [US] /bjʊˈrɑː.krə-/ *noun* [C or U] MAINLY DISAPPROVING a system for controlling or managing a country, company or organization that is operated by a large number of officials who are employed to follow rules carefully: *I had to deal with the university's bureaucracy before I could change from one course to another.*

bureaucrat /ˈbjʊə.rə.kræt/ [US] /ˈbjʊr.ə-/ *noun* [C] someone working in a bureaucracy: *It turned out she was one of those* ***faceless*** *bureaucrats who control our lives.*

bureaucratic /ˌbjʊə.rəˈkræt.ɪk/ [US] /ˌbjʊr.əˈkræt̬-/ *adj*: *I had a lot of bureaucratic hassle* (= long and difficult dealings with officials) *trying to get the information I needed.* ○ *The company was inefficient because it was highly bureaucratic.*

ˌbureau de ˈchange *noun* [C] an office where you can change the money of one country for that of another

burgeon /ˈbɜː.dʒən/ [US] /ˈbɝː-/ *verb* [I] LITERARY to develop or grow quickly: *Love burgeoned between them.*

burgeoning /ˈbɜː.dʒən.ɪŋ/ [US] /ˈbɝː-/ *adj*: *The company hoped to profit from the burgeoning* (= quickly developing) *communications industry.*

burger /ˈbɜː.gər/ [US] /ˈbɝː.gɚ/ *noun* [C] meat or other food pressed into a round, flat shape and fried: *a burger and chips* ○ *a hamburger* ○ *a veggieburger*

burgher /ˈbɜː.gər/ [US] /ˈbɝː.gɚ/ *noun* [C] OLD-FASHIONED OR HUMOROUS a person who lives in a city

burglar /ˈbɜː.glər/ [US] /ˈbɝː.glɚ/ *noun* [C] a person who illegally enters buildings and steals things

burglary /ˈbɜː.glər.i/ [US] /ˈbɝː.glɚ-/ *noun* [C or U] the crime of illegally entering a building and stealing things

burgle /ˈbɜː.gl̩/ [US] /ˈbɝː-/ *verb* [T] (US USUALLY **burglarize**) to illegally enter a building and steal things: *When they got back from their holiday they found that their home had been burgled.*

ˈburglar aˌlarm *noun* [C] a device on a building that gives a warning such as making a loud noise or flashing a light, or informs the police, if someone tries to illegally enter the building

burial /ˈber.i.əl/ *noun* [C or U] the act of putting a dead body into the ground, or the ceremony connected with this: *We went back to Ireland for my uncle's burial.* ➲See also **bury**.

ˈburial ˌground *noun* [C] an area of land where dead bodies are buried, especially a long time ago

burk /bɜːk/ [US] /bɝːk/ *noun* [C] ANOTHER SPELLING OF **berk**

burlap /ˈbɜː.læp/ [US] /ˈbɝː-/ *noun* [U] US FOR **hessian**

burlesque /bɜːˈlesk/ [US] /bɝː-/ *noun* **1** [C or U] a type of writing or acting that tries to make something serious seem ridiculous **2** [U] US a theatrical entertainment in the US in the late 19th and early 20th centuries that had amusing acts and a STRIPTEASE (= a performance in which someone removes their clothes)

burly /ˈbɜː.li/ [US] /ˈbɝː-/ *adj* describes a man who is large and strong: *a burly policeman*

burn [BE ON FIRE] /bɜːn/ [US] /bɝːn/ *verb* **burnt** or **burned**, **burnt** or **burned** **1** [I] to be on fire, or to produce flames: *The wood was wet and would not burn.* ○ *Helplessly we watched our house burning.* ○ *A fire was burning brightly in the fireplace.* **2** [I] If your face burns, it feels very hot: *His face burned* ***with*** *embarrassment/shame/anger.* **3** [+ *to* infinitive] to want to do something very much: *She was burning to tell us her news.*

• **burn the candle at both ends** to work or do other things from early in the morning until late at night and so get very little rest

• **burn the midnight oil** to work late into the night

burner /ˈbɜː.nər/ [US] /ˈbɝː.nɚ/ *noun* [C] the part of a cooker, light, etc. that produces flame or heat

burning /ˈbɜː.nɪŋ/ [US] /ˈbɝː-/ *adj* **1** on fire **2** A burning desire, need, etc., is one that is very strong: *a burning ambition* ○ *He spoke of his burning desire to play for England.* **3 burning issue/question** a subject or question that must be dealt with or answered quickly

burn [PRODUCE LIGHT] /bɜːn/ [US] /bɝːn/ *verb* [I] **burnt** or **burned**, **burnt** or **burned** to produce light: *I saw a light burning in her window.*

burn [DAMAGE] /bɜːn/ [US] /bɝːn/ *verb* **burnt** or **burned**, **burnt** or **burned** **1** [I or T] to (cause something to) be hurt, damaged or destroyed by fire or extreme heat: *He was badly burnt in the blaze.* ○ *She burnt his old love letters.* ○ *The brandy burned* (= felt too hot on) *my throat.* ○ *On her first day in the Caribbean Josie was badly burned* (= her skin became red and painful from too much sun). ○ *Fair-skinned people burn easily in the sun.* ○ *Unable to escape, six people were burnt* ***alive***/*burnt* ***to death*** (= died by burning) *in the building.* ○ *The vegetables were burnt* ***to a crisp*** (= badly burnt). **2** [T always passive] to cause emotional pain to someone

• **burn a hole in *sb's* pocket** If money is burning a hole in your pocket, you are very eager to spend it.

• **burn *sb* at the stake** to kill someone by tying them to a post and burning them

• **burn *your* boats/bridges** If you are in a situation and you burn your boats/bridges, you destroy all possible ways of going back to that situation.

• **burn *sth* to the ground** to completely destroy a building by fire: *The building was burned to the ground ten years ago.*

• **get/have *your* fingers burnt** (ALSO **burn *your* fingers**) INFORMAL to suffer unpleasant results of an action, especially loss of money, so you do not want to do the same thing again: *She'd invested extensively in stocks and got her fingers burnt when the market collapsed.*

burn /bɜːn/ [US] /bɝːn/ *noun* [C] a place where fire or heat has hurt or damaged something: *One rescue worker caught in the explosion sustained severe burns.* ○ *I noticed a cigarette burn in the carpet.* ➲See also **heartburn**; **sunburn**.

burning /ˈbɜː.nɪŋ/ [US] /ˈbɝː-/ *adj*: *Suddenly she felt a burning* ***(sensation)*** (= feeling of heat) *in her throat.*

burnt /bɜːnt/ [US] /bɝːnt/ *adj* destroyed or made black by fire or heat

burn [COPY] /bɜːn/ [US] /bɝːn/ *verb* [T] **burnt** or **burned**, **burnt** or **burned** to copy information, recorded music, images, etc. onto a COMPACT DISC: *Burn your favourite songs or your important files* ***onto*** *CDs.*

burn [STREAM] /bɜːn/ [US] /bɝːn/ *noun* [C] SCOTTISH ENGLISH a small stream

PHRASAL VERBS WITH **burn** ▼

▲ **burn *(sth)* down** *phrasal verb* [M] to destroy something, especially a building, by fire, or to be destroyed by fire: *He tried to burn down the school by setting fire to papers on a noticeboard.*

▲ **burn *sth* off/up** *phrasal verb* [M] to use or get rid of energy or fat by doing a lot of physical exercise: *Running is an excellent way to burn off excess calories.*

▲ **burn out** [FIRE] *phrasal verb* If a fire burns out, it stops producing flames because nothing remains that can burn.

▲ **burn out** [BREAK] *phrasal verb* If something such as a motor burns out, it stops working because of damage from heat: *It looks like the starter motor on the car has burnt out.*

▲ **burn *yourself* out** [BECOME TIRED] *phrasal verb* [R] to be forced to stop working because you have become ill or very tired from working too hard: *Stop working so hard – you'll burn yourself out.* ➲See also **burn-out**.

▲ **burn up** [FEVER] *phrasal verb* INFORMAL to have a bad fever: *"You're burning up!" she said, touching his forehead.*

▲ **burn *(sth)* up** [DESTROY] *phrasal verb* [M] to destroy something completely with fire or heat, or to be destroyed completely by fire or heat: *Meteorites often burn up in the atmosphere before they reach the earth.*

▲ **burn up with *sth*** *phrasal verb* If you burn up with an emotion, you feel that emotion so strongly that you cannot act in a reasonable way: *He was burnt up with jealousy and suspicion.*

▲ **burn with** ***sth*** *phrasal verb* If you burn with an emotion, you feel that emotion very strongly: *They were both burning with desire.*

burnish /ˈbɜː.nɪʃ/ [US] /ˈbɝː-/ *verb* [T] **1** LITERARY to rub metal until it is smooth and shiny **2** If you burnish something such as your public image, you take action to improve it and make it more attractive: *The company is currently trying to burnish its socially responsible image.*

burnished /ˈbɜː.nɪʃt/ [US] /ˈbɝː-/ *adj* LITERARY smooth and shiny

burn-out /ˈbɜːn.aʊt/ [US] /ˈbɝːn-/ *noun* [U] extreme tiredness usually caused by working too much: *employees complaining of/suffering burn-out*

ˈburn ˌrate *noun* [C] the speed at which a company spends the money that is available to it when it begins trading: *It is estimated that the company will last 10 years based on the current burn rate.*

burnt /bɜːnt/ [US] /bɝːnt/ *past simple and past participle of* **burn**

ˌburnt ˈoffering *noun* [C] **1** something, often an animal, that is burned in honour of a god **2** UK HUMOROUS a meal that has been spoiled by burning

burnt-out /ˌbɜːntˈaʊt/ [US] /ˌbɝːnt-/ *adj* describes a building or vehicle which has been badly damaged by fire: *After the fire the factory was completely burnt-out/just a burnt-out shell.*

ˌburnt siˈenna *noun* [U] a reddish brown colour

burp /bɜːp/ [US] /bɝːp/ *verb* **1** [I] to allow air from the stomach to come out through the mouth in a noisy way **2** [T] to gently rub a baby's back to help air to come out of its stomach **burp** /bɜːp/ [US] /bɝːp/ *noun* [C]

burr [SOUND] /bɜːʳ/ [US] /bɝː/ *noun* [C usually sing] a way of speaking English in which the 'r' sound is longer and more noticeable than usual: *He spoke in a soft West Country burr.*

burr [SEED], **bur** /bɜːʳ/ [US] /bɝː/ *noun* [C] a very small round seed container that sticks to clothes and to animals' fur because it is covered in little hooks

burrito /bəˈriː.təʊ/ [US] /-ˈriː.t̬oʊ/ *noun* [C] *plural* **burritos** a type of Mexican food made by folding a TORTILLA (= thin round bread) and putting meat, beans and cheese inside it

burrow /ˈbʌr.əʊ/ [US] /ˈbɝː.oʊ/ *noun* [C] a hole in the ground dug by an animal such as a rabbit, especially to live in

burrow /ˈbʌr.əʊ/ [US] /ˈbɝː.oʊ/ *verb* **1** [I usually + adv or prep] to dig a hole in the ground, especially to live in: *Rats had burrowed* ***into*** *the bank of the river.* **2** [T + adv or prep] to move yourself into a position where you can feel warm, comfortable or safe: *Suddenly shy, our young daughter burrowed her head* ***into*** *my shoulder.* **3** [I + adv or prep] to search for something, as if by digging: *I burrowed* ***through*** *the clothes in the drawer looking for a clean pair of socks.*

bursar /ˈbɜː.səʳ/ [US] /ˈbɝː.sɚ/ *noun* [C] the person in a college, school or university who is responsible for controlling its money

bursary /ˈbɜː.sᵊr.i/ [US] /ˈbɝː.sɚ-/ *noun* [C] UK a sum of money given to a person by an organization, such as a university, to pay for them to study

burst /bɜːst/ [US] /bɝːst/ *verb* **burst, burst 1** [I or T] to break open or apart suddenly, or to make something do this: *Balloons make me nervous – I hate it when they burst.* ○ *The river was threatening to burst its* ***banks.*** ○ *Suddenly the door burst* ***open*** (= opened suddenly and forcefully) *and police officers carrying guns rushed in.* ○ FIGURATIVE HUMOROUS *If I eat any more cake I'll burst* (= I cannot eat anything else)*!* **2** [I] to feel a strong emotion, or strong desire to do something: *I knew they were bursting* ***with*** *curiosity but I said nothing.* ○ [+ to infinitive] INFORMAL *I'm bursting* ***to*** *go to the loo!* ○ *Tom was bursting* ***to*** *tell everyone the news.*

• **burst at the seams** INFORMAL to be completely full: *When all the family come home the house is bursting at the seams.*

• **burst into song/tears/laughter** to suddenly begin to sing/cry/laugh: *Much to my surprise Ben suddenly burst into song.*

• **burst into flames** to suddenly burn fiercely, producing a lot of flames: *Smoke started pouring out from underneath, then the truck burst into flames.*

burst /bɜːst/ [US] /bɝːst/ *noun* [C] **1** when something breaks open and what is inside breaks out: *a burst in the water pipe* **2** a sudden increase in something, especially for a short period: *a burst* ***of speed/applause/laughter***

PHRASAL VERBS WITH **burst** ▼

▲ **burst in/into** ***(somewhere)*** *phrasal verb* to enter a room or building suddenly and without warning: *The side door of the pub flew open and three men burst in.*

▲ **burst in on** ***sb/sth*** *phrasal verb* to enter a room suddenly and without warning, interrupting the people or activity inside: *Katya burst in on him without warning.*

▲ **burst out** *phrasal verb* to suddenly say something loudly: *"Don't go!" he burst out.*

• **burst out laughing/crying** to suddenly start laughing/crying: *I walked in and everyone burst out laughing.*

burton /ˈbɜː.tᵊn/ [US] /ˈbɝː.t̬ᵊn/ *noun* UK OLD-FASHIONED INFORMAL **gone for a burton** spoiled or lost: *That's our quiet evening in gone for a burton.*

bury /ˈber.i/ *verb* [T] **1** to put a dead body into the ground, or to put something into a hole in the ground and cover it: *His father is buried* ***in*** *the cemetery on the hill.* ○ *The dog trotted off to bury its bone.* ○ *If an avalanche strikes, skiers can be buried* ***alive*** *by snow.* ○ *buried* ***treasure*** ➲See also **burial**. **2** to put something in a place where it is difficult or impossible to find or see: *I found the article buried* ***(away)*** *in the business section of the newspaper.* ○ *She buried her face* ***in*** *her hands and began to sob.* **3** to intentionally forget an unpleasant experience: *He'd had to bury his pain over the years.* **4** OLD-FASHIONED If someone says they buried someone, usually a close relative, they mean that the person died: *She buried both her parents last year.*

• **bury the hatchet** to stop an argument and become friends again: *Can't you two just bury the hatchet?*

bus /bʌs/ *noun* [C] *plural* **buses** or US ALSO **busses** a large vehicle in which people are driven from one place to another: *You should* ***take the bus/go by*** *bus* (= travel by bus) *if you want to see the sights.* ➲See also **minibus**; **omnibus** TRANSPORT; **trolleybus**. ➲See picture **Cars and Trucks** on page Centre 13

bus /bʌs/ *verb* [T] **-ss-** or US USUALLY **-s- 1** to take people somewhere by bus: *Demonstrators were bussed in from all parts of the country to attend the protest rally.* **2** US to take children by bus to school in another area every day

busboy, **bus boy** /ˈbʌs.bɔɪ/ *noun* [C] US a person who helps someone serve in a restaurant, especially by removing dirty dishes and bringing clean ones

busby /ˈbʌz.bi/ *noun* [C] a fur hat worn by some British soldiers on ceremonial occasions

ˈbus conˌductor *noun* [C] the person on some buses whose job is to take your money and give you a ticket

bush [PLANT] /bʊʃ/ *noun* [C] a plant with many small branches growing either directly from the ground or from a hard woody stem, giving the plant a rounded shape: *a rose bush*

the bush [AREA OF LAND] *noun* [S] (especially in Australia and Africa) an area of land covered with bushes and trees which has never been farmed and where there are very few people

bushed /bʊʃt/ *adj* [after v] INFORMAL very tired

bushel /ˈbʊʃ.ᵊl/ *noun* [C] a unit of measurement equal to approximately 36.4 litres in Britain or 35.2 litres in the US: *a bushel of wheat*

ˈbush ˌfire *noun* [C] a fire burning in THE BUSH (= wild area of land) that is difficult to control and sometimes spreads quickly

bushman /ˈbʊʃ.mən/ *noun* [C] MAINLY AUS a person who lives in THE BUSH (= wild area of land)

bushranger /ˈbʊʃˌreɪn.dʒəʳ/ [US] /-dʒɚ/ *noun* [C] AUS OLD-FASHIONED a criminal or thief who lived in THE BUSH (= wild area of land)

,**bush 'telegraph** *noun* [S] *UK OLD-FASHIONED HUMOROUS* the informal way in which information quickly spreads from person to person

bushy /ˈbʊʃ.i/ *adj* describes hair or fur that is very thick: *a squirrel's bushy **tail*** ○ *bushy **eyebrows***

busily /ˈbɪz.ɪ.li/ *adv* ➲See at **busy** DOING THINGS.

business SELLING /ˈbɪz.nɪs/ *noun* [C or U] the activity of buying and selling goods and services, or a particular company that does this, or work you do to earn money: *My brother's **in** business.* ○ *He's **in the** frozen food business.* ○ *The two brothers established/set up/started up a clothes retailing business.* ○ *Our firm **does** a lot of business **with** overseas customers.* ○ *Eventually they found a consultant they felt they could **do** business **with** (= with whom they could work well).* ○ *Currently, there are fewer firms **in** business (= operating) in the area than ever before.* ○ *This new tax will put a lot of small firms **out of** business (= they will stop operating).* ○ *She **set up in** business (= started her own company) as a management consultant.* ○ *How is business (= Are you selling much) at the moment?* ○ *Business is good/brisk/booming/ flourishing (= I'm selling a lot).* ○ *Business is bad/slack/ quiet (= I'm not selling much).* ○ *I'm in Baltimore **on** business.* ○ *a business appointment*

business-to-business /ˌbɪz.nɪs.təˈbɪz.nɪs/ *adj* [before n] (*ABBREVIATION* **B2B**) describing or involving arrangements or trade between different businesses, rather than between businesses and the general public

business-to-consumer /ˌbɪz.nɪs.tə.kənˈsjuː.məʳ/ ⑩ /-ˈsuː.mɚ/ *adj* [before n] (*ABBREVIATION* **B2C**) describing or involving the sale of goods or services to individual customers for their own use, rather than to businesses

• **be in business** *INFORMAL* to be ready and able to start doing something that you planned: *Once we get the computer installed we'll be in business.*

• **get down to business** to start talking about the subject to be discussed: *If the introductions are over I'd like to get down to business.*

• **not be in the business of** If a person or organization is not in the business of doing something considered wrong, they do not normally do it: *The intelligence service is not in the business of routinely monitoring the activities of law-abiding citizens.*

• **(It's) business as usual.** *SAYING* said when things are continuing as they always do, despite a difficult situation

• **Business before pleasure.** *SAYING* said to emphasize that you believe business is more important than entertainment and enjoyment

business MATTER /ˈbɪz.nɪs/ *noun* [S or U] a situation or activity, often one that you are giving your opinion about: *Arranging a trip abroad is **a** time-consuming business.* ○ *These killings are **a** dreadful business.* ○ *I **make it** my business (= I feel it is my particular duty) to check the monthly accounts.* ○ *We've got some **unfinished** business to discuss (= We still have something important to discuss).*

the '**business** *noun* [S] *UK SLANG* extremely good: *That new defender is the business!*

• **What a business!** used to mean that something was annoying and caused a lot of trouble for you: *It took ages to sort out the documentation needed to get into the country – what a business!*

• **do the business 1** *INFORMAL* to do what is wanted or needed in a situation: *As long as he does the business on the football field, the club is happy with him.* **2** *UK SLANG* to have sex

business THINGS YOU DO /ˈbɪz.nɪs/ *noun* [U] the things that you do or the matters which relate only to you: *I got on with **the** business **of** filling in the form.* ○ *What she does with her life is her business.*

• **have no business doing sth** to have no right to do something: *You had no business reading my private letters.*

• **like nobody's business** very quickly or very much: *He was scribbling away like nobody's business.*

• **be none of sb's business** If something is none of someone's business, they do not need to know about it, although they want to, because it does not affect them: *Stop pestering me, it's none of your business!*

'**business ,class** *noun* [U], *adv* travelling conditions on an aircraft that are better than the conditions you get when you travel more cheaply: *Do you usually travel business class?*

'**business ,end** *noun* [S] *INFORMAL* The business end of something, such as a knife or a gun, is the end which does the work or damage rather than the handle.

businesslike /ˈbɪz.nɪs.laɪk/ *adj* getting things done in a quick and practical way: *The meeting was brief and businesslike.*

businessman /ˈbɪz.nɪs.mən/ *noun* [C] a man who works in business, especially if he has a high position in a company: *He was a successful businessman before becoming a writer.*

'**business ,park** *noun* [C] an area that is specially designed to have business offices, small factories, etc.

'**business ,plan** *noun* [C] a detailed plan describing the future plans of a business

businesswoman /ˈbɪz.nɪs.wʊm.ən/ *noun* [C] a woman who works in business, especially if she has a high position in a company: *She's a good/shrewd businesswoman who's popular with her staff.*

busk /bʌsk/ *verb* [I] *UK* to play music or sing in a public place so that the people who are there will give money

busker /ˈbʌs.kəʳ/ ⑩ /ˈbʌs.kɚ/ *noun* [C]

'**bus ,lane** *noun* [C] a specially marked wide strip on a road, on which only buses are allowed to travel

busman's holiday /ˌbʌs.mənzˈhɒl.ɪ.deɪ/ ⑩ /-ˈhɑː.lɪ-/ *noun* [S] *HUMOROUS* a holiday where you do something similar to your usual work instead of having a rest from it

bus-shelter /ˈbʌs.ʃel.təʳ/ ⑩ /-t̬ɚ/ *noun* [C] a place to wait for buses that has a roof

'**bus ,station** *noun* [C] a place where buses start and end their journeys

'**bus ,stop** *noun* [C] a place, usually marked by a pole with a sign, where a bus stops to allow passengers to get on and off

bust BREAK /bʌst/ *verb* [T] **bust** or *US* **busted**, **bust** or *US* **busted** *INFORMAL* to break something: *Oh no! I've bust his CD player.* **bust** /bʌst/ *adj* [after v] (*US ALSO* **busted**) *I think my watch is bust.*

• **go bust** If a company goes bust, it is forced to close because it is financially unsuccessful: *More than twenty companies in the district went bust during the last three months.*

bust ARREST /bʌst/ *verb* [T] **bust** or *US* **busted**, **bust** or *US* **busted** *SLANG* When the police bust a person they arrest him or her, or when they bust a building or a place they arrest people in it who they believe are breaking the law: *The police busted him because they think he's involved with a terrorist group.*

bust /bʌst/ *noun* [C] *SLANG* an occasion when police arrest people who are thought to have broken the law: *In their latest **drugs** bust police entered a warehouse where cocaine dealers were meeting.*

bust HEAD /bʌst/ *noun* [C] a statue of the head and shoulders of a person: *There was a bust **of** Mahler on his desk.*

bust BREASTS /bʌst/ *noun* [C] a woman's breasts, or the measurement around a woman's breasts and back: *I couldn't find anything in the shop in my bust size.*

busty /ˈbʌs.ti/ *adj* *INFORMAL* A busty woman has large breasts.

▲ **bust up** *phrasal verb* *MAINLY US INFORMAL* to end a relationship after an angry argument: *She's bust up with Carlo.* ➲See also **bust-up**.

buster DISLIKED PERSON /ˈbʌs.təʳ/ ⑩ /-t̬ɚ/ *noun* [as form of address] *US INFORMAL* used to address a man or a boy you do not like: *Cut it out, buster!*

-**buster** DESTROY /-bʌs.təʳ/ ⑩ /-t̬ɚ/ *suffix* a person or thing intended to destroy the stated thing: *crime-busters*

bustle BE BUSY /ˈbʌs.l̩/ *verb* [I + adv or prep] to do things in a hurried and busy way: *Thora bustled **about** the flat, getting everything ready.*

bustle /ˈbʌs.l̩/ *noun* [U] *I sat in a café, watching the **(hustle and)** bustle (= busy activity) of the street outside.*

bustling /ˈbʌs.lɪŋ/ *adj*: *This used to be a bustling* (= full of busy activity) *town but a lot of people have moved away over recent years.* ○ *The house, usually bustling **with** activity, was strangely silent.*

bustle [DRESS] /ˈbʌs.l̩/ *noun* [C] a frame worn under a dress or skirt by women in the late 19th century to make the skirt stick out

bust-up /ˈbʌst.ʌp/ *noun* [C] *UK INFORMAL* a serious argument, especially one which ends a relationship: *She **had** a big bust-up **with** her brother-in-law.*

busy [DOING THINGS] /ˈbɪz.i/ *adj* **1** If you are busy, you are working hard, or giving your attention to a particular thing: *Mum was busy in the kitchen.* ○ *The kids are busy **with** their homework.* ○ *She's busy writing out the wedding invitations.* ○ *I've got plenty of jobs to **keep** you busy.* ○ *He was **too** busy talking **to** notice us come in.* **2** A busy place is full of activity or people: *a busy restaurant* ○ *Their house is near a very busy road.* **3** In a busy period, you have a lot of things to do: *I've got a busy week ahead of me.* ○ *Have a rest – you've had a busy day.* **4** (*UK ALSO* **engaged**) If a telephone line is busy, someone is using it: *I tried calling you but the line was busy.*
busily /ˈbɪz.ɪ.li/ *adv*: *I was busily preparing for their arrival.*
• **ˈbusy yourself** to make the time pass by doing something: *I busied myself with tidying up my desk.*

busy [WITH PATTERNS] /ˈbɪz.i/ *adj DISAPPROVING* having too much decoration or too many colours: *The jacket was a bit busy for my tastes – I'd prefer something a bit plainer.*

busybody /ˈbɪz.iˌbɒd.i/ [US] /-ˌbɑː.di/ *noun* [C] *INFORMAL* a person who is too interested in things that do not involve them: *Some interfering busybody had rung the police.*

but [DIFFERENCE] *STRONG* /bʌt/, *WEAK* /bət/ *conjunction* used to introduce an added statement, usually something that it different from what you have said before: *She's very hard-working but not very imaginative.* ○ *This is not caused by evil, but by simple ignorance.* ○ *The play's good, but not that good – I've seen better.* ○ *I'm sorry, but I think you're wrong when you say she did it deliberately.* ○ *Call me old-fashioned, but I like handwritten letters.* ○ *I can understand his unhappiness. But to attempt suicide!* ○ *"She said she's leaving." "But why?"* ○ *You can invite Keith to the party, but please don't ask that friend of his.* ○ *We must not complain about the problem, but* (= instead we must) *help to put it right.* ○ *She's not a painter but a writer* (= She is a writer, not a painter). ○ *She's **not only** a painter but **also** a writer* (= She is both). ○ *He said he hadn't been there, but **then*** (= it is not surprising that) *he would say that.* ○ *I think it's true, but **then*** (= it should be understood that), *I'm no expert.*
buts /bʌts/ *plural noun* **no buts (about it)** used to emphasize that something will happen even if the person you are talking to does not want it to: *We're going to visit your aunt tomorrow and there'll be no buts about it.*

but [EXCEPT] *STRONG* /bʌt/, *WEAK* /bət/ *prep, conjunction* except: *Eventually, **all** but **one** of them promised to come to his leaving party.* ○ *He's **anything** but violent* (= not violent in any way). ○ *I'd have crashed the car but **for** your warning.* ○ *This is the **last** episode but **one*** (= one before the last) *of this drama serial.* ○ *She's one of those guests who does **nothing** but complain.* ○ *This car has been **nothing** but trouble – it's always breaking down!*

but [ONLY] *STRONG* /bʌt/, *WEAK* /bət/ *adv* **1** *FORMAL* only; just: *She's but a young girl!* **2** used to give force to a statement: *Everyone, but everyone, will be there.*

butane /ˈbjuː.teɪn/ *noun* [U] a chemical containing carbon that is used as a fuel

butch /bʊtʃ/ *adj* (of a woman) looking or behaving like a man, or (of a man) being very strong and muscular, and behaving in a traditionally male way

butcher [ANIMALS] /ˈbʊtʃ.əʳ/ [US] /-ɚ/ *noun* [C] **1** a person who sells meat in a shop **2** (*UK ALSO* **butcher's**) a shop where butchers work
• **have a butcher's** *UK SLANG* to look at something: *Let's have a butcher's **at** your present, then.*
butcher /ˈbʊtʃ.əʳ/ [US] /-ɚ/ *verb* [T] to cut an animal into pieces of meat

butcher [PEOPLE] /ˈbʊtʃ.əʳ/ [US] /-ɚ/ *noun* [C] someone who murders a lot of people, especially in a cruel way
butcher /ˈbʊtʃ.əʳ/ [US] /-ɚ/ *verb* [T] to kill someone in a very violent way

butchery /ˈbʊtʃ.ᵊr.i/ [US] /-ɚ-/ *noun* [U] **1** the preparation of meat for sale **2** cruel killing

butler /ˈbʌt.ləʳ/ [US] /-lɚ/ *noun* [C] the most important male servant in a house, usually responsible for organizing the other servants

butt [THICK END] /bʌt/ *noun* [C] the thick end of a rifle handle: *They struck him with their rifle butts.*

butt [CIGARETTE] /bʌt/ *noun* [C] the part of a finished cigarette that has not been smoked

butt [BOTTOM] /bʌt/ *noun* [C] *US SLANG FOR* bottom: *She told him to **get off** his butt and do something useful.*

butt [HIT] /bʌt/ *verb* [I or T] to hit something or someone hard with the head or the horns
▲ **butt in** *phrasal verb INFORMAL* to interrupt a conversation or discussion or someone who is talking: *He kept on butting in with silly comments.*

butt [PERSON] /bʌt/ *noun* **be the butt of *sb's* jokes** to be a person who is joked about or laughed at: *He was fed up with being the butt of their jokes.*

butt [CONTAINER] /bʌt/ *noun* [C] a large container used to store liquids

butter /ˈbʌt.əʳ/ [US] /ˈbʌt̬.ɚ/ *noun* [U] a pale yellow, fatty solid made from cream, that is spread on bread or used in cooking: *We were served scones with butter and jam.* ○ *Have some **bread and** butter* (= bread spread with butter). ○ *a butter **dish***
• **butter wouldn't melt in *sb's* mouth** when someone looks as if they would never do anything wrong, although you feel they might: *Tommy looked as if butter wouldn't melt in his mouth.*
butter /ˈbʌt.əʳ/ [US] /ˈbʌt̬.ɚ/ *verb* [T] to spread butter on something **buttered** /ˈbʌt.əd/ [US] /ˈbʌt̬.ɚd/ *adj*: *buttered toast* **buttery** /ˈbʌt.ᵊr.i/ [US] /ˈbʌt̬.ɚ-/ *adj*
▲ **butter *sb* up** *phrasal verb* [M] *INFORMAL* to be very kind or friendly to someone or try to please them, so that they will do what you want them to do: *You'll have to butter them up a bit before they'll agree.*

ˈbutter ˌbean *UK noun* [C usually pl] (*US* **lima bean**) a large, flat, creamy yellow bean

buttercup /ˈbʌt.ə.kʌp/ [US] /ˈbʌt̬.ɚ-/ *noun* [C] a small, bright, yellow wild flower ➲See picture **Flowers and Plants** on page Centre 3

butterfingers /ˈbʌt.əˌfɪŋ.gəz/ [US] /ˈbʌt̬.ɚˌfɪŋ.gɚz/ *noun* [S] *HUMOROUS* a person who drops things they are carrying or trying to catch: [as form of address] *"Butterfingers!" she called as I dropped the hot plates.*

butterfly /ˈbʌt.ə.flaɪ/ [US] /ˈbʌt̬.ɚ-/ *noun* [C] **1** a type of insect with large often brightly coloured wings **2** *DISAPPROVING* a person who is not responsible or serious, and who is likely to change activities easily or only be interested in pleasure: *She's such a **social** butterfly.* **3** the small metal part put on the back of a STUD (= piece of jewellery worn in the ear) that keeps it in place
• **have butterflies (in *your* stomach)** *INFORMAL* to feel very nervous, usually about something you are going to do: *I had terrible butterflies before I gave that talk in Venice.*

ˈbutterfly ˌstroke *noun* [S or U] (*ALSO* **the butterfly**) a way of swimming on your front by kicking with your legs while raising your arms together out of the water and then bringing them down in front of you

buttermilk /ˈbʌt.ə.mɪlk/ [US] /ˈbʌt̬.ɚ-/ *noun* [U] the liquid that is left after taking the fat from cream to make butter

butterscotch /ˈbʌt.ə.skɒtʃ/ [US] /ˈbʌt̬.ɚ.skɑːtʃ/ *noun* [C or U] a hard, light-brown coloured, sweet food made by boiling butter and sugar together

ˌbutt ˈnaked *adj US SLANG* completely naked

buttock /ˈbʌt.ək/ [US] /ˈbʌt̬-/ *noun* [C usually pl] either side of a person's bottom ➲See picture **The Body** on page Centre 5

button /ˈbʌt.ᵊn/ [US] /ˈbʌt̬-/ *noun* [C] **1** a small, usually circular object used to fasten something, for example a shirt or coat: *I **did up/undid*** (= fastened/unfastened) *the buttons on my blouse.* **2** a small, sometimes circular

[B]

object which you press to operate a device or a machine, or an area on a computer screen which looks and acts like one of these: *He inserted the cassette and pressed the 'play' button.*

• **at the push of a button** very easily: *You can't expect to get everything you need at the push of a button.*

• **right on the button** exactly correct: *She was right on the button when she said I'd regret moving out.*

button /ˈbʌt.ᵊn/ [US] /ˈbʌt̬-/ *verb* **[I or T]** to fasten something, usually a piece of clothing, using buttons: *Button **(up)** your coat, it's cold out.*

• **button it** *INFORMAL* a rude way of telling someone to stop talking: *Button it, OK! I'm trying to think.*

ˌbutton-down ˈcollar *noun* **[C]** a collar on a shirt that has the pointed ends fastened to the shirt by buttons

buttoned-down /ˌbʌt.ᵊndˈdaʊn/ [US] /ˌbʌt̬-/ *adj* **[before n]** (*ALSO* **button-down**) *US* formal and old-fashioned or boring: *a buttoned-down accountant/lawyer* ○ *How well will Mr. Landman's laid-back attitude merge with the more button-down **style** at Hughes Electronics Corp.?*

button-fly /ˈbʌt.ᵊn.flaɪ/ [US] /ˈbʌt̬-/ *noun* **[C]** Button-fly trousers or trousers with a button-fly, are trousers which fasten at the front with buttons.

buttonhole [HOLE] /ˈbʌt.ᵊn.həʊl/ [US] /ˈbʌt.ᵊn.hoʊl/ *noun* **[C]** **1** a hole that a button is pushed through to fasten a shirt, coat, etc. **2** *MAINLY UK* a flower that a man wears in the buttonhole of, or pinned to, his jacket on a special occasion such as a WEDDING (= a marriage ceremony)

buttonhole [MAKE LISTEN] /ˈbʌt.ᵊn.həʊl/ [US] /ˈbʌt̬.ᵊn.hoʊl/ *verb* **[T]** to stop someone and make them listen to you: *Greg buttonholed me about sales figures when I came out of the meeting.*

button-through /ˈbʌt.ᵊn.θruː/ [US] /ˈbʌt̬-/ *adj* **[before n]** describes a dress or skirt fastened with buttons from the top to the bottom

buttress /ˈbʌt.rəs/ *noun* **[C]** a structure made of stone or brick, which sticks out from and supports a wall of a building

buttress /ˈbʌt.rəs/ *verb* **[T]** **1** to build buttresses to support a building or structure: *It was decided to buttress the crumbling walls.* **2** to make support for an idea or argument stronger by providing a good reason for it: *The arguments for change are buttressed by events elsewhere.*

butty /ˈbʌt.i/ [US] /ˈbʌt̬-/ *noun* **[C]** *NORTHERN ENGLISH INFORMAL FOR* a **sandwich** (= two pieces of bread with food between them)

buxom /ˈbʌk.sᵊm/ *adj* (of a woman) healthy-looking and slightly fat, with large breasts

buy [PAY FOR] /baɪ/ *verb* **[I or T]** **bought, bought** to obtain something by paying money for it: *Eventually she had saved enough money to buy a small car.* ○ **[+ two objects]** *He bought his mother some flowers/He bought some flowers **for** his mother.* ○ *There are more people buying at this time of the year so prices are high.* ○ *The company was set up to buy and sell shares on behalf of investors.* ○ *I bought my camera **from**/(INFORMAL) **off** a friend of mine.* ○ *UK We bought **in*** (= bought for future use) *lots of tinned food in case of heavy snow.* ○ *McDowell was trying to buy **into** the newspaper business* (= buy a part of it to have some control over it). ○ *What will we have to do to buy her **silence*** (= to make her not tell anyone what she knows)*?*

• ***sb* has bought it** *SLANG* used to say that someone has been killed: *"Marvin's bought it!" screamed the serjeant.*

• **buy time** to do something in order to be allowed more time: *He tried to buy time by saying he hadn't been well.*

buy /baɪ/ *noun* **a good/bad buy** to be worth/not be worth the price: *This jacket is a really good buy, at £20.*

buyer /ˈbaɪ.əʳ/ [US] /-ɚ/ *noun* **[C]** **1** someone who buys something expensive such as a house: *He's still looking for a buyer **for** his house.* **2** someone whose job it is to decide what will be bought by a company: *She's the buyer for a stylish boutique in Dublin.*

buy [BELIEVE] /baɪ/ *verb* **[T]** **bought, bought** *SLANG* to believe that something is true: *She'll never buy that story about you getting lost!*

PHRASAL VERBS WITH **buy** ▼

▲ **buy into *sth*** *phrasal verb DISAPPROVING* to completely believe in a set of ideas: *I don't buy into all that New Age stuff.*

▲ **buy *sb* off** *phrasal verb* **[M]** to pay someone so that they do not cause you any trouble: *They tried to buy the guard at the bank off but he told the police and the gang were arrested.*

▲ **buy *sb* out** [BUSINESS] *phrasal verb* **[M]** to buy a part of a company or building from someone else so that you own all of it: *Allied Chemicals have been trying to buy out their competitor's share in the target company.*

▲ **buy *yourself* out** [ARMY] *phrasal verb* **[R]** *UK* If you buy yourself out of the armed forces, you pay a sum of money so that you can leave earlier than you had previously agreed to.

▲ **buy *sth* up** *phrasal verb* **[M]** To buy something up is to buy large amounts of it, or all that is available: *He bought up all the land in the surrounding area.*

buyback /ˈbaɪ.bæk/ *noun* **[C or U]** when a business or person sells something, especially SHARES (= equal parts of its ownership), and then buys them again according to a fixed agreement: *His company have just announced a $1 billion stock buyback.*

buyer's market /ˌbaɪ.əzˈmɑː.kɪt/ [US] /-ɚzˈmɑːr-/ *noun* **[S]** a time when there are more goods for sale than there are people to buy them, so prices tend to be low

buyout /ˈbaɪ.aʊt/ *noun* **[C]** (in business) a situation where a person or group buys all the shares belonging to a company and so gets control of it: *a management buyout*

buzz /bʌz/ *verb* **1** **[I]** to make a continuous low sound such as the one a bee makes: *I can hear something buzzing.* **2** **[I usually + adv or prep]** to be busy and and full of energy: *The place was buzzing **(with** excitement).* ○ *Reporters were buzzing **around**, trying to get the full story.* **3 head/mind is buzzing** If your head/mind is buzzing, you are thinking about many different things at the same time. **4** **[I or T]** to press a buzzer in order to get someone's attention: *I buzzed him but there was no answer.* ○ *The first person to buzz may answer.* **5** **[T]** *INFORMAL* If an aircraft buzzes a place or people, it flies over them very low and fast.

buzz /bʌz/ *noun* **[S]** **1** a continuous low sound: *I heard a buzz and then saw the plane in the distance.* **2** *INFORMAL* a feeling of excitement, energy and pleasure: *I love cycling fast – it **gives me a** real buzz.* ○ *I **get a** buzz **out of** public speaking.*

• **give *sb* a buzz** *INFORMAL* to telephone someone: *I'll give you a buzz next week.*

buzzer /ˈbʌz.əʳ/ [US] /-ɚ/ *noun* **[C]** an electronic device that makes a buzzing sound: *I pressed the buzzer and after a while someone came to the door.*

▲ **buzz off** *phrasal verb INFORMAL* **1** to go away: *I've got some stuff to do at home, so I'm going to buzz off now.* **2** If someone says buzz off to another person, they are telling them to go away in a rude way: *Buzz off, I'm busy!*

buzzard /ˈbʌz.əd/ [US] /-ɚd/ *noun* **[C]** a large European bird that is a type of HAWK, or a type of North American VULTURE that feeds on the flesh of dead animals

buzzword /ˈbʌz.wɜːd/ [US] /-wɝːd/ *noun* **[C]** a word or expression from a particular subject area, that has become fashionable by being used a lot, especially on television and in the newspapers: *'Diversity' is the new buzzword in education.*

by [CAUSE] /baɪ/ *prep* used to show the person or thing that does something: *The motorcycle was driven by a tiny bald man.* ○ *We were amazed by what she told us.* ○ *I'm reading some short stories (written) by Chekhov.* ○ *The book was translated by a well-known author.* ○ *I felt frightened by the anger in his voice.*

by [METHOD] /baɪ/ *prep* used to show how something is done: *They travelled across Europe by train/car.* ○ *She did the decorating **(all)** by herself* (= alone, without help from anyone). ○ *We went in by* (= through) *the front door.* ○ *Do you wish to be paid in cash or by cheque?* ○ *He learned English by listen**ing** to the radio.* ○ *Suddenly, she grabbed him by the arm* (= took hold of this part of his body). ○ *I refuse to live by* (= following) *their rules.*

by [NOT LATER THAN] /baɪ/ *prep* not later than; at or before: *She had promised to be back by five o'clock.* ○ *The application must be in by the 31st to be accepted.* ○ *By the time I got to the station the train had already gone.*

by [MEASUREMENT] /baɪ/ *prep* used to show measurements or amounts: *Our office floor space measured twelve metres by ten* (= was twelve metres in one direction and ten in the other). ○ *Their wages were increased by 12%.* ○ *Freelance workers are paid by the hour* (= for every hour they work). ○ *These telephones have sold by the thousand.*

by [DURING] /baɪ/ *prep* during: *We travelled by night and rested by day.*

• **by and by** *OLD-FASHIONED* after a short period: *By and by a man appeared.*

by [NEAR] /baɪ/ *prep, adv* near, beside or (in distance or time) past: *A small child stood sullenly by her side.* ○ *He wanted to keep her close by him always.* ○ *The policewoman walked by* (= past) *(them) without saying a word.* ○ *The years flew by.*

by [PERSONAL INFORMATION] /baɪ/ **by nature/profession/trade, etc.** used when describing someone's character/job, etc: *She is, by nature, a sunny, positive sort of a person.* ○ *He's a plumber by trade.* ○ *She was, by profession, a lawyer.*

by [PERMISSION] /baɪ/ **be all right/fine by *sb*** If something is all right/fine by someone, they agree that it can happen: *"I'd prefer to go later." "That's fine by me."* ○ *If it's all right by you, I'd like to leave now.*

bye(-bye) /ˈbaɪ.baɪ/ *exclamation INFORMAL* goodbye: *Are you going? Bye then.* ○ *Bye-bye, see you tomorrow.*

• **go (to) bye-byes** *MAINLY UK INFORMAL* an expression used by or to young children, meaning 'go to sleep': *It's getting late – it's time for you to go to bye-byes.*

by-election /ˈbaɪ.ɪˌlek.ʃᵊn/ *noun* [C] in the UK, an election which happens at a different time from a main election, to choose a member of parliament or representative to replace one who has died or left their job

bygone /ˈbaɪ.gɒn/ [US] /-gɑːn/ *adj* [before n] belonging to or happening in a past time: *a bygone era*

bygones /ˈbaɪ.gɒnz/ [US] /-gɑːnz/ *plural noun* **let bygones be bygones** used to tell someone they should forget about unpleasant things that happened in the past, and especially to forgive and forget something bad that someone has done to them: *Forget about the argument you two had, just let bygones be bygones and be friends again.*

bylaw, **bye-law** /ˈbaɪ.lɔː/ [US] /-lɑː/ *noun* [C] **1** a law made by local government that only relates to its particular region **2** *US* a rule which governs the members of an organization

by-line /ˈbaɪ.laɪn/ *noun* [C] *SPECIALIZED* a line at the top of a newspaper or magazine article giving the writer's name

BYOB /ˌbiː.waɪ.əʊˈbiː/ [US] /-oʊ-/ *WRITTEN ABBREVIATION FOR* bring your own bottle: used on a party invitation to request that guests bring their own alcoholic drinks

bypass /ˈbaɪ.pɑːs/ [US] /-pæs/ *verb* [T] **1** to avoid something by going around it: *We were in a hurry so we decided to bypass Canterbury because we knew there'd be a lot of traffic.* **2** to ignore a rule or official authority: *They bypassed the committee and went straight to senior management.*

bypass /ˈbaɪ.pɑːs/ [US] /-pæs/ *noun* [C] a road built around a town or village so that traffic does not need to travel through it

ˈbypass (opeˌration) *noun* [C] a medical operation in which the flow of a person's blood is changed to avoid a diseased part of their heart: *a triple bypass operation*

byplay /ˈbaɪ.pleɪ/ *noun* [U] things that happen, especially in a play, at the same time as the main action but that are less important than it

by-product /ˈbaɪˌprɒd.ʌkt/ [US] /-ˌprɑː.dəkt/ *noun* [C] something that is produced as a result of making something else, or something unexpected that happens as a result of something: *Buttermilk is a by-product **of** making butter.* ○ *Illness is one of the by-products **of** overcrowded housing.*

byre /baɪəʳ/ [US] /baɪr/ *noun* [C] *UK OLD-FASHIONED* a building in which cattle are kept; a **cowshed**

bystander /ˈbaɪˌstæn.dəʳ/ [US] /-dɚ/ *noun* [C] a person who is standing near and watching something that is happening but is not taking part in it: *Many **innocent** bystanders were injured by the explosion.*

byte /baɪt/ *noun* [C] *SPECIALIZED* a unit of computer information, consisting of a group of (usually eight) BITS ➲See also **gigabyte**; **kilobyte**; **megabyte**.

byway /ˈbaɪ.weɪ/ *noun* [C] a small road that not many cars or people travel on

byword /ˈbaɪ.wɜːd/ [US] /-wɝːd/ *noun* [C] a person or thing that is very closely connected with a particular quality: *Their shops are a byword **for** good value.*

byzantine /bɪˈzæn.taɪn/ /ˈbɪz.ᵊn.tiːn/ *adj FORMAL DISAPPROVING* difficult to understand and complicated: *rules of byzantine complexity*

C

[C]

C [LETTER] *(plural* **C's** or **Cs**), **c** *(plural* **c's** or **cs**) /siː/ *noun* **[C]** the 3rd letter of the English alphabet: *Does she spell her name with a C or with a K?*

C [MUSIC] /siː/ *noun* **[C or U]** *plural* **C's** or **Cs** a note in Western music: *This song is in* ***(the key of)*** *C.*

C [MARK] /siː/ *noun* **[C or U]** *plural* **C's** or **Cs** a mark in an exam or for a piece of work which shows that your work is average: *Rachel got (a) C for her French exam.*

C [NUMBER] /siː/ *noun* **[C]** the sign used in the Roman system for the number 100

C [TEMPERATURE] /siː/ *noun* **[after n]** *ABBREVIATION FOR* **Celsius**: *The temperature today reached 25°C.*

C [COMPUTER LANGUAGE] /siː/ *noun* a computer programming language

C++ /ˌsiː.plʌsˈplʌs/ *noun* an OBJECT-ORIENTED version of C

c *prep* (*ALSO* **ca**) *ABBREVIATION FOR* **circa**

cab [PART OF VEHICLE] /kæb/ *noun* **[C]** the separate front part of a large vehicle, such as a truck, bus or train, in which the driver sits

cab [VEHICLE] /kæb/ *noun* **[C]** **1** a taxi: *It'll save time if we go* ***by*** *cab.* ➲See also **minicab**. **2** in the past, a vehicle pulled by a horse, used as a taxi

cabal /kəˈbæl/ /-ˈbɑːl/ *noun* **[C]** *DISAPPROVING* a small group of people who plan secretly to take action, especially political action: *He was assassinated by a cabal* ***of*** *aides within his own regime.*

cabaret /ˈkæb.ə.reɪ/ [US] /-ɚ.eɪ/ *noun* **[C or U]** a performance of popular music, singing or dancing, especially in a restaurant or bar: *a cabaret* ***act****.*

cabbage /ˈkæb.ɪdʒ/ *noun* **1** **[C or U]** a large round vegetable with large green, white or purple leaves, which can be eaten cooked or raw: *a savoy cabbage* ○ *red/white cabbage* ➲See picture **Vegetables** on page Centre 2 **2** **[C]** *UK OFFENSIVE* a person who has lost all their powers of thought or speech usually as the result of a serious accident or illness

cabbie, **cabby** /ˈkæb.i/ *noun* **[C]** *INFORMAL* a driver of a TAXI (= car that you pay to travel in)

caber /ˈkeɪ.bəʳ/ [US] /-bɚ/ *noun* **[C]** a long heavy wooden pole which is thrown as a test of strength in traditional sports competitions in Scotland: ***tossing*** (= throwing) *the caber*

cabin [HOUSE] /ˈkæb.ɪn/ *noun* **[C]** a small, simple house made of wood: *a log cabin*

cabin [SHIP] /ˈkæb.ɪn/ *noun* **[C]** a small room where you sleep in a ship

cabin [AIRCRAFT] /ˈkæb.ɪn/ *noun* **[C]** the area where passengers sit in an aircraft

ˈcabin ˌboy *noun* **[C]** *OLD-FASHIONED* a boy who is a servant on a ship

ˈcabin ˌcrew *group noun* **[C]** (*ALSO* **cabin staff**) in an aircraft, the people whose job it is to take care of the passengers

ˈcabin ˌcruiser *noun* **[C]** a boat powered by a motor, with one or more small rooms for sleeping in

cabinet [FURNITURE] /ˈkæb.ɪ.nət/ *noun* **[C]** a piece of furniture with shelves, cupboards, or drawers, which is used for storing or showing things: *Valuable pieces of china were on display in a glass-fronted cabinet.* ○ *a* ***bathroom/filing*** *cabinet*

COMMON LEARNER ERROR

cabinet **or** office?

Cabinet cannot be used to mean a room where people work. In English the word for this is office.

There will be a meeting at 9.00 in my office.
~~*There will be a meeting at 9.00 in my cabinet.*~~

Cabinet [GOVERNMENT], **cabinet** /ˈkæb.ɪ.nət/ *group noun* **[C usually sing]** a small group of the most important people elected to government, who make the main decisions about what should happen: *The Cabinet meet/meets every Thursday.* ○ *a cabinet* ***minister****.* ○ *The Prime Minister has announced a cabinet* ***reshuffle*** (= changes in the Cabinet).

ˈcabinet ˌmaker *noun* **[C]** a person who makes or repairs good quality furniture

ˈcabin ˌfever *noun* **[U]** when you feel angry and bored because you have been inside for too long: *The rain had kept me indoors all weekend and I was beginning to get cabin fever.*

cable [WIRE] /ˈkeɪ.bl̩/ *noun* **[C or U]** a wire, covered by plastic, that carries electricity, telephone signals, etc: *a length of cable* ○ *The road has been dug up in order to* ***lay*** *cables.* ○ *overhead power cables*

cable [SYSTEM] /ˈkeɪ.bl̩/ *noun* **[U]** the system of sending television programmes or telephone signals along wires under the ground: *The office has gone over to cable.* ○ *cable TV* ○ *This channel is only available* ***on*** *cable.*

ˈcable ˌcar *noun* **[C]** **1** a vehicle which hangs from and is moved by a CABLE (= thick strong wire), and transports people up steep slopes **2** *US* a vehicle on a CABLE RAILWAY

ˈcable ˌrailway *noun* **[C]** *US* a transport system that uses CABLES (= thick strong wires) under the road to pull passenger vehicles up steep slopes

ˈcable ˌstitch *noun* **[U]** a pattern of wool used in knitting, which looks like twisted CABLES

ˌcable (TˈV) *noun* **[U]** (*ALSO* **cable television**) a system of sending television pictures and sound along CABLES (= wires buried under the ground): *Do you have cable?*

caboodle /kəˈbuː.dl̩/ *noun INFORMAL* **the whole (kit and) caboodle** the whole of something, including everything that is connected to it: *I like everything about summer – the light, the warmth, the clothes – the whole caboodle.*

caboose /kəˈbuːs/ *noun* **[C]** *US FOR* **guard's van**

ˈcab ˌstand *noun* **[C]** *US FOR* **taxi rank**

cacao /kəˈkaʊ/ *noun* **[U]** the seeds of a tropical tree, from which chocolate and COCOA are made: *cacao beans*

cache /kæʃ/ *noun* **[C]** a hidden store of things, or the place where they are kept: *an arms cache* ○ *a cache* ***of*** *explosives/weapons/drugs*

ˌcache (ˈmemory) *noun* **[C or U]** an area or type of computer MEMORY in which information that is often in use can be stored temporarily and accessed especially quickly: *256Kb secondary cache*

cachet /ˈkæʃ.eɪ/ [US] /-ˈ-/ *noun* **[S or U]** *FORMAL* a quality which marks someone or something as special and worth respect and admiration: *This type of jacket used to have* ***a certain*** *cachet.*

cack-handed /ˌkækˈhæn.dɪd/ *adj UK SLANG DISAPPROVING* describes someone who often drops or breaks things or does things badly: *That's a cack-handed way of going about it!*

cackle /ˈkæk.l̩/ *verb* **[I]** **1** to make the loud, unpleasant sound of a chicken: *The hens cackled in alarm.* **2** *DISAPPROVING* to laugh in a loud, high voice: *A group of women were cackling in a corner.* ○ *a cackling witch*
cackle /ˈkæk.l̩/ *noun* **[C]**

cacophony /kəˈkɒf.ə.ni/ [US] /-ˈkɑː.fə-/ *noun* **[S]** an unpleasant mixture of loud sounds: *What a cacophony!* ○ *As we entered the farmyard we were met with* ***a*** *cacophony* ***of*** *animal sounds.* **cacophonous** /kəˈkɒf.ə.nəs/ [US] /-ˈkɑː.fə-/ *adj*

cactus /ˈkæk.təs/ *noun* **[C]** *plural* **cacti** or **cactuses** any of many types of desert plant usually with sharp spines and thick stems for storing water

cad /kæd/ *noun* **[C]** *OLD-FASHIONED* a man who behaves badly or dishonestly, especially to women: *He's a cad* ***and a bounder*** *– I'm not in the least surprised he let you down.*

cadaver /kəˈdæv.əʳ/ [US] /-ɚ/ *noun* **[C]** *SPECIALIZED* a dead human body
cadaverous /kəˈdæv.ᵊr.əs/ [US] /-ɚ-/ *adj* looking pale, thin and ill: *cadaverous features*

caddie, **caddy** /ˈkæd.i/ *noun* **[C]** a person who carries the equipment for someone who is playing golf ➲See picture **Sports** on page Centre 10

caddie (**caddying, caddied, caddied**), **caddy** /'kæd.i/ *verb* [I] to be a caddie for someone

caddy /'kæd.i/ *noun* [C] a small container, especially one for storing tea leaves: *tea caddy*

cadence [VOICE] /'keɪ.dᵊnts/ *noun* [C] the regular rise and fall of the voice

cadence [MUSIC] /'keɪ.dᵊnts/ *noun* [C] *SPECIALIZED* a set of CHORDS (= different notes played together) at the end of a piece of music

cadet /kə'det/ *noun* [C] a student in the armed forces or the police

cadge /kædʒ/ *verb* [T] *INFORMAL OFTEN DISAPPROVING* to (try to) get something from someone else without paying for it: *Can I cadge a lift home?* ○ *He's always cadging free meals and free trips* ***from/off*** *his clients.* **cadger** /'kædʒ.əʳ/ [US] /-ɚ/ *noun* [C]

cadmium /'kæd.mi.əm/ *noun* [U] a soft bluish white metallic element

cadre /'kɑː.dəʳ/ [US] /-dɚ/ *group noun* [C] a small group of trained people who form the basic unit of a military, political or business organization
cadre /'kɑː.dəʳ/ [US] /-dɚ/ *noun* [C] a member of such a group

caesarean (section), *US USUALLY* **cesarean** /sɪˌzeə.ri.ən'sek.ʃᵊn/ [US] /-ˌzer.i-/ *noun* [C or U] an operation in which a woman's womb is cut open to allow a baby to be born: *I had to have a caesarean.* ○ *The baby was born* ***by*** *caesarean.* ○ *a caesarean* ***birth/delivery***

café, cafe /'kæf.eɪ/ *noun* [C] (*UK INFORMAL* **caff**) a restaurant where only small meals and drinks that usually do not contain alcohol are served: *There's a little café on the corner that serves very good coffee.*

cafeteria /ˌkæf.ə'tɪə.ri.ə/ [US] /-'tɪr.i-/ *noun* [C] a restaurant (often in a factory, a college or an office building) where people collect food and drink from a serving area and take it to a table themselves after paying for it

cafetiere /ˌkæf.ə'tjeəʳ/ [US] /-'tjer/ *noun* [C] a glass container for making coffee, in which hot water is poured onto coffee and then a FILTER (= net) is pushed down into the container to keep the solids at the bottom ➲See picture **In the Kitchen** on page Centre 16

caff /kæf/ *noun* [C] *UK INFORMAL FOR* **café**

caffeine /'kæf.iːn/ *noun* [U] a chemical, found for example in tea and coffee, which is a STIMULANT (= something which makes people more active)

caftan, kaftan /'kæf.tæn/ *noun* [C] a long, loose piece of clothing with wide sleeves, of the type worn in the Middle East

cage /keɪdʒ/ *noun* [C] a space surrounded on all sides by bars or wire, in which animals or birds are kept **cage** /keɪdʒ/ *verb* [T usually passive] *caged birds/animals* ○ *Sam's been prowling about* ***like a*** *caged* ***animal*** *all morning.*

cagey /'keɪ.dʒi/ *adj* **cagier, cagiest** *INFORMAL* unwilling to give information: *He was very cagey* ***about*** *what happened at the meeting.* **cagily** /'keɪ.dʒɪ.li/ *adv* **caginess** /'keɪ.dʒɪ.nəs/ *noun* [U]

cagoule, kagoule /kə'guːl/ *noun* [C] *UK* a light waterproof jacket with a HOOD (= head cover) which protects the wearer against wet and windy weather: *Bad weather is likely, so please wear walking boots and a cagoule.*

cahoots /kə'huːts/ *plural noun INFORMAL* **in cahoots (with)** acting together with others for an illegal or dishonest purpose: *a banker and a government minister were in cahoots over a property deal* ○ *It's reckoned that someone in the government was in cahoots with the assassin.*

caiman /'keɪ.mən/ *noun* [C] *ANOTHER SPELLING OF* **cayman**

cairn /keən/ [US] /kern/ *noun* [C] a small pile of stones made, especially on mountains, to mark a place or as a MEMORIAL (= an object to make people remember someone or something)

cajole /kə'dʒəʊl/ [US] /-'dʒoʊl/ *verb* [I or T] to persuade someone to do something they might not want to do, by pleasant talk and (sometimes false) promises: *He really knows how to cajole people* ***into*** *doing what he wants.* ○ *I managed to cajole her* ***out of*** *leaving too early.* ○ *The most effective technique is to cajole rather than to threaten.*

Cajun /'keɪ.dʒᵊn/ *noun* [C] a person who lives in the US state of Louisiana and whose relations in the past were French-speaking Canadians **Cajun** /'keɪ.dʒᵊn/ *adj*: *Cajun cooking/food* ○ *Lafayette is the home of Cajun music/dance.*

cake [FOOD] /keɪk/ *noun* [C or U] a sweet food made with a mixture of flour, eggs, fat and sugar: *Would you like a piece of/a slice of/some cake.* ○ *chocolate/sponge cake* ○ *a birthday/christmas cake* ○ *cream cakes* ○ *He* ***made/baked*** *a delicious cake.* ➲See also **oatcake, pancake**.
• **the slice/share of the cake** the amount of money, goods, etc., available: *Everyone should have a fair slice of the cake.*
• **have *your* cake and eat it** to have or do two things at the same time that are impossible to have or do at the same time: *You can't have your cake and eat it – if you want more local services, you can't expect to pay less tax.*

cake [SHAPE] /keɪk/ *noun* [C] a small flat object made by pressing together a soft substance: *fish/potato cakes* ○ *a cake* ***of*** *soap*

cake [COVER] /keɪk/ *verb* [T usually passive] to cover something or someone thickly with a substance that then dries out: *The men were caked* ***in*** *layers of filth and grime.* ○ *boots caked* ***with*** *mud*

cakewalk /'keik.wɔːk/ [US] /-wɑːk/ *noun* [S] *US INFORMAL* something which is very easy to achieve, or a one-sided competitive event where the opposition gives up without a fight: *The Superbowl was a cakewalk* ***for*** *the Forty-Niners.*

calabash /'kæl.ə.bæʃ/ *noun* [C] (a tropical plant which produces) a large fruit, the outside of which becomes hard when dried and can be used as a container

calamine (lotion) /ˌkæl.ə.maɪn'ləʊ.ʃᵊn/ [US] /-'loʊ-/ *noun* [U] a pink liquid used to reduce pain on sore skin

calamity /kə'læm.ɪ.ti/ [US] /-ə.t̬i/ *noun* [C] a serious accident or bad event causing damage or suffering: *A series of calamities ruined them – floods, a failed harvest and the death of a son.* **calamitous** /kə'læm.ɪ.təs/ [US] /-t̬əs/ *adj* **calamitously** /kə'læm.ɪ.tə.sli/ [US] /-t̬ə-/ *adv*

calcify /'kæl.sɪ.faɪ/ *verb* [I or T] to become hard or make something hard, especially by the addition of substances containing CALCIUM

calcium /'kæl.si.ᵊm/ *noun* [U] a chemical element which is present in teeth, bones and chalk

calculate /'kæl.kjʊ.leɪt/ *verb* [T] to judge the number or amount of something by using the information that you already have, and adding, multiplying, subtracting or dividing numbers: *The cost of the damage caused by the recent storms has been calculated* ***as/at*** *over £5 million.* ○ *The new tax system would be calculated* ***on*** *the value of property owned by an individual.* ○ [+ question word] *At some stage we need to calculate* ***when*** *the project will be finished.* ○ [+ that] *He's calculated* ***that*** *it would take him two years to save up enough for a car.* **calculation** /ˌkæl.kjʊ'leɪ.ʃᵊn/ *noun* [C or U] *The calculations that you* ***did/made*** *contained a few inaccuracies.*
calculator /'kæl.kjʊ.leɪ.təʳ/ [US] /-t̬ɚ/ *noun* [C] a small electronic device which is used for doing calculations: *a* ***pocket*** *calculator* ➲See picture **In the Office** on page Centre 15
▲ **calculate on *sth*** *phrasal verb* to expect or depend on a particular amount or time: *We're calculating on about 30 guests.*

calculated /'kæl.kjʊ.leɪ.tɪd/ [US] /-t̬ɪd/ *adj* planned or arranged in order to produce a particular effect: *It was a cruel, calculated crime with absolutely no justification.* ○ [+ to infinitive] *It's a policy that was hardly calculated to* (= will not) *win votes.*

ˌcalculated 'risk *noun* [C] a risk which you consider worth taking because the result, if it is successful, will be so good: *The director took a calculated risk in giving the film's main role to an unknown actor.*

calculating /'kæl.kjʊ.leɪ.tɪŋ/ [US] /-t̬ɪŋ/ *adj* tending to control situations for your own advantage in a way that is slightly unpleasant and causes people not to trust you: *In the film she's depicted as a very* ***cold and*** *calculating character.* **calculation** /ˌkæl.kjʊ'leɪ.ʃᵊn/ *noun* [U] *There's an element of calculation in his behaviour that makes me distrust him.*

calculus /ˈkæl.kjʊ.ləs/ *noun* [U] *SPECIALIZED* an area of advanced mathematics in which continually changing values are studied

caldron /ˈkɔːl.drən/ [US] /ˈkɑːl-/ *noun* [C] *US FOR* **cauldron**

calendar /ˈkæl.ɪn.dəʳ/ [US] /-dɚ/ *noun* [C] **1** a printed table showing all the days, weeks and months of the year **2** the system used to measure and arrange the days, weeks, months and special events of the year according to a belief system or tradition: *the Christian/Jewish/Chinese calendar* **3** a list of events and dates within a particular year that are important for an organization or for the people involved in a particular activity: *the political/school/sporting calendar*

ˈcalendar ˌmonth *noun* [C] one of the twelve named months that the year is divided into: *Your salary will be paid on the third week of each calendar month.*

ˈcalendar ˌyear *noun* [C] a period of 365 or 366 days, starting on January 1st and ending on December 31st

calf [ANIMAL] /kɑːf/ [US] /kæf/ *noun* [C] *plural* **calves** a young cow, or the young of various other large mammals such as elephants and whales ➲See also **calve**.

• **in calf** If a cow is in calf, it is pregnant.

calf [LEG] /kɑːf/ [US] /kæf/ *noun* [C] *plural* **calves** the thick curved part at the back of the human leg between the knee and the foot: *She's been unable to play since January because of a torn calf* ***muscle***. ➲See picture **The Body** on page Centre 5

calf-length /ˈkɑːf.leŋkθ/ [US] /kæf-/ *adj* describes clothing or boots that end at the middle point between the foot and the knee: *a calf-length skirt*

calfskin /ˈkɑːf.skɪn/ [US] /ˈkæf-/ *noun* [U] leather made from the skin of a young cow: *calfskin boots*

calibrated /ˈkæl.ɪ.breɪ.tɪd/ [US] /-t̬ɪd/ *adj SPECIALIZED* describes tools or other devices that are adjusted or marked for making accurate measurements: *a calibrated stick for measuring the amount of oil in an engine* **calibrate** /ˈkæl.ɪ.breɪt/ *verb* [T] **calibration** /ˌkæl.ɪˈbreɪ.ʃən/ *noun* [C or U]

calibre [QUALITY] *UK, US* **caliber** /ˈkæl.ɪ.bəʳ/ [US] /-bɚ/ *noun* [U] the degree of quality or excellence of someone or something: *If teaching paid more it might attract people* ***of (a) higher*** *calibre.* ○ *The competition entries were* ***of*** *such (a)* ***high*** *calibre that judging them was very difficult.*

calibre [MEASUREMENT] *UK, US* **caliber** /ˈkæl.ɪ.bəʳ/ [US] /-bɚ/ *noun* [C or U] the width of the inside of a pipe, especially of the long cylindrical part of a gun, or the width of a bullet

calico /ˈkæl.ɪ.kəʊ/ [US] /-koʊ/ *noun* [U] a heavy plain cloth made from cotton

calif /ˈkeɪ.lɪf/ *noun* [C] *ANOTHER SPELLING OF* **caliph**

calipers /ˈkæl.ɪ.pəz/ [US] /-pɚz/ *plural noun US FOR* **callipers** TOOL

caliph, calif, kalif, khalif /ˈkeɪ.lɪf/ *noun* [C] a Muslim ruler

calisthenics /ˌkæl.ɪsˈθen.ɪks/ *group noun* [U] *US FOR* **callisthenics**

call [NAME] /kɔːl/ [US] /kɑːl/ *verb* [T + obj + n] to give someone or something a name, or to know or address someone by a particular name: *They've called the twins Katherine and Thomas.* ○ *What's that actor called that we saw in the film last night?* ○ *His real name is Jonathan, but they've always called him 'Johnny'.* ○ *What's her new novel called?* ○ *I wish he wouldn't keep calling me 'dear' – it's so patronising!*

• **call *sb* names** If a person, especially a child, calls someone names, he or she addresses that person with a name which is intended to be offensive: *Tom's worried that if he wears glasses at school the other children will call him names.*

call [TELEPHONE] /kɔːl/ [US] /kɑːl/ *verb* [I or T] to telephone someone: *He called (you) last night when you were out.* ○ *She called (me) this morning at the office and we had a brief chat.* ○ *I've been calling all morning but I can't get through.* ○ *Do you think we should call the police?*

• **call collect** *US* (*US ALSO AND UK* **reverse (the) charges**) to make a telephone call which is paid for by the person who receives it

call /kɔːl/ [US] /kɑːl/ *noun* [C] when you use the telephone: *I got a call* ***from*** *an old college friend last night.* ○ *If there are any calls* ***for*** *me, could you write them down next to the telephone?* ○ *I've just got a couple of calls to* ***make***. ○ *That decorator you rang about painting the house – did he ever* ***return*** *your call?* ○ *The radio station* ***received*** *a lot of calls complaining about the show's bad language.* ○ *Before six o'clock, calls are charged at peak rate.*

caller /ˈkɔː.ləʳ/ [US] /ˈkɑː.lɚ/ *noun* [C] someone who makes a telephone call, especially a member of the public who telephones a radio or television programme while it is being broadcast: *I'd just like to comment on what your previous caller was saying.*

call [VISIT] /kɔːl/ [US] /kɑːl/ *verb* [I] to visit someone, especially for a short time: *The electrician must have called* ***(round)*** *this morning when we were out – there's a note on the door mat.*

call /kɔːl/ [US] /kɑːl/ *noun* [C] a short, especially official visit, usually made by someone whose job is connected with health: *Doctor Seward is out* ***on a*** *call this morning.* ○ *The nurse has got a few calls to* ***make*** *this afternoon.* ○ *SLIGHTLY OLD-FASHIONED I thought I'd* ***pay*** *a call* ***on*** (= visit) *an old friend of mine this weekend.*

• **on call** Some types of workers, especially doctors, are described as being on call if they are available to make official visits at any time when they are needed, whether they are at home or at work: *She's a doctor, so she's often on call at the weekend.*

caller /ˈkɔː.ləʳ/ [US] /ˈkɑː.lɚ/ *noun* [C] a visitor

call [SHOUT/CRY] /kɔːl/ [US] /kɑːl/ *verb* [I or T] to say something in a loud voice, especially in order to attract someone's attention, or (of animals) to make a loud, high sound, especially to another animal: *Someone in the crowd called* ***(out)*** *his name.* ○ *Did you call?* ○ [+ speech] *"Hey, you! Come over here!" she called.* ○ *The blackbird called* ***to*** *its mate.*

• **call *sb's* bluff** to make someone prove that what they are saying is true, or to make someone prove that they will really do what they say they will do, because you do not believe them

• **call *your* shot** *US* to state clearly your intentions

• **call the shots** (*ALSO* **call the tune**) to be in the position of being able to make the decisions which will influence a situation

call /kɔːl/ [US] /kɑːl/ *noun* **1** [C] when an animal makes a sound or when someone shouts something: *The whale has a very distinctive call.* ○ *She could hear calls* ***for help*** *from inside the burning building.* ○ *I'll be in the next room, so* ***give*** *me a call if you need any help.* **2** [U] when people want or need a particular thing: *There's* ***not much*** *call* ***for*** *fur coats these days.* ○ *FORMAL I certainly don't think there's any call* ***for*** *that sort of language, young lady!* **3** [C] a demand for something to happen: *Management have so far ignored the union's calls* ***for*** *stricter safety regulations.*

• **call of nature** *HUMOROUS* the need to use the toilet

call [ASK TO COME] /kɔːl/ [US] /kɑːl/ *verb* [I or T] to ask someone to come to you: *She called me* ***over*** *to where she was sitting.* ○ *I keep the bedroom door open in case the children call* ***(for)*** *me in the night.* ○ *I was called* ***to*** *an emergency meeting this morning.* ○ *At school she was always being called* ***into*** *the headteacher's office.*

• **call/bring *sth* to mind** to remember something: *Her name is familiar, but I can't quite call to mind where I've heard it.*

• **call into question** *FORMAL* to cause doubts about something: *The fact that a party can be voted into power by a minority of the electorate calls into question the country's electoral system.*

call [CONSIDER] /kɔːl/ [US] /kɑːl/ *verb* [T + obj + n] to consider someone or something to be: *He knows a lot of people, but only one or two that he'd call close friends.* ○ *One sandwich and a lettuce leaf – I don't call that a meal!* ○ *I'm not calling you a liar – I'm just suggesting that you misunderstood the facts of the situation.*

• **call it quits** *INFORMAL* to stop doing something, or to agree with someone that a debt has been paid and that no one owes anything more: *I paid for last week's shopping and you paid for this week's, so let's call it quits.*

• **call it a day** *INFORMAL* to stop the work you are doing: *I'm getting a bit tired now – shall we call it a day?*
• **call a spade a spade** *INFORMAL* to say the truth about something, even if it is not polite or pleasant
• **call *sth your* own** to consider something as belonging to you: *I don't aspire to anything very grand – I just want a place I can call my own.*

call [DECIDE ON] /kɔːl/ [US] /kɑːl/ *verb* [T] to decide officially to have a particular event or take particular action: *The managing director has called* ***a meeting*** *to discuss pay levels.* ○ *The papers are predicting that the Prime Minister will call* ***an election*** *in the spring.* ○ *It's reckoned that the unions will call* ***a strike*** *if management will not agree to their demands.* ○ *They had to call* ***a halt to*** (= end) *the match because of the heavy rain.*
• **call for order** (*ALSO* **call *sth* to order**) to ask people in a meeting to stop talking so that the meeting can continue: *She called for order/called the meeting to order.*

PHRASAL VERBS WITH **call**

▲ **call back** [RETURN] *phrasal verb* to return to a place in order to see someone or collect something: *She said she'd call back later to pick up that report.*
▲ **call *sb* back** [TELEPHONE] *phrasal verb* to telephone someone again, or to telephone someone who called you earlier: *I'm a bit busy – can I call you back later?*
▲ **call by** *phrasal verb* to visit somewhere for a short while on your way to somewhere else: *I just thought I'd call by on my way into town.*
▲ **call for *sb*** [COLLECT] *phrasal verb* to go to a place in order to collect someone: *I'll call for you at eight.*
▲ **call for *sth*** [DEMAND] *phrasal verb* to demand that something happens: *Members have called for his resignation.*
▲ **call for *sth*** [DESERVE] *phrasal verb* to need or deserve a particular action, remark or quality: *This calls for a celebration!* ○ *It's the sort of work that calls for a high level of concentration.* ○ *He told you that you were an idiot? Well, I don't think that was called for* (= I think it was rude and not deserved)*!*
▲ **call forth *sth*** *phrasal verb FORMAL* to cause something to exist: *The proposed shopping centre has called forth an angry response from local residents.*
▲ **call *sb* in** [ASK FOR HELP] *phrasal verb* [M] to ask someone to come to help in a difficult situation: *A new team of detectives were called in to conduct a fresh inquiry.*
▲ **call *sth* in** [DEMAND MONEY] *phrasal verb* [M] If a bank calls in money, it demands that you pay back the money it has lent to you: *He needs to make the business work before the bank calls in the loan.*
▲ **call *sth* off** [ACTIVITY] *phrasal verb* [M] to decide that a planned event, especially a sports event, will not happen, or to end an activity because it is no longer useful or possible: *Tomorrow's match has been called off because of the icy weather.* ○ *The police have called off the search for the missing child until dawn tomorrow.*
▲ **call *sb/sth* off** [ATTACK] *phrasal verb* [M] to order a dog, or sometimes a person, to stop attacking someone or something: *I shouted to him to call his dog off, but he just laughed at me.* ○ *Call off your thugs, and I'll show you where the money is.*
▲ **call (in) on *sb*** [VISIT] *phrasal verb* to visit someone for a short time: *I thought we might call in on your mother on our way – I've got some magazines for her.*
▲ **call on *sb*** [ASK] *phrasal verb* [+ **to** infinitive] to ask someone in a formal way to do something: *They're calling on all men and boys over the age of 14 to join the army.* ○ *FORMAL I now call on everyone to raise a glass to the happy couple.*
▲ **call on *sth*** [USE] *phrasal verb FORMAL* to use something, especially a quality that you have, in order to achieve something: *She would have to call on all her strength if she was to survive the next few months.*
▲ **call *sb* up** [TELEPHONE] *phrasal verb* [M] *MAINLY US* to telephone someone: *My dad called me up to tell me the good news.*
▲ **call *sb* up** [ORDER TO JOIN] *phrasal verb* [M usually passive] to order someone to join a military organization or to ask someone to join an official, especially national, team: *He was called up when the war began.* ○ *Lucie Saint was called up for the final against Brazil.*

call-up /ˈkɔːl.ʌp/ [US] /ˈkɑːl-/ *noun* [C usually sing] **1** (*US ALSO* **draft**) an order to join a military organization: *She was very upset when her boyfriend received his call-up* ***(papers)***. **2** an invitation to play in an official, especially national, team: *Le Tissier was delighted when he received his England call-up .*
▲ **call *sth* up** [COMPUTING] *phrasal verb* [M] to find and show information on a computer screen: *You can use the search facility to call up all the occurrences of a particular word in a document.*

callanetics /kæl.əˈnet.ɪks/ [US] /-ˈnet̬-/ *noun* [U] *UK TRADEMARK* a system of physical exercise which involves frequently repeated small movements of the muscles and is intended to make the body firmer and more attractively shaped

ˈcall ˌbox [PHONE] *noun* [C] *UK* a **phone box**

ˈcall ˌbox [EMERGENCY] *noun* [C] *US* a small box next to a FREEWAY (= motorway) containing a telephone to use after an accident or other emergency

ˈcall ˌcentre *noun* [C] *UK* a large office in which a company's employees provide information to its customers, or sell or advertise its goods or services by telephone

ˈcall ˌgirl *noun* [C] a female prostitute who arranges her meetings with men over the telephone

calligraphy /kəˈlɪg.rə.fi/ *noun* [U] (the art of producing) beautiful writing, often created with a special pen or brush: *There's some wonderful calligraphy in these old manuscripts.*

call-in /ˈkɔːl.ɪn/ [US] /ˈkɑːl-/ *noun* [C] *US FOR* **phone-in**

calling /ˈkɔː.lɪŋ/ [US] /ˈkɑː-/ *noun* [C] *FORMAL* a strong desire to do a job, usually one which is socially valuable: *I'm glad she's going into medicine. It's a very worthy calling.*

callipers [TOOL] *UK, US* **calipers** /ˈkæl.ɪ.pəz/ [US] /-pɚz/ *plural noun* a device for measuring widths or distances, consisting of two long thin pieces of metal fixed together at one end

callipers [LEG SUPPORT] *UK* /ˈkæl.ɪ.pəz/ [US] /-pɚz/ *plural noun* (*US* **braces**) metal supports which are fastened to the legs of people who have difficulties with walking

callisthenics *UK, US* **calisthenics** /ˌkæl.ɪsˈθen.ɪks/ *group noun* [U] (a system of) simple physical exercises that are done to make the body firm, able to stretch easily and more attractive

callous /ˈkæl.əs/ *adj* unkind or cruel; without sympathy or feeling for other people: *It might sound callous, but I don't care if he's homeless. He's not living with me!* **callously** /ˈkæl.ə.sli/ *adv* **callousness** /ˈkæl.ə.snəs/ *noun* [U]

callow /ˈkæl.əʊ/ [US] /-oʊ/ *adj LITERARY DISAPPROVING* describes someone, especially a young person, who behaves in a way that shows a lack of experience, confidence or judgment: *Mark was just a callow* ***youth*** *of sixteen when he arrived in Paris.*

callus /ˈkæl.əs/ *noun* [C] an area of hard thickened skin, especially on the feet or hands: *He had workman's hands which were rough and covered with calluses.*

calm /kɑːm/ *adj* **1** peaceful and quiet; without hurried movement, anxiety or noise: *After a night of fighting, the streets are now calm.* ○ *He has a very calm manner.* ○ *Now* ***keep*** *calm everyone, the police are on their way.* **2** describes weather which is not windy, or the sea or a lake when it is still and has no waves
calm /kɑːm/ *verb* [T] to stop someone feeling upset, angry or excited: *He tried to calm the screaming baby by rocking it back and forth.*
• **calm *sb's* fears** to make someone feel less anxious about something
calmly /ˈkɑːm.li/ *adv* in a quiet or relaxed way: *She reacted surprisingly calmly to the news of his death.*
calmness /ˈkɑːm.nəs/ *noun* [U] (*LITERARY* **calm**) *It was the calm of the countryside that he loved so much.*
• **the calm before the storm** a quiet or peaceful period before a period during which there is great activity, argument or unpleasantness: *I like to get everything done before the guests arrive and relax for a moment in the calm before the storm.*
▲ **calm (*sb*) down** *phrasal verb* [M] to stop feeling upset, angry or excited, or to stop someone feeling this way: [R]

She sat down and took a few deep breaths to calm herself down. ○ *She was angry at first but we managed to calm her down.* ○ *Calm down, for goodness sake. It's nothing to get excited about!*

Calor gas /ˈkæ.lə,gæs/ [US] /-lɚ-/ *noun* [U] *UK TRADEMARK* a type of gas which is sold in metal containers and can be taken to places where there is no gas supply, and used for heating and cooking: *We took a calor gas* ***stove*** *for cooking on when we went camping.*

calorie [FOOD] /ˈkæl.ᵊr.i/ [US] /-ɚ-/ *noun* [C] a unit of energy which is used as a measurement for the amount of energy which food provides: *There are about fifty calories in an apple.* ○ *An athlete in training needs a lot of calories.* ○ *This drink can only help you to lose weight as a part of a calorie-***controlled diet**. ○ *He found calorie-***counting** *the best way of losing weight.*

calorific /ˌkæl.əˈrɪf.ɪk/ *adj*: *Fatty foods have a high calorific* ***value***. ○ *Although it's only a quick snack, a hamburger is very calorific* (= it contains a lot of calories.)

calorie [HEAT] /ˈkæl.ᵊr.i/ [US] /-ɚ-/ *noun* [C] *SPECIALIZED* a unit of heat energy

calumny /ˈkæl.əm.ni/ *noun* [C or U] *FORMAL* (the act of making) a statement about someone which is not true and is intended to damage the reputation of that person: *He was subjected to the most vicious calumny, but he never complained and never sued.*

calvados /ˈkæl.və.dɒs/ [US] /-doʊs/ *noun* [U] a type of brandy made from apples, produced in northern France

calve /kɑːv/ *verb* [I] When a cow calves, it gives birth to a CALF (= a young cow): *Four cows calved overnight.*

calves /kɑːvz/ *plural of* **calf**

Calvinist /ˈkæl.vɪ.nɪst/ *adj* (*ALSO* **Calvinistic**) **1** relating to the Christian teachings of John Calvin, especially the belief that God controls what happens on Earth: *Calvinist doctrine* **2** having severe moral standards and considering pleasure to be wrong or not neccessary: *Her parents have very Calvinist attitudes.* **Calvinism** /ˈkæl.vɪ.nɪ.zᵊm/ *noun* [U] **Calvinist** /ˈkæl.vɪ.nɪst/ *noun* [C]

calypso /kəˈlɪp.səʊ/ [US] /-soʊ/ *noun* [C] *plural* **calypsos** or **calypsoes** a type of popular West Indian song whose words, often invented as the song is sung, usually deal with a subject of interest at the present time

camaraderie /ˌkæm.əˈrɑː.dᵊr.i/ [US] /-dɚ-/ *noun* [S or U] *SLIGHTLY FORMAL* a feeling of friendliness towards people with whom you work or share an experience: *When you've been climbing alone for hours, there's a tremendous sense of camaraderie when you meet another climber.*

camber /ˈkæm.bəʳ/ [US] /-bɚ/ *noun* [C or U] a gradual slope down from the middle of a road to each edge, which helps water to flow off it

camcorder /ˈkæm,kɔː.dəʳ/ [US] /-ˌkɔːr.dɚ/ *noun* [C] a combination of a small video camera and recording device, in a single unit which can be held easily in one hand

came /keɪm/ *past simple of* **come**

camel [ANIMAL] /ˈkæm.ᵊl/ *noun* [C] a large animal with a long neck, that lives in the desert and has one or two HUMPS (= large raised areas of flesh) on its back ➲See also DROMEDARY. ➲See picture **Animals and Birds** on page Centre 4

camel [CLOTH] /ˈkæm.ᵊl/ *noun* [U] (*ALSO* **camel hair**) a soft, pale brown woollen cloth used to make coats

camellia /kəˈmiː.li.ə/ *noun* [C] a bush with dark shiny leaves and large white, pink or red flowers which are similar to ROSES

Camembert /ˈkæm.ᵊm.beəʳ/ [US] /-ber/ *noun* [C or U] a soft French cheese with a white outside and a creamy yellow inside

cameo [PERFORMANCE] /ˈkæm.i.əʊ/ [US] /-oʊ/ *noun* [C] *plural* **cameos** a small but noticeable part in a film or play, performed by a famous actor: *He appears briefly towards the end of the film in a cameo* ***role*** *as a priest.*

cameo [JEWELLERY] /ˈkæm.i.əʊ/ [US] /-oʊ/ *noun* [C] *plural* **cameos** a piece of usually oval jewellery on which there is a head or other shape of one colour on a background of a noticeably different colour: *a cameo* ***brooch***

camera /ˈkæm.rə/ *noun* [C] **1** a device for taking photographs or making films or television programmes: *I forgot to take my camera with me to Portugal, so I couldn't take any photos.* ○ *Television camera* ***crews*** *broadcast the event all round the world.* ○ *It was said of Marilyn Monroe that the camera loved her* (= that she looked very attractive on film and in photographs). **2 on camera** appearing on a piece of film: *They were caught on camera as they brutally attacked a man.*

cameraman /ˈkæm.rə.mæn/ /-mən/ *noun* [C] a person who operates a camera when films or television programmes are being made

camera-shy /ˈkæm.rə.ʃaɪ/ *adj* [after v] If someone is camera-shy, they dislike having their photograph taken.

ˈcamera ˌwork *noun* [U] the way in which cameras are used in films: *The camera work in some of these animal documentaries is fantastic.*

camiknickers /ˈkæm.iˌnɪk.əz/ [US] /-ɚz/ *plural noun UK* a piece of women's underwear consisting of a light part to cover the top half of the body, connected to a pair of KNICKERS

camisole /ˈkæm.ɪ.səʊl/ [US] /-soʊl/ *noun* [C] a light piece of women's underwear for the top half of the body, with thin straps that go over the shoulders

camomile, **chamomile** /ˈkæm.ə.maɪl/ *noun* [U] a sweet smelling plant whose white and yellow flowers have uses in medicine and are also used to make tea: *camomile* ***tea***

camouflage /ˈkæm.ə.flɑːʒ/ *noun* **1** [U] the use of leaves, branches, paints and clothes for hiding soldiers or military equipment so that they look part of their surroundings: *a camouflage jacket* **2** [S or U] the way that the colour or shape of an animal or plant appears to mix with its surroundings to prevent it from being seen by attackers: *The lizard's light brown skin acts as* ***(a)*** *camouflage in the desert sand.* **3** [S or U] something that is meant to hide something, or behaviour that is intended to hide the truth: *Using smoke as* ***(a)*** *camouflage, the army advanced up the hill.* ○ *He believed that her kindness was merely a camouflage for her real intentions.*

camouflage /ˈkæm.ə.flɑːʒ/ *verb* [T] [R] *The troops had camouflaged themselves so effectively that the enemy didn't notice them approaching.*

camp [TENTS/BUILDINGS] /kæmp/ *noun* **1** [C or U] a place where people stay in tents or other temporary structures: *We* ***pitched/set up*** *camp* (= put up our tents) *by the lakeside.* **2** [C] an area where people are kept temporarily for a particular reason: *a* ***labour/prison/refugee*** *camp* **3** [C or U] a place where soldiers stay when they are training or fighting a war: *an army camp*

camp /kæmp/ *verb* [I] to put up a tent and stay in it for a short while, for example while on holiday: *We camped on one of the lower slopes of the mountain.*

• **camp out** to sleep outside in a tent

camping /ˈkæm.pɪŋ/ *noun* [U] when you stay in a tent on holiday: *We used to* ***go*** *camping in Spain when I was a child.* ○ *camping* ***equipment***

camper /ˈkæm.pəʳ/ [US] /-pɚ/ *noun* [C] **1** a person who stays in a tent or in a HOLIDAY CAMP on holiday **2** (*UK ALSO* **camper van**) a **motorhome 3** (*ALSO* **trailer**) *US FOR* **caravan** VEHICLE

camp [STYLE] /kæmp/ *adj INFORMAL* **1** (of a man) behaving and dressing in a way that some people think is typical of a HOMOSEXUAL: *What's the name of that amazingly camp actor with the high voice and a funny walk?* **2** using bold colours, loud sounds, unusual behaviour, etc. in an amusing way: *Their shows are always incredibly camp and flamboyant.*

camp [OPINION] /kæmp/ *group noun* [C] a group of people who share an opinion, especially a political one: *The pro-abortion camp are fighting to decriminalize abortion.* ○ *The party is divided into two distinct camps over the legislation.*

▲ **camp it up** *phrasal verb INFORMAL* If an actor camps it up, he or she gives an artificial and often amusing performance in which emotions are expressed too strongly and the movements of the hands and body are more noticeable than they would usually be.

campaign /kæm'peɪn/ *noun* [C] **1** a planned group of especially political, business or military activities which are intended to achieve a particular aim: *The protests were part of their campaign* ***against*** *the proposed building development in the area.* ○ *This is the latest act of terrorism in a long-standing and bloody campaign* ***of violence.*** ○ *The endless public appearances are an inevitable part of an* ***election*** *campaign.* ○ *She's the campaign* ***organizer*** *for the Labour Party.* ○ *The government have just* ***launched*** (= begun) *their annual Christmas campaign* ***to*** *stop drunken driving.* ○ *a controversial new* ***advertising*** *campaign* **2** a group of connected actions or movements that forms part of a war: *a bombing campaign*

campaign /kæm'peɪn/ *verb* [I] to organize a series of activities to try to achieve something: [+ *to* infinitive] *They've been campaigning for years* ***to*** *get him out of prison.* ○ *He's spending a lot of his time at the moment campaigning* ***for/on behalf of*** *the Conservative Party.* ○ *They're busy campaigning* ***against*** *the building of a new motorway near here.*

campaigner /ˌkæm'peɪ.nəʳ/ [US] /-nɚ/ *noun* [C] a person who takes part in organized activities which are intended to change something in society: *an animal rights campaigner* ○ *She's a campaigner* ***for*** *Friends of the Earth.*

cam'paign ˌtrail *noun* [C usually sing] a series of planned events in different places attended or given by a politician who is trying to be elected: *She went* ***on the*** *campaign trail around the Southern states with Clinton before the 1992 election.*

campanology /ˌkæm.pə'nɒl.ə.dʒi/ [US] /-'nɑː.lə-/ *noun* [U] SPECIALIZED the art or skill of ringing bells to make music **campanologist** /ˌkæm.pə'nɒl.ə.dʒɪst/ [US] /-nɑː.lə-/ *noun* [C]

'camp ˌbed *UK noun* [C] (*US* **cot**) a light bed which can be folded so that it can be easily carried and stored

'camper ˌvan *noun* [C] *UK* a **motorhome**

campfire /'kæmp.faɪəʳ/ [US] /-faɪr/ *noun* [C] an outside fire which is made and used by people who are staying outside or in tents

'camp ˌfollower *noun* [C] a person who is interested in and supports a particular political party or other organization but is not a member of it

campground /'kæmp.graʊnd/ *noun* [C] *US* a piece of land where people on holiday can camp, usually with toilets and places for washing

camphor /'kæm.fəʳ/ [US] /-fɚ/ *noun* [U] a white or colourless substance with a strong smell, which is sometimes used in medicine

'camping ˌground *noun* [C] *AUS FOR* **campground**

campsite /'kæmp.saɪt/ *noun* [C] **1** (*AUS* **camping ground,** *US ALSO* **campground**) a piece of land where people on holiday can camp, usually with toilets and places for washing: *The campsite is in a beautiful location next to the beach.* **2** *US* a place for one tent at a place where people stay in tents: *Our tent was so large that they charged us for two campsites.*

campus /'kæm.pəs/ *noun* [C or U] the buildings of a college or university and the land that surrounds them: *There's accommodation for about five hundred students* ***on*** *campus.*

campy /'kæm.pi/ *adj* MAINLY *US* describes an activity, or someone's behaviour or appearance, that is amusing because it is obviously intended to be strange or shocking: *The result is a decidedly mixed bag of campy humor, wild-eyed fantasy and high-tech special effects.*

camshaft /'kæm.ʃɑːft/ [US] /-ʃæft/ *noun* [C] a device which causes the valves of an engine to open or close at the correct time

can [CONTAINER] /kæn/ *noun* [C] **1** (*UK ALSO* **tin**) a closed metal container, especially a cylindrical one, in which some types of drink and food are sold: *a can of soup/beans.* ✻ NOTE: In British English, *can* and *tin* both refer to the metal container that food comes in, but only *can* refers to the metal container that drink comes in. **2** (*UK ALSO* **tin**) the amount of food or drink that is contained in a can: *You'll need a can of tuna for this recipe.* **3** a metal container, especially one with a lid, handle and shaped opening for pouring: *an* ***oil*** *can* ○ *a can of paint*

• **in the can** INFORMAL If a film is in the can, filming has been completed and it is ready to be prepared for showing to the public.

• **can of worms** INFORMAL a situation which causes a lot of problems for you when you start to deal with it: *Corruption is a serious problem, but nobody has yet been willing to* ***open*** *up that can of worms.*

can /kæn/ *verb* [T] **-nn- 1** to put food and drink into a closed metal container without air: *He works in a factory where they can fruit.* **2** MAINLY *US* INFORMAL to stop doing something or making noise: *Hey, can* ***it,*** *would you? I'm trying to sleep.*

canned /kænd/ *adj* preserved and sold in a can: *canned* (*UK ALSO* ***tinned***) *fruit/tomatoes*

cannery /'kæn.ᵊr.i/ [US] /'-ɚ-/ *noun* [C] a factory where food is put into cans

the can [PRISON] *noun* [S] *US INFORMAL FOR* **prison**: *He spent ten years* ***in*** *the can for armed robbery.*

the can [TOILET] *noun* [S] *US INFORMAL FOR* **toilet**

can [ABILITY] STRONG /kæn/, WEAK /kən/ *modal verb* to be able to: *Can you drive?* ○ *She can speak four languages.* ○ *Can you read that sign from this distance?* ○ *The doctors are doing all that they can, but she's still not breathing properly.* ○ *Do the best you can – I realize the circumstances are not ideal.* ○ *If the party is awful, we can* ***always*** *leave* (= that would be one possible solution to our problem). ○ *"She's really furious about it." "Can you blame her* (= I'm not surprised)?*"*

• **can do** *US* INFORMAL used to say that you can and will do something: *"Will you mail this letter for me, please?" "Can do."* ○ *"I need you to pick up the kids today." "Sorry, no can do* (= no I can't).*"*

COMMON LEARNER ERROR

can/could or **be able to?**

Be able to means the same as **can**, but it is used in different kinds of sentences. **Be able to** is used after modal and auxiliary verbs, for example when you use the verb **will** in order to talk about the future.

I'm afraid I won't be able to come to your party.

~~*I'm afraid I won't can come to your party.*~~

When you form the simple past with **could** it refers to a general ability.

I could swim before I was three.

When you form the simple past with **was/were able to** it refers to something you managed to do on a particular occasion.

A man was able to swim out to the girl and save her.

can [PERMISSION] STRONG /kæn/, WEAK /kən/ *modal verb* **1** to be allowed to: *Can I use your bike, John?* ○ *You can park over there.* ○ *You can have a piece of cake after you've eaten your vegetables!* **2** INFORMAL sometimes used to tell someone angrily to do something: *If you carry on being horrible to your sister, Sophie, you can just go to bed!*

USAGE

can, could or **may?**

Can is used in standard spoken English when asking for permission. **Could** is slightly more formal. Both of these are acceptable in most forms of written English, although in very formal writing, such as official instructions, **may** is usually used instead.

Persons under 14 unaccompanied by an adult may not enter.

can [REQUEST] STRONG /kæn/, WEAK /kən/ *modal verb* used to request something: *If you see Adrian, can you tell him I'm in London next weekend?* ○ *Can you make a little less noise, please? I'm trying to work.*

can [POSSIBILITY] STRONG /kæn/, WEAK /kən/ *modal verb* used to express possibility: *You can get stamps from the local newsagents.* ○ *You can get very nasty skin diseases from bathing in dirty water.* ○ *Smoking can cause cancer.* ○ *Noise can be quite a problem when you're living in a flat.* ○ *He can be really annoying at times* (= He is sometimes very annoying).

can [OFFER] STRONG /kæn/, WEAK /kən/ *modal verb* used in polite offers of help: *Can I help you with those bags?*

○ *I'm afraid Ms Ferguson has already left the office. Can I be of any help?*

Canadian /kə'neɪ.di.ən/ *adj* from, belonging to or relating to Canada

Canadian /kə'neɪ.di.ən/ *noun* [C] a person from Canada

canal /kə'næl/ *noun* [C] a long channel of water which is artificially made either for boats to travel along or for taking water from one area to another: *The Panama Canal provides a crucial shipping link between the Atlantic and Pacific oceans.* ⊃See also **alimentary canal**.

ca'nal ,boat *noun* [C] (*ALSO* **narrow boat**) a long narrow boat which is used on a canal

canapé /'kæn.ə.peɪ/ *noun* [C usually plural] a small thin biscuit or piece of bread which has savoury food on top, such as cheese, fish or meat, and is served with drinks, especially at a party

canard /'kæn.ɑːd/ ⑩ /kə'nɑːrd/ *noun* [C] *LITERARY* a false report or piece of information which is intended to deceive people

canary /kə'neə.ri/ ⑩ /-'ner.i/ *noun* [C] a small yellow bird which is well known for its singing, and is sometimes kept as a pet in a cage

canasta /kə'næs.tə/ *noun* [U] a card game for two to six people which is played with two sets of cards

cancan /'kæn.kæn/ *noun* [C] a fast dance, originally performed in France in the 19th century, in which a row of women on a stage kick their legs high and lift their skirts

cancel /'kænt.sᵊl/ *verb* -ll- or *US USUALLY* -l- **1** [I or T] to decide that an organized event will not happen, or to stop an order for goods or services that you no longer want: *They've had to cancel tomorrow's football match because of the bad weather.* ○ *The 7.10 train to London has been cancelled.* ○ *to cancel a magazine subscription* **2** [T] to mark a stamp to show that it has been used and cannot be used again

cancellation /ˌkænt.sᵊl'eɪ.ʃᵊn/ *noun* [C or U] when someone decides that an organized event will not happen or stops an order for something: *Many trains are subject to cancellation because of the flooding.* ○ *The theatre tickets were sold out, so we waited to see if there were any cancellations* (= unwanted returned tickets).

▲ **cancel** *sth* **out** *phrasal verb* [M] to remove the effect of one thing by doing another thing which has the opposite effect: *This month's pay cheque will cancel out his debt, but it won't give him any extra money.*

cancer DISEASE /'kænt.səʳ/ ⑩ /-sɚ/ *noun* **1** [C or U] a serious disease that is caused when cells in the body grow in a way that is uncontrolled and not normal, killing normal cells and often causing death: *He died of liver cancer.* ○ *cancer of the cervix/stomach* ○ *breast/bowel/lung cancer* ○ *cancer cells* ○ *a cancer patient* ○ *It was a secondary cancer.* ⊃See also **carcinogen**. **2** [C] a harmful activity that spreads quickly: *Drug abuse is a cancer which is destroying our society.* **cancerous** /'kænt.sᵊr.əs/ ⑩ /-sɚ-/ *adj: a cancerous growth/tumour*

Cancer SIGN /'kænt.səʳ/ ⑩ /-sɚ/ *noun* [C or U] the fourth sign of the zodiac, relating to the period from 22 June to 22 July and represented by a crab, or a person born during this period

candelabra /ˌkæn.dəl'ɑː.brə/ *noun* [C] *plural* **candelabra** or **candelabras** a decorative holder for several candles or lights

candid /'kæn.dɪd/ *adj APPROVING* truthful and honest, especially about something difficult or painful: *The two presidents have had candid talks about the current crisis.* ○ *To be candid with you, I think you're making a dreadful mistake.* ⊃See also **candour**. **candidly** /'kæn.dɪd.li/ *adv*

candida /'kæn.dɪ.də/ *noun* [U] *SPECIALIZED* a type of fungus which can cause an infection, especially in the VAGINA or mouth

candidate /'kæn.dɪ.dət/ /-deɪt/ *noun* [C] **1** a person who is competing to get a job or elected position: *There are three candidates standing in the election.* **2** a person or thing considered likely to receive or experience something: *The English Department is a likely candidate for staff cuts.* **3** *UK* someone who is taking an exam:

Candidates must write their names on the top page of the exam paper.

candidacy /'kæn.dɪ.də.si/ *noun* [C usually sing; U] (*UK ALSO* **candidature**) *She is expected to announce officially her candidacy* (= the fact that she is a candidate) *for president early next week.*

,candied 'peel *noun* [U] the skin of lemons and oranges which is preserved with sugar and used for making cakes

candle /'kæn.dl̩/ *noun* [C] a usually cylindrical piece of wax with a WICK (= piece of string) in the middle of it which produces light as it slowly burns: *Shall I light a candle?*

candlelight /'kæn.dl̩.laɪt/ *noun* [U] the light that a candle produces when it is burning **candlelit** /'kæn.dl̩.lɪt/ *adj* [before n] *a candlelit dinner*

candlestick /'kæn.dl̩.stɪk/ *noun* [C] a holder for one or more candles

can-do /ˌkæn'duː/ *adj* [before n] *US* If someone has a can-do character or approach to a problem, they are very positive about their ability to achieve success: *Her can-do attitude is what made her our choice for the job.*

candour *UK, US* **candor** /'kæn.dəʳ/ ⑩ /-dɚ/ *noun* [U] the quality of being truthful and honest, especially about a difficult or embarrassing subject: *"We really don't know what to do about it," she said with surprising candour.* ⊃See also **candid**.

candy /'kæn.di/ *noun* [C or U] *US* a sweet food made from sugar or chocolate, or a piece of this: *a candy bar* ○ *a box of candy*

candied /'kæn.did/ *adj* preserved with sugar: *candied fruit*

candy-ass /'kæn.di.æs/ *noun* [C] *US OFFENSIVE* a cowardly person

candyfloss *UK, US* **cotton candy**, *AUS* **fairy floss** /'kæn.di.flɒs/ ⑩ /-flɑːs/ *noun* [U] a large soft ball of white or pink sugar in the form of thin threads, which is usually sold on a stick and eaten at fairs and amusement parks

candy-striped /'kæn.di.straɪpt/ *adj* Something that is candy-striped has narrow strips of white and a bright colour such as pink: *a candy-striped shirt*

cane /keɪn/ *noun* **1** [C or U] the long, hard, hollow stem of particular plants such as BAMBOO, sometimes used to make furniture or support other plants in the garden **2** [C] a long stick used especially by old, ill or blind people to help them walk **3** [S] a long, thin stick used in the past as a school punishment

cane /keɪn/ *verb* [T] to hit a child at school with a stick as a punishment

canine /'keɪ.naɪn/ *adj* of or relating to dogs: *The city's canine population* (= The number of dogs in the city) *has grown dramatically over recent years.*

'canine (,tooth) *noun* [C] one of four pointed teeth in the human mouth ⊃Compare **incisor**; **molar**.

canister /'kæn.ɪ.stəʳ/ ⑩ /-stɚ/ *noun* [C] a metal, usually cylindrical, container for gases or dry things: *The police fired tear gas canisters into the crowd.*

canker TREES /'kæŋ.kəʳ/ ⑩ /-kɚ/ *noun* [C or U] *SPECIALIZED* a disease which attacks the wood of trees

canker ANIMALS /'kæŋ.kəʳ/ ⑩ /-kɚ/ *noun* [U] *SPECIALIZED* a disease affecting the ears and mouth of animals and humans

canker EVIL /'kæŋ.kəʳ/ ⑩ /-kɚ/ *noun* [C usually sing] *FORMAL* something evil that spreads through a person's mind, an organization or a society: *Poverty is a canker eating away at the heart of society.*

cannabis /'kæn.ə.bɪs/ *noun* [U] a usually illegal drug which is made from the dried leaves and flowers of the HEMP plant, and produces a feeling of pleasant relaxation when smoked or eaten: *Are you in favour of the legalization of cannabis?*

,canned 'laughter *noun* [U] *DISAPPROVING* recordings of laughter that have been added to a humorous radio or television programme when something amusing has been said or done

,canned 'music *noun* [U] *DISAPPROVING* **Muzak**

cannelloni, **canneloni** /ˌkæn.əlˈəʊ.ni/ [US] /-ˈoʊ-/ *noun* [U] tubes of pasta usually filled with cheese or meat and covered with sauce

cannibal /ˈkæn.ɪ.bəl/ *noun* [C] a person who eats human flesh, or an animal which eats the flesh of animals of its own type **cannibalism** /ˈkæn.ɪ.bəl.ɪ.zəm/ *noun* [U] **cannibalistic** /ˌkæn.ɪ.bəlˈɪs.tɪk/ *adj*

cannibalize, *UK USUALLY* **-ise** /ˈkæn.ɪ.bəl.aɪz/ *verb* [T] to take parts from a machine or vehicle in order to make or repair another machine or vehicle: *He bought an old engine and cannibalized it for spare parts.*

cannon [GUN] /ˈkæn.ən/ *noun* [C] *plural* **cannon** or **cannons** **1** a large, powerful gun fixed to two or four wheels, which fires heavy stone or metal balls, and which was used in the past **2** a gun attached to an aircraft

cannon [KNOCK] /ˈkæn.ən/ *verb* [I usually + adv or prep] *UK* to knock or hit against someone or something suddenly and forcefully as you are running: *I was rushing along with my head down when I cannoned **into** an old lady walking the other way.*

cannonade /ˌkæn.əˈneɪd/ *noun* [C] a period of continuous heavy firing of large guns, especially as part of an attack

ˈcannon ˌball *noun* [C] a heavy metal or stone ball fired from a cannon

ˈcannon ˌfodder *noun* [U] If you describe soldiers as cannon fodder, you mean that they are not considered important by their officers and are sent into war without their leaders caring if they die.

cannot /ˈkæn.ɒt/ [US] /-ɑːt/ *modal verb* can not; the negative form of the verb **can**: *I cannot predict what will happen next year.*
• **cannot but** *FORMAL* used to say that something will certainly happen: *If we persevere, we cannot but succeed.*

canny [CLEVER] /ˈkæn.i/ *adj* thinking quickly and cleverly, especially in business or financial matters: *These salesmen are a canny lot.* **cannily** /ˈkæn.ɪ.li/ *adv*

canny [PLEASANT] /ˈkæn.i/ *adj NORTHERN AND SCOTTISH ENGLISH* good or pleasant: *a canny lad*

canoe /kəˈnuː/ *noun* [C] **1** a small light narrow boat, pointed at both ends and moved using a PADDLE (= a short pole with a flat blade) ➲See picture **Planes, Ships and Boats** on page Centre 14 **2** *UK FOR* **kayak**
canoe /kəˈnuː/ *verb* [I usually + adv or prep] **canoeing**, **canoed**, **canoed** to travel in a canoe **canoeing** /kəˈnuː.ɪŋ/ *noun* [U] *They died in a canoeing accident.* **canoeist** /kəˈnuː.ɪst/ *noun* [C]

canon [PRIEST] /ˈkæn.ən/ *noun* [C] a Christian priest with special duties in a cathedral

canon [STANDARD] /ˈkæn.ən/ *noun* [C usually pl] *FORMAL OR SPECIALIZED* a rule, principle or law, especially in the Christian Church **canonical** /kəˈnɒn.ɪ.kəl/ [US] /-ˈnɑː.nɪ-/ *adj*

canon [WRITINGS] /ˈkæn.ən/ *noun* [C usually sing] *SPECIALIZED* all the writings or other works known to be by a particular person: *the Shakespearean canon*

canonize, *UK USUALLY* **-ise** /ˈkæn.ə.naɪz/ *verb* [T] (in the Roman Catholic Church) to officially announce that a dead person is a saint

canoodle /kəˈnuː.dl̩/ *verb* [I] *OLD-FASHIONED INFORMAL* If two people canoodle, they kiss and hold each other in a sexual way.

ˈcan ˌopener *noun* [C] (*UK ALSO* **tin opener**) a tool for opening metal containers of food ➲See picture **In the Kitchen** on page Centre 16

canopy /ˈkæn.ə.pi/ *noun* [C] **1** a cover fixed over a seat or bed, etc. for shelter or decoration **2** the branches and leaves that spread out at the top of a group of trees forming a type of roof **3** the transparent part in a military aircraft which covers the place where the pilot sits **4** the large circular piece of cloth that is the main part of a parachute

cant /kænt/ *noun* [U] **1** statements on especially religious or moral subjects which are not sincerely believed by the person making them: *Shelley's friendship with Byron was rooted in their shared contempt for cant and hypocrisy.* **2** special words used by a particular group of people such as thieves, lawyers or priests, often in order to keep things secret

can't /kɑːnt/ [US] /kænt/ *short form of* **1** cannot: *Speak up! I can't hear you.* **2** often used to suggest that someone should do a particular thing, especially when it seems the obvious thing to do: *Can't you just take the dress back to the shop if it doesn't fit?*

cantaloupe, **cantaloup** /ˈkæn.tə.luːp/ [US] /-t̬ə.loʊp/ *noun* [C or U] (*AUS ALSO* **rockmelon**) a type of MELON (= large fruit with a thick skin) that is round and has yellow or green skin and sweet orange flesh

cantankerous /ˌkænˈtæŋ.kər.əs/ [US] /-kɚ-/ *adj* arguing and complaining a lot: *He's getting a bit cantankerous in his old age.*

cantata /kænˈtɑː.tə/ [US] /kənˈtɑː.t̬ə/ *noun* [C] a short musical work, with words usually based on a religious subject ➲Compare **oratorio**.

canteen [RESTAURANT] /kænˈtiːn/ *noun* [C] a place in a factory, office, etc. where food and meals are sold, often at a lower than usual price

canteen [KITCHEN EQUIPMENT] /kænˈtiːn/ *noun* [C] *UK* (a small flat case containing) a complete set of knives, forks and spoons: *We're giving them a canteen **of cutlery** as a wedding present.*

canteen [CONTAINER] /kænˈtiːn/ *noun* [C] a small container for carrying water or another drink, used especially by soldiers or travellers

canter /ˈkæn.təʳ/ [US] /-t̬ɚ/ *verb* [I] If a horse canters, it moves at a quite fast but easy and comfortable speed: *The horsemen cantered round the field a few times.* **canter** /ˈkæn.təʳ/ [US] /-tɚ/ *noun* [C usually sing] *The horses set off **at** a canter.*

cantilever /ˈkæn.tɪ.liː.vəʳ/ [US] /-t̬ɪ.liː.vɚ/ *noun* [C] *SPECIALIZED* a long bar or beam which is fixed at only one end to a vertical support and is used to hold a structure such as an arch, bridge or shelf in position: *a cantilever bridge*

canton /ˈkæn.tɒn/ [US] /-tɑːn/ *noun* [C] a political region or local government area in some countries, especially one of the 23 political regions into which Switzerland is divided

Cantonese /kæn.təˈniːz/ *noun* [U] one of the two main types of the Chinese language, spoken in the south of China and used as an official language in Hong Kong

cantor /ˈkæn.tɔːʳ/ [US] /-tɔːr/ *noun* [C] **1** an official of a Jewish SYNAGOGUE (= religious building) who sings and leads prayers **2** someone who formally leads the singing in a Christian church choir

canvas /ˈkæn.vəs/ *noun* **1** [U] strong, rough cloth used for making tents, sails, bags, strong clothes, etc. **2** [C] a piece of canvas used by artists for painting on, usually with oil paints, or the painting itself: *These two canvases by Hockney would sell for £500 000.*
• **under canvas** in a tent: *I love sleeping under canvas.*

canvass [OBTAIN SUPPORT] /ˈkæn.vəs/ *verb* [I or T] to try to obtain political support or votes, especially by visiting all the houses in an area: *I've been out canvassing **for** the Labour Party every evening this week.* **canvass** /ˈkæn.vəs/ *noun* [C] **canvasser** /ˈkæn.və.səʳ/ [US] /-sɚ/ *noun* [C]

canvass [ASK] /ˈkæn.vəs/ *verb* [T] to try to discover information or opinions by asking people: *The council has been canvassing local **opinion**/local people to get their thoughts on the proposed housing development.*

canvass [SUGGEST] /ˈkæn.vəs/ *verb* [T] *UK FORMAL* to suggest an idea or plan for consideration: *Wind and wave power are now being seriously canvassed as the solution to our energy problems.*

canyon /ˈkæn.jən/ *noun* [C] a large valley with very steep sides and usually a river flowing along the bottom

canyoning /ˈkæn.jə.nɪŋ/ *noun* [U] a sport which involves jumping into a mountain stream which is flowing very fast and being carried down the stream while you float on your back

cap [HAT] /kæp/ *noun* [C] **1** a soft flat hat which has a curved part sticking out at the front, often worn as part of a uniform ➲See pictures **Clothes** on page Centre 6, **Hairstyles and Hats** on page Centre 8 **2** a thin waterproof hat that stops your hair getting wet: *a **shower/***

***swimming** cap* **3** *UK* a cap given to someone who plays for their national team in a particular sport, or a player who receives this: *Davis has 17 Scottish caps* (= has played for Scotland 17 times). ○ *The team contains five international caps.*

• **go cap in hand to *sb*** to ask someone in a polite and sincere way for something, especially money or forgiveness

C

cap /kæp/ *verb* **be capped** to play for your national team in a particular sport: *She's been capped **for** Scotland nine times.*

cap [LIMIT] /kæp/ *verb* **[T often passive] -pp-** to put a limit on the amount of money that can be charged or spent in connection with a particular activity: *High spending councils have all been (rate/charge) capped.* ○ *Our mortgage is capped at 8.75% for five years.*

cap /kæp/ *noun* **[C]** *Central government has imposed a cap* (= limit) ***on** local tax increases.*

cap [COVER] /kæp/ *noun* **[C]** **1** a small usually protective lid or cover: *The camera has a **lens** cap to protect the lens surface.* **2** an artificial protective covering on a tooth

cap /kæp/ *verb* **[T] -pp-** *The mountain was capped **with*** (= The top of it was covered by) *snow.* ○ *have your teeth capped* (= protected with an artificial covering)

• **to cap it all** used when you mention something in addition to all the other (bad) things that have happened: *It's been a terrible week and now, to cap it all, I've got a cold.*

-capped /-kæpt/ *suffix* with a top covered in the way mentioned: *a snow-capped mountain*

cap [BIRTH CONTROL] /kæp/ *noun* **[C]** *UK* **diaphragm**

cap [EXPLOSIVE] /kæp/ *noun* **[C]** a very small amount of explosive powder in a paper container, used especially in toy guns to produce a loud noise

capable /ˈkeɪ.pə.bl̩/ *adj* **1** able to do things effectively and skilfully, and to achieve results: *She's a very capable woman/worker/judge.* ○ *We need to get an assistant who's capable and efficient.* **2 capable of sth/doing sth** having the ability, power or qualities to be able to do something: *Only the Democratic Party is capable of running the country.* ○ *A force 10 wind is capable of blowing the roofs off houses.* ○ *When she's drunk she's capable of saying* (= likely to say) *awful, rude things.* ○ *I think your plan is capable of being* (= could be) *improved.* ➲The opposite is **incapable**.

• **in *sb's* capable hands** *HUMOROUS* being dealt with by the person mentioned: *I'm going away next week, so I'll be **leaving** everything in your capable hands.*

-capable /-keɪ.pə.bl̩/ *suffix*: *These are nuclear-capable aircraft* (= They can carry nuclear weapons).

capability /ˌkeɪ.pəˈbɪl.ɪ.ti/ [US] /-ə.t̬i/ *noun* **[C or U]** *These tests are beyond the capability* (= ability) *of an average 12-year-old.* ○ **[+ to infinitive]** *With the new machines we finally have the capability* (= power) ***to** do the job properly.* ○ *Several countries are trying to develop a **nuclear** capability* (= weapons needed to fight a nuclear war).

capably /ˈkeɪ.pə.bli/ *adv*: *She drove very capably.*

capacious /kəˈpeɪ.ʃəs/ *adj FORMAL* able to contain a lot; having lots of space: *a capacious pocket/handbag*

capacitor /kəˈpæs.ɪ.təʳ/ [US] /-t̬ɚ/ *noun* **[C]** *SPECIALIZED* a device which collects and stores electricity, and is an important part of electronic equipment such as televisions and radios

capacity [AMOUNT] /kəˈpæs.ə.ti/ [US] /-t̬i/ *noun* **[C or S or U]** the total amount that can be contained or produced, or (especially of a person or organization) the ability to do a particular thing: *The stadium has a **seating** capacity of 50 000.* ○ *The game was watched by a capacity **crowd/audience** of 50 000* (= the place was completely full). ○ *She has a great capacity **for** hard work.* ○ *The purchase of 500 tanks is part of a strategy to increase military capacity by 25% over the next five years.* ○ **[+ to infinitive]** *It seems to be **beyond** his capacity **to*** (= He seems to be unable to) *follow simple instructions.* ○ *Do you think it's **within** his capacity **to*** (= Do you think he'll be able to) *do the job without making a mess of it?* ○ *The generators each have a capacity **of*** (= can produce) *1000 kilowatts.* ○ *The larger cars have bigger capacity engines* (= the engines are bigger and more powerful). ○ *All our factories are working **at (full)** capacity* (= are producing goods as fast as possible). ○ *We are running **below** capacity* (= not producing as many goods as we are able to) *because of cancelled orders.* ○ *He suffered a stroke in 1988, which left him unable to speak, but his **mental** capacity* (= his ability to think and remember) *wasn't affected.* ➲See also **capacious**.

capacity [POSITION] /kəˈpæs.ə.ti/ [US] /-t̬i/ *noun* **[S]** *FORMAL* a particular position or job: *In his capacity **as** secretary of the residents association, he regularly attends meetings of the community policing committee.* ○ *She was speaking in her capacity **as** a novelist, rather than as a television presenter.*

cape [LAND] /keɪp/ *noun* **[C]** a very large piece of land sticking out into the sea: *the Cape of Good Hope*

cape [COAT] /keɪp/ *noun* **[C]** a type of loose coat without sleeves, which is fastened at the neck and hangs from the shoulders

caped /keɪpt/ *adj* wearing a cape

caper [JUMP] /ˈkeɪ.pəʳ/ [US] /-pɚ/ *verb* **[I + adv or prep]** to run and jump about in an energetic, happy way

caper [ACTIVITY] /ˈkeɪ.pəʳ/ [US] /-pɚ/ *noun* **[C]** an illegal, unusual or amusing activity: *The whole incident started as an innocent caper.*

caper [FOOD] /ˈkeɪ.pəʳ/ [US] /-pɚ/ *noun* **[C usually pl]** a small dark green flower BUD which is used in sauces to give a slightly sour taste to food

capillary /kəˈpɪl.ᵊr.i/ [US] /-ɚ-/ *noun* **[C]** *SPECIALIZED* a very thin tube, especially one of the smaller tubes that carry blood around the body

capital [CITY] /ˈkæp.ɪ.tᵊl/ [US] /-t̬ᵊl/ *noun* **[C]** **1** a city which is the centre of government of a country or smaller political area: *Australia's capital city is Canberra.* **2** the most important place for a particular business or activity: *London used to be the financial capital of the world.*

capital [MONEY] /ˈkæp.ɪ.tᵊl/ [US] /-t̬ᵊl/ *noun* **[U]** wealth, especially a large amount of money used for producing more wealth or for starting a new business: *She leaves her capital untouched in the bank and lives off the interest.* ○ *We've **put** £20 000 capital **into** the business, but we're unlikely to see any return for a few years.*

• **make capital out of *sth*** to use a situation to obtain an advantage for yourself: *The Opposition is making a lot of **political** capital out of the Government's failure to invest in education.*

capitalize, *UK USUALLY* **-ise** /ˈkæp.ɪ.tᵊl.aɪz/ [US] /-t̬ᵊl-/ *verb* **[T often passive]** to supply money to a business so that it can develop or operate as it should

capitalization, *UK USUALLY* **-isation** /ˌkæp.ɪ.tᵊl.aɪˈzeɪ.ʃᵊn/ [US] /-t̬ᵊl-/ *noun* **[S or U]** the total value of a company's shares on a STOCK EXCHANGE

capital [LETTER] /ˈkæp.ɪ.tᵊl/ [US] /-t̬ᵊl/ *noun* **[C]** a letter of the alphabet in the form and larger size that is used at the beginning of sentences and names: *print in capitals*

capital /ˈkæp.ɪ.tᵊl/ [US] /-t̬ᵊl/ *adj*: *Do you write 'calvinist' with a capital 'C'?*

• **with a capital *A, B, etc.*** said after the name of a particular quality to say that it is very strong, using its first letter: *He's trouble with a capital T!*

capitalize, *UK USUALLY* **-ise** /ˈkæp.ɪ.tᵊl.aɪz/ [US] /-t̬ᵊl-/ *verb* **[T]** to write a letter of the alphabet as a capital, or to write the first letter of a word as a capital: *The names of political parties are always capitalized, e.g. the Green Party.* **capitalization**, *UK USUALLY* **-isation** /ˌkæp.ɪ.tᵊl.aɪˈzeɪ.ʃᵊn/ [US] /-t̬ᵊl-/ *noun* **[U]**

capital [EXCELLENT] /ˈkæp.ɪ.tᵊl/ [US] /-t̬ᵊl/ *adj UK OLD-FASHIONED* very good or excellent: *That's a capital **idea**!*

capital [DEATH] /ˈkæp.ɪ.tᵊl/ [US] /-t̬ᵊl/ *adj* **capital crime/offence** a crime that can be punished by death: *In some countries, importing drugs is a capital offence.*

capital [COLUMN] /ˈkæp.ɪ.tᵊl/ [US] /-t̬ᵊl/ *noun* **[C]** *SPECIALIZED* the top part of a column

ˌcapital ˈassets *plural noun* the buildings and machines owned by a business or other organization

ˌcapital ˈgains *plural noun* profits made by selling property or an investment

ˌcapital ˈgains ˌtax *noun* **[U]** (*ALSO* **CDT**) tax on the profits made from selling something you own

ˌcapital inˈtensive *adj* describes an industry, business or process that needs a lot of money to buy buildings and equipment in order to start operating: *As agriculture became more capital intensive, many farm labourers moved to the towns and cities to look for work.*

,capital in'vestment *noun* [U] (*ALSO* **capital expenditure**) money which is spent on buildings and equipment to increase the effectiveness of a business

capitalism /ˈkæp.ɪ.t^əl.ɪ.z^əm/ ⓤ /-t̬^əl-/ *noun* [U] an economic, political and social system based on private ownership of property, business and industry, and directed towards making the greatest possible profits for successful organizations and people ⊃Compare **communism**; **socialism**. **capitalist** /ˈkæp.ɪ.t^əl.ɪst/ ⓤ /-t̬^əl-/ *adj* (*ALSO* **capitalistic**) *a capitalist economy/country/ system*

capitalist /ˈkæp.ɪ.t^əl.ɪst/ ⓤ /-t̬^əl-/ *noun* [C] **1** someone who supports capitalism **2** someone who has great wealth invested in a business

▲ **capitalize on** *sth*, UK USUALLY **-ise** *phrasal verb* to use a situation to your own advantage: *She capitalized on her knowledge and experience to get a new and better paid job.*

,capital 'letter *noun* [C] a letter of the alphabet in the form and larger size that is used at the beginning of sentences and names

,capital 'punishment *noun* [U] (*ALSO* **the death pen-alty**) punishment by death, as ordered by a legal system

capitation /ˌkæp.ɪˈteɪ.ʃ^ən/ *noun* [C or U] SPECIALIZED a tax, charge or amount which is fixed at the same level for everyone: *Doctors receive capitation of £13.85 per patient.*

Capitol /ˈkæp.ɪ.t^əl/ ⓤ /-t̬^əl/ *noun* **1 the Capitol** the build-ing in which the US Congress meets **2** [C usually sing] a building in which a US state government meets: *the Oklahoma State Capitol*

capitulate /kəˈpɪt.jʊ.leɪt/ *verb* [I] **1** to accept military defeat: *Their forces capitulated five hours after the Allied bombardment of the city began.* **2** to accept something or agree to do something unwillingly: *The sports minister today capitulated to calls for his resignation.* **capitula-tion** /kə,pɪt.jʊˈleɪ.ʃ^ən/ *noun* [C or U]

cappuccino /ˌkæp.ʊˈtʃiː.nəʊ/ ⓤ /-noʊ/ *noun* [C or U] plural **cappuccinos** (a cup of) coffee made with heated milk which is served with a thick mass of bubbles and often powdered chocolate on the top

caprice /kəˈpriːs/ *noun* [C or U] LITERARY (the tendency to have) a sudden and usually foolish desire to have or do something, or a sudden and foolish change of mind or behaviour; a **whim**: *The $300 million palace was built to satisfy the caprice of one man.* **capricious** /kəˈprɪʃ.əs/ *adj: a capricious child* ○ *He was a cruel and capricious tyrant.* **capriciously** /kəˈprɪʃ.ə.sli/ *adv* **capriciousness** /kəˈprɪʃ.ə.snəs/ *noun* [U]

Capricorn /ˈkæp.rɪ.kɔːn/ ⓤ /-kɔːrn/ *noun* [C or U] the tenth sign of the zodiac, relating to the period from 23 December to 20 January and represented by a goat, or a person born during this period

capsicum /ˈkæp.sɪ.kəm/ *noun* [C or U] SPECIALIZED a **pepper** VEGETABLE

capsize /kæpˈsaɪz/ *verb* [I or T] to (cause a boat or ship to) turn upside down accidentally while on water: *A huge wave capsized the yacht.* ○ *When the boat capsized we were trapped underneath it.*

capstan /ˈkæp.stən/ *noun* [C] **1** a machine with a spin-ning vertical cylinder which is used, especially on ships, for pulling heavy objects with a rope **2** a thin spinning cylinder in a TAPE RECORDER (= a machine that records and plays back sound) which pulls the tape through the machine

capsule MEDICINE /ˈkæp.sjuːl/ ⓤ /-s^əl/ *noun* [C] a small container with medicine inside which you swallow

capsule SPACECRAFT /ˈkæp.sjuːl/ ⓤ /-s^əl/ *noun* [C] the part of a spacecraft in which the people on it live

captain /ˈkæp.tɪn/ ⓤ /-t^ən/ *noun* [C] **1** the person in charge of a ship or an aircraft, or the leader of a sports team: *This is your captain speaking. We expect to be land-ing at London Heathrow in an hour's time.* ○ *It's unusual to have a goalkeeper as (the) captain of a football team.* **2** an officer's rank in the army or navy, or in the US air force, or in the US police and fire departments

captain /ˈkæp.tɪn/ ⓤ /-t^ən/ *verb* [T] to lead and be the captain of a team, military group, ship or aircraft: *He captained the England cricket team for 5 years.* **captaincy** /ˈkæp.tɪn.si/ ⓤ /-t^ən-/ *noun* [C or U]

,captain of 'industry *noun* [C] a person who has an important job in industry and who can influence company and national planning: *In a speech to captains of industry, she predicted economic growth of 3.5% next year.*

caption /ˈkæp.ʃ^ən/ *noun* [C] a short piece of text under a picture in a book, magazine or newspaper which describes the picture or explains what the people in it are doing or saying

captious /ˈkæp.ʃəs/ *adj* FORMAL tending to express criti-cisms about unimportant matters

captivate /ˈkæp.tɪ.veɪt/ *verb* [T] to hold the attention of someone by being extremely interesting, exciting, charming or attractive: *With her beauty and charm, she captivated film audiences everywhere.* **captivating** /ˈkæp.tɪ.veɪ.tɪŋ/ ⓤ /-t̬ɪŋ/ *adj: a captivating performance*

captive /ˈkæp.tɪv/ *noun* [C] a person or animal whose ability to move or act freely is limited by being in an en-closed space; a prisoner, especially a person held by the enemy during a war: *When the town was recaptured, we found soldiers who had been captives for several years.* **captive** /ˈkæp.tɪv/ *adj: captive soldiers*

● **hold/take** *sb* **captive** to keep someone as a prisoner or make someone a prisoner: *The terrorists were holding several British diplomats captive.*

captivity /kæpˈtɪv.ɪ.ti/ ⓤ /-ə.t̬i/ *noun* [U] when a person or animal is kept somewhere and is not allowed to leave: *All the hostages, when released* **from** *captivity, looked remarkably fit and well.* ○ *Animals bred* **in** *captivity would probably not survive if they were released into the wild.*

,captive 'audience *noun* [C] a group of people who listen to or watch someone or something because they can not leave

captor /ˈkæp.tə^r/ ⓤ /-tɚ/ *noun* [C] a person who has captured a person or animal and refuses to release them

capture /ˈkæp.tʃə^r/ ⓤ /-tʃɚ/ *verb* [T] **1** to take someone as a prisoner, or to take something into your possession, especially by force: *Two of the soldiers were killed and the rest were captured.* ○ *Rebel forces captured the city after a week-long battle.* **2** to represent or describe some-thing very accurately using words or images: *It would be impossible to capture her beauty in a painting.* **3** to record or take a picture of something using a camera: *A passer-by captured the whole incident* **on film**. **4** If some-thing captures your imagination or attention, you feel very interested and excited by it: *The American drive to land a man on the Moon captured the* **imagination/ attention** *of the whole world.* **5** to succeed in getting something when you are competing with other people: *The Democratic Party captured 70% of the vote.* **6** SPECIALIZED If a computer or similar machine captures information, it takes it in and stores it. **capture** /ˈkæp.-tʃə^r/ ⓤ /-tʃɚ/ *noun* [S or U] *They witnessed* **the capture of** *the city by rebel troops.*

car /kɑː^r/ ⓤ /kɑːr/ *noun* [C] **1** a road vehicle with an engine, four wheels, and seats for a small number of people: *They don't have a car.* ○ *Where did you park your car?* ○ *It's quicker* **by** *car.* ○ *a car chase/accident/factory* ⊃See pictures **Car** on page Centre 12, **Cars and Trucks** on page Centre 13 **2** a part of a train used for a special purpose: *a* **restaurant/sleeping** *car*

carafe /kəˈræf/ *noun* [C] a tall glass container with a wide round bottom for serving wine or water in a restaurant, or the amount contained in this

caramel /ˈkær.ə.m^əl/ ⓤ /ˈkɑːr.məl/ /ˈker.ə-/ *noun* **1** [U] burnt sugar used to give flavour and a brown colour to food **2** [C or U] a sticky brown sweet made from sugar which has been heated with milk, butter or cream in hot water: *chocolates with caramel centres*

caramelize, UK USUALLY **-ise** /ˈkær.ə.m^əl.aɪz/ ⓤ /ˈkɑːr.-məl-/ /ˈker.ə-/ *verb* **1** [I] If sugar caramelizes, it turns into caramel. **2** [T] to cook a food with sugar so that the food becomes sweet and often brown: *caramelized onions/ carrots*

carapace /ˈkær.ə.peɪs/ [US] /ˈker-/ *noun* [C] *SPECIALIZED* a hard shell that covers and protects animals such as CRABS and TURTLES

carat /ˈkær.ət/ [US] /ˈker-/ *noun* [C] **1** a unit for measuring the weight of jewels **2** *UK* (*US* **karat**) a unit for measuring the purity of gold: *24-carat gold is the purest.*

caravan [VEHICLE] /ˈkær.ə.væn/ [US] /ˈker-/ *noun* [C] **1** *UK* (*US* **trailer**) a wheeled vehicle for living or travelling in, especially for holidays, which contains beds and cooking equipment and can be pulled by a car ➲See picture **Cars and Trucks** on page Centre 13 **2** *UK* a painted wooden vehicle that is pulled by a horse and in which people live: *a gypsy caravan*

caravanning *UK* /ˈkær.ə.væn.ɪŋ/ [US] /ˈker-/ *noun* [U] (*US* **trailer camping**) going on holiday in a caravan

caravan [GROUP] /ˈkær.ə.væn/ [US] /ˈker-/ *noun* [C] a group of people with vehicles or animals who travel together for safety through a dangerous area, especially across a desert on CAMELS

ˈcaravan ˌsite *UK noun* [C] (*US* **trailer park,** *AUS* **caravan park**) an area of ground where CARAVANS can be parked, especially by people spending their holidays in them

caraway /ˈkær.ə.weɪ/ [US] /ˈker-/ *noun* [U] a short plant or its small seed-like fruits which have a flavour similar to but weaker than ANISEED and are used in food, especially for making bread or cake: *caraway* ***seeds***

carbine /ˈkɑː.baɪn/ [US] /ˈkɑːr-/ *noun* [C] *SPECIALIZED* a short light RIFLE (= gun), originally used by soldiers on horses

carbohydrate /ˌkɑː.bəʊˈhaɪ.dreɪt/ [US] /ˌkɑːr-/ *noun* [C or U] one of several substances such as sugar or starch, which provide the body with energy, or foods containing these substances such as bread, potatoes, pasta and rice

carbolic acid /kɑːˌbɒl.ɪkˈæs.ɪd/ [US] /kɑːrˌbɑː.lɪk-/ *noun* [U] a liquid which destroys bacteria, and is used for cleaning injuries or surfaces to prevent disease

carbolic soap /kɑːˌbɒl.ɪkˈsəʊp/ [US] /kɑːrˌbɑː.lɪkˈsoʊp/ *noun* [U] a strong soap made from COAL TAR

ˈcar ˌbomb *noun* [C] a bomb put inside a car and left to explode in a public place

carbon /ˈkɑː.bən/ [US] /ˈkɑːr-/ *noun* [U] a simple chemical substance, which exists in its pure form as diamond or GRAPHITE, and is an important part of other substances such as coal and oil, as well as being contained in all plants and animals

carboniferous /ˌkɑː.bəˈnɪf.ər.əs/ [US] /ˌkɑːr.bəˈnɪf.ɚ-/ *adj* **1** *SPECIALIZED* containing or producing carbon: *carboniferous rocks* **2 Carboniferous** relating to the period of Earth's history during which coal was formed: *the Carboniferous period*

carbonize, *UK USUALLY* **-ise** /ˈkɑː.bən.aɪz/ [US] /ˈkɑːr-/ *verb* [I or T] *SPECIALIZED* to change or be changed to carbon by burning

carbonated /ˈkɑː.bən.eɪ.tɪd/ [US] /ˈkɑːr.bən.eɪ.t̬ɪd/ *adj* A carbonated drink is fizzy because it contains CARBON DIOXIDE: *carbonated drinks/water*

ˌcarbon (ˈcopy) [DOCUMENT] *noun* [C] a copy of a document, made with carbon paper

ˌcarbon ˈcopy [SAME APPEARANCE] *noun* [C] a person or thing that is very similar to or exactly like another person or thing: *She's a carbon copy* ***of*** *her mother.*

ˌcarbon ˈdating *noun* [U] a method of calculating the age of extremely old objects by measuring the amount of a particular type of carbon in them

ˌcarbon diˈoxide *noun* [U] the gas formed when carbon is burned, or when people or animals breathe out: *carbon dioxide emissions*

carbon monoxide /ˌkɑː.bən.məˈnɒk.saɪd/ [US] /ˌkɑːr.bən.məˈnɑː-/ *noun* [U] the poisonous gas formed by the burning of carbon, especially in the form of car fuel

ˈcarbon ˌpaper *noun* [U] thin paper with a covering of carbon or other dark-coloured substance on one side, which is used between sheets of writing to make copies

ˈcarbon ˌsink *noun* [C] *SPECIALIZED* an area of forest which is large enough to absorb important and noticeable amounts of CARBON DIOXIDE from the Earth's atmosphere and therefore to reduce the effect of GLOBAL WARMING

ˈcarbon ˌtax *noun* [C] *SPECIALIZED* a tax on the use of oil, coal etc. which produce GREENHOUSE GASES which harm the atmosphere

ˌcar ˈboot ˌsale *UK noun* [C] (*US* **swap meet**) an event in a public place where people sell their unwanted possessions, often from the backs of their cars

carbuncle [SWELLING] /ˈkɑː.bʌŋ.kl̩/ [US] /ˈkɑːr-/ *noun* [C] *SPECIALIZED* a large painful swelling under the skin

carbuncle [JEWEL] /ˈkɑː.bʌŋ.kl̩/ [US] /ˈkɑːr-/ *noun* [C] a dark red jewel

carburettor *UK, US* **carburetor** /ˌkɑː.bəˈret.əʳ/ [US] /ˌkɑːr.bəˈreɪ.t̬ɚ/ *noun* [C] the part of an engine which mixes fuel and air, producing the gas which is burnt to provide the power needed to operate the vehicle or machine

carcass /ˈkɑː.kəs/ [US] /ˈkɑːr-/ *noun* [C] **1** (*UK ALSO* **carcase**) the body of a dead animal, especially a large one that is soon to be cut up as meat or eaten by wild animals: *Vultures flew around in the sky waiting to pick at the rotting carcass* ***of*** *the deer.* ○ *SLANG Move your great carcass* (= your body) *out of that chair!* **2** the frame of an old or broken object, car, ship, etc: *Carcasses of burnt-out vehicles lined the roads near the scene of the worst fighting.*

carcinogen /kɑːˈsɪn.ə.dʒən/ [US] /kɑːr-/ *noun* [C] a substance which causes cancer: *The American government classifies both asbestos and environmental tobacco smoke as class one carcinogens.*

carcinogenic /ˌkɑː.sən.əʊˈdʒen.ɪk/ [US] /ˌkɑːr.sən.oʊ-/ *adj* describes a substance which causes cancer

carcinoma /kɑː.sɪˈnəʊ.mə/ [US] /kɑːr.sɪˈnoʊ-/ *noun* [C] *SPECIALIZED* a diseased growth which forms on or inside the body; a **tumour**

card [STIFF PAPER] /kɑːd/ [US] /kɑːrd/ *noun* [C or U] (a piece of) thick stiff paper ➲See also **phone card**; **railcard**; **scorecard**.

card [GAME] /kɑːd/ [US] /kɑːrd/ *noun* [C] (*ALSO* **playing card**) one of a set of 52 small rectangular pieces of stiff paper each with a number and one of four signs printed on it, used in games: *After dinner, Ted got out a* ***pack****/(US ALSO)* ***deck*** *of cards* ○ *John* ***shuffled*** (= mixed up) *the cards before he* ***dealt*** *them* ***(out)*** (= gave them to the players). ○ *Whist is my favourite card* ***game***. ○ *a card table*

• **have a card up *your* sleeve** to have an advantage that other people do not know about: *Well, Alan, England have definitely been the weaker side in the first half, but I think they've still got one or two cards up their sleeve.*

• **keep/hold *your* cards close to *your* chest** to be very secretive about your intended actions: *You never quite know what Barry's going to do next – he keeps his cards very close to his chest.*

• ***your*** **best/strongest/trump card** your main advantage over other people

• **put/lay *your* cards on the table** to be honest about your feelings and intentions: *I thought it was time I laid my cards on the table, so I told him that I had no intention of marrying him.*

• **be on the cards** *UK* (*US* **be in the cards**) to be likely to happen: *"So you think there'll be an election next year." "I think it's on the cards."*

cards /kɑːdz/ [US] /kɑːrdz/ *plural noun* any of a range of games played with cards, such as POKER, WHIST and BRIDGE: *I've never been much good at cards.* ○ *Shall we* ***have a game of/play*** *cards?*

card [PERMISSION] /kɑːd/ [US] /kɑːrd/ *noun* [C] a small rectangular piece of card or plastic, often with your signature, photograph or other information proving who you are, which allows you to do something, such as make a payment, obtain money from a bank or enter a particular place: *I don't have any cash – can I* ***put*** *this* ***on*** (= pay using) *my* ***(credit/charge)*** *card?* ○ *A lot of shops won't accept cheques unless you have a* ***(cheque/****UK ALSO* ***banker's)*** *card with you.* ○ *The bank's closed now, but I can get some money out with my* ***(cash)*** *card.* ○ *I don't have any change for the phone but I do have a* ***(phone)*** *card, if that's of any use.* ○ *You usually have to show your (membership) card at the door.* ➲See also **cardholder**.

card /kɑːd/ [US] /kɑːrd/ *verb* [T] *US* to ask someone to show you a document, especially an IDENTITY CARD, in order to prove how old they are

card [GREETINGS] /kɑːd/ [US] /kɑːrd/ *noun* **[C]** **1** a rectangular piece of stiff paper, folded in half, with a picture on the front and often a message printed inside, sent on a special occasion: *anniversary/get-well cards* ○ *It's Steve's birthday on Thursday – I must* ***send*** *him a card.* **2** a **postcard**

card [INFORMATION] /kɑːd/ [US] /kɑːrd/ *noun* **[C]** a small rectangular piece of stiff paper with information printed on it, especially a person's job title, business address and telephone number: *Here, let me give you my* ***(business)*** *card.* ➲See picture **In the Office** on page Centre 15

card [PERSON] /kɑːd/ [US] /kɑːrd/ *noun* **[C]** *OLD-FASHIONED INFORMAL* an amusing or strange person: *You're such a card, Patrick!*

cardamom, *UK ALSO* **cardamum**, *US ALSO* **cardamon** /ˈkɑː.də.məm/ [US] /ˈkɑːr-/ *noun* **[C or U]** an Indian plant, the seeds of which are used as a spice, especially in Asian food: *cardamom seeds* ○ *Add two teaspoonfuls of ground cardamom.*

cardboard /ˈkɑːd.bɔːd/ [US] /ˈkɑːrd.bɔːrd/ *noun* **[U]** material like very thick stiff paper, usually pale brown in colour, which is used especially for making boxes: *a cardboard* ***box***.

cardboard /ˈkɑːd.bɔːd/ [US] /ˈkɑːrd.bɔːrd/ *adj DISAPPROVING* relating to something, usually a character in a film or play, that does not seem to be real or interesting: *I've never enjoyed his plays – somehow all his characters are all cardboard.*

card-carrying member /ˌkɑːd.kær.i.ɪŋˈmem.bəʳ/ [US] /ˌkɑːrd.ker.i.ɪŋˈmem.bɚ/ *noun* **[C]** A card-carrying member of an organization is an active and involved member: *My brother's a card-carrying member of the Communist Party.*

cardholder /ˈkɑːdˌhəʊl.dəʳ/ [US] /ˈkɑːrdˌhoʊl.dɚ/ *noun* **[C]** someone who has been given permission to use a card which allows them to do something, especially a cheque card or a credit card

cardi- /kɑː.di-/ [US] /kɑːr-/ *prefix SPECIALIZED* **cardio-**

cardiac /ˈkɑː.di.æk/ [US] /ˈkɑːr-/ *adj* of the heart or heart disease: *cardiac* ***arrest*** (= a condition in which the heart stops beating)

cardigan /ˈkɑː.dɪ.gən/ [US] /ˈkɑːr-/ *noun* **[C]** (*UK INFORMAL* **cardy**, *ALSO* **cardie**) a woollen piece of clothing which covers the upper part of the body and the arms, fastening at the front with buttons, and usually worn over other clothes ➲See picture **Clothes** on page Centre 6

cardinal [PRIEST] /ˈkɑː.dɪ.nəl/ [US] /ˈkɑːr-/ *noun* **[C]** a priest of very high rank in the Roman Catholic Church: *Cardinals elect and advise the Pope.*

cardinal [IMPORTANT] /ˈkɑː.dɪ.nəl/ [US] /ˈkɑːr-/ *adj* **[before n]** of great importance; main: *a cardinal rule/error/sin*

cardinal [BIRD] /ˈkɑː.dɪ.nəl/ [US] /ˈkɑːr-/ *noun* **[C]** a North American bird, the male of which has bright red feathers

ˌcardinal (ˈnumber) *noun* **[C]** a number which represents amount, such as 1, 2, 3, rather than order, such as 1st, 2nd, 3rd ➲Compare **ordinal (number)**.

ˌcardinal ˈpoint *noun* **[C]** one of the four main points of the compass: north, south, east and west

ˈcard ˌindex *noun* **[C]** a box for storing cards in a particular order

cardio- /kɑː.di.əʊ-/ [US] /-oʊ-/ *prefix* (*ALSO* **cardi-**) of the heart: *cardiovascular*

cardiography /ˌkɑː.diˈɒg.rə.fi/ [US] /ˌkɑːr.diˈɑː.grə-/ *noun* **[U]** *SPECIALIZED* the use of a machine to record the beating of the heart

cardiograph /ˈkɑː.di.ə.græf/ /-grɑːf/ [US] /ˈkɑːr.di.ə.græf/ *noun* **[C]** *SPECIALIZED* a machine for recording the beating of the heart

cardiogram /ˈkɑː.di.ə.græm/ [US] /ˈkɑːr-/ *noun* **[C]** *SPECIALIZED* the picture drawn by a cardiograph, which shows a record of the heart's activity

cardiology /ˌkɑː.diˈɒl.ə.gi/ [US] /ˌkɑːr.diˈɑː.lə-/ *noun* **[U]** *SPECIALIZED* the study and treatment of medical conditions of the heart

cardiologist /ˌkɑː.diˈɒl.ə.dʒɪst/ [US] /ˌkɑːr.diˈɑː.lə-/ *noun* **[C]** *SPECIALIZED* a heart specialist

cardiovascular /ˌkɑː.di.əʊˈvæs.kjʊ.ləʳ/ [US] /ˌkɑːr.di.oʊˈvæs.kjə.lɚ/ *adj SPECIALIZED* relating to the heart and blood VESSELS (= tubes that carry blood around the body): *cardiovascular disease*

cardphone /ˈkɑːd.fəʊn/ [US] /ˈkɑːrd.foʊn/ *noun* **[C]** a public telephone which you operate using a special card instead of coins

cardsharp /ˈkɑːd.ʃɑːp/ [US] /ˈkɑːrd.ʃɑːrp/ *noun* **[C]** a person who earns money by playing cards dishonestly

ˈcard ˌvote *noun* **[C]** (*ALSO* **block vote**) *UK* a way of voting in which your vote represents other members of your organization, especially at TRADE UNION meetings

cardy, **cardie** /ˈkɑː.di/ [US] /ˈkɑːr-/ *noun* **[C]** *UK INFORMAL FOR* **cardigan**

care [PROTECTION] /keəʳ/ [US] /ker/ *noun* **[U]** **1** the process of protecting and looking after someone or something: *The standard of care at our local hospital is excellent.* ○ *Mira's going to be very weak for a long time after the operation, so she'll need a lot of care.* ○ *Nurseries are responsible for the children* ***in*** *their care.* **2** used as a combining form: *skin care/healthcare/childcare*

• **care in the community** *UK* when people with mental illness or reduced mental ability are allowed to continue living in their own homes, with treatment and help, and are not kept in hospital

• **take care of** ***sb/sth*** to look after someone or something: *Take* ***good*** *care of that girl of yours, Patrick – she's very special.* ○ *Don't worry about me, I can take care of myself* (= I do not need anyone else to protect me).

• **take care of** ***sth*** to deal with something: *If you can sort out the drink for the party, I'll take care of the food.* ○ *All the travel arrangements have been taken care of.* ○ *No, you paid for dinner last time, let me take care of* (= pay for) *it.*

• **take care (of yourself)** used when saying goodbye to someone: *"Bye, Melissa." "Goodbye Rozzie, take care."*

• **in care** (*ALSO* **take/put into care**) *UK* Children who are in care or who have been taken/put into care are not living with their natural parents but instead with a national or local government organization or another family: *Both children were taken into care when their parents died.*

care [ATTENTION] /keəʳ/ [US] /ker/ *noun* **[U]** serious attention, especially to the details of a situation or something: *She painted the window frames* ***with*** *great care so that no paint got onto the glass.* ○ *You need to* ***take*** *a bit more care* ***with*** *your spelling.* ○ *The roads are icy, so drive* ***with*** *care.* ○ ***Take*** *care on these busy roads* (= Drive with attention so that you do not have an accident). ○ **[+ to infinitive]** ***Take*** *care not* ***to*** (= Make certain that you do not) *spill your coffee.* ○ **[+ that]** ***Take*** *care* (= Make certain) ***that*** *you don't fall.* ○ *The parcel had a label on it saying* ***'Handle with*** *care'.*

careful /ˈkeə.fəl/ [US] /ˈker-/ *adj* giving a lot of attention to what you are doing so that you do not have an accident, make a mistake, or damage something: ***Be careful with*** *the glasses.* ○ ***Be careful where*** *you put that hot pan.* ○ ***Be*** *careful* ***to*** *look both ways when you cross the road.* ○ *Michael is a very careful worker.* ○ *After careful consideration of your proposal, I regret to say that we are unable to accept it.* ○ *He's in a really foul temper so be careful* ***(about/of)*** *what you say to him.*

carefully /ˈkeə.fəl.i/ [US] /ˈker-/ *adv* with great attention: *She carefully folded the letter and put it in her pocket.* ○ *Drive carefully on those icy roads.*

careless /ˈkeə.ləs/ [US] /ˈker-/ *adj* not taking or showing enough care and attention: *My son's teacher says that his work is often rather careless.* ○ *He made a careless* (= without thinking) *remark about her appearance that really upset her.* **carelessly** /ˈkeə.lə.sli/ [US] /ˈker-/ *adv*: *He told me off for driving carelessly.* **carelessness** /ˈkeə.lə.snəs/ [US] /ˈker-/ *noun* **[U]**

care [WORRY] /keəʳ/ [US] /ker/ *noun* **[C or U]** a feeling of worry or anxiety: *She seemed weighed down by all her cares.*

• **have all the cares of the world on** ***your*** **shoulders** to be very worried by many different problems: *You look as if you have all the cares of the world on your shoulders.*

• **without a care in the world** (*ALSO* **not a care in the world**) without any worries: *Look at her, not a care in the world!*

care /keəʳ/ US /ker/ *verb* [I] to think that something is important and to feel interested in it or upset about it: *She's never cared very much **about** her appearance.* ○ [+ question word] *I really don't care **whether** we go out or not.* ○ *I don't care **how** much it costs, just buy it.* ○ *"Was Lorna happy about the arrangements?" "I **don't know and** I don't care."* ○ *Your parents are only doing this because they care **about** (= love) you.*

• *I couldn't care less* INFORMAL used to emphasize rudely that you are not interested in or worried about something or someone: *"Mike's really fed up about it." "I couldn't care less."*

• *for all I care* INFORMAL used to say that you are not interested in or worried about what someone else is doing: *You can go to the match with Paula, for all I care.*

• *as if I care* INFORMAL used to say that you are not interested in or worried about something that has happened or that someone has said: *He said he didn't approve of what I'd done, as if I cared.*

• *Who cares?* INFORMAL used to emphasize rudely that you do not think something is important: *"It looks as if Scotland are going to win." "Who cares?".*

careless /ˈkeə.ləs/ US /ˈker-/ *adj* LITERARY relaxed, natural and free from anxiety ➔See also **carefree**. **carelessly** /ˈkeə.lə.sli/ US /ˈker-/ *adv* **carelessness** /ˈkeə.lə.snəs/ US /ˈker-/ *noun* [U]

care [WANT] /keəʳ/ US /ker/ *verb* [I] FORMAL used in polite offers and suggestions: *Would you care **for** a drink?* ○ [+ to infinitive] *Would you care **to** join us for dinner?*

PHRASAL VERBS WITH **care** ▼

▲ **care for** *sb* [LOOK AFTER] *phrasal verb* to look after someone or something, especially someone who is young, old or ill: *The children are being cared for by a relative.* ○ *She can't go out to work because she has to stay at home to care for her elderly mother.* ○ *It's good to know that the dogs will be well cared for while we're away.*

▲ **care for** *sb* [LIKE] *phrasal verb* FORMAL to feel affectionate and often romantic towards someone: *You know I care for you, Peter.*

▲ **not care for** *sb/sth* [DISLIKE] *phrasal verb* SLIGHTLY FORMAL to not like something or someone: *I have to say I don't much care for modern music.* ○ *Your father thought she was nice but Camille and I didn't care for her.*

careen /kəˈriːn/ *verb* [I + adv or prep] MAINLY US to go forward quickly while moving from side to side: *The driver lost control of his car when the brakes failed, and it went careening **down** the hill.*

career [JOB] /kəˈrɪəʳ/ US /-ˈrɪr/ *noun* [C] the job or series of jobs that you do during your working life, especially if you continue to get better jobs and earn more money: *He's hoping for a career in the police force/**as** a police officer.* ○ *When he retires he will be able to look back over a **brilliant** career (= a working life which has been very successful).* ○ *It helps if you can move a few rungs up the career **ladder** before taking time off to have a baby.* ○ *I took this new job because I felt that the career **prospects** were much better.* ○ *Elaine has become a real career **woman/girl** (= is interested in and spends most of her time on her job).* ○ *Judith is very career-**minded/-oriented** (= gives a lot of attention to her job).*

careerist /kəˈrɪə.rɪst/ US /-ˈrɪr.ɪst/ *noun* [C] OFTEN DISAPPROVING someone who thinks that their career is more important than anything else, and who will do anything to be successful in it

careers UK /kəˈrɪəz/ US /-ˈrɪrz/ *adj* [before n] (US **career**) relating to advice about jobs and training: *a careers adviser/officer*

COMMON LEARNER ERROR

career

Many learners make mistakes when spelling the word **career** (the jobs that you have during your working life). Note that the correct spelling has '-reer' at the end of the word.

Connors had a long and successful career in the police force.

career [MOVE] /kəˈrɪəʳ/ US /-ˈrɪr/ *verb* [I usually + adv or prep] (especially of a vehicle) to move fast and uncontrollably: *The coach careered **down** a slope and collided with a bank.*

carefree /ˈkeə.friː/ US /ˈker-/ *adj* having no problems or worries: *I remember my carefree student days.*

careful /ˈkeə.fºl/ US /ˈker-/ *adj* ➔See at **care** ATTENTION

caregiver /ˈkeə.gɪv.əʳ/ US /ˈker.gɪv.ɚ/ *noun* [C] MAINLY US OR SPECIALIZED **carer**

careless /ˈkeə.ləs/ US /ˈker-/ *adj* ➔See at **care** ATTENTION, **care** WORRY

carer UK /ˈkeə.rəʳ/ US /ˈker.ɚ/ *noun* [C] (US **caregiver**, US **caretaker**) someone who looks after a person who is young, old or ill

caress /kəˈres/ *verb* [I or T] to touch or kiss someone in a gentle and loving way: *Gently he caressed her cheek.* **caress** /kəˈres/ *noun* [C]

caretaker [BUILDING WORKER] UK /ˈkeə.teɪ.kəʳ/ US /ˈker.teɪ.kɚ/ *noun* [C] (US AND SCOTTISH ENGLISH **janitor**, US ALSO **custodian**) a person employed to take care of a large building, such as a school, and who deals with the cleaning, repairs, etc. **caretaking** /ˈkeə.teɪ.kɪŋ/ US /ˈker-/ *noun* [U] *caretaking staff/duties*

caretaker [GIVES CARE] /ˈkeə.teɪ.kəʳ/ US /ˈker.teɪ.kɚ/ *noun* [C] US FOR **carer**

caretaker 'government *noun* [C] UK a government that has power for a short period of time until a new one is chosen

careworn /ˈkeə.wɔːn/ US /ˈker.wɔːrn/ *adj* appearing tired, worried and unhappy: *Her mother, who couldn't have been much more than thirty, looked old and careworn.*

carfare /ˈkɑː.feəʳ/ US /ˈkɑːr.fer/ *noun* [U] MAINLY US the money paid by a passenger for travelling in a bus, taxi, etc: *You'll need a couple of dollars for carfare.*

car ˌferry *noun* [C] a ship designed for carrying vehicles and passengers

cargo /ˈkɑː.gəʊ/ US /ˈkɑːr.goʊ/ *noun* [C or U] *plural* **cargoes** or **cargos** the goods carried by a ship, aircraft or other large vehicle: *a cargo ship/plane* ○ *The ship was carrying a cargo **of** wool from England to France.*

cargo ˌpants *plural noun* loose trousers with large pockets on the outside of the legs

carhop /ˈkɑː.hɒp/ US /ˈkɑːr.hɑːp/ *noun* [C] US INFORMAL a person who serves food at a DRIVE-IN restaurant (= a restaurant in which people eat their meals in their cars)

the ˌCaribbean (ˈSea) *noun* [S] the sea which is east of Central America and north of South America: *The hurricane is centered over the eastern Caribbean.*

the Carib'bean *noun* [S] the islands and countries which border the Caribbean: *They're holidaying somewhere in the Caribbean.* **Caribbean** /ˌkær.ɪˈbiː.ªn/ /kəˈrɪb.i-/ US /ˌker.ɪˈbiː-/ *adj: Caribbean food*

caribou /ˈkær.ɪ.buː/ US /ˈker-/ *noun* [C] *plural* **caribous** or **caribou** a N. American REINDEER (= a large deer with long branch-like horns)

caricature /ˈkær.ɪ.kə.tʃʊəʳ/ US /ˈker.ɪ.kə.tʃʊr/ *noun* [C or U] (the art of making) a drawing or written or spoken description of someone, which makes part of their appearance or character more noticeable than it really is, and which usually makes them look ridiculous: *The characters in his early novels are a lot subtler than the overblown caricatures in his more recent work.* ○ FIGURATIVE *Over the years he's become a grotesque caricature **of** himself.* **caricature** /ˌkær.ɪ.kəˈtʃʊəʳ/ US /ˌker.ɪ.kəˈtʃʊr/ *verb* [T] *Charles Dickens caricatured lawyers (= represented them in a way which made them look ridiculous) in several of his novels.* **caricaturist** /ˌkær.ɪ.kəˈtʃʊə.rɪst/ US /ˌker.ɪ.kəˈtʃʊr.ɪst/ *noun* [C] a person who creates caricatures

caries /ˈkeə.riːz/ US /ˈker.iːz/ *noun* [U] SPECIALIZED decay in the teeth or bones

carillon /kəˈrɪl.jən/ US /ˈkæ.rə.lɑːn/ *noun* [C] (a tune played on) a set of bells, usually hung in a tower

caring /ˈkeə.rɪŋ/ US /ˈker.ɪŋ/ *adj* describes someone who is kind and gives emotional support to others: *I've always thought of Jo as a very caring person.*

ˌcaring proˈfession *noun* [C] UK a job such as nursing, which involves caring for people

carjacking /'kɑː.dʒæk.ɪŋ/ ⓤ /'kɑːr-/ noun [C or U] the crime of stealing someone's car while they are in it by using physical force or threats **carjacker** /'kɑː.dʒæk.əʳ/ ⓤ /'kɑːr.dʒæk.ɚ/ noun [C]

carmine /'kɑː.maɪn/ ⓤ /'kɑːr-/ adj, noun [U] (of a) deep bright red colour

carnage /'kɑː.nɪdʒ/ ⓤ /'kɑːr-/ noun [U] the violent killing of large numbers of people, especially in war: *The Battle of the Somme was a scene of dreadful carnage.*

carnal /'kɑː.nəl/ ⓤ /'kɑːr-/ adj FORMAL relating to the physical feelings and desires of the body; sexual: *carnal desires* **carnality** /kɑːˈnæl.ɪ.ti/ ⓤ /kɑːrˈnæl.ə.t̬i/ noun [U]

,carnal 'knowledge noun [U] FORMAL sex

carnation /kɑːˈneɪ.ʃən/ ⓤ /kɑːr-/ noun [C] (a plant with) a small flower with a sweet smell, which is usually white, pink, or red ➋See picture **Flowers and Plants** on page Centre 3

carnival /'kɑː.nɪ.vəl/ ⓤ /'kɑːr-/ noun **1** [C/U] (a special occasion or period of) public enjoyment and entertainment involving wearing unusual clothes, dancing, and eating and drinking, usually held in the roads of a city: *There's a real carnival atmosphere in the streets.* **2** [C] US FOR **funfair** and **fête** EVENT

carnivore /'kɑː.nɪ.vɔːʳ/ ⓤ /'kɑːr.nɪ.vɔːr/ noun [C] an animal that eats meat: *Lions and tigers are carnivores.* ○ HUMOROUS *I did mostly vegetarian food but put a couple of meat dishes out for the carnivores* (= people who eat meat). ➋Compare **herbivore**. **carnivorous** /kɑːˈnɪv.ᵊr.əs/ ⓤ /kɑːrˈnɪv.ɚ-/ adj

carob /'kær.əb/ ⓤ /'ker-/ noun [C or U] (the dark brown bean-like seeds of) a Mediterranean tree: *Carob is sometimes used in sweet foods as a healthier alternative to chocolate.*

carol /'kær.əl/ ⓤ /'ker-/ noun [C] a happy or religious song, usually one sung at Christmas: *a carol concert* ○ *'Silent Night' is my favourite (Christmas) carol.*

carol /'kær.əl/ ⓤ /'ker-/ verb [I] -ll- or US USUALLY -l- to sing songs, especially carols, in a loud and joyful way

'carol ,singer UK noun [C] (US **caroler**) a member of a group of people who go from house to house singing carols at Christmas **carol-singing** UK /'kær.əl.sɪŋ.ɪŋ/ ⓤ /'ker-/ noun [U] (US **caroling**)

carotene /'kær.ə.tiːn/ ⓤ /'ker-/ noun [U] an orange-yellow or red PIGMENT (= substance which gives colour) contained in some foods

carouse /kəˈraʊz/ verb [I] LITERARY OR HUMOROUS to enjoy yourself by drinking alcohol and speaking and laughing loudly in a group of people: *We'd been up carousing till the early hours and were exhausted.*

carousel AMUSEMENT /ˌkær.ʊˈsel/ ⓤ /ˌker.ə-/ noun [C] MAINLY US FOR **merry-go-round**

carousel AIRPORT /ˌkær.ʊˈsel/ ⓤ /ˌker.ə-/ noun [C] a continuous moving strip on which airport passengers' bags are put for collection

Carousel CONTAINER /ˌkær.ʊˈsel/ ⓤ /ˌker.ə-/ noun [C] TRADEMARK a circular device in which SLIDES (= small pieces of photographic film) for a PROJECTOR are held

carp COMPLAIN /kɑːp/ ⓤ /kɑːrp/ verb [I] to complain continually about unimportant matters: *I can't stand the way he's always carping.*

carp FISH /kɑːp/ ⓤ /kɑːrp/ noun [C or U] plural **carp** a large edible fish which lives in lakes and rivers

carpal tunnel syndrome /ˌkɑː.pᵊlˈtʌn.ᵊl. sɪn.drəʊm/ ⓤ /ˌkɑːr.pᵊlˈtʌn.ᵊl.sɪndroʊm/ noun [U] SPECIALIZED a medical condition of pain and weakness in the hand, caused by repeated pressure on a nerve in the wrist

'car ,park AREA UK noun [C] (US **parking lot**) an area of ground for parking cars

'car ,park BUILDING UK noun [C] (US **parking garage**) a building for parking cars

carpenter /'kɑː.pɪn.təʳ/ ⓤ /'kɑːr.pɪn.t̬ɚ/ noun [C] a person whose job is making and repairing wooden objects and structures ➋Compare **joiner**.

carpentry /'kɑː.pɪn.tri/ ⓤ /'kɑːr-/ noun [U] the skill of making and repairing wooden objects

carpet COVERING /'kɑː.pɪt/ ⓤ /'kɑːr-/ noun **1** [C or U] (a shaped piece of) thick woven material used for covering floors: *We've just had a new carpet fitted/laid in our*

bedroom. ○ UK *We've got fitted* (= cut to fit exactly) *carpets in the bedrooms.* **2** [S] a layer of something that covers the ground: *a carpet of snow* ○ *Our lawn is a carpet of daisies.*

• **be on the carpet** MAINLY US to be in trouble with someone in authority

carpet /'kɑː.pɪt/ ⓤ /'kɑːr-/ verb [T] to cover something with carpet: *We need to carpet the stairs.*

carpeted /'kɑː.pə.tɪd/ ⓤ /'kɑːr.pə.t̬ɪd/ adj covered with carpet

• **be carpeted with sth** to be covered with something: *In spring this area is carpeted with bluebells.*

carpeting /'kɑː.pɪ.tɪŋ/ ⓤ /'kɑːr.pɪ.t̬ɪŋ/ noun [U] material for making carpets

carpet CRITICIZE /'kɑː.pɪt/ ⓤ /'kɑːr-/ verb [T] UK INFORMAL to severely criticize someone who has made a mistake

carpetbagger POLITICS /'kɑː.pɪt.bæg.əʳ/ ⓤ /'kɑːr.pɪt.bæg.ɚ/ noun [C] MAINLY US DISAPPROVING someone who tries to become a politician in a place away from their home because they think there is a greater chance of succeeding there

carpetbagger MONEY /'kɑː.pɪt.bæg.əʳ/ ⓤ /'kɑːr.pɪt.bæg.ɚ/ noun [C] UK DISAPPROVING someone who invests in a financial organization that is owned by its members, in order to make a profit if it is sold: *Thousands of carpetbaggers have invested in the building society, hoping that it will become a public company.*

'carpet ,bombing noun [U] the act of dropping a lot of bombs all over a particular area so that it will be destroyed

'carpet ,slipper noun [C usually pl] UK FOR **slipper**

'carpet ,sweeper noun [C] a machine with a brush fixed to the bottom of it for cleaning carpets

'car ,phone noun [C] a telephone which is kept and used in a car and is connected to the telephone system by radio

'car ,pool PEOPLE group noun [C] a group of people who travel together, especially to work or school, usually in a different member's car each day **car-pooling** /'kɑː.puː.lɪŋ/ ⓤ /'kɑːr-/ noun [U]

'car ,pool CARS group noun [C] a group of cars owned by a company or other organization which can be used by any of its employees

carport /'kɑː.pɔːt/ ⓤ /'kɑːr.pɔːrt/ noun [C] a shelter for cars, which has a roof and one or more open sides, and which can be built against the side of a house

carriage VEHICLE /'kær.ɪdʒ/ ⓤ /'ker-/ noun [C] **1** a vehicle with four wheels, which is usually pulled by horses and was used especially in the past: *a horse-drawn carriage* **2** UK any of the separate parts of a train in which the passengers sit: *a railway carriage*

carriage TRANSPORTING /'kær.ɪdʒ/ ⓤ /'ker-/ noun [U] UK (the cost of) transporting goods: *That will be £150, carriage included.*

carriage BODY MOVEMENT /'kær.ɪdʒ/ ⓤ /'ker-/ noun [U] FORMAL the way in which a person moves or keeps their body when they are standing, sitting or walking

'carriage ,clock noun [C] a small, rectangular, decorative clock with a metal handle on top

carriageway /'kær.ɪdʒ.weɪ/ ⓤ /'ker-/ noun [C] UK one of the two halves of a motorway or other wide road

'carrier (,bag) UK noun [C] (US **shopping bag**) a large plastic or paper bag with handles, used to put your shopping in

'carrier ,pigeon noun [C] a pigeon which is trained to carry messages

carrion /'kær.i.ən/ ⓤ /'ker-/ noun [U] dead or decaying flesh

carrot VEGETABLE /'kær.ət/ ⓤ /'ker-/ noun [C or U] a long pointed orange root eaten as a vegetable ➋See picture **Vegetables** on page Centre 2

carroty /'kær.ə.ti/ ⓤ /'ker.ə.t̬i/ adj: *Leo has bright carroty* (= orange) *hair.*

carrot REWARD /'kær.ət/ ⓤ /'ker-/ noun [C] INFORMAL something that is offered to someone in order to encourage them to do something

• **carrot and stick** a system in which you are rewarded for some actions and threatened with punishment for

C

others: *Sometimes I just have to resort to the carrot and stick approach with my children.*

carry [TRANSPORT] /'kær.i/ [US] /'ker-/ *verb* [I or T] to transport or take something from one place to another: *Would you like me to carry your bag for you?* ○ *She carried her tired child upstairs **to** bed.* ○ *These books are too heavy for me to carry.* ○ *The bus that was involved in the accident was carrying children **to** school.* ○ *The Brooklyn Bridge carries traffic across the East River **from** Brooklyn **to** Manhattan.* ○ *Police think that the body was carried **down** the river* (= was transported by the flow of the river). ○ *Underground cables carry electricity **to** all parts of the city.* ○ *We only had a small suitcase, so we were able to carry it **onto** the plane.* ○ *Rubbish left on the beach during the day is carried **away*** (= removed) *at night by the tide.* ○ *Thieves broke the shop window and carried **off*** (= removed) *jewellery worth thousands of pounds.* ○ *Robson injured his leg in the second half of the match and had to be carried **off**.*

• **carry the can** *UK INFORMAL* to take the blame or responsibility for something that is wrong or has not succeeded: *As usual, I was left to carry the can.*

• **carry a torch for *sb*** *INFORMAL* to be in love with someone: *Terry has been carrying a torch for Liz for years, but she seems not to notice.*

carrier /'kær.i.əʳ/ [US] /'ker.i.ɚ/ *noun* [C] **1** a person or thing that carries something **2** a company which operates aircraft **3** used as a combining form, especially in phrases which refer to military vehicles of a type which carry other vehicles or groups of soldiers: *an armoured troop-carrier* ○ *a freight carrier* **4** *INFORMAL FOR* **aircraft carrier**

carry [HAVE WITH YOU] /'kær.i/ [US] /'ker-/ *verb* [T] to have something with you all the time: *Police officers in Britain do not usually carry guns.* ○ *FIGURATIVE He will carry the **memory** of the accident with him* (= will remember the accident) *for ever.*

carry [SPREAD] /'kær.i/ [US] /'ker-/ *verb* [T] to take something from one person or thing and give it to another person or thing; to spread: *Malaria is a disease carried by mosquitoes.*

carrier /'kær.i.əʳ/ [US] /'ker.i.ɚ/ *noun* [C] someone who does not suffer from a disease but has the infection or faulty gene that causes it and can give the disease to someone else: *There are an estimated 1.5 million HIV carriers in the country.*

carry [HAVE] /'kær.i/ [US] /'ker-/ *verb* [T] to have something as a part, quality or result: *All cigarette packets carry a government health warning.* ○ *Our cars carry a twelve-month guarantee.* ○ *His speech carried so much **conviction** that I had to agree with him.* ○ *In some countries, murder carries the death penalty.* ○ *I'm afraid my opinion doesn't carry any **weight** with* (= influence) *my boss.* ○ US *The salesclerk said they didn't carry* (= have a supply of) *sportswear.*

carry [SUPPORT WEIGHT] /'kær.i/ [US] /'ker-/ *verb* [T] to support the weight of something without moving or breaking: *The weight of the cathedral roof is carried by two rows of pillars.*

carry [KEEP IN OPERATION] /'kær.i/ [US] /'ker-/ *verb* [T] to support, keep in operation, or make a success: *We can no longer afford to carry people who don't work as hard as they should.* ○ *Luckily they had a very strong actor in the main part and he managed to carry the whole play* (= make a success of it through his own performance).

carry [WIN] /'kær.i/ [US] /'ker-/ *verb* [T] to win the support, agreement or sympathy of a group of people: *The management's plans to reorganize the company won't succeed unless they can carry the workforce with them.*

carry [APPROVE] /'kær.i/ [US] /'ker-/ *verb* [T usually passive] to give approval, especially by voting: *The **motion/proposal/resolution/bill** was carried **by** 210 votes to 160.*

carry [BROADCAST] /'kær.i/ [US] /'ker-/ *verb* [T] (of a newspaper, radio or television broadcast) to contain particular information: *This morning's newspapers all carry the same story on their front page.*

carry [REACH] /'kær.i/ [US] /'ker-/ *verb* [I] to be able to reach or travel a particular distance: *The sound of the explosion carried for miles.* ○ *The ball carried high into the air and landed the other side of the fence.*

carry [DEVELOP] /'kær.i/ [US] /'ker-/ *verb* [T usually + adv or prep] to develop; to continue: *Lenin carried Marx's ideas a stage further by putting them into practice.* ○ *If we carry this argument **to** its logical conclusion, we realise that further investment is not a good idea.* ○ *She carries tidiness **to** extremes/**to** its limits* (= She is too tidy). ○ *We must end here, but we can carry today's discussion **forward** at our next meeting.* ○ *He always carries his jokes too far* (= he continues making jokes when he should have stopped).

carry [MATHEMATICS] /'kær.i/ [US] /'ker-/ *verb* [T] to put a number into another column when doing addition

carry [BE PREGNANT WITH] /'kær.i/ [US] /'ker-/ *verb* [T] to be pregnant with a child: *It was quite a shock to learn that she was carrying twins.* ○ *I was enormous when I was carrying Josh.*

'carry ˌyourself [MOVE BODY] /'kær.i/ [US] /'ker-/ *verb* [R] to move your body in a particular way: *You can tell she's a dancer from the way that she carries herself.*

PHRASAL VERBS WITH **carry** ▼

▲ **carry *sb* away** *phrasal verb* **1 be/get carried away** to become so excited about something that you do not control what you say or do: *There's far too much food – I'm afraid I got a bit carried away.* ○ *The manager warned his young players not to get carried away by the emotion of the occasion.* **2** [M] to cause someone to become very excited and to lose control: *The crowd were carried away by his passionate speech.*

▲ **carry *sth* forward/over** *phrasal verb* [M] to include an amount of money in a later set of calculations: *The balance in our account for June includes £5000 carried over from May.*

▲ **carry *sth* off** *phrasal verb* [M] to succeed in doing or achieving something difficult: *I thought he carried off the part of Hamlet with great skill.* ○ *She was nervous about giving a talk to her colleagues, but she carried **it** off very well.*

▲ **carry *(sth)* on** [CONTINUE] *phrasal verb* [M] to continue doing something, or to cause something to continue: *Let's carry on this discussion at some other time.* ○ *Carry on **the good work**!* ○ *Sorry to interrupt, do carry on (**with** what you were saying).* ○ *You just have to carry on as if nothing's happened.* ○ [+ v-ing] *Steve just carried on playing on his computer.* ○ *Daphne is carrying on the family tradition by becoming a lawyer.*

▲ **carry on** [BEHAVE] *phrasal verb INFORMAL* to behave in an uncontrolled, excited or anxious way: *The children have been carrying on all day.*

carry-on /'kær.i.ɒn/ [US] /'ker.i.ɑːn/ /ˌ--'-/ *noun* [S] *UK INFORMAL* a show of annoyance, anxiety, dissatisfaction or excitement, usually one which is greater than the situation deserves: *There was a real carry-on when Pat was found kissing Ashley.*

carrying-on /ˌkær.i.ɪŋ'ɒn/ [US] /ˌker.i.ɪŋ'ɑːn/ *noun* [C or U] *plural* **carryings-on** dishonest or immoral activity: *The company seems to have been involved in some rather dishonest carrying-on.* ○ *The newspapers were full of the Minister's carryings-on.*

▲ **carry on** [HAVE SEX] *phrasal verb OLD-FASHIONED INFORMAL* to have a sexual relationship: *Is it true that Rachel and Marcus have been carrying on (**with** each other)?*

▲ **carry *sth* out** *phrasal verb* [M] to do or complete something, especially that you have said you would do or that you have been told to do: *Nigel is carrying out research on early Christian art.* ○ *The hospital is carrying out tests to find out what's wrong with her.* ○ *Our soldiers carried out a successful attack last night.* ○ *It is hoped that the kidnappers will not carry out their threat to kill the hostages.* ○ *Don't blame me, I'm only carrying out my orders/instructions.*

▲ **carry *sth* over** [DO LATER] *phrasal verb* [M] to use or do something at a later time than planned: *The performance has had to be carried over **to/till** next week because the repairs to the theatre aren't finished yet.*

▲ **carry *(sth)* over** [EXIST/AFFECT] *phrasal verb* [M] If something from one situation carries over or is carried over into another situation, it is allowed to exist in or affect the other situation: *I try not to let my problems at work carry over **into** my private life.*

▲ **carry** *sb* **through** (*sth*) HELP *phrasal verb* to help someone be able to deal with a difficult situation: *The soldiers' courage carried them through.*

▲ **carry** *sth* **through** COMPLETE *phrasal verb* [M] to complete something successfully: *It is doubtful whether it will be possible to carry through the education reforms as quickly as the government hopes.*

carryall /ˈkær.i.ɔːl/ ⓤ /ˈker.i.ɑːl/ *noun* [C] *US FOR* **holdall**

carrycot *UK* /ˈkær.i.kɒt/ ⓤ /ˈker.i.kɑːt/ *noun* [C] (*US* **bassinet**) a container shaped like a rectangular box with two handles, in which a baby can be carried

carrying ,charge *noun* [C usually sing] *US* an extra charge added when you buy goods by making regular small payments for them until the full amount owed has been paid

carry-on /ˈkær.i.ɒn/ ⓤ /ˈker.i.ɑːn/ *adj* [before n] *MAINLY US* relating to items that you take onto a plane with you: *All carry-on **luggage** must be stored under your seat or in the overhead compartments.*

carryout /ˈkær.i.aʊt/ ⓤ /ˈker-/ *noun* [C or U], *adj US AND SCOTTISH ENGLISH FOR* **takeaway**

carsick /ˈkɑː.sɪk/ ⓤ /ˈkɑːr-/ *adj* feeling that you want to vomit because of the movement of a car **carsickness** /ˈkɑːˌsɪk.nəs/ ⓤ /ˈkɑːr-/ *noun* [U]

cart VEHICLE /kɑːt/ ⓤ /kɑːrt/ *noun* [C] **1** a vehicle with either two or four wheels which is pulled by a horse, and which is used for carrying goods: *a **horse and** cart.* **2** *US FOR* **trolley** FOR CARRYING

● **put the cart before the horse** to do things in the wrong order: *Aren't you putting the cart before the horse by deciding what to wear for the wedding before you've even been invited to it?*

carter /ˈkɑː.təʳ/ ⓤ /ˈkɑːr.t̬ɚ/ *noun* [C] *OLD USE* a person who drives a cart

cart TAKE /kɑːt/ ⓤ /kɑːrt/ *verb* [T + adv or prep] to take something or someone somewhere, especially using a lot of effort: *We carted all the rubbish to the bottom of the garden and burned it.* ○ *Council workers have carted **away** all the dead leaves that had collected at the side of the road.* ○ *INFORMAL I've been carting (= carrying) these letters **around** with me all week, and I still haven't posted them.* ○ *INFORMAL The drunks who had been sleeping in the park were carted **off** (= taken by force) to the police station.*

carte blanche /ˌkɑːtˈblɑːʃ/ ⓤ /ˌkɑːrtˈblɑːnʃ/ *noun* [S or U] complete freedom to do something: [+ to infinitive] *Her husband has **given** her carte blanche **to** redecorate the living room.*

cartel /kɑːˈtel/ ⓤ /kɑːr-/ *noun* [C] a group of similar independent companies who join together to control prices and limit competition: *an oil cartel*

carthorse /ˈkɑːt.hɔːs/ ⓤ /ˈkɑːrt.hɔːrs/ *noun* [C] a large strong horse used for pulling CARTS

cartilage /ˈkɑː.tᵊl.ɪdʒ/ ⓤ /ˈkɑːr.t̬ᵊl/ *noun* [C or U] (a piece of) a type of strong stretchy tissue found in humans in the joints and other places such as the nose, throat and ears: *He has a **torn** cartilage in his knee.*

cartload /ˈkɑːt.ləʊd/ ⓤ /ˈkɑːrt.loʊd/ *noun* [C] **1** the amount that a CART holds **2** *INFORMAL* a large amount of something: *We threw out cartloads **of** rubbish when we moved house.*

cartography /kɑːˈtɒg.rə.fi/ ⓤ /kɑːrˈtɑː.grə-/ *noun* [U] the science or art of making or drawing maps **cartographer** /kɑːˈtɒg.rə.fəʳ/ ⓤ /kɑːrˈtɑː.grə.fɚ/ *noun* [C] someone who makes or draws maps

carton /ˈkɑː.tᵊn/ ⓤ /ˈkɑːr.t̬ᵊn/ *noun* [C] a box made from thick cardboard, for storing goods, or a container made from cardboard or plastic, in which milk or fruit juice, etc. is sold: *a carton **of** orange juice*

cartoon DRAWING /kɑːˈtuːn/ ⓤ /kɑːr-/ *noun* [C] **1** a drawing, especially in a newspaper or magazine, that tells a joke or makes an amusing political criticism **2** *SPECIALIZED* in art, a drawing made especially in preparation for a painting **cartoonist** /kɑːˈtuː.nɪst/ ⓤ /kɑːr-/ *noun* [C] a person who draws cartoons

cartoon FILM /kɑːˈtuːn/ ⓤ /kɑːr-/ *noun* [C] a film made using characters and images which are drawn rather than real, and which is usually amusing

cartridge /ˈkɑː.trɪdʒ/ ⓤ /ˈkɑːr-/ *noun* [C] **1** a small part with a particular purpose, used in a larger piece of equipment, which can be easily replaced with another similar part: *an ink/printer/video game cartridge* **2** a small tube containing an explosive substance and a bullet for use in a gun

cartridge ,paper *noun* [U] thick strong paper for drawing or writing on

cartridge ,pen *noun* [C] a pen in which there is an ink-filled plastic cartridge which can be replaced when it is empty

cart ,track *noun* [C] *UK* a narrow road with a rough surface that is usually made of earth

cartwheel /ˈkɑːt.wiːl/ ⓤ /ˈkɑːrt-/ *noun* [C] a fast skilful movement like a wheel turning, in which you throw yourself sideways onto one hand, then onto both hands with your arms and legs straight and your legs pointing up, before landing on your feet again **cartwheel** /ˈkɑːt.wiːl/ ⓤ /ˈkɑːrt-/ *verb* [I]

carve /kɑːv/ ⓤ /kɑːrv/ *verb* [I or T] **1** to make something by cutting into especially wood or stone, or to cut into the surface of stone, wood, etc: *This totem pole is carved **from/out of** a single tree trunk.* ○ *He carved her name **on** a tree.* ○ *Some of the tunnels in the cliff are natural, some were carved **out** (= cut into the rock) by soldiers for defensive purposes.* **2** to cut thin pieces from a large piece of cooked meat: *Would you like me to carve (the chicken)?*

● **carved in stone** *INFORMAL* If a suggestion, plan, rule, etc. is carved in stone, it cannot be changed: *These proposals are for discussion, they're not carved in stone.*

carver /ˈkɑː.vəʳ/ ⓤ /-ˌkɑːr.vɚ/ *noun* [C] (*ALSO* **electric carver**) a knife which has a blade that is moved very quickly by electricity, and is used for cutting cooked meat

carving /ˈkɑː.vɪŋ/ ⓤ /ˈkɑːr-/ *noun* [C or U] a shape or pattern cut into wood or stone or the skill of doing this: *wooden/stone carvings*

PHRASAL VERBS WITH **carve** ▼

▲ **carve** *sth* **out** (**for** *yourself*) *phrasal verb* to successfully create or obtain something, especially a work position, by working for it: *He hopes to carve out **a niche** for himself as a leading researcher in his field of study.* ○ *She carved out a reputation for herself as an aggressive businesswoman.*

▲ **carve** *sth* **up** DIVIDE *phrasal verb* [M] *DISAPPROVING* to divide something into smaller parts: *The Nazi-Soviet pact carved up the Baltic states in 1939.*

▲ **carve** *sb* **up** DRIVE *phrasal verb* *UK INFORMAL* to drive past someone in a car and then suddenly drive in front of them: *Some idiot carved us up on the way over here – I don't know how he missed us!*

carvery /ˈkɑː.vᵊr.i/ ⓤ /ˈkɑːr.vɚ-/ *noun* [C] a restaurant where you eat meat that is cut for you at a special table

carving ,knife *noun* [C] a large knife used for cutting cooked meat

car ,wash *noun* [C] a machine which you can drive through to have your car cleaned automatically

Casanova /ˌkæs.əˈnəʊ.və/ ⓤ /ˌkæs.əˈnoʊ-/ *noun* [C] *INFORMAL DISAPPROVING* a man who has had a lot of sexual relationships

cascade /kæsˈkeɪd/ *noun* [C] **1** a small waterfall, often one of a group **2** a large amount of something which hangs down: *A cascade **of** golden hair fell down his back.* **cascade** /kæsˈkeɪd/ *verb* [I usually + adv or prep] to fall quickly and in large amounts: *Coins cascaded **from/out** of the fruit machine.*

case SITUATION /keɪs/ *noun* [C] a particular situation or example of something: *Over a hundred people were injured, in several cases seriously.* ○ *Jobs are hard to find but **in** his case that's not the problem because he has so much experience.* ○ *I wouldn't normally agree but I'll make an exception **in this** case.* ○ *The number of new cases **of** the illness appears to be declining.* ○ *We have lots of applications from people who want to study here and in* *each case we consider the candidate very carefully.* ○ *She was suffering from an **extreme** case of sunburn.*

● **a case in point** an example which shows that what you are saying is true or helps to explain why you are saying it: *Lack of communication causes serious problems and their marriage is a case in point.*

● **as the case might be** (*ALSO* **whatever the case might be**) one of the stated possibilities which is true: *When the election is called in April, or June, as the case might be, we shall be ready for it.*

● **in the case of** with reference to, or in the situation of: *The law will apply equally to men and women except in the case of maternity leave.*

● **in that case** because of the mentioned situation: *There's no coffee left? In that case I'll have tea.*

● **(not) the case** (not) true: *If that is the case then I will be very disappointed.*

● **in any case** also: *I don't want to go and in any case, I haven't been invited.*

● **(just) in case** because of a possibility of something happening, being needed, etc: *I don't think I'll need any money but I'll bring some just in case.* ○ *Bring a map in case you get lost.*

● **a case of** used when a situation is of a particular type: *She doesn't want to work full-time, it's a case of having to.*

case PROBLEM /keɪs/ *noun* [C] **1** a problem, a series of events or a person being dealt with by police, doctors, lawyers, etc: *Several social workers have looked into the child's case.* ○ *The detective **on the case** (= responsible for solving it) has been suspended from duty.* ○ *When he first went for treatment at the hospital he seemed to be a **hopeless** case (= a person who could not be cured).* **2** LEGAL a matter to be decided by a judge in a court of law: *a murder case* ○ *The case will go before the European Court next month.* ○ *She accused her employer of unlawful dismissal and **won/lost** her case.*

● **be on the case** INFORMAL to be doing what needs to be done in a particular situation: *"We need to book a flight before it's too late." "Don't worry, I'm on the case."*

case ARGUMENT /keɪs/ *noun* [S] arguments, facts and reasons in support of or against something: *There's a good case **for/against** bringing in new regulations.* ○ *The case **against** cigarette advertising is becoming stronger all the time.* ○ *She's very busy so don't **overstate** the case – just give her the essentials.*

● **make a case for** *sth* (*UK ALSO* **make out a case for** *sth*) to argue that something is the best thing to do, giving your reasons: *We will only publish a new edition if you can make a convincing case for it.*

case CONTAINER /keɪs/ *noun* [C] **1** a container or box for storing things in ⊃See also **bookcase**; **briefcase**; **pillowcase**. **2 a case of wine, etc.** a box holding twelve bottles of wine or another type of alcoholic drink, or the twelve bottles and their contents

cased /keɪst/ *adj* covered in a tight case: *These are the electrical connectors, cased in waterproof plastic.*

casing /ˈkeɪ.sɪŋ/ *noun* [C or U] a covering

case GRAMMAR /keɪs/ *noun* [C or U] SPECIALIZED any of the various types to which a noun can belong, according to the work it does in a sentence, usually shown by a special word ending: *the accusative/dative case*

case LOOK AT /keɪs/ *verb* SLANG **case the joint** to look at a place with the intention of stealing from it later: *He looked around shiftily, as if he was casing the joint.*

case ˌhistory *noun* [C] a record of a person's health, development or behaviour, kept by an official such as a doctor: *The report was written after analysing data from the case histories of thousands of patients.*

ˈcase ˌlaw *noun* [U] LEGAL law based on decisions that have been made by judges in the past

caseload /ˈkeɪs.ləʊd/ ⑩ /-loʊd/ *noun* [C] the amount of work which someone, especially a doctor or lawyer has to do in a period of time: *a heavy caseload*

casement (window) /ˌkeɪ.smənt ˈwɪn.dəʊ/ ⑩ /-doʊ/ *noun* [C] a type of window that is fixed on one side and opens like a door

ˈcase ˌstudy *noun* [C] a detailed account giving information about the development of a person, group or

thing, especially in order to show general principles: *This is an interesting psychiatric case study of a child with extreme behavioural difficulties.*

cash /kæʃ/ *noun* [U] money in the form of notes and coins, rather than cheques or CREDIT CARDS: *Do you have any cash on you?* ○ *Will you pay by credit card or **in** cash?* ○ *He says he wants cash **in advance** before he'll do the job.* ○ INFORMAL *I'm a bit **short of/strapped for** cash* (= I do not have much money) *at the moment.* ⊃See also **COD** PAYMENT.

cash /kæʃ/ *verb* [T] to exchange a cheque, etc. for cash: *Would you cash a cheque for me?*

cashless /ˈkæʃ.ləs/ *adj* using or operating with CREDIT and DEBIT cards and electronic systems, not money in the form of coins or notes: *a cashless society*

PHRASAL VERBS WITH **cash** ▼

▲ **cash in on** *sth phrasal verb* to get money or another advantage from an event or situation, often in an unfair way: *Her family have been accused of cashing in on her death.*

▲ **cash up** *phrasal verb* to count all the money taken by a shop or business at the end of each day: *She cashed up and realized there was £10 missing from the till.*

ˌcash and ˈcarry *noun* [C] a large shop where people, usually from another business, can buy large amounts of goods cheaply, taking them away immediately

cashback PAYMENT /ˈkæʃ.bæk/ *noun* [U] UK a system in which banks or businesses encourage people to buy something by giving them money after they have bought it: *The major banks are offering cashback deals of up to £5000 on their mortgages.*

cashback MONEY /ˈkæʃ.bæk/ *noun* [U] UK an amount of money that a shop, usually a SUPERMARKET, enables you to take from your bank account when you pay for something with a bank card: *£20 cashback*

ˈcash ˌcard UK *noun* [C] (*US* **ATM card**) a special plastic card given to you by a bank, that allows you to take money out of your bank account using a CASH MACHINE

ˈcash ˌcrop *noun* [C] a crop that is grown mainly to be sold, rather than used by the people who grew it or those living in the area it is grown in

ˈcash ˌdesk *noun* [C] UK the place in a shop where you can pay for the things that you buy

ˈcash disˌpenser *noun* [C] UK a **cash machine**

cashew (nut) /ˈkæʃ.uː.nʌt/ /kəˈʃuː-/ *noun* [C] a small edible nut from a tropical American tree

ˈcash ˌflow, **cashflow** *noun* [U] the amount of money moving into and out of a business: *Small traders often have short-term cash-flow problems.*

cashier PERSON /kæʃˈɪəʳ/ ⑩ /-ˈɪr/ *noun* [C] a person whose job is to receive and pay out money in a shop, bank, restaurant, etc.

cashier DISMISS /kæʃˈɪəʳ/ ⑩ /-ˈɪr/ *verb* [T] to officially dismiss a person from a military organization, especially making them lose their honour at the same time

ˈcash maˌchine MAINLY UK *noun* [C] (*US USUALLY* **ATM**, *AUS* **automatic teller machine**) a machine, usually in a wall outside a bank, from which you can take money out of your bank account using a special card

cashmere /ˈkæʃ.mɪəʳ/ ⑩ /-mɪr/ /-ˈ-/ *noun* [U] very soft, expensive woollen material that is made from the hair of goats from Kashmir

cashpoint /ˈkæʃ.pɔɪnt/ *noun* [C] UK a **cash machine**

ˈcash ˌregister *noun* [C] a machine in a shop or other business that records sales and into which money received is put

cash-strapped *adj* not having enough money: *cash-strapped universities*

casing /ˈkeɪ.sɪŋ/ *noun* [C] ⊃See at **case** CONTAINER

casino /kəˈsiː.nəʊ/ ⑩ /-noʊ/ *noun* [C] *plural* **casinos** a building where games, especially ROULETTE and card games are played for money

cask /kɑːsk/ ⑩ /kæsk/ *noun* [C] a strong, round, wooden container used for storing liquid: *a cask of water/wine*

casket /ˈkɑː.skɪt/ ⑩ /ˈkæs.kɪt/ *noun* [C] **1** a small decorative box, especially one used to keep jewellery in **2** *US FOR* **coffin**

cassava /kəˈsɑː.və/ *noun* [U] a South American plant with large roots, or a type of flour made from these roots

casserole /ˈkæs.ᵊr.əʊl/ [US] /-ə.roʊl/ *noun* [C or U] a dish made by cooking meat, vegetables or other foods in liquid inside a heavy container at low heat, or the heavy, deep container with a lid used in cooking such dishes: *lamb casserole*

cassette /kəˈset/ *noun* [C] a flat rectangular device containing a very long strip of magnetic material that is used to record sound and/or pictures, or a machine that uses such devices: *a video cassette* ○ *an audio cassette*

casˈsette ˌplayer *noun* [C] a machine that can play CASSETTES but not record them

casˈsette reˌcorder *noun* [C] a machine that can play and record CASSETTES

cassock /ˈkæs.ək/ *noun* [C] a long, loose, usually black piece of clothing worn especially by priests

cast [LIGHT] /kɑːst/ [US] /kæst/ *verb* [T usually + adv or prep] **cast, cast 1** to send light or SHADOW (= an area of darkness) in a particular direction: *The moon cast a white light into the room.* ○ *The tree cast a shadow* ***over/on*** *his face.* ○ *FIGURATIVE Her arrival cast a shadow* ***over/on*** *the party* (= made it less pleasant). **2 cast light on *sth*** to provide an explanation for a situation or problem, or information that makes it easier to understand: *The discovery of the dinosaur skeleton has cast light on why they became extinct.*

cast [LOOK] /kɑːst/ [US] /kæst/ **cast a look/glance/smile/ etc.** to look/smile/etc. in a particular direction: *She cast a quick look in the rear mirror.*

• **cast an/your eye over *sth*** to look briefly at something: *Could you cast an eye over this report for me?*

cast [THROW] /kɑːst/ [US] /kæst/ *verb* **cast, cast 1** [T + adv or prep] *LITERARY* to throw something: *The knight cast the sword far out into the lake.* **2** [T] (in fishing) to throw something, such as a line, into the water to catch fish with: *He cast the line to the middle of the river.*

• **cast *your* net wide** to include many people or things when you are looking for something

• **cast pearls before swine** to offer something valuable or good to someone who does not know its value: *I'm afraid you're casting pearls before swine with your good advice – he won't listen.*

cast [DOUBT] /kɑːst/ [US] /kæst/ **1 cast doubt/suspicion on *sb/sth*** to make people feel less sure about or have less trust in something or someone: *New evidence has cast doubt on the guilty verdict.* **2** *FORMAL* **cast aspersions on *sb/sth*** to make critical or damaging remarks or judgments about someone or something: *His opponents cast aspersions on his patriotism.*

cast [REMEMBER] /kɑːst/ [US] /kæst/ **cast *your* mind back** to try to remember: *If you cast your mind back, you might recall that I never promised to go.*

cast [ACTORS] /kɑːst/ [US] /kæst/ *verb* [T] **cast, cast** to choose actors to play particular parts in a play, film or show: *He was often cast* ***as*** *the villain.* ○ *In her latest film she was cast* ***against type*** (= played a different character than the one she usually played or might be expected to play). ○ *FIGURATIVE They like to cast the opposing political party* ***as*** (= to say that they are) *the party of high taxes.* ➲See also **typecast**.

cast /kɑːst/ [US] /kæst/ *group noun* [C] the actors in a film, play or show: *After the final performance, the director threw a party for the cast.* ○ *Part of the film's success lies in the strength of the* ***supporting*** *cast* (= the actors who were not playing the main parts).

cast [SHAPE] /kɑːst/ [US] /kæst/ *verb* [T] **cast, cast** to make an object by pouring hot liquid, such as melted metal, into a shaped container where it becomes hard

• **be cast in the same mould** to be very similar in character to someone else: *Everyone who works for that firm seems to be cast in the same mould.*

cast /kɑːst/ [US] /kæst/ *noun* [C] **1** an object made by pouring hot liquid into a container and leaving it to become solid **2** a **plaster cast**

cast [VOTE] /kɑːst/ [US] /kæst/ *verb* **cast a/your vote** to vote: *All the votes in the election have now been cast and the counting has begun.*

cast [MAGIC] /kɑːst/ [US] /kæst/ **cast a spell** to use words thought to be magic, especially in order to have an effect on someone: *The old woman cast a spell* ***on*** *the prince and he turned into a frog.* ○ *FIGURATIVE At 17 jazz cast its spell* ***on*** *me* (= I started to like it very much).

cast [SKIN] /kɑːst/ [US] /kæst/ *verb* [T] **cast, cast** If a snake casts its skin, the outer layer of old skin comes off its body.

PHRASAL VERBS WITH **cast**

▲ **cast around/about** *phrasal verb* to look around for something: *Fashion editors are always casting around* ***for*** *words to describe colours.*

▲ **cast *sb/sth* aside/off** *phrasal verb* [M] *FORMAL* to get rid of someone or something: *You must cast aside all thoughts of revenge.*

▲ **cast off** [LEAVE] *phrasal verb* If a boat casts off, it leaves the SHORE: *The ship was scheduled to cast off at 8pm.*

▲ **cast off** [FINISH] *phrasal verb SPECIALIZED* in knitting, to use special stitches to finish the item you are making

▲ **cast on** *phrasal verb SPECIALIZED* in knitting, to make special stitches to start the item you are making

▲ **cast *sb/sth* out** *phrasal verb* [M] *LITERARY OR OLD USE* to get rid of someone or something, especially forcefully: *Cast out by his family, he was forced to fend for himself.*

castanets /ˌkæs.təˈnets/ *plural noun* a musical instrument consisting of two small pieces of wood tied together by string and knocked against each other in the hand to make a noise

castaway /ˈkɑː.stə.weɪ/ [US] /ˈkæs.tə-/ *noun* [C] a person who has escaped from a ship that has sunk, and managed to get to an island or country where there are few or no other people

caste /kɑːst/ [US] /kæst/ *noun* [C or U] a system of dividing Hindu society into classes, or any of these classes: *the caste* ***system***

castellated /ˈkæs.tɪ.leɪ.tɪd/ [US] /-t̬ɪd/ *adj SPECIALIZED* describes a building that is made to look like a castle by having towers and BATTLEMENTS (= a wall with regular spaces in it)

caster /ˈkɑː.stəʳ/ [US] /ˈkæs.tɚ/ *noun* [C] (*ALSO* **castor**) a small wheel, usually one of a set, that is fixed to the bottom (of the leg) of a piece of furniture so that it can be moved easily

ˈcaster ˌsugar *noun* [U] *UK* white sugar with very small grains, often used in cooking

castigate /ˈkæs.tɪ.geɪt/ *verb* [T] *FORMAL* to criticize someone or something severely: *Health inspectors castigated the kitchen staff* ***for*** *poor standards of cleanliness.*

ˈcasting ˌcouch *noun* [C usually sing] *HUMOROUS* If you say that someone has got a good part in a film or play by using the casting couch, you mean that they had sex with important people in order to get the part.

ˌcasting ˈvote *noun* [S] a single vote given by the person in charge of a meeting if the number of votes about something is equal, and which therefore decides the matter

ˌcast ˈiron *noun* [U] a type of hard iron that will not bend easily and is made into shapes by being poured into a MOULD when melted

cast-iron /kɑːstˈaɪən/ [US] /kæstˈaɪrn/ *adj* **1 cast-iron guarantee/alibi/etc.** a guarantee/alibi/etc. that can be trusted completely: *Can you give me a cast-iron guarantee that the work will be completed on time?* **2** [before n] very strong: *I have a cast-iron stomach, I can eat anything.*

castle /ˈkɑː.sl̩/ [US] /ˈkæs.l̩/ *noun* [C] **1** a large strong building, built in the past by a ruler or important person to protect the people inside from attack **2** *INFORMAL FOR* **rook** GAME PIECE

• **castles in the air** plans that have very little chance of happening

castle /ˈkɑː.sl̩/ [US] /ˈkæs.l̩/ *verb* [I] *SPECIALIZED* in chess, to make a special move which puts your king in a more protected place at the side of the board

cast-offs /ˈkɑːst.ɒfs/ [US] /ˈkæst.ɑːfs/ *plural noun* things, usually clothes, that you no longer want: *I always had to wear my sister's cast-offs as a child.* **cast-off** /ˈkɑːst.ɒf/ [US] /ˈkæst.ɑːf/ *adj* [before n] *cast-off clothes*

castor /'kɑː.stə^r/ ⓤⓈ /'kæs.tə/ *noun* [C] ANOTHER SPELLING OF **caster**

ˌcastor ˈoil *noun* [U] a thick usually yellow oil, used especially as a medicine to help people excrete the contents of their bowels

castrate /kæs'treɪt/ *verb* [T] to remove the testicles of a male animal or human **castration** /kæs'treɪ.ʃ^ən/ *noun* [U]

casual NOT INTERESTED /'kæʒ.ju.əl/ *adj* not taking or not seeming to take much interest; not caring: *The psychologist's* **attitude** *seemed far too casual, even brutal.* ○ *Security around the conference hotel seemed almost casual.* ○ *Although close to tears, she tried to make her voice sound casual.* **casually** /'kæʒ.ju.ə.li/ *adv*

casual TEMPORARY /'kæʒ.ju.əl/ *adj* [before n] not regular or fixed; temporary: *casual* **labour/labourers/workers** ○ *casual* **sex** **casually** /'kæʒ.ju.ə.li/ *adv*

casual CHANCE /'kæʒ.ju.əl/ *adj* [before n] not serious or considered; (done) by chance: *It was just a casual* **comment***, I didn't mean it to be taken so seriously.* ○ *To a casual* **observer***, everything might appear normal.* **casually** /'kæʒ.ju.ə.li/ *adv*

casual INFORMAL /'kæʒ.ju.əl/ *adj* describes clothes that are not formal or not suitable for special occasions: *casual* **clothes** **casually** /'kæʒ.ju.ə.li/ *adv*: *She was dressed casually in shorts and a T-shirt.*

casualty INJURED /'kæʒ.ju.əl.ti/ *noun* [C] a person injured or killed in a serious accident or war: *The train was derailed but there were no casualties, police said.* ○ *The rebels* **suffered heavy** *casualties.*

casualty BADLY AFFECTED /'kæʒ.ju.əl.ti/ *noun* [C] a person or thing that suffers as a result of something else happening: *She lost her job in 1989, a casualty* **of** *the recession.* ○ *The first casualty* **of** *the reorganization will be the bus service, which will be stopped altogether.*

casualty HOSPITAL /'kæʒ.ju.əl.ti/ *noun* [U] (US **emergency room**) UK the part of a hospital where people who are hurt in accidents or suddenly become ill are taken for urgent treatment: *She had to be rushed* **to** *casualty.*

casuistry /'kæz.ju.ɪ.stri/ *noun* [U] FORMAL the use of clever arguments to trick people

cat /kæt/ *noun* [C] a small four-legged furry animal with a tail and claws, usually kept as a pet or for catching mice, or any member of the group of similar animals such as the lion

● **be the cat's whiskers** UK OLD-FASHIONED to be better than everyone else

● **fight like cat and dog** INFORMAL to argue violently all the time: *As kids we used to fight like cat and dog.*

● **Has the cat got your tongue?** INFORMAL something you say to someone when you are annoyed because they will not speak: *What's the matter? Has the cat got your tongue?*

● **let the cat out of the bag** to let a secret be known, usually without intending to: *I was trying to keep the party a secret, but Mel went and let the cat out of the bag.*

● **like a cat on a hot tin roof** (UK OLD-FASHIONED **like a cat on hot bricks**) describes someone who is in a state of extreme nervous anxiety

● **look like something the cat brought/dragged in** INFORMAL to look very untidy and dirty

● **not have a cat in hell's chance** (MAINLY US **not have a snowball's chance in hell**) INFORMAL to be completely unable to achieve something: *They haven't a cat in hell's chance* **of** *getting over the mountain in weather like this.*

● **play cat and mouse** to try to defeat someone by tricking them into making a mistake so that you have an advantage over them: *The 32-year-old actress spent a large proportion of the week playing cat and mouse with the press.*

● **put/set the cat among the pigeons** UK to say or do something that causes trouble or makes a lot of people very angry

● **While the cat's away, the mice will play.** SAYING said when the person who is in charge of a place is not there, and the people there behave badly

cattery /'kæt.^ər.i/ ⓤⓈ /'kæt.ə-/ *noun* [C] a place where cats are taken care of while their owners are away or where cats are bred for sale

cataclysm /'kæt.ə.klɪ.z^əm/ ⓤⓈ /'kæt-/ *noun* [C] LITERARY a great destructive event or sudden violent change **cataclysmic** /ˌkæt.ə'klɪz.mɪk/ ⓤⓈ /ˌkæt-/ *adj: These countries are on the brink of cataclysmic famine.*

catacomb /'kæt.ə.kuːm/ ⓤⓈ /'kæt-/ *noun* [C usually pl] a series of underground passages and rooms where bodies were buried in the past: *They went down into catacombs beneath the church.*

Catalan /'kæt.ə.læn/ ⓤⓈ /'kæt-/ *noun* [U] a language spoken in a region of Spain

catalepsy /'kæt.ə.lep.si/ ⓤⓈ /'kæt-/ *noun* [U] a medical condition in which a person's body becomes stiff and stops moving, as if dead **cataleptic** /ˌkæt.ə'lep.tɪk/ ⓤⓈ /ˌkæt-/ *adj*

catalogue LIST, US USUALLY **catalog** /'kæt.^əl.ɒg/ ⓤⓈ /'kæt.^əl.ɑːg/ *noun* [C] **1** a book with a list of all the goods that you can buy from a shop: *a* **mail-order** *catalogue* **2** a list of all the books, paintings, etc. that exist in a place **catalogue** /'kæt.^əl.ɒg/ ⓤⓈ /'kæt.^əl.ɑːg/ *verb* [T] to record something, especially in a list: *Many plants become extinct before they have even been catalogued.*

catalogue BAD EVENTS, US USUALLY **catalog** /'kæt.^əl.ɒg/ ⓤⓈ /'kæt.^əl.ɑːg/ *noun* [S] A catalogue of unwanted events is a series of them: *The whole holiday was* **a catalogue of** *disasters.* ○ *a catalogue of errors/crimes/complaints*

catalysis /kə'tæl.ə.sɪs/ *noun* [U] SPECIALIZED the process of making a chemical reaction happen more quickly by using a CATALYST **catalytic** /ˌkæt.ə'lɪ.tɪk/ ⓤⓈ /ˌkæt.ə'lɪ.tɪk/ *adj*

catalyst /'kæt.^əl.ɪst/ ⓤⓈ /'kæt-/ *noun* [C] **1** SPECIALIZED something that makes a chemical reaction happen more quickly without itself being changed **2** an event or person that causes great change: *The high suicide rate* **acted as** *a catalyst* **for** *change in the prison system.*

ˌcatalytic con'verter *noun* [C] SPECIALIZED a device on a car that reduces the amount of poisonous gas that is released from the EXHAUST

catamaran /'kæt.ə.mə.ræn/ ⓤⓈ /'kæt-/ *noun* [C] a sailing boat that has two parallel HULLS (= floating parts) held together by a single DECK (= flat surface)

catapult /'kæt.ə.pʌlt/ ⓤⓈ /'kæt-/ *noun* [C] **1** a device which can throw objects at a high speed: *In the past, armies used catapults to hurl heavy stones at enemy fortifications.* ○ *On that type of aircraft carrier, a catapult was used to help launch aircraft.* **2** UK (US **slingshot**, AUS ALSO **shanghai**) a Y-shaped stick or piece of metal with a piece of elastic fixed to the top parts, used especially by children for shooting small stones **catapult** /'kæt.ə.pʌlt/ ⓤⓈ /'kæt-/ *verb* [T usually + adv or prep] **1** to throw someone or something with great force: *When the two vehicles collided, he was catapulted* **forwards***.* **2** **be catapulted into** *sth* to suddenly experience a particular state, such as fame: *The award for best actress meant that almost overnight she was catapulted* **into** *the limelight.*

cataract DISEASE /'kæt.ə.rækt/ ⓤⓈ /'kæt-/ *noun* [C] a disease in which an area of the eye becomes cloudy so that a person cannot see correctly, or the area diseased in this way

cataract WATER FEATURE /'kæt.ə.rækt/ ⓤⓈ /'kæt-/ *noun* [C] LITERARY a large waterfall

catarrh /kə'tɑː^r/ ⓤⓈ /-'tɑːr/ *noun* [U] a condition in which a lot of mucus is produced in the nose and throat, especially when a person has an infection, or the mucus produced

catastrophe /kə'tæs.trə.fi/ *noun* [C] **1** a sudden event that causes very great trouble or destruction: *They were warned of the ecological catastrophe to come.* **2** a bad situation: *The emigration of scientists is a catastrophe for the country.* **catastrophic** /ˌkæt.ə'strɒf.ɪk/ ⓤⓈ /ˌkæt.ə-'strɑː.fɪk/ *adj: An unchecked increase in the use of fossil fuels could have catastrophic results for the planet.*

catatonic /ˌkæt.ə'tɒn.ɪk/ ⓤⓈ /ˌkæt.ə'tɑː.nɪk/ *adj* describes someone who is stiff and not moving or reacting, as if dead

ˈcat ˌburglar *noun* [C] a thief who enters and leaves a building by climbing up walls to an upper window, door, etc.

catcall /ˈkæt.kɔːl/ [US] /-kɑːl/ *noun* [C] a loud shout or WHISTLE (= high sound) expressing disapproval, especially made by people in a crowd

catch [TAKE HOLD] /kætʃ/ *verb* [I or T] **caught, caught** to take hold of something, especially something that is moving through the air: *I managed to catch the glass before it hit the ground.* ○ *We saw the eagle swoop from the sky to catch its prey.* ○ *Our dog ran past me and out of the house before I could catch it.* ○ *He caught* ***hold of*** *my arm.* ○ *We placed saucepans on the floor to catch* (= collect) *the drops of water coming through the roof.* ○ *UK SPECIALIZED The batsman was caught* ***(out)*** (= someone in the other team caught the ball when he hit it).

• **get caught up in** ***sth*** to become involved in something, often without wanting to: *They were having an argument and somehow I got caught up in it.*

• **catch** ***your*** **breath** to stop breathing for a moment, or to begin to breathe correctly again after running or other exercise: *I had to sit down and catch my breath.*

• **catch the sun** *UK* If you have caught the sun, the sun has made your skin a slightly darker brown or red colour: *You've caught the sun on the back of your neck.*

• **catch a few rays** (*ALSO* **catch some rays**) *INFORMAL* to stay outside in the sun for a period of time: *I'm going out to catch a few rays before lunch.*

• **catch the light** If something catches the light, a light shines on it and makes it look shiny.

catcher /ˈkætʃ.əʳ/ [US] /ˈketʃ.ɚ/ *noun* [C] in baseball, the player who catches the ball if the BATTER fails to hit it

catch [STOP ESCAPING] /kætʃ/ *verb* [T] **caught, caught** to find and stop a person or animal that is trying to escape: *Great pressure was put on the police to catch the terrorists as soon as possible.* ○ [+ v-ing] *Two armed men were caught* ***trying*** *to cross the frontier at night.* ○ *They were happy because they had caught a lot of fish that day.* ○ *FIGURATIVE I can see you're busy right now, so I'll catch you* (= speak to you) *later.*

catch /kætʃ/ *noun* **1** [C] an amount of fish caught: *The fishermen were disappointed with their catch that day.* **2** [S] *INFORMAL* a person who is considered to be very suitable for a relationship: *Her new boyfriend's not much of a catch really, is he?*

catch [STICK] /kætʃ/ *verb* [I or T] **caught, caught** to stick somewhere, or to make something stick somewhere: *The sleeve of my jacket (got) caught* ***on*** *the door handle and ripped.* ○ *Her hair got caught* ***(up) in*** *her hair dryer.*

catch [NOTICE] /kætʃ/ *verb* [T] **caught, caught** to discover, see or become aware of something, especially someone doing something wrong: [+ v-ing] *He caught her* ***reading*** *his old love letters.* ○ *If the virus is caught* (= discovered) *in time, most patients can be successfully treated.* ○ *I caught* ***sight of****/caught* ***a glimpse of*** (= saw for a moment) *a red coat in the crowd.*

• **catch** ***your*** **eye 1** to get someone's attention: *A sudden movement caught my eye.* **2** to get someone's attention, especially by looking at them: *I tried to catch the waiter's eye, so we could order.* **3** to be attractive or different enough to be noticed by someone: *It was the unusual colour of his jacket that caught my eye.*

• **catch** ***sb*** **napping** *INFORMAL* If someone is caught napping, something happens to them which they are not prepared for: *The goalkeeper was caught napping and the ball went straight in.*

• **catch** ***sb*** **red-handed** to discover someone while they are in the act of doing something bad or illegal: *He was caught red-handed* ***taking*** *money from the till.*

• **catch** ***sb*** **with** ***their*** **pants/trousers down 1** to discover someone doing something that they want to keep secret, usually something sexual **2** to ask someone unexpectedly to do or say something that they are not prepared for

• **be caught without** ***sth*** to not have something, especially when it is needed: *He doesn't like to be caught without any biscuits in the house.*

• **you won't catch** ***sb doing sth*** said to mean that you will certainly not see someone doing a particular thing or in a particular place: *You won't catch me at work after four o'clock.* ○ *You won't catch Carla eating in a cheap restaurant, oh no.*

catch [BE IN TIME] /kætʃ/ *verb* [T] **caught, caught** to manage to be in time to see or do something: *I went home a bit early to catch the beginning of the programme.* ○ *You'll have to run if you want to catch* ***the post*** (= send a letter before the post has been collected).

catch [HEAR/SEE] /kætʃ/ *verb* [T] **caught, caught** to manage to hear something: *I couldn't catch what the announcer said, with all the other noise going on.*

catch [TRAVEL] /kætʃ/ *verb* [T] **caught, caught** to travel or be able to travel on an aircraft, train, bus, etc: *He always catches the 10.30am train to work.* ○ *She was worried that she'd arrive too late to catch the last bus home.*

catch [BECOME INFECTED] /kætʃ/ *verb* [T] **caught, caught** to get an illness, especially one caused by bacteria or a virus: *He caught* ***a cold*** *on holiday.* ○ *A lot of children in the school caught measles last term.*

catching /ˈkætʃ.ɪŋ/ *adj* [after v] *INFORMAL Flu is catching* (= able to be given to someone else), *so stay away from work.*

catch [HIT] /kætʃ/ *verb* [T] **caught, caught** to hit something, especially unintentionally: *His head caught the edge of the table as he fell.* ○ *Medical teams were caught* ***in the crossfire*** *of the opposing armies.*

catch [BURN] /kætʃ/ *verb* [I] **caught, caught** to begin to burn: *This wood's too wet, the fire won't catch.*

• **catch fire** to start burning: *For reasons which are not yet known, the factory caught fire late yesterday evening.*

catch [PROBLEM] /kætʃ/ *noun* [S] a hidden problem or disadvantage: *Free food? It sounds too good to be true.* ***What's the*** *catch?*

catch [FASTENING DEVICE] /kætʃ/ *noun* [C] a small device on a door, window, bag, etc. that keeps it fastened

PHRASAL VERBS WITH **catch** ▼

▲ **catch on** [BECOME POPULAR] *phrasal verb* to become fashionable or popular: *I wonder if the game will ever catch on with young people?*

▲ **catch on** [UNDERSTAND] *phrasal verb INFORMAL* to understand, especially after a long time: *He doesn't take hints very easily, but he'll catch on* ***(to*** *what you're saying) eventually.*

▲ **catch** ***sb*** **out** [SHOW WRONG] *phrasal verb* [M] *INFORMAL* to show that someone is doing wrong: *I suspected he wasn't telling me the truth, and one day I caught him out when I found some letters he'd written.*

▲ **catch** ***sb*** **out** [TRICK] *phrasal verb* [M] *INFORMAL* to trick someone into making a mistake: *The examiner will try to catch you out, so stay calm and think carefully before you speak.*

▲ **catch** ***sb*** **out** [CAUSE DIFFICULTY] *phrasal verb* [M] *INFORMAL* to put someone in a difficult situation: *A lot of people were caught out* ***by*** *the sudden change in the weather.*

▲ **catch** ***(sb)*** **up** [REACH SOMEONE] *phrasal verb* to reach someone in front of you by going faster than them: *I ran after her and managed to catch up* ***with*** *her.* ○ *UK Go on to the shops without me, I'll catch you up.*

▲ **catch up** [REACH SAME STANDARD] *phrasal verb* to reach the same quality or standard as someone or something else: *Will Western industry ever catch up* ***with*** *Japanese innovations?* ○ *He was off school for a while and is finding it hard to catch up.*

▲ **catch up** [DO SOMETHING] *phrasal verb* to do something you did not have time to do earlier: *She's staying late at the office to catch up* ***with/on*** *some reports.*

▲ **catch up** [DISCUSS] *phrasal verb* to learn or discuss the latest news: *Let's go for a coffee – I need to catch up* ***on*** *all the gossip.*

▲ **catch up with** ***sb*** [CAUSE PROBLEMS] *phrasal verb* If something bad that you have done or that has been happening to you catches up with you, it begins to cause problems for you: *His lies will catch up with him one day.*

▲ **catch up with** ***sb*** [PUNISH] *phrasal verb* If someone in authority catches up with you, they discover that you have been doing something wrong and often punish you for it: *They had been selling stolen cars for years before the police caught up with them.*

catch-all /ˈkætʃ.ɔːl/ [US] /-ɑːl/ *adj* [before n] general and intended to include everything: *'South London' is a catch-*

all ***phrase/term*** *for anywhere south of the river.* **catch-all** /ˈkætʃ.ɔːl/ [US] /-ɑːl/ *noun* [C] a very general description

catchment area /ˈkætʃ.mənt,eə.ri.ə/ [US] /ˈketʃ.mənt,er.i-/ *noun* [C] the area served by a school or hospital

catchphrase /ˈkætʃ.freɪz/ *noun* [C] a phrase which is often repeated by and therefore becomes connected with a particular organization or person, especially someone famous such as a television entertainer

Catch-22 /,kætʃ.twen.tiˈtuː/ *noun* [S or U] an impossible situation where you are prevented from doing one thing until you have done another thing, but you cannot do the other thing until you have done the first thing: *a Catch-22* ***situation***

catchword /ˈkætʃ.wɜːd/ [US] /-wɝːd/ *noun* [C] a word or phrase which is often repeated by, or becomes connected with a particular organization, especially a political group

catchy /ˈkætʃ.i/ *adj* (especially of a tune or song) pleasing and easy to remember: *a catchy tune* ○ *a song with catchy lyrics* ○ *a catchy name/slogan for the new product*

catechism /ˈkæt.ə.kɪ.zᵊm/ [US] /ˈkæt̬-/ *noun* [C usually sing] an established group of questions and answers, especially about a set of Christian beliefs

categorical /,kæt.əˈgɒr.ɪ.kᵊl/ [US] /,kæt̬.əˈgɑːr-/ *adj* without any doubt or possibility of being changed; certain: *a categorical statement/reply/assurance* **categorically** /,kæt.əˈgɒr.ɪ.kli/ [US] /,kæt̬.əˈgɑː.rɪ-/ *adv*: *He categorically* ***refused*** *to take part in the project.*

category /ˈkæt.ə.gri/ [US] /ˈkæt̬-/ *noun* [C] (in a system for dividing things according to appearance, quality, etc.) a type, or a group of things having some features that are the same: *There are three categories of accommodation – standard, executive and deluxe.*

categorize, *UK USUALLY* **-ise** /ˈkæt.ə.gᵊr.aɪz/ [US] /ˈkæt̬.ə.gə.raɪz/ *verb* [T] to put people or things into groups with the same features: *The books are categorized* ***into*** *beginner and advanced.* ○ *I would categorize this* ***as*** *a very early example of Tudor art.* **categorization**, *UK USUALLY* **-isation** /,kæt.ə.gᵊr.aɪˈzeɪ.ʃᵊn/ [US] /,kæt̬.ə.gə.raɪ-/ *noun* [U]

cater /ˈkeɪ.təʳ/ [US] /-t̬ɚ/ *verb* [I or T] to provide, and sometimes serve, food: *I'm catering* ***for*** *twelve on Sunday, all the family are coming.* ○ *Which firm will be catering at the wedding reception?* ○ *US Who catered your party?* **caterer** /ˈkeɪ.tᵊr.əʳ/ [US] /-t̬ɚ.ɚ/ *noun* [C] **catering** /ˈkeɪ.tᵊr.ɪŋ/ [US] /-t̬ɚ-/ *adj* [before n] *a high-class catering company*

PHRASAL VERBS WITH **cater**

▲ **cater for** ***sb/sth*** *phrasal verb MAINLY UK* to provide what is wanted or needed by someone or something: *The club caters for children between the ages of 4 and 12.*

▲ **cater to** ***sb/sth*** *phrasal verb* to try to satisfy a need, especially an unpopular or generally unacceptable need: *This legislation simply caters to racism.*

caterpillar /ˈkæt.ə.pɪl.əʳ/ [US] /ˈkæt̬.ɚ.pɪl.ɚ/ *noun* [C] a small, long animal with many legs, which feeds on the leaves of plants, and develops into a BUTTERFLY or MOTH

ˈcaterpillar ,track *noun* [C] *TRADEMARK* a belt of metal plates around the sets of wheels on each side of a vehicle that enables movement over rough ground

ˈcaterpillar ,tractor *noun* [C] a heavy vehicle fitted with a caterpillar track

caterwaul /ˈkæt.ə.wɔːl/ [US] /ˈkæt̬.ɚ.wɑːl/ *verb* [I] (of a person or animal) to make a high unpleasant noise like a cat

catfish /ˈkæt.fɪʃ/ *noun* [C] a fish with a flat head and long hairs around its mouth, which lives in rivers or lakes

catgut /ˈkæt.gʌt/ *noun* [U] strong cord, made from the dried intestines of animals, especially sheep, which is used for the strings of musical instruments

catharsis /kəˈθɑː.sɪs/ [US] /-ˈθɑːr-/ *noun* [C or U] *plural* **catharses** the process of releasing strong emotions through a particular activity or experience, such as writing or theatre, which helps you to understand those emotions **cathartic** /kəˈθɑː.tɪk/ [US] /-ˈθɑːr.t̬ɪk/ *adj*: *a cathartic* ***experience***

cathedral /kəˈθiː.drəl/ *noun* [C] a very large, usually stone, building for Christian worship, which is the largest and most important church of a DIOCESE (= area): *Salisbury Cathedral*

catherine wheel /ˈkæθ.rɪn,wiːl/ /-ᵊr.ɪn-/ [US] /ˈkeθ.ɚ.ɪn-/ *noun* [C] a round firework which is fixed to a stick and which spins round

catheter /ˈkæθ.ɪ.təʳ/ [US] /-t̬ɚ/ *noun* [C] *SPECIALIZED* a long, very thin tube used to take liquids out of the body

cathode /ˈkæθ.əʊd/ [US] /-oʊd/ *noun* [C] *SPECIALIZED* the negative part of an electrical CELL at which electrons enter a system ➲Compare **anode**.

Catholic [RELIGIOUS PERSON] /ˈkæθ.ᵊl.ɪk/ *noun* [C], *adj* (a) **Roman Catholic**: *Is he (a) Catholic?* ○ *a Catholic school/church* ➲See also **the Roman Catholic Church**. **Catholicism** /kəˈθɒl.ɪ.sɪ.zᵊm/ [US] /-θɑː.lɪ-/ *noun* [U] ➲See **Roman Catholicism** at **the Roman Catholic Church**

catholic [VARIED] /ˈkæθ.ᵊl.ɪk/ *adj FORMAL* including many different types of thing: *As a young person he had more catholic* ***tastes*** *than he does now.*

catkin /ˈkæt.kɪn/ *noun* [C] a group of small flowers hanging like short pieces of string from the branches of particular trees in the spring: *birch/willow/hazel catkins*

catnap /ˈkæt.næp/ *noun* [C] a short sleep **catnap** /ˈkæt.-næp/ *verb* [I] **-pp-**

cat-o'-nine-tails /,kæt.əˈnaɪn.teɪlz/ [US] /,kæt̬-/ *noun* [S] (*INFORMAL* **cat**) a whip made from rope that has nine ends, and was used especially in the past for hitting people to punish them

cat's cradle /,kætsˈkreɪ.dl̩/ *noun* [C or U] in children's games, a special pattern or series of patterns made by weaving string around the fingers of both hands

cat's eyes *UK* /ˈkæt.saɪz/ *plural noun* (*US* **reflectors**) small pieces of glass or plastic that are put along the middle and sometimes the sides of a road, to reflect the lights of a car, in order to show the driver where to drive when it is dark

catsuit /ˈkæt.suːt/ *noun* [C] *UK* a piece of women's clothing that fits tightly and covers the whole body, arms and legs

catsup /ˈkæt.səp/ *noun* [C or U] *US FOR* **ketchup**

cattle /ˈkæt.l̩/ [US] /ˈkæt̬-/ *plural noun* large farm animals kept for their milk or meat; cows and bulls: ***beef/dairy*** *cattle*

ˈcattle ,grid *noun* [C] a set of bars over a hole in the road which allows vehicles to cross, but not cattle

catty /ˈkæt.i/ [US] /ˈkæt̬-/ *adj* describes words, especially speech, which are unkind because they are intended to hurt someone: *She's always making catty* ***remarks*** *about her sister.* **cattily** /ˈkæt.ɪ.li/ [US] /ˈkæt̬.ə-/ *adv* **cattiness** /ˈkæt.ɪ.nəs/ [US] /ˈkæt̬-/ *noun* [U]

catwalk /ˈkæt.wɔːk/ [US] /-wɑːk/ *noun* [C] **1** the long, narrow stage that MODELS walk along in a FASHION SHOW **2** a narrow path, raised above the ground, often built for workers to walk on outside a building that is being built or repaired

Caucasian /kɔːˈkeɪ.ʒᵊn/ [US] /kɑː-/ *adj* belonging to the races of people who have skin that is of a pale colour: *The chief suspect for the robbery is a Caucasian male.* **Caucasian** /kɔːˈkeɪ.ʒᵊn/ [US] /kɑː-/ *noun* [C]

caucus /ˈkɔː.kəs/ [US] /ˈkɑː-/ *noun* [C] **1** (a meeting of) a small group of people in a political party or organization who have a lot of influence, or who have similar interests **2** in the US, a meeting held to decide which CANDIDATE a political group will support in an election

caught /kɔːt/ [US] /kɑːt/ *past simple and past participle of* **catch**

cauldron, *MAINLY US* **caldron** /ˈkɔːl.drᵊn/ [US] /ˈkɑːl-/ *noun* [C] *OLD USE OR LITERARY* a large round container for cooking in, usually supported over a fire

cauliflower /ˈkɒl.ɪ,flaʊ.əʳ/ [US] /ˈkɑː.lɪ,flaʊr/ *noun* [C or U] (*UK INFORMAL* **cauli**) a large round white vegetable which is eaten cooked or raw ➲See picture **Vegetables** on page Centre 2

ˌcauliflower ˈcheese *noun* [U] *UK* a dish of cooked cauliflower in a thick white sauce made with cheese

ˌcauliflower ˈear *noun* [C] a swollen, badly shaped ear caused by repeated hitting

causative /ˈkɔː.zə.tɪv/ [US] /ˈkɑː.zə.t̬ɪv/ *adj FORMAL* acting as the cause of something: *Smoking is a causative **factor** in the development of several serious diseases, including lung cancer.*

cause [REASON] /kɔːz/ [US] /kɑːz/ *noun* **1** [C or U] the reason why something, especially something bad, happens: *The police are still trying to establish the cause **of** the fire.* ○ *She had died of natural causes.* ○ *I wouldn't tell you **without (good)** cause* (= if there was not a (good) reason). ○ *I believe we have/there is **just** cause* (= a fair reason) ***for** taking this action.* **2** [U] a reason to feel something or to behave in a particular way: *He's never given me any cause **for** concern.*

cause /kɔːz/ [US] /kɑːz/ *verb* [T] to make something happen, especially something bad: *The difficult driving conditions caused several accidents.* ○ [+ obj + **to** infinitive] *The bright light caused her **to** blink.* ○ *Most heart attacks are caused **by** blood clots.* ○ [+ two objects] *I hope the children haven't caused you too much trouble.*

causal /ˈkɔː.zəl/ [US] /ˈkɑː-/ *adj FORMAL* **causal relationship/link/etc.** a relationship/link/etc. between two things in which one causes the other: *Is there a causal relationship between violence on television and violent behaviour?*

causality /kɔːˈzæl.ɪ.ti/ [US] /kɑːˈzæl.ə.t̬i/ *noun* [U] *FORMAL* the principle that there is a cause for everything that happens

causation /kɔːˈzeɪ.ʃən/ [US] /kɑː-/ *noun* [U] *FORMAL* the process of causing something to happen or exist

cause [PRINCIPLE] /kɔːz/ [US] /kɑːz/ *noun* [C] a socially valuable principle which is strongly supported by some people: *They are fighting for a cause – the liberation of their people.* ○ *I'll sponsor you for £10 – it's all in a **good** cause.*

cause célèbre /ˌkɔːz.selˈeb.rə/ [US] /ˌkɑːz-/ *noun* [C] *plural* **causes célèbres** an event, such as a famous legal trial, which attracts a lot of public attention

causeway /ˈkɔːz.weɪ/ [US] /ˈkɑːz-/ *noun* [C] a raised path, especially across a wet area

caustic [CHEMICAL] /ˈkɔː.stɪk/ [US] /ˈkɑː-/ *adj* describes a chemical that burns or destroys things, especially anything made of living cells: *a caustic substance*

caustic [WORDS] /ˈkɔː.stɪk/ [US] /ˈkɑː-/ *adj* describes a remark or way of speaking that is hurtful, critical or intentionally unkind: *caustic comments* ○ *She's famous in the office for her caustic wit.* **caustically** /ˈkɔː.stɪ.kli/ [US] /ˈkɑː-/ *adv*

ˌcaustic ˈsoda *noun* [U] a caustic chemical used in industrial processes such as soap and paper production, and in powerful cleaning substances

cauterize, *UK USUALLY* **-ise** /ˈkɔː.tər.aɪz/ [US] /ˈkɑː.t̬ɚ-/ *verb* [T] *SPECIALIZED* to burn an injury to stop bleeding and prevent infection

caution [CARE] /ˈkɔː.ʃən/ [US] /ˈkɑː-/ *noun* [U] great care and attention: *We need to **proceed with/exercise** caution* (= be careful in taking action, making decisions, etc.) ○ *They **treated** the story of his escape **with** (some/great/extreme) caution* (= thought that it might not be true).

cautious /ˈkɔː.ʃəs/ [US] /ˈkɑː-/ *adj* **1** describes someone who avoids risks: *He's a cautious driver.* **2** describes something which is careful, well considered and sometimes slow or uncertain: *a cautious approach* ○ *cautious criticism*

• **cautious optimism** a feeling that you can be generally hopeful about a situation even though you do not expect complete success or improvement

cautiously /ˈkɔː.ʃə.sli/ [US] /ˈkɑː-/ *adv* in a cautious way

cautiousness /ˈkɔː.ʃə.snəs/ [US] /ˈkɑː-/ *noun* [U]

caution [WARNING] /ˈkɔː.ʃən/ [US] /ˈkɑː-/ *noun* **1** [C] *UK* a spoken warning given by a police officer or official to someone who has broken the law: *As it was her first offence, she was only given a caution.* **2** [C or U] advice or a warning: *Just a **word of** caution – the cheaper models probably aren't worth buying.*

caution /ˈkɔː.ʃən/ [US] /ˈkɑː-/ *verb* [T] **1** If the police caution someone, they give them an official warning. **2** *FORMAL* to warn someone: *The newspaper cautioned its readers **against** buying shares without getting good advice first.*

cautionary /ˈkɔː.ʃən.ər.i/ /-ri/ [US] /ˈkɑː.ʃən.er.i/ *adj FORMAL* giving a warning

ˌcautionary ˈtale *noun* [C] a story which gives a warning: *Her story is a cautionary tale for women travelling alone.*

C

cavalcade /ˌkæv.əlˈkeɪd/ *noun* [C] a line of people, vehicles, horses, etc. following a particular route as part of a ceremony

cavalier [WITHOUT CARE] /ˌkæv.əlˈɪər/ [US] /-ˈɪr/ *adj DISAPPROVING* thoughtless and not caring about other people's feelings or safety: *That's a rather cavalier **attitude**.*

Cavalier [PERSON] /ˌkæv.əlˈɪər/ [US] /-ˈɪr/ *noun* [C] a supporter of the king in the English Civil War in the 1640s

cavalry /ˈkæv.əl.ri/ *group noun* [U] the group of soldiers in an army who fight in TANKS, or (especially in the past) on horses ➲Compare **infantry**. **cavalryman** /ˈkæv.əl.ri.mən/ /-mæn/ *noun* [C]

cave /keɪv/ *noun* [C] a large hole in the side of a hill, cliff or mountain, or one that is underground

cave /keɪv/ *verb*

PHRASAL VERBS WITH **cave** ▼

▲ **cave in** [FALL] *phrasal verb* If a ceiling, roof or other structure caves in, it breaks and falls into the space below: *Because of the explosion, the roof of the building caved in, trapping several people.*

▲ **cave in** [AGREE] *phrasal verb INFORMAL* to agree to something that you were against before, after someone has persuaded you or threatened you: *At first, they refused to sign the agreement, but they caved in when they heard another firm was being approached.*

caveat /ˈkæv.i.æt/ *noun* [C] *FORMAL* a warning to consider something before acting further, or a statement which limits a more general statement; a **proviso**: *He agreed to the interview, with the caveat that he could approve the final article.*

caveat emptor /ˌkæv.i.ætˈemp.tɔːr/ [US] /-ɔːr/ *FORMAL* used for saying that buyers must take responsibility for the quality of goods that they are buying

caveman /ˈkeɪv.mæn/ *noun* [C] **1** someone who lived in a cave in the early stages of the development of human society **2** *INFORMAL* a modern man who is very rude or violent towards other people, especially women

cavern /ˈkæv.ən/ [US] /-ɚn/ *noun* [C] a large cave

cavernous /ˈkæv.ən.əs/ [US] /-ɚn-/ *adj* If something is cavernous, there is a very large open space inside it: *a cavernous 4000-seat theatre*

caviar, **caviare** /ˈkæv.i.ɑːr/ [US] /-ɑːr/ /ˌ--ˈ-/ *noun* [U] the eggs of various large fish, especially the STURGEON, which are eaten as food and are usually very expensive

cavil /ˈkæv.əl/ *verb* [I] **-ll-** or *US USUALLY* **-l-** *FORMAL* to make unreasonable complaints, especially about things that are not important

caving *UK* /ˈkeɪ.vɪŋ/ *noun* [U] (*US* **spelunking**) the sport of walking and climbing in caves ➲See also **potholing**.

caver *UK* /ˈkeɪ.vər/ [US] /-vɚ/ *noun* [C] (*US* **spelunker**) a person who walks and climbs in caves as a sport

cavity /ˈkæv.ɪ.ti/ [US] /-ə.t̬i/ *noun* [C] **1** a hole, or an empty space between two surfaces: *The gold was hidden in a secret cavity.* **2** a hole in a tooth

ˌcavity ˈwall *noun* [C] a wall of a building formed from two walls with a space, usually for air, between them. It is made in this way to keep out water and cold air.

cavort /kəˈvɔːt/ [US] /-ˈvɔːrt/ *verb* [I] to jump or move around in a playful way, sometimes noisily, and often in a sexual way: *They were spotted cavorting beside the swimming pool.*

caw /kɔː/ [US] /kɑː/ *noun* [C] the loud, rough cry of a bird such as a crow **caw** /kɔː/ [US] /kɑː/ *verb* [I]

cayenne pepper /ˌkeɪ.enˈpep.ər/ [US] /-ɚ/ *noun* [U] a red powder made from a type of pepper and used to give a hot taste to food

cayman, caiman /ˈkeɪ.mən/ *noun* [C] an animal similar to an ALLIGATOR

CB /ˌsiːˈbiː/ *noun* [U] *ABBREVIATION FOR* **Citizens' Band (radio)** (= a local radio system used especially by drivers to speak to each other)

CBS /ˌsiː.biːˈes/ *group noun* [U] *ABBREVIATION FOR* Columbia Broadcasting System: an organization that broadcasts on television in the US

cc [MEASURE] /ˌsiːˈsiː/ *noun ABBREVIATION FOR* cubic centimetre: *a 750cc motorcycle*

cc [COPIES] /ˌsiːˈsiː/ *noun ABBREVIATION FOR* **carbon copy**: written at the end of a business letter or in an email before the names of the people who will receive a copy

CCTV /ˌsiː.siː.tiːˈviː/ *ABBREVIATION FOR* **closed-circuit television**: a system which sends television signals to a limited number of screens, and is often used in shops as protection against thieves: *CCTV cameras*

CD /ˌsiːˈdiː/ *noun* [C] *ABBREVIATION FOR* **compact disc**: a small plastic disc with a metallic surface on which information, especially high quality sound, is recorded

ˌCˈD ˌplayer *noun* [C] a machine that is used for playing music CDS

CD-ROM /ˌsiː.diːˈrɒm/ [US] /-ˈrɑːm/ *noun* [C or U] *ABBREVIATION FOR* compact disc read-only memory: a compact disc that holds large amounts of information that can be read by a computer but cannot be changed: *Cambridge dictionaries are available* ***on*** *CD-ROM.* ➲See picture **In the Office** on page Centre 15

CD-RW /ˌsiː.diː.ɑːˈdʌb.l̩.juː/ [US] /-ɑːr-/ *noun* [C] *ABBREVIATION FOR* compact disc re-writable: an empty COMPACT DISC which you can use to record information on and read information from, using a special type of DRIVE (= computer device): *This software allows you to write files from compatible CD-RW drives.*

cease /siːs/ *verb* [I or T] *SLIGHTLY FORMAL* to stop something: *Whether the protests will cease remains to be seen.* ○ *The company has decided to cease all UK operations after this year.* ○ [+ **to** infinitive] *Workplace nurseries will cease* ***to*** *be liable for tax.*
cease /siːs/ *noun SLIGHTLY FORMAL* **without cease** without stopping ➲See also **cessation**.
ceaseless /ˈsiː.sləs/ *adj* continuous **ceaselessly** /ˈsiː.slə.sli/ *adv*

ceasefire /ˈsiːs.faɪəʳ/ [US] /-faɪr/ *noun* [C usually sing] an agreement, usually between two armies, to stop fighting to allow discussions about peace: *declare a ceasefire*

cedar /ˈsiː.dəʳ/ [US] /-dɚ/ *noun* **1** [C] a tall wide evergreen tree **2** [U] (*ALSO* **cedarwood**) the wood of this tree

cede /siːd/ *verb* [T] *FORMAL* to give something such as ownership to someone else, especially unwillingly or because forced to do so: *Hong Kong was ceded* ***to*** *Britain after the Opium War.*

cedilla /sɪˈdɪl.ə/ *noun* [C] (used when writing some languages) a mark made under a letter, especially c, which is then written as ç to show that the letter has a special sound

Ceefax /ˈsiː.fæks/ *noun* [U] *UK TRADEMARK* in Britain, a system of giving written information on television, provided by the BBC

ceilidh /ˈkeɪ.li/ *noun* [C] a special event at which people dance to traditional music, especially in Scotland and Ireland

ceiling /ˈsiː.lɪŋ/ *noun* **1** [C] the inner surface of a room which you can see when you look above you **2** [C usually sing] an upper limit, usually relating to money: *They have* ***imposed/set*** *a ceiling on pay rises.* ➲See also **glass ceiling**.

celeb /sɪˈleb/ *noun* [C] *INFORMAL SHORT FOR* **celebrity**: *A number of celebs attended the party.*

celebrate [ENJOY AN OCCASION] /ˈsel.ɪ.breɪt/ *verb* [I or T] to take part in special enjoyable activities in order to show that a particular occasion is important: *We always celebrate our wedding anniversary* ***by*** *going out to dinner.* ○ *If this plan works, we'll celebrate* ***in style*** (= in a special way). **celebratory** /ˌsel.ɪˈbreɪ.tᵊr.i/ [US] /-t̬ɚ-/ *adj*: *When we heard she'd got the job, we all went off for a celebratory drink.*
celebration /ˌsel.ɪˈbreɪ.ʃᵊn/ *noun* [C or U] a special social event, such as a party, when you celebrate something, or the act of celebrating something: *There were lively New Year celebrations all over town.* ○ *Such good news* ***calls for*** (= deserves) *a celebration!* ○ *Let's buy some champagne* ***in*** *celebration* ***of*** *her safe arrival.*

celebrate [PRAISE] /ˈsel.ɪ.breɪt/ *verb* [T] *FORMAL* to express admiration and approval for something or someone: *His work celebrates the energy and enthusiasm of the young.*
celebrated /ˈsel.ɪ.breɪ.tɪd/ [US] /-t̬ɪd/ *adj* famous for some special quality or ability: *a celebrated opera singer/city/novel* ➲Compare **notorious**.

celebrate [LEAD A CEREMONY] /ˈsel.ɪ.breɪt/ *verb* [T] to lead or take part in a religious ceremony: *to celebrate Mass*
celebrant /ˈsel.ɪ.brənt/ *noun* [C] a person who takes part in or the priest who leads a religious ceremony

celebrity /sɪˈleb.rɪ.ti/ [US] /-t̬i/ *noun* **1** [C] someone who is famous, especially in the entertainment business **2** [U] the state of being famous

celeriac /səˈler.i.æk/ *noun* [U] a type of CELERY (= a vegetable) with a large round white edible root ➲See picture **Vegetables** on page Centre 2

celerity /səˈler.ɪ.ti/ [US] /-t̬i/ *noun* [U] *FORMAL* speed

celery /ˈsel.ᵊr.i/ [US] /-ɚ-/ *noun* [U] a vegetable with long thin whitish or pale green stems which can be eaten raw or cooked: *a stick of celery* ➲See picture **Vegetables** on page Centre 2

celestial /sɪˈles.ti.ᵊl/ [US] /-tʃᵊl/ *adj FORMAL* of or from the sky or outside this world: *The moon is a celestial body.*

celibate /ˈsel.ɪ.bət/ *adj* not having sexual activity, especially because of making a religious promise to do this **celibacy** /ˈsel.ɪ.bə.si/ *noun* [U]
celibate /ˈsel.ɪ.bət/ *noun* [C] *FORMAL* a person who does not have sex

cell [ROOM] /sel/ *noun* [C] a small bare room, especially in a prison or a monastery or convent

cell [ORGANISM] /sel/ *noun* [C] the smallest basic unit of a plant or animal **-celled** /-seld/ *suffix*: *a single-celled life form* **cellular** /ˈsel.jʊ.ləʳ/ [US] /-lɚ/ *adj*

cell [PART] /sel/ *noun* [C] a small part of something: *the cells of a honeycomb*
cellular /ˈsel.jʊ.ləʳ/ [US] /-lɚ/ *adj*: *The organization has a cellular structure* (= is made of many small groups that work independently).

cell [ELECTRICAL DEVICE] /sel/ *noun* [C] a device for producing electrical energy from chemical energy

cellar /ˈsel.əʳ/ [US] /-ɚ/ *noun* [C] a room under the ground floor of a building, usually used for storage

cellmate /ˈsel.meɪt/ *noun* [C] the person with whom a prisoner shares a prison cell

cello (*plural* **cellos**) /ˈtʃel.əʊ/ [US] /-oʊ/ *noun* [C] (*FORMAL* **violoncello**) a wooden musical instrument with four strings, that is held vertically between the legs and is played by moving a bow across the strings
cellist /ˈtʃel.ɪst/ *noun* [C] a cello player

Cellophane /ˈsel.ə.feɪn/ *noun* [U] *TRADEMARK* thin, quite stiff, transparent material used for covering goods, especially flowers and food

cellphone /ˈsel.fəʊn/ [US] /-foʊn/ *noun* [C] (*ALSO* **cellular phone**) a **mobile (phone)** ➲See picture **In the Office** on page Centre 15

cellulite /ˈsel.jʊ.laɪt/ *noun* [U] fat in the human body, especially in the upper legs, which makes the surface of the skin appear lumpy

celluloid /ˈsel.jʊ.lɔɪd/ *noun* [U] **1** *OLD-FASHIONED* films or the cinema generally: *Critics called it 'The most seductive image of woman ever committed to celluloid'* (= put in a film). **2** a type of plastic used to make many items, especially, in the past, photographic film

cellulose /ˈsel.jʊ.ləʊs/ [US] /-loʊs/ *noun* [U] the main substance in the cell walls of plants, also used in making paper, artificial fibres and plastics

Celsius /ˈsel.si.əs/ *noun* [U], *adj* (*ALSO* **centigrade**, *WRITTEN ABBREVIATION* **C**) (of) a measurement of temperature on a standard in which 0° is the temperature at which water freezes, and 100° the temperature at which it boils: *Are the temperatures given* ***in*** *Celsius or Fahrenheit?* ○ *The sample was heated to (a temperature of) 80°C.* ➲Compare **Fahrenheit**.

Celtic /ˈkel.tɪk/ /ˈsel-/ *adj* of an ancient European people whose modern relatives include the Irish, Scots, Welsh and Bretons, or of their language or culture: *Celtic art*

cement [BUILDING MATERIAL] /sɪˈment/ *noun* [U] a grey powder which is mixed with water and sand to make MORTAR or with water, sand and small stones to make concrete: *a bag of cement* ○ *a cement factory*
cement /sɪˈment/ *verb* [T] **1** to put cement on a surface **2** to make something such as an agreement or friendship stronger: *The university's exchange scheme for teachers has cemented its links with many other academic institutions.*

cement [GLUE] /sɪˈment/ *noun* [U] a substance which sticks things together: *Dentists use cement to hold crowns and bridges in place.* **cement** /sɪˈment/ *verb* [T]

ceˈment ˌmixer *noun* [C] a machine which has a large cylindrical container which turns round and round, in which cement, water and small stones are mixed to make concrete

cemetery /ˈsem.ə.tri/ [US] /-ter.i/ *noun* [C] an area of ground in which dead bodies are buried, especially one which is not next to a church

cenotaph /ˈsen.əʊ.tɑːf/ /-tæf/ *noun* [C] a public MONUMENT (= special statue or building) built in memory of particular people who died in war, often with their names written on it

censor /ˈsent.səʳ/ [US] /-sɚ/ *noun* [C] a person whose job is to read books, watch films, etc. in order to remove anything offensive from them, or who reads private letters, especially sent during war or from prison, to remove parts considered unsuitable **censor** /ˈsent.səʳ/ [US] /-sɚ/ *verb* [T] *The book was heavily censored when first published.* **censorship** /ˈsent.sə.ʃɪp/ [US] /-sɚ-/ *noun* [U] *censorship of the press*

censure /ˈsen.ʃəʳ/ [US] /-ʃɚ/ *noun* [U] FORMAL strong criticism or disapproval: *His dishonest behaviour came under severe censure.* **censure** /ˈsen.ʃəʳ/ [US] /-ʃɚ/ *verb* [T] *Ministers were censured **for** their lack of decisiveness during the crisis.*

census /ˈsent.səs/ *noun* [C] a count for official purposes, especially one to count the number of people living in a country and to obtain information about them: *We have a census in this country every ten years.* ○ *She was stopped in her car for a traffic census.*

cent /sent/ *noun* [C] a unit of money worth 0.01 of the US dollar and of the main monetary unit of many countries, or a coin with this value

centaur /ˈsen.tɔːʳ/ [US] /-tɔːr/ *noun* [C] a creature in ancient Greek stories, which has a human's upper body and the lower body and legs of a horse

centenarian /ˌsen.təˈneə.ri.ən/ [US] /-t̬əˈner.i-/ *noun* [C] someone who is a hundred years old or more

centenary /senˈtiː.nᵊr.i/ /-ˈten.ᵊr-/ [US] /-ˈten.ɚ-/ *noun* [C] (US USUALLY ALSO **centennial**) (the day or year that is) 100 years after an important event; the 100th ANNIVERSARY: *centenary celebrations* ○ *Next year is the centenary **of** her death.* ⊃See also **bicentenary**; **tercentenary**.

center /ˈsen.təʳ/ [US] /-t̬ɚ/ *noun, verb* US FOR **centre**

centerfold /ˈsen.tə.fəʊld/ [US] /-t̬ɚ.foʊld/ *noun* [C] US FOR **centrefold**

centerpiece /ˈsen.tə.piːs/ [US] /-t̬ɚ-/ *noun* [C] US FOR **centrepiece**

centi- /sen.ti-/ [US] /-t̬i-/ *prefix* 0.01 of the stated unit: *a centimetre* ○ *a centilitre*

centigrade /ˈsen.tɪ.greɪd/ [US] /-t̬ɪ-/ *noun* [U], *adj* **Celsius**

centigram /ˈsen.tɪ.græm/ [US] /-t̬ɪ-/ *noun* [C] (UK ALSO **centigramme**) a unit of mass equal to 0.01 of a gram

centilitre UK, US **centiliter** /ˈsen.tiˌliː.təʳ/ [US] /-t̬iˌliː.t̬ɚ/ *noun* [C] (WRITTEN ABBREVIATION **cl**) a unit of measurement of liquid equal to 0.01 of a litre

centimetre UK, US **centimeter** /ˈsen.tɪˌmiː.təʳ/ [US] /-t̬ɪˌmiː.t̬ɚ/ *noun* [C] (WRITTEN ABBREVIATION **cm**) a unit of length equal to 0.01 of a metre

centipede /ˈsen.tɪ.piːd/ [US] /-t̬ɪ-/ *noun* [C] a small, long, thin animal with many legs

central [NEAR THE MIDDLE] /ˈsen.trəl/ *adj* in, at, from or near the centre or most important part of something: *central Europe/London* ○ *Of course, you pay more for premises with a central location* (= in or near the centre of a town). ⊃See also **centre** MIDDLE. **centrally** /ˈsen.trə.li/ *adv*: *centrally located*
centralism /ˈsen.trə.lɪ.zᵊm/ *noun* [U] the principle or action of putting something under central control
centralize, UK ALSO **-ise** /ˈsen.trə.laɪz/ *verb* [T] to remove authority in a system, company, country, etc. from local places to one central place so that the whole system, etc. is under central control: *Payment of bills is now centralized* (= organized at one place instead of several). **centralization**, UK ALSO **-isation** /ˌsen.trəˈlaɪzeɪ.ʃᵊn/ *noun* [U]

central [IMPORTANT] /ˈsen.trəl/ *adj* main or important: *a central role* ○ *Community involvement is central **to** our plan.*
centrality /senˈtræl.ɪ.ti/ [US] /-ə.t̬i/ *noun* [U] importance

ˌcentral ˈbank *noun* [C] a bank that provides services to a national government, puts the official financial plans of that government into operation, and controls the amount of money in the economy

ˌcentral ˈgovernment *noun* [U] national government from a single important city rather than local government

ˌcentral ˈheating *noun* [U] a system of heating buildings by warming air or water at one place and then sending it to different rooms in pipes

ˌcentral ˈnervous ˌsystem *noun* [U] the main system of nerve control in a living thing, consisting of the brain and the main nerves connected to it

ˌcentral reserˈvation UK *noun* [C usually sing] (US **median strip**) the narrow piece of land between the two halves of a large road

centre [MIDDLE] UK, US **center** /ˈsen.təʳ/ [US] /-t̬ɚ/ *noun* [C] the middle point or part: *There was a large table in the centre of the room.* ○ *the **town** centre* ⊃See also **central** NEAR THE MIDDLE.
• **centre of attention** the person or thing that everyone is most interested in and pays most attention to: *She's the centre of attention everywhere she goes.*
centre UK, US **center** /ˈsen.təʳ/ [US] /-t̬ɚ/ *group noun* [S], *adj* in politics, the people in a group who hold opinions which are not extreme but are between two opposites: *His political views are known to be **left of/right of** centre.*
centre UK, US **center** /ˈsen.təʳ/ [US] /-t̬ɚ/ *verb* [T] to put something in the middle of an area: *Centre* (= Put at equal distances from the left and right sides of the page) *all the headings in this document.*

centre [PLACE] UK, US **center** /ˈsen.təʳ/ [US] /-t̬ɚ/ *noun* [C] a place or building, especially one where a particular activity happens: *a sports/leisure/health centre* ○ *a garden/shopping centre* ○ *Grants will be given to establish centres **of excellence*** (= places where a particular activity is done extremely well) *in this field of research.*
▲ **centre around/on *sth*** *phrasal verb* to have something as the main subject of discussion or interest: *The discussion centred around reducing waste.*

centrefold UK, US **centerfold** /ˈsen.tə.fəʊld/ [US] /-t̬ɚ.foʊld/ *noun* [C] a large photograph that covers the two pages opposite each other in the middle of a magazine, usually of a young woman with few or no clothes on, or the person who appears in such a picture

ˌcentre ˈforward *noun* [C] in particular team sports, the person who is in the middle of the front row of players who try to score goals

ˌcentre of ˈgravity *noun* [C usually sing] *plural* **centres of gravity** the point in an object where its weight is balanced

centrepiece [IMPORTANT PART] UK, US **centerpiece** /ˈsen.tə.piːs/ [US] /-t̬ɚ-/ *noun* [C] the most important or attractive part or feature of something: *The reduction of crime levels is the centrepiece **of** the president's domestic policies.* ○ *The centrepiece **of** the shopping centre is a giant fountain.*

centrepiece [DECORATION] UK, US **centerpiece** /ˈsen.tə.piːs/ [US] /-t̬ɚ-/ *noun* [C] a decorative object put in the centre of a table, especially for a formal meal

centre-spread /ˌsen.təˈspred/ [US] /-t̬ɚ-/ *noun* [C] the two pages opposite each other in the middle of a newspaper

[C]

or magazine, which deal only with one particular subject and include many pictures: *Tomorrow's edition will include a centre-spread on the Spanish royal family.*

centre 'stage *noun* [U] **1** the middle of a theatre stage **2** a situation in which someone or something receives a lot of attention: *In the eighties he **took** centre stage in his party's struggle with the unions.*

-centric /-sen.trɪk/ *suffix* having the stated thing as your main interest: *Eurocentric* **-centrism** /-sen.trɪ.zᵊm/ *suffix*

centrifugal /ˌsen.trɪ'fjuː.gᵊl/ *adj* (of a turning object) tending to move away from the point around which it is turning: *centrifugal force*

centrifuge /'sen.trɪ.fjuːdʒ/ *noun* [C] a machine which turns a container round very quickly, causing the solids and liquids inside it to separate by centrifugal action

centripetal /ˌsen.trɪ'piː.tᵊl/ ⓤ /-tᵊl/ *adj* SPECIALIZED (of a turning object) tending to move towards the point around which it is turning: *centripetal force*

centrist /'sen.trɪst/ *adj* supporting the centre of the range of political opinions **centrist** /'sen.trɪst/ *noun* [C]

centurion /sen'tjʊə.ri.ən/ ⓤ /-'tʊr.i-/ *noun* [C] an officer in the army of ancient Rome, who was responsible for 100 soldiers

century /'sen.tʃᵊr.i/ ⓤ /-tʃɚ-/ *noun* [C] **1** a period of 100 years: *The city centre has scarcely changed in over a century.* ○ *This sculpture must be centuries old.* ○ *Her medical career spanned half a century.* ⊃Compare **millennium**. **2** a period of 100 years counted from what is believed to be the year of the birth of Jesus Christ: *Rome was founded in the eighth century BC* (= before Christ). ○ *He's an expert on fifteenth century Italian art.* **3** a score of 100 RUNS in cricket
• **the turn of the century** the time when one century ends and another begins: *Queen Victoria died at the turn of the century.*

CEO /ˌsiː.iː'əʊ/ ⓤ /-'oʊ/ *noun* [C] ABBREVIATION FOR **chief executive officer**: the person with the most important position in a company

ceramics /sɪ'ræm.ɪks/ *noun* [U] the production of objects by shaping pieces of clay which are then hardened by baking

ceramics /sɪ'ræm.ɪks/ *plural noun* the objects produced by shaping and heating clay, especially when considered as art **ceramic** /sɪ'ræm.ɪk/ *adj: ceramic tiles*

cereal /'sɪə.ri.əl/ ⓤ /'sɪr.i-/ *noun* [C or U] **1** a plant which is cultivated to produce grain: *cereal crops* **2** a food that is made from grain and eaten with milk, especially in the morning

cerebral /'ser.ɪ.brᵊl/ *adj* **1** SPECIALIZED relating to the brain **2** FORMAL demanding careful reasoning and mental effort rather than feelings: *She makes cerebral films that deal with important social issues.*

cerebral palsy /ˌser.ə.brᵊl'pɔːl.zi/ *noun* [U] a physical condition involving permanent tightening of the muscles which is caused by damage to the brain around or before the time of birth

cerebrum /sɪ'riː.brəm/ *noun* [C] *plural* **cerebrums** or **cerebra** SPECIALIZED the front part of the brain, which is involved with thought, decision, emotion and character

ceremony FORMAL ACTS /'ser.ɪ.mə.ni/ *noun* [C or U] (FORMAL **ceremonial**) (a set of) formal acts, often fixed and traditional, performed on important social or religious occasions: *a wedding/graduation ceremony* **ceremonial** /ˌser.ɪ'məʊ.ni.əl/ ⓤ /-'moʊ-/ *adj: ceremonial occasions/duties* **ceremonially** /ˌser.ɪ'məʊ.ni.ə.li/ ⓤ /-'moʊ-/ *adv*

ceremony FORMAL BEHAVIOUR /'ser.ɪ.mə.ni/ *noun* [U] very formal and polite behaviour: *She arrived at the airport without the **pomp and** ceremony that usually accompanies important politicians.* ○ *I handed her my letter of resignation **without** ceremony* (= in an informal way).

ceremonious /ˌser.ɪ'məʊ.ni.əs/ ⓤ /-'moʊ-/ *adj* describes behaviour that is very or too formal or polite **ceremoniously** /ˌser.ɪ'məʊ.ni.ə.sli/ ⓤ /-'moʊ-/ *adv: He shook hands ceremoniously with each of his supporters as they arrived.*

cerise /sə'riːs/ *adj, noun* [U] (having) a dark reddish pink colour

cert CERTAIN THING /sɜːt/ ⓤ /sɝːt/ *noun* [C usually sing] UK INFORMAL something or someone that is thought to be certain to happen or be successful: *With all her experience she's a **dead** cert **for** *(= is certain to get) *the job.* ○ [+ **to** infinitive] *The Russian team is a cert **to** win the gold medal.*

cert. DOCUMENT /sɜːt/ ⓤ /sɝːt/ *noun* [C] WRITTEN ABBREVIATION FOR **certificate**

certain IN NO DOUBT /'sɜː.tᵊn/ ⓤ /'sɝː-/ *adj* **1** having no doubt or knowing exactly that something is true, or known to be true, correct, exact or effective: [+ (*that*)] *Are you absolutely certain (**that**) you gave them the right number?* ○ *I **feel** certain (**that**) you're doing the right thing.* ○ *You should **make** certain (**that**) everyone understands the instructions.* ○ *The police **seem** certain (**that**) they will find the people responsible for the attack.* ○ [+ question word] *I'm not certain **how** much it will cost.* ○ *He was quite certain **about/of** his attacker's identity.* ○ *One thing is certain – she won't resign willingly.* **2 know/say for certain** to know or state something without doubt: *I don't know for certain if she's coming.* ○ *I can't say for certain how long I'll be there.*

certainly /'sɜː.tᵊn.li/ ⓤ /'sɝː.-/ *adv* **1** used to reply emphatically or to emphasize something and show that there is no doubt about it: *She certainly had a friend called Mark, but I don't know whether he was her boyfriend.* ○ *"This is rather a difficult question." "Yes, it's certainly not easy."* ○ *"Do you think more money should be given to education?" "Certainly!"* ○ *"Had you forgotten about our anniversary?" "Certainly not! I've reserved a table at Michel's restaurant for this evening."* **2** used when agreeing or disagreeing strongly to a request: *"Could you lend me £10?" "Certainly."* ○ *"Did you take any money out of my purse?" "Certainly not!"*

certainty /'sɜː.tᵊn.ti/ ⓤ /'sɝː.-/ *noun* **1** [C] something which cannot be doubted: *There are few absolute certainties in life.* **2** [U] the state of being completely confident or having no doubt about something: *I'm unable to answer that question **with** any certainty.*

certain EXTREMELY LIKELY /'sɜː.tᵊn/ ⓤ /'sɝː-/ *adj* impossible to avoid or extremely likely: [+ **to** infinitive] *The population explosion is certain **to** cause widespread famine.* ○ *Oil prices are certain **to** rise following the agreement to limit production.* ○ *After all his hard work, he's certain **to** pass his exams.* ○ *The team looks almost certain **to** win the match.* ○ [+ (*that*)] *It is virtually certain (**that**) she will win the gold medal.* ○ *Even if a ceasefire can be agreed, how can they **make** certain (**that**) neither side breaks it?* ○ *Cancer sufferers no longer face certain death as they once did.* ○ *This scandal will mean certain defeat for the party in the election.* **certainly** /'sɜː.tᵊn.li/ ⓤ /'sɝː-/ *adv: She will certainly win the election if the opinion polls are accurate.*

certainty /'sɜː.tᵊn.ti/ ⓤ /'sɝː-/ *noun* [C] something which is very likely to happen: *Joan will win – that's a certainty.* ○ [+ **to** infinitive] *Joan is a certainty **to** win.*

certain PARTICULAR /'sɜː.tᵊn/ ⓤ /'sɝː-/ *determiner* particular but not named or described: *We have certain reasons for our decision, which have to remain confidential.* ○ *Do you think war is justifiable in certain circumstances?* ○ *The song has a certain appeal, but I'm not sure what it is.* ○ *Certain members of the audience may disagree with what I'm about to say.*

certain /'sɜː.tᵊn/ ⓤ /'sɝː-/ *pronoun* FORMAL *Certain* (= Some) **of** *the candidates were well below the usual standard, but others were very good indeed.*

certain NAMED /'sɜː.tᵊn/ ⓤ /'sɝː-/ *adj* [before n] FORMAL named but neither famous nor known well: *I had lunch today with a certain George Michael – not the George Michael, I should explain.*

certain LIMITED /'sɜː.tᵊn/ ⓤ /'sɝː-/ *adj* [before n] limited: *I like modern art to a certain **extent/degree**, but I don't like the really experimental stuff.*

certificate /sə'tɪf.ɪ.kət/ ⓤ /sɚ-/ *noun* [C] **1** an official document which states that the information on it is true: *a birth/marriage/death certificate* ○ *a doctor's/medical certificate* **2** the qualification that you receive when you are successful in an exam: *She has a*

Certificate in Drama Education.

ˌcertified ˈmail *noun* [U] *US FOR* **recorded delivery**

ˌcertified ˌpublic acˈcountant *noun* [C] (*ABBREVIATION* **CPA**) *US FOR* **chartered** accountant (= an accountant who has received special training)

certify /ˈsɜː.tɪ.faɪ/ [US] /ˈsɝː.t̬ə-/ *verb* **1** [I or T] to state something officially, usually in writing, especially that something is true or correct: [+ (*that*)] *I hereby certify* ***(that)*** *the above information is true and accurate.* ○ [+ n or adj] *The driver was certified* ***(as)*** *dead on arrival at the hospital.* ○ *The meat has been certified* ***(as)*** *fit for human consumption.* **2** [T] to state officially that someone is mentally ill: *As a young man, he had been certified and sent to a hospital for the mentally ill.* **certification** /ˌsɜː.tɪ.fɪˈkeɪ.ʃᵊn/ [US] /ˌsɝː.t̬ə-/ *noun* [U]

certified /ˈsɜː.tɪ.faɪd/ [US] /ˈsɝː.t̬ə-/ *adj* [before n] having a document that proves that you have successfully completed a course of training: *a certified teacher/nurse*

certifiable /ˈsɜː.tɪ.faɪ.ə.bl/ [US] /ˈsɝː.t̬ə-/ *adj* **1** mentally ill **2** *INFORMAL* behaving in a foolish or stupid way: *Simon's washing his car again – that man's certifiable!*

certitude /ˈsɜː.tɪ.tjuːd/ [US] /ˈsɝː.t̬ə.tuːd/ *noun* [U] *FORMAL* certainty or confidence: *It is impossible to predict the outcome of the negotiations with any degree of certitude.*

ˌcervical ˈsmear *noun* [C] a medical test in which some cells are taken from a woman's CERVIX (= the opening of her womb) and then tested to discover if she has cancer

cervix /ˈsɜː.vɪks/ [US] /ˈsɝː-/ *noun* [C] *plural* **cervixes** or **cervices** *SPECIALIZED* the narrow lower part of the womb, which leads into the vagina **cervical** /səˈvaɪ.kᵊl/ /ˈsɜː.vɪ-/ [US] /ˈsɝː.vɪ-/ *adj*: *cervical cancer/screening*

cesarean /sɪˈzeə.ri.ən/ [US] /-zer.i-/ *noun* [C], *adj US FOR* **caesarean (section)**

cessation /sesˈeɪ.ʃᵊn/ *noun* [C or U] *FORMAL* ending or stopping: *Religious leaders have called for a total cessation* ***of*** *the bombing campaign.* ➲See also **cease**.

cesspit /ˈses.pɪt/ *noun* [C] **1** (*ALSO* **cesspool**) a large underground hole or container which is used for collecting and storing excrement, urine and dirty water **2** *DISAPPROVING* a situation that causes disgust

c'est la vie /ˌseɪ.læˈviː/ *exclamation* used to say that situations of that type happen in life, and you cannot do anything about them: *I can't go to the football on Saturday – I've got to work. Oh well, c'est la vie.*

cetacean /sɪˈteɪ.ʃᵊn/ *noun* [C] *SPECIALIZED* any of various types of mammal, such as the whale, that live in the sea like fish **cetacean** /sɪˈteɪ.ʃᵊn/ *adj*

cf., cf *FORMAL* used in writing when you want the reader to make a comparison between the subject being discussed and something else

CFC /ˌsiː.efˈsiː/ *noun* [C] *ABBREVIATION FOR* chlorofluorocarbon: a gas used in fridges and, in the past, in AEROSOLS (= a metal container in which liquids are kept under pressure and forced out in drops): *CFCs cause damage to the ozone layer.*

cha-cha(-cha) /ˈtʃɑː.tʃɑː/ /ˌtʃɑː.tʃɑːˈtʃɑː/ *noun* [C] (a piece of music written for) an energetic modern dance, originally from South America, involving small fast steps and movement of the bottom from side to side

chafe [RUB] /tʃeɪf/ *verb* [I or T] to make or become damaged or sore by rubbing: *The bracelet was so tight that it started to chafe (my wrist).*

chafe [BE ANNOYED] /tʃeɪf/ *verb* [I usually + adv or prep] to be or become annoyed or lose patience because of rules or limits: *We have been chafing* ***under*** *petty regulations for too long.*

chaff /tʃɑːf/ [US] /tʃæf/ *noun* [U] the outer layer which is separated from grains such as wheat before they are used as food, or dried grass and stems when used to feed cattle

chaffinch /ˈtʃæf.ɪntʃ/ *noun* [C] a common small European bird

chagrin /ˈʃæg.rɪn/ *noun* [U] *FORMAL* disappointment or annoyance, especially when caused by a failure or mistake: *My children have never shown an interest in music, much* ***to*** *my chagrin.* **chagrined** /ˈʃæg.rɪnd/ *adj*

chain [RINGS] /tʃeɪn/ *noun* [C or U] (a length of) rings usually made of metal which are connected together and used for fastening, pulling, supporting, or limiting freedom, or as jewellery: *The gates were locked with a padlock and a heavy steel chain.* ○ *Put the chain on the door if you are alone in the house.* ○ *Mary was wearing a beautiful silver chain around her neck.*

• **in chains** tied with chains: *The hostages were kept in chains for 23 hours a day.*

chains /tʃeɪnz/ *plural noun* a fact or situation that limits a person's freedom: *At last the country has freed itself from the chains* ***of*** *the authoritarian regime.*

chain /tʃeɪn/ *verb* [T usually + adv or prep] to fasten someone or something using a chain: *It's so cruel to keep a pony chained* ***up*** *like that all the time.* ○ *They chained themselves* ***to*** *lampposts in protest at the judge's decision.* ○ *FIGURATIVE I don't want a job where I'm chained* ***to*** *a desk for eight hours a day.*

chain [CONNECTED THINGS] /tʃeɪn/ *noun* [C] a set of connected or related things: *She has built up a chain of 180 bookshops across the country.* ○ *We witnessed a remarkable chain* ***of events*** *in eastern Europe in 1989.*

ˈchain ˌletter *noun* [C] a letter which is sent to several people who are each asked to send copies to several others, and which sometimes threatens that bad things will happen if they do not send these copies

chain-link fence /ˌtʃeɪn.lɪŋkˈfents/ *noun* [C] *US* a fence made of strong wire netting

ˈchain ˌmail *noun* [U] (*ALSO* **mail**) small metal rings that have been joined together to look like cloth. It was used in the past to protect the body of a soldier from injury when fighting.

ˌchain reˈaction *noun* [C] a set of related events in which each event causes the next one, or a chemical reaction in which each change causes another: *The war risked setting off a perilous chain reaction that would endanger the whole world.*

ˈchain ˌsaw *noun* [C] a large saw with a motor, that has teeth-like parts fitted onto a continuous chain, and which is used especially for cutting trees

chain-smoke /ˈtʃeɪn.sməʊk/ [US] /-smoʊk/ *verb* [I] to smoke cigarettes one after another: *Joan's under a lot of pressure these days – she's been chain-smoking ever since her divorce.* **ˈchain ˌsmoker** *noun* [C]

ˈchain ˌstitch *noun* [U] a decorative sewing method in which each stitch is connected to the next so that they form a chain

ˈchain ˌstore *noun* [C] (one of) a group of shops which belong to a single company, having the same appearance and selling similar goods

chair [FURNITURE] /tʃeəʳ/ [US] /tʃer/ *noun* [C] a seat for one person, which has a back, usually four legs, and sometimes two arms ➲See also **armchair** CHAIR; **deckchair**; **pushchair**; **wheelchair**. ➲See picture **In the Office** on page Centre 15

• **the chair** *INFORMAL FOR* **the electric chair**

chair [TITLE] /tʃeəʳ/ [US] /tʃer/ *noun* [C] (the official position of) a person in charge of a meeting or organization, or a position in an official group, or the person in charge of or having an important position in a college or university department: *All questions should be addressed to the chair.* **chair** /tʃeəʳ/ [US] /tʃer/ *verb* [T] *Would you like to chair tomorrow's meeting?*

ˈchair ˌlift *noun* [C] a set of chairs hanging from a moving wire powered by a motor, which carries people, especially people who are going skiing, up and down mountains

chairman, chair, chairperson /ˈtʃeə.mən/ *noun* [C] a person in charge of a meeting or organization

chairmanship /ˈtʃeə.mən.ʃɪp/ [US] /ˈtʃer-/ *noun* [C usually sing] *His chairmanship* (= The period when he was in charge) *lasted a year.*

chairwoman /ˈtʃeəˌwʊm.ən/ [US] /ˈtʃer-/ *noun* [C] a female chairman

chaise longue /ˌʃezˈlɔ̃ːŋ/ *noun* [C] (*US ALSO* **chaise lounge**) a long low seat, with an arm at one side and usually a low back along half of its length, which a person can stretch out their legs on

chakra /'tʃæk.rə/ *noun* [C] SPECIALIZED in YOGA and traditional Indian medicine, one of the seven centres of energy in the human body

chalet /'ʃæl.eɪ/ *noun* [C] a small wooden house found in mountainous areas, especially in Switzerland, or a house built in a similar style, especially as used by people on holiday

chalice /'tʃæl.ɪs/ *noun* [C] **1** in Christian ceremonies, a large, decorative, gold or silver cup from which wine is drunk **2** in magic, a cup representing the element of water

chalk /tʃɔːk/ US /tʃɑːk/ *noun* [C or U] a type of soft white rock, or (a stick of) this rock or a similar substance used for writing or drawing

• **be like chalk and cheese** UK If two people are like chalk and cheese they are completely different from each other: *My brother and I are like chalk and cheese.*

chalk /tʃɔːk/ US /tʃɑːk/ *verb* [I or T] to write something with a piece of chalk

chalky /'tʃɔː.ki/ US /'tʃɑː-/ *adj*: *The soil in this area is very chalky* (= contains chalk). **chalkiness** /'tʃɔː.kɪ.nəs/ US /'tʃɑː-/ *noun* [U]

▲ **chalk** *sth* **up** *phrasal verb* [M] to achieve something, such as a victory, or to score points in a game: *Today's victory is the fifth that the Irish team has chalked up this year.* ○ *It was doubtful whether the Conservatives could chalk up a fourth successive election victory, but they did.*

• **chalk** *sth* **up to experience** to accept failure and learn from a particular experience: *"So your new job didn't work out very well?" "No, it didn't, but never mind – chalk it up to experience."*

chalkboard /'tʃɔːk.bɔːd/ US /'tʃɑːk.bɔːrd/ *noun* [C] US FOR **blackboard**

challenge DIFFICULT JOB /'tʃæl.ɪndʒ/ *noun* [C or U] (the situation of being faced with) something needing great mental or physical effort in order to be done successfully and which therefore tests a person's ability: *Finding a solution to this problem is one of the greatest challenges faced by scientists today.* ○ *You know me – I like a challenge.* ○ *It's going to be a difficult job but I'm sure she'll rise to the challenge.*

challenge /'tʃæl.ɪndʒ/ *verb* [T] to test someone's ability or determination

challenging /'tʃæl.ɪn.dʒɪŋ/ *adj* difficult, in a way that tests your ability or determination: *This has been a challenging time for us all.*

challenge INVITATION /'tʃæl.ɪndʒ/ *noun* [C] an invitation to compete or take part, especially in a game or argument: *"I bet you can't eat all that food on your plate." "Is that a challenge?"* ○ [+ to infinitive] *She issued a challenge to her rival candidates to take part in a public debate.*

challenge /'tʃæl.ɪndʒ/ *verb* [T] *Tina has challenged me to a game of poker*

challenger /'tʃæl.ɪn.dʒər/ US /-dʒɚ/ *noun* [C] someone who tries to win a competition, fight or sports event from someone who has previously won it

challenge EXPRESSION OF DOUBT /'tʃæl.ɪndʒ/ *noun* [C or U] a questioning of whether something is true or legal: *The result of the vote poses a serious challenge to the government's credibility.* ○ *Because of the way this research was conducted, its findings are open to challenge.* **challenge** /'tʃæl.ɪndʒ/ *verb* [T] *Children challenge their parents' authority far more nowadays than they did in the past.*

challenge INSTRUCTION /'tʃæl.ɪndʒ/ *noun* [C] an instruction given by a soldier or guard at a border or gate, telling a person to stand still and state their name and reasons for being there **challenge** /'tʃæl.ɪndʒ/ *verb* [T]

challenge REFUSAL /'tʃæl.ɪndʒ/ *noun* [C] LEGAL a refusal to accept someone as a member of a jury: *A challenge to a member of the jury should be made before the trial begins.* **challenge** /'tʃæl.ɪndʒ/ *verb* [T]

chamber BEDROOM /'tʃeɪm.bər/ US /-bɚ/ *noun* [C] OLD USE a room in a house, especially a bedroom

chamber ROOM /'tʃeɪm.bər/ US /-bɚ/ *noun* [C] FORMAL a room used for a special or official purpose, or a group of people who form (part of) a parliament: *Meetings of the council are held in the council chamber.* ○ *a torture chamber* ○ *There are two chambers in the British parliament – the House of Commons is the lower chamber, and*

the House of Lords is the upper chamber.

• **in chambers** UK LEGAL If a trial is in chambers, it happens in a court room without the presence of the public, newspaper reporters, etc.

chambers /'tʃeɪm.bəz/ US /-bɚz/ *plural noun* a judge's private office. A judge may have legal discussions with lawyers in private in his or her chambers.

chamber SPACE /'tʃeɪm.bər/ US /-bɚ/ *noun* [C] SPECIALIZED an enclosed space in a machine, plant or animal: *The human heart has four chambers.*

chambermaid /'tʃeɪm.bə.meɪd/ US /-bɚ-/ *noun* [C] a woman employed in a hotel to clean and tidy bedrooms

chamber music *noun* [U] classical music written for a small group of musicians so that it can be performed easily in a small room, or, in the past, in a private home

chamber of commerce *noun* [C] *plural* **chambers of commerce** an organization consisting of people in business, who work together to improve business in their town or local area

chamber orchestra *noun* [C] a small orchestra that performs classical music

chamber pot *noun* [C] a large, round, bowl-shaped container, which in the past was kept under a bed and used as a toilet at night or during an illness

chameleon /kə'miː.li.ən/ *noun* [C] **1** a lizard that changes its skin colour to match its surroundings so that it cannot be seen **2** a person who changes their opinions or behaviour to please other people

chamois /'ʃæm.wɑː/ *noun* [C] *plural* **chamois** a small animal which looks like a goat and which lives in the mountains of Europe and southwest Asia

chamois ('leather), shammy ('leather) /'ʃæm.i/ *noun* [C or U] (a piece of) soft leather used for cleaning and making things shine, or (a piece of) cotton cloth made to feel like leather

champ BITE /tʃæmp/ *verb* [I or T] to **chomp**

• **champ at the bit** (US ALSO **chomp at the bit**) to be eager and not willing to wait to do something

champ CHAMPION /tʃæmp/ *noun* [C] INFORMAL FOR **champion** WINNER

champagne /ʃæm'peɪn/ *noun* [U] (UK OLD-FASHIONED INFORMAL **champers**) an expensive white or pink fizzy wine made in the Champagne area of Eastern France, or, more generally, any similar wine. Champagne is often drunk to celebrate something: *We always celebrate our wedding anniversary with a bottle of champagne.* ○ *The champagne corks were popping* (= Bottles of champagne were opened) *when Guy got his new job.*

champagne flute *noun* [C] (ALSO **flute**) a tall, narrow glass with a long stem, which is used for drinking champagne

champagne socialist *noun* [C] DISAPPROVING a rich person who claims to support a fair society in which everyone has equal rights and the rich help the poor, but who may not behave in this way

champion WINNER /'tʃæm.pi.ən/ *noun* [C] (INFORMAL **champ**) someone or something, especially a person or animal, that has beaten all other competitors in a competition: *an Olympic champion* ○ *She is the world champion for the third year in succession.* ○ *The defending champion will play his first match of the tournament tomorrow.* ○ *Who are the reigning European football champions?*

championship /'tʃæm.pi.ən.ʃɪp/ *noun* [C] **1** a high-level competition to decide who is the best, especially in a sport: *the British Diving Championship* ○ *The world championships will be held in Scotland next year.* ○ *He has been playing championship tennis for three years now.* **2** the position of being a champion: *She has held the championship for the past three years.*

champion SUPPORT /'tʃæm.pi.ən/ *noun* [C] a person who enthusiastically supports, defends or fights for a person, belief, right or principle: *She has long been a champion of prisoners' rights/the disabled/free speech.* **champion** /'tʃæm.pi.ən/ *verb* [T] *He has championed constitutional reform for many years.* **championship** /'tʃæm.pi.ən.ʃɪp/ *noun* [U]

champion GOOD /'tʃæm.pi.ən/ *adj, exclamation* INFORMAL, MAINLY NORTHERN ENGLISH excellent

chance LUCK /tʃɑːnts/ ⓤ /tʃænts/ *noun* [U] the force that causes things to happen without any known cause or reason for doing so: *Roulette is a game of chance.* ○ *I got this job completely by chance.* [+ (*that*)] *It was pure/sheer chance (that) we met.* ○ *We must double-check everything and leave nothing to chance.*

• **by any chance** used to ask a question or request in a polite way: *Are you Hungarian, by any chance?* ○ *Could you lend me a couple of pounds, by any chance?* ○ *You wouldn't, by any chance, have a calculator on you, would you?*

chance /tʃɑːnts/ ⓤ /tʃænts/ *verb* [I] OLD-FASHIONED OR LITERARY to happen or do something by chance: [+ *to* infinitive] *They chanced to be in the restaurant when I arrived.* ○ *I chanced on/upon* (= found unexpectedly) *some old love letters in a drawer.* ○ *Ten years after leaving school, we chanced on/upon* (= unexpectedly met) *each other in Regent Street.*

COMMON LEARNER ERROR

chance or lucky?

Chance is not used when you are talking about good things that happen. In this situation use 'lucky'.

We were lucky because the weather was perfect.
~~We had the chance because the weather was perfect.~~

---

chance LIKELIHOOD /tʃɑːnts/ ⓤ /tʃænts/ *noun* [S] likelihood; the level of possibility that something will happen: *You'd have a better chance/more chance of passing your exams if you worked a bit harder.* ○ [+ (*that*)] *There's a good chance (that) I'll have this essay finished by tomorrow.* ○ *There's a slim/slight chance (that) I might have to go to Manchester next week.* ○ *If we hurry, there's still an outside* (= very small) *chance of catching the plane.* ○ *"Is there any chance of speaking to him?"* *"Not a/No chance, I'm afraid."* ○ *I don't think I stand/have a chance of winning.* ○ UK *John thinks they're in with a chance* (= they have a possibility of doing or getting what they want).

chances /tʃɑːnt.sɪz/ ⓤ /tʃænt-/ *plural noun*: *Her resignation has improved my chances of* (= the likelihood that I will get) *promotion.* ○ *What are her chances of survival?* ○ [+ *that*] *What are the chances* (= How likely is it) *that they'll win?*

• **(the) chances are** INFORMAL it is likely: *Chances are (that) they'll be late anyway.*

• **not give much for *sb's* chances** to not believe someone will succeed: *I wouldn't give much for his chances in the next race.*

chance OPPORTUNITY /tʃɑːnts/ ⓤ /tʃænts/ *noun* [C] an occasion which allows something to be done; an opportunity: *I didn't get/have a chance to speak to her.* ○ [+ *to* infinitive] *If you give me a chance to speak, I'll explain.* ○ *Society has to give prisoners a second chance when they come out of jail.* ○ *He left and I missed my chance to say goodbye to him.* ○ *I'd go now given half a chance* (= If I had the slightest opportunity).

• **chance would be a fine thing** UK INFORMAL said when you would very much like something to happen but there is no possibility that it will: *"You should relax a bit more." "Chance would be a fine thing."*

chance RISK /tʃɑːnts/ ⓤ /tʃænts/ *noun* [C] a possibility that something negative will happen; a risk: *I'm delivering my work by hand – I'm not taking any chances.* ○ *There's a chance of injury in almost any sport.*

chance /tʃɑːnts/ ⓤ /tʃænts/ *verb* [T] *You'd be a fool to chance* (= risk) *your life savings on a single investment.*

• **chance *your* arm** to take a chance in order to get something that you want: *Aren't you chancing your arm a bit giving up a secure job to start up a business?*

chancy /tʃɑːnt.si/ ⓤ /tʃænt-/ *adj* INFORMAL risky: *Investing on the Stock Exchange is a chancy business.*

chancel /tʃɑːnt.sᵊl/ ⓤ /tʃænt-/ *noun* [C] the part of a church containing the ALTAR, where the priests and choir sit

chancellor /tʃɑːnt.sᵊl.əʳ/ ⓤ /tʃænt.sᵊl.ɚ/ *noun* [C] a person in a position of the highest or high rank, especially in a government or university: *Helmut Kohl became the first Chancellor of a united Germany in 1990.* ○ *A for-*

mer politician has been appointed Chancellor of the university. **chancellorship** /tʃɑːnt.sᵊl.ə.ʃɪp/ ⓤ /tʃænt.sᵊl.-ɚ-/ *noun* [S]

chancellery /tʃɑːnt.sᵊl.ᵊr.i/ ⓤ /tʃænt.sᵊl.ɚ-/ *noun* [C] a building or room where a chancellor works or lives, or the people who work in a chancellor's offices

Chancellor of the Exchequer /ˌtʃɑːnt.sᵊl.ə.rəv.ðɪ.-eks'tʃek.əʳ/ ⓤ /ˌtʃænt.sᵊl.ɚ.əv.ðɪ.eks'tʃek.ɚ/ *noun* the person in the British Government who is responsible for deciding tax levels and how much money the Government can spend

chandelier /ˌʃæn.dəˈlɪəʳ/ ⓤ /-ˈlɪr/ *noun* [C] a decorative light which hangs from the ceiling and has several branch-like parts for holding BULBS or, especially in the past, candles

chandler /tʃɑːnd.ləʳ/ ⓤ /tʃænd.lɚ/ *noun* [C] a person who trades in supplies for ships

change BECOME DIFFERENT /tʃeɪndʒ/ *verb* 1 [I or T] to make or become different, or to exchange one thing for another thing, especially of a similar type: *I almost didn't recognize him – she'd changed so much.* ○ *That was twenty years ago and things have changed since then.* ○ *Nothing changes, does it – I've been away two years and the office still looks exactly the same.* ○ *People have changed their diets a lot over the past few years.* ○ *I'm going to change my hair style.* ○ *I had to change those trousers I bought for* (= take them back to the shop in order to get) *a bigger pair.* ○ *She's just changed jobs.* ○ *Let's change the subject* (= talk about something different). 2 [I] When the wind or the tide (= the rise and fall of the sea) changes, it starts to move in a different direction: *The tide is starting to change.*

• **change for the better** to improve: *Her attitude has definitely changed for the better since she started this new job.*

• **change hands** to go from one owner to another: *That Italian restaurant is nowhere near as good since it changed hands.*

• **change *your* mind** to form a new opinion or make a new decision about something which is different from your old one: *If you change your mind about coming tonight, just give me a call.* ○ *When I first met him I didn't like him but I've changed my mind.*

• **change places** to be in someone else's situation: *I wouldn't change places with him for the world!*

• **change (*your*) tack** to try a different method to deal with the same problem: *I've written twice and received no reply, so I might change tack and call her.*

• **change *your* tune** DISAPPROVING to change your opinion completely, especially because you know it will bring you an advantage: *He was against the idea to start with, but he soon changed his tune when he realized how much money he'd get.*

• **change *your* ways** to improve the bad parts of your behaviour: *If he wants to carry on living here, he's going to have to change his ways and learn to be a bit more tidy.*

• **Plus ça change (plus c'est la même chose).** SAYING The more things change, the more they stay the same. Used when a change does not result in an improvement in a situation: *What's the point in voting? Plus ça change...*

change /tʃeɪndʒ/ *noun* 1 [C or U] when something becomes different, or the result of something becoming different: *Let me know if there's any change in the situation.* ○ *We're living in a time of great change.* ○ *We need a change of government.* ○ *a change in lifestyle* ○ *They've made a lot of changes to the house.* ○ *The new management will make fundamental/radical/sweeping changes* (= do things in a very different way). 2 [S] something which is pleasant or interesting because it is unusual or new: *It's nice to see her smile for a change.* ○ *"Shall we eat in the garden?" "Why not – it'll make a change."* ○ *We've always had a red car – it's time we had a change!*

• **change of scene** a new situation: *She'd been with the same company for too many years and felt she needed a change of scene, so she applied for a job as a stage manager.*

• **change of heart** If someone has a change of heart, they change their opinion or the way they feel about something: *She was going to sell her house but had a change of heart at the last minute.*

• **the change (of life)** *OLD-FASHIONED FOR* the **menopause**: *She's **going through** the change.*

• **A change is as good as a rest.** *UK SAYING* You can benefit as much from changing the work you do as from having a rest.

changeable /ˈtʃeɪn.dʒə.bl̩/ *adj* describes something that often changes: *The weather in Britain is notoriously changeable.* ○ *His moods are very changeable.*

changed /tʃeɪndʒd/ *adj* **a changed man/woman** someone whose behaviour and character has changed a lot, especially improved: *He's a changed man since he met Debbie.*

changing /ˈtʃeɪn.dʒɪŋ/ *adj* in a state of becoming different: *the rapidly changing world of politics* ○ *changing attitudes towards childcare* ○ *changing circumstances*

changeless /ˈtʃeɪndʒ.ləs/ *adj LITERARY* describes something that never seems to change: *Surrounded by this changeless landscape, one can imagine the world as it was many thousands of years ago.*

COMMON LEARNER ERROR

change (noun) + preposition

When you use **change** as a noun, be careful to use the correct preposition. Use **change in** to describe a gradual change from one situation to a different one.

There has been a change in the attitude of local people over the last few months.

~~*There has been a change on the attitude of local people over the last few months.*~~

Use **change of** when something such as an address or job is being replaced by a different one.

Can you give me your change of address?

Use **change to** in order to describe a change which someone makes so that something is different but not completely different.

We may have to make some changes to the design.

~~*We may have to make some changes in the design.*~~

change [CLOTHES/BEDS] /tʃeɪndʒ/ *verb* **[I or T]** to remove one set of clothes and put a different set on yourself or a young child, especially a baby, or to remove dirty sheets from a bed and put clean ones on it: *You don't need to change – you look great as you are.* ○ *I'll just change **into*** (= get dressed in) *something a bit smarter.* ○ *Give me five minutes to change **out of*** (= remove) *my work clothes and I'll come out with you.* ○ *How often do you think he changes his shirt?* ○ *Could you change the **baby**/the baby's (UK) **nappy** (US **diaper**)?* ○ *I've changed the **sheets**/the **bed*** (= the sheets on the bed) *in the guest room.*

change *noun* **[C]** **1** the action of putting on different clothes: *Imagine a 3-day journey without a wash or a change of clothes.* **2 a change of clothes** a set of clothes that is additional to the ones that you are wearing: *You'll need a change of clothes if you're staying overnight.*

change [MONEY] /tʃeɪndʒ/ *verb* **[T]** to get or give money in exchange for money, either because you want it in smaller units, or because you want the same value in foreign money: *Could you change a £10 note (**for** two fives), please?* ○ *Could you change a £5 note **for** me?* ○ *I need to change my dollars **for/into** English money.*

change /tʃeɪndʒ/ *noun* **[U]** **1** money which is coins rather than notes: *She gave me £5 **in** change.* ○ *My dad always used to carry a lot of **loose/small** change* (= coins) *in his pocket.* **2** smaller units of money given in exchange for larger units of the same amount: *Have you got change for a twenty-dollar bill?* **3** the money which is returned to someone who has paid for something which costs less than the amount that they gave: *I think you've given me the **wrong** change.*

change [TRANSPORT] /tʃeɪndʒ/ *verb* **[I or T]** to get off a train, bus, etc. and catch another in order to continue a journey: *I had to change (trains) twice to get there.* ○ *Change at Peterborough for York.* **change** /tʃeɪndʒ/ *noun* **[C]** *I hate journeys where you've got a lot of changes, especially if you're carrying luggage.*

change [SPEED] /tʃeɪndʒ/ *verb* **[I or T]** (*US USUALLY* **shift**) to put a vehicle into a different gear, usually in order to change the speed at which it is moving: *to change **gear*** ○ *I changed **into** fourth (gear).* ○ *UK Change **down** (US **Downshift**) to go round the corner.*

PHRASAL VERBS WITH **change** ▼

▲ **change over** *phrasal verb* to stop using or having one thing and to start using or having something else: *We've just changed over **from** gas central heating **to** electric.*

▲ **change *sth* round/around** *phrasal verb* **[M]** to move objects such as furniture into different positions: *The room looks very different since you've changed the furniture round.*

changeling /ˈtʃeɪndʒ.lɪŋ/ *noun* **[C]** (especially in stories) a baby who is secretly used to take the place of another baby

changeover /ˈtʃeɪndʒˌəʊ.vəʳ/ [US] /-ˌoʊ.vɚ/ *noun* **[C usually sing]** a complete change from one system or method to another: *The changeover **to** the new taxation system has created a lot of problems.*

ˈchanging ˌroom *noun* **[C]** a room where people can change their clothes, for example before and after sports or, in a shop, where people can try on clothes before buying them

channel [TELEVISION] /ˈtʃæn.əl/ *noun* **[C]** a television station: *a cable/terrestrial channel* ○ *a music/movie/news/shopping/sports channel* ○ *the news **on** Channel 4* ○ *She **switched/turned to** another channel to watch the football.*

channel [PASSAGE] /ˈtʃæn.əl/ *noun* **[C]** a passage for water or other liquids to flow along, or a part of a river or other area of water which is deep and wide enough to provide a route for ships to travel along: *There are **drainage/irrigation** channels all over this flat agricultural land.* ○ *The boats all have to pass through this narrow channel.*

• **the (English) Channel** the area of sea which separates England from France: *We're going to have a day-trip across the Channel.* ○ *We took the car to France overnight on a **(cross-)**channel ferry.*

channel [AIRPORT/PORT] /ˈtʃæn.əl/ *noun* **[C]** a route or way out of an airport or port where travellers' bags are examined: *If you have nothing to declare, go through the **green** channel.* ○ *Goods to declare – use the **red** channel.*

channel [COMMUNICATING] /ˈtʃæn.əl/ *noun* **[C]** a way of communicating with people or getting something done: *We must open the channels **of communication** between the two countries.* ○ *The government pursued every **diplomatic/official** channel to free the hostages.* ○ *Complaints should be made through the **proper/usual** channels.*

channel [DIRECT] /ˈtʃæn.əl/ *verb* **[T]** **-ll-** or *US USUALLY* **-l-** to direct something into a particular place or situation: *Ditches were constructed to channel **water** away from the buildings.* ○ *If she could only channel all that **energy into** something useful.* ○ *A lot of **money** has been channelled **into** research in that particular field.*

channel-hopping /ˈtʃæn.əl̩.hɒ.pɪŋ/ [US] /-ˌhɑː-/ *noun* **[U]** quickly changing from one T.V. channel to another to find something you want to watch

the ˌChannel ˈTunnel *noun* **[S]** (*INFORMAL* **the Chunnel**) the three long passages under the English Channel between England and France

chant /tʃɑːnt/ [US] /tʃænt/ *verb* **[I or T]** to repeat or sing a word or phrase continuously, or to sing a religious prayer or song to a simple tune: *The crowd were chanting the name of their football team.* ○ *Demonstrators chanted anti-government slogans in the square.* ○ *We could hear the monks chanting.*

chant /tʃɑːnt/ [US] /tʃænt/ *noun* **[C]** a word or phrase that is repeated many times: *The fans started to sing the familiar **football** chant, "Here we go, here we go, here we go!".*

chanteuse /ˌʃɑːnˈtɜːz/ *noun* **[C]** *LITERARY* a female singer, especially one who sings on the stage in a theatre or bar

chanty, *US* **chantey** /ˈʃæn.ti/ *noun* **[C]** a **shanty** SONG

Chanukah /ˈhɑː.nə.kə/ *noun* [C or U] **Hanukkah**

chaos /ˈkeɪ.ɒs/ ⓤ /-ɑːs/ *noun* [U] a state of total confusion and lack of order: *Snow and ice have caused chaos on the roads.* ○ *Ever since our secretary walked out, the office has been in a state of total/utter chaos.* ○ *We muddled up the name labels and chaos ensued* (= resulted).
 chaotic /keɪˈɒt.ɪk/ ⓤ /-ˈɑː.t̬ɪk/ *adj* in a state of chaos: *The house is a bit chaotic at the moment – we've got all these extra people staying and we're still decorating.* ○ *He's a chaotic sort of a person – always trying to do twenty things at once.* **chaotically** /keɪˈɒt.ɪ.kli/ ⓤ /-ˈɑː.t̬ɪ-/ *adv*

ˈchaos ˌtheory *noun* [U] a scientific theory about situations that obey particular laws but appear to have little or no order: *A frequent metaphor for one aspect of chaos theory is called the Butterfly Effect – butterflies flapping their wings in the Amazon affect the weather in Chicago.*

chap [MAN] /tʃæp/ *noun* [C] (*ALSO* **chappie**, *ALSO* **chappy**) UK INFORMAL OLD-FASHIONED a man: *He's a friendly sort of a chap.*

chap. [BOOK] *noun* [C] WRITTEN ABBREVIATION FOR **chapter**
BOOK: *Chap. 21*

chapati (*plural* **chapatis** or **chapaties**) /tʃəˈpæ.ti/ ⓤ /-t̬i/ *noun* [C] (*ALSO* **chapatti**) a type of flat round Indian bread made without yeast

chapel /ˈtʃæp.əl/ *noun* [C] **1** a room within a larger building, which is used for Christian worship: *The college/hospital/prison has its own chapel.* ○ *Two of the cathedral's chapels were added later – the Lady Chapel and the Chapel of St Paul.* **2** MAINLY UK a building which is used for Christian worship by Christians who do not belong to the Church of England or the Roman Catholic Church

chaperone, **chaperon** /ˈʃæp.ə.rəʊn/ ⓤ /-roʊn/ *noun* [C] **1** (especially in the past) an older person, especially a woman, who goes with and takes care of a younger woman who is not married when she is in public: HUMOROUS *She's asked me to go to the cinema with her and Andrew, I think as a sort of chaperone.* **2** a female nurse who is in the same room when a female patient is examined by a male doctor, or a police officer who protects a person injured by a criminal when they are in public **3** US an older person who is present at a social event for young people to encourage correct behaviour: *Several parents acted as chaperones for the school disco.*
 chaperone, **chaperon** /ˈʃæp.ə.rəʊn/ ⓤ /-ə.roʊn/ *verb* [T] MAINLY HUMOROUS *Do you trust him on your own or do you want me to chaperone you* (= go with you)*?* ○ US *Several parents volunteered to chaperone class bus trips.*

chaplain /ˈtʃæp.lɪn/ *noun* [C] a Christian official who is responsible for the religious needs of an organization: *the college/hospital/prison chaplain*
 chaplaincy /ˈtʃæp.lɪnt.si/ *noun* [C] the job of a chaplain, or a building or office where a chaplain works

chapped /tʃæpt/ *adj* describes skin which is sore, rough and cracked, especially caused by cold weather: *chapped lips* ○ *She'd been working outside all winter and her hands were red and chapped.* **chap** /tʃæp/ *verb* [I or T] -pp- *The cold wind had chapped her lips.*

chappy, **chappie** /ˈtʃæp.i/ *noun* [C] UK OLD-FASHIONED INFORMAL a **chap** MAN

chaps /tʃæps/ *plural noun* protective leather clothing worn over trousers by cowboys when riding a horse

chapter [BOOK] /ˈtʃæp.təʳ/ ⓤ /-t̬ɚ/ *noun* [C] (*WRITTEN ABBREVIATION* **chap.**) any of the separate parts into which a book or other piece of text is divided, usually numbered or given a title: *Read Chapter 10 before class tomorrow.*
● **give/quote** *sth/sb* **chapter and verse** to give exact information about something, especially something in a book: *I can't quote you chapter and verse but I think it's a line from 'Macbeth'.*

chapter [PERIOD] /ˈtʃæp.təʳ/ ⓤ /-t̬ɚ/ *noun* [C] a period which is part of a larger amount of time during which something happens: *The whole period leading up to the revolution is an interesting chapter in British history.* ○ *That chapter of my life closed when I had a serious riding accident.*

● **be a chapter of accidents** UK to be a series of unpleasant events: *The whole trip was a chapter of accidents.*

chapter [SOCIETY] /ˈtʃæp.təʳ/ ⓤ /-t̬ɚ/ *noun* [C] US OR FORMAL a local division of a larger organization: *The local chapter of the League of Women Voters meets at the library.*

char [BURN] /tʃɑːʳ/ ⓤ /tʃɑːr/ *verb* [I or T] -rr- to burn and become black or to burn something so that it becomes black: *For easy peeling, grill the peppers until the skin starts to char.*
 charred /tʃɑːd/ ⓤ /tʃɑːrd/ *adj* burnt and black: *charred meat* ○ *The charred body of a man was found by police in a burnt-out car last night.*

char [CLEAN] /tʃɑːʳ/ ⓤ /tʃɑːr/ *verb* [I] -rr- UK OLD-FASHIONED to clean and tidy a house or office for payment
 char /tʃɑːʳ/ ⓤ /tʃɑːr/ *noun* [C] UK OLD-FASHIONED INFORMAL **charwoman**

charabanc /ˈʃær.ə.bæŋ/ ⓤ /ˈʃer-/ *noun* [C] (*ALSO* **chara**) UK OLD-FASHIONED a large old-fashioned bus, especially one used by groups for visiting places of interest

character [QUALITY] /ˈkær.ɪk.təʳ/ ⓤ /ˈker.ɪk.tɚ/ *noun* **1** [C or U] the particular combination of qualities in a person or place that makes them different from others: *Politeness is traditionally part of the British character.* ○ *It would be very out of character* (= not typical) *of her to lie.* ○ *One of the joys of being a parent is watching the child's character develop.* ○ *The idea was to modernize various aspects of the house without changing its essential character.* ○ *It's not in his character to be* (= he is not usually) *jealous.* **2** [U] qualities which are interesting and unusual: *a hotel of character* ○ *I'd prefer an old place with a bit of character.* ○ *Old books are said to give a room character.* ○ *As people grow older, their faces acquire more character.* **3** [U] the quality of being determined and able to deal with difficult situations: *She has such strength of character.*
 characteristic /ˌkær.ɪk.təˈrɪs.tɪk/ ⓤ /ˌker-/ *adj* typical of a person or thing: *With the hospitality so characteristic of these people, they opened their house to over fifty guests.* ○ *She behaved with characteristic dignity.* ○ *The creamy richness is characteristic of the cheese from this region.*
 characteristic /ˌkær.ɪk.təˈrɪs.tɪk/ ⓤ /ˌker-/ *noun* [C] a typical or noticeable quality of someone or something: *Unfortunately a big nose is a family characteristic.* ○ *Sentimentality seems a characteristic of all the writers of that period.* ○ *The male bird displays* (= has) *several characteristics which distinguish him from the female.*
 characteristically /ˌkær.ɪk.təˈrɪs.tɪ.kli/ ⓤ /ˌker-/ *adv*: *She gave a characteristically skilful performance.*
 characterize, UK USUALLY **-ise** /ˈkær.ɪk.tə.raɪz/ ⓤ /ˈker.ɪk.tɚ.aɪz/ *verb* [T] **1** Something which characterizes another thing is typical of it: *Bright colours and bold strokes characterize his early paintings.* **2** to describe something by stating its main qualities: *In her essay, she characterizes the whole era as a period of radical change.*
 characterization, UK USUALLY **-isation** /ˌkær.ɪk.tə.raɪˈzeɪ.ʃən/ ⓤ /ˌker.ɪk.tɚ.ɪ-/ *noun* [C]
 characterless /ˈkær.ɪk.tə.ləs/ ⓤ /ˈker.ɪk.tɚ-/ *adj* describes something or someone who lacks interest or style and does not possess any unusual qualities: *It's just one of those characterless modern cities.* ○ *a perfect but characterless face*

character [PERSON] /ˈkær.ɪk.təʳ/ ⓤ /ˈker.ɪk.tɚ/ *noun* [C] **1** a person, especially when you are describing a particular quality that they have: *She's a curious character – I don't really know what to think of her.* ○ *There were one or two strange-looking characters hanging around the bar.* **2** INFORMAL someone whose behaviour is different from most people's, especially in a way that is interesting or amusing: *He's quite a character/a real character, is Ted – he's seventy now and still riding that motorbike.*

character [REPRESENTATION] /ˈkær.ɪk.təʳ/ ⓤ /ˈker.ɪk.tɚ/ *noun* [C] a person represented in a film, play or story: *The film revolves around three main characters.* ○ *She had Mickey Mouse or some other cartoon/Disney character on her sweater.* ○ *He made his name as a character actor* (= an actor who plays unusual and often humorous people).

characterization, *UK USUALLY* **-isation** /ˌkær.ɪk.tə.raɪˈzeɪ.ʃən/ [US] /ˌker.ɪk.tə.rɪ-/ *noun* [U] the way that people are represented in a film, play or book so that they seem real and natural: *The plots in her books are very strong but there's almost no characterization.* ○ *The film's characterization of the artist* ***as*** *a complete drunk has annoyed a lot of people.*

character [MARK] /ˈkær.ɪk.təʳ/ [US] /ˈker.ɪk.tɚ/ *noun* [C] a letter, number or other mark or sign used in writing or printing, or the space one of these takes: ***a string of*** *characters* (= a line of marks) ○ *The address was written in* ***Chinese/Japanese*** *characters* (= systems of writing). ○ *The computer screen on this laptop is 66 characters* (= spaces) *wide.*

ˈcharacter assassinˌation *noun* [C or U] an intentional attempt to spoil the reputation of a person by criticizing them severely, especially unfairly, in the newspapers or on television

ˈcharacter ˌreference *noun* [C] a written statement of a person's good qualities, written by someone who knows the person well, which is sent to a future employer

charade /ʃəˈrɑːd/ [US] /-ˈreɪd/ *noun* [C] an act or event which is clearly false: *Everyone knew who was going to get the job from the start – the interviews were just a charade.*

charades /ʃəˈrɑːdz/ [US] /-ˈreɪdz/ *noun* [U] a team game in which each member tries to communicate to the others a particular word or phrase that they have been given, by expressing each syllable or word using silent actions

charcoal /ˈtʃɑː.kəʊl/ [US] /ˈtʃɑːr.koʊl/ *noun* [U] a hard black substance similar to coal which can be used as fuel or, in the form of sticks, as something to draw with: *charcoal for the barbecue* ○ *I prefer sketching* ***in*** *charcoal to pencil.* ○ *a charcoal* ***drawing*** ○ *The uniform is charcoal* ***(grey)*** (= dark grey) *and red.*

Chardonnay /ˈʃɑː.də.neɪ/ *noun* [C or U] a type of white wine, or the type of grape from which the wine is made

charge [MONEY] /tʃɑːdʒ/ [US] /tʃɑːrdʒ/ *verb* [I or T] **1** to ask an amount of money for something, especially a service or activity: ***How much/What*** *do you charge* ***for*** *a haircut and blow-dry?* ○ *The bank charged* ***commission*** *to change my traveller's cheques.* ○ [+ two objects] *They charge you $20 just to get in the nightclub.* ○ *The local museum doesn't charge for admission.* **2 charge** ***sth*** **to** ***your*** **account** If you charge something you have bought to your account, the amount you have spent is recorded and you pay for it at a later time: *Charge the bill to my account, please.* ○ *Shall we charge the flowers to your account?*

charge /tʃɑːdʒ/ [US] /tʃɑːrdʒ/ *noun* [C or U] the amount of money that you have to pay for something, especially for an activity or service: *Is there a charge* ***for*** *children or do they go free?* ○ *There's an* ***admission*** *charge of £5.* ○ *They fixed my watch* ***free of*** *charge.*

chargeable /ˈtʃɑː.dʒə.bl̩/ [US] /ˈtʃɑːr-/ *adj* Something is chargeable if you have to pay tax on it: *chargeable earnings/income* ○ *earnings/income chargeable* ***to*** *tax*

charge [ACCUSE FORMALLY] /tʃɑːdʒ/ [US] /tʃɑːrdʒ/ *verb* [T] **1** (of the police) to make a formal statement saying that someone is accused of a crime: *She's been charged* ***with*** *murder.* ○ *She is charged* ***with*** *murder****ing*** *her husband.* **2** *FORMAL* to publicly accuse someone of doing something bad: *The paper charged her* ***with*** *us****ing*** *the company's money for her own purposes.*

charge /tʃɑːdʒ/ [US] /tʃɑːrdʒ/ *noun* [C] **1** *LEGAL* a formal police statement saying that someone is accused of a crime: *The 19-year-old will be appearing in court on Thursday where she will face* ***criminal*** *charges.* ○ *He has been arrested* ***on*** *a charge* ***of*** *murder.* ○ *The police* ***brought a*** *charge of theft* ***against*** *him.* ○ *The police have had to* ***drop*** (= stop) *charges* ***against*** *her because they couldn't find any evidence.* ○ *He claimed he had been arrested on a* ***trumped up*** (= false) *charge.* **2** *FORMAL* when you accuse someone of something bad: [+ **that**] *The president responded angrily to the charge* ***that*** *she had lost touch with her country's people.* ○ *Her refusal to condemn the violence* ***laid/left*** *her* ***open to the*** *charge* ***of*** *positive support for the campaign* (= allowed people to say that she supported it).

charge [MOVE FORWARD] /tʃɑːdʒ/ [US] /tʃɑːrdʒ/ *verb* **1** [I or T] to move forward quickly and violently, especially towards something which has caused difficulty or annoyance: *The bull lowered its horns and charged.* ○ *The violence began when the police charged* ***(at)*** *a crowd of demonstrators.* **2** [I + adv or prep] *INFORMAL* to hurry from one place to another: *I've been charging* ***about/around*** *all day and I'm exhausted.* ○ *He came charging* ***up*** *the stairs to tell me the good news.*

charge /tʃɑːdʒ/ [US] /tʃɑːrdʒ/ *noun* [C] an attack in which people or animals suddenly run forwards: *a charge* ***of*** *buffalo/elephants* ○ *a police charge*

charge [CONTROL] /tʃɑːdʒ/ [US] /tʃɑːrdʒ/ *noun* **1** [U] responsibility for controlling or caring for something: *Her ex-husband* ***has*** *charge* ***of*** *the children during the week and she has them at the weekend.* ○ *His boss asked him to* ***take*** *charge* ***of*** *the office for a few days while she was away.* **2 in charge** being the person who has control of or is responsible for someone or something: *Who will be in charge* ***of*** *the department when Sophie leaves?* ○ *I* ***left*** *Jack in charge of the suitcases while I went to get the tickets.* **3** [C] *OLD-FASHIONED* a person, especially a child, who is in your care and for whom you are responsible

charge [ORDER] /tʃɑːdʒ/ [US] /tʃɑːrdʒ/ *verb* **1** [T often passive] *FORMAL* to order someone to do something: *He was charged* ***with*** *tak****ing*** *care of the premises.* **2** [T] *US LEGAL* When a judge charges a jury, the judge explains the details of the law to them. **charge** /tʃɑːdʒ/ [US] /tʃɑːrdʒ/ *noun* [C] *FORMAL*

charge [SUPPLY ENERGY] /tʃɑːdʒ/ [US] /tʃɑːrdʒ/ *verb* [I or T] *SPECIALIZED* to put electricity into an electrical device such as a battery: *She drove the car round the block to charge* ***(up)*** *its batteries.* ○ *It's not working – I don't think the battery is charging.*

charge /tʃɑːdʒ/ [US] /tʃɑːrdʒ/ *noun* [C usually sing] **1** *SPECIALIZED* the amount of electricity that an electrical device stores or that a substance carries **2** *UK* **on charge** If something is on charge, you are putting an amount of electricity into it: *Is it all right to leave/put the battery on charge overnight?* **charged** /tʃɑːdʒd/ [US] /tʃɑːrdʒd/ *adj*: *electrically charged particles/ions* ➲See also **charged**.

charge [EXPLOSIVE] /tʃɑːdʒ/ [US] /tʃɑːrdʒ/ *noun* [C] the amount of explosive to be fired at one time, or the bullet or other explosive object fired from a gun

charge /tʃɑːdʒ/ [US] /tʃɑːrdʒ/ *verb* [T] to load a gun with enough explosive to fire it once

ˈcharge acˌcount *noun* [C] *US FOR* **credit account**

ˈcharge ˌcard *noun* [C] a small, plastic card that you get from a particular shop and use to buy goods from it that you can pay for later

charged /tʃɑːdʒd/ *adj* (of arguments or subjects) causing strong feelings and differences of opinion or, more generally, filled with emotion or excitement: *Abortion is a* ***highly*** *charged issue.* ○ *He spoke in a voice charged* ***with*** *emotion.* ➲See also **charged** at **charge** SUPPLY ENERGY.

chargé (d'affaires) /ˌʃɑː.ʒeɪ.dæfˈeəʳ/ [US] /ˌʃɑːr.ʒeɪ.dæfˈer/ *noun* [C] *plural* **chargés (d'affaires)** a person who represents the leader of his or her government, either temporarily while the AMBASSADOR is away, or permanently in a country where there is no ambassador: *the Belgian chargé d'affaires/the chargé d'affaires* ***for*** *Belgium*

ˈcharge ˌnurse *noun* [C] *UK* a male nurse who is responsible for a particular part of a hospital. He is the male equal of a SISTER.

charger /ˈtʃɑː.dʒəʳ/ [US] /ˈtʃɑːr.dʒɚ/ *noun* [C] *OLD USE OR LITERARY* a soldier's large strong horse

ˈcharge ˌsheet *noun* [C] *UK* an official document on which a police officer records the details of a crime of which a person is accused ➲Compare **rap sheet**.

chargrilled /ˈtʃɑː.grɪld/ [US] /ˈtʃɑːr-/ *adj* describes food that is cooked over or under direct heat so that its surface becomes slightly black: *chargrilled tuna steaks*

chariot /ˈtʃær.i.ət/ [US] /ˈtʃer-/ *noun* [C] a two-wheeled vehicle that was used in ancient times for racing and fighting and was pulled by a horse

charioteer /ˌtʃær.i.əˈtɪəʳ/ [US] /ˌtʃer.i.əˈtɪr/ *noun* [C] a person who drives a chariot

charisma /kəˈrɪz.mə/ *noun* [U] a special power which some people possess naturally which makes them able to influence other people and attract their attention and admiration: *On screen Garbo had this great charisma so that you couldn't take your eyes off her.* ○ *How did a man of so little personal charisma get to be prime minister?* **charismatic** /ˌkær.ɪzˈmæt.ɪk/ ⓤ /-ˈmæt-/ *adj: Few were able to resist this charismatic and persuasive leader.*

charismatic /ˌkær.ɪzˈmæt.ɪk/ ⓤ /-ˈmæt-/ *adj* belonging or relating to various groups within the Christian Church who believe that God gives people special powers, such as the ability to heal others and to speak to him in a special language: *the charismatic movement*

charitable /ˈtʃær.ɪ.tə.bl̩/ ⓤ /ˈtʃer.ɪ.tə-/ *adj* kind, and not judging other people in a severe way: *Some critics said the show was good in parts – those less charitable said the whole thing was a disaster.* **charitably** /ˈtʃær.ɪ.tə.bli/ ⓤ /ˈtʃer.ɪ.tə-/ *adv: She described him, rather charitably, as quiet whereas I would have said he was boring.* **charity** /ˈtʃær.ɪ.ti/ ⓤ /ˈtʃer.ɪ.ti/ *noun* [U] FORMAL

charity /ˈtʃær.ɪ.ti/ ⓤ /ˈtʃer.ɪ.ti/ *noun* [C or U] a system of giving money, food or help free to those who are in need because they are ill, poor or homeless, or any organization which is established to provide money or help in this way: *She does a lot of work for charity.* ○ *People tend to give to* (= give money to) *charity at Christmas time.* ○ *Proceeds from the sale of these cards will go to* (= be given to) *local charities.* ○ *UNICEF is an international charity.* ○ *They did a charity performance on the first night, to raise money for AIDS research.*

• **Charity begins at home.** *SAYING* You should take care of your family and other people who live close to you before helping people who are living further away or in another country.

charitable /ˈtʃær.ɪ.tə.bl̩/ ⓤ /ˈtʃer.ɪ.tə-/ *adj* [before n] giving money, food or help free to those who are in need because they are ill, poor or homeless: *a charitable foundation/organization/trust* ○ *The entire organization is funded by charitable donations.* ○ *The school has charitable status* (= It is officially a charity).

'**charity ˌshop** *noun* [C] a shop in which a charity sells all types of used goods which are given by the public, or in which they sell new goods, to make money for the work of the charity

charlady /ˈtʃɑːˌleɪ.di/ ⓤ /ˈtʃɑːr-/ *noun* [C] UK OLD-FASHIONED a **charwoman**

charlatan /ˈʃɑː.lə.tʰn/ ⓤ /ˈʃɑːr.lə.tʰn/ *noun* [C] DISAPPROVING a person who pretends to have skills or knowledge that they do not have, especially in medicine

Charleston /ˈtʃɑːl.stən/ ⓤ /ˈtʃɑːrl-/ *noun* [C or U] a fast energetic dance that was popular in the 1920s

charley horse /ˈtʃɑː.liˌhɔːs/ ⓤ /ˈtʃɑːr.liˌhɔːrs/ *noun* [C] *plural* **charley horses** US INFORMAL a CRAMP (= a sudden painful tightening of a muscle) in your arm or leg

charlie /ˈtʃɑː.li/ ⓤ /ˈtʃɑːr-/ *noun* [C] UK OLD-FASHIONED INFORMAL a foolish person: *He looked a right charlie in that hat!*

charm ATTRACTION /tʃɑːm/ ⓤ /tʃɑːrm/ *noun* [C or U] a quality which makes you like or feel attracted to someone or something: *a woman of great charm* ○ *It's a town with a lot of old-world charm.* ○ *Even as a young boy he knew how to turn on the charm* (= be pleasant intentionally) *when he wanted something.* ○ *I had to use all my charms to get them to lend us the hall.*

charm /tʃɑːm/ ⓤ /tʃɑːrm/ *verb* [T often passive] to attract someone or persuade someone to do something because of your charm: *We were charmed by his boyish manner.*

• **charm the pants off sb** SLANG to make someone like you very much, especially when they meet you for the first time: *"How did your sister's boyfriend get on with your mum?" "Oh, he charmed the pants off her."*

charmed /tʃɑːmd/ ⓤ /tʃɑːrmd/ *adj: He said he would be charmed* (= very pleased) *if a woman gave him flowers.*

charmer /ˈtʃɑː.məʳ/ ⓤ /ˈtʃɑːr.məʳ/ *noun* [C] **1** a person who has good qualities that make you like them: *Ruth's a little charmer – you'll never meet a more likeable child.* **2** a person who uses their attractiveness to influence other people, usually for their own purposes: *He's a real charmer is Paul – you want to be careful with him!*

charmless /ˈtʃɑːm.ləs/ ⓤ /ˈtʃɑːrm-/ *adj* DISAPPROVING *I've always found him a most charmless* (= unpleasant and without charm) *individual.*

charming /ˈtʃɑː.mɪŋ/ ⓤ /ˈtʃɑːr-/ *adj* **1** pleasant and attractive: *We had dinner with our director and his charming wife.* ○ *What a charming street this is.* **2** DISAPPROVING describes people who use their attractiveness to influence people or to make other people like them: *He's very charming but I wouldn't trust him.* **3** DISAPPROVING, OFTEN HUMOROUS used to show that you do not approve of what someone has said or done: *"Shut up, will you, I'm trying to watch TV!" "Oh, charming!"*

charmingly /ˈtʃɑː.mɪŋ.li/ ⓤ /ˈtʃɑːr-/ *adv* APPROVING

charm JEWELLERY /tʃɑːm/ ⓤ /tʃɑːrm/ *noun* [C] a small, especially gold or silver, object worn on a chain as jewellery

charm LUCKY OBJECT /tʃɑːm/ ⓤ /tʃɑːrm/ *noun* [C] an object or saying which is thought to possess magical powers, such as the ability to bring good luck: *He keeps a rabbit's paw as a lucky/good luck charm.*

charmed /tʃɑːmd/ ⓤ /tʃɑːrmd/ *adj* **lead/live a charmed life** to be very lucky in life, often escaping dangerous situations without being hurt

'**charm ˌbracelet** *noun* [C] a chain which is worn round the wrist and to which small, especially gold or silver, objects are fixed

'**charm oˌfensive** *noun* [C usually sing] an intentional attempt to achieve something by using charm: *to launch* (= start) *a charm offensive*

charnel (house) /ˈtʃɑː.nʰlhaʊs/ ⓤ /ˈtʃɑːr-/ *noun* [C] OLD USE a building where the bodies of dead people are kept

chart /tʃɑːt/ ⓤ /tʃɑːrt/ *noun* [C] **1** a drawing which shows information in a simple way, often using lines and curves to show amounts: *There is a chart on the classroom wall showing the relative heights of all the children.* ○ *The sales chart shows a distinct decline in the past few months.* ○ *the TV weather chart* ➲See also **the charts**. ➲See picture **In the Office** on page Centre 15 **2** a detailed map of an area of water: *a naval chart*

chart /tʃɑːt/ ⓤ /tʃɑːrt/ *verb* [T] **1** to show something on a chart: *We need some sort of graph on which we can chart our progress.* ○ *The map charts the course of the river where it splits into two.* **2** to watch something with careful attention or to record something in detail: *A global study has just been started to chart the effects of climate change.* ➲See also **chart** at **the charts**. **3** MAINLY US to arrange a plan of action: *The local branch of the party is meeting to chart their election campaign.*

charter OFFICIAL PAPER /ˈtʃɑː.təʳ/ ⓤ /ˈtʃɑːr.təʳ/ *noun* [C] a formal statement of the rights of a country's people, or of an organization or a particular social group, which is agreed by or demanded from a ruler or government: *a charter of rights* ○ *Education is one of the basic human rights written into the United Nations Charter.* ○ *The Government have produced a Citizen's/Parents'/Patients' Charter.*

charter /ˈtʃɑː.təʳ/ ⓤ /ˈtʃɑːr.təʳ/ *verb* [T] *Cambridge University Press was chartered* (= officially accepted by the government) *in 1534.*

charter RENT /ˈtʃɑː.təʳ/ ⓤ /ˈtʃɑːr.təʳ/ *verb* [T] to rent a vehicle, especially an aircraft, for a special use and not as part of a regular service: *They've chartered a plane to take delegates to the conference.*

charter /ˈtʃɑː.təʳ/ ⓤ /ˈtʃɑːr.təʳ/ *noun* [U] the renting of a vehicle: *boats for charter* ○ *a charter flight* ○ *a major charter operator*

chartered /ˈtʃɑː.təd/ ⓤ /ˈtʃɑːr.təd/ *adj* [before n] rented for a particular purpose: *a small chartered plane* ○ *They spent their annual holiday on a chartered yacht in the Caribbean.*

chartered /ˈtʃɑː.təd/ ⓤ /ˈtʃɑːr.təd/ *adj* UK (of people who do particular jobs) having successfully completed the necessary training and examinations: *He's a chartered surveyor/accountant.*

Chartreuse /ʃɑːˈtrɜːz/ ⓤ /ʃɑːrˈtruːz/ *noun* [U] TRADEMARK a strong French green or yellow alcoholic drink

the charts *plural noun* the numbered lists produced each week of the records with the highest sales: *the*

dance charts ○ *It's been number one* ***in*** *the charts for six weeks.*
chart /tʃɑːt/ [US] /tʃɑːrt/ *verb* [I] *INFORMAL* *Their first record didn't even chart* (= enter the charts).

charwoman /ˈtʃɑːˌwʊ.mən/ [US] /ˈtʃɑːr-/ *noun* [C] (*ALSO* **charlady,** *INFORMAL* **char**) *UK OLD-FASHIONED* a woman whose job is to clean and tidy an office or private house

chary /ˈtʃeə.ri/ [US] /ˈtʃer.i/ *adj* uncertain and afraid to take risks; unwilling to take action: *I'm a bit chary* ***of using*** *a travel agency that doesn't have official registration.*

chase [FOLLOW] /tʃeɪs/ *verb* **1** [I or T] to hurry after someone or something in order to catch them: *The police car was going so fast, it must have been chasing someone.* ○ *She was chasing* ***(after)*** *a man who had snatched her bag.* **2** [T] to try to get something that is difficult to obtain: *It's depressing how many people there are chasing so few jobs.* ○ *After years of chasing her* ***dreams****, she finally got a part in a film.* **3** [I or T] to try very hard to persuade someone to have a relationship with you: *She's always chasing* ***(after)*** *men.* **4** [I usually + adv or prep] to hurry or run in various directions: *She couldn't study with the children chasing* ***around*** *the house.*
• **chase the dragon** *SLANG* to take the drug heroin, by smoking it
• **be chasing *your* tail** to be busy doing a lot of things but achieving very little
chase /tʃeɪs/ *noun* [C] **1** when you go after someone or something very quickly in order to catch them: *a tedious film with endless* ***car/police*** *chases* **2 the chase** the sport of hunting animals: *Asked why he went fox-hunting, he replied that he loved* ***the thrill of*** *the chase.*
• **give chase** to go after a criminal quickly in order to catch them
▲ **chase *sb* up** *phrasal verb* [M] *INFORMAL* to ask someone to do something that they have said they would do but that they have not yet done: *If you don't hear from the builders this week, make sure you chase them up.* ○ *I must chase my flatmate up about those bills and see if she paid them.*

chase [GET RID OF] /tʃeɪs/ *verb* [T + adv or prep] to run after a person or an animal in a threatening way in order to make them leave: *He used to chase the children* ***away*** *from his apple trees.* ○ *She's always chasing cats* ***out*** *of the garden to protect her precious birds.*

chaser /ˈtʃeɪ.səʳ/ [US] /-sɚ/ *noun* [C] **1** *UK* a small alcoholic drink which is drunk after a weaker alcoholic drink: *beer with a* ***whisky*** *chaser* **2** *US* a drink with little or no alcohol in it which is drunk after a small strong alcoholic drink: *whisky with a beer chaser* ○ *tequila with a grapefruit-juice chaser*

chasm /ˈkæz.ᵊm/ *noun* [C] **1** a very deep narrow opening in rock, earth or ice: *They leaned over the rails and peered down into the dizzying chasm below.* **2** *FORMAL* a very large difference between two opinions or groups of people: *There is still a vast economic chasm* ***between*** *developed and developing countries.*

chassis /ˈʃæs.i/ *noun* [C] *plural* **chassis** /ˈʃæsiz/ the frame of a vehicle, usually including the wheels and engine, onto which the metal covering is fixed: *The car's lightweight chassis is made from aluminium sheets.*

chaste /tʃeɪst/ *adj FORMAL* **1** not having had sex, or only having a sexual relationship with the person whom you are married to: *In the past, a woman needed to be chaste to make a good marriage.* ○ *They exchanged a few chaste kisses* (= not expressing sexual desire). **2** describes decoration or style that is very simple and smooth: *I like the simple, chaste lines of their architecture.*
chastity /ˈtʃæs.tə.ti/ [US] /-t̬i/ *noun* [U] the state of not having sexual relationships or never having had sex: *As a monk, he took vows of chastity, poverty and obedience.*

chasten /ˈtʃeɪ.sᵊn/ *verb* [T usually passive] *FORMAL* to make someone aware that they have failed or done something wrong and make them want to improve: *He was chastened by the defeat and determined to worker harder in future.*

chastise /tʃæsˈtaɪz/ *verb* [T] *FORMAL* to criticize someone severely: *Charity organizations have chastised the Government* ***for*** *not do****ing*** *enough to prevent the latest famine in Africa.* **chastisement** /tʃæsˈtaɪz.mənt/ *noun* [U]

ˈchastity ˌbelt *noun* [C] a device that some women were forced to wear in the past to prevent them from having sex. It had a part that went between the woman's legs and a lock so that it could not be removed.

chat /tʃæt/ *verb* [I] **-tt- 1** to talk to someone in a friendly informal way: *She spends hours on the phone chatting* ***to*** *her friends.* ○ *We were just chatting* ***about*** *what we did last weekend.* ○ *Whenever I walk in, I always find the two of them chatting* ***away*** (= talking eagerly). **2** to take part in a discussion with someone on the Internet
chat /tʃæt/ *noun* [C or U] a friendly, informal conversation: *Why don't you give me a call and we'll* ***have*** *a chat?* ○ *I had a chat* ***with*** *my boss today* ***about*** *a possible salary increase.* ○ *It was the usual* ***idle*** *chat* (= conversation about unimportant things). ➲See also **chit-chat**.
chatty /ˈtʃæt.i/ [US] /ˈtʃæt̬-/ *adj INFORMAL* **1** liking to talk a lot in a friendly, informal way **2** If a piece of writing is chatty, it is informal: *a chatty letter/style*
▲ **chat *sb* up** *phrasal verb* [M] *UK INFORMAL* to talk to someone in a way that shows them that you are sexually attracted to them: *He spent all evening chatting her up and buying her drinks.*

chateau /ˈʃæt.əʊ/ [US] /ʃætˈoʊ/ *noun* [C] *plural* **chateaux** a large house or castle in France

chatline /ˈtʃæt.laɪn/ *noun* [C] *UK* a telephone service where callers can speak to other callers for fun: *He ran up an enormous phone bill by ringing up chatlines all the time.*

ˈchat ˌroom *noun* [C] a part of the Internet where you can use email to discuss a subject with other people

ˈchat ˌshow *noun* [C] (*ALSO* **talk show**) *UK* an informal television or radio programme on which famous people are asked questions about themselves and their work

chattel /ˈtʃæt.ᵊl/ [US] /ˈtʃæt̬-/ *noun* [C] *OLD USE OR FORMAL* a personal possession: *He treated his wife as little more than a chattel.* ○ ***goods and*** *chattels*

chatter /ˈtʃæt.əʳ/ [US] /ˈtʃæt̬.ɚ/ *verb* [I] **1** to talk for a long time about things that are not important: *She spent the morning chattering* ***away*** *to her friends.* ○ *He chattered* ***on*** *about nothing in particular.* **2** If animals chatter, they make quick repeated noises: *The gun shot made the monkeys chatter in alarm.* **3** If your teeth chatter, they knock together repeatedly because you are very cold or frightened: *I could hardly talk, my teeth were chattering so much.*
chatter /ˈtʃæt.əʳ/ [US] /ˈtʃæt̬.ɚ/ *noun* [U] **1** conversation about things that are not important: *I can't concentrate with Ann's constant chatter.* **2** the quick repeated noises that some animals make: *He could hear the chatter of birds in the trees overhead.*

chatterbox /ˈtʃæt.ə.bɒks/ [US] /ˈtʃæt̬.ɚ.bɑːks/ *noun* [C] *INFORMAL* a person, especially a child, who talks a lot: *Your sister's a real chatterbox!*

the ˈchattering ˌclasses *plural noun UK INFORMAL DISAPPROVING* well-educated middle-class people who enjoy discussing political, cultural and social matters and who express opinions on a lot of subjects

chatty /ˈtʃæt.i/ [US] /ˈtʃæt̬-/ *adj INFORMAL* ➲See at **chat**.

chat-up line *UK* /ˈtʃæt.ʌpˌlaɪn/ [US] /ˈtʃæt̬-/ *noun* [C] (*US* **come-on line**) *INFORMAL* a remark which someone makes to a person whom they are sexually attracted to in order to make their sexual interest known to them and start a conversation with them: *"Have you been here before?" "That's one of the oldest chat-up lines I've ever heard!"*

chauffeur /ˈʃəʊ.fəʳ/ [US] /ʃoʊˈfɝː/ *noun* [C] someone whose job is to drive a car for a rich or important person: *As company director, she has a chauffeur-driven limousine to take her everywhere.*
chauffeur /ˈʃəʊ.fəʳ/ [US] /ʃoʊˈfɝː/ *verb* [T] to drive someone somewhere: *His mother spoils him terribly and chauffeurs him* ***(around/about)*** *everywhere.*

chauvinism /ˈʃəʊ.vɪ.nɪ.zᵊm/ [US] /ˈʃoʊ-/ *noun* [U] *DISAPPROVING* **1** the strong and unreasonable belief that your own country or race is the best or most important: *The war stimulated an intense national chauvinism.* **2** (*ALSO* **male chauvinism**) the belief that women are naturally less important, intelligent or able than men **chauvinist**

/ˈʃəʊ.vɪ.nɪst/ ⑤ /ˈʃoʊ-/ *noun* [C] *She called him a (male) chauvinist because of his insistence on calling all women 'girls'.* chauvinist /ˈʃəʊ.vɪ.nɪst/ ⑤ /ˈʃoʊ-/ *adj* (ALSO chauvinistic) *The crowd was enthusiastically singing chauvinistic patriotic songs.* ○ *It is a deeply chauvinist community where the few women who have jobs are ridiculed.* chauvinistically /ˌʃəʊ.vɪˈnɪs.tɪ.kli/ ⑤ /ˌʃoʊ-/ *adv*

cheap /tʃiːp/ *adj* **1** costing little money or less than is usual or expected: *I got a cheap flight at the last minute.* ○ *Food is usually cheaper in supermarkets.* ○ *Children and the elderly are entitled to cheap train tickets.* ○ *The scheme is simple and cheap to operate.* ○ *During times of mass unemployment, there's a pool of cheap labour for employers to draw from.* ○ FIGURATIVE *In a war, human life becomes very cheap* (= seems to be of little value). **2** If a shop or restaurant is cheap, it charges low prices: *I go to the cheapest hairdresser's in town.* **3** DISAPPROVING describes goods that are both low in quality and low in price: *I bought some cheap wine for cooking with.* ○ *He bought some cheap shoes that fell apart after a couple of months.* **4** US (UK **mean**) unwilling to spend money: *He's so cheap he didn't even buy me a card for my birthday.* **5** DISAPPROVING If you describe the way a person is dressed as cheap, you mean that it is very obvious that they are trying to sexually attract other people. **6** DISAPPROVING unpleasant and unkind: *I wish you'd stop making cheap jokes about my friends.*
• **cheap and cheerful** UK cheap but good or enjoyable: *There's a restaurant round the corner that serves cheap and cheerful food.*
• **cheap and nasty** UK costing little and of very bad quality
• **cheap at half the price** HUMOROUS very expensive
• **on the cheap** INFORMAL If you get goods on the cheap, you obtain them for a low price, often from someone you know who works in the company or business that produces them.
cheap /tʃiːp/ *adv*: *I got some shoes cheap* (= for little money) *in the sale.* ○ *There were some chairs in the market going cheap* (= they were not expensive).
• **not come cheap** If you say that something does not come cheap, you mean that it is of good quality and is therefore expensive: *If you want a qualified accountant, their services don't come cheap.*
cheapen /ˈtʃiː.pən/ *verb* [T] **1** to reduce the price: *This has had the effect of cheapening UK exports.* **2** DISAPPROVING to make someone or something seem less valuable or important so that people respect them less: *She felt that the photos were exploitative and cheapened her.*
cheaply /ˈtʃiː.pli/ *adv* for a low price: *The shop round the corner does shoe repairs very cheaply.*
cheapness /ˈtʃiːp.nəs/ *noun* [U] the low price: *The relative cheapness of foreign travel means that more people are going abroad than ever before.*
cheapo /ˈtʃiː.pəʊ/ ⑤ /-poʊ/ *adj* [before n] INFORMAL low in price and often low in quality: *We stayed in a cheapo hotel to save money.*

'cheap ˌrate *noun* [C] the amount charged for a service which is lower than usual because there is not so much demand for the service at that time: *Cheap rate for overseas telephone calls is from 8pm to 8am.* cheap-rate /ˈtʃiː.p.reɪt/ *adj*: *cheap-rate calls*

cheapskate /ˈtʃiːp.skeɪt/ *noun* [C] INFORMAL DISAPPROVING a person who is unwilling to spend money: *My dad's such a cheapskate that he's put a lock on the telephone.*

cheat /tʃiːt/ *verb* [I or T] to behave in a dishonest way in order to get what you want: *Anyone caught cheating will be immediately disqualified from the exam.* ○ *He cheats at cards?* ○ *She cheated in the test by copying from the boy in front.* ○ *I suspect he cheats the taxman* (= avoids paying taxes by using illegal methods).
• **cheat death** LITERARY to succeed in staying alive in an extremely dangerous situation: *As a racing driver, he was involved in many serious crashes and had cheated death on several occasions.*
cheat /tʃiːt/ *noun* **1** [C] a person who behaves in a dishonest way: *Trouble broke out in the match when one of the players called the other team a cheat.* **2** [S] something dishonest which makes people believe that

something is true when it is not: *You can use cocoa powder to make the cake rather than chocolate – it's a bit of a cheat, but nobody notices the difference.* **3** [C] a collection of instructions or special information which someone can use to help them play a computer game more successfully: *the latest game/desktop cheats* ○ *cheat codes*

PHRASAL VERBS WITH **cheat** ▼

▲ **cheat on** sb *phrasal verb* INFORMAL If you cheat on your husband, wife or usual sexual partner, you secretly have a sexual relationship with someone else: *She found out that he'd been cheating on her.*

▲ **cheat** sb **out of** sth *phrasal verb* to unfairly prevent someone from obtaining or achieving something which should belong to them: *She claimed that her cousin had cheated her out of her inheritance.*

check EXAMINE /tʃek/ *verb* [I or T] to make certain that something or someone is correct, safe or suitable by examining it or them quickly: *You should always check your oil, water and tyres before taking your car on a long trip.* ○ *Customs stopped us and checked* (= searched) *our bags for alcohol and cigarettes.* ○ *After I'd finished the exam, I checked my answers for mistakes.* ○ *The doctor will call next week to check on your progress.* ○ *My wife checks on* (= visits) *our elderly neighbour every few days to make sure that he's alright.* ○ [+ (that)] *I always check (that) I've shut the windows before I leave the house.* ○ [+ question word] *I rang them yesterday to check when they were arriving.* ○ *He double-checked all the doors* (= checked them all twice) *before leaving the house.* ○ [+ to infinitive] *If you're near the garage, could you check to see* (= ask) *if the car's ready?* ○ *If you're unsure of your legal rights, I would check with* (= ask) *a lawyer.* ⇒See also **crosscheck**.
check /tʃek/ *noun* [C] an examination of something in order to make certain that it is correct or the way it should be: *The soldiers gave their equipment a final check before setting off.* ○ *"I can't find my keys." "Have another check in/through your jacket pockets."* ○ *Security checks have become really strict at the airport.* ○ *The police are carrying out spot checks on* (= quick examinations of a limited number of) *drivers over the Christmas period to test for alcohol levels.* ○ *It's my job to keep a check on stock levels.* ○ *I'll just run a check on* (= find information about) *that name for you in the computer.*
checker /ˈtʃek.əʳ/ ⑤ /-ɚ/ *noun* [C] US a **cashier** PERSON

check STOP /tʃek/ *verb* [T] to stop someone from doing or saying something, or to prevent something from increasing or continuing: *They have begun to vaccinate children in an attempt to check the spread of the disease.*
check /tʃek/ *noun* **hold/keep** sth **in check** to limit something: *We must find ways of keeping our expenditure in check.*
• **checks and balances** rules intended to prevent one person or group from having too much power within an organization: *A system of checks and balances exists to ensure that our government is truly democratic.*

check LEAVE /tʃek/ *verb* [T] US to leave something with someone at a particular place, so that they can take care of it for a short time: *It was hot so we checked our coats before going round the gallery.*

check PATTERN /tʃek/ *noun* [C or U] a pattern of squares formed by lines of different colours crossing each other: *a shirt with a pattern of blue and yellow checks* ○ *a grey check suit* checked /tʃekt/ *adj*: *a red and white checked tablecloth*

check AGREE /tʃek/ *verb* [I] MAINLY US If information checks, it agrees with other information: *Her statement checks with most of the eye-witness reports.*

check MARK /tʃek/ *verb* [I or T], *noun* [C] US FOR **tick** MARK

check MONEY /tʃek/ *noun* [C] US FOR **cheque**

check RESTAURANT /tʃek/ *noun* [C] US FOR **bill** REQUEST FOR PAYMENT: *Can I have the check, please?*

check YES /tʃek/ *exclamation* US used to say yes to someone who is making certain that all the items on a list have been dealt with or included: *"Did you bring your sleeping bag?" "Check* (= Yes).*" "Pillow?" "Check."*

C

PHRASAL VERBS WITH **check**

▲ **check in** [AIRPORT] *phrasal verb* to show your ticket at an airport so that you can be told where you will be sitting and so that your bags can be put on the aircraft: *Passengers are requested to check in two hours before the flight.*

check-in /ˈtʃek.ɪn/ *noun* [C] the place at an airport where you show your ticket so that you can be told where you will be sitting: *A representative from the tour company will meet you at the check-in.* ○ *I'll meet you at the check-in desk.*

▲ **check in/check into *sth*** [HOTEL] *phrasal verb* to say who you are when you arrive at a hotel so that you can be given a key for your room: *Please would you check in **at** the reception desk and sign your name in the book.*

▲ **check *sth* off** *phrasal verb* [M] *US* to mark names or items on a list as correct or as having been dealt with: *He checked off their names on the list as they got on the coach.*

▲ **check out** [LEAVE] *phrasal verb* to leave a hotel after paying and returning your room key: *We checked out (**of/from** our hotel) at 5 a.m. to catch a 7 a.m. flight.*

▲ **check *sth* out** [EXAMINE] *phrasal verb* [M] *INFORMAL* to examine something or get more information about it in order to be certain that it is true, safe or suitable: *We'll need to check out his story.*

▲ **check *sth* out** [GO TO SEE] *phrasal verb* [M] *INFORMAL* to go to a place in order to see what it is like: *I'm going to check out that new club.*

▲ **check *sth* out** [BORROW] *phrasal verb* [M] *MAINLY US* to borrow books from a library

▲ **check up on *sb*** *phrasal verb* to try to discover what someone is doing in order to be certain that they are doing what they should be doing: *My mum checks up on me most evenings to see that I've done my homework.*

checkbook /ˈtʃek.bʊk/ *noun* [C] *US FOR* **chequebook**

checkered /ˈtʃek.əd/ [US] /-ɚd/ *adj US FOR* **chequered**

checkers /ˈtʃek.əz/ [US] /-ɚz/ *noun* [U] *US FOR* **draughts**

ˈ**checking ac**ˌ**count** *noun* [C] *US FOR* **current account**

checklist /ˈtʃek.lɪst/ *noun* [C] a list of things that you must think about, or that you must remember to do: *I have a checklist of things that I must do today.*

checkmate /ˈtʃek.meɪt/ *noun* [U] **1** a winning position in chess in which you have put the other player's king under a direct attack from which it cannot escape **2** a situation in which someone has been defeated or a plan cannot develop or continue ➲Compare **stalemate**.
checkmate /ˈtʃek.meɪt/ *verb* [T] *My Dad can always checkmate me within twenty moves.*

checkout /ˈtʃek.aʊt/ *noun* [C] the place in a shop, especially a large food shop, where you pay for your goods: *Your fruit and vegetables will be weighed at the checkout.* ○ *She works **on** the checkout at the local supermarket.* ➲See also **check out**.

checkpoint /ˈtʃek.pɔɪnt/ *noun* [C] a place where people are stopped and questioned and vehicles are examined, especially at a border between two countries: *Checkpoint Charlie used to be the most famous border crossing between East and West Berlin.*

checkroom /ˈtʃek.ruːm/ /-rʊm/ *noun* [C] *US FOR* **cloakroom** (= a room in a public building where you can leave your coat, bag, etc. while you are in the building)

checkup /ˈtʃek.ʌp/ *noun* [C] a medical examination to test your general state of health: *She goes to her doctor for regular checkups.* ○ *a dental checkup* ➲See also **check up on**.

cheddar /ˈtʃed.əʳ/ [US] /-ɚ/ *noun* [U] a hard British cheese: *Do you prefer **mild** or **mature** cheddar?*

cheek [BODY PART] /tʃiːk/ *noun* [C] the soft part of your face which is below your eye and between your mouth and ear: *The tears ran down her cheeks.* ○ *rosy cheeks* ○ *He embraced her, kissing her on both cheeks.* ➲See picture **The Body** on page Centre 5
• **cheek by jowl** very close together: *The poor lived cheek by jowl in industrial mining towns in Victorian England.*
-cheeked /-tʃiːkt/ *suffix* **red-/rosy-cheeked** having red cheeks

cheek [BEHAVIOUR] /tʃiːk/ *noun* [S or U] *UK* rudeness or lack of respect: *He told me off for being late when he arrived half an hour after me. What **a** cheek!* ○ [+ to infinitive] *She's got some cheek **to** take your car without asking.* ○ *He **had the** cheek **to** ask me to pay for her!* ○ *She's always getting into trouble for **giving** her teachers cheek* (= being rude to them).
cheek /tʃiːk/ *verb* [T] *UK INFORMAL* to be rude to someone: *He's always getting into trouble for cheeking his teachers.*
cheeky /ˈtʃiː.ki/ *adj UK* slightly rude or showing a lack of respect, but often in a funny way: *She's got such a cheeky grin.* ○ *Don't be so cheeky!* **cheekily** /ˈtʃiː.kɪ.li/ *adv*
cheekiness /ˈtʃiː.kɪ.nəs/ *noun* [U]

cheek [BOTTOM] /tʃiːk/ *noun* [C] *INFORMAL* either of the two halves of your bottom

cheekbone /ˈtʃiːk.bəʊn/ [US] /-boʊn/ *noun* [C usually pl] one of the two bones at the top of your cheeks, just below your eye and towards your ear: *She has the **high** cheekbones of a supermodel.*

cheep /tʃiːp/ *noun* [C] the high weak cry made by a young bird **cheep** /tʃiːp/ *verb* [I]

cheer /tʃɪəʳ/ [US] /tʃɪr/ *verb* [I] to give a loud shout of approval or encouragement: *Everyone cheered as the winners received their medals.* ○ *He was cheering **for** the other side.*
cheer /tʃɪəʳ/ [US] /tʃɪr/ *noun* **1** [C] a loud shout of approval or encouragement: *Her speech was received with cheers and a standing ovation.* ○ *His victory in the 400m earned him the biggest cheer of the afternoon.* ○ ***Three** cheers for the winning team* (= Let's give them three shouts of approval)*!* **2** [U] *FORMAL OR OLD-FASHIONED* a feeling of happiness: *The victory in the by-election has brought great cheer to the Liberal Democrats.*
• **be of good cheer** *OLD USE* to be happy
cheering /ˈtʃɪə.rɪŋ/ [US] /ˈtʃɪr-/ *noun* [U] shouts of encouragement and approval
cheering /ˈtʃɪə.rɪŋ/ [US] /ˈtʃɪr-/ *adj* describes something that encourages you and makes you feel happier: *We received some cheering news.*

PHRASAL VERBS WITH **cheer**

▲ **cheer *sb* on** *phrasal verb* [M] to shout loudly in order to encourage someone in a competition: *As the runners went by, we cheered them on.*

▲ **cheer *(sb)* up** [HAPPIER] *phrasal verb* [M] If someone cheers up, or something cheers them up, they start to feel happier: *She was ill so I sent her some flowers to cheer her up.* ○ *He cheered up **at** the prospect of a meal.* ○ *Cheer up! It's not that bad!* ○ [R] *She went shopping to cheer herself up.*

▲ **cheer *sth* up** [MORE ATTRACTIVE] *phrasal verb* [M] to make a place look brighter or more attractive: *A coat of paint and new curtains would really cheer the kitchen up.*

cheerful /ˈtʃɪə.fᵊl/ [US] /ˈtʃɪr-/ *adj* **1** happy and positive: *He's usually fairly cheerful.* ○ *You're in a cheerful mood this morning.* ○ *She manages to stay cheerful* (= happy and positive) *despite everything.* **2** describes a place or thing that is bright and pleasant and makes you feel positive and happy: *The doctor's waiting room was bright and cheerful with yellow walls and curtains.* ○ *Turn that dreadful wailing music off and put on something cheerful.*
cheerfully /ˈtʃɪə.fᵊl.i/ [US] /ˈtʃɪr-/ *adv*: *She walked down the road, whistling cheerfully.* ○ *HUMOROUS By the end of the evening I could cheerfully have* (= I would like to have) *punched him.* **cheerfulness** /ˈtʃɪə.fᵊl.nəs/ [US] /ˈtʃɪr-/ *noun* [U]

cheerio /ˌtʃɪə.riˈəʊ/ [US] /ˌtʃɪr.iˈoʊ/ *exclamation UK OLD-FASHIONED* goodbye: *Cheerio! Have a good trip!*

cheerleader /ˈtʃɪəˌliː.dəʳ/ [US] /ˈtʃɪrˌliː.dɚ/ *noun* [C] (especially in America) a person, usually a woman or girl, who leads the crowd in shouting encouragement and supporting a team at a sports event: *She was a cheerleader **for** the Dallas Cowboys.*

cheerless /ˈtʃɪə.ləs/ [US] /ˈtʃɪr-/ *adj* not bright or pleasant and making you feel sad: *a cold and cheerless winter afternoon* ○ *a bare, cheerless apartment* **cheerlessness** /ˈtʃɪə.lə.snəs/ [US] /ˈtʃɪr-/ *noun* [U]

Cheers! /tʃɪəz/ [US] /tʃɪrz/ *exclamation* **1** a friendly expression said just before you drink an alcoholic drink: *Cheers! Your good health.* **2** *UK INFORMAL* used to mean 'thank you': *"I've bought you a drink." "Cheers, mate."* **3** *UK INFORMAL* used to mean 'goodbye': *"Bye." "Cheers, see you next week."*

cheery /ˈtʃɪə.ri/ [US] /ˈtʃɪr.i/ *adj* bright and happy: *She walked in with a cheery "Good morning!"* ○ *He gave us a cheery wave as we drove past.* **cheerily** /ˈtʃɪə.rɪ.li/ [US] /ˈtʃɪr.ɪ-/ *adv*: *He waved cheerily.* **cheeriness** /ˈtʃɪə.rɪ.nəs/ [US] /ˈtʃɪr.ɪ-/ *noun* [U]

cheese /tʃiːz/ *noun* [C or U] a food made from milk, which can either be firm or soft and is usually yellow or white in colour: *Would you like a slice/piece of cheese with your bread?* ○ ***goat's*** *cheese* ○ *You need 250g of* ***grated*** *cheese for this recipe.* ○ *I like* ***soft*** *French cheeses such as Brie and Camembert.* ○ *I prefer* ***hard*** *cheeses, like Cheddar.* ○ *cheese and biscuits*
• **say cheese** something that someone who is taking a photograph of you tells you to say so that your mouth makes the shape of a smile
• **Hard/Tough cheese!** *UK* (*US* **Stiff cheese!**) *INFORMAL* something that you say to or about someone to whom something bad has happened in order to show that you have no sympathy for them: *So he's fed up because he's got to get up early one morning in seven, is he? Well hard cheese!*

cheesy /ˈtʃiː.zi/ *adj* **1** tasting like or of cheese: *cheesy snacks* **2** *UK INFORMAL* If someone's feet, shoes or socks are cheesy, they smell unpleasant: *Someone here's got cheesy feet!* ➲See also **cheesy**.

cheese /tʃiːz/ *verb*
▲ **cheese** *sb* **off** *phrasal verb* [M] *UK INFORMAL* to annoy someone: *Her attitude to the whole thing really cheeses me off!*
cheesed off /ˌtʃiːzdˈɒf/ [US] /-ˈɑːf/ *adj* [after v] *UK INFORMAL* annoyed and disappointed with something or someone: *She's a bit cheesed off* ***with*** *her job.*

ˌcheese ˈbiscuit *UK noun* [C] (*US* **cracker**) a savoury biscuit that is eaten with cheese or contains cheese

cheeseboard /ˈtʃiːz.bɔːd/ [US] /-bɔːrd/ *noun* [C] a board on which several different types of cheese are arranged for you to choose from at the end of a meal, or cheese served in this way

cheeseburger /ˈtʃiːzˌbɜː.gəʳ/ [US] /-ˌbɝː.gɚ/ *noun* [C] a HAMBURGER (= round, flat shape made of meat, eaten between bread) with a slice of melted cheese

cheesecake [FOOD] /ˈtʃiːz.keɪk/ *noun* [C or U] a cake made from a layer of biscuit, or a sweet pastry base, covered with soft cheese, eggs, sugar and sometimes fruit: *lemon/almond cheesecake*

cheesecake [WOMEN] /ˈtʃiːz.keɪk/ *noun* [U] *MAINLY US OLD-FASHIONED SLANG* photographs of sexually attractive young women wearing very few clothes, or the women who appear in such photographs ➲Compare **beefcake**.

cheesecloth /ˈtʃiːz.klɒθ/ [US] /-klɑːθ/ *noun* [U] thin rough cotton cloth which is woven loosely

ˈcheese ˌknife *noun* [C] a small knife with a curved blade that ends in two sharp points, which is used to cut and pick up a piece of cheese

cheeseparing /ˈtʃiːzˌpeə.rɪŋ/ [US] /-ˌper.ɪŋ/ *noun* [U] *DISAPPROVING* unwillingness to spend money

cheesy /ˈtʃiː.zi/ *adj* **1** *INFORMAL* clearly of cheap quality or in bad style: *cheesy hotel music* ○ *cheesy adverts* **2** *UK INFORMAL* describes a wide smile which is not sincere: *She gave a cheesy* ***grin*** *to the cameras.* ➲See also **cheesy** at **cheese**.

cheetah /ˈtʃiː.tə/ [US] /-t̬ə/ *noun* [C] a wild animal of the cat family, with yellowish brown fur and black spots, which can run faster than any other animal: *Cheetahs are mainly found in Africa.*

chef /ʃef/ *noun* [C] a skilled and trained cook who works in a hotel or restaurant, especially the most important cook: *He is one of the top chefs in Britain.* ○ *She is* ***head-chef*** *at the Waldorf-Astoria.*

chef d'oeuvre /ˌʃeɪˈdɜː.vrə/ [US] /-ˈɝː-/ *noun* [C] *plural* **chefs d'oeuvre** *FORMAL* an artist or writer's greatest piece of work: *The Decameron is widely regarded as Boccaccio's chef d'oeuvre.*

chemical /ˈkem.ɪ.kəl/ *noun* [C] any basic substance which is used in or produced by a reaction involving changes to atoms or molecules: *The government has pledged to reduce the amount of chemicals used in food production.* ○ *Each year, factories release millions of tonnes of* ***toxic*** (= poisonous) *chemicals into the atmosphere.*
chemical /ˈkem.ɪ.kəl/ *adj* relating to chemicals: *The chemical* ***industry*** *produces such things as petrochemicals, drugs, paint and rubber.* **chemically** /ˈkem.ɪ.kli/ *adv*: *The fund provides money to clean up chemically polluted industrial sites.*

ˌchemical enginˈeering *noun* [U] the design and operation of machinery used in industrial chemical processes

ˌchemical eˈquation *noun* [C] a symbolic representation of the changes which happen in a chemical reaction

ˌchemical ˈformula *noun* [C] the representation of a substance using the symbols of its elements: *H_2O is the chemical formula for water.*

ˌchemical reˈaction *noun* [C] a process in which the atomic or MOLECULAR structure of a substance is changed

ˌchemical ˈwarfare *noun* [U] the use of poisonous gases and other harmful chemicals against enemy forces

ˌchemical ˈweapon *noun* [C] a substance, such as a poisonous gas rather than an explosive, which can be used to kill or injure people

chemise /ʃəˈmiːz/ *noun* [C] a loose piece of clothing for women, which covers the top part of the body, and which is worn under other clothes

chemist [SCIENCE] /ˈkem.ɪst/ *noun* [C] a person who studies chemistry, or a scientist who works with chemicals or studies their reactions

chemist [MEDICINE] *UK* /ˈkem.ɪst/ *noun* [C] **1** (*US* **druggist,** *ALSO* **pharmacist**) a person whose job is to prepare and sell medicines in a shop **2** (*UK ALSO* **chemist's,** *US* **drugstore,** *ALSO* **pharmacy**) a shop where you can buy medicines, make-up and products used for washing yourself ➲See usage note at **pharmacy**.

chemistry /ˈkem.ɪ.stri/ *noun* [U] **1** (the part of science which studies) the basic characteristics of substances and the different ways in which they react or combine with other substances: *She studied chemistry and physics at college.* ○ *A team of scientists has been studying the chemistry* ***of*** *the ozone layer.* ○ *a chemistry department/laboratory* **2** *INFORMAL* understanding and attraction between two people: *There was an immediate* ***sexual*** *chemistry* ***between*** *us the first time we met.*

chemotherapy /ˌkiː.məʊˈθer.ə.pi/ [US] /-moʊ-/ *noun* [U] the treatment of diseases using chemicals: *Chemotherapy is often used in the treatment of cancer.*

chenille /ʃəˈniːl/ *noun* [U] a thick soft thread which is used for decorating cloth, or the material which is made from this: *a chenille jumper/bedspread*

cheque *UK, US* **check** /tʃek/ *noun* [C] a printed form, used instead of money, to make payments from your bank account: *I* ***wrote*** *him a cheque* ***for*** *£50.* ○ *I don't have any cash on me, so could I pay* ***with*** *a/****by*** *cheque?* ○ *Who should I* ***make out*** *this cheque* ***to*** (= Whose name should I write on it)*?* ○ *Please make your cheques* ***payable to*** *The Brighter Toyshop Ltd* (= Please write this name on them).

chequebook *UK* /ˈtʃek.bʊk/ *noun* [C] (*US* **checkbook**) a book of cheques with your name printed on them which is given to you by your bank to make payments with
• **ˌcheque book ˈjournalism** *UK* (*US* **check book journalism**) *DISAPPROVING* when a newspaper persuades someone involved in a news story to give their report of events by paying them a lot of money

ˌcheque guaranˈtee ˌcard *UK noun* [C] (*UK ALSO* **cheque card,** *US* **check guarantee card**) a small plastic card which you have to show when you pay for something by cheque and which is proof that your bank will pay the money you owe

chequered [VARIED] *UK* /ˈtʃek.əd/ [US] /-ɚd/ *adj* (*US* **checkered**) having had both successful and unsuccessful periods in your past: *He's had a chequered business* ***career***.

chequered PATTERN UK /'tʃek.əd/ US /-ɚd/ adj (US **check-ered**) having a pattern of squares in two or more colours: *red and white chequered tablecloths*

the ,chequered 'flag noun [S] (US **the checkered flag**) the black and white flag which is waved to show that a car has won a race: *Three minutes from the chequered flag, Mansell was in the lead by 2.25 seconds.*

cherish /'tʃer.ɪʃ/ verb [T] **1** to love, protect and care for someone or something that is important to you: *Although I cherish my children, I do allow them their independence.* ○ *Her most cherished possession is a 1926 letter from F. Scott Fitzgerald.* ○ *Freedom of speech is a cherished* (= carefully protected) *right in this country.* **2** to keep hopes, memories or ideas in your mind because they are important to you and bring you pleasure: *I cherish the memories of the time we spent together.*

cheroot /ʃə'ruːt/ noun [C] a short thin CIGAR with both ends cut flat

cherry /'tʃer.i/ noun [C] a small, round, soft red or black fruit with a single hard seed in the middle, or the tree on which the fruit grows ⊃See picture **Fruit** on page Centre 1

cherry /'tʃer.i/ adj (ALSO **cherry-red**) bright red: *cherry-red lips*

cherub /'tʃer.əb/ noun [C] *plural* **cherubs** or FORMAL **cherubim 1** an ANGEL that is represented in art as a beautiful, fat, naked child with small wings **2** INFORMAL APPROVING a beautiful and well-behaved child

cherubic /tʃə'ruː.bɪk/ adj having a round, attractive face like that of a child: *a blonde-haired child with a cherubic face*

chervil /'tʃɜː.vɪl/ US /'tʃɝː-/ noun [U] a herb used in cooking which has delicate, feathery leaves and a flavour like LIQUORICE

chess /tʃes/ noun [U] a game played by two people on a square board, in which each player has 16 pieces that can be moved on the board in different ways

chessboard /'tʃes.bɔːd/ US /-bɔːrd/ noun [C] a square board divided into 64 smaller squares, half of which are light and half dark in colour, which is used for playing the game of chess or DRAUGHTS

chess ,set noun [C] the pieces used to play chess and the board on which the game is played

chest BODY PART /tʃest/ noun [C] the upper front part of the body of humans and some animals, between the stomach and the neck, enclosing the heart and lungs: *He was shot in the chest at point blank range.* ○ *He folded his arms across his chest.* ○ *His shirt was open to the waist revealing a very hairy chest.* ○ *She went to the doctor complaining of chest pains.* ⊃See picture **The Body** on page Centre 5
• **get sth off your chest** INFORMAL to tell someone about something that has been worrying you or making you feel guilty for a long time: *I had spent two months worrying about it and I was glad to get it off my chest.*
-chested /-tʃes.tɪd/ suffix: *He was bare-chested* (= The top half of his body was naked). ○ *She is rather flat-chested* (= She has small breasts).

chesty /'tʃes.ti/ adj MAINLY UK having or relating to a lot of mucus (= thick liquid) in the lungs: *a chesty cough*

chest BOX /tʃest/ noun [C] a large strong box, usually made of wood, which is used for storing valuable goods or possessions or for moving possessions from one place to another: *Her books and clothes were packed into chests and shipped across to Canada.*

chestnut /'tʃes.nʌt/ noun **1** [C] a large shiny reddish-brown nut, or the tree on which the nuts grow: *A man in the street was selling bags of roast chestnuts.* ○ *a 200-year-old chestnut tree* ⊃See also **horse chestnut**. **2** [C] a brown horse **3** [U] a reddish-brown colour
• **old chestnut** INFORMAL a subject, idea or joke which has been discussed or repeated so often that it is not funny any more: *I wondered whether there might, after all, be some truth in the old chestnut that one's school days are the happiest of one's life.*

chestnut /'tʃes.nʌt/ adj reddish-brown in colour

,chest of 'drawers (*plural* **chests of drawers**) noun [C] (US ALSO **bureau**) a piece of furniture with drawers in which you keep things such as clothes

chevron /'ʃev.rᵊn/ /-rɒn/ noun [C] a shape like a V or an upside down V, used especially on the sleeve of a police or military uniform to show the wearer's rank, or on road signs in Britain to show a severe bend in the road

chew /tʃuː/ verb [I or T] **1** to crush food into smaller, softer pieces with the teeth so that it can be swallowed: *This meat is difficult to chew.* ○ *You don't chew your food enough – that's why you get indigestion.* **2** to bite something with your teeth, usually in order to taste its flavour: *Would you like some gum to chew?* ○ *She gave the children some sweets to chew (on) during the long car journey.* ○ *She sat in the dentist's waiting room, nervously chewing (at)* (= biting) *her nails.*
• **chew the fat** INFORMAL to talk with someone in an informal and friendly way: *We sat in a bar most of the evening just chewing the fat.*

chew /tʃuː/ noun [C] **1** an act of chewing something **2** a hard sweet that gets softer the more you chew it

chewy /'tʃuː.i/ adj describes food that needs to be chewed a lot before it is swallowed: *The meat was tasteless and chewy.*

PHRASAL VERBS WITH **chew** ▼

▲ **chew sb out** phrasal verb [M] US INFORMAL to tell someone angrily that they have done something wrong: *The coach chewed his team out for playing so badly.*

▲ **chew sth over** phrasal verb [M] INFORMAL to think about or discuss something carefully for a long time: *I've been chewing the problem over since last week.*

▲ **chew sth up** phrasal verb [M] If a machine chews up something that you have put inside it, it damages or destroys it: *Your tape deck has chewed up my favourite cassette!*

'chewing ,gum noun [U] a sweet that you keep in your mouth and chew to get its flavour, but which you do not swallow: *Would you like a piece/stick of chewing gum?*

chiaroscuro /kiˌɑː.rə'skʊə.rəʊ/ US /-ˌɑːr.ə'skjʊr.oʊ/ noun [U] SPECIALIZED the use of areas of light and darkness in a painting: *Caravaggio is famous for his use of chiaroscuro.*

chic /ʃiːk/ adj stylish and fashionable: *I like your haircut – it's very chic.* ○ *a chic restaurant* **chic** /ʃiːk/ noun [U] *British politicians are not renowned for their chic.*

chicane /ʃɪ'keɪn/ noun [C] SPECIALIZED a piece of road with severe bends like an 'S', which forces drivers to go more slowly, especially in motor racing

chicanery /ʃɪ'keɪ.nᵊr.i/ US /-nɚ-/ noun [U] FORMAL clever, dishonest talk or behaviour which is used to deceive people: *The investigation revealed political chicanery and corruption at the highest levels.*

Chicano /tʃɪ'kɑː.nəʊ/ US /-noʊ/ noun [C] *plural* **Chicanos** INFORMAL someone living in the US who was born in Mexico or whose parents came from Mexico

chichi /'ʃiː.ʃi/ adj INFORMAL DISAPPROVING trying too hard to be decorated in a stylish or attractive way and therefore lacking any real style or beauty: *They live in a rather chichi part of town.*

chick BIRD /tʃɪk/ noun [C] a baby bird, especially a young chicken

chick WOMAN /tʃɪk/ noun [C] SLANG a young woman. This word is considered offensive by many women.

chicken BIRD /'tʃɪk.ɪn/ noun [C or U] a type of bird kept on a farm for its eggs or its meat, or the meat of this bird which is cooked and eaten: *In battery farms, chickens are kept in tiny cages.* ○ *A male chicken is called a cock and a female chicken is called a hen.* ○ *We're having roast/fried chicken for dinner.*
• **a chicken and egg situation** INFORMAL a situation in which it is impossible to say which of two things existed first and which caused the other one

chicken PERSON /'tʃɪk.ɪn/ noun [C] INFORMAL a **coward**: *Jump, you chicken!*
• **play chicken** SLANG to play dangerous games in order to discover who is the bravest: *They would play chicken by driving head-on at each other until one of them lost their nerve and swerved out of the way.*

chicken /'tʃɪk.ɪn/ adj [after v] CHILD'S WORD cowardly: *Why won't you jump? Are you chicken?*

chicken /ˈtʃɪk.ɪn/ *verb*
▲ **chicken out** *phrasal verb SLANG DISAPPROVING* to decide not to do something because you are too frightened: *I was going to go bungee jumping, but I chickened out.*

chickenfeed /ˈtʃɪk.ɪn.fiːd/ *noun* [U] *INFORMAL* a small and unimportant amount of money: *They're losing $200 000 on this deal, but that's chickenfeed* ***to/for*** *a company with yearly profits of $25 million.*

chickenpox /ˈtʃɪk.ɪn.pɒks/ [US] /-pɑːks/ *noun* [U] an infectious disease that causes a slight fever and red spots on the skin: *Chickenpox is a very common disease among children.*

chickenshit /ˈtʃɪk.ɪn.ʃɪt/ *noun* [C], *adj US SLANG DISAPPROVING FOR* **chicken** (= coward): *C'mon, don't be such a chickenshit — just go up and ask her to dance.*

ˈchicken ˌwire *noun* [U] netting made of metal wire, which was originally used to make enclosures for chickens

ˈchick ˌflick *noun* [C] *INFORMAL HUMOROUS* a film about relationships, romance, etc. that attracts mainly women

chickpea *UK* /ˈtʃɪk.piː/ *noun* [C] (*US* **garbanzo bean**) a hard pale brown round bean which can be cooked and eaten: *Chickpeas are used to make houmous and felafel.*

chicory /ˈtʃɪk.ᵊr.i/ [US] /-ɚ-/ *noun* [U] **1** (*US ALSO* **endive,** *AUS ALSO* **witlof**) a vegetable with bitter-tasting white leaves eaten raw in salads **2** a powder made from the root of this plant and added to or used instead of coffee

chide /tʃaɪd/ *verb* [T] *FORMAL* to speak to someone severely because they have behaved badly: *She chided him* ***for*** *his bad manners.*

chief [PERSON IN CHARGE] /tʃiːf/ *noun* [C] the person in charge of a group or organization, or the ruler of a tribe: *a police chief* ○ *A new chief* ***of*** *the security forces has just been appointed.* ○ [as form of address] *UK HUMOROUS Can you sign this form for me, chief?*
• **too many chiefs and not enough Indians** *INFORMAL* too many managers and not enough people to do the work
chief /tʃiːf/ *adj* [before n] highest in rank: *the chief fire officer* ○ *the government's chief medical officer*

COMMON LEARNER ERROR

chief or boss/manager?

Chief can only be used to mean 'a person in charge of other people' in a few particular senses, such as in the police.

a police chief

Chief can also be used as an adjective in the names of some important jobs.

A new Chief Executive Officer has been appointed this week.

More common words for 'a person in charge of other people in a company' are **boss**, which is slightly informal, and **manager**.

I asked my boss/manager if I could have a week off.
~~*I asked my chief if I could have a week off.*~~

chief [MOST IMPORTANT] /tʃiːf/ *adj* [before n] most important or main: *The chief problem we have in the area now is the spread of disease.* ○ *The weather was our chief reason for coming here.* ○ *Our chief expenditure is on raw materials.*
chiefly /ˈtʃiː.fli/ *adv* mainly: *magazines intended chiefly for teenagers*

ˌchief ˈconstable *noun* [C usually sing] in Britain, the police officer in charge of the police in a particular area

ˌchief eˈxecutive *noun* [C usually sing] the person with the most important position in a company: *She's the chief executive of one of the country's largest charities.*

the ˌChief Eˈxecutive *noun* [S] *US* the president of the United States

ˌchief eˈxecutive ˌofficer *noun* [C] (*ABBREVIATION* **CEO**) the person with the most important position in a company

ˌchief ˈjustice *noun* [C usually sing] the most important judge of a court of law, especially a very important court in a country

ˌchief of ˈstaff *noun* [C] one of the highest-ranking officers in the armed forces

chieftain /ˈtʃiːf.tᵊn/ *noun* [C] the leader of a tribe

chiffon [CLOTH] /ˈʃɪf.ɒn/ [US] /ʃɪˈfɑːn/ *noun* [U] a very thin, almost transparent cloth of silk or NYLON

chiffon [FOOD] /ˈʃɪf.ɒn/ [US] /ʃɪˈfɑːn/ *adj* [before n] *US* made light, especially by adding the clear part of eggs which have been beaten: *lemon chiffon pie*

chignon /ˈʃiː.njɒ̃/ [US] /-njɑːn/ *noun* [C] a woman's hairstyle where the hair is arranged in a knot or roll at the back of her head

chihuahua /tʃɪˈwɑː.wə/ *noun* [C] a very small dog with large eyes and smooth hair

chilblain /ˈtʃɪl.bleɪn/ *noun* [C] a painful red swelling on the toes or fingers, caused by cold weather

child /tʃaɪld/ *noun* [C] *plural* **children 1** a boy or girl from the time of birth until he or she is an adult, or a son or daughter of any age: *an eight-year-old child* ○ *As a child I didn't eat vegetables.* ○ *A small group of children waited outside the door.* ○ *Both her children are now married with children of their own.* ○ *Jan is married with three* ***young*** *children.* ○ *They campaign for the rights of the* ***unborn*** *child.* ➲See also **brainchild**. **2** *DISAPPROVING* an adult who behaves badly, like a badly behaved child: *He's such a child if he doesn't get his own way.* **3 a child of *sth*** someone who has been very influenced by a particular period or situation: *Me, I'm a child of the sixties.*
• **be child's play** *INFORMAL* to be very easy: *Using computers nowadays is child's play compared to how difficult they were to use twenty years ago.*
• **(great) with child** *OLD USE* (very) pregnant
• **Children should be seen and not heard.** *SAYING* said to emphasize that you think children should behave well and be quiet
childhood /ˈtʃaɪld.hʊd/ *noun* [C or U] the time when someone is a child: *She had an unhappy childhood.* ○ *Childhood is not always a happy time.* ➲Compare **boyhood** at **boy**; **girlhood** at **girl**.
childish /ˈtʃaɪl.dɪʃ/ *adj* **1** typical of a child: *childish handwriting* **2** *DISAPPROVING* If an adult is childish, they behave badly in a way that would be expected of a child: *He wasn't enjoying the occasion so he thought he'd spoil it for everyone else – it was very childish of him.* ➲Compare with **childlike**. **childishly** /ˈtʃaɪl.dɪʃ.li/ *adv DISAPPROVING*
childishness /ˈtʃaɪl.dɪʃ.nəs/ *noun* [U]
childless /ˈtʃaɪld.ləs/ *adj* without children: *Couples who are childless can feel excluded from the rest of society.*
childlessness /ˈtʃaɪld.lə.snəs/ *noun* [U]
childlike /ˈtʃaɪld.laɪk/ *adj* (of adults) showing the good qualities that children have, such as trusting people, being honest and enthusiastic: *a childlike innocence/quality* ○ *All her life she had a childlike trust in other people.* ➲Compare with **childish**.

ˈchild aˌbuse *noun* [U] when adults intentionally treat children in a cruel or violent way

childbearing /ˈtʃaɪldˌbeə.rɪŋ/ [US] /-ˌber.ɪŋ/ *noun* [U] the process of having babies: *The survey is only concerned with women of childbearing* ***age***.

ˌchild ˈbenefit *noun* [U] *UK* money received regularly by families from the government to help pay for the costs of caring for children

childbirth /ˈtʃaɪld.bɜːθ/ [US] /-bɝːθ/ *noun* [U] the act of giving birth to a baby: *A great number of women used to die* ***in*** *childbirth.*

childcare /ˈtʃaɪld.keəʳ/ [US] /-ker/ *noun* [U] care for children provided by either the government, an organization or a person, while parents are at work or are absent for another reason: *What childcare facilities does your company offer?* ○ *Without the adequate provision of childcare, many women who wish to work are unable to do so.*

child-centred /ˈtʃaɪldˌsen.təd/ [US] /-t̬ɚd/ *adj* describes ways of teaching and treating children in which the child's needs and desires are the most important thing: *a child-centred approach to parenting*

child-free /ˈtʃaɪld.friː/ *adj* describes people who choose not to have children, or a place or situation without children: *a child-free couple/hotel/lifestyle*

childminder *UK* /ˈtʃaɪldˌmaɪn.dəʳ/ [US] /-dɚ/ *noun* [C] (*US* **babysitter**) a person, usually a woman, whose job is to take care of other people's children in her own home: *a registered childminder* **childminding** *UK* /ˈtʃaɪldˌmaɪn.-

dɪŋ/ *noun* [U] (*US* **babysitting**) **childmind** /ˈtʃaɪld.maɪnd/ *verb* [I or T] (*US* **babysit**)

ˈ**child moˌlester** *noun* [C] a person who tries to have sex with children

ˈ**child ˌprodigy** *noun* [C] a young child who has very great ability in something: *A child prodigy, he made his first professional tour as a pianist at the age of six.*

childproof /ˈtʃaɪld.pruːf/ *adj* describes containers and locks that cannot be opened or operated by a child: *Most bottles of bleach have childproof lids.*

child-rearing /ˈtʃaɪldˌrɪə.rɪŋ/ [US] /-ˈrɪr-/ *noun* [U] the practice of looking after children until they are old enough to look after themselves: *Why shouldn't a woman have a job after years of child-rearing?*

children /ˈtʃɪl.drən/ *plural of* **child**

children's home /ˈtʃɪl.drənzˌhəʊm/ [US] /-ˌhoʊm/ *noun* [C] a place where children are cared for if their parents are dead or unable to take care of them

ˈ**child supˌport** *noun* [U] money that someone gives the mother or father of their children when they do not live with them ➲See also **maintenance** at **maintain** PROVIDE.

chill /tʃɪl/ *verb* [I or T] to (cause to) become cold but not freeze: *I've put the beer in the fridge to chill.* ○ *Chill the wine before serving.*

• **chill *sb* to the bone/marrow** to frighten someone very much: *This is a film that will chill you to the marrow.*

chill /tʃɪl/ *noun* **1** [S] a feeling of cold: *There was a chill in the air this morning.* **2** [C] a slight fever: *Don't go out with wet hair, you might* ***catch*** *a chill.* **3** [S] a sudden unpleasant feeling, especially of fear: *I suddenly realized, with a chill of apprehension, the danger of the task ahead.*

• **take the chill off *sth*** to make something slightly less cold: *We lit the fire to take the chill off the room.*

• **send chills down/up *sb's* spine** to make someone feel very frightened: *His words sent a chill down her spine.*

• **the chill wind of *sth*** *LITERARY* the problems caused by something: *Many more businesses are feeling the chill wind of the recession.*

chilly /ˈtʃɪl.i/ *adj* (*LITERARY* **chill**) (of weather, conditions in a room, or parts of the body) cold: *The bathroom* ***gets*** *chilly in the winter.* ○ *I felt a bit chilly so I put on a jacket.* ○ *a chilly October day*

chilling /ˈtʃɪl.ɪŋ/ *adj* frightening: *a chilling tale* ○ *The monument stands as a chilling reminder of man's inhumanity to man.* **chillingly** /ˈtʃɪl.ɪŋ.li/ *adv*

▲ **chill out** *phrasal verb* (*ALSO* **chill**) *INFORMAL* to relax completely, or not allow things to upset you: *I'm just chilling out in front of the TV.* ○ *Chill out, Dad. The train doesn't leave for another hour!*

chilled /tʃɪld/ *adj INFORMAL* relaxed, not worrying about anything: *Me, I'm feeling pretty chilled.*

chilli *UK (plural* **chillies**), *US* **chili** /ˈtʃɪl.i/ *noun* [C or U] the small red or green seed case from particular types of pepper plant that is used to make some foods very hot and spicy

chilli con carne /ˌtʃɪl.i.kɒnˈkɑː.ni/ [US] /-kɑːnˈkɑːr-/ *noun* [U] a spicy dish of meat, onions and CHILLIES or chilli powder and usually beans

ˈ**chilli ˌpowder** *noun* [U] a dark red powder made from dried CHILLIES and other spices, that is used for flavouring particular foods

ˈ**chill ˌroom** *noun* [C] **1** (*ALSO* **chill-out room**) a room that people can use to relax in, for example at a dance club or office: *The club has three rooms, a chill room and two dance floors.* **2** a WEB PAGE (= area on the Internet) containing relaxing music and images, etc. **3** a storage room that is kept cold, usually used for keeping food fresh

chilly /ˈtʃɪl.i/ *adj* unfriendly: *I went to see the sales manager but got a rather chilly reception.* ➲See also **chilly** at **chill**.

chime /tʃaɪm/ *verb* [I or T] (of bells) to make a clear ringing sound: *In the square the church bells chimed.*

chime /tʃaɪm/ *noun* [C] *I was woken up by the chimes* (= ringing sounds) *of the cathedral bells.*

chimes /tʃaɪmz/ *plural noun* a set of small bells, or objects that make ringing sounds: *wind chimes*

▲ **chime in** *phrasal verb INFORMAL* to interrupt or speak in a conversation, usually to agree with what has been said: *"It's very difficult, I said. "Impossible," she chimed in.* ○ *Andy chimed in* ***with*** *his view of the situation.*

chimera /kaɪˈmɪə.rə/ [US] /-ˈmɪr.ə/ *noun* [C] *FORMAL* a hope or dream that is extremely unlikely ever to come true: *Is the ideal of banishing hunger throughout the world just a chimera?* **chimerical** /kaɪˈmer.ɪ.kəl/ *adj*

chimney [PIPE] /ˈtʃɪm.ni/ *noun* [C] a hollow structure that allows the smoke from a fire inside a building to escape to the air outside: *Factory chimneys belched dense white smoke into the sky.*

chimney [PASSAGE] /ˈtʃɪm.ni/ *noun* [C] *SPECIALIZED* a narrow vertical passage in the rock of a cliff or mountain, through which a person can climb

ˈ**chimney ˌbreast** *noun* [C] the part of a wall in a room which is built around a chimney and into which a fireplace is built

chimney pot /ˈtʃɪm.ni.pɒt/ [US] /-pɑːt/ *noun* [C] a short pipe, often made of clay, fixed to the top of a chimney

chimney stack /ˈtʃɪm.ni.stæk/ *noun* [C] *UK* the part of a chimney that sticks out above a roof

ˈ**chimney ˌsweep** *noun* [C] (*INFORMAL* **sweep**) a person whose job is to clean inside chimneys, usually using a set of brushes with a very long handle

chimpanzee /ˌtʃɪm.pænˈziː/ *noun* [C] (*INFORMAL* **chimp**) a small, very intelligent African ape with black or brown fur

chin /tʃɪn/ *noun* [C] the part of a person's face below their mouth: *To keep the helmet in position, fasten the strap beneath the chin.* ○ *She sat behind the table, her chin resting in her hands.* ➲See picture **The Body** on page Centre 5

• **Chin up!** *INFORMAL* something you say to someone in a difficult situation in order to encourage them to be brave and try not to be sad: *Chin up! It'll soon be the weekend.*

• **take it on the chin** *INFORMAL* to accept unpleasant events bravely and without complaining

-chinned /-tʃɪnd/ *suffix* having a particular type of chin: *square-chinned*

china /ˈtʃaɪ.nə/ *noun* [U] clay of a high quality that is shaped and then heated to make it permanently hard, or objects made from this, such as cups and plates: *china plates*

Chinatown /ˈtʃaɪ.nə.taʊn/ *noun* [C or U] an area of a city outside China where many Chinese people live and there are a lot of Chinese restaurants and shops

chinchilla /tʃɪnˈtʃɪl.ə/ *noun* [C] a small South American animal with very soft, pale grey fur that is highly valued

Chinese /tʃaɪˈniːz/ /ˈ--/ *adj* of or from China: *A Chinese theatre company will be performing in the drama festival.*

Chinese chequers /ˌtʃaɪ.niːzˈtʃek.əz/ [US] /-ɚz/ *noun* [U] a game played on a star-shaped board where small balls are moved from hole to hole

Chinese gooseberry /ˌtʃaɪ.niːzˈgʊz.bər.i/ *noun* [C] a **kiwi (fruit)**

Chinese lantern /ˌtʃaɪ.niːzˈlæn.tən/ [US] /-tɚn/ *noun* [C] a folding decoration made from thin coloured paper

Chinese puzzle /ˌtʃaɪ.niːzˈpʌz.l̩/ *noun* [C] **1** a game where you have to solve the problem of fitting many different pieces together, especially boxes inside other boxes **2** a situation that is complicated and difficult to understand

chink [CRACK] /tʃɪŋk/ *noun* [C] a small narrow crack or opening: *I peered through a chink in the curtains and saw them all inside.*

• **chink in *sb's* armour** a fault in someone's character or argument that may cause problems for them: *A single chink in our armour at the negotiating table means we could lose out badly.*

chink [SOUND] /tʃɪŋk/ *noun* [C usually sing] a light ringing sound; a **clink**: *On a hot day it's lovely to hear the chink of ice in a glass.* **chink** /tʃɪŋk/ *verb* [I] *The coins chinked lightly in his pocket as he walked along.*

Chink [PERSON] /tʃɪŋk/ *noun* [C] (*UK ALSO* **Chinky**) *OFFENSIVE* a Chinese person

Chinky /ˈtʃɪŋ.ki/ *noun* [C] *UK SLANG* an offensive word for a restaurant serving Chinese food

chinless *MAINLY UK* /ˈtʃɪn.ləs/ *adj* (*US USUALLY* **weak-chinned**) having a very small chin, sometimes thought of as a sign of a weak character

ˌchinless ˈwonder *noun* [C] *UK INFORMAL* a foolish man, typically of high social class

chinos /ˈtʃiː.nəʊz/ [US] /-noʊz/ *plural noun* loose cotton trousers, usually of a light brown colour ➲See picture **Clothes** on page Centre 6

ˈchin ˌrest *noun* [C] the part of an instrument, such as a violin, on which a person puts their chin for support while playing

chinstrap /ˈtʃɪn.stræp/ *noun* [C] a strap that goes around the lower part of a person's head to keep a protective hat, especially a helmet, in place

chintz /tʃɪnts/ *noun* [U] cotton cloth, usually with patterns of flowers, that has a slightly shiny appearance **chintzy** /ˈtʃɪnt.si/ *adj*: *I find their house a bit too chintzy* (= decorated with lots of chintz).

chintzy /ˈtʃɪnt.si/ *adj US* (of things) cheap and of low quality, or (of people) not willing to spend money: *It's a chintzy hat, you can't expect it to last for long.* ○ *Don't be so chintzy, the whole evening will only cost you 10 bucks.*

chinwag /ˈtʃɪn.wæg/ *noun* [C] *INFORMAL* a long and pleasant conversation between friends: *We had a* ***good*** *chinwag over a bottle of wine.*

chip [FRIED FOOD] /tʃɪp/ *noun* [C usually pl] **1** *UK* (*US* **french fry**) a long thin piece of potato that is fried and usually eaten hot: *fish and chips* ○ *beans/egg/sausage and chips* ○ *oven chips* (= chips that are baked in a cooker) **2** *US FOR* **crisp** POTATO: *a bag of chips* **3** a thin slice of fried maize, BANANA or other food which is eaten cold: *banana chips*

chip [PIECE] /tʃɪp/ *noun* [C] a small piece that has been broken off a larger object, or the mark left on an object such as a cup, plate, etc. where a small piece has been broken off it: *wood chips* ○ *Polly fell and knocked a chip* ***out of*** *her front tooth.* ○ *This mug's got a chip* ***in it/out of*** *it.*

• **a chip off the old block** *INFORMAL* someone who is very similar in character to their father or mother

• **have a chip on *your* shoulder** *INFORMAL* to seem angry all the time because you think you have been treated unfairly or feel you are not as good as other people: *He's got a chip on his shoulder about not having been to university.*

chip /tʃɪp/ *verb* [I or T] **-pp-** to accidentally break a small piece off something: *I wish my nail polish wouldn't keep chipping.* ○ *He's chipped a bone in his wrist.* **chipped** /tʃɪpt/ *adj*: *a chipped glass* ○ *All the plates were old and chipped.*

chip [COMPUTER PART] /tʃɪp/ *noun* [C] (*ALSO* **microchip**) *SPECIALIZED* a very small piece of SEMICONDUCTOR, especially in a computer, that contains extremely small electronic circuits and devices, and can perform particular operations: *a silicon chip*

chip [PLASTIC COIN] /tʃɪp/ *noun* [C] a small plastic disc used to represent a particular amount of money in gambling: *FIGURATIVE The hostages are being held as a* ***bargaining*** *chip by terrorist organizations.*

• **when the chips are down** *INFORMAL* when you are in a very difficult or dangerous situation, especially that makes you understand the true value of people or things: *One day when the chips are down, you will know who your true friends are.*

• **have had *your* chips** *UK INFORMAL* to have lost your position, importance or power

PHRASAL VERBS WITH **chip** ▼

▲ **chip (sth) in** [PAY] *phrasal verb* [M] *INFORMAL* to give some money when several people are giving money to pay for something together: *They all chipped in fifty pounds and bought their mother a trip to Greece.*

▲ **chip in** [INTERRUPT] *phrasal verb MAINLY UK INFORMAL* to interrupt a conversation in order to say something: *I'll start and you can all chip in* ***with*** *your comments.*

chipboard /ˈtʃɪp.bɔːd/ [US] /-bɔːrd/ *noun* [U] hard material made from small pieces of wood mixed with glue, often used instead of wood in making furniture because it is cheaper: *veneered chipboard*

chipmunk /ˈtʃɪp.mʌŋk/ *noun* [C] a small furry North American animal with dark strips along its back

chipolata, chippolata /ˌtʃɪp.əˈlɑː.tə/ [US] /-t̬ə/ *noun* [C] *UK* a small thin sausage

chipper /ˈtʃɪp.əʳ/ [US] /-ɚ/ *adj INFORMAL* very happy: *You seem mighty chipper this morning – what's up?*

chipping /ˈtʃɪp.ɪŋ/ *noun* [C usually pl] *UK* a small piece of stone, put in road surfaces or under railway tracks

ˈchip ˌshop *noun* [C] (*INFORMAL* **chippy**) *UK* a shop that sells fried fish, potatoes and other foods, which you take away to eat

chiropodist /kɪˈrɒp.ə.dɪst/ /ʃɪ-/ [US] /-ˈrɑː.pə-/ *noun* [C] a person whose job is to treat problems and diseases of people's feet **chiropody** /kɪˈrɒp.ə.di/ /ʃɪ-/ [US] /-ˈrɑː.pə-/ *noun* [U]

chiropractor /ˈkaɪ.rəʊ.præk.təʳ/ [US] /-roʊ.præk.tɚ/ *noun* [C] a person whose job is to treat diseases by adjusting a person's joints, especially those in the back **chiropractic** /ˌkaɪᵊ.rəʊˈpræk.tɪk/ [US] /-roʊ-/ *noun* [U] the system of treatment used by a chiropractor

chirp /tʃɜːp/ [US] /tʃɝːp/ *verb* **1** [I] (*ALSO* **chirrup**) (especially of a bird) to make a short high sound or sounds **2** [+ speech] to say something with a high, happy voice: *"Morning!" she chirped.*

chirpy /ˈtʃɜː.pi/ [US] /ˈtʃɝː-/ *adj* happy and active: *She seemed quite chirpy this morning.* **chirpily** /ˈtʃɜː.pɪ.li/ [US] /ˈtʃɝː-/ *adv* **chirpiness** /ˈtʃɜː.pi.nəs/ [US] /ˈtʃɝː-/ *noun* [U]

chisel /ˈtʃɪz.ᵊl/ *noun* [C] a tool with a long metal blade that has a sharp edge for cutting wood, stone, etc. **chisel** /ˈtʃɪz.ᵊl/ *verb* [T] **-ll-** or *US USUALLY* **-l-** to use a chisel: *She chiselled a figure* ***out of*** *the marble.* **chiselled**, *US USUALLY* **chiseled** /ˈtʃɪz.ᵊld/ *adj*: *She brought with her a young man with finely chiselled* ***features*** (= strong, sharp and attractive nose, mouth, chin, etc.)

chit [NOTE] /tʃɪt/ *noun* [C] *UK OLD-FASHIONED* an official note giving information or showing a sum of money that is owed or has been paid: *a chit for the dry cleaner's*

chit [GIRL] /tʃɪt/ *noun* [C] *OLD-FASHIONED DISAPPROVING* a young and foolish girl: *just a chit* ***of a girl***

chit-chat /ˈtʃɪt.tʃæt/ *noun* [U] *INFORMAL* informal conversation about unimportant matters: *"What did you talk about?" "Oh, just chit-chat."* **chit-chat** /ˈtʃɪt.tʃæt/ *verb* [I] *We were just chit-chatting about this and that.*

chivalrous /ˈʃɪv.ᵊl.rəs/ *adj* A chivalrous man is polite, honourable and kind towards women. **chivalrously** /ˈʃɪv.ᵊl.rə.sli/ *adv*: *"After you," he said chivalrously, holding open the door.* **chivalry** /ˈʃɪv.ᵊl.ri/ *noun* [U] **1** very polite and honourable behaviour, especially shown by men towards women **2** the system of behaviour followed by knights in the medieval period of history, that put a high value on purity, honour, kindness and bravery: *the age of chivalry*

chives /tʃaɪvz/ *plural noun* a plant with long thin leaves and purple flowers, or its leaves when cut into small pieces and used in cooking to give a flavour similar to onions

chivvy /ˈtʃɪv.i/ *verb* [T usually + adv or prep] *UK INFORMAL* to encourage someone to do something they do not want to do: *He kept putting off writing the report so I had to chivvy him* ***along.*** ○ *I had to chivvy him* ***into*** *writing the report.*

chloride /ˈklɔː.raɪd/ [US] /ˈklɔːr.aɪd/ *noun* [C or U] *SPECIALIZED* a chemical compound that is a mixture of CHLORINE and another substance: *Sodium chloride is the chemical name for common salt.*

chlorine /ˈklɔː.riːn/ [US] /ˈklɔːr.iːn/ *noun* [U] a greenish-yellow gas with a strong smell, which is added to water in order to kill organisms that might cause infection: *The chlorine in the pool makes my eyes sore.* **chlorinate** /ˈklɔː.rɪ.neɪt/ [US] /ˈklɔːr.ɪ-/ *verb* [T] to add chlorine to water in order to kill organisms that might cause infection **chlorinated** /ˈklɔː.rɪ.neɪ.tɪd/ [US] /ˈklɔːr.ɪ.neɪ.t̬ɪd/ *adj*: *chlorinated swimming pools*

C

chloroform /ˈklɒr.ə.fɔːm/ [US] /ˈklɔːr.ə.fɔːrm/ *noun* [U] a colourless liquid with a sweet smell that makes you unconscious if you breathe it in

chlorophyll, *US ALSO* **chlorophyl** /ˈklɒr.ə.fɪl/ [US] /ˈklɔːr.ə-/ *noun* [U] the green substance in plants, that allows them to use the energy from the sun

chocaholic /ˌtʃɒk.əˈhɒl.ɪk/ [US] /ˌtʃɑː.kəˈhɑː.lɪk/ *noun* [C] *ANOTHER SPELLING OF* chocoholic

choccy /ˈtʃɒk.i/ [US] /ˈtʃɑːk-/ *noun* [C or U] *UK INFORMAL* chocolate: *choccy bickies*

choc-ice /ˈtʃɒk.aɪs/ [US] /ˈtʃɑːk-/ *noun* [C] *UK* a small block of ICE CREAM (= a sweet, very cold food) covered in a thin layer of chocolate

chock /tʃɒk/ [US] /tʃɑːk/ *noun* [C] a block of wood that can be put under a wheel or a heavy object to prevent it from moving

chocka /ˈtʃɒk.ə/ [US] /tʃɑːk-/ *adj* [after v] *UK SLANG FOR* **chock-a-block**

chock-a-block /ˌtʃɒk.əˈblɒk/ /ˈ---/ [US] /ˈtʃɑːk.ə.blɑːk/ *adj* [after v] *INFORMAL* describes a place that is very full of people or things: *The streets were chock-a-block **(with** cars).*

chocker /ˈtʃɒk.ə/ [US] /tʃɑːk-/ *adj* (*ALSO* **chockers**) *UK SLANG FOR* **chock-a-block**

chock-full /tʃɒkˈfʊl/ [US] /tʃɑːk-/ *adj* [after v] *INFORMAL* completely full: *The whole room was chock-full **of** books.*

chocoholic /ˌtʃɒk.əˈhɒl.ɪk/ [US] /ˌtʃɑː.kəˈhɑː.lɪk/ *noun* [C] (*ALSO* **chocaholic**) *INFORMAL HUMOROUS* a person who loves chocolate and eats a lot of it

chocolate /ˈtʃɒk.lət/ [US] /ˈtʃɑːk-/ *noun* **1** [C or U] a sweet, usually brown, food made from CACAO seeds, that is usually sold in a block, or a small sweet made from this: *a bar of chocolate* ○ *chocolate biscuits/mousse* ○ *milk/dark/white chocolate* ○ *I took her a **box of** chocolates.* **2** [C or U] *UK ALSO FOR* **hot chocolate** **3** [U] a dark brown colour

chocolate-box /ˈtʃɒk.lət.bɒks/ [US] /ˈtʃɑːk.lət.bɑːks/ *adj* [before n] *UK* describes something that looks very attractive, but is traditional and boring: *a chocolate-box village*

choice [ACT] /tʃɔɪs/ *noun* [C or S or U] an act or the possibility of choosing: *If the product doesn't work, you are given the choice of a refund or a replacement.* ○ *It's a difficult choice to **make**.* ○ *It's your choice/The choice is yours* (= only you can decide). ○ *It was a choice **between** pain now or pain later, so I chose pain later.* ○ *Now you know all the facts, you can make an **informed** choice.* ○ *I'd prefer not to work but I do**n't have much** choice* (= this is not possible). ○ *He **had no** choice **but to** accept* (= He had to accept). ○ *Is she single **by** choice?*

choice [VARIETY] /tʃɔɪs/ *noun* [S or U] the range of different things from which you can choose: *There wasn't much choice on the menu.* ○ *The evening menu offers a **wide** choice of dishes.* ○ *The dress is available **in a** choice **of** colours.*

choice [PERSON/THING] /tʃɔɪs/ *noun* [C] a person or thing that has been chosen or that can be chosen: *Harvard was not his **first** choice.* ○ *He wouldn't be my choice **as** a friend.* ○ *This type of nursery care may well be the best choice **for** your child.*

choice [SPLENDID] /tʃɔɪs/ *adj* of high quality: *I had the most expensive dish on the menu - a choice fillet of fish.*

choir /kwaɪəʳ/ [US] /kwaɪr/ *group noun* [C] a group of people who sing together, especially in a church: *He sings **in** the church choir.* ○ *choir **practice*** ➲See also **choral**; **chorister**.

choirboy /ˈkwaɪə.bɔɪ/ [US] /ˈkwaɪr-/ *noun* [C] a boy who sings in a church choir

choirmaster /ˈkwaɪəˌmɑː.stəʳ/ [US] /ˈkwaɪrˌmæs.tɚ/ *noun* [C] a person who trains a choir and is in control of their singing when they perform

choke [STOP BREATHING] /tʃəʊk/ [US] /tʃoʊk/ *verb* **1** [I or T] If you choke, or if something chokes you, you stop breathing because something is blocking your throat: *She choked **to death** on a fish bone.* ○ *Children can choke **on** peanuts.* ○ *Peanuts can choke a small child.* **2** [T] to make someone stop breathing by pressing their throat with the hands

choke [DEVICE] /tʃəʊk/ [US] /tʃoʊk/ *noun* [C or U] a device in a motor vehicle, that changes the amount of air going into the engine, allowing more fuel compared to air to go in and therefore making the engine easier to start

choke [FILL] /tʃəʊk/ [US] /tʃoʊk/ *verb* [T usually passive] (*ALSO* **choke up**) to fill something such as a road or pipe, so that nothing can pass through: *At lunchtime the streets were choked with traffic.*

choke [FAIL] /tʃəʊk/ [US] /tʃoʊk/ *verb* [I] (*ALSO* **choke it**) *INFORMAL* (usually in sports) to fail to do something at a time when it is urgent, usually because you suddenly lose confidence: *He could score points at will during the qualifying matches, but in the final he completely choked.*

▲ **choke *sth* back** *phrasal verb* [M] If you choke back feelings or tears, you force yourself not to show how angry or upset you are: *Choking back my anger, I tried to speak calmly.* ○ *"John has had an accident," she said, choking back **the tears**.*

choked /tʃəʊkt/ [US] /tʃoʊkt/ *adj* [after v] unable to speak because you are upset: *She tried to say a few words but found herself choked.*

choker /ˈtʃəʊ.kəʳ/ [US] /ˈtʃoʊ.kɚ/ *noun* [C] a narrow strip of cloth or a NECKLACE that fits very closely around a woman's neck: *a pearl choker*

cholera /ˈkɒl.ᵊr.ə/ [US] /ˈkɑː.lɚ-/ *noun* [U] a serious infection of the bowels caused by drinking infected water or eating infected food, causing DIARRHOEA, vomiting and often death

choleric /kɒlˈer.ɪk/ [US] /kəˈler-/ *adj FORMAL* very angry or easily annoyed

cholesterol /kəˈles.tᵊr.ɒl/ [US] /-tə.rɑːl/ *noun* [U] a fatty substance that is found in the body tissue and blood of all animals, and which is thought to be part of the cause of heart disease if there is too much of it: *an oil which is high in polyunsaturates and low in cholesterol*

chomp /tʃɒmp/ [US] /tʃɑːmp/ *verb* [I or T] (*ALSO* **champ**) *INFORMAL* to chew food noisily: *He was chomping **away** on a bar of chocolate.* ○ *There she sat, happily chomping her breakfast.*

choo-choo /ˈtʃuː.tʃuː/ *noun* [C] *plural* **choo-choos** *CHILD'S WORD* a train

chook /tʃʊk/ *noun* [C] *AUS INFORMAL* a chicken

choose /tʃuːz/ *verb* [I or T] **chose**, **chosen** to decide what you want from a range of things or possibilities: *She had to choose **between** the two men in her life.* ○ *Danny, come here and choose your ice cream.* ○ *He chose a shirt **from** the many in his wardrobe.* ○ [+ question word] *It's difficult choosing where to live.* ○ [+ two objects] *I've chosen Luis a present/I've chosen a present **for** Luis.* ○ *Yesterday the selectors chose Dales **as** the team's new captain.* ○ [+ obj + to infinitive] *The firm's directors chose Emma **to** be the new production manager.* ○ [+ *to* infinitive] *Katie chose* (= decided) ***to** stay away from work that day.*

● **little/not much to choose between** When there is little to choose between two or more things, they are (all) very similar.

choosy /ˈtʃuː.zi/ *adj INFORMAL* difficult to please because you are very exact about what you like: *She's very choosy **about** what she eats and drinks.*

chop [CUT] /tʃɒp/ [US] /tʃɑːp/ *verb* [T] **-pp- 1** to cut something into pieces with an axe, knife or other sharp instrument: *He was chopping wood in the yard.* ○ *Add some fresh parsley, finely chopped.* ○ *Chop **(up)** the onions and carrots roughly.* ○ *INFORMAL Laura had her hair chopped* (= cut) *yesterday.* ➲See picture **In the Kitchen** on page Centre 16 **2** If something is chopped in finance or business, it is stopped or reduced: *Because of lack of funding many long-term research projects are being chopped.*

● **chop and change** *UK* to keep changing your ideas, opinions, activities or job: *After six months of chopping and changing, we've decided to go back to our old system.*

chop /tʃɒp/ [US] /tʃɑːp/ *noun* [C] an act of cutting something with an axe, knife or other sharp instrument

the chop *noun* [S] **1** *MAINLY UK* (*US USUALLY* **the axe**) when your job is taken away from you, either because you have done something wrong or as a way of saving money: *If you're late for work again, you'll be **for** the chop.* ○ *Anyone stepping out of line is liable to **get** the chop.* ○ *Hundreds of workers at the factory have already* been ***given*** *the chop.* **2** the ending of a factory, school, etc. or plan: *When the reorganization occurs, the smaller shipyards will be the first* ***for*** *the chop.* ○ *Many of these special schools are* ***facing*** *the chop.*

chop [MEAT] /tʃɒp/ [US] /tʃɑːp/ *noun* [C] a small piece of meat with a bone still in it: *a lamb/pork chop*

PHRASAL VERBS WITH **chop**

▲ **chop *sth* down** *phrasal verb* [M] to cut through something to make it fall down: *Most of the diseased trees were chopped down last year.*

▲ **chop *sth* off** *phrasal verb* [M] to cut off part of something with a sharp tool: *Two of his fingers were chopped off in the accident.*

chop-chop /ˌtʃɒpˈtʃɒp/ [US] /ˌtʃɑːpˈtʃɑːp/ *exclamation* INFORMAL used to tell someone to hurry: *Come on, chop-chop, we're late!*

chophouse /ˈtʃɒp.haʊs/ [US] /ˈtʃɑːp-/ *noun* [C] a restaurant that mainly serves thick slices of meat such as STEAKS and CHOPS

chopper [AIRCRAFT] /ˈtʃɒp.əʳ/ [US] /ˈtʃɑː.pɚ/ *noun* [C] INFORMAL FOR **helicopter**

chopper [TOOL] /ˈtʃɒp.əʳ/ [US] /ˈtʃɑː.pɚ/ *noun* [C] a small axe held in one hand

chopper [PENIS] /ˈtʃɒp.əʳ/ [US] /ˈtʃɑː.pɚ/ *noun* [C] UK SLANG FOR penis

choppers /ˈtʃɒp.əz/ [US] /ˈtʃɑː.pɚz/ *plural noun* SLANG teeth, especially a set of artificial teeth

choppy /ˈtʃɒp.i/ [US] /ˈtʃɑː.pi/ *adj* (of sea, lakes or rivers) with lots of small, rough waves caused by the wind

chops /tʃɒps/ [US] /tʃɑːps/ *plural noun* INFORMAL the area of the face surrounding the mouth of a person or an animal: *a dog* ***licking*** *its chops* ○ *I'll give him a smack in the chops if he doesn't shut up.*

chopstick /ˈtʃɒp.stɪk/ [US] /ˈtʃɑːp-/ *noun* [C usually pl] one of a pair of narrow sticks that are used for eating East Asian food

chop suey /ˌtʃɒpˈsuː.i/ [US] /ˌtʃɑːp-/ *noun* [U] a Chinese-style dish made from small pieces of meat and vegetables, especially BEANSPROUTS, cooked together

choral /ˈkɔː.rᵊl/ [US] /ˈkɔːr.ᵊl/ *adj* of (music sung by) a choir or a CHORUS: *choral music* ○ *a choral society*

chorale /kɒrˈɑːl/ /kəˈrɑːl/ *noun* [C] a formal song written to be sung by a choir, especially in a church

chord /kɔːd/ [US] /kɔːrd/ *noun* [C] three or more musical notes played at the same time

chore /tʃɔːʳ/ [US] /tʃɔːr/ *noun* [C] a job or piece of work which is often boring or unpleasant but needs to be done regularly: *I'll go shopping when I've* ***done my*** *chores* (= done the jobs in or around the house). ○ *I find writing reports a real chore* (= very boring).

choreography /ˌkɒr.iˈɒg.rə.fi/ [US] /ˌkɔːr.iˈɑː.grə-/ *noun* [U] the skill of combining movements into dances to be performed: *a flamboyant style of choreography* **choreograph** /ˈkɒr.i.ə.grɑːf/ [US] /ˈkɔːr.i.ə.græf/ *verb* [T] *The ballet was choreographed by Ashton.* **choreographer** /ˌkɒr.iˈɒg.rə.fəʳ/ [US] /ˌkɔːr.iˈɑː.grə.fɚ/ *noun* [C] *Ballanchine, the well-known choreographer*

chorister /ˈkɒr.ɪ.stəʳ/ [US] /ˈkɔːr.ɪ.stɚ/ *noun* [C] one of a group of people who sing together in a choir, either in a cathedral or in a special school connected to a university

chortle /ˈtʃɔː.tl̩/ [US] /ˈtʃɔːr.t̬l̩/ *verb* [I] to laugh, showing pleasure and satisfaction, often at someone else's bad luck: *She chortled* ***with*** *glee at the news.* **chortle** /ˈtʃɔː.tl̩/ [US] /ˈtʃɔːr.t̬l̩/ *noun* [C] *I thought I heard a chortle at the back of the room.*

chorus [SONG PART] /ˈkɔː.rəs/ [US] /ˈkɔːr.əs/ *noun* [C] part of a song which is repeated several times, usually after each VERSE (= set of lines), or a piece of music written to be sung by a choir: *I'll sing the verses and I'd like you all to* ***join in*** *the chorus.* ○ *The choir will be performing the Hallelujah Chorus at the concert.* ○ *They burst into* ***a*** *chorus* ***of*** (= they sang the song) *Happy Birthday.*

chorus [SINGING GROUP] /ˈkɔː.rəs/ [US] /ˈkɔːr.əs/ *group noun* [C] a group of people who are trained to sing together: *He sings with the Los Angeles Gay Men's Chorus.* ➲See also **choral**.

chorus [THEATRE GROUP] /ˈkɔː.rəs/ [US] /ˈkɔːr.əs/ *group noun* **1** [C] a group of performers who, as a team, have a supporting position singing or dancing in a show: *She quickly left the chorus for a starring role.* ○ *a chorus* ***girl*** **2** [S] SPECIALIZED a group of male actors in ancient Greek plays who explained or gave opinions on what was happening in the play using music, poetry and dance

chorus [SPEAK TOGETHER] /ˈkɔː.rəs/ [US] /ˈkɔːr.əs/ *verb* [T + speech] LITERARY (of a group of people) to say similar things at the same time; to speak together: *"Not now," the children chorused* ***in unison***, *"we're watching TV."* **chorus** /ˈkɔː.rəs/ [US] /ˈkɔːr.əs/ *noun* [C usually sing] *The newcomers added their voices to the chorus expressing delight at the result.* ○ *There was* ***a*** *chorus* ***of*** *disapproval/complaint/condemnation at his words* (= everyone complained together).

ˈchorus ˌline *group noun* [C usually sing] a row of people dancing and sometimes singing in an entertainment

chose /tʃəʊz/ [US] /tʃoʊz/ *past simple of* **choose**

chosen /ˈtʃəʊ.zᵊn/ [US] /ˈtʃoʊ-/ *past participle of* **choose**

• **the ˌchosen ˈfew** a small group of people who are treated better than other people, often when they do not deserve it: *There's a staff canteen for everyone and there's a smarter restaurant for the chosen few.*

choux pastry /ˌʃuːˈpeɪ.stri/ *noun* [U] a type of pastry made with eggs, which when cooked forms a hollow case for filling with cream or other thick liquids

chow /tʃaʊ/ *noun* [U] OLD-FASHIONED SLANG food; something to eat

chowder /ˈtʃaʊ.dəʳ/ [US] /-dɚ/ *noun* [U] MAINLY US a type of thick soup usually made from fish or other sea creatures: *clam chowder*

chow mein /ˌtʃaʊˈmeɪn/ *noun* [C or U] a Chinese dish consisting of vegetables, meat and long, thin pasta all fried together

Christ /kraɪst/ *noun* ➲See **Jesus (Christ)**. ➲See also **Christian**.

christen /ˈkrɪs.ᵊn/ *verb* [T] **1** to give a baby a name at a Christian ceremony and make him or her a member of the Christian Church: *She's being christened in June.* ○ [+ n] *She was christened Maria.* **2** to use something for the first time: *I'm going to christen my new walking boots on Saturday.* **3** to give a person a name based on a characteristic that they have: *We christened him 'Slowcoach' because he took so long to do anything.* **christening** /ˈkrɪs.ᵊn.ɪŋ/ *noun* [C] a Christian ceremony at which a baby is given a name and made a member of the Christian Church: *We're going to my nephew's christening on Saturday.*

Christendom /ˈkrɪs.ᵊn.dəm/ *noun* [U] OLD USE Christian people or countries as a whole: *All Christendom responded to the call.*

Christian /ˈkrɪs.tʃən/ /-ti.ən/ *adj* **1** of or belonging to the religion based on the teachings of Jesus Christ: *a Christian charity/organization* ○ *the Christian faith* **2** describes a person or action that is good, kind, helpful, etc. **Christian** /ˈkrɪs.tʃən/ /-ti.ən/ *noun* [C] someone who believes in and follows the teachings of Jesus Christ **Christianity** /ˌkrɪs.tiˈæn.ɪ.ti/ [US] /-tʃiˈæn.ə.t̬i/ *noun* [U] a religion based on belief in God and the life and teachings of Jesus Christ, and on the Bible

the ˈChristian ˌEra *noun* [S] the period of time which begins with the birth of Jesus Christ

ˈChristian ˌname *noun* [C] in Western countries, the first name and not the family name ➲Compare **first name**.

ˌChristian ˈScience *noun* [U] a religion which considers that illness can be cured by religious belief, making medicine unnecessary

Christmas /ˈkrɪs.məs/ *noun* [C or U] (the period just before and after) 25 December, a Christian holy day which celebrates the birth of Christ: *We're going to my mother's for Christmas.* ○ *Happy Christmas!* ○ *We had a lovely Christmas.* ○ *the Christmas holidays* **Christmassy** /ˈkrɪs.mə.si/ *adj* INFORMAL typical of Christmas, or happy because it is Christmas: *It looks very Christmassy in here with the tree and all the decorations.* ○ *I'd feel more Christmassy if it were snowing.*

'**Christmas** ,**cake** *noun* [C or U] *UK* a cake containing a lot of dried fruit and nuts and covered with ICING, which is eaten at Christmas

'**Christmas** ,**card** *noun* [C] a decorated card that you send to someone at Christmas

,**Christmas** '**carol** *noun* [C] a traditional or religious song that people sing at Christmas

,**Christmas** '**cracker** *UK noun* [C] (*US* **bonbon**) a tube of brightly coloured paper given at Christmas parties, which makes a noise when pulled apart by two people and contains a small present, a paper hat and a joke

,**Christmas** '**Day** *noun* [C or U] December 25th: *We spent Christmas Day with Ben's parents.*

,**Christmas** '**Eve** *noun* [C or U] December 24th, the day before Christmas Day

,**Christmas** '**pudding** *noun* [C or U] *UK* a sweet dark food containing dried fruit, which is eaten at the end of the meal in the UK during Christmas

,**Christmas** '**stocking** *noun* [C] a large sock which children leave out when they go to bed on CHRISTMAS EVE so that it can be filled with small presents

Christmastime /'krɪs.məs.taɪm/ *noun* [U] (*OLD USE* **Christmastide**) the period just before and after Christmas Day

'**Christmas** ,**tree** *noun* [C] a real or artificial FIR tree which is decorated with things such as coloured balls and kept in the home at Christmas

chromatic COLOUR /krəʊ'mæt.ɪk/ US /kroʊ'mæṭ-/ *adj* [before n] SPECIALIZED relating to colours: *a chromatic range/combination*

chromatic MUSIC /krəʊ'mæt.ɪk/ US /kroʊ'mæṭ-/ *adj* SPECIALIZED belonging or relating to a musical scale in which the notes follow each other in SEMITONES: *the chromatic scale* (= 12 half-tone notes played in order)

chrome /krəʊm/ US /kroʊm/ *noun* [U] **chromium**: *office furnishings in glass, leather and chrome*

,**chrome** '**yellow** *noun* [U], *adj* bright yellow

chromium /'krəʊ.mi.əm/ US /'kroʊ-/ *noun* [U] a hard blue-grey element used in combination with other substances to form a shiny covering on objects

chromosome /'krəʊ.mə.səʊm/ US /'kroʊ.mə.soʊm/ *noun* [C] any of the rod-like structures found in all living cells, containing the chemical patterns which control what an animal or plant is like: *X and Y chromosomes* ○ *sex chromosomes* **chromosomal** /krəʊ.mə'səʊ.məl/ US /kroʊ.-mə'soʊ-/ *adj: chromosomal abnormalities/defects*

chronic /'krɒn.ɪk/ US /'krɑː.nɪk/ *adj* **1** (especially of a disease or something bad) continuing for a long time: *chronic diseases/conditions* ○ *chronic arthritis/pain* ○ *a chronic invalid* ○ *There is a chronic **shortage** of teachers.* **2** *UK INFORMAL* very bad: *The acting was chronic.* **chronically** /'krɒn.ɪ.kli/ US /'krɑː.nɪ-/ *adv*: *care for the chronically ill*

,**chronic fa'tigue ,syndrome** *noun* [U] (*UK ALSO* **ME**) an illness, sometimes lasting for several years, in which a person's muscles and joints hurt and they are generally very tired

chronicle /'krɒn.ɪ.kl̩/ US /'krɑː.nɪ-/ *noun* [C] **1** a written record of historical events: *the Anglo-Saxon Chronicle* ○ *a chronicle of the French Revolution* **2** part of the name of a newspaper: *the Hampshire Chronicle* **chronicle** /'krɒn.ɪ.kl̩/ US /'krɑː.nɪ-/ *verb* [T] to make a record or give details of something: *The book chronicles the writer's coming to terms with his illness.* **chronicler** /'krɒn.ɪ.klə'/ US /'krɑː.nɪ.klə/ *noun* [C]

chronograph /'krɒn.ə.grɑːf/ US /'krɑː.nə.græf/ *noun* [C] SPECIALIZED a piece of equipment which measures and records periods of time

chronology /krə'nɒl.ə.dʒi/ US /-'nɑː.lə-/ *noun* [C or U] the order in which a series of events happened, or a list or explanation of these events in the order in which they happened: *I'm not sure of the chronology of events.* **chronological** /,krɒn.ə'lɒdʒ.ɪ.kəl/ US /-'lɑː.dʒɪ-/ *adj*: *Give me the dates in chronological order.* **chronologically** /,krɒn.ə'lɒdʒ.ɪ.kli/ US /-'lɑː.dʒɪ-/ *adv*

chronometer /krə'nɒm.ɪ.tə'/ US /-'nɑː.mɪ.ṭə/ *noun* [C] SPECIALIZED a piece of equipment which measures time very accurately

chrysalis /'krɪs.ə.lɪs/ *noun* [C] *plural* **chrysalises** an insect covered by a hard protective case at the stage of development before it becomes a MOTH or BUTTERFLY with wings, or the case itself

chrysanthemum /krɪ'sænt.θə.məm/ *noun* [C] any of several types of garden plant, including some with many small flowers and some with few but very large flowers ⊃See picture **Flowers and Plants** on page Centre 3

chubby /'tʃʌb.i/ *adj* (especially of children) fat in a pleasant and attractive way: *chubby legs* ○ *chubby cheeks* **chubbiness** /'tʃʌb.ɪ.nəs/ *noun* [U]

chuck THROW /tʃʌk/ *verb* [T often + adv or prep] INFORMAL to throw something carelessly: *Chuck it over there/into the corner.* ○ [+ two objects] *Chuck me the keys.*
• **chuck** *sb* **under the chin** to touch especially a younger person in a friendly way under the chin: *"Cheer up," she said and chucked the little girl under the chin.*

chuck END /tʃʌk/ *verb* [T] *UK OLD-FASHIONED INFORMAL* to end your romantic relationship with someone: *He's just chucked his girlfriend.*

chuck PERSON /tʃʌk/ *noun* (*ALSO* **chuckie**) NORTHERN ENGLISH INFORMAL a friendly form of address: *"All right, then, chuck?"*

chuck MACHINE /tʃʌk/ *noun* [C] SPECIALIZED a device for holding an object firmly in a machine

PHRASAL VERBS WITH **chuck** ▼

▲ **chuck** *sth* **away/out** *phrasal verb* [M] INFORMAL to throw something away: *I've chucked out all my old clothes.*

▲ **chuck** *sth* **in** *phrasal verb* [M] INFORMAL to stop doing something which was a regular job or activity: *I've decided to chuck in my job.*

▲ **chuck** *sb* **out** *phrasal verb* [M] INFORMAL to force someone to leave a place: *He'd been chucked out of a club for fighting.*

chuckle /'tʃʌk.l̩/ *verb* [I] to laugh quietly: *She was chuckling as she read the letter.* **chuckle** /'tʃʌk.l̩/ *noun* [C] *He gave a chuckle in response to her question.*

,**chuck** '**steak** *noun* [C] a piece of meat cut from the shoulder area of a cow

chuffed /tʃʌft/ *adj* [after v] *UK INFORMAL* pleased or happy: *He was really chuffed with his present.*

chug /tʃʌg/ *verb* [I usually + adv or prep] **-gg-** to make the sound of an engine or motor, or to move making this sound: *The lorry chugged up the hill.* **chug** /tʃʌg/ *noun* [C often sing] *We heard the chug of the boat's engine in the distance.*

chum /tʃʌm/ *noun* [C] *OLD-FASHIONED INFORMAL* a friend: *They were old school/college chums.* ○ [as form of address] *That's all right by me, chum.*

chummy /'tʃʌm.i/ *adj* INFORMAL friendly: *They're very chummy with their neighbours.*

chum /tʃʌm/ *verb*

▲ **chum up** *phrasal verb* *UK OLD-FASHIONED INFORMAL* to become friends: *She chummed up with some girls from Bristol on holiday.*

chump /tʃʌmp/ *noun* [C] *OLD-FASHIONED INFORMAL* a foolish or stupid person: [as form of address] *You chump! Why did you tell her that?*
• **be off** *your* **chump** *UK OLD-FASHIONED INFORMAL* to be extremely silly or stupid

chunder /'tʃʌn.də'/ US /-də/ *verb* [I] *MAINLY AUS INFORMAL* to vomit: *He rushed out of the bar and chundered in the street.* **chunder** /'tʃʌn.də'/ US /-də/ *noun* [U] *I nearly stepped in a pool of chunder.*

chunk /tʃʌŋk/ *noun* [C] **1** a roughly cut lump: *a chunk of cheese/meat* ○ *pineapple/tuna chunks* **2** INFORMAL a part of something, especially a large part: *a chunk of text* ○ *a substantial chunk of our profits* ○ *Three hours is quite a chunk out of my working day.*

chunky /'tʃʌŋ.ki/ *adj* **1** describes clothes that are thick and heavy, or jewellery made of large pieces: *a chunky sweater* ○ *a chunky necklace* **2** APPROVING describes a person who is short and heavy

the Chunnel /ðə'tʃʌn.əl/ *noun* [S] INFORMAL FOR the **Channel Tunnel**

chunter /ˈtʃʌn.tər/ ⑩ /-t̬ər/ *verb* [I] *UK INFORMAL* to complain, especially in a low voice: *Al was chuntering (on) about being the last to know what was happening.*

chupatti /tʃəˈpæ.ti/ ⑩ /-t̬i/ *noun* [C] a **chapati**

church BUILDING /tʃɜːtʃ/ ⑩ /tʃɝːtʃ/ *noun* [C] a building for Christian religious activities: *The town has four churches.* ○ *a church spire/tower* ○ *a church hall* (= a building belonging to a church, with a large room for meetings)

church ORGANIZATION /tʃɜːtʃ/ ⑩ /tʃɝːtʃ/ *noun* **1** [C or U] an official Christian religious organization: *All the local churches were represented at the memorial service.* ○ *He went on a walking trip with some of his friends from church.* **2** [U] when this organization meets as a group of people: *I'll see her after church.* ○ *They* **go to church** *every Sunday.* ○ *church* **services**
• **the Church** Christian religious organizations: *Some people think the Church shouldn't interfere in politics.*
• **go into/enter the church** to become a priest: *He was in his thirties when he decided to enter the church.*

churchgoer /ˈtʃɜːtʃˌgəʊ.ər/ ⑩ /ˈtʃɝːtʃˌgoʊ.ɚ/ *noun* [C] a person who goes regularly to church: *He's never been a regular churchgoer.* **churchgoing** /ˈtʃɜːtʃˌgəʊ.ɪŋ/ ⑩ /ˈtʃɝːtʃˌgoʊ-/ *noun* [U] *Churchgoing in Britain is declining.*

churchman /ˈtʃɜːtʃ.mən/ /-mæn/ ⑩ /ˈtʃɝːtʃ-/ *noun* [C] a man who is actively involved in the church, especially as a priest or other official

the Church of England /ˌtʃɜːtʃ.əvˈɪŋ.glənd/ ⑩ /ˌtʃɝːtʃ-/ *noun* [S] (*ABBREVIATION* **C of E**) the official church in England: *a Church of England bishop/vicar* ○ *The Queen is the head of the Church of England.*

churchwoman /ˈtʃɜːtʃˌwʊm.ən/ ⑩ /ˈtʃɝːtʃ-/ *noun* [C] a woman who is actively involved in the church or who is a priest or official in a church

churchy /ˈtʃɜː.tʃi/ ⑩ /ˈtʃɝː-/ *adj INFORMAL DISAPPROVING* looking like or suitable for a church: *churchy music*

churchyard /ˈtʃɜːtʃ.jɑːd/ ⑩ /ˈtʃɝːtʃ.jɑːrd/ *noun* [C] an area of land around a church, where dead bodies are buried

churlish /ˈtʃɜː.lɪʃ/ ⑩ /ˈtʃɝː-/ *adj* rude, unfriendly and unpleasant: *They invited me to dinner and I thought* **it would be** *churlish* **to** *refuse.* **churlishly** /ˈtʃɜː.lɪʃ.li/ ⑩ /ˈtʃɝː-/ *adv* **churlishness** /ˈtʃɜː.lɪʃ.nəs/ /ˈtʃɝːr-/ *noun* [U]

churn MOVE/MIX /tʃɜːn/ ⑩ /tʃɝːn/ *verb* **1** [T] (*ALSO* **churn up**) to mix something, especially a liquid, with great force: *The sea was churned up by heavy winds.* **2** [T] to mix milk until it becomes butter **3** [I] If your stomach is churning, you feel ill, usually because you are nervous: *I had my driving test that morning and my stomach was churning.*

churn CONTAINER /tʃɜːn/ ⑩ /tʃɝːn/ *noun* [C] a large container for transporting milk or for making milk into butter: *a milk churn* ○ *a butter churn*
▲ **churn** *sth* **out** *phrasal verb* [M] *INFORMAL* to produce large amounts of something quickly, usually something of low quality: *They churn out thousands of pairs of these shoes every week.* ○ *She churns out a new bestselling novel every year.*

churn (rate) /tʃɜːn/ ⑩ /tʃɝːn/ *noun* [S or U] *SPECIALIZED* the number of customers who decide to stop using a service offered by one company and to use another company, usually because it offers a better service or price: *Internet and cable television companies suffer from a high churn rate.*

chute SLIDE /ʃuːt/ *noun* [C] a narrow, steep slope down which objects or people can slide: *a water chute* ○ *a laundry chute* ○ *a garbage/rubbish chute* ○ *an emergency chute*

chute CLOTH DEVICE /ʃuːt/ *noun* [C] *INFORMAL FOR* **parachute**

chutes and ladders *plural noun US TRADEMARK FOR* **snakes and ladders**

chutney /ˈtʃʌt.ni/ *noun* [C or U] a mixture containing fruit, spices, sugar and vinegar, eaten cold with especially meat or cheese: *tomato and apple chutney* ○ *mango chutney*

chutzpah /ˈhʊt.spə/ *noun* [U] *APPROVING* imaginative and shocking behaviour, involving taking risks but not feeling guilt

the CIA /ˌðə.siː.aɪˈeɪ/ *group noun* [S] *ABBREVIATION FOR* the Central Intelligence Agency: a US government organization which secretly collects information about other countries

ciao /tʃaʊ/ *exclamation INFORMAL* used for saying 'goodbye' and less often 'hello'

cicada /sɪˈkɑː.də/ *noun* [C] *plural* **cicadas** a large insect found in warm countries, which produces a high continuous sound

CID /ˌsiː.aɪˈdiː/ *group noun* [S or U] *ABBREVIATION FOR* Criminal Investigation Department: the part of a UK police force which does not wear uniform and is responsible for discovering who has committed crimes

cider /ˈsaɪ.dər/ ⑩ /-dɚ/ *noun* [U] **1** *UK* (*US* **hard cider**, *AUS* **rough cider**) an alcoholic drink made from apples **2** *US* (*US AND UK* **apple juice**, *AUS* **sweet cider**) juice from crushed apples, used as a drink or to make vinegar

cig /sɪg/ *noun* [C] *INFORMAL* a cigarette

cigar /sɪˈgɑːr/ ⑩ /-gɑːr/ *noun* [C] a tube made from dried and rolled tobacco leaves, which people smoke: *an after-dinner cigar and brandy*

cigarette /ˌsɪg.əˈret/ ⑩ /-ɚ-/ *noun* [C] a small paper tube filled with cut pieces of tobacco, which people smoke: *a packet of cigarettes* ○ *She* **lit** *a cigarette.*

cigarette end *noun* [C] (*ALSO* **cigarette butt**) the part of a cigarette which is left after it has been smoked: *The floor was littered with cigarette ends.*

cigarette holder *noun* [C] a tube that someone uses for holding a cigarette while they are smoking it

cigarette lighter *noun* [C] a device which produces a small flame

cigarette paper *noun* [C] a thin piece of paper used in making a cigarette, especially by someone who makes their own

ciggie, ciggy /ˈsɪg.i/ *noun* [C] *INFORMAL* a cigarette

cilantro /sɪˈlæn.trəʊ/ ⑩ /-troʊ/ *noun* [U] *US* the leaves of the CORIANDER plant, used to add flavour to food

C-in-C /ˌsiː.ɪnˈsiː/ *noun* [C] *ABBREVIATION FOR* **commander-in-chief**

cinch /sɪntʃ/ *noun* [S] *INFORMAL* something which is very easy and is therefore a certainty: *The exam was a cinch.*

cinder /ˈsɪn.dər/ ⑩ /-dɚ/ *noun* [C] a small piece of partly burnt coal or wood: *The cake was* **burnt to a cinder** (= burnt black).

cinder block *noun* [C] *US* a small light block made of concrete mixed with burnt coal which is used in building

Cinderella /ˌsɪn.dəˈrel.ə/ ⑩ /-dəˈrel-/ *noun* [S] **1** someone or something that is given little attention or care, especially less than they deserve: *Mental health has long been considered the Cinderella of the health service.* **2** a girl in a traditional story who was badly treated by her sisters but who met and married a PRINCE

cinema *MAINLY UK* /ˈsɪn.ə.mə/ *noun* [C] (*US USUALLY* **movie theater**) a theatre where people pay to watch films: *The town no longer has a cinema.* ○ *a cinema ticket*

the cinema *MAINLY UK* *noun* [S or U] (*US USUALLY* **the movies**) the business of making films: *He was well-known for his work in the cinema.*
• **go to the cinema** (*US, AUS ALSO* **go to the movies**) to go to watch a film

cinematic /ˌsɪn.əˈmæt.ɪk/ ⑩ /-ˈmæt̬-/ *adj SPECIALIZED* relating to the cinema: *The cinematic effects in her films are clearly borrowed from the great film-makers of the past.*

cinemagoer *UK* /ˈsɪn.ə.məˌgəʊ.ər/ ⑩ /-ˌgoʊ.ɚ/ *noun* [C] (*US* **moviegoer**) a person who regularly goes to watch films at the cinema **cinemagoing** *UK* /ˈsɪn.ə.məˌgəʊ.ɪŋ/ ⑩ /-ˌgoʊ.ɪŋ/ *noun* [U], *adj* [before n] (*US* **moviegoing**) *Cinemagoing is still popular with the young.* ○ *the cinemagoing public*

cinematography /ˌsɪn.ə.məˈtɒg.rə.fi/ ⑩ /-ˈtɑː.grə-/ *noun* [U] *SPECIALIZED* the art and methods of film photography **cinematographer** /ˌsɪn.ə.məˈtɒg.rə.fər/ ⑩ /-ˈtɑː.grə.fɚ/ *noun* [C]

cinnamon /ˈsɪn.ə.mən/ noun [U] the BARK (= hard outer covering) of a tropical tree, or a brown powder made from this, used as a spice to give a particular taste to food, especially sweet food: *a cinnamon stick*

cipher SECRET LANGUAGE, **cypher** /ˈsaɪ.fər/ ⓤ /-fɚ/ noun [C or U] SPECIALIZED a system of writing that prevents most people from understanding the message; a **code**: *The message was written in cipher.*

cipher PERSON /ˈsaɪ.fər/ ⓤ /-fɚ/ noun [C] FORMAL DISAPPROVING a person or group of people without power, but used by others for their own purposes, or someone who is not important: *The interim government is a mere cipher for military rule.*

cipher NUMBER /ˈsaɪ.fər/ ⓤ /-fɚ/ noun [C] US a zero: *If you have no children, enter a cipher in the space on the form.*

circa /ˈsɜː.kə/ ⓤ /ˈsɜː-/ prep (WRITTEN ABBREVIATION **c** or **ca**) FORMAL (used especially with years) approximately: *He was born circa 1600.*

circle SHAPE /ˈsɜː.kl̩/ ⓤ /ˈsɜː-/ noun [C] a continuous curved line, the points of which are always the same distance away from a fixed central point, or the area enclosed by such a line: *Coloured paper was cut into circles, squares and triangles.* ○ *We sat in a circle.*
● **go/run round in circles** to keep doing or talking about the same thing without achieving anything: *The discussion kept going round in circles.* ○ *I've been running round in circles trying to get all the reports finished before the meeting.*

circle /ˈsɜː.kl̩/ ⓤ /ˈsɜː-/ verb **1** [I or T] to move in a circle, often around something: *The plane circled for an hour before receiving permission to land.* ○ *Security staff circled the grounds of the house with guard dogs every hour.* **2** [T] to draw a circle around something: *Circle the answer you think is correct.* ⊃See also **encircle**.

circular /ˈsɜː.kjʊ.lər/ ⓤ /ˈsɜː.kjʊ.lɚ/ adj **1** shaped like a circle: *a circular flowerbed/tablecloth* ⊃See also **circular**. **2** describes an argument which keeps returning to the same points and is not effective **circularity** /ˌsɜː.kjʊˈlær.ɪ.ti/ ⓤ /ˌsɜː.kjʊˈler.ɪ.t̬i/ noun [U] *the circularity of political arguments*

circle GROUP /ˈsɜː.kl̩/ ⓤ /ˈsɜː-/ noun [C] a group of people with family, work or social connections: *The subject was never discussed outside the family circle.* ○ *She's not one of my close circle of friends.* ○ *We never meet these days – we move in different circles* (= do not have the same group of friends).

the 'circle UPPER FLOOR noun [S] UK an upper floor in a theatre or cinema where people sit to watch the performance: *Shall I get seats in the circle or in the stalls?* ⊃Compare **gallery** RAISED AREA; **the stalls** THEATRE.

circuit CLOSED SYSTEM /ˈsɜː.kɪt/ ⓤ /ˈsɜː-/ noun [C] a closed system of wires or pipes through which electricity or liquid can flow: *A defect was found in the water-cooling/electrical circuit.*

circuitry /ˈsɜː.kɪ.tri/ ⓤ /ˈsɜː-/ noun [U] the circuits that an electrical or electronic device contains, considered as a single system: *The circuitry in this fighter aircraft has been protected against strong magnetic fields.*

circuit TRACK /ˈsɜː.kɪt/ ⓤ /ˈsɜː-/ noun [C] something shaped approximately like a circle, especially a route, path or sports track which starts and ends in the same place: *They test the car tyres on a motor racing circuit.* ○ *We made a leisurely circuit of the city walls before lunch.*

circuit VISITS /ˈsɜː.kɪt/ ⓤ /ˈsɜː-/ noun [C or U] **1** a regular pattern of visits or the places visited: *They first met each other on the tennis circuit* (= while at different tennis competitions). ○ *He was a familiar figure on the lecture circuit.* **2** LEGAL a particular area containing different courts which a judge visits: *The judge had served for many years on the North-east Circuit.* ○ *a circuit judge*

'circuit ,board noun [C] SPECIALIZED a set of electrical connections made by thin lines of metal fixed onto a surface

'circuit ,breaker noun [C] a safety device which stops the flow of current to an electrical system when there is a fault ⊃Compare **fuse** SAFETY PART.

circuitous /sɜːˈkjuː.ɪ.təs/ ⓤ /sɜːˈkjuː.ɪ.t̬əs/ adj FORMAL not straight or direct: *a circuitous route/path* ○ *a*

circuitous (= long and indirect) *explanation* **circuitously** /sɜːˈkjuː.ɪ.tə.sli/ ⓤ /sɜːˈkjuː.ɪ.t̬ə-/ adv

'circuit ,training noun [U] a type of sports training which involves sets of different exercises done in order one after the other

circular /ˈsɜː.kjʊ.lər/ ⓤ /ˈsɜː.kjʊ.lɚ/ noun [C] a letter or notice sent to a large number of people: *Circulars and other junk mail go straight in the bin.* ⊃See also **circular** at **circle** SHAPE.

circulate /ˈsɜː.kjʊ.leɪt/ ⓤ /ˈsɜː-/ verb [I or T] to move around or through something, or to make something move around or through something: *Hot water circulates through the heating system.* ○ *I try to circulate* (= move around and talk to a lot of people) *at a party and not just stay with the friends I came with.* ○ *I've circulated a good luck card for everyone to sign.*

circulation /ˌsɜː.kjʊˈleɪ.ʃən/ ⓤ /ˌsɜː-/ noun **1** [U] when something such as information, money or goods passes from one person to another: *Police have warned that there are a lot of fake £50 notes in circulation.* ○ *Add her name to the circulation list for this report* (= the people who will be given it to read). ○ FIGURATIVE *I hear she's out of circulation/back in circulation* (= taking part/not taking part in social activities) *after her accident.* **2** [C usually sing] the number of people to whom a newspaper or magazine is regularly sold: *The paper has a circulation of 150 000.* **3** [U] the movement of blood around the body: *Exercise helps to improve circulation.*

circumcise /ˈsɜː.kəm.saɪz/ ⓤ /ˈsɜː-/ verb [T] to cut the protecting loose skin off a boy's penis, or to cut away a girl's CLITORIS and the skin around it, for medical, traditional or religious reasons **circumcision** /ˌsɜː.kəmˈsɪʒ.ən/ ⓤ /ˌsɜː-/ noun [C or U]

circumference /səˈkʌm.fə.r.ən ts/ ⓤ /sɚˈkʌm.fɚ-/ noun [C or U] **1** the distance around a circle, or the distance around the widest part of a circular or round object; the line enclosing a circular space: *the circumference of a circle/an orange* ○ *Draw a circle 30 centimetres in circumference.* **2** the **circumference** the outside edge of an area of any size or shape

circumflex /ˈsɜː.kəm.fleks/ ⓤ /ˈsɜː-/ noun [C] a sign (^) over a letter, especially a vowel, which shows that it has a different pronunciation from the letter without a sign over it

circumlocution /ˌsɜː.kəm.ləˈkjuː.ʃən/ ⓤ /ˌsɜː-/ noun [C or U] FORMAL (an example of) an indirect way of saying something, especially something unpleasant: *'Economical with the truth' is a circumlocution for 'lying'.* ○ *Politicians are experts in circumlocution.* **circumlocutory** /ˌsɜː.kəm.ləˈkjuː.tər.i/ ⓤ /ˌsɜː.kəm-ˈlə.kjuː.t̬ɚ-/ adj

circumnavigate /ˌsɜː.kəmˈnæv.ɪ.geɪt/ ⓤ /ˌsɜː-/ verb [T] FORMAL to sail all the way around something: *They circumnavigated Cape Horn Island in canoes.* **circumnavigation** /ˌsɜː.kəmˌnæv.ɪˈgeɪ.ʃən/ ⓤ /ˌsɜː-/ noun [C or U] *a circumnavigation of the globe from west to east*

circumscribe /ˈsɜː.kəm.skraɪb/ ⓤ /--/ /ˈsɜː-/ verb **1** [T often passive] FORMAL to limit something: *Their movements have been severely circumscribed since the laws came into effect.* ○ *There followed a series of tightly circumscribed visits to military installations.* **2** [T] SPECIALIZED If you circumscribe a triangle, square etc., you draw a circle which encloses it and touches each of its corners.

circumspect /ˈsɜː.kəm.spekt/ ⓤ /ˈsɜː-/ adj FORMAL careful not to take risks: *Officials were circumspect about what the talks had achieved.* **circumspection** /ˌsɜː.kəm-ˈspek.ʃən/ ⓤ /ˌsɜː-/ noun [U] *This is a very sensitive case requiring extreme circumspection.* **circumspectly** /ˈsɜː.kəm.spekt.li/ ⓤ /ˈsɜː-/ adv

circumstance /ˈsɜː.kəm.stɑːnts/ ⓤ /ˈsɜː.kəm.stænts/ noun **1** [C usually pl] a fact or event that makes a situation the way it is: *I think she coped very well under the circumstances.* ○ *Obviously we can't deal with the problem until we know all the circumstances.* ○ *She died in suspicious circumstances.* ○ *We oppose capital punishment in/under any circumstances.* ○ *Under no circumstances should you* (= You must not) *approach the man.* ○ *The meeting has been cancelled due to circumstances beyond our control.* **2** [U] FORMAL events that change your life, over which you have no control: *They were victims of circumstance.* ◦ *We were obliged to go by force of circumstance.* **3 circumstances** how much money someone has: *Grants are available depending on your circumstances.* ◦ *By now she was alone and living in reduced circumstances* (= with little money).

circumstantial /ˌsɜː.kəmˈstɑːn.tʃ³l/ ⓤ /ˌsɜː.kəmˈstæn-/ *adj* containing information, especially about a crime, which makes you think something is true but does not definitely prove it: *circumstantial evidence* ◦ *The case against her was circumstantial.*

circumvent /ˌsɜː.kəmˈvent/ ⓤ /ˌsɜː-/ *verb* [T] FORMAL to avoid something, especially cleverly or illegally: *Ships were registered abroad to circumvent employment and safety regulations.* **circumvention** /ˌsɜː.kəmˈven.tʃ³n/ ⓤ /ˌsɜː-/ *noun* [U]

circus ENTERTAINMENT /ˈsɜː.kəs/ ⓤ /ˈsɜː-/ *noun* **1** [C or S] a group of travelling entertainers including ACROBATS (= people skilled in difficult physical movements), or those who work with trained animals, or a performance by such people usually in a large tent: *She ran away to join the circus.* ◦ *The horses trotted into the circus ring* (= the large circle, with seats all round, in which a circus performs). ◦ *The children loved being taken to the circus.* **2** [S] DISAPPROVING a lot of activity and interest caused by an event or situation: *the media circus surrounding the case*

circus ROAD /ˈsɜː.kəs/ ⓤ /ˈsɜː-/ *noun* [C] UK an open circular area where several roads join: *Piccadilly Circus* ◦ *Oxford Circus*

cirrhosis /sɪˈrəʊ.sɪs/ ⓤ /-ˈroʊ-/ *noun* [U] a serious disease of the liver which usually causes death: *The commonest cause of cirrhosis is alcohol consumption.* ◦ *cirrhosis of the liver*

cirrus /ˈsɪr.əs/ *noun* [U] SPECIALIZED a type of light feathery cloud that is seen high in the sky ⊃Compare **cumulus**; **nimbus**.

cissy /ˈsɪs.i/ *noun* [C], *adj* **sissy**

cistern /ˈsɪs.tən/ ⓤ /-tən/ *noun* [C] a container in which water is stored, especially one connected to a toilet or in the roof of a house

citadel /ˈsɪt.ə.del/ ⓤ /ˈsɪt̬-/ *noun* [C] **1** a strong castle in or near a city, where people can shelter from danger, especially during a war: *The town has a 14th century citadel overlooking the river.* **2** LITERARY a powerful organization in which finding a job is difficult for someone who does not know people who work there: *At the age of 32, she managed to enter one of the citadels of high fashion.*

cite GIVE EXAMPLE /saɪt/ *verb* [T] FORMAL to mention something as proof for a theory or as a reason why something has happened, or to speak or write words taken from a particular writer or written work: *She cited three reasons why people get into debt.* ◦ *The company cited a 12% decline in new orders as evidence that overall demand for its products was falling.* ◦ *She cites both T.S. Eliot and Virginia Woolf in her article.*
citation /saɪˈteɪ.ʃ³n/ *noun* [C] a word or piece of writing taken from a written work: *All citations are taken from the 1973 edition of the text.*

cite NAME /saɪt/ *verb* [T] LEGAL to officially name or mention someone or something in a court of law, or to officially request someone to appear in a court of law: *The lawyer cited two similar cases.* ◦ *He has been cited as the co-respondent in the divorce case.*
citation /saɪˈteɪ.ʃ³n/ *noun* [C] LEGAL an official request for someone to appear in a court of law: *The court issued a contempt citation against city council members who refused to comply with a court order.*

cite PRAISE /saɪt/ *verb* [T] FORMAL to praise someone in the armed forces publicly because of their bravery: *He was cited for bravery.*
citation /saɪˈteɪ.ʃ³n/ *noun* [C] official praise for a person in the armed forces for bravery: *The four soldiers are to receive citations from the President for their brave actions.*

citizen /ˈsɪt.ɪ.z³n/ ⓤ /ˈsɪt̬-/ *noun* [C] a person who is a member of a particular country and who has rights because of being born there or because of being given

rights, or a person who lives in a particular town or city: *The interests of British citizens living abroad are protected by the British Embassy.* ◦ *He applied to become an American citizen.* ◦ *The citizens of Moscow woke up this morning to find they had a new government.* ◦ *Old people are just treated like second-class citizens* (= unimportant people). ◦ *He reassured people that law-abiding citizens* (= people who do not break the law) *would have nothing to fear from the enquiries.*
the citizenry /ðəˈsɪt.ɪ.z³n.ri/ ⓤ /-ˈsɪt̬-/ *group noun* [S] FORMAL the group of people who live in a particular city, town, area or country: *The country's citizenry is/are more politically aware than in the past.*
citizenship /ˈsɪt.ɪ.z³n.ʃɪp/ ⓤ /ˈsɪt̬-/ *noun* [U] **1** the state of being a member of a particular country and having rights because of it: *He was granted Canadian citizenship.* ◦ *He holds joint citizenship in Sweden and Peru.* **2** the state of living in a particular area or town and behaving in a way that other people who live there expect of you

Citizens Ad'vice ˌBureau *noun* [C] (ABBREVIATION **CAB**) offices in the UK which give you free advice about your problems and are usually run by people who do not get paid for their work

Citizens' Band (radio) TRADEMARK /ˌsɪt.ɪ.z³nzˈbænd/ ⓤ /ˌsɪt̬-/ *noun* [C or U] (ALSO **CB (radio)**) a radio communication system for members of the public: *Long-distance truck drivers often use CB radio to talk to each other.*

citric 'acid *noun* [U] a weak acid found in many types of fruit, especially oranges and lemons

citrus /ˈsɪt.rəs/ *noun* [C] *plural* **citrus** or **citruses** any of a group of plants which produce juicy acidic fruits: *The field was planted with citrus trees.* ◦ *Oranges, lemons, limes and grapefruit are types of citrus fruit.* **citric** /ˈsɪt.rɪk/ *adj*: *a wine with a sharp, citric flavour*

city TOWN /ˈsɪt.i/ ⓤ /ˈsɪt̬-/ *noun* [C] **1** a large town: *Many of the world's cities have populations of more than 5 million.* ◦ *Wellington is the capital city* (= centre of government) *of New Zealand.* **2** any town in the UK which has a cathedral: *The city of Ely has about 10,000 inhabitants.*

the 'City FINANCIAL CENTRE *noun* [S] **1** the business centre of London where the large financial organizations are, such as the Bank of England: *He works in the City.* ◦ *a City analyst* **2** the financial organizations as a group and the people who work for them: *The City acted swiftly to the news of a fall in the value of sterling.*

ˌcity 'centre *noun* [C] UK the central part of a city: *It's impossible to park in the city centre.* ⊃Compare **downtown**.

ˌcity 'council *noun* [C] the local government of a city
ˌcity 'councillor *noun* [C] *City councillors have voted to pedestrianize the city centre.*

'city ˌdesk *noun* [C usually sing] **1** UK the department of a newspaper that deals with financial and business news **2** US the department of a newspaper that deals with local news

ˌcity 'fathers *plural noun* OLD-FASHIONED members of the governing group of a city

ˌcity 'hall *noun* [C] MAINLY US a building used as offices by people working for a city government ⊃Compare **town hall**.
ˌCity 'Hall *noun* [U] MAINLY US the government of a city: *You will have to apply to City Hall for a building permit.*

ˌcity 'slicker *noun* [C] INFORMAL DISAPPROVING a person who knows how to deal with the problems of living in a city, and who pretends to know more about fashion and culture than people who live in the countryside

city-state /ˌsɪt.iˈsteɪt/ ⓤ /ˌsɪt̬-/ *noun* [C] in the ancient world, a city and the area around it with an independent government: *Rome, Carthage and Athens were some of the great city-states of the ancient world.*

citywide /ˈsɪt.i.waɪd/ ⓤ /ˈsɪt̬-/ /ˌ--ˈ-/ *adj, adv* MAINLY US existing or happening in all parts of the city: *a citywide outbreak of crimes against vehicles* ◦ *This office is one of forty-six citywide.*

civet /ˈsɪv.ɪt/ *noun* **1** [C] a small cat-like animal from Africa and southern Asia **2** [U] a strong-smelling substance obtained from this animal, which is used for making perfume

civic /'sɪv.ɪk/ *adj* [before n] of a town or city or the people who live in it: *The Prime Minister met many civic* **leaders**, *including the mayor and the leaders of the immigrant communities.* ○ *She felt it was her civic* **duty** (= her duty as a person living in the town) *to tell the police.* ○ *The opera house is a great source of civic* **pride**.

civics /'sɪv.ɪks/ *noun* [U] MAINLY US the study of the way in which a local government works and of the rights and duties of the people who live in the city

civil ⟨ORDINARY⟩ /'sɪv.ºl/ *adj* [before n] not military or religious, or relating to the ordinary people of a country: *Helicopters are mainly used for military rather than civil use.* ○ *After ten years of military dictatorship, the country now has a civil* **government**. ○ *We weren't married in church, but we had a civil* **ceremony** *in a registry office.*

civil ⟨POLITE⟩ /'sɪv.ºl/ *adj* polite and formal: *His manner was civil, though not particularly friendly.*

• **Keep a civil tongue in** *your* **head!** OLD-FASHIONED used to tell someone to stop being rude

• **not have a civil word to say about** *sb* to not be able to think of anything good to say about someone

civilly /'sɪv.ɪl.li/ *adv*: *He greeted us civilly* (= politely).

civility /sɪˈvɪl.ɪ.ti/ ⓤ /-t̬i/ *noun* [C or U] *She greeted them* **with** *civility* (= politeness), *but not much warmth.* ○ *After a few civilities* (= polite remarks), *they got down to business.*

civil ⟨LAW⟩ /'sɪv.ºl/ *adj* [before n] LEGAL relating to private arguments between people or organizations rather than criminal matters: *The matter would be better dealt with in the civil* **court** *rather than by an expensive criminal proceeding.*

civil 'action *noun* [C] an official complaint made by a person or company in a law court against someone who is said to have done something to harm them, and which is dealt with by a judge: *She* **brought** *a civil action* **against** *her former employer.*

civil de'fence *noun* [U] the organizing and training of ordinary people to protect themselves or their property from an enemy attack during a war

civil diso'bedience *noun* [U] a refusal by a group of people to obey laws or pay taxes, as a peaceful way of expressing their disapproval of those laws or taxes and in order to persuade the government to change them: *Gandhi and Martin Luther King both led campaigns of civil disobedience to try to persuade the authorities to change their policies.*

civil engin'eering *noun* [U] the planning and building of things not used for worship or war, such as roads, bridges and public buildings

civil engin'eer *noun* [C] someone whose job is to plan and build public buildings, roads, bridges, etc.

civilian /sɪˈvɪl.i.ən/ *noun* [C] a person who is not a member of the police or the armed forces: *The bomb killed four soldiers and three civilians.* **civilian** /sɪˈvɪl.i.ən/ *adj*: *The army has been criticized for attacking the unarmed civilian* **population**.

civilization, UK USUALLY **-isation** /ˌsɪv.ºl.aɪˈzeɪ.ʃºn/ *noun* **1** [C or U] human society with its highly developed social organizations, or the culture and way of life of a society or country at a particular period in time: *Some people think that nuclear war would mean the end of civilization.* ○ *Cuzco was the centre of one of the world's most famous civilizations, that of the Incas.* ⊃See also **civilization** at **civilize**. **2** [U] MAINLY HUMOROUS a place that has comfortable living conditions: *How does it feel to be back in civilization after all those weeks in a tent?*

COMMON LEARNER ERROR

civilization or culture?

When you are talking about the way of life, customs and beliefs of a particular society, you usually use **culture** for modern societies and **civilization** for ancient societies.

The city centre was packed with thousands of tourists of different races and cultures.

~~The city centre was packed with thousands of tourists of different races and civilizations.~~

---

civilize, UK USUALLY **-ise** /'sɪv.ɪ.laɪz/ *verb* [T] **1** to educate a society so that its culture becomes more developed: *The Romans set out to civilize the Ancient Britons.* **2** to improve someone's behaviour: *I like to think I had a civilizing effect on my younger brothers.* **civilization**, UK USUALLY **-isation** /ˌsɪv.ɪ.laɪˈzeɪ.ʃºn/ *noun* [U] *The civilization of Britain by the Romans took years to complete.* ⊃See also **civilization**.

civilized, UK USUALLY **-ised** /'sɪv.ɪ.laɪzd/ *adj* **1** describes a society or country that has a highly developed system of government, culture and way of life and that treats the people who live there fairly: *A fair justice system is a fundamental part of a civilized society.* ○ *The terrorist attack on the UN building has shocked the civilized world.* **2** If a person or their behaviour is civilized, they are polite and behave in a calm and reasonable way: *Let's discuss this like civilized people* (= politely and calmly). **3** describes a pleasant or comfortable place or thing: *"This is all very civilized," he said, settling himself down in a chair by the fire.*

civil 'law *noun* [U] the part of the legal system which relates to personal matters, such as marriage and property, rather than criminal matters

civil 'liberties *plural noun* the rights of a person to do, think and say what they want if this does not harm other people: *The introduction of identity cards has been opposed by the campaign for civil liberties.*

civil 'list *noun* [C usually sing] UK the amount of money allowed by Parliament for the expenses of the king or queen and royal family in doing their duties

civil 'rights *plural noun* the rights that each person has in a society, whatever their race, sex or religion: *Civil rights include freedom, equality in law and in employment, and the right to vote.*

civil 'servant *noun* [C] a person who works in the Civil Service

the Civil 'Service *group noun* [S] the government departments responsible for putting central government plans into action: *The British Civil Service is supposed to be non-political.*

civil 'war *noun* [C] a war fought by different groups of people living in the same country: *The Spanish Civil War lasted from 1936 to 1939.*

civvies /'sɪv.iz/ *plural noun* OLD-FASHIONED INFORMAL ordinary clothes which are not part of a uniform: *I didn't realize he was a soldier because he was in civvies.*

civvy street /ˌsɪv.iˈstriːt/ *noun* [U] UK OLD-FASHIONED INFORMAL ordinary life which is not connected with the armed forces: *How does it feel to be back in civvy street?*

CJD /ˌsiː.dʒeɪˈdiː/ *noun* [U] ABBREVIATION FOR Creutzfeldt-Jakob disease: a fatal disease that damages the brain and the main nerves connected to it: *When it was first realised that BSE could lead to* **new variant** *CJD, the European Commission banned the sale of all British beef.*

cl WRITTEN ABBREVIATION FOR **centilitre**: *a 75 cl bottle*

clack /klæk/ *noun* [C usually sing] a short sharp noise made by two hard objects being hit together: *He could hear the clack of high heels walking past in the corridor.* **clack** /klæk/ *verb* [I] *Her typewriter clacked noisily as she typed out the letter.*

clad /klæd/ *adj* LITERARY (of people) dressed, or (of things) covered: *A strange figure appeared in the doorway, clad in white.* ○ *an ivy-clad wall* ○ *an armour-clad vehicle* **cladding** /'klæd.ɪŋ/ *noun* [U] protective material which covers the surface of something: *The pipes froze because the cladding had fallen off.*

clag /klæg/ *noun* [U] AUS a type of glue

claim ⟨SAY⟩ /kleɪm/ *verb* **1** [T] to say that something is true or is a fact, although you cannot prove it and other people might not believe it: [+ (*that*)] *The company claims* (*that*) *it is not responsible for the pollution in the river.* ○ [+ *to* infinitive] *He claims* **to** *have met the President, but I don't believe him.* ○ *All parties have claimed* **success** *in yesterday's elections.* ○ *An unknown terrorist group has claimed* **responsibility** *for this morning's bomb attack.*

2 [T] If an organization or group claims a particular number of members, that number of people are believed to belong to it.

• **claim the moral high ground** to say that you are morally better than someone else

claim /kleɪm/ *noun* [C] a statement that something is true or is a fact, although other people might not believe it: *He said the police assaulted him while he was in custody, a claim which the police deny.* ○ [+ that] *The government's claim* ***that*** *it would reduce taxes proved false.* ○ *Can you give any evidence to* ***support*** *your claim?* ○ *He* ***made*** *wild claims* ***about*** *being able to cure cancer.*

• **make no claim to be** ***sth*** to not be trying to make people believe that you are a particular thing: *I make no claim to be a brilliant pianist, but I can play a few tunes.*

• ***sb's/sth's*** **claim to fame** a reason why someone or something is famous: *This little town's only claim to fame is that the President was born here.*

claim [DEMAND] /kleɪm/ *verb* **1** [T] to ask for something of value because you think it belongs to you or because you think you have a right to it: *The police said that if no one claims the watch, you can keep it.* ○ *When King Richard III died, Henry VII claimed the English throne.* **2** [I or T] to make a written demand for money from a government or organization because you think you have a right to it: *The number of people claiming unemployment* ***benefit*** *has risen sharply this month.* ○ *Don't forget to claim* ***(for)*** *your travelling expenses after the interview.* ○ *When my bike was stolen, I claimed* ***on*** *the insurance and got £150 back.* ○ *UK If the shop won't give me a replacement TV, I'll claim my money back.*

• **claim damages** to make an official request for money after an accident, from the person who caused your injuries

• **claim** ***sb's*** **life** If a violent event or fighting or a disease claims someone's life, it kills them: *The war has claimed thousands of lives.*

claim /kleɪm/ *noun* [C] **1** a written request asking an organization to pay you a sum of money which you believe they owe you: *After her house was burgled, she* ***made*** *a claim* ***on*** *her insurance.* ○ *Please* ***submit*** *your claim* ***for*** *travelling expenses to the accounts department.* **2** a right to have something or obtain something from someone: *She has no* ***rightful*** *claim* ***to*** *the title.* ○ *Our neighbours have no claim to* (= cannot say that they own) *that strip of land between our houses.* ○ *My ex-wife has* ***no*** *claims* ***on*** *me* (= has no right to any of my money).

claimant /ˈkleɪ.mənt/ *noun* [C] a person who asks for something which they believe belongs to them or which they have a right to

ˈclaim ˌform *noun* [C] an official document which you use to request a sum of money from an organization, when you think you are owed it

clairvoyant /ˌkleəˈvɔɪ.ənt/ [US] /ˌkler-/ *noun* [C] a person who claims to have powers to see the future or see things which other people cannot see: *She went to see a clairvoyant who said he could communicate with her dead husband.* **clairvoyant** /ˌkleəˈvɔɪ.ənt/ [US] /ˌkler-/ *adj* **clairvoyance** /ˌkleəˈvɔɪ.ənts/ [US] /ˌkler-/ *noun* [U]

clam /klæm/ *noun* [C] a type of sea creature with a shell in two parts that can close together tightly, and a soft body which can be eaten

clam /klæm/ *verb*

▲ **clam up** *phrasal verb* (*ALSO* **shut up like a clam**) *INFORMAL* to go silent suddenly, usually because you are embarrassed or nervous, or do not want to talk about a particular subject: *He just clams up if you ask him about his childhood.*

clambake /ˈklæm.beɪk/ *noun* [C] *US* an event in which SEAFOOD is cooked and eaten outside, usually beside the sea

clamber /ˈklæm.bəʳ/ [US] /-bɚ/ *verb* [I usually + adv or prep] to climb up, across or into somewhere with difficulty, using the hands and the feet: *They clambered* ***over/up*** *the rocks.* ○ *I clambered* ***into/onto*** *the bus.* ○ *She clambered* ***into*** *bed.* **clamber** /ˈklæm.bəʳ/ [US] /-bɚ/ *noun* [C usually sing] *I was worn out after my clamber up the hillside.*

clammy /ˈklæm.i/ *adj* sticky and slightly wet in an unpleasant way: *My hands felt all clammy.* ○ *It was a hot, clammy day.* **clamminess** /ˈklæm.ɪ.nəs/ *noun* [U]

clamour *UK*, *US* **clamor** /ˈklæm.əʳ/ [US] /-ɚ/ *verb* [I] to make a loud complaint or demand: *The children were all clamouring* ***for*** *attention.* ○ [+ to infinitive] *She clamours* ***to*** *go home as soon as she gets to school.*

clamour *UK*, *US* **clamor** /ˈklæm.əʳ/ [US] /-ɚ/ *noun* [S or U] **1** a loud complaint about something or a demand for something: *After the bombing, there was* ***a*** *public clamour* ***for*** *vengeance.* **2** *FORMAL* loud noise, especially made by people's voices: *the clamour* ***of*** *the city* ○ *a clamour* ***of*** *voices*

clamorous /ˈklæm.ᵊr.əs/ [US] /-ɚ-/ *adj LITERARY* **1** making loud demands or complaints **2** making a lot of noise: *clamorous, excited* ***voices***

clamp /klæmp/ *noun* [C] a device, made of wood or metal, which is used to hold two things together tightly: *Carefully* ***tighten*** *the clamp until it firmly supports the pipette in a vertical position.*

clamp /klæmp/ *verb* **1** [T usually + adv or prep] to fasten two thing together, using a clamp: *Clamp the two pieces of wood* ***(together)*** *for 15 minutes.* **2** [T + adv or prep] If you clamp something in a particular place, you hold it there tightly: *He clamped his hand* ***over*** *her mouth.* ○ *A heavy iron chain was clamped* ***around*** *his wrists.* **3** [T] *MAINLY UK* If the police or another person in authority clamps a vehicle, they fix a metal device to one of its wheels, usually because it is parked illegally. The device is usually only removed when the owner pays an amount of money: *When I finally got back, I found my car had been clamped.* ➲See also **wheel clamp**.

▲ **clamp down on** ***sth*** *phrasal verb* to take strong action to stop or limit a harmful or unwanted activity: *The government is clamping down on teenage drinking.*

clampdown /ˈklæmp.daʊn/ *noun* [C] a sudden action taken by a government or people in authority to stop or limit a particular activity: *Following the military coup, there has been a clampdown* ***on*** *press reporting in the capital.*

clan /klæn/ *group noun* **1** [C] a group of families, especially in Scotland, who originate from the same family and have the same name ➲See also **clansman**. **2** [C + sing or pl v] *INFORMAL* a person's relatives: *Is/Are the whole clan coming to visit you for Christmas?*

clannish /ˈklæn.ɪʃ/ *adj DISAPPROVING* describes members of a group of people or society who are friendly to each other, but not to people outside the group **clannishness** /ˈklæn.ɪʃ.nəs/ *noun* [U]

clandestine /klænˈdes.tɪn/ *adj FORMAL* planned or done in secret, especially describing something that is not officially allowed: *The group held weekly clandestine meetings in a church.* ○ *He has been having a clandestine affair with his secretary for three years.* ○ *She undertook several clandestine operations for the CIA.* **clandestinely** /klænˈdes.tɪn.li/ *adv*

clang /klæŋ/ *verb* [I or T] to make a loud deep ringing sound like that of metal being hit, or to cause something to make this sound: *He woke up to hear the sound of bells clanging in the distance.* ○ [+ obj + adj] *She clanged the metal gate shut behind her.* **clang** /klæŋ/ *noun* [C usually sing] *The bell made a resounding clang.*

clanger /ˈklæŋ.əʳ/ [US] /-ɚ/ *noun* [C] *MAINLY UK INFORMAL* something that you say by accident that embarrasses or upsets someone: *Claire* ***dropped*** (= said) *a clanger by joking about his dog that's been dead for three months.*

clank /klæŋk/ *verb* [I or T] to make a short loud sound like that of metal objects hitting each other, or to cause something to make this sound: *My bike chain was clanking in an alarming way as I pedalled along.* ○ *Whenever their team scored a goal, they leapt up and down clanking their beer cans together.* **clank** /klæŋk/ *noun* [C usually sing] *I heard the clank of buckets as they went to milk the cows.*

clansman /ˈklænz.mən/ *noun* [C] a member of a Scottish CLAN

clanswoman /ˈklænzˌwʊm.ən/ *noun* [C] a female member of a Scottish CLAN

clap [MAKE NOISE] /klæp/ *verb* [I or T] **-pp- 1** to make a short loud noise by hitting your hands together: *"When I clap my hands, you must stand still," said the teacher.* ○ *The*

C

band played a familiar tune which had everyone clapping ***along.*** ○ *The audience clapped* ***in time to*** *the music.* **2** to clap your hands repeatedly to show that you like or admire someone or have enjoyed a performance: *The audience clapped and cheered when she stood up to speak.* ○ *We all clapped his performance enthusiastically.*

clap /klæp/ *noun* **1** [S] when you clap your hands continuously to show that you like or admire someone or something: *Let's give* ***a*** *big clap* ***to/for*** *our winning contestant!* **2** [C] a sudden loud noise made by thunder: *There was* ***a*** *clap* ***of*** *thunder and then it started to pour with rain.*

clap [PUT QUICKLY] /klæp/ *verb* [T + adv or prep] **-pp-** to put a person or thing somewhere quickly or suddenly: *She clapped her hand* ***over*** *her mouth to try to stop herself from laughing.* ○ *The police clapped him* ***into/in*** *prison for possession of drugs.*

clap [HIT] /klæp/ *verb* [T + adv or prep] **-pp-** to hit someone lightly on the shoulder or back in a friendly way, especially to express pleasure at what they have done: *He clapped his daughter* ***on*** *the back and told her how proud of her he was.* **clap** /klæp/ *noun* [C] *He gave me a friendly clap* ***on*** *the shoulder and said, "Well done!"*

the clap [DISEASE] /ðə'klæp/ *noun* [S] SLANG FOR **gonorrhoea**: *a nasty dose of the clap*

clapboard /'klæp.bɔːd/ [US] /-bɔːrd/ *noun* **1** [U] US a series of boards fixed horizontally to the outside of a building, with each board partly covering the one below, to protect the building from the weather: *The town of Rockport is full of rows of white clapboard houses.* **2** [C] US FOR **clapperboard**

clapped-out /ˌklæpt'aʊt/ *adj* MAINLY UK INFORMAL **1** describes machines which are old and no longer work well: *She drives a clapped-out old Mini.* **2** describes people who are very tired or unhealthy: *I felt too clapped-out to go to aerobics last night.*

clapper /'klæp.əʳ/ [US] /-ɚ/ *noun* [C] a piece of metal which hangs inside a bell and makes the bell ring when it hits the sides

• **like the clappers** UK OLD-FASHIONED INFORMAL extremely fast: *You'll have to* ***run*** *like the clappers if you want to catch your train.*

clapperboard /'klæp.ə.bɔːd/ [US] /-ɚ.bɔːrd/ *noun* [C] (US USUALLY **clapboard**) SPECIALIZED a device used by people making films, which consists of a board with two parts which are hit together at the start of filming

claptrap /'klæp.træp/ *noun* [U] INFORMAL DISAPPROVING foolish, meaningless talk which should not be believed: *Don't believe a word of what he says. It's just* ***a load of*** *claptrap.*

claret /'klær.ət/ [US] /'kler-/ *noun* **1** [C or U] red wine made in the region near Bordeaux in France **2** [U] a colour that is between dark red and purple

clarify [EXPLAIN] /'klær.ɪ.faɪ/ [US] /'kler-/ *verb* [T] to make something clear or easier to understand by giving more details or a simpler explanation: *Could you clarify the first point please? I don't understand it completely.* ○ *The* ***position*** *of all shareholders will be clarified next month when we finalize our proposals.*

clarification /ˌklær.ɪ.fɪ'keɪ.ʃᵊn/ [US] /ˌkler-/ *noun* [C or U] *Some further clarification* (= explanation) *of your position is needed.*

clarity /'klær.ɪ.ti/ [US] /'kler.ɪ.t̬i/ *noun* [U] **1** the quality of being clear and easy to understand: *There has been a call for greater clarity in this area of the law.* **2** the quality of being easy or see or hear: *She was phoning from Australia, but I was amazed at the clarity of her voice.* **3** the ability to think clearly and not be confused: *He has shown great clarity* ***of mind.*** ○ *mental clarity*

clarify [COOKING] /'klær.ɪ.faɪ/ [US] /'kler-/ *verb* [T] SPECIALIZED to remove water and unwanted substances from fat, such as butter, by heating it **clarified** /'klær.ɪ.faɪd/ [US] /'kler-/ *adj*: *You often use clarified* ***butter*** *when making curry.*

clarinet /ˌklær.ɪ'net/ [US] /ˌkler-/ *noun* [C] a tube-shaped musical instrument which is played by blowing through a single reed and pressing the metal keys to produce different notes

clarinettist, clarinetist /ˌklær.ɪ'net.ɪst/ [US] /ˌkler.ɪ'net̬-/ *noun* [C] a person who plays the clarinet

clarion call /'klær.i.ən,kɔːl/ [US] /'kler.i.ən,kɑːl/ *noun* [C usually sing] LITERARY a very clear message or instruction about what action is needed: *to issue/sound a clarion call* ***for*** *change*

clash [FIGHT] /klæʃ/ *verb* **1** [I usually + adv or prep] to fight or argue: *Students clashed* ***with*** *police after demonstrations at five universities.* ○ *The government and the opposition parties have clashed* ***over*** *the cuts in defence spending.* **2** [I] If two opinions, statements or qualities clash, they are very different from each other: *This latest statement from the White House clashes* ***with*** *important aspects of US foreign policy.*

clash /klæʃ/ *noun* **1** [C] a fight or argument between people: *Rioters hurled rocks and petrol bombs in clashes* ***with*** *police at the weekend.* ○ *There were violent clashes* ***between*** *the police and demonstrators in the city centre.* **2** [C usually sing] a situation in which people's opinions or qualities are very different from and opposed to each other: *a clash of opinions/loyalties/personalities*

clash [COMPETE] /klæʃ/ *verb* [I] If two people or teams clash in a sports competition or race, they compete seriously against each other.

clash /klæʃ/ *noun* [C] a sports competition or race between two people or teams

clash [NOT ATTRACTIVE] /klæʃ/ *verb* [I not continuous] If colours or styles clash, they look ugly or wrong together: *I like red and orange together, though lots of people think they clash.* **clash** /klæʃ/ *noun* [C]

clash [HAPPEN TOGETHER] /klæʃ/ *verb* [I not continuous] UK If two events clash, they happen at the same time in a way that is inconvenient: *Her party clashes* ***with*** *my brother's wedding, so I won't be able to go.* **clash** /klæʃ/ *noun* [C] *In the new timetable, there's a clash* ***between*** *history and physics.*

clash [LOUD NOISE] /klæʃ/ *verb* [I or T] to make a loud metallic noise, or to cause something to make this noise: *The saucepans clashed as he piled them into the sink.* ○ *She clashed the cymbals together.* **clash** /klæʃ/ *noun* [C] *a clash of cymbals*

clasp /klɑːsp/ [US] /klæsp/ *verb* [T] to hold someone or something firmly in your hands or arms: *He was clasping the vase tightly, terrified of dropping it.* ○ *Lie on your back, clasp your knees and pull them down towards your chest.* ○ *She clasped her son* ***in*** *her arms.*

clasp /klɑːsp/ [US] /klæsp/ *noun* **1** [S] a tight hold with your hand or arms: *She held the child's hand in a* ***firm*** *clasp as they crossed the road.* **2** [C] a small metal device which is used to fasten a belt, bag or a piece of jewellery

'clasp ˌknife *noun* [C] (US USUALLY **pocketknife**) a knife with one or more folding blades

class [TEACHING GROUP] /klɑːs/ [US] /klæs/ *group noun* [C] **1** a group of students who are taught together at school, college or university: *Which class are you in this year?* ○ *She gave the whole class extra homework for a week.* ○ *My class* (= The people in my class) *was/were rather noisy this morning.* ○ [as form of address] *Okay, class, settle down and open your books.* **2** a period of time in which students are taught something: *My last class ends at 4 o'clock.* ○ *I was told off for talking* ***in*** *class.* ○ *Who* ***takes/teaches*** *your environmental studies class?* ○ *I missed my aerobics class yesterday.* ○ *Classes have been cancelled today because of a staff meeting.*

class /klɑːs/ [US] /klæs/ *noun* MAINLY US **the class of '98/ '99, etc.** a group of students who successfully completed their studies in a particular year

COMMON LEARNER ERROR

class or classroom?

Class cannot be used to mean the room where a lesson happens. For this meaning you must use **classroom**.

Every classroom in the entire school has its own electronic whiteboard.

~~*Every class in the entire school has its own electronic whiteboard.*~~

class [ECONOMIC GROUP] /klɑːs/ [US] /klæs/ *noun* [C or U] a group of people within society who have the same economic and social position: *The Labour Party has lost a lot of* *support among the **working** class.* ○ *She belongs to the rich American **upper** class.* ○ *We live in a **middle** class neighbourhood.* ○ *She comes from an **upper middle** class background.* ○ *He was a member of the **ruling** classes.* ○ *She's studying the class **structure** of Japan.* ➲See also **underclass**.

classless /ˈklɑː.sləs/ [US] /ˈklæs.ləs/ *adj* **1** not belonging to a particular social class: *Her accent is classless.* **2** having no different social classes: *The prime minister claims that he wants to create a classless **society**.*

class [RANK] /klɑːs/ [US] /klæs/ *noun* [C] **1** a group into which goods, services or people are put according to their standard: *Whenever I travel by train, I always travel **first** class.* ○ ***first/second** class mail* ○ *a **business/economy** class ticket* ○ *All the vegetables we sell are Class A.* ○ *When it comes to mathematics, he's in **a different** class **to** his peers.* **2** UK in Britain, the standard which someone has reached in their university degree: *What class of degree did you get?* ○ *He graduated with a second-class honours degree in physics.*

• **be in a class of *your* own** to be the best at a particular activity: *As a long-distance runner, she's in a class of her own.*

• **be in a class by itself/of its own** to be something of such a high quality that nothing can be compared to it

• **be out of *your* class** to be much better at doing something than you: *I can't play chess with him. He's completely out of my class!*

class /klɑːs/ [US] /klæs/ *verb* [T] to consider someone or something to belong to a particular group because of their qualities: *I'm 17, but I'm still classed **as** a child when I travel by bus.* ○ *I would class her **among/with** the top ten American novelists.*

class /klɑːs/ [US] /klæs/ *adj* INFORMAL very good: *a class act* ○ *He's a class golfer.*

class [STYLE] /klɑːs/ [US] /klæs/ *noun* [U] the quality of being stylish or fashionable: *She's got real class.* **classy** /ˈklɑː.si/ [US] /ˈklæs.i/ *adj*: *That's one classy vehicle you've got there.*

class [BIOLOGY] /klɑːs/ [US] /klæs/ *noun* [C] SPECIALIZED a group of related plants or animals, in the general CLASSIFICATION of plants and animals

class-conscious /ˈklɑːs.kɒn.tʃəs/ [US] /ˈklæs.kɑːn-/ *adj* very aware of the differences between the various social classes or of belonging to a particular social class: *America is perceived of as being less class-conscious than Britain.*

classic [HIGH QUALITY] /ˈklæs.ɪk/ *adj* **1** having a high quality or standard against which other things are judged: *Have you ever read Fielding's classic **novel** 'Tom Jones'?* ○ *Another classic goal there from Corley!* **2** INFORMAL extremely or unusually funny, bad or annoying: *Then she fell over backwards into the flowerbed – it was absolutely classic!* ○ *That was classic! That van-driver signalled right, and then turned left.* ➲See also **classic** TYPICAL.

classic /ˈklæs.ɪk/ *noun* [C] a piece of writing, a musical recording or a film which is well-known and of a high standard and lasting value: *Jane Austen's 'Pride and Prejudice' is a classic **of** English literature.* ○ *Many of the Rolling Stones' records have become rock classics.* ➲See also **the classics**.

classic [TRADITIONAL] /ˈklæs.ɪk/ *adj* having a simple, traditional style which is always fashionable: *She wore a classic navy suit.*

classic /ˈklæs.ɪk/ *noun* [C] a piece of clothing which is always fashionable: *A long wool coat is a classic no wardrobe should be without.*

classical /ˈklæs.ɪ.kəl/ *adj* describes something that is attractive because it has a simple, traditional style: *I love the classical lines of his dress designs.* ➲See also **classical**. **classically** /ˈklæs.ɪ.kli/ *adv*: *a classically beautiful face*

classic [TYPICAL] /ˈklæs.ɪk/ *adj* **1** having all the characteristics or qualities that you expect: *He's a classic **example** of a kid who's clever but lazy.* ○ *He had all the classic **symptoms** of the disease.* **2** INFORMAL DISAPPROVING bad or unpleasant, but not particularly surprising or unexpected: *It's classic – you arrive at the station on time and find that the train's left early.*

classically /ˈklæs.ɪ.kli/ *adv*: *The dress combines stylish lines with an attractive floral print for a classically feminine look.*

classical [CULTURE] /ˈklæs.ɪ.kəl/ *adj* belonging to or relating to the culture of ancient Rome and Greece: *the classical world* ○ *classical literature* ➲See also **classics**; **classicism**; **neoclassical**.

classical [MUSIC] /ˈklæs.ɪ.kəl/ *adj* describes music that is considered to be part of a long especially formal tradition and to be of lasting value: *Do you prefer classical music like Mozart and Mahler, or pop?*

classical [TRADITIONAL] /ˈklæs.ɪ.kəl/ *adj* traditional in style or form, or based on methods developed over a long period of time: *Does she study classical ballet or modern ballet?* ○ *He is one of our greatest classical actors.* **classically** /ˈklæs.ɪ.kli/ *adv*: *She is a classically trained dancer.*

Classicism /ˈklæs.ɪ.sɪ.zəm/ *noun* [U] SPECIALIZED a style in painting, sculpture and building, based on particular standards in Greek and Roman art, which was especially popular during the 18th and 19th centuries in Europe: *Ingres and Delacroix were two famous exponents of Classicism.* ➲See also **neoclassicism**. Compare **romanticism**.

classics /ˈklæs.ɪks/ *noun* [U] the study of ancient Greek and Roman culture, especially their languages and literature: *She **studied/read** classics at Cambridge.* ○ *a classics scholar.* ➲See also **classical** CULTURE.

classicist /ˈklæs.ɪ.sɪst/ *noun* [C] a person who studies ancient Greek or Roman culture

the 'classics *plural noun* the most famous works of literature: *I spent my childhood **reading** the classics.*

classified /ˈklæs.ɪ.faɪd/ *adj* describes information that is officially stated to be secret: *These documents contain classified **material**.*

ˌclassified 'ad *noun* [C] (ALSO **classified**) INFORMAL a small advertisement that you put in a newspaper or a magazine, usually because you want to sell or buy something or to find or offer a job

classify /ˈklæs.ɪ.faɪ/ *verb* [T] to divide things into groups according to their type: *The books in the library are classified **by/according to** subject.* ○ *Biologists classify animals and plants **into** different groups.* **classifiable** /ˈklæs.ɪ.faɪ.ə.bl̩/ *adj* **classification** /ˌklæs.ɪ.fɪˈkeɪ.ʃən/ *noun* [C or U] *Do you understand the system of classification used in ornithology?*

classmate /ˈklɑːs.meɪt/ [US] /ˈklæs-/ *noun* [C] someone who is in the same class as you at school

classroom /ˈklɑːs.ruːm/ /-rʊm/ [US] /ˈklæs-/ *noun* [C] a room in a school or college where groups of students are taught

• **in the classroom** **1** being taught by a teacher: *Students learning computer studies spend two days each week in a computer lab and four days in the classroom.* **2** teaching CLASSES of students in school or college: *There are also no promotions within the school, so that teachers remain in the classroom throughout their careers.*

ˌclass 'struggle *noun* [S or U] in MARXISM, a continuing fight between the CAPITALIST class and the working class for political and economic power

classy /ˈklɑː.si/ [US] /ˈklæs.i/ *adj* ➲See at **class** STYLE

clatter /ˈklæt.əʳ/ [US] /ˈklæt̬.ɚ/ *verb* [I or T] to make continuous loud noises by hitting hard objects against each other, or to cause objects to do this: *Don't clatter the dishes – you'll wake the baby up.* ○ *He was clattering **away** on his old typewriter.* **clatter** /ˈklæt.əʳ/ [US] /ˈklæt̬.ɚ/ *noun* [S] *the clatter of dishes in the kitchen*

clause [GRAMMAR] /klɔːz/ [US] /klɑːz/ *noun* [C] SPECIALIZED a group of words, consisting of a subject and a FINITE form of a verb (= the form that shows the tense and subject of the verb), which might or might not be a sentence: *In the sentence 'I can't cook very well but I make quite good omelettes', both 'I can't cook very well' and 'I make quite good omelettes' are **main/independent** clauses* (= they are of equal importance and could each exist as a separate sentence). ○ *In the sentence 'I'll get you some stamps if I go to town', 'if I go to town' is a **subordinate/dependent** clause* (= it is not equal to the main part of the sentence and could not exist as a separate sentence).

clause [LEGAL DOCUMENT] /klɔːz/ [US] /klɑːz/ *noun* [C] *SPECIALIZED* a particular part of a written legal document, for example a law passed by Parliament or a CONTRACT (= an agreement): *They have* ***added/deleted/ amended*** *a clause in the contract which says the company can make people redundant for economic reasons.* ○ *Clause 4 of the constitution is thought to be the most important section.*

C

claustrophobia /ˌklɒs.trəˈfəʊ.bi.ə/ [US] /ˌklɑː.strəˈfoʊ-/ *noun* [U] fear of being in enclosed spaces: *He* ***suffers from*** *claustrophobia so he never travels on underground trains.* ➲Compare **agoraphobia**.

claustrophobic /ˌklɒs.trəˈfəʊ.bɪk/ [US] /ˌklɑː.strəˈfoʊ-/ *adj* **1** describes a place which is small and enclosed, and makes you feel uncomfortable when you are in it: *My room's a bit claustrophobic.* **2** *SPECIALIZED* describes a person suffering from a fear of being in enclosed spaces

claustrophobic /ˌklɒs.trəˈfəʊ.bɪk/ [US] /ˌklɑː.strəˈfoʊ-/ *noun* [C] *SPECIALIZED* a claustrophobic person

clavichord /ˈklæv.ɪ.kɔːd/ [US] /-kɔːrd/ *noun* [C] an early keyboard instrument in which the strings are hit by pieces of metal when the keys are pressed

clavicle /ˈklæv.ɪ.kl/ *noun* [C] *SPECIALIZED FOR* **collarbone** ➲See picture **The Body** on page Centre 5

claw /klɔː/ [US] /klɑː/ *noun* [C] **1** one of the sharp curved nails at the end of each of the toes of some animals and birds: *Our cat likes to* ***sharpen*** *her claws on the legs of the dining table.* ➲See picture **Animals and Birds** on page Centre 4 **2** one of the two pointed parts, used for holding things, at the end of the legs of some insects and sea creatures: *Keep your fingers away from the crab's claws when you pick it up.*

• **get** ***your*** **claws into** ***sb*** *INFORMAL DISAPPROVING* **1** to find a way of influencing or controlling someone: *If the loan company gets its claws into you, you'll still be paying off this debt when you're 50.* **2** If a woman gets her claws into a man, she manages to start a relationship with him, often because she wants to control him or get something from him: *If she gets her claws into that young man, she'll ruin his political career.*

claw /klɔː/ [US] /klɑː/ *verb* [I or T] to use claws to tear something or someone: *He was seriously injured when one of the lions clawed his back.* ○ *When our cat is hungry, she starts clawing* ***at*** *my legs.*

• **claw** ***your*** **way** ***(somewhere)*** to move forwards with difficulty, especially by using stiff curved fingers to remove the things that are in your way: *The rescuers could hear the sound of the trapped people desperately trying to claw their way* ***through*** *the rubble.* ○ *FIGURATIVE Sidney ruthlessly clawed his way* ***(up) from*** *the position of junior clerk* ***to*** *chairman of the company* (= He achieved success with effort and by hurting other people).

▲ **claw** ***sth*** **back** *phrasal verb* [M] **1** to obtain possession of something again with difficulty: *The airline is beginning to claw back some of the business it lost after the bomb explosion.* **2** *MAINLY UK* If the government, for example, claws back money, it takes money back in one way that it has already given in another way: *We got a government grant for setting up our business, but they clawed it all back again in taxes.*

clay /kleɪ/ *noun* [U] thick, heavy earth that is soft when wet, and hard when dry or baked, used for making bricks and containers

clayey /ˈkleɪ.i/ *adj* containing a lot of clay: *clayey soil*

ˌclay ˈpigeon *noun* [C] a disc made of clay which is fired into the air to be shot at for sport: *clay-pigeon shooting*

clean [NOT DIRTY] /kliːn/ *adj* not dirty: *a clean white shirt* ○ *clean air/water* ○ *Make sure your hands are clean before you have your dinner.* ○ *Hospitals need to be kept* ***spotlessly*** (= extremely) *clean.*

• **(as) clean as a (new) pin** (*ALSO* **(as) clean as a whistle**) *OLD-FASHIONED* extremely clean

• **ˌclean bill of ˈhealth** *INFORMAL* **1** when a doctor says that someone is healthy: *He's been* ***given*** *a clean bill of health by the doctor.* **2** when someone in authority says that a particular thing is in good condition: *Of 30 countries inspected for airline safety, only 17 received a clean bill of health.*

clean /kliːn/ *verb* **1** [T] to remove dirt from something: *I'm going to clean the windows this morning.* ○ *You should always clean your teeth after meals.* ○ *Would you clean the fingermarks* ***from/off*** *the door?* ○ *He asked her to help him clean* ***out*** *the stables.* ➲See also **clean up** MAKE CLEAN. **2** [I usually + adv or prep] to become clean: *This carpet doesn't clean very well.* ○ *I hope these bloodstains will clean* ***off*** *my shirt.* **3** [T] to prepare a fish or an animal killed for food by removing the inside parts of it that are not eaten

clean /kliːn/ *noun* [S] when something is cleaned: *These windows need a really thorough clean.* ➲See also **clean up** MAKE CLEAN.

cleaner /ˈkliː.nəʳ/ [US] /-nɚ/ *noun* **1** [C] a person whose job is to clean houses, offices, public places, etc: *Chris has an evening job as an office cleaner.* **2** [C or U] a substance used for cleaning things: *We've run out of floor cleaner.*

cleaner's /ˈkliː.nəz/ [US] /-nɚz/ *noun* [C] *plural* **cleaners** a shop where clothes that cannot be washed in an ordinary washing machine are cleaned: *Could you pick up my suit from the cleaner's for me, please?* ➲See also **dry cleaner's**.

• **take** ***sb*** **to the cleaner's** *INFORMAL* **1** to get a lot of money from someone, usually by cheating them: *Paul was really taken to the cleaner's* ***on*** *that deal.* **2** to defeat someone by a very large amount: *In the second half, United were really taken to the cleaner's, and they finally lost the match 6-1.*

cleaning /ˈkliː.nɪŋ/ *noun* [U] when you remove the dirt from things and places, especially in a house: *It's your turn to* ***do the*** *cleaning.* ○ *Joan has a cleaning job.*

cleanness /ˈkliːn.nəs/ *noun* [U] how clean something is ➲See also **cleanliness**.

clean [HONEST] /kliːn/ *adj* **1** honest or fair, or showing that you have not done anything illegal: *a good clean* ***fight/ contest*** ○ *The judge took the defendant's clean* ***record*** (= the absence of previous involvement in crime) *into account when passing sentence.* ○ *I've always had a clean* ***driving licence.*** **2** *SLANG* not doing anything illegal, or not having or carrying illegal drugs or stolen goods: *The police busted Pete last night, but he was clean.*

• **come clean** to tell the truth about something that you have been keeping secret: *I thought it was time to come clean* ***(with*** *everybody)* ***about*** *what I'd been doing.*

• **make a clean breast of it** to tell the truth about something: *Julia finally made a clean breast of it and admitted that she had stolen the money.*

cleanly /ˈkliːn.li/ *adv* fairly and honestly: *The election campaign was not conducted very cleanly.*

clean [MORAL] /kliːn/ *adj* **1** morally acceptable: *It's all* ***good*** *clean* ***fun.*** ○ *clean* ***living*** **2** not about sex: *Can't you think of any clean* ***jokes?***

• **clean up** ***your*** **act** to start to obey certain laws or generally accepted standards of behaviour: *You're going to have to clean up your act if you're serious about keeping your job.*

clean [NOT ROUGH] /kliːn/ *adj* having no rough edges, and smooth, straight or equally balanced: *I've broken my leg, but the doctor says that it's a clean* ***break,*** *so it should heal easily.* ○ *A good clean hit from Botham sent the ball straight out to the boundary.* ○ *What he liked about the car was its clean* ***lines.*** ○ *I tried to make a clean* ***cut,*** *but the knife wasn't sharp enough.*

cleanly /ˈkliːn.li/ *adv* **1** with smooth straight edges: *The plate* ***broke*** *cleanly in half.* **2** equally: *Opinions were* ***split*** *cleanly between men and women.*

clean [COMPLETE] /kliːn/ *adj* [before n] complete: *It's better for both of us if we* ***make a*** *clean* ***break (of it)*** (= end our relationship completely). ○ *Sara says she needs a clean* ***break with*** *the past.* ○ *The new prime minister is expected to* ***make a*** *clean* ***sweep*** (= a complete change) **of** *the government.*

clean /kliːn/ *adv* completely: *I clean* ***forgot*** *that I was supposed to be meeting Lucy last night.* ○ *He's been cheating his customers for years, and* ***getting*** *clean* ***away*** *with it.* ○ *The bullet went clean* ***through*** *his shoulder.*

clean [NOTHING ON] /kliːn/ *adj* [before n] When something you write on is clean, there is nothing on it or it is not

yet used: *Take a clean sheet of paper.*
● **a clean sheet/slate** INFORMAL when people decide to forget your past behaviour, usually because it was not good: *You were very lazy last term, but we'll start again with a clean sheet this term.* ➔See also **wipe the slate clean** at **wipe**.

PHRASAL VERBS WITH **clean** ▼

▲ **clean** *sth* **out** CLEAN *phrasal verb* [M] to take everything out of a room, car, container, etc. and clean the inside of it: *I found these photos while I was cleaning out my cupboards.*

▲ **clean** *sb/sth* **out** STEAL *phrasal verb* [M] INFORMAL to use or steal all of someone's money or space: *Buying our new house has completely cleaned us out.* ○ *Richard came home for the weekend and completely cleaned us out of food.* ○ *The burglars cleaned out the shop.*

▲ **clean** *sb/sth* **up** MAKE CLEAN *phrasal verb* [M] to make a person or place clean and tidy: *We'll go out as soon as I've cleaned up the kitchen.* ○ *I need to clean up (= myself or the place where I am) before we go out.* ○ [R] *Clean yourself up a bit before dinner.*
clean-up /ˈkliːn/ *noun* [S] *It's time you gave your bedroom a good clean-up.* ○ *Residents have called for a clean-up campaign to keep their streets free from rubbish.*

▲ **clean** *(sth)* **up** MONEY *phrasal verb* [M] SLANG to win a lot of money: *We cleaned up at the poker table last night.*

▲ **clean** *sth* **up** CRIME *phrasal verb* [M] to stop illegal or dishonest activity in a place or organization: *We need a mayor who is tough enough to clean up this town.*

▲ **clean** *sth* **up** LIMIT IMMORAL BEHAVIOUR *phrasal verb* [M] to stop or limit the violence, sex or immoral behaviour shown or contained in programmes or books, magazines, etc., to make them more acceptable: *Some people think that television should be cleaned up.*

▲ **clean up after** *sb* to remove dirt or problems that someone has made: *I'm fed up with cleaning up after you all the time.*

ˌclean ˈbowled *adj* [after v] If you are clean bowled in the sport of cricket, the ball touches the WICKET without you hitting it.

clean-cut /ˌkliːnˈkʌt/ *adj* APPROVING describes a man who is tidy in appearance and behaves well: *Julie's fiancé is a nice clean-cut young man.*

clean-limbed /ˌkliːnˈlɪmd/ *adj* APPROVING healthy-looking and active: *The school sports field swarmed with clean-limbed young people eager for the day's events.*

cleanliness /ˈklen.lɪ.nəs/ *noun* [U] the state of being clean, or the practice of keeping things clean

cleanse /klenz/ *verb* [T] **1** to make something completely clean: *Cleanse the cut/wound thoroughly before you bandage it.* **2** to make someone or something morally clean or pure: *to cleanse the thoughts of our hearts* ○ *Roman Catholics go to confession to be cleansed of their sins.* ○ FIGURATIVE *The mayor has promised to cleanse the city of drug dealers* (= to remove them from the city).

cleanser /ˈklen.zəʳ/ US /-zɚ/ *noun* [C or U] a substance used for cleaning, especially your face: *I use cleanser on my face every night.* ○ *Kitchen cleansers are all more or less the same.*

cleansing /ˈklen.zɪŋ/ *adj* [before n] describes something that cleans or is used for cleaning: *a cleansing cream/lotion*

clean-shaven /ˌkliːnˈʃeɪ.vʲən/ *adj* describes a man who has no hair on the lower part of his face

clear ABLE TO BE UNDERSTOOD /klɪəʳ/ US /klɪr/ *adj* easy to understand, hear, read or see: *clear instructions/directions* ○ *Can we make the sound any clearer?* ○ *These books have lovely clear print.* ○ *Our new television has a very clear picture.*
● **(as) clear as a bell** very easy to hear: *Clear as a bell, from the back of the theatre came a child's voice saying, "I want to go home".*
● **(as) clear as day** very easy to understand: *The instructions were as clear as day.*
● **(as) clear as mud** HUMOROUS very difficult to understand: *His instructions were as clear as mud.*
● **Do I make myself clear?** (ALSO **Is that clear?**) something you say in order to emphasize what you have just said,

or to express your authority: *I will not tolerate this behaviour any longer. Do I make myself clear?*
clearly /ˈklɪə.li/ US /ˈklɪr-/ *adv* in a way that is easy to see, hear, read or understand

clear CERTAIN /klɪəʳ/ US /klɪr/ *adj* certain, having no doubt, or obvious: *He isn't at all clear about what he wants to do with his life.* ○ [+ *that*] *It is rapidly becoming clear (to me) (that) I'm not suited to being a teacher.* ○ [+ question word] *It isn't clear how long the strike will go on for.* ○ *It's a clear case of corruption.* ○ *You've made your position quite clear* (= there is no doubt about what you think).
● **(as) clear as day** certain: *It's as clear as day that the government is going to win the election.*
clearly /ˈklɪə.li/ US /ˈklɪr-/ *adv* used to show that you think something is obvious or certain: *The accident was clearly the lorry driver's fault.* ○ *Clearly, you should tell her the truth.*

clear NOT CONFUSED /klɪəʳ/ US /klɪr/ *adj* free from confusion; able to think quickly and well: *Marie is good at making decisions because she's a very clear thinker.*
clear /klɪəʳ/ US /klɪr/ *verb* [T] *I need to get some fresh air to clear my head* (= to make me able to think well).
clearly /ˈklɪə.li/ US /ˈklɪr-/ *adv* When you think clearly, you are not confused.

clear NOT GUILTY /klɪəʳ/ US /klɪr/ *adj* free from guilt: *to have a clear conscience*
● **be in the clear** to not be guilty of a crime: *The police breathalysed Andy last night, but he was in the clear.*
clear /klɪəʳ/ US /klɪr/ *verb* [T] to prove that someone is not guilty of something that they were accused of: *After many years in prison, the men were finally cleared of the bombings.*

clear NOT TROUBLED /klɪəʳ/ US /klɪr/ *adj* [after v] not troubled; without difficulties: *This is the first time in his life that he's been clear of* (= without) *debt.*
● **be in the clear** to have no problems after being in a difficult situation: *The X-rays showed that she's in the clear.*
clear /klɪəʳ/ US /klɪr/ *verb* **clear your debts/clear yourself of debts** to pay back all the money that you owe

clear NOT BLOCKED /klɪəʳ/ US /klɪr/ *adj* **1** not covered or blocked by anything: *We have a clear view of the ocean from our hotel window.* ○ *The journey was quite quick because the road was clear* (= there was not much traffic on it). ○ *I always like to leave my desk clear* (= with no work on it) *at the end of the day.* **2** not busy or filled by any planned activity: *The only time I have clear next week is Tuesday afternoon.* ○ *We've got two clear* (= whole) *weeks in which to finish the decorating.*
clear /klɪəʳ/ US /klɪr/ *verb* [I or T] to remove or get rid of whatever is blocking or filling something, or to stop being blocked or full: *It took several hours to clear the road after the accident.* ○ *I'll make the coffee if you'll clear the table.* ○ *If you use this nasal spray, your nose should clear a bit.* ○ *After my aunt died, we arranged for her house to be cleared* (= for the furniture to be removed from it). ○ *If you press this key, the computer screen will clear* (= the text and pictures will be removed from it). ○ *Shops are currently holding sales to clear their summer stock* (= get rid of goods by selling them cheaply). ○ *Paul helped his elderly neighbour by clearing her path of snow/clearing snow from her path.* ○ *Could you clear your things off/from the sofa?* ○ *I never leave work until I've cleared my in-tray* (= have finished the work that needs to be done).
● **clear the decks** INFORMAL to remove unnecessary things so that you are ready for action: *Let's clear the decks and then we can start cooking dinner.*
● **clear your throat** to give a small cough: *She cleared her throat nervously before she began to speak.*
● **clear the way** to make it possible for something to happen: *We've got a loan from the bank which has cleared the way for us to buy a house.*
clearance /ˈklɪə.rɒnts/ US /ˈklɪr.ʲənts/ *noun* [S or U] **1** when waste or things you do not want are removed from a place: *house/slum clearance* **2** when goods are offered for sale cheaply so that people will be encouraged to buy them and there will be space for new goods: *We bought our new carpet at a clearance sale.*

C

clearing /ˈklɪə.rɪŋ/ (US) /ˈklɪr.ɪŋ/ *noun* [C] an area in a wood or forest from which trees and bushes have been removed

clear [PURE] /klɪəʳ/ (US) /klɪr/ *adj* **1** not cloudy, foggy or marked, but pure or easy to see through: *clear glass* ○ *The* ***water*** *in the lake is so clear that you can see the bottom.* ○ *We could see hundreds of stars in the clear desert* ***sky****.* ○ *She has a beautifully clear* ***skin/ complexion*** (= with no marks or spots). ○ *The* ***weather*** *is expected to remain clear for the next few days.* ○ *You can see the mountains from here on a clear* ***day****.* **2** describes a pleasant, pure sound: *the clear sound of the flute* **3** describes something that you remember easily: *I have clear* ***memories*** *of visiting my grandfather's farm as a child.*

clear /klɪəʳ/ (US) /klɪr/ *verb* [I or T] to become clear or make something clear: *The children enjoyed stirring the mud at the bottom of the pond, then watching the water slowly clear* (= become easy to see through) *again.* ○ *Your skin would clear* (= become free of spots) *if you had a healthier diet.* ○ *After the thunderstorm, the sky cleared* (= stopped being cloudy). ○ *The fog is expected to have cleared* ***(away)*** (= gone) *by midday.*

• **clear the air 1** to make the air cooler, fresher and more comfortable: *The rain has helped clear the air.* **2** to remove the bad feelings between people: *I had a massive argument with Sue yesterday, but at least it has cleared the air.*

clear [LEFT] /klɪəʳ/ (US) /klɪr/ *adj* describes a sum of money that is left after all necessary payments have been made: *The school summer fair made a clear* ***profit*** *of £500.* ○ *Bill earns a clear $200 a week/earns $200 a week clear.*

clear /klɪəʳ/ (US) /klɪr/ *verb* [T] *Bill clears $200 a week* (= has $200 left each week after he has paid taxes and all other necessary payments).

clear [NOT TOUCHING] /klɪəʳ/ (US) /klɪr/ *adj* not touching something, or away from something: *Only one competitor made a clear jump of the highest fence* (= jumped over it without touching it). ○ *When we're clear* ***of*** *the main road, we'll stop for our picnic.*

clear /klɪəʳ/ (US) /klɪr/ *adv* not touching, or away from: *Stand clear* ***of*** *the doors, please.* ○ *Make sure you park clear* ***of*** *the kerb.* ○ *The children were saved from the fire only because a neighbour pulled them clear.*

• **steer/stay/keep clear** to avoid something or someone: *His parents warned him to steer clear* ***of*** *trouble.*

clearance /ˈklɪə.rənts/ (US) /ˈklɪr.ᵊnts/ *noun* [C or U] the distance or space that is needed for one thing to avoid touching another thing: *It was difficult getting the piano through the doorway because we only had a clearance* ***of*** *a few centimetres.* ○ *High vehicles must take an alternative route because of* ***low*** *clearance under the bridge.*

clear /klɪəʳ/ (US) /klɪr/ *verb* [T] to jump or go over something without touching it: *The horse cleared the fence with inches to spare.*

clear [CHEQUE] /klɪəʳ/ (US) /klɪr/ *verb* [I or T] to (cause a cheque to) go from one bank to another through a central organization, so that money can be paid to the person to whom it is owed: *It usually takes four to five working days for a cheque to clear.* **clearance** /ˈklɪə.rənts/ (US) /ˈklɪr.ᵊnts/ *noun* [U] *Clearance (of a cheque) can take up to a week.*

clear [OFFICIAL PERMISSION] /klɪəʳ/ (US) /klɪr/ *verb* [T] **1** to give official permission for something: *Despite local opposition, the plans for the new supermarket have been cleared by the council.* ○ *Ladies and gentlemen, air-traffic control has now cleared the plane* ***for*** *take-off.* ○ *I don't know if I can get the car tonight – I'll have to clear it* ***with*** *Mum.* **2** to satisfy the official conditions of something: *Before you can enter the country, you have to clear* ***customs****.*

clearance /ˈklɪə.rənts/ (US) /ˈklɪr.ᵊnts/ *noun* [U] when you have official permission for something or have satisfied the official conditions of something: *The plane will be taking off as soon as it gets clearance.* ○ *To visit the prison, you'll need* ***security*** *clearance.*

PHRASAL VERBS WITH **clear**

▲ **clear *sth* away** *phrasal verb* [M] to make a place tidy by removing things from it or putting them where they should be: *I want you to clear all these toys away before bedtime.*

▲ **clear *sb* off *sth*** *phrasal verb* to make someone go away from somewhere: *The police used dogs to clear the campers off the village green.*

▲ **clear off** *phrasal verb* used to tell someone to go away in a rude way: *"Clear off or I'll call the police!"*

▲ **clear *sth* out** [TIDY] *phrasal verb* [M] to tidy a place by getting rid of things that you do not want: *If we clear out the spare room, you can use it as a study.*

clear-out /ˈklɪə.raʊt/ (US) /ˈklɪr.aʊt/ *noun* [C usually sing] MAINLY UK *We need to give the garage a* ***good*** *clear-out* (= to tidy it and get rid of the things in it that are no longer wanted).

▲ **clear out** [LEAVE] *phrasal verb* INFORMAL to leave a place: *I hear Daphne's finally told her husband to clear out* (= to leave home). ○ *My landlord's given me a week to clear out* ***of*** *my flat.*

▲ **clear *(sth)* up** [PLACE] *phrasal verb* [M] MAINLY UK to make a place tidy by removing things from it or putting them where they should be: *Dad was clearing up in the kitchen.* ○ *I'm tired of always having to clear up* ***after*** *you* (= tidy your things).

▲ **clear *sth* up** [PROBLEM] *phrasal verb* [M] to give or find an explanation for something, or to deal with a problem or argument: *They never cleared up the* ***mystery*** *of the missing money.* ○ *After twenty years, the case has finally been cleared up.*

▲ **clear *(sth)* up** [ILLNESS] *phrasal verb* If an illness clears up, or if medicine clears an illness up, the illness goes away: *You won't be able to go swimming tomorrow if your cold hasn't cleared up.* ○ *These pills should clear your rash up.*

▲ **clear up** [WEATHER] *phrasal verb* INFORMAL If the weather clears up, the cloud and rain disappears: *I hope it clears up in time for the picnic.*

clear-cut /ˌklɪəˈkʌt/ (US) /ˌklɪr-/ *adj* clear or obvious without needing any evidence or proof: *She has clear-cut evidence that the company cheated her.*

ˌclear ˈhead *noun* [C usually sing] the ability to think clearly: *I won't have another drink, thanks. I need to* ***have a*** *clear head for my meeting in the morning.*

clear-headed /ˌklɪəˈhed.ɪd/ (US) /ˌklɪr-/ *adj* able to think clearly

ˈclearing ˌbank *noun* [C] a bank which exchanges cheques with other banks through a central organization called a **clearing house**

ˈclearing ˌhouse *noun* [C] a central office used by banks to collect and send out money and cheques

clear-sighted /ˌklɪəˈsaɪt.ɪd/ (US) /ˌklɪr-/ *adj* having a good understanding of a particular subject and the ability to make good judgements about it: *Simon has a clear-sighted vision of the company's future.*

clearway /ˈklɪə.weɪ/ (US) /ˈklɪr-/ *noun* [C] UK a road on which you are only allowed to stop if your car stops working

cleat /kliːt/ *noun* [C] **1** US FOR **stud** BOOT **2** US a boot that is worn for playing football, baseball, etc.

cleavage [BODY AREA] /ˈkliː.vɪdʒ/ *noun* [C or U] the narrow space between a woman's breasts, that is seen when she wears a piece of clothing which does not cover the top of them: *Clare was wearing a low-cut dress which showed off her cleavage.*

cleavage [DISAGREEMENT] /ˈkliː.vɪdʒ/ *noun* [C or U] FORMAL (a) division or disagreement: *There is a marked cleavage* ***between*** *the parties about the government's defence policy.*

cleave /kliːv/ *verb* [I] **cleaved** or US ALSO **clove**, **cleaved** or **cloven** LITERARY OR OLD USE to separate or divide, or cause something to separate or divide, often violently: *With one blow of the knight's axe, he clove the rock* ***in twain*** (= into two pieces).

cleaver /ˈkliː.vəʳ/ (US) /-vɚ/ *noun* [C] a heavy knife with a large square blade: *a meat cleaver*

▲ **cleave to *sth*** *phrasal verb* LITERARY **1** to stick or hold firmly onto something: *The ancient ivy cleaved to the ruined castle walls.* **2** to continue to believe firmly in something: *People in the remote mountain villages still cleave to their old traditions.*

clef /klef/ *noun* [C] a sign put at the beginning of a line of music to show how high or low the notes are: *the bass/treble/alto clef*

cleft /kleft/ *noun* [C] an opening or crack, especially in a rock or the ground: *Eagles often nest in a cleft **in** the rocks.*

ˌcleft ˈlip *noun* [C] an upper lip which does not join in the middle because it did not develop normally before birth: *Bobby was born with a cleft lip.*

ˌcleft ˈpalate *noun* [C] an opening in the top of the mouth caused when a baby does not develop normally before it is born

ˌcleft ˈstick *noun* UK **be in a cleft stick** to be in a situation where it is very difficult to decide what to do, usually because both of your two choices of action would cause problems: *UN troops are in a cleft stick: something has to be done for the civilian population, yet to retaliate would surely be the spark to ignite all-out war.*

clematis /ˈklem.ə.tɪs/ [US] /-t̬əs/ *noun* [C or U] *plural* **clematis** a climbing plant with flat white, pink or purple flowers

clemency /ˈklem.ənt.si/ *noun* [U] FORMAL kindness when giving a punishment: *The jury passed a verdict of guilty, with an appeal to the judge for clemency.*

clement /ˈklem.ᵊnt/ *adj* FORMAL describes weather which is pleasant or not severe: *It's very clement for the time of year.* **clemency** /ˈklem.ənt.si/ *noun* [U]

clementine /ˈklem.ən.tiːn/ *noun* [C] a fruit like a small orange

clench /klentʃ/ *verb* [T] to close or hold something very tightly, often in a determined or angry way: *The old man clenched his **fist** and waved it angrily at us.* ○ *With a knife clenched **in/between** his teeth, he climbed up the tree to cut some coconuts.* ○ *"Get out of here," she said through clenched **teeth**.*

clergy /ˈklɜː.dʒi/ [US] /ˈklɝː-/ *plural noun* priests, especially in the Christian Church: *We were surprised when he announced he wanted to **join the** clergy* (= become a priest).

clergyman /ˈklɜː.dʒɪ.mən/ [US] /ˈklɝː-/ *noun* [C] a man who is a member of the clergy

clergywoman /ˈklɜː.dʒɪˌwʊm.ən/ [US] /ˈklɝː-/ *noun* [C] a woman who is a member of the clergy

cleric /ˈkler.ɪk/ *noun* [C] a priest: *a Buddhist/Catholic/Muslim cleric*

ˌclerical ˈcollar *noun* [C] a stiff white piece of material that is worn round the neck as part of a priest's clothing

clerk /klɑːk/ [US] /klɝːk/ *noun* [C] **1** a person who works in an office, dealing with records or performing general office duties: *a **filing** clerk* ○ *a junior **office** clerk* **2** US a hotel employee who welcomes the guests on arrival: *The **(desk)** clerk checked us in and gave us our key.* **3** US someone who sells things in a shop: *Take your purchases to the **(sales)** clerk, and he will wrap them for you.*

clerk /klɑːk/ [US] /klɝːk/ *verb* [I] *Debbie has a summer job clerking* (= working as a clerk) *in an office.*

clerical /ˈkler.ɪ.kᵊl/ *adj* relating to work done in an office: *a clerical **job*** (= a job performing general office duties). ○ *a clerical **error*** (= a mistake made in the office)

clever /ˈklev.əʳ/ [US] /-ɚ/ *adj* **1** having or showing the ability to learn and understand things quickly and easily: *Judy has never been very clever, but she tries hard.* ○ *Fiona is very clever **at** physics.* ○ *Charlie has a clever **idea/plan** for getting us out of our present difficulties.* **2** skilful: *My mother is very clever **with** her hands.* **3** well-designed: *I've got a clever little gadget for opening jars.*

• **clever dick/clogs** UK INFORMAL DISAPPROVING someone who shows that they are clever, in a way which annoys other people: *If you're such a clever dick, you finish the crossword puzzle.*

• **be too clever by half** to be too confident of your own intelligence in a way that annoys other people: *She was too clever by half – always correcting the teacher or coming back with a smart answer.*

cleverly /ˈklev.ᵊl.i/ [US] /-ɚ.li/ *adv* in a clever or skilful way: *I thought you handled the situation very cleverly.*

cleverness /ˈklev.ə.nəs/ [US] /-ɚ-/ *noun* [U] ability to understand and learn quickly and easily

clever-clever /ˈklev.əˌklev.əʳ/ [US] /-ɚˌklev.ɚ/ *adj* UK INFORMAL DISAPPROVING trying too hard to seem clever: *I wish Jon would make some constructive proposals instead of just making clever-clever remarks.*

cliché /ˈkliː.ʃeɪ/ [US] /-ˈ-/ *noun* [C or U] a comment that is very often made and is therefore not original and not interesting: *My wedding day – and I know it's a cliché – was just the happiest day of my life.* **clichéd** /ˈkliː.ʃeɪd/ *adj*: *He made some clichéd remark about the birth of his first child completely changing his life.*

cliché-ridden /ˈkliː.ʃeɪˌrɪd.ᵊn/ [US] /-ˈ-ˌ--/ *adj* containing a lot of clichés: *a cliché-ridden speech*

click [SOUND] /klɪk/ *verb* [I or T] to make a short, sharp sound, or to make something do this: *The door clicked shut behind her.* ○ *Can you hear that strange clicking noise?* ○ *Paul clicked his **fingers*** (= moved his thumb against his middle finger to make a short sharp sound) *to attract the waiter's attention.* ○ *Soldiers click their **heels*** (= bring them sharply together) *when they stand to attention.* **click** /klɪk/ *noun* [C] *The soldier gave a click **of** his heels as he saluted.*

click [BECOME FRIENDLY] /klɪk/ *verb* [I] INFORMAL to become friendly or popular: *Liz and I really clicked the first time we met.* ○ *The new daytime soap opera has yet to show signs that it's clicking **with** the television audience.*

click [BECOME CLEAR] /klɪk/ *verb* [I] INFORMAL to be understood, or become clear suddenly: *Suddenly everything clicked and I realized where I'd met him.* ○ [+ question word] *As he talked about his schooldays, **it** suddenly clicked **where** I had met him before.* ○ [+ that] *So it's finally clicked **that** you're going to have to get yourself a job, has it?* ○ *In the last act of the play, everything clicks **into place**.*

click [OPERATE] /klɪk/ *verb* [I or T] SPECIALIZED to (cause a computer instruction to) operate by pressing a button on the MOUSE (= small control device) of a computer: *If you want to open a file, click twice **on** the icon for it.* ○ *When you have selected the file you want, click the 'Open' box.*

clickable /ˈklɪk.ə.bl̩/ *adj* describes a word or image on a computer screen which you can click on to make further information appear or a new process begin: *To find your nearest UK school, we have a clickable map dividing the UK into regions.*

client [CUSTOMER] /ˈklaɪ.ᵊnt/ *noun* [C] a customer or someone who receives services: *Mr Black has been a client **of** this firm for many years.* ○ *We always aim to give our clients personal attention.*

clientele /ˌkliː.ɒnˈtel/ [US] /-ɑːn-/ *group noun* [S] all the customers of a business when they are considered as a group: *The nightclub has a very fashionable clientele.*

client [COMPUTER] /ˈklaɪ.ᵊnt/ *noun* [C] a computer that is connected to a SERVER (= large central computer) from which it obtains information

client-server /ˌklaɪ.ᵊntˈsɜː.vəʳ/ [US] /-ˈsɝː.vɚ/ *adj* [before n] using or consisting of several computers which are connected to a SERVER (= large central computer) from which they obtain information: *client-server **systems/applications***

ˌclient ˈstate *noun* [C] a country which gets support and protection from another larger and more powerful country

cliff /klɪf/ *noun* [C] a high area of rock with a very steep side, often on a coast: *Keep away from the edge of the cliff – you might fall.* ○ *the cliff edge*

cliffhanger /ˈklɪfˌhæŋ.əʳ/ [US] /-ɚ/ *noun* [C] a story or a situation which is exciting because its ending or result is uncertain until it happens: *Many of Hitchcock's films are real cliffhangers.* ○ *It looks as if the election is going to be a cliffhanger.*

clifftop /ˈklɪf.tɒp/ [US] /-tɑːp/ *noun* [C] an area of ground at the top of a cliff: *We stayed in a marvellous clifftop hotel.*

climate [WEATHER] /ˈklaɪ.mət/ *noun* [C or U] the general weather conditions usually found in a particular place: *a hot/dry/harsh climate* ○ *The Mediterranean climate is good for growing citrus fruits and grapes.* ○ *When we retire, we're going to move to a warmer climate* (= an

area where the climate is warmer).
climatic /klaɪˈmæt.ɪk/ [US] /-ˈmæt̬-/ *adj*: *Some parts of the world seem to be experiencing climatic changes* (= changes in general weather conditions).
climatology /ˌklaɪ.məˈtɒl.ə.dʒi/ [US] /-ˈtɑː.lə-/ *noun* [U] the scientific study of general weather conditions

C

climate [SITUATION] /ˈklaɪ.mət/ *noun* [C] the general development of a situation, or the situation, feelings and opinions that exist at a particular time: *the political/social climate* ○ *I don't think we should expand our business in the current* ***economic*** *climate.* ○ *Terrorism* ***creates*** *a climate* ***of*** *fear.*

climax /ˈklaɪ.mæks/ *noun* [C] **1** the most important or exciting point in a story or situation, which usually happens near the end: *The climax* ***of*** *the air show was a daring flying display.* ○ *The election campaign* ***reaches*** *its climax next week.* ➲See also **anticlimax**. **2** the highest point of sexual pleasure
climax /ˈklaɪ.mæks/ *verb* [I] **1** to reach the most important or exciting part: *The show climaxed* ***with*** *all the performers singing on stage together.* ○ *The Olympics climaxed* ***in*** *a spectacular closing ceremony.* **2** to reach the highest point of sexual pleasure
climactic /klaɪˈmæk.tɪk/ *adj*: *The third movement of the symphony ends in a climactic crescendo* (= has a loud and exciting ending).

climb [RISE] /klaɪm/ *verb* **1** [I] to go up, or to go towards the top of something: *The plane climbed quickly* ***to*** *a height of 30 000 feet.* ○ *As it leaves the village, the road climbs steeply* ***up*** *the mountain.* ○ *The sun climbed higher in the sky.* **2** [I or T] to use your legs, or your legs and hands, to go up or onto the top of something: *to climb the stairs/mountain* ○ *I hate climbing ladders.* ○ *We're going climbing* (= climbing mountains as a sport) *in Scotland next weekend.* **3** [I] If a price, number, or amount climbs, it increases: *Our costs have climbed rapidly in the last few years.* **4** [I] to move into a higher social position, or to improve your position at work: *He quickly climbed to the top of his profession.*
• **be climbing the walls** to suffer unpleasant feelings, such as anxiety, in an extreme way: *to be climbing the walls* ***with*** *boredom/anger/frustration* ○ *When Joely went missing, we were practically climbing the walls.*
climb /klaɪm/ *noun* [C] **1** an act or process of climbing: *We were very tired after our climb.* ○ *The climb* ***down*** *the mountain took longer than the climb* ***up***. ○ *I've* ***made*** *three climbs so far this year.* ○ *Her climb* ***to*** *power has been very rapid.* **2** a place or object to be climbed: *The north face of the Eiger is a very difficult climb.*
climber /ˈklaɪ.məʳ/ [US] /-mɚ/ *noun* [C] someone who climbs mountains for sport
climbing /ˈklaɪ.mɪŋ/ *noun* [U] the sport of climbing mountains: *Chris has just taken up climbing.* ○ *He needs some climbing boots.* ➲See picture **Sports** on page Centre 10

climb [GROW] /klaɪm/ *verb* [I] to grow upwards: *There's masses of ivy climbing* ***up/over*** *the walls of our house.*
climber /ˈklaɪ.məʳ/ [US] /-mɚ/ *noun* [C] a plant which grows up a supporting surface **climbing** /ˈklaɪ.mɪŋ/ *adj* [before n] *I need some climbing* ***plants*** *that will grow on a north-facing wall.*

climb [MOVE] /klaɪm/ *verb* [I usually + adv or prep] to move into or out of a small space awkwardly or with difficulty or effort: *They climbed* ***into*** *the truck and drove away.* ○ *We can't stop Tom climbing* ***out of*** *his cot.*
▲ **climb down** *phrasal verb* UK to change your opinion or admit that you were wrong: *The government has been forced to climb down* ***over*** *the issue of increased taxes.*
climbdown /ˈklaɪm.daʊn/ *noun* [C] *Saying she was wrong was a difficult climbdown for Sarah.*

ˈclimbing ˌframe UK *noun* [C] (US **jungle gym**) a large frame made of bars that children can climb on

climes /klaɪmz/ *plural noun* LITERARY a place where the weather is different in a particular way: *We're off to* ***sunnier*** *climes next week.*

clinch [WIN] /klɪntʃ/ *verb* [T] INFORMAL to finally get or win something: *I hear he finally clinched the* ***deal*** *to buy the land he wanted.*

clinch [DECIDE] /klɪntʃ/ *verb* INFORMAL **clinch it** to make someone decide what to do after a lot of consideration or discussion: *When they said the job would involve travelling to Paris, that clinched it* ***(for*** *her)* (= that made her certain that she wanted the job).
clincher /ˈklɪn.tʃəʳ/ [US] /-tʃɚ/ *noun* [C usually sing] *It was the offer of a large discount on the TV that was the real clincher* (= the fact that made us decide to buy it).

clinch [HOLD] /klɪntʃ/ *noun* [C] the position two people are in when they are holding each other tightly in their arms, when fighting or showing affection

cling [HOLD] /klɪŋ/ *verb* [I + adv or prep] **clung, clung** to stick onto or hold something or someone tightly, or to refuse to stop holding them: *We got so wet that our clothes clung* ***to*** *us.* ○ *They clung* ***together*** *in terror as the screams grew louder.* ○ *One little girl was clinging* ***onto*** *a cuddly toy.* ○ *She clung* ***to*** *the handrail as she walked down the slippery steps.* **clingy** /ˈklɪŋ.i/ *adj*: *clingy material* ○ *a clingy skirt*

cling [STAY CLOSE] /klɪŋ/ *verb* **clung, clung 1** [I usually + adv or prep] to stay close or near: *The road clings* ***to*** (= closely follows) *the coastline for several miles, then it turns inland.* **2** [I] DISAPPROVING to stay close to someone who is caring for you, in a dependent way: *Jenny is the kind of child who always clings whenever she's taken to a new place.* **clinging** /ˈklɪŋ.ɪŋ/ *adj* (ALSO **clingy**) DISAPPROVING *Jimmy is a very clingy child.*

PHRASAL VERBS WITH **cling** ▼

▲ **cling (on) to *sth*** *phrasal verb* to try very hard to keep something: *He clung on to power for another ten years.*
▲ **cling to *sth*** *phrasal verb* to refuse to stop believing or hoping for something: *She clings to the hope that her husband will come back to her.*

clingfilm UK /ˈklɪŋ.fɪlm/ *noun* [U] (US **plastic wrap**) thin, transparent, plastic material, used for wrapping food to keep it fresh: *Could you put some clingfilm over the salad?*

clinic /ˈklɪn.ɪk/ *noun* [C] a building, often part of a hospital, to which people can go for medical care or advice: *Bring your baby to the clinic and we'll take a look at her.* ○ *Antenatal clinics provide care for pregnant women.*
• **hold a clinic 1** to be available at a particular place to provide medical care to members of the public: *Dr Clark holds a clinic on Tuesday mornings.* **2** UK to be available at a particular place to provide advice to members of the public: *Our MP holds a clinic every Friday evening.*

clinical [MEDICAL] /ˈklɪn.ɪ.kəl/ *adj* describes medical work or teaching that relates to the examination and treatment of ill people: *clinical tests/training* ○ *the Department of Clinical Medicine* ○ *Clinical* ***trials*** *of the new drug may take five years.*
clinically /ˈklɪn.ɪ.kli/ *adv*: *This toothpaste has been clinically proven* (= has been shown in experiments) *to protect your teeth.* ○ *Doctors pronounced him clinically* ***dead*** (= judged him to be dead by examining his body) *at the scene of the accident.*
clinician /klɪˈnɪʃ.ən/ *noun* [C] SPECIALIZED someone, such as a doctor, who is qualified in an area of highly skilled health work

clinical [WITHOUT EMOTION] /ˈklɪn.ɪ.kəl/ *adj* **1** DISAPPROVING expressing no emotion or feelings: *She seems to have a very clinical attitude towards her children.* **2** lacking in character and warmth: *We were going to paint our kitchen white, but we decided that would look too clinical.*
clinically /ˈklɪn.ɪ.kli/ *adv* DISAPPROVING *Should doctors always remain clinically detached from* (= express no emotion towards) *their patients?*

ˌclinical deˈpression *noun* [U] a mental illness which causes feelings of sadness and loss of hope, changes in sleeping and eating habits, loss of interest in your usual activities, and pains which have no physical explanation **ˌclinically deˈpressed** *adj*

ˌclinical therˈmometer *noun* [C] a device used for measuring the body temperature of a person or animal

clink [SOUND] /klɪŋk/ *verb* [I or T] to (cause something to) make a short ringing sound like pieces of glass or metal knocking lightly together: *The ice clinked as she dropped* it into the glass. ○ *We all clinked our **glasses** together and drank to a happy new year.* **clink** /klɪŋk/ *noun* [S] *I could hear **the** clink of coins in his pocket.* **clinking** /'klɪŋ.kɪŋ/ *noun* [S] *the clinking of glasses*

clink PRISON /klɪŋk/ *noun* [S or U] INFORMAL prison: *Everyone always said Joe would end up in (the) clink.*

clinker /'klɪŋ.kəʳ/ US /-kɚ/ *noun* **1** [U] the ASH (= powder) and rough hard lumps that remain after coal has been burned **2** [C] US OLD-FASHIONED SLANG a mistake, especially a wrong musical note

clip FASTENER /klɪp/ *noun* [C] a small usually metal or plastic object used for fastening things together or holding them in position: *a paper/hair/tie clip* ○ *The wires were fastened together with a plastic clip.*

clip /klɪp/ *verb* [I or T; usually + adv or prep] -pp- to fasten something with a clip: *You can always tell a real bow tie from one that clips **on**.* ○ *When you've finished your work sheets, clip them **together** and hand them in to me.*

clip FILM/TELEVISION /klɪp/ *noun* [C] a short part of a film or television programme: *I've seen a clip **from** the film.*

clip CUT /klɪp/ *verb* [T] -pp- **1** to cut something with scissors or a similar sharp tool, especially to make it tidier: *I'm going to clip the hedge this weekend.* ○ *When the guard came to clip my train ticket (= make a hole in it to show that it had been used), I couldn't find it.* ○ *I'm always clipping recipes **out of** magazines.* **2** to reduce something by the stated amount: *Christie has clipped a tenth of a second **off** the record.*

• **clip** *sb's* **wings** to limit someone's freedom

clip /klɪp/ *noun* [S] when you cut something in order to make it tidy: *That hedge needs a clip.*

clippers /'klɪp.əz/ US /-ɚz/ *plural noun* a device for cutting especially nails, hair, wire or bushes

clipping /'klɪp.ɪŋ/ *noun* **1** [C usually pl] a piece that has been cut off something: *grass/nail clippings* **2** [C] an article cut from a newspaper: *A friend recently sent me a **newspaper** clipping about someone we were at school with.*

clip HIT /klɪp/ *verb* [T] -pp- to hit something or someone with a short sharp movement: *He clipped the edge of the kerb with his front tyre.* ○ UK OLD-FASHIONED *I'll clip you **round the ear** (= hit the side of your head to punish you) in a minute, if you're not careful.* **clip** /klɪp/ *noun* [C usually sing]

• **clip** *sb* **round/on the ear** UK OLD-FASHIONED a quick hit on the side of someone's head: *You do that once more and you'll **get** a clip round the ear, my lad.*

clip SPEED /klɪp/ *noun* US INFORMAL **at a fast/good clip** fast: *We set off at a good clip, but we gradually slowed down.*

clip GUN PART /klɪp/ *noun* [C] a container which is fastened to a gun, from which bullets go into the gun for firing

clip **art** , UK USUALLY **clipart** *noun* [U] small pictures which are stored on your computer and can be easily added to a document: *The site links to about 24 other sites offering clip art.* ○ *a clipart collection/library*

clipboard WRITING SURFACE /'klɪp.bɔːd/ US /-bɔːrd/ *noun* [C] a board with a CLIP (= fastener) at the top which holds sheets of paper in position, and which provides a surface for writing on: *A woman with a clipboard stopped us in the street to ask us some questions.*

clipboard COMPUTING /'klɪp.bɔːd/ US /-bɔːrd/ *noun* [C usually sing] an area for storing information temporarily in a computer when you are moving it from one position or document to another: *You draw the shape somewhere on your worksheet, click on it and copy it to the clipboard.*

clip-clop /'klɪp.klɒp/ US /-klɑːp/ *noun* [C usually sing] a sound like that of horses' HOOVES on a hard surface: *the clip-clop **of** horses coming up the road*

clip-clop /'klɪp.klɒp/ US /-klɑːp/ *verb* [I] -pp- *We heard horses clip-clopping (= making a sound with their feet) along the road.*

clip **joint** *noun* [C] INFORMAL DISAPPROVING a bar or nightclub where customers are charged too much for food and drink of low quality

clip-on /'klɪp.ɒn/ US /-ɑːn/ *adj* [before n] describes something that is fastened with a clip: *clip-on earrings/sunglasses* **clip-on** /'klɪp.ɒn/ US /-ɑːn/ *noun* [C usually pl]

They only had earrings for pierced ears, but I wanted clip-ons.

clipped SPEAKING /klɪpt/ *adj* with words pronounced quickly and sharply, sometimes with parts missing, or in a very brief and unfriendly way: *I heard the clipped **tones** of his secretary saying "I have Mr Watson for you."*

clipped TIDY /klɪpt/ *adj* cut short and tidy: *a clipped beard/moustache*

clique /kliːk/ US /klɪk/ *group noun* [C] DISAPPROVING a small group of people who spend their time together and do not welcome other people into that group: *Our golf club is run by a very unfriendly clique **(of people)**.* ○ *There's a clique at work that never talks/who never talk to anyone else.*

cliquey (**cliquier**, **cliquiest**) /'kliː.ki/ *adj* (ALSO **cliquish**) DISAPPROVING *I decided not to join the tennis club because I found it very cliquey (= because new members were not made to feel welcome).*

clitoris /'klɪt.ˀr.ɪs/ US /'klɪt̬.ɚ-/ *noun* [C] a sexual organ above the vagina which can give a woman sexual pleasure when it is touched **clitoral** /'klɪt.ˀr.ˀl/ US /'klɪt̬.-ɚ-/ *adj*

cloak PIECE OF CLOTHING /kləʊk/ US /kloʊk/ *noun* [C] a loose outer piece of clothing without sleeves, which fastens at the neck, and is worn instead of a coat

cloak HIDE /kləʊk/ US /kloʊk/ *noun* [S or U] something which hides, covers or keeps something else secret: *The restaurant he owned was just a cloak **for** (= hid) his drug-dealing activities.* ○ *They left the house under cloak **of** darkness.*

cloak /kləʊk/ US /kloʊk/ *verb* [T] *He has always kept his love affairs cloaked **in** secrecy (= kept them secret).* ○ *The river is often cloaked **in** (= covered by) mist in the early morning.*

cloak-and-dagger /ˌkləʊk.ən'dæg.əʳ/ US /ˌkloʊk.ən-'dæg.ɚ/ *adj* describes an exciting story involving secrecy and mystery, often about SPIES, or something which makes you think of this: *I'm tired of all these cloak-and-dagger (= secretive) meetings – let's discuss the issues openly.*

cloakroom /'kləʊk.rʊm/ /-ruːm/ US /'kloʊk-/ *noun* [C] **1** (US ALSO **checkroom**) a room in a public building such as a restaurant, theatre, etc. where coats, bags, and other personal items can be left while their owners are in the building **2** UK POLITE WORD FOR toilet, especially one in a public building: *I went to the cloakroom in the first interval.*

clobber HIT /'klɒb.əʳ/ US /'klɑː.bɚ/ *verb* [T] INFORMAL **1** to hit someone or something hard and repeatedly: *If you do that again, I'll clobber you **(one)**.* **2** to punish someone: *The government is proposing new measures to clobber tax dodgers.* **3** to harm someone financially: *The new supermarket is really going to clobber the small local shops.*

clobber DEFEAT /'klɒb.əʳ/ US /'klɑː.bɚ/ *verb* [T] to defeat completely: *The government clobbered the opposition's proposals.*

clobber POSSESSIONS /'klɒb.əʳ/ US /'klɑː.bɚ/ *noun* [U] UK INFORMAL possessions, especially those that you carry around with you, or clothes: *I've got far too much clobber in my handbag.* ○ *Did you bring all your tennis clobber?*

cloche COVER /klɒʃ/ US /kloʊʃ/ *noun* [C] (ALSO **cold frame**) a piece of clear material, sometimes on a frame, used to cover plants for a short time, usually to protect them from cold weather or to help them grow faster

cloche HAT /klɒʃ/ US /kloʊʃ/ *noun* [C] a woman's hat which is shaped like a bell and fits closely around the head, popular in the 1920s

clock TIME /klɒk/ US /klɑːk/ *noun* [C] a device for measuring and showing time, which is usually found in or on a building and is not worn by a person: *We have an antique clock on our mantelpiece.* ○ *The town-hall clock **says** (= shows that the time is) 9 o'clock.* ○ *I think the kitchen clock is **fast/slow** (= is showing a later/earlier time than it should).* ○ *The clock began to **strike** twelve.* ○ *She **set** her clock (= put it to the right time) by the time signal on the radio.*

• **against the clock 1** If you do something against the clock, you do it as fast as possible and try to finish it

before a certain time. **2** When people do something against the clock, the time they take to do it is recorded, in order to find which person or attempt is the fastest.
• **be watching the clock** (*ALSO* **have/keep *your* eye on the clock**) to be looking to see what the time is, usually because you are bored or eager to leave: *I had a train to catch, so I was watching the clock all through the meeting.*
• **put/turn the clocks back** *UK* (*US* **set/turn the clocks back**) to change the time on your clocks to an hour earlier, at an officially chosen time of year: *Don't forget to turn the clocks back tonight.*
• **put/turn the clocks forward** (*US ALSO* **set the clocks ahead**) to change the time on your clocks to an hour later, at an officially chosen time of year
• **put/turn the clock back** to make things the same as they were at an earlier time: *The court's decision on this case will turn the clock back fifty years.* ○ *If I could turn the clock back and do things differently, I would.*
• **round/around the clock** all day and all night: *Doctors and nurses **worked** round the clock to help those injured in the train crash.* ○ *She needed round-the-clock nursing.*
• **turn back the clock** to remember or imagine times in the past: *Now we're going to turn back the clock with some rock 'n' roll from the 1950s.*
clock /klɒk/ [US] /klɑːk/ *verb* [T] to take a particular time exactly to do or complete something: *He clocked 10 seconds in the 100 metres* (= He ran it in 10 seconds).

the clock [SPEED] *noun* [S] **1** a SPEEDOMETER (= a device that measures speed): *I was only doing 30 mph **on** the clock.* **2** a MILEOMETER (= a device for recording distance travelled): *My car's only got 10 000 miles **on** the clock.*
clock /klɒk/ [US] /klɑːk/ *verb* [T] to show or reach a particular speed or distance on a measuring device: [+ v-ing] *The police clocked him doing 80 mph in a 50 mph area.* ○ *Jim's car has clocked (up)* (= travelled) *40 000 miles in less than two years.*

clock [HIT] /klɒk/ [US] /klɑːk/ *verb* [T] *UK INFORMAL* to hit someone, especially on the head or face: *Then the other guy turned round and clocked him **one*** (= hit him).

PHRASAL VERBS WITH ˌ**clock**

▲ **clock in** *phrasal verb* (*UK ALSO* **clock on**) *INFORMAL* to record the time you arrive at work on a special machine: *What time did you clock in this morning?* ○ *Clocking-in time is 9.00 a.m.*
▲ **clock out** *phrasal verb* (*UK ALSO* **clock off**) *INFORMAL* to leave work, especially by recording the time you leave on a special machine
▲ **clock *sth* up** *phrasal verb* [M] *MAINLY UK INFORMAL* to win or achieve a large number of similar things: *The Australians have clocked up three gold medals and two silvers in the swimming events.*

ˌ**clock ˈradio** *noun* [C] a **radio alarm (clock)**

ˈ**clock ˌtower** *noun* [C] a tower which has a clock at the top of it

clock-watching /ˈklɒkˌwɒtʃ.ɪŋ/ [US] /ˈklɑːkˌwɑːtʃ-/ *noun* [U] *DISAPPROVING* when you continually look to see what time it is in order to see how much longer you have to work **clock-watcher** /ˈklɒkˌwɒtʃ.əʳ/ [US] /ˈklɑːkˌwɑːtʃ.ɚ/ *noun* [C]

clockwise /ˈklɒk.waɪz/ [US] /ˈklɑːk-/ *adj, adv* in the direction in which the pointers of a clock move: *Turn the knob clockwise/in a clockwise direction.* * NOTE: The opposite is *(UK)* **anti-clockwise** or *(US)* **counterclockwise**.

clockwork /ˈklɒk.wɜːk/ [US] /ˈklɑːk.wɝːk/ *noun* [U] a system of springs and wheels that you wind with a key or handle to make some clocks, toys and other devices operate: *a clockwork train/mouse*
• **like clockwork** (*ALSO* **(as) regular as clockwork**) very regularly, or at exactly the planned times: *Since the recent improvements to the service, the buses are running like clockwork.* ○ *My daughter always calls me every Friday evening, (as) regular as clockwork.*
• **run/go like clockwork** to happen exactly as planned, without any trouble: *The party went like clockwork.*

clod [LUMP] /klɒd/ [US] /klɑːd/ *noun* [C] a lump of earth or clay: *Their hooves threw up clods **of** earth as they galloped across the field.*

clod [PERSON] /klɒd/ [US] /klɑːd/ *noun* [C] *OLD-FASHIONED* a stupid person: *Don't be such a clod!*

clodhopper [PERSON] /ˈklɒdˌhɒp.əʳ/ [US] /ˈklɑːdˌhɑː.pɚ/ *noun* [C] *INFORMAL* an awkward or clumsy person: *Look where you're going, you **great** clodhopper.* **clodhopping** /ˈklɒdˌhɒp.ɪŋ/ [US] /ˈklɑːdˌhɑː.pɪŋ/ *adj* [before n] *You clodhopping idiot!*

clodhopper [SHOE] /ˈklɒdˌhɒp.əʳ/ [US] /ˈklɑːdˌhɑː.pɚ/ *noun* [C] *INFORMAL* a heavy shoe: *You're not coming in the house in those **great** clodhoppers.* **clodhopping** /ˈklɒdˌhɒp.ɪŋ/ [US] /ˈklɑːdˌhɑː.pɪŋ/ *adj* [before n] *big clodhopping shoes*

clog [BLOCK] /klɒg/ [US] /klɑːg/ *verb* [I or T] **-gg-** to (cause something to) become blocked or filled so that movement or activity is difficult: *The roads are clogged **with** holiday traffic.* ○ *Eating too much fat causes your arteries to clog **(up)**.* ○ *Leaves are clogging **(up)** the drain.*
clogged /klɒgd/ [US] /klɑːgd/ *adj* blocked: *clogged pipes*

clog [SHOE] /klɒg/ [US] /klɑːg/ *noun* [C usually pl] a type of shoe made of wood, or with the top part made of leather and the bottom part of wood

cloister /ˈklɔɪ.stəʳ/ [US] /-stɚ/ *noun* [C usually pl] a covered stone passage around the four sides of a COURTYARD (= a square or rectangular space), especially in a religious building such as a church or monastery
cloistered /ˈklɔɪ.stəd/ [US] /-stɚd/ *adj* surrounded by covered passages: *a cloistered courtyard*

cloistered /ˈklɔɪ.stəd/ [US] /-stɚd/ *adj* separated from and having little contact with the outside world: *These academics lead such a cloistered **life/existence**.*

clone /kləʊn/ [US] /kloʊn/ *noun* [C] **1** a plant or animal which has the same genes as the original from which it was produced **2** *INFORMAL DISAPPROVING* someone or something that looks very much like someone or something else: *Most people saw her as just another blond-haired, red-lipped Marilyn Monroe clone.* **3** *SPECIALIZED* a computer that operates in a very similar way to the one that it was copied from
clone /kləʊn/ [US] /kloʊn/ *verb* [T] to create a clone of a plant or animal: *Scientists have already cloned a sheep.* ○ *Experiments to try to clone human embryos have met with hostility from some sections of the public.* **cloning** /ˈkləʊ.nɪŋ/ [US] /ˈkloʊ-/ *noun* [U] *animal/human cloning*

close [NOT OPEN] /kləʊz/ [US] /kloʊz/ *verb* **1** [I or T] to (cause something to) change from being open to not being open: *Could you close the **door/window** please?* ○ *Close your **eyes** – I've got a surprise for you.* ➲See Note **open** or **switch on?** at **open** NOT CLOSED. **2** [I] When a shop, restaurant or public place closes, people cannot go into it: *The banks had closed **(to** customers) so I couldn't get any money out.* ○ *The museum closes **at** 5.30.* ○ *We can't get a drink! It's after **(pub)** closing **time**.*
• **close *your* eyes to *sth*** to ignore something bad and pretend it is not happening: *She closed her eyes to **the fact** that her son was stealing.*
• **close ranks** When the members of a group or organization close ranks, they make an effort to stay united, especially in order to defend themselves from severe criticism: *In the past, the party would have closed ranks around its leader and defended him loyally.*
closed /kləʊzd/ [US] /kloʊzd/ *adj* **1** not open: *It might be less draughty if the door were closed.* **2** not open for business: *All the shops were closed, so we couldn't buy any food.*
• **behind closed doors** If something happens behind closed doors, it is hidden or kept secret from public view: *The deal was negotiated behind closed doors.*

close [END] /kləʊz/ [US] /kloʊz/ *verb* [I or T] **1** to (cause something to) end: *The play closed **with** the tragic death of both hero and heroine.* ○ *She closed the meeting with a short speech.* ○ *The pound closed **at*** (= was worth) *$1.47 at the end of the day's trading.* **2** to (cause a business, organization or business arrangement) to stop operating: *I closed that bank **account** when I came to London.* ○ *The **factory** closed over ten years ago.*
• **close a deal** to make a successful business arrangement with someone: *We closed a deal **with** a major supermarket.*

closed /kləʊzd/ ⓤ /kloʊzd/ *adj* completed and therefore not able to be discussed further: *"The matter is closed,"* said the health minister.

close /kləʊz/ ⓤ /kloʊz/ *noun* [S] the end of something, or when you end it: *I tried to **bring** the conversation **to a** close.* ○ *"Let's **draw** this meeting **to a** close, gentlemen,"* said the chairman.

closure /'kləʊ.ʒəʳ/ ⓤ /'kloʊ.ʒɚ/ *noun* **1** [C] when a business, organization, etc. stops operating: *factory/branch closures* ○ *The unions fought hard against the government's programme of pit closures.* **2** [U] the feeling or act of bringing an unpleasant situation, time or experience to an end, so that you are able to start new activities: *a sense of closure* ○ *to **achieve/reach** closure*

close NEAR /kləʊs/ ⓤ /kloʊs/ *adj, adv* not distant in position or time: *Don't get too close to that dog, Rosie.* ○ *I hate people standing too close **to** me.* ○ *As Christmas gets closer, the shops get more and more crowded.* ○ *Emma looked close **to** tears* (= almost going to cry).
• **at close quarters/range** (from) a short distance away: *When you see famous people at close quarters, they always appear much smaller than you imagined them.* ○ *He was shot at close range.*
• **be close to the bone** If something you say or write is close to the bone, it is close to the truth in a way that might offend some people.
• **be too close for comfort** HUMOROUS to be so close to you that you feel worried or frightened: *His mother lives in the next street to us, which is a little too close for comfort.*
closeness /'kləʊ.snəs/ ⓤ /'kloʊ-/ *noun* [U] being close

close RELATIONSHIP /kləʊs/ ⓤ /kloʊs/ *adj* **1** having direct family connections or shared beliefs, support and sympathy: *There weren't many people at the funeral – just close **family/relatives**.* ○ *They're a worrying political party because of their close **links/ties** with terrorist groups.* ○ *In those early months, there's a very close **bond** between mother and child.* ○ *a close community* **2** describes people who know each other very well and like each other a lot, or who see and talk to each other a lot: *Mira is one of my closest **friends**.* ○ *Her relationship isn't good with her father, but she's very close **to** her mother.* ○ *My brother and I have become much closer over the years.* **closely** /'kləʊ.sli/ ⓤ /'kloʊ-/ *adv*: *English and German are closely **related**.* ○ *Both politicians have been closely **associated** with the movement for some time.* **closeness** /'kləʊ.snəs/ ⓤ /'kloʊ-/ *noun* [U] *A special closeness is supposed to exist between twins.*

close SIMILAR /kləʊs/ ⓤ /kloʊs/ *adj* having only a small difference: *The election results were so close they had to vote again.* ○ *He came second in the race, but it was very close.* ○ *The youngest boys are so close **in** age they look like twins.* ○ *Both children bear a very close **resemblance** to their father.*
• **close on/to** almost: *I think there are close on three million unemployed at present.*

close SECRETIVE /kləʊs/ ⓤ /kloʊs/ *adj* unwilling to talk about things to other people: *He's so close **about** his past – it seems like he's hiding something.* **closely** /'kləʊ.sli/ ⓤ /'kloʊ-/ *adv*: *a closely **guarded** secret*

close LACKING AIR /kləʊs/ ⓤ /kloʊs/ *adj* describes weather or air conditions in which it is difficult to breathe and is uncomfortably warm: *Can I open the window? It's very close in here.* **closeness** /'kləʊ.snəs/ ⓤ /'kloʊ-/ *noun* [U]

close ROAD /kləʊs/ ⓤ /kloʊs/ *noun* [C] UK a road, usually with private houses, which vehicles can only enter from one end: *He lives at 83 Barker Close.*

PHRASAL VERBS WITH **close** ▼

▲ **close** *(sth)* **down** *phrasal verb* [M] If a business or organization closes down or someone closes it down, it stops operating: *All the mines in this area were closed down in the 80's.* ○ *Our local butcher is closing down.*
▲ **close in** *phrasal verb* to gradually get nearer to someone, usually in order to attack them: *The advancing soldiers closed in **on** the town.* ○ *The hunt chased the fox until it was too tired and weak to run and then closed in **for the kill**.*
▲ **close** *sth* **off** *phrasal verb* [M] to put something across the entrance of a place to stop people from entering:

Police quickly closed off the area.

close-by /ˌkləʊs'baɪ/ ⓤ /ˌkloʊs-/ *adv* near: *Shall we call in on Miranda? You know she lives quite close-by.*

close 'call *noun* [C] a **close shave**

close-cropped /ˌkləʊs'krɒpt/ ⓤ /ˌkloʊs'krɑːpt/ *adj* describes hair or grass that has been cut very short

closed 'book *noun* [S] INFORMAL a subject about which you know or understand nothing: *I'm afraid physics will always be a closed book **to** me.*

closed-circuit television /ˌkləʊzd.sɜː.kɪt'tel.ɪ.vɪʒ.ᵊn/ ⓤ /ˌkloʊzd.sɜːkɪt'tel.ə-/ *noun* [U] (ABBREVIATION **CCTV**) a system which sends television signals to a limited number of screens and is often used in shops as protection against thieves

closed ˌseason *noun* [S] US FOR **close season**

closed 'shop *noun* [C usually sing] a place of work where you have to belong to a particular TRADE UNION (= organization of workers)

close-fitting /ˌkləʊs'fɪt.ɪŋ/ ⓤ /ˌkloʊs'fɪt.ɪŋ/ *adj* describes clothing that fits very tightly

close-grained /ˌkləʊs'greɪnd/ ⓤ /ˌkloʊs-/ *adj* describes wood that has a pattern of narrow rings or lines

close-knit /ˌkləʊs'nɪt/ ⓤ /ˌkloʊs-/ *adj* describes a group of people in which everyone helps and supports each other: *a close-knit family/community*

close-out US /'kləʊz.aʊt/ ⓤ /'kloʊz-/ *noun* [C] (AUS **sell-off**) when the price of goods in a shop or factory is reduced so they can be sold quickly

close ˌseason UK *noun* [S] (MAINLY US **closed season**) a period of the year in which the killing of a particular type of animal, for example birds or fish, is not permitted: *This is the close season **for** salmon.* ➲Compare **open season**.

close-set /ˌkləʊs'set/ ⓤ /ˌkloʊs-/ *adj* describes eyes or teeth that are very close to each other

close 'shave *noun* [C] (ALSO **close call**) when you come extremely close to a dangerous or unpleasant situation or only just manage to avoid it: *I had a close shave this morning, – some idiot almost knocked me off my bike.*

closet CUPBOARD /'klɒz.ɪt/ ⓤ /'klɑː.zɪt/ *noun* [C] MAINLY US a cupboard or a small room with a door, used for storing things, especially clothes: *a bedroom/linen/storage closet*
• **come out of the closet** to admit to your family, friends or the public, after a period of secrecy, that you are homosexual

closet /'klɒz.ɪt/ ⓤ /'klɑː.zɪt/ *adj* [before n] describes a belief, activity or feeling which is kept secret from the public, usually because you are frightened of the results of it becoming known: *a closet alcoholic/homosexual* ○ *Dole portrayed the president in campaign speeches as a 'closet liberal'.*

closet STAY /'klɒz.ɪt/ ⓤ /'klɑː.zɪt/ *verb* [T usually passive] to put yourself in a place, especially an enclosed space, and stay there: [R] *Two weeks before my exams I closeted myself (away) in my room with my books and I didn't speak to anyone.* ○ *The President is closeted **with** (= having a private meeting with) his advisers.*

close-up /'kləʊs.ʌp/ ⓤ /'kloʊs-/ *noun* [C] a photograph taken from a short distance that gives a very detailed picture: *She took a stunning close-up **of** him.*

clot LUMP /klɒt/ ⓤ /klɑːt/ *noun* [C] an almost solid lump: *He had a **blood** clot removed from his brain.*

clot /klɒt/ ⓤ /klɑːt/ *verb* [I] -tt- to form clots: *He was rushed into hospital because his blood wasn't clotting properly.* ○ *an anti-(blood) clotting agent*

clot PERSON /klɒt/ ⓤ /klɑːt/ *noun* [C] UK OLD-FASHIONED INFORMAL a stupid person: *Look what you've done, you clot!*

cloth /klɒθ/ ⓤ /klɑːθ/ *noun* **1** [U] (a type of) woven material: *a piece/length of cloth* **2** [C] a small piece of material, used in cleaning to remove dirt, dust or liquid: *a washing-up cloth*

clothe /kləʊð/ ⓤ /kloʊð/ *verb* [T] to provide someone with clothes: *It costs a lot to **feed** and clothe five children.*

clothed /kləʊðd/ ⓤ /kloʊðd/ *adj* wearing clothes: *Bathers must be **fully** clothed before entering the restaurant.*

clothes /kləʊðz/ [US] /kloʊðz/ *plural noun* things such as dresses and trousers that you wear to cover, protect or decorate your body: *She usually* ***wears*** *smart/casual clothes.* ○ *I'm just* ***putting*** *my clothes* ***on.*** ○ ***Take*** *your clothes* ***off*** *and get in the bath.* ○ ***designer*** *clothes* ○ *a clothes shop* ➲See picture **Clothes** on page Centre 6

COMMON LEARNER ERROR

clothes

Remember that **clothes** is always plural. If you want to talk about one particular thing that you wear, use the name of the particular item or use 'piece/item of clothing'.

I need some new clothes.
That's a lovely shirt.
The police took away an item of clothing belonging to the suspect.

'clothes ,basket *noun* [C] a container that you put clothes in when they need washing

'clothes ,brush *noun* [C] a brush for removing dust and dirt from clothes

'clothes ,hanger *noun* [C] a **hanger**

'clothes ,horse [FRAME] *noun* [C] a frame on which wet clothes can be hung to dry, usually used inside the house

'clothes ,horse [PERSON] *noun* [C] *SLIGHTLY DISAPPROVING* a person, especially a woman, who is employed to wear expensive and fashionable clothes

'clothes ,line *noun* [C] a length of rope or string from which wet clothes are hung, usually outside, to dry

'clothes ,peg *UK noun* [C] (*US* **clothes pin**) a device used for holding clothes onto a clothes line while they dry

clothing /'kləʊ.ðɪŋ/ [US] /'kloʊ-/ *noun* [U] *FORMAL* clothes, especially of a type made to protect the wearer against heat, water or machinery: ***Protective*** *clothing must be worn.* ○ *You can only take three* ***articles/items of*** *clothing into the changing room.*

,clotted 'cream *noun* [U] a thick cream with soft lumps in it, made especially in southwest England

cloud /klaʊd/ *noun* **1** [C or U] a usually grey or white mass in the sky, made of very small floating drops of water: *Do you think those are* ***rain*** *clouds on the horizon?* ○ *The sky was a perfect blue – not a cloud in sight.* ○ *There was so much cloud, we couldn't see anything.* ○ *Dark clouds massed on the horizon.* **2** [C] a mass of something such as dust or smoke that looks like a cloud: *On the eastern horizon, a huge cloud* ***of*** *smoke from burning oil tanks stretched across the sky.* ○ *The initial cloud* ***of*** *tear gas had hardly cleared before shots were fired.*

• **a cloud on the horizon** something which threatens to cause problems or unhappiness in the future: *The only cloud on the horizon is the physics exam in June.*

• **be on cloud nine** *INFORMAL* to be extremely happy and excited: *"Was Helen pleased about getting that job?" "Pleased? She was on cloud nine!"*

• **be under a cloud** to not be trusted or popular because people think you have done something bad: *The cabinet minister left his office under a cloud after a fraud scandal.*

• **Every cloud has a silver lining.** *SAYING* said to emphasize that every difficult or unpleasant situation has some advantage

cloud /klaʊd/ *verb* **1** [I or T] If something transparent clouds, or if something clouds it, it becomes hard to see through. **2** [T] to make someone confused, or make something harder to understand: *When it came to explaining the lipstick on his collar, he found that drink had clouded* (= confused) *his* ***memory.***

cloudless /'klaʊd.ləs/ *adj* with no clouds: *a cloudless sky/night*

cloudy /'klaʊ.di/ *adj* **1** with clouds: *a cloudy sky/day* ○ *Scotland will be cloudy with wintry showers.* **2** not transparent: *The beer was cloudy and dark.*

PHRASAL VERBS WITH **cloud** ▼

▲ **cloud over** [SKY] *phrasal verb* If the sky clouds over, it becomes covered with clouds.

▲ **cloud over** [FACE] *phrasal verb* If a person's face clouds over, they suddenly look unhappy or worried: *At the mention of her dead husband, her face clouded over.*

'cloud ,bank *noun* [C] a big low mass of cloud

cloud-burst /'klaʊd.bɜːst/ [US] /-bɝːst/ *noun* [C] a sudden heavy fall of rain

cloud-cuckoo-land /,klaʊd'kʊk.uː.lænd/ *DISAPPROVING* **live/be in cloud-cuckoo-land** to not be realistic but to think that things which are completely impossible might happen: *When referees make contentious decisions players are going to be upset, and anyone who thinks otherwise is living in cloud-cuckoo-land.*

clout [HIT] /klaʊt/ *verb* [T] *INFORMAL* to hit someone or something with the hand or with a heavy object: *Quigley clouted me smartly across the side of the head.* **clout** /klaʊt/ *noun* [C] *If the photocopier stops working, just* ***give*** *it* ***a*** *clout.*

clout [POWER] /klaʊt/ *noun* [U] power and influence over other people or events: *The queen may have privilege but she* ***has*** *no real* ***political*** *clout.*

clove [PLANT PART] /kləʊv/ [US] /kloʊv/ *noun* [C] a small separate part of a BULB of GARLIC (= plant used in cooking): *This recipe takes four cloves of garlic.* ➲See picture **Vegetables** on page Centre 2

clove [SPICE] /kləʊv/ [US] /kloʊv/ *noun* [C or U] a small dark-brown dried flower of an evergreen tree, which is used as a spice: *The ham was studded with cloves.* ○ *sweet spices such as ginger and clove*

clove [DIVIDE] /kləʊv/ [US] /kloʊv/ *past simple of* **cleave**

cloven /'kləʊ.vᵊn/ [US] /'kloʊ-/ *past participle of* **cleave**

cloven /'kləʊ.vᵊn/ [US] /'kloʊ-/ *adj* describes something, especially an animal's HOOF, which is divided into two parts: *The devil was painted with horns and cloven* ***hooves.***

clover /'kləʊ.vəʳ/ [US] /'kloʊ.vɚ/ *noun* [U] a small plant with three round leaves on each stem, often fed to cows ➲See picture **Flowers and Plants** on page Centre 3

• **live/be in clover** to enjoy a life of wealth and comfort: *With the income from the family estate, she's in clover.*

clown /klaʊn/ *noun* [C] **1** an entertainer who wears amusing clothes, has a painted face, and makes people laugh by performing tricks and behaving foolishly **2** someone who behaves foolishly, often intentionally

clown /klaʊn/ *verb* [I usually + adv or prep] to act stupidly, often to make other people laugh: *Left alone, the class threw books, pulled faces and generally clowned* ***around.***

cloying /'klɔɪ.ɪŋ/ *adj* **1** *LITERARY DISAPPROVING* too sweet and therefore unpleasant: *This is a wonderful wine – honeyed and rich without being remotely cloying.* **2** *DISAPPROVING* too good or kind, or expressing feelings of love in a way that is not sincere: *She criticized the cloying sentimentality of the film.* **cloyingly** /'klɔɪ.ɪŋ.li/ *adv*: *cloyingly sweet*

club [GROUP] /klʌb/ *group noun* [C] **1** an organization of people with a common purpose or interest, who meet regularly and take part in shared activities: *I've just* ***joined*** *the local golf/squash/tennis club.* ○ *Visitors must be accompanied by club* ***members.*** **2** *US FOR* **team**: *The Orioles are an exciting club this year.*

club /klʌb/ *noun* [C] a building in which a club meets

• **in the club** *UK OLD-FASHIONED SLANG* pregnant

club [GOLF] /klʌb/ *noun* [C] a long, thin stick used in the game of golf to hit the ball: *a set of* ***golf*** *clubs* ➲See picture **Sports** on page Centre 10

club [WEAPON] /klʌb/ *noun* [C] a heavy stick used as a weapon

club /klʌb/ *verb* [T] **-bb-** to beat a person or an animal, usually repeatedly, with a heavy stick or object: *He was clubbed over the head.* ○ *The alligators are then clubbed* ***to death.***

club [CARD] /klʌb/ *noun* [C] a playing card showing the black sign with three leaves

clubs /klʌbz/ *group noun* [U] one of the four suits in playing cards: *the three of clubs*

club [DANCE] /klʌb/ *noun* [C] a nightclub: *I went to that new club that's just opened.*

clubbing /'klʌb.ɪŋ/ *noun* **go clubbing** to go to nightclubs: *Roz and I went clubbing last weekend.*

▲ **club together** *phrasal verb* If a group of people club together, they share the cost of something between them: *If we club together, we'll be able to get her the complete dinner set.*

clubhouse /ˈklʌb.haʊs/ *noun* [C] a building where members of a club meet and have social events

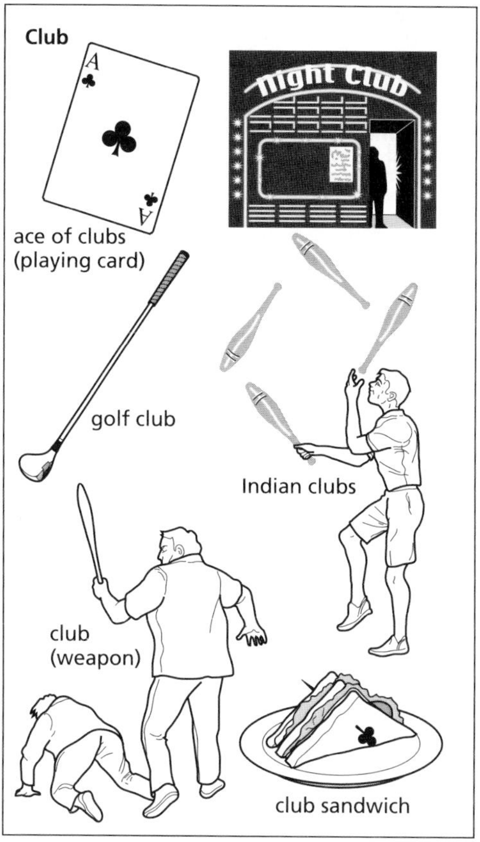
Club
Night Club
ace of clubs (playing card)
golf club
Indian clubs
club (weapon)
club sandwich

clubland /ˈklʌb.lænd/ *noun* [U] the places where people go to drink and dance at night, or the people who work and spend time there: *London clubland* ○ *the clubland scene*

ˌ**club ˈsandwich** *noun* [C] a sandwich made from three pieces of bread with meat, egg, cheese, salad or other cold food between them

ˌ**club ˈ(soda)** *noun* [C or U] *US FOR* **soda water**

cluck /klʌk/ *verb* **1** [I] to make the low interrupted noise that a chicken makes **2** [I or T] *INFORMAL* to express disapproval or other emotion by making a short sharp sound with your tongue: *to cluck **in** disapproval/amazement* ○ *She shakes her head, smiles, and clucks her tongue.* **3** [I] *INFORMAL* to express an unnecessary amount of sympathy, anxiety or approval towards someone: *The attendants clucked and fussed **over** passengers.*

clue /kluː/ *noun* [C] a sign or some information which helps you to find the answer to a problem, question or mystery: *Police are still **looking for** clues in their search for the missing girl.* ○ *I'm never going to guess the answer if you don't **give** me a clue.*

• **not have a clue** *INFORMAL* to be completely unable to guess, understand, or deal with something: *"Who invented algebra?" "I haven't a clue."* ○ *Don't ask your father which key to press – he hasn't got a clue **about** computers.*

clueless /ˈkluː.ləs/ *adj INFORMAL* having no knowledge of something, or of things in general: *Most people are completely clueless **about** tide directions and weather conditions.*

clue /kluː/ *verb* **clueing, clued, clued**

▲ **clue *sb* in** *US phrasal verb* [M] (*UK* **clue *sb* up**) to give someone information that is necessary or new: *He'd been out of the country for weeks, so I clued him in **on** all that's been happening.*

clued up /ˌkluːdˈʌp/ *adj* [after v] *UK* having a special and detailed knowledge of something: *Ben's more clued up **on/about** the cinema than I am.*

clump [GROUP] /klʌmp/ *noun* [C] a group, especially of trees or flowers: *a clump of grass/daffodils*

clump /klʌmp/ *verb* [I or T] to form a group, or to put things into a group: *As it started to rain, everyone clumped **together** in doorways.*

clump [WALK NOISILY] /klʌmp/ *verb* [I + adv or prep] to walk noisily with slow, heavy steps: *She clumped **around** the room/**up** the stairs in her boots.*

clump /klʌmp/ *noun* [C usually sing] *We could hear the clump* (= loud sound) *of his feet on the wooden floor.*

clump [LUMP] /klʌmp/ *noun* [C] a solid mass of something such as earth: *There were big clumps **of** soil on his boots.*

clumsy /ˈklʌm.zi/ *adj* **1** awkward in movement or manner: *The first mobile phones were heavy and clumsy to use, but nowadays they are much easier to handle.* ○ *My attempts to apologize were very clumsy* (= not said well). **2** describes someone who often has accidents because they do not behave in a careful, controlled way: *That's the third glass you've smashed this week, – you're so clumsy!* **clumsily** /ˈklʌm.zi.li/ *adv* **clumsiness** /ˈklʌm.zi.nəs/ *noun* [U]

clung /klʌŋ/ *past simple and past participle of* **cling**

clunk /klʌŋk/ *noun* [C usually sing] a deep low often metallic sound made by two objects hitting each other: *He shut the van door with a clunk.*

cluster /ˈklʌs.tər/ [US] /-tɚ/ *group noun* [C] a group of similar things that are close together, sometimes surrounding something: *Have a look at the cluster **of** galaxies in this photograph.* ○ *There was a cluster **of** fans around him, asking for autographs.* **cluster** /ˈklʌs.tər/ [US] /-tɚ/ *verb* [I] *People clustered **around** the noticeboard to read the exam results.*

ˈ**cluster ˌbomb** *noun* [C] an explosive device which throws out smaller bombs when it explodes

clutch [HOLD] /klʌtʃ/ *verb* [I or T] to take or try to take hold of something tightly, usually in fear, anxiety or pain: *Silent and pale, she clutched **(onto)** her mother's hand.* ○ *Clutching the money **to** his chest, he hurried to the bank.* ○ *He collapsed, clutching his stomach.*

ˈ**clutches** /ˈklʌtʃ.ɪz/ *plural noun HUMOROUS* **sb's clutches** the control of someone: *He **is in**/**has fallen into** the clutches **of** that woman.*

clutch [MACHINE PART] /klʌtʃ/ *noun* [C usually sing] **1** a device which allows turning movement to be sent from one part of a machine to another: *I've booked the car into the garage because the clutch is **slipping**.* ➲See picture **Car** on page Centre 12 **2** the PEDAL or handle in a vehicle that is used to operate the engine's clutch: ***Push the** clutch **in**, put the car into gear, rev the engine and then gently **let the** clutch **out**.*

clutch [GROUP] /klʌtʃ/ *group noun* [C] **1** a small group of eggs produced by the same bird, especially in a nest **2** a small group of people or things: *a fresh clutch **of** students*

▲ **clutch at *sth*** *phrasal verb* to try very hard to hold something: *Feeling herself fall, she clutched at a branch.*

ˈ**clutch ˌbag** *noun* [C] a small flat bag without a handle, carried by women, especially on formal occasions

clutter /ˈklʌt.ər/ [US] /ˈklʌt̬.ɚ/ *noun* [U] (a lot of objects in) a state of untidiness: *Sorry about the clutter in the kitchen.* ○ *My desk is covered in/full of clutter.*

clutter /ˈklʌt.ər/ [US] /ˈklʌt̬.ɚ/ *verb* [T] to fill something in an untidy or badly organized way: *The kids always clutter the hall **(up) with** school bags and coats and stuff.* ○ *Every shelf is cluttered **with** ornaments.* ○ *FIGURATIVE I try not to clutter **(up)** my mind with useless information.* **cluttered** /ˈklʌt.əd/ [US] /ˈklʌt̬.ɚd/ *adj*: *a cluttered desk/room*

cm *WRITTEN ABBREVIATION FOR* **centimetre**: *a piece of glass 22 cm by 35 cm*

C

c'mon /kə'mɒn/ ⑩ /-mɑːn/ *short form of* come on: *Oh c'mon, you don't really mean that!*

CND /ˌsiː.en'diː/ *noun* [U] *ABBREVIATION FOR* Campaign for Nuclear Disarmament: a British organization which opposes the development and use of nuclear weapons

CNN /ˌsiː.en'en/ *group noun* [U] *ABBREVIATION FOR* Cable News Network: a US organization that broadcasts news on television internationally

C-note /'siː.nəʊt/ ⑩ /-nəʊt/ *noun* [C] *US SLANG* a piece of paper money with the value of 100 dollars

CO [OFFICER] /ˌsiː'əʊ/ ⑩ /-'oʊ/ *noun* [C] *ABBREVIATION FOR* Commanding Officer: a person in charge of a military unit

Co. [BUSINESS] /kəʊ/ ⑩ /koʊ/ *noun* [U] *ABBREVIATION FOR* **company** BUSINESS: *Peters, Stynes & Co.*
• **and co.** *INFORMAL* and other people: *K Branagh and co. have achieved great success in a very short time.*

Co. [AREA] *noun* [U] *ABBREVIATION FOR* county, when used in names: *Co. Durham*

co- [TOGETHER] /kəʊ-/ ⑩ /koʊ-/ *prefix* together; with: *co-ownership* ○ *a co-writer/co-author* ○ *Appalling poverty and great wealth co-exist in the city.*

c/o [LETTERS] /ˌsiː'əʊ/ ⑩ /-'oʊ/ *ABBREVIATION FOR* care of: used in addresses when the person you are writing to is staying at someone else's home: *Sylvia Mendez, c/o Ann Smith, 12 Glastonbury Lane, Bickerton*

coach [VEHICLE] /kəʊtʃ/ ⑩ /koʊtʃ/ *noun* [C] **1** (*US USUALLY* **bus**) a long motor vehicle with comfortable seats, used to take groups of people on journeys: *We're going to the airport by coach.* ○ *a coach trip* ⊃See picture **Cars and Trucks** on page Centre 13 **2** an old-fashioned carriage pulled by horses, now used mainly in official or royal ceremonies **3** *UK* (*US* **car**) a carriage in a train

coach [TEACH] /kəʊtʃ/ ⑩ /koʊtʃ/ *verb* [I or T] to give special classes in sports or a school subject, especially privately, to one person or a small group: *She coaches students in French, usually for exams.*
coach /kəʊtʃ/ ⑩ /koʊtʃ/ *noun* [C] someone whose job is to teach people to improve at a sport, skill, or school subject: *a tennis/maths coach* **coaching** /'kəʊ.tʃɪŋ/ ⑩ /'koʊ-/ *noun* [U] *You're very behind in your English – why don't you get some extra coaching?*

coach [TRAVEL] /kəʊtʃ/ ⑩ /koʊtʃ/ *noun* [U], *adv* *US* the cheapest type of seats on a plane or train: *Even the company's director flies coach most of the time.*

coach ˌstation *noun* [C] *UK* a place where COACHES (= vehicles) arrive and leave from

coachwork /'kəʊtʃ.wɜːk/ ⑩ /'koʊtʃ.wɜːrk/ *noun* [U] *UK* the body of a car or other vehicle, especially the outside painted surface

coagulate /kəʊ'æg.jʊ.leɪt/ ⑩ /koʊ-/ *verb* [I or T] to change from liquid to a more solid state, or to cause something to do this: *The sauce coagulated as it cooled down.* ○ *The venom of this snake coagulates the blood.*

coal /kəʊl/ ⑩ /koʊl/ *noun* [C or U] a hard, black substance which is dug from the earth in lumps, and can be burnt to produce heat or power, or a single piece of this: *How much coal was mined here?* ○ *a burning/red hot coal*
• **haul/drag sb over the coals** to speak angrily to someone because they have done something you disapprove of: *He was hauled over the coals for coming in late for work.*
• **carry/take coals to Newcastle** *UK* to supply something to a place or person that already has a lot of that particular thing: *Exporting pine to Scandinavia seems a bit like carrying coals to Newcastle.*

coal 'black *adj* pure black: *She stared into his coal-black eyes.*

coal ˌbunker *noun* [C] a large container, especially outside a house, for storing coal

coalesce /kəʊ.ə'les/ ⑩ /koʊ-/ *verb* [I] *FORMAL* If two or more things coalesce, they come or grow together to form one thing or system.
coalescence /kəʊ.ə'les.ᵊnts/ ⑩ /koʊ-/ *noun* [U] *FORMAL* the process of coalescing

coalface /'kəʊl.feɪs/ ⑩ /'koʊl-/ *noun* [C] the surface from which coal is cut
• **at the coalface** *UK* doing the work involved in a job, in real working conditions, rather than planning or talk-

ing about it: *At the coalface with a deadline looming, you sometimes feel under a lot of pressure.*

coalfield /'kəʊl.fiːld/ ⑩ /'koʊl-/ *noun* [C] an area where there is a lot of coal in the ground

coal-fired /'kəʊl.faɪəd/ ⑩ /'koʊl.faɪrd/ *adj* fuelled by coal: *a coal-fired boiler*

coalition /kəʊ.ə'lɪʃ.ᵊn/ ⑩ /koʊ-/ *noun* [C or U] the union of different political parties or groups for a particular purpose, usually for a limited time: *Government by coalition has its own peculiar set of problems.* ○ *By forming a coalition, the rebels and the opposition parties defeated the government.* ○ *a coalition government*

coal ˌmine *noun* [C] the deep hole or system of holes under the ground from which coal is removed
coal ˌminer *noun* [C] a person who works in a coal mine removing coal from the ground **coal ˌmining** *noun* [U]

coal ˌscuttle *noun* [C] a container with a handle in which coal is kept inside a house

coal ˌtar *noun* [U] a sticky black substance made from coal which is used to make various chemical products

coarse [ROUGH] /kɔːs/ ⑩ /kɔːrs/ *adj* rough and not smooth or soft, or not in very small pieces: *coarse sand/breadcrumbs* ○ *Linen is a coarse-grained fabric.*
coarsen /'kɔː.sᵊn/ ⑩ /'kɔːr-/ *verb* [I or T] to become coarse or cause something to become coarse **coarseness** /'kɔː.snəs/ ⑩ /'kɔːr-/ *noun* [U] *The coarseness of the cloth irritated her skin.*

coarse [RUDE] /kɔːs/ ⑩ /kɔːrs/ *adj* rude and offensive: *a coarse joke* ○ *coarse language* **coarsely** /'kɔː.sli/ ⑩ /'kɔːr-/ *adv* **coarseness** /'kɔː.snəs/ ⑩ /'kɔːr-/ *noun* [U] *She can't abide coarseness and stupidity.*

coast [LAND] /kəʊst/ ⑩ /koʊst/ *noun* [C] the land next to or close to the sea: *Rimini is a thriving holiday resort on the east coast of Italy.* ○ *The accident happened three miles off the coast* (= in the sea three miles from land). ○ *We spent a week by/on the coast* (= by the sea).
• **the coast is clear** it is safe to do something or go somewhere because no one is watching or listening who would prevent you or catch you: *You can come out now, the coast is clear.*
• **coast to coast** from one side of the country to the other: *We travelled across America coast to coast.*
coastal /'kəʊ.stᵊl/ ⑩ /'koʊst-/ *adj* situated on, or relating to the coast: *a coastal town*

coast [MOVE] /kəʊst/ ⑩ /koʊst/ *verb* [I] **1** to move forward in a vehicle without using the engine, usually down a hill: *At the top of the hill I switched off the engine and we just coasted down the other side.* **2** to progress or succeed without any effort or difficulty: *While I struggled, my sister coasted through school with top grades.*

coaster [OBJECT] /'kəʊ.stəʳ/ ⑩ /'koʊ.stɚ/ *noun* [C] a small piece of wood, plastic or other material that you put a glass or cup on to protect a surface from heat or liquid

coaster [BOAT] /'kəʊ.stəʳ/ ⑩ /'koʊ.stɚ/ *noun* [C] a ship which sails between ports along a coast

coastguard /'kəʊst.gɑːd/ ⑩ /'koʊst.gɑːrd/ *noun* [C] an official who is employed to watch the sea near to a coast for ships that are in danger or involved with illegal activities
the 'coast,guard *group noun* [S] the official organization which coastguards belong to

coastline /'kəʊst.laɪn/ ⑩ /'koʊst-/ *noun* [C or U] the particular shape of the coast, especially as seen from above, from the sea, or on a map

coat [CLOTHING] /kəʊt/ ⑩ /koʊt/ *noun* [C] **1** an outer piece of clothing with sleeves which is worn over other clothes, usually for warmth: *Do your coat up, Joe, or you'll freeze.* ○ *We need a coat hook on the back of this door.* ⊃See picture **Clothes** on page Centre 6 **2** used as a combining form: *an overcoat* ○ *a raincoat*

coat [ANIMAL] /kəʊt/ ⑩ /koʊt/ *noun* [C] the hair, wool or fur covering an animal: *a thick/glossy/matted coat* **-coated** /-kəʊ.tɪd/ ⑩ /-koʊ.t̬ɪd/ *suffix*: *a smooth-coated dog*

coat [COVER] /kəʊt/ ⑩ /koʊt/ *verb* [T] to cover something with a layer of a particular substance: *When the biscuits are cool, you coat them in/with melted chocolate.* **coat** /kəʊt/ ⑩ /koʊt/ *noun* [C] (*ALSO* **coating**) *I'll give the walls a* quick coat *of* paint. ○ *two coats of varnish* ○ *a thick coating of chocolate*

coated /ˈkəʊ.tɪd/ ⓤ /ˈkoʊ.t̬ɪd/ *adj* thickly covered: *Your trousers are coated in mud!* -coated /-kəʊ.tɪd/ ⓤ /-koʊ.t̬ɪd/ *suffix*: *sugar*-coated almonds

'coat ,hanger *noun* [C] a hanger

,coat of 'arms *noun* [C] *plural* coats of arms a special SHIELD or shield-shaped pattern which is the sign of a family, university or city

coat-tails /ˈkəʊt.teɪlz/ ⓤ /ˈkoʊt-/ *plural noun* the long divided pieces of cloth that hang down from the back of an old-fashioned, formal type of man's jacket ⊃See also tailcoat.

coax /kəʊks/ ⓤ /koʊks/ *verb* [T] to persuade someone gently to do something or go somewhere, by being kind and patient, or by appearing to be: *Perhaps you could coax your father into taking you to the station.* ○ *He has some information I want, so I'm going to try to coax it out of him over a drink.* ○ *A mother was coaxing her reluctant child into the water.* ○ *a coaxing voice* coaxing /ˈkəʊk.sɪŋ/ ⓤ /ˈkoʊk-/ *noun* [U] *A bit of gentle coaxing is all that's required and he'll come, I'm sure.* coaxingly /ˈkəʊk.sɪŋ.li/ ⓤ /ˈkoʊk-/ *adv*

cob HORSE /kɒb/ ⓤ /kɑːb/ *noun* [C] a strong horse with short legs ⊃See also corn on the cob.

cob BIRD /kɒb/ ⓤ /kɑːb/ *noun* [C] a male swan

cob BREAD /kɒb/ ⓤ /kɑːb/ *noun* [C] *UK* a round loaf of bread

cobalt /ˈkəʊ.bɒlt/ ⓤ /ˈkoʊ.bɑːlt/ *noun* [U] a hard silvery white metal used in metal mixtures and for colouring materials blue

,cobalt ('blue) *adj, noun* [U] (having) a deep blue or greenish-blue colour

cobber /ˈkɒb.əʳ/ ⓤ /ˈkɑː.bɚ/ *noun* [C] *AUS OLD-FASHIONED INFORMAL* (used especially by a man speaking to or about another man) a friend

cobble /ˈkɒb.l̩/ ⓤ /ˈkɑː.bl̩/ *noun* [C usually pl] (*ALSO* cobblestone) a rounded stone used on the surface of an old-fashioned road: *The cart rumbled over the cobbles.*

cobbled /ˈkɒb.l̩d/ ⓤ /ˈkɑː.bl̩d/ *adj* made of cobbles: *cobbled streets*

cobble /ˈkɒb.l̩/ ⓤ /ˈkɑː.bl̩/ *verb*

▲ cobble *sth* together *phrasal verb* [M] to do or make something quickly and not very carefully: *I just had to cobble this meal together from what I had in the fridge.*

cobbler /ˈkɒb.ləʳ/ ⓤ /ˈkɑː.blɚ/ *noun* [C] a person who repairs shoes

cobblers /ˈkɒb.ləz/ ⓤ /ˈkɑː.blɚz/ *noun* [U] *UK SLANG* nonsense or lies: *a load of old cobblers*

cobnut /ˈkɒb.nʌt/ ⓤ /ˈkɑː.bʌt/ *noun* [C] a hazelnut

cobra /ˈkəʊ.brə/ ⓤ /ˈkoʊ-/ *noun* [C] a poisonous snake from Africa or southern Asia which makes itself look bigger and more threatening by spreading the skin at the back of its head

cobweb /ˈkɒb.web/ ⓤ /ˈkɑː-/ *noun* [C] a net-like structure of sticky silk threads made by a spider for catching insects

Coca Cola /ˌkəʊ.kəˈkəʊ.lə/ ⓤ /ˌkoʊ.kəˈkoʊ.lə/ *noun* [C or U] (*INFORMAL* Coke) *TRADEMARK* a fizzy sweet dark-brown drink

cocaine /kəʊˈkeɪn/ ⓤ /koʊ-/ *noun* [U] a drug used in medicine to prevent pain and also used illegally, often in the form of white powder which is breathed in through the nose

coccyx /ˈkɒk.sɪks/ ⓤ /ˈkɑːk-/ *noun* [C] *plural* coccyxes or coccyges *SPECIALIZED* a small triangular bone at the base of the spine of humans and some apes

cochineal /ˌkɒtʃ.ɪˈniːl/ ⓤ /ˈkɑː.tʃ.ɪ-/ *noun* [U] a bright red substance used as a food colouring, made from a type of small South American insect

cochlea /ˈkɒk.li.ə/ ⓤ /ˈkɑːk-/ *noun* [C] *plural* cochleae or cochleas *SPECIALIZED* a twisted tube inside the inner ear which is the main organ of hearing

cock BIRD /kɒk/ ⓤ /kɑːk/ *noun* [C] (*US ALSO* rooster) **1** an adult male chicken: *The cock started to crow.* **2** used with the name of a bird to refer to the adult male of that type: *a cock robin* ○ *a cock pheasant*

cock PENIS /kɒk/ ⓤ /kɑːk/ *noun* [C] *OFFENSIVE* a penis

cock TURN /kɒk/ ⓤ /kɑːk/ *verb* [T] to move a part of your body upwards or in a particular direction: *He cocked his head on one side with a slight frown.* ○ *The dog cocked its leg against a tree.* ○ *to cock an ear/eyebrow* cocked /kɒkt/ ⓤ /kɑːkt/ *adj*: *Her hat was cocked at a jaunty angle.*

cock PREPARE GUN /kɒk/ ⓤ /kɑːk/ *verb* [T] to push the necessary piece of a gun up into position so that it is ready for firing: *The marksman cocked his rifle and took aim.*

cock FORM OF ADDRESS /kɒk/ ⓤ /kɑːk/ *noun* (*ALSO* cocker) *UK OLD-FASHIONED INFORMAL* an affectionate form of address, used especially by a man talking to another man: *Wotcher, cock! How's things?*

cock SHOW LACK OF RESPECT /kɒk/ ⓤ /kɑːk/ *verb UK* cock a snook at *sb/sth* to do something intentionally to show a lack of respect for someone or something: *He could seldom resist an opportunity to cock a snook at traditional English life.*

▲ cock *sth* up *phrasal verb* [M] *UK SLANG* to do something wrong or badly: *David cocked up the arrangements and we ended up missing the reception.* ○ *"How did the exam go?" "Terrible – I panicked and really cocked it up."*

cock-up /ˈkɒk.ʌp/ ⓤ /ˈkɑːk-/ *noun* [C] *Gerry's made a right cock-up with/of those figures?* ○ *So it was delivered to the wrong place? What a cock-up!*

cockade /kɒkˈeɪd/ ⓤ /kɑːˈkeɪd/ *noun* [C] a decorative knot of cloth worn in the hat, often for ceremonial purposes, to show rank

cock-a-doodle-doo /ˌkɒk.ə.duː.dl̩ˈduː/ ⓤ /ˌkɑːk-/ *noun* [C] *CHILD'S WORD* the long call which the COCK (= adult male chicken) makes

cock-a-hoop /ˌkɒk.əˈhuːp/ ⓤ /ˌkɑːk-/ *adj* [after v] extremely happy and excited about something: *Graeme was cock-a-hoop when Hibs won the championship.*

cock-a-leekie /ˌkɒk.əˈliː.ki/ ⓤ /ˌkɑːk-/ *noun* [U] a soup, originally from Scotland, made from boiled chicken and vegetables

cockamamie /ˌkɒk.əˈmeɪ.mi/ ⓤ /ˌkɑːk-/ *adj US SLANG* ridiculous or foolish: *He had some cockamamie idea about turning waste paper into animal food.*

cock-and-bull story /ˌkɒk.ənd.bʊlˈstɔː.ri/ ⓤ /ˌkɑːk.ənd-ˈbʊlstɔːr.i/ *noun* [C] *INFORMAL DISAPPROVING* a story which is obviously not true, especially one given as an excuse: *He gave me some cock-and-bull story about having to be at his cousin's engagement party.*

cockatoo /ˌkɒk.əˈtuː/ ⓤ /ˈkɑːk.kə.tuː/ *noun* [C] *plural* cockatoos or cockatoo an Australian bird with a decorative CREST (= growth of feathers) on its head and a powerful beak

cockchafer /ˈkɒk.tʃeɪ.fəʳ/ ⓤ /ˈkɑːk.tʃeɪ.fɚ/ *noun* [C] a type of European beetle which causes damage to trees

cockerel /ˈkɒk.ˀr.ˀl/ /-rəl/ ⓤ /ˈkɑː.kɚ-/ *noun* [C] a young male chicken

,cocker 'spaniel *noun* [C] a breed of dog with long ears, short legs, and fur that is white and brown or white and black

cockeyed SLOPING /ˌkɒkˈaɪd/ ⓤ /ˌkɑːk-/ *adj INFORMAL* not straight, but sloping to one side: *Would you straighten that picture over there? – It's a bit cockeyed.*

cockeyed RIDICULOUS /ˌkɒkˈaɪd/ ⓤ /ˌkɑːk-/ *adj* describes a plan or idea that is ridiculous, unsuitable or unlikely to be successful: *The government has dreamed up some cockeyed scheme for getting unemployed youngsters back into work.*

'cock ,fight *noun* [C] an activity, illegal in Britain, in which people watch as two male chickens attack each other and bet on which one will win

cockle /ˈkɒk.l̩/ ⓤ /ˈkɑː.kl̩/ *noun* [C] a small rounded edible sea creature with a shell, common in Europe

Cockney /ˈkɒk.ni/ ⓤ /ˈkɑːk-/ *noun* **1** [U] the type of speech used in East London, especially the poorer part: *You won't hear much real Cockney spoken unless you go to the East End.* **2** [C] a person from East London, who speaks Cockney Cockney /ˈkɒk.ni/ ⓤ /ˈkɑːk-/ *adj*: *a Cockney accent*

,Cockney 'rhyming ,slang *noun* [U] slang which is used instead of a word or phrase and which rhymes

C

with it: *In Cockney rhyming slang, 'apples and pears' means 'stairs'.*

cockpit /ˈkɒk.pɪt/ [US] /ˈkɑːk-/ *noun* [C] the small enclosed space where the pilot sits in an aircraft, or where the driver sits in a racing car ➲See picture **Planes, Ships and Boats** on page Centre 14

cockroach /ˈkɒk.rəʊtʃ/ [US] /ˈkɑːk.roʊtʃ/ *noun* [C] a flat brown or black insect sometimes found in the home

cockscomb /ˈkɒks.kəʊm/ [US] /ˈkɑːks.koʊm/ *noun* [C] (*ALSO* **comb**) the soft red growth on the head of a male chicken

cocksure /ˌkɒkˈʃɔːʳ/ [US] /ˌkɑːkˈʃɝː/ *adj INFORMAL DISAPPROVING* too confident, in a way that is slightly unpleasant or rude: *a cocksure young man*

cocktail [DRINK] /ˈkɒk.teɪl/ [US] /ˈkɑːk-/ *noun* [C] a drink, usually an alcoholic one, made by mixing two or more drinks together: *We were all in the bar* ***sipping*** *cocktails.* ○ *a champagne cocktail*

cocktail [MIXTURE] /ˈkɒk.teɪl/ [US] /ˈkɑːk-/ *noun* [C usually sing] a mixture of different things, often an unexpected, dangerous or exciting one: *The inquest heard that the guitarist died from a cocktail* ***of*** *drink and drugs.* ○ *Cars produce a* ***lethal*** *cocktail* ***of*** *gasses.*

cocktail [DISH] /ˈkɒk.teɪl/ [US] /ˈkɑːk-/ *noun* [C or U] a cold dish, often eaten at the start of a meal, consisting of small pieces of food: *fruit cocktail* ○ *a prawn/seafood cocktail*

ˈcocktail ˌdress *noun* [C] a dress worn for a special social occasion in the evening, such as a party or dance

ˈcocktail ˌlounge *noun* [C] a large comfortable room in a hotel where you can meet people and be served alcoholic drinks

ˈcocktail ˌparty *noun* [C] a formal party with alcoholic drinks, usually in the early evening

ˈcocktail ˌstick *noun* [C] a small pointed wooden or plastic stick on which small pieces of food, such as cheese or sausage, are served to guests at parties

cocky /ˈkɒk.i/ [US] /ˈkɑː.ki/ *adj INFORMAL DISAPPROVING* describes a young person who is confident in a way that is unpleasant and sometimes rude: *He's a bit cocky for my liking.*

cocoa /ˈkəʊ.kəʊ/ [US] /ˈkoʊ.koʊ/ *noun* [U] **1** a dark brown powder made from COCOA BEANS, used to make chocolate and add a chocolate flavour to food and drink **2** a sweet chocolate drink that is made with cocoa powder: *a nice hot mug of cocoa*

ˈcocoa ˌbean *noun* [C] the seed of the tropical CACAO tree

ˈcocoa ˌbutter *noun* [U] a fatty substance from the COCOA BEAN used in some foods and also in products for the skin and hair

coconut /ˈkəʊ.kə.nʌt/ [US] /ˈkoʊ-/ *noun* **1** [C] a large nut-like fruit with a woody brown shell containing hard white edible flesh and a white liquid ➲See picture **Fruit** on page Centre 1 **2** [U] the white flesh of the coconut, often used in cooking: ***grated/shredded*** *coconut*

ˈcoconut ˌshy *noun* [C] *UK* a game at a fair where you throw balls at a row of COCONUTS and try to knock them down to win them

cocoon [COVER] /kəˈkuːn/ *noun* [C] the covering made of soft smooth threads that encloses and protects particular insects during the PUPA stage as they develop into adult form

cocoon [PROTECTED PLACE] /kəˈkuːn/ *noun* [C usually sing] a safe quiet place: *the warm, safe cocoon of childhood*

cocoon /kəˈkuːn/ *verb* [T usually passive] to protect someone or something from pain or unpleasantness: *As a student you're cocooned* ***against/from*** *the real world.*

cod [FISH] /kɒd/ [US] /kɑːd/ *noun* [C or U] *plural* **cod** a large sea fish which can be eaten: *Cod and chips, please.*

COD [PAYMENT] /ˌsiː.əʊˈdiː/ [US] /-oʊˈ-/ *adv ABBREVIATION FOR* cash on delivery: payment will be made when goods are delivered

coda /ˈkəʊ.də/ [US] /ˈkoʊ-/ *noun* [C] **1** *SPECIALIZED* a piece of music at the end of a longer piece of music, which is usually separate from the basic structure: *The coda is often more technically difficult than the rest of the piece.* **2** *FORMAL* the final or additional part of a speech, event or piece of writing: *In a coda* ***to*** *the main exhibition are various works which were once attributed to Rembrandt.*

coddle [COOK] /ˈkɒd.l̩/ [US] /ˈkɑː.dl̩/ *verb* [T] to cook food, especially eggs, in water just below boiling temperature: *coddled eggs*

coddle [PROTECT] /ˈkɒd.l̩/ [US] /ˈkɑː.dl̩/ *verb* [T] to protect someone or something too much: *The steel industry is coddled by trade protection and massive subsidies.*

code [LANGUAGE] /kəʊd/ [US] /koʊd/ *noun* [C or U] a system of words, letters or signs which is used to represent a message in secret form, or a system of numbers, letters or signals which is used to represent something in a shorter or more convenient form: *The message was written* ***in*** *code.* ○ *She managed to* ***decipher/break/crack*** (= succeed in understanding) *the code.* ○ *Each entry in this dictionary has a grammar code.*

code /kəʊd/ [US] /koʊd/ *verb* [T] to represent a message in code so that it can only be understood by the person who is meant to receive it

coded /kəʊd.ɪd/ [US] /koʊd-/ *adj* written or sent in code: *a coded message/warning*

code [LAW] /kəʊd/ [US] /koʊd/ *noun* [C] **1** a set of rules which are accepted as general principles, or a set of written rules which state how people in a particular organization or country should behave: *Clinics will be subject to a new code* ***of conduct*** *and stronger controls by local authorities.* **2** a set of principles that are accepted and used by society or a particular group of people: *a moral code* ○ *a code of behaviour/ethics*

codeine /ˈkəʊ.diːn/ [US] /ˈkoʊ-/ *noun* [U] a drug made from OPIUM which is used to reduce pain

ˈcode ˌname *noun* [C] a special word or name which is used instead of the real name of someone or something to keep the real name secret: *Her code name is 'Running Bear'.* **code-name** /ˈkəʊd.neɪm/ [US] /ˈkoʊd-/ *verb* [T] *We've code-named the new project 'Entropy'.*

ˌcode of ˈpractice *noun* [C] a set of standards agreed on by a group of people who do a particular job

codex /ˈkəʊ.deks/ [US] /ˈkoʊ-/ *noun* [C] *plural* **codices** *SPECIALIZED* an ancient book which was written by hand

codger /ˈkɒdʒ.əʳ/ [US] /ˈkɑː.dʒɚ/ *noun* [C] *INFORMAL* an old man, especially one who is strange or amusing in some way: *A couple of* ***old*** *codgers were sitting on the park bench, grumbling about the children.*

codicil /ˈkəʊ.dɪ.sɪl/ [US] /ˈkɑː-/ *noun* [C] *LEGAL* an instruction which is added to a will

codify /ˈkəʊ.dɪ.faɪ/ [US] /ˈkɑː-/ *verb* [T] *FORMAL* to arrange something, such as laws or rules, into a system

cod-liver oil /ˌkɒd.lɪv.əˈrɔɪl/ [US] /ˌkɑːd-/ *noun* [U] a thick yellow oily substance that contains vitamins A and D, which some people take to keep healthy

codpiece /ˈkɒd.piːs/ [US] /ˈkɑːd-/ *noun* [C] *OLD USE* a small bag-like piece of clothing in 15th and 16th-century fashion, which covered the opening at the front of men's trousers

codswallop /ˈkɒdzˌwɒl.əp/ [US] /ˈkɑːdzˌwɑː.ləp/ *noun* [U] *UK SLANG* nonsense: *What* ***a load of*** *codswallop!*

co-ed /ˌkəʊˈed/ [US] /ˌkoʊ-/ *adj INFORMAL FOR* **co-educational**

co-ed /ˌkəʊˈed/ [US] /ˌkoʊ-/ *noun* [C] *US OLD-FASHIONED INFORMAL* a female student in a college with male and female students

co-educational /ˌkəʊ.ed.jʊˈkeɪ.ʃᵊn.ᵊl/ [US] /ˌkoʊ-/ *adj* (*INFORMAL* **co-ed**) having male and female students being taught together in the same school or college rather than separately: *Girls tend to do better academically in single-sex schools than in co-educational ones.*

co-education /ˌkəʊ.ed.jʊˈkeɪ.ʃᵊn/ [US] /ˌkoʊ-/ *noun* [U] the teaching of male and female students together

coefficient /ˌkəʊ.ɪˈfɪʃ.ᵊnt/ [US] /ˌkoʊ-/ *noun* [C] *SPECIALIZED* a value, in mathematics, that appears in front of and multiplies another value: *In* $2x + 4y = 7$, *2 is* ***the*** *coefficient* ***of*** *x.*

coeliac disease /ˌsiː.liː.æk.dɪˈziːz/ *noun* [U] a medical condition in which the intestine reacts badly to a type of protein contained in GLUTEN (= a protein found in wheat, etc.): *People with coeliac disease need to keep to a gluten-free diet.*

coequal /ˌkəʊˈiːˌkwəl/ ⓤ /ˌkoʊ-/ *adj FORMAL* equal in rank, ability or power to another person or thing **coequal** /ˌkəʊˈiːˌkwəl/ ⓤ /ˌkoʊ-/ *noun* [C]

coerce /kəʊˈɜːs/ ⓤ /koʊˈɜːs/ *verb* [T] *FORMAL* to persuade someone forcefully to do something which they are unwilling to do: *The court heard that the six defendants had been coerced into making a confession.* **coercion** /kəʊˈɜːʃ°n/ ⓤ /koʊˈɜː-/ *noun* [U] *He claimed the police had used coercion, threats and promises to illegally obtain the statement.*

coercive /kəʊˈɜːsɪv/ ⓤ /koʊˈɜː-/ *adj* using force to persuade people to do things which they are unwilling to do: *The president relied on the coercive powers of the military.* ○ *coercive measures/tactics*

coeval /kəʊˈiːvºl/ ⓤ /koʊ-/ *adj FORMAL* of the same age or existing at the same time as another person or thing: *The abundant reef growth on Gotland was shown to be coeval with that in Estonia.* **coeval** /kəʊˈiːvºl/ ⓤ /koʊ-/ *noun* [C] *FORMAL* someone or something coeval

co-exist, **coexist** /ˌkəʊ.ɪɡˈzɪst/ ⓤ /ˌkoʊ-/ *verb* [I] to live or exist together at the same time or in the same place: *He does not believe that modern medicine can co-exist with faith-healing.* **coexistence** /ˌkəʊ.ɪɡˈzɪs.tºnts/ ⓤ /ˌkoʊ-/ *noun* [U] *The two communities enjoyed a period of peaceful coexistence.*

C of E *adj, noun* [U] *ABBREVIATION FOR* **the Church of England:** *a C of E service*

coffee /ˈkɒf.i/ ⓤ /ˈkɑː.fi/ *noun* [C or U] a dark brown powder with a strong flavour and smell that is made by crushing COFFEE BEANS, or a hot drink made from this powder: *decaffeinated coffee* ○ *fresh/instant coffee* ○ *a cup of coffee* ○ *Would you get some coffee when you go shopping?* ○ *If I drink too much coffee, I can't sleep.* ○ *Can I get you a coffee* (= cup of coffee)? ○ *I'd like a black coffee* (= a cup of coffee without milk)*, please.* ○ *Do you take* (= drink) *your coffee white* (= with milk)*?*

coffee bean *noun* [C] a seed of a tropical bush which is heated until it is brown and then crushed to make coffee

coffee break *noun* [C] a short rest from work in the morning or afternoon

coffee cake *noun* [C or U] **1** *UK* a cake that is flavoured with coffee **2** *US* a type of sweet bread which is made with nuts or fruit

coffee grinder *noun* [C] (*ALSO* **coffee mill**) a machine that crushes coffee beans to make coffee powder

coffee house *noun* [C] a restaurant, especially in central and northern Europe, where people have coffee or other drinks, cakes, and small meals

coffee morning *noun* [C] *UK* a social event where people meet to talk, drink coffee and eat cakes, often giving money to a charity or other organization

coffee pot *noun* [C] a container with a handle and shaped opening, for making and serving coffee in

coffee shop *noun* [C] **1** (*UK ALSO* **coffee bar**) a small informal restaurant where drinks and small meals are served, sometimes in a larger shop or building: *the hospital/theatre coffee shop* **2** a shop where different types of coffee are sold, either to drink or as beans or powder

coffee table *noun* [C] a small low table on which coffee is served or books and magazines are arranged

coffee-table book /ˈkɒf.i.teɪ.blˌbʊk/ ⓤ /ˈkɑː.fi-/ *noun* [C] a large expensive book with a lot of pictures, which is meant to be looked at rather than read

coffer /ˈkɒf.əʳ/ ⓤ /ˈkɑː.fɚ/ *noun* [C] a large strong box in which money or valuable objects are kept **coffers** /ˈkɒf.əz/ ⓤ /ˈkɑː.fɚz/ *plural noun* the money that an organization has in its bank accounts and available to spend: *government/party coffers*

cofferdam /ˈkɒf.ə.dæm/ ⓤ /ˈkɑː.fɚ-/ *noun* [C] *SPECIALIZED* a large box filled with air which allows people to work under water, for example while building bridges

coffin /ˈkɒf.ɪn/ ⓤ /ˈkɑː.fɪn/ *noun* [C] (*US ALSO* **casket**) a long box in which a dead person is buried or burnt

cog /kɒɡ/ ⓤ /kɑːɡ/ *noun* [C] **1** one of the tooth-like parts around the edge of a wheel in a machine which fits between those of a similar wheel, causing both wheels to move **2** (*ALSO* **cogwheel**) a wheel with cogs around its edge, used to turn another wheel or part in a machine
● **a cog in a/the machine** *DISAPPROVING* a member of a large organization whose job, although necessary, makes them feel unimportant: *I decided to set up my own business because I was tired of just being a cog in a machine.*

cogent /ˈkəʊ.dʒºnt/ ⓤ /ˈkoʊ-/ *adj FORMAL* describes an argument or reason, etc. that is clearly expressed and persuasive **cogently** /ˈkəʊ.dʒºnt.li/ ⓤ /ˈkoʊ-/ *adv*: *She argued most cogently for a relaxation of the sanctions.* **cogency** /ˈkəʊ.dʒºnt.si/ ⓤ /ˈkoʊ-/ *noun* [U]

cogitate /ˈkɒdʒ.ɪ.teɪt/ ⓤ /ˈkɑː.dʒɪ-/ *verb* [I] *FORMAL* to spend time thinking very carefully about a subject **cogitation** /ˌkɒdʒ.ɪˈteɪ.ʃºn/ ⓤ /ˌkɑː.dʒɪ-/ *noun* [C or U]

cognac /ˈkɒn.jæk/ ⓤ /ˈkoʊ.njæk/ *noun* [C or U] high quality brandy made in western France, or a glass of this: *a bottle of cognac* ○ *Would you like another cognac?*

cognate /ˈkɒɡ.neɪt/ ⓤ /ˈkɑːɡ-/ *adj SPECIALIZED* describes languages and words that have the same origin, or that are related and in some way similar: *The Italian word 'mangiare'* (= to eat) *is cognate with the French 'manger'.* **cognate** /ˈkɒɡ.neɪt/ ⓤ /ˈkɑːɡ-/ *noun* [C] *SPECIALIZED* a word that has the same origin, or that is related in some way, to a word in another language

cognitive /ˈkɒɡ.nɪ.tɪv/ ⓤ /ˈkɑːɡ.nɪ.tɪv/ *adj* [before n] *SPECIALIZED* connected with thinking or conscious mental processes: *Some of her cognitive functions have been impaired.* ○ *cognitive behaviour/development* ○ *cognitive therapy/psychology*

cognition /kɒɡˈnɪʃ.ºn/ ⓤ /kɑːɡ-/ *noun* [U] *FORMAL OR SPECIALIZED* when you think or use a conscious mental process: *a book on human learning, memory and cognition*

cognizance /ˈkɒɡ.nɪ.zºnts/ ⓤ /ˈkɑːɡ-/ *noun FORMAL OR LEGAL* **take cognizance of sth** to take notice of and consider something, especially when judging: *The lawyer asked the jury to take cognizance of the defendant's generosity in giving to charity.*
cognizant /ˈkɒɡ.nɪ.zºnt/ ⓤ /ˈkɑːɡ-/ *adj FORMAL* Unfortunately, we were not cognizant of (= did not know about) *the full facts.*

cognoscenti /ˌkɒn.jəʊˈʃen.tiː/ ⓤ /ˌkɑː.njə-/ *plural noun FORMAL* a group of people who have a great knowledge and understanding of a particular subject, especially one of the arts: *Not being one of the cognoscenti, I failed to understand the ballet's subtler points.*

cogwheel /ˈkɒɡ.wiːl/ ⓤ /ˈkɑːɡ-/ *noun* [C] ➲See at **cog**.

cohabit /kəʊˈhæb.ɪt/ ⓤ /koʊ-/ *verb* [I] *FORMAL* If two people, especially a man and a woman who are not married, cohabit, they live together and have a sexual relationship: *About 23% of men and women aged 25 to 34 told researchers they had previously cohabited with a partner without it leading to marriage.* ○ *cohabiting couples*
cohabitant *FORMAL* /kəʊˈhæb.ɪ.tºnt/ ⓤ /koʊˈhæb.ɪ.t̬ºnt/ *noun* [C] (*FORMAL* **cohabitee**) the official term for someone who lives in the same house, apartment, etc. as someone else: *Is Mr Jones one of the cohabitants at this address?*
cohabitation /kəʊˌhæb.ɪˈteɪ.ʃºn/ ⓤ /koʊ-/ *noun* [U] *FORMAL* a cohabitation agreement

cohere /kəʊˈhɪəʳ/ ⓤ /koʊˈhɪr/ *verb* [I] *FORMAL* **1** If an argument or theory coheres, all the different stages fit together to form a persuasive whole. **2** to unite or to hold together as a unit: *His vision is of a world that coheres through human connection rather than rules.*

cohesion /kəʊˈhiː.ʒºn/ ⓤ /koʊˈhiː-/ *noun* [U] (*ALSO* **cohesiveness**) *FORMAL* when the members of a group or society are united: *social/national cohesion* ○ *The lack of cohesion within the party lost them votes in the election.*

cohesive /kəʊˈhiː.sɪv/ ⓤ /koʊ-/ *adj FORMAL* united and working together effectively: *a cohesive group* ○ *cohesive forces*

coherent /kəʊˈhɪə.rºnt/ ⓤ /koʊˈhɪr.ºnt/ *adj* **1** If an argument, set of ideas or a plan is coherent, it is clear and carefully considered, and each part of it connects or follows in a natural or sensible way. **2** If someone is coherent, you can understand what they say: *When she calmed down, she was more coherent* (= able to speak clearly and be understood).

coherence /kəʊˈhɪə.rənts/ ⑩ /koʊˈhɪr.³nts/ *noun* [U] the quality of cohering or being coherent: *There was no coherence between the first and the second half of the film.* **coherently** /kəʊˈhɪə.rənt.li/ ⑩ /koʊˈhɪr.³nt-/ *adv*

cohort /ˈkəʊ.hɔːt/ ⑩ /ˈkoʊ.hɔːrt/ *group noun* [C] **1** SPECIALIZED a group of people who share a characteristic, usually age: *This study followed up a cohort of 386 patients aged 65 + for six months after their discharge home.* **2** DISAPPROVING a group of people who support a particular person, usually a leader: *The Mayor and his cohorts have abused their positions of power.*

coiffed /kwɒft/ ⑩ /kwɑːft/ *adj* OFTEN HUMOROUS describes hair that is carefully arranged in an attractive style: *How do those TV mothers always manage to look so immaculately coiffed as they do the housework?*

coiffure /kwɑːˈfjʊər/ ⑩ /kwɑːˈfjʊr/ *noun* [C] FORMAL the style in which someone's hair is cut and arranged: *The star appeared on stage in a black leather outfit and a 1950s coiffure.*

coil CIRCLE /kɔɪl/ *noun* [C] **1** a length of rope, hair or wire, arranged into a series of circles, one above the other: *A coil of rope lay on the beach.* ○ FIGURATIVE *A coil of thick blue smoke rose up from his pipe.* **2** SPECIALIZED a twisted length of wire through which an electric current travels **coil** /kɔɪl/ *verb* [I or T] *She coiled her hair into a neat bun on top of her head.* ○ [R] *The snake coiled itself tightly around the deer.* **coiled** /kɔɪld/ *adj: a coiled spring*

coil MEDICAL /kɔɪl/ *noun* [C] UK INFORMAL an IUD (= a medical device to stop a woman becoming pregnant)

coin MONEY /kɔɪn/ *noun* **1** [C] a small round piece of metal, usually silver or copper coloured, which is used as money: *a 10p/ten pence coin* ○ *a pound coin* ○ *a ten-cent coin* ○ *gold coins* ○ *I asked for ten pounds in 20p coins.* ○ *That machine doesn't take 50p coins.* **2** [U] money in the form of metal coins **coin** /kɔɪn/ *verb* UK INFORMAL **coining it (in)** to be earning a lot of money quickly

coinage /ˈkɔɪ.nɪdʒ/ *noun* [U] a set of coins of different values used in a country's money system: *decimal coinage*

coin INVENT /kɔɪn/ *verb* [T] to invent a new word or expression, or to use one in a particular way for the first time: *Allen Ginsberg coined the term "flower power".*
● **to coin a phrase** HUMOROUS something you say before using an expression that has been very popular or used too much: *I was, to coin a phrase, gobsmacked!*
coinage /ˈkɔɪ.nɪdʒ/ *noun* [C or U] (the invention of) a new word or phrase in a language: *The expression 'boy band' is a nineties coinage.*

coincide /ˌkəʊ.ɪnˈsaɪd/ ⑩ /ˌkoʊ-/ *verb* [I] **1** to happen at or near the same time: *I timed my holiday to coincide with the children's school holiday.* ○ *If the heavy rain had coincided with an extreme high tide, serious flooding would have resulted.* **2** to be the same or similar: *Our views coincide on a range of subjects.* ○ *If our schedules coincide, we'll go to Spain together.*

coincidence /kəʊˈɪnt.sɪ.dənts/ ⑩ /koʊ-/ *noun* **1** [C] an occasion when two or more similar things happen at the same time, especially in a way that is unlikely and surprising: *You chose exactly the same wallpaper as us – what a coincidence!* ○ *Is it just a coincidence that the wife of the man who ran the competition won first prize?* ○ *a series of strange/amazing coincidences* **2** [U] chance or luck: *Just by coincidence, I met my old school-mate again fifty years later.* ○ [+ that] *It was pure/sheer coincidence that I remembered his phone number.* ○ *By some strange coincidence, he was passing the house just when it happened.*
coincidental /kəʊˌɪnt.sɪˈden.t³l/ ⑩ /koʊˌɪnt.sɪˈden.t³l/ *adj* happening by coincidence **coincidentally** /kəʊˌɪnt.sɪˈden.t³l.i/ ⑩ /koʊˌɪnt.sɪˈden.t³l.i/ *adv: The highest scorers, coincidentally, were all women.*

coitus /ˈkɔɪ.təs/ ⑩ /-t̬əs/ *noun* [U] SPECIALIZED the sexual act in which a man puts his penis into a woman's vagina **coital** /ˈkɔɪ.t³l/ ⑩ /-t̬³l/ *adj*

coitus interruptus /ˌkɔɪ.təs.ɪn.tə³rʌp.təs/ ⑩ /-təs.ɪn.tə-/ *noun* [U] a method of preventing pregnancy in which the man removes his penis from the woman's vagina before sperm is released

Coke DRINK /kəʊk/ ⑩ /koʊk/ *noun* [C or U] INFORMAL TRADEMARK FOR **Coca Cola**

coke FUEL /kəʊk/ ⑩ /koʊk/ *noun* [U] the solid grey substance that is left after coal is heated and the gas and TAR removed, which is burnt as a fuel

coke DRUG /kəʊk/ ⑩ /koʊk/ *noun* [U] SLANG FOR **cocaine**

Col. RANK, **Col** *noun* [C] WRITTEN ABBREVIATION FOR **colonel**: *Col. (Angus) Ferguson*

col. PRINTING, **col** /kɒl/ ⑩ /kɑːl/ *noun* [C] ABBREVIATION FOR **column** PRINTING

col- TOGETHER /kɒl-/ ⑩ /kɑːl-/ *prefix* together; with: *colleagues*

cola /ˈkəʊ.lə/ ⑩ /koʊ-/ *noun* [C or U] a sweet fizzy brown drink which does not contain alcohol: *Coke and Pepsi are types of cola.*

colander /ˈkʌl.ɪn.dər/ ⑩ /ˈkɑː.lən.dər/ *noun* [C] a bowl with small holes in it which is used for washing food or for emptying food into when it has been cooked in water: *After four minutes, pour the pasta into a colander to drain.* ⊃See picture **In the Kitchen** on page Centre 16

cold LOW TEMPERATURE /kəʊld/ ⑩ /koʊld/ *adj* at a low temperature, especially when compared to the temperature of the human body, and not hot or warm: *a cold day/house* ○ *cold food/water* ○ *cold hands* ○ *cold weather* ○ *My feet are so cold.* ○ *It's freezing cold today.* ○ *You'll feel cold if you don't wear a coat.*
● **be (as) cold as ice** to be extremely cold: *Feel my toes – they're as cold as ice.*
● **be cold comfort** When being told a particular thing about a bad situation is cold comfort, it does not make you feel better although it is intended to.
● **in cold blood** If someone kills in cold blood, they kill in a way that seems especially cruel because they show no emotion.
● **get cold feet** to suddenly become too frightened to do something you had planned to do, especially something important such as getting married
● **give sb the cold shoulder** (ALSO **cold-shoulder sb**) to be intentionally unfriendly to someone and give them no attention: *I tried to be pleasant to her but she gave me the cold shoulder.*
● **You're getting colder.** said by children playing a guessing or searching game to tell the person who is guessing or searching that they are getting further away from the answer or hidden object
● **pour/throw cold water on sth** to criticize someone's opinions or ideas and stop people believing them or being excited about them
● **Cold hands, warm heart.** SAYING said to someone with cold hands in order to stop them being embarrassed
cold /kəʊld/ ⑩ /koʊld/ *noun* [S or U] cold weather or temperatures: *Don't stand out there in the cold, come in here and get warm.* ○ *Old people tend to feel the cold* (= feel uncomfortable in cold temperatures) *more than the young.* ○ *My feet were numb with cold.*

cold UNFRIENDLY /kəʊld/ ⑩ /koʊld/ *adj* not showing affection, kindness or emotion and not friendly: *His handshake was cold, and his eyes lifeless.* ○ *He stared into her cold blue eyes.* ○ *She would never feel welcome in this city with its cold, unsmiling inhabitants.* ○ *The school was a cold, unwelcoming place.*
coldly /ˈkəʊld.li/ ⑩ /ˈkoʊld-/ *adv* in an unfriendly way and without emotion: *"That's your problem," she said coldly.* **coldness** /ˈkəʊld.nəs/ ⑩ /ˈkoʊld-/ *noun* [U] *It was the coldness of her manner that struck me.*

cold ILLNESS /kəʊld/ ⑩ /koʊld/ *noun* [C] a common infection especially in the nose and throat which often causes a cough, a slight fever and sometimes some pain in the muscles: *I've got a cold.* ○ *She caught a cold at school.* ○ UK INFORMAL *Don't come near me – I've got a stinking/streaming cold* (= extremely bad cold).

cold-blooded /ˌkəʊldˈblʌd.ɪd/ ⑩ /ˌkoʊld-/ *adj* **1** describes animals that can only control their body heat by taking in heat from the outside or by being very active: *Snakes and lizards are cold-blooded animals.*

⊃Compare **warm-blooded**. **2** showing great cruelty and no sympathy for other people: *a cold-blooded murder*

,**cold 'calling** *noun* [U] when a person in business telephones or visits a possible customer to try to sell them something without being asked by the customer to do so **cold-call** /ˌkəʊldˈkɔːl/ ⓤ /ˌkoʊldˈkɑːl/ *verb* [T] *We were cold-called by a company offering savings on our phone bill.*

'**cold ,cream** *noun* [U] a thick white oily substance used to clean the skin and stop it from becoming too dry

'**cold ,cuts** *plural noun* MAINLY US thin flat slices of cold meat

,**cold 'fish** *noun* [S] someone who seems unfriendly and who does not share their feelings

'**cold ,frame** *noun* [C] a glass or plastic box, with a top which can be left open, into which young plants are put for a short time, especially in order to help them grow faster or to protect them from cold weather

,**cold 'front** *noun* [C] the weather condition in which an advancing mass of cold air pushes into a mass of warm air resulting in a fall in temperature

cold-hearted /ˌkəʊldˈhɑːtɪd/ ⓤ /ˌkoʊldˈhɑːrtɪd/ *adj* DIS-APPROVING showing no understanding for or regret at another person's suffering: *a cold-hearted killer*

'**cold ,snap** *noun* [C] a short period of cold weather

'**cold ,sore** *noun* [C] a painful red swelling on especially the lips or nose which is caused by a virus

,**cold 'storage** *noun* [U] If something, usually food, is kept in cold storage, it is put in artificially cold conditions, usually to preserve it.

,**cold 'sweat** *noun* [C] a state of uncontrollable anxiety and fear: *I **break out in** a cold sweat* (= become extremely anxious) *just thinking about public speaking.*

,**cold 'turkey** *noun* [U] SLANG the period of extreme suffering which comes immediately after a person has stopped taking a drug on which they are dependent: *Six years ago she **went** cold turkey on* (= stopped completely) *a three-pack-a-day smoking habit.*

,**cold 'war** *noun* [C] a state of extreme unfriendliness existing between countries, especially with opposing political systems, which expresses itself not through fighting but through political pressure and threats. The expression is usually used of the relationship between the US and the Soviet Union after the Second World War.

coleslaw /ˈkəʊl.slɔː/ ⓤ /ˈkoʊl.slɑː/ *noun* [U] cold raw cabbage, carrot and onion, cut into long thin strips and covered in a thick creamy cold sauce

coley /ˈkəʊ.li/ ⓤ /ˈkoʊ-/ *noun* [C or U] *plural* **coley** a fish that lives in the North Atlantic, or the flesh of this fish eaten as food

colic /ˈkɒl.ɪk/ ⓤ /ˈkɑː.lɪk/ *noun* [U] a severe but not continuous pain in the bottom part of the stomach or bowels, especially of babies **colicky** /ˈkɒl.ɪ.ki/ ⓤ /ˈkɑː.lɪ-/ *adj*: *a colicky baby*

colitis /kəʊˈlaɪ.təs/ ⓤ /koʊˈlaɪ.təs/ *noun* [U] an illness of the COLON (= part of the bowels) in which the contents of the bowels are excreted too frequently

collaborate WORK WITH /kəˈlæb.ə.reɪt/ *verb* [I] to work with someone else for a special purpose: *Two writers collaborated **on** the script for the film.* ○ *A German company collaborated **with** a Swiss firm **to** develop the product.* ○ *The British and Italian police collaborated **in** catching the terrorists.*

collaboration /kəˌlæb.əˈreɪ.ʃ°n/ *noun* [C or U] when two or more people work together to create or achieve the same thing: *The two playwrights worked **in close** collaboration (**with** each other) on the script.* ○ *The new airport is a collaboration **between** two of the best architects in the country.* **collaborator** /kəˈlæb.ə.reɪ.tə°/ ⓤ /-t̬ə-/ *noun* [C] *a new production by Andrew Davies and collaborators*

collaborative /kəˈlæb.°r.ə.tɪv/ ⓤ /-ɚ.ə.t̬ɪv/ *adj* [before n] involving two or more people working together for a special purpose: *The presentation was a collaborative **effort** by all the children in the class.*

collaborate SUPPORT AN ENEMY /kəˈlæb.ə.reɪt/ *verb* [I] DIS-APPROVING to work with an enemy who has taken control

of your own country: *Anyone who was suspected of collaborating **with** the occupying forces was arrested.* **collaboration** /kəˌlæb.əˈreɪ.ʃ°n/ *noun* [U] *She was accused of collaboration.* **collaborator** /kəˈlæb.ə.reɪ.tə°/ ⓤ /-t̬ə-/ *noun* [C] *wartime collaborators* ○ *a Nazi collaborator*

collage /ˈkɒl.ɑːʒ/ ⓤ /ˈkɑː.lɑːʒ/ *noun* [C or U] (the art of making) a picture in which various materials or objects, for example paper, cloth or photographs, are stuck onto a larger surface: *The children made a collage of postcards.* ⊃Compare **assemblage**.

collagen /ˈkɒl.ə.dʒen/ ⓤ /ˈkɑː.lə-/ *noun* [U] a protein found especially in the joints of humans and animals

• **collagen implant/injection** an injection of collagen into the lips or skin to make the lips appear larger or the skin appear younger and smoother

collapse FALL /kəˈlæps/ *verb* **1** [I] to fall down suddenly because of pressure or lack of strength or support: *Thousands of buildings collapsed in the earthquake.* ○ *The chair collapsed **under** her weight.* ○ FIGURATIVE *He thought his whole world had collapsed when his wife died.* **2** [I] If someone collapses they fall down because they are ill or weak: *He collapsed and died of a heart attack.* **3** [I or T] to fold something into a smaller shape, usually so it can be stored, or (especially of furniture) to fold in this way: *All chairs collapse for easy storage.*

collapse /kəˈlæps/ *noun* [S or U] when a person or structure becomes too weak to stand and suddenly falls: *He was taken to hospital after his collapse on the pitch.* ○ *the collapse of a tower block during the earthquake*

collapsible /kəˈlæp.sɪ.bl̩/ *adj* describes furniture that can be folded, usually so it can be put or stored in a smaller space: *collapsible chairs*

collapsed /kəˈlæpst/ *adj* describes a lung or BLOOD VESSEL (= tube which carries blood in the body) which is not able to work because disease or injury has caused it to become flat

collapse FAIL /kəˈlæps/ *verb* [I] (of people and business) to suffer the sudden inability to continue or work correctly: *Lots of people lost their jobs when the property market collapsed.* ○ *Talks between management and unions have collapsed.* ○ *Share prices collapsed* (= became lower suddenly) *after news of poor trading.*

collapse /kəˈlæps/ *noun* [C or U] the sudden failure of a system, organization, business, etc: *I don't know what caused the collapse **of** her marriage.* ○ *A poor economy has caused the collapse **of** thousands of small businesses.* ○ *Negotiations between the two countries are **on the brink/verge of** collapse* (= very soon going to fail). ○ *He **suffered a mental/nervous** collapse after ten years' teaching.*

collar NECK /ˈkɒl.ə°/ ⓤ /ˈkɑː.lə-/ *noun* [C] **1** the part around the neck of a piece of clothing, usually sewn on and sometimes made of different material: *a shirt collar* ○ *a fur collar* ○ *a dress with a big collar* **2** a strap made of leather or other strong material which is put around the neck of an animal, especially a dog or cat: *I grabbed the dog by the collar and dragged it out of the room.* **3** a type of NECKLACE (= a piece of jewellery worn around the neck): *a diamond collar* **4** SPECIALIZED an area around the neck of an animal which is coloured differently from the other parts of the body: *The bird has grey feathers with a lighter collar.* **5** SPECIALIZED a strip of strong material that is put round a pipe or a piece of machinery to make it stronger or to join two parts together

collar CATCH /ˈkɒl.ə°/ ⓤ /ˈkɑː.lə-/ *verb* [T] **1** INFORMAL to catch and hold someone so that they cannot escape: *She was collared by the police at the airport.* **2** to find someone and stop them going somewhere, often so that you can talk to them about something: *I was collared by Pete as I was coming out of the meeting this morning.*

collarbone /ˈkɒl.ə.bəʊn/ ⓤ /ˈkɑː.lə-.boʊn/ *noun* [C] (SPECIALIZED **clavicle**) a bone between your shoulder and neck on each side of your body ⊃See picture **The Body** on page Centre 5

collate /kəˈleɪt/ *verb* [T] **1** FORMAL to bring together different pieces of written information so that the similarities and differences can be seen: *to collate data/ information* **2** to collect and arrange the sheets of a report, book, etc., in the correct order: *The photocopier will collate the documents for you.*

collation /kə'leɪ.ʃ°n/ *noun* [C or U] the act or an example of collating ⊃See also **collation**.

collateral MONEY /kə'læt.°r.°l/ US /-'læt̬.ɚ-/ *noun* [U] SPECIALIZED valuable property owned by someone who wants to borrow money which they agree will become the property of the company or person who lends the money if the debt is not paid back: *She used/put up her house as collateral for a loan.*

collateral CONNECTED /kə'læt.°r.°l/ US /-'læt̬.ɚ-/ *adj* FORMAL connected but additional and less important, or of the same family although not directly related: *collateral senses of a word* ○ *a collateral branch of the family*

col,lateral 'damage *noun* [U] during a war, the unintentional deaths and injuries of people who are not soldiers, and damage that is caused to their homes, hospitals, schools, etc.

collation /kə'leɪ.ʃ°n/ *noun* [C] FORMAL a meal, especially one left ready for people to serve themselves ⊃See also **collation** at **collate**.

colleague /'kɒl.iːg/ US /'kɑː.liːg/ *noun* [C] one of a group of people who work together: *We're entertaining some colleagues of Ben's tonight.*

collect GATHER /kə'lekt/ *verb* **1** [I or T] to gather together from a variety of places or over a period of time: *A large crowd of reporters collected outside the Prime Minister's house.* ○ *After the party I collected (up) twenty bottles from various parts of the house.* ○ *We're collecting (money) for the homeless.* ○ *These china ornaments just collect dust.* **2** [T] to get and keep things of one type such as stamps or coins as a hobby: *She collects dolls.* ○ *So when did you start collecting antique glass?*

collected /kə'lek.tɪd/ *adj* [before n] brought together in one book or series of books: *His collected poems were published in 1928.*

collection /kə'lek.ʃ°n/ *noun* [C] **1** a group of objects of one type that have been collected by one person or in one place: *a private art collection* ○ *a valuable stamp collection* **2** an amount of money collected from several people, or the act of collecting money: *We're having a collection for Tom's retirement present.* **3** a lot of things or people: *There's quite a collection of toothbrushes in the bathroom.* **4** a range of new clothes produced by one clothes DESIGNER: *Kenzo's summer/winter collection.*

collector /kə'lek.tə'/ US /-tɚ/ *noun* [C] someone who collects objects because they are beautiful, valuable or interesting: *a keen stamp/antiques collector* ○ *a collector of modern art*

collectable, collectible /kə'lek.tə.bl̩/ *adj* describes something that is considered to be worth collecting as a hobby: *Comics from the early sixties are highly collectable at the moment.*

collectable, collectible /kə'lek.tə.bl̩/ *noun* [C] any object which people want to collect as a hobby

collect GET /kə'lekt/ *verb* [T] UK to go to a place and bring someone or something away from: *Your shoes will be repaired and ready for you to collect on Thursday.* ○ *I'll collect you from the station.*

collection /kə'lek.ʃ°n/ *noun* [C or U] when something is taken away from a place: *The photos will be ready for collection on Tuesday afternoon.* ○ *Which day is the rubbish collection?* ○ UK *There are three collections a day from the post box on the corner.*

collector /kə'lek.tə'/ US /-tɚ/ *noun* [C] someone whose job is to collect tickets or money from people: *a tax/ticket collector*

collect CONTROL /kə'lekt/ *verb* FORMAL **collect yourself/ your thoughts** to get control of your feelings and thoughts, especially after shock, surprise or laughter: *I was so stunned by what he'd said I had to collect myself before I could reply.*

collected /kə'lek.tɪd/ *adj* showing control over your feelings: *She appeared calm and collected.*

collect PRAYER /kə'lekt/ *noun* [C] a short prayer which is said during some Christian religious ceremonies

collect TELEPHONE /kə'lekt/ *adj, adv* US When you telephone collect or make a collect telephone call, the person you telephone pays for the call: *I'd like to make a*

collect *call.* ○ *She called me collect.*

collective /kə'lek.tɪv/ *adj* [before n] of or shared by every member of a group of people: *a collective decision/effort* ○ *collective responsibility/leadership*

collective /kə'lek.tɪv/ *noun* [C] an organization or business which is owned and controlled by the people who work in it

collectively /kə'lek.tɪv.li/ *adv* as a group: *She has a staff of four who collectively earn almost $200 000.*

collectivism /kə'lek.tɪ.vɪ.z°m/ US /-t̬ə-/ *noun* [U] SPECIALIZED a theory or political system based on the principle that all of the farms, factories and other places of work in a country should be owned by or for all the people in that country

col,lective 'bargaining *noun* [U] the system in which employees talk as a group with their employers to try to agree on matters such as pay and working conditions

col,lective 'farm *noun* [C] (originally in countries which had a communist system of government), a large farm or group of farms owned by the state but controlled by the workers

col,lective 'noun *noun* [C] SPECIALIZED a noun which describes a group of things or people as a unit: *'Family' and 'flock' are examples of collective nouns.*

collector's item /kə,lek.təz-/ US /-tɚz-/ *noun* [C] (ALSO **collector's piece**) an object which is very valuable to a person who collects those objects as a hobby because it is so rare or beautiful

colleen /kɒl'iːn/ US /kɑː'liːn/ *noun* [C] **1** IRISH ENGLISH a girl or young woman **2** US a girl from Ireland

college EDUCATION /'kɒl.ɪdʒ/ US /'kɑː.lɪdʒ/ *noun* **1** [C or U] any place for specialized education after the age of 16 where people study or train to get knowledge and/or skills: *a teacher training college* ○ *a secretarial college* ○ *a Naval college* ○ UK *a sixth form college* ○ *She's at art college.* **2** [C or U] US university: *You have to go to* (= study at) *college for a lot of years if you want to be a doctor.* **3** [C] one of the separate and named parts into which some universities are divided: *King's College, Cambridge* ○ *I attended the College of Arts and Sciences at New York University.* ○ *Cambridge has some very fine old colleges* (= college buildings). **4** [C] in Britain and Australia, used in the names of some schools for children, especially those where education is paid for: *Cheltenham Ladies' College*

collegiate /kə'liː.dʒi.ət/ US /-dʒɪt/ *adj* **1** of or belonging to a college or its students: *a collegiate theatre* ○ *collegiate sports* **2** UK formed of colleges: *Oxford and Cambridge are both collegiate universities.*

college GROUP /'kɒl.ɪdʒ/ US /'kɑː.lɪdʒ/ *noun* [C] a group of people with a particular job, purpose, duty or power who are organized into a group for sharing ideas, making decisions, etc: *the Royal College of Medicine/Nursing*

collide /kə'laɪd/ *verb* [I] (especially of moving objects) to hit something violently: *The two vans collided at the crossroads.* ○ *It was predicted that a comet would collide with one of the planets.*

collie /'kɒl.i/ US /'kɑː.li/ *noun* [C] any of several breeds of long-haired dog which are bred for controlling sheep

colliery /'kɒl.i.°r.i/ US /'kɑː.ljɚ-/ *noun* [C] a coal mine and all the buildings, machines, etc. connected with it

collier /'kɒl.i.ə'/ US /'kɑː.ljɚ/ *noun* [C] **1** FORMAL a coal miner ⊃See at **coal mine**. **2** a ship used for carrying coal

collision /kə'lɪʒ.°n/ *noun* **1** [C or U] an accident that happens when two vehicles hit each other with force: *There has been a collision on the southbound stretch of the motorway.* ○ *Two drivers were killed in a head-on* (= direct) *collision between a car and a taxi last night.* ○ *The cyclist was in collision with a bus.* **2** [C] a strong disagreement: *There was a collision of interests/opinions.*

● **be on a collision course** If two or more people or groups are on a collision course, they are doing or saying things which are certain to cause a serious disagreement or fight between them: *All attempts at diplomacy have broken down and the two states now appear to be on a collision course.*

collocate /ˈkɒl.əʊ.keɪt/ ⓤ /ˈkɑː.lə-/ *verb* [I] *SPECIALIZED* (of words and phrases) to be used frequently together in a way that sounds correct to people who have spoken the language all their lives, but might not be expected from the meaning

collocation /ˌkɒl.əʊˈkeɪ.ʃⁿn/ ⓤ /ˌkɑː.lə-/ *noun SPECIALIZED* **1** [C] (*ALSO* **collocate**) a word or phrase which is frequently used with another word or phrase, in a way that sounds correct to people who have spoken the language all their lives, but might not be expected from the meaning: *In the phrase 'a hard frost', 'hard' is a collocation of 'frost' and 'strong' would not sound natural.* **2** [C] the combination of words formed when two or more words are frequently used together in a way that sounds correct: *The phrase 'a hard frost' is a collocation.* **3** [U] the frequent use of some words and phrases with others, especially in a way which is difficult to guess

colloquial /kəˈləʊ.kwi. əl/ ⓤ /-ˈloʊ-/ *adj SPECIALIZED* (of words and expressions) informal and more suitable for use in speech than in writing: *colloquial speech*

colloquialism /kəˈləʊ.kwi. əl.ɪ.zⁿm/ ⓤ /-ˈloʊ-/ *noun* [C] an informal word or expression which is more suitable for use in speech than in writing **colloquially** /kəˈləʊ.kwi.ᵊl.i/ ⓤ /-ˈloʊ-/ *adv*

colloquy /ˈkɒl.ə.kwi/ ⓤ /ˈkɑː.lə-/ *noun* [C] *FORMAL* a formal conversation

collude /kəˈluːd/ *verb* [I] *FORMAL* to act together secretly or illegally in order to deceive or cheat someone: *It was suspected that the police had colluded **with** the witnesses.*

collusion /kəˈluː.ʒⁿn/ *noun* [U] *FORMAL* It is thought that they worked **in** collusion **with** (= secretly together with) *the terrorist network.* **collusive** /kəˈluː.sɪv/ *adj*: *The report concluded that there was no evidence of collusive behaviour between the banks.*

the collywobbles /ðəˈkɒl.iˌwɒb.lz/ ⓤ /-ˈkɑː.liˌwɑː-/ *plural noun UK INFORMAL* an uncomfortable feeling in the stomach caused by feelings of nervousness or slight fear: *I've **got** the collywobbles **about** my exam this afternoon.*

cologne /kəˈləʊn/ ⓤ /-ˈloʊn/ *noun* [U] (*ALSO* **eau de cologne**) a type of perfume

colon BODY PART /ˈkəʊ.lɒn/ ⓤ /ˈkoʊ.lən/ *noun* [C] the lower and bigger half of the bowels in which water is removed from excrement

colon SIGN /ˈkəʊ.lɒn/ ⓤ /ˈkoʊ.lən/ *noun* [C] the sign (:) used in writing, especially to introduce a list of things or a sentence or phrase taken from somewhere else

colón /kɒlˈɒn/ ⓤ /kəˈloʊn/ *noun* [C] the standard unit of money used in Costa Rica and El Salvador

colonel /ˈkɜː.nⁿl/ ⓤ /ˈkɝː-/ *noun* [C] (*WRITTEN ABBREVIATION* **Col.**) an officer of high rank in the army or air force: *Colonel Marcus Furlong* ○ *Colonel is the military rank between lieutenant-colonel and brigadier.*

Colonel Blimp *noun* [C] *UK OLD-FASHIONED* an old man who has old-fashioned ideas and believes he is very important

colonnade /ˌkɒl.əˈneɪd/ ⓤ /ˌkɑː.lə-/ *noun* [C] a row of columns separated from each other by an equal distance

colony /ˈkɒl.ə.ni/ ⓤ /ˈkɑː.lə-/ *noun* [C] **1** a country or area controlled politically by a more powerful and often distant country: *Australia and New Zealand are **former** British colonies.* **2** a group of people who live in a colony **3** a group of people with a shared interest or job who live together in a way that is separate from other people: *an artists' colony* ○ *a nudist colony* **4** *SPECIALIZED* a group of animals, insects or plants of the same type that live together: *a colony of ants/termites/bacteria*

colonial /kəˈləʊ.ni.əl/ ⓤ /-ˈloʊ-/ *adj* **1** [before n] relating to a colony or colonialism: *Turkey was once an important colonial power.* ○ *Various parts of Africa have suffered **under** colonial **rule**.* **2** describes furniture or buildings in the style of a period when some countries were colonies: *colonial architecture* ○ *colonial-style houses*

colonial /kəˈləʊ.ni.ᵊl/ ⓤ /-ˈloʊ-/ *noun* [C] a person from another country who lives in a colony, especially as part of its system of government

colonialism /kəˈləʊ.ni.ə.lɪ.zⁿm/ ⓤ /-ˈloʊ-/ *noun* [U] the belief in and support for the system of one country controlling another

colonialist /kəˈləʊ.ni.ᵊl.ɪst/ ⓤ /-ˈloʊ-/ *noun* [C] a supporter of colonialism **colonialist** /kəˈləʊ.ni.ᵊl.ɪst/ ⓤ /-ˈloʊ-/ *adj: the colonialist powers* ○ *colonialist ideology*

colonist /ˈkɒl.ə.nɪst/ ⓤ /ˈkɑː.lə-/ *noun* [C] someone who lives in or goes to live in a country or area that is a colony

colonize, *UK USUALLY* **-ise** /ˈkɒl.ə.naɪz/ ⓤ /ˈkɑː.lə-/ *verb* [T *often passive*] to send people to live in and govern another country: *Peru was colonized by the Spanish in the sixteenth century.* **colonization**, *UK USUALLY* **-isation** /ˌkɒl.ə.naɪˈzeɪ.ʃⁿn/ ⓤ /ˌkɑː.lə-/ *noun* [U]

color /ˈkʌl.ər/ ⓤ /-ɚ/ *noun US FOR* colour

coloration /ˌkʌl.əˈreɪ.ʃⁿn/ *noun* [U] *SPECIALIZED* the presence of colour on an animal or plant and the pattern which the colour makes

color line *noun* [C usually sing] *US FOR* **colour bar**

colossus /kəˈlɒs.əs/ ⓤ /-ˈlɑː.səs/ *noun* [C] *plural* **colossuses** or **colossi 1** a person or thing of great size, influence or ability: *She has been described as the creative colossus of the literary world.* **2** a very large statue or building: *the Colossus of Rhodes*

colossal /kəˈlɒs.ᵊl/ ⓤ /-ˈlɑː.sⁿl/ *adj* extremely large: *In the centre of the hall stood a colossal wooden statue, decorated in ivory and gold.* ○ *They were asking a colossal amount of money for the house.*

colour APPEARANCE *UK*, *US* **color** /ˈkʌl.ər/ ⓤ /-ɚ/ *noun* **1** [C or U] red, blue, green, yellow, etc: *What's your favourite colour?* ○ *She wears a lot of bright colours.* ○ *What colour are your eyes?* ○ *Does the shirt come **in** any other colour?* ○ *I like rich jewel colours, such as purple, blue and green.* ○ *Are the photos **in** colour or black and white?* **2** [U] the pleasant effect of a bright colour or of a lot of colours together: *I think we need a bit of colour in this room.* ○ *Red and yellow peppers give a little colour to the sauce.* ○ *LITERARY The whole garden was **ablaze with/a riot of** colour* (= full of different bright colours). **3** [C] a substance, such as a paint or DYE, which you add to something to give it a particular colour: *I put my new green shirt in a hot wash and the colour **ran*** (= the colour came out of the material). **4** [U] interesting or exciting qualities or details: *We added your story for a bit of local colour.* ○ *Michael was there so that added a bit of colour to the evening's proceedings.* **5** [U] a pink colour in someone's face, often showing good health or showing feelings such as embarrassment or excitement: *That walk has **put some** colour **in your cheeks**.* ○ *I watched the colour **drain from** her face as she heard the news.* ○ *She has a high colour* (= The natural colour of her face is red).

colour *UK*, *US* **color** /ˈkʌl.ər/ ⓤ /-ɚ/ *adj* Colour television, photography or printing shows things in all their colours, not just in black and white.

colour *UK*, *US* **color** /ˈkʌl.ər/ ⓤ /-ɚ/ *verb* **1** [I or T] to become a particular colour, or to make something a particular colour: *Do you think he colours his hair?* ○ *He drew a heart and coloured it red.* ○ *Fry the onions till they start to colour.* **2** [I] to become red in the face because you are embarrassed **3** [T *often passive*] If something colours your opinion of something, it influences your opinion in a negative way: *I'm sure my views on marriage are coloured by my parents' divorce.* ○ *I'm trying not to let my judgement be coloured by that one incident.*

coloured *UK*, *US* **colored** /ˈkʌl.əd/ ⓤ /-ɚd/ *adj* having or producing a colour or colours: *coloured lights/pencils*

coloureds *UK*, *US* **coloreds** /ˈkʌl.ədz/ ⓤ /-ɚdz/ *plural noun* clothes that are any colour except white

-coloured *UK*, *US* **-colored** /-ˈkʌl.əd/ ⓤ /-ɚd/ *suffix* of the colour or colours described: *a multi-coloured scarf* ○ *brightly-coloured flowers* ○ *flesh-coloured tights*

colourful *UK*, *US* **colorful** /ˈkʌl.ə.fⁿl/ ⓤ /-ɚ-/ *adj* **1** having bright colours or a lot of different colours: *a colourful painting* ○ *colourful costumes* **2** interesting and exciting: *a colourful character* ○ *The town, of course, has a very colourful history/past.* ○ *The old city around the cathedral is the most colourful part of town.* **colourfully** *UK*, *US* **colorfully** /ˈkʌl.ə.fⁿl.i/ ⓤ /-ɚ-/ *adv*

colouring *UK, US* **coloring** /ˈkʌl.ᵊr.ɪŋ/ [US] /-ɚ-/ *noun* **1** [S] the combined effect of a person's hair, skin and eye colour: *Their colouring is so totally different that you would never think they were sisters.* **2** [C or U] a substance that is added to food or drink to change its colour artificially: *It says on the label that no preservatives or* ***artificial*** *colourings have been added.*

colourless *UK, US* **colorless** /ˈkʌl.ə.ləs/ [US] /-ɚ-/ *adj* **1** having no colour: *Water and glass are colourless.* ○ *Carbon monoxide is a colourless, odourless, poisonous gas.* **2** not exciting or not interesting: *It is a rather grey, colourless city, with few interesting sights or historical monuments.*

colour [RACE] *UK, US* **color** /ˈkʌl.əʳ/ [US] /-ɚ/ *noun* [C or U] the natural colour of a person's skin which shows which race they belong to: *She felt she had not been given the job because of her colour.* ○ *There should be no discrimination on the grounds of colour.*

coloured *UK, US* **colored** /ˈkʌl.əd/ [US] /-ɚd/ *adj* **1** *OLD-FASHIONED* used to describe a person who has black or brown skin. This word is now considered offensive by most people: *Coloured* ***people*** *were not allowed to use the same facilities as whites.* **2** in South Africa, describes a person of mixed race: *In the recent elections, the National Party was given a lot of support from the coloured population.*

coloured *UK, US* **colored** /ˈkʌl.əd/ [US] /-ɚd/ *noun* [C] **1** *OLD-FASHIONED* a person who has black or brown skin. This word is now considered offensive by most people. **2** in South Africa, a person of mixed race

▲ **colour *sth* in** *phrasal verb* [M] *UK* to fill an area with colour using paint, coloured pencils, etc: *Rosie drew an elephant and coloured it in.*

ˈcolour ˌbar *UK noun* [C usually sing] (*US* **color barrier**) a social and legal system in which people of different races are separated and not given the same rights and opportunities

colour-blind /ˈkʌl.ə.blaɪnd/ [US] /-ɚ-/ *adj* unable to see the difference between particular colours, especially green and red

colour-coded /ˈkʌl.əˌkəʊ.dɪd/ [US] /-ɚˌkoʊ-/ *adj* If a set of objects such as books or wires are colour-coded, they are marked with different colours so that people can recognize them as being different or separate.

colour-fast /ˈkʌl.ə.fɑːst/ [US] /-ɚ.fæst/ *adj* If a piece of clothing or material is colour-fast, its colour will not change or lose brightness when it is washed.

ˈcolour ˌprejudice *noun* [U] an unreasonable dislike of people who have a different skin colour which results in the unfair treatment of members of different races

colours *UK, US* **colors** /ˈkʌl.əz/ [US] /-ɚz/ *plural noun* **1** (at school, college or university) an honour given to people who have been chosen for a sports team, which is often represented by a special symbol on a shirt or tie: *She was awarded her colours* ***for*** *hockey/her hockey colours at the end of term.* **2** the official flag of a country, ship or military group: *The military parade passed through the streets, with each regiment proudly displaying its regimental colours.*

• **show *sb* in their true colours** to show what someone's real character is, especially when it is unpleasant

• **see *sb's* true colours** to see someone's real character for the first time, especially when it is unpleasant: *It was only when they started to work together that she began to see his true colours.*

ˈcolour ˌscheme *noun* [C] *UK* a combination of colours that has been chosen for a particular room

ˈcolour ˌsupplement *noun* [C] *MAINLY UK* a magazine with colour pictures which is given free with a newspaper, especially on Saturdays and Sundays

colourway /ˈkʌl.ə.weɪ/ [US] /-ɚ-/ *noun* [C] *UK SPECIALIZED* a combination of colours in which cloth or paper is printed: *The sweaters are available* ***in*** *two colourways: grey/pink or blue/white*

colt [HORSE] /kəʊlt/ [US] /koʊlt/ *noun* [C] a young male horse under the age of four ➲Compare **filly**.

coltish /ˈkəʊl.tɪʃ/ [US] /ˈkoʊl-/ *adj* describes a person who is young and energetic but awkward: *coltish limbs*

Colt [GUN] /kəʊlt/ [US] /koʊlt/ *noun* [C] *TRADEMARK* (the name of the maker of) a small American gun

columbine /ˈkɒl.əm.baɪn/ [US] /ˈkɑː.ləm-/ *noun* [C] a plant which has brightly-coloured flowers with five pointed petals that hang down

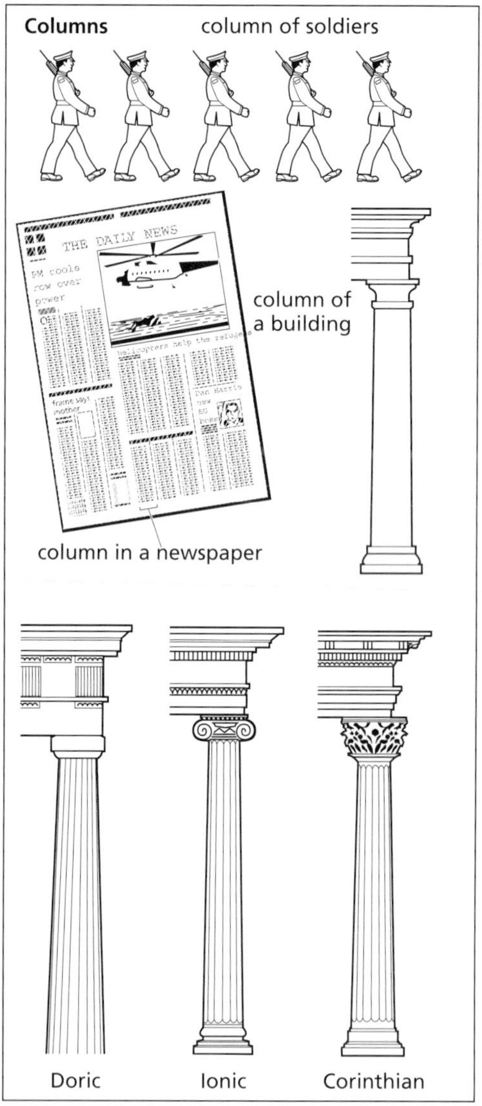
Columns
column of soldiers
column of a building
column in a newspaper
Doric
Ionic
Corinthian

column [BUILDING] /ˈkɒl.əm/ [US] /ˈkɑː.ləm/ *noun* [C] **1** a tall vertical stone post which is used as a support for a roof or in classical buildings for decoration, or which stands alone as a MONUMENT (= as a symbol of respect for a special person or event): *The roof of the temple was held up by a row of thick stone columns.* ○ *Nelson's Column in Trafalgar Square* ➲See also **spinal column**. **2 column of *sth*** something with a tall narrow shape: *A column of smoke rose from the chimney.* **3** a line of moving people or vehicles: *a column of refugees*

column [PRINTING] /ˈkɒl.əm/ [US] /ˈkɑː.ləm/ *noun* [C] **1** one of several vertical blocks of print into which a page of a newspaper or magazine is divided: *I didn't have time to read the whole article – just the first column.* **2** a piece of writing in a newspaper or magazine which is always written by the same person and which appears regularly, usually on a particular subject: *She writes a weekly* ***fashion/gossip*** *column for the Evening*

Standard. **3** any vertical block of words or numbers: *Add the column of figures and divide the sum by three.*

columnist /ˈkɒl.əm.nɪst/ ⓤ /ˈkɑː.ləm.nɪst/ *noun* [C] someone who writes a regular article for a newspaper or magazine: *a gossip/sports columnist* ○ *She's a columnist for USA Today.*

com- /kɒm-/ ⓤ /kɑːm-/ *prefix* together; with: *combination* ○ *community* ○ *companions*

.com /ˌdɒtˈkɒm/ ⓤ /ˌdɑːtˈkɑːm/ *INTERNET ABBREVIATION FOR* company: used in some Internet addresses which belong to companies or businesses: *www.yahoo.com*

coma /ˈkəʊ.mə/ ⓤ /ˈkoʊ-/ *noun* [C] a state of unconsciousness from which a person cannot be woken, which is caused by damage to the brain after an accident or illness: *He's been in a coma for the past six weeks.* ○ *She went into a deep coma after taking an overdose of sleeping pills.*

comatose /ˈkəʊ.mə.təʊs/ ⓤ /ˈkoʊ.mə.toʊs/ *adj* **1** *SPECIALIZED* in a coma **2** *INFORMAL* very tired or in a deep sleep because of extreme tiredness, hard work or too much alcohol: *By midnight I was virtually comatose.*

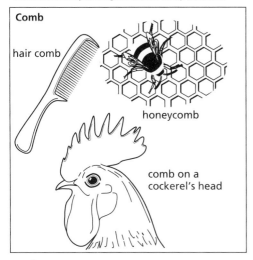

Comb

hair comb

honeycomb

comb on a
cockerel's head

comb FOR HAIR /kəʊm/ ⓤ /koʊm/ *noun* [C] **1** a flat piece of plastic, wood or metal with a thin row of long narrow parts along one side, which you use to tidy and arrange your hair **2** a small comb-shaped object which women put in their hair to hold their hair away from their face or for decoration

comb /kəʊm/ ⓤ /koʊm/ *verb* [T] to tidy your hair using a comb: *She combed her hair and put on some lipstick.* ○ *I've been trying to comb out (= remove using a comb) the knots in her hair.*

comb SEARCH /kəʊm/ ⓤ /koʊm/ *verb* [T] to search a place or an area very carefully in order to find something: *The police combed the whole area for evidence.* ○ *Investigators combed through the wreckage.*

comb CHICKEN /kəʊm/ ⓤ /koʊm/ *noun* [C] a soft red growth on a chicken's head ➔See **cockscomb**.

combat /ˈkɒm.bæt/ ⓤ /ˈkɑːm-/ *noun* **1** [C or U] a fight, especially during a war: *There was fierce combat between the two sides.* ○ *No one knew how many troops had died in combat.* ○ *The soldiers were engaged in hand-to-hand combat.* ○ *armed combat (= fighting with weapons)* ○ *unarmed combat (= fighting without weapons)* **2** [C] a fight between two people or things: *The film explores the combat between good and evil.*

combat /kəmˈbæt/ ⓤ /ˈkɑːm.bæt/ *verb* [T] to try to stop something unpleasant or harmful from happening or increasing: *to combat crime/terrorism/inflation/disease* ○ *The government is spending millions of dollars in its attempt to combat drug abuse.* ○ *I have to combat this constant desire to eat chocolate.*

combatant /ˈkɒm.bə.tˤnt/ ⓤ /ˈkɑːm.bə.tˤnt/ *noun* [C] *FORMAL* a person who fights in a war

combative /ˈkɒm.bə.tɪv/ ⓤ /ˈkɑːm.bə.t̬ɪv/ *adj* *FORMAL* eager to fight or argue: *The prime minister was in a combative mood, twice accusing the opposition of gross incompetence.*

combat trousers *plural noun* (*ALSO* **combats**) loose trousers made of strong material with large pockets on the outside of the legs: *British Army camouflage-pattern combat trousers*

combine /kəmˈbaɪn/ *verb* **1** [I or T] to (cause to) exist together, or join together to make a single thing or group: *None of us has much money so let's combine what we've got.* ○ *Sickness, combined with (= together with) terrible weather, contrived to ruin the trip.* ○ *The two countries combined against their common enemy.* ○ [+ to infinitive] *These normally harmless substances combine to form a highly poisonous gas.* **2** [T] If someone combines two or more qualities, they possess both of those qualities: *As a writer, he combined wit and/with passion.* **3** [T] to do two activities at the same time: *She manages to successfully combine family life and/with a career.*

combine /ˈkɒm.baɪn/ ⓤ /ˈkɑːm-/ *group noun* [C] a group of people or organizations acting together in business: *They had earlier that year established a newspaper combine.*

combination /ˌkɒm.bɪˈneɪ.ʃ°n/ ⓤ /ˌkɑːm-/ *noun* **1** [C or U] a mixture obtained when two or more things are combined: *Strawberries and cream – a perfect combination.* ○ *A combination of tiredness and boredom caused me to fall asleep.* ○ *This drug can be safely used in combination with other medicines.* ○ *Her experience and energy are a winning combination (= a successful mixture) in business.* **2** [C] *SPECIALIZED* an arrangement in a different order: *From the letters X Y Z, we can get three combinations of two letters: XY, XZ, and YZ.* **3** [C] a set of letters or numbers in a particular order which can be used to open some types of locks: *a combination lock*

combine (**'harvester**) *noun* [C] a large farming machine which cuts the plant, separates the seed from the stem and cleans the grain as it moves across a field

com'bining ,form *noun* [C] *SPECIALIZED* a word or group of letters which is added to the beginning or end of words to change or add meaning: *The combining form 'Anglo', which means English, combines to make various words, including Anglo-American and Anglophile.*

combo MUSICIANS /ˈkɒm.bəʊ/ ⓤ /ˈkɑːm.boʊ/ *group noun* [C] *plural* **combos** *INFORMAL* a small group of musicians who play dance and jazz music

combo MIXTURE /ˈkɒm.bəʊ/ ⓤ /ˈkɑːm.boʊ/ *noun* [C] *plural* **combos** *INFORMAL* a combination of different things: *That's a funny combo – pink and orange.* ○ *I'll have the burrito and taco combo, please.*

combustion /kəmˈbʌs.tʃ°n/ *noun* [U] **1** the process of burning **2** *SPECIALIZED* the chemical process in which substances mix with oxygen in the air to produce heat and light

combustible /kəmˈbʌs.tɪ.bl̩/ *adj* *FORMAL* able to burn easily: *Wood and coal are both combustible substances.*

com'bustion ,chamber *noun* [C] an enclosed space in which combustion happens

come MOVE TO SPEAKER /kʌm/ *verb* [I] **came**, **come** to move or travel towards the speaker or with the speaker: *Are you coming with me?* ○ *There's a car coming!* ○ *Can you come to my party?* ○ *Here comes Adam.* ○ *She's come 500 km (= has travelled 500km) to be here with us tonight.* ○ *If you're ever in Oxford, come and visit us.* ○ *We came by car.* ○ *Your father will come for (= to collect) you at 4 o'clock.* ○ *Come forward a bit and stand on the line.* ○ *I've come straight from the airport.* ○ *The door opened and a nurse came into the room.* ○ [+ to infinitive] *A man's coming to mend the boiler this afternoon.* ○ *As he came towards me, I could see he'd been crying.* ○ *He thought we'd been picking his apples and came after (= chased) us with a stick.* ○ [+ v-ing] *He came rushing over when I fell.*

● **as it comes** *UK* If someone asks how they should prepare your drink and you say as it comes, you mean that any way they prepare it will be acceptable: *"How do you like your coffee?" "Oh, as it comes."*

- **Come again?** *INFORMAL* used to ask someone to repeat something that you have not heard or understood
- **come and go** to exist or happen somewhere for a short time and then go away: *The feeling of nausea comes and goes.*
- **come from behind** to succeed in winning after being in a losing position in a game: *England came from behind to beat Scotland 2-1.*
- **come the** *sth DISAPPROVING* to pretend to be or feel something: *Don't come the poor little innocent **with** me!*
- **come to pass** *OLD USE* to happen: *It came to pass that their love for each other grew and grew.*
- **come to** *your* **attention/notice** If something comes to your attention, you notice it: *It has recently come to my attention that some of the younger boys are not using the toilets for the proper purpose.*
- **come to that** *INFORMAL* in fact: *"I owe you a fiver, don't I?" "Yes, and come to that, you never paid me back the other money I lent you."*
- **had it coming (to *you*)** *INFORMAL* If someone had it coming, something bad happened to them which they deserved: *He's been sacked but, with all that time he took off, he had it coming really.*
- **how come?** *INFORMAL* used to ask how or why something has happened: *So how come you missed the train?* ○ *"We had to stop in Birmingham." "How come?"*
- **be as crazy/rich, etc. as they come** to be very crazy/rich, etc: *He's as mean as they come.*
- **not know whether you are coming or going** to be in a very confused state: *I'm so busy, I don't know whether I'm coming or going.*

come [MOVE TO LISTENER] /kʌm/ *verb* [I] **came, come** to move or travel in the direction of the person being spoken to: *"Sal, are you ready?" "Coming."* ○ *I'll come **and** pick you up in the car if you like.* ○ *I've come **for** (= come to collect) your census form.* ○ [+ *to* infinitive] *I've come **to** read the gas meter.*

come [ARRIVE] /kʌm/ *verb* [I] **came, come** to get to a particular place: *Has she come yet?* ○ *When does the post come?* ○ *Hasn't his train come **in** yet?*

comings /'kʌm.ɪŋz/ *plural noun* **the comings and goings** the movements of people arriving at places and leaving places: *I sometimes just look out the window and watch the comings and goings of everyone in the street.*

come [LEAVE] /kʌm/ *verb* [I + adv or prep] **came, come** to leave a place: *I had to come **away from** the party early.* ○ *The police watched him come **out** of the house.*

come [EXIST] /kʌm/ *verb* [I + adv or prep; not continuous] **came, come** to exist or be available: *Do these trousers come **in** any other colour?* ○ *Runners come **in** all shapes and sizes – fat and thin, short and tall.* ○ *This cuddly baby doll comes **with** her own blanket and bottle.* ○ *They're the best sunglasses you can buy, but they **don't** come **cheap** (= they are expensive).*

come [HAPPEN] /kʌm/ *verb* [I] **came, come** to happen: *Spring has come early.* ○ *The announcement came at a bad time.* ○ *Her resignation came **as** quite a shock.* ○ *INFORMAL* **Come** Monday morning (= When it is Monday morning) *you'll regret staying up all night.* ○ *I'm afraid those days are gone and they'll never come **again**.*
- **the days/week(s)/year(s) to come** the following or next days/week(s)/year(s): *What are your plans for the year to come (= next year)?*

coming /'kʌm.ɪŋ/ *adj* [before n] happening soon: *We look forward to greater success in the coming year.* ○ *I'll be back **this** coming Friday.*

come [ORDER] /kʌm/ *verb* **come after/first/last, etc.** to have or achieve a particular position in a race, competition, list, etc: *She (UK) came second/(US) came **in** second in the 100m race.* ○ *Z comes **after** Y in the alphabet.* ○ *Which king came **after** Edward?* ○ *April comes **before** May.* ○ *I know the first verse of the song, but I don't know what comes **next**.*

come [START] /kʌm/ *verb* **come to do** *sth* to start to do something: *I've come to like her over the months.* ○ *It used to hold paper bags, but gradually came to be used for magazines.* ○ *How did that phrase come to mean (= develop so that it means) that?*

come [CHANGE] /kʌm/ *verb* [L] **came, come** to change or develop so as to be in a different position or condition: *Those pictures will have to come **down** (= be removed from the wall).* ○ *He pulled the knob and it just came **off** (in his hand).* ○ *How many times have you come **off** that horse?* ○ *She punched him in the mouth and two of his teeth came **out**.* ○ *Can you get this cork to come **out** of the bottle?* ○ *When does the heating come **on** (= start working)?* ○ [+ adj] *A wire has come **loose** at the back.* ○ *The door came **open** for no apparent reason.*

come [SEX] /kʌm/ *verb* [I] **came, come** *SLANG* to have an ORGASM

come /kʌm/ *noun* [U] *SLANG* **semen** (= the liquid containing sperm)

PHRASAL VERBS WITH **come** ▼

▲ **come about** *phrasal verb* to happen, or start to happen: *How did the problem come about in the first place?*

▲ **come across** *sth* [FIND] *phrasal verb* to find something by chance: *He came across some of his old love letters in his wife's drawer.*

▲ **come across** [BEHAVE] *phrasal verb* to behave in a way which makes people believe that you have a particular characteristic: *She comes across really well (= creates a positive image) on television.* ○ *He comes across **as** a bit of a bore in interview.*

▲ **come across** [EXPRESS] *phrasal verb* If an idea or emotion comes across in writing, film, music or when someone is speaking, it is expressed clearly and people notice it: *What comes across in his later poetry is a great sense of sadness.*

▲ **come along** [ARRIVE] *phrasal verb* to arrive or appear at a place: *You go now and I'll come along later.* ○ *You wait half an hour for a bus, then three come along at once!*

▲ **come along** [GO WITH SOMEONE] *phrasal verb* **1** to go somewhere with someone: *We're going to the cinema. Do you want to come along?* **2** *UK* used to tell someone to hurry: *Come along – we don't want to be late!*

▲ **come along** [EXIST] *phrasal verb* to start to exist: *I gave up climbing when my first child came along.*

▲ **come along** [DEVELOP] *phrasal verb* If something is coming along, it is developing or improving: *Hassan's English is really coming along.*

▲ **come apart** *phrasal verb* to separate into several pieces: *I picked up the book and it came apart in my hands.* ○ *My boots are coming apart at the seams.*

▲ **come around** *phrasal verb us for* **come round**

▲ **come at** *sb phrasal verb* to move towards someone in order to attack them: *He came at me **with** a knife.*

▲ **come away** *phrasal verb* If something comes away from something else, it becomes separated from it: *I just opened the drawer as usual and the handle came away in my hand.* ○ *The paper has started to come away **from** the walls.*

▲ **come back** [RETURN] *phrasal verb* to return to a place: *I'll come back and pick you up in half an hour.* ○ *We've just come back **from** Amsterdam.*

▲ **come back** [FASHION] *phrasal verb* If a style or a fashion comes back, it becomes popular again after being unpopular for a period of time: *Padded shoulders are coming back, apparently.* ○ *Long hair on men seems to be coming back **into** fashion.*

comeback /'kʌm.bæk/ *noun* [C] a successful attempt to get power, importance or fame again after a period of having lost it: *She's trying to **make a** comeback with her first album for twenty years.*

▲ **come back to** *sb phrasal verb* If something comes back to you, you start to remember it: *I can't think of her name – it'll come back to me later.* ○ *It's all coming back to me!*

▲ **come before** *sth/sb* [IMPORTANCE] *phrasal verb* to be more important than, or to be treated as more important than, another thing or person: *My children will always come before my career.*

▲ **come before** *sth/sb* [COURT] *phrasal verb LEGAL* If a legal case comes before a court of law or a judge, it is dealt with by them, and when someone comes before a court or judge, they are present while their case is dealt with.

▲ **come between** ***sth*** [STOP] *phrasal verb* to stop someone from doing something that they like doing: *Nothing comes between Jim and his food.* * NOTE: This sense is usually used in negative sentences.

▲ **come between** ***sb*** [RELATIONSHIP] *phrasal verb* If something comes between two people, it harms their relationship: *Don't let one little quarrel come between you.*

▲ **come by** ***sth*** [OBTAIN] *phrasal verb* to obtain something, using effort, by chance or in a way that has not been explained: *Cheap organic food is still difficult to come by.* ○ *I'd like to know how she came by that black eye.*

▲ **come by** ***(somewhere)*** [VISIT] *phrasal verb* to visit a place for a short time, often when you are going somewhere else: *I'll come by (the office/your house) one day this week and we can have a chat.*

▲ **come down** [LAND] *phrasal verb* to fall and land on the ground: *A lot of trees came down in the storm.* ○ *Our plane came down in a field.* ○ *The snow came down during the night.*

▲ **come down** [LOWER LEVEL] *phrasal verb* **1** If a price or a level comes down, it becomes lower: *House prices have come down recently.* ○ *Inflation is coming down.* **2** *INFORMAL* to feel less excited after a very enjoyable experience: *The whole weekend was so wonderful I haven't come down yet.*

comedown /ˈkʌm.daʊn/ *noun* [S] *INFORMAL* a situation that is not as good as the one you were in before: *These days he plays to audiences of a hundred or fewer which is* ***a bit of a*** *comedown after Wembley Stadium.*

▲ **come down** [SUPPORT] *phrasal verb* [+ adv or prep] to decide that you support a particular person or side in an argument, etc: *The government has come down* ***on the side of*** *military action.*

▲ **come down** [DRUGS] *phrasal verb INFORMAL* If a person comes down from a drug, they stop feeling its effects.

▲ **come down** [UNIVERSITY] *phrasal verb UK OLD-FASHIONED* If you come down (from a college or university, especially Oxford or Cambridge University), you leave your studies either permanently or for a short time.

▲ **come down** [TRAVEL SOUTH] *phrasal verb* [I] to go to a place which is south of where you live: *My boyfriend's coming down* ***from*** *Scotland this weekend.* ○ *They don't come down* ***to*** *London much because it's too tiring with the kids.*

▲ **come down on** ***sb/sth*** *phrasal verb* to punish or criticize a person or activity very strongly: *They're coming down* ***heavily*** *on people* ***for*** *not paying their licence fees.* ○ *The authorities plan to come down* ***hard*** *on truancy in future.*

• **come down on** ***sb*** **like a ton of bricks** to punish someone very quickly and severely: *Do that once more and I'll come down on you like a ton of bricks!*

▲ **come down to** ***sth*** *phrasal verb* If a situation or decision comes down to something, that is the thing that influences it most: *What* ***it all*** *comes down to is your incredible insecurity.* ○ ***It all*** *comes down to money in the end.* ○ [+ question word] *Eventually our choice of hotel will come down to how much we can afford.*

▲ **come down with** ***sth*** *phrasal verb* to start to suffer from an illness, especially one that is not serious: *I think I'm coming down with flu.*

▲ **come forward** *phrasal verb* to offer to give help or information: *No witnesses to the accident have come forward yet, despite the police's appeal.* ○ *Nobody has yet come forward* ***with*** *any information relating to the girl's death.*

▲ **come from** ***somewhere/sth*** [ORIGINATE] *phrasal verb* to be born, obtained from, or made in a particular place: *She comes from Italy.* ○ *Some of the best wines come from France.* ○ *Does that quote come from Shakespeare?* ○ *She could hear banging coming from the room upstairs.* ○ *Where will the money for the project come from?*

▲ **come from** ***sth*** [BE CAUSED] *phrasal verb* to be caused by something: *"I feel awful." "That comes from eating too much."*

▲ **come in** [ENTER] *phrasal verb* to enter a room or building: *Do you want to come in for a cup of tea?* ○ *Hi, come in – lovely to see you!*

▲ **come in** [FASHION] *phrasal verb* If a fashion or product comes in, it becomes available or popular: *Flared trousers first came in during the seventies.*

▲ **come in** [BE USEFUL] *phrasal verb* **come in handy/useful, etc.** to be useful for a particular purpose: *Keep it, it might come in useful.* ○ *His money will come in handy when I want to travel.*

▲ **come in** [BE RECEIVED] *phrasal verb* **1** When news or information comes in, it is received: *Reports are just coming in of a major oil spillage in the North Sea.* **2** If you have money coming in, you receive it as income: *With Dave unemployed, we haven't got much money coming in at the moment.*

▲ **come in** [BE INVOLVED] *phrasal verb INFORMAL* to become involved in a situation, story or plan: *We need expert advice, and that's where you come in.*

▲ **come in** [RACE] *phrasal verb* **come in first/second, etc.** to finish a race in first, second, etc. position

▲ **come in** [SEA] *phrasal verb* When the sea or the TIDE comes in, the water moves forwards to cover more of the beach. ➲Compare **go out** SEA.

▲ **come in for** ***sth*** *phrasal verb* to receive blame or criticism: *The director has come in for a lot of criticism over his handling of the affair.*

▲ **come into** ***sth*** [MONEY] *phrasal verb* If someone comes into money, property or a title, they receive it as a result of the death of a relative: *She came into a bit of money when her grandfather died.*

▲ **come into** ***sth*** [INFLUENCE] *phrasal verb* If a particular emotion or quality comes into a situation, it influences that situation: *She married for money – love didn't come into* ***it***. * NOTE: This sense is usually used in negative sentences.

▲ **come of** ***sth*** *phrasal verb* to happen as a result of something: *Did anything come of all those job applications?*

▲ **come off** [SUCCEED] *phrasal verb INFORMAL* to happen as planned or to succeed: *There was some sort of property deal that didn't come off.* ○ *I tried telling a few jokes but they didn't come off* (= no one laughed).

▲ **come off** [FINISH] *phrasal verb* **come off better/worse/badly/well** to finish in a particular condition after a fight, argument, etc., especially compared to someone else: *The smaller dog actually came off better, with only a few scratches.* ○ *I always come off worse when we argue.*

▲ **come off** ***sth*** [STOP USING] *phrasal verb MAINLY UK* If you come off medicine or drugs, you stop using them: *He's come off the tablets because they were making him dizzy.*

• **Come off it!** *INFORMAL* used to tell someone that you do not believe what they are saying is true, or that you strongly disagree with them: *Ask Simon to cook the meal? Come off it, he can hardly boil an egg!*

▲ **come off** ***sth*** [COMPLETE] *phrasal verb US* to have recently completed a period of time when something very successful or very difficult happened: *The company was coming off one of its best years ever.*

▲ **come on** [START] *phrasal verb* **1** to start to happen or work: *The heating comes on at six in the morning.* **2** If you have got an illness coming on, it is starting gradually: *I think I've got a cold coming on.* **3** *UK INFORMAL* If a woman comes on, her period (= the bleeding from the womb that happens every month) starts.

▲ **come on** said to encourage someone to do something, especially to hurry or try harder, or to tell you something: *Come on – we're going to be late if you don't hurry!* ○ *Come on! Push harder!* ○ *Come on, Annabelle, you can tell me. I won't tell anyone.*

• **come on** *INFORMAL* used to tell someone that you do not believe them or that you disagree with them, or to show that you are angry with them: *Oh come on, Ian, you made the same excuse last week!*

▲ **come on/along** [MAKE PROGRESS] *phrasal verb* to make progress: *Your piano playing has really come on since I last heard you play.* ○ *How's your English coming on?*

▲ **come on** [SEXUAL INTEREST] *phrasal verb INFORMAL* to make your sexual interest known to someone: *Then his wife left the room and he started coming on* ***to*** *me.* ○ *She was coming on* ***strong*** *and I, naturally, responded.*

come-on /ˈkʌm.ɒn/ [US] /-ɑːn/ *noun* [C] *MAINLY US INFORMAL* **1** a remark that shows someone that you are sexually interested in them: *He was* ***giving me the*** *come-on.* **2** something which someone who is selling a product uses to interest a customer

C

▲ **come on** [APPEAR] *phrasal verb* to be seen on stage in a play, or in a scene in a film or television programme, or to be heard in a radio programme: *There was great applause when the Russian ballerina came on.*

▲ **come out** [BE PUBLISHED] *phrasal verb* If a book, record, film, etc. comes out, it becomes available for people to buy or see: *When does their new album come out?*

▲ **come out** [APPEAR] *phrasal verb* When the sun, moon or stars come out, they appear in the sky: *The clouds finally parted and the sun came out.*

▲ **come out** [BECOME KNOWN] *phrasal verb* **1** If something comes out, it becomes known publicly after it has been kept secret: *After her death, it came out that she'd lied about her age.* ○ *When the truth came out, there was public outrage.* **2** If information or results come out, they are given to people: *The exam results come out in August.*

▲ **come out** [SOCIAL EVENT] *phrasal verb* UK to go somewhere with someone for a social event: *Would you like to come out for a drink sometime?*

▲ **come out** [RESULT] *phrasal verb* [+ adv or prep or adj] If you describe how something or someone comes out at the end of a process or activity, you say what condition they are in or what they have achieved: *She came out of the divorce settlement a rich woman.* ○ *These figures have come out wrong! I don't understand it.* ○ *Your painting has come out really well.* ○ *He hasn't exactly come out of the scandal with his reputation enhanced.*

▲ **come out** [BE REMOVED] *phrasal verb* If dirt or a mark comes out, it disappears from something when it is cleaned: *Did the red wine stain come out?*

▲ **come out** [PHOTO] *phrasal verb* If a photo or part of a photo comes out, the picture can be seen clearly: *The photos didn't come out because the room was so dark.* ○ *He's in the picture, but his face hasn't come out very clearly.*

▲ **come out** [GIVE OPINION] *phrasal verb* [+ adv or prep] to express an opinion: *In the survey politicians came out overwhelmingly **in favour of** capital punishment.* ○ *Some of the members supported the changes, but the majority came out **against**.*

▲ **come out** [BE SAID] *phrasal verb* If something you say comes out in a particular way, that is how you say it: *I didn't mean to be rude – it just came out like that.* ○ *When I tried to tell her that I loved her it just came out **all wrong**.*

▲ **come out** [HOMOSEXUAL] *phrasal verb* to tell people that you are homosexual, often after a period of secrecy

▲ **come out** [STOP WORKING] *phrasal verb* UK If workers come out, they stop working because of a disagreement: *The postal workers have come out in support of their pay claim.*

▲ **come out** [OPEN] *phrasal verb* When flowers come out, they open: *Daffodils come out in spring.*

▲ **come out in** *sth phrasal verb* If you come out in something, such as spots, they appear on your skin: *This heat has made me come out in an itchy red rash.*

▲ **come out of** *sth phrasal verb* If something comes out of a process or event, it is one of the results: *I hope something good can come out of this mess.*

▲ **come out with** *sth phrasal verb* to say something suddenly and unexpectedly: *He comes out with the strangest things!* ○ *She comes out with some good ideas though.*

▲ **come over** [MOVE] *phrasal verb* to come to a place, move from one place to another, or move towards someone: *Come over here!* ○ *Are your family coming over from Greece for the wedding?*

▲ **come over** [SEEM] *phrasal verb* to seem to be a particular type of person: *I watched the interview and felt he came over **as** quite arrogant.*

▲ **come over** [FEEL] *phrasal verb* [L only + adj] UK to be influenced suddenly and unexpectedly by a strange feeling: *I stood up too quickly and came over **all** dizzy/faint/peculiar.*

▲ **come over** *sb phrasal verb* to influence someone suddenly to behave in a particular way: *I'm sorry! That was a stupid thing to say – I don't know **what** came over me.* ○ HUMOROUS *He gave you a present! **What's** come over him?*

▲ **come round** [VISIT] UK *phrasal verb* (US **come around**) to visit someone in their home: *Come round tonight and we'll watch a video.*

▲ **come round** [CHANGE YOUR MIND] UK *phrasal verb* (US **come around**) to change your opinion of something, often influenced by another person's opinion: *He'll come round **to** my point of view, given a bit of time.* ○ *Do you still dislike your office, or have you come round **to** thinking it's all right?*

▲ **come round** [EVENT] UK *phrasal verb* (MAINLY US **come around**) If an event that happens regularly comes round/around, it happens at its usual time: *Christmas comes round so quickly!*

▲ **come round** [BECOME CONSCIOUS] UK *phrasal verb* (US **come around**) to become conscious again after an accident or operation: *She hasn't come round **from** the anaesthetic yet.*

▲ **come through** [INFORMATION] *phrasal verb* If a piece of information or a document comes through, you receive it: *Have the test results come through yet?* ○ *My visa still hasn't come through.*

▲ **come through** [EMOTION] *phrasal verb* If an emotion comes through, other people can notice it: *His nervousness came through when he spoke.*

▲ **come through** (*sth*) [DIFFICULT SITUATION] *phrasal verb* to manage to get to the end of a difficult or dangerous situation: *We've had some hard times, but we've come through.*

▲ **come to** [BECOME CONSCIOUS] *phrasal verb* to become conscious again after an accident or operation: *Has he come to yet?*

▲ **come to** *sb* [REMEMBER] *phrasal verb* If a thought or idea comes to you, you suddenly remember or start to think about it: *I can't remember his name – it'll come to me in a minute.*

▲ **come to** *sth* [REACH] *phrasal verb* to reach a particular point or state: *His hair comes right **down** to his shoulders.* ○ *He's tiny, he doesn't even come **up** to my chest!* ○ *And now I come to* (= I will mention) *my main point.* ○ *The war had just come to **an end*** (= ended). ○ *The car spun off the road, turned over twice and came to **rest*** (= stopped moving) *in a field.* ○ *We may have to sell the house, but I hope it won't come to **that**.*

● **come to nothing** If plans come to nothing, they fail: *So much effort and planning and it's all come to nothing.*

▲ **come to** *sth* [TOTAL] *phrasal verb* to be a particular total when numbers or amounts are added together: *That comes to £25.*

▲ **come to** *sth* [DECIDE] *phrasal verb* If you come to a decision, arrangement etc., you make a decision or decide what to think about something: *We haven't come to a decision on the matter yet.* ○ *Have you come to any conclusions about the story yet?*

▲ **come under** *sth* [EXPERIENCE] *phrasal verb* If you come under something, you are suddenly caused to experience or suffer it: *Our armies have come under heavy bombardment.* ○ *The government are coming under pressure to change the law.*

▲ **come under** *sth* [BOOK] *phrasal verb* If a piece of information comes under a particular part of a list, book, or collection of things, you can find it in that part: *Swimming pools usually come under 'leisure centres' in the telephone directory.*

▲ **come under** *sth* [ORGANIZATION] *phrasal verb* to be controlled or dealt with by an official organization or a particular part of it: *Playground guidelines come under the Department of Health and Safety.*

▲ **come up** [MOVE TOWARDS] *phrasal verb* to move towards someone: *A young girl came up **to** me and asked for money.*

▲ **come up** [BE MENTIONED] *phrasal verb* to be mentioned or talked about in conversation: *What points came up at the meeting?*

▲ **come up** [OPPORTUNITY] *phrasal verb* If a job or opportunity comes up, it becomes available: *A position has come up in the accounts department.*

▲ **come up** [HAPPEN] *phrasal verb* **1** to happen, usually unexpectedly: *I've got to go – something has just come up at home and I'm needed there.* **2 be coming up** to be happening soon: *My exams are coming up soon.*

▲ **come up** RISE *phrasal verb* When the sun or moon comes up, it rises.

▲ **come up** COMPUTER *phrasal verb* If information comes up on a computer screen, it appears there.

▲ **come up against** *sth phrasal verb* to have to deal with a problem: *If you come up against difficulties, let me know and I'll help out.*

▲ **come up to** *sth phrasal verb* to reach the usual or necessary standard: *The essay didn't come up to his usual standards.* ○ *The food didn't come up to my expectations.*

▲ **come up with** *sth phrasal verb* to suggest or think of an idea or plan: *She's come up with some amazing scheme to double their income.*

▲ **come upon** *sth phrasal verb FORMAL* to find something or meet someone unexpectedly: *I came upon this book in the attic – would you like it?*

comedy /ˈkɒm.ə.di/ ⓤ /ˈkɑː.mə-/ *noun* **1** [C] a (type of) film, play or book which is intentionally amusing either in its characters or its action: *His latest film is described as a 'romantic comedy'.* ○ *I prefer Shakespeare's comedies to his tragedies.* **2** [U] the amusing parts of a situation: *The vicar's forgetting his lines in the middle of the speech provided some good comedy.*

• **comedy of manners** a type of comedy in which the social behaviour of a particular group of people is made to appear foolish

comedian /kəˈmiː.di.ən/ *noun* [C] (*FEMALE ALSO* **comedienne**) a person whose job is to make people laugh by telling jokes and amusing stories or by copying the behaviour or speech of famous people: *a stand-up comedian*

come-hither /kʌmˈhɪð.ər/ ⓤ /-ɚ/ *adj* [before n] *OLD-FASHIONED INFORMAL* describes a way of looking at someone that shows you are sexually interested in them: *come-hither eyes*

comely /ˈkʌm.li/ *adj OLD-FASHIONED OR LITERARY* describes a woman who is attractive in appearance

'come-on ,line *noun* [C] *US FOR* **chat-up line**

comestibles /kəˈmes.tɪ.blz/ *plural noun FORMAL* things which are to be eaten

comet /ˈkɒm.ɪt/ ⓤ /ˈkɑː.mɪt/ *noun* [C] an object that moves around the sun, usually at a great distance from it, that is seen only rarely from Earth as a bright line in the sky

come-uppance /kʌmˈʌp.ənts/ ⓤ /kəˈmʌp-/ *noun* [S] *INFORMAL HUMOROUS* a person's bad luck that is considered to be a fair and deserved punishment for something bad that they have done: *She'll get her come-uppance, don't worry.*

comfort /ˈkʌm.fət/ ⓤ /-fɚt/ *noun* **1** [U] a pleasant feeling of being relaxed and free from pain: *She evidently dresses for comfort.* ○ *It's a little too hot for comfort.* ○ *Now you can watch the latest films in the comfort of your own room.* **2** [C or U] when you feel better after feeling sad or worried, or something that makes you feel better in this way: *The letters that people wrote after his death gave me a lot of comfort.* ○ *It's some comfort to his wife* (= It makes her feel less sad) *to know that he died instantly and didn't suffer.* ○ *I've got to take an exam too, if it's any comfort* (= if it makes you feel better to know that we share the same problem or bad luck). ○ *I know she goes out a lot at night, but I draw/take comfort from the fact that she's always with friends.* ○ *He's a great comfort to his mother.* **3** [U] when you have a pleasant life with enough money for everything that you need: *He could retire now and live in comfort for the rest of his life.* **4** [C usually pl] something that makes your life easy and pleasant: *After the trip, it was nice getting back to a few home comforts.* ○ *She's always liked her creature comforts* (= the type of pleasure found in the house, for example warmth, food, etc.).

• **comfort eat** to eat because you are feeling anxious or upset and not because you are hungry **'comfort ,eating** *noun* [U]

comfort /ˈkʌm.fət/ ⓤ /-fɚt/ *verb* [T] to make someone feel better when they are sad or anxious: *The girl's mother was at home today, being comforted by relatives.*

comforting /ˈkʌm.fə.tɪŋ/ ⓤ /-fɚ.tɪŋ/ *adj* making you feel less sad or anxious: *I found her words very comforting.* ○ *Hot soup is very comforting on a cold winter's day.*

comfortingly /ˈkʌm.fə.tɪŋ.li/ ⓤ /-fɚ.tɪŋ-/ *adv* in a way that makes you feel less sad or anxious: *"It'll be all right," she said comfortingly.*

comfortless /ˈkʌm.fət.ləs/ ⓤ /-fɚt-/ *adj FORMAL* without anything that gives physical comfort

comfortable /ˈkʌmp.fə.tə.bḷ/ ⓤ /-fɚ.tə-/ *adj* **1** describes furniture and clothes that provide a pleasant feeling and that do not give you any physical problems: *a comfortable bed/sofa* ○ *comfortable shoes/trousers* **2** relaxed and free from pain: *Are you comfortable or shall I turn the heat down?* ○ *I don't feel comfortable in high heels.* ○ *Do sit down and make yourself comfortable.* **3** If you are comfortable with a situation, you do not have any worries about it: *I'm not comfortable with the idea of leaving her on her own.* **4** describes an ill or injured person in hospital who is not feeling too much pain **5** having enough money for a good standard of living: *They're not fabulously rich or anything, but they're quite comfortable.* **6** If you win a game or competition by a comfortable amount, you win easily: *a comfortable lead/victory*

comfortably /ˈkʌmf.tə.bli/ *adv* **1** in a comfortable way: *Are you sitting comfortably? Then I'll begin.* **2** without financial or other problems: *We could live fairly comfortably on Edward's salary.*

• **comfortably off** having enough money to lead a good life

'comfort ,break *noun* [C] *UK* a short pause in a meeting to allow people to go to a toilet: *Shall we have a comfort break?*

comforter *US* /ˈkʌm.fə.tər/ ⓤ /-tɚ/ *noun* [C] (*UK* **duvet**) a large soft flat bag filled with feathers or artificial material used on a bed

'comfort ,food *noun* [C or U] the type of food which people eat when they are sad or anxious, often sweet food or food that people ate as children

'comfort ,station *noun* [C] *US OLD-FASHIONED* a public toilet

'comfort ,stop *noun* [C] *UK* a short pause in a journey to allow passengers to go to a toilet

comfy /ˈkʌm.fi/ *adj INFORMAL FOR* **comfortable**: *a comfy chair*

comic MAGAZINE /ˈkɒm.ɪk/ ⓤ /ˈkɑː.mɪk/ *noun* [C] (*US ALSO* **comic book**) a magazine, especially for children, which contains a set of stories told in pictures with a small amount of writing

comic PERSON /ˈkɒm.ɪk/ ⓤ /ˈkɑː.mɪk/ *noun* [C] someone who entertains people by telling jokes

comic AMUSING /ˈkɒm.ɪk/ ⓤ /ˈkɑː.mɪk/ *adj* making you want to laugh; amusing: *a comic actor/performance/ writer*

comical /ˈkɒm.ɪ.kᵊl/ ⓤ /ˈkɑː.mɪ-/ *adj* funny in a strange or silly way: *He looked so comical in that hat.* **comically** /ˈkɒm.ɪ.kli/ ⓤ /ˈkɑː.mɪ-/ *adv*

,comic 'opera *noun* [C or U] a play that is amusing and in which there is a lot of music and singing

'comic ,strip *noun* [C] (*ALSO* **cartoon strip**) a short series of amusing drawings with a small amount of writing which is usually published in a newspaper

comma /ˈkɒm.ə/ ⓤ /ˈkɑː.mə/ *noun* [C] the (,) punctuation mark that is used in writing to separate parts of a sentence showing a slight pause, or to separate the various single items in a list

command ORDER /kəˈmɑːnd/ ⓤ /-ˈmænd/ *noun* **1** [C] an order, especially one given by a soldier: *You will run forward at* (= when you hear) *my command.* ○ *When I give the command, fire!* ○ *He hated being in the army because he had to obey commands.* **2** [U] control over someone or something and responsibility for them: *Colonel Sailing has command over/is in command of the Guards Regiment.* ○ *General Haig took command of the British Expeditionary Force in 1915.* ○ *The soldiers were under the command of a tough sergeant-major.*

• **at your command 1** If you have particular qualities at your command, you are able to use them effectively: *As a writer, she has both style and humour at her command.*

2 *HUMOROUS* If someone says that they are at your command, they mean they are willing to do what you ask: *"I can't reach my zip – could you unfasten it, please?" "I'm at your command!"*

• **be in command (of *yourself*)** to be calm and completely in control of your behaviour and emotions: *Suntanned and relaxed, looking calmly about the room, he appeared completely in command.*

command /kə'mɑːnd/ [US] /-'mænd/ *verb* **1** [I or T] to give someone an order: [+ *to* infinitive] *The officer commanded his men **to** shoot.* ○ [+ **that**] *He commanded **that** the troops (should) cross the water.* **2** [I or T] to control someone or something and tell them what to do: *Colonel Sailing commands the Guards Regiment.* **3** [T] to deserve and get something good, such as attention, respect, or a lot of money: *She was one of those teachers who just commanded **respect**.* ○ *She commands one of the highest fees per film in Hollywood.*

commanding /kə'mɑːn.dɪŋ/ [US] /-'mæn-/ *adj* **1** [before n] having the authority to give orders: *a commanding officer* **2** describes a voice or manner which seems to have authority and therefore demands your attention: *his commanding presence* **3** [before n] in a very successful position and likely to win or succeed: *He has a commanding **lead** in the championships.*

command [COMPUTER] /kə'mɑːnd/ [US] /-'mænd/ *noun* [C] an instruction to a computer to perform a particular action

command [KNOWLEDGE] /kə'mɑːnd/ [US] /-'mænd/ *noun* [S or U] a great knowledge of a subject and an ability to use that knowledge: *She **has an** impressive command **of** the English language.*

Command [SOLDIERS] /kə'mɑːnd/ [US] /-'mænd/ *noun* [C] a group of soldiers or an area controlled by a commander: *Western Command*

command [VIEW] /kə'mɑːnd/ [US] /-'mænd/ *verb* [T] *FORMAL* to give a view: *The master bedroom commands a **view** of rolling green hills.* **command** /kə'mɑːnd/ [US] /-'mænd/ *noun* [S] *a fine castle with its command of the surrounding countryside*

commanding /kə'mɑːn.dɪŋ/ [US] /-'mæn-/ *adj FORMAL* **a commanding position/view** a position or view from which a lot of land can be seen: *The house occupies a commanding position at the top of the valley.*

commandant /'kɒm.ən.dænt/ [US] /'kɑː-/ *noun* [C] an officer who is in charge of a military organization or establishment, such as a prison for soldiers used during a war

commandeer /ˌkɒm.ən'dɪər/ [US] /ˌkɑː.mən'dɪr/ *verb* [T] to take possession of or control private property by force or for military use

commander /kə'mɑːn.dər/ [US] /-'mæn.dɚ/ *noun* [C] an officer who is in charge of a military operation, or an officer of a particular rank in the British Royal Navy

commander-in-chief /kəˌmɑːn.dər.ɪn'tʃiːf/ [US] /-ˌmæn.dɚ-/ *noun* [C] (*ABBREVIATION* **C-in-C**) a commander in charge of all the armed forces of a country or of all the forces fighting in a particular area or operation

commandment /kə'mɑːnd.mənt/ [US] /-'mænd-/ *noun* [C] **1** any of the ten very important rules of behaviour which are stated in the OLD TESTAMENT (= first part) of the Bible **2** *LITERARY* an order

commando /kə'mɑːn.dəʊ/ [US] /-'mæn.doʊ/ *noun* [C] *plural* **commandos** or **commandoes** (a member of) a small group of soldiers that are specially trained to make attacks on enemy areas which are particularly dangerous or difficult to attack

com'mand perˌformance *noun* [C] a special performance of a play or film which is given because a royal or very important person has requested it

comme il faut /ˌkɒm.iːl'fəʊ/ [US] /ˌkɑː.miːl'foʊ/ *adj* [after v] *FORMAL* behaving or dressing in the right way in public according to formal rules of social behaviour: *Trust me – it's not comme il faut to wear a pink tie to a funeral.*

commemorate /kə'mem.ə.reɪt/ *verb* [T] to remember officially and give respect to a great person or event, especially by a public ceremony or by making a statue or special building: *Gathered all together in this church, we commemorate those who lost their lives in the great war.* ○ *A statue has been built to commemorate the 100th anniversary of the poet's birthday.*

commemoration /kəˌmem.ə'reɪ.ʃən/ *noun* [C or U] something which is done to remember officially and give respect to a great person or event: *A set of stamps has been commissioned **in** commemoration **of** Independence Day.* ○ *Thousands of veterans will take part in a commemoration of the battle.* **commemorative** /kə'mem.ər.ə.tɪv/ [US] /-ɚ.ə.t̬ɪv/ *adj*: *a commemorative statue/stamp/service/plaque*

commence /kə'ments/ *verb* [I or T] *FORMAL* to begin something: *We will commence building work in August of next year.* ○ *Shall we let the meeting commence, gentlemen?* ○ [+ *v-ing*] *Unfortunately, he commenced speak**ing** before all the guests had finished eating.*

commencement /kə'ment.smənt/ *noun* **1** [C or U] *FORMAL* the beginning of something: *Would passengers please put out cigarettes before the commencement of the flight.* **2** [C] *US* a ceremony at which students formally receive their degrees

commend /kə'mend/ *verb* [T] to formally praise someone or something: *The judge commended her **for/on** her bravery.* ○ *For a low-budget film, it has much to commend it* (= it deserves praise). ○ *It says on the back cover of the book '**highly** commended'.*

commendable /kə'men.də.bl/ *adj FORMAL* deserving praise: *commendable efforts / behaviour / bravery*

commendably /kə'men.də.bli/ *adv*

commendation /ˌkɒm.en'deɪ.ʃən/ [US] /ˌkɑː.mən-/ *noun* [C or U] *FORMAL* praise, or an official statement which praises someone: *Several of the firefighters received commendation **for** their bravery.*

commensurate /kə'ment.sjər.ət/ [US] /-sjɚ-/ *adj FORMAL* in a correct and suitable amount compared to something else: *a salary that is commensurate **with** skills and experience*

comment /'kɒm.ent/ [US] /'kɑː.ment/ *noun* [C or U] something that you say or write that expresses your opinion: *I don't want any comments **on/about** my new haircut, thank you!* ○ *He made negative comments to the press.* ○ *I suppose his criticism was **fair** comment* (= a reasonable opinion). ○ *She was asked about the pay increase but made **no** comment* (= did not give an opinion).

• **No comment.** used to say that you do not want to answer someone's question

comment /'kɒm.ent/ [US] /'kɑː.ment/ *verb* [I or T] to make a comment: *My mum always comments **on** what I'm wearing.* ○ [+ **that**] *He commented **that** the two essays were rather similar.* ○ *The official **refused to/declined to** comment on the matter.*

commentary /'kɒm.ən.tri/ [US] /'kɑː.mən.ter-/ *noun* [C or U] **1** a spoken description of an event on the radio or television that is broadcast as the event happens: *The commentary **on** the Olympic games was much better on the other channel.* **2** a set of written remarks on an event, book or person which explains its subject or expresses an opinion on it: *There's a good arts coverage in the newspaper, but not much political commentary.* **3** **running commentary** (a) continuous description of events as they are happening

'commentary ˌbox *noun* [C] a room or place for a radio or television reporter at a special event, especially a sports competition, from which they report what is happening: *Let's return now to the commentary box to see what's happening in this exciting final.*

commentator /'kɒm.ən.teɪ.tər/ [US] /'kɑː.mən.teɪ.t̬ɚ/ *noun* [C] a reporter for radio or television who provides a spoken description of and remarks on an event, especially a sports competition, as it happens: *a radio commentator* ○ *a sports/football commentator.* **commentate** /'kɒm.ən.teɪt/ [US] /'kɑː.mən-/ *verb* [I] *She commentates **on** the tennis each year at Wimbledon.*

commerce /'kɒm.ɜːs/ [US] /'kɑː.mɝːs/ *noun* [U] the activities involved in buying and selling things: *the world of commerce and industry*

commercial /kə'mɜː.ʃəl/ [US] /-'mɝː-/ *adj* **1** related to buying and selling things: *a commercial organization/venture/success* ○ *commercial law* ○ *The commercial future of the company looks very promising.* **2** *DISAPPROVING* describes a record, film, book, etc. that has been produced with the aim of making money and as a result lacks artistic value **3** [before n] describes a product that can be bought by or is intended to be bought by the general public

commercialize *UK USUALLY* **-ise** /kə'mɜː.ʃəl.aɪz/ [US] /-'mɝː-/ *verb* [T usually passive] to organize something to make a profit **commercialized** *UK USUALLY* **-ised** *DISAPPROVING* /kə'mɜː.ʃəl.aɪzd/ [US] /-'mɝː-/ *adj*: *It's a pity Christmas has become so commercialized.* **commercialization** *UK USUALLY* **-isation** /kəˌmɜː.ʃəl.aɪ'zeɪ.ʃən/ [US] /-ˌmɝː-/ *noun* [U] *The commercialization of football has turned it from a sport into a business.*

commercialism /kə'mɜː.ʃəl.ɪ.zəm/ [US] /-'mɝː-/ *noun* [U] the principles and activity of commerce, especially those connected with profit and not quality or morality

commercially /kə'mɜː.ʃəl.i/ [US] /-'mɝː-/ *adv*: *Does the market research show that the product will succeed commercially* (= make a profit)? ○ *The drug won't be commercially* ***available*** (= able to be bought) *until it has been thoroughly tested.*

commercial /kə'mɜː.ʃəl/ [US] /-'mɝː-/ *noun* [C] an advertisement which is broadcast on television or radio: *a commercial break*

commercial /kə'mɜː.ʃəl/ [US] /-'mɝː-/ *adj* [before n] describes radio or television that is paid for by advertisements which are broadcast between and during programmes

commie /'kɒm.i/ [US] /'kɑː.mi/ *noun* [C], *adj INFORMAL DISAPPROVING FOR* **communist**

commiserate /kə'mɪz.ə.reɪt/ *verb* [I] to express sympathy to someone about some bad luck: *I began by commiserating* ***with*** *her* ***over*** *the defeat.* **commiseration** /kəˌmɪz.ə'reɪ.ʃən/ *noun* [U] *She gave me a look of commiseration as I entered the room.*

commiserations /kəˌmɪz.ə'reɪ.ʃənz/ *plural noun* an expression of sympathy for someone, especially someone who has lost a competition: *Commiserations* ***on*** *losing the match!* ○ *Our commiserations* ***to*** *the losing side!*

commissar /'kɒm.ɪ.sɑːr/ [US] /'kɑː.mɪ.sɑːr/ /ˌ--'-/ *noun* [C] (in the Soviet Union until 1946) the official title of the head of a government department, or an official responsible for political education, especially in a military group

commissariat /ˌkɒm.ɪ'seə.ri.ət/ [US] /ˌkɑː.mə'ser-/ *group noun* [C] a military department which supplies food and equipment

commissary /'kɒm.ɪ.sər.i/ [US] /'kɑː.mə.ser-/ *noun* [C] *US* a shop which supplies food and goods, especially to people in the army or in prison

commission [WORK] /kə'mɪʃ.ən/ *verb* [T] to formally choose someone to do a special piece of work: *The newspaper commissioned a series of articles on the worst excesses of the fashion industry.*

commission /kə'mɪʃ.ən/ *noun* [C] a request to do a special piece of work: [+ *to* infinitive] *She's just got a commission* ***to*** *paint Sir Ellis Pike's wife.* ○ *Do you* ***do/take*** *commissions?*

commission [PAYMENT] /kə'mɪʃ.ən/ *noun* [C or U] a (system of) payment to someone who sells goods which is directly related to the amount of goods sold: *Is she paid a regular wage or is it* ***on/by*** *commission only?* ○ *She* ***gets*** *a 15% commission* ***on*** *every machine she sells.*

commission [GROUP] /kə'mɪʃ.ən/ *group noun* [C] a group of people who have been formally chosen to discover information about a problem or examine the reasons why the problem exists: *a commission* ***on*** *alcohol abuse/racial tension* ○ *The government have* ***set up/established*** *a commission to investigate the problem of inner city violence.*

commission [MILITARY] /kə'mɪʃ.ən/ *verb* [T usually passive] to give someone the official authority to be an officer in the armed forces: *Grandfather was commissioned* ***as*** *Group Captain in the RAF just before the war.*

commission /kə'mɪʃ.ən/ *noun* [C] the official authority to be an officer in the armed forces

• **in commission** If something, such as a machine or a military ship, is in commission it is working and ready for use.

• **out of commission** If something, such as a machine or a military ship, is out of commission it is broken or not available to be used.

commission [CRIME] /kə'mɪʃ.ən/ *noun* [U] *FORMAL OR LEGAL* the act of committing a crime: *the commission of the crime/offence/murder*

commissionaire /kəˌmɪʃ.ən'eər/ [US] /-'er/ *noun* [C] *MAINLY UK* a person wearing a uniform who stands at the entrance of a hotel, theatre, etc. and whose job is to open the door for guests and generally be helpful to them when they arrive

comˌmissioned 'officer *noun* [C] a type of officer in the armed forces ➲See also **NCO**.

commissioner /kə'mɪʃ.ən.ər/ [US] /-ɚ/ *noun* [C] an important official who has responsibility in a government department or another organization: *There is a commissioner in charge of the London police force.*

commit [CRIME] /kə'mɪt/ *verb* [T] **-tt-** to do something illegal or something that is considered wrong: *He was sent to prison for a crime that he didn't commit.* ○ *to commit adultery/murder* ○ *to commit an offence*

• **commit suicide** If a person commits suicide, they kill themselves.

commit [PROMISE] /kə'mɪt/ *verb* [I or T] **-tt- 1** to promise or give your loyalty, time or money to a particular principle, person or plan of action: [R] *Like so many men, he has problems committing himself* ***to*** *a relationship.* ○ *The government must commit itself* ***to*** *improv****ing*** *health care.* ○ *Once we have committed* ***to*** *this course of action there is no going back.* **2** **commit** ***yourself*** to express an opinion or to make a decision that you tell people about: *I think I can come but I won't commit myself till I know for sure.*

• **commit** ***sth*** **to memory** to make certain that you remember something

• **commit** ***sth*** **to paper** to write something down: *Perhaps we should commit these ideas to paper before we forget them.*

committed /kə'mɪt.ɪd/ [US] /-'mɪt̬-/ *adj* **1** loyal and willing to give your time and energy to something that you believe in: *a committed socialist/Christian/teacher* **2** [after v] having promised to be involved in a plan of action: *We are committed* ***to*** *withdraw****ing*** *our troops by the end of the year.*

commitment /kə'mɪt.mənt/ *noun* **1** [C or U] when you are willing to give your time and energy to something that you believe in, or a promise or firm decision to do something: *her commitment* ***to*** *left-wing politics/the cause of feminism/the company* ○ *She is known chiefly for her commitment* ***to*** *nuclear disarmament.* ○ *I'd like to thank the staff for having shown such commitment.* ○ *Try the product out in the comfort of your own home with absolutely no commitment* ***to*** *buy!* **2** [C] something that you must do or deal with that takes your time: *family/work commitments* ○ *I've got too many commitments at the moment to do an evening class.* ○ *Children are such a commitment.*

commit [SEND] /kə'mɪt/ *verb* [T] **-tt-** *FORMAL* to send someone officially to prison or hospital: *He's been committed* ***to*** *prison for fraud.*

committal /kə'mɪt.əl/ [US] /-'mɪt̬-/ *noun* [U] *SPECIALIZED* the process of sending someone to a prison or mental hospital: *The psychiatric team decided that committal would not be beneficial in her case.*

committee /kə'mɪt.i/ [US] /-'mɪt̬-/ *group noun* [C] a small group of people chosen to represent a larger organization and either make decisions or gather information for it: *She* ***sits on/is on*** *the school's development committee.* ○ *The local council have just set up a committee to study recycling.* ○ *a committee* ***meeting***

commode /kə'məʊd/ [US] /-'moʊd/ *noun* [C] a piece of furniture that looks like a chair but has a container in the seat which people who are ill or old can use as a toilet

commodious /kə'məʊ.di.əs/ [US] /-'moʊ-/ *adj FORMAL* describes a room or house that has a lot of space

commodity /kə'mɒd.ə.ti/ [US] /-'mɑː.də.t̬i/ *noun* [C] **1** a substance or product that can be traded, bought or sold: *The country's most valuable commodities include tin and*

C

diamonds. ○ *the international commodities market* **2** a valuable quality: *If you're going into teaching, energy is a necessary commodity.*

commodore /ˈkɒm.ə.dɔːʳ/ [US] /ˈkɑː.mə.dɔːr/ *noun* [C] an officer of high rank in the navy, or the person in charge of a sailing organization

C

common [USUAL] /ˈkɒm.ən/ [US] /ˈkɑː.mən/ *adj* **1** the same in a lot of places or for a lot of people: *It's quite common to see couples who dress alike.* ○ *The surname 'Smith' is very common in Britain.* **2 common courtesy/decency** the basic level of politeness which you expect from someone **3 common knowledge** a fact that everyone knows: [+ *that*] *It's common knowledge that they live together.*

• **the common man** ordinary people: *How can anyone so privileged have any understanding of the common man?*

• **the common touch** the ability of an important or rich person to communicate well with and understand ordinary people: *It was always said of the Princess that she had the common touch and that was why she was so well loved by the people.*

commonly /ˈkɒm.ən.li/ [US] /ˈkɑː.mən-/ *adv* often or usually: *Elbow injuries are commonly found among tennis players.*

common [SHARED] /ˈkɒm.ən/ [US] /ˈkɑː.mən/ *adj* belonging to or shared by two or more people or things: *a common goal/interest* ○ *English has some features common* ***to*** *many languages.* ➲See also **common ground**.

• **for the common good** If something is done for the common good it is done to help everyone.

• **make common cause with *sb*** *FORMAL* to act together with someone in order to achieve something: *Environment protesters have made common cause with local people to stop the motorway being built.*

common /ˈkɒm.ən/ [US] /ˈkɑː.mən/ *noun* **1 have *sth* in common** to share interests, experiences or other characteristics with someone or something: *We don't really have much in common.* **2 in common with *sb/sth*** in the same way as someone or something: *In common with many mothers, she feels torn between her family and her work.*

common [LAND] /ˈkɒm.ən/ [US] /ˈkɑː.mən/ *noun* [C] (*US ALSO* **commons**) an area of grass which everyone is allowed to use, usually in or near a village

common [LOW CLASS] /ˈkɒm.ən/ [US] /ˈkɑː.mən/ *adj DISAPPROVING* typical of a low social class: *My mum thinks dyed blonde hair is a bit common.* **commonly** /ˈkɒm.ən.-li/ [US] /ˈkɑː.mən-/ *adv*

commoner /ˈkɒm.ən.əʳ/ [US] /ˈkɑː.mən.ɚ/ *noun* [C] a person who is not born into a position of high social rank: *The princess's children have no titles because their father is a commoner.*

the ˌcommon ˈcold *noun* [S] a slight illness which a lot of people catch, causing a cough, sore throat and blocked nose

ˌcommon deˈnominator [NUMBER] *noun* [C] *SPECIALIZED* a number which can be divided exactly by all the DENOMINATORS (= numbers under the line) in a group of fractions: *12 is a common denominator* ***of*** *⅓ and ¼.*

ˌcommon deˈnominator [SIMILARITY] *noun* [C] something that is the same for all the members of a group and might bring them together: *The common denominator was that we had all worked for the same company.*

ˌcommon ˈground *noun* [U] shared interests, beliefs or opinions between two people or groups of people who disagree about most other subjects: *It seems increasingly unlikely that the two sides will find any common ground.*

ˌcommon ˈlaw *noun* [U] the legal system in England and most of the US which has developed over a period of time from old customs and court decisions, rather than laws made in Parliament

common-law /ˈkɒm.ən.lɔː/ [US] /ˈkɑː.mən.lɑː/ *adj* **common-law husband/wife** someone who is not officially a wife or husband but is considered to be one because she or he has been living with their partner for a long time

the ˌCommon ˈMarket *noun* [S] *OLD-FASHIONED* **the European Union** or **the European Community**

ˌcommon ˈnoun *noun* [C] *SPECIALIZED* a noun that is the name of a group of similar things, such as 'table' or 'book', and not of a single person, place or thing ➲Compare **proper noun**.

ˌcommon-or-ˈgarden *adj UK INFORMAL* very ordinary: *It's a common-or-garden washing machine with just the basic functions, but it works perfectly well.*

commonplace [ORDINARY] /ˈkɒm.ən.pleɪs/ [US] /ˈkɑː.mən-/ *adj* happening frequently or often seen or experienced and so not considered to be special: *Home computers are increasingly commonplace.*

commonplace [REMARK] /ˈkɒm.ən.pleɪs/ [US] /ˈkɑː.mən-/ *noun* [C] *FORMAL* a boring remark which is used very often and does not have much meaning: *We exchanged commonplaces about the weather over cups of tea.*

ˈcommon ˌroom *noun* [C] *MAINLY UK* a room in a school or college where students or teachers can sit together and talk when they are not working

the ˈCommons *noun* [S] **the House of Commons**: *The bill was defeated in the Commons by 249 votes to 131.* ○ *a Commons committee*

ˌcommon ˈsense *noun* [U] the basic level of practical knowledge and judgment that we all need to help us live in a reasonable and safe way: *Windsurfing is perfectly safe as long as you have/use some common sense.* ○ *a matter of common sense* **commonsensical** /ˌkɒm.ən-ˈsen.sɪ.kəl/ [US] /ˌkɑː.mən-/ *adj*: *He described the report as 'rigorous and commonsensical'.*

commonwealth /ˈkɒm.ən.welθ/ [US] /ˈkɑː.mən-/ *noun* [C] **1** a country or part of a country that is governed by its people or representatives elected by its people **2** *FORMAL* a group of countries with the same political or economic aims

the ˌCommonwealth (of ˈNations) *noun* [S] an organization of independent countries which in the past belonged to the British Empire and now still have friendly and practical connections with each other

commotion /kəˈməʊ.ʃən/ [US] /-ˈmoʊ-/ *noun* [S or U] a sudden short period of noise, confusion or excited movement: *His arrival* ***caused*** *quite a commotion.* ○ *He looked up to see what all the commotion was about.*

communal /ˈkɒm.jʊ.nəl/ /kəˈmjuː-/ [US] /ˈkɑː.mjə-/ *adj* **1** belonging to or used by a group of people rather than one single person: *communal facilities/food/property* ○ *We each have a separate bedroom but share a communal kitchen.* **2** based on differences or disagreements within a larger social group: *Communal riots/disturbances have once again broken out between the two ethnic groups.* **3** describes a society in which everyone lives and works together and the ownership of property and possessions is shared **communally** /kəˈmjuː.nəl.i/ *adv*

commune [GROUP] /ˈkɒm.juːn/ [US] /ˈkɑː.mjuːn/ *group noun* [C] a group of families or single people who live and work together sharing possessions and responsibilities: *She left her husband to* ***join*** *a women's commune.*

commune [GOVERNMENT] /ˈkɒm.juːn/ [US] /ˈkɑː.mjuːn/ *noun* [C] in some countries, a unit of local government

commune [GET CLOSE] /kəˈmjuːn/ *verb* [I] *FORMAL* to get very close to someone or something by exchanging feelings or thoughts: *Lying naked in the grass, among the trees and birds, he felt he had communed* ***with*** *nature.*

communion /kəˈmjuː.ni.ən/ *noun* [U] *FORMAL* a close relationship with someone in which feelings and thoughts are exchanged: *It was a spiritual communion that he found with her.* ○ *He lived* ***in*** *close communion* ***with*** *nature/God.* ➲See also **Communion**.

communion /kəˈmjuː.ni.ən/ *group noun* [C] *LITERARY* a group of people who are united by the same especially religious beliefs: *The author has a vision of an emerging worldwide Christian communion.* ➲See also **Communion**.

communicant /kəˈmjuː.nɪ.kənt/ *noun* [C] a person who is involved in HOLY COMMUNION (= a Christian religious ceremony), and is therefore considered to be an active member of a church

communicate /kə'mjuː.nɪ.keɪt/ *verb* **1** [I or T] to share information with others by speaking, writing, moving your body or using other signals: *We can now communicate instantly* ***with*** *people on the other side of the world.* ○ *Unable to speak a word of the language, he communicated* ***with*** (= using) *his hands.* ○ *Has the news been communicated* ***to*** *the staff yet?* ○ *As an actor he could communicate a whole range of emotions.* **2** [I] to talk about your thoughts and feelings, and help other people to understand them: *I find I just can't communicate* ***with*** *her.* **3** [T] SPECIALIZED to pass a disease from one person or animal to another **4** [I] FORMAL If one room communicates with another, it connects with it through a door: *The bedroom communicates* ***with*** *both toilet and hall.* ○ *communicating rooms*

communicable /kə'mjuː.nɪ.kə.bl̩/ *adj* FORMAL able to be given from one person to another: *In this period, there were 974 outbreaks of communicable* ***disease*** *attributed to the consumption of raw milk.* ○ *communicable ideas/emotions*

communication /kəˌmjuː.nɪ'keɪ.ʃən/ *noun* **1** [U] the act of communicating with people: *Television is an increasingly important* ***means of*** *communication.* ○ *We are* ***in*** *direct communication* ***with*** *Moscow.* ○ *With an hour's walk to the nearest telephone, communication is difficult.* ○ *There's very little communication* ***between*** *mother and daughter* (= they do not have a good relationship). ○ *a course on communication skills* **2** [C] FORMAL a message or a letter: *We received your communication of 11th March and are sorry to inform you that we won't be attending the conference.*

communications /kəˌmjuː.nɪ'keɪ.ʃənz/ *plural noun* **1** the various methods of sending information between people and places, especially official systems such as post systems, radio, telephone, etc: *the communications industry* **2** ways of moving between one place and another: *Its commercial success as a city is partly due to its excellent rail and road communications.*

communicator /kə'mjuː.nɪ.keɪ.tə^r/ [US] /-t̬ɚ/ *noun* [C] someone who is able to tell people about their ideas and emotions in a way that other people understand: *Obviously teachers have to be good communicators.*

communicative /kə'mjuː.nɪ.kə.tɪv/ [US] /-t̬ɪv/ *adj* **1** willing to talk to people and give them information: *He was in a bad mood at breakfast and wasn't very communicative.* **2** relating to communication: *The communicative ability of the whale is thought to be highly developed.*

COMMON LEARNER ERROR

communications or **public transport?**

Communications is not usually used to talk about how you travel from place to place. It is usually used to talk about phones, radio and TV.

Public transport is the normal phrase for trains, buses, etc. that everyone can use. In the US, the phrase for this is **public transportation**.

We live on the edge of the city and the public transport is terrible.
~~*We live on the edge of the city and the communication is terrible.*~~

communi'cation ˌcord UK *noun* [C] (US **emergency cord**) a chain in a train carriage which a passenger can pull in an emergency to stop the train

communi'cations ˌsatellite *noun* [C] an artificial object in space used to send out television, radio and telephone signals around the earth's surface

Communion /kə'mjuː.ni.ən/ *noun* [U] (FORMAL **Holy Communion**) a Christian ceremony based on Jesus Christ's last meal with his DISCIPLES (= the twelve men who were his followers) ➲See also **communion** at **commune** GET CLOSE.

communiqué /kə'mjuː.nɪ.keɪ/ *noun* [C] an official piece of news or an announcement, especially to the public or newspapers: *The palace have* ***issued*** *a communiqué denying the rumour.*

communism, Communism /'kɒm.jʊ.nɪ.zəm/ [US] /'kɑː.mjə-/ *noun* [U] the belief in a society without different classes in which the methods of production are owned and controlled by all its members and everyone works as much as they can and receives what they need ➲Compare **capitalism**; **socialism**. **communist, Communist** /'kɒm.jʊ.nɪst/ [US] /'kɑː.mjə-/ *adj, noun: the Communist party* ○ *communist ideology* ○ *Was she ever a Communist?*

community /kə'mjuː.nə.ti/ [US] /-t̬i/ *group noun* [C] **1** the people living in one particular area or people who are considered as a unit because of their common interests, background or nationality: *He's well-known in the* ***local*** *community.* ○ *There's a large* ***black/white/Jewish*** *community living in this area.* ○ *Her speech caused outrage among the* ***gay*** *community.* ○ *Drug trafficking is a matter of considerable concern for the entire* ***international*** *community* (= all the countries of the world). ○ *There's a real* ***sense of*** *community* (= caring and friendly feeling) *in this neighbourhood.* **2** SPECIALIZED a group of animals or plants that live or grow together **3** **the community** the general public: *Unlike the present government, we believe in* ***serving*** *the community.*

com'munity ˌcentre *noun* [C] a place where people who live in an area can meet each other and play sports, take courses, etc.

com'munity ˌchest *noun* [C] US an amount of money which has been given and collected by the people of a particular area to help people who are old or ill and in need of help

com'munity ˌcollege *noun* [C] **1** UK a school for children between the ages of 11 and 18 which also provides a variety of classes, sports, etc. for adults from the local area **2** US a two-year college where students can learn a skill or prepare to enter a university

com'munity ˌservice *noun* [U] work that people do to help other people without payment, and which young criminals whose crime was not serious enough for them to be put in prison are sometimes ordered to do

commute [TRAVEL] /kə'mjuːt/ *verb* [I] to make the same journey regularly between work and home: *It's exhausting commuting* ***from*** *Brighton* ***to*** *London every day.*

commute /kə'mjuːt/ *noun* [C] INFORMAL *It's at least an hour's commute to work.*

commuter /kə'mjuː.tə^r/ [US] /-t̬ɚ/ *noun* [C] someone who regularly travels between work and home: *The train was packed with commuters.*

commute [CHANGE] /kə'mjuːt/ *verb* [T] **1** FORMAL to change one thing into another: *People used to believe that you could commute base metals* ***into*** *gold.* **2** SPECIALIZED to exchange one type of payment for a different type: *I think I'll commute my life insurance* ***into*** *an annuity.* **3** LEGAL to change a punishment to one that is less severe: *Her sentence was commuted* ***from*** *death* ***to*** *life imprisonment.*

commutation /ˌkɒm.jʊ'teɪ.ʃən/ [US] /ˌkɑː.mjə-/ *noun* [U] LEGAL when a punishment is changed to one that is less severe: *His execution became certain when the state board refused his request for commutation.*

com'muter ˌtrain *noun* [C] a train service especially for people travelling between home and work

compact [CLOSE TOGETHER] /kəm'pækt/ *adj* consisting of parts that are positioned together closely or in a tidy way, using very little space: *compact soil/sand* ○ *a compact camera/bag* ○ *What a compact office! How did you fit so much into so little space?*

compact /kəm'pækt/ *verb* [T] FORMAL to press something together in a tight and solid way: *Cars had compacted the snow until it was like ice.* **compactly** /kəm'pækt.li/ *adv* **compactness** /kəm'pækt.nəs/ *noun* [U]

compact [CASE] /'kɒm.pækt/ [US] /'kɑːm-/ *noun* [C] a small flat case which contains women's face powder: *a powder compact*

compact [CAR] /'kɒm.pækt/ [US] /'kɑːm-/ *noun* [C] US a small car

compact [AGREEMENT] /'kɒm.pækt/ [US] /'kɑːm-/ *noun* [C] FORMAL a formal agreement between two or more people, organizations or countries: [+ **to** infinitive] *They made a compact not* ***to*** *reveal any details.*

ˌcompact 'disc *noun* [C] a **CD**

companion [PERSON] /kəm'pæn.jən/ *noun* [C] **1** a person you spend a lot of time with either because you are friends or because you are travelling together: *The dog has been her* ***constant*** *companion these past ten years.*

○ *a travelling companion* **2** OLD USE in the past, a young woman who was paid to care for and provide friendship for an old or ill woman, especially while she was travelling

companionable /kəm'pæn.jən.ə.bl̩/ *adj* friendly and pleasant to be with

companionship /kəm'pæn.jən.ʃɪp/ *noun* [U] *I lived on my own for a while but I missed the companionship of* (= enjoyment of being with) *others.*

companion [OBJECT] /kəm'pæn.jən/ *noun* [C] OLD-FASHIONED either of two matching objects: *I've still got one of the candlesticks but I've lost its companion.*

companion [BOOK] /kəm'pæn.jən/ *noun* [C] used in the title of the type of book which gives you information on a particular subject or tells you how to do something: *the Music Lover's Companion*

companionway /kəm'pæn.jən.weɪ/ *noun* [C] SPECIALIZED the steps which lead from one DECK (= level) of a ship to another

company [BUSINESS] /'kʌm.pə.ni/ *noun* [C] an organization which sells goods or services in order to make money: *He works for a software company/a company that makes software.* ○ *I work for Duggan and Company.* ○ *No smoking is company **policy**.*

company [OTHER PEOPLE] /'kʌm.pə.ni/ *noun* [U] when you are with a person or people, or the person or people you are with: *I just enjoy his company.* ○ *It was a long journey and I was grateful for his company.* ○ *I enjoy my **own** company* (= I like being alone). ○ *I travelled **in the** company **of*** (= with) *two teachers as far as Istanbul.* ○ *I'd rather you didn't mention it when we're **in** company* (= with other people). ○ *I didn't realize you **had** company* (= were with someone/people). ○ *Margot came to stay for a week as company **for** my mother while I was away.* ○ *With only her thoughts for company* (= Being alone), *she walked slowly along the seafront.* ➲See also **accompany** GO WITH. See Note **society or company?** at **society** PEOPLE.

• **be good company** to be pleasant and amusing to be with: *You'll like Rosie – she's good company.*

• **be in good company** to have the same problem as many other people: *"I can't play tennis – I'm hopeless at it!" "Oh well, you're in good company."*

• **for company** If you do something for company, you do it to make you feel as if you are not alone: *I usually have the radio on for company.*

• **keep *sb* company** to stay with someone so that they are not alone: *I'll keep you company till the train comes.*

• **the company *you* keep** the influence of the people that you spend time with: *"Where does he pick up words like that?" "It's the company he keeps."* ○ *He's been keeping bad company* (= spending time with unsuitable people).

company [THEATRICAL GROUP] /'kʌm.pə.ni/ *noun* [C] a group of actors, singers or dancers who perform together: *She's in the Royal National Theatre Company.* ○ *I'd like to thank the director, the choreographer and the other members of the company for being so supportive.*

company [GROUP] /'kʌm.pə.ni/ *group noun* [C] a large group of soldiers. especially a division of a BATTALION

ˌcompany 'car *noun* [C] a car owned by a company or other organization which is used by an employee for his or her work

'company ˌtown *noun* [C] US a city or town in which most of the workers are employed by a single organization

comparative /kəm'pær.ə.tɪv/ Ⓤⓢ /-'per.ə.t̬ɪv/ *noun* [C] SPECIALIZED the form of an adjective or adverb that expresses a difference in amount, in number, in degree or quality: *'Fatter' is the comparative **of** 'fat'.* ○ *'More difficult' is the comparative **of** 'difficult'.* ➲See also **comparative** at **compare** EXAMINE DIFFERENCES. **comparative** /kəm'pær.ə.tɪv/ Ⓤⓢ /-'per.ə.t̬ɪv/ *adj*: *The comparative form of 'slow' is 'slower'.*

compare [EXAMINE DIFFERENCES] /kəm'peəʳ/ Ⓤⓢ /-per/ *verb* [T] to examine or look for the difference between two or more things: *If you compare house prices in the two areas, it's quite amazing how different they are.* ○ *That seems expensive – have you compared prices in other shops?* ○ *Compare some recent work **with** your older stuff and you'll see how much you've improved.* ○ *This road is quite busy compared **to/with** ours.* ○ *Children seem to learn more interesting things compared **to/with** when we were at school.* ＊ NOTE: Both *compared to* and *compared with* are widely used, although many speakers of British English do not consider *compared to* acceptable.

• **compare notes** If two people compare notes, they tell each other what they think about something they have both done: *We'd both been out with the same man at different points in our lives so it was interesting to compare notes.*

comparative /kəm'pær.ə.tɪv/ Ⓤⓢ /-'per.ə.t̬ɪv/ *adj* **1** comparing different things: *She's carrying out a comparative study of health in inner cities and rural areas.* ➲See also **comparative**. **2 comparative comfort/freedom/silence** a situation which is comfortable/free/silent, etc. when compared to another situation or what is normal: *I enjoyed the comparative calm of his flat after the busy office.*

comparatively /kəm'pær.ə.tɪv.li/ Ⓤⓢ /-'per.ə.t̬ɪv-/ *adv* as compared to something else: *We couldn't afford it and yet we're comparatively well-off* (= we are richer than most people). ○ *Comparatively **speaking**, this machine is easy to use.*

comparison /kəm'pær.ɪ.sᵊn/ Ⓤⓢ /-'per-/ *noun* [C or U] when two or more people or things are compared: *They **made a** comparison of different countries' eating habits.* ○ ***By/In** comparison **with** the French, the British eat far less fish.*

compare [CONSIDER SIMILARITIES] /kəm'peəʳ/ Ⓤⓢ /-per/ *verb* [T] **1** to judge, suggest or consider that something is similar or of equal quality to something else: *The poet compares his lover's tongue **to** a razor blade.* ○ *Still only twenty-five, she has been compared **to** the greatest dancer of all time.* ○ *People have compared me **to** Elizabeth Taylor.* ○ *You can't compare the two cities – they're totally different.* **2 does not compare** If something or someone does not compare with something or someone else, the second thing is very much better than the first: *Instant coffee just doesn't compare **with** freshly ground coffee.* **3 compare favourably** If something compares favourably with something else, it is better than it: *The hotel certainly compared favourably **with** the one we stayed in last year.*

compare /kəm'peəʳ/ Ⓤⓢ /-per/ *noun* LITERARY **beyond compare** so good that everyone or everything else is of worse quality: *Her beauty is beyond compare.*

comparable /'kɒm.pᵊr.ə.bl̩/ Ⓤⓢ /'kɑːm.pɚ-/ *adj* similar in size, amount or quality to something else: *The girls are of comparable ages.* ○ *Our prices are comparable **to/with** those in other shops.* ○ *The two experiences aren't comparable.* **comparably** /'kɒm.pᵊr.ə.bli/ Ⓤⓢ /'kɑːm.pɚ-/ *adv*: *comparably priced tickets*

comparison /kəm'pær.ɪ.sᵊn/ Ⓤⓢ /-'per-/ *noun* [C or U] when something is considered similar or of equal quality to something else: *She **drew a** comparison **between** life in the army and life in prison.* ○ *To my mind **there's no** comparison between the two restaurants* (= one is much better than the other). ○ *He's a good writer but he doesn't **bear/stand** comparison **with** Shakespeare* (= he is not nearly as good as Shakespeare).

compartment /kəm'pɑːt.mənt/ Ⓤⓢ /-'pɑːrt-/ *noun* [C] **1** one of the separate areas inside a vehicle, especially a train: *a first class compartment* **2** a separate part of a piece of furniture, equipment or container with a particular purpose: *a fridge with a small freezer compartment* ○ *the sleeping/inner compartment in a tent*

compartmentalize, UK USUALLY **-ise** /ˌkɒm.pɑːt-'men.tᵊl.aɪz/ Ⓤⓢ /ˌkɑːm.pɑːrt'men.t̬ᵊl-/ *verb* [T] to separate something into parts and not allow those parts to mix together: *His life was carefully compartmentalized, with his work in one city and his social life in another.*

compass [DEVICE] /'kʌm.pəs/ *noun* [C] a device for finding direction which has a freely moving needle that always points to magnetic north

compass [LIMIT] /'kʌm.pəs/ *noun* [U] FORMAL a particular range (of ability, activity, interest, etc.): *It's a musical instrument made of brass, somewhat like a cornet and with a similar compass.* ○ *The discussion went **beyond the** compass **of** my brain.*

compasses /'kʌm.pə.sɪz/ *plural noun* a V-shaped device which is used for drawing circles or measuring distances on maps

compassion /kəm'pæʃ.ᵊn/ *noun* [U] APPROVING a strong feeling of sympathy and sadness for the suffering or bad luck of others and a desire to help them: *I was hoping she might show a little compassion.*

compassionate /kəm'pæʃ.ᵊn.ət/ *adj* APPROVING showing compassion: *The public's response to the crisis appeal was generous and compassionate.* **compassionately** /kəm'pæʃ.ᵊn.ət.li/ *adv*

com,passionate 'leave *noun* [U] UK a period of time that a company allows you not to come to work because a member of your family has died or is ill

com'passion fa,tigue *noun* [U] when people stop caring about a problem that is affecting lots of people and stop giving money to them because the problem has been continued for too long

'compass ,point *noun* [C] any of the 32 marks on the compass that show direction

compatible /kəm'pæt.ɪ.bl̩/ ⓤ /-'pæt̬-/ *adj* able to exist, live together, or work successfully with something or someone else: *It was when we started living together that we found we just weren't compatible.* ○ *This software may not be compatible* **with** *older operating systems.* ○ *Such policies are not compatible* **with** *democratic government.* ○ *Are their two blood groups compatible* (= can blood from one person be given to the other person)? **compatibility** /kəm,pæt.ə'bɪl.ɪ.ti/ ⓤ /-,pæt̬.ə'bɪl.ə.t̬i/ *noun* [U] **compatibly** /kəm'pæt.ɪ.bli/ ⓤ /-'pæt̬-/ *adv*

compatriot /kəm'pæt.ri.ət/ ⓤ /-'peɪ.tri-/ *noun* [C] **1** FORMAL a person who comes from the same country **2** US a friend or someone you work with

compel /kəm'pel/ *verb* [T] -ll- **1** to force someone to do something: [+ to infinitive] *As a school boy he was compelled to wear shorts even in winter.* ○ FORMAL *The new circumstances compelled a change in policy.* ⊃See also **compulsion** FORCE. **2** FORMAL to produce a strong feeling or reaction, sometimes unwillingly: *Over the years her work has compelled universal admiration and trust.*

compelled /kəm'peld/ *adj* [after v] [+ to infinitive] *He felt compelled to* (= He felt he had to) *report the incident.*

compelling /kəm'pel.ɪŋ/ *adj* **1** If a reason, argument, etc. is compelling, it makes you believe it or accept it because it is so strong: *compelling evidence* ○ *It's a fairly compelling argument for going.* **2** very exciting and interesting and making you want to watch or listen: *I found the whole film very compelling.* ○ *a compelling story*

compendium /kəm'pen.di.əm/ *noun* [C] *plural* **compendiums** or **compendia** a short but complete account of a particular subject, especially in the form of a book: *the Gardener's Compendium*

compensate PAY MONEY /'kɒm.pən.seɪt/ ⓤ /'kɑːm-/ *verb* [T] to pay someone money in exchange for something that has been lost or damaged or for some inconvenience: *Victims of the crash will be compensated for their injuries.*

compensation /,kɒm.pen'seɪ.ʃᵊn/ ⓤ /,kɑːm-/ *noun* [U] money that is paid to someone in exchange for something that has been lost or damaged or for some inconvenience: *She received £40 000 in compensation for a lost eye.* ○ *You should claim/seek compensation.* ○ *a compensation claim* **compensatory** /,kɒm.pən'seɪt.ᵊri/ ⓤ /kəm'pen.sə,tɔːri/ *adj*: MAINLY US *He was awarded $3 million in compensatory damages.*

compensate EXCHANGE /'kɒm.pən.seɪt/ ⓤ /'kɑːm-/ *verb* [I] to provide something good or useful in place of or to make someone feel better about something that has failed or been lost or missed: *Nothing will ever compensate for his lost childhood.* ○ *His enthusiasm more than compensates for his lack of experience.* ○ *I took her swimming to compensate for having missed out on the cinema.* ○ *We were late and I was driving fast to compensate.*

compensation /,kɒm.pen'seɪ.ʃᵊn/ ⓤ /,kɑːm-/ *noun* [C or U] something that makes you feel better when you have suffered something bad: *I have to spend three months of the year away from home – but there are compensations*

like the chance to meet new people. ○ *Free food was no compensation for a very boring evening.*

compere UK /'kɒm.peəʳ/ ⓤ /'kɑːm.per/ *noun* [C] (US **emcee**) a person whose job is to introduce acts in a television, radio or stage show: *He started his career as a TV compere.*

compere UK /'kɒm.peəʳ/ ⓤ /'kɑːm.per/ *verb* [I or T] (US **emcee**) to act as a compere: *She comperes that awful game show on Saturday night.*

compete /kəm'piːt/ *verb* [I] **1** to try to be more successful than someone or something else: *It's difficult for a small supermarket to compete* **against/with** *the big supermarkets.* ○ *Both girls compete* **for** *their father's attention.* ○ FIGURATIVE *Turn the music down – I'm not competing* **against/with** *that noise* (= I can't/won't try to speak louder than that music)! **2** to take part in a race or competition: *Are you competing* **in** *the 100 metres?* ○ *The two athletes are competing* **for** *the gold medal.*

competition /,kɒm.pə'tɪʃ.ᵊn/ ⓤ /,kɑːm-/ *noun* **1** [U] when someone is trying to win something or be more successful than someone else: *Competition for jobs is intense.* ○ *There's a lot of competition* **between** *computer companies.* ○ *The two companies are* **in** *competition* **with** *each other.* ○ [+ to infinitive] *There's fierce competition* **to** *join the Special Branch.* ○ *Foreign competition* (= similar products from other countries) *had reduced their sales.* ○ *Why are you jealous of her? She's* **no** *competition!* **2** [C] an organized event in which people try to win a prize by being the best, fastest, etc: *a swimming/chess competition* ○ *She's* **entered** *a crossword competition.* ○ HUMOROUS *You don't need to eat so quickly! It's not a competition.*

the compe'tition *noun* [S] the person or people you are trying to be better than: *The competition on the track looked fierce and her heart sank.*

competitor /kəm'pet.ɪ.təʳ/ ⓤ /-'pet̬.ɪ.t̬ɚ/ *noun* [C] a person, team or company that is competing against others: *Their prices are better than any of their competitors.* ○ *How many competitors took part in the race?*

competitive /kəm'pet.ɪ.tɪv/ ⓤ /-'pet̬.ə.t̬ɪv/ *adj* **1** involving competition: *competitive sports* ○ *a highly competitive industry* ○ *Acting is very competitive – you've got to really push yourself if you want to succeed.* **2** wanting very much to win or be more successful than other people: *You're very competitive – it's meant to be a friendly match!* ○ *I could never play team sports – I lack the competitive* **spirit** (= strong desire to beat others). **3** Competitive prices, services, etc. are as good as or better than other prices, services, etc. **competitively** /kəm'pet.ɪ.tɪv.li/ ⓤ /-'pet̬.ə.t̬ɪv-/ *adv*: *competitively priced goods* **competitiveness** /kəm'pet.ɪ.tɪv.nəs/ ⓤ /-'pet̬.ə.t̬ɪv-/ *noun* [U]

competence /'kɒm.pɪ.tᵊnts/ ⓤ /'kɑːm.pə.t̬ᵊnts/ *noun* [U] (ALSO **competency**) the ability to do something well: *Her competence as a teacher is unquestionable.* ○ *He reached a reasonable level of competence* **in** *his English.* ✳ NOTE: the opposite is **incompetence**.

competent /'kɒm.pɪ.tᵊnt/ ⓤ /'kɑːm.pə.t̬ᵊnt/ *adj* able to do something well: *a competent secretary/horse-rider/cook* ○ *I wouldn't say he was brilliant but he is competent* **at** *his job.* ✳ NOTE: The opposite is **incompetent**. **competently** /'kɒm.pɪ.tᵊnt.li/ ⓤ /'kɑːm.pə.t̬ᵊnt-/ *adv*: *I thought she played the role very competently.*

compile GATHER TOGETHER /kəm'paɪl/ *verb* [T] to collect information from a variety of places and arrange it in a book, report or list: *We're compiling some facts and figures for a documentary on the subject.*

compilation /,kɒm.pɪ'leɪ.ʃᵊn/ ⓤ /,kɑːm-/ *noun* **1** [U] the act of compiling something: *A team of four were involved in the compilation of the book.* **2** [C] a book, CD, etc. that has been made from several separate parts: *a compilation of their greatest hits* **compiler** /kəm'paɪ.ləʳ/ ⓤ /-lɚ/ *noun* [C] *a dictionary compiler*

compile CHANGE INSTRUCTIONS /kəm'paɪl/ *verb* [T] SPECIALIZED to change a computer program into a machine language

compiler /kəm'paɪ.ləʳ/ ⓤ /-lɚ/ *noun* [C] SPECIALIZED *She ran her code through the compiler* (= program that changes instructions into machine language).

complacency /kəmˈpleɪ.sᵊnt.si/ *noun* [U] (*ALSO* **complacence**) *DISAPPROVING* a feeling of calm satisfaction with your own abilities or situation that prevents you from trying harder: *What annoys me about these girls is their complacency – they seem to have no desire to expand their horizons.* ○ *There's no* ***room for*** *complacency if we want to stay in this competition!*

complacent /kəmˈplei.sᵊnt/ *adj DISAPPROVING* feeling so satisfied with your own abilities or situation that you feel you do not need to try any harder: *a complacent smile/attitude* ○ *We can't afford to become complacent about any of our products.* **complacently** /kəmˈpleɪ.sᵊnt.li/ *adv*

complain /kəmˈpleɪn/ *verb* [I] **1** to say that something is wrong or not satisfactory: *Lots of people have complained* ***about*** *the noise.* ○ *You're always complaining!* ○ [+ **that**] *He complained* ***that*** *his boss was useless and he had too much work.* **2** to tell someone formally that something is wrong: *If the service was so bad why didn't you complain* ***to*** *the manager?* **complainingly** /kəmˈpleɪ.nɪŋ.li/ *adv*: *"You always walk too fast for me," she said complainingly.*

complainant /kəmˈpleɪ.nənt/ *noun* [C] *LEGAL* a person who makes a formal complaint in a court of law

complaint /kəmˈpleɪnt/ *noun* **1** [C or U] when someone says that something is wrong or not satisfactory: *We've received a complaint from one of our listeners* ***about*** *offensive language.* ○ *I've* ***made a*** *complaint* (= formally complained) ***to*** *the police about the noise.* ○ [+ **that**] *We've had complaints* ***that*** *you've been playing your radio too loud.* ○ *Do you have any* ***grounds for*** *complaint* (= reason to formally complain)? **2** [C] an illness: *a heart/stomach complaint*

COMMON LEARNER ERROR

complain about something

Many learners wrongly use prepositions like 'for' or 'on' after the verb **complain**. The correct preposition is 'about'.

I am writing to complain about the trip I took last month.
~~*I am writing to complain for the trip I took last month.*~~

▲ **complain of** ***sth*** *phrasal verb* to tell other people that something is making you feel ill: *She's been complaining of a bad back recently.*

complaisance /kəmˈpleɪ.zᵊnts/ [US] /-sᵊnts/ *noun* [U] *FORMAL* a willingness to please others by being polite and fitting in with plans **complaisant** /kəmˈpleɪ.zᵊnt/ [US] /-sᵊnt/ *adj*

complement /ˈkɒm.plɪ.ment/ [US] /ˈkɑːm-/ *verb* [T] to make something else seem better or more attractive when combining with it: *Strawberries and cream complement* ***each other*** *perfectly.* ○ *The music complements her voice perfectly.* * NOTE: Do not confuse with **compliment**.

complementary /ˌkɒm.plɪˈmen.tᵊr.i/ [US] /ˈkɑːm.plɪˈmen.t̬ɚ-/ *adj* useful or attractive together: *complementary colours/flavours/skills* ○ *My family and my job both play an important part in my life, fulfilling separate but complementary needs.*

compleˌmentary ˈangle *noun* [C usually pl] one of two angles which together add up to 90°

compleˌmentary ˈmedicine *noun* [U] a wide range of treatments for medical conditions which people use instead of or in addition to ordinary medicine: *Acupuncture, reflexology and homeopathy are all forms of complementary medicine.*

complete [PERFECT] /kəmˈpliːt/ *verb* [T] **1** to make whole or perfect: *Complete the sentence with one of the adjectives provided.* ○ *He only needs two more cards to complete the set.* ○ *All she needed to complete her happiness was a baby.* **2** to write all the details asked for on a form or other document: *Have you completed your application form yet?*

complete /kəmˈpliːt/ *adj* with all the parts: *the complete works of Oscar Wilde* ○ *The report comes complete* ***with*** (= including) *diagrams and colour photographs.* ○ *Sun, sand and romance – her holiday was complete.*

completeness /kəmˈpliːt.nəs/ *noun* [U] *For the sake of completeness* (= So that nothing is omitted), *I should also mention two other minor developments.*

complete [FINISH] /kəmˈpliːt/ *verb* [T] to finish doing something: *He's just completed filming his 17th feature film.* ○ *The palace took over twenty years to complete.* ○ *She will complete her studies in France.*

completion /kəmˈpliː.ʃᵊn/ *noun* [U] when something that you are doing or making is finished: *You'll be paid* ***on*** *completion* ***of*** *the project.* ○ *The road repair work is* ***nearing*** *completion* (= almost finished).

complete [VERY GREAT] /kəmˈpliːt/ *adj* [before n] very great or to the largest degree possible: *The man's a complete fool!* ○ *I need a break, a complete change of scene.* ○ *I made a complete* ***and utter*** *mess of it!*

completely /kəmˈpliːt.li/ *adv* in every way or as much as possible: *I agree with you completely.* ○ *She's completely mad.* ○ *He'd completely changed – I didn't recognize him.*

complex [HAVING MANY PARTS] /ˈkɒm.pleks/ /kəmˈpleks/ [US] /ˈkɑːm-/ *adj* **1** involving a lot of different but related parts: *a complex molecule/carbohydrate* ○ *a complex network of roads* ○ *a complex procedure* ○ *The company has a complex organizational structure.* **2** difficult to understand or find an answer to because of having many different parts: *It's a very complex issue to which there is no straightforward answer.* ○ *The film's plot was so complex that I couldn't follow it.* **complexity** /kəmˈplek.sɪ.ti/ [US] /-sə.t̬i/ *noun* [C or U] *a problem of great complexity* ○ *There are a lot of complexities surrounding this issue.*

complex [BUILDING] /ˈkɒm.pleks/ [US] /ˈkɑːm-/ *noun* [C] a large building with various connected rooms or a related group of buildings: *a shopping/sports and leisure complex* ○ *US They live in a large apartment complex.*

complex [BAD FEELING] /ˈkɒm.pleks/ [US] /ˈkɑːm-/ *noun* [C] a particular anxiety or unconscious fear which a person has, especially as a result of an unpleasant experience that they have had in the past or because they have a low opinion of their own worth, and which influences their behaviour: *an inferiority complex* ○ *I think he's* ***got*** *a complex* ***about*** *being bald.* ○ *Don't go on about her weight – you'll* ***give*** *her a complex!*

complexion [FACE] /kəmˈplek.ʃᵊn/ *noun* [C] the natural appearance of the skin on a person's face, especially its colour or quality: *a dark/fair complexion* ○ *a healthy/clear/spotty complexion*

complexion [CHARACTER] /kəmˈplek.ʃᵊn/ *noun* [C] the general character of something: *These are radical changes which will alter the complexion* ***of*** *the British contemporary dance scene.* ○ *What Pablo has just said* ***puts an*** *entirely/completely* ***new*** *complexion* ***on*** (= changes) *things.*

ˌcomplex ˈsentence *noun* [C] *SPECIALIZED* in grammar, a sentence which contains a main part and one or more other parts

ˌcomplex ˈword *noun* [C] *SPECIALIZED* a word consisting of a main part and one or more other parts

compliance /kəmˈplaɪ.ənts/ *noun* [U] ➲See **comply**.

compliant /kəmˈplaɪ.ənt/ *adj* ➲See **comply**.

complicate /ˈkɒm.plɪ.keɪt/ [US] /ˈkɑːm-/ *verb* [T] **1** to make something more difficult to deal with, do or understand: *It will only complicate the situation if we invite his old girlfriend as well.* ○ *The rescue operation has been complicated by bad weather.* ○ *These new rules have complicated the tax system even further.* **2** If one illness complicates another illness, it makes the other illness worse: *The breathing problem has now been complicated by a chest infection.*

complicated /ˈkɒm.plɪ.keɪ.tɪd/ [US] /ˈkɑːm.plɪ.keɪ.t̬ɪd/ *adj* involving a lot of different parts, in a way that is difficult to understand: *complicated instructions* ○ *I had to fill in this really complicated form.* ○ *The rules are rather complicated to follow.* ○ *The relationship is a bit complicated. He's my mother's cousin's daughter's child.*

complication /ˌkɒm.plɪˈkeɪ.ʃᵊn/ [US] /ˌkɑːm-/ *noun* **1** [C or U] something which makes a situation more difficult, or when it does this: *Dave couldn't find his passport at the airport and then there were* ***further*** *complications when*

Fiona lost her baggage. ○ *If any complications **arise**, let me know and I'll help.* **2** [C] an additional medical problem which makes it more difficult to treat an existing illness: *If there are no complications, the doctor says that she'll be able to come home within two weeks.*

complicity /kəm'plɪs.ɪ.ti/ ⓤ /-ə.t̬i/ *noun* [U] *FORMAL* involvement in a crime or some activity that is wrong: *She is suspected of complicity **in** the fraud.*

compliment /'kɒm.plɪ.mənt/ ⓤ /'kɑːm-/ *noun* **1** [C] a remark that expresses approval, admiration or respect: *She complained that her husband never **paid** her any compliments any more.* ○ *I **take it as** a compliment* (= I am pleased) *when people say I look like my mother.* ○ *Are you **fishing for*** (= trying to get) *compliments?* ✳ NOTE: Do not confuse with **complement**. **2** [S] an action which expresses approval or respect: *You should **take it as** a compliment when I fall asleep in your company – it means I'm relaxed.* ○ *Thank you so much for your help – I hope one day I'll be able to **return/repay the** compliment* (= do something good for you).

compliments /'kɒm.plɪ.mənts/ ⓤ /'kɑːm-/ *plural noun FORMAL* **1 My compliments...** an expression of your appreciation or respect: *That was an excellent meal! My compliments **to** the chef.* **2 with your compliments** If you give something to someone with your compliments, you give it to them free: *We enclose a copy of our latest brochure, with our compliments.*

compliment /'kɒm.plɪ.mənt/ ⓤ /'kɑːm-/ *verb* [T] to praise or express admiration for someone: *I was just complimenting Robert **on** his wonderful food.* ○ *I must compliment you **on** your handling of a very difficult situation.*

complimentary /ˌkɒm.plɪ'men.t̬ər.i/ ⓤ /ˌkɑːm.plɪ'men.-t̬ɚ-/ *adj* **1** praising or expressing admiration for someone: *The reviews of his latest film have been highly complimentary.* ○ *She wasn't very complimentary **about** your performance, was she?* ○ *Our guests said some very complimentary things about the meal I'd cooked.* ✳ NOTE: The opposite is **uncomplimentary**. **2** If tickets, books, etc. are complimentary, they are given free, especially by a business.

'compliment(s) ˌslip *noun* [C] a piece of paper printed with the name and address of a company, which is sent with a parcel in place of a letter

comply /kəm'plaɪ/ *verb* [I] *FORMAL* to act according to an order, set of rules or request: *He's been ordered to have the dog destroyed because it's dangerous, but he refuses to comply.* ○ *There are serious penalties for failure to comply **with** the regulations.*

compliance /kəm'plaɪ.ənts/ *noun* [U] **1** *FORMAL* when people obey an order, rule or request: *It is the job of the inspectors to enforce compliance **with** the regulations.* ○ *The company said that it had always acted in compliance **with** environmental laws.* **2** *MAINLY DISAPPROVING* the tendency to be too willing to do what other people want you to do: *It's his compliance that amazes me.*

compliant /kəm'plaɪ.ənt/ *adj FORMAL* willing to do what other people want you to do: *a compliant child*

component /kəm'pəʊ.nənt/ ⓤ /-'poʊ-/ *noun* [C] a part which combines with other parts to form something bigger: *television/aircraft/computer components* ○ *The factory supplies electrical components for cars.* ○ *The course has four main components: business law, finance, computing and management skills.* ○ *Fresh fruit and vegetables are an **essential** component **of** a healthy diet.* ○ *The control of inflation is a **key** component **of** the government's economic policy.*

com'port yourself BEHAVE *verb* [R] *FORMAL* to behave: *She comported herself with great dignity at her husband's funeral.* **comportment** /kəm'pɔːt.mənt/ ⓤ /-'pɔːrt-/ *noun* [U] *This scandal raises new questions about the president's private comportment and true character.*

comport BE SIMILAR /kəm'pɔːt/ ⓤ /-'pɔːrt/ *verb* [I] *US FORMAL* If an idea or statement, etc. comports, it matches or is similar to something else: *The findings of this research do not comport **with** accepted theory.*

compose PRODUCE ART /kəm'pəʊz/ ⓤ /-'poʊz/ *verb* [I or T] to produce music, poetry or formal writing: *Prokofiev started composing at the age of five.* ○ *The music was* specially composed **for** the film. ○ *a piece of music composed **for** the flute* ○ *He composed this poem **for** his wife.* ○ *FORMAL My lawyer is going to compose a letter of complaint.*

composer /kəm'pəʊ.zər/ ⓤ /-'poʊ.zɚ/ *noun* [C] a person who writes music, especially classical music

composition /ˌkɒm.pə'zɪʃ.ᵊn/ ⓤ /ˌkɑːm-/ *noun* **1** [C] a piece of music that someone has written: *This concerto is one of her earlier/later compositions.* **2** [U] the process or skill of writing music: *At music school I studied piano and composition.* **3** [C] the way that people or things are arranged in a painting or photograph: *a group composition* **4** [C or U] *OLD-FASHIONED* a short piece of writing about a particular subject, done by a student: *a 200-word composition*

COMMON LEARNER ERROR

compose or dial?

Compose cannot be used when you are talking about pressing the buttons on a telephone when you want to phone someone. The correct verb to use is **dial**.

If you're phoning from Geneva, you'll need to dial the code 021.

~~If you're phoning from Geneva, you'll need to compose the code 021.~~

---

compose FORMED FROM /kəm'pəʊzd/ ⓤ /-'poʊzd/ *verb* **1 be composed of sth** to be formed from various things: *Air is composed mainly of nitrogen and oxygen.* ○ *The committee is composed of MPs, doctors, academics and members of the public.* ○ *The audience was composed largely of young people.* **2** [T] to be the parts that something is made of: *At that time, women composed only 1.6% of the US forces.*

composition /ˌkɒm.pə'zɪʃ.ᵊn/ ⓤ /ˌkɑːm-/ *noun* [U] the parts, substances, etc. that something is made of: *the composition of the atmosphere*

compose CALM /kəm'pəʊz/ ⓤ /-'poʊz/ *verb* **1 compose yourself** to make yourself calm again after being angry or upset: *She finally stopped crying and composed herself.* **2 compose your features/thoughts** to try to make yourself look or feel calm after being angry or upset: *I tried to compose my features into a smile.* ○ *He took a minute or two to compose his thoughts before he replied.*

composed /kəm'pəʊzd/ ⓤ /-'poʊzd/ *adj* calm and in control of your emotions: *She looked remarkably composed throughout the funeral.* **composedly** /kəm'pəʊ.zɪd.li/ ⓤ /-'poʊ-/ *adv*

composure /kəm'pəʊ.ʒər/ ⓤ /-'poʊ.ʒɚ/ *noun* [U] calmness and control: *I didn't want to **lose** my composure in front of her.*

compose ARRANGE TEXT /kəm'pəʊz/ ⓤ /-'poʊz/ *verb* [T] *SPECIALIZED* to arrange words, sentences, pages, etc. in preparation for printing

composite /'kɒm.pə.zɪt/ ⓤ /ˌkɑːm-/ *noun* [C] something which is made of various different parts: *The main character in her latest novel is a composite **of** several public figures of that era.* ○ *Scientists have put together a composite picture of what the Earth's crust is like.*

compositor /kəm'pɒz.ɪ.tər/ ⓤ /-'pɑː.zɪ.t̬ɚ/ *noun* [C] a person whose job is to arrange the letters, words, sentences, etc. of a book or a magazine before it is printed

compos mentis /ˌkɒm.pɒs'men.tɪs/ ⓤ /ˌkɑːm.pəs-'men.t̬əs/ *adj* [after v] *HUMOROUS* able to think clearly and be in control of and responsible for your actions; mentally healthy: *She was quite old at the time but still compos mentis.*

compost /'kɒm.pɒst/ ⓤ /'kɑːm.pɑːst/ *noun* [U] decaying plant material which is added to earth to improve its quality **compost** /'kɒm.pɒst/ ⓤ /'kɑːm.pɑːst/ /-'-/ *verb* [T]

compôte /'kɒm.pɒt/ ⓤ /'kɑːm.poʊt/ *noun* [C or U] a sweet dish made of cooked fruit

compound COMBINATION /'kɒm.paʊnd/ ⓤ /'kɑːm-/ *noun* **1** [C] a chemical that combines two or more elements: *Salt is a compound **of** sodium and chlorine.* ○ *Many fertilizers contain nitrogen compounds.* **2** [C] *FORMAL* something consisting of two or more different parts: *Then there was his manner, a curious compound of humour and severity.* **3** [C] in grammar, a word which combines two or sometimes more different words. Often, the meaning of the compound cannot be discovered by knowing the meaning of the different words that form it. Compounds can be written either as one word or as separate words: *'Bodyguard' and 'floppy disk' are two examples of compounds.*

compound /ˈkɒm.paʊnd/ [US] /ˈkɑːm-/ *adj* **1** consisting of two or more parts: *Many insects have compound* ***eyes.*** **2** used to refer to a system of paying interest in which interest is paid both on the original amount of money invested or borrowed and on any interest which that original amount has collected over a period of time: *compound interest ○ The investment fund has achieved annual compound returns of 18.2%.*

compound /kəmˈpaʊnd/ [US] /ˈkɑːm.paʊnd/ *verb* [T] to mix two things together: *Most tyres are made of rubber compounded* ***with*** *other chemicals and materials.*

compound [WORSEN] /kəmˈpaʊnd/ [US] /ˈkɑːm.paʊnd/ *verb* [T often passive] to make a problem or difficult situation worse: *Her terror was compounded by the feeling that she was being watched. ○ His financial problems were compounded when he unexpectedly lost his job. ○ Severe drought has compounded food shortages in the region.*

compound [AREA] /ˈkɒm.paʊnd/ [US] /ˈkɑːm-/ *noun* [C] an enclosed area which contains a group of buildings: *The gates opened and the troops marched into their compound. ○ The embassy compound has been closed to the public because of a bomb threat.*

ˌcompound ˈfracture *noun* [C] when a bone breaks or cracks and cuts through the surrounding flesh ➲Compare **simple fracture**.

ˌcompound ˈleaf *noun* [C] a type of leaf which is formed from a number of smaller leaves all joined to one stem

comprehend /ˌkɒm.prɪˈhend/ [US] /ˌkɑːm-/ *verb* [I or T; not continuous] SLIGHTLY FORMAL to understand something completely: *I fail to comprehend their attitude. ○ He doesn't seem to comprehend the scale of the problem ○* [+ question word] *I'll never comprehend* ***why*** *she did what she did. ○* [+ that] *I don't think he* ***fully*** *comprehends* ***that*** *she won't be here to help him.*

comprehensible /ˌkɒm.prɪˈhent.sɪ.bl̩/ [US] /ˌkɑːm-/ *adj* able to be understood: *It's written in clear, comprehensible English. ○ Her writing is barely comprehensible* ***to*** *me.* * NOTE: The opposite is **incomprehensible**.

comprehensibly /ˌkɒm.prɪˈhent.sɪ.bli/ [US] /ˌkɑːm-/ *adv*

comprehensibility /ˌkɒm.prɪ.hent.sɪˈbɪl.ɪ.ti/ [US] /ˌkɑːm.prə.hent.səˈbɪl.ə.t̬i/ *noun* [U]

comprehension /ˌkɒm.prɪˈhen.tʃən/ [US] /ˌkɑːm-/ *noun* **1** [U] the ability to understand completely and be aware of a situation, facts, etc: *He has no comprehension* ***of*** *the size of the problem. ○ How she manages to fit so much into a working day is* ***beyond*** *my comprehension* (= I cannot understand it). **2** [C or U] UK a test to find out how well students understand written or spoken language: *a* ***listening/reading*** *comprehension*

comprehensive /ˌkɒm.prɪˈhent.sɪv/ [US] /ˌkɑːm-/ *adj* complete and including everything that is necessary: *We offer you a comprehensive training in all aspects of the business. ○ Is this list comprehensive or are there some names missing? ○ He has written a* ***fully*** *comprehensive guide to Rome.*

comprehensively /ˌkɒm.prɪˈhent.sɪv.li/ [US] /ˌkɑːm-/ *adv* completely: *a comprehensively illustrated book ○ The plan was comprehensively rejected.*

compreˌhensive inˈsurance *noun* [U] insurance which financially protects any other vehicles and people that are involved in a car accident with you, in addition to yourself

compreˈhensive (ˌschool) *noun* [C] UK a school in Britain for children above the age of eleven in which children of all abilities are taught: *the local comprehensive ○ a comprehensive (school) education*

compress [REDUCE SIZE] /kəmˈpres/ *verb* [T] **1** to press something into a smaller space: *Firmly compress the soil in the pot so that the plant is secure. ○ compressed air* **2** to make information, a piece of writing, etc. shorter: *The course compresses two year's training* ***into*** *six intensive months. ○ I managed to compress ten pages of notes* ***into*** *four paragraphs.* **3** to make a computer file use less space when it is stored in the MEMORY of a computer or on a disk, by using a special program: *to compress data/files* **compressible** /kəmˈpres.ɪ.bl̩/ *adj*: *compressible gas*

compression /kəmˈpreʃ.ən/ *noun* [U] the action of compressing or being compressed

compress [CLOTH] /ˈkɒm.pres/ [US] /ˈkɑːm-/ *noun* [C] a thick soft piece of cloth which is pressed to a part of a person's body to stop bleeding or to reduce pain or swelling: *a cold/hot compress*

compressor /kəmˈpres.əʳ/ [US] /-ɚ/ *noun* [C] a (part of a) machine which presses gas or air into less space

comprise /kəmˈpraɪz/ *verb* [T; L only + n; not continuous] FORMAL to have as parts or members, or to be those parts or members: *The course comprises a class book, a practice book and an audio tape. ○ The class is comprised mainly* ***of*** *Italian and French students. ○ Italian students comprise 60%* ***of*** *the class.*

compromise [AGREEMENT] /ˈkɒm.prə.maɪz/ [US] /ˈkɑːm-/ *noun* [C or U] an agreement in an argument in which the people involved reduce their demands or change their opinion in order to agree: *It is hoped that a compromise will be* ***reached*** *in today's talks. ○ In a compromise* ***between*** *management and unions, a 4% pay rise was agreed in return for an increase in productivity. ○ The government has said that there will be no compromise* ***with*** *terrorists.*

compromise /ˈkɒm.prə.maɪz/ [US] /ˈkɑːm-/ *verb* [I] to accept that you will reduce your demands or change your opinion in order to reach an agreement with someone: *Party unity is threatened when members will not compromise. ○ Well, you want $400 and I say $300, so let's compromise* ***at/on*** *$350.*

compromise [LOWER STANDARDS] /ˈkɒm.prə.maɪz/ [US] /ˈkɑːm-/ *verb* [T] DISAPPROVING to allow your principles to be weakened or your standards or morals to be lowered: *Don't compromise your* ***beliefs/principles*** *for the sake of being accepted. ○ If we back down on this issue, our* ***reputation*** *will be compromised. ○* [R] *His political career ended when he compromised himself by accepting bribes.*

compromising /ˈkɒm.prə.maɪ.zɪŋ/ [US] /ˈkɑːm-/ *adj* causing damage to the reputation of someone, especially making known that they have had a sexual relationship with someone who is considered unsuitable: *Photographs were published of her in a compromising* ***position/situation*** *with her bodyguard.*

comptroller /kənˈtrəʊ.ləʳ/ [US] /-ˈtroʊ.lɚ/ *noun* [C] MAINLY US FORMAL a CONTROLLER, especially in titles of public finance officials and organizations: *Office of the Comptroller and Auditor General*

compulsion [DESIRE] /kəmˈpʌl.ʃən/ *noun* [C] a very strong or uncontrollable desire (to do something repeatedly): *For many people, dieting is a compulsion. ○* [+ to infinitive] *I seem to* ***have*** *a* ***constant*** *compulsion* ***to*** *eat.*

compulsive /kəmˈpʌl.sɪv/ *adj* **1** doing something a lot and unable to stop doing it: *a compulsive liar/thief/eater ○ compulsive gambling ○ a compulsive eating disorder* **2** describes a film, play, sports event, book, etc. that is so interesting or exciting that you do not want to stop watching or reading it: *I always find programmes about hospitals compulsive* ***viewing****. ○ Her latest book is compulsive* ***reading****/a compulsive* ***read****.*

compulsively /kəmˈpʌl.sɪv.li/ *adv* too much and in a way that shows you are unable to stop: *She exercises/cleans/works compulsively.* **compulsiveness** /kəmˈpʌl.sɪv.nəs/ *noun* [U]

compulsion [FORCE] /kəmˈpʌl.ʃən/ *noun* [S or U] a force that makes you do something: *He seems to be driven by some kind of inner compulsion. ○* [+ to infinitive] *We were* ***under no*** *compulsion* ***to*** *attend. ○ Don't feel* ***under any*** *compulsion* ***to*** *take me with you.* ➲See also **compel**.

compulsory /kəmˈpʌl.sər.i/ [US] /-sɚ-/ *adj* If something is compulsory, you must do it because of a rule or law: *Swimming was compulsory at my school. ○ Wearing seat belts in cars is compulsory by law.* **compulsorily** /kəmˈpʌl.sər.ɪ.li/ [US] /-sɚ-/ *adv*: *Patients can now be compulsorily detained in hospital only under tightly drawn criteria.*

compunction /kəmˈpʌŋk.ʃən/ *noun* [U] *FORMAL* a slight feeling of guilt for something you have done or might do: *I wouldn't have any compunction* ***about*** *telling him to leave.*

compute /kəmˈpjuːt/ *verb* [T] *FORMAL* to calculate an answer or amount by using a machine: *Compute the ratio of the object's height to its weight.* **computation** /ˌkɒm.pjʊˈteɪ.ʃən/ [US] /ˌkɑːm.pjə-/ *noun* [C or U]

computer /kəmˈpjuː.təʳ/ [US] /-t̬ɚ/ *noun* [C or U] an electronic machine which is used for storing, organizing and finding words, numbers and pictures, for doing calculations and for controlling other machines: *a personal/home computer* ○ *All our customer orders are handled* ***by*** *computer.* ○ *We've put all our records* ***on*** *computer.* ○ *Is she computer-****literate*** (= does she know how to use a computer)? ○ *computer software/hardware* ○ *computer graphics* ○ *a computer program* ➲See picture **In the Office** on page Centre 15

computerize, *UK USUALLY* **-ise** /kəmˈpjuː.tər.aɪz/ [US] /-t̬ə.raɪz/ *verb* [T] to use a computer to do something that was done by people or other machines before: *They've just computerized the whole system.* **computerization**, *UK USUALLY* **-isation** /kəmˌpjuː.tər.aɪˈzeɪ.ʃən/ [US] /-t̬ɚ-/ *noun* [U]

computing /kəmˈpjuː.tɪŋ/ [US] /-t̬ɪŋ/ *noun* [U] the study of or use of computers: *a degree in computing*

comˈputer ˌdating *noun* [U] a way of helping people find suitable romantic partners by using a computer to match them with people of similar interests

comˈputer ˌgame *noun* [C] a game which is played on a computer, in which the pictures that appear on the screen are controlled by pressing keys or moving a JOYSTICK

comˈputer ˌscience *noun* [U] the study of computers and how they can be used

comrade [FRIEND] /ˈkɒm.reɪd/ [US] /ˈkɑːm.ræd/ *noun* [C] (*UK* **comrade-in-arms**) *OLD-FASHIONED* a friend, especially one with whom you been involved in difficult or dangerous, usually military, activities: *Many of his comrades were killed in the battle.*

comradely /ˈkɒm.ræd.li/ [US] /ˈkɑːm-/ *adj* like a comrade: *He gave me a comradely slap on the back.*

comradeship /ˈkɒm.reɪd.ʃɪp/ [US] /ˈkɑːm-/ *noun* [U] the feeling of friendship between people who live or work together, especially in a difficult situation

comrade [POLITICAL MEMBER] /ˈkɒm.reɪd/ [US] /ˈkɑːm.ræd/ *noun* [C] a member of the same political group, especially a communist or SOCIALIST group or a trade union: *I know my opinion is shared by many of my comrades in the Labour movement.* ○ [as form of address] *Welcome to the conference, comrades.* **comradely** /ˈkɒm.ræd.li/ [US] /ˈkɑːm-/ *adj*

con [TRICK] /kɒn/ [US] /kɑːn/ *verb* [T] **-nn-** *INFORMAL* to make someone believe something false, usually so that they will give you their money or possessions: *She felt she had been conned* ***into*** *buy****ing*** *the car.* ○ *Thieves conned him* ***out of*** *his life savings.* ○ *He managed to con £20* ***out of*** *them* (= get that amount from them by deceiving them).

con /kɒn/ [US] /kɑːn/ *noun* [C] *INFORMAL* a trick to get someone's money, or make them do what you want: *It's a con – you get half the food for twice the price!* ○ *a con trick*

con [DISADVANTAGE] /kɒn/ [US] /kɑːn/ *noun* [C usually pl] *INFORMAL* a disadvantage or a reason for not doing something: *One of the cons of buying a bigger car is that it costs more to run.* ○ *You have to weigh up all the* ***pros and*** *cons of the matter before you make a decision.*

con [PRISONER] /kɒn/ [US] /kɑːn/ *noun* [C] *SLANG* a **convict**

Con. [POLITICS] *adj ABBREVIATION FOR* **Conservative** POLITICAL PARTY

con- [TOGETHER] /kən-/ [US] /kɑːn-/ *prefix* together; with: *conspiracy* ○ *consortium*

ˈcon ˌartist *noun* [C] (*ALSO* **con man**) a person who deceives other people by making them believe something false or making them give money away

concave /ˈkɒŋ.keɪv/ [US] /ˈkɑːn-/ *adj* curving in: *a concave lens* ➲Compare **convex**. **concavity** /ˌkɒnˈkæv.ɪ.ti/ [US] /ˌkɑːn.kæv.ə.t̬i/ *noun* [C or U] *SPECIALIZED*

conceal /kənˈsiːl/ *verb* [T] to prevent something from being seen or known about; to hide something: *The listening device was concealed in a pen.* ○ *I tried to conceal my surprise when she told me her age.* ○ *It was said that the police concealed vital evidence.* ○ *Is there something you're concealing* ***from*** *me?*

concealment /kənˈsiːl.mənt/ *noun* [U] when something is hidden: *the concealment* ***of*** *evidence/facts/weapons*

concede /kənˈsiːd/ *verb* **1** [T] to admit, often unwillingly, that something is true: [+ (*that*)] *The Government has conceded* ***(that)*** *the new tax policy has been a disaster.* ○ [+ speech] *"Well okay, perhaps I was a little hard on her," he conceded.* ➲See also **concession** SOMETHING ALLOWED. **2** [T] to allow someone to have something, even though you do not want to: *The president is not expected to concede these reforms.* ○ *He is not willing to concede any of his power/authority.* ○ *Britain conceded* (= allowed) *independence* ***to*** *India in 1948.* **3** [I or T] to admit that you have lost in a competition: *He kept on arguing and wouldn't concede* ***defeat.*** ○ *She conceded even before all the votes had been counted.* **4 concede a goal/point** to fail to stop an opposing team or person from winning a point or game: *The team conceded two goals (****to*** *the other side) in the first five minutes of the game.*

conceit [PRIDE] /kənˈsiːt/ *noun* [U] when you are too proud of yourself and your actions: *The conceit of that man is incredible!*

conceited /kənˈsiː.tɪd/ [US] /-t̬ɪd/ *adj DISAPPROVING* too proud of yourself and your actions and abilities: *Without wishing to sound conceited, I am the best salesperson in the company.* **conceitedly** /kənˈsiː.tɪd.li/ [US] /-t̬ɪd-/ *adv*

conceit [COMPARISON] /kənˈsiːt/ *noun* [C] *LITERARY* a clever or surprising comparison, especially in a poem

conceive [IMAGINE] /kənˈsiːv/ *verb* [I or T] to imagine something: *I think my uncle still conceives* ***of*** *me* ***as*** *a four-year-old.* ○ *He couldn't conceive* ***of*** *a time when he would have no job.* ○ [+ question word] *I can't conceive* (= It is too shocking to imagine) ***how*** *anyone could behave so cruelly.* ○ [+ that] *I find it hard to conceive* (= It is too shocking to imagine) ***that*** *people are still treated so badly.*

conceivable /kənˈsiː.və.bl̩/ *adj* possible to imagine or to believe: *Books on every conceivable subject lined one wall.* ○ *It's* ***just*** *conceivable* (= possible although difficult to imagine) ***(that)*** *the hospital made a mistake.*

conceivably /kənˈsiː.və.bli/ *adv*: *She could conceivably* (= possibly) *have already left.*

conceive [INVENT] /kənˈsiːv/ *verb* [T] to invent a plan or an idea: *He conceived the plot for this film while he was still a student.* ○ *The exhibition was conceived by the museum's director.* ➲See also **concept** and **conception**.

conceive [BECOME PREGNANT] /kənˈsiːv/ *verb* [I or T] to become pregnant, or to cause a baby to begin to form: *Do you know exactly when you conceived?* ○ *The baby was conceived in March, so will be born in December.* ➲See also **conception** BABY.

concentrate [GIVE ATTENTION] /ˈkɒnt.sən.treɪt/ [US] /ˈkɑːnt-/ *verb* [I or T] to direct your mental powers or your efforts towards a particular activity, subject or problem: *Come on, concentrate! We haven't got all day to do this.* ○ *I can't concentrate* ***on*** *my work with all that noise.* ○ *I find running concentrates* ***the mind*** (= helps me to think). ○ *I'm going to concentrate* ***on*** *my writing for a while.* ○ *The company is concentrating (its resources)* ***on*** *developing new products.*

concentrated /ˈkɒn.sən.treɪ.tɪd/ [US] /ˈkɑːn.sən.treɪ.t̬ɪd/ *adj* [before n] using a lot of effort to succeed at one particular thing: *The company is making a concentrated effort to broaden its market.*

concentration /ˌkɒnt.sənˈtreɪ.ʃən/ [US] /ˌkɑːnt-/ *noun* [U] the ability to think carefully about something you are doing and nothing else: *The noise outside made concentration difficult.* ○ *There was a look of* ***intense*** *concentration on her face.* ○ *I find that yoga improves my* ***powers of*** *concentration.* ○ *I found it hard to follow what the teacher was saying, and eventually I* ***lost*** *concentration.* ○ *The government's concentration* ***on*** *tax reduction has won them a lot of support.*

concentrate [COME TOGETHER] /ˈkɒnt.sən.treɪt/ [US] /ˈkɑːnt-/ *verb* [T usually passive or I; usually + adv or prep] to bring or come together in a large number or amount in one particular area: *Most of the country's population is con-*

C

centrated in the north. ○ In the dry season, the animals tend to concentrate in the areas where there is water.

concentration /ˌkɒnt.sᵊnˈtreɪ.ʃᵊn/ [US] /ˌkɑːnt-/ *noun* [C or U] **1** a large number or amount of something in the same place: *There is a heavy concentration* ***of*** *troops in the area.* **2** *SPECIALIZED* the exact amount of one particular substance that is found in another substance: *a concentration of one part per million* ○ *High concentrations* ***of*** *toxic elements were found in the polluted areas of the sea.*

concentrate [REMOVE WATER] /ˈkɒnt.sᵊn.treɪt/ [US] /ˈkɑːnt-/ *verb* [T] *SPECIALIZED* to make a liquid or substance stronger and reduce its size by removing water from it

concentrate /ˈkɒn.sᵊn.treɪt/ [US] /ˈkɑːn-/ *noun* [C or U] **1** a liquid from which some of the water has been removed: *fruit-juice concentrate* **2** an ORE from which rock has been removed: *a mineral concentrate*

concentrated /ˈkɒnt.sᵊn.treɪ.tɪd/ [US] /ˈkɑːnt.sᵊn.treɪ.t̬ɪd/ *adj* having had some liquid removed: *concentrated orange juice*

concenˈtration ˌcamp *noun* [C] a prison where people are kept in extremely bad conditions, especially for political reasons: *Nazi concentration camps*

concentric /kənˈsen.trɪk/ *adj* describes circles and rings that have the same centre: *a concentric pattern/arrangement*

concept /ˈkɒn.sept/ [US] /ˈkɑːn-/ *noun* [C] a principle or idea: *The very concept* ***of*** *free speech is unknown to them.* ○ *It is very difficult to define the concept* ***of*** *beauty.* ○ *I failed to grasp the film's central concept.* ○ *Kleenbrite is a whole* ***new*** *concept* ***in*** *toothpaste!*

• **not have any concept/have no concept of *sth*** to not understand about something: *I don't think you have any concept of the pain you have caused her.*

conceptual /kənˈsep.tju.əl/ *adj* based on ideas or principles: *The main weakness of the proposal is conceptual.*

conceptualize, *UK USUALLY* **-ise** /kənˈsep.tju.ə.laɪz/ *verb* [I or T] *FORMAL* to form an idea or principle in your mind: *He argued that morality could be conceptualized* (= thought about) ***as*** *a series of principles based on human reason.*

conception [IDEA] /kənˈsep.ʃᵊn/ *noun* [C or U] an idea of what something or someone is like, or a basic understanding of a situation or a principle: *People from different cultures have different conceptions* ***of*** *the world.* ○ *She has a conception* ***of*** *people as being basically good.* ○ *I thought the book's writing was dreadful, and its conception* (= the ideas on which it was based) *even worse.* ○ *He has absolutely* ***no*** *conception* ***of*** *how a successful business should run.*

conception [BABY] /kənˈsep.ʃᵊn/ *noun* [U] the process of a sperm and an egg joining and causing a baby to start to form: *at/from the moment of conception*

concern [INVOLVE] /kənˈsɜːn/ [US] /-ˈsɝːn/ *verb* [T] **1** to be important to someone or to involve someone directly: *Matters of pollution and the environment concern us all.* ○ *What I have to say to Amy doesn't concern you.* **2** *FORMAL* If a story, film or article concerns a particular subject, person, etc., it is about that person or subject: *The film concerns a woman who goes to China as a missionary.* **3** [R] to become involved with something, or worried about something: *There's no need for you to concern your****self with*** *what happened.* ○ *Don't concern your****self***. *She'll be home soon.*

• **To whom it may concern** something you write at the start of a formal letter or notice when you do not know exactly who it should be addressed to

concern /kənˈsɜːn/ [US] /-ˈsɝːn/ *noun* [C or U] something that involves or affects you or is important to you: *What were the major concerns* ***of*** *the writers from this period?* ○ *I don't want to hear about it – it's no concern* ***of*** *mine!* ○ *"What's happening?" "That's* ***none of/not any of*** *your concern."*

• **be of concern** to be important: *The results of the election are of concern* ***to*** *us all.*

concerned /kənˈsɜːnd/ [US] /-ˈsɝːnd/ *adj* [after v] involved in something or affected by it: *I'd like to thank everyone concerned for making the occasion run so smoothly.* ○ *It was quite a shock for* ***all/everyone*** *concerned.* ○ *Her job is something concerned* ***with*** *computers.* ○ *I'm not very good* ***where*** *money is concerned* (= when dealing with money).

• **be concerned with *sth/sb*** to be about a particular thing or person: *Today's lesson is concerned with punctuation.*

• **as far as *sb* is concerned** in a particular person's opinion: *As far as I'm concerned, feng shui is a load of rubbish.*

• **as far as *sth* is concerned** if we are discussing or thinking about a particular thing: *As far as unemployment's concerned, a change of government would be a good idea.*

concerning /kənˈsɜː.nɪŋ/ [US] /-ˈsɝː-/ *prep SLIGHTLY FORMAL* about: *I've had a letter from the tax authorities concerning my tax payments.*

concern [WORRY] /kənˈsɜːn/ [US] /-ˈsɝːn/ *verb* [T] to cause anxiety to someone: *The state of my father's health concerns us* ***greatly***. ○ [+ that] ***It*** *concerns me* ***that*** *he hasn't been in contact.*

concern /kənˈsɜːn/ [US] /-ˈsɝːn/ *noun* [C or U] **1** a feeling of worry or nervousness, or something that worries you: *Concern* ***for*** *the safety of the two missing teenagers is* ***growing***. ○ *There's a lot of public concern* ***about/over*** *dangerous toxins recently found in food.* ○ [+ that] *My concern is* ***that*** *you're not getting enough work done.* **2** something that is important to you, or when something is important: [+ to infinitive] *His concern* ***to*** *appear sophisticated amused everyone.* ○ *The company's* ***sole*** *concern is* ***to*** *ensure the safety of its employees.* ○ *There's* ***a matter of*** *some concern that I have to discuss with you.*

concerned /kənˈsɜːnd/ [US] /-ˈsɝːnd/ *adj* worried: *I'm a bit concerned* ***about/for*** *your health.* ○ [+ (that)] *Aren't you concerned* ***(that)*** *she might tell someone?* ○ [+ to infinitive] *He was concerned* ***to*** *hear that two of his trusted workers were leaving.* ○ *Concerned parents have complained about the dangerous playground.*

concern [BUSINESS] /kənˈsɜːn/ [US] /-ˈsɝːn/ *noun* [C] a company: *a family concern* ○ *It started slowly, but the company is now a* ***going*** *concern* (= doing business effectively).

concert /ˈkɒn.sət/ [US] /ˈkɑːn.sɚt/ *noun* [C] a performance of music by one or more musicians or singers: *a pop/classical concert* ○ *a school concert*

• **in concert 1** playing or singing with other musicians in a public performance: *She was appearing in concert at Carnegie Hall.* **2** *FORMAL* together: *If the member countries would* ***act*** *in concert, the problem might be solved more easily.*

concerted /kənˈsɜː.tɪd/ [US] /-ˈsɝː.t̬ɪd/ *adj* [usually before n] **1** planned or done together for a shared purpose: *The richer countries of the world should take concerted* ***action*** *to help the poorer countries.* ○ *The D-Day invasion was a concerted* ***exercise*** *by the armed forces of Britain, the US and Canada.* **2** describes an effort or attempt that is determined and serious: *There has been a concerted campaign against the proposals.* ○ *He's making a concerted* ***effort*** *to improve his appearance.*

concert-goer /ˈkɒn.sət‚gəʊ.əʳ/ [US] /ˈkɑːn.sɚt‚goʊ.ɚ/ *noun* [C] a person who often goes to concerts

ˌconcert ˈgrand *noun* [C] the biggest type of GRAND PIANO, usually used for concerts

ˈconcert ˌhall *noun* [C] a large building in which concerts are performed

concertina /ˌkɒn.səˈtiː.nə/ [US] /ˌkɑːn.sɚ-/ *noun* [C] a musical instrument with a folding middle part, which you play by pushing both ends inwards with the hands and pressing buttons

concertina /ˌkɒn.səˈtiː.nə/ [US] /ˌkɑːn.sɚ-/ *verb* [I or T] *UK* to fold, crush or squeeze together: *In the accident, several cars concertinaed* ***into*** *each other.* ○ *FIGURATIVE Could we concertina the three meetings* ***into*** *one morning?*

concerto /kənˈtʃɜː.təʊ/ [US] /-ˈtʃer.t̬oʊ/ *noun* [C] *plural* **concertos** or **concerti** a long piece of music for one or more main SOLO instruments and an orchestra: *a violin/piano concerto* ○ *Mozart's concerto* ***for*** *flute and harp*

concession [SOMETHING ALLOWED] /kənˈseʃ.ᵊn/ *noun* **1** [C or U] something which is allowed or given up, often in order to end a disagreement, or the act of allowing or giving this: *Both sides involved in the conflict* ***made*** *some concessions in yesterday's talks.* ○ *He stated firmly that no* *concessions will be* ***made to*** *the strikers.* ➲See also **concede**. **2** [U] when someone admits defeat: *The former president's concession came even before all the votes had been counted.* ○ *a concession speech*

concession [LOWER PRICE] /kən'seʃ.ᵊn/ *noun* [C] *UK* a reduction in the usual price of something, which is available to students or young, old or unemployed people: *You can get travel concessions if you are under 26.* **concessionary** /kən'seʃ.ᵊn.ᵊr.i/ [US] /-er-/ *adj*: *a concessionary fare/ticket*

concession [RIGHT] /kən'seʃ.ᵊn/ *noun* [C] **1** a special right to property or land **2** the right to sell a product in a particular area

concessionaire /kən,seʃ.ᵊn'eəʳ/ [US] /-'er/ *noun* [C] someone who has been given a concession to sell or do something

concessive clause /kən,ses.ɪv'klɔːz/ [US] /-'klɑːz/ *noun* [C] *SPECIALIZED* a clause, often beginning with 'though' or 'although', which expresses an idea that suggests the opposite of the main part of the sentence: *The sentence 'Although he's quiet, he's not shy' begins with a concessive clause.*

conch /kɒntʃ/ /kɒŋk/ [US] /kɑːntʃ/ /kɑːŋk/ *noun* [C] a large SPIRAL shell, or the tropical snail-like sea animal which lives in it

conchie /'kɒn.ʃi/ [US] /'kɑːn-/ *noun* [C] *OLD-FASHIONED INFORMAL FOR* **conscientious objector** (= someone who refuses to work in the armed forces for moral or religious reasons)

concierge /,kɒn.si'eəʒ/ [US] /kɑːn.si'erʒ/ *noun* [C] **1** a person who is employed to take care of an apartment building, especially in France **2** someone who is employed in a hotel to help guests arrange things, such as theatre tickets and visits to restaurants

conciliate /kən'sɪl.i.eɪt/ *verb* [I or T] to end a disagreement or someone's anger by acting in a friendly way or slightly changing your opinions, or to satisfy someone who disagrees with you by acting in this way: *An independent adviser has been brought in to conciliate* ***between*** *the two sides involved in the conflict.* ○ *These changes have been made in an attempt to conciliate critics of the plan.* **conciliation** /kən,sɪl.i'eɪ.ʃᵊn/ *noun* [U] *FORMAL* *All attempts at conciliation failed and the dispute continued.* **conciliatory** /kən'sɪl.i.ə.tri/ [US] /-tɔːr.i/ *adj*: *a conciliatory gesture/remark*

concise /kən'saɪs/ *adj* short and clear, expressing what needs to be said without unnecessary words: *Make your answers clear and concise.* **concisely** /kən'saɪ.sli/ *adv* **conciseness** /kən'saɪ.snəs/ *noun* [U] (*ALSO* **concision**)

conclave /'kɒŋ.kleɪv/ [US] /'kɑːn-/ *noun* [C] *FORMAL* a private meeting at which the discussions are kept secret

conclude /kən'kluːd/ *verb* **1** [I or T] to end a speech, meeting or piece of writing: *She concluded the speech* ***by*** *remind****ing*** *us of our responsibility.* ○ *Before I conclude, I'd like to thank you all for coming.* ○ *The concert concluded* ***with*** *a rousing chorus.* **2** [T] to judge or decide something after some consideration: [+ **that**] *The jury concluded* ***from*** *the evidence* ***that*** *the defendant was innocent.* ○ *We talked late into the night, but nothing was concluded.* **3** [T] to complete an official agreement or task, or arrange a business deal

concluding /kən'kluː.dɪŋ/ *adj* [**before n**] last in a series of things: *Don't miss tonight's concluding episode.*

conclusion /kən'kluː.ʒᵊn/ *noun* **1** [C] the final part of something: *I found the conclusion of the film rather irritating.* **2** [C] the opinion you have after considering all the information about something: *Did you* ***come to/ reach/draw*** *any conclusions at the meeting this morning?* ○ [+ **that**] *At first I thought he was a bit shy, but I've* ***come to*** *the conclusion* ***that*** *he's simply unfriendly!* **3** [U] when something is arranged or agreed formally: *the conclusion of the deal/treaty*

• **in conclusion** *FORMAL* finally: *In conclusion, I would like to thank our guest speaker.*

conclusive /kən'kluː.sɪv/ *adj* proving that something is true, or ending any uncertainty: *They had conclusive* ***evidence/proof*** *of her guilt.* ○ *a conclusive argument*
* NOTE: The opposite is **inconclusive**.

conclusively /kən'kluː.sɪv.li/ *adv* without any doubt: *It is impossible to* ***demonstrate/prove*** *conclusively that the factory is responsible for the pollution.*

concoct /kən'kɒkt/ [US] /-'kɑːkt/ *verb* [T] **1** to make something, usually food, by adding several different parts together, often in a way that is original or not planned: *He concocted the most amazing dish from all sorts of unlikely ingredients.* **2** to invent an excuse, explanation or story in order to deceive someone: *He concocted a story about working late at the office.*

concoction /kən'kɒk.ʃᵊn/ [US] /-'kɑːk-/ *noun* [C or U] the result or process of concocting something

concomitant /kən'kɒm.ɪ.tᵊnt/ [US] /-'kɑː.mə.t̬ᵊnt/ *noun* [C] *FORMAL* something that happens with something else and is connected with it: *Loss of memory is a natural concomitant* ***of*** *old age.*

concomitant /kən'kɒm.ɪ.tᵊnt/ [US] /-'kɑː.mə.t̬ᵊnt/ *adj FORMAL* happening and connected with another thing: *Any increase in students meant a concomitant increase in funding.* **concomitantly** /kən'kɒm.ɪ.tᵊnt.li/ [US] /-'kɑː.mə.t̬ᵊnt-/ *adv*

concord /'kɒŋ.kɔːd/ [US] /'kɑːŋ.kɔːrd/ *noun* [U] **1** *FORMAL* agreement and peace between countries and people: *nations living* ***in*** *concord* ➲Compare **discord** DISAGREEMENT. **2** *SPECIALIZED* when the words in a sentence match each other according to the rules of grammar, for example when the verb is plural because the subject of the sentence is plural

concordance /kən'kɔː.dᵊnts/ [US] /-'kɔːr-/ *noun* **1** [C] *SPECIALIZED* a book or list which is an alphabetical collection of the words used in a book or a writer's work, with information about where the words can be found and in which sentences: *a Shakespeare concordance* **2** [U] *FORMAL* when there is agreement or similarity between things: *Last Thursday's show produced moments of inspired concordance* ***between*** *the dance forms.*

concordat /kən'kɔː.dæt/ [US] /-'kɔr-/ *noun* [C] *SPECIALIZED* a formal agreement, especially on religious matters, between the Roman Catholic Church and a particular country

concourse /'kɒŋ.kɔːs/ [US] /'kɑːn.kɔːrs/ *noun* [C] a large space or room in a public building such as a station or airport which people gather in or pass through: *There's a ticket machine in the main concourse.*

concrete [HARD MATERIAL] /'kɒŋ.kriːt/ [US] /'kɑːn-/ *noun* [U] a very hard building material made by mixing together cement, sand, small stones and water: *reinforced concrete* ○ *a concrete floor/path* ○ *a grey concrete building*

concrete /'kɒŋ.kriːt/ [US] /'kɑːn-/ *verb* [T] to cover something in concrete: *Why did you concrete* ***over*** *that nice garden?*

concrete [CERTAIN] /'kɒŋ.kriːt/ [US] /'kɑːn-/ *adj* clear and certain, or real and existing in a form that can be seen or felt: *They think she killed her husband, but they've no concrete* ***evidence***. ○ *We've got a general idea of what we want, but nothing concrete at the moment.*

,concrete 'jungle *noun* [**C usually sing**] an ugly grey area of a city where people live in closely crowded apartment buildings and there is little space and no trees or grass

'concrete ,mixer *noun* [C] a **cement mixer**

,concrete 'noun *noun* [C] a noun which refers to a material object ➲Compare **abstract noun**.

concubine /'kɒŋ.kjʊ.baɪn/ [US] /'kɑːn-/ *noun* [C] a woman who, in some societies, lives and has sex with a man she is not married to, and has a lower social rank than his wife or wives

concur /kən'kɜːʳ/ [US] /-'kɝː/ *verb* [I] **-rr-** *FORMAL* **1** to agree with someone or have the same opinion as someone else: *The new report concurs* ***with*** *previous findings.* ○ [+ **that**] *The board concurred* ***that*** *the editor should have full control over editorial matters.* ○ [+ **speech**] *"I think you're absolutely right," concurred Chris.* **2** If two or more events concur, they happen at the same time.

concurrence /kən'kʌr.ᵊnts/ [US] /-'kɝː-/ *noun* [U] *FORMAL* when people, things or events concur

concurrent /kən'kʌr.ᵊnt/ [US] /-'kɝː-/ *adj* happening or existing at the same time: *The judge imposed concurrent sentences totalling 14 years for the attacks on the girls.*

C

concurrently /kənˈkʌr.ᵊnt.li/ [US] /-ˈkɝː-/ *adv*: *Her two dramas are being shown concurrently* (= at the same time) *by rival television stations.*

concussion /kənˈkʌʃ.ᵊn/ *noun* [U] temporary damage to the brain caused by a fall or hit on the head or by violent shaking: *He's been a bit dizzy and confused since the accident. Do you think it's mild concussion?* **concuss** /kənˈkʌs/ *verb* [T often passive] to give someone concussion **concussed** /kənˈkʌst/ *adj* suffering from concussion: *I hit my head and was concussed for several days.*

condemn /kənˈdem/ *verb* [T] to criticize something or someone strongly, usually for moral reasons: *The terrorist action has been condemned* ***as*** *an act of barbarism and cowardice.* ○ *The film was condemned* ***for*** *its sexism.* **condemnation** /ˌkɒn.dəmˈneɪ.ʃᵊn/ [US] /ˌkɑːn-/ *noun* [C or U] when you condemn something or someone: *The shooting of the policeman has received universal condemnation.* **condemnatory** /kənˈdem.nə.tri/ [US] /kənˈdem.nə.tɔːr.i/ *adj*: *a condemnatory speech/tone*

condemned /kənˈdemd/ *adj* **1** A condemned person is someone who is going to be killed, especially as a punishment for having committed a very serious crime, such as murder. **2** describes a building that has been officially judged not safe for people to live in or to use, or food that has been officially judged not safe to eat

PHRASAL VERBS WITH **condemn** ▼

▲ **condemn *sb* to *(do) sth*** [PUNISH] *phrasal verb* to say what the punishment of someone who has committed a serious crime will be: *She was condemned to* ***death*** *and executed two weeks later.* ○ [often passive] *They were condemned to spend the rest of their lives in prison.*

▲ **condemn *sb* to *sth*** [MAKE SUFFER] *phrasal verb* to make someone suffer in a particular way: *Poor education condemns many young people to low-paid jobs.*

conˌdemned ˈcell *noun* [C] a room in a prison for someone who is going to be killed as a legal punishment

condensation /ˌkɒn.denˈseɪ.ʃᵊn/ [US] /ˌkɑːn-/ *noun* [U] **1** the drops of water that appear on cold windows or other surfaces, as a result of hot air or steam becoming cool: *We get a lot of condensation on the walls in the winter.* **2** *SPECIALIZED* the act or process of changing from a gas to a liquid or solid state **condense** /kənˈdents/ *verb* [I or T] *Water vapour in the air condenses into fog.*

condense /kənˈdents/ *verb* [T] **1** to reduce something, such as a speech or piece of writing, in length: *I condensed ten pages of comments* ***into/to*** *two.* **2** to make a liquid thicker by removing some of the water **condensed** /kənˈdentst/ *adj*: *condensed soup*

conˌdensed ˈmilk *noun* [U] a thick and very sweet milk from which water has been removed

condenser /kənˈden.səʳ/ [US] /-sɚ/ *noun* [C] *SPECIALIZED* a piece of equipment that reduces gases to their liquid or solid form

condescend /ˌkɒn.dɪˈsend/ [US] /ˌkɑːn-/ *verb USUALLY HUMOROUS* **condescend to do *sth*** If you condescend to do something, you agree to do something which you do not consider to be good enough for your social position: *I wonder if Michael will condescend to visit us?*

▲ **condescend to *sb*** *phrasal verb* to treat someone as if you are better or more important than them: *He explains things without condescending to his audience.* **condescending** /ˌkɒn.dɪˈsen.dɪŋ/ [US] /ˌkɑːn-/ *adj*: *DISAPPROVING I hate the way he's so condescending to his staff!* **condescendingly** /ˌkɒn.dɪˈsen.dɪŋ.li/ [US] /ˌkɑːn-/ *adv* **condescension** /ˌkɒn.dɪˈsent.ʃᵊn/ [US] /ˌkɑːn-/ *noun* [U]

condiment /ˈkɒn.dɪ.mənt/ [US] /ˈkɑːn-/ *noun* [C] *FORMAL* a substance, such as salt, that you add to food to improve its taste

condition [STATE] /kənˈdɪʃ.ᵊn/ *noun* **1** [S or U] the particular state that something or someone is in: *Mum's still got our pram – it's very old, but it's* ***in*** *perfect condition.* ○ *They left the flat in a terrible condition – there was mess everywhere.* ○ *The hospital say her condition* (= state of health) *is improving slowly.* ○ *He's* ***in no*** *condition* (= He is too ill or too drunk) ***to*** *drive home.* ➲See also **condition** at **conditioner**. **2** [C] any of a variety of diseases: *to suffer from a heart/skin condition* ○ *a medical condition*

• **out of condition** not healthy enough for hard physical exercise, as a result of not taking part in sport or other physical activities

conditions /kənˈdɪʃ.ᵊnz/ *plural noun* the physical situation that someone or something is in and affected by: ***weather*** *conditions* ○ ***working*** *conditions* ○ *The prisoners were kept* ***in*** *the most appalling conditions.* ○ ***Under*** *what conditions do plants grow best?*

COMMON LEARNER ERROR

condition or **health?**

Condition is not usually used to describe how healthy or fit someone is. The correct words to use are **health** or **fitness**.

After a few weeks at the gym you should notice an improvement in your health and fitness.

~~*After a few weeks on the diet you should notice an improvement in your condition.*~~

condition [AGREED LIMITATION] /kənˈdɪʃ.ᵊn/ *noun* [C] an arrangement that must exist before something else can happen: *One of the conditions in the contract is that we don't build on the land.* ○ *We're not in a position to* ***make/set*** *any conditions – we'll have to accept what they offer us.* ○ ***Under*** *the conditions of the agreement, she must vacate the house on 12 July.*

• **on (the) condition that** only if: *I'll come to the party on the condition that you don't wear those ridiculous trousers!*

conditional /kənˈdɪʃ.ᵊn.ᵊl/ *adj* describes an offer or agreement that depends on something else being done: *The offer of a place on the nursing course is conditional* ***on/upon*** *my passing all three exams.* ＊ NOTE: The opposite is **unconditional**. **conditionally** /kənˈdɪʃ.ᵊn.ᵊl.i/ *adv*

condition [INFLUENCE] /kənˈdɪʃ.ᵊn/ *verb* [T] to train or influence a person or animal mentally so that they do or expect a particular thing without thinking about it: *a conditioned reflex/response* ○ [+ to infinitive] *Pavlov conditioned dogs to salivate at the sound of a bell.* ○ *Women were conditioned* ***to*** *expect lower wages than men.* **conditioning** /kənˈdɪʃ.ᵊn.ɪŋ/ *noun* [U] *Conditioning starts as soon as boys are given guns to play with and girls are given dolls.*

conditional [SENTENCE FORM] /kənˈdɪʃ.ᵊn.ᵊl/ *adj, noun* [C] *SPECIALIZED* (relating to) a sentence, often starting with 'if' or 'unless', in which one half expresses something which is dependent on the other half: *a conditional clause* ○ *'If I won a lot of money, I'd go travelling' is an example of a conditional (sentence).*

conditional [VERB FORM] /kənˈdɪʃ.ᵊn.ᵊl/ *adj, noun* [S] *SPECIALIZED* (a form of a verb) expressing the idea that one thing is dependent on another thing: *In English,* ***the*** *conditional is expressed by 'would'.*

conditioner /kənˈdɪʃ.ᵊn.əʳ/ [US] /-ɚ/ *noun* [C or U] **1** a thick often creamy liquid which you put on and wash off your hair after you have washed it, to improve the quality and appearance of your hair **2** a thick liquid which you wash clothes in to soften them: ***fabric*** *conditioner* **condition** /kənˈdɪʃ.ᵊn/ *verb* [T] to try to improve the quality or appearance of your hair, skin, etc. by putting a conditioner on it

condo /ˈkɒn.dəʊ/ [US] /ˈkɑːn.doʊ/ *noun* [C] *US INFORMAL* a **condominium**

condolence /kənˈdəʊ.lənts/ [US] /-ˈdoʊ-/ *noun* [C usually pl; U] sympathy and sadness for the family or close friends of a person who has recently died, or an expression of this, especially in written form: *a letter of condolence* ○ *Dignitaries from all over the world came to* ***offer*** *their condolences.*

condom /ˈkɒn.dɒm/ [US] /ˈkɑːn.dəm/ *noun* [C] (*UK ALSO* **sheath,** *US SLANG ALSO* **rubber**) a thin rubber covering that a man can wear on his penis during sex to stop a woman becoming pregnant or to protect him or his partner against infectious diseases

condominium [BUILDING] /ˌkɒn.dəˈmɪn.i.ᵊm/ [US] /ˌkɑːn-/ *noun* [C] **1** *US* an apartment building in which each apartment is owned separately by the people living in it, but also containing shared areas **2** (*INFORMAL* **condo**) an apartment in a condominium

condone /kənˈdəʊn/ ⓤ /-ˈdoʊn/ *verb* [T] to accept or allow behaviour that is wrong: *If the government is seen to condone **violence**, the bloodshed will never stop.*

condor /ˈkɒn.dɔːʳ/ ⓤ /ˈkɑːn.dɔːr/ *noun* [C] a type of VULTURE (= a large bird which feeds on dead animals) from South America

conducive /kənˈdjuː.sɪv/ ⓤ /-ˈduː-/ *adj* providing the right conditions for something good to happen or exist: *Such a noisy environment was not conducive **to** a good night's sleep.* ○ *This is a more conducive atmosphere **for** studying.*

conduct ORGANIZE /kənˈdʌkt/ *verb* [T] to organize and perform a particular activity: *We are conducting a survey to find out what our customers think of their local bus service.* ○ *The experiments were conducted by scientists in New York.* ○ *How you choose to conduct your private life is your own business!*

conduct /ˈkɒn.dʌkt/ ⓤ /ˈkɑːn-/ *noun* [U] FORMAL the way in which an activity is organized and performed: *He was criticized for his conduct of the inquiry.*

conduct SHOW WAY /kənˈdʌkt/ *verb* **1** [T usually + adv or prep] FORMAL to lead someone to a particular place: *May I conduct you **to** your table, sir, or would you prefer to have a drink at the bar first?* ○ *The protesters were conducted from the courtroom by two police officers.* **2** [T] If you conduct a tour of a place, you take people round it and show it to them: *A guide conducts **tours** of the cathedral every afternoon at 2.00.* ○ *a conducted **tour** of the palace*

conduct MUSIC /kənˈdʌkt/ *verb* [I or T] to direct the performance of musicians or a piece of music: *The orchestra was conducted by Mira Shapur.* ○ *Who's conducting at tonight's concert?* **conductor** /kənˈdʌk.təʳ/ ⓤ /-t̬ɚ/ *noun* [C] *The conductor raised his baton.* ○ *a guest conductor*

conˈduct yourself BEHAVIOUR /kənˈdʌkt/ *verb* [R] to behave in a particular way, especially in a public or a formal situation, or to organize the way in which you live in a particular way: *How should I conduct myself at these dinners? I know nothing about etiquette.*

conduct /ˈkɒn.dʌkt/ ⓤ /ˈkɑːn-/ *noun* [U] behaviour: *bad/ excellent/disgraceful conduct* ○ *The club has a strict **code** (= set of rules) of conduct.*

conduct ALLOW THROUGH /kənˈdʌkt/ *verb* [T] to allow electricity or heat to go through: *Copper conducts electricity, but plastic does not.* **conduction** /kənˈdʌk.ʃən/ *noun* [U] *the conduction of electricity* **conductive** /kənˈdʌk.tɪv/ ⓤ /-t̬ɪv/ *adj*: *Aluminium is a conductive metal.* **conductivity** /ˌkɒn.dʌkˈtɪv.ɪ.ti/ ⓤ /ˌkɑːn.dʌkˈtɪv.ə.t̬i/ *noun* [U] *a high level of conductivity* **conductor** /kənˈdʌk.təʳ/ ⓤ /-t̬ɚ/ *noun* [C] *Metal is a good conductor of heat.*

conductor /kənˈdʌk.təʳ/ ⓤ /-t̬ɚ/ *noun* [C] someone whose job is to sell tickets on a bus, train or other public vehicle ➨See also **conductor** at **conduct** ALLOW THROUGH, **conduct** MUSIC.

conduit /ˈkɒn.djuː.ɪt/ ⓤ /ˈkɑːn.duː-/ *noun* [C] a pipe or passage for water or electrical wires to go through

cone SHAPE /kəʊn/ ⓤ /koʊn/ *noun* [C] a shape with a flat, round or oval base and a top which narrows to a point: *a **traffic** cone* **conical** /ˈkɒn.ɪ.kəl/ ⓤ /ˈkɑː.nɪ-/ *adj* shaped like a cone: *a conical flask*

cone TREE /kəʊn/ ⓤ /koʊn/ *noun* [C] the hard oval-shaped fruit of a CONIFER

cone FOOD /kəʊn/ ⓤ /koʊn/ *noun* [C] an edible container made of very light thin biscuit, or one of these containing ICE CREAM: *an ice cream cone*

cone /kəʊn/ ⓤ /koʊn/ *verb*

▲ **cone** *sth* **off** *phrasal verb* to prevent traffic from using a road or area by putting special objects that are shaped like cones on it: *Part of the road had been coned off for repair work.*

coney /ˈkəʊ.ni/ ⓤ /ˈkoʊ-/ *noun* [C or U] ANOTHER SPELLING OF **cony**

confab /ˈkɒn.fæb/ ⓤ /ˈkɑːn-/ *noun* [C usually sing] OLD-FASHIONED HUMOROUS an informal discussion, usually about one particular subject: *They had a quick confab to decide on a possible design.*

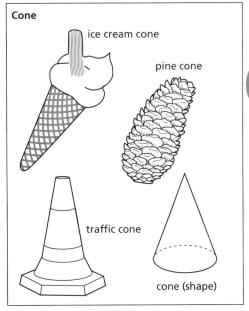

Cone

ice cream cone

pine cone

traffic cone

cone (shape)

confection /kənˈfek.ʃən/ *noun* [C] FORMAL a decorated cake or unusual sweet dish

confectioners' sugar /kənˌfek.ʃən.əzˈʃʊg.əʳ/ ⓤ /-ɚzˈʃʊg.ɚ/ *noun* [U] US FOR **icing sugar**

confectionery /kənˈfek.ʃən.ri/ ⓤ /-er.i/ *noun* [U] SWEETS (= small pieces of sweet food, made with sugar) or chocolates **confectioner** /kənˈfek.ʃən.əʳ/ ⓤ /-ɚ/ *noun* [C] a company or person that makes or sells SWEETS or chocolates

confederacy /kənˈfed.ʳr.ə.si/ ⓤ /-ɚ-/ *group noun* [C] a union of states or people who have combined together for a particular purpose, usually related to politics or trade

confederate /kənˈfed.ʳr.ət/ ⓤ /-ɚ-/ *adj* united in or part of a confederacy: *confederate states*

confederate /kənˈfed.ʳr.ət/ ⓤ /-ɚ-/ *noun* [C] FORMAL someone you work together with in a secret, sometimes illegal, activity

confederation /kənˌfed.əˈreɪ.ʃən/ *group noun* [C] an organization consisting of different groups of people working together for business or political reasons: *the Confederation of British Industry*

confer TALK /kənˈfɜːʳ/ ⓤ /-ˈfɜː-/ *verb* [I] -rr- to exchange ideas on a particular subject, often in order to reach a decision on what action to take: *I should like some time to confer **with** my lawyer.*

confer GIVE /kənˈfɜːʳ/ ⓤ /-ˈfɜː-/ *verb* [T] -rr- to give an official title, honour, or advantage to someone: *An honorary doctorate was conferred **on** him by Edinburgh University.*

conference /ˈkɒn.fʳr.ənts/ ⓤ /ˈkɑːn.fɚ-/ *noun* [C] an event, sometimes lasting a few days, at which there are a group of talks on a particular subject, or a meeting in which especially business matters are discussed formally: *a conference **on** women's rights* ○ *They frequently **hold** conferences at that hotel.* ○ *I'm speaking at/ attending a conference next week.* ○ *Should I book the conference **room** for the meeting?*

● **be in conference** FORMAL to be in a meeting: *Ms O'Neill isn't available at present. She's in conference.*

confess /kənˈfes/ *verb* [I or T] **1** to admit that you have done something wrong or something that you feel guilty or bad about: [+ that] *She confessed **to** her husband **that** she had sold her wedding ring.* ○ *He confessed **to** sleeping/having slept through most of the film.* ○ *He has confessed **to** the murder.* ○ [+ (that)] *I **have to** confess **(that)**, when I first met your husband, I didn't think he was very bright.* ○ *I found it all very confusing, I **must***

confess. ○ [R] *The director confessed him**self** (to be)* *puzzled by the company's losses.* **2** in the Christian religion, especially the Roman Catholic Church, to tell God or a priest what you have done wrong so that you can be forgiven: *to confess your sins*

confession /kənˈfeʃ.ᵊn/ *noun* [C or U] **1** when you admit that you have done something wrong or illegal: *I've got a bit of a confession to **make** – I've lost that book you lent me.* ○ *I can't ask for help. It feels like a confession of failure.* ○ *Confession is the first stage of coming to terms with what you've done.* ○ *He **made** a full confession to the police.* **2** when a Christian tells God or, especially in the Roman Catholic Church, tells a priest formally and privately, what they have done wrong so that they can be forgiven: *Have you been to confession recently?* ○ *The priest **heard** his confession.*

confessional /kənˈfeʃ.ᵊn.ᵊl/ *noun* [C] a small enclosed box-like room in a church, especially a Roman Catholic church, which people enter privately to confess to a priest

confessor /kənˈfes.əʳ/ US /-ɚ/ *noun* [C] a priest to whom someone can confess

confetti /kənˈfet.i/ US /-ˈfet̬-/ *noun* [U] small pieces of coloured paper which you throw at a celebration, especially over two people who have just been married

confidant /ˈkɒn.fɪ.dænt/ US /ˈkɑːn.fə-/ *noun* [C] (*FEMALE ALSO* **confidante**) a person you trust and share your feelings and secrets with: *a **close** confidant*

confide /kənˈfaɪd/ *verb* [I or T] to tell something secret or personal to someone whom you trust not to tell anyone else: [+ that] *He confided (to her) that his hair was not his own.* ○ [+ speech] *"My husband doesn't know yet, but I'm going to leave him,"* she confided. **confiding** /kənˈfaɪ.dɪŋ/ *adj*: *a confiding tone/whisper* **confidingly** /kənˈfaɪ.dɪŋ.li/ *adv*: *She spoke in a low voice, leaning towards him confidingly.*

▲ **confide in** *sb phrasal verb* to share your feelings and secrets with someone because you trust them not to tell other people: *She's nice, but I don't feel I can confide in her.*

confidence [CERTAINTY] /ˈkɒn.fɪ.dᵊnts/ US /ˈkɑːn-/ *noun* [U] the quality of being certain of your abilities or of having trust in people, plans, or the future: [+ to infinitive] *He's got the confidence to walk into a room of strangers and immediately start a conversation.* ○ *She's very timid, – completely lacking in (self-)confidence.* ○ *I **have every/ complete** confidence **in** her. She'll be perfect for the job.* ○ [+ that] *I don't share your confidence **that** the market will improve next year.*

confident /ˈkɒn.fɪ.dᵊnt/ US /ˈkɑːn-/ *adj* having confidence: *Be a bit more confident **in** yourself!* ○ *They don't sound confident **about** the future of the industry.* ○ *I'm confident **of** his skills as a manager.* ○ [+ that] *Are you confident **that** enough people will attend the event?* ○ *It was a confident performance.* **confidently** /ˈkɒn.fɪ.dᵊnt.li/ US /ˈkɑːn-/ *adv*: *Try to act confidently, even if you feel nervous.* ○ *Can we confidently rely on him to get the job done?*

confidence [SECRET] /ˈkɒn.fɪ.dᵊnts/ US /ˈkɑːn-/ *noun* [C] a secret that you tell someone: *They talked endlessly, **exchanging** confidences.*

● **in confidence** If you tell something to someone in confidence, you do not want them to tell anyone else.

● **take** *sb* **into** *your* **confidence** to share your secrets with someone, trusting them not to tell other people: *I should never have taken him into my confidence.*

ˈconfidence ˌtrick *noun* [C] a **con** TRICK

ˈconfidence ˌtrickster *noun* [C] a **con artist**

confidential /ˌkɒn.fɪˈden.tʃᵊl/ US /ˌkɑːn-/ *adj* secret, often in a formal, business or military situation: *All information will be treated as **strictly** confidential.* **confidentially** /ˌkɒn.fɪˈden.tʃᵊl.i/ US /ˌkɑːn-/ *adv*: *Can I speak to you confidentially?* ○ *All information supplied will be treated confidentially.*

confidentiality ɒʃ /ˌkɒn.fɪ.den.tʃiˈæl.ɪ.ti/ US /ˌkɑːn.fɪ.den.tʃiˈæl.ə.t̬i/ *noun* [U] when something is confidential: *patient/client confidentiality* ○ *All replies will be treated with complete confidentiality.*

configuration /kənˌfɪg.əˈreɪ.ʃᵊn/ *noun* **1** [C] *FORMAL OR SPECIALIZED* the particular arrangement or pattern of a group of related things **2** [C or U] the way in which all the equipment that makes up a computer system is set to operate, or when you adjust or change a computer system in a particular way

configure /kənˈfɪg.əʳ/ US /kənˈfɪg.ɚ/ *verb* [T] to adjust something or change the controls on a computer or other device so that it can be used in a particular way: [+ to infinitive] *Some software can be configured **to** prevent children from giving out their phone numbers on the Internet.*

confine /kənˈfaɪn/ *verb* **1** [T] to limit an activity, person or problem in some way: *Let's confine our discussion **to** the matter in question, please!* ○ *Please confine your use of the telephone **to** business calls.* ○ *By closing the infected farms we're hoping to confine the disease **to** the north of the region* (= stop it from spreading to other areas). **2** [T usually passive] to keep someone in an enclosed place, often by force: *The hostages had been confined for so long that they couldn't cope with the outside world.*

● **be confined to** *somewhere/sth* to exist only in a particular area or group of people: *We know that the illness is not confined to any one group in society.* ○ *This attitude seems to be confined to the upper classes.*

confinement /kənˈfaɪn.mənt/ *noun* **1** [U] when a person or animal is kept somewhere, usually by force: *She spent most of those years under house arrest or **close** confinement.* **2** [C or U] *OLD-FASHIONED OR FORMAL* **labour** (= when a woman gives birth to a baby)

confines /ˈkɒn.faɪnz/ US /ˈkɑːn-/ *plural noun FORMAL* the outer limits of something: *the **narrow** confines of a religious life* ○ *within/beyond the confines of the city*

confirm [MAKE CERTAIN] /kənˈfɜːm/ US /-ˈfɝːm/ *verb* [I or T] to make an arrangement or meeting certain, often by telephone or writing: [+ that] *Six people have confirmed **that** they will be attending and ten haven't replied yet.* ○ *Flights should be confirmed 48 hours before departure.* ○ *I've accepted the job over the phone, but I haven't confirmed in writing yet.*

confirmation /ˌkɒn.fəˈmeɪ.ʃᵊn/ US /ˌkɑːn.fɚ-/ *noun* [C or U] a statement, often written, that an arrangement or meeting is certain: *a letter of confirmation* ○ *We've only had five confirmations for the conference so far.* ○ *We will send you **written** confirmation **of** our offer shortly.*

confirm [PROVE TRUE] /kənˈfɜːm/ US /-ˈfɝːm/ *verb* [T] to give certainty to a belief or an opinion which was previously not completely certain: [+ question word] *The smell of cigarette smoke confirmed **what** he had suspected: there had been a party in his absence.* ○ [+ (that)] *Her announcement confirmed (that) she would be resigning as Prime Minister.* ○ *The leader's speech was impressive and confirmed her faith in the party.*

confirmation /ˌkɒn.fəˈmeɪ.ʃᵊn/ US /ˌkɑːn.fɚ-/ *noun* [U] a statement or proof that something is true: *We are still awaiting confirmation **of** the exact number of casualties.* ○ *Her confession was no surprise to him, – just the confirmation of a long-held suspicion.*

confirm [RELIGION] /kənˈfɜːm/ US /-ˈfɝːm/ *verb* [T] to accept someone formally as a full member of the Christian Church at a special ceremony

confirmation /ˌkɒn.fəˈmeɪ.ʃᵊn/ US /ˌkɑːn.fɚ-/ *noun* [C or U] when someone is confirmed into the Christian Church

confirmed /kənˈfɜːmd/ US /-fɝːmd/ *adj* [before n] describes someone who has had a particular habit or way of life for a long time and is unlikely to change: *a confirmed bachelor/atheist/tea drinker*

confiscate /ˈkɒn.fɪ.skeɪt/ US /ˈkɑːn-/ *verb* [T] to take a possession away from someone when you have the right to do so, usually as a punishment and often for a limited period, after which it is returned to the owner: *Miss Edwards has confiscated my comics till the end of term!* ○ *His passport was confiscated by the police to prevent him from leaving the country.* **confiscation** /ˌkɒn.fɪˈskeɪ.ʃᵊn/ US /ˌkɑːn-/ *noun* [C or U] *There was a record number of confiscations by customs officers last year.*

conflagration /ˌkɒn.fləˈgreɪ.ʃᵊn/ US /ˌkɑːn-/ *noun* [C] *FORMAL* **1** a large destructive fire **2** a large and violent event, such as a war, involving a lot of people: *They may succeed in turning a little local difficulty into a full-blown regional conflagration.*

conflate /kən'fleɪt/ *verb* [T] to combine two or more separate things, especially pieces of text, to form a whole: *She succeeded in conflating the three plays to produce a fresh new work.* **conflation** /kən'fleɪ.ʃən/ *noun* [C or U]

conflict /'kɒn.flɪkt/ [US] /'kɑːn-/ *noun* [C or U] **1** an active disagreement between people with opposing opinions or principles: *There was a lot of conflict* ***between*** *him and his father.* ○ *It was an unpopular policy and caused a number of conflicts within the party.* ○ *His outspoken views would frequently* ***bring*** *him* ***into*** *conflict* ***with*** *the president.* **2** fighting between two or more groups of people or countries: *We wish to avoid conflict between our countries if at all possible.*

conflict /kən'flɪkt/ *verb* [I] If beliefs, needs, or facts, etc. conflict, they are very different and cannot easily exist together or both be true: *The results of the new research would seem to conflict* ***with*** *existing theories.*

conflicted /kən'flɪk.tɪd/ *adj* [after v] confused or anxious because you cannot choose between very different ideas, feelings or beliefs, and do not know what to do or believe: *It seems that politicians, like ordinary citizens, are conflicted* ***about*** *gambling.*

conflicting /kən'flɪk.tɪŋ/ *adj* describes beliefs, needs, facts, etc. that are different and opposing: *conflicting opinions/ideas/advice* ○ *She was troubled by the conflicting* ***interests*** (= interests which are difficult to combine) *of a career and a family.* ○ *The jury heard conflicting* ***evidence*** *from three different witnesses.*

confluence /'kɒn.fluː.ənts/ [US] /'kɑːn-/ *noun* [C] *SPECIALIZED* the place where two rivers flow together and become one larger river

conform /kən'fɔːm/ [US] /-'fɔːrm/ *verb* [I] to behave according to the usual standards of behaviour which are expected by a group or society: *At our school, you were required to conform, and there was no place for originality.*

conformist /kən'fɔː.mɪst/ [US] /-'fɔːr-/ *noun* [C] *OFTEN DISAPPROVING* someone who conforms **conformist** /kən'fɔː.mɪst/ [US] /-'fɔːr-/ *adj* **conformity** /kən'fɔː.mɪ.ti/ [US] /-'fɔːr.mə.ṭi/ *noun* [U] *It's depressing how much conformity there is in such young children.*

▲ **conform to/with** ***sth*** *phrasal verb* to obey a rule or reach the necessary stated standard, or to do things in a traditional way: *Before buying a pram, make sure that it conforms to the official safety standards.* ○ *Members must conform to a strict dress code.*

confound /kən'faʊnd/ *verb* [T] to confuse and greatly surprise someone, so that they are unable to explain or deal with a situation: *An elderly man from Hull has confounded doctors* ***by*** *recovering after he was officially declared dead.* ○ *The dancer confounded her critics* ***with*** *a remarkable follow-up album.*

confounded /kən'faʊn.dɪd/ *adj* [before n] *OLD-FASHIONED INFORMAL* used to express annoyance: *What a confounded nuisance!*

confront /kən'frʌnt/ *verb* [T] to face, meet or deal with a difficult situation or person: *As she left the court, she was confronted by angry crowds who tried to block her way.* ○ *It's an issue we'll have to confront at some point, no matter how unpleasant it is.* ○ *I thought I would remain calm, but when I was confronted* ***with/by*** *the TV camera, I became very nervous.*

confrontation /ˌkɒn.frʌn'teɪ.ʃən/ [US] /ˌkɑːn.frən-/ *noun* [C or U] a fight or argument: *She actually enjoys confrontation, whereas I prefer a quiet life.* ○ *There were violent confrontations between police and demonstrators.* **confrontational** /ˌkɒn.frʌn'teɪ.ʃən.əl/ [US] /ˌkɑːn.frən-/ *adj*: *He's got a rather aggressive, confrontational manner.*

▲ **confront** ***sb*** **with** ***sth*** *phrasal verb* to tell someone what they do not want to hear, often because it is something bad that they have done or because it needs an explanation: *I know it's her that made the error, but I don't want to confront her with it in case she breaks down.*

confuse /kən'fjuːz/ *verb* [T] **1** to mix up someone's mind or ideas, or to make something difficult to understand: *You're confusing him! Tell him slowly and one thing at a time.* ○ *Stop confusing the issue* (= making the problem unnecessarily difficult)*!* **2** to mix up two separate things or people in your mind, imagining that they are one: *You're confusing me* ***with*** *my sister, – she's the one studying drama.* ○ *It's easy to confuse his films, because he tends to use the same actors.*

confused /kən'fjuːzd/ *adj* **1** unable to think clearly or to understand something: *Grandfather gets quite confused sometimes, and doesn't even know what day it is.* ○ *I'm a bit confused. Was that her husband or her son she was with?* **2** not clear and therefore difficult to understand: *Your essay gets a bit confused halfway through when you introduce too many ideas at once.*

confusing /kən'fjuː.zɪŋ/ *adj* describes something that makes you feel confused because it is difficult to understand: *We've got two people called Paul James working here, so it's a bit confusing!* ○ *The instructions are terribly confusing. Could you help me with them, please?*

confusion /kən'fjuː.ʒən/ *noun* **1** [C or U] when people do not understand what is happening, what they should do or who someone or something is: *There seems to be some confusion* ***over*** *who is actually giving the talk.* ○ *To avoid confusion, the twins never wore the same clothes.* **2** [U] a situation, often with a lot of activity and noise, in which people do not know what to do: *In the confusion after the bomb blast, I lost my bag and wasn't able to stop and look for it.*

confute /kən'fjuːt/ *verb* [T] *FORMAL* to prove a person or an argument to be wrong

conga /'kɒŋ.gə/ [US] /'kɑːŋ-/ *noun* [C] **1** a Latin American dance in which a chain of people hold each other around the waist and follow the leader around using simple steps and kicks **2** a piece of music for the conga

congeal /kən'dʒiːl/ *verb* [I] to change from a liquid or soft state to a thick or solid state: *The blood had congealed in thick black clots.* **congealed** /kən'dʒiːld/ *adj*: *congealed fat*

congenial /kən'dʒiː.ni.əl/ *adj* friendly and pleasant: *congenial company/surroundings*

congenital /kən'dʒen.ɪ.təl/ [US] /-ṭəl/ *adj* **1** *SPECIALIZED* describes a disease or condition that exists at or from birth: *a congenital abnormality/disease* **2** describes someone who always shows a particular bad quality: *a congenital* ***liar***

conger eel /ˌkɒŋ.gə'riːl/ [US] /ˌkɑŋ.gɚ-/ *noun* [C] a long powerful snake-like sea fish

congested /kən'dʒes.tɪd/ *adj* **1** too blocked or crowded and causing difficulties **2** describes roads and towns where there is too much traffic and movement is made difficult **3** describes someone who cannot breathe through their nose because it is blocked, usually during an infection **4** describes lungs or other body parts that have become too full of blood or other liquid **congestion** /kən'dʒes.tʃən/ *noun* [U] *The* ***(traffic)*** *congestion in the city gets even worse during the summer.* ○ *This spray helps to ease* ***nasal*** *congestion.*

conglomerate [COMPANY] /kən'glɒm.ər.ət/ [US] /-'glɑː.mɚ-/ *noun* [C] a company that owns several smaller businesses whose products or services are usually very different: *a financial/industrial conglomerate*

conglomerate [ROCK] /kən'glɒmər.ət/ [US] /-'glɑː.mɚ-/ *noun* [C or U] *SPECIALIZED* a rock which consists of small rounded stones that are held together by clay and sand

conglomeration /kənˌglɒm.ər'eɪ.ʃən/ [US] /-ˌglɑː.mə'reɪ-/ *group noun* [C usually sing] a large group or mass of different things all gathered together in an untidy or unusual way: *There were a strange conglomeration* ***of*** *objects on the mantelpiece.*

congrats /kən'græts/ *exclamation, plural noun INFORMAL* **congratulations**

congratulate /kən'græt.jʊ.leɪt/ *verb* [T] to praise someone and say that you approve of or are pleased about a special or unusual achievement: *I was just congratulating Ceri* ***on*** *winning/****on*** *having won her race.* **congratulation** /kənˌgræt.jʊ'leɪ.ʃən/ *noun* [U] *He sent her a note of congratulation on her election victory.*

congratulations /kənˌgræt.jʊ'leɪ.ʃənz/ *exclamation, plural noun* something that you say when you want to congratulate someone: *"I passed my driving test yesterday." "Did you? Congratulations!"* ○ *Congratulations* ***on*** *your engagement!* **congratulatory** /kənˌgræt.jʊ'leɪ.tər.i/ [US] /-'grætʃ.əl.ə.tɔːr.i/ *adj*: *a congratulatory speech*

C

congregate /ˈkɒŋ.ɡrɪ.ɡeɪt/ [US] /ˈkɑːŋ-/ *verb* [I] to gather together in a large group of people or animals: *A crowd congregated* ***around*** *the entrance to the theatre, hoping to catch a glimpse of the stars of the show.*

congregation /ˌkɒŋ.ɡrɪˈɡeɪ.ʃᵊn/ [US] /ˌkɑːŋ-/ *group noun* [C] a group of people gathered together in a religious building for worship and prayer: *The vicar asked the congregation to kneel.* **congregational** /ˌkɒŋ.ɡrɪˈɡeɪ.ʃᵊn.ᵊl/ [US] /ˌkɑːŋ-/ *adj: congregational singing*

congress [MEETING] /ˈkɒŋ.ɡres/ [US] /ˈkɑːŋ-/ *group noun* [C] a large formal meeting of representatives from countries or societies at which ideas are discussed and information is exchanged: *an international/medical congress* ○ *the congress* ***of*** *the Australian Council of Trade Unions*

Congress [US POLITICIANS] /ˈkɒŋ.ɡres/ [US] /ˈkɑːŋ-/ *group noun* [S] the elected group of politicians in the US who are responsible for making the law, consisting of the Senate and the House of Representatives: *Congress has rejected the recent presidential proposal on firearms.*

congressional /kəŋˈɡreʃ.ᵊn.ᵊl/ *adj* [before n] belonging or related to the US Congress: *a congressional committee* ○ *congressional elections*

congressman /ˈkɒŋ.ɡres.mən/ [US] /ˈkɑːŋ-/ *noun* [C] a man who belongs to a congress, especially a member of the US House of Representatives

congresswoman /ˈkɒŋ.ɡresˌwʊm.ən/ [US] /ˈkɑːŋ-/ *noun* [C] a woman who belongs to a congress, especially a member of the US House of Representatives

congruent /ˈkɒŋ.ɡru.ənt/ [US] /ˈkɑːŋ-/ *adj* SPECIALIZED describes a shape in mathematics that has the same shape and size as another: *congruent triangles* **congruence** /ˈkɒŋ.ɡru.ᵊnts/ [US] /ˈkɑːŋ-/ *noun* [U]

conical /ˈkɒn.ɪ.kᵊl/ [US] /ˈkɑː.nɪ-/ *adj* ➲See at **cone** SHAPE.

conifer /ˈkɒn.ɪ.fəʳ/ [US] /ˈkɑː.nɪ.fɚ/ *noun* [C] one of various types of evergreen tree which produce fruit in the form of cones **coniferous** /kəˈnɪf.ᵊr.əs/ [US] /-ɚ-/ *adj: a coniferous forest*

conj *noun* [C] WRITTEN ABBREVIATION FOR **conjunction** CONNECTING WORD

conjecture /kənˈdʒek.tʃəʳ/ [US] /-tʃɚ/ *noun* [C or U] (the forming of) a guess about something based on how it seems and not on proof: *There's been a lot of conjecture in the papers recently* ***about*** *the royal marriage.*

conjecture /kənˈdʒek.tʃəʳ/ [US] /-tʃɚ/ *verb* [I] FORMAL to guess, based on the appearance of a situation and not on proof: *We'll never know exactly how she died; we can only conjecture.* ○ [+ that] *He conjectured* ***that*** *the company would soon be in financial difficulties.* **conjectural** /kənˈdʒek.tʃᵊr.ᵊl/ [US] /-tʃɚ-/ *adj*

conjoined /kənˈdʒɔɪnd/ *adj* FORMAL joined together

conˌjoined ˈtwins *plural noun* (OLD-FASHIONED **Siamese twins**) two people with the same mother who were born at the same time, with some part of their bodies joined together

conjugal /ˈkɒn.dʒʊ.ɡᵊl/ [US] /ˈkɑːn-/ *adj* FORMAL connected with marriage or the relationship between husband and wife, especially their sexual relationship: *conjugal happiness* ○ *Some prisoners who want to start a family are to be permitted conjugal* ***visits.***

ˌconjugal ˈrights *plural noun* OFTEN HUMOROUS the right to have sex with the person you are married to: *He complained that he had been denied his conjugal rights.*

conjugate /ˈkɒn.dʒʊ.ɡeɪt/ [US] /ˈkɑːn-/ *verb* [I or T] SPECIALIZED If a verb conjugates, it has different forms depending on number, tense, etc., and if you conjugate a verb, you list its various forms: *The verb 'to be' conjugates irregularly.*

conjugation /ˌkɒn.dʒʊˈɡeɪ.ʃᵊn/ [US] /ˌkɑːn-/ *noun* SPECIALIZED **1** [C] a group of verbs that conjugate in the same way **2** [U] when or how you conjugate a verb

conjunction [CONNECTING WORD] /kənˈdʒʌŋk.ʃᵊn/ *noun* [C] (WRITTEN ABBREVIATION **conj**) a word such as 'and', 'but', 'while' or 'although' that connects words, phrases and clauses in a sentence

conjunction [COMBINATION] /kənˈdʒʌŋk.ʃᵊn/ *noun* (FORMAL **conjuncture**) [C or U] **1** when events or conditions combine or happen together: *An unfortunate conjunction of circumstances led to his downfall.* ○ *There is a team of writers working* ***in*** *conjunction* ***(with*** *each other) on the book.* **2** SPECIALIZED in astrology, when two planets appear to be in the same portion of the sky as seen from Earth: *Mars and Venus will be* ***in*** *exact conjunction on the first of September.*

conjunctivitis /kənˌdʒʌŋk.tɪˈvaɪ.tɪs/ [US] /-t̬ɪs/ *noun* [U] a painful infection of the eyes which makes them red and makes the eyelids swollen and sticky

conjure /ˈkʌn.dʒəʳ/ [US] /-dʒɚ/ *verb* [I or T] to make something appear by magic, or as if by magic: *In an instant, the magician had conjured* ***(up)*** *a white dove from his hat.*

conjurer, conjuror /ˈkʌn.dʒᵊr.əʳ/ [US] /-dʒɚ.ɚ/ *noun* [C] a person who performs magic to entertain people

PHRASAL VERBS WITH **conjure** ▼

▲ **conjure *sth* up** [THINK OF] *phrasal verb* [M] to make a picture or idea appear in someone's mind: *The glittering ceremony conjured up images of Russia's imperial past.* ○ *For some people, the word 'England' may still conjure up images of pretty gardens and tea parties.*

▲ **conjure *sth* up** [CREATE] *phrasal verb* [M] to make something in a quick and clever way, especially food: *How am I expected to conjure up a meal for six of his friends with almost nothing in the fridge?*

▲ **conjure *sb/sth* up** [ASK TO APPEAR] *phrasal verb* [M] to ask the spirit of a dead person or an imaginary being to appear, by using special words

ˈconjuring ˌtrick *noun* [C] a trick in which something is made to appear as if by magic, often using a quick movement of the hand

conk [NOSE] /kɒŋk/ [US] /kɑːŋk/ *noun* [C] UK INFORMAL HUMOROUS a nose

conk [HIT] /kɒŋk/ [US] /kɑːŋk/ *verb* [T] INFORMAL HUMOROUS to hit someone, usually on the head with a heavy object

▲ **conk out** *phrasal verb* INFORMAL **1** If vehicles and other machines conk out, they stop working or fail suddenly: *I was just two miles from home when my motorbike conked out!* **2** to go to sleep very quickly, or to suddenly become unconscious: *After a six-hour flight and a long day of meetings, it's not surprising you conked out.*

conker /ˈkɒŋ.kəʳ/ [US] /ˈkɑːŋ.kɚ/ *noun* [C] MAINLY UK the shiny brown poisonous nut of a HORSE CHESTNUT tree

conkers /ˈkɒŋ.kəz/ [US] /ˈkɑːŋ.kɚz/ *noun* [U] UK a children's game in which you have a conker with a string through it and try to break another child's conker by hitting it with yours

ˈcon ˌman, **conman** *noun* [C] a **con artist**

connect [JOIN] /kəˈnekt/ *verb* [I or T] to join or be joined with something else: *Can I connect my printer* ***to*** *your computer?* ○ *Where does the cooker connect* ***(up) to*** *the electricity?* ○ *Has the telephone/electricity/gas been connected* (= switched on or joined to the main supply) *in your new place yet?*

connected /kəˈnek.tɪd/ *adj* joined together: *The TV won't work if the aerial's not connected.*

connecting /kəˈnek.tɪŋ/ *adj* joining or being joined: *There's a connecting corridor between the buildings.* ○ *connecting rooms*

connection /kəˈnek.ʃᵊn/ *noun* **1** [C or U] when something joins or is joined to something else, or the part or process that enables this: *The electricity company guarantees connection within 24 hours.* ○ *It's no wonder your shaver isn't working. There's a loose connection* (= a connecting wire has become loose) *in the plug.* **2** [C] when people or things are joined or connected in some way

connections /kəˈnek.ʃᵊn/ *plural noun* the people you know and who can help you: *He only got the job because of his connections!* ○ *He has important connections in Washington.*

connector /kəˈnek.təʳ/ [US] /-tɚ/ *noun* [C] SPECIALIZED a device at the end of a wire in an item of electrical equipment, which holds the wire in position: *electrical connectors*

connect [RELATE] /kəˈnekt/ *verb* [T] to consider or show a person or thing to be related to someone or something else: *She's an actress I connect* ***with*** *the theatre rather than films.* ○ *Police are connecting the break-in* ***with*** *other recent thefts in the area.* **connected** /kəˈnek.tɪd/

adj: *They're not blood relations, – they're only connected by marriage.* ○ *He was connected in some way **with** that fraud scandal a couple of years back.* ⮣See also **well-connected**.

connection /kəˈnek.ʃən/ *noun* [C] *The connection **between** smoking **and** heart disease is well known.* ○ *They're sisters, are they? I knew that their surname was the same, but I never **made** (= thought of) the connection.*
• **in connection with** on the subject of: *They want to talk to you in connection with an unpaid tax bill.*

connect TELEPHONE /kəˈnekt/ *verb* [T] to make it possible for you to speak to someone else by telephone: *Could you connect me **with/to** a number in Paris, please? I can't seem to get through.* connection /kəˈnek.ʃən/ *noun* [C] *Sorry, could you repeat that? This is a very **bad** connection.*

connect TRANSPORT /kəˈnekt/ *verb* [I] If two public transport vehicles connect, they arrive at suitable times to allow passengers to get off one and onto another: *Your flight arrives in Malaga at ten o'clock where it connects **with** a coach service to your hotel.* ○ *There's a connecting train service between the airport and the city.* connection /kəˈnek.ʃən/ *noun* [C] *If the flight is late, we'll **miss** our connection.*

connective tissue /kəˌnek.tɪvˈtɪʃ.uː/ /-ˈtɪs.juː/ *noun* [U] SPECIALIZED the strong stretchy material that acts as a support around the organs in the body and is also found in the joints

connive /kəˈnaɪv/ *verb* [I] **1** to plan secretly and dishonestly for something to happen which will be to your advantage: *Civil servants and ministers were accused of conniving **with** the company **in** the supply of arms to Sierra Leone.* ○ [+ to infinitive] *They connived **to** break the school rules at every opportunity.* **2** to allow something bad to happen although you know about it: *She had murdered or connived **at** the murder of one of her lovers.* ○ *He called for checks to discover whether corrupt officials are being bribed to connive **in** shoddy construction.*
connivance /kəˈnaɪ.vənts/ *noun* [U] when someone connives, especially by being aware of something bad that is happening and allowing it to continue: *Their appalling treatment of their child could only have happened **with** the connivance **of** their neighbours.*
conniving /kəˈnaɪ.vɪŋ/ *adj* describes a person who deceives others for their own advantage: *He's a conniving bastard!*

connoisseur /ˌkɒn.əˈsɜːʳ/ US /ˌkɑː.nəˈsɝː/ *noun* [C] a person who knows a lot about and enjoys one of the arts, or food, drink, etc. and can judge quality and skill in that subject: *a wine/art connoisseur* ○ *a connoisseur **of** ballet/cigars*

connotation /ˌkɒn.əˈteɪ.ʃən/ US /ˌkɑː.nə-/ *noun* [C] a feeling or idea that is suggested by a particular word although it is not necessarily a part of the word's meaning, or something suggested by an object or situation: *The word 'lady' has connotations **of** refinement and excessive femininity that some women find offensive.* connote /kəˈnəʊt/ US /-ˈnoʊt/ *verb* [T] FORMAL *To me, chocolate connotes pleasure and indulgence.*

connubial /kəˈnjuː.bi.əl/ US /-ˈnuː-/ *adj* FORMAL connected with marriage: *connubial bliss*

conquer /ˈkɒŋ.kəʳ/ US /ˈkɑː.ŋ.kɚ/ *verb* [T] **1** to take control or possession of foreign land, or a group of people, by force: *The Spanish conquered the New World in the 16th century.* ○ *The English were conquered by the Normans in 1066.* **2** to deal with or successfully fight against a problem or an unreasonable fear: *He has finally conquered his **fear** of spiders.* ○ *It may be many years before this dreadful disease is conquered.*
conqueror /ˈkɒŋ.kəʳ.əʳ/ US /ˈkɑː.ŋ.kɚ.ɚ/ *noun* [C] someone who has conquered a country or its people
conquest /ˈkɒŋ.kwest/ US /ˈkɑː.ŋ-/ *noun* **1** [C or U] when someone conquers a country, area or situation **2** [C] HUMOROUS someone you have had sex with but probably not a relationship: *I was determined not to become just another of his conquests.*

conquistador /kɒnˈkwɪs.tə.dɔːʳ/ US /kɑːnˈkiː.stə.dɔːr/ *noun* [C] OLD USE one of the Spanish people who travelled to America in the 16th century and took control of Mexico and Peru

conscience /ˈkɒn.tʃənts/ US /ˈkɑː.n-/ *noun* [C or U] the part of you that judges the morality of your own actions and makes you feel guilty about bad things that you have done or things you feel responsible for: *a **guilty** conscience* ○ *a **question/matter** of conscience* ○ *You didn't do anything wrong, – you should have a **clear** conscience* (= not feel guilty). ○ *My conscience would really trouble me if I wore a fur coat.* ○ *He's got no conscience at all* (= does not feel guilty) **about** *leaving me to do the housework.*
• **be/weigh on your conscience** to make you feel guilty: *I ignored an old woman who asked me for money in the street yesterday, and it's been on my conscience ever since.*
• **in all conscience** UK (US **in good conscience**) SLIGHTLY FORMAL without feeling guilty: *You couldn't, in all conscience, ask her to pay the whole bill!*

conscience-stricken /ˈkɒn.tʃənts.strɪk.ən/ US /ˈkɑː.n-/ *adj* feeling much regret for something that you have done wrong

conscientious /ˌkɒn.ʃiˈent.ʃəs/ US /ˌkɑː.n-/ *adj* putting a lot of effort into your work: *a conscientious student* conscientiously /ˌkɒn.ʃiˈent.ʃə.sli/ US /ˌkɑː.n-/ *adv* conscientiousness /ˌkɒn.ʃiˈent.ʃə.snəs/ US /ˌkɑː.nt-/ *noun* [U]

consci,entious ob'jector *noun* [C] a person who refuses to work in the armed forces for moral or religious reasons

conscious AWAKE /ˈkɒn.tʃəs/ US /ˈkɑː.n-/ *adj* awake, thinking and aware of what is happening around you: *He's still conscious but he's fairly badly injured.* ○ *They've brought her out of the operating theatre, but she's not fully conscious yet.* ○ FIGURATIVE HUMOROUS *"Can I speak to Isobel, please?" "She's still in bed. I'll just go and see if she's conscious* (= awake) *yet."* ✳ NOTE: The opposite is **unconscious**. consciousness /ˈkɒn.tʃə.snəs/ US /ˈkɑː.n-/ *noun* [U] *He **lost** consciousness after his accident and never **recovered/regained** it.*

conscious AWARE OF /ˈkɒn.tʃəs/ US /ˈkɑː.n-/ *adj* be **conscious of sth/sb** to be aware of the existence or presence of a particular thing or person: *The tooth doesn't exactly hurt, but I'm conscious of it* (= I can feel it) *all the time.* ○ [+ v-ing] *I think she's very conscious of **being** the only person in the office who didn't have a university education.* ○ [+ that] *He gradually became conscious (of the fact) **that** everyone else was wearing a suit.* ✪See also **subconscious**.
consciousness /ˈkɒn.tʃə.snəs/ US /ˈkɑː.n-/ *noun* [U] awareness: [+ that] *Her consciousness **that** she's different makes her feel uneasy.* ○ *Working in an unemployment office had helped to **raise** his political consciousness.*

conscious INTENTIONAL /ˈkɒn.tʃəs/ US /ˈkɑː.n-/ *adj* determined and intentional: *He's obviously making a conscious **effort** to be nice to me at the moment.* ○ *It wasn't a conscious **decision** to lose weight. It just happened.* consciously /ˈkɒn.tʃə.sli/ US /ˈkɑː.n-/ *adv*: *I don't think she's consciously rude to people – it's just her manner.*

-conscious -krb.tʃəs/ ʊf /-kɑː.n-/ *suffix* used after nouns and adverbs to mean 'aware of and worried about a particular thing', or 'thinking that something is important': *fashion-conscious teenagers* ○ *the health-conscious consumer* ○ *He's never been especially politically conscious.* ✪See also **self-conscious**.

'consciousness ,raising *noun* [U] the attempt to increase people's knowledge of and interest in social and political matters

conscript /kənˈskrɪpt/ *verb* [T] (US USUALLY **draft**) to force someone by law to serve in one of the armed forces: *He was conscripted **into** the army at the age of 18.* conscript /ˈkɒn.skrɪpt/ US /ˈkɑː.n-/ *noun* [C] (US USUALLY **draftee**) *Over half the army was composed of conscripts.* ✪Compare **volunteer**. conscript /ˈkɒn.skrɪpt/ US /ˈkɑː.n-/ *adj* [before n] *a conscript army* conscription /kənˈskrɪp.ʃən/ *noun* [U] *He's been worried that the government will introduce conscription ever since the war began.*

consecrate /ˈkɒnt.sɪ.kreɪt/ US /ˈkɑː.nt-/ *verb* [T] **1** to officially make something holy and able to be used for religious ceremonies: *The new cathedral was completed* *and consecrated in 1962.* **2** to officially give someone the title of bishop in the Christian Church in a religious ceremony **consecrated** /ˈkɒnt.sɪ.kreɪ.tɪd/ [US] /ˈkɑːnt.sɪ.kreɪ.t̬ɪd/ *adj*: *consecrated bread/wine/ground* **consecration** /ˌkɒnt.sɪˈkreɪ.ʃən/ [US] /ˌkɑːnt-/ *noun* [U] *the consecration of the new bishop*

C

consecutive /kənˈsek.jʊ.tɪv/ [US] /-t̬ɪv/ *adj* describes events, numbers, etc. that follow one after another without an interruption: *This is the fifth consecutive weekend that I've spent working, and I'm a bit fed up with it.* **consecutively** /kənˈsek.jʊ.tɪv.li/ [US] /-t̬ɪv-/ *adv*: *Tickets are numbered consecutively.*

consensual /ˌkɒnˈsen.sju.əl/ [US] /ˌkɑːn-/ *adj* FORMAL OR LEGAL with the willing agreement of all the people involved: *The woman alleged rape, but Reeves insisted it was consensual.* ○ *consensual sex*

consensus /kənˈsent.səs/ *noun* [S or U] a generally accepted opinion or decision among a group of people: *The **general** consensus in the office is that he's useless at his job.* ○ *Could we **reach** a consensus **on** this matter? Let's take a vote.*

consent /kənˈsent/ *noun* [U] SLIGHTLY FORMAL permission or agreement: *They can't publish your name without your consent.* ○ *You can only come on the trip if your parents **give** their consent.*

• **by common consent** most people agree: *Her latest film, by common consent, is her best yet.*

consent /kənˈsent/ *verb* [I] to agree to do something, or to allow someone to do something: [+ to infinitive] *Very reluctantly, I've consented **to** lend her my car.* ○ *My aunt never married because her father wouldn't consent **to** her marriage.*

conˌsenting ˈadult *noun* [C] SLIGHTLY FORMAL a person who is considered old enough, and therefore responsible enough, to decide if they want sex and who they want to have sex with

consequence /ˈkɒnt.sɪ.kwənts/ [US] /ˈkɑːnt-/ *noun* [C] an often bad or inconvenient result of a particular action or situation: *Not making a will can have **serious** consequences for the people you might wish to benefit.* ○ *Scientists think it unlikely that any species will actually become extinct **as a** consequence **of** the oil spill.* ○ *I told the hairdresser to do what she wanted to my hair, and **look at the** consequences!* ○ *Well, if you insist on eating so much, you'll have to **suffer/take*** (= accept and deal with) *the consequences!*

• **of little/no consequence** (ALSO **not of any/much consequence**) not important: *The money was of little consequence to Tony.*

consequent /ˈkɒnt.sɪ.kwənt/ [US] /ˈkɑːnt-/ *adj* (ALSO **consequential**) happening as a result of something: *Our use of harmful chemicals and the consequent damage to the environment is a very serious matter.*

consequently /ˈkɒnt.sɪ.kwənt.li/ [US] /ˈkɑːnt-/ *adv* as a result: *I spent most of my money in the first week and consequently had very little to eat by the end of the holiday.*

conservative [AGAINST CHANGE] /kənˈsɜː.və.tɪv/ [US] /-ˈsɝː.və.t̬ɪv/ *adj* **1** tending not to like or trust change, especially sudden change: *a conservative society/outlook* ○ *Older people tend to be quite conservative and a bit suspicious of any supposed advances.* ➲Compare **liberal** SOCIETY. **2** If you are conservative in your appearance, you tend not to like fashionable or modern clothes or hairstyles: *He's a very conservative dresser – he always looks like he's wearing his father's clothes!* **conservatively** /kənˈsɜː.və.tɪv.li/ [US] /-ˈsɝː.və.t̬ɪv-/ *adv*: *I dress more conservatively for the office.* **conservatism** /kənˈsɜː.və.tɪ.zəm/ [US] /-ˈsɝː.və.t̬ɪ-/ *noun* [U]

Conservative [POLITICAL PARTY] /kənˈsɜː.və.tɪv/ [US] /-ˈsɝː.və.t̬ɪv/ *adj* (ALSO **Tory**) belonging to or supporting the British political party which opposes sudden social change, high taxation and government involvement in industry: *the Conservative Party* ○ *Conservative policies* ○ *a Conservative MP/government* ○ *Did you **vote** Conservative at the last election?*

Conservative /kənˈsɜː.və.tɪv/ [US] /-ˈsɝː.və.t̬ɪv/ *noun* [C] (ALSO **Tory**) *She's a **staunch*** (= very loyal) *Conservative.*

Conservatism /kənˈsɜː.və.tɪ.zəm/ [US] /-ˈsɝː.və.t̬ɪ-/ *noun* [U] Conservative actions and beliefs

conservative [LOW] /kənˈsɜː.və.tɪv/ [US] /-ˈsɝː.və.t̬ɪv/ *adj* A conservative guess or calculation is likely to be less than the real amount: *If I said there were three million unemployed, that would be a conservative **estimate**.* **conservatively** /kənˈsɜː.və.tɪv/ [US] /-ˈsɝː.və.t̬ɪv/ *adv*: *The costs of cleaning up the bay are estimated, conservatively, at $1 billion.*

conservatory [SCHOOL] /kənˈsɜː.və.tri/ [US] /-ˈsɝː.və.tɔː.ri/ *noun* [C] (UK ALSO **conservatoire**) a school for the teaching of music or sometimes acting or art

conservatory [ROOM] /kənˈsɜː.və.tri/ [US] /-ˈsɝː.və.tɔː.ri/ *noun* [C] (US ALSO **solarium**) a glass room, usually connected to a house, in which plants are grown and kept

conserve [KEEP] /kənˈsɜːv/ [US] /-ˈsɝːv/ *verb* [T] to keep and protect something from damage, change or waste: *To conserve electricity, we are cutting down on our central heating.* ○ *The nationalists are very keen to conserve their customs and language.* ○ *I'm not being lazy – I'm just conserving my **energy/strength** for later.*

conservation /ˌkɒnt.səˈveɪ.ʃən/ [US] /ˌkɑːnt.sɚ-/ *noun* [U] **1** the protection of plants and animals, natural areas, and interesting and important structures and buildings, especially from the damaging effects of human activity: *wildlife conservation* ○ *a conservation area* **2** carefully using valuable natural substances that exist in limited amounts in order to make certain that they will be available for as long a time as possible: *the conservation of coal/gas/oil reserves* ○ ***Energy** conservation reduces your fuel bills and helps the environment.* **conservationist** /ˌkɒnt.səˈveɪ.ʃən.ɪst/ [US] /ˌkɑːnt.sɚ-/ *noun* [C] *Conservationists are fighting to save our hedgerows.*

conserve [FOOD] /ˈkɒn.sɜːv/ [US] /ˈkɑːn.sɝːv/ *noun* [C or U] FORMAL a type of jam in which the fruit is whole or in large pieces: *apricot/strawberry conserve*

consider [POSSIBILITY] /kənˈsɪd.əʳ/ [US] /-ɚ/ *verb* [I or T] to spend time thinking about a possibility or making a decision: *Don't make any decisions before you've considered the matter.* ○ [+ question word] *Have you considered **what** you'll do if you don't get the job?* ○ [+ v-ing] *We're considering sell**ing** the house.* ○ *She's being considered **for** the job.* ○ *I'd like some time to consider before I make a decision.*

considered /kənˈsɪd.əd/ [US] /-ɚd/ *adj* **considered opinion/view/decision** an opinion or decision that someone has reached after a lot of thought: [+ that] *It is **my** considered opinion **that** he should be promoted.*

consideration /kənˌsɪd.əˈreɪ.ʃən/ *noun* [U] when you think about something carefully: *After some consideration, we've decided to sell the house.* ○ *The whole matter needs (to be given) careful consideration.*

consider [SUBJECT/FACT] /kənˈsɪd.əʳ/ [US] /-ɚ/ *verb* [T] to give attention to a particular subject or fact when judging something else: *You've got to consider the time element when planning the whole project.* ○ [+ question word] *If you consider **how** long he's been learning the piano, he's not very good.* **consideration** /kənˌsɪd.əˈreɪ.ʃən/ *noun* [C or U] *It may be fairly cheap to buy, but you've got to **take into** consideration the money you'll spend on repairs.* ○ *Comfort/Safety is an important consideration.*

considering /kənˈsɪd.ər.ɪŋ/ [US] /-ɚ-/ *prep, conjunction, adv* used to mention a particular condition or fact about something, usually a disadvantageous one: *Considering the weather, we got here quite quickly.* ○ *She did well to find the way, considering she'd only been there once before.*

consider [CARE ABOUT] /kənˈsɪd.əʳ/ [US] /-ɚ/ *verb* [T] to care about or respect other people or their feelings and wishes: *Have you considered your mother and how she's going to feel about you leaving?* ○ *She never considers anyone but herself – she's totally selfish!*

considerate /kənˈsɪd.ər.ət/ [US] /-ɚ-/ *adj* kind and helpful: *It wasn't very considerate of you to drink all the milk.*
* NOTE: The opposite is **inconsiderate**.

consideration /kənˌsɪd.əˈreɪ.ʃən/ *noun* **1** [U] when you are kind to people or think about their feelings: *You've got no consideration **for** others!* ○ *Could you turn your music down and **show** a little consideration **for** the neighbours!* ○ *We didn't publish the details, **out of** consideration **for** the victim's family.* **2** [C] OLD-FASHIONED OR HUMOROUS a payment for a service: *For **a small** con-*

sideration, madam, I'll show you the way there myself.

consider OPINION /kən'sɪd.əʳ/ US /-ɚ-/ *verb* [T often + obj + (to be) n or adj] to believe someone or something to be, or think of them as: *He is currently considered (to be) the best British athlete.* ○ *We don't consider her suitable for the job.* ○ [passive + obj + to infinitive] *It is considered bad manners in some cultures to speak with your mouth full of food.* ○ [R] *I consider myself lucky that I only hurt my arm in the accident.* ○ *Do you consider him a friend of yours?* ○ [+ (that)] *She considers (that) she has done enough to help already.*
● **be highly/well considered** to be very much admired: *I've never enjoyed her books, but I know she's very highly considered.*

considerable /kən'sɪd.ᵊr.ə.bl̩/ US /-ɚ-/ *adj* large or of noticeable importance: *The fire caused considerable damage to the church.* **considerably** /kən'sɪd.ᵊr.ə.bli/ US /-ɚ-/ *adv*: *He's considerably fatter than he was when I knew him.*

considerate /kən'sɪd.ᵊr.ət/ US /-ɚ-/ *adj* ⊃See at **consider** CARE ABOUT.

consideration /kən,sɪd.ə'reɪ.ʃᵊn/ *noun* ⊃See at **consider** POSSIBILITY, SUBJECT/FACT, CARE ABOUT

consign /kən'saɪn/ *verb* [T] FORMAL to send something to someone: *The goods have been consigned to you by air.*

consignee /ˌkɒn.saɪ'niː/ US /ˌkɑːn-/ *noun* [C] FORMAL *Goods must be signed for by the consignee* (= the person to whom they are sent).

consignment /kən'saɪn.mənt/ *noun* [C] an amount of goods that is sent somewhere: *The most recent consignment of cloth was faulty.*
● **on consignment** If goods are on consignment, the person or company that receives them will only pay for them after they have been sold.
▲ **consign sb/sth to sth** *phrasal verb* [often passive] FORMAL to get rid of someone or something or to put them in an unpleasant place or situation: *to be consigned to prison* ○ *After the financial disaster, she was consigned to a life of poverty.*

consist /kən'sɪst/ *verb*

PHRASAL VERBS WITH **consist** ▼

▲ **consist in sth** *phrasal verb* [L not continuous] FORMAL to have something as a major and essential part or quality: *The beauty of air travel consists in its speed and ease.*
▲ **consist of sth** *phrasal verb* [L not continuous] to be made of or formed from something: *The team consists of four Europeans and two Americans.* ○ *It's a simple dish to prepare, consisting mainly of rice and vegetables.*

consistency SUBSTANCE /kən'sɪs.tᵊnt.si/ *noun* [C or U] the physical nature of a substance, especially a thick liquid, for example by being thick or thin, smooth or lumpy: *She loved the creamy consistency of fresh paint.* ○ *Melt the chocolate to a **pouring** (= easy to pour) consistency.*

consistency NOT VARIED /kən'sɪs.tᵊnt.si/ *noun* [U] when someone always behaves or performs in a similar way, or when something always happens in a similar way: *They've won a few matches this season but they lack consistency.* ✻ NOTE: The opposite is **inconsistency.**

consistent NOT VARYING /kən'sɪs.tᵊnt/ *adj* always behaving or happening in a similar, especially positive, way: *There has been a consistent improvement in her attitude.* ○ *Her work is sometimes good, but the problem is she's not consistent.* ✻ NOTE: The opposite is **inconsistent.** **consistently** /kən'sɪs.tᵊnt.li/ *adv*: *The President has consistently denied the rumours.*

consistent AGREEING /kən'sɪs.tᵊnt/ *adj* [after v] in agreement with other facts or with typical or previous behaviour, or having the same principles as something else: *What the witness said in court was not consistent with the statement he made to the police.* ○ *We do not consider his behaviour to be consistent with the holding of a high-ranking job.*

conso'lation ˌprize *noun* [C] a small prize given to someone who has taken part in a competition, but who has not won

console COMFORT /kən'səʊl/ US /-'soʊl/ *verb* [T] to make someone who is sad or disappointed feel better by giving them comfort or sympathy: *He tried to console her, but*

---

she kept saying it was all her own fault. ○ *I tried to console her with a box of chocolates.* ○ *I was consoling Liz on having broken up with her boyfriend.* **consolation** /ˌkɒn.sə'leɪ.ʃᵊn/ US /ˌkɑːn-/ *noun* [C or U] *If it's (of) any consolation (to you), you're not the only one he was rude to.* ○ *I didn't know what to say – I just offered a few **words of** consolation.* **consolatory** /kən'sɒl.ə.tri/ US /-'sɑː.lə.tɔːr.i/ *adj* FORMAL *a consolatory remark*

console MACHINE /'kɒn.səʊl/ US /-soʊl/ *noun* [C] a surface on which you find the controls for a piece of electrical equipment or a machine: *a computer console*

consolidate /kən'sɒl.ɪ.deɪt/ US /-'sɑː.lɪ-/ *verb* [I or T] **1** to become, or cause something to become, stronger and more certain: *The success of their major product consolidated the firm's position in the market.* ○ *She hoped that marriage would consolidate their relationship.* ○ *The party consolidated its hold on power during its term of office.* ○ *The company has been expanding rapidly and I feel it's now time to consolidate* (= stop growing and make our present position stronger). **2** to combine several things, especially businesses, so that they become more effective, or to be combined in this way: *The two firms consolidated to form a single company.* **consolidated** /kən'sɒl.ɪ.deɪ.tɪd/ US /-'sɑː.lɪ.deɪ.t̬ɪd/ *adj*: *consolidated trading/accounts* **consolidation** /kən,sɒl.ɪ'deɪ.ʃᵊn/ US /-,sɑː.lɪ-/ *noun* [C or U] *The company is entering a period of consolidation* (= becoming better and stronger at what it does). ○ *We have seen a similar consolidation* (= joining together) *of booksellers and distributors.*

consommé /kən'sɒm.eɪ/ US /ˌkɑːn.t̬.sə'meɪ/ *noun* [U] a thin clear soup

consonant /'kɒn.sə.nənt/ US /'kɑːn-/ *noun* [C] one of the speech sounds or letters of the alphabet which is not a vowel. Consonants are pronounced by stopping the air from flowing freely through the mouth, especially by closing the lips or touching the teeth with the tongue. ⊃Compare **vowel.**

consort BE TOGETHER /kən'sɔːt/ US /-'sɔːrt/ *verb* [I + adv or prep] to spend a lot of time in the company of a particular group of people, especially people whose character is not approved of: *They claimed he had been consorting with drug dealers.*

consort PARTNER /'kɒn.sɔːt/ US /'kɑːn.sɔːrt/ *noun* [C] a wife or husband, especially of a ruler

consortium /kən'sɔː.ti.əm/ US /-'sɔːr.t̬i-/ *noun* [C] *plural* **consortiums** or **consortia** an organization of several businesses or banks joining together as a group for a shared purpose: *a consortium of textile manufacturers*

conspicuous /kən'spɪk.ju.əs/ *adj* very noticeable or tending to attract attention, often in a way that is not wanted: *In China, her blonde hair was conspicuous.* ○ *He tried not to look conspicuous and moved slowly along the back of the room.* ✻ NOTE: The opposite is **inconspicuous.**
● **be conspicuous by your absence** MAINLY HUMOROUS to be absent when you should be present, in a way that other people notice: *Why wasn't Stephen at the meeting, then? He was conspicuous by his absence.*
conspicuously /kən'spɪk.ju.ə.sli/ *adv* in a way that is conspicuous: *The temple's grand white arches rose conspicuously over the dirty decaying city.* **conspicuousness** /kən'spɪk.ju.ə.snəs/ *noun* [U]

conˌspicuous conˈsumption *noun* [U] DISAPPROVING when people spend a lot of money intentionally so that other people notice and admire them for their wealth

conspiracy /kən'spɪr.ə.si/ *noun* [C or U] when people secretly plan together to do something bad or illegal: *The three men are accused of conspiracy.* ○ [+ to infinitive] *She has been charged with conspiracy to murder.* ○ *I think there was a conspiracy to keep me out of the committee.*
● **conˌspiracy of ˈsilence** a general agreement to keep silent about a subject for the purpose of secrecy

conˈspiracy ˌtheory *noun* [C] a belief that an unpleasant event or situation is the result of a secret plan made by powerful people

conspirator /kən'spɪr.ə.təʳ/ US /-t̬ɚ/ *noun* [C] someone who conspires with other people to do something

conspiratorial /kən,spɪr.ə'tɔː.ri.əl/ /-'tɔːr.i-/ *adj* **1** relating to a secret plan to do something bad, illegal or against someone's wishes **2** showing that you share a secret: *They exchanged conspiratorial glances.* **conspiratorially** /kən,spɪr.ə'tɔː.ri.ᵊl.i/ /-'tɔːr.i-/ *adv*: *She heard them whispering conspiratorially in the bedroom.*

conspire /kən'spaɪəʳ/ /-'spaɪr/ *verb* [I] to plan secretly with other people to do something bad, illegal or against someone's wishes: [+ *to* infinitive] *He felt that his colleagues were conspiring together to remove him from his job.* ○ *As girls, the sisters used to conspire with each other against their brother.*

▲ **conspire against** *sth phrasal verb* (ALSO **conspire to do** *sth*) If events or conditions conspire against something or conspire to do something, they combine in such a way that they spoil your plans: *The weather had conspired to ruin their day out.* ○ *I'd planned a romantic evening together, but circumstances conspired against it – friends arrived unexpectedly and then Dave was called out to an emergency.*

constable /'kʌn.stə.bl/ /'kɑːnt-/ *noun* [C] a British police officer of the lowest rank

constabulary /kən'stæb.jʊ.lə.ri/ /-je.ler.i/ *group noun* [C] the British police force for a particular area

constant STAYING SAME /'kɒnt.stᵊnt/ /'kɑːnt-/ *adj* staying the same, or not getting less or more: *We've kept up a fairly constant speed.* ○ *The fridge keeps food at a constant temperature*.

constant /'kɒnt.stᵊnt/ /'kɑːnt-/ *noun* [C] SPECIALIZED a particular number or amount that never changes **constancy** *noun* [U] FORMAL

constant FREQUENT /'kɒnt.stᵊnt/ /'kɑːnt-/ *adj* happening a lot or all the time: *He's in constant trouble with the police.* ○ *machines that are in constant use*

constantly /'kɒnt.stᵊnt.li/ /'kɑːnt-/ *adv* all the time or frequently: *He's constantly changing his mind.* ○ *She has the television on constantly.*

constant LOYAL /'kɒnt.stᵊnt/ /'kɑːnt-/ *adj* describes a companion or friend who is loyal to you **constancy** /'kɒnt.stᵊnt.si/ /'kɑːnt-/ *noun* [U] FORMAL *Never doubt the constancy of my love for you.*

constellation /,kɒnt.stə'leɪ.ʃᵊn/ /,kɑːnt-/ *noun* [C] **1** any of the groups of stars in the sky which seem from Earth to form a pattern and have been given names **2** OFTEN HUMOROUS a group of famous or admired people gathered in one place: *At our annual ceremony we had a whole constellation of film stars/directors.*

consternation /,kɒnt.stə'neɪ.ʃᵊn/ /,kɑːnt.stɚ-/ *noun* [U] a feeling of anxiety, shock or confusion: *The prospect of so much work filled him with consternation.* ○ *To his consternation, when he got to the airport he found he'd forgotten his passport.*

constipated /'kɒnt.stɪ.peɪ.tɪd/ /'kɑːnt.stɪ.peɪ.ṭɪd/ *adj* unable to empty your bowels as often as you should: *If you ate more fibre you wouldn't get constipated.* **constipation** /,kɒnt.stɪ'peɪ.ʃᵊn/ /,kɑːnt-/ *noun* [U] to get/have/suffer from constipation

constituency /kən'stɪt.ju.ənt.si/ *noun* [C] (the group of voters belonging to) any of the official areas of a country that elect someone to represent them nationally: *a rural/urban constituency*

constituent /kən'stɪt.ju.ənt/ *noun* [C] a voter in a particular area of the country: *The senator worked hard, always talking to his constituents and hearing their problems.*

constituent /kən'stɪt.ju.ənt/ *noun* [C] one of the parts that a substance or combination is made of: *What are the basic constituents of the mixture?* **constituent** /kən'stɪt.ju.ənt/ *adj* [before n] *Let's look at the constituent parts of this sentence.*

constitute FORM PART OF /'kɒn.stɪ.tjuːt/ /'kɑːn.stɪ.tuːt/ *verb* [L not continuous] to form or make something: *Women constitute about 10% of Parliament.* ○ *The under-18s constitute nearly 25% of the town's population.*

constitution /,kɒn.stɪ'tjuː.ʃᵊn/ /,kɑːn.stɪ'tuː-/ *noun* [C] how something is formed from different CONSTITUENTS (= parts): *the constitution of a chemical compound*

constitute BE CONSIDERED AS /'kɒn.stɪ.tjuːt/ /'kɑːn.stɪ.tuːt/ *verb* [L only + n; not continuous] FORMAL to be or be considered as something: *This latest defeat constitutes a major setback for the government.*

constitution LAWS /,kɒn.stɪ'tjuː.ʃᵊn/ /,kɑːn.stɪ'tuː-/ *noun* [C] (a written document which forms) the set of political principles by which a state or organization is governed, especially in relation to the rights of the people it governs: *Britain has no written constitution.* ○ *The Constitution of the United States* ○ *Under* (= As part of) *the union constitution, a new committee must be elected each year.*

constitutional /,kɒn.stɪ'tjuː.ʃᵊn.ᵊl/ /,kɑːn.stɪ'tuː-/ *adj* allowed by or contained in a constitution: *Such a policy would not be constitutional.* ○ *Freedom of speech should be a constitutional right.* ✻ NOTE: The opposite is **unconstitutional**.

constitutionally /,kɒn.stɪ'tjuː.ʃᵊn.ᵊl.i/ /,kɑːn.stɪ.'tuː-/ *adv* according to the rules in the constitution: *There was some doubt as to whether the government were behaving constitutionally.*

constitutionality /,kɒn.stɪ.tjuː.ʃᵊn'æl.ɪ.ti/ /,kɑːn.stɪ.tuː.ʃᵊn'æl.ə.ṭi/ *noun* [U] US the quality of being allowed by or contained in a constitution: *The judge chose to ignore questions of the constitutionality of the Senator's actions.*

constitution HEALTH /,kɒn.stɪ'tjuː.ʃᵊn/ /,kɑːn.stɪ-'tuː-/ *noun* [C] the general state of someone's health: *He has a very strong constitution.* **constitutional** /,kɒn.stɪ'tjuː.ʃᵊn.ᵊl/ /,kɑːn.stɪ.stɪ'tuː-/ *adj: constitutional weakness*

constitutional /,kɒn.stɪ'tjuː.ʃᵊn.ᵊl/ /,kɑːn.stɪ'tuː-/ *noun* [C] OLD-FASHIONED HUMOROUS a walk that you frequently do to keep yourself healthy: *She's nearly 86 and still takes a constitutional every morning.*

constitutionally /,kɒn.stɪ'tjuː.ʃᵊn.ᵊl.i/ /,kɑːn.stɪ'tuː-/ *adv* in a way that relates to or is caused by your general health or your character: *constitutionally weak* ○ HUMOROUS *She seems constitutionally unable to make decisions.*

constitutional 'monarchy *noun* [C] a system in which the king or queen's power is severely limited, because they act on the advice of the politicians who form the government

constraint /kən'streɪnt/ *noun* **1** [C] something which controls what you do by keeping you within particular limits: *The constraints of politeness wouldn't allow her to say what she really thought about his cooking.* ○ *Financial constraints on the company are preventing them from employing new staff.* **2** [U] FORMAL unnatural behaviour which is sometimes the result of forcing yourself to act in a particular way: *She tried to appear friendly, but her constraint was obvious.*

● **under constraint** FORMAL If you do something under constraint, you do it only because you have been forced to: *They confessed, but only under severe constraint.*

constrain /kən'streɪn/ *verb* [T often passive] to control and limit something: *The country's progress was constrained by a leader who refused to look forward.*

constrained /kən'streɪnd/ *adj* **1** **constrained to do** *sth* forced to do something against your will: *Don't feel constrained to do what he says – he's got no authority.* **2** describes behaviour that is forced and unnatural: *a constrained voice/manner*

constrict /kən'strɪkt/ *verb* **1** [I or T] to become tighter and narrower, or to make something become tighter and narrower: *He hated wearing a tie – he felt it constricted his breathing.* ○ *If you're going dancing, you don't want to wear anything that constricts your movements.* ○ *The drug causes the blood vessels to constrict.* **2** [T] to limit an action or behaviour: *Too many rules had constricted her lifestyle.*

constriction /kən'strɪk.ʃᵊn/ *noun* [C] *The constrictions* (= limitations) *of prison life were inhuman.* ○ *He felt a constriction* (= tight feeling) *in his chest.*

construct /kən'strʌkt/ *verb* [T] to build something or put together different parts to form something whole: *to construct a new bridge/building* ○ *The walls are constructed of concrete.* ○ *to construct a story/sentence/argument*

construct /'kɒn.strʌkt/ /'kɑːn-/ *noun* [C] FORMAL an idea or an imaginary situation: *His reputation as an eccentric is largely a media construct.*

construction /kən'strʌk.ʃᵊn/ *noun* **1** [U] the work of building or making something, especially buildings, bridges, etc: *She works **in** construction/in **the** construction **industry**.* ○ *The bridge is a marvellous work of engineering and construction.* ○ *This website is currently **under** construction* (= being created). ➲See also **construction** at **construe**. **2** [U] the particular type of structure, materials, etc. that something has: *The bridge is of lightweight construction.* **3** [C] a building: *What's that concrete and metal construction over there?* **4** [C] *SPECIALIZED* the way in which the words in a sentence or phrase are arranged: *The writer has used several complex grammatical constructions.* **5** *FORMAL* **put a construction on *sth*** to understand something in a particular way: *How can they put such a damning construction on a perfectly innocent phrase?* **constructor** /kən'strʌk.təʳ/ [US] /-t̬ɚ/ *noun* [C] *The firm produces kits for amateur car constructors.*

constructive /kən'strʌk.tɪv/ *adj* If advice, criticism or actions are constructive, they are useful and intended to help or improve something: *She criticised my writing, but in a way that was very constructive – I learned a lot from her.* ○ *If you don't have anything constructive to say, I'd rather you kept quiet.* **constructively** /kən'strʌk.tɪv.li/ *adv*

con,structive dis'missal *noun* [C or U] *MAINLY UK* actions taken by an employer that intentionally make working conditions for an employee difficult or unfair so that the employee feels forced to leave their job

construe /kən'struː/ *verb FORMAL* **construe *sth* as *sth*** to understand the meaning, especially of other people's actions and statements, in a particular way: *Any change in plan would be construed as indecision.* **construction** /kən'strʌk.ʃᵊn/ *noun* [C] *I don't want them to **put** the wrong construction **on** my actions.* ➲See also **construction** at **construct**.

consul /'kɒnt.sᵊl/ [US] /'kɑːnt-/ *noun* [C] an official chosen by a government to live in a foreign city, in order to take care of people from the official's own country who travel or live there, and to protect the trade interests of that government: *the British Consul*

consular /'kɒnt.sjʊ.ləʳ/ [US] /'kɑːnt.sjə.lɚ/ *adj* [before n] relating to a consul or a consulate: *the consular office*

consulate /'kɒn.sjʊ.lət/ [US] /'kɑːn.sjə-/ *noun* [C] the office where a consul works: *the Cuban consulate in Mexico city*

consult /kən'sʌlt/ *verb* **1** [T] to get information or advice from a person, book, etc. with special knowledge on a particular subject: *If the symptoms get worse, consult your doctor.* ○ *I'm not quite sure how to get there – I'd better consult a map.* **2** [I or T] to discuss something with someone before you make a decision: *Why didn't you consult me about this?* ○ *This afternoon the Prime Minister was consulting **with** his advisors and we are expecting an announcement shortly.*

consultancy /kən'sʌl.tᵊnt.si/ *noun* **1** [C] a company that gives specialist advice on a particular subject: *a management/financial/recruitment consultancy* **2** [U] the activity of giving advice on a particular subject

consultant /kən'sʌl.tᵊnt/ *noun* [C] **1** someone who advises people on a particular subject: *a management/financial/computer consultant* ○ *a firm of public relations consultants* **2** *UK* a **specialist** (= doctor with special training and knowledge in a particular area of medicine)

consultation /ˌkɒn.sʌl'teɪ.ʃᵊn/ [US] /ˌkɑːn-/ *noun* **1** [C] a meeting to discuss something or to get advice: *After consultations **with** our accountants, we've decided how to cut costs within the company.* **2** [U] when you discuss something with someone in order to get their advice or opinion about it: *He chose his study course **in** consultation **with** his parents and teachers.*

consultative /kən'sʌl.tə.tɪv/ [US] /-t̬ə.t̬ɪv/ *adj* A consultative group or document gives advice about something: *She works for the firm in a consultative capacity.* ○ *to set up a consultative committee*

consulting /kən'sʌl.tɪŋ/ [US] /-t̬ɪŋ/ *adj* [before n] giving advice on a particular subject: *a consulting lawyer/engineer*

con,sulting 'room *noun* [C] an office where a doctor talks to and examines patients

consume /kən'sjuːm/ [US] /-'suːm/ *verb* [T] **1** to use fuel, energy or time, especially in large amounts: *Our high living standards cause our present population to consume 25 percent of the world's oil.* **2** *FORMAL* to eat or drink, especially a lot of something: *He consumes vast quantities of chips with every meal.* **3** If a fire consumes something, it destroys it completely. **4 be consumed by/with *sth*** to have so much of a feeling that it affects everything you do: *He was consumed with jealousy.* ○ *As a teenager, I was consumed by passion for the boy next door.*

C

consumables /kən'sjuː.mə.bl̩z/ [US] /-suː-/ *plural noun* goods, especially food, or services which people buy regularly because they are quickly used and need to be replaced quite often: *At this hospital we use up bandages, disposable gloves and other consumables at an alarming rate.*

consumer /kən'sjuː.məʳ/ [US] /-'suː.mɚ/ *noun* [C] a person who buys goods or services for their own use: *The new telephone rates will affect all consumers including businesses.* ○ *consumer rights/advice*

consumerism /kən'sjuː.mə.rɪ.zᵊm/ [US] /-'suː.mɚ.ɪ-/ *noun* [U] **1** the state of advanced industrial society in which a lot of goods are bought and sold **2** *DISAPPROVING* when too much attention is given to buying and owning things: *He disliked Christmas and its **rampant** (= extreme) consumerism.*

consuming /kən'sjuː.mɪŋ/ [US] /-'suː-/ *adj* describes an emotion that is very strong: *Running is a consuming **passion** with him.*

consumption /kən'sʌmp.ʃᵊn/ *noun* [U] **1** the amount used or eaten: *As a nation, our consumption of junk food is horrifying.* ○ *We need to cut down on our fuel consumption by having fewer cars on the road.* ➲See also **consumption**. **2** when someone uses, eats, or drinks something: *The meat was clearly **unfit for human** consumption* (= not suitable for people to eat). ○ *These products are not for national consumption, but for export.* **3** when information, entertainment, etc. is intended for a particular group of people: *This memo is for **internal** consumption only.* ○ *The movie was not intended for **public** consumption.*

consumer durables /kən,sjuː.mə'djʊə.rə.bl̩z/ [US] /-ˌsuː.mɚ'dʊr.ə-/ *plural noun* goods that last a long time and are not intended to be bought very frequently, such as televisions and cars

con,sumer 'price ,index *noun* [C usually sing] (*ABBREVIATION* **CPI**) *US FOR* **retail price index**

con,sumer pro'tection *noun* [U] the protection of buyers of goods and services against low quality or dangerous products and advertisements that deceive people

con'sumer so,ciety *noun* [C] a society in which people frequently buy new goods, especially goods which are not essential, and which places a high value on owning many things

consummate [COMPLETE] /'kɒn.sə.mət/ [US] /'kɑːn-/ *adj* [before n] *FORMAL* perfect, or complete in every way: *a life of consummate happiness* ○ *He's a consummate athlete/gentleman/liar.*

consummate /'kɒn.sjʊ.meɪt/ [US] /'kɑːn.sə-/ *verb* [T] *FORMAL* to make something complete or perfect **consummation** /ˌkɒn.sjʊ'meɪ.ʃᵊn/ [US] /ˌkɑːn.sə-/ *noun* [U]

consummate [HAVE SEX] /'kɒn.sjʊ.meɪt/ [US] /'kɑːn.sə-/ *verb* [T] *LEGAL* to make a marriage or romantic relationship complete by having sex: *The marriage was never consummated.* **consummation** /ˌkɒn.sjʊ'meɪ.ʃᵊn/ [US] /ˌkɑːn.sə-/ *noun* [U]

consumption /kən'sʌmp.ʃᵊn/ *noun* [U] *OLD-FASHIONED FOR* **tuberculosis** (= a serious disease of the lungs) ➲See also **consumption** at **consume**. **consumptive** /kən'sʌmp.tɪv/ *adj, noun* [C] *OLD-FASHIONED She didn't live very long – she was (a) consumptive.*

cont. /kən'tɪn.juːd/ *adj* (*ALSO* **contd**) *WRITTEN ABBREVIATION FOR* **continued** ➲See at **continue**.

contact [COMMUNICATION] /'kɒn.tækt/ [US] /'kɑːn-/ *noun* [U] communication with someone, especially by speaking

[C]

or writing to them regularly: *"Have you been* ***in*** *contact* ***with*** *Andrew recently?" "Only by telephone."* ○ *I'm still* ***in*** *contact* ***with*** *her – we write a couple of times a year.* ○ *There isn't enough contact* ***between*** *teachers and parents.* ○ *I've been busy at home and have hardly* ***had*** *any contact* ***with*** *the outside world.* ○ *I'd hate to* ***lose*** *contact* ***with*** *my old school friends.* ○ *She finally* ***made*** *contact* ***with*** *him in Italy.* ○ *Air traffic control* ***lost*** *radio contact* ***with*** *the pilot of the aircraft ten minutes before the accident.* ○ *The school likes to have a contact* ***number*** (= telephone number, esp. for emergencies) *for parents during school hours.*

contact /ˈkɒn.tækt/ [US] /ˈkɑːn-/ *verb* [T] to communicate with someone by telephoning them or sending them a letter, email, etc: *I tried to contact him at his office, but he wasn't in.* ○ *You can contact me* (UK) ***on***/(US) ***at*** (= speak to me by telephoning) *388 9146.* ○ *Unless the money is returned, we shall shortly be contacting our legal department.* **contactable** /kənˈtæk.tə.bl̩/ *adj*: *Is he contactable at his home number?*

COMMON LEARNER ERROR

contact with

Remember to use the preposition 'with' when you use the phrases 'make/be in/keep in/lose contact with' someone.

When you live abroad it's important not to lose contact with friends and family at home.
~~*When you live abroad it's important not to lose contact to friends and family at home.*~~

contact [TOUCH] /ˈkɒn.tækt/ [US] /ˈkɑːn-/ *noun* [U] when two people or things touch each other: *Don't let that glue* ***come into*** *contact* ***with*** *your skin.* ○ *Have you been* ***in*** *contact* ***with*** (= touched or been very near) *anyone with the disease?* ○ *He hates* ***physical*** *contact of any sort – he doesn't even like to shake your hand.*

contact [PERSON] /ˈkɒn.tækt/ [US] /ˈkɑːn-/ *noun* [C] a person, especially in a high position, who can give you useful information or introductions which will help you at work or socially: *I don't really know how she got the job, but I suspect her mother's got contacts.* ○ *If you need more stationery, I've got a good contact in a local printing firm.* ○ *We're* ***building up*** (= increasing the number of) *our contacts in the business.*

contact [ELECTRICITY] /ˈkɒn.tækt/ [US] /ˈkɑːn-/ *noun* [C] a part in a circuit which completes the circuit when it touches another part

ˌcontact ˈlens *noun* [C] a small round curved piece of transparent plastic which is worn on the surface of your eye to improve your sight: *I usually wear contact lenses, but I sometimes wear glasses when my eyes are tired.*

ˌcontact ˈsport *noun* [C] a sport such as rugby and American football in which players are allowed to touch each other when, for example, they are trying to get the ball

contagious /kənˈteɪ.dʒəs/ *adj* **1** describes a disease that can be caught by touching someone with the disease or a piece of infected clothing: *The infection is* ***highly*** *contagious, so don't let anyone else use your towel.* **2** describes someone who has a contagious disease: *Keep him off school till he stops being contagious.* **3** A contagious feeling spreads quickly among people: *Fear is contagious.*

contagion /kənˈteɪ.dʒən/ *noun* [U] FORMAL when a disease is spread by touching someone or something: *The doctor says there's no chance/danger of contagion.*

contain [HOLD] /kənˈteɪn/ *verb* [T not continuous] to have something inside or include something as a part: *How much liquid do you think this bottle contains?* ○ *I've lost a file containing a lot of important documents.* ○ *Try to avoid foods which contain a lot of fat.* ○ *The allegations contained* ***in*** *this report are very serious.*

container /kənˈteɪ.nəʳ/ [US] /-nɚ/ *noun* [C] **1** a hollow object, such as a box or a bottle, which can be used for holding something, especially to carry or store it: *an airtight container* ○ *a plastic drinks container* **2** SPECIALIZED a very large metal box used for transporting goods: *a container ship/lorry*

containerize, UK USUALLY **-ise** /kənˈteɪ.nəʳ.aɪz/ [US] /-nə.raɪz/ *verb* [T] to put goods in a large metal box for transport, or to make a port, ship, etc. suitable for this method of transport: *containerized goods*

COMMON LEARNER ERROR

contain or include?

Use **contain** to talk about objects which have something else inside them.

This folder contains important letters.
This soup contains garlic and onions.

Use **include** to say that something or someone is a part of something else but that there are other parts as well.

The team includes two new players.
The price of the ticket includes insurance and tax.

contain [CONTROL] /kənˈteɪn/ *verb* **1** [T not continuous] to keep something harmful within limits and not allow it to spread: *Farms in the area have been closed off in an attempt to contain the disease.* ○ *More police were sent to help contain the violence.* **2** [T often in negatives] to control or hide a strong emotion, such as excitement or anger: *She could no longer contain her anger and shouted at him uncontrollably.* ○ HUMOROUS *Contain yourself! It's not that exciting.*

containment /kənˈteɪn.mənt/ *noun* [U] **1** SPECIALIZED when something or someone harmful is controlled and limited: *Containment of crowd violence was the police's main concern.* **2** an attempt to keep another country's political power within limits without having a war with them: *The government is pursuing a policy of containment.*

contaminate /kənˈtæm.ɪ.neɪt/ *verb* [T] to spoil the purity of something or make it poisonous: *Much of the coast has been contaminated by nuclear waste.* ○ *The food which had been contaminated was destroyed.*

contaminant /kənˈtæm.ɪ.nənt/ *noun* [C] SPECIALIZED a substance that spoils the purity of something or makes it poisonous: *Make sure that all equipment is clean and free of contaminants.* **contaminated** /kənˈtæm.ɪ.neɪ.tɪd/ [US] /-t̬ɪd/ *adj*: *The infection was probably caused by swimming in contaminated water/water contaminated* ***with*** *sewage.*

contamination /kənˌtæm.ɪˈneɪ.ʃən/ *noun* [U] *The water supply is being tested for contamination* (= the presence of unwanted or dangerous substances).

contd /kənˈtɪn.juːd/ *adj* (ALSO **cont.**) WRITTEN ABBREVIATION FOR **continued** ➲See at **continue**.

contemplate /ˈkɒn.təm.pleɪt/ [US] /ˈkɑːn.t̬əm-/ *verb* [I or T] to spend time considering a possible future action, or to consider one particular thing for a long time in a serious and quiet way: [+ v-ing] *I'm contemplating going abroad for a year.* ○ *You're not contemplating a change of job, are you?* ○ *It's* ***too*** *awful/horrific/dangerous* ***to*** *contemplate.* **contemplation** /ˌkɒn.təmˈpleɪ.ʃən/ [US] /ˌkɑːn.t̬əm-/ *noun* [U] *She was staring out over the lake,* ***lost in*** *contemplation.* ○ *The nuns have an hour for silent contemplation every morning.* **contemplative** /kənˈtem.plə.tɪv/ [US] /-t̬ɪv/ *adj*: *Her mood was calm and contemplative.* **contemplatively** /kənˈtem.plə.tɪv.li/ [US] /-t̬ɪv-/ *adv*

contemporaneous /kənˌtem.pəˈreɪ.ni.əs/ *adj* FORMAL happening or existing at the same period of time: *The two events were more or less contemporaneous, with only months between them.* **contemporaneously** /kənˌtem.pəˈreɪ.ni.ə.sli/ *adv*

contemporary [EXISTING NOW] /kənˈtem.pəʳ.əʳ.i/ [US] /-pə.rer-/ *adj* existing or happening now: *contemporary music/literature/art/fashion* ○ *Although it was written hundreds of years ago, it still has a contemporary* (= modern) *feel to it.*

contemporary [OF SAME PERIOD] /kənˈtem.pəʳ.əʳ.i/ [US] /-pə.rer-/ *adj* belonging to the same or a stated period in the past: *Almost all of the contemporary accounts of the event have been lost.* ○ *Most of the writers he was contemporary* ***with*** *were interested in the same subjects.*

contemporary /kənˈtem.pəʳ.əʳ.i/ [US] /-pə.rer-/ *noun* [C] **1** someone living during the same period as someone else:

Was he a contemporary of Shakespeare's? **2** a person who is of the same age as you: *She didn't mix with her contemporaries, prefering the company of older people.*

contempt [DISRESPECT] /kən'tempt/ *noun* [U] a strong feeling of combined dislike and lack of respect: *At school she had complete contempt **for** all her teachers.* ○ *You should **treat** those remarks **with** the contempt that they deserve.* ○ *She's **beneath** contempt* (= I have no respect for her)*!*

• **hold *sb/sth* in contempt** to feel contempt for someone or something

contemptible /kən'temp.tɪ.bl̩/ *adj* deserving contempt: *Her behaviour was contemptible.* **contemptibly** /kən'temp.tɪ.bli/ *adv*

contemptuous /kən'temp.tju.əs/ *adj* expressing contempt: *a contemptuous manner/laugh* ○ *He was very contemptuous **of** 'popular' writers, whom he described as having no talent.* **contemptuously** /kən'temp.tju.ə.sli/ *adv*: *The waiter smiled contemptuously at anyone who didn't know which wine to order.*

con,tempt (of 'court) [DISOBEYING] /kən'tempt/ *noun* [U] *LEGAL* behaviour that is illegal because it does not obey or respect the rules of a law court: *The tobacco companies may be guilty of contempt of court for refusing to produce the documents.*

contend [COMPETE] /kən'tend/ *verb* [I] to compete in order to win something: *There are three world-class tennis players contending **for** this title.* ○ *He's contending **against** someone with twice his experience.*

contender /kən'ten.də^{r}/ [US] /-dɚ/ *noun* [C] someone who competes with other people to try to win something: *Now aged 42, he is no longer considered a serious contender **for** the title.*

contention /kən'ten.tʃ^{ə}n/ **be in/out of contention for *sth*** to be able/not able to achieve or win something, especially in sport: *This decisive defeat puts them out of contention for this year's championship finals.* ➲See also **contention** DISAGREEMENT, **contention** OPINION.

contend [CLAIM] /kən'tend/ *verb* [T + (*that*)] *FORMAL* to state something is true or is a fact: *The lawyer contended **(that)** her client had never been near the scene of the crime.*

▲ **contend with *sth*** *phrasal verb* to have to deal with a difficult or unpleasant situation: *At the age of nine, he had the death of both parents to contend with.* ○ *We don't need a computer failure to contend with as well as all our other problems.*

content [HAPPY] /kən'tent/ *adj* [after v] pleased with your situation and not hoping for change or improvement: *He seems fairly content **with** (his) life.* ○ [+ **to** infinitive] *They're content **to** socialize with a very small circle of people.*

• **not content with *sth/doing sth*** *MAINLY HUMOROUS* in addition to something wrong or unpleasant you have done: *Not content with having upset my parents, he then insulted my sister!*

content /kən'tent/ *verb* [T] to make someone content: *You're quite easily contented, aren't you?* ○ *My explanation seemed to content him.*

contented /kən'ten.tɪd/ [US] /-t̬ɪd/ *adj*: *She smiled a contented **smile**.* ○ *He won't be contented* (= satisfied) *until he's upset everyone in the office.* **contentedly** /kən'ten.tɪd.li/ [US] /-t̬ɪd-/ *adv*: *Finishing her meal, she sat back and sighed contentedly.* **contentment** /kən'tent.mənt/ *noun* [U] (*ALSO* **content**) *His face wore a look of pure contentment.*

content [SUBJECT] /'kɒn.tent/ [US] /'kɑːn-/ *noun* [S or U] the ideas that are contained in a piece of writing, a speech or a film: *It's a very stylish and beautiful film, but it lacks content.* ○ *We've discussed the unusual form of the book – now, what about the content?*

content [AMOUNT] /'kɒn.tent/ [US] /'kɑːn-/ *noun* [S] the amount of a particular substance contained in something: *Chocolate has a **high** fat content.* ➲See also **contents**.

▲ **content *yourself* with *sth*** *phrasal verb* to do something or have something although it is not exactly what you want: *I wanted to take two weeks' holiday, but had to content myself with one because the office was so busy.*

contention [DISAGREEMENT] /kən'tent.ʃ^{ə}n/ *noun* [U] the disagreement that results from opposing arguments: *There's a lot of contention about that issue – for every person firmly in favour, there's someone fiercely against it.* ○ *The matter has been settled – it's no longer **in** contention.* ➲See also **contention** at **contend** COMPETE.

contentious /kən'ten.ʃəs/ *adj* causing or likely to cause disagreement: *a contentious decision/policy/issue/subject* ○ *She has some rather contentious **views** on education.* **contentiousness** /kən'ten.ʃə.snəs/ *noun* [U]

contention [OPINION] /kən'tent.ʃ^{ə}n/ *noun* [C] *SLIGHTLY FORMAL* an opinion expressed in an argument: [+ *that*] *It is her contention **that** exercise is more important than diet if you want to lose weight.* ➲See also **contention** at **contend** COMPETE.

contents /'kɒn.tents/ [US] /'kɑːn-/ *plural noun* **1** everything that is contained within something: *The contents **of** his bag spilled all over the floor.* ○ *He hardly needed to open the letter because he already knew the contents.* **2** the list of items or parts contained in a magazine or book, with the number of the page they begin on

contest [COMPETITION] /'kɒn.test/ [US] /'kɑːn-/ *noun* [C] a competition to do better than other people, usually in which prizes are given: *a dance/sports contest* ○ *She's won a lot of **beauty** contests.*

contest /kən'test/ *verb* [T] to compete for something: *The medal is being keenly contested by eight gymnasts.*

contestant /kən'tes.t^{ə}nt/ [US] /-t̬^{ə}nt/ *noun* [C] someone who competes in a contest: *In tonight's quiz, our contestants have come from all over the country.*

contest [ATTEMPT] /'kɒn.test/ [US] /'kɑːn-/ *noun* [C] an attempt, usually against difficulties, to win an election or to get power or control: *The contest **for** deputy leadership of the party is gathering speed.*

contest /kən'test/ *verb* [T] to attempt to win an election or to get power or control: *She stands a good chance, since only two people are contesting the seat and the other candidate is very unpopular.*

contestant /kən'tes.t^{ə}nt/ *noun* [C] someone who attempts to win an election or get power or control: *Two main candidates are emerging as contestants **for** the presidency.*

contest [ARGUE] /kən'test/ *verb* [T] If you contest a formal statement, a claim, a judge's decision, or a legal case, you say formally that it is wrong or unfair and try to have it changed: *We will certainly contest any claims made against the safety of our products.*

context [CAUSE OF EVENT] /'kɒn.tekst/ [US] /'kɑːn-/ *noun* [C] the situation within which something exists or happens, and that can help explain it: *It is important to see all the fighting and bloodshed in his plays **in** historical context.* ○ *This small battle is very important **in the** context **of** Scottish history.*

contextual /kən'tek.stju.əl/ *adj FORMAL* related to the context **contextually** /kən'tek.stju.ə.li/ *adv*

contextualize, *UK USUALLY* **-ise** /kən'tek.stju.ə.laɪz/ *verb* [T] *FORMAL* to consider something in its context: *We must contextualize the problem before we can understand its origin.*

context [TEXT/SPEECH] /'kɒn.tekst/ [US] /'kɑːn-/ *noun* [C] the text or speech that comes immediately before and after a particular phrase or piece of text and helps to explain its meaning: *In this exercise, a word is blanked out and you have to guess what it is by looking at the context.*

• **out of context** If words are used out of context, only a small separate part of what was originally said or written is reported, which causes their meaning to be unclear or not understood: *The papers took my remarks completely out of context.*

contextual /kən'tek.stjʊəl/ *adj SPECIALIZED* related to the context: *It's impossible to understand the nuances of an isolated word without some contextual clues.* **contextually** /kən'tek.stjʊə.li/ *adv*

contextualize, *UK USUALLY* **-ise** /kən'tek.stjʊə.laɪz/ *verb* [T] *SPECIALIZED* to consider in context

contiguous /kən'tɪg.ju.əs/ *adj FORMAL* next to or touching another, usually similar, thing: *The two states are contiguous **with/to** each other, but the laws are quite different.* **contiguity** /ˌkɒn.tɪ'gjuː.ɪ.ti/ [US] /ˌkɑːn.t̬ə'gjuː.ə.t̬i/ *noun* [U]

continent LAND /ˈkɒn.tɪ.nənt/ US /ˈkɑːn.t̬ᵊn.ənt/ *noun* [C] one of the seven large land masses on the Earth's surface, surrounded, or mainly surrounded, by sea and usually consisting of various countries: *the North American continent* ○ *Asia and Africa are the two biggest continents.* **continental** /ˌkɒn.tɪˈnen.t̬ᵊl/ US /ˌkɑːn.t̬ᵊnˈen.-t̬ᵊl/ *adj: continental waters*

the ˈContinent EUROPE *noun* [S] MAINLY UK Europe, especially western Europe but not including the British Isles: *He found driving **on** the Continent very different to Britain.* **Continental, continental** /ˌkɒn.tɪˈnen.t̬ᵊl/ US /ˌkɑːn.t̬ᵊnˈen.t̬ᵊl/ *adj: She preferred the continental way of life.*
Continental, continental /ˌkɒn.tɪˈnen.t̬ᵊl/ US /ˌkɑːn.t̬ᵊn-ˈen.t̬ᵊl/ *noun* [C] MAINLY UK OLD-FASHIONED someone who comes from Europe but not the British Isles

continent CONTROL /ˈkɒn.tɪ.nənt/ US /ˈkɑːn.t̬ᵊn.ənt/ *adj* **1** SPECIALIZED able to control when you urinate and empty your bowels ＊ NOTE: The opposite is **incontinent**. **2** OLD USE able to control your sexual desires **continence** /ˈkɒn.tɪ.nənts/ US /ˈkɑːn.t̬ᵊn.ənts/ *noun* [U]

ˌcontinental ˈbreakfast *noun* [C] a simple morning meal consisting of fruit juice, coffee, and bread with butter and jam

ˌcontinental ˈdrift *noun* [U] SPECIALIZED the very slow movement of continents over the Earth's surface

ˌcontinental ˈquilt *noun* [C] UK OLD-FASHIONED a **duvet**

ˌcontinental ˈshelf *noun* [C usually sing] SPECIALIZED the area of the bottom of the sea near the coast of a continent, where the sea is not very deep

contingency /kənˈtɪn.dʒᵊnt.si/ *noun* [C] FORMAL something that might possibly happen in the future, usually causing problems or making further arrangements necessary: *You must be able to deal with all possible contingencies.* ○ *Have you made any contingency **plans**?*

contingent GROUP /kənˈtɪn.dʒᵊnt/ *group noun* [C] a group of people representing an organization or country, or a part of a military force: *The French contingent certainly made their presence known at this year's conference.* ○ *a large contingent of voluntary soldiers*

contingent DEPENDING /kənˈtɪn.dʒᵊnt/ *adj* FORMAL **contingent on/upon** *sth* depending on something else in the future in order to happen: *Outdoor arrangements are, as ever, contingent on the weather and we have other plans in the event of rain.* ○ *Our success is contingent upon your support.*

continue /kənˈtɪn.juː/ *verb* **1** [I or T] to keep happening, existing or doing something, or to cause something or someone to do this: [+ *to* infinitive] *It's said that as the boat went down the band continued **to** play.* ○ [+ *v-ing*] *If she continues drink**ing** like that, I'll have to carry her home.* ○ *Do you intend to continue **(with)** your studies?* ○ *If the rain continues, we'll have to cancel tonight's plans.* ○ *Sally Palmer will be continuing **as** chairperson this autumn.* ○ *The article continues/is continued **on** page ten.* **2** [I] to start to do something again after a pause: *After stopping for a quick drink, they continued **on** their way.* ○ [+ *v-ing*] *He paused for a moment to listen and then continued eat**ing**.* ○ *The president continued **by** saying that his country was a free country and would always remain so.* ○ [+ speech] *"I don't like your weather!" she shouted, "and I don't like your food."*
continual /kənˈtɪn.ju.əl/ *adj* happening repeatedly, usually in an annoying or inconvenient way: *I've had continual **problems** with this car ever since I bought it.* ○ *I'm sorry – I can't work with these continual interruptions.* **continually** /kənˈtɪn.ju.ə.li/ *adv: They argue continually.*
continuous /kənˈtɪn.ju.əs/ *adj* without a pause or interruption: *continuous pain* ○ *My computer makes a continuous low buzzing noise.* ○ *A continuous white line* (= line without spaces) *in the middle of the road means no overtaking.* **continuously** /kənˈtɪn.ju.ə.sli/ *adv: You can't work continuously for six hours without a break!* **continuation** /kənˌtɪn.juˈeɪ.ʃᵊn/ *noun* [C or U] (FORMAL **continuance**) *The continuation of the strike caused a lot of poverty.* ○ *It's just a continuation of the bigger river, but called by a different name.*

continued /kənˈtɪn.juːd/ *adj* **1** [before n] (ALSO **continuing**) still happening, existing or done: *Continued fighting in the city is causing great concern.* **2** (WRITTEN ABBREVIATION **cont.**) often used at the bottom of a page to show that the story, article, etc., is not finished: *continued on page 7*

continuity /ˌkɒn.tɪˈnjuː.ɪ.ti/ US /ˌkɑːn.t̬ᵊnˈuː.ə.t̬i/ *noun* [U] **1** when something continues for a long period of time without being changed or stopped: *There has been no continuity in that class – they've had a succession of different teachers.* **2** SPECIALIZED the way in which film and television broadcasts are joined together so that the action happens without any pause or change

conˌtinuous asˈsessment *noun* [U] the system in which the quality of a student's work is judged by various pieces of course work and not by one final examination

continuum /kənˈtɪn.ju.əm/ *noun* [C] *plural* **continua** or **continuums** SPECIALIZED something that changes in character gradually or in very slight stages without any clear dividing points: *It's not 'left-wing or right-wing' - political opinion is a long continuum.*

contort /kənˈtɔːt/ US /-ˈtɔːrt/ *verb* [I or T] to (cause something to) twist or bend violently and unnaturally into a different shape or form: *His face contorted **with** bitterness and rage.* **contorted** /kənˈtɔː.tɪd/ US /-ˈtɔːr.t̬ɪd/ *adj: contorted limbs/branches* **contortion** /kənˈtɔː.ʃᵊn/ US /-ˈtɔːr-/ *noun* [C or U] *facial/bodily contortions*
contortionist /kənˈtɔː.ʃᵊn.ɪst/ US /-ˈtɔːr-/ *noun* [C] someone who can twist their body into shapes and positions that ordinary people cannot

contour /ˈkɒn.tɔːr/ US /-ˈkɑːn.tʊr/ *noun* [C] the shape of a mass of land or other object, especially its surface or the shape formed by its outer edge: *the rugged contour of the coast* ○ *He studied the contours of her face.* ○ *Her latest collection of swimwear shows off the contours of the human body to perfection.*

ˈcontour (ˌline) *noun* [C] SPECIALIZED a line on a map that joins points of equal height or depth, in a way that shows high and low areas of land: *a 400 ft contour line* ○ *This map has contours marked at 250m intervals.*

contraband /ˈkɒn.trə.bænd/ US /ˈkɑːn-/ *noun* [U] goods which are brought into or taken out of the country secretly and illegally: *The lorry contained thousands of pounds worth of contraband.* **contraband** /ˈkɒn.trə.bænd/ US /ˈkɑːn-/ *adj: contraband cigarettes/goods*

contraception /ˌkɒn.trəˈsep.ʃᵊn/ US /ˌkɑːn-/ *noun* [U] (the use of) any of various methods intended to prevent a woman becoming pregnant: *They offer impartial advice on contraception.* ○ *What is the most reliable **form/method** of contraception?*
contraceptive /ˌkɒn.trəˈsep.tɪv/ US /ˌkɑːn-/ *noun* [C] any of various devices or drugs intended to prevent pregnancy: *The clinic provides a free supply of contraceptives on request.* **contraceptive** /ˌkɒn.trəˈsep.tɪv/ US /ˌkɑːn-/ *adj: a contraceptive device/pill*

contract AGREEMENT /ˈkɒn.trækt/ US /ˈkɑːn-/ *noun* [C] a legal document that states and explains a formal agreement between two different people or groups, or the agreement itself: *a contract of employment* ○ *a temporary/building contract* ○ *They could take legal action against you if you **break (the terms of)** the contract.* ○ *My solicitor is **drawing up** (= writing) a contract.* ○ *Don't **sign/enter into** any contract before examining its conditions carefully.* ○ [+ *to* infinitive] *They're the firm of architects who **won** the contract **to** design the National Museum extension.*
● **be under contract** to have formally agreed to work for a company or person on a stated job for a stated period of time
contract /kənˈtrækt/ *verb* [I or T] to make a legal agreement with someone to do work or to have work done for you: [+ *to* infinitive] *They have just contracted our company **to** build shelters for the homeless.* **contractual** /kən-ˈtræk.tju.ᵊl/ *adj: contractual conditions/terms* ○ *Are you **under a** contractual **obligation** to any other company?* **contractually** /kənˈtræk.tju.ᵊl.i/ *adv: They are contractually **bound/obliged** to finish the work.*

contract [SHORTEN] /kən'trækt/ *verb* [I or T] to make or become shorter or narrower or generally smaller: *In spoken English, 'do not' often contracts **to** 'don't.'* ○ *As it cooled, the metal contracted.*
contractile /kən'træk.taɪl/ [US] /-t̬əl/ *adj* SPECIALIZED describes body tissue that is able to contract, or something that causes this to happen
contraction /kən'træk.ʃən/ *noun* **1** [U] when something becomes smaller or shorter: *Cold causes contraction of the metal.* ○ *The contraction of this muscle raises the lower arm.* **2** [C] one of the very strong and usually painful movements of the muscles in the womb that help to push the baby out of the mother's body during the process of birth: *She was **having** regular strong contractions every four minutes.* **3** [C] a shortened form of a word or combination of words which is often used instead of the full form in spoken English: *'Won't' is a contraction of 'will not'.*

contract [BECOME ILL] /kən'trækt/ *verb* [T] SLIGHTLY FORMAL to catch, or become ill with, a disease: *He contracted malaria while he was travelling.*

PHRASAL VERBS WITH **contract** ▼

▲ **contract in/out** *phrasal verb* UK to formally agree to take part/stop taking part in an official plan or system: *Have you contracted in **to** the pension scheme?*
▲ **contract *sth* out** *phrasal verb* [M] to formally arrange for other people to do a particular job: *The government contracted out hospital cleaning **to** private companies.*

contractor /kən'træk.təʳ/ [US] /'kɑːn.træk.tɚ/ *noun* [C] a person or company that arranges to supply materials or workers, for building or for moving goods

contradict /ˌkɒn.trə'dɪkt/ [US] /ˌkɑːn-/ *verb* [I or T] (of people) to state the opposite of what someone else has said, or (of one fact or statement) to be so different from another fact or statement that one of them must be wrong: *If you're both going to lie, at least stick to the same story and don't contradict each other!* ○ [R] *He kept contradicting him**self** when we were arguing – I think he was a bit confused.* ○ *How dare you contradict (me)!* ○ *Recent evidence has tended to contradict established theories on this subject.* **contradiction** /ˌkɒn.trə'dɪk.ʃən/ [US] /ˌkɑːn-/ *noun* [C or U] *You say that you're good friends and yet you don't trust him. Isn't that a bit of a contradiction?*
• **a contradiction in terms** a combination of words which is nonsense because some of the words suggest the opposite of some of the others: *Many people think that an honest politician is a contradiction in terms.*
contradictory /ˌkɒn.trə'dɪk.tər.i/ [US] /ˌkɑːn.trə'dɪk.tɚ-/ *adj* If two or more facts, pieces of advice, etc. are contradictory, they are very different from each other: *I keep getting contradictory advice – some people tell me to keep it warm and some tell me to put ice on it.*

contraflow /'kɒn.trə.fləʊ/ [US] /'kɑːn.trə.floʊ/ *noun* [C] MAINLY UK a temporary traffic arrangement, usually on a motorway, in which traffic travelling in both directions uses one side of the road while the other side is being repaired: *A contraflow is **in operation/in force** between junctions 13 and 14 on the motorway.*

contraindication /ˌkɒn.trəˌɪn.dɪ'keɪ.ʃən/ [US] /ˌkɑːn-/ *noun* [C] SPECIALIZED a sign that someone should not continue with a particular medicine or treatment because it is or might be harmful

contralto /kən'træl.təʊ/ [US] /-t̬oʊ/ *noun* [C] *plural* **contraltos** or **contralti** a woman singer with the lowest female singing voice, or this type of voice

contraption /kən'træp.ʃən/ *noun* [C] a device or machine that looks awkward or old-fashioned, especially one that you do not know how to use: *Whatever's that **strange** contraption you've got in the garage?*

contrapuntal /ˌkɒn.trə'pʌn.təl/ [US] /ˌkɑːn.trə'pʌn.t̬əl/ *adj* SPECIALIZED describes music in which two or more separate tunes happen at the same time

the 'contrary [OPPOSITE] *noun* [S] the opposite: *I was worried that it might be too difficult for me but I found the contrary.*
• **on the contrary** used to show that you think or feel the opposite of what has just been stated: *"Didn't you find the film exciting?" "On the contrary, I nearly fell asleep half way through it!"*
• **to the contrary** saying or showing the opposite: *For a long time it was thought to be a harmless substance, but we now have **proof/evidence** to the contrary.*
contrary /'kɒn.trə.ri/ [US] /'kɑːn.trɚ-/ *adj* opposite: *a contrary point of view* ○ *Contrary **to** all our expectations, he's found a well-paid job and a nice girlfriend.*
• **contrary to popular opinion** in a different way from what most people believe: *Contrary to popular opinion, I don't dye my hair!*

contrary [UNREASONABLE] /kən'treə.ri/ [US] /-'trer.i/ *adj* describes a person who intentionally wants to disagree with and annoy other people: *He doesn't really mean it – he's just being contrary.* **contrariness** /kən'treə.ri.nəs/ [US] /-'trer.i-/ *noun* [U]

contrast /'kɒn.trɑːst/ [US] /'kɑːn.træst/ *noun* [C or U] an obvious difference between two or more things: *I like the contrast **of** the white trousers **with** the black jacket.* ○ *The antique furnishing provides an unusual contrast **to** the modernity of the building.* ○ *There's a **marked** contrast **between** his character **and** hers.* ○ *Their economy has expanded enormously, while ours, **by/in** contrast, has declined.* ○ *The amount spent on defence is **in stark/sharp*** (= in very noticeable) *contrast **to** that spent on housing and health.* ○ *I love his use of contrast* (= strong differences between light and darkness) *in his later photographs.*
contrast /kən'trɑːst/ [US] /-træst/ *verb* **1** [T] to compare two people or things in order to show the differences between them: *If you contrast some of her early writing **with** her later work, you can see just how much she improved.* **2** [I] If one thing contrasts with another, it is very different from it: *The styles of the two film makers contrast quite dramatically.* ○ *The sharpness of the lemons contrasts **with** the sweetness of the honey.*
contrasting /kən'trɑː.stɪŋ/ [US] /-'træs.tɪŋ/ *adj* very different: *contrasting colours/flavours* ○ *the contrasting attitudes of different age-groups*

contravene /ˌkɒn.trə'viːn/ [US] /ˌkɑːn-/ *verb* [T] FORMAL to do something that a law or rule does not permit, or to break a law or rule: *This contravenes the Race Relations Act.* **contravention** /ˌkɒn.trə'ven.tʃən/ [US] /ˌkɑːn-/ *noun* [C or U] *By accepting the money, she was **in** contravention **of** company regulations.*

contretemps /'kɒn.trə.tɒ̃/ [US] /'kɑːn.trə.tɑ̃ː/ *noun* [C] *plural* **contretemps** a small argument or unlucky event, often happening in public and causing social embarrassment: *There was a slight contretemps **between** Richard and some bloke at the bar.* ○ *Have you got over your little contretemps **with** the neighbour yet, or are you still not speaking?*

contribute /kən'trɪb.juːt/ /'kɒn.trɪ.bjuːt/ [US] /'kɑːn-/ *verb* [I or T] **1** to give something, especially money, in order to provide or achieve something together with other people: *Aren't you going to contribute **towards** Jack's leaving present?* ○ *Come to the meeting if you feel you have something to contribute.* ○ *Her family have contributed £50,000 **to** the fund.* **2** to write articles for a newspaper, magazine or book: *She contributes **to** several magazines.*
contributor /kən'trɪb.jʊ.təʳ/ [US] /-jə.t̬ɚ/ *noun* [C] **1** a person who gives something, especially money, in order to provide or achieve something together with other people: *At the back of the programme, there is a list of contributors **to** the theatre appeal.* **2** someone who writes articles for a newspaper, magazine or book
contribution /ˌkɒn.trɪ'bjuː.ʃən/ [US] /ˌkɑːn-/ *noun* [C or U] something that you do or give to help produce or achieve something together with other people, or to help make something successful: *All contributions* (= presents of money), *no matter how small, will be much appreciated.* ○ *All contributions* (= articles to be printed) ***for** the school magazine must be received by August 1st.* ○ *This invention **made a** major contribution **to** road safety.* ○ *She didn't **make** much of **a** contribution* (= She did not say much) *at today's meeting, did she?*
contributory /kən'trɪb.jʊ.tri/ [US] /-jə.tɔːr.i/ *adj* **1** describes something that you contribute to: *The company offers a contributory* (UK) ***pension scheme**/*(US)

pension plan (= one to which both the employee and employer contribute). ✳ NOTE: The opposite is **non-contributory**. **2** helping to cause something: *Too little exercise is a contributory **factor** in heart disease.*
▲ **contribute to** *sth phrasal verb* to help to cause an event or situation: *Smoking certainly contributed to his early death.*

con,tributory 'negligence *noun* [U] *UK LEGAL* when it is decided in court that a person who has been hurt in an accident was partly responsible for their own injuries because they failed to act in a way that could have prevented the accident or the injuries

contrite /'kɒn.traɪt/ ⓤ /'kɑːn-/ *adj FORMAL* feeling great regret and guilt for something bad that you have done: *a contrite apology/expression* **contritely** /kən'traɪt.li/ *adv* **contrition** /kən'trɪʃ.ᵊn/ *noun* [U]

contrive /kən'traɪv/ *verb* [T] **1** to arrange a situation or event, or arrange for something to happen, using clever planning: *Couldn't you contrive a meeting between them? I think they'd be ideally suited.* ○ [+ to infinitive] *Somehow she contrived **to** get tickets for the concert.* **2** to invent and/or make a device or other object in a clever and possibly unusual way: *Do you think you could contrive something for hanging my clothes on until I can get a wardrobe?*
contrivance /kən'traɪ.vᵊnts/ *noun* [C or U] *FORMAL* when someone contrives something: *DISAPPROVING Because of the timing, I'm sure the salary freeze is a deliberate contrivance, not a coincidence.* ○ *I think the meeting happened more by contrivance than chance.*
contrived /kən'traɪvd/ *adj DISAPPROVING* **1** clever rather than honest: *His excuse sounded a bit contrived.* **2** artificial and difficult to believe: *I enjoyed the film, but felt the ending was a bit contrived.*

control /kən'trəʊl/ ⓤ /-'troʊl/ *verb* [T] -ll- to order, limit, instruct or rule something, or someone's actions or behaviour: *If you can't control your dog, put it on a lead!* ○ *You're going to have to learn to control your temper.* ○ *The temperature is controlled by a thermostat.* ○ *The laws controlling drugs are very strict in this country.* ○ *The government is trying to control spending.*
control /kən'trəʊl/ ⓤ /-'troʊl/ *noun* **1** [C or U] when you control something or someone, or the power to do this: *She's got no control **over** that child – it's terrible.* ○ *He wants the government to **impose** strict controls **on** dog ownership.* ○ *The dictator **took** control **of** the country in 1933.* ○ *He felt he was **losing** control **of** events.* ○ *You need to stay **in** control **of** your emotions.* ○ *The car skidded and **went out of** control, crashing into an oncoming truck.* ○ *There was nothing we could do about it – the situation was **out of/beyond/outside** our control.* ○ *She criticized the police's methods of **crowd** control.* **2** [C] a switch or other device used to operate a machine such as a vehicle: *The main instruments are in the centre of the control **panel**.* ○ *Captain Firth sat **at the** controls **of** the aircraft.* **3** [C] *SPECIALIZED* in an experiment, an object or system which is not changed so that you can compare it with similar objects or systems which are intentionally changed
● **under control** being dealt with or limited successfully: *It seems that the disease is now under control.* ○ *Everything is under control, sir.* ○ *It took them two hours to **bring/get** the fire under control.*
controller /kən'trəʊ.lə^r/ ⓤ /-'troʊ.lɚ/ *noun* [C] a person who controls something, or someone who is responsible for what a particular organization does: *an air-traffic controller* ○ *That was the year he became Controller of Radio 4.*

con'trol ,freak *noun* [C] *INFORMAL DISAPPROVING* someone who is determined to make things happen exactly in the way they want and who tries to make other people do what they want

con'trol (,key) *noun* [C usually sing] (WRITTEN ABBREVIATION **Ctrl**) a key on a computer keyboard that you press at the same time as other keys to make the keyboard operate in a particular way: *Press and hold down the control key while you press '9'.* ○ *I pressed control Alt Delete but nothing happened.*

con'trol ,tower *noun* [C] a building at an airport from which air traffic is watched and directed

controversy /'kɒn.trə.vɜː.si/ /kən'trɒv.ə-/ ⓤ /'kɑːn.trə.vɜː-/ *noun* [C or U] a lot of disagreement or argument about something, usually because it affects or is important to many people: *There was a big controversy **surrounding/over** the use of drugs in athletics.* ○ *The policy has caused **fierce/heated** controversy ever since it was introduced.*
controversial /,kɒn.trə'vɜː.ʃᵊl/ ⓤ /,kɑːn.trə'vɜː-/ *adj* causing disagreement or discussion: *a controversial issue/decision/speech/figure* ○ *The book was very controversial.* **controversially** /,kɒn.trə'vɜː.ʃᵊ.li/ ⓤ /,kɑːn.trə'vɜː-/ *adv*

contusion /kən'tjuː.ʒᵊn/ ⓤ /-'tuː-/ *noun* [C] *SPECIALIZED* **bruise**
contuse /kən'tjuːz/ ⓤ /-'tuːz/ *verb* [I or T] *SPECIALIZED* to **bruise**

conundrum /kə'nʌn.drəm/ *noun* [C] **1** a problem that is difficult to deal with: *Arranging childcare over the school holidays can be quite a conundrum for working parents.* **2** a trick question, often involving an amusing use of words that have two meanings

conurbation /,kɒn.ə'beɪ.ʃᵊn/ ⓤ /,kɑː.nɚ-/ *noun* [C] *FORMAL* a city area containing a large number of people, formed by various towns growing and joining together: *the conurbations of Tokyo and Osaka*

convalesce /,kɒn.və'les/ ⓤ /,kɑːn-/ *verb* [I] to rest in order to get better after an illness: *After your operation, you'll need to convalesce for a week or more.*
convalescence /,kɒn.və'les.ᵊnts/ ⓤ /,kɑːn-/ *noun* [S or U] a period in which you convalesce
convalescent /,kɒn.və'les.ᵊnt/ ⓤ /,kɑːn-/ *adj* (for or relating to) convalescing: *a convalescent **home/hospital***
convalescent /,kɒn.və'les.ᵊnt/ ⓤ /,kɑːn-/ *noun* [C] someone who is getting better after a serious injury: *Most convalescents prefer to be cared for at home rather than in a hospital.*

convection /kən'vek.ʃᵊn/ *noun* [U] *SPECIALIZED* the flow of heat through a gas or a liquid: *Warm air rises by the process of convection.*

convector /kən'vek.tə^r/ ⓤ /-tɚ/ *noun* [C] a device which warms a room by causing a current of hot air

convene /kən'viːn/ *verb* [I or T] *FORMAL* to arrange (a group of people for) a meeting, or to meet for a meeting: *The Prime Minister convened (a meeting of) his ministers to discuss the matter.* ○ *The council will be convening on the morning of the 25th.*
convenor /kən'viː.nə^r/ ⓤ /-nɚ/ *noun* [C] (ALSO **convener**) a high-ranking British TRADE UNION official who works in a particular factory

convenience /kən'viː.ni.ᵊnts/ *noun* **1** [C] a device or machine, usually in the house, which operates quickly and needs little effort: *The house has every modern convenience.* **2** [C usually pl] (ALSO **public convenience**) *FORMAL* a public toilet

con'venience ,food *noun* [U] food that is almost ready to eat when it is bought and can be prepared quickly and easily

convenient /kən'viː.ni.ᵊnt/ *adj* **1** suitable for your purposes and needs and causing the least difficulty: *Our local shop has very convenient opening hours.* ○ *A bike's a very convenient way of getting around.* ○ [+ that] *It's very convenient that you live near the office.* ○ [+ to infinitive] *I find it convenient to be able to do my banking by phone.* ○ *What time would it be convenient **for** me to come round?* ✳ NOTE: The opposite is **inconvenient**. **2** near or easy to get to or use: *a very convenient bus service* ○ *Our new flat is very convenient **for** (= near to) the kids' school.*
conveniently /kən'viː.ni.ᵊnt.li/ *adv: The house is conveniently situated near the station and the shops.* ○ *HUMOROUS I asked her to tidy the kitchen but of course she conveniently forgot* (= she forgot because she did not want to do it).
convenience /kən'viː.ni.ᵊnts/ *noun* [U] when something is convenient: *I like the convenience of living so near work.* ○ *Just for convenience, I'm going to live at my mother's place until my new house is ready.*
● **at your convenience** when you want: *The goods will be delivered at your convenience.*

• **at *your* earliest convenience** as soon as you like or can: *Please return the completed form at your earliest convenience.*

COMMON LEARNER ERROR

convenient (spelling)

Many learners make mistakes when spelling this word. One way to remember the correct spelling is that the 'e' of the second syllable is pronounced with a 'long e' sound as in the word 'me'.

Well, 6am is not convenient for me.

convent /'kɒn.vənt/ [US] /'kɑːn-/ *noun* [C] a building in which nuns live ➲Compare **monastery**.
• **enter a convent** to become a nun

convention [CUSTOM] /kən'ven*t*.ʃən/ *noun* **1** [C or U] (an example of) a usual or accepted way of behaving, especially in social situations, often following an old way of thinking or a custom in one particular society: *They* ***defied/flouted/broke with*** *convention by giving up their jobs and becoming self-sufficient.* ○ *Convention* ***dictates that*** *it is the man who asks the woman to marry him and not the reverse.* ○ *In many countries, it is the/a convention to wear black at funerals.* **2** [C] a common way of showing something in art or writing: *an artistic convention*

conventional /kən'ven*t*.ʃən.əl/ *adj* **1** traditional and ordinary: *conventional behaviour/attitudes/clothes* ○ *conventional medicine/farming* ○ *a conventional wedding* ○ DISAPPROVING *I find his art rather dull and conventional.* ✻ NOTE: The opposite is **unconventional**. **2** describes weapons which are not nuclear, or methods of fighting a war that do not involve nuclear weapons: *conventional weapons/bombs* **conventionally** /kən'ven*t*.ʃən.əl.i/ *adv* **conventionality** /kən,ven*t*.ʃən'æl.ɪ.ti/ [US] /-ə.ţi/ *noun* [U]

convention [MEETING] /kən'ven*t*.ʃən/ *noun* [C] a large formal meeting of people who do a particular job or have a similar interest, or a large meeting for a political party: *the national Democratic convention* ○ *Where are they* ***holding*** *their party convention?*

convention [AGREEMENT] /kən'ven.*t*ʃən/ *noun* [C] a formal agreement between country leaders, politicians and states on a matter which involves them all: *the Geneva Convention* ○ *a convention on human rights*

'convent ,school *noun* [C] a school in which the teachers are nuns

converge /kən'vɜːdʒ/ [US] /-'vɝːdʒ/ *verb* [I] **1** If lines, roads or paths converge, they move towards the same point where they join or meet: *The paths all converge* ***at*** *the main gate of the park.* ○ *Due to roadworks, three lanes of traffic have to converge* ***into*** *two.* ➲Compare **diverge**. **2** If ideas and opinions converge, they gradually become similar. **3** to come from other places to meet in a particular place: *Ambulances, police cars and fire engines all converged* ***on*** *the scene.* ○ *100 000 people are expected to converge* ***on*** *the town for the festival.* **convergence** /kən'vɜː.dʒən*t*s/ [US] /-'vɝː-/ *noun* [C or U] *a convergence* ***of*** *interests/opinions/ideas* **convergent** /kən'vɜː.dʒənt/ [US] /-'vɝː-/ *adj*: *convergent lines/opinions*

conversant /kən'vɜː.sənt/ [US] /-'vɝː-/ *adj* FORMAL **be conversant with** ***sth*** to be familiar with, and have knowledge or experience of the facts or rules of something: *I'm not conversant with the rules of chess.*

conversation /,kɒn.və'seɪ.ʃən/ [US] /,kɑːn.vɚ-/ *noun* [C or U] (a) talk between two or more people in which thoughts, feelings and ideas are expressed, questions are asked and answered, or news and information are exchanged: *She* ***had*** *a strange conversation* ***with*** *the bloke who's moved in upstairs.* ○ *It's impossible to* ***hold/carry on*** *a conversation with all this noise going on!* ○ *I* ***struck up*** (= started) *an interesting conversation* ***with*** *your uncle.* ○ *Because of television, many people have lost the art of conversation* (= talking to each other). ○ *Whenever I'm in a social situation with my boss, we seem to* ***run out of*** *conversation* (= things to say to each other) *after two minutes!*
• **make conversation** to say things to someone whom you do not know well, in order to be polite: *I was just trying to make conversation.*

conversational /,kɒn.və'seɪ.ʃən.əl/ [US] /,kɑːn.vɚ-/ *adj* relating to or like a conversation: *a conversational style of writing* ○ *He seems to lack basic conversational skills.*

conversationalist /,kɒn.və'seɪ.ʃən.əl.ɪst/ [US] /,kɑːn.vɚ-/ *noun* [C] someone who enjoys or is good at talking with people **converse** /kən'vɜːs/ [US] /-'vɝːs/ *verb* [I] FORMAL *She's so shy that conversing* ***with*** *her can be quite difficult.* ➲See also **converse**.

conver'sation ,piece *noun* [C] an unusual object which causes people to start talking

converse /'kɒn.vɜːs/ /kən'vɜːs/ [US] /'kɑːn.vɝːs/ /kən'vɜːrs/ *adj* FORMAL opposite: *a converse effect/opinion/argument* ➲See also **converse** at **conversation**.

the 'converse *noun* [S] FORMAL the opposite: *In the US, you drive on the right hand side of the road, but in Britain the converse applies.* ○ *However, the converse of this theory may also be true.*

conversely /kən'vɜː.sli/ /'kɒn.vɜː-/ [US] /kən'vɝː-/ /'kɑːn.vɜːr-/ *adv* in an opposite way

conversion /kən'vɜː.ʃən/ [US] /kən'vɝː.ʃən/ *noun* [C] in rugby, an attempt to score more points after a TRY SPORT, by kicking the ball over the bar and between the two posts

convert /kən'vɜːt/ [US] /-'vɝːt/ *verb* [I or T] to (cause something or someone to) change in form, character or opinion: *Could we convert the small bedroom* ***into*** *a second bathroom?* ○ *What's the formula for converting pounds* ***into*** *kilos?* ○ *He converted* ***to*** (= starting believing in) *Catholicism when he got married.* ○ *I used not to like exercise, but my sister has converted me* ***(to*** *it).*

convert /'kɒn.vɜːt/ [US] /'kɑːn.vɝːt/ *noun* [C] someone who changes their beliefs, habits, or way of living: *a Christian/Buddhist convert* ○ *a convert* ***to*** *vegetarianism/wholemeal bread*

conversion /kən'vɜː.ʃən/ /-ʒən/ [US] /-'vɝː-/ *noun* **1** [C or U] when someone or something is converted: *Her conversion* ***to*** *Buddhism/Islam was a very gradual process.* ○ *He used to be very right-wing, but he's* ***undergone*** *something of a conversion recently.* ○ *Solar power is the conversion* ***of*** *the sun's energy* ***into*** *heat and electricity.* **2** [C] a place for living in that has been changed from its previous use: *a barn/factory conversion*

convertible /kən'vɜː.tɪ.bl̩/ [US] /-'vɝː.ţɪ-/ *adj* **1** able to be arranged in a different way and used for a different purpose: *a convertible sofa-bed* **2** SPECIALIZED describes a type of money that can be easily exchanged into other types of money: *a convertible currency/bond*

convertible /kən'vɜː.tɪ.bl̩/ [US] /-'vɝː.ţə-/ *noun* [C] (ALSO **soft top**) a car with a soft roof which can be folded back: *a Volkswagen convertible* ➲See picture **Cars and Trucks** on page Centre 13

converter /kən'vɜː.təʳ/ [US] /-'vɝː.ţɚ/ *noun* [C] (ALSO **convertor**) a machine or device that changes something into a different form

convex /'kɒn.veks/ [US] /'kɑːn-/ /kən'veks/ *adj* curved or swelling out: *a convex lens/mirror* ➲Compare **concave**.

convey [COMMUNICATE] /kən'veɪ/ *verb* [T] to express a thought, feeling or idea so that it is understood by other people: *His poetry conveys a great sense of religious devotion.* ○ *If you see James, do convey my apologies* ***(to*** *him).* ○ [+ question word] *I tried to convey in my speech* ***how*** *grateful we all were for his help.* ○ *You don't want to convey the impression* ***that*** *we're not interested.*

convey [TAKE] /kən'veɪ/ *verb* [T] to take or carry someone or something to a particular place: *The goods are usually conveyed by sea.* ○ *Could you convey a message* ***to*** *Mr Merrick for me, please?*

conveyance /kən'veɪ.ən*t*s/ *noun* **1** [U] FORMAL when something is moved from one place to another: *the conveyance of water* **2** [C] OLD-FASHIONED a **vehicle** MACHINE or method of transport: *a horse-drawn/public conveyance*

conveyancing /kən'veɪ.ən*t*.sɪŋ/ *noun* [U] LEGAL the process of moving the legal ownership of property or land from one person to another: *When we bought our house, we did our own conveyancing instead of using a lawyer.*

conveyance /kən'veɪ.ənts/ *noun* [C] a legal document which officially gives to someone else the rights to land or property

conveyor (belt) /kən'veɪ.ə,belt/ ⓤ /-ɚ-/ *noun* [C] a continuous moving strip or surface that is used for transporting a load of objects from one place to another

convict /kən'vɪkt/ *verb* [T usually passive] to decide officially in a court of law that someone is guilty of a crime: *He has twice been convicted **of** robbery/arson.* ⊃Compare **acquit**. **convicted** /kən'vɪk.tɪd/ *adj*: *a convicted murderer*

convict /'kɒn.vɪkt/ ⓤ /'kɑːn-/ *noun* [C] someone who is in prison because they are guilty of a crime: *an escaped convict*

conviction [CRIME] /kən'vɪk.ʃən/ *noun* [C or U] when someone is officially found to be guilty of a particular crime: *As it was her first conviction **for** stealing, she was given a less severe sentence.* ○ *He has a long record of previous convictions **for** similar offences.* ○ *The conviction **of** the three demonstrators has caused public outrage locally.*
✻ NOTE: Compare **acquittal**.

conviction [OPINION] /kən'vɪk.ʃən/ *noun* **1** [C or U] a strong opinion or belief: *religious/moral convictions* ○ *a **deep/strong/lifelong** conviction* ○ [+ that] *It's my personal conviction **that** all rapists should be locked away for life.* **2** [U] a feeling of certainty about something: *He said he was enjoying his new job, but his voice **lacked** conviction.*

convince /kən'vɪnts/ *verb* [T] to persuade someone or make them certain: *He managed to convince the jury **of** his innocence.* ○ [+ (that)] *It's useless trying to convince her **(that)** she doesn't need to lose any weight.* ○ [+ to infinitive] *I hope this will convince you **to** change your mind.*

convinced /kən'vɪntst/ *adj* **1** certain: *My boyfriend says I'd enjoy a walking holiday, but I'm not convinced.* ○ [+ (that)] *I'm convinced **(that)** she is lying.* **2** certain of your beliefs: *a convinced Christian/atheist* ○ *a convinced socialist*

convincing /kən'vɪnt.sɪŋ/ *adj* **1** able to make you believe that something is true or right: *a convincing argument/explanation* ○ *convincing evidence* ○ *I didn't find the ending of the film very convincing.* **2 a convincing win/victory** a win or victory in which the person or team that wins is much better than the person or team they are competing against: *They won a convincing victory.* **convincingly** /kən'vɪnt.sɪŋ.li/ *adv*: *She spoke convincingly of the need for a more humane prison system.*

convivial /kən'vɪv.i.əl/ *adj* friendly and making you feel happy and welcome: *a convivial atmosphere/host* **convivially** /kən'vɪv.i.ə.li/ *adv* **conviviality** /kən,vɪv.i'æl.ɪ.ti/ ⓤ /-ə.t̬i/ *noun* [U]

convocation /,kɒn.və'keɪ.ʃən/ ⓤ /,kɑːn-/ *noun* FORMAL **1** [C] a large formal meeting, especially of church officials or of (previous) members of some British colleges: *a university convocation* **2** [U] the act of arranging a convocation

convoluted /'kɒn.və.luː.tɪd/ ⓤ /'kɑːn.və.luː.t̬ɪd/ *adj* **1** very twisted: *a very convoluted route/knot* **2** describes sentences, explanations and arguments, etc. that are unreasonably long and difficult to understand: *His grammar explanations are terribly convoluted.* ○ *Her book is full of long convoluted sentences.* **convolution** /,kɒn.və'luː.ʃən/ ⓤ /,kɑːn-/ *noun* [C usually pl] an intricate pattern of endless convolutions ○ *It's a good film, but the plot has so many convolutions that you really have to concentrate.*

convoy /'kɒn.vɔɪ/ ⓤ /'kɑːn-/ *noun* [C] a group of vehicles or ships which travel together, especially for protection: *A convoy of trucks containing supplies was sent to the famine area.*
● **in convoy** travelling one behind another in a row: *Shall we all drive to the party in convoy so we don't get lost?*

convoy /'kɒn.vɔɪ/ ⓤ /'kɑːn-/ *verb* [T] to travel with a vehicle or group of people to make certain that they arrive safely: *Two tanks convoyed the trucks across the border.*

convulse /kən'vʌls/ *verb* [I or T] to (cause to) shake violently with sudden uncontrolled movements: *to convulse **with** pain* ○ *A racking cough convulsed her whole body.*
● **be convulsed with laughter/rage,** etc. to laugh or feel anger, etc. uncontrollably

convulsion /kən'vʌl.ʃən/ *noun* [C usually pl] a sudden uncontrollable movement of the muscles in your body, caused by illness or drugs: *She **went into** convulsions and had to be rushed to hospital.*
● **be in convulsions** INFORMAL to be laughing uncontrollably

convulsive /kən'vʌl.sɪv/ *adj* describes sudden uncontrollable movements of the muscles in your body: *convulsive spasms*

cony /'kəʊ.ni/ ⓤ /'koʊ-/ *noun* [C or U] (ALSO **coney**) OLD USE a rabbit, or the fur of a rabbit

coo /kuː/ *verb* [I] **cooing, cooed, cooed 1** When birds such as DOVES and PIGEONS coo, they make a low soft call. **2** to speak in a soft, gentle or loving way: *The baby lay in his cot, cooing and gurgling.* ○ *It's sickening the way she coos **over** those cats of hers.* ○ [+ speech] *"How wonderful to see you again, darling," she cooed.*

cook [HEAT] /kʊk/ *verb* [I or T] When you cook food, you prepare it to be eaten by heating it in a particular way, such as baking or boiling, and when food cooks, it is heated until it is ready to eat: *I don't cook meat very often.* ○ [+ two objects] *He cooked us an enormous meal./He cooked an enormous meal **for** us.* ○ *Let the fish cook for half an hour before you add the wine.*
● **be cooking** US INFORMAL to be making good progress or doing something well: *"Look! I've found the missing puzzle pieces." "Now we're cooking!"* ○ *Jean's new band was really cooking at the party last night.*
● **cook sb's goose** to do something that spoils someone's plans and prevents them from succeeding: *Just tell her we can't - that'll cook her goose.*
● **What's cooking?** OLD-FASHIONED SLANG used to ask about what is happening or what someone is planning: *I just saw the police arrive – what's cooking?*

cook /kʊk/ *noun* [C] someone who prepares and cooks food: *She's a wonderful cook.*
● **Too many cooks spoil the broth.** UK (US **Too many cooks spoil the soup.**) SAYING said when there are too many people doing the same piece of work at the same time, so that the final result will be spoiled

cooked /kʊkt/ *adj* not raw: *cooked meat/vegetables* ○ *Is that cake cooked properly in the middle?*

cooker /'kʊk.ə/ ⓤ /-ɚ-/ *noun* [C] **1** MAINLY UK (US **stove**) a large box-shaped device which is used to cook and heat food either by putting the food inside or by putting it on the top: *a gas/electric cooker* **2** UK INFORMAL a **cooking apple**

cookery /'kʊk.ºr.i/ ⓤ /-ɚ-/ *noun* [U] UK the skill or activity of preparing and cooking food: *cookery classes* ○ *cookery books*

cooking /'kʊk.ɪŋ/ *noun* [U] preparing or cooking food: *My mother always hated cooking.* ○ *Who **does** the cooking in your house?* ○ *I love my dad's cooking* (= the food that he cooks).

cooking /'kʊk.ɪŋ/ *adj* [before n] suitable for cooking with: *cooking apples* ○ *cooking oil*

cook [CHANGE] /kʊk/ *verb* [T] INFORMAL to change evidence, written facts or records in order to deceive people
● **cook the books** INFORMAL to change numbers dishonestly in the accounts of an organization, especially in order to steal money from it
▲ **cook sth up** *phrasal verb* [M] INFORMAL to invent a story, plan, etc., usually dishonestly: *She'd cooked up some weird scheme that was going to earn her a fortune.* ○ *I had to cook up an excuse about my car breaking down.*

cookbook /'kʊk.bʊk/ *noun* [C] (UK ALSO **cookery book**) a book containing RECIPES which tell you how to prepare and cook particular dishes

cooked breakfast *noun* [C] UK a dish eaten in the morning consisting of fried eggs, BACON, sausages and toast

cookie [BISCUIT], **cooky** /'kʊk.i/ *noun* [C] MAINLY US a sweet biscuit: *chocolate-chip cookies*
● **That's the way the cookie crumbles.** SAYING said when something slightly unlucky has happened but it could not have been prevented and so must be accepted

cookie [TYPE OF PERSON] /'kʊk.i/ *noun* [C] US INFORMAL a person of the type mentioned: *She's a **smart/tough** cookie.*

cookie [COMPUTING] /ˈkʊk.i/ *noun* [C] SPECIALIZED a piece of information stored on your computer which contains information about all the Internet documents that you have looked at

ˈcookie ˌcutter *noun* [C] MAINLY US a sharp metal or plastic device used to cut COOKIES (= sweet biscuits) into shapes before they are cooked

cookie-cutter /ˈkʊk.iˌkʌt.əʳ/ [US] /-ɚ/ *adj* US DISAPPROVING similar to other things of the same type, especially in a way that shows a lack of imagination: *a row of cookie-cutter houses*

ˈcooking ˌapple *noun* [C] (UK INFORMAL **cooker**) a sour and usually large apple which is used in cooking ➲Compare **eating apple**.

cookout /ˈkʊk.aʊt/ *noun* [C] MAINLY US INFORMAL a meal cooked and eaten outside, especially as part of a party

cool [COLD] /kuːl/ *adj* **1** slightly cold; of a low temperature: *cool water* ○ *cool weather* **2** slightly cold in a pleasant way: *It was a lovely cool evening.* ○ *How do you manage to look so cool in this hot weather?* **3** describes colours, such as blue or green, that make you feel calm and relaxed: *The bedroom was painted a lovely cool blue.* **4** describes a temperature which is slightly too cold: ***It's** a bit cool in here, isn't it? I think I'll close the window.*

cool /kuːl/ *verb* [I or T] to cause something to become cool: *Leave the cake to cool for an hour before cutting it.* ○ *He took off his shoes to cool* (= make colder) *his sweaty feet.*

the cool *noun* [S] the pleasant, slightly cold temperature of a place: *He loved the cool **of** the early morning.* ○ *She left the midday sun for the cool of the shade.*

cooler /ˈkuː.ləʳ/ [US] /-lɚ/ *noun* [C] **1** US FOR **cool box**: *We've brought a cooler full of beer with us.* **2** MAINLY US a cold drink, usually of wine, fruit juice and fizzy water: *a wine/fruit cooler*

cooling /ˈkuː.lɪŋ/ *adj* causing you to feel less warm or hot: *a cooling breeze/drink/swim* **coolness** /ˈkuːl.nəs/ *noun* [U] *There's a slight coolness in the air – do you think it's going to rain?*

cool [CALM] /kuːl/ *adj* calm and not anxious or frightened; not influenced by strong feeling of any type: *He was very cool and calm about the mishap, and didn't shout or lose his temper.* ○ ***Stay/Keep** cool* (= Do not become angry or excited).

• **be cool with *sth*** MAINLY US INFORMAL to be happy to accept a situation or suggestion: *Yeah, we could leave later – I'm cool with that.*

• **cool customer** INFORMAL someone who stays calm and does not show their emotions, even in a difficult situation

• **keep a cool head** to stay calm in a difficult situation: *I don't know how you manage to keep **such** a cool head in such a hectic, stressful office!*

• **(as) cool as a cucumber** very calm or very calmly, especially when this is surprising: *She walked in as cool as a cucumber, as if nothing had happened.*

cool /kuːl/ *noun* [U] INFORMAL a person's ability to stay calm and not become angry or excited: ***keep** your cool* ○ *He really **lost** his cool when he heard about what happened.*

cool /kuːl/ *verb* [I] (ALSO **cool off**) If a feeling cools, it starts to become less strong: *They were desperately in love to begin with, but I think it's starting to cool off now.* ○ *Their interest in the project seems to be cooling.*

• **cool it** SLANG used to tell someone to become calm, rather than be violent: *Just cool it everyone, fighting won't solve anything.*

coolness /kuːl/ *noun* [U] the ability to stay calm and act in a reasonable way even in difficult situations: *Her coolness in an emergency was admirable.*

cool [UNFRIENDLY] /kuːl/ *adj* unfriendly or not showing affection or interest in something or someone: *She was decidedly cool **towards** me.* ○ *I got a rather cool **reception/welcome** this evening. What do you think I've done wrong?*

coolly /ˈkuːl.li/ *adv* in an unfriendly way: *"How did he receive your suggestion?" "Rather coolly – I don't think he was too keen."*

coolness /ˈkuːl.nəs/ *noun* [U] lack of warm feelings and friendliness: *I noticed a certain coolness between your parents.*

cool [FASHIONABLE] /kuːl/ *adj* INFORMAL fashionable or attractive: *Angie's got some cool new sunglasses.* ○ *Now I know it won't **look** very cool, but this hat will keep the sun out of your eyes.*

cool [GOOD] /kuːl/ *adj, exclamation* INFORMAL excellent; very good: *"So how was the concert?" "It was cool!"* ○ *"Do you want to come with us?" "Yeah, cool!"*

PHRASAL VERBS WITH **cool**

▲ **cool *(sb/sth)* down/off** [BECOME LESS HOT] *phrasal verb* [M] to become less hot, or to make someone or something become less hot: *She waited until her coffee had cooled down before taking a sip.* ○ *We went for a swim to cool off.*

▲ **cool *(sb)* down/off** [BECOME CALM] *phrasal verb* [M] to stop feeling angry after an argument, or to stop someone else feeling angry after an argument: *Leave her to cool off and then talk to her.*

coolant /ˈkuː.lənt/ *noun* [C or U] SPECIALIZED (a) specially prepared liquid which is used to stop a machine from getting too hot while it is operating

ˈcool ˌbag UK *noun* [C] (US **cooler bag**) a bag made of a thick INSULATING material that keeps food and drink cold when you are travelling

ˈcool ˌbox UK *noun* [C] (US **cooler**) a box-like container with a lid, which is used for making or keeping food and drinks cool

ˈcooler ˌbag *noun* [C] US FOR **cool bag**

coolheaded /ˌkuːlˈhed.ɪd/ *adj* having the ability to stay calm and think clearly in difficult situations

coolie /ˈkuː.li/ *noun* [C] OFFENSIVE OLD-FASHIONED an unskilled and cheaply employed worker in Asia

cooling-off period /ˌkuː.lɪŋˈɒfˌpɪə.ri.əd/ [US] /-ˈɑːfˌpɪr.i-/ *noun* [C usually sing] an agreed length of time in which someone can decide not to buy something they have agreed to buy, or a period in which two groups who are arguing can try to improve the situation before taking further action: *There is a twenty-day cooling-off period in which the investor can choose to back out of the contract.*

ˈcooling ˌtower *noun* [C] a tall hollow structure which is used in industrial processes to reduce the temperature of especially water, so that it can be used (again) to cool other parts of the system

coon /kuːn/ *noun* [C] OFFENSIVE a black person

coop /kuːp/ *noun* [C] a cage where small animals are kept, especially chickens

cooped up /ˌkuːptˈʌp/ *adj* If you are cooped up somewhere, you are in a small enclosed space from which you cannot escape, or you feel as if you are: *Cooped up in a small dark cell, the prisoner hadn't seen daylight for five years.* ○ *It's such a tiny office – don't you ever feel cooped up here?*

coop /kuːp/ *verb*

▲ **coop *sb/sth* up** *phrasal verb* [M] to keep someone or something in an enclosed space: *I feel like I've been cooped up in this flat for days.*

cooperate, UK ALSO **co-operate** /kəʊˈɒp.ᵊr.eɪt/ [US] /koʊˈɑː.pə.reɪt/ *verb* [I] to act or work together for a particular purpose, or to help someone willingly when help is requested: *I find it very hard to dress my two-year-old when she refuses to cooperate.* ○ *The two companies have cooperated **in** joint ventures for the past several years.* ○ *The Spanish authorities cooperated **with** the British police **in** finding the terrorists.*

cooperation, UK ALSO **co-operation** /kəʊˌɒp.ᵊrˈeɪ.ʃᵊn/ [US] /koʊˌɑː.pəˈreɪ-/ *noun* [U] when you work together with someone or do what they ask you: *This documentary was made with the cooperation of British Rail.* ○ *There's very little cooperation **between** the two countries.* ○ *The company produces computers **in** cooperation **with** a German firm.*

cooperative, UK ALSO **co-operative** /kəʊˈɒp.ᵊr.ə.tɪv/ [US] /koʊˈɑː.pɚ.ə.t̬ɪv/ *adj* willing to help or do what people ask: *I've asked them not to play their music so loudly, but* *they're not being very cooperative.* ✻ NOTE: The opposite is **uncooperative**.

cooperative, *UK ALSO* **co-operative** /kəʊˈɒp.ᵊr.ə.tɪv/ [US] /koʊˈɑː.pɚ.ə.t̬ɪv/ *noun* [C] (*ABBREVIATION* **co-op**) a company that is owned and managed by the people who work in it: *The magazine is run by a cooperative.* **cooperatively**, *UK ALSO* **co-operatively** /kəʊˈɒp.ᵊr.ə.tɪv.li/ [US] /koʊˈɑː.pɚ.ə.t̬ɪv-/ *adv*

co-opt /kəʊˈɒpt/ [US] /koʊˈɑːpt/ *verb* [T] **1** (of an elected group) to make someone a member through the choice of the present members: *She was co-opted* ***on to*** *the committee last June.* **2** to include someone in something, often against their will: *Although he was reluctant to get involved, he was co-opted* ***onto*** *the committee in 1998.* **3** to use someone else's ideas: *Rock 'n' roll music was largely co-opted from the blues.*

coordinate [COMBINE], *UK ALSO* **co-ordinate** /kəʊˈɔː.dɪ.neɪt/ [US] /koʊˈɔːr-/ *verb* [T] to make various different things work effectively as a whole: *We need someone to co-ordinate the whole campaign.* ○ *A number of charities are coordinating their efforts to distribute food to the region.* **coordinated** /kəʊˈɔː.dɪ.neɪ.tɪd/ [US] /koʊˈɔːr.dɪ.neɪ.t̬ɪd/ *adj* **1** effectively organized: *The rebel troops have launched a coordinated attack on government soldiers.* **2** If a person is coordinated, they move in a very easy and controlled way, especially when playing sports or dancing: *I wasn't a very coordinated child.* **coordination** /kəʊˌɔː.dɪˈneɪ.ʃᵊn/ [US] /koʊˌɔːr-/ *noun* [U] **1** the act of making all the people involved in a plan or activity work together in an organized way: *There's absolutely no coordination* ***between*** *the different groups – nobody knows what anyone else is doing.* **2** the ability to make your arms, legs and other body parts move in a controlled way: *Gymnastics is a sport that requires a considerable level of coordination.* **coordinator** /kəʊˈɔː.dɪ.neɪ.təʳ/ [US] /koʊˈɔːr.dɪ.neɪ.t̬ɚ/ *noun* [C] someone whose job is to make different groups work together in an organized way to achieve something: *We've just appointed a coordinator who will oversee the whole project.*

coordinate [POINT] /kəʊˈɔː.dɪ.nət/ [US] /koʊˈɔːr-/ *noun* [C usually pl] one of a pair of numbers and/or letters that show the exact position of a point on a map or GRAPH

coordinate [MATCH] /kəʊˈɔː.dɪ.neɪt/ [US] /koʊˈɔːr-/ *verb* [I] to match; to look attractive together: *The bed linen coordinates with the bedroom curtains.* ○ *a coordinating jacket and skirt* **coordinated** /kəʊˈɔː.dɪ.neɪ.tɪd/ [US] /koʊˈɔːr.dɪ.neɪ.t̬ɪd/ *adj*: *colour-coordinated decor* ○ *The colour scheme of their living room is carefully coordinated* (= arranged so that the colours match). **coordinates** /kəʊˈɔː.dɪ.nəts/ [US] /koʊˈɔːr-/ *plural noun* clothes, especially for women, which are made in matching colours or styles so that they can be worn together

coot [BIRD] /kuːt/ *noun* [C] a small dark bird which lives near rivers and lakes

coot [PERSON] /kuːt/ *noun* [C] *US INFORMAL* a person, especially one who is not very clever: *He's a sweet* ***old*** *coot.*

cop [CRIME] /kɒp/ [US] /kɑːp/ *verb* [T] **-pp-** *UK SLANG* to arrest someone for a crime: *He was copped* ***for*** *driving without a licence last week.*

• **cop it** *UK INFORMAL* to be punished or spoken to severely because you have done something wrong: *You'll really cop it if your parents find out you've been stealing.*

cop /kɒp/ [US] /kɑːp/ *noun* [S] ➲See **it's a fair cop** at **fair** RIGHT.

cop [TAKE] /kɒp/ [US] /kɑːp/ *verb* [T] **-pp-** *SLANG* to take or hold: *Cop* ***(hold of)*** *that, would you – I can't carry both myself.*

• **cop a feel** *US SLANG* to touch someone in a sexual way without their permission

• **cop a plea** *US* to admit to having committed a crime in order to avoid being punished for a more serious crime

cop [OFFICER] /kɒp/ [US] /kɑːp/ *noun* [C] (*UK OLD-FASHIONED* **copper**) *INFORMAL* a **police officer**: *Quick, run – there's a cop coming!*

cop [QUALITY] /kɒp/ [US] /kɑːp/ *SLANG* **not much cop** not very good: *His last book wasn't much cop.*

▲ **cop out** *phrasal verb SLANG* to avoid doing something that you should do or that you have promised to do because you are frightened, shy, or you think it is too difficult: *She copped out* ***of*** *the parachute jump at the last minute with some feeble excuse.*

cope /kəʊp/ [US] /koʊp/ *verb* [I] to deal successfully with a difficult situation: *It must be difficult to cope* ***with*** *three small children and a job.* ○ *The tyres on my car don't cope very well on wet roads.* ○ *He had so much pressure on him in his job that eventually he just couldn't cope.*

copier /ˈkɒp.i.əʳ/ [US] /ˈkɑː.pi.ɚ/ *noun* [C] a PHOTOCOPIER (= machine which makes copies of documents using a photographic process)

copilot /ˈkəʊˌpaɪ.lət/ [US] /ˈkoʊ-/ *noun* [C] (*ALSO* **co-pilot**) a pilot who helps the main pilot on an aircraft

copious /ˈkəʊ.pi.əs/ [US] /ˈkoʊ-/ *adj* in large amounts; more than enough: *They drank copious* ***amounts*** *of wine.* ○ *He took copious notes during the lecture.* **copiously** /ˈkəʊ.pi.ə.sli/ [US] /ˈkoʊ-/ *adv*: *We ate and drank copiously at the party.*

cop-out /ˈkɒp.aʊt/ [US] /ˈkɑːp-/ *noun* [C usually sing] *SLANG* a way of avoiding doing something difficult or unpleasant that you should do, or the excuse that you use to do this: *She always thought that having a family instead of a career was a cop-out.*

copper [METAL] /ˈkɒp.əʳ/ [US] /ˈkɑː.pɚ/ *noun* **1** [U] a reddish brown metal used especially for making wire and coins, or the reddish brown colour of this metal: *copper wire/pipes* ○ *a copper alloy* ○ *Rosie's hair shone copper* (= reddish brown) *in the sunlight.* **2** [C usually pl] *UK INFORMAL* a brown coin of low value: *I gave him a few coppers.* **coppery** /ˈkɒp.ᵊr.i/ [US] /ˈkɑː.pɚ.i/ *adj* reddish-brown: *The leaves on the trees have started to turn a rich coppery colour.*

copper [OFFICER] /ˈkɒp.əʳ/ [US] /ˈkɑː.pɚ/ *noun* [C] *UK OLD-FASHIONED INFORMAL* a **police officer**

ˌcopper ˈbeech *noun* [C] a type of tree with reddish-brown leaves

copper-bottomed /ˌkɒp.əˈbɒt.ᵊmd/ [US] /ˌkɑː.pɚˈbɑː.t̬ᵊmd/ *adj* **1** *UK* describes a plan, deal or investment that can be trusted completely because it is safe and certain to succeed **2** having a base made of copper: *a copper-bottomed saucepan*

copperplate /ˈkɒp.ə.pleɪt/ [US] /ˈkɑː.pɚ-/ *noun* [U] an old-fashioned decorative style of writing with long flowing letters

coppice /ˈkɒp.ɪs/ [US] /kɑː.pɪs/ *noun* [C] an area of closely planted trees, especially one in which the trees are cut back regularly to provide wood: *a hazel/willow coppice* **coppice** /ˈkɒp.ɪs/ [US] /ˈkɑː.pɪs/ *verb* [T] *SPECIALIZED* to cut trees or bushes back in order to form a small, closely planted area

copse /kɒps/ [US] /kɑːps/ *noun* [C] a **coppice**

ˈcop ˌshop *noun* [C] *UK INFORMAL* a **police station**

Coptic /ˈkɒp.tɪk/ [US] /ˈkɑːp-/ *adj* of or connected with the ancient Christian Church of Egypt, which is now based in Egypt and Ethiopia: *a Coptic monastery*

copula /ˈkɒp.jʊ.lə/ [US] /ˈkɑː.pjə-/ *noun* [C] *SPECIALIZED* a type of verb, of which the most common is 'be', which joins the subject of the verb with a COMPLEMENT (= word that describes the subject): *In the sentence 'You smell nice', 'smell' is a copula.*

copulate /ˈkɒp.jʊ.leɪt/ [US] /ˈkɑː.pjə-/ *verb* [I] *SPECIALIZED* to have sex **copulation** /ˌkɒp.jʊˈleɪ.ʃᵊn/ [US] /ˌkɑː.pjə-/ *noun* [U]

copy [PRODUCE] /ˈkɒp.i/ [US] /ˈkɑː.pi/ *verb* [I or T] to produce something so that it is the same as an original piece of work, or to behave, dress, speak, etc. in a way that is intended to be like someone else, for example, because you admire them: *They've copied the basic design* ***from*** *the Japanese model and added a few of their own refinements.* ○ *Patricia's going to copy her novel onto disk and send it to me.* ○ *He tends to copy his brother* ***in*** *the way he dresses.* ○ *DISAPPROVING He was always copying* ***from/off*** *other children* (= cheating by copying), *but never got caught.* **copy** /ˈkɒp.i/ [US] /ˈkɑː.pi/ *noun* [C] **1** something that has been made to be exactly like something else: *This painting is only a copy – the original hangs in the Louvre.* ○ *I* *always* **keep** *a copy* **of** *any official or important letters that I send off.* ○ *Could you* **make** *a copy* **of** (= use a special machine to copy) *this for tomorrow's meeting, please?* **2** a single book, newspaper, record or other printed or recorded item of which many have been produced: *Have you got a copy of last Saturday's 'Guardian', by any chance?*

copy TEXT /'kɒp.i/ ⓤ /'kɑː.pi/ *noun* [U] written text which is to be printed, or text which is intended to help with the sale of a product: *We need someone who can write good copy for our publicity department.*

PHRASAL VERBS WITH **copy**   ▼

▲ **copy** *sth* **down** *phrasal verb* [M] to write something that someone has said or written so that you can remember it

▲ **copy** *sth* **out** *phrasal verb* [M] UK If you copy out a piece of writing, you write it out again on a piece of paper: *Copy out the poem on page six.*

copybook /'kɒp.i.bʊk/ ⓤ /'kɑː.pi-/ *adj* [before n] UK APPROV-ING agreeing exactly with what is expected or with the rules that are connected with a situation: *a copybook musical performance* ○ *a copybook military exercise*

copycat /'kɒp.i.kæt/ ⓤ /'kɑː.pi-/ *noun* [C] CHILD'S WORD someone who lacks their own ideas and does or says exactly the same as someone else: *You're just a copycat!*

copycat /'kɒp.i.kæt/ ⓤ /'kɑː.pi-/ *adj* **1** done or made to be very similar to something else: *In the market you can buy affordable copycat* (= very similar) *versions of expensive perfumes.* **2** describes a crime that is believed to have been influenced by another, often famous, crime because it is so similar: *copycat murders*

copyright /'kɒp.i.raɪt/ ⓤ /'kɑː.pi-/ *noun* [C or U] the legal right to control the production and selling of a book, play, film, photograph or piece of music: *Who* **owns/holds** *the copyright* **on** *this article?* ○ *His work is no longer protected* **by** *copyright.* ○ *The symbol* © *shows that something is protected by copyright.* **copyright** /'kɒp.i.raɪt/ ⓤ /'kɑː.pi-/ *verb* [T]

copywriter /'kɒp.i,raɪ.tər/ ⓤ /'kɑː.pi,raɪ.t̬ɚ/ *noun* [C] someone who writes the words for advertisements

coquette /kɒk'et/ ⓤ /kou'ket/ *noun* [C] LITERARY a woman whose behaviour is intended to attract sexual attention by being playful and charming **coquettish** /kɒk'et.ɪʃ/ ⓤ /kou'ket̬.ɪʃ/ *adj*: *She greeted him with a coquettish smile.* **coquettishly** /kɒk'et.ɪʃ.li/ ⓤ /kou'ket̬-/ *adv* **coquetry** /'kɒk.ɪ.tri/ ⓤ /'kou.kə-/ *noun* [U]

cor EXPRESSING INTEREST /kɔːr/ ⓤ /kɔːr/ *exclamation* UK SLANG an expression of interest and admiration or surprise: *Cor! Did you see him in the blue swimming trunks?*

● **Cor blimey!** UK OLD-FASHIONED SLANG a way of expressing surprise or annoyance: *Cor blimey, I didn't see you there!*

cor- TOGETHER /kər/ ⓤ /kɚ/ *prefix* together; with: *to correspond*

coracle /'kɒr.ə.kl̩/ ⓤ /'kɔːr-/ *noun* [C] a small round boat which is made by stretching animal skin over a wooden frame

coral /'kɒr.əl/ ⓤ /'kɔːr-/ *noun* [U] a rock-like substance, formed in the sea by groups of particular types of small animal, that is often used in jewellery: *a coral bracelet/necklace*

coral /'kɒr.əl/ ⓤ /'kɔːr-/ *adj* pinkish orange in colour: *Paul wore pale grey trousers with a coral T-shirt and black jacket.*

,**coral** '**reef** *noun* [C] a bank of coral, the top of which can sometimes be seen just above the sea

cor anglais (*plural* **cors anglais**) /,kɔː.rɒŋ'gleɪ/ ⓤ /,kɔːr.ɑːŋ-/ *noun* [C] (US **English horn**) a musical instrument like an OBOE but with a lower sound

cord ROPE/WIRE /kɔːd/ ⓤ /kɔːrd/ *noun* [C or U] **1** (a length of) rope or string made of twisted threads: *Where's the cord that ties back the curtains?* ○ *Have you got some cord that I can tie this parcel up with?* **2** (UK ALSO **flex**) a piece of wire covered in plastic, used to connect electrical equipment to a power supply: *an* **extension** *cord* ○ *a telephone cord*

cordless /'kɔːd.ləs/ ⓤ /'kɔːrd-/ *adj* describes an electrical tool or piece of equipment that operates without needing to be permanently connected by a wire to

an outside electrical supply: *a cordless telephone/drill/iron*

cord CLOTH /kɔːd/ ⓤ /kɔːrd/ *noun* [U] UK **corduroy**: *a cord shirt/jacket* ⊃See also **cords**.

cordial FRIENDLY /'kɔː.di.əl/ ⓤ /'kɔːr.dʒəl/ *adj* friendly, but formal and polite: *a cordial smile/greeting/welcome/reception* ○ *Relations between the two leaders are said to be cordial.* **cordially** /'kɔː.di.ə.li/ ⓤ /'kɔːr.dʒə-/ *adv* FORMAL *You are cordially* **invited** *to attend our annual wine-tasting evening.* **cordiality** /,kɔː.di'æl.ɪ.ti/ ⓤ /,kɔːr'dʒæl.ə.t̬i/ *noun* [U]

cordial DRINK /'kɔː.di.əl/ ⓤ /'kɔːr.dʒəl/ *noun* [U] **1** UK a sweet fruit-based drink to which water is usually added: *lime cordial* **2** US **liqueur**

cordial STRONG /'kɔː.di.əl/ ⓤ /'kɔːr.dʒəl/ *adj* FORMAL (of a feeling, especially dislike) strong: *The two statesmen are known to have a cordial* **dislike** *for each other.* **cordially** /'kɔː.di.ə.li/ ⓤ /'kɔːr.dʒə.li/ *adv*: *On a personal level, they came to be cordially* **disliked.**

cordite /'kɔː.daɪt/ ⓤ /'kɔːr-/ *noun* [U] SPECIALIZED a type of explosive, especially used in bullets

cordon /'kɔː.dən/ ⓤ /'kɔːr-/ *noun* [C] a line of police, soldiers, vehicles, etc. positioned around a particular area in order to prevent people from entering it: *There was a* **police** *cordon around the building.*

cordon /'kɔː.dən/ ⓤ /'kɔːr-/ *verb*

▲ **cordon** *sth/somewhere* **off** *phrasal verb* [M] If people in authority, such as the police, cordon off a building or area, they put something around it in order to stop people from entering it: *They've cordoned off the whole area because of a suspected bomb.*

cordon bleu /,kɔː.dɒ'blɜː/ ⓤ /,kɔːrdɑː-/ *adj* **1** describes food prepared to the highest standard: *cordon bleu cuisine* **2** describes people who are able to cook food to the highest standard: *a cordon bleu chef*

cords /kɔːdz/ ⓤ /kɔːrdz/ *plural noun* trousers made of CORDUROY material

corduroy /'kɔː.də.rɔɪ/ ⓤ /'kɔːr-/ *noun* [U] a thick cotton material with soft raised parallel lines in one direction, used especially for making clothes

core CENTRE /kɔːr/ ⓤ /kɔːr/ *noun* [C] **1** the hard central part of some fruits, such as apples, which contains the seeds: *Don't throw your apple core on the floor!* ⊃See picture **Fruit** on page Centre 1 **2** the centre of a planet: *The earth's core is a hot, molten mix of iron and nickel.* **3** SPECIALIZED The core of a NUCLEAR REACTOR (= a device in which atoms are changed to produce energy) is the place where FISSION (= splitting of atoms) happens. **4** SPECIALIZED a long thin cylindrical mass of material taken out of the earth for study

● **to the core 1** in every part: *He's a Conservative to the core.* **2** to an extreme degree: *I was shocked to the core.*

core /kɔːr/ ⓤ /kɔːr/ *verb* [T] to remove the core from a piece of fruit: *Peel and core the pears before cooking them.*

core IMPORTANT PART /kɔːr/ ⓤ /kɔːr/ *noun* [S or U] **1** the basic and most important part of something: *The basic lack of government funding is* **at the** *core of the problem.* **2** **core value/belief/issue, etc.** a value, belief, etc. which is basic and more important than any other: *The final status negotiations would focus on the core issues of the peace process.* **3** **core business/operations/activities** the most important or largest part of a company's business activities, which it depends on in order to continue trading: *The company's core operations include entertainment and aviation.* **4** **core curriculum/subjects/courses** the most important parts of a course of study, that all students must do

co-respondent /,kəʊ.rɪ'spɒn.dənt/ ⓤ /,kou.rə'spɑːn-/ *noun* [C] LEGAL the person with whom a married person is said to have committed ADULTERY (= sex outside marriage): *He was* **cited/named** *as co-respondent in the divorce.* ⊃Compare **respondent** at **respond**.

corgi /'kɔː.gi/ ⓤ /'kɔːr-/ *noun* [C] a breed of dog with a long strong body, short legs and a pointed nose

coriander /,kɒr.i'æn.dər/ ⓤ /'kɔːr.i.æn.dɚ/ *noun* [U] a plant whose leaves or seeds are added to food to give a special flavour

C

Corinthian /kəˈrɪnt.θi.ən/ *adj* of or copying the most decorated of the three styles of ancient Greek building: *Corinthian columns* ⊃Compare **Doric**; **Ionic**.

cork /kɔːk/ [US] /kɔːrk/ *noun* **1** [U] the light soft bark of a Mediterranean tree **2** [C] a short cylindrical piece of cork, or sometimes plastic or rubber, which is put into the top of a bottle, especially a wine bottle, to close it: *I can't get the cork out of the bottle – can you try?*

cork /kɔːk/ [US] /kɔːrk/ *verb* [T] to close a bottle by putting a cork in it: *If you've drunk enough, I'll cork the bottle and we can have the rest later.*

corkage /ˈkɔː.kɪdʒ/ [US] /ˈkɔːr-/ *noun* [U] the charge made by some restaurants for serving wine that has been bought from somewhere else

corked /kɔːkt/ [US] /kɔːrkt/ *adj* Wine is described as being corked if its taste has been spoiled by the cork.

▲ **cork *sth* up** *phrasal verb* [M] *INFORMAL* to not allow yourself to express your anger, anxiety or sadness

corker /ˈkɔː.kəʳ/ [US] /ˈkɔːr.kɚ/ *noun* [C] *INFORMAL MAINLY HUMOROUS* a person or thing that is especially good, attractive or amusing: *She told an absolute corker of a story about a priest she'd mistaken for an ex-lover.*

corkscrew /ˈkɔː.k.skruː/ [US] /ˈkɔːrk-/ *noun* [C] a device for removing CORKS from bottles, which consists of a handle with a twisted metal rod to screw into the cork and pull it out

corkscrew /ˈkɔːk.skruː/ [US] /ˈkɔːrk-/ *adj* [before n] tightly twisted or curled: *Her daughter's hair is a mass of wonderful red corkscrew curls.*

corm /kɔːm/ [US] /kɔːrm/ *noun* [C] *SPECIALIZED* the short underground growth of particular plants from which the new stem grows each year

cormorant /ˈkɔː.məʳr.ənt/ [US] /ˈkɔːr.mɚ-/ *noun* [C] a large black sea bird with a long neck and body

corn [FOOD] /kɔːn/ [US] /kɔːrn/ *noun* [U] **1** *UK* (the seeds of) plants, such as wheat, maize, oats and barley: *a sheaf of corn* ○ *grains of corn* **2** *US* the seeds of the maize plant, or the plant itself ⊃See picture **Vegetables** on page Centre 2

corn [AREA OF SKIN] /kɔːn/ [US] /kɔːrn/ *noun* [C] a small painful area of hard skin that forms on the foot, especially on the toes

corn [EMOTION] /kɔːn/ [US] /kɔːrn/ *noun* [U] *MAINLY US SLANG* something which is old-fashioned, boring, or done to cause emotion: *Everyone says it's a great movie, but I think it's **just** corn.*

cornball /ˈkɔːn.bɔːl/ [US] /ˈkɔːrn.bɑːl/ *adj US* describes a joke, film, story etc. which lacks new ideas and sincerity, or is too often repeated and therefore not amusing or interesting: *the usual cornball romantic comedy*

ˈcorn ˌbread *noun* [U] *US* a type of bread made from maize

ˈcorn ˌchips *noun* [C usually pl] *US* thin flat crisp pieces of food made from crushed maize: *I love corn chips and beer.*

corncob /ˈkɔːn.kɒb/ [US] /ˈkɔːrn.kɑːb/ *noun* [C] the cylindrical part of the maize plant on which the grain grows

corncrake /ˈkɔːn.kreɪk/ [US] /ˈkɔːrn-/ *noun* [C] a European bird with a loud cry

cornea /kɔːˈni.ə/ [US] /ˈkɔːr.ni-/ *noun* [C] the transparent outer covering of the eye

corned beef /ˌkɔːndˈbiːf/ [US] /ˌkɔːrnd-/ *noun* [U] cooked beef which has been preserved in salty water and spices, and which is often sold in TINS (= metal containers)

corner /ˈkɔː.nəʳ/ [US] /ˈkɔːr.nɚ/ *noun* [C] **1** the point, area or line which is formed by the meeting of two lines, surfaces, roads, etc: *You drive round corners too fast – just slow down a bit!* ○ *There's a postbox **on** the corner* (= the place where the street crosses another). ○ *Click the icon **in** the bottom right-hand corner of the screen.* ○ *I've got a bruise where I hit my leg against the corner of the table.* ○ *They only live **just around/round the** corner* (= very close although not in the same road) *– so we see them all the time.* ○ *They live in a **remote** corner **of*** (= place where there are very few people or buildings in) *Scotland, miles from the nearest shop.* **2** a kick in football or a shot in hockey that is taken from the corner of the playing area

• **(just) around the corner** not far away, or going to happen (very) soon: *There's a great restaurant just around the corner.* ○ *Everything is a bit depressing at the moment, but I carry on in the belief that good times are just around the corner.*

• **all/the four corners of the world/earth** many different distant parts of the world: *She had invited relatives from the four corners of the world to her 80th birthday party.*

• **out of/from the corner of *your* eye** If you see something out of/from the corner of your eye, you see it but not clearly because it happens to the side of you: *I saw something move out of the corner of my eye.*

• **corner on a market** If a company has a corner on a particular market, it is more successful than any other company at selling the particular type of product.

• **be in a tight corner** to be in a difficult situation

corner /ˈkɔː.nəʳ/ [US] /ˈkɔːr.nɚ/ *verb* **1** [I] If a vehicle corners well, badly, etc., it drives around corners in the stated way: *It's a powerful car, but it doesn't corner **well**.* **2** [T] to force a person or an animal into a place or situation from which they cannot easily escape: *Once the police had cornered her in the basement, she gave herself up.*

• **corner the market** If a company corners the market for a particular type of product, it is more successful than any other company at selling the product: *They've more or less cornered the fast-food market – they're in every big city in the world.*

-cornered /-kɔː.nəd/ [US] /-kɔːr.nɚd/ *suffix* having the number of corners mentioned: *a three-cornered hat*

ˈcorner ˌshop *noun* [C] *UK* a small shop, especially on a corner of a road, which sells common foods and other objects that are useful in the house

cornerstone /ˈkɔː.nə.stəʊn/ [US] /ˈkɔːr.nɚ.stoʊn/ *noun* [C] **1** a stone in a corner of a building, especially one with the date when the building was made or other writing on it **2** something of great importance which everything else depends on: *In most countries, the family unit is still the cornerstone of society.*

cornet [CONE] /ˈkɔː.nɪt/ [US] /ˈkɔːr-/ *noun* [C] *UK* a **cone** FOOD

cornet [INSTRUMENT] /ˈkɔː.nɪt/ [US] /kɔːr-/ *noun* [C] a musical instrument made from metal, usually brass, that you play by blowing into it

cornfield /ˈkɔːn.fiːld/ [US] /ˈkɔːrn-/ *noun* [C] a field which is used for growing corn

cornflakes /ˈkɔːn.fleɪks/ [US] /ˈkɔːrn-/ *plural noun* small thin yellowish-orange pieces of dry food made from crushed maize, often eaten with milk and sugar in the morning: *a bowl of cornflakes*

cornflour *UK* /ˈkɔːn.flaʊəʳ/ [US] /ˈkɔːrn.flaʊr/ *noun* [U] (*US* **cornstarch**) a white flour made from maize, used in cooking, especially for making liquids thicker

cornflower /ˈkɔːn.flaʊəʳ/ [US] /ˈkɔːrn.flaʊɚ/ *noun* [C] a plant that grows in fields and gardens, usually with blue flowers

cornice /ˈkɔː.nɪs/ [US] /ˈkɔːr-/ *noun* [C] a decorative border found where the ceiling meets the walls in some rooms and also along the top of some walls and buildings

Cornish pasty /ˌkɔː.nɪʃˈpæs.ti/ [US] /ˈkɔːr-/ *noun* [C] *UK* a piece of pastry baked with a mixture of meat and vegetables inside it, usually for one person to eat

cornmeal /ˈkɔːn.mɪəl/ [US] /ˈkɔːrn-/ *noun* [U] rough yellow flour made from maize, used to make bread, TORTILLAS, etc.

ˈcorn ˌoil *noun* [U] oil made from maize, which is often used for cooking

corn on the cob /ˌkɔː.n.ɒn.ðəˈkɒb/ [US] /ˌkɔːrn.ɑːn.ðəˈkɑːb/ *noun* [U] the cylinder-like part of the maize plant which is cooked with the sweet yellow or white grains on it ⊃See picture **Vegetables** on page Centre 2

cornrow /ˈkɔːn.rəʊ/ [US] /ˈkɔːrn.roʊ/ *noun* [C] *MAINLY US* one of many strips of hair twisted together close to the head in thin rows: *Tyler likes her hair in cornrows, but braiding it takes a long time.* ⊃See picture **Hairstyles and Hats** on page Centre 8 **cornrow** /ˈkɔːn.rəʊ/ [US] /ˈkɔːrn.roʊ/ *verb* [T] *Paul cornrowed her hair.*

cornstarch /ˈkɔːn.stɑːtʃ/ US /ˈkɔːrn.stɑːrtʃ/ noun [U] US FOR **cornflour**

corn ˈsyrup noun [U] a thick sweet liquid made from maize

cornucopia /ˌkɔː.njʊˈkəʊ.pi.ə/ US /ˌkɔːr.njəˈkoʊ-/ noun [S] FORMAL a large amount of something; a great supply: *The table held a veritable cornucopia **of** every kind of food or drink you could want.*

corny /ˈkɔː.ni/ US /ˈkɔːr-/ adj INFORMAL (especially of jokes, films, stories, etc.) lacking new ideas and sincerity; too often repeated and therefore not amusing or interesting: *corny **jokes** ○ I couldn't watch the whole movie – it was just too corny.*

corollary /kəˈrɒl.ᵊr.i/ US /-ˈrɑː.lə-/ noun [C] FORMAL something that results from something else: *Unfortunately, violence is the inevitable corollary **of** such a revolutionary change in society.*

corona /kəˈrəʊ.nə/ US /-ˈroʊ-/ noun [C usually sing] plural **coronas** or **coronae** a circle of light that can sometimes be seen around the moon at night, or around the sun during an ECLIPSE (= a situation when the moon is positioned exactly between the sun and the Earth)

coronary /ˈkɒr.ᵊn.ᵊr.i/ US /ˈkɔːr.ə.ner-/ noun [C] (SPECIALIZED **coronary thrombosis**) an extremely dangerous medical condition in which the flow of blood to the heart is blocked by a blood CLOT (= a lump of blood): *He's in hospital after **having** a coronary last week.*

coronary /ˈkɒr.ᵊn.ᵊr.i/ US /ˈkɔːr.ə.ner-/ adj SPECIALIZED relating to the arteries that supply blood to the muscles of the heart: *Regular exercise reduces the risk of coronary **heart disease**.*

coronation /ˌkɒr.əˈneɪ.ʃᵊn/ US /ˌkɔːr-/ noun [C] a ceremony at which a person is made king or queen

coroner /ˈkɒr.ə.nəʳ/ US /ˈkɔːr.ᵊn.ɚ/ noun [C] an official who examines the reasons for a person's death, especially if it was violent or unexpected

coronet /ˈkɒr.ə.nət/ US /ˌkɔːr-/ /--'-/ noun [C] a small CROWN (= circular decoration for the head)

Corp. BUSINESS noun [C] WRITTEN ABBREVIATION FOR **corporation** BUSINESS

Corp. RANK noun [C] WRITTEN ABBREVIATION FOR **corporal** RANK

corpora /ˈkɔː.pᵊr.ə/ US /ˈkɔːr.pɚ-/ plural of **corpus**

corporal BODILY /ˈkɔː.pᵊr.ᵊl/ US /ˈkɔːr.pɚ-/ adj FORMAL of or relating to the body

corporal RANK /ˈkɔː.pᵊr.ᵊl/ US /ˈkɔːr.pɚ-/ noun [C] (WRITTEN ABBREVIATION **Corp.**) a person of low rank in an army or an air force

corporal ˈpunishment noun [U] the physical punishment of people, especially of children, by hitting them

corporate /ˈkɔː.pᵊr.ət/ US /ˈkɔːr.pɚ-/ adj **1** [before n] relating to a large company: *corporate finance ○ a corporate merger ○ corporate executives* **2** FORMAL of or shared by a whole group and not just of a single member: *All adults take corporate **responsibility** for the upbringing of the tribe's children.*

corporate ˈimage noun [C] the way in which a company is seen and understood by people in general

corporation BUSINESS /ˌkɔː.pᵊrˈeɪ.ʃᵊn/ US /ˌkɔːr.pəˈreɪ-/ group noun [C] (WRITTEN ABBREVIATION **Corp.**) a large company or group of companies that is controlled together as a single organization: *a multinational corporation ○ the British Broadcasting Corporation ○ She didn't want to work for a big corporation where everything was so impersonal.*

corporation LOCAL ORGANIZATION /ˌkɔː.pᵊrˈeɪ.ʃᵊn/ US /ˌkɔːr.pəˈreɪ-/ group noun [C] MAINLY UK the organization in a particular town or city which is responsible for services such as cleaning roads: *a municipal corporation*

corpoˈration ˌtax noun [U] UK tax paid by businesses on their profits

corporeal /kɔːˈpɔː.ri.əl/ US /kɔːrˈpɔːr.i-/ adj FORMAL physical and not spiritual; of the body **corporeally** /kɔːˈpɔː.ri.ə.li/ US /kɔːrˈpɔːr.i-/ adv

corps MILITARY UNIT /kɔːʳ/ US /kɔːr/ group noun [C] plural **corps** a military unit trained to perform particular duties: *the Royal Army Medical Corps ○ the intelligence corps*

corps GROUP /kɔːʳ/ US /kɔːr/ group noun [C] plural **corps** a group of people who are connected because they are involved in a particular activity: *the diplomatic corps ○ the press corps ○ A corps of technicians is/are accompanying the band on their tour.*

corps de ˈballet group noun [S] the members of a group of ballet dancers who dance together, especially those who are not the main dancers

corpse /kɔːps/ US /kɔːrps/ noun [C] a dead body, usually of a person

corpulent /ˈkɔː.pjʊ.lənt/ US /ˈkɔːr-/ adj FORMAL fat: *a corpulent gentleman* **corpulence** /ˈkɔː.pjʊ.lənts/ US /ˈkɔːr-/ noun [U]

corpus /ˈkɔː.pəs/ US /ˈkɔːr-/ noun [C] plural **corpuses** or **corpora** the collection of a single writer's work or of writing about a particular subject, or a large amount of written and sometimes spoken material collected to show the state of a language

corpuscle /ˈkɔː.pʌs.l̩/ US /ˈkɔːr-/ noun [C] SPECIALIZED any of the red or white cells in the blood

corral /kəˈrɑːl/ US /-ˈræl/ noun [C] an area surrounded by a fence for keeping horses or cattle in, especially in North America

corral /kəˈrɑːl/ US /-ˈræl/ verb [T] -ll- **1** to guide horses or cattle into a corral **2** to gather a group of people together and keep them in one place, especially in order to control them: *Police corralled most of the demonstrators in a small area near the station.*

correct /kəˈrekt/ adj **1** right and not wrong; in agreement with the true facts or with what is generally accepted: *a correct answer ○ "Is that the correct spelling?" "I don't know – look it up in a dictionary." ○ It's not correct **to** describe them as 'students'. ○ FORMAL "Your name is Angela Black?" "That is correct."* ✳ NOTE: The opposite is **incorrect**. **2** taking or showing great care to behave or speak in a way that is generally accepted and approved of: *He's very correct **in** his dress/speech/manner, isn't he?*

correct /kəˈrekt/ verb [T] **1** to show or tell someone that something is wrong and to make it right: *Students said it was helpful if the teacher corrected their pronunciation. ○ I've got thirty exam papers to correct.* **2** If a medical treatment corrects a particular condition, it cures the condition or makes it easier to manage: *glasses to correct poor vision ○ a chair which corrects bad posture*

● **correct me if I'm wrong but...** said as a polite and slightly formal way of disagreeing with someone: *Correct me if I'm wrong, but I think we arranged the meeting for the 12th of December.* **correctly** /kəˈrekt.li/ adv: *Have I pronounced your name correctly?*

correctness /kəˈrekt.nəs/ noun [U] *He speaks with such correctness (= care) that it sometimes sounds very formal.*

correction /kəˈrek.ʃᵊn/ noun **1** [C or U] a change made to something in order to correct or improve it, or when you make such a change: *She was disappointed to see her essay returned with a mass of corrections in red ink.* ⊃See also **corrections**. **2** [U] OLD USE punishment of a type that was intended to improve bad behaviour

corrective /kəˈrek.tɪv/ adj **1** intended to improve a situation: *corrective measures/action* **2** describes something that is intended to cure a medical condition: *corrective surgery*

COMMON LEARNER ERROR

correct or **right**?

Correct means 'accurate' or 'without mistakes'.

All the details were correct.

Right is another word for 'correct'. It also means 'suitable' or 'morally acceptable'.

She was careful to choose the right word.
I don't think it's right for parents to hit their children.

Remember that **correct** does not mean 'good'.

The hotel was cheap but good.
~~The hotel was cheap but correct.~~

C

cor'rectional ,center noun [C] (ALSO **correctional facility**) US FOR **prison**

corrections /kəˈrek.ʃᵊnz/ plural noun US FORMAL the set of methods available to the authorities for punishing and treating people who have committed crimes: *a corrections officer* ⊃See also **correction** at **correct**.
correctional /kəˈrek.ʃᵊn.ᵊl/ adj: *a correctional program* ○ *correctional personnel*

correlation /ˌkɒr.əˈleɪ.ʃᵊn/ ⑩ /ˌkɔːr-/ noun [C or U] a connection between two or more things, often one in which one of them causes or influences the other: *There's a high correlation between smoking and lung cancer.*
correlate /ˈkɒr.ə.leɪt/ ⑩ /ˈkɔːr-/ verb [T] *Stress levels and heart disease are strongly correlated* (= connected).

correspond MATCH /ˌkɒr.ɪˈspɒnd/ ⑩ /ˌkɔːr.ɪˈspɑːnd/ verb [I] to match or be similar or equal: *The money I've saved corresponds roughly to the amount I need for my course.* ○ *The American FBI corresponds to the British MI5.* ○ *His story of what happened that night didn't correspond with the witness's version.*
correspondence /ˌkɒr.ɪˈspɒn.dᵊnts/ ⑩ /ˌkɔːr.ɪˈspɑːn-/ noun [C usually sing; U] *The survey found no correspondence between crime and unemployment rates.*
corresponding /ˌkɒr.ɪˈspɒn.dɪŋ/ ⑩ /ˌkɔːr.ɪˈspɑːn-/ adj similar, or resulting from something else: *Company losses were 50 per cent worse than in the corresponding period last year.* ○ *As the course becomes more difficult, there's usually a corresponding drop in attendance.*
correspondingly /ˌkɒr.ɪˈspɒn.dɪŋ.li/ ⑩ /ˌkɔːr.ɪˈspɑːn-/ adv: *The cost of living in the city is more expensive, but salaries are supposed to be correspondingly higher.*

correspond WRITE /ˌkɒr.ɪˈspɒnd/ ⑩ /ˌkɔːr.ɪˈspɑːnd/ verb [I] to communicate by writing a letter or sending an EMAIL: *I've been corresponding with several experts in the field.*
correspondence /ˌkɒr.ɪˈspɒn.dᵊnts/ ⑩ /ˌkɔːr.ɪˈspɑːn-/ noun [U] **1** letters, especially official or business letters: *Any further correspondence should be sent to my new address.* **2** the action of writing, receiving and reading letters, especially between two people: *Her correspondence with Jim lasted many years.*
correspondent /ˌkɒr.ɪˈspɒn.dᵊnt/ ⑩ /ˌkɔːr.ɪˈspɑːn-/ noun [C] FORMAL someone who writes letters: *I'm a terrible correspondent – I never seem to get the time to write.*

corres'pondence ,course noun [C] a course of study in which you study at home, receiving and sending off work by post, email, etc.

correspondent /ˌkɒr.ɪˈspɒn.dᵊnt/ ⑩ /ˌkɔːr.ɪˈspɑːn-/ noun [C] a person employed by a newspaper, a television station, etc. to report on a particular subject or send reports from a foreign country: *a war correspondent* ○ *the education correspondent for the Guardian*

corridor PASSAGE /ˈkɒr.ɪ.dɔːʳ/ ⑩ /ˈkɔːr.ɪ.dɚ/ noun [C] a long passage in a building or train, especially with rooms on either side: *Her office is at the end of the corridor.*

• **the corridors of power** the higher levels of government where the most important decisions are made

corridor LAND /ˈkɒr.ɪ.dɔːʳ/ ⑩ /ˈkɔːr.ɪ.dɚ/ noun [C] a long piece of one country's land which goes through another country: *the Polish corridor*

corroborate /kəˈrɒb.ə.reɪt/ ⑩ /ˈrɑː.bə-/ verb [T] FORMAL to add proof or certainty to an account, statement, idea, etc. with new information: *Recent research seems to corroborate his theory.* corroboration /kəˌrɒb.əˈreɪ.ʃᵊn/ ⑩ /ˌrɑː.bə-/ noun [U] *Without corroboration from forensic tests, it will be difficult to prove that the suspect is guilty.* corroborating /kəˈrɒb.ᵊr.eɪ.tɪŋ/ ⑩ /ˈrɑː.bə.reɪ.t̬ɪŋ/ adj (ALSO **corroborative**) *corroborating evidence/reports*

corrode /kəˈrəʊd/ ⑩ /ˈroʊd/ verb [I or T] If metal corrodes, or if something corrodes it, it is slowly damaged by something such as rain or water: *Steel tends to corrode faster in a salty atmosphere, such as by the sea.* corrosion /kəˈrəʊ.ʒᵊn/ ⑩ /ˈroʊ-/ noun [U] *There was a lot of corrosion on the bottom of the car.* ○ *FIGURATIVE We are witnessing the corrosion of moral standards within our society.*
corrosive /kəˈrəʊ.sɪv/ ⑩ /ˈroʊ-/ adj **1** A corrosive substance causes damage by chemical action: *a highly*

corrosive acid **2** harmful and causing bad, bitter feelings: *the corrosive influence of racism* corrosively /kəˈrəʊ.sɪv.li/ ⑩ /ˈroʊ-/ adv

corrugated /ˈkɒr.ə.geɪ.tɪd/ ⑩ /ˈkɔːr.ə.geɪ.tɪd/ adj (especially of sheets of iron or cardboard) having parallel rows of folds which look like a series of waves when seen from the edge: *The roof is made from sheets of corrugated iron.*

corrupt IMMORAL /kəˈrʌpt/ adj **1** dishonestly using your position or power to your own advantage, especially for money: *Both companies are under investigation for corrupt practices.* ○ *The whole system was corrupt – every official she approached wanted money before helping her.* **2** morally bad: *a corrupt society*
corrupt /kəˈrʌpt/ verb [T] to make someone or something become dishonest or immoral: *The study claimed that violence on television corrupts the minds of children.* corruptible /kəˈrʌp.tɪ.bl̩/ adj: *Perhaps some systems of government are more corruptible than others.* corruption /kəˈrʌp.ʃᵊn/ noun **1** [U] illegal, immoral or dishonest behaviour, especially by people in positions of power: *The film is about a young police-officer and his struggle to expose corruption in the force.* ○ *Political corruption is widespread throughout the country.* **2** [C] in language, a word whose original form has been changed: *The swear word 'bloody' is wrongly thought by some to be a corruption of the words 'by our Lady.'*

corrupt COMPUTER /kəˈrʌpt/ adj When information on a computer becomes corrupt, it is spoilt and cannot be properly used because it has become changed in wrong ways: *corrupt data* ○ *a corrupt file* corrupt /kəˈrʌpt/ verb [T] *Most of the data on the hard drive was corrupted by the power cut.* corruption /kəˈrʌp.ʃᵊn/ noun [U] *data corruption*

corsage /kɔːˈsɑːʒ/ ⑩ /kɔːr-/ noun [C] a small decorative group of flowers which a woman pins to her clothes or ties around her wrist, usually for a special occasion

corset /ˈkɔː.sɪt/ ⑩ /ˈkɔːr-/ noun [C] a tight piece of underwear worn on the middle part of a woman's body to make her waist appear smaller, especially in the past

cortege /kɔːˈteʒ/ ⑩ /kɔːr-/ noun [C] a slowly moving line of people or cars at a funeral

cortex /ˈkɔː.teks/ ⑩ /ˈkɔːr-/ noun [C] plural **cortices** SPECIALIZED the outer layer, especially of the brain and other organs: *the cerebral cortex*

cortisone /ˈkɔː.tɪ.zəʊn/ ⑩ /ˈkɔːr.tə.zoʊn/ noun [U] a particular hormone which is used medically, especially for treating ARTHRITIS (= a painful condition of the joints) and skin problems

coruscating /ˈkɒr.ə.skeɪ.tɪŋ/ ⑩ /ˈkɔːr.ə.skeɪ.t̬ɪŋ/ adj **1** LITERARY flashing brightly **2** FORMAL extremely clever and exciting or amusing: *He's not known for his coruscating wit.*

cos BECAUSE /kəz/ conjunction (ALSO **'cos**) NOT STANDARD FOR **because**: *You can cook dinner tonight cos I did it last night.*

cos MATHEMATICS /kɒz/ ⑩ /kɑːz/ ABBREVIATION FOR **cosine**

cosh UK /kɒʃ/ ⑩ /kɑːʃ/ noun [C] (US **blackjack**) a short heavy stick made of metal or rubber used as a weapon
cosh /kɒʃ/ ⑩ /kɑːʃ/ verb [T] UK *He was coshed* (= hit with a cosh) *outside the pub.*

cosignatory /ˌkəʊˈsɪg.nə.tᵊr.i/ ⑩ /ˌkoʊˈsɪg.nə.tɔːr-/ noun [C] FORMAL one of two or more people who sign an official agreement or document

cosily /ˈkəʊ.zɪ.li/ ⑩ /ˈkoʊ-/ adv ⊃See at **cosy**.

cosine /ˈkəʊ.saɪn/ ⑩ /ˈkoʊ-/ noun [C] (WRITTEN ABBREVIATION **cos**) SPECIALIZED (in a triangle that has one angle of 90°) the ratio of the length of the side next to an angle less than 90°, divided by the length of the HYPOTENUSE (= the side opposite the 90° angle) ⊃Compare **sine**; **tangent** TRIANGLE.

'cos (,lettuce) UK noun [C] (US **romaine**) a type of lettuce with long narrow leaves

cosmetic /kɒzˈmet.ɪk/ ⑩ /kɑːzˈmet̬-/ adj DISAPPROVING describes changes, etc. that are intended to make you believe that something is better when, in reality, the problem has not been solved; SUPERFICIAL: *They were offered a few cosmetic improvements to their working con-*

ditions, but nothing of significance. cosmetically /kɒz-ˈmet.ɪ.kli/ ⓤ /kɑːzˈmeṭ-/ adv

cosmetics /kɒzˈmet.ɪks/ ⓤ /kɑːzˈmeṭ-/ plural noun substances that you put on your face or body which are intended to improve its appearance: We sell a wide range of cosmetics and toiletries at a very reasonable price. cosmetic /kɒzˈmet.ɪk/ ⓤ /kɑːzˈmeṭ-/ adj [before n] a cosmetic cream

cosˌmetic ˈsurgery noun [U] any medical operation which is intended to improve a person's appearance

cosmonaut /ˈkɒz.mə.nɔːt/ ⓤ /ˈkɑːz.mə.nɑːt/ noun [C] an astronaut from the former Soviet Union

cosmopolitan /ˌkɒz.məˈpɒl.ɪ.tⁿn/ ⓤ /ˌkɑːz.məˈpɑː.lɪ.t̬ⁿn/ adj USUALLY APPROVING containing or having experience of people and things from many different parts of the world: New York is a highly cosmopolitan city. cosmopolitan /ˌkɒz.məˈpɒl.ɪ.tⁿn/ ⓤ /ˌkɑːz.məˈpɑː.lɪ.t̬ⁿn/ noun [C] USUALLY APPROVING Lisa is a real cosmopolitan (= she has experience of many different parts of the world).

the cosmos /ðəˈkɒz.mɒs/ ⓤ /-ˈkɑːz.moʊs/ noun [S] the universe considered as a system with an order and pattern cosmological /ˌkɒz.məˈlɒdʒ.ɪ.kⁿl/ ⓤ /ˌkɑːz.məˈlɑː.dʒɪ-/ adj (ALSO **cosmologic**) cosmology /kɒzˈmɒl.ə.dʒi/ ⓤ /kɑːzˈmɑː.lə-/ noun [C or U] the study of the nature and origin of the universe, or a theory about it

cosmic /ˈkɒz.mɪk/ ⓤ /ˈkɑːz-/ adj **1** relating to the universe and the natural processes that happen in it: cosmic dust/radiation **2** INFORMAL very great: The earthquake was a disaster of cosmic proportions/scale. cosmically /ˈkɒz.mɪ.kli/ ⓤ /ˈkɑːz-/ adv

Cossack /ˈkɒs.æk/ ⓤ /ˈkɑː.sæk/ noun [C] one of a group of people from Russia with a famous history of fighting and bravery

cosset /ˈkɒs.ɪt/ ⓤ /ˈkɑː.sɪt/ verb [T] -t- or UK ALSO -tt- to give a lot of attention to making someone comfortable and to protecting them from anything unpleasant: Children need to be cosseted. ○ DISAPPROVING The country has been cosseted (= too protected) by the government for so long that people have forgotten how to take responsibility for themselves.

cossie **cozzie** /ˈkɒz.i/ ⓤ /ˈkɑː.zi/ noun [C] UK INFORMAL FOR swimming costume

cost MONEY /kɒst/ ⓤ /kɑːst/ noun [U] the amount of money needed to buy, do or make something: When you buy a new computer, you usually get software included at no extra cost (= for no additional money). ○ For many parents, two salaries are essential to **cover** the cost of (= pay for) school fees. ○ The supermarket chain announced that it was **cutting** the cost (= reducing the price) of all its fresh and frozen meat. ○ It's difficult for most people to cope with the **rising** cost **of** (= increasing price of) healthcare. ○ I was able to buy the damaged goods **at** cost (= for only the amount of money needed to produce or get the goods, with no money added for profit).

costs /kɒsts/ ⓤ /kɑːsts/ plural noun the cost of something: We need to **cut** our advertising costs. ○ The **estimated** costs of the building project are well over £1 million.

cost /kɒst/ ⓤ /kɑːst/ verb [T] cost, cost If something costs an amount of money, you must pay that amount to buy or do it: "How much does this book cost (= What is the price of this book)?" ○ **It** costs a lot **to** buy a house in London. ○ [+ two objects] The trip will cost you $1000.

• cost an arm and a leg/a small fortune (UK ALSO cost a bomb/the earth/a packet) to be extremely expensive: I'd love to buy a Rolls-Royce, but they cost an arm and a leg.

• it'll cost **you** INFORMAL it will be very expensive: It'll cost you to have your roof mended.

• cost **sb** dear to cause someone to spend a lot of money or lose money: Buying that second-hand car without having it checked by a mechanic first cost us dear. ➔See also cost **sb** dear at cost SOMETHING GIVEN.

cost /kɒst/ ⓤ /kɑːst/ verb [T] cost, costed to calculate the future cost of something: How carefully did you cost the materials for the new fence and gate? ○ Has your scheme been properly costed (**out**)?

costing /ˈkɒs.tɪŋ/ ⓤ /ˈkɑː.stɪŋ/ noun [C often pl; U] (a) calculation of the future cost of something such as a possible product: We'll need accurate costings before we can agree to fund the scheme.

costly /ˈkɒst.li/ ⓤ /ˈkɑːst-/ adj expensive: a costly item ○ a costly purchase ○ DISAPPROVING The project was subject to several costly **delays/setbacks**. costliness /ˈkɒst.lɪ.nəs/ ⓤ /ˈkɑːst-/ noun [U]

cost SOMETHING GIVEN /kɒst/ ⓤ /kɑːst/ noun [S or U] something which is given, needed or lost in order to obtain a particular thing: We were going to paint the house ourselves, but when we considered the cost **in** time and effort, we decided to get a painter to do it for us. ○ The driver managed not to hit the child who ran in front of his car, but only **at the** cost **of** injuring himself. ○ She has finally got the job she wanted, but **at** great personal cost (= she has had to give up other things that were important to her). ○ It's not worth getting into an argument with Tim, as I learned **to my** cost (= from my unpleasant experience of having done so).

• at all cost(s) (ALSO at any cost) If something must be done or avoided at all costs, it must be done or avoided whatever happens: Security during the president's visit must be maintained at all costs. ○ He wanted her at any cost, even if it meant giving up everything he had.

cost /kɒst/ ⓤ /kɑːst/ verb [T] cost, cost to cause someone to lose or destroy something valuable: Drinking and driving costs lives (= can cause accidents in which people die). ○ [+ two objects] His affairs cost him his marriage (= his marriage ended because of them).

• cost **sb** dear If something that someone does, especially something stupid, costs them dear, it causes them a lot of problems: Later that year he attacked a photographer, an incident that cost him dear. ➔See also cost **sb** dear at cost MONEY.

costly /ˈkɒst.li/ ⓤ /ˈkɑːst-/ adj: Building this bridge has already been too costly in terms of lives (= people have been killed while working on it). costliness /ˈkɒst.lɪ.nəs/ ⓤ /ˈkɑːst-/ noun [U]

co-star /ˈkəʊ.stɑːʳ/ ⓤ /ˈkoʊ.stɑːr/ noun [C] a famous actor appearing with another famous actor in a film or a play, both of whom have parts of equal importance: The co-stars of 'Casablanca' are Ingrid Bergman and Humphrey Bogart. co-star /ˈkəʊ.stɑːʳ/ ⓤ /ˈkoʊ.stɑːr/ verb [I or T] -rr- Katherine Hepburn co-starred **with** Spencer Tracy in many films.

cost-cutting noun [U] actions which are taken to reduce the amount that is spent on a service or within an organization: The recovery was achieved in the old-fashioned way with cost-cutting and price increases. ○ a cost-cutting exercise ○ cost-cutting measures

cost-effective /ˌkɒst.ɪˈfek.tɪv/ ⓤ /ˌkɑːst-/ adj If an activity is cost-effective, it is good value for the amount of money paid: It wouldn't be cost-effective to buy an expensive new computer when all you want to do is word processing.

cost of ˈliving noun [S] the amount of money that a person needs to live on: The increase in interest rates will **raise** the cost of living.

cost of ˈliving ˌindex noun [C usually sing] US FOR retail price index

ˈcost ˌprice noun [C] the price that it cost to make an item, without a profit being added: We were able to buy the furniture from a friend **at** cost price.

costume /ˈkɒs.tjuːm/ ⓤ /ˈkɑː.stuːm/ noun **1** [C or U] the set of clothes typical of a particular country or period of history, or suitable for a particular activity: Singers performing Mozart's operas often **dress in**/wear **historical** costume. ○ The dancers leading the procession were **in** colourful and elaborate costumes. ○ UK The shop has a good selection of bikinis and **bathing/swimming** costumes. **2** [C] (UK ALSO **fancy-dress costume**) a set of clothes worn in order to look like someone or something else, especially for a party or as part of an entertainment: Our host was wearing a clown costume. ○ The children were dressed in **halloween** costumes.

costumier /kɒsˈtjuː.mi.eɪ/ ⓤ /kɑːˈstuː-/ noun [C] a person who makes and rents out costumes, especially for theatrical use

C

'costume ˌdrama *noun* [C or U] a film, especially on television, about a period in the past, or films of this type

'costume ˌjewellery *noun* [U] cheap jewellery made to look as if it is expensive

cosy *UK, US* **cozy** /'kəʊ.zi/ [US] /'koʊ-/ *adj* **1** comfortable and pleasant, especially (of a building) because small and warm: *This room is* ***nice and*** *cosy in the winter.* ○ *He showed me into a cosy* ***little*** *room.* **2** DISAPPROVING describes a situation which is convenient for those involved but not always honest or legal: *He has some cosy arrangement/deal with his supplier, which means he's able to sell his goods more cheaply.*
cosy *UK, US* **cozy** /'kəʊ.zi/ [US] /'koʊ-/ *noun* [C] a cover that you put on a TEAPOT or a boiled egg to keep it warm: *a tea cosy* ○ *an egg cosy*
cosily *UK, US* **cozily** /'kəʊ.zɪ.li/ [US] /'koʊ-/ *adv*: *The children are cosily* (= warmly and comfortably) *tucked up in bed.*

cot /kɒt/ [US] /kɑːt/ *noun* [C] **1** *UK* (*US* **crib**) a small bed for a baby or young child with high bars round the sides so that the child cannot fall out **2** *US FOR* **camp bed**

'cot ˌdeath *noun* [C or U] (*SPECIALIZED* **SIDS**) the sudden death of a baby while it is sleeping for no obvious reason

coterie /'kəʊ.tᵊr.i/ [US] /'koʊ.t̬ɚ-/ *group noun* [C] a small group of people with shared interests who often do not want other people to join them: *a coterie* ***of*** *writers*

coterminous /ˌkəʊ'tɜː.mɪ.nəs/ [US] /ˌkoʊ'tɝː-/ *adj FORMAL* having or meeting at a shared border or limit: *France is coterminous* ***with*** *Italy.* **coterminously** /ˌkəʊ'tɜː.mɪ.nə.sli/ [US] /ˌkoʊ'tɝː-/ *adv*

cottage /'kɒt.ɪdʒ/ [US] /'kɑː.t̬ɪdʒ/ *noun* [C] a small house, usually in the countryside: *They live in an idyllic* ***country/thatched*** *cottage, with roses round the door.*
cottager /'kɒt.ɪ.dʒəʳ/ [US] /'kɑː.t̬ɪ.dʒɚ/ *noun* [C] *OLD USE* a person who lives in a cottage

ˌcottage 'cheese *noun* [U] soft white lumpy cheese made from sour milk

ˌcottage 'industry *noun* [C] a small business run from home

ˌcottage 'loaf *noun* [C] *UK* a loaf of bread which has a smaller round part on top of a larger round part

ˌcottage 'pie *noun* [C or U] a dish consisting of a layer of small pieces of meat covered with a thick layer of MASHED POTATO

cottaging /'kɒt.ɪ.dʒɪŋ/ [US] /'kɑː.t̬ɪ-/ *noun* [U] *UK SLANG* sexual activity in a public toilet between men who are not involved in a lasting relationship with each other

cotton /'kɒt.ᵊn/ [US] /'kɑː.t̬ᵊn/ *noun* [U] **1** the fibre which grows around the seeds of a tall plant which is cultivated especially in the US, China and India: *a bale of cotton* **2** thread or cloth made from the fibres of the cotton plant: *a shirt made of pure cotton* ○ *She looked pretty in a simple cotton dress.* ○ *UK a reel of cotton* (= thread) **3** *US FOR* **cotton wool** **cottony** /'kɒt.ᵊn.i/ [US] /'kɑː.t̬ᵊn-/ *adj*

cotton /'kɒt.ᵊn/ [US] /'kɑː.t̬ᵊn/ *verb*
▲ **cotton on** *phrasal verb UK INFORMAL* to begin to understand a situation or fact: *I'd only just cottoned on* ***to*** *the fact that they were having a relationship.*

'cotton ˌbud *UK noun* [C] (*US TRADEMARK* **Q-tip**) a short stick with a small amount of cotton on each end that is used for cleaning, especially the ears

ˌcotton 'candy *noun* [U] *US FOR* **candyfloss**

'cotton ˌgin *noun* [C] a machine used for separating the fibres of the cotton plant from the seeds

cotton-picking /'kɒt.ᵊnˌpɪ.kɪŋ/ [US] /'kɑː.t̬ᵊn-/ *adj* [before n] *US INFORMAL* used to add emphasis when you are slightly annoyed: *Just wait one cotton-picking minute, will you?*

cottonwood /'kɒt.ᵊn.wʊd/ [US] /'kɑː.t̬ᵊn-/ *noun* [C] a North American tree whose seeds are covered with hairs that look like cotton

ˌcotton 'wool *UK noun* [U] (*US* **cotton**) cotton in the form of a soft mass, usually used for cleaning your skin: *cotton wool balls/pads*

couch [SEAT] /kaʊtʃ/ *noun* [C] a **sofa**

couch [BED] /kaʊtʃ/ *noun* [C] a type of high bed, especially one in a doctor's office

couch [EXPRESS] /kaʊtʃ/ *verb FORMAL* **couch *sth* in/as *sth*** to express something in a particular way: [often passive] *I don't understand this form – it's all couched* ***in*** *legal terminology.*

couchette /kuː'ʃet/ *noun* [C] a bed in a train or on a boat which can either be folded away or used as an ordinary seat during the day

'couch poˌtato *noun* [C] *INFORMAL DISAPPROVING* a person who watches a lot of television and does not have an active style of life

cougar *MAINLY US* /'kuː.gəʳ/ [US] /-gɚ/ *noun* [C] (*MAINLY UK* **puma**) a large brown wild cat that lives in North and South America

cough /kɒf/ [US] /kɑːf/ *verb* [I] **1** to force air out of your lungs through your throat with a short loud sound: *The smoke made me cough.* ○ *I coughed all night long.* **2** to make a sound like a cough: *The car engine coughed a few times, but wouldn't start.*
cough /kɒf/ [US] /kɑːf/ *noun* [C] **1** when you cough, or the sound this makes: *a dry cough* (= one which does not produce mucus) ○ *a hacking* (= very bad and loud) *cough* **2** an illness that makes you cough a lot: *a smoker's cough* ○ *Emily has a very bad/nasty cough* (= has been coughing frequently as part of an illness).

PHRASAL VERBS WITH **cough** ▼

▲ **cough *sth* up** [COUGH] *phrasal verb* [M] to make something come out of your throat or lungs when you cough: *Doctors were worried when she started to cough up blood.*
▲ **cough *(sth)* up** [PRODUCE] *phrasal verb* [M] *SLANG* to produce money or information unwillingly: *I've just had to cough up £10 for a parking fine.*

'coughing ˌfit *noun* [C] a sudden period of coughing

'cough ˌmedicine *noun* [C or U] (*ALSO* **cough mixture**) medicine in the form of a liquid that helps a cough get better

'cough ˌsweet *UK noun* [C] (*US* **cough drop**, *AUS* **cough lolly**) a hard, sweet piece of medicine that you suck on to help a cough get better

.co.uk /dɒtˌkəʊ.dɒt.juː'keɪ/ [US] /dɑːtˌkoʊ.dɑːt-/ *INTERNET ABBREVIATION* the last part of an Internet address that belongs to a British company

could [CAN] *STRONG* /kʊd/, *WEAK* /kəd/ *past simple of* **can**, used to talk about what someone or something was able or allowed to do: *When I was younger I could stay up all night and not get tired.* ○ *It was so noisy that we couldn't hear ourselves speak.* ○ *You said we could watch television when we've finished our homework.* ○ *We asked if the computer could access the Internet.* ➲See Note **can/could or be able to?** at **can** ABILITY.

could [PERMISSION] *STRONG* /kʊd/, *WEAK* /kəd/ *modal verb* used as a more polite form of 'can' when asking for permission: *Could I speak to Mr Davis, please?* ○ *Excuse me, could I just say something?*

could [REQUEST] *STRONG* /kʊd/, *WEAK* /kəd/ *modal verb* used as a more polite form of 'can' when asking someone to provide something or do something: *Could you lend me £5?* ○ *Could you possibly turn that music down a little, please?*

could [POSSIBILITY] *STRONG* /kʊd/, *WEAK* /kəd/ *modal verb* used to express possibility, especially slight or uncertain possibility: *A lot of crime could be prevented.* ○ *She could arrive anytime now.* ○ *This new drug could be an important step in the fight against cancer.* ○ *Be careful with that stick – it could* ***have*** *gone in my eye!*

could [SUGGEST] *STRONG* /kʊd/, *WEAK* /kəd/ *modal verb* used for making a suggestion: *We could go for a drink after work tomorrow, if you like.* ○ *You could* ***always*** *call Susie and see if she might babysit.*
• **could do with *sth*** *INFORMAL* If you could do with something, you want it very much: *I could do with a rest.*

could [SHOULD] *STRONG* /kʊd/, *WEAK* /kəd/ *modal verb* used for saying, especially angrily, what you think someone else should do: *Well, you could try to look a little more enthusiastic!* ○ *I waited ages for you – you could've said that you weren't coming!*

couldn't /'kʊd.ªnt/ *short form of* could not: *I couldn't find my keys this morning.*

could've /'kʊd.ªv/ *short form of* could have: *It could've been much worse, you know.*

coulis /'ku:.li/ *noun* [C or U] *plural* **coulis** a liquid made by cooking and crushing fruit: *raspberry coulis*

council /'kaʊnt.sªl/ *group noun* [C] **1** a group of people elected or chosen to make decisions or give advice on a particular subject, to represent a particular group of people, or to run a particular organization: *the United Nations Security Council* ○ *This play is supported by a grant from the local arts council.* **2** the group of people elected to govern a particular area, town or city, and organize services for it: *Edinburgh City Council* ○ *The* **local** *council has/have decided not to allocate funds for the project.* ○ *The* **town/city** *council is/are responsible for keeping the streets clean.*
councillor, *US* **councilor** /'kaʊnt.sªl.ªr/ ⓤ /-ɚ/ *noun* [C] (*US ALSO* **councilman, councilwoman**) an elected member of a local government: *a town/city/county/local councillor* ○ *Councillor Moore*

'council e,state *UK noun* [C] (*US* **housing project**) an area of a city in which there are council houses and flats: *She was brought up in a council estate in Liverpool.*

'council ,house/'flat *noun* [C] *UK* a house/flat owned by the council and rented to people

'council ,housing *UK noun* [U] (*US* **public housing**) houses or flats owned by the government for which the rent is lower than homes that are privately owned

,council of 'war *noun* [C] *UK* a meeting held to decide what action to take in a serious or difficult situation: *Parents are holding a council of war to decide what to do about the threatened closure of the school.*

counsel /'kaʊnt.sªl/ *verb* [T] **-ll-** or *US USUALLY* **-l-** to give advice, especially on social or personal problems: *The police have provided experts to counsel local people affected by the tragedy.* ○ *My job involves counselling unemployed people* **on/about** *how to find work.*
counsel /'kaʊnt.sªl/ *noun* **1** [U] *FORMAL* advice: *I should have listened to my father's wise counsel, and saved some money instead of spending it all.* **2** [C] *LEGAL* one or more of the lawyers taking part in a law case: *The judge addressed counsel.* ○ *Counsel* **for the defence** (= the lawyer giving advice to the accused person) *argued convincingly that his client was not guilty.*
● **keep** *your* **own counsel** to not say what your opinions are: *I'd love to know what Anna thinks about things, but she always keeps her own counsel.*
counselling, *US USUALLY* **counseling** /'kaʊnt.sªl.ɪŋ/ *noun* [U] the job or process of listening to someone and giving them advice about their problems: *a counselling* **service**
counsellor, *US USUALLY* **counselor** /'kaʊnt.sªl.ªr/ ⓤ /-ɚ/ *noun* [C] someone who is trained to listen to people and give them advice about their problems: *The college now has a counsellor to help students with both personal and work problems.* ○ *a* **marriage-guidance** *counsellor*
counselor /'kaʊnt.sªl.ªr/ ⓤ /-ɚ/ *noun* [C] *US* **1** a lawyer: [as form of address] *I don't think that question is relevant, counselor.* **2** someone who looks after children at a summer camp

count NUMBER /kaʊnt/ *verb* [I or T] to say the names of numbers one after the other in order, or to calculate the number of people or things in a group: *Let's count* **out loud** (= speak the words) *from one to ten.* ○ *The teachers counted the students as they got on to the coach.* ○ *Count your money carefully to make sure it's all there.* ○ [+ question word] *We need to count* **who's** *here, so we can make sure that no one's missing.* ○ *There'll be eight for dinner, counting* (= including) *ourselves.* ○ *We're still waiting for the votes to be counted* (up).
● **count** *your* **blessings** to be grateful for the good things in your life, often to stop yourself becoming too unhappy about the bad things
● **count the cost** to start to understand how badly something has affected you: *I didn't read the contract fully before I signed it but I'm counting the cost now.*

● **count heads** to count the number of people present somewhere: *There look to be about fifty people present - I haven't counted heads yet.*
● **could count on (the fingers of) one hand** If you could count something on (the fingers of) one hand, it happens very rarely or exists in very small numbers: *I could count the number of times he's paid for a round of drinks on the fingers of one hand.*
● **Don't count your chickens before they're hatched.** *SAYING* said to emphasize that you cannot depend on something happening before it has happened
count /kaʊnt/ *noun* [C] **1** the act of counting, or the total number of things counted: *Early vote counts show Mr Adams in the lead.* ○ *We had 450 members* **at the last** *count* (= when they were last counted). **2** a scientifically measured amount of something: *a high pollen count* ○ *a low blood/sperm count*
● **on the count of 3/4/5, etc.** when a particular number is reached: *On the count of three, I'd like you all to stand up.*
● **be out for the count** to be sleeping, especially heavily: *It looks like Ben's out for the count.*
● **keep count** *UK* to record how many of something there is, or how many time something has happened: *I'm trying to lose weight, so I'm keeping count of the number of calories I eat every day.*
● **lose count** to not be able to remember how many times something has happened: *I've lost count of how many times she's been late for work this month.*
countable /'kaʊn.tə.bl̩/ ⓤ /-t̬ə-/ *adj SPECIALIZED* describes a noun that has both plural and singular forms: *An example of a countable noun is 'table', and an example of an uncountable noun is 'money'.* ⊃Compare **uncountable**.
counter /'kaʊn.tər/ ⓤ /'kaʊn.t̬ɚ/ *noun* [C] a person or machine that counts ⊃See also **Geiger counter**.

count CONSIDER /kaʊnt/ *verb* [I or T] to consider or be considered as: [R] *I count myself fortunate to have had such a good education.* ○ *I've had three jobs in the last five years, but one of them was unpaid, so it doesn't count* (= cannot be considered as a real job). ○ *I've always counted Lucy* **among** *my closest friends.* ○ *I didn't think his grudging remarks really counted* **as** *an apology.*

count VALUE /kaʊnt/ *verb* [I] to have value or importance; to **matter**: *I've always believed that happiness counts more than money.* ○ *My opinion doesn't count* **for** *anything around here* (= no one values my opinion).

count MAN /kaʊnt/ *noun* [C] a European man of the same social rank as an English EARL ⊃See also **countess**.

count CRIME /kaʊnt/ *noun* [C] *LEGAL* a particular crime which a person is accused of: *The prisoner was found guilty* **on** *two counts* **of** *murder.*

count OPINION /kaʊnt/ *noun* [C] an opinion in a discussion or argument: *I'm afraid I disagree with you* **on** *all/ several counts* (= I disagree with all/several of your opinions).

PHRASAL VERBS WITH **count** ▼

▲ **count against** *sb/sth phrasal verb* to make someone or something more likely to fail: *Gail's qualified for the job, but her lack of experience will count against her.*
▲ **count** *sb* **in** *phrasal verb* [M] *INFORMAL* to include someone in an activity or arrangement: *"Do you want to come swimming tomorrow?" "Yes, count me in."*
▲ **count on** *sb* DEPEND *phrasal verb* to be confident that you can depend on someone: *You can always count on Michael in a crisis.* ○ [+ to infinitive] *I can count on my parents* **to** *help me.*
▲ **count on** *sth* EXPECT *phrasal verb* to expect something to happen and make plans based on it: [+ v-ing] *I'm counting on the meeting finishing on time, or I'll miss my train.* ○ *Sorry I'm late, I didn't count on being held up in the traffic.* ○ *There's never a taxi when you want one – that's the one thing you can count on!*
▲ **count** *sth* **out** MONEY *phrasal verb* [M] to count coins or notes one by one as you put them down: *She counted out five crisp new $100 bills.*
▲ **count** *sb* **out** OMIT *phrasal verb INFORMAL* to keep someone out or omit them from an activity or arrangement:

Scuba diving? Oh no, count me out - I hate water!

▲ **count sb out** BOXING *phrasal verb* [often passive] In a boxing competition, the REFEREE counts someone out by counting to ten when they fall to the floor and announcing that they have lost the fight if they fail to get up before the ten seconds is over: *Cooper was counted out in the final round.*

▲ **count towards** *sth phrasal verb* to be part of what is needed to complete or achieve something: *The work that the students do during the year will count towards their final degrees.*

countable ˌ**noun** *noun* [C] a **count noun**

countdown /ˈkaʊnt.daʊn/ *noun* **1** [C] the act of counting backwards to zero: *The countdown **to** the rocket launch will begin at 9.00 am.* **2** [S] a short period of time leading to an important event: *The countdown **to** the election has already begun.*

countenance FACE /ˈkaʊn.tə.nənts/ ⑩ /-tⁿn.ənts/ *noun* [C or U] *FORMAL* the appearance or expression of someone's face: *He was of noble countenance.*

countenance APPROVE OF /ˈkaʊn.tə.nənts/ ⑩ /-tⁿn.ənts/ *verb* [T] *FORMAL* to find acceptable; to approve of or give support to: *The school will not countenance bad behaviour.*

countenance /ˈkaʊn.tə.nənts/ ⑩ /-tⁿn.ənts/ *noun* [U] *FORMAL* We will not **give/lend** countenance (= approval) **to** any kind of terrorism.

counter SURFACE /ˈkaʊn.təʳ/ ⑩ /-t̬ɚ/ *noun* [C] **1** a long flat narrow table or table in a shop, bank, restaurant, etc. at which people are served: *There was nobody **behind/on** the counter when I went into the bank, and I had to wait to be served.* ○ *You will find sausages **on** the meat counter/rolls **on** the bread counter.* **2** *MAINLY US* a **work-top** (= flat surface in a kitchen, on which food can be prepared): *We stacked the dirty plates on the **kitchen** counter.*

• **over the counter** Drugs that are bought over the counter are bought in a shop without first visiting a doctor: *You can buy most cold remedies over the counter.* ○ *All these medicines are available over the counter*

• **under the counter** Things bought under the counter are bought secretly and illegally: *He'd managed to get cigarettes under the counter.*

counter OBJECT /ˈkaʊn.təʳ/ ⑩ /-t̬ɚ/ *noun* [C] (*US ALSO* **piece**) a small object used to mark someone's place in some games played on boards

counter OPPOSE /ˈkaʊn.təʳ/ ⑩ /-t̬ɚ/ *verb* [I or T] to react to something with an opposing opinion or action; to defend yourself against something: *The Prime Minister countered the opposition's claims about health service cuts **by** saying that the government had increased spending in this area.* ○ *When criticisms were made of the school's performance, the parents' group countered **with** details of its examination results.* ○ *Extra police have been moved into the area to counter the risk of violence.*

counter /ˈkaʊn.təʳ/ ⑩ /-t̬ɚ/ *adv* in a way that opposes: *Bob's decision not to take the job **ran** counter **to** his family's expectations.*

counter- /ˈkaʊn.təʳ-/ ⑩ /-t̬ɚ-/ *prefix* as a reaction to or in opposition to

counteract /ˌkaʊn.təˈrækt/ ⑩ /-t̬ɚˈækt/ *verb* [T] to reduce or remove the effect of something unwanted by producing an opposite effect: *Drinking a lot of water counteracts the dehydrating **effects** of hot weather.*

counter-argument /ˌkaʊn.tə.rɑː.ˌgjuː.mənt/ ⑩ /-t̬ɚ.ˌɑːr-/ *noun* [C] an argument against another argument, idea or suggestion

counterattack /ˈkaʊn.tə.rə.tæk/ ⑩ /-t̬ɚ.ə-/ *noun* [C] an attack intended to stop or oppose an attack by an enemy or competitor: *The Republicans have **launched** a strong counterattack against the Democrats' manifesto.* **counterattack** /ˌkaʊn.tə.rəˈtæk/ ⑩ /-t̬ɚ.ə-/ *verb* [I or T] *The air force counterattacked and repelled the invasion.*

counterbalance /ˈkaʊn.təˌbæl.ənts/ ⑩ /-t̬ɚ/ *verb* [T] to have an equal but opposite effect on something so that it does not have too much of a particular characteristic: *The ugliness of the resort is counterbalanced by the excellence of the skiing.* **counterbalance** /ˈkaʊn.təˌbæl.ənts/ ⑩ /-t̬ɚ-/ *noun* [C usually sing] *Her calm nature served*

*as a natural counterbalance **to** his excitable personality.*

counterclockwise /ˌkaʊn.təˈklɒk.waɪz/ ⑩ /-t̬ɚˈklɑː.kwaɪz/ *adj, adv US FOR* **anti-clockwise**

counter-culture /ˈkaʊn.tə.kʌl.tʃəʳ/ ⑩ /-t̬ɚ.kʌl.tʃɚ/ *noun* [C or U] a way of life and a set of ideas that are completely different from those accepted by most of society, or the group of people who live this way

counter-espionage /ˌkaʊn.tə'res.pi.ə.nɑːʒ/ ⑩ /-t̬ɚ'es-/ *noun* [U] secret action taken by a country to prevent another country from discovering its military, industrial or political secrets

counterfeit /ˈkaʊn.tə.fɪt/ ⑩ /-t̬ɚ-/ *adj* made to look like the original of something, usually for dishonest or illegal purposes: *counterfeit jewellery/passports/coins* **counterfeit** /ˈkaʊn.tə.fɪt/ ⑩ /-t̬ɚ-/ *noun* [C] *This watch may be a counterfeit, but it looks just like the original.* **counterfeit** /ˈkaʊn.tə.fɪt/ ⑩ /-t̬ɚ-/ *verb* [T] *Two women and a man have been convicted of counterfeiting $100 bills.* **counterfeiter** /ˈkaʊn.tə.fɪ.təʳ/ ⑩ /t̬ɚ.fɪ.t̬ɚ/ *noun* [C]

counterfoil *UK* /ˈkaʊn.tə.fɔɪl/ ⑩ /-t̬ɚ-/ *noun* [C] (*MAINLY US* **stub**) the part of a ticket, cheque, etc. which is kept as a record of payment

counterinsurgency /ˌkaʊn.tə.rɪnˈsɜː.dʒⁿnt.si/ ⑩ /-t̬ɚ.ɪnˈsɝː-/ *noun* [U] military action taken by a government to prevent attacks by small groups of soldiers or fighters that are opposed to it ⊃Compare **insurgency** at **insurgent**.

counterintelligence /ˌkaʊn.tə.rɪnˈtel.ɪ.dʒənts/ ⑩ /-t̬ɚ.ɪn-/ *noun* [U] secret action taken by a country to prevent another country from discovering its military, industrial or political secrets

counter-intuitive /ˌkaʊn.tə.rɪnˈtjuː.ɪ.tɪv/ ⑩ /-t̬ɚ.ɪnˈtuː.ɪ.t̬ɪv/ *adj* describes something that does not happen in the way you would expect it to: *Steering a yacht is counter-intuitive – you push the tiller the opposite way to the way you want to go.*

countermand /ˌkaʊn.təˈmɑːnd/ ⑩ /-t̬ɚˈmænd/ *verb* [T] *FORMAL* to change an order that has been already given, especially by giving a new order

countermeasure /ˈkaʊn.təˌmeʒ.əʳ/ ⑩ /-t̬ɚˌmeʒ.ɚ/ *noun* [C] an action taken against an unwanted action or situation: *The Chancellor's countermeasures **against** inflation have been completely ineffective.*

counteroffensive /ˌkaʊn.tə.rəˈfent.sɪv/ ⑩ /-t̬ɚ.ə-/ *noun* [C] a set of attacks which defend against enemy attacks

counterpane /ˈkaʊn.tə.peɪn/ ⑩ /-t̬ɚ-/ *noun* [C] *UK OLD-FASHIONED* a **bedspread**

counterpart /ˈkaʊn.tə.pɑːt/ ⑩ /-t̬ɚ.pɑːrt/ *noun* [C] a person or thing which has the same purpose as another one in a different place or organization: *The Prime Minister is to meet his European counterparts to discuss the war against drugs.*

counterpoint /ˈkaʊn.tə.pɔɪnt/ ⑩ /-t̬ɚ-/ *noun* [U] the combination of two or more different tunes played at the same time

counterproductive /ˌkaʊn.tə.prəˈdʌk.tɪv/ ⑩ /-t̬ɚ-/ *adj* having an effect which is opposite to the one that is intended or desired: *Improved safety measures in cars can be counterproductive as they encourage people to drive faster.*

counter-revolution /ˌkaʊn.tə.rev.əˈluː.ʃⁿn/ ⑩ /-t̬ɚ-/ *noun* [C] a political activity which happens as a reaction or in opposition to an earlier political change **counter-revolutionary** /ˌkaʊn.tə.rev.əˈluː.ʃⁿn.ᵊr.i/ ⑩ /-t̬ɚ.rev.əˈluː.ʃⁿn.ᵊr.er-/ *noun* [C], *adj*: *She was tried and executed for being a counter-revolutionary.* ○ *counter-revolutionary activities/literature*

countersign /ˈkaʊn.tə.saɪn/ ⑩ /-t̬ɚ-/ *verb* [T] *SPECIALIZED* to write your name on a document which already has the signature of another person, especially in order to show that you are certain that the first person is who they say they are

counter-suit /ˈkaʊn.tə.sjuːt/ ⑩ /-t̬ɚ.suːt/ *noun* [C] a legal claim that you make as a reaction to a claim made against you

countertenor /ˌkaʊn.təˈten.əʳ/ ⑩ /-t̬ɚˈten.ɚ/ *noun* [C] (*ALSO* **male alto**) a man with a singing voice which is higher than usual for a TENOR and similar to a low female voice

countervailing /ˌkaʊn.tə'veɪ.lɪŋ/ [US] /-t̬ɚ-/ *adj* **[before n]** *FORMAL* having equal force but an opposite effect: *There was nobody strong enough to lead an effective countervailing* ***force*** *against the dictator.* ○ *a countervailing argument*

counterweight /'kaʊntə,weɪt/ *noun* **[C]** a weight that is as heavy as something else so that the two objects can balance

countess /'kaʊn.tes/ [US] /-t̬əs/ *noun* **[C]** a woman of high social rank, or the wife of a COUNT or EARL: *the Countess of Abingdon*

countless /'kaʊnt.ləs/ *adj* very many; too many to be counted: *There are countless arguments against this ridiculous proposal.* ○ *I've heard it played countless* ***times*** *on the radio.*

'count ˌnoun *noun* **[C]** (*ALSO* **countable noun**) *SPECIALIZED* a noun that can be used in the singular and the plural: *Count nouns are shown in this dictionary with* **[C]**.

country [POLITICAL UNIT] /'kʌn.tri/ *noun* **[C]** **1** an area of land that has its own government, army, etc: *Which is the largest country in Europe?* ○ *Sri Lanka is my native country, but I've been living in Belgium for the past five years.* ○ *The climate is cooler in the east of the country.* ○ *European countries* ○ *He had betrayed his country and that was the punishment.*

USAGE

country, land, nation, or **state?**

Country is the most general of these words. It usually means an area of land with its own government and people.

China, Japan, and other countries in Asia

Nation is used to talk about a country, especially when you mean the people or the culture of that country.

The whole nation celebrated the 100th anniversary of independence.

State is used to talk about a country as a political or official area. Some countries are divided into political units that are also called states.

Belgium became an independent state in 1830.
The USA is divided into more than 50 states.
the state of Florida

Land means an area of ground, especially when used for farming or building. It can also be used to mean a country, but this is a literary usage.

We bought some land to build a house on.
He told stories of distant lands.

---

2 the country all the people who live in a country: *The whole country celebrated the signing of the peace treaty.*
• **go to the country** *UK* to have an election: *The Prime Minister has decided to go to the country.*

country [NATURAL LAND] /'kʌn.tri/ *noun* **[S or U]** land which is not in towns, cities or industrial areas and is either used for farming or left in its natural condition: *He lives out* ***in the*** *country somewhere.* ○ *Would you prefer to live* ***in the*** *country instead of a town?* ○ *Country life isn't always as peaceful as city-dwellers think.* ○ *It's often quicker to travel* ***across*** *country and avoid the major roads altogether.*

countrified /'kʌn.trɪ.faɪd/ *adj* describes a person or thing that belongs to, or is suited to, the countryside: *I thought myself very sophisticated compared with my countrified relatives.* ○ *DISAPPROVING Their house was decorated in a style that was rather tasteless and countrified* (= artificially like something seen in the countryside).

country [LAND] /'kʌn.tri/ *noun* **[U]** an area of land considered in relation to a particular feature: *Stratford-on-Avon is the capital of Shakespeare country.* ○ *The empty roads make this area good cycling country.*

ˌcountry (and 'western) *noun* **[U]** (*ALSO* **country music**) popular music which is based on a type of traditional music from the western and southern US: *the enduring appeal of country and western.*

'country ˌclub *noun* **[C]** a sports or social organization based in the countryside, often one which does not allow membership to people who are considered to be unsuitable because of their social position, job or lack of wealth

ˌcountry 'dance *noun* **[C]** a traditional British dance for several pairs of male and female dancers who are arranged in circles, squares or long rows

ˌcountry 'house *noun* **[C]** a large traditional house in the countryside, especially one which has belonged to the same family for many years: *Through the trees we could see a beautiful Georgian country house.*

countryman [FROM YOUR COUNTRY] /'kʌn.trɪ.mən/ *noun* **[C]** a person from your own country: *Didn't he feel guilty about betraying his* ***fellow*** *countrymen and women?*

countryman [FROM THE COUNTRYSIDE] /'kʌn.trɪ.mən/ *noun* **[C]** *UK* someone who lives in or who comes from the countryside and not a town

'country ˌmusic *noun* **[U]** **country (and western)**

ˌcountry 'seat *noun* **[C]** *UK* a country house and a large piece of land surrounding it: *Lady Castleton has a flat near Westminster, but her country seat is in Yorkshire.*

countryside /'kʌn.trɪ.saɪd/ *noun* **[S or U]** land not in towns, cities or industrial areas, which is either used for farming or left in its natural condition: *The countryside around there is lovely.* ○ *The mansion is set in 90 acres of beautiful, unspoilt countryside.* ○ *Every summer thousands of people flock to the countryside.* ➲See Note **nature, the environment and the counryside** at **nature** LIFE.

countrywide /ˌkʌn.tri'waɪd/ *adj, adv* existing in or involving all parts of a country: *a countrywide epidemic* ○ *Countrywide protests against the government* ○ *The bank has three branches in Norwich, and over three hundred countrywide.*

countrywoman /'kʌn.trɪˌwʊm.ən/ *noun* **[C]** a female COUNTRYMAN

county /'kaʊn.ti/ [US] /-t̬i/ *noun* **[C]** (*WRITTEN ABBREVIATION* **Co.**) a political division of the UK or Ireland, forming the largest unit of local government, or the largest political division of a state in the US: *County Antrim* ○ *A county usually consists of several towns and the rural areas which surround them.* ○ *Rutland used to be the smallest county in England, but in 1974 it became part of Leicestershire.* ○ *Texas is divided into 254 counties.*

county /'kaʊn.ti/ [US] /-t̬i/ *adj UK USUALLY DISAPPROVING* describes someone who behaves in a way that is typical of rich people with a high social position who live in large houses in the countryside: *She mixes with a very county set.*

ˌcounty 'council *group noun* **[C]** *UK* an elected group of people which forms the government of a county: *Northumberland County Council*

ˌcounty 'court *noun* **[C]** a local law court in England and in some parts of the US, which deals with cases that do not involve serious crime

ˌcounty 'fair *noun* **[C]** a large public event that happens every summer in US counties, with RIDES, games and competitions for the best animal, best cooked dish, etc: *She won first prize for her raspberry jam at the Mitchell County Fair.*

ˌcounty 'town *UK noun* **[C]** (*US* **county seat**) the most important town or city in a county, especially the one where the local government is based: *Cambridge is the county town of Cambridgeshire.*

countywide /ˌkaʊn.ti'waɪd/ [US] /-t̬i-/ *adj, adv MAINLY US* existing in or involving all parts of a county: *a countywide survey* ○ *Countywide, examination results have improved by an average of eight per cent.*

coup /kuː/ *noun* **[C]** an unexpectedly successful achievement: *It was a tremendous coup for the local paper to get an exclusive interview with Prince Charles.* ○ *I got him to come to a party which was something of a coup.*

coup de grâce /ˌkuː.də'grɑːs/ *noun* **[S]** *FORMAL* an action which ends something that has been gradually worsening or which kills a person or animal in order to end their suffering: *Jane's affair was the coup de grâce **to** her disintegrating marriage.*

coup (d'état) /ˌkuː.deɪˈtɑː/ *noun* [C] *plural* **coups (d'état)** a sudden illegal, often violent, taking of government power, especially by (part of) an army: *a **military** coup*

coupé /ˈkuː.peɪ/ [US] /kuˈpeɪ/ *noun* [C] a car with a fixed roof, two doors, two or four seats, and usually a sloping back

C

couple [SOME] /ˈkʌp.l̩/ *noun* [S] two or a few things that are similar or the same, or two or a few people who are in some way connected: *The doctor said my leg should be better in **a** couple **of** days.* ○ ***A** couple **of** people objected to the proposal, but the vast majority approved of it.* ○ *We'll have to wait **another** couple **of** hours for the paint to dry.* ○ *She'll be retiring in **a** couple **more** years.* ○ *The weather's been terrible for **the last** couple **of** days.* ○ *Many economists expect unemployment to fall over **the next** couple **of** months.* ○ *I'm sorry I didn't phone you, but I've been very busy over **the past** couple **of** weeks.*

couple [TWO PEOPLE] /ˈkʌp.l̩/ *group noun* [C] two people who are married or in a romantic or sexual relationship, or two people who are together for a particular purpose: *a **married** couple* ○ *An **elderly** couple (UK) live/(US) lives next door.* ○ *Should the government do more to help **young** couples buy their own homes?* ○ *The couple skated spectacularly throughout the competition.*

couple [JOIN] /ˈkʌp.l̩/ *verb* [T usually passive; usually + adv or prep] to join or combine: *The sleeping car and restaurant car were coupled **together**.* ○ *High inflation coupled **with** low output spells disaster for the Government in the election.*

coupling /ˈkʌp.lɪŋ/ *noun* [C] a device which joins two things together: *The carriage at the end of the train was left stranded when the coupling broke.*

couple [HAVE SEX] /ˈkʌp.l̩/ *verb* [I] *FORMAL* When two people or two animals couple, they have sex.

couplet /ˈkʌp.lət/ *noun* [C] two lines of poetry next to each other, especially ones which rhyme and have the same length and rhythm: *a **rhyming** couplet*

coupon /ˈkuː.pɒn/ [US] /-pɑːn/ *noun* [C] **1** a piece of paper which can be used to obtain something without paying for it or at a reduced price: *If you **collect** ten coupons from the newspaper, you can get a free beach towel.* **2** a piece of paper, especially a part of an advertisement in a newspaper or magazine, which a reader can send to an organization in order to obtain information about its products or services: *To find out more about our products, fill in the coupon and send it to us at the address given below.*

courage /ˈkʌr.ɪdʒ/ [US] /ˈkɝː-/ *noun* [U] the ability to control your fear in a dangerous or difficult situation: *They showed great courage when they found out about their baby's disability.* ○ [+ to infinitive] *People should have **the** courage **to** stand up for their beliefs.* ○ *It took me ages to **summon/pluck up** the courage **to** ask for a promotion.*

• **have the courage of *your* convictions** to be brave and confident enough to do what you believe in: *Although many of his policies were unpopular, he had the courage of his convictions to see them through.*

courageous /kəˈreɪ.dʒəs/ *adj* having or showing courage: *It was a courageous decision to resign in protest at the company's pollution record.* ○ *It was courageous **of** her to challenge the managing director's decision.*

courageously /kəˈreɪ.dʒə.sli/ *adv*

courgette *UK* /kɔːˈʒet/ [US] /kʊr-/ *noun* [C] (*US* **zucchini**) a long thin vegetable with a dark green skin. It is a type of small MARROW. ➲See picture **Vegetables** on page Centre 2

courier [MESSAGE] /ˈkʊr.i.əʳ/ [US] /-i.ɚ/ *noun* [C] a person who carries important messages or documents for someone else: *I want to have this package delivered by motorcycle courier.*

courier [HOLIDAY] /ˈkʊr.i.əʳ/ [US] /-i.ɚ/ *noun* [C] *UK* a person who looks after a group of people on holiday especially by giving them advice on what to do, what to see, etc.

course [DIRECTION] /kɔːs/ [US] /kɔːrs/ *noun* [C usually sing; U] the direction in which a vehicle, especially an aircraft, spacecraft or ship, moves, or the path along which a river flows: *The pilot avoided a collision by **changing** course.* ○ *Changing the course of the river would cause serious environmental damage to the whole valley.* ○ *FIGURATIVE The debate completely changed course after Liz made her speech.*

• **on course** likely to happen, or likely to succeed as planned: *Because of the recession, we're on course **for/to have** record unemployment levels.*

course [DEVELOPMENT] /kɔːs/ [US] /kɔːrs/ *noun* [S] the often gradual development of something, or the way something happens, or a way of doing something: *Did the scandal have any effect on the course of the election?* ○ ***During the/In the** course **of*** (= During) *the interview it became clear that he was not suitable for the job.* ○ *What would be an appropriate course **(of action)** in such a situation?* ○ *If our rivals are spending more on advertising, we'll have to follow the same course.* ○ *The defendants are also accused of attempting to pervert the course of justice.*

• **in the course of time** *UK* after a period of time: *I expect they plan to have children in the course of time.*

• **in/with the course of time** gradually: *With the course of time, I've learned to live with my disability.*

• **of course 1** *INFORMAL* used to say 'yes' or to give someone permission to do something: *"Can you help me?" "Of course."* ○ *May I have a look at your newspaper?" "Of course you can."* ○ *"Have you written your English essay yet?" "Of course, I finished it last week."* **2** used to show that what you are saying is obvious or already known: *The Second World War ended, of course, in 1945.* **3** used to show that a situation or a piece of information is not surprising: *We arrived at the restaurant 30 minutes late so, of course, our reservation had been cancelled.*

• **of course not** used to emphasize that you disagree or that something is not true: *"Where did you get the money? Did you steal it?" "Of course not. I borrowed it from Carol."*

course [CLASSES] /kɔːs/ [US] /kɔːrs/ *noun* [C] a set of classes or a plan of study on a particular subject, usually resulting in an exam or qualification: *Tim **did** a three-year course **in** linguistics at Newcastle.* ○ *They're going away **on** a training course next week.* ○ *I'd like to (UK) **do**/(US) **take** a writing course when I retire.*

course [MEDICAL TREATMENT] /kɔːs/ [US] /kɔːrs/ *noun* [C] a fixed number of regular medical treatments: *My doctor's **put** me **on** a course **of** antibiotics.* ○ *She needed a six-month course of physiotherapy after she broke her leg.*

course [SPORTS AREA] /kɔːs/ [US] /kɔːrs/ *noun* [C] an area of land or water used for a sports event: *a golf course/cross-country course* ➲See also **racecourse**.

course [MEAL] /kɔːs/ [US] /kɔːrs/ *noun* [C] a part of a meal which is served separately from the other parts: *a four-course lunch* ○ *A traditional British **main** course consists of a meat dish with potatoes and other vegetables.*

course [LAYER] /kɔːs/ [US] /kɔːrs/ *noun* [C] *SPECIALIZED* a continuous horizontal layer of bricks or other building material

course [FLOW] /kɔːs/ [US] /kɔːrs/ *verb* [I usually + adv or prep] to flow quickly or in large amounts: *Tears were coursing **down** his cheeks.* ○ *You could almost hear the blood coursing **through** her veins as she passed the finishing line.* ○ *FIGURATIVE A new wave of idealism is coursing **through** our schools.*

coursebook /ˈkɔːs.bʊk/ [US] /ˈkɔːrs-/ *noun* [C] *UK* a book used by students when they do a particular course of study

coursework /ˈkɔːs.wɜːk/ [US] /ˈkɔːrs.wɝːk/ *noun* [U] work set at regular periods as part of an educational course

coursing /ˈkɔː.sɪŋ/ [US] /ˈkɔːr-/ *noun* [U] *UK* a sport in which rabbits are chased by dogs

court [LAW] /kɔːt/ [US] /kɔːrt/ *noun* [C usually sing; U] **1** (a large room in) a building where trials and other legal cases happen, or the people present in such a room, especially the officials and those deciding whether someone is guilty: *Protestors gathered outside the court to await the verdict.* ○ *He's due to appear **in** court again on Monday.* ○ *Please describe to the court exactly what you saw.* ○ *the European Court of Human Rights* ○ *The lack of evidence means that the case is unlikely to **go to** court.* **2 take *sb* to court** to take legal action against someone: *She's* *threatening to take me to court for not paying the bill on time.* **3 settle (a case) out of court** to solve a case without taking legal action: *The newspaper has agreed to settle out of court.*

court SPORT /kɔːt/ US /kɔːrt/ *noun* [C] an area marked out on the ground which is used for playing sports such as tennis and basketball: *a tennis/volleyball/basketball/squash court* ○ *They were penalized for having too many players on the court.*

court AREA /kɔːt/ US /kɔːrt/ *noun* [C] **1** an area or a short road, which is not covered by a roof and is mostly or completely surrounded by buildings: *You really should go and see the lovely medieval court in the castle.* **2** MAINLY UK **Court** used in the names of some roads, and buildings containing apartments

court ROYALTY /kɔːt/ US /kɔːrt/ *noun* [C or U] the official home of a queen or king: *the courts of Renaissance Europe* ○ *He quickly lost his popularity at court.*

court *group noun* [S] the important people who live in the official home of a queen or king or who work for or advise them

court PLEASE /kɔːt/ US /kɔːrt/ *verb* [T] to try to please someone because you want them to join you: *Adams is being courted by a number of football clubs.*

court TRY TO GET /kɔːt/ US /kɔːrt/ *verb* [T] to try to get something, especially attention or support from other people: *She courts publicity by inviting journalists to extravagant parties.*

court RISK /kɔːt/ US /kɔːrt/ *verb* [T] to risk something unpleasant, especially by behaving stupidly or carelessly: *Drinking and driving is simply courting disaster.*

court RELATIONSHIP /kɔːt/ US /kɔːrt/ *verb* [I or T] OLD-FASHIONED to have a romantic relationship with someone that you hope to marry: *They courted for two years before getting married.*

courtship /ˈkɔːt.ʃɪp/ US /ˈkɔːrt-/ *noun* [C or U] OLD-FASHIONED OR FORMAL the time when people have a romantic relationship with the intention of getting married: *They had a passionate courtship and a long, loving marriage.*

courteous /ˈkɜː.ti.əs/ US /ˈkɜːr.ti-/ *adj* polite and respectful; WELL-MANNERED: *Although she often disagreed with me, she was always courteous.* **courteously** /ˈkɜː.ti.ə.sli/ US /ˈkɜːr.ti-/ *adv*: *He's always behaved courteously toward my family.*

courtesan /ˌkɔː.tɪˈzæn/ /---/ US /ˈkɔːr.tɪ-/ *noun* [C] a woman, usually with a high social position, who in the past had sexual relationships with rich or important men in exchange for money

courtesy /ˈkɜː.tə.si/ US /ˈkɜːr.tə-/ *noun* [C or U] polite behaviour, or a polite action or remark: *You might get on better with your parents if you showed them some courtesy.* ○ [+ to infinitive] *He could at least have had the courtesy to say sorry.* ○ *The President welcomed the Queen with the usual courtesies.*

● **(by) courtesy of 1** by permission of: *Phil Collins appears on the album courtesy of Virgin Records.* **2** because of: *Did the Conservatives win courtesy of the division of the opposition vote between Labour and the Liberal Democrats?*

courthouse /ˈkɔːt.haʊs/ US /ˈkɔːrt-/ *noun* [C] US a building which contains law courts: *a county/federal courthouse*

courtier /ˈkɔː.ti.əʳ/ US /ˈkɔːr.ti.ɚ/ *noun* [C] a companion of a queen, king or other ruler in their official home, especially in the past: *Many of the courtiers were upset by the princess's resistance to tradition.*

courtly /ˈkɔːt.li/ US /ˈkɔːrt-/ *adj* polite, graceful and formal in behaviour **courtliness** /ˈkɔːt.lɪ.nəs/ US /ˈkɔːrt-/ *noun* [U]

court ˈmartial *noun* [C] *plural* **court martials** or FORMAL **courts martial** (a trial in) a military court for members of the armed forces **court-martial** /ˌkɔːtˈmɑː.ʃəl/ US /ˈkɔːrt-ˌmɑːr-/ *verb* [T] *She is likely to be court-martialled for disobeying her commanding officer.*

court of inˈquiry *group noun* [C] UK a group of people, often with specialist knowledge or skill, who have been brought together in order to examine the causes of an accident

court ˈorder *noun* [C] an instruction given by a court telling someone what they can or cannot do

courtroom /ˈkɔːt.rʊm/ /-ruːm/ US /ˈkɔːrt-/ *noun* [C] a room where a court of law meets: *The accused entered the courtroom handcuffed to two police officers.* ○ *It was a courtroom drama set in the 1960s.*

ˈcourt ˌshoe UK *noun* [C] (US **pump**) a type of plain shoe with a raised heel and no fastenings which is worn by women

courtyard /ˈkɔːt.jɑːd/ US /ˈkɔːrt.jɑːrd/ *noun* [C] an area of flat ground outside which is partly or completely enclosed by the walls of a building

couscous /ˈkuːs.kuːs/ *noun* [U] a food, originally from North Africa, consisting of crushed wheat, which is often served with meat or vegetables

cousin /ˈkʌz.ᵊn/ *noun* [C] (ALSO **first cousin**) **1** a child of a person's aunt or uncle, or, more generally, a distant relative: *My brother's wife and I both had babies around the same time, so the cousins are very close in age.* ○ *Many of our distant cousins, whom we hadn't seen for years, came to my sister's wedding.* **2** a member of a group of people with similar origins: *We Americans owe a great deal to our European cousins.*

couture /kuːˈtjʊəʳ/ US /-ˈtʊr/ *noun* [U] (ALSO **haute couture**) the designing, making and selling of expensive fashionable clothing, or the clothes themselves: *a couture show/collection/house* **couturier** /kuːˈtjʊə.ri.eɪ/ US /-ˈtʊr.i-/ *noun* [C] *In 1960, Pierre Cardin became the first couturier to design men's clothes.*

cove COAST /kəʊv/ US /koʊv/ *noun* [C] a curved part of a coast which partly encloses an area of water; a small BAY

cove MAN /kəʊv/ US /koʊv/ *noun* [C] UK OLD-FASHIONED a man: *He's an odd-looking cove.*

coven /ˈkʌv.ᵊn/ *group noun* [C] a group or meeting of witches

covenant /ˈkʌv.ᵊn.ᵊnt/ *noun* [C] **1** a formal agreement between two or more people; a promise: *The contract contained a restrictive covenant against building on the land.* **2** UK SPECIALIZED a formal agreement to pay a fixed sum of money regularly, especially to a charity **covenant** /ˈkʌv.ᵊn.ᵊnt/ *verb* [T] *5% of our profits are covenanted to charity.*

cover PLACE OVER /ˈkʌv.əʳ/ US /-ɚ/ *verb* [T] to put or spread something over something, or to lie on the surface of something: *The light was so bright that I had to cover my eyes.* ○ *Snow covered the hillsides.* ○ *She covered him (up) with a blanket.* ○ *Cover the meat with a layer of cheese.* ○ *The bandages were covered with/in blood.* ○ *How much of the Earth's surface is covered by/with water?*

● **cover your ass/butt/backside, etc.** US OFFENSIVE (ALSO **cover yourself**) to do something to protect yourself from blame or criticism in the future: *He'd do anything to cover his ass, including lie, cheat and murder.* ○ *I kept copies of my expense receipts, just to cover myself.*

-covered /-kʌv.əd/ US /-ɚd/ *suffix* covered in the way mentioned: *snow-covered hills*

cover /ˈkʌv.əʳ/ US /-ɚ/ *noun* [C] **1** something which is put on or over something else, usually to protect it, to keep something in, etc: *I keep my computer printer under a protective plastic cover.* ○ *Remove the packaging and pierce the film cover before microwaving.* **2** the stiff outside part of a book or magazine, usually made of thick paper or cardboard and often shiny: *Who should we put on the cover of the magazine this month?* ○ *Paperback books have soft covers.*

covers /ˈkʌv.əz/ US /-ɚz/ *plural noun* the blankets, SHEETS, etc. on a bed: *Martha threw back the covers and bounced out of bed.*

● **read sth from cover to cover** to read a book or magazine, etc. all the way through from the beginning to the end

● **send sth under plain/separate cover** FORMAL to send something in a plain/separate envelope

covering /ˈkʌv.ᵊr.ɪŋ/ US /-ɚ-/ *noun* [C] a layer of something that covers something else: *a light covering of snow*

cover TRAVEL /ˈkʌv.əʳ/ US /-ɚ/ *verb* [T] to travel a particular distance: *We covered 400km in three hours.*

cover DEAL WITH /ˈkʌv.əʳ/ US /-ɚ/ *verb* [T] to deal with or direct attention to something: *This leaflet covers what we've just discussed in more detail.* ○ *Do these parking restrictions cover residents as well as visitors?* ○ *The new office will cover the whole of Scotland.*

coverage /ˈkʌv.əʳ.ɪdʒ/ US /-ɚ-/ *noun* [U] *These books give very good grammar coverage* (= They deal with grammar very well).

cover REPORT /ˈkʌv.əʳ/ US /-ɚ/ *verb* [T] to report the news about a particular important event: *She's covering the American election for BBC television.*

coverage /ˈkʌv.əʳ.ɪdʒ/ US /-ɚ-/ *noun* [U] the reporting of a particular important event or subject: *What did you think of the BBC's election coverage?*

cover BE ENOUGH /ˈkʌv.əʳ/ US /-ɚ/ *verb* [T] to be enough money to pay for something: *The selling price barely covered the cost of the raw materials.* ○ *Would £50 cover your expenses?*

cover PROTECT /ˈkʌv.əʳ/ US /-ɚ/ *verb* [T] to protect someone against loss, damage, accident or having something stolen, by having insurance: *Does your travel insurance cover you against/for the loss or theft of cash?*

cover UK /ˈkʌv.əʳ/ US /-ɚ/ *noun* [U] (US **coverage**) financial protection so that you get money if something bad happens: *I've got £20 000 worth of cover for the contents of my house.* ○ *Have you got cover for accidental damage?*

cover SHELTER /ˈkʌv.əʳ/ US /-ɚ/ *noun* [U] **1** shelter or protection in an unpleasant or dangerous situation: *We took cover from the storm in a bus shelter.* ○ *The burglar broke into the house under cover of darkness.* **2** plants, especially bushes, that are used as shelter by animals

cover GIVE ARMED PROTECTION /ˈkʌv.əʳ/ US /-ɚ/ *verb* [T] **1** to aim a gun or shoot at someone to discourage them from shooting or escaping, or to protect someone else: *The police officer was covered by her colleagues while she ran towards the gunman's hideout.* **2** When soldiers or police officers cover a place such as a road or building, they are in a position from which they can watch and defend it: *We've got all the exits covered, so they've no chance of escape.*

cover /ˈkʌv.əʳ/ US /-ɚ/ *noun* [U] *We needed more cover* (= protection) *from the enemy aircraft.*

cover DO SOMEONE'S JOB /ˈkʌv.əʳ/ US /-ɚ/ *verb* [I or T] to do someone else's job or duty when they are absent: *I'm going to the doctor's tomorrow, so do you think you could cover my shift for me?* ○ *Sorry, I'm already covering for someone else.*

cover RECORD /ˈkʌv.əʳ/ US /-ɚ/ *verb* [T] to make a recording of a song or tune which has already been recorded by someone else: *I think more singers have covered 'Yesterday' than any other song.* ˈ**cover** (ˌ**version**) *noun* [C] *How many cover versions have been made of 'My Way'?*

▲ **cover** *sth* **up** *phrasal verb* [M] to stop people discovering the truth about something bad: *The company tried to cover up its employment of illegal immigrants.*

cover-up /ˈkʌv.ə.rʌp/ US /-ɚ.ʌp/ *noun* [C] an attempt to prevent the public discovering information about a serious crime or mistake: *Allegations of a cover-up of the effects of industrial pollution have been strongly denied by the Environment Minister.*

coveralls /ˈkʌv.ə.rɔːlz/ US /-ɚ.ɑːlz/ *plural noun* US FOR **boiler suit**

ˈ**cover** ˌ**charge** *noun* [C usually sing] a charge which is sometimes added to the amount that a customer pays for food, drinks and service in a restaurant, or which is added in a nightclub to pay for entertainment

ˈ**cover** ˌ**girl** *noun* [C] an attractive, often famous, woman whose photograph appears on the front of a magazine

ˈ**covering** ˌ**letter/ˌnote** *noun* [C] (US **cover letter/note**) a letter or note which contains information about the thing it is sent with: *Please send a covering letter with your application form.*

coverlet /ˈkʌv.ə.lət/ US /-ɚ-/ *noun* [C] a **bedspread**

ˈ**cover** ˌ**note** *noun* [C] UK SPECIALIZED a document which is used temporarily as proof that someone is INSURED until the final official document is available

ˈ**cover** ˌ**story** *noun* [C usually sing] a report or article connected with the picture on the front of a magazine

covert /ˈkəʊ.vɜːt/ US /ˈkoʊ.vɝːt/ /-ˈ-ˈ-/ *adj* hidden or secret: *covert actions* ○ *The government was accused of covert military operations against the regime.* ➔Compare **overt**.

covert /ˈkʌv.ət/ US /-ɚt/ *noun* [C] a group of bushes and small trees growing close together in which animals can hide, especially from hunters

covertly /ˈkʌv.ət.li/ US /-ɚt-/ *adv* secretly, or in a hidden way: *Terrorists have been operating covertly in England for several years.*

covet /ˈkʌv.ɪt/ *verb* [T] FORMAL to desire something strongly, especially something which belongs to someone else: *She always coveted power but never quite achieved it.* ○ *The Booker Prize is the most coveted British literary award.*

covetable /ˈkʌv.ɪ.tə.bl̩/ US /-t̬ə-/ *adj* UK FORMAL very desirable

covetous /ˈkʌv.ɪ.təs/ US /-t̬əs/ *adj* FORMAL DISAPPROVING desiring something too much, especially something that belongs to someone else: *Western companies are casting covetous eyes on the bargain-priced companies of eastern Europe.* **covetously** /ˈkʌv.ɪ.tə.sli/ US /-t̬ə-/ *adv*: *The boys looked covetously at the shiny new motorcycles.* **covetousness** /ˈkʌv.ɪ.tə.snəs/ US /-t̬ə-/ *noun* [U]

cow ANIMAL /kaʊ/ *noun* [C] **1** a large female farm animal kept to produce meat and milk: *a dairy cow* **2** the adult female of some mammals, such as elephants, whales and seals: *a cow elephant*

● **till/until the cows come home** for a very long time: *I could sit here and argue with you till the cows come home, but it wouldn't solve anything.*

cow WOMAN /kaʊ/ *noun* [C] UK OFFENSIVE an unkind or unpleasant woman: *You stupid cow!*

cow UNPLEASANT THING /kaʊ/ *noun* [S] AUS INFORMAL something difficult or unpleasant: *It's been a cow of a day.*

cow FRIGHTEN /kaʊ/ *verb* [T usually passive] to frighten someone into doing something, using threats or violence: *The protesters refused to be cowed into submission by the army.*

coward /ˈkaʊ.əd/ US /ˈkaʊ.ɚd/ *noun* [C] DISAPPROVING a person who is too eager to avoid danger, difficulty or pain: *I'm too much of a coward to confront her.* ○ *They branded her a coward for informing on her colleagues during the interrogation.* **cowardice** /ˈkaʊ.ə.dɪs/ US /-ɚ-/ *noun* [U] *You can accuse me of cowardice, but I still wouldn't volunteer to fight in a war.* **cowardly** /ˈkaʊ.əd.li/ US /-ɚd-/ *adj*: *This was a particularly brutal and cowardly attack.* ○ *They are guilty of a cowardly failure to address the problem.*

cowbell /ˈkaʊ.bel/ *noun* [C] a bell which is hung from a cow's neck so that the cow can be found, or a metal musical instrument in the shape of a bell which is hit with a stick

cowboy FARM WORKER /ˈkaʊ.bɔɪ/ *noun* [C] (ALSO **cowhand**) a person, especially in the western US, whose job is to take care of cattle, and who usually rides a horse, or a similar character in a film: *The ranch employed ten or twelve cowboys.* ○ *He was wearing cowboy boots and a cowboy hat.* ○ *I don't much like cowboy films/movies.*

cowboy DISHONEST PERSON /ˈkaʊ.bɔɪ/ *noun* [C] UK INFORMAL someone who is not honest, careful or skilful in their trade or business, or someone who ignores rules that most people obey and is therefore not considered to be responsible: *Those builders are a bunch of cowboys – they made a terrible job of our extension.*

ˈ**cowboy** ˌ**film** UK *noun* [C] (US **cowboy movie**) a film based on invented stories about cowboys and life in the west of the US in the past

ˈ**cowboy** ˌ**hat** *noun* [C] a hat with a wide, curving lower edge, especially worn by cowboys

cowcatcher /ˈkaʊˌkætʃ.əʳ/ US /-ɚ/ *noun* [C] US a strong metal frame fixed to the front of a train which pushes objects off the track as the train moves forward

cower /ˈkaʊ.əʳ/ US /ˈkaʊ.ɚ/ *verb* [I] to lower your head or body in fear, often while moving backwards: *Stop cowering! I'm not going to hit you.*

cowgirl /ˈkaʊ.gɜːrl/ *noun* [C] a female COWBOY FARM WORKER

cowherd /ˈkaʊ.hɜːd/ US /-hɝːd/ *noun* [C] a person employed to take care of cattle

cowhide /ˈkaʊ.haɪd/ *noun* [C or U] (leather made from) the skin of a cow: *a cowhide briefcase*

cowl /kaʊl/ *noun* [C] **1** a large loose covering for the head and sometimes shoulders, but not the face, which is worn especially by monks **2** a metal cover on the top of a chimney which helps smoke go up it and prevents wind blowing down it

cowling /ˈkaʊ.lɪŋ/ *noun* [C] a metal cover for an engine, especially an aircraft engine

cowlick /ˈkaʊ.lɪk/ *noun* [C] a bit of hair that always sticks out on someone's head

cowman /ˈkaʊ.mən/ /-mæn/ *noun* [C] **1** *UK* a male COWHERD **2** *US* a man who owns cattle

co-worker /ˌkəʊˈwɜː.kəʳ/ [US] /ˌkoʊˈwɝː.kɚ/ *noun* [C] a person working with another worker, especially as a partner or helper

ˈcow ˌparsley *UK noun* [U] (*US* **Queen Anne's lace**) a wild plant with delicate white flowers

cowpat /ˈkaʊ.pæt/ *noun* [C] a round flat mass of excrement from a cow

cowpox /ˈkaʊ.pɒks/ [US] /-pɑːks/ *noun* [U] a disease in cattle

cowrie, **cowry** /ˈkaʊ.ri/ [US] /ˈkaʊr.i/ *noun* [C] a small sea animal with a soft body and a brightly-coloured shell, or the shell itself used in the past as money in parts of Africa and southern Asia: *a cowrie **shell***

co-write /ˈkəʊ.raɪt/ [US] /ˈkoʊ-/ /-ˈ-/ *verb* [T] **co-wrote**, **co-written** to write something with someone else, especially a popular song or tune, or something for television or the cinema: *Lennon and McCartney co-wrote most of the Beatles' songs.* **co-writer** /ˈkəʊˌraɪ.təʳ/ [US] /ˈkoʊˌraɪ.t̬ɚ/ *noun* [C] *Flanagan and McCulloch were co-writers **on** the television series 'Sleepers'.*

cowshed /ˈkaʊ.ʃed/ *noun* [C] a building where cows are kept while they are MILKED (= have milk taken from them), or where they are kept during winter or bad weather

cowslip /ˈkaʊ.slɪp/ *noun* [C] a small plant with yellow flowers that smell sweet

cox /kɒks/ [US] /kɑːks/ *noun* [C] (*FORMAL* **coxswain**) the person who sits at the back of a rowing boat and controls which direction it moves in: *Coxes are often small, light people.* **cox** /kɒks/ [US] /kɑːks/ *verb* [I or T] *She coxed **for** her college for three seasons.* ○ *He coxed the winning eight.*

coy [SECRETIVE] /kɔɪ/ *adj* intentionally secretive: *She's very coy **about** her age.* **coyly** /ˈkɔɪ.li/ *adv* **coyness** *noun* [U]

coy [MODEST] /kɔɪ/ *adj* (especially of women) being or pretending to be shy, modest, childish or lacking in confidence: *She gave me a coy look from under her schoolgirl's fringe.* **coyly** /ˈkɔɪ.li/ *adv*: *She smiled coyly.* **coyness** /ˈkɔɪ.nəs/ *noun* [U]

coyote /kaɪˈəʊ.ti/ [US] /-ˈoʊ.t̬i/ *noun* [C] a small dog-like wild animal which lives in North America

coypu /ˈkɔɪ.puː/ *noun* [C] *plural* **coypus** or **coypu** a South American animal that lives near water and is valuable for its fur

cozily /ˈkəʊ.zɪ.li/ [US] /ˈkoʊ-/ *adv US FOR* **cosily**, see at **cosy**

cozy /ˈkəʊ.zi/ [US] /ˈkoʊ-/ *adj*, *noun* [C] *US FOR* **cosy**

cozzie /ˈkɒz.i/ [US] /ˈkɑː.zi/ *noun* [C] *UK INFORMAL FOR* **swimming costume**

CPR /ˌsiː.piːˈɑːʳ/ [US] /-ˈɑːr/ *noun* [U] *ABBREVIATION FOR* cardiopulmonary resuscitation: a method used to keep someone alive in a medical emergency, in which you blow into their mouth then press on their chest and then repeat the process: *to administer/perform CPR*

CPU /ˌsiː.piːˈjuː/ *noun* [C] *ABBREVIATION FOR* central processing unit: the electronic system that performs the basic operations of a computer ➲See picture **In the Office** on page Centre 15

crab /kræb/ *noun* [C or U] a sea animal that has five pairs of legs and a round flat body covered by a shell, or its flesh eaten as food: *We walked along the beach collecting small crabs in a bucket.* ○ *All the shops on the seafront had crab for sale.* ○ *This crab **meat/salad** is delicious!*

the Crab *noun* [S] the star sign CANCER

crabwise /ˈkræb.waɪz/ *adv UK* If you move crabwise, you move sideways or in a careful and indirect manner.

ˈcrab ˌapple *noun* [C] (*UK ALSO* **crab**) (the small sour fruit of) a small tree which has attractive flowers: *a crab apple tree*

crabbed /kræbd/ /ˈkræb.ɪd/ *adj OLD-FASHIONED* describes writing that is written too closely together and therefore difficult to read

crabby /ˈkræb.i/ *adj* (*OLD-FASHIONED* **crabbed**) *INFORMAL* easily annoyed and complaining: *You're very crabby today. What's upset you?* **crabbily** /ˈkræb.ɪ.li/ *adv* **crabbiness** /ˈkræb.ɪ.nəs/ *noun* [U]

crabgrass /ˈkræb.grɑːs/ [US] /-græs/ *noun* [U] *US* a type of weed

crabs /kræbz/ *plural noun* (*ALSO* **crab lice**) small insects that can live in the hair around the sex organs

crack [BREAK] /kræk/ *verb* **1** [I or T] to break something so that it does not separate, but very thin lines appear on its surface, or to become broken in this way: *A stone hit the window and cracked the glass.* ○ *I cracked my tooth as I fell.* ○ *The walls cracked and the roof collapsed in the earthquake.* ➲See also **cracked**. **2** [I] *INFORMAL* to become mentally and physically weak: *Stress and overwork are causing teachers to crack **(up)**.* **3** [I] *INFORMAL* to fail as a result of problems: *Their relationship began to crack **(up)** after their child died.* **4** [I] If somebody cracks, they weaken and agree that they have been defeated: *He cracked during questioning and told us where to find the stolen goods.*

crack /kræk/ *noun* [C] **1** a very narrow space between parts of something: *Cracks had appeared in the dry ground.* ○ *We peered through the crack in the floorboards.* ○ *FIGURATIVE Cracks began to show in his facade of self-confidence.* **2** **(just) a crack** so that there is a (very) small space: *She opened the door just a crack to listen to the conversation.*

• **at the crack of dawn** very early in the morning, especially at the time at which the sun first appears: *We'll have to leave at the crack of dawn.*

crack [GET INTO] /kræk/ *verb* [T] **1** to break something open, especially in order to reach or use what is inside: *Crack three **eggs** into a bowl and mix them together.* ○ *He cracked **(open)** the **nuts** with his hands.* **2** to find a solution to a problem: *They cracked the **code** and read the secret message.* ○ *UK I've been trying to solve this problem all week, but I still haven't cracked it.* **3** (*ALSO* **crack into** ***sth***) to get into someone else's computer system without permission and obtain information or do something illegal **4** *INFORMAL* to copy computer programs or recorded material illegally

crack /kræk/ *noun* [C] *INFORMAL* a method of cracking someone else's computer system: *Find cracks for your shareware programs.*

crack [HIT] /kræk/ *verb* [I or T; usually + adv or prep] to hit something or someone: *I cracked my head **on/against** the door.* ○ *They cracked him **over** the head with a baseball bat.*

crack [SOUND] /kræk/ *verb* **1** [I or T] to make a sudden, short noise, or to cause something to make this noise: *The whip cracked over the horses' heads.* ○ *He's always cracking his **knuckles*** (= pulling the joints of his fingers to make a noise). **2** [I] If a voice cracks, its sound changes because the person is upset: *Her voice cracked **with** emotion as she told the story.*

• **crack the whip** to use your authority to make someone else behave better or work harder: *We were two months behind schedule, so I decided it was time to crack the whip.*

• **get cracking** to start doing something quickly: *Get cracking* (= Hurry), *or we'll miss the train.* ○ *I'd better get cracking **with** these letters before I go home.*

crack /kræk/ *noun* [C] a sudden loud sound: *the crack of a rifle/whip/breaking branch*

crack [DRUG] /kræk/ *noun* [U] (*ALSO* **crack cocaine**) *SLANG* a pure and powerful form of the drug COCAINE: *Several kilos of crack were found in her luggage.* ○ *a crack addict*

crack [JOKE] /kræk/ *verb* [T] to make a joke or clever remark: *He's always cracking **jokes**.*

crack /kræk/ *noun* [C] a **wisecrack**

crack [ENJOYABLE TIME] /kræk/ *noun* [U] ➲See at **craic**.

crack [GOOD] /kræk/ *adj* **[before n]** excellent, of highest quality: *a crack regiment* ○ *crack troops*
cracking /ˈkræk.ɪŋ/ *adj* UK INFORMAL extremely good: *He scored with a cracking shot into the back of the goal.* ○ *The marathon began at a cracking* (= very fast) *pace.*

crack [ATTEMPT] /kræk/ *noun* **[C usually sing]** INFORMAL an attempt; a try: *It was her first crack **at** beating the record.* ○ *It's not something I've done before, but I'll (UK) **have**/(US) **take** a crack **at** it.*

PHRASAL VERBS WITH **crack**

▲ **crack down** *phrasal verb* to start dealing with bad or illegal behaviour in a more severe way: *The library is cracking down **on** people who lose their books.*
crackdown /ˈkræk.daʊn/ *noun* **[C]** *There has been a series of government crackdowns **on** safety in factories.*

▲ **crack up** [BECOME ILL] *phrasal verb* INFORMAL to become mentally ill: *I think she's cracking up.*

▲ **crack *(sb)* up** [LAUGH] *phrasal verb* **[M]** INFORMAL to suddenly laugh a lot, or to make someone suddenly laugh a lot: *I took one look at her and cracked up.* ○ *There's something about that guy's face that just cracks me up.*

cracked /krækt/ *adj* **1** If something is cracked, it is damaged with one or more thin lines on its surface: *a cracked mirror/window* ○ *cracked plates* **2 crackers**
• **not be all *it's* cracked up to be** INFORMAL to not be as good as claimed: *This new radio station's not all it's cracked up to be.* ➲See also **crack up**.

cracker [FOOD] /ˈkræk.əʳ/ [US] /-ɚ/ *noun* **[C]** a thin flat crisp biscuit, especially one eaten with cheese

cracker [DEVICE] UK /ˈkræk.əʳ/ [US] /-ɚ/ *noun* **[C]** (AUS USUALLY **bonbon**) a paper tube with small toys, small pieces of sweet food, etc. inside, which is covered with bright paper and makes a short sharp sound when both ends are pulled: *Who wants to **pull** a cracker with me?* ○ *a **Christmas** cracker*

cracker [GOOD THING] /ˈkræk.əʳ/ [US] /-ɚ/ *noun* **[S]** UK INFORMAL a person or thing that is very good or has a special exciting quality: *She's written five books, and every one a cracker.*

crackers /ˈkræk.əz/ [US] /-ɚz/ *adj* **[after v]** (ALSO **cracked**) INFORMAL foolish, stupid or slightly mentally ill

ˈ**crack** ˌ**head** *noun* **[C]** SLANG a person who cannot stop using CRACK (= an illegal drug)

ˈ**crack** ˌ**house** *noun* **[C]** SLANG a house or flat where people use, sell or buy CRACK (= an illegal drug)

crackle /ˈkræk.l̩/ *verb* **[I]** to make a lot of short, dry, sharp sounds: *The radio started to crackle.* ○ *The logs crackled and popped in the fireplace.* **crackle** /ˈkræk.l̩/ *noun* **[C or U]** *the crackle of burning logs* **crackling** /ˈkræk.lɪŋ/ *noun* **[U]** *We could hear the crackling of a fire.* **crackly** /ˈkræk.li/ *adj*: *a crackly voice*

crackling /ˈkræk.lɪŋ/ *noun* **[U]** (US ALSO **cracklings**) the crisp skin of cooked PORK (= meat from a pig)

crackpot /ˈkræk.pɒt/ [US] /-pɑːt/ *noun* **[C]** INFORMAL a person who is foolish or stupid **crackpot** /ˈkræk.pɒt/ [US] /-pɑːt/ *adj*: *crackpot ideas*

cradle [BED] /ˈkreɪ.dl̩/ *noun* **[C]** a small bed for a baby, especially one that swings from side to side: *The nurse **rocked** the cradle.*
• **the cradle of *sth*** LITERARY the place where something started: *Fossil records indicate that Africa was the cradle of early human evolution.* ○ *the cradle of civilisation*
• **from (the) cradle to (the) grave** for all of a person's life: *She lived in the same village from the cradle to the grave.*
• **The hand that rocks the cradle (rules the world).** SAYING said to emphasize that women have a strong influence on events through their children

cradle [EQUIPMENT] UK /ˈkreɪ.dl̩/ *noun* **[C]** (US **scaffold**) a frame which hangs on the side of a building, ship, etc. for people to work from

cradle [SUPPORT] /ˈkreɪ.dl̩/ *verb* **[T]** to hold something or someone gently, especially by supporting with the arms: *She cradled him tenderly **in** her **arms**.*

ˈ**cradle** ˌ**snatcher** UK *noun* **[C]** (US **cradle robber**) HUMOROUS OR DISAPPROVING a person whose sexual partner is much younger than they are

craft [SKILL] /krɑːft/ [US] /kræft/ *noun* **[C or U]** *plural* **crafts** (a job or activity needing) skill and experience, especially in relation to making objects: *the craft of furniture making/boat building/glass blowing* ○ *political/literary craft* ○ *rural/ancient/traditional crafts* ○ *craft workers* (= skilled workers) **craft** /krɑːft/ [US] /kræft/ *verb* **[T often passive]** *These bracelets were crafted by native Americans.* ○ *a beautifully crafted silver brooch*
craftsman /ˈkrɑːfts.mən/ [US] /ˈkræfts-/ *noun* **[C]** a person who is skilled in a particular craft: *The plates are hand painted by our finest craftsmen.*
craftswoman /ˈkrɑːftsˌwʊm.ən/ [US] /ˈkræfts-/ *noun* **[C]** a female craftsman
craftsmanship /ˈkrɑːfts.mən.ʃɪp/ [US] /ˈkræfts-/ *noun* **[U]** skill at making things: *The jewellery showed exquisite craftsmanship.*

craft [VEHICLE] /krɑːft/ [US] /kræft/ *noun* **[C]** *plural* **craft** a vehicle for travelling on water or through the air: *naval/civilian/patrol/rescue craft* ○ *Eighteen craft* (= boats) *set out in the race.* ➲See also **aircraft**; **hovercraft**; **spacecraft**.

ˈ**craft** ˌ**fair** *noun* **[C]** an event where people sell decorative objects that they have made by hand

ˈ**craft** ˌ**shop** *noun* **[C]** a shop that sells the materials and tools used for making decorative objects by hand, or the decorative objects themselves

crafty /ˈkrɑːf.ti/ [US] /ˈkræf.ti/ *adj* clever, especially in a dishonest or secretive way: *I've had a crafty idea for getting round the regulations.* ○ *She was a crafty old woman.* **craftily** /ˈkrɑːf.tɪ.li/ [US] /ˈkræf-/ *adv* **craftiness** /ˈkrɑːf.tɪ.nəs/ [US] /ˈkræf-/ *noun* **[U]**

crag /kræg/ *noun* **[C]** a high rough mass of rock which sticks out from the land around it
craggy /ˈkræg.i/ *adj* **1** having many crags: *a craggy coastline* **2** describe a man's face that is quite roughly formed and has loose skin but is also attractive: *a craggy face* ○ *craggy features*

craic /kræk/ *noun* **[U]** (ALSO **crack**) IRISH ENGLISH enjoyable time spent with other people, especially when the conversation is entertaining and amusing: *The boys went driving round the town just **for the** craic.*

cram [PUSH] /kræm/ *verb* **[T usually + adv or prep] -mm-** INFORMAL to force a lot of things into a small space, or to do many things in a short period of time: *Eight children were crammed **into** the back of the car.* ○ *I managed to cram three countries **into** a week's business trip.* ○ *The room was packed and we were crammed **against** the door.*
crammed /kræmd/ *adj*: *a crammed train/room* ○ *The platform was crammed **with**/crammed **full of** people trying to board the train.*

cram [LEARN] /kræm/ *verb* **[I] -mm-** to try to learn a lot very quickly before an exam: *She's cramming **for** her history exam.*
crammer /ˈkræm.əʳ/ [US] /-ɚ/ *noun* **[C]** UK OLD-FASHIONED INFORMAL a school or a book which helps you to learn quickly
▲ **cram *sth* down** *phrasal verb* **[M]** INFORMAL to eat a lot of something quickly: *I just had time to cram down a few biscuits before we left.*

cramp [PAIN] /kræmp/ *noun* **[C or U]** a sudden painful tightening in a muscle, often after a lot of exercise, which limits movement: *Several runners needed treatment for (UK) cramp/(US) cramps and exhaustion.* ○ *I've got (UK) cramp/(US) a cramp in my foot.* ○ ***stomach** cramps*
cramps /kræmps/ *plural noun* pains in the lower stomach caused by a woman's period

cramp [LIMIT] /kræmp/ *verb* **[T]** to limit someone, especially to prevent them from enjoying a full life: *Worry and lack of money cramp the lives of the unemployed.*
• **cramp *sb's* style** INFORMAL HUMOROUS to prevent someone from enjoying themselves as much as they would like, especially by going somewhere with them
cramped /kræmpt/ *adj* not having enough space or time: *a cramped room/house* ○ *We have six desks in this room, so we're rather cramped (**for** space).* ○ *Meeting you before the end of the month will be difficult, because I have a very cramped schedule until then.*

crampon /ˈkræm.pɒn/ [US] /-pɑːn/ *noun* **[C]** a metal frame with sharp points which is fixed to the bottom of a boot to make walking on ice or snow easier

cranberry /ˈkræn.bᵊr.i/ [US] /-ber-/ *noun* [C] a small round red fruit with a sour taste

crane [MACHINE] /kreɪn/ *noun* [C] a tall metal structure with a long horizontal part which is used for lifting and moving heavy objects: *The crane lifted the container off the ship.*

crane [BIRD] /kreɪn/ *noun* [C] a tall bird with long thin legs and a long neck

crane [STRETCH] /kreɪn/ *verb* [I usually + adv or prep; T] to stretch in order to look at something: *He craned* ***forward*** *to see the procession.* ○ *Mike was craning his* ***neck*** *to get the first glimpse of the car.*

ˈcrane ˌfly *noun* [C] a flying insect with a narrow body and very long legs

cranium /ˈkreɪ.ni.əm/ *noun* [C] *plural* **craniums** or **crania** *SPECIALIZED* the hard bone case in animals and humans, which gives the head its shape and protects the brain ➲See picture **The Body** on page Centre 5

cranial /ˈkreɪ.ni.əl/ *adj SPECIALIZED* of the SKULL

crank [STRANGE PERSON] /kræŋk/ *noun* [C] *INFORMAL* a person who has strange or unusual ideas and beliefs **cranky** /ˈkræŋ.ki/ *adj*: *She's a member of a group that promotes cranky ideas about food and exercise.*

crank [UNPLEASANT PERSON] /kræŋk/ *noun* [C] *US INFORMAL* an unpleasant and easily annoyed person: *She's always a crank first thing in the morning.* **cranky** /ˈkræŋ.ki/ *adj*: *a cranky baby* ○ *He's been cranky all day.*

crank [EQUIPMENT] /kræŋk/ *noun* [C] a device which allows movement to go between parts of a machine or which changes backward and forward movement into circular movement: *a crank handle*

crank /kræŋk/ *verb*

PHRASAL VERBS WITH **crank** ▼

▲ **crank** ***sth*** **out** *phrasal verb* [M] *US INFORMAL* to produce something with no special care or effort: *Like clockwork, he cranks out a new book every year.*

▲ **crank** ***sth*** **up** *phrasal verb* [M] *INFORMAL* to increase or improve something: *crank up the volume/pressure*

ˌcrank ˈcaller *noun* [C] someone who makes unpleasant telephone calls to people whom they do not know

crankshaft /ˈkræŋk.ʃɑːft/ [US] /-ʃæft/ *noun* [C] a long metal rod, especially one in a car engine, that helps the engine turn the wheels: *a crankshaft bearing*

cranny /ˈkræn.i/ *noun* [C] a small narrow opening in something solid: *There were small plants growing in every* ***nook and*** *cranny of the wall.*

crap [EXCREMENT] /kræp/ *noun* [S or U] *OFFENSIVE* excrement, or when an animal or person produces excrement: *I stepped in a pile of crap.* ○ *That dog's just (UK)* ***had****/(US)* ***taken*** *a crap on my lawn.* **crap** /kræp/ *verb* [I] -pp- *The dog crapped right in the middle of the street.*

crapper /ˈkræp.əʳ/ [US] /-ɚ/ *noun* [C] *OFFENSIVE* a toilet

crap [BAD] /kræp/ *noun* [U] *INFORMAL OR OFFENSIVE* something which is worthless, useless, nonsense or of bad quality: *I can't believe she's trying to pass off this crap as art!* ○ *I've only read one novel by him and it was* ***a load of*** *crap.*

crap /kræp/ *adj* **1** *INFORMAL OR OFFENSIVE* of very bad quality: *A bad film? It was crap!* ○ *UK He watches a lot of crap TV.* **2** *UK INFORMAL OR OFFENSIVE* not skilled or not organized: *He's totally crap* ***at*** *football.* ○ *I meant to call him and invite him, but I've been a bit crap* ***about*** *asking people.*

▲ **crap on** *phrasal verb OFFENSIVE* to talk for a long time in a boring way: *I had to listen to Mikey crapping on about his music collection.*

crape /kreɪp/ *noun* [U] *UK FOR* **crepe** CLOTH

crappy /ˈkræp.i/ *adj OFFENSIVE* unpleasant or of very bad quality: *He's had a series of crappy jobs.*

craps /kræps/ *noun* [U] (*ALSO* **crap**) *US* a game played with dice for money

crash [ACCIDENT] /kræʃ/ *verb* [I or T] to have an accident, especially one which damages a vehicle: *We skidded on the ice and crashed (****into*** *another car).* ○ *The plane crashed* ***into*** *a mountainside.* ○ *Her brother borrowed her motorbike and crashed it.*

crash /kræʃ/ *noun* [C] an accident, especially one which damages a vehicle: *a car crash* ○ *She* ***had*** *a crash on the way to work.* ○ *They were only slightly injured in the crash.*

crash [MAKE A NOISE] /kræʃ/ *verb* [I or T; usually + adv or prep] to hit something, often making a loud noise or causing damage: *We could hear waves crashing* ***on/against*** *the shore.* ○ *Suddenly, cymbals crashed and the orchestra began playing.* ○ *A dog* ***came*** *crashing through the bushes.* ○ *Without warning, the tree crashed through the roof.*

crash /kræʃ/ *noun* [C] a sudden loud noise made when something breaks or falls: *I heard a loud crash in the kitchen.* ○ *The vase landed on the floor with a crash.*

crashing /ˈkræʃ.ɪŋ/ *noun* [U] *I could hear crashing* (= loud noises) *in the next room.*

crash [FAIL] /kræʃ/ *verb* [I] **1** If something such as a business crashes, it suddenly fails or becomes unsuccessful: *Investors were seriously worried when the stock market began to crash.* **2** If a computer or system crashes, it suddenly stops operating: *My laptop's crashed again.*

• **crash and burn** *INFORMAL* to fail very suddenly, obviously and completely: *In this business, new products often crash and burn.*

crash /kræʃ/ *noun* [C] **1** when the value of a country's businesses suddenly falls by a large amount: *They lost a lot of money in the Stock Market crash.* **2** when a computer or system suddenly stops operating: *a computer crash*

crash [QUICK] /kræʃ/ *adj* [before n] *INFORMAL* quick and complete, or short and difficult: *The company undertook a crash program of machine replacement.* ➲See also **crash course**.

crash [SLEEP] /kræʃ/ *verb* [I] *INFORMAL* to sleep at someone else's house for the night, especially when you have not planned it: *They crashed on my floor after the party.* ➲See also **crash out** SLEEP.

crash [ENTER WITHOUT PERMISSION] /kræʃ/ *verb* [T] *INFORMAL* to go to a party or other event without an invitation: *We tried to crash the party, but the bouncers wouldn't let us in.* ➲See also **gatecrash**.

PHRASAL VERBS WITH **crash** ▼

▲ **crash out** [SLEEP] *phrasal verb INFORMAL* to go to sleep very quickly because you are very tired: *I just want to go home and crash out.*

▲ **crash out** [LOSE] *phrasal verb UK INFORMAL* to lose in a sports competition when you were expected to win: *He crashed out* ***of*** *the French Open in the second round.*

ˈcrash ˌbarrier *noun* [C] *UK* a strong fence which separates the two sides of a large road or which is built at a dangerous place at the edge of a road, to help prevent accidents

ˈcrash ˌcourse *noun* [C] a course that teaches you a lot of basic facts in a very short time: *I did/took a crash course* ***in*** *French before my trip to Paris.*

ˌcrash ˈdiet *noun* [C] a way of losing body weight quickly by eating very little

ˈcrash ˌhelmet *noun* [C] a hard hat which covers and protects the whole head, worn especially by motorcyclists ➲See picture **Hairstyles and Hats** on page Centre 8

ˌcrashing ˈbore *noun* [C] *INFORMAL* someone or something that is extremely boring: *I love his books, but in person he's a crashing bore.*

crash-land /ˈkræʃ.lænd/ *verb* [I or T] to land an aircraft suddenly because of an emergency, sometimes resulting in serious damage or injuries: *The jet crash-landed and burst into flames.* **crash-landing** /ˈkræʃ.læn.dɪŋ/ *noun* [C] *The pilot attempted a crash-landing on the beach.*

crass /kræs/ *adj* without consideration for how other people might feel; stupid: *a crass remark* ○ *crass behaviour/ignorance* ○ *a crass error of judgment* ○ *He made crass comments about her worn-out clothes.* **crassly** /ˈkræs.li/ *adv* **crassness** /ˈkræs.nəs/ *noun* [U]

crate /kreɪt/ *noun* [C] a box made of wood, plastic or metal, especially one divided into parts to hold bottles: *a milk crate* ○ *a crate of empty bottles* ○ *a packing crate*

C

C

crate /kreɪt/ *verb* [T] to put something into a crate, especially in order to move it

crater /ˈkreɪ.təʳ/ [US] /-t̬ɚ/ *noun* [C] the round hole at the top of a volcano, or a hole similar to this: *the huge crater of Vesuvius* ○ *a bomb crater* ○ *With a good telescope, you can see craters on the moon.* **cratered** /ˈkreɪ.təd/ [US] /-t̬ɚd/ *adj*: *a cratered surface*

cravat /krəˈvæt/ *noun* [C] a wide straight piece of material worn loosely tied in the open neck of a shirt

craven /ˈkreɪ.vᵊn/ *adj* FORMAL extremely cowardly: *a craven act of terrorism*

craving /ˈkreɪ.vɪŋ/ *noun* [C] a strong or uncontrollable desire: *I have a craving **for** chocolate.* **crave** /kreɪv/ *verb* [T] *Many young children crave **attention**.*

crawl [MOVE] /krɔːl/ [US] /krɑːl/ *verb* [I] to move slowly or with difficulty, especially (of a person) with the body stretched out along the ground or on hands and knees: *The child crawled **across** the floor.* ○ *The injured soldier crawled to safety.* ○ *The lorry crawled noisily up the hill.* ○ *Megan has just learned to crawl.*
crawl /krɔːl/ [US] /krɑːl/ *noun* [S] a very slow speed: *Traffic moved forward **at a** crawl.*
crawler /ˈkrɔː.ləʳ/ [US] /ˈkrɑː.lɚ/ *noun* [C] **1** UK a baby who has not yet learned to walk **2** something that crawls, such as a slow-moving vehicle

crawl [TRY TO PLEASE] /krɔːl/ [US] /krɑːl/ *verb* [I] INFORMAL DISAPPROVING to try hard to please in order to get an advantage: *I don't like people who crawl.* ○ UK *He crawled **to** the group leader because he wanted a promotion.*
• **crawl back (to *sb*)** to admit that you were wrong and ask someone for forgiveness or for something that you refused in the past: *Don't **come** crawling back to me when she throws you out!*
crawler /ˈkrɔː.ləʳ/ [US] /ˈkrɑː.lɚ/ *noun* [C] UK INFORMAL DISAPPROVING a person who tries hard to please others in order to get an advantage

crawl [FILL] /krɔːl/ [US] /krɑːl/ *verb* INFORMAL **be crawling with *sth*** to be completely covered with or full of a particular type of thing: *The kitchen floor was crawling with ants.*

crawl [SWIMMING] /krɔːl/ [US] /krɑːl/ *noun* [S or U] a style of swimming in which you move your arms over your head and kick with straight legs

crayfish (*plural* **crayfish** or **crayfishes**) /ˈkreɪ.fɪʃ/ *noun* [C or U] (US ALSO **crawfish**) a small animal which lives in rivers and is similar to a LOBSTER, or its flesh eaten as food

crayon /ˈkreɪ.ɒn/ [US] /-ɑːn/ *noun* [C] a small stick of coloured wax used for drawing or writing: *wax crayons* ○ *children's crayons*
crayon /ˈkreɪ.ɒn/ [US] /-ɑːn/ *verb* [I or T] UK to draw something with a crayon: *When I left her she was busy crayoning.*

craze /kreɪz/ *noun* [C usually sing] an activity, object or idea that is extremely popular, usually for a short time: *Cycling shorts were **the latest** craze/**(all)** the craze that year.* ○ *The craze **for** health foods has become big business.*

crazed /kreɪzd/ *adj* behaving in a wild or strange way, especially because of strong emotions or extreme pain: *a crazed expression* ○ *He became crazed **with** anger/jealousy/pain.* ○ *The horses bolted, crazed **with** fear.*

crazy /ˈkreɪ.zi/ *adj* **1** stupid or not sensible: *It's a crazy idea.* ○ *You're crazy **to** buy a house without seeing it.* **2** annoyed or angry: *The constant noise **drove** me crazy* (= made me become angry). **3** mentally ill: *I seriously think she'll **go** crazy if she doesn't have a holiday soon.*
• **be crazy about *sb/sth*** to be very interested in something or love someone very much: *Both my sons are crazy about old motorbikes.* ○ *Lorna is completely crazy about her boyfriend.*
• **like crazy** INFORMAL If you do something like crazy, you do a lot of it or do it very quickly: *They were working like crazy to get the job done on time.*
crazy /ˈkreɪ.zi/ *noun* [C] US SLANG a person who behaves in a way that is stupid or not sensible, especially one who is mentally ill: *There's some old crazy over there shouting and spitting at people.* **crazily** /ˈkreɪ.zɪ.li/ *adv* **craziness** /ˈkreɪ.zɪ.nəs/ *noun* [U]

ˌcrazy ˈpaving *noun* [U] UK a hard surface for paths made with broken pieces of stone or concrete

creak /kriːk/ *verb* [I] When a door or floorboard, etc. creaks, it makes a long low sound when it moves or is moved: *The door creaked on its hinges.* ○ *I heard the floorboards creak as he crept closer.*
creak /kriːk/ *noun* [C] a noise made when something creaks: *I heard a creak on the stairs.*
creaky /ˈkriː.ki/ *adj* **1** describes something that creaks: *a creaky hinge/chair/bed* ○ *creaky floorboards* **2** UK describes something that is old-fashioned and not now effective: *the creaky legal system* **creakily** /ˈkriː.kɪ.li/ *adv* **creakiness** /ˈkriː.kɪ.nəs/ *noun* [U]

cream /kriːm/ *noun* **1** [U] the thick yellowish-white liquid that forms on the top of milk: *strawberries and cream* ○ *Do you like cream in your coffee?* ○ UK *a cream cake* (= cake with cream in it) **2** [U] the colour of cream **3** [C] a type of sweet which is soft inside: *chocolate/peppermint creams* **4** [C or U] a soft substance that you rub into your skin: ***face/hand** cream* ○ *moisturizing cream* ○ *Put some **sun** cream on to protect your face.* **5** [U] a thick liquid used for cleaning things: *cream cleaner* **6 cream of mushroom/tomato, etc. soup** soup that has been made into a smooth thick liquid and usually has cream in it
• **the cream of *sth*** the best of a particular group of things or people: *The cream of this year's graduates have gone abroad for jobs.*
cream /kriːm/ *adj* having a yellow-white colour: *a cream shirt*
cream /kriːm/ *verb* [T] to make food into a smooth thick liquid: *Cream the butter and sugar together.*
creamy /ˈkriː.mi/ *adj* like cream or containing cream: *The chocolate mousse was smooth and creamy.* ○ *a creamy sauce* **creaminess** /ˈkriː.mɪ.nəs/ *noun* [U]
▲ **cream *sth/sb* off** *phrasal verb* [M] to remove the best part of something or the best people in a group and use them for your own advantage: *They had a plan to cream off the brightest children and put them in separate schools.*

ˌcream ˈcheese *noun* [C or U] (a) soft white cheese which you spread rather than cut

ˌcream ˈcracker *noun* [C] UK a hard biscuit which is not sweet and is often eaten with cheese

creamer /ˈkriː.məʳ/ [US] /-mɚ/ *noun* **1** [U] a powder which is added to hot drinks instead of milk or cream: *I've run out of milk – would you like some creamer instead?* **2** [C] US a small container for serving cream in

ˌcream of ˈtartar *noun* [U] a white powder used in baking

ˌcream ˈsoda *noun* [C or U] US (a) fizzy drink flavoured with VANILLA

ˌcream ˈtea *noun* [C] MAINLY UK a light meal of SCONES (= small bread-like cakes) with jam and cream

crease [FOLD] /kriːs/ *noun* [C] a line on cloth or paper where it has been folded or crushed: *He ironed a crease down the front of each trouser leg.*
crease /kriːs/ *verb* [I or T] If cloth, paper, etc. creases, or if you crease it, it gets a line in it where it has been folded or crushed: *The seatbelt has creased my blouse.* ○ *It's a nice dress, but it creases very easily.*
creased /kriːst/ *adj* with a crease: *creased trousers*

crease [CRICKET] /kriːs/ *noun* [S] UK SPECIALIZED a line marked on the ground where the player stands to hit the ball in cricket
▲ **crease *(sb)* up** *phrasal verb* UK INFORMAL to laugh a lot, or make someone else laugh a lot: *The look on his face just creased me up.*

create [MAKE] /kriˈeɪt/ *verb* [T] to make something new, especially to invent something: *Charles Schulz created the characters 'Snoopy' and 'Charlie Brown'.* ○ *The Bible says that God created the world.* ○ *He created a wonderful meal **from** very few ingredients.* ○ *It's important to create a good impression when you meet a new client.*
creation /kriˈeɪ.ʃᵊn/ *noun* [C or U] the act of creating something, or the thing that is created: *the creation **of** a new political party* ○ *Their policies are all towards the creation **of** wealth.* ○ *This 25-foot-high sculpture is her latest creation.* ○ *The fashion magazines were full of the latest Paris creations* (= fashionable new clothes).

the Cre'ation *noun* [S] in the Bible, the making of the world by God
creationist /kri'eɪ.ʃən.ɪst/ *noun* [C] a person who believes that the world was made by God exactly as described in the Bible
creator /kri'eɪ.tər/ [US] /-t̬ɚ/ *noun* [C] someone who has invented something: *He's the creator **of** a successful cartoon series.* ○ *Who was the creator **of** the miniskirt?*
the Cre'ator *noun* [S] God

create [BE ANGRY] /kri'eɪt/ *verb* [I] *UK OLD-FASHIONED* to show that you are angry: *If she sees you with an ice cream she'll only start creating.*

creative /kri'eɪ.tɪv/ [US] /-t̬ɪv/ *adj* producing or using original and unusual ideas: *a creative person/artist/designer/programmer* ○ *creative talents/powers/abilities* ○ *creative thinking*
creative /kri'eɪ.tɪv/ [US] /-t̬ɪv/ *noun* [C] *SPECIALIZED* an employee whose imagination and artistic skills are very important for a company: *Several leading creatives are involved in the advertising campaign.* **creatively** /kri'eɪ.tɪv.li/ [US] /-t̬ɪv-/ *adv* **creativity** /ˌkriː.eɪ'tɪv.ɪ.ti/ [US] /-'t̬ɪv.ə.t̬i/ *noun* [U] (*ALSO* **creativeness**) *Too many rules might deaden creativity.* ○ *Creativity, ingenuity and flair are the songwriter's real talents.*

cre,ative ac'counting *noun* [U] *DISAPPROVING* when you find ways of explaining how money has been spent, which keep hidden what has really happened to it

creature /'kriː.tʃər/ [US] /-tʃɚ/ *noun* [C] **1** any large or small living thing which can move independently; an animal: *Rain forests are filled with amazing creatures.* ○ *Don't all **living** creatures have certain rights?* ○ *Blue whales are the largest creatures ever to have lived.* **2** used to refer to a life form that is unusual, unknown or imaginary: *The unicorn is a mythical creature.* ○ *The film was about creatures from outer space.* ○ *The duck-billed platypus is a truly bizarre creature.* **3** used to refer to a person when an opinion is being expressed about them: *John is a strange/weak/pathetic creature.* ○ *A lovely blonde creature* (= a beautiful blonde woman) *walked into the room.*
• **be the creature of *sb/sth*** *FORMAL DISAPPROVING* to do everything that you are asked to do by a particular person or organization, without question: *He had become the creature of the secret police.*
• **creature of habit** someone who always does the same thing in the same way: *My father's such a creature of habit – he always has to have a biscuit and a cup of tea at bedtime.*

,creature 'comforts *plural noun* things that make life more pleasant, such as good food and a comfortable place to live

creche /kreʃ/ *noun* [C] **1** *MAINLY UK* a place where young children are cared for during the day while their parents do something else, especially work, study or shop: *Does your employer provide a creche?* **2** *US* (*UK* **crib**) a model of the people and animals present at the birth of Jesus, which is used as a decoration at Christmas

cred /kred/ *noun* [U] *UK SLANG* **street-cred**

credence /'kriː.dənts/ *noun* [U] *FORMAL* acceptance, support or belief that something is true: *I'm not prepared to **give** credence **to** anonymous complaints.* ○ *His bruises **added/lent** credence **to** his statement that he had been beaten.*

credentials /krɪ'den.tʃəlz/ *plural noun* the abilities and experience which make someone suitable for a particular job or activity, or proof of someone's abilities and experience: *All the candidates had excellent academic credentials.* ○ *She was asked to show her press credentials.*

credi'bility ,gap *noun* [S] a difference between what is promised and what really happens

credible /'kred.ɪ.bl̩/ *adj* able to be believed or trusted: *They haven't produced any credible **evidence** for convicting him.* ○ *The story of what had happened to her was **barely*** (= only just) *credible.* **credibly** /'kred.ɪ.bli/ *adv*: *The family in the television programme could not be credibly compared with a real one.*
credibility /ˌkred.ə'bɪl.ɪ.ti/ [US] /-ə.t̬i/ *noun* [U] when someone can be believed or trusted: *His arrest for lewd behaviour seriously damaged his credibility **as** a religious leader.* ○ *He complained that we had tried to undermine his credibility within the company.*

credit [PRAISE] /'kred.ɪt/ *noun* [U] **1** praise, approval or honour: *She got no credit for solving the problem.* ○ *Her boss **took** credit **for** it/**took** (all) **the** credit instead.* ○ ***To** her (great) credit, she admitted she was wrong.* ○ *I **gave** him credit **for*** (= thought that he would have) *better judgment than he showed.* **2 be a credit to *sb/sth*** to do something that makes a person, group or organization feel proud or receive praise: *She is a credit to her family.*
do your family/parents/teacher, etc. credit to cause someone who has been or is responsible for you to receive praise by your good behaviour or successful actions: *She does her teachers credit.*
• **all credit to *sb*** used to show that you think a person deserves a lot of praise for something that they have done: *All credit to her, she did it all herself.*
• **credit where credit's due** an expression which means that you should praise someone who deserves it, although you might dislike some things about them: *I don't especially like the woman but, credit where credit's due, she's very efficient.*
creditable /'kred.ɪ.tə.bl̩/ [US] /-t̬ə-/ *adj* deserving of praise, trust or respect: *Our team came in a creditable third in the competition.* ○ *The other, less creditable, reason for their decision was personal gain.*

credit [PAYMENT] /'kred.ɪt/ *noun* [U] a method of paying for goods or services at a later time, usually paying interest as well as the original money: *They decided to buy the car **on** credit.* ○ *The shop was offering six months' **(interest-free)** credit **on** electrical goods.* ⊃Compare **debit**.
creditor /'kred.ɪ.tər/ [US] /-t̬ɚ/ *noun* [C] someone to whom money is owed: *The company couldn't pay its creditors.* ⊃Compare **debtor** at **debt**.

credit [HAVING MONEY] /'kred.ɪt/ *noun* [C or U] money in your bank account: *I was relieved to see from my statement that my account was **in** credit.*
credit /'kred.ɪt/ *verb* [T] *They credited my account **with** $20* (= put $20 into my account) *after I pointed out the mistake.*

credit [BELIEVE] /'kred.ɪt/ *verb* [T not continuous] to believe something which seems unlikely to be true: *He even tried to pretend he was a film star's son – can you credit it?* ○ ***It** was hard **to** credit some of the stories we heard about her.*

credit [COURSE UNIT] /'kred.ɪt/ *noun* [C] a unit which represents a successfully completed part of an educational course: *He's already got a credit/three credits in earth science.*
▲ **credit *sb* with *sth*** *phrasal verb* **1** to consider that someone has a particular quality: *I had credited them with more integrity than they showed.* **2** to say that someone is responsible for something good: *She is credited with making the business a success.*

'credit ac,count *UK noun* [C] (*US* **charge account**) a formal agreement between a shop or other business and a customer, in which the customer can take goods and pay the shop or business for them at a later time

'credit ,card *noun* [C] a small plastic card which can be used as a method of payment, the money being taken from you at a later time

'credit ,note *noun* [C] *UK* a piece of paper given by a shop when you return something you do not want, which allows you to buy other goods of the same value

'credit ,rating *noun* [C usually sing] a calculation of someone's ability to pay back money which they have borrowed

the 'credits *plural noun* a list of people who helped to make a film or a television or radio programme, which is shown or announced at the beginning or the end of it

'credit ,squeeze *UK noun* [C] (*US* **credit crunch**) *INFORMAL* a period of economic difficulty when it is difficult to borrow money from banks

'credit ,terms *plural noun* the arrangements made for giving credit, especially the amount of money, the period of borrowing, etc.

C

creditworthy /'kred.ɪt,wɜː.ði/ /-,wɜː-/ adj describes someone who has enough money or property for banks and other organizations to be willing to lend them money: *The bank refused to give him a loan, saying that he wasn't creditworthy.* **creditworthiness** /'kred.ɪt-,wɜː.ðɪ.nəs/ /-,wɜː-/ noun [U]

credulous /'kred.jʊ.ləs/ adj SLIGHTLY FORMAL too willing to believe what you are told; easily deceived **credulously** /'kred.jʊ.lə.sli/ adv
credulity /krə'djuː.lə.ti/ /-'duː.lə.t̬i/ noun [U] (ALSO **credulousness**) SLIGHTLY FORMAL willingness to believe that something is real or true

creed /kriːd/ noun [C] (ALSO **credo**) FORMAL a set of beliefs which expresses a particular opinion and influences the way you live
● **the Creed** SPECIALIZED a short formal statement of Christian religious belief, said in church

creek /kriːk/ noun [C] **1** UK a narrow area of water that flows into the land from the sea, a lake, etc. **2** US a stream or narrow river
● **up the creek** INFORMAL in trouble: *If any more people resign, we'll be really up the creek.*

creep MOVE SLOWLY /kriːp/ verb [I usually + adv or prep] crept, crept to move slowly, quietly and carefully, usually in order to avoid being noticed: *She turned off the light and crept through the door.* ○ *Someone was creeping around outside my window.* ○ *The spider crept up the wall.* ○ *The traffic was creeping along at a snail's pace.*
creeping /'kriː.pɪŋ/ adj [before n] DISAPPROVING happening, developing or moving slowly or gradually: *We are totally against any form of creeping Socialism.*

creep PERSON /kriːp/ noun [C] **1** UK INFORMAL someone who tries to make someone more important like them by being very polite and helpful in a way that is not sincere: *Making coffee for the boss again? You creep!* **2** INFORMAL an unpleasant person, especially a man: *He was a real creep - he was always staring at me in the canteen.* ○ [as form of address] *Leave me alone, you creep!*

PHRASAL VERBS WITH **creep** ▼

▲ **creep in/creep into** sth phrasal verb **1** MAINLY UK If mistakes creep in or creep into a piece of text, they are included despite efforts not to include them: *A few mistakes always creep in during the editing process.* ○ *One or two typing errors crept into the report.* **2** to gradually start to be noticeable: *Doubts began to creep into my mind about the likely success of the project.*

▲ **creep over** sb phrasal verb If a bad feeling creeps over someone, they gradually start to feel it: *A dangerous tiredness crept over her as she drove.*

▲ **creep up** phrasal verb If the value or amount of something creeps up, it slowly increases: *Over the last year, the rate of inflation has crept up to almost 7%.*

▲ **creep up on/behind** sb SURPRISE phrasal verb to surprise someone by moving closer to them without them seeing or hearing you: *Don't creep up on me like that!* ○ *We crept up behind her and yelled "Boo!"*

▲ **creep up on** sb EXPERIENCE phrasal verb If a feeling or state creeps up on someone, they start to experience it so gradually that they are not aware of it: *It was only after I turned 60 that old age began to creep up on me.*

creeper /'kriː.pər/ /-pɚ/ noun [C] a plant that grows along the ground, or up walls or trees
creeping plant noun [C] a plant that grows along the ground

creepy /'kriː.pi/ adj INFORMAL strange or unnatural and making you feel frightened: *a creepy film* ○ *a creepy smile*
creeps /kriːps/ plural noun INFORMAL **give** sb **the creeps** to cause someone to have uncomfortable feelings of nervousness or fear: *Living next to a graveyard would give me the creeps.*

creepy-crawly /,kriː.pi'krɔː.li/ /-'krɑː.li/ noun [C] INFORMAL a small insect that gives you a feeling of fear and disgust

cremate /krɪ'meɪt/ /'kriː.meɪt/ verb [T] to burn a dead person's body, usually as part of a funeral ceremony
cremation /krɪ'meɪ.ʃən/ noun [C or U] *My dad's cremation was a sad affair.*

crematorium (plural **crematoriums** or **crematoria**) /,krem.ə'tɔː.ri.əm/ /-'tɔːr.i-/ noun [C] (US ALSO **crematory**) a building where dead people's bodies are burnt, usually as part of a funeral ceremony

crème brûlée /,krem.bruː'leɪ/ noun [C or U] a sweet food made from CUSTARD (= a sweet soft food made from milk, eggs and sugar), with hard burnt sugar on top

crème caramel /,krem.kær.ə'mel/ /-ker-/ noun [C or U] a sweet food made from CUSTARD (= a sweet soft food made from milk, eggs and sugar) with soft brown liquid sugar on top

the crème de la crème /ðə,krem.də.lɑː'krem/ noun [S] the best people in a group or the best type of a particular thing: *She was hoping to attract the crème de la crème of the art world to her exhibition.*

crème de menthe /,krem.də'mɑːntθ/ noun [U] a sweet mint-flavoured alcoholic drink

crenellated, US USUALLY **crenelated** /'kren.ªl.eɪ.tɪd/ /-t̬ɪd/ adj SPECIALIZED having BATTLEMENTS (= castle walls with regular spaces along the top) **crenellations**, US USUALLY **crenelations** /,kren.ªl'eɪ.ʃªnz/ plural noun

creole LANGUAGE /kri'əʊl/ /-'oʊl/ noun [C or U] a language that has developed from a mixture of languages: *creole-speaking tribes*
Creole /kri'əʊl/ /-'oʊl/ noun [C or U] an American or West Indian language, which is a combination of a European language and another language and which is a main language in the southern US and in the Caribbean

creole PERSON /kri'əʊl/ /-'oʊl/ noun [C] a person of mixed African and European origin who speaks Creole
Creole /kri'əʊl/ /-'oʊl/ noun [C] someone who is related to the first Europeans who came to the West Indies or the southern US **Creole** /kri'əʊl/ /-'oʊl/ adj: *I love Creole cooking, so hot and spicy.*

creosote /'kriː.ə.səʊt/ /-soʊt/ noun [U] a thick brown oily liquid, used especially for preserving wood
creosote /'kriː.ə.səʊt/ /-soʊt/ verb [T] *James and I creosoted (= put creosote on) the fence.*

crepe FOOD, **crêpe** /krep/ noun [C] MAINLY US a thin light PANCAKE

crepe CLOTH, **crêpe**, UK ALSO **crape** /kreɪp/ noun [U] thin cloth with a WRINKLED (= uneven and having fine lines) surface: *a black crepe dress* ○ *a crepe jacket*

crepe RUBBER, **crêpe** /kreɪp/ noun [U] a strong type of rubber with an uneven surface, used especially for making the bottom of shoes: *crepe-soled shoes*

crepe paper noun [U] thin, usually brightly coloured paper, used especially for making party decorations

crêpe suzette /,krep.suː'zet/ noun [C or U] a sweet orange-flavoured pancake, covered with LIQUEUR or brandy which is set on fire just before you eat it

crept /krept/ past simple and past participle of **creep**

crepuscular /krɪ'pʌs.kjʊ.lər/ /-lɚ/ adj LITERARY relating to or like the time of day just before the sun comes up, or just after it goes down; not bright

crescendo /krɪ'ʃen.dəʊ/ /-doʊ/ noun [C usually sing] plural **crescendos 1** a gradual increase in loudness, or the moment when a noise or piece of music is at its loudest: *The music reached a crescendo.* **2** an increase in excitement, danger or action: *There has been a rising crescendo of violence in the region.*

crescent /'kres.ªnt/ noun [C] **1** (something with) a curved shape that has two narrow pointed ends, like the moon when it is less than half of a circle: *The moon was a brightly shining crescent.* **2** a row of houses or a road built in a curve: *They live at 15 Park Crescent.* **crescent** /'kres.ªnt/ adj: *the crescent moon*

cress /kres/ noun [U] any of various plants with small green leaves, used especially in salads: *egg and cress sandwiches* ⊃See also **watercress**.

crest TOP /krest/ noun [C] **1** the top or highest part of something such as a wave or a hill: *the crest of a hill/wave* **2** a growth of feathers, fur or skin along the top of the heads of some animals **3** a decoration, usually made of feathers or animal hair, on the top of a soldier's hat, especially in the past

• **be riding/on the crest of a wave** to be very successful for a limited period of time: *Mrs Singh is still riding the crest of a wave **of** popularity.*

crested /'kres.tɪd/ *adj* A crested bird has a growth of feathers on its head: *a crested grebe*

crest PICTURE /krest/ *noun* [C] a formal picture that is used by a family, town, organization, etc. as their particular sign: *a royal crest* **crested** /'kres.tɪd/ *adj: crested writing paper*

crestfallen /'krest.ˌfɔː.lᵊn/ ⑥ /-ˌfɑː-/ *adj* disappointed and sad because of having failed unexpectedly in something: *He looked crestfallen at their decision, but did not argue.*

cretin /'kret.ɪn/ ⑥ /'kriː.tᵊn/ *noun* [C] OFFENSIVE a very stupid person **cretinous** /'kret.ɪ.nəs/ ⑥ /'kriː.tᵊn-/ *adj*

Creutzfeldt-Jakob disease /ˌkrɔɪts.felt'jæk.ɒb.-dɪˌziːz/ ⑥ /-ˌjɑː.kɑːb-/ *noun* [U] (ABBREVIATION **CJD**) a fatal disease that damages the brain and the main nerves connected to it

crevasse /krə'væs/ *noun* [C] a very deep crack in the thick ice of a GLACIER

crevice /'krev.ɪs/ *noun* [C] a small narrow crack or space, especially in the surface of rock

crew /kruː/ *noun* **1** [C + sing or pl v] a group of people who work together, especially all those who work on and operate a ship, aircraft, etc: *an ambulance/lifeboat crew* ○ *a TV/film/camera crew* ○ *The aircraft **has/carries** a crew of seven.* ➔See also **aircrew**. **2** [C] the people who work on a ship, aircraft, etc. who are not officers: *Apart from the 10 officers, a crew of 90 looks after the 300 passengers.*

crew /kruː/ *verb* [I or T] If you crew a boat, or crew for someone on their boat, you help to sail it.

'crew ˌcut *noun* [C] a hairstyle in which the hair is cut very short ➔See picture **Hairstyles and Hats** on page Centre 8

crewmember /'kruː.ˌmem.bər/ ⑥ /-bɚ/ *noun* [C] (ALSO **crewman**) a member of a group of people who work together, especially on a ship: *All crewmembers should return to the ship by 6 a.m.*

'crew ˌneck *noun* [C] a round neck hole on a jumper, or a jumper with a neck hole in this shape

crib BED /krɪb/ *noun* [C] US FOR **cot** (= a small bed for a baby)

crib MODEL UK /krɪb/ *noun* [C] (US **creche**) a model of the people and animals present at the birth of Jesus, used as a decoration at Christmas

crib COPY /krɪb/ *verb* [I or T] -bb- INFORMAL DISAPPROVING to copy someone else's work, especially dishonestly: *I got chucked out of the exam for cribbing **from** the guy in front.*

crib HOME /krɪb/ *noun* [C] US SLANG Someone's crib is their home or the place where they are currently living.

'crib ˌdeath *noun* [C or U] US FOR **cot death**

'crib ˌsheet *noun* [C] (US **crib notes**) INFORMAL a piece of paper that contains notes or information, used for cheating during an exam

crick /krɪk/ *noun* [C] a painful, usually sudden stiffness in a group of muscles in the neck or back: *I got a crick in my neck from painting the ceiling.* **crick** /krɪk/ *verb* [T] *I cricked my neck while I was painting the ceiling.*

cricket GAME /'krɪk.ɪt/ *noun* [U] a sport in which two teams of eleven players try to score runs by hitting a small hard leather-covered ball with a bat, and running between two sets of small wooden posts: *a cricket ball/bat* ➔See picture **Sports** on page Centre 10

• **not cricket** UK OLD-FASHIONED OR HUMOROUS If someone's behaviour or actions are not cricket, they are not honourable or moral: *It's simply not cricket to flirt with another man's wife.*

cricketer /'krɪk.ɪ.tər/ ⑥ /-t̬ɚ/ *noun* [C] a cricket player

cricketing /'krɪk.ɪ.tɪŋ/ ⑥ /-t̬ɪŋ/ *adj* [before n] relating to cricket: *the cricketing **world***

cricket INSECT /'krɪk.ɪt/ *noun* [C] a brown or black insect which makes short loud noises by rubbing its wings together

cri de coeur /ˌkriː.də'kɜːr/ ⑥ /-'kɝː/ *noun* [C usually sing] *plural* **cris de coeur** an urgent and strongly felt request

for help from someone in a very bad situation

cried /kraɪd/ *past simple and past participle of* **cry**

crikey /'kraɪ.ki/ *exclamation* UK OLD-FASHIONED INFORMAL an expression of surprise

crime /kraɪm/ *noun* **1** [U] illegal activities: *a life of crime* ○ *rising crime* ○ *crime prevention* ○ **petty** (= unimportant) *crime/**serious** crime* **2** [C] an illegal act: *He has admitted **committing** several crimes, including two murders.* ○ *The defendant is **accused of/charged with** a range of crimes, from theft to murder.* ○ *A knife was found at **the scene of the** crime* (= the place where the crime happened). ○ *Bombing civilians is a crime **against humanity*** (= a cruel crime against many people). **3** [S] an immoral or very foolish act or situation: *To have hundreds of homeless people sleeping in the streets of a rich city like London is **a** crime .* ○ *It would be **a** crime* (= a waste) *to spend such a beautiful day indoors.*

• **Crime doesn't pay.** SAYING said to emphasize that you believe criminals are always punished for their crimes

ˌcrime of 'passion *noun* [C] a crime committed because of very strong emotional feelings, especially in connection with a sexual relationship

'crime ˌwave *noun* [C usually sing] a sudden increase in the number of crimes

criminal /'krɪm.ɪ.nəl/ *noun* [C] someone who commits a crime: *a dangerous/violent criminal*

criminal /'krɪm.ɪ.nəl/ *adj* **1** [before n] relating to crime: *criminal activity* ○ *a criminal act/offence* ○ *criminal behaviour* ○ *a criminal investigation* **2** very bad or morally wrong: *It's criminal **to** charge so much for a book.* ○ *The way we waste this planet's resources is criminal.* **criminality** /ˌkrɪm.ɪ'næl.ɪ.ti/ ⑥ /-ə.t̬i/ *noun* [U] **criminally** /'krɪm.ɪ.nə.li/ *adv*

criminalize, UK USUALLY **-ise** /'krɪm.ɪ.nə.laɪz/ *verb* [T] *The law has criminalized* (= made illegal) *prostitution but not got rid of it.*

'criminal ˌcourt *noun* [C] a law court which deals with criminal cases

ˌcriminal 'damage *noun* [U] serious damage which is against the law

ˌcriminal 'justice ˌsystem *noun* [S] the process by which people who are accused of crimes are judged in court

ˌcriminal 'law *noun* [U] the part of the legal system which relates to punishing people who break the law

ˌcriminal 'record *noun* [C] an official record of the crimes that a person has committed: *They fired him when they found out he had a criminal record.*

criminology /ˌkrɪm.ɪ'nɒl.ə.dʒi/ ⑥ /-'nɑː.lə-/ *noun* [U] the scientific study of crime and criminals **criminologist** /ˌkrɪm.ɪ'nɒl.ə.dʒɪst/ ⑥ /-'nɑː.lə-/ *noun* [C] someone who studies crime and criminals

crimp /krɪmp/ *verb* [T] to press cloth, paper, etc. into small folds along its edges, or to press hair into a series of folds using a heated instrument

Crimplene /'krɪm.pliːn/ *noun* [U] UK TRADEMARK an artificial cloth, used for clothes, that does not easily CREASE (= develop unwanted folds and lines)

crimson /'krɪm.zᵊn/ *adj* **1** having a dark deep red colour **2** **go/turn crimson** If you go/turn crimson, your face becomes red because you are so embarrassed or angy: *She went crimson **with** embarrassment.* **crimson** /'krɪm.zᵊn/ *noun* [U] a dark deep red colour

cringe /krɪndʒ/ *verb* [I] **1** to suddenly move away from someone or something because you are frightened **2** INFORMAL to feel very embarrassed: *I cringed **at** the sight of my dad dancing.*

cringe-making /'krɪndʒ.ˌmeɪ.kɪŋ/ *adj* UK INFORMAL describes someone or something that is so bad that you feel embarrassed: *Then there were his cringe-making attempts at humour.*

crinkle /'krɪŋ.kl̩/ *verb* [I or T] to become covered in many little lines and folds, or to cause something to do this: *She crinkled **(up)** her nose in distaste.* **crinkle** /'krɪŋ.kl̩/ *noun* [C] **crinkled** /'krɪŋ.kl̩d/ *adj* **crinkly** /'krɪŋ.kli/ *adj*

crinoline /'krɪn.ᵊl.ɪn/ *noun* [C] a stiff frame worn, especially in the 19th century, under a woman's skirt to give it a full appearance

cripes /kraɪps/ *exclamation* OLD-FASHIONED INFORMAL an expression of surprise

cripple /ˈkrɪp.l̩/ *noun* [C] **1** OFFENSIVE OLD-FASHIONED a person who cannot use their arms or legs in a normal way **2** INFORMAL **emotional cripple** someone who finds it difficult to have or express feelings
cripple /ˈkrɪp.l̩/ *verb* [T] **1** to injure someone so that they are unable to walk or move properly **2** to cause serious damage to someone or something, making them weak and ineffective: *a country crippled by war* **crippled** /ˈkrɪp.l̩d/ *adj*: *Will she be crippled **for life**?* **crippling** /ˈkrɪp.l̩ɪŋ/ /-lɪŋ/ *adj*: *A crippling attack of malaria kept him in bed for months.* ○ *crippling debts*

crisis /ˈkraɪ.sɪs/ *noun plural* **crises** **1** [C or U] a situation that has reached an extremely difficult or dangerous point; a time of great disagreement, uncertainty or suffering: *crisis talks* ○ *The country's leadership is **in crisis**.* ○ *an economic/financial crisis* ○ *I've got a family crisis on my hands – my 16-year-old sister is pregnant.* ○ *A mediator has been called in to **resolve** the crisis.* **2** [C] a moment during a serious illness when there is the possibility of suddenly getting either a lot better or a lot worse: *He's passed the crisis – the fever's started to go down.* **3** **crisis of confidence** a sudden loss of confidence: *With inflation at 500%, the country faces a crisis of confidence.*

crisp [HARD] /krɪsp/ *adj* MAINLY APPROVING **1** hard enough to be broken easily **2** describes cooked foods, such as pastry and biscuits, that are well cooked so that they are just dry and hard enough **3** describes fruit or vegetables that are fresh and firm: *a crisp apple* **4** describes paper or cloth that is stiff and smooth: *a crisp new £5 note/a crisp white tablecloth* **5** describes sound or an image that is very clear: *Now that we have cable, we get a wonderfully crisp picture, even on our old TV.* **6** describes weather that is cold, dry and bright: *a wonderful crisp spring morning* **7** describes air that is cold, dry and fresh: *I breathed in deeply the crisp mountain air.* **8** describes a way of speaking, writing or behaving that is quick, confident and effective: *a crisp reply* ○ *a crisp, efficient manner* **crisply** /ˈkrɪs.pli/ *adv* **crispness** /ˈkrɪsp.nəs/ *noun* [U]

crisp [POTATO] UK /krɪsp/ *noun* [C usually pl] (US **(potato) chip**) a very thin, often round piece of fried potato, sometimes flavoured, and sold especially in plastic bags: ***a packet of** salt and vinegar crisps*

crisp [SWEET FOOD] /krɪsp/ *noun* [C] US FOR **crumble** SWEET FOOD

crispbread /ˈkrɪsp.bred/ *noun* [C or U] UK a hard dry flat savoury type of food similar to a biscuit, often eaten instead of bread by people trying to lose weight

crispy /ˈkrɪs.pi/ *adj* APPROVING describes food that is hard enough to be broken easily: *crispy bacon*

criss-cross /ˈkrɪs.krɒs/ [US] /-krɑːs/ *verb* [I or T] to move or exist in a pattern of lines crossing something or each other: *This area of the city is criss-crossed by railway lines.* **criss-cross** /ˈkrɪs.krɒs/ [US] /-krɑːs/ *adj*

criterion /kraɪˈtɪə.ri.ən/ [US] /-ˈtɪr.i-/ *noun* [C] *plural* **criteria** a standard by which you judge, decide about or deal with something: *The Health Service should not be judged by financial criteria alone.*

critic /ˈkrɪt.ɪk/ [US] /ˈkrɪt̬-/ *noun* [C] **1** someone who says that they do not approve of someone or something: *Her critics say she is leading the party to disaster.* ○ *He's his own worst critic* (= He judges himself severely). **2** someone whose job is to give their opinion about something, especially films, books, music, etc: *She's a film/theatre critic for the 'Irish Times'.* ○ *The play has been well received by the critics.*

critical [NOT PLEASED] /ˈkrɪt.ɪ.kᵊl/ [US] /ˈkrɪt̬-/ *adj* saying that someone or something is bad or wrong: *a critical report* ○ *The report is **highly** critical **of** safety standards at the factory.*

critical [GIVING OPINIONS] /ˈkrɪt.ɪ.kᵊl/ [US] /ˈkrɪt̬-/ *adj* giving opinions or judgements on books, plays, films, etc: *She has written a major critical appraisal/study of Saul Bellow's novels.* ○ *His last film **won/received** critical **acclaim*** (= was praised by film critics). **critically** /ˈkrɪt.ɪ.kli/ [US] /ˈkrɪt̬-/ *adv*: *a critically **acclaimed** TV series*

critical [IMPORTANT] /ˈkrɪt.ɪ.kᵊl/ [US] /ˈkrɪt̬-/ *adj* of the greatest importance to the way things might happen: *The President's support is critical (**to** this project).* ○ *a critical decision*

critical [SERIOUS] /ˈkrɪt.ɪ.kᵊl/ [US] /ˈkrɪt̬-/ *adj* extremely serious or dangerous: *Both drivers are critical/in a critical **condition*** (= so badly hurt that they might die) *after the 120mph crash.* **critically** /ˈkrɪt.ɪ.kli/ [US] /ˈkrɪt̬-/ *adv*: *They were both critically **injured** in the crash.*

criticism /ˈkrɪt.ɪ.sɪ.zᵊm/ [US] /ˈkrɪt̬-/ *noun* [C or U] **1** when you say that something or someone is bad; disapproval: *The designs for the new mosque have attracted widespread criticism.* ○ *I have a few criticisms to make **of/about** your speech.* **2** when you give your opinion or judgment about the good or bad qualities of something or someone, especially books, films, etc: ***literary** criticism* ○ *If you've got any **constructive*** (= positive) *criticism of the project, I'd be glad to hear it.*

criticize, UK USUALLY **-ise** /ˈkrɪt.ɪ.saɪz/ [US] /ˈkrɪt̬-/ *verb* **1** [I; T often passive] to express disapproval of someone or something: *The government is being widely criticized in the press **for failing** to limit air pollution.* ○ *We'll get nowhere if all you can do is criticize.* **2** [T] to give an opinion or judgement about a book, film, etc: *We're a group of artists who meet to discuss things and criticize each other's work.*

critique /krɪˈtiːk/ *noun* [C] a report of something such as a political situation or system or a person's work or ideas, which examines it and provides an often negative judgment: *a Marxist critique **of** neo-liberal economic policy*

critter /ˈkrɪt.əʳ/ [US] /ˈkrɪt̬.ɚ/ *noun* [C] (ALSO **crittur**) US NOT STANDARD a creature

croak [SOUND] /krəʊk/ [US] /kroʊk/ *verb* [I or T] **1** When animals such as frogs and crows croak, they call making deep rough sounds. **2** When you croak because you have a sore or dry throat, you speak with a rough voice. **croak** /krəʊk/ [US] /kroʊk/ *noun* [C]

croak [DIE] /krəʊk/ [US] /kroʊk/ *verb* [I] OLD-FASHIONED SLANG to die

crochet /ˈkrəʊ.ʃeɪ/ [US] /kroʊˈʃeɪ/ *verb* [I or T] to make clothes and other items using wool and a special needle with a hook at one end **crochet** /ˈkrəʊ.ʃeɪ/ [US] /kroʊˈʃeɪ/ *noun* [U] **crocheted** /ˈkrəʊ.ʃeɪd/ [US] /kroʊˈʃeɪd/ *adj*

ˈcrochet ˌhook *noun* [C] a needle with a hook at one end which is used to crochet with

crock [CONTAINER] /krɒk/ [US] /krɑːk/ *noun* [C] a container, usually one made of clay: *He keeps his coffee in an earthenware crock.*
• **a crock (of shit)** US INFORMAL OR OFFENSIVE something that is not true or useful: *His presentation was a crock of shit.*

crock [CAR OR PERSON] /krɒk/ [US] /krɑːk/ *noun* [C] UK OLD-FASHIONED SLANG an old person or car

crockery /ˈkrɒk.ᵊr.i/ [US] /ˈkrɑː.kɚ-/ *noun* [U] UK OLD-FASHIONED cups, plates, bowls, etc., used to serve food and drink, especially made of CHINA ➲Compare **cutlery**.

crocodile (*plural* **crocodiles** or **crocodile**) /ˈkrɒk.ə.daɪl/ [US] /ˈkrɑː.kə-/ *noun* [C] **1** (INFORMAL **croc**) a large hard-skinned reptile that lives in and near rivers and lakes in the hot wet parts of the world. It is like an ALLIGATOR, but it usually has a longer and narrower nose: *a crocodile-infested swamp* ➲See picture **Animals and Birds** on page Centre 4 **2** UK INFORMAL a line of people, especially children, who are walking in pairs

ˈcrocodile ˌtears *plural noun* tears that you cry when you are not really sad or sorry

crocus /ˈkrəʊ.kəs/ [US] /ˈkroʊ-/ *noun* [C] a small yellow, white or purple spring flower

croft /krɒft/ [US] /krɑːft/ *noun* [C] UK (especially in Scotland) a very small farm around a house, or the house itself **crofter** /ˈkrɒf.təʳ/ [US] /ˈkrɑːf.tɚ/ *noun* [C] someone who lives and works on a croft

croissant /ˈkwæs.ɒ̃/ [US] /kwɑːˈsɑ̃ː/ *noun* [C] a piece of light CRESCENT-shaped pastry, usually eaten in the morning

crone /krəʊn/ [US] /kroʊn/ *noun* [C] an unpleasant or ugly old woman

crony /ˈkrəʊ.ni/ [US] /ˈkroʊ-/ *noun* [C] *INFORMAL* a friend, or a person who works for someone in authority, especially one who is willing to give and receive dishonest help: *The General and his cronies are now awaiting trial for drug-smuggling.*

crook [CRIMINAL] /krʊk/ *noun* [C] *INFORMAL* a very dishonest person, especially a criminal or a cheat: *These politicians are just a bunch of crooks.*
crooked /ˈkrʊk.ɪd/ *adj INFORMAL* dishonest: *crooked police officers*

crook [BEND] /krʊk/ *noun* **the crook of *your* arm** the inside part of your arm where it bends
crook /krʊk/ *verb* [T] *OLD-FASHIONED She delicately crooked* (= bent) *her little finger as she picked up her tea cup.*

crook [STICK] /krʊk/ *noun* [C] a long stick with a curved end, especially one carried by a SHEPHERD or a bishop

crook [BAD] /krʊk/ *adj AUS INFORMAL* bad or ill

crooked /ˈkrʊk.ɪd/ *adj* not forming a straight line; having many sharp bends: *You have to drive slowly on these crooked country roads.* ○ *His front teeth are crooked.*
crookedly /ˈkrʊk.ɪd.li/ *adv*: *She smiled crookedly at me, turned and left.*

croon /kruːn/ *verb* [I or T] to sing or talk in a sweet low voice full of emotion
crooner /ˈkruː.nəʳ/ [US] /-nɚ/ *noun* [C] *OLD-FASHIONED* a singer, especially a man, who sings slow love songs

crop [PLANT] /krɒp/ [US] /krɑːp/ *noun* **1** [C] (the total amount gathered of) a plant such as a grain, fruit or vegetable grown in large amounts: *The main crops grown for export are coffee and rice.* ○ *a* ***bumper*** (= very good) *potato crop* **2** [C usually sing] *INFORMAL* a group of people or things with something in common, that exist at a particular time: *The judges will select the best from this year's crop* ***of*** *first novels.*
crop /krɒp/ [US] /krɑːp/ *verb* **-pp- 1** [I usually + adv or prep] If a plant crops, it produces fruit, flowers, etc: *The carrots have cropped* (= grown) *well this year.* **2** [T usually passive] to grow crops on land: *The land is intensively-cropped.*

crop [CUT] /krɒp/ [US] /krɑːp/ *verb* [T] **-pp- 1** to make something shorter or smaller, especially by cutting: *He had his hair cropped when he went into the army.* **2** When animals such as sheep or horses crop grass or other plants, they eat the top parts. **3** to cut off some or all of the edges from a photograph, leaving only the most important part
crop /krɒp/ [US] /krɑːp/ *noun* [C] a short hair cut: *She's had a very short crop.*

crop [THROAT] /krɒp/ [US] /krɑːp/ *noun* [C] a bag-like part of the throat in many birds where food is stored before going into the stomach

crop [STICK] /krɒp/ [US] /krɑːp/ *noun* [C] a short stick used to control a horse by hitting it

▲ **crop up** *phrasal verb INFORMAL* to happen or appear unexpectedly: *Her name keeps cropping up* ***in*** *conversation.*

cropper /ˈkrɒp.əʳ/ [US] /ˈkrɑː.pɚ/ *noun INFORMAL* **come a cropper** to fail badly, or to fall from a horse or have a bad accident in a vehicle: *Having reached the final, the British have come a cropper against the more experienced German team.* ○ *She came an almighty cropper when her back wheels hit an icy patch.*

ˈcrop roˌtation *noun* [U] a method of farming where a number of different plants are grown one after the other on a field so that the earth stays healthy and FERTILE

ˈcrop ˌspraying *noun* [U] (*ALSO* **crop dusting**) a way of covering crops with chemicals in order to kill harmful insects and diseases, sometimes from an aircraft

ˈcrop ˌtop *noun* [C] a piece of clothing for a woman's top half which does not cover the stomach

croquet /ˈkrəʊ.keɪ/ [US] /kroʊˈkeɪ/ *noun* [U] a game in which two, three or four players use MALLETS (= long wooden hammers) to hit wooden balls through small metal HOOPS (= arches) fixed into the grass

croquette /krəˈket/ [US] /kroʊ-/ *noun* [C] a small rounded mass of food, such as meat, fish or potato, that has been cut into small pieces, pressed together, covered in breadcrumbs and fried

crore /krɔːʳ/ [US] /krɔːr/ *determiner, noun INDIAN ENGLISH* ten million: *This year's profits were more than Rs 164.7 crore.*

crosier, crozier /ˈkrəʊ.zi.əʳ/ [US] /ˈkroʊ.zi.ɚ/ *noun* [C] a long stick with a decorative end that is curved or in the shape of a cross, carried by bishops

cross [GO ACROSS] /krɒs/ [US] /krɑːs/ *verb* [I or T] to go across from one side of something to the other: *It's not a good place to cross the road.* ○ *Look both ways before you cross* ***over*** (= cross the road). ○ *Cross the bridge and turn right at the first set of traffic lights.* ○ *They crossed* ***from*** *Albania* ***into*** *Greece.*
• **cross *sb's* hand/palm with silver** to give someone money so that they will tell you what will happen to you in the future
• **cross *your* mind** If something crosses your mind, you think of it: *It crossed my mind yesterday that you must be a bit short of staff – shall I send someone to help out?* ○ *It never once crossed my mind that she might be unhappy.*
• **I'll/We'll cross that bridge when I/we come/get to it.** an expression which means you will not worry about a possible future problem but will deal with it if it happens
cross- /krɒs-/ [US] /krɑːs-/ *prefix* going across a particular thing: *a cross-****Channel*** *ferry* (= one that sails from Britain to France, Belgium or Holland)
crossing /ˈkrɒs.ɪŋ/ [US] /ˈkrɑː.sɪŋ/ *noun* [C] **1** a place where something such as a road can be crossed safely, or a place where a road and a railway meet and cross each other: *a border/river crossing* **2** a journey across something such as a sea, from one side to the other: *We had a really rough crossing – I was sick three times.*

cross [ARMS/FINGERS/LEGS] /krɒs/ [US] /krɑːs/ *verb* **cross *your* arms/fingers/legs** to put one of your arms/fingers/legs over the top of the other: *She sat down and crossed her legs.*
• **cross *your* fingers** to hope very much that something will happen: *I'm just going to cross my fingers and hope it works.*
• **cross swords** to have an argument with someone

cross [MARK] /krɒs/ [US] /krɑːs/ *noun* [C] **1** a written mark (x), usually used to show where something is, or that something has been written incorrectly **2** an object in the shape of a cross (†) used as a symbol of Christianity: *Christ died on the Cross.* ○ *She wears a gold cross round her neck.* ○ *The priest* ***made the sign of the*** *cross* (= moved his or her hand down and then across the chest) *over the dead bodies.* **3** a medal in the shape of a cross: *In Britain, the Victoria Cross is awarded for acts of great bravery during wartime.*
• **a (heavy) cross to bear** an unpleasant or painful situation or person that you must accept and deal with, although you find it very difficult
cross /krɒs/ [US] /krɑːs/ *verb* [T] *UK SPECIALIZED* to draw two lines across the middle of a cheque to show that it must be paid into a bank account: *a crossed cheque*
• **cross *yourself*** When Christians cross themselves, they move their hand down and then across their face or chest, making the shape of a cross.
• **Cross my heart (and hope to die).** *SAYING* said to show that what you have just said or promised is completely true or sincere

cross [ANNOYED] /krɒs/ [US] /krɑːs/ *adj* annoyed or angry: *My Dad gets cross (****with*** *me) if I leave the kitchen in a mess.*
crossly /ˈkrɒs.li/ [US] /ˈkrɑː.sli/ *adv*: *"He's so unreliable!" she said crossly.*
cross /krɒs/ [US] /krɑːs/ *verb* [T] to annoy someone by not doing or saying what they want: *I wouldn't cross him if I were you, not if you value your life.*

cross [MIXTURE] /krɒs/ [US] /krɑːs/ *noun* [C] a mixture of two different things which have been combined to produce something new: *Police dogs are often a cross* ***between*** *a retriever and an alsatian.* ➲See also **crossbreed**.
cross /krɒs/ [US] /krɑːs/ *verb* [T] If you cross a plant or animal with another of a different type, you cause them to breed together in order to produce a new variety.

PHRASAL VERBS WITH **cross** ▼

▲ **cross *sb/sth* off (*sth*)** *phrasal verb* to remove someone or something, such as a name, from a list by drawing a line through it: *Did you cross her name off the guest list?*
▲ **cross *sth* out** *phrasal verb* [M] to draw a line through something you have written, usually because it is

wrong: *If you think it's wrong, cross it out and write it again.*

crossbar /ˈkrɒs.bɑːʳ/ [US] /ˈkrɑːs.bɑːr/ *noun* [C] a horizontal bar, either the part that forms the top of a goal, or the part of a bicycle between the seat and the HANDLEBARS

crossbones /ˈkrɒs.bəʊnz/ [US] /ˈkrɑːs.boʊnz/ *noun* ➲See at **skull and crossbones**.

C

cross-border /ˈkrɒs.ˌbɔː.dəʳ/ [US] /ˈkrɑːs.ˌbɔːr.dɚ/ *adj* [before n] between different countries, or involving people from different countries: *cross-border trade*

crossbow /ˈkrɒs.bəʊ/ [US] /ˈkrɑːs.boʊ/ *noun* [C] a weapon used, especially in the past, for shooting a short arrow with great force

crossbreed /ˈkrɒs.briːd/ [US] /ˈkrɑːs-/ *noun* [C] an animal or plant that is a mixture of breeds and is therefore a new variety **crossbreed** /ˈkrɒs.briːd/ [US] /ˈkrɑːs-/ *verb* [I or T] **crossbred** /ˈkrɒs.bred/ [US] /ˈkrɑːs-/ *adj*

crosscheck /ˈkrɒs.tʃek/ [US] /ˈkrɑːs-/ /-ˈ-/ *verb* [I or T] to make certain that information, a calculation, etc. is correct, by asking a different person or using a different method of calculation

cross-country [SPORTS] /ˌkrɒsˈkʌn.tri/ [US] /ˌkrɑːs-/ *adj* describes sports in which competitors travel long distances through the countryside: *cross-country skiing/running*

cross-country [DIRECTION] /ˌkrɒsˈkʌn.tri/ [US] /ˌkrɑːs-/ *adv* across the length of a country: *After high school, we bought a camper van and travelled cross-country for two months.*

cross-dressing /ˌkrɒsˈdres.ɪŋ/ [US] /ˌkrɑːs-/ *noun* [U] the practice of wearing the clothes of the opposite sex: *There's a lot of cross-dressing in British pantomimes, where men dress up as Dames and a woman plays the part of the young hero.* **cross-dresser** /ˌkrɒsˈdres.əʳ/ [US] /ˌkrɑːsˈdres.ɚ/ *noun* [C]

cross-examine /ˌkrɒs.ɪɡˈzæm.ɪn/ [US] /ˌkrɑːs-/ *verb* [T] (*ALSO* **cross-question**) to ask detailed questions of someone, especially a WITNESS in a trial, in order to discover if they have been telling the truth **cross-examination** /ˌkrɒs.ɪɡˌzæm.ɪˈneɪ.ʃᵊn/ [US] /ˌkrɑːs-/ *noun* [C usually sing; U] ***Under*** *cross-examination, the witness admitted her evidence had been mostly lies.* **cross-examiner** /ˌkrɒs.ɪɡˈzæm.ɪ.nəʳ/ [US] /ˌkrɑː.sɪɡˈzæm.ɪ.nɚ/ *noun* [C]

cross-eyed /ˌkrɒsˈaɪd/ [US] /ˌkrɑːs-/ *adj* having eyes that look in towards the nose

cross-fertilization, *UK USUALLY* **-isation** /ˌkrɒs.fɜː.tɪ.laɪˈzeɪ.ʃᵊn/ [US] /ˌkrɑːs.fɝː.t̬ə.lɪ-/ *noun* [U] the mixing of the ideas, customs, etc. of different places or groups of people, to benefit all

crossfire /ˈkrɒs.faɪəʳ/ [US] /ˈkrɑːs.faɪr/ *noun* [U] bullets fired towards you from different directions: *One boat of refugees was* ***caught in (the)*** *naval crossfire and sunk.*
- **caught in the crossfire** to be involved in a situation where people around you are arguing: *The Health Minister, who resigned today, claims she is an innocent victim caught in the crossfire of the current battle over inflation.*

cross-hatching /ˈkrɒsˌhætʃ.ɪŋ/ [US] /ˈkrɑːs-/ *noun* [U] two groups of parallel lines which are drawn close together across each other, especially at an angle of 90°, on parts of a picture to show differences of light and darkness **cross-hatched** /ˈkrɒs.hætʃt/ [US] /ˈkrɑːs-/ *adj* **cross-hatch** /ˈkrɒs.hætʃ/ [US] /ˈkrɑːs-/ *verb* [I or T] (*ALSO* **hatch**)

cross-legged /ˌkrɒsˈlegd/ /-ɪd/ [US] /ˌkrɑːs-/ *adv* having your feet crossed over each other, but your knees wide apart, usually while sitting on the floor

crossover /ˈkrɒs.əʊ.vəʳ/ [US] /ˈkrɑːs.oʊ.vɚ/ *noun* [C] the process or result of changing from one activity or style to another: *a crossover artist/album*

ˌcross ˈpurposes *adv* **at cross purposes** If two or more people are at cross purposes, they do not understand each other because they are talking about different subjects without realizing this: *I think we've been talking at cross purposes – I meant next year, not this year.*

cross-question /ˌkrɒsˈkwes.tʃᵊn/ [US] /ˌkrɑːs-/ *verb* [T] to **cross-examine**

cross-reference /ˌkrɒsˈref.ᵊr.ənts/ [US] /ˌkrɑːsˈref.ɚ-/ *noun* [C] a note in a book that tells you to look somewhere else in the book for more information about something **cross-refer** /ˌkrɒs.rɪˈfɜːʳ/ [US] /ˌkrɑːs.rɪˈfɝː/ *verb* [T] *The main entry also cross-refers you* ***to*** *the appendix on page 259.*

crossroads /ˈkrɒs.rəʊdz/ [US] /ˈkrɑːs.roʊdz/ *noun* [C] *plural* **crossroads** a place where two roads meet and cross each other
- **be at a crossroads** to be at a stage in your life when you have to make a very important decision

cross-section /ˈkrɒs.sek.ʃᵊn/ [US] /ˈkrɑːs-/ /ˌ-ˈ--/ *noun* [C] **1** something that has been cut in half so that you can see the inside, or a model or picture of this: *a cross-section of the human heart* **2** a small group which is representative of all the different types within the total group: *The demonstrators seemed to be* ***from*** *a complete cross-section of society – male and female, old and young, rich and poor.*

cross-stitch /ˈkrɒs.stɪtʃ/ [US] /ˈkrɑːs-/ *noun* [U] a decorative style of sewing which uses stitches which cross each other to form an X

cross-training /ˈkrɒsˌtreɪ.nɪŋ/ [US] /ˈkrɑːs-/ *noun* [U] exercise which strengthens your whole body by combining several different activities: *a cross-training program* **cross-trainer** /ˈkrɒsˌtreɪ.nəʳ/ [US] /ˈkrɑːsˌtreɪ.nɚ/ *noun* **1** [C] (*ALSO* **elliptical trainer**) a piece of exercise equipment designed to exercise all of the body's main groups of muscles **2** [C usually pl] (*ALSO* **cross-training shoe**) a sports shoe that is suitable for wearing in the GYM (= a room or building where you can exercise) and also for running and other sports

crosswalk /ˈkrɒs.wɔːk/ [US] /ˈkrɑːs.wɑːk/ *noun* [C] *US FOR* **pedestrian crossing**

crosswind /ˈkrɒs.wɪnd/ [US] /ˈkrɑːs-/ *noun* [C] a wind blowing at an angle to the direction of travel of a vehicle

crosswise /ˈkrɒs.waɪz/ [US] /ˈkrɑːs-/ *adv, adj* crossing something, especially at an angle of 90°

crossword (puzzle) /ˈkrɒs.wɜːdˌpʌz.l̩/ [US] /ˈkrɑːs.wɝːd-/ *noun* [C] a game in which you write words which are the answers to questions in a pattern of black and white squares: *I* ***do*** *the Times crossword every morning.*

crotch /krɒtʃ/ [US] /krɑːtʃ/ *noun* [C] (*ALSO* **crutch**) the part of your body where your legs join at the top, or the part of trousers or underwear which covers this area **crotchless** /ˈkrɒtʃ.ləs/ [US] /ˈkrɑːtʃ-/ *adj* describes underwear that has no part covering the area where your legs join at the top

crotchet /ˈkrɒtʃ.ət/ [US] /ˈkrɑː.tʃət/ *noun* [C] (*MAINLY US* **quarter note**) *SPECIALIZED* a musical note with a time value equal to two QUAVERS or half a MINIM

crotchety /ˈkrɒtʃ.ɪ.ti/ [US] /ˈkrɑː.tʃə.t̬i/ *adj INFORMAL* bad-tempered and easily annoyed: *By the time the meal began, the youngest children were getting tired and crotchety.*

crouch /kraʊtʃ/ *verb* [I] to bend your knees and lower yourself so that you are close to the ground and leaning forward slightly: *She saw him coming and crouched* ***(down)*** *behind a bush.* **crouch** /kraʊtʃ/ *noun* [S]

croup /kruːp/ *noun* [U] a children's illness in which they have noisy, difficult breathing and cough a lot

croupier /ˈkruː.pi.eɪ/ *noun* [C] a person who works in a CASINO (= a place where people risk money in games) who is responsible for a particular table and whose job is to collect and pay out money and give out playing cards, etc.

crouton /ˈkruː.tɒ̃/ [US] /-t̬ɑːn/ *noun* [C usually pl] a small square piece of bread that is fried or TOASTED (= heated until it is crisp and brown) and which is added to soup or a salad just before you eat it

crow [BIRD] /krəʊ/ [US] /kroʊ/ *noun* [C] a large black bird with a loud unpleasant cry
- **as the crow flies** describes a distance when measured in a straight line between two points or places

crow [CRY] /krəʊ/ [US] /kroʊ/ *verb* [I] **crowed** or *UK ALSO* **crew**, **crowed** or *UK ALSO* **crew** **1** When a COCK (= an adult male chicken) crows, it makes a very long and loud sharp cry: *We were woken at dawn by a cock crowing repeatedly.* **2** When a baby crows, it makes sudden cries of happiness. **3** *DISAPPROVING* to talk in a proud and annoying way about something you have done: *He's always crowing **about** his latest triumph.*

crowbar /ˈkrəʊ.bɑːʳ/ [US] /ˈkroʊ.bɑːr/ *noun* [C] a heavy iron bar with a bent end that is used to help lift heavy objects off the ground or to force things open: *The thieves forced one of the shop windows open with a crowbar.*

crowd /kraʊd/ *group noun* **1** [C] a large group of people who have gathered together: *A crowd of about 15 000 attended the concert.* **2** [S] INFORMAL a group of friends or a group of people with similar interests: *She goes about with a friendly crowd.* ○ *"Who was there?" "Oh, the usual crowd, Dave, Mike and Fiona."*

• **follow the crowd** DISAPPROVING to do what most other people do: *Think for yourself, don't just follow the crowd.*

crowd /kraʊd/ *verb* [T] INFORMAL to make someone feel uncomfortable by standing too close to them or by continually watching them: *I need some time to do this work properly, so don't crowd me.*

PHRASAL VERBS WITH **crowd**

▲ **crowd *(sth)* into *sth*** *phrasal verb* If people crowd or are crowded into a place, they fill it completely: *Hordes of commuters crowded into the train.*

▲ **crowd *sb/sth* out** *phrasal verb* [M] to not allow a person or thing any space to grow or develop: *Small local businesses have been crowded out by large multinationals.*

▲ **crowd round/around *(sb/sth)*** *phrasal verb* to gather closely in a crowd around someone or something: *As soon as he appeared, reporters crowded round.*

crowded /ˈkraʊ.dɪd/ *adj* If a place is crowded, it is full of people: *By ten o'clock the bar was crowded.*

crowd-puller /ˈkraʊdˌpʊl.əʳ/ [US] /-ɚ/ *noun* [C] a person or thing that attracts a lot of attention and that people will pay to see

crown [HEAD COVERING] /kraʊn/ *noun* [C] **1** a circular decoration for the head, usually made of gold and jewels, and worn by a king or queen at official ceremonies ➲See picture **Hairstyles and Hats** on page Centre 8 **2 the Crown** the royal governing power of a country that has a king or queen **3** the winning of a sports competition: *He plans to defend his Olympic crown.*

crown /kraʊn/ *verb* [T] **1** to put a crown on someone's head in an official ceremony that makes them king or queen: *Queen Elizabeth II was crowned (queen)* (= made queen in a special ceremony) *in 1953.* ➲See also **coronation. 2** If an event or achievement crowns something, it is the best or most successful part of it: *an acting career crowned by her final Oscar-winning performance*

crowning /ˈkraʊ.nɪŋ/ *adj*: *the crowning **achievement*** (= the greatest achievement) *of her long career* ○ *Walking on the moon was his crowning **glory*** (= his most important achievement).

crown [TOP PART] /kraʊn/ *noun* [C] the top part of a head, hat or hill: *A pink ribbon had been tied around the crown of the hat.*

crown /kraʊn/ *verb* [T] **1** FORMAL If something crowns something else, it is on or around the top of it: *The church was crowned with golden domes.* **2** SLANG to hit someone on the head

• **to crown it all** UK INFORMAL used to say that something is the worst thing to happen in a series of unpleasant events: *I had lost my ticket, was soaked to the skin, and, to crown it all, discovered that my purse had been stolen.*

crown [TOOTH] /kraʊn/ *noun* [C] an artificial piece used to cover a damaged tooth

crown /kraʊn/ *verb* [T] *She's had her two front teeth crowned* (= fitted with crowns).

crown [COIN] /kraʊn/ *noun* [C] a British coin which is no longer used

ˌcrown ˈcolony *noun* [C] an area or country which is politically controlled by Britain and which has a British GOVERNOR

ˌcrown ˈcourt *noun* [C] UK LEGAL a law court in England or Wales where criminal cases are judged by a judge and jury

ˌcrowned ˈhead *noun* [C usually pl] FORMAL a king or queen: *Most of the crowned heads of Europe have been entertained in this palace.*

ˌcrown ˈjewels *plural noun* the crown and other jewels worn at important official ceremonies by the king or queen

ˌcrown ˈprince *noun* [C] the man who will be king of a country when the ruling king or queen dies

ˌcrown prinˈcess *noun* [C] the woman who will be queen of a country when the ruling king or queen dies, or is the wife of a crown prince

ˌcrown ˈprosecutor *noun* [C] UK LEGAL an official who is responsible for trying to prove in a law court that people accused of crimes are guilty

crow's feet /ˈkrəʊz.fiːt/ [US] /ˈkroʊz-/ *plural noun* narrow lines around the outside corners of your eyes, that appear when you get older

crow's nest /ˈkrəʊz.nest/ [US] /ˈkroʊz-/ *noun* [C usually sing] a small enclosed space near the top of a ship's mast, from which a person can see in all directions

crozier /ˈkrəʊ.zi.əʳ/ [US] /ˈkroʊ.zi.ɚ/ *noun* [C] a **crosier**

crucial /ˈkruː.ʃəl/ *adj* extremely important or necessary: *a crucial decision/question* ○ *Her work has been crucial **to** the project's success.* ○ [+ **that**] *It is crucial **that** the problem is tackled immediately.* **crucially** /ˈkruː.ʃəl.i/ *adv*

crucible /ˈkruː.sɪ.bl̩/ *noun* [C] **1** a container in which metals or other substances can be heated to very high temperatures **2** FORMAL a severe test **3** FORMAL a place or situation in which different cultures or styles can mix together to produce something new and exciting

crucifix /ˈkruː.sɪ.fɪks/ *noun* [C] a model or picture representing Jesus Christ on a cross: *She always wears a small gold crucifix round her neck.*

crucifixion /ˌkruː.sɪˈfɪk.ʃən/ *noun* [C or U] **1** when someone is crucified **2 the Crucifixion** the death of Christ on a cross

cruciform /ˈkruː.sɪ.fɔːm/ [US] /-fɔːrm/ *adj* FORMAL in the shape of a cross

crucify /ˈkruː.sɪ.faɪ/ *verb* [T] **1** to kill someone by tying or nailing them to a cross and leaving them there to die **2** INFORMAL to severely punish or damage someone or something: *He's going to crucify me when he finds out what I've done!*

crud /krʌd/ *noun* [U] INFORMAL something dirty and unpleasant **cruddy** /ˈkrʌd.i/ *adj*

crude [SIMPLE] /kruːd/ *adj* simple and not skilfully done or made: *a crude device/weapon* **crudely** /ˈkruːd.li/ *adv*: *a crudely made bomb* **crudeness** /ˈkruːd.nəs/ *noun* [U] (ALSO **crudity**)

crude [RUDE] /kruːd/ *adj* rude and offensive: *a crude remark/comment* **crudely** /ˈkruːd.li/ *adv* **crudeness** /ˈkruːd.nəs/ *noun* [U] (ALSO **crudity**)

ˌcrude (ˈoil) *noun* [U] oil in a natural state that has not yet been treated

crudités /ˈkruː.dɪ.teɪz/ [US] /ˌkruː.dɪˈteɪz/ *plural noun* small pieces of raw vegetables, often served with a DIP (= a cold thick creamy sauce) before a meal

cruel /ˈkruː.əl/ /krʊəl/ *adj* **crueller, cruellest** or **crueler, cruelest 1** extremely unkind and unpleasant and causing pain to people or animals intentionally: *Don't tease him about his weight – it's cruel.* ○ *Children can be very cruel to each other.* **2** causing suffering: *His death was a cruel **blow**.*

• **be cruel to be kind** to do or say something that causes someone pain because you believe that it will help them

cruelly /ˈkruː.ə.li/ /ˈkrʊəl.i/ *adv* in a cruel way

cruelty /ˈkruː.əl.ti/ /ˈkrʊəl-/ [US] /-t̬i/ *noun* [C or U] cruel behaviour or a cruel action: *The farmer was accused of cruelty **to** animals.*

cruet /ˈkruː.ɪt/ *noun* [C] **1** UK a container that holds smaller containers of salt and pepper, etc., used when having a meal **2** US a glass bottle which holds oil or vinegar for use during a meal

cruise /kruːz/ *noun* [C] a journey on a large ship for pleasure, during which you visit several places

cruise /kruːz/ *verb* **1** [I] to travel on ships for pleasure **2** [I] If a ship or aircraft cruises, it travels at a continuous speed. **3** [I or T] SLANG to go around public places looking for someone to have sex with: *He spends the weekends cruising the bars.* **cruising** /'kruː.zɪŋ/ *noun* [U] *Mediterranean/luxury cruising* ○ *a popular cruising area/ground*

cruise 'missile *noun* [C] a missile which can be directed by a computer during its flight and which sometimes carries nuclear explosives

cruiser WAR SHIP /'kruː.zəʳ/ US /-zɚ/ *noun* [C] a large fast ship used in war

cruiser PLEASURE BOAT /'kruː.zəʳ/ US /-zɚ/ *noun* [C] a boat with an engine and a CABIN in which people sail for pleasure

cruise ship *noun* [C] (*ALSO* **cruise liner**) a large ship like a hotel, which people travel on for pleasure ○See picture **Planes, Ships and Boats** on page Centre 14

crumb /krʌm/ *noun* [C] **1** a very small piece of bread, cake or biscuit ○See also **breadcrumbs**. **2** a small amount of something: *a crumb of* **hope/comfort**

crumble BREAK /'krʌm.bl̩/ *verb* **1** [I or T] to break, or cause something to break, into small pieces: *She nervously crumbled the bread between her fingers.* ○ *The cliffs on which the houses are built are starting to crumble.* **2** [I] to weaken in strength and influence: *Support for the government is crumbling.*

crumbly /'krʌm.bli/ /-bl̩.i/ *adj* breaking easily into small pieces: *bread with a crumbly texture*

crumble SWEET FOOD *UK* /'krʌm.bl̩/ *noun* [C or U] (*US* **crisp**) a sweet dish made from fruit covered in a mixture of flour, butter and sugar rubbed together into small pieces, which is baked and eaten hot: *apple/rhubarb crumble*

crumbs /krʌmz/ *exclamation UK OLD-FASHIONED INFORMAL* an expression of surprise or worry

crummy /'krʌm.i/ *adj INFORMAL* of very bad quality: *a crummy old carpet*

crumpet BREAD /'krʌm.pɪt/ *noun* [C] a small round bread-like cake with holes in one side that is eaten hot with butter

crumpet WOMAN /'krʌm.pɪt/ *noun* [U] *UK SLANG* one or more people, usually women, who are sexually attractive: *a nice bit of crumpet*

crumple /'krʌm.pl̩/ *verb* **1** [I or T] to become, or cause something to become, full of irregular folds: *This shirt crumples easily* **2** [I] If someone's face crumples, it becomes full of lines because of a strong emotion: *Her face crumpled with laughter.* **3** [I] If someone crumples, they fall to the ground suddenly: *The bullet hit him and he crumpled into a heap on the floor.* **crumpled** /'krʌm.pl̩d/ *adj: crumpled clothes* ○ *the crumpled charm of linen*

▲ **crumple** *sth* **up** *phrasal verb* [M] to crush a piece of paper until all of it is folded: *Sylvie crumpled up the letter and threw it in the bin.*

crumple zone *noun* [C] *UK* a part of a car that is designed to crumple easily in an accident and so protect the people inside from being hit too hard: *The car has front and rear crumple zones and two side-impact protection bars.*

crunch SOUND /krʌntʃ/ *verb* [I or T] to crush hard food loudly between the teeth, or to make a sound as if something is being crushed or broken: *She was crunching noisily on an apple.* ○ *The gravel crunched underfoot as we walked up to the house.* **crunch** /krʌntʃ/ *noun* [C usually sing] *The woods were silent apart from the crunch of our feet in the snow.*

crunchy /'krʌn.tʃi/ *adj* describes food that is firm and makes a loud noise when it is eaten: *crunchy vegetables*

the crunch DIFFICULTY *noun* [S] *INFORMAL* a difficult situation which forces you to make a decision or do something: *The crunch* **came** *when she was forced to choose between her marriage and her career.*

● **if/when it comes to the crunch** when a situation becomes extremely serious and a decision must be made: *If it comes to the crunch and you and your husband do split up, you can always stay with us.*

crusade /kruː'seɪd/ *noun* **1** [C] a long and determined attempt to achieve something which you believe in strongly: *They have been involved in a crusade* **for** *racial equality.* ○ *a* **moral** *crusade against drugs* **2** [C often pl] (*ALSO* **Crusade**) a holy war fought by the Christ-

ians against the Muslims, often in Palestine, in the 11th, 12th, 13th and 17th centuries

crusade /kruː'seɪd/ *verb* [I] to make an effort to achieve something which you believe in strongly: *She crusaded* **against** *sex and violence on television.* **crusader** /kruː'seɪ.dəʳ/ US /-dɚ/ *noun* [C] *He caught the public imagination as a crusader* **against** *corruption.*

crush PRESS /krʌʃ/ *verb* [T] **1** to press something very hard so that it is broken or its shape is destroyed: *The package had been badly crushed in the post.* ○ *Add three cloves of crushed garlic.* ○ *His arm was badly crushed in the car accident.* **2** to press paper or cloth so that it becomes full of irregular folds and is no longer flat: *My dress got all crushed in my suitcase.* **3** If people are crushed against other people or things, they are pressed against them: *Tragedy struck when several people were crushed* **to death** *in the crowd.*

crush /krʌʃ/ *noun* [S] a crowd of people forced to stand close together: *I had to struggle through the crush to get to the door.* ○ *You can come in our car, but it'll be a bit of a crush* (= there will be a lot of people in it).

crush SHOCK /krʌʃ/ *verb* [T usually passive] to upset or shock someone badly: *He was crushed by the news of the accident.*

crushing /'krʌʃ.ɪŋ/ *adj: The news came as a crushing* (= severe) *blow.*

crush DESTROY /krʌʃ/ *verb* [T] to defeat someone completely: *The president called upon the army to help crush the rebellion.* ○ *France crushed Wales by 36 to 3 in last Saturday's match in Paris.*

crushing /'krʌʃ.ɪŋ/ *adj: Their army had suffered a crushing* (= severe) *defeat.*

crush ATTRACTION /krʌʃ/ *noun* [C] *INFORMAL* a strong but temporary attraction for someone: *She has a crush* **on** *one of her teachers at school.*

crush barrier *noun* [C] a strong fence that is used to divide a large crowd, for example at a football game, to stop them from being pressed too close together

crust /krʌst/ *noun* **1** [C or U] a hard outer covering of something: *pie crust* (= the cooked pastry on top of it) ○ *the Earth's crust* **2** [C] the outside layer of a loaf of bread: *Could you cut the crusts off the sandwiches, please?* **crusted** /'krʌs.tɪd/ *adj: crusted with mud*

crusty /'krʌs.ti/ *adj* having a hard outer layer: *fresh, crusty bread* ○See also **crusty**.

crustacean /krʌs'teɪ.ʃən/ *noun* [C] any of various types of animal which live in water and have a hard outer shell

crusty EASILY ANNOYED /'krʌs.ti/ *adj* (especially of older people) complaining and easily annoyed: *a crusty old man* ○See also **crusty** at **crust**.

crusty PERSON /'krʌs.ti/ *noun* [C] *UK INFORMAL* a young person who does not live in a way that society considers normal, typically with untidy or dirty clothes and hair, and no regular job or permanent home: *Lots of crusties came into town for the festival.*

crutch /krʌtʃ/ *noun* **1** [C usually pl] a stick with a piece that fits under the arm, which you lean on for support if you have difficulty in walking because of a foot or leg injury: *Martin broke his leg playing football and has been on crutches for the past six weeks.* **2** [S] *OFTEN DISAPPROVING* something that provides help and support and which you depend on, often too much: *As an atheist, he believes that religion is just an* **emotional** *crutch for the insecure.* **3** [C] **crotch**

the crux /ðə'krʌks/ *noun* [S] the most important or serious part of a matter, problem or argument: *The crux of the country's economic problems is its foreign debt.* ○ *The issue of an arms embargo will be at the crux of the negotiations in Geneva.*

cry PRODUCE TEARS /kraɪ/ *verb* [I or T] to produce tears as the result of a strong emotion, such as unhappiness or pain: *I could hear someone crying in the next room.* ○ *"There, there, don't cry," she said.* ○ *We all laughed until we cried.* ○ *She cried bitter tears when she got the letter.* ○ *He cried* **for joy** *when he heard that his son had been found alive and well.*

● **cry yourself to sleep** to cry for a long time until you start to sleep

• **cry *your* eyes out** to cry a lot: *I was so upset that day, I cried my eyes out.*
• **It's no use crying over spilt milk.** *SAYING* said to emphasize that it is useless to regret something which has already happened: *It's no use crying over spilt milk, – he's spent all the money, and there's nothing you can do about it.*
cry /kraɪ/ *noun* [S] a period of crying: *"Go on, have a **good** cry", he said, stroking her hair.* **crying** /ˈkraɪ.ɪŋ/ *noun* [U] *She could hear crying coming from the next room.*

cry [SHOUT] /kraɪ/ *verb* [I or T] to call out loudly: [+ speech] *"Look out!" she cried.*

COMMON LEARNER ERROR

cry, scream or **shout?**

Cry is usually only used with speech.

'Get me out of here!' she cried.

The most common words used to mean 'to call out loudly' are **scream** or **shout**. **Scream** is usually something you do when you are frightened or being attacked and is often just sounds not words.

As he grabbed her arm, she screamed and tried to get away.
~~*As he grabbed her arm, she cried and tried to get away.*~~

Shout is a more general word for 'to call out loudly'.

Alex shouted something to me across the street.
~~*Alex cried something to me across the street.*~~

• **For crying out loud!** *INFORMAL* said when you are annoyed, and to emphasize what you are saying: *Oh, for crying out loud, why won't you listen to me!*
• **cry foul** to say that something which has happened is unfair or illegal: *The opposition parties have cried foul **at** the president's act, seeing it as a violation of democracy.*
• **cry wolf** *DISAPPROVING* to ask for help when you do not need it: *If you cry wolf too often, people will stop believing that you need help.*
cry /kraɪ/ *noun* [C] **1** a loud high sound that expresses an emotion: *a cry of despair* **2** a shout made to attract people's attention: *They were wakened by cries of 'Fire!' from the next room.* **3** the noise that a bird or animal makes
• **in full cry** talking continuously about something in a noisy or eager way: *The opposition was in full cry in Parliament last night **over** the proposed changes to the education bill.*
• **cry for help** a way of saying that you need help: *Most suicide attempts are really a cry for help.*

PHRASAL VERBS WITH **cry**

▲ **cry off** *phrasal verb INFORMAL* to decide not to do something that you have arranged to do: *She usually says she'll be there and then cries off at the last minute.*
▲ **cry out** *phrasal verb* to shout or make a loud noise because you are frightened, hurt, etc: *She cried out in pain as the bullet grazed her shoulder.*
▲ **cry out against *sth*** *phrasal verb* to complain loudly about something that you do not approve of: *Women's rights groups have cried out against the proposed cut in benefit paid to single mothers.*
▲ **cry out for *sth*** *phrasal verb* to need a particular thing very much: *The country is crying out for a change in leadership.*

cry-baby /ˈkraɪ.beɪ.bi/ *noun* [C] *INFORMAL DISAPPROVING* someone, usually a child, who cries a lot without good reason: *Don't be such a cry-baby – it's only a scratch.*

crying /ˈkraɪ.ɪŋ/ *adj* [before n] very serious and needing urgent attention: *There's a crying **need** for a better education system.* ➲See also **crying** at **cry** PRODUCE TEARS.
• **it's a crying shame** *OLD-FASHIONED* something that you say when you think a situation is wrong: *It's a crying shame **that** she's paid so little for what she does.*

cryonics /ˌkraɪˈɒn.ɪks/ [US] /-ˈɑː.nɪks/ *noun* [U] the process of storing a dead body by freezing it until science has advanced to such a degree that it is able to bring that person back to life

crypt /krɪpt/ *noun* [C] a room under the floor of a church where bodies are often buried

cryptic /ˈkrɪp.tɪk/ *adj* mysterious and difficult to understand: *I received a cryptic message through the post.* **cryptically** /ˈkrɪp.tɪ.kli/ *adv*

cryptic crossword /ˌkrɪp.tɪkˈkrɒs.wɜːd/ [US] /ˈkrɑːs.wɝːd/ *noun* [C] a type of CROSSWORD (= word game) which has difficult clues that are not obvious in their meaning

crypto- /krɪp.təʊ-/ [US] /-toʊ-/ *prefix* hidden or secret: *The minister accused his opponent of being a crypto-communist.*

crystal [SHAPE] /ˈkrɪs.təl/ *noun* [C] *SPECIALIZED* a piece of a substance which has become solid, with a regular shape: *When sea water is allowed to evaporate, salt crystals are deposited.* ○ *Cirrus clouds are composed of ice crystals.* **crystalline** /ˈkrɪs.təl.aɪn/ *adj*: *crystalline deposits*
crystallize, *UK USUALLY* **-ise** /ˈkrɪs.təl.aɪz/ *verb SPECIALIZED* **1** [I] If a liquid crystallizes, it turns into crystals. **2** [T] If something crystallizes your thoughts or opinions, it makes them clear and fixed: *The event helped to crystallize my thoughts.* **crystallization**, *UK USUALLY* **-isation** /ˌkrɪs.təl.aɪˈzeɪ.ʃən/ *noun* [U]

crystal [ROCK] /ˈkrɪs.təl/ *noun* [C or U] clear transparent rock which is used in jewellery, or a piece of this: *a pair of crystal earrings*
• **crystal clear 1** extremely clear: *crystal clear water* **2** very easy to understand: *The evidence is now crystal clear.* ○ *She made it crystal clear **that** she was in charge.*
crystalline /ˈkrɪs.təl.aɪn/ [US] /-lən/ *adj LITERARY* clear and bright like crystal: *Her singing voice has a pure, crystalline quality.*

crystal [GLASS] /ˈkrɪs.təl/ *noun* **1** [U] transparent glass of very high quality, usually with its surface cut into delicate patterns: *a crystal vase* **2** [C] *US* a transparent glass, or plastic cover for a watch or clock

ˌcrystal ˈball *noun* [C usually sing] a transparent glass ball used by someone who claims they can discover what will happen to you in the future by looking into it

crystallized, *UK USUALLY* **-ised** /ˈkrɪs.təl.aɪzd/ *noun* [C] SOAKED (= left to become completely wet) in melted sugar which has then become hard: *crystallized **fruit***

the CSA /ðəˌsiː.esˈeɪ/ *noun ABBREVIATION FOR* the Child Support Agency: a British government organization that makes parents who do not live with their children continue to pay for their living costs

CSE /ˌsiː.esˈiː/ *noun* [C or U] *ABBREVIATION FOR* Certificate of Secondary Education: a former system of British examinations taken in various subjects, usually at the age of 16 ➲Compare **GCSE**.

ˈc-ˌsection *noun* [C] a **caesarean (section)** (= operation in which a woman's womb is cut open to allow a baby to be born)

ˌCS ˌgas *noun* [U] a gas that causes painful breathing and tears, which is used by the army or police to control a person or crowd in a violent situation

CU, **cu** *INTERNET ABBREVIATION FOR* see you: used when saying goodbye at the end of an email or TEXT MESSAGE (= text sent by telephone) to a friend

cub /kʌb/ *noun* [C] a young lion, bear, wolf, etc. ➲See also **cub (scout)**.

cubbyhole /ˈkʌb.i.həʊl/ [US] /-hoʊl/ *noun* [C] a very small room or space for storing things

cube [SHAPE] /kjuːb/ *noun* [C] a solid object with six square sides of equal size: *Cut the cheese into small cubes.*
cube /kjuːb/ *verb* [T] to cut food into cubes

cube [NUMBER] /kjuːb/ *noun* [C] *SPECIALIZED* the number made by multiplying a number twice by itself
cube /kjuːb/ *verb* [T] *SPECIALIZED* If you cube a number, you multiply it twice by itself: *2 cubed (= 2 x 2 x 2) equals 8, and is written 2^3.*
cubic /ˈkjuː.bɪk/ *adj SPECIALIZED* used in units of volume to show when the length of something has been multiplied by its width and height

ˌcube ˈroot *noun* [C] *SPECIALIZED* The cube root of a number is another number that, when multiplied by itself twice, makes the first number: *The cube root of 125 is 5, because 5 x 5 x 5 = 125.*

cubicle /ˈkjuː.bɪ.kl/ *noun* [C] a small space with walls or curtains around it, that is separate from the rest of a room and where you can be private when taking clothes off, etc: *a shower cubicle* ○ *I was getting undressed in one of the cubicles.*

Cubism /ˈkjuː.bɪ.zᵊm/ *noun* [U] a style of modern art in which an object or person is shown as a set of GEOMETRIC shapes and as if seen from many different angles at the same time **Cubist** /ˈkjuː.bɪst/ *adj, noun* [C]

cuboid /ˈkjuː.bɔɪd/ *noun* [C] *SPECIALIZED* a solid object with six rectangular sides

cuboid /ˈkjuː.bɔɪd/ *adj* approximately in the shape of a CUBE (= a solid object with six square sides of equal size)

ˌcub reˈporter *noun* [C] a young person being trained to write articles for a newspaper

ˌcub (ˈscout) *noun* [C] a boy aged between 8 and 11 years old who is a member of the international organization called the Scouts

cuckold /ˈkʌk.əʊld/ [US] /-oʊld/ *noun* [C] *OLD-FASHIONED DISAPPROVING* a man whose wife deceives him by having a sexual relationship with another man

cuckold /ˈkʌk.əʊld/ [US] /-oʊld/ *verb* [T] *OLD-FASHIONED DISAPPROVING* If a man or woman is cuckolded, their wife or husband has a sexual relationship with another person.

cuckoo [BIRD] /ˈkʊk.uː/ *noun* [C] *plural* **cuckoos** a grey bird with a two-note call that sounds similar to its name, which puts its eggs in other birds' nests

cuckoo [FOOLISH] /ˈkʊk.uː/ *adj INFORMAL* foolish

ˈcuckoo ˌclock *noun* [C] a decorative clock that has a little wooden bird inside it which comes out every hour and makes a quick two-note call

cucumber /ˈkjuː.kʌm.bəʳ/ [US] /-bɚ/ *noun* [C or U] a long thin pale-green vegetable with dark green skin, usually eaten raw in salads ➲See picture **Vegetables** on page Centre 2

cud /kʌd/ *noun* [U] food that has been eaten by an animal with more than one stomach, such as a cow, and that comes back into the animal's mouth to be chewed again before going into the second stomach: *a cow chewing the cud*

• **chew the cud** *INFORMAL* to think slowly and carefully about something: *He sat for a moment chewing the cud before he spoke.*

cuddle /ˈkʌd.l̩/ *verb* [I or T] to put your arms around someone and hold them in a loving way, or (of two people) to hold each other close for affection or comfort: *She cuddled the baby and eventually it stopped crying.* ○ *They sat in the back row of the cinema kissing and cuddling.* **cuddle** /ˈkʌd.l̩/ *noun* [C] *Come here and give me a cuddle.*

cuddly /ˈkʌd.l̩i/ *adj APPROVING* liking to cuddle, or making you want to cuddle: *a very cuddly child*

▲ **cuddle up** *phrasal verb INFORMAL* to sit or lie very close to someone and put your arms around them: *We cuddled up together and tried to get warm.* ○ *She cuddled up **to** her mother.*

ˌcuddly ˈtoy *noun* [C] *UK* a toy animal that is soft and covered in fur

cudgel /ˈkʌdʒ.ᵊl/ *noun* [C] a short heavy stick used for hitting people

• **take up the cudgels for/against *sb/sth*** *UK OLD-FASHIONED* to argue strongly in support of, or against, someone or something: *Relatives have taken up the cudgels for two British women accused of murder.*

cudgel /ˈkʌdʒ.ᵊl/ *verb* [T] **-ll-** or *US USUALLY* **-l-** to hit someone with a cudgel

• **cudgel *your* brains** *UK OLD-FASHIONED* to think very hard or try to remember something you have forgotten

cue [SIGNAL] /kjuː/ *noun* [C] **1** a word or action in a play or film, which is used as a signal by a performer to begin saying or doing something **2** a signal for someone to do something: [+ *to* infinitive] *They started washing up, so that was our cue **to** leave the party.*

• **on cue** If something happens on cue, it happens just after someone has said or thought it would happen: *I was just wondering where Sarah was, when, right on cue, she came in.*

• **take *your* cue from *sb*** to take notice of someone's words or behaviour so that you know what you should do: *She watched his lips carefully and took her cue from him.*

• **take *your* cue from *sth/sb*** to be greatly influenced by something or someone: *The architects took their cue for the design of the new pub from the nearby Jacobean house, Aston Hall.*

cue (**cueing, cued, cued**) /kjuː/ *verb* [T] (*ALSO* **cue in**) to give someone a signal to do something: *With a nod of his head, the drummer cued the lead singer **in**.*

cue [STICK] /kjuː/ *noun* [C] a long thin wooden pole with a small piece of leather at one end, which is used for hitting the ball in games such as billiards or snooker

cuff [MATERIAL] /kʌf/ *noun* [C] **1** the thicker material at the end of a sleeve nearest the hand **2** *US* (*UK* **turn-up**) the part of a trouser leg that is turned up

• **off the cuff** If you speak off the cuff, you say something without having prepared or thought about your words first: *I hadn't prepared a speech so I just said a few words off the cuff.* ○ *an off-the-cuff remark*

cuff [HIT] /kʌf/ *verb* [T] to hit someone with your hand in a light, joking way: *His brother cuffed him playfully round the head.* **cuff** /kʌf/ *noun* [C] *She gave him a playful cuff on the shoulder.*

ˈcuff ˌlink *noun* [C] a small decorative object used to fasten shirt cuffs

cuffs /kʌfs/ *plural noun INFORMAL FOR* **handcuffs**

cuff /kʌf/ *verb* [T] *INFORMAL He was led out of the dock with his hands cuffed* (= in HANDCUFFS) *behind his back.*

cuisine /kwɪˈziːn/ *noun* [U] a style of cooking: *French cuisine* ➲See also **haute cuisine**; **nouvelle cuisine**.

cul-de-sac /ˈkʌl.də.sæk/ *noun* [C] **1** a short road which is blocked off at one end **2** a situation which leads nowhere: *an intellectual cul-de-sac*

culinary /ˈkʌl.ɪ.nᵊr.i/ [US] /ˈkʌl.ə.ner-/ *adj SLIGHTLY FORMAL* connected with cooking or kitchens: *the culinary **delights*** (= pleasant tasting food) *of Beijing* ○ *My culinary **skills** are rather limited, I'm afraid* (= I am not very good at cooking)*!*

cull /kʌl/ *verb* [T] When people cull animals, they kill them, especially the weaker members of a particular group of them, in order to reduce or limit their number: *The plan to cull large numbers of baby seals has angered environmental groups.* **cull** /kʌl/ *noun* [C] *the annual red deer cull*

▲ **cull *sth* from *sth*** *phrasal verb* [often passive] to collect ideas or information from various places: *Here are a few facts and figures I've culled from the week's papers.*

cullender /ˈkʌl.ɪn.dəʳ/ [US] /ˈkɑː.lən.dɚ/ *noun* [C] *ANOTHER SPELLING OF* **colander**

culminate /ˈkʌl.mɪ.neɪt/ *verb* **culminate in/with *sth*** If an event or series of events culminates in something, it ends with it, having developed until it reaches this point: *My arguments with the boss got worse and worse, and it all culminated in my deciding to change jobs.* ○ *Their many years of research have finally culminated in a cure for the disease.* **culmination** /ˌkʌl.mɪˈneɪ.ʃᵊn/ *noun* [U] *Winning first prize was **the** culmination **of** years of practice and hard work.*

culottes /kʊˈlɒts/ [US] /kjəˈlɑːts/ *plural noun* women's short trousers which look like a skirt: *a pair of culottes*

culpable /ˈkʌl.pə.bl̩/ *adj FORMAL* deserving to be blamed or considered responsible for something bad: *He was **held** culpable* (= blamed) ***for** all that had happened.*

culpability /ˌkʌl.pəˈbɪl.ɪ.ti/ [US] /-ə.t̬i/ *noun* [U] *After the accident, the company refused to **accept** culpability.*

culpably /ˈkʌl.pə.bli/ *adv*

culprit /ˈkʌl.prɪt/ *noun* [C] **1** someone who has done something wrong: *Police hope the public will help them to find the culprits.* **2** a fact or situation that is the reason for something bad happening: *Children in this country are getting much too fat, and sugar and sweets are the main culprits.*

cult [RELIGION] /kʌlt/ *noun* [C] **1** a religious group, often living together, whose beliefs are considered extreme or strange by many people: *Their son ran away from home and joined a **religious** cult.* **2** a particular system of religious belief: *the Hindu cult **of** Shiva*

cult [POPULARITY] /kʌlt/ *noun* [S] someone or something that has become very popular with a particular group of people: *the cult of celebrity* ➲See also **personality cult**.

cult /kʌlt/ *adj* **[before n]** liked very much by a particular group of people: *The singer had a cult* ***following*** *in the 1970's.* ○ *a cult* ***figure/movie***

cultivate /ˈkʌl.tɪ.veɪt/ [US] /-t̬ə-/ *verb* **[T] 1** to prepare land and grow crops on it, or to grow a particular crop: *Most of the land there is too poor to cultivate.* ○ *The villagers cultivate mostly maize and beans.* **2** to try to develop and improve something: *She has cultivated* ***an image*** *as a tough negotiator.* **3** If you cultivate a relationship, you make a special effort to establish and develop it, because you think it might be useful to you: *The new Prime Minister is cultivating relationships with old Eastern Bloc countries.*
cultivable /ˈkʌl.tɪ.və.bl̩/ [US] /-t̬ə-/ *adj*: *Most of the island isn't cultivable* (= can't be cultivated) – *the soil is too rocky and dry.*
cultivated /ˈkʌl.tɪ.veɪ.tɪd/ [US] /-t̬ə.veɪ.t̬ɪd/ *adj* describes land which is cultivated: *cultivated fields/soil/land*
cultivation /ˌkʌl.tɪˈveɪ.ʃᵊn/ [US] /-t̬ə-/ *noun* **[U]**

cultivated /ˈkʌl.tɪ.veɪ.tɪd/ [US] /-t̬ə.veɪ.t̬ɪd/ *adj* describes someone who has had a good education and knows a lot about and likes art, music, painting, etc.

culture [WAY OF LIFE] /ˈkʌl.tʃəʳ/ [US] /-tʃɚ/ *noun* **[C or U]** the way of life, especially the general customs and beliefs, of a particular group of people at a particular time: *youth/working-class culture* ○ *She's studying modern Japanese language and culture.* ➲See Note **civilization or culture?** at **civilization**. See also **subculture**.
cultural /ˈkʌl.tʃᵊr.ᵊl/ [US] /-tʃɚ-/ *adj* relating to the habits, traditions and beliefs of a society: *The USA is often accused of cultural imperialism.* ○ *Australia has its own cultural* ***identity****, which is very different from that of Britain.* ○ *cultural* ***diversity/differences*** ○ *cultural* ***heritage*** (= ways of living and thinking that have existed for a long time in a society) **culturally** /ˈkʌl.tʃᵊr.ᵊl.i/ [US] /-tʃɚ-/ *adv*: *a culturally diverse society*

culture [ART] /ˈkʌl.tʃəʳ/ [US] /-tʃɚ/ *noun* **[U]** music, art, theatre, literature, etc: *You won't find much culture in this sleepy little town, I'm afraid!* ○ ***popular*** *culture* (= the books, music, etc. liked by most people)
cultural /ˈkʌl.tʃᵊr.ᵊl/ [US] /-tʃɚ-/ *adj* relating to music, art, theatre, literature, etc: *cultural* ***activities*** ○ *a cultural* ***centre*** (= a place with a lot of museums, theatres, etc.) ○ *a cultural desert/wasteland* (= a place without museums, theatres, etc.)
cultured /ˈkʌl.tʃəd/ [US] /-tʃɚd/ *adj* describes someone who has had a good education and knows a lot about art, music, literature, etc.

culture [GROW] /ˈkʌl.tʃəʳ/ [US] /-tʃɚ/ *noun* **[C or U]** *SPECIALIZED* cells, tissues, organs or organisms grown for scientific purposes, or the breeding and keeping of particular living things in order to get the substances they produce
culture /ˈkʌl.tʃəʳ/ [US] /-tʃɚ/ *verb* **[T]**

ˌcultured ˈpearl *noun* **[C]** a PEARL (= round white jewel) that has been formed artificially

ˈculture ˌshock *noun* **[C]** a feeling of confusion felt by someone visiting a country or place that they do not know: *It was a real culture shock to find herself in London after living on a small island.*

ˈculture ˌvulture *noun* **[C]** *INFORMAL* someone who is very interested in the arts: *He's a bit of a culture vulture – always out at galleries and theatres.*

culvert /ˈkʌl.vət/ [US] /-vɚt/ *noun* **[C]** a pipe for waste water that crosses under roads, railways, etc.

-cum- /-kʌm-/ *preposition* used to join two nouns, showing that a person or thing does two things or has two purposes; combined with: *This is my bedroom-cum-study.*

cumbersome /ˈkʌm.bə.səm/ [US] /-bɚ-/ *adj* awkward because of being large, heavy or ineffective: *cumbersome equipment* ○ *cumbersome* ***bureaucracy***

cumin /ˈkjuː.mɪn/ *noun* **[U]** (a plant with) seeds that smell pleasant and are used as a spice, especially in Indian and Middle Eastern cooking

cummerbund /ˈkʌm.ə.bʌnd/ [US] /-ɚ-/ *noun* **[C]** a wide piece of cloth worn round the waist, especially by men, as part of formal or Middle Eastern clothing

cumquat /ˈkʌm.kwɒt/ [US] /-kwɑːt/ *noun* **[C]** a **kumquat**

cumulative /ˈkjuː.mjʊ.lə.tɪv/ [US] /-t̬ɪv/ *adj* increasing by one addition after another: *The cumulative* ***effect*** *of using so many chemicals on the land could be disastrous.*
cumulatively /ˈkjuː.mjʊ.lə.tɪv.li/ [US] /-t̬ɪv-/ *adv*

cumulus /ˈkjuː.mjʊ.ləs/ *noun* **[U]** *SPECIALIZED* a type of tall white cloud with a wide flat base and rounded shape ➲Compare **cirrus**; **nimbus**.

cuneiform /ˈkjuː.nɪ.fɔːm/ [US] /-fɔːrm/ *adj* of a form of writing used for over 3 000 years until the 1st century BC in the ancient countries of the Middle East
cuneiform /ˈkjuː.nɪ.fɔːm/ [US] /-fɔːrm/ *noun* **[U]**

cunnilingus /ˌkʌn.ɪˈlɪŋ.gəs/ *noun* **[U]** the sexual activity of moving the tongue across the female sex organs in order to give pleasure and excitement ➲Compare **fellatio**.

cunning [CLEVER] /ˈkʌn.ɪŋ/ *adj* describes people who are clever at planning something so that they get what they want, especially by tricking other people, or things that are cleverly made for a particular purpose: *a cunning* ***plan/ploy*** ○ *He's a very cunning man.* **cunning** /ˈkʌn.ɪŋ/ *noun* **[U]** *We need to* ***show*** *a bit of cunning if we want to trick the enemy.* **cunningly** /ˈkʌn.ɪŋ.li/ *adv*

cunning [ATTRACTIVE] /ˈkʌn.ɪŋ/ *adj US OLD-FASHIONED* attractive; CUTE: *a cunning little child/puppy/kitten*

cunt [PERSON] /kʌnt/ *noun* **[C]** *OFFENSIVE* a very unpleasant or stupid person: *You stupid cunt!* ○ *He's a right cunt.*

cunt [SEXUAL ORGANS] /kʌnt/ *noun* **[C]** *OFFENSIVE* the outer female sex organ; the vagina

cup [DRINKING CONTAINER] /kʌp/ *noun* **[C] 1** a small round container, often with a handle, used for drinking tea, coffee, etc: *a cup and saucer* ○ *a plastic/paper cup* ○ *a coffee cup/teacup* **2** *US* a container which holds nearly a quarter of a litre of liquid, used for measuring in cookery
• **not be *sb's* cup of tea** If something or someone is not your cup of tea, they are not the type of thing or person that you like: *Thanks for inviting me, but ballet isn't really my cup of tea.*
cupful /ˈkʌp.fʊl/ *noun* **[C]** *plural* **cupfuls** or *US ALSO* **cupsful** *Add two cupfuls of milk* (= the amount held by a cup) *to the mixture.*

cup [SPORT] /kʌp/ *noun* **[C]** a specially designed cup, usually with two handles and often made of silver, which is given as a prize in a sports competition, or a game or match in which the winner receives such a cup: *Sheila won this cup in the school squash championship.* ○ *The Davis Cup is an important international tennis championship.*

cup [CONTAINER] /kʌp/ *noun* **[C] 1** a bowl-shaped container: *an egg cup* **2** the size of the two parts that support the breasts in a woman's BRA (= item of underwear): *"What size bra do you wear?" "A 'C' cup."* **3** *US* (*UK* **box**) a curved piece of hard plastic which is worn by men while playing sports to protect their outer sex organs
cup /kʌp/ *verb* **[T] -pp-** *She gently cupped the small injured bird* ***in*** *her* ***hands*** (= held her hands in the shape of a cup around it).

cup [DRINK] /kʌp/ *noun* **[C or U]** a mixture of several types of drink, often including one which is alcoholic, which is often drunk at parties and usually served from a bowl: *a strawberry/cider cup*

cupboard /ˈkʌb.əd/ [US] /-ɚd/ *noun* **[C]** a piece of furniture or a small part of a room with a door or doors behind which there is space for storing things, usually on shelves: *a kitchen cupboard* ○ *a built-in cupboard* ○ *Is there plenty of cupboard* ***space*** (= Are there many cupboards) *in your new house?* ➲See picture **In the Kitchen** on page Centre 16
• **the cupboard is bare** used to say that there is no food in a house or that there is no money, etc. available: *I'd like to help you out with your expenses, Paul, but I'm afraid the cupboard is bare.*

ˈcupboard ˌlove *noun* **[U]** affection shown by someone, typically a child or an animal, in order to get what they want

cupcake /ˈkʌp.keɪk/ *noun* **[C]** *MAINLY US FOR* **fairy cake**

ˌcup ˈfinal *noun* **[C]** *UK* the last game in a competition between teams, usually in football or rugby, for a CUP SPORT: *Manchester United has won the FA* (= Football

Association) *Cup Final for the last two years in a row.*

ˈcup ˌholder *noun* [C] In a team sport, the cup holders are the team which won the cup for the competition held during the previous year or season: *The cup holders began their defence of the trophy in fine style.*

C

Cupid /ˈkjuː.pɪd/ *noun* the ancient Roman god of love, represented by a naked baby boy who has wings and shoots arrows at people to make them start to love each other

cupid /ˈkjuː.pɪd/ *noun* [C] a statue or painting of a little boy looking like Cupid

cupidity /kjuːˈpɪd.ɪ.ti/ [US] /-ə.t̬i/ *noun* [U] FORMAL a great desire, especially for money or possessions

cupola /ˈkjuː.pəl.ə/ *noun* [C] a small DOME (= round roof) on top of a building

cuppa /ˈkʌp.ə/ *noun* [C] MAINLY UK INFORMAL a cup of tea: *Make us a cuppa, will you, love?*

ˈcup ˌtie *noun* [C] UK a game between two teams trying to win a cup, especially in football

cur /kɜːʳ/ [US] /kɝː/ *noun* [C] LITERARY **1** a MONGREL (= dog of mixed type), especially one that is frightening or fierce **2** a person who is thought to be worthless or cowardly

curable /ˈkjʊə.rə.bl̩/ [US] /ˈkjʊr-/ *adj* describes a disease that can be cured: *Many illnesses which once killed are today curable.* ✱ NOTE: The opposite is **incurable**. **curability** /ˌkjʊə.rəˈbɪl.ɪ.ti/ [US] /ˌkjʊr.əˈbɪl.ə.t̬i/ *noun* [U]

curaçao /ˈkjʊə.rə.səʊ/ [US] /ˈkjʊr.ə.soʊ/ *noun* [U] an orange-flavoured LIQUEUR (= type of strong alcoholic drink)

curate /ˈkjʊə.rət/ [US] /ˈkjʊr.ət/ *noun* [C] a priest of the lowest rank, especially in the Church of England, whose job is to help the VICAR (= priest of a particular church area)

• **curate's egg** UK something that is partly good but mainly bad: *The film is a bit of a curate's egg.*

curacy /ˈkjʊə.rə.si/ [US] /ˈkjʊr.ə-/ *noun* [C] a job or period of time as a curate: *He's got a curacy in the North of England.*

curative /ˈkjʊə.rə.tɪv/ [US] /ˈkjʊr.ə.t̬ɪv/ *adj* able to cure or cause to get better: *Do you believe in the curative* ***powers*** *of the local mineral water?*

curator /kjʊˈreɪ.təʳ/ [US] /kjɝːˈeɪ.t̬ɚ/ *noun* [C] a person in charge of a museum, library, etc.

curb [CONTROL] /kɜːb/ [US] /kɝːb/ *verb* [T] to control or limit something that is not desirable: *The Government should act to curb tax evasion.* **curb** /kɜːb/ [US] /kɝːb/ *noun* [C] *You must try to put a curb* ***on*** *your bad temper/spending habits.*

curb [EDGE] /kɜːb/ [US] /kɝːb/ *noun* [C] US SPELLING OF **kerb**

curbside /ˈkɜːb.saɪd/ [US] /ˈkɝːb-/ *noun* [U], *adj* [before n] US SPELLING OF **kerbside**

curd /kɜːd/ [US] /kɝːd/ *noun* [U] (ALSO **curds**) the solid substance which forms when milk turns sour

ˌcurd ˈcheese *noun* [U] (ALSO **curds**) MAINLY UK a soft smooth white cheese without a strong taste

curdle /ˈkɜː.dl̩/ [US] /ˈkɝː-/ *verb* [I or T] If a liquid curdles, or you curdle it, it gets thicker and develops lumps.

• **make *sb's* blood curdle** (ALSO **curdle *sb's* blood**) to fill someone with fear: *The strange sound made his blood curdle.* ➲See also **blood-curdling**.

cure [MAKE WELL] /kjʊəʳ/ [US] /kjʊr/ *verb* [T] **1** to make someone with an illness healthy again: *At one time the doctors couldn't cure TB/cure people* ***of*** *TB.* **2** to solve a problem: *Finance Ministers meet this week to discuss how to cure inflation.*

cure /kjʊəʳ/ [US] /kjʊr/ *noun* [C] **1** something that makes someone with an illness healthy again: *There's still no cure* ***for*** *cancer.* ○ *There is* ***no known*** *cure* ***for*** *this disease* (= a cure has not yet been found). **2** a solution to a problem: *The best cure* ***for*** *boredom is hard work!*

cure [PRESERVE] /kjʊəʳ/ [US] /kjʊr/ *verb* [T] to treat food, tobacco, etc. with smoke or salt, etc. in order to stop it decaying: *cured meats*

▲ **cure *sb* of *sth*** *phrasal verb* to stop someone doing or wanting something bad: *I ate so much of it one day I was sick and that cured me of my addiction.*

cure-all /ˈkjʊə.rɔːl/ [US] /ˈkjʊr.ɑːl/ *noun* [C] something that people think will solve any problem or cure any illness: *a cure-all wonder drug*

curfew /ˈkɜː.fjuː/ [US] /ˈkɝː-/ *noun* [C or U] a rule that everyone must stay at home between particular times, usually at night, especially during a war or a period of political trouble: *to impose/lift a curfew* ○ *a midnight curfew* ○ *He was shot for* ***breaking*** (= not obeying) *the curfew.* ○ *You'll be in trouble if you get home after curfew.*

the Curia /ðəˈkjʊə.ri.ə/ [US] /-ˈkjʊr.i-/ *noun* [S] SPECIALIZED the government and court of the Roman Catholic Church, with the Pope in the highest position

curio /ˈkjʊə.ri.əʊ/ [US] /ˈkjʊr.i.oʊ/ *noun* [C] *plural* **curios** an unusual object: *a shop full of antiques and curios*

curiosity [INTEREST] /ˌkjʊə.riˈɒs.ɪ.ti/ [US] /ˌkjʊr.iˈɑː.sə.t̬i/ *noun* [U] an eager desire to know or learn about something: *to* ***arouse/excite/satisfy*** *someone's curiosity* ○ *I'm* ***burning with*** *curiosity – you must tell me who's won!* ○ *She decided to call her ex-boyfriend* ***out of*** *curiosity.* ○ *"Why do you ask?" "Oh, just* ***idle*** *curiosity* (= for no particular reason)."

• **Curiosity killed the cat.** SAYING said to warn someone not to ask too many questions about something

curiosity [STRANGE OBJECT] /ˌkjʊə.riˈɒs.ɪ.ti/ [US] /ˌkjʊr.iˈɑː.sə.t̬i/ *noun* [C] something that is interesting because it is rare and unusual: *Cars like mine are curiosities nowadays.* ○ *I kept this old pot for its curiosity* ***value*** (= the interest it has because it is unusual).

curious [INTERESTED] /ˈkjʊə.ri.əs/ [US] /ˈkjʊr.i-/ *adj* interested in learning about people or things around you: *I was curious to know what would happen next.* ○ *Babies are curious* ***about*** *everything around them.* ○ *"Why did you ask?" "I was just curious."* **curiously** /ˈkjʊə.ri.ə.sli/ [US] /ˈkjʊr.i-/ *adv*

curious [STRANGE] /ˈkjʊə.ri.əs/ [US] /ˈkjʊr.i-/ *adj* strange and unusual; PECULIAR: *There was a curious-****looking*** *man standing outside.* ○ *A curious thing happened to me yesterday.* ○ *It's curious* ***(that)*** *Billy hasn't phoned when he promised he would.*

curiously /ˈkjʊə.ri.ə.sli/ [US] /ˈkjʊr.i-/ *adv*: *Curiously* (= Strangely), *there didn't seem to be a bank in the town.*

curl /kɜːl/ [US] /kɝːl/ *noun* [C or U] a piece of hair which grows or has been formed into a curving shape, or something that is the same shape as this: *tight/loose curls* ○ *Her hair fell* ***in*** *curls over her shoulders.* ○ *Curls of smoke were rising from the chimney.* ➲Compare **wave** HAIR CURVES.

curl /kɜːl/ [US] /kɝːl/ *verb* [I or T] to make something into the shape of a curl, or to grow or change into this shape: *Does your hair curl* ***naturally****, or is it permed?* ○ *A new baby will automatically curl its fingers* ***round*** *any object it touches.*

• **curl up and die** INFORMAL to feel very ashamed and sorry: *I just wanted to curl up and die when I spilt coffee on their new carpet!*

• **curl *your* lip** to show by an upwards movement of one side of your mouth that you feel no respect for something or someone: *Her lip curled at what he said.*

curly /ˈkɜː.li/ [US] /ˈkɝː-/ *adj* having curls or a curved shape: *He has blond curly hair.* ○ *These pigs all have curly tails.* ➲See picture **Hairstyles and Hats** on page Centre 8

PHRASAL VERBS WITH **curl** ▼

▲ **curl up** [POSITION] *phrasal verb* to sit or lie in a position with your arms and legs close to your body: *She curled up on the sofa to watch TV.*

▲ **curl up** [EDGES] *phrasal verb* If something flat, such as paper, curls up, the edges start to curve up.

curler /ˈkɜː.ləʳ/ [US] /ˈkɝː.lɚ/ *noun* [C] (ALSO **roller**) a small plastic tube that you wind hair around to make it curl

curlew /ˈkɜː.ljuː/ [US] /ˈkɝː-/ *noun* [C] a large brownish coloured bird with long legs and a very long curved beak, which is usually seen near water

curling /ˈkɜː.lɪŋ/ [US] /ˈkɝː-/ *noun* [U] a game played on ice in which special flat round stones are slid towards a mark

curmudgeon /kəˈmʌdʒ.ən/ [US] /kɚ-/ *noun* [C] OLD-FASHIONED a bad-tempered old person **curmudgeonly** /kəˈmʌdʒ.ən.li/ [US] /kɚ-/ *adj*

currant [DRY FRUIT] /ˈkʌr.ᵊnt/ [US] /ˈkɝː-/ *noun* [C] a small black dried grape without seeds, used especially in cakes: *currant buns*

currant [FRUIT] /ˈkʌr.ᵊnt/ [US] /ˈkɝː-/ *noun* [C] a small round fruit which grows on bushes and is eaten fresh or cooked: *blackcurrants/redcurrants* ○ *currant* ***bushes***.
* NOTE: This word is often used in compounds.

currency [MONEY] /ˈkʌr.ᵊnt.si/ [US] /ˈkɝː-/ *noun* [C or U] the money that is used in a particular country at a particular time: *foreign currency*

currency [ACCEPTANCE] /ˈkʌr.ᵊnt.si/ [US] /ˈkɝː-/ *noun* [U] the state of being commonly known or accepted, or of being used in many places: *His ideas* ***enjoyed wide*** *currency during the last century.* ○ *Many informal expressions are* ***gaining*** *currency in serious newspapers.*

current [NOW] /ˈkʌr.ᵊnt/ [US] /ˈkɝː-/ *adj* of the present time: *Have you seen the current* ***issue*** *of* (= the most recently published) *Vogue magazine?* ○ *The word 'thou'* (= you) *is no longer* ***in*** *current* ***use***. ➲See Note **actual or current?** at **actual**. **currently** /ˈkʌr.ᵊnt.li/ [US] /ˈkɝː-/ *adv*: *The Director is currently having talks in the USA.*

current [MOVEMENT] /ˈkʌr.ᵊnt/ [US] /ˈkɝː-/ *noun* [C] **1** a movement of water, air or electricity, in a particular direction: *to swim against/with the current* ○ *He was swept out to sea by the* ***strong*** *current.* ○ *Switch off the electric current before touching that machine.* **2** a particular opinion or feeling that a group of people have: *There is a growing current of support for green issues among voters.*

ˈcurrent acˌcount *UK noun* [C] (*US* **checking account**) a bank account that you can take money from at any time and which usually earns little or no interest

ˌcurrent afˈfairs *plural noun* political news about events happening now

curriculum /kəˈrɪk.jʊ.ləm/ *noun* [C] *plural* **curricula** or **curriculums** the group of subjects studied in a school, college, etc: *the school curriculum* ➲See also **the national curriculum**. Compare **syllabus**. **curricular** /kəˈrɪk.jʊ.ləʳ/ [US] /-lɚ/ *adj SPECIALIZED*

curriculum vitae /kəˌrɪk.jʊ.ləmˈviː.taɪ/ *noun* [C] *plural* **curriculum vitaes** or **curricula vitae** *FORMAL* a **CV**

curry [FOOD] /ˈkʌr.i/ [US] /ˈkɝː-/ *noun* [C or U] a dish, originally from India, consisting of meat or vegetables cooked in a spicy sauce: *a hot* (= very spicy) *curry* ○ *a mild* (= slightly spicy) *curry* ○ *vegetable/chicken/lamb curry* ○ *curry sauce* **curried** /ˈkʌr.id/ [US] /ˈkɝː-/ *adj*: *curried eggs/fish*
curry /ˈkʌr.i/ [US] /ˈkɝː-/ *verb* [T] *Let's curry* (= make a curry with) *the leftover meat.*

curry [OBTAIN] /ˈkʌr.i/ [US] /ˈkɝː-/ *verb DISAPPROVING* **curry favour** to praise someone, especially someone in authority, in a way that is not sincere, in order to obtain some advantage for yourself: *He's always trying to curry favour* ***with*** *the boss.*

ˌcurry ˈpaste *noun* [C or U] a soft mixture of spices and oil, used to flavour CURRIES

ˈcurry ˌpowder *noun* [U] a dry mixture of spices used to flavour CURRIES

curse [SPEAK ANGRILY] /kɜːs/ [US] /kɝːs/ *verb* [I or T] to say a word or an expression which is not polite and shows that you are very angry: *We could hear him cursing and swearing as he tried to get the door open.* ○ *I could curse her* ***for*** *losing my key!*
curse /kɜːs/ [US] /kɝːs/ *noun* [C] a rude word or phrase
cursed /kɜːst/ /ˈkɜː.sɪd/ [US] /ˈkɝːst/ *adj* [before n] *OLD-FASHIONED It's a cursed* (= annoying) *nuisance, having to work late every evening!* ➲See also **accursed**.

curse [PERFORM MAGIC] /kɜːs/ [US] /kɝːs/ *noun* [C] magic words which are intended to bring bad luck to someone: *In the story, a wicked witch* ***put a*** *curse* ***on*** *the princess for 100 years.* **curse** /kɜːs/ [US] /kɝːs/ *verb* [T] *Things were going so badly – it was as if I'd been cursed.* **cursed** /kɜːst/ [US] /kɝːst/ *adj*: *HUMOROUS I'm sure this car is cursed – it never starts when I need it.*

curse [TROUBLE] /kɜːs/ [US] /kɝːs/ *noun* [C] a cause of trouble and unhappiness: *Noise is the curse of modern city life.* **cursed** /kɜːst/ [US] /kɝːst/ *adj*: *In recent years I've been cursed* ***with*** *worsening eyesight.*

the curse [BLEEDING] *noun* [S] *OLD-FASHIONED INFORMAL* a woman's **period** BLEEDING

cursive /ˈkɜː.sɪv/ [US] /ˈkɝː-/ *adj SPECIALIZED* describes writing that is written with rounded letters which are joined together

cursor /ˈkɜː.səʳ/ [US] /ˈkɝː.sɚ/ *noun* [C] a MARKER (= small sign), usually an arrow or a vertical line, on a computer screen which moves to show the point where work is being done: *You can* ***move*** *the cursor either by using the mouse or by using the arrow keys on the keyboard.*

cursory /ˈkɜː.sᵊr.i/ [US] /ˈkɝː.sɚ-/ *adj* quick and probably not detailed: *a cursory glance/look* ○ *a cursory examination* **cursorily** /ˈkɜː.sᵊr.ᵊl.i/ [US] /ˈkɝː.sɚ-/ *adv*: *He glanced cursorily at the letter, then gave it to me.*

curt /kɜːt/ [US] /kɝːt/ *adj DISAPPROVING* If someone's manner or speech is curt, it is rude as a result of being very brief: *to give a curt nod/reply* ○ *The boss was rather curt* ***with*** *him.* **curtly** /ˈkɜːt.li/ [US] /ˈkɝːt-/ *adv*: *Steve answered curtly and turned his back on me.* **curtness** /ˈkɜːt.nəs/ [US] /ˈkɝːt-/ *noun* [U] *Claire's curtness made him wonder what he'd done wrong.*

curtail /kəˈteɪl/ [US] /kɚ-/ *verb* [T] to stop something before it is finished, or to reduce or limit something: *to curtail your holiday/spending* ○ *The last government* ***severely*** *curtailed trade union rights.* **curtailment** /kəˈteɪl.mənt/ [US] /kɚ-/ *noun* [C or U]

curtain /ˈkɜː.tᵊn/ [US] /ˈkɝː.t̬ᵊn/ *noun* [C] **1** a piece of material, especially cloth, which hangs across a window or opening to make a room or part of a room dark or private: *Heavy curtains blocked out the sunlight.* ○ ***draw*** (= open or close) *the curtains* **2** a thick layer of something which makes it difficult to see anything behind it: *They could see nothing through the curtain of rain/smoke.* **3** the large screen of heavy material in a theatre which separates the stage from the area where people are watching
• **be curtains for *sb*** *INFORMAL* used to say someone will die or have to stop doing something: *It'll be curtains for him, if he doesn't do what I tell him!*

ˈcurtain ˌcall *noun* [C] when actors come to the front of the stage at the end of a performance and the people watching clap to show their enjoyment

ˈcurtain ˌrail *noun* [C] a fixed strip of plastic or metal from which a curtain hangs

ˈcurtain ˌraiser *noun* [C] **1** a small event that happens before a bigger one and is a preparation for it **2** a short play sometimes performed before the main play

curtsy, curtsey /ˈkɜːt.si/ [US] /ˈkɝːt-/ *verb* [I] When a girl or woman curtsies, she bends quickly at the knees, with one foot in front of the other, while holding her skirt, especially to show respect to a king or queen, etc: *She curtseyed* ***to*** *the Queen.* ➲Compare **bow** BEND. **curtsy, curtsey** /ˈkɜːt.si/ [US] /ˈkɝːt-/ *noun* [C]

curvaceous /kɜːˈveɪ.ʃəs/ [US] /kɝː-/ *adj* describes a woman who has a body with attractive curves

curvature /ˈkɜː.və.tʃəʳ/ [US] /ˈkɝː.və.tʃɚ/ *noun* [C or U] *SPECIALIZED* the state of being curved or bent: *the curvature of the earth's surface* ○ *a pronounced curvature of the spine*

curve /kɜːv/ [US] /kɝːv/ *noun* [C] a line which bends continuously and has no straight parts: *a curve* ***in*** *the road* ○ *the curve of a graph*
curve /kɜːv/ [US] /kɝːv/ *verb* [I] to form a curve or move in the shape of a curve: *The road curves* ***round*** *to the left.*
curved /kɜːvd/ [US] /kɝːvd/ *adj*: *a curved surface*
curvy /ˈkɜː.vi/ [US] /ˈkɝː-/ *adj* containing a lot of curves: *a curvy line*

ˈcurve ˌball *noun* [C] *US* When you throw a curve ball in the sport of baseball, the ball curves as it moves towards the player with the bat.

cushion /ˈkʊʃ.ᵊn/ *noun* [C] **1** a bag made of cloth, plastic or leather which is filled with soft material, often has an attractive cover, and is used especially on chairs for sitting or leaning on: *She sank back* ***against/into*** *the cushions.* ➲See also **pincushion**. Compare **pillow**. **2** *SPECIALIZED* **cushion of air** a layer of air often used to support a machine or vehicle: *A hovercraft travels on a cushion of air.*

C

C

cushion /ˈkʊʃ.ᵊn/ *verb* [T] *The soft grass cushioned his* ***fall*** (= made it hurt less).
• **cushion the blow** to make a bad situation less serious: *He's lost his job, but the redundancy money will cushion the blow.*

cushy /ˈkʊʃ.i/ *adj* INFORMAL DISAPPROVING very easy: *a cushy job* ○ UK *a cushy* ***number*** (= an easy job or situation)

cusp /kʌsp/ *noun* [S] the dividing line between two very different things: ***on the*** *cusp* ***of*** *adulthood*

cuspidor /ˈkʌs.pɪ.dɔːʳ/ [US] /-dɔːr/ *noun* [C] US FOR **spittoon**

cuss [SWEAR] /kʌs/ *verb* [I] MAINLY US OLD-FASHIONED INFORMAL to say words which are not polite because you are angry; to **curse**

cuss [PERSON] /kʌs/ *noun* [C] US OLD-FASHIONED INFORMAL a person of the bad type mentioned: *Tom's an* ***awkward/stupid/irritable (old)*** *cuss!*

cussed /ˈkʌs.ɪd/ *adj* DISAPPROVING describes people who are unwilling to be helpful, or things that are annoying: *He's just* ***plain*** *cussed: he's only doing it because I asked him not to!* ○ *It's a cussed nuisance.* **cussedly** /ˈkʌs.ɪd.li/ *adv* **cussedness** /ˈkʌs.ɪd.nəs/ *noun* [U] *He refused to help* ***out of sheer/pure*** *cussedness.*

custard /ˈkʌs.təd/ [US] /-tɚd/ *noun* [U] a (usually warm) sweet sauce made from eggs, milk and sugar and poured over sweet dishes: *apple pie and custard*

ˌcustard ˈpie *noun* [C] UK a flat open pastry container filled with artificial custard, thrown at people's faces on the stage to make people laugh

ˈcustard ˌpowder *noun* [U] UK a yellowish powder which you combine with milk and sugar to make custard

custodian /kʌsˈtəʊ.di.ən/ [US] /-ˈtoʊ-/ *noun* [C] **1** FORMAL a person with responsibility for protecting or taking care of something or keeping something in good condition: *the custodian* ***of*** *a museum/castle* **2** FORMAL someone who tries to protect particular ideas or principles: *She sees herself as a custodian* ***of*** *the public's morals.* **3** US FOR **caretaker** BUILDING WORKER

custody [CARE] /ˈkʌs.tə.di/ *noun* [U] the legal right or duty to care for someone or something, especially a child after its parents have separated or died: *The court* ***awarded/granted/gave*** *custody* ***of*** *the child to the father.* ○ *The mother* ***got/received*** *custody (****of*** *the child).* ○ *The parents were given* ***joint*** *custody (****of*** *the child).* **custodial** /kʌsˈtəʊ.di.əl/ [US] /-ˈtoʊ-/ *adj*: *custodial care*

custody [PRISON] /ˈkʌs.tə.di/ *noun* [U] the state of being kept in prison, especially while waiting to go to court for trial: *You will be* ***remanded in*** *custody until your trial.*
custodial /kʌsˈtəʊ.di.əl/ [US] /-ˈtoʊ-/ *adj*: **custodial sentence** a period of time that someone must stay in prison

custom [TRADITION] /ˈkʌs.təm/ *noun* [C or U] a way of behaving or a belief which has been established for a long time: *a local/ancient custom* ○ [+ *to* infinitive] *In my country, it's* ***the*** *custom (****for*** *women)* ***to*** *get married in white.* **customary** /ˈkʌs.tə.mᵊr.i/ [US] /-mer-/ *adj* [+ *to* infinitive] *In my village,* ***it*** *is customary* ***for*** *a girl* ***to*** *take her mother's name.*

custom [USUAL ACTIVITY] /ˈkʌs.təm/ *noun* [S] something you usually do: *He left the house at nine exactly,* ***as is*** *his custom.*
customary /ˈkʌs.tə.mᵊr.i/ [US] /-mer-/ *adj*: *She's not her customary* (= usual) *cheerful self today.* **customarily** /kʌs.təˈmer.ɪ.li/ *adv*

custom [TRADE] /ˈkʌs.təm/ *noun* [U] the support given to a business, especially a shop, by the people who buy things or services from it: *Most of our custom comes from tourists nowadays.* ○ *If we don't give good service, people will* ***take*** *their custom* ***elsewhere.***

custom- /kʌs.təm-/ *prefix* used before another word to mean 'specially designed for a particular person or purpose': *custom-designed* ○ *custom-built software*

custom-built /ˌkʌs.təmˈbɪlt/ *adj* If a car, machine, etc. is custom-built, it is made according to the needs of a particular buyer.

customer /ˈkʌs.tə.məʳ/ [US] /-mɚ/ *noun* [C] a person who buys goods or a service: *a satisfied customer* ○ *Mrs. Wilson is one of our* ***regular*** *customers.*
• **The customer is always right.** SAYING said to emphasize that in business, it is very important not to disagree with a customer or make them angry

ˌcustomer ˈservices *plural noun* the part of an organization which answers customers' questions, exchanges goods which have been damaged, etc.

customize, UK USUALLY **-ise** /ˈkʌs.tə.maɪz/ *verb* [T] to make or change something according to the buyer's or user's needs **customized**, UK USUALLY **-ised** /ˈkʌs.tə.maɪzd/ *adj*: *The company specializes in customized computer systems.*

custom-made /ˌkʌs.təmˈmeɪd/ *adj* If an article of clothing is custom-made, it is specially made for a particular buyer: *custom-made shoes*

customs /ˈkʌs.təmz/ *plural noun* the place at a port, airport or border where travellers' bags are looked at to find out if any goods are being carried illegally: *to* ***go through*** *customs*

ˌCustoms and ˈExcise *group noun* [U] a UK government department which collects taxes, especially on goods leaving or entering the country

ˈcustoms ˌofficer *noun* [C] a person whose job is to look inside travellers' bags to make certain they are not taking goods into a country without paying taxes

cut [USE KNIFE] /kʌt/ *verb* [I or T] **cutting, cut, cut** to break the surface of something, or to divide or make something smaller, using a sharp tool, especially a knife: *cut a slice of bread* ○ *I've cut myself/my hand* ***on*** *that glass/****with*** *that knife.* ○ *Cut the meat* ***up*** *into small pieces.* ○ *This knife doesn't cut very well, it's not sharp enough.* ○ *Where did you* ***have*** *your* ***hair cut?*** ○ [+ obj + adj] *Firefighters had to cut the trapped driver* ***loose/free*** (= cut the metal, etc. to allow the driver to get out of the car) *using special equipment.* ○ *He fell off the swing and cut his head* ***open*** (= got a deep cut in his head). ○ *He cut the cake* ***in/into*** *six (pieces) and gave each child a slice.*
• **not be cut out for *sth*** to not be the right type of person for something: *I'm not cut out for an office job.*
• **cut both/two ways** If you say something cuts both/two ways, you think it has both a good and a bad side.
• **cut it/things fine** to allow very little time for something: *She arrived ten minutes before her flight, so she was cutting it* ***a bit*** *fine.*
• **cut a fine figure** (ALSO **cut quite a figure/dash**) OLD-FASHIONED to cause people to admire you because of your appearance: *The young soldier cut a fine figure in his smart new uniform.*
• **cut no ice with *sb*** to not cause someone to change their opinion or decision: *I've heard her excuses and they cut no ice with me.*
• **you could cut the atmosphere with a knife** used to describe a situation in which everyone is feeling very angry or nervous and you feel that something unpleasant could soon happen
• **cut loose** US to behave in an uncontrolled, wild way
• **can't cut it** (ALSO **can't cut the mustard**) US to not be able to deal with problems or difficulties satisfactorily: *If he can't cut it, then we'll get someone else to do the job.*
• **cut off *your* nose to spite *your* face** to do something because you are angry, even if it will cause trouble for you
• **cut (*sb*) to the quick** to greatly hurt someone's feelings: *Her thoughtless remark cut him to the quick.*
• **be cut up** UK to be upset: *Philip was very cut up* ***about*** *his grandmother's death.*
• **cut up rough** UK to become very angry, and often violent
• **cut *sb* some slack** INFORMAL to not judge someone as severely as you usually would because they are having problems at the present time: *"Andrew's late again." "Cut him some slack – his wife's just had a baby."*
• **cut a swathe through *sth*** to destroy a large part of something or kill many of a group of people: *The storm cut a swathe through the village.*
• **You should cut your coat according to your cloth.** UK SAYING said to emphasize that someone should do the best they can with the limited money they have

cut /kʌt/ *noun* **1** [C] an injury made when the skin is cut with something sharp: *a deep cut* **2** [C] a piece of meat cut from a particular part of an animal: *Sirloin is the most expensive cut* ***of*** *beef.* **3** [S] the shape into which something is cut: *I don't like* ***the*** *cut* ***of*** *these jeans.* **4** [S] *INFORMAL* a share of something, usually money: *When am I going to get my cut?*
• **a cut above** someone who is of a higher social class: *She thinks she's a cut above her neighbours.*
• **cut and thrust** lively arguments: *She enjoys the cut and thrust of party politics.*
cutters /ˈkʌt.əz/ [US] /-ɚz/ *plural noun* a tool for cutting something: *wire cutters* ○ *bolt cutters*

cut [REDUCE] /kʌt/ *verb* [T] **cutting, cut, cut** to make something shorter, lower, smaller, etc: *to cut prices/costs* ○ *to cut overtime/wages*
• **cut sb down to size** to show someone that they are not as clever or important as they think they are: *Someone should cut that man down to size!*
• **cut *your* losses** to avoid losing any more money than you have already lost: *Let's cut our losses and sell the business before prices drop even further.*
• **to cut a long story short** to not tell all the details: *To cut a long story short, I got the job.*
cut /kʌt/ *noun* [C] a reduction in the number, amount or rate of something: *a cut* ***in*** *expenditure/interest rates/hospital waiting lists*
cuts /kʌts/ *plural noun* reductions in public spending: *Students and workers were out on the streets protesting against the cuts.*

cut [REMOVE] /kʌt/ *verb* [T] **cutting, cut, cut** to remove something from something else: *The sex scenes had been cut* ***out of*** *the English version of the film.*
• **cut sb out of *your* will** to decide not to leave someone any of your money or possessions when you die, because you are angry with them
• **cut and paste** to move words or pictures from one place to another in a computer document
• **cut the ground from under *sb's* feet** to make someone or their ideas seems less good, especially by doing something before them or better than them
cut /kʌt/ *noun* [C] when a part is removed from a book, film, etc., or a part that is removed: *The film contains some very violent scenes, so some cuts were* ***made*** *when it was shown on television.*

cut [MISS] /kʌt/ *verb* [T] **cutting, cut, cut** *MAINLY US INFORMAL* to not go, especially to a place where you should be: *Your son has been cutting* ***classes***.

cut [STOP SUDDENLY] /kʌt/ *verb* [I or T] **cutting, cut, cut** to stop or interrupt something: *to cut an engine/a motor* ○ *"Cut! (= Stop filming!)" shouted the director.*
• **cut sb short** to stop someone from talking before they have finished what they were saying: *He started to explain, but she cut him short, saying she had to catch a bus.*
• **Cut it/that out!** *INFORMAL* used to tell someone to stop talking or stop behaving in an annoying way: ***Just*** *cut it out! I've had enough of your silly jokes.*
• **Cut the crap!** *OFFENSIVE* a rude way of telling someone to stop saying things that are not true or not important: *Just cut the crap, will you, and tell me where I'm going wrong.*
• **cut sb dead** to pretend you do not know someone in order to show you are angry: *I said "Good Morning" but he just cut me dead.*

cut [GROW TEETH] /kʌt/ *verb* **cut a tooth** (of a baby) to grow a new tooth: *The baby's cutting a tooth. That's why she's crying all the time.*
• **cut *your* political/professional, etc. teeth** to get your first experience of the type mentioned: *The Prime Minister cut her political teeth* ***on*** *student debates.*

cut [CROSS] /kʌt/ *verb* [I usually + adv or prep] **cutting, cut, cut** to go through or across a place, especially in order to get somewhere quickly: *to cut* ***through*** *an alleyway/passage*
• **cut a corner** *UK* to fail to keep to your own side of the road when going round a corner
• **cut corners** to do something in the easiest, cheapest or fastest way

cut [CARDS] /kʌt/ *verb* [I or T] **cutting, cut, cut** to choose a playing card by dividing a pile of cards into two parts: *Who's going to cut the cards?*

cut [RECORD] /kʌt/ *verb* [T] **cutting, cut, cut** to record music or speech on a record: *When did Elvis cut his first record?*

PHRASAL VERBS WITH **cut**

▲ **cut across *sth*** [CROSS] *phrasal verb* to go straight from one side of an area to another instead of going round: *If we cut across the field, it'll save time.*
▲ **cut across *sth*** [AFFECT] *phrasal verb* If a problem or subject cuts across different groups of people, all of those groups are affected by or interested in it: *Support for environmental issues cuts across traditional party lines.*
▲ **cut back/down** *phrasal verb* to do less of something or use something in smaller amounts: *The government has announced plans to cut back* ***on*** *defence spending by 10% next year.* ○ *I'm trying to cut down* ***on*** *caffeine.*
cutback /ˈkʌt.bæk/ *noun* [C] a reduction in something, made in order to save money: *The closure of the Manchester printing factory is the company's biggest single cutback so far.*
▲ **cut *sth* down** *phrasal verb* to make a tree or other plant fall to the ground by cutting it near the bottom
▲ **cut in** [TALK] *phrasal verb* to interrupt what someone is saying by saying something yourself: *I was just talking to Jan, when Dave cut in (****on*** *us/our conversation).*
▲ **cut in** [DRIVE] *phrasal verb* to make a sudden sideways movement to position your car in front of another car, not leaving a safe distance between the two vehicles: *Did you see that white car cut in (****on*** *us/****in front of*** *us)?*
➲See also **cut up** DRIVE BADLY.
▲ **cut in** [DANCE] *phrasal verb* to interrupt two people who are dancing in order to dance with one of them: *She was dancing with Jack, when Tom suddenly cut in.*
▲ **cut *sb* in** [GAME] *phrasal verb* to permit someone to take part in something, for example a game or business: *Shall we cut you in (****on*** *the deal/game)?*
▲ **cut into *sth*** *phrasal verb* If an activity cuts into a period of time, it fills part of it, often a large part of it: *I don't like doing the shopping on a Saturday afternoon because it cuts into my weekend.*
▲ **cut off** [REMOVE] *phrasal verb* [M] to remove a part of something to make it smaller or shorter, using a sharp tool such as a knife: *Remember to cut off the fat before you fry the steak.*
cutoffs /ˈkʌt.ɒfs/ [US] /ˈkʌt̬.ɑːfs/ *plural noun* (*ALSO* **cutoff jeans**) a pair of jeans which has had parts of the legs removed
▲ **cut *sth* off** [STOP] *phrasal verb* [M] to stop providing something such as electricity, supplies, etc: *If this bill is not paid within five days, your gas supply will be cut off.* ○ *The aim was to cut off the enemy's escape route/supplies.*
▲ **cut *sb* off** *phrasal verb* [M] *US* If someone serving drinks in a bar cuts you off, they stop serving you alcoholic drinks because they think you have drunk too many: *I'm glad the bartender cut Tommy off – he's already had too much to drink.*
cutoff /ˈkʌt.ɒf/ [US] /ˈkʌt̬.ɑːf/ *noun* [C] **1** the act of stopping the supply of something: *The US has announced a cutoff* ***of*** *military aid to the country.* **2** a fixed point or level at which you stop including people or things: *March 31 is the cutoff* ***date*** *for applications to be accepted.*
▲ **cut *sb* off** [PHONE] *phrasal verb* [usually passive] to stop people from continuing a telephone conversation by breaking the telephone connection: *We were cut off before she could give me directions.*
▲ **cut *sb/sth* off** [SEPARATE] *phrasal verb* [M] to cause a person or place to become separate, or cause someone to be or feel alone: *When his wife died, he cut himself off* ***from*** *other people.* ○ *Many villages have been cut off* ***by*** *the heavy snow.*
▲ **cut *sth* out** [REMOVE] *phrasal verb* [M] to remove something or form a shape by cutting, usually from paper or cloth: *She cut out his picture from the magazine.*
▲ **cut *sth* out** [STOP EATING] *phrasal verb* [M] to stop eating or drinking something, usually to improve your health: *Since my heart attack, I've cut fatty foods out altogether.*

C

▲ **cut *sb* out** [NOT INCLUDE] *phrasal verb* to not allow someone to share something or be included in something: *They cut me out **of** the conversation.*
▲ **cut out** [STOP WORKING] *phrasal verb* If an engine, machine or piece of equipment cuts out, it suddenly stops working: *One of the plane's engines cut out, so they had to land with only one.*
▲ **cut out** [DRIVE] *phrasal verb US* to make a sudden sideways movement out of a line of traffic: *Don't cut out when everyone is going fast.*
▲ **cut through *sth*** *phrasal verb* If you cut through something difficult that usually causes problems, you quickly understand it or deal with it so that it does not cause problems for you: *She always manages to cut through the complex theory and get at the facts.*
▲ **cut *sth* up** [SEPARATE] *phrasal verb* [M] to cut something into pieces
▲ **cut *sb* up** [DRIVE BADLY] *UK phrasal verb* [M] (*US* **cut *sb* off**) to suddenly move your car sideways in front of another car which was in front of you, leaving too little space: *I **got/was** cut up several times on the motorway this morning – I've never seen such dangerous driving!*
▲ **cut up** [BEHAVE STRANGELY] *phrasal verb US* to behave in a very active and silly way in order to make people laugh: *I hate it when Jane cuts up in class.*
cutup /ˈkʌt.ʌp/ [US] /ˈkʌt̬-/ *noun* [C] *US* someone who behaves in an active and silly way in order to make people laugh: *It's hard to believe Sally was a cutup in school – she's so quiet now.*

ˌcut and ˈdried *adj* already decided and unlikely to be changed: *We need a cut-and-dried decision by the end of the week.*

cute [CHARMING] /kjuːt/ *adj* **1** (especially of something or someone small or young) charming and attractive: *He's got a really cute baby brother.* **2** *MAINLY US* sexually attractive **cutely** /ˈkjuːt.li/ *adv* **cuteness** /ˈkjuːt.nəs/ *noun* [U]

cute [CLEVER] /kjuːt/ *adj US* wishing to seem clever, sometimes in a rude or unpleasant way: *Don't be cute with me, Vicki.*

cutesy /ˈkjuːt.si/ *adj INFORMAL DISAPPROVING* artificially attractive and charming, especially in a childish way: *She sent me one of those awful birthday cards with a cutesy kitten on it.*

ˌcut ˈglass *noun* [U] glass with a decorative pattern cut into the surface: *a cut-glass bowl*

cuticle /ˈkjuː.tɪ.kl̩/ [US] /-t̬ɪ-/ *noun* [C] the thin skin at the base of the nails on the fingers and toes

cutie, cutey /ˈkjuː.ti/ [US] /-t̬i/ *noun* [C] (*ALSO* **cutiepie**) *MAINLY US INFORMAL* a woman or girl whom you consider attractive or feel affection for: *His daughter is a real cutie.* ○ [as form of address] *Hi there, cutie, we were just talking about you.*

cutlass /ˈkʌt.ləs/ *noun* [C] a curved sword with a single sharp edge, especially as used in the past by PIRATES

cutlery *UK* /ˈkʌt.lə.ri/ [US] /-lɚ.i/ *noun* [U] (*US USUALLY* **silverware**) knives, forks and spoons used for eating food ➲Compare **crockery**.

cutlet [PIECE OF MEAT] /ˈkʌt.lət/ *noun* [C] a small piece of meat still joined to the bone, especially from the animal's neck or ribs: ***lamb** cutlets*

cutlet [SAVOURY FOOD] /ˈkʌt.lət/ *noun* [C] small pieces of vegetables, nuts, fish or meat which have been pressed into a round flat shape: *a **nut** cutlet*

ˌcut ˈlunch *noun* [C] *AUS FOR* **packed lunch**

cutout [SHAPE] /ˈkʌt.aʊt/ [US] /ˈkʌt̬-/ *noun* [C] a shape that has been cut out from something, especially a flat one that can stand vertically: *a life-size cutout **of** the president*

cutout [SAFETY DEVICE] /ˈkʌt.aʊt/ [US] /ˈkʌt̬-/ *noun* [C] a device which, for safety reasons, stops or interrupts a circuit, used, for example, in a motor or engine: *a cutout **fuse/switch***

cut-price /ˌkʌtˈpraɪs/ *adj* [before n] **1** describes something that costs less than its usual price: *cut-price airline tickets* **2** A cut-price shop sells things at lower prices than other shops.

cut-rate /ˈkʌt.reɪt/ *adj* [before n] charged at a lower rate than usual: *We get cut-rate electricity for six hours each night.*

cut-throat *MAINLY UK* /ˈkʌt.θrəʊt/ [US] /-θroʊt/ *adj* (*US ALSO* **cutthroat**) fierce; not involving consideration or care about any harm caused to others: *the cut-throat **world** of journalism* ○ *The advertising world can be a very cut-throat **business**.*

ˌcut-throat ˈrazor *UK noun* [C] (*US* **straight razor**) a type of old-fashioned razor with a long blade that folds out from the handle

cutting [ARTICLE] /ˈkʌt.ɪŋ/ [US] /ˈkʌt̬-/ *noun* [C] (*US ALSO* **clipping**) an article which has been cut from a newspaper or magazine

cutting [PLANT] /ˈkʌt.ɪŋ/ [US] /ˈkʌt̬-/ *noun* [C] a piece cut off from a plant which can be used to grow another plant of the same type in a different place

cutting [PASSAGE] /ˈkʌt.ɪŋ/ [US] /ˈkʌt̬-/ *noun* [C] (*US* **cut**) a deep narrow passage made through a hill for a road, railway or canal

cutting [UNKIND] /ˈkʌt.ɪŋ/ [US] /ˈkʌt̬-/ *adj* unkind and intending to upset someone: *a cutting remark/comment* ○ *He can be very cutting when he chooses to be!*

the ˌcutting ˈedge *noun* [S] the most recent stage of development in a particular type of work or activity: *a company **at** the cutting edge **of** mobile communications technology*
cutting-edge /ˌkʌt.ɪŋˈedʒ/ [US] /ˌkʌt̬-/ *adj* [before n] very modern and with all the newest features: *cutting-edge design/technology*

cuttlefish /ˈkʌt.l̩.fɪʃ/ [US] /ˈkʌt̬-/ *noun* [C] *plural* **cuttlefish** or **cuttlefishes** a sea animal with eight arms and two TENTACLES, which has a wide flattened shell inside its body, and lives in coastal waters near the bottom of the sea

CV /ˌsiːˈviː/ *noun* [C] **1** *MAINLY UK* (*US USUALLY* **résumé**) a short written description of your education, qualifications, previous employment and sometimes also your personal interests, which you send to an employer when you are trying to get a job; CURRICULUM VITAE **2** *US* a written description of the previous employment of someone who is looking for a job at a college or university: *Applicants interested in applying for the position should submit their CVs to the Anatomy Department no later than February 15.*

cwt *WRITTEN ABBREVIATION FOR* **hundredweight**

cyan /ˈsaɪ.ən/ *adj, noun* [U] (of) a deep greenish blue colour, one of the three main colours that are used in colour printing and photography

cyanide /ˈsaɪə.naɪd/ *noun* [U] an extremely powerful poison

cyber- /saɪ.bər-/ [US] /-bɚ-/ *prefix* involving, using or relating to computers, especially the Internet: *cybercrime* ○ *cyberculture*

cybercafé /ˈsaɪ.bəˌkæf.eɪ/ [US] /-bɚ-/ *noun* [C] a small informal restaurant where you can pay to use the Internet

cyberfraud /ˈsaɪ.bə.frɔːd/ [US] /-bɚ.frɑːd/ *noun* [U] when someone uses the Internet to obtain money or goods, etc. from people illegally by deceiving them

cybernetics /ˌsaɪ.bəˈnet.ɪks/ [US] /-bɚˈnet̬-/ *noun* [U] the scientific study of how information is communicated in machines and electronic devices in comparison with how information is communicated in the brain and nervous system

cyberpet /ˈsaɪ.bə.pet/ [US] /-bɚ-/ *noun* [C] (*TRADEMARK* **Tamagotchi**) an electronic toy that behaves like a pet

cyberpunk /ˈsaɪ.bə.pʌŋk/ [US] /-bɚ-/ *noun* [U] *US* literature about an imaginary society controlled by computers: *cyberpunk science fiction*

cybersex /ˈsaɪ.bə.seks/ [US] /-bɚ-/ *noun* [U] any sexual entertainment or activity that involves using the Internet

cyberspace /ˈsaɪ.bə.speɪs/ [US] /-bɚ-/ *noun* [U] *INFORMAL* the Internet considered as an imaginary area without limits where you can meet people and discover information about any subject: *You can find the answer to almost any question in cyberspace.*

C

cybersquatting /ˈsaɪ.bəˌskwɒt.ɪŋ/ [US] /-bɚˌskwɑː.t̬ɪŋ/ *noun* [U] when someone pays to officially take a famous name as an Internet address, so that they can later sell it for a high price to the person or organization with that name **cybersquat** /ˈsaɪ.bə.skwɒt/ [US] /-bɚ.skwɑːt/ *verb* [I] **cybersquatter** /ˈsaɪ.bəˌskwɒt.əʳ/ [US] /-bɚˌskwɑː.t̬ɚ/ *noun* [C]

cyberterrorism /ˈsaɪ.bəˌter.ə.rɪ.zəm/ [US] /-bɚˌter.ɚ.ɪ-/ *noun* [U] when people use the Internet to damage or destroy computer systems for political or other reasons **cyberterrorist** /ˈsaɪ.bəˌter.ə.rɪst/ [US] /-bɚˌter.ɚ.ɪst/ *noun* [C] someone who takes part in cyberterrorism: *Unidentified cyberterrorists gained access to e-mails and financial details of customers.*

cybrary /ˈsaɪ.brə.ri/ *noun* [C] a collection of pieces of writing, images, etc., often relating to literature or educational subjects, that can be accessed on the Internet **cybrarian** /saɪˈbreə.ri.ən/ [US] /saɪˈbre-/ *noun* [C] a person who creates and is responsible for a cybrary, or a person who works in a library and uses the Internet and computers as part of their job

cyclamen /ˈsɪk.lə.mən/ *noun* [C] a small plant with white, pink, purple or red flowers whose petals turn backwards, and which has green and silver leaves

cycle [BICYCLE] /ˈsaɪ.kl̩/ *noun* [C] a bicycle **cycle** /ˈsaɪ.kl̩/ *verb* [I] to ride a bicycle **cycling** /ˈsaɪ.klɪŋ/ *noun* [U] *We did a lot of cycling in France last year.* **cyclist** /ˈsaɪ.klɪst/ *noun* [C] someone who rides a bicycle

cycle [SERIES] /ˈsaɪ.kl̩/ *noun* [C] **1** a group of events which happen in a particular order, one following the other, and which are often repeated: *the life cycle of a moth* **2** one in a series of movements that a machine performs: *the spin cycle* **cyclical** /ˈsaɪ.klɪ.kəl/ /ˈsɪk.lɪ-/ *adj* (*ALSO* **cyclic**) *Changes in the economy have followed a cyclical pattern.*

cycle [PLAYS/POEMS] /ˈsaɪ.kl̩/ *group noun* [C] a group of plays, poems, etc. written by one person and connected with each other by dealing with the same characters or ideas: *It's one in a cycle of plays that are being performed on successive evenings.*

ˈcycle ˌclips *plural noun* thin straps which you wear around the bottom of your trousers when you are riding a bicycle to prevent the trousers from becoming caught in the bicycle's chain

ˈcycle ˌhelmet *noun* [C] (*ALSO* **cycling helmet**) a hard hat which you wear on your head to protect it if you have an accident while you are riding a bicycle

ˈcycle ˌlane/ˌpath *noun* [C] *UK* a part of the road or a special path for the use of people riding bicycles

ˈcycle ˌrack *UK noun* [C] (*US* **bike rack**) a row of holders where bicycles can be left

ˈcycling ˌshorts *plural noun* (*ALSO* **cycle shorts**) short tight trousers worn by people involved in cycling sports

cyclone /ˈsaɪ.kləʊn/ [US] /-kloʊn/ *noun* [C] a violent tropical storm or wind in which the air moves very fast in a circular direction

Cyclops /ˈsaɪ.klɒps/ [US] /-klɑːps/ *noun* in ancient Greek stories, a GIANT (= extremely tall creature) with one eye

cygnet /ˈsɪg.nət/ *noun* [C] a young SWAN (= large white bird with a long neck)

cylinder [SHAPE] /ˈsɪl.ɪn.dəʳ/ [US] /-dɚ/ *noun* [C] a solid or hollow tube with long straight sides and two equal-sized circular ends, or an object shaped like this, often used as a container: *Deep-sea divers carry cylinders* (= containers) *of oxygen on their backs.* **cylindrical** /sɪˈlɪn.drɪ.kəl/ *adj* having the shape of a cylinder

cylinder [ENGINE PART] /ˈsɪl.ɪn.dəʳ/ [US] /-dɚ/ *noun* [C] the tube-shaped device, found especially in an engine, inside which the part of the engine which causes the fuel to produce power moves up and down: *a six-cylinder engine*

cymbal /ˈsɪm.bəl/ *noun* [C usually pl] a flat round musical instrument made of brass, which makes a loud noise when hit with a stick or against another cymbal

cynic /ˈsɪn.ɪk/ *noun* [C] *DISAPPROVING* a person who believes that people are only interested in themselves and are not sincere: *I'm too much of a cynic to believe that he'll keep his promise.* ○ *A cynic might say that the government has only taken this measure because it is concerned about its declining popularity.* **cynicism** /ˈsɪn.ɪ.sɪ.zəm/ *noun* [U] *He's often been accused of cynicism in his attitude towards politics.*

cynical /ˈsɪn.ɪ.kəl/ *adj DISAPPROVING* **1** believing that people are only interested in themselves and are not sincere: *I think she takes a rather cynical* ***view*** *of men.* ○ *I've always been* ***deeply*** *cynical* ***about*** *politicians.* **2** describes a tendency to use someone's feelings or emotions to your own advantage: *She works in that most cynical of industries – advertising.* ○ *He praises my cooking but it's just a cynical ploy to get me to make his meals.* **cynically** /ˈsɪn.ɪ.kli/ *adv*

cynosure /ˈsaɪ.nə.sjʊəʳ/ [US] /-ʃʊr/ *noun* [C] *LITERARY* a person or thing having a quality of excellence or great beauty which attracts a lot of attention

cypher /ˈsaɪ.fəʳ/ [US] /-fɚ/ *noun* [C or U] *ANOTHER SPELLING OF* **cipher** SECRET LANGUAGE

cypress /ˈsaɪ.prəs/ *noun* [C] a type of CONIFER (= evergreen tree)

Cyrillic /sɪˈrɪl.ɪk/ *adj, noun* [U] (written in, or relating to) the alphabet used in some Slavonic languages, such as Russian

cyst /sɪst/ *noun* [C] a round growth, just under the skin or deeper in the body, which contains liquid: *He had a cyst removed from near his eye.*

cystic fibrosis /ˌsɪs.tɪk.faɪˈbrəʊ.sɪs/ [US] /-ˈbroʊ-/ *noun* [U] a serious disease which causes blockages in the lungs and other organs, such as the liver and the PANCREAS

cystitis /sɪˈstaɪ.tɪs/ [US] /-t̬ɪs/ *noun* [U] a disease, especially of women, in which the bladder becomes infected and there is pain when urinating

cytology /saɪˈtɒl.ə.dʒi/ [US] /-ˈtɑː.lə-/ *noun* [U] the scientific study of cells from living things

cytoplasm /ˈsaɪ.təʊ.plæz.əm/ [US] /-t̬ə-/ *noun* [U] *SPECIALIZED* the substance inside a cell which surrounds the cell's nucleus

czar /zɑːʳ/ [US] /zɑːr/ *noun* [C] *MAINLY US FOR* **tsar**

D

D LETTER (*plural* **D's** or **Ds**), **d** (*plural* **d's** or **ds**) /diː/ *noun* [C] the 4th letter of the English alphabet

D NUMBER, **d** /diː/ *noun* [C] the sign used in the Roman system for the number 500

D MUSIC /diː/ *noun* [C or U] *plural* **D's** or **Ds** a note in Western music: *in (the key of) D*

d. ABBREVIATION FOR died: used when giving the dates of someone's birth and death: *John Winston Lennon (b. 9 October 1940, Liverpool, d. 8 December 1980, New York).*

'd /əd/ *short form of* **1** would: *I asked if she'd like to come tonight.* **2** had: *If you'd told me what was wrong I could have helped.*

DA /ˌdiːˈeɪ/ *noun* [C] *US ABBREVIATION FOR* **district attorney**

dab /dæb/ *verb* [I or T] **-bb-** to touch something with quick light touches, or to put a substance on something with quick light touches: *She dabbed at her eyes with a tissue.* ○ *She dabbed a little perfume behind her ears.*

dab /dæb/ *noun* [C] a small amount of a substance, or a light touch: *Can't you just put a dab of paint over the mark and cover it up?* ○ *I'll give that stain a quick dab with a wet cloth.*

dabble TRY /ˈdæb.l̩/ *verb* [I] to take a slight and not very serious interest in a subject, or try a particular activity for a short period: *He first dabbled in politics when he was at law school.* ○ *She dabbled with drugs at university.* **dabbler** /ˈdæb.lə[r]/ ⓤ /-lɚ/ *noun* [C]

dabble MOVE IN WATER /ˈdæb.l̩/ *verb* [T] to put part of your body, such as your hand or foot, into the water of a pool or stream, etc. and move it about

dab hand *noun* [C] *UK INFORMAL* someone who is very good at a particular activity: *Binns was a dab hand at cricket and played for his county in his youth.* ○ *Carlo's a dab hand in the kitchen* (= good at cooking), *isn't he?*

dachshund /ˈdæk.sᵊnd/ ⓤ /ˈdɑːks.hʊnd/ *noun* [C] (*INFORMAL* **sausage dog**, *US INFORMAL* **wiener dog**) a small dog with a long body and short legs

Dacron /ˈdæk.rɒn/ ⓤ /-rɑːn/ *noun* [U] *US TRADEMARK* (cloth made from) an artificial fibre

dad /dæd/ *noun* [C] *INFORMAL* a father: *It was lovely to see your mum and dad at the school concert last night.* ○ [as form of address] *Can you give me a lift back from the cinema tonight, Dad?*

daddy /ˈdæd.i/ *noun* [C] a word for 'father', used especially by children: *Mummy and Daddy are taking me to the circus on Saturday.*

daddy longlegs /ˌdæd.iˈlɒŋ.legz/ ⓤ /-ˈlɑːŋ-/ *noun* [C] *plural* **daddy longlegs** *INFORMAL FOR* **crane fly**

dado rail /ˈdeɪ.dəʊ.reɪl/ ⓤ /-doʊ-/ *noun* [C] a long thin piece of decorative wood fixed about one metre above the floor along all the walls of a room

daffodil /ˈdæf.ə.dɪl/ *noun* [C] a yellow bell-shaped flower with a long stem which is commonly seen in the spring ⊃See picture **Flowers and Plants** on page Centre 3

daffy /ˈdæf.i/ *adj INFORMAL* strange or unusual, sometimes in an amusing way

daft /dɑːft/ ⓤ /dæft/ *adj INFORMAL* silly or stupid: *You daft idiot!* ○ *It was a pretty daft idea anyway.* ○ *Don't be daft – let me pay – you paid last time.*
● **be (as) daft as a brush** *UK INFORMAL* to be very silly: *He's a nice enough boy, but he's as daft as a brush.*

dag /dæg/ *noun* [C] *AUS INFORMAL* a person who looks unattractive or who behaves in an unattractive way

dagger /ˈdæg.ə[r]/ ⓤ /-ɚ/ *noun* [C] a short pointed knife which is sharp on both sides, used especially in the past as a weapon
● **(at) daggers drawn** If two people, countries, etc. are at daggers drawn, they are in a state of extreme unfriendliness and do not trust each other: *The two sides have been at daggers drawn for some months now with no sign of improvement in relations.*

daggy /ˈdæg.i/ *adj AUS INFORMAL* (of a person or their clothes) untidy or dirty

dago /ˈdeɪ.gəʊ/ ⓤ /-goʊ/ *noun* [C] *plural* **dagoes** or **dagos** OFFENSIVE a person from Spain, Portugal, Italy or South America

daguerreotype /dəˈger.ə.taɪp/ *noun* [C] the first successfully produced type of photograph

dahlia /ˈdeɪ.li.ə/ ⓤ /ˈdeɪl.jə/ *noun* [C] a brightly coloured garden flower with long thin petals in a circular or ball-like shape

the Dáil /ðəˈdɔɪl/ *noun* [S] one of the two law-making bodies which together make up the parliament in the Republic of Ireland

daily EVERY DAY /ˈdeɪ.li/ *adv, adj* happening on or relating to every day: *Take the tablets twice daily.* ○ *Exercise has become part of my daily routine.* ○ *We back up our computer files at work on a daily basis.* ○ *She's looking forward to retiring and ending the daily grind* (= hard, boring work or duty) *of working in an office.*

daily PERSON /ˈdeɪ.li/ *noun* [C] *UK OLD-FASHIONED INFORMAL* a person who is employed to clean someone else's home

daily bread *noun* [U] *INFORMAL* the money you need to pay for essential things, such as food

daily (paper) *noun* [C] a newspaper which is published every day of the week except Sunday: *UK The story was covered in all the national dailies.*

dainty /ˈdeɪn.ti/ ⓤ /-t̬i/ *adj* small and graceful: *She was a small, dainty child, unlike her sister who was large and had big feet.* ○ *We were given tea, and some dainty little cakes.* **daintily** /ˈdeɪn.tɪ.li/ ⓤ /-t̬ɪ-/ *adv: She skipped daintily down the street, holding her father's hand.* ○ *He handed round a plate of tiny sandwiches, daintily arranged in rings.* **daintiness** /ˈdeɪn.tɪ.nəs/ ⓤ /-t̬ɪ-/ *noun* [U]

daiquiri /ˈdæk.ɪ.ri/ ⓤ /-ɚ.i/ *noun* [C or U] an alcoholic drink made with RUM, lime juice, sugar and ice

dairy /ˈdeə.ri/ ⓤ /ˈder.i/ *noun* [C] a place on a farm where milk and cream are kept and cheese and butter are made, or a company which supplies milk and products made from milk

dairy /ˈdeə.ri/ ⓤ /ˈder.i/ *adj* used to refer to cows that are used for producing milk, rather than meat, or to foods which are made from milk, such as cream, butter and cheese: *dairy cattle* ○ *dairy farmers* ○ *dairy products*

dairy farm *noun* [C] (*US ALSO* **dairy**) a farm which only produces milk and products made from milk

dais /ˈdeɪ.ɪs/ /deɪs/ *noun* [C] a raised surface at one end of a meeting room which someone can stand on when speaking to a group

daisy /ˈdeɪ.zi/ *noun* [C] a small flower with white petals and a yellow centre, which often grows in grass ⊃See picture **Flowers and Plants** on page Centre 3

the Dalai Lama /ðəˌdæl.aɪˈlɑː.mə/ *noun* [S] the leader of the Tibetan Buddhist religion

dale /deɪl/ *noun* [C] **1** *LITERARY OR NORTHERN ENGLISH* a valley **2 the (Yorkshire) Dales** an area of northern England in which there are a lot of hills and valleys

dalliance RELATIONSHIP /ˈdæl.i.ənts/ *noun* [C or U] *MAINLY HUMOROUS* (involvement in) a short sexual relationship with someone for whom your feelings are not lasting or strong

dalliance INVOLVEMENT /ˈdæl.i.ənts/ *noun* [C or U] an interest or involvement in an activity or belief which only lasts for a very short period: *The 1970s witnessed the first of the pop-star's dalliances with communism.*

dally /ˈdæl.i/ *verb* [I] *OLD-FASHIONED* to waste time or do something slowly ⊃See also **dillydally**.

PHRASAL VERBS WITH **dally** ▼

▲ **dally with** *sb* ROMANCE *phrasal verb* (*ALSO* **dally with** *sb's* **affections**) to be romantically or sexually involved with someone, usually for a short time, without really caring for them: *It's cruel the way she just dallies with his affections.*

▲ **dally with** *sth* IDEAS *phrasal verb* to consider or imagine an idea, subject or plan, but not in a serious way: *He had occasionally dallied with the idea of starting his own business, but he had never actually done anything about it.*

dalmatian /dælˈmeɪ.ʃᵊn/ *noun* [C] a big dog with short white fur and dark spots

dam /dæm/ *noun* [C] a wall built across a river which stops the river's flow and collects the water, especially to make a RESERVOIR (= an artificial lake) which provides water for an area: *The Aswan High Dam is on the river Nile in Egypt.* ➲Compare **dyke** WALL.

dam /dæm/ *verb* [T] **-mm-** to build a dam across a river in order to store the water

▲ **dam *sth* up** *phrasal verb* [M] to build a dam across a river in order to store water

damage /ˈdæm.ɪdʒ/ *verb* [T] to harm or spoil something: *Many buildings were badly damaged during the war.* ○ *It was a political scandal which damaged a lot of reputations.*

damage /ˈdæm.ɪdʒ/ *noun* [U] harm or injury: *Strong winds had caused serious damage **to** the roof.* ○ *Recent discoveries about corruption have **done** serious damage **to** the company's reputation.* ○ *The doctors were worried that he might have suffered **brain** damage.*

damaged /ˈdæm.ɪdʒd/ *adj* harmed or spoilt: *They're selling off damaged goods at reduced prices.* ○ *Both the cars involved in the accident looked badly damaged.*

damaging /ˈdæm.ɪ.dʒɪŋ/ *adj* causing harm: *Many chemicals have a damaging **effect** on the environment.* ○ *These are very damaging allegations.*

• **What's the damage?** *INFORMAL HUMOROUS* used to ask how much something has cost you

• **the damage is done** said to mean that it is too late to improve a bad situation: *I didn't even know I'd offended her till Colin told me and then it was too late – the damage was done.*

ˈdamage limiˌtation *noun* [U] the process of limiting the damaging effects of an action or mistake, or the attempt in war to use careful planning to avoid unnecessary death: *The government is involved in a damage limitation **exercise** to minimize the effects of the scandal.*

damages /ˈdæm.ɪ.dʒɪz/ *plural noun LEGAL* money which is paid to someone by a person or organization who has been responsible for causing them some injury or loss: *The politician was **awarded** £50 000 damages over false allegations made by the newspaper.* ○ *The police have been ordered to **pay** substantial damages to the families of the two dead boys.*

damask /ˈdæm.əsk/ *noun* [U] a type of heavy cloth which has a pattern woven into it that is the same colour as the background: *a white damask tablecloth*

dame [WOMAN] /deɪm/ *noun* [C] *US OLD-FASHIONED SLANG* a woman

Dame [TITLE] /deɪm/ *noun* [C] a title used in front of a woman's name which is given in Britain as a special honour, usually for valuable work done over a long period, or a woman having this honour: *Dame Judy Dench* ➲Compare **knight**.

dame [CHARACTER] /deɪm/ *noun* [C] *UK* the amusing character of an older woman in a PANTOMIME (= musical play for children) who is usually played by a man

damn [EXPRESSION] /dæm/ *exclamation* (*ALSO* **damn it,** *ALSO* **dammit**) *INFORMAL* an expression of anger or annoyance: *Damn, I've spilt coffee down my blouse!* ➲See also **goddamn**.

• **not give/care a damn** *INFORMAL* used as a way of saying you do not care about something, especially the annoying things that someone else is doing or saying: *He can think what he likes about me – I don't give a damn!*

damn /dæm/ *adj* [before n] (*ALSO* **damned**) *INFORMAL* used to express anger or annoyance with someone or something: *Damn **fool**!*

damn /dæm/ *verb INFORMAL* **damn you/them/it/etc.** used to express anger or annoyance with someone or something: *You got the last ticket – damn you, I wanted that!*

• **I'm damned if** *INFORMAL* used to say that you will certainly not do something: *I'm polite to his ex-wife when I meet her, but I'm damned if I'm going to invite her round for dinner.*

• **(Well) I'll be damned!** *INFORMAL* an expression of complete surprise: *She's marrying a man who she met two months ago? - Well, I'll be damned!*

damnable /ˈdæm.nə.bl̩/ *adj OLD-FASHIONED INFORMAL* very annoying: *This damnable car! It just won't start on cold mornings!* **damnably** /ˈdæm.nə.bli/ *adv*

damnedest /ˈdæm.dɪst/ *noun INFORMAL* **do *your* damnedest** to try very hard: *I don't know if I'll succeed, but I'll do my damnedest.*

damnedest /ˈdæm.dɪst/ *adj* [before n] *MAINLY US* very surprising or unusual: *Well that's the damnedest excuse I've ever heard!*

damn [VERY] /dæm/ *adv INFORMAL* used, especially when you are annoyed, to mean 'very': *He **knew** damn **well** how much trouble it would cause.* ○ *Next time he can damn **well** do it himself!* ○ *You were damn lucky not to have been killed!*

• **damn all** *UK INFORMAL* nothing: *I know damn all about computers.*

damn [BLAME] /dæm/ *verb* [T] to blame or strongly criticize something or someone: *The inquiry into the disaster damns the company **for** its lack of safety precautions.*

• **damned if *you* do and damned if *you* don't** used to say that you cannot escape being criticized, whatever you decide to do

• **damn *sb* with faint praise** to praise someone so slightly that it suggests you do not really admire them

damning /ˈdæm.ɪŋ/ *adj* describes a report, finding, remark, etc. which is very critical or which shows clearly that someone is wrong, guilty or has behaved very badly: *He made some fairly damning remarks about the government's refusal to deal with the problem.* ○ *The two men were convicted on some extremely damning **evidence**.*

damn [PUNISH] /dæm/ *verb* [T usually passive] (especially of God) to force someone to stay in hell and be punished forever: *As a child she was taught that she would be damned for her sins.*

damnation /dæmˈneɪ.ʃᵊn/ *noun* [U] the act of sending someone to hell or the state of being in hell: *He believed that he would be condemned to **eternal** damnation for what he had done.*

the damned /ðəˈdæmd/ *plural noun* the people who have been sent to hell after their death

Damocles /ˈdæm.ə.kliːz/ *noun* ➲See **sword of Damocles** at **sword**.

damp /dæmp/ *adj* slightly wet, especially in a way that is not pleasant or comfortable: *The grass is still damp.* ○ *This shirt still feels a bit damp.* ○ *It was a damp, misty morning.*

damp /dæmp/ *noun* [U] *UK* when something is slightly wet: *Is that a patch of damp on the wall?* ○ *The whole house smells of damp.*

dampen /ˈdæm.pən/ *verb* [T] **1** (*ALSO* **damp**) to make something slightly wet: *Rain had dampened the tent so we left it to dry in the afternoon sun.* **2** to make feelings, especially of excitement or enjoyment, less strong: *Nothing you can say will dampen her **enthusiasm**.* ○ *I didn't want to dampen his **spirits**.*

dampness /ˈdæmp.nəs/ *noun* [U] (*UK ALSO* **damp**) when something is slightly wet: *It's the dampness in the air that is bad for your lungs.*

damp /dæmp/ *verb*

PHRASAL VERBS WITH **damp**

▲ **damp *sth* down** [FIRE] *phrasal verb* [M] to make a fire burn more slowly: *Water was pumped from a nearby lake in an attempt to damp down the flames.*

▲ **damp *sth* down** [FEELING] *phrasal verb* [M] to make a strong feeling be felt less strongly: *He had tried to damp down speculation about the state of his marriage.*

ˈdamp ˌcourse *noun* [C] (*ALSO* **damp-proof course**) *UK* a layer of material which is put in the bottom of a wall in order to stop water rising through the bricks

damper /ˈdæm.pəʳ/ [US] /-pɚ/ *noun INFORMAL* **put a damper/dampener on *sth*** to stop an occasion from being enjoyable: *Both the kids were ill while we were in Boston, so that rather put a damper on things.*

ˌdamp ˈsquib *noun* [C] *UK* an event which is not as exciting or popular as people thought it would be: *After all that media attention, the whole event turned out to be* *a bit of a damp squib, with very few people attending.*

damsel /ˈdæm.zᵊl/ *noun* [C] *OLD USE* a young woman who is not married

• **a damsel in distress** *HUMOROUS* a young woman who is in trouble and needs a man's help

damson /ˈdæm.zᵊn/ *noun* [C] the sour dark-blue fruit of a type of PLUM tree: *damson jam*

dance /dɑːnts/ [US] /dænts/ *verb* **1** [I or T] to move the body and feet to music: *We danced all night.* ○ *We* ***went*** *dancing at a nightclub.* ○ *What sort of music do you like dancing* ***to****?* ○ *Who was she dancing* ***with*** *at the party last night?* ○ *Can you dance the tango?* **2** [I] *LITERARY* to move quickly and lightly: *The daffodils were dancing in the breeze.* ○ *She watched the sunlight dancing on the water's surface.*

• **dance attendance on *sb*** *UK* to do everything that someone asks you to and treat them as if they are special: *I can't stand the way she has to have someone dancing attendance on her the whole time.*

• **be dancing in the streets** *INFORMAL* to be extremely happy about something that has happened: *Few people will be dancing in the streets* ***about*** *a two per cent pay rise.*

• **dance to *sb's* tune** to do what someone wants

dance /dɑːnts/ [US] /dænts/ *noun* **1** [C] when you move your feet and body to music: *We* ***had a*** *dance.* ○ *a dance* ***class*** **2** [C] a particular series of movements which you perform to music or the type of music which is connected with it: *The band played a slow dance.* **3** [C] a social occasion at which people dance, especially a formal occasion in a large room: *They're having an end-of-term dinner-dance.* **4** [U] the art of performing dances, especially as a form of entertainment: *The performers tell the story through song and dance.*

dancer /ˈdɑːnt.səʳ/ [US] /ˈdænt.sɚ/ *noun* [C] someone who dances either as a job or for pleasure: *He's a dancer in the Royal Ballet.* ○ *I never knew you were such a good dancer.*

ˈdance ˌfloor *noun* [C] an area of a DISCO, restaurant, etc. which is specially for dancing: *Have you seen him* ***on*** *the dance floor* (= dancing)*?*

ˈdance ˌhall *noun* [C] especially in the past, a special building or large room for dancing in

ˈdance ˌstudio *noun* [C] a place where people can pay for dance classes

ˌD and ˈC *noun* [C] *SPECIALIZED ABBREVIATION FOR* dilatation and curettage: an operation in which the inside surface of a woman's womb is removed for medical reasons

dandelion /ˈdæn.dɪ.laɪ.ən/ [US] /-də-/ *noun* [C] a common small bright-yellow wild flower which has a lot of long thin petals arranged in a circular pattern around a round centre: *The children took turns blowing the dandelion* ***clock*** (= the mass of white threads to which the seeds are attached). ➲See picture **Flowers and Plants** on page Centre 3

dandle /ˈdæn.dḷ/ *verb* [T] *OLD-FASHIONED* to hold a baby or child on your knee and move it up and down in a playful way

dandruff /ˈdæn.drʌf/ [US] /-drəf/ *noun* [U] small white bits of dead skin from the head which gather in the hair or fall on the clothes

dandy [MAN] /ˈdæn.di/ *noun* [C] a man, especially in the past, who dressed in expensive, fashionable clothes and was very interested in his own appearance: *an upper-class dandy*

dandified /ˈdæn.dɪ.faɪd/ [US] /-də-/ *adj* looking like a dandy: *An embroidered silk waistcoat contributed to his dandified appearance.*

dandy [GOOD] /ˈdæn.di/ *adj* (*ALSO* **jim-dandy**) *US OLD-FASHIONED* very good: *"Shall we meet at six?" "Sure, that's just dandy."*

danger /ˈdeɪn.dʒəʳ/ [US] /-dʒɚ/ *noun* **1** [C or U] the possibility of harm or death to someone: *Danger! Keep out!* ○ *He drove so fast that I really felt my life was* ***in*** *danger.* ○ *The doctors say he is now* ***out of*** *danger* (= is not expected to die although he has been extremely ill). ○ *the dangers of rock-climbing* **2 danger of *sth*** the possibility that something bad will happen: *If there's any danger of seeing Gary at the party, I'm not going.* ○ *If he carries on like this he's* ***in*** *danger* ***of*** *losing his job.* **3** [C] something or someone that may harm you: *Icy roads are a danger* ***to*** *drivers.* ○ *The judge described him as a danger* ***to*** *society.*

• **There's no danger of that!** *HUMOROUS* said to mean that something definitely will not happen: *"Bye – don't work too hard!" "There's no danger of that!"*

ˈdanger ˌlist *noun* **be on/off the danger list** to be expected/no longer expected to die from serious injury or illness

ˈdanger ˌmoney *UK noun* [U] (*US* **hazardous-duty pay**) extra money that is paid to someone because their job is dangerous

dangerous /ˈdeɪn.dʒᵊr.əs/ [US] /-dʒɚ-/ *adj* describes a person, animal or activity that could harm you: *dangerous chemicals* ○ *I've never played ice hockey – it's far too dangerous.* ○ [+ to infinitive] ***It's*** *dangerous* ***to*** *take more than the recommended dose of tablets.* **dangerously** /ˈdeɪn.dʒᵊr.ə.sli/ [US] /-dʒɚ-/ *adv*: *She drives dangerously.* ○ *He likes to* ***live*** *dangerously.* ➲See also **endanger**.

dangle /ˈdæŋ.gḷ/ *verb* **1** [I or T] to hang loosely, or to hold something so that it hangs loosely: *Loose electric wires were dangling* ***from*** *the wall.* ○ *He dangled the puppet in front of the children.* **2** [T] to offer someone something that they want in order to persuade them to do something: *I've tried dangling all sorts of offers* ***before*** *him/****in front of*** *him to get him to work harder at school, but nothing works.*

dangly /ˈdæŋ.gli/ *adj* hanging loosely: *dangly* ***earrings***

Danish /ˈdeɪ.nɪʃ/ *adj* from, belonging to or relating to Denmark

Danish /ˈdeɪ.nɪʃ/ *noun* [U] the language of Denmark

ˌDanish ˈpastry *noun* [C] (*US USUALLY* **Danish**) a type of cake for one person, consisting of sweet pastry, often with fruit inside

dank /dæŋk/ *adj* (especially of buildings and air) wet, cold and unpleasant: *a dank, dark cellar* ○ *In the cathedral vaults the air was dank and stale.* **dankness** /ˈdæŋk.nəs/ *noun* [U]

Daoism /ˈdaʊ.ɪ.zᵊm/ *noun* [U] **Taoism**

dapper /ˈdæp.əʳ/ [US] /-ɚ/ *adj* describes a man who is dressed in a fashionable and tidy way: *Hercule Poirot is the dapper detective of the Agatha Christie novels.*

dappled /ˈdæp.ḷd/ *adj* marked with spots of colour that are lighter or darker than the main colour, or marked with areas of light and darkness: *a dappled pony.* ○ *The dappled sunlight fell across her face as she lay beneath the tree.*

dare [BE BRAVE/RUDE] /deəʳ/ [US] /der/ *verb* [I not continuous] to be brave enough to do something difficult or dangerous, or to be rude or foolish enough to do something that you have no right to do: *I was going to ask if his dog was any better, but I didn't dare in case it had died.* ○ [+ (to) infinitive] *Everyone in the office complains that he smells awful, but nobody dares* ***(to)*** *mention it to him.* ○ [+ (to) infinitive] *Dare you tell him the news?* ○ *Do you dare* ***(to)*** *tell him the news?* ○ *I wouldn't dare have a party in my flat in case the neighbours complained.* ○ *I daren't/don't dare think how much it's going to cost.* ○ *I'd never dare* ***(to)*** *talk to my mother the way Ben talks to his.* ○ [+ to infinitive] *He was under attack for daring* ***to*** *criticize the Prime Minister.* ➲See also **daresay**.

How dare she/you, *etc.*! used to express anger about something someone has done: *How dare you use my car without asking!* ○ *How dare he tell me what to do!*

• **don't you dare** *MAINLY HUMOROUS* used to tell someone angrily not to do something: *"I think I'll just walk my dirty shoes over your nice clean floor." "Don't you dare!"* ○ *Don't you dare go without me!*

dare [ASK] /deəʳ/ [US] /der/ *verb* [T] to ask someone to do something which involves risk: *Wear the low-cut blouse with your pink shorts – go on, I dare you!* ○ [+ to infinitive] *I dare you* ***to*** *ask him to dance.*

dare /deəʳ/ [US] /der/ *noun* [C] something you do because someone dares you to: *He jumped in the river at twelve o'clock last night (UK)* ***as/for****/(US)* ***on*** *a dare.*

daredevil /ˈdeəˌdev.ᵊl/ [US] /ˈder-/ *noun* [C] *INFORMAL* a person who does dangerous things and takes risks

daredevil /ˈdeəˌdev.əl/ [US] /ˈder-/ *adj* [before n] *racing-car drivers doing daredevil stunts*

daren't /deənt/ [US] /dernt/ *short form of* dare(s) not: *I daren't tell him – he'll be so angry.*

daresay /ˌdeəˈseɪ/ [US] /ˌder-/ /ˈ--/ *verb* **I daresay/I dare say** used to say that you agree or think that something is true: *"She's got a lot of admirers." "I daresay – she's very beautiful."* ○ *He gets paid a lot of money, but I daresay* ***(that)*** *he earns it.*

daring /ˈdeə.rɪŋ/ [US] /ˈder.ɪŋ/ *adj* brave and taking risks: *a daring escape* ○ *This is a daring new film* (= one showing willingness to risk criticism) *by one of our most original modern directors.* ○ *She was wearing a rather daring* (= sexually exciting) *skirt that only just covered her bottom.* **daringly** /ˈdeə.rɪŋ.li/ [US] /ˈder.ɪŋ-/ *adv*: *a daringly short skirt*

dark [WITHOUT LIGHT] /dɑːk/ [US] /dɑːrk/ *adj* **1** with little or no light: *It was too dark to see properly.* ○ *What time does it* ***get*** *dark in the summer?* ○ *Our bedroom was very dark until we put a larger window in.* **2** nearer to black than white in colour: *dark blue/green* ○ *dark clouds* ○ *She has dark hair.* ○ *He was tall, dark* (= with black/brown hair) *and handsome.*

• **The darkest hour is just before the dawn.** *SAYING* said to emphasize that things often seem at their worst just before they get better

dark /dɑːk/ [US] /dɑːrk/ *noun* **1 the dark** when there is no light somewhere: *Cats can see in the dark.* ○ *I've always been afraid of the dark.* **2 before/after dark** before/after the sun has gone down: *It isn't safe to leave the house after dark.* ○ *I want to be home before dark.*

• **be in the dark** to not know about something that other people know about

darken /ˈdɑː.kən/ [US] /ˈdɑːr-/ *verb* [I] to become dark: *The sky darkened as thick smoke billowed from the blazing oil well.*

• **not darken** ***sb's*** **door** *LITERARY* used to tell someone to never come back to a place: *Never darken my door again!*

darkened /ˈdɑː.kənd/ [US] /ˈdɑːr-/ *adj*: *We crept slowly along the darkened* (= without light) *corridor.* **darkly** /ˈdɑː.kli/ [US] /ˈdɑːr-/ *adv*: *His figure could be seen darkly on the foggy moor.* **darkness** /ˈdɑːk.nəs/ [US] /ˈdɑːrk-/ *noun* [U] *The city centre was* ***plunged into*** *darkness by the power cut.*

dark [SAD] /dɑːk/ [US] /dɑːrk/ *adj* [before n] sad and without hope: *Her husband's sudden death was the start of a dark chapter in her life.* ○ *This environmental report contains more dark predictions about the future of the Earth.*

dark [EVIL] /dɑːk/ [US] /dɑːrk/ *adj* evil or threatening: *There's a darker side to his character.* **darkly** /ˈdɑː.kli/ [US] /ˈdɑːr-/ *adv*: *"Don't come any closer," she said darkly.*

dark [SECRET] /dɑːk/ [US] /dɑːrk/ *adj* secret or hidden: *I've just been promoted, but* ***keep*** *it dark – I don't want everyone to know just yet.*

the ˈdark ˌages *plural noun* **1 the Dark Ages** the period in European history from the end of the Roman empire in AD 476 to about AD 1000 **2** *DISAPPROVING* a time in the past considered to be not advanced and when people were unwilling to accept the beliefs or opinions of others: *This repressive law takes gay rights* ***back to*** *the dark ages.*

ˌdark ˈchocolate *noun* [C or U] (*UK ALSO* **plain chocolate**) dark brown chocolate that has been made without milk

ˌdark ˈglasses *plural noun* glasses with dark LENSES (= pieces of glass)

ˌdark ˈhorse [SECRETIVE] *noun* [C usually sing] *UK* a person who keeps their interests and ideas secret, especially someone who has a surprising ability or skill: *Anna's such a dark horse – I had no idea she'd published a novel.*

ˌdark ˈhorse [WINNER] *noun* [C usually sing] *US* a horse or a politician who wins a race or competition although no one expected them to

darkie, *US USUALLY* **darky** /ˈdɑː.ki/ [US] /ˈdɑːr-/ *noun* [C] *OFFENSIVE OLD-FASHIONED* a person who has black or brown skin

darkroom /ˈdɑːk.rʊm/ /-ruːm/ [US] /ˈdɑːrk-/ *noun* [C] a specially lit room where photographic film is processed

darling /ˈdɑː.lɪŋ/ [US] /ˈdɑːr-/ *noun* [C] a person who is greatly loved or liked: *Oh darling, I do love you.* ○ *Here's your change, darling.* ○ *In spite of his unpopularity in the USSR, Gorbachev remained* ***a/the*** *darling* ***of*** (= very popular with) *the West right to the end.* * NOTE: This is used as a form of address between people who love each other and people who are being friendly. As a friendly form of address it is not usually used between men.

darling /ˈdɑː.lɪŋ/ [US] /ˈdɑːr-/ *adj* [before n] **1** *OLD-FASHIONED* loved very much; used when addressing someone you love, for example in a letter: *Darling Martha, It was lovely to see you at the weekend.* **2** very attractive: *They've just bought a darling little cottage.*

darn [REPAIR] /dɑːn/ [US] /dɑːrn/ *verb* [T] to repair a hole or a piece of clothing with long stitches across the hole and other stitches woven across them: *She still darns the holes in her socks.* **darn** /dɑːn/ [US] /dɑːrn/ *noun* [C]

darning /ˈdɑː.nɪŋ/ [US] /ˈdɑːr-/ *noun* [U] *I don't think I'll ever finish that darning* (= collection of things needing to be darned).

darn [EXPRESSION] /dɑːn/ [US] /dɑːrn/ *exclamation INFORMAL* used instead of DAMN to express annoyance: *Darn* ***it****! There goes my bus!* **darn** /dɑːn/ [US] /dɑːrn/ *adj* [before n], *adv* (*ALSO* **darned**) *Getting off the bus while it was moving was a darn stupid thing to do.*

ˈdarning ˌneedle *noun* [C] a special large needle used for darning, or for sewing thick cloth

dart [WEAPON] /dɑːt/ [US] /dɑːrt/ *noun* [C] a small thin object with a sharp point which is thrown by hand in a game, or fired from a gun or blown from a tube when used as a weapon ➲Compare **arrow**.

darts /dɑːts/ [US] /dɑːrts/ *noun* [U] a game in which darts are thrown at a circular board. The number of points won depends on where the darts land on the board: *a* ***game of*** *darts* ○ *a darts tournament*

dart [MOVE QUICKLY] /dɑːt/ [US] /dɑːrt/ *verb* [I + adv or prep] **1** to move quickly or suddenly: *I darted behind the sofa and hid.* **2 dart a glance/look at** ***sb*** to look quickly at someone: *She darted an angry look at me and I shut up.*

dart /dɑːt/ [US] /dɑːrt/ *noun* [C usually sing] *We* ***made*** *a dart* ***for*** (= moved quickly towards) *the exit.*

dart [SEWN FOLD] /dɑːt/ [US] /dɑːrt/ *noun* [C] a small fold becoming narrower towards one end which is sewn into a piece of clothing to make it fit better

dartboard /ˈdɑːt.bɔːd/ [US] /ˈdɑːrt.bɔːrd/ *noun* [C] a circular board which DARTS are thrown at in a game

dash [MOVE QUICKLY] /dæʃ/ *verb* [I] to go somewhere quickly: *I've been dashing* ***around*** *all day.* ○ *I must dash – I've got to be home by seven.*

dash /dæʃ/ *noun* **1** [S] when you run somewhere very quickly: *I* ***made a*** *dash* ***for*** *the toilets.* ○ *There was a* ***mad*** *dash for the exit.* ○ *As soon as the rain dies down I'm going to* ***make a*** *dash* ***for it*** (= run somewhere very fast). **2** [C usually sing] *MAINLY US* a race over a short distance: *Who won the 100-yard dash?*

dash [HIT] /dæʃ/ *verb* [I or T usually + prep] to hit with great force, especially causing damage: *The tidal wave dashed the ship* ***against*** *the rocks.* ○ *Waves dashed* ***against*** *the cliffs.*

• **dash** ***sb's*** **hopes** to destroy someone's hopes: *Saturday's 2-0 defeat dashed their hopes of reaching the final.*

dash [SMALL AMOUNT] /dæʃ/ *noun* **a dash** a small amount of something, especially liquid food, that is added to something else: *"Cream with your coffee, Madam?" "Yes please – just a dash."* ○ *FIGURATIVE a youthful ambiance with a dash of* (= small amount of) *sophistication*

dash [PUNCTUATION] /dæʃ/ *noun* [C] **1** the – punctuation mark that can be used to separate parts of a sentence ➲Compare **hyphen**. **2** a long sound or flash of light which is used with DOTS to send messages in MORSE (CODE)

dash [STYLE] /dæʃ/ *noun* [U] *OLD-FASHIONED* style and confidence

dash [ANNOYANCE] /dæʃ/ *exclamation UK OLD-FASHIONED INFORMAL* used to express annoyance: *Oh dash* ***(it)****! I've left my umbrella in the office.*

▲ **dash** ***sth*** **off** *phrasal verb* [M] to write something quickly, putting little effort into it: *She dashed the letter off in five minutes.*

dashboard /ˈdæʃ.bɔːd/ [US] /-bɔːrd/ *noun* [C] (*MAINLY US* **dash,** *UK OLD-FASHIONED* **fascia**) the part of a car which contains some of the controls used for driving and the devices for measuring speed and distance ➲See picture **Car** on page Centre 12

dashed /dæʃt/ *adj* **[before n]**, *adv MAINLY UK OLD-FASHIONED* extremely: *Dashed decent of you, old boy!*

dashing /ˈdæʃ.ɪŋ/ *adj OLD-FASHIONED* attractive in a confident, exciting and stylish way: *a dashing young soldier* **dashingly** /ˈdæʃ.ɪŋ.li/ *adv*

dastardly /ˈdæs.təd.li/ [US] /-tɚd-/ *adj OLD-FASHIONED OR HUMOROUS* evil and cruel: *It's the story of a woman who plots a dastardly revenge on her unfaithful lover.*

D

DAT /dæt/ *noun* **[C or U]** *ABBREVIATION FOR* **digital audio tape**

data /ˈdeɪ.tə/ [US] /-t̬ə/ *group noun* **[U]** information, especially facts or numbers, collected for examination and consideration and used to help decision-making, or information in an electronic form that can be stored and processed by a computer: *The data was/were collected by various researchers.* ○ *Now the data is being transferred from magnetic tape to hard disk.*

ˈdata ˌbank *noun* **[C]** a large collection of information which can be searched through quickly, especially by a computer

database /ˈdeɪ.tə.beɪs/ [US] /-t̬ə-/ *noun* **[C]** a large amount of information stored in a computer system in such a way that it can be easily looked at or changed: *We're linked to the on-line database at our head office.*

ˈdata ˌcapture *noun* **[U]** any method of collecting information and then changing it into a form which can be processed by a computer

dataglove /ˈdeɪ.tə.glʌv/ [US] /-t̬ə-/ *noun* **[C]** an electronic glove which sends information about the hand movements of the person wearing it to a computer

ˈdata ˌprocessing *noun* **[U]** the use of a computer to perform calculations on data: *a data-processing bureau*

date [DAY] /deɪt/ *noun* **[C]** **1** a numbered day in a month, often given with a combination of the name of the day, the month and the year: *What's the date (today)?/What date is it?/What's today's date?* ○ *Today's date is (Friday) the 24th of June/June the 24th (1994).* ○ *What is your date **of birth**?* ○ *The **closing** date for applications is the end of this month.* ○ *We've agreed to meet again at a later date.* ○ *I'd like to fix a date for our next meeting.* ○ *I've **made a** date* (= agreed a date and time) *to see her about the house.* ➲See also **out-of-date** and **up-to-date**. **2** a particular year: *The date on the coin is 1789.* ○ *Albert Einstein's dates are 1879 to 1955* (= he was born in 1879 and died in 1955). **3** a month and a year: *The (UK) **expiry**/(US) **expiration** date of this certificate is August 2005.* **4** a performance: *They've just finished an exhausting 75-date European tour.*

• **to date** *FORMAL* up to the present time: *This novel is his best work to date.*

date /deɪt/ *verb* **[T]** **1** to say how long something has existed or when it was made: *Archaeologists have been unable to date these fossils.* ○ *An antique dealer had dated the vase **at*** (= said that it was made in) *1734.* **2** to write the day's date on something you have written or made: **[+ obj + n]** *Thank you for your letter dated August 30th.*

date [MEETING] /deɪt/ *noun* **[C]** **1** a social meeting planned in advance, such as one between two people who are or might become sexual partners: *He's asked her out **on a** date.* ○ *She has a **hot** date* (= an exciting meeting) *tonight.* **2** *US* a person you have a romantic meeting with: *Who's your date for the prom?*

• **it's a date** *INFORMAL* used to say that a particular time is a suitable time to meet: *"I can't make it at seven o'clock. How about nine-thirty?" "Sure, it's a date."*

date /deɪt/ *verb* **[I or T]** *MAINLY US* to regularly spend time with someone you have a romantic relationship with: *They were dating for five years before they got married.* ○ *How long have you been dating Nicky?*

date [AGE] /deɪt/ *verb* **[I or T]** to stop being fashionable or become old-fashioned, or to show the age of a person or thing: *Some James Bond films have dated more quickly than others.* ○ *I can remember watching live TV coverage of the first lunar landing, so that dates me* (= shows how old I am).

dated /ˈdeɪ.tɪd/ [US] /-t̬ɪd/ *adj* old-fashioned: *Spy thrillers with plots based on the Cold War look particularly dated nowadays.*

▲ **date back** *phrasal verb* to have existed a particular length of time or since a particular time: *This tradition dates back **to** medieval times.*

date [FRUIT] /deɪt/ *noun* **[C]** the sweet fruit of various types of palm tree ➲See picture **Fruit** on page Centre 1

dateline /ˈdeɪt.laɪn/ *noun* **[C]** the line in a newspaper article which tells the place and date of writing ➲Compare **by-line** and **headline**.

ˈdate ˌrape *noun* **[C or U]** (a case of) RAPE which happens during a date or social event in which the attacker is already known to the person who is attacked

ˈdating ˌagency *UK noun* **[C]** (*US* **dating service**) an organization which introduces people with similar interests to each other, especially people who want to start a personal or sexual relationship with someone: *She met her husband through a dating agency.*

dative /ˈdeɪ.tɪv/ [US] /-t̬ɪv/ *noun* **[C or U]** the form of a noun, pronoun or adjective which in some languages marks the INDIRECT OBJECT of a verb that has two objects **dative** /ˈdeɪ.tɪv/ [US] /-t̬ɪv/ *adj*: *the dative case*

daub /dɔːb/ [US] /dɑːb/ *verb* **[T]** to spread a thick or sticky liquid on something or to cover something with a thick or sticky liquid, often quickly or carelessly: *The walls had been daubed **with** graffiti.* ○ *The baby had daubed butter all **over** its hair and face.*

daub /dɔːb/ [US] /dɑːb/ *noun* **[C]** **1** an area of thick or sticky liquid on something: *a daub of red paint* **2** a badly-painted picture

daughter /ˈdɔː.təʳ/ [US] /ˈdɑː.t̬ɚ/ *noun* **[C]** your female child: *Liz and Phil have a daughter and three sons.* ➲See also **stepdaughter**.

daughter-in-law /ˈdɔː.tər.ɪn,lɔː/ [US] /ˈdɑː.t̬ɚ.ɪn,lɑː/ *noun* **[C]** *plural* **daughters-in-law** your son's wife

daunt /dɔːnt/ [US] /dɑːnt/ *verb* **[T often passive]** to make someone feel slightly frightened or worried about their ability to achieve something; to discourage: *She was not at all daunted by the size of the problem.*

• **nothing daunted** *MAINLY UK* not discouraged: *She was rejected the first time she applied to the university, but, nothing daunted, reapplied the following year and was accepted.*

daunting /ˈdɔːn.tɪŋ/ [US] /ˈdɑːn.t̬ɪŋ/ *adj* making you feel slightly frightened or worried about your ability to achieve something: *In spite of unification, the country was still faced with the daunting prospect of overcoming four decades of division.*

dauntless /ˈdɔːnt.ləs/ [US] /ˈdɑːnt-/ *adj LITERARY* showing determination and a lack of fear: *In spite of the scale of the famine, the relief workers struggled on with dauntless optimism and commitment.*

dawdle /ˈdɔː.dl̩/ [US] /ˈdɑː-/ *verb* **[I]** to do something or go somewhere very slowly, taking more time than is necessary: *Stop dawdling! You'll be late for school!*

dawn [EARLY MORNING] /dɔːn/ [US] /dɑːn/ *noun* **[C or U]** **1** the period in the day when light from the sun begins to appear in the sky: *We woke **at** dawn.* ○ *We left as dawn was **breaking*** (= starting). ○ *We left at the **break of** dawn.* ○ *Twenty-three people were arrested and large quantities of heroin were seized in a dawn **raid*** (= a sudden entering of a building by police officers, in an attempt to catch people involved in illegal activities). **2** *LITERARY* **the dawn of sth** the start of a period of time or the beginning of something new: *The fall of the Berlin Wall marked the dawn **of a new era** in European history.*

• **from dawn to dusk** from early morning until night: *We worked from dawn to dusk, seven days a week.*

dawn /dɔːn/ [US] /dɑːn/ *verb* **[I]** If a day or period of time dawns, it begins: *He left the house just as the day was dawning.* ○ *As 1990 dawned, few people could have predicted the dramatic changes that were to take place in eastern Europe during that year.*

dawn [BECOME KNOWN] /dɔːn/ [US] /dɑːn/ *verb* **[I]** to become known or obvious: *Gradually the truth about him dawned.* ○ **[+ that]** ***It** eventually dawned **that** he wouldn't be coming back.*

▲ **dawn on *sb*** *phrasal verb* If a fact dawns on you, you become aware of it after a period of not being aware of it: [+ **that**] *I was about to pay for the shopping when* ***it*** *suddenly dawned on me* ***that*** *I'd left my cheque book at home.*

ˌdawn ˈchorus *noun* [S] MAINLY UK the singing of birds together, which happens just before dawn

day /deɪ/ *noun* [C] **1** a period of 24 hours, especially from 12 o'clock one night to 12 o'clock the next night: *January has 31 days.* ○ *the days of the week* ○ *He runs five miles every day.* ○ *It took us almost a day to get here.* ○ *I saw him* ***the*** *day* ***before yesterday****.* ○ *We leave* ***the*** *day* ***after tomorrow****.* ○ *He was last seen alive five days* ***ago****.* ○ *They haven't been seen* ***for*** *days* (= for several days). ○ *I'll be seeing Pat* ***in a few*** *days/****in a few*** *days'* ***time****.* ○ *How's your day been* (= Have you enjoyed today)*?* ○ *Have a nice day!* ○ *I must get some sleep – I've got* ***a big*** *day* (= an important day) *tomorrow.* **2** used to refer to the period in 24 hours when it is naturally light: *a bright, sunny day* ○ *It's rained* ***all*** *day today.* ○ *These animals sleep in the day and hunt at night.* **3** the time that you usually spend at work or at school: *a normal working day* ○ *I work a seven-hour day.* ○ *We're having to work a six-day week to cope with demand.* ○ *She's at home today – she's having a day* ***off****.*

• **one/some day** at some time in the future: *I'd love to go to China some/one day.*

• **all in a day's work** If something difficult, unpleasant or strange is all in a day's work for someone, it is a usual part of their job: *When you're a nurse, cleaning up vomit is all in a day's work.*

• **any day now** very soon, especially within the next few days: *The baby's due any day now.*

• **the best/happiest days of *your* life** the most pleasant time you will ever have: *Adults are fond of telling children that their years at school are the best days of their life.*

• **by day** when it is naturally light: *I prefer travelling by day.*

• **day after day** repeatedly, every day: *The same problems keep coming up day after day.*

• **day and night** all the time: *You can hear the traffic from your room day and night.*

• ***sb's/sth's*** **days are numbered** If someone or something's days are numbered, they will not exist for much longer: *The latest opinion polls suggest that his days* ***as*** *leader are numbered.*

• **day by day** every day, or more and more as each day passes: *Day by day he became weaker.*

• **day in day out** (especially of something boring) done or happening every day for a long period of time: *I have to do the same boring jobs day in day out.*

• **(from) day to day** If something changes (from) day to day, it changes often: *The symptoms of the disease change from day to day.*

• **have had *its/your* day** to be much less popular than before: *She sold a lot of books in the 1960's, but she's had her day.*

• **in all my (born) days** in all of my life: *I've never seen anything so strange in all my born days.*

• **in my day** when I was young: *Children take so much for granted nowadays – in my day a new bike was really special.*

• **in this day and age** at the present time: *You can't afford to run businesses inefficiently in this day and age.*

• **in those days** in the past: *In those days people used to write a lot more letters.*

• **make *sb's* day** to make someone happy: *Seeing Adrian again after such a long time really made my day.*

• **not be *sb's* day** If it is not your day, you are having a difficult or unpleasant day: *This really isn't my day – my wallet was stolen this morning and now I've lost my car keys.*

• **one of these days** some time in the near future: *You're going to get into serious trouble one of these days.*

• **one of those days** a bad day, full of problems: *It's just been one of those days.*

• **that'll be the day** something you say in order to show you think something is unlikely to happen: *"Mike says he's going to give up smoking." "That'll be the day!"*

• **the other day** a few days ago: *Didn't I see you in the post office the other day?*

• **the days** a period in history: *How did people communicate in the days before email?*

• **these days** used to talk about the present time, in comparison with the past: *Vegetarianism is very popular these days.*

• **those were the days** something you say which means life was better at the time in the past that you are talking about: *We were young and madly in love. Ah, those were the days!*

• **to the day** exactly: *She died ten years ago to the day.*

• **to this day** until now: *To this day nobody knows what happened to him.*

COMMON LEARNER ERROR

day

Be careful to use the correct preposition with the word **day**. You usually need to use the preposition **on**.

On the second day of our holiday we went to the beach.
~~*In the second day of our holiday we went to the beach.*~~

ˈdayˌ boy *noun* [C] a male DAY PUPIL

daybreak /ˈdeɪ.breɪk/ *noun* [U] **dawn** EARLY MORNING

ˈday ˌcare *noun* [U] care or education provided during the day, especially for young children or old people: *a day care centre for the elderly*

daydream /ˈdeɪ.driːm/ *noun* [C usually sing] a set of pleasant thoughts about something you would prefer to be doing or something you would like to achieve in the future: *He never paid attention in class and seemed to be* ***in a*** *permanent daydream.* ○ *I was just enjoying a daydream* ***about*** *winning the Nobel Prize for literature.* **daydream** /ˈdeɪ.driːm/ *verb* [I] *Stop daydreaming and get on with your work!* **daydreamer** /ˈdeɪˌdriː.mə^r/ [US] /-mɚ/ *noun* [C]

ˈday ˌgirl *noun* [C] a female DAY PUPIL

Day-Glo /ˈdeɪ.gləʊ/ [US] /-gloʊ/ *adj* TRADEMARK in or of a colour which seems to shine unusually brightly in ordinary light: *Day-glo swimsuits*

daylight /ˈdeɪ.laɪt/ *noun* [U] (the period when there is) natural light from the sun: *The colours look much better in daylight.*

ˌdaylight ˈrobbery *noun* [U] (US ALSO **highway robbery**) INFORMAL a situation in which you are charged a lot too much for something: *£4 for an orange juice? That's just daylight robbery!*

daylights /ˈdeɪ.laɪts/ *plural noun* INFORMAL **beat/knock the (living) daylights out of *sb*** to hit someone very hard, many times: *I'll knock the living daylights out of him if he says that again!*

• **frighten/scare, etc. the (living) daylights out of *sb*** INFORMAL to frighten someone very much: *Don't jump out on me like that! You scared the living daylights out of me!*

ˌdaylight ˈsaving ˌtime UK AND US *noun* [U] (AUS **daylight saving**) the time set usually one hour later in summer so that there is a longer period of daylight in the evening

ˈday ˌnursery *noun* [C] a place where young children are looked after, especially while their parents are working

the ˌDay of Aˈtonement *noun* [U] **Yom Kippur**

the ˌDay of ˈJudgment *noun* [U] **Judgment Day**

ˌday of ˈreckoning *noun* [S] a time when the effect of a past mistake is experienced or when a crime is punished

ˈday ˌpupil UK *noun* [C] (US **day student**) a student who sleeps at home and studies at a school where some of the other students live ➲Compare **boarder** at **board** STAY.

ˈday reˌlease *noun* [U] UK a system in which people who work can study one day a week at a college: *My boss wants me to do a day-release course in computing.*

ˌday reˈturn *noun* [C] UK a ticket which can only be used for travelling to a place and back to where you started in a single day: *a day return to London*

ˈday ˌschool *noun* [C] a private school whose students return home in the evening

ˈday ˌstudent *noun* [C] US FOR **day pupil**

D

daytime /ˈdeɪ.taɪm/ *noun* [U] the period between the time when the sun rises and the time it goes down, or the part of the day which is neither evening nor night: *I tend to sleep **in/during** the daytime and study at night.* ○ *a regular daytime job* ○ *a daytime telephone number* ○ *daytime television*

day-to-day /ˌdeɪ.təˈdeɪ/ *adj* [before n] happening every day as a regular part of your job or life: *day-to-day problems/responsibilities*

ˈday ˌtrip /ˈdeɪ.trɪp/ *noun* [C] a visit to a place in which you go there and come back on the same day: *Do you fancy coming **on** a day trip to Bath next Saturday?* **day-tripper** /ˈdeɪ.trɪp.əʳ/ [US] /-ɚ/ *noun* [C] *The coast is full of day-trippers at this time of year.*

dazed /deɪzd/ *adj* very confused and unable to think clearly because you are shocked or have hit your head: *You're looking rather dazed – is anything wrong?* ○ *a dazed expression*

daze /deɪz/ *noun* **in a daze** unable to think clearly: *She was wandering around in a daze this morning.*

dazzle /ˈdæz.l̩/ *verb* **1** [T] If light dazzles you, it makes you unable to see for a short time: *I was dazzled by the sunlight.* **2** [T usually passive] If you are dazzled by someone or something, you think they are extremely good and exciting: *I was dazzled by his charm and good looks.*

dazzling /ˈdæz.lɪŋ/ *adj* **1** A dazzling light is so bright that you cannot see for a short time after looking at it: *a dazzling white light* **2** extremely attractive or exciting: *dazzling good looks* ○ *a dazzling smile* ○ *a dazzling performance/display* **dazzlingly** /ˈdæz.lɪŋ.li/ *adv*: *a dazzlingly inventive author*

DBMS /ˌdiː.biː.emˈes/ *noun* [C] *ABBREVIATION FOR* database management system: a set of computer programs for allowing large amounts of information to be put into a computer and for organizing it so that it can be searched, examined or printed easily and quickly

DC [ELECTRICITY] /ˌdiːˈsiː/ *noun* [U] *ABBREVIATION FOR* direct current: electrical current which always flows in one direction ➲Compare **AC** ELECTRICITY.

DC [UNITED STATES] /ˌdiːˈsiː/ *noun* [U] *ABBREVIATION FOR* the District of Columbia: an area of the eastern US which has the same borders as the US capital, Washington, and which is not part of a US state

D-Day /ˈdiː.deɪ/ *noun* [U] **1** the day during the Second World War when the Allies began their INVASION of Europe by attacking the coast of northern France: *The D-Day landings began on 6 June 1944, when Allied forces invaded Normandy.* **2** a day when something important will happen: *After four hectic weeks of electioneering, candidates are preparing themselves for D-Day* (= election day) *tomorrow.*

DDT /ˌdiː.diːˈtiː/ *noun* [U] a poisonous chemical for killing insects

de- /diː-/ /dɪ-/ *prefix* used to add the meaning 'opposite', 'remove' or 'reduce' to a noun or verb: *the deforestation of the rainforests* ○ *the denationalization of the coal industry* ○ *Once you've written a computer program, you have to debug* (= remove the errors from) *it.*

deacon /ˈdiː.kən/ *noun* [C] (in some church groups) a church official, either male or female, who is below a priest in rank and who performs some of the duties of a priest

deaconess /ˌdiː.kəˈnes/ [US] /ˈdiː.kᵊn.əs/ *noun* [C] (in some church groups) a woman who performs particular duties in a church but who is not a deacon

deactivate /ˌdiˈæk.tɪ.veɪt/ *verb* [T] to cause something to be no longer active or effective: *All chemical weapons facilities will be deactivated.* **deactivation** /ˌdiː.æk.tɪˈveɪ.ʃᵊn/ [US] /diˌæk-/ *noun* [U]

dead [NOT LIVING] /ded/ *adj* **1** not now living: *She's been dead for twenty years now.* ○ *The motorcyclist was dead **on arrival** at the hospital.* ○ *He was **shot** dead* (= killed by shooting) *outside his home.* ➲See Note **died or dead?** at **die** STOP LIVING. **2** *MAINLY UK* If a part of your body is dead, you cannot feel it: *I've been sitting with my legs crossed for so long, my right leg has gone dead.* **3** *UK* describes empty glasses and bottles that were previously full **4** In some sports, if a ball is dead, it is outside the area of play.

• **be as dead as a doornail** *INFORMAL* to be clearly and obviously dead

• **be (as) dead as a/the dodo** *INFORMAL* to not be important or popular any longer: *Who cares about Socialism any more? Socialism's as dead as the dodo.*

• **be dead on *your* feet** to be very tired

• **be dead in the water** If something is dead in the water, it has failed and it seems impossible that it will be successful in the future: *So how does a government revive an economy that is dead in the water?*

• **be dead to the world** to be sleeping: *"Is Georgie up yet?" "I doubt it – she was dead to the world ten minutes ago."*

• **over my dead body** If you say something will happen over your dead body, you mean that you will do everything you can to prevent it: *"Joe says he's going to buy a motorbike." "Over my dead body!"*

• **Dead men tell no tales.** *SAYING* People who are dead cannot tell secrets: *I think they killed him because he knew too much. Dead men tell no tales.*

dead /ded/ *plural noun* dead people: *Three children were among **the** dead.* ○ *A ceasefire has been called to allow the survivors to bury their dead.*

• **come back from the dead** (*ALSO* **rise from the dead**) to be successful or popular again after a period of not being successful or popular: *This was a company that had risen from the dead.*

• **in the dead of night/winter** in the middle of night/winter: *The fire broke out in the dead of night.*

deaden /ˈded.ᵊn/ *verb* [T] to make something less painful or less strong: *Morphine is often used to deaden the pain of serious injuries.* ○ *Double glazing has helped to deaden the noise from the motorway.*

deadly /ˈded.li/ *adj* likely to cause death: *a deadly virus* ○ *a deadly weapon* ➲See also **deadly** at **dead** BORING and **dead** COMPLETE.

dead [BORING] /ded/ *adj* If a place is dead, it is too quiet and nothing interesting happens there: *The city centre's quite lively during the day, but it's totally dead at night.*

deadly /ˈded.li/ *adj* *INFORMAL* extremely boring: *The party was deadly.*

dead [EQUIPMENT] /ded/ *adj* If a piece of equipment is dead, it is not working: *a dead battery* ○ *The phone suddenly **went** dead.*

dead [COMPLETE] /ded/ *adj* [before n], *adv* complete(ly): *The conductor waited for dead **silence** before commencing the performance.* ○ *You won't be able to change his mind – he's dead **against** the plan.* ○ *INFORMAL I'm dead **certain** I left my purse on the desk.* ○ *INFORMAL I'm dead* (= very) *hungry.* ○ *INFORMAL The exam was dead* (= very) ***easy**.* ○ *UK INFORMAL "How was the film?" "It was dead good."* ○ *The post office is dead* (= straight) ***ahead**.* ○ *Aim for the dead* (= exact) *centre of the target.* ○ *I always try to arrive dead* (= exactly) ***on time**.* ○ *Martha's dead **set on** having* (= very much wants to have) *a new bike for her birthday.* ○ *He's dead **set against*** (= completely opposed to) *living in the city.*

deadly /ˈded.li/ *adj, adv*: *They have been deadly* (= extreme) ***enemies** ever since Mark stole Greg's girlfriend.* ○ *I thought she was joking but she was deadly* (= completely) ***serious**.*

ˌdead ˈair *noun* [U] *US* an unintentional period of silence during a radio or television broadcast

deadbeat [PERSON] /ˈded.biːt/ *noun* [C] *MAINLY US INFORMAL* a person who is not willing to work, does not behave in a responsible way and does not fit into ordinary society: *He's a **real** deadbeat who's never had a proper job.* ○ [as form of address] *Come off it, deadbeat, you're never going to get anywhere.*

deadbeat [IN DEBT] /ˈded.biːt/ *adj* [before n], *noun* [C] *MAINLY US INFORMAL* (a person or company) not willing to pay debts: *The new law is aimed at deadbeat landlords who owe $22 million.*

deadbolt /ˈded.bəʊlt/ [US] /-boʊlt/ *noun* [C] *US FOR* **mortise lock**

ˌdead ˈcat ˌbounce *noun* [S] *SPECIALIZED* a temporary increase in the value of the shares of a company after there has been a large decrease in their value: *Are we witnessing a genuine recovery in the share price, or is it just a dead cat bounce?*

ˌdead ˈduck *noun* [C usually sing] *INFORMAL* someone or something that is very unlikely to be successful, especially because of a mistake or bad judgment: *Thanks to the lack of market research, the project was a dead duck right from the start.*

ˌdead ˈend *noun* **1** [C] a road which is closed at one end, and therefore does not lead anywhere **2** [S] a situation that has no hope of advancement: *Negotiators have reached a dead end in their attempts to find a peaceful solution.*

ˌdead-end ˈjob *noun* [C] a job in which there is no chance of being raised to a better, more important job

deadhead [PERSON] /ˈded.hed/ *noun* [C] *INFORMAL* a person who is boring or stupid

deadhead [PLANTS] /ˌdedˈhed/ *verb* [T] to remove old flowers from a plant

ˌdead ˈheat *noun* [C] a competition in which two or more competitors finish at exactly the same time or with exactly the same result: *The race ended* ***in*** *a dead heat.* ○ *The opinion polls show the three election candidates* ***in*** *a dead heat (****with*** *each other).*

ˌdead ˈlanguage *noun* [C] a language which is no longer spoken by anyone as their main language: *Latin is a dead language.*

ˌdead ˈletter [MAIL] *noun* [C] a letter that cannot be delivered to the address written on it and cannot be returned to the person who sent it: *the dead-letter office*

ˌdead ˈletter [LAW/AGREEMENT] *noun* [C usually sing] a law or agreement which is no longer effective: *The ceasefire treaty was a dead letter as soon as it was signed, as neither side ever had any intention of keeping to it.*

deadline /ˈded.laɪn/ *noun* [C] a time or day by which something must be done: *There's no way I can* ***meet*** *that deadline.* ○ *We're working to a* ***tight*** *deadline* (= We do not have much time to finish the work). ○ *I'm afraid you've* ***missed*** *the deadline – the deadline* ***for*** *applications was May 30th.*

deadlock /ˈded.lɒk/ [US] /-lɑːk/ *noun* [S or U] a situation in which agreement in an argument cannot be reached because neither side will change its demands or accept any of the demands of the other side; STALEMATE: *Somebody will have to compromise if we are to* ***break*** (= end) *the deadlock* ***between*** *the two warring factions.* ○ *Once again the talks have* ***ended in*** *deadlock.* ○ *Deadlock* ***over*** *wage levels has prevented an agreement being reached.* **deadlocked** /ˈded.lɒkt/ [US] /-lɑːkt/ *adj*: *The dispute has now been deadlocked for several months.*

ˌdead ˈloss *noun* [S] *INFORMAL* **1** an activity or process that is not at all effective or successful: *Yesterday's meeting was a dead loss – nothing was decided.* **2** a completely useless or unskilled person: *I was a dead loss at languages at school.* ○ *John was a dead loss – he just stood there and did nothing.*

deadly nightshade /ˌded.liˈnaɪt.ʃeɪd/ *noun* [C or U] (*ALSO* **belladonna**) a very poisonous plant with small black shiny fruits, which grows in Europe, North Africa and West Asia

deadpan /ˈded.pæn/ *adj* looking or seeming serious when you are telling a joke: *a deadpan expression/voice*

ˌdead ˈreckoning *noun* [U] a way of calculating the position of a ship or aircraft using only information about the direction and distance it has travelled from a known point

ˌdead ˈringer *noun* [C usually sing] someone or something which looks very similar to someone or something else: *He's a dead ringer* ***for*** *Bono from U2.*

ˌdead ˈweight *noun* [C usually sing] the heaviness of a person or object that cannot or does not move by itself: *She may be small but, when I have to carry her upstairs after she's fallen asleep, she's a dead weight/(US ALSO) she is dead weight.*

ˌdead ˈwood *noun* [U] people or things which are no longer useful: *She cleared out the dead wood as soon as she took over the company.*

deaf /def/ *adj* **1** unable to hear, either completely or partly: *He's been totally/partially deaf since birth.* **2** *DISAPPROVING* unwilling to listen: *The local council has remained deaf* ***to*** *all the objections to its proposals.*

• **(as) deaf as a post** *INFORMAL* completely deaf: *Grandad's as deaf as a post.*

• **There's none so deaf as those who will not hear.** *SAYING* said about someone who has been given advice which they have chosen to ignore, or who has been told something which they do not want to believe

the deaf *plural noun* people who are unable to hear: *Many of the TV programmes are broadcast with subtitles for the deaf.*

deafen /ˈdef.ᵊn/ *verb* [T] If a very loud noise deafens you, it makes you deaf, or makes you temporarily unable to hear the other sounds near you: *The explosion permanently deafened her in her right ear.*

deafening /ˈdef.ᵊn.ɪŋ/ *adj* extremely loud: *The music was deafening.* **deafness** /ˈdef.nəs/ *noun* [U]

ˈdeaf ˌaid *noun* [C] *UK* a **hearing aid**

deaf-mute /ˌdefˈmjuːt/ *noun* [C] a person who can neither hear nor speak

deal [SHARE OUT] /diːl/ *verb* [I or T] **dealt, dealt** to give or share out something, especially playing cards: *Whose turn is it to deal?* ○ *Would you like to deal* ***(out)*** *the cards?* ○ [+ two objects] *Deal them five cards each./Deal five cards* ***to*** *each of them.* ○ *We have only a small amount of food and clothing to deal* ***out to*** *each refugee.*

• **deal a blow to *sb/sth*** (*ALSO* **deal *sb/sth* a blow**) to cause someone or something, usually a plan or hope, to fail or to be affected very badly: *The latest trade figures have dealt a severe blow to hopes of an early economic recovery.*

deal /diːl/ *noun* [C] when someone deals, especially cards: *It's your deal* (= turn to deal).

deal [DO BUSINESS] /diːl/ *verb* [I or T] **dealt, dealt** to do business: *We only deal* ***with*** *companies which have a good credit record.* ○ *SLANG How long had she been dealing* (= selling drugs) *before she was arrested?* ○ *SLANG He was suspected of dealing* (= selling) *cocaine.*

deal /diːl/ *noun* [C] an agreement or an arrangement, especially in business: *a business deal* ○ *The unions and management have* ***made*** *a two-year pay and productivity deal.* ○ *I'll* ***make/do*** *a deal* ***with*** *you – you wash the car and I'll let you use it tonight.* ○ *She got* ***a good*** *deal* (= paid a low price) ***on*** *her new house.* ○ *Is industry* ***getting*** *a* ***raw/rough*** *deal from* (= being unfairly/badly treated by) *the EU?* **dealer** /ˈdiː.ləʳ/ [US] /-lɚ/ *noun* [C] *a second-hand car dealer* ○ *an antiques dealer* ○ *drug dealers* **dealership** /ˈdiː.lə.ʃɪp/ [US] /-lɚ-/ *noun* [C] *Their company has just won the dealership* ***for*** *Rolls-Royce* (= permission from Rolls-Royce to sell their products). **dealings** /ˈdiː.lɪŋz/ *plural noun* activities involving other people, especially in business: *Have you* ***had*** *any dealings* ***with*** *their Paris office?*

deal [AMOUNT] /diːl/ *noun* **a good/great deal** a large amount; much: *She spends a good deal of her time in Glasgow.* ○ *A great deal of effort has gone into making the software reliable.* ○ *They still need a great deal more money to finish the project.*

PHRASAL VERBS WITH **deal**

▲ **deal in *sth*** *phrasal verb* to buy and sell particular goods as a business: *They mainly deal in rare books.*

▲ **deal with *sth*** [TAKE ACTION] *phrasal verb* to take action in order to achieve something or in order to solve a problem: *How do you intend to deal with this problem?* ○ *General enquiries are dealt with by our head office.*

▲ **deal with *sth*** [BE ABOUT] *phrasal verb* to be about or be on the subject of something: *Her new film deals with the relationship between a woman and her sick daughter.* ○ *The author has tried to deal with* (= write about) *a very difficult subject.*

▲ **deal with *sb*** [TALK TO] *phrasal verb* to talk to someone or meet someone, especially as part of your job: *She's used to dealing with difficult customers.*

dealt /delt/ *past simple and past participle of* **deal**

dean [COLLEGE] /diːn/ *noun* [C] **1** a high-ranking official in a college or university who is responsible for the organization of a department or departments: *She is the new dean of the Faculty of Social Sciences.* ○ *the Dean of Medicine* **2** *US* someone among a group of people who has worked the longest in the particular job or activity they share, and who is their unofficial leader: *Parsons is*

D

the dean of the TV news correspondents at Channel Nine.

dean CHURCH /diːn/ *noun* [C] a high-ranking priest in the Church of England or the Roman Catholic Church, who is in charge of managing a large church or cathedral

dear LOVED /dɪə^r/ US /dɪr/ *adj* **1** loved or greatly liked: *She was a very dear friend.* ○ *He was very dear to me.* ○ *This place is very dear to me – we came here on our honeymoon.* ○ *What a dear (= very attractive) little kitten!* ○ **My dear Gina** *– how lovely to see you!* **2** used at the beginning of a letter to greet the person you are writing to: *Dear Kerry/Mum and Dad/Ms Smith/Sir*
● **for dear life** If you do something for dear life, you do it with as much effort as possible, usually to avoid danger: *As the ship began to tilt, we clung on for dear life.*

dear /dɪə^r/ US /dɪr/ *noun* **1** [C usually sing] INFORMAL a kind person: *Annie's such a dear – she's brought me breakfast in bed every morning this week.* **2** [as form of address] used to address someone you love or are being friendly to, not used between men: *Here's your receipt, dear.* ○ *Would you like a drink, dear?* ○ *Lovely to see you, my dear.*

dearly /'dɪə.li/ US /'dɪr-/ *adv:* very much: *She will be dearly missed by her family and friends.* ○ *We would dearly love to sell our flat and move to the country.*

dear EXPENSIVE /dɪə^r/ US /dɪr/ *adj* costing too much; expensive: *The food was good but very dear.* **dearly** /'dɪə.li/ US /'dɪr-/ *adv:* *dearly priced*
● **pay dearly** to suffer greatly as a result of a particular action or event: *If you refuse to cooperate with us, you will pay dearly for it.*

dear EXPRESSION /dɪə^r/ US /dɪr/ *exclamation* (ALSO **dearie**) INFORMAL used in expressions of annoyance, disappointment, sadness or surprise: *Oh dear! I've lost my keys again.* ○ *Dear me, it's already four-thirty and I said I'd be home by five!* ○ *Dearie me, what a mess!*

dearest /'dɪə.rɪst/ US /'dɪr.ɪst/ *adj* OLD-FASHIONED used when writing to someone you love: *'Dearest Kitty,' she wrote.*

dearest /'dɪə.rɪst/ US /'dɪr.ɪst/ *noun* [C] OLD-FASHIONED used when writing or speaking to someone you love: *Come, my dearest, it's getting late.*

Dear 'John (,letter) *noun* [C] a letter written to end a romantic relationship

dearth /dɜːθ/ US /dɝːθ/ *noun* [S] FORMAL an amount or supply which is not large enough; a lack: *a dearth of new homes in the region*

deary, **dearie** /'dɪə.ri/ US /'dɪr.i/ *noun* [as form of address] OLD-FASHIONED a friendly form of address, not used between men: *Here's your change, dearie.*

death /deθ/ *noun* [C or U] the end of life: *The disease causes thousands of deaths a year.* ○ *Do you believe in life after death?* ○ *He never got over the death of his daughter.* ○ *death threats*
● **to death** until you die: *The animals burned to death in the barn.* ○ *He choked to death on a fish bone.* ○ *The traitor was put to death (= killed as a punishment).*
● **bored/frightened, etc. to death** extremely bored/frightened, etc.
● **the death of** *sth* the cause of the end of life, or the end or destruction of something: *The failure of the family business was the death of him.* ○ *That child will be the death of me (= is always doing something which upsets me)!*
● **catch your death of cold** INFORMAL to catch a very bad COLD (= illness) because you are not wearing warm or dry clothes, etc.
● **be at death's door** INFORMAL to be very ill
● **look/feel like death warmed up/over** UK (US **look/feel like death warmed over**) INFORMAL to look/feel very ill: *He shouldn't be working when he's so ill – he looks like death warmed up!*
● **be in at the death** UK to be present at the important time when something comes to an end

deathbed /'deθ.bed/ *noun* [C usually sing] OLD USE the bed that someone dies in or is dying in: *She spoke to her family from her deathbed.*
● **be on your deathbed** to be dying

death-defying /'deθ.dɪ.faɪ.ɪŋ/ *adj* [before n] very dangerous: *a death-defying leap from an aircraft*

'death ,duty *noun* [U] UK the unofficial name for tax on a person's money and possessions when they die

'death ,knell *noun* [S] a warning of the end of something: *The opening of the superstore will sound/toll the death knell for (= cause the failure of) hundreds of small independent shops.*

deathless /'deθ.ləs/ *adj* LITERARY lasting forever and never to be forgotten. ✻ NOTE: often used humorously about writing of a low quality: *his deathless prose*

deathly /'deθ.li/ *adj, adv* extreme in a way that is unpleasant: *After he had spoken, a deathly silence/hush fell on the room.* ○ *She went deathly pale.*

'death ,mask *noun* [C] a model of a dead person's face made by pressing wax onto the face

the 'death ,penalty *noun* [S] the legal punishment of death for a crime: *She would like to see the return of the death penalty in Britain.*

death 'row *noun* MAINLY US **on death row** in prison and waiting to be killed as a punishment for a crime

'death ,sentence *noun* [C usually sing] a legal punishment of a crime by death: *In some countries, drug-smuggling still carries the death sentence.*

death's head /'deθs.hed/ *noun* [C] a picture of a human SKULL (= the hard structure of the head) used as a warning of danger or to frighten

'death ,squad *group noun* [C] an unofficial armed group who look for and illegally kill particular people, especially the enemies of a political party

'death ,throes *plural noun* LITERARY the process of dying or ending in a very painful or unpleasant way: *Mercutio, fatally stabbed, staggers round the stage in his death throes.* ○ *The government was in its death throes.*

'death ,toll *noun* [C usually sing] the number of people who die because of an event such as a war or an accident: *The day after the explosion the death toll had risen to 90.*

'death ,trap *noun* [C usually sing] something that is very dangerous and could cause death: *The car he met me in was a death trap.*

'death ,warrant *noun* [C] an official document which says that someone must be killed as a punishment

deathwatch beetle /,deθ.wɒtʃ'biː.tl/ US /-wɑːtʃ'biːtl/ *noun* [C] an insect which eats wood, especially in old houses, causing serious damage

'death ,wish *noun* [S] a desire for death: *The chances he takes, you'd think he had a death wish.*

deb /deb/ *noun* [C] INFORMAL FOR **debutante**

debacle /deɪ'bɑː.kl/ *noun* [C or U] a complete failure, especially because of bad planning and organization: *The collapse of the company was described as the greatest financial debacle in US history.*

debar /dɪ'bɑː^r/ US /diː'bɑːr/ *verb* [T] **-rr-** FORMAL to stop someone from doing something by law or by official agreement: *He was debarred from the club for unacceptable behaviour.*

debase /dɪ'beɪs/ *verb* [T] to reduce the quality or value of something: *Some argue that money has debased football.* ○ *Our world view has become debased. We no longer have a sense of the sacred.* **debasement** /dɪ'beɪs.mənt/ *noun* [U]

debatable /dɪ'beɪ.tə.bl/ US /-ţə-/ *adj* not clear, not certain, not fixed; possibly not true: [+ question word] *It's debatable whether a university degree helps at all.* ○ *The value of some of the experiments is debatable.*

debate /dɪ'beɪt/ *noun* [C or U] (a) serious discussion of a subject in which many people take part: *Education is the current focus of public debate.* ○ *How we proceed from here is a matter for debate.* ○ *Over the year we have had several debates about future policy.*

debate /dɪ'beɪt/ *verb* **1** [I or T] to discuss a subject in a formal way: *In Parliament today, MPs debated the Finance Bill.* ○ *They had been debating for several hours without reaching a conclusion.* ○ [+ question word] *The authorities debated whether to build a new car park.* **2** [T] to try to make a decision about something: [+ question word] *We debated whether to take the earlier train.* ○ *I'm still debating what colour to paint the walls.* **debater**

/dɪˈbeɪ.təʳ/ [US] /-t̬ɚ/ *noun* [C] *She was a good speaker and an excellent debater.*

debauched /dɪˈbɔːtʃt/ [US] /-ˈbɑːtʃt/ *adj* weakened or destroyed by bad sexual behaviour, drinking too much alcohol, taking drugs, etc: *his debauched lifestyle*
debauchee /ˌdeb.ɔːˈtʃiː/ [US] /-ɑːˈʃiː/ *noun* [C] a debauched person: *He gave a convincing stage performance as the unpleasant young debauchee.* **debauchery** /dɪˈbɔː.tʃəʳ.i/ [US] /-ˈbɑː.tʃɚ-/ *noun* [U] *a life of debauchery*

debilitate /dɪˈbɪl.ɪ.teɪt/ *verb* [T] *FORMAL* to make someone or something physically weak: *Chemotherapy exhausted and debilitated him.* **debilitating** /dɪˈbɪl.ɪ.teɪ.tɪŋ/ [US] /-teɪ.t̬ɪŋ/ *adj*: *a debilitating **condition/disease***
debility /dɪˈbɪl.ɪ.ti/ [US] /-ə.t̬i/ *noun* [U] *FORMAL* physical weakness

debit /ˈdeb.ɪt/ *noun* [C or U] (a record of) money taken out of a bank account: *The account was **in** debit at the end of the month* (= more money had been spent than was in the account at that time). ➲Compare **credit** PAYMENT.
debit /ˈdeb.ɪt/ *verb* [T] *The bank debited my account./The bank debited the money **from** my account.*

ˈdebit ˌcard *noun* [C] a small plastic card which can be used as a method of payment, the money being taken from your bank account automatically: *I paid with my debit card.*

ˈdebit ˌcolumn *noun* [C] the list of numbers which shows amounts of money which have been spent from an account

debonair /ˌdeb.əˈneəʳ/ [US] /-ˈner/ *adj SLIGHTLY OLD-FASHIONED* (especially of men) charming, confident and carefully dressed: *a debonair appearance/manner* ○ *a debonair young man*

debrief /ˌdiːˈbriːf/ *verb* [T] to question someone in detail about work they have done for you: *The pilots were thoroughly debriefed after every mission.* ○ *a debriefing **session***

debris /ˈdeb.riː/ /ˈdeɪ.briː/ [US] /dəˈbriː/ *noun* [U] broken or torn pieces of something larger: *Debris from the aircraft was scattered over a large area.*

debt /det/ *noun* [C or U] something, especially money, which is owed to someone else, or the state of owing something: *He managed to **pay off** his debts in two years.* ○ *The firm **ran up** huge debts.* ○ *They are **in** debt **to*** (= owe money to) *the bank.* ○ *He **ran/got into** debt* (= borrowed money) *after he lost his job.* ○ *The company is **deep in** debt* (= owes a lot of money). ➲See also **indebted** GRATEFUL; **indebted** OWING.
debtor /ˈdet.əʳ/ [US] /ˈdet̬.ɚ/ *noun* [C] someone who owes money ➲Compare **creditor** at **credit** PAYMENT.

debug [REMOVE MISTAKES] /ˌdiːˈbʌg/ *verb* [T] **-gg-** to remove BUGS (= mistakes) from a computer program: *to debug a program*

debug [REMOVE DEVICES] /ˌdiːˈbʌg/ *verb* [T] **-gg-** to look for and remove BUGS (= hidden listening or recording devices) from a place: *Security officers had debugged the room before the meeting.*

debunk /ˌdiːˈbʌŋk/ *verb* [T] *INFORMAL* to show that something is less important, less good or less true than it has been made to appear: *The writer's aim was to debunk the **myth** that had grown up around the actress.*

debut /ˈdeɪ.bjuː/ *noun* [C] when someone performs or presents something to the public for the first time: *She **made** her professional stage debut in Swan Lake.* ○ *He started as an actor, **making** his debut **as** a director in 1990.* ○ *her debut* (= first) *album*
debut /ˈdeɪ.bjuː/ *verb* [I usually + adv or prep] to perform or be introduced to the public for the first time: *The programme debuted last year to great acclaim.*

debutante /ˈdeb.juː.tɒnt/ [US] /-tɑːnt/ *noun* [C] (*INFORMAL* **deb**) a rich young woman who, especially in the past in Britain, went to a number of social events as a way of being introduced to other young people of high social rank: *a debutantes' ball*

Dec *noun WRITTEN ABBREVIATION FOR* **December**

decade /ˈdek.eɪd/ /-ˈ-/ *noun* [C] a period of ten years, especially a period such as 1860 to 1869, or 1990 to 1999

decadence /ˈdek.ə.dənts/ *noun* [U] low moral standards and behaviour: *Western decadence* **decadent** /ˈdek.ə.dənt/ *adj*: *a decadent society* ○ *the decadent court surrounding the king* ○ *HUMOROUS Champagne and chocolates for breakfast – how decadent!*

decaf /ˈdiː.kæf/ *noun* [C or U] *INFORMAL FOR* decaffeinated coffee: *a cup of decaf*

decaffeinated /diːˈkæf.ɪ.neɪ.tɪd/ [US] /dɪˈkæf.ɪ.neɪ.t̬ɪd/ *adj* describes coffee or tea from which the CAFFEINE (= a chemical substance) has been removed

decal /ˈdiː.kæl/ [US] /-ˈ-/ *noun* [C] *MAINLY US* a picture or design printed on special paper, that can be put onto another surface, such as metal or glass

the Decalogue /ðəˈdek.ə.lɒg/ [US] /-lɑːg/ *noun* [S] *SPECIALIZED* the rules of behaviour God gave to Israel through Moses on Mount Sinai; the **Ten Commandments**

decamp /diːˈkæmp/ *verb* [I] *INFORMAL* to leave suddenly and unexpectedly, usually without telling anyone: *He decamped from the hotel with someone else's luggage.*

decant /dɪˈkænt/ *verb* [T] to pour a liquid from one container into another
decanter /dɪˈkæn.təʳ/ [US] /-t̬ɚ/ *noun* [C] a decorative glass container for wine and other alcoholic drinks, with a part that fits into the top: *a cut-glass sherry decanter*

decapitate /dɪˈkæp.ɪ.teɪt/ *verb* [T] to cut off the head of a person **decapitation** /dɪˌkæp.ɪˈteɪ.ʃən/ *noun* [U]

decathlon /dɪˈkæθ.lɒn/ [US] /-lɑːn/ *noun* [C] a competition in which a male athlete competes in ten sports events ➲Compare **biathlon**; **heptathlon**; **pentathlon**.
decathlete /dɪˈkæθ.liːt/ *noun* [C] a man who competes in a decathlon

decay /dɪˈkeɪ/ *verb* [I or T] to (cause something to) become gradually damaged, worse or less: *Sugar makes your teeth decay.* ○ *The role of the extended family has been decaying for some time.* ○ *Pollution has decayed the surface of the stonework on the front of the cathedral.* ○ *the smell of decaying meat*
decay /dɪˈkeɪ/ *noun* [U] when something decays: *environmental/industrial/moral/urban decay* ○ *dental/tooth decay* ○ *The buildings had started to **fall into** decay.* ○ *This industry has been **in** decay for some time.*

decease /dɪˈsiːs/ *noun* [U] *FORMAL* a person's death: *The house will not be yours till after your mother's decease.*

deceased /dɪˈsiːst/ *adj FORMAL* **1** dead: *the recently deceased Member of Parliament* **2 the deceased** a person who has recently died or people who have recently died: *The deceased shot her mother before killing herself.* ○ *Five of the deceased were employed by the club.*

deceit /dɪˈsiːt/ *noun* [C or U] (an act of) keeping the truth hidden, especially to get an advantage: *The story is about theft, fraud and deceit on an incredible scale.* ○ *When the newspapers published the full story, all his earlier deceits were revealed.* **deceitful** /dɪˈsiːt.fəl/ *adj*: *deceitful behaviour* **deceitfully** /dɪˈsiːt.fə.li/ *adv* **deceitfulness** /dɪˈsiːt.fəl.nəs/ *noun* [U]

deceive /dɪˈsiːv/ *verb* [T] **1** to persuade someone that something false is the truth; to keep the truth hidden from someone for your own advantage; to trick: *The company deceived customers by selling old computers as new ones.* ○ *The sound of the door closing deceived me **into** thinking they had gone out.* ➲See also **deception**. **2 deceive yourself** to refuse to accept the truth: *She thinks he'll come back, but she's deceiving herself.*
• **Are my eyes deceiving me?** something you say when you cannot believe what you see: *Is that snow in May, or are my eyes deceiving me?*
deceiver /dɪˈsiː.vəʳ/ [US] /-vɚ/ *noun* [C] someone who deceives people

decelerate /ˌdiːˈsel.əʳ.eɪt/ [US] /-ə.reɪt/ *verb* [I] to go more slowly; to reduce speed: *The car decelerated at the sight of the police car.* ➲Compare **accelerate** MOVE FASTER.

December /dɪˈsem.bəʳ/ [US] /-bɚ/ *noun* [C or U] (*WRITTEN ABBREVIATION* **Dec**) the twelfth and last month of the year, after November and before January: *23(rd) December/December 23(rd)* ○ *We went to Mexico **on** the twelfth of December/December the twelfth/(MAINLY US) December twelfth.* ○ *Their baby was born **last**/is expected **next** December.* ○ *My parents got married **in/during** December.* ○ *It was one of the coldest Decembers ever.*

decent /ˈdiː.sənt/ *adj* **1** socially acceptable or good: *Everyone should be entitled to a decent wage/standard of* *living.* ○ *I thought he was a decent sort of person.* ○ *It was very decent* (= kind) ***of** you **to** help.* ○ *It made quite a decent-sized* (= large) *hole.* ○ *After the recent scandal, the priest is expected to **do the** decent **thing** and resign from his position.* **2** INFORMAL dressed or wearing clothes: *Are you decent yet?* ○ *You can come in now, I'm decent.*

decency /ˈdiː.sᵊnt.si/ *noun* [U] behaviour that is good, moral and acceptable in society: *a sense of decency* ○ [+ to infinitive] *She didn't even **have the** decency **to** apologize.*

the decencies /ðəˈdiː.sᵊnt.siz/ *plural noun* UK OLD-FASHIONED the acceptable or expected ways of doing something: *I hate going to funerals, but you must **observe** the decencies* (= it is something you should do).

decently /ˈdiː.sᵊnt.li/ *adv*

decentralize, UK USUALLY **-ise** /ˌdiːˈsen.trə.laɪz/ *verb* [I or T] to move the control of an organization or government from a single place to several smaller ones: *We decentralized our operations last year and opened several regional offices.* ○ *Modern technology has made it easy for us to decentralize.* **decentralization**, UK USUALLY **-isation** /ˌdiː.sen.trə.laɪˈzeɪ.ʃᵊn/ *noun* [U] *the decentralization of power*

deception /dɪˈsep.ʃᵊn/ *noun* [C or U] when people hide the truth, especially to get an advantage: *He was found guilty of obtaining money by deception.* ➲See also **deceive**.

deceptive /dɪˈsep.tɪv/ *adj* making you believe something that is not true: *It's deceptive – from the outside the building looks small, but inside it's quite big.*

deceptively /dɪˈsep.tɪv.li/ *adv*: *The plan seemed deceptively simple* (= It seemed simple but was not in fact).

deceptiveness /dɪˈsep.tɪv.nəs/ *noun* [U]

decibel /ˈdes.ɪ.bel/ *noun* [C] a unit for measuring the loudness of sound: *The typical lawn mower makes about 90 decibels of noise.*

decide /dɪˈsaɪd/ *verb* **1** [I or T] to choose something, especially after thinking carefully about several possibilities: *They have to decide by next Friday.* ○ *I don't mind which one we have – you decide.* ○ [+ to infinitive] *In the end, we decided **to** go to the theatre.* ○ [+ (that)] *She decided **(that)** she would retire to the country.* ○ [+ question word] *I can't decide **what** to do.* ○ *He can't decide **whether** to buy it.* ○ *The committee decided **in favour of*** (= made a formal judgment to choose) *the cheapest option.* **2** [T] to be the reason or situation that makes a particular result happen: *The weather decided the outcome of the cricket match.* ○ *Tim's mistake decided the game* (= caused him to lose).

decision /dɪˈsɪʒ.ᵊn/ *noun* [C] a choice that you make about something after thinking about several possibilities: *She has had to **make** some very difficult decisions.* ○ *The company will **reach/come to/make** a decision shortly.* ○ *Let me have a/your decision* (= Tell me what you have decided) *by next week.* ○ [+ to infinitive] *It was his decision **to** leave.* ○ *The decision **about/on** whether he is innocent or guilty rests with the jury.* ○ *We need to take a lot of factors into account in our decision-**making**.* ○ [+ that] *I accepted his decision **that** he wished to die with dignity.* ➲See also **decision**.

▲ **decide on** ***sth/sb*** *phrasal verb* to choose something or someone after careful thought: *I've decided on blue for the bathroom.*

decided /dɪˈsaɪ.dɪd/ *adj* [before n] FORMAL certain, obvious or easy to notice: *She had a decided advantage over her opponent.*

decidedly /dɪˈsaɪ.dɪd.li/ *adv*: *He was decidedly* (= very obviously) *careful about what he told me.* ○ *An agreement is looking decidedly difficult according to the newspapers.*

decider /dɪˈsaɪ.dəʳ/ [US] /-dɚ/ *noun* [C] INFORMAL a final game or competition which allows one person or team to win, or the winning point scored: *They lost what was regarded as the championship decider at Leeds.* ○ *Jones scored the decider in the final minute.*

deciding /dɪˈsaɪ.dɪŋ/ *adj* [before n] A deciding event or action is more important than the rest because the final result, decision or choice is changed by it: *The environmental argument was a deciding **factor**.* ○ *The chairperson always has the deciding **vote**.* ○ *Glennon scored the deciding goal in the final minute of the match.*

deciduous /dɪˈsɪd.ju.əs/ *adj* SPECIALIZED A deciduous tree loses its leaves in autumn and grows new ones in the spring. ➲Compare **evergreen**.

decimal /ˈdes.ɪ.məl/ *adj* relating to or expressed in a system of counting based on the number ten: *If you calculate the result **to** two decimal **places*** (= give two numbers after the decimal point, as in 3.65), *that should minimize any possible errors.*

decimal /ˈdes.ɪ.məl/ *noun* [C] (SPECIALIZED **decimal fraction**) a number expressed using a system of counting based on the number ten: *Three fifths expressed as a decimal is 0.6.*

decimalization, UK USUALLY **-isation** /ˌdes.ɪ.mə.laɪˈzeɪ.ʃᵊn/ *noun* [U] the changing of a system or number to a decimal form

ˌdecimal ˈcurrency *noun* [C or U] a money system in which a smaller unit can be multiplied by ten or a hundred to make up a bigger unit: *The UK and United States both have decimal currencies.*

ˌdecimal ˈplace *noun* [C] the position of a number after a DECIMAL POINT: *The number is accurate to three decimal places.* ○ *Pi expressed to five decimal places is 3.14159.*

ˌdecimal ˈpoint *noun* [C] the . between the two parts of a decimal. In some countries a comma (,) is used instead: *To divide by ten, move the decimal point one place to the left.*

ˈdecimal ˌsystem *noun* [S] a system of counting based on the number ten, with numbers from 0 to 9

decimate /ˈdes.ɪ.meɪt/ *verb* [T usually passive] to kill a large number of something, or to reduce something severely: *Populations of endangered animals have been decimated.*

decipher /dɪˈsaɪ.fəʳ/ [US] /-fɚ/ *verb* [T] to discover the meaning of something written badly or in a difficult or hidden way: *Can you decipher the writing on this envelope?*

decision /dɪˈsɪʒ.ᵊn/ *noun* [U] APPROVING the ability to decide quickly and without pausing because of uncertainty: *She **acted with** decision, closing the bank account and phoning the police.* ➲See also **decision** at **decide**. **decisiveness** /dɪˈsaɪ.sɪv.nəs/ *noun* [U]

decisive /dɪˈsaɪ.sɪv/ *adj* **1** able to make decisions quickly and confidently, or showing this quality: *You need to be more decisive.* ○ *a decisive reply* ✱ NOTE: The opposite is **indecisive**. **2** strongly affecting how a situation will progess or end: *These results could prove decisive in establishing the criminal's identity.* ○ *a decisive role* ○ *a decisive victory*

decisively /dɪˈsaɪ.sɪv.li/ *adv*: *If we had acted earlier and more decisively* (= more quickly and effectively) *it might not have come to this.*

deck [FLOOR] /dek/ *noun* [C] **1** a flat area for walking on, especially one built across the space between the sides of a boat or a bus; a type of floor: *We sat **on** deck until it was dark.* ○ *The upper/top deck of the bus was always full of people smoking.* ➲See also **quarterdeck**; **sundeck**. ➲See picture **Planes, Ships and Boats** on page Centre 14 **2** US a raised area without a roof, which is attached to a house, similar to a BALCONY

• **below decks** on a level of a ship below the main deck: *Our cabin was below decks.*

deck [SET OF CARDS] /dek/ *noun* [C] (ALSO **pack**) MAINLY US a set of cards used for playing card games: *a new deck **of** cards*

deck [DECORATE] /dek/ *verb* [T] to decorate or add something to something to make an effect: *The room was decked **with** flowers.* ○ *The wedding guests were decked **out in** their finery* (= wearing their best clothes). ➲See also **bedeck**.

deck [HIT] /dek/ *verb* [T] SLANG to hit someone, especially to hit someone and knock them down: *Do that again and I'll deck you.*

deckchair /ˈdek.tʃeəʳ/ [US] /-tʃer/ *noun* [C] a folding chair for use outside, especially on the beach, on a ship or in a park, with a long strip of material which forms a low seat when the chair is open

deckhand /ˈdek.hænd/ *noun* [C] a person, usually unskilled, who works on a ship, but who does not serve the passengers or work in the engine room

decking /ˈdek.ɪŋ/ *noun* [U] a floor outside made of wood, or the long pieces of wood used to make this floor

declaim /dɪˈkleɪm/ *verb* [I or T] *FORMAL* to express something with strong feeling, especially in a loud voice or with forceful language: [+ speech] *"The end of the world is at hand!" the poster declaimed.* ○ *She declaimed* ***against*** *the evils of capitalism.* **declamation** /ˌdek.ləˈmeɪ.ʃᵊn/ *noun* [C or U] *He subjected us to half an hour of impassioned declamation* ***against*** *the new motorway.* ○ *Declamations* ***against*** *the press are common enough.* **declamatory** /dɪˈklæm.ə.tᵊr.i/ [US] /-tɔːr-/ *adj*: *a declamatory style*

declaration /ˌdek.ləˈreɪ.ʃᵊn/ *noun* [C] an announcement, often one that is written and official: *Members of Parliament must* ***make*** *a declaration of their business interests.* ○ *As witnesses to the accident, we were asked to* ***make*** *written declarations of what we had seen.* ○ *The company made a declaration* ***of intent*** *to follow an equal opportunities policy.*

declare [EXPRESS] /dɪˈkleəʳ/ [US] /-ˈkler/ *verb* [T] **1** to announce something clearly, firmly, publicly or officially: *They declared their support for the proposal* [+ (*that*)] *She declared (that) it was the best chocolate cake she had ever tasted.* ○ [+ obj + (*to be*) n or adj] *They declared themselves (to be) bankrupt.* ○ [+ speech] *"I won't do it!" he declared.* ○ *America declared* ***war on*** *Japan in 1941* (= announced officially that it was at war). ○ *FIGURATIVE The government have declared* ***war on*** (= publicly announced their opposition to) *the drug dealers.* ○ *The country declared* ***independence*** *in 1952* (= announced that it was no longer under the control of another country). **2** to officially tell someone the value of goods you have bought, or the amount of money you have earned because you might have to pay tax: *Nothing to declare.* ○ *Goods to declare.*
• **I declare** *OLD-FASHIONED* used to express surprise: *Well, I declare!*
declared /dɪˈkleəd/ [US] /-ˈklerd/ *adj*: *He is a declared supporter of* (= publicly supports) *the scheme.* ○ *It has always been my declared intention* (= I have always said I intend) *to sail round the world.*

declare [STOP] /dɪˈkleəʳ/ [US] /-ˈkler/ *verb* [I] If a cricket team declares, they stop batting because they think they already have enough runs to win: *Pakistan declared* ***at*** *350 for 7, leaving Australia to make an unlikely 5 runs an over to win.* **declaration** /ˌdek.ləˈreɪ.ʃᵊn/ *noun* [C] *a cleverly timed declaration*
▲ **declare for/against** ***sth*** *phrasal verb* to give/not give someone or something your public support: *She declared for the new airport plan.*

declassify /ˌdiːˈklæs.ɪ.faɪ/ *verb* [T] to say officially that especially political or military information is no longer secret: *Many government documents are declassified after 50 years.* **declassification** /ˌdiː.klæs.ɪ.fɪˈkeɪ.ʃᵊn/ *noun* [U]

decline [GO DOWN] /dɪˈklaɪn/ *verb* [I] to gradually become less, worse, or lower: *His interest in the project declined after his wife died.* ○ *The party's popularity has declined in the opinion polls.* ○ *FORMAL The land declines sharply away from the house.*
• ***sb's*** **declining years** the last years of someone's life: *He became very forgetful in his declining years.*
decline /dɪˈklaɪn/ *noun* [S or U] when something becomes less in amount, importance, quality or strength: *industrial decline* ○ *Home cooking seems to be* ***on the/in*** *decline* (= not so many people are doing it). ○ *a decline* ***in*** *the number of unemployed* ○ *She seemed to be recovering and then she went into a decline.*

decline [REFUSE] /dɪˈklaɪn/ *verb* [I or T] *FORMAL* to refuse: *I invited him to the meeting but he declined.* ○ *He declined my offer.* ○ [+ to infinitive] *They declined* ***to*** *tell me how they had got my address.*

decode /diːˈkəʊd/ [US] /-ˈkoʊd/ *verb* **1** [T] to discover the meaning of information given in a secret or complicated way: *Decoding the paintings is not difficult once you know what the component parts symbolise.* ➲Compare **encode**. **2** [I or T] *SPECIALIZED* to understand the meaning of a word or phrase in a foreign language in the correct way: *Grammatical information helps learners to decode sentences.*

decoder /diːˈkəʊd.əʳ/ [US] /-ˈkoʊd.ɚ/ *noun* [C] *SPECIALIZED* a piece of equipment that allows you to receive particular television signals: *You need a decoder to get these channels.*

decolletage /ˌdeɪ.kɒl.ɪˈtɑːʒ/ [US] /-ˌkɑː.ləˈtɑːʒ/ *noun* [C or U] (the shoulders and chest of a woman's body shown by) the low top edge of a dress

decolonization, *UK USUALLY* **-isation** /diːˌkɒl.ə.naɪˈzeɪ.ʃᵊn/ *noun* [U] the giving of political independence to a country that was previously a COLONY (= controlled by another country)

decommission /ˌdiː.kəˈmɪʃ.ᵊn/ *verb* [T] to take equipment or weapons out of use: *The government has decided to decommission two battleships.* ○ *It would cost $300 million to decommission the nuclear installation.*

decompose /ˌdiː.kəmˈpəʊz/ [US] /-ˈpoʊz/ *verb* [I or T] **1** to decay, or to cause something to decay: *The body must have been decomposing for several weeks.* **2** *SPECIALIZED* to break, or to break something, into smaller parts: *Microbes decompose organic waste into a mixture of methane and carbon dioxide.* **decomposition** /ˌdiː.kɒm.pəˈzɪʃ.ᵊn/ [US] /-kɑːm-/ *noun* [U] *The corpse was in an advanced stage of decomposition.*

decompress /ˌdiː.kəmˈpres/ *verb* [I or T] to return to the original size or air pressure, or to cause something to do this: *The computer chip compresses and decompresses a colour image in less than a second.* ○ *If a plane window breaks the cabin will rapidly decompress.*
decompression /ˌdiː.kəmˈpreʃ.ᵊn/ *noun* [U]

decomˈpression ˌchamber *noun* [C] a small room in which a very high air pressure is reduced slowly to the normal level to prevent or treat DECOMPRESSION SICKNESS

decomˈpression ˌsickness *noun* [U] *SPECIALIZED* **the bends** (= a serious medical condition caused by returning too quickly to the surface of the sea when DIVING with breathing equipment)

decongestant /ˌdiː.kᵊnˈdʒes.tᵊnt/ *noun* [C] a medicine which helps you to breathe more easily, especially when you have a cold

decontaminate /ˌdiː.kᵊnˈtæm.ɪ.neɪt/ *verb* [T] to remove dangerous substances from something: *Estimates of the amount of money needed to decontaminate the heavily polluted chemical installations vary.*
decontamination /ˌdiː.kᵊn.tæm.ɪˈneɪ.ʃᵊn/ *noun* [U]

decontrol /ˌdiː.kᵊnˈtrəʊl/ [US] /-ˈtroʊl/ *verb* [T] **-ll-** to remove official control on something, especially prices and businesses: *Prices have been decontrolled and markets are flourishing.*

decor /ˈdeɪ.kɔːʳ/ /ˈdek.ɔːʳ/ [US] /deɪˈkɔːr/ *noun* [S or U] the colour, style and arrangement of the objects in a room: *elegant decor*

decorate [MAKE ATTRACTIVE] /ˈdek.ə.reɪt/ *verb* **1** [T] to add something to an object or place, especially in order to make it more attractive: *They decorated the wedding car* ***with*** *ribbons and flowers.* **2** [I or T] to paint the inside or outside of a house or put paper on the inside walls: *We're going to decorate the kitchen next week.* ○ *I hate the smell of paint when I'm decorating.*
decoration /ˌdek.əˈreɪ.ʃᵊn/ *noun* **1** [C or U] when you make something look more attractive by putting things on it or around it, or something that you use to do this: *Christmas/party/table/cake decorations* ○ *He's good at cake decoration.* **2** [U] when the walls or other surfaces of rooms or buildings are covered with paint or paper: *This place is badly in need of decoration.*
decorative /ˈdek.ᵊr.ə.tɪv/ [US] /-ɚ.ə.t̬ɪv/ *adj* made to look attractive: *a decorative display of plants and flowers* ○ *a mirror in a decorative frame* **decoratively** /ˈdek.ᵊr.ə.tɪv.li/ [US] /-ɚ.ə.t̬ɪv-/ *adv*: *A shawl was arranged decoratively over the back of the chair.*
decorator /ˈdek.ᵊr.eɪ.təʳ/ [US] /-ɚ.eɪ.t̬ɚ/ *noun* [C] a person whose job is to paint the inside or outside of buildings and to do other related work: *a firm of painters and decorators*

decorate [HONOUR] /ˈdek.ə.reɪt/ *verb* [T] to reward or honour a person by giving them something, especially a medal: *They were decorated* ***for*** *their part in the rescue.* **decoration** /ˌdek.əˈreɪ.ʃᵊn/ *noun* [C] *The Victoria Cross* *and George Cross are British decorations **for** bravery.*

decorous /ˈdek.ə.rəs/ ⓤ /-ɚ.əs/ *adj FORMAL* behaving politely and in a controlled way: *His manner, as ever, was decorous.* **decorously** /ˈdek.ə.rə.sli/ ⓤ /-ɚ.ə-/ *adv*

decorum /dɪˈkɔː.rəm/ ⓤ /-ˈkɔːr.əm/ *noun* [U] *FORMAL* behaviour that is controlled, calm and polite: *As young ladies we were expected to **act/behave with** proper decorum.*

decoy /ˈdiː.kɔɪ/ *noun* [C] something or someone used to trick or confuse other people or animals into doing something, especially something dangerous: *They used a girl hitch-hiker as the decoy to get him to stop.* **decoy** /dɪˈkɔɪ/ *verb* [T]

decrease /dɪˈkriːs/ ⓤ /ˈdiː.kriːs/ *verb* [I or T] to become less, or to make something become less: *Our share of the market has decreased sharply this year.* ○ *We have decreased our involvement in children's books.* ✳ NOTE: The opposite is **increase**. **decrease** /ˈdiː.kriːs/ *noun* [C or U] *There has been a steady decrease **in** the number of visitors.* ○ *I haven't noticed much decrease **in** interest.*

decree /dɪˈkriː/ *noun* [C or U] *FORMAL* an official statement that something must happen: *The decree stopped short of a full declaration of independence.* ○ *More than 200 people were freed **by** military decree.* **decree** /dɪˈkriː/ *verb* [T] *They decreed an end to discrimination on grounds of age.* ○ [+ that] *The local council has decreed **that** the hospital should close.*

de,cree 'absolute *noun* [S] *LEGAL* the final stage of a legal agreement to end a marriage, when people become free to marry again

decree nisi /dɪˌkriːˈnaɪ.saɪ/ /-si/ *noun* [S] *LEGAL* the first stage of a legal agreement to end a marriage

decrepit /dɪˈkrep.ɪt/ *adj* in very bad condition because of being old, or not having been cared for, or having been used a lot: *Most of the buildings were old and decrepit.* ○ *A decrepit old man sat on a park bench.* **decrepitude** /dɪˈkrep.ɪ.tjuːd/ ⓤ /-tuːd/ *noun* [U] *FORMAL a state of decrepitude*

decriminalize, UK USUALLY **-ise** /ˌdiːˈkrɪm.ɪ.nə.laɪz/ *verb* [T] to stop something from being illegal: *the campaign to decriminalize cannabis* **decriminalization**, UK USUALLY **-isation** /ˌdiːˈkrɪm.ɪ.nə.laɪˈzeɪ.ʃən/ *noun* [U]

decry /dɪˈkraɪ/ *verb* [T] *FORMAL* to criticize something as bad, worthless or unnecessary; to **condemn**: *She decried the appalling state of the British film industry.*

decrypt /diːˈkrɪpt/ *verb* [T] to change electronic information or signals that were stored, written or sent in the form of a secret CODE (= system of letters, numbers or symbols) back into a form that you can understand and use normally: *Messages encrypted using the public key can be decrypted only by someone with the private key.*

dedicate /ˈded.ɪ.keɪt/ *verb* [T] **1** to give completely your energy, time, etc: *He has dedicated his life **to** scientific research.* ○ [R] *The new President said she would dedicate herself **to** protecting the rights of the old, the sick and the homeless.* **2** If you dedicate a book, play, performance, etc. to someone or something, you publicly say that it is in their honour: *The book is dedicated **to** the author's husband.* **3** *FORMAL* When a building, especially a religious building, is dedicated, there is a ceremony at which it is formally opened for use and its particular purpose is stated: *The church was dedicated on 1st March 1805 **to** the local Saint Jude.*

dedicated /ˈded.ɪ.keɪ.tɪd/ ⓤ /-tɪd/ *adj* **1** believing that something is very important and giving a lot of time and energy to it: *a dedicated father/teacher* ○ *She's completely dedicated **to** her work.* ○ *The Green Party is dedicated **to** protecting the environment.* **2** *SPECIALIZED* designed to be used for one particular purpose: *a dedicated computer* ○ *a dedicated sports channel*

dedication /ˌded.ɪˈkeɪ.ʃən/ *noun* **1** [U] when you give a lot of time and energy to something because it is important: *He has always shown great dedication **to** the cause.* ○ *She thanked the staff for their dedication and enthusiasm.* **2** [C] a statement which says in whose honour something has been written, made, performed, etc: *The dedication at the front of the book read 'For my Father'.* **3** [C] a ceremony in which a building, especially a

religious building, is opened for use and its purpose is stated

deduce /dɪˈdjuːs/ ⓤ /-ˈduːs/ *verb* [T] to reach an answer or a decision by thinking carefully about the known facts: *We cannot deduce very much **from** these figures.* ○ [+ that] *The police have deduced **that** he must have left his apartment yesterday evening.*

deducible /dɪˈdjuː.sɪ.bl/ ⓤ /-ˈduː-/ *adj FORMAL* able to be deduced

deduction /dɪˈdʌk.ʃən/ *noun* [C or U] *Through a process of deduction* (= thinking carefully about the known facts), *the detectives discovered the identity of the killer.* ○ *All we can do is make deductions **from** (= form answers by thinking carefully about) the available facts.* ➔See also **deduction** at **deduct**. **deductive** /dɪˈdʌk.tɪv/ *adj: a deductive argument* ○ *deductive logic/reasoning*

deduct /dɪˈdʌkt/ *verb* [T] to take away an amount or part from a total: *The player had **points** deducted (**from** his score) for arguing with the referee.*

deductible, AUS ALSO **deductable** /dɪˈdʌk.tɪ.bl/ ⓤ /-tə-/ *adj*: *Expenses like office telephone bills are **tax** deductible* (= you do not have to pay tax on them).

deduction /dɪˈdʌk.ʃən/ *noun* [C or U] when an amount or a part of something is taken away from a total, or the amount that is taken: *The interest I receive on my savings account is paid after the deduction **of** tax.* ○ *After deductions* (= expenses on which tax does not have to be paid), *his taxable income is $30 000.* ➔See also **deduction** at **deduce**.

deed ACTION /diːd/ *noun* [C] an intentional act, especially a very bad or very good one: *It seems to me that a lot of evil deeds are **done** in the name of religion.* ○ *She's always helping people and **doing** other good deeds.*

deed DOCUMENT /diːd/ *noun* [C] *LEGAL* a legal document which is an official record of an agreement or official proof of ownership of land or of a building

'deed ,box *noun* [C usually sing] a metal box that can be locked, in which important documents are kept

'deed ,poll *noun* [S or U] in Britain, a type of legal document, especially one that allows someone to officially change their name: *He changed his name **by** deed poll.*

deejay /ˈdiː.dʒeɪ/ *noun* [C] *INFORMAL* a **disc jockey**

deem /diːm/ *verb* [T not continuous] *FORMAL* to consider or judge something in a particular way: [+ obj + n or adj] *The area has now been deemed safe.* ○ *We will provide help whenever you deem it appropriate.* ○ [+ obj + to infinitive] *Anyone not paying the registration fee by 31 March will be deemed to have withdrawn from the scheme.*

deep DOWN /diːp/ *adj, adv* going or being a long way down from the top or surface, or being of a particular distance from the top to the bottom: *a deep well/mine* ○ *a deep river/sea* ○ *a deep cut* ○ *The hole is so deep you can't see the bottom.* ○ *The water's not deep here – look, I can touch the bottom.* ○ *Drill 20 holes, each 5 cm deep.* ○ *The water's only ankle/knee/waist-deep, so we'll be able to get across the river easily.* ○ *He thrust his hands deep **in(to)** his pockets.* ○ *The submarine sailed deep **under** the ice cap.* ○ *Take a few deep **breaths** (= breaths that fill the lungs with air) and calm down.* ➔See also **depth** DISTANCE DOWN.
- **deep in thought** thinking very hard: *She sat, not listening, but deep in thought.*
- **be in deep water** (ALSO **get into deep water**) to be in or get into serious trouble: *The government is in deep water over its plans for tax increases.*
- **go off the deep end** *INFORMAL* to get very angry about something or lose control of yourself
- **jump in at the deep end** (ALSO **throw sb in at the deep end**) If you jump or are thrown in at the deep end, you start doing something new and difficult without help or preparation.
- **run/go deep** If a feeling or problem runs deep, it is strong or serious and has existed for a long time: *The anger runs deep on both sides.*

the deep *noun* [S] *LITERARY* the sea or the ocean

deepen /ˈdiː.pən/ *verb* [I or T] to make something deeper, or to become deeper: *One way of preventing further flooding would be to deepen the river bed.* ○ *The sea bed deepens here **to** 5000 metres.*

deep [FRONT TO BACK] /diːp/ *adj* **1** If something is deep, it has a large distance between its edges, especially between its front and back edges: *Is the alcove deep enough for bookshelves?* ○ *The wardrobe is 2 m high, 1 m wide and 60 cm deep.* ○ *By midnight, there were customers standing six deep* (= in six rows) *at the bar.* ➲See also **depth** DISTANCE BACKWARDS. **2 deep in/inside/within *sth*** near the middle of something, and a long distance from its edges: *Little Red Riding Hood's grandmother lived in a house deep in the forest.*

deep [STRONGLY FELT] /diːp/ *adj* very strongly felt or experienced and usually lasting a long time: *Their son has been a deep disappointment to them.* ○ *We're in deep trouble.* ○ *She fell into a lovely deep sleep.* ➲See also **depth** STRENGTH.

deepen /ˈdiː.pᵊn/ *verb* [I or T] to become more strongly felt or experienced or to make something this way: *Over the years, her love for him deepened.* ○ *The economic crisis is deepening.* ○ *We must try not to deepen* (= make more strongly felt) *existing splits within the party.*

deepening /ˈdiː.pᵊn.ɪŋ/ *adj*: *They felt a deepening* (= increasing) *sense of despair.*

deeply /ˈdiː.pli/ *adv* extremely: *I'm deeply grateful to you.* ○ *He found her comments deeply irritating/offensive.* ○ *We don't want to get too deeply involved with these people.* ○ *After 20 years of marriage, they're still deeply in love.*

deep [COMPLICATED] /diːp/ *adj* showing or needing serious thought; not easy to understand: *His films are generally a bit deep for me.* ➲See also **depth** SERIOUSNESS.

deepen /ˈdiː.pᵊn/ *verb* [I or T] *It certainly helped to deepen* (= make more serious) *my understanding of the situation.*

deep [LOW] /diːp/ *adj* (of a sound) low: *a wonderfully deep voice* ➲See also **depth** LOW SOUND. Compare **high** SOUND.

deepen /ˈdiː.pᵊn/ *verb* [I] *Boys' voices deepen* (= become lower) *in their early to mid-teens.*

deep [DARK] /diːp/ *adj* (of a colour) strong and dark: *The sky was deep blue.* ➲See also **depth** DARKNESS.

deepen /ˈdiː.pᵊn/ *verb* [I] *The shadows deepened* (= got darker) *as the evening drew on.*

deep-down /ˌdiːpˈdaʊn/ *adv, adj* felt strongly and often hidden from other people: *a deep-down certainty* ○ *Deep-down, I know you love me really.*

ˌdeep ˈfreeze *noun* [C] a **freezer**

deep-fry /ˈdiːp.fraɪ/ *verb* [T] to fry food in a deep pan in which the food is completely covered by oil **deep-fried** /ˈdiːp.fraɪd/ *adj*: *deep-fried chicken/chips*

deep-seated /ˌdiːpˈsiː.tɪd/ [US] /-t̬ɪd/ *adj* (ALSO **deep(ly)-rooted**) strongly felt or believed and very difficult to change or get rid of: *a deep-seated faith in God*

deep-set /ˌdiːpˈset/ *adj* describes eyes that are far back in the bones of the face

the ˌDeep ˈSouth *noun* [S] the part of the US that is furthest to the south and east, including Alabama, Georgia, Louisiana, Mississippi and South and North Carolina

ˌdeep ˌvein thromˈbosis *noun* [U] (ABBREVIATION **DVT**) a serious medical condition in which a blood CLOT (= a sticky lump of blood) forms in the veins of the legs or lungs

deer /dɪəʳ/ [US] /dɪr/ *noun* [C] *plural* **deer** a quite large four-legged animal which eats grass and leaves. The male has ANTLERS (= wide branch-like horns). The female is called a HIND or a DOE and the male a STAG or BUCK: *a **herd of** deer* ➲See also **reindeer**.

deerstalker /ˈdɪəˌstɔː.kəʳ/ [US] /ˈdɪrˌstɑː-/ *noun* [C] a soft hat with two PEAKS (= flat curved parts that stick out), one at the back and one at the front, and coverings for the ears, which are usually worn turned up: *Sherlock Holmes's deerstalker*

de-escalate /ˌdiːˈes.kə.leɪt/ *verb* [I or T] to (cause to) become less dangerous or difficult: *The government has taken these measures in an attempt to de-escalate the conflict.* ○ *There are signs that the confrontation is beginning to de-escalate.*

deface /dɪˈfeɪs/ *verb* [T] to damage and spoil the appearance of something by writing or drawing on it: *He was fined for defacing library books.*

de facto /ˌdeɪˈfæk.təʊ/ [US] /-toʊ/ *adj* [before n], *adv* FORMAL existing in fact, although not necessarily intended, legal or accepted: *The city is rapidly becoming the de facto centre of the financial world.* ○ *He's her de facto husband though they're not actually married.* ○ *English is de facto the common language of much of the world today.* ○ *If it is on British soil then it is de facto British.* ➲Compare **de jure**.

de facto /ˌdeɪˈfæk.təʊ/ [US] /-toʊ/ *noun* [C] AUS a person with whom someone lives as a wife or a husband, although they are not married: *They've invited Joanne and her de facto for lunch on Sunday.*

defame /dɪˈfeɪm/ *verb* [T] FORMAL to damage the reputation of a person or group by saying or writing bad things about them which are not true: *Mr Turnock claimed the editorial had defamed him.* ➲Compare **libel**; **slander**. **defamation** /ˌdef.əˈmeɪ.ʃᵊn/ *noun* [U] *He is suing for defamation **of character**.* **defamatory** /dɪˈfæm.ə.tᵊr.i/ [US] /-tɔːr-/ *adj*: *He claims the remarks were **highly** defamatory.*

default [FAIL] /dɪˈfɒlt/ [US] /-ˈfɑːlt/ *verb* [I] to fail to do something, such as pay a debt, that you legally have to do: *People who default **on** their mortgage repayments may have their home repossessed.*

default /dɪˈfɒlt/ [US] /-ˈfɑːlt/ *noun* [C or U] *Defaults **on** loan repayments have reached 52 000 a month.* ○ *Any default **on** your mortgage repayments may mean you will lose your house.* ○ *Since they refuse to reply, I think we've won the argument **by** default* (= because of their failure to act). ○ ***The default rate*** (= the number of people failing to do something) *is estimated at 1 in 10 of tax payers.*

default [RESULT] /dɪˈfɒlt/ [US] /-ˈfɑːlt/ *noun* [U] what exists or happens if you do not change it intentionally by performing an action: *Unless something else happens, the default is to meet at the hotel at 7.00 p.m.* ○ *The computer will take '0' as the default **value**, unless you type in something different.* ○ FORMAL ***In** default **of*** (= Because there is not) *any better alternative, we will have to proceed with the original plan.*

▲ **default to *sth*** *phrasal verb* If a computer defaults to a way of operating, it automatically uses it, unless you intentionally change it.

defeat /dɪˈfiːt/ *verb* [T] **1** to win a victory over someone in a fight, war or competition: *Napoleon was defeated by the Duke of Wellington at the battle of Waterloo.* ○ *If we can defeat the Italian team, we'll be through to the final.* ➲See also **self-defeating**. **2** to cause someone or something to fail: *The proposal to change the rules was **narrowly*** (= only just) *defeated by 201 votes to 196.* ○ *Our ambitions for this tournament have been defeated by the weather.* ○ *I'm afraid anything that involves language learning has always defeated me* (= I have been unable to do it).

defeat /dɪˈfiːt/ *noun* [C or U] when someone loses against someone else in a fight or competition, or when someone or something is made to fail: *At the last General Election, they **suffered** a **crushing/humiliating** defeat.* ○ *After their defeat in battle, the soldiers surrendered.* ○ *She **admitted/conceded** defeat well before all the votes had been counted.* ➲Compare **victory**.

• **admit defeat** to accept that you cannot do something: *I thought I could mend the radio myself, but I've had to admit defeat.*

defeatism /dɪˈfiː.tɪ.zᵊm/ [US] /-t̬ɪ-/ *noun* [U] DISAPPROVING a way of thinking or behaving that shows that you lack any hope and expect to fail: *There is a spirit of defeatism among some members of the party.* **defeatist** /dɪˈfiː.tɪst/ [US] /-t̬ɪst/ *adj*: *Being defeatist will get us nowhere.* ○ *He's got such a defeatist attitude.* **defeatist** /dɪˈfiː.tɪst/ [US] /-t̬ɪst/ *noun* [C] *I can't believe it – you're such a defeatist!*

defecate /ˈdef.ə.keɪt/ *verb* [I] FORMAL to excrete the contents of the bowels **defecation** /ˌdef.əˈkeɪ.ʃᵊn/ *noun* [U]

defect [FAULT] /ˈdiː.fekt/ *noun* [C] **1** a fault, problem or lack in something or someone that spoils them or causes them not to work correctly: *All R45 aircraft have been grounded, after a defect **in** the engine cooling system was discovered.* ○ *There are so many defects **in** our education system.* ○ *It's a **character** defect **in** her that she can't ever accept that she's in the wrong.* **2** a physical condition in which something is wrong with a part of someone's body: *She suffers from a heart/sight/speech defect.* ○ *The drug has been shown to cause* ***birth*** *defects.* ○ *Cystic fibrosis is caused by a* ***genetic*** *defect.*

defective /dɪˈfek.tɪv/ *adj* describes something that has a fault in it and does not work correctly: *defective brakes* ○ *defective hearing/eyesight* ○ *a defective gene* ○ *I think that argument/theory is defective.*

defect [LEAVE] /dɪˈfekt/ *verb* [I] to leave a country, political party, etc., especially in order to join an opposing one: *When the national hockey team visited America, half the players defected.* ○ *The British spy, Kim Philby, defected* ***to*** *the Soviet Union/defected* ***from*** *Britain in 1963.* **defection** /dɪˈfek.ʃən/ *noun* [C or U] *Over the years there were hundreds of defections* ***to*** *the West/defections* ***from*** *the East.* ○ *Recent changes in policy have resulted in large-scale defection* ***from*** *the party.* **defector** /dɪˈfek.təʳ/ [US] /-tɚ/ *noun* [C] *She was one of many Communist Party defectors.*

deˈfence ˌmechanism *UK, US* **defense mechanism** *noun* [C] an automatic way of behaving or thinking by which you protect yourself from something, especially from feeling unpleasant emotions: *Arrogance is often a defence mechanism.*

defend /dɪˈfend/ *verb* **1** [T] to protect someone or something against attack or criticism: *How can we defend our homeland if we don't have an army?* ○ *White blood cells help defend the body* ***against*** *infection.* ○ *They are fighting to defend their* ***beliefs/interests/rights.*** ○ *He vigorously defended his point of view.* ○ *The Bank of England intervened this morning to defend the pound* (= stop it from losing value). ○ *The Prime Minister was asked how he could defend* (= explain his support for) *a policy that increased unemployment.* ○ *He will be defending* (= trying not to lose) *his title at the European Championships next week.* ○ [R] *I'm going to karate lessons to learn how to defend myself.* ○ *I can't afford a lawyer so I shall defend myself* (= argue my own case in a law court). ➲Compare **attack**. **2** [I] to try to prevent the opposing player or players from scoring points, goals, etc. in a sport: *The defending champion will play her first match of the tournament tomorrow.*

defence *UK, US* **defense** /dɪˈfents/ *noun* **1** [C or U] (a) protection or support against attack, criticism or infection: *The rebels' only form of defence* ***against*** *the soldiers' guns was sticks and stones.* ○ *The war has ended but government spending on defence* (= the country's army, navy and air force) *is still increasing.* ○ *When Helen criticized me, Chris* ***came/rushed to*** *my defence* (= quickly supported me). ○ *The book is a closely argued defence* ***of*** (= something that supports) *the economic theory of Keynes.* ○ *The towers were once an important part of the city's defences.* ○ *A good diet helps build the body's natural defences.* ➲See also **self-defence**. **2** [S or U] (an) argument or explanation which you use to prove that you are not guilty of something: *The judge remarked that ignorance was not a valid defence.* ○ *She said that she didn't want a lawyer and was going to* ***conduct*** *her own defence.* ○ *All I can say,* ***in*** *defence* ***of*** *my actions, is that I had little choice.* **3** [S or U] in some sports, the part of a team which tries to prevent the other team from scoring goals or points: *a strong defence* ○ *I play (UK)* ***in****/(US)* ***on*** *defence.*

• **the defence** *LEGAL* the person or people in a law case who have been accused of doing something illegal, and their lawyer(s): *a witness for the defence* ○ *a defence lawyer*

defenceless *UK* /dɪˈfent.sləs/ *adj* (*US* **defenseless**) describes people, animals, places or things that are weak and unable to protect themselves from attack: *a small defenceless child* ○ *a defenceless city* ○ *They were quite defenceless* ***against*** *the enemy bombs.* **defencelessness** *UK* /dɪˈfent.slə.snəs/ *noun* [U] (*US* **defenselessness**)

defendant /dɪˈfen.dənt/ *noun* [C] *LEGAL* a person in a law case who is accused of having done something illegal ➲Compare **plaintiff**.

defender /dɪˈfen.dəʳ/ [US] /-dɚ/ *noun* [C] **1** someone who protects a place against attack, or who believes in and supports a person, idea, plan, etc: *The city's defenders were outnumbered by the besieging army.* ○ *So far they have found few defenders* ***of*** *their point of view on campus.* **2** someone in a sports team who tries to prevent the other team from scoring points, goals, etc: *The Brazilian attack put France's defenders under pressure.*

defensible /dɪˈfent.sɪ.bl̩/ *adj* (*US ALSO* **defendable**) able to be protected from attack, or able to be supported by argument: *A city built on an island is easily defensible.* ○ *High petrol taxes are defensible on ecological grounds.*

defensive /dɪˈfent.sɪv/ *adj* **1** used to protect against attack: *These are purely defensive weapons, not designed for attack.* ✻ NOTE: The opposite is **offensive**. **2** too quick to protect yourself from being criticized **3** in a sports event, trying to prevent the opposing player or players from scoring points, goals, etc: *He's currently the best defensive player on the team.*

defensive /dɪˈfent.sɪv/ *noun* **on the defensive** ready to protect yourself because you are expecting to be criticized or attacked **defensively** /dɪˈfent.sɪv.li/ *adv* **defensiveness** /dɪˈfent.sɪv.nəs/ *noun* [U]

defer /dɪˈfɜːʳ/ [US] /-ˈfɝː/ *verb* [T] **-rr-** to delay something until a later time; to **postpone**: *My bank has agreed to defer the* ***repayments*** *on my loan while I'm still a student.* ○ [+ v-ing] *Can we defer making a decision until next week* **deferment** /dɪˈfɜː.mənt/ [US] /-ˈfɝː-/ *noun* [C or U] (*ALSO* **deferral**)

▲ **defer to** ***sb/sth*** *phrasal verb FORMAL* to allow someone or something to make decisions for you or tell you what to do, even if you disagree with them, because of your respect for them or because of their higher rank, authority, knowledge, etc: *I have to defer to my boss* ***on*** *important decisions.* ○ *I defer to* (= accept) *your judgment.*

deference /ˈdef.ər.ənts/ [US] /-ɚ-/ *noun* [U] *FORMAL* respect and politeness: *He* ***treats*** *her* ***with*** *such deference.* ○ *She covered her head* ***out of/in*** *deference* ***to*** (= because of a polite respect for) *Muslim custom.*

deferential /ˌdef.əˈren.tʃəl/ *adj* respectful and polite: *She is always extremely deferential* ***to/towards*** *anyone in authority.* **deferentially** /ˌdef.əˈren.tʃəl.i/ *adv*: *They bowed deferentially as she came into the room.*

defiance /dɪˈfaɪ.ənts/ *noun* [U] ➲See at **defy**.

defiant /dɪˈfaɪ.ənt/ *adj* ➲See at **defy**.

defibrillator /ˌdiːˈfɪb.rɪ.leɪ.təʳ/ [US] /-t̬ɚ/ *noun* [C] *SPECIALIZED* a machine used especially in hospitals, which uses an electric current to stop any irregular and dangerous activity of the heart's muscles: *Defibrillators are used to restore normal rhythm to the heart.*

deficiency /dɪˈfɪʃ.ənt.si/ *noun* [C or U] (a) lack of what is needed: *Pregnant women often suffer from iron deficiency.* ○ *Deficiencies* ***in*** *the education system have been much in the news.*

deficient /dɪˈfɪʃ.ənt/ *adj* **1** lacking: *A diet deficient* ***in*** *vitamin D may cause the disease rickets.* **2** not good enough: *His theory is deficient in several respects.* **deficiently** /dɪˈfɪʃ.ənt.li/ *adv*

deˈficiency disˌease *noun* [C] a disease which is caused by not eating enough of particular types of food that are necessary for good health: *deficiency diseases, for example scurvy*

deficit /ˈdef.ɪ.sɪt/ *noun* [C] the total amount by which money spent is more than money received: *The country is running a balance-of-payments/budget/trade deficit* ***of*** *$250 million.* ○ *The UK's deficit* ***in*** *manufactured goods fell slightly in the last three months.*

defile [SPOIL] /dɪˈfaɪl/ *verb* [T] *FORMAL* to spoil the beauty, importance, purity, etc. of something or someone: *It's a shame that such a beautiful area has been defiled by a rubbish dump.* ○ *The soldiers deliberately defiled all the holy places.* **defilement** /dɪˈfaɪl.mənt/ *noun* [U]

defile [VALLEY] /dɪˈfaɪl/ *noun* [C] *LITERARY* a very narrow valley between two mountains

define [EXPLAIN] /dɪˈfaɪn/ *verb* [T] **1** to say what the meaning of something, especially a word, is: *In this dictionary 'reality' is defined* ***as*** *'the state of things as they are, rather than as they are imagined to be'.* ○ *Before I answer your question, could you define your* ***terms*** *a little more* (= explain what you mean by the words you have used)*?* ➲See also **well-defined**. **2** to explain and state the meaning and exact limits of something: *Your rights and* responsibilities are defined in the citizens' charter. ○ Your role in the project will be strictly defined (= limited to particular areas). ○ I'd hate to feel that I was defined **by** (= that my life got its meaning and importance only from) *my job.* **definable** /dɪˈfaɪ.nə.bl̩/ adj: definable rules of grammar/syntax

definition /ˌdef.ɪˈnɪʃ.ᵊn/ noun [C] **1** a statement that explains the meaning of a word or phrase: *a dictionary definition* ○ *What is the definition **of** 'mood'?* **2** a description of the features and limits of something: *The legal definition **of** what is and what is not pornography is very unsatisfactory.*
• **by definition** because of its own features: *Psychology is by definition an inexact science.*

define CLEARLY SHOW /dɪˈfaɪn/ verb [T] to show clearly the edge of something: *The outline of the castle on the hill was clearly defined **against** the evening sky.*

definition /ˌdef.ɪˈnɪʃ.ᵊn/ noun [U] how clear an image or sound is: *The photograph rather lacks definition.*

de**ˌfining ˈmoment** noun [C] the point at which a situation is clearly seen to start to change: *The end of the Cold War was a defining moment for the world in more ways than one.*

definite /ˈdef.ɪ.nət/ adj fixed, certain or clear: *The date for the meeting is now definite: 5th March.* ○ *She has very definite opinions.* ○ *We need a definite answer by tomorrow.* ○ *"Are you sure I'm invited too?" "Yes, Roger was quite definite **about** it on the phone."* ○ *There's been a definite improvement in your English since you arrived.*

definite /ˈdef.ɪ.nət/ noun [C] INFORMAL something that is certain to happen: *Let's make the 9th a definite – we'll have a curry and then go to the movies.* ○ *She's a definite **for** the Olympic team.*

definitely /ˈdef.ɪ.nət.li/ adv without any doubt: *Have you definitely decided to go to America?* ○ *He definitely said he'd be here.* ○ *"Are you going to have children?" "Oh, definitely (= without any doubt)."* ○ *"Is she not coming, then?" "No, definitely not."*

ˌdefinite ˈarticle noun [C] SPECIALIZED the grammatical name for the word 'the' in English, or the words in other languages which have a similar use ⊃Compare **indefinite article.**

definitive /dɪˈfɪn.ɪ.tɪv/ adj not able to be questioned or improved; final, complete, or best: *a definitive judgment/ruling* ○ *There are no definitive **answers/solutions** to this problem.* ○ *The police have no definitive **proof** of her guilt.* ○ *He's written the definitive (= best and most complete) guide to Britain's Lake District.*
definitively /dɪˈfɪn.ɪ.tɪv.li/ adv

deflate MAKE SMALLER /dɪˈfleɪt/ verb **1** [I or T] If something which has air or gas inside it deflates, or is deflated, it becomes smaller because it loses the air or gas: *to deflate a balloon/tyre* **2** [T often passive] to cause something to become weaker: *The party's ambitions have been rather deflated by the two recent by-election defeats.* **3** [T often passive] to make someone lose confidence or feel less important: *They were totally deflated by losing the match.*
deflated /dɪˈfleɪ.tɪd/ adj feeling less confident and positive than before: *Her criticism left me feeling a bit deflated.*

deflate REDUCE MONEY SUPPLY /dɪˈfleɪt/ verb [T] to reduce the supply of money in an economy
deflation /dɪˈfleɪ.ʃᵊn/ noun [U] **1** a reduction of the supply of money in an economy, and therefore a reduction of economic activity, which is often part of an intentional government plan to reduce prices ⊃Compare **inflation; reflation** at **reflate. 2** a reduction in value: *There has been a deflation **in/of** property values.*
deflationary /dɪˈfleɪ.ʃᵊn.ᵊr.i/ US /-er.i/ adj: a deflationary budget/policy

deflect /dɪˈflekt/ verb [I or T] to (cause to) change direction: *The crowd cheered as the goalkeeper deflected the shot.* ○ *He deflected the ball **away from** the goal.* ○ *The Prime Minister deflected mounting **criticism** today by announcing tax cuts.* ○ *The ball deflected **off** my hockey stick, straight into the goal.*
deflection /dɪˈflek.ʃᵊn/ noun [C or U] *The second goal was from a deflection (= a change of direction) **off** the Liverpool captain.* ○ *The journalists were frustrated by her constant deflection **of** their questions.*

deflower /ˌdiːˈflaʊ.ər/ US /-ɚ/ verb [T] LITERARY to have sex with a woman who has never had sex before

defog /ˌdiːˈfɒg/ US /-ˈfɑːg/ verb [T] -gg- US FOR **demist**
defogger /ˌdiːˈfɒg.ər/ US /-ˈfɑː.gɚ/ noun [C] US FOR **demister**

defoliate /ˌdiːˈfəʊ.li.eɪt/ US /-ˈfoʊ-/ verb [T] to make the leaves drop off a plant, especially by using strong chemicals
defoliant /ˌdiːˈfəʊ.li.ənt/ US /-ˈfoʊ-/ noun [C or U] a chemical which is used to make the leaves drop off plants **defoliation** /ˌdiː.fəʊ.liˈeɪ.ʃᵊn/ US /-foʊ-/ noun [U]

deforestation /diːˌfɒr.ɪˈsteɪ.ʃᵊn/ US /-ˌfɔːr-/ noun [U] the cutting down of trees in a large area; the destruction of forests by people: *Deforestation is destroying large areas of tropical rain forest.* **deforest** /ˌdiːˈfɒr.ɪst/ US /-ˈfɔːr-/ verb [T]

deform /dɪˈfɔːm/ US /-ˈfɔːrm/ verb **1** [T] to spoil the usual and true shape of something: *Age deforms the spine.* **2** [I] SPECIALIZED If something deforms, its usual shape changes and becomes spoiled: *These plastics deform at temperatures of over 90°C.*
deformed /dɪˈfɔːmd/ US /-ˈfɔːrmd/ adj with a shape that has not developed normally: *deformed hands*
deformation /ˌdef.əˈmeɪ.ʃᵊn/ US /-ɚ-/ noun [U] *The deformation **of** the bones was caused by poor diet.*
deformity /dɪˈfɔː.mɪ.ti/ US /-ˈfɔːr.mə.ti/ noun [C or U] when a part of the body has not developed in the normal way or with the normal shape

defraud /dɪˈfrɔːd/ US /-ˈfrɑːd/ verb [T] to take something illegally from a person, company, etc., or to prevent someone from having something that is legally theirs by deceiving them: *He was found guilty of defrauding the Internal Revenue Service.* ○ *They are both charged with conspiracy to defraud an insurance company **of** $20 000.*

defray /dɪˈfreɪ/ verb [T] FORMAL (especially of an organization) to pay the cost of something: *The company will defray all your expenses, including car hire.*

defrock /ˌdiːˈfrɒk/ US /-ˈfrɑːk/ verb [T] OLD USE OR HUMOROUS to dismiss a priest, usually because of bad behaviour

defrost /ˌdiːˈfrɒst/ US /-ˈfrɑːst/ verb [I or T] to (cause to) become free of ice, or to (cause to) become no longer frozen: *When you get a build-up of ice in your freezer, you know it's time to defrost it.* ○ *Defrost the chicken thoroughly before cooking.* ○ *Leave the chicken to defrost.*
defroster /ˌdiːˈfrɒs.tər/ US /-ˈfrɑː.stɚ/ noun [C] US FOR a **demister.** ⊃See at **demist.**

deft /deft/ adj skilful, clever or quick: *Her movements were deft and quick.* ○ *She answered the journalist's questions with a deft touch.* ○ *He's very deft **at** handling awkward situations.*
deftly /ˈdeft.li/ adv: *He deftly (= skilfully) caught the ball.* **deftness** /ˈdeft.nəs/ noun [U]

defunct /dɪˈfʌŋkt/ adj FORMAL no longer existing, living, or working correctly: *members of a **now** defunct communist organization* ○ HUMOROUS *I think this kettle is defunct!*

defuse /ˌdiːˈfjuːz/ verb [T] to make a difficult or dangerous situation calmer by reducing or removing its cause, or to prevent a bomb from exploding: *The two groups will meet next week to try to defuse the crisis/situation/tension.* ○ *Bomb disposal experts have defused a 110-pound bomb at Victoria Station.*

defy /dɪˈfaɪ/ verb [T] **1** to refuse to obey, or to act or be against, a person, decision, law, situation, etc: *children openly defying their teachers* ○ *A few workers have defied the majority decision and gone into work despite the strike.* ○ *The fact that aircraft don't fall out of the sky always seems to me to defy (= act against) the **law** of gravity.* ○ *A forest fire raging in the south of France is defying (= is not changed by) all attempts to control it.* **2** **defy belief/description/explanation** to be extreme or very strange and therefore impossible to believe/describe/explain: *The chaos at the airport defies description.* **3** **defy sb to do** sth to tell someone to do something that you think will be impossible: *I defy you to prove your accusations.* ○ *I defy you to tell where I've painted over the scratch on my car.*

defiance /dɪˈfaɪ.ᵊnts/ noun [U] when you refuse to obey someone or something: *The demonstration is a pointless*

D

***act/gesture** of defiance **against** the government.* ○ ***In** defiance **of** the ceasefire, rebel troops are again firing on the capital.*

defiant /dɪˈfaɪ.ənt/ *adj* **1** proudly refusing to obey authority: *a defiant attitude/gesture* ○ *The protesters blocking the entrance to the offices remained defiant this morning.* **2** not willing to accept criticism or disapproval: *The Prime Minister was in defiant mood in the House of Commons yesterday.* **defiantly** /dɪˈfaɪ.ənt.li/ *adv*: *A group of prisoners stood on the roof, defiantly waving banners and throwing stones.*

degenerate /dɪˈdʒen.ə.reɪt/ *verb* [I] to become worse in quality: *Educational standards are degenerating year by year because of a lack of funds.* ○ *What was intended as a peaceful demonstration rapidly degenerated **into** violence.*

degenerate /dɪˈdʒen.ər.ət/ [US] /-ɚ-/ *adj* having low standards of behaviour: *a degenerate young man*

degenerate /dɪˈdʒen.ər.ət/ [US] /-ɚ-/ *noun* [C] FORMAL DISAPPROVING someone with low standards of behaviour: *They're just **moral** degenerates with no sense of decency.*

degeneration /dɪˌdʒen.əˈreɪ.ʃən/ *noun* [S or U] the process by which something gets worse: *There has been a gradual degeneration **of** the judicial system in the last few years.* ○ *High blood pressure can cause degeneration **of** the heart muscles.*

degenerative /dɪˈdʒen.ər.ə.tɪv/ [US] /-ɚ.ə.t̬ɪv/ *adj* describes an illness in which the body or a part of the body gradually stops working: *a degenerative disease/condition*

degrade [MAKE WORTHLESS] /dɪˈgreɪd/ *verb* [T] to cause people to feel that they or other people are worthless and do not have the respect or good opinion of others: *Pornography degrades women.*

degrading /dɪˈgreɪ.dɪŋ/ *adj* causing people to feel that they are worthless: [+ to infinitive] ***It** is so degrading **to** have to ask for money.* ○ *No one should have to suffer such degrading treatment.* **degradation** /ˌdeg.rəˈdeɪ.ʃən/ *noun* [U] FORMAL *the misery and degradation of prison life*

degrade [SPOIL] /dɪˈgreɪd/ *verb* **1** [T] to spoil or destroy the beauty or quality of something: *Every day the environment is further degraded by toxic wastes.* **2** [I or T] SPECIALIZED If the quality of something electrical or electronic degrades or is degraded, it becomes less good or less correct. **degradation** /ˌdeg.rəˈdeɪ.ʃən/ *noun* [U] *environmental degradation*

degrade [CHANGE STRUCTURE] /dɪˈgreɪd/ *verb* [I] SPECIALIZED (of a substance) to change into a more simple chemical structure: *These chemicals quickly degrade **into** harmless compounds.* ➲See also **biodegrade** at **biodegradable**. **degradable** /dɪˈgreɪ.də.bl̩/ *adj*: *These bags are made of degradable plastic.* ➲See also **biodegradable**.

degree [AMOUNT] /dɪˈgriː/ *noun* [C usually sing; U] (an) amount or level of something: *This job demands a high degree **of** skill.* ○ *There isn't the slightest degree **of** doubt that he's innocent.* ○ *I have to warn you that there's **a** degree **of*** (= some) *danger involved in this.* ○ *The number of terrorist attacks has increased **to** a terrifying degree.* ○ *There was some degree **of** truth in what she said.* ○ ***To what** degree do you think we will be providing a better service?* ○ *"That's really bad." "Well, it's all a **matter/question of** degree* (= there are other things better and other things worse)*."*

• **by degrees** gradually: *The economy seems to be improving by degrees.*

• **to a/some degree** partly: *To some degree I think that's right, but there are other factors which affect the situation.*

-degree /-dɪ.griː/ *suffix*: *She suffered **first-/second-/third**-degree* (= least serious/serious/very serious) *burns on her legs.* ○ US *He's being charged with **first**-degree* (= the most serious type of) ***murder**.*

degree [UNIT] /dɪˈgriː/ *noun* [C] (WRITTEN ABBREVIATION **deg.**) any of various units of measurement, especially of temperature or angles, usually shown by the symbol (°) written after a number: *a difference of three degrees* ○ *Water boils at 212° **Fahrenheit** and 100° **Celsius/Centigrade**.* ○ *A right angle is an angle of 90°.* ○ *New York is on a **latitude of** 41°N and a **longitude of** 74°W.*

degree [COURSE] /dɪˈgriː/ *noun* [C] a course of study at a college or university, or the qualification given to a student who has completed this: *"What degree did you **do** at York?" "Geography."* ○ *She's **got** a physics degree/a degree **in** physics **from** Oxford.* ○ MAINLY US *She's **got** a **bachelor's/master's** degree **in** history **from** Yale.*

dehumanize, UK USUALLY **-ise** /ˌdiːˈhjuː.mə.naɪz/ *verb* [T] to remove from a person the special human qualities of independent thought, feeling for other people, etc: *It's a totalitarian regime that reduces and dehumanizes its population.*

dehydrate /ˌdiː.haɪˈdreɪt/ *verb* [I or T] to (cause to) lose water: *Air travel dehydrates the body.* ○ *You'll dehydrate* (= lose water from your body) *very quickly in this heat, if you don't drink lots of water.* **dehydration** /ˌdiː.haɪˈdreɪ.ʃən/ *noun* [U] *More than 11 000 children die every day around the world because of dehydration caused by diarrhoea.*

de-ice /ˌdiːˈaɪs/ *verb* [T] to remove ice from something: *to de-ice the car*

de-icer /ˌdiːˈaɪ.səʳ/ [US] /-sɚ/ *noun* [C] a substance for removing ice

deify /ˈdeɪ.ɪ.faɪ/ *verb* [T] **1** to make someone or something into a god: *The Romans used to deify their emperors.* **2** DISAPPROVING to consider someone or something to be more important than anything else: *Elvis Presley was deified by his fans.* **deification** /ˌdeɪ.ɪ.fɪˈkeɪ.ʃən/ [US] /ˌdiː.ə-/ *noun* [U]

deign /deɪn/ *verb* DISAPPROVING **deign to do sth** to do something unwillingly and in a way that shows that you think you are too important to do it: *If she deigns to reply to my letter, I'll be extremely surprised.*

deindustrialization, UK USUALLY **-isation** /diː.ɪnˌdʌs.tri.əl.aɪˈzeɪ.ʃən/ *noun* [U] the process by which a country or area stops having industry as its main SOURCE (= cause) of work or income: *the deindustrialization of America/the North East of England*

deism /ˈdeɪ.ɪ.zəm/ *noun* [U] the belief in a single god who does not act to influence events, and whose existence has no connection with religions, religious buildings, or religious books, etc.

deity /ˈdeɪ.ɪ.ti/ [US] /ˈdiː.ə.t̬i/ *noun* [C] a god or goddess: *Ares and Aphrodite were the ancient Greek deities of war and love.*

the 'Deity *noun* [S] FORMAL God

déjà vu /ˌdeɪ.ʒɑːˈvuː/ *noun* [U] the strange feeling that in some way you have experienced already what is happening now: *When I met her, I had a strange **feeling of** déjà vu.* ○ DISAPPROVING *The movie has a strong **sense of** déjà vu about it* (= is similar to other films and does not contain new ideas).

dejected /dɪˈdʒek.tɪd/ *adj* unhappy, disappointed or lacking hope: *She looked a bit dejected when she was told that she hadn't got the job.* **dejectedly** /dɪˈdʒek.tɪd.li/ *adv* **dejection** /dɪˈdʒek.ʃən/ *noun* [U]

de jure /ˌdeɪˈdʒʊə.reɪ/ /ˌdiː-/ [US] /-ˈdʒʊr.i/ *adj* [before n], *adv* FORMAL having a right or existence as stated by law: *The country has de facto independence now, and it will soon be recognized de jure by the world's governments.* ○ *The President aims to create a de jure one-party state.* ➲Compare **de facto**.

delay /dɪˈleɪ/ *verb* **1** [I or T] to make something happen at a later time than originally planned or expected: *My plane was delayed by an hour.* ○ *Could we delay the meeting a few days?* ○ [+ v-ing] *I think we should delay deciding about this until next year.* **2** [T] to cause someone or something to be slow or late: *I was delayed by traffic.* **3** [I] to not act quickly or immediately: *If you delay now, the opportunity might be lost.*

delay /dɪˈleɪ/ *noun* [C or U] when you have to wait longer than expected for something to happen, or the time that you have to wait: *This situation needs to be tackled **without** delay.* ○ *Long delays are predicted on the motorway because of the accident.* ○ *There has been a delay **in** the book's publication.*

delayed /dɪˈleɪd/ *adj* [before n] happening at a later time than expected or intended: *Officials said that the reason for the large number of delayed trains was the bad weather conditions.* ○ *The protests are a delayed reaction to last week's announcement.* ○ *He's suffering from delayed **shock**.*

de'laying ˌtactics *plural noun* actions that are intended to make something happen more slowly, in order to gain an advantage

delectable /dɪˈlek.tə.bl̩/ *adj* beautiful; giving great pleasure: *a delectable cheesecake* **delectably** /dɪˈlek.tə.bli/ *adv*

delectation /ˌdiː.lekˈteɪ.ʃən/ *noun* [U] FORMAL great pleasure and amusement

delegate [CHOSEN PERSON] /ˈdel.ɪ.gət/ *noun* [C] a person chosen or elected by a group to speak, vote, etc. for them, especially at a meeting: *Delegates have voted in favour of the motion.* ○ *Each union elects several delegates* ***to*** *the annual conference.*

delegate /ˈdel.ɪ.geɪt/ *verb* [T + obj + *to* infinitive] *A group of four teachers were delegated* (= chosen) ***to*** *represent the school at the union conference.*

delegation /ˌdel.ɪˈgeɪ.ʃən/ *group noun* [C] a group of delegates: *A delegation from Spain has/have arrived for a month.*

delegate [GIVE] /ˈdel.ɪ.geɪt/ *verb* [I or T] to give a particular job, duty, right, etc. to someone else so that they do it for you: *As a boss you have to delegate (responsibilities* ***to*** *your staff).* ○ *Authority to make financial decisions has been delegated* ***to*** *a special committee.* **delegation** /ˌdel.ɪˈgeɪ.ʃən/ *noun* [U] *Delegation* ***of*** *responsibility is a key part of a manager's job.*

delete /dɪˈliːt/ *verb* [I or T] to remove or draw a line through something, especially a written word or words: *They insisted that all expletives be deleted* ***from*** *the article.* ○ *Here is a list of possible answers. Please delete* (= draw a line through them) *as appropriate.*

deletion /dɪˈliː.ʃən/ *noun* [C or U] *In 1982, the management ordered the deletion* (= removal and loss) *of all computer files on this subject.* ○ *There have been some deletions* (= words have been removed) ***from*** *this text.*

deleterious /ˌdel.ɪˈtɪə.ri.əs/ [US] /-ˈtɪr.i-/ *adj* FORMAL harmful: *These drugs have a proven deleterious* ***effect*** *on the nervous system.* **deleteriously** /ˌdel.ɪˈtɪə.ri.ə.sli/ [US] /-ˈtɪr.i-/ *adv*

Delhi belly /ˈde.li.be.li/ *noun* [U] INFORMAL a stomach illness often caught by people visiting India and caused by drinking dirty water or eating food which has not been washed

deli /ˈdel.i/ *noun* [C] INFORMAL FOR **delicatessen**

deliberate [INTENTIONAL] /dɪˈlɪb.ər.ət/ [US] /-ɚ-/ *adj* **1** (often of something bad) intentional or planned: *a deliberate attack/insult/lie* ○ *We made a deliberate decision to live apart for a while.* **2** describes a movement, action or thought which is done carefully without hurrying: *From her slow, deliberate speech I guessed she must be drunk.*

deliberately /dɪˈlɪb.ər.ət.li/ [US] /-ɚ-/ *adv*: *I'm sure he says these things deliberately* (= intentionally) *to annoy me.* ○ *Calmly and deliberately* (= slowly and carefully), *she poured petrol over the car and set it alight.* **deliberation** /dɪˌlɪb.əˈreɪ.ʃən/ *noun* [U] *Slowly and with deliberation she turned to me and told me to get out.*

deliberate [CONSIDER] /dɪˈlɪb.ə.reɪt/ *verb* [I or T] FORMAL to think or talk seriously and carefully about something: *The jury took five days to deliberate* ***on*** *the case.* ○ *The committee has deliberated the question at great length.* ○ [+ question word] *He's deliberating* ***wh****ether or not to accept the new job that he's been offered.*

deliberation /dɪˌlɪb.əˈreɪ.ʃən/ *noun* [C or U] FORMAL consideration or discussion of something: *After much deliberation, she decided to accept their offer.* ○ *After five days of deliberations, the jury decided on a verdict of not guilty.*

delicacy /ˈdel.ɪ.kə.si/ *noun* [C] something especially rare or expensive that is good to eat: *In some parts of the world, sheep's eyes are considered a* ***great*** *delicacy.* ➲See also **delicacy** at **delicate** EASILY DAMAGED and **delicate** SOFT.

delicate [EASILY DAMAGED] /ˈdel.ɪ.kət/ *adj* **1** needing careful treatment, especially because easily damaged: *Peaches have delicate skins which are easily bruised.* ○ *Delicate plants need to be kept in a greenhouse during the winter.* ○ *delicate china* ○ *Molly's* ***health*** *has always been delicate* (= She becomes ill easily). **2 delicate situation/matter/point, etc.** a situation or matter, etc. that needs to be dealt with carefully in order to avoid trouble or offence: *I need to speak to you about a rather delicate matter.* ○ *The pay negotiations have reached a delicate point/stage.* ○ *Teachers need to strike a delicate* (= carefully achieved) *balance between instructing their pupils and letting them discover things for themselves.* **3** able to measure very small changes: *Weather-forecasters have extremely delicate* ***equipment*** *which helps them predict what the weather is going to be like.* **4** needing to be done carefully: *Repairing damaged nerves is a very delicate* ***operation/process****.*

delicately /ˈdel.ɪ.kət.li/ *adv*: *I thought you handled the situation very delicately* (= in a way that avoided causing offence). ○ *We received a delicately worded refusal of our invitation.*

delicacy /ˈdel.ɪ.kə.si/ *noun* [U] *I have a matter of some delicacy* (= needing to be dealt with carefully in order not to cause trouble or offence) *that I'd like to raise.* ○ *I don't think you quite appreciate the delicacy* ***of*** *the situation.* ➲See also **delicacy**; **delicacy** at **delicate** SOFT.

delicate [SOFT] /ˈdel.ɪ.kət/ *adj* pleasantly soft or light; not strong: *a rose with a delicate scent* ○ *a delicate shade of pink* ○ *We chose a delicate floral pattern for our bedroom curtains.* **delicacy** /ˈdel.ɪ.kə.si/ *noun* [U] *This region produces wines of great delicacy.* ➲See also **delicacy**; **delicacy** at **delicate** EASILY DAMAGED. **delicately** /ˈdel.ɪ.kət.li/ *adv*: *The pudding was delicately flavoured with vanilla.*

delicatessen /ˌdel.ɪ.kəˈtes.ən/ *noun* [C] (INFORMAL **deli**) a small shop that sells high quality foods, such as types of cheese and cold cooked meat, which often come from other countries

delicious /dɪˈlɪʃ.əs/ *adj* **1** having a very pleasant taste or smell: *a delicious cake* ○ *The delicious smell of freshly-made coffee came from the kitchen.* ○ *This wine is delicious.* **2** describes a situation or activity that gives you great pleasure: *I've got some delicious gossip.*

deliciously /dɪˈlɪʃ.ə.sli/ *adv* **1** with a very pleasant taste or smell: *a deliciously garlicky potato cake* **2** very pleasantly: *As she dived into the pool, the water felt deliciously cool on her skin.* **deliciousness** /dɪˈlɪʃ.ə.snəs/ *noun* [U]

delight /dɪˈlaɪt/ *noun* [C or U] (something or someone that gives) great pleasure, satisfaction or happiness: *My sister's little boy is a real delight.* ○ *I read your letter* ***with*** *great delight.* ○ *The children squealed* ***in*** *delight when they saw all the presents under the Christmas tree.* ○ *He seems to* ***take*** *great delight* ***in*** (= enjoys) *teasing his sister.*

• **the delights of sth** the pleasures of something: *We're just discovering the delights of being retired.*

delight /dɪˈlaɪt/ *verb* [T] to give someone great pleasure or satisfaction: *Peter's success at college delighted his family.*

▲ **delight in *sth*** *phrasal verb* to get a lot of pleasure from something, especially something unpleasant: *Some people delight in the misfortunes of others.* ○ *My brother always delights in tell****ing*** *me when I make a mistake.*

delighted /dɪˈlaɪ.tɪd/ [US] /-t̬ɪd/ *adj* very pleased: *a delighted audience* ○ *We're delighted* ***with*** *our new house.* ○ *I was delighted* ***at/by*** *your news.* ○ [+ that] *I'm* ***absolutely*** *delighted* ***that*** *you can come.* ○ [+ *to* infinitive] *We'd be delighted* ***to*** *come to dinner on Friday.*

delightedly /dɪˈlaɪ.tɪd.li/ [US] /-t̬ɪd-/ *adv*

delightful /dɪˈlaɪt.fəl/ *adj* very pleasant, attractive or enjoyable: *Our new neighbours are delightful.* ○ *Thank you for a delightful evening.* **delightfully** /dɪˈlaɪt.fəl.i/ *adv*

delimit /ˌdiːˈlɪm.ɪt/ *verb* [T] FORMAL to mark or describe the limits of something: *Police powers are delimited by law.*

delineate /dɪˈlɪn.i.eɪt/ *verb* [T] FORMAL to describe or mark the edge of something: *The main characters are clearly delineated in the first chapter of the book.* ○ *The boundary of the car park is delineated* (= its edges are marked) *by a low brick wall.* **delineation** /dɪˌlɪn.iˈeɪ.ʃən/ *noun* [C or U]

delinquent /dɪˈlɪŋ.kwənt/ *noun* [C] a person, usually young, who behaves in a way that is illegal or unacceptable to most people: ***juvenile*** *delinquents*

D

delinquency /dɪˈlɪŋ.kwᵊnt.si/ *noun* **1** [U] behaviour, especially of a young person, that is is illegal or unacceptable to most people: *There is a high rate of **juvenile** delinquency in this area.* **2** [C] *FORMAL* an unacceptable or illegal action: *His past delinquencies have made it difficult for him to get a job.*
delinquent /dɪˈlɪŋ.kwᵊnt/ *adj* **1** being or behaving in ways that are illegal or not acceptable: *delinquent teenagers* ○ *They are carrying out research on the causes of delinquent behaviour among young people.* **2** *US FORMAL* late (in paying money owed): *She has been delinquent **in** paying her taxes.*

D

delirious /dɪˈlɪr.i.əs/ *adj* unable to think or speak clearly because of fever, excitement or mental confusion: *She had a high temperature and was delirious.*
deliriously /dɪˈlɪr.i.ə.sli/ *adv*: *Kate and Peter are deliriously **happy*** (= extremely happy) *together.*
delirium /dɪˈlɪr.i.əm/ *noun* [U] *fever accompanied by delirium* ○ *I've never seen such delirium* (= excited happiness) *at a football match before.*

delirium tremens /dɪˌlɪr.i.əmˈtrem.ənz/ /-ˈtriː-/ *noun* [U] *FORMAL FOR* **the DTs**

deliver [TAKE] /dɪˈlɪv.əʳ/ [US] /-ɚ/ *verb* [T] to take goods, letters, parcels etc. to people's houses or places of work: *Mail is delivered **to** our office twice a day.* ○ *The shop is delivering our new bed on Thursday.*
delivery /dɪˈlɪv.ᵊr.i/ [US] /-ɚ-/ *noun* [C or U] *We get two deliveries **of** mail* (= it is delivered twice) *a day.* ○ *You can pay for the carpet **on** delivery* (= when it is delivered). ○ *We expect to **take** delivery **of*** (= receive) *our new car next week.* ○ *a delivery **van***

deliver [GIVE] /dɪˈlɪv.əʳ/ [US] /-ɚ/ *verb* [T] to give, direct or aim something: *The priest delivered a passionate **sermon/speech** against war.* ○ *The jury delivered a **verdict** of not guilty.* ○ *The police said that it was the **blow** that had been delivered* (= given) ***to** her head that had killed her.* ○ *The bowler tripped as he was delivering the ball* (= throwing it towards the person with the bat).
delivery /dɪˈlɪv.ᵊr.i/ [US] /-ɚ-/ *noun* **1** [S] the way in which someone speaks in public: *the actor's delivery* **2** [C or U] in some sports, such as cricket or baseball, the act of throwing the ball towards the person with the bat, in order for that person to try to hit the ball: *That was a good delivery from Thompson.* ○ *The pitcher is famous for the speed of his delivery.*

deliver [GIVE BIRTH] /dɪˈlɪv.əʳ/ [US] /-ɚ/ *verb* [T] to (help) give birth to a baby: *She delivered her third child at home.* ○ *The baby was delivered by a midwife.* ○ *FORMAL The princess has been delivered **of*** (= has given birth to) *a healthy baby boy.*
delivery /dɪˈlɪv.ᵊr.i/ [US] /-ɚ-/ *noun* [C] a birth

deliver [SAVE] /dɪˈlɪv.əʳ/ [US] /-ɚ/ *verb* [T] *FORMAL* to save someone from a painful or bad experience: *Is there nothing that can be done to deliver these starving people **from** their suffering?* **deliverance** /dɪˈlɪv.ᵊr.ᵊnts/ [US] /-ɚ-/ *noun* [U] *We pray for deliverance **from** our sins.* **deliverer** /dɪˈlɪv.ᵊr.əʳ/ [US] /-ɚ.ɚ/ *noun* [C] *Moses was the deliverer **of** the Israelites from Egypt.*

deliver [PRODUCE] /dɪˈlɪv.əʳ/ [US] /-ɚ/ *verb* [I or T] to achieve or produce; to fulfil something promised: *The government has failed to deliver (what it promised).* ○ *MAINLY US The Republicans are relying on their agricultural policies to deliver the farmers' vote* (= to persuade farmers to vote for them). **deliverable** /dɪˈlɪv.ᵊr.ə.bl̩/ [US] /-ɚ-/ *adj*

deliveryman /dɪˈlɪv.ᵊr.i.mæn/ [US] /-ɚ-/ *noun* [C] a man who delivers goods to people's houses or places of work

deˈlivery ˌroom *noun* [C usually sing] a room in a hospital in which babies are born

delouse /ˌdiːˈlaʊs/ *verb* [T] to remove LICE (= a type of very small insect) from the body, hair or clothing of a person or the fur of an animal

delphinium /delˈfɪn.i.əm/ *noun* [C] (*ALSO* **larkspur**) a tall garden plant with blue flowers

delta /ˈdel.tə/ [US] /-t̬ə/ *noun* [C] an area of low flat land, sometimes shaped approximately like a triangle, where a river divides into several smaller rivers before flowing into the sea: *the Mississippi delta* ○ *the delta **of** the Nile*

delude /dɪˈluːd/ *verb* [T] to make someone believe something that is not true; to deceive: [R] *He's deluding himself if he thinks he's going to be promoted this year.*
deluded /dɪˈluː.dɪd/ *adj* believing things that are not real or true: *Poor deluded girl, she thinks he's going to marry her.*

deluge /ˈdel.juːdʒ/ *noun* [C] **1** a very large amount of rain or water: *This little stream can become a deluge when it rains heavily.* **2 a deluge of sth** a lot of something: *The newspaper received a deluge of complaints/letters/phone calls about the article.*
deluge /ˈdel.juːdʒ/ *verb* [T usually passive] to cover something with a lot of water: *The city was deluged when the river burst its banks.* ○ *FIGURATIVE We've been deluged **with*** (= have received a lot of) *replies to our advertisement.*

delusion /dɪˈluː.ʒᵊn/ *noun* [C or U] when someone believes something that is not true: [+ that] *He's **under** the delusion **that** he will be promoted this year.*
• **delusions of grandeur** the belief that you are more important or powerful than you really are
delusive /dɪˈluː.sɪv/ *adj* (*ALSO* **delusory**) false **delusively** /dɪˈluː.sɪv.li/ *adv*

deluxe, de luxe /dɪˈlʌks/ *adj* [usually before n] luxurious and of very high quality: *a deluxe hotel in Paris*

delve /delv/ *verb* [I] to search, especially as if by digging, in order to find a thing or information: *She delved **into** her pocket to find some change.*
▲ **delve into *sth*** *phrasal verb* to examine something carefully in order to discover more information about someone or something: *It's not always a good idea to delve too deeply into someone's past.*

Dem /dem/ *noun* [C] *ABBREVIATION FOR* **Democrat**, see at **democracy**

demagogue, *US ALSO* **demagog** /ˈdem.ə.gɒg/ [US] /-gɑːg/ *noun* [C] *DISAPPROVING* a person, especially a political leader, who wins support by exciting people's emotions rather than by having good ideas **demagogic** /ˌdem.əˈgɒg.ɪk/ [US] /-ˈgɑː-/ *adj* **demagogically** /ˌdem.əˈgɒg.ɪ.kli/ [US] /-ˈgɑː-/ *adv* **demagoguery** /ˌdem.əˈgɒg.ə.ri/ [US] /-ˈgɑː.gɚ.i/ *noun* [U]

demand /dɪˈmɑːnd/ [US] /-ˈmænd/ *verb* [T] **1** to ask for something forcefully, in a way that shows that a refusal is not expected: *I demanded an explanation.* ○ *The car workers' union is demanding a 7% pay rise this year.* ○ *He has always demanded the highest standards of behaviour **from** his children.* ○ [+ speech] *"And where do you think you're going?" demanded the police officer.* ○ [+ to infinitive] *I demand **to** see the manager.* ○ [+ that] *She demanded **that** he return the books he borrowed from her.* **2** to need something such as time, effort, or a particular quality: *This is a very difficult piece of music to play – it demands a lot of concentration.* ○ *He seems to lack many of the qualities demanded **of*** (= needed by) *a successful politician.*
demand /dɪˈmɑːnd/ [US] /-ˈmænd/ *noun* **1** [C] a strong request: *You can't give in to children's demands all the time.* ○ *The government is unlikely to agree to the rebels' demands **for** independence.* ○ *UK They received a **final** demand* (= a last request) ***for** payment.* **2** [C or U] a need for something to be sold or supplied: *There was little demand **for** tickets.* ○ *Good teachers are always **in (great)** demand* (= are always needed).
demands /dɪˈmɑːndz/ [US] /-ˈmændz/ *plural noun* the difficult things that you have to do: *The demands **of** nursing are too great for a lot of people.* ○ *His new job **makes** a lot of demands **on** him* (= he has to work very hard).
demanding /dɪˈmɑːn.dɪŋ/ [US] /-ˈmæn-/ *adj* needing a lot of time, attention or energy: *She's a very demanding child.* ○ *a demanding job/task*

COMMON LEARNER ERROR

demand or **ask?**

Be careful when using the word **demand**. It is stronger than the word **ask** and it sounds as if you are forcing someone to do something.

He asked the teacher to repeat the question.
~~*He demanded the teacher to repeat the question.*~~

demarcate /ˈdiː.mɑː.keɪt/ [US] /ˌdiːˈmɑːr-/ *verb* [T] (*US ALSO* **demark**) to show the limits of something: *Parking spaces are demarcated by white lines.* ○ *Responsibilities within the department are clearly demarcated.* **demarcation** /ˌdiː.mɑːˈkeɪ.ʃᵊn/ [US] /-mɑːr-/ *noun* [C or U] (*US ALSO* **demarkation**) *The river serves as the* ***line of*** *demarcation* (= the line showing the separation) ***between*** *the two counties.* ○ *In some schools, there is little demarcation* ***between*** *subjects* (= subjects are not taught separately). ○ *On this map, demarcations* ***between*** (= the limits of) *regions are shown with dotted lines.*

demarˈcation ˌdispute *noun* [C] *UK* a disagreement between TRADE UNIONS (= organizations of workers) about what types of work should be done by the members of each of them

demean /dɪˈmiːn/ *verb* [T] to cause someone to become less respected: *The entire family was demeaned by his behaviour.* ○ [R] *I wouldn't demean myself by asking my parents for money.* **demeaning** /dɪˈmiː.nɪŋ/ *adj*: *That advertisement is demeaning* ***to*** *women.* ○ [+ to infinitive] ***It*** *was very demeaning* ***to*** *be criticized in front of all my colleagues.*

demeanour *UK*, *US* **demeanor** /dɪˈmiː.nəʳ/ [US] /-nɚ/ *noun* [U] *FORMAL* a way of looking and behaving: *There was nothing* ***in*** *his demeanour that suggested he was anxious.* ○ *She* ***has*** *the demeanour* ***of*** *a woman who is contented with her life.*

demented /dɪˈmen.tɪd/ [US] /-t̬ɪd/ *adj* **1** unable to think or act clearly because you are extremely worried, angry or excited by something: *She was nearly demented* ***with*** *worry when her son didn't come home.* **2** *OLD-FASHIONED OR INFORMAL* mentally ill: *The man is demented – he's going to wreck the whole operation.* **dementedly** /dɪˈmen.tɪd.li/ [US] /-t̬ɪd-/ *adv*

dementia /dɪˈmen.tʃə/ *noun* [U] *SPECIALIZED* a medical condition that affects especially old people, causing gradual worsening of the memory and other mental abilities, and leading to confused behaviour: *The most common form of dementia is Alzheimer's disease.*

demerara (sugar) /ˌdem.əˌreə.rəˈʃʊg.əʳ/ [US] /-ˌrɑːr.əˈʃʊg.ɚ/ *noun* [U] rough pale brown sugar

demerit /ˌdiːˈmer.ɪt/ *noun* [C] **1** *FORMAL* a fault or disadvantage: *We need to consider the merits and demerits* ***of*** *the plan.* **2** *US* a mark given to someone, especially a student in a school, because they have done something wrong or broken a rule: *She got three demerits* ***for*** *lateness on this term's report.*

demigod /ˈdem.i.gɒd/ [US] /-gɑːd/ *noun* [C] (in ancient stories) a being who is partly human and partly a god: *Some football players become like demigods to their fans.*

demilitarize, *UK USUALLY* **-ise** /ˌdiːˈmɪl.ɪ.tᵊr.aɪz/ [US] /-t̬ɚ-/ *verb* [T] to remove military forces from an area: *A demilitarized* ***zone*** *has been created on the border between the warring countries.* **demilitarization**, *UK USUALLY* **-isation** /diːˌmɪl.ɪ.tᵊr.aɪˈzeɪ.ʃᵊn/ [US] /-t̬ɚ-/ *noun* [C or U]

demise /dɪˈmaɪz/ *noun* [S] *FORMAL* **1** death **2** the end of something that was previously considered to be powerful, such as a business, industry or system: *The demise* ***of*** *the company was sudden and unexpected.*

demist *UK* /ˌdiːˈmɪst/ *verb* [T] (*US* **defrost**, *ALSO* **defog**) to remove the mist from the window of a car, usually by blowing air over it **demister** *UK* /ˌdiːˈmɪs.təʳ/ [US] /-tɚ/ *noun* [C] (*US* **defroster**, *ALSO* **defogger**) a device for removing mist from a car window

demo [MARCH] /ˈdem.əʊ/ [US] /-oʊ/ *noun* [C] *plural* **demos** *UK INFORMAL FOR* **demonstration** (= a political march), see at **demonstrate** MARCH: *I went on lots of demos as a student.*

demo [EXAMPLE] /ˈdem.əʊ/ [US] /-oʊ/ *noun* [C] *plural* **demos** **1** an example of a product, especially a computer program or piece of recorded music, given or shown to someone to try to make them buy it: *a software demo* ○ *A team of music industry figures will select bands and soloists from demo* ***tapes.*** **2** *INFORMAL FOR* **demonstration** (= when you show people how something works or how to do something): *a cookery demo* ➲See at **demonstrate** SHOW.

demo /ˈdem.əʊ/ [US] /-oʊ/ *verb* [T] to show something and explain how it works, or to show or produce a demo: *to demo a new piece of software* ○ *They've just completed a Christmas single and are also demoing lots of new songs.*

demob /ˌdiːˈmɒb/ [US] /-ˈmɑːb/ *verb* [T] **-bb-** *INFORMAL FOR* **demobilize** **demob** /ˌdiːˈmɒb/ [US] /-ˈmɑːb/ *noun* [U] *INFORMAL FOR* **demobilization**

demobilize, *UK USUALLY* **-ise** /ˌdiːˈməʊ.bɪ.laɪz/ [US] /-ˈmoʊ-/ *verb* [T] *FORMAL* to release someone from one of the armed forces, especially at the end of a war: *He was demobilized in March 1946.* **demobilization**, *UK USUALLY* **-isation** /diːˌməʊ.bɪ.laɪˈzeɪ.ʃᵊn/ [US] /-ˌmoʊ-/ *noun* [U]

democracy /dɪˈmɒk.rə.si/ [US] /-ˈmɑː.krə-/ *noun* **1** [U] the belief in freedom and equality between people, or a system of government based on this belief, in which power is either held by elected representatives or directly by the people themselves: *The government has promised to uphold the principles of democracy.* ○ *The early 1990s saw the spread of democracy in Eastern Europe.* **2** [C] a country in which power is held by elected representatives: *Few of the Western democracies still have a royal family.* **democrat** /ˈdem.ə.kræt/ *noun* [C] a person who believes in democracy **Democrat** /ˈdem.ə.kræt/ *noun* [C] (*WRITTEN ABBREVIATION* **Dem**) in the US, a member or supporter of the DEMOCRATIC PARTY **democratic** /ˌdem.əˈkræt.ɪk/ [US] /-ˈkræt̬-/ *adj*: *We must accept the results of a democratic election* (= an election in which all people can vote). ○ *Do you think Australia is a more democratic country* (= there is greater social equality there) *than Britain?* **democratically** /ˌdem.əˈkræt.ɪ.kli/ [US] /-ˈkræt̬-/ *adv*: *We need to decide this democratically* (= based on the wishes of most of the people). ○ *Boris Yeltsin was Russia's first democratically elected president.* **democratize**, *UK USUALLY* **-ise** /dɪˈmɒk.rə.taɪz/ [US] /-ˈmɑː.krə-/ *verb* [T] *It's about time we democratized* (= made democratic) *the organization of this company.* **democratization**, *UK USUALLY* **-isation** /dɪˌmɒk.rə.taɪˈzeɪ.ʃᵊn/ [US] /-ˌmɑː.krə.t̬ɪ-/ *noun* [U]

the Demoˈcratic ˌParty *group noun* [S] one of the two main political parties in the US

demography /dɪˈmɒg.rə.fi/ [US] /-ˈmɑː.grə-/ *noun* [U] **1** the study of changes in the number of births, marriages, deaths, etc. in a particular area during a period of time: *historical demography* **2** The demography of an area is the number and characteristics of the people who live in an area, in relation to their age, sex, whether they are married or not, etc: *The increase in the number of young people leaving to work in the cities has had a dramatic impact on the demography of the villages.* **demographer** /dɪˈmɒg.rə.fəʳ/ [US] /-ˈmɑː.grə.fɚ/ *noun* [C] a person who studies changes in numbers of births, marriages, deaths, etc. in an area over a period of time **demographic** /ˌdem.əˈgræf.ɪk/ *adj*: *There have been monumental social and demographic changes in the country.* ○ *Current demographic* ***trends*** *suggest that there will be fewer school leavers coming into the workforce in ten years' time.* **demographics** /ˌdem.əˈgræf.ɪks/ *plural noun* the quantity and characteristics of the people who live in a particular area, especially in relation to their age, how much money they have and what they spend it on: ***The*** *demographics* ***of*** *the country have changed dramatically in recent years.* ○ *No one has exact demographics on* (= information about the quantity and characteristics of the people who live in) *the area.*

demolish /dɪˈmɒl.ɪʃ/ [US] /-ˈmɑː.lɪʃ/ *verb* [T] **1** to completely destroy a building, especially in order to use the land for something else: *A number of houses were demolished so that the supermarket could be built.* **2** to say or prove that an argument or theory is wrong: *He completely demolished all her arguments.* **3** *HUMOROUS* to quickly eat all the food you have been given: *Joe demolished an enormous plateful of sausages and chips.* **4** to easily defeat someone: *In a surprise result, Hibs demolished Rangers 5-0.*

D

D

demolition /ˌdem.əˈlɪʃ.ᵊn/ *noun* [C or U] when something such as a building is destroyed: *the demolition of dangerous buildings*

demoˈlition ˌderby *noun* [C] a car race in which the drivers drive their cars into other cars intentionally, with the winner being the last car still able to move

demon /ˈdiː.mən/ *noun* **1** [C] an evil spirit **2** [C usually sing] *APPROVING* a person who does a particular activity with great skill or energy: *She works like a demon.* ○ *Stefan has a demon serve.* **3** [C] a negative feeling such as guilt or regret which causes you to behave badly: *She had her demons and, later in life, they drove her to drink.*

• **the demon drink** (*US* **the demon alcohol**) *HUMOROUS* alcohol and its unpleasant effects

demoniacal /ˌdiː.məˈnaɪ.ə.kᵊl/ *adj* (*ALSO* **demoniac**) *FORMAL* wild and evil: *A demoniacal light had entered his eyes.* **demoniacally** /ˌdiː.məˈnaɪ.ə.kli/ *adv*

demonic /dɪˈmɒn.ɪk/ *US* /-ˈmɑː.nɪk/ *adj* wild and evil: *He had a demonic (= cruel) gleam in his eye.* **demonically** /dɪˈmɒn.ɪ.kli/ *US* /-ˈmɑː.nɪ-/ *adv*

demonize, *UK USUALLY* **-ise** /ˈdiː.mə.naɪz/ *verb* [T] to try to make someone or a group of people seem as if they are completely evil: *During the 1930s and 40s, the Nazis used racist propaganda in an attempt to demonize the Jews.*

demonology /ˌdiː.məˈnɒl.ə.dʒi/ *US* /-ˈnɑː.lə-/ *noun* [U] the study of demons and other evil creatures

demonstrate [SHOW] /ˈdem.ən.streɪt/ *verb* [T] **1** to show; to make clear: *These figures clearly demonstrate the size of the economic problem facing the country.* ○ [+ that] *Research has demonstrated that babies can recognize their mother's voice very soon after birth.* ○ *These problems demonstrate the importance of strategic planning.* **2** to show something and explain how it works: *He's got a job demonstrating kitchen equipment in a department store.* ○ [+ question word] *The teacher demonstrated how to use the equipment.*

demonstrable /dɪˈmɒnt.strə.bl̩/ *US* /-ˈmɑːnt-/ *adj*: able to be proved: *The report contains numerous demonstrable errors.* **demonstrability** /dɪˌmɒnt.strəˈbɪl.ɪ.ti/ *US* /-ˌmɑːnt.strəˈbɪl.ə.ti/ *noun* [U] **demonstrably** /dɪˈmɒnt.strə.bli/ *US* /-ˈmɑːnt-/ *adv*: *That's demonstrably untrue!*

demonstration /ˌdem.ənˈstreɪ.ʃᵊn/ *noun* [C or U] when you show someone how to do something, or how something works: *This disaster is a clear demonstration of (= makes clear) the need for tighter controls.* ○ *Let me give you a demonstration of how the camera works.* ○ *She told us how easy it was to use the computer, then by way of demonstration simply pressed a few keys on the keyboard.* ○ *We're going to a cookery demonstration tonight.*

demonstrative /dɪˈmɒnt.strə.tɪv/ *US* /-ˈmɑːnt.strə.tɪv/ *adj FORMAL* The findings of this survey are demonstrative of (= show) the need for further research. ➝See also **demonstrative**; **demonstrative** at **demonstrate** EXPRESS.

demonstrator /ˈdem.ən.streɪ.tər/ *US* /-t̬ɚ/ *noun* [C] a person who explains how something works or how to do something: *There was a special stand in the shop where a demonstrator was showing how the food processor worked.*

demonstrate [EXPRESS] /ˈdem.ən.streɪt/ *verb* [T] to express or show that you have a particular feeling, quality or ability: *He has demonstrated a genuine interest in the project.* ○ *His answer demonstrated a complete lack of understanding of the question.*

demonstration /ˌdem.ənˈstreɪ.ʃᵊn/ *noun* [C or U] a way of expressing a feeling or a quality: *Huge crowds followed the funeral procession in a public demonstration of grief.* ○ *There has been little demonstration (= expression) of support for the proposal so far.*

demonstrative /dɪˈmɒnt.strə.tɪv/ *US* /-ˈmɑːnt.strə.tɪv/ *adj* If you are demonstrative, you show your feelings or behave affectionately: *We're a very demonstrative family.* ➝See also **demonstrative**; **demonstrative** at **demonstrate** SHOW. **demonstratively** /dɪˈmɒnt.strə.tɪv.li/ *US* /-ˈmɑːnt.strə.tɪv.li/ *adv* **demonstrativeness** /dɪˈmɒnt.strə.tɪv.nəs/ *US* /-ˈmɑːnt.strə.tɪv.nəs/ *noun* [U]

demonstrate [MARCH] /ˈdem.ən.streɪt/ *verb* [I] to make a public expression of dissatisfaction, especially by marching or having a meeting: *Thousands of people gathered to demonstrate against the new proposals.*

demonstration /ˌdem.ənˈstreɪ.ʃᵊn/ *noun* [C] (*INFORMAL* **demo**) when a group of people march or stand together to show that they disagree with or support something or someone: *The students are holding a demonstration to protest against the increase in their fees.* ○ *Protesters staged an anti-war demonstration in front of the US embassy.*

demonstrator /ˈdem.ən.streɪ.tər/ *US* /-t̬ɚ/ *noun* [C] a person who marches or stands with a group of people to show that they disagree with or support something or someone: *Police arrested several of the demonstrators.*

demonstrative /dɪˈmɒnt.strə.tɪv/ *US* /-ˈmɑːnt.strə.tɪv/ *adj* describes words such as 'this', 'that', 'these' and 'those' that show which person or thing is being referred to: *In the sentence 'This is my brother', 'this' is a demonstrative pronoun.* ➝See also **demonstrative** at **demonstrate** SHOW and **demonstrate** EXPRESS.

demoralize, *UK USUALLY* **-ise** /dɪˈmɒr.ə.laɪz/ *US* /-ˈmɔːr-/ *verb* [T] to weaken the confidence of someone or something: *Losing several matches in succession had completely demoralized the team.*

demoralized, *UK USUALLY* **-ised** /dɪˈmɒr.ə.laɪz/ *US* /-ˈmɔːr-/ *adj* having lost your confidence, enthusiasm, and hope: *After the game, the players were tired and demoralized.* **demoralizing**, *UK USUALLY* **-ising** /dɪˈmɒr.ə.laɪ.zɪŋ/ *US* /-ˈmɔːr-/ *adj*: *Being out of work for a long time is very demoralizing.* **demoralization**, *UK USUALLY* **-isation** /dɪˌmɒr.ᵊl.aɪˈzeɪ.ʃᵊn/ *US* /-ˌmɔːr-/ *noun* [U]

demote /dɪˈməʊt/ *US* /-ˈmoʊt/ *verb* [T] to lower someone or something in rank or position: *The captain was demoted (to sergeant) for failing to fulfil his duties.* ✻ NOTE: The opposite is **promote**. **demotion** /dɪˈməʊ.ʃᵊn/ *US* /-ˈmoʊ-/ *noun* [C or U]

demotic /dɪˈmɒt.ɪk/ *US* /-ˈmɑː.t̬ɪk/ *adj FORMAL* (of or in a form of language) used by ordinary people

demotivate /ˌdiːˈməʊ.tɪ.veɪt/ *US* /-ˈmoʊ.t̬ɪ-/ *verb* [T] to make someone less enthusiastic about a job: *She was very demotivated by being told she had little chance of being promoted.* **demotivating** /ˌdiːˈməʊ.tɪ.veɪ.tɪŋ/ *US* /-ˈmoʊ.t̬ɪ.veɪ.t̬ɪŋ/ *adj*: *Constant criticism can be very demotivating.*

demur /dɪˈmɜːr/ *US* /-ˈmɜː-/ *verb* [I] **-rr-** *FORMAL* to express disagreement or refusal to do something: *The lawyer requested a break in the court case, but the judge demurred.* **demur** /dɪˈmɜːr/ *US* /-ˈmɜː-/ *noun* [U] *She agreed to his request without demur.*

demure /dɪˈmjʊər/ *US* /-ˈmjʊr/ *adj* (especially of women and children) quiet and well behaved: *She gave him a demure smile.* **demurely** /dɪˈmjʊə.li/ *US* /-ˈmjʊr-/ *adv*: *She sat with her hands folded demurely in her lap.* **demureness** /dɪˈmjʊə.nəs/ *US* /-ˈmjʊr-/ *noun* [U]

demystify /ˌdiːˈmɪs.tɪ.faɪ/ *verb* [T] to make something easier to understand: *What I need is a book that will demystify the workings of a car engine for me.*

demythologize, *UK USUALLY* **-ise** /ˌdiː.mɪˈθɒl.ə.dʒaɪz/ *US* /-ˈθɑː.lə-/ *verb* [T] to provide an explanation of something, or to present something, in a way which removes any mystery surrounding it

den /den/ *noun* [C] **1** the home of particular types of wild animal **2** a rough structure, usually built outside from pieces of wood, cardboard, etc., in which children play **3** *MAINLY US* a room in a house or apartment, which is used for activities not involving work: *The kids are watching television in the den.* **4** a place where people secretly plan or take part in immoral or illegal activities: *a drug/drinking/vice den* ○ *OFTEN HUMOROUS a den of thieves/iniquity*

denationalize, *UK USUALLY* **-ise** /ˌdiːˈnæʃ.ᵊn.ᵊl.aɪz/ *verb* [T] to change an industry from public to private ownership **denationalization**, *UK USUALLY* **-isation** /diːˌnæʃ.ᵊn.ᵊl.aɪˈzeɪ.ʃᵊn/ *noun* [C or U]

deniable /dɪˈnaɪ.ə.bl̩/ *adj* ➝See at **deny** NOT TRUE.

denial /dɪˈnaɪ.əl/ *noun* ➝See at **deny**.

denier /ˈden.i.ər/ *US* /-jɚ/ *noun* [U] *MAINLY UK* a measure of the thickness of the weave of NYLON, silk, etc. thread, especially that which is used in making stockings or tights

denigrate /ˈden.ɪ.greɪt/ *verb* [T] to say that someone or something is not good or important: *You shouldn't denigrate people just because they have different beliefs from you.* **denigration** /ˌden.ɪˈgreɪ.ʃən/ *noun* [U]

denim /ˈden.ɪm/ *noun* [U] a thick strong cotton cloth, often blue in colour, used especially for making JEANS: *a denim jacket and jeans*

denims /ˈden.ɪmz/ *plural noun* UK INFORMAL *He's usually in denims* (= clothes made of denim).

denizen /ˈden.ɪ.zən/ *noun* [C] LITERARY an animal, plant or person that lives in or is often in a particular place: *Deer, foxes and squirrels are among the denizens* **of** *the forest.*

denomination [RELIGIOUS GROUP] /dɪˌnɒm.ɪˈneɪ.ʃən/ [US] /-ˌnɑː.mə-/ *group noun* [C] a religious group which has slightly different beliefs from other groups which share the same religion: *Protestantism and Roman Catholicism are both denominations of the Christian faith.*

denominational /dɪˌnɒm.ɪˈneɪ.ʃən.əl/ [US] /-ˌnɑː.mə-/ *adj* connected with a particular religious denomination

* NOTE: The opposite is **nondenominational**.

denomination [VALUE] /dɪˌnɒm.ɪˈneɪ.ʃən/ [US] /-ˌnɑː.mə-/ *noun* [C] a unit of value, especially of money: *It always takes time to get used to the different denominations* **of** *coins when you go to a foreign country.*

denominator /dɪˈnɒm.ɪ.neɪ.təʳ/ [US] /-ˈnɑː.mə.neɪ.t̬ɚ/ *noun* [C] the number below the line in a fraction: *In the fraction* $\frac{3}{4}$*, 4 is the denominator.* ➲Compare **numerator**.

denote /dɪˈnəʊt/ [US] /-ˈnoʊt/ *verb* [T] to represent something: *The colour red is used to denote passion or danger.*

denouement /deɪˈnuː.mɒ̃/ [US] /-mɑ̃ː/ *noun* [C] the end of a story, in which everything is explained, or the end result of a situation

denounce [CRITICIZE] /dɪˈnaʊnts/ *verb* [T] to criticize something or someone strongly and publicly: *The government's economic policy has been denounced on all sides.* ○ *We must denounce injustice and oppression.*

denunciation /dɪˌnʌnt.siˈeɪ.ʃən/ *noun* [C or U] public criticism of something or someone

denounce [ACCUSE] /dɪˈnaʊnts/ *verb* [T] to accuse someone publicly of being something bad; to give information against: *His former colleagues have denounced him* **as** *a spy.* **denunciation** /dɪˌnʌnt.siˈeɪ.ʃən/ *noun* [C or U]

dense [THICK] /dents/ *adj* **1** thick; close together; difficult to go or see through: *dense* ***fog*** ○ *a dense forest* ○ *The body was found hidden in dense* ***undergrowth***. ○ *a book with dense print* (= with the words printed small and close together) **2** INFORMAL stupid: *We've got some really dense people in our class.*

densely /ˈdent.sli/ *adv*: *England was once a densely wooded country* (= a lot of trees grew close together there). ○ *Mexico City is one of the most densely* ***populated*** *cities in the world* (= a lot of people live close together there). ○ *His books tend to be rather densely written* (= contain a lot of information and ideas and are difficult to understand).

density /ˈdent.sɪ.ti/ [US] /-sə.t̬i/ *noun* [C or U] (ALSO **denseness**) the number of people or things in a place when compared with the size of the place: *The area has a* ***high/low*** *population density.* ○ *We were unable to move because of the density* ***of*** *the crowd.*

dense [MATTER] /dents/ *adj* SPECIALIZED (of a substance) containing a lot of matter in a small space: *Plutonium is very dense.*

density /ˈdent.sɪ.ti/ [US] /-sə.t̬i/ *noun* [C or U] SPECIALIZED the relationship between the mass of a substance and its size: *Lead* ***has*** *a* ***high*** *density.* ○ *Aluminium is* ***low in*** *density.*

dent /dent/ *noun* [C] a small hollow mark in the surface of something, caused by pressure or being hit: *a dent in the door of a car*

• **make/put a dent in** ***sth*** to reduce an amount of money: *The holiday made a big dent in our savings.*

dent /dent/ *verb* [T] **1** to make a small hollow mark in the surface of something: *I dropped a hammer on the floor, and it dented the floorboard.* **2** If you dent someone's confidence or pride, you make them feel less confident or proud: *His confidence was* ***badly*** *dented when he didn't get into the football team.*

dental /ˈden.təl/ [US] /-t̬əl/ *adj* relating to the teeth: *dental decay/treatment*

ˈdental ˌfloss *noun* [U] a type of thread which is used for cleaning between the teeth

ˈdental hyˌgienist *noun* [C] a person who works with a dentist and cleans people's teeth to keep them healthy

ˈdental pracˌtitioner/ˌsurgeon *noun* [C] FORMAL a dentist

dentist /ˈden.tɪst/ [US] /-t̬ɪst/ *noun* [C] a person whose job is treating people's teeth: *You should have your teeth checked by a dentist at least twice a year.*

dentistry /ˈden.tɪ.stri/ [US] /-t̬ɪ-/ *noun* [U] the work of a dentist

dentist's /ˈden.tɪsts/ [US] /-t̬ɪsts/ *noun* [C] *plural* **dentists** *I've got to go to the dentist's* (= the place where a dentist works) *on Friday.*

dentures /ˈden.tʃəz/ [US] /-tʃɚz/ *plural noun* false teeth fixed to a small piece of plastic or similar material, which fits inside the mouth of someone who does not have their own teeth: *a set of dentures*

denude /dɪˈnjuːd/ [US] /-ˈnuːd/ *verb* [T] **1** to remove the covering of something, especially land: *The countryside has been denuded by war.* ○ *Drought and years of heavy grazing by sheep have completely denuded the hills* ***of*** *grass.* **2** to remove a valuable possession or quality: *Any further cuts in the country's armed forces would leave its* ***defences*** *dangerously denuded.*

ˌDenver ˈboot *noun* [C] (ALSO **boot**) US a **wheel clamp**

deny [NOT TRUE] /dɪˈnaɪ/ *verb* [T] to say that something is not true: *He will not confirm or deny the* ***allegations***. ○ [+ **that**] *Neil denies* ***that*** *he broke the window, but I'm sure he did.* ○ [+ **v-ing**] *Neil denies break****ing*** *the window.*

• **there's no denying** it is true: *There's no denying* ***that*** *this has been a difficult year for the company.*

deniable /dɪˈnaɪ.ə.bl̩/ *adj* possible to deny: *The facts are simply not deniable.*

denial /dɪˈnaɪ.əl/ *noun* [C] a statement that something is not true: *The prime minister* ***issued*** *a denial* ***of*** *the report that she is about to resign.* ○ [+ **that**] *Officials did not believe the runner's denial* ***that*** *he had taken drugs.*

deny [REFUSE] /dɪˈnaɪ/ *verb* [T] to not allow someone to have or do something: *Her request for time off work was denied.* ○ *No one should be denied a good education./A good education should be denied* ***to*** *no one.* ○ [+ **two objects**] *The goalkeeper denied him his third goal.* ○ *I was denied the opportunity of learning French at school.*

deˈny ***yourself*** /dɪˈnaɪ/ *verb* [R] to not allow yourself to have or do things: *Many parents deny themselves so that their children can have the best.*

denial /dɪˈnaɪ.əl/ *noun* [U] when someone is not allowed to do or have something: ***a*** *gross denial* ***of*** *justice* ➲See also **self-denial**.

deny [NOT ADMIT] /dɪˈnaɪ/ *verb* [T] to not admit that you have knowledge, responsibility, feelings, etc: *He denied all responsibility for the rumours which have been circulating.* ○ *Even under torture, he refused to deny his beliefs/faith.*

denial /dɪˈnaɪ.əl/ *noun* [C] *His denial* ***of*** *responsibility for the accident was unconvincing.* ○ *If I did what you ask, it would be a denial* ***of*** *everything I stand for* (= believe in).

deodorant /diˈəʊ.dər.ənt/ [US] /-ˈoʊ.dɚ-/ *noun* [C or U] a substance that you put on your body to prevent or hide unpleasant smells

dep. WRITTEN ABBREVIATION FOR **depart** or **departure** (used in TIMETABLES to show the time at which a bus, train or aircraft leaves a place): *Flight BA174, dep. Heathrow 07.45.*

depart /dɪˈpɑːt/ [US] /-ˈpɑːrt/ *verb* [I] FORMAL to go away or leave, especially on a journey: *The plane departs at 6.00 a.m.* ○ *The train for London departs* ***from*** *Platform 2.*

• **depart this life** FORMAL to die: *In loving memory of my dear husband, who departed this life on May 5, 1978.*

departed /dɪˈpɑː.tɪd/ [US] /-ˈpɑːr.t̬ɪd/ *adj* **1** LITERARY describes something that happened in the past and is finished: *The old man talked about the departed triumphs of his youth.* **2** LITERARY dead: *We will always remember our* ***dear*** *departed friends.* **3** FORMAL **the departed** a person who has died, or people who have died: *Let us remember the departed.*

D

departure /dɪˈpɑː.tʃəʳ/ [US] /-ˈpɑːr.tʃɚ/ *noun* [C or U] **1** when a person or vehicle, etc. leaves somewhere: *There are several departures* (= buses, trains, ships or aircraft leaving) ***for*** *Paris every day.* ○ *Our departure was delayed because of bad weather.* ○ *departure time* **2** when someone leaves a job: *Everyone in the office was surprised by Graham's sudden departure.* **3** a change from what is expected, or from what has happened before: *There can be no departure* ***from*** *the rules.* ○ *Selling men's clothing is a* ***new*** *departure* (= type of activity) *for the shop.*

▲ **depart from** ***sth*** *phrasal verb* FORMAL to be different from the usual or expected way of doing or thinking about something: *I see no reason for us to depart from our usual practice.* ○ *At this point in the speech, the minister departed from his prepared text.*

department /dɪˈpɑːt.mənt/ [US] /-ˈpɑːrt-/ *group noun* [C] (*WRITTEN ABBREVIATION* **dept**) a part of an organization such as a school, business or government which deals with a particular area of study or work: *the geography department/the department* ***of*** *geography* ○ *The accounts department is/are having a Christmas party this week.* ○ *the Department* ***of*** *Health and Social Security*

• **be** ***sb's*** **department** INFORMAL to be a particular person's area of responsibility: *Wasn't buying the tickets your department, Kev?*

• **in the** ***brain/looks*** **department** HUMOROUS in intelligence/attractiveness: *He's a bit lacking in the brain department.*

departmental /ˌdiː.pɑːtˈmen.təl/ [US] /-pɑːrtˈmen.t̬əl/ *adj* relating to a department: *Janet is now a departmental head/manager.* ○ *a departmental meeting*

deˈpartment ˌstore *noun* [C] a large shop divided into several different parts, each of which sells different things

deˈparture ˌlounge *noun* [C usually sing] the area in an airport where passengers wait before getting onto an aircraft

depend /dɪˈpend/ *verb* [I] to be decided by or to vary according to the stated thing: *Whether or not we go to Spain for our holiday depends* ***on*** *the cost.* ○ [+ question word] *I might go to the cinema tomorrow – **it** depends **what** time I get home from work.*

• **it (all) depends** INFORMAL it is not decided yet: *"Are you going to Emma's party?" "I don't know, it depends – we might be going away that weekend."*

dependent /dɪˈpen.dənt/ *adj* **dependent on/upon** ***sth*** influenced or decided by something: *Whether I go to university or not is dependent on what exam grades I get.* ⊃See also **dependent**.

COMMON LEARNER ERROR

depend on something

Remember that the correct preposition after **depend** is 'on'.

I might go sailing on Friday, it depends on the weather.
~~*I might go sailing on Friday, it depends from the weather.*~~

PHRASAL VERBS WITH **depend** ▼

▲ **depend on/upon** ***sb/sth*** [TRUST] *phrasal verb* to trust someone or something and know that they will help you or do what you want or expect them to do: *You can always depend on Michael in a crisis.* ○ [+ to infinitive] *I'm depending on you* ***to*** *keep your promise.* ○ [+ v-ing] *You can't always depend on the trains arriv**ing** on time.* ○ HUMOROUS *You can depend on Jane* ***to*** *be late* (= she is always late).

• **(you can) depend on/upon it** you can be certain: *You haven't heard the last of this, depend upon it.*

▲ **depend on/upon** ***sb/sth*** [SUPPORT] *phrasal verb* to need something, or need the help and support of someone or something, in order to live or continue as before: *Charities depend on people supporting their activities.* ○ *The country depends* ***heavily*** *on foreign aid.* ○ *Elaine depends upon Bob completely* ***for*** *her happiness.*

dependable /dɪˈpen.də.bl/ *adj* If someone or something is dependable, you can trust them or have confidence in them: *I need someone dependable to look after the children while I'm at work.* ○ *a dependable car* **dependably** /dɪˈpen.də.bli/ *adv* **dependability** /dɪˌpen.dəˈbɪl.ɪ.ti/ [US] /-ə.t̬i/ *noun* [U] *The car offers value for money, comfort and dependability.*

dependant, MAINLY US **dependent** /dɪˈpen.dənt/ *noun* [C] someone who depends on you for financial support, such as a child or family member who does not work: *My pension will provide for my dependants.*

dependence, US ALSO **dependance** /dɪˈpen.dənts/ *noun* [S or U] (*ALSO* **dependency**) when you need something or someone all the time, especially in order to continue existing or operating: *The company needs to reduce its dependence* ***on*** *just one particular product.* ○ *Drug dependence led to her early death.* ○ *She has developed* ***a*** *deep dependence* ***on*** *him* (= she needs him emotionally).

dependency /dɪˈpen.dənt.si/ *noun* [C] a country which is supported and governed by another country

dependent /dɪˈpen.dənt/ *adj* **1** needing the support of something or someone in order to continue existing or operating: *He has three dependent children.* ○ *It's very easy to become dependent* ***on*** *sleeping pills.* **2** describes a grammatical clause which cannot form a separate sentence but can form a sentence when it is joined to a main clause

depersonalize, UK USUALLY **-ise** /ˌdiːˈpɜː.sən.əl.aɪz/ [US] /-ˈpɝː-/ *verb* [T] to remove from a person, organization, object, etc. the qualities or features which make them particular or special: *He thinks that wearing school uniform depersonalizes children.*

depict /dɪˈpɪkt/ *verb* [T] to represent or show something in a picture or story: *Her paintings depict the lives of ordinary people in the last century.* ○ *In the book, he depicts his father* ***as*** *a tyrant.* ○ [+ v-ing] *People were shocked by the advertisement which depicted a woman beat**ing** her husband.* **depiction** /dɪˈpɪk.ʃən/ *noun* [C or U] *The painter's depictions* ***of*** *the horror of war won her a worldwide reputation.* ○ *I disapprove of the depiction* ***of*** *violence on television.*

depilatory /dɪˈpɪl.ə.tər.i/ [US] /-tɔːr-/ *noun* [C] a substance used for removing unwanted hair from the human body **depilatory** /dɪˈpɪl.ə.tər.i/ [US] /-tɔːr-/ *adj*: *I use a depilatory* ***cream*** *under my arms.*

deplane /ˌdiːˈpleɪn/ *verb* [I] US to leave an aircraft: *Would all passengers please deplane by the rear doors.*

deplete /dɪˈpliːt/ *verb* [T] to reduce something in size or amount, especially supplies of energy, money or similar: *If we continue to deplete the Earth's natural resources, we will cause serious damage to the environment.* ○ *The illness depletes the body* ***of*** *important vitamins.* ○ HUMOROUS *That last holiday has seriously depleted my bank account!*

depleted /dɪˈpliː.tɪd/ [US] /-t̬ɪd/ *adj* reduced: *Measures have been taken to protect the world's depleted elephant population.* ○ *physically/emotionally depleted* (= weakened)

depletion /dɪˈpliː.ʃən/ *noun* [S or U] (a) reduction: *the depletion* ***of*** *the ozone layer* ○ *Increased expenditure has caused a depletion* ***in*** *our capital/funds.*

deplore /dɪˈplɔːʳ/ [US] /-ˈplɔːr/ *verb* [T not continuous] FORMAL to say or think that something is very bad: *We deeply deplore the loss of life.* ○ *He said that he deplored all violence.* ○ UK *The attitude of the Minister is* ***to be*** *deplored* (= is very bad).

deplorable /dɪˈplɔː.rə.bl/ [US] /-ˈplɔːr.ə-/ *adj* FORMAL very bad: *I thought his behaviour absolutely deplorable.* ○ *They are forced to live in deplorable conditions.* **deplorably** /dɪˈplɔː.rə.bli/ [US] /-ˈplɔːr.ə-/ *adv*: *He behaved deplorably.*

deploy /dɪˈplɔɪ/ *verb* [T] **1** to use something or someone, especially in an effective way: *The company is reconsidering the way in which it deploys its* ***resources/staff.*** ○ *My job doesn't really allow me fully to deploy my skills/talents.* **2** to move soldiers or equipment to a place where they can be used when they are needed: *The decision has been made to deploy extra* ***troops****/more powerful* ***weapons.*** **deployment** /dɪˈplɔɪ.mənt/ *noun* [U] *The Chief of Police ordered the deployment* ***of*** *2 000 troops to try to stop the rioting.* ○ *the deployment* ***of*** *nuclear weapons*

depopulate /ˌdiːˈpɒp.jʊ.leɪt/ [US] /-ˈpɑː.pjə-/ *verb* [T] to cause a country or area to have fewer people living in it: *The region was depopulated by disease/famine/war.* **depopulation** /diːˌpɒp.jʊˈleɪ.ʃᵊn/ [US] /-ˌpɑː.pjə-/ *noun* [U] *rural depopulation/depopulation **of** the rural areas*

deport /dɪˈpɔːt/ [US] /-ˈpɔːrt/ *verb* [T] to force someone to leave a country, especially someone who has no legal right to be there or who has broken the law: *Thousands of illegal immigrants are caught and deported every year.* ○ *The refugees were deported back to their country of origin.* **deportation** /ˌdiː.pɔːˈteɪ.ʃᵊn/ [US] /-pɔːr-/ *noun* [C or U] *There were **mass** deportations in the 1930s, when thousands of people were forced to leave the country.* **deportee** /ˌdiː.pɔːˈtiː/ [US] /-pɔːr-/ *noun* [C] a person who has been, or is waiting to be, deported

depor'tation ˌorder *noun* [C] an official document stating that someone must be made to leave the country

deportment /dɪˈpɔːt.mənt/ [US] /-ˈpɔːrt-/ *noun* [U] *FORMAL* **1** the way a person walks and stands: *to have good/bad deportment* ○ *speech and deportment lessons* **2** the way a person behaves: *Throughout the ordeal of her husband's funeral, Mrs Kennedy was a model of deportment* (= behaved in a controlled and calm way).

depose /dɪˈpəʊz/ [US] /-ˈpoʊz/ *verb* [T] to remove someone important from a powerful position: *Margaret Thatcher was deposed **as** leader of the British Conservative Party in 1991.* ○ *King Charles I was deposed **from** the English throne in 1646.* **deposition** /ˌdep.əˈzɪʃ.ᵊn/ *noun* [U] *FORMAL Crowds celebrated the dictator's deposition.* ➲See also **deposition**.

deposit [LEAVE] /dɪˈpɒz.ɪt/ [US] /-ˈpɑː.zɪt/ *verb* [T usually + adv or prep] to leave something somewhere: *The flood waters fell, depositing mud over the whole area.* ○ *The bus deposited me miles from anywhere.* ○ *The cuckoo deposits* (= puts) *her eggs in other birds' nests.* ○ *I deposited my luggage in a locker at the station.*
deposit /dɪˈpɒz.ɪt/ [US] /-ˈpɑː.zɪt/ *noun* **1** [C or U] a substance or layer that is left, usually after a liquid is removed: *Decant the wine carefully, so that you leave the deposit in the bottom of the bottle.* ○ *In hard-water areas, a chalky deposit often forms in pipes and kettles.* ○ *The flood left a thick deposit **of** mud over the entire ground floor of the house.* **2** [C] *SPECIALIZED* a layer which has formed under the ground, especially over a long period: *mineral/oil/coal deposits*

deposit [STORE MONEY] /dɪˈpɒz.ɪt/ [US] /-ˈpɑː.zɪt/ *verb* [T] **1** to put something valuable, especially money, in a bank or SAFE (= strong box or cupboard with locks): *There's a night safe outside the bank, so you can deposit money whenever you wish.* ○ *I deposited £500 **in** my account this morning.* **2** to pay someone a sum of money when you make an agreement with them to pay for or buy something, which either will be returned to you later, if the agreed arrangement is kept, or which forms part of the total payment: *When we moved in, we had to deposit $1000 **with** the landlord in case we broke any of his things.* ○ *You deposit 20% now and pay the rest when the car is delivered.*
deposit /dɪˈpɒz.ɪt/ [US] /-ˈpɑː.zɪt/ *noun* [C] **1** a payment: *To open an account, you need to **make** a minimum deposit **of** $500.* **2** a sum of money which is given in advance as part of a total payment for something: *The shop assistant says if I **leave** £10 **as** a deposit, they'll keep the dress for me.* ○ *We **paid/put** a deposit **of** £10 000 **on** the house, and paid the balance four weeks later.* **3** a sum of money which you pay when you rent something, and which is returned to you when you return the thing you have rented: *It costs £1000 a week to hire the yacht, plus a £120 **refundable/returnable** deposit.* ○ *You pay a 10p deposit/deposit of 10p **on** the bottle, which you get back when you return the empty bottle.*
depositor /dɪˈpɒz.ɪ.təʳ/ [US] /-ˈpɑː.zə.t̬ɚ/ *noun* [C] someone who deposits money

de'posit acˌcount *UK noun* [C] (*US* **savings account**) a bank account in which you usually leave money for a long time and which pays you interest

deposition /ˌdep.əˈzɪʃ.ᵊn/ *noun* [C] *LEGAL* a formal written statement made or used in a court of law: *Before the court case, we had to **file/give** a deposition.* ○ *Our lawyer **took** a deposition from us.* ○ *a **sworn** deposition* ➲See also **deposition** at **depose**.

depository /dɪˈpɒz.ɪ.tᵊr.i/ [US] /-ˈpɑː.zə.tɔːr-/ *noun* [C] a place, especially a large building, for storing things: *The government is having difficulty finding a safe depository **for** nuclear waste.*

depot /ˈdep.əʊ/ [US] /ˈdiː.poʊ/ *noun* [C] **1** a building where supplies or vehicles, especially buses, are kept: *an arms/weapons depot* ○ *a fuel/storage depot* ○ *a bus depot* **2** *US* a bus station or train station

depraved /dɪˈpreɪvd/ *adj* morally bad or evil: *a depraved character/mind* ○ *Someone who can kill a child like that must be totally depraved.*
deprave /dɪˈpreɪv/ *verb* [T] *FORMAL* to make someone depraved
depravity /dɪˈpræv.ə.ti/ [US] /-t̬i/ *noun* [U] the state of being morally bad

deprecate [DISAPPROVE] /ˈdep.rɪ.keɪt/ *verb* [T not continuous] *FORMAL* to not approve of something or say that you do not approve of something: *We deprecate this use of company funds for political purposes.* **deprecating** /ˈdep.rɪ.keɪ.tɪŋ/ [US] /-t̬ɪŋ/ *adj* (*ALSO* **deprecatory**) *The teacher gave the boys a deprecating stare.* **deprecatingly** /ˈdep.rɪ.keɪ.tɪŋ.li/ [US] /-t̬ɪŋ-/ *adv* **deprecation** /ˌdep.rɪˈkeɪ.ʃᵊn/ *noun* [U]

deprecate [NOT VALUE] /ˈdep.rɪ.keɪt/ *verb* [T] *FORMAL* to say that you think something is of little value or importance: *He always deprecates my achievements.*
deprecating /ˈdep.rɪ.keɪ.tɪŋ/ [US] /-t̬ɪŋ/ *adj* (*ALSO* **deprecatory**) **1** showing that you think something is of little value or importance: *Her deprecating smile clearly showed that she thought I'd said something stupid.* ➲See also **self-deprecating**. **2** showing that you feel embarrassed, especially by praise: *She reacted to his compliments with a deprecating laugh.* **deprecatingly** /ˈdep.rɪ.keɪ.tɪŋ.li/ [US] /-t̬ɪŋ-/ *adv* **deprecation** /ˌdep.rɪˈkeɪ.ʃᵊn/ *noun* [U]

depreciate /dɪˈpriː.ʃi.eɪt/ *verb* [I or T] to (cause something to) lose value, especially over time: *Our car depreciated **(by)** £1500 in the first year we owned it.* ○ *Since they set up a builder's yard next door, our house has depreciated **in value**.* ➲Compare **appreciate** INCREASE.
depreciation /dɪˌpriː.ʃiˈeɪ.ʃᵊn/ *noun* [U] when something loses value

depredation /ˌdep.rəˈdeɪ.ʃᵊn/ *noun* [C usually pl; U] *FORMAL* (an act causing) damage or destruction: *The entire area has suffered the depredations **of** war.* ○ *Depredation **of*** (= Damage done to) *the environment is destroying hundreds of species each year.*

depress [CAUSE SADNESS] /dɪˈpres/ *verb* [T] to cause someone to feel unhappy and without hope for the future: *This weather depresses me.* ○ [+ v-ing] *Doesn't **it** depress you listen**ing** to the news these days?* ○ [+ to infinitive] ***It** depresses me **to** think that I'll probably still be doing exactly the same job in ten years' time.*
depressant /dɪˈpres.ᵊnt/ *noun* [C] a substance which causes you to feel unhappy and without hope: *Alcohol is a depressant.* **depressant** /dɪˈpres.ᵊnt/ *adj*: *These drugs have a depressant effect.*
depressed /dɪˈprest/ *adj* unhappy and without hope for the future: *He seemed a bit depressed **about** his work situation.* ○ *She became **deeply** depressed when her husband died.*
depressing /dɪˈpres.ɪŋ/ *adj* making you feel unhappy and without hope for the future: *I find this weather so depressing.* ○ *Her letter made depressing reading.* ○ [+ v-ing] ***It** was very depressing watch**ing** the news on television tonight.* ○ [+ to infinitive] ***It**'s depressing **to** think that we've got five more years of this government!* **depressingly** /dɪˈpres.ɪŋ.li/ *adv*: *My score was depressingly low.* ○ *The story was depressingly **familiar**.*

depress [REDUCE] /dɪˈpres/ *verb* [T] **1** to reduce the value of something, especially money: *A surplus of corn has helped depress the grain **market**/grain **prices**.* ○ *The rise in the value of the dollar has depressed the company's **earnings/profits** this year.* **2** to reduce the amount of activity in something, especially a business operation: *High interest rates are continuing to depress the **economy**.* **3** to lower the level or amount of something: *This drug helps depress high hormone levels.*

depressed /dɪ'prest/ *adj* showing a lack of money or business activity: *In a depressed market, it's difficult to sell goods unless you lower your prices.* ○ *an economically depressed area*

depress PRESS DOWN /dɪ'pres/ *verb* [T] SLIGHTLY FORMAL to press down or lower: *Slowly depress the accelerator/brake pedal.*

depression UNHAPPINESS /dɪ'preʃ.ᵊn/ *noun* **1** [U] a feeling of unhappiness and lack of hope for the future: *I was overwhelmed by feelings of depression.* **2** [C or U] a mental illness in which a person is very unhappy and anxious for long periods and cannot have a normal life during these periods: *Tiredness, loss of appetite and sleeping problems are all classic symptoms of depression.* ○ *If you suffer from depression, it's best to get professional help.* ⊃See also **clinical depression**.

depressive /dɪ'pres.ɪv/ *noun* [C] a person who often suffers from depression **depressive** /dɪ'pres.ɪv/ *adj*: *a depressive personality* ○ *a depressive disorder/illness*

depression NO ACTIVITY /dɪ'preʃ.ᵊn/ *noun* [C] a period in which there is very little business activity and not many jobs: *The stock market crash marked the start of a severe depression.*

depression WEATHER /dɪ'preʃ.ᵊn/ *noun* [C] SPECIALIZED an area where the air pressure is low: *The deep depression over the mid-Atlantic will gradually move eastwards during the day.*

depression HOLE /dɪ'preʃ.ᵊn/ *noun* [C] a part in a surface which is slightly lower than the rest: *There was a depression in the sand where he'd been lying.*

depressurize, UK USUALLY **-ise** /ˌdiː'preʃ.ə.raɪz/ *verb* [I or T] SPECIALIZED to (cause an enclosed space, especially the inside of an aircraft to) become lower in air pressure: *If the cabin depressurizes, oxygen masks will automatically drop down.*

deprive /dɪ'praɪv/ *verb* [T] to take something, especially something necessary or pleasant, away from someone: *He claimed that he had been deprived of his freedom/rights.* ○ *You can't function properly when you're deprived of sleep.*
• **deprive** *sb* **of** *your* **company** HUMOROUS to prevent someone from being with someone else: *Where have you been? We've been deprived of your company for far too long!*

deprivation /ˌdep.rɪ'veɪ.ʃᵊn/ *noun* [C or U] when you do not have things or conditions that are usually considered necessary for a pleasant life: *They used sleep deprivation as a form of torture.* ○ *There is awful deprivation in the shanty towns.* ○ *There were food shortages and other deprivations during the Civil War.*

deprived /dɪ'praɪvd/ *adj* not having the things that are necessary for a pleasant life, such as enough money, food or good living conditions: *She had a deprived childhood/comes from a deprived background.* ○ *a deprived area*

dept /dɪ'pɑːt.mənt/ ⓤ /dɪ'pɑːrt-/ *noun* WRITTEN ABBREVIATION FOR **department**

depth DISTANCE DOWN /depθ/ *noun* [C or U] the distance down either from the top of something to the bottom, or to a distance below the top surface of something: *the depth of a lake/pond* ○ *There are very few fish at depths* (= distances below the surface) *below 3000 metres.* ○ *The river froze to a depth of over a metre.* ⊃See also **deep** DOWN.
• **out of** *your* **depth 1** not having the knowledge, experience, or skills to deal with a particular subject or situation: *I was out of my depth in the advanced class, so I moved to the intermediate class.* **2** in water that is so deep that it goes over your head when you are standing: *I'm not a strong swimmer so I prefer not to go out of my depth.*
the depths *plural noun* LITERARY the lowest part of the sea: *The ship sank slowly to the depths of the ocean.*

depth DISTANCE BACKWARDS /depθ/ *noun* [C or U] the distance from the front to the back of something: *Measure the depth of the cupboard/shelf.* ⊃See also **deep** FRONT TO BACK.
• **in the depth(s) of** *somewhere* in the middle of somewhere, and a long distance from its edges: *a house in the depths of the forest*

• **in the depth(s) of winter** in the middle of winter

depth STRENGTH /depθ/ *noun* [C or U] when a feeling, state or characteristic is strong, extreme or detailed: *He spoke with great depth of feeling.* ○ *I was amazed at the depth of her knowledge.* ⊃See also **deep** STRONGLY FELT.
• **in the depth(s) of** *sth* **1** experiencing an extreme and negative emotion: *He was in the depths of despair/depression about losing his job.* **2** during the worst period of a bad situation: *The company was started in the depth of the recession of the 1930s.*

depth SERIOUSNESS /depθ/ *noun* [C or U] when you have serious qualities or the ability to think seriously about something: *Terry lacks depth – he's a very superficial person.* ○ *Her writing shows astonishing depth.* ○ *Jo has hidden depths* (= serious qualities that you do not see immediately). ⊃See also **deep** COMPLICATED.
• **in depth** in a serious and detailed way: *I'd like to look at this question in some depth.*

depth LOW SOUND /depθ/ *noun* [U] the quality of having a low sound: *The depth of his voice makes him sound older than he is.* ⊃See also **deep** LOW.

depth DARKNESS /depθ/ *noun* [U] when something, especially a colour, has the quality of being dark and strong: *I love the depth of colour in her early paintings.* ⊃See also **deep** DARK.

'depth ˌcharge *noun* [C] a bomb which explodes under water

deputation /ˌdep.jʊ'teɪ.ʃᵊn/ *group noun* [C] a group of people sent to speak or act for others: *They sent a deputation to Parliament.* ○ *The deputation from the EU arrives/arrive tomorrow.* ○ *a deputation of local government officials* ○ *She was sent on a deputation to see the Pope.*

depute /dɪ'pjuːt/ *verb* [T] FORMAL to ask someone to act or speak for you: [+ *to* infinitive] *I've deputed Lara Brown to speak for me at the conference.*

deputy /'dep.jʊ.ti/ ⓤ /-t̬i/ *noun* [C] a person who is given the power to do something instead of another person, or the person whose rank is immediately below that of the leader of an organization: *I'd like you to meet Ann Gregory, my deputy.* ○ *I'm acting as deputy while the boss is away.* ○ *She's deputy (head) of a large North London school.* ○ *the deputy chairperson/manager/(US) sheriff/etc.*

deputize, UK USUALLY **-ise** /'dep.jʊ.taɪz/ *verb* [I] *I'm deputizing for* (= doing the job of) *the director during his absence.*

derail /ˌdiː'reɪl/ *verb* **1** [I or T] If a train derails or is derailed, it comes off the railway tracks. **2** [T] to prevent a plan or process from succeeding: *Renewed fighting threatens to derail the peace talks.* **derailment** /ˌdiː'reɪl.mənt/ *noun* [C] *There's been a derailment just outside Crewe, and many people are feared dead.*

deranged /dɪ'reɪndʒd/ *adj* completely unable to think clearly or behave in a controlled way, especially because of mental illness: *a deranged criminal/mind/personality* ○ *to be mentally deranged* **derangement** /dɪ'reɪndʒ.mənt/ *noun* [U]

derby SPORTING EVENT /'dɑː.bi/ ⓤ /'dɝː-/ *noun* [C] **1** a sports event between teams in the same area: *a local derby between Manchester United and Manchester City* **2** MAINLY US a sports event in which any competitor can take part: *the annual New Hampshire fishing derby*
Derby /'dɑː.bi/ ⓤ /'dɝː-/ *noun* [C usually sing] a type of horse race: *the Epsom/Kentucky Derby*

derby HAT /'dɑː.bi/ ⓤ /'dɝː-/ *noun* [C] US FOR **bowler (hat)**

deregulate /ˌdiː'reg.jʊ.leɪt/ *verb* [T] to remove national or local government controls or rules from a business or other activity: *The government plans to deregulate the banking industry/the bus system.* **deregulation** /ˌdiː.reg.jʊ'leɪ.ʃᵊn/ *noun* [U] *Couldn't the deregulation of broadcasting lead to a lowering of standards?*

derelict IN BAD CONDITION /'der.ə.lɪkt/ *adj* describes buildings or places that are not cared for and are in bad condition: *a derelict site* ○ *The theatre has been left to stand/lie derelict.* **dereliction** /ˌder.ə'lɪk.ʃᵊn/ *noun* [U] *The old railway cottages were in a state of dereliction.* ⊃See also **dereliction**.

derelict [PERSON] /ˈder.ə.lɪkt/ *noun* [C] *FORMAL* a person who has no home or money and often lives outside

dereliction /ˌder.əˈlɪk.ʃən/ *noun* [C or U] (a) failure to do what you should do: *What you did was a grave dereliction **of duty**.* ➲See also **dereliction** at **derelict** IN BAD CONDITION.

deride /dɪˈraɪd/ *verb* [T] *FORMAL* to laugh at someone or something in a way which shows you think they are ridiculous or of no value: *He derided my singing **as** pathetic.* ○ *This building, once derided by critics, is now a major tourist attraction.*

derision /dɪˈrɪʒ.ən/ *noun* [U] *FORMAL* when someone or something is laughed at and considered ridiculous or of no value: *They treated his suggestion **with** derision.* ○ *Her speech was met with **hoots/howls of** derision.*

derisive /dɪˈraɪ.sɪv/ *adj* (*ALSO* **derisory**) *FORMAL* showing derision: *derisive laughter* ○ *a derisive comment/remark* ➲See also **derisory**. **derisively** /dɪˈraɪ.sɪv.li/ *adv*

de rigueur /də.rɪˈgɜːr/ [US] /-ˈgɝː/ *adj* [after v] *FORMAL* demanded by fashion, custom, etc: *Where I work, smart suits are de rigueur **for** the women.*

derisory /dɪˈraɪ.sər.i/ [US] /-ɚ.i/ *adj* *FORMAL DISAPPROVING* describes an amount that is so small it is ridiculous: *We were awarded a derisory sum.* ➲See also **derisive** at **deride**.

derive /dɪˈraɪv/ *verb* **derive *sth* from *sth*** to get or obtain something from something else: *The institute derives all its money from foreign investments.* ○ *She derives great pleasure/satisfaction from playing the violin.*

▲ **derive from *sth*** *phrasal verb* [often passive] to come from something: *The English word 'olive' is derived from the Latin word 'oliva'.*

derivation /ˌder.ɪˈveɪ.ʃən/ *noun* [C or U] the origin of something, such as a word, from which another form has developed, or the new form itself

derivative /dɪˈrɪv.ə.tɪv/ [US] /-t̬ɪv/ *adj* *DISAPPROVING* If something is derivative, it is not the result of new ideas, but has been developed from something else: *His painting/style is terribly derivative.*

derivative /dɪˈrɪv.ɪ.tɪv/ [US] /-ə.t̬ɪv/ *noun* [C] *SPECIALIZED* a form of something, such as a word, made or developed from another form: *'Detestable' is a derivative **of** 'detest'.*

dermatitis /ˌdɜː.məˈtaɪ.təs/ [US] /ˌdɝː.məˈtaɪ.t̬əs/ *noun* [U] *SPECIALIZED* a disease in which the skin is red and painful

dermatology /ˌdɜː.məˈtɒl.ə.dʒi/ [US] /ˌdɝː.məˈtɑː.lə-/ *noun* [U] the scientific study of the skin and its diseases

dermatologist /ˌdɜː.məˈtɒl.ə.dʒɪst/ [US] /ˌdɝː.məˈtɑː.lə-/ *noun* [C] a doctor who studies and treats skin diseases

derogatory /dɪˈrɒg.ə.tər.i/ /-tri/ [US] /-ˈrɑː.gə.tɔːr-/ *adj* showing strong disapproval and not showing respect: *He made some derogatory **comment/remark** about her appearance.*

derrick /ˈder.ɪk/ *noun* [C] *SPECIALIZED* **1** a type of CRANE (= machine with an arm-like part) used for moving things on and off ships **2** a tower above an OIL WELL which supports the DRILL (= machine for making a hole in the ground)

derrière /ˈder.i.eər/ [US] /-ˈer/ *noun* [C] *HUMOROUS* a person's bottom

derring-do /ˌder.ɪŋˈduː/ *noun* [U] *OLD-FASHIONED OR HUMOROUS* brave action taken without considering the danger involved: ***deeds/feats of** derring-do*

derv /dɜːv/ [US] /dɝːv/ *noun* [U] *UK* a type of liquid fuel used especially in trucks

dervish /ˈdɜː.vɪʃ/ [US] /ˈdɝː-/ *noun* [C] a member of a Muslim religious group which has an energetic dance as part of its worship: *The children were spinning around like **whirling** dervishes.*

desalinate /ˌdiːˈsæl.ɪ.neɪt/ *verb* [T] to remove salt from sea water

desalination /ˌdiː.sæl.ɪˈneɪ.ʃən/ [US] /diːˌsæl-/ *noun* [U] *a desalination **plant*** (= factory)

descale /ˌdiːˈskeɪl/ *verb* [T] to remove SCALE (= a layer of hard white material) from something: *This kettle needs descaling.*

descant /ˈdes.kænt/ *noun* [C] a part of a piece of music which is sung or played at the same time as the main tune, but higher: *Shall I sing the descant in the last verse?*

descend [POSITION] /dɪˈsend/ *verb* **1** [I or T] *FORMAL* to go or come down: *The path descended steeply into the valley.* ○ *Jane descended the stairs.* **2** [I] *LITERARY* If darkness or night descends, it becomes dark and day changes to night.

descent /dɪˈsent/ *noun* [C or U] a movement down: *The plane began (to **make**) its **final** descent into the airport.* ○ *There is a steep descent* (= way down, such as a path) *to the village below.*

descend [NEGATIVE MOOD] /dɪˈsend/ *verb* [I] *LITERARY* **1** If a negative or bad feeling descends, it is felt everywhere in a place or by everyone at the same time: *A feeling of despair descended (**on** us) as we realized that we were completely lost.* **2** If a condition, usually a negative condition, descends, it quickly develops in every part of a place: *Silence descended **on** the room/**over** the countryside.*

descent /dɪˈsent/ *noun* [S or U] a change in someone's behaviour, or in a situation, from good to bad: *His descent **into** crime was rapid.*

PHRASAL VERBS WITH **descend** ▼

▲ **descend from *sth*** *phrasal verb* **1** to have developed from something that existed in the past: *All living creatures are thought to descend from an organism that came into being three billion years ago.* **2 be descended from *sb*** to be related to a particular person or group of people who lived in the past: *Her father is descended from Greek royalty.* ○ *Humans are descended from* (= developed from) *ape-like creatures.*

▲ **descend into *sth*** *phrasal verb* *FORMAL* If a situation descends into a particular state, it becomes worse: *The demonstrations in the capital rapidly descended into anarchy.*

▲ **descend on/upon *sb/sth*** *phrasal verb* If a group of people descend on a place or person, they arrive, usually without warning or without being invited: *Sorry to descend on you like this, but we had no time to phone.* ○ *The police descended on the house in the early hours of the morning.*

▲ **descend to *sth*** *phrasal verb* to behave badly in a way that other people would not expect you to: *I never thought she would descend to steal**ing**.*

descendant /dɪˈsen.dənt/ *noun* [C] a person who is related to someone and who lives after them, such as their child or grandchild: *He has no descendants.* ○ *They claim to be descendants **of** a French duke.* ○ *We owe it to our descendants* (= people younger than us who will live after we have died) *to leave them a clean world to live in.* ➲Compare **ancestor**.

descent [RELATION] /dɪˈsent/ *noun* [U] the state or fact of being related to a particular person or group of people who lived in the past: *She's a woman **of** mixed/French descent.* ○ *They trace their **line of** descent back to a French duke.* ○ *He claims **direct** descent **from** Mohammed.* ➲See also **descent** at **descend** POSITION and **descend** NEGATIVE MOOD.

descent [ARRIVAL] /dɪˈsent/ *noun* [U] *MAINLY HUMOROUS* when a group of people arrive somewhere, usually suddenly or unexpectedly: *We're preparing for the yearly descent of thousands of visitors **on** the village for the pop festival.*

describe /dɪˈskraɪb/ *verb* [T] **1** to say or write what someone or something is like: *Could you describe your attacker?* ○ *He described the painting **in detail**.* ○ [+ question word] *Let me describe (**to** you) **how** it happened.* ○ *She described Gary **as** shy.* **2** *FORMAL* If you describe a shape, you draw it or move in a direction that follows the line of it: *He used compasses to describe a circle.*

description /dɪˈskrɪp.ʃən/ *noun* [C or U] something that tells you what something or someone is like: *Write a description **of** your favourite seaside resort.* ○ *She has **given** the police a very **detailed/full** description **of** the robber.* ○ *A girl **answering*** (= matching) *the description **of** the missing teenager was spotted in Hull.* ○ *Your essay contains too much description, and not enough discussion of the issues.*

• **of every description** of all types: *Boats of every description were entering the harbour.*
• **be beyond description** (*ALSO* **defy description**) to be something that you cannot describe accurately because of its great size, quality or level: *Her beauty is beyond description.* ○ *The mess in Bart's room defies description* (= is very bad)*!*
descriptive /dɪ'skrɪp.tɪv/ *adj* describing something, especially in a detailed, interesting way: *a descriptive essay/passage*

D

desecrate /'des.ɪ.kreɪt/ *verb* [T] to damage or show a lack of respect towards something holy or highly respected: *The mosque/shrine was desecrated by vandals.* ○ *It's a crime to desecrate the country's flag.* **desecration** /ˌdes.ɪ'kreɪ.ʃᵊn/ *noun* [U] *People were horrified at the desecration **of** the cemetery.*
desegregate /ˌdiː'seg.rɪ.geɪt/ *verb* [T] to end SEGREGATION (= separation) between races, or sexes, in an organization: *President Truman desegregated the American armed forces in 1948.* ○ *Plans to desegregate the schools/universities met with opposition.* **desegregation** /ˌdiː.seg.rɪ'geɪ.ʃᵊn/ *noun* [U]
deselect /ˌdiː.sə'lekt/ *verb* [T often passive] *UK SPECIALIZED* to choose, as a local political party, not to have the person who already represents your party as your CANDIDATE at the next election
desensitize, *UK USUALLY* **-ise** /ˌdiː'sent.sɪ.taɪz/ *verb* [T] to cause someone to experience something, usually an emotion or a pain, less strongly than before: *Seeing too much violence on television can desensitize people **to** it.* **desensitization**, *UK USUALLY* **-isation** /diˌsent.sɪ.taɪ'zeɪ.ʃᵊn/ *noun* [U]
desert [RUN AWAY] /dɪ'zɜːt/ [US] /-'zɝːt/ *verb* [I or T] to leave the armed forces without permission and with no intention of returning: *Soldiers who deserted and were caught were shot.* ○ *How many people desert **from** the army each year?*
deserter /dɪ'zɜː.təʳ/ [US] /-'zɝː.t̬ɚ/ *noun* [C] a person who leaves the armed forces without permission **desertion** /dɪ'zɜː.ʃᵊn/ [US] /-'zɝː-/ *noun* [C or U] *During the war, desertion was punishable by death.* ○ *There were thousands of desertions in the last weeks of the war.* ○ *FIGURATIVE There have been **mass** desertions **from*** (= a lot of people have left) *the party in recent months.*
desert [LEAVE BEHIND] /dɪ'zɜːt/ [US] /-'zɝːt/ *verb* [T] **1** to leave someone without help or in a difficult situation and not come back: *He deserted his wife and family **for** another woman.* **2** If a quality deserts you, you suddenly and temporarily lose it: *All my confidence/courage deserted me when I walked into the exam room.* **deserted** /dɪ'zɜː.tɪd/ [US] /-'zɝː.t̬ɪd/ *adj: a deserted wife*
desertion /dɪ'zɜː.ʃᵊn/ [US] /-'zɝː-/ *noun* [U] *Roger got his divorce on the grounds of desertion* (= because his wife had left him).
desert [AREA] /'dez.ət/ [US] /-ɚt/ *noun* [C or U] **1** an area, often covered with sand or rocks, where there is very little rain and not many plants: *They were lost **in** the desert for nine days.* ○ *We had to cross a large area of arid, featureless desert.* ○ *the desert sun* **2** *DISAPPROVING* **cultural/intellectual, etc. desert** a place that is considered to lack any cultural/intellectual, etc. quality or interest: *This town is a cultural/intellectual desert.*
desertification /dɪˌzɜː.tɪ.fɪ'keɪ.ʃᵊn/ [US] /-ˌzɝː.t̬ə-/ *noun* [U] *SPECIALIZED* the process by which land changes into desert
deserted /dɪ'zɜː.tɪd/ [US] /-'zɝː.t̬ɪd/ *adj* If a place is deserted, there are no people in it: *a deserted building/street* ○ *The coastal resorts are deserted* (= do not have many visitors) *in winter.* ➲See also **deserted** at **desert** LEAVE BEHIND.
ˌdesert 'island *noun* [C] an island, especially in a warm region, where no people live
deserts /dɪ'zɜːts/ [US] /-'zɝːts/ *plural noun* **get *your* just deserts** to get what you deserve: *I'd say he got his just deserts **for** not sticking around to help with the children.*
deserve /dɪ'zɜːv/ [US] /-'zɝːv/ *verb* [T not continuous] to have earned or to be given something because of the way you have behaved or the qualities you have: *After all that hard work, you deserve a holiday.* ○ *Chris deserves our special **thanks** for all his efforts.* ○ *I hope they get the **punishment** they deserve.* ○ [+ to infinitive] *They certainly deserved **to** win that match.*
• ***She/He* deserves a medal** *HUMOROUS* said when you admire someone for dealing with a difficult person or situation for a long time: *She deserves a medal **for** putting up with that husband of hers.*
• ***He/She* deserves whatever/everything *he/she* gets.** said if you think someone should have to suffer because of their bad behaviour: *After all the harm she's done, she deserves whatever she gets.*
deserved /dɪ'zɜːvd/ [US] /-'zɝːvd/ *adj* describes something that you earn or are given because of your behaviour or qualities: *a **well-**deserved holiday/rest* ○ *Their victory was **richly/thoroughly** deserved.*
deservedly /dɪ'zɜː.vɪd.li/ [US] /-'zɝː-/ *adv: He won the award for best actor, **and** deservedly **so*** (= he deserved it).
deserving /dɪ'zɜː.vɪŋ/ [US] /-'zɝː-/ *adj* If people or things are deserving, they should be helped because they have good qualities: *a deserving **cause/charity***
• **be deserving of *sth*** *FORMAL* to deserve to get something: *His efforts are certainly deserving of praise.*
desiccated /'des.ɪ.keɪ.tɪd/ [US] /-t̬ɪd/ *adj* dried: *100g of desiccated* (= dried and broken into small pieces) ***coconut***
desiccation /ˌdes.ɪ'keɪ.ʃᵊn/ *noun* [U] *SPECIALIZED* the process of becoming completely dried
design [PLAN] /dɪ'zaɪn/ *verb* [I or T] to make or draw plans for something, for example clothes or buildings: *Who designed this building/dress/furniture?* ○ *This range of clothing is specially designed **for** shorter women.*
design /dɪ'zaɪn/ *noun* **1** [C] a drawing or set of drawings showing how a building or product is to be made and how it will work and look: *Have you seen the designs **for** the new shopping centre?* **2** [U] (*ALSO* **designing**) the art of making plans or drawings for something: *She's an expert on kitchen/software design.* ○ *He's studying design at college.* **3** [S or U] the way in which something is planned and made: *I don't like the design **of** this kettle.* ○ *The building was originally Victorian **in** design.* ○ *a serious design **fault*** ○ *The car has some excellent design **features**.*
designer /dɪ'zaɪ.nəʳ/ [US] /-nɚ/ *noun* [C] a person who imagines how something could be made and draws plans for it: *a fashion/software/theatrical designer*
designer /dɪ'zaɪ.nəʳ/ [US] /-nɚ/ *adj* [before n] made by a famous or fashionable designer: *designer jeans/sunglasses* ○ *I can't afford designer **labels**/designer **label** clothes.*
design [INTEND] /dɪ'zaɪn/ *verb* [T usually passive] to intend: *This dictionary is designed **for** advanced learners of English.* ○ [+ to infinitive] *These measures are designed **to** reduce pollution.*
design /dɪ'zaɪn/ *noun* **by design** intentionally: *I'm sure he ignored you by accident and not by design.*
design [PATTERN] /dɪ'zaɪn/ *noun* [C] a pattern used to decorate something: *a floral/abstract design* ○ *I like the design **on** your sweatshirt.*
designate /'dez.ɪg.neɪt/ *verb* [T] **1** to choose someone officially to do a particular job: *Traditionally, the president designates his or her successor.* ○ *Thompson has been designated **(as/to be)** team captain.* ○ *She has been designated **to** organize the meeting.* **2** to state officially that a place or thing has a particular character or purpose: *This area of the park has been **specially** designated **for** children.* ○ *They officially designated the area **(as)** unsuitable for human habitation.*
designate /'dez.ɪg.nət/ /-neɪt/ *adj* [after n] used after the title of a particular official job to refer to someone chosen to do that job, but who has not yet started doing it: *the Secretary General/Managing Director designate* ➲Compare **-elect** at **elect**.
designation /ˌdez.ɪg'neɪ.ʃᵊn/ *noun* **1** [C] an official title or name: *What's her official designation now she's been promoted?* **2** [U] when a place or thing is designated: *The area qualifies for designation **as** a site of special scientific interest.*
designer /dɪ'zaɪ.nəʳ/ [US] /-nɚ/ *noun* ➲See at **design** PLAN.

de'signer ˌdrug *noun* [C] any of various strong drugs that has been changed to give it a similar effect to an illegal drug such as COCAINE

deˌsigner 'stubble *noun* [U] a beard that has grown for one or two days and is then kept at this length in order to look fashionable

designs /dɪ'zaɪnz/ *plural noun* plans, often ones which are not honest, to get something or someone for yourself: *to **have** territorial designs (**on** neighbouring countries)* ○ HUMOROUS *I think Alan **has** designs **on/upon** your job/wife!*
designing /dɪ'zaɪ.nɪŋ/ *adj* [before n] FORMAL describes someone who tries to get what they want for themselves, usually dishonestly

desire [WANT] /dɪ'zaɪəʳ/ Ⓤⓢ /-'zaɪr/ *verb* [T not continuous] FORMAL to want something, especially strongly: *I desire only to be left in peace.* ○ *The hotel had everything you could possibly desire.* ○ *What does her Ladyship desire me **to** do/desire **of** me?* ○ [+ to infinitive] *The President desires **to** meet the new Prime Minister.*
desire /dɪ'zaɪəʳ/ Ⓤⓢ /-'zaɪr/ *noun* [C or U] a strong feeling that you want something: *I certainly **have no** desire to have children.* ○ *There is a strong desire **for** peace among the people.* ○ *He needed to **satisfy** his desire **for** revenge.* ○ [+ to infinitive] *She **had** a **burning/strong** desire **to** go back to her home country before she died.* ○ *Several people have **expressed** a desire **to** see the report.*
• ***sb's* heart's desire** something that you want very much
desirable /dɪ'zaɪə.rə.bl̩/ Ⓤⓢ /-'zaɪr.ə-/ *adj* worth having and wanted by most people: *It's regarded as a **highly** desirable job.* ○ *The house is in a very desirable area of the city.* **desirably** /dɪ'zaɪə.rə.bli/ Ⓤⓢ /dɪ'zaɪr.ə-/ *adv* **desirability** /dɪˌzaɪə.rə'bɪl.ɪ.ti/ Ⓤⓢ /-ˌzaɪr.ə'bɪl.ə.t̬i/ *noun* [U] *Too much emphasis is placed on the desirability **of** being thin.*
desired /dɪ'zaɪəd/ Ⓤⓢ /-'zaɪrd/ *adj* that is wanted: *His words had the desired **effect**.*
desirous /dɪ'zaɪə.rəs/ Ⓤⓢ /də'zaɪr.əs/ *adj* [after v] OLD-FASHIONED FORMAL wanting something: *The duke is desirous **of** meet**ing** you.*

desire [SEXUAL NEED] /dɪ'zaɪəʳ/ Ⓤⓢ /-'zaɪr/ *noun* [U] FORMAL the strong feeling that you want to have sex with someone: *sexual desire* ○ *Beatrice was the **object of** Dante's desire.*
desirable /dɪ'zaɪə.rə.bl̩/ Ⓤⓢ /dɪ'zaɪr.ə-/ *adj* sexually attractive: *a **highly** desirable man*
desirability /dɪˌzaɪə.rə'bɪl.ɪ.ti/ Ⓤⓢ /dɪˌzaɪr.ə'bɪl.ə.t̬i/ *noun* [U] sexual attractiveness: *She need have no doubts about her desirability.*
desire /dɪ'zaɪəʳ/ Ⓤⓢ /dɪ'zaɪr/ *verb* [T not continuous] FORMAL to feel desire for someone

desist /dɪ'sɪst/ *verb* [I] FORMAL to stop doing something, especially something that someone else does not want you to do: *The soldiers have been ordered to desist **from** firing their guns.* ○ *The high winds are expected to desist tomorrow.*

desk [TABLE] /desk/ *noun* [C] a type of table that you can work at, often one with drawers: *a office/school desk* ○ *She sat **at** her desk writing letters.* ○ *He had a pile of papers **on** his desk.* ○ *The report arrived on/landed on/reached my desk* (= I received it) *this morning.* ➲See picture **In the Office** on page Centre 15

desk [SERVICE AREA] /desk/ *noun* [C] a place, often with a COUNTER (= a long flat narrow surface), especially in a hotel or airport, where you can get information or service: *a check-in/information/reception desk*

desk [NEWSPAPER OFFICE] /desk/ *noun* [C] an office which deals with a particular type of news for a newspaper or broadcasting company: *the foreign/sports desk* ○ *Now let's hear from Sue at our travel desk.*

desk-bound /'desk.baʊnd/ *adj* describes someone who has to work in an office, sitting at a desk

'desk ˌclerk *noun* [C] US someone who is employed to welcome hotel guests when they arrive

'desk ˌjob *noun* [C] a job working in an office

'desk ˌtidy UK *noun* [C] (US **desk organizer**) a container for holding pens, pencils, etc. that is kept on top of a desk

desktop [COMPUTING] /'desk.tɒp/ Ⓤⓢ /-tɑːp/ *noun* [C] **1** a view on a computer screen which is intended to represent the top of a desk and which contains ICONS (= small symbols or pictures) that represent files, programs and other features of the computer: *The menu bar with its windows is one of the features of the desktop.* **2** (ALSO **desktop computer**) a type of computer that is small enough to fit on the top of a desk ➲Compare **laptop (computer)**, **notebook (computer)**, **palmtop (computer)**. **desktop** /'desk.tɒp/ Ⓤⓢ /-tɑːp/ *adj* [before n] *a desktop device/printer/system*

desktop [FURNITURE] /'desk.tɒp/ Ⓤⓢ /-tɑːp/ *noun* [C usually sing] the top of a desk

ˌdesktop 'publishing *noun* [U] (ABBREVIATION **DTP**) the production of finished page designs for books or other printed material, using a small computer and printer

desolate [EMPTY] /'des.əl.ət/ *adj* describes a place that is unattractive and empty, with no people or nothing pleasant in it: *The house stood in a bleak and desolate landscape.* **desolation** /ˌdes.əl'eɪ.ʃən/ *noun* [U] *a **scene of** desolation*

desolate [SAD] /'des.əl.ət/ *adj* extremely sad and feeling alone: *She **felt** desolate when her closest friend moved away.* **desolated** /'des.əl.eɪ.tɪd/ Ⓤⓢ /-t̬ɪd/ *adj* [after v] *She was desolated **at** the loss of her sister.* **desolately** /'des.əl.ət.li/ *adv* **desolation** /ˌdes.əl'eɪ.ʃən/ *noun* [U] *a feeling of utter desolation*

despair /dɪ'speəʳ/ Ⓤⓢ /-'sper/ *noun* [U] the feeling that there is no hope and that you can do nothing to improve a difficult or troubling situation: *a **mood/sense of** despair* ○ *They're **in (the depths of)** despair **over/about** the money they've lost.* ○ ***To** her teacher's despair, Nicole never does the work that she's told to do.* ○ *Their fourth year without rain **drove** many farmers **to*** (= caused them to feel) *despair.*
• **be the despair of *sb*** to cause someone such difficulties that they do not know how to deal with you: *He's the despair of his parents because he shows no interest in getting a job.*
despair /dɪ'speəʳ/ Ⓤⓢ /-'sper/ *verb* [I] to feel despair about something or someone: *Don't despair! We'll find a way out!* ○ *I despair **at/over** the policies of this government.* ○ *They began to despair **of** ever be**ing** rescued.* **despairing** /dɪ'speə.rɪŋ/ Ⓤⓢ /-'sper.ɪŋ/ *adj*: *a despairing glance/cry* **despairingly** /dɪ'speə.rɪŋ.li/ Ⓤⓢ /-'sper.ɪŋ-/ *adv*: *He rubbed his hand despairingly over his face.*

despatch /dɪ'spætʃ/ *noun, verb* **dispatch**

desperado /ˌdes.pə'rɑː.dəʊ/ Ⓤⓢ /-doʊ/ *noun* [C] *plural* **desperados** or **desperadoes** someone who willingly does risky, dangerous and often criminal things: *a gang of desperados*

desperate [RISKY] /'des.pər.ət/ Ⓤⓢ /-pɚ-/ *adj* **1** feeling that you have no hope and are ready to do anything to change the bad situation you are in: *The doctors made one last desperate **attempt/effort** to save the boy's life.* ○ *Desperate **measures** are needed to deal with the growing drug problem.* ○ *They made a desperate **plea** for help.* **2** willing to be violent, and therefore dangerous: *This man is desperate and should not be approached as he may have a gun.* **desperately** /'des.pər.ət.li/ Ⓤⓢ /-pɚ-/ *adv*: *They fought desperately for their lives.*
desperation /ˌdes.pə'reɪ.ʃən/ *noun* [U] the feeling that you have when you are in such a bad situation that you are willing to take risks in order to change it: *There was a note of desperation in his voice.* ○ ***In** desperation, they jumped out of the window to escape the fire.* ○ ***an act of** desperation*

desperate [SERIOUS] /'des.pər.ət/ Ⓤⓢ /-pɚ-/ *adj* **1** very serious or bad: *desperate poverty* ○ *a desperate **shortage** of food/supplies* ○ *The **situation** is desperate – we have no food, very little water and no medical supplies.* **2** very great or extreme: *The earthquake survivors are in desperate need of help.* ○ *He has a desperate desire to succeed.* ○ INFORMAL *I'm in a desperate hurry.*
desperately /'des.pər.ət.li/ Ⓤⓢ /-pɚ-/ *adv* extremely or very much: *He was desperately ill.* ○ *I'm not desperately keen on watching football.* ○ *He was desperately in love with her.* ○ *They desperately wanted a child.*

desperate [WANTING] /'des.pər.ət/ Ⓤⓢ /-pɚ-/ *adj* [usually after v] needing or wanting something very much: *They are*

D

desperate for help. ○ HUMOROUS *I'm desperate for a drink!* ○ [+ *to* infinitive] *He was desperate to tell someone his good news.* **desperation** /ˌdes.pəˈreɪ.ʃən/ *noun* [U]

despise /dɪˈspaɪz/ *verb* [T not continuous] to feel a strong dislike for someone or something because you think they are bad or worthless: *The two groups despise each other.* ○ *She despised him for the way he treated her sister.* ○ [R] *He despised himself for being such a coward.*

despicable /dɪˈspɪk.ə.bl̩/ *adj*: very unpleasant or bad, causing strong feelings of dislike: *despicable behaviour* ○ *He's a despicable human being!* ○ *It was despicable of her to lie about her friend.* despicably /dɪˈspɪk.ə.bli/ *adv*: *I think you behaved despicably.*

despite /dɪˈspaɪt/ *prep* without taking any notice of or being influenced by; not prevented by: *I still enjoyed the week despite the weather.* ○ *Despite repeated assurances that the product is safe, many people have stopped buying it.* ○ [+ v-ing] *He managed to eat a big lunch despite having eaten an enormous breakfast.*

despite /dɪˈspaɪt/ *prep* **despite yourself** If you do something despite yourself, you do it although you do not want to or although you know you should not: *He laughed despite himself.* ○ *She took the money from her mother's purse, despite herself.*

despoil /dɪˈspɔɪl/ ⑩ /ˌdiː-/ *verb* [T] FORMAL to make a place less attractive especially by taking things away from it by force: *Many of the tombs had been despoiled.*

despondent /dɪˈspɒn.dənt/ ⑩ /-ˈspɑːn-/ *adj* unhappy and discouraged because you feel you are in a difficult situation: *He became/grew increasingly despondent when she failed to return his phone calls.* ○ *She started to feel despondent about ever finding a job.* despondently /dɪˈspɒn.dənt.li/ ⑩ /-ˈspɑːn-/ *adv*: *"It's hopeless," he said, shaking his head despondently.* despondency /dɪˈspɒn.dənt.si/ ⑩ /-ˈspɑːn-/ *noun* [U] *A mood of despondency had set in.*

despot /ˈdes.pɒt/ ⑩ /-pɑːt/ *noun* [C] a person, especially a ruler, who has unlimited power over other people, and often uses it unfairly and cruelly: *an evil despot* ○ *The king was regarded as having been a enlightened despot.* ⊃See also **tyrant** at **tyranny**. despotic /dɪˈspɒt.ɪk/ ⑩ /des'pɑː.tɪk/ *adj*: *a despotic government/regime* despotically /dɪˈspɒt.ɪ.kli/ ⑩ /des'pɑː.t̬ɪ-/ *adv* despotism /ˈdes.pə.tɪ.zᵊm/ ⑩ /-tɪ-/ *noun* [U] *After years of despotism, the country is now moving towards democracy.*

des res /ˌdezˈrez/ *noun* [C] UK INFORMAL HUMOROUS a very desirable RESIDENCE (= house or apartment): *She's got a nice little des res in Chelsea.*

dessert /dɪˈzɜːt/ ⑩ /-ˈzɝːt/ *noun* [C or U] sweet food eaten at the end of a meal: *a dessert fork/spoon* ○ *For dessert there's apple pie, cheesecake or fruit.* ○ *If you make the main course, I'll make a dessert.*

dessertspoon /dɪˈzɜːt.spuːn/ ⑩ /-ˈzɝːt-/ *noun* [C] **1** a medium-sized spoon, used especially for eating sweet food at the end of a meal ⊃Compare **teaspoon**; **tablespoon**. **2** the amount that a dessertspoon holds, used for measuring food in cooking: *Add one dessertspoon of sugar.* dessertspoonful /dɪˈzɜːt.spuːn.fʊl/ ⑩ /-ˈzɝːt-/ *noun* [C] *plural* **dessertspoonsful** or **dessertspoonfuls** the amount that a dessertspoon holds

des'sert ˌwine *noun* [C or U] a sweet wine, especially for drinking with sweet food

destabilize, UK USUALLY **-ise** /ˌdiːˈsteɪ.bᵊl.aɪz/ *verb* [T] to make a government, area or political unit lose power or control, or to make a political or economic situation less strong or safe, by causing changes and problems: *They uncovered a plot to destabilize the government.* ○ *The conflict destabilized the whole region.* ○ *Further increases in imports could destabilize the economy.* **destabilization**, UK USUALLY **-isation** /ˌdiːˌsteɪ.bᵊl.aɪˈzeɪ.ʃən/ *noun* [U] **destabilizing**, UK USUALLY **-ising** /ˌdiːˈsteɪ.bᵊl.aɪ.zɪŋ/ *adj* [before n] *The conflict had a seriously destabilizing effect on the region.*

destination /ˌdes.tɪˈneɪ.ʃən/ *noun* [C] the place where someone is going or where something is being sent or taken: *We arrived at our destination tired and hungry.* ○ *His letter never reached its destination.* ○ *The*

Caribbean is a popular tourist/(UK) *holiday/*(US) *vacation destination.*

destined /ˈdes.tɪnd/ *adj* **1** intended (for a particular purpose): *The money was destined for the relief of poverty, but was diverted by corrupt officials.* ○ *These cars are destined for the European market.* **2** travelling or being sent to somewhere: *Customs officers have seized nearly a ton of heroin destined for New York.* **3** controlled by a force which some people believe controls what happens, and which cannot be influenced by people: *She is destined for an extremely successful career.* ○ [+ *to* infinitive] *These plans are destined to fail.* ○ [+ *that*] *Do you think it was destined that we should one day meet?*

destiny /ˈdes.tɪ.ni/ *noun* **1** [C] the things that will happen in the future: *The destiny of our nation depends on this vote!* ○ *She felt that her destiny had been shaped by her gender.* ○ *People want to control/determine/take charge of their own destinies.* **2** [U] the force that some people think controls what happens in the future, and which cannot be influenced by people: *You can't fight destiny.* ○ *He is a tragic victim of destiny.*

destitute /ˈdes.tɪ.tjuːt/ ⑩ /-tɪ.tuːt/ *adj* without money, food, a home or possessions: *The floods left thousands of people destitute.* **destitution** /ˌdes.tɪˈtjuː.ʃən/ ⑩ /-ˈtuː-/ *noun* [U] *Destitution has become a major problem in the capital.*

destroy /dɪˈstrɔɪ/ *verb* [T] **1** to damage something so badly that it does not exist or cannot be used: *Most of the old part of the city was destroyed by bombs during the war.* ○ *The accident seemed to have completely/totally destroyed his confidence.* **2** to kill an animal because it is ill, in pain or dangerous

destroyer /dɪˈstrɔɪ.əʳ/ ⑩ /-ɚ/ *noun* [C] **1** a small fast military ship **2** LITERARY a person or thing that destroys something

destruction /dɪˈstrʌk.ʃən/ *noun* [U] when something is destroyed: *Many people are very concerned about the destruction of the rainforests.* ○ *Unusually high winds left a trail of destruction over southern Britain.* ○ *weapons of mass destruction* (= those which kill or hurt large numbers of people) destructive /dɪˈstrʌk.tɪv/ *adj*: *the destructive power of nuclear weapons* ○ *I worry about the destructive effect that violent films may have on children.* ○ *Lack of trust is very destructive in a relationship.* destructively /dɪˈstrʌk.tɪv.li/ *adv* destructiveness /dɪˈstrʌk.tɪv.nəs/ *noun* [U]

desultory /ˈdes.ᵊl.tᵊr.i/ ⑩ /-tɔːr-/ *adj* FORMAL without a clear plan or purpose and showing little effort or interest: *She made a desultory attempt at conversation.* ○ *He wandered around, clearing up in a desultory way.* desultorily /ˈdes.ᵊl.tᵊr.ᵊl.i/ ⑩ /-tɔːr-/ *adv*

detach /dɪˈtætʃ/ *verb* [T] to separate or remove something from something else that it is connected to: *You can detach the hood if you prefer the coat without it.* ○ *Detach the lower part of the form from this letter and return it to the above address.* ⊃Compare **attach** CONNECT.

detachable /dɪˈtætʃ.ə.bl̩/ *adj* able to be detached: *a detachable collar/hood*

detached /dɪˈtætʃt/ *adj* **1** separated: *The label became detached from your parcel.* **2** describes a house that is not connected to any other building ⊃Compare **semidetached**. **3** describes someone who does not show any emotional involvement or interest in a situation: *She seemed a bit detached, as if her mind were on other things.* ○ *Throughout the novel, the story is seen through the eyes of a detached observer.*

detachment /dɪˈtætʃ.mənt/ *noun* [U] to have an **air of detachment** (= not being involved)

detachment /dɪˈtætʃ.mənt/ *group noun* [C] a group of soldiers who are separated from the main group in order to perform a particular duty: *a military detachment* ○ *A detachment of Italian soldiers was sent to the area.*

detail INFORMATION /ˈdiː.teɪl/ ⑩ /-ˈ-/ *noun* **1** [C] a single piece of information or fact about something: *She insisted on telling me every single detail of what they did to her in hospital.* ○ *We don't know the full/precise details of the story yet.* ○ *She refused to disclose/divulge any details about/of the plan.* **2** [U] the small features of something that you only notice when you look carefully: *I was just admiring the detail in the doll's house – even the tins of food have labels on them.* ○ *It's his **eye for** (=* ability to notice) *detail that distinguishes him as a painter.* **3** [C] an unimportant part of something: *As far as Tony's concerned, he's getting that car and finding the money to pay for it is just a detail.*

details /'diː.teɪlz/ ⑥ /-'-/ *plural noun* information about someone or something: *Can I have your details (=* name and address, etc.), *please?* ○ *I've sent off for the details **of** a job I saw advertised in the paper.* ○ *A police officer **took down** the details **of** what happened.*

● **in detail** including or considering all the information about something or every part of something: *We haven't **discussed** the matter in detail yet.* ○ *The book **described** her sufferings in graphic detail.* ○ *He talked in **great** detail about the curtains he's chosen for his lounge.*

● **go into detail** to tell or include all the facts about something: *I won't go into detail over the phone, but I've been having a few health problems recently.*

detail /'diː.teɪl/ ⑥ /-'-/ *verb* [T] to describe something completely, giving all the facts: [+ question word] *Can you produce a report detailing **wh**at we've spent on the project so far?*

detailed /'diː.teɪld/ ⑥ /-'-/ *adj* giving a lot of information with many details: *A witness gave a detailed **description** of the man.*

detail ORDER /'diː.teɪl/ ⑥ /-'-/ *verb* [T + **to** infinitive; often passive] to order someone, often a small group of soldiers or workers, to perform a particular duty: *Four soldiers were detailed **to** check the road for troops.*

detail /'diː.teɪl/ ⑥ /-'-/ *group noun* [C] a group of people who have been given a particular duty

detain /dɪ'teɪn/ *verb* [T often passive] **1** to force someone officially to stay in a place: *A suspect has been detained by the police for further questioning.* ○ *Several of the injured were detained overnight in hospital.* **2** to delay someone for a short length of time: *I'm sorry I'm late – I was **unavoidably** detained.*

● **detain** *sb* **at His/Her Majesty's pleasure** UK LEGAL to keep someone in prison for as long as the authorities feel is necessary

detainee /ˌdiː.teɪ'niː/ *noun* [C] a person who has been officially ordered to stay in a prison or similar place, especially for political reasons: *a political detainee*

detention /dɪ'ten.tʃən/ *noun* **1** [U] when someone is officially detained: *Concern has been expressed about the death **in** detention of a number of political prisoners.* **2** [C or U] a form of punishment in which school children are made to stay at school for a short time after classes have ended: *She's had four detentions this term.*

detect /dɪ'tekt/ *verb* [T] **1** to notice something that is partly hidden or not clear or to discover something, especially using a special method: *Some sounds cannot be detected by the human ear.* ○ *Financial experts have detected signs that the economy is beginning to improve.* **2** to discover something, usually using special equipment: *High levels of lead were detected in the atmosphere.* ○ *Radar equipment is used to detect (=* find the position of) *enemy aircraft.* **detectable** /dɪ'tek.tə.bl̩/ *adj:* *There has been no detectable change in the patient's condition.*

detection /dɪ'tek.ʃən/ *noun* [U] **1** when someone notices or discovers something: *Early detection **of** the cancer improves the chances of successful treatment.* ○ *bomb detection* **2** when the police discover information about crimes: *a low/high **crime** detection rate*

detector /dɪ'tek.tər/ ⑥ /-tɚ/ *noun* [C] a device used to find particular substances or things, or measure their level: *a metal/smoke detector*

detective /dɪ'tek.tɪv/ *noun* [C] **1** someone whose job is to discover information about crimes and find out who is responsible for them: *a private detective* ○ *detective stories* **2** used as part of the title of particular ranks in the police force: *Detective Sergeant Lewis*

de'tective ˌwork *noun* [U] when you search for information about something, often over a long period: *After a lot of detective work, I managed to find out where he was living.*

detente, **détente** /deɪ'tɒnt/ ⑥ /-'tɑːnt/ *noun* [U] FORMAL an improvement in the relationship between two

countries which in the past were not friendly and did not trust each other: *The talks are aimed at furthering detente **between** the two countries.*

detention /dɪ'ten.tʃən/ *noun* [C or U] ⊃See at **detain**

de'tention ˌcentre UK, US **detention center** *noun* [C] **1** a type of prison where young people can be kept for short periods of time **2** a place where people who have entered a country without the necessary documents can be kept for short periods of time

deter /dɪ'tɜːr/ ⑥ /-'tɜː-/ *verb* [T] **-rr-** to prevent or discourage someone from doing something by making it difficult for them to do it or by threatening bad results if they do it: *These measures are designed to deter an enemy attack.* ○ *High prices are deterring many young people **from** buying houses.*

deterrent /dɪ'ter.ənt/ *noun* [C] something which deters people from doing something: *a nuclear deterrent* ○ *Tougher prison sentences may **act/serve as** (=* be) *a deterrent **to** other would-be offenders.* **deterrent** /dɪ'ter.ənt/ *adj: a deterrent effect*

detergent /dɪ'tɜː.dʒənt/ ⑥ /-'tɜː-/ *noun* [C or U] a chemical substance in the form of a powder or a liquid for removing dirt from clothes or dishes, etc.

deteriorate /dɪ'tɪə.ri.ə.reɪt/ ⑥ /-'tɪr.i-/ *verb* [I] to become worse: *She was taken into hospital last week when her **condition** suddenly deteriorated.* ○ *The political **situation** in the region has deteriorated rapidly.* **deterioration** /dɪ,tɪə.ri.ə'reɪ.ʃən/ ⑥ /-,tɪr.i-/ *noun* [C or U] *We've seen a continuing deterioration **in** relations between the two countries.*

determine DECIDE /dɪ'tɜː.mɪn/ ⑥ /-'tɜː-/ *verb* [T often passive] to control or influence something directly, or to decide what will happen: *The number of staff we can take on will be determined by how much money we're allowed to spend.* ○ *Your health is determined in part by what you eat.* ○ *Eye colour is genetically determined.* ○ [+ question word] FORMAL *A pitch inspection will determine **wh**ether or not the match will be played.* ○ *People should be allowed to determine their own future.* ⊃See also **determine** at **determined**.

determination /dɪ,tɜː.mɪ'neɪ.ʃən/ ⑥ /-,tɜː-/ *noun* [U] FORMAL the process of controlling, influencing or deciding something: *The determination of policy is not your business – your job is to implement it.*

determine DISCOVER /dɪ'tɜː.mɪn/ ⑥ /-'tɜː-/ *verb* [T] FORMAL to discover the facts or truth about something: *The police never actually determined the cause of death.* ○ [+ question word] *It is the responsibility of the court to determine **wh**ether these men are innocent.* ○ [+ that] *The jury determined **that** the men were guilty.*

determined /dɪ'tɜː.mɪnd/ ⑥ /-'tɜː-/ *adj* wanting to do something very much and not letting anyone or any difficulties stop you: [+ **to** infinitive] *I'm determined **to** get this piece of work finished today.* ○ *She's sure to get the job she wants – she's a very determined person.* **determinedly** /dɪ'tɜː.mɪnd.li/ ⑥ /-'tɜː-/ *adv: He continued determinedly despite his injury.* **determine** /dɪ'tɜː.mɪn/ ⑥ /-'tɜː-/ *verb* FORMAL [+ that] *She determined **that** one day she would be an actor.* ○ [+ **to** infinitive] *On leaving jail, Joe determined **to** reform.* ⊃See also **determine** DECIDE.

determination /dɪ,tɜː.mɪ'neɪ.ʃən/ ⑥ /-,tɜː-/ *noun* [U] the ability to continue trying to do something, although it is very difficult: *a man of fierce/ruthless determination* ○ [+ **to** infinitive] *She has a great determination **to** succeed.* ⊃See also **self-determination**.

determiner /dɪ'tɜː.mɪ.nər/ ⑥ /-'tɜː.mɪ.nɚ/ *noun* [C] SPECIALIZED in grammar, a word which is used before a noun to show which particular example of the noun you are referring to: *In the phrases 'my first boyfriend' and 'that strange woman', the words 'my' and 'that' are determiners.*

determinism /dɪ'tɜː.mɪ.nɪ.zəm/ ⑥ /-'tɜː-/ *noun* [U] SPECIALIZED the theory that everything which happens must happen as it does and could not have happened any other way

deterrent /dɪ'ter.ənt/ *noun, adj* ⊃See at **deter**.

detest /dɪ'test/ *verb* [T not continuous] to hate someone or something very much: *I detest any kind of cruelty.* ○ [+ v-

[D]

ing] *I detest having to get up when it's dark outside.* ○ *her detested older brother*

detestable /dɪˈtes.tə.bl/ *adj FORMAL* describes people or things that you hate very much: *a detestable coward* **detestably** /dɪˈtes.tə.bli/ *adv* **detestation** /ˌdiː.tesˈteɪ.ʃᵊn/ *noun* [U] *FORMAL*

dethrone /diˈθrəʊn/ [US] /-ˈθroʊn/ *verb* [T] **1** to remove a king or queen from their position of power **2** to beat someone who is the best at something, especially a sport, and become the best yourself: *The world champion was dethroned by a young Swedish challenger.*

detonate /ˈdet.ᵊn.eɪt/ [US] /ˈdet̬-/ *verb* [I or T] to (cause something to) explode: *The device detonated unexpectedly.* ○ *A remote control device was used to detonate the bomb.*

detonator /ˈdet.ᵊn.eɪ.təʳ/ [US] /ˈdet̬.ᵊn.eɪ.t̬ɚ/ *noun* [C] a small amount of explosive in a bomb which explodes first and causes a larger explosion, or an electrical device which is used from a distance to make a bomb explode

detonation /ˌdet.ᵊnˈeɪ.ʃᵊn/ [US] /ˌdet̬-/ *noun* [C or U] when something is detonated: *Underground nuclear detonations are believed to have been carried out.*

detour /ˈdiː.tɔːʳ/ [US] /-tʊr/ *noun* [C] a different or indirect route to a place, that is used to avoid a problem or to visit somewhere or do something: *You'd be wise to* ***make/****(US ALSO)* ***take*** *a detour to avoid the roadworks.*

detour /ˈdiː.tɔːʳ/ [US] /-tʊr/ *verb* [I or T] *MAINLY US* *We had to detour around the town centre, so it took us longer than usual.*

detox /ˈdiː.tɒks/ [US] /-tɑːks/ *noun* [S or U] **1** when you stop taking unhealthy or harmful foods, drinks or drugs into your body for a period of time, in order to improve your health: *She went on a 48-hour detox, eating nothing but grapes.* ○ *a detox diet* **2** medical treatment in a special hospital to stop someone drinking too much alcohol or taking harmful drugs: *He'd spent 18 months* ***in*** *detox/at a detox centre fighting drug addiction.*

detox /ˈdiː.tɒks/ [US] /-tɑːks/ *verb* [I or T] **1** to stop taking unhealthy or harmful foods, drinks and other substances into your body for a period of time, in order to improve your health: *If you have skin problems or feel sluggish and run-down, then it may be time to detox.* **2** to have medical treatment in a special hospital in order to stop drinking too much alcohol or taking harmful drugs

detoxification /diːˌtɒk.sɪ.fɪˈkeɪ.ʃᵊn/ [US] /-ˌtɑːk-/ *noun* [U] the process of removing harmful chemicals from something **detoxify** /diːˈtɒk.sɪ.faɪ/ [US] /-ˈtɑːk-/ *verb* [I or T]

detract /dɪˈtrækt/ *verb*

▲ **detract from** ***sth*** *phrasal verb* [not continuous] to make something seem less valuable or less deserving of admiration than it really is or was thought to be: *All that make-up she wears actually detracts from her beauty, I think.*

detractor /dɪˈtræk.təʳ/ [US] /-tɚ/ *noun* [C] someone who criticizes something or someone, often unfairly: *His detractors claim that his fierce temper makes him unsuitable for party leadership.*

detriment /ˈdet.rɪ.mənt/ *noun* [U] *FORMAL* harm or damage: *Are you sure that I can follow this diet* ***without*** *detriment* ***to*** *my health?* ○ *She was very involved with sports at college,* ***to the*** *detriment* ***of*** (= harming) *her studies.* **detrimental** /ˌdet.rɪˈmen.tᵊl/ [US] /-t̬ᵊl/ *adj*: *These chemicals have a detrimental* ***effect/impact*** *on the environment.* ○ *Their decision could be detrimental* ***to*** *the future of the company.*

detritus /dɪˈtraɪ.təs/ [US] /-t̬əs/ *noun* [U] **1** *FORMAL* waste material or rubbish, especially that left after a particular event: *The stadium was littered with the detritus* ***of*** *yesterday's rock concert.* **2** *SPECIALIZED* a loose mass of decaying material

de trop /dəˈtrəʊ/ [US] /-ˈtroʊ/ *adj* [after v] *FORMAL* unnecessary, unwanted or more than is suitable: *I thought her remarks about Roger's recent problems were rather de trop.*

deuce /djuːs/ [US] /duːs/ *noun* [U] **1** the score in tennis when both players have 40 points **2** the word for 'two' in some card and dice games **3** *OLD-FASHIONED INFORMAL* **the deuce** used in questions to express annoyance or surprise: *What the deuce do you think you're doing?*

deus ex machina /ˌdeɪ.əs.eksˈmæk.ɪ.nə/ [US] /-ˈmɑː.kɪ-/ *noun* [S] *FORMAL* an artificial or very unlikely end to a story or event, which solves or removes any problems too easily

Deutschmark /ˈdɔɪtʃ.mɑːk/ [US] /-mɑːrk/ *noun* [C] (*ALSO* **mark**, *ABBREVIATION* **DM**) the standard unit of money used in Germany before the euro

devalue [MONEY] /ˌdiːˈvæl.juː/ *verb* [I or T] to reduce the rate at which money can be exchanged for foreign money: *Last year Mexico was forced to devalue the peso.*

devaluation /ˌdiː.væl.juˈeɪ.ʃᵊn/ *noun* [C or U] *The devaluation* ***of*** *the dollar had a strong effect on the financial markets.*

devalue [NOT VALUE] /ˌdiːˈvæl.juː/ *verb* [T] to cause someone or something not to be valued or considered important: *I don't want to devalue your achievement, but you seem to have passed your exam without really doing any work.*

devastate /ˈdev.ə.steɪt/ *verb* [T] **1** to destroy a place or thing completely or cause great damage **2** to make someone feel very shocked and upset

devastated /ˈdev.ə.steɪ.tɪd/ [US] /-t̬ɪd/ *adj* **1** completely destroyed: *Thousands of people have left their devastated villages and fled to the mountains.* **2** very shocked and upset: *She was utterly devastated when her husband died.*

devastating /ˈdev.ə.steɪ.tɪŋ/ [US] /-t̬ɪŋ/ *adj* **1** causing a lot of damage or destruction: *If the bomb had exploded in the main shopping area, it would have been devastating.* ○ *The drought has had devastating* ***consequences/effects.*** **2** making someone very shocked and upset: *devastating news* **3** describes a personal quality that has a powerful effect: *She had a devastating beauty/charm/smile that few men could resist.* **devastatingly** /ˈdev.ə.steɪ.tɪŋ.li/ [US] /-t̬ɪŋ-/ *adv*: *devastatingly beautiful/powerful*

devastation /ˌdev.əˈsteɪ.ʃᵊn/ *noun* [U] *If disease is allowed to spread, it will cause widespread devastation.* ○ *The storm left behind it a* ***trail of*** *devastation.* ○ *She had a look of utter devastation* (= extreme shock and sadness) *on her face.*

develop [GROW] /dɪˈvel.əp/ *verb* [I or T] to (cause something to) grow or change into a more advanced, larger or stronger form: *It became clear that he wasn't developing like all the other little boys.* ○ *The fear is that these minor clashes may develop* ***into*** *all-out confrontation.* ○ *Over time, their acquaintance developed* ***into*** *a lasting friendship.* ○ *This exercise is designed to develop the shoulder and back muscles.* ○ *I'm looking for a job which will enable me to develop my skills/talents.*

developed /dɪˈvel.əpt/ *adj* advanced or powerful: *Sharks have a* ***highly*** *developed sense of smell.* ○ *less developed nations* ➲See also **well-developed**.

developer /dɪˈvel.ə.pəʳ/ [US] /-pɚ/ *noun* [C] someone, especially a child, whose physical or mental development can be described in a particular way: *Tom was a* ***late/slow*** *developer.*

developing /dɪˈvel.ə.pɪŋ/ *adj* [before n] growing or becoming stronger or more advanced ➲See also **developing**.

development /dɪˈvel.əp.mənt/ *noun* **1** [U] when someone or something grows or changes and becomes more advanced: *healthy growth and development* ○ *The programme traced the development* ***of*** *popular music through the ages.* ○ *The region suffers from under-/over-development* (= having too little/much industry). ○ *a development project* (= one to help improve industry) *in Pakistan* **2** [C] a recent event which is the latest in a series of related events: *an important development in the fuel crisis* ○ *Phone me if there are any new developments.* ➲See also **development** at **develop** START

developmental /dɪˌvel.əpˈmen.tᵊl/ [US] /-t̬ᵊl/ *adj*: *a developmental process/problem*

develop [START] /dɪˈvel.əp/ *verb* **1** [T] to invent something or bring something into existence: *We must develop a new policy/strategy to deal with the problem.* ○ *The company is spending $650 million on developing new products/technology.* **2** [I] to start to happen or exist: *Large cracks began to develop in the wall.* **3** [I or T] If you develop an illness or problem, or if it develops, you start to suffer from it: *The study showed that one in twelve women is likely to develop breast cancer.* ○ *She's developed some very strange habits lately.* **4** [T] to build houses, factories, shops, etc. on a piece of land: *They're planning to develop the whole site* ***into*** *a shopping complex.*

developer /dɪˈvel.ə.pəʳ/ [US] /-pɚ/ *noun* [C] a person or company that makes money from buying land, building new houses, shops or offices, or by changing existing buildings to sell or rent: *a* ***property*** *developer*

development /dɪˈvel.əp.mənt/ *noun* **1** [U] the process of developing something new: *Mr Berkowitz is in charge of* ***product*** *development.* **2** [C] an area on which new buildings are built in order to make a profit: *a* ***housing*** *development* ➲See also **development** at **develop** GROW.

develop [PROCESS FILM] /dɪˈvel.əp/ *verb* [I or T] to make photographs or NEGATIVES from a film: *I haven't had my holiday photos developed yet.*

developer /dɪˈvel.ə.pəʳ/ [US] /-pɚ/ *noun* [C or U] a chemical used for developing photographs or films

developing /dɪˈvel.ə.pɪŋ/ *adj* describes a country or area of the world which is poorer and has less advanced industries, especially in Africa, Latin America or Asia: *the developing world/countries/nations* ➲See also **developing** at **develop** GROW.

deˈvelopment ˌarea *noun* [C] *UK* an area of high numbers of people without jobs where the government encourages new industries to start so that more jobs will be created

deviant /ˈdiː.vi.ənt/ *adj* (*US ALSO* **deviate**) describes a person or behaviour that is not usual and is generally considered to be unacceptable

deviant /ˈdiː.vi.ənt/ *noun* [C] someone whose behaviour, especially sexual behaviour, is deviant: *a sexual deviant*

deviance /ˈdiː.vi.ənts/ *noun* [U]

deviate /ˈdiː.vi.eɪt/ *verb* [I] **1** to do something which is different from the usual or common way of behaving: *The recent pattern of weather deviates* ***from*** *the norm for this time of year.* **2** to go in a different direction: *The path follows the river closely, occasionally deviating round a clump of trees.* **deviation** /ˌdiː.viˈeɪ.ʃən/ *noun* [C or U] *Any deviation* ***from*** *the party's faith is seen as betrayal.*

device [OBJECT] /dɪˈvaɪs/ *noun* [C] an object or machine which has been invented to fulfil a particular purpose: *a contraceptive/electronic device* ○ *Rescuers used a special device* ***for*** *finding people trapped in collapsed buildings.*

device [METHOD] /dɪˈvaɪs/ *noun* [C] a method which is used to produce a desired effect: *a literary/rhetorical device* ○ *A trademark can be a powerful marketing device.* ○ [+ to infinitive] *Her cool manner is just a device* ***to*** *avoid having to talk to people.*

device [BOMB] /dɪˈvaɪs/ *noun* [C] a bomb or other explosive: *an explosive/incendiary/nuclear device*

devil /ˈdev.əl/ *noun* [C] **1** an evil being, often represented in human form but with a tail and horns **2** *INFORMAL* someone, especially a child, who behaves badly: *Those* ***little/young*** *devils broke my window.* **3** *INFORMAL HUMOROUS* a person who enjoys doing things people might disapprove of: *"I'm going to wear a short black skirt and thigh-length boots." "Ooh, you devil!"* ○ *Have another slice of cake – go on,* ***be*** *a devil!* **4** *INFORMAL* used with an adjective to describe someone and express your opinion about something that has happened to them: *I hear you've got a new car, you* ***lucky*** *devil!* ○ *He's been ill for weeks,* ***poor*** *devil.*

the ˈDevil *noun* [S] a powerful evil force and the enemy of God in Christianity and Judaism

• **the/a devil of a** *OLD-FASHIONED* an extremely difficult or serious type of: *a devil of a mess/problem* ○ *We had the devil of a* ***job/time*** *trying to find this place!*

• **go to the devil** *OLD-FASHIONED* something you say to someone annoying or bad to tell them to go away forever

• **speak/talk of the devil** something you say when the person you were talking about appears unexpectedly: *Did you hear what happened to Anna yesterday – oh, speak of the devil, here she is.*

• **what/where/how/why the devil** *OLD-FASHIONED INFORMAL* used to give emphasis to a question: *What the devil are you doing?* ○ *Where the devil have you been?*

• **be between the devil and the deep blue sea** to have two choices but both of them are equally unpleasant or inconvenient

• **(to) give the devil his due** said when you admit that someone you do not like or admire does have particular good qualities: *I don't like the man but – give the devil his due – he works incredibly hard.*

devilish /ˈdev.əl.ɪʃ/ *adj* **1** evil or morally bad: *a devilish plot* **2** morally bad but in an attractive way: *a devilish grin* **3** extremely difficult or clever: *devilish cunning*

devilishly /ˈdev.əl.ɪʃ.li/ *adv* extremely: *That's a devilishly* ***difficult*** *question.*

devilment /ˈdev.əl.mənt/ *noun* [U] (*ALSO* **devilry**) *OLD-FASHIONED* behaviour that intentionally causes trouble but is usually intended to be playful or amusing: *He's up to some kind of devilment again, I'll be bound.*

devil-may-care /ˌdev.əl.meɪˈkeəʳ/ [US] /-ˈker/ *adj* not worrying or caring about the results of your actions: *He has a rather devil-may-care* ***attitude*** *to his studies.*

devil's advocate /ˌdev.əlzˈæd.və.kət/ *noun* [C usually sing] someone who pretends, in an argument or discussion, to be against an idea or plan which a lot of people support, in order to make people discuss and consider it in more detail: *I don't really believe all that – I was just* ***playing*** *devil's advocate.*

devil's food cake /ˈdev.əlz.fuːdˌkeɪk/ *noun* [C or U] *MAINLY US* a strong-tasting dark chocolate cake

devious /ˈdiː.vi.əs/ *adj* **1** describes people or plans and methods that are dishonest, often in a complicated way, but often also clever and successful: *You have to be a bit devious if you're going to succeed in business.* ○ *a devious scheme* **2** indirect: *He took a rather devious route which avoids the city centre.* **deviously** /ˈdiː.vi.ə.sli/ *adv* **deviousness** /ˈdiː.vi.ə.snəs/ *noun* [U]

devise /dɪˈvaɪz/ *verb* [T] to invent a plan, system, object, etc., usually cleverly or imaginatively: *He's good at devising language games that you can play with students in class.* ○ *The cartoon characters Snoopy and Charlie Brown were devised by Charles M. Schultz.*

devoid /dɪˈvɔɪd/ *adj FORMAL* **be devoid of** ***sth*** to lack or be without something that is necessary or usual: *Their apartment is devoid of* ***all*** *comforts.* ○ *He seems to be devoid of compassion.*

devolution /ˌdiː.vəˈluː.ʃən/ *noun* [U] the moving of power or responsibility from a main organization to a lower level, or from a central government to a regional government: *The majority of people in the province are in favour of devolution.*

devolve /dɪˈvɒlv/ [US] /-ˈvɑːlv/ *verb* [T] to (cause power or responsibility to) be given to other people: *To be a good manager, you must know how to devolve responsibility downwards.* ○ *FORMAL Those duties will necessarily devolve* ***on/upon*** *me.*

▲ **devolve** ***sth*** **to** ***sb*** *phrasal verb FORMAL* to give power or responsibility to a person or organization at a lower or more local level: *The local education authorities have devolved financial control to individual schools.*

devote /dɪˈvəʊt/ [US] /-ˈvoʊt/ *verb*

▲ **devote** ***sth*** **to** ***sth/sb*** *phrasal verb* **1** to give all of something, especially your time, effort or love, or yourself, to something you believe in or to a person: *He left government to devote more* ***time*** *to his family.* ○ *She has devoted all her* ***energies/life*** *to the care of homeless people.* ○ [R] *At the age of 25, he decided to devote him****self*** *to God.* **2** [often passive] to use a space, area, time, etc. for a particular purpose: *Over half his speech was devoted to the issue of unemployment.* ○ *The report recommends that more* ***resources*** *be devoted to teach****ing*** *four year olds.*

devoted /dɪˈvəʊ.tɪd/ [US] /-ˈvoʊ.t̬ɪd/ *adj* extremely loving and loyal: *a devoted fan/husband* ○ *Lucy is devoted* ***to*** *her cats.* **devotedly** /dɪˈvəʊ.tɪd.li/ [US] /-ˈvoʊ.t̬ɪd-/ *adv*

devotion /dɪˈvəʊ.ʃən/ [US] /-ˈvoʊ-/ *noun* [U] **1** loyalty and love or care for someone or something: *He inspired respect and devotion from his pupils.* ○ *She will be remembered for her selfless/unstinting devotion* ***to*** *the cause.* **2** religious worship: *He knelt* ***in*** *humble devotion.*

D

devotional /dɪ'vəʊ.ʃᵊn.ᵊl/ ⓤ /-'voʊ-/ adj connected with the act of religious worship: *devotional music/poems/practices*

devotions /dɪ'vəʊ.ʃᵊnz/ ⓤ /-'voʊ-/ plural noun acts of religious worship, especially prayers

devotee /ˌdev.ə'tiː/ noun [C] a person who strongly admires a particular person or is extremely interested in a subject: *He is a great devotee of the Prime Minister.* ○ *devotees of cricket*

devour /dɪ'vaʊᵊ/ ⓤ /-'vaʊɚ/ verb [T] **1** to eat something eagerly and in large amounts so that nothing is left: *The young cubs hungrily devoured the deer.* **2** LITERARY to destroy something completely: *The flames quickly devoured the building.* **3** to read books or literature quickly and eagerly: *She's a very keen reader – she devours one book after another.*

● **be devoured by** *sth* to feel an emotion, especially a bad emotion, very strongly so that it strongly influences your behaviour: *He was devoured by jealousy/hatred.*

devouring /dɪ'vaʊə.rɪŋ/ ⓤ /-'vaʊɚ.ɪŋ/ adj [before n] LITERARY describes an emotion that is extremely strong and usually destructive: *She is driven by a devouring ambition/passion.*

devout /dɪ'vaʊt/ adj believing strongly in a religion and obeying all its rules or principles: *a devout Buddhist/Christian/churchgoer*

devoutly /dɪ'vaʊt.li/ adv **1** in a very religious way: *a devoutly Catholic family* **2** FORMAL sincerely and strongly: *He devoutly hoped that they would reach a peaceful agreement.* **devoutness** /dɪ'vaʊt.nəs/ noun [U]

dew /djuː/ ⓤ /duː/ noun [U] drops of water that form on the ground and other surfaces outside during the night **dewy** /'djuː.i/ ⓤ /'duː-/ adj: *a dewy morning*

dewdrop /'djuː.drɒp/ ⓤ /'duː.drɑːp/ noun [C] a drop of DEW

dewlap /'djuː.læp/ ⓤ /'duː-/ noun [C] a fold of loose skin which hangs under the throat of a cow or a dog

dewy-eyed /ˌdjuː.i'aɪd/ ⓤ /ˌduː-/ adj **1** having eyes that are wet with tears because you feel emotional: *dewy-eyed nostalgia* **2** innocent and lacking experience of life: *a dewy-eyed bride* ○ *dewy-eyed innocence*

dexterity /dek'ster.ə.ti/ ⓤ /-t̬i/ noun [U] the ability to perform a difficult action quickly and skilfully with the hands, or the ability to think quickly and effectively: *He caught the ball with great dexterity.* ○ *He answered the journalists' questions with all the dexterity of a politician.* **dexterous, dextrous** /'dek.stᵊr.əs/ ⓤ /-stɚ-/ adj: *a dexterous movement* **dexterously, dextrously** /'dek.stᵊr.ə.sli/ ⓤ /-stɚ-/ adv

dextrose /'dek.strəʊs/ ⓤ /-stroʊs/ noun [U] SPECIALIZED a type of naturally-produced sugar found in fruits, honey, etc.

dhoti /'dəʊ.ti/ ⓤ /'doʊ.t̬i/ noun [C] a loose piece of clothing wrapped around the lower half of the body, worn by men in India

diabetes /ˌdaɪə'biː.tiːz/ ⓤ /-t̬əs/ noun [U] a disease in which the body cannot control the level of sugar in the blood

diabetic /ˌdaɪə'bet.ɪk/ ⓤ /-'bet̬-/ adj **1** relating to diabetes: *a diabetic coma* **2** made for diabetic people to eat: *diabetic chocolate/jam*

diabetic /ˌdaɪə'bet.ɪk/ ⓤ /-'bet̬-/ noun [C] a person who has diabetes

diabolical /ˌdaɪə'bɒl.ɪ.kᵊl/ ⓤ /-'bɑː.lɪ.kᵊl/ adj (US ALSO **diabolic**) **1** INFORMAL extremely bad or shocking: *Conditions in the prison were diabolical.* ○ *His driving is diabolical!* **2** evil, or caused by THE DEVIL

diabolically /ˌdaɪə'bɒl.ɪ.kli/ ⓤ /-'bɑː.lɪ-/ adv: *diabolically* (= extremely) *clever/wicked*

diadem /'daɪə.dem/ noun [C] a small CROWN (= circular decoration for the head) with jewels in it

diagnose /'daɪə.gnəʊz/ ⓤ /ˌdaɪə.əg'noʊz/ verb [T] to recognize and name the exact character of a disease or a problem, by making an examination: *The specialist diagnosed cancer.* ○ *His condition was diagnosed as some sort of blood disorder.* ○ *She was diagnosed with/as having diabetes.* ○ *The electrician has diagnosed a fault in the wiring.*

diagnosis /ˌdaɪ.əg'nəʊ.sɪs/ ⓤ /-'noʊ-/ noun [C or U] plural **diagnoses** a judgment about what a particular illness or problem is, made after making an examination: *"What was the diagnosis?" "Arthritis in both joints."* ○ *The doctor has made an initial diagnosis, but there'll be an additional examination by a specialist.* ○ *Diagnosis of the disease* (= saying what it is) *is difficult in the early stages.* **diagnostic** /ˌdaɪ.əg'nɒs.tɪk/ ⓤ /-'nɑː.stɪk/ adj: *diagnostic techniques/tests*

diagonal /daɪ'æg.ᵊn.ᵊl/ adj **1** A diagonal line is straight and sloping, not horizontal or vertical, for example joining two opposite corners of a square or other four-sided flat shape: *The book has a diagonal black stripe on the cover.* **2** moving in a diagonal line: *Peters received a diagonal pass and headed the ball into the net.* **diagonally** /daɪ'æg.ᵊn.ᵊl.i/ adv: *It's quickest if you cut diagonally across the park.*

diagonal /daɪ'æg.ᵊn.ᵊl/ noun [C] SPECIALIZED a straight line which joins two opposite corners of a four-sided flat shape, such as a square

diagram /'daɪ.ə.græm/ noun [C] a simple plan which represents a machine, system or idea, etc., often drawn to explain how it works: *The teacher drew a diagram showing how the blood flows through the heart.* **diagrammatic** /ˌdaɪ.ə.grə'mæt.ɪk/ ⓤ /-'mæt̬-/ adj

diagrammatically /ˌdaɪ.ə.grə'mæt.ɪ.kli/ ⓤ /-'mæt̬-/ adv using diagrams: *She explained the whole problem diagrammatically.*

dial TELEPHONE /'daɪ.əl/ verb [I or T] **-ll-** or US USUALLY **-l-** to operate a telephone or make a telephone call to someone by pressing a particular series of numbered buttons, or moving a numbered disc, on the telephone: *Can I dial this number direct, or do I have to go through the operator?* ○ *Dial 0 for the switchboard.*

dial /'daɪ.əl/ noun [C] the numbered disc on old-fashioned telephones which you turn when you make a telephone call

dial MEASURING DEVICE /'daɪ.əl/ noun [C] **1** the part of a machine or device which shows you a measurement of something such as speed or time: *Can you read what it says on the dial?* ○ *The dial of/on his watch* (= the part of it which has the numbers on it) *had a picture of Mickey Mouse on it.* **2** a device on an instrument which you move in order to control or adjust it: *You turn this dial to find a different radio station.*

dialect /'daɪ.ə.lekt/ noun [C or U] a form of a language that people speak in a particular part of a country, containing some different words and grammar, etc: *a regional dialect* ○ *The poem is written in northern dialect.*

dialectic /ˌdaɪ.ə'lek.tɪk/ noun [U] (ALSO **dialectics**) SPECIALIZED a way of discovering what is true by considering opposite theories **dialectical** /ˌdaɪ.ə'lek.tɪ.kᵊl/ adj

dialling code UK noun [C] (US **area code**) a series of numbers used before the main telephone number when you telephone someone outside your own town or area

dialling tone UK noun [C usually sing] (US **dial tone**) a continuous sound which tells you that a telephone is connected to the telephone system and is ready to be used

dialogue US ALSO **dialog** /'daɪ.ə.lɒg/ ⓤ /-lɑːg/ noun [C or U] **1** (a) conversation which is written for a book, play or film: *The play contained some very snappy/witty dialogue.* ○ *Act Two begins with a short dialogue between father and son.* **2** formal talks between opposing countries, political groups, etc: *The rebel leaders stated that they are willing to enter into dialogue with the government.* ○ *The two sides have at last begun to engage in a constructive dialogue.*

dial-up /'daɪ.əl.ʌp/ adj [before n] Dial-up computer systems and devices and Internet services use a telephone line to connect them: *a dial-up connection* ○ *dial-up access/networking* ○ *a dial-up account/modem*

dialysis /daɪ'æl.ə.sɪs/ noun [U] SPECIALIZED a process of separating dissolved substances by putting them through a thin piece of skin-like material, especially to make pure the blood of people whose kidneys are not working correctly: *a dialysis machine* ○ *kidney dialysis* ○ *She is on* (= being treated by) *dialysis.*

diamanté /diːəˈmɒn.teɪ/ ⓤ /-ˈmɑːn.t̬eɪ/ *noun* [U] artificial jewels which shine brightly: *a diamanté brooch/ diamanté earrings*

diameter /daɪˈæm.ɪ.tə^r/ ⓤ /-ə.t̬ə/ *noun* [C or U] (the length of) a straight line that reaches from one point on the edge of a round shape or object, through its centre, to a point on the opposite edge: *The diameter measures twice the radius.* ○ *The pond is six feet in diameter.*

diametrically /ˌdaɪ.əˈmet.rɪ.kʰl.i/ *adv* completely: *The two politicians have diametrically opposite points of view/are diametrically opposed.*

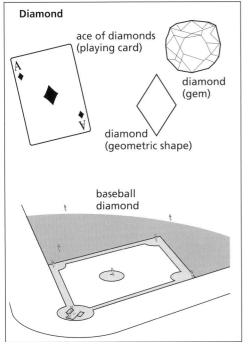

Diamond

ace of diamonds (playing card)

diamond (gem)

diamond (geometric shape)

baseball diamond

diamond /ˈdaɪə.mənd/ *noun* **1** [C or U] an extremely hard valuable stone which is used in jewellery, and in industry for cutting hard things: *a diamond ring/necklace* ○ *The tiara was set with diamonds and rubies.* ○ *He had worked in the diamond mines of South Africa.* ○ *diamond-tipped saw blades* **2** [C or U] a shape with four straight sides of equal length, forming two opposite angles which are wide and two which are narrow: *Joe's socks had diamond patterns on them.* **3** [C] a card, with a red diamond shape on it, which belongs to one of the four suits in a set of playing cards: *the six of diamonds* **4** [C] the square part of a field on which baseball is played, which is marked off by the four BASES, or the whole field on which the game is played ➲See picture **Sports** on page Centre 10

diamond in the 'rough *noun* [C usually sing] US FOR **rough diamond**

diamond 'jubilee *noun* [C usually sing] MAINLY UK the day exactly 60 years after an important occasion, or a special event to celebrate this

diamond 'wedding (anni,versary) *noun* [C] the day exactly 60 years after a marriage, often celebrated with a party

diaper /ˈdaɪ.pə^r/ ⓤ /-pə/ *noun* [C] US FOR **nappy**

diaphanous /daɪˈæf.ʰn.əs/ *adj* LITERARY describes a substance, especially cloth, which is so delicate and thin that you can see through it: *a diaphanous silk veil*

diaphragm MUSCLE /ˈdaɪ.ə.fræm/ *noun* [C] the muscle which separates the chest from the lower part of the body

diaphragm BIRTH CONTROL /ˈdaɪ.ə.fræm/ *noun* [C] a circular rubber device which a woman puts inside her vagina before having sex, to prevent herself from becoming pregnant

diaphragm COVER /ˈdaɪ.ə.fræm/ *noun* [C] SPECIALIZED any thin piece of material stretched across an opening

diarrhoea, MAINLY US **diarrhea** /ˌdaɪ.əˈriː.ə/ *noun* [U] an illness in which the body's solid waste is more liquid than usual and comes out of the body more often: *diarrhoea and sickness* ○ *an attack of diarrhoea*

diary /ˈdaɪə.ri/ ⓤ /ˈdaɪr.i/ *noun* [C] a book with a separate space or page for each day, in which you write down your future arrangements, meetings, etc. or one used to record your thoughts and feelings or what has happened on that day: *Don't forgot to write/enter the date of the meeting in your diary.* ○ *I've never kept* (= written about what has happened to me in) *a diary.*

diarist /ˈdaɪə.rɪst/ *noun* [C] someone who is known for writing or having written a diary: *Anne Frank was a famous diarist of the Second World War.*

diaspora /daɪˈæs.pʰr.ə/ ⓤ /-pə-/ *noun* [U] FORMAL the spreading of people from one original country to other countries

the Di'aspora *group noun* [U] the Jews living in different parts of the world outside Israel, or the various places outside Israel in which they live

diatonic /ˌdaɪ.əˈtɒn.ɪk/ ⓤ /-ˈtɑː.nɪk/ *adj* SPECIALIZED belonging or relating to a major or minor musical scale consisting of five full TONES and two SEMITONES

diatribe /ˈdaɪ.ə.traɪb/ *noun* [C] FORMAL an angry speech or piece of writing which severely criticizes something or someone: *He launched into a long diatribe against the government's policies.*

dibs /dɪbz/ *plural noun* US INFORMAL **dibs on sth** a right to have or obtain something from someone, or to use something: *Dibs on the front seat!* ○ *Cablevision might have first dibs on buying the rest of the property.*

dice GAME /daɪs/ (*plural* **dice**) *noun* **1** [C] (US ALSO OR OLD-FASHIONED **die**) a small CUBE (= object with six equal square sides) with a different number of spots on each side, used in games involving chance: *We need two dice to play the game.* ○ *You roll/throw the dice and whoever gets the highest score goes first.* **2** [U] any game involving chance in which dice are thrown: *Let's play dice.*

• **no dice** US INFORMAL something that people say when you may not or cannot do something: *I asked if we could go to the party, but Mom said no dice.*

dice /daɪs/ *verb* **dice with death** to do something extremely dangerous and foolish: *You're dicing with death driving at that speed on icy roads.*

dice CUT /daɪs/ *verb* [T] to cut food into small squares: *Peel and dice the potatoes.* ○ *diced carrots*

dicey /ˈdaɪ.si/ *adj* dicier, diciest MAINLY UK INFORMAL slightly dangerous or uncertain: *The company's finances look a bit dicey.*

dichotomy /daɪˈkɒt.ə.mi/ ⓤ /-ˈkɑː.t̬ə-/ *noun* [C usually sing] FORMAL a difference between two completely opposite ideas or things: *There is often a dichotomy between what politicians say and what they do.*

dick PENIS /dɪk/ *noun* [C] OFFENSIVE a penis

dick PERSON /dɪk/ *noun* [C] **1** OFFENSIVE a stupid man: *That guy is such a dick.* **2** US OLD-FASHIONED INFORMAL a **detective** (= someone whose job is to discover facts about a crime): *a private dick*

dickens /ˈdɪk.ɪnz/ *plural noun* OLD-FASHIONED INFORMAL **the dickens** used in questions to express annoyance or surprise: *What the dickens are you doing with that paint?*

Dickensian /dɪˈken.zi.ən/ *adj* **1** relating to or similar to something described in the books of the 19th century British writer, Charles Dickens, especially living or working conditions that are below an acceptable standard: *The bathrooms in this hotel are positively Dickensian – no hot water and grime everywhere.* **2** written by or in the style of Charles Dickens

dicker /ˈdɪk.ə^r/ ⓤ /-ə-/ *verb* [I] US to argue with someone, especially about the price of goods: *She dickered with the driver over the fare.*

dickey, dicky, dickie /ˈdɪk.i/ *noun* [C] a piece of clothing worn around the neck to fill the space left by an open collar

dickhead /ˈdɪk.hed/ *noun* [C] *OFFENSIVE* a stupid person: *You dickhead – you've dented the back of my car!*

dicky /ˈdɪk.i/ *adj UK INFORMAL* weak, especially in health, and likely to fail or suffer from problems: *Grandad's got a dicky **heart**.*

dickybird /ˈdɪk.i.bɜːd/ [US] /-bɝːd/ *noun* [C] *UK CHILD'S WORD* a small bird

• **not a dickybird** *OLD-FASHIONED INFORMAL* nothing at all: *We haven't **heard** a dickybird from* (= spoken to or received a letter from) *Riza recently.*

ˈdicky (ˌbow) *noun* [C] *UK INFORMAL FOR* **bow tie**

dicta /ˈdɪk.tə/ *plural of* **dictum**

Dictaphone /ˈdɪk.tə.fəʊn/ [US] /-foʊn/ *noun* [C] *TRADEMARK* a machine used in an office to record spoken words and later repeat them aloud so that they can be written down ➲See picture **In the Office** on page Centre 15

dictate [GIVE ORDERS] /dɪkˈteɪt/ [US] /ˈ--/ *verb* **1** [I or T] to give orders, or state something exactly, with total authority: *The UN will dictate the terms of troop withdrawal from the region.* ○ [+ question word] *He disagrees with the government dictating **what** children are taught in schools.* ○ [+ that] *The tennis club rules dictate **that** suitable footwear must be worn on the courts.* **2** [T] to influence something or make it necessary: *The party's change of policy has been dictated by its need to win back the support of voters.* ○ [+ that] *I wanted to take a year off, but my financial situation dictated **that** I got a job.*

dictate /ˈdɪk.teɪt/ *noun* [C usually pl] *FORMAL* an order which should be obeyed, often one which you give to yourself: *the dictates **of** conscience/common sense* ➲Compare **diktat**.

dictator /dɪkˈteɪ.təʳ/ [US] /ˈdɪk.teɪ.t̬ɚ/ *noun* [C] **1** *MAINLY DISAPPROVING* a leader who has complete power in a country and has not been elected by the people **2** *HUMOROUS OR DISAPPROVING* a person who gives orders and behaves as if they have complete power: *My boss is a bit of a dictator.* **dictatorial** /ˌdɪk.təˈtɔː.ri.əl/ [US] /-ˈtɔːr.i-/ *adj DISAPPROVING a dictatorial ruler/government* ○ *Her father is very dictatorial.*

dictatorship /dɪkˈteɪ.tə.ʃɪp/ [US] /-t̬ɚ-/ *noun* **1** [C] a country ruled by a dictator: *a **military** dictatorship* **2** [U] the state of being, or being ruled by, a dictator: *The dictatorship **of** General Franco lasted for nearly 40 years.*

dictate [SPEAK] /dɪkˈteɪt/ [US] /ˈ--/ *verb* [I or T] to speak something aloud for a person or machine to record the words said, so that they can be written down: *I dictated my order over the phone.* ○ *She spent the morning dictating letters **to** her secretary.*

dictation /dɪkˈteɪ.ʃᵊn/ *noun* **1** [U] when someone dictates something for someone else to write down: *I'll ask my assistant to **take** dictation* (= write down what I say). **2** [C] a test in which a piece of writing is dictated to students learning a foreign language, to test their ability to hear and write the language correctly: *Our French dictation lasted half an hour.*

▲ **dictate to *sb*** *phrasal verb* to tell someone what to do: *The President is so powerful that he is able to dictate to the government.* ○ *I will not be dictated to like that!*

diction /ˈdɪk.ʃᵊn/ *noun* [U] the manner in which words are pronounced: *It is very helpful for a language teacher to have good diction.*

dictionary /ˈdɪk.ʃᵊn.ᵊr.i/ [US] /-er.i/ *noun* [C] **1** a book that contains a list of words in alphabetical order with their meanings explained or written in another language, or a similar product for use on a computer: *a French-English/English-French dictionary* ○ *a bilingual/monolingual dictionary* ○ *To check how a word is spelt, look it up in a dictionary.* **2** a book which gives information about a particular subject, in which the entries are given in alphabetical order: *a biographical/science dictionary* ○ *a dictionary **of** quotations*

dictum /ˈdɪk.tᵊm/ *noun* [C] *plural* **dicta** or **dictums** a short statement, especially one expressing advice or a general truth: *He followed the famous American dictum, 'Don't get mad, get even'.*

did /dɪd/ *past simple of* **do**

didactic /daɪˈdæk.tɪk/ *adj MAINLY DISAPPROVING* **1** intended to teach, especially in a way that is too determined or eager, and often fixed and unwilling to change: *a didactic approach to teaching* **2** intended to teach people a moral: *didactic literature* **didactically** /daɪˈdæk.tɪ.kli/ *adv*

diddle [CHEAT] /ˈdɪd.l̩/ *verb* [T] *INFORMAL* to obtain money from someone in a way which is not honest: *He diddled me! He said that there were six in a bag, but there were only five.* ○ *I checked the bill and realized the restaurant had diddled me **out of** £5.*

diddly /ˈdɪd.l̩.i/ *noun* [U] (*ALSO* **diddly-squat**) *US INFORMAL* anything: *He hasn't done diddly all day.* ○ *There's no point in asking Ellen – she doesn't know diddly.*

diddums! /ˈdɪd.ᵊmz/ *exclamation UK HUMOROUS* something you say to show that you feel no sympathy for someone who is behaving like a child: *He called you a bad name, did he? Ah, diddums!*

didgeridoo /ˌdɪdʒ.ə.riˈduː/ [US] /-ɚ.i-/ *noun* [C] *plural* **didgeridoos** a long wooden wind instrument played by Australian Aborigines to produce a long deep sound

didn't /ˈdɪd.ᵊnt/ *short form of* did not: *We didn't arrive at our hotel until after midnight.*

die [STOP LIVING] /daɪ/ *verb* [I] **dying, died, died 1** to stop living or existing, either suddenly or slowly: *Twelve people died in the accident.* ○ *She died **of/from** hunger/cancer/a heart attack/her injuries.* ○ *It is a brave person who will die **for** their beliefs.* ○ *I should like to die **in my sleep*** (= while I am sleeping). ○ *Many people have a fear of dying.* ○ *Our love will never die.* ○ *She will not tell anyone – the secret will die with her.* ➲See also **death**. **2 die a natural/violent, etc. death** to die naturally, violently, etc: *He died a violent death.* ○ *My grandmother died a natural death* (= did not die of illness or because she was killed), *as she would have wanted.* **3** *INFORMAL* If a machine stops working, or if an object cannot be used or repaired any more, usually because it is very old, people sometimes say it has died: *The engine just died **on** us.* ○ *HUMOROUS He wore his jeans until they died.*

• **die hard** If a belief or way of behaving dies hard, it takes a long time to disappear, and is not given up easily: *Old habits die hard.* ➲See also **diehard**.

• **almost/nearly die of *sth*** (*ALSO* **could have died of *sth***) to feel a particular feeling extremely strongly: *I almost/could have died of embarrassment.*

• **die a/the death** *UK* (*US* **die a natural death**) to fail and end: *The play, like so many before it, died the death after a week.*

• **or die in the attempt** said when someone would do anything to achieve what they want to achieve: *She'll finish the race or die in the attempt.*

• **be dying for/to do *sth*** to be extremely eager to have or do something: *I'm dying to hear your news.* ○ *I'm dying for a cup of tea.*

• **do or die** said when you are in a situation in which you must take a big risk in order to avoid failure: *On Tuesday, **it's** do or die in the match against Brazil.*

• **to die for** *INFORMAL* excellent or extremely desirable: *She has a figure to die for.* ○ *That chocolate cake is to die for.*

• **Never say die.** *SAYING* said to encourage people to keep trying

dying /ˈdaɪ.ɪŋ/ *adj* **1** very ill and likely to die soon: *She nursed her dying husband for months.* **2** describes a tradition or industry which is becoming noticeably less common or important **3** happening at the time someone dies, or connected with that time: *Beethoven's dying **words** are said to have been "I shall hear in heaven".* **4** **the dying** people who are about to die: *These nurses specialize in the care of the dying.*

• **to/until *my* dying day** as long as I live: *I'll remember your kindness to my dying day.*

COMMON LEARNER ERROR

died or dead?

Do not confuse the verb and adjective. **Died** is the simple past and past participle of the verb 'die'.

Her father died last year.

Dead is an adjective which means 'not alive'.

Her father is dead.

~~*Her father is died.*~~

die [TOOL] /daɪ/ *noun* [C] a shaped piece or MOULD (= hollow container) made of metal or other hard material, used to shape or put a pattern on metal or plastic

die [GAME] /daɪ/ *noun* [C] *OLD USE OR US FOR* **dice** GAME

• **the die is cast** said when a situation is certain to develop in a particular way because decisions have been taken which cannot be changed: *From the moment the negotiations failed, the die was cast and war was inevitable.*

PHRASAL VERBS WITH **die** ▼

▲ **die away** *phrasal verb* If something, especially a sound, dies away, it gradually becomes reduced until it stops existing or disappears: *The sound of his footsteps gradually died away.*

▲ **die down** *phrasal verb* If a sound or activity dies down, it becomes quieter or less obvious: *It was several minutes before the applause died down.*

▲ **die off** *phrasal verb* If a group of plants, animals or people dies off, all of that group dies over a period of time.

▲ **die out** *phrasal verb* to become less common and finally stop existing: *Dinosaurs died out millions of years ago.* ○ *It's a custom which is beginning to die out.*

die-cast /ˈdaɪ.kɑːst/ [US] /-kæst/ *verb* [T] to make something by pouring liquid metal, plastic, etc., usually under pressure, into a MOULD (= hollow container) **die-cast** /ˈdaɪ.kɑːst/ [US] /-kæst/ *adj*: *a die-cast toy*

diehard, **die-hard** /ˈdaɪ.hɑːd/ [US] /-hɑːrd/ *noun* [C] *DISAPPROVING* someone who is unwilling to change or give up their ideas or ways of behaving, even when there are good reasons to do so: *a diehard conservative/fan* ➲See also **die hard** at **die** STOP LIVING.

diesel /ˈdiː.zəl/ *noun* **1** [U] a type of heavy oil used as fuel: *a diesel engine* ○ *My new car* **runs on** (= uses) *diesel.* **2** [C] any vehicle, especially a train, which has a diesel engine

diet /ˈdaɪ.ət/ *noun* **1** [C or U] the food and drink usually taken by a person or group: *Diet varies between different countries in the world.* ○ *a* ***healthy/balanced/varied*** *diet* ○ *Rice is the* ***staple*** *diet* (= most important food) *of many people in China.* ○ *The children seem to exist on a diet* ***of*** *burgers and chips.* **2** [C] when someone eats less food, or only particular types of food, because they want to become thinner or for medical reasons: *I'm* ***going on*** *a diet next week and hope to lose two kilos before Christmas.* ○ *a* ***crash/strict/calorie-controlled*** *diet* ○ *The doctor put me* ***on*** *a low-salt diet to reduce my blood pressure.* **3** [S] a particular type of thing that you experience or do regularly, or a limited range of activities: *He was brought up on a diet* ***of*** *political propaganda from birth.* ○ *The TV only offers a diet* ***of*** *comedies and old movies every evening.*

diet /ˈdaɪ.ət/ *verb* [I] to limit the food and/or drink which you take, especially in order to lose weight: *You should be able to reduce your weight by careful dieting.*

diet /ˈdaɪ.ət/ *adj* [before n] describes food or drink that contains much less sugar or fat than the usual type, and is often sweetened artificially: *diet cola*

dietary /ˈdaɪ.ə.tər.i/ /-tri/ [US] /-ter-/ *adj* relating to your diet: *Dietary* ***habits*** *can be very difficult to change.* ○ *Do you have any special dietary* ***requirements****?*

dieter /ˈdaɪ.ə.təʳ/ [US] /-t̬ɚ/ *noun* [C] someone who is trying to lose weight by dieting

ˌdietary ˈfibre *noun* [U] **fibre** FOOD

dietician, **dietitian** /ˌdaɪ.əˈtɪʃ.ən/ *noun* [C] a person who scientifically studies, and gives advice about, food and eating

dietetics /ˌdaɪ.əˈtet.ɪks/ [US] /-ˈtet̬-/ *noun* [U] the scientific study of the food that people eat and its effects on health

differ /ˈdɪf.əʳ/ [US] /-ɚ/ *verb* [I] **1** to be not like something or someone else, either physically or in another way: *The twins look alike, but they differ* ***in*** *temperament.* ○ *His views differ considerably* ***from*** *those of his parents.* ○ *The findings of the various studies differ* ***significantly/markedly/radically****.* ○ *The incidence of the illness differs greatly* ***between*** *men and women.* **2** *FORMAL* to disagree: *Economists differ* ***on*** *the cause of inflation.* ○ *I* ***beg to*** *differ* ***with*** *you on that point.*

difference /ˈdɪf.ər.ənts/ [US] /-ɚ-/ *noun* **1** [C or U] the way in which two or more things which you are comparing are not the same: *What's the difference* ***between*** *an ape and a monkey?* ○ *Is there any significant difference* ***in*** *quality* ***between*** *these two items?* **2** [C usually pl] a disagreement: *They had an awful row several years ago, but now they've* ***settled/resolved*** *their differences.*

• **have a difference of opinion** to disagree: *They had a difference of opinion* ***about/over*** *their child's education.*

• **make a (big) difference** (*ALSO* **make all the difference**) to improve a situation (greatly): *Exercise can make a big difference* ***to*** *your state of health.* ○ *Putting up some new wallpaper has made all the difference* ***to*** *the place.*

• **not make any difference** (*ALSO* **not make the slightest difference**) to not change a situation in any way: *You can ask him again if you like, but it won't make any difference – he'll still say no.* ○ *It makes no difference* ***where*** *you put the aerial, the TV picture's still lousy.*

• **with a difference** describes something unusual, and more interesting or better than other things of the same type: *Try new Cremetti – the ice cream with a difference.*

different /ˈdɪf.ər.ənt/ [US] /-ɚ-/ *adj* **1** not the same: *She seems to wear something different every day.* ○ *He's different now that he's been to college.* ○ *We're reading a different book this week.* ○ *Emily is* ***very/completely/entirely*** *different* ***from*** *her sister.* ○ *Emily and her sister are quite* (= completely) *different.* ○ *There are many different* ***types/kinds*** *of bacteria.* ✻ NOTE: *Different from* is used in British and American English. *Different than* is also used in American English. *Different to* is also used in British English, but some people consider this to be incorrect. **2** *INFORMAL* describes something or someone you think is unusual or shows bad judgment: *What do I think of your purple shoes? Well, they're certainly different.* **differently** /ˈdɪf.ər.ənt.li/ [US] /-ɚ-/ *adv*

COMMON LEARNER ERROR

difference

Be careful to use the correct preposition. You talk about the **difference between** two things when you are comparing them.

What's the difference between a cup and a mug?

You talk about the **difference in** something or someone when you want to say how something or someone has changed.

Have you noticed a difference in him since last year?

differential /ˌdɪf.əˈren.tʃəl/ *noun* [C] **1** an amount of difference between things which are compared: *a* ***price*** *differential* ○ *The* ***pay*** *differential* ***between*** *workers and management is too great.* **2** a **differential gear**

differential /ˌdɪf.əˈren.tʃəl/ *adj* based on a difference: *We have a differential salary structure based on employees' experience.* **differentially** /ˌdɪf.əˈren.tʃəl.i/ *adv*

difˌferential ˈcalculus *noun* [U] *SPECIALIZED* the branch of CALCULUS in which rates of change and connected quantities are calculated

difˌferential ˈgear *noun* [C] *SPECIALIZED* a device fitted to the AXLE of a vehicle that allows the wheels to turn at different rates when going round a corner

differentiate /ˌdɪf.əˈren.tʃi.eɪt/ *verb* **1** [I or T] to show or find the difference between things which are compared: *We do not differentiate* ***between*** *our workers on the basis of their background or ethnic origin.* **2** [T] to make someone or something different: *The slate roof differentiates this house* ***from*** *others in the area.*

differentiation /ˌdɪf.ər.en.tʃiˈeɪ.ʃən/ [US] /-ə.ren-/ *noun* **1** [C] when you differentiate: *a differentiation between mental illness and mental handicap* **2** [U] the process of becoming or making something different: *Product differentiation is essential to the future of the company.*

difficult /ˈdɪf.ɪ.kəlt/ *adj* **1** needing skill or effort; not easy: *a difficult problem/choice/task/language* ○ [+ to infinitive] ***It*** *will be very difficult* ***to*** *prove that they are guilty.* ○ *Many things make* ***it*** *difficult* ***for*** *women* ***to*** *reach the top in US business.* ○ [+ v-ing] *He finds* ***it*** *extremely difficult be****ing*** *a single parent.* **2** not friendly, easy to deal with, or behaving well: *The manager is difficult* ***to*** *deal with/a difficult person* ***to*** *deal with.* ○ *His wife is a very difficult person.* ○ *Please children, don't be so difficult!*

D

difficulty /ˈdɪf.ɪ.kəl.ti/ [US] /-t̬i/ *noun* **1** [U] when something is not easy to do or understand: *We finished the job, but only* ***with*** *great difficulty.* ○ *The difficulty* ***of*** *the task excited them.* ○ *People with asthma have difficulty* ***in*** *breathing.* ○ [+ v-ing] *She* ***had*** *great difficulty* ***finding*** *a job.* **2** [C] a problem: *to* ***have*** *financial/personal difficulties* ○ *children with* ***learning*** *difficulties* ○ *People learning a new language often* ***encounter*** *some difficulties at first.* ○ *An unforeseen difficulty has* ***arisen.***
• **be in difficulties** *UK* (*US* **be in difficulty**) to have problems or be in a difficult situation: *A ship is in difficulties off the coast of Ireland.*

COMMON LEARNER ERROR

have difficulty (in) doing something

You can say you **have difficulty doing** something or **have difficulty in doing** something.

She has difficulty walking.
She has difficulty in walking.
~~*She has difficulty to walk.*~~

diffident /ˈdɪf.ɪ.dənt/ *adj* shy and not confident of your abilities: *a diffident manner* ○ *You shouldn't be so diffident* ***about*** *your achievements – you've done really well!* **diffidence** /ˈdɪf.ɪ.dənts/ *noun* [U] **diffidently** /ˈdɪf.ɪ.dənt.li/ *adv*

diffraction /dɪˈfræk.ʃən/ *noun* [U] *SPECIALIZED* (a pattern caused by) a change in the direction of light, water or sound waves
diffract /dɪˈfrækt/ *verb* [T] to separate light into coloured strips or into light and dark strips

diffuse /dɪˈfjuːz/ *verb* [I or T] **1** to (cause something to) spread in many directions: *Television is a powerful means of diffusing knowledge.* **2** to (cause a gas or liquid to) spread through or into a surrounding substance by mixing with it: *Oxygen diffuses from the lungs* ***into*** *the bloodstream.* ○ *The drop of red dye diffused slowly in the water.*
diffuse /dɪˈfjuːs/ *adj* **1** spread out and not directed in one place: *a diffuse light* ○ *The company has become large and diffuse.* **2** *DISAPPROVING* not clear or easy to understand: *a diffuse literary style* **diffusely** /dɪˈfjuːs.li/ *adv* **diffusion** /dɪˈfjuː.ʒən/ *noun* [U] *the process of diffusion in gases/liquids/solids*

dig [MOVE EARTH] /dɪg/ *verb* **digging, dug, dug 1** [I or T] to break up and move earth using a tool, a machine or your hands: *Digging (in) the garden is good exercise.* **2** [T] to form a hole by moving earth: *The tunnel was dug with the aid of heavy machinery.* ○ *The dog was digging a hole to hide its bone in.*
• **dig *yourself* into a hole** *INFORMAL* to get yourself into a difficult situation: *The government has really dug itself into a hole with its economic policies.*
• **dig *your* own grave** to do something which causes you harm, sometimes serious harm: *She dug her own grave when she made fun of the boss.*
• **dig *your* heels in** to refuse to change your plans or ideas, especially when someone is trying to persuade you to do so
dig /dɪg/ *noun* [C] the careful removal of earth and objects from an area of historical interest: *an* ***archaeological*** *dig* ➲See also **digs**.
digger /ˈdɪg.əʳ/ [US] /-ɚ/ *noun* [C] **1** a machine used for digging: *a mechanical digger* **2** *AUS* a person who mines for gold ➲See also **gold digger**.

dig [SEARCH] /dɪg/ *verb* [I usually + adv or prep] **digging, dug, dug** to search for an object or information or to find it after looking: *He dug* ***into*** *his pocket and took out a few coins.* ○ *As I dug* ***deeper into*** *his past* (= found out more about it), *I realized that there was a lot about this man that I didn't know.*

dig [PRESS] /dɪg/ *verb* **dig *sb* in the ribs** to push the side of someone's body quickly with your ELBOW (= the middle part of the arm where it bends), often as a way of sharing a private joke with them or to get their attention

dig [REMARK] /dɪg/ *noun* [C] a remark which is intended to criticize, embarrass or make a joke about someone: *He's always* ***having/taking/making*** *digs* ***at*** *me.* ➲See also **digs**.

dig [APPROVE] /dɪg/ *verb* [T] **digging, dug, dug** *OLD-FASHIONED SLANG* to like or understand something: *Hey, I really dig those shoes!* ○ *You dig my meaning, man?*

PHRASAL VERBS WITH **dig** ▼

▲ **dig *(yourself)* in** [PROTECT] *phrasal verb* [R] to make arrangements to protect yourself from an attack by the enemy in a war situation, for example by digging TRENCHES
▲ **dig in** [EAT] *phrasal verb INFORMAL* to start eating: *The food's going cold – dig in!*
▲ **dig *(sth)* into *sb/sth*** *phrasal verb* to press or push, or to press or push an object, hard into someone or something: *A stone was digging into my heel.* ○ *She dug her fingernails into my wrist.*
▲ **dig *sb/sth* out** [GET OUT] *phrasal verb* [M] to get someone or something out of somewhere by digging: *Firefighters helped to dig out the people trapped in the snowdrift.* ○ *The doctor used a sharp instrument to dig a piece of glass out of my finger.*
▲ **dig *sth* out** [FIND] *phrasal verb* [M] *INFORMAL* to find something that you have not seen or used for a long time: *Mum dug out some old family photos to show me.*
▲ **dig *sth* up** [TAKE OUT] *phrasal verb* [M] to take something out of the ground by digging: *It's time we dug up those potatoes.*
▲ **dig *sth* up** [BREAK GROUND] *phrasal verb* [M] to break the ground or to make a hole in it with a tool, machine, etc: *They're digging up the road outside to repair the electricity cables.*
▲ **dig *sth* up** [INFORMATION] *phrasal verb* [M] to discover secret or forgotten facts by searching very carefully: *I've been doing some research on our family history and I've dug up some interesting information.* ○ *She's one of those journalists who's always trying to dig up* ***dirt on*** (= private details about) *celebrities.*

digest [EAT] /daɪˈdʒest/ *verb* [I or T] to change food in your stomach into substances that your body can use: *I find that I don't digest meat easily.* ○ *Sit still and allow your meal to digest.*
digestion /daɪˈdʒes.tʃən/ *noun* [C or U] when your body digests food, or your ability to digest food: *a poor/good/strong digestion* ○ *Discover how eating raw food helps balance your body and* ***aids*** *digestion.* **digestive** /daɪˈdʒes.tɪv/ *adj*: *the digestive process*

digest [UNDERSTAND] /daɪˈdʒest/ *verb* [T] to read or hear new information and take the necessary time to understand it: *This chapter is so difficult to digest, I shall have to read it again later.*
digest /ˈdaɪ.dʒest/ *noun* [C] a short written report providing the most important parts of a larger piece of writing, or one containing recent news: *A digest* ***of*** *the research findings is now available.* ○ *The company publishes a monthly digest of its activities.*

diˌgestive (ˈbiscuit) *noun* [C] *UK* a slightly sweet biscuit made from WHOLEMEAL flour

diˈgestive ˌsystem *noun* [C usually sing] the organs in your body that digest food

Digibox /ˈdɪdʒ.ɪ.bɒks/ [US] /-bɑːks/ *noun* [C] *TRADEMARK* an electronic device that makes it possible to watch DIGITAL broadcasts on ordinary televisions

digit [NUMBER] /ˈdɪdʒ.ɪt/ *noun* [C] any one of the ten numbers 0 to 9: *The number 345 contains three digits.*
digital /ˈdɪdʒ.ɪ.təl/ [US] /-t̬əl/ *adj* **1** describes information, music, an image, etc. that is recorded or broadcast using computer technology: *digital data* ○ *a digital recording* ○ *a digital camera* ○ *digital TV* ○ *digital compact/audio cassettes* **2** showing information in the form of an electronic display: *a digital clock/display* ○ *a digital watch* **digitally** /ˈdɪdʒ.ɪ.təl.i/ *adv*: *Sound and pictures can be stored digitally, as on a CD.*
digitize, *UK USUALLY* **-ise** /ˈdɪdʒ.ɪ.taɪz/ *verb* [T] to put information into the form of a series of the numbers 0 and 1, usually so that it can be processed by a computer

digit [FINGER] /ˈdɪdʒ.ɪt/ *noun* [C] *SPECIALIZED* a finger, thumb or toe

ˌdigital ˈaudio ˌtape *noun* [C or U] (*ABBREVIATION* **DAT**) a magnetic tape used to record high-quality sound by storing information as a series of the numbers 0 and 1 ➲See also **magnetic tape**.

ˌdigital ˈcamera *noun* [C] a type of camera that records images which can be viewed on a computer

dignify /ˈdɪg.nɪ.faɪ/ *verb* [T] **1** to cause something to be valued and respected **2** to cause something to be valued and respected when that is not deserved: *I'm not even going to dignify that stupid question **with** an answer.*

dignified /ˈdɪg.nɪ.faɪd/ *adj* controlled, graceful, serious and calm, and therefore deserving respect: *a tall dignified woman* ○ *He has maintained a dignified **silence** about the rumours.* ○ *The defeated candidate gave a dignified speech in which he congratulated his rival.*

dignitary /ˈdɪg.nɪ.tᵊr.i/ [US] /-nə.ter-/ *noun* [C] a person who has an important position in a society: *Several foreign dignitaries attended the ceremony.*

dignity /ˈdɪg.nɪ.ti/ [US] /-ə.t̬i/ *noun* [U] **1** calm, serious and controlled behaviour that makes people respect you: *He is a man of dignity and calm determination.* ○ *She has **a** quiet dignity about her.* ○ *He longs for a society in which the dignity **of** all people is recognized.* ○ *I think everyone should be able to die with dignity.* **2** the opinion that you have of the standard of your own importance and value: *How could you wear something so indecent? Have you no dignity?* ○ *In hospital, she felt stripped of all her dignity.*

• **beneath** ***your*** **dignity** If something is beneath your dignity, you feel that you are too important to do it: *Cleaning of any description he felt was beneath his dignity.*

digress /daɪˈgres/ *verb* [I] to move away from the main subject you are writing or talking about and to write or talk about something else: *But I digress. To get back to what I was saying, this poem reflects the poet's love of nature and his religious beliefs.* ○ *The lecturer temporarily digressed **from** her subject to deal with a related theory.* **digression** /daɪˈgreʃ.ᵊn/ *noun* [C or U] *Talking about money now would be a digression **from** the main purpose of this meeting.*

digs /dɪgz/ *plural noun* MAINLY UK INFORMAL FOR **lodgings**: *Many students in London have to live **in** digs.*

dike /daɪk/ *noun* [C] ANOTHER SPELLING OF **dyke**

diktat /ˈdɪk.tæt/ *noun* [C or U] DISAPPROVING an order which must be obeyed, or when you give such an order: *The coach issued a diktat that all team members must attend early-morning practice.* ○ *The occupying force ruled by diktat.*

dilapidated /dɪˈlæp.ɪ.deɪ.tɪd/ [US] /-t̬ɪd/ *adj* describes something old and in poor condition: *The hotel we stayed in was really dilapidated.* ○ *a dilapidated old car/shed* **dilapidation** /dɪˌlæp.ɪˈdeɪ.ʃᵊn/ *noun* [U] *The farmhouse fell into **a state of** dilapidation.*

dilate /daɪˈleɪt/ [US] /ˈ--/ *verb* [I or T] MAINLY SPECIALIZED to (cause a part of the body to) become wider or further open: *The pupils of the eyes dilate as darkness increases.* ○ *This drug will dilate the arteries.* **dilation** /daɪˈleɪ.ʃᵊn/ *noun* [U]

dilatory /ˈdɪl.ə.tri/ [US] /-tɔːr.i/ *adj* FORMAL slow and likely to cause delay: *dilatory behaviour/tactics* ○ *British institutions have been dilatory **in** cutting credit card charges.*

dildo /ˈdɪl.dəʊ/ [US] /-doʊ/ *noun* [C] *plural* **dildos** an object shaped like and used in place of a penis, for giving sexual pleasure

dilemma /daɪˈlem.ə/ *noun* [C] a situation in which a difficult choice has to be made between two different things you could do: *The President is clearly **in** a dilemma **about/over** how to tackle the crisis.* ○ *She **faces** the dilemma **of** disobey**ing** her father or los**ing** the man she loves.* ○ *a **moral/ethical** dilemma*

dilettante /ˌdɪl.əˈtæn.ti/ *noun* [C] *plural* **dilettantes** or **dilettanti** USUALLY DISAPPROVING a person who is or seems to be interested in a subject, but whose understanding of it is not very deep: *He's a bit of a dilettante as far as wine is concerned.*

diligent /ˈdɪl.ɪ.dʒᵊnt/ *adj* **1** APPROVING careful and using a lot of effort: *a diligent student* ○ *Leo is very diligent **in/about** his work.* ○ *Their lawyer was extremely diligent **in** prepar**ing** their case.* **2** done in a careful and detailed way: *The discovery was made after years of diligent research.* **diligence** /ˈdɪl.ɪ.dʒᵊnts/ *noun* [U] *She hoped that her diligence would be noticed at work.* **diligently** /ˈdɪl.ɪ.dʒᵊnt.li/ *adv*

dill /dɪl/ *noun* [U] a herb whose seeds and thin feathery leaves are used in cooking: *dill pickles* ○ *1 tsp fresh dill, chopped*

dillydally /ˈdɪl.iˌdæl.i/ /ˌ--ˈ--/ *verb* [I] OLD-FASHIONED INFORMAL to waste time, especially by being slow, or by not being able to make a decision: *Don't dillydally – just get your things and let's go!*

dilute /daɪˈluːt/ *verb* [T] **1** to make a liquid weaker by mixing in something else: *Dilute the juice (**with** water) before you drink it.* **2** to reduce the strength of a feeling, action, etc: *These measures are designed to dilute public fears about the product's safety.*

dilute /daɪˈluːt/ *adj* (US USUALLY **diluted**) made weaker by diluting: *dilute hydrochloric acid* **dilution** /daɪˈluː.ʃᵊn/ *noun* [C or U] *The drug's effectiveness is increased by dilution.* ○ *a dilution of standards*

dim /dɪm/ *adj* **dimmer, dimmest 1** not giving or having much light: *The lamp gave out a dim light.* ○ *He sat in a dim corner of the waiting-room.* ○ *We could see a dim* (= not easily seen) *shape in the fog.* **2** LITERARY If your eyes are dim, you cannot see very well. **3 a dim memory/recollection, etc.** something that you remember slightly, but not very well: *I had a dim recollection **of** having met her before.* **4** INFORMAL not very clever: *He's a nice chap, but a little dim.* ○ *Don't be dim.* **5** not likely to succeed: *The company's prospects for the future are rather dim.*

• **take a dim view of** ***sth*** to disapprove of something: *I take a dim view of this kind of behaviour.*

dim /dɪm/ *verb* [I or T] **-mm- 1** to (make something) become less bright: *Someone dimmed the lights.* ○ *The lights dimmed and the curtains opened.* **2** LITERARY to (make a positive feeling or quality) less strong: *Our hopes/expectations dimmed as the hours passed.* **dimly** /ˈdɪm.li/ *adv*: *The room was dimly lit.* ○ *I dimly remembered seeing the film before.* **dimness** /ˈdɪm.nəs/ *noun* [U]

dime /daɪm/ *noun* [C] an American or Canadian coin which has the value of ten cents

• **be a dime a dozen** US (UK ALSO **be two/ten a penny**) to be common and/or of very little value: *Books like this are a dime a dozen.*

dimension /ˌdaɪˈmen.tʃᵊn/ *noun* **1** [C often pl] a measurement of something in a particular direction, especially its height, length or width: *Please specify the dimensions* (= the height, length and width) ***of** the room.* ○ *a building of vast dimensions* (= size) **2** [C] a part or feature or way of considering something: *His personality has several dimensions.* ○ *These weapons add a **new** dimension to modern warfare.* ○ *There is a spiritual dimension to her poetry.*

-dimensional /-daɪ.men*t*.ʃᵊn.ᵊl/ *suffix*: *a three-dimensional* (= having three measurements in different directions) *figure*

diminish /dɪˈmɪn.ɪʃ/ *verb* [I or T] to reduce or be reduced in size or importance: *I don't want to diminish her achievements, but she did have a lot of help.* ○ *These memories will not be diminished by time.* ○ *What he did has seriously diminished him in many people's eyes.* ○ *We've seen our house diminish **greatly/sharply/substantially** in value over the last six months.* **diminution** /ˌdɪm.ɪˈnjuː.ʃᵊn/ [US] /-əˈnuː-/ *noun* [C or U] FORMAL *Regular exercise can result in a general diminution **in** stress levels.* ○ *The company suffered a diminution in profits.*

diˌminished responsiˈbility *noun* [U] (US **diminished capacity**) LEGAL the condition in which someone's mental state, etc. causes them not to be in full control of their actions: *The accused pleaded not guilty **on grounds of** diminished responsibility.*

diminutive /dɪˈmɪn.jʊ.tɪv/ [US] /-t̬ɪv/ *adj* very small: *He's a diminutive figure, less than five feet tall.*

ˌdimmer (ˈswitch) *noun* [C] a device for varying the brightness of an electric light, which is often combined with a switch to turn the light on and off

D

dimple /'dɪm.pl̩/ *noun* [C] a small hollow place, especially one which appears on a person's face when they smile: *Freddie was an angelic-looking child with blond curly hair, blue eyes and dimples.* ○ *The pane of glass had a small dimple in it.* dimpled /'dɪm.pl̩d/ *adj*: *dimpled cheeks*

dimwit /'dɪm.wɪt/ *noun* [C] INFORMAL a stupid person: *I've forgotten what I came in here for – I'm such a dimwit!* ○ *Look where you're going, dimwit!*

dim-witted /ˌdɪm'wɪt.ɪd/ US /-'wɪt̬-/ *adj* stupid: *Marilyn was portrayed as some sort of dim-witted, floozy blonde.*

din /dɪn/ *noun* [S] a loud unpleasant confused noise which lasts for a long time: *the din of the traffic* ○ *I had to shout to make myself heard above the din.* ○ *The children were making a terrible din.*

din /dɪn/ *verb* -nn-
▲ **din** *sth* **into** *sb phrasal verb* to say something forcefully and repeatedly to someone so that they remember it: *It was dinned into me that I mustn't be late.*

dinar /'diː.nɑːr/ /-'-/ US /diː'nɑr / ˌdiː.nɑːr/ /diːˌnɑːr/ *noun* [C] the standard unit of money used in Algeria, Bahrain, Iraq, Jordan, Kuwait, Libya, Tunisia and Bosnia-Herzogovina

dine /daɪn/ *verb* [I] FORMAL to eat the main meal of the day, usually in the evening: *I hate dining alone.* ○ *We dined by candlelight.* ○ *He once dined with the President of France.*

PHRASAL VERBS WITH **dine** ▼

▲ **dine on/upon** *sth phrasal verb* FORMAL to eat something as a meal: *We dined on salmon and strawberries.*

▲ **dine out** *phrasal verb* FORMAL to go to a restaurant to eat your evening meal: *We rarely dine out these days.*

▲ **dine out on** *sth phrasal verb* MAINLY UK to entertain people, especially at a meal, by telling them about an experience you have had: *For months I've been dining out on the story of what happened when my house got flooded.*

diner /'daɪ.nər/ US /-nə/ *noun* [C] **1** someone who is eating a meal, especially in a restaurant **2** MAINLY US a small restaurant at the side of the road

dingbat /'dɪŋ.bæt/ *noun* [C] SLANG a stupid or easily confused person: *Edith may seem like a dingbat, but she's quite clever really.*

ding-dong SOUND /'dɪŋ.dɒŋ/ US /-dɑːŋ/ *noun* [U] a written representation of the sound a bell makes

ding-dong ARGUMENT /'dɪŋ.dɒŋ/ US /-dɑːŋ/ *noun* [S] MAINLY UK INFORMAL a noisy argument or fight: *They had a real ding-dong in the middle of the restaurant.*

dinghy /'dɪŋ.gi/ *noun* [C] **1** a small open boat: *an inflatable/motorized dinghy* ○ *He was transferred to the ship by dinghy.* **2** a small sailing boat: *a dinghy race*

dingo /'dɪŋ.gəʊ/ US /-goʊ/ *noun* [C] *plural* dingoes a type of wild dog found in Australia

dingy /'dɪn.dʒi/ *adj* dark and often also dirty: *a dingy room/corridor* ○ *Her hair was a dingy brown colour.* dingily /'dɪn.dʒɪ.li/ *adv*

dining car *noun* [C usually sing] (UK ALSO restaurant car) a part of a train in which passengers are served meals

dining hall *noun* [C usually sing] a large room attached to a school or other building, where many people can eat at the same time

dining room *noun* [C] a room in which meals are eaten

dining table *noun* [C] a table at which meals are eaten ⊃Compare **the dinner table**.

dinky /'dɪn.ki/ *adj* INFORMAL small: UK APPROVING She's got *dinky little* (= small and charming) *feet.* ○ US DISAPPROVING *They live in a dinky* (= small and without charm) *one-room apartment.*

dinner /'dɪn.ər/ US /-ə/ *noun* **1** [C or U] the main meal of the day, usually the meal you eat in the evening but sometimes, in Britain, the meal eaten in the middle of the day: *We were just having (our) dinner.* ○ *We had some friends round for dinner on Saturday.* ○ *a romantic candlelit dinner* ⊃Compare **lunch**. **2** [C usually sing] a formal social occasion in the evening at which a meal is

served: *They held a dinner to celebrate his retirement.* ○ *a charity/society dinner*

dinner dance *noun* [C] a social occasion in the evening, at which there is a meal and dancing

dinner jacket UK *noun* [C] (ABBREVIATION DJ, US tuxedo) a man's black or white jacket worn at formal social events, usually in the evening, with matching trousers and a BOW TIE

dinner party *noun* [C] a formal evening meal to which a small number of people are invited: *I'm having/giving a dinner party next week.*

dinner service *noun* [C] (ALSO dinner set) a complete set of plates and dishes with the same design, used when serving a meal to several people

the dinner table *noun* [S] the table at which the main meal of the day is served, or the occasion when this meal is served: *They sat round the dinner table, arguing about politics.* ○ *No reading at the dinner table!* ○ *We usually talk about the day's events over the dinner table.* ⊃Compare **dining table**.

dinnertime /'dɪn.ə.taɪm/ US /-ə-/ *noun* [U] the time at which the main meal of the day is eaten: *I didn't get home till after dinnertime.*

dinosaur /'daɪ.nə.sɔːr/ US /-sɔːr/ *noun* [C] **1** a type of reptile which stopped existing about 60 000 000 years ago. There were many different types of dinosaur, some of which were extremely large. **2** an old-fashioned person or thing that people no longer consider to be useful: *This typewriter's a bit of a dinosaur, isn't it?*

dint BECAUSE OF /dɪnt/ *noun* FORMAL **by dint of** as a result of: *She got what she wanted by dint of pleading and threatening.*

dint MARK *noun* [C] a small hollow mark in the surface of something, caused by pressure or being hit

diocese /'daɪ.ə.sɪs/ *noun* [C] *plural* dioceses in the Roman Catholic Church and the Anglican Church, an area controlled by a bishop diocesan /daɪ'ɒs.ɪ.zən/ US /-'ɑː.sə-/ *adj*

diode /'daɪ.əʊd/ US /-oʊd/ *noun* [C] SPECIALIZED a device which controls an electric current so that it can only flow in one direction

dioxide /daɪ'ɒk.saɪd/ US /-'ɑːk-/ *noun* [U] SPECIALIZED a chemical substance consisting of two atoms of oxygen combined with one atom of another element: *carbon/sulphur dioxide*

dioxin /daɪ'ɒk.sɪn/ US /-'ɑːk-/ *noun* [C or U] a poisonous chemical of a type produced when substances used for killing plants are made: *Highly toxic dioxins were released into the air.*

dip PUT INTO /dɪp/ *verb* [T] -pp- **1** to put something briefly into a liquid: *Dip the fish in the batter, then drop it into the hot oil.* ○ *She dipped her toe into the pool to see how cold it was.* **2** to put sheep briefly into a container of liquid containing chemicals which kill harmful insects on the sheep's bodies
● **dip a/your toe in (the water)** to start very carefully to do or become involved in something that you are not experienced at

dip /dɪp/ *noun* **1** [C or U] a cold thick creamy sauce which you eat by dipping pieces of raw vegetable or biscuits, etc. into it: *cheese/salsa dip* **2** [C usually sing] a quick swim: *a dip in the sea/pool* **3** [C or U] a special liquid used for cleaning, etc: *a silver dip* ○ *sheep dip* **4** [C usually sing] a brief consideration of a subject: *We begin our dip into local history by examining the town's origins.*

dip DROP /dɪp/ *verb* -pp- **1** [I] to go down to a lower level: *As you turn the corner, the road dips suddenly.* ○ *House prices dipped in the first three months of the year.* ○ *The sun dipped below the horizon.* **2** [T] UK to make the beam from the lights at the front of a vehicle point downwards: *You'll dazzle oncoming drivers if you don't dip your headlights.* dip /dɪp/ *noun* [C usually sing] *a dip in the road* ○ *a dip in temperature*

PHRASAL VERBS WITH **dip** ▼

▲ **dip (sth) in/dip (sth) into** *sth phrasal verb* to put your hand into a container and take something out: *We all dipped into the box of chocolates.* ○ *He dipped his hand in his pocket and brought out a few coins.*

▲ **dip into** *sth* BOOK *phrasal verb* UK to read small parts of a book or magazine: *It's the sort of book you can just dip into now and again.*

▲ **dip into** *sth* MONEY *phrasal verb* to spend part of a supply of money that you have been keeping or saving: *I've had to dip into my savings to pay for the repairs.*

diphtheria /dɪfˈθɪə.ri.ə/ /dɪp-/ ⓤ /-ˈθɪr.i-/ *noun* [U] a serious infectious disease that causes fever and difficulty in breathing and swallowing

diphthong /ˈdɪf.θɒŋ/ /ˈdɪp-/ ⓤ /-θɑːŋ/ *noun* [C] SPECIALIZED a vowel sound in which the tongue changes position to produce the sound of two vowels

diploma /dɪˈpləʊ.mə/ ⓤ /-ˈploʊ-/ *noun* [C] a document given by a college or university to show that you have passed a particular examination or completed a course: *a diploma in business studies* ○ *US a high school diploma*

diplomacy /dɪˈpləʊ.mə.si/ ⓤ /-ˈploʊ-/ *noun* [U] **1** the management of relationships between countries: *Diplomacy has so far failed to bring an end to the fighting.* **2** APPROVING skill in dealing with people without offending or upsetting them: *It took all her tact and diplomacy to persuade him not to resign.*

diplomat /ˈdɪp.lə.mæt/ *noun* [C] **1** (OLD-FASHIONED **diplomatist**) an official whose job is to represent one country in another, and who usually works in an EMBASSY: *a Spanish/British diplomat* **2** APPROVING a person who is skilled at dealing with difficult situations in a way which does not offend people

diplomatic /ˌdɪp.ləˈmæt.ɪk/ ⓤ /-ˈmæt̬-/ *adj* **1** involving the management of the relationships between countries: *diplomatic negotiations* **2** APPROVING acting in a way that does not cause offence: *Ask him nicely – be diplomatic.* **diplomatically** /ˌdɪp.ləˈmæt.ɪ.kli/ ⓤ /-ˈmæt̬-/ *adv*

diplo,matic 'bag *noun* [C usually sing] a container in which letters are sent between countries' representatives in other countries, and which is not examined by CUSTOMS officials

diplo'matic ,corps *group noun* [C usually sing] all the people who work in one country as representatives of another country

,diplomatic im'munity *noun* [U] the special rights that DIPLOMATS (= government officials) have while working in a country that is not their own, such as freedom from legal action: *He did not have to pay his speeding fine because he pleaded diplomatic immunity.*

,diplomatic re'lations *plural noun* the arrangement between two countries by which each has representatives in the other country: *Britain threatened to break off diplomatic relations.*

the ,diplomatic 'service *group noun* [S] the government department that employs people to represent their country in other parts of the world

dippy /ˈdɪp.i/ *adj* INFORMAL silly: *You dippy thing!* ○ *That's the dippiest thing I ever heard!*

dipsomania /ˌdɪp.səˈmeɪ.ni.ə/ *noun* [U] an uncontrollable need to drink alcohol

dipsomaniac /ˌdɪp.səˈmeɪ.ni.æk/ *noun* [C] (INFORMAL **dipso**) someone suffering from dipsomania

dipstick MEASURE /ˈdɪp.stɪk/ *noun* [C] a long thin stick for measuring the amount of liquid in a container, especially the oil in a car engine

dipstick PERSON /ˈdɪp.stɪk/ *noun* [C] SLANG a silly person

dip-switch UK /ˈdɪp.swɪtʃ/ *noun* [C] (US **dimmer switch**) a switch for temporarily reducing the brightness of the lights of a vehicle

dire /daɪəʳ/ ⓤ /daɪr/ *adj* **1** very serious or extreme: *These people are in dire need of help.* ○ *He gave a dire warning that an earthquake was imminent.* ○ *This decision will have dire consequences for local people.* **2** INFORMAL very bad: *I thought that film was dire!*

direct STRAIGHT /daɪˈrekt/ *adj* **1** going in a straight line towards somewhere or someone without stopping or changing direction: *a direct route/line* ○ *Is there a direct train to Edinburgh?* **2** without anyone or anything else being involved or between: *She decided to take direct control of the project.* ○ *He denied that he had any direct involvement in the deal.* ○ *Have you any direct experience of this kind of work?* ○ *He left as a direct*

result/consequence of what she said. ○ *There is a direct link/connection between smoking and lung cancer.* **3** **direct light/heat** strong light or heat that has nothing protecting and separating you from it: *This plant should be kept out of direct sunlight.* **4** **direct relation/ relative/descendant** a relative who is related to you through one of your parents, not through an aunt or uncle, etc: *Diana is a direct descendant of Robert Peel.*

direct /daɪˈrekt/ *adv*: *Does this train go direct* (= so that I do not have to change trains) *to Edinburgh?* ○ *Can I dial this number direct* (= without anything or anyone else being involved) *or do I have to go through the switchboard?*

directly /daɪˈrekt.li/ *adv*: *Our hotel room was directly above* (= there was nothing between it and) *a building site.* ○ *The disease is directly* (= in a way not influenced by other causes) *linked to poor drainage systems.* ○ *The sun shone directly* (= in a way not blocked by anything else) *in my eyes.*

direct COMPLETE /daɪˈrekt/ *adj* complete: *a direct contrast* ○ *She's very thoughtful – the direct opposite of her sister.*

direct HONEST /daɪˈrekt/ *adj* describes someone who says what they think in a very honest way without worrying about other people's opinions: *I like her open and direct manner.*

directly /daɪˈrekt.li/ *adv* honestly, even when it might make people feel uncomfortable: *Let me answer that question directly.* ○ *"Did you tell him to go?" "Not directly, no."* **directness** /daɪˈrekt.nəs/ *noun* [U]

direct AIM /daɪˈrekt/ *verb* [T usually + adv or prep] to aim in a particular direction: *Was that remark directed at/ towards me?* ○ *Criticism was directed against/at the manufacturers of the product.*

direct SAY WHERE /daɪˈrekt/ *verb* [T] to tell someone how to get somewhere: *Could you direct me to the airport?* ○ *I couldn't find the station, so I asked someone if they could direct me.*

directions /daɪˈrek.ʃ°nz/ *plural noun* instructions that you give to someone about how to find a particular place: *Can you give me directions to your house?* ○ *"Did you have any difficulty finding the theatre?" "No, your directions were excellent."*

direct CONTROL /daɪˈrekt/ *verb* **1** [T] to control or be in charge of an activity, organization, etc: *There was a police officer directing the traffic.* ○ *She directs a large charity.* **2** [I or T] to be in charge of a film or play and tell the actors how to play their parts: *He wanted to give up acting and start directing (his own films).* ○ *'Jaws' was directed by Steven Spielberg.* ⊃Compare **produce** FILM/ BROADCASTING.

direction /daɪˈrek.ʃ°n/ *noun* [U] control or instruction: *The project was under the direction of a well-known academic.*

director /daɪˈrek.təʳ/ *noun* [C] **1** a manager of an organization, company, college, etc: *the board of directors* ○ *She has become the director of the new information centre.* **2** a person who is in charge of a film or play and tells the actors how to play their parts: *a famous film/movie director* ⊃Compare **producer** at **produce** FILM/BROADCASTING; **produce** RECORDING.

directorate /daɪˈrek.t°r.ət/ *noun* [C] a department or organization which is responsible for one particular thing: *the Norwegian fish and game directorate* ○ *the directorate of corporate development*

directorate /daɪˈrek.t°r.ət/ *group noun* [C] a group of directors **directorial** /ˌdɪr.ekˈtɔː.ri.əl/ ⓤ /-ˈtɔːr.i-/ *adj*: *Is she ready for directorial responsibility?*

directorship /daɪˈrek.tə.ʃɪp/ *noun* [C] the position of being a director: *He holds several company directorships.*

direct ORDER /daɪˈrekt/ *verb* [T + obj + to infinitive] FORMAL to order someone, especially officially: *The judge directed the defendant to remain silent.*

directions /daɪˈrek.ʃ°nz/ *plural noun* information or orders telling you what to do: *I couldn't understand the directions on the packet.* ○ *He will be giving/issuing directions to judges on sentencing in the next few days.*

directive /daɪˈrek.tɪv/ ⓤ /-t̬ɪv/ *noun* [C] FORMAL an official instruction: *The boss issued a directive about not using the fax machine.*

ˌdirect ˈaction *noun* [U] the use of strikes, violence or protests as a way of trying to get what you want, instead of talking

ˌdirect ˈdebit *noun* [C or U] *UK* an arrangement for making payments, usually to an organization, in which your bank moves money from your account into the organization's account at regular times: *I pay my electricity bill* ***by*** *direct debit.* ➲Compare **standing order**.

ˌdirect deˈposit *noun* [U] *US* an arrangement in which money is moved electronically into a bank account: *I get paid by direct deposit.*

diˌrect ˈhit *noun* [C] an explosion or injury caused when a bomb or bullet hits an object accurately: *The house suffered a direct hit.*

direction /daɪˈrek.ʃən/ *noun* [C] **1** the position towards which someone or something moves or faces: *"No, go that way," I said, pointing* ***in*** *the opposite direction.* ○ *He was going* ***in*** *the direction* ***of*** *the bedroom.* ○ *They drove away in opposite directions.* **2** ***sb's*** **direction** the area or position which someone is in: *She keeps looking* ***in*** *my direction.*

• **lack direction** to not know what you really want to do: *She seems to lack direction in her life.*

• **sense of direction** ability to find places or to know which direction to go: *a* ***good*** *sense of direction* ○ *Which way is it? – I* ***have*** *no/a lousy sense of direction!*

directional /daɪˈrek.ʃən.əl/ *adj* SPECIALIZED describes radio equipment that receives or gives stronger signals in particular directions

directionless /daɪˈrek.ʃən.ləs/ *adj* not knowing what you want to do

directly /daɪˈrekt.li/ *adv* **1** OLD-FASHIONED OR FORMAL very soon: *Dr Schwarz will be with you directly.* **2** OLD-FASHIONED immediately: *When you get home you're going directly to bed.*

directly /daɪˈrekt.li/ *conjunction* **1** FORMAL immediately after: *Directly he was paid, he went out shopping.* **2** SLIGHTLY FORMAL as soon as: *I'll be with you directly I've finished this letter.*

ˌdirect ˈmail *noun* [U] MAINLY US when companies or organizations write to people to try to persuade them to buy their product or give money, etc.

ˌdirect ˈobject *noun* [C] SPECIALIZED The direct object of a TRANSITIVE verb is the person or thing that is affected by the action of the verb. ➲Compare **indirect object**.

diˌrector ˈgeneral *noun* [C usually sing] the person who is in charge of a big organization

Diˌrector of ˌPublic Proseˈcutions *noun* [S] *UK* the official title of the lawyer who works for the government and who decides whether someone formally accused of committing a crime should be made to appear in a court of law

directory /dɪˈrek.tər.i/ /daɪ-/ [US] /-tɚ.i/ *noun* [C] a book which gives a list of names, addresses or other facts: *a business directory* ○ *a directory* ***of*** *hotels* ○ *Look up their number in the telephone directory.*

Diˌrectory Enˈquiries *UK group noun* [U] (*US* **Directory Assistance**) a service which you can telephone in order to find out someone's telephone number

ˌdirect ˈspeech *noun* [U] (*US ALSO* **direct discourse**) SPECIALIZED When you use direct speech, you repeat what someone has said using exactly the words they used: *'She said, "If it rains, I won't go out."' is an example of the use of direct speech.* ➲Compare **indirect speech**.

ˌdirect ˈtax *noun* [C usually sing] the money that a person must pay to the government themselves, such as income tax, rather than through someone else ➲Compare **indirect tax**. **ˌdirect taxˈation** *noun* [U]

dirge /dɜːdʒ/ [US] /dɝːdʒ/ *noun* [C] a slow sad song or piece of music, sometimes played because someone has died

dirham /ˈdɪ.ræm/ [US] /dɪrˈhæm/ *noun* [C] the standard unit of money used in the United Arab Emirates and Morocco

dirk /dɜːk/ [US] /dɝːk/ *noun* [C] a type of DAGGER (= small pointed knife) used as a weapon in Scotland in the past

dirndl (skirt) /ˌdɜːn.dlˈˌskɜːt/ [US] /ˌdɝːn.dlˈskɝːrt/ *noun* [C] a wide skirt tightly gathered at the waist

dirt /dɜːt/ [US] /dɝːt/ *noun* [U] **1** dust, earth or any substance that makes a surface not clean: *His coat was covered with dirt.* **2** MAINLY US loose earth on the ground: *After I'd finished gardening, there was dirt from the flower beds all over the path.* **3** INFORMAL excrement: *I got some* ***dog*** *dirt on my shoes.* **4** INFORMAL unpleasant or bad details about someone's private life, which are repeated or published to stop other people admiring them: *Journalists are always* ***digging for*** (= trying to discover) *dirt.*

dirty /ˈdɜː.ti/ [US] /ˈdɝː.t̬i/ *adj* **1** not clean: *Her face was dirty and tear-stained.* **2** INFORMAL unfair, dishonest or unkind: *She played a dirty* ***trick*** *on me by telling me Diane was having a party when she wasn't.* ○ *The airline admitted being involved in a dirty* ***tricks*** *campaign to win customers from their rival.* ○ *That's a dirty lie!* **3** INFORMAL describes something that is connected with sex, in a way that many people think is offensive: *a dirty* ***magazine/film/joke*** ○ *You've got a really dirty* ***mind!***

• **do the dirty on** ***sb*** *UK INFORMAL* to behave unfairly towards someone, usually without their knowledge: *He can't forgive her for doing the dirty on him and having an affair with his best friend.*

• **do** ***sb's*** **dirty work** to do something unpleasant or difficult for someone else because they do not want to do it themselves: *Tell her yourself – I'm not going to do your dirty work for you.*

• **give** ***sb*** **a dirty look** to look at someone in a disapproving way: *He gave me a really dirty look.*

dirty /ˈdɜː.ti/ [US] /ˈdɝː.t̬i/ *verb* [T] to make something dirty: *Don't sit on the floor – you might dirty your dress.*

• **dirty your hands** to become involved in something unfair or immoral: *He refused to dirty his hands by lying about what had happened.*

dirtiness /ˈdɜː.ti.nəs/ [US] /ˈdɝː.t̬i-/ *noun* [U] when something is dirty: *I don't mind untidiness – it's dirtiness I can't stand.*

dirty /ˈdɜː.ti/ [US] /ˈdɝː.t̬i/ *adv* **dirty great/big** very great/big: *The power station's nothing but a dirty great blot on the landscape.*

• **play dirty** INFORMAL to behave dishonestly, especially by cheating in a game: *Dez likes football but he plays dirty.*

ˌdirt ˈcheap *adj, adv* very cheap

ˌdirt ˈpoor *adj US* very poor

ˌdirt ˈroad *noun* [C] (*UK* **dirt track**) a road in the countryside made from earth: *We drove up a narrow dirt track to their house.*

ˈdirty ˌbomb *noun* [C] a bomb which has RADIOACTIVE material added to it so that it causes more damage and POLLUTION

ˌdirty ˌold ˈman *noun* [C] DISAPPROVING OR HUMOROUS an older man who has an unpleasantly strong interest in sex

ˌdirty weekˈend *noun* [C usually sing] MAINLY UK when two people go away together for a weekend to have sex, especially in a secret way because they are not married to each other

ˌdirty ˈword *noun* **1** [C] a word that is connected with sex and which many people consider offensive **2** [S] a word or an expression that refers to something that many people do not approve of: *For the environmentally aware, 'disposable' has become a dirty word.*

dis- /dɪs-/ *prefix* added to the front of some words to form their opposites: *to disagree* ○ *a dishonest person* ➲Compare **in-** LACKING; **non-**; **un-**.

dis /dɪs/ *verb* [T] *US SLANG* **diss**

disability /ˌdɪs.əˈbɪl.ɪ.ti/ [US] /-ə.t̬i/ *noun* [C or U] an illness, injury or condition that makes it difficult for someone to do the things that other people do: *a physical/learning disability* ○ *She is deaf, but refuses to let her disability prevent her from doing what she wants to do.* ○ *Trying to change attitudes to disability is an uphill struggle.* ➲Compare **inability**.

disabled /dɪˈseɪ.bl̩d/ *adj* **1** lacking one or more of the physical or mental abilities that most people have: *The accident left him severely disabled.* **2** [before n] specially relating to or intended for disabled people: *The library does not have disabled* ***access***.

the disabled *plural noun* people who are disabled: *It is often very difficult for the disabled to find jobs.*
disable /dɪˈseɪ.bl/ *verb* **1** [T often passive] to cause someone to have an illness, injury or condition that makes it difficult for them to do the things that other people do: *She was disabled in the accident.* **2** [T] to stop something such as (part of) a machine, system or weapon from working: *These guns will destroy or disable any incoming missile.* ○ *Disable the alarm system and then enter the building.* **disabling** /dɪˈseɪ.blɪŋ/ *adj*: *a disabling illness/disease*

disabuse /ˌdɪs.əˈbjuːz/ *verb* [T] FORMAL to cause someone no longer to have a wrong idea: *He thought that all women liked children, but she soon disabused him* ***of*** *that (idea/notion).*

disadvantage /ˌdɪs.ədˈvɑːn.tɪdʒ/ [US] /-ˈvæn.t̬ɪdʒ/ *noun* [C or U] a condition or situation which causes problems, especially one which causes something or someone to be less successful than other things or people: *One disadvantage of living in the town is the lack of safe places for the children to play.* ○ *We need to consider whether the disadvantages of the plan outweigh the advantages.*
• **at a disadvantage** in a situation in which you are less likely to succeed than others: *He's at a disadvantage being so shy.* ○ *This new law* ***places/puts*** *poorer families at a distinct disadvantage.*
disadvantage /ˌdɪs.ədˈvɑːn.tɪdʒ/ [US] /-ˈvæn.t̬ɪdʒ/ *verb* [T] to cause someone or something to be less successful than most other people or things: *Teachers claim such measures could unfairly disadvantage ethnic minorities.*
disadvantaged /ˌdɪs.ədˈvɑːn.tɪdʒd/ [US] /-ˈvæn.t̬ɪdʒd/ *adj* lacking the standard of living conditions, education, etc. that most people have: *A new educational programme has been set up for economically disadvantaged children.*
the disadˈvantaged *plural noun* people who do not have good living conditions, a good standard of education, etc., considered as a group: *These measures are intended to help the disadvantaged.* **disadvantageous** /ˌdɪsˌæd.vənˈteɪ.dʒəs/ [US] /-væn-/ *adj*

disaffected /ˌdɪs.əˈfek.tɪd/ *adj* **1** no longer supporting or being satisfied with an organization or idea: *The party needs to take steps to attract disaffected voters.* **2** describes young people who are no longer satisfied with society's values: *The teacher said that he found it difficult to cope with a class of disaffected* ***teenagers***. ○ *disaffected youth* **disaffection** /ˌdɪs.əˈfek.ʃən/ *noun* [U] *a growing disaffection with the country's political leaders*

disafforest /ˌdɪs.əˈfɒr.ɪst/ [US] /-ˈfɔːr-/ *verb* [T] to **deforest**

disagree /ˌdɪs.əˈgriː/ *verb* [I] **1** to not have the same opinion, idea, etc.; to not agree: *I'm afraid I have to disagree* ***with*** *you* ***(on*** *that issue).* ○ [+ that] *Few people would disagree* ***that*** *something should be done to reduce the level of crime in the area.* ○ *I* ***profoundly/strongly*** *disagree* ***with*** (= do not accept) *the decision that has been taken.* **2** If two or more statements, ideas, sets of numbers, etc. disagree, they are not the same.
disagreement /ˌdɪs.əˈgriː.mənt/ *noun* [C or U] *We had a disagreement* (= argument) ***about/over*** *the fee for the work.* ○ *Literary critics were* ***in*** *total disagreement* (= did not have the same opinions) ***(about*** *the value of the book).*
▲ **disagree with** ***sb*** *phrasal verb* If a type of food disagrees with you, it makes you feel slightly ill or uncomfortable: *Spicy food disagrees with me.*

disagreeable /ˌdɪs.əˈgriː.ə.bl/ *adj* FORMAL unpleasant: *a rather disagreeable young man* ○ *She said some very disagreeable things.* **disagreeably** /ˌdɪs.əˈgriː.ə.bli/ *adv*

disallow /ˌdɪs.əˈlaʊ/ *verb* [T] to state officially that something cannot be accepted because it has not been done in the correct way; to not allow something: *The England team had two goals disallowed.*

disappear /ˌdɪs.əˈpɪəʳ/ [US] /-ˈpɪr/ *verb* [I] If people or things disappear, they go somewhere where they cannot be seen or found: *The search was called off for the sailors who disappeared in the storm.* ○ *This is a way of life that is fast disappearing.* ○ *I can't find my keys anywhere – they've completely disappeared.* ○ *The sun disappeared* ***behind*** *a cloud.* ○ *We looked for her but she had disappeared* ***into*** *the crowd.* ○ *The film is about a girl who* ***mysteriously*** *disappeared while on a picnic at Hanging Rock.* ○ *I don't know how it's possible for a person to disappear* ***without trace***.
the disapˈpeared *plural noun* people who have been killed by a government or army, usually for political reasons, and whose bodies have not been found
disappearance /ˌdɪs.əˈpɪə.rənts/ [US] /-ˈpɪr.ənts/ *noun* [C or U] when someone or something disappears: *A man was being questioned in connection with her disappearance.*

disappoint /ˌdɪs.əˈpɔɪnt/ *verb* [I or T] to fail to satisfy someone or their hopes, desires, etc.; to cause someone to feel unhappy: *I'm sorry to disappoint you, but I'm afraid I can't come after all.* ○ *We don't want to disappoint the fans.*
disappointed /ˌdɪs.əˈpɔɪn.tɪd/ [US] /-t̬ɪd/ *adj* unhappy because someone or something was not as good as you hoped or expected, or because something did not happen: *We were* ***deeply*** *disappointed* ***at/about*** *the result.* ○ *His parents were* ***bitterly*** *disappointed* ***in/with*** *him.* ○ [+ (that)] *She was disappointed* ***(that)*** *they hadn't phoned.* ○ [+ to infinitive] *He was disappointed* ***to*** *find they'd already gone.* ○ *If you're expecting Dad to let you borrow his car, you're going to be* ***sorely*** *disappointed.* **disappointedly** /ˌdɪs.əˈpɔɪn.tɪd.li/ [US] /-t̬ɪd-/ *adv*
disappointing /ˌdɪs.əˈpɔɪn.tɪŋ/ [US] /-t̬ɪŋ/ *adj*: making you feel disappointed: *What a disappointing result!* ○ *The response to our advertisement has been somewhat disappointing.* **disappointingly** /ˌdɪs.əˈpɔɪn.tɪŋ.li/ [US] /-t̬ɪŋ-/ *adv*: *The team played very disappointingly.*
disappointment /ˌdɪs.əˈpɔɪnt.mənt/ *noun* **1** [U] the feeling of being disappointed: *Book early to avoid disappointment.* ○ ***To*** *my* ***(great)*** *disappointment* (= sadness), *he decided to leave.* **2** [C usually sing] something or someone that is not what you were hoping it would be: *The party turned out to be a huge disappointment.* ○ *I'm afraid I've been rather a disappointment* ***to*** *my parents.*

COMMON LEARNER ERROR

disappoint (spelling)

Many learners make mistakes when spelling this word. The correct spelling has 's' and 'pp'.

I was so disappointed.
The film was rather disappointing.

disapprobation /ˌdɪs.æp.rəˈbeɪ.ʃən/ [US] /ˌdɪsˌæp-/ *noun* [U] FORMAL strong feelings of not approving of something or someone: *She feared her father's disapprobation.*

disapprove /ˌdɪs.əˈpruːv/ *verb* [I] to feel that something or someone is bad, wrong etc.; to not approve: *The survey showed that 32% of respondents approve, 54% disapprove and the rest are undecided.* ○ *I* ***strongly*** *disapprove* ***of*** *under-age drinking.*
disapproval /ˌdɪs.əˈpruː.vəl/ *noun* [U] when you feel that something or someone is bad or wrong: *Although they said nothing, she could sense their disapproval* ***of*** *her suggestion.* ○ *There was a note of disapproval in the teacher's voice.*
disapproving /ˌdɪs.əˈpruː.vɪŋ/ *adj* showing that you feel something or someone is bad or wrong: *a disapproving look* **disapprovingly** /ˌdɪs.əˈpruː.vɪŋ.li/ *adv*: *They looked at her disapprovingly.*

disarm [REMOVE WEAPONS] /dɪˈsɑːm/ [US] /-ˈsɑːrm/ *verb* [I or T] to take weapons away from someone, or to give up weapons or armies: *With one movement, she disarmed the man and pinned him against the wall.* ○ *Many politicians argued that this was no time to disarm* (= give up the country's weapons and army). ○ *Experts successfully managed to disarm the* ***bomb*** (= stop it from exploding).
disarmament /dɪˈsɑː.mə.mənt/ [US] /-ˈsɑːr-/ *noun* [U] *She said she supported* ***nuclear*** *disarmament* (= the act of reducing or giving up these weapons.)

disarm [CHARM] /dɪˈsɑːm/ [US] /-ˈsɑːrm/ *verb* [T] to make someone like you, especially when they had not expected to: *His frankness completely disarmed her.* **disarming** /dɪˈsɑː.mɪŋ/ [US] /-ˈsɑːr-/ *adj* APPROVING *He displayed a disarming honesty by telling them about his father's bankruptcy.*

disarrange /ˌdɪs.əˈreɪndʒ/ *verb* [T] FORMAL to make something untidy

disarray /ˌdɪs.əˈreɪ/ *noun* [U] *FORMAL* the state of being confused and lacking in organization or of being untidy: *Ever since the oil crisis, the industry has been **in (a state of)** disarray.* ○ *The news had **thrown** his plans **into** disarray.* ○ *Her clothes and hair were **in** disarray* (= were untidy).

disassociate /ˌdɪs.əˈsəʊ.si.eɪt/ [US] /-ˈsoʊ-/ *verb* [T] to **dissociate**

D

disaster /dɪˈzɑː.stəʳ/ [US] /-ˈzæs.tɚ/ *noun* [C or U] **1** (an event which results in) great harm, damage or death, or serious difficulty: *An inquiry was ordered into the recent rail disaster* (= a serious train accident). ○ *It would be a disaster **for** me if I lost my job.* ○ *This is one of the worst **natural** disasters ever to **befall** the area.* ○ *Heavy and prolonged rain can **spell** disaster **for** many plants.* ○ *Everything was going smoothly until suddenly disaster **struck**.* ○ *Inviting James and Ivan to dinner on the same evening was a **recipe for** disaster* (= caused a very difficult situation) – *they always argue with each other.* **2** *INFORMAL* **be a disaster** to be very unsuccessful or extremely bad: *The evening was a complete disaster.* ○ *As an engineer, he was a disaster.*

disastrous /dɪˈzɑː.strəs/ [US] /-ˈzæs.trəs/ *adj*: extremely bad or unsuccessful: *Such a war would be disastrous **for** the country.* ○ *This decision will have a disastrous impact on foreign policy.* ○ *His first attempt was disastrous.* **disastrously** /dɪˈzɑː.strə.sli/ [US] /-ˈzæs.trə-/ *adv*: *Things began to go disastrously wrong.*

diˈsaster ˌarea *noun* **1** [C usually sing] a place where a very serious accident, such as an earthquake, has happened **2** [S] *HUMOROUS* an extremely untidy, dirty or badly organized place: *After the party, the house was a complete disaster area.*

disavow /ˌdɪs.əˈvaʊ/ *verb* [T] *FORMAL* to say that you know nothing about something, or that you have no responsibility for or connection with something: *They were quick to disavow the rumour.* ○ *She tried to disavow her past.* **disavowal** /ˌdɪs.əˈvaʊ.əl/ *noun* [C]

disband /dɪsˈbænd/ *verb* [I] to stop being a group: *She formed a political group which disbanded a year later.*

disbar /dɪsˈbɑːʳ/ [US] /-ˈbɑːr/ *verb* [T] **-rr-** *LEGAL* to make someone unable to continue working as a lawyer, especially because they have done something wrong

disbelief /ˌdɪs.bɪˈliːf/ *noun* [U] the refusal to believe that something is true: *His response was one of complete disbelief.* ○ *She shook her head **in** disbelief.*

disbelieve /ˌdɪs.bɪˈliːv/ *verb* [I or T] *FORMAL* *Do you disbelieve* (= not believe) *me?* ○ *They said that they disbelieved the evidence.*

disburse /dɪsˈbɜːs/ [US] /-ˈbɝːs/ *verb* [T] *FORMAL* to pay out money, usually from an amount that has been collected for a particular purpose: *The local authorities annually disburse between £50m and £100m on arts projects.*

disc, *US ALSO* **disk** /dɪsk/ *noun* [C] **1** a circular flat object: *The dog's name was engraved on a little metal disc attached to its collar.* ⊃See also **CD**; **disk**. **2** a small piece of CARTILAGE (= a strong elastic body tissue) between the bones in your back **3** a musical record or a COMPACT DISC

discard /dɪˈskɑːd/ [US] /-ˈskɑːrd/ *verb* **1** [T] to throw something away or get rid of it because you no longer want or need it: *Discarded food containers and bottles littered the streets.* **2** [I or T] to get rid of a card you are holding during a card game

discard /dɪˈskɑːd/ [US] /-ˈskɑːrd/ *noun* [C] in a card game, a card that you have got rid of

ˈdisc ˌbrake *noun* [C] a type of brake where two pieces of material are pressed against a metal disc which is fixed to a wheel

discern /dɪˈsɜːn/ [US] /-ˈsɝːn/ *verb* [T] *FORMAL* to see, recognize or understand something that is not clear: *I could just discern a figure in the darkness.* ○ *It is difficult to discern any pattern in these figures.*

discernible, *US ALSO* **discernable** /dɪˈsɜː.nɪ.bl̩/ [US] /-ˈsɝː-/ *adj* *FORMAL* *The influence of Rodin is discernible* (= can be seen) *in the younger artist.* ○ *There is no discernible reason* (= one that can be understood) *why this should be the case.* **discernibly** /dɪˈsɜː.nɪ.bli/ [US] /-ˈsɝː-/ *adv*

discerning /dɪˈsɜː.nɪŋ/ [US] /-ˈsɝː-/ *adj* *FORMAL APPROVING* showing good judgement, especially about style and quality: *a discerning customer*

discernment /dɪˈsɜːn.mənt/ [US] /-ˈsɝːn-/ *noun* [U] *FORMAL APPROVING* the ability to judge people and things well: *It's clear that you are a person of discernment.*

discharge [ALLOW TO LEAVE] /dɪsˈtʃɑːdʒ/ [US] /-ˈtʃɑːrdʒ/ *verb* [T] to allow someone officially to leave somewhere, especially a hospital or a court of law: *Patients were discharged **from** hospital because the beds were needed by other people.* ○ *A peace protester was **conditionally** discharged for twelve months* (= allowed to go free only if they do not commit a crime again for this period of time). ○ *More than half of all prisoners discharged* (= allowed to leave prison) *are reconvicted within two years.*

discharge /ˈdɪs.tʃɑːdʒ/ [US] /-tʃɑːrdʒ/ *noun* [C or U] *The judge **gave** him a one-year **conditional** discharge.* ○ *The soldier **received** a **dishonourable** discharge for a disciplinary offence.*

discharge [SEND OUT] /dɪsˈtʃɑːdʒ/ [US] /-ˈtʃɑːrdʒ/ *verb* [I or T] to send out a substance, especially waste liquid or gas: *Large amounts of dangerous waste are discharged daily by the factory.* ○ *The oil which discharged **into** the sea seriously harmed a lot of birds and animals.*

discharge /ˈdɪs.tʃɑːdʒ/ [US] /-tʃɑːrdʒ/ *noun* [C or U] **1** when waste liquid or gas is sent out: *Thousands of fish were killed as a result of a discharge **of** poisonous chemicals from a nearby factory.* **2** liquid matter, which is often infected, that comes from a part of the body: *vaginal discharge*

discharge [PERFORM] /dɪsˈtʃɑːdʒ/ [US] /-ˈtʃɑːrdʒ/ *verb* [T] *FORMAL* **1** to perform a duty, especially an official one: *If the authority is to discharge its legal **duty** to house the homeless, it needs government support.* **2 discharge a debt** to pay a debt completely

discharge [FIRE] /dɪsˈtʃɑːdʒ/ [US] /-ˈtʃɑːrdʒ/ *verb* [T] *FORMAL* to fire a gun, or to fire a shot from a gun: *The police stated that some fifty rounds had been discharged.* **discharge** /ˈdɪs.tʃɑːdʒ/ [US] /-tʃɑːrdʒ/ *noun* [C]

disciple /dɪˈsaɪ.pl̩/ *noun* [C] a person who believes in the ideas and principles of someone famous and tries to live the way they do or did: *an ardent disciple **of** the prime minister*

the Diˈsciples *plural noun* the twelve men who followed Jesus Christ during his life

discipline [TRAINING] /ˈdɪs.ə.plɪn/ *noun* [U] **1** training which produces obedience or self-control, often in the form of rules, and punishments if these are broken, or the obedience or self-control produced by this training: *parental/military/school discipline* ○ *There should be better discipline in schools.* ○ *I don't have enough **(self)** discipline to save money.* **2 (good) discipline** the ability to control yourself or other people, even in difficult situations: *Maintaining classroom discipline* (= control of the students) *is the first task of every teacher.*

discipline /ˈdɪs.ə.plɪn/ *verb* **1** [T] to punish someone: *A senior civil servant has been disciplined **for** revealing secret government plans to the media.* **2** [T or R] to teach someone to behave in a controlled way: [+ *to* infinitive] *I'm trying to discipline myself **to** eat less chocolate.*

disciplined /ˈdɪs.ə.plɪnd/ *adj* behaving in a very controlled way: *France play with more flair and inventiveness, whereas England are a more disciplined side.* ○ *Those children are well disciplined.*

disciplinarian /ˌdɪs.ə.plɪˈneə.ri.ən/ [US] /-ˈner.i-/ *noun* [C] *MAINLY DISAPPROVING* someone who believes in keeping complete control of the people he or she is in charge of, especially by giving severe punishments: *a strict disciplinarian*

disciplinary /ˌdɪs.əˈplɪn.ər.i/ [US] /ˈdɪs.ə.plɪ.ner-/ *adj*: *disciplinary **measures/action*** (= punishment)

discipline [SUBJECT] /ˈdɪs.ə.plɪn/ *noun* [C] a particular area of study, especially a subject studied at a college or university

ˈdisc ˌjockey *noun* [C] (*ABBREVIATION* **DJ**) someone who plays records and talks on the radio or at an event where people dance to recorded popular music, such as a DISCO

disclaim /dɪˈskleɪm/ *verb* [T] *FORMAL* to say that you have no responsibility for, or knowledge of, something that has happened or been done: *We disclaim all responsibility for this disaster.*

disclaimer /dɪˈskleɪ.məʳ/ [US] /-mɚ/ *noun* [C] **1** *FORMAL* a formal statement saying that you are not legally responsible for something, such as the information given in a book or on the Internet, or that you have no direct involvement in it **2** *SPECIALIZED* a formal statement giving up your legal claim to something or ending your connection with it

disclose /dɪˈskləʊz/ [US] /-ˈsklouz/ *verb* [I or T] *FORMAL* to make something known publicly, or to show something that was hidden: *Several companies have disclosed profits of over £200 million.* ○ [+ that] *The police have disclosed* ***that*** *two officers are under internal investigation.* **disclosure** /dɪˈskləʊ.ʒəʳ/ [US] /-ˈsklou.ʒɚ/ *noun* [C or U] *Any public disclosure* ***of*** *this information would be very damaging to the company.* ○ *The newspaper made damaging disclosures* ***of*** *management incompetence.*

disco (*plural* **discos**) /ˈdɪs.kəʊ/ [US] /-kou/ *noun* [C] (*OLD-FASHIONED* **discotheque**) an event where people dance to modern recorded music for entertainment, or a place where this often happens: *disco music/lights*

discolour *UK, US* **discolor** /dɪˈskʌl.əʳ/ [US] /-ɚ/ *verb* [I or T] to (cause something to) change from the original colour and therefore to look unpleasant: *The coal fire had discoloured the paintwork.* **discoloration** /dɪˌskʌl.əˈreɪ.ʃᵊn/ *noun* [C or U]

discoloured *UK, US* **discolored** /dɪˈskʌl.əd/ [US] /-ɚd/ *adj* describes something that has become a less attractive colour than it was originally: *discoloured teeth*

discomfit /dɪˈskʌmp.fɪt/ *verb* [T] *FORMAL* to make someone feel uncomfortable, especially mentally **discomfiture** /dɪˈskʌmp.fɪ.tʃəʳ/ [US] /-tʃɚ/ *noun* [U] *She turned away to hide her discomfiture.*

discomfort /dɪˈskʌmp.fət/ [US] /-fɚt/ *noun* [C or U] a feeling of being uncomfortable physically or mentally, or something that causes this: *You may feel* ***a little*** *discomfort for a few days after the operation.*

disconcert /ˌdɪs.kənˈsɜːt/ [US] /-ˈsɝːt/ *verb* **1** [I or T] to make someone feel suddenly uncertain and worried: *The whole experience had disconcerted him.* **2** worried by something and uncertain: *I was a little disconcerted by his reply.* **disconcerting** /ˌdɪs.kənˈsɜː.tɪŋ/ [US] /-ˈsɝː.t̬ɪŋ/ *adj*: *There was a disconcerting silence.* **disconcertingly** /ˌdɪs.kənˈsɜː.tɪŋ.li/ [US] /-ˈsɝː.t̬ɪŋ-/ *adv*

disconnect /ˌdɪs.kəˈnekt/ *verb* [T] **1** to unfasten something, especially to break the connection between a supply of electricity, gas, water, etc. and a device or piece of equipment: *Never try to mend a broken machine without disconnecting it* ***from*** *the electricity supply.* **2** to stop supplying electricity/gas/water/telephone services, especially because money has not been paid **3** If you are disconnected while speaking on the telephone, the telephone connection is suddenly broken and you can no longer continue your conversation. **disconnection** /ˌdɪs.kəˈnek.ʃᵊn/ *noun* [C or U]

disconnected /ˌdɪs.kəˈnek.tɪd/ *adj* If ideas or remarks, etc. or the different parts of something are disconnected, they are not well joined together and it is difficult to see their purpose or pattern: *disconnected thoughts*

disconsolate /dɪˈskɒnt.sᵊl.ət/ [US] /-ˈskɑːnt-/ *adj* *FORMAL* extremely sad and disappointed: *The team were disconsolate after losing what should have been an easy game.* **disconsolately** /dɪˈskɒnt.sᵊl.ət.li/ [US] /-ˈskɑːnt-/ *adv*

discontent /ˌdɪs.kənˈtent/ *noun* [U] (*ALSO* **discontentment**) a feeling of wanting better treatment or an improved situation: *Discontent* ***among*** *junior ranks was rapidly spreading.* ○ *There was* ***widespread*** *discontent* ***at/about/over/with*** *the plan.* **discontented** /ˌdɪs.kənˈten.tɪd/ [US] /ˌdɪs.kənˈten.t̬ɪd/ *adj* **discontentedly** /ˌdɪs.kənˈten.tɪd.li/ [US] /ˌdɪs.kənˈten.t̬ɪd-/ *adv*

discontinue /ˌdɪs.kənˈtɪn.juː/ *verb* [T] *FORMAL* to stop doing or providing something: *The bank is discontinuing its Saturday service.* **discontinuation** /ˌdɪs.kənˌtɪn.juˈeɪ.ʃᵊn/ *noun* [U] (*ALSO* **discontinuance**)

discontinued /ˌdɪs.kənˈtɪn.juːd/ *adj* describes a product or service that is no longer being produced or offered: *a discontinued line*

discontinuous /ˌdɪs.kənˈtɪn.ju.əs/ *adj* *FORMAL* with breaks, or stopping and starting again: *a discontinuous process* **discontinuity** /ˌdɪs.kɒn.tɪˈnjuː.ɪ.ti/ [US] /-kɑːn.təˈnuː.ə.t̬i/ *noun* [C or U]

discord [DISAGREEMENT] /ˈdɪs.kɔːd/ [US] /-kɔːrd/ *noun* [U] *FORMAL* a lack of agreement or shared opinions: *marital discord* ○ *A* ***note of*** *discord has crept into relations between the two countries.* ➲Compare **concord**.

discordant /dɪˈskɔː.dᵊnt/ [US] /-ˈskɔːr-/ *adj* *FORMAL* **strike a discordant note** to look or sound different or wrong compared with everything else: *The contemporary dialogue for me struck a slightly discordant note.*

discord [SOUND] /ˈdɪs.kɔːd/ [US] /-kɔːrd/ *noun* [C or U] *SPECIALIZED* a group of musical notes which give an unpleasant sound when played together **discordant** /dɪˈskɔː.dᵊnt/ [US] /-ˈskɔːr-/ *adj*

discotheque /ˈdɪs.kə.tek/ *noun* [C] *OLD-FASHIONED* a **disco**

discount [REDUCTION] /ˈdɪs.kaʊnt/ *noun* [C] a reduction in the usual price: *They usually* ***give*** *you a discount if you buy multiple copies.* ○ *They offer a 10 percent discount* ***on*** *rail travel for students.* **discount** /dɪˈskaʊnt/ *verb* [T often passive] *discounted goods/rates*

discount [NOT CONSIDER] /dɪˈskaʊnt/ *verb* [T] to decide that something or someone is not worth consideration or attention: *You shouldn't discount the possibility of him coming back.*

ˈdiscount ˌstore *noun* [C] a shop which sells its goods at cheap prices

ˈdiscount ˌwarehouse *noun* [C] a large shop, usually not in the centre of a town, which sells goods at cheap prices, especially large goods or large quantities of goods

discourage [MAKE LESS CONFIDENT] /dɪˈskʌr.ɪdʒ/ [US] /-ˈskɝː-/ *verb* [T] to make someone feel less confident, enthusiastic and positive about something, or less willing to do something: *The thought of how much work she had to do discouraged her.* * NOTE: The opposite is **encourage**.

discouraged /dɪˈskʌr.ɪdʒd/ [US] /-ˈskɝː-/ *adj* having lost your confidence or enthusiasm for something: *I think he felt discouraged because of all the criticism he'd received.*

discouraging /dɪˈskʌr.ɪ.dʒɪŋ/ [US] /-ˈskɝː-/ *adj*: *discouraging results* **discouragement** /dɪˈskʌr.ɪdʒ.mənt/ [US] /-ˈskɝː-/ *noun* [C or U] *a feeling of discouragement*

discourage [PREVENT] /dɪˈskʌr.ɪdʒ/ [US] /-ˈskɝː-/ *verb* [T] to prevent or try to prevent something happening or someone doing something, by making things difficult or unpleasant, or by showing disapproval: *a campaign to discourage people* ***from*** *smok****ing*** ○ *The authorities have put tanks on the streets to discourage any protest.* * NOTE: The opposite is **encourage**. **discouragement** /dɪˈskʌr.ɪdʒ.mənt/ [US] /-ˈskɝː-/ *noun* [U]

discourse /ˈdɪs.kɔːs/ [US] /-kɔːrs/ *noun* *FORMAL* **1** [U] communication in speech or writing **2** [C] a speech or piece of writing about a particular, usually serious, subject: *a discourse* ***on/upon*** *the nature of life after death*

discourteous /dɪˈskɜː.ti.əs/ [US] /-ˈskɝː.t̬i-/ *adj* *FORMAL* rude and not considering other people's feelings; not polite: *According to the customer survey, 6% said employees were unhelpful and discourteous.* **discourtesy** /dɪˈskɜː.tə.si/ [US] /-ˈskɝː.t̬ə-/ *noun* [C or U]

discover /dɪˈskʌv.əʳ/ [US] /-ɚ/ *verb* **1** [T] to find information, a place or an object, especially for the first time: *Who discovered America?* ○ *We searched all morning for the missing papers and finally discovered them in a drawer.* ○ [+ question word] *Scientists have discovered* ***how*** *to predict an earthquake.* ○ [+ (that)] *She discovered* ***(that)*** *her husband was having an affair.* ○ [+ to infinitive] *Following a routine checkup, Mrs Mason was discovered* ***to*** *have heart disease.* ○ [+ obj + v-ing] *The boss discovered him* (= unexpectedly found him) *steal****ing*** *money from the till.* **2** [T often passive] to notice that a person has a special talent or quality and to help them to become successful: *Los Angeles is full of beautiful girls working as waitresses, hoping to be discovered by a movie agent.* **discoverer** /dɪˈskʌv.ᵊr.əʳ/ [US] /-ɚ.ɚ/ *noun* [C] *Jim Watson and Francis*

*Crick were the discoverers **of** DNA.* **discovery** /dɪ-'skʌv.ªr.i/ ⓤ /-ɚ-/ *noun* [C or U] *the discovery **of** electricity* ○ *Leonardo **made** many scientific discoveries.* ○ *a journey/voyage of discovery* ○ *The discovery **of** a body in the undergrowth started a murder enquiry.*

discredit /dɪ'skred.ɪt/ *verb* [T] FORMAL to cause people to stop respecting someone or believing in an idea or person: *Evidence of links with drug dealers has discredited the President.* ○ *discredited theories* **discredit** /dɪ'skred.ɪt/ *noun* [U] *The stupid behaviour of one pupil has **brought** discredit **on** the whole school.* ○ *To her discredit, she never admitted her role in the scandal.* **discreditable** /dɪ'skred.ɪ.tə.bļ/ ⓤ /-ə.t̬ə-/ *adj* **discreditably** /dɪ'skred.ɪ.tə.bli/ ⓤ /-ə.t̬ə-/ *adv*

discreet /dɪ'skriːt/ *adj* careful not to cause embarrassment or attract too much attention, especially by keeping something secret: *The family made discreet enquiries about his background.* ○ *They are very good assistants, very discreet – they wouldn't go shouting to the press about anything they discovered while working for you.* * NOTE: Do not confuse with **discrete**. **discreetly** /dɪ'skriːt.li/ *adv*

discretion /dɪ'skreʃ.ªn/ *noun* [U] **1** the ability to behave without causing embarrassment or attracting too much attention, especially by keeping information secret: *"Can you trust him with this?" "Yes, he's **the soul of** discretion* (= he will not tell other people).*" **2** FORMAL the right or ability to decide something: *Students can be expelled **at the** discretion of the headteacher* (= if the headteacher decides it).* ○ *I leave the decision **to your** discretion* (= to your good judgment).

● **Discretion is the better part of valour.** SAYING said when you believe it is wise to be careful and avoid unnecessary risks

discretionary /dɪ'skreʃ.ªn.ªr.i/ ⓤ /-er-/ *adj* FORMAL decided by officials and not fixed by rules: *a discretionary grant* ○ *Judges have great discretionary powers.*

discrepancy /dɪ'skrep.ªnt.si/ *noun* [C or U] FORMAL (a) difference between two things that should be the same: *There is some discrepancy **between** the two accounts.* ○ *The committee is reportedly unhappy about the discrepancy in numbers.*

discrete /dɪ'skriːt/ *adj* having a clear independent shape or form; separate: *These small companies now have their own discrete identity.* * NOTE: Do not confuse with **discreet**.

discriminate TREAT DIFFERENTLY /dɪ'skrɪm.ɪ.neɪt/ *verb* [I] to treat a person or particular group of people differently, especially in a worse way from the way in which you treat other people, because of their skin colour, religion, sex, etc: *She felt she had been discriminated **against** because of her age.* ○ *In order to increase the number of female representatives, the selection committee decided to discriminate **in favour of** women for three years.* **discrimination** /dɪ,skrɪm.ɪ'neɪ.ʃªn/ *noun* [U] *racial/sex discrimination* ○ *Until 1986 most companies would not even allow women to take the examinations, but such blatant discrimination is now disappearing.* **discriminatory** /dɪ'skrɪm.ɪ.nə.tªr.i/ ⓤ /dɪ-'skrɪm.ɪ.nə.tɔːr-/ *adj: discriminatory legislation/laws/practices*

discriminate SEE A DIFFERENCE /dɪ'skrɪm.ɪ.neɪt/ *verb* [I + adv or prep] FORMAL to be able to see the difference between two things or people: *Police dogs can discriminate **between** the different smells.* **discriminating** /dɪ'skrɪm.ɪ.neɪ.tɪŋ/ ⓤ /-t̬ɪŋ/ *adj* FORMAL APPROVING able to know and act on the difference between good and bad: *They're discriminating shoppers.* ○ *a discriminating palate* **discrimination** /dɪ,skrɪm.ɪ-'neɪ.ʃªn/ *noun* [U] FORMAL

discursive /dɪ'skɜː.sɪv/ ⓤ /-skɜː-/ *adj* FORMAL MAINLY DISAPPROVING talking about or dealing with subjects which are only slightly connected with the main subject for longer than necessary: *a discursive writer/essay/speech*

discus /'dɪs.kəs/ *noun* [C] **1** a heavy plate-shaped object which is thrown as part of a sports event **2 the discus** the event or sport in which a discus is thrown as far as possible ⊃See picture **Sports** on page Centre 10

discuss /dɪ'skʌs/ *verb* [T] **1** to talk about a subject with someone and tell each other your ideas or opinions: *The police want to discuss these recent racist attacks **with** local people.* **2** to talk or write about a subject in detail, especially considering different ideas and opinions related to it: *The later chapters discuss the effects on the environment.*

discussion /dɪ'skʌʃ.ªn/ *noun* [C or U] when people talk about something and tell each other their ideas or opinions: *I can say nothing – the matter is still **under** discussion* (= being considered).* ○ *a discussion group/document* ○ *Management are **holding/having** discussions **with** the union about possible redundancies.*

COMMON LEARNER ERROR

discuss

Discuss is not followed by a preposition.

We discussed the plans for the wedding.

~~We discussed about the plans for the wedding.~~

You can, however, **discuss** something **with** someone.

Can I discuss this report with you?

---

disdain /dɪs'deɪn/ *noun* [U] FORMAL when you dislike someone or something and think that they do not deserve your interest or respect: *He regards the political process **with** disdain.*

disdain /dɪs'deɪn/ *verb* [T] FORMAL **1** to feel disdain for someone or something: *The older musicians disdain the new, rock-influenced music.* **2 disdain to do** *sth* to refuse to do something because you feel too important to do it **disdainful** /dɪs'deɪn.fªl/ *adj: a disdainful expression* **disdainfully** /dɪs'deɪn.fªl.i/ *adv*

disease /dɪ'ziːz/ *noun* **1** [C or U] (an) illness of people, animals, plants, etc., caused by infection or a failure of health rather than by an accident: *a contagious/infectious disease* ○ *a common/rare/incurable/fatal disease* ○ *They reported a sudden **outbreak of** the disease in the south of the country.* ○ *The first **symptom of** the disease is a very high temperature.* ○ *She has **caught/contracted*** (= begun to have) *a lung disease/disease of the lungs.* ○ *Starvation and disease have killed thousands of refugees.* **2** [C] something that is considered very bad in people or society: *The real disease affecting the country is inflation.* **diseased** /dɪ'ziːzd/ *adj: a diseased lung/kidney* ○ *diseased brain tissue* ○ *Farmers were dumping or burying the diseased animals/carcasses.* ○ *The bush looked badly diseased, with black marks on all the leaves.* ○ *a diseased mind/imagination* ○ *a diseased society*

disembark /,dɪs.ɪm'bɑːk/ ⓤ /-'bɑːrk/ *verb* [I] FORMAL to leave a ship, aircraft, etc. after a journey **disembarkation** /,dɪs.ɪm.bɑː'keɪ.ʃªn/ ⓤ /-'bɑːrk-/ *noun* [U]

disembodied /,dɪs.ɪm'bɒd.id/ ⓤ /-'bɑː.did/ *adj* seeming not to have a body or not to be connected to a body: *a disembodied voice*

disembowel /,dɪs.ɪm'bau.əl/ *verb* [T] -ll- or US USUALLY -l- to remove the stomach and bowels from a dead animal, or to kill a person in this way, especially in the past as a punishment

disenchanted /,dɪs.ɪn'tʃɑːn.tɪd/ ⓤ /-'tʃæn.t̬ɪd/ *adj* no longer believing in the value of something, especially having learned of the problems with it: *Many voters have **become** disenchanted **with** the government.* **disenchantment** /,dɪs.ɪn'tʃɑːnt.mənt/ ⓤ /-'tʃænt-/ *noun* [U] *There is (a) growing disenchantment **with** the way the country/school/club is being run.*

disenfranchise /,dɪs.ɪn'fræn.tʃaɪz/ *verb* [T] (ALSO **disfranchise**) to take away power or opportunities, especially the right to vote, from a person or group

disenfranchised /,dɪs.ɪn'fræn.tʃaɪzd/ *adj* not having the right to vote, or a similar right, or having had that right taken away: *disenfranchised youth/communities/voters*

disengage /,dɪs.ɪn'geɪdʒ/ *verb* **1** [I or T] to become separated from something, or to make two things become separate from each other: *They recognized that the country would revive only if it thoroughly disengaged **from** the chaos of the old regime.* ○ *The number-one rule for being a good colleague is to disengage your emotions* *from the working relationship.* ○ [R] *Both children, disengaging themselves from their game, came to her side.* **2** [T] If you disengage the CLUTCH of a car, you stop the power produced by the engine being connected to the wheels. **disengagement** /ˌdɪs.ɪnˈɡeɪdʒ.mənt/ *noun* [U]

disentangle /ˌdɪs.ɪnˈtæŋ.ɡl̩/ *verb* [T] to separate things that have become joined or confused: *It's difficult to disentangle hard fact from myth, or truth from lies.* ○ *I tried to disentangle the wires under my desk.*

disestablish /ˌdɪs.ɪˈstæb.lɪʃ/ *verb* [T] FORMAL to take away official support and position from a CHURCH ORGANIZATION or similar organized group **disestablishment** /ˌdɪs.ɪˈstæb.lɪʃ.mənt/ *noun* [U]

disfavour UK, US **disfavor** /dɪsˈfeɪ.vər/ ⓤ /-vɚ/ *noun* [U] FORMAL a feeling of dislike or disapproval: *She sat down, regarding the plate in front of her with disfavour.*

disfigure /dɪsˈfɪɡ.ər/ ⓤ /-jɚ/ *verb* [T] to spoil the appearance of something or someone, especially their face, completely: *She was horribly disfigured by burns.* ○ *This part of the old town has been disfigured by ugly new buildings.*

disfranchise /dɪsˈfræn.tʃaɪz/ *verb* [T] MAINLY US to **disenfranchise**

disgorge /dɪsˈɡɔːdʒ/ ⓤ /-ˈɡɔːrdʒ/ *verb* [T] **1** LITERARY to release large amounts of liquid, gas or other contents: *The pipe was found to be disgorging dangerous chemicals into the sea.* **2** LITERARY to let many people out of a place or vehicle at the same time: *The delayed commuter train disgorged hundreds of angry passengers.* **3** FORMAL to force something up from the stomach and out through the mouth: *Flies disgorge digestive fluid onto their food to soften it up.* **4** LITERARY to unwillingly release information or money: *The judge has forced EXIP to disgorge $400 000 in illegal profits.*

disgrace /dɪsˈɡreɪs/ *noun* [U] **1** embarrassment and the loss of other people's respect, or behaviour which causes this: *They were sent home in disgrace.* ○ *He brought disgrace on the whole team by falsifying the results.* **2** **be a disgrace** to be a very bad situation: *Three families living in one room – it's a disgrace!* ○ [+ that] *It's a disgrace that the government spends so much on guns and so little on education.* **3** **be a disgrace to sb/sth** to be so bad or unacceptable that you make people lose respect for the group or activity you are connected to: *You're a disgrace (to the family) – what a way to behave!*

disgrace /dɪsˈɡreɪs/ *verb* [T] to make people stop respecting you or your family, team, etc. by doing something very bad: *You have disgraced us all with your behaviour.*

disgraced /dɪsˈɡreɪst/ *adj*: *a disgraced politician*

disgraceful /dɪsˈɡreɪs.fəl/ *adj* very bad: *disgraceful behaviour/conduct* ○ *a disgraceful situation* ○ *She thought that their attitude was absolutely disgraceful.* ○ [+ that] *It is disgraceful that children can get hold of drugs at school.* **disgracefully** /dɪsˈɡreɪs.fəl.i/ *adv*: *You've behaved disgracefully.*

disgruntled /dɪsˈɡrʌn.tl̩d/ ⓤ /-t̬l̩d/ *adj* unhappy, annoyed and disappointed about something: *A disgruntled former employee is being blamed for the explosion.* ○ *The players were disgruntled with the umpire.*

disguise /dɪsˈɡaɪz/ *verb* [T] **1** to give a new appearance to a person or thing, especially in order to hide its true form: [R] *He disguised himself by shaving his head and wearing a false beard.* ○ *Minor skin imperfections can usually be disguised with a spot of make-up.* ○ *We tried to disguise the fact that it was just a school hall by putting up coloured lights and balloons.* **2** to hide an opinion, a feeling, etc.: *I couldn't disguise my disappointment.* **disguise** /dɪsˈɡaɪz/ *noun* [C or U] *He put on a large hat and glasses as a disguise and hoped no one would recognise him.*

• **in disguise** If people, objects or activities are in disguise, they appear to be something which they are not, especially intentionally: *She usually goes out in disguise to avoid being bothered by the public.* ○ *He claims that most Western aid to the Third World is just colonialism in disguise.*

disguised /dɪsˈɡaɪzd/ *adj* having an appearance that hides the true form: *In Shakespeare's play 'Twelfth Night', Duke Orsino falls in love with the disguised Viola.* ○ *In the book, the author gives a thinly* (= only slightly) *disguised account of his own early teaching experiences.*

disgust /dɪsˈɡʌst/ *noun* [U] strong feeling of disapproval and dislike at a situation or person's behaviour, etc: *She walked out in disgust.* ○ *We are demonstrating to show our anger and disgust at the treatment of refugees.* ○ *He resigned from the committee in disgust at the corruption.* ○ *Beresford, much to his disgust, was fined for illegal parking.*

disgust /dɪsˈɡʌst/ *verb* [T not continuous] to make you feel extreme dislike or disapproval: *Doesn't all this violence on TV disgust you?*

disgusted /dɪsˈɡʌs.tɪd/ *adj* feeling extreme dislike or disapproval of something: *She was disgusted at the way they treated their children.* ○ *I'm totally disgusted with your behaviour.* **disgustedly** /dɪsˈɡʌs.tɪd.li/ *adv*

disgusting /dɪsˈɡʌs.tɪŋ/ *adj* extremely unpleasant or unacceptable: *It's disgusting that there are no schools or hospitals for these people.* ○ *Passengers were kept for hours in a disgusting waiting room.* **disgustingly** /dɪsˈɡʌs.tɪŋ.li/ *adv*

dish CONTAINER /dɪʃ/ *noun* [C] a container, flatter than a bowl and sometimes with a lid, from which food can be served or which can be used for cooking: *an oven-proof dish* ⊃See also **satellite dish**.

the 'dishes *plural noun* all the plates, glasses, knives, forks, etc. that have been used during a meal: *Have you done/washed the dishes?*

dish FOOD /dɪʃ/ *noun* [C] food prepared in a particular way as part of a meal: *a chicken/vegetarian dish*

dish ATTRACTIVE PERSON /dɪʃ/ *noun* [S] OLD-FASHIONED a sexually attractive person: *He's gorgeous – what a dish!*

dishy /ˈdɪʃ.i/ *adj* UK SLANG *What a dishy guy.*

dish SPOIL REPUTATION /dɪʃ/ *verb* **dish the dirt** to tell people unpleasant or shocking personal information about someone: *She agreed to dish the dirt on her ex-husband for a fee of fifty thousand pounds.*

PHRASAL VERBS WITH **dish** ▼

▲ **dish sth out** GIVE *phrasal verb* [M] INFORMAL to give or say things to people without thinking about it carefully: *Doctors are short of time to listen and are therefore keen to dish out drugs whenever they can.* ○ *He's very keen to dish out criticism.*

• **they can dish it out but they can't take it** INFORMAL OLD-FASHIONED said when someone often criticizes other people but does not like it when people do the same to them

▲ **dish sth out** GIVE FOOD *phrasal verb* [M] INFORMAL to give or serve food to people: *Jon, could you dish the carrots out for me, please?*

▲ **dish (sth) up** *phrasal verb* [M] UK INFORMAL to produce or serve a meal: *Come to the table everybody – I'm ready to dish (supper) up.* ○ *What's the canteen dishing up for us today?*

▲ **dish sth up** *phrasal verb* [M] to produce something: *The offer is better than anything the other airlines can dish up.*

disharmony /dɪsˈhɑː.mə.ni/ ⓤ /-ˈhɑːr-/ *noun* [U] FORMAL when there is disagreement and unpleasantness between people: *racial disharmony*

dishcloth /ˈdɪʃ.klɒθ/ ⓤ /-klɑːθ/ *noun* [C] a cloth for washing and cleaning dirty plates, cups, forks, etc.

dishearten /dɪsˈhɑː.tən/ ⓤ /-ˈhɑːr.tən/ *verb* [T] to make a person lose confidence, hope and energy; to discourage **disheartened** /dɪsˈhɑː.tənd/ ⓤ /-ˈhɑːr.tən-/ *adj*: *She was very disheartened by the results of the test.* **disheartening** /dɪsˈhɑː.tən.ɪŋ/ ⓤ /-ˈhɑːr.tən-/ *adj*: *disheartening news*

dishevelled, US USUALLY **disheveled** /dɪˈʃev.əld/ *adj* (of people or their appearance) very untidy: *dishevelled hair/clothes/appearance* ○ *He ran in looking rather dishevelled.*

dishonest /dɪˈsɒn.ɪst/ ⓤ /-ˈsɑː.nɪst/ *adj* not honest: *a dishonest lawyer* ○ *a dishonest way of making money* ○ *morally dishonest* ○ *intellectually dishonest* ○ *He's been dishonest in his dealings with us/about his past.* **dishonestly** /dɪˈsɒn.ɪst.li/ ⓤ /-ˈsɑː.nɪst-/ *adv*: *The money was dishonestly obtained.* ○ *She's been accused of acting dis-*

honestly. **dishonesty** /dɪˈsɒn.ɪ.sti/ [US] /-ˈsɑː.nə-/ *noun* [U] *Her dishonesty landed her in prison.*

dishonour *UK, US* **dishonor** /dɪˈsɒn.əʳ/ [US] /-ˈsɑː.nɚ/ *noun* [U] *FORMAL* a feeling of embarrassment and loss of people's respect, or when you experience this: *Some of the leaders of the coup took their lives rather than face dishonour.* ○ *It was no dishonour to finish out of the medals in the most memorable 100 metres race ever seen.*

dishonour *UK, US* **dishonor** /dɪˈsɒn.əʳ/ [US] /-ˈsɑː.n/ *verb* [T] *FORMAL* **1** to cause someone or something to lose respect: *He felt that he had dishonoured his country.* **2** If you dishonour a promise or agreement, you do not do what you said you would do: *We suspect he means to dishonour the* ***agreement*** *made three years ago.* **dishonourable** *UK, US* **dishonorable** /dɪˈsɒn.ᵊr.ə.bl̩/ [US] /-ˈsɑː.nɚ-/ *adj*: *dishonourable actions*

dishtowel /ˈdɪʃ.taʊəl/ *noun* [C] *US FOR* **tea towel**

dishwasher /ˈdɪʃˌwɒʃ.əʳ/ [US] /-ˌwɑː.ʃɚ/ *noun* [C] **1** a machine that washes dirty plates, cups, forks, etc. ➲See picture **In the Kitchen** on page Centre 16 **2** a person who washes dishes

dishwater /ˈdɪʃˌwɔː.təʳ/ [US] /-ˌwɑː.t̬ɚ/ *noun* [U] water in which dirty plates, cups, forks, etc. have been washed
• **like dishwater** *INFORMAL DISAPPROVING* describes a drink or liquid which is unpleasant because it is watery and has very little flavour: *This soup/tea* ***tastes*** *like dishwater.*

dishy /ˈdɪʃ.i/ *adj SLANG* ➲See at **dish** ATTRACTIVE PERSON.

disillusion /ˌdɪs.ɪˈluː.ʒᵊn/ *verb* [T] to disappoint someone by telling them the unpleasant truth about something or someone that they had a good opinion of, or respected: ***I hate to/I'm sorry to*** *disillusion you, but pregnancy is not always wonderful – I was sick every day for six months.* **disillusioned** /ˌdɪs.ɪˈluː.ʒᵊnd/ *adj*: *He's become a disillusioned man.* ○ *All the other teachers are thoroughly disillusioned* ***with*** *their colleague.* **disillusionment** /ˌdɪs.ɪˈluː.ʒᵊn.mənt/ *noun* [U] (*ALSO* **disillusion**) *There is increasing disillusionment* ***with*** *the government.*

disincentive /ˌdɪs.ɪnˈsen.tɪv/ [US] /-t̬ɪv/ *noun* [C] something that discourages people from doing something or working hard: *High taxes are a disincentive* ***to*** *business.*

disinclination /ˌdɪs.ɪŋ.klɪˈneɪ.ʃᵊn/ *noun* [S or U] a feeling of not wanting to do something: [+ *to* infinitive] *I have a strong disinclination* ***to*** *do any work.* **disinclined** /ˌdɪs.ɪŋˈklaɪnd/ *adj* **be/feel disinclined to** ***do sth***: *I am/feel disinclined to offer him a job if he hasn't got a degree.*

disinfect /ˌdɪs.ɪnˈfekt/ *verb* [T] to clean something using chemicals that kill bacteria and other very small living things that cause disease: *disinfect the toilets/a wound*

disinfectant /ˌdɪs.ɪnˈfek.tᵊnt/ [US] /-t̬ᵊnt/ *noun* [C or U] a substance which contains chemicals that kill bacteria and is used especially for cleaning surfaces in toilets and kitchens

disinformation /ˌdɪs.ɪn.fəˈmeɪ.ʃən/ [US] /-fɚ-/ *noun* [U] false information spread in order to deceive people: *They claimed there was an official disinformation campaign by the government.*

disingenuous /ˌdɪs.ɪnˈdʒen.ju.əs/ *adj FORMAL* (of a person or their behaviour) slightly dishonest; not speaking the complete truth: *It was disingenuous of her to claim she had no financial interest in the case.*

disinherit /ˌdɪs.ɪnˈher.ɪt/ *verb* [T] to prevent someone, especially a son or daughter who has made you angry, from receiving any of your property after your death: *Her father said he'd disinherit her if she married Stephen.*

disintegrate /dɪˈsɪn.tɪ.greɪt/ [US] /-t̬ə-/ *verb* [I] **1** to become weaker or be destroyed by breaking into small pieces: *The spacecraft disintegrated as it entered the Earth's atmosphere.* ○ *The Ottoman Empire disintegrated* ***into*** *lots of small states.* **2** to become much worse: *The situation disintegrated* ***into*** *chaos.* **disintegration** /dɪˌsɪn.tɪˈgreɪ.ʃᵊn/ [US] /ˌdɪs.ɪn.t̬ə-/ *noun* [U] *social disintegration* ○ *the gradual disintegration* ***of*** *family values*

disinter /ˌdɪs.ɪnˈtɜːʳ/ [US] /-ˈtɝː/ *verb* [T] -rr- **1** to dig up a dead body from the ground **2** to find and use something that has not been seen or used for a long time

disinterest [NOT INTERESTED] /dɪsˈɪn.tᵊr.est/ [US] /-t̬ɚ-/ *noun* [U] lack of interest: *Some kids become high-achievers to compensate for their parents' disinterest.*

disinterest [NOT INVOLVED] /dɪsˈɪn.tᵊr.est/ [US] /-t̬ɚ-/ *noun* [U] *FORMAL* when you have no involvement in or receive no special advantage or benefit from a situation or event: *Their close and financially rewarding relationship was sufficient to call into question the independence and disinterest of the directors.*

disinterested /dɪˈsɪn.trə.stɪd/ *adj* having no personal involvement or receiving no personal advantage, and therefore free to act fairly: *a disinterested observer/judgment* ○ *a piece of disinterested advice* ✱ NOTE: **Disinterested** is sometimes used to mean 'not interested', but many people consider this use to be incorrect. ➲Compare **uninterested**.

disinvest /ˌdɪs.ɪnˈvest/ *verb* [I] (*US ALSO* **divest**) to sell your SHARES in a company or to stop taking part in a business activity **disinvestment** /ˌdɪs.ɪnˈvest.mənt/ *noun* [U] (*US ALSO* **divestiture,** *US ALSO* **divestment**)

disjointed /dɪsˈdʒɔɪn.tɪd/ [US] /-t̬ɪd/ *adj* (especially of words or ideas) not well connected or well ordered: *The script was disjointed and hard to follow.*

disk, *UK ALSO* **disc** /dɪsk/ *noun* [C] a flat circular device, usually inside a square container, which has a magnetic covering and is used for storing computer information ➲See also **disc**; **floppy (disk)**; **hard disk**.

ˈdisk ˌdrive *noun* [C] a piece of computer equipment that allows information to be stored on and read from a disk

diskette /dɪsˈket/ *noun* [C] a small flat square object made of plastic that you put in your computer to record and store information electronically

dislike /dɪˈslaɪk/ *verb* [T] to not like someone or something: *Why do you dislike her so much?* ○ [+ v-*ing*] *I dislike walk****ing*** *and I hate the countryside.*

dislike /dɪˈslaɪk/ *noun* **1** [S or U] a feeling of not liking something or someone: *She has a dislike of cold weather.* ○ *I'm afraid Dad* ***took*** *an instant dislike* ***to*** (= decided he does not like) *this new boyfriend of yours.* **2** [C usually pl] something that you do not like: *His main dislikes about work are the noise and dust in the factory.*

dislocate /ˈdɪs.ləʊ.keɪt/ [US] /dɪˈsloʊ-/ *verb* [T] **1** to force a bone suddenly out of its correct position: *She dislocated her knee falling down some steps.* **2** to have a negative effect on the working of something **dislocated** /ˈdɪs.ləʊ.keɪ.tɪd/ [US] /-loʊ.keɪ.t̬ɪd/ *adj*: *a dislocated hip* **dislocation** /ˌdɪs.ləʊˈkeɪ.ʃᵊn/ [US] /-loʊ-/ *noun* [C or U] *Snow has caused serious dislocation* ***of/to*** *train services.*

dislodge /dɪˈslɒdʒ/ [US] /-ˈslɑːdʒ/ *verb* [T] to remove something or someone, especially by force, from a fixed position: *The earthquake dislodged stones* ***from*** *the walls and the roof.* ○ *We need two wins to dislodge the French team* ***from*** *first place.*

disloyal /ˌdɪsˈlɔɪ.əl/ *adj* not loyal; not supporting someone that you should support: *His sisters thought that his autobiography was disloyal* ***to*** *the family.*

dismal /ˈdɪz.məl/ *adj* **1** sad and without hope: *a dismal expression* **2** *INFORMAL* very bad: *The acting was dismal, wasn't it?* ○ *What dismal weather!* **dismally** /ˈdɪz.mə.li/ *adv*

dismantle /dɪˈsmæn.tl̩/ [US] /-t̬l̩/ *verb* **1** [I or T] to take a machine apart or to come apart into separate pieces: *She dismantled the washing machine to see what the problem was, but couldn't put it back together again.* ○ *The good thing about the bike is that it dismantles if you want to put it in the back of the car.* **2** [T] to get rid of a system or organization, usually over a period of time: *Unions accuse the government of dismantling the National Health Service.*

dismay /dɪˈsmeɪ/ *noun* [U] a feeling of unhappiness and disappointment: *Aid workers were said to have been* ***filled with*** *dismay by the appalling conditions that the refugees were living in.* ○ *The supporters watched* ***in/with*** *dismay as their team lost 6-0.* ○ *She discovered,* ***to*** *her dismay, that her exam was a whole month earlier than she'd expected.* **dismay** /dɪˈsmeɪ/ *verb* [T] **dismayed** /dɪˈsmeɪd/ *adj*: *I was dismayed to discover that he'd lied.*

dismember /dɪˈsmem.bəʳ/ [US] /-bɚ/ *verb* [T] **1** to cut, tear or pull the arms and legs off a human body: *The police found the dismembered body of a young man in the*

D

murderer's freezer. **2** LITERARY to divide a country or an empire into different parts: *The UN protested at the dismembering of Bosnia.* **dismemberment** /dɪˈsmem.bə.mənt/ ⓤ /-bɚ.mənt/ *noun* [U] LITERARY *the dismemberment of the empire*

dismiss FORGET /dɪˈsmɪs/ *verb* [T] to decide that something or someone is not important and not worth considering: *I think he'd dismissed me as an idiot within five minutes of meeting me.* ○ *Let's not just dismiss the idea before we've even thought about it.* ○ *Just dismiss those thoughts from your mind – they're crazy and not worth thinking about.* **dismissal** /dɪˈsmɪs.ᵊl/ *noun* [U] **dismissive** /dɪˈsmɪs.ɪv/ *adj*: *He's so dismissive of anybody else's suggestions.* ○ *a dismissive attitude* **dismissively** /dɪˈsmɪs.ɪv.li/ *adv*

dismiss END JOB /dɪˈsmɪs/ *verb* [T often passive] to remove someone from their job, especially because they have done something wrong: *He has been dismissed from his job for incompetence.*
dismissal /dɪˈsmɪs.ᵊl/ *noun* [C or U] when an employer officially makes someone leave their job: *unfair/wrongful dismissal*

dismiss SEND AWAY /dɪˈsmɪs/ *verb* [T] **1** to formally ask or order someone to leave: *The teacher dismissed the class early because she had a meeting.* **2** When a judge dismisses a court case, he or she formally stops the trial, often because there is not enough proof of someone's guilt: *The defending lawyer asked that the charge against his client be dismissed.*

dismount /dɪˈsmaʊnt/ *verb* [I] to get off a horse, bicycle or motorcycle

disobedient /ˌdɪs.əʊˈbiː.di.ənt/ ⓤ /-əˈ-/ *adj* refusing to do what someone in authority tells you to do: *a disobedient child* **disobediently** /ˌdɪs.əʊˈbiː.di.ənt.li/ ⓤ /-əˈ-/ *adv* **disobedience** /ˌdɪs.əʊˈbiː.di.ənts/ ⓤ /-əˈ-/ *noun* [U]

disobey /ˌdɪs.əʊˈbeɪ/ ⓤ /-əˈ-/ *verb* [I or T] to refuse to do something that you are told to do; to not obey: *How dare you disobey me!* ○ *disobey orders*

disobliging /ˌdɪs.əˈblaɪ.dʒɪŋ/ *adj* FORMAL unwilling to help or do what you are asked to do

disorder CONFUSION /dɪˈsɔː.də⁽ʳ⁾/ ⓤ /-ˈsɔːr.dɚ/ *noun* [U] a state of untidiness or lack of organization: *The whole office was in a state of disorder.* ○ *The opposition party have been in such disorder for so long that they pose no real threat to the present government.* **disorderly** /dɪˈsɔː.dᵊl.i/ ⓤ /-ˈsɔːr.dɚ.li/ *adj*: *It's a disorderly sort of a house with books and papers lying around everywhere.*

disorder ILLNESS /dɪˈsɔː.də⁽ʳ⁾/ ⓤ /-ˈsɔːr.dɚ/ *noun* [C or U] an illness of the mind or body: *a blood disorder* ○ *The family have a history of mental disorder.*

disorder ANGRY SITUATION /dɪˈsɔː.də⁽ʳ⁾/ ⓤ /-ˈsɔːr.dɚ/ *noun* [U] an angry, possibly violent, expression of dissatisfaction by crowds of people, especially about a political matter: *The trial was kept secret because of the risk of public disorder.* **disorderly** /dɪˈsɔː.dᵊl.i/ ⓤ /-ˈsɔːr.dɚ.li/ *adj*: *The police feared that the crowd were becoming disorderly and so they moved in with horses.*

disorganized , UK USUALLY -ised /dɪˈsɔː.gə.naɪzd/ ⓤ /-ˈsɔːr-/ *adj* **1** badly planned and lacking order: *The whole conference was totally disorganized – nobody knew what they were supposed to be doing.* **2** not good at planning or organizing things: *He's impossible to work for – he's so disorganized.* **disorganization** , UK USUALLY -isation /dɪˌsɔː.gə.naɪˈzeɪ.ʃᵊn/ ⓤ /-ˌsɔːr-/ *noun* [U]

disorientate /dɪˈsɔː.ri.ən.teɪt/ ⓤ /-ˈsɔːr.i-/ *verb* [T] (US USUALLY **disorient**) to make someone confused about where they are and where they are going **disorientating** /dɪˈsɔː.ri.ən.teɪ.tɪŋ/ ⓤ /-ˈsɔːr.i-/ *adj* (US USUALLY **disorienting**)

disoriented /dɪˈsɔː.ri.ən.tɪd/ ⓤ /-ˈsɔːr.i.ən.t̬ɪd/ *adj* (UK ALSO **disorientated**) confused and not knowing where to go or what to do: *Whales become disoriented in shallow water.*

disown /dɪˈsəʊn/ ⓤ /-ˈsoʊn/ *verb* [T not continuous] to make it known that you no longer have any connection with someone that you were closely connected with: *It's a story set in the last century about a girl whose parents disowned her when she married a foreigner.*

disparage /dɪˈspær.ɪdʒ/ ⓤ /-ˈsper-/ *verb* [T] to criticize someone or something in a way that shows you do not respect or value them: *The actor's work for charity has recently been disparaged in the press as an attempt to get publicity.*
disparaging /dɪˈspær.ɪ.dʒɪŋ/ ⓤ /-ˈsper-/ *adj* critical, in a way that shows you do not respect or value someone: *disparaging remarks* **disparagingly** /dɪˈspær.ɪ.dʒɪŋ.li/ ⓤ /-ˈsper-/ *adv* **disparagement** /dɪˈspær.ɪdʒ.mənt/ ⓤ /-ˈsper-/ *noun* [U]

disparate /ˈdɪs.pᵊr.ət/ ⓤ /-pɚ.ət/ *adj* FORMAL different in every way: *The two cultures were so utterly disparate that she found it hard to adapt from one to the other.*

disparity /dɪˈspær.ə.ti/ ⓤ /-ˈper.ə.t̬i/ *noun* [C or U] SLIGHTLY FORMAL a lack of equality and similarity, especially in a way that is not fair: *the growing disparity between rich and poor*

dispassionate /dɪˈspæʃ.ᵊn.ət/ *adj* able to think clearly or make good decisions because not influenced by emotions: *In all the media hysteria, there was one journalist whose comments were clear-sighted and dispassionate.* **dispassionately** /dɪˈspæʃ.ᵊn.ət.li/ *adv*

dispatch , UK ALSO **despatch** /dɪˈspætʃ/ *verb* [T] **1** to send something, especially goods or a message, somewhere for a particular purpose: *Two loads of woollen cloth were dispatched to the factory on December 12th.* **2** LITERARY OR OLD-FASHIONED to kill someone: *In the film's last five minutes, our handsome hero manages to dispatch another five villains.*
dispatch , UK ALSO **despatch** /dɪˈspætʃ/ *noun* **1** [U] when someone or something is sent somewhere: *the dispatch of troops* **2** [C] a newspaper report sent by someone in a foreign country, often communicating war news, or an official report, often on a military matter: *In her latest dispatch, Clare Duggan, our war correspondent, reported an increase in fighting.*
• **be mentioned in dispatches** UK to be highly praised for actions you have performed as a soldier: *Sergeant Havers was mentioned in dispatches for his courage.*
• **with dispatch** OLD-FASHIONED FORMAL quickly and effectively

disˈpatch ˌbox *noun* [C] UK in Britain, the box on a table in the House of Commons which important politicians stand next to when they are formally speaking to the Members of Parliament

disˈpatch ˌrider *noun* [C] UK someone who travels between companies riding a motorcycle or bicycle, delivering documents and packages as quickly as possible

dispel /dɪˈspel/ *verb* [T] -ll- to remove fears, doubts and false ideas, usually by proving them wrong or unnecessary: *I'd like to start the speech by dispelling a few rumours that have been spreading recently.*

dispensable /dɪˈspent.sə.bl̩/ *adj* additional to your needs and therefore not necessary; that can be got rid of: *It seemed the soldiers were regarded as dispensable – their deaths just didn't matter.* ✻ NOTE: The opposite is **indispensable**.

dispensation PERMISSION /ˌdɪs.penˈseɪ.ʃᵊn/ *noun* [C or U] FORMAL special permission, especially from the Church, to do something that is not usually allowed: *The couple have requested (a) special dispensation from the Church to allow them to marry.*

dispensation SYSTEM /ˌdɪs.penˈseɪ.ʃᵊn/ *noun* [C] FORMAL a political or religious system controlling a country at a particular time

dispense PROVIDE /dɪˈspents/ *verb* [T] to give out things, especially products, services or amounts of money, to people: *There is a vending machine on the platform that dispenses snacks.*
dispenser /dɪˈspent.sə⁽ʳ⁾/ ⓤ /-sɚ/ *noun* [C] a machine or container that you can get something from: *a cash/soap/drinks dispenser*

dispense GIVE OUT MEDICINE /dɪˈspents/ *verb* [T] to prepare and give out medicine: UK *a dispensing chemist*
dispensary /dɪˈspent.sᵊr.i/ ⓤ /-sɚ.i/ *noun* [C] a place where medicines are prepared and given out, often in a hospital

▲ **dispense with** *sth/sb phrasal verb* to get rid of something or someone or stop using them because you do not need them: *They've had to dispense with a lot of luxuries since Mike lost his job.*

dis'**pensing op,tician** UK *noun* [C] (US **optician**) a person whose job is fitting and selling glasses and CONTACT LENSES to correct sight problems, but who does not examine people's eyes ⊃Compare **optician**.

disperse /dɪˈspɜːs/ US /-ˈspɝːs/ *verb* [I or T] to scatter or move away over a large area, or to make something do this: *When the rain came down the crowds started to disperse.* ○ *Police dispersed the crowd that had gathered around the building.* **dispersal** /dɪˈspɜː.səl/ US /-ˈspɝː-/ *noun* [U]

dispersion /dɪˈspɜː.ʃən/ US /-ˈspɝː-/ *noun* [U] **1** FORMAL dispersal **2** SPECIALIZED the separation of light into different colours

dispirited /dɪˈspɪr.ɪ.tɪd/ US /-t̬ɪd/ *adj* not feeling hopeful about a particular situation or problem: *The troops were dispirited and disorganised.* **dispiriting** /dɪˈspɪr.ɪ.tɪŋ/ US /-t̬ɪŋ/ *adj*: *It was a bit dispiriting to see so few people arriving for the meeting.*

displace /dɪˈspleɪs/ *verb* [T] to force something or someone out of its usual or original position: *The building of a new dam will displace thousands of people who live in this area.* **displaced** /dɪˈspleɪst/ *adj*

displacement /dɪˈspleɪs.mənt/ *noun* [U] **1** when people are forced to leave the place where they normally live: *The recent famine in these parts has caused the displacement of tens of thousands of people.* **2** SPECIALIZED the weight of liquid that is forced out of position by an object which is floating on or in it

dis,**placed** '**person** *noun* [C] *plural* **displaced persons** someone who has been forced to leave their home, especially because of war or a natural DISASTER (= something that causes a lot of damage), such as an earthquake, flood, etc.

dis'**placement ac,tivity** *noun* [C or U] SPECIALIZED an unnecessary activity that you only do because you are trying to delay doing a more difficult or unpleasant activity: *When I was studying for my exams I used to clean the house as a sort of displacement activity.*

display [ARRANGE] /dɪˈspleɪ/ *verb* [T] to arrange something or a collection of things so that they can be seen by the public: *Family photographs were displayed on the wall.*

display /dɪˈspleɪ/ *noun* **1** [C or U] a collection of objects or pictures arranged for people to look at, or a performance or show for people to watch: *There's an Egyptian art collection on display (= being shown) at the museum at the moment.* ○ *a firework display* **2** [C] when something is shown electronically such as on a computer screen: *The display problems might be due to a shortage of disk space.*

display [SHOW] /dɪˈspleɪ/ *verb* [T] to show a feeling: *The British traditionally tend to not display much emotion in public.* **display** /dɪˈspleɪ/ *noun* [C or U] *There's never much (of a) display of affection between them.*

displease /dɪˈspliːz/ *verb* [T] FORMAL to cause someone to be annoyed or unhappy: *I wouldn't want to do anything to displease him.* **displeased** /dɪˈspliːzd/ *adj* **displeasure** /dɪˈspleʒ.ər/ US /-ɚ/ *noun* [U] *Employees have publicly criticized the company's plans, much to the displeasure of the management.*

disport /dɪˈspɔːt/ US /-ˈspɔːrt/ *verb* OLD USE OR HUMOROUS **disport yourself** to amuse yourself, especially by doing physical activity

disposable /dɪˈspəʊ.zə.bl̩/ US /-ˈspoʊ-/ *adj* describes an item that is intended to be thrown away after use: *disposable nappies* ○ *a disposable camera*

disposable /dɪˈspəʊ.zə.bl̩/ US /-ˈspoʊ-/ *noun* [C usually pl] a disposable product, especially a disposable NAPPY: *paper/plastic/medical disposables* ○ *Do you use disposables or washable nappies?*

dis,**posable** '**income** *noun* [U] the money which you can spend as you want and not the money which you spend on taxes, food and other basic needs

dispose /dɪˈspəʊz/ US /-ˈspoʊz/ *verb* FORMAL **dispose sb to/towards sb/sth** to make someone feel a particular way towards someone or something: *His rudeness when*

we first met didn't dispose me very kindly **to/towards** him.

disposed /dɪˈspəʊzd/ US /-ˈspoʊzd/ *adj* FORMAL **1 be disposed to do sth** to be willing or likely to do something: [+ to infinitive] *After all the trouble she put me to, I didn't feel disposed to (= I did not want to) help her.* **2 be well/favourably/etc. disposed to/towards sth/sb** to like or approve of something or someone: *She seems favourably disposed towards the idea.*

▲ **dispose of sb/sth** *phrasal verb* to get rid of someone or something or deal with something so that the matter is finished: *How did they dispose of the body?* ○ *It took a mere five minutes for the world champion to dispose of (= defeat) his opponent.*

disposal /dɪˈspəʊ.zəl/ US /-ˈspoʊ-/ *noun* [U] when you get rid of something, especially by throwing it away: *waste disposal* ○ *the disposal of hazardous substances*

• **at sb's disposal** FORMAL available to be used by someone: *I would take you if I could, but I don't have a car at my disposal this week.* ○ *Having sold the house she had a large sum of money at her disposal (= to spend as she wanted).*

disposition /ˌdɪs.pəˈzɪʃ.ən/ *noun* **1** [C usually sing] the particular type of character which a person naturally has: *She is of a nervous/cheerful/sunny disposition.* **2** [S + to infinitive] FORMAL a natural tendency to do something, or to have or develop something: *a disposition to deceive*

dispossess /ˌdɪs.pəˈzes/ *verb* [T] FORMAL to take property, especially buildings or land, away from someone or a group of people: *A lot of people were dispossessed of their homes during the civil war.* ⊃Compare **repossess**. **dispossessed** /ˌdɪs.pəˈzest/ *adj*

the ,**dispos'sessed** *plural noun* FORMAL dispossessed people: *the poor and the dispossessed* **dispossession** /ˌdɪs.pəˈzeʃ.ən/ *noun* [U]

disproportionate /ˌdɪs.prəˈpɔː.ʃən.ət/ US /-ˈpɔːr-/ *adj* too large or too small in comparison to something else, or not deserving its importance or influence: *There are a disproportionate number of girls in the class.* ○ *The country's great influence in the world is disproportionate to its relatively small size.* **disproportion** /ˌdɪs.prəˈpɔː.ʃən/ US /-ˈpɔːr-/ *noun* [U] FORMAL **disproportionately** /ˌdɪs.prəˈpɔː.ʃən.ət.li/ US /-ˈpɔːr-/ *adv*

disprove /dɪˈspruːv/ *verb* [T] to prove that something is not true: *The allegations have been disproved.*

dispute /dɪˈspjuːt/ /ˈdɪs.pjuːt/ *noun* [C or U] an argument or disagreement, especially an official one between, for example, workers and employers or two bordering countries: *a bitter/long-running dispute* ○ *a border dispute* ○ *a pay/legal/trade dispute* ○ *They have been unable to settle/resolve the dispute over working conditions.* ○ *The unions are in dispute with management over pay.*

• **beyond (all) dispute** certainly: *He is beyond all dispute the finest actor in Hollywood today.*

• **in dispute** being doubted: *I don't think her ability is in dispute, what I question is her attitude.*

• **open to dispute** not certain: *He says it's the best musical equipment you can buy, but I think that's open to dispute.*

dispute /dɪˈspjuːt/ *verb* [I or T] to disagree with something that someone says: *Few would dispute his status as the finest artist of the period.* ○ *The circumstances of her death have been hotly disputed.* ○ [+ (that)] *I don't dispute (that) Lucas' films are entertaining, but they haven't got much depth.* **disputed** /dɪˈspjuː.tɪd/ US /-t̬ɪd/ *adj*: *a disputed border/goal* ○ *disputed territory*

disputable /dɪˈspjuː.tə.bl̩/ US /-t̬ə-/ *adj* not certain: *It's claimed that they produce the best athletes in the world but I think that's disputable.*

disputation /ˌdɪs.pjuˈteɪ.ʃən/ US /-pjuː-/ *noun* [C or U] OLD USE (a) disagreement

disputatious /ˌdɪs.pjuˈteɪ.ʃəs/ US /-pjuː-/ *adj* OLD USE *He's a disputatious young man (= he argues a lot).*

disqualify /dɪˈskwɒl.ɪ.faɪ/ US /-ˈskwɑː.lə-/ *verb* [T] to stop someone from being in a competition or doing something because they are unsuitable or they have done something wrong: *He's been disqualified from driving for a year.* ○ *Two top athletes have been disqualified from the championship after positive drug tests.* **disqualification** /dɪˌskwɒl.ɪ.fɪˈkeɪ.ʃən/ US /-ˌskwɑː.lə-/ *noun* [C or U] *The fans' bad behaviour has resulted in the disqualification of* *their football team* ***from*** *the championship.*

disquieting /dɪˈskwaɪə.tɪŋ/ [US] /-t̬ɪŋ/ *adj* FORMAL causing anxiety: *The disquieting situation between these two neighbouring countries looks set to continue.*

disquiet /dɪˈskwaɪət/ *noun* [U] FORMAL anxiety: *The leader's decline in popularity is causing disquiet among supporters.*

disquisition /ˌdɪs.kwɪˈzɪʃ.ən/ *noun* [C] FORMAL a long and detailed explanation of a particular subject

disregard /ˌdɪs.rɪˈɡɑːd/ [US] /-ˈɡɑːrd/ *noun* [U] lack of consideration or respect for something: *What amazes me is her complete disregard* ***for*** *anyone else's opinion.*

disregard /ˌdɪs.rɪˈɡɑːd/ [US] /-ˈɡɑːrd/ *verb* [T] to ignore something: *He told us to disregard everything we'd learned so far and start again.*

disrepair /ˌdɪs.rɪˈpeəʳ/ [US] /-ˈper/ *noun* [U] the state of being broken or old and needing to be repaired: *The building has* ***fallen into*** *disrepair over the years.*

disreputable /dɪsˈrep.jʊ.tə.bl̩/ [US] /-jə.t̬ə-/ *adj* not trusted or respected; thought to have a bad character: *Some of the more disreputable newspapers made false claims about her private life.* ○ *a disreputable young man*

disreputably /dɪsˈrep.jʊ.tə.bli/ [US] /-jə.t̬ə-/ *adv*

disrepute /ˌdɪs.rɪˈpjuːt/ *noun* [U] the state of not being trusted or respected: *Involvement with terrorist groups* ***brought*** *the political party* ***into*** *disrepute.* ○ *The legal profession has* ***fallen into*** *disrepute.*

disrespect /ˌdɪs.rɪˈspekt/ *noun* [U] **1** lack of respect: *a disrespect for authority* **2 no disrespect to *sb*** used before you criticize someone in order not to sound rude: *No disrespect to Julie, but this department worked perfectly well before she started here.* **disrespectful** /ˌdɪs.rɪˈspekt.fəl/ *adj*: *disrespectful behaviour* **disrespectfully** /ˌdɪs.rɪˈspekt.fəl.i/ *adv*

disrobe /dɪsˈrəʊb/ [US] /-ˈroʊb/ *verb* [I] FORMAL OR HUMOROUS to remove your clothes, especially an outer or ceremonial piece of clothing

disrupt /dɪsˈrʌpt/ *verb* [T] to prevent something, especially a system, process or event, from continuing as usual or as expected: *A heavy fall of snow had disrupted the city's transport system.* ○ *The meeting was disrupted by a group of protesters who shouted and threw fruit at the speaker.* **disruption** /dɪsˈrʌp.ʃən/ *noun* [C or U] *The accident on the main road through town is causing widespread disruption for motorists.*

disruptive /dɪsˈrʌp.tɪv/ *adj* causing trouble and therefore stopping something from continuing as usual: *His teacher described him as a noisy, disruptive* ***influence*** *in class.* **disruptively** /dɪsˈrʌp.tɪv.li/ *adv*

diss, dis /dɪs/ *verb* [T] US SLANG to speak or behave rudely to someone or to show them no respect: *Don't diss me, man!*

dissatisfied /ˌdɪsˈsæt.ɪs.faɪd/ [US] /-ˈsæt̬.əs-/ *adj* not pleased with something; feeling that something is not as good as it should be: *If you're dissatisfied* ***with*** *the service, why don't you complain to the hotel manager?* **dissatisfaction** /dɪsˌsæt.ɪsˈfæk.ʃən/ [US] /ˌdɪs.sæt̬.əs-/ *noun* [U] *At the moment she's experiencing a lot of dissatisfaction* ***with*** *her job.*

dissect /daɪˈsekt/ *verb* [T] **1** to cut open something, especially a dead body or a plant, and study its structure: *In biology classes at school we used to dissect rats.* **2** to examine or consider something in detail: *He's the sort of person who watches a film and then dissects it for hours.* **dissection** /daɪˈsek.ʃən/ *noun* [C or U] *The novel is really a dissection of nationalism.*

dissemble /dɪˈsem.bl̩/ *verb* [I] FORMAL to hide your real intentions and feelings or the facts: *He accused the government of dissembling.*

disseminate /dɪˈsem.ɪ.neɪt/ *verb* [T] FORMAL to spread or give out something, especially news, information, ideas, etc., to a lot of people: *One of the organization's aims is to disseminate information about the disease.* **dissemination** /dɪˌsem.ɪˈneɪ.ʃən/ *noun* [U] *the dissemination of information*

dissension /dɪˈsen.tʃən/ *noun* [U] SLIGHTLY FORMAL arguments and disagreement, especially in an organization, group, political party, etc: *There are signs of dissension* ***within*** *the ruling political party.*

dissent /dɪˈsent/ *noun* [U] SLIGHTLY FORMAL strong difference of opinion on a particular subject; disagreement, especially about an official suggestion or plan or a popular belief: *When the time came to approve the proposal, there were one or two* ***voices of*** *dissent.* ➲Compare **assent**.

dissent /dɪˈsent/ *verb* [I] SLIGHTLY FORMAL to disagree with other people about something: *Anyone wishing to dissent* ***from*** *the motion should now raise their hand.*

dissenter /dɪˈsen.təʳ/ [US] /-t̬ɚ/ *noun* [C] SLIGHTLY FORMAL someone who dissents

dissenting /dɪˈsen.tɪŋ/ [US] /-t̬ɪŋ/ *adj* SLIGHTLY FORMAL *The jury found it an easy decision to make – in fact there was only one dissenting* ***voice*** (= person who disagreed).

dissertation /ˌdɪs.əˈteɪ.ʃən/ [US] /-ɚ-/ *noun* [C] a long piece of writing on a particular subject, especially one that is done as a part of a course at college or university: *Ann did her dissertation* ***on*** *Baudelaire.*

disservice /ˌdɪsˈsɜː.vɪs/ [US] /-ˈsɝː-/ *noun* [S] an action which harms something or someone: *She has* ***done*** *a great disservice* ***to*** *her cause by suggesting that violence is justifiable.*

dissident /ˈdɪs.ɪ.dənt/ *noun* [C] a person who publicly disagrees with and criticizes their government: *political dissidents* **dissident** /ˈdɪs.ɪ.dənt/ *adj*: *a dissident group/writer* **dissidence** /ˈdɪs.ɪ.dənts/ *noun* [U]

dissimilar /ˌdɪsˈsɪm.ɪ.ləʳ/ [US] /-lɚ/ *adj* different: *The new house is* ***not*** *dissimilar* (= is similar) ***to*** *our old one except that it's a bit bigger.*

dissipate /ˈdɪs.ɪ.peɪt/ *verb* [I or T] FORMAL to (cause to) gradually disappear or waste: *The heat gradually dissipates into the atmosphere.* ○ *His anger dissipated as the situation became clear.*

dissipated /ˈdɪs.ɪ.peɪ.tɪd/ [US] /-t̬ɪd/ *adj* FORMAL DISAPPROVING spending too much time enjoying physical pleasures and harmful activities such as drinking too much alcohol: *He recalled his dissipated youth spent in nightclubs and bars.* **dissipation** /ˌdɪs.ɪˈpeɪ.ʃən/ *noun* [U] FORMAL

dissociate /dɪˈsəʊ.ʃi.eɪt/ [US] /-ˈsoʊ-/ *verb* [T] (ALSO **disassociate**) to consider as separate and not related: *I can't dissociate the man* ***from*** *his political opinions – they're one and the same thing.* **dissociation** /dɪˌsəʊ.ʃiˈeɪ.ʃən/ [US] /-ˌsoʊ-/ *noun* [U]

▲ **dissociate *yourself* from *sth*** *phrasal verb* [R] to make it publicly known that you are not in any way connected to, or responsible for someone or something, often to avoid blame or embarrassment: *Most party members are keen to dissociate themselves from the extremists.*

dissolute /ˈdɪs.ə.luːt/ *adj* LITERARY (of a person) living in a way that other people strongly disapprove of; immoral: *He led a dissolute life, drinking and womanising till his death.* **dissolutely** /ˈdɪs.ə.luːt.li/ *adv* **dissoluteness** /ˈdɪs.ə.luːt.nəs/ *noun* [U]

dissolve [BE ABSORBED] /dɪˈzɒlv/ [US] /-ˈzɑːlv/ *verb* [I or T] (of a solid) to be absorbed by a liquid, especially when mixed, or (of a liquid) to absorb a solid: *Dissolve two spoons of powder* ***in*** *warm water.* ○ *Nitric acid will dissolve most animal tissue.*

dissolve [END] /dɪˈzɒlv/ [US] /-ˈzɑːlv/ *verb* **1** [T often passive] to end an official organization or a legal arrangement: *Parliament has been dissolved.* ○ *Their marriage was dissolved in 1968.* **2** [I] to disappear: *The tension in the office just dissolves when she walks out.* **dissolution** /ˌdɪs.əˈluː.ʃən/ *noun* [U] *the dissolution of parliament*

▲ **dissolve into *sth*** *phrasal verb* **dissolve into tears/laughter** to suddenly start to cry or laugh: *When she saw his photograph, she dissolved into tears.*

dissonance /ˈdɪs.ən.ənts/ [US] /-ə.nənts/ *noun* [U] **1** SPECIALIZED a combination of sounds or musical notes that are not pleasant when heard together: *the jarring dissonance of Klein's musical score* **2** FORMAL disagreement **dissonant** /ˈdɪs.ən.ənt/ [US] /-ə.nənt/ *adj* SPECIALIZED OR FORMAL

dissuade /dɪˈsweɪd/ *verb* [T] to persuade someone not to do something: *I tried to dissuade her* ***from*** *leaving.*

distance [SPACE] /ˈdɪs.tənts/ *noun* [C or U] the amount of space between two places: *What's the distance* ***between*** *Madrid and Barcelona/****from*** *Madrid* ***to*** *Barcelona?* ○ *He*

travels quite a distance (= a long way) *to work every day.* ○ *Does she live* ***within walking*** *distance of her parents?*
• **at/from a distance** from a place that is not near: *From a distance he looks a bit like James Bond.*
• **go the distance** to manage to continue until the end of a competition
• **in the distance** at a point which is far away: *On a clear day you can see the temple in the distance.*
• **keep** ***your*** **distance** to avoid going near someone or something, or to avoid getting too friendly with people: *I've tried being friendly but she keeps her distance.*
distant /ˈdɪs.tᵊnt/ *adj* far away: *a distant country* ○ *She could hear the distant sound of fireworks exploding.*
• **in the distant past/future** far away in the past or future: *At some point in the distant future I would like to have my own house.*
• **in the not-too-distant future** quite soon: *They plan to have children in the not-too-distant future.*
distantly /ˈdɪs.tᵊnt.li/ *adv* far away: *He heard, distantly, the sound of the sea.* ○ *They're distantly related.*

distance [MANNER] /ˈdɪs.tᵊnts/ *noun* [S or U] behaviour that shows little interest or friendliness: *I noticed a certain distance* ***between*** *father and son.*
distant /ˈdɪs.tᵊnt/ *adj* describes someone who does not show much emotion and is not friendly: *She seemed cold and distant.*
distantly /ˈdɪs.tᵊnt.li/ *adv* in an unfriendly way, showing no emotion: *Sam smiled, distantly.*

distance /ˈdɪs.tᵊnts/ *verb*
▲ **distance** ***yourself*** **from** ***sth*** *phrasal verb* [R] to become or seem less involved or connected with something: *The leader has recently distanced himself from the extremists in the party.*

ˈdistance ˌlearning *noun* [U] a way of studying, especially for a degree, where you study mostly at home, receiving and sending off work by post

distaste /dɪˈsteɪst/ *noun* [U] a dislike of something which you find unpleasant or immoral: *His distaste* ***for*** *publicity of any sort is well known.* ○ *She looked at the advertisement with distaste before walking quickly on.*
distasteful /dɪˈsteɪst.fᵊl/ *adj*: *He found the subject of their conversation very distasteful.* **distastefully** /dɪˈsteɪst.fᵊl.i/ *adv* **distastefulness** /dɪˈsteɪst.fᵊl.nəs/ *noun* [U]

distemper [PAINT] /dɪˈstem.pəʳ/ [US] /-pɚ/ *noun* [U] a type of paint that is mixed with water and glue, used especially in the past for painting walls

distemper [DISEASE] /dɪˈstem.pəʳ/ [US] /-pɚ/ *noun* [U] a type of infectious disease that can be caught by animals, especially dogs

distend /dɪˈstend/ *verb* [I] (usually of the stomach or other part of the body) to swell and become large (as if) by pressure from inside: *In the refugee centres we saw many children whose stomachs were distended because of lack of food.* **distension** /dɪˈsten.tʃᵊn/ *noun* [U] SPECIALIZED

distil [LIQUID] (-ll-), US USUALLY **distill** /dɪˈstɪl/ *verb* [T] to make a liquid stronger or purer by heating it until it changes to a gas and then cooling it so that it changes back into a liquid: *distilled water* ○ *Some strong alcoholic drinks such as whisky are made by distilling.*
distillation /ˌdɪs.tɪˈleɪ.ʃᵊn/ *noun* [C or U]
distiller /dɪˈstɪl.əʳ/ [US] /-ɚ/ *noun* [C] a person or a company that makes strong alcoholic drinks by the process of distilling
distillery /dɪˈstɪl.ᵊr.i/ [US] /-ɚ.i/ *noun* [C] a factory where strong alcoholic drinks are produced by the process of distilling: *a whisky distillery*

distil [INFORMATION] /dɪˈstɪl/ *verb* [T usually passive] -ll- LITERARY to get or show only the most important part of something: *Over 80 hours of footage have been distilled* ***into*** *these 40 minutes.* **distillation** /ˌdɪs.tɪˈleɪ.ʃᵊn/ *noun* [C or U]

distinct [DIFFERENT] /dɪˈstɪŋkt/ *adj* clearly separate and different (from something else): *The two concepts are quite distinct* ***(from*** *each other).* ○ *There are two distinct factions within the one political party.*
• **as distinct from** rather than: *She's a personal assistant as distinct from a secretary.*

distinct [NOTICEABLE] /dɪˈstɪŋkt/ *adj* [before n] clearly noticeable; that certainly exists: *There's a distinct smell of cigarettes in here.* **distinctly** /dɪˈstɪŋkt.li/ *adv*: *I distinctly remember asking him not to tell her about the new sales figures.*

distinction [DIFFERENCE] /dɪˈstɪŋk.ʃᵊn/ *noun* [C or U] a difference between two similar things: *There's a* ***clear*** *distinction* ***between*** *the dialects spoken in the two regions.* ○ *This company* ***makes*** *no distinction* ***between*** *the sexes.*

distinction [EXCELLENCE] /dɪˈstɪŋk.ʃᵊn/ *noun* **1** [U] excellence: *a writer/scientist/wine* ***of*** *distinction* **2** [C] a mark given to students who produce work of an excellent standard

distinction [SPECIAL] /dɪˈstɪŋk.ʃᵊn/ *noun* [S] the quality of being special or different: *She* ***has the*** *distinction* ***of being*** *one of the few people to have an honorary degree conferred on her by the university this year.*

distinctive /dɪˈstɪŋk.tɪv/ *adj* Something that is distinctive is easy to recognize because it is different from other things: *a distinctive smell/taste* ○ *She's got a very distinctive voice.* **distinctively** /dɪˈstɪŋk.tɪv.li/ *adv* **distinctiveness** /dɪˈstɪŋk.tɪv.nəs/ *noun* [U]

distinguish /dɪˈstɪŋ.gwɪʃ/ *verb* [I or T; not continuous] **1** to notice or understand the difference between two things, or to make one person or thing seem different from another: *He's colour-blind and can't distinguish (the difference)* ***between*** *red and green easily.* ○ *I sometimes have difficulty distinguishing Spanish* ***from*** *Portuguese.* ○ *It's important to distinguish* ***between*** *business and pleasure.* ○ *It's not the beauty so much as the range of his voice that distinguishes him* ***from*** *other tenors.* **2** **distinguish** ***yourself*** to do something so well that you are admired and praised for it: *He distinguished himself in British theatre at a very early age.* **distinguishable** /dɪˈstɪŋ.gwɪ.ʃə.bl/ *adj*: *There are at least twenty distinguishable dialects of the language just on the south island.*
distinguishing /dɪˈstɪŋ.gwɪ.ʃɪŋ/ *adj*: *The main distinguishing* (= different and noticeable) ***feature*** *of the new car is its fast acceleration.*

distinguished /dɪˈstɪŋ.gwɪʃt/ *adj* **1** describes a respected and admired person, or their work: *a distinguished writer/director/politician* ○ *a distinguished career* **2** describes a person, especially an older person, who looks formal, stylish or wise: *I think grey hair on a man can look very distinguished.*

distort /dɪˈstɔːt/ [US] /-ˈstɔːrt/ *verb* [T] to change something from its usual, original, natural or intended meaning, condition or shape: *My original statement has been completely distorted by the media.* **distorted** /dɪˈstɔː.tɪd/ [US] /-ˈstɔːr.t̬ɪd/ *adj*: *This report gives a somewhat distorted impression of what actually happened.* ○ *The music just gets distorted when you play it so loud.* ○ *His face was distorted in agony.* **distortion** /dɪˈstɔː.ʃᵊn/ [US] /-ˈstɔːr-/ *noun* [C or U] *a gross distortion* ***of*** *the facts*

distract /dɪˈstrækt/ *verb* [T] to make someone stop giving their attention to something: *Don't distract her* ***(from*** *her studies).* ○ *He tried to distract* ***attention from*** *his own illegal activities.* **distracting** /dɪˈstræk.tɪŋ/ *adj*: *Please turn your music down – it's very distracting.* **distraction** /dɪˈstræk.ʃᵊn/ *noun* [C or U] *I can turn the television off if you find it a distraction.* ➲See also **distraction** at **distracted**.

distracted /dɪˈstræk.tɪd/ *adj* nervous, anxious or confused because you are worried about something: *Gill seems rather distracted at the moment – I think she's worried about her exams.* **distractedly** /dɪˈstræk.tɪd.li/ *adv*
distraction /dɪˈstræk.ʃᵊn/ *noun* [U] *His lessons bore me* ***to*** *distraction* (= bore me very much). ○ *That dreadful noise is* ***driving*** *me* ***to*** *distraction* (= annoying me so much that it will make me angry). ➲See also **distraction** at **distract**.

distraught /dɪˈstrɔːt/ [US] /-ˈstrɑːt/ *adj* extremely worried, anxious or upset: *The missing child's distraught parents made an emotional appeal for information on TV.*

distress /dɪˈstres/ *noun* [U] **1** a feeling of extreme worry, sadness or pain: *She claimed that the way she had been treated at work had caused her extreme emotional and psychological distress.* ○ *Many of the horses were showing signs of distress at the end of the race.* **2** when you are suffering or are in great danger and therefore in urgent need of help: *Six people were rescued by helicopter from a fishing boat* **in** *distress off the Cornish coast.* ○ *a distress* **signal**

distress /dɪˈstres/ *verb* [T] to make someone feel very upset or worried: *I hope I haven't distressed you with all these personal questions.*

distressed /dɪˈstrest/ *adj*: *She was* **deeply** *distressed by the news of his death.* ○ *The government is taking steps to stimulate business development in* **(economically)** *distressed areas* (= those in economic difficulty). **distressing** /dɪˈstres.ɪŋ/ *adj* (US USUALLY **distressful**) *The television reports about the famine were particularly distressing.* ○ *It was* **deeply** *distressing for him* **to** *see his wife in such pain.* **distressingly** /dɪˈstres.ɪŋ.li/ *adv*

distribute /dɪˈstrɪb.juːt/ /ˈdɪs.trɪ.bjuːt/ [US] /-jʊt/ *verb* [T] to give something out to several people, or to spread or supply something: *The books will be distributed free* **to** *local schools.* ○ *Several people were arrested for distributing racist leaflets/pamphlets* **(to** *the spectators).* ○ *The company aims eventually to distribute* (= supply for sale) *its products* **throughout** *the European Union.*

distribution /ˌdɪs.trɪˈbjuː.ʃᵊn/ *noun* [C or U] *We must find a way of achieving* **a** *more* **equitable** *distribution* (= sharing) *of resources/wealth.* ○ *Has the Channel Tunnel improved the distribution* (= supplying for sale) **of** *goods* **between** *the British Isles and mainland Europe?* ○ *an unfair distribution of wealth* ○ *distribution costs*

distributor [GOODS] /dɪˈstrɪb.jʊ.təʳ/ [US] /-jə.t̬ɚ/ *noun* [C] a person or organization that supplies goods to shops and companies: *a film distributor*

distributor [ENGINE] /dɪˈstrɪb.jʊ.təʳ/ [US] /-jə.t̬ɚ/ *noun* [C] a device in a petrol engine which sends electricity to each of the SPARK PLUGS (= devices which cause the engine to start) in the necessary order

district /ˈdɪs.trɪkt/ *noun* [C] an area of a country or town which has fixed borders that are used for official purposes, or which has a particular feature that makes it different from surrounding areas: *South Cambridgeshire District Council* ○ *the fashion district of New York* ○ *the Lake District/the Peak District*

ˌdistrict atˈtorney *noun* [C] (ABBREVIATION **DA**) a lawyer whose job is to represent the government in a particular area of the US

ˌdistrict ˈnurse *noun* [C] UK a person who is employed in a particular area to care for people who are ill or injured, often visiting them in their homes

distrust /dɪˈstrʌst/ *noun* [U] when you do not trust someone or something: *The two groups have existed in a state of* **mutual** *distrust for centuries.* ○ *She has* **a (deep)** *distrust of journalists.* **distrust** /dɪˈstrʌst/ *verb* [T] *In spite of its election success, the government is still* **deeply** *distrusted on key health and education issues.* **distrustful** /dɪˈstrʌst.fᵊl/ *adj*

disturb [INTERRUPT] /dɪˈstɜːb/ [US] /-ˈstɝːb/ *verb* [T] to interrupt what someone is doing: *Please don't disturb Georgina – she's trying to do her homework.* ○ *I'm sorry to disturb you so late, but my car's broken down and I was wondering if I could use your phone.*

• **disturb the peace** to break the law by behaving unpleasantly and noisily in public: *Several England supporters were arrested and charged with disturbing the peace after the match.*

disturbance /dɪˈstɜː.bᵊnts/ [US] /-ˈstɝː-/ *noun* [C or U] *Residents are fed up with the disturbance caused by the nightclub.* ○ *Phone calls are the biggest disturbance at work.* ○ *There was a minor disturbance* (= violent event in public) *during the demonstration, but nobody was injured.*

• **cause a disturbance** to break the law by fighting or behaving extremely noisily in public

disturb [WORRY] /dɪˈstɜːb/ [US] /-ˈstɝːb/ *verb* [T] to cause someone to be anxious or upset: *Some scenes are violent and may disturb younger viewers.*

disturbing /dɪˈstɜː.bɪŋ/ [US] /-ˈstɝː-/ *adj* making you feel worried or upset: *The Home Secretary described the latest crime figures as 'disturbing'.* ○ *The following programme contains scenes that may be disturbing* **to** *some viewers.* **disturbingly** /dɪˈstɜː.bɪŋ.li/ [US] /-ˈstɝː-/ *adv*: *Pollution has reached disturbingly high levels in some urban areas.*

disturb [MOVE] /dɪˈstɜːb/ [US] /-ˈstɝːb/ *verb* [T] to move or change something from its usual position, arrangement, condition or shape: *The thief had disturbed the documents in her filing cabinet, but nothing had been taken.*

disturbed /dɪˈstɜːbd/ [US] /-ˈstɝːbd/ *adj* not thinking or behaving normally because of mental or emotional problems: *a centre for* **emotionally/mentally** *disturbed teenagers*

disunite /ˌdɪs.juːˈnaɪt/ *verb* [T] to cause people to disagree so much that they can no longer work together effectively: *A publicly disunited party stands little chance of winning the election.* **disunity** /dɪˈsjuː.nɪ.ti/ [US] /-nə.t̬i/ *noun* [U]

disuse /dɪˈsjuːs/ *noun* [U] the condition of not being used (any longer): *The church was recently restored after decades of disuse.* **disused** /dɪˈsjuːzd/ *adj*: *Many disused railway lines have become public footpaths.*

disyllabic /ˌdaɪ.sɪˈlæb.ɪk/ *adj* SPECIALIZED (of a word) having two syllables

ditch [CHANNEL] /dɪtʃ/ *noun* [C] a long narrow open channel dug into the ground usually at the side of a road or field, which is used especially for supplying or removing water, or for dividing land

ditch [GET RID OF] /dɪtʃ/ *verb* [T] INFORMAL to get rid of something or someone that is no longer wanted: *The getaway car had been ditched a couple of kilometres away from the scene of the robbery.* ○ *Did you know that Sarah has ditched* (= ended her relationship with) *her boyfriend?*

ditch [AIRCRAFT] /dɪtʃ/ *verb* [I or T] to land an aircraft in water in an emergency

dither /ˈdɪð.əʳ/ [US] /-ɚ/ *verb* [I] DISAPPROVING to be unable to make a decision about doing something: *Stop dithering and choose which one you want!* ○ *She's still dithering* **over** *whether to accept the job she's just been offered.*

dither /ˈdɪð.əʳ/ [US] /-ɚ/ *noun* DISAPPROVING **be in a dither about sth** to be very nervous, excited or confused about something: *Gideon is in a bit of a dither about what to wear for the interview.* **ditherer** /ˈdɪð.ə.rəʳ/ [US] /-ɚ.ɚ/ *noun* [C]

ditransitive /ˌdaɪˈtrænt.sə.tɪv/ [US] /-t̬ɪv/ *adj* SPECIALIZED describes a verb which can be followed by two objects, one of which has the action of the verb done to it and the other of which has the action of the verb directed towards it. In this dictionary, ditransitive verbs are shown with the label [+ two objects]: *In the sentence 'I sent Victoria a letter', 'send' is ditransitive.*

ˈditto (ˌmark) *noun* [C usually sing] a symbol (") which means 'the same' and is used in a list to avoid writing again the word which is written immediately above it

ditto /ˈdɪt.əʊ/ [US] /ˈdɪt̬.oʊ/ *adv* used to agree with something that has just been said, or to avoid repeating something that has been said: *"I hate these reality TV shows" "Ditto. What's on the other side?"* ○ *Local residents are opposed to the proposal. Ditto many members of the council* (= They are also).

ditty /ˈdɪt.i/ [US] /ˈdɪt̬-/ *noun* [C] a short simple song

diuretic /ˌdaɪ.jʊəˈret.ɪk/ [US] /-jəˈret̬-/ *noun* [C] SPECIALIZED a substance which causes an increase in the production of urine **diuretic** /ˌdaɪ.jʊəˈret.ɪk/ [US] /-jəˈret̬-/ *adj*

diurnal /ˌdaɪˈɜː.nəl/ [US] /-ˈɝː-/ *adj* SPECIALIZED happening over a period of a day, or being active or happening during the day rather than at night ➲Compare **nocturnal**. **diurnally** /ˌdaɪˈɜː.nə.li/ [US] /-ˈɝː-/ *adv*

div /dɪv/ *noun* UK INFORMAL a **divvy**

diva /ˈdiː.və/ *noun* [C] a very successful and famous female singer: *an Italian opera diva* ○ *a pop diva*

Divali /dɪˈvɑː.li/ *noun* [C or U] DIWALI (= a Hindu festival)

divan /dɪˈvæn/ *noun* [C] **1** a sofa with no back or arms **2** (ALSO **divan bed**) UK a bed consisting of a mattress and a base, with no boards at either end

dive [MOVE DOWN] /daɪv/ *verb* [I] **dived** or US ALSO **dove, dived** or US ALSO **dove 1** to jump into water, especially with your head and arms going in first, or to move down under the water: *Look at those children diving* **for** *oysters over there!* ○ *They ran to the pool, dived* **in**, *and swam to the other side.* ○ *Mark dived* **off** *the bridge* **into**

D

the river. ○ *The submarine dived just in time to avoid the enemy attack.* **Ɔ**See also **nosedive**. **2** to swim under water, usually with breathing equipment **3** to go down very quickly: *The plane dived towards the ground and exploded in a ball of flame.* ○ *The goalkeeper dived for the ball* (= tried to catch the ball by jumping towards it and falling on the ground.)

dive /daɪv/ *noun* [C] *the best dive of the competition* ○ *The goalkeeper made a valiant dive for* (= jump towards) *the ball, but couldn't stop it going in the net.*

diver /ˈdaɪ.vəʳ/ ⓤ /-vɚ/ *noun* [C] a person who dives as a sport, or who works or searches for things under water using special breathing equipment: *He was a diver on a North Sea oil rig.* **diving** /ˈdaɪ.vɪŋ/ *noun* [U]

dive BECOME LESS /daɪv/ *verb* [I] **dived** or *US ALSO* **dove, dived** or *US ALSO* **dove** to fall in value suddenly and by a large amount: *The company's shares dived by 90p to 165p on the stock market yesterday.* **dive** /daɪv/ *noun* [S] *The firm's profits took a dive last month.*

dive MOVE QUICKLY /daɪv/ *verb* [I or T] **dived** or *US ALSO* **dove, dived** or *US ALSO* **dove** to move quickly, often in order to avoid something: *They dived for cover when they heard the shooting start.* **dive** /daɪv/ *noun* [S]

dive PLACE /daɪv/ *noun* [C] *INFORMAL* a restaurant, hotel, bar or place for entertainment or social activities that is unpleasant because of the condition of the building or the type of people that go there: *I know this place is a bit of a dive, but the drink's cheap and the food's great.*

▲ **dive in/dive into** *sth phrasal verb* to start doing something suddenly and energetically, often without stopping to think: *If neighbouring countries are having a war, you can't just dive in.*

ˈdive ˌbomber *noun* [C] a military aircraft designed to dive quickly before dropping its bombs on a target
dive-bomb /ˈdaɪv.bɒm/ ⓤ /-bɑːm/ *verb* [I or T] to drop bombs on something or someone from a dive bomber

diverge /ˌdaɪˈvɜːdʒ/ ⓤ /dɪˈvɝːdʒ/ *verb* [I] to follow a different direction, or to be or become different: *They walked along the road together until they reached the village, but then their paths diverged.* ○ *Although the two organizations have worked together for many years, their objectives have diverged recently.* ✳ NOTE: The opposite is **converge**. **divergence** /ˌdaɪˈvɜː.dʒ°nts/ ⓤ /dɪˈvɝː-/ *noun* [C or U] *The divergence between the incomes of the rich and the poor countries seems to be increasing.* ○ *Recently published figures show a divergence from previous trends.* **divergent** /ˌdaɪˈvɜː.dʒ°nt/ ⓤ /dɪˈvɝː-/ *adj: They hold widely divergent opinions on controversial issues like abortion.*

divers /ˈdaɪ.vəz/ ⓤ /-vɚz/ *adj* [before n] *OLD USE* various or several

diverse /daɪˈvɜːs/ ⓤ /dɪˈvɝːs/ *adj* varied or different: *Students from countries as diverse as Colombia and Lithuania use Cambridge textbooks when they learn English.* ○ *New York is a very culturally/ethnically diverse city.*

diversify /daɪˈvɜː.sɪ.faɪ/ ⓤ /dɪˈvɝː-/ *verb* **1** [I] to become more varied or different: *Millions of years ago, changes in the Earth's climate caused animal and plant life to diversify.* **2** [I or T] If a business diversifies, it starts making new products or offering new services: *Many wheat farmers have begun to diversify into other forms of agriculture.* **diversification** /daɪˌvɜː.sɪ.fɪˈkeɪ.ʃ°n/ ⓤ /dɪˌvɝː-/ *noun* [U]

diversity /daɪˈvɜː.sɪ.ti/ ⓤ /dɪˈvɝː.sə.t̬i/ *noun* [S or U] when many different types of things or people are included in something: *Does television adequately reflect the ethnic and cultural diversity of the country?* ○ *There is a wide diversity of opinion on the question of unilateral disarmament.*

divert CHANGE DIRECTION /daɪˈvɜːt/ ⓤ /dɪˈvɝːt/ *verb* [T] **1** to cause something or someone to change direction: *Traffic will be diverted through the side streets while the main road is resurfaced.* ○ *Our flight had to be diverted to Stansted because of the storm.* **2** to use something for a different purpose: *Should more funds/money/ resources be diverted from roads into railways?*

diversion /daɪˈvɜː.ʃ°n/ ⓤ /dɪˈvɝː-/ *noun* **1** [C] *UK* (*US* **detour**) a different route that is used because a road is

closed: *Traffic diversions will be kept to a minimum throughout the festival.* **2** [C or U] when something is sent somewhere different from where it was originally intended to go: *the diversion of money to other projects*

divert TAKE ATTENTION AWAY /daɪˈvɜːt/ ⓤ /dɪˈvɝːt/ *verb* [T] **1** to take someone's attention away from something: *The war has diverted attention (away) from the country's economic problems.* **2** *FORMAL* to entertain someone: *It's a marvellous game for diverting restless children on long car journeys.*

diversion /daɪˈvɜː.ʃ°n/ ⓤ /dɪˈvɝː-/ *noun* [C] **1** something that takes your attention away from something else: *Shoplifters often work in pairs, with one creating a diversion* (= an action that takes someone's attention away from something) *to distract the shop assistants while the other steals the goods.* **2** *FORMAL* an activity you do for entertainment: *Reading is a pleasant diversion.* **diversionary** /daɪˈvɜː.ʃ°n.°r.i/ ⓤ /dɪˈvɝː.ʒ°n.er.i/ *adj: The proposal was dismissed as a diversionary tactic intended to distract attention from the real problems.*

divest /daɪˈvest/ *verb* [I or T] *MAINLY US* to sell something, especially a business or a part of a business: *The company is divesting its less profitable business operations.* ○ [R] *She has divested herself of* (= sold) *some of her share-holdings.*

▲ **divest sb of** *sth phrasal verb FORMAL* to take something off or away from someone or yourself: *There is a growing movement to divest the monarchy of its remaining constitutional power.* ○ [R] *She divested herself of her cumbersome attire.*

divide SEPARATE /dɪˈvaɪd/ *verb* **1** [I or T] to (cause to) separate into parts or groups: *At the end of the lecture, I'd like all the students to divide into small discussion groups.* ○ *After World War Two, Germany was divided into two separate countries.* **2** [T] to share: *I think we should divide (up) the costs equally among/between us.* **3** [T] If something divides two areas, it marks the edge or limit of them: *There's a narrow alley which divides our house from the one next door.* ○ *This path marks the dividing line between my land and my neighbour's.* **4** [T] to use different amounts of something for different purposes or activities: *She divides her time between her apartment in New York and her cottage in Yorkshire.* **5** [T often passive] to cause a group of people to disagree about something: *The party is divided on/over the issue of capital punishment.*

● **divide and rule** when you keep yourself in a position of power by causing disagreements among other people so that they are unable to question your power
divide /dɪˈvaɪd/ *noun* [C] a difference or separation: *Because of debt repayments, the divide between rich and poor countries is continuing to grow.*

divide CALCULATE /dɪˈvaɪd/ *verb* **1** **divide sth by sth** to calculate the number of times by which one number fits (exactly) into another: *10 divided by 5 is/equals 2.* **Ɔ**Compare **multiply**; **subtract**. **2** **divide (sth) into sth** If a number divides into another number, it fits (exactly) into it when multiplied a particular number of times: *What do you get if you divide 6 into 18?* ○ *2 divides into 10 five times.* **divisible** /dɪˈvɪz.ɪ.bl̩/ *adj* (*US ALSO* **dividable**) *A prime number is a whole number greater than 1 which is exactly divisible by itself and 1 but no other number.* **division** /dɪˈvɪʒ.°n/ *noun* [U] when you calculate how many times one number goes into another **divisor** /dɪˈvaɪ.zəʳ/ ⓤ /-zɚ/ *noun* [C] *When you divide 21 by 7, 7 is the divisor.*

diˌvided ˈhighway *noun* [C] *US FOR* **dual carriageway**
dividend /ˈdɪv.ɪ.dend/ /-dənd/ *noun* [C] (a part of) the profit of a company that is paid to the people who own shares in it: *Dividends will be sent to shareholders on March 31.*

dividers /dɪˈvaɪ.dəz/ ⓤ /-dɚz/ *plural noun UK* a piece of equipment used in mathematics consisting of two parts which are joined at one end and have sharp points at the other and which are used for measuring lines and angles and for marking positions along lines

divine GOD-LIKE /dɪˈvaɪn/ *adj* connected with a god, or like a god: *The Ayatollah described the earthquake in Iran as a divine test.* ○ *Some fans seem to regard* *footballers as divine beings.* ○ *England have fallen so far behind in the championship that their only hope of victory is divine* ***intervention*** (= help from God). ○ *Just because you've been promoted that doesn't give you a divine* ***right*** (= one like that of a god) *to tell us all what to do.*

divine [SPLENDID] /dɪˈvaɪn/ *adj OLD-FASHIONED* extremely good, pleasant or enjoyable: *We had a perfectly divine time in Switzerland.* ○ *Their new house is quite divine!* **divinely** /dɪˈvaɪn.li/ *adv*

divine [GUESS] /dɪˈvaɪn/ *verb* [T] to guess something: [+ *that*] *I divined* ***from*** *his grim expression* ***that*** *the news was not good.*

divination /ˌdɪv.ɪˈneɪ.ʃən/ *noun* [U] the skill or act of saying what will happen in the future or discovering something that is unknown or secret by magical methods

divine [SEARCH] /dɪˈvaɪn/ *verb* [I or T] to search for water or minerals underground by holding horizontally in your hands a Y-shaped rod or stick, the end of which suddenly points down slightly when water or minerals are below it: *a divining* ***rod***

diviner /dɪˈvaɪ.nəʳ/ [US] /-nɚ/ *noun* [C] (*ALSO* **dowser**) a person who divines for water or minerals

diving /ˈdaɪ.vɪŋ/ *noun* [U] ➲See at **dive** MOVE DOWN.

ˈdiving ˌbell *noun* [C] a bell-shaped metal container without a base which is supplied with air so that a person can work in deep water

ˈdiving ˌboard *noun* [C] a (high) board that sticks out over a swimming pool, from which people can dive into water below

divinity /dɪˈvɪn.ɪ.ti/ [US] /-ə.t̬i/ *noun* **1** [U] the state of being a god: *How can you be a Christian and dispute the divinity of Jesus?* **2** [C] a god or goddess **3** *OLD-FASHIONED* **Divinity** the study of religion: *She has a Doctorate in Divinity from York University.*

divisible /dɪˈvɪz.ɪ.bl̩/ *adj* ➲See at **divide** CALCULATE.

division /dɪˈvɪʒ.ən/ *noun* **1** [U] when something is separated into parts or groups, or the way that it is separated: *the equal division of labour between workers* **2** [C] a separate part of an army or large organization: *the sales division* **3** [C or U] when people disagree about something: *Disagreements about defence cuts have opened up* ***deep*** *divisions* (= disagreements) ***within*** *the military.* ○ *Division* (= Disagreement) ***within*** *the party will limit its chances at the election.* **4** [C] a group of teams which play against each other in a particular sport: *Norwich are currently top of Division one.* **divisional** /dɪˈvɪʒ.ən.əl/ *adj*: *the divisional commander/headquarters*

diˈvision ˌlobby *noun* [C] *UK SPECIALIZED* one of two rooms to which a British Member of Parliament must go according to whether they are voting for or against a suggested law

diˌvision of ˈlabour *noun* [U] a way of organizing work, especially making things, so that it is done as a set of separate processes by different (groups of) people: *Society is challenging the traditional sexual division of labour.*

divisive /dɪˈvaɪ.sɪv/ *adj* describes something that causes great and sometimes unfriendly disagreement within a group of people: *The Vietnam war was an extremely divisive issue in the US.* **divisively** /dɪˈvaɪ.sɪv.li/ *adv* **divisiveness** /dɪˈvaɪ.sɪv.nəs/ *noun* [U]

divorce [PEOPLE] /dɪˈvɔːs/ [US] /-ˈvɔːrs/ *verb* [I or T] to end your marriage by an official or legal process: *She's divorcing her husband.*

divorce /dɪˈvɔːs/ [US] /-ˈvɔːrs/ *noun* [C or U] when a marriage is ended by an official or legal process: *The last I heard they were* ***getting a*** *divorce.* ○ *Divorce is on the increase.* ○ *Ellie wants a divorce.* ○ *What are the chances of a marriage* ***ending in*** *divorce?*

divorced /dɪˈvɔːst/ [US] /-ˈvɔːrst/ *adj* married in the past but not now married: *She's divorced.* ○ *They* ***got*** *divorced after only six months of marriage.*

divorcee /dɪˌvɔːˈsiː/ [US] /dəˌvɔːrˈseɪ/ *noun* [C] someone who is divorced and who has not married again

divorce [SUBJECTS] /dɪˈvɔːs/ [US] /-ˈvɔːrs/ *verb* [T] to separate two subjects: *How can you divorce the issues of environmental protection and overpopulation?*

divorce /dɪˈvɔːs/ [US] /-ˈvɔːrs/ *noun* [C] *FORMAL* a separation: *Why is there such a divorce* ***between*** *the arts and the sciences in this country's schools?*

divorced /dɪˈvɔːst/ [US] /-ˈvɔːrst/ *adj* not based on or affected by something: *Sometimes politicians seem to be divorced* ***from*** *reality.*

divulge /daɪˈvʌldʒ/ *verb* [T] to make something secret known: *Journalists do not divulge their sources.* ○ [+ question word] *The managing director refused to divulge* ***how*** *much she earned.*

divvy /ˈdɪv.i/ *noun* [C] (*ALSO* **div**) *UK INFORMAL* a stupid person: *Don't be such a divvy!*

divvy /ˌdɪv.i/ *verb*

▲ **divvy *sth* up** *phrasal verb* [M] *MAINLY US INFORMAL* to share something between a number of people: *They haven't yet decided how to divvy up the proceeds from the sale.*

Diwali, **Divali** /dɪˈwɑː.li/ *noun* [C or U] a Hindu festival in October/November that is a celebration of light and of hopes for the following year

dixieland /ˈdɪk.si.lænd/ *noun* [U] a style of traditional jazz music with a two-beat rhythm, which originally began in New Orleans in the US in the 1920s

DIY /ˌdiː.aɪˈwaɪ/ *noun* [U] *UK ABBREVIATION FOR* do-it-yourself: the activity of decorating or repairing your home, or making things for your home yourself, rather than paying someone else to do it for you: *a DIY enthusiast* ○ *a DIY superstore*

dizzy [FEELING] /ˈdɪz.i/ *adj* feeling as if everything is spinning round and being unable to balance and about to fall down: *You'll make yourself dizzy spinning around like that!* ○ *Going without sleep for a long time makes me feel dizzy and light-headed.* ○ *I felt quite dizzy* ***with*** *excitement as I went up to collect the award.*

• **the dizzy heights of *sth*** *HUMOROUS* a very important position: *Do you think Tess will* ***reach*** *the dizzy heights of Senior Editor before she's 30?*

dizzily /ˈdɪz.ɪ.li/ *adv* in a dizzy way or a way that makes you feel dizzy: *The skyscrapers towered dizzily above us.*

dizziness /ˈdɪz.ɪ.nəs/ *noun* [U]

dizzying /ˈdɪz.i.ɪŋ/ *adj* causing you to feel dizzy: *a dizzying display of acrobatics*

dizzy [QUALITY] /ˈdɪz.i/ *adj* **1** [before n] confusing and very fast: *Who could have predicted the dizzy* ***pace*** *of change in the country?* **2** *INFORMAL* describes a person who is silly, especially a woman: *In the film, she played the part of a dizzy* ***blonde***. **dizzily** /ˈdɪz.ɪ.li/ *adv*

dizzying /ˈdɪz.i.ɪŋ/ *adj* very fast or confusing: *The dizzying* ***pace*** *of political change in the country caught many people by surprise.* **dizzyingly** /ˈdɪz.i.ɪŋ.li/ *adv*

DJ [PERSON], **deejay** /ˌdiːˈdʒeɪ/ /ˈ--/ *noun* [C] *ABBREVIATION FOR* **disc jockey**

DJ [CLOTHING] /ˈdiː.dʒeɪ/ *noun* [C] *UK ABBREVIATION FOR* **dinner jacket**

DMs /ˌdiːˈemz/ *plural noun ABBREVIATION FOR* **Dr Martens**

DNA /ˌdiː.enˈeɪ/ *noun* [U] *SPECIALIZED* deoxyribonucleic acid: the chemical at the centre of the cells of living things, which controls the structure and purpose of each cell and carries the genetic information during reproduction

do [FOR QUESTIONS/NEGATIVES] *WEAK* /də, du/, *STRONG* /duː/ *auxiliary verb* **did, done** used with another verb to form questions and negative sentences, including negative orders, and sometimes in AFFIRMATIVE sentences for reasons of style: *Where do you work?* ○ *What does she like to eat?* ○ *Why did you do that?* ○ *Why don't we have lunch together on Friday?* ○ *Doesn't Matthew look old these days?* ○ *"Didn't you realise she was deaf?" "No I didn't."/"Of course I did."* ○ *Not only did I speak to her, I even got her autograph!* ○ *FORMAL Never did I hear such a terrible noise.* ○ *Don't (you) speak to me like that!* ○ *UK Don't let's argue about it* (= Let's not argue about it). ○ *FORMAL So quietly did she speak* (= She spoke so quietly) *that I could scarcely hear her.* ○ ***Little*** *does he know* (= He knows nothing about it),

D

D

Forms of the verb **to do**.

This is a table of all the usual forms of the irregular verb **to do**.

present tense	past tense
I do	I did
you do	you did
he/she/it does	he/she/it did
we do	we did
you do	you did
they do	they did

past participle

done	I have done my homework.

present participle

doing	I am doing my homework

short negative forms

don't	doesn't	didn't

Don't you want any cake?

---

but we're flying to Geneva next weekend to celebrate his birthday. ○ *"I want three cakes, two chocolate bars and an ice cream." "Do you now/indeed? (= That is surprising or unreasonable)."*

do FOR EMPHASIS /duː/ *auxiliary verb* [+ infinitive without *to*] did used to give extra force to the main verb: *Do shut up, Georgia, and get on with your homework.* ○ *Do write and let me know how you're getting on.* ○ *"Can I buy stamps here?" "Well, we do sell them, but we haven't got any at the moment."* ○ *He cooks a lot does Alex. He does far more than me.*

do TO AVOID REPEATING *WEAK* /də, dʊ/, *STRONG* /duː/ *auxiliary verb* did, done **1** used to avoid repeating a verb or verb phrase: *She runs much faster than he does.* ○ *Maria looks much healthier than she did.* ○ *"I don't like intense heat." "Nor/Neither do I."* ○ *"I hate intense heat." "So do I."* ○ *"You left your umbrella." "So I did. I'm becoming so forgetful these days."* ○ *"Would you mind tidying up the kitchen?" (MAINLY UK) "I have done already./I already have done."* ○ *"May I join you?" "Please do!"* ○ *"Who said that?" "I did."* ○ *"Tilly speaks fluent Japanese." "Does she really?"* ○ *"I thought I'd take a day off school today." "Oh no you don't (= I'm not going to let you do that)!"* **2** used instead of the main verb in questions that are added to the end of a sentence to check information: *You met him at our dinner party, didn't you?* ○ *You don't understand the question, do you?* **3** used instead of the main verb in questions that are added to the end of a sentence as a way of expressing surprise: *So Susannah and Guy finally got married, did they?*

do PERFORM /duː/ *verb* [T] did, done **1** to perform, take part in or achieve something: *That was a really stupid thing to do.* ○ *Why were you sent home from school early? What have you done now?* ○ *What are you doing over the weekend?* ○ *The only thing we can do now is wait and see what happens.* ○ *You should be able to do it by yourself/on your own.* ○ *What have you done (= caused to happen) to her?* ○ *What (on earth) were you doing in the library (= Why were you there and what action were you performing) at two o'clock in the morning?* ○ *What are these toys doing here (= Why are they here)?* ○ *What do you do (for a living) (= What is your job)?* ○ *What can I do for you (= How can I help you)?* ○ *What have you done with (= Where have you put) my coat? Have you hidden it?* ○ *She just hasn't known what to do with herself (= how to keep herself busy) since she retired.* **2 do sth about sth** to take action to deal with something: *It's a global problem – what can individuals do about it?*

• **do well/badly by *sb*** FORMAL to treat someone well or badly

• **do something/nothing, etc. for/to *sb*** INFORMAL to have/not have a strong and positive effect on someone, or to be/not be something or someone that they like or enjoy: *Watching that film really did something to me.* ○ *You really do something for me (= I find you sexually attractive), you know.* ○ *Chopin has never really done it/anything for me.*

• **do it** INFORMAL to have sex

• **That does it!** said when someone or something goes beyond the limit of what is acceptable: *That does it! I will not tolerate that sort of behaviour in this class.*

• **That's done it!** INFORMAL said when someone or something has caused damage or a difficulty: *"That's done it!" said Anna as she looked at the damage. "Now I really will have to get a new car."*

• **to do with** connected with: *"Why did you want to talk to me?" "Well, it's to do with a complaint that's been made about your work."* ○ *"But I didn't have any money." "What has that got to do with it? You still shouldn't have taken my purse without asking me."* ○ *She's refused to have anything (more) to do with him since he was arrested for drinking and driving.* ○ *"I thought I should tell you I saw your son smoking today." "Mind your own business, would you? It has nothing to do with you what my son does!"*

• **What's done is done.** SAYING said when you cannot change something that has already happened

doable /ˈduː.ə.bl̩/ *adj* If something is doable, it can be achieved or performed: *This project may be difficult, but I still think it's doable.*

doer /ˈduː.ər/ US /-ɚ/ *noun* [C] ◆someone who gets actively involved in something, rather than just thinking or talking about it: *There are too many thinkers and not enough doers in this office.*

do's /duːz/ *plural noun* **do's and don'ts** rules about actions and activities which people should or should not perform or take part in: *At my school we had to put up with a lot of do's and don'ts that were completely pointless.*

do or **make**?

Do usually means to perform an activity or job.

I should do more exercise.

~~I should make more exercise.~~

Make usually means to create or produce something.

Did you make the dress yourself ?

~~Did you do the dress yourself?~~

---

do ACT /duː/ *verb* [I or T] did, done to act or take action: *Stop arguing with me, Daryl, and do as you're told!* ○ *She told me not to ask any questions, just to do as she did.* ○ *"Was it wrong of me to go to the police?" "Oh no, I'm sure you did right/did the right thing."* ○ *You'd do well to take some professional advice on this matter.*

doing /ˈduː.ɪŋ/ *noun* [U] *Is this your doing? (= Did you do this?)* ○ *It was none of my doing.* ○ *Running a marathon takes some/a lot of doing (= is difficult to do and needs a lot of effort).* ◆See also **deed** ACTION.

doings /ˈduː.ɪŋz/ *plural noun: We'd like the doings (= activities) of government ministers to be more public.*

do DEAL WITH /duː/ *verb* did, done **1** [T] to deal with; to be responsible for: *Lucia is going to do the publicity for the school play.* ○ *If they ask any awkward questions, just let me do the talking.* **2** [I] If you say that you have done with something or someone, or have done performing a particular action, you mean that you have finished what you were doing with something or someone, or what you were saying to someone, or that you have finished the action: *Have you done with those scissors yet?* ○ *Where the hell are you going? I haven't done with you yet.* ○ [+ v-ing] *I haven't done talking to you yet.*

• **can't be doing with *sth*** UK INFORMAL to be unable to bear something, or to have no patience with it: *I can't be doing with all this shouting and screaming.*

• **Do as you would be done by.** *SAYING* said to show that you believe in treating others as you would like them to treat you

done /dʌn/ *adj* [after v] finished: *The washing-up's done, but I've left the drying for you.*

• **done deal** a plan that has been formally arranged or agreed and that is now certain to happen: *Although it has yet to happen, cross-border consolidation of Europe's banking industry is regarded as a done deal.*

do STUDY /duː/ *verb* [T] **did**, **done** to study a subject: *Diane did anthropology at university.*

do SOLVE /duː/ *verb* [T] **did**, **done** to solve, or find the answer to something: *to do a puzzle* ○ *I've never been able to do crosswords.*

do MAKE /duː/ *verb* [T] **did**, **done** to make, produce or create something: *I can't come out tonight – I've got to do my history essay.* ○ [+ two objects] *Can you do me 20 photocopies of this report/do 20 photocopies of this report for me?*

do CLEAN/MAKE TIDY /duː/ *verb* [I or T] **did**, **done** to clean or tidy, or make something look attractive: *I want to do* (= clean) *the living room this afternoon.* ○ *I cooked the dinner so you can do* (= wash) *the dishes.* ○ *do your* **hair/make-up/nails**

do ARRANGE /duː/ *verb* [T] **did**, **done** to arrange something: *You've done those flowers beautifully.* ○ *Can anyone here do* (= tie) *bow-ties?*

do VISIT /duː/ *verb* [T] **did**, **done** *INFORMAL* to visit the interesting places in a town or country, or to look around an interesting place: *We didn't manage to do Nice when we were in France.*

do TRAVEL /duː/ *verb* [T] **did**, **done 1** to travel a particular distance or to travel at a particular speed: *It's an old car and it's done over 80 000 miles.* ○ *My new car does 50 miles to the gallon/30 km to the litre* (= uses one GALLON of fuel to travel 50 miles, or one litre to travel 30 km). ○ *We were doing 150 (km an hour) along the motorway.* **2** to complete a journey: *We did the journey to Wales in five hours.*

do BE ACCEPTABLE /duː/ *verb* [I or T] **did**, **done** to be acceptable, suitable or enough (for): *Will this room do or would you prefer one with a shower?* ○ *This kind of behaviour just won't do.* ○ [+ to infinitive] *It doesn't do to criticize your parents.* ○ *I haven't got any grapefruit juice, but I've got some orange juice. Will that do (you)?* ○ *"Is that enough potato, or would you like some more?" "That'll do* (= be enough for) *me, thanks."*

• **That'll do!** used to tell someone to stop behaving badly: *That'll do, Timothy! Please just sit down and keep quiet.*

• **That will never do!** *OLD-FASHIONED* used to say that a situation is wrong and unacceptable: *"The dinner was excellent except that they served red wine with the chicken." "Dear me! That will never do!"*

do CAUSE TO HAVE /duː/ *verb* [T] **did**, **done** to provide or sell something, or to cause someone to have something: *There's a special offer on and they're doing three for the price of two.* ○ *Do you do travel insurance as well as flights?* ○ *The pub only does food at lunchtimes, not in the evenings.*

do COOK /duː/ *verb* [T] **did**, **done** to cook or prepare food: *Who's doing the food for your party?* ○ [+ two objects] *I'll do you some scrambled eggs.*

done /dʌn/ *adj* [after v] *Are the vegetables done* (= Have they finished cooking) *yet?* ○ *"How would you like your steak done?" "Well-done* (= Cooked for a long time), *please."* ⊃Compare **medium** VALUE; **rare** COOKED.

do PLAY /duː/ *verb* [T] **did**, **done** to perform a play or to play the part of a character: *The children are doing a play at the end of term.* ○ *She's done all the important Shakespearean roles apart from Lady Macbeth.* ○ *I hope she doesn't do a Helen* (= do what Helen did) *and get divorced six months after her wedding.*

do STEAL /duː/ *verb* [T] **did**, **done** *INFORMAL* to enter a building illegally and steal from it: *Our house was done while we were away.*

do CHEAT /duː/ *verb* [T] **did**, **done** *INFORMAL* to cheat someone: *Fifty bucks for that old bike! You've been done! I wouldn't give you more than ten.* ○ *He did me for a thousand quid for that car.*

do PRISON /duː/ *verb* [T] **did**, **done** *INFORMAL* to spend time in prison: *He did three years for his part in the robbery.* ○ *If you're not careful you'll end up doing time again.*

do PUNISH /duː/ *verb* [T] **did**, **done** *MAINLY UK INFORMAL* to punish someone: *If you mess with me again, I'll do you good and proper.* ○ *I got done* (= stopped by the police) *for speeding on my way home last night.*

do TAKE /duː/ *verb* [T] **did**, **done** *INFORMAL* to take an illegal drug: *How long have you been doing heroin?* ○ *I don't do drugs.*

do HAPPEN /duː/ *verb* [I] *INFORMAL* to happen: *This town is so boring in the evening – there's never anything doing.*

do MANAGE /duː/ *verb* [I usually + adv] **did**, **done** to develop or continue with the stated amount of success; to manage: **How** *is Mary doing in her new job/school?* ○ *Both the new mother and her baby are doing very* **well**. ○ *Are your roses doing* **all right** *this year?* ○ *Many shops are doing* **badly** *because of the economic situation.* ○ *I did rather* **well** *when I traded in my car – they gave me a good price for it.* ○ *Alexa has done* **well for herself** (= has achieved great personal success) *getting such a highly paid job.*

do TREATMENT /duː/ *noun* [C] *plural* **dos** *UK INFORMAL* a way of treating people. *There are no special privileges for the managers – we believe in* **fair** *dos all round* (= equal treatment for everyone) *in this company.* ○ *It's a* **poor** *do* (= a bad, unfair situation) *when a so-called developed country can't even provide homes for all its citizens.*

do PARTY /duː/ *noun* [C] *plural* **dos** *MAINLY UK INFORMAL* a party or other social event: *Julie's having a* **bit of a** *do for her fortieth birthday.* ○ *It was one of those dos where nobody really knew each other.*

do HAIR /duː/ *noun* [C] *plural* **dos** *US FOR* **hairdo**

PHRASAL VERBS WITH do ▼

▲ **do away with** *sth* GET RID OF *phrasal verb* to get rid of something or stop using something: *These ridiculous rules and regulations should have been done away with years ago.* ○ *Computerization has enabled us to do away with a lot of paperwork.* ○ *How on earth could they do away with a lovely old building like that and put a car park there instead?*

▲ **do away with** *sb* KILL *phrasal verb* *INFORMAL* to murder someone

▲ **do** *sb* **down** *phrasal verb* to criticize someone in order to make them feel ashamed or to make other people lose respect for them: *She felt that everyone in the meeting was trying to do her down.* ○ [R] *Stop doing yourself down.*

▲ **do for** *sb/sth* HARM *phrasal verb* *UK OLD-FASHIONED INFORMAL* to seriously damage something, or to seriously hurt or kill someone: *Driving on those rough roads has really done for my car.*

done for /ˈdʌn.fɔːʳ/ ⓤ /-fɔːr/ *adj* **1 be done for** to be about to die or suffer greatly because of a serious difficulty or danger: *We all thought we were done for when the boat started to sink.* **2** *INFORMAL* very tired: *I'm really done for – I'm going to bed.*

▲ **do** *sth* **for** *sb/sth* CURE *phrasal verb* If a doctor of medicine does something for someone or their illness, they make them better: *Can you do* **anything** *for my bad back, doctor?* ○ *These pills I've been taking have done* **nothing** *for me.*

▲ **do** *sb* **in** KILL *phrasal verb* *SLANG* to attack or kill someone: *They threatened to do me in if I didn't pay up by Friday.*

▲ **do yourself** '**in** *phrasal verb* [R] *SLANG* to kill yourself: *She threatened to do herself in when her husband ran off with her best friend.*

▲ **do** *sb* '**in** TIRE *phrasal verb* *INFORMAL* to make someone extremely tired: *That hockey match really did me in.*

done in /dʌn.ɪn/ [after v] (*US* **all done in**) *INFORMAL* too tired to do any more: *I was/felt really done in after the match.*

▲ **do** *sth* **out** CLEAN *phrasal verb* [M] *UK INFORMAL* to clean or tidy something: *I'd like you to do out your room before Chris comes to stay.*

▲ **do** *sth* **out** DECORATE *phrasal verb* [M] to decorate something: *They did the room out* **with** *balloons and streamers ready for the party.* ○ *We've had the bathroom done out* **in** *pale yellow.*

▲ **do** *sb* **out of** *sth* CHEAT *phrasal verb* INFORMAL to stop someone from getting or keeping something, especially in a dishonest or unfair way: *Thousands of pensioners have been done out of millions of pounds as a result of the changes.*

▲ **do** *sb* **over** ATTACK *phrasal verb* [M] MAINLY UK INFORMAL to attack someone violently: *They said they'd do me over if I refused to drive the getaway car.*

▲ **do** *sth* **over** DO AGAIN *phrasal verb* US to do something again because you did not do it well the first time: *This essay's the worst you've ever done. I think you should do it over.*

▲ **do** *(sth)* **up** FASTEN *phrasal verb* [M] to fasten something or become fastened: *Can you help me to do up my dress?* ○ *Do your shoes/laces up before you trip over.* ○ *These trousers must have shrunk – I can't do the zip up.* ○ *Why won't this zip do up?* ✳ NOTE: The opposite is **undo**.

▲ **do** *sth* **up** BUILDING *phrasal verb* [M] to repair or decorate a building so that it looks attractive: *I'd like to buy a run-down cottage that I can do up.*

▲ **do** *sth* **up** WRAP *phrasal verb* [M] to wrap something in paper: *She always does her presents up beautifully in gold and silver paper.*

▲ **do without** *(sth)* *phrasal verb* to manage without having something: *There's no mayonnaise left, so I'm afraid you'll just have to do without.* ○ *Thank you Kate, we can do without language like that* (= we don't want to hear your rude language).

dob /dɒb/ US /dɑːb/ *verb* **-bb-**

▲ **dob** *sb* **in** *verb* [I or T] INFORMAL to secretly tell someone in authority that someone else has done something wrong: *Who was it who dobbed me in (to the teacher)?*

dobber /'dɒb.əʳ/ US /'dɑː.bəʳ/ *noun* [C] AUS INFORMAL DISAPPROVING a person who secretly tells someone in authority that someone else has done something wrong

doc /dɒk/ US /dɑːk/ *noun* [C] INFORMAL a doctor: [as form of address] *You see, doc, I haven't been sleeping at all well recently.*

docile /'dəʊ.saɪl/ US /'dɑː.sᵊl/ *adj* quiet and easy to influence, persuade or control: *The once docile population has finally risen up against the ruthless regime.*

docility /dəʊ'sɪl.ɪ.ti/ US /dɑː'sɪl.ə.t̬i/ *noun* [U]

dock FOR SHIPS /dɒk/ US /dɑːk/ *noun* [C] **1** a specially enclosed area of water in a port that is used for loading and unloading or repairing ships ✪Compare **harbour** WATER. **2** US a long platform built over water where passengers can get on or off a boat or where goods can be loaded and unloaded **docks** /dɒks/ US /dɑːks/ *plural noun*: *The strike has led to the cancellation of some ferry services and left hundreds of passengers stranded at the docks.*

dock /dɒk/ US /dɑːk/ *verb* [I or T] If a ship docks, it arrives at a dock and if someone docks a ship, they bring it into a dock: *Hundreds of people turned up to see the ship dock at Southampton.* ○ *The Russians and Americans docked* (= joined together in space) *(their spacecraft) just after one o'clock this morning.*

docker /'dɒk.əʳ/ US /'dɑː.kəʳ/ *noun* [C] (ALSO **dockworker**) a person who works at a port, loading and unloading ships

the dock LAW *noun* [S] MAINLY UK the place in a criminal law court where the accused person sits or stands during the trial: *The defendant seemed nervous as he left the dock and stepped up to the witness box.* ○ *The company will find itself in the dock* (= in court) *if it continues to ignore the pollution regulations.*

dock REMOVE /dɒk/ US /dɑːk/ *verb* [T] to remove part of something, especially money: *The University has docked lecturers' pay/wages by 20% because of their refusal to mark examination papers.* ○ *The lambs' tails are docked* (= cut short) *for hygiene reasons.*

dock PLANT /dɒk/ US /dɑːk/ *noun* [C or U] a common wild plant with large wide leaves which grows in some northern countries such as Britain: *Rubbing dock leaves on nettle stings helps to relieve the pain.*

docket /'dɒk.ɪt/ US /'dɑː.kɪt/ *noun* [C] **1** UK an official document describing something that is being delivered or transported and giving details of where it is coming from and where it is going to **2** US a list of cases to be

dealt with in a law court, or an AGENDA in business

dockland /'dɒk.lænd/ /-lənd/ US /'dɑː.k-/ *noun* [C or U] UK the area that surrounds the DOCKS in a port: *Hundreds of millions of pounds are needed to redevelop large areas of derelict dockland.*

the dockside /ðə'dɒk.saɪd/ US /-'dɑː.k-/ *noun* [S] the area next to a DOCK where goods can be stored before loading or after unloading

dockyard /'dɒk.jɑːd/ US /'dɑː.kjɑːrd/ *noun* [C] (ALSO **shipyard**) a place where ships are built, maintained and repaired

Doc Martens /,dɒk'mɑː.tɪnz/ US /,dɑː.k'mɑːr.t̬ənz/ *plural noun* INFORMAL FOR **Dr Martens**

doctor MEDICINE /'dɒk.təʳ/ US /'dɑː.k.təʳ/ *noun* [C] **1** (WRITTEN ABBREVIATION **Dr**) a person with a medical degree whose job is to treat people who are ill or hurt: *The doctor prescribed some pills.* ○ *You should see a doctor about that cough.* ○ [as form of address] *Good morning, Doctor Smith/Doctor.* **2 the doctor's** the place where the doctor works: *He went to the doctor's this morning for a checkup.*

• **just what the doctor ordered** exactly what is wanted or needed: *Ooh thank you, a nice cup of tea. Just what the doctor ordered.*

doctor EDUCATION /'dɒk.təʳ/ US /'dɑː.k.təʳ/ *noun* [C] (WRITTEN ABBREVIATION **Dr**) a person who has the highest degree from a college or university **doctoral** /'dɒk.tᵊr.ᵊl/ US /'dɑː.k.təʳ-/ *adj* [before n] *a doctoral dissertation*

doctorate /'dɒk.tᵊr.ət/ US /'dɑː.k.təʳ-/ *noun* [C] the highest degree from a university: *She has a doctorate in physics from Norwich.*

doctor CHANGE /'dɒk.təʳ/ US /'dɑː.k.təʳ/ *verb* [T] **1** to change a document in order to deceive people: *He was found to have provided the court with doctored evidence.* **2** to secretly put a harmful or poisonous substance into food or drink: *Bottles of lemonade doctored with rat poison were discovered in the kitchen.* **3** UK INFORMAL to remove the sexual organs of an animal in order to prevent it from having babies

doctor's orders /,dɒk.təʳ'zɔː.dəz/ US /,dɑː.k.təʳ'zɔːr.dəʳz/ *plural noun* MAINLY HUMOROUS used to mean that you must do something because your doctor has told you to do it: *I have to have a week off work – it's doctor's orders!*

doctrine /'dɒk.trɪn/ US /'dɑː.k-/ *noun* [C or U] a belief or set of beliefs, especially political or religious, taught and accepted by a particular group: *Christian doctrine* ○ *The president said he would not go against sound military doctrine.*

doctrinaire /,dɒk.trɪ'neəʳ/ US /,dɑː.k.trə'ner/ *adj* FORMAL DISAPPROVING *These principles are doctrinaire* (= based too much on fixed beliefs that do not consider practical problems).

doctrinal /dɒk'traɪ.nᵊl/ US /'dɑː.k.trɪ-/ *adj* FORMAL relating to doctrine: *a doctrinal matter/approach*

docudrama /'dɒk.jʊ.drɑː.mə/ US /'dɑː.kjʊ.drɑː.mə/ *noun* [C or U] a television programme whose story is based on an event or situation that really happened although it is not intended to be accurate in every detail

document /'dɒk.jʊ.mənt/ US /'dɑː.kjʊ-/ *noun* [C] **1** a paper or set of papers with written or printed information, especially of an official type: *official/ confidential/legal documents* ○ *They are charged with using forged documents.* **2** a text that is written and stored on a computer: *I'll send you the document by email.*

document /'dɒk.jʊ.mənt/ /-ment/ US /'dɑː.kjʊ-/ *verb* [T] to record the details of an event, a process, etc: *His interest in cricket has been well-documented* (= recorded and written about) *by the media.*

documentary /,dɒk.jʊ'men.tᵊr.i/ US /,dɑː.kjʊ'men.t̬əʳ-/ *adj* [before n] *Human rights campaigners have discovered documentary evidence* (= written proof) *of torture.* ✪See also **documentary**.

documentation /,dɒk.jʊ.men'teɪ.ʃᵊn/ US /,dɑː.kjʊ-/ *noun* [U] **1** pieces of paper containing official information: *Passengers without proper documentation* (= official papers saying who they are) *will not be allowed to travel.* **2** the instructions for using a computer device or program

documentary /ˌdɒk.jʊˈmen.tᵊr.i/ [US] /ˌdɑː.kjəˈmen.t̬ɚ-/ *noun* [C] a film or television or radio programme that gives facts and information about a subject: *The documentary took a fresh look at the life of Darwin.* ○ *They showed a documentary* **on** *animal communication.* **documentary** /ˌdɒk.jʊˈmen.tᵊr.i/ [US] /ˌdɑː.kjəˈmen.t̬ɚ-/ *adj* [before n] *Most of her films have a documentary style.* ➲See also **documentary** at **document**.

docusoap /ˈdɒ.kjuː.səʊp/ [US] /ˈdɑː.kjuː.soʊp/ *noun* [C] an entertaining programme about the lives of real people, especially people who live in the same place or do the same job: *Have you seen the new docusoap about driving instructors?*

doddery /ˈdɒd.ᵊr.i/ [US] /ˈdɑː.dɚ-/ *adj* (ALSO **doddering**) INFORMAL weak and unable to walk properly, usually because you are old: *a doddery old man*

doddle /ˈdɒd.l̩/ [US] /ˈdɑː.dl̩/ *noun* [S] UK INFORMAL something that is very easy to do: *The exam was a doddle.*

dodge /dɒdʒ/ [US] /dɑːdʒ/ *verb* **1** [I or T] to avoid being hit by something by moving quickly to one side: *He dodged to avoid the hurtling bicycle.* **2** [T] to avoid something unpleasant: *The minister dodged questions about his relationship with the actress.*

dodge /dɒdʒ/ [US] /dɑːdʒ/ *noun* [C] INFORMAL a clever dishonest way of avoiding something: *They bought another car as a* ***tax*** *dodge* (= a way to avoid paying tax).

dodger /ˈdɒdʒ.əʳ/ [US] /ˈdɑː.dʒɚ/ *noun* [C] a person who avoids doing what they should do: *a* ***tax*** *dodger* (= someone who avoids paying tax).

dodgem (car) /ˈdɒdʒ.əm.kɑːʳ/ [US] /ˈdɑː.dʒəm.kɑːr/ *noun* [C usually pl] TRADEMARK a small electric car driven for entertainment in a special enclosed space where the aim is to try to hit other cars

dodgy /ˈdɒdʒ.i/ [US] /ˈdɑː.dʒi/ *adj* UK INFORMAL **1** dishonest: *a dodgy deal* ○ *They got involved with a dodgy businessman and lost all their savings.* **2** unable to be depended on or risky: *The weather might be a bit dodgy at this time of year.* ○ *I can't come in to work today – I've got a bit of a dodgy stomach.* ○ *It was a dodgy situation.* **3** likely to break or cause pain: *Careful – that chair's a bit dodgy.* ○ *Ever since the war I've had this dodgy leg.*

dodo /ˈdəʊ.dəʊ/ [US] /ˈdoʊ.doʊ/ *noun* [C] *plural* **dodos** a large bird, unable to fly, that no longer exists

doe /dəʊ/ [US] /doʊ/ *noun* [C] the female of animals such as the deer or rabbit ➲Compare **buck** ANIMAL.

doer /ˈduː.əʳ/ [US] /-ɚ/ *noun* [C] ➲See at **do** PERFORM.

does STRONG /dʌz/, WEAK /dəz/ *he/she/it form of* **do**

doesn't /ˈdʌz.ᵊnt/ *short form of* does not: *Doesn't she look lovely in that hat?*

doff /dɒf/ [US] /dɑːf/ *verb* [T] OLD-FASHIONED to remove your hat, usually to show respect ➲Compare **don** PUT ON.

• **doff *your* hat to *sb or sth*** LITERARY to show respect to someone or something: *The song doffs its hat to the best soul traditions.*

dog [ANIMAL] /dɒg/ [US] /dɑːg/ *noun* [C] a common four-legged animal, especially kept by people as a pet or to hunt or guard things: *my pet dog* ○ *wild dogs* ○ *dog food* ○ *We could hear dogs barking in the distance.*

• **dog-eat-dog** DISAPPROVING describes a situation in which people will do anything to be successful, even if what they do harms other people: *It's a dog-eat-dog* ***world*** *out there.*

• **a dog in the manger** someone who keeps something that they do not want in order to prevent someone else from getting it

• **a dog's breakfast** UK INFORMAL something or someone that looks extremely untidy, or something that is very badly done

• **a dog's life** a very unhappy and unpleasant life

• **done up/dressed up like a dog's dinner** UK INFORMAL wearing very formal or decorative clothes in a way that attracts attention

• **go to the dogs** If a country or organization is going to the dogs, it is becoming very much less successful than it was in the past.

• **put on the dog** US INFORMAL to act as if you are more important than you are

• **Every dog has its day.** SAYING said to emphasize that everyone is successful or happy at some time in their life

• **Give a dog a bad name.** UK SAYING said when someone has been accused of behaving badly in the past, with the result that people expect them to behave like that in the future

• **Let sleeping dogs lie.** SAYING said to warn someone that they should not talk about a bad situation that most people have forgotten about

• **You can't teach an old dog new tricks.** SAYING said to mean that it is very difficult to teach someone new skills or to change their habits or character

D

dog [PERSON] /dɒg/ [US] /dɑːg/ *noun* [C] **1** SLANG a man who is unpleasant or not to be trusted: *He tried to steal my money, the* ***dirty*** *dog.* **2** OFFENSIVE an unattractive woman

dog [FOLLOW] /dɒg/ [US] /dɑːg/ *verb* [T] **-gg-** to follow someone closely and continually: *Reporters dogged him for answers.* ➲See also **dogged**.

dog [PROBLEM] /dɒg/ [US] /dɑːg/ *verb* [T] **-gg-** to cause difficulties: *Technical problems dogged our trip from the outset.*

ˈdog ˌbiscuit *noun* [C] a hard baked biscuit for dogs

dogcatcher /ˈdɒgˌkætʃ.əʳ/ [US] /ˈdɑːgˌkætʃ.ɚ/ *noun* [C] a person whose job is to catch homeless dogs and cats and take them to an official place where they are kept in cages

ˈdog ˌcollar [DOG] *noun* [C] a strap worn around a dog's neck

ˈdog ˌcollar [PRIEST] *noun* [C] INFORMAL FOR **clerical collar**

ˈdog ˌdays *plural noun* the hottest days of the summer

dog-eared /ˈdɒg.ɪəd/ [US] /ˈdɑːg.ɪrd/ *adj* A book or paper that is dog-eared has the pages turned down at the corners as a result of a lot of use.

dogfight /ˈdɒg.faɪt/ [US] /ˈdɑːg-/ *noun* [C] **1** a fight between two military aircraft in which they fly very fast and very close to each other **2** a fight between dogs, usually organized as an illegal entertainment

dogfish /ˈdɒg.fɪʃ/ [US] /ˈdɑːg-/ *noun* [C] *plural* **dogfish** or **dogfishes** a type of small SHARK

dogged /ˈdɒg.ɪd/ [US] /ˈdɑː.gɪd/ *adj* very determined to do something, even if it is very difficult: *Her ambition and dogged determination ensured that she rose to the top of her profession.* **doggedly** /ˈdɒg.ɪd.li/ [US] /ˈdɑː.gɪd-/ *adv*: *I kept at it, doggedly and patiently until finally I could skate.* **doggedness** /ˈdɒg.ɪd.nəs/ [US] /ˈdɑː.gɪd-/ *noun* [U]

doggerel /ˈdɒg.ᵊr.ᵊl/ [US] /ˈdɑː.gɚ-/ *noun* [U] poetry that is silly or worthless

doggone /ˈdɒg.ɒn/ [US] /ˈdɑː.gɑːn/ *adj* [before n], *exclamation* US INFORMAL used to express annoyance: *Doggone* ***(it)****, where's that letter?* ○ *That doggone washing machine's broken again.*

doggy, **doggie** /ˈdɒg.i/ [US] /ˈdɑː.gi/ *noun* [C] CHILD'S WORD a dog

ˈdoggy ˌbag *noun* [C] a small bag that a restaurant provides so that you can take home any food you have not finished

ˈdoggy ˌpaddle *noun* [U] (US ALSO **dog paddle**) a simple swimming action in which a person moves their arms and legs up and down in quick movements under the water

doghouse /ˈdɒg.haʊs/ [US] /ˈdɑːg-/ *noun* [C] US FOR **kennel** (= a small shelter for a dog to sleep in)

• **in the doghouse** UK AND US INFORMAL If you are in the doghouse, someone is annoyed with you and shows their disapproval: *I'm in the doghouse – I broke Sara's favourite vase this morning.*

dogie /ˈdəʊ.gi/ [US] /ˈdoʊ-/ *noun* [C] US a CALF (= young cow) that has no mother

dogleg /ˈdɒg.leg/ [US] /ˈdɑːg-/ *noun* [C] a sharp bend, especially in a road or on a GOLF COURSE

dogma /ˈdɒg.mə/ [US] /ˈdɑːg-/ *noun* [C or U] DISAPPROVING a fixed, especially religious, belief or set of beliefs that people are expected to accept without any doubts

dogmatic /dɒɡˈmæt.ɪk/ [US] /dɑːɡˈmæt̬-/ *adj* DISAPPROVING If someone is dogmatic, they are certain that they are right and that everyone else is wrong. **dogmatically** /dɒɡˈmæt.ɪ.kli/ [US] /dɑːɡˈmæt̬-/ *adv*

dogmatism /ˈdɒɡ.mə.tɪ.zᵊm/ [US] /ˈdɑːɡ.mə.t̬ɪ-/ *noun* [U] DISAPPROVING stating your opinions in a strong way and not accepting anyone else's opinions: *There is a note of dogmatism in the book.*

dogmatist /ˈdɒɡ.mə.tɪst/ [US] /ˈdɑːɡ.mə.t̬ɪst/ *noun* [C] DISAPPROVING a person who believes too strongly that their personal opinions or beliefs are correct

do-gooder /ˈduːˌɡʊd.əʳ/ [US] /-ɚ/ *noun* [C] MAINLY DISAPPROVING someone who does things that they think will help other people, although the other people might not find their actions helpful

dogsbody /ˈdɒɡz.bɒd.i/ [US] /ˈdɑːɡz.bɑː.di/ *noun* [C] UK INFORMAL a person who has to do all the boring or unpleasant jobs that other people do not want to do

dogsled /ˈdɒɡ.sled/ [US] /ˈdɑːɡ-/ *noun* [C] US a SLEDGE pulled by dogs

ˈdog ˌtag *noun* [C] US a small piece of metal worn round the neck by members of the US armed forces with their name and number on it

dog-tired /ˌdɒɡˈtaɪəd/ [US] /ˌdɑːɡˈtaɪrd/ *adj* INFORMAL extremely tired

dogwood /ˈdɒɡ.wʊd/ [US] /ˈdɑːɡ-/ *noun* [C or U] a flowering bush, growing either wild or in gardens

d'oh, d'uh /dəʊ/ [US] /doʊ/ *exclamation* INFORMAL used when you feel stupid, usually after doing something silly, or to show that you think what someone else has done or said is stupid: *I forgot to turn it on. D'oh!*

doily /ˈdɔɪ.li/ *noun* [C] a small piece of paper or cloth with a pattern of little holes in it, used as a decoration on a plate or under a cake

doing /ˈduː.ɪŋ/ *noun* ➲See at **do** ACT.

doings /ˈduː.ɪŋz/ *noun* [C] *plural* **doings** UK INFORMAL anything, especially a small object, whose name you have forgotten or do not know: *I'm looking for a doings to hold up a curtain rail that's fallen down.* ➲See also **doings** at **do** ACT.

doings /ˈduː.ɪŋz/ *plural noun* UK someone's activities: *The doings **of** the British royal family have always been of interest to the media.*

do-it-yourself /ˌduː.ɪt.jəˈself/ [US] /-jɚ-/ *noun* [U] **DIY**

Dolby /ˈdɒl.bi/ [US] /ˈdɑːl-/ *noun* [U] TRADEMARK an electronic system for reducing unwanted noise on sound recordings

the doldrums /ðəˈdɒl.drəmz/ [US] /-ˈdoʊl-/ *plural noun* **1** INFORMAL **in the doldrums** unsuccessful or showing no activity or development: *Her career was in the doldrums during those years.* **2** UK INFORMAL **in the doldrums** sad and with no energy or enthusiasm

the dole /ðəˈdəʊl/ [US] /-ˈdoʊl/ *noun* [S] UK INFORMAL the money that the government gives to people who are unemployed: *Young people **on*** (= receiving) *the dole are often bored and frustrated.* ○ *If I can't find any work within a month, I'll have to **go on** the dole.*

dole /dəʊl/ [US] /doʊl/ *verb*

▲ **dole *sth* out** *phrasal verb* [M] INFORMAL to give something, usually money, to several people

doleful /ˈdəʊl.fᵊl/ [US] /ˈdoʊl-/ *adj* very sad: *a doleful expression* **dolefully** /ˈdəʊl.fᵊl.i/ [US] /ˈdoʊl-/ *adv*

doll /dɒl/ [US] /dɑːl/ *noun* [C] a child's toy in the shape of a small person or baby

doll /dɒl/ [US] /dɑːl/ *verb*

▲ **doll *yourself* up** *phrasal verb* [R] DISAPPROVING If a woman dolls herself up, she tries to make herself more attractive by putting on make-up and special clothes: *I'm not going to doll myself up just to go to the shops.*

dolled up /ˌdɒldˈʌp/ [US] /ˌdɑːld-/ *adj* [after v] INFORMAL *She spent two hours **getting** dolled up for the party.*

dollar /ˈdɒl.əʳ/ [US] /ˈdɑː.lɚ/ *noun* [C] **1** (SYMBOL **$**) the standard unit of money used in the US, Canada, Australia, New Zealand and other countries: *Can I borrow ten dollars?* ○ *The suitcase was full of dollar **bills*** (= notes). **2 the dollar** the value of the US dollar, used in comparing the values of different types of money from around the world: *In the financial markets today, the dollar **rose against/fell against*** (= was worth more than/less than) *the pound.*

ˈdollar ˌsign *noun* [C] the symbol $

dollop /ˈdɒl.əp/ [US] /ˈdɑː.ləp/ *noun* [C] a small amount of something soft, especially food: *a dollop **of** ice cream/whipped cream*

doll's house UK /ˈdɒlzˌhaʊs/ [US] /ˈdɑːlz-/ *noun* [C] (US **dollhouse**) a toy that is a very small house, often with furniture and small dolls in it

dolly /ˈdɒl.i/ [US] /ˈdɑː.li/ *noun* [C] CHILD'S WORD a **doll**

ˈdolly ˌbird *noun* [C] UK OLD-FASHIONED INFORMAL a young woman who is thought of as attractive but not very intelligent

dolmen /ˈdɒl.men/ [US] /ˈdoʊl-/ *noun* [C] SPECIALIZED a group of stones consisting of one large flat stone supported by several vertical ones, built in ancient times

dolorous /ˈdɒl.ᵊr.əs/ [US] /ˈdoʊ.lɚ-/ *adj* LITERARY sad, or causing sadness or emotional suffering

dolphin /ˈdɒl.fɪn/ [US] /ˈdɑːl-/ *noun* [C] a sea mammal that is large, smooth and grey, with a long pointed mouth

dolt /dəʊlt/ [US] /doʊlt/ *noun* [C] DISAPPROVING a stupid person

domain [AREA] /dəʊˈmeɪn/ [US] /doʊ-/ *noun* [C] an area of interest or an area over which a person has control: *She treated the business as her private domain.* ○ *These documents are **in the public** domain* (= available to everybody).

domain [INTERNET] /dəʊˈmeɪn/ [US] /doʊˈmeɪn/ *noun* [C] a part of the Internet that belongs to a person or organization where they can access EMAIL or display documents on the Internet

doˈmain ˌname *noun* [C] SPECIALIZED the part of an EMAIL or WEBSITE address on the Internet that shows the name of the organization that the address belongs to

dome /dəʊm/ [US] /doʊm/ *noun* [C] **1** a rounded roof on a building or a room, or a building with such a roof **2** a shape like one-half of a ball: *Gerald had a long grey beard and a shiny bald dome* (= head).

domed /dəʊmd/ [US] /doʊmd/ *adj* shaped like a dome or covered with a dome

domestic [HOME] /dəˈmes.tɪk/ *adj* belonging or relating to the home, house or family: *domestic chores/duties/arrangements*

domesticated /dəˈmes.tɪ.keɪ.tɪd/ [US] /-t̬ɪd/ *adj* able or willing to do cleaning, cooking and other jobs in the home, and to look after children: *Since they had their baby they've both become quite domesticated.*

domestic /dəˈmes.tɪk/ *noun* [C] (ALSO **domestic help**) OLD-FASHIONED someone paid to do work, such as cleaning and cooking, in someone else's house **domestically** /dəˈmes.tɪ.kli/ *adv*

domesticity /ˌdəʊ.mesˈtɪs.ɪ.ti/ [US] /ˌdoʊ.mesˈtɪs.ə.t̬i/ *noun* [U] life at home looking after your house and family: *She married young and settled happily into domesticity.*

domestic [COUNTRY] /dəˈmes.tɪk/ *adj* relating to a person's own country: *domestic airlines/flights* ○ *Domestic opinion had turned against the war.*

domestically /dəˈmes.tɪ.kli/ *adv*: *Such a policy would be unacceptable both domestically and internationally.*

doˌmestic ˈanimal *noun* [C] an animal that is not wild and is kept as a pet or to produce food

doˌmestic apˈpliance *noun* [C] a large piece of electrical equipment used in the home, especially in the kitchen: *We stock a wide range of domestic appliances, including fridges, freezers and dishwashers.*

domesticate /dəˈmes.tɪ.keɪt/ *verb* [T often passive] to bring animals or plants under human control in order to provide food, power or companionship: *Dogs were probably the first animals to be domesticated.*

doˌmestic ˈscience *noun* [U] UK OLD-FASHIONED FOR **home economics**

domicile /ˈdɒm.ɪ.saɪl/ [US] /ˈdɑː.mə-/ *noun* [C] FORMAL OR LEGAL the place where a person lives

domiciled /ˈdɒm.ɪ.saɪld/ [US] /ˈdɑː.mə-/ *adj* [after v] FORMAL OR LEGAL *He was domiciled* (= living) ***in** Saudi Arabia during the 1980s.*

dominant /ˈdɒm.ɪ.nənt/ [US] /ˈdɑː.mə-/ *adj* **1** more important, strong or noticeable than anything else of the same type: *a dominant military power* ○ *Unemployment will be a dominant **issue** at the next election.* **2** SPECIALIZED **dominant gene** a gene which always produces a particular characteristic in a person, plant or animal **dominance** /ˈdɒm.ɪ.nənts/ (US) /ˈdɑː.mə-/ *noun* [U] *Music companies have profited from the dominance of CDs over vinyl records.*

dominate /ˈdɒm.ɪ.neɪt/ (US) /ˈdɑː.mə-/ *verb* [I or T] OFTEN DISAPPROVING to have control over a place or a person, or to be the most important person or thing: *He refuses to let others speak and dominates every meeting.* ○ *They work as a group – no one person is allowed to dominate.*
dominating /ˈdɒm.ɪ.neɪ.tɪŋ/ (US) /ˈdɑː.mə.neɪ.t̬ɪŋ/ *adj: a dominating personality*
domination /ˌdɒm.ɪˈneɪ.ʃən/ (US) /ˌdɑː.mə-/ *noun* [U] *The film was about a group of robots set on world domination* (= control of all countries).

dominatrix /ˌdɒm.ɪˈneɪ.trɪks/ (US) /ˌdɑː.mə-/ *noun* [C] *plural* **dominatrices** a woman who has power or control over her partner in a sexual relationship

domineering /ˌdɒm.ɪˈnɪə.rɪŋ/ (US) /ˌdɑː.məˈnɪr.ɪŋ/ *adj* DISAPPROVING having a strong tendency to control other people without taking their feelings into consideration: *She found him arrogant and domineering.*

Dominican /dəˈmɪn.ɪ.kən/ (US) /doʊ-/ *noun* [C] a monk who belongs to a Christian religious group that was established by Saint Dominic **Dominican** /dəˈmɪn.ɪ.kən/ (US) /doʊ-/ *adj*

dominion /dəˈmɪn.jən/ *noun* FORMAL **1** [U] control over a country or people: *God **has** dominion **over*** (= controls) *all his creatures.* **2** [C] the land that belongs to a ruler: *The chief's son would inherit all his dominions.*

domino /ˈdɒm.ɪ.nəʊ/ (US) /ˈdɑː.mə.noʊ/ *noun* [C] *plural* **dominoes** a small, rectangular object with spots on it, that is used in a game
dominoes /ˈdɒm.ɪ.nəʊz/ (US) /ˈdɑː.mɪ.noʊz/ *noun* [U] a game using DOMINOES: *A group of old men sat **playing** dominoes.*

the ˈdomino efˌfect *noun* [S] when something, usually something bad, happens and causes other similar events to happen, like each of a set of dominoes knocking the next one over

don [TEACHER] /dɒn/ (US) /dɑːn/ *noun* [C] UK a LECTURER (= college teacher), especially at Oxford or Cambridge University in England
donnish /ˈdɒn.ɪʃ/ (US) /ˈdɑː.nɪʃ/ *adj* UK intelligent, often in a way that is too serious: *He was a thin, donnish-looking man in a tweed jacket and sandals.*

don [PUT ON] /dɒn/ (US) /dɑːn/ *verb* [T] -nn- FORMAL to put on a piece of clothing: *He donned his finest coat and hat.* ➲Compare **doff**.

donate /dəʊˈneɪt/ (US) /ˈdoʊ.neɪt/ *verb* **1** [I or T] to give money or goods to help a person or organization: *An anonymous businesswoman donated one million dollars **to** the charity.* ○ *Please donate generously.* ➲See also **donor**. **2** [T] to allow some of your blood or a part of your body to be used for medical purposes: *The appeal for people to donate blood was very successful.*
donation /dəʊˈneɪ.ʃən/ (US) /doʊˈneɪ-/ *noun* [C or U] when money or goods are given to help a person or organization: *donations of food and money* ○ *I'd like to **make** a small donation in my mother's name.*

done /dʌn/ *past participle of* **do**
• **Done!** said to show that you accept someone's offer or that you agree to something: *"I'll give you twenty quid for all five of them." "Done!"*

Don Juan /ˌdɒnˈdʒuː.ən/ /-ˈhwɑːn/ (US) /ˌdɑːn-/ *noun* [C] a man who has had sex with a lot of women

donkey /ˈdɒŋ.ki/ (US) /ˈdɑːŋ-/ *noun* [C] an animal like a small horse with long ears
• **donkey's years** UK INFORMAL a very long time: *She's been in the same job **for** donkey's years.* ○ *We've known each other for donkey's years.*
• **do (all) the donkey work** UK INFORMAL to do the hard boring part of a job: *Why should I do all the donkey work while you sit around doing nothing?*

ˈdonkey ˌjacket *noun* [C] UK a type of thick jacket, usually dark blue, often worn by men who work outside

donor /ˈdəʊ.nəʳ/ (US) /ˈdoʊ.nɚ/ *noun* [C] **1** a person who gives some of their blood or a part of their body to help someone who is ill: *a blood donor* ○ *a kidney donor* ➲See also **donate**. **2** a person who gives money or goods to an organization: *Thanks to a large gift from an anonymous donor, the charity was able to continue its work.*

ˈdonor ˌcard *noun* [C] a card you can carry that says you want doctors to use parts of your body to help ill people when you die

don't /dəʊnt/ (US) /doʊnt/ *short form of* do not: *Don't do that – it hurts!*
don'ts /dəʊnts/ (US) /doʊnts/ *plural noun* ➲See **do's and don'ts** at DO PERFORM.

donut /ˈdəʊ.nʌt/ (US) /ˈdoʊ-/ *noun* US FOR **doughnut**

doodah UK /ˈduː.dɑː/ *noun* [C] (US **doodad**) INFORMAL anything whose name you cannot remember or do not know: *Have you got the doodah, you know, the thing you attach to the end of this?*

doodle /ˈduː.dl̩/ *verb* [I] to draw pictures or patterns while thinking about something else or when you are bored: *She'd doodled all over her textbooks.* **doodle** /ˈduː.dl̩/ *noun* [C]

doohickey /duːˈhɪk.i/ *noun* [C] US INFORMAL any small object whose name you cannot remember

doom /duːm/ *noun* [U] death, destruction or any very bad situation that cannot be avoided: *A sense of doom hung over the entire country.* ○ *The newspapers are always full of doom **and gloom*** (= bad news and unhappiness) *these days.*
doom /duːm/ *verb* [T usually passive] to make someone or something certain to do or experience something unpleasant, or to make something bad certain to happen: [+ to infinitive] *Are we doomed **to** repeat the mistakes of the past?* ○ *Mounting debts doomed the factory **to** closure.*
doomed /duːmd/ *adj* certain to fail, die or be destroyed: *This is a doomed city.*

doomsday /ˈduːmz.deɪ/ *noun* [U] the end of the world, or a time when something very bad will happen: *Ecologists predict a doomsday **scenario*** (= a time when death and destruction will happen) *if the amount of pollution continues to increase at the present rate.* ○ *You could talk **till/until** doomsday* (= for a very long time), *but they will never change their minds.*

doona /ˈduː.nə/ *noun* [C] AUS TRADEMARK a large soft flat bag filled with feathers or artificial material used on a bed

door /dɔːʳ/ (US) /dɔːr/ *noun* [C] **1** a flat object, often fixed at one edge, that is used to close the entrance of something such as a room or building, or the entrance itself: *the front door* ○ *the back door* ○ *a car door* ○ *a sliding door* ○ *The door **to** his bedroom was locked.* ○ *We could hear someone knocking **at/on** the door.* ○ *Could you **open/close/shut** the door, please?* ○ *She asked me to **answer** the door* (= go and open the door because someone had just knocked on it or rung the bell). **2 be on the door** to work at the entrance of a building, collecting tickets or preventing particular people from entering **3** used to refer to a house or other building: *Sam only lives a few doors **(away/up/down) from** us.* ○ *The people **next** door **(to us)*** (= living in the house next to us) *aren't very friendly.*
• **open the door to/close the door on** ***sth*** to make something possible/impossible: *These discussions may well open the door to a peaceful solution.*
• **out of doors** outside in the open air
• **close/shut the door on** ***sth*** to make it impossible for something to happen, especially a plan or a solution to a problem: *There are fears that this latest move might have closed the door on a peaceful solution.*
• **shut/close the stable/barn door after the horse has bolted** to be so late in taking action to prevent something bad happening that the bad event has already happened

doorbell /ˈdɔː.bel/ (US) /ˈdɔːr-/ *noun* [C] a bell operated by a button on or next to the door of a house, which you ring to tell the people inside that you are there

doorframe /ˈdɔː.freɪm/ (US) /ˈdɔːr-/ *noun* [C] the rectangular frame that surrounds an opening into which a door fits

D

doorjamb /ˈdɔː.dʒæm/ [US] /ˈdɔːr-/ *noun* [C] *US FOR* **doorpost**

doorknob /ˈdɔː.nɒb/ [US] /ˈdɔːr.nɑːb/ *noun* [C] a round handle that you turn to open a door

doorknocker /ˈdɔːˌnɒk.əʳ/ [US] /ˈdɔːrˌnɑː.kɚ/ *noun* [C] a **knocker**

doorman /ˈdɔː.mən/ [US] /ˈdɔːr-/ *noun* [C] a person whose job is to stand by the door of a hotel or public building and allow people to go in or out, and to open their car doors, etc.

doormat /ˈdɔː.mæt/ [US] /ˈdɔːr-/ *noun* [C] **1** a piece of thick material placed on the floor by a door, used to clean your shoes on when you go into a building **2** *INFORMAL DISAPPROVING* a person who accepts being treated badly and does not complain: *He may be selfish and insensitive, but she is a bit of a doormat.*

doornail /ˈdɔː.neɪl/ [US] /ˈdɔːr-/ *noun* [C] See **be as dead as a doornail** at **dead** NOT LIVING.

doorpost /ˈdɔː.pəʊst/ [US] /ˈdɔːr.poʊst/ *noun* [C] (*US ALSO* **doorjamb**) one of the two vertical posts on either side of an opening into which a door fits

doorstep /ˈdɔː.step/ [US] /ˈdɔːr-/ *noun* [C] **1** a step in front of an outside door: *Don't keep her* **on** *the doorstep* (= outside the door)*, Jamie, invite her in.* **2** *UK* a very thick piece of bread

• **on *sb's* doorstep** *INFORMAL* very close to where someone is or lives: *There's a lovely park right on our doorstep.*

doorstep /ˈdɔː.step/ [US] /ˈdɔːr-/ *verb* [T often passive] **-pp-** *UK DISAPPROVING* If you are doorstepped by JOURNALISTS, they come to your house and ask you to speak or answer questions, even if you do not want to them to: *He complained about being constantly doorstepped by the press.*

doorstop /ˈdɔː.stɒp/ [US] /ˈdɔːr.stɑːp/ *noun* [C] a heavy object that is used to keep a door open

door-to-door [ALL HOMES] /ˌdɔː.təˈdɔːʳ/ [US] /ˌdɔːr.t̬əˈdɔːr/ *adj* [before n], *adv* going from one house or building in an area to another: *He was a door-to-door* **salesman** *before he became an actor.* ○ *She sells cosmetics door-to-door.*

door-to-door [WHOLE JOURNEY] /ˌdɔː.təˈdɔːʳ/ [US] /ˌdɔːr.t̬əˈdɔːr/ *adv* including all the stages of a journey from the beginning to the end: *My journey from Cambridge to Paris takes five hours door-to-door.*

doorway /ˈdɔː.weɪ/ [US] /ˈdɔːr-/ *noun* [C] the space in a wall where a door opens, or a covered area just outside a door

dope [DRUG] /dəʊp/ [US] /doʊp/ *noun* [U] *INFORMAL* cannabis, or, more generally, any type of illegal drug: *They were arrested for* **smoking/selling/buying** *dope.*

dope /dəʊp/ [US] /doʊp/ *verb* [T] to give a person or an animal drugs in order to make them perform better or worse in a competition: *They were arrested for doping racehorses.*

dope /dəʊp/ [US] /doʊp/ *verb* [T] to give a person or an animal a drug to make them want to sleep: *We always have to dope* **up** *our cat for long car journeys.*

ˌdoped (ˈup) *adj* under the influence of drugs: *They were too doped up to notice what was happening.*

dopey /ˈdəʊ.pi/ [US] /ˈdoʊ-/ *adj* **dopier, dopiest** *He'd taken a sleeping tablet the night before and still felt dopey* (= wanting sleep and moving slowly).

dope [PERSON] /dəʊp/ [US] /doʊp/ *noun* [C] a silly person: *You shouldn't have told him, you dope!*

dopey /ˈdəʊ.pi/ [US] /ˈdoʊ-/ *adj* **dopier, dopiest** *He's nice, but a bit dopey* (= silly).

ˈdope ˌtest *noun* [C] an official test to discover whether a person or an animal taking part in a competition has been given any drugs to make their performance better or worse

doppelgänger /ˈdɒp.əlˌgæŋ.əʳ/ [US] /ˈdɑː.pəlˌgæŋ.ɚ/ *noun* [C] a spirit that looks exactly like a living person, or a person who looks exactly like someone else but who is not related to them

Doppler effect /ˈdɒp.lə.rɪˌfekt/ [US] /ˈdɑː.plɚ.ɪ-/ *noun* [U] (*ALSO* **Doppler shift**) *SPECIALIZED* a change that seems to happen in the rate of sound or light wave production of an object when its movement changes in relation to another object

Doric /ˈdɒr.ɪk/ [US] /ˈdɔːr-/ *adj* of or copying the simplest of the classical styles of ancient Greek building: *a Doric column* ➲Compare **Corinthian**; **Ionic**.

dork /dɔːk/ [US] /dɔːrk/ *noun* [C] *SLANG* a stupid awkward person

dormant /ˈdɔː.mənt/ [US] /ˈdɔːr-/ *adj* **1** describes something that is not active or growing, but which has the ability to be active at a later time: *The long-dormant volcano has recently shown signs of erupting.* ○ *These investments have remained dormant for several years.* **2 lie dormant** If something lies dormant, it is not active: *Her talent might have lain dormant had it not been for her aunt's encouragement.*

dormer (window) /ˌdɔː.məˈwɪn.dəʊ/ [US] /ˌdɔːr.mɚˈwɪn.doʊ/ *noun* [C] a window sticking out from a sloping roof

dormitory [ROOM] /ˈdɔː.mɪ.tᵊr.i/ [US] /ˈdɔːr.mə.tɔːr-/ *noun* [C] (*INFORMAL* **dorm**) *UK* a large room containing many beds, especially in a BOARDING school or university

dormitory [BUILDING] /ˈdɔː.mɪ.tᵊr.i/ [US] /ˈdɔːr.mə.tɔːr-/ *noun* [C] (*INFORMAL* **dorm**) *US* a large building at a college or university where students live

ˈdormitory ˌtown *UK noun* [C] (*AUS* **dormitory suburb,** *US* **bedroom community**) a place from which many people travel in order to work in a bigger town or city

dormouse /ˈdɔː.maʊs/ [US] /ˈdɔːr-/ *noun* [C] *plural* **dormice** a small animal which looks like a mouse with a long furry tail

dorsal /ˈdɔː.sᵊl/ [US] /ˈdɔːr-/ *adj* [before n] *SPECIALIZED* of, on or near the back of an animal: *a shark's dorsal **fin*** ➲Compare **ventral**.

dory /ˈdɔː.ri/ [US] /ˈdɔːr.i/ *noun* [C] a **John Dory**

DOS /dɒs/ [US] /dɑːs/ *noun* [U] *TRADEMARK ABBREVIATION FOR* disk operating system: (= a type of operating system for computers)

dosage /ˈdəʊ.sɪdʒ/ [US] /ˈdoʊ-/ *noun* [C usually sing] *FORMAL* the amount of medicine that you should take at one time: *"What's the dosage?" "One spoonful three times a day."* ○ *You mustn't exceed the* **recommended** *dosage.*

dose /dəʊs/ [US] /doʊs/ *noun* [C] **1** a measured amount of something such as medicine: *a high/low dose* ○ *a dose* **of** *penicillin* ○ *The label says to take one dose three times a day.* ○ *Twenty or thirty of these pills would be a* **lethal** *dose* (= enough to kill you). **2** an amount or experience of something bad or unpleasant: *The government received a hefty dose* **of** *bad news this week.* ○ *She's got a nasty dose* **of** *flu.*

• **in small doses** for short periods of time: *I can only stand opera in small doses.*

• **like a dose of salts** *UK INFORMAL* very quickly: *The medicine went through me like a dose of salts.*

dose /dəʊs/ [US] /doʊs/ *verb* [T] to give someone a measured amount of medicine: *INFORMAL He dosed* **himself (up) with** *valium to calm his nerves.*

dosh /dɒʃ/ [US] /dɑːʃ/ *noun* [U] *UK SLANG* money

doss /dɒs/ [US] /dɑːs/ *verb* [I usually + adv or prep] *UK SLANG* **1** to sleep outside or in an empty building because you have no home and no money: *She was dossing in doorways until the police picked her up.* ➲See also **dosshouse**. **2** (*ALSO* **doss down**) to sleep somewhere without a bed: *Can I doss down at your house tonight, after the party?*

▲ **doss about/around** *phrasal verb UK SLANG* to spend your time doing very little: *Come on, Peter, stop dossing around and get some work done.*

a doss /əˈdɒs/ *noun* [S] *UK SLANG* an activity that is easy or does not need hard work

dosser /ˈdɒs.əʳ/ [US] /ˈdɑː.sɚ/ *noun* [C] *UK SLANG* **1** someone who has no home and no money **2** a very lazy person

dosshouse *UK* /ˈdɒs.haʊs/ [US] /ˈdɑːs-/ *noun* [C] (*US* **flophouse**) *SLANG* an extremely cheap hotel for poor homeless people in a city

dossier /ˈdɒs.i.eɪ/ /-əʳ/ [US] /ˈdɑː.si.eɪ/ *noun* [C] a set of papers containing information about a person, often a criminal, or on any subject: *The secret service probably has a dossier* **on** *all of us.*

dot /dɒt/ [US] /dɑːt/ *noun* **1** [C] a very small round mark: *The full stop at the end of this sentence is a dot.* ○ *Her skirt was blue with white dots.* **2** [U] the spoken form of a

FULL STOP in an Internet or email address, or some computer files: *"What's the web address?" "www dot cambridge dot org"*.

• **on the dot** exactly at the stated or expected time: *The plane landed at two o'clock on the dot.* ○ UK *She came promptly on the dot of eleven.*

• **the year dot** UK INFORMAL a very long time ago: *I've known Peter since the year dot.*

dot /dɒt/ ⓤ /dɑːt/ *verb* -**tt**- **1** [T] to put a dot or dots on something: *Your handwriting is difficult to read because you don't dot your i's.* **2** [T often passive] to be spread across an area, or to spread many similar things across an area: *We have offices dotted about/all over the region.* ○ *The countryside is dotted with beautiful churches.*

• **dot the i's and cross the t's** to pay a great deal of attention to the details of something, especially when you are trying to complete a task: *The negotiations are nearly finished, but we still have to dot the i's and cross the t's.*

dotage /'dəʊ.tɪdʒ/ ⓤ /'doʊ.tɪdʒ/ *noun* [U] old age, especially with some loss of mental ability

dot.com, **dotcom** /ˌdɒtˈkɒm/ ⓤ /ˌdɑːtˈkɑːm/ *noun* [C] a company that does most of its business on the Internet: *A survey found that 20 of the top 150 European dot.coms could run out of cash within a year.* **dot.com**, **dotcom** *adj* [before n]: *a dot.com firm/millionaire*

dote /dəʊt/ ⓤ /doʊt/ *verb*

▲ **dote on** *sb phrasal verb* to love someone completely and believe they are perfect: *He dotes on the new baby.*

doting /'dəʊ.tɪŋ/ ⓤ /'doʊ.tɪŋ/ *adj* [before n] showing that you love someone very much: *We saw photographs of the doting father with the baby on his knee.*

dot-matrix printer /ˌdɒtˌmeɪ.trɪksˈprɪn.tə^r/ ⓤ /ˌdɑːt-ˈmeɪ.trɪksˌprɪn.tɚ/ *noun* [C] SPECIALIZED a computer printer that forms letters, numbers and other symbols from dots

dotted 'line *noun* [C] a line of dots: *Footpaths are shown on the map as dotted red lines.* ○ *Cut along the dotted line.*

dotty /'dɒt.i/ ⓤ /'dɑː.t̬i/ *adj* **1** UK INFORMAL slightly strange or mentally ill: *a dotty old woman* **2** UK OLD-FASHIONED **be dotty about** *sb/sth* to like or love someone or something very much or be very interested in them: *Jean's absolutely dotty about cats.* **dottiness** /'dɒt.ɪ.nəs/ ⓤ /'dɑː.t̬ɪ-/ *noun* [U]

double TWICE /'dʌb.l̩/ *adj* twice the size, amount, price, etc., or consisting of two similar things together: *I ordered a double espresso* (= two standard amounts in one cup). ○ *Go through the double doors and turn left.* ○ *The word 'cool' has a double 'o' in the middle.* ○ *Everything he says has a double meaning* (= has two possible meanings). ○ *This painkiller is double strength* (= has twice the medicine as normal). ○ UK *Sabiha's telephone number is double three, one, five, double seven* (= 331577).

double /'dʌb.l̩/ *noun, predeterminer* something that is twice the amount, size, strength, etc. of something else: *I paid double* (= twice as much) *for those trousers before the sale.* ○ *Electrical goods are almost double the price they were a few years ago.* ○ *"Would you like another whiskey?" "Yes. Make it a double* (= two standard amounts in one glass)."

double /'dʌb.l̩/ *noun* [C] US in baseball, a hit that allows the BATTER (= person who hits the ball) to reach second BASE

• **see double** to have a problem with your eyes so that you see two of everything, usually because you are drunk or ill: *I started seeing double, then I fainted.*

• **at/on the double** OLD-FASHIONED INFORMAL very quickly and without any delay

• **double or quits** UK (US **double or nothing**) (in games where money is risked) an agreement that the player who owes money will owe twice as much if they lose, but will owe nothing if they win

double /'dʌb.l̩/ *adv* in two parts or layers: *Fold the blanket double* (= so that it is in two layers) *and then you won't be cold.* ○ *They were bent double* (= Their heads and shoulders were bent far forward and down) *from decades of labour in the fields.*

double /'dʌb.l̩/ *verb* [I or T] to become twice as much or as many, or to make something twice as much or many: *The government aims to double the number of students in*

higher education within 25 years. ○ *Company profits have doubled since the introduction of new technology.*

doubly /'dʌb.li/ *adv* twice as much, or very much more: *Losing both the Cup and the League is doubly disappointing* (= disappointing in two ways).

double PERSON /'dʌb.l̩/ *noun* [C usually sing] a person who looks exactly the same as someone else: *Hey Tony, I met someone at a party last week who was your double.*

PHRASAL VERBS WITH **double** ▼

▲ **double (up) as** *sth phrasal verb* to be also used as something else: *The kitchen table doubles as my desk when I'm writing.* ○ *Our spare bedroom doubles up as a study for Dan when he's working at home.*

▲ **double back** *phrasal verb* to turn and go back in the direction you have come from: *We realized we had taken the wrong road and had to double back.*

▲ **double** *(sb)* **up/over** BEND *phrasal verb* If you double up/over, or if something doubles you up/over, you suddenly bend forwards and down, usually because of pain or laughter: *Most of the crowd doubled up with laughter at every joke.* ○ *She was doubled up/over with the pain in her stomach.*

▲ **double up** SHARE *phrasal verb* to share something, especially a room, with someone else: *Terry will have to double up with Bill in the front bedroom.*

double 'agent *noun* [C] a person employed by a government to discover secret information about enemy countries, but who is really working for one of these enemy countries

double-barreled TWO PURPOSES /ˌdʌb.l̩ˈbær.^əld/ *adj* US having two purposes: *It was a double-barreled question.*

double-barrelled GUN /ˌdʌb.l̩ˈbær.^əld/ *adj* [before n] describes a gun that has two barrels: *a double-barrelled shotgun*

double-barrelled 'name *noun* [C] UK a family name with two joined parts, such as Harvey-Jones

double 'bass *noun* [C] (INFORMAL **bass fiddle**) the largest musical instrument of the violin family, which plays very low notes

double 'bed *noun* [C] a bed big enough for two people to sleep in

double 'bill *noun* [C] a cinema or theatre performance that consists of two main items

double 'bind *noun* [C usually sing] a difficult situation in which, whatever action you decide to take, you cannot escape unpleasant results: *The headteacher is caught in a double bind because whether she expels the boy or lets him off, she still gets blamed.*

double-blind /ˌdʌb.l̩ˈblaɪnd/ *adj* describes a study or TRIAL, especially in medicine, in which two groups of people are studied, for example with one group taking a new drug and one group taking something else, but neither the people in the study nor the doctor knows which person is in which group

double 'bluff *noun* [C] UK a clever attempt to deceive someone, especially by telling them the truth when they think you are telling lies

double-book /ˌdʌb.l̩ˈbʊk/ *verb* [I; T often passive] to promise the same room, seat, ticket, etc. to different people: *The room was double-booked so they had to give us a different one.*

double-breasted /ˌdʌb.l̩ˈbres.tɪd/ *adj* A double-breasted jacket or coat has two sets of buttons and two wide parts at the front, one of which covers the other when the buttons are fastened.

double-check /ˌdʌb.l̩ˈtʃek/ *verb* [T] If you double-check something, you make certain it is correct or safe, usually by examining it again.

double 'chin *noun* [C] a fold of skin between the face and neck which is caused by a layer of fat developing under the chin

double-click /ˌdʌb.l̩ˈklɪk/ *verb* [I or T] (in computing) to press the MOUSE (= control device) twice in order to tell the computer to do something: *Double-click (on) the icon to start the program.*

double 'cream UK *noun* [U] (US **heavy cream**) very thick cream

D

double-cross /ˌdʌb.l'krɒs/ ⓤ /-ˌ'krɑːs/ *verb* [T] to deceive someone by working only for your own advantage in the (usually illegal) activities you have planned together: *The diamond thief double-crossed his partners and gave them only worthless fake jewels.* **double-cross** /ˌdʌb.l'krɒs/ ⓤ /-ˌ'krɑːs/ *noun* [C] *They set up a double-cross to cheat him of his money.*

double-dealing /ˌdʌb.l'diː.lɪŋ/ *noun* [U] dishonesty and actions intended to deceive: *The local business community has been destroyed by corruption, cheating and double-dealing.*

double-decker (bus) /ˌdʌb.lˌdek.ə'bʌs/ ⓤ /-ɚ-/ *noun* [C] a tall bus with two levels

double-decker (sandwich) /ˌdʌb.lˌdek.ə'sænd.wɪdʒ/ ⓤ /-ɚ'sænd.wɪtʃ/ *noun* [C] a sandwich made with three pieces of bread with food such as cold meat or cheese between them

double-dip /ˌdʌb.l'dɪp/ *verb* [I] *US* to get money from two places at the same time, often in a way that is not legal

double 'Dutch NONSENSE *noun* [U] *UK INFORMAL* talk or writing that is nonsense or that you cannot understand

double 'Dutch GAME *noun* [U] a game played in the US by jumping over a rope

double-edged /ˌdʌb.lˌ'edʒd/ *adj* describes something that acts in two ways, often with one negative and one positive effect: *She paid me the double-edged compliment of saying my work was "excellent for a beginner".* ○ *The government's programme to grow cash crops for export is a double-edged **sword** because it has created a local food shortage.* ⊃See also **two-edged**.

double entendre /ˌduː.bl.ɑːn'tɑːn.drə/ *noun* [C] a word or phrase that might be understood in two ways, one of which is usually sexual

double 'fault *noun* [C] (in tennis and some other games) two mistakes made one after the other by a player who is beginning a game by hitting the ball

double 'feature *noun* [C] the showing of two different films, one after the other in a cinema

double-glazing /ˌdʌb.l'gleɪ.zɪŋ/ *noun* [U] windows that have two layers of glass to keep a building warm or to reduce noise from outside **double-glaze** /ˌdʌb.l'gleɪz/ *verb* [T]

double-header /ˌdʌb.l'hed.əʳ/ ⓤ /-ɚ-/ *noun* [C] two games of baseball or football played one after the other

double 'helix *noun* [U] *SPECIALIZED* the structure of a DNA molecule

double 'jeopardy *noun* [U] the act of putting someone on trial twice for the same offence

double-jointed /ˌdʌb.l'dʒɔɪn.tɪd/ ⓤ /-t̬ɪd/ *adj* able to move your joints in an unusual way so that, for example, you can bend your fingers or legs backwards as well as forwards

double 'negative *noun* [C] in grammar, the use of two negatives (= words that mean 'no') in the same phrase or sentence: *The phrase 'a not unfamiliar situation' is an example of a double negative.*

double-park /ˌdʌb.lˌ'pɑːk/ ⓤ /-ˌ'pɑːrk/ *verb* [I or T] to park a car illegally next to a car that is already parked at the side of the road

double 'play *noun* [C] when two players are put out in baseball after the ball is hit once

double-quick /ˌdʌb.l'kwɪk/ *adv* *UK INFORMAL* very quickly: *She left the room double-quick when I started singing.*

● **in double-quick time** *UK INFORMAL* very quickly; as quickly as possible: *I shouted and he was gone in double quick time.*

double 'room *noun* [C] (*INFORMAL* **double**) a room in a hotel for two people

doubles /'dʌb.lz/ *noun* [U] a game of tennis or a similar sport between two teams of two people: *men's/women's/mixed doubles* ○ *Who won the men's doubles at Wimbledon this year?* ⊃Compare **singles** at **single** ONE.

double-space /ˌdʌb.l'speɪs/ *verb* [T] If you double-space lines of text on a typewriter or computer, you put an empty line between each line of writing. **double-spacing** /ˌdʌb.l'speɪ.sɪŋ/ *noun* [U]

double-speak /'dʌb.l.spiːk/ *noun* [U] *UK FOR* **double-talk**

double 'standard *noun* [C] a rule or standard of good behaviour which, unfairly, some people are expected to follow or achieve but other people are not: *The Government is being accused of **(having)** double standards in the way it is so tough on law and order yet allows its own MPs to escape prosecution for fraud.* ✳ NOTE: In British English this word is usually a plural noun, but in American English it is usually a singular noun.

doublet /'dʌb.lɪt/ *noun* [C] a short tight jacket worn by European men in the 15th, 16th and 17th centuries

double 'take *noun* *INFORMAL* **do a double take** to look at someone or something and then look again because you suddenly recognize them or notice that something unusual is happening: *I did a double take – I couldn't believe it was her.*

double-talk /'dʌb.l.tɔːk/ ⓤ /-tɑːk/ *noun* [U] (*UK ALSO* **double-speak**) language that has no real meaning or has more than one meaning and is intended to hide the truth: *He accused the ambassador of diplomatic double-talk.*

double-team /'dʌb.l.tiːm/ *verb* [T] in basketball, to have two members of a team trying to prevent an opposing player from scoring: *They double-teamed Jordan in the second half.*

double 'time *noun* [U] If you are paid double time, you are paid twice the usual amount for the time which you spend working, usually because you are working at the WEEKEND (= Saturday and Sunday) or on an official holiday.

double 'trouble *noun* [U] *INFORMAL* a situation in which there is twice the number of problems that usually exist: *Having twins usually means double trouble for the parents.*

double 'vision *noun* [U] when you see two of everything, usually with one image partly covering the other: *He suffered headaches and double vision after hitting his head in the accident.*

double whammy /ˌdʌb.l'wæm.i/ *noun* [C usually sing] *INFORMAL* a situation when two unpleasant things happen at almost the same time: *Britain's farmers have faced the double whammy of a rising pound and falling agricultural prices.*

double 'yellow ˌline *noun* [C usually pl] in Britain, two lines of yellow paint which are put along the side of a road to show that vehicles may never be parked there: *It's an offence to park on double yellow lines.* ⊃See also **yellow line**.

doubt /daʊt/ *noun* [C or U] (a feeling of) uncertainty about something, especially about how good or true it is: *I'm **having** doubts **about** his ability to do the job.* ○ *If there's any doubt **about** the rocket's engines, we ought to cancel the launch.* ○ *The prosecution has to establish his guilt* (*UK*) **beyond (reasonable) doubt**/(*US*) **beyond a (reasonable) doubt**. ○ *This latest scandal has **raised** doubts **about** his suitability for the post.* ○ [+ *(that)*] *I never had any doubt **(that)** you would win.* ○ *He's the most attractive man in the building, **no** doubt **about that/it**.*

● **cast doubt on sth** to make something seem uncertain: *Witnesses have cast doubt on the suspect's innocence.*

● **in doubt** If the future or success of someone or something is in doubt, it is unlikely to continue or to be successful: *The future of the stadium is in doubt because of a lack of money.*

● **no doubt** used to emphasize that what you are saying is true or likely to happen: *We will, no doubt, discuss these issues again at the next meeting.* ○ *No doubt you'll want to unpack and have a rest before dinner.*

● **without (a) doubt** used to emphasize your opinion: *She is without (a) doubt the best student I have ever taught.* ⊃See also **undoubtedly** at **undoubted**.

doubt /daʊt/ *verb* [T] **1** to not feel certain or confident about something or to think that something is not probable: *I doubt **whether/if** I can finish the work on time.* ○ [+ *that*] *They had begun to doubt **that** it could be completed in time.* ○ *He may come back tomorrow with the money, but I very much doubt it.* ○ *I don't doubt his abilities.* **2 doubt sb/doubt sb's word** to not trust someone or believe what they say: *He's never lied to me before, so I have no reason to doubt his word.*

doubter /ˈdaʊ.tə^r/ [US] /-t̬ɚ/ *noun* [C] someone who doubts: *critics and doubters*

doubtful /ˈdaʊt.f^{ə}l/ *adj* **1** If you are doubtful about something, you are uncertain about it: *The teacher is doubtful* ***about*** *hav****ing*** *parents working as classroom assistants.* **2** If a situation is doubtful, it is unlikely to happen or to be successful: ***It*** *is doubtful* ***whether/if*** *they ever reached the summit before they died.* ○ ***It*** *was doubtful* ***that*** *the money would ever be found again.*

doubtfully /ˈdaʊt.f^{ə}l.i/ *adv*: *"Are you telling me the truth?" he asked doubtfully.*

doubtless /ˈdaʊt.ləs/ *adv* FORMAL used to mean that you are certain that something will happen or is true: *They will doubtless protest, but there's nothing they can do.* ○ *Doubtless you will have heard the news already.*

doubting Thomas /ˌdaʊ.tɪŋˈtɒm.əs/ [US] /-t̬ɪŋˈtɑː.məs/ *noun* [C usually sing] a person who refuses to believe anything until they are shown proof

douche /duːʃ/ *verb* [I or T] to put a liquid, usually water, into the vagina in order to wash it or treat it medically

douche /duːʃ/ *noun* [C]

dough [FLOUR] /dəʊ/ [US] /doʊ/ *noun* [C or U] flour mixed with water and often yeast, fat or sugar so that it is ready for baking: *bread dough* ○ *pastry dough* ○ *She* ***kneaded*** *the dough and left it to rise.*

doughy /ˈdəʊ.i/ [US] /ˈdoʊ-/ *adj* soft, thick and sticky, like dough

dough [MONEY] /dəʊ/ [US] /doʊ/ *noun* [U] OLD-FASHIONED SLANG money: *I don't want to work but I need the dough.*

doughnut, US ALSO **donut** /ˈdəʊ.nʌt/ [US] /ˈdoʊ-/ *noun* [C] a small circular cake, fried in hot fat, either with a hole in the middle or filled with jam: *a (UK)* ***jam/****(US)* ***jelly*** *doughnut*

doughty /ˈdaʊ.ti/ [US] /-t̬i/ *adj* LITERARY determined, brave and unwilling ever to admit defeat: *She has been for many years a doughty campaigner for women's rights.*

dour /dʊə^r/ [US] /dʊr/ *adj* (usually of a person's appearance or manner) unfriendly, unhappy and very serious: *The normally dour Mr James was photographed smiling and joking with friends.* **dourly** /ˈdʊə.li/ [US] /ˈdʊr-/ *adv*

douse [MAKE WET], **dowse** /daʊs/ *verb* [T] to make something or someone wet by throwing a lot of liquid over them: *We watched as demonstrators doused a car* ***in/with*** *petrol and set it alight.*

douse [STOP BURNING], **dowse** /daʊs/ *verb* [T] to stop a fire or light from burning or shining, especially by putting water on it or by covering it with something

dove [BIRD] /dʌv/ *noun* [C] a white or grey bird, often used as a symbol of peace

dove [PERSON] /dʌv/ *noun* [C] a person in politics who prefers to solve problems using peaceful methods instead of force or violence ➲Compare **hawk** PERSON.

dove [DIVE] /dəʊv/ [US] /doʊv/ MAINLY US *past simple of* **dive**

dovecote, **dovecot** /ˈdʌv.kəʊt/ [US] /-koʊt/ *noun* [C] a small building for DOVES or similar birds to live in

dovetail /ˈdʌv.teɪl/ *verb* [I or T] to cause something to fit exactly together: *Their results dovetail nicely* ***with*** *ours.* ○ *We've tried to dovetail our plans* ***with*** *theirs.*

ˈdovetail (ˌjoint) *noun* [C] SPECIALIZED a type of joint used to fix two pieces of wood firmly together

dowager /ˈdaʊə.dʒə^r/ [US] /-dʒɚ/ *noun* [C] **1** SPECIALIZED a woman of high social rank whose husband is dead but who has a title and property because of her marriage to him: *a dowager queen* **2** LITERARY an old woman who is, or behaves as if she is, of high social rank

dowdy /ˈdaʊ.di/ *adj* DISAPPROVING (especially of clothes or the person wearing them) not attractive or fashionable: *a dowdy skirt* ○ *She looked dowdy and plain in that outfit.*

the Dow Jones (industrial) average /ðəˌdaʊ.dʒəʊnz.ɪnˌdʌs.tri.əlˈæv.^{ə}r.ɪdʒ/ [US] /-dʒoʊnz.ɪnˌdʌs.tri.əlˈæv.ɚ-/ *noun* [S] (ALSO **Dow Jones, the Dow**) an INDEX (= a system for comparing values) of the prices of shares in the 30 most important companies on the New York Stock Exchange ➲Compare **the FTSE 100 (Index)**; **the Nikkei (index)**.

down [LOWER POSITION] /daʊn/ *prep, adv* **1** in or towards a low or lower position, from a higher one: *Is this (UK) lift/(US) elevator going down?* ○ *I slid down the hill.* ○ *Don't look down! You'll get dizzy.* ○ *Aikiko fell down some stairs and broke her wrist.* ○ *The sun's going down and it'll be dark soon.* ○ *The space capsule came down in the ocean.* ○ *I bent down to look under the bed.* **2** moving from above and onto a surface: *Just as I was sitting down to watch TV, the phone rang.* ○ *Why don't you lie down on the sofa for a while?* ○ *This box is really heavy – can we put it down (on the floor) for a minute?* ○ *Get down off that table immediately, you silly girl!* ○ *The terrorists forced everybody to lie face down* (= with the front part of the body below) *on the floor.* **3** inside your stomach: *You'll feel better once you've got some hot soup down you.* ○ *He's getting weak because he can't keep anything down.*

down /daʊn/ *adv* If you burn/cut/knock something or someone down, you cause them to fall to the ground, usually damaged, destroyed or injured: *The house burned down many years ago.* ○ *These trees will have to be cut down to make way for the new road.* ○ UK *She was knocked down by a car and killed instantly.*

down /daʊn/ *adv, adj* **1** firmly in place or into position: *I put the loose floorboard back and nailed it down.* ○ *He held my arms down by my sides.* **2** from an older person to a younger one: *The necklace has been passed/handed down through seven generations.* ○ *These myths have come down to us from prehistoric times.* ➲See also **go down** BE REMEMBERED.

• **Down with** ***sb/sth*****!** something you say, write or shout to show your opposition to someone or something, and to demand that they are removed from power or destroyed

• **(right) down to** even including the following minor things or people: *Amalie was dressed completely in black, right down to black lipstick and a black earring.* ○ *Everyone,* ***from*** *the Director down to the secretaries, was questioned by the police.*

• **down the drain** (AUS ALSO **down the gurgler**) INFORMAL If work or money is or goes down the drain, it is spoiled or wasted: *If the factory closes, that will be a million pounds' worth of investment down the drain.*

• **down the toilet** (UK ALSO **down the pan**) INFORMAL If something is or goes down the toilet, it is wasted or spoiled: *After the drugs scandal, his career went down the toilet.*

• **down under** UK AND US INFORMAL (in or to) Australia or New Zealand: *She was born in Scotland, but she's been living down under for 22 years.*

• **kick/hit** ***sb*** **when** ***they are*** **down** to take unfair advantage of someone when they are in a weak position: *It's typical of the boss to kick someone when they're down.*

down /daʊn/ *verb* [T] **1** to cause something or someone to fall to the ground: *We downed three enemy planes with our missiles.* ○ *The ice storm has downed trees and power lines all over the region.* **2** to eat or drink something quickly: *He'd downed four beers before I'd finished one.*

• **down tools** UK to refuse to continue working, especially because you are dissatisfied with the amount you are being paid or with your working conditions: *The printers are threatening to down tools if the pay offer is not increased to 8%.*

down [LOWER LEVEL] /daʊn/ *adv* in or towards a lower level, a smaller amount or a simpler state: *The rate of inflation is finally going down.* ○ *Turn the TV down – it's way too loud!* ○ *The nurse bandaged my sprained ankle to keep the swelling down* (= to limit the swelling). ○ *If you wait a few months, the price will come down.* ○ *Milan were three goals down* (= losing by three goals) *at half-time.* ○ *The number of students at this school has* ***gone*** *down* ***from*** *500 last year* ***to*** *410.*

• **be down on** ***sb*** INFORMAL to criticize someone: *It's not fair of the boss to be so down on a new employee.*

• **come/go down in the world** MAINLY UK to lose the money and high social rank that you had in the past: *Fancy her taking a job like that – she's certainly come down in the world!*

• **One/Two, etc. down, one/two. etc. to go.** an expression which is used to mean that you have done or dealt with the first number of things and have yet to do or deal with the second number of things: *"Have you done your essays?" "Two down, three to go."*

down /daʊn/ *noun UK INFORMAL* **have a down on sb** to dislike someone, often unfairly: *Why do you have a down on him? I think he seems really nice.*

down DISTANT /daʊn/ *adv* **1** used, especially with prepositions, to emphasize that a place is distant from you or from somewhere considered to be central: *I'll meet you down at the club after work.* ○ *He has a house down by the harbour.* ○ *I'm going down to the shop to buy some milk.* ◔See also **down** TO. **2** in or towards the south: *Things are much more expensive down (in the) south.* ○ *My parents live down in Florida, but they come up to Chicago every summer.* ○ *We're moving down to London.*

• **down** *sb's* **way** in the (distant) place where someone lives: *Down our way people don't take much interest in politics.*

down ALONG /daʊn/ *prep* along: *We drove down the motorway as far as Bristol.* ○ *Her office is down the corridor on the right.* ○ *They sailed the boat down the river* (= towards the sea).

• **down the road/line/track** in the future: *We have an idea to develop a talking book, but a marketable product is a long way down the road.*

down TO /daʊn/ *prep UK NOT STANDARD* to: *I went down the pub with my mates.* ◔Compare **up** TO.

down IN WRITING /daʊn/ *adv* in writing or on paper: *I'll write it down now so I won't forget.* ○ *Do you have it down in writing/on paper, or was it just a verbal agreement?* ○ *I've got/put you down for* (= have written that you want) *three tickets each.* ○ *The police officers were taking down the names of witnesses.*

down UNHAPPY /daʊn/ *adj* unhappy; unable to feel excited or energetic about anything: *She's been really down since her husband died.* ○ *I've been (feeling) a bit down this week.*

down MONEY /daʊn/ *adv* at the time of buying: *I gave him £1000 down, and paid the rest in instalments.*

down NOT IN OPERATION /daʊn/ *adj* [after v] *SPECIALIZED* (of a system or machine, especially a computer) not in operation or not working, usually only for a limited period of time: *The network will be down for an hour for routine maintenance.* ○ *The whole system's gone down.* ◔See also **downtime**.

down FEATHERS /daʊn/ *noun* **1** [U] small soft feathers, especially those from a young bird: *goose/duck down* ○ *a down jacket/pillow/sleeping bag* (= a jacket/pillow/sleeping bag filled with down) **2** [S or U] very soft fine hair

downy /'daʊ.ni/ *adj* **1** filled with feathers: *a downy nest* **2** covered with soft fine hair: *a tiny baby's downy head*

down DEFEAT /daʊn/ *verb* [T] *US* to defeat someone, especially in sport: *The Yankees downed the Red Sox 7-0 last night.*

down- LOWER OR WORSE /daʊn/ *prefix* at or towards the end or the lower or worse part: *downhill* ○ *downriver* ○ *down-market* ○ *the downside*

down-and-out /ˌdaʊn.ə'naʊt/ *adj* having no luck, no money and no opportunities: *a down-and-out loser* ○ *Nobody loves you when you're down and out.* **down-and-out** /ˌdaʊn.ə'naʊt/ *noun* [C] *UK*

down-at-heel *UK* /ˌdaʊn.ət'hiːl/ *adj* (*US* **down-at-the-heel**) wearing old clothes, or in a bad condition, because of a lack of money: *She had a decidedly down-at-heel appearance.* ○ *He worked in a grungy, down-at-the-heel cafe.*

downbeat /'daʊn.biːt/ *adj INFORMAL* quiet and without much excitement: *The actual signing of the treaty was a downbeat affair without any ceremony.* ○ *The band seemed rather downbeat, even unconcerned about their success.* ◔Compare **upbeat**.

downcast UNHAPPY /'daʊn.kɑːst/ ⓤ /-kæst/ /ˌ-'-/ *adj FORMAL* sad and without hope: *I thought you were looking a little downcast this morning.*

downcast EYES DOWN /'daʊn.kɑːst/ ⓤ /-kæst/ /ˌ-'-/ *adj* If someone's eyes are downcast, they are looking down.

downer EXPERIENCE /'daʊ.nəʳ/ ⓤ /-nɚ/ *noun* [C usually sing] *INFORMAL* an event or experience which makes you very unhappy: *You lost your job? That's a real downer!*

downer DRUG /'daʊ.nəʳ/ ⓤ /-nɚ/ *noun* [C] *INFORMAL* a drug that makes you feel calmer ◔Compare **upper** DRUG.

downfall /'daʊn.fɔːl/ ⓤ /-fɑːl/ *noun* [S] (something that causes) the usually sudden destruction of a person, organization or government and their loss of power, money or health: *Rampant corruption brought about the downfall of the government.* ○ *In the end, it was the continual drinking that was his downfall.*

downgrade /ˌdaʊn'greɪd/ *verb* [T] to reduce someone or something to a lower rank or position, or to make something less important or less valued: *My job's been downgraded to that of ordinary editor.* ○ *We mustn't let management downgrade the importance of safety at work.* ◔Compare **upgrade**.

downhearted /ˌdaʊn'hɑː.tɪd/ ⓤ /-'hɑːr.t̬ɪd/ *adj* unhappy and lacking in hope, especially because of a disappointment or failure: *After hearing the news of the defeat, she told supporters not to be downhearted.*

downhill /ˌdaʊn'hɪl/ /'--/ *adv, adj* (moving) towards the bottom of a hill: *It's so much easier running downhill!* ○ *The route is all downhill from here to the finish.* ◔Compare **uphill**.

• **be (all) downhill** to be much easier: *Once we get the preparation done, it'll be downhill all the way.* ○ *If I can just get through the training period, it'll be all downhill from here.*

• **go downhill** to gradually become worse: *After his wife died, his health started to go downhill.*

downhill 'skiing *noun* [U] skiing down slopes, rather than along level ground

'Downing ,Street *noun* [U] the road in central London where the official home of the British Prime Minister is situated: *The Prime Minister lives at 10 Downing Street.*

'Downing ,Street *group noun* [U] the British government or the British Prime Minister: *The announcement took Washington and Paris by surprise, but Downing Street had been expecting it.*

down 'jacket *noun* [C] *US* a warm jacket filled with the soft feathers of a duck or a goose

download /ˌdaʊn'ləʊd/ /'--/ ⓤ /-'loʊd/ *verb* [I or T] to copy or move programs or information into a computer's memory, especially from the Internet or a larger computer

download /'daʊn.ləʊd/ ⓤ /-loʊd/ *noun* [C] a computer program or information that has been or can be downloaded

downloadable /ˌdaʊn'ləʊd.ə.bl̩/ ⓤ /-'loʊd-/ *adj* able to be downloaded: *downloadable documents/files/images* ○ *downloadable software/music*

downmarket *UK* /ˌdaʊn'mɑː.kɪt/ ⓤ /'daʊn,mɑːr-/ *adj* (*US* **downscale**) *DISAPPROVING* cheap in quality and price: *a downmarket tabloid newspaper* ◔Compare **upmarket**. **downmarket** /ˌdaʊn'mɑː.kɪt/ ⓤ /'daʊn,mɑːr-/ *adv*: *This catalogue has gone downmarket since the last time I bought something from it.*

down 'payment, downpayment *noun* [C] an amount of money that you pay at the time that you buy something, but which is only a part of the total cost of that thing. You usually pay the rest of the cost over a period of time: *I've made/put a down payment on a new TV and video.*

downplay /ˌdaʊn'pleɪ/ *verb* [T] to make something seem less important or less bad than it really is: *The government has been trying to downplay the crisis.*

downpour /'daʊn.pɔːʳ/ ⓤ /-pɔːr/ *noun* [C usually sing] a lot of rain in a short time

downright /'daʊn.raɪt/ *adj* [before n], *adv INFORMAL* (especially of something bad) extremely or very great: *She's being downright difficult and obstructive.* ○ *I think the way she's been treated is a downright disgrace.* ○ *These working conditions are unhealthy, if not downright* (= and probably extremely) *dangerous.*

downriver /ˌdaʊn'rɪv.əʳ/ ⓤ /-ɚ/ *adv, adj* **downstream**

downs /daʊnz/ *plural noun UK* low hills covered in grass, especially used in the names of two such areas in southeast England: *the North Downs* ○ *the South Downs*

downscale /'daʊn.skeɪl/ *adj US FOR* **downmarket**

downshift [WAY OF LIVING] /ˈdaʊn.ʃɪft/ *verb* [I] to leave a job that is highly paid and difficult in order to do something that gives you more time and satisfaction but less money **downshifting** /ˈdaʊn.ʃɪf.tɪŋ/ *noun* [U] *The trend towards downshifting, where employees swap the stress of corporate life for more quality time, tempted 6% of the UK workforce last year.*

downshift [VEHICLE] /ˈdaʊn.ʃɪft/ *verb* [I] *US* to change to a lower gear when driving, to reduce power and speed

downside /ˈdaʊn.saɪd/ *noun* [S] the disadvantage of a situation: *The downside of living here, of course, is that it is expensive.* ○ *Unemployment, inflation and greater inequality are often the downside of a market economy.* ➲Compare **upside**.

downsize /ˈdaʊn.saɪz/ *verb* [I or T] If you downsize a company or organization, you make it smaller by reducing the number of people working for it, and if it downsizes, it becomes smaller in this way: *to downsize your workforce/company* ○ *The plight of the Asian economy is forcing businesses to downsize.* **downsizing** /ˈdaʊn.saɪ.zɪŋ/ *noun* [U] ***corporate** downsizing*

downspout /ˈdaʊn.spaʊt/ *noun* [C] *US* a pipe that carries rain water from the roof of a building; a **drainpipe**

Down's syndrome /ˈdaʊnzˌsɪn.drəʊm/ [US] /-droʊm/ *noun* [U] a genetic condition in which a person is born with lower than average mental ability, a flat face, and sloping eyes

downstage /ˌdaʊnˈsteɪdʒ/ [US] /ˈ--/ *adv, adj* towards or at the front of the stage in a theatre ➲Compare **upstage** THEATRE AREA.

downstairs /ˌdaʊnˈsteəz/ [US] /-ˈsterz/ *adv* to or on a lower floor of a building, especially the ground floor: *I went downstairs to answer the phone.* ➲Compare **upstairs**. **downstairs** /ˌdaʊnˈsteəz/ [US] /-ˈsterz/ *adj*: *a downstairs bathroom* **the downˈstairs** *noun* [S] *We've finished decorating upstairs but the downstairs still needs some work.*

downstream /ˌdaʊnˈstriːm/ *adv, adj* in the direction a river or stream is flowing: *The current carried her downstream.* ➲Compare **upstream**.

downswing /ˈdaʊn.swɪŋ/ *noun* [C usually sing] a **downturn**

downtime /ˈdaʊn.taɪm/ *noun* [U] the time during which a machine, especially a computer, is not working or is not able to be used

down-to-earth /ˌdaʊn.tuːˈɜːθ/ [US] /-ˈɝːθ/ *adj APPROVING* practical and sensible: *She's a down-to-earth sort of woman with no pretensions.*

downtown /ˌdaʊnˈtaʊn/ *adj* [before n], *adv US* in or to the central part of a city: *downtown Los Angeles* ○ *a downtown address* ○ *I work downtown, but I live in the suburbs.* **downtown** /ˌdaʊnˈtaʊn/ *noun* [U] *US The hotel is situated two miles north of downtown.* ➲Compare **uptown**.

downtrodden /ˈdaʊnˌtrɒd.ən/ [US] /-ˌtrɑː.dən/ *adj* badly and unfairly treated: *the downtrodden masses*

downturn /ˈdaʊn.tɜːn/ [US] /-tɝːn/ *noun* [C usually sing] a reduction in the amount or success of something, such as a country's economic activity: *the continuing economic downturn* ○ *There is evidence of a downturn **in** the housing market.* ➲Compare **upturn**.

ˌdown ˈvest *noun* [C] *US* a short warm jacket without sleeves which is filled with the soft feathers of a duck or a goose

downwards /ˈdaʊn.wədz/ [US] /-wɚdz/ *adv* (*US ALSO* **downward**) towards a lower position: *The road slopes gently downwards for a mile or two.* ○ *The water filters downwards through the rock for hundreds of feet.* ○ *He was lying **face** downwards on the pavement.* ○ *Casualty figures were **revised** downwards (= reduced) after the war had ended.* ➲Compare **upwards** at **upward**. **downward** /ˈdaʊn.wəd/ [US] /-wɚd/ *adj*: *a downward trend* ○ *The country's economy is on a downward **spiral**.* ➲Compare **upward**.

downwind /ˌdaʊnˈwɪnd/ *adv, adj* in the direction in which the wind blows; with the wind behind: *The smoke drifted downwind.* ○ *They live downwind **of** a pig-farm and sometimes the smell is awful.* ➲Compare **upwind**.

downy /ˈdaʊ.ni/ *adj* ➲See at **down** FEATHERS.

dowry /ˈdaʊ.ri/ *noun* [C] in some societies, an amount of money or property which a woman's parents give to the man she marries

dowse /daʊz/ *verb* [I] to **divine** SEARCH

doyen /ˈdɔɪ.en/ /dwaɪˈen/ *noun* [C usually sing] the oldest, most experienced, and often most respected person of all the people involved in a particular type of work

doyenne /dɔɪˈen/ /dwaɪˈen/ *noun* [C usually sing] the oldest, most experienced, and often most respected woman involved in a particular type of work: *The party was held in honour of Vivienne Westwood, that doyenne **of** British fashion.*

doze /dəʊz/ [US] /doʊz/ *verb* [I] to have a short sleep, especially during the day: *My cat likes dozing in front of the fire.* **doze** /dəʊz/ [US] /doʊz/ *noun* [S] *MAINLY UK He's just **having a** little doze on the settee.*

dozy /ˈdəʊ.zi/ [US] /ˈdoʊ-/ *adj* **1** *INFORMAL* tired and wanting to sleep: *Drinking a beer at lunchtime makes me feel dozy all afternoon.* **2** *UK INFORMAL* mentally slow and tending not to notice what is happening around you: *He'd have driven straight into me if I hadn't seen him first – the dozy idiot!* **dozily** /ˈdəʊ.zɪ.li/ [US] /ˈdoʊ-/ *adv* **doziness** /ˈdəʊ.zɪ.nəs/ [US] /ˈdoʊ-/ *noun* [U]

▲ **doze off** *phrasal verb INFORMAL* If you doze off, you start to sleep, especially during the day: *The office was so hot I nearly dozed off at my desk.*

dozen /ˈdʌz.ən/ *noun* [C], *determiner* twelve: *a dozen eggs* ○ *This recipe makes three dozen cookies.* ○ *Could you get me **half a** dozen (= six) eggs when you go to the shop?* ○ *INFORMAL I've spoken to him dozens **of** (= many) times, but I still don't know his name!* ○ *The refugees arrived **by the** dozen/**in their** dozens (= in large numbers).*

• **nineteen/ten to the dozen** *UK INFORMAL* If you are talking nineteen/ten to the dozen, you are talking very quickly and without stopping.

DPhil /ˌdiːˈfɪl/ *noun* [C] a **PhD**

Dr /ˈdɒk.təʳ/ [US] /ˈdɑːk.tɚ/ *noun* [before n] *WRITTEN ABBREVIATION FOR* Doctor: *An appointment has been made for you to see Dr Fiasco on July 19th at 2.30 p.m.*

drab /dræb/ *adj* **drabber, drabbest** *DISAPPROVING* boring, especially in appearance; lacking colour and excitement: *She walked through the city centre with its drab, grey buildings and felt depressed.* ○ *I feel so drab in this grey uniform.* **drabness** /ˈdræb.nəs/ *noun* [U] *It's the unrelieved drabness of big industrial cities that depresses me.*

drabs /dræbz/ *plural noun* **in dribs and drabs** in small amounts, a few at a time

drachma /ˈdræk.mə/ *noun* [C] the standard unit of money used in Greece before they started using the euro

draconian /drəˈkəʊ.ni.ən/ [US] /-ˈkoʊ-/ *adj FORMAL* describes laws, government actions, etc. which are unreasonably severe; going beyond what is right or necessary: *draconian laws/methods* ○ *He criticized the draconian **measures** taken by the police in controlling the demonstrators.*

draft [PLAN] /drɑːft/ [US] /dræft/ *noun* [C] a piece of text, a formal suggestion or a drawing in its original state, often containing the main ideas and intentions but not the developed form: *This is only a **rough** draft – the finished article will have pictures as well.* ○ *She asked me to check the **(first)** draft of her proposal.* **draft** /drɑːft/ [US] /dræft/ *verb* [T] *Draft a proposal for the project and we can discuss it at the meeting.* **draft** /drɑːft/ [US] /dræft/ *adj* [before n] *a draft plan/bill/proposal*

the draft [MILITARY] *MAINLY US noun* [S] (*UK* **conscription**) the system of ordering people by law to join the armed forces: *He avoided the draft because of a foot injury.* **draft** *MAINLY US* /drɑːft/ [US] /dræft/ *verb* [T usually passive] (*UK* **conscript**) *He was drafted **(into** the army) at eighteen.* **draftee** /ˌdrɑːfˈtiː/ [US] /ˌdræfˈt̬iː/ *noun* [C] *US* a person who has been ordered by law to join the armed forces

draft [MONEY] /drɑːft/ [US] /dræft/ *noun* [C] a written order for money to be paid by a bank, especially to another bank: *I arranged for some money to be sent from London to Madrid by **banker's** draft.*

draft [COLD AIR] /drɑːft/ [US] /dræft/ *noun* [C] *US FOR* **draught** COLD AIR

drafty /ˈdrɑːf.ti/ [US] /ˈdræf.t̬i/ *adj* US FOR **draughty**, see at **draught** COLD AIR

▲ **draft *sb* in** *phrasal verb* [M] UK to bring someone somewhere to do a particular job: *Every Christmas thousands of people are drafted in to help with the post.*

ˈdraft ˌdodger *noun* [C] MAINLY US a person who has disobeyed an official order to join the armed forces

draftsman /ˈdrɑːfts.mən/ [US] /ˈdræfts-/ *noun* [C] **1** US FOR **draughtsman 2** (US ALSO **drafter**) someone who writes legal documents

D

draftswoman /ˈdrɑːftsˌwʊm.ən/ [US] /ˈdræfts-/ *noun* [C] **1** US FOR **draughtswoman 2** a woman who writes legal documents

drag [PULL] /dræg/ *verb* **-gg- 1** [T] to move something by pulling it along a surface, usually the ground: *Pick the chair up instead of dragging it behind you!* ○ *She dragged the canoe down to the water.* **2** [T + adv or prep] to make someone go somewhere they do not want to go: *She had to drag her child **away** from the toy shop.* ○ *I really had to drag myself **out** of bed this morning.* **3** [T] to move something on a computer screen using a **mouse** DEVICE **4** [T] If you drag a subject into a conversation, etc. you begin to talk about it even if it is not connected with what you are talking about: *She's always dragging sex **into** the conversation.* **5** [T] to pull nets or hooks along the bottom of a river or lake in order to find something: *They found the man's body after dragging the canal.*

• **drag *your* heels/feet** to do something slowly because you do not want to do it: *I suspect the government is dragging its heels over this issue.*

• **drag *sb's* name through the mire/mud** to damage someone's reputation by saying extremely insulting things about them

• **drag and drop** If you drag and drop something on a computer screen, you move it from one area to another using the MOUSE DEVICE.

drag /dræg/ *noun* [S or U] SPECIALIZED the force that acts against the forward movement of something which is passing through a gas or a liquid: *Engineers are always looking for ways to minimize drag in new aircraft.*

• **be a drag on *sb/sth*** INFORMAL to slow down or limit the development of someone or something: *She didn't want a husband who would **be a** drag **on** her career.*

drag [BORING] /dræg/ *noun* [S] SLANG something which is inconvenient and boring or unpleasant: *Filling in forms is **such a** drag!* ○ *I've got to go to the dentist's again – what **a** drag!*

drag /dræg/ *verb* [I] **-gg-** *The first half of the film was interesting but the second half dragged **(on)*** (= seemed to go slowly because it was boring).

drag [SUCK] /dræg/ *noun* [C] SLANG the action of taking in air through a cigarette: *Taking a deep drag **of/on** his cigarette he closed his eyes and sighed.*

drag [CLOTHES] /dræg/ *noun* [U] INFORMAL (especially of a man) dressing in clothes of the opposite sex, often for humorous entertainment: *a man **in** drag*

PHRASAL VERBS WITH **drag** ▼

▲ **drag *sb* away** *phrasal verb* INFORMAL to make someone leave a place or stop doing what they are doing so that they can go somewhere else or do something else: *I'm ready to go home now but I don't want to drag you away if you're enjoying yourself.* ○ *I'll bring Tom, if I can drag him away from the football.*

▲ **drag *sb* down** *phrasal verb* UK If an unpleasant situation drags someone down, it makes them feel unhappy or ill: *All that stress at work had begun to drag him down.*

▲ **drag *sb* into *sth*** *phrasal verb* to force someone to become involved in an unpleasant or difficult situation: *Don't drag me into your argument! It's nothing to do with me.*

▲ **drag *sth* out** *phrasal verb* [M] to cause an event to continue for more time than is necessary or convenient: *I don't want to drag this meeting out too long, so could we run through the main points quickly?*

▲ **drag *sth* out of *sb*** *verb* to force someone to say something, especially when they do not want to: *You never tell me how you feel – I always have to drag it out of you.*

dragnet /ˈdræg.net/ *noun* [C] **1** a series of actions taken by the police which are intended to catch criminals: *The police have widened their dragnet in their search for the killer.* **2** a heavy net that is pulled along the bottom of a river or area of water when searching for something

dragon /ˈdræg.ən/ *noun* [C] **1** a large fierce imaginary animal, usually represented with wings, a long tail and fire coming out of its mouth **2** INFORMAL an unfriendly and frightening woman: *She's a real **old** dragon.* **3** AUS any of various types of lizard

dragonfly /ˈdræg.ən.flaɪ/ *noun* [C] a large insect with a long thin brightly-coloured body and two pairs of transparent wings

dragoon /drəˈguːn/ *noun* [C] in the past, a soldier who rode on a horse and carried a gun

dragoon /drəˈguːn/ *verb*

▲ **dragoon *sb* into *sth*** *phrasal verb* [T often passive] to force or persuade someone to do something unpleasant: [+ v-ing] *I've been dragooned into giv**ing** the after-dinner speech.*

ˈdrag ˌqueen *noun* [C] a man, often a homosexual, dressed as a woman

ˈdrag ˌrace *noun* [C] US a car race over a very short distance **ˈdrag ˌracing** *noun* [U]

dragster /ˈdræg.stəʳ/ [US] /-stɚ/ *noun* [C] a long narrow fast car which has been specially built to take part in drag races

drain [REMOVE LIQUID] /dreɪn/ *verb* [I or T] If you drain something, you remove the liquid from it, usually by pouring it away or allowing it to flow away, and if something drains, liquid flows away or out of it: *Drain the pasta thoroughly.* ○ *We drained the pond and filled it with fresh water.* ○ *Drain **(off)** any liquid that is left in the rice.* ○ *Don't bother drying the pans – just leave them to drain.*

drain /dreɪn/ *noun* [C] **1** a pipe or channel which is used to carry away waste matter and water from a building, or an opening in the road which rain water can flow down: *I think the kitchen drain is blocked.* ○ *She accidentally dropped her ring down a drain in the road.* **2** US FOR **plughole**

drains /dreɪnz/ *plural noun* UK the system of pipes, openings in the ground or other devices that are used for carrying away waste matter and water: *There was an unpleasant smell coming from the drains.*

drainage /ˈdreɪ.nɪdʒ/ *noun* [U] **1** the system of water or waste liquids flowing away from somewhere into the ground or down pipes: *drainage channels/ditches/ systems* **2** the ability of soil to allow water to flow away: *These plants need a sunny spot with good drainage.*

drain [MAKE TIRED] /dreɪn/ *verb* [T] to make someone very tired: *The long journey completely drained me.*

drain /dreɪn/ *noun* [S] *I think looking after her elderly mother is quite a drain **on** her energy* (= makes her very tired).

drained /dreɪnd/ *adj*: *You look completely drained* (= very tired) *– why don't you go to bed?* ○ *It was one of those films that leaves you **emotionally** drained.*

drain [REDUCE] /dreɪn/ *verb* **1** [I or T] to reduce or cause something to reduce: *The long war had drained the resources of both countries.* ○ *War drains a nation **of** its youth and its wealth* (= uses them until they are gone). **2** If the blood/colour drains from someone's face, or if their face drains (of blood/colour), they turn very pale, often because they are shocked or ill: *The colour drained **from** his **face/cheeks** when they told him the results.*

drain /dreɪn/ *noun* [S] something that uses more of your energy, money or time than you want to give: *Having a big mortgage is a real drain **on** your earnings.*

drain [DRINK] /dreɪn/ *verb* [T] If you drain a glass or cup, you drink all the liquid in it.

▲ **drain *(sth)* away** *phrasal verb* [M] If energy, colour, excitement, etc. drains away, it disappears completely, and if something drains it away, it completely removes it: *Stretching out her tired limbs, she felt the tensions of the day drain away.*

drainer /ˈdreɪn.əʳ/ [US] /-ɚ/ *noun* [C] a **draining board**

ˈdraining ˌboard UK *noun* [C usually sing] (US **drainboard**) the place next to a sink where plates, knives, forks, etc. are left to dry after they have been washed ➲See picture

In the Kitchen on page Centre 16

drainpipe /'dreɪn.paɪp/ noun [C] a pipe that carries waste water or SEWAGE away from buildings

drake /dreɪk/ noun [C] a male duck

dram /dræm/ noun [C] MAINLY SCOTTISH ENGLISH a small amount of a strong alcoholic drink, especially whisky: *a dram **of** whisky*

drama THEATRE /'drɑː.mə/ ⑩ /'dræm.ə/ noun **1** [C or U] a play in a theatre or on television or radio, or plays and acting generally: *She's been in several **television** dramas.* ○ *He's the drama critic for the Times.* ○ *She studied English and drama at college.* **2** used in expressions which refer to the type of play or film: *a courtroom drama* ○ *a historical drama*

dramatic /drə'mæt.ɪk/ ⑩ /-'mæt̬-/ adj relating to plays and acting: *She bought me the complete dramatic works* (= texts to be performed) *of Brecht for my birthday.* ○ *the Royal Academy of Dramatic Arts*

dramatically /drə'mæt.ɪ.kli/ ⑩ /-'mæt̬-/ adv: *She swept her hair back dramatically* (= as if acting in a play).

dramatist /'dræm.ə.tɪst/ ⑩ /-t̬ɪst/ noun [C] a person who writes plays

dramatize, UK USUALLY **-ise** /'dræm.ə.taɪz/ verb [T] When writers dramatize books, stories, poems, etc., they write them again in a form which can be performed. **2** used in expressions

dramatization, UK USUALLY **-isation** /ˌdræm.ə.taɪˈzeɪ.ʃən/ noun [C] *a dramatization of a novel*

drama EXCITEMENT /'drɑː.mə/ ⑩ /'dræm.ə/ noun **1** [C] an event or situation, especially an unexpected one, in which there is anxiety or excitement and usually a lot of action: *We had a little drama last night when the oil in the pan caught fire.* **2** [U] the excitement and energy that is created by a lot of action and arguments: *As a lawyer, he positively revelled in the drama of the courtroom.*

dramatic /drə'mæt.ɪk/ ⑩ /-'mæt̬-/ adj very sudden or noticeable, or full of action and excitement: *a dramatic change/improvement* ○ *We watched scenes of the dramatic* (= exciting) *rescue on the news.*

dramatically /drə'mæt.ɪ.kli/ ⑩ /-'mæt̬-/ adv: *Your life changes dramatically* (= very suddenly and noticeably) *when you have a baby.*

dramatize, UK USUALLY **-ise** /'dræm.ə.taɪz/ verb [T] DISAPPROVING If someone dramatizes a report of what has happened to them, they make the story seem more exciting, important or dangerous than it really is.

'drama ˌqueen noun [C] DISAPPROVING someone who gets far too upset or angry over small problems: *God, he's such a drama queen! I've never seen such a fuss.*

dramatis personae /drəˌmɑː.tɪs.pɜːˈsəʊ.naɪ/ ⑩ /ˌdræm.ə.t̬ɪs.pɜːˈsoʊ-/ plural noun FORMAL all the characters in a play

drank /dræŋk/ past simple of **drink**

drape /dreɪp/ verb **1** **drape** *sth* **across/on/over, etc.** to put something such as cloth or a piece of clothing loosely over something: *He draped his jacket over the back of the chair and sat down to eat.* ○ *She draped the scarf loosely around her shoulders.* **2** **be draped in/with** *sth* to be loosely covered with a cloth: *The coffins were all draped with the national flag.*
• **draped all over** *sb* USUALLY HUMOROUS very close to someone and with your arms around them: *I saw him last night in the pub with some woman draped all over him.*

drape /dreɪp/ noun [C or U] the way in which cloth folds or hangs as it covers something: *She liked the heavy drape of velvet.* ⊃See also **drapes**.

draper /'dreɪ.pər/ ⑩ /-pɚ/ noun [C] UK OLD-FASHIONED someone who, in the past, owned a shop selling cloth, curtains, etc.

drapery /'dreɪ.pər.i/ ⑩ /-pɚ-/ noun [U] **1** cloth hanging or arranged in folds **2** UK (US **dry goods**) OLD-FASHIONED cloth, pins, thread, etc. used for sewing

drapes /dreɪps/ plural noun (ALSO **draperies**) US heavy curtains made with thick cloth

drastic /'dræs.tɪk/ adj (especially of actions) severe and sudden or having very noticeable effects: *drastic measures* ○ *Many employees have had to take drastic cuts in pay.* **drastically** /'dræs.tɪ.kli/ adv: *Our budget has been drastically reduced.*

drat (it) /'dræt.ɪt/ ⑩ /'dræt̬-/ exclamation OLD-FASHIONED INFORMAL used to express slight annoyance: *Oh drat! I've lost her telephone number!*

draught COLD AIR UK, US **draft** /drɑːft/ ⑩ /dræft/ noun [C] a current of unpleasantly cold air blowing through a room **draughty** UK, US **drafty** /'drɑːf.ti/ ⑩ /'dræf.t̬i/ adj: *a draughty old house*

draught BEER UK, US **draft** /drɑːft/ ⑩ /dræft/ adj [before n] (of drinks such as beer) stored in and served from large containers, especially barrels: *draught beer/lager/cider* **draught** UK, US **draft** /drɑːft/ ⑩ /dræft/ noun [U] *Is the lager **on** draught or is it bottled?*

draught ANIMALS UK, US **draft** /drɑːft/ ⑩ /dræft/ adj [before n] (of animals) used for pulling heavy loads, vehicles, etc: *a draught horse*

draught BOATS UK, US **draft** /drɑːft/ ⑩ /dræft/ noun [C] SPECIALIZED the depth of water needed for a boat to be able to float: *A punt has a shallow draught.*

draughts UK /drɑːfts/ ⑩ /dræfts/ noun [U] (US **checkers**) a game for two people, each with twelve circular pieces which they move on a board with black and white squares

draughtsman UK, US **draftsman** /'drɑːfts.mən/ ⑩ /'dræfts-/ noun [C] **1** someone whose job is to do detailed drawings of machines, new buildings, etc. **2** someone who draws well

draughtswoman /'drɑːfts.wʊm.ən/ ⑩ /'dræfts-/ noun [C] UK a female draughtsman

draw PICTURE /drɔː/ ⑩ /drɑː/ verb [I or T] drew, drawn to make a picture of something or someone with a pencil or pen: *Jonathon can draw brilliantly.* ○ *The children drew pictures of their families.* ○ *Draw a line at the bottom of the page.*
• **draw the line** to never do something because you think it is wrong: *I swear quite a lot but even I draw the line **at** saying certain words.*

drawing /'drɔː.ɪŋ/ ⑩ /'drɑː-/ noun [C or U] the act of making a picture with a pencil or pen, or a picture made in this way: *Rosie loves drawing.* ○ *She gave me a beautiful drawing **of** a horse.*

draw MOVE /drɔː/ ⑩ /drɑː/ verb [I + adv or prep] drew, drawn **1** to move in a particular direction, especially in a vehicle: *The train slowly drew **into** the station/drew **in**.* ○ *As we drew **alongside** (= reached) the black car, I suddenly recognized my ex-boyfriend at the wheel.* ○ *Montgomery drew **level with** Greene in the 100 metres final, but never passed him.* **2** **draw near/close, etc.** to become nearer in space or time: *As Christmas draws nearer, the shops start to get unbearably crowded.* ○ *As she drew closer I realized that I knew her.* **3** **draw to a close/an end** to gradually finish: *As the evening drew to a close, people started reaching for their coats.*

draw ATTRACT /drɔː/ ⑩ /drɑː/ verb [T] drew, drawn to attract attention or interest: *He's an excellent speaker who always draws a crowd.* ○ *Does he wear those ridiculous clothes to draw **attention**?* ○ *Could I draw your **attention** to item number three on the agenda?*
• **draw your eye(s)** to attract your attention: *Her eyes were immediately drawn **to** the tall blond man standing at the bar.*

draw /drɔː/ ⑩ /drɑː/ noun [C usually sing] someone or something that a lot of people are interested in: *We need someone at the event who'll be a **big** draw and attract the paying public.*

draw PULL /drɔː/ ⑩ /drɑː/ verb [T + adv or prep] drew, drawn **1** to pull or direct something in a particular direction: *She drew her coat tightly around her shoulders.* ○ *The crowd watched as the referee drew the player **aside/to one side** and (UK ALSO) **to one side** and spoke to him.* **2** **draw the curtains** to pull curtains so that they are either together or apart
• **draw a veil over** *sth* UK If you draw a veil over a particular subject, you do not speak about it because it is unpleasant and you do not want to think about it: *Yes, well I think we'll just draw a veil over what went on last night.*

draw CHOOSE /drɔː/ ⑩ /drɑː/ verb [I or T] drew, drawn to choose a number, card, etc. from several numbers, cards, etc. without first seeing it, in a competition or a

game: *I was dealt two aces and I drew a third.*
• **draw a blank** INFORMAL to fail to get an answer or a result: *He asked me for my phone number and I drew a blank – I just couldn't remember it.*

draw UK /drɔː/ US /drɑː/ *noun* [C] (US ALSO **drawing**) a competition that is decided by choosing a particular ticket or number

draw EQUAL /drɔː/ US /drɑː/ *noun* [C] a situation in which each team in a game has equal points and neither side wins /drɔː/ US /drɑː/ verb [I] **drew**, **drawn** *Coventry drew 1-1 with Manchester United in the semi-finals.*

draw MAKE /drɔː/ US /drɑː/ *verb* [T] **drew**, **drawn** **1** FORMAL to make or show a comparison between things: *You can't really draw a* **comparison** *between the two cases – they're entirely different.* ○ *It's sometimes very difficult to draw a clear* **distinction** *between the meanings of different words.* **2 draw a conclusion** to consider the facts of a situation and make a decision about what is true, correct, likely to happen, etc: *I'd seen them together so often I drew the logical conclusion that they were husband and wife.*

draw TAKE OUT /drɔː/ US /drɑː/ *verb* [T] **drew**, **drawn** **1** to take something out of a container or your pocket, especially a weapon: *Suddenly he drew a* **gun/knife** *and held it to my throat.* **2** to cause a substance, especially blood, to come out of a body: *He bit me so hard that it drew* **blood***.*

draw USE /drɔː/ US /drɑː/ *verb* [T] **drew**, **drawn** to get a feeling, idea, etc. from something or someone: *She drew comfort* **from** *the fact that he died peacefully.*

draw INTO LUNGS /drɔː/ US /drɑː/ *verb* [I or T] **drew**, **drawn** to take air or smoke into your lungs: *She drew a deep* **breath** *and plunged into the water.*
• **draw breath** UK to pause for a moment to let your breathing become calmer and easier

draw CAUSE /drɔː/ US /drɑː/ *verb* [T] **drew**, **drawn** If something draws a reaction, people react in the stated way: *Her speech last night in the Senate drew an angry* **response***.*

draw TAKE MONEY /drɔː/ US /drɑː/ *verb* [T + prep] **drew**, **drawn** to get money from a bank, account, etc. so that you can use it: *Alison drew some* **money out** *of her account to pay for our trip.*

draw RECEIVE MONEY /drɔː/ US /drɑː/ *verb* [T] **drew**, **drawn** to receive money regularly, especially as an employee or from the government: *He's been drawing a pension for ten years.*

PHRASAL VERBS WITH **draw** ▼

▲ **draw back** *phrasal verb* to move away from someone or something, usually because you are surprised or frightened: *She leaned forward to stroke the dog but quickly drew back when she saw its teeth.*

▲ **draw in** *phrasal verb* UK If days, evenings or nights draw in, it becomes darker earlier because autumn or winter is coming.

▲ **draw** sb **into** sth *phrasal verb* to make someone become involved in a difficult or unpleasant situation: *They tried to draw me into their argument but I refused.*

▲ **draw** sth **off** *phrasal verb* [M] to remove a small amount of liquid from a larger amount, especially by letting it flow through a pipe: *She drew off a little of her home-made wine just to taste.*

▲ **draw on** sth *phrasal verb* to use information or your knowledge of something to help you do something: *His novels draw heavily on his childhood.* ○ *She had a wealth of experience to draw on.*

▲ **draw** sth **out** LENGTHEN *phrasal verb* [M] to cause something to last longer than is usual or necessary: *The director drew the meeting out for another hour with a series of tedious questions.*
drawn-out /ˌdrɔːnˈaʊt/ US /ˌdrɑːn-/ *adj*: *This trouble with the unions has been a* **long** *drawn-out affair.*

▲ **draw** sb **out** ENCOURAGE *phrasal verb* [M] to help someone to express their thoughts and feelings more easily by making them feel less nervous: *Like all good interviewers he manages to draw people out of themselves.*

▲ **draw** sth **up** PREPARE *phrasal verb* [M] to prepare something, usually something official, in writing: *I've drawn up a list of candidates that I'd like to interview.*

▲ **draw** sth **up** MOVE *phrasal verb* [M] to move a chair near to someone or something: *Draw up a chair and I'll tell you all about it.*

▲ **draw** yourself **up** STRAIGHTEN *phrasal verb* to make yourself look bigger by standing straight with your shoulders back, usually to try to seem more important: *Like a lot of short men, he tends to draw himself up to his full height in public.*

drawback /ˈdrɔː.bæk/ US /ˈdrɑː-/ *noun* [C] a disadvantage or the negative part of a situation: *One of the drawbacks of living with someone is having to share a bathroom.*

drawbridge /ˈdrɔː.brɪdʒ/ US /ˈdrɑː-/ *noun* [C] a bridge that can be raised or lowered in order to protect a castle from attack or to allow big boats to go under it

drawer /drɔːʳ/ US /drɑː/ *noun* [C] a box-shaped container without a top which is part of a piece of furniture. It slides in and out to open and close and is used for keeping things in: *I keep my socks* **in** *the bottom drawer.* ○ *I don't like to go rummaging through other people's drawers.*

drawers /drɔːz/ US /drɑːz/ *plural noun* OLD-FASHIONED **underpants**

'drawing ˌboard *noun* [C] a large flat table, often with a top that can be moved into different positions, which is used as a desk for drawing or designing something
• **go back to the drawing board** to start planning a piece of work again because the first plan failed

'drawing ˌpin UK *noun* [C] (US **thumbtack**) a short sharp pin with a flat round top used especially for putting up notices

'drawing ˌroom *noun* [C] FORMAL a comfortable room in a large house used for relaxing or for entertaining guests

drawl /drɔːl/ US /drɑːl/ *noun* [S] a slow way of speaking in which the vowel sounds are lengthened and words are not separated clearly: *a southern/Texan/mid-Atlantic drawl* **drawl** /drɔːl/ US /drɑːl/ *verb* [I or T] [+ speech] *"Hey, what's the rush? Slow down baby," he drawled.*

drawn DRAW /drɔːn/ US /drɑːn/ *past participle of* **draw**

drawn TIRED /drɔːn/ US /drɑːn/ *adj* (usually of the face) very tired and showing suffering: *She looked pale and drawn after her ordeal.*

drawn-out /ˌdrɔːnˈaʊt/ US /ˌdrɑːn-/ *adj* ↪See at **draw out** LENGTHEN.

drawstring /ˈdrɔː.strɪŋ/ US /ˈdrɑː-/ *noun* [C] a cord or string which goes through an opening especially in the top of a bag or the waist of a piece of clothing and can be pulled to fasten, tighten or loosen it

dray /dreɪ/ *noun* [C] a large low carriage with four wheels which is pulled by horses

dread /dred/ *verb* [T] to feel extremely anxious or frightened about something that is going to happen or that might happen: *He's dreading his driving test – he's sure he's going to fail.* ○ [+ v-ing] *I'm dreading having to meet his parents.*
• **dread to think** used to say that you do not want to think about something because it is too worrying: *I dread to think what would happen if he was left to cope on his own.*
dread /dred/ *noun* [U] a strong feeling of fear or worry: *The prospect of working full-time fills me with dread.* ○ *I live in dread of bumping into her in the street.* **dreaded** /ˈdred.ɪd/ *adj* [before n] HUMOROUS *I've got my dreaded cousin coming to stay!* **dread** /dred/ *adj* [before n] FORMAL *The dread spectre of civil war looms over the country.*

ˌdreaded ˈlurgy *noun* [S] UK INFORMAL a humorous way of speaking of any illness which is not very serious but is easily caught

dreadful /ˈdred.fªl/ *adj* very bad, of very low quality, or shocking and very sad: *The food was bad and the service was dreadful.* ○ *I was beginning to think I'd made a dreadful* **mistake***.* ○ *The news report was so dreadful that I just had to switch it off.*

dreadfully /ˈdred.fªl.i/ *adv* **1** extremely badly: *She behaved dreadfully.* **2** MAINLY UK extremely: *He was dreadfully upset.* ○ *I'm dreadfully sorry – I really am.*

dreadlocks /'dred.lɒks/ ⓤⓢ /-lɑːks/ *plural noun* a hairstyle in which the hair hangs in long thick twisted lengths ➷See picture **Hairstyles and Hats** on page Centre 8

dream ⓈⓁⒺⒺⓅ /driːm/ *noun* [C] a series of events or images that happen in your mind when you are sleeping: *a good/bad dream* ○ *a recurring dream* ○ *I had a very odd dream **about** you last night.* ○ [+ **that**] *Paul had a dream **that** he won the lottery.* dreamless /'driːm.ləs/ *adj*: *I sank into a deep, dreamless sleep.*

• **in a dream** *UK* not aware of what is happening around you because other thoughts are filling your mind: *I'm sorry, I didn't hear what you were saying – I was in a dream.*

dream /driːm/ *verb* [I or T] dreamed or dreamt, dreamed or dreamt **1** to experience events and images in your mind while you are sleeping: *What did you dream **about** last night?* ○ *I often dream **about/of** flying.* ○ [+ **that**] *I dreamed **that** I was having a baby.* **2** *MAINLY UK* to imagine that you have heard, done or seen something when you have not: *Did you say that you were going tonight or did I dream it?* ○ *I thought I'd bought some polish and it seems I haven't – I must have been dreaming.*

• **wouldn't dream of** *sth/doing sth* used to say that you would not do something because you think it is wrong or silly: *My father is very generous, but I wouldn't dream of actually asking him for money!*

dreamily /'driː.mɪ.li/ *adv* If you say or do something dreamily, you do it as if you are not completely awake and are thinking of pleasant things: *"We had the most wonderful evening boating on the lake," she said dreamily.*

dreamlike /'driːm.laɪk/ *adj* as if in a dream and therefore not real: *There's a dreamlike quality to the final stages of the film.*

dreamy /'driː.mi/ *adj* **1** seeming to be in a dream and not paying attention to what is happening around you: *She gets this dreamy expression on her face when she talks about food.* **2** very pleasant or attractive: *The film opens with a dreamy shot of a sunset.* ○ *OLD-FASHIONED He has these dreamy blue eyes.*

dream ⒽⓄⓅⒺ /driːm/ *noun* [C] something that you want to happen very much but that is not very likely: *It's always been my dream to have flying lessons.* ○ *Winning all that money was a dream **come true**.*

dream /driːm/ *adj* **dream holiday/house/job, etc.** the perfect holiday/house/job, etc, that you want more than any other

• **work/go like a dream** to work or go extremely well, without any problems: *The whole plan went like a dream.* ○ *He let me drive his new car last night – it goes like a dream.*

• **of your dreams** the best that you can imagine: *Win the house of your dreams in our fantastic competition!*

• **be (living) in a dream world** *DISAPPROVING* to have hopes and ideas which are not practical or realistic: *If he thinks I'll forgive him, he's living in a dream world.*

dream /driːm/ *verb* [I] dreamed or dreamt, dreamed or dreamt to imagine something that you would like to happen: *I dream **of** living on a tropical island.* ○ [+ **that**] *He **never** dreamed **that** one day he would become President.*

• **dream on** *INFORMAL* used to tell someone that what they are hoping for is not likely to happen or to be true: *"Watch. All I have to do is wink at her, and she'll come over here." "Dream on, Dave!"*

dreamer /'driː.məʳ/ ⓤⓢ /-mɚ/ *noun* [C] a person who spends a lot of time thinking about or planning enjoyable events that are not likely to happen

---

PHRASAL VERBS WITH **dream** ▼

▲ **dream about/of** *sth phrasal verb* to think about something that you want very much: *I dream of one day working for myself and not having a boss.*

▲ **dream** *sth* **up** *phrasal verb* [M] to invent something very imaginative and usually silly: *This is the latest ploy dreamt up by advertising companies to sell their new products.*

dreamboat /'driːm.bəʊt/ ⓤⓢ /-boʊt/ *noun* [C] *OLD-FASHIONED* a very physically attractive person

dream ˌteam *noun* [C usually sing] a group of people who have been specially chosen to work together and are considered to be the best at what they do: *a dream team of lawyers/heart specialists/baseball players*

dream ˌticket *noun* [C usually sing] a perfect combination, especially a combination of two politicians working for one party in an election: *Kennedy and Johnson were the first 'dream ticket'.*

dreary /'drɪə.ri/ ⓤⓢ /'drɪr.i/ *adj* boring and making you feel unhappy: *a dreary little town* ○ *She had spent another dreary day in the office.* drearily /'drɪə.rə.li/ ⓤⓢ /'drɪr.ə.l-/ *adv* dreariness /'drɪə.rɪ.nəs/ ⓤⓢ /'drɪr.ɪ-/ *noun* [U]

dredge ⓇⒺⓂⓄⓋⒺ /dredʒ/ *verb* [T] **1** to remove unwanted things from the bottom of a river, lake, etc. using a sucking or other device: *They have to dredge the canal regularly to keep it open.* **2** to search an area of water by dredging: *The police are dredging the lake **for** his body.* ○ *They dredged **up** (= brought to the surface) the man's clothes but not his body.*

dredger /'dredʒ.əʳ/ ⓤⓢ /-ɚ/ *noun* [C] (*ALSO* **dredge**) a boat or a device which is used to dredge rivers, lakes, etc.

dredge ⓈⒸⒶⓉⓉⒺⓇ /dredʒ/ *verb* [T] to scatter flour, sugar, etc. on food: *Lightly dredge the cake **with** icing sugar.*

▲ **dredge** *sth* **up** *phrasal verb* [M] to talk about something bad or unpleasant that happened in the past: *The article dredged up details of her unhappy childhood.*

dregs /dregz/ *plural noun* the solid bits that sink to the bottom of some liquids, such as wine or coffee, which are not usually drunk: *In one swift go, she had drunk her coffee down **to the** dregs* (= finished it).

• **the dregs of society/humanity** a group of people in society whom you consider to be immoral and worthless: *People tend to regard drug addicts as the dregs of society.*

drench /drentʃ/ *verb* [T often passive] to make someone or something extremely wet: *A sudden thunderstorm had drenched us **to the** skin.* ○ *The athletes were drenched **in/with** sweat.*

dress ⓅⒾⒺⒸⒺ ⓄⒻ ⒸⓁⓄⓉⒽⒾⓃⒼ /dres/ *noun* [C] a piece of clothing for women or girls which covers the top half of the body and hangs down over the legs: *a long/short dress* ○ *a wedding dress* ➷See picture **Clothes** on page Centre 6

dress ⓅⓊⓉ ⓄⓃ ⒸⓁⓄⓉⒽⒺⓈ /dres/ *verb* **1** [I or T] to put clothes on yourself or someone else, especially a child: *My husband dresses the children while I make breakfast.* ○ *He left very early and had to dress in the dark.* **2** [I + adv or prep] to wear a particular type of clothes: *I have to dress quite smartly for work.* ○ *Patricia always dresses **in** black* (= wears black clothes). **3** **dress for dinner** to put on formal clothes for a meal: *It's the sort of hotel where you're expected to dress for dinner.*

dress /dres/ *adj* [before n] describes men's suits, shirts or other clothes of the type that are worn at formal occasions: *a white dress shirt and bow tie*

dress /dres/ *noun* [U] used, especially in combination, to refer to clothes of a particular type, especially those worn in particular situations: *The queen, in full ceremonial dress, presided over the ceremony.*

dresser /'dres.əʳ/ ⓤⓢ /-ɚ/ *noun* [C] **1** used in phrases which describe the type of clothes that someone wears: *She was always a very stylish dresser.* ○ *He's a very snappy* (= stylish and modern) *dresser.* **2** *SPECIALIZED* a person who works in the theatre or in films, helping the actors to put on their clothes ➷See also **dresser**.

dressy /'dres.i/ *adj* **1** describes clothes which are suitable for formal occasions: *I need something a bit more dressy for the wedding.* **2** describes an occasion at which people wear very formal clothes: *a dressy affair/occasion*

dress ⓈⒶⓁⒶⒹ /dres/ *verb* [T] **1** to add a liquid, especially a mixture of oil and vinegar, to a salad for additional flavour: *a dressed salad* **2** to prepare meat, chicken, fish, and especially crab so it can be eaten: *a whole dressed crab*

dressing /'dres.ɪŋ/ *noun* [C or U] a liquid mixture, often containing oil, vinegar and herbs, which is added to food, especially salads

dress [INJURY] /dres/ *verb* [T] to treat an injury by cleaning it and putting medicine or a protective covering on it: *Clean and dress the wound immediately.*
dressing /ˈdres.ɪŋ/ *noun* [C] a protective covering which is put on a wound or an area of damaged skin

dress [SHOP WINDOW] /dres/ *verb* [T] to decorate a shop window usually with an arrangement of the shop's goods: *They're dressing Harrods' windows for Christmas.*

PHRASAL VERBS WITH **dress**

▲ **dress down** *phrasal verb* If you dress down for an occasion, you intentionally wear informal clothes of the type that will not attract attention: *She always makes a point of dressing down on her first date with a man.*

▲ **dress up** [WEAR FORMAL CLOTHES] *phrasal verb* to put on formal clothes for a special occasion: *You don't need to dress up just to go to the pub – jeans and a T-shirt will do.*

▲ **dress up** [CHANGE APPEARANCE] *phrasal verb* to put on special clothes in order to change your appearance: *Small children usually love dressing up **in** their mothers' clothes.* ○ *He dressed up **as** a cowboy for the party.*

▲ **dress *sth* up** [ADD SOMETHING] *phrasal verb* [M] If you dress something up, you add something to it in order to make it seem more interesting or pleasing than it really is: *I thought I'd dress up the frozen pizza **with** a few extra tomatoes and olives.* ○ *Politicians tried to dress up the bill **as** a bold new strategy for combatting poverty.*

dressage /ˈdres.ɑːʒ/ Ⓤⓢ /-ˈ-/ *noun* [U] the training of a horse to perform special, carefully controlled movements as directed by the rider, or the performance of these movements as a sport or in a competition: *a dressage competition*

ˈdress ˌcircle *noun* [C usually sing] *UK* the first level of seats above the main floor in a theatre

ˈdress ˌcode *noun* [C usually sing] **1** *UK* an accepted way of dressing for a particular occasion or in a particular social group: *Most evenings there's a party and the dress code is strict – black tie only.* **2** *US* a set of rules for what you can wear: *My school had a very strict dress code.*

dressed /drest/ *adj* [after v] **1** wearing clothes and not naked: *I usually **get** dressed before I eat breakfast.* ○ *He was dressed **in** a dark grey suit.* ○ *They arrived early and I wasn't fully dressed* (= didn't have all my clothes on). **2** wearing clothing of a particular type: *a well-dressed/casually dressed man*

• **dressed (up) to the nines** *INFORMAL* to be wearing fashionable or formal clothes for a special occasion: *Jackie went out dressed to the nines.*

• **dressed to kill** intentionally wearing clothes that attract sexual attention and admiration

dresser /ˈdres.əʳ/ Ⓤⓢ /-ɚ/ *noun* [C] **1** *UK* a tall piece of furniture with cupboards below and shelves on the top half: *a kitchen dresser* **2** *US* a piece of bedroom furniture with drawers, usually with a mirror on top, used especially for keeping clothes in ➲See also **dresser** at **dress** PUT ON CLOTHES.

dressing-down /ˌdres.ɪŋˈdaʊn/ *noun* [S] an act of speaking angrily to someone because they have done something wrong: *She **gave** me a dressing-down for getting there late.*

ˈdressing ˌgown *MAINLY UK noun* [C] (*US USUALLY* **bathrobe**) a long loose piece of clothing, like a coat, which you wear informally inside the house

ˈdressing ˌroom *noun* [C] a room, especially in a theatre, in which actors put on clothes and make-up

ˈdressing ˌtable *MAINLY UK noun* [C] (*US USUALLY* **vanity**) a piece of bedroom furniture like a table with a mirror and drawers

dressmaker /ˈdresˌmeɪ.kəʳ/ Ⓤⓢ /-kɚ/ *noun* [C] someone who makes women's clothes, especially as a job
dressmaking /ˈdresˌmeɪ.kɪŋ/ *noun* [U]

ˈdress reˌhearsal *noun* [C] the last time a play, opera, dance, etc. is practised before the real performance and is performed with the clothes, stage and lighting exactly as they will be for the real performance

ˈdress ˌsense *noun* [U] the ability to dress well in attractive combinations of clothes that suit you

dressy /ˈdres.i/ *adj* ➲See at **dress** PUT ON CLOTHES.

drew /druː/ *past simple of* **draw**

dribble [FLOW SLOWLY] /ˈdrɪb.l̩/ *verb* [I or T] to (cause a liquid to) flow very slowly in small amounts: *The water was barely dribbling **out of** the tap.* ○ *Dribble the remaining olive oil over the tomatoes.* **dribble** /ˈdrɪb.l̩/ *noun* [C or U] *The flow of water was reduced to a dribble.*

dribble [FROM MOUTH] /ˈdrɪb.l̩/ *verb* [I or T] to have liquid slowly come out of your mouth: *Babies dribble constantly.* **dribble** /ˈdrɪb.l̩/ *noun* [C or U] *There was dribble all over her chin.* ○ *a dribble of saliva*

dribble [MOVE BALL] /ˈdrɪb.l̩/ *verb* [I or T] (in football or hockey) to move a ball along the ground with repeated small kicks or hits, or (in basketball) to move a ball by repeatedly hitting it against the floor with your hand: *He dribbled the ball to the edge of the pitch.* ○ *His speed allows him to easily dribble past defenders.* **dribble** /ˈdrɪb.l̩/ *noun* [C] *Brinkworth's attempted dribble through the Milan defence was stopped by Ponti's tackle.*
dribbler /ˈdrɪb.l̩.əʳ/ Ⓤⓢ /-ɚ/ *noun* [C] *He's a good dribbler.*
dribbling /ˈdrɪb.l̩.ɪŋ/ *noun* [U]

dribs /drɪbz/ *plural noun UK* **in dribs and drabs** in small amounts, a few at a time: *The information has been released in dribs and drabs.*

dried /draɪd/ *past simple and past participle of* **dry** NOT WET

ˌdried ˈfruit *noun* [C or U] fruit which has been dried to preserve it

ˌdried ˈmilk *noun* [U] milk in the form of a powder which you must add water to before you can drink

drier /ˈdraɪ.əʳ/ Ⓤⓢ /-ɚ/ *comparative of* **dry** ➲See also **dryer**.

driest /ˈdraɪ.əst/ *superlative of* **dry**

drift [MOVE] /drɪft/ *verb* [I usually + adv or prep] to move slowly, especially as a result of outside forces, with no control over direction: *No one noticed that the boat had begun to drift **out** to sea.* ○ *A mist drifted **in** from the marshes.* ○ *After the band stopped playing, people drifted **away** in twos and threes.* ○ *FIGURATIVE The talk drifted **aimlessly** from one subject to another.*
drift /drɪft/ *noun* **1** [C] a pile of snow or something similar, formed by the wind: *The snow lay in deep drifts.* **2** [S or U] a general development or change in a situation: *The downward drift in copper prices looks set to continue.*
drifter /ˈdrɪf.təʳ/ Ⓤⓢ /-tɚ/ *noun* [C] *DISAPPROVING* someone who moves from one place to another or from one job to another without any real purpose

drift [MEANING] /drɪft/ *noun* [S] the general meaning without the details: *The **general** drift **of** the article was that society doesn't value older people.*

• **catch/get *sb's* drift** *INFORMAL* to understand the general meaning of what someone is saying

• **if you ˌcatch/ˌget my ˈdrift** *INFORMAL* used to say that you have left out information or your opinion from what you have just said, but that you expect the person listening to understand it anyway: *She's married, but she doesn't act as if she is, if you get my drift.*

PHRASAL VERBS WITH **drift**

▲ **drift apart** *phrasal verb* If two people drift apart, they gradually become less friendly and their relationship ends.

▲ **drift off** *phrasal verb* to gradually start to sleep: *I couldn't help drifting off in the middle of that lecture – it was so boring!*

driftnet /ˈdrɪft.net/ *noun* [C] a very large fishing net which hangs in the sea from devices floating on the surface

driftwood /ˈdrɪft.wʊd/ *noun* [U] wood which is floating on the sea or brought onto the beach by the sea

drill [TOOL] /drɪl/ *noun* [C] a tool or machine which makes holes: *an electric/pneumatic drill* ○ *a dentist's drill* ○ *a drill **bit*** (= the sharp part of the drill which cuts the hole) **drill** /drɪl/ *verb* [I or T] *Drill three holes in the wall for the screws.* ○ *They are going to drill **for** oil nearby.*

drill [REGULAR ACTIVITY] /drɪl/ *noun* [C] an activity which practises a particular skill and often involves repeating the same thing several times, especially a military exercise intended to train soldiers: *In some of these*

schools, army-style drills are used to instil a sense of discipline. ○ *a spelling/pronunciation drill*
• **what's the drill for *sth*?** *INFORMAL* used to ask what the usual, correct way of doing or getting something is: *What's the drill for getting money after four o'clock?*
drill /drɪl/ *verb* **1** **[I or T]** to practise something, especially military exercises, or to make someone do this: *We watched the soldiers drilling on the parade ground.* **2** **[T usually + adv or prep]** to tell someone something repeatedly to make them remember it: *It was drilled* ***into*** *us at an early age that we should always say 'please' and 'thank you'.* ○ *He drilled the children* ***in*** *what they should say.*

drily /ˈdraɪ.li/ *adv* ➲See at **dry** BORING.

drink [LIQUID] /drɪŋk/ *noun* **[C or U]** (an amount of) liquid which is taken into the body through the mouth: *Would you like a drink* ***of*** *water/tea/juice?* ○ *They'd had no food or drink for two days.* **drink** /drɪŋk/ *verb* **[I or T]** **drank, drunk** *He drank three glasses of water.* ○ *The animals came down to the waterhole to drink.*
drinkable /ˈdrɪŋ.kə.bl̩/ *adj* **1** clean and safe to drink: *Is the water drinkable?* **2** pleasant tasting: *"What's the wine like?" "Oh, it's nice – very drinkable."* **drinker** /ˈdrɪŋ.kəʳ/ [US] /-kɚ/ *noun* **[C]** *I'm a tea drinker really – I don't like coffee.*
drinking /ˈdrɪŋ.kɪŋ/ *noun* **[U]** the act of taking liquid in through your mouth: *This water is not for drinking.*

drink [ALCOHOL] /drɪŋk/ *noun* **[C or U]** alcoholic liquid: *Have we got time for a quick drink?* ○ *Whose turn is it to buy the drinks?* ○ *UK We ran out of drink at the party.*
• **take to drink** *OLD-FASHIONED* to start drinking alcohol frequently, often because of a personal problem: *He took to drink after his wife left him.*
drinks /drɪŋks/ *plural noun* a party at which you have drinks, especially alcoholic drinks: *Come for drinks on Saturday.* ○ *UK We're having a small drinks* ***party*** *for one of our colleagues who's leaving next week.*
drink /drɪŋk/ *verb* **[I]** **drank, drunk** to drink alcohol: *"Would you like a glass of wine?" "No thanks, I don't drink."* ○ *I didn't drink at all while I was pregnant.*
• **drink like a fish** *INFORMAL* to drink too much alcohol
• **drink *sb* under the table** *INFORMAL* to drink a lot more alcohol than someone else: *Now I like a few beers but Lucy can drink me under the table.*
drinking /ˈdrɪŋ.kɪŋ/ *noun* **[U]** when someone drinks alcohol: *I've* ***done*** *a lot of drinking since dad died.* ○ *Drinking* ***and driving*** *is dangerous.* ○ *The doctor told me to change my drinking* ***habits*** (= not to drink so much alcohol).
drinker /ˈdrɪŋ.kəʳ/ [US] /-kɚ/ *noun* **[C]** someone who drinks alcohol: *He's a* ***heavy/light*** *drinker* (= drinks/does not drink a lot of alcohol). ○ *I'm not much of a drinker* (= I don't drink much alcohol).

PHRASAL VERBS WITH **drink** ▼

▲ **drink *sth* in** *phrasal verb* **[M]** to listen to, look at, or experience something very attentively and with great enjoyment: *They drank in the words of their leader.*
▲ **drink to *sth*** *phrasal verb* If two or more people drink to something or someone, they hold their glasses up at the same time and then drink from them as a celebration, or to show respect or good wishes: *"Here's to a prosperous future then." "I'll drink to* ***that****!"*
▲ **drink *(sth)* up** *phrasal verb* **[M]** to finish your drink completely: *Drink up! It's time to go.*

drink-driving *UK* /ˌdrɪŋkˈdraɪ.vɪŋ/ *noun* **[U]** (*US* **drunk-driving**) driving a vehicle after drinking too much alcohol: *He was jailed for four months for drink-driving.*

ˈdrinking ˌfountain *noun* **[C]** a device, usually in a public place, which supplies water for drinking

ˈdrinking ˌproblem *noun* **[S]** (*UK ALSO* **drink problem**) the regular drinking of too much alcohol: *I suspect he* ***has*** *a drinking problem.*

drinking-up time /ˌdrɪŋ.kɪŋˈʌp.taɪm/ *noun* **[U]** *UK* the short time allowed in a pub for people to finish their drinks before it closes

ˈdrinking ˌwater *noun* **[U]** water that is suitable for drinking

ˈdrink ˌproblem *noun* **[S]** *UK FOR* **drinking problem**

ˈdrinks maˌchine *UK noun* **[C]** (*US USUALLY* **vending machine**) a machine which sells drinks ➲See picture **In the Office** on page Centre 15

drip [LIQUID] /drɪp/ *verb* **-pp-** **1** **[I or T]** If a liquid drips, it falls in drops, or you make it fall in drops: *Water dripped* ***down*** *the wall.* ○ *She dripped paint on the carpet.* **2** **[I]** to produce drops of liquid: *Watch out – the candle's dripping.*
drip /drɪp/ *noun* **1** **[C]** a drop of liquid: *drips of paint/sweat* **2** **[S]** the sound or action of liquid falling in drops: *All I could hear was* ***the*** *drip of the rain from the roof.* **3** **[C]** *UK* (*ALSO* **IV**) a method of slowly giving someone liquid medicine or food through a tube into one of their veins, or a piece of equipment for doing this: *He was* ***on*** *a drip for three days.*
dripping /ˈdrɪp.ɪŋ/ *adj* **[after v]** very wet: *It's so hot outside – I'm absolutely dripping* ***(wet)****.* ○ *Jim had just been on a run and was dripping* ***with*** *sweat.*

drip [PERSON] /drɪp/ *noun* **[C]** *INFORMAL DISAPPROVING* a boring person without a strong character: *He's pleasant enough, but he's such a drip!* **drippy** /ˈdrɪp.i/ *adj INFORMAL* *Where's that drippy brother of yours?*

ˈdrip ˌcoffee *noun* **[C or U]** *US FOR* **filter/filtered coffee**

drip-dry /ˈdrɪp.draɪ/ *adj* Drip-dry clothing can be hung up to dry and does not need to be ironed: *a drip-dry shirt*
drip-dry /ˌdrɪpˈdraɪ/ *verb* **[I or T]** to dry a piece of clothing by hanging it up so that the water runs out of it: *If I were you, I'd hang that sweater on the line and let it drip-dry.*

dripping /ˈdrɪp.ɪŋ/ *noun* **[U]** (*US USUALLY* **drippings**) the fat that has come out of meat during cooking: *beef dripping*

drive [USE VEHICLE] /draɪv/ *verb* **[I or T]** **drove, driven** to move or travel on land in a motor vehicle, especially as the person controlling the vehicle's movement: *I'm learning to drive.* ○ *"Are you going by train?" "No, I'm driving."* ○ *She drives a red sports car.* ○ *They're driving to Scotland on Tuesday.* ○ *We saw their car outside the house and drove* ***on/past/away****.* ○ *I drove my daughter to school.* ➲Compare **ride**.
• **drive a coach and horses through *sth*** *UK* to completely destroy a rule, an argument or a plan
• **driving while intoxicated** (*ABBREVIATION* **DWI**) *US LEGAL* the crime of operating a motor vehicle after having drunk more alcohol than you are legally allowed to: *Smith was arrested and charged with DWI.*
drive /draɪv/ *noun* **1** **[C]** a journey in a car: *It's a long drive from Glasgow to London.* ○ *Shall we* ***go for a*** *drive this afternoon?* **2** **[U]** the system used to power a vehicle: *a car with* ***left-hand/right-hand*** *drive* (= in which the driver sits in the seat on the left/right). ○ *a* ***four-wheel*** *drive vehicle* **-driven** /-drɪv.ᵊn/ *suffix*: *He arrived every morning by* ***chauffeur****-driven car.*
driver /ˈdraɪ.vəʳ/ [US] /-vɚ/ *noun* **[C]** someone who drives a vehicle: *a bus/lorry/truck/taxi driver* ○ *The driver* ***of*** *the van was killed in the accident.* **driving** /ˈdraɪ.vɪŋ/ *noun* **[U]** *a driving lesson/school/test* ○ *She has to* ***do*** *a lot of driving in her job.*
• **be in the driving seat** *UK* (*US* **be in the driver's seat**) to be in charge or in control of a situation

COMMON LEARNER ERROR

drive or **ride?**

You **drive** a car, truck, bus or train.
She drives a blue estate car.
You **ride** a bicycle, motorcycle or horse.
My brother is learning to ride a bicycle.
~~*My brother is learning to drive a bicycle.*~~

drive [FORCE] /draɪv/ *verb* **[T]** **drove, driven** **1** to force someone or something to go somewhere or do something: *They used dogs to drive the sheep into a pen.* ○ *By the end of the year, most of the occupying troops had been driven from the city.* ○ *For the second time in ten years, the government has driven the economy into deep and damaging recession.* ○ *A post had been driven* (= hit hard) *into the ground near the tree.* ○ **[+ to infinitive]** *In the end, it was his violent behaviour that drove her* ***to*** *leave home.* **2** to force someone or something into a particular state, often an unpleasant one: *In the course of history, love has driven men and women **to** strange extremes.*

• **drive** *sb* **to drink** *HUMOROUS* to make someone extremely anxious or unhappy: *These children will drive me to drink!*

• **drive** *sb* **mad/crazy, etc.** *INFORMAL* to make someone extremely annoyed: *My mother-in-law has been staying with us this past week and she' driving me crazy.* ○ *He leaves dirty clothes all over the floor and it's driving me mad.*

• **drive** *sb* **wild** *INFORMAL* to make you very excited, especially sexually: *When he runs his fingers through my hair, it drives me wild!*

• **drive a hard bargain** *INFORMAL* to expect a lot in exchange for what you pay or do

• **drive** *your* **message/point home** to state something in a very forceful and effective way: *The speaker really drove his message home, repeating his main point several times.*

• **drive a wedge between** *sb* to damage the good relationship that two people or groups of people have: *It would be silly to let things which have happened in the past drive a wedge between us now.*

drive PROVIDE POWER /draɪv/ *verb* [T] **drove**, **driven 1** to provide the power to keep a machine working, or to make something happen: *The engine drives the wheels.* ○ *Water drives the turbines which produce electricity.* **2** If you drive a ball, you hit it hard so that it travels a long way: *Slater drove the ball **down** the fairway.*

drive /draɪv/ *noun* **1** [U] energy and determination to achieve things: *We are looking for someone with drive and ambition.* ○ [+ **to** infinitive] *He has the drive **to** succeed.* ○ *Later on in life the **sex** drive tends to diminish.* **2** [C] (in sport) a powerful hit which sends a ball a long way

driven /ˈdrɪv.ən/ *adj* describes someone who is so determined to achieve something or be successful that all their behaviour is directed towards this aim: *Like most of the lawyers that I know, Rachel is driven.*

-driven /-drɪv.ən/ *suffix*: *The new ships, propelled by gas turbines, require less maintenance than older, steam-driven ones.* ○ *The fact remains that there are some public services that cannot be entirely **market**-driven* (= controlled by economic forces).

driver /ˈdraɪ.vəʳ/ ⓤ /-vɚ/ *noun* [C] a type of CLUB (= long thin stick) with a wooden head, used in golf

driving /ˈdraɪ.vɪŋ/ *adj* [before n] **1** strong and powerful and therefore causing things to happen: *Driving **ambition** is what most great leaders have in common.* ○ *She was always the driving **force** behind the scheme.* **2** **driving rain/snow** rain/snow that is falling fast and being blown by the wind: *Driving snow brought more problems on the roads last night.*

drive ROAD /draɪv/ *noun* **1** [C] (*ALSO* **driveway**) a short private road which leads from a public road to a house: *I parked **in** the drive.* **2** used in the names of some roads, especially roads containing houses: *12 Cotswold Drive*

drive PLANNED EFFORT /draɪv/ *noun* [C] a planned effort to achieve something: *The latest promotional material is all part of a **recruitment** drive.* ○ *I'm meant to be **on** an **economy** drive at the moment, so I'm trying not to spend too much.*

drive COMPUTING /draɪv/ *noun* [C] a device for storing computer information: *a disk/tape drive* ○ *a floppy/hard drive*

PHRASAL VERBS WITH **drive** ▼

▲ **drive at** *sth phrasal verb INFORMAL* **be driving at** If you ask someone what they are driving at, you ask them what they really mean: *I don't see what you're driving at.*

▲ **drive off** *phrasal verb* to leave in a car: *I got in the car and drove off.*

drive-in /ˈdraɪv.ɪn/ *adj* [before n] *MAINLY US* A drive-in bank, cinema, restaurant, etc. is one that you can use or visit without getting out of your car.

drive-in /ˈdraɪv.ɪn/ *noun* [C] a cinema or restaurant that you can visit without getting out of your car

drivel /ˈdrɪv.əl/ *noun* [U] *DISAPPROVING* nonsense or boring and useless information: *You don't believe the drivel you read in the papers, do you?* ○ *You're **talking** drivel as*

usual! **drivelling** /ˈdrɪv.əl.ɪŋ/ *adj*: *Who was that drivelling **idiot** on the radio this morning?*

driver /ˈdraɪ.vəʳ/ ⓤ /ˈdraɪ.vɚ/ *noun* [C] *SPECIALIZED* a computer program that enables a computer to use other pieces of equipment such as a printer

drive ˌshaft *noun* [C] (in a vehicle) a rod that spins round and takes the power from the engine to the wheels

driveway /ˈdraɪv.weɪ/ *noun* [C] a **drive** ROAD

driving /ˈdraɪ.vɪŋ/ *noun* [U] ⊃See at **drive** PROVIDE POWER.

driving ˌlicence *UK noun* [C] (*US* **driver's license**, *AUS* **driver's licence**) official permission for someone to drive a car, received after passing a driving test, or a document showing this

drizzle RAIN /ˈdrɪz.l̩/ *noun* [U] rain in very small light drops: *Tomorrow will be cloudy with outbreaks of rain and drizzle.* **drizzle** /ˈdrɪz.l̩/ *verb* [I] *It's been drizzling all day.* **drizzly** /ˈdrɪz.li/ *adj*: *a drizzly afternoon*

drizzle POUR /ˈdrɪz.l̩/ *verb* [T] to pour liquid slowly over something, especially in a thin line or in small drops: *Drizzle the syrup **over** the warm cake.* **drizzle** /ˈdrɪz.l̩/ *noun* [S] *Serve the pasta hot with a drizzle of olive oil.*

Dr Martens *TRADEMARK* /ˌdɒk.təˈmɑː.tɪnz/ ⓤ /ˌdɑːk.təˈmɑːr.tənz/ *plural noun* (*ALSO* **Doc Martens,** *ALSO* **DMs**) (a pair of) a type of strong, heavy-looking shoes or boots, with LACES and thick rubber soles

droll /drəʊl/ ⓤ /droʊl/ *adj* amusing, especially in an unusual way: *a droll remark/expression/person* **drolly** /ˈdrəʊ.li/ ⓤ /ˈdroʊ.li/ *adv*

dromedary /ˈdrɒm.ə.dəʳ.i/ ⓤ /ˈdrɑː.mə.der-/ *noun* [C] a type of CAMEL (= a large animal that lives in the desert) with one HUMP (= raised area) on its back

drone NOISE /drəʊn/ ⓤ /droʊn/ *noun* [S] a low continuous noise which does not change its note: *the drone **of** an engine* ○ *Outside the tent I could hear **the** constant drone **of** insects.* ○ ***The** drone **of** his voice made me feel sleepy.* **drone** /drəʊn/ ⓤ /droʊn/ *verb* [I] *An airplane droned in the background.*

▲ **drone on** *phrasal verb DISAPPROVING* to talk for a long time in a boring way: *He was droning on (**and on**) **about** his operation.*

drone BEE /drəʊn/ ⓤ /droʊn/ *noun* [C] a male bee

drool /druːl/ *verb* [I] to allow saliva to flow out of your mouth: *The dog lay drooling on the mat.* ○ *I drooled all over my pillow.*

drool /druːl/ *noun* [U] saliva which has come out of your mouth uncontrollably

▲ **drool over** *sb/sth phrasal verb* to show extreme and sometimes foolish pleasure while looking at someone or something: *Roz and I sat by the swimming pool, drooling over all the gorgeous young men.* ○ *I left Sara in the shop drooling over a green silk dress.*

droop /druːp/ *verb* [I] **1** to bend or hang down heavily: *The flowers were drooping in the heat.* ○ *I can see you're tired because your eyelids have started to droop.* **2** If your SPIRITS (= feelings of happiness) droop, you start to feel less happy and energetic. **drooping** /ˈdruː.pɪŋ/ *adj*: *drooping branches* ○ *Bloodhounds have drooping eyes and floppy ears.* **droopy** /ˈdruː.pi/ *adj INFORMAL* *He had a long droopy **moustache**.*

drop FALL /drɒp/ ⓤ /drɑːp/ *verb* [I or T] -**pp**- to fall or to allow something to fall: *She dropped her keys.* ○ *I'm always dropping things.* ○ *Amanda dropped her sunglasses **in/into** the fountain.* ○ *The book dropped **from/off** the shelf.* ○ *Don't drop it!/Don't let it drop!*

• **be fit/ready to drop** *INFORMAL* to be extremely tired: *I'd just walked ten miles and was ready to drop.*

• **drop dead** to die suddenly and unexpectedly: *He dropped dead on the squash court at the age of 43.*

• **Drop dead!** *SLANG* a rude way of telling someone that you are angry with them and want them to go away or be quiet: *Oh, just drop dead!*

• **drop-dead gorgeous** *INFORMAL* extremely attractive: *He's not drop-dead gorgeous or anything, but he's quite nice.*

• **drop** *sb* **a line** *INFORMAL* to write someone a letter, especially a short informal one: *Just drop me a line when you've decided on a date.*

• **drop (*sb*) a hint** *INFORMAL* to tell someone something in an indirect way: *Margaret dropped a hint that she'd like to come to the party.*
• **drop a brick/clanger** *UK* to do or say something which makes you feel embarrassed
• **drop *your* aitches/h's** *UK* to not pronounce the letter *h* at the beginning of words in which it should be pronounced
drop /drɒp/ [US] /drɑːp/ *noun* [C] when things such as supplies, medicine, etc. are delivered, often by dropping them from an aircraft: *a food drop* ○ *The helicopter **made** a drop of much-needed supplies to the stranded hikers.*
• **at the drop of a hat** If you do something at the drop of a hat, you do it immediately without stopping to think about it: *People will file lawsuits at the drop of a hat these days.*

drop [LOWER] /drɒp/ [US] /drɑːp/ *verb* [I or T] **-pp-** to move to a lower level, or cause something to move to a lower level: *The water level in the flooded region has finally begun to drop.* ○ *The land drops **(away)*** (= slopes down) *sharply behind the barrier.* ○ *We've had to drop our prices because of the recession.*
drop /drɒp/ [US] /drɑːp/ *noun* [C usually sing] **1** the distance from one thing to something lower: *There's a drop **of** two metres from the window to the ground.* **2** a reduction in the amount or level of something: *The recent drop **in** magazine subscriptions is causing some concern.*

drop [STOP] /drɒp/ [US] /drɑːp/ *verb* [T] **-pp- 1** to stop doing or planning something, especially an activity: *I'm going to drop yoga and do aerobics instead.* ○ *Can you drop what you're doing and help me with this report?* **2** to stop including someone in a group or team: *He's been dropped **from** the team because of injury.*
• **drop it/the subject** to stop talking about something, especially because it is upsetting or annoying: *I don't want to talk about it anymore – let's drop the subject.*
• **drop everything** to stop whatever you are doing: *We just dropped everything and rushed to the hospital.*
• **drop *sb/sth* like a hot potato** *INFORMAL* to quickly stop being involved with someone or something because you do not now like them or you think they will cause problems for you: *He dropped the plan like a hot potato when he realized how much it would cost him.*

drop [TAKE] /drɒp/ [US] /drɑːp/ *verb* [T + adv/prep] **-pp-** to take someone to a particular place, usually in a car and leave them there: *They dropped me **off** at the main entrance.* ○ *I dropped him **at** the library and went shopping.*

drop [SMALL AMOUNT] /drɒp/ [US] /drɑːp/ *noun* **1** [C] a small round shaped amount of liquid: *I thought I felt a drop **of** rain.* ○ *There were little drops **of** paint on the kitchen floor.* **2** [S] a small amount of liquid you can drink: *I'll have a drop **more** juice, please.* ○ *"Would you like some more?" "**Just** a drop, please."* **3** [C] *MAINLY UK* a small piece of sweet food made of sugar: *fruit/pear drops* ○ *chocolate drops*
• **a drop too much (to drink)** *MAINLY UK* too much alcohol to drink
• **a drop in the ocean** *UK* (*US* **a drop in the bucket**) a very small amount compared to the amount needed: *My letter of protest was just a drop in the ocean.*
droplet /ˈdrɒp.lət/ [US] /ˈdrɑːp-/ *noun* [C] a small drop of liquid
dropper /ˈdrɒp.əʳ/ [US] /ˈdrɑː.pɚ/ *noun* [C] a small tube with a rubber container at one end which is filled with air and allows liquid to be given out in separate drops
drops /drɒps/ [US] /drɑːps/ *plural noun* liquid medicine given in very small amounts: *eye/nose/ear drops*

PHRASAL VERBS WITH **drop** ▼

▲ **drop behind** *phrasal verb* to get further behind or away from something or someone: *As the pace quickened, Pepe began to drop behind.* ○ *She stopped going to classes and dropped behind in her schoolwork.*
▲ **drop by/in** *phrasal verb INFORMAL* to visit someone: *I dropped in **on** George on my way home from school.* ○ *Drop by and pick up that book sometime.*
▲ **drop off** [SLEEP] *phrasal verb* to start to sleep
▲ **drop off** [DECREASE] *phrasal verb* If the amount, number or quality of something drops off, it becomes less: *The demand for mobile phones shows no signs of dropping off.*
▲ **drop *sb/sth* off** [TAKE] *phrasal verb* [M] *INFORMAL* to take someone or something to a particular place, usually by car, as you travel to a different place: *We dropped our luggage off at the hotel and went sightseeing.*
▲ **drop out** *phrasal verb* **1** to not do something that you were going to do, or to stop doing something before you have completely finished: *He dropped out of the race after two laps.* **2** If a student drops out, they stop going to classes before they have finished their course.
dropout /ˈdrɒp.aʊt/ [US] /ˈdrɑːp-/ *noun* [C] a person who leaves school, college or university before finishing a course, or a person who lives in an unusual way: *a high school/college dropout* ○ *He was a loner and a dropout.*

ˈdrop ˌkick *noun* [C] in rugby, a kick in which the ball is dropped to the ground before being kicked

drop-leaf table /ˌdrɒp.liːfˈteɪ.bl/ [US] /ˌdrɑːp-/ *noun* [C] a table whose sides can be folded down so that the table fits into a smaller space

droppings /ˈdrɒp.ɪŋz/ [US] /ˈdrɑː.pɪŋz/ *plural noun* excrement produced by animals and birds

dross /drɒs/ [US] /drɑːs/ *noun* [U] *MAINLY UK* something useless or worthless: *So much of what's on TV is pure dross.* ○ *We read all the manuscripts but 95% are dross.*

drought /draʊt/ *noun* [C or U] a long period when there is little or no rain: *This year (a) severe drought has ruined the crops.*

drove [DRIVE] /drəʊv/ [US] /droʊv/ *past simple of* **drive**

drove [TAKE ANIMALS] /drəʊv/ [US] /droʊv/ *verb* [T] **drove, drove** *UK SPECIALIZED* to move farm animals on foot from one place to another
drove /drəʊv/ [US] /droʊv/ *noun* [C] *MAINLY UK* a large group of animals, especially cattle or sheep, moving from one place to another **drover** /ˈdrəʊ.vəʳ/ [US] /ˈdroʊ.vɚ/ *noun* [C] *The drover walked alongside the oxen, gently tapping them with his stick.*

droves /drəʊvz/ [US] /droʊvz/ *plural noun* a large group, especially of people, moving towards a place: *Every summer droves of sightseers crowd the city.* ○ *Fans came **in** droves/(UK ALSO) **in their** droves to see her concerts.*

drown [DIE] /draʊn/ *verb* [I or T] to (cause to) die by being unable to breathe under water: *He drowned in a boating accident.* ○ *Many animals were drowned by the tidal wave.*
• **drown *your* sorrows** to drink alcohol in order to forget your problems
• **look like a drowned rat** *INFORMAL* to be very wet, especially because you have been in heavy rain
• **A drowning man will clutch at a straw.** *SAYING* said about someone who is in a very difficult situation, and who will take any available opportunity to improve it

drown [COVER] /draʊn/ *verb* [T] to cover or be covered, especially with a liquid: *A whole valley was drowned when the river was dammed.* ○ *DISAPPROVING He drowned his food **in/with** tomato sauce.*

PHRASAL VERBS WITH **drown** ▼

▲ **drown in *sth*** *phrasal verb* to have more of something than you are able to deal with: *I'm drowning in unpaid bills.*
▲ **drown *sth* out** *phrasal verb* [M] *INFORMAL* If a loud noise drowns out another noise, it prevents it from being heard.

drowsy /ˈdraʊ.zi/ *adj* being in a state between sleeping and being awake: *The room is so warm it's making me feel drowsy.* **drowsily** /ˈdraʊ.zi.li/ *adv* **drowsiness** /ˈdraʊ.zɪ.nəs/ *noun* [U] *Seasickness tablets often cause drowsiness.*

drubbing /ˈdrʌb.ɪŋ/ *noun* [C usually sing] *UK INFORMAL* a beating or serious defeat, especially in a sports competition: *Nottingham Forest **got/received/took** a severe drubbing at the hands of Manchester United.*

drudgery /ˈdrʌdʒ.ᵊr.i/ [US] /-ɚ-/ *noun* [U] hard boring work: *the drudgery of housework* **drudge** /drʌdʒ/ *noun* [C] *I feel like a real drudge – I've done nothing but clean all day!*

drug [MEDICINE] /drʌg/ *noun* [C] any natural or artificially made chemical which is used as a medicine: *anti-*

cancer/fertility/pain-killing drugs ○ *a **prescription** drug* ○ *drug therapy* ○ *He **takes** several drugs for his condition.*

drug /drʌg/ *verb* [T] -gg- to give someone or something a chemical which causes a loss of feeling or unconsciousness: *The killer confessed that he often drugged his victims before he killed them.* ○ *She was heavily drugged to ease the pain.* ○ INFORMAL *We visited her in hospital but she was drugged **to the eyeballs** (= had been given a lot of drugs) and I don't think she even knew we were there.*

druggist /ˈdrʌg.ɪst/ *noun* [C] US FOR **chemist** MEDICINE

drug ILLEGAL SUBSTANCE /drʌg/ *noun* [C] **1** any natural or artificially made chemical which is taken for pleasure, to improve someone's performance of an activity, or because a person cannot stop using it: *illegal drugs* ○ *a drug **addict*** ○ *drug **addiction/abuse*** ○ *She began to suspect that her son was **on/taking/doing** drugs.* ○ *She was suspected of being a drug **dealer**/(UK ALSO) drugs **dealer** (= someone who sells drugs).* ○ *His son died of a drug/(UK ALSO) drugs **overdose**.* **2** any activity that you cannot stop doing: *Work is a drug **for** him.*

druggie /ˈdrʌg.i/ *noun* [C] INFORMAL a person who frequently uses illegal drugs

drugstore /ˈdrʌg.stɔːr/ ⑤ /-stɔːr/ *noun* [C] US FOR **chemist** (= a shop where you can buy medicines, make-up, sweets, cigarettes, etc.)

druid /ˈdruː.ɪd/ *noun* [C] a priest of a religion followed in Britain, Ireland and France, especially in ancient times

drum INSTRUMENT /drʌm/ *noun* [C] a musical instrument, especially one made from a skin stretched over the end of a hollow tube or bowl, played by hitting with the hand or a stick: *a bass/snare/kettle drum* ○ *They danced to the **beat** of the drums* (= sound of the drums being hit).

● bang/beat the drum UK to speak enthusiastically about a belief or idea in order to persuade other people to support it too: *Labour are banging the drum for a united Europe.*

drum /drʌm/ *verb* [I or T] -mm- to hit a surface regularly and make a sound like a drum, or to make something do this: *She drummed her fingers impatiently **on** the table.* ○ *The rain drummed loudly **on** the roof.*

drummer /ˈdrʌm.əʳ/ ⑤ /-ɚ/ *noun* [C] someone who plays a drum or a set of drums, especially in a music group

drum CONTAINER /drʌm/ *noun* [C] **1** a large tube-like container: *an oil drum* ○ *a five-gallon plastic drum* ○ *a drum **of** radioactive waste* **2** the hollow metal cylinder in a washing machine into which clothes and other items are put for washing

---

PHRASAL VERBS WITH **drum** ▼

▲ drum *sth* into *sb* *phrasal verb* to teach something to someone by repeating it to them frequently: *The importance of good manners was drummed into us at an early age.*

▲ drum *sb* out of *sth* *phrasal verb* to force someone to leave a job, group, etc., often because they have behaved in a way which is not considered honourable: *The minister was drummed out of office when it was discovered that he had been taking bribes.*

▲ drum *sth* up *phrasal verb* [M] to increase interest in something or support for something: *He was trying to drum up some enthusiasm for the project.*

drumbeat /ˈdrʌm.biːt/ *noun* [C] (the sound of) a single hit on a drum

'drum ˌkit *noun* [C] (US ALSO **drum set**) a set of drums and CYMBALS played by one person

'drum maˌchine *noun* [C] an electronic machine which produces the sound of drums

ˌdrum 'major *noun* [C] the person who leads a marching musical group

ˌdrum majoˈrette *noun* [C] (ALSO **majorette**) MAINLY US a girl or young woman who leads a marching musical group

drum'n'bass, drum and bass /ˌdrʌm.ən'beɪs/ *noun* [U] UK a type of popular dance music with a fast strong drum rhythm and low range of musical notes

drumstick MUSIC /ˈdrʌm.stɪk/ *noun* [C] a stick for beating a drum

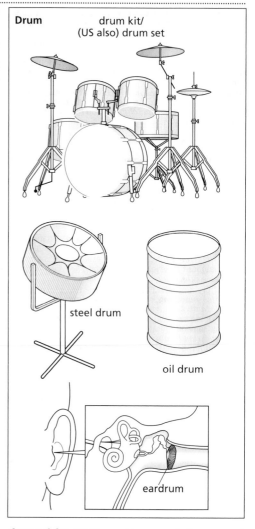

Drum drum kit/ (US also) drum set

steel drum

oil drum

eardrum

drumstick FOOD /ˈdrʌm.stɪk/ *noun* [C] the lower part of the leg of a chicken or similar bird eaten as food: *chicken drumsticks*

drunk DRINK /drʌŋk/ *noun* (US ALSO **drank**) **drink**

drunk TOO MUCH ALCOHOL /drʌŋk/ *adj* [after v] **1** unable to speak or act in the usual way because of having had too much alcohol: *I **got** completely drunk at my sister's wedding.* ○ *I'd had a couple of glasses of wine but I certainly wasn't drunk.* ○ UK *He came home last night **blind** (= extremely) drunk.* **2** LEGAL **drunk and disorderly** the crime of behaving badly in public after drinking too much alcohol **3 drunk with power** having a strong and unreasonable feeling of being able to control other people

● drunk as a lord UK (US **drunk as a skunk**) INFORMAL extremely drunk: *Andy staggered in last night drunk as a lord.*

drunk /drʌŋk/ *noun* [C] (ALSO **drunkard**) DISAPPROVING a person who drinks large amounts of alcohol very frequently and is unable to give up the habit

drunken /ˈdrʌŋ.kən/ *adj* [before n] DISAPPROVING **1** describes someone who is (often) under the influence of alcohol: *She was convicted of murdering her drunken and allegedly violent husband.* ○ *Just before midnight, the square filled up with drunken revellers.* **2** describes a situation in which a lot of alcohol has been drunk: *a drunken **brawl*** ○ *He came home and fell into a drunken* *stupor* (= sleep). **drunkenly** /ˈdrʌŋ.kən.li/ *adv*: *He staggered drunkenly toward the door.* **drunkenness** /ˈdrʌŋ.kən.nəs/ *noun* [U]

drunk-driving /ˌdrʌŋkˈdraɪ.vɪŋ/ *noun* [U] *US FOR* **drink-driving**

dry [NOT WET] /draɪ/ *adj* **drier, driest** or **dryer, dryest 1** describes something that has no water or other liquid in, on, or around it: *I hung his wet trousers on the radiator, but they're not dry yet.* ○ *These plants grow well in dry soil/a dry climate.* ○ *This cake's a bit dry – I think I overcooked it.* **2** *UK* **the dry** a place where the conditions are not wet, especially when compared to somewhere where the conditions are wet: *You're soaked – come into the dry.* **3 run dry** If a river or other area of water runs dry, the water gradually disappears from it: *By this time all the wells had run dry.* **4** describes hair or skin that lacks the natural oils that make it soft and smooth: *a shampoo for dry hair* **5** describes bread when it is plain, without butter, jam, etc: *All I was offered was a piece of dry bread and an apple!*

• **as dry as a bone** (*ALSO* **bone-dry**) extremely dry: *I don't think he's been watering these plants – the soil is as dry as a bone.*

• **There wasn't a dry eye in the house.** used to mean that all the people at a particular place felt very emotional about what they had seen or heard and many of them were crying

dry /draɪ/ *verb* [I or T] to become dry, or to make something become dry: *Will this paint dry by tomorrow?* ○ *Hang the clothes up to dry.* ○ *The fruit is dried in the sun.*

• **dry *your* eyes** to stop crying: *Come on, Rosie, dry your eyes and we'll go and find daddy.*

• **dry the dishes** (*UK ALSO* **dry up (the dishes),** *UK* **do the drying (up)**) to dry plates, knives, forks, etc. after they have been washed

dried /draɪd/ *adj* Dried food or plants have had all their liquid removed, especially in order to preserve them: *dried apricots/bananas/mushrooms* ○ *dried* ***flowers***

dryness /ˈdraɪ.nəs/ *noun* [U] *The meat was juicy with no hint of dryness.*

dry [BORING] /draɪ/ *adj* **drier, driest** or **dryer, dryest** *DISAPPROVING* If a book, talk, subject is dry, it is not interesting.

dry [NO ALCOHOL] /draɪ/ *adj* without alcoholic drinks: *a dry wedding* ○ *a dry bar* ○ *a dry state* (= a part of a country which does not allow alcohol)

dry [NOT SWEET] /draɪ/ *adj* **drier, driest** or **dryer, dryest** If wine or another alcoholic drink is dry, it does not taste sweet: *dry cider/martini/sherry/wine* ○ *On the whole, I prefer dry wines to sweet ones.* **dryness** /ˈdraɪ.nəs/ *noun* [U] *The wine has just enough dryness to balance its fruitiness.*

dry [HUMOUR] /draɪ/ *adj* **drier, driest** or **dryer, dryest** *APPROVING* Dry humour is very amusing in a way which is clever and not loud or obvious: *a dry* ***sense of humour*** ○ *a dry wit* **drily, dryly** /ˈdraɪ.li/ *adv*: *"I know it sounds silly, but when I get to the beach I feel like a kid again." "We noticed," she said drily.*

PHRASAL VERBS WITH **dry**

▲ **dry *(sb/sth)* off** [M] *phrasal verb* to make someone or something dry, or to become dry, especially on the surface: *I dried myself off and got dressed.*

▲ **dry *(sth)* out** [SUBSTANCE] *phrasal verb* to make something dry, or to become dry: *If you don't keep food covered, it dries out.*

▲ **dry out** [PERSON] *phrasal verb INFORMAL* Someone who dries out stops being dependent on alcohol: *He went to a clinic in Arizona to dry out.*

▲ **dry *sth* up** [PLATES] *phrasal verb* [M] *MAINLY UK* to dry plates, cups, etc. with a cloth after they have been washed

▲ **dry up** [WATER] *phrasal verb* If a river, lake, etc. dries up, the water in it disappears.

▲ **dry up** [END] *phrasal verb* If a supply of something dries up, it ends: *His main source of work had dried up, leaving him short of money.*

ˌdry ˈclean *verb* [I] to clean clothes with chemicals, not water: *This dress has to be dry cleaned.*

dry cleaner's /ˌdraɪˈkliː.nəz/ [US] /-nɚz/ *noun* [C] a shop where clothes are cleaned with chemicals **ˌdry ˈcleaning** *noun* [U]

ˌdry ˈdock *noun* [C] an enclosed area of water which can be emptied and used for repairing ships

dryer, drier /ˈdraɪ.əʳ/ [US] /-ɚ/ *noun* [C] a machine that dries things: *a hair dryer* ○ *a grain dryer* ○ *Put those damp clothes in the (tumble) dryer.*

dry-eyed /ˌdraɪˈaɪd/ *adj* If someone is dry-eyed, they are not crying, especially in a situation in which you might expect them to be crying: *She accused me of being unfeeling because I left the cinema dry-eyed.*

ˈdry ˌgoods [FOOD] *plural noun* food, such as coffee and flour, that is solid and dry

ˈdry ˌgoods [CLOTH] *plural noun US FOR* **drapery** (= cloth, pins, thread, etc. used for sewing) ➲See at **drape**.

ˌdry ˈice *noun* [U] frozen CARBON DIOXIDE, used for preserving things by keeping them very cold and for producing a gas that looks like smoke in musical and theatrical performances

ˌdry ˈland *noun* [U] land and not sea or water: *We sailed for three days before we saw dry land.*

ˌdry ˈrot *noun* [U] a disease caused by a fungus which destroys wood in houses and boats, etc.

ˌdry ˈrun *noun* [C] *INFORMAL* a **dummy run**

dry-stone wall /ˌdraɪ.stəʊnˈwɔːl/ [US] /-stoʊnˈwɑːl/ *noun* [C] a wall made with stones which fit together firmly without being stuck together with MORTAR

the DTs /ðəˌdiːˈtiːz/ *plural noun INFORMAL ABBREVIATION FOR* delirium tremens: a physical condition, caused by drinking too much alcohol over a long period, in which someone shakes uncontrollably and sees imaginary things: *He's got a bad case of the DTs.*

dual /ˈdjuː.əl/ [US] /ˈduː.ᵊl/ *adj* [before n] **1** with two parts, or combining two things: *This room has a dual* ***purpose****, serving as both a study and a dining room.* ○ *the dual* ***role*** *of chairman and chief executive* **2 dual controls** two sets of controls in a car, one for the person who is learning to drive and one for the teacher **3 dual nationality/citizenship** the nationality of two countries at the same time: *dual British and American nationality*

dualism /ˈdjuː.ə.lɪ.zᵊm/ [US] /ˈduː.ᵊl.ɪ-/ *noun* [U] *FORMAL* the belief that things are divided into two often very different or opposing parts: *Western dualism values mind over body.*

duality /djuːˈæl.ə.ti/ [US] /duːˈæl.ə.ṭi/ *noun* [U] *FORMAL* the state of combining two different things: *His poems reveal the duality of his nature, the joy and hope, the fear and despair.*

ˌdual ˈcarriageway *UK noun* [C] (*US* **divided highway**) a road which has an area of land in the middle, dividing the rows of traffic which are moving in opposite directions

dual-purpose /ˌdjuː.əlˈpɜː.pəs/ [US] /ˌduː.ᵊlˈpɝː-/ *adj* able to be used to do two things: *a dual-purpose lawn-raking and leaf-collecting machine*

dub [NAME] /dʌb/ *verb* [T + n] **-bb-** to give something or someone a particular name, especially describing what you think of them: *She was dubbed by the newspapers 'The Angel of Death'.*

dub [SOUNDS] /dʌb/ *verb* [T] **-bb-** to change the sounds and speech on a film or television programme, especially to a different language: *I'd rather watch a film with subtitles than one dubbed* ***into*** *English.* ○ *To conceal his identity, the man's voice has been dubbed* ***over*** (= an actor speaks his words).

dub [STYLE] /dʌb/ *noun* [U] a style of music or poetry connected with REGGAE in which the main part of the tune is removed and various special effects are added

dubious /ˈdjuː.bi.əs/ [US] /ˈduː-/ *adj* **1** thought not to be completely true or not able to be trusted: *These claims are dubious and not scientifically proven.* ○ *He has been associated with some dubious characters.* ○ *Ruth Ellis has the dubious (= bad)* ***distinction*** *of being the last woman to be hanged in Britain.* **2** feeling doubt or uncertainty: *I'm dubious* ***about*** *his promises to change his ways.* **dubiously** /ˈdjuː.bi.əs.li/ [US] /ˈduː-/ *adv*

D

ducal /ˈdjuː.kəl/ [US] /ˈduː-/ *adj* of or connected with a duke

duchess /ˈdʌtʃ.es/ *noun* [C] (the title of) a woman who is married to a duke or who has the rank of duke: *the Duchess of Kent*

duchy /ˈdʌtʃ.i/ *noun* [C] the area of land owned or ruled by a DUKE or DUCHESS

D

duck [BIRD] /dʌk/ *noun* **1** [C] a bird that lives by water, has WEBBED feet (= feet with skin between the toes), a short neck and a large beak ➲See picture **Animals and Birds** on page Centre 4 **2** [U] the meat of this bird
• **take to *sth* like a duck to water** *INFORMAL* to discover when you start to do something for the first time that you have a natural ability to do it: *He took to fatherhood like a duck to water.*

duck [MOVE] /dʌk/ *verb* **1** [I or T] to move your head or the top part of your body quickly down, especially to avoid being hit: *I saw the ball hurtling towards me and ducked **(down)**.* ○ *Duck your head or you'll bang it on the door-frame.* **2** [T] to push someone underwater for a short time: *The boys were splashing about and ducking each other in the pool.* **3** [I + adv/prep] to move quickly to a place, especially in order not to be seen: *When he saw them coming, he ducked **into** a doorway.*
▲ **duck out of *sth*** *phrasal verb INFORMAL* to avoid doing something: *You can't duck out of your responsibilities.*
ducking /ˈdʌk.ɪŋ/ *noun* [C] an act or period of going below the surface of water: *The boat turned over and we all **got/had** a ducking.*

duck [PERSON] /dʌk/ *noun* [C] (*ALSO* **ducks**) *UK OLD-FASHIONED INFORMAL* an affectionate way of addressing someone you like: *Come and sit beside me, duck.*

ˌduck-billed ˈplatypus *noun* [C] a **platypus**

duckling /ˈdʌk.lɪŋ/ *noun* [C or U] a young duck, or its flesh when used as food

duckweed /ˈdʌk.wiːd/ *noun* [U] a plant that grows on the surface of some pools

duct /dʌkt/ *noun* [C] a tube or pipe that carries liquid or air, especially in and out of buildings or through the body: *Most office buildings have dozens of **air** ducts and vents.* ○ *People with blocked **tear** ducts cannot cry.*

ductile /ˈdʌk.taɪl/ [US] /-tɪl/ *adj SPECIALIZED* describes metals that can be bent easily

ductless gland /ˌdʌkt.ləsˈglænd/ *noun* [C] *SPECIALIZED* an **endocrine gland**

dud /dʌd/ *noun* [C] *INFORMAL* something that has no value or that does not work: *Are there any more batteries? This one's a dud.* ○ *He's made eleven films in the last twenty years and not one a dud.*
dud /dʌd/ *adj INFORMAL A customer had tried to pass off a dud **cheque*** (= one for which a bank will not give money).

dude /duːd/ *noun* [C] *MAINLY US SLANG* a man: *Some dude just asked me if I knew you.* ○ [as form of address] *Dude, where were you last night?* ○ *Jason was one **cool** dude.*

ˈdude ˌranch *noun* [C] a holiday farm in the US that offers activities such as riding horses and camping

dudgeon /ˈdʌdʒ.ən/ *noun LITERARY* **in high dudgeon** If you do something in high dudgeon, you do it angrily, usually because of the way you have been treated: *After waiting over an hour for them, he drove off in high dudgeon.*

due [OWED] /djuː/ [US] /duː/ *adj* owed as a debt or as a right: *The rent is due* (= should be paid) *at the end of the month.* ○ *Fifty pounds is (MAINLY UK) due **to** me/(MAINLY US) due me by the people I worked for last month.* ○ *Our thanks are due **to** everyone.* ○ *UK LEGAL He was found to have been driving without due* (= the necessary) ***care and attention**.*
due /djuː/ [US] /duː/ *noun* **give *sb* their due** said when you are praising someone for something good they have done, although you dislike other things about them: *He failed again, but to give him his due, he did try hard.*
dues /djuːz/ [US] /duːz/ *plural noun* the official payments that you make to an organization you belong to: *Members of the society pay $1000 in annual dues.*

due [EXPECTED] /djuː/ [US] /duː/ *adj* expected to happen, arrive, etc. at a particular time: *What time is the next bus due?* ○ *The next meeting is due **to** be held in three months' time.* ○ *Their first baby is due in January.*
• **in due course** *FORMAL* at a suitable time in the future: *You will receive notification of the results in due course.*

due [STRAIGHT] /djuː/ [US] /duː/ *adv* in a direction that is straight towards the north, south, east or west: *From here, you go due east until you get to a forest.*

due [RESULTING] /djuː/ [US] /duː/ *adj* **due to** because of: *A lot of her unhappiness is due to boredom.* ○ *Due to wet leaves on the line, this train will arrive an hour late.*

duel /ˈdjuː.əl/ [US] /ˈduː.əl/ *noun* **1** [C] a formal fight in the past, using guns or swords, arranged between two people as a way of deciding an argument: *The two men **fought** a duel **over** the lady.* ○ *The composer Strauss was once **challenged to** a duel.* **2** [C usually sing] a difficult competition in which both sides show a lot of effort: *The two yachts are **locked in** a duel **for** the championship title.* **duel** /ˈdjuː.əl/ [US] /ˈduː.əl/ *verb* [I]
duelling, *US USUALLY* **dueling** /ˈdjuː.ə.lɪŋ/ [US] /ˈduː-/ *noun* [U] the activity of fighting duels: *FIGURATIVE Eventually, the duelling* (= arguing) *politicians agreed to end their quarrel.*

duet /djuˈet/ [US] /duː-/ *noun* [C] a song or other piece of music sung or played by two people

duff [BAD] /dʌf/ *adj UK INFORMAL* bad, useless or not working: *He's directed so many films that you might expect a few duff ones.*

duff [BOTTOM] /dʌf/ *noun* [C] *US INFORMAL* a person's bottom: ***Get off** your duff and start working.*
▲ **duff *sb* up** *phrasal verb* [M] *UK INFORMAL* to hit someone repeatedly: *Two of the robbers threatened to duff the witness up if he went to the police.*

duffel bag, **duffle bag** /ˈdʌf.lˌbæg/ *noun* [C] a strong bag with thick string at the top that is used to close it and carry it

duffel coat, **duffle coat** /ˈdʌf.lˌkəʊt/ [US] /-ˌkoʊt/ *noun* [C] a coat made of thick wool which has TOGGLE (= solid tube-shaped) fasteners and usually has a HOOD (= head cover)

duffer /ˈdʌf.əʳ/ [US] /-ɚ/ *noun* [C] *OLD-FASHIONED* a person who lacks skill or is slow to learn

dug /dʌg/ *past simple and past participle of* **dig**

dugout /ˈdʌg.aʊt/ *noun* [C] **1** a shelter, usually for soldiers, made by digging a hole in the ground and covering it **2** a shelter for the members of a team beside a sports field

ˌdugout (caˈnoe) *noun* [C] a small light boat made by cutting out the middle of a tree trunk

duke /djuːk/ [US] /duːk/ *noun* [C] a man of very high rank in a country, or the ruler of a small independent country
dukedom /ˈdjuːk.dəm/ [US] /ˈduːk-/ *noun* [C] the rank of a duke, or the land owned by a duke

dulcet /ˈdʌl.sət/ *adj* **1** *LITERARY* describes sounds that are soft and pleasant to listen to **2** *HUMOROUS* ***sb's* dulcet tones** a person's voice

dulcimer /ˈdʌl.sɪ.məʳ/ [US] /-mɚ/ *noun* [C] a musical instrument, consisting of a wooden box with wire strings stretched over it, played by hitting the strings with a pair of light hammers

dull [BORING] /dʌl/ *adj* not interesting or exciting in any way; boring: *She wrote dull, respectable articles for the local newspaper.* ○ *He's pleasant enough, but **deadly** dull* (= very boring).
• **be (as) dull as ditchwater** *INFORMAL* to be very boring
dullness /ˈdʌl.nəs/ *noun* [U] when something is boring
dully /ˈdʌl.li/ *adv*

dull [NOT BRIGHT] /dʌl/ *adj* not clear, bright or shiny; dark: *We could just see a dull **glow** given off by the fire's last embers.* ○ *The first day of our holiday was dull* (= cloudy). **dully** /ˈdʌl.li/ *adv*: *The car lights glowed dully through the mist.*

dull [NOT SHARP] /dʌl/ *adj* **1** describes a sound or pain that is not sharp or clear: *I heard a dull **thud** from the kitchen and realized she must have fainted.* ○ *The dull rumble of traffic woke her.* ○ *She felt a dull **ache** at the back of her head.* **2** *OLD-FASHIONED* not intelligent
dull /dʌl/ *verb* [T] to make something less severe: *Homeless children sniff glue to dull their hunger pains.* **dully** /ˈdʌl.li/ *adv*: *My arm still ached dully.*

dullard /ˈdʌl.əd/ [US] /-ɚd/ *noun* [C] *OLD-FASHIONED* a stupid person

duly /ˈdjuː.li/ [US] /ˈduː-/ *adv* in the correct way or at the correct time; as expected: *He knew he had been wrong, and duly apologized.* ○ *She asked for his autograph and he duly* ***obliged*** *by signing her programme.*

dumb [SILENT] /dʌm/ *adj* permanently or temporarily unable to speak: *He's been deaf and dumb since birth.* ○ *She was* ***struck*** *dumb by what she had seen.*

dumbly /ˈdʌm.li/ *adv* without speaking: *She stared dumbly into space.* **dumbness** /ˈdʌm.nəs/ *noun* [U]

dumb [STUPID] /dʌm/ *adj MAINLY US INFORMAL* stupid and annoying: *Are they brave or just dumb?* ○ *What a dumb idea!*

dumb /dʌm/ *verb*

▲ **ˌdumb *sth* ˈdown** *phrasal verb* [M] *INFORMAL DISAPPROVING* to make something simpler and easier for people to understand, especially in order to make it more popular: *The General Synod accused broadcasters of dumbing down religious programmes.*

dumbing down /ˌdʌm.ɪŋˈdaʊn/ *noun* [U] *the dumbing down of British television*

dumbbell [WEIGHT] /ˈdʌm.bel/ *noun* [C] a short bar with a weight on each end that you lift up and down to strengthen your arm and shoulder muscles

dumbbell [PERSON] /ˈdʌm.bel/ *noun* [C] *US FOR* **dummy** STUPID PERSON

dumbfounded /ˌdʌmˈfaʊn.dɪd/ *adj* (*ALSO* **dumbstruck**) so shocked that you cannot speak: *He was dumbfounded* ***by*** *the allegations.*

ˈdumb ˌshow *noun* [C or U] *UK* the use of hand movements and not speech in order to communicate what you mean, or an example of this

ˌdumb ˈwaiter *noun* [C] a small LIFT (= device used to move things from one level of a building to another) used especially in restaurants to deliver food from the kitchen

dum-dum (bullet) /ˈdʌm.dʌmˌbʊl.ɪt/ *noun* [C] a bullet with a soft front that increases in size when it hits someone, causing serious injuries

dummy [MODEL] /ˈdʌm.i/ *noun* [C] a large model of a human, especially one used to show clothes in a shop: *a* ***shop*** *dummy* ○ *a ventriloquist's dummy*

dummy [NOT REAL] /ˈdʌm.i/ *noun* [C] **1** something that is not real and is used for practice or to deceive: *The device is not a real bomb but a dummy.* **2** (in some sports, especially football) when you pretend to hit the ball in a particular direction but do not, in order to deceive the other players

dummy /ˈdʌm.i/ *adj* [before n] not real: *an enormous dummy perfume bottle in the shop window*

dummy [FOR BABY] *UK* /ˈdʌm.i/ *noun* [C] (*US* **pacifier**) a smooth rubber or plastic object that is given to a baby to suck in order to comfort it and make it stop crying

dummy [STUPID PERSON] /ˈdʌm.i/ *noun* [C] (*US ALSO* **dumbbell**) *INFORMAL* a stupid or silly person: *Only a dummy would ignore the safety warnings.*

ˌdummy ˈrun *noun* [C] (*ALSO* **dry run**) *INFORMAL* a practice of a particular activity or performance: *The local elections can be seen as a dummy run* ***for*** *the national election next year.*

dump /dʌmp/ *verb* [T] **1** to put down or drop something in a careless way: *He came in with four shopping bags and dumped them on the table.* **2** to get rid of something unwanted, especially by leaving it in a place where it is not allowed to be: *The tax was so unpopular that the government decided to dump it.* ○ *Several old cars had been dumped near the beach.* ○ *Toxic chemicals continue to be dumped in the North Sea.* **3** to sell unwanted goods very cheaply, usually in other countries: *They accused the West of dumping out-of-date medicines* ***on*** *Third World countries.* **4** *INFORMAL* to suddenly end a romantic relationship you have been having with someone: *If he's so awful, why don't you just dump him?* **5** *SPECIALIZED* to move information from a computer's memory to a storage device

dump /dʌmp/ *noun* [C] **1** (*ALSO* **rubbish dump**) a place where people are allowed to leave their rubbish: *I need to clear out the shed and take everything I don't want to the dump.* **2** *INFORMAL* a very unpleasant and untidy place: *His room is an absolute dump!* **3** a place where things of a particular type are stored, especially by an army: *an ammunition/arms/weapons/food dump*

• **have/take a dump** *OFFENSIVE* to excrete the contents of the bowels

dumping /ˈdʌm.pɪŋ/ *noun* [U] the act of dumping something: *They have promised to limit the dumping* ***of*** *sewage sludge in the sea.*

dumper truck *UK* /ˈdʌm.pəˌtrʌk/ [US] /-pɚ-/ *noun* [C] (*US* **dump truck,** *AUS* **tip truck**) a large truck for transporting heavy loads, with a back part which can be raised at one end so that its contents fall out ➲See picture **Cars and Trucks** on page Centre 13

ˈdumping ˌground *noun* [C usually sing] a place where something unwanted is left: *Most people do not want this country to become a dumping ground* ***for*** *toxic waste.*

dumpling /ˈdʌm.plɪŋ/ *noun* [C] **1** a small ball of DOUGH (= flour and water mixed together) cooked and eaten with meat and vegetables **2** a small amount of fruit covered in a sweet DOUGH and baked: *apple dumplings*

dumps /dʌmps/ *plural noun INFORMAL* **(down) in the dumps** unhappy: *She's a bit down in the dumps because she's got to take her exams again.*

Dumpster /ˈdʌmp.stəʳ/ [US] /-stɚ/ *noun* [C] *US TRADEMARK FOR* **skip** CONTAINER

ˈdump ˌtruck *noun* [C] *US FOR* **dumper truck** ➲See picture **Cars and Trucks** on page Centre 13

dumpy /ˈdʌm.pi/ *adj* short and fat: *a dumpy little woman*

dun /dʌn/ *adj* of a greyish brown colour

dunce /dʌnts/ *noun* [C] *DISAPPROVING* a person who is slow to learn or stupid, especially at school

dunce's cap /ˈdʌnt.sɪzˌkæp/ *noun* [C usually sing] (*US USUALLY* **dunce cap**) a tall paper hat with a pointed end that in the past a child had to wear in school if they had made many mistakes in their work

dunderhead /ˈdʌn.də.hed/ [US] /-dɚ-/ *noun* [C] *OLD-FASHIONED INFORMAL* a stupid person

dune /djuːn/ [US] /duːn/ *noun* [C] a small hill of sand beside a beach or in a desert

dung /dʌŋ/ *noun* [U] solid excrement from animals, especially cattle and horses; MANURE

dungarees /ˌdʌŋ.gəˈriːz/ *plural noun* **1** *UK* (*US* **overalls**) a pair of trousers with an extra piece of cloth that covers the chest and is held in place by a strap over each shoulder ➲See picture **Clothes** on page Centre 6 **2** *US OLD-FASHIONED* trousers made of denim

dungeon /ˈdʌn.dʒᵊn/ *noun* [C] an underground prison, especially in a castle

dunk /dʌŋk/ *verb* [T] **1** to put a biscuit, bread, etc. into a liquid such as tea or soup for a short time before eating it: *She dunked a biscuit* ***in*** *her tea.* **2** *US* to **slam-dunk**

dunno /dəˈnəʊ/ [US] /-ˈnoʊ/ *NOT STANDARD short form of* I don't know: *"Where are we exactly?" "Dunno."*

dunny /ˈdʌn.i/ *noun* [C] *AUS INFORMAL FOR* **toilet** CONTAINER

duo /ˈdjuː.əʊ/ [US] /ˈduː.oʊ/ *noun* [C] *plural* **duos** a pair, especially of singers, musicians or other performers: *the comedy duo Laurel and Hardy*

duodenum /ˌdjuː.əʊˈdiː.nəm/ [US] /ˌduː.ə-/ *noun* [C] *plural* **duodenums** or **duodena** *SPECIALIZED* the first part of the bowel just below the stomach

duodenal /ˌdjuː.əʊˈdiː.nəl/ [US] /ˌduː.ə-/ *adj SPECIALIZED* relating to the duodenum: *Drugs have been developed to cure some duodenal* ***ulcers.***

dupe /djuːp/ [US] /duːp/ *verb* [T] to deceive someone, usually making them do something they did not intend to do: *The girls were duped by drug smugglers* ***into*** *carrying heroin for them.*

dupe /djuːp/ [US] /duːp/ *noun* [C] someone who has been tricked: *an innocent dupe*

duplex [ROOMS] /ˈdjuː.pleks/ [US] /ˈduː-/ *noun* [C] a set of rooms for living in that are on two floors of a building

duplex [TWO HOUSES] /ˈdjuː.pleks/ [US] /ˈduː-/ *noun* [C] *AUS* a pair of small houses on a single floor that are joined together

duplicate /ˈdjuː.plɪ.keɪt/ [US] /ˈduː-/ *verb* [T] to make an exact copy of something: *Can you duplicate (= use a special machine to copy) this document for me?*

D

○ *Parenthood is an experience nothing else can duplicate.*

duplicate /ˈdjuː.plɪ.kət/ ⓤ /ˈduː-/ *adj* [before n] being an exact copy of something: *The thieves were equipped with duplicate keys to the safe.*

duplicate /ˈdjuː.plɪ.kət/ ⓤ /ˈduː-/ *noun* [C] something that is an exact copy of something else: *I lost the original form so they sent me a duplicate.*

duplication /ˌdjuː.plɪˈkeɪ.ʃ°n/ ⓤ /ˌduː-/ *noun* [U] the act or process of duplicating something

duplicity /djuˈplɪs.ɪ.ti/ ⓤ /duːˈplɪs.ə.t̬i/ *noun* [U] FORMAL lack of honesty, especially by saying different things to two people: *They were accused of duplicity in their dealings with both sides.*

duplicitous /djuˈplɪs.ɪ.təs/ ⓤ /duːˈplɪs.ə.t̬əs/ *adj* FORMAL involving duplicity: *a duplicitous traitor/spy/politician*

durable /ˈdjʊə.rə.bl̩/ ⓤ /ˈdʊr.ə-/ *adj* able to last a long time without becoming damaged: *The machines have to be made of durable materials.* ○ *The resolution calls for a durable peace settlement.* **durability** /ˌdjʊə.rəˈbɪl.ɪ.ti/ ⓤ /ˌdʊr.əˈbɪl.ə.t̬i/ *noun* [U] *the durability of the materials used*

duration /djʊəˈreɪ.ʃ°n/ ⓤ /duː-/ *noun* [U] the length of time that something lasts: *He planned a stay of two years' duration.*

• **for the duration** for as long as something lasts: *I suppose we're stuck with each other for the duration (of the journey).*

duress /djʊˈres/ ⓤ /duː-/ *noun* [U] FORMAL threats used to force a person to do something: *He claimed that he signed the confession under duress.*

Durex /ˈdjʊə.reks/ ⓤ /ˈdʊr.eks/ *noun* [C] UK TRADEMARK a type of condom

during THROUGH /ˈdjʊə.rɪŋ/ ⓤ /ˈdʊr.ɪŋ/ *prep* from the beginning to the end of a particular period; **throughout**: *They work during the night and sleep by day.* ○ *There were huge advances in aviation technology during World War Two.* ⊃Compare **while** DURING.

during AT SOME TIME IN /ˈdjʊə.rɪŋ/ ⓤ /ˈdʊr.ɪŋ/ *prep* at some time between the beginning and the end of a period: *I woke up several times during the night.* ○ *The programme will be shown on television during the weekend.*

COMMON LEARNER ERROR

during or **for**?

Use **during** to talk about a period of time when something happens.
I'm at work during the day, so it's better to phone in the evening.
Please don't take photos during the performance.

Use **for** to say how long something happens or continues, for example 'for two hours', 'for three days'.
I've been in Cambridge for six months now.
We waited for an hour and then left.
~~We waited during an hour and then left.~~

---

durum wheat /ˈdjʊə.rəm.wiːt/ ⓤ /ˈdʊr-/ *noun* [U] a type of wheat which is used to make pasta

dusk /dʌsk/ *noun* [U] the time before night when it is not yet dark: *As dusk fell, bats began to fly between the trees.*

dusky /ˈdʌs.ki/ *adj* LITERARY dark in colour: *In autumn, the leaves turn a dusky red.*

dust /dʌst/ *noun* [U] dry dirt in the form of powder that covers surfaces inside a building, or very small dry pieces of earth, sand or other substances: *The furniture was covered in dust and cobwebs.* ○ *A cloud of dust rose in the air as the car roared past.* ○ *Many miners have suffered from the effects of coal dust in their lungs.*

• **turn to dust** LITERARY to become worthless: *Every promise they have made has turned to dust.*

• **the dust settles** If the dust settles after an argument or big change, the situation becomes calmer: *We thought we'd let the dust settle before discussing the other matter.*

dust /dʌst/ *verb* **1** [I or T] to use a cloth to remove dust from the surface of something: *I was dusting the mantelpiece when I noticed a crack.* **2** [T] to cover something with a fine powder: *Dust the top of the cake with icing sugar.*

• **be done and dusted** UK INFORMAL to be complete and finished: *By now the deal was done and dusted.*

▲ **dust sth off** *phrasal verb* [M] (UK ALSO **dust down**) to prepare something for use, especially after it has not been

used for a long time: *They brought out the old ambulances, dusted them down and put them back into service.*

duster /ˈdʌs.tər/ ⓤ /-tɚ/ *noun* [C] a piece of cloth that is used for removing dust from furniture, books, surfaces, etc.

dusty /ˈdʌs.ti/ *adj* **1** covered in dust: *Heaps of dusty books lay on the floor.* ○ *We drove along the dusty road.* **2** slightly grey in colour: *dusty pink*

dustbin UK /ˈdʌst.bɪn/ *noun* [C] (US **garbage can**, US ALSO **trash can**) a large container for rubbish from a house or other building, usually made of strong plastic or metal and kept outside

• **consign sth to the dustbin** to get rid of something: *Fox hunting, he claimed, should be consigned to the dustbin of history.*

dustbin ˌbag/ˈliner UK *noun* [C] (US **garbage/trash bag**, US **trash can liner**) a plastic bag put inside a dustbin to hold the waste and keep the container clean

dustbowl /ˈdʌst.bəʊl/ ⓤ /-boʊl/ *noun* [C] an area of land where the earth is very dry and where the air is often full of dust

dustcart UK /ˈdʌst.kɑːt/ ⓤ /-kɑːrt/ *noun* [C] (US **garbage truck**) a large vehicle that is driven from one house to another to collect rubbish from the DUSTBINS outside ⊃See picture **Cars and Trucks** on page Centre 13

dust ˌjacket *noun* [C] a paper cover for a book, usually with the title of the book and the name of the author printed on it

dustman UK /ˈdʌst.mən/ *noun* [C] (US **garbageman**, UK FORMAL **refuse collector**) a person whose job it is to empty people's DUSTBINS and take the rubbish away

dustpan /ˈdʌst.pæn/ *noun* [C] a flat container with a handle into which you brush dust and dirt

dustsheet /ˈdʌst.ʃiːt/ *noun* [C] a large piece of cloth that is put over furniture to protect it from dust

dust-up /ˈdʌs.tʌp/ *noun* [C usually sing] OLD-FASHIONED a fight or argument

dusty /ˈdʌs.ti/ ⓤ /-t̬i/ *adj* ⊃See at **dust**.

Dutch /dʌtʃ/ *adj* from, belonging to or relating to the Netherlands

• **go Dutch** INFORMAL to agree to share the cost of something, especially a meal

Dutch /dʌtʃ/ *noun* [U] the language of the Netherlands
✱ NOTE: This language is also spoken in Belgium, where it is called Flemish.

Dutch ˈcap *noun* [C] a **diaphragm** BIRTH CONTROL

Dutch ˈcourage UK *noun* [U] (US **liquid courage**) the confidence some people get from drinking alcohol before they do something frightening

Dutch ˈelm diˌsease *noun* [U] a disease that slowly kills ELM trees

Dutchman /ˈdʌtʃ.mən/ *noun* [C] a man who comes from the Netherlands

• **I'm a Dutchman** UK HUMOROUS said after describing or hearing something that is very obviously not true: *If that's his real hair, then I'm a Dutchman.*

duty RESPONSIBILITY /ˈdjuː.ti/ ⓤ /ˈduː.t̬i/ *noun* [C or U] something that you have to do because it is part of your job, or something that you feel is the right thing to do: *The duty of the agency is to act in the best interests of the child.* ○ [+ to infinitive] *I felt it was my duty to tell them the truth.* ○ *You have a duty to yourself to take a holiday now and then.* ○ *He only went to see her out of duty (= because he thought he should).* ○ *You should report for duty (= arrive at work) at 8 am on Monday.* ○ *What time are you off/on duty (= When do you finish/start work) tomorrow?*

• **be duty bound to do sth** to have to do something because it is your duty: *We are duty bound to justify how we spend our funds.*

dutiful /ˈdjuː.tɪ.f°l/ ⓤ /ˈduː.t̬ɪ-/ *adj* doing everything that you should do: *a dutiful son/husband* **dutifully** /ˈdjuː.tɪ.f°l.i/ ⓤ /ˈduː.t̬ɪ-/ *adv*

duty TAX /ˈdjuː.ti/ ⓤ /ˈduː.t̬i/ *noun* [C or U] a tax paid to the government, especially on things that you bring into a country: *There's a high duty on alcohol.*

dutiable /ˈdjuː.ti.ə.bl̩/ ⓤ /ˈduː.t̬i-/ *adj* SPECIALIZED describes goods on which duty must be paid

duty-free /ˌdjuːˈtiˈfriː/ ⓤ /ˌduː.ti-/ *adj* Duty-free goods are luxury goods bought in special shops in airports, on ships, etc. on which you do not pay government tax: *He bought his wife some duty-free perfume.* ○ *I almost missed my flight because there was a long queue in the duty-free* **shop**. **duty-free** /ˌdjuːˈtiˈfriː/ ⓤ /ˌduː.ti-/ *noun* [U] *We can* **buy** *our duty-free while we're waiting at the airport.*

duvet UK /ˈduː.veɪ/ ⓤ /-ˈ-/ *noun* [C] (UK ALSO **continental quilt**, US **comforter**) a large soft flat bag filled with feathers or artificial material used on a bed

'**duvet ˌcover** *noun* [C] a cover for a duvet

DVD /ˌdiː.viːˈdiː/ *noun* [C] ABBREVIATION FOR digital versatile disc or digital video disc: a disc used for storing and playing music, films or information: *I got a DVD of 'Mary Poppins' for Christmas.* ○ *Is the film available on DVD?* ○ *a DVD drive/player*

DVT /ˌdiː.viːˈtiː/ *noun* [U] ABBREVIATION FOR **deep vein thrombosis**

dwarf /dwɔːf/ ⓤ /dwɔːrf/ *noun* [C] *plural* **dwarfs** or **dwarves** **1** in stories for children, a creature like a little man with magical powers: *Snow White and the Seven Dwarves* **2** OFTEN OFFENSIVE a person who is much smaller than the usual size

dwarf /dwɔːf/ ⓤ /dwɔːrf/ *adj* [before n] very small: *You can grow dwarf conifers in pots on the patio.*

dwarf /dwɔːf/ ⓤ /dwɔːrf/ *verb* [T] If one thing dwarfs another, it makes it seem much bigger by comparison: *The new skyscraper will dwarf all those near it.* ○ *This new financial crisis may well dwarf most that have gone before.*

dweeb /dwiːb/ *noun* [C] US SLANG DISAPPROVING a person who is physically and socially awkward and lacks confidence: *What a dweeb! Why doesn't she dump him?*

dwell /dwel/ *verb* [I usually + adv or prep] **dwelt** or **dwelled**, **dwelt** or **dwelled** FORMAL to live in a place or in a particular way: *She dwelt in remote parts of Asia for many years.*

▲ **dwell on** *sth phrasal verb* to keep thinking or talking about something, especially something bad or unpleasant: *In his speech, he dwelt on the plight of the sick and the hungry.*

dweller /ˈdwel.əʳ/ ⓤ /-ɚ/ *noun* **city/town/cave, etc. dweller** a person who lives in a city, town, cave, etc.

dwelling /ˈdwel.ɪŋ/ *noun* [C] FORMAL a house or place to live in: *There is an estimated shortfall of some five million dwellings across the country.*

DWI /ˌdiː.dʌb.ļ.juːˈaɪ/ US ABBREVIATION FOR **driving while intoxicated**; see at **drive** USE VEHICLE

dwindle /ˈdwɪn.dļ/ *verb* [I] to become smaller in size or amount, or fewer in number: *The community has dwindled to a tenth of its former size in the last two years.* ○ *Her hopes of success in the race dwindled last night as the weather became worse.* **dwindling** /ˈdwɪn.dļ.ɪŋ/ *adj*: *dwindling numbers/supplies*

dye /daɪ/ *verb* [T] **dyeing**, **dyed**, **dyed** to change the colour of something using a special liquid: *For a change, why not dye your T-shirts?* ○ [+ obj + adj] *He's dyed his hair black.*

dye /daɪ/ *noun* [C or U] a substance used to change the colour of something: *She dipped the material into the dye.* ○ *There are dozens of different dyes to choose from.*

dyed-in-the-wool /ˌdaɪ.dɪn.ðəˈwʊl/ If someone has dyed-in-the-wool opinions, they hold them strongly and will not change them: *He's a dyed-in-the-wool traditionalist where cooking is concerned – he won't have any modern gadgets in the kitchen.*

dyke WALL, **dike** /daɪk/ *noun* [C] a wall built to prevent the sea or a river from flooding an area, or a channel dug to take water away from an area ⊃Compare **dam**.

dyke WOMAN, **dike** /daɪk/ *noun* [C] SLANG a homosexual woman; a LESBIAN. Many people consider this word offensive.

dynamic /daɪˈnæm.ɪk/ *adj* having a lot of ideas and enthusiasm; energetic and forceful: *She's young and dynamic and will be a great addition to the team.* ○ *We need a dynamic expansion of trade with other countries.* **dynamically** /daɪˈnæm.ɪ.kli/ *adv* **dynamism** /ˈdaɪ.nə.mɪ.zᵊm/ *noun* [U] the quality of being dynamic: *She has a freshness and dynamism about her.*

dynamics /daɪˈnæm.ɪks/ *plural noun* **1** forces that produce movement: *This software is used for modelling atmospheric dynamics.* **2** forces or processes that produce change inside a group or system: *The fight for the leadership gave a fascinating insight into the group's dynamics.* **3** SPECIALIZED changes in loudness in a piece of music

dynamics /daɪˈnæm.ɪks/ *noun* [U] SPECIALIZED the scientific study of the forces that produce movement **dynamic** /daɪˈnæm.ɪk/ *adj*: *a dynamic force* **dynamically** /daɪˈnæm.ɪ.kli/ *adv*: *dynamically stable*

dynamite /ˈdaɪ.nə.maɪt/ *noun* [U] **1** a type of explosive: *a stick of dynamite* **2** INFORMAL something that causes or may cause great shock or excitement: *The issue of unemployment is **political** dynamite* (= could cause big political problems) *for the government.*

dynamite /ˈdaɪ.nə.maɪt/ *verb* [T] *The rebels had dynamited the railway line* (= destroyed it with dynamite).

dynamo /ˈdaɪ.nə.məʊ/ ⓤ /-moʊ/ *noun plural* **dynamos** **1** [C] a device which changes energy of movement into electrical energy: *A dynamo on a bicycle will power a pair of lights while the wheels are going round.* **2** [C usually sing] an energetic force: *Onstage she is a **human** dynamo, spending the hour in perpetual motion.*

dynasty /ˈdɪn.ə.sti/ ⓤ /ˈdaɪ.nə-/ *noun* [C] a series of rulers or leaders who are all from the same family, or a period when a country is ruled by them: *The Mogul dynasty ruled over India for centuries.* **dynastic** /daɪˈnæs.tɪk/ *adj* FORMAL

d'you STRONG /djuː/, WEAK /djə/ INFORMAL short form of do you: *D'you come here often?*

dysentery /ˈdɪs.ᵊn.tᵊr.i/ /-tri/ ⓤ /-ter-/ *noun* [U] a disease of the bowels which causes the contents to be excreted much more often and in a more liquid form than usual. It is caused by an infection which is spread by dirty water or food.

dysfunction /dɪsˈfʌŋk.ʃᵊn/ *noun* [C] SPECIALIZED a problem or fault in a part of the body or a machine: *There appears to be a dysfunction in the patient's respiratory system.* **dysfunctional** /dɪsˈfʌŋk.ʃᵊn.əl/ *adj* SPECIALIZED not behaving or working normally: *a dysfunctional family*

dyslexia /dɪˈslek.si.ə/ *noun* [U] a difficulty with reading and writing caused by the brain's inability to see the difference between some letter shapes **dyslexic** /dɪˈslek.sɪk/ *adj, noun* [C] (someone) having dyslexia

dyspepsia /dɪˈspep.si.ə/ *noun* [U] SPECIALIZED pain in the stomach; INDIGESTION **dyspeptic** /dɪˈspep.tɪk/ *adj* **1** SPECIALIZED having problems with digestion **2** LITERARY always angry or easily annoyed

E

E LETTER (*plural* **E's** or **Es**), **e** (*plural* **e's** or **es**) /iː/ *noun* [C] the 5th letter of the English alphabet

E EAST *noun* [U], *adj* WRITTEN ABBREVIATION FOR **east** or **eastern**

E MUSIC /iː/ *noun* [C or U] *plural* **E's** or **Es** a note in Western music: *The piece is in E/**the key of** E.* ○ *The bottom string on a guitar is an E.*

E MARK /iː/ *noun plural* **E's** or **Es** **1** [C or U] MAINLY UK a mark in an exam or for a piece of work that shows the work is considered to be very bad: *You might have to take the course again if you get many more Es.* **2** [C] US a mark in an exam or for a piece of work that shows the work is considered to be excellent

E DRUG /iː/ *noun* [C or U] *plural* **E's** or **Es** INFORMAL ABBREVIATION FOR **ecstasy** DRUG

e- /iː/ *prefix* ABBREVIATION FOR **electronic** ELECTRICAL: *e-commerce* ○ *email*

each /iːtʃ/ *pronoun, determiner* every thing, person, etc. in a group of two or more, considered separately: *When you run, each foot leaves the ground before the other comes down.* ○ *There are five leaflets – please take one of each.* ○ *Each of the companies supports a local charity.* ○ *Each and every one of the flowers has its own colour and smell.* ○ *We each* (= Every one of us) *wanted the bedroom with the balcony, so we tossed a coin to decide.* ○ *The bill comes to £79, so that's about £10 each.*

• **each to his/their own** (MAINLY US **to each their own**) used to say that everyone likes different things: *You actually like modern jazz, do you? Each to their own.*

• **each way** If you put a sum of money each way on a horse race, you will win money if the horse you have chosen comes first, second or third.

each 'other *pronoun* (ALSO **one another**) used to show that each person in a group of two or more people does something to the others: *They kept looking at each other and smiling.* ○ *They're always wearing each other's clothes.* ○ *Why are you always arguing with each other?* ○ *They're so happy together – they were made for each other* (= are perfectly matched).

eager /ˈiːɡəʳ/ ⑩ /-ɡɚ/ *adj* wanting very much to do or have something, especially something interesting or enjoyable: *the children's eager faces* ○ *She sounded very eager to meet you.* ○ *They crowded round the spokesperson, eager for any news.*

eagerly /ˈiːɡə.li/ ⑩ /-ɡɚ-/ *adv* in an eager way: *an eagerly awaited announcement*

eagerness /ˈiːɡə.nəs/ ⑩ /-ɡɚ-/ *noun* [S or U often + *to* infinitive] *In their eagerness to* (= Wanting so much to) *find a solution, they may have overlooked certain financial difficulties.*

eager 'beaver *noun* [C] INFORMAL a person who is willing to work very hard

eagle /ˈiː.ɡl̩/ *noun* [C] a large strong bird with a curved beak which eats meat and can see very well ⊃See picture **Animals and Birds** on page Centre 4

eagle ,eye *noun* [C usually sing] If someone has an eagle eye, they notice everything, even very small details: *We sat down and started the exam under the eagle eye of the teacher.* **eagle-eyed** /ˌiː.ɡlˈaɪd/ *adj*: *My eagle-eyed mother noticed that some cakes had gone missing.*

-ean /-i.ən/ *suffix* ⊃See at **-an** BELONG TO.

ear BODY PART /ɪəʳ/ ⑩ /ɪr/ *noun* [C] either of the two organs, one on each side of the head, by which people or animals hear sounds, or the piece of skin and tissue outside the head connected to this organ: *The hearing in my left ear's not so good.* ○ *She leant over and whispered something in his ear.* ⊃See also **aural**. ⊃See picture **The Body** on page Centre 5

• **be all ears** to be waiting eagerly to hear about something: *I'm all ears – tell us what they had to say.*

• **close your ears** to stop listening: *I tried to close my ears to the sounds coming from next door.*

• **have/keep *your* ear to the ground** to pay attention to everything that is happening around you and to what people are saying

• *your* **ears must be burning** INFORMAL something that you say to someone who is being talked about: *All this talk about Emma – her ears must be burning!*

• **ears are flapping** INFORMAL If you say that someone's ears are flapping, you mean that they are trying to hear what you are saying, although they are not part of your conversation.

• **go in one ear and out the other** INFORMAL If you say that something you hear goes in one ear and out the other, you mean you quickly forget it: *If I have to listen to something I don't understand, it just goes in one ear and out the other.*

• **have good ears** to have good hearing

• **have an ear for** *sth* If someone has an ear for music or languages, they are good at hearing, repeating or understanding these sounds: *She's never had much of an ear for languages.*

• **have the ear of** *sb* If someone has the ear of an important person, their ideas are listened to and considered important by that person.

• **be out on *your* ear** INFORMAL to be forced to leave a job or place, especially because you have done something wrong

• **be up to *your* ears in** *sth* to be very busy, or to have more of something than you can manage: *I'm up to my ears in work.* ○ *She's up to her ears in debt.*

-eared /-ɪəd/ ⑩ /-ɪrd/ *suffix* with ears of a particular type: *a long-eared rabbit*

ear PLANT PART /ɪəʳ/ ⑩ /ɪr/ *noun* [C] the flowering part of a grass-like plant such as wheat, which later contains the grains which are used as food: *an ear of corn*

earache /ˈɪə.reɪk/ ⑩ /ˈɪr.eɪk/ *noun* [C or U] a pain in the inside part of your ear

earbashing /ˈɪəˌbæʃ.ɪŋ/ ⑩ /ˈɪr-/ *noun* [S] UK INFORMAL angry words spoken to someone who has done something wrong: *I got an earbashing from Sam for being late.*

eardrops /ˈɪə.drɒps/ ⑩ /ˈɪr.drɑːps/ *plural noun* liquid medicine put into the ears, usually to cure an ear infection

eardrum /ˈɪə.drʌm/ ⑩ /ˈɪr-/ *noun* [C] a thin piece of skin inside the ear that moves backwards and forwards very quickly when sound waves reach it, allowing you to hear sounds

earflaps /ˈɪə.flæps/ ⑩ /ˈɪr-/ *plural noun* the two pieces of material or fur on some hats which can be pulled down to cover the ears

earful /ˈɪə.fʊl/ ⑩ /ˈɪr-/ *noun* INFORMAL **give *sb* an earful** to angrily complain to someone

earl /ɜːl/ ⑩ /ɝːl/ *noun* [C] (the title of) a British man of high social rank, between a MARQUIS and a VISCOUNT: *the Earl of Northumberland*

earldom /ˈɜːl.dəm/ ⑩ /ˈɝːl-/ *noun* [C] the rank or lands of an earl or COUNTESS

earlobe /ˈɪə.ləʊb/ ⑩ /ˈɪr.loʊb/ *noun* [C] (ALSO **lobe**) the soft round part at the bottom of the ear

early /ˈɜː.li/ ⑩ /ˈɝː-/ *adj, adv* **earlier, earliest** near the beginning of a period of time, or before the usual, expected or planned time: *If you finish early you can go home.* ○ *If you arrived earlier, you'd have more time.* ○ *I like being a little early for interviews.* ○ *They scored two goals early (on) in the game.* ○ *I hate having to get up early (in the morning).* ○ *I'm going to have an early night* (= go to sleep before my usual time). ○ *She was a poet living in the early fifteenth century.* ○ *He learned to read at the early age of three.* ○ *It's rather early to be sowing carrot seeds, isn't it?* ○ *Mercedes were pioneers during the early days/years of car manufacture.* ○ *My earliest* (= first) *memory is of being shown around our new house.* ○ *These are some of my early* (= first) *attempts at sculpture.* ○ *Here's a dish I prepared earlier* (= I made a short time ago). ⊃Compare **late** NEAR THE END; **late** AFTER.

• **It's early days.** UK said when you think it is too soon to make a judgment about the likely result of something because a lot might still happen or change: *Our progress has been fairly slow so far, but it's early days.*

• **drive/send** *sb* **to an early grave** to cause someone to die young: *Sometimes I think these children are going to drive me to an early grave!*

• **at the earliest** used after a date or time to show that something will not happen before then: *I'm very busy, so I won't be with you till 4 o'clock at the earliest.*

• **Early to bed and early to rise (makes a man healthy, wealthy and wise).** *SAYING* This means that someone who gets enough sleep and starts work early in the day will have a successful life.

• **The early bird catches the worm.** *SAYING* said to advise someone that they will gain an advantage if they do something immediately or before anyone else does it

early ˌbird *noun* [C] *HUMOROUS* a person who gets up or arrives early

ˌEarly 'Childhood ˌEducation *noun* [U] (*ABBREVIATION* **ECE**) *US* the study of the education of children from two to seven years of age

ˌearly 'music *noun* [U] Western music of THE MIDDLE AGES or THE RENAISSANCE, written before about 1600

early 'warning ˌsystem *noun* [C] a military system of RADAR stations intended to give a warning as soon as enemy aircraft or bombs approach

earmark /ˈɪə.mɑːk/ ⓤ /ˈɪr.mɑːrk/ *verb* [T often passive] to keep or intend something for a particular purpose: *Five billion dollars of this year's budget is already earmarked for hospital improvements.*

earmuffs /ˈɪə.mʌfs/ ⓤ /ˈɪr-/ *plural noun* a pair of small pieces of furry material worn over the ears with a strap that goes over the head to keep them on

earn /ɜːn/ ⓤ /ɜːn/ *verb* [I or T] **1** to receive money as payment for work that you do: *I earn $30 000 a year.* ∘ *How much do you earn, if you don't mind me asking?* ∘ *You can't expect to earn **a living** (= be paid enough money to live on) from your painting.* ∘ [+ two objects] *Coffee exports earn* (= give) *Brazil many millions of pounds a year./ Brazil earns many millions of pounds a year **from** coffee exports.* **2** to get something that you deserve: *It's been a tough six months and I feel I've earned a few weeks off.* ⊃See also **well-earned**.

earner /ˈɜː.nə^r/ ⓤ /ˈɜːːnɚ/ *noun* [C] someone or something that earns money: *In most of these cases, the woman is the sole earner in the family.* ∘ *INFORMAL That hamburger stand is **a nice little** earner* (= makes a lot of money).

earnings /ˈɜː.nɪŋz/ ⓤ /ˈɜːː-/ *plural noun* the amount of money that someone is paid for the work they do: *Average earnings for skilled workers are rising.*

earnest /ˈɜː.nɪst/ ⓤ /ˈɜːː-/ *adj* **1** serious or determined, especially too serious and unable to find your own actions amusing: *He was a very earnest young man.* **2 in deadly earnest** completely serious: *These fanatics are in deadly earnest when they say they want to destroy all forms of government.* **3 in earnest** When something begins in earnest, it has already started but is now being done in a serious and complete way: *The election campaign has begun in earnest.* **4 be in earnest** to be speaking honestly: *I thought he was joking – I didn't realize he was in earnest.* **earnestly** /ˈɜː.nɪst.li/ ⓤ /ˈɜːː-/ *adv* **earnestness** /ˈɜː.nɪst.nəs/ ⓤ /ˈɜːː-/ *noun* [U]

earphones /ˈɪə.fəʊnz/ ⓤ /ˈɪr.foʊnz/ *plural noun* a piece of electronic equipment that you put on your ears so that you can listen privately to radio, recorded music, etc: *a pair/set of earphones*

earpiece /ˈɪə.piːs/ ⓤ /ˈɪr-/ *noun* [C] the part of a telephone that you hold next to your ear ⊃See picture **In the Office** on page Centre 15

earplug /ˈɪə.plʌg/ ⓤ /ˈɪr-/ *noun* [C usually pl] a small piece of soft material such as wax, cotton or plastic which you put into your ear to keep out noise or water

earring /ˈɪə.rɪŋ/ ⓤ /ˈɪr.ɪŋ/ *noun* [C] a piece of jewellery, usually one of a pair, worn in a hole in the ear or fixed to the ear by a fastener: *gold earrings* ∘ *a pair of dangly earrings* ∘ *He was **wearing** an earring in his left ear.*

earshot /ˈɪə.ʃɒt/ ⓤ /ˈɪr.ʃɑːt/ *noun* [U] the range of distance within which it is possible to be heard or to hear what someone is saying: *I don't think you should say anything while the boss is still **in/within** earshot.* ∘ *Wait till she's **out of** earshot before you say anything.*

ear-splitting /ˈɪə.ˌsplɪt.ɪŋ/ ⓤ /ˈɪr.ˌsplɪt-/ *adj* (*ALSO* **ear-piercing**) describes a sound that is so loud or high that it hurts your ears: *an ear-splitting explosion* ∘ *ear-piercing screams*

Earth PLANET /ɜːθ/ ⓤ /ɜːθ/ *noun* [S or U] the planet third in order of distance from the Sun, between VENUS and MARS; the world on which we live: *The Earth takes approximately 365¼ days to go round the Sun.* ∘ *The Circus has been described as the greatest show **on** earth* (= in the world).

• **come back down to earth** (*ALSO* **bring** *sb* **back down to earth**) to start dealing with life and problems again after you have had a very exciting time, or to make someone do this: *The realization of how little work I'd done for the exams brought me abruptly back down to earth.*

• **like nothing (else) on earth** very strange, unusual or unpleasant: *With his make-up and strange clothes, he looked like nothing on earth.*

• **how/what/why, etc. on earth** *INFORMAL* used when you are extremely surprised, confused or angry about something: *How on earth did this happen?* ∘ *Why on earth didn't you tell me before?*

• **cost/charge, etc. the earth** to cost/charge, etc. a lot of money: *They charge the earth just for a cup of coffee.*

• **the earth moved** *INFORMAL* If someone says the earth moved, they are joking about how good a sexual experience was.

earth SUBSTANCE /ɜːθ/ ⓤ /ɜːθ/ *noun* [U] the usually brown, heavy and loose substance of which a large part of the surface of the ground is made, and in which plants can grow; the land surface of the Earth rather than the sky or sea: *The ploughed earth looked rich and dark and fertile.* ⊃See also **earthen**.

earthy /ˈɜː.θi/ ⓤ /ˈɜːː-/ *adj* like or relating to earth: *an earthy smell* ⊃Compare **earthy**.

earth WIRE *UK* /ɜːθ/ ⓤ /ɜːθ/ *noun* [C usually sing] (*US* **ground**) a wire that makes a connection between a piece of electrical equipment and the ground, so the user is protected from feeling an electric shock if the equipment develops a fault

earth *UK* /ɜːθ/ ⓤ /ɜːθ/ *verb* [T usually passive] (*US* **ground**) to put an earth between a piece of electrical equipment and the ground: *You could get a nasty shock from that water heater if it isn't earthed properly.*

earth HOLE /ɜːθ/ ⓤ /ɜːθ/ *noun* [C] a hole in the ground where an animal such as a fox lives

earthbound /ˈɜːθ.baʊnd/ ⓤ /ˈɜːθ-/ *adj* **1** unable to leave the surface of the earth: *The space shuttle remained earthbound because of a technical fault.* **2** not exciting or imaginative: *an uninspired and earthbound performance*

earthen /ˈɜː.θ^ən/ ⓤ /ˈɜːː-/ *adj* made of earth or of baked clay: *an earthen casserole dish*

earthenware /ˈɜː.θ^ən.weə^r/ ⓤ /ˈɜːr.θ^ən.wer/ *adj* made of quite rough clay, often shaped with the hands: *earthenware mugs/bowls*

earthenware /ˈɜː.θ^ən.weə^r/ ⓤ /ˈɜːr.θ^ən.wer/ *noun* [U] plates, bowls, cups, etc. that are made of rough clay

earthiness /ˈɜː.θɪ.nəs/ ⓤ /ˈɜːː-/ *noun* [U] ⊃See at **earthy**.

earthling /ˈɜːθ.lɪŋ/ ⓤ /ˈɜːθ-/ *noun* [C] in stories, a human being, especially when talked to or talked about by a creature from another planet

earthly /ˈɜːθ.li/ ⓤ /ˈɜːθ-/ *adj* **1** *LITERARY* happening in or related to this world and this physical life, not in heaven or relating to a spiritual life: *his earthly existence* ∘ *earthly powers* **2** used in questions or negatives to mean possible: *What earthly **reason** can she have for being so horrible to you?*

'earth ˌmother *noun* [C] *INFORMAL* a woman who seems full of emotional and spiritual awareness, and seems suited to having and loving children

earthquake /ˈɜːθ.kweɪk/ ⓤ /ˈɜːθ-/ *noun* [C] a sudden violent movement of the Earth's surface, sometimes causing great damage: *In 1906 an earthquake destroyed much of San Francisco.*

'earth ˌscience *noun* [C or U] the scientific study of the structure, age, etc. of the Earth

earth-shattering /ˈɜːθˌʃæt.ər.ɪŋ/ [US] /ˈɜːrθˌʃæt̬-/ *adj* (ALSO **earth-shaking**) extremely important or very surprising: *an earth-shattering discovery*

ˈearth ˌtone *noun* [C usually pl] (ALSO **earth colour**) a rich dark colour which contains some brown

earthwards /ˈɜːθ.wədz/ [US] /ˈɝːθ.wɚdz/ *adv* (ALSO **earthward**) towards the Earth, from the air or from space: *The plane began to spiral earthwards.* **earthward** /ˈɜːθ.wəd/ [US] /ˈɝːθ.wɚd/ *adj*: *an earthward descent*

earthwork /ˈɜːθ.wɜːk/ [US] /ˈɝːθ.wɜːrk/ *noun* [C usually pl] a bank of earth made, especially in the past, for defence against enemy attack

earthworm /ˈɜːθ.wɜːm/ [US] /ˈɝːθ.wɜːrm/ *noun* [C] a common type of worm, which moves through the earth

earthy /ˈɜː.θi/ [US] /ˈɝː-/ *adj* referring to sex and the human body in a direct way: *She has an earthy sense of humour.* ➲Compare **earthy** at **earth** SUBSTANCE. **earthiness** /ˈɜː.θɪ.nəs/ [US] /ˈɝː-/ *noun* [U] *I like the earthiness of her writing.*

earwig /ˈɪə.wɪɡ/ [US] /ˈɪr-/ *noun* [C] a small insect with two PINCERS (= curved pointed parts) at the back end of its body

ease [MAKE LESS] /iːz/ *verb* [I or T] to make or become less severe, difficult, unpleasant, painful, etc: *To ease the problem of overcrowding, new prisons will be built.* ○ *These pills should ease the pain.* ○ *After the arrival of the United Nations soldiers, tension in the area began to ease.*

• **ease *your* mind** to stop you from worrying: *If it will ease your mind, I'll have a word with Charlotte for you.*

ease [MOVE] /iːz/ *verb* [T + adv or prep] to move or to make something move slowly and carefully in a particular direction or into a particular position: *She eased the key **into** the lock, anxious not to wake anyone.* ○ *I eased myself out of the chair.*

ease [NO DIFFICULTY] /iːz/ *noun* [U] when you experience no difficulty, effort, pain, etc: *She won the 400m race **with** ease.* ○ *The doors are extra-wide **for** ease **of** access* (= so that people can get in without difficulty). ➲See also **easy** NOT DIFFICULT.

• **at *(your)* ease** relaxed: *He felt completely at ease.* ○ *She soon **put/set** me at ease* (= made me relaxed).

• **at ease** (ALSO **standing at ease**) If someone, especially a soldier is at ease, they are standing with their feet apart and their hands behind their back.

PHRASAL VERBS WITH **ease**

▲ **ease up/off** [STOP] *phrasal verb* to gradually stop or become less: *At last the rain began to ease off.*

▲ **ease up/off** [WORK LESS] *phrasal verb* to start to work less or do things with less energy: *As he got older, he started to ease up a little.*

▲ **ease up/off** [TREAT LESS SEVERELY] *phrasal verb* to start to treat someone less severely: *I wish his supervisor would ease up **on** him a bit.*

▲ **ease *sb* out** *phrasal verb* [M] to try to make someone leave a job or powerful position: *The head teacher was eased out **of** his job after teachers and parents accused him of being autocratic.*

easel /ˈiː.zəl/ *noun* [C] a wooden frame, usually with three legs, that holds a picture, especially one which an artist is painting or drawing

easily /ˈiː.zɪ.li/ *adv* ➲See at **easy** NOT DIFFICULT

easiness /ˈiː.zɪ.nəs/ *noun* [U] ➲See at **easy** NOT DIFFICULT

east /iːst/ *noun* [U] **1** (ALSO **East**) (WRITTEN ABBREVIATION **E**) the direction from which the sun rises in the morning, opposite to the west: *The points of the compass are North, South, East and West.* ○ *Which way is east?* **2 the east** the part of an area or country which is in this direction: *Most of the country, except the east, is rural.* ○ *Her home is **in** the east **of** France.* ○ *According to the map, the village lies about 10 km **to** the east **of** here.* **3 the East** those countries in Europe which had communist governments before the 1990s: *The collapse of Communism changed East-West relations for ever.* **4 the East** Asia, especially its eastern and southern parts: *She spent her childhood in the East – mostly in China and Japan.*

east /iːst/ *adj* **1** (ALSO **East**) (WRITTEN ABBREVIATION **E**) in or forming the east part of something: *Cambridge is in East Anglia.* ○ *The east wall of the mosque is covered with a beautiful mosaic.* **2** An east wind is a wind coming from the east.

east, East /iːst/ *adv*: *We'll drive east for a few more miles, then turn south.* ○ *They were the first people to travel east **of** the mountains* (= into the area beyond and to the east of the mountains). ○ *We walked **due*** (= directly) *east for two kilometres.* ○ *The garden **faces** east, so we'll get the morning sun.*

• **back east** US to or in the east of the US: *Helen lived in Oregon for two years before moving back east.*

eastbound /ˈiːst.baʊnd/ *adj, adv* going or leading towards the east: *an eastbound train*

easterly /ˈiː.stəl.i/ [US] /-stɚ.li/ *adj* in or towards the east, or blowing from the east: *They were travelling in an easterly direction.* ○ *The town is in the most easterly part of the country.* ○ *an easterly **wind***

easterly /ˈiː.stəl.i/ [US] /-stɚ.li/ *noun* [C] a wind that blows from the east

eastern, Eastern /ˈiː.stən/ [US] /-stɚn/ *adj* (WRITTEN ABBREVIATION **E**) in or from the east part of an area: *The eastern part of the country is very mountainous.* ○ *Until about 1991, the Eastern **bloc** was the Soviet Union and the communist countries of Eastern Europe.* ○ *Buddhism and other Eastern* (= Asian) *religions fascinate me.*

easterner, Easterner /ˈiː.stən.əʳ/ [US] /-ɚ/ *noun* [C] a person born or living in the eastern part of a country, especially the US

easternmost /ˈiː.stənˌməʊst/ [US] /-stɚnˌmoʊst/ *adj* furthest towards the east: *Lowestoft is the easternmost town in Great Britain.*

eastward /ˈiːst.wəd/ [US] /-wɚd/ *adj* towards the east: *The eastward route might be quicker.*

eastwards /ˈiːst.wədz/ [US] /-wɚdz/ *adv* (ALSO **eastward**) towards the east: *The storm is moving slowly eastwards.*

the ˌEast ˈCoast *noun* [S] in the US, the part of the country near the Atlantic Ocean, including cities such as New York, Boston and Philadelphia

the ˌEast ˈEnd *noun* [S] an area in the east of London

Eastender /iːstˈen.dəʳ/ [US] /-dɚ/ *noun* [C] someone who lives in the east of London

Easter /ˈiː.stəʳ/ [US] /-stɚ/ *noun* [C or U] a Christian religious holiday to celebrate Jesus Christ's return to life after he was killed: *I get two weeks off school **at** Easter.*

ˈEaster ˌegg *noun* [C] a chocolate in the shape of an egg, given as a gift at EASTER

ˌEastern ˈStandard ˌTime *noun* [U] the time on the eastern coast of the United States and Canada

ˌEaster ˈSunday, Easter Day *noun* [C usually sing] the day on which Easter is celebrated

easy [NOT DIFFICULT] /ˈiː.zi/ *adj* not difficult; needing little effort: *an easy exam* ○ *Would a ten o'clock appointment be easier **for** you?* ○ ***It's** easy **to** see why he's so popular.* ○ *She's very easy **to** talk to.* ○ *The easiest thing **to** do would be for us to take the train home.* ○ ***It** isn't easy being a parent.* ○ *Getting into the film business is **no** easy **matter**.* ○ *I don't trust that easy* (= relaxed) *charm of his.* ○ SLANG *My car can do 250kph, easy.* ➲See also **ease** NO DIFFICULTY.

• **(as) easy as pie ABC/anything/falling off a log** INFORMAL extremely easy

• **easier said than done** INFORMAL said when something seems like a good idea but it would be difficult to do: *"Why don't you just ask Simon to pay?" "That's easier said than done."*

• **the easiest thing in the world** INFORMAL extremely easy: *Making bread is the easiest thing in the world.*

• **be easy game/meat** (US **be an easy mark**) SLANG to be easily deceived: *Old ladies living alone are easy game **for** con-men.*

easily /ˈiː.zɪ.li/ *adv* **1** with no difficulty or effort: *I can easily be home early tonight, if you want.* ○ *Ever since the illness I get tired very easily* (= more quickly than usual). **2** without doubt: *For me, Venice is easily the most beautiful city in Europe.* **easiness** /ˈiː.zi.nəs/ *noun* [U]

easy [COMFORTABLE] /ˈiː.zi/ *adj* comfortable or calm; free from worry, pain, etc: *They both retired and went off to* *lead an easy life in the Bahamas.* ○ *I don't feel easy* **about** *leaving him alone in the house all day.* ○ *With the harvest finished, I was able to relax* **with an** *easy* **mind/ conscience**.

• **easy come, easy go** INFORMAL said when something, especially money, is easily obtained and then soon spent or lost: *I lost £500 in a card game last night, but that's life – easy come, easy go.*

• **Easy does it!** INFORMAL used to tell someone to do something slowly and carefully

• **easy on the eye/ear** pleasant to look at/listen to: *Her paintings are very easy on the eye.*

• **go easy** INFORMAL **1** to not take or use too much of something: *Go easy* **on/with** *the cream – I haven't had any yet.* **2** to treat someone in a gentle way and not criticize them or punish them: *Go easy* **on** *the new students.*

• **I'm easy.** INFORMAL used to say that you do not mind which choice is made: *"Shall we go to the Indian restaurant, or would you prefer Chinese food?" "I'm easy."*

• **take it/things easy** to relax and not use too much energy: *I wasn't feeling too good, so I thought I'd take it easy for a couple of days.*

• **on easy street** OLD-FASHIONED INFORMAL rich

ˈeasy ˌchair *noun* [C] a big soft comfortable chair with arms

easy-going /ˌiː.ziˈɡəʊ.ɪŋ/ [US] /-ˈɡoʊ-/ *adj* APPROVING relaxed and not easily upset or worried: *an easy-going attitude/manner* ○ *a friendly, easy-going type of guy*

ˌeasy ˈlistening *adj* describes music that is not complicated, serious or difficult

ˌeasy ˈmoney *noun* [U] INFORMAL money that is easily and sometimes dishonestly earned

ˌeasy ˈoption *noun* [C] (UK ALSO **soft option**) a decision or choice that is easy to make: *We'll have to make some tough decisions – there are no easy options.*

easy-peasy /ˌiː.ziˈpiː.zi/ *adj* UK INFORMAL OR CHILD'S WORD very easy

an ˌeasy ˈtouch *noun* [S] INFORMAL someone whom you can easily persuade or deceive into giving you something, usually money

eat (**ate, eaten**) /iːt/ *verb* [I or T] to put or take food into the mouth, chew it, and swallow it: *Do you eat meat?* ○ *When I've got a cold, I don't feel like eating.* ○ *We usually eat* (= have a meal) *at about 7 o'clock.*

• **(I'm so hungry), I could eat a horse.** HUMOROUS used to say that you are extremely hungry

• **eat like a horse** INFORMAL to always eat a lot of food: *She's so thin yet she eats like a horse.*

• **eat *sb* for breakfast** INFORMAL to be able to very easily control or defeat someone: *He eats people like you for breakfast.*

• **eat *sb* out of house and home** HUMOROUS to eat a lot of the food someone has in their house

• **have *sb* eating out of *your* hand** INFORMAL to easily make someone do or think what you want: *Within two minutes of walking into the classroom, she had the kids eating out of her hand.*

• **eat *your* heart out** HUMOROUS If someone says eat your heart out followed by the name of a famous person, they are joking that they are even better than that person: *I'm singing in the village production of Tosca next month – eat your heart out Pavarotti!*

• **eat humble pie** (US ALSO **eat crow**) INFORMAL to admit that you were wrong: *After boasting that his company could outperform the industry's best, he's been forced to eat humble pie.*

• **I'll eat my hat** OLD-FASHIONED used to say that you are sure something will not happen: *If she actually marries him I'll eat my hat.*

• **eat *your* words** to admit that something you said before was wrong: *Sam said it would never sell, but when he sees these sales figures he'll have to eat his words.*

• **What's eating *sb*?** INFORMAL used to ask why someone seems angry or upset: *Jack's in a strange mood – I wonder what's eating him.*

• **eaten up with/by *sth*** INFORMAL If someone is eaten up with/by a negative emotion, they are experiencing it very strongly: *He was so eaten up with guilt, he became ill.*

eatable /ˈiː.tə.bl̩/ [US] /-t̬ə-/ *adj* describes food that is good enough to eat, though not excellent ➲Compare **edible**.

eater /ˈiː.təʳ/ [US] /-t̬ɚ/ *noun* **a big/good/small eater** someone who always eats a lot/very little

eatery /ˈiː.tᵊr.i/ [US] /-t̬ɚ.ri/ *noun* [C] INFORMAL a restaurant: *We met in a little eatery just off the main road.*

eats /iːts/ *plural noun* INFORMAL a small amount of food: *Would you like some eats?*

PHRASAL VERBS WITH **eat** ▼

▲ **eat away at *sth*** [DAMAGE] *phrasal verb* to gradually damage or destroy something

▲ **eat away at *sb*** [MAKE UNHAPPY] *phrasal verb* If a bad memory or feeling eats away at someone, it makes them feel more and more unhappy.

▲ **eat in** *phrasal verb* to have a meal at home rather than in a restaurant

▲ **eat into *sth*** *phrasal verb* to use or take away a large part of something valuable, such as money or time: *The high cost of living in London is eating into my savings.*

▲ **eat out** *phrasal verb* to eat in a restaurant: *When I lived in Spain, I used to eat out all the time.*

▲ **eat *(sth)* up** [FOOD] *phrasal verb* [M] to eat all the food that you have been given: *Be a good boy and eat up your vegetables.*

▲ **eat up *sth*** [USE] *phrasal verb* to use or take away a large part of something valuable: *A big old car like that eats up petrol.*

ˈeating ˌapple *noun* [C] an apple that can be eaten raw, rather than cooked ➲Compare **cooking apple**.

ˈeating disˌorder *noun* [C] a mental illness in which people eat far too little or far too much food and are unhappy with their bodies

ˌeau de coˈlogne *noun* [C or U] a pleasant smelling liquid which you put on your body to make yourself smell fresh

eaves /iːvz/ *plural noun* the edge of a roof that sticks out over the top of a wall

eavesdrop /ˈiːvz.drɒp/ [US] /-drɑːp/ *verb* [I] **-pp-** to listen to someone's private conversation without them knowing: *He was eavesdropping* **on** *our conversation.* **eavesdropper** /ˈiːvz.drɒp.əʳ/ [US] /-drɑː.pɚ/ *noun* [C]

ebb [WATER] /eb/ *verb* [I] When the sea or tide ebbs, it moves away from the coast and falls to a lower level.

ebb /eb/ *noun* **the ebb** the tide when it is moving away from the coast: *We'll sail* **on** *the ebb.*

• **ebb and flow** the way in which the level of something regularly becomes higher or lower in a situation: *You have to accept the ebb and flow* **of** *love in a relationship.*

• **at a low ebb** in a bad or weak state: *Consumer confidence is currently at a low ebb.* ○ *I was recently divorced and feeling at a very low ebb.*

ebb [FEELING] /eb/ *verb* [I] If a physical or emotional feeling ebbs, it becomes less strong or disappears: *He could feel his* ***strength*** *ebbing* ***(away)***.

ˈebb ˌtide *noun* [C usually sing] the regular movement of the sea away from the coast

Ebola /ɪˈbəʊ.lə/ [US] /-ˈboʊ-/ *noun* [U] an infectious and very serious disease with fever and internal bleeding: *the Ebola virus*

Ebonics /ɪˈbɒn.ɪks/ [US] /ɪˈbɑː.nɪks/ *noun* [U] a type of English spoken by some African-Americans

ebony [WOOD] /ˈeb.ᵊn.i/ *noun* [U] a very hard dark-coloured wood of a tropical tree, used especially for making furniture

ebony [BLACK] /ˈeb.ᵊn.i/ *adj* LITERARY black: *her ebony hair*

e-book /ˈiː.bʊk/ *noun* [C] an **electronic book**

ebullient /ɪbˈʊl.i.ᵊnt/ *adj* very energetic, positive and happy: *He wasn't his usual ebullient self.* **ebulliently** /ɪbˈʊl.i.ᵊnt.li/ *adv* **ebullience** /ɪˈbʊl.i.ᵊnts/ *noun* [U]

e-business /ˈiːˌbɪz.nɪs/ *noun* [C or U] the business of buying and selling goods and services on the Internet, or a particular company which does this

the EC /ðiˌiːˈsiː/ *group noun* [S] ABBREVIATION FOR **the European Community**

E

[E]

e-cash /ˈiː.kæʃ/ *noun* [U] money from a special bank account which is used to buy goods and services over the Internet by sending information from your computer

eccentric [STRANGE] /ekˈsen.trɪk/ *adj* strange or unusual, sometimes in an amusing way: *eccentric behaviour* ○ *eccentric clothes* **eccentric** /ekˈsen.trɪk/ *noun* [C] *My mother's a bit of an eccentric.* **eccentrically** /ekˈsen.trɪ.kli/ *adv*

eccentricity /ˌek.senˈtrɪs.ɪ.ti/ [US] /-t̬i/ *noun* **1** [U] the state of being eccentric: *His eccentricity now extends to never washing or changing his clothes.* **2** [C] an eccentric action: *Her eccentricities get stranger by the day.*

eccentric [NOT CIRCULAR] /ekˈsen.trɪk/ *adj* not perfectly circular

ecclesiastical /ɪˌkliː.ziˈæs.tɪk.əl/ *adj* (*ALSO* **ecclesiastic**) *SLIGHTLY FORMAL* belonging to or connected with the Christian religion

ecclesiastic /ɪˌkliː.ziˈæs.tɪk/ *noun* [C] *FORMAL OR OLD-FASHIONED* a Christian priest or official

ECE /ˌiː.siːˈiː/ *noun* [U] *US ABBREVIATION FOR* **Early Childhood Education**

ECG /ˌiː.siːˈdʒiː/ *noun* [C] *ABBREVIATION FOR* **electrocardiogram** or **electrocardiograph**

echelon /ˈeʃ.ə.lɒn/ [US] /-lɑːn/ *noun* [C] **1** a particular level or group of people within an organization such as an army or company: *These salary increases will affect only the highest echelons of local government.* ○ *the upper echelons of society* **2** *SPECIALIZED* a special arrangement of soldiers, aircraft or ships

echidna /ɪˈkɪd.nə/ *noun* [C] a small Australian mammal which has a protective covering of spines, a long nose and eats ANTS and TERMITES

echo /ˈek.əʊ/ [US] /-oʊ/ *noun* [C] *plural* **echoes** **1** a sound that is heard after it has been reflected off a surface such as a wall or a cliff: *The echoes of his scream sounded in the cave for several seconds.* ○ *Thick carpet would reduce the echo in this hallway.* **2** a detail that is similar to and makes you remember something else: *There are echoes **of** Mozart in her first piano compositions.*

echo /ˈek.əʊ/ [US] /-oʊ/ *verb* **echoing, echoed, echoed** **1** [I] If a sound echoes or a place echoes with a sound, you hear the sound again because you are in a large, empty space: *The sound of footsteps echoed **round** the hall.* ○ *Suddenly, the building echoed **with** the sound of gunfire.* **2** [T] to repeat details that are similar to, and make you think of something else: *The design of the church echoes that of St. Paul's Cathedral.* ○ *I've heard the Prime Minister's view echoed throughout the party.*

• **echo down/through the ages** to continue to have a particular effect for a long time: *The ideas of Plato have echoed through the ages.*

ˈecho ˌsounder *noun* [C] a piece of equipment, especially on a ship, which uses sound waves to discover water depth or the position of an object in the water

éclair /ɪˈkleər/ [US] /-kler/ *noun* [C] a small thin cake made of pastry, with cream inside and usually chocolate on top

éclat /eɪˈklɑː/ *noun* [U] *LITERARY* a strong and stylish effect: *She broke onto the music scene with great éclat.*

eclectic /ɪˈklek.tɪk/ *adj FORMAL* Methods, beliefs, ideas, etc. that are eclectic, combine whatever seem the best or most useful things from many different areas or systems, rather than following a single system: *an eclectic style/approach* ○ *an eclectic taste in literature* **eclectically** /ɪˈklek.tɪ.kli/ *adv* **eclecticism** /ɪˈklek.tɪ.sɪ.zəm/ *noun* [U]

eclipse [SIGHT] /ɪˈklɪps/ *noun* [C] when the sun disappears from view, either completely or partly, while the moon is moving between it and the Earth, or when the moon darkens while the SHADOW (= darkness) of the Earth moves over it: *a solar/lunar eclipse* ○ *On Wednesday there will be a **total/partial** eclipse **of** the sun.*

eclipse /ɪˈklɪps/ *verb* [T] to make an eclipse of the moon or sun: *The moon will be totally eclipsed at 12.10 pm.*

eclipse [IMPORTANCE] /ɪˈklɪps/ *noun* [S or U] *LITERARY* when something becomes less important: *The eclipse **of** the ruling political party was inevitable.* ○ *His remarkable contribution to literature has been too long **in** eclipse.*

eclipse /ɪˈklɪps/ *verb* [T often passive] to make another person or thing seem much less important, good or famous: *The economy has eclipsed all other issues during this election campaign.*

eco- /iː.kəʊ-/ [US] /-koʊ-/ *prefix* connected with the environment

eco-friendly /ˈiː.kəʊˌfrend.li/ [US] /-koʊ-/ *adj UK* describes a product that has been designed to do the least possible damage to the environment: *eco-friendly washing powder*

eco-label /ˈiː.kəʊˌleɪ.bəl/ [US] /-koʊ-/ *noun* [C] an official symbol which shows that a product has been designed to do less harm to the environment than similar products **eco-labelling** *UK*, *US* **eco-labeling** /ˈiː.kəʊˌleɪ.bəl.ɪŋ/ [US] /-koʊ-/ *noun* [U]

E coli /ˌiːˈkəʊ.laɪ/ [US] /ˌiːˈkoʊ.laɪ/ *noun* [U] *ABBREVIATION FOR* Escherichia coli: a BACTERIUM (= small organism) that can exist in food which has not been cooked enough and can cause serious illness or death

ecology /ɪˈkɒl.ə.dʒi/ [US] /-ˈkɑː.lə-/ *noun* [U] the relationships between the air, land, water, animals, plants, etc., usually of a particular area, or the scientific study of this: *The oil spill caused terrible damage to the fragile ecology **of** the coast.* ○ *She hopes to study ecology at college.*

ecological /ˌiː.kəˈlɒdʒ.ɪ.kəl/ [US] /-ˈlɑː.dʒɪ-/ *adj* relating to ecology or the environment: *The destruction of the rain forests is an ecological disaster that threatens the future of life on Earth.*

ecologically /ˌiː.kəˈlɒdʒ.ɪ.kli/ [US] /-ˈlɑː.dʒɪ-/ *adv*: *It's an ecologically **friendly/sound*** (= not harmful) *means of transportation.*

ecologist /ɪˈkɒl.ə.dʒɪst/ [US] /-ˈkɑː.lə-/ *noun* [C] a person who studies the natural relationships between the air, land, water, animals, plants, etc.

e-commerce /ˌiːˈkɒm.ɜːs/ [US] /ˌiːˈkɑː.mɝːs/ *noun* [U] the business of buying and selling goods and services on the Internet

econometrics /ɪˌkɒn.əˈmet.rɪks/ [US] /-ˌkɑː.nə-/ *noun* [U] *SPECIALIZED* the testing of the performance of economies and economic theories using mathematical methods **econometric** /ɪˌkɒn.əˈmet.rɪk/ [US] /-ˌkɑː.nə-/ *adj*

economy [SAVING MONEY] /ɪˈkɒn.ə.mi/ [US] /-ˈkɑː.nə-/ *noun* [C or U] the intentional saving of money or, less commonly, the saving of time, energy, words, etc: *They've had to **make** economies since Colin lost his job.* ○ *This can be done by machines with more speed and economy.* ○ *She writes with such economy – I've never known a writer say so much in so few words.*

economic /ˌiː.kəˈnɒm.ɪk/ [US] /-ˈnɑː.mɪk/ /ek.ə-/ *adj*: making a profit, or likely to make a profit: *We had to close our London office – with the rent so high it just wasn't economic.*

economical /ˌiː.kəˈnɒm.ɪ.kəl/ [US] /-ˈnɑː.mɪ-/ /ek.ə-/ *adj* not using a lot of fuel, money, etc: *There's increasing demand for cars which are more economical **on** fuel.* ○ *What's the most economical way of heating this building?*

• **economical with the truth** *HUMOROUS* avoiding stating the true facts of a situation, or lying about it

economically /ˌiː.kəˈnɒm.ɪ.kli/ [US] /-ˈnɑː.mɪ-/ /ek.ə-/ *adv* using little money, time, etc: *As a student she lived very economically, rarely going out and buying very few clothes.*

economize, *UK USUALLY* **-ise** /ɪˈkɒn.ə.maɪz/ [US] /-ˈkɑː.nə-/ *verb* [I] to try to save money by reducing the amount that you are spending: *You could economize **on** food by not eating in restaurants all the time.* ○ *A lot of companies are trying to economize by not taking on new staff.*

COMMON LEARNER ERROR

economic, economical or **financial?**

Economic describes something that is connected to the economy of a country.

economic growth/policy/advisors
~~*economical growth/policy/advisors*~~

Economical describes something that saves you money, especially by using less fuel, etc. than normal.

New cars tend to be more economical because their engines use less petrol.

Financial relates to a supply of money and can be used in connection with individuals.

She's a single mum who doesn't receive any financial support from the child's father.

~~She's a single mum who doesn't receive any economical support from the child's father.~~

---

economy [SYSTEM] /ɪˈkɒn.ə.mi/ /-ˈkɑː.nə-/ *noun* [C] the system of trade and industry by which the wealth of a country is made and used: *the global economy* ○ *the German/US economy* ○ *the state of the economy* ○ *a weak/strong economy* ○ *Tourism contributes millions of pounds to the country's economy.*
economic /iː.kəˈnɒm.ɪk/ /ek.ə-/ /-ˈnɑː.mɪk/ *adj* [before n] relating to trade, industry and money: *The country has been in a very poor economic state ever since the decline of its two major industries.* ○ *The government's economic* **policies** *have led us into the worst recession for years.*
economically /ˌiː.kəˈnɒm.ɪ.kli/ /ek.ə-/ /-ˈnɑː.mɪk-/ *adv*: *Economically the country has been improving steadily these past ten years.*
economics /ˌiː.kəˈnɒm.ɪks/ /ek.ə-/ /-ˈnɑː.mɪks/ *noun* [U] the way in which trade, industry or money is organized, or the study of this: *Their ideas sound fine in principle but they haven't worked out the economics behind the policies.* ○ *She's in her third year of economics at York university.*
economist /ɪˈkɒn.ə.mɪst/ /-ˈkɑː.nə-/ *noun* [C] a person who studies or has a special knowledge of economics

e'conomy ,class *noun* [U], *adv* (using) the cheapest and least comfortable type of seats on an aircraft: *They always* **fly** *economy class.*

e'conomy ,drive *noun* [C usually sing] an attempt to save money by spending as little as possible: *I don't think we'll be going anywhere expensive – Guy's* **on** *an economy drive.*

e'conomy ,pack *noun* [C] a larger amount of goods that you buy for a lower price

economy-sized /ɪˈkɒn.ə.mi.saɪzd/ /-ˈkɑː.nə-/ *adj* describes an amount of goods which is larger than normal and can be bought for a lower price

ecosystem /ˈiː.kəʊˌsɪs.təm/ /-koʊ-/ *noun* [C] all the living things in an area and the way they affect each other and the environment: *Pollution can have disastrous effects on the delicately balanced ecosystem.*

ecotourism /ˈiː.kəʊˌtʊə.rɪ.zᵊm/ /ˈiː.koʊ.tʊ.rɪ.zᵊm/ *noun* [U] the business of organizing holidays to places that people do not usually visit in a way which helps local people and does not damage the environment

eco-warrior /ˈiː.kəʊˌwɒr.i.ə/ /-koʊˌwɔːr.i.ɚ/ *noun* [C] *UK* a person who argues against and tries to stop activities which damage the environment

ecstasy [EMOTION] /ˈek.stə.si/ *noun* [C or U] a state of extreme happiness, especially when feeling pleasure: *sexual ecstasy* ○ *She threw her head back as if* **in** *ecstasy.*
● **be/go into ecstasies about/over** *sth INFORMAL* to be or become very excited about something: *She went into ecstasies about the food there.*
ecstatic /ɪkˈstæt.ɪk/ /-ˈstæt̬-/ *adj* extremely happy: *The new president was greeted by an ecstatic crowd.* **ecstatically** /ɪkˈstæt.ɪ.kli/ /-ˈstæt̬-/ *adv*

ecstasy [DRUG] /ˈek.stə.si/ *noun* [U] (*ALSO* **E**) a powerful drug which makes you feel very active and can cause you to HALLUCINATE (= see or hear things that do not exist)

ECT /ˌiː.siːˈtiː/ *noun* [U] *ABBREVIATION FOR* **electroconvulsive therapy**

ectopic pregnancy /ek.tɒp.ɪkˈpreg.nənt.si/ /-ˌtɑː.pɪk-/ *noun* [C] the development of the EMBRYO outside the usual position within the womb, usually inside one of the FALLOPIAN TUBES

ectoplasm /ˈek.tə.plæz.ᵊm/ /-toʊ-/ *noun* [U] **1** *SPECIALIZED* the outer layer of particular types of cell **2** a substance which is believed to surround ghosts and other creatures that are connected with spiritual activities

ECU /ˈek.juː/ /ˈeɪ.kjuː/ *noun* [C] *ABBREVIATION FOR* European Currency Unit: the former official unit of money used in

the European Union, which was replaced by the euro in 1999 ⊃Compare **EMS**; **EMU**.

ecumenical /ˌiː.kjʊˈmen.ɪk.ᵊl/ /ˌek.jʊ-/ *adj* *FORMAL* tending to support and encourage unity between the various types of the Christian religion: *an ecumenical service*
ecumenicism /ˌiː.kjʊˈmen.ɪ.sɪ.zᵊm/ /ˌek.jʊ-/ *noun* [U]

eczema /ˈek.sɪ.mə/ *noun* [U] a skin condition in which areas of the skin become red, rough and sore and make you want to rub them: *As a young boy he suffered from eczema.*

-ed /-t/ /-d/ /-ɪd/ /-əd/ *suffix* (*ALSO* **-d**) used to form the past simple and past participle of regular verbs: *called* ○ *asked* ○ *looked* ○ *started* ○ *played* ○ *returned* ○ *worked*

Edam /ˈiː.dæm/ *noun* [C or U] hard, yellow cheese covered with red wax which comes from the Netherlands

eddy /ˈed.i/ *verb* [I] If water, wind, smoke, etc. eddies, it moves fast in a circle: *The water eddied around in a whirlpool.* **eddy** /ˈed.i/ *noun* [C] *The bend in the river had caused an eddy of fast swirling water.*

Eden /ˈiː.dᵊn/ *noun* [S] (*ALSO* **the Garden of Eden**) in the Bible, the garden where the first human beings, Adam and Eve, lived in perfect happiness before they disobeyed God and were ordered by Him to leave

edge [OUTER POINT] /edʒ/ *noun* **1** [C] the outer or furthest point of something: *He'd piped fresh cream around the edge* **of** *the cake.* ○ *They built the church on the edge of the village.* ○ *A man was standing at the water's edge with a small boy.* ○ *I caught* (= hit) *my leg on the edge of the table as I walked past.* **2** [C usually sing] the point just before something very different and noticeable happens: *The company is* **on** *the edge* **of** *collapse.* ○ *The government had* **brought** *the country* **to** *the edge of a catastrophe.*
edged /edʒd/ *adj* having something around the edge: *He bought a white tablecloth edged* **with** *a pretty pattern.* (= with a pattern around the outside) ○ *a lace-edged collar*
edging /ˈedʒ.ɪŋ/ *noun* [C or U] something which is put around the outside of something, usually to decorate it: *a tablecloth with (a) dark edging*

edge [BLADE] /edʒ/ *noun* [C] the side of a blade which cuts, or any sharp part of an object which could cut: *Careful with that open tin – it's got a very sharp edge.*
● **take the edge off** *sth* to make something unpleasant have less of an effect on someone: *Have an apple – it'll take the edge off your hunger.* ○ *His apology took the edge off her anger.*
-edged /-edʒd/ *suffix* having a particular type of edge: *a double-edged blade*

edge [MOVE] /edʒ/ *verb* [I or T; + adv or prep] to move slowly with gradual movements or in gradual stages, or to make someone or something move in this way: *A long line of traffic edged* **its** *way forward.* ○ *Inflation has edged* **up** *to 5% over the last two years.* ○ *Those who disagreed with the director's viewpoint were gradually edged* **out** *of* (= forced to leave) *the company.*

edge [ANGER/NERVOUSNESS] /edʒ/ *noun* [U] a small but noticeable amount of annoyance in someone's voice: *There's a definite edge* **to/in** *her voice when she talks to her husband.*
● **on edge** nervous and not relaxed: *Is something wrong? You seem a bit on edge this morning.*
edgy /ˈedʒ.i/ *adj* *INFORMAL* nervous or anxious **edgily** /ˈedʒ.ɪ.li/ *adv*

edge [ADVANTAGE] /edʒ/ *noun* [S] an advantage over other people: *In terms of experience, she definitely* **had** *the edge* **over** *the other people that we interviewed.*

edgeways /ˈedʒ.weɪz/ *adv* See **not get a word in edgeways** at **word** LANGUAGE UNIT.

edible /ˈed.ɪ.bl̩/ *adj* suitable or safe for eating: *Only the leaves of the plant are edible.* ⊃Compare **eatable** at **eat**. ✳ NOTE: The opposite is **inedible**.

edict /ˈiː.dɪkt/ *noun* [C] *FORMAL* an official order, especially one which is given in a forceful and unfair way: *Most shops are ignoring the government's edict against Sunday trading.*

edification /ˌed.ɪ.fɪˈkeɪ.ʃᵊn/ *noun* [U] *FORMAL* the improvement of the mind and understanding, especially by learning: *I tend to watch the television for pleasure rather than edification.*

edify /ˈed.ɪ.faɪ/ *verb* [T] *FORMAL* to improve someone's mind

edifying /ˈed.ɪ.faɪ.ɪŋ/ *adj HUMOROUS OR FORMAL* improving your mind: *Being left in a bar all afternoon with a load of football supporters is not the most edifying of experiences.*

edifice /ˈed.ɪ.fɪs/ *noun* [C] **1** *FORMAL* a large building, especially a splendid one: *The town hall is the only edifice surviving from the fifteenth century.* **2** a system which has been established for a long time: *It looks as if the whole political edifice of the country is about to collapse.*

edit /ˈed.ɪt/ *verb* [T] **1** to prepare a text or film for printing or viewing by correcting mistakes and deciding what will be removed and what will be kept in, etc: *Janet edited books for a variety of publishers.* ○ *The film's 129 minutes were edited* ***down*** *from 150 hours of footage.* **2** to be in charge of the reports in a newspaper or magazine, etc: *He edits a national newspaper.* **editing** /ˈed.ɪ.tɪŋ/ [US] /-t̬ɪŋ/ *noun* [U] *Doing the filming for the documentary took two months, but editing took another four.*

editor /ˈed.ɪ.təʳ/ [US] /-t̬ɚ/ *noun* [C] a person who corrects or changes pieces of text or films before they are printed or shown, or a person who is in charge of a newspaper or magazine: *She's a senior editor in the reference department of a publishing company.* ○ *Who is the current editor of the Times?*

editorial /ˌed.ɪˈtɔː.ri.əl/ [US] /-əˈtɔːr.i-/ *adj* relating to editors or editing, or to the editor of a newspaper or magazine: *editorial staff* ○ *Editorial decisions are generally made by senior editors.* ○ *It's plain reporting of the facts – there's not much editorial content* (= opinion).

editorial /ˌed.ɪˈtɔː.ri.əl/ [US] /-əˈtɔːr.i-/ *noun* [C] (*UK ALSO* **leader, leading article**) an article in a newspaper which expresses the editor's opinion on a subject of particular interest at the present time: *All the papers deal with the same subject in their editorials.*

editorialize, *UK USUALLY* **-ise** /ˌed.ɪˈtɔː.ri.ə.laɪz/ [US] /-əˈtɔːr.i-/ *verb* [I] *DISAPPROVING* to express a personal opinion, especially when you should be giving a report of the facts only

▲ **edit *sth* out** *phrasal verb* [M] to remove something before it is broadcast or printed: *Most of the violent scenes were edited out for television.*

edition /ɪˈdɪʃ.ən/ *noun* [C] **1** a particular form in which a book, magazine or newspaper is published: *the paperback/hardback edition of the dictionary* ○ *The regional editions of the paper contain specific information for that area.* **2** a single broadcast of a series of radio or television programmes: *This morning's edition of 'Women's Hour' is at the earlier time of a quarter to ten.* **3** the total number of copies of a particular book, newspaper, etc. that are published at the same time: *She collects* ***first*** *editions of nineteenth century authors.* **4** *US* one of a series of repeated events: *The 77th edition of the Indianapolis 500 was held before an estimated 450 000 fans.*

.edu /dɒt,iː.diːˈjuː/ [US] /dɑːt-/ *INTERNET ABBREVIATION FOR* education: used to show that an Internet address belongs to a university or college: *To contact our Australian branch, email us at info@cambridge.edu.au.*

educate /ˈed.jʊ.keɪt/ *verb* [T] to teach someone, especially using the formal system of school, college or university: *The form says he was educated in Africa.* ○ *How much does it cost to educate a child privately?* ○ *The government say they are trying to do more to educate the public* ***about*** *the consequences of drug abuse.*

educated /ˈed.jʊ.keɪ.tɪd/ [US] /-t̬ɪd/ *adj*: having learned a lot at school or university and having a good level of knowledge: *She was probably the most* ***highly*** *educated prime minister of this century.*

education /ˌed.jʊˈkeɪ.ʃən/ *noun* [S or U] the process of teaching or learning in a school or college, or the knowledge that you get from this: *As a child he* ***received*** *most of his education at home.* ○ *It's a country which places great importance on education.* ○ *She lectures in education* (= the study of education) *at the teacher training college.* ○ *It's important for children to get a good education.*

educational /ˌed.jʊˈkeɪ.ʃən.əl/ *adj* providing education or relating to education: *Reducing the size of classes may improve educational standards.* ○ *She seems to have spent all her life studying in educational* ***establishments.*** ○ *HUMOROUS My father has never been to a rock concert before – it'll be an educational* ***experience*** *for him* (= a new experience from which he can learn). **educationally** /ˌed.jʊˈkeɪ.ʃən.əl.i/ *adv*: *The woman who committed the crime was educationally disadvantaged.*

educationalist /ˌed.jʊˈkeɪ.ʃən.əl.ɪst/ *noun* [C] (*ALSO* **educationist**) a person who has a special knowledge of the principles and methods of teaching

educative /ˈed.jʊ.kə.tɪv/ [US] /-keɪ.t̬ɪv/ *adj* providing education: *Very few activities at this age have no educative value at all.*

educator /ˈed.jʊ.keɪ.təʳ/ [US] /-t̬ɚ/ *noun* [C] *MAINLY US* a person who teaches people

ˌeducated ˈguess *noun* [C usually sing] a guess which is made using judgment and a particular level of knowledge and is therefore more likely to be correct

Edwardian /edˈwɔː.di.ən/ [US] /-ˈwɔːr-/ *adj* from the period when Edward VII was king of England (1901-10): *Edwardian architecture/clothes*

Edwardian /edˈwɔː.di.ən/ [US] /-ˈwɔːr-/ *noun* [C] a person from this period

-ee [OBJECT] /-iː/ /-i/ *suffix* added to a verb to form a noun which refers to the person to whom the action of the verb is being done: *an employee* (= someone who is employed) ○ *the payee* (= a person to whom money is paid) ○ *an interviewee* (= someone who is being INTERVIEWED for a job)

-ee [CONDITION] /-iː/ /-i/ *suffix* added to an adjective, noun or verb to refer to a person who is in that condition or state: *a refugee* (= someone who has taken REFUGE) ○ *an escapee* (= someone who has escaped)

the EEC /ðiˌiː.iːˈsiː/ *noun* [S] the European Economic Community: an organization formed in 1958 by a group of European countries in order to establish agreed aims, especially in farming and trade, between its member countries. This organization developed into the European Community, which became the European Union in 1994.

EEG /ˌiː.iːˈdʒiː/ *noun* [C] *ABBREVIATION FOR* **electroencephalogram** or **electroencephalograph**

eek /iːk/ *exclamation INFORMAL MAINLY HUMOROUS* an expression of anxiety or slight fear

eel /iːl/ *noun* [C] a long, thin snake-like fish, some types of which are eaten

eerie /ˈɪə.ri/ [US] /ˈɪr.i/ *adj* strange in a frightening and mysterious way: *She heard the eerie noise of the wind howling through the trees.* ○ *He had the eerie* ***feeling*** *that he had met this stranger before.* **eerily** /ˈɪə.rɪ.li/ [US] /ˈɪr.ɪ-/ *adv*: *Her voice was eerily similar to her dead grandmother's.* **eeriness** /ˈɪə.rɪ.nəs/ [US] /ˈɪr.ɪ-/ *noun* [U]

eff /ef/ *verb UK INFORMAL* **eff and blind** to swear, using words that are considered offensive by some people

effing /ˈef.ɪŋ/ *adj* [before n] *UK SLANG* used to add force to an expression. Some people might consider this offensive: *He's such an effing nuisance!*

▲ **Eff off!** *phrasal verb OFFENSIVE* something that is said in order to tell someone rudely to go away ✱ NOTE: Although offensive, this is less offensive than **fuck off**.

efface [REMOVE] /ɪˈfeɪs/ *verb* [T] *FORMAL* to remove something intentionally: *The whole country had tried to efface the memory of the old dictatorship.*

efˈface *yourself* [MODEST] /ɪˈfeɪs/ *verb* [R] *FORMAL* to behave in a modest way and treat as unimportant the good things that you have achieved, often because you lack confidence ➲See also **self-effacing**.

effect [RESULT] /ɪˈfekt/ *noun* [C or U] **1** the result of a particular influence: *The radiation leak has had a disastrous effect* ***on/upon*** *the environment.* ○ *I tried taking tablets for the headache but they didn't have any effect.* ○ *I think I'm suffering from the effects of too little sleep.* ○ *She has a lot of confidence which she uses* ***to good*** *effect* (= to her advantage) *in interviews.* ➲See Note **affect or effect?** at **affect**. See also **after effects**. **2 take effect** to produce or achieve the results you want: *They had to wait ten minutes for the anaesthetic to take effect before* *they stitched up the cut.* **3** *MAINLY DISAPPROVING* **for effect** If you say or do something for effect, you intentionally do it to shock people or attract their attention: *I get the impression that she uses bad language in meetings for effect.* **4 in effect** in fact, or in practice: *So in effect the government have lowered taxes for the rich and raised them for the poor.* ➲See also **effect** USE.

• **to that effect** (*ALSO* **to the effect that**) used to express that what you are reporting is only a short and general form of what was really said: *She said she was unhappy, or* ***words*** *to that effect.* ○ *He said something to the effect that he would have to change jobs if the situation continued.*

effective /ɪ'fek.tɪv/ *adj* **1** successful or achieving the results that you want: *It's an extremely effective cure for a headache.* ○ *The lighting for the production made a very effective use of shadow.* ○ *She's a very effective teacher.* * NOTE: The opposite is **ineffective**. **2** [before n] in fact, although not officially: *Although she's not officially our boss, she's in effective control of the office.* ➲See also **effective** at **effect** USE.

effectively /ɪ'fek.tɪv.li/ *adv* **1** in a way that is successful and achieves what you want: *The tablets work more effectively if you take a hot drink after them.* **2** used when you describe what the real result of a situation is: *His wife left him when the children were small, so he effectively brought up the family himself.* ○ *Effectively, we have to start again from scratch.*

effectiveness /ɪ'fek.tɪv.nəs/ *noun* [U] *There are doubts about the effectiveness of the new drug* (= how successful it is) *in treating the disease.*

effectual /ɪ'fek.tju.əl/ *adj FORMAL* effective and successful: *They wish to promote a real and effectual understanding between the two countries.* **effectually** /ɪ'fek.tju.əl.i/ *adv*

effect [USE] /ɪ'fekt/ *noun* [U] use: *The present system of payment will remain* ***in*** *effect* (= be used) *until the end of the rental agreement.* ○ *When do the new driving laws* ***come into*** *effect?* ○ *The new salary increases will* ***take*** *effect* (= begin) *from January onwards.* **effective** /ɪ'fek.tɪv/ *adj*: *The new laws will become effective next month.* ➲See also **effective** at **effect** RESULT.

effect [ACHIEVE] /ɪ'fekt/ *verb* [T] *FORMAL* to achieve something and cause it to happen: *As a political party they are trying to effect a change in the way that we think about our environment.* ➲See note **affect** or **effect** at **affect** INFLUENCE.

effects [FILM] /ɪ'fekts/ *plural noun* (*ALSO* **special effects**) lighting, sounds and objects which are specially produced for the stage or a film and are intended to make something which does not exist seem real: *This is a movie worth seeing for its effects alone.*

effects [POSSESSIONS] /ɪ'fekts/ *plural noun SPECIALIZED* a person's possessions, especially after their death: *It says on the form that the insurance covers all* ***personal*** *effects.*

effeminate /ɪ'fem.ɪ.nət/ *adj DISAPPROVING* describes a man who behaves or looks similar to a woman: *He's got a very effeminate manner/voice.* **effeminacy** /ɪ'fem.ɪ.nə.si/ *noun* [U] *FORMAL*

effervescent [FIZZY] /ˌef.ə'ves.ᵊnt/ [US] /-ɚ-/ *adj* describes a liquid that produces bubbles of gas: *effervescent vitamin C tablets*

effervesce /ˌef.ə'ves/ [US] /-ɚ-/ *verb* [I] *SPECIALIZED* If a liquid effervesces, it produces small bubbles. **effervescence** /ˌef.ə'ves.ᵊnts/ [US] /-ɚ-/ *noun* [U]

effervescent [ACTIVE] /ˌef.ə'ves.ənt/ [US] /-ɚ-/ *adj* full of energy, positive and active: *She's one of those effervescent personalities that you often see presenting TV game shows.*

effete /ɪ'fiːt/ *adj* **1** *LITERARY DISAPPROVING* weak and lacking power: *With nothing to do all day the aristocracy had grown effete and lazy.* **2** *DISAPPROVING* more typical of a woman than of a man

efficacy /'ef.ɪ.kə.si/ *noun* [U] *FORMAL* an ability, especially of a medicine or a method of achieving something, to produce the intended result; effectiveness: *They recently ran a series of tests to measure the efficacy of the drug.*

efficacious /ˌef.ɪ'keɪ.ʃəs/ *adj FORMAL* able to produce the intended result; effective

efficient /ɪ'fɪʃ.ᵊnt/ *adj* working or operating quickly and effectively in an organized way: *The city's transport system is one of the most efficient in Europe.* ○ *We need someone really efficient who can organize the office and make it run smoothly.* * NOTE: The opposite is **inefficient**.

efficiently /ɪ'fɪʃ.ᵊnt.li/ *adv*: *She runs the business very efficiently.*

efficiency /ɪ'fɪʃ.ᵊnt.si/ *noun* [U] **1** when someone or something uses time and energy well, without wasting any: *What is so impressive about their society is the efficiency of the public services.* ○ *energy efficiency* **2** *SPECIALIZED* the difference between the amount of energy that is put into a machine in the form of fuel, effort, etc. and the amount that comes out of it in the form of movement

effigy /'ef.ɪ.dʒi/ *noun* [C] a model or other object which represents someone, especially one of a hated person which is hung or burnt in a public place: *Crowds marched through the streets carrying burning effigies of the president.*

efflorescence /ˌef.lə'res.ᵊnts/ *noun* [U] **1** *SPECIALIZED* the period when flowers start to appear on a plant **2** *LITERARY* the production of a lot of art, especially of a high quality

effluent /'ef.lu.ənt/ *noun* [C or U] *SPECIALIZED* liquid waste that is sent out from factories or places where SEWAGE is dealt with, usually flowing into the sea or rivers: *Effluents from local factories are finding their way into the river.*

effort /'ef.ət/ [US] /-ɚt/ *noun* **1** [C or U] physical or mental activity needed to achieve something: [+ to infinitive] *If we could all* ***make*** *an effort* ***to*** *keep this office tidier it would help.* ○ *You can't expect to have any friends if you don't* ***make*** *any effort with people.* ○ ***In*** *their efforts* ***to*** *reduce crime the government expanded the police force.* ○ *He's jogging round the park every morning in an effort* ***to*** *get fit for the football season.* ○ *It takes a long time to prepare the dish but the results are so good that it's* ***worth the*** *effort.* **2** [C] the result of an attempt to produce something, especially when its quality is low or uncertain: *Do you want to have a look at his exam paper? It's a fairly poor effort.*

effortless /'ef.ət.ləs/ [US] /-ɚt-/ *adj APPROVING* seeming not to need any effort: *When you watch her dance it looks so effortless.* ○ *He was an actor of effortless charm.* **effortlessly** /'ef.ət.lə.sli/ [US] /-ɚt-/ *adv*: *She runs so effortlessly as if it's the easiest thing in the world.* **effortlessness** /'ef.ət.lə.snəs/ [US] /-ɚt-/ *noun* [U]

effrontery /ɪ'frʌn.tᵊr.i/ [US] /-t̬ɚ-/ *noun* [U] *FORMAL* extreme rudeness and lack of ability to understand that your behaviour is not acceptable to other people: *He was silent all through the meal and then had the effrontery to complain that I looked bored!*

effusion /ɪ'fjuː.ʒᵊn/ *noun* [C usually sing] *LITERARY* a sudden and uncontrolled expression of strong emotion: *an effusion* ***of*** *anger and despair*

effusive /ɪ'fjuː.sɪv/ *adj FORMAL* expressing welcome, approval or pleasure in a way that shows very strong feeling: *They gave us such an effusive welcome it was quite embarrassing.* **effusively** /ɪ'fjuː.sɪv.li/ *adv*

E-fit, **e-fit** /'iː.fɪt/ *noun* [C] *MAINLY UK* a picture of a person who is believed to have committed a crime or who is missing, created on a computer using the description of someone who saw them: *An e-fit of the man prompted hundreds of calls after its release on Tuesday.* ○ *Detectives issued computerized E-fit* ***pictures*** *of two men they want to question.*

EFL /ˌiː.ef'el/ *noun* [U] *ABBREVIATION FOR* English as a Foreign Language: the teaching of English to students whose first language is not English: *Which bookshop has the largest selection of EFL materials?* ➲Compare **ESL**.

e.g., **eg** /iː'dʒiː/ *ABBREVIATION FOR* exempli gratia: a Latin phrase which means 'for example'. It can be pronounced as 'e.g.' or 'for example': *You should eat more food that contains a lot of fibre, e.g. fruit, vegetables and bread.*

egalitarian /ɪˌgæl.ɪ'teə.ri.ən/ [US] /-'ter.i-/ *adj FORMAL* believing that all people are equally important and should have the same rights and opportunities in life: *an egalitarian society* ○ *The party's principles are basically egalitarian.*

egalitarian /ɪˌgæl.ɪˈteə.ri.ən/ ⑩ /-ˈter.i-/ *noun* [C] FORMAL a person who has egalitarian beliefs: *Ford is no egalitarian.*

egalitarianism /ɪˌgæl.ɪˈteə.ri.ən.ɪ.zᵊm/ ⑩ /-ˈter.i-/ *noun* [U] FORMAL the belief in and actions taken according to egalitarian principles

egg REPRODUCTION /eg/ *noun* [C] **1** an oval object, often with a hard shell, which is produced by female birds and particular reptiles and insects, and contains a baby animal which comes out when it is developed: *The cuckoo lays her egg in another bird's nest.* ○ *After fourteen days the eggs hatch.* **2** a cell produced by a woman or female animal from which a baby might develop if it combines with sperm from a male: *Identical twins develop from a single fertilized egg which then splits into two.*

egg FOOD /eg/ *noun* **1** [C or U] the oval object with a hard shell which is produced by female birds, especially chickens, and which is eaten as food: *a hard-boiled/soft-boiled egg* ○ *How do you like your eggs – fried or boiled?* **2** [C] an object which is made in the shape of a bird's egg: *a chocolate/marble egg*
• **egg on sb's face** INFORMAL If someone has or gets egg on their face, they look stupid because of something that they have done: *This latest scandal has left the government with egg on its face.*
• **put all your eggs in one basket** INFORMAL to depend for your success on a single person or plan of action: *I'm applying for several jobs because I don't really want to put all my eggs in one basket.*

eggy /ˈeg.i/ *adj* INFORMAL tasting or smelling of eggs

egg /eg/ *verb*
▲ **egg sb on** *phrasal verb* [M] to strongly encourage someone to do something which might not be a very good idea: *Don't egg him on! He gets himself into enough trouble without your encouragement.*

egg-and-spoon race /ˌeg.ᵊndˈspuːn.reɪs/ *noun* [C] a race in which people run with an egg balanced on a spoon

egg cup *noun* [C] a small container used to hold a boiled egg while you eat it

egghead /ˈeg.hed/ *noun* [C] HUMOROUS DISAPPROVING a person, especially a man, who is very clever and interested only in studying and other mental activities

eggplant /ˈeg.plɑːnt/ ⑩ /-plænt/ *noun* [C] US FOR **aubergine** ⊃See picture **Vegetables** on page Centre 2

egg roll *noun* [C] US FOR **spring roll**

eggshell /ˈeg.ʃel/ *noun* [C or U] the hard outside covering of an egg

egg timer *noun* [C] a device which helps you judge when a boiled egg has been cooked long enough to be eaten

egg white *noun* [C or U] the transparent part of an egg which turns white when it is cooked

egg yolk *noun* [C or U] the yellow part of an egg

ego /ˈiː.gəʊ/ ⑩ /ˈiː.goʊ/ *noun* [C] *plural* **egos 1** MAINLY DISAPPROVING your idea or opinion of yourself, or a great feeling of your own importance and ability: *That man has such an enormous ego – I've never known anyone so full of themselves!* ○ *I'm glad she got the job – she needed something to boost/bolster her ego* (= give her confidence). ⊃See also **alter ego**; **superego**. **2** SPECIALIZED in PSYCHOANALYSIS, the part of a person's mind which tries to match the hidden desires of the ID (= part of unconscious mind) with the demands of reality

egocentric /ˌiː.gəʊˈsen.trɪk/ ⑩ /-goʊ-/ *adj* MAINLY DISAPPROVING describes someone who is selfish, thinking only of themselves: *Babies are entirely egocentric, concerned only with when they will next be fed.* **egocentrically** /ˌiː.gəʊˈsen.trɪ.kli/ ⑩ /-goʊ-/ *adv* **egocentricity** /ˌiː.gəʊ.senˈtrɪs.ɪ.ti/ ⑩ /-goʊ.senˈtrɪs.ə.ţi/ *noun* [U]

egomania /ˌiː.gəʊˈmeɪ.ni.ə/ ⑩ /-goʊ-/ *noun* [U] DISAPPROVING when a person considers themselves to be very important and able to do anything that they want to do

egomaniac /ˌiː.gəʊˈmeɪ.ni.æk/ ⑩ /-goʊ-/ *noun* [C] DISAPPROVING a person who considers themselves to be

extremely important and able to do anything that they want to do

egotism /ˈiː.gəʊ.tɪ.zᵊm/ ⑩ /-goʊ-/ *noun* [U] (ALSO **egoism**) DISAPPROVING the tendency to think only about yourself and consider yourself better and more important than other people: *Finding herself world-famous by the time she was eighteen only encouraged the actress's egotism.*

egotist /ˈiː.gəʊ.tɪst/ ⑩ /-goʊ-/ *noun* [C] (ALSO **egoist**) DISAPPROVING a person who considers themselves to be better or more important than other people: *Politicians are notorious egotists.* **egotistic**, **egotistical** /ˌiː.gəʊˈtɪs.tɪ.kᵊl/ ⑩ /-goʊ-/ *adj*

ego trip *noun* [C] DISAPPROVING something that you do because it makes you feel important and also shows other people how important you are: *He was on another one of his ego trips, directing and taking the main part in a film.*

egregious /ɪˈgriː.dʒəs/ *adj* FORMAL DISAPPROVING often of mistakes, extremely and noticeably bad: *It was an egregious error for a statesman to show such ignorance.*

Egyptian /ɪˈdʒɪp.ʃᵊn/ /iː-/ *adj* from, belonging to or relating to Egypt: *Egyptian art*

eh /eɪ/ *exclamation* (US USUALLY **huh**) INFORMAL used to express surprise or confusion, to ask someone to repeat what they have said, or as a way of getting someone to give some type of reaction to a statement that you have made: *"Janet's leaving her husband." "Eh?"* ○ *"Did you hear what I said?" "Eh? Say it again – I wasn't listening."* ○ *Going overseas again, eh? It's a nice life for some!*

Eid /iːd/ *noun* [C or U] the name of two Muslim festivals. The more important of these is called Eid Al Fitr and is celebrated to mark the end of RAMADAN.

eiderdown /ˈaɪ.də.daʊn/ ⑩ /-dɚ-/ *noun* [C] a thick covering for on top of the bed, filled with soft feathers or warm material, used especially in the past

eight /eɪt/ *determiner, pronoun, noun* the number 8: *six, seven, eight, nine, ten* ○ *We've got eight people coming to dinner.*

eighth /eɪtθ/ *determiner, pronoun, adj, adv, noun* [S] 8th written as a word: *He finished eighth in the race.* ○ *Bob's birthday is on the eighth (of June).*

eighth /eɪtθ/ *noun* [C] one of eight equal parts of something

eighteen /eɪˈtiːn/ /ˈ--/ *determiner, pronoun, noun* the number 18: *seventeen, eighteen, nineteen*

eighteenth /eɪˈtiːnθ/ /ˈ--/ *determiner, pronoun, adj, adv, noun* 18th written as a word

eighth note *noun* [C] US FOR **quaver** MUSICAL NOTE

eighty /ˈeɪ.ti/ ⑩ /-ţi/ *determiner, pronoun, noun* the number 80: *seventy, eighty, ninety* ○ *They've invited eighty (guests) to the wedding.*

eighties /ˈeɪ.tiz/ ⑩ /-ţiz/ *plural noun* A person's eighties are the period in which they are aged between 80 and 89: *My grandmother is in her eighties.*

the 'eighties *plural noun* **1** the range of temperature between 80° and 89° Fahrenheit: *The temperature is expected to be in the eighties tomorrow.* **2** the period of years between 80 and 89 in any century: *Margaret Thatcher was the British Prime Minister for most of the eighties* (= between 1980 and 1989).

eightieth /ˈeɪ.ti.əθ/ ⑩ /-ţi-/ *determiner, pronoun, adj, adv, noun* 80th written as a word

either ALSO /ˈaɪ.ðəʳ/ /ˈiː-/ ⑩ /-ðɚ/ *adv* used in negative sentences instead of 'also' or 'too': *I don't eat meat and my husband doesn't either.* ○ *"I've never been to the States." "I haven't either."* ○ *They do really good food at that restaurant and it's not very expensive either.*

either CHOICE /ˈaɪ.ðəʳ/ /ˈiː-/ ⑩ /-ðɚ/ *determiner, pronoun, conjunction* used when referring to a choice between two possibilities: *Either candidate would be ideal for the job.* ○ *"Do you prefer pork or beef?" "I don't like either."* ○ *"Would you like the metal or plastic one?" "Either will do."* ○ *You can get there by train or bus – either way/in either case it'll take an hour.* ○ *We can either eat now or after the show – it's up to you.* ○ *Either you leave now or I call the police!*

either BOTH /ˈaɪ.ðəʳ/ /ˈiː-/ ⑩ /-ðɚ/ *determiner* both: *Unfortunately I was sitting at the table with smokers on either side of me.*

either-or /ˌaɪ.ðər'ɔːʳ/ /ˌiː-/ [US] /-ðɚ'ɔːr/ *adj* [before n] describes a situation in which there is a choice between two different plans of action, but both together are not possible: *It's an either-or* ***situation*** *– we can buy a new car this year or we can go on holiday but we can't do both.*

ejaculate [SPERM] /ɪ'dʒæk.jʊ.leɪt/ *verb* [I or T] of a man or male animal, to produce a sudden flow of sperm from the penis or similar reproductive part **ejaculation** /ɪˌdʒæk.jʊ'leɪ.ʃᵊn/ *noun* [C or U]

ejaculate [SAY] /ɪ'dʒæk.jʊ.leɪt/ *verb* [T] *OLD-FASHIONED OR HUMOROUS* to shout or say something suddenly, sometimes unexpectedly: [+ speech] *"You've got my umbrella!" he ejaculated.* **ejaculation** /ɪˌdʒæk.jʊ'leɪ.ʃᵊn/ *noun* [C]

eject /ɪ'dʒekt/ *verb* **1** [T often passive] to force someone to leave a particular place: *A number of football fans had been ejected* ***from*** *the bar for causing trouble.* **2** [T] *US* (*UK* **send off**) to order a sports player to leave the playing area during a game because they have done something wrong **3** [I] to leave an aircraft in an emergency by being pushed while still in your seat **4** [I or T] to come out of a machine when a button is pressed, or to make something do this: *How do you eject the tape?* ○ *The coffee machine suddenly ejected a handful of coins.*

ejection /ɪ'dʒekt.ʃᵊn/ *noun* [C or U] the act of ejecting someone or something

e'jection ˌseat *noun* [C] (*ALSO* **ejector seat**) a seat which can throw out the person flying an aircraft if they suddenly have to leave it because they are in danger

eke /iːk/ *verb*

▲ **eke *sth* out** *phrasal verb* [M] to use something slowly or carefully because you only have a small amount of it: *There wasn't much food left, but we just managed to eke it out.* ○ *He managed to eke out* ***a living*** (= earn just enough to live on) *one summer by selling drinks on a beach.*

EKG /ˌiː.keɪ.'dʒiː/ *noun* [C] *US FOR* **ECG**

elaborate [DETAILED] /ɪ'læb.ᵊr.ət/ [US] /-ɚ-/ *adj* containing a lot of careful detail or many detailed parts: *You want a plain blouse to go with that skirt – nothing too elaborate.* ○ *They're making the most elaborate preparations for the wedding.* ○ *He came out with such an elaborate excuse that I didn't quite believe him.* **elaborately** /ɪ'læb.ᵊr.ət.li/ [US] /'-ɚ-/ *adv*: *It was the most elaborately decorated cake – all sugar flowers and bows.*

elaborate [EXPLAIN] /ɪ'læb.ə.reɪt/ *verb* [I] *SLIGHTLY FORMAL* to add more information to or explain something that you have said: *The minister said he was resigning, but refused to elaborate* ***on*** *his reasons for doing so.*

elaboration /ɪˌlæb.ə'reɪ.ʃᵊn/ *noun* [C or U] the act of explaining something: *This point needs greater elaboration.*

élan /eɪ'læn/ *noun* [U] *LITERARY APPROVING* a combination of style and energetic confidence, especially in performances or manner: *She dances the role with such élan.* ○ *As a prime minister, she had a certain élan.*

elapse /ɪ'læps/ *verb* [I] *FORMAL* If time elapses, it goes past: *Four years had elapsed since he left college and still he hadn't found a job.*

elastic /ɪ'læs.tɪk/ *adj* **1** describes material that is able to stretch and be returned to its original shape or size: *A lot of sportswear is made of very elastic material.* **2** able or likely to be changed: *The project has only just started so any plans are still very elastic.* ○ *In this country, time is an elastic concept.*

elastic /ɪ'læs.tɪk/ *noun* [U] a type of rubber that is able to stretch and be returned to its original shape or size: *His trousers were held up with a piece of elastic.*

elasticated *UK* /ɪ'læs.tɪ.keɪ.tɪd/ [US] /-t̬ɪd/ *adj* (*US* **elasticized,** *AUS* **elasticised**) Clothes or parts of clothes that are elasticated have threads of elastic in them: *a dress with an elasticated waist*

elasticity /ˌɪl.æs'tɪs.ɪ.ti/ [US] /-ə.t̬i/ *noun* [U] **1** the ability to stretch: *As the skin grows older it loses its elasticity.* **2** the ability to change: *There is some elasticity in our plans – nothing has been firmly decided yet.*

eˌlastic 'band *noun* [C] *UK FOR* **rubber band**

Elastoplast /ɪ'læs.tə.plæst/ *noun* [C or U] *UK TRADEMARK* a common type of PLASTER (= a small piece of sticky material to cover and protect a cut in the skin)

elated /ɪ'leɪ.tɪd/ [US] /-t̬ɪd/ *adj* extremely happy and excited, often because something has happened or been achieved: *The prince was reported to be elated* ***at/by*** *the birth of his new daughter.*

elation /ɪ'leɪ.ʃᵊn/ *noun* [U] a state of extreme happiness or excitement: *There's a sense of elation at having completed a race of such length.*

elbow /'el.bəʊ/ [US] /-boʊ/ *noun* [C] the part in the middle of the arm where it bends, or the part of a piece of clothing which covers this area: *Her arm was bandaged from the elbow to the fingers.* ○ *The sleeve of his shirt was torn* ***at the*** *elbow.* ⊃See picture **The Body** on page Centre 5

• **at *sb's* elbow** close beside and a little behind someone: *During the visit, the interpreter was always at her elbow.*

• **give *sb* the elbow** *UK INFORMAL* to end your romantic relationship with someone

elbow /'el.bəʊ/ [US] /-boʊ/ *verb* [T usually + adv or prep] **1** *DISAPPROVING* to push someone rudely with your elbows so that you can move or have more space: *He elbowed* ***his way to*** *the front of the crowd.* ○ *They elbowed the onlookers aside.* **2** to hit someone with your elbow, sometimes as a sign to make them notice or remember something: *She elbowed me* ***in the ribs*** *before I could say anything.*

▲ **elbow *sb* out** *phrasal verb* [M often passive] to force someone or something out of a position or job: *He resigned before he was elbowed out.*

'elbow ˌgrease *noun* [U] *INFORMAL* a lot of physical effort: *The polish needs a certain amount of elbow grease to apply.*

'elbow ˌroom *noun* [U] **1** space to move around in: *We were tightly squashed in at dinner, with very little elbow room.* **2** freedom to do what you want: *At first the management gave the new director plenty of elbow room.*

elder /'el.dəʳ/ [US] /-dɚ/ *noun* [C] **1** an older person, especially one with a respected position in society: *You should listen to the advice of your elders.* ○ *They consulted the* ***village*** *elders.* ○ *FORMAL She is* ***my*** *elder* ***by*** *three years* (= three years older than me). **2** an official of a religious group: *a* ***church*** *elder*

elder /'el.dəʳ/ [US] /-dɚ/ *adj* **1 elder sister/brother/son/daughter** a sister/brother/son/daughter who is older than the other sister(s), brother(s), etc. **2 the elder** the older person of two people: *Of the two brothers Harvey is the elder.* **3 the elder** used after someone's name to show that they are the older of two people who have the same name, especially a father and son: *William Pitt the elder*

COMMON LEARNER ERROR

elder/eldest or older/oldest?

Elder and **eldest** are only used before nouns, usually when comparing members of a family.

My elder sister is a teacher.

The comparative and superlative forms of the adjective **old** are **older** and **oldest**.

My sister is three years older than me.

elderberry /'el.dəˌber.i/ [US] /-dɚ-/ *noun* [C] (*ALSO* **elder (tree)**) a small tree which grows wild or in gardens and has large flat groups of white flowers, or its nearly black fruit which can be used in cooking or making wine: *elderberry wine*

elderly /'el.dᵊl.i/ [US] /-dɚ.li/ *adj* *POLITE WORD FOR* old: *elderly relatives/parents* ⊃See Note **old or elderly?** at **old** EXISTED MANY YEARS.

the 'elderly *plural noun* old people considered as a group: *The city is building new housing for the elderly.*

ˌelder 'statesman *noun* [C] a respected leader, often one who no longer has an active job, who is thought of as having good advice to give: *He is one of the medical profession's elder statesmen.*

eldest /'el.dɪst/ *adj* [before n] **1** being the oldest of three or more people, especially within a family: *Her eldest child is nearly 14.* **2 the eldest** a person who is the oldest of three of more people: *He was the eldest of four kids.*

the 'eldest *noun* [S] the oldest child in a family: *My eldest is at college.*

E

elect /ɪˈlekt/ *verb* [T] **1** to decide on or choose, especially to choose a person for a particular job, by voting: *The Government is elected for a five-year term of office.* ○ [+ obj + as + n] *We elected him* ***as*** *our representative.* ○ [+ obj + n] *She was elected Chair of the Board of Governors.* ○ [+ obj + to infinitive] *The group elected one of its members* ***to*** *be their spokesperson.* **2** FORMAL **elect to do *sth*** to choose to do a particular thing: *She elected to take early retirement instead of moving to the new location.*

the eˈlect *plural noun* **1** FORMAL in the Bible, people who are chosen by God **2** HUMOROUS any group of people who have been specially chosen for their particular qualities

-elect /-ɪ.lekt/ *suffix* **president-elect/prime minister-elect, etc.** the person who has been voted to be president, prime minster, etc. but has not yet started work: *The President-elect has been preparing to take office in January.* ➲Compare **designate**.

election /ɪˈlek.ʃᵊn/ *noun* [C or U] a time when people vote in order to choose someone for a political or official job: *The Government is expected to* ***call*** *an election* (= allow the country to vote) *very soon.* ○ *Local government elections will take place in May.* ○ *The first election results have started to come in.* ➲See also **by-election**; **general election**.

electioneering /ɪˌlek.ʃəˈnɪə.rɪŋ/ [US] /-ˈnɪr.ɪŋ/ *noun* [U] MAINLY DISAPPROVING the activity of trying to persuade people to vote for a particular political party: *The M.P.'s speech was dismissed by her opponents as crude electioneering.*

elective /ɪˈlek.tɪv/ *adj* FORMAL voted for or chosen: *an elective office* ○ *elective surgery*

elector /ɪˈlek.təʳ/ [US] /-tɚ/ *noun* [C] a person who votes: *At this election many eighteen-year-olds will become electors for the first time.*

electoral /ɪˈlek.tᵊr.ᵊl/ [US] /-tɚ-/ *adj* [before n] relating to an election: *the electoral system* ○ *electoral law/reform/gains/defeat* **electorally** /ɪˈlek.tᵊr.ə.li/ [US] /-tɚ-/ *adv*

electorate /ɪˈlek.tᵊr.ət/ [US] /-tɚ-/ *group noun* [C usually sing] all the people who are allowed to vote: *The present voting system distorts the wishes of the electorate.*

eˈlection camˌpaign *noun* [C] the period of weeks immediately before an election when politicians try to persuade people to vote for them

ˈelection ˌday *noun* [C usually sing] (UK ALSO **polling day**) the day when people vote in an election

eˌlective dicˈtatorship *noun* [C] UK DISAPPROVING a government which is elected but which has won so many votes that it can do what it likes

eˌlectoral ˈcollege *noun* [C] a group of people whose job is to choose a political or religious leader

eˌlectoral ˈregister *noun* [C] (ALSO **electoral roll**) UK the official list of people who are allowed to vote

electric [POWER] /ɪˈlek.trɪk/ *adj* using electricity for power: *an electric blanket/car/kettle/light*

electrical /ɪˈlek.trɪ.kᵊl/ *adj* related to electricity: *electrical equipment/goods/devices* ○ *an electrical fuse/circuit/fault* **electrically** /ɪˈlek.trɪ.kli/ *adv*: *an electrically powered car*

electrician /ˌɪl.ekˈtrɪʃ.ᵊn/ *noun* [C] a person who puts in and maintains electrical wires

electrics /ɪˈlek.trɪks/ *plural noun* UK the electrical system of something, especially a car: *I think the fault is in the electrics.*

electrify /ɪˈlek.trɪ.faɪ/ *verb* [T] to make a machine or system operate using electricity when it did not before: *The east coast railway line has been electrified.*

electrification /ɪˌlek.trɪ.fɪˈkeɪ.ʃᵊn/ *noun* [U] *the electrification of the railways* ○ *electrification technology*

electric [EXCITEMENT] /ɪˈlek.trɪk/ *adj* very exciting and producing strong feelings: *an electric performance/atmosphere*

electrify /ɪˈlek.trɪ.faɪ/ *verb* [T] to make a person or group extremely excited by what you say or do: *She electrified her audience with her vivid stories.*

electrifying /ɪˈlek.trɪ.faɪ.ɪŋ/ *adj* very exciting: *an electrifying performance*

eˌlectrical enginˈeer *noun* [C] a trained specialist in electrical systems, especially those which power and control machines or are involved in communication

eˌlectrical ˈstorm *noun* [C] (UK ALSO **electric storm**) a storm with thunder and lightning

the eˌlectric ˈchair *noun* [S] in some parts of the US, a special chair which is used to kill a criminal with a current of electricity

eˌlectric ˈfence *noun* [C] a fence which produces a small electric current, usually to keep animals in a particular area

eˌlectric ˈheater *noun* [C] (UK ALSO **electric fire**) a device which uses electricity to produce heat, for example from metal bars which become red and hot when the current is switched on

electricity /ˌɪl.ekˈtrɪs.ɪ.ti/ [US] /-ə.t̬i/ *noun* [U] a form of energy, produced in various ways, which provides power to devices that create light, heat, etc: *The electricity has been turned off.* ○ *an electricity generating company* ○ *powered/heated by electricity* ○ *an electricity bill*

eˌlectric ˈshock *noun* [C] (ALSO **shock**) a sudden painful feeling that you get when electricity flows through your body: *He* ***got*** *an electric shock from one of the wires.*

electrocardiogram /ɪˌlek.trəˈkɑː.di.ə.græm/ [US] /-ˈkɑːr-/ *noun* [C] (ABBREVIATION **ECG**) SPECIALIZED a drawing or image made by an electrocardiograph

electrocardiograph /ɪˌlek.trəˈkɑː.di.ə.græf/ /-grɑːf/ [US] /-ˈkɑːrdi.ə.græf/ *noun* [C] (ABBREVIATION **ECG**) SPECIALIZED a machine that records the electrical activity of the heart as it beats

electroconvulsive therapy /ɪˌlek.trəʊ.kᵊnˈvʌl.sɪv ˌθer.ə.pi/ [US] /-troʊ-/ *noun* [U] (ABBREVIATION **ECT**) SPECIALIZED the treatment of particular MENTAL ILLNESSES (= diseases which affect the mind) which involves sending an electric current through the brain

electrocute /ɪˈlek.trə.kjuːt/ *verb* [T often passive] to kill someone by causing electricity to flow through their body: *He was electrocuted when he touched the bare wires.* **electrocution** /ɪˌlek.trəˈkjuː.ʃᵊn/ *noun* [C or U]

electrode /ɪˈlek.trəʊd/ [US] /-troʊd/ *noun* [C] the point at which an electric current enters or leaves something, for example, a battery

electroencephalogram /ɪˌlek.trəʊ.enˈsef.ə.lə.græm/ [US] /-troʊ-/ *noun* [C] (ABBREVIATION **EEG**) SPECIALIZED a drawing or electronic image made by an electroencephalograph

electroencephalograph /ɪˌlek.trəʊ.enˈsef.ə.lə.græf/ /-grɑːf/ [US] /-troʊ-/ *noun* [C] (ABBREVIATION **EEG**) SPECIALIZED a machine that records the electrical activity of the brain

electrolysis /ˌɪl.ekˈtrɒl.ə.sɪs/ [US] /-ˈtrɑː.lə-/ *noun* [U] **1** the use of an electric current to cause chemical change in a liquid **2** the process of using a very small electric current to remove hair and stop it from growing back

electrolyte /ɪˈlek.trə.laɪt/ *noun* [C] SPECIALIZED a substance, usually a liquid, which electricity can go through or which breaks into its parts when electricity goes through it

electromagnetism /ɪˌlek.trəʊˈmæg.nə.tɪ.zᵊm/ [US] /-troʊ-/ *noun* [U] SPECIALIZED the science of MAGNETISM and electrical currents

electromagnetic /ɪˌlek.trəʊ.mægˈnet.ɪk/ [US] /-troʊ.mægˈnet̬-/ *adj* having magnetic and electrical parts: *an electromagnetic wave*

electromagnet /ɪˌlek.trəʊˈmæg.nə.tɪ.zᵊm/ [US] /-troʊˈmæg.nə.t̬ɪ-/ *noun* [C] SPECIALIZED a device made from a piece of iron that becomes magnetic when a changing current is passed through the wire that goes round it

electron /ɪˈlek.trɒn/ [US] /-trɑːn/ *noun* [C] an extremely small piece of matter with a negative electrical charge ➲Compare **neutron**; **proton**.

electronic [ELECTRICAL] /ˌɪl.ekˈtrɒn.ɪk/ [US] /-ˈtrɑː.nɪk/ *adj* (especially of equipment), using, based on or used in a system of operation which involves the control of electric current by various devices: *an electronic keyboard/game* ○ *electronic components/devices*

electronics /ˌɪl.ekˈtrɒn.ɪks/ [US] /-ˈtrɑː.nɪks/ *noun* [U] the scientific study of electric current and the technology that uses it: *a degree in electronics* ○ *the electronics industry* **electronically** /ˌɪl.ekˈtrɒn.ɪ.kli/ [US] /-ˈtrɑː.nɪ-/ *adv*:

electronically generated graphics ○ *electronically stored information*

electronic [COMPUTING] /ˌɪl.ekˈtrɒn.ɪk/ ⓤ /-ˈtrɑː.nɪk/ *adj* relating to computers or something that is done by computers: *electronic communication/cash* ○ *electronic publishing*

elec,tronic 'banking *noun* [U] (*ALSO* **e-banking**) when customers use the Internet to organize, examine and make changes to their bank accounts and investments, etc. electronically, or when banks operate accounts and services in this way: *electronic banking* **services**

elec,tronic 'book *noun* [C] **1** (*ALSO* **e-book**) a book that is published in electronic form, for example on the Internet or on a disk, and not printed on paper: *electronic book publishing* ○ *an e-book publisher* **2** (*ALSO* **e-book (reader/player)**) a small electronic device with a screen which allows you to read an electronic book, perform searches, add notes, etc: *Buyers can download his latest novel to read on a computer, personal organiser or electronic book.*

elec,tronic 'mail *noun* [U] *FORMAL* **email**

elec,tronic 'mail,box *noun* [C] a computer file where e-mails are stored

elec,tronic 'organizer *noun* [C] an electronic device in which information is stored, such as names, addresses, telephone numbers and dates of meetings, and which people use to help them organize their time

elec,tronic 'publishing *noun* [U] the business of publishing information that is read using a computer: *an electronic publishing company/course*

elec,tronic 'tagging *noun* [U] the use of an electronic device which is attached to a person who has committed a crime, so that the police know where they are

e,lectron 'microscope *noun* [C] a device which sends electrons through objects which are too small to be seen easily, to produce a picture which is more detailed than that produced by ordinary microscopes

electroshock therapy /ɪˌlek.trəʊˈʃɒkˈθer.ə.pi/ ⓤ /-troʊˈʃaːk-/ *noun* [U] *US* **electroconvulsive therapy**

electrostatic /ɪˌlek.trəʊˈstæt.ɪk/ ⓤ /-troʊˈstæt-/ *adj SPECIALIZED* connected with or caused by electricity which does not move in a current but is attracted to the surface of some objects: *an electrostatic charge*

elegant /ˈel.ɪ.gənt/ *adj* **1** graceful and attractive in appearance or behaviour: *an elegant woman* ○ *a very elegant suit* ○ *an elegant dining room* **2** describes an idea, plan or solution that is clever but simple, and therefore attractive **elegantly** /ˈel.ɪ.gənt.li/ *adv*: *elegantly dressed* **elegance** /ˈel.ɪ.gənts/ *noun* [U] *It was her natural elegance that struck me.* ○ *the elegance of her clothes*

elegy /ˈel.ə.dʒi/ *noun* [C] a sad poem or song, especially remembering someone who has died or something in the past: *Gray's 'Elegy in a Country Churchyard' is a famous English poem.* **elegiac** /ˌel.ɪˈdʒaɪ.ək/ ⓤ /ɪˈliː.dʒi.æk/ *adj LITERARY* relating to an elegy

element [PART] /ˈel.ɪ.mənt/ *noun* [C] a part of something: *List the elements which make up a perfect dinner party.* ○ *The film had all the elements of a good thriller.* ○ *We weren't even taught the elements of* (= basic information about) *physics at school.*

element [AMOUNT] /ˈel.ɪ.mənt/ *noun* **an element of** *sth* a small amount of an emotion or quality: *There was certainly an element of truth in what she said.* ○ *Don't you think there's an element of jealousy in all of this?* ○ *We walked quietly up to the door to preserve the element of surprise.*

element [SIMPLE SUBSTANCE] /ˈel.ɪ.mənt/ *noun* [C] **1** a simple substance which cannot be reduced to smaller chemical parts: *Aluminium is an element.* **2** *OLD USE* earth, air, fire and water from which people believed everything else was made

• **be in** *your* **element** to be happy because you are doing what you like or can do best: *Kate, of course, was in her element, making all the arrangements.*

• **be out of** *your* **element** to be unhappy and feel uncomfortable in a particular situation

element [HEAT] /ˈel.ɪ.mənt/ *noun* [C] the part of an electrical device which produces heat: *a heating element* ○ *The kettle needs a new element.*

elemental /ˌel.ɪˈmen.təl/ *adj* **1** *LITERARY* showing the strong power of nature: *elemental force/fury* **2** basic or most simple, but strong: *elemental needs/desires/feelings*

elementary /ˌel.ɪˈmen.tər.i/ ⓤ /-tɚ-/ *adj* **1** basic: *I have an elementary knowledge of physics.* ○ *They made some elementary mistakes.* ○ *Millions of travellers fail to take even the most elementary of precautions.* **2** relating to the early stages of studying a subject: *This book contains a series of elementary exercises for learners.*

ele,mentary 'particle *noun* [C] *SPECIALIZED* one of the most simple parts of all matter, such as an electron, a PROTON or a NEUTRON

ele'mentary ,school *noun* [C] *UK OLD-FASHIONED OR US* a school which provides the first part of a child's education, usually for children between five and eleven years old

the 'elements *plural noun* *MAINLY HUMOROUS* the weather, usually bad weather: *We decided to **brave** the elements and go for a walk* (= go for a walk despite the bad weather).

elephant /ˈel.ɪ.fənt/ *noun* [C] a very large grey mammal which has a TRUNK (= long nose) with which it can pick things up ⊃See picture **Animals and Birds** on page Centre 4

elephantine /ˌel.ɪˈfæn.taɪn/ *adj FORMAL* very large: *She's so tiny she makes me feel elephantine.*

elevate /ˈel.ɪ.veɪt/ *verb* [T] **1** *FORMAL* to raise something or lift something up: *The platform was elevated by means of hydraulic legs.* **2** to make someone or something more important or to improve something: *They want to elevate the status of teachers.* ○ *These factors helped to elevate the town into the list of the ten most attractive in the country.* **3** *FORMAL* **be elevated to** *sth* to be given a higher rank or social position: *He has been elevated to deputy manager.* ○ *She was elevated to the peerage* (= was given the title 'Lady').

elevated /ˈel.ɪ.veɪ.tɪd/ ⓤ /-tɪd/ *adj* **1** raised: *The doctor said I was to keep my leg elevated.* ○ *There is an elevated area at the back of the building.* **2** high or important: *She holds a more elevated position in the company.* **3** [before n] greater than is normal or reasonable: *He has a rather elevated idea of his own importance.* **4** [before n] *FORMAL* literary or formal: *an elevated style/tone* ○ *the elevated language of the Psalms*

elevation /ˌel.ɪˈveɪ.ʃən/ *noun FORMAL* **1** [C or U] the height of a place above the level of the sea: *Atmospheric pressure varies with elevation and temperature.* ○ *The crop is not grown at high elevations/above an elevation of 1000 metres.* **2** [C] a hill: *The flagpole stands on a small elevation in front of the building.* **3** [U] when someone or something is given a more important position: *His elevation to the presidency of the new republic was generally popular.*

elevation /ˌel.ɪˈveɪ.ʃən/ *noun* [C] *SPECIALIZED* the front or side of a building as shown on a drawing: *This plan shows the front, side and back elevations of the new supermarket.*

elevator /ˈel.ɪ.veɪ.tər/ ⓤ /-tɚ/ *noun* [C] **1** *US* (*UK* **lift**) a small room which carries people or goods up and down in tall buildings **2** a moving strip which can be used for unloading goods from a ship, putting bags onto an aircraft, moving grain into a store etc.

'elevator ,music *noun* [U] *US FOR* **Muzak**

eleven /ɪˈlev.ən/ *determiner, pronoun, noun* the number 11: *nine, ten, eleven, twelve* ○ *There are eleven girls in my class and fifteen boys.*

eleven /ɪˈlev.ən/ *group noun* [C] a team of eleven players **elevenses** /ɪˈlev.ən.zɪz/ *plural noun UK INFORMAL* a drink and a small amount to eat between breakfast and lunch **eleventh** /ɪˈlev.ənθ/ *determiner, pronoun, adj, adv, noun* 11th written as a word

• **the eleventh hour** the last moment or almost too late: *We only received the official signatures **at** the eleventh hour.*

eleventh-hour /ɪˈlev.ənθˌaʊər/ ⓤ /-ˌaʊr/ *adj*: *an eleventh-hour decision by the union to call off the strike*

the eleven-plus /ɪˌlev.ᵊnˈplʌs/ *noun* [S] *UK* in some parts of Britain, an exam taken by children aged eleven which affects what type of school they go to next

elf /elf/ *noun* [C] *plural* **elves** a small person with pointed ears who has magic powers in children's stories
elfin /ˈel.fɪn/ *adj* descibes a person who is small and delicate: *Her features were small, almost elfin.*

elicit /ɪˈlɪs.ɪt/ *verb* [T] *FORMAL* to obtain or produce something, especially information or a reaction: *Have you managed to elicit a response* ***from*** *them yet?* ○ *The questionnaire was intended to elicit information on eating habits.* ○ *They were able to elicit the support of the public.*

E

eligible /ˈel.ɪ.dʒə.bl/ *adj* **1** having the necessary qualities or fulfilling the necessary conditions: *Are you eligible* ***for*** *early retirement/maternity leave?* ○ *You might be eligible for a grant.* ○ *Only people over 18 are eligible* ***to*** *vote.* **2** describes someone who is not married and is desirable as a marriage partner, especially because they are rich and attractive: *I can think of several eligible* ***bachelors*** *of my acquaintance.* **eligibility** /ˌel.ɪ.dʒəˈbɪl.ɪ.ti/ [US] /-ə.t̬i/ *noun* [U] *I'll have to check her eligibility to take part.* ○ *The eligibility rules prevent under-18s being in the team.*

eliminate /ɪˈlɪm.ɪ.neɪt/ *verb* **1** [T] to remove or take away: *A move towards healthy eating could help eliminate heart disease.* ○ *We eliminated the possibility that it could have been an accident.* ○ *The police eliminated him* ***from*** *their enquiries.* **2** [T often passive] to defeat someone so that they cannot continue in a competition: *He was eliminated in the third round of the competition.* **3** [T] *SLANG* to murder: *A police officer was accused of helping a drug gang eliminate rivals.*
elimination /ɪˌlɪm.ɪˈneɪ.ʃᵊn/ *noun* [U] the removal of something: *the elimination of disease/pain* ○ *their elimination from the competition*
• **by a process of elimination** by removing from several possible answers the ones which are unlikely to be correct until only one is left: *We eventually found the answer by a process of elimination.*
eliminator /ɪˈlɪm.ɪ.neɪ.təʳ/ [US] /-t̬ɚ/ *noun* [C] *UK* a part of a competition in any game or sport where one person or team plays against another to decide which of them will continue to the next stage and which will be removed from the competition

elimiˈnation ˌtournament *noun* [C] *US FOR* **knock-out** COMPETITION

elite /ɪˈliːt/ *group noun* [C] the richest, most powerful, best educated or most highly trained group in a society: *the country's educated elite* ○ *a member of the elite* ○ *DISAPPROVING A powerful and corrupt elite has bled this country dry.*
elite /ɪˈliːt/ *adj* [before n] *Elite* (= A group of excellent) *troops were airlifted to the trouble zone.*
elitism /ɪˈliː.tɪ.zᵊm/ *noun* [U] *MAINLY DISAPPROVING* when things are organized for the benefit of a few people with special interests or abilities: *The accusation of elitism seems unfair as the festival presents a wide range of music, with something to please everyone.*
elitist /ɪˈliː.tɪst/ *adj DISAPPROVING* based on elitism: *Many remember sport at school as elitist, focusing only on those who were good at it.*

elixir /ɪˈlɪk.sɪəʳ/ [US] /-sjɚ/ *noun* [C usually sing] *LITERARY* a substance, usually a liquid, with a magical power to cure, improve or preserve: *It's yet another health product claiming to be the elixir* ***of life/youth*** (= something to make you live longer/stay young).

Elizabethan /ɪˌlɪz.əˈbiː.θᵊn/ *adj* from the period when Queen Elizabeth I was the ruler of England (1558-1603)
Elizabethan /ɪˌlɪz.əˈbiː.θᵊn/ *noun* [C] a person living during this period: *Sir Francis Drake was a famous Elizabethan.*

elk /elk/ *noun* [C] *plural* **elks** or **elk** **1** a large deer with a lot of hair on its neck which lives in the forests of the northern US and Canada **2** *UK OLD-FASHIONED FOR* **moose** (= a large deer with large flat horns and a long nose)

ellipse /ɪˈlɪps/ *noun* [C] an oval; a flattened circle
elliptical /ɪˈlɪp.tɪ.kᵊl/ *adj* (*ALSO* **elliptic**) having an oval shape ➲See also **elliptical** at **ellipsis** LANGUAGE.

ellipsis [LANGUAGE] /ɪˈlɪp.sɪs/ *noun* [C or U] *plural* **ellipses** *SPECIALIZED* when words are left out of a sentence but the sentence can still be understood: *An example of ellipsis is "What percentage was left?" "Twenty"* (= 20 per cent).
elliptical /ɪˈlɪp.tɪ.kᵊl/ *adj FORMAL* Elliptical language has parts missing, so that it is sometimes difficult to understand: *His message was written in a deliberately elliptical style.* **elliptically** /ɪˈlɪp.tɪ.kli/ *adv*

ellipsis [PRINTED MARK] /ɪˈlɪp.sɪs/ *noun* [C] *plural* **ellipses** *SPECIALIZED* three dots in a printed text which show where one or more words have been intentionally omitted

elm /elm/ *noun* [C or U] a large tree which loses its leaves in winter, or the wood from this tree

El Nino /elˈniːn.jəʊ/ [US] /-joʊ/ *noun* [U] an unusual ocean current along the coast of Peru every 2-10 years, which kills large numbers of sea organisms and causes noticeable and often severe changes in weather conditions in many areas of the world: *the El Nino weather pattern/system/phenomenon* ○ *Rains came late to the region because of El Nino.*

elocution /ˌel.əˈkjuː.ʃᵊn/ *noun* [U] the art of careful public speaking, using clear pronunciation and good breathing to control the voice: *classes in elocution*

elongate /ˈiː.lɒŋ.geɪt/ [US] /ɪˈlɑːŋ-/ *verb* [I or T] to become or make something become longer, and often thinner: *The cells elongate as they take in water.*
elongated /ˈiː.lɒŋ.geɪ.tɪd/ [US] /ɪˈlɑːŋ.geɪ.t̬ɪd/ *adj* (*SPECIALIZED* **elongate**) longer and thinner than usual: *In the photo her face was slightly elongated.* **elongation** /ˌiː.lɒŋˈgeɪ.ʃᵊn/ [US] /ɪˌlɑːŋ-/ *noun* [U]

elope /ɪˈləʊp/ [US] /-ˈloʊp/ *verb* [I] to leave home secretly in order to get married without the permission of parents: *She eloped* ***with*** *an Army officer.* **elopement** /ɪˈləʊp.mənt/ [US] /-ˈloʊp-/ *noun* [C]

eloquent /ˈel.ə.kwᵊnt/ *adj* giving a clear, strong message: *She made an eloquent appeal for action before it was too late.* ○ *The pictures were an eloquent reminder of the power of the volcano.* **eloquently** /ˈel.ə.kwᵊnt.li/ *adv*: *He spoke eloquently.* **eloquence** /ˈel.ə.kwᵊnts/ *noun* [U] *She was renowned for her eloquence and beauty.*

else /els/ *adv* used after words beginning with any-, every-, no- and some-, or after how, what, where, who, why but not which, to mean other, another, different, additional: *Everybody else has* (= All the other people have) *agreed except for you.* ○ *If it doesn't work, try something else* (= something different). ○ *Let's go before they ask us to visit anyone else* (= another person). ○ *It's not my bag. It must be someone else's* (= it must belong to another person). ○ *The book isn't here. Where else* (= In what other place) *should I look?* ○ *He came to see you. Why else* (= For what other reason) *would he come?* ○ *After I'd thanked them I didn't know what else* (= what other things) *to say.*
• **or else 1** used to say what will happen if another thing does not happen: *We must be there by six, or else we'll miss the beginning.* **2** used to compare two different things or situations: *She's either really talkative and you can't shut her up or else she's silent.* **3** *INFORMAL* used as a threat, sometimes humorously: *He'd better find it quickly, or else* (= or I will punish him in some way)*!*

elsewhere /elsˈweəʳ/ [US] /-ˈwer/ /ˈ--/ *adv* at, in, from, or to another place or other places; anywhere or somewhere else: *The report looks at economic growth in Europe and elsewhere.* ○ *They couldn't find what they wanted and decided to look elsewhere.*

ELT /ˌiː.elˈtiː/ *noun* [U] *ABBREVIATION FOR* English Language Teaching: the teaching of English to speakers of other languages

elucidate /ɪˈluː.sɪ.deɪt/ *verb* [I or T] *FORMAL* to explain or make clear: *I don't understand. You'll have to elucidate.* ○ *The reasons for the change in weather conditions have been elucidated by several scientists.* **elucidation** /ɪˌluː.sɪˈdeɪ.ʃᵊn/ *noun* [U] *These figures need elucidation.*

elude [NOT ACHIEVE] /ɪˈluːd/ *verb* [T] *FORMAL* If something that you want eludes you, you do not succeed in achieving it: *The gold medal continues to elude her.* ○ *They had minor breakthroughs but real success eluded them.*

elude [NOT BE CAUGHT] /ɪˈluːd/ *verb* [T] to not be caught by someone: *They eluded the police by fleeing abroad.*

elude [NOT REMEMBER] /ɪˈluːd/ *verb* [T] FORMAL If a piece of information eludes you, you cannot remember it: *I know who you mean but her name eludes me.*

elusive /ɪˈluː.sɪv/ *adj* difficult to describe, find, achieve or remember: *The answers to these questions remain as elusive as ever.* ○ *Success, however, remained elusive for her.* ○ *elusive memories* **elusively** /ɪˈluː.sɪv.li/ *adv* **elusiveness** /ɪˈluː.sɪv.nəs/ *noun* [U]

elves /elvz/ *plural of* **elf**

em- /ɪm-/ /em-/ *prefix* ➲See at **en-** CAUSE.

'em /əm/ INFORMAL *short form of* them: *Tell 'em to go away.*

emaciated /ɪˈmeɪ.si.eɪ.tɪd/ [US] /-t̬ɪd/ *adj* FORMAL very thin and weak, usually because of illness or extreme hunger: *There were pictures of emaciated children on the cover of the magazine.* **emaciation** /ɪˌmeɪ.siˈeɪ.ʃᵊn/ *noun* [U]

email, e-mail /ˈiː.meɪl/ *noun* **1** [U] the system for using computers to send messages over the Internet: *You can contact us* ***by*** *email or fax.* ○ *What's your email* ***address****?* **2** [C] a message or document sent using this system: *I got an email from Danielle last week.*

email, e-mail /ˈiː.meɪl/ *verb* [T] to send an email to someone: *Email me when you've got time.* ○ [+ two objects] *Has he emailed you that list of addresses yet?*

emanate /ˈem.ə.neɪt/ *verb* [T] FORMAL to express a quality or feeling through the way that you look and behave: *Her face emanated sadness.* **emanation** /ˌem.əˈneɪ.ʃᵊn/ *noun* [C or U]

▲ **emanate from/through** ***sth/sb*** *phrasal verb* FORMAL to come out of or be produced by something or someone: *Angry voices emanated from the room.*

emancipated /ɪˈmænt.sɪ.peɪ.tɪd/ [US] /-t̬ɪd/ *adj* not limited socially or politically: *We live in more emancipated times.* ○ *The twenties and sixties are often regarded as the most emancipated decades.* **emancipate** /ɪˈmænt.sɪ.peɪt/ *verb* [T] **emancipation** /ɪˌmænt.sɪˈpeɪ.ʃᵊn/ *noun* [U] *women's/female emancipation* ○ *black emancipation*

emasculate /ɪˈmæs.kjʊ.leɪt/ *verb* [T] **1** FORMAL to weaken or to reduce the effectiveness of something: *They were accused of trying to emasculate the report's recommendations.* **2** FORMAL to make a man feel less male by taking away his power and confidence: *A lot of men would feel emasculated if they stayed at home while their wives went out to work.* **3** SPECIALIZED to remove the male parts of something **emasculation** /ɪˌmæs.kjʊˈleɪ.ʃᵊn/ *noun* [U] FORMAL

embalm /ɪmˈbɑːm/ *verb* [T] to use chemicals to prevent a dead body from decaying **embalmer** /ɪmˈbɑː.məʳ/ *noun* [C]

embankment /ɪmˈbæŋk.mənt/ *noun* [C] an artificial slope made of earth and/or stones: *a river/road/railway embankment*

embargo /ɪmˈbɑː.gəʊ/ [US] /-goʊ/ *noun* [C] *plural* **embargoes** an order to temporarily stop something, especially trading or giving information: *They have* ***put*** *an embargo* ***on*** *imports of clothing.* ○ *The police asked for a* ***news*** *embargo while they tried to find the kidnapper.*

embargo /ɪmˈbɑː.gəʊ/ [US] /-goʊ/ *verb* [T] **embargoing, embargoed, embargoed** to officially stop trading with another country: *They are planning to embargo oil imports.*

embark /ɪmˈbɑːk/ [US] /-bɑːrk/ *verb* [I] FORMAL to go onto a ship: *We embarked at Liverpool for New York.* * NOTE: The opposite is **disembark**. **embarkation** /ˌem.bɑːˈkeɪ.ʃᵊn/ [US] /-bɑːr-/ *noun* [C or U] *You'll be asked for those documents* ***on*** *embarkation.*

▲ **embark on/upon** ***sth*** *phrasal verb* to start something new or important: *We're embarking upon a new project later this year.*

embarrass /ɪmˈbær.əs/ [US] /-ˈber-/ *verb* [T] to cause someone to feel anxious or uncomfortable: *You're embarrassing him with your compliments!* ○ *I didn't want to embarrass her in front of her friends.*

embarrassed /ɪmˈbær.əst/ [US] /-ˈber-/ *adj* **1** feeling ashamed or shy: *She felt embarrassed* ***about*** *undressing in front of the doctor.* ○ [+ to infinitive] *I was too embarrassed to admit that I was scared.* **2** HUMOROUS **financially embarrassed** having no money

embarrassing /ɪmˈbær.ə.sɪŋ/ [US] /-ˈber-/ *adj* making you feel embarrassed: *an embarrassing situation* ○ *It's embarrassing* ***to*** *be caught telling a lie.* ○ *My most embarrassing moment was trying to introduce a woman whose name I couldn't remember.* **embarrassingly** /ɪmˈbær.ə.sɪŋ.li/ [US] /-ˈber-/ *adv*: *an embarrassingly poor performance/loud voice*

embarrassment /ɪmˈbær.ə.smənt/ [US] /-ˈber-/ *noun* [C or U] when you feel embarrassed, or something that makes you feel embarrassed: *She blushed with embarrassment.* ○ *My parents are* ***an*** *embarrassment* ***to*** *me!*

COMMON LEARNER ERROR

embarrass (spelling)

Many learners make mistakes when spelling this word. The correct spelling has 'rr' and 'ss'.

Oh, her jokes are so embarrassing!

COMMON LEARNER ERROR

embarrassing or **annoying?**

Someone or something that is **embarrassing** makes you feel uncomfortable and ashamed in front of other people. Something or someone that is annoying makes you feel slightly angry.

It's quite embarrassing when your child starts yelling in public.

Something or someone that is **annoying** makes you feel slightly angry.

There's nothing more annoying than missing a good film on TV.

~~*There's nothing more embarrassing than missing a good film on TV.*~~

• **an embarrassment of riches** FORMAL so many good things or people that it is impossible to decide which of them you want

embassy /ˈem.bə.si/ *noun* [C] **1** the group of people who represent their country in a foreign country: *We used to be friendly with some people who worked* ***at*** *the Swedish Embassy.* **2** the building that these people work in: *The Ambassador held a reception at the embassy.*

embattled /ɪmˈbæt.l̩d/ [US] /-ˈbæt̬-/ *adj* having a lot of problems or difficulties: *an embattled government* ○ *embattled teachers*

embed (-dd-), US ALSO **imbed** (-dd-) /ɪmˈbed/ *verb* [T] to fix something firmly into a substance

embedded, US ALSO **imbedded** /ɪmˈbed.ɪd/ *adj* **1** fixed into the surface of something: *The thorn was embedded* ***in*** *her thumb.* **2** If an emotion, attitude, etc. is embedded in someone or something, it is a very strong or important part of them: *A sense of guilt was deeply embedded* ***in*** *my conscience.*

embellish /ɪmˈbel.ɪʃ/ *verb* [T] to make something more beautiful or interesting by adding something to it: *The ceiling was embellished* ***with*** *flowers and leaves.* ○ *He couldn't resist embellishing the story of his accident a little.* **embellishment** /ɪmˈbel.ɪʃ.mənt/ *noun* [C or U]

ember /ˈem.bəʳ/ [US] /-bɚ/ *noun* [C usually pl] a piece of wood or coal, etc. which continues to burn after a fire has no more flames: *We sat by the* ***glowing/dying*** *embers of the fire.*

embezzle /ɪmˈbez.l̩/ *verb* [I or T] to secretly take money that is in your care or that belongs to an organization or business you work for: *She embezzled thousands of dollars* ***from*** *the charity.* **embezzlement** /ɪmˈbez.l̩.mənt/ *noun* [U] *They were arrested for embezzlement* ***of*** *company funds.* **embezzler** /ɪmˈbez.ləʳ/ [US] /-lɚ/ *noun* [C]

embittered /ɪmˈbɪt.əd/ [US] /-ˈbɪt̬.ɚd/ *adj* very angry about unfair things that have happened to you: *They ignored all her pleas and she became very embittered.* ○ *He died a disillusioned and embittered old man.* **embitter** /ɪmˈbɪt.əʳ/ [US] /-ˈbɪt̬.ɚ/ *verb* [T]

emblazon /ɪmˈbleɪ.zᵊn/ *verb* [T usually passive] (ALSO **blazon**) to print or decorate something in a very noticeable way: *Her name was emblazoned* ***across*** *the front of the theatre.* ○ *cars emblazoned* ***with*** *the company logo*

emblem /ˈem.bləm/ *noun* [C] a picture of an object which is used to represent a particular person, group or idea: *A rose is the national emblem* ***of*** *England.*

E

emblematic /ˌem.bləˈmæt.ɪk/ ⑥ /-ˈmæt̬-/ *adj FORMAL* representing a particular person, group or idea: *A sword is emblematic* ***of*** *power gained by violence.* **emblematically** /ˌem.bləˈmæt.ɪ.kli/ ⑥ /-ˈmæt̬-/ *adv*

embody /ɪmˈbɒd.i/ ⑥ /-ˈbɑː.di/ *verb* [T] *FORMAL* **1** to represent a quality or an idea exactly: *She embodied good sportsmanship on the playing field.* **2** to include as part of something: *Kennett embodied in one man an unusual range of science, music and religion.* **embodiment** /ɪmˈbɒd.ɪ.mənt/ ⑥ /-ˈbɑː.dɪ-/ *noun* **the embodiment of** *sth* someone or something that represents a quality or an idea exactly: *He was the embodiment of the English gentleman.* ○ *She was portrayed in the papers as the embodiment of evil.*

embolden /ɪmˈbəʊl.dᵊn/ ⑥ /-ˈboʊl-/ *verb* [T] *FORMAL* to make someone brave: *Emboldened by drink, he walked over to speak to her.*

embolism /ˈem.bə.lɪ.zᵊm/ *noun* [C] *SPECIALIZED* a bubble of air, a lump of hardened blood or a small piece of fat which causes a blockage in a tube carrying blood around the body

emboss /ɪmˈbɒs/ ⑥ /-ˈbɑːs/ *verb* [T] to decorate an object, especially with letters, using special tools which make a raised mark on its surface: *She handed me a business card with her name neatly embossed on it.*

embrace [HOLD] /ɪmˈbreɪs/ *verb* [I or T] *LITERARY* to hold someone tightly with both arms to express love, liking or sympathy, or when greeting or leaving someone: *She saw them embrace on the station platform.* ○ *He leant over to embrace the child.*

embrace [INCLUDE] /ɪmˈbreɪs/ *verb* [T] *FORMAL* to include something, often as one of a number of things: *Linguistics embraces a diverse range of subjects such as phonetics and stylistics.*

embrace [ACCEPT] /ɪmˈbreɪs/ *verb* [T] *FORMAL* to accept something enthusiastically: *This was an opportunity that he would embrace.*

embrocation /ˌem.brəʊˈkeɪ.ʃᵊn/ ⑥ /-broʊ-/ *noun* [C] *MAINLY UK FORMAL* a liquid that is rubbed onto the body to reduce pain or stiffness in muscles

embroider [DECORATE] /ɪmˈbrɔɪ.dəʳ/ ⑥ /-dɚ/ *verb* [I or T] to decorate cloth or clothing with patterns or pictures consisting of stitches that are sewn directly onto the material: *I am embroidering this picture for my mother.* **embroidery** /ɪmˈbrɔɪ.dᵊr.i/ ⑥ /-dɚ-/ *noun* [C or U] *Let me show you Pat's embroideries.* ○ *I'm no good at embroidery.*

embroider [ADD] /ɪmˈbrɔɪ.dəʳ/ ⑥ /-dɚ/ *verb* [I or T] to make a story more entertaining by adding imaginary details to it: *Naturally, I embroidered the tale a little to make it more interesting.* **embroidery** /ɪmˈbrɔɪ.dᵊr.i/ ⑥ /-dɚ-/ *noun* [U]

embroil /ɪmˈbrɔɪl/ *verb* [T] to cause someone to become involved in an argument or a difficult situation: [R] *She had no desire to embroil herself* ***in*** *lengthy lawsuits with the tabloid newspapers.* ○ *The United Nations was reluctant to get its forces embroiled* ***in*** *civil war.*

embryo /ˈem.bri.əʊ/ ⑥ /-oʊ/ *noun* [C] *plural* **embryos** an animal that is developing either in its mother's womb or in an egg, or a plant that is developing in a seed: *Between the eighth week of development and birth a human embryo is called a foetus.*
• **in embryo** *FORMAL* developing and not yet complete: *The department's plans for enlargement are still in embryo.* **embryonic** /ˌem.briˈɒn.ɪk/ ⑥ /-ˈɑː.nɪk/ *adj* **1** relating to an embryo **2** [usually before n] *FORMAL* starting to develop: *The project is still at an embryonic* ***stage.***

embryology /ˌem.briˈɒl.ə.dʒi/ ⑥ /-ˈɑː.lə-/ *noun* [U] the study of animal development between the FERTILIZATION of the egg and the time when the animal is born **embryologist** /ˌem.briˈɒl.ə.dʒɪst/ ⑥ /-ˈɑː.lə-/ *noun* [C]

emcee /emˈsiː/ *noun* [C], *verb* *US FOR* **MC** (= Master of Ceremonies)

emend /ɪˈmend/ *verb* [T] to correct or improve a text: *The text is currently being emended and will be published shortly.* **emendation** /ˌiː.menˈdeɪ.ʃᵊn/ *noun* [C or U]

emerald [STONE] /ˈem.ə.rᵊld/ *noun* [C or U] a bright green transparent precious stone which is often used in jewellery

emerald ('green) [COLOUR] *noun* [U] a bright green colour **emerald ('green)** *adj*: *emerald green eyes*

the Emerald 'Isle *noun* [S] *LITERARY* Ireland

emerge [APPEAR] /ɪˈmɜːdʒ/ ⑥ /-ˈmɝːdʒ/ *verb* [I] **1** to appear by coming out of something or out from behind something: *She emerged* ***from*** *the sea, blue with cold.* **2** to come to the end of a difficult period or experience: *The Prince emerged unscathed* ***from*** *the scandal.* **emergence** /ɪˈmɜː.dʒᵊnts/ ⑥ /-ˈmɝː-/ *noun* [U] the process of appearing: *The emergence of small Japanese cars in the 1970s challenged the US and European manufacturers.* **emerging** /ɪˈmɜː.dʒɪŋ/ ⑥ /-ˈmɝː-/ *adj* [before n] (*FORMAL* **emergent**) starting to exist: *Western governments should be giving more aid to the emerging democracies of the Third World.* ○ *emergent economies/markets*

emerge [BECOME KNOWN] /ɪˈmɜːdʒ/ ⑥ /-ˈmɝːdʒ/ *verb* [I] to become known, especially as a result of examination or questioning: *The facts behind the scandal are sure to emerge eventually.* ○ [+ that] *It has emerged* ***that*** *secret talks had been going on between the two companies before the takeover was announced.* ○ *She's the most exciting British singer to emerge on the pop scene for a decade.*

emergency /ɪˈmɜː.dʒᵊnt.si/ ⑥ /-ˈmɝː-/ *noun* [C or U] something dangerous or serious, such as an accident, which happens suddenly or unexpectedly and needs immediate action in order to avoid harmful results: *How much disabled people escape* ***in*** *an emergency? ○ Is the emergency* ***exit*** *suitable for wheelchairs? ○ The pilot of the aircraft was forced to make an emergency* ***landing*** *on Lake Geneva.*

e'mergency ,brake *noun US FOR* **handbrake** ⟳See picture **Car** on page Centre 12

e'mergency ,room *noun* (*ABBREVIATION* **ER**) *US FOR* **casualty** HOSPITAL

e,mergency 'services *plural noun MAINLY UK* the organizations that deal with accidents and urgent problems such as fire, illness or crime

emeritus /ɪˈmer.ɪ.təs/ ⑥ /-t̬əs/ *adj* [before or after n] no longer having a position, especially in a college or university, but keeping the title of the position: *She became Emeritus Professor of Linguistics when she retired.*

emery /ˈem.ᵊr.i/ ⑥ /-ɚ-/ *noun* [U] a very hard dark grey substance, usually in the form of a powder, which is used to smooth or shape things

'emery ,board *noun* [C] a thin piece of cardboard with a rough surface used to shape FINGERNAILS

emetic /ɪˈmet.ɪk/ ⑥ /-ˈmet̬-/ *noun* [C] *SPECIALIZED* a substance, especially a medicine, that causes vomiting **emetic** /ɪˈmet.ɪk/ ⑥ /-ˈmet̬-/ *adj*

emigrate /ˈem.ɪ.greɪt/ *verb* [I] to leave a country permanently and go to live in another one: *Millions of Germans emigrated* ***from*** *Europe to America in the nineteenth century.* ○ *How long ago did your parents emigrate?* **emigration** /ˌem.ɪˈgreɪ.ʃᵊn/ *noun* [C or U]

emigrant /ˈem.ɪ.grənt/ *noun* [C] a person who emigrates ⟳Compare **immigrant**.

émigré, emigré /ˈem.ɪ.greɪ/ *noun* [C] someone who has had to leave their country permanently, usually for political reasons

eminence [RESPECT] /ˈem.ɪ.nənts/ *noun* [U] the state of being famous, respected or important: *his eminence as a film director* **eminent** /ˈem.ɪ.nənt/ *adj* famous, respected or important: *an eminent historian*

Eminence [PRIEST] /ˈem.ɪ.nənts/ *noun* [C] the title of a CARDINAL (= priest of very high rank in the Roman Catholic Church)

eminently /ˈem.ɪ.nənt.li/ *adv FORMAL* very and obviously: *He is eminently qualified for the job.* ○ *an eminently readable book*

emir /emˈɪəʳ/ ⑥ /-ˈɪr/ *noun* [C] a ruler of particular Muslim countries in the Middle East: *the Emir of Kuwait*

emirate /ˈem.ɪ.rət/ *noun* [C] a country ruled by an emir

emissary /ˈem.ɪ.sᵊr.i/ ⑥ /-ser-/ *noun* [C] *FORMAL* a person sent by one government or political leader to another to deliver messages or to take part in discussions: *The*

Foreign Secretary has flown to China as the personal emissary of the Prime Minister.

emit /ɪ'mɪt/ *verb* [T] **-tt-** to send out a beam, noise, smell or gas: *The alarm emits infra-red rays which are used to detect any intruder.* ○ *The machine emits a high-pitched sound when you press the button.*

emission /ɪ'mɪʃ.ᵊn/ *noun* **1** [U] when gas, heat, light, etc. is sent out: *The Green Party have called for a substantial reduction in the emission of greenhouse gases by the UK.* **2** [C] an amount of gas, heat, light, etc. that is sent out: *The increased use of natural gas will help reduce carbon dioxide emissions.*

Emmy /'em.i/ *noun* [C] TRADEMARK one of a set of American prizes given each year to actors and other people involved in making television programmes: *She won this year's Emmy for best screenplay for a mini-series.*

emollient /ɪ'mɒl.i.ənt/ [US] /-'mɑː.li-/ *noun* [C] a cream or liquid which makes dry or sore skin softer or less painful

emollient /ɪ'mɒl.i.ənt/ [US] /-'mɑː.li-/ *adj* **1** helping dry, sore skin: *an emollient cream* **2** FORMAL calming and avoiding argument: *an emollient mood/tone*

emolument /ɪ'mɒl.jʊ.mənt/ [US] /-'mɑːl-/ *noun* [C] UK VERY FORMAL a payment in money or some other form that is made for work that has been done

emoticon /ɪ'məʊ.tɪ.kɒn/ [US] /ɪ'moʊ.t̬ɪ.kɑːn/ *noun* [C] (ALSO **smiley**) a sideways image of a face formed by keyboard symbols, which is used in emails to express a particular emotion

emotion /ɪ'məʊ.ʃᵊn/ [US] /-'moʊ-/ *noun* [C or U] a strong feeling such as love or anger, or strong feelings in general: *Like a lot of men, he finds it hard to express his emotions.* ○ *My mother was overcome with emotion and burst into tears.*

emotional /ɪ'məʊ.ʃᵊn.ᵊl/ [US] /-'moʊ-/ *adj* **1** relating to the emotions: *a child's emotional development* ○ *My doctor said the problem was more emotional than physical.* ○ *Amnesia can be caused by emotional trauma.* **2** having and expressing strong feelings: *He's a very emotional man.* ○ *I felt quite emotional during the wedding ceremony.* ○ *He became very emotional when I told him I was pregnant.* ○ *The President has made an emotional* (= full of emotion) *plea for the killing to stop.* **3 emotional blackmail** when someone tries to control your emotions in order to make you do something, especially by making you feel guilty

emotionally /ɪ'məʊ.ʃᵊn.ᵊl.i/ [US] /-'moʊ-/ *adv*: *She spoke emotionally about her experiences as a war correspondent.* ○ *Many children have become emotionally **disturbed** as a result of the abuse they have suffered.* ○ *an emotionally **charged*** (= causing strong feelings) *issue*

emotionalism /ɪ'məʊ.ʃᵊn.ᵊl.ɪ.zᵊm/ [US] /-'moʊ-/ *noun* [U] DISAPPROVING showing too much emotion

e,motional in'telligence *noun* [U] the ability to understand the way people feel and react and to use this skill to make good judgments and to avoid or solve problems: *Individuals with even a small degree of emotional intelligence are a dream to work for.*

emotionless /ɪ'məʊ.ʃᵊn.ləs/ [US] /-'moʊ-/ *adj* not showing emotion

emotive /ɪ'məʊ.tɪv/ [US] /-'moʊ.t̬ɪv/ *adj* causing strong feelings: *Animal experimentation is a highly emotive **issue**.* **emotively** /ɪ'məʊ.tɪv.li/ [US] /-'moʊ.t̬ɪv-/ *adv*

empanel (-ll- or US USUALLY -l-), **impanel** /ɪm'pæn.ᵊl/ *verb* [T] SPECIALIZED in a law court, to choose the people who will form the jury for a trial

empathy /'em.pə.θi/ *noun* [U] the ability to share someone else's feelings or experiences by imagining what it would be like to be in their situation ➲Compare **sympathy** UNDERSTANDING. **empathetic** /,em.pə'θet.ɪk/ [US] /-'θet̬-/ *adj*

empathize, UK USUALLY **-ise** /'em.pə.θaɪz/ *verb* [I] to be able to understand how someone else feels: *It's very easy to empathize **with** the characters in her books.* ➲Compare **sympathize** at **sympathy** UNDERSTANDING.

emperor /'em.pᵊr.əʳ/ [US] /-pɚ.ɚ/ *noun* [C] a male ruler of an empire ➲See also **empress**.

emphasize /'emp.fə.saɪz/ *verb* [T] **1** (UK USUALLY **-ise**) to show or state that something is particularly important or worth giving attention to: [+ question word] *I'd just like to emphasize **how** important it is for people to learn foreign languages.* ○ [+ that] *He emphasized **that** all the people taking part in the research were volunteers.* ○ *You can use italics or capitals to emphasize a word in a piece of writing.* **2** to make something more obvious: *Tight jeans will only emphasize any extra weight that you are carrying.*

emphasis /'emp.fə.sɪs/ *noun* [C or U] *plural* **emphases** **1** the particular importance or attention that you give to something: *I think we should put as much emphasis **on** preventing disease as we do on curing it.* ○ *Schools here **put/place/lay** great emphasis **on** written work and grammar.* **2** the extra force that you give to a word or part of a word when you are saying it: *The emphasis is **on** the final syllable.* ○ *Where do you **put** the emphasis in the word 'controversy'?*

emphatic /emp'fæt.ɪk/ [US] /-'fæt̬-/ *adj* done or said in a strong way and without any doubt: *Poland reached the final of the championship yesterday with an emphatic 5-0 **victory** over Italy.* ○ *The minister has issued an emphatic rejection of the accusation.* **emphatically** /emp'fæt.ɪ.kli/ [US] /-'fæt̬-/ *adv*: *Johnson has emphatically denied the allegations against him.*

emphysema /,emp.fə'siː.mə/ *noun* [U] a condition in which the small bags in the lungs become filled with too much air, causing breathing difficulties and heart problems: *Heavy cigarette smoking often causes emphysema.*

empire [COUNTRIES] /'em.paɪəʳ/ [US] /-paɪr/ *noun* [C] a group of countries ruled by a single person, government or country: *the Holy Roman Empire* ➲See also **imperial** EMPIRE.

empire [ORGANIZATION] /'em.paɪəʳ/ [US] /-paɪr/ *noun* [C] a very large and important business or organization: *In the space of just ten years, her company has grown from one small shop to a multi-million-pound empire.*

empirical /ɪm'pɪr.ɪ.kᵊl/ *adj* based on what is experienced or seen rather than on theory: *This theory needs to be backed up with solid empirical **data/evidence**.* ○ *Empirical **studies** show that some forms of alternative medicine are extremely effective.* **empirically** /ɪm'pɪr.ɪ.kli/ *adv*

empiricism /ɪm'pɪr.ɪ.sɪ.zᵊm/ *noun* [U] the belief in using empirical methods **empiricist** /ɪm'pɪr.ɪ.sɪst/ *noun* [C]

emplacement /ɪm'pleɪ.smənt/ *noun* [C] SPECIALIZED a position specially prepared for large pieces of military equipment

employ [PROVIDE JOB] /ɪm'plɔɪ/ *verb* [T] to have someone work or do a job for you and pay them for it: *How many people does your company employ?* ○ *Can't we employ someone **as** an assistant to help with all this paperwork?* ○ [+ to infinitive] *We've employed a market researcher **to** find out what people really want from a cable TV system.* ○ *More people are now employed in service industries than in manufacturing.*

employ /ɪm'plɔɪ/ *noun* FORMAL **be in sb's employ** to be working for someone

employable /ɪm'plɔɪ.ə.bl̩/ *adj* having enough skills and abilities for someone to employ you: *Computer skills make you far more employable.*

employee /ɪm'plɔɪ.iː/ /,--'-/ *noun* [C] someone who is paid to work for someone else: *The number of employees in the company has trebled over the past decade.* ○ *She's a former council employee/employee of the council.*

employer /ɪm'plɔɪ.əʳ/ [US] /-ɚ/ *noun* [C] a person or organization that employs people: *We need a reference from your former employer.*

employment /ɪm'plɔɪ.mənt/ *noun* [S or U] **1** when someone is paid to work for a company or organization: *Employment levels are unlikely to rise significantly before the end of next year.* ○ *How long have you been looking for employment?* **2** FORMAL **be in employment** to have a job: *Are you in employment at the moment?*

employ [USE] /ɪm'plɔɪ/ *verb* [T] FORMAL to use something: *Sophisticated statistical analysis was employed to obtain these results.*

E

employment /ɪm'plɔɪ.mənt/ *noun* [U] *FORMAL* use: *How can you justify the employment **of** capital punishment?*

employ [SPEND TIME] /ɪm'plɔɪ/ *verb FORMAL* **be employed in doing *sth*** to spend time doing something: *He was busily employed in lacing up his shoes.*

em'ployment ˌagency *noun* [C] a business that finds suitable people to work for other businesses

emporium /ɪm'pɔː.ri.əm/ [US] /-pɔːr.i-/ *noun* [C] *plural* **emporia** or **emporiums** *OLD-FASHIONED* a large shop selling a large range of goods, or a shop selling a particular type of goods: *a video/ice cream/antiques emporium*

empower /ɪm'paʊəʳ/ [US] /-'paʊr/ *verb* [T] to give someone official authority or the freedom to do something: [+ *to* infinitive] *This amendment empowers the president **to** declare an emergency for a wide range of reasons.* ○ *The first step in empowering the poorest sections of society is making sure they vote.*

empowering /ɪm'paʊə.rɪŋ/ [US] /-'paur.ɪŋ/ *adj* Something that is empowering makes you more confident and makes you feel you are in control of your life: *For me, learning to drive was an empowering experience.*

empowerment /ɪm'paʊə.mənt/ [US] /-'paʊr-/ *noun* [U]

empress /'em.prəs/ *noun* [C] a female ruler of an empire, or the wife of a male ruler of an empire ➲See also **emperor**.

empty [NOTHING IN] /'emp.ti/ *adj* not containing any things or people: *an empty house/street* ○ *Shall I take the empty bottles for recycling?* ○ *The train was empty* (= There were no passengers) *by the time it reached London.*

• **on an empty stomach** without eating anything: *You shouldn't go to work on an empty stomach.*

empty /'emp.ti/ *verb* **1** [T] to remove everything from inside something: *I emptied the closet and put my belongings into the black overnight case.* ○ *Would you mind emptying **(out)** your pockets?* ○ *Empty the soup **into** a saucepan and simmer gently for ten minutes.* ○ *She quickly emptied her glass* (= drank its contents) *and ordered another drink.* **2** [I] to become empty: *The place emptied pretty quickly when the fight started.*

▲ **empty into *sth*** *phrasal verb* If a river empties into a larger area of water, the water from it flows into that larger area: *The River Tees empties into the North Sea.*

empty /'emp.ti/ *noun* [C usually pl] an empty drinks bottle: *Don't forget to take the empties to the bottle bank.*

emptily /'emp.tɪ.li/ *adv*

emptiness /'emp.tɪ.nəs/ *noun* [U] empty space: *He gazed out over the emptiness of the moors.*

empty [NOT SINCERE] /'emp.ti/ *adj* [usually before n] not sincere or without any real meaning: *empty threats/rhetoric* ○ *They're just empty **promises**.* **emptiness** /'emp.tɪ.nəs/ *noun* [U]

empty [WITHOUT PURPOSE] /'emp.ti/ *adj* without purpose or interest: *He says his life has been completely empty since his wife died.* ○ *I felt empty, like a part of me had died.* **emptiness** *noun* [U] *I was left with a horrible feeling of emptiness.*

ˌempty 'calories *plural noun* energy obtained from food containing no NUTRIENTS (= substances which help you to be healthy)

empty-handed /ˌemp.ti'hæn.dɪd/ *adj* [after v] without bringing or taking anything: *We can't go to the party empty-handed.*

empty-headed /ˌemp.ti'hed.ɪd/ *adj* [after v] silly, foolish or lacking good judgment

the ˌEM'S [MONEY] *noun* [S] *ABBREVIATION FOR* the European Monetary System: a system for limiting changes in the values of the different types of money used in countries in the European Union ➲Compare **ECU**; **EMU**.

EMS [TELEPHONE] /ˌiː.em'es/ *noun* [U] *ABBREVIATION FOR* enhanced messaging service: a system for sending text messages from one MOBILE PHONE (= a telephone that you can carry with you) to another

emu /'iː.mjuː/ *noun* [C] *plural* **emu** or **emus** a large Australian bird with a long neck and grey or brown feathers, which cannot fly but has long legs and can run quickly: *Emus grow to almost two metres and can run at nearly 50 kph.*

EMU /ˌiː.em'juː/ *noun* [U] *ABBREVIATION FOR* European Monetary Union: the process within the European Union which is intended to result in a united economic system ➲Compare **ECU**; **EMS**.

emulate /'em.jʊ.leɪt/ *verb* [T] *FORMAL* to copy something achieved by someone else and try to do it as well as they have: *They hope to emulate the success of other software companies.* ○ *Fitzgerald is keen to emulate Martin's record of three successive world titles.* **emulation** /ˌem.jʊ'leɪ.ʃᵊn/ *noun* [C or U]

emulsion /ɪ'mʌl.ʃᵊn/ *noun* [C or U] **1** a mixture that results when one liquid is added to another and is mixed with it but does not dissolve into it: *Mixing oil and vinegar together produces an emulsion.* **2** a water-based paint which is not shiny when dry: *emulsion paint*

emulsify /ɪ'mʌl.sɪ.faɪ/ *verb* [I or T] If two liquids emulsify or are emulsified, they combine and become a smooth mixture.

emulsifier /ɪ'mʌl.sɪ.faɪ.əʳ/ [US] /-ɚ/ *noun* [C] a substance which forms or preserves an emulsion and is often added to processed foods to prevent particular parts separating

en- [CAUSE], /ɪn-/ /en-/ *BEFORE B OR P* **em-** /ɪm-/ em-/ *prefix* **1** used to form verbs which mean to put into or onto something: *encase* ○ *encircle* ○ *endanger* **2** used to form verbs which mean to cause to be something: *enable* ○ *endear* ○ *enlarge* ○ *enrich* **3** used to form verbs which mean to provide with something: *empower*

-en [INCREASE] /-ᵊn/ *suffix* used to form verbs which mean to increase the stated quality: *Sweeten to taste with honey or brown sugar.* ○ *I've had to loosen my belt.*

enable /ɪ'neɪ.bl̩/ *verb* [T] to make someone able to do something, or to make something possible: [+ *to* infinitive] *Computerization should enable us **to** cut production costs by half.*

enabled /ɪ'neɪ.bl̩d/ *adj, suffix* **1** provided with a particular type of equipment or technology, or having the necessary or correct system, device or arrangement to use it: *WAP-enabled mobile phones* ○ *Their aim is to make sure that every home and business becomes **Internet** enabled in the next 10 years.* **2** operated or made possible by the use of a particular thing: *voice-enabled software*

enabler /ɪ'neɪ.bləʳ/ [US] /-blɚ/ *noun* [C] a person or organization that allows other people to do things themselves instead of doing things for them

enact [MAKE LAW] /ɪ'nækt/ *verb* [T often passive] *SPECIALIZED* to put something into action, especially to change something into a law: *A package of economic sanctions is to be enacted against the country.* **enactment** /ɪ'nækt.mənt/ *noun* [C or U]

enact [PERFORM] /ɪ'nækt/ *verb* [T] *FORMAL* to perform a story or play: *The stories are enacted using music, dance and mime.* **enactment** /ɪ'nækt.mənt/ *noun* [C or U]

enamel /ɪ'næm.ᵊl/ *noun* **1** [C or U] a glass-like substance used for decoration or protection which is melted onto clay, metal and glass objects and then left to cool and harden, or an object covered with this substance **2** a type of paint which forms a shiny surface when dry **3** the hard white shiny substance which forms the covering of a tooth

enamel /ɪ'næm.ᵊl/ *verb* [T] **-ll-** or *US USUALLY* **-l-** to cover something with enamel

enamoured *UK, US* **enamored** /ɪ'næm.əd/ [US] /-ɚd/ *adj* [after v] *FORMAL* liking a lot: *I have to say I'm not exactly enamoured **with/of** this part of the country.*

en bloc /ˌɒ̃'blɒk/ [US] /ˌɑ̃ː'blɑːk/ *adv FORMAL* all together in a united group: *The ruling committee resigned en bloc to make way for a new election.*

encampment /ɪn'kæmp.mənt/ *noun* [C] a group of tents or temporary shelters put in one place: *Many people are living in encampments around the city with no electricity or running water.*

encamp *MAINLY UK* /ɪn'kæmp/ *verb* [I or T] (*US USUALLY* **camp**) *FORMAL* to make an encampment or put someone in an encampment

encapsulate /ɪn'kæp.sjʊ.leɪt/ *verb* [T] to express or show the most important facts about something: *It was very difficult to encapsulate the story of the revolution **in** a* *single one-hour documentary.* ○ *She encapsulates the stereotyped image that the British have of Americans.* **encapsulation** /ɪnˌkæp.sjʊˈleɪ.ʃən/ *noun* [C or U]

encase /ɪnˈkeɪs/ *verb* [T] to cover or enclose something or someone completely: *The nuclear waste is encased* ***in*** *concrete before being sent for storage in disused mines.*

-ence [ACTION], **-ance** /-ənts/ *suffix* used to form nouns which refer to an action or series of actions: *violence* (= violent actions) ○ *a performance* (= act of performing)

-ence [STATE], **-ance** /-ənts/ *suffix* used to form nouns which describe a state or quality: *her long absence* (= period during which she was absent)

enchant [PLEASE] /ɪnˈtʃɑːnt/ [US] /-ˈtʃænt/ *verb* [T] to charm or please someone greatly: *The audience was clearly enchanted by her performance.*
enchanting /ɪnˈtʃɑː.nɪŋ/ [US] /-ˈtʃæn.t̬ɪŋ/ *adj* very pleasant: *It's described in the guide book as 'an enchanting medieval city'.* **enchantment** /ɪnˈtʃɑːnt.mənt/ [US] /-ˈtʃænt-/ *noun* [C or U]

enchant [MAGIC] /ɪnˈtʃɑːnt/ [US] /-ˈtʃænt/ *verb* [T] to have a magical effect on someone or something
enchanted /ɪnˈtʃɑːn.tɪd/ [US] /-ˈtʃæn.t̬ɪd/ *adj* affected by magic or seeming to be affected by magic: *They met in Paris one enchanted afternoon in early autumn.* **enchanter** /ɪnˈtʃɑːn.təʳ/ [US] /-ˈtʃæn.t̬ɚ/ *noun* [C] **enchantment** /ɪnˈtʃɑːnt.mənt/ [US] /-ˈtʃænt-/ *noun* [C or U] *spells and enchantments*
enchantress /ɪnˈtʃɑːn.trəs/ [US] /-ˈtʃæn-/ *noun* [C] **1** a woman with magical powers **2** LITERARY an extremely attractive and interesting woman

enchilada /ˌen.tʃɪˈlɑː.də/ *noun* [C] a type of food originally from Mexico consisting of a thin pancake that is fried, filled with meat and covered with a very spicy sauce

encircle /ɪnˈsɜː.kl̩/ [US] /-ˈsɝː-/ *verb* [T] to surround something, forming a circle around it: *The house is encircled by a high fence.* ○ *Villaverde is one of the high-rise districts that encircle Madrid.*

enclave /ˈeŋ.kleɪv/ [US] /ˈɑːŋ-/ *noun* [C] a part of a country that is surrounded by another country, or a group of people who are different from the people living in the surrounding area: *Campione d'Italia is an Italian enclave in Switzerland.*

enclose [SURROUND] /ɪnˈkləʊz/ [US] /-ˈkloʊz/ *verb* [T] to surround: *The park that encloses the monument has recently been enlarged.*
enclosed /ɪnˈkləʊzd/ [US] /-ˈkloʊzd/ *adj* surrounded by walls, objects or structures: *He doesn't like enclosed spaces.*
enclosure /ɪnˈkləʊ.ʒəʳ/ [US] /-ˈkloʊ.ʒɚ/ *noun* **1** [C] an enclosed area: *the members enclosure* **2** [C or U] when people enclose land: *An early example of privatization was the enclosure* ***of*** *public land for private use by wealthy landlords.*

enclose [SEND] /ɪnˈkləʊz/ [US] /-ˈkloʊz/ *verb* [T] to send something in the same envelope or parcel as something else: *Please enclose a curriculum vitae with your letter of application.* ○ FORMAL *Please find enclosed a cheque in settlement of your invoice.*
enclosure /ɪnˈkləʊ.ʒəʳ/ [US] /-ˈkloʊ.ʒɚ/ *noun* [C] something that is put in the same envelope or parcel as something else

encode /ɪnˈkəʊd/ [US] /-ˈkoʊd/ *verb* **1** [T often passive] to change something into a system for sending messages secretly, or to represent complicated information in a simple or brief way: *Many satellite broadcasts are encoded so that they can only be received by people who have paid to see them.* ○ *Some music CDs are now encoded with information about the performers and their music.* **2** [I or T] SPECIALIZED to use a word or phrase in a foreign language in the correct way: *Grammatical information helps learners to encode sentences.* ➲Compare **decode**.

encompass /ɪnˈkʌm.pəs/ *verb* [T] FORMAL to include, especially a variety of things: *The festival is to encompass everything from music, theatre and ballet to literature, cinema and the visual arts.*

encore /ˈɒŋ.kɔːʳ/ [US] /ˈɑːŋ.kɔːr/ *noun* [C] an extra song or piece of music that is performed at the end of a show because the audience shout for it: *We were shouting for an encore.* ○ *They did old hits* ***as/for*** *an encore.*
Encore! /ˈɒŋ.kɔːʳ/ [US] /ˈɑːŋ.kɔːr/ *exclamation* shouted at the end of a performance to get the performer to sing or play more

encounter [EXPERIENCE] /ɪnˈkaʊn.təʳ/ [US] /-t̬ɚ/ *verb* [T] to experience, especially something unpleasant: *When did you first encounter these difficulties?* ○ *The army is reported to be encountering considerable resistance.*

encounter [MEET] /ɪnˈkaʊn.təʳ/ [US] /-t̬ɚ/ *verb* [T] FORMAL to meet someone unexpectedly: *On their way home, they encountered a woman selling flowers.*
encounter /ɪnˈkaʊn.təʳ/ [US] /-t̬ɚ/ *noun* [C] **1** a meeting, especially one that happens by chance: *I had a rather alarming encounter* ***with*** *a wild pig.* ○ *This meeting will be the first encounter* ***between*** *the party leaders since the election.* **2** an occasion when people have sex, usually with someone they have not met before **3** an occasion when two teams play against each other: *In their last encounter* ***with*** *Italy, England won 3-2.*

encourage /ɪnˈkʌr.ɪdʒ/ [US] /-ˈkɝː-/ *verb* [T] **1** to make someone more likely to do something, or to make something more likely to happen: [+ *to* infinitive] *We were encouraged* ***to*** *learn foreign languages at school.* ○ *The council is encouraging the development of the property for both employment and recreation.* **2** to talk or behave in a way that gives someone confidence to do something: *They've always encouraged me* ***in*** *everything I've wanted to do.*
encouraged /ɪnˈkʌr.ɪdʒd/ [US] /-ˈkɝː-/ *adj* [after v] having more confidence or hope about something: *She felt encouraged by their promise of support.*
encouraging /ɪnˈkʌr.ɪ.dʒɪŋ/ [US] /-ˈkɝː-/ *adj* making you feel more confidence or hope: *There was a lot of positive feedback which was very encouraging.* **encouragingly** /ɪnˈkʌr.ɪ.dʒɪŋ.li/ [US] /-ˈkɝː-/ *adv*: *My mother smiled encouragingly at me as I went up on stage.*
encouragement /ɪnˈkʌr.ɪdʒ.mənt/ [US] /-ˈkɝː-/ *noun* [C or U] **1** when someone talks or behaves in a way that gives you confidence to do something: *Children need lots of encouragement from their parents.* ○ *I could never have achieved this without the encouragement* ***of*** *my husband and family.* **2** words or behaviour that make something more likely to happen: *The armed forces are now* ***giving*** *positive encouragement to applications from Asians and black people.*

encroach /ɪnˈkrəʊtʃ/ [US] /-ˈkroʊtʃ/ *verb*
▲ **encroach on/upon *sth*** *phrasal verb* **1** to gradually take away someone else's rights, or to take control of someone's time, work, etc: *What the government is proposing encroaches on the rights of individuals.* ○ *I resent it that my job is starting to encroach on my family life.* **2** to gradually cover more and more of an area of land: *They have promised that the development will not encroach on public land.*
encroachment /ɪnˈkrəʊtʃ.mənt/ [US] /-ˈkroʊtʃ-/ *noun* [C or U] *The new censorship laws are serious encroachments* ***on*** *freedom of expression.*

encrustation /ˌɪn.krʌsˈteɪ.ʃən/ *noun* [C] US FOR **incrustation**

encrusted /ɪnˈkrʌs.tɪd/ *adj* covered with something hard or decorative: *She arrived home with her knees encrusted* ***with*** *mud.* ○ *The manuscript is bound in gold and silver and encrusted* ***with*** *jewels.*

encrypt /ɪnˈkrɪpt/ *verb* [T usually passive] to change electronic information or signals into a secret CODE (= system of letters, numbers or symbols) that people cannot understand or use on normal equipment: *Your financial information is fully encrypted and cannot be accessed.* **encryption** /ɪnˈkrɪp.ʃən/ *noun* [U]

encumber /ɪnˈkʌm.bəʳ/ [US] /-bɚ/ *verb* [T] FORMAL to weigh someone or something down, or to make it difficult for someone to do something: *Today, thankfully, women tennis players are not encumbered* ***with/by*** *long, heavy skirts and high-necked blouses.* **encumbrance** /ɪnˈkʌm.brənts/ *noun* [C] *When you're walking 30 miles a day, the fewer encumbrances the better.*

-ency, **-ancy** /-ənt.si/ *suffix* used to form nouns showing a state or quality: *her long presidency* (= time during which she was President) ○ *a difficult pregnancy* (= time during which a woman is pregnant)

encyclopedia, encyclopaedia /ɪnˌsaɪ.kləˈpiː.di.ə/ *noun* [C] a book or set of books containing many articles arranged in alphabetical order which deal either with the whole of human knowledge or with a particular part of it: *The Cambridge Encyclopedia of Language*
encyclopedic, encyclopaedic /ɪnˌsaɪ.kləˈpiː.dɪk/ *adj* **1** containing a lot of information **2** covering a large range of knowledge, often in great detail: *her encyclopedic knowledge of France*

E

end [LAST POINT] /end/ *noun* **1** [C] the point in space or time beyond which something no longer exists, or a part of something that includes this point: *This cable should have a plug* ***at*** *one end and a socket at the other.* ○ *We damaged* ***the*** *end* ***of*** *the piano when we moved it.* ○ *Get to* ***the*** *end* ***of*** *the queue and wait your turn like everyone else.* ○ *Is it safe to stand the computer on (its) end?* ○ *The end of the film was much more exciting than I'd expected.* ○ *This latest injury must surely mean that her tennis career is now* ***at an*** *end* (= finished). ○ *The statement said there would be* ***no*** *end* ***to*** *the violence until the terrorists' demands were met.* **2** [S] POLITE WORD FOR death: *We were all by her bedside when the end finally* ***came.*** ○ *He* ***met his*** *end* (= died) *in a shoot-out with the police.* **3** [C] either of the two halves of a sports field: *The teams change ends at half-time so that neither side has an unfair advantage.* **4** [C] US one of the two players in American football who begin play furthest from the ball
• **in the end** finally, after something has been thought about or discussed a lot: *We were thinking about going to Switzerland, but in the end we went to Austria.*
• **no end** very much: *It would please Granny no end if you wrote to her occasionally.*
• **no end of** ***sth*** a lot of: *If you don't want the job, there's no end of people willing to take your place.*
• **for hours/days, etc. on end** for hours, days, etc. without stopping: *He used to lock himself in his bedroom for hours on end and refuse to talk to anyone.*
• **come to an end** to finish: *Everyone wishes the war would come to an end soon.*
• **keep/hold** ***your*** **end up** UK to continue to deal with difficulties bravely and successfully
• **make ends meet** to have just enough money to pay for the things that you need
• **put an end to** ***sth*** to make something stop happening or existing: *How can we put an end to the fighting?*
• **at the end of the day** UK something that you say before you give the most important fact of a situation: *Of course I'll listen to what she has to say but at the end of the day, it's my decision.*
• **the end of the line/road** the point where it is no longer possible to continue with a process or activity: *We've struggled on for as long as we could, but now we're* ***at*** *the end of the line.* ○ *When the bank refused to lend us any more money we realised we'd* ***reached*** *the end of the road.*
• **end of story** INFORMAL something you say when you think that the opinion you have just expressed about something is correct and that there is no other way of thinking about it: *This woman is innocent – end of story.*
• **not be the end of the world** INFORMAL If something is not the end of the world, it will not cause very serious problems: *I'm really hoping to win, but it won't be the end of the world if I don't.*

end /end/ *verb* [I or T] to finish or stop, or to make something finish or stop: *When is your meeting due to end?* ○ *Her resignation ends months of speculation about her future.* ○ *Their marriage ended in 1991.* ○ *The match ended* ***in*** *a draw.* ○ *I'd like to end* ***with*** *a song from my first album.* ○ *She ended her speech on an optimistic note.*
• **end it all** USUALLY HUMOROUS to kill yourself: *And if this doesn't work, I'm just going to end it all.*
ending /ˈen.dɪŋ/ *noun* [C] **1** the last part of a story: *People want love stories with* ***happy*** *endings.* **2** a part added to the end of a word: *To make the plural of 'dog', you add the plural ending '-s'.*
endless /ˈend.ləs/ *adj* never finishing or seeming never to finish: *We used to have endless arguments about politics.* ○ *He seems to think that I have an endless supply of money.* ○ *The possibilities are endless.* **endlessly** /ˈend.ləs.li/ *adv*: *I find myself endlessly repeating the same phrases.*

end [SMALL PART] /end/ *noun* [C] a small unwanted part of something that is left after most of it has been used: *The floor was covered in cigarette ends.*

end [AIM] /end/ *noun* [C] an aim, intention or purpose: *Do you have a particular end in mind?*
• **to this end** with this aim: *He wanted science students to take an interest in the arts, and to this end he ran literature classes at his home on Sunday afternoons.*
• **The end justifies the means.** SAYING said about a situation in which the final aim is so important that any way of achieving it is acceptable

end [TYPE OF ACTIVITY] /end/ *noun* [S] **1** INFORMAL the parts of a task or process connected with one particular type of activity or person: *Rick's more involved with the financial end* ***of things.*** **2** **sb's end of the bargain/deal, etc.** the area of activity for which someone is responsible: *We've kept our end of the deal – let's see if they keep theirs.*
▲ **end up** *phrasal verb* to finally be in a particular place or situation: *They're travelling across Europe by train and are planning to end up* ***in*** *Moscow.* ○ *Much of this meat will probably end up* ***as*** *dog food.* ○ [L] *She'll end up penniless if she carries on spending like that.* ○ [+ v-ing] *After working her way around the world, she ended up teach****ing*** *English as a foreign language.*

endanger /ɪnˈdeɪn.dʒəʳ/ Ⓤⓢ /-dʒɚ/ *verb* [T] to put someone or something at risk or in danger of being harmed, damaged or destroyed: *He would never do anything to endanger the lives of his children.* ○ *We must be careful not to do anything that might endanger the economic recovery.*
endangered /ɪnˈdeɪn.dʒəd/ Ⓤⓢ /-dʒɚd/ *adj* **endangered birds/plants/species** animals or plants which may soon not exist because there are very few now alive

endear /ɪnˈdɪəʳ/ Ⓤⓢ /-dɪr/ *verb*
▲ **endear** ***sb*** **to** ***sb*** *phrasal verb* to cause someone to be liked by someone: [R] *She is unlikely to endear herself to her colleagues with such an aggressive approach.*
endearing /ɪnˈdɪə.rɪŋ/ Ⓤⓢ /-ˈdɪr.ɪŋ/ *adj* making someone like you: *She laughs at herself a lot which is always endearing.* **endearingly** /ɪnˈdɪə.rɪŋ.li/ Ⓤⓢ /-ˈdɪr.ɪŋ-/ *adv* **endearment** /ɪnˈdɪə.mənt/ Ⓤⓢ /-ˈdɪr-/ *noun* [C or U]

endeavour UK, US **endeavor** /enˈdev.əʳ/ Ⓤⓢ /-ɚ/ *verb* [I + to infinitive] to try to do something: *Engineers are endeavouring* ***to*** *locate the source of the problem.*
endeavour UK, US **endeavor** /enˈdev.əʳ/ Ⓤⓢ /-ɚ/ *noun* [C or U] an attempt to do something: *In spite of our best endeavours, it has proven impossible to contact her.* ○ *Crossing the North Pole on foot was an amazing feat of human endeavour.* ○ *artistic endeavour*

endemic /enˈdem.ɪk/ *adj* especially of a disease or a condition, regularly found and very common among a particular group or in a particular area: *Malaria is endemic* ***in*** *many of the hotter regions of the world.* ○ *The disease is endemic* ***among*** *British sheep/****to*** *many British flocks.* ○ *There is endemic* ***racism/poverty/violence*** *in many of the country's cities.*

endgame /ˈend.geɪm/ *noun* [C usually sing] the last stage of a process, especially one involving discussion: *A fevered diplomatic endgame is now under way to find a peaceful solution to the crisis.*

endive /ˈen.daɪv/ *noun* [C or U] **1** UK a plant with curly green leaves which are eaten raw in salads **2** US FOR **chicory**

endless /ˈend.ləs/ *adj* ➲See at **end** LAST POINT

endocrine gland /ˈen.də.kraɪnˌglænd/ *noun* [C] (ALSO **ductless gland**) SPECIALIZED any of the organs of the body, such as the PITUITARY GLAND or the OVARIES, which produce and release hormones into the blood to be carried around the body

end-of-season *adj* [before n] describes a sports event which happens at the end of a SEASON (= the part of a year in which sport is played): *the end-of-season play-offs*

end-of-terrace /ˌend.əvˈter.əs/ *adj* [before n] UK describes a house at the end of a row of similar houses which are joined together

endorphin /enˈdɔː.fɪn/ Ⓤⓢ /-ˈdɔːr-/ *noun* [C] SPECIALIZED a chemical naturally released in the brain to reduce pain, and which in large amounts can make you feel relaxed and/or energetic

endorse SUPPORT /ɪnˈdɔːs/ ⓤ /-ˈdɔːrs/ *verb* [T] **1** to make a public statement of your approval or support for something or someone: *The National Executive is expected to endorse these recommendations.* ○ FORMAL *I fully endorse* (= agree with) *everything the Chairperson has said.* **2** to appear in an advertisement, saying that you use and like a particular product: *They paid $2 million to the world champion to endorse their new aftershave.* **endorsement** /ɪnˈdɔːsmənt/ ⓤ /-ˈdɔːr-/ *noun* [C or U]

endorse GIVE PERMISSION /ɪnˈdɔːs/ ⓤ /-ˈdɔːrs/ *verb* [T] to write something in order to give permission for something, especially your signature on the back of a cheque, in order to make it able to be paid to someone else **endorsement** /ɪnˈdɔːsmənt/ ⓤ /-ˈdɔːr-/ *noun* [U]

endorse PUNISH /ɪnˈdɔːs/ ⓤ /-ˈdɔːrs/ *verb* [T] UK to officially record on a DRIVING LICENCE that the driver has been found guilty of driving in an illegal way **endorsement** /ɪnˈdɔːsmənt/ ⓤ /-ˈdɔːr-/ *noun* [C] *He's got a couple of endorsements **on** his licence already.*

endoscope /ˈen.dəʊˌskəʊp/ ⓤ /-doʊˌskoʊp/ *noun* [C] SPECIALIZED a long thin medical device which is used to examine the hollow organs of the body such as the lungs **endoscopy** /enˈdɒs.kə.pi/ ⓤ /-ˈdɑː.skə-/ *noun* [C or U] SPECIALIZED a medical examination of a hollow organ of the body

endow /ɪnˈdaʊ/ *verb* [T] to give a large amount of money to pay for creating a college or hospital, etc. or to provide an income for it: *The state of Michigan has endowed three institutes to do research for industry.* ○ *This hospital was endowed by the citizens of Strasbourg in the 16th century.*

• **be endowed with** *sth* to have a particular quality or feature: *Some lucky people are endowed with both brains and beauty.* ○ *Sardinia is generously endowed with prehistoric sites.* ⊃See also **well-endowed**.

endowment /ɪnˈdaʊ.mənt/ *noun* **1** [C or U] money that is given to a college or hospital, etc. in order to provide it with an income, or the giving of this money: *The school has received an endowment of £50 000 to buy new books for the library.* **2** [C] something that you have from birth, often a quality: *There are tests which can establish a baby's genetic endowment.*

en,dowment 'mortgage *noun* [C] an arrangement in which you have an ENDOWMENT POLICY which provides the money you need in order to buy a house

en,dowment 'policy *noun* [C] an agreement where you pay money regularly so that you will receive a large agreed sum of money at an agreed later date or when you die

'end ,product *noun* [C usually sing] something that is produced by an activity, especially by an industrial process: *Every stage of production from obtaining raw materials to recycling end products is monitored for its environmental effects.*

,end re'sult *noun* [C usually sing] a result of a series of events or a long process: *The end result of these changes will be more bureaucracy and fewer resources.*

endure EXPERIENCE /ɪnˈdjʊəʳ/ ⓤ /-ˈdʊr/ *verb* [T] to suffer something difficult, unpleasant or painful: *We had to endure a nine-hour delay at the airport.* ○ *She's already had to endure three painful operations on her leg.* **endurable** /ɪnˈdjʊə.rə.bl̩/ ⓤ /-ˈdʊr.ə-/ *adj*
endurance /ɪnˈdjʊə.rᵊnts/ ⓤ /-ˈdʊr.ᵊnts/ *noun* [U] the ability to keep doing something difficult, unpleasant or painful for a long time: *Running a marathon is a test of human endurance.* ○ *The pain was bad beyond endurance.*

endure CONTINUE /ɪnˈdjʊəʳ/ ⓤ /-ˈdʊr/ *verb* [I] FORMAL to continue to exist for a long time: *The political system established in 1400 endured until about 1650.*
enduring /ɪnˈdjʊə.rɪŋ/ ⓤ /-ˈdʊr.ɪŋ/ *adj* existing for a long time: *the enduring appeal of cartoons* ○ *I shall be left with many enduring memories of the time I spent in India.*

,end 'user *noun* [C] the person or organization that uses something rather than an organization which trades in

it: *The software can be modified to suit the particular needs of the end user.*

endways /ˈend.weɪz/ *adv* (US ALSO **endwise**) with the end, rather than the side, facing or touching: *Looking at the sofa endways (**on**), I don't think it'll go through the door.*

enema /ˈen.ə.mə/ *noun* [C] cleaning or treatment of the bowels by filling them with a liquid through the anus

enemy /ˈen.ə.mi/ *noun* **1** [C] a person who hates or opposes another person and tries to harm them or stop them from doing something: *He's **made** a few enemies in this company.* ○ *Max stole Lee's girlfriend and they've been enemies ever since.* ○ *political enemies* **2** [C usually sing] a country, or the armed forces of a country which is at war with another country: *The enemy had succeeded in stopping our supplies from getting through.* ○ *an attack by enemy aircraft* ○ *enemy forces/territory* **3** LITERARY the enemy of *sth* something that harms something else: *Familiarity is the enemy of desire.*

energy STRENGTH /ˈen.ə.dʒi/ ⓤ /-ɚ-/ *noun* [U] the power and ability to be physically and mentally active: *Since I started eating more healthily I've got so much more energy.* ○ *I was going to go out this evening, but I just haven't got the energy.* ○ [+ to infinitive] *I didn't even have **the** energy to get out of bed.* ○ APPROVING *Her writing is full of passion and energy* (= enthusiasm).
energies /ˈen.ə.dʒiz/ ⓤ /-ɚ-/ *plural noun* the total of all your power and ability to be mentally and physically active: *I'm going to channel all my energies into getting a better job.*
energetic /ˌen.əˈdʒet.ɪk/ ⓤ /-ɚˈdʒeţ-/ *adj* having or involving a lot of energy: *an energetic young woman* ○ *I tried aerobics but it was too energetic for me.* **energetically** /ˌen.əˈdʒet.ɪ.kli/ ⓤ /-ɚˈdʒeţ-/ *adv*
energize, UK USUALLY **-ise** /ˈen.ə.dʒaɪz/ ⓤ /-ɚ-/ *verb* [T] to make someone feel energetic or eager: *I felt very energized after my holiday.*

energy POWER /ˈen.ə.dʒi/ ⓤ /-ɚ-/ *noun* [U] the power from something such as electricity or oil, which can do work, such as providing light and heat: *The energy generated by the windmill drives all the drainage pumps.* ○ *energy conservation/efficiency.* ○ *nuclear energy*

enervating /ˈen.ə.veɪ.tɪŋ/ ⓤ /-ɚ.veɪ.ţɪŋ/ *adj* FORMAL causing you to feel weak and lacking in energy: *I find this heat very enervating.* **enervate** /ˈen.ə.veɪt/ ⓤ /-ɚ-/ *verb* [T] LITERARY

enfant terrible /ˌɑ̃ː.fɑ̃ː.terˈiː.blə/ *noun* [C] *plural* **enfants terribles** FORMAL a famous or successful person who likes to shock people: *In the seventies he was the enfant terrible **of** the theatre.*

enfeeble /ɪnˈfiː.bl̩/ *verb* [T] FORMAL to make someone or something very weak **enfeebled** /ɪnˈfiː.bl̩d/ *adj*

enfold /ɪnˈfəʊld/ ⓤ /-ˈfoʊld/ *verb* [T] LITERARY to closely hold or completely cover someone or something: *He enfolded her **in** his arms.*

enforce /ɪnˈfɔːs/ ⓤ /-ˈfɔːrs/ *verb* [T] to make people obey a law, or to make a particular situation happen or be accepted: *It isn't always easy for the police to enforce speed limits.* ○ *The new teacher had failed to enforce any sort of discipline.* **enforceable** /ɪnˈfɔː.sə.bl̩/ ⓤ /-ˈfɔːr-/ *adj*
enforcement /ɪnˈfɔː.smənt/ ⓤ /-ˈfɔːr-/ *noun* [U] *law enforcement*

enfranchise /ɪnˈfræn.tʃaɪz/ *verb* [T] FORMAL to give a person or group of people the right to vote in elections: *Women in Britain were first enfranchised in 1918.* **enfranchisement** /ɪnˈfræn.tʃaɪz.mənt/ *noun* [U]

engage INTEREST /ɪnˈgeɪdʒ/ *verb* [T] FORMAL to interest someone in something and keep them thinking about it: *The debate about food safety has engaged the whole nation.* ○ *If a book doesn't engage my **interest** in the first few pages, I don't usually carry on reading it.*

engage FIT TOGETHER /ɪnˈgeɪdʒ/ *verb* [I or T] to make one part of a machine fit into and move together with another part of a machine: *When the large cog wheel engages (**with** the smaller one), the mill stone will start to go round.*

engage BEGIN FIGHTING /ɪnˈgeɪdʒ/ *verb* [I or T] SPECIALIZED to attack or begin to fight someone: *Enemy planes engaged the troops as they advanced into the mountains.*

engagement /ɪnˈɡeɪdʒ.mənt/ *noun* [C or U] SPECIALIZED the act of beginning to fight someone, or a period of time in a war ⊃See also **engagement** at **engaged** MARRIAGE; **engagement**.

engage EMPLOY /ɪnˈɡeɪdʒ/ *verb* [T] MAINLY UK FORMAL to employ someone to: [+ to infinitive] *I have engaged a secretary to deal with all my paperwork.* ○ *We're engaging the services of a professional administrator.*

▲ **engage in** *sth phrasal verb* FORMAL to take part in something: *The two governments have agreed to engage in a comprehensive dialogue to resolve the problem.*

● **engage** *sb* **in conservation** FORMAL to start a conversation with someone: *Once Mrs Kirkpatrick engages you in conversation, you're stuck with her for half an hour.*

engaged MARRIAGE /ɪnˈɡeɪdʒd/ *adj* having formally agreed to marry: *Debbie and Chris have just got engaged.* ○ *She was engaged to some guy in the army.* ○ FORMAL *They're engaged to be married in June.* **engagement** /ɪnˈɡeɪdʒ.mənt/ *noun* [C] *They announced their engagement at the party on Saturday.* ○ *an engagement party* ⊃See also **engagement** at **engage** BEGIN FIGHTING; **engagement**.

engaged IN USE /ɪnˈɡeɪdʒd/ *adj* If a telephone or public toilet is engaged, someone is already using it: *Every time I ring her, she/the phone/the number is engaged.* ○ UK *I've been trying to call him all evening, but I keep getting the engaged tone/(AUS) engaged signal (US busy signal).* use. ○ *The sign on the toilet door said 'Engaged'.* ⊃Compare **vacant** EMPTY.

engaged INVOLVED/BUSY /ɪnˈɡeɪdʒd/ *adj* [after v] **1** involved in something: *They've been engaged in a legal battle with the council for several months.* ○ *She's part of a team of scientists who are engaged on/upon cancer research.* **2** FORMAL busy doing something: *I'd come to the meeting on Tuesday but I'm afraid I'm otherwise engaged* (= doing something else).

engagement /ɪnˈɡeɪdʒ.mənt/ *noun* [C] FORMAL an arrangement to meet someone or do something at a particular time: *a dinner engagement* ○ *I'm afraid I have a previous/prior engagement* (= another arrangement already made). ⊃See also **engagement** at **engage** BEGIN FIGHTING; **engaged** MARRIAGE.

enˈgagement ˌring *noun* [C] a ring, usually with precious stones in it, which a man gives to a woman as a formal sign that they have decided to get married

engaging /ɪnˈɡeɪ.dʒɪŋ/ *adj* APPROVING pleasant, attractive and charming: *an engaging smile/manner/person*

engender /ɪnˈdʒen.dəʳ/ ⓊⓈ /-dɚ/ *verb* [T] FORMAL to make people have a particular feeling or make a situation start to exist: *Her latest book has engendered a lot of controversy.* ○ *The minister's speech did not engender confidence in his judgment.*

engine /ˈen.dʒɪn/ *noun* [C] **1** a machine that uses the energy from liquid fuel or steam to produce movement: *a jet engine* ○ *a car engine* ○ *My car's been having engine trouble recently.* ⊃See picture **Planes, Ships and Boats** on page Centre 14 **2** (ALSO **locomotive**) the part of a railway train that pulls it along **-engined** /-en.dʒɪnd/ *suffix*: *twin-engined* ○ *jet-engined*

ˈengine ˌdriver UK *noun* [C] (US USUALLY **engineer**) a train driver

engineer PERSON /ˌen.dʒɪˈnɪəʳ/ ⓊⓈ /-ˈnɪr/ *noun* [C] **1** a person whose job is to design or build machines, engines or electrical equipment, or things such as roads, railways or bridges, using scientific principles: *a civil engineer* ○ *a mechanical/structural engineer* ○ *a software engineer* **2** a person whose job is to repair or control machines, engines or electrical equipment: *a computer engineer* ○ *The engineer is coming to repair our phone tomorrow morning.* **3** US an **engine driver**

engineer /ˌen.dʒɪˈnɪəʳ/ ⓊⓈ /-ˈnɪr/ *verb* [T] to design and build something using scientific principles

engineering /ˌen.dʒɪˈnɪə.rɪŋ/ ⓊⓈ /-ˈnɪr.ɪŋ/ *noun* [U] the work of an engineer, or the study of this work: *Richard studied engineering at Manchester University.*

engineer ARRANGE /ˌen.dʒɪˈnɪəʳ/ ⓊⓈ /-ˈnɪr/ *verb* [T] to arrange cleverly and often secretly for something to happen, especially something that is to your advantage:

Left-wing groups engineered a coup against the military government. ○ *I'm trying to engineer a meeting between them.*

English /ˈɪŋ.ɡlɪʃ/ *noun* [U] the language that is spoken in the UK, the US, and in many other countries: *American/British English* ○ *Do you speak English?*

English /ˈɪŋ.ɡlɪʃ/ *adj* **1** in or relating to the English language: *an English teacher* ○ *an English translation* **2** relating to or from England: *English films/food/people* ○ *English law* ○ *Is she English?* **3 the English** the people of England

ˌEnglish ˈbreakfast *noun* [C or U] UK a meal eaten in the morning consisting of cooked food such as fried eggs, tomatoes, BACON and toast

Englishman /ˈɪŋ.ɡlɪʃ.mən/ *noun* [C] a man who comes from England

● **An Englishman's home is his castle.** UK OLD-FASHIONED SAYING used to show that English people believe that they should be able to control what happens in their own homes, and that no one else should tell them what to do there

ˌEnglish ˈmuffin *noun* [C] US FOR **muffin** BREAD

Englishwoman /ˈɪŋ.ɡlɪʃˌwʊm.ən/ *noun* [C] a woman who comes from England

engorged /ɪnˈɡɔːdʒ/ ⓊⓈ /-ˈɡɔːrdʒ/ *adj* SPECIALIZED describes a part of the body that has become swollen or filled with a liquid, especially blood **engorgement** /ɪnˈɡɔːdʒ.mənt/ ⓊⓈ /-ˈɡɔːrdʒ-/ *noun* [U]

engrave /ɪnˈɡreɪv/ *verb* [T] to cut words, pictures or patterns into the surface of metal, stone, etc: *The jeweller skillfully engraved the initials on the ring.* ○ *The bracelet was engraved with his name and date of birth.*

● **be engraved on your memory/mind** to be very difficult to forget: *That last conversation we had is engraved on my memory forever.*

engraver /ɪnˈɡreɪ.vəʳ/ ⓊⓈ /-vɚ/ *noun* [C] a person whose job is to engrave things

engraving /ɪnˈɡreɪ.vɪŋ/ *noun* **1** [U] the activity of engraving **2** [C] a picture printed onto paper from a piece of wood or metal into which the design has been cut

engrossed /ɪnˈɡrəʊst/ ⓊⓈ /-ˈɡroʊst/ *adj* giving all your attention to something; absorbed: *She was so engrossed by/in the book that she forgot the cakes in the oven.* ○ *They were so engrossed in/with what they were doing that they didn't hear me come in.*

engrossing /ɪnˈɡrəʊ.sɪŋ/ ⓊⓈ /-ˈɡroʊ-/ *adj* very interesting and needing all your attention: *an engrossing book/story*

engulf /ɪnˈɡʌlf/ *verb* [T] to surround and cover something or someone completely: *The flames rapidly engulfed the house.* ○ *Northern areas of the country were engulfed by/in a snowstorm last night.* ○ *The war is threatening to engulf the entire region.*

enhance /ɪnˈhɑːnts/ ⓊⓈ /-ˈhænts/ *verb* [T] to improve the quality, amount or strength of something: *These scandals will not enhance the organization's reputation/image.* **enhancement** /ɪnˈhɑːnt.smənt/ ⓊⓈ /-ˈhænt-/ *noun* [C or U]

enhancer /ɪnˈhɑːnt.səʳ/ ⓊⓈ /-ˈhænt.sɚ/ *noun* [C] something which is used to improve the quality of something. Enhancer is usually used as a combining form: *Music can be a mood enhancer.* ○ *I don't like to use artificial flavour enhancers in my cooking.* **-enhancing** /-ɪn.hɑːnt.sɪŋ/ ⓊⓈ /-hænt-/ *suffix*: *Several athletes tested positive for illegal performance-enhancing drugs.*

enigma /ɪˈnɪɡ.mə/ *noun* [C] something that is mysterious and seems impossible to understand completely: *She is a bit of an enigma.* ○ *The newspapers were full of stories about the enigma of Lord Lucan's disappearance.*

enigmatic /ˌen.ɪɡˈmæt.ɪk/ ⓊⓈ /-ˈmæt̬-/ *adj* mysterious and impossible to understand completely: *The Mona Lisa has a famously enigmatic smile.* ○ *He left an enigmatic message on my answering machine.* **enigmatically** /ˌen.ɪɡˈmæt.ɪ.kli/ ⓊⓈ /-ˈmæt̬-/ *adv*: "Who was that?" "Just a man I know," she said enigmatically.

enjoin /ɪnˈdʒɔɪn/ *verb* [T] **1** FORMAL to instruct someone to do something or to behave in a particular way: [+ to infinitive] *We were all enjoined to be on our best behaviour.* ○ *He enjoined* (= suggested) *caution.* **2** US LEGAL to legally force someone to do something or stop doing something

enjoy [PLEASURE] /ɪn'dʒɔɪ/ *verb* [T] to get pleasure from something: *I really enjoyed that film/book/concert/party/meal.* ○ [+ v-ing] *I want to travel because I enjoy meet**ing** people and see**ing** new places.*

en'joy yourself /ɪn'dʒɔɪ/ *verb* [R] **1** to get pleasure from the situation which you are in: *I don't think Marie is enjoying herself very much at school.* ○ *Come on, why aren't you dancing? Enjoy yourselves!* **2** *INFORMAL* **Enjoy!** something you say to someone when you have given them something and you want them to enjoy it: *Here are your drinks. Enjoy!*

enjoyable /ɪn'dʒɔɪ.ə.bl̩/ *adj* An enjoyable event or experience gives you pleasure: *a very enjoyable game/film* ○ *Thank you for a most enjoyable evening.*

enjoyment /ɪn'dʒɔɪ.mənt/ *noun* [U] when you enjoy something: *Knowing the ending already didn't spoil my enjoyment of the film.*

COMMON LEARNER ERROR

enjoy doing something

When **enjoy** is followed by a verb, the verb must be in the **-ing** form.

My parents enjoy walking in the mountains.
~~*My parents enjoy to walk in the mountains.*~~

enjoy [BENEFIT] /ɪn'dʒɔɪ/ *verb* [T] to have the benefit of something: *Even though he's 86, he enjoys excellent health.*

enlarge /ɪn'lɑːdʒ/ [US] /-'lɑːrdʒ/ *verb* **1** [I or T] to become bigger or to make something bigger: *They've enlarged the kitchen by building over part of the garden.* ○ *Symptoms of the disease include an enlarged spleen or liver.* **2** [T] to print a bigger copy of a photograph or document

enlargement /ɪn'lɑːdʒ.mənt/ [US] /-'lɑːrdʒ-/ *noun* **1** [S or U] when something is enlarged: *I am pleased to announce the enlargement of the History Department by three new teachers.* **2** [C] something, especially a photograph, that has been enlarged: *I had an enlargement of my graduation photo done for my grandparents.*

enlarger /ɪn'lɑː.dʒəʳ/ [US] /-'lɑːr.dʒɚ/ *noun* [C] a piece of equipment used especially by photographers to make pictures or photographs bigger

▲ **enlarge on/upon *sth*** *phrasal verb FORMAL* to give more details about something you have said or written: *Would you care to enlarge on what you've just said?*

enlighten /ɪn'laɪ.tᵊn/ [US] /-t̬ᵊn/ *verb* [I or T] to provide someone with information and understanding; to explain the true facts about something to someone: *Should the function of children's television be to entertain or to enlighten?* ○ *I don't understand this. Could you enlighten me?*

enlightened /ɪn'laɪ.tᵊnd/ [US] /-t̬ᵊnd/ *adj APPROVING* **1** showing understanding, acting in a positive way, and not following old-fashioned or false beliefs: *The school has an enlightened policy of teaching boys to cook.* ○ *These days she's much more enlightened in her views on education.* **2** knowing the truth about existence: *Buddha was an enlightened being.*

enlightening /ɪn'laɪ.tᵊn.ɪŋ/ [US] /-t̬ᵊn-/ *adj* giving you more information and understanding of something: *That was a very enlightening programme.* ○ *The instruction manual that came with my new computer wasn't very enlightening **about** how to operate it.*

enlightenment /ɪn'laɪ.tᵊn.mənt/ [US] /-t̬ᵊn-/ *noun* [U] **1** the state of understanding something: *Can you give me any enlightenment **on** what happened?* **2** in Hinduism and Buddhism, the highest spiritual state that can be achieved **3 the Enlightenment** the period in the 18th century in Europe, when many people began to emphasize the importance of science and reason, rather than religion and tradition

enlist [JOIN] /ɪn'lɪst/ *verb* [I] to join the armed forces: *They both enlisted (**in** the navy) a year before the war broke out.*

enlisted /ɪn'lɪst.ɪd/ *adj* [before n] *US* An enlisted man/woman is a member of the armed forces who is not an officer. **enlistment** /ɪn'lɪst.mənt/ *noun* [C or U]

enlist [ASK FOR HELP] /ɪn'lɪst/ *verb* [T] *SLIGHTLY FORMAL* to ask for and get help or support from someone: *We've got to enlist some people to help prepare the food.* ○ *The organization has enlisted the support of many famous people in raising money to help homeless children.*

enliven /ɪn'laɪ.vᵊn/ *verb* [T] to make something more interesting: *The game was much enlivened when both teams scored within five minutes of each other.*

en masse /ˌɒ̃ 'mæs/ [US] /ˌɑ̃ː-/ *adv* If a group of people do something en masse, they do it together and at the same time: *The shop's 85 workers have resigned en masse.*

enmesh /en'meʃ/ *verb* [T] to catch or involve someone in something unpleasant or dangerous from which it is difficult to escape: *The whales are caught by being enmeshed **in** nets.* ○ *She has become enmeshed **in** a tangle of drugs and petty crime.*

enmity /'en.mɪ.ti/ [US] /-t̬i/ *noun* [C or U] a feeling of hate: *She denied any personal enmity **towards** him.* ○ *Bitter historical enmities underlie the present violence.*

ennoble /ɪ'nəʊ.bl̩/ [US] /-'noʊ-/ *verb* [T] **1** to make someone a member of the NOBILITY (= highest social rank) **2** *LITERARY* to make something or someone more admirable: *He has this theory that suffering can ennoble a person's character.*

ennui /ˌɒn'wiː/ [US] /ˌɑːn-/ *noun* [U] *LITERARY* a feeling of boredom and mental tiredness caused by having nothing interesting or exciting to do: *The whole country seems to be affected by the ennui of winter.*

enormity [SIZE] /ɪ'nɔː.mɪ.ti/ [US] /-'nɔːr.mə.t̬i/ *noun* [U] very great size or importance: *Nobody fully understands the enormity and complexity **of** the task of reviving the country's economy.* ○ *I don't think you really realize the enormity **of** the problem.*

enormity [EVIL ACT] /ɪ'nɔː.mɪ.ti/ [US] /-'nɔːr.mə.t̬i/ *noun* [C or U] *FORMAL* an extremely evil act or the quality of being extremely evil

enormous /ɪ'nɔː.məs/ [US] /-'nɔːr-/ *adj* extremely large: *an enormous car/house* ○ *He earns an enormous salary.* ○ *I was absolutely enormous when I was pregnant.* ○ *You've been an enormous help.*

enormously /ɪ'nɔː.mə.sli/ [US] /-'nɔːr-/ *adv* extremely or very much: *She worked enormously hard on the project.* ○ *The show was enormously popular.* **enormousness** /ɪ'nɔː.mə.snəs/ [US] /-'nɔːr-/ *noun* [U]

enough /ɪ'nʌf/ *determiner, pronoun, adv* **1** as much as is necessary; in the amount or to the degree needed: *Is there enough cake/Are there enough cakes **for** everyone?* ○ *There are 25 textbooks per class. That should be enough.* ○ *Have you had enough (**to** eat)?* ○ *I know enough about art **to** recognize a masterpiece when I see one.* ○ *He's tall enough to change the bulb without getting on a chair.* **2** as much as or more than is wanted: [+ to infinitive] *I've got enough work **to** do at the moment, without being given any more.* ○ *Half an hour in his company is **quite** enough!* ○ *Stop. You've made enough **of a*** (= a lot of) *mess already.* ○ *You've drunk **more than** enough* (= too much) *already.* ○ *I've **seen/heard** enough now* (= I do not want to see/hear any more). ○ *I've **had** enough **of** your excuses* (= I want them to stop). ○ *Enough **of this**/* *(US) Enough **already*** (= Stop)*! I don't want to discuss it any more.*

enough /ɪ'nʌf/ *adv* **1** used after an adjective, adverb or verb to mean to the necessary degree: *Is the water hot enough yet?* ○ *I don't think he's really experienced enough for this sort of job.* ○ *She told me it was brand new and I was stupid enough **to** believe her.* ○ *FORMAL Would you be **good** enough **to** take my bag upstairs for me?* **2** used after an adjective or adverb to mean quite: *He's bad enough, but his brother is far worse.* ○ *She's gone away for six months, but strangely/oddly/funnily enough* (= surprisingly), *her boyfriend doesn't seem too unhappy about it.*

• **Enough is enough** something you say when you want something to stop: *Enough is enough – I don't want to argue with you any more.*

• **enough said** *INFORMAL* something you say to tell someone that you understand what they have said and that they do not need to say any more: *"Someone has to explain the situation to her." "Enough said."*

• **have had enough** to want something to stop because it is annoying you: *I've had enough – I'm going home.*

E

E

• **That's enough** used to tell someone to stop behaving badly: *That's enough, Peter. Give those toys back, please.*

en passant /ˌɒ̃'pæs.ɒ̃/ [US] /ˌɑ̃ː.pæ'sɑ̃ː/ *adv FORMAL* If you say something en passant, you mention something briefly while talking about something else: *She mentioned, en passant, that she'd been in Brighton the previous week.*

enquire /ɪn'kwaɪəʳ/ [US] /-'kwaɪr/ *verb* [I or T] *UK* to **inquire**

enquiry /ɪn'kwaɪə.ri/ [US] /'ɪn.kwə.ri/ *noun* [C or U] *UK* **inquiry**

enrage /ɪn'reɪdʒ/ *verb* [T often passive] to cause someone to become very angry: *Plans to build a new nightclub in the neighbourhood have enraged local residents.* ○ *He was so enraged* ***at*** *the article about him that he sued the newspaper.*

enraptured /ɪn'ræp.tʃəd/ [US] /-tʃɚd/ *adj LITERARY* filled with great pleasure or extremely pleased by something: *The audience was enraptured by the young soloist's performance.*

enrich /ɪn'rɪtʃ/ *verb* **1** [T] to improve the quality of something by adding something else: *Fertilizer helps to enrich the soil.* ○ *My life was greatly enriched by knowing her.* **2** [T often R] to make something or someone richer: *He claimed that the large stores were enriching themselves at the expense of their customers.* **enrichment** /ɪn'rɪtʃ.mənt/ *noun* [U]

enrol *UK* (-ll-), *US USUALLY* **enroll** /ɪn'rəʊl/ [US] /-'roʊl/ *verb* [I or T] to put yourself or someone else onto the official list of members of a course, college or group: *Is it too late to enrol* ***at*** *the college?* ○ *I enrolled* ***for/in/on*** *the modern art course.* ○ *He is enrolled as a part-time student.* ○ *They want to enrol their children in their local school.* **enrolment** *UK, US USUALLY* **enrollment** /ɪn'rəʊl.mənt/ [US] /-'roʊl-/ *noun* [C or U]

en route, *US ALSO* **enroute** /ˌɒ̃'ruːt/ /ˌɒn-/ [US] /ˌɑ̃ːn-/ *adv* on the way to or from somewhere: *I stopped en route (****to*** *the party) and got some wine.* ○ *The bomb exploded while the plane was en route* ***from*** *Paris* ***to*** *Tokyo.*

ensconce ***yourself*** /ɪn'skɒnts/ [US] /-'skɑːnts/ *verb* [R] *LITERARY* to make yourself very comfortable or safe in a place or position: *After dinner, I ensconced myself* ***in*** *a deep armchair with a book.*

ensconced /ɪn'skɒntst/ [US] /-'skɑːntst/ *adj* [after v] *LITERARY* positioned safely or comfortably somewhere: *The Prime Minister is now* ***firmly*** *ensconced* ***in*** *Downing Street with a large majority.*

ensemble /ˌɒn'sɒm.bl̩/ [US] /ˌɑːn'sɑːm-/ *group noun* [C] a group of things or people acting or taken together as a whole, especially a group of musicians who regularly play together: *The Mozart Ensemble is/are playing at the Wigmore Hall tonight.* ○ *She bought a dress and matching hat, gloves and shoes – in fact the whole ensemble.*

enshrine /ɪn'ʃraɪn/ *verb* [T usually + adv or prep] *FORMAL* **1** to contain or keep as if in a holy place: *Almost two and a half million war dead are enshrined at Yasukuni.* ○ *A lot of memories are enshrined* ***in*** *this photograph album.* **2 be enshrined in** ***sth*** If a political or social right is enshrined in something, it is protected by being included in it: *The right of freedom of speech is enshrined* ***in*** *law/* ***in*** *the constitution.*

enshroud /ɪn'ʃraʊd/ *verb* [T] **1** *LITERARY* to cover something so that it cannot be seen clearly: *The planet Venus is enshrouded* ***in*** *thick clouds.* **2** to keep the whole of something in an unclear, uncertain, or unknown state: *The commission's report has dispelled much of the uncertainty that has enshrouded the telephone industry since the Telecommunications Act was signed.*

ensign /'en.sᵊn/ *noun* [C] a flag on a ship that shows which country the ship belongs to

enslave /ɪn'sleɪv/ *verb* [T often passive] **1** to control and keep someone forcefully in a bad situation, or to make a slave of someone: *Women in this region were enslaved by poverty.* ○ *The early settlers enslaved or killed much of the native population.* **2** *LITERARY* to control someone's actions, thoughts, emotions, or life completely: *We are increasingly enslaved by technology.* ○ *Guilt enslaved her.* **enslavement** /ɪn'sleɪv.mənt/ *noun* [U]

ensnare /ɪn'sneəʳ/ [US] /-'sner/ *verb* [T] *LITERARY* to catch or get control of something or someone: *Spiders ensnare flies and other insects in their webs.* ○ *They wanted to make a formal complaint about their doctor, but ended up ensnared* ***in*** *the complexities of the legal system.*

ensue /ɪn'sjuː/ [US] /-'suː/ *verb* [I] *FORMAL* to happen after something else, especially as a result of it: *The police officer said that he had placed the man under arrest and that a scuffle had ensued.*

ensuing /ɪn'sjuː.ɪŋ/ [US] /-'suː-/ *adj* [before n] happening after something and because of it: *An argument broke out and in the ensuing fight, a gun went off.* ○ *He lost his job and in the ensuing months became more and more depressed.*

en suite, en-suite, ensuite /ˌɒ̃'swiːt/ [US] /ˌɑ̃ː-/ *adj, adv* describes a bathroom which is directly connected to a bedroom or a bedroom which is connected to a bathroom: *I want a hotel room with an en suite bathroom.* ○ *All four bedrooms in their new house are en suite.*

en suite, en-suite, ensuite /ˌɒ̃'swiːt/ [US] /ˌɑ̃ː-/ *noun* [C] a bathroom directly connected to a bedroom

ensure, *US ALSO* **insure** /ɪn'ʃɔːʳ/ [US] /-'ʃʊr/ *verb* [T] to make something certain to happen: *The airline is taking steps to ensure safety on its aircraft.* ○ [+ (that)] *The role of the police is to ensure* ***(that)*** *the law is obeyed.* ○ [+ two objects] *Their 2-0 victory today has ensured the Italian team a place in the Cup Final/ensured a place in the Cup Final* ***for*** *the Italian team.*

entail /ɪn'teɪl/ *verb* [T] *FORMAL* to make something necessary, or to involve something: *Such a large investment inevitably entails some risk.* ○ [+ v-ing] *Repairing the roof will entail spending a lot of money.*

entangle /ɪn'tæŋ.gl̩/ *verb* [T usually passive] **1** to cause something to become caught in something such as a net or ropes: *The dolphin had become entangled* ***in/with*** *the fishing nets.* **2 entangled in/with** ***sth/sb*** involved with something or someone in a way that makes it difficult to escape: *He went to the shop to buy bread, and got entangled* ***in/with*** *a carnival parade.* ○ *The mayor and the city council are anxious to avoid getting entangled* ***in*** *the controversy.* ○ *She seems to be romantically entangled* ***with*** *some artist in Rome.*

entanglement /ɪn'tæŋ.gl̩.mənt/ *noun* **1** [C] a situation or relationship that you are involved in and that is difficult to escape from: *The book describes the complex emotional and sexual entanglements between the members of the group.* **2** [C usually pl] *UK SPECIALIZED* a fence made of wire with sharp points on it, intended to make it difficult for enemy soldiers to go across an area of land

entente (cordiale) /ˌɒn.tɒntˌkɔː.di'ɑːl/ [US] /ˌɑːn.tɑːntˌkɔːr-/ *noun* [S or U] a friendly agreement or relationship between two countries

enter [GO IN] /'en.təʳ/ [US] /-t̬ɚ/ *verb* [I or T] to come or go into a particular place: *The police entered (the building)* ***through/by*** *the side door.* ○ *You will begin to feel sleepy as the drug enters the* ***bloodstream***. ➲See also **entrance**; **entry** WAY IN.

COMMON LEARNER ERROR

enter a place

The verb **enter** is not followed by a preposition.

I entered the classroom.
~~*I entered in the classroom.*~~

Be careful not to use **enter** when you are talking about getting into a vehicle.

She got into the car.
~~*She entered the car.*~~

enter [INFORMATION] /'en.təʳ/ [US] /-t̬ɚ/ *verb* [T] **1** to put information into a computer, book or document: *You have to enter a password to access the database.* ➲See also **entry** INFORMATION. **2** *FORMAL* to make a particular type of statement officially: *The prisoner entered a* ***plea*** *of not guilty.*

enter /'en.təʳ/ [US] /-t̬ɚ/ *noun* [S] the key on a computer keyboard which is used to say that the words or numbers on the screen are correct, or to say that an instruction should be performed, or to move down a line on the screen: *Move the cursor to where it says 'New File' and press enter.*

enter COMPETITION /ˈen.tər/ US /-t̬ɚ/ *verb* [I or T] to be included in a competition, race or exam, or to arrange for someone else to do this: *Both men have been entered for/in the 100 metres in Paris next month.* ○ *All three companies have entered the race to develop a new system.* ○ *Are you going to enter the photography competition?* ➔See also **entry** COMPETITION.

enter ORGANIZATION /ˈen.tər/ US /-t̬ɚ/ *verb* [T] to become a member of a particular organization, or to start working in a particular type of job: *Ms Doughty entered politics/Parliament after a career in banking.*

enter PERIOD /ˈen.tər/ US /-t̬ɚ/ *verb* [T] to begin a period of time: *The project is entering its final stages.* ○ *The violence is now entering its third week.*

▲ **enter into** *sth phrasal verb FORMAL* to start to become involved in something, especially a discussion or agreement: *They refuse to enter into any discussion on this matter.*

● **not enter into** *sth* If you say that something does not enter into something else, it is not an important or necessary part of it: *The Council's opinion doesn't enter into it – it's up to us to make the decision.*

enteritis /ˌen.təˈraɪ.təs/ US /-t̬əˈraɪ.t̬əs/ *noun* [U] ➔See **gastroenteritis.**

enterprise /ˈen.tə.praɪz/ US /-t̬ɚ-/ *noun* **1** [C or U] an organization, especially a business, or a difficult and important plan, especially one that will earn money: *Don't forget this is a commercial enterprise – we're here to make money.* ○ *Those were the years of private enterprise* (= businesses being run privately, rather than by the government), *when lots of small businesses were started.* ○ *Her latest enterprise* (= plan) *is to climb Mount Everest.* **2** [U] eagerness to do something new and clever, despite any risks: *They've showed a lot of enterprise in setting up this project.* ○ *We need someone with enterprise and imagination to design a marketing strategy.*

enterprising /ˈen.tə.praɪ.zɪŋ/ US /-t̬ɚ-/ *adj* good at thinking of and doing new and difficult things, especially things that will make money: *The business was started by a couple of enterprising young women.* ○ *That was very enterprising of you, Vijay!*

ˈenterprise ˌculture *noun* [S or U] a society in which personal achievement, the creation of wealth and the development of private business is encouraged

ˈenterprise ˌzone *noun* [C] an area with economic problems that has been given financial help by the government to encourage the growth of new businesses

entertain AMUSE /en.təˈteɪn/ US /-t̬ɚ-/ *verb* [I or T] to keep a group of people interested or amused: *We hired a magician to entertain the children.* ○ *Most children's television programmes aim to educate and entertain at the same time.*

entertainer /en.təˈteɪ.nər/ US /-t̬əˈteɪ.nɚ/ *noun* [C] someone whose job is to entertain people by singing, telling jokes, etc.

entertaining /en.təˈteɪ.nɪŋ/ US /-t̬ɚ-/ *adj* amusing and enjoyable: *an entertaining story/film* ○ *His books aren't particularly well-written, but they're always entertaining.* **entertainingly** /en.təˈteɪ.nɪŋ.li/ US /-t̬ɚ-/ *adv*

entertainment /en.təˈteɪn.mənt/ US /-t̬ɚ-/ *noun* [C or U] shows, films, television, or other performances or activities that entertain people, or a performance of this type: *There's not much in the way of entertainment in this town – just the cinema and a couple of pubs.* ○ *FORMAL This season's entertainments include five new plays and several concerts of Chinese and Indian music.*

entertain INVITE /en.təˈteɪn/ US /-t̬ɚ-/ *verb* [I or T] to invite someone to your house and give food and drink to them: *We entertain a lot of people, mainly business associates of my wife's.* ○ *Now that I live on my own, I don't entertain much.* **entertaining** /en.təˈteɪ.nɪŋ/ US /-t̬ɚ-/ *noun* [U] We do a lot of entertaining.

entertain THINK ABOUT /ˌen.təˈteɪn/ US /-t̬ɚ-/ *verb* [T not continuous] *FORMAL* to hold in your mind or to be willing to consider or accept: *The General refused to entertain the possibility of defeat.*

enthral UK (-ll-), US USUALLY **enthrall** /ɪnˈθrɔːl/ US /-ˈθrɑːl/ *verb* [I or T] to keep someone completely interested: *The baseball game completely enthralled the crowd.* ○ *The audience were enthralled for two hours by a sparkling, dramatic performance.* ○ *They listened enthralled to what he was saying.*

enthralling /ɪnˈθrɔː.lɪŋ/ US /-ˈθrɑː-/ *adj* keeping someone's interest and attention completely: *I found your book absolutely enthralling!*

enthrone /ɪnˈθrəʊn/ US /-ˈθroʊn/ *verb* **1** [T] *FORMAL* to put a king, queen, etc. through the ceremony of sitting on a THRONE (= ceremonial chair) in order to mark the official beginning of their period in power **2** [T often passive] *HUMOROUS* to be positioned somewhere where you look or feel important: *She sat in the dining room, enthroned on an old high-backed chair.* **enthronement** /ɪnˈθrəʊn.mənt/ US /-ˈθroʊn-/ *noun* [C or U]

enthusiasm /ɪnˈθjuː.zi.æz.ᵊm/ US /-ˈθuː-/ *noun* **1** [U] a feeling of energetic interest in a particular subject or activity and an eagerness to be involved in it: *One of the good things about teaching young children is their enthusiasm.* ○ *After the accident he lost his enthusiasm for the sport.* ○ *I just can't work up* (= start to feel) *any enthusiasm for the whole project.* **2** [C] a subject or activity that interests you very much: *One of his greatest enthusiasms was yoga.*

enthuse /ɪnˈθjuːz/ US /-ˈθuːz/ *verb* **1** [I] to express excitement about something or great interest in it: *He was enthusing over a wonderful restaurant he'd been to.* ○ [+ speech] *"She's the best leader that this country has ever known!" he enthused.* **2** [T] to give your feeling of excitement and interest in a particular subject to other people: *He was passionately interested in classical music but failed to enthuse his children (with it).*

enthusiast /ɪnˈθjuː.zi.æst/ US /-ˈθuː-/ *noun* [C] a person who is very interested in and involved with a particular subject or activity: *a keep-fit enthusiast* ○ *a model-aircraft enthusiast*

enthusiastic /ɪnˌθjuː.ziˈæs.tɪk/ US /-ˌθuː-/ *adj* showing enthusiasm: *You don't seem very enthusiastic about the party – don't you want to go tonight?* **enthusiastically** /ɪnˌθjuː.ziˈæs.tɪ.kli/ US /-ˌθuː-/ *adv*

entice /ɪnˈtaɪs/ *verb* [T] to persuade someone to do something by offering them something pleasant: *The adverts entice the customer into buying things they don't really want.* ○ *People are being enticed away from the profession by higher salaries elsewhere.* ○ [+ to infinitive] *A smell of coffee in the doorway enticed people to enter the shop.* **enticement** /ɪnˈtaɪs.mənt/ *noun* [C or U] *One of the enticements of the job is the company car.*

enticing /ɪnˈtaɪ.sɪŋ/ *adj* Something which is enticing attracts you to it by offering you advantages or pleasure: *an enticing smile* ○ *an enticing job offer* **enticingly** /ɪnˈtaɪ.sɪŋ.li/ *adv*

entire /ɪnˈtaɪər/ US /-ˈtaɪr/ *adj* [before n] whole or complete, with nothing missing: *Between them they ate an entire cake.* ○ *He'd spent the entire journey asleep.* ○ *They got an entire set of silver cutlery as a wedding present.*

entirely /ɪnˈtaɪə.li/ US /-ˈtaɪr-/ *adv* completely: *I admit it was entirely my fault.* ○ *The company is run almost entirely by middle-aged men.*

entirety /ɪnˈtaɪə.rɪ.ti/ US /-ˈtaɪr.ɪ.t̬i/ *noun* *FORMAL* **in its entirety** with all parts included: *I've never actually read the book in its entirety.*

entitle ALLOW /ɪnˈtaɪ.tl̩/ US /-t̬l̩/ *verb* [T] to give someone the right to do or have something: *Being unemployed entitles you to free medical treatment.* ○ [+ to infinitive] *The employer is entitled to ask for references.*

entitled /ɪnˈtaɪ.tl̩d/ US /-t̬l̩d/ *adj* [+ to infinitive] *I felt entitled* (= I felt I had the right) *to know how my own money is being spent!*

entitlement /ɪnˈtaɪ.tl̩.mənt/ US /-t̬l̩-/ *noun* [C or U] something that you have right to do or have, or when you have the right to do or have something: *pension/holiday entitlements* ○ *Managers have generous leave entitlement.*

entitle GIVE TITLE /ɪnˈtaɪ.tl̩/ US /-t̬l̩/ *verb* [T] to give a title to a book, film, etc: *Her latest novel, entitled 'The Forgotten Sex', is out this week.*

entity /ˈen.tɪ.ti/ US /-t̬ə.t̬i/ *noun* [C] *FORMAL* something which exists apart from other things, having its own independent existence: *The museums work closely together, but are separate legal entities.* ○ *He regarded the north of the country as a separate cultural entity.*

entomb /ɪnˈtuːm/ *verb* [T often passive] *FORMAL* to bury someone or something: *The nuclear waste has been entombed* ***in*** *concrete many metres under the ground.*

entomology /ˌen.təˈmɒl.ə.dʒi/ [US] /-t̬əˈmɑː.lə-/ *noun* [U] *SPECIALIZED* the scientific study of insects **entomologist** /ˌen.təˈmɒl.ə.dʒɪst/ [US] /-t̬əˈmɑː.lə-/ *noun* [C]

entourage /ˈɒn.tʊ.rɑːʒ/ [US] /ˌɑːn.tʊˈrɑːʒ/ *group noun* [C usually sing] the group of people who travel with and work for an important or famous person: *The rock-star arrived in London with her usual entourage of dancers and backing singers.*

entrails /ˈen.treɪlz/ *plural noun* the intestines and other inside organs of an animal or person, when they are outside the body: *pig entrails* ○ *FIGURATIVE The sofa's entrails* (= pieces of material from inside) *were sticking out in places.*

entrance /ˈen.trənts/ *noun* **1** [C] a door, gate, etc. by which you can enter a building or place: *There are two entrances – one at the front and one round the back.* ➲See also **enter** GO IN; **entry** WAY IN. Compare **exit**. **2** [C usually sing] when an actor or dancer comes onto a stage: *He* ***makes*** *a spectacular entrance in act two draped in a gold sheet.* **3** [C usually sing] the act of a person coming into a room in an ordinary situation, although often because there is something noticeable about it: *I noticed her entrance because she slipped and fell in the doorway.* **4** [U] the right to enter a place: *The management reserve the right to* ***refuse*** *entrance.*

entrant /ˈen.trənt/ *noun* [C] **1** a person who becomes a member of a group or organization: *new entrants to the school/company* **2** a person who takes part in a competition or an examination: *All entrants complete two three-hour papers.*

entranced /ɪnˈtrɑːntst/ [US] /-ˈtræntst/ *adj LITERARY* If you are entranced by someone or something, you cannot stop watching them because they are very interesting or very beautiful: *The children sat silent on the carpet, entranced* ***by*** *the puppet show.* **entrance** /ɪnˈtrɑːnts/ [US] /-ˈtrænts/ *verb* [T] *She entranced them with her intellect and the joy of her company.* **entrancing** /ɪnˈtrɑːnt.sɪŋ/ [US] /-ˈtrænt-/ *adj*: *This countryside provides you with some of the most entrancing views.*

ˈentrance exˌam *noun* [C] an exam which you take to decide if you can be accepted into a school, etc.

ˈentrance ˌfee *noun* [C] an amount of money that you pay in order to be allowed into a cinema, theatre, etc.

entrap /ɪnˈtræp/ *verb* [T] **-pp-** *FORMAL* to cause someone to do something that they would not usually do, by unfair methods: *I firmly believe my son has been entrapped by this cult.*

entrapment /ɪnˈtræp.mənt/ *noun* [U] *FORMAL* the practice of causing someone to do something they would not usually do by tricking them: *The police have been accused of using entrapment to bring charges against suspects.*

entreaty /ɪnˈtriː.ti/ [US] /-t̬i/ *noun* [C] an attempt to persuade someone to do something: *She refused to become involved with him despite his passionate entreaties.*

entreat /ɪnˈtriːt/ *verb* [T] to try very hard to persuade someone to do something: [+ *to* infinitive] *We would spend every meal time entreating the child* ***to*** *eat her vegetables.*

entrée [FOOD] /ˈɒn.treɪ/ [US] /ˈɑːn-/ *noun* [C] **1** *US* the main dish of a meal **2** *UK* at very formal meals, a small dish served just before the main part

entrée [ENTRY] /ˈɒn.treɪ/ [US] /ˈɑːn-/ *noun* [C or U] the right to join a group of people or enter a place

entrench /ɪnˈtrentʃ/ *verb* [T] *MAINLY DISAPPROVING* to establish something, especially an idea or a problem, firmly so that it cannot be changed: [R] *The government's main task was to prevent inflation from entrenching itself.*

entrenched /ɪnˈtrentʃt/ *adj MAINLY DISAPPROVING* Entrenched ideas are so fixed or have existed for so long that they cannot be changed: *It's very difficult to change attitudes that have become so* ***deeply*** *entrenched over the years.* ○ *The organization was often criticized for being too entrenched* ***in*** *its views.*

entrenchment /ɪnˈtrentʃ.mənt/ *noun* [U] *MAINLY DISAPPROVING* the process by which ideas become fixed and cannot be changed: *There has been a shift in opinion on the issue after a decade of entrenchment.*

entre nous /ˌɒn.trəˈnuː/ [US] /ˌɑːn-/ *adv, adj* [after v] *FORMAL* used when telling someone something that is secret and should not be told to anyone else: *He told me – and this is* ***strictly*** *entre nous – that he's going to ask Ruth to marry him.*

entrepreneur /ˌɒn.trə.prəˈnɜːʳ/ [US] /ˌɑːn.trə.prəˈnɝː/ *noun* [C] someone who starts their own business, especially when this involves risks: *He was one of the entrepreneurs of the eighties who made their money in property.* **entrepreneurial** /ˌɒn.trə.prəˈnɜː.ri.əl/ [US] /ˌɑːn.trə.prəˈnɝː.i-/ *adj*: *She'll make money – she's got that entrepreneurial* ***spirit***.

entropy /ˈen.trə.pi/ *noun* [U] *SPECIALIZED* the amount of order or lack of order in a system

entrust /ɪnˈtrʌst/ *verb* [T + adv or prep] to give someone a thing or a duty for which they are responsible: *He didn't look like the sort of man you should entrust your luggage* ***to***. ○ *Two senior officials have been entrusted* ***with*** *organizing the auction.*

entry [WAY IN] /ˈen.tri/ *noun* **1** [C or U] when you enter a place or join a particular society or organization: *A flock of sheep blocked our entry* ***to*** *the village.* ○ *I can't go down that street – there's a 'No entry' sign.* ○ *The actress's entry* ***into*** *the world of politics surprised most people.* ○ *She* ***made*** *her entry to the ceremony surrounded by a group of photographers.* ○ *The burglars* ***gained*** *entry by a top window.* ➲See also **entrance**; **enter** GO IN. **2** [C] a door, gate, etc. by which you enter a place: *I'll wait for you at the entry to the park.*

entry [COMPETITION] /ˈen.tri/ *noun* [C or U] a piece of work that you do in order to take part in a competition, or the act of taking part in a competition: *There have been a fantastic number of entries for this year's poetry competition.* ○ *the* ***winning*** *entries* ○ *Entry* ***to*** *the competition is restricted to those who have a ticket.* ○ *Have you filled in your entry* ***form*** *yet?* ➲See also **enter** COMPETITION.

entry [INFORMATION] /ˈen.tri/ *noun* [C] a separate piece of information that is recorded in a book, computer, etc: *They've updated a lot of the entries in the most recent edition of the encyclopaedia.* ○ *As his illness progressed, he* ***made*** *fewer entries in his diary.* ➲See also **enter** INFORMATION.

ˈentry ˌlevel *noun* [U] the lowest level of an organization, type of work, etc: *E-commerce is presenting a lot of new jobs at entry level.*

entry-level /ˈen.tri,lev.əl/ *adj* [before n] **1** at or relating to the lowest level of an organization, type of work, etc: *entry-level* ***jobs/workers/salaries*** **2** describes a device that is basic and less expensive or technical than other types and therefore suitable for someone who has not used or bought one before: *an entry-level* ***model/machine/PC***

entryphone /ˈen.tri.fəʊn/ [US] /-foʊn/ *noun* [C] *UK* a telephone at the entrance to a large building which people speak into when they want to speak to someone who is inside the building

entryway /ˈen.tri.weɪ/ *noun* [C] *US FOR* **passage** CONNECTING WAY

entwine /ɪnˈtwaɪn/ *verb* [T often passive] to twist something together or around something: *The picture captures the two lovers with their arms entwined.*

entwined /ɪnˈtwaɪnd/ closely connected or unable to be separated: *The fates of both countries seem somehow entwined.*

ˈE ˌnumber *noun* [C] An E number is any of a variety of numbers with the letter E in front of them which are used on containers of food in the European Union to show which particular approved chemical has been added to the food.

enumerate /ɪˈnjuː.mə.reɪt/ [US] /-ˈnuː.mə.eɪt/ *verb* [T] *FORMAL* to name things separately, one by one: *He enumerated the benefits of the insurance scheme.* **enumeration** /ɪˌnjuː.məˈreɪ.ʃən/ [US] /-ˌnuː-/ *noun* [U]

enunciate [PRONOUNCE] /ɪˈnʌnt.si.eɪt/ *verb* [I or T] *FORMAL* to pronounce words or parts of words clearly: *He doesn't* *enunciate (his words) very clearly.* **enunciation** /ɪ.nʌn.-si'eɪ.ʃ°n/ *noun* [C or U]

enunciate EXPLAIN /ɪ'nʌnt.si.eɪt/ *verb* [T] FORMAL to state and explain a plan or principle clearly or formally: *In the speech, the leader enunciated his party's proposals for tax reform.*

envelop /ɪn'vel.əp/ *verb* [T] LITERARY to cover or surround something completely: *The graveyard looked ghostly, enveloped in mist.*

envelope /'en.və.ləʊp/ ⓤ /'ɑːn.və.loʊp/ *noun* [C] a flat, usually square or rectangular, paper container for a letter
• **on the back of an envelope** in a hurried way, without much detail: *The prices were very roughly calculated – it looked as though he'd done them on the back of an envelope.*

enviable /'en.vi.ə.bl̩/ *adj* ⊃See at **envy**.

envious /'en.vi.əs/ *adj* ⊃See at **envy**.

environment SURROUNDINGS /ɪn'vaɪə.rən.mənt/ ⓤ /-'vaɪr.ən-/ *noun* [C] the conditions that you live or work in and the way that they influence how you feel or how effectively you can work: *The office is quite bright and airy – it's a pleasant **working** environment.* ○ *As a parent you try to create a stable **home** environment for your children to grow up in.*

the en'vironment NATURE *noun* [S] the air, water and land in or on which people, animals and plants live: *Certain chemicals have been banned because of their damaging effect on the environment.* ○ *We're not doing enough to protect the environment from pollution.* ⊃See Note **nature, the environment and the countryside** at **nature** LIFE.

environmental /ɪn,vaɪə.rən.'men.t°l/ ⓤ /-,vaɪr.ən-'men.t̬°l/ *adj* relating to the environment: *People are becoming far more aware of environmental issues.*

environmentally /ɪn,vaɪə.rən'men.t°l.i/ ⓤ /-,vaɪr.ən-'men.t̬°l-/ *adv* **environmentally friendly** not harmful to the environment: *environmentally-friendly washing powder*

environmentalism /ɪn,vaɪə.rən'men.t°l.ɪ.z°m/ ⓤ /-,vaɪr.-ən'men.t̬°l-/ *noun* [U] an interest in or the study of the environment, in order to protect it from damage by human activities

environmentalist /ɪn,vaɪə.rən'men.t°l.ɪst/ ⓤ /-,vaɪr.ən-'men.t̬°l-/ *noun* [C] a person who is interested in or studies the environment and who tries to protect it from being damaged by human activities

environs /ɪn'vaɪə.rənz/ ⓤ /-'vaɪr.ənz/ *plural noun* FORMAL the area surrounding a place, especially a town

envisage /ɪn'vɪz.ɪdʒ/ *verb* [T] (*US ALSO* **envision**) SLIGHTLY FORMAL **1** to imagine or expect as a likely or desirable possibility in the future: *Train fare increases of 5% are envisaged for the next year.* ○ [+ that] *It's envisaged that the building will start at the end of this year.* ○ [+ v-ing] *When do you envisage finishing the project?* ○ [+ question word] *It's hard to envisage how it could have happened.* **2** to form a mental picture of something or someone you have never seen: *He wasn't what I'd expected – I'd envisaged someone much taller.*

envoy /'en.vɔɪ/ *noun* [C] someone who is sent as a representative from one government or organization to another: *a United Nations special envoy*

envy /'en.vi/ *verb* [T] to wish that you had something that another person has: *I envy her ability to talk to people she's never met before.* ○ [+ two objects] *I don't envy you the job of cooking for all those people.*

envy /'en.vi/ *noun* [U] the feeling that you wish you had something that someone else has: *I watched with envy as she set off for the airport.* ⊃Compare **jealousy** at **jealous** UNHAPPY.
• **be the envy of** *sb* to be liked and wanted by a lot of people: *Her hair is the envy of the office.*

enviable /'en.vi.ə.bl̩/ *adj* If someone is in an enviable situation, you wish you were also in that situation: *She's in the enviable position of being able to choose who she works for.* **enviably** /'en.vi.ə.bli/ *adv*

envious /'en.vi.əs/ *adj* wishing you had what another person has: *I'm very envious of your new coat – it's lovely.* ⊃Compare **jealous** UNHAPPY. **enviously** /'en.vi.ə.sli/

adv: I was looking enviously at your plate, wishing I'd had the fish. **enviousness** /'en.vi.ə.snəs/ *noun* [U]

enzyme /'en.zaɪm/ *noun* [C] any of a group of chemical substances which are produced by living cells and which cause particular chemical reactions to happen while not being changed themselves: *An enzyme in the saliva of the mouth starts the process of breaking down the food.*

eon, UK ALSO **aeon** /'iː.ɒn/ ⓤ /-ɑːn/ *noun* [C] a period of time which is so long that it cannot be measured: INFORMAL *I've been waiting eons for my new computer.*

epaulet, **epaulette** /,ep.ə'let/ *noun* [C] a decorative part on the shoulder of a piece of clothing, especially on a military coat, shirt, etc.

épée /'ep.eɪ/ ⓤ /ep'eɪ/ *noun* [C] a thin sword used in the sport of FENCING (= sword fighting) which is heavier than a FOIL (= light, bendable sword) and has a larger, rounded part for protecting the hand of the user

EPG /,iː.piː'dʒiː/ *noun* [C] ABBREVIATION FOR electronic programme guide: a list on a television screen that says which programmes are going to be broadcast on which stations

ephemeral /ɪ'fem.°r.°l/ ⓤ /-ɚ-/ *adj* lasting for only a short time: *Fame in the world of rock and pop is largely ephemeral.*

ephemera /ɪ'fem.°r.ə/ ⓤ /-ɚ-/ *plural noun* the type of objects which, when they were produced, were not intended to last a long time or were specially produced for one occasion: *Amongst other pop ephemera, the auction will be selling off rock stars' stage clothes.*

epic /'ep.ɪk/ *noun* [C] a film, poem or book which is long and contains a lot of action, usually dealing with a historical subject: *It's one of those old Hollywood epics with a cast of thousands.*

epic /'ep.ɪk/ *adj* **1** in the style of an epic: *an epic film about the Roman Empire* **2** describes events that happen over a long period and involve a lot of action and difficulty: *an epic journey/struggle* **3** INFORMAL extremely large: *The problem of inflation has reached epic proportions.*

epicentre UK, US **epicenter** /'ep.ɪ.sen.tə'/ ⓤ /-t̬ɚ/ *noun* [C] SPECIALIZED the point on the Earth's surface directly above an earthquake or atomic explosion

epicure /'ep.ɪ.kjʊə'/ ⓤ /-kjʊr/ *noun* [C] (*ALSO* **epicurean**) FORMAL a person who enjoys food and drink of a high quality; a **gourmet**

epicurean /,ep.ɪ'kjʊə.ri.°n/ ⓤ /-'kjʊr.i-/ *adj* FORMAL getting pleasure from food and drink of a high quality

epidemic /,ep.ɪ'dem.ɪk/ *noun* **1** [C] the appearance of a particular disease in a large number of people at the same time: *a flu/AIDS epidemic* **2** [C usually sing] a particular problem that seriously affects many people at the same time: *a crime/unemployment epidemic*

epidemic /,ep.ɪ'dem.ɪk/ *adj*: *Poverty in this country has reached epidemic proportions* (= has an effect on many people). ○ *Crime and poverty are epidemic in the city.*

epidermis /,ep.ɪ'dɜː.mɪs/ ⓤ /-'dɝː-/ *noun* [S or U] SPECIALIZED the thin outer layer of the skin

epidural /,ep.ɪ'djʊə.rəl/ ⓤ /-'dʊr.°l/ *noun* [C] when an ANAESTHETIC (= substance which stops you feeling pain) is put into the nerves in a person's lower back with a special needle: *They gave my wife an epidural when she was giving birth.*

epiglottis /,ep.ɪ'glɒt.ɪs/ ⓤ /-'glɑː.t̬ɪs/ *noun* [C] SPECIALIZED a small flat part at the back of the tongue which closes when you swallow to prevent food from entering the tube which goes to the lungs

epigram /'ep.ɪ.græm/ *noun* [C] a short saying or poem which expresses an idea in a way that is clever and amusing: *One of Oscar Wilde's most frequently quoted epigrams is "I can resist everything except temptation".* **epigrammatic** /,ep.ɪ.grə'mæt.ɪk/ ⓤ /-'mæt̬-/ *adj*

epigraph /'ep.ɪ.grɑːf/ ⓤ /-græf/ *noun* [C] SPECIALIZED a saying or a part of a poem, play or book put at the beginning of a piece of writing to give the reader some idea of what the piece is about

epilepsy /'ep.ɪ.lep.si/ *noun* [U] a condition of the brain which causes a person to lose consciousness for short periods or to move in a violent and uncontrolled way:

*She can't drive because she **suffers from/has** epilepsy.* **epileptic** /ˌep.ɪˈlep.tɪk/ *adj, noun* [C] *an epileptic fit* ○ *He takes medication because he's an epileptic.*

epilogue, *US ALSO* **epilog** /ˈep.ɪ.lɒg/ [US] /-lɑːg/ *noun* [C] a speech or piece of text which is added to the end of a play or book, often giving a short statement about what happens to the characters after the play or book finishes ➲Compare **prologue**.

Epiphany [HOLY DAY] /ɪˈpɪf.ən.i/ *noun* [C or U] January 6, a Christian holy day which, in the Western church, celebrates the coming of the three MAGI (= important visitors) to see the baby Jesus Christ, and in the Eastern church, the baptism of Christ

epiphany [UNDERSTANDING] /ɪˈpɪf.ən.i/ *noun* [C or U] *LITERARY* when you suddenly feel that you understand, or suddenly become aware of, something that is very important to you or a powerful religious experience

episcopal /ɪˈpɪs.kə.pəl/ *adj FORMAL* of a bishop, or of a church which is directed by bishops **Episcopalian** /ɪˌpɪs.kəˈpeɪ.li.ən/ *adj, noun* [C] *He is (an) Episcopalian* (= belongs to the Episcopal church).

the Eˌpiscopal ˈChurch *noun* [S] a part of the Anglican Church, especially in Scotland and the US

episode [EVENT] /ˈep.ɪ.səʊd/ [US] /-soʊd/ *noun* [C] a single event or group of related events: *This latest episode in the fraud scandal has shocked a lot of people.* ○ *The drugs, the divorce and the depression – it's an episode in his life that he wants to forget.* **episodic** /ˌep.ɪˈsɒd.ɪk/ [US] /-ˈsɑː.dɪk/ *adj FORMAL* happening only sometimes and not regularly: *The war between these two countries has been long-drawn-out and episodic.*

episode [PART OF STORY] /ˈep.ɪ.səʊd/ [US] /-soʊd/ *noun* [C] one of the single parts into which a story is divided, especially when it is broadcast on the television or radio **episodic** /ˌep.ɪˈsɒd.ɪk/ [US] /-ˈsɑː.dɪk/ *adj FORMAL*

epistemology /ɪˌpɪs.təˈmɒl.ə.dʒi/ [US] /-ˈmɑː.lə-/ *noun* [U] *SPECIALIZED* the part of PHILOSOPHY that is about the study of how we know things

epistle /ɪˈpɪs.l̩/ *noun* [C] **1** *FORMAL* a letter: *HUMOROUS Many thanks for your **lengthy** epistle which arrived in this morning's post.* **2** one of the letters written to the early Christians by the APOSTLES (= the first followers of Jesus Christ) **epistolary** /ɪˈpɪs.təl.ər.i/ [US] /-er-/ *adj FORMAL*

epitaph /ˈep.ɪ.tɑːf/ [US] /-tæf/ *noun* [C] a short piece of writing or a poem about a dead person, especially one written on their GRAVESTONE

• **be your epitaph** to be something, especially something you say, that other people will remember you for

epithet /ˈep.ɪ.θet/ *noun* [C] *FORMAL* an adjective added to a person's name or a phrase used instead of it, usually to criticize or praise them: *The opera-singer's 104-kilo frame has earned him the epithet of 'Man Mountain' in the press.*

epitome /ɪˈpɪt.ə.mi/ [US] /-ˈpɪt̬-/ *noun* **the epitome of** ***sth*** the typical or highest example of a stated quality, as shown by a particular person or thing: *Even now in her sixties, she is the epitome of French elegance.* **epitomize**, *UK USUALLY* **-ise** /ɪˈpɪt.ə.maɪz/ [US] /-ˈpɪt̬-/ *verb* [T] to be a perfect example of a quality or type of thing: *With little equipment and unsuitable footwear, she epitomizes the inexperienced and unprepared mountain walker.*

epoch /ˈiː.pɒk/ [US] /-pɑːk/ *noun* [C] *plural* **epochs** a long period of time, especially one in which there are new advances and great change: *The president said that his country was moving into a new epoch which would be one of lasting peace.*

epoch-making /ˈiː.pɒkˌmeɪ.kɪŋ/ [US] /-pɑːk-/ *adj* [after v] An event might be described as epoch-making if it has a great effect on the future.

eponymous /ɪˈpɒn.ɪ.məs/ [US] /-ˈpɑː.nɪ-/ *adj* [before n] *LITERARY* An eponymous character in a play, book, etc. has the same name as the title. **eponym** /ˈep.ə.nɪm/ *noun* [C] *FORMAL* the name of an object or activity which is also the name of the person who first produced the object or did the activity

eˌpoxy ˈresin *noun* [C or U] a type of strong glue for sticking things together and covering surfaces

epoxy /ɪˈpɒk.si/ [US] /-ˈpɑːk-/ *verb* [T] *US INFORMAL I epoxied* (= stuck together) *the broken chair.*

Epsom salts /ˌep.səmˈsɒlts/ [US] /-ˈsɑːlts/ *plural noun* a bitter white powder that is mixed with water to make a drink that helps people pass solid waste

equable /ˈek.wə.bl̩/ *adj* not changing suddenly; always being pleasant: *Graham has a fairly equable **temperament** – I haven't often seen him really angry.* ○ *The south of the country enjoys an equable **climate**.* **equably** /ˈek.wə.bli/ *adv: As a manager she deals with problems reasonably and equably, never losing her temper.*

equal [SAME] /ˈiː.kwəl/ *adj* the same in amount, number or size, or the same in importance and deserving the same treatment: *All people are equal, deserving the same rights as each other.* ○ *They've got a long way to go before they achieve equal **pay/status** for men and women.* ○ *One litre is equal **to** 1.76 imperial pints.* ○ *One box may look bigger than the other, but in fact they are roughly* (= almost) *equal **in** volume.* **equal** /ˈiː.kwəl/ *noun* [C] *The good thing about her as a boss is that she treats us all as equals.* ○ *Throughout her marriage she never considered her husband as her intellectual equal.* ○ *As an all-round athlete he **has no equal*** (= no-one else is as good). **equal** /ˈiː.kwəl/ *verb* [L only + n; T] **-ll-** or *US USUALLY* **-l-** *Sixteen ounces equals one pound.* ○ *We raised over $500 for charity last year and we're hoping to equal that this year.* **equality** /ɪˈkwɒl.ɪ.ti/ [US] /-ˈkwɑː.lə.t̬i/ *noun* [U] the right of different groups of people to have a similar social position and receive the same treatment: *equality between the sexes* ○ ***racial** equality* **equalize**, *UK USUALLY* **-ise** /ˈiː.kwə.laɪz/ *verb* **1** [T] to make things or people equal: *They are putting pressure on the government to equalize state pension ages between men and women.* **2** [I] *UK* to get the point in a game or competition that makes your score the same as that of the other team or player: *Spain managed to equalize in the last minute of the game.* **equalization**, *UK USUALLY* **-isation** /ˌiː.kwə.laɪˈzeɪ.ʃən/ *noun* [U] **equalizer**, *UK USUALLY* **-iser** /ˈiː.kwə.laɪ.zər/ [US] /-zɚ/ *noun* [C] *UK* the point in a game or competition which gives both teams or players the same score: *He **scored** an equalizer during the closing minutes of the match.* **equally** /ˈiː.kwə.li/ *adv* to the same degree or level, or into amounts or parts that are the same: *You looked equally nice in both dresses – I wouldn't know which one to advise you to buy.* ○ *The inheritance money was shared equally among the three sisters.*

equal [ABLE] /ˈiː.kwəl/ *adj* [after v] *FORMAL* skilled or brave enough for a difficult duty or piece of work: *It's a challenging job but I'm sure you'll **prove** equal **to** it.* ○ *Is he equal **to the task**?*

ˌequal opporˈtunity *noun* [C or U] (*ALSO* **equal opportunities**) the principle of treating all people the same, and not being influenced by a person's sex, race, religion, etc: *The advert said 'We are an equal opportunities employer'.*

ˈequal ˌsign, **equals sign** *noun* [C] the symbol =, used to show that two things are the same in value, size, meaning, etc.

equanimity /ˌek.wəˈnɪm.ɪ.ti/ [US] /-t̬i/ *noun* [U] *FORMAL* calmness and self-control, especially after a shock or disappointment or in a difficult situation: *He received the news of his mother's death **with** remarkable equanimity.* ○ *Three years after the tragedy she has only just begun to regain her equanimity.*

equate /ɪˈkweɪt/ *verb* [T] to consider one thing to be the same as or equal to another thing: *He complained that there was a tendency to equate right-wing politics **with** self-interest.* **equation** /ɪˈkweɪ.ʒən/ *noun* [U] *There is a tendency in films to **make** the equation **between** violence and excitement.*

▲ **equate to** ***sth*** *phrasal verb* to be the same in amount, number or size: *The price of such goods in those days equates to about $50 a kilo at current prices.*

equation /ɪˈkweɪ.ʒən/ *noun* **1** [C] a mathematical statement in which you show that two amounts are equal using mathematical symbols: *In the equation $3x - 3 = 15$, $x = 6$.* **2** [C usually sing] a difficult problem which can only be understood if all the different influences are considered: *Managing the economy is a complex equation **of** controlling inflation and reducing unemployment.*

equator /ɪˈkweɪ.təʳ/ [US] /-t̬ɚ/ *noun* [S] an imaginary line drawn around the middle of the Earth an equal distance from the North Pole and the South Pole: *Singapore **is/lies on** the Equator.* **equatorial** /ˌek.wəˈtɔː.ri.əl/ [US] /-ˈtɔːr.i-/ *adj*: *equatorial Africa* ○ *The equatorial climate of the Amazonian rain forests is hot and wet.*

equerry /ˈek.wə.ri/ [US] /-wɚ.i/ *noun* [C] an officer who works for a particular member of a royal family to help them in their official duties: *an equerry **to** the Queen*

equestrian /ɪˈkwes.tri.ən/ *adj* connected with the riding of horses: *They plan to hold the Olympics' equestrian **events** in another part of the city.*
equestrian /ɪˈkwes.tri.ən/ *noun* [C] *FORMAL* a person who rides horses, especially as a job or very skilfully

equi- /ek.wɪ-/ *prefix* equal or equally

equidistant /ˌek.wɪˈdɪs.tənt/ /ˌiː.kwɪ-/ *adj* equally distant or close: *London is roughly equidistant **from** Oxford and Cambridge.*

equilateral /ˌiː.kwɪˈlæt.ər.əl/ /ˌek.wɪ-/ [US] /-læt̬-/ *adj* describes a shape whose sides are all the same length: *an equilateral triangle*

equilibrium /ˌiː.kwɪˈlɪb.ri.əm/ /ˌek.wɪ-/ *noun* [S or U] *SLIGHTLY FORMAL* **1** a state of balance: *The disease destroys much of the inner-ear, disturbing the animal's equilibrium.* ○ *the country's economic equilibrium* **2** a state of mental calmness: *Yoga is said to restore one's inner equilibrium.*

equine /ˈek.waɪn/ *adj FORMAL* connected with horses, or appearing similar to a horse: *equine flu* ○ *The portraits showed an aristocratic family with long equine faces.*

equinox /ˈek.wɪ.nɒks/ [US] /-nɑːks/ *noun* [C] either of the two occasions in the year when day and night are of equal length: *the vernal/autumn equinox*

equip [PROVIDE] /ɪˈkwɪp/ *verb* [T] **-pp-** to provide a person or a place with objects that are necessary for a particular purpose: *It's going to cost $4 million to equip the hospital.* ○ *All the police officers were equipped **with** shields to defend themselves against the rioters.* **equipped** /ɪˈkwɪpt/ *adj*: *Their schools are very poorly equipped.*
equipment /ɪˈkwɪp.mənt/ *noun* [U] **1** the set of necessary tools, clothing etc. for a particular purpose: *office/camping/kitchen equipment* ○ *electrical equipment* **2** *FORMAL* the act of equipping a person or place

COMMON LEARNER ERROR

Equipment not equipments

Remember **equipment** is uncountable.

Have you packed all the camping equipment?
~~*Have you packed all the camping equipments?*~~

equip [PREPARE] /ɪˈkwɪp/ *verb* [T] **-pp-** to give someone the skills they need to do a particular thing: *The course aims to equip people **with** the skills necessary for a job in this technological age.* ○ *A degree in the history of art is very nice but it doesn't exactly equip you **for** many jobs.* **equipped** /ɪˈkwɪpt/ *adj* [+ **to** infinitive] *Many consider him the leader best equipped **to** be prime minister.* ○ *Not being a specialist in the subject I don't feel very well-equipped **to** answer such questions.*

equitable /ˈek.wɪ.tə.bl̩/ [US] /-t̬ə-/ *adj FORMAL* fair and reasonable; treating everyone in the same way: *an equitable tax system* **equitably** /ˈek.wɪ.tə.bli/ [US] /-t̬ə-/ *adv*: *If the law is to be effective it must be applied equitably.*
equity /ˈek.wɪ.ti/ [US] /-t̬i/ *noun* [U] **1** *FORMAL* when everyone is treated fairly and equally: *a society based on equity and social justice* * NOTE: The opposite of equity is **inequity**. **2** *LEGAL* in English-speaking countries, a system of justice which allows a fair judgment of a case where the laws that already exist are not satisfactory

equity /ˈek.wɪ.ti/ [US] /-t̬i/ *noun* **1** [C or U] *SPECIALIZED* the value of a company, which is divided into many equal parts owned by the SHAREHOLDERS, or one of the equal parts into which the value of a company is divided: *He sold his equity in the company last year.* ○ *The rights give holders the opportunity to purchase additional equity interests in the company at a big discount.* **2** [U] the value of a property after you have paid any MORTGAGE or other charges relating to it

equivalent /ɪˈkwɪv.əl.ənt/ *adj* having the same amount, value, purpose, qualities, etc: *She's doing the equivalent job in the new company but for more money.* ○ *Is $50 equivalent **to** about £30?* **equivalent** /ɪˈkwɪv.əl.ənt/ *noun* [C usually sing] *There is no English equivalent **for** 'bon appetit' so we have adopted the French expression.* ○ *Ten thousand people a year die of the disease – that's the equivalent **of** the population of this town.* **equivalence** /ɪˈkwɪv.əl.ənts/ *noun* [U] *FORMAL* *There's a general equivalence between the two concepts.*

equivocal /ɪˈkwɪv.ə.kəl/ *adj FORMAL* unclear and seeming to have two opposing meanings, or confusing and able to be understood in two different ways: *His words to the press were deliberately equivocal – he didn't deny the reports but neither did he confirm them.* * NOTE: The opposite is **unequivocal**. **equivocally** /ɪˈkwɪv.ə.kli/ *adv*
equivocate /ɪˈkwɪv.ə.keɪt/ *verb* [I] *FORMAL* to speak in a way that is intentionally unclear and confusing to other people, especially to hide the truth: *She accused the minister of equivocating, claiming that he had deliberately avoided telling the public how bad the problem really was.* **equivocation** /ɪˌkwɪv.əˈkeɪ.ʃən/ *noun* [U] *He answered openly and honestly without hesitation or equivocation.*

ER [THE QUEEN] /ˌiːˈɑːʳ/ [US] /-ˈɑːr/ *ABBREVIATION FOR* Elizabeth Regina: Queen Elizabeth II of England (1952-)

ER [HOSPITAL] /ˌiːˈɑːʳ/ [US] /-ˈɑːr/ *noun* [C usually sing] *US ABBREVIATION FOR* **emergency room**

er [SOUND] /ɜːʳ/ [US] /ɝː/ *exclamation* the sound that people frequently make when they pause in the middle of what they are saying or pause before they speak, often because they are deciding what to say: *"What time shall we meet this evening?" "Er, eightish?"* ○ *"Is he handsome?" "Er, well – he's got a nice friendly sort of face though he's not exactly handsome."*

-er [PERFORMER] /-əʳ/ [US] /-ɚ/ *suffix* (*ALSO* **-or**) added to some verbs to form nouns which refer to people or things that do that particular activity: *a singer* (= a person who sings) ○ *a swimmer* (= a person who swims) ○ *a dishwasher* (= a machine or person that washes dishes) ○ *an actor* (= a person who acts)

-er [SPECIALIST] /-əʳ/ [US] /-ɚ/ *suffix* added to the names of particular subjects to form nouns which refer to people who have knowledge about or are studying that subject: *a philosopher* (= a person who knows about/studies philosophy) ○ *an astronomer* (= a person who knows about/studies astronomy)

-er [FROM A PLACE] /-əʳ/ [US] /-ɚ/ *suffix* added to the names of particular places to form nouns referring to people who come from those places: *a Londoner* (= a person who comes from London) ○ *a northerner* (= a person who comes from the north)

-er [INVOLVED WITH] /-əʳ/ [US] /-ɚ/ *suffix* added to nouns or adjectives to form nouns referring to people who are connected or involved with that particular thing: *a pensioner* (= a person who receives a PENSION) ○ *first graders* (= children who are in the first GRADE of an American school)

-er [CHARACTERISTICS] /-əʳ/ [US] /-ɚ/ *suffix* added to nouns to form nouns or adjectives referring to people or things which have those particular characteristics: *a double-decker* (= a bus with two DECKS) ○ *a big-spender* (= someone who spends a lot of money)

era /ˈɪə.rə/ [US] /ˈɪr.ə/ *noun* [C] a period of time that is marked by particular events or stages of development: *the Clinton era* ○ *a **bygone*** (= past) *era* ○ *the post-war era* ○ *They had worked for peace during the long era **of** conflict.* ○ *The fall of the Berlin wall marked **the end of an** era.*

eradicate /ɪˈræd.ɪ.keɪt/ *verb* [T] *FORMAL* to get rid of completely or destroy something bad: *The government claims to be doing all it can to eradicate corruption.* ○ *The disease which once claimed millions of lives has now been eradicated.* **eradication** /ɪˌræd.ɪˈkeɪ.ʃən/ *noun* [U]

E

erase [MARK] *MAINLY US* /ɪ'reɪz/ [US] /-'reɪs/ *verb* [T] (*UK USUALLY* **rub out**) to remove something, especially a pencil mark by rubbing it: *It's in pencil so you can just erase anything that's wrong.*
erasure /ɪ'reɪ.ʒəʳ/ [US] /-ʒɚ/ *noun* [C] *MAINLY US* an act of erasing something: *There are a few gaps in the text where I* ***made*** *some erasures.*

erase [SOMETHING RECORDED] /ɪ'reɪz/ [US] /-'reɪs/ *verb* [T] to remove recordings or information from a magnetic tape or disc: *A virus erased my hard disk.*

erase [SOMETHING PAST] /ɪ'reɪz/ [US] /-'reɪs/ *verb* [T] **1** to cause a feeling or memory, or a time to be completely forgotten: *Tiger Woods is determined to erase the* ***memory of*** *a disappointing Cup debut two years ago.* ○ *Taylor wants a convincing victory to erase* ***doubts*** *about his team's ability to reach the World Cup finals.* ○ *One election cannot erase 65 years of a corrupt one-party political process.* **2** *LITERARY* to remove or destroy someone or something, or anything showing that they existed or happened: *The President said NATO expansion will finally erase the boundary line in Europe artificially created by the Cold War.* ○ *Years of hard living had blurred but not erased her girlhood beauty.* ○ *He was a man of mystery – erased from the history books.*

eraser /ɪ'reɪ.zəʳ/ [US] /-'reɪ.sɚ/ *noun* [C] (*UK USUALLY* **rubber**) a small piece of rubber used to remove the marks made by a pencil: *If you draw or write in pencil you can always rub out your mistakes with an eraser.* ➲See picture **In the Office** on page Centre 15

ere /eəʳ/ [US] /er/ *prep, conjunction LITERARY OR OLD USE* before: *I shall be back ere nightfall.*

erect [BUILD] /ɪ'rekt/ *verb* [T] *FORMAL* to build a building, wall or other structure: *The war memorial was erected in 1950.* ○ *The soldiers had erected barricades to protect themselves.*
erection /ɪ'rek.ʃᵊn/ *noun* **1** [U] *FORMAL* the act of building or making a structure: *They approved the erection of an electrified fence around the prison.* **2** [C] *MAINLY HUMOROUS* a building: *This splendid if extraordinary erection from the last century is a local landmark.*

erect [MAKE VERTICAL] /ɪ'rekt/ *verb* [T] *FORMAL* to raise something to a vertical position: *They erected a marquee to accommodate 500 wedding guests.*
erect /ɪ'rekt/ *adj* **1** standing with your back and neck very straight: *He's very tall and erect for his 78 years.* **2** When a part of the body, especially soft tissue, is erect, it is harder and bigger than usual, often pointing out or up: *an erect penis* ○ *erect nipples*
erectile /ɪ'rek.taɪl/ [US] /-təl/ *adj SPECIALIZED* Body tissue or parts of the body which are erectile are able to be filled with blood, making them larger and harder than usual.
erection /ɪ'rek.ʃᵊn/ *noun* [C] When a man has an erection, his penis is temporarily harder and bigger than usual and points up: *to get/have an erection*

ergo /'ɜː.gəʊ/ [US] /'er.goʊ/ *adv FORMAL* therefore

ergonomics /ˌɜː.gə'nɒm.ɪks/ [US] /ˌɝː.gə'nɑː.mɪks/ *noun* [U] the scientific study of people and their working conditions, especially done in order to improve effectiveness: *A specialist in ergonomics will work with the team designing the production line in our new factory.* ○ *The ergonomics of the new office furniture have reduced eye-strain and back problems among the computer users.* **ergonomic** /ˌɜː.gə'nɒm.ɪk/ [US] /ˌɝː.gə'nɑː.mɪk/ *adj*: *ergonomic design/features* **ergonomically** /ˌɜː.gə'nɒm.ɪ.kli/ [US] /ˌɝː.gə'nɑː.mɪ-/ *adv*

ermine /'ɜː.mɪn/ [US] /'ɝː-/ *noun* [U] expensive white fur with black spots that is the winter fur of the STOAT (= a small mammal) and is used to decorate formal clothes worn by kings, queens, judges, etc.

erode /ɪ'rəʊd/ [US] /-'roʊd/ *verb* [I or T] **1** to rub or be rubbed away gradually: *Wind and rain have eroded the statues into shapeless lumps of stone.* ○ *The cliffs are eroding several feet a year.* **2** to slowly reduce or destroy: *His behaviour over the last few months has eroded my confidence in his judgement.* **erosion** /ɪ'rəʊ.ʒᵊn/ [US] /-'roʊ-/ *noun* [U] *soil/coastal erosion*

erogenous /ɪ'rɒdʒ.ɪ.nəs/ [US] /ɪ'rɑː.dʒə-/ *adj* of areas of the body, able to feel sexual pleasure: *erogenous zones*

erotic /ɪ'rɒt.ɪk/ [US] /-'rɑː.t̬ɪk/ *adj* related to sexual desire and pleasure: *an erotic film* ○ *erotic dreams/feelings*
erotica /ɪ'rɒt.ɪ.kə/ [US] /-'rɑː.t̬ɪ-/ *noun* [U] books, pictures, etc. which produce sexual desire and pleasure **erotically** /ɪ'rɒt.ɪ.kli/ [US] /-rɑː.t̬ɪ-/ *adv*
eroticism /ɪ'rɒt.ɪ.sɪ.zᵊm/ [US] /-'rɑː.t̬ə-/ *noun* [U] the quality of a picture, book, film, etc. being erotic: *The play's eroticism shocked audiences when it was first performed.*

err /ɜːʳ/ /eəʳ/ [US] /ɝː/ /er/ *verb* [I] *FORMAL* to make a mistake or to do something wrong: *He erred in agreeing to her appointment.*
• **err on the side of caution** to be especially careful rather than taking a risk or making a mistake: *Twenty-five people have replied to the invitation, but I've erred on the side of caution and put out 30 chairs.*
• **To err is human (to forgive divine).** *SAYING* something that you say which means that it is natural for people to make mistakes and it is important to forgive people when they do

errand /'er.ənd/ *noun* [C] a short journey either to take a message or to deliver or collect something: *I'll meet you at six, I've got some errands to* ***do/run*** *first.*
• **errand of mercy** *LITERARY* an act of bringing help

'errand ˌboy *noun* [C] *OLD-FASHIONED* a boy or young man employed by a shop or business to take messages, deliver goods, etc.

errant /'er.ənt/ *adj* [before n] *FORMAL* behaving wrongly in some way, especially by leaving home: *an errant husband* ○ *errant children*

errata /ɪ'rɑː.tə/ [US] /-t̬ə/ *plural of* **erratum**: *a list of errata*

erratic /ɪ'ræt.ɪk/ [US] /-'ræt̬-/ *adj* irregular, uncertain or without organization in movement or behaviour: *He drove in an erratic course down the road.* ○ *She can be very erratic, one day she is friendly and the next she'll hardly speak to you.* **erratically** /ɪ'ræt.ɪ.kli/ [US] /-'ræt̬-/ *adv*: *In her study, books were arranged erratically on chairs, tables and shelves.* ○ *The machine is working erratically – there must be a loose connection.*

erratum /ɪ'rɑː.təm/ [US] /-t̬əm/ *noun* [C] *plural* **errata** *FORMAL* a mistake in a printed or written document

erroneous /ɪ'rəʊ.ni.əs/ [US] /-'roʊ-/ *adj FORMAL* wrong or false: *an erroneous belief/impression* **erroneously** /ɪ'rəʊ.ni.ə.sli/ [US] /-'roʊ-/ *adv*

error /'er.əʳ/ [US] /-ɚ/ *noun* [C or U] a mistake: *He admitted that he'd made an error.* ○ *The letter contains a number of typing errors.* ○ ***Human*** *error has been blamed for the air crash.* ○ *With something as delicate as brain surgery, there is little* ***margin for*** *error* (= you must not make mistakes). ➲See Note **fault or mistake/error?** at **fault** MISTAKE.
• **error of judgment** a wrong decision: *Not telling the staff before they read the news in the papers was an error of judgment.*
• **see the error of *your* ways** to understand that you were wrong to behave in a particular way and start to behave differently

ersatz /'eə.zæts/ [US] /'er.zɑːts/ *adj DISAPPROVING* used instead of something else, usually because the other thing is too expensive or rare: *I'm allowed to eat ersatz chocolate made from carob beans, but it's a poor substitute for the real thing.*

erstwhile /'ɜːst.waɪl/ [US] /'ɝːst-/ *adj* [before n] *FORMAL* former

erudite /'er.ʊ.daɪt/ *adj FORMAL* having or containing a lot of specialist knowledge: *He's the author of an erudite book on Scottish history.* **erudition** /ˌer.ʊ'dɪʃ.ᵊn/ *noun* [U] *a work of great erudition*

erupt /ɪ'rʌpt/ *verb* [I] to explode or burst out suddenly: *At the end of a hot summer, violence erupted in the inner cities.* ○ *Since the* ***volcano*** *last erupted, many houses have been built in a dangerous position on its slopes.* ○ *Two days after he'd been exposed to the substance, a painful rash erupted* (= suddenly appeared) *on his neck.* ○ *Her back erupted* ***in*** *small red spots.* **eruption** /ɪ'rʌp.ʃᵊn/ *noun* [C or U] *a volcanic eruption* ○ *There was a violent eruption of anti-government feeling.*

escalate /'es.kə.leɪt/ *verb* [I or T] to make or become greater or more serious: *The decision to escalate UN involvement has been taken in the hopes of a swift end to the* hostilities. ○ *His financial problems escalated after he became unemployed.* ○ *The escalating rate of inflation will almost certainly bring escalating prices.* **escalation** /ˌes.kəˈleɪ.ʃᵊn/ *noun* [C **or** U] *It's difficult to explain the recent escalation in/of violent crime.*

escalator /ˈes.kə.leɪ.təʳ/ ⓤ /-t̬ɚ/ *noun* [C] a set of stairs moved up or down by electric power on which people can stand and be taken from one level of a building to another, especially in shops, railway stations and airports: *I'll meet you by the up/down escalator on the second floor.*

escalope /ˈes.kə.lɒp/ ⓤ /ɪˈskɑː.ləp/ *noun* [C] a thin piece of meat without bones: *veal/turkey escalopes*

escapade /ˈes.kə.peɪd/ *noun* [C] an act involving some danger, risk or excitement because it is different from usual or expected behaviour: *Her latest escapade was to camp outside a department store on the night before the sale.*

escape /ɪˈskeɪp/ *verb* **1** [I **or** T] to get free from something, or to avoid something: *Two prisoners have escaped.* ○ *A lion has escaped from its cage.* ○ *She was lucky to escape serious injury.* ○ *He narrowly* (= only just) *escaped a fine.* ○ *His name escapes me* (= I have forgotten his name). ○ *Nothing important escapes her notice/ attention.* **2** [I] SPECIALIZED to press the key on a computer keyboard which allows you to leave a particular screen and return to the previous one or to interrupt a process: *Escape from this window and return to the main menu.*
• **There's no escaping the fact** used to mean that something is certain: *There's no escaping the fact (that) we won't be able to complete these orders without extra staff.*

escape /ɪˈskeɪp/ *noun* **1** [C **or** U] when someone succeeds in getting out of a place or a dangerous or bad situation: *He made it on the back of a motorbike.* ○ *an escape route* ○ *They had a narrow escape* (= only just avoided injury or death) *when their car crashed.* **2** [C] an accidental loss: *an escape of radioactivity* **3** [S] something that helps you to forget about your usual life or problems: *Romantic novels provide an escape from reality.*

escaped /ɪˈskeɪpt/ *adj* [before n] having got free: *an escaped prisoner*

escapee /ɪˌskeɪˈpiː/ *noun* [C] a person who has escaped from a place: *The escapees were recaptured after three days on the run.*

eˈscape ˌhatch *noun* [C] the part of a SUBMARINE through which people can leave when it is under water

eˈscape (ˌkey) *noun* [C usually sing] (WRITTEN ABBREVIATION **Esc**) SPECIALIZED the key on a computer keyboard which allows you to leave a particular screen and return to the previous one or to interrupt a process: *Press Esc to return to the main menu.*

escapism /ɪˈskeɪ.pɪ.zᵊm/ *noun* [U] when someone avoids an unpleasant or boring life, especially by thinking, reading, etc. about more exciting but impossible activities: *These adventure films are pure escapism. For many people going on holiday is a form of escapism.* **escapist** /ɪˈskeɪ.pɪst/ *noun* [C], *adj*: *escapist literature*

escapology /ˌes.kəˈpɒl.ə.dʒi/ ⓤ /-ˈpɑː.lə-/ *noun* [U] the activity of escaping from chains, boxes, etc. usually as part of an entertainment **escapologist** /ˌes.kəˈpɒl.ə.-dʒɪst/ ⓤ /-ˈpɑː.lə-/ *noun* [C] (US USUALLY **escape artist**)

escarpment /ɪˈskɑːp.mənt/ ⓤ /-ˈskɑːrp-/ *noun* [C] a steep slope or cliff, such as one which marks the edge of a range of hills

eschew /ɪsˈtʃuː/ *verb* [T] FORMAL to avoid something intentionally, or to give something up: *We won't have discussions with this group unless they eschew violence.*

escort GO WITH /ˈes.kɔːt/ ⓤ /-kɔːrt/ /-ˈ-/ *verb* [T] **1** to go with someone or a vehicle especially to make certain that they arrive safely or that they leave a place: *Several little boats escorted the sailing ship into the harbour.* ○ *Security guards escorted the intruders from the building.* ○ *The police escorted her to the airport, and made sure that she left the country.* **2** to go with someone and show them a place: *People on the tour will be escorted by an expert on archaeology.*

escort /ˈes.kɔːt/ ⓤ /-kɔːrt/ /-ˈ-/ *noun* **1** [C] a person who goes somewhere with another person as a helper or a guard: *The members of the jury left the court with a police escort.* **2** [U] the state of having someone with you who gives you protection or guards you: *The prisoners were transported under military escort.*

escort SOCIAL COMPANION /ˈes.kɔːt/ ⓤ /ˈes.kɔːrt/ *noun* [C] **1** a person who goes with another person, usually someone of the opposite sex, to a social event: *"But I can't go to the dance without an escort," she protested.* **2** someone, often a young woman, who is paid to go out to social events with another person: *He hired an escort girl to go to the dinner with him.*

escort /ˈes.kɔːt/ ⓤ /-kɔːrt/ *verb* [T] FORMAL to go to a social event with someone, especially a person of the opposite sex: *Who will be escorting her to the ball?*

eˈscort ˌagency *noun* [C] (ALSO **escort service**) a business which supplies people who work as escorts

escrow /ˈes.krəʊ/ ⓤ /-kroʊ/ *noun* [U] SPECIALIZED an agreement between two people or organizations in which money or property is kept by a third person or organization until a particular condition is completed: *The money was placed in escrow.*

escudo /esˈkuː.dəʊ/ ⓤ /-doʊ/ *noun* [C] the standard unit of money used in Portugal before they started using the euro, and in Cape Verde

Eskimo (*plural* **Eskimos** or **Eskimo**) /ˈes.kɪ.məʊ/ ⓤ /-kə.moʊ/ *noun* [C] (CANADIAN ENGLISH **Inuit**) a member of one of the Native American tribes who live in the very cold northern areas of North America, Russia and Greenland * NOTE: Many people consider this term offensive, and prefer the word **Inuit**.

ESL /ˌiː.esˈel/ *noun* [U] ABBREVIATION FOR English as a Second Language: the teaching of English to speakers of other languages who live in a country where English is an official or important language ➔Compare **EFL**.

esophagus /ɪˈsɒf.ə.gəs/ ⓤ /-ˈsɑː.fə-/ *noun* [C] US FOR **oesophagus**

esoteric /ˌiː.səʊˈter.ɪk/ ⓤ /ˌes.ə-/ *adj* very unusual, understood or liked by only a small number of people, especially those with special knowledge: *He has an esoteric collection of old toys and games.* ○ DISAPPROVING OR HUMOROUS *She has a rather esoteric taste in clothes.*

ESP /ˌiː.esˈpiː/ *noun* [U] ABBREVIATION FOR **extrasensory perception**

esp, **esp.** *adv* WRITTEN ABBREVIATION FOR **especially**

especial /ɪˈspeʃ.ᵊl/ *adj* [before n] FORMAL special

especially /ɪˈspeʃ.ᵊl.i/ *adv* (ALSO **specially**) very much; particularly; for a particular reason: *She's not especially interested in sport.* ○ *I chose this especially for your new house.* ○ *They invited her to speak especially because of her experience in inner cities.* ➔See Note **specially or especially?** at **special** PARTICULAR.

Esperanto /ˌes.pᵊrˈæn.təʊ/ ⓤ /-pəˈræn.toʊ/ *noun* [U] an artificial language, made by combining features of several European languages, intended as a form of international communication

espionage /ˈes.pi.ə.nɑːʒ/ *noun* [U] the discovering of secrets, especially political or military information of another country or the industrial information of a business: *military/industrial espionage* ➔See also **spy** SECRET PERSON.

esplanade /ˈes.plə.neɪd/ ⓤ /-nɑːd/ *noun* [C] OLD-FASHIONED a wide level path for walking along, often by the sea

espouse /esˈpaʊz/ *verb* [T] FORMAL to become involved with or support an activity or opinion: *Vegetarianism is one cause she does not espouse.* **espousal** /esˈpaʊ.zᵊl/ *noun* [S **or** U] *Espousal of such liberal ideas won't make her very popular around here.*

espresso /esˈpres.əʊ/ ⓤ /-oʊ/ *noun* [C **or** U] *plural* **espressos** strong coffee, or a cup of this, made by forcing hot water through crushed coffee beans and served without milk: *Do you like espresso?* ○ *Would you prefer an espresso or a cappuccino?*

esprit de corps /esˌpriː.dəˈkɔːʳ/ ⓤ /-ˈkɔːr/ *noun* [U] FORMAL the feelings, such as pride and loyalty, shared by members of a group of people: *His leadership kept the team's esprit de corps intact during difficult periods.*

espy /es'paɪ/ *verb* [T] *OLD-FASHIONED* to suddenly or unexpectedly see something, especially something a long distance away: *She suddenly espied someone waving at her from the window.*

Esq *noun* [after n] **1** *MAINLY UK FORMAL ABBREVIATION FOR* Esquire: a title added after a man's name on envelopes and official documents. If Esq is used, Mr is not used before the name. **2** *US ABBREVIATION* usually used only after the full name of a man or woman who is a lawyer: *Address it to my lawyer, Steven A. Neil, Esq./Gloria Neil, Esq.*

-esque /-esk/ *suffix* like or in the style of someone or their work: *Dali-esque* ○ *Leonardo-esque* ○ *Working there was like being trapped in a Kafkaesque nightmare.*

E

essay [WRITING] *UK* /'es.eɪ/ *noun* [C] (*US* **paper**) a short piece of writing on a particular subject, especially one done by students as part of the work for a course: *For homework I want you to write an essay **on** endangered species.*
essayist /'es.eɪ.ɪst/ *noun* [C] a person who writes essays that are published: *a political essayist*

essay [ATTEMPT] /e'seɪ/ *verb* [T] *OLD-FASHIONED* to try to do something: *The procedure was first essayed in 1923.*

essence [SMELL/TASTE] /'es.ᵊnts/ *noun* [C or U] a strong liquid, usually from a plant or flower, that is used to add a flavour or smell to something: *vanilla essence* ○ *essence of violets*

essence [IMPORTANCE] /'es.ᵊnts/ *noun* [S or U] the basic or most important idea or quality of something: *The essence of his argument was that education should continue throughout life.* ○ *Yet change is the very essence of life.*
• **in essence** *FORMAL* relating to the most important characteristics or ideas of something: *In essence, both sides agree on the issue.*
• **be of the essence** *FORMAL* to be the most important thing: *In any of these discussions, of course, honesty is of the essence.* ○ *Time is of the essence.*

essential /ɪ'sen.tʃᵊl/ *adj* necessary; needed: *Government support will be essential if the project is to succeed.* ○ *There is essential work to be done before the building can be re-occupied.* ○ *Water is essential **for/to** living things.* ○ ***It** is essential **(that)** our prices remain competitive.* ○ *For the experiment to be valid, it is essential **to** record the data accurately.*
essential /ɪ'sen.tʃᵊl/ *noun* [C usually pl] a basic thing that you cannot live without: *Because I live in a remote village, I regard my car as an essential.* ○ *When we go on holiday, we only take **the bare** essentials.* ○ *This leaflet will give you the essentials **of** how to use the word processor.*
essentially /ɪ'sen.tʃᵊl.i/ *adv* relating to the most important characteristics or ideas of something: *It's essentially a dictionary but it differs in one or two respects.* ○ *What he's saying is essentially true.*

es,sential 'oil *noun* [C] an oil, usually with a strong smell, which is taken from a plant and is used to make perfume, or for rubbing into a person's body during MASSAGE: *Lavender, peppermint, and jasmine are essential oils which are widely available.*

es,sential 'services *plural noun* basic public needs, such as water, gas and electricity, which are often supplied to people's houses

est [JUDGED], **est.** *adj ABBREVIATION FOR* **estimated**: *the town of Brownford (est population 14 000)*

Est [STARTED], **Est.** *adj ABBREVIATION FOR* established: *P. R. Jones & Co, Est 1920*

establish [START] /ɪ'stæb.lɪʃ/ *verb* [T often passive] to start a company or organization that will continue for a long time: *The brewery was established in 1822.* ○ *These methods of working were established in the last century.*
establish *yourself* *verb* [R] to be in a successful position over a long period of time: *He has established himself as the leading candidate in the election.* **establishment** /ɪ'stæb.lɪʃ.mənt/ *noun* [U] *Since its establishment two years ago, the advice centre has seen over 500 people a week.* ○ *The establishment **of** new areas of employment is a priority.* ➲See also **establishment**.

establish [ACCEPT] /ɪ'stæb.lɪʃ/ *verb* [T] to cause to be accepted in or familiar with a place, position, etc: *His reputation for carelessness was established long before the latest problems arose.* ○ *He's established himself **as** a dependable source of information.* ○ *After three months we were well established **in/at** our new house/new jobs.*
established /ɪ'stæb.lɪʃt/ *adj*: *There are established procedures for dealing with emergencies.*

establish [DISCOVER] /ɪ'stæb.lɪʃ/ *verb* [T] *FORMAL* to discover or get proof of something: *Before we take any action we must establish the facts/truth.* ○ [+ question word] *Can you establish **what** time she left home/**whether** she has left home.* ○ [+ (that)] *We have established **(that)** she was born in 1900.*

the e'stablished 'church *noun* the official religion of a country: *In Britain, the Queen is the head of the established church.*

establishment /ɪ'stæb.lɪʃ.mənt/ *noun* [C] a business or other organization, or the place where an organization operates: *an educational/financial/religious establishment* ➲See also **establishment** at **establish** START.
• **the establishment** the important and powerful people who control a country or an organization, especially those who support the existing situation: *Critics said judges were on the side of the establishment.*

estate [PROPERTY] /ɪ'steɪt/ *noun* [C] **1** a large area of land in the country which is owned by a family or an organization and is often farmed: *It's a typical **country** estate with a large house for the owner, farm buildings and estate workers' houses.* **2** *LEGAL* everything that a person owns when they die: *She **left** her entire estate to her niece.*

estate [BUILDINGS] /ɪ'steɪt/ *noun* [C] *UK* a group of houses or factories built in a planned way: *a housing estate* ○ *an industrial estate* (= a group of factories)

estate [STATE] /ɪ'steɪt/ *noun* [U] *OLD USE* a state of being: *the holy estate of marriage*

es'tate ,agency *UK noun* [C] (*US* **real estate office,** *US* **realty office**) a business that arranges the selling, renting or management of homes, land and buildings for their owners

es'tate ,agent *UK noun* [C] (*US* **real estate agent, realtor**) someone who works for an estate agency

es'tate (,car) *UK noun* [C] (*US* **station wagon**) a car with a lot of space behind the back seat and an extra door at the back for loading large items ➲See picture **Cars and Trucks** on page Centre 13

esteem /ɪ'stiːm/ *noun* [U] *FORMAL* respect for or a good opinion of someone: *There has been a drop in public esteem **for** teachers.* ○ *Because of their achievements they were **held in*** (= given) ***(high)*** *esteem.*
esteem /ɪ'stiːm/ *verb* [T not continuous] to respect someone or have a good opinion of them: *Her work is highly esteemed by all her colleagues.* ○ [+ obj + n or adj] *OLD-FASHIONED I would esteem* (= consider) ***it a favour*** *if you would accompany me.*

esthetic /es'θet.ɪk/ [US] /-'θeṭ-/ *adj MAINLY US FOR* **aesthetic**
esthete /'iːs.θiːt/ *noun* [C] *MAINLY US*

estimable /'es.tɪ.mə.bl̩/ *adj FORMAL* of a person or their behaviour, producing a good opinion; very good: *He writes estimable poetry under a pseudonym.* ○ *Her performance under such stressful conditions was estimable.*

estimate /'es.tɪ.mət/ *noun* [C] a guess of what the size, value, amount, cost, etc. of something might be: *The number of people who applied for the course was 120 compared with an initial estimate **of** between 50 and 100.* ○ *We'll accept the lowest of three estimates **for** the building work.* ○ *a **conservative*** (= low) *estimate* ○ *a **rough*** (= not exact) *estimate*
estimate /'es.tɪ.meɪt/ *verb* [T] to guess the cost, size, value, etc. of something: *Government sources estimate a long-term 50% increase in rail fares.* ○ [+ (that)] *They estimate **(that)** the journey will take at least two weeks.* ○ [+ question word] ***It** was difficult to estimate **how** many trees had been destroyed.* **estimated** /'es.tɪ.meɪ.tɪd/ [US] /-ṭɪd/ *adj*: *an estimated cost/value*

estimation /,es.tɪ'meɪ.ʃᵊn/ *noun* [S] your opinion of someone or something: ***In** my estimation a lot of other banks are going to have the same problem.* ○ *He **sank in***

my estimation (= My opinion of him fell) *when I saw how he treated his wife.*

estranged /ɪˈstreɪndʒd/ *adj* **1** describes a husband or wife who is not now living with the person they are married to: *his estranged wife* **2** FORMAL If you are estranged from your family or friends then you have seriously argued with them and are no longer friendly with them: *It's sad to see someone estranged from their parents.*

estrangement /ɪˈstreɪndʒ.mənt/ *noun* [C or U] FORMAL (a period) when you are estranged from someone

estrogen /ˈiː.strə.dʒən/ *noun* [U] MAINLY US FOR **oestrogen**

estuary /ˈes.tjʊə.ri/ ⓤ /-tu.er.i/ *noun* [C] the wide part of a river at the place where it joins the sea: *the Thames estuary* ○ *the Rance estuary* **estuarine** /ˈes.tjʊə.ri:n/ /-tjʊr.i:n/ *adj* SPECIALIZED *estuarine species*

Estuary ˈEnglish *noun* [U] a type of English spoken in south-east England which is a mixture of standard English and London English

ETA /ˌiː.tiːˈeɪ/ *noun* [S] ABBREVIATION FOR estimated time of arrival: the time you expect to arrive: *What's your ETA?*

e-tailer /ˈiː.teɪ.ləʳ/ ⓤ /-lɚ/ *noun* [C] UK a business that uses the Internet to sell its products: *a music/wine/ electrical e-tailer* **e-tailing** /ˈiː.teɪ.lɪŋ/ ⓤ /-lɚ/ *noun* [U]

et al. /et ˈæl/ SPECIALIZED ABBREVIATION FOR et alia: and others. It is used in formal writing to avoid a long list of names of people who have written something together: *The method is described in an article by Feynman et al.*

etc., etc ABBREVIATION FOR et cetera: and other similar things. It is used to avoid giving a complete list: *We saw lots of lions, tigers, elephants, etc.*

etch /etʃ/ *verb* [T] to cut a pattern, picture, etc. into a smooth surface, especially on metal or glass, using acid or sometimes a sharp instrument: *He etched his name on a piece of glass.*

● **be etched on/in your memory** to be something that you will continue to remember: *The scene will be etched on my memory forever.*

● **be etched somewhere, be etched with sth** LITERARY If a feeling, emotion or shape is etched somewhere, it can be seen there very clearly: *His face was etched with pain.* ○ *Confusion and sadness were etched on their faces.* ○ *The foothills of the Himalayas were sharply etched against the pale blue sky.*

etcher /ˈetʃ.əʳ/ ⓤ /-ɚ/ *noun* [C] a person who makes etchings

etching /ˈetʃ.ɪŋ/ *noun* **1** [U] the practice of etching **2** [C] a picture produced by printing from a metal plate which has been etched with acid

eternal /ɪˈtɜː.nəl/ ⓤ /-ˈtɜː.-/ *adj* lasting forever or for a very long time: *The company is engaged in the eternal search for a product that will lead the market.* ○ *Will you two never stop your eternal arguing!*

● **Hope springs eternal.** SAYING said when you are hopeful that something will happen although it seems unlikely

eternally /ɪˈtɜː.nəl.i/ ⓤ /-ˈtɜː.-/ *adv: the eternally changing seasons* ○ *eternally weary/sad/cheerful* ○ FORMAL *I'd be eternally* (= very or always) *grateful if you could arrange it.*

eˌternal ˈstudent *noun* [C usually sing] HUMOROUS someone who tries to avoid getting a job for as long as possible by taking more educational courses

eternity /ɪˈtɜː.nɪ.ti/ ⓤ /-ˈtɜː.nə.t̬i/ *noun* [U] **1** time which never ends or which has no limits: *They haven't been given these rights for (all) eternity – they should justify having them just like most other people have to.* ○ *Religions gain some of their worldly power by claiming they have the key to eternity* (= a state of existence outside normal life). **2 an eternity** a very long time: *The film went on for what seemed like an eternity.* ○ *Nine months is a long time for anyone, but it's an eternity for the very young.*

ethanol /ˈeθ.ə.nɒl/ ⓤ /-nɑːl/ *noun* [U] (ALSO **ethyl alcohol**) a chemical compound which is a type of alcohol

ether MEDICAL /ˈiː.θəʳ/ ⓤ /-θɚ/ *noun* [U] a colourless liquid used, especially in the past, as an ANAESTHETIC to make people sleep before a medical operation

the ˈether SKY, **the aether** *noun* [S] OLD USE the clear sky; the upper air, or the AIRWAVES

ethereal /ɪˈθɪə.ri.əl/ ⓤ /-ˈθɪr.i-/ *adj* light and delicate, especially in an unnatural way: *an ethereal being* ○ *ethereal beauty* **ethereally** /ɪˈθɪə.ri.ə.li/ ⓤ /-ˈθɪr.i-/ *adv*

ethic /ˈeθ.ɪk/ *noun* [C usually pl] a system of accepted beliefs which control behaviour, especially such a system based on morals: *the (Protestant) work ethic* ○ *The ethics of journalism are much debated.* ○ *He said he was bound by a scientist's code of ethics.* ○ *Publication of the article was a breach of ethics.* **ethical** /ˈeθ.ɪ.kəl/ *adj*: *ethical problems/standards* ○ *ethical practice* ○ *We are a moral, ethical people and therefore we do not approve of their activities.* **ethically** /ˈeθ.ɪ.kli/ *adv*: *This action is ethically questionable.*

ethics /ˈeθ.ɪks/ *noun* [U] the study of what is morally right and what is not

ethnic /ˈeθ.nɪk/ *adj* **1** of a national or racial group of people: *A question on ethnic origin was included in the census.* ○ *The factory's workforce reflects the ethnic mix from which it draws its labour.* ○ *Conflicts between the different ethnic groups in the country exploded into civil war.* **2** from a different race or interesting because characteristic of an ethnic group which is very different from those that are common in western culture: *ethnic food* ○ *ethnic costume*

ethnic /ˈeθ.nɪk/ *noun* [C] US a person belonging to an ethnic group **ethnically** /ˈeθ.nɪ.kli/ *adv*: *ethnically related communities* **ethnicity** /eθˈnɪs.ɪ.ti/ ⓤ /-ə.t̬i/ *noun* [U] FORMAL

ethnic ˈcleansing *noun* [U] the organized attempt by one racial or political group to completely remove from a country or area anyone who belongs to another particular racial group, using violence and often murder to achieve this

ethnic miˈnority *noun* [C] a national or racial group living in a country or area which contains a larger group of people of a different race or nationality

ethnocentric /ˌeθ.nəʊˈsen.trɪk/ ⓤ /-noʊ-/ *adj* believing that the people, customs and traditions of your own race or nationality are better than those of other races **ethnocentrism** /ˌeθ.nəʊˈsen.trɪ.zᵊm/ ⓤ /-noʊ-/ *noun* [U]

ethnography /eθˈnɒg.rə.fi/ ⓤ /-ˈnɑː.grə-/ *noun* [C or U] a scientific description of the culture of a society by someone who has lived in it, or a book containing this: *One of the aims of ethnography is to contribute to an understanding of the human race.* ○ *Malinowski wrote several ethnographies of the Trobriand Islands.* **ethnographic** /ˌeθ.nəʊˈgræf.ɪk/ ⓤ /-noʊ-/ *adj* (ALSO **ethnographical**) **ethnographically** /ˌeθ.nəʊˈgræf.ɪ.kli/ ⓤ /-noʊ-/ *adv* **ethnographer** /eθˈnɒg.rə.fəʳ/ ⓤ /-ˈnɑː.grə.fɚ/ *noun* [C]

ethnology /eθˈnɒl.ə.dʒi/ ⓤ /-ˈnɑː.lə-/ *noun* [U] comparative and historical study of different societies and cultures **ethnologic** /ˌeθ.nəʊˈlɒdʒ.ɪ.kᵊl/ ⓤ /-noʊˈlɑː.-dʒɪ-/ *adj* (ALSO **ethnological**) **ethnologically** /ˌeθ.nəʊˈlɒdʒ.ɪ.kli/ ⓤ /-noʊˈlɑː.dʒɪ.kli/ *adv* **ethnologist** /eθˈnɒl.ə.dʒɪst/ ⓤ /-ˈnɑː.lə-/ *noun* [C]

ethos /ˈiː.θɒs/ ⓤ /-θɑːs/ *noun* [S] the set of beliefs, ideas, etc. about social behaviour and relationships of a person or group: *national ethos* ○ *working-class ethos* ○ *The ethos of the traditional family firm is under threat.*

ethyl ˈalcohol *noun* [U] ethanol

etiolated /ˈiː.ti.əʊ.leɪ.tɪd/ ⓤ /-ə.leɪ.t̬ɪd/ *adj* SPECIALIZED especially of plants, pale and weak

etiology /ˌiː.tiˈɒl.ə.dʒi/ ⓤ /-ˈɑː.lə-/ *noun* [U] the scientific study of the cause of diseases

etiquette /ˈet.ɪ.ket/ ⓤ /ˈet̬.ɪ.kət/ *noun* [U] the set of rules or customs which control accepted behaviour in particular social groups or social situations: *(Social) etiquette dictates that men cannot sit while women are standing.* ○ *Diplomatic etiquette forbids calling for the death of a national leader.*

etymology /ˌet.ɪˈmɒl.ə.dʒi/ ⓤ /-ˈmɑː.lə-/ *noun* [C or U] the study of the origin and history of words, or a study of this type relating to one particular word: *At university she developed an interest in etymology.* ○ *A list of selected words and their etymologies is printed at the back of the book.* **etymological** /ˌet.ɪ.məˈlɒdʒ.ɪ.kᵊl/ ⓤ /-ˈlɑː.dʒɪ-/ *adj* **etymologically** /ˌet.ɪ.məˈlɒdʒ.ɪ.kli/ ⓤ /-ˈlɑː.dʒɪ-/ *adv* **etymologist** /ˌet.ɪˈmɒl.ə.dʒɪst/ ⓤ /-ˈmɑː.lə-/ *noun* [C]

E

E

the EU /ˌðiːiːˈjuː/ *group noun* [S] *ABBREVIATION FOR* **the European Union**

eucalyptus (tree) /ˌjuː.kᵊlˈɪp.təs.triː/ *noun* [C or U] (*ALSO* **gum (tree)**) any of several types of tree, found especially in Australia, which produce an oil with a strong smell used in medicine and industry: *eucalyptus oil*

Eucharist /ˈjuːkᵊr.ɪst/ *noun* [S or U] the Christian ceremony based on Jesus Christ's last meal with his DIS-CIPLES (= the twelve men who were his followers), or the holy bread and wine used in this ceremony ⊃See also **Communion**. **eucharistic** /ˌjuː.kᵊrˈɪs.tɪk/ *adj*

eugenics /juːˈdʒen.ɪks/ *noun* [U] *SPECIALIZED* the study of methods of improving humans by allowing only care-fully chosen people to reproduce: *Eugenics was the central, and most controversial, part of his social philosophy.* **eugenic** /juːˈdʒen.ɪk/ *adj*

eulogy /ˈjuː.lə.dʒi/ *noun* [C or U] *FORMAL* a speech, piece of writing, poem, etc. containing great praise, especially for someone who recently died or stopped working: *He was the most self-effacing of men – the last thing he would have relished was a eulogy.* ○ *The song was a eulogy to the joys of travelling.* **eulogist** /ˈjuː.lə.dʒɪst/ *noun* [C] **eu-logistic** /ˌjuː.ləˈdʒɪs.tɪk/ *adj*

eulogize, *UK USUALLY* **-ise** /ˈjuː.lə.dʒaɪz/ *verb* [T; I usually + adv or prep] *FORMAL* to praise someone or something in a speech or piece of writing: *Critics everywhere have eu-logized her new novel.* ○ *They eulogized over the breath-taking views.*

eunuch /ˈjuː.nək/ *noun* [C] *plural* **eunuchs** a man who has had his testicles removed

euphemism /ˈjuː.fə.mɪ.zᵊm/ *noun* [C or U] a word or phrase used to avoid saying an unpleasant or offensive word: *'Senior citizen' is a euphemism for 'old person'.* ○ *The article made so much use of euphemism that often its meaning was unclear.* **euphemistic** /ˌjuː.fəˈmɪs.tɪk/ *adj* **euphemistically** /ˌjuː.fəˈmɪs.tɪ.kli/ *adv*

euphonious /juːˈfəʊ.ni.əs/ ⑧ /-ˈfoʊ-/ *adj* *FORMAL* having a pleasant sound

euphonium /juːˈfəʊ.ni.əm/ ⑧ /-ˈfoʊ-/ *noun* [C] a large musical instrument made from brass, that you play by blowing into it

euphoria /juːˈfɔː.ri.ə/ ⑧ /-ˈfɔːr.i-/ *noun* [U] extreme happiness, sometimes more than is reasonable in a particular situation: *They were in a state of euphoria for days after they won the prize.*

euphoric /juːˈfɒr.ɪk/ ⑧ /-ˈfɑːr-/ *adj* extremely happy and excited: *a euphoric mood* **euphorically** /juːˈfɒr.ɪ.kli/ ⑧ /-ˈfɑːr-/ *adv*

Eurasian /jʊəˈreɪ.ʒᵊn/ ⑧ /jʊ-/ *adj* **1** describes a person with one European parent and one Asian parent **2** of or connected with Europe and Asia considered as a unit: *Eurasian languages* **Eurasian** /jʊəˈreɪ.ʒᵊn/ ⑧ /jʊ-/ *noun* [C]

eureka /jʊəˈriː.kə/ *exclamation* *OFTEN HUMOROUS* used to show that you have been successful in something you were trying to do: *"Eureka!" she shouted as the engine started.*

Euro [EUROPE] /jʊə.rəʊ-/ ⑧ /jʊr.oʊ-/ *adj* [before n], *prefix* of or connected with Europe, especially of the European Union: *the Euro elections* ○ *a Euro-MP* (= Member of the European Parliament)

euro [MONEY], **Euro** /ˈjʊə.rəʊ/ ⑧ /ˈjʊ.roʊ/ *noun* [C] the unit of money used in most European Union countries

Eurocheque /ˈjuː.rəʊ.tʃek/ ⑧ /-roʊ-/ *noun* [C] a cheque that can be used in particular banks or shops in Europe

Eurocrat /ˈjuː.rəʊ.kræt/ ⑧ /-roʊ-/ *noun* [C] an official, especially an important one, of the European Union

Euroland /ˈjʊə.rəʊ.lænd/ ⑧ /ˈjʊ.roʊ.lænd/ *noun* [U] (*ALSO* **the Eurozone**) *INFORMAL* the countries belonging to the European Union which use the Euro as their unit of money. In 2002 not all of the European Union countries were using the Euro.

Europe /ˈjʊə.rəp/ ⑧ /ˈjʊ-/ *noun* [U] **1** the continent that is to the east of the Atlantic Ocean, to the north of the Mediterranean and to the west of Asia **2** the European Union **3** *UK* the continent of Europe without including the UK

European /ˌjʊə.rəˈpiː.ən/ ⑧ /ˌjʊr.ə-/ *adj* of or from Europe

European /ˌjʊə.rəˈpiː.ən/ ⑧ /ˌjʊr.ə-/ *noun* [C] someone who comes from Europe

the Euro,pean Com'munity *group noun* [S] (*ABBREVIATION* **the EC**) the organization through which particular European governments made decisions and agreed on shared action in social and economic matters until November 1993, when it became the EUROPEAN UNION

Euro'pean ,plan *noun* [U] *US* when the price of a room in a hotel does not include meals

the Euro,pean 'Union *group noun* [S] (*ABBREVIATION* **the EU**) the organization, since November 1993, through which European governments who choose to be members make decisions and agree on shared action in social and economic matters

Eurosceptic /ˈjʊə.rəʊˌskep.tɪk/ ⑧ /ˈjʊ.roʊ-/ *noun* [C] *UK* a person, especially a politician, who opposes closer con-nections between Britain and the European Union

euthanasia /ˌjuː.θəˈneɪ.ʒə/ *noun* [U] the act of killing someone who is very ill or very old so that they do not suffer any more: *Although some people campaign for the right to euthanasia, it is still illegal in most countries.*

evacuate /ɪˈvæk.ju.eɪt/ *verb* [I or T] to move people from a dangerous place to somewhere safe: *The police evacuated the village shortly before the explosion.* ○ *A thousand people were evacuated from their homes following the floods.* ○ *When toxic fumes began to drift toward our homes, we were told to evacuate.* **evacuation** /ɪˌvæk.juˈeɪ.ʃᵊn/ *noun* [C or U] *The evacuation of civilians remains out of the question while the fighting continues.* ○ *The first evacuations came ten days after the disaster.*

evacuee /ɪˌvæk.juˈiː/ *noun* [C] someone who is evacuated from a dangerous place, especially during a war: *Thousands of evacuees crossed the border to safety this morning.*

evade /ɪˈveɪd/ *verb* [T] **1** *SLIGHTLY FORMAL* to avoid or escape from someone or something: *Just give me an answer and stop evading the question!* ○ *The police have assured the public that the escaped prisoners will not evade recapture for long.* ○ *She leant forward to kiss him but he evaded her by pretending to sneeze.* ○ *An Olympic gold medal is the only thing that has evaded her in her remarkable career.* ○ [+ v-ing] *He can't evade doing military service forever.* **2** **evade the issue/question, etc.** to intentionally not talk about something or not answer something

evasion /ɪˈveɪ.ʒᵊn/ *noun* [C or U] when you avoid some-thing or someone: *Her speech was full of excuses and eva-sions and never properly addressed the issue.* ○ *tax eva-sion* (= illegally not paying tax)

evasive /ɪˈveɪ.sɪv/ *adj* done in order to avoid something or someone: *By the time the pilot realised how close the plane was to the building, it was too late to take evasive action.* ○ *The Minister was her usual evasive self, skil-fully dodging reporters' questions about her possible resignation.* **evasively** /ɪˈveɪ.sɪv.li/ *adv* **evasiveness** /ɪ-ˈveɪ.sɪv.nəs/ *noun* [U]

evaluate /ɪˈvæl.ju.eɪt/ *verb* [T] to judge or calculate the quality, importance, amount or value of something: *It's impossible to evaluate these results without knowing more about the research methods employed.* ○ [+ question word] *We shall need to evaluate how the new material stands up to wear and tear.* **evaluation** /ɪˌvæl.juˈeɪ.ʃᵊn/ *noun* [C or U] *Evaluation of this new treatment cannot take place until all the data has been collected.* **evaluative** /ɪ-ˈvæl.ju.ə.tɪv/ ⑧ /-eɪ.t̬ɪv/ *adj* *FORMAL* *evaluative research*

evanescent /ˌiː.vəˈnes.ᵊnt/ ⑧ /ˌev.ə-/ *adj* *FORMAL* lasting for only a short time, then disappearing quickly and being forgotten **evanescence** /ˌiː.vəˈnes.ᵊnts/ ⑧ /ˌev.ə-/ *noun* [U]

evangelical [RELIGION] /ˌiː.vænˈdʒel.ɪ.kᵊl/ *adj* belonging to one of the Protestant Churches or Christian groups which believe biblical teaching and persuading other people to join them to be extremely important: *the Evangelical movement* **evangelical** /ˌiː.vænˈdʒel.ɪ.kᵊl/ *noun* [C] *The new Archbishop is an evangelical.* **evangelicalism** /ˌiː.vænˈdʒel.ɪ.kᵊl.ɪ.zᵊm/ *noun* [U]

evangelical [OPINIONS] /ˌiː.vænˈdʒel.ɪ.kᵊl/ *adj* having very strong beliefs and often trying to persuade other people to have the same beliefs: *Why is it that people who've*

given up smoking become so evangelical and intolerant of other smokers?
evangelize /ɪˈvæn.dʒə.laɪz/ *verb* [I] to talk about how good you think something is: *I wish she would stop evangelizing about the virtues of free market economics.*

evangelist /ɪˈvæn.dʒə.lɪst/ *noun* [C] **1** a person who tries to persuade people to become Christians, often by travelling around and organizing religious meetings ➲See also **televangelist** at **televangelism**. **2 Evangelist** one of the writers of the four books in the Bible about Jesus Christ **evangelism** /ɪˈvæn.dʒə.lɪ.zᵊm/ *noun* [U] **evangelistic** /ɪˌvæn.dʒəˈlɪs.tɪk/ *adj*
evangelize, *UK USUALLY* **-ise** /ɪˈvæn.dʒə.laɪz/ *verb* [T] to try to persuade people to become Christians

evaporate /ɪˈvæp.ᵊr.eɪt/ [US] /-ɚ-/ *verb* **1** [I or T] to cause a liquid to change to a gas, especially by heating: *The high concentration of sugars forms a syrup when the sap evaporates.* ○ *Plants keep cool during the summer by evaporating water from their leaves.* **2** [I] to disappear: *Halfway through the film reality evaporates and we enter a world of pure fantasy.* **evaporation** /ɪˌvæp.əˈreɪ.ʃᵊn/ *noun* [U]

eˌvaporated ˈmilk *noun* [U] milk that has been thickened by removing some of the water from it, and which is used in sweet dishes

evasion /ɪˈveɪ.ʒᵊn/ *noun* ➲See at **evade**.
evasive /ɪˈveɪ.sɪv/ *adj* ➲See at **evade**.

eve [DAY BEFORE] /iːv/ *noun* **1** [S] the period or day before an important event: *Mr Hurd was speaking to Arab journalists in London* ***on the*** *eve* ***of*** *his visit to Jordan and Saudi Arabia.* ○ ***Christmas/New Year's*** *Eve* **2** [S or U] *OLD USE* the evening

Eve [WOMAN] /iːv/ *noun* [S] the first woman, according to the biblical story of how the world was made

even [SURPRISE] /ˈiː.vᵊn/ *adv* used to show that something is surprising, unusual, unexpected, or extreme: *I don't even know where it is.* ○ *Everyone I know likes the smell of bacon – even Mike does and he's a vegetarian.* ○ *We were all on time – even Chris and he's usually late for everything.* ○ *It's a very difficult job – it might even take a year to finish it.* ○ *"I never cry." "Not even when you hurt yourself really badly?"* ○ *Even with a load of electronic gadgetry, you still need some musical ability to write a successful song.*
• **even as** at the same time as: *I tried to reason with him, but even as I started to explain what had happened he stood up to leave.*
• **even if** whether or not: *Even if you take a taxi, you'll still miss your train.*
• **even now/then** despite something: *I've thought about it so much, but even now I can't believe how lucky I was to survive the accident.* ○ *I gave Jim very clear instructions, but even then he managed to make a mess of it.*
• **even so** despite what has just been said: *I had a terrible headache, but even so I went to the concert.* ○ *An immediate interest cut might give a small boost to the economy. Even so, any recovery is likely to be very slow.*
• **even though** although: *Even though he left school at 16, he still managed to become prime minister.*

even [EMPHASIS] /ˈiː.vᵊn/ *adv* used to emphasize a comparison: *The next 36 hours will be even colder with snow showers becoming more widespread.* ○ *Any devaluation of sterling would make it even more difficult to keep inflation low.*

even [MORE EXACTLY] /ˈiː.vᵊn/ *adv* used when you want to be more exact or detailed about something you have just said: *I find some of his habits rather unpleasant, disgusting even.* ○ *She has always been very kind to me, even generous on occasion.*

even [FLAT] /ˈiː.vᵊn/ *adj* flat and smooth, or on the same level: *We resurfaced the kitchen floor because it wasn't even.*
• **on an even keel** regular and well-balanced and not likely to change suddenly: *The new manager succeeded in putting the business back on an even keel.*

even [CONTINUOUS] /ˈiː.vᵊn/ *adj* continuous or regular: *You should try to work at an even rate instead of taking it easy one day and working flat out the next.*
evenly /ˈiː.vᵊn.li/ *adv* If you say something evenly, you speak without showing emotion in your voice although you are angry or not satisfied in some way: *"We are not terrorists," he said evenly. "We are freedom fighters."*

even [EQUAL] /ˈiː.vᵊn/ *adj* equal or equally balanced: *Both sides played well – it was a very even contest.* ○ *The weather forecast said that there's an even chance of thunderstorms tonight* (= that it is equally likely that there will or will not be storms).
• **get even with** ***sb*** *INFORMAL* to do something equally bad to someone who has done something bad to you
evenly /ˈiː.vᵊn.li/ *adv* in or into equal amounts: *Divide the mixture evenly between the baking pans.* ○ *Congress is still evenly divided on the issue.*
evens /ˈiː.vᵊnz/ *adj* **1** *UK* (*US* **even**) equally likely to happen as to not happen: *The chances of her getting the job are about evens.* **2** describes a bet on something where the risk is equally balanced and which will pay back twice the amount of money that is paid, if it is successful: *an even bet* ○ *If I were having a bet I'd take even* ***money*** *on United.*
even /ˈiː.vᵊn/ *verb* [T] to make two things equal: *Sheila was awarded a scholarship in Chemistry, and now her brother has evened* ***the score*** *with a scholarship in Economics.* ○ *The whisky industry is campaigning for the taxes on different alcoholic drinks to be evened* ***up***.
▲ **even** ***(sth)*** **out** *phrasal verb* [M] to become equal, or to make something equal: *The university has a system designed to even out the differences between rich and poor colleges.*

even [NUMBER] /ˈiː.vᵊn/ *adj* forming a whole number which can be divided exactly by two: *6 is an even number and 7 is an odd number.*

even-handed /ˌiː.vᵊnˈhæn.dɪd/ *adj* treating everyone fairly and equally: *Several broadcasters have been criticized for failing to give even-handed treatment to all the parties during the election campaign.*

evening /ˈiːv.nɪŋ/ *noun* [C or U] the part of the day between the end of the afternoon and night: *a chilly evening* ○ *I work in a restaurant and only get one evening* ***off*** *a week.* ○ *Thank you for such a lovely evening.* ○ *I always go to see a film* ***on*** *Friday evenings.* ○ ***In the*** *evenings, I like to relax.* ○ *I'm working late* ***this*** *evening.* ○ *What are you doing* ***tomorrow*** *evening?* ○ *It poured down* ***all*** *evening and most of the night as well.* ○ *What time do you usually get home* ***in the*** *evening?*
evenings /ˈiːv.nɪŋz/ *adv MAINLY US What time do you get home evenings* (= in the evening)*?* ○ *I work evenings.*

ˈevening ˌclass *noun* [C] a class intended for adults rather than children which happens in the evening: *Pat teaches evening classes* ***in*** *yoga and relaxation.* ○ *I've been going to evening classes to improve my German.*

ˈevening ˌdress *noun* **1** [U] special clothing worn for formal events, such as special evening meals: *The invitation says to wear evening dress.* **2** [C] a long dress worn by a woman to a formal party or dinner

ˌevening ˈprimrose *noun* [C or U] a plant with pale yellow flowers. Its seeds are used to make an oil which is used to treat various medical conditions: *evening primrose oil*

the ˌevening ˈstar *noun* [S] a planet, especially Venus, which can be seen shining brightly in the west just after the sun has gone down

evensong /ˈiː.vən.sɒŋ/ [US] /-ˌsɑːŋ/ *noun* [U] the evening ceremony of the Church of England or the Roman Catholic Church

event /ɪˈvent/ *noun* [C] **1** anything that happens, especially something important or unusual: *This year's Olympic Games will be the biggest ever sporting event.* ○ *Susannah's party was the* ***social*** *event of the year.* ○ *The police are trying to determine the* ***series of*** *events that led up to the murder.* **2** one of a set of races or competitions: *The women's 200 metre event will be followed by the men's 100 metres.*
• **in the event** *UK* used to emphasize that what happened was not what you expected: *We had expected to arrive an hour late, but in the event we were early.*

• **in the event of *sth*** if something happens: *In the event of a strike, the army will take over responsibility for fire-fighting.*
• **in any event** (*UK ALSO* **at all events**) whatever happens: *I might go home next month, but in any event, I'll be home for Christmas.*
• **in either event** in either of two situations: *I can't decide whether to accept the Cambridge or the London job, but in either event I'll have to move house.*
• **in that event** if that happens: *There's a possibility of my flight being delayed. In that event I'll phone to let you know.*

eventful /ɪˈvent.fᵊl/ *adj* full of interesting or important events: *Her time at university was the most eventful period of her life.* ○ *We had quite an eventful journey.*

even-tempered /ˌiː.vᵊnˈtem.pəd/ [US] /-pɚd/ *adj APPROVING* always calm and never angry or too excited about anything

eventide /ˈiː.vᵊn.taɪd/ *noun* **[C or U]** *LITERARY* evening

eventual /ɪˈven.tju.ᵊl/ *adj* **[before n]** happening or existing at a later time or at the end, especially after a lot of effort, problems, etc: *The Dukes were the eventual winners of the competition.* ○ *Although the original budget for the project was $1 billion, the eventual cost is likely to be 50% higher.*

eventually /ɪˈven.tju.ᵊl.i/ *adv* in the end, especially after a long time or a lot of effort, problems, etc: *Although she had been ill for a long time, it still came as a shock when she eventually died.* ○ *It might take him ages but he'll do it eventually.*

COMMON LEARNER ERROR

eventual/eventually

These words have only a single meaning 'in the end, especially after a long time or a lot of effort, problems, etc.' but learners often use them wrongly in other ways. Be careful not to use **eventually** like 'finally' at the end of a list of points in an argument.

Firstly...Secondly...Thirdly...Finally...
~~*Firstly...Secondly...Thirdly...Eventually...*~~

Eventually also cannot be used to mean 'possible' or 'possibly'.

It would be lovely if the children could see and, if possible, touch the animals.
~~*It would be lovely if the children could see and, eventually, touch the animals.*~~

Eventually also cannot be used to mean 'in fact'.

He confessed that in fact he had never sent the letter.
~~*He confessed that he eventually had never sent the letter.*~~

eventuality /ɪˌven.tjuˈæl.ɪ.ti/ [US] /-ə.t̬i/ *noun* **[C]** something unpleasant or unexpected that might happen or exist in the future: *We've tried to anticipate the most likely problems, but it's impossible to be prepared for all eventualities/every eventuality.* ○ *I'm looking for a travel insurance policy that will cover me for* ***any*** *eventuality.*

ever [AT ANY TIME] /ˈev.əʳ/ [US] /-ɚ/ *adv* at any time: *Nothing ever happens here in the evenings.* ○ *Have you ever been to London?* ○ *If you're ever/If ever you're in Cambridge, do give me a ring.* ○ *He* ***hardly*** *ever* (= almost never) *washes the dishes and he* ***rarely, if*** *ever,* (= probably never) *does any cleaning.* ○ *When there's a James Bond film on TV, I* ***never*** *ever miss it.* ○ ***If*** *ever there was a cause for celebration, this peace treaty was it.* ○ *The smell is worse* ***than*** *ever.* ○ *I thought she was famous, but none of my friends have ever heard of her.*
• **if ever there was one** (*ALSO* **if ever I saw one**) used to emphasize that what you are saying is true: *It was a brilliant performance if ever there was one.*
• **better/bigger/more, etc. than ever** better/bigger/more than at any time before: *We are spending more than ever on education.*
• **as big/fast/good, etc. as ever** as big/fast/good as at any time before: *The restaurants are as good as ever and no more expensive.*

ever [ALWAYS] /ˈev.əʳ/ [US] /-ɚ/ *adv* continually: *Manchester United's record in cup competitions grows ever* ***more*** *impressive.* ○ *The ever-****increasing*** *demand for private cars could be halted by more investment in public transport.* ○ *nuclear devastation was an ever-****present*** *threat* ○ *After nine years in Cambridge, Susannah and Guy moved to Watlington, where they lived* ***happily ever after.***
• **ever since** continually since that time: *He's been depressed ever since he got divorced.*
• **as ever** in the same way as always: *As ever, I was the last to find out.*
• **Yours ever** (*ALSO* **Ever yours**) *UK SLIGHTLY FORMAL* used at the end of a letter as a way of saying goodbye to someone you know well: *I'm looking forward to seeing you all next month. Yours ever, Yvonne.*

ever [EMPHASIS] /ˈev.əʳ/ [US] /-ɚ/ *adv* **1** used for emphasizing an adjective: *The orchestra is to perform its last ever concert/last concert ever tomorrow night at the Albert Hall.* ○ *Yesterday the company announced its* ***first*** *ever fall in profits.* ○ *Was she ever a fast runner!* (= She was a very fast runner!) ○ *"Are you looking forward to your vacation?" "Am I ever!* (= Yes, very much!)*"* **2** in questions, used to emphasize the question word: *How ever did he manage that?* ○ *What ever have you done to him?* ○ *Why ever would anyone/Why would anyone ever want to hurt her?* **3** *UK SLIGHTLY INFORMAL* **ever so/ever such a** very/a very: *She's ever so pretty.* ○ *She's ever such a pretty girl.*

evergreen /ˈev.ə.griːn/ [US] /-ɚ-/ *adj* **1** describes a plant, bush, or tree which has leaves for the whole year ➲Compare **deciduous**. **2** always seeming fresh or remaining popular: *that evergreen TV series 'The Good Life'*

evergreen /ˈev.ə.griːn/ [US] /-ɚ-/ *noun* **[C]** a plant, bush or tree which has leaves for the whole year

everlasting /ˌev.əˈlɑː.stɪŋ/ [US] /-ɚˈlæs.tɪŋ/ *adj* lasting forever or for a long time: *I wish someone would invent an everlasting light bulb.* ○ *Their contributions to science have earned them an everlasting place in history.*

evermore /ˌev.əˈmɔːʳ/ [US] /-ɚˈmɔːr/ *adv LITERARY* always in the future: *Their name will live on* ***for*** *evermore.*

every [ALL] /ˈev.ri/ *determiner* used when referring to all the members of a group of three or more: *The police want to interview every employee about the theft.* ○ *The show will be broadcast every weekday morning between 9 and 10.* ○ *We're open every day except Sunday.* ○ *I've been out every night this week.* ○ *Every time I go to London I get caught in a traffic jam.* ○ *Ten pence is donated to charity for every bottle sold.* ○ *These paintings may look like the real thing, but* ***(each and)*** *every* ***one*** *of them is a fake.* ○ *That salmon was very expensive so make sure you eat up every* ***(single) bit.***
• **every bit as** equally as: *Opponents of the war are considered every bit as patriotic as supporters.*
• **on/at every corner** in many places along the streets of a town or city: *After the match, police were stationed on every corner.*
• **every minute** describes the whole period that something lasted: *"Did you like the concert?" "Yes, I enjoyed every minute* ***of*** *it."*
• **every last** every: *We can catch the vast majority of people, but hunting down every last tax dodger is virtually impossible.*
• **every which way** *US* in all directions: *The game was hindered by a fierce wind that swept the ball every which way.*
• **in every way** in all ways: *This movie is in every way a masterpiece of cinematography.*
• ***(your)*** **every need** all the things that you need or want: *There'll be an assistant there to see to your every need.*
• ***(your)*** **every word** all the things that you say: *She's such a fascinating lecturer – I was hanging on to her every word.*
• ***(your)*** **every move** everything that you do: *I'd hate to be someone really famous with the press reporting my every move.* ○ *After that, she was watching his every move.*

COMMON LEARNER ERROR

every

When **every** is followed by **body**, **one**, **thing**, or **where**, you write the words together as one word.

Everybody needs to bring something to eat.
Can everyone see the blackboard?

Have you got everything you need?
~~*Have you got every thing you need?*~~
I've looked everywhere for it.
~~*I've looked every where for it.*~~

In other situations you write **every** as a separate word.

You have to take your membership card every time you go.
Do you go jogging every morning?

---

every [REPEATED] /ˈev.ri/ *determiner* used to show that something is repeated regularly: *Computers can perform millions of calculations every second.* ○ *Every four minutes a car is stolen in this city.* ○ *Every day in the United States 25 people are murdered with handguns.* ○ *Every **few** kilometres we passed a burnt out jeep or truck at the side of the road.* ○ *The conference takes place every **other/second** year.*
• **every now and again/then** sometimes but not often: *Every now and again/then they'll have a beer together.*
• **every so often** sometimes but not often: *Every so often I treat myself to a meal in an expensive restaurant.*

every [GREATEST] /ˈev.ri/ *determiner* the greatest possible or that can be imagined: *I'd like to wish you every success in your new job/happiness in your new home.* ○ *She has every reason to be unhappy after losing her job and her home.* ○ *You had every opportunity to make a complaint.* ○ *Every effort is being made to minimise civilian casualties.* ○ *She has every right to be proud of her tremendous achievements.*

everybody /ˈev.riˌbɒd.i/ [US] /-ˌbɑː.di/ *pronoun* **everyone**

everyday /ˈev.ri.deɪ/ *adj* ordinary, typical or usual: *The documentary offers an insight into the everyday lives of millions of ordinary Russian citizens.* ○ *Death was an everyday occurrence during the Civil War.*

everyone /ˈev.ri.wʌn/ *pronoun* (*ALSO* **everybody**) every person: *Would everyone who wishes to attend the dinner let me know by Friday afternoon?* ○ *Everyone has their own ideas about the best way to bring up children.* ○ *I've received replies from everybody but Jane.* ○ *Do you agree with the principle that everyone should pay something towards the cost of health care?* ○ *Everyone knows who stole it, but they're all afraid to tell anyone.* ○ *Everyone involved in the accident has been questioned by the police.* ○ *Goodbye, everybody – I'll see you next week.* ○ *I'm sorry, but you'll just have to wait your turn like everybody **else**.*

everyplace /ˈev.ri.pleɪs/ *adv US INFORMAL* everywhere

everything /ˈev.ri.θɪŋ/ *pronoun* all things: *You can't blame him for everything.* ○ *She's obsessed with Elvis Presley and collects **anything and** everything connected with him.* ○ *Jane's been unfaithful to Jim three times, but he still loves her **in spite of** everything.* ○ *Money isn't everything* (= the most important thing). ○ *His children are everything **to** him* (= the most important part of his life). ○ *Have you been crying? Is everything all right?* ○ *The thieves took everything.* ○ *We did everything we could to save her but she died.* ○ *We shall do everything **necessary** to bring the murderer to justice.* ○ *They're very busy with their new house and everything* (= all the things connected with it).
• **everything but/except the kitchen sink** *HUMOROUS* a much larger number of things than is necessary: *We're only going on vacation for a week, but John will insist on taking everything but the kitchen sink.*

everywhere /ˈev.ri.weəʳ/ [US] /-wer/ *adv* (*US INFORMAL* **everyplace**) to, at or in all places or the whole of a place: *His children go everywhere with him.* ○ *Everywhere looks so grey and depressing in winter.* ○ *I looked everywhere for my keys.* ○ *Reasonable people everywhere will be outraged by this atrocity.* ○ *We had to stay in the sleaziest hotel in town as everywhere **else*** (= all other places) *was fully booked.*

evict /ɪˈvɪkt/ *verb* [T] to force someone to leave somewhere: *Tenants who fall behind in their rent risk being evicted.* ○ *He was evicted **from** the pub for drunken and violent behaviour.* **eviction** /ɪˈvɪk.ʃᵊn/ *noun* [C or U] *After falling behind with his mortgage repayments he now faces eviction **from** his home.* ○ *In this economically depressed area, evictions are common.*

evidence /ˈev.ɪ.dᵊnts/ *noun* [U] one or more reasons for believing that something is or is not true: *The police have found no evidence **of** a terrorist link with the murder.* ○ [+ **to** infinitive] *There is no scientific evidence **to** suggest that underwater births are dangerous.* ○ [+ **that**] *Is there any scientific evidence **that** a person's character is reflected in their handwriting?* ○ *Several experts are to **give** evidence on the subject.* ○ *There is only **circumstantial** evidence against her, so she is unlikely to be convicted.* ○ *Campaigners now have compelling **documentary** evidence of the human rights abuses that they had been alleging for several years.* ○ ***Fresh** evidence suggests that the statement had been fabricated.* ○ *The traces of petrol found on his clothing provided the **forensic** evidence proving that he had started the fire deliberately.* ○ ***All the** evidence points to a substantial rise in traffic over the next few years.* ○ *There is growing/mounting/increasing evidence **that** people whose diets are rich in vitamins are less likely to develop some types of cancer.* **evidenced** /ˈev.ɪ.dᵊntst/ *adj MAINLY US His desire to win an Olympic medal is evidenced **by** his performances throughout this season.*

evident /ˈev.ɪ.dᵊnt/ *adj SLIGHTLY FORMAL* easily seen or understood; obvious: *The full extent of the damage only became evident the following morning.* ○ ***From** the smell **it** was evident **that** the drains had been blocked for several days.* ○ *Harry's courage during his illness was evident **to** everyone.* ○ *Her love for him was evident **in** all that she did.* ➲See also **self-evident**. **evidently** /ˈev.ɪ.dᵊnt.li/ *adv*: *She should have been here two hours ago so she's evidently decided not to come after all.* ○ *He was evidently upset by the news of the accident.*

COMMON LEARNER ERROR

evident or **obvious?**

evident is more formal than **obvious**. It is usually better to choose the word **obvious**.

The advantages of living close to where you work are obvious.
~~*The advantages of living close to where you work are evident.*~~

---

evil /ˈiː.vəl/ *adj* **1** immoral, cruel, or very unpleasant: *an evil dictator* ○ *These people are just evil.* **2** If the weather or a smell is evil, it is very unpleasant.
• **the ˌevil ˈeye** a magical power to injure or harm people by looking at them

evil /ˈiː.vəl/ *noun* [C or U] something that is very bad and harmful: *Each new leader would blame his predecessor for all the evils of the past.* ○ *Drug-addiction is one of today's great social evils.* ○ *For the sake of long-term peace, the military option is the **lesser** evil/the **lesser of two** evils* (= the less unpleasant of two bad choices). ○ *the battle between good and evil*

evildoer /ˈiː.vəlduː.əʳ/ [US] /-ɚ/ *noun* [C] someone who does something evil: *The government has blamed the protests on a handful of evildoers.*

evince /ɪˈvɪnts/ *verb* [T] *FORMAL* to make obvious or show clearly: *They have never evinced any readiness or ability to negotiate.* ○ *In all the years I knew her, she never evinced any desire to do such a thing.*

eviscerate /ɪˈvɪs.ə.reɪt/ *verb* [T] *SPECIALIZED* to remove one or all of the organs from the inside of a body **evisceration** /ɪˌvɪs.əˈreɪ.ʃᵊn/ *noun* [U]

evoke /ɪˈvəʊk/ [US] /-ˈvoʊk/ *verb* [T] to make someone remember something or feel an emotion: *That smell always evokes memories of my old school.* ○ *a detergent designed to evoke the fresh smell of summer meadows* **evocation** /ˌiː.vəʊˈkeɪ.ʃᵊn/ [US] /ˌev.ə-/ *noun* [C or U] **evocative** /ɪˈvɒk.ə.tɪv/ [US] /-ˈvɑː.kə.t̬ɪv/ *adj* making you remember or imagine something pleasant: *evocative music* ○ *a sound evocative **of** the sea* **evocatively** /ɪˈvɒk.ə.tɪv.li/ [US] /-ˈvɑː.kə.t̬ɪv-/ *adv*

evolve /ɪˈvɒlv/ [US] /-ˈvɑːlv/ *verb* [I or T] to develop gradually, or to cause something or someone to develop gradually: *Humans evolved **from** apes.* ○ *The company has evolved over the years **into** a multi-million dollar organization.* ○ *Bacteria are evolving resistance to antibiotics.* **evolution** /ˌiː.vəˈluː.ʃᵊn/ /ˌev.ə-/ *noun* [U] the way in which living things change and develop over millions of years, or a gradual process of change and development: *Darwin's theory of evolution* ○ *the evolution of language*

evolutionary /ˌiː.vəˈluː.ʃ⁾n.⁾r.i/ /ˌev.ə'-/ ⓊⓈ /-er-/ *adj*: *The change has been evolutionary* (= gradual) *rather than revolutionary.*

ewe /juː/ *noun* [C] a female sheep, especially an adult one: *ewe's milk*

ex- /eks-/ *prefix* used to show that someone is no longer what they were: *ex-prisoners* ○ *ex-policemen* ○ *my ex-husband* ○ *my ex-girlfriend*

    ex /eks/ *noun* [C] INFORMAL Someone's ex is a person who was their wife, husband or lover in the past: *Is she still in touch with her ex?*

exacerbate /ɪgˈzæs.ə.beɪt/ ⓊⓈ /-ɚ-/ *verb* [T] to make something which is already bad worse: *This attack will exacerbate the already tense relations between the two communities.* **exacerbation** /ɪgˌzæs.ə'beɪ.ʃ⁾n/ ⓊⓈ /-ɚ-/ *noun* [U]

exact CORRECT /ɪgˈzækt/ *adj* in great detail, or complete, correct or true in every way; **precise**: *The exact distance is 1.838 metres.* ○ *The exact time of the accident was 2.43 pm.* ○ *"I still owe you £7, don't I?" "Actually, it's £7.30 to be exact."* ○ *The exact location of the factory has yet to be decided.* ○ *Unlike astronomy, astrology cannot be described as an exact science.*

    exactly /ɪgˈzækt.li/ *adv* **1** used when you are giving or asking for information that is completely correct: *The journey took exactly three hours.* ○ *That'll be £15 exactly, please.* ○ *It tastes exactly the same as the real thing, but has half the fat.* ○ *The town centre looks exactly as it did when it was built in 1877.* ○ *He's not exactly* (= not what I would describe as) *good-looking, but he has a certain attraction.* ○ *"So you gave her your Walkman?" "Not exactly* (= That is not completely true), *I lent it to her."* ○ *"What you seem to be saying is that more should be invested in the road system and less in the railways." "Exactly* (= That is completely correct)." **2** used to emphasize what you are saying: *Do exactly what I tell you and no-one will get hurt!* ○ *Exactly how do you propose to achieve this?* ○ *What exactly do you mean?*

    exactness /ɪgˈzækt.nəs/ *noun* [U] (FORMAL **exactitude**)

exact OBTAIN /ɪgˈzækt/ *verb* [T] FORMAL to demand and obtain something, sometimes using force, threats or persuasion, or to make something necessary: *to exact revenge on someone* ○ *The blackmailers exacted a total of $100 000 from their victims.* ○ *Heart surgery exacts tremendous skill and concentration.*

    exacting /ɪgˈzæk.tɪŋ/ *adj* demanding a lot of effort, care or attention: *an exacting training schedule* ○ *exacting standards*

exaggerate /ɪgˈzædʒ.ə.reɪt/ ⓊⓈ /-ɚ.eɪt/ *verb* [I or T] to make something seem larger, more important, better or worse than it really is: *The threat of attack has been greatly exaggerated.* ○ *Don't exaggerate – it wasn't that expensive.* ○ *I'm not exaggerating – it was the worst meal I've ever eaten in my life.* **exaggerated** /ɪgˈzædʒ.ə.reɪ.tɪd/ ⓊⓈ /-ɚ.eɪ.tɪd/ *adj*: *exaggerated reports of the problem* **exaggeratedly** /ɪgˈzædʒ.ə.reɪ.tɪd.li/ ⓊⓈ /-ɚ.eɪ.tɪd-/ *adv* **exaggeration** /ɪgˌzædʒ.əˈreɪ.ʃ⁾n/ *noun* [C or U] when someone makes something seem larger, more important, better or worse than it really is: *Sal reckons over sixty people were there but I think that's a slight exaggeration.* ○ [+ to infinitive] *It would be no exaggeration to say that her work has saved lives.*

exalt /ɪgˈzɒlt/ ⓊⓈ /-ˈzɑːlt/ *verb* [T] **1** FORMAL to raise someone to a higher rank or more powerful position **2** OLD USE to praise someone a lot

    exalted /ɪgˈzɒl.tɪd/ ⓊⓈ /-ˈzɑːl.tɪd/ *adj*: *She rose to the exalted* (= very high) *post of Foreign Secretary after only three years in the government.*

exaltation /ˌeg.zɒlˈteɪ.ʃ⁾n/ ⓊⓈ /-zɑːl-/ *noun* [U] FORMAL a very strong feeling of happiness

    exalted /ɪgˈzɒl.tɪd/ ⓊⓈ /-ˈzɑːl.tɪd/ *adj* FORMAL extremely happy

exam /ɪgˈzæm/ *noun* [C] (FORMAL **examination**) a test of a student's knowledge or skill in a particular subject which results in a qualification if the student is successful: *How many pupils are taking the geography exam this term?* ○ *I failed my physics exam, but I passed chemistry.* ○ *an examination paper* ○ *exam results*

examine /ɪgˈzæm.ɪn/ *verb* [T] to test someone's knowledge or skill in a particular subject: *We were examined on European history.* ○ UK *You'll be examined in three main areas; speaking, listening and reading comprehension.* ➲See also **examine**.

    examiner /ɪgˈzæm.ɪ.nəʳ/ ⓊⓈ /-nɚ/ *noun* [C] *The candidates listed below have failed to satisfy the examiners* (= people judging and marking exams).

COMMON LEARNER ERROR

take/sit an exam

To **take an exam** means to do an official test. 'Sit' is slightly more formal than 'take' in this phrase and is only used in UK English.

We have to take an exam at the end of the course.
~~We have to write an exam at the end of the course.~~

examine /ɪgˈzæm.ɪn/ *verb* [T] to look at or consider a person or thing carefully and in detail in order to discover something about them: *Forensic scientists are examining the wreckage for clues about the cause of the explosion.* ○ *The council is to examine ways of reducing traffic in the city centre.* ○ *The research examined the effects of alcohol on long-term memory.* ○ [+ question word] *We need to examine how an accident like this can be avoided in the future.* ○ *A psychiatrist was examined* (= asked questions) *on the mental state of the defendant.* ➲See also **examine** at **exam**.

    examination /ɪgˌzæm.ɪˈneɪ.ʃ⁾n/ *noun* [C or U] when someone looks at or considers something carefully in order to discover something: *a post-mortem examination* ○ *I had to have/undergo a medical examination when I started my pension scheme.* ○ *The evidence is still under examination* (= being examined). ○ *I thought it was paint at first, but on closer examination I realised it was dried blood.* ➲See also **examination** at **exam**.

example TYPICAL CASE /ɪgˈzɑːm.pl̩/ ⓊⓈ /-ˈzæm-/ *noun* [C] **1** something which is typical of the group of things that it is a member of: *Could you give me an example of the improvements you have mentioned?* ○ *This painting is a marvellous example of her work.* ➲See also **exemplify**. **2** a way of helping someone to understand something by showing them how it is used: *Study the examples first of all, then attempt the exercises on the next page.*

    • **for example** used when giving an example of the type of thing you mean: *Offices can easily become more environmentally-friendly by, for example, using recycled paper.* ✳ NOTE: **for example** is sometimes shortened to the Latin abbreviation **e.g.**

example BEHAVIOUR /ɪgˈzɑːm.pl̩/ ⓊⓈ /-ˈzæm-/ *noun* [C] a person or their behaviour when considered for their suitability to be copied: *He's a very good example to the rest of the class.* ○ *He's decided to follow the example of his father and study law.*

    • **set an example** to behave in a way that other people should copy: *You should be setting a good example to your younger brother.*

example PUNISHMENT /ɪgˈzɑːm.pl̩/ ⓊⓈ /-ˈzæm-/ *noun* [C] (a person who receives) a punishment which is intended to warn others against doing the thing that is being punished: *The judge made an example of him and gave him the maximum possible sentence.*

exasperate /ɪgˈzɑː.spə.reɪt/ ⓊⓈ /-ˈzæs.pɚ.eɪt/ *verb* [T] to make someone very annoyed, usually when they can do nothing to solve a problem

    exasperated /ɪgˈzɑː.spə.reɪ.tɪd/ ⓊⓈ /-ˈzæs.pɚ.eɪ.tɪd/ *adj* annoyed: *He's becoming increasingly exasperated with the situation.* **exasperatedly** /ɪgˈzɑː.spə.rei.tɪd.li/ ⓊⓈ /-ˈzæs.pɚ.eɪ.tɪd-/ *adv*

    exasperating /ɪgˈzɑː.spə.reɪ.tɪŋ/ ⓊⓈ /-ˈzæs.pɚ.eɪ.tɪŋ/ *adj* extremely annoying: *It's so exasperating when he won't listen to a word that I say.* **exasperatingly** /ɪgˈzɑː.spə.reɪ.tɪŋ.li/ ⓊⓈ /-ˈzæs.pɚ.eɪ.tɪŋ-/ *adv*

    exasperation /ɪgˌzɑː.spəˈreɪ.ʃ⁾n/ ⓊⓈ /-ˈzæs.pə-/ *noun* [U] annoyance: *There is growing exasperation within the government at the failure of these policies to reduce unemployment.* ○ *After ten hours of fruitless negotiations, he stormed out of the meeting in exasperation.*

ex cathedra /ˌeks.kəˈθiː.drə/ *adj* [before n], *adv* FORMAL with complete authority, or said by the Pope to be true and so accepted by all members of the Roman Catholic Church

excavate /ˈek.skə.veɪt/ *verb* [I or T] **1** to remove earth that is covering very old objects buried in the ground in order to discover things about the past: *Tintagel Castle, the reputed birthplace of King Arthur, is being excavated professionally for the first time in more than 50 years.* **2** to dig a hole or channel in the ground, especially with a machine: *In tin mining today, workers excavate tunnels horizontally from a vertical shaft.* **excavation** /ˌeks.kəˈveɪ.ʃᵊn/ *noun* [C or U] *Excavation on the site is likely to continue for several years.* ○ *She has taken part in several excavations of Roman settlements across Europe.*
excavator *UK* /ˈek.skə.veɪ.təʳ/ [US] /-t̬ɚ/ *noun* [C] (*US* **steam shovel**) a large powerful machine with a container connected to a long arm that is used for digging up the ground

exceed /ɪkˈsiːd/ *verb* [T] to be greater than a number or amount, or to go beyond a permitted limit: *The final cost should not exceed $5000.* ○ *The success of our campaign has exceeded our wildest expectations.* ○ *She was found guilty on three charges of exceeding the speed limit.*

exceedingly /ɪkˈsiː.dɪŋ.li/ *adv FORMAL* to a very great degree; extremely: *He was clever, handsome and exceedingly rich.*

excel /ɪkˈsel/ *verb* [I] **-ll-** to be extremely good at something: *Rebecca always excelled* ***in*** *languages at school.*
excel *yourself* *verb* [R] to do something better than you usually do: *The British team have excelled themselves this year to reach the finals.*

Excellency /ˈek.sᵊl.ənt.si/ *noun* **your Excellency/his Excellency** (the title of) someone in an important official position, especially someone, such as an AMBASSADOR, who represents their government in a foreign country: *His Excellency will be pleased to see you now.*

excellent /ˈek.sᵊl.ᵊnt/ *adj* extremely good: *The food was excellent.* ○ *Her car is in excellent condition.* ○ *The fall in interest rates is excellent news for borrowers.* ○ *"Our sales are up for the third year in a row." "Excellent.* (= I'm extremely pleased.)*"* **excellently** /ˈek.sᵊl.ᵊnt.li/ *adv*
excellence /ˈek.sᵊl.ᵊnts/ *noun* [U] the quality of being excellent: *The school is noted for its academic excellence.*

except /ɪkˈsept/ *prep, conjunction* not including; but not: *The museum is open daily except Monday(s).* ○ *The government has few options except to keep interest rates high.* ○ *It's cool and quiet everywhere except in the kitchen.* ○ *Everyone was there except* ***for*** *Sally.* ○ *There is nothing to indicate the building's past, except* ***(for)*** *the fireplace.* ○ *They look very similar except* ***that*** *one is a little taller.*
excepted /ɪkˈsept.ɪd/ *adj* [after n] *FORMAL* not included: *I can't stand academics –* ***present company*** *excepted* (= not including those who are being talked to).
excepting /ɪkˈsep.tɪŋ/ *prep, conjunction FORMAL* not including: *All the people who were on the aircraft have now been identified, excepting one.*
exception /ɪkˈsep.ʃᵊn/ *noun* [C or U] someone or something that is not included in a rule, group or list or that does not behave in the expected way: *Men are usually quite good at map-reading but Tim is the exception.* ○ *There are exceptions* ***to*** *every rule.* ○ *I like all kinds of films* ***with the*** *exception* ***of*** (= but not) *horror films.* ○ *Her books are always entertaining and this one is* ***no*** *exception.* ○ *You must report here every Tuesday* ***without*** *exception.*
• **make an exception** to not treat someone or something according to the usual rules: *We don't usually accept late applications, but in this case we will make an exception.*
• **take exception to *sth/sb*** to be offended or made angry by something or someone: *Why did you take exception to what he said? He was only joking.*
• **the exception that proves the rule** something that emphasizes the general truth of a statement by disagreeing with it: *Most company directors are middle-aged men, but this 28-year-old woman is an exception that proves the rule.*

exceptionable /ɪkˈsep.ʃᵊn.ə.bl̩/ *adj FORMAL* offensive or upsetting: *exceptionable behaviour*

exceptional /ɪkˈsep.ʃᵊn.ᵊl/ *adj APPROVING* much greater than usual, especially in skill, intelligence, quality, etc: *an exceptional student* ○ *exceptional powers of concentration* ○ *The company has shown exceptional growth over the past two years.* **exceptionally** /ɪkˈsep.ʃᵊn.ᵊl.i/ *adv*: *an exceptionally fine portrait*

excerpt /ˈek.sɜːpt/ [US] /-sɝːpt/ *noun* [C] a short part taken from a speech, book, film, etc: *An excerpt* ***from*** *her new thriller will appear in this weekend's magazine.* **excerpt** /ekˈsɜːpt/ [US] /-ˈsɝːpt/ /ˈ--/ *verb* [T] *MAINLY US This passage of text has been excerpted* ***from*** *her latest novel.*

excess /ekˈses/ /ˈ--/ *noun* [S or U] an amount which is more than acceptable, expected or reasonable: *An excess* ***of*** *enthusiasm is not always a good thing.* ○ *They both eat* ***to*** *excess* (= too much). ○ *There will be an increase in tax for those earning* ***in*** *excess* ***of*** (= more than) *twice the national average wage.*
excess /ekˈses/ /ˈ--/ *adj* [before n] extra: *Cut off any excess pastry and put it to one side.*
excesses /ekˈses.ɪz/ *plural noun* actions far beyond the limit of what is acceptable: *For many years people were trying to escape the excesses* (= cruel actions) *of the junta.* ○ *As for shoes, her excesses* (= the large number she owned) *were well known.*
excessive /ekˈses.ɪv/ *adj* too much: *Excessive exercise can sometimes cause health problems.* ○ *Any more pudding would simply be excessive.* **excessively** /ekˈses.ɪv.li/ *adv*: *She was polite but not excessively so.* ○ *I don't drink excessively.*

exˌcess ˈbaggage *noun* [U] (*UK ALSO* **excess luggage**) bags which weigh more than the allowed amount for an individual passenger, or the money you are charged to take them onto an aircraft: *We had to pay excess baggage.* ○ *He arrived with 88 pounds of excess baggage.*

exchange /ɪksˈtʃeɪndʒ/ *verb* [T] to give something to someone and receive something from them: *It's traditional for the two teams to exchange shirts after the game.* ○ *I exchanged those trousers* ***for*** *a larger size.* ○ *Every month the group meets so its members can exchange their views/opinions* (= have a discussion). ○ *We exchanged greetings before the meeting.* ○ *We can exchange addresses when we see each other.* ○ *Exchanging houses* (= going to live in someone else's house while they live in yours) *for a few weeks is a good way of having a holiday.*
• **exchange words** to speak with someone: *We exchanged words after the meeting.*
exchange /ɪksˈtʃeɪndʒ/ *noun* **1** [C or U] when you give something to someone and they give you something else: *an exchange of ideas/information* ○ *They were given food and shelter* ***in*** *exchange* ***for*** *work.* ○ *She proposes an exchange of contracts at two o'clock.* ○ *Several people were killed during the exchange of gunfire.* **2** [C] a short conversation or argument: *There was a brief exchange between the two leaders.* **exchangeable** /ɪksˈtʃeɪn.dʒə.bl̩/ *adj*: *Goods are exchangeable as long as they are returned in good condition.*

exˈchange ˌrate *noun* [C] (*ALSO* **rate of exchange**) the rate at which the money of one country can be changed for the money of another country

the Exchequer /ðiː.ɪksˈtʃek.əʳ/ [US] /-ɚ/ *noun* [S] the government department which receives and gives out public money, in Britain and some other countries

excise [TAX] /ˈek.saɪz/ *noun* [U] a tax made by a government on some types of goods produced and used within their own country: *The excise* ***(duty) on*** *beer was increased under the last government.*

excise [REMOVE] /ekˈsaɪz/ [US] /ˈ--/ *verb* [T] *FORMAL* to remove, especially by cutting: *During a three-hour operation six tumours were excised* ***from*** *the wall of the patient's stomach.* ○ *The official censors have excised the controversial sections of the report.* **excision** /ekˈsɪʒ.ᵊn/ *noun* [C or U]

excite [MAKE HAPPY] /ɪkˈsaɪt/ *verb* [T] to make someone have strong feelings of happiness and enthusiasm: *Nothing about my life excites me at present.*
excitable /ɪkˈsaɪ.tə.bl̩/ [US] /-t̬ə-/ *adj* easily and often becoming excited: *an excitable child*

E

excited /ɪkˈsaɪ.tɪd/ ⑥ /-t̬ɪd/ *adj* feeling very happy and enthusiastic: *Are you getting excited **about** your holiday?* ○ *An excited crowd waited for the singer to arrive.*
• **be nothing to get excited about** to not be unusually good: *It's a competent enough first novel but nothing to get excited about.*

excitedly /ɪkˈsaɪ.tɪd.li/ ⑥ /-t̬ɪd-/ *adv* in an excited way: *She ran excitedly down the hall to greet her cousins.*

exciting /ɪkˈsaɪ.tɪŋ/ ⑥ /-t̬ɪŋ/ *adj* making you feel excited: *an exciting film/soundtrack* ○ *You're going to Africa? How exciting!* ○ *It was a really exciting match.* **excitingly** /ɪkˈsaɪ.tɪŋ.li/ ⑥ /-t̬ɪŋ-/ *adv*

excitement /ɪkˈsaɪt.mənt/ *noun* [C or U] a feeling of being excited, or an exciting event: *Robin's heart was pounding with excitement.* ○ *If you want excitement, you should try parachuting.* ○ *the excitements of the previous day*

excite CAUSE REACTION /ɪkˈsaɪt/ *verb* [T] FORMAL to cause a particular reaction in someone: *This product has excited a great deal of media interest.* ○ *The statement excited new speculation that a senior minister may be about to resign.*

excl ABBREVIATION FOR **excluding** or **exclusive**, see at **exclude** ✳ NOTE: This abbreviation is used mainly in advertisements.

exclaim /ɪkˈskleɪm/ *verb* [I] to say or shout something suddenly because of surprise, fear, pleasure, etc: [+ speech] *"You can't leave now!" she exclaimed.* ○ *"Rubbish!" he exclaimed in disgust.* ○ *She exclaimed **in** delight upon hearing the news.*

exclamation /ˌek.skləˈmeɪ.ʃən/ *noun* [C] something you say or shout suddenly because of surprise, fear, pleasure, etc: *an exclamation of delight*

excla·mation ˌmark *noun* [C] (*US* **exclamation point**) the ! punctuation mark that is written immediately after an exclamation

exclude /ɪkˈskluːd/ *verb* [T] to keep out or omit something or someone: *Women are still excluded **from** the club.* ○ *Microbes must, as far as possible, be excluded **from** the room during an operation.* ○ *Tom has been excluded **from** school* (= he is not allowed to go to school) *for bad behaviour.* ○ *The price excludes local taxes.* ○ *We can't exclude the possibility that he is dead.* ➔Compare **include**.

excluding /ɪkˈskluː.dɪŋ/ *prep* not including: *The aircraft carries 461 people excluding the crew and cabin staff.*

exclusion /ɪkˈskluː.ʒən/ *noun* [C or U] when someone or something is not allowed to take part in an activity or to enter a place: *her exclusion **from** the list of Oscar nominees* ○ *the exclusion of disruptive pupils from school*
• **to the exclusion of** If you do something to the exclusion of something else, you do it so much that you do not have time for anything else.

exclusive /ɪkˈskluː.sɪv/ *adj* **1 exclusive of sth** not including something: *Is the total exclusive of service charges?* **2 mutually exclusive** not possible at the same time: *Some people think that uncontrolled economic growth and environmental stability are mutually exclusive.* ➔See also **exclusive**.

exclusive /ɪkˈskluː.sɪv/ *adj* **1** limited to only one person or group of people: *This room is for the exclusive use of guests.* ○ *an exclusive interview* **2** expensive and only for people who are rich or of a high social class: *an exclusive private club* ○ *an apartment in an exclusive part of town*

exclusive /ɪkˈskluː.sɪv/ *noun* [C] a story which is printed in one newspaper or magazine and no others: *The newspaper published an exclusive about the escape.*

exclusively /ɪkˈskluː.sɪv.li/ *adv* only: *This offer is available exclusively to our established customers.* ○ *an exclusively female audience* **exclusiveness** /ɪkˈskluː.sɪv.nəs/ *noun* [U] **exclusivity** /ˌek.skluːˈsɪv.ɪ.ti/ ⑥ /-ə.t̬i/ *noun* [U]

excommunicate /ˌek.skəˈmjuː.nɪ.keɪt/ *verb* [T] When the Christian Church, especially the Roman Catholic Church, excommunicates someone, it refuses to give them COMMUNION and does not allow them to be involved in the Church. **excommunication** /ˌek.skəˌmjuː.nɪˈkeɪ.ʃən/ *noun* [C or U]

excoriate /ekˈskɔː.ri.eɪt/ ⑥ /-ˈskɔːr.i-/ *verb* [T] FORMAL to state the opinion that a play, a book, a political action, etc. is very bad: *His latest novel received excoriating*

reviews. ○ *The President excoriated the Western press for their biased views.*

excrescence /ekˈskres.ənts/ *noun* [C] **1** FORMAL an unusual growth on an animal or one of its organs or on a plant **2** LITERARY something considered to be very ugly: *The new office development is an excrescence **on** the face of the city.*

excrete /ɪkˈskriːt/ *verb* [I or T] FORMAL to get rid of waste material such as excrement or urine from the body: *Most toxins are naturally excreted from the body.* **excretion** /ɪkˈskriː.ʃən/ *noun* [C or U] *Excretion is one of several activities common to both plants and animals.*

excrement /ˈek.skrɪ.mənt/ *noun* [U] FORMAL the solid waste which is released from the bowels of a person or animal: *human excrement*

excreta /ɪkˈskriː.tə/ ⑥ /-t̬ə/ *noun* [U] FORMAL the waste material produced by a body, especially solid waste

excruciating /ɪkˈskruː.ʃi.eɪ.tɪŋ/ ⑥ /-t̬ɪŋ/ *adj* **1** extremely painful: *an excruciating pain in the lower back* **2** extremely boring or embarrassing: *excruciating boredom* ○ *His confession, when it came, was excruciating.* **excruciatingly** /ɪkˈskruː.ʃi.eɪ.tɪŋ.li/ ⑥ /-t̬ɪŋ-/ *adv*: *excruciatingly painful/uncomfortable* ○ *excruciatingly embarrassing/boring/funny*

exculpate /ˈek.skʌl.peɪt/ *verb* [T] FORMAL to remove blame from someone: *The pilot of the aircraft will surely be exculpated when all the facts are known.* **exculpatory** /ek.skʌlˈpeɪ.t̬ər.i/ ⑥ /-tɔːr.i/ *adj*

excursion /ɪkˈskɜː.ʃən/ ⑥ /-ˈskɜː-/ *noun* [C] **1** a short journey usually made for pleasure, often by a group of people: *This year's annual excursion will be **to** Lincoln.* ○ *Next week we're going **on** an excursion.* **2 excursion into sth** a brief involvement in a new activity: *A teacher by profession, this is her first excursion into writing for the theatre.*

excuse FORGIVE /ɪkˈskjuːz/ *verb* [T] to forgive someone: *Please excuse me **for** arriving late – the bus was delayed.* ○ *Nothing can excuse that sort of behaviour.* ○ *No amount of financial recompense can excuse the way in which the company carried out its policy.* ○ *We cannot excuse him **for** these crimes.* ○ *I asked the teacher if I could be excused **from** (= allowed not to do) football practice as my knee still hurt.* ○ *Please excuse me from* (= allow me to miss) *the rest of the meeting – I've just received a telephone call which requires my immediate attention.*
• **Excuse me 1** a polite way of attracting the attention, especially of someone you don't know: *Excuse me, does this bus go to Oxford Street?* **2** used to politely ask someone to move so that you can walk past them: *Excuse me, can I just get past?* **3** used to tell someone politely that you are leaving: *Excuse me a moment, I'll be with you shortly.* **4** used to say sorry for something you have accidentally done: *Did I take your seat? Do excuse me.* **5** said before disagreeing with someone: *Excuse me but aren't you forgetting something?* **6** *US* (*UK* **Pardon?/I beg your pardon?**) used to politely ask someone to repeat something they have said because you have not heard it

excusable /ɪkˈskjuː.zə.bl/ *adj* deserving to be forgiven: *Considering her difficult childhood her behaviour is excusable.* ✳ NOTE: The opposite is **inexcusable**.

excuse EXPLANATION /ɪkˈskjuːs/ *noun* [C] **1** a reason that you give to explain why you did something wrong: *He'd better have a **good** excuse **for** being late.* ○ *I've never known him to miss a meeting – I'm sure he'll **have** an excuse.* ○ *There's **no** excuse **for** that sort of behaviour.* **2** a false reason that you give to explain why you do something: [+ to infinitive] *She was just looking for an excuse to call him.* ○ *Any excuse **for** a holiday!*
• **make your excuses** to explain why you cannot be present somewhere: *Please make my excuses at the meeting on Friday.*
• **make excuses** to give false reasons why you cannot do something: *You're always making excuses **for** not helping me.*
• **a miserable/poor, etc. excuse for sth** a very bad example of something: *It was a miserable excuse for a meal.*

ex-directory *UK* /ˌeks.daɪˈrek.tri/ ⑥ /-tɔːr.i/ *adj* (*US* **unlisted**) describes a telephone number that is not in the public telephone DIRECTORY (= book that lists numbers) and is not given to people who ask for it from the telephone company: *We've **gone** ex-directory because we were receiving so many unwanted calls.*

execrable /ˈek.sə.krə.bl̩/ *adj* FORMAL very bad: *an execrable performance* ○ *She's always had execrable taste in men.* **execrably** /ˈek.sə.krə.bli/ *adv*: *He was treated execrably.*

execute [DO] /ˈek.sɪ.kjuːt/ *verb* [T] **1** FORMAL to do or perform something, especially in a planned way: *to execute a deal/plan* ○ *The whole play was executed with great precision.* **2** LEGAL **execute a will** If you execute someone's will, you deal with their money, property, etc., according to the instructions in it.

execution /ˌek.sɪˈkjuː.ʃᵊn/ *noun* [U] when something is done or performed, especially in a planned way: *Sometimes **in the** execution **of** their duty the police have to use firearms.* ○ *Although the original idea was good, its execution has been disappointing.*

executor /ɪɡˈzek.jʊ.təʳ/ [US] /-jə.t̬ɚ/ *noun* [C] LEGAL a person who executes the wishes expressed in a will

execute [KILL] /ˈek.sɪ.kjuːt/ *verb* [T] to kill someone as a legal punishment: *He was executed for murder.*

execution /ˌek.sɪˈkjuː.ʃᵊn/ *noun* [C or U] when someone is killed as a legal punishment: *Execution is still the penalty in some states for murder.* ○ *The executions will be carried out by a firing squad.*

executioner /ˌek.sɪˈkjuː.ʃᵊn.əʳ/ [US] /-ɚ/ *noun* [C] someone who performs executions

executive /ɪɡˈzek.jʊ.tɪv/ [US] /-jə.t̬ɪv/ *noun* [C] **1** (INFORMAL **exec**) someone in a high position, especially in business, who makes decisions and puts them into action: *She is now a senior executive having worked her way up through the company.* **2 the executive** the part of a government that is responsible for making certain that laws and decisions are put into action **3** a group of people who run a business or an organization: *The executive of the health workers' union accepted the proposed pay increase on behalf of their members.*

executive /ɪɡˈzek.jʊ.tɪv/ [US] /-jə.t̬ɪv/ *adj* [before n] relating to making decisions and managing businesses, or suitable for people with important jobs in business: *His executive skills will be very useful to the company.* ○ *executive cars* ○ *an executive suite*

exegesis /ˌek.sɪˈdʒiː.sɪs/ *noun* [C or U] *plural* **exegeses** SPECIALIZED an explanation of a text, especially from the Bible, after its careful study

exemplar /ɪɡˈzem.plɑːʳ/ [US] /-plɑːr/ *noun* [C] FORMAL a typical or good example of something: *It is an exemplar **of** a house of the period.*

exemplary /ɪɡˈzem.plə.ri/ [US] /-plɚ.i/ *adj* **1** very good and suitable to be copied by other people: *His tact was exemplary, especially considering the circumstances.* **2** [before n] describes a punishment that is severe and intended as a warning to others: *The judge awarded exemplary damages.*

exemplify /ɪɡˈzem.plɪ.faɪ/ *verb* [T] to be or give a typical example of something: *This painting perfectly exemplifies the naturalistic style which was so popular at the time.* **exemplification** /ɪɡˌzem.plɪ.fɪˈkeɪ.ʃᵊn/ *noun* [C or U]

exempt /ɪɡˈzempt/ *verb* [T] to excuse someone or something from a duty, payment, etc: *Small businesses have been exempted **from** the tax increase.*

exempt /ɪɡˈzempt/ *adj* with special permission not to do or pay something: *Goods exempt **from** this tax include books and children's clothes.* ○ *Pregnant women are exempt **from** dental charges under the current health system.* **exemption** /ɪɡˈzemp.ʃᵊn/ *noun* [C or U] *Candidates with a qualification in Chemistry have exemption from this course.*

exercise [HEALTHY ACTIVITY] /ˈek.sə.saɪz/ [US] /-sɚ-/ *noun* [C or U] physical activity that you do to make your body strong and healthy: *Swimming is my favourite form of exercise.* ○ *You really should **take** more **exercise**.* ○ *I **do** stomach exercises most days.*

exercise /ˈek.sə.saɪz/ [US] /-sɚ-/ *verb* **1** [I or T] to do physical activities to make your body strong and healthy: *She exercises most evenings usually by running.* ○ *A work-out in the gym will exercise all the major muscle groups.* **2** [T] If you exercise an animal, you make it walk or run so that it stays strong and healthy: *Now he's retired he spends most afternoons exercising his dogs.*

• **exercise *your* mind** FORMAL to worry you: *The whole situation is exercising our minds greatly.*

exercise [PRACTISING] /ˈek.sə.saɪz/ [US] /-sɚ-/ *noun* [C] **1** an action or actions intended to improve something or make something happen: *Ships from eight navies will be taking part in an exercise in the Pacific to improve their efficiency in combat.* ○ *It would be a useful exercise for you to say the speech aloud several times.* ○ *an exercise **in** public relations* **2** a short piece of written work which you do to practise something you are learning: *The book has exercises at the end of every chapter.*

exercises /ˈek.sə.saɪ.zɪz/ [US] /-sɚ-/ *plural noun* US FORMAL a ceremony which includes speeches and usually traditional music or activities: *graduation/inaugural exercises*

exercise [USE] /ˈek.sə.saɪz/ [US] /-sɚ-/ *verb* [T] FORMAL to use something: *I exercised my democratic right by not voting in the election.* ○ *Always exercise **caution** when handling radioactive substances.* ○ *We've decided to exercise the **option*** (= use the part of a legal agreement) *to buy the house we now lease.*

exercise /ˈek.sə.saɪz/ [US] /-sɚ-/ *noun* [U] *The exercise **of*** (= use of) *restraint may well be difficult.*

ˈexercise ˌbike *noun* [C] a machine for taking exercise which looks similar to and is used like a bicycle but does not move from one place

exert [USE] /ɪɡˈzɜːt/ [US] /-ˈzɝːt/ *verb* [T] to use something such as authority, power, influence, etc. in order to make something happen: *If you were to exert your **influence** they might change their decision.* ○ *Some managers exert considerable **pressure on** their staff to work extra hours without being paid.* **exertion** /ɪɡˈzɜː.ʃᵊn/ [US] /-ˈzɝː-/ *noun* [U]

exert *yourself* [MAKE AN EFFORT] *verb* [R] to make a mental or physical effort: *I was too tired to exert myself.*

exertion /ɪɡˈzɜː.ʃᵊn/ [US] /-ˈzɝː-/ *noun* [C or U] when you make a lot of mental or physical effort: *I get out of breath with any kind of **physical** exertion.* ○ *We were exhausted after our exertions.*

exfoliate /ɪksˈfəʊ.li.eɪt/ [US] /-ˈfoʊ-/ *verb* [I or T] to remove dead skin cells from the surface of the skin, in order to improve the appearance **exfoliation** /eksˌfəʊ.liˈeɪ.ʃᵊn/ [US] /-ˌfoʊ-/ *noun* [U]

exfoliant *noun* [C or U] a substance with which you exfoliate

ex gratia /eksˈɡreɪ.ʃə/ *adj, adv* FORMAL An ex gratia payment is not necessary, especially legally, but is made to show good intentions: *Ex gratia payments were made to all those who had been affected by the spillage.*

exhale /eksˈheɪl/ [US] /ˈ--/ *verb* [I or T] FORMAL to send air out of your lungs: *Take a deep breath in then exhale into the mouthpiece.* ➲Compare **inhale**. **exhalation** /ˌeks.*h*əˈleɪ.ʃᵊn/ *noun* [C or U]

exhaust [TIRE] /ɪɡˈzɔːst/ [US] /-ˈzɑːst/ *verb* [T] to make someone extremely tired: *The long journey exhausted the children.* ○ *I've exhausted myself with all that cleaning.*

exhausted /ɪɡˈzɔː.stɪd/ [US] /-ˈzɑː-/ *adj* extremely tired: *Exhausted, they fell asleep.* ○ *By the time they reached the summit they were exhausted.*

exhausting /ɪɡˈzɔː.stɪŋ/ [US] /-ˈzɑː-/ *adj* making you feel extremely tired: *I've had an exhausting day.*

exhaustion /ɪɡˈzɔːs.tʃᵊn/ [US] /-ˈzɑː-/ *noun* [U] when you are extremely tired: *She felt ill with/from exhaustion.*

exhaust [USE] /ɪɡˈzɔːst/ [US] /-ˈzɑːst/ *verb* [T] to use something completely: *How long will it be before the world's fuel supplies are exhausted?* ○ *I'm afraid he's exhausted my patience.* ○ *We seem to have exhausted this topic of conversation* (= we have nothing new to say about it).

exhaustible /ɪɡˈzɔː.stɪ.bl̩/ [US] /-ˈzɑː-/ *adj*: *It is clear that many of the Earth's resources are exhaustible* (= will be used completely and disappear).

exhaustive /ɪɡˈzɔː.stɪv/ [US] /-ˈzɑː-/ *adj* complete: *an exhaustive study/report* **exhaustively** /ɪɡˈzɔː.stɪv.li/ [US] /-ˈzɑː-/ *adv*: *The survey was exhaustively documented.*

exhaust [GAS] /ɪɡˈzɔːst/ [US] /-ˈzɑːst/ *noun* [U] the waste gas from an engine, especially a car's, or the pipe the gas

E

flows through: *Car exhaust is the main reason for the city's pollution.* ➲See picture **Car** on page Centre 12

ex'haust ˌpipe *noun* [C] (*US USUALLY* **tailpipe**) the pipe at the back of a vehicle through which waste gas escapes from the engine

exhibit /ɪg'zɪb.ɪt/ *verb* [I or T] to show something publicly: *He frequently exhibits at the art gallery.* ○ *In the summer the academy will exhibit several prints which are rarely seen.* ○ *He exhibited great self-control considering her rudeness.*

exhibit /ɪg'zɪb.ɪt/ *noun* [C] **1** an object such as a painting that is shown to the public: *The museum has a fascinating collection of exhibits ranging from Iron Age pottery to Inuit clothing.* **2** *LEGAL* an item used as evidence in a trial: *Is exhibit C the weapon which you say was used?*

exhibition /ˌek.sɪ'bɪʃ.ᵊn/ *noun* [C or U] when objects such as paintings are shown to the public, or when someone shows a particular skill or quality to the public: *The photographs will be* ***on*** *exhibition until the end of the month.* ○ *There's a new exhibition of sculpture on at the city gallery.* ○ *The athlete's third, and winning, jump was an exhibition of skill and strength.*

• **make an exhibition of *yourself*** *DISAPPROVING* to do something stupid in public: *I hope I didn't make an exhibition of myself last night.*

exhibitionism /ˌek.sɪ'bɪʃ.ᵊn.ɪ.zᵊm/ *noun* [U] **1** *DISAPPROVING* behaviour which tries to attract attention: *It's exhibitionism to flaunt wealth so blatantly.* **2** *FORMAL* when someone shows their sexual organs in public

exhibitionist /ˌek.sɪ'bɪʃ.ᵊn.ɪst/ *noun* [C] **1** someone who tries to attract attention to themselves by their behaviour: *I have an exhibitionist streak that comes out on the dance floor.* **2** someone who shows their sexual organs in public

exhibitor /ɪg'zɪb.ɪ.təʳ/ [US] /-t̬ɚ/ *noun* [C] someone who has made or owns something, especially a work of art, shown in an exhibition: *Many of the exhibitors will be at the gallery to meet the public.*

exhi'bition ˌmatch *noun* [C] a single sports game that is not part of a larger competition, in which the players show their skills

exhilarate /ɪg'zɪl.ə.reɪt/ *verb* [T] to give someone strong feelings of happiness and excitement

exhilaration /ɪgˌzɪl.ə'reɪ.ʃᵊn/ *noun* [U] excitement and happiness

exhilarated /ɪg'zɪl.ə.reɪ.tɪd/ [US] /-t̬ɪd/ *adj* very excited and happy: *At the end of the race I was exhilarated.*

exhilarating /ɪg'zɪl.ə.reɪ.tɪŋ/ [US] /-t̬ɪŋ/ *adj* making you feel very excited and happy: *an exhilarating walk in the mountains*

exhort /ɪg'zɔːt/ [US] /-'zɔːrt/ *verb* [T + *to* infinitive] *FORMAL* to strongly encourage or try to persuade someone to do something: *The governor exhorted the prisoners not* ***to*** *riot.* **exhortation** /ˌeg.zɔː'teɪ.ʃᵊn/ [US] /-zɔːr-/ *noun* [C or U] *Despite the exhortations of the union leaders the workers voted to strike.* ○ *The book is essentially an exhortation* ***to*** *religious tolerance.*

exhume /eks'hjuːm/ [US] /eg'zuːm/ *verb* [T] *FORMAL* to remove a dead body from the ground after it has been buried **exhumation** /ˌeks.hjuː'meɪ.ʃᵊn/ *noun* [C or U]

ex-husband /ˌeks'hʌz.bənd/ *noun* [C] A woman's ex-husband is a man that she was married to but is not now married to.

exigency /'ek.sɪ.dʒᵊnt.si/ *noun* [C or U] *FORMAL* the difficulties of a situation, especially one which causes urgent demands: *the exigencies of war* ○ *Economic exigency obliged the government to act.*

exigent /'ek.sɪ.dʒᵊnt/ *adj FORMAL* needing urgent attention, or demanding too much from other people: *an exigent problem* ○ *an exigent manager*

exile /'ek.saɪl/ /'eg.zaɪl/ *noun* **1** [U] the condition of someone being sent or kept away from their own country, village, etc., especially for political reasons: *The king* ***went into*** *exile because of the political situation in his country.* ○ *The deposed leaders are currently* ***in*** *exile in the neighbouring country.* **2** [C] a person who is sent or kept away from their own country, etc. ➲See also **tax exile**. **exile** /'ek.saɪl/ /'eg.zaɪl/ *verb* [T] *The monarch was exiled because of the coup.* **exiled** /'ek.saɪld/ /'eg.zaɪld/ *adj: the exiled king*

exist /ɪg'zɪst/ *verb* [I] **1** to be, or to be real: *I don't think ghosts exist.* ○ *Poverty still exists in this country.* **2** to live, or to live in difficult conditions: *Some species exist in this small area of forest and nowhere else on Earth.* ○ *Few people can exist without water for more than a week.* ○ *No-one can be expected to exist* ***on*** *such a low salary.*

existence /ɪg'zɪs.tᵊnts/ *noun* **1** [U] when something or someone exists: *Many people question the existence* ***of*** *God.* ○ *Modern cosmology believes the Universe to have* ***come into*** *existence about fifteen billion years ago.* ○ *The theatre company that they started is still* ***in*** *existence today.* **2** [C usually sing] a particular way of life: *She has a miserable existence living with him.*

existent /ɪg'zɪs.tᵊnt/ *adj FORMAL* existing now: *This carving is believed to be the only existent image of Saint Frideswide.*

existing /ɪg'zɪs.tɪŋ/ *adj* [before n] *The existing laws* (= laws which exist at the present time) *covering libel in this country are thought by many to be inadequate.* ○ *Under the existing* (= present) *conditions many children are going hungry.*

existentialism /ˌeg.zɪ'sten.tʃᵊl.ɪ.zᵊm/ *noun* [U] *SPECIALIZED* the modern system of belief made famous by Jean Paul Sartre in the 1940s in which the world is meaningless and each person is alone and completely responsible for their own actions, by which they make their own character **existential** /ˌeg.zɪ'sten.tʃᵊl/ *adj* (*ALSO* **existentialist**) *an existential/existentialist argument/philosopher* **existentialist** /ˌeg.zɪ'sten.tʃᵊl.ɪst/ *noun* [C]

exit /'ek.sɪt/ /'eg.zɪt/ *noun* [C] **1** the door through which you might leave a building or large vehicle, or the act of leaving especially a theatre stage: *a fire exit* (= a door you can escape through if there is a fire) ○ *an* ***emergency*** *exit* ○ *He saw Emma arrive and* ***made*** *a quick exit.* ○ *She* ***made*** *her exit from the stage to rapturous applause.* ➲Compare **entrance**. **2** a smaller road used to leave a main road: *Come off the motorway at the Duxford exit.* **exit** /'ek.sɪt/ /'eg.zɪt/ *verb* [I or T] *I exited quickly before anyone could see me.* ○ *Please exit the theatre by the side doors.*

'exit ˌpoll *noun* [C] the organized questioning of people as they leave a POLLING STATION (= place at which people vote) about how they voted, to try to discover who will win the election

Exocet /'ek.sə.set/ [US] /-soʊ-/ *noun* [C] *TRADEMARK* a missile which can be accurately directed over short distances, used especially against enemy ships

exodus /'ek.sə.dəs/ *noun* [S] **1** the movement of a lot of people from a place: *There has been a* ***mass*** *exodus of workers* ***from*** *the villages to the towns.* ○ *There is always an exodus* ***to*** *the coast at holiday times.* **2 Exodus** the second book of the Bible telling of Moses and the journey of the Israelites out of Egypt

ex officio /ˌeks.ə'fɪʃ.i.əʊ/ [US] /-oʊ/ *adj, adv FORMAL* because of a person's position in a formal group: *The cabinet will also attend the meeting ex-officio.*

exonerate /ɪg'zɒn.ə.reɪt/ [US] /-'zɑː.nɚ.eɪt/ *verb* [T] *FORMAL* to show or state that someone or something is not guilty of something: *The report exonerated the crew* ***from*** *all responsibility for the collision.* **exoneration** /ɪgˌzɒn.ə'reɪ.ʃᵊn/ [US] /-ˌzɑː.nə-/ *noun* [U]

exorbitant /ɪg'zɔː.bɪ.tᵊnt/ [US] /-'zɔːr.bə.t̬ᵊnt/ *adj* Exorbitant prices and demands, etc. are much too large: *The bill for dinner was exorbitant.*

exorcize, *UK ALSO* **exorcise** /'ek.sɔː.saɪz/ [US] /-sɔːr-/ *verb* [T] **1** to force an evil spirit to leave a person or place by using prayers or magic: *After the priest exorcized the spirit/house/child, apparently, the strange noises stopped.* **2** to remove the bad effects of a frightening or upsetting event: *It will take a long time to exorcise the memory of the accident.* **exorcism** /'ek.sɔː.sɪ.zᵊm/ [US] /-sɔːr-/ *noun* [C or U] **exorcist** /'ek.sɔː.sɪst/ [US] /-sɔːr-/ *noun* [C]

exotic /ɪg'zɒt.ɪk/ [US] /-'zɑː.t̬ɪk/ *adj* unusual and often exciting because of coming (or seeming to come) from a distant, especially tropical country: *exotic flowers/food/ designs*

exotica /ɪgˈzɒt.ɪ.kə/ ⓤ /-ˈzɑː.t̬ɪ-/ *plural noun* unusual objects, often ones that have come from a distant country: *Collectors of eighteenth century exotica are our main customers.* **exoticism** /ɪgˈzɒt.ɪ.sɪ.zᵊm/ ⓤ /-ˈzɑː.t̬ɪ-/ *noun* [U]

e,xotic 'dancer *noun* [C] a performer who removes her or his clothes in a sexually exciting way

expand /ɪkˈspænd/ *verb* [I or T] to increase in size, number or importance, or to make something increase in this way: *The air in the balloon expands when heated.* ○ *They expanded their retail operations significantly during the 1980s.*

expandable /ɪkˈspæn.də.bļ/ *adj* able to increase in size: *pregnancy trousers with expandable waists*

expansion /ɪkˈspæn.tʃᵊn/ *noun* [C or U] when something increases in size, number or importance: *the rapid expansion of the software industry* ○ *Expansion into new areas of research is possible.* ○ *an expansion of industry*

expansionism /ɪkˈspæn.tʃᵊn.ɪ.zᵊm/ *noun* [U] DISAPPROVING increasing the amount of land ruled by a country, or the business performed by a company: *As a consequence of expansionism by some European countries, many ancient cultures have suffered.* **expansionist** /ɪkˈspæn.tʃᵊn.ɪst/ *noun* [C], *adj*

▲ **expand on** *sth phrasal verb* to give more details about something you have said or written: *She mentioned a few ideas, but she didn't expand on them.*

ex,panded poly'styrene *noun* [U] a light plastic containing gas used for wrapping things in before putting them in boxes

expanse /ɪkˈspæns/ *noun* [C] a large, open area of land, sea or sky: *She gazed at the immense expanse of the sea.* ○ *vast expanses of sand and pine*

expansive /ɪkˈspæn.sɪv/ *adj* covering a large area: *There was an expansive view from the window.* ○ *"All this is mine," she said with an expansive* (= using big movements) *arm gesture.* **expansively** /ɪkˈspæn.sɪv.li/ *adv*

expansive /ɪkˈspæn.sɪv/ *adj* FORMAL very happy to talk to people in a friendly way: *He was in an expansive mood on the night of the party.* **expansively** /ɪkˈspæn.sɪv.li/ *adv* **expansiveness** /ɪkˈspæn.sɪv.nəs/ *noun* [U]

expatiate /ekˈspeɪ.ʃi.eɪt/ *verb* [I] FORMAL DISAPPROVING to speak or write about something in great detail or for a long time: *She expatiated on/upon her work for the duration of the meal.*

expatriate /ekˈspæt.ri.ət/ ⓤ /-ˈspeɪ.tri-/ *noun* [C] (INFORMAL **expat**) someone who does not live in their own country: *A large community of expatriates has settled there.* **expatriate** /ekˈspæt.ri.ət/ ⓤ /-ˈspeɪ.tri-/ *adj*: *an expatriate Scot*

expatriate /ekˈspæt.ri.eɪt/ ⓤ /-ˈspeɪ.tri-/ *verb* [T] FORMAL to use force or law to remove someone from their own country: *The new leaders expatriated the ruling family.*

expect THINK /ɪkˈspekt/ *verb* [T] to think or believe something will happen, or someone will arrive: *We are expecting a lot of applicants for the job.* ○ [+ (that)] *I expect (that) you'll find it somewhere in your bedroom.* ○ *I expect (that) he'd have left anyway.* ○ [+ to infinitive] *He didn't expect to see me.* ○ *The financial performance of the business is fully expected* (= almost certain) *to improve.* ○ *We were half expecting you not to come back.* ⊃See Note **attend** or **wait/expect?** at **attend** BE PRESENT. **expected** /ɪkˈspek.tɪd/ *adj* [before n] *The expected counter-attack never happened.*

• **(only) to be expected** normal and what usually happens: *All parents of small children get tired. It's to be expected.*

expectancy /ɪkˈspek.tᵊnt.si/ *noun* [U] when you think that something exciting or pleasant is going to happen: *There was a general air of expectancy in the crowd.* ⊃See also **life expectancy**.

expectant /ɪkˈspek.tᵊnt/ *adj* thinking that something pleasant or exciting is going to happen: *the children's expectant faces* **expectantly** /ɪkˈspek.tᵊnt.li/ *adv*: *Roland heard the rustle of biscuit wrappers and looked up at John expectantly.*

expectation /ˌek.spekˈteɪ.ʃᵊn/ *noun* **1** [C usually pl] when you expect good things to happen in the future: *The holiday lived up to all our expectations* (= was as good as we were expecting). ○ *I have high expectations for this job* (= I believe it will be good). ○ *We did so well – beyond all* (= better than) *our expectations.* ○ *I think she had unrealistic expectations of motherhood.* **2** [C or U] when you expect something to happen: *Considering the injuries he's had there can be little expectation of him winning the race.* ○ *Our expectations are that the UK will cut its interest rate.*

• **against/contrary to all expectations** different from what is expected: *Contrary to all expectations, she was accepted by the academy.*

expect DEMAND /ɪkˈspekt/ *verb* [T] to think that someone should behave in a particular way or do a particular thing: *I expect punctuality from my students.* ○ [+ to infinitive] *Borrowers are expected to* (= should) *return books on time.*

expect BE PREGNANT /ɪkˈspekt/ *verb* **be expecting (a baby)** to be pregnant: *She shouldn't be lifting those boxes if she's expecting.* ○ *Kate and Dom are expecting a baby.*

expectant /ɪkˈspek.tᵊnt/ *adj* [before n] describes a woman who is pregnant or a man whose partner is pregnant: *expectant mothers/fathers/couples*

expectorant /ɪkˈspek.tᵊr.ᵊnt/ *noun* [C] a type of cough medicine used to loosen PHLEGM (= thick liquid) from the lungs

expectorate /ɪkˈspek.tᵊr.eɪt/ ⓤ /-tɚ-/ *verb* [I] SPECIALIZED to bring up liquid from the throat or lungs and force it out of the mouth

expedience /ɪkˈspiː.di.ᵊnts/ *noun* [U] (ALSO **expediency**) FORMAL when something is helpful or useful in a particular situation, but sometimes not morally acceptable: *As a matter of expedience, we will not be taking on any new staff this year.* ○ *I think this government operates on the basis of expediency, not of principle.*

expedient /ɪkˈspiː.di.ᵊnt/ *adj* FORMAL helpful or useful in a particular situation, but sometimes not morally acceptable: *It might be expedient not to pay him until the work is finished.* ○ *The management has taken a series of expedient measures to improve the company's financial situation.*

expedient /ɪkˈspiː.di.ᵊnt/ *noun* [C] FORMAL an action that is expedient: *a political expedient* **expediently** /ɪkˈspiː.di.ᵊnt.li/ *adv*

expedite /ˈek.spə.daɪt/ *verb* [T] FORMAL to cause to be done more quickly; to hurry: *Something needs to be done to expedite the process.*

expedition /ˌek.spəˈdɪʃ.ᵊn/ *noun* [U] FORMAL speed in doing something: *We will deal with your order with the greatest possible expedition.*

expeditious /ˌek.spəˈdɪʃ.əs/ *adj* FORMAL quick: *The bank was expeditious in replying to my letter.* **expeditiously** /ˌek.spəˈdɪʃ.ə.sli/ *adv*

expedition /ˌek.spəˈdɪʃ.ᵊn/ *noun* [C] **1** an organized journey for a particular purpose: *We're going on a shopping expedition on Saturday.* ○ *Scott died while he was on an expedition to the Antarctic in 1912.* **2** the people, vehicles, animals, etc. taking part in an expedition: *The British expedition to Mount Everest is leaving next month.*

expeditionary /ˌek.spəˈdɪʃ.ᵊn.ᵊr.i/ ⓤ /-er-/ *adj* **expeditionary force/unit** a group of soldiers sent to another country to fight in a war

expel /ɪkˈspel/ *verb* [T] -ll- to force to leave; to remove: *The new government has expelled all foreign diplomats.* ○ *My brother was expelled from school for bad behaviour.* ○ *When you breathe out, you expel air from your lungs.* ⊃See also **expulsion**.

expend /ɪkˈspend/ *verb* [T] SLIGHTLY FORMAL to use or spend especially time, effort or money: *You expend so much effort for so little return.* ○ *Governments expend a lot of resources on war.*

expendable /ɪkˈspen.də.bļ/ *adj* If someone or something is expendable, people can do something or deal with a situation without them: *No one likes to think that they're expendable.*

expenditure /ɪk'spen.dɪ.tʃəʳ/ [US] /-tʃɚ/ *noun* **1** [C or U] the total amount of money that a government or person spends: *It's part of a drive to cut government expenditure.* ○ *The government's annual expenditure* ***on*** *arms has been reduced.* **2** [U] the act of using or spending energy, time or money: *The expenditure of effort* ***on*** *this project has been enormous.*

expense /ɪk'spents/ *noun* **1** [U] when you spend or use money, time or effort: *Buying a bigger car has proved to be well* ***worth the*** *expense.* ○ *We've just had a new garage built* ***at*** *great expense.* ○ *We went on holiday* ***at*** *my father's expense* (= he paid for it). ○ *It's silly to* ***go to the*** *expense* ***of*** (= spend money on) *buying new clothes when you don't really need them.* **2** [C] something which causes you to spend money: *Our biggest expense this year was our summer holiday.* ○ *We need to cut down on our expenses.*

• **blow/hang the expense** *UK INFORMAL* used for saying that you want something so much that you do not care how much it costs: *I'm going to book a holiday. Blow the expense!*

• **no expense is spared** If no expense is spared in arranging something, a lot of money is spent to make it extremely good: *No expense was spared in making the guests feel comfortable.*

• **at the expense of *sb*** (*ALSO* **at *sb's* expense**) making another person look foolish: *Would you stop making jokes at my expense?*

expenses /ɪk'spent.sɪz/ *plural noun* money that you spend when you are doing your job, that your employer will pay back to you: *I need to get my expenses approved.* ○ *UK Don't worry about the cost of lunch – it's* ***on*** *expenses.*

• **all expenses paid** If something is all expenses paid, it means that you do not have to pay for anything yourself: *She's going on a trip to New York, all expenses paid.* ○ *an all expenses paid trip to New York*

expensive /ɪk'spent.sɪv/ *adj* costing a lot of money: *Rolls Royces are very expensive.* ○ *Big houses are expensive* ***to*** *maintain.* ○ *She has expensive* ***tastes*** (= she likes things that cost a lot of money).

expensively /ɪk'spent.sɪv.li/ *adv*: *Sarah is always very expensively dressed* (= she wears clothes that cost a lot of money).

ex'pense ac,count *noun* [C] an arrangement in which your employer will pay for the things you need to buy while doing your job: *I can* ***put*** *this lunch* ***on my*** *expense account.* ○ *expense-account fraud*

experience /ɪk'spɪə.ri.ᵊnts/ [US] /-'spɪr.i-/ *noun* **1** [U] (the process of getting) knowledge or skill which is obtained from doing, seeing or feeling things: *Do you have any experience* ***of*** *working with kids* (= Have you ever worked with them)*?* ○ *The best way to learn is* ***by*** *experience* (= by doing things). ○ *I know* ***from*** *experience that Tony never keeps his promises.* ○ *I don't think she has the experience* ***for*** *the job* (= enough knowledge and skill for it). ○ ***In my*** *experience, people generally smile back if you smile at them.* ○ *The experience* ***of*** *pain* (= what pain feels like) *varies from one person to another.* ○ *There's nothing we can do about it now, we'll just have to* ***put it down to*** *experience* (= consider it as a mistake we can learn from). **2** [C] something that happens to you that affects how you feel: *I had a rather unpleasant experience at the dentist's.* ○ *It was interesting hearing about his experiences as a policeman.* ○ *I did meet him once and it was an experience I shall never forget.*

experience /ɪk'spɪə.ri.ᵊnts/ [US] /-'spɪr.i-/ *verb* [T] If you experience something, it happens to you, or you feel it: *We experienced a lot of difficulty in selling our house.* ○ *New companies often experience a loss in their first few years.* ○ *It was the worst pain I'd ever experienced.*

experienced /ɪk'spɪə.ri.ᵊntst/ [US] /-'spɪr.i-/ *adj APPROVING* having skill or knowledge because you have done something many times: *an experienced teacher* ○ *She is very experienced* ***in*** *marketing.*

experiential /ɪk,spɪə.ri'en.tʃᵊl/ [US] /-,spɪr.i-/ *adj FORMAL* based on experience: *experiential learning*

experiment /ɪk'sper.ɪ.mənt/ *noun* [C or U] a test done in order to learn something or to discover whether something works or is true: *Some people believe that experiments* ***on*** *animals should be banned.* ○ [+ to infinitive] *Scientists are* ***conducting/carrying out/doing*** *experiments* ***to*** *test the effectiveness of the new drug.* ○ *I've bought a different kind of coffee this week* ***as*** *an experiment* (= in order to see what it is like). ○ *We can only find the best solution* ***by*** *experiment.*

experiment /ɪk'sper.ɪ.ment/ *verb* [I] to try something in order to discover what it is like: *Things would never change if people weren't prepared to experiment* (= to try doing something different). ○ *The school is experimenting* ***with*** (= trying) *new teaching methods.* ○ *Experimenting* ***on*** *mice can give us an idea of the effect of the disease in humans.*

experimental /ɪk,sper.ɪ'men.tᵊl/ [US] /-t̬ᵊl/ *adj* relating to tests, especially scientific ones: *The drug is still at the experimental stage* (= is still being tested). ○ *The changes to the distribution system are purely experimental at the moment.* ○ *experimental* ***psychology*** **experimentally** /ɪk,sper.ɪ'men.tᵊl.i/ [US] /-t̬ᵊl-/ *adv*

experimentation /ɪk,sper.ɪ.men'teɪ.ʃᵊn/ *noun* [U] *Children need the opportunity for experimentation* (= for trying things). ○ *Extensive experimentation* (= testing) *is needed before new drugs can be sold.* **experimenter** /ɪk'sper.ɪ.men.təʳ/ [US] /-t̬ɚ/ *noun* [C]

expert /'ek.spɜːt/ [US] /-spɝːt/ *noun* [C] a person with a high level of knowledge or skill; a specialist: *a gardening/medical expert* ○ *My mother is an expert* ***at*** *dress-making* (= she does it very well). **expert** /'ek.spɜːt/ [US] /-spɝːt/ *adj* [before n] *The centre provides expert* ***advice*** *for people with financial problems.* ○ *What's your expert* ***opinion****?*

expertise /,ek.spɜː'tiːz/ [US] /-spɝː-/ *noun* [U] a high level of knowledge or skill: *We admired the expertise with which he prepared the meal.* ○ *I have no expertise* ***in*** *sewing/sewing expertise.* ○ *She has considerable expertise* ***in*** *French history.* **expertly** /'ek.spɜːt.li/ [US] /-spɝːt-/ *adv*: *He carved the roast expertly.*

'expert ,system *noun* [C] a computer system which asks questions and gives answers that have been thought of by a human expert

expiate /'ek.spi.eɪt/ *verb* [T] *FORMAL* to show regret for bad behaviour by doing something to express that you are sorry and by accepting punishment: *to expiate a crime/sin* **expiation** /,ek.spi'eɪ.ʃᵊn/ *noun* [U] *the expiation of a sin*

expire [END] /ɪk'spaɪəʳ/ [US] /-'spaɪr/ *verb* [I] If something which lasts for a fixed length of time expires, it comes to an end or stops being in use: *Our television license expires next month.* ○ *The contract between the two companies will expire at the end of the year.*

expiry *UK* /,ek.spɪ'reɪ.ʃᵊn/ *noun* [U] (*US* **expiration**) *the expiry of a lease/visa* ○ *What is the expiry/expiration* ***date*** *of your credit card* (= What is the last date on which it can be used)*?*

expire [DIE] /ɪk'spaɪəʳ/ [US] /-'spaɪr/ *verb* [I] *LITERARY* to die

explain /ɪk'spleɪn/ *verb* [I or T] to make something clear or easy to understand by describing or giving information about it: *If there's anything you don't understand, I'll be happy to explain.* ○ *The teacher explained the rules* ***to*** *the children.* ○ [+ question word] *Our guide explained* ***wh****ere the cathedral was.* ○ *He explained* ***how*** *the machine worked.* ○ *Please could you explain* ***why*** *you're so late.* ○ [+ that] *She explained* ***that*** *she was going to stay with her sister.* ○ [+ speech] *"Someone must have hit the wrong button," an official explained.* ○ [R] *Molly asked the teacher if she could explain herself a bit more clearly* (= say more clearly what she meant). ○ *No one has been able to explain* (= give the reason for) *the accident.*

explain *yourself* *verb* [R] to give reasons for your behaviour: *He hadn't been home for three days so I asked him to explain himself.*

explaining /ɪk'spleɪ.nɪŋ/ *noun* [U] when you have to explain or give a good reason for your actions: *You'll* ***have*** *a lot of explaining* ***to do*** *when dad finds out what happened.*

explanation /,ek.splə'neɪ.ʃᵊn/ *noun* [C or U] the details or reasons that someone gives to make something clear or easy to understand: *Could you* ***give*** *me a quick explanation* ***of*** *how it works?* ○ *What was her explanation* ***for*** *why she was late?* ○ [+ that] *The judge didn't believe his*

*explanation **that** he had stolen the money in order to give it to charity.* ○ *He said, **by way of** explanation, that he hadn't seen the traffic light change to red.*
explanatory /ɪk'splæn.ə.tri/ [US] /-tɔːr.i/ *adj* giving an explanation about something: *There are explanatory notes with the diagram.* ⊃See also **self-explanatory**.
▲ **explain *sth* away** *phrasal verb* **[M]** to avoid blame for something that has happened by making it seem unimportant or not your fault: *I don't know how you're going to explain away that dent you made in your dad's car.*

expletive /ɪk'spliː.tɪv/ [US] /'ek.splə.t̬ɪv/ *noun* **[C]** FORMAL a swear word: *She dropped the book on her foot and **let out** a row/string of expletives.*

explicable /ek'splɪk.ə.bl̩/ *adj* able to be explained: *Under the circumstances, what he said was quite explicable.* **explicably** /ek'splɪk.ə.bli/ *adv*

explicate /'ek.splɪ.keɪt/ *verb* **[T]** FORMAL to explain especially a piece of writing or an idea in detail: *This is a book which clearly explicates Marx's later writings.* **explication** /ˌek.splɪ'keɪ.ʃᵊn/ *noun* **[C or U]**

explicit /ɪk'splɪs.ɪt/ *adj* **1** clear and exact: *I gave her very explicit directions how to get here.* ○ *She was very explicit **about*** (= said very clearly and exactly) *what she thought was wrong with the plans.* ○ *I wasn't aware that I would be paying – you certainly didn't **make** it explicit* (= state it clearly). ⊃Compare **implicit**. **2** showing or talking about sex or violence in a very detailed way: *a sexually explicit film*
explicitly /ɪk'splɪs.ɪt.li/ *adv*: *I told you quite explicitly* (= clearly) *to be home by midnight.* **explicitness** /ɪk'splɪs.ɪt.nəs/ *noun* **[U]**

explode [BURST] /ɪk'spləʊd/ [US] /-'sploʊd/ *verb* **[I or T]** to (cause to) burst violently: *A **bomb** exploded at one of London's busiest railway stations this morning.* ○ *He was driving so fast that his car tyre exploded.* ⊃Compare **implode**.
explosion /ɪk'spləʊ.ʒᵊn/ [US] /-'sploʊ-/ *noun* **[C or U]** when something such as a bomb explodes: *The fire was thought to have been caused by a gas explosion.* ○ *The explosion* (= the intentional exploding) ***of** nuclear devices in the Bikini Atoll was stopped in 1958.*
explosive /ɪk'spləʊ.sɪv/ [US] /-'sploʊ-/ *noun* **[C or U]** a substance or piece of equipment that can cause explosions
explosive /ɪk'spləʊ.sɪv/ [US] /-'sploʊ-/ *adj* **1** exploding or able to explode easily: *Certain gases are **highly** explosive.* ○ *An explosive **device*** (= a bomb) *was found at one of London's busiest stations this morning.* **2** very loud and sudden, like an explosion: *There was an explosive clap of thunder overhead.* **explosively** /ɪk'spləʊ.sɪv.li/ [US] /-'sploʊ-/ *adv*

explode [EMOTION] /ɪk'spləʊd/ [US] /-'sploʊd/ *verb* **[I]** to react suddenly with a strong expression of emotion: **[+ speech]** *"What on earth do you think you're doing?" she exploded* (= said angrily). ○ *The children exploded **into** giggles* (= suddenly started laughing uncontrollably).
explosion /ɪk'spləʊ.ʒᵊn/ [US] /-'sploʊ-/ *noun* **[C]** a sudden strong expression of emotion: *There was an explosion **of** applause from the audience at the end of the performance.*
explosive /ɪk'spləʊ.sɪv.li/ [US] /-'sploʊ.sɪv-/ *adj* describes a situation or emotion in which strong feelings are loudly or violently expressed: *The **situation** in the poorer parts of some of America's major cities has become very explosive.* ○ *Capital punishment is an explosive **issue**.* ○ *She has an explosive **temper**.* **explosively** /ɪk'spləʊ.sɪv.li/ [US] /-'sploʊ-/ *adv* **explosiveness** /ɪk'spləʊ.sɪv.nəs/ [US] /-'sploʊ-/ *noun* **[U]**

explode [INCREASE] /ɪk'spləʊd/ [US] /-'sploʊd/ *verb* **[I]** to increase very quickly: *The population has exploded in the last ten years.*
explosion /ɪk'spləʊ.ʒᵊn/ [US] /-'sploʊ-/ *noun* **[C]** when the number of something increases very quickly: *The government has had to take measures to halt the **population** explosion.* **explosive** /ɪk'spləʊ.sɪv/ [US] /-'sploʊ-/ *adj*: *The last few years have seen an explosive increase in the number of homeless people on our streets.*
▲ **explode into *sth*** *phrasal verb* to suddenly change into something powerful or exciting: *London's parks have exploded into colour* (= become very colourful because many flowers have opened) *in the last week.*

explode [PROVE FALSE] /ɪk'spləʊd/ [US] /-'sploʊd/ *verb* **[T]** to show something to be wrong: *This book finally explodes some of the **myths** about the origin of the universe.*
explosion /ɪk'spləʊ.ʒᵊn/ [US] /-'sploʊ-/ *noun* **[S]**

exploit [USE WELL] /ɪk'splɔɪt/ *verb* **[T]** to use something for advantage: *We need to make sure that we exploit our **resources** as fully as possible.*
exploitable /ɪk'splɔɪ.tə.bl̩/ [US] /-t̬ə-/ *adj*: *The coal mine is no longer commercially exploitable* (= can no longer be used for profit).
exploitation /ˌek.splɔɪ'teɪ.ʃᵊn/ *noun* **[U]** *Britain's exploitation **of*** (= its use of) *its natural gas reserves began after the Second World War.*

exploit [USE UNFAIRLY] /ɪk'splɔɪt/ *verb* **[T]** to use someone or something unfairly for your own advantage: *Laws exist to stop companies exploiting their employees.*
exploitable /ɪk'splɔɪ.tə.bl̩/ [US] /-t̬ə-/ *adj*: *The lack of jobs in this area means that the workforce is easily exploitable* (= employers can use workers unfairly for their own advantage).
exploitation /ˌek.splɔɪ'teɪ.ʃᵊn/ *noun* **[U]** when someone uses someone else unfairly for their own advantage: *Marx wrote about the exploitation **of** the workers.*
exploitative /ɪk'splɔɪ.tə.tɪv/ [US] /-t̬ə.t̬ɪv/ *adj* using someone else unfairly for your own advantage
exploiter /ɪk'splɔɪ.təʳ/ [US] /-t̬ɚ/ *noun* **[C]** someone who uses other people or things for his or her own profit or advantage

exploit [ACT] /'ek.splɔɪt/ *noun* **[C usually pl]** something unusual, brave or funny that someone has done: *She was telling me about her exploits while travelling around Africa.*

explore /ɪk'splɔːʳ/ [US] /-'splɔːr/ *verb* **[I or T]** to search and discover (about something): *to explore space* ○ *The best way to explore the countryside is on foot.* ○ *Let's explore this **issue/idea** more fully* (= examine it carefully in order to discover more about it). ○ *The children have gone exploring in the woods.*
exploration /ˌek.splə'reɪ.ʃᵊn/ [US] /-splɚ'reɪ-/ *noun* **[C or U]** *Livingstone was the first European to make an exploration **of** the Zambezi river* (= to travel to it in order to discover more about it). ○ *We need to carry out a full exploration* (= examination) ***of** all the alternatives.* ○ *The exploration* (= search) ***for** new sources of energy is vital for the future of our planet.*
exploratory /ek'splɒr.ə.tri/ [US] /-'splɑː.rə.tɔːr.i/ *adj* in order to discover more about something: *an exploratory expedition to Antarctica* ○ *She's having some exploratory tests done to find out what's causing the illness.* ○ *We're having an exploratory meeting next week to talk about* (= a meeting in order to examine) *the possibility of merging the two companies.*
explorer /ɪk'splɔː.rəʳ/ [US] /-rɚ/ *noun* **[C]** someone who travels to places where no one has ever been in order to find out what is there: *Magellan was a famous sixteenth-century explorer.*

expo /'ek.spəʊ/ [US] /-spoʊ/ *noun* **[C]** an **exposition** SHOW

exponent [PERSON] /ɪk'spəʊ.nənt/ [US] /-'spoʊ-/ *noun* **[C]** a person who supports an idea or belief or performs an activity: *Adam Smith was an exponent **of** free trade.* ○ *Jaqueline du Pré was a leading exponent **of** cello-playing.*

exponent [NUMBER] /ɪk'spəʊ.nᵊnt/ [US] /-'spoʊ-/ *noun* **[C]** SPECIALIZED a number or sign which shows how many times another number is to be multiplied by itself: *In 6^4 and y^n, 4 and n are the exponents.*

exponential /ˌek.spəʊ'nen.tʃᵊl/ [US] /-spoʊ-/ *adj* **1** SPECIALIZED containing an EXPONENT (= number or sign which shows how many times another number is to be multiplied by itself): *6^4 is an exponential expression.* **2** FORMAL describes a rate of increase which becomes quicker and quicker as the thing that increases becomes larger: *We are looking for exponential growth in our investment.* ○ *There has been an exponential increase in the world population this century.* **exponentially** /ˌek.spəʊ'nen.tʃᵊl.i/ [US] /-spoʊ-/ *adv* FORMAL *Malthus wrote about the risks involved in the world's population increasing exponentially.*

E

export /ɪkˈspɔːt/ ⑩ /ˈek.spɔːrt/ *verb* **1** [I or T] to send goods to another country for sale: *French cheeses are exported* **to** *many different countries.* ○ *Our clothes sell so well in this country that we have no need to export.* ⊃Compare **import** BRING IN. **2** [T] to put something from one country into use in other countries: *American culture has been exported all over the world.* **3** [T] If you export information from a computer, you copy a large amount of it either to a different part of the computer's storage space or to another form of storage such as a FLOPPY DISK, so that it can be used for a different purpose.

export /ˈek.spɔːt/ ⑩ /-spɔːrt/ *noun* [C or U] a product that you sell in another country, or the business of sending goods to another country in order to sell them there: *Coffee is one of Brazil's main exports.* ○ *We plan to increase our exports over the next five years.* ○ *The export of ivory is now strictly controlled.* ○ *India grows tea for export.* ○ *We are planning to develop our export* **market/ trade**.

exportable /ɪkˈspɔː.tə.bl̩/ ⑩ /-ˈspɔːr.tə-/ *adj*: *The value of the new television technology to the company is that it is highly exportable* (= can be sold in other countries).

exportation /ˌek.spɔːˈteɪ.ʃən/ ⑩ /-spɔːr-/ *noun* [U] *These crates have been packed* **for exportation** (= to be sent for sale in other countries).

exporter /ɪkˈspɔː.tər/ ⑩ /-ˈspɔːr.tə/ *noun* [C] a person, country or business that sells goods to another country: *Japan is a major exporter* **of** *cars.*

exposé /ek'spəʊ.zeɪ/ ⑩ /ˌek.spəˈzeɪ/ *noun* [C] a public report of the facts about a situation, especially one that is shocking or has been kept secret: *Today's newspaper contains a searing exposé* **of** *police corruption.*

expose /ɪkˈspəʊz/ ⑩ /-ˈspoʊz/ *verb* [T] **1** to remove what is covering something so that it can be seen: *The plaster on the walls has been removed to expose the original bricks underneath.* ○ *He damaged his leg so badly in the accident that the bone was exposed.* ○ *This photograph was* **under-/over-**exposed (= too little/too much light was allowed to reach the film). **2** to make public something bad or dishonest: *The review exposed widespread corruption in the police force.* ○ *The newspaper story exposed him* **as** (= showed that he was) *a liar.* **3 expose yourself** If a man exposes himself, he shows his sexual organs in a public place to people he does not know.

exposed /ɪkˈspəʊzd/ ⑩ /-ˈspoʊzd/ *adj* having no protection from bad weather: *The house is in a very exposed position.*

▲ **expose** *sb* **to** *sth phrasal verb* [usually passive] to make it likely that someone will experience something harmful or unpleasant: *About 800, 000 children are exposed to poisons each year.* ○ *It is feared that people living near the power station may have been exposed to radiation.*

exposition EXPLANATION /ˌek.spəˈzɪʃ.ən/ *noun* [C or U] FORMAL a clear and full explanation of an idea or theory: *It purports to be an exposition of Catholic social teaching.*

exposition SHOW /ˌek.spəˈzɪʃ.ən/ *noun* [C] (ALSO **expo**) a show in which industrial goods, works of art, etc. are shown to the public: *the San Francisco exposition* ○ *Expo 92* (= a show that happened in 1992)

expostulate /ɪkˈspɒs.tjʊ.leɪt/ ⑩ /-ˈspɑː.stjʊ-/ *verb* [I] FORMAL to express disagreement or complaint: *Walter expostulated* **with** *the waiter* **about** *the size of the bill.* **expostulation** /ɪkˌspɒs.tjʊˈleɪ.ʃən/ ⑩ /-ˌspɑː.stjʊ-/ *noun* [C or U]

exposure EXPERIENCE /ɪkˈspəʊ.ʒər/ ⑩ /-ˈspoʊ.ʒə/ *noun* [C or U] when someone experiences something or is affected by it because they are in a particular situation or place: *You should always limit your exposure* **to** *the sun.* ○ *Even a brief exposure* **to** *radiation is very dangerous.*

exposure MADE PUBLIC /ɪkˈspəʊ.ʒər/ ⑩ /-ˈspoʊ.ʒə/ *noun* [C or U] when something bad that someone has done is made public: *The exposure* **of** *the minister's love affair forced him to resign.*

exposure ATTENTION /ɪkˈspəʊ.ʒər/ ⑩ /-ˈspoʊ.ʒə/ *noun* [U] when an event or information is often discussed in newspapers and on the television, etc: *His last film got so much exposure in the press.*

exposure ILLNESS /ɪkˈspəʊ.ʒər/ ⑩ /-ˈspoʊ.ʒə/ *noun* [U] a serious medical condition that is caused by being out-side in very cold weather: *All the members of the expedition to the South Pole died of exposure.*

exposure PHOTOGRAPH /ɪkˈspəʊ.ʒər/ ⑩ /-ˈspoʊ.ʒə/ *noun* [C] a single photograph on a piece of film, or the amount of time a piece of film is open to the light when making a photograph: *There are twenty-four exposures on this film.*

exposure DIRECTION /ɪkˈspəʊ.ʒər/ ⑩ /-ˈspoʊ.ʒə/ *noun* [S] the direction in which something faces: *Our dining room has a northern exposure* (= faces north), *so it's rather cold.*

expound /ɪkˈspaʊnd/ *verb* [I or T] FORMAL to give a detailed explanation of something: *He's always expound-ing* **on** *what's wrong with the world.* ○ *She uses her news-paper column to expound her views on environmental issues.*

express SHOW /ɪkˈspres/ *verb* [T] **1** to show a feeling, opinion or fact: *Her eyes expressed deep sadness.* ○ *I would like to express my thanks for your kindness.* ○ *Words can't express* **how** *happy I am.* ○ *These figures are expressed* **as** *a percentage of the total.* **2 express yourself** to communicate what you think or feel, by speaking or writing, or in some other way: *I'm afraid I'm not expressing myself very clearly.* ○ *Children often express themselves in painting.*

expression /ɪkˈspreʃ.ən/ *noun* **1** [C or U] when you say what you think or show how you feel using words or actions: *He wrote her a poem as an expression* **of** *his love.* ○ *We've received a lot of expressions* **of** *support for our campaign.* ○ *Freedom of expression is a basic human right.* ○ *It's better to* **give** *expression* **to** (= show) *your anger, rather than hiding it.* ○ FORMAL *His sadness at the death of his wife* **found** *expression* (= was shown) *in his music.* ○ *She plays the violin with great expression* (= feeling). ⊃See also **expression** WORDS. **2** [C] the look on someone's face, showing what they feel or think: *I could tell from her expression that something serious had happened.* ○ *Mark always has such a miserable expres-sion on his face.*

expressionless /ɪkˈspreʃ.ən.ləs/ *adj* not showing what someone thinks or feels: *He has such an expressionless* **face/voice**.

expressive /ɪkˈspres.ɪv/ *adj* **1** showing what someone thinks or feels: *an expressive face* ○ *expressive hands* **2** FORMAL **be expressive of** *sth* showing a particular feel-ing: *The final movement of Beethoven's Ninth Symphony is expressive of joy.* **expressively** /ɪkˈspres.ɪv.li/ *adv*: *She danced the part of Giselle very expressively.* **expressive-ness** /ɪkˈspres.ɪv.nəs/ *noun* [U]

express FAST /ɪkˈspres/ *adj* [before n] moving or being sent fast: *Please send this letter by express* **delivery**. ○ *an express* **train** ○ *The dry cleaners offer a normal or an express* **service**.

express /ɪkˈspres/ *noun* [C or U] *The quickest way to get here is to take the uptown express* (= the fast train). ○ *the Orient Express* ○ *This parcel needs to be sent* **by** *express* (= a service which delivers fast).

express /ɪkˈspres/ *adv*: *Send this parcel express* (= by a service which delivers fast).

express /ɪkˈspres/ *verb* [T] *Your order will be expressed* (= delivered fast) **to** *you within 24 hours.*

express CLEAR /ɪkˈspres/ *adj* [before n] clearly and in-tentionally stated: *It is my express wish that after my death, my books be given to my old college library.* ○ *The lawyer argued that the accused had gone to the victim's house with the express purpose of killing her.*

expressly /ɪkˈspres.li/ *adv*: *I expressly* (= clearly) *told you to be home by midnight.* ○ *The farmer put up the fence expressly to stop* (= with the intention of stopping) *people walking across his field.*

expression WORDS /ɪkˈspreʃ.ən/ *noun* [C] a word or group of words used in a particular situation or by particular people: *He uses a lot of unusual expressions.* ○ *'A can of worms' is an expression which means 'a difficult situa-tion'.* ⊃See also **expression** at **express** SHOW.

expression NUMBERS /ɪkˈspreʃ.ən/ *noun* [C] in mathe-matics, a symbol or group of symbols which represent an amount: $4xy^2$ *is an expression.*

Expressionism /ɪkˈspreʃ.ᵊn.ɪ.zᵊm/ *noun* [U] a style of art, music or writing, found particularly in the 1900s, which expresses people's states of mind **Expressionist** /ɪkˈspreʃ.ᵊn.ɪst/ *adj, noun* [C] *Edvard Munch's "The Scream" is a famous Expressionist painting.*

expresso /esˈpres.əʊ/ ⓤⓢ /-oʊ/ *noun* [C or U] **espresso**

expressway /ɪkˈspres.weɪ/ *noun* [C] *US* a wide road built for fast moving traffic travelling long distances, with a limited number of points at which drivers can enter and leave it

expropriate /ɪkˈsprəʊ.pri.eɪt/ ⓤⓢ /-ˈsprəʊ-/ *verb* [T] *FORMAL* to take away money or property especially for public use without payment to the owner, or for personal use illegally: *He was discovered to have been expropriating company funds.* **expropriator** /ɪkˈsprəʊ.pri.eɪ.təʳ/ ⓤⓢ /-ˈsprəʊ.pri.eɪ.t̬əʳ/ *noun* [C] **expropriation** /ɪkˌsprəʊ.priˈeɪ.ʃᵊn/ ⓤⓢ /-ˌsprəʊ-/ *noun* [C or U]

expulsion /ɪkˈspʌl.ʃᵊn/ *noun* [C or U] (the act of) forcing someone, or being forced, to leave somewhere: *They threatened him with expulsion **from** school.* ○ *This is the second expulsion **of** a club member this year.* ⊃See also **expel**.

expunge /ɪkˈspʌndʒ/ *verb* [T] *FORMAL* **1** to rub off or remove information from a piece of writing: *His name has been expunged **from** the list of members.* **2** to cause something to be forgotten: *She has been unable to expunge the details of the accident **from** her **memory**.*

expurgate /ˈek.spə.geɪt/ ⓤⓢ /-spɚ-/ *verb* [T usually passive] *FORMAL* to remove parts of a piece of writing that are considered likely to cause offence: *The book was expurgated to make it suitable for children.* **expurgated** /ˈek.spə.geɪ.tɪd/ ⓤⓢ /-spɚ.geɪ.t̬ɪd/ *adj: Only an expurgated **version** of the novel has been published so far.* **expurgation** /ˌek.spəˈgeɪ.ʃᵊn/ ⓤⓢ /-spɚ-/ *noun* [C or U]

exquisite BEAUTIFUL /ɪkˈskwɪz.ɪt/ *adj* very beautiful; delicate: *an exquisite piece of china* ○ *Look at this exquisite painting.* ○ *She has exquisite taste.* **exquisitely** /ɪkˈskwɪz.ɪt.li/ *adv: Their house is exquisitely (= beautifully) furnished.* **exquisiteness** /ɪkˈskwɪz.ɪt.nəs/ *noun* [U]

exquisite SHARP /ɪkˈskwɪz.ɪt/ *adj* LITERARY describes feelings such as pleasure or pain that are extremely strong, or qualities that are extremely good; great: *exquisite joy* ○ *The pain was quite exquisite.* ○ *a vase of exquisite workmanship* ○ *A good comedian needs to have an exquisite sense of timing.* **exquisitely** /ɪkˈskwɪz.ɪt.li/ *adv:* **exquisiteness** /ɪkˈskwɪz.ɪt.nəs/ *noun* [U]

ex-serviceman /ˌeksˈsɜː.vɪs.mən/ ⓤⓢ /-ˈsɚ-/ *noun* [C] a man who was a member of the armed services in the past

ex-servicewoman /ˌeksˈsɜː.vɪs.wʊm.ən/ ⓤⓢ /-ˈsɚ-/ *noun* [C] a woman who was a member of the armed services in the past

extant /ekˈstænt/ /ˈek.stənt/ *adj* FORMAL describes something very old that is still existing: *We have some extant parish records from the sixteenth century.*

extemporaneous /ek.stem.pəˈreɪ.ni.əs/ *adj* FORMAL done or said without advance preparation or thought: *an extemporaneous speech*

extempore /ekˈstem.pᵊr.i/ *adj, adv* FORMAL done or said without advance preparation or thought: *an extempore performance* ○ *At the audition, the actors were asked to perform extempore.*

extemporize, *UK USUALLY* **-ise** /ɪkˈstem.pᵊr.aɪz/ ⓤⓢ /-pɚ.aɪz/ *verb* [I] FORMAL to speak or perform without advance preparation or thought: *I'd lost my notes and had to extemporize.*

extend REACH /ɪkˈstend/ *verb* [T; I usually + adv or prep] to (cause something to) reach, stretch or continue; to add to something in order to make it bigger or longer: *The Sahara Desert extends (= reaches) **for** miles.* ○ *The path extends (= continues) **beyond** the end of the road.* ○ *Rain is expected to extend **to** (= reach) all parts of the country by this evening.* ○ *The effects of this legislation will extend (= reach) further than the government intends.* ○ *Parking restrictions do not extend **to** (= include) disabled people.* ○ *We've extended a washing line (= made it reach) between two trees in the garden.* ○ *We're planning to extend our publishing of children's books (= increase*

it). ○ *He extended his hand as a greeting (= held out his hand for someone to shake it).* ○ *The government has produced a series of leaflets designed to extend (= increase) public awareness of the dangers of AIDS.* ○ *We have plans to extend our house (= to make it bigger).* ○ *The pub has recently extended its opening hours (= made them longer).* ○ *I need to extend my visa (= make it last longer).*

extendable /ɪkˈsten.də.bl̩/ *adj* describes something that can be made longer: *an extendable ladder* ○ *The lease on the office is extendable.*

extended /ɪkˈsten.dɪd/ *adj* [before n] long or longer than usual: *They're going on an extended holiday to Australia.* ○ *There was an extended news bulletin because of the plane crash.*

extension /ɪkˈsten.tʃᵊn/ *noun* [C or U] *Martin Luther King, Jr, campaigned for the extension of civil rights to (= for them to include) black people.* ○ *The extension (= increasing) **of** police powers in the province has been heavily criticized.* ○ *His report contained serious criticisms of the finance director, and, **by** extension (= therefore), of the entire board of management.* ○ *The article is an extension **of** (= takes further) the ideas Professor Fox developed in an earlier book.* ○ *We're building an extension (= adding a new room or rooms) **to/on** our house.* ○ *I've applied for an extension **to** my visa (= asked for it to last longer).* ○ *They are hoping to get an extension **of** their loan (= to be given a longer period of time in which to pay it back).*

extend OFFER /ɪkˈstend/ *verb* [T] SLIGHTLY FORMAL to offer or give: *I should like to extend my thanks **to** you for your kindness.* ○ *The chairperson extended a warm welcome **to** the guest speaker.* ○ *The government is extending (= giving) aid to people who have been affected by the earthquake.* ○ [+ two objects] *The bank has agreed to extend us money/extend money **to** us (= lend us money) to buy our house.* **extension** /ɪkˈsten.tʃᵊn/ *noun* [U]

extend USE ABILITY /ɪkˈstend/ *verb* [T] to cause someone to use all their ability: *She feels that her job doesn't extend her enough.*

ex,tended 'family *group noun* [C usually sing] a family unit which includes grandmothers, grandfathers, aunts and uncles, etc. in addition to parents and children ⊃Compare **nuclear family**.

extension /ɪkˈsten.tʃᵊn/ *noun* [C] any of two or more telephones in the same house which share the same number, or any of a number of telephones connected to a SWITCHBOARD in a large building such as an office: *We have an extension in our bedroom.* ○ *When you call, ask for extension 3276.* ⊃See also **extension** at extend REACH; **extend** OFFER.

ex'tension ,cord *US noun* [C] (*UK* **extension lead**) an additional wire used to take electricity to a piece of electrical equipment when it is an extra distance from the nearest SOCKET

extensive /ɪkˈsten.sɪv/ *adj* covering a large area; having a great range: *a school with extensive grounds* ○ *extensive repairs to the motorway* ○ *Her knowledge of music is extensive (= she knows a lot about music).* ○ *The wedding received extensive coverage in the newspapers.* **extensively** /ɪkˈsten.sɪv.li/ *adv: The house was extensively (= a large part of it was) rebuilt after the fire.* ○ *The side effects of the new drug are being extensively researched (= are being studied in detail).*

extent /ɪkˈstent/ *noun* [S or U] area or length; amount: *From the top of the Empire State Building, you can see **the** full extent of Manhattan (= the area it covers).* ○ *We don't yet know **the** extent of his injuries (= how bad his injuries are).* ○ *Rosie's teacher was impressed by **the** extent **of** her knowledge (= how much she knew).* ○ *The River Nile is over 6500 kilometres **in** extent (= length).*

● **to the extent of** so strongly that: *Some people hold their beliefs very strongly, even to the extent of being prepared to go to prison for them.*

● **to the extent that** to a particular degree or stage, often causing particular results: *Sales have fallen badly this year, to the extent that we will have to close some of our shops.*

● **to the same extent** to the same degree as; as much as: *The rich will not benefit from the proposed changes to the* *tax system to the same extent as the lower paid.*

● **to some extent** partly: *To some extent, she was responsible for the accident.*

● **to such an extent** so much: *The car was damaged to such an extent that it couldn't be repaired.*

● **to what extent** how much: *To what extent will the budget have to be modified? ○ To what extent do you think he's aware of the problem?*

extenuate /ɪkˈsten.ju.eɪt/ *verb* [T] FORMAL to cause a wrong act to be judged less seriously by giving reasons for it: *He was unable to say anything that might have extenuated his behaviour.*

extenuating /ɪkˈsten.juː.eɪ.tɪŋ/ US /-t̬ɪŋ/ *adj* [before n] SLIGHTLY FORMAL *She was found guilty of theft, but because of extenuating* **circumstances** (= a situation which made her crime seem less serious) *was not sent to prison.*

extenuation /ɪkˌsten.juˈeɪ.ʃən/ *noun* [U] FORMAL *Her plea of ignorance of the law* **in extenuation of** (= as an excuse for) *her crime was not accepted.*

exterior /ɪkˈstɪə.ri.ər/ US /-ˈstɪr.i.ɚ/ *adj* outer; on or from the outside: *In some of the villages the exterior walls of the houses are painted pink. ○ Exterior* **to** *the main house there is a small building that could be used as an office or studio.* ⸰See also **external**. Compare **interior**.

exterior /ɪkˈstɪə.ri.ər/ US /-ˈstɪr.i.ɚ/ *noun* [C] the outside part of something or someone: *The Palace of Fontainebleau has a very grand exterior. ○ The exterior* **of** *the house needs painting. ○ There are shutters* **on** *the exterior* **of** *the windows. ○ Behind that cold exterior there's a passionate man.*

exterminate /ɪkˈstɜː.mɪ.neɪt/ US /-ˈstɜ˞ː-/ *verb* [T] to kill all the animals or people in a particular place or of a particular type: *Once cockroaches get into a building, it's very difficult to exterminate them. ○ Millions of Jewish people were exterminated in concentration camps in the Second World War.*

extermination /ɪkˌstɜː.mɪˈneɪ.ʃən/ US /-ˌstɜ˞ː-/ *noun* [U] *International measures have been taken to prevent the extermination of the whale* (= all of them being killed).

exterminator /ɪkˈstɜː.mɪ.neɪ.tər/ US /-ˈstɜ˞ː.mɪ.neɪ.t̬ɚ/ *noun* [C]

external /ɪkˈstɜː.nəl/ US /-ˈstɜ˞ː-/ *adj* of, on, for or coming from the outside: *the external walls of the house ○ Female kangaroos carry their young in pouches that are external* **to** *their bodies. ○ This cream is* **for** *external use* only (= it must not be put inside the body). *○ In later years, his paintings began to show a number of external influences* (= influences coming from other people). *○ Most news magazines have a section devoted to external affairs* (= foreign news). *○ You shouldn't judge people by their external* **appearances** (= what they appear to be like). ⸰See also **exterior**. Compare **internal**. **externally** /ɪkˈstɜː.nə.li/ US /-ˈstɜ˞ː-/ *adv: The inside of the house is in good condition, but externally it's in need of repair. ○ Externally, she appeared calm, but inside she was furious.*

externalize, UK USUALLY **-ise** /ɪkˈstɜː.nə.laɪz/ US /-ˈstɜ˞ː-/ *verb* [T] SPECIALIZED to express feelings, especially bad feelings, such as anger: *You have to learn to externalize your anger.* **externalization**, UK USUALLY **-isation** /ɪk-ˌstɜː.nə.laɪˈzeɪ.ʃən/ US /-ˌstɜ˞ː-/ *noun* [C or U] *the externalization of negative feelings*

externals /ɪkˈstɜː.nəlz/ US /-ˈstɜ˞ː-/ *plural noun* the appearance of something or someone: *It's easy to be misled by externals.*

ex͵ternal exami͵nation *noun* [C] an examination arranged by people outside a student's own school, college or university

ex͵ternal ex͵aminer *noun* [C] someone from outside a student's own school, college or university who judges an examination

extinct /ɪkˈstɪŋkt/ *adj* **1** not now existing: *There is concern that the giant panda will soon* **become** *extinct. ○ Many tribes became extinct when they came into contact with Western illnesses. ○ A lot of trades have become extinct because of the development of technology.* **2** An extinct volcano is one that is not now ACTIVE (= will not explode again).

extinction /ɪkˈstɪŋk.ʃən/ *noun* [U] *The extinction of the dinosaurs occurred* (= they stopped existing) *millions of years ago. ○ Many species of plants and animals are* **in danger of/threatened with** *extinction* (= being destroyed so that they no longer exist). *○ Some people predict the extinction* **of** *family life as we know it today.*

extinguish /ɪkˈstɪŋ.gwɪʃ/ *verb* [T] **1** to stop a fire or a light burning: *It took the firefighters several hours to extinguish the flames. ○ to extinguish a cigarette* **2** LITERARY to stop or get rid of an idea or feeling: *Nothing could extinguish his love for her.*

extinguisher /ɪkˈstɪŋ.gwɪ.ʃər/ US /-ɚ/ *noun* [C] a **fire extinguisher**

extirpate /ˈek.stə.peɪt/ US /-stɚ-/ *verb* [T] FORMAL to remove or destroy something completely **extirpation** /ˌek.stəˈpeɪ.ʃən/ US /-stɚ-/ *noun* [U]

extol (-ll-) /ɪkˈstəʊl/ US /-ˈstoʊl/ *verb* [T] FORMAL to praise something or someone highly: *His book extolling the benefits of vegetarianism sold thousands of copies. ○ She is forever extolling* **the virtues of** *her children.*

extort /ɪkˈstɔːt/ US /-ˈstɔːrt/ *verb* [T] to obtain something by force or threat, or with difficulty: *He had been extorting money* **from** *the old lady for years. ○ Police have not so far been able to extort a confession* **from** *the people accused of the bombing.*

extortion /ɪkˈstɔː.ʃən/ US /-ˈstɔːr-/ *noun* [U] *He was found guilty of obtaining the money by extortion* (= by forceful methods).

extortioner /ɪkˈstɔː.ʃən.ər/ US /-ˈstɔːr.ʃən.ɚ/ *noun* [C] (ALSO **extortionist**) a person who obtains something by force or threat

extortionate /ɪkˈstɔː.ʃən.ət/ US /-ˈstɔːr-/ *adj* DISAPPROVING extremely expensive: *The price of books nowadays is extortionate.* **extortionately** /ɪkˈstɔː.ʃən.ət.li/ US /-ˈstɔːr-/ *adv: First-class travel is extortionately expensive.*

extra MORE /ˈek.strə/ *adj* additional: *If you need any extra help, just call me. ○ Recently he's been working an extra two hours a day. ○ The price includes travel and accommodation but meals are extra* (= there is an additional charge for meals).

extra /ˈek.strə/ *adv* more: *They pay her extra to work nights. ○ We agreed on a price but afterwards they wanted £10 extra. ○ I worked extra hard* (= more than usual) *on that essay.*

extra /ˈek.strə/ *noun* [C] something that costs more when you buy goods or pay for a service: *Seat-belts are included as standard but electric windows are an* **optional** *extra.*

extra FILMS /ˈek.strə/ *noun* [C] a person in a film who does not have a speaking part and who is usually part of the background, for example, in a crowd

extra- OUTSIDE /ek.strə-/ *prefix* outside or in addition to: *extraterrestrial beings* (= imaginary creatures which come from outside the planet Earth) *○ an extramarital affair* (= a sexual relationship of a married person with someone other than their husband or wife) *○ extracurricular activities* (= activities which are not part of the usual school or college course)

extract /ɪkˈstrækt/ *verb* [T] **1** to remove or take out something: *They used to extract iron ore* **from** *this site. ○ The oil which is extracted* **from** *olives is used for cooking. ○ The tooth was eventually extracted.* **2** to make someone give you something when they do not want to: *After much persuasion they managed to extract the information* **from** *him.*

extract /ˈek.strækt/ *noun* **1** [C or U] a substance taken from a plant, flower, etc. and used especially in food or medicine: *malt/yeast extract ○ The cream contained extracts* **of/from** *several plants.* **2** [C] a particular part of a book, poem, etc. that is chosen so that it can be used in a discussion, article, etc: *They published an extract* **from** *his autobiography.*

extraction /ɪkˈstræk.ʃən/ *noun* **1** [U] the process of removing something, especially by force: *The extraction* **of** *minerals has damaged the countryside.* **2** [C] SPECIALIZED the removal of a tooth: *She had two extractions.* **3** **be of French/German/Chinese, etc. extraction** to be from a family that originally came from another country

extractor /ɪkˈstræk.tə^r/ ⓤ /-tɚ/ *noun* [C] a machine used to extract something: *a juice extractor*

extracurricular /ˌek.strə.kəˈrɪk.jʊ.lə^r/ ⓤ /-jə.lɚ/ *adj* **1** describes an activity or subject that is not part of the usual school or college course **2** *HUMOROUS* used to refer to something a person does secretly or unofficially not within their normal work or relationship, especially a sexual relationship: *He detailed the future president's extracurricular activities while governor.*

extradite /ˈek.strə.daɪt/ *verb* [T] to make someone return for trial to another country where they have been accused of doing something illegal: *He will be extradited to Britain from France.*
  extraditable /ˈek.strə.daɪ.tə.bl̩/ ⓤ /-t̬ə-/ *adj* describes a crime for which a person can be extradited, or a person who can be extradited: *an extraditable crime/offence*
  extradition /ˌek.strəˈdɪʃ.^ən/ *noun* [C or U] *They have applied for his extradition to Ireland.* ○ *an extradition treaty*

extramarital /ˌek.strəˈmær.ɪ.t^əl/ ⓤ /-ə.t^əl/ *adj* describes a married person's sexual relationship with someone who is not their husband or wife: *an extramarital affair*

extramural *MAINLY UK* /ˌek.strəˈmjʊə.r^əl/ ⓤ /-ˈmjʊr.^əl/ *adj* (*US USUALLY* **extension**) organized especially by a college or university, etc. for people who are not students there: *extramural classes/courses*

extraneous /ɪkˈstreɪ.ni.əs/ *adj* not directly connected with or related to something: *extraneous information* ○ *These questions are extraneous to the issue being discussed.*

extranet /ˈeks.trə.net/ *noun* [C] a system of computers that enables particular organizations to communicate with each other and share information: *The extranet will link the company with its customers and suppliers.*

extraordinary /ɪkˈstrɔː.dɪn.^ər.i/ ⓤ /-ˈstrɔːr.d^ən.er-/ *adj* **1** very unusual, special, unexpected or strange: *He told the extraordinary story of his escape.* ○ *Her voice had an extraordinary hypnotic quality.* ○ *an extraordinary coincidence* **2 extraordinary meeting** a special meeting which happens between regular meetings
  extraordinarily /ɪkˈstrɔː.dɪn.^ər.^əl.i/ ⓤ /-ˈstrɔːr.d^ən.er-/ *adv* very; unusually: *She is, it must be said, extraordinarily beautiful.*

extrapolate /ɪkˈstræp.ə.leɪt/ *verb* [I or T] to guess or think about what might happen from information that is already known: *You can't really extrapolate a trend from such a small sample.* **extrapolation** /ɪkˌstræp.ə-ˈleɪ.ʃ^ən/ *noun* [C or U]

extrasensory /ˌek.strəˈsent.s^ər.i/ ⓤ /-sɚ-/ *adj* without the use of hearing, seeing, touch, taste and smell

extrasensory per'ception *noun* [U] (*ABBREVIATION* **ESP**) the ability to know things without using hearing, seeing, touch, taste or smell

extraterrestrial /ˌek.strə.təˈres.tri.^əl/ *adj* (coming from) outside the planet Earth: *extraterrestrial beings*

extraterritorial /ˌek.strə.ter.ɪˈtɔː.ri.^əl/ ⓤ /-ˈtɔːr.i-/ *adj* outside (the laws of) a country: *extraterritorial possessions*

extra 'time *UK noun* [U] (*US* **overtime**) a period of time in a football game in which play continues if neither team has won in the usual time allowed for the game

extravagant /ɪkˈstræv.ə.g^ənt/ *adj* spending, using or doing more than necessary in an uncontrolled way: *the extravagant lifestyle of a movie star* ○ *That was very extravagant of you to buy strawberries out of season.* ○ *He rarely used taxis, which he regarded as extravagant.* ○ *His children made extravagant* (= very great) *demands on his time and money.* ○ *The product does not live up to the extravagant* (= very great and not realistic) *claims of the advertisers.* **extravagantly** /ɪk-ˈstræv.ə.g^ənt.li/ *adv*
  extravagance /ɪkˈstræv.ə.g^ənts/ *noun* [C or U] *I think she was shocked by my extravagance.* ○ *Perfume is my greatest extravagance* (= something I don't need which I spend a lot of money on).

extravaganza /ɪkˌstræv.ə.ˈgæn.zə/ *noun* [C] a large, exciting and expensive event or entertainment: *a musical/dance extravaganza* ○ *a 3-hour extravaganza of country music*

extreme GREAT /ɪkˈstriːm/ *adj* very large in amount or degree: *extreme pain/stupidity/wealth*
  extreme /ɪkˈstriːm/ *noun* [C] the largest possible amount or degree of something: *I've never witnessed such extremes of wealth and poverty.* ○ *Most people I know work fairly hard but she takes it to extremes.* ○ *My moods seem to go from one extreme to another* (= my moods often change from very bad to very good).
  ● **in the extreme** used for emphasis; extremely: *Some of the scenes were unpleasant in the extreme.*
  extremely /ɪkˈstriːm.li/ *adv* very: *They played extremely well.* ○ *She's extremely beautiful.*

extreme BAD /ɪkˈstriːm/ *adj* very severe or bad: *extreme weather conditions* ○ *In extreme cases, the disease can lead to blindness.* **extreme** /ɪkˈstriːm/ *noun* [C]

extreme BELIEFS /ɪkˈstriːm/ *adj* describes beliefs and political parties which most people consider unreasonable and unacceptable: *He has rather extreme views.* ○ *He's on the extreme right-wing of the party.*
  extremism /ɪkˈstriː.mɪ.z^əm/ *noun* [U] *political extremism* (= extreme political opinions)
  extremist /ɪkˈstriː.mɪst/ *noun* [C], *adj*: *a group of extremists* (= people with extreme opinions) ○ *extremist tendencies*

extreme FURTHEST POINT /ɪkˈstriːm/ *adj* [before n] at the furthest point, especially from the centre: *They live in the extreme south of the island.*
  extremity /ɪkˈstrem.ɪ.ti/ ⓤ /-ə.t̬i/ *noun* [C] the furthest point, especially from the centre: *The wood lies at the southern extremity of the estate.*

ex'treme 'sport *noun* [C] a sport that is very dangerous and exciting

extremities /ɪkˈstrem.ɪ.tiz/ ⓤ /-ə.t̬iz/ *plural noun FORMAL* the parts of the human body furthest from the heart, for example, the fingers, toes and nose

extricate /ˈek.strɪ.keɪt/ *verb* [T] *FORMAL* to remove or set free something with difficulty: *It took hours to extricate the car from the sand.* ○ *I tried to extricate myself from the situation but it was impossible.* **extrication** /ˌek.strɪ-ˈkeɪ.ʃ^ən/ *noun* [U]

extrovert, **extravert** /ˈek.strə.vɜːt/ ⓤ /-vɝːt/ *noun* [C] an energetic, happy person who enjoys being with other people: *Most sales people are extroverts.* ➔Compare **introvert**. **extrovert**, **extravert** /ˈek.strə.vɜːt/ ⓤ /-vɝːt/ *adj*: *an extrovert personality*

extrude /ɪkˈstruːd/ *verb* [T] *SPECIALIZED* to form something by forcing or pushing it out, especially through a small opening: *extruded aluminium rods* **extrusion** /ɪkˈstruː.ʒ^ən/ *noun* [U]

exuberant /ɪgˈzjuː.b^ər.^ənt/ ⓤ /-ˈzuː.bɚ-/ *adj* **1** (especially of people and their behaviour) very energetic: *Young and exuberant, he symbolises Italy's new vitality.* **2** (of plants) strong and growing quickly **exuberance** /ɪgˈzjuː.b^ər.^ənts/ ⓤ /-ˈzuː.bɚ-/ *noun* [U]

exude /ɪgˈzjuːd/ ⓤ /-ˈzuːd/ *verb* [T] **1** If you exude love, confidence, pain, etc., you show that you have a lot of that feeling: *She just exudes confidence.* **2** to produce a smell or liquid substance from inside: *Some trees exude from their bark a sap that repels insect parasites.*

exult /ɪgˈzʌlt/ *verb* [I] *FORMAL* to express great pleasure or happiness, especially at someone else's defeat or failure: *They exulted at/over their victory.* ○ *She seems to exult in her power.*
  exultant /ɪgˈzʌl.t^ənt/ *adj FORMAL* very happy, especially at someone else's defeat or failure: *an exultant cheer* ○ *an exultant crowd* **exultantly** /ɪgˈzʌl.t^ənt.li/ *adv* **exultation** /ˌeg.z^əlˈteɪ.ʃ^ən/ *noun* [U] *FORMAL*

ex-wife /ˌeksˈwaɪf/ *noun* [C] A man's ex-wife is a woman that he was married to but is not now married to.

eye ORGAN /aɪ/ *noun* [C] **1** one of the two organs in your face, which you use to see with: *He has no sight in his left eye.* ○ *She's got beautiful green eyes.* ○ *He closed his eyes and went to sleep.* ➔See picture **The Body** on page Centre 5 **2** a dark spot on a potato or similar plant part, from which a new stem and leaves will grow
  ● **be all eyes** to watch someone or something with a lot of interest: *We were all eyes as the Princess emerged from the car.*

E

• **as far as the eye can/could see** for a long distance until something is so far away and small it cannot be seen any more: *The road stretched into the distance as far as the eye could see.*

• **before your very eyes** while you are watching: *Then, before my very eyes, she disappeared.*

• **have an eye in the back of your head** to know everything that is happening around you: *Parents of young children need to have eyes in the back of their heads.*

• **keep your eye in** UK to continue to be good at a sport or other activity by practising it: *I try to play regularly to keep my eye in.*

• **have an eye for sth** to be good at noticing a particular type of thing: *She has an eye for detail.*

• **have your eye on sth** to have seen something that you want and intend to get: *She's had her eye on a bike for some time.*

• **have an eye to/for the main chance** UK Someone who has an eye to/for the main chance is always ready to use a situation to their own advantage.

• **in sb's eyes** in someone's opinion: *And although she was probably just an ordinary-looking kid, in my eyes she was the most beautiful child on the face of the planet.*

• **keep your/an eye on sth/sb** to watch or look after something or someone: *Will you keep your eye on my suitcase while I go to get the tickets?*

• **clap/lay/set eyes on sb/sth** to see someone or something for the first time: *Everyone keeps talking about Patrick in the accounts department, but I've never clapped eyes on the man.*

• **make eyes at sb** OLD-FASHIONED to look at someone with sexual interest: *She was making eyes at him all evening.*

• **be one in the eye for sb** UK to be a disappointment or defeat for someone: *His promotion was one in the eye for his rivals.*

• **roll your eyes** to move your eyes upwards as a way of showing that you are annoyed or bored after someone has done or said something

• **not take your eyes off sb/sth** to not stop looking at someone or something: *He was so handsome – I couldn't take my eyes off him.*

• **be more to sth than meets the eye** If there is more to something than meets the eye, it is more difficult to understand or involves more things than you thought at the beginning.

• **to my eye** used when giving your opinion about the appearance of something or someone: *You see, to my eye, she looks better without make-up.*

• **be up to your eyes in sth** to be very busy doing something: *I'm up to my eyes in school reports this week.*

• **with your eyes shut 1** If someone could do something with their eyes shut, they could do it very easily because they have done it many times: *I could do that journey with my eyes shut.* **2** noticing nothing: *Half the time you go around with your eyes shut.*

• **keep your/an eye out for sb/sth** INFORMAL to watch carefully for someone or something to appear: *Keep your eye out for signposts to Yosemite.*

• **keep your eyes peeled/skinned** to watch carefully for someone or something: *Keep your eyes peeled for Polly and Maisie.*

• **with your eyes open** knowing about all the problems there could be with something you want to do: *I went into this marriage with my eyes open.*

• **sb's eyes are bigger than their belly/stomach** HUMOROUS something that you say when someone has taken more food than they can eat

• **An eye for an eye (and a tooth for a tooth).** SAYING said to show that you believe if someone does something wrong, they should be punished by having the same thing done to them

-eyed /-aɪd/ *suffix* with the eyes described: *a brown-eyed baby girl* ○ *She was wide-eyed in amazement.*

eye HOLE /aɪ/ *noun* [C] the hole in a needle through which you put the thread

eye LOOK AT /aɪ/ *verb* [T] **eyeing** or US ALSO **eying**, **eyed**, **eyed** to look at someone or something with interest: *I could see her eyeing my lunch.* ○ *She eyed me warily.*

▲ **eye sb up** *phrasal verb* [M] INFORMAL to look at someone with sexual interest: *That guy in the grey jacket has been eyeing you up all evening.*

▲ **eye sth up** *phrasal verb* [T] to look closely at something that you are interested in: *I saw you eyeing up that chocolate cake.*

eyeball /'aɪ.bɔːl/ US /-bɑːl/ *noun* [C] the whole eye, including the part that cannot usually be seen

• **eyeball to eyeball** If you are eyeball to eyeball with an enemy or someone you are arguing with, you deal with them in a direct way.

• **be up to your eyeballs in sth** to be very busy with something: *I'm up to my eyeballs in reports.*

eyeball /'aɪ.bɔːl/ US /-bɑːl/ *verb* [T] INFORMAL to look closely at someone: *He eyeballed me across the bar.*

eyebrow /'aɪ.braʊ/ *noun* [C] the line of short hairs above each eye in humans: *Do you **pluck** your eyebrows* (= remove some of the hairs to change their shape)? ○ *He's got really **bushy** (= thick) eyebrows.* ⊃See picture **The Body** on page Centre 5

• **raise your eyebrows** to show surprise by moving your eyebrows upwards

eye-catching /'aɪ.kætʃ.ɪŋ/ *adj* particularly attractive or noticeable: *an eye-catching poster*

'eye ˌcontact *noun* [U] when two people look at each other's eyes at the same time: *He's very shy and never **makes** eye contact.* ○ *If you're telling the truth, why are you **avoiding** eye contact with me?*

eyeful /'aɪ.fʊl/ *noun* **1** [C] an amount of something, usually dust or dirt, which has entered the eye: *As the lorry went past, I got an eyeful **of** grit.* **2** [S] INFORMAL a very noticeable or attractive sight, often a sexually attractive person: *She's quite an eyeful.*

• **get an eyeful** INFORMAL to look at something or someone: *Hey, get an eyeful of this!*

eyeglasses /'aɪ.glɑː.sɪz/ US /-ˌglæs.ɪz/ *plural noun* US **glasses**

eyehole /'aɪ.həʊl/ US /-hoʊl/ *noun* [C] UK FOR **peephole**

eying , US ALSO **eying** /'aɪ.ɪŋ/ *present participle of* **eye**

eyelash /'aɪ.læʃ/ *noun* [C] any of the short hairs which grow along the edges of the eye: *long eyelashes* ○ *false eyelashes* ⊃See picture **The Body** on page Centre 5

eyelet /'aɪ.lət/ *noun* [C] a small hole in material, the edge of which is protected by a ring of metal, through which a piece of string, a SHOELACE, etc. is put to fasten something

'eye ˌlevel *noun* [U] If something is at eye level, it is positioned at approximately the same height as your eyes.

eyelid /'aɪ.lɪd/ *noun* [C] either of the two pieces of skin which can close over each eye ⊃See picture **The Body** on page Centre 5

eyeliner /'aɪ.laɪ.nə^r/ US /-nɚ/ *noun* [C or U] a coloured substance, usually contained in a pencil, which is put in a line just above or below the eyes in order to make them look more attractive

eye-opener /'aɪ.əʊ.p^ən.ə^r/ US /-ˌoʊ.p^ən.ɚ/ *noun* [C usually sing] something that surprises you and teaches you new facts about life, people, etc: *Living in another country can be a real eye-opener.*

eye-patch /'aɪ.pætʃ/ *noun* [C] a covering worn over the eye to protect it if it is damaged or sore

eyepiece /'aɪ.piːs/ *noun* [C] the part of a piece of equipment, for example a microscope, through which you look

'eye ˌshadow *noun* [C or U] a coloured cream or powder which is put around the eyes to make them look larger or more attractive

eyesight /'aɪ.saɪt/ *noun* [U] the ability to see: *good/bad/poor eyesight* ○ *You need to have your eyesight tested.*

'eye ˌsocket *noun* [C] one of the two round, low areas on each side of the nose which contain the eyes

eyesore /'aɪ.sɔː^r/ US /-sɔːr/ *noun* [C] an unpleasant or ugly sight in a public place: *They think the new library building is an eyesore.*

eyestrain /'aɪ.streɪn/ *noun* [U] tired or painful eyes as a result of too much reading, looking at a computer screen, etc.

eyetooth /ˈaɪ.tuːθ/ *noun* [C] *plural* **eyeteeth** either of the two pointed teeth which are found one on each side at the top of the mouth; a **canine (tooth)**

• **give *your* eyeteeth for *sth*** If you would give your eyeteeth for something, you would like it very much: *Most women would give their eyeteeth for hair like yours.*

eyewash [LIQUID] /ˈaɪ.wɒʃ/ [US] /-wɑːʃ/ *noun* [C or U] a liquid used to clean the eyes

eyewash [NONSENSE] /ˈaɪ.wɒʃ/ [US] /-wɑːʃ/ *noun* [U] *OLD-FASHIONED INFORMAL* nonsense or something which is not true

eyewitness /ˈaɪˌwɪt.nəs/ *noun* [C] a person who saw something happen, for example a crime or an accident: *According to an eyewitness* ***account****, the thieves abandoned their vehicle near the scene of the robbery and then ran off.*

eyrie /ˈɪə.ri/ [US] /ˈɪr.i/ *noun* [C] **1** (*MAINLY US* **aerie**) the nest of an eagle or other large bird which eats meat, usually built in a high, distant place **2** a room or apartment that is high up in a building: *I interviewed the chairman of the company in his seventh-floor eyrie.*

e-zine /ˈiː.ziːn/ *noun* [C] a ZINE (= small magazine) that is available on the Internet

E

F

F LETTER (*plural* **F's** or **Fs**), **f** (*plural* **f's** or **fs**) /ef/ *noun* [C] the 6th letter of the English alphabet

F MUSIC /ef/ *noun* [C or U] *plural* **F's** or **Fs** a note in Western music: *The song is in (the key of) F.* ○ *Play an F followed by a G.*

F TEMPERATURE *noun* [after n] ABBREVIATION FOR **Fahrenheit**: *Yesterday the temperature was 90°F.*

f2f INTERNET ABBREVIATION FOR face to face: used in an e-mail or CHAT ROOM to describe a situation where you meet and talk to someone, rather than communicate electronically

the FA /ˌði.efˈeɪ/ *noun* [S] ABBREVIATION FOR the Football Association: the national organization for football in England

fab /fæb/ *adj* INFORMAL FOR **fabulous** GOOD: *I bought some fab jeans on Saturday.*

fable /ˈfeɪ.bl̩/ *noun* [C or U] a short story which tells a general truth or is only partly based on fact, or literature of this type: *the fable of the tortoise and the hare*

fabled /ˈfeɪ.bl̩d/ *adj* [before n] LITERARY describes something or someone who has been made very famous, especially by having many stories written about them: *the fabled film director Cecil B. De Mille*

fabric CLOTH /ˈfæb.rɪk/ *noun* [C or U] (a type of) cloth or woven material: *dress fabric* ○ *seats upholstered in hard-wearing fabric* ○ *cotton/woollen fabrics*

fabric STRUCTURE /ˈfæb.rɪk/ *noun* **the fabric of sth** the structure or parts especially of a social unit or a building: *the fabric of society* ○ *Unhappiness was woven into the natural fabric of people's lives.* ○ *We must invest in the fabric of our hospitals and start rebuilding them.*

fabricate /ˈfæb.rɪ.keɪt/ *verb* [T] to invent or produce something false in order to deceive: *He was late, so he fabricated an excuse to avoid trouble.* ○ *He claims that the police fabricated evidence against him.* **fabrication** /ˌfæb.rɪˈkeɪ.ʃən/ *noun* [C or U] *The evidence he gave in court was a complete fabrication.*

fabulous GOOD /ˈfæb.jʊ.ləs/ *adj* very good; excellent: *She looked absolutely fabulous in her dress.* ○ *They've got a fabulous apartment in the centre of Paris.* ○ *We had a fabulous time at the party.* **fabulously** /ˈfæb.jʊ.lə.sli/ *adv*: *fabulously* (= extremely) *rich/wealthy*

fabulous NOT REAL /ˈfæb.jʊ.ləs/ *adj* imaginary, not existing in real life: *The unicorn is a fabulous creature/beast.*

facade /fəˈsɑːd/ *noun* **1** [C] (*ALSO* **façade**) the front of a building, especially a large or attractive building: *the gallery's elegant 18th century facade* **2** [S] a false appearance that is more pleasant than the reality: *Behind that amiable facade, he's a deeply unpleasant man.* ○ *We are fed up with this facade of democracy.*

face HEAD /feɪs/ *noun* [C] **1** the front of the head, where the eyes, nose and mouth are: *She's got a long, thin face.* ○ *She had a puzzled expression on her face.* **2** an expression on someone's face: *I was greeted by smiling faces.* ○ *He had a face like thunder* (= He looked very angry). **3** **make/pull a face** to make a strange expression with your face, usually to show that you do not like someone or something: *"This tastes horrible," said Tom, pulling a face at his glass.* ○ *I was pulling silly faces to make the baby laugh.*

• **sb's face falls** If someone's face falls, they suddenly look very disappointed: *Her face fell when she heard he wasn't coming.*

• **to sb's face** If you say something unpleasant to someone's face, you say it to them directly, when you are with them: *If you've got something to say, say it to my face.*

• **in the face of sth** despite having to deal with a difficult situation or problem: *She left home in the face of strong opposition from her parents.*

• **sb's face doesn't fit** UK INFORMAL If someone's face doesn't fit, their appearance or personality are not suitable for a job or other activity.

• **Get out of my face!** SLANG a rude way of telling someone that they are annoying you and should stop: *I said no! Now get out of my face!*

• **be in your face** SLANG to be shocking and annoying in a way that is difficult to ignore: *dance music that is aggressive, sexy and in your face*

• **be in your face** US INFORMAL If someone is in your face, they criticize you all the time: *One of the managers is always in my face.*

• **have a face like the back end of a bus** UK INFORMAL to be very ugly

-faced /-feɪst/ *suffix* with the face described: *round-faced* (= having a round face) ○ *sad-faced* (= having a sad face) ○ *red-faced* (= embarrassed)

face FRONT /feɪs/ *noun* [C] **1** the front or surface of an object: *the north face of a mountain* ○ *the west face of the building* **2** the front of a clock or watch which has the numbers or marks which show what time it is: *a watch face with Roman numerals*

• **the face of sth** what you can see of something or what shows: *Poor quality is the unacceptable face of increased productivity.*

• **disappear off the face of the earth** (*ALSO* **be wiped off the face of the earth**) to disappear completely: *The whole tribe seem to have disappeared off the face of the earth.*

• **on the face of sth** used when you are describing how a situation seems on the surface: *On the face of it, it seems like a bargain, but I bet there are hidden costs.*

• **take sth at face value** to accept something for what it appears to be rather than studying it more closely: *I took the offer at face value. I didn't think they might be trying to trick me.*

face /feɪs/ *verb* [T] If you face a building, you put an extra layer in front of what is already there: *The house was built of wood but faced in/with brick.* **facing** /ˈfeɪ.sɪŋ/ *noun* **1** [C] an outer layer covering a wall, etc: *The wall was built of rubble with a facing of stone.* **2** [C or U] an extra layer of material sewn to the inside edge of a piece of clothing to strengthen it, or to cover the outside, especially of collars and the ends of sleeves, for decoration: *A blue jacket with white facing*

face TURN TOWARDS /feɪs/ *verb* [I usually + adv or prep; T] to turn or be turned towards something physically; to be opposite: *The terrace faces towards the sea/faces south.* ○ *Their houses face each other across the street.* **-facing** /-feɪ.sɪŋ/ *suffix*: *Most avalanche accidents occur on north- and east-facing slopes.*

face RESPECT /feɪs/ *noun* [U] the respect and honour of others: *He thinks he would lose face if he admitted the mistake.* ○ *She tried to save face by inventing a story about being overseas at the time.*

face DEAL WITH /feɪs/ *verb* [T] **1** If you face a problem, or a problem faces you, you have to deal with it: *This is one of the many problems faced by working mothers.* ○ *Passengers could face long delays.* ○ *You're faced with a very difficult choice there.* **2** to accept that something unpleasant is true and start to deal with the situation: *I think Phil has to face the fact that she no longer loves him.* ○ *We have to face facts here – we simply don't have enough money.* ○ *He's dying but he refuses to face the truth.* **3** **can't face sth/doing sth** to not want to do or deal with something unpleasant: *I can't face walking up all those steps again.* ○ *I know I've got to tell her but I can't face it.*

• **face the music** to accept criticism or punishment for something you have done

▲ **face up to sth** *phrasal verb* to accept that a difficult situation exists: *She's going to have to face up to the fact that he's not going to marry her.*

facecloth UK /ˈfeɪs.klɒθ/ US /-klɑːθ/ *noun* [C] (US **washcloth**, AUS **face washer**) a small cloth used to wash the body, especially the face and hands

face ˌcream *noun* [C or U] cream which you put on your face to make the skin softer and less dry

faceless /ˈfeɪ.sləs/ *adj* DISAPPROVING lacking any clear characteristics and therefore not interesting: *faceless bureaucrats*

facelift /'feɪs.lɪft/ *noun* **1** [C] a medical treatment which tightens loose skin to make the face look younger **2** [S] treatment to improve something, for example a building, to make it look more attractive: *The bank is planning to give its 1930s building a complete facelift.*

'face ˌpack *noun* [C] a cream-like substance which is left on the face to dry and is then removed, in order to clean and tighten the skin

'face ˌpowder *noun* [U] skin-coloured powder used on the face to make it look less shiny and more attractive

face-saving /'feɪsˌseɪ.vɪŋ/ *adj* [before n] done so that other people will continue to respect you: *a face-saving exercise/gesture*

facet /'fæs.ɪt/ *noun* [C] **1** one part of a subject, situation, etc. that has many parts: *She has so many facets to her personality.* **2** one of the small flat surfaces cut on a precious stone
-faceted /-fæs.ɪ.tɪd/ [US] /-t̬ɪd/ *suffix* **multi-/many-faceted** having many different parts: *a multi-faceted personality*

facetious /fə'siː.ʃəs/ *adj* DISAPPROVING not serious about a serious subject, in an attempt to be amusing or to appear clever: *facetious remarks* ○ *He's just being facetious.* **facetiously** /fə'siː.ʃə.sli/ *adv* **facetiousness** /fə'siː.ʃə.snəs/ *noun* [U]

face-to-face /ˌfeɪs.tə'feɪs/ *adv, adj* [before n] directly, meeting someone in the same place: *We've spoken on the phone but never face-to-face.* ○ *She* **came** *face-to-face with the gunman as he strode into the playground.*

ˌface 'value *noun* [C usually sing] the value or price which is shown on, for example, a stamp, a coin or a bank note

facial [OF THE FACE] /'feɪ.ʃəl/ *adj* of or on the face: *facial hair* ○ *facial cleansers and moisturizers* ○ *facial expressions*

facial [BEAUTY TREATMENT] /'feɪ.ʃəl/ *noun* [C] a beauty treatment which cleans and improves the skin of the face with CREAMS (= thick liquids) and gentle rubbing: *Beauty treatments range from an eyelash tint at £8 to a deep cleansing facial costing £58.*

facile /'fæs.aɪl/ *adj* describes a remark or theory which is too simple and has not been thought about enough: *a facile explanation* ○ *We must avoid facile recriminations about who was to blame.*

facilitate /fə'sɪl.ɪ.teɪt/ *verb* [T] FORMAL to make possible or easier: *The new ramp will facilitate the entry of wheelchairs.* ○ *The current structure does not facilitate efficient work flow.* **facilitator** /fə'sɪl.ɪ.teɪ.təʳ/ [US] /-t̬ɚ/ *noun* [C] *I see my role as that of a facilitator, enabling other people to work in the way that suits them best.*

facility [ABILITY] /fə'sɪl.ɪ.ti/ [US] /-ə.t̬i/ *noun* [C or U] an ability, feature or quality: *His facility* **for** *languages is astonishing.* ○ *a phone with a memory facility*

facility [BUILDING] /fə'sɪl.ɪ.ti/ [US] /-ə.t̬i/ *noun* [C] a place, especially including buildings, where a particular activity happens: *a nuclear research facility* ○ *a military facility* ○ *a new sports facility*
facilities /fə'sɪl.ɪ.tiz/ [US] /-ə.t̬iz/ *plural noun* the buildings, equipment and services provided for a particular purpose: *shopping facilities* ○ *medical facilities* ○ *sports facilities*

-facing /-feɪ.sɪŋ/ *suffix* ➲See at **face** TURN TOWARDS

facsimile /fæk'sɪm.ɪ.li/ *noun* [C] **1** an exact copy, especially of a document: *a facsimile* **of** *the original manuscript* **2** FORMAL a **fax**

fact /fækt/ *noun* [C or U] something which is known to have happened or to exist, especially something for which proof exists, or about which there is information: *No decision will be made till we know all the facts.* ○ *I don't know all the facts* **about** *the case.* ○ *I'm not angry that you took my car – it's just the fact* **that** *you didn't ask me first.* ○ *He knew* **for a** *fact that Natalie was lying.* ○ *It's sometimes hard to separate fact from fiction in what she says.*
• **a fact of life** something unpleasant which cannot be avoided: *Going bald is just a fact of life.*
• **as a matter of fact** (ALSO **in (actual) fact**) used to add emphasis to what you are saying, or to show that it is the opposite of or different from what went before: *No I don't work. In fact, I've never had a job.* ○ *"Have you always lived here?" "As a matter of fact* (= The truth is) *I've only lived here for the last three years".*
• **facts and figures** exact detailed information: *We are getting some facts and figures together and we will then have a full board meeting.*
• **the facts of life** details about sexual activity and the way that babies are born
factual /'fæk.tjuəl/ *adj* using or consisting of facts: *She gave a clear, factual account of the attack.* **factually** /'fæk.tjuə.li/ *adv*: *factually accurate*

fact-finding /'fæktˌfaɪn.dɪŋ/ *adj* [before n] done in order to discover information for your company, government, etc: *a fact-finding mission/trip*

faction /'fæk.ʃən/ *noun* [C] MAINLY DISAPPROVING a group within a larger group, especially one with slightly different ideas from the main group: *the left-wing faction of the party* **factional** /'fæk.ʃən.əl/ *adj*: *factional leaders* **factionalism** /'fæk.ʃən.əl.ɪ.zəm/ *noun* [U] *Factionalism was tearing the party and the country apart.*

factitious /fæk'tɪʃ.əs/ *adj* FORMAL false or artificial: *He has invented a wholly factitious story about his past.*

factor [FACT] /'fæk.təʳ/ [US] /-tɚ/ *noun* [C] a fact or situation which influences the result of something: *People's voting habits are influenced by political, social and economic factors.* ○ *Heavy snow was a* **contributing** *factor* **in** *the accident.* ○ *Price will be a* **major/crucial** *factor* **in** *the success of this new product.* ○ *The economy is regarded as the* **decisive/key** *factor which will determine the outcome of the general election.* ○ INFORMAL *The film's success is largely due to its* **feel-good** *factor* (= its ability to make people feel happy).

factor [NUMBER] /'fæk.təʳ/ [US] /-tɚ/ *noun* [C] SPECIALIZED **1** in mathematics, any whole number which is produced when you divide a larger number by another whole number: *Two, three, four and six are all factors of twelve.* **2** a particular level on some systems of measurement: *a factor 20 suntan cream* ○ *a wind chill factor of -20*
• **by a factor of** If an amount becomes larger or smaller by a factor of a particular number, it becomes that number of times larger or smaller: *Cases of leukaemia in the area near the nuclear reactor have risen by a factor of four.*
factorize, UK USUALLY **-ise** /'fæk.tər.aɪz/ [US] /-tə.raɪz/ *verb* [T] (ALSO **factor**) SPECIALIZED If you factorize a number, you divide it into factors.

factor /'fæk.təʳ/ [US] /-tɚ/ *verb*
▲ **factor *sth* in** *phrasal verb* (ALSO **factor *sth* into *sth***) to include something when you are doing a calculation, or when you are trying to understand something: *People are earning more, but when inflation is factored in, they are no better off.* ○ *The age of the patients and their overall health must be factored into the results.*

factory /'fæk.tər.i/ [US] /-t̬ɚ.i/ *noun* [C] a building or set of buildings where large amounts of goods are made using machines: *a car/shoe/textile factory* ○ *a factory worker/manager*

ˌfactory 'farming *noun* [U] a system of farming in which a lot of animals are kept in a small enclosed area, in order to produce a large amount of meat, eggs or milk as cheaply as possible: *a campaign against factory farming* **factory-farmed** /'fæk.tər.i.fɑːmd/ [US] /-t̬ɚ.i.fɑːrmd/ *adj*: *I think free-range chickens taste much better than factory-farmed ones.*

ˌfactory 'floor *noun* [C] the area where the ordinary workers in a factory work: *The company has been criticized for the lack of safety measures on the factory floor.*
• **on the factory floor** by ordinary workers rather than managers: *That sort of decision should be taken on the factory floor.*

factotum /fæk'təʊ.təm/ [US] /-'toʊ.t̬əm/ *noun* [C] FORMAL a person employed to do all types of jobs for someone: *She was a* **general** *factotum at the restaurant – washing dishes, cleaning the floors and polishing the furniture.*

factsheet /'fækt.ʃiːt/ *noun* [C] a written document containing information for the public: *A set of factsheets accompanies the TV series.*

faculty [COLLEGE] /'fæk.əl.ti/ [US] /-t̬i/ *noun* [C] **1** a group of departments in a college which specialize in a

F

particular subject or group of subjects: *the Arts/Law Faculty* ○ *the Faculty of Science* **2** US the people who teach in a department in a college

faculty [ABILITY] /ˈfæk.əl.ti/ [US] /-t̬i/ *noun* **1** [C usually pl] a natural ability to hear, see, think, move, etc: *Even at the age of 100, she still* ***had*** *all her faculties.* ○ *Is he* ***in command/possession of*** *all his faculties* (= Can he still hear, speak, see and think clearly)? **2** [C] a special ability to do a particular thing: *She has a faculty* ***for*** *inspiring confidence in people.* ○ *Studying has certainly* ***sharpened*** *my* ***critical*** *faculties* (= taught me to think carefully about things using my judgment).

the FA Cup /ˌef.eɪˈkʌp/ *noun* [S] a competition for teams that belong to the Football Association, or the silver cup which is given as a prize in this competition: *Manchester United are hoping to win the FA Cup this year.* ○ *It's the FA Cup* ***final*** *next week.* ○ *last season's FA Cup* ***finalists***

F

fad /fæd/ *noun* [C] a style, activity or interest which is very popular for a short period of time: *the latest health fad* ○ *There was a fad* ***for*** *wearing ripped jeans a few years ago.*

faddy /ˈfæd.i/ *adj* (ALSO **faddish**) having a tendency to like or dislike particular things, especially food, for no good reason: *I was a really faddy eater when I was young.* **faddily** /ˈfæd.ɪ.li/ *adv* (ALSO **faddishly**) **faddiness** /ˈfæd.ɪ.nəs/ *noun* [U] (ALSO **faddishness**)

fade /feɪd/ *verb* [I or T] to (cause to) lose colour, brightness or strength gradually: *If you hang your clothes out in the bright sun, they will fade.* ○ *My suntan is already fading.* ○ *They arrived home just as the light was fading* (= as it was going dark). ○ *The sun had faded the bright blue walls.*

• **be fading away/fast** to be growing weaker and thinner and to be likely to die soon

faded /ˈfeɪ.dɪd/ *adj* less bright in colour than before: *faded* ***jeans*** ○ *faded curtains/wallpaper* ○ FIGURATIVE *a faded beauty* (= a woman who was beautiful in the past)

PHRASAL VERBS WITH **fade** ▼

▲ **fade away** *phrasal verb* to slowly disappear, lose importance or become weaker: *The voices became louder and closer and then faded away again.* ○ *As the years passed, the memories faded away.*

▲ **fade *(sth)* in** *phrasal verb* [I or M] If the picture or sound of a film or recording fades in, or someone fades it in, it becomes gradually stronger.

▲ **fade *(sth)* out** *phrasal verb* [I or M] If the picture or sound of a film or recording fades out or someone fades it out, it becomes gradually weaker.

faeces, MAINLY US **feces** /ˈfiː.siːz/ *plural noun* FORMAL the solid waste excreted from the body of a human or animal through the bowels: *The disease is spread by the contamination of food and water by faeces.* **faecal**, MAINLY US **fecal** /ˈfiː.kəl/ *adj*: *faecal matter*

faff /fæf/ *noun* UK INFORMAL **be a faff** to need a lot of effort or cause inconvenience: *Stripping the walls was a real faff.*

faff /fæf/ *verb*

▲ **faff about/around** *phrasal verb* UK INFORMAL to spend your time doing a lot of unimportant things instead of the thing that you should be doing: *I wish you'd stop faffing about and do something useful!*

fag [CIGARETTE] /fæg/ *noun* [C] UK SLANG a cigarette: *a packet of fags* ○ *She's gone outside for a quick fag.* ○ *There were fag* ***ends*** *all over the floor.*

• **the fag end of *sth*** UK INFORMAL the last, and often worst, part of something: *We always used to go on holiday at the fag end of the holiday season.*

fag [HOMOSEXUAL] /fæg/ *noun* [C] US SLANG an offensive word for a homosexual man

fag [TROUBLE] /fæg/ *noun* MAINLY UK INFORMAL **be a fag** to be boring and tiring to do: *It's such a fag to have to make your bed every morning.*

ˌfagged (ˈout) *adj* MAINLY UK INFORMAL tired and bored

• **can't be fagged** UK INFORMAL If you can't be fagged to do something, you are unwilling to make the effort that is needed to do it: *I can't be fagged* ***to*** *walk all the way there.*

fag [YOUNG BOY] /fæg/ *noun* [C] UK OLD-FASHIONED (at some large British private schools) a younger boy who has to do jobs for an older boy

fag /fæg/ *verb* [I] **-gg-** UK OLD-FASHIONED If a younger boy fags for an older boy at a British private school, he does jobs for him.

faggot [HOMOSEXUAL] /ˈfæg.ət/ *noun* [C] (INFORMAL **fag**) MAINLY US SLANG a homosexual man. This word is considered offensive when it is used by people who are not homosexual.

faggot [WOOD], US ALSO **fagot** /ˈfæg.ət/ *noun* [C usually pl] OLD-FASHIONED sticks of wood, tied together, which are used as fuel for a fire

faggot [FOOD] /ˈfæg.ət/ *noun* [C usually pl] UK a ball of meat mixed with bread and herbs, which is fried or cooked in sauce

ˈfag ˌhag *noun* [C] SLANG a woman who likes to spend time with homosexual men

Fahrenheit /ˈfær.ən.haɪt/ *adj, noun* [U] (WRITTEN ABBREVIATION **F**) of a measurement of temperature on a standard in which 32° is the temperature at which water freezes and 212° that at which it boils: *Shall I give you the temperature in Celsius or* ***in*** *Fahrenheit?* ○ *It was 80°F in the shade.* ○ *Data are recorded in* ***degrees*** *Fahrenheit.* ➲Compare **Celsius**.

fail [NOT SUCCEED] /feɪl/ *verb* [I] to not succeed in what you are trying to achieve or are expected to do: *She moved to London in the hope of finding work as a model, but failed.* ○ *This method of growing tomatoes never fails.* ○ *He failed* ***in*** *his attempt to break the record.* ○ [+ to infinitive] *She failed* ***to*** *reach the Wimbledon Final this year.* ○ *The reluctance of either side to compromise means that the talks are* ***doomed to*** (= will certainly) *fail.*

• **if all else fails** if none of our plans succeed: *If all else fails, we can always spend the holidays at home.*

failed /feɪld/ *adj* [before n] having not succeeded: *a failed actress/writer* ○ *She has two failed marriages behind her.*

failure /ˈfeɪ.ljəʳ/ [US] /-ljɚ/ *noun* [C or U] when someone or something does not succeed: *The meeting was a* ***complete/total*** *failure.* ○ *I'm a bit of a failure* ***at*** *making* (= I cannot make) *cakes.* ○ *I* ***feel such a*** *failure* (= so unsuccessful). ○ *Their attempt to climb the Eiger* ***ended in*** *failure.* ○ *The whole project was* ***doomed to*** *failure right from the start* (= It could never have succeeded). ➲See also **failure** at **fail** NOT DO, **fail** STOP.

fail [NOT DO] /feɪl/ *verb* [I] to not do something which you should do: [+ to infinitive] *He failed* ***to*** *arrive on time.* ○ *The club had been promised a grant from the council, but the money failed* ***to*** (= did not) *materialize.* ○ *You couldn't fail* ***to*** *be* (= It is impossible that you would not be) *affected by the film.* ○ *I'd be failing* ***in*** *my duty if I didn't tell you about the risks involved in the project.*

• **fail to see/understand** used when you do not accept something: *I fail to see* ***why*** *you can't work on a Saturday.*

• **without fail 1** If you do something without fail, you always do it: *I go to the gym every Monday and Wednesday, without fail.* **2** used to tell someone that they must do something: *Be there at nine o'clock, without fail.*

failure /ˈfeɪ.ljəʳ/ [US] /-ljɚ/ *noun* [U + to infinitive] when you do not do something that you must do or are expected to do: *His failure* ***to*** *return her phone call told her that something was wrong.* ○ *Failure* ***to*** *keep the chemical at the right temperature could lead to an explosion.* ➲See also **failure** at **fail** NOT SUCCEED, **fail** STOP.

fail [NOT HELP] /feɪl/ *verb* [T] to not help someone when they expected you to: *He failed her when she most needed him.* ○ *When I looked down and saw how far I had to jump, my* ***courage*** *failed me* (= I felt very frightened).

fail [EXAMINATION] /feɪl/ *verb* [I or T] to be unsuccessful, or to judge that someone has been unsuccessful in a test or examination: *I passed in history but failed* ***in*** *chemistry.* ○ *A lot of people fail their driving test the first time.* ○ *The examiners failed him because he hadn't answered enough questions.*

fail /feɪl/ *noun* [C] an unsuccessful result in a course, test or examination: *John* ***got*** *three passes and four fails in his exams.*

fail [STOP] /feɪl/ *verb* **[I]** **1** to become weaker or stop working completely: *If my eyesight fails, I'll have to stop doing this job.* ○ *The brakes failed and the car crashed into a tree.* ○ *After talking non-stop for two hours, her voice started to fail.* ○ *The old man was failing* ***fast*** (= He was dying). **2** If a business fails, it is unable to continue because of money problems.

failing /ˈfeɪ.lɪŋ/ *adj* becoming weaker or less successful: *a failing business* ○ *failing eyesight* ○ *In the failing light, it was hard to read the signposts.* ➲See also **failing** WEAKNESS, **failing** WITHOUT.

failure /ˈfeɪ.ljəʳ/ [US] /-ljɚ/ *noun* **[C or U]** when something does not work, or stops working as well as it should: *He died of* ***heart/liver*** *failure.* ○ *The accident was caused by the failure of the reactor's cooling system.* ○ *The number of* ***business*** *failures rose steeply last year.* ○ *After three* ***crop*** *failures in a row, the people face starvation.* ➲See also **failure** at **fail** NOT SUCCEED, **fail** NOT DO.

failing [WEAKNESS] /ˈfeɪ.lɪŋ/ *noun* **[C]** a fault or weakness: *His one big failing is that he never says he's sorry.* ➲See also **failing** at **fail** STOP.

failing [WITHOUT] /ˈfeɪ.lɪŋ/ *prep* if that is not possible: *Give her a book, or failing* ***that****, buy her something to wear.* ○ *Appointments are available on the 2nd and the 6th of this month but failing either of those, we could fit you in on the 15th.*

fail-safe /ˈfeɪ.l.seɪf/ *adj* **1** very unlikely to fail: *a fail-safe plan* **2** If something is fail-safe, it has been designed so that if one part of it does not work, the whole thing does not become dangerous: *a fail-safe device/mechanism*

faint [SLIGHT] /feɪnt/ *adj* not strong or clear; slight: *a faint sound/noise/smell* ○ *The lamp gave out a faint glow.* ○ *She gave me a faint smile of recognition.* ○ *There's not the faintest hope of ever finding him.* ○ *She bears a faint resemblance to my sister.* ○ *I have a faint* ***suspicion*** *that you may be right!*

• **not have the faintest idea** INFORMAL used to emphasize that you do not know something: *"Is she going to stay?" "I haven't the faintest idea."* ○ *I haven't the faintest idea what you're talking about!*

faintly /ˈfeɪnt.li/ *adv*: *She seemed faintly* (= slightly) *embarrassed to see us there.* ○ *A light flickered faintly* (= with little strength) *in the distance.*

faintness /ˈfeɪnt.nəs/ *noun* **[U]** the quality of not being strong or clear: *The faintness of the handwriting made the manuscript difficult to read.*

faint [LOSE CONSCIOUSNESS] /feɪnt/ *verb* **[I]** to suddenly become unconscious for a short time, usually falling down: *He faints at the sight of blood.* ○ *I nearly fainted in the heat.* ○ *She took one look at the hypodermic needle and fainted* ***(dead) away*** (= lost consciousness immediately).

faint /feɪnt/ *adj* **feel faint** to feel weak, as if you are about to lose consciousness: *She felt faint with hunger.*

faint /feɪnt/ *noun* **[S]** when someone suddenly becomes unconscious: *On receiving the news, she* ***fell into a dead faint****.*

faintness /ˈfeɪnt.nəs/ *noun* **[U]** the feeling that you are about to lose consciousness: *Faintness and morning sickness can be signs that you are pregnant.*

faint-hearted /ˌfeɪntˈhɑː.tɪd/ [US] /-ˈhɑːr.t̬ɪd/ *adj* **[before n]** describes someone who is not confident or brave and dislikes taking unnecessary risks: *The terrorist threat in the region has kept faint-hearted tourists away.*

the faint-hearted *plural noun* people who are not brave: *The drive along the winding coast road is* ***not for*** *the faint-hearted.*

fair [RIGHT] /feəʳ/ [US] /fer/ *adj* **1** treating someone in a way that is right or reasonable, or treating a group of people equally and not allowing personal opinions to influence your judgment: *a fair trial* ○ *Why should I have to do all the cleaning? It's not fair!* ○ *It's not fair* ***on*** *Joe* (= It is not right) *to make him do all the work!* ○ *It's not fair* ***that*** *she's allowed to go and I'm not!* ○ *It's not fair* ***to*** *blame me for everything!* ○ *She's* ***scrupulously*** *fair* ***with*** *all her employees* (= she treats them all equally). ○ *She claims her article was a fair* ***comment*** *on* (= a reasonable thing to say about) *a matter of public interest.* ○ *He offered to do all the cleaning if I did all the cooking, which seemed like a fair* (= reasonable) ***deal****.* **2** If something, such as a price or share, is fair, it is reasonable and is what you expect or deserve: *I thought it was a fair* ***price*** *that she was offering.* ○ *I'm willing to do my fair* (= equal) ***share*** *of the work.* ○ *All the workers want is a fair* ***wage*** *for the work that they do.* **3** If a game or competition is fair, it is done according to the rules: *It was a fair fight.*

• **it's only fair** it is the right way to treat someone and what they deserve: *I think it's only fair to tell you that we have had over 300 applications for this job.*

• **it's fair to say** it is true to say: *I think it's fair to say* ***(that)*** *you've done less of the work than I have.*

• **to be fair** considering everything that has an effect on the situation, so that a fair judgement can be made: *He's done the job badly but, to be fair, I gave him very little time to do it.*

• **by fair means or foul** If you try to achieve something by fair means or foul, you use any method you can to achieve it, even if it is not honest or fair.

• **it's a fair cop** UK INFORMAL something you say when someone has caught you doing something wrong and you agree that you were wrong

• **fair enough** UK INFORMAL something you say to show that you understand why someone has done or said something: *"I'm just annoyed with him because he's behaved so badly." "Fair enough."*

• **Fair's fair** (ALSO **fair do's**) INFORMAL something that you say when you want someone to behave reasonably or treat you the same as other people: *Come on, it's my turn. Fair's fair!*

• **a fair hearing** an opportunity to explain something or give your opinions, without other people trying to influence the situation: *He didn't feel he* ***got*** *a fair hearing in court.*

• **fair and square** **1** in an honest way and without any doubt: *We won the match fair and square.* **2** (US **squarely**) UK If you hit someone fair and square on a particular part of their body, you hit them hard, exactly on that part: *He hit me fair and square on the nose.*

• **a fair crack of the whip** UK (US **a fair shake**) an equal chance to do something: *It's only right that all the candidates should be given a fair crack of the whip.*

• **All's fair in love and war.** SAYING in love and war you do not have to obey the usual rules about reasonable behaviour

fairly /ˈfeə.li/ [US] /ˈfer-/ *adv* If you do something fairly, you do it in a way which is right and reasonable and treats people equally: *He claimed that he hadn't been* ***treated*** *fairly by his employers.* ○ *Officials will ensure that the election is carried out fairly.* ➲See also **fairly** at **fair** QUITE LARGE.

• **fairly and squarely** (US **squarely**) completely: *She lays the blame for the recession fairly and squarely on the government.*

fairness /ˈfeə.nəs/ [US] /ˈfer-/ *noun* **[U]** the quality of treating people equally or in a way that is right or reasonable: *He had a real sense of fairness and hated injustice.* ○ *The ban on media reporting during the election has made some people question the fairness of the election* (= ask whether it was fair). ➲See also **fairness** at **fair** BEAUTIFUL.

• **in (all) fairness** considering everything that has an effect on the situation, so that a fair judgement can be made: *In all fairness, he has been a hard worker.* ○ *In fairness* ***to*** *Diana, she has at least been honest with you.*

fair [PALE] /feəʳ/ [US] /fer/ *adj* (of skin) pale, or (of hair) pale yellow or golden: *She's got fair hair and blue eyes.* ○ *a fair complexion* ○ *My sister's dark and my brother's fair* (= He has fair hair). ○ *He's fair-****haired****.* ○ *All my family are fair-****skinned****.*

fair [AVERAGE] /feəʳ/ [US] /fer/ *adj* **[after v]** neither very good nor very bad: *Films are rated on a scale of poor, fair, good and excellent.* ○ *I was fair* ***at*** *science but it was never my thing.*

• **fair to middling** INFORMAL not very good but not bad: *"What's your French like?" "Oh, fair to middling."*

fair [QUITE LARGE] /feəʳ/ [US] /fer/ *adj* **[before n]** quite large: *We've had a fair* ***amount*** *of rain this week.* ○ *We've had a fair* ***number*** *of applicants.* ○ *It's a fair-****sized*** *garden.*

○ *We've come a long way, but there's still a fair **way*** (= quite a long distance) *to go.*

fairly /ˈfeə.li/ ⓤ /ˈfer-/ *adv* **1** more than average, but less than very: *She's fairly tall.* ○ *I'm fairly sure that this is the right address.* ○ *We get on fairly well.* ○ *I saw her fairly recently.* ➪See also **fairly** at **fair** RIGHT. **2** LITERARY used to emphasize figurative expressions which describe what people or objects are doing: *The answer fairly jumps off the page at you!* ○ *The dog fairly flew out of the door to greet him.*

fair QUITE GOOD /feəʳ/ ⓤ /fer/ *adj* [before n] (of an idea, guess or chance) good, but not excellent: *I think I've got a fair **idea** of* (= I understand reasonably well) *what you want.* ○ *She's got a fair **chance** of winning* (= There is a reasonable chance that she will win).

fair WEATHER /feəʳ/ ⓤ /fer/ *adj* (of weather) pleasant and dry: *Fair weather was forecast for the following day.*

fair BEAUTIFUL /feəʳ/ ⓤ /fer/ *adj* OLD USE (of a woman) beautiful: *a fair maiden*
• **with *your* own fair hand(s)** HUMOROUS used to say that you have made something yourself: *"Where did you get this cake?" "I made it with my own fair hands."*
fairness /ˈfeə.nəs/ ⓤ /ˈfer-/ *noun* [U] OLD USE beauty ➪See also **fairness** at **fair** RIGHT.

fair PUBLIC EVENT /feəʳ/ ⓤ /fer/ *noun* [C] **1** a large public event where goods are bought and sold, usually from tables which have been specially arranged for the event, and where there is often entertainment: *I bought a wooden salad bowl at the local **craft** fair.* **2** (UK ALSO **funfair**, US ALSO **carnival**) an outside event where you can ride large machines for pleasure and play games to win prizes **3** a large show at which people who work in a particular industry meet, and sell and advertise their products: *a book/antiques/toy fair* ○ *a trade fair* **4** a public event in the countryside where farm animals and farm products are sold: *a cattle/agricultural fair* ○ *US a county/state fair* **5** MAINLY US FOR **fête** EVENT

fair ˈcopy *noun* [C usually sing] the final, corrected copy of a piece of written work

fair dinkum /ˌfeəˈdɪŋ.kəm/ ⓤ /ˌfer-/ *adj* [after v], *adv*, *exclamation* AUS INFORMAL honest(ly) or real(ly): *They beat us fair dinkum.*

fair ˈgame *noun* [U] someone or something that should be allowed to be criticized: *Many journalists consider the royal family fair game.*

fair ˈgo *exclamation* AUS INFORMAL something you say when you want someone to act in a reasonable way: *Fair go mate, let the others have a turn!*

fairground /ˈfeə.graʊnd/ ⓤ /ˈfer-/ *noun* [C] a large outside area used for a fair: *There was a small fairground just by the river, with a carousel, a roller coaster and a Ferris wheel.*

fair-haired boy /ˌfeə.heədˈbɔɪ/ ⓤ /ˌfer.herd-/ *noun* [C] US FOR **blue-eyed boy**

fairisle /ˈfeə.raɪl/ ⓤ /ˈfer-/ *adj* (ALSO **Fair Isle**) (of knitted clothing) made with a special pattern typical of one of Scotland's Shetland Islands: *a fairisle cardigan*

fair-minded /ˌfeəˈmaɪn.dɪd/ ⓤ /ˌfer-/ *adj* treating everyone equally: *a fair-minded employer*

fair ˈplay *noun* [U] **1** in sport, when players or teams play according to the rules and no one has an unfair advantage ➪See also **play fair** at **play** GAME. **2** UK fair and honest treatment of people: *The committee's job is to ensure fair play between all the political parties and candidates during the election.*

the ˈfair ˌsex *noun* OLD-FASHIONED OR HUMOROUS women in general

fair ˈtrade, **fairtrade** *noun* [U] a way of buying and selling products that makes certain that the original producer receives a fair price: *Fair trade, say Oxfam, is about giving poor people power.* ○ *fair trade coffee/chocolate* **ˌfairly ˈtraded** *adv*: *fairly traded bananas*

fairway /ˈfeə.weɪ/ ⓤ /ˈfer-/ *noun* [C] SPECIALIZED in golf, the area of short grass between the TEE (= place where you first hit the ball) and the GREEN (= place where the ball should enter a hole): *He completely missed the fairway from his tee shot, and his ball ended up in the bushes.*

fair-weather friend /ˌfeə.weð.əˈfrend/ ⓤ /ˌfer.weð.ɚ-/ *noun* [C usually sing] DISAPPROVING someone who is a good friend when it is easy for them to be one and who stops when you are having problems

fairy IMAGINARY CREATURE /ˈfeə.ri/ ⓤ /ˈfer.i/ *noun* [C] an imaginary creature with magical powers, usually represented as a very small person with wings: *Do you believe in fairies?* ○ *She used to think there were fairies at the bottom of her garden.*

fairy HOMOSEXUAL /ˈfeə.ri/ ⓤ /ˈfer.i/ *noun* [C] OFFENSIVE a homosexual man

ˈfairy ˌcake UK *noun* [C] (US **cupcake**) a small light cake, often with ICING on top

ˌfairy ˈgodmother *noun* [C usually sing] **1** a magical character in some children's stories who helps someone who is in trouble: *Cinderella's fairy godmother helped her go to the ball.* **2** someone who unexpectedly arrives to solve your problems or make good things happen to you: *The company **played** fairy godmother by deciding to sponsor the club for a further five years.*

fairyland /ˈfeə.ri.lænd/ ⓤ /ˈfer.i-/ *noun* **1** [U] the place where FAIRIES (= imaginary creatures) are said to live **2** [S] APPROVING a beautiful place with a charming or special quality: *It had snowed heavily during the night and in the morning the garden was a white fairyland.*

ˈfairy ˌlights *plural noun* UK small electric lights on a string used as decoration, especially on trees at Christmas

ˈfairy ˌtale *noun* [C] (ALSO **fairy story**) a traditional story written for children which usually involves imaginary creatures and magic
fairy-tale, **fairytale** /ˈfeə.ri.teɪl/ ⓤ /ˈfer.i-/ *adj* [before n] APPROVING having a special and charming or beautiful quality, like something in a fairy tale: *They had a fairy-tale **wedding**.* ○ *Sadly, there was no fairytale happy ending to the story.*

fait accompli /ˌfet.əˈkɒmˈpliː/ ⓤ /ˌfeɪ.tə.kɑːm-/ *noun* [C] *plural* **faits accomplis** an action which has already been done and which cannot be changed: *The policy change was **presented** to us **as** a fait accompli, without consultation or discussion.*

faith TRUST /feɪθ/ *noun* [U] great trust or confidence in something or someone: *She **has** no faith **in** modern medicine.* ○ *You'll cope – I have **great** faith in you.* ○ *After the trial, his family said they had **lost** all faith **in** the judicial system.* ○ *Ministers must start keeping their promises if they want to **restore** faith **in** the government.*
• **accept/take *sth* on faith** to be willing to believe something without proof
• **put/place *your* faith in *sth/sb*** to make a decision to trust something or someone: *Some people put their faith in strong leaders rather than sound policies.*
• **keep faith with *sth/sb*** to continue to support something or someone, or to do what you promised to do in a particular thing: *Despite the continuing recession, the government has asked people to keep faith with its reforms.* ○ *The company has not kept faith with its promise to invest in training.*

faithful /ˈfeɪθ.fəl/ *adj* **1** loyal: *a faithful **friend*** ○ *They are faithful supporters of the Labour Party.* ○ *His faithful old dog accompanied him everywhere he went.* **2** true or not changing any of the details, facts, style, etc. of the original: *She gave a faithful **account** of what had happened on that night.* ○ *I have tried to keep my translation as faithful as possible **to** the original book.* **3** If your husband, wife or partner is faithful, they do not have a sexual relationship with anyone else: *Was your wife faithful during your marriage?* ○ *He was faithful **to** his wife throughout their 30-year marriage.* **4 faithful to *sth*** continuing to support or follow something: *He remained faithful to the president's regime when so many others spoke out against it.* ○ *Despite persecution, she remained faithful to her beliefs.*

faithful /ˈfeɪθ.fəl/ *noun* [C] someone who continues to support someone or something: *He gave a rousing speech to a room full of **party** faithfuls.*

the faithful *group noun* **the faithful** people who are always loyal to a particular group or organization, especially a political party: *They asked for donations from the **party** faithful.*

faithfully /ˈfeɪθ.fᵊl.i/ *adv* **1** *He served the family faithfully* (= in a loyal way) *for 40 years.* ○ *I always follow the instructions on medicine bottles faithfully* (= exactly). ○ *She **promised** faithfully* (= made a firm promise) *that she would never leave him.* **2** *MAINLY UK* **Yours faithfully** used at the end of a formal letter beginning with 'Dear Sir' or 'Dear Madam'

faithfulness /ˈfeɪθ.fᵊl.nəs/ *noun* [U] the quality of being faithful to someone or something: *The bishop stressed the importance of faithfulness **in** marriage.*

faithless /ˈfeɪθ.ləs/ *adj* **1** not loyal and not able to be trusted **2** not faithful sexually to your marriage partner or usual sexual partner: *a faithless husband* **faithlessly** /ˈfeɪθ.lə.sli/ *adv* **faithlessness** /ˈfeɪθ.lə.snəs/ *noun* [U]

faith [RELIGION] /feɪθ/ *noun* **1** [C] a particular religion: *the Muslim/Christian/Jewish/Buddhist faith* ○ *They were persecuted for their faith.* ○ *He was forced to **practise** his faith in secret.* ○ *a **multi-**faith society* ○ *They were brought up in **the true** faith* (= the religion which the speaker believes is the only true one). **2** [U] strong belief in God or a particular religion: *Even in the bad times she never **lost** her faith.* ○ *Her faith **in** God was shattered when her baby died.* ○ *It's my faith that keeps me going.*

faithful /ˈfeɪθ.fᵊl/ *adj* following a particular religion: *faithful Christians* ○ *faithful **followers** of Buddhism*

the ˈfaithful *plural noun* the followers of a particular religion: *We heard bells calling the faithful to prayer.*

faithless /ˈfeɪθ.ləs/ *adj* with no religious faith

faithlessness /ˈfeɪθ.lə.snəs/ *noun* [U]

ˈfaith ˌhealer *noun* [C] a person who heals using the power of prayer and belief **ˈfaith ˌhealing** *noun* [U] *Despite all the advances in modern medicine, demand for alternative therapies and faith healing keeps growing.*

fajita /fəˈhiː.tə/ *noun* [C] a Mexican dish of meat and vegetables cut into strips, cooked and wrapped inside a TORTILLA (= thin, round bread)

fake [OBJECT] /feɪk/ *noun* [C] **1** an object which is made to look real or valuable in order to deceive people: *Experts revealed that the painting was a fake.* ○ *The gun in his hand was a fake.* **2** someone who is not what or whom they say they are: *After working for ten years as a doctor, he was exposed as a fake.*

fake /feɪk/ *adj* not real, but made to look or seem real: *He was charged with possessing a fake passport.* ○ *fake fur/blood* ○ *a fake suntan*

fake /feɪk/ *verb* [T] to make an object look real or valuable in order to deceive people: *to fake a document/signature* **faker** /ˈfeɪ.kəʳ/ Ⓤⓢ /-kɚ/ *noun* [C]

fake [FEELING] /feɪk/ *verb* [I or T] to pretend that you have a feeling or illness: *to fake surprise* ○ *to fake an orgasm* ○ *She didn't want to go out, so she faked a headache.* ○ *He faked a heart attack and persuaded prison staff to take him to hospital.* ○ *He isn't really crying, he's just faking.*

fakir, faqir /ˈfeɪ.kɪəʳ/ Ⓤⓢ /fəˈkɪr/ *noun* [C] a member of an Islamic religious group, or a Hindu holy man

falafel /fəˈlæf.ᵊl/ Ⓤⓢ /-ˈlɑː.fᵊl/ *noun* [C or U] **felafel**

falcon /ˈfɒl.kᵊn/ Ⓤⓢ /ˈfɑːl-/ *noun* [C] a bird with pointed wings and a long tail which can be trained to hunt other birds and small animals

falconer /ˈfɒl.kᵊn.əʳ/ Ⓤⓢ /ˈfɑːl.kə.nɚ/ *noun* [C] a person who keeps and often trains falcons for hunting

falconry /ˈfɒl.kᵊn.ri/ Ⓤⓢ /ˈfɑːl-/ *noun* [U] the sport of hunting small animals and birds using falcons: *a falconry display/course/centre*

fall [ACCIDENT] /fɔːl/ Ⓤⓢ /fɑːl/ *verb* [I] **fell, fallen** to suddenly go down onto the ground or towards the ground unintentionally or accidentally: *The path's very steep, so be careful you don't fall.* ○ *He fell badly and broke his leg.* ○ *Athletes have to learn how to fall without hurting themselves.* ○ *She fell under a bus and was killed instantly.* ○ *The horse fell at the first fence.* ○ *I fell **down** the stairs and injured my back.* ○ *She had fallen, it appeared, **from** a great height.* ○ *The water's deep here, so don't fall **in**!* ○ *He fell **into** the river and drowned.* ○ *If you fell **off** the roof, you'd kill yourself.* ○ *He was leaning out of the window and fell **out**.* ○ *She fell five metres **to** the bottom of the ravine.* ○ *He fell **to** his **death** climbing the Matterhorn.*

• **fall about (laughing)** *UK INFORMAL* to laugh uncontrollably: *We fell about when we heard her reply.*

• **fall between two stools** If something falls between two stools, it fails to achieve either of two aims: *The grammar guide falls between two stools – it's too difficult for a beginner but not detailed enough for an advanced student.*

• **fall by the wayside** If someone falls by the wayside, they fail to finish an activity, and if something falls by the wayside, people stop doing it, making it, or using it : *So why does one company survive a recession while its competitors fall by the wayside?*

• **fall foul of *sth*** to break a rule or law, especially unintentionally: *Manufacturers may fall foul of the new government guidelines.*

• **fall foul of *sb*** to have a disagreement with someone: *Things were going well for her till she fell foul of the director.*

• **fall flat** If a joke, idea or suggestion falls flat, it does not have the intended effect: *He made several jokes and each of them fell flat.*

• **fall flat on *your* face** *INFORMAL* to fall and land with your face down: *Poor Kathy fell flat on her face in the mud.*

• **fall from grace** when you do something which makes people in authority stop liking you or admiring you: *The Finance Minister's fall from grace gave the tabloid press great satisfaction.*

• **fall in love** to be very attracted to someone and begin to love them: *They met and fell **madly** in love.* ○ *He fell in love **with** a young German student.* ○ *I thought I was falling in love.*

• **fall into place 1** When things fall into place, they happen in a satisfactory way, without problems: *If you plan the project well, then everything should fall into place.* **2** When events or details that you did not understand before fall into place, they become easy to understand: *Once I discovered that the woman whom he had been dancing with was his daughter, everything fell into place.*

• **fall into the/someone's trap** to make a mistake or get into a difficult situation by doing something or by trusting someone: *Don't fall into the trap **of** thinking you can learn a foreign language without doing any work.* ○ *We fell right into the enemy's trap.*

• **fall into the wrong hands** If something falls into the wrong hands, a dangerous person or an enemy starts to own or control it: *There are fears that the weapons might fall into the wrong hands.*

• **fall into *sb's* arms** *LITERARY* When people fall into each other's arms, they hold each other tightly with both arms, to show their love for each other.

• **nearly/almost fall off *your* chair** *INFORMAL* to be extremely surprised: *She nearly fell off her chair when she heard her exam result.* ➲See also **fall off**.

• **fall on deaf ears** If a suggestion or warning falls on deaf ears, no one listens to it: *Their appeals to release the hostages fell on deaf ears.*

• **fall on hard times** to lose your money and start to have a difficult life: *The scheme is designed to help children whose parents have fallen on hard times.*

• **fall over *your*self** *UK* (*US* **fall all over *your*self**) to be very eager to do something: *Publishers are falling over themselves **to** produce non-fiction for five to seven-year-olds.*

• **fall prey/victim to *sth/sb*** to suddenly begin to suffer as a result of something or someone bad: *Police fear that more pensioners could fall prey to the thieves.*

• **fall short** to fail to reach a desired or expected amount or standard, causing disappointment: *August car sales fell short **of** the industry's expectations.*

fall /fɔːl/ Ⓤⓢ /fɑːl/ *noun* [C usually sing] when someone or something falls down to the ground, usually unintentionally or accidentally: *He **had/took** a nasty fall and hurt his back.* ○ *the fall of the Berlin Wall* (= when the Berlin Wall was destroyed) ➲See also **fall** at **fall** COME DOWN, **fall** LOWER, **fall** BE DEFEATED.

• **take a/the fall for *sb*** US INFORMAL to accept the blame for something another person did: *I wasn't going to take the fall for him.*

fallen /ˈfɔː.lən/ [US] /ˈfɑː-/ *adj* **[before n]** lying on the ground, after falling down: *A fallen tree was blocking the road.* ➲See also **fallen** at **fall** COME DOWN, **fall** BE DEFEATED.

COMMON LEARNER ERROR

fall or **feel?**

The past forms of the verbs **fall** and **feel** are often confused by learners. The past tense of **fall** is 'fell'.

He fell off the roof and broke his leg.

The past tense of **feel** is 'felt'.

I felt very nervous.

---

fall [COME DOWN] /fɔːl/ [US] /fɑːl/ *verb* **[I] fell, fallen 1** to come down onto the ground or from a high position to a lower position: *The snow had been falling steadily all day.* ○ *You can tell it's autumn because the leaves have started to fall.* ○ *She fell* **into** *bed, completely exhausted.* ○ *A bomb fell* **on** *the church and destroyed it.* ○ *A huge meteor fell* **to** *earth in the middle of the desert.* ○ *He begged for mercy as the blows fell* **on** *him* (= as he was being hit). ➲See also **fall on/upon**; **fall to**. **2** When the curtain falls in the theatre, it comes down because the play or performance has ended: *The audience was still laughing as the curtain fell.*

fall /fɔːl/ [US] /fɑːl/ *noun* **[C usually sing]** when something moves down onto the ground or from a higher position to a lower position: *a heavy fall of snow* ➲See also **rainfall**. See also **fall** at **fall** ACCIDENT, **fall** LOWER, **fall** BE DEFEATED.

falls /fɔːlz/ [US] /fɑːlz/ *plural noun* often used in place names to mean a very wide waterfall, often made of many separate waterfalls: *Niagara Falls*

fallen /ˈfɔː.lən/ [US] /ˈfɑː-/ *adj* **[before n]** having dropped down: *fallen leaves* ➲See also **fallen** at **fall** ACCIDENT, **fall** BE DEFEATED.

fall [LOWER] /fɔːl/ [US] /fɑːl/ *verb* **[I] fell, fallen 1** to become lower in size, amount or strength: *Demand for new cars has fallen due to the recession.* ○ *The standard of his work has fallen during the year.* ○ *Salaries in the public sector are expected to fall by 15% this year.* ○ *The temperature could fall* **below** *zero overnight.* ○ *Average temperatures fell* **by** *ten degrees.* ○ *The pound has fallen* **to** *its lowest-ever level against the dollar.* ○ *When the teacher walked in, the children's voices fell* **to a whisper** (= they became very quiet). ○ *Share prices fell* **sharply** *this week.* ➲See also **fall back**; **fall to** DUTY; **fall to** START. **2 face/spirits fall** If your face falls, you suddenly look unhappy or disappointed, and if your spirits fall, you suddenly feel unhappy or disappointed: *His spirits fell when he saw the distance he still had to go.* ○ *As she read her exam results, her face fell.*

fall /fɔːl/ [US] /fɑːl/ *noun* **[C usually sing]** when the size, amount or strength of something gets lower: *a fall* **in** *the price of petrol/the unemployment rate* ○ *We could hear the rise and fall of voices in the other room.* ○ *There was a fall* **in** *support for the Republican party at the last election.* ➲See also **fall** at **fall** ACCIDENT, **fall** COME DOWN, **fall** BE DEFEATED.

falling /ˈfɔː.lɪŋ/ [US] /fɑː-/ *adj* describes something that is becoming lower in size, amount or strength: *falling birth/interest rates* ○ *Parents had complained about falling standards at the school.*

fall [BECOME] /fɔːl/ [US] /fɑːl/ *verb* **[I + adv or prep; L] fell, fallen** to change to a particular condition from a different one: *He always falls* **asleep** *after drinking red wine.* ○ *Your rent falls* **due** (= must be paid) *on the first of the month.* ○ *She suddenly fell* **ill**. ○ *The book fell* **open** (= opened by chance) *at the page on Venice.* ○ *The government has fallen strangely* **silent** *on the subject of tax cuts after all its promises at the last election.* ○ ***Silence*** *fell* **on** *the group of men* (= They became silent) *as they received the news.* ○ *She fell* **under** *the influence of* (= began to be influenced by) *an older student.*

fall [BE DEFEATED] /fɔːl/ [US] /fɑːl/ *verb* **[I] fell, fallen 1** to be beaten or defeated: *The government finally fell after losing the support of the centre parties.* ○ *The president fell* ***from power*** *during the military coup.* **2** If a place falls in a war or an election, an enemy army or a different political party obtains control of it: *Rome fell* **to** *the Vandals in 455 AD.* ○ *The constituency fell* **to** *Labour at the last election, after ten years of Conservative rule.* **3** LITERARY If soldiers fall while fighting, they are killed: *Many brave men fell in the fight to save the city.* ○ *During the war, he saw many of his comrades fall* **in battle**.

fall /fɔːl/ [US] /fɑːl/ *noun* **[C usually sing]** when someone is defeated or loses their power: *the fall of Rome* ○ *The army took control of the city after the president's fall from power.* ➲See also **fall** at **fall** ACCIDENT, **fall** COME DOWN, **fall** LOWER.

the 'fallen *plural noun* FORMAL soldiers who have died in a war: *a statue in memory of the fallen in the two world wars*

fall [HAPPEN] /fɔːl/ [US] /fɑːl/ *verb* **[I] fell, fallen** to come at a particular time or happen in a particular place: *Easter falls late this year.* ○ *My birthday will fall* **on** *a Friday this year.* ○ ***Night/Darkness*** *had fallen by the time we got back to the camp.* ○ *In the word 'table', the accent falls* **on** *the first syllable.* ○ *The Treasury has still not decided where the cuts will fall.*

fall [BELONG TO] /fɔːl/ [US] /fɑːl/ *verb* **[I usually + adv or prep] fell, fallen** to belong to a particular group, subject or area: *The material falls* **into** *three categories.* ○ *Matters of discipline fall* **outside** *my area of responsibility.*

fall [HANG DOWN] /fɔːl/ [US] /fɑːl/ *verb* **[I usually + adv or prep] fell, fallen** to hang down loosely: *The boy's hair fell* **around** *his shoulders in golden curls.* ○ *The veil fell almost* **to** *her waist.*

fall [SEASON] US /fɔːl/ [US] /fɑːl/ *noun* **[C or U]** (UK **autumn**) the season after summer and before winter, when fruits and crops become ripe and the leaves fall off the trees: *Next fall we'll be back in New York.* ○ *They met* **in the fall of** *1992.*

PHRASAL VERBS WITH **fall** ▼

▲ **fall apart** [BREAK] *phrasal verb* to break into pieces: *My poor old boots are falling apart.*

▲ **fall apart** [STOP WORKING] *phrasal verb* **1** If an organization, system or agreement falls apart, it fails or stops working effectively: *The deal fell apart because of a lack of financing.* ○ *Their marriage fell apart when she found out about her husband's affair.* **2** INFORMAL to experience serious emotional problems that make you unable to think or act in the usual way: *After his wife died, he began to fall apart.*

▲ **fall away** [PART] *phrasal verb* If parts of something fall away, they break off and drop to the ground: *On the bathroom ceiling, some pieces of plaster had fallen away.* ○ *The rear sections of the rocket fell away.*

▲ **fall away/off** [AMOUNT] *phrasal verb* to become smaller or lower in amount or rate: *Membership of the club has fallen away in recent months.*

▲ **fall away** [LAND] *phrasal verb* If land falls away, it slopes down suddenly: *On the other side of the hill, the land falls away* **sharply**.

▲ **fall back** *phrasal verb* **1** LITERARY to move back suddenly from someone or something, often because you are frightened: *She fell back* **in** *horror/disgust.* **2** If an army falls back, it moves away from an enemy army in order to avoid fighting them: *The infantry fell back* **in** *disarray.*

▲ **fall back on *sth*** *phrasal verb* to use something for help because no other choice is available: *When the business failed, we had to fall back on our savings.* ○ *If I lose my job, I'll have nothing to fall back on.*

fallback /ˈfɔːl.bæk/ [US] /ˈfɑːl-/ *adj* **[before n]** describes a plan or position which can be used if other plans do not succeed or other things are not available: *Do we have a fallback* **position** *for these negotiations?*

▲ **fall behind** *phrasal verb* to fail to do something fast enough or on time: *He was ill for six weeks and fell behind* **with** *his schoolwork.* ○ *I've fallen behind* **with** *the mortgage payments.*

▲ **fall down** [FALL] *phrasal verb* **1** to fall to the ground: *Our apple tree fell down in the storm.* ○ *He stumbled and fell down.* **2** If a building is falling down, it is in a very bad condition and there is a risk that it will break into pieces and drop to the ground: *Many buildings in the old part of the city are falling down, and the goverment has no money to repair them.*

▲ **fall down** FAIL *phrasal verb* to fail: *Where do you think the plan falls down?*

▲ **fall down on sth** *phrasal verb* to not be good at something in comparison with another thing: *I'm quite good at speaking Chinese, but I fall down on the written work.*

▲ **fall for sb** LOVE *phrasal verb* INFORMAL to suddenly have strong romantic feelings about someone: *She always falls for unsuitable men.* ○ *He's fallen for her in a big way.*

▲ **fall for sth** BE TRICKED *phrasal verb* INFORMAL to be tricked into believing something that is not true: *He told me he owned a mansion in Spain and I fell for it.*

● **I'm not falling for that one!** INFORMAL said when you recognize a trick and refuse to be deceived by it: *"Lend me a fiver and I'll buy you a drink." "Oh no, I'm not falling for that one."*

▲ **fall in** ROOF *phrasal verb* If a roof or ceiling falls in, it drops to the ground because it is damaged: *Ten miners were trapped underground when the roof of the tunnel fell in.*

▲ **fall in** SOLDIERS *phrasal verb* If soldiers fall in, they move into a line, one beside the other: *"Company, fall in!" shouted the sergeant-major.* ○ *He started to march away, and the others fell in* **behind** *him.* ↪Compare **fall out** SOLDIERS.

● **fall in/into line** If a person in an organization falls in/into line, they start to follow the rules and behave according to expected standards of behaviour: *Teachers who fail to fall in line* **with** *the new regulations may face dismissal.*

▲ **fall in with sb** PERSON *phrasal verb* INFORMAL to become friendly with someone: *She fell in with a strange crowd of people at university.*

▲ **fall in with sth** PLAN *phrasal verb* INFORMAL to accept and support a plan or suggestion: *It seemed like a good idea so we just fell in with it.*

▲ **fall into sth** START *phrasal verb* to start doing something, often without intending to: *We've fallen into the* **habit** *of getting up late on Saturday mornings.* ○ *I fell into my job quite by accident.* ○ *She fell into a conversation with a man at the bar.*

▲ **fall into sth** CONDITION *phrasal verb* to gradually get into a particular condition, especially to get into a bad condition as a result of not being taken care of: *Over the years the house had fallen into disrepair.* ○ *The old school fell into* **disuse** *(= people stopped using it).*

▲ **fall off** *phrasal verb* If the amount, rate or quality of something falls off, it becomes smaller or lower: *Sales have been falling off recently.*

falling-off /ˌfɔː.lɪŋˈɒf/ ⓤ /ˌfɑː-/ *noun* [S] *Travel agencies have recorded a falling-off in (= a lower rate of) bookings this summer.*

▲ **fall on/upon sb** ATTACK *phrasal verb* LITERARY to attack someone suddenly and unexpectedly: *The soldiers fell on the villagers and seized all their weapons.*

▲ **fall on/upon sth** EAT *phrasal verb* LITERARY to start to eat food eagerly: *They fell on the bread as if they hadn't eaten for days.*

▲ **fall on/upon sth** NOTICE *phrasal verb* LITERARY If your eyes fall on something, or your sight, or it. falls on something, you see and notice it: *Her gaze fell upon a small box at the back of the shop.*

▲ **fall on sb** GUILTY *phrasal verb* **suspicion falls on sb** When suspicion falls on a particular person, people think that they may be guilty of doing something bad: *He was the last person to see the woman alive, and suspicion immediately fell on him.*

▲ **fall out** ARGUE *phrasal verb* INFORMAL to argue with someone and stop being friendly with them: *He left home after falling out with his parents.* ○ *She'd fallen out with her boyfriend* **over** *his ex-girlfriend.*

falling-out /ˌfɔː.lɪŋˈaʊt/ ⓤ /ˌfɑː-/ *noun* [S] INFORMAL an argument: *Rachel and Fi have* **had** *a falling-out and they're not speaking to each other.*

▲ **fall out** SOLDIERS *phrasal verb* If soldiers fall out, they move out of a line: *"Fall out, men!" shouted the sergeant-major.* ↪Compare **fall in** SOLDIERS.

▲ **fall out** SEPARATE *phrasal verb* If a tooth or your hair falls out, it becomes loose and separates from your mouth or head: *Her baby teeth are starting to fall out.* ○ *A side effect of the treatment is that your hair starts to fall out.*

▲ **fall over** DROP DOWN *phrasal verb* **1** If someone falls over, they fall to the ground: *She tripped and fell over.* **2** If something falls over, it falls onto its side: *If you make the cake too high, it'll fall over.*

▲ **fall over sth/sb** COVER *phrasal verb* LITERARY to cover something or someone: *A shadow fell over her work and she looked up to see who was there.*

▲ **fall through** *phrasal verb* to fail to happen: *We found a buyer for our house, but then the sale fell through.*

▲ **fall to sb** DUTY *phrasal verb* to be or become the duty or job of someone: *The worst job fell to me.*

● **it falls to you** FORMAL it is your duty: *It falls to me to thank you for all you have done for the association.*

▲ **fall to** START *phrasal verb* LITERARY to begin doing something energetically: *There was a lot of work to do, so they fell to immediately.*

fallacy /ˈfæl.ə.si/ *noun* [C] FORMAL an idea that a lot of people think is true but which is false: [+ *that*] *It is a common fallacy that women are worse drivers than men.*

fallacious /fəˈleɪ.ʃəs/ *adj* FORMAL not correct: *His argument is based on fallacious reasoning.* **fallaciously** /fəˈleɪ.ʃə.sli/ *adv* **fallaciousness** /fəˈleɪ.ʃə.snəs/ *noun* [U]

fallen 'woman *noun* [C] OLD-FASHIONED DISAPPROVING a woman who has lost her good reputation by having sex with someone before she is married

'fall ˌguy *noun* [C usually sing] MAINLY US SLANG a person who is falsely blamed for something that has gone wrong, or for a crime that they have not committed: *The governor was looking for a fall guy to take the blame for the corruption scandal.*

fallible /ˈfæl.ɪ.bl̩/ *adj* **1** able or likely to make mistakes: *We place our trust in doctors, but even they are fallible.* ✻ NOTE: The opposite is **infallible**. **2** A fallible object or system is likely not to work satisfactorily: *This method is more fallible than most because it depends on careful and accurate timing.* **fallibility** /ˌfæl.ɪˈbɪl.ɪ.ti/ ⓤ /-ə.t̬i/ *noun* [U] *The play deals with the fallibility of human nature.*

ˌfalling 'star *noun* [C] INFORMAL FOR **meteor**

fallopian tube /fəˌləʊ.pi.ənˈtjuːb/ ⓤ /-ˌloʊ.pi.ənˈtuːb/ *noun* [C usually pl] SPECIALIZED either of the two tubes in a woman's body along which eggs travel from the OVARIES to the womb

fallout /ˈfɔːl.aʊt/ ⓤ /ˈfɑːl-/ *noun* [U] **1** the radioactive dust in the air after a nuclear explosion: *Cancer deaths caused by fallout* **from** *weapons testing could rise to 2.4 million over the next few centuries.* **2** the unpleasant results or effects of an action or event: *The* **political** *fallout of the revelations has been immense.*

'fallout ˌshelter *noun* [C] a strong building, usually under the ground, intended to keep people safe from the dust in the air after a nuclear explosion

fallow /ˈfæl.əʊ/ ⓤ /-oʊ/ *adj* **1** describes land that is not planted with crops, in order to improve the quality of the soil: *Farmers are eligible for government support if they let a certain amount of land lie* **fallow**. **2** describes a period of time in which very little happens: *August is a fallow* **period** *in British politics.*

'fallow ˌdeer *noun* [C] plural **fallow deer** a small deer of Europe and Asia which is grey in winter and pale brown with white spots in summer

false NOT REAL /fɒls/ ⓤ /fɑːls/ *adj* not real, but made to look or seem real: *false eyelashes/teeth* ○ *Modern office buildings have false floors, under which computer and telephone wires can be laid.*

false NOT TRUE /fɒls/ ⓤ /fɑːls/ *adj* DISAPPROVING not true, but made to seem true in order to deceive people: *She was charged with giving false evidence in court.* ○ *When she was stopped by the police for speeding, she gave them a false* **name** *and address.* ○ *He assumed a false* **identity** *(= pretended he was someone else) in order to escape from the police.*

● **under false pretences** If you do something under false pretences, you lie about who you are, what you are doing, or what you intend to do, in order to obtain something: *He was deported for entering the country under false pretences.* ○ *If you're not going to offer me a job, then you've brought me here under false pretences* (= you have deceived me in order to make me come here).

falsehood /ˈfɒls.hʊd/ [US] /ˈfɑːls-/ *noun* FORMAL **1** [U] lying: *She doesn't seem to understand the difference between truth and falsehood.* **2** [C] a lie or a statement which is not correct

falsely /ˈfɒl.sli/ [US] /ˈfɑːl-/ *adv* in a way that is not true: *He claimed, falsely, that he was married.*

falsify /ˈfɒl.sɪ.faɪ/ [US] /ˈfɑːl-/ *verb* [T] DISAPPROVING to change something, such as a document, in order to deceive people: *The certificate had clearly been falsified.* **falsification** /ˌfɒl.sɪ.fɪˈkeɪ.ʃᵊn/ [US] /ˌfɑːl-/ *noun* [U] *falsification of evidence*

false [NOT CORRECT] /fɒls/ [US] /fɑːls/ *adj* not correct: *"Three plus three is seven. True or false?" "False."* ○ *The news report about the explosion turned out to be false.* ○ *You'll get a false **impression/idea** of the town if you only visit the university.*

falsely /ˈfɒl.sli/ [US] /ˈfɑːl-/ *adv* wrongly: *She was falsely accused of shoplifting.*

falsity /ˈfɒl.sə.ti/ [US] /ˈfɑːl.sə.t̬i/ *noun* [U] (ALSO **falseness**) when something is not correct

false [NOT SINCERE] /fɒls/ [US] /fɑːls/ *adj* DISAPPROVING not sincere or expressing real emotions: *a false smile/laugh* ○ *I didn't like her – she seemed a bit false.*

falsely /ˈfɒl.sli/ [US] /ˈfɑːl-/ *adv* DISAPPROVING in a way that is not sincere: *She tends to adopt a falsely cheerful tone when she's upset about something.* **falseness** /ˈfɒl.snəs/ [US] /ˈfɑːl-/ *noun* [U] (ALSO **falsity**) *She left her career in television, saying she hated the falsity of it all.*

false [NOT LOYAL] /fɒls/ [US] /fɑːls/ *adj* LITERARY DISAPPROVING A false friend is not loyal or cannot be trusted.

ˌfalse aˈlarm *noun* [C] an occasion when people believe incorrectly that something dangerous or unpleasant is happening or will happen: *Three fire engines rushed to the school only to discover it was a false alarm.* ○ *She thought she was pregnant, but it turned out to be a false alarm* (= she discovered she was not).

ˌfalse ˈdawn *noun* [C usually sing] something which seems to show that a successful period is beginning or that a situation is improving when it is not: *The increase in sales at the end of the year proved to be a false dawn.*

ˌfalse eˈconomy *noun* [C usually sing] an action which saves money at the beginning but which, over a longer period of time, results in more money being wasted than being saved: *Buying cheap white goods is just a false economy – they're twice as likely to break down.*

ˌfalse ˈfriend *noun* [C] a word which is often confused with a word in another language because the two words look or sound similar, but which has a different meaning: *The French word 'actuellement' and the English word 'actually' are false friends.*

ˌfalse ˈhopes *plural noun* confident feelings about something that might not be true: *I don't want to **raise** any false hopes, but I believe your son is still alive.*

ˌfalse imˈprisonment *noun* [C usually sing] LEGAL the limiting of someone's freedom without the authority or right to do so: *He brought civil proceedings against the police for false imprisonment.*

ˌfalse ˈmodesty *noun* [U] when a person pretends to have a low opinion of their own abilities or achievements: *He shows great pride in his work and has no false modesty about his success.*

ˌfalse ˈmove *noun* [C usually sing] an unwise action which is likely to have an unpleasant or dangerous effect: *We can't afford to **make** any false moves once we're in enemy territory.* ○ *"One false move and you're dead!* (= I will kill you)*" shouted the gunman.*

ˌfalse ˈstart [RACE] *noun* [C usually sing] when one competitor in a race starts too early, before the official signal to begin: *If an athlete **makes** a false start, the race must be restarted.*

ˌfalse ˈstart [PROBLEM] *noun* [C usually sing] an attempt to do something which fails because you are not ready or not able to do it: *We had a couple of false starts because of computer problems, but now the project is really under way.*

falsetto /fɔːlˈset.əʊ/ [US] /fɑːlˈset̬.oʊ/ *noun* [C] *plural* **falsettos** a form of singing or speaking by men using an extremely high voice: **falsetto** /fɔːlˈset.əʊ/ [US] /fɑːlˈset̬.oʊ/ *adj, adv*: *The lead singer has a falsetto voice.* ○ *to sing falsetto*

falsies /ˈfɒl.siːz/ [US] /ˈfɑːl-/ *plural noun* INFORMAL thick soft pieces of material which can be worn inside a woman's clothing to make her breasts look bigger

falter /ˈfɒl.təʳ/ [US] /ˈfɑːl.t̬ɚ/ *verb* [I] **1** to lose strength or purpose and stop, or almost stop: *The dinner party conversation faltered for a moment.* ○ *Her friends never faltered in their belief in her.* ○ *Nigel's voice faltered and he stopped speaking.* **2** to move awkwardly as if you might fall: *The nurse saw him falter and made him lean on her.* **faltering** /ˈfɒl.tᵊr.ɪŋ/ [US] /ˈfɑːl.t̬ɚ-/ *adj*: *She took a few faltering steps.* ○ *This legislation is designed to stimulate the faltering economy.* **falteringly** /ˈfɒl.tᵊr.ɪŋ.li/ [US] /ˈfɑːl.t̬ɚ-/ *adv*

fame /feɪm/ *noun* [U] when you are known or recognized by many people because of your achievements, skills, etc: *She first **rose to** fame as a singer at the age of 16.* ○ *She moved to London in search of fame **and fortune**.* ○ *The town's fame rests on its beautiful 14th-century abbey.* ➲See also **famous**.

famed /feɪmd/ *adj* known or familiar to many people: *It's a city famed **for** its ski slopes and casinos.* ○ *His famed calmness temporarily deserted him.*

familiar [EASY TO RECOGNIZE] /fəˈmɪl.i.əʳ/ [US] /ˈ-jɚ/ *adj* easy to recognize because of being seen, met, heard, etc. before: *There were one or two familiar **faces*** (= people I knew). ○ *The house looked strangely familiar, though she knew she'd never been there before.* ○ *The street was familiar **to** me.*

• **be familiar with *sth/sb*** to know something or someone well: *I'm sorry, I'm not familiar with your poetry.*

familiarity /fəˌmɪl.iˈær.ə.ti/ [US] /-ˈer.ə.t̬i/ *noun* [U] a good knowledge of something, or the fact that you know it so well: *Ellen's familiarity **with** pop music is astonishing.* ○ *I love the familiarity of my old chair.* ➲See also **familiarity** at **familiar** FRIENDLY.

• **Familiarity breeds contempt.** SAYING said about someone you know very well and have stopped respecting because you have seen all their bad qualities

familiar [FRIENDLY] /fəˈmɪl.i.əʳ/ [US] /-jɚ/ *adj* informal and friendly, sometimes in a way that is not respectful to someone who is not a relative or close friend: *"That'll be five pounds, dear", he said in an irritatingly familiar way.* ○ *He doesn't like to be too familiar **with** his staff.*

• **be on familiar terms** to have a close and informal relationship: *We had met before, but we were hardly* (= not) *on familiar terms.*

familiarly /fəˈmɪl.i.ə.li/ [US] /-jɚ.li/ *adv*: *Henry Channon, known familiarly* (= by his friends) *as 'Chips'*

familiarity /fəˌmɪl.iˈær.ə.ti/ [US] /-ˈer.ə.t̬i/ *noun* [U] friendly and informal behaviour: *His excessive familiarity offended her.* ➲See also **familiarity** at **familiar** EASY TO RECOGNIZE.

familiar [COMPANION] /fəˈmɪl.i.əʳ/ [US] /-jɚ/ *noun* [C] OLD USE a close friend, or a spirit in the shape of a cat, bird or other animal that is the close companion of a witch

familiarize /fəˈmɪl.i.ᵊr.aɪz/ *verb*

▲ **familiarize *yourself* with *sth***, UK USUALLY **-ise** *phrasal verb* [R] to learn about something: *We spent a few minutes familiarizing ourselves with the day's schedule.*

family [SOCIAL GROUP] /ˈfæm.ᵊl.i/ *group noun* **1** [C or U] a group of people who are related to each other, such as a mother, a father, and their children: *A new family has/have moved in next door.* ○ *I come from a large family – I have three brothers and two sisters.* ○ *He hasn't any family.* ○ *He's American but his family* (= relatives in the past) *come/comes from Ireland.* ○ *This film is good family entertainment* (= something that can be enjoyed by parents and children together). ○ *How does family **life*** (= being married, having children, etc.) *suit you?* **2** [C usually sing; U] the children of a family: *Women shouldn't have to choose between career and family* (= having children). ○ *Paul and Alison are hoping to **start** a family* (=

have children) soon. ○ *My dad died when we were small so my mum **raised** the family on her own.* **3** [C] a pair of adult animals and their babies: *We've got a family **of** squirrels living in our garden.*
• **be in the family way** *OLD-FASHIONED INFORMAL* to be pregnant

family [BIOLOGICAL GROUP] /ˈfæm.əl.i/ *noun* [C] *SPECIALIZED* a large group of related types of animal or plant: *The lion is a member of the cat family.*

ˌfamily ˈcredit *noun* [U] a payment made by the government in Britain to families with a low income

ˌfamily ˈdoctor *noun* [C] a **GP**

ˈfamily ˌman *noun* [C] a man who has a wife and children, or who enjoys spending a lot of time with them

ˈfamily ˌname *noun* [C] a **surname**

ˌfamily ˈplanning *noun* [U] the use of CONTRACEPTION (= any of various methods intended to prevent a woman becoming pregnant) to control how many children you have and when you have them: *a family-planning clinic*

ˌfamily ˈtree *noun* [C] a drawing that shows the relationships between the different members of a family, especially over a long period of time

famine /ˈfæm.ɪn/ *noun* [C or U] when there is not enough food for a great number of people, causing illness and death, or a particular period when this happens: *Another crop failure could result in **widespread** famine.* ○ *There were reports of refugees **dying of** famine.* ○ *Thousands of people emigrated during the Irish potato famine of 1845-46.*

famished /ˈfæm.ɪʃt/ *adj INFORMAL* extremely hungry: *Have some dinner with us – you must be famished!*

famous /ˈfeɪ.məs/ *adj* known and recognized by many people: *a famous actress/building* ○ *Marie Curie is famous **for** her contribution to science.* ○ *a city famous for its nightlife*
• **famous last words** *INFORMAL* said when someone makes a definite statement which is shown very soon, and in an embarrassing way, to be wrong: *I told him categorically that we could never be anything more than friends. Famous last words! Within a few months we were engaged.*

famously /ˈfeɪ.mə.sli/ *adv* in a famous way: *He's designed dresses for many celebrities, most famously the Queen.*

famously /ˈfeɪ.mə.sli/ *adv OLD-FASHIONED* extremely well: *We **got along** famously.*

fan [AIR] /fæn/ *noun* [C] a device that is used to move the air around, either an object made of folded paper or other material that you wave with your hand, or an electric device with wide blades that spin round: *There was no air conditioning, just a ceiling fan turning slowly.*
fan /fæn/ *verb* [T] **-nn- 1** to wave a fan, or something that acts as a fan, in front of your face: [R] *It was so hot in the car that I tried to fan myself **with** the road map.* ○ *She sat down and began fanning her face.* **2** to blow air at a fire to make it burn more strongly

fan [MAKE WORSE] /fæn/ *verb* [T] **-nn-** *LITERARY* to encourage bad emotions or behaviour to get worse: *to fan the violence/hatred* ○ *The newspapers deliberately fanned the public's **fears** of losing their jobs.*
• **fan the flames** to make a dangerous or unpleasant mood or situation worse: *His speeches fanned the flames **of** racial tension.*

fan [PERSON] /fæn/ *noun* [C] someone who admires and supports a person, sport, sports team, etc: *More than 15, 000 Liverpool fans attended Saturday's game.* ○ *He's a big fan **of** country music.* ○ *I'm pleased to meet you – I'm a great fan **of** your work.*
▲ **fan out** *phrasal verb* If a group of people fan out, they move in different directions from a single point.

fanatic /fəˈnæt.ɪk/ [US] /-ˈnæt̬-/ *noun* [C] a person whose strong admiration for something is considered to be extreme or unreasonable: *a fitness/film fanatic*
fanatical /fəˈnæt.ɪ.kəl/ [US] /-ˈnæt̬-/ *adj*: *His enthusiasm for aerobics was almost fanatical.* ○ *Gary's fanatical **about** football.* **fanatically** /fəˈnæt.ɪ.kli/ [US] /-ˈnæt̬-/ *adv*: *The band has a fanatically loyal British following.* **fanaticism** /fəˈnæt.ɪ.sɪ.zəm/ [US] /-ˈnæt̬-/ *noun* [U]

ˈfan ˌbelt *noun* [C] a strip of material that moves round continuously to make a fan turn and keep an engine cool

fanciable /ˈfænt.si.ə.bl/ *adj UK INFORMAL* sexually attractive: *This Ben bloke – is he fanciable?*

ˈfan ˌclub *noun* [C] an organization for people who admire the same music star, football team, etc.

fancy [LIKE] /ˈfænt.si/ *verb* [T] **1** *MAINLY UK* to want to have or do something: *Do you fancy a drink this evening?* ○ [+ v-ing] *I didn't fancy swimming in that water.* **2** *MAINLY UK INFORMAL* to be sexually attracted to someone: *He could tell she fancied him.*
fancy *yourself* *verb* [R] *MAINLY UK DISAPPROVING* to think you are very attractive or important: *That Dave really fancies himself, doesn't he?*
fancy /ˈfænt.si/ *noun* **passing fancy** something that you like very much for a short period: *But for me, parachuting was no passing fancy.*
• **take a fancy to *sth/sb*** to start liking something or someone very much: *Laura's taken a fancy to Japanese food.*
• **take/tickle *your* fancy** *INFORMAL* If something takes/tickles your fancy, you like it and want to have or do it: *I looked in a lot of clothes shops but nothing really tickled my fancy.*
fancier /ˈfænt.si.əʳ/ [US] /-ɚ/ *noun* [C] someone who has an interest in and breeds a particular animal or plant: *a pigeon fancier*

fancy [IMAGINE] /ˈfænt.si/ *verb* [I or T] to imagine or think that something is so: [(+ that)] *UK I fancied **(that)** I saw something moving in the corner.* ○ [R] *He fancies himself **as** a bit of a singer.* ○ [+ to infinitive] *Who do you fancy **to** win the Cup this year?* ○ *UK OLD-FASHIONED This isn't the first time this has happened, I fancy.*
• **fancy!** (*ALSO* **fancy that!**) *UK OLD-FASHIONED* an expression of surprise: *"They have eight children." "Fancy that!*
• **fancy *sb's* chances** *MAINLY UK* to think that someone is likely to succeed: *I don't fancy his chances **of** getting his novel published.*
fancied /ˈfænt.sid/ *adj MAINLY UK* expected or thought likely to succeed: *She is the most fancied candidate for the next election.*
fancy /ˈfænt.si/ *noun* [U] *LITERARY* the imagination ➲See **flight of fancy** at **flight** MOVEMENT.
fanciful /ˈfænt.sɪ.fəl/ *adj* not realistic: *He has some fanciful notion about converting one room of his apartment into a gallery.* **fancifully** /ˈfænt.sɪ.fəl.i/ *adv*

fancy [DECORATIVE] /ˈfænt.si/ *adj* **1** decorative or complicated: *I wanted a simple black dress, nothing fancy.* ○ *The decor was rather fancy for my tastes.* ○ *fancy cakes* **2** *INFORMAL* expensive: *We stayed in a fancy hotel near the Champs-Élysées.* ○ *a fancy restaurant*

ˌfancy ˈdress *noun* [U] *UK* the special clothes that you wear for a party where everyone dresses as a particular type of character or thing: *a fancy-dress **party*** ○ *I thought he was **in** fancy dress.*

fancy-free /ˌfænt.siˈfriː/ *adj* [after v] (*ALSO* **footloose and fancy-free**) free to do what you like and go where you like because you have no responsibilities such as a family or a relationship

ˈfancy ˌman/ˌwoman *noun* [C] *OLD-FASHIONED* a lover

fandango /fænˈdæŋ.gəʊ/ [US] /-goʊ/ *noun* [C] *plural* **fandangos** a fast Spanish dance performed by a man and a woman dancing close together

fanfare /ˈfæn.feəʳ/ [US] /-fer/ *noun* [C] a loud short piece of music played, usually on a TRUMPET and to introduce the arrival of someone important

fang /fæŋ/ *noun* [C] a long sharp tooth: *The dog growled and bared its fangs.*

ˈfan ˌheater *noun* [C] an electrically powered machine which blows heated air into a room

fanlight /ˈfæn.laɪt/ *noun* [C] (*US USUALLY* **transom (window)**) a small window over the top of a door

ˈfan ˌmail *noun* [U] letters that are sent to a famous person by people who admire that person

fanny /ˈfæn.i/ *noun* [C] **1** *UK OFFENSIVE* a woman's sexual organs **2** *US OLD-FASHIONED INFORMAL* a person's bottom

ˈfanny ˌpack *US noun* [C] (*UK* **bumbag**) a small bag fixed to a long strap which you fasten around your waist, and which is used for carrying money, keys, etc.

F

fantasia /fænˈteɪ.zi.ə/ *noun* [C] a piece of music with no fixed form, or one consisting of tunes that many people know or recognize

fantastic [GOOD] /fænˈtæs.tɪk/ *adj* INFORMAL extremely good: *You look fantastic in that dress.* ○ *We had a fantastic time.* ○ *They've won a holiday? How fantastic!*
fantastically /fænˈtæs.tɪ.kli/ *adv* extremely well

fantastic [NOT REAL] /fænˈtæs.tɪk/ *adj* **1** (ALSO **fantastical**) strange and imaginary, or not reasonable: *He drew fantastic animals with two heads and large wings.* ○ *fantastical tales* (= about imaginary things) **2** very unusual, strange or unexpected: *It seemed fantastic that they still remembered her 50 years later.* **fantastically** /fænˈtæs.tɪ.kli/ *adv*

fantastic [LARGE] /fænˈtæs.tɪk/ *adj* A fantastic amount is very large: *She must be earning a fantastic amount of money.*
fantastically /fænˈtæs.tɪ.kli/ *adv* extremely: *They're fantastically rich.* ○ *They're doing fantastically well this season.*

fantasy /ˈfæn.tə.si/ *noun* [C or U] a pleasant situation that you enjoy thinking about, but which is unlikely to happen, or the activity of thinking itself: *Steve's favourite fantasy was to own a big house and a flashy car.* ○ *sexual fantasies* ○ *She retreated into a world of fantasy/a fantasy world, where she could be anything she wanted.*
fantasist /ˈfæn.tə.sɪst/ *noun* [C] someone who often has fantasies, or someone who confuses fantasy and reality
fantasize, UK USUALLY **-ise** /ˈfæn.tə.saɪz/ *verb* [I or T] to think about something very pleasant that is unlikely to happen: *He fantasized about winning the Nobel Prize.* ○ [+ that] *As a child Emma fantasized that she would do something heroic.*

fanzine /ˈfæn.ziːn/ *noun* [C] a magazine written by people who admire a sports team, musicians, etc., for other people with the same special interest ⊃See also **fan** PERSON.

FAQ /ˌef.eɪˈkjuː/ *noun* [C] ABBREVIATION FOR frequently asked question: a question in a list of questions and answers intended to help people understand a particular subject: *If you have any problems, consult the FAQs on our website.*

far [DISTANCE] /fɑːʳ/ ⑩ /fɑːr/ *adv* **farther**, **farthest**, or **further**, **furthest** at, to or from a great distance in space or time: *How far is it from Australia to New Zealand?* ○ *Is the station far away?* ○ *She doesn't live far from here.* ○ *He felt lonely and far from home.* ○ *One day, perhaps far in/into the future, you'll regret what you've done.*
● **as far as it goes** used to say that something has good qualities but could be better: *It's a good essay as far as it goes.*
● **as/so far as I know** used to say what you think is true, although you do not know all the facts: *He isn't coming today, as far as I know.*
● **as/so far as I'm concerned** used to say what your personal opinion is about something: *She can come whenever she likes, as far as I'm concerned.*
● **as/so far as I can tell** used to say what you have noticed or understood: *There's been no change, as far as I can tell.*
● **far be it from me to** I certainly would not: *Far be it from me to tell you how to run your life.*
● **far from sth** certainly not something: *The situation is far from clear.*
● **far from it** certainly not: *He's not handsome – far from it.*
● **from far and wide** from a large number of places: *People came from far and wide to see the house.*
● **go far** INFORMAL to be very successful in the future: *She's a very talented writer – I'm sure she'll go far.*
● **go too far** INFORMAL to behave in a way that upsets or annoys people: *It's all very well having a joke but sometimes you go too far.*
● **so far** until now: *So far we've made thirty-two thousand pounds.*
● **so far so good** used to say that an activity has gone well until now: *I've found a tin of beans. So far so good, but where is the opener?*

far /fɑːʳ/ ⑩ /fɑːr/ *adj* **farther**, **farthest** or **further**, **furthest** **1** describes something distant, or the part of something that is most distant from the centre or from you: *The station isn't far – we could easily walk it.* ○ [before n] *The children ran to the far side/corner of the room.* **2 far left/right** refers to political groups whose opinions are very extreme: *supporters of the far left*
● **be a far cry from sth** to be completely different from something: *This flat is a far cry from the house they had before.*

COMMON LEARNER ERROR

far

Be careful with the way that you use the word **far** when describing distances. You can use it in questions or in negative sentences.

How far is Cambridge from London?
It isn't far from my apartment to the school.

You should not use **far** when giving the exact distance between two places. You just need to give the distance and the preposition 'from'.

I live in a small village 30 kilometres from Bologna.
~~I live in a small village 30 kilometres far from Bologna.~~

far [AMOUNT] /fɑːʳ/ ⑩ /fɑːr/ *adv* very much: *This car is far better than our old one.* ○ *It cost far more (money) than I could afford.* ○ *He loses his temper far too often.* ○ *I'd rather/sooner go to the theatre than watch a video.*
● **by far** by a great amount: *They are by far the best students in the class.*

faraway /ˌfɑː.rəˈweɪ/ /ˈ---/ ⑩ /ˌfɑːr.ə-/ *adj* [before n] **1** LITERARY distant: *They travelled to faraway lands/places.* **2** describes a person's expression which shows that they are not thinking about what is happening around them: *There was a faraway look in his eyes.*

farce [PLAY] /fɑːs/ ⑩ /fɑːrs/ *noun* **1** [C] a humorous play or film where the characters become involved in unlikely situations **2** [U] the style of writing or acting in this type of play: *The play suddenly changes from farce to tragedy.*

farce [SITUATION] /fɑːs/ ⑩ /fɑːrs/ *noun* [C] DISAPPROVING a ridiculous or meaningless situation or action: *No one had prepared anything so the meeting was a bit of a farce.* **farcical** /ˈfɑː.sɪ.kᵊl/ ⑩ /ˈfɑːr-/ *adj*: *The whole situation has become farcical.* **farcically** /ˈfɑː.sɪ.kli/ ⑩ /ˈfɑːr-/ *adv*

fare [PAYMENT] /feəʳ/ ⑩ /fer/ *noun* [C] **1** the money that you pay for a journey on a vehicle such as a bus or train: *Train fares are going up again.* **2** someone who pays to be driven somewhere in a taxi

fare [MANAGE] /feəʳ/ ⑩ /fer/ *verb* [I usually + adv or prep] SLIGHTLY OLD-FASHIONED to succeed or be treated in the stated way: *How did you fare in your exams?* ○ *Low-paid workers will fare badly/well under this government.*

fare [FOOD] /feəʳ/ ⑩ /fer/ *noun* [U] SLIGHTLY OLD-FASHIONED the type of food that is served in a restaurant: *a pub serving traditional British fare*

the ˌFar ˈEast *group noun* [S] the countries of East Asia, including China, Japan, North and South Korea and Indonesia ⊃Compare **the Middle East**.

farewell /ˌfeəˈwel/ ⑩ /ˌfer-/ *exclamation* OLD-FASHIONED OR FORMAL goodbye
farewell /ˌfeəˈwel/ ⑩ /ˌfer-/ *noun* [C] FORMAL when someone says goodbye: *We said our sad farewells and got on the bus.* ○ *He bid us both a fond* (= affectionate) *farewell.* ○ *a farewell party*

far-fetched /ˌfɑːˈfetʃt/ ⑩ /ˌfɑːr-/ *adj* very unlikely to be true, and difficult to believe: *a far-fetched idea/story*

far-flung /ˌfɑːˈflʌŋ/ ⑩ /ˌfɑːr-/ *adj* LITERARY describes places that are a great distance away, or something that is spread over a very large area: *The news spread to all corners of our far-flung empire.*

far-gone /ˌfɑːˈɡɒn/ ⑩ /ˌfɑːrˈɡɑːn/ *adj* INFORMAL very drunk, ill, or in some other advanced and bad state: *He was so far-gone that he could hardly walk.*

farm /fɑːm/ ⑩ /fɑːrm/ *noun* [C] **1** an area of land, together with house and buildings, used for growing crops and/or keeping animals as a business: *a dairy/arable farm* ○ *farm animals* ○ *fresh farm produce* ○ *farm workers* **2** a place where a particular type of animal is raised in large numbers to be sold: *a sheep/fish/mink farm*

farm /fɑːm/ [US] /fɑːrm/ *verb* [T] to use land for growing crops and/or raising animals as a business: *The Stamfords have farmed this land for over a hundred years.*

farmer /ˈfɑː.məʳ/ [US] /ˈfɑːr.mɚ/ *noun* [C] someone who owns or takes care of a farm: *a dairy/sheep farmer*

farming /ˈfɑː.mɪŋ/ [US] /ˈfɑːr-/ *noun* [U] the activity of working on a farm or organizing the work there

PHRASAL VERBS WITH **farm**

▲ **farm *sth* out** [WORK] *phrasal verb* [M] to give work to other people to do: *Magazines often farm out articles **to** freelance journalists.*

▲ **farm *sb* out** [CHILD] *phrasal verb* [M] *DISAPPROVING* to arrange for another person to look after someone, especially your child: *Almost since birth, their baby has been farmed out **to** nannies and nurseries.*

farmers' market /ˈfɑː.məz,mɑː.kɪt/ [US] /ˈfɑːr.mɚz,mɑːr-/ *noun* [C] a regular event in a town or city when farmers come to sell their fruit, vegetables, eggs, meat, etc. directly to customers

farmhand /ˈfɑːm.hænd/ [US] /ˈfɑːrm-/ *noun* [C] a person who is paid to work on a farm

farmhouse [HOUSE] /ˈfɑːm.haʊs/ [US] /ˈfɑːrm-/ *noun* [C] the main house on a farm where the FARMER lives

farmhouse [FOOD] /ˈfɑːm.haʊs/ [US] /ˈfɑːrm-/ *adj* [before n] describes food that is made using traditional methods: *farmhouse cheddar*

farmland /ˈfɑːm.lænd/ [US] /ˈfɑːrm-/ *noun* [U] land that is used for or is suitable for farming

farmstead /ˈfɑːm.sted/ [US] /ˈfɑːrm-/ *noun* [C] *US* the house belonging to a farm and the buildings around it

farmyard /ˈfɑːm.jɑːd/ [US] /ˈfɑːrm.jɑːrd/ *noun* [C] (*US USUALLY* **barnyard**) an area surrounded by or near farm buildings: *farmyard animals/smells*

far-off /ˌfɑːˈrɒf/ [US] /-ˈrɑːf/ *adj* **1** describes a time that is a long way from the present, or in the distant past or future: *some point in the far-off future* **2** describes a place that is a great distance away

far-out [STRANGE] /ˌfɑːˈraʊt/ *adj SLANG* strange and unusual: *I've seen the video – it's pretty far-out.*

far-out [EXCELLENT] /ˌfɑːˈraʊt/ *exclamation OLD-FASHIONED SLANG* excellent: *You got the job? Far-out!*

farrago /fəˈrɑː.gəʊ/ [US] /-goʊ/ *noun* [C] *plural* **farragos** or *US* **farragoes** *FORMAL DISAPPROVING* a confused mixture: *He told us a farrago **of** lies.*

far-reaching /ˌfɑːˈriː.tʃɪŋ/ [US] /ˌfɑːr-/ *adj* Something far-reaching has a great influence on many people or things: *These new laws will have far-reaching benefits for all working mothers.*

farrier /ˈfær.i.əʳ/ [US] /-ɚ/ *noun* [C] *SPECIALIZED* a person who makes and fits metal plates for horses' feet

far-sighted [WISE] /ˌfɑːˈsaɪ.tɪd/ [US] /ˌfɑːrˈsaɪ.t̬ɪd/ *adj UK* having good judgment about what will be needed in the future and making wise decisions based on this: *Buying those shares was a very far-sighted move – they must be worth ten times their original value now.*

far-sighted [SEEING] *US* /ˌfɑːˈsaɪ.tɪd/ [US] /ˌfɑːrˈsaɪ.t̬ɪd/ *adj* (*UK* **long-sighted**) describes someone who has difficulty seeing things that are close: *I'm so far-sighted, I can't read the newspaper without my glasses.*

fart [GAS] /fɑːt/ [US] /fɑːrt/ *verb* [I] *VERY INFORMAL* to release gas from the bowels through the bottom

fart /fɑːt/ [US] /fɑːrt/ *noun* [C] *VERY INFORMAL* an escape of gas from the bowels: *to do a fart*

fart [PERSON] /fɑːt/ [US] /fɑːrt/ *noun* [C] *OFFENSIVE* a boring, annoying or unpleasant person: *He's a pompous **old** fart.*

▲ **fart about/around** *phrasal verb UK OFFENSIVE* to waste time doing silly or useless things: *Stop farting about and help me tidy up.*

farther /ˈfɑː.ðəʳ/ [US] /ˈfɑːr.ðɚ/ *adv, comparative of* **far** DISTANCE; to a greater distance: *How much farther is it to the airport?* ○ *The fog's so thick, I can't see farther **than** about ten metres.* ➲See Note **further or farther?** at **further** GREATER DISTANCE. **farther** /ˈfɑː.ðəʳ/ [US] /ˈfɑːr.ðɚ/ *adj*: *It was farther to the shops **than** I expected.* ○ *He swam to the farther side of the lake.*

farthest /ˈfɑː.ðɪst/ [US] /ˈfɑːr-/ *adv, superlative of* **far** DISTANCE: *What's the farthest you've ever run?* ➲See usage note at **furthest**. **farthest** /ˈfɑː.ðɪst/ /ˈfɑː-/ *adj*: *The farthest landmark visible is about 30km away.*

farthing /ˈfɑː.ðɪŋ/ [US] /ˈfɑːr-/ *noun* [C] a coin worth a quarter of a PENNY in old British money

fascia [VEHICLE] /ˈfeɪ.ʃə/ *noun* [C] *UK FORMAL* the DASHBOARD in a motor vehicle

fascia [SHOP] /ˈfeɪ.ʃə/ *noun* [C] the sign above the window of a shop, where the shop's name is written

fascinate /ˈfæs.ɪ.neɪt/ *verb* [T] to interest someone a lot: *Science has always fascinated me.* ○ *Anything to do with aeroplanes and flying fascinates him.*

fascinated /ˈfæs.ɪ.neɪ.tɪd/ [US] /-t̬ɪd/ *adj* extremely interested: *We watched fascinated as he cleaned and repaired the watch.* ○ *I was fascinated **to** hear about his travels in Bhután.* ○ *They were absolutely fascinated by the game.*

fascinating /ˈfæs.ɪ.neɪ.tɪŋ/ [US] /-t̬ɪŋ/ *adj* extremely interesting: *The book offers a fascinating glimpse of the lives of the rich and famous.* ○ *I found the whole film fascinating.*

fascination /ˌfæs.ɪˈneɪ.ʃən/ *noun* [S or U] when you find someone or something fascinating: *Miller's fascination **with** medieval art dates from her childhood.* ○ *Mass murders **hold** a gruesome fascination **for** the public.*

Fascism /ˈfæʃ.ɪ.zəm/ *noun* [U] a political system based on a very powerful leader, state control and extreme pride in country and race, and in which political opposition is not allowed **fascist** /ˈfæʃ.ɪst/ *adj* (*ALSO* **fascistic**) *fascist groups* ○ *a fascist dictator/regime*

fascist /ˈfæʃ.ɪst/ *noun* [C] **1** someone who supports fascism **2** a person of the far RIGHT in politics **3** *DISAPPROVING* someone who does not allow any opposition: *He reckons all policemen are fascists and bullies.*

fashion [CLOTHING] /ˈfæʃ.ən/ *noun* [C or U] a style that is popular at a particular time, especially in clothes, hair, make-up, etc: *Long hair is back **in** fashion for men.* ○ *Fur coats have gone **out of** fashion.* ○ *a programme with features on pop music, sport and fashion* ○ *She buys all **the latest** fashion magazines.* ○ *There was a fashion for keeping reptiles as pets.*

• **follow (a) fashion** to do what is popular at the time

fashionable /ˈfæʃ.ən.ə.bl/ *adj* **1** popular at a particular time: *a fashionable nightclub/restaurant* ○ *fashionable ideas/clothes* ○ ***It's** not fashionable **to** wear short skirts at the moment.* **2** wearing clothes, doing things and going to places that are in fashion: *A fashionable couple posed elegantly at the next table.* **fashionably** /ˈfæʃ.ən.ə.bli/ *adv*: *fashionably dressed*

fashion [MANNER] /ˈfæʃ.ən/ *noun* [S] a way of doing things: *The rebel army behaved in a brutal fashion.*

• **after a fashion** If you can do something after a fashion, you can do it, but not well: *I can cook, after a fashion.*

fashion [MAKE] /ˈfæʃ.ən/ *verb* [T] *FORMAL* to make something using your hands: *He fashioned a hat for himself **from/out of** newspaper.*

fashion-conscious /ˈfæʃ.ənˌkɒn.tʃəs/ [US] /-ˌkɑːn-/ *adj* interested in the latest fashions and in wearing fashionable clothes: *your average fashion-conscious teenager*

ˈfashion ˌshow *noun* [C] a show for the public where MODELS wear new styles of clothes

ˈfashion ˌstatement *noun* [C] clothes that you wear or something else that you own in order to attract attention and show other people the type of person you are: *I thought I'd be bold and **make** a fashion statement.*

ˈfashion ˌvictim *noun* [C] someone who always wears very fashionable clothes even if the clothes sometimes make them look silly

fast [QUICK] /fɑːst/ [US] /fæst/ *adj* **1** moving or happening quickly, or able to move or happen quickly: *fast cars* ○ *a fast swimmer* ○ *Computers are getting faster all the time.* ○ *The fast train* (= one that stops at fewer stations and travels quickly) *to London takes less than an hour.* **2** If your watch or clock is fast, it shows a time that is later than the correct time. **3** *SPECIALIZED* describes photographic film which allows you to take pictures when

F

there is not much light or when things are moving quickly

• **fast and furious** describes something that is full of speed and excitement: *It's not a relaxing film – it's pretty fast and furious.*

fast /fɑːst/ ⓤ /fæst/ *adv* quickly: *The accident was caused by people driving too fast in bad conditions.* ○ *You'll have to act fast.* ○ *Children's publishing is a fast-growing business.*

• **as fast as your legs would carry you** as quickly as possible: *He scuttled back into the house as fast as his legs would carry him.*

fast FIXED /fɑːst/ ⓤ /fæst/ *adv, adj* firmly fixed: *The glue had set and my hand was **stuck** fast.* ○ *He tried to get away, but she held him fast.*

• **hold/stand fast** to firmly remain in the same position or maintain the same opinion: *The rebels are standing fast and refuse to be defeated.* ○ *He held fast **to** his principles.*

fast /fɑːst/ ⓤ /fæst/ *adj* If the colour of an item of clothing is fast, the colour does not come out of the cloth when it is washed.

fastness /ˈfɑːst.nəs/ ⓤ /ˈfæst-/ *noun* [U] how fast (= fixed) something is: *Test clothes for **colour** fastness before washing.*

fast NOT EAT /fɑːst/ ⓤ /fæst/ *noun* [C] a period of time when you eat no food: *Hundreds of prisoners began a fast in protest about prison conditions.* **fast** /fɑːst/ ⓤ /fæst/ *verb* [I] *One day a week he fasts for health reasons.*

fast IMMORAL /fɑːst/ ⓤ /fæst/ *adj* OLD-FASHIONED DISAPPROVING without moral principles: *a fast crowd* ○ *a fast woman*

fastball /ˈfɑːst.bɔːl/ ⓤ /ˈfæst.bɑːl/ *noun* [C] US a type of high-speed throw in baseball: *The pitcher wound up and let loose a fastball.*

fasten /ˈfɑː.sⁿn/ ⓤ /ˈfæs.ⁿn/ *verb* [I or T] **1** to (cause something to) become firmly fixed together, or in position, or closed: *Make sure your seat belt is securely fastened.* ○ *This shirt fastens at the back.* **2 fasten *sth* on/to/together, etc.** to fix one thing to another: *I fastened the sticker to the windscreen.*

fastener /ˈfɑː.sⁿn.əʳ/ ⓤ /ˈfæs.ⁿn.ɚ/ *noun* [C] a button, zip or other device for temporarily joining together the parts of things such as clothes

fastening /ˈfɑː.sⁿn.ɪŋ/ ⓤ /ˈfæs-/ *noun* [C] a device on a window, door, box, etc. for keeping it closed

▲ **fasten on/upon *sth*** *phrasal verb* to give attention to something, because it is of special interest or often because you think it is the cause of a problem: *The tabloid newspapers have fastened on popular psychology.* ○ *My mind fastened on his admission that he was an agent.*

fast food *noun* [U] hot food such as a BURGER that is quick to cook or is already cooked and is therefore served very quickly in a restaurant

fast food restaurant /ˌfɑːstˈfuːd.res.trɒnt/ ⓤ /ˌfæstˈfuːd.res.tə.rɑːnt/ *noun* [C] a restaurant that serves fast food such as BURGERS

fast-forward /ˌfɑːstˈfɔː.wəd/ ⓤ /ˌfæstˈfɔːr.wɚd/ *verb* [I or T] If you fast-forward a recording, or if it fast-forwards, you make it play at very high speed so that you get to the end or a later part more quickly: *I hate this song – I'll fast-forward to the next one.* ○ *The tape jammed while I was fast-forwarding it.*

the fast-forward *noun* [S] the part of a piece of electronic equipment that allows you to fast-forward

fastidious /fæsˈtɪd.i.əs/ *adj* **1** giving too much attention to small details and wanting everything to be correct and perfect: *He is very fastidious **about** how a suitcase should be packed.* **2** having a strong dislike of anything dirty or unpleasant: *They were too fastidious to eat in a fast-food restaurant.* **fastidiously** /fæsˈtɪd.i.ə.sli/ *adv*: *fastidiously clean/dressed* **fastidiousness** /fæsˈtɪd.i.ə.snəs/ *noun* [U]

fast lane *noun* [S] the part of a main road, such as a motorway, where vehicles travel at the fastest speed

• **life in the fast lane** a way of living which is full of excitement, activity and often danger: *Parties, drugs,*

and a stream of glamorous women – his was a life in the fast lane.

fastness /ˈfɑːst.nəs/ ⓤ /ˈfæst-/ *noun* [C] LITERARY a safe place, such as a FORTRESS: *a mountain fastness*

fast-talk /ˈfɑːst.tɔːk/ ⓤ /ˈfæst.tɑːk/ *verb* [T] MAINLY US DISAPPROVING to persuade people with a lot of quick, clever, but usually dishonest talk: *He fast-talked his way **into** a powerful job.*

fast-talker /ˈfɑːst.tɔː.kəʳ/ ⓤ /ˈfæst.tɑː.kɚ/ *noun* [C] INFORMAL DISAPPROVING someone who is good at persuading people to do what he or she wants

fast track *noun* [S] the quickest, but usually most competitive, route to success or advancement: *A degree in computer science offers a fast track to the top.* **fast-track** /ˈfɑːst.træk/ ⓤ /ˈfæst-/ *adj* [before n] *fast-track opportunities* ○ *They've introduced a fast-track **system** for brighter pupils which will allow thousands to take their GCSE exams two years early.*

fat BIG /fæt/ *adj* **fatter**, **fattest 1** having a lot of flesh on the body: *Like most women, she thinks she's fat.* ○ *I have horrible fat thighs.* ○ *He eats all the time but he never **gets** fat.* **2** thick or large: *He lifted a fat volume down from the shelf.* ○ *Some producers of mineral water have made fat profits.*

fatness /ˈfæt.nəs/ *noun* [U] when someone or something is fat: *Fatness often runs in families.*

fatty /ˈfæt.i/ ⓤ /ˈfæt̬-/ *noun* [C] (*ALSO* **fatso**) INFORMAL DISAPPROVING OR HUMOROUS a fat person

fat SUBSTANCE /fæt/ *noun* **1** [U] the substance under the skin of humans and animals that stores energy and keeps them warm: *body fat* ○ *Women have a layer of subcutaneous fat (= fat under the skin), which provides them with better insulation than men.* **2** [C or U] a solid or liquid substance obtained from animals or plants and used especially in cooking: *This product contains no animal fat.* ○ *I only use vegetable fats in cooking.*

• **live off the fat of the land** to be rich enough to enjoy the best of everything

• **The fat is in the fire.** INFORMAL said when something has been said or done that will cause a lot of trouble

fatty /ˈfæt.i/ ⓤ /ˈfæt̬-/ *adj* containing a lot of fat: *Goose is a very fatty meat.*

fat NO /fæt/ *adj* [before n] INFORMAL used in some phrases to mean very little or none: *A fat **lot** of use you are (= You are not useful in any way)!* ○ *He knows it upsets me, but a fat **lot** he cares (= he doesn't care).*

• **fat chance** INFORMAL used to say that you definitely do not think that something is likely to happen: *"Perhaps they'll invite you." "Fat chance (of that)!"*

fatal /ˈfeɪ.tⁿl/ ⓤ /-t̬ⁿl/ *adj* **1** A fatal illness or accident, etc. causes death: *This illness is fatal in almost all cases.* ○ *the fatal shooting of an unarmed 15-year-old* **2** very serious and having an important bad effect on the future: *He made the fatal **mistake/error** of believing what they told him.* ○ *It just shows how you should never say how well things are going for you – it's fatal (= it causes bad things to happen).*

fatally /ˈfeɪ.tⁿl.i/ ⓤ /-t̬ⁿl.i/ *adv*: *Several people were injured, two fatally (= they died as a result).*

fatality /fəˈtæl.ə.ti/ ⓤ /-t̬i/ *noun* [C] a death caused by an accident or by violence, or someone who has died in either of these ways: *Britain has thousands of road fatalities (= deaths on roads) every year.* ○ *The first fatalities of the war were civilians.*

fatalism /ˈfeɪ.tⁿl.ɪ.zⁿm/ ⓤ /-t̬ⁿl-/ *noun* [U] the belief that people cannot change the way events will happen and that events, especially bad ones, cannot be avoided **fatalist** /ˈfeɪ.tⁿl.ɪst/ ⓤ /-t̬ⁿl-/ *noun* [C] **fatalistic** /ˌfeɪ.tⁿl-ˈɪs.tɪk/ ⓤ /-t̬ⁿl-/ *adj*: *Being fatalistic about your chances will do no good.* **fatalistically** /ˌfeɪ.tⁿl-ˈɪs.tɪ.kli/ ⓤ /-t̬ⁿl-/ *adv*

fat cat *noun* [C often pl] DISAPPROVING someone who has a lot of money, especially someone in charge of a company who has the power to increase their own pay: *The report criticised boardroom fat cats who award themselves huge pay increases.* ○ *fat cat bosses/directors*

fate /feɪt/ *noun* **1** [C usually sing] what happens to a particular person or thing, especially something final or negative, such as death or defeat: *We want to **decide** our* *own fate.* ○ *His fate is now in the hands of the jury.* ○ *The disciples were terrified that they would **suffer/meet** the same fate as Jesus.* **2** [U] a power that some people believe causes and controls all events, so that you cannot change or control the way things will happen: *When we met again by chance in Cairo, I felt it must be fate.* ○ *Fate has brought us together.*

• **a fate worse than death** INFORMAL HUMOROUS something you do not want to experience because it is so unpleasant: *When you're 16, an evening at home with your parents seems like a fate worse than death.*

• **the Fates** three goddesses whom the ancient Greeks believed controlled people's lives and decided when people must die

fated /ˈfeɪ.tɪd/ [US] /-t̬ɪd/ *adj* [after v] not able to be avoided because planned by a power that controls events: [+ *that*] *It seemed fated **that** we would get married.* ○ [+ to infinitive] *She says she was fated **to** become a writer.*

fateful /ˈfeɪt.fəl/ *adj* [before n] having an important and usually negative effect on the future: *the fateful **day** of President Kennedy's assassination* ○ *He made the fateful decision to send in the troops.*

fat-free /ˌfætˈfriː/ *adj* describes food that contains no fat

fathead /ˈfæt.hed/ *noun* [C] INFORMAL a stupid person

fatheaded /ˌfætˈhed.ɪd/ *adj*

father [PARENT] /ˈfɑː.ðəʳ/ [US] /-ðɚ/ *noun* [C] a male parent: *My father took me to watch the football every Saturday.*

• **the father of *sth*** the man who began something or first made something important: *Freud was the father of psychiatry.*

father /ˈfɑː.ðəʳ/ [US] /-ðɚ/ *verb* [T] to become the father of a child by making a woman pregnant: *He's fathered three children.*

fatherhood /ˈfɑː.ðə.hʊd/ [US] /-ðɚ-/ *noun* [U] the state or time of being a father: *Fatherhood is a lifelong responsibility.*

fatherless /ˈfɑː.ðə.ləs/ [US] /-ðɚ-/ *adj* without a father: *fatherless children*

fatherly /ˈfɑː.ðəl.i/ [US] /-ðɚ.li/ *adj* describes a man or male behaviour typical of a kind and caring father: *fatherly **advice***

Father [PRIEST] /ˈfɑː.ðəʳ/ [US] /-ðɚ/ *noun* [C] **1** (*WRITTEN ABBREVIATION* **Fr**) (the title of) a Christian priest, especially a Roman Catholic or Orthodox priest: *Father O'Reilly* ○ [as form of address] *Are you giving a sermon, Father?* **2** a name for the Christian God: *God the Father* ○ *Our Father, who art in heaven...*

ˌFather ˈChristmas *noun* MAINLY UK an imaginary old man with long white hair and a beard and a red coat who is believed by children to bring them presents at Christmas, or a person who dresses as this character for children

ˈfather ˌfigure *noun* [C] an older man whom you treat like a father, especially by asking for his advice, help or support

father-in-law /ˈfɑː.ðəʳ.ɪn.lɔː/ [US] /-ðɚ.ɪn.lɑː/ *noun* [C] *plural* **fathers-in-law** the father of the person you are married to

fatherland /ˈfɑː.ðə.lænd/ [US] /-ðɚ-/ *noun* [C usually sing] (*ALSO* **motherland**) the country in which you were born, or the country with which you feel most connected

fathom [MEASUREMENT] /ˈfæð.əm/ *noun* [C] a unit for measuring the depth of water, equal to 1.8 metres or 6 feet

fathomless /ˈfæð.əm.ləs/ *adj* LITERARY too deep to be measured: *a fathomless ocean* ○ FIGURATIVE *She gazed into the fathomless **depths** of his brown eyes.*

fathom [UNDERSTAND] /ˈfæð.əm/ *verb* [T] **1** to discover the meaning of something: *For years people have been trying to fathom **(out)** the mysteries of the whale's song.* **2** to understand someone or why someone acts as they do: *I can't fathom her at all.*

fathomless /ˈfæð.əm.ləs/ *adj* LITERARY impossible to understand: *I'm afraid it's a fathomless mystery.*

fatigue /fəˈtiːg/ *noun* [U] **1** FORMAL extreme tiredness: *She was **suffering from** fatigue and a stress-related illness.* **2** SPECIALIZED weakness in something, such as a metal part or structure, often caused by repeated bending: *The crash was caused by **metal** fatigue in one of the propeller blades.* ➲See also **compassion fatigue**.

fatigue /fəˈtiːg/ *verb* [T] OLD USE OR FORMAL to make someone extremely tired: *The journey had fatigued him.*

fatigued /fəˈtiːgd/ *adj* [after v] FORMAL tired

fatiguing /fəˈtiː.gɪŋ/ *adj* FORMAL OR OLD-FASHIONED tiring: *Loading and unloading ships is dirty and fatiguing work.*

fatigues /fəˈtiːgz/ *plural noun* **1** SPECIALIZED a loose brownish green uniform worn by soldiers: ***army** fatigues* **2** work such as cleaning or cooking, done by soldiers, often as punishment: *Get dressed right now or you'll find yourself **on** fatigues.*

fatness /ˈfæt.nəs/ *noun* [U] ➲See at **fat** BIG.

fatso /ˈfæt.səʊ/ [US] /-soʊ/ *noun* [C] INFORMAL DISAPPROVING a fat person: *Hey, fatso!*

fatted /ˈfæt.ɪd/ [US] /ˈfæt̬-/ *adj* ➲See **kill the fatted calf** at **kill**.

fatten /ˈfæt.ən/ [US] /ˈfæt̬-/ *verb*

▲ **fatten *sb/sth* up** *phrasal verb* [M] to give an animal or a thin person lots of food so that they become fatter: *These cattle are being fattened up for slaughter.* ○ HUMOROUS *You're just trying to fatten me up.*

fattening /ˈfæt.ən.ɪŋ/ [US] /ˈfæt̬-/ *adj* describes food that contains a lot of fat, sugar, etc. that would quickly make you fatter if you ate a lot of it: *fattening food, such as cheese and chocolate*

ˌfatty ˈacid *noun* [C] any of a group of chemicals, most of which are involved in cell operation in the body

fatuous /ˈfæt.ju.əs/ *adj* FORMAL stupid, not correct, or not carefully thought about: *a fatuous idea/remark* **fatuously** /ˈfæt.ju.ə.sli/ *adv* **fatuousness** /ˈfæt.ju.əs.nəs/ *noun* [U]

fatwa /ˈfæt.wɑː/ *noun* [C] an official statement or order from an Islamic religious leader

faucet /ˈfɔː.sɪt/ [US] /ˈfɑː-/ *noun* [C] US FOR **tap** DEVICE ➲See picture **In the Kitchen** on page Centre 16

fault [MISTAKE] /fɒlt/ [US] /fɑːlt/ *noun* **1** [U] a mistake, especially something for which you are to blame: *It's not my fault she didn't come!* ○ *She believes it was the doctor's fault that Peter died.* ○ *The fault **was/lay with** the organizers, who failed to make the necessary arrangements for dealing with so many people.* ○ ***Through no** fault **of his own**, he spent a week locked up in jail.* **2** [C] a weakness in a person's character: *He has many faults, but dishonesty isn't one of them.* **3** [C] a broken part or weakness in a machine or system: *The car has a serious design fault.* ○ *I think it's got an **electrical** fault.* ○ *For all its faults, our transport system is still better than that in many other countries.* **4** [C] a mistake made when hitting the ball over the net, in tennis or a similar game, to begin a game

• **be at fault** to have done something wrong: *Her doctor was at fault **for/in** not sending her straight to a specialist.*

• **find fault with *sb/sth*** to criticize someone or something, especially without good reasons: *He's always finding fault with my work.*

• **be kind/generous, etc. to a fault** to be extremely kind/generous, etc: *She's a really sweet person and she's generous to a fault.*

fault /fɒlt/ [US] /fɑːlt/ *verb* **1** [T] to find a reason to criticize someone or something: *I can't fault the way they dealt with the complaint.* ○ *I can't fault you **on** your logic.* **2** [I] to hit a fault in tennis and other similar games: *That's the fourth serve he's faulted **on** today.*

faultless /ˈfɒlt.ləs/ [US] /ˈfɑːlt-/ *adj* APPROVING perfect and without any mistakes: *a faultless performance* ○ *speaking faultless French* **faultlessly** /ˈfɒlt.lə.sli/ [US] /ˈfɑːlt-/ *adv*

faulty /ˈfɒl.ti/ [US] /ˈfɑːl.t̬i/ *adj* A faulty machine or device is not perfectly made or does not work correctly: *faulty wiring/brakes*

COMMON LEARNER ERROR

fault or **mistake/error?**

Use **fault** when explaining who is responsible for something bad.

It's my fault that the car was stolen. I left the window open.

~~*It's my mistake the car was stolen. I left the window open.*~~

F

Use **mistake** or **error** for talking about something that you did or thought which was wrong. **Error** is slightly more formal than **mistake**.

I still make lots of mistakes in my essays.
We lost a week's work due to a computer error.
~~I still make lots of faults in my essays.~~

***

fault CRACK /fɒlt/ ⑤ /fɑːlt/ *noun* [C] SPECIALIZED a crack in the Earth's surface where the rock has divided into two parts which move against each other: *Surveyors say the fault line is capable of generating a major earthquake once in a hundred years.*

faun /fɔːn/ ⑤ /fɑːn/ *noun* [C] an imaginary creature which is like a small man with a goat's back legs, tail, ears and horns

fauna /ˈfɔːnə/ ⑤ /ˈfɑː-/ *group noun* [U] SPECIALIZED all the animals that live wild in a particular area: *an expedition to explore the flora and fauna of Hornchurch Wood*

faux /fəʊ/ ⑤ /foʊ/ *adj* [before n] not real, but made to look or seem real; false: *faux fur* ○ *a faux-brick wall*

faux pas /ˌfəʊˈpɑː/ ⑤ /ˌfoʊ-/ *noun* [C] *plural* **faux pas** words or behaviour that are a social mistake or not polite: *I made some remark about his wife's family then realized I'd made a serious faux pas.*

fave /feɪv/ *noun* [C], *adj* INFORMAL FOR **favourite**: *"Does anyone want a sweet?" "Ooh thanks, they're my faves."*

favour SUPPORT *UK, US* **favor** /ˈfeɪvər/ ⑤ /-vər/ *noun* [U] the support or approval of something or someone: *These plans are unlikely to find favour unless the cost is reduced.* ○ *The Council voted in favour of a £200 million housing development.* ○ *She is out of favour (= unpopular) with her colleagues.* ○ *Her economic theories are in favour (= popular) with the current government.* ○ *He sent her presents in an attempt to win her favour.*
• **in your favour** When something is in your favour, it gives you an advantage: *This candidate has a lot in her favour, especially her experience of teaching.*
• **find in sb's favour** If a judge finds in someone's favour, they say that they are not guilty.

favour *UK, US* **favor** /ˈfeɪvər/ ⑤ /-vər/ *verb* [T] **1** to support or prefer one particular possibility: *These are the running shoes favoured by marathon runners.* ○ *In the survey, a majority of people favoured higher taxes and better public services over (= rather than) tax cuts.* ○ [+ v-ing] *I generally favour travelling by night, when the roads are quiet.* **2** to give an advantage to someone or something, in an unfair way: *A strong wind will favour the bigger boats.* ○ *She always felt that her parents favoured her brother.*

favourable *UK, US* **favorable** /ˈfeɪvərəbl/ ⑤ /-vər-/ *adj* **1** showing that you like or approve of someone or something: *We have had a favourable response to the plan so far.* ✻ NOTE: The opposite of favourable is **unfavourable**. **2** making you support or approve of someone or something: *She made a very favourable impression on us.* **3** giving you an advantage or more chance of success: *favourable weather conditions*

favourably *UK, US* **favorably** /ˈfeɪvərəbli/ ⑤ /-vər-/ *adv*: *Our products compare favourably with (= are as good as, or better than) all the leading brands.*

favoured *UK, US* **favored** /ˈfeɪvəd/ ⑤ /-vərd/ *adj*

favour KIND ACT *UK, US* **favor** /ˈfeɪvər/ ⑤ /-vər/ *noun* **1** [C] a kind action that you do for someone: *She rang up to ask me a favour.* ○ *Could you do me a favour – would you feed my cat this weekend?* **2** [C usually pl] when you favour someone by giving them an advantage, such as money or a good job: *Several politicians were accused of dispensing favours to people who voted for them.*
• **Do me/us a favour!** INFORMAL something you say in answer to a ridiculous and impossible suggestion: *"Why don't you tell the police what happened?" "Oh, do me a favour!"*
• **be free with your favours** OLD-FASHIONED to be willing to have sex with lots of people: *She's rather too free with her favours, from what I hear.*
▲ **favour sb with sth** *phrasal verb* FORMAL to be polite and kind enough to give something to someone: *I've no idea what is happening – David has not favoured me with an explanation.*

favourite *UK, US* **favorite** /ˈfeɪvᵊr.ɪt/ *adj* [before n] best liked or most enjoyed: *"What's your favourite colour?" "Green."* ○ *my favourite restaurant/book/song*

favourite *UK, US* **favorite** /ˈfeɪvᵊr.ɪt/ *noun* [C] **1** a favourite thing: *How clever of you to buy chocolate chip cookies – they're my favourites.* **2** a person who is treated with special kindness by someone in authority: *the teacher's favourite* **3** the person or animal most people expect to win a race or competition: *Great Gold is the favourite in the 2.00 race at Epsom.* ○ [+ to infinitive] *Brazil are favourites to win this year's World Cup.*

favouritism *UK, US* **favoritism** /ˈfeɪvᵊr.ɪ.tɪ.zᵊm/ *noun* [U] DISAPPROVING unfair support shown to one person or group, especially by someone in authority: *A parent must be careful not to show favouritism towards any one of their children.*

favourite 'son *UK, US* **favorite son** *noun* [S] a famous person, especially a politician, who is supported and praised by people in the area they come from

fawn DEER /fɔːn/ ⑤ /fɑːn/ *noun* [C] a young deer

fawn BROWN /fɔːn/ ⑤ /fɑːn/ *adj, noun* [U] (having) a pale yellowish brown colour

fawn /fɔːn/ ⑤ /fɑːn/ *verb*

PHRASAL VERBS WITH **fawn** ▼

▲ **fawn on/upon sb** *phrasal verb* If an animal such as a dog fawns on/upon you, it is very friendly towards you and rubs itself against you.

▲ **fawn over/on sb** *phrasal verb* DISAPPROVING to praise someone too much and give them a lot of attention which is not sincere in order to get a positive reaction: *I hate waiters who fawn over you.*

fawning /ˈfɔː.nɪŋ/ ⑤ /ˈfɑː-/ *adj*: *a fawning young man*

fax /fæks/ *noun* **1** [C] (a copy of) a document that travels in electronic form along a telephone line and is then printed on paper: *I'll send you a fax with the details of the proposal.* **2** [C or U] (ALSO **fax machine**) a device or system used to send and receive documents in electronic form along a telephone line: *I'll send you the agenda by fax.* ○ *Have you got a fax at home?* �‌See picture **In the Office** on page Centre 15

fax /fæks/ *verb* [T] to send a document using a fax machine: *I'll fax it (through/over/across) to you.* ○ [+ two objects] *Fax me your reply/Fax your reply to me.*

faze /feɪz/ *verb* [T not continuous] INFORMAL to surprise and worry someone: *No one is fazed by the sight of guns here any more.*

the FBI /ˌðiː.ef.biːˈaɪ/ *group noun* [S] ABBREVIATION FOR the Federal Bureau of Investigation: one of the national police forces in the US controlled by the central government

fear /fɪər/ ⑤ /fɪr/ *noun* [C or U] an unpleasant emotion or thought that you have when you are frightened or worried by something dangerous, painful or bad that is happening or might happen: *Trembling with fear, she handed over the money to the gunman.* ○ *Even when the waves grew big, the boy showed no (signs of) fear.* ○ *I have a fear of heights.* ○ *The low profit figures simply confirmed my worst fears.* ○ [+ that] *There are fears that the disease will spread to other countries.*
• **be in fear of your life** to be frightened that you might be killed: *Lakisha sat inside, in fear of her life, until the police came.*
• **be no fear of sth** INFORMAL to be no possibility that a particular thing will happen: *Malcolm knows the city well, so there's no fear of us getting lost (= we will not get lost).*
• **for fear that/of sth** because you are worried that a particular thing might happen: *They wouldn't let their cat outside for fear (that) it would get run over.* ○ *I didn't want to move for fear of waking her up.*
• **No fear!** UK SLANG certainly not: *"Are you coming to the concert?" "No fear!"*
• **put the fear of God into you** to frighten you a lot
• **without fear or favour** in an equal and fair way: *The appointments are supposed to be made without fear or favour.*

fear /fɪər/ ⑤ /fɪr/ *verb* **1** [T not continuous] to be frightened of something or someone unpleasant: *Most older employ-*

ees fear unemployment. ○ *What do you fear most?* **2** [not continuous] *FORMAL* to be worried or frightened that something bad might happen or might have happened: [+ (that)] *Police fear* ***(that)*** *the couple may have drowned.* ○ [+ (that)] *FORMAL* ***It is*** *feared* ***(that)*** *as many as two hundred passengers may have died in the crash.* ○ *We huddled together, fearing we might be killed.* ○ [+ to infinitive] *Fearing* ***to*** *go herself, she sent her son to find out the news.* **3 I fear** *FORMAL* used to give someone news of something bad that has happened or might happen: [+ (that)] *I fear* ***(that)*** *she's already left.*

• **never fear** (*ALSO* **fear not**) *OLD USE OR HUMOROUS* do not worry: *Never fear, I'll take good care of him.*

fearful /ˈfɪə.fᵊl/ [US] /ˈfɪr-/ *adj* **1** *SLIGHTLY FORMAL* frightened or worried about something: *He hesitated before ringing her, fearful* ***of*** *what she might say.* ○ *She's fearful* ***(that)*** *she may lose custody of her children.* **2** *UK OLD-FASHIONED* very bad: *a fearful argument* ○ *a fearful temper*

fearfully /ˈfɪə.fᵊl.i/ [US] /ˈfɪr-/ *adv* **1** with fear: *Fearfully, he walked closer to the edge.* **2** *UK OLD-FASHIONED* extremely: *These cakes are fearfully good.* **fearfulness** /ˈfɪə.fᵊl.nəs/ [US] /ˈfɪr-/ *noun* [U]

fearless /ˈfɪə.ləs/ [US] /ˈfɪr-/ *adj* having no fear: *a fearless fighter* **fearlessly** /ˈfɪə.lə.sli/ [US] /ˈfɪr-/ *adv*: *They fought fearlessly against the invading armies.* **fearlessness** /ˈfɪə.lə.snəs/ [US] /ˈfɪr-/ *noun* [U]

fearsome /ˈfɪə.səm/ [US] /ˈfɪr-/ *adj FORMAL* frightening: *a fearsome reputation* ○ *a fearsome display of violence* **fearsomely** /ˈfɪə.səm.li/ [US] /ˈfɪr-/ *adv*

▲ **fear for *sb/sth*** *phrasal verb FORMAL* to be worried about something, or to be worried that someone is in danger: *Her parents fear for her safety.*

feasible /ˈfiː.zə.bl̩/ *adj SLIGHTLY FORMAL* **1** able to be made, done or achieved: *With the extra resources, the scheme now seems feasible.* ○ [+ to infinitive] *It may be feasible to clone human beings, but is it ethical?* **2** possible or reasonable: ***It's*** *quite feasible* ***(that)*** *we'll get the money.*

feasibly /ˈfiː.zə.bli/ *adv*

feasibility /ˌfiː.zəˈbɪl.ɪ.ti/ [US] /-ə.t̬i/ *noun* [U] whether something is feasible: *We're looking at the feasibility* ***of*** *building a shopping centre there.* ○ *to carry out/conduct a feasibility* ***study***

feast [FOOD] /fiːst/ *noun* **1** [C] a special meal with very good food or a large meal for many people: *"What a feast!" she said, surveying all the dishes on the table.* ○ *a wedding feast* **2** [S] a very enjoyable experience for the senses, especially a visual or musical experience: *a* ***visual*** *feast* ○ *His food is a feast* ***for the eyes*** *as well as the palate.* **3** [S] a collection of something to be enjoyed: *The team contains a veritable feast* ***of*** *international talent.*

feast [CELEBRATION] /fiːst/ *noun* [C] a day on which a religious event or person is remembered and celebrated: *the Feast of St James/the Passover* ○ *a Muslim feast day*

feast /fiːst/ *verb*

▲ **feast on *sth*** *phrasal verb LITERARY* to eat a lot of good food and enjoy it very much: *We feasted on smoked salmon and champagne.*

• **feast *your* eyes on *sth/sb*** *LITERARY* to look at someone or something with great enjoyment: *As you cruise the waterways, feast your eyes on the gorgeous views of the illuminated city.*

feat /fiːt/ *noun* [C] something difficult needing a lot of skill, strength, bravery, etc. to achieve it: *The Eiffel Tower is a remarkable feat* ***of*** *engineering.* ○ *She's performed remarkable feats of organization for the office.*

• **be no mean feat** *INFORMAL* to be a great achievement: *Getting the job finished in under a week was no mean feat.*

feather /ˈfeð.əʳ/ [US] /-ɚ/ *noun* [C] one of the many soft light things which cover a bird's body, consisting of a long thin central part with hair-like material along each side: *peacock/ostrich feathers* ○ *feather* ***pillows*** (= those containing feathers) ○ *The bird* ***ruffled*** *its feathers.*

• **be (as) light as a feather** to be very light in weight

• **a feather in *your* cap** an achievement to be proud of: *It's a real feather in our cap to be representing Britain in this contest.*

feather /ˈfeð.əʳ/ [US] /-ɚ/ *verb* [T] *SPECIALIZED* to turn OARS (= poles with flat ends used to move a boat), so that the flat parts are horizontal above the water while you prepare for the next pull

• **feather *your* own nest** *MAINLY DISAPPROVING* to make yourself rich, especially in a way that is selfish or dishonest

feathered /ˈfeð.əd/ [US] /-ɚd/ *adj* having feathers: *HUMOROUS our feathered* ***friends*** (= birds)

feathery /ˈfeð.ᵊr.i/ [US] /-ɚ.i/ *adj* soft or delicate, or made of many very small and delicate pieces: *feathery clouds/foliage/leaves* ○ *feathery blond hair*

featherbed /ˌfeð.əˈbed/ [US] /-ɚ-/ *verb* [T] **-dd-** *DISAPPROVING* to protect someone, especially a group of workers, too much and make things easy for them **featherbedding** /ˌfeð.əˈbed.ɪŋ/ [US] /-ɚ-/ *noun* [U] *The taxpayer was forced to fund the featherbedding of a privatised Railtrack.*

ˌfeather ˈboa *noun* [C] a long thin item of clothing made of feathers, and worn around the neck, especially by women

featherbrained /ˈfeð.ə.breɪnd/ [US] /-ɚ-/ *adj* silly or often forgetting things

ˌfeather ˈduster *noun* [C] a stick with feathers fixed to one end, used for cleaning dust from delicate objects

featherweight /ˈfeð.ə.weɪt/ [US] /-ɚ-/ *noun* [C] a boxer who weighs more than a BANTAMWEIGHT but less than a LIGHTWEIGHT

feature [QUALITY] /ˈfiː.tʃəʳ/ [US] /-tʃɚ/ *noun* **1** [C] a typical quality or an important part of something: *The town's main features are its beautiful mosque and ancient marketplace.* ○ *Our latest model of phone has several new features.* ○ *A unique feature of these rock shelters was that they were dry.* **2** [C] a part of a building or of an area of land: *a geographical feature* ○ *This tour takes in the area's best-known natural features, including the Gullfoss waterfall.* ○ *The most striking feature of the house was a huge two-storey room running the entire breadth and height of the building.* **3** [C usually pl] one of the parts of someone's face, such as their eyes or nose, that you notice when you look at them: *He has wonderful strong features.* ○ ***regular*** (= even and attractive) *features* ○ *Her eyes are her* ***best*** *feature.*

feature /ˈfiː.tʃəʳ/ [US] /-tʃɚ/ *verb* [I + adv or prep; T] *SLIGHTLY FORMAL* to include someone or something as an important part: *The film features James Dean as a disaffected teenager.* ○ *This week's broadcast features a report on victims of domestic violence.* ○ *It's an Australian company whose logo features a red kangaroo.*

featureless /ˈfiː.tʃə.ləs/ [US] /-tʃɚ-/ *adj* looking the same in every part, usually in a way that most people consider to be boring: *a featureless desert* ○ *a grey featureless landscape*

feature [ARTICLE] /ˈfiː.tʃəʳ/ [US] /-tʃɚ/ *noun* [C] a special article in a newspaper or magazine, or a part of a television or radio broadcast, that deals with a particular subject: *a double-page feature* ***on*** *global warming*

ˈfeature (ˌfilm) *noun* [C] a film that is usually 90 or more minutes long

feature-length /ˈfiː.tʃə.leŋkθ/ [US] /-tʃɚ-/ *adj* [before n] describes a film or television play that is 90 or more minutes long

febrile [ACTIVE] /ˈfiː.braɪl/ [US] /ˈfeb.rɪl/ *adj LITERARY* extremely active, or too excited, imaginative or emotional: *She sang with febrile intensity.* ○ *He has a febrile* ***imagination.***

febrile [FEVER] /ˈfiː.braɪl/ [US] /ˈfeb.rɪl/ *adj SPECIALIZED* caused by a fever: *febrile* ***convulsions***

February /ˈfeb.ru.ᵊr.i/ [US] /-ruː.er-/ *noun* [C or U] (*WRITTEN ABBREVIATION* **Feb**) the second month of the year, after January and before March: *28(th) February/February 28(th)* ○ *I was born* ***on*** *the fifth of February/February the fifth/(MAINLY US) February fifth.* ○ *We moved house* ***last*** *February/are moving house* ***next*** *February.* ○ *Building work is expected to start* ***in*** *February.* ○ *It was a dull, cold February.*

feces /ˈfiː.siːz/ *plural noun MAINLY US FOR* **faeces**

feckless /ˈfek.ləs/ *adj FORMAL* describes people or behaviour with no energy and enthusiasm: *He was portrayed as a feckless drunk.*

fecund /'fek.ənd/ *adj FORMAL* **1** able to produce a lot of crops, fruit, babies, young animals, etc: *fecund nature/ soil* **2** active and productive: *a fecund career/ imagination* **fecundity** /fe'kʌn.də.ti/ ⓤ /-ṭi/ *noun* [U] *FORMAL*

fed FEED /fed/ *past simple and past participle of* **feed**

Fed OFFICER /fed/ *noun* [C] *US INFORMAL* a police officer or other representative of the central government: *The Feds completely screwed up the arrest.*

federal 'holiday *noun* [C] *US FOR* **national holiday**

the ˌFederal Re'serve *noun* [S] (*INFORMAL* **the Fed**) the CENTRAL BANK of the United States of America

federation /ˌfed.ər'eɪ.ʃən/ ⓤ /-ə'reɪ-/ *noun* **1** [C] a group of organizations, countries, regions, etc. that have joined together to form a larger organization or government: *The United States is a federation of 50 individual states.* **2** [U] the act of forming a federation: *The federation of the six original Australian states took place in 1901.* ○ *He's against European federation.*

federal /'fed.ər.ºl/ ⓤ /-ɚ.ºl/ *adj* **1** [before n] relating to the central government, and not to the government of a region, of some countries such as the United States: *the federal government* ○ *a federal agency/employee* **2** A federal system of government consists of a group of regions that is controlled by a central government. **federalism** /'fed.ər.ºl.ɪ.zºm/ ⓤ /-ɚ-/ *noun* [U] the system of giving power to a central authority **federalist** /'fed.ər.ºl.ɪst/ ⓤ /-ɚ-/ *noun* [C] someone who supports a federal system of government **federate** /'fed.ºr.eɪt/ ⓤ /-ə.reɪt/ *verb* [I or T] to join to form a federation

fedora /fə'dɔː.rə/ ⓤ /-'dɔːr.ə/ *noun* [C] a man's hat, like a TRILBY but with a wider brim ⊃See picture **Hairstyles and Hats** on page Centre 8

ˌfed 'up *adj* [after v] *INFORMAL* bored, annoyed or disappointed, especially by something that you have experienced for too long: *I'm fed up **with** my job.* ○ *He got fed up with all the travelling he had to do.*
• **fed up to the back teeth** *MAINLY UK INFORMAL* very fed up: *I'm fed up to the back teeth **with/of** being criticized all the time.*

fee /fiː/ *noun* [C] an amount of money paid for a particular piece of work or for a particular right or service: *legal fees* ○ *university fees* ○ *an entrance/ registration fee* ○ *We couldn't afford to pay the lawyer's fee.*

feeble /'fiː.bl̩/ *adj* **1** weak and without energy, strength or power: *He was a feeble, helpless old man.* ○ *The little lamp gave only a feeble light.* ○ *Opposition to the plan was rather feeble.* **2** not effective or good: *a feeble joke/ excuse* **feebly** /'fiː.bli/ *adv*

feeble-minded /ˌfiː.bl̩'maɪn.dɪd/ *adj* without an ordinary level of intelligence or unable to act or think in an intelligent way

feed GIVE FOOD /fiːd/ *verb* **fed, fed 1** [T] to give food to a person, group or animal: *I usually feed the neighbour's cat while she's away.* ○ *Let's feed the kids first and have our dinner after.* ○ [+ two objects] *Do you feed your chickens corn?* ○ *If you feed your dog on cakes and biscuits, it's not surprising he's so fat.* ○ *The kids love feeding bread to the ducks.* **2** [I or T] If a baby or animal feeds, it eats or drinks milk: *The baby only feeds once a night at the moment, thank goodness.* ○ [R] *Most babies can feed themselves by the time they're a year old.* **3** [T] to be enough food for a group of people or animals: *This amount of pasta won't feed ten people.* **4** [T] to produce or supply enough food for someone or something: [R] *If agriculture were given priority, the country would easily be able to feed itself.* ○ *Feed the world/starving.* **5** [T] to give a plant substances that will help it grow: *Don't forget to feed the tomatoes.*
• **be like feeding time at the zoo** *HUMOROUS* to be very noisy, untidy and lacking order: *Tea-time in our house is like feeding time at the zoo!*

feed /fiːd/ *noun* **1** [C] *UK* (*US* **feeding**) when a baby has something to eat or drink: *The baby had a feed an hour ago, so she can't be hungry.* **2** [U] food eaten by animals that are not kept as pets: *cattle/animal feed* ⊃See also **chickenfeed**. **3** [C] *OLD-FASHIONED* a large meal

feeder /'fiː.dəʳ/ ⓤ /-dɚ/ *noun* [C] **1** a baby or animal that eats in a particular way: *a messy/slow feeder* **2** a container for giving food to animals: *a bird feeder* **3** *OLD-FASHIONED* a BIB for a young child

feed PUT /fiːd/ *verb* **fed, fed 1** [I or T; usually + adv or prep] to supply something to a person or thing, or put something into a machine or system, especially in a regular or continuous way: *The vegetables are fed **into** the machine at this end.* ○ *The images are fed **over** satellite networks to broadcasters throughout the world.* ○ [+ two objects] *A member of the princess's staff had been feeding the newspaper information/feeding information **to** the newspaper.* ○ *Several small streams feed **into** (= join) the river near here.* **2** [T] to put fuel on or inside something that burns, to keep it burning: *Remember to feed the fire while I'm out.*
• **feed sb a line** *DISAPPROVING* to tell someone something that is not completely true, often as an excuse: *She fed me a line about not having budgeted for pay increases this year.*

feed /fiːd/ *noun* [C] the part of a machine through which it is supplied with fuel or with something else that it needs: *the car's oil feed* ○ *the printer's paper feed* **feeder** /'fiː.dəʳ/ ⓤ /-dɚ/ *adj* [before n] describes something that leads to or supplies a larger thing of the same type: *a feeder **road*** ○ *a feeder school*

PHRASAL VERBS WITH **feed** ▼

▲ **feed off/on** *sth phrasal verb* to increase because of something, or to use something to succeed or get advantages: *Fascism feeds off poverty.*

▲ **feed sb/sth up** *phrasal verb* [M] to make a person or animal healthier or fatter by giving them lots of food: *You've lost a lot of weight – you need feeding up a bit.*

feedback OPINION /'fiːd.bæk/ *noun* [U] information or statements of opinion about something, such as a new product, that provide an idea of whether it is successful or liked: *Have you **had** any feedback from customers about the new soap?* ○ *positive/negative feedback*

feedback NOISE /'fiːd.bæk/ *noun* [U] the sudden, high, unpleasant noise sometimes produced by an AMPLIFIER when sound it produces is put back into it: *Jimi Hendrix loved to fling his guitar around to get weird and wonderful sounds from the feedback.*

feedbag /'fiːd.bæg/ *noun* [C] *US FOR* **nosebag**

feel EXPERIENCE /fiːl/ *verb* [L or T] **felt, felt** to experience something physical or emotional: *"How are you feeling?" "Not too bad, but I've still got a slight headache."* ○ *How would you feel about moving to a different city?* ○ *He's still feeling a bit weak after his operation.* ○ *My eyes feel really sore.* ○ *I never feel safe when I'm being driven by Richard.* ○ *Never in her life had she felt so happy.* ○ *My suitcase began to feel really heavy after a while.* ○ *I felt* (= thought that I was) *a complete idiot/such a fool.* ○ *She felt his hot breath on her neck.* ○ [+ obj + v-ing] *I could feel the sweat trickling down my back.* ○ *By midday, we were really feeling* (= suffering from) *the heat.* ⊃See Note **fall or feel?** at **fall** ACCIDENT.
• **feel like** *sth* **1** to have a desire for something, or to want to do something, at a particular moment: *I feel like (going for) a swim.* ○ *I feel like (having) a nice cool glass of lemonade.* ○ *"Are you coming to aerobics?" "No, I don't feel like it today."* **2** [+ v-ing] to want to do something that you do not do: *He was so rude I felt like slapping his face.*
• **feel your age** to become aware that you are no longer young: *Everybody there looked under twenty and I really felt my age.*
• **feel the cold** to get cold quicker and more often than most people: *As you get older, you tend to feel the cold more.*
• **feel free** If someone tells you to feel free to do something, they mean that you can do it if you want to: *Feel free to help yourself to coffee.*
• **feel it in your bones** to believe something strongly although you cannot explain why: *It's going to be a good summer – I can feel it in my bones.*
• **not feel a thing** *INFORMAL* to not feel any pain: *"Did it hurt?" "Not at all – I didn't feel a thing."*

feeling /ˈfiː.lɪŋ/ *noun* **[C or U] 1** when you feel something physical: *I had a tingling feeling in my fingers.* ○ *I've got this strange feeling **in** my stomach.* ○ *My toes were so cold that I'd lost all feeling in them.* **2** emotion: *The feeling **of** loneliness suddenly overwhelmed him.* ○ *There's a feeling **of** dissatisfaction with the government.* ○ **[+ that]** *I got the feeling **that** I was not welcome.* ○ *Her performance seemed to me completely lacking in feeling.* ↻See Note **sentiments** or **feelings?** at **sentiment**.

• **bad feeling** *UK* (*US* **bad feelings**) when people are upset or angry with each other: *I'd like to complain to the neighbours about the noise, but I don't want to cause any bad feeling **(between** us).*

feelingly /ˈfiː.lɪŋ.li/ *adv* with deep and sincere emotion: *"I've just had enough!" she said feelingly.*

feelings /ˈfiː.lɪŋz/ *plural noun* emotions, especially those influenced by other people: *Some people say that dogs have feelings.* ○ *I wanted to **spare** his feelings* (= not to upset him), *so I didn't tell him what she'd said about him.*

• **hurt *sb's* feelings** to upset someone by criticizing them or by refusing something that they have offered you

feel [TOUCH] /fiːl/ *verb* **[I or T] felt, felt** to touch something in order to discover something about it: **[+ question word]** *Just feel **how** cold my hands are!* ○ *He gently felt the softness of the baby's cheek.* ○ *I was feeling **(around)*** (= searching with my hand) *in my bag **for** the keys.*

• **feel *your* way 1** to judge where you are going by touching with your hands instead of looking: *The room was so dark, I had to feel my way along the wall to the door.* **2** to act slowly and carefully because you are not certain how to do something: *It's my first month in the job so I'm still feeling my way.*

feel /fiːl/ *noun* **1 [S]** the way that something feels: *She loved the feel of silk against her skin.* **2 [C]** *MAINLY UK INFORMAL* the action of touching something: *Is that shirt silk? Ooh, let me **have a** feel!*

feel [OPINION] /fiːl/ *verb* **[I or T] felt, felt** to have the opinion, or consider: **[+ (that)]** *I feel **(that)** I should be doing more to help her.* ○ **[R + (to infinitive) + adj]** *He had always felt himself **(to be)** inferior to his brothers.* ○ *Do you feel very strongly* (= have strong opinions) *about this?* ○ *I feel certain I'm right.*

feeling /ˈfiː.lɪŋ/ *noun* **[C]** opinion: *My feeling is that we had better act quickly or it will be too late.*

feel [CHARACTER] /fiːl/ *noun* **[S]** (*ALSO* **feeling**) the character of a place or situation: *I like the decoration – it's got quite a Spanish feel **to** it.* ○ *There was **a** feel of mystery about the place.* ○ *We were there for such a short time, we didn't really **get** the feel **of*** (= get to know) *the place.*

feel [UNDERSTANDING] /fiːl/ *noun* (*ALSO* **feeling**) **a feel for *sth*** a natural understanding or ability, especially in a subject or activity: *She has a real feel for language.* ○ *I tried learning the piano, but I never had much of a feel for it.*

• **get the feel of *sth*** to learn how to do something, usually a new activity: *Once you get the feel of it, using a mouse is easy.*

PHRASAL VERBS WITH **feel** ▼

▲ **feel for *sb*** *phrasal verb* to experience sympathy and sadness for someone because they are suffering: *I know what it's like to be lonely, so I do feel for her.*

▲ **feel *sb* up** *phrasal verb* **[M]** *SLANG* to touch someone sexually, especially someone you do not know, for your own excitement: *That's the second time she's been felt up on the Metro.*

feeler /ˈfiː.ləʳ/ Ⓤⓢ /-lɚ/ *noun* **[C usually pl]** one of the two long parts on an insect's head with which it touches things in order to discover what is around it

• **put out feelers** to make informal suggestions as a way of testing other people's opinions on something before any decisions are made

feelgood /ˈfiːl̩gʊd/ *adj* **[before n]** causing happy and positive feelings about life: *a feelgood movie* ○ *With the housing market picking up and consumer spending buoyant, it appears that **the** feelgood **factor*** (= a happy and positive feeling felt by people generally) *has returned.*

fee-paying /ˈfiːˌpeɪ.ɪŋ/ *adj UK* describes a school where parents pay the school directly for their children's education

feet /fiːt/ *plural of* **foot**

feign /feɪn/ *verb* **[T]** to pretend to feel something, usually an emotion: *You know how everyone feigns surprise when you tell them how old you are.* ○ *She responded to his remarks with feigned amusement.*

feint /feɪnt/ *verb* **[I or T]** (especially in football or boxing) to pretend to move, or to make a move, in a particular direction in order to deceive a competitor: **[+ *to* infinitive]** *Callas feinted **to** pass the ball and then shot it into the net.* ○ *He feinted a shot to the left.* **feint** /feɪnt/ *noun* **[C]** *He produced a brilliant feint, passed two defenders, and smashed the ball into the net.*

feisty /ˈfaɪ.sti/ *adj* active, forceful and full of determination: *a feisty lady* ○ *He launched a feisty attack on the government.*

felafel, falafel /fəˈlæf.əl/ Ⓤⓢ /-ˈlɑː.fəl/ *noun* **[C or U]** fried balls of spicy food made from CHICKPEAS (= pale brown round seeds)

felicity [HAPPINESS] /fəˈlɪs.ɪ.ti/ Ⓤⓢ /-ə.t̬i/ *noun* **[U]** *LITERARY* happiness, luck, or a condition which produces positive results: *the dubious felicity of marriage*

felicity [SUITABLE] /fəˈlɪs.ɪ.ti/ Ⓤⓢ /-ə.t̬i/ *noun LITERARY* **1 [U]** when words or remarks are suitable and express what was intended: *As a songwriter, he combined great linguistic felicity with an ear for a tune.* **2 [C usually pl]** a word or remark which is suitable or right and expresses well the intended thought or feeling: *Her article contained one or two verbal felicities which will stay in my mind for years.*

felicitous /fəˈlɪs.ɪ.təs/ Ⓤⓢ /-t̬əs/ *adj LITERARY* suitable or right and expressing well the intended thought or feeling: *He summed up Jack's achievements in one or two felicitous **phrases**.* ✻ NOTE: The opposite of felicitous is **infelicitous**. **felicitously** /fəˈlɪs.ɪ.tə.sli/ Ⓤⓢ /-t̬ə-/ *adv: a felicitously phrased speech*

feline /ˈfiː.laɪn/ *adj* **1** belonging or relating to the cat family: *feline leukaemia* **2** *MAINLY APPROVING* appearing or behaving like a cat: *She had pretty, almost feline features.*

feline /ˈfiː.laɪn/ *noun* **[C]** *SPECIALIZED* a member of the cat family: *a wildlife park with tigers and various other felines*

fell [FALL] /fel/ *past simple of* **fall**

fell [CUT DOWN] /fel/ *verb* **[T] 1** to cut down a tree: *A great number of trees were felled to provide space for grazing.* **2** to knock someone down, especially in sports: *The boxer was felled by a punch to the head.*

fell [EVIL] /fel/ *adj LITERARY OR OLD USE* evil, or cruel

• **at/in one fell swoop** If you do something at/in one fell swoop, you do it all at the same time: *I got all my Christmas shopping done in one fell swoop.*

fella /ˈfel.ə/ *noun* **[C]** *NOT STANDARD* **1** a man: *There were a couple of fellas leaning up by the bar.* **2** a male sexual partner or boyfriend: *Was she with her fella?*

fellatio /fəˈleɪ.ʃi.əʊ/ Ⓤⓢ /-oʊ/ *noun* **[U]** the sexual activity of sucking or moving the tongue across the penis in order to give pleasure and excitement ↻Compare **cunnilingus**.

feller /ˈfel.əʳ/ Ⓤⓢ /-ɚ/ *noun* **[C]** *ANOTHER SPELLING OF* **fella**

fellow [MAN] /ˈfel.əʊ/ /-oʊ/ *noun* **[C]** *INFORMAL* a man, used especially in the past by people in a higher social class: *He seemed like a decent sort of a fellow.*

fellow [MEMBER] /ˈfel.əʊ/ Ⓤⓢ /-oʊ/ *noun* **[C] 1** a member of a group of high-ranking teachers at a particular college or university or of particular ACADEMIC societies: *Georgia's a fellow of Clare College, Cambridge.* **2** a member of an official organization for a particular subject or job: *He's a fellow of the Royal Institute of Chartered Surveyors.*

fellow [SHARED] /ˈfel.əʊ/ Ⓤⓢ /-oʊ/ *adj* **[before n]** describes someone who has the same job or interests as you, or is in the same situation as you: *She introduced me to some of her fellow students.* ○ *Our fellow travellers were mostly Spanish-speaking tourists.*

ˌfellow ˈfeeling *noun* **[U]** an understanding or sympathy that you feel for another person because you have a shared experience: *There was a fellow feeling between everyone who had lived through the war.*

ˌ**fellow 'man/'men** *noun* ***your* fellow man/men** people generally or the people living around you: *He had very little love for his fellow men.*

fellowship [GROUP] /ˈfel.əʊ.ʃɪp/ [US] /-oʊ-/ *noun* **1** [C] *FORMAL* a group of people or an organization with the same purpose: *the National Schizophrenia Fellowship* ○ *the American Fellowship of Reconciliation* **2** [U] *OLD-FASHIONED* a friendly feeling that exists between people who have a shared interest or are doing something as a group: *He enjoyed the fellowship of other actors in the company.* ○ *Christian fellowship*

fellowship [EDUCATION] /ˈfel.əʊ.ʃɪp/ [US] /-oʊ-/ *noun* [C] **1** the position of a FELLOW (= high-ranking teacher at a college): *He's been* ***elected to*** *a fellowship at Merton College.* **2** an amount of money that is given to POSTGRADUATES to enable them to study a subject at an advanced level: *She's applied for a* ***research*** *fellowship.*

fells /felz/ *plural noun* mountains, hills or other areas of high land, especially in northwest England **fell** /fel/ *adj* [before n] *We went fell* ***walking*** *last weekend.*

felony /ˈfel.ə.ni/ *noun* [C or U] *UK OLD-FASHIONED OR US LEGAL* (an example of) serious crime which can be punished by one or more years in prison: *a felony charge* ○ *He was convicted of felony.*

felon /ˈfel.ən/ *noun* [C] *LEGAL* a person who is guilty of a serious crime

felt [FEEL] /felt/ *past simple and past participle of* **feel**

felt [CLOTH] /felt/ *noun* [U] a type of thick soft cloth made from a pressed mass of wool and hair: *a felt hat*

felt-tip (pen) /ˌfelt.tɪpˈpen/ *noun* [C] (*UK ALSO* **fibre-tip (pen)**) a pen which has a writing point made of felt

fem *adj ABBREVIATION FOR* **feminine** GRAMMAR or FEMALE

female [SEX] /ˈfiː.meɪl/ *adj* **1** belonging or relating to women, or the sex that can give birth to young or produce eggs: *She was voted the best female vocalist.* ○ *Female lions do not have manes.* ➲See also **feminine** FEMALE. Compare **male** SEX. **2** describes plants which produce flowers that will later develop into fruit

female /ˈfiː.meɪl/ *noun* [C] **1** a female animal or person: *The kitten was actually a female, not a male.* ○ *Females* (= women) *represent 40% of the country's workforce.* **2** used to refer to a woman in a way that shows a lack of respect: *I suspect the doctor thought I was just another hysterical female.* **femaleness** /ˈfiː.meɪl.nəs/ *noun* [U]

female [CONNECTING PART] /ˈfiː.meɪl/ *adj SPECIALIZED* describes a piece of equipment that has a hole or space into which another part can be fitted: *a female plug/connector* ➲Compare **male** CONNECTING PART.

feminine [FEMALE] /ˈfem.ɪ.nɪn/ *adj* acting, or having qualities which are traditionally considered to be suitable for a woman: *With his long dark eyelashes, he looked almost feminine.* ○ *The current style in evening wear is soft, romantic and feminine.* ○ *Her clothes are always very feminine.* ➲Compare **masculine** MALE.

femininity /ˌfem.əˈnɪn.ɪ.ti/ [US] /-ə.t̬i/ *noun* [U] *USUALLY APPROVING Long hair was traditionally regarded as a sign of femininity.*

feminine [GRAMMAR] /ˈfem.ɪ.nɪn/ *adj* **1** (*WRITTEN ABBREVIATION* **fem, f**) belonging to the group of nouns which, in some languages, are not masculine or NEUTER: *In French, 'table' is feminine.* **2** describes a particular form of a noun in English, such as 'actress', which refers only to a female person. These feminine forms are now being used less often.

feminism /ˈfem.ɪ.nɪ.zᵊm/ *noun* [U] the belief that women should be allowed the same rights, power and opportunities as men and be treated in the same way, or the set of activities intended to achieve this state: *She had a lifelong commitment to feminism.*

feminist /ˈfem.ɪ.nɪst/ *noun* [C] a person who believes in feminism, often being involved in activities that are intended to achieve change: *All her life she was an ardent feminist.* ○ *a radical feminist* **feminist** /ˈfem.ɪ.nɪst/ *adj*: *the feminist movement* ○ *feminist issues/literature*

femme fatale /ˌfæm.fəˈtɑːl/ *noun* [C] *plural* **femmes fatales** a woman who is very attractive in a mysterious way, usually leading people into danger or causing their destruction

femur /ˈfiː.məʳ/ [US] /-mɚ/ *noun* [C] *plural* **femurs** or **femora** *SPECIALIZED* the long bone in the upper part of the leg ➲See picture **The Body** on page Centre 5

fen /fen/ *noun* [C or U] (*ALSO* **fenland**) an area of low flat wet land: *areas of marsh and fen* ○ *The road to Ely leads out across the fens.*

fence [STRUCTURE] /fents/ *noun* [C] a structure which divides two areas of land, similar to a wall but made of wood or wire and supported with posts

fencing /ˈfent.sɪŋ/ *noun* [U] fences, or the materials used to make fences: *wire/wooden fencing*

fence [FIGHT] /fents/ *verb* [I] to fight as a sport with a long thin sword

fencer /ˈfent.səʳ/ [US] /-sɚ/ *noun* [C] a person who fences as a sport

fencing /ˈfent.sɪŋ/ *noun* [U] the sport of fighting with long thin swords: *a fencing tournament/mask* ○ *I did a bit of fencing while I was at college.*

fence [CRIMINAL] /fents/ *noun* [C] *OLD-FASHIONED SLANG* a person who buys and sells stolen goods

PHRASAL VERBS WITH **fence**

▲ **fence *sth* in** [AREA] *phrasal verb* [M] to build a fence around an area: *She would need to fence in the field if she was to keep a horse there.*

▲ **fence *sb* in** [PERSON] *phrasal verb* [often passive] *INFORMAL* to limit someone's activity in an annoying or discouraging way: *I feel a bit fenced in at work because my boss won't let me apply for promotion.*

▲ **fence *sth* off** *phrasal verb* [M] to separate an area with a fence in order to stop people or animals from entering it: *The hill had been fenced off to stop animals grazing on it.*

ˈ**fence ˌmending** /ˈfentsˌmen.dɪŋ/ *noun* [U] when you try to improve the relationship between two opposing sides in a disagreement and help them to agree: *Fence-building is what she is best at; she's a wonderful listener.*

fence-mending /ˈfentsˌmen.dɪŋ/ *adj* [before n] *The UN Secretary General is on a fence-mending mission.*

ˈ**fence ˌsitter** *noun* [C] *DISAPPROVING* someone who supports both sides in a disagreement because they cannot make a decision or do not want to annoy or offend either side ˈ**fence ˌsitting** *noun* [U]

fend /fend/ *verb*

PHRASAL VERBS WITH **fend**

▲ **fend for *yourself*** *phrasal verb* [R] to take care of and provide for yourself without depending on anyone else: *Now that the children are old enough to fend for themselves, we can go away on holiday by ourselves.*

▲ **fend *sb* off** *phrasal verb* [M] to push or send away an attacker or other unwanted person: *He managed to fend off his attackers with a stick.* ○ *She spent the entire evening fending off unwanted admirers.*

▲ **fend *sth* off** *phrasal verb* [M] to avoid dealing with something that is unpleasant or difficult to deal with: *Somehow she managed to fend off the awkward questions.*

fender [FIRE] /ˈfen.dəʳ/ [US] /-dɚ/ *noun* [C] a low metal frame around an open fireplace which stops the coal or wood from falling out

fender [CAR] /ˈfen.dəʳ/ [US] /-dɚ/ *noun* [C] *US FOR* **wing** PART OF CAR or MUDGUARD ➲See picture **Car** on page Centre 12

ˈ**fender ˌbender** *US noun* [C] (*UK* **prang**) *INFORMAL* a road accident in which the vehicles involved are only slightly damaged

feng shui /ˌfeŋˈʃuːi/ /ˌfʊŋˈʃweɪ/ *noun* [U] an ancient Chinese belief that the way your house is built and the way that you arrange objects affects your success, health, and happiness: *It's* ***good*** *feng shui to have a healthy, loving animal in your home.* ○ *a feng shui consultant*

fennel /ˈfen.ᵊl/ *noun* [U] a plant with a large rounded base that is eaten as a vegetable and small pale leaves that are used as a herb ➲See picture **Vegetables** on page Centre 2

fenugreek /ˈfen.ʊ.griːk/ *noun* [U] a plant with hard yellowish brown seeds used as a spice in Indian cooking

feral /ˈfer.əl/ *adj* existing in a wild state, especially describing an animal that was previously kept by people: *feral dogs/cats*

ferment [CHANGE CHEMICALLY] /fəˈment/ [US] /fɚ-/ *verb* [I or T] to (cause something to) change chemically through the action of living substances, such as yeast or bacteria: *You make wine by leaving grape juice to ferment until all the sugar has turned to alcohol.* **fermentation** /ˌfɜː.menˈteɪ.ʃən/ [US] /ˌfɝː-/ *noun* [U]

ferment [CONFUSION] /ˈfɜː.ment/ [US] /ˈfɝː-/ *noun* [U] LITERARY a state of confusion, change, and lack of order or fighting: *The resignation of the president has left the country **in** ferment.*

fern /fɜːn/ [US] /fɝːn/ *noun* [C] a green plant with long stems, feathery leaves and no flowers

ferocious /fəˈrəʊ.ʃəs/ [US] /-ˈroʊ-/ *adj* fierce and violent: *a ferocious dog* ○ *a ferocious battle* ○ *She's got a ferocious* (= very bad) *temper.* ○ *The president came in for some ferocious criticism.* **ferociously** /fəˈrəʊ.ʃə.sli/ [US] /-ˈroʊ-/ *adv*: *A female lion defends her young ferociously.* **ferocity** /fəˈrɒs.ə.ti/ [US] /-ˈrɑː.sə.t̬i/ *noun* [U] (ALSO **ferociousness**) *The ferocity of the attack shocked a lot of people.*

ferret [ANIMAL] /ˈfer.ɪt/ *noun* [C] a small yellowish white animal with a long body, bred for hunting rabbits and other small animals

ferret [SEARCH] /ˈfer.ɪt/ *verb* INFORMAL **1** [I + adv or prep] to search for something by moving things around with your hands, especially in a drawer, bag or other enclosed space: *I was just ferreting **around** in my drawer for my passport.* **2** [I] to search for something or someone, by looking in many places or asking many questions: *After a bit of ferreting, I managed to find his address.*

▲ **ferret *sth* out** *phrasal verb* [M] to find out a piece of information or find someone or something, after looking in many places or asking many questions: [+ question word] *I know his name but I haven't yet managed to ferret out **where** he lives.*

Ferris wheel /ˈfer.ɪsˌwiːl/ *noun* [C] MAINLY US FOR **big wheel**

ferrous /ˈfer.əs/ *adj* SPECIALIZED containing or relating to iron: *ferrous metals/compounds*

ˈferry (ˌboat) *noun* [C] a boat or ship for taking passengers and often vehicles across an area of water, especially as a regular service: *a car ferry* ○ *We're going across to France **by/on the** ferry.* ○ *We **took** the ferry to Calais.* ➲See picture **Planes, Ships and Boats** on page Centre 14

ferry /ˈfer.i/ *verb* [T usually + adv or prep] to transport people or goods in a vehicle, especially regularly and often: *I spend most of my time ferrying the children **about**.*

fertile [LAND] /ˈfɜː.taɪl/ [US] /ˈfɝː.t̬əl/ *adj* describes land that can produce a large number of good quality crops ➲Compare **barren**.

• **fertile ground for *sth*** a situation or place which produces good results or a lot of ideas: *British politics remains very fertile ground for comedy.*

fertility /fəˈtɪl.ɪ.ti/ [US] /fɚˈtɪl.ə.t̬i/ *noun* [U] the quality of being fertile: *the fertility of the soil*

fertilize, UK USUALLY **-ise** /ˈfɜː.tɪ.laɪz/ [US] /ˈfɝː.t̬əl.aɪz/ *verb* [T] to spread a natural or chemical substance on land or plants, in order to make the plants grow well

fertilizer, UK USUALLY **-iser** /ˈfɜː.tɪ.laɪ.zəʳ/ [US] /ˈfɝː.t̬əl.aɪ-/ *noun* [C or U] a natural or chemical substance which is spread on the land or given to plants, to make plants grow well: *organic fertilizer* ○ *a liquid/chemical fertilizer*

fertile [REPRODUCTION] /ˈfɜː.taɪl/ [US] /ˈfɝː.t̬əl/ *adj* **1** describes animals or plants that are able to produce (a lot of) young or fruit: *People get less fertile as they get older.* ✻ NOTE: The opposite is **infertile**. **2** describes a seed or egg that is able to develop into a new plant or animal **fertility** /fəˈtɪl.ɪ.ti/ [US] /fɚˈtɪl.ə.t̬i/ *noun* [U] *a fertility symbol* ○ *declining fertility **rates***

fertilize, UK USUALLY **-ise** /ˈfɜː.tɪ.laɪz/ [US] /ˈfɝː.t̬əl.aɪz/ *verb* [T] to cause an egg or seed to start to develop into a new young animal or plant by joining it with a male cell: *Bees fertilize the flowers by bringing pollen.* ○ *Once an egg is fertilized by the sperm, it becomes an embryo.* **fertilization**, UK USUALLY **-isation** /ˌfɜː.tɪ.laɪˈzeɪ.ʃən/ [US] /ˌfɝː.t̬əl.aɪ-/ *noun* [U] *In humans, fertilization is more likely to occur at certain times of the month.*

fertile [IMAGINATIVE] /ˈfɜː.taɪl/ [US] /ˈfɝː.t̬əl/ *adj* A fertile mind or imagination is active and produces a lot of interesting and unusual ideas. **fertility** /fəˈtɪl.ɪ.ti/ [US] /fɚˈtɪl.ə.t̬i/ *noun* [U] LITERARY

fervent /ˈfɜː.vənt/ [US] /ˈfɝː-/ *adj* (ALSO **fervid**) FORMAL describes beliefs that are strongly and sincerely felt or people who have strong and sincere beliefs: *a fervent supporter of the communist party* ○ *It is his fervent **hope** that a peaceful solution will soon be found.* **fervently** /ˈfɜː.vənt.li/ [US] /ˈfɝː-/ *adv*: *The nationalists **believe** fervently in independence for their country.* **fervour** UK, US **fervor** /ˈfɜː.vəʳ/ [US] /ˈfɝː.vɚ/ *noun* [U] (FORMAL **fervency**) *nationalist/religious fervour*

fess /fes/ *verb*

▲ **fess up** *phrasal verb* [I] INFORMAL to admit that you have done something that someone else will not like: *Fess up – it was you who ate that last piece of cake, wasn't it?*

fest /fest/ *noun, suffix* **a beer/film/jazz, etc. fest** a special event where people can enjoy a particular activity or thing

fester [INJURY] /ˈfes.təʳ/ [US] /-tɚ/ *verb* [I] If a cut or other injury festers, it becomes infected and produces pus: *a festering sore*

fester [FEELING] /ˈfes.təʳ/ [US] /-tɚ/ *verb* [I] If an argument or bad feeling festers, it continues so that feelings of hate or dissatisfaction increase: *It's better to expressed your anger than let it fester inside you.* ○ *a festering argument/dispute*

festival /ˈfes.tɪ.vəl/ *noun* [C] **1** a special day or period, usually in memory of a religious event, with its own social activities, food or ceremonies: *a Jewish/Christian/Hindu festival* **2** an organized set of special events, such as musical performances: *a folk/pop/rock festival* ○ *The Brighton Festival is **held** every year around May time.* ○ *the Cannes Film Festival*

festive /ˈfes.tɪv/ *adj* having or producing happy and enjoyable feelings suitable for a festival or other special social occasion: *a festive mood/occasion* ○ *The hall looked very festive with its coloured lights and Christmas tree.*

festivity /fesˈtɪv.ɪ.ti/ [US] /-ə.t̬i/ *noun* [U] when people are happy and celebrating

festivities /fesˈtɪv.ɪ.tiz/ [US] /-ə.t̬iz/ *plural noun* the parties, meals and other social activities with which people celebrate a special occasion: *"Come in and **join the** festivities – what will you have to drink?"*

the ˈfestive ˌseason *noun* [S] UK the period around Christmas and New Year

festoon /fesˈtuːn/ *noun* [C] a decorative chain made of coloured paper, flowers, etc. hung in a curve between two points

festoon /fesˈtuːn/ *verb* [T] to decorate a room or other place for a special occasion by hanging coloured paper, lights or flowers around it, especially in curves: *The hall was festooned **with** Christmas lights and holly.*

fetal /ˈfiː.təl/ [US] /-t̬əl/ *adj* US FOR **foetal** ➲See at **foetus**.

fetch [GET] /fetʃ/ *verb* [T] to go to another place to get something or someone and bring them back: [+ two objects] *Could you fetch me my glasses/fetch my glasses **for** me from the other room, please?* ○ *I have to fetch my mother from the station.*

• **fetch and carry for *sb*** to do boring, unskilled jobs for someone, as if you were their servant

▲ **fetch up** *phrasal verb* MAINLY US INFORMAL to arrive somewhere, especially unintentionally: *After a whole hour of driving, we fetched up back where we started.*

fetch [SELL] /fetʃ/ *verb* [T] to be sold for a particular amount of money: *The paintings fetched over a million dollars.* ○ *The house didn't fetch as much as she was hoping it would.*

fetching /ˈfetʃ.ɪŋ/ *adj* A fetching person or piece of clothing is attractive: *a rather fetching off-the-shoulder*

dress ○ *You* ***look*** *very fetching in your green shorts.*
fetchingly /ˈfetʃ.ɪŋ.li/ *adv*

fête [EVENT] *UK* /feɪt/ *noun* [C] (*US* **fair**) a public event, often held outside, where you can take part in competitions and buy small items and food, often organized to collect money for a particular purpose: *a summer fête* ○ *They're holding the* ***village*** *fête on the green.*

fête [PRAISE] /feɪt/ *verb* [T] to praise or to welcome someone publicly because of their achievements: *She was fêted by audiences both in her own country and abroad.*

fetid, foetid /ˈfet.ɪd/ Ⓤⓢ /ˈfeṭ-/ *adj* FORMAL smelling extremely bad and STALE: *fetid air/breath*

fetish [INTEREST] /ˈfet.ɪʃ/ Ⓤⓢ /ˈfeṭ-/ *noun* [C] **1** a sexual interest in an object or a part of the body other than the sexual organs: *a rubber/foot fetish* ○ *He has a fetish* ***about/for*** *high-heels.* **2** an activity or object which you are so interested in that you spend an unreasonable amount of time thinking about it or doing it: *She* ***makes a*** *fetish* ***of*** *organization – it's quite obsessive.* ○ *He* ***has*** *a fetish* ***for/about*** *cleanliness.*
fetishist /ˈfet.ɪ.ʃɪst/ Ⓤⓢ /ˈfeṭ-/ *noun* [C] a person who has a particular fetish: *a foot fetishist* **fetishistic** /ˌfet.ɪˈʃɪs.tɪk/ Ⓤⓢ /ˌfeṭ-/ *adj* **fetishism** /ˈfet.ɪ.ʃɪ.zᵊm/ Ⓤⓢ /ˈfeṭ-/ *noun* [U]

fetish [RELIGIOUS OBJECT] /ˈfet.ɪʃ/ Ⓤⓢ /ˈfeṭ-/ *noun* [C] SPECIALIZED an object which is worshipped in some societies because it is believed to possess a spirit or special magical powers **fetishism** /ˈfet.ɪ.ʃɪ.zᵊm/ Ⓤⓢ /ˈfeṭ-/ *noun* [U] **fetishistic** /ˌfet.ɪˈʃɪs.tɪk/ Ⓤⓢ /ˌfeṭ-/ *adj*: *fetishistic religions*

fetlock /ˈfet.lɒk/ Ⓤⓢ /-lɑːk/ *noun* [C] SPECIALIZED the part of a horse's leg at the back, just above the foot, where longer hair grows

fetter /ˈfet.əʳ/ Ⓤⓢ /ˈfeṭ.ɚ/ *verb* [T] **1** LITERARY to keep someone within limits or stop their advance: *He felt fettered* ***by*** *a nine-to-five office existence.* **2** to tie someone to a place by putting chains around their ankles
fetters /ˈfet.əz/ Ⓤⓢ /ˈfeṭ.ɚz/ *plural noun* **1** OLD USE a pair of chains which were tied round the legs of prisoners to prevent them from escaping **2** LITERARY something which severely limits you: *the fetters* ***of*** *motherhood*

fettle /ˈfet.l̩/ Ⓤⓢ /ˈfeṭ-/ OLD-FASHIONED INFORMAL **in fine/good fettle** healthy or strong, or in good condition: *"How was Jane?" "Oh, she was in fine fettle."*

fetus /ˈfiː.təs/ Ⓤⓢ /-ṭəs/ *noun* [C] US FOR **foetus**

feud /fjuːd/ *noun* [C] an argument which has existed for a long time between two people or groups, causing a lot of anger or violence: *a* ***family*** *feud* ○ *a 10-year-old feud* ***between*** *the two countries* ○ *a bitter feud* ***over*** *land* **feud** /fjuːd/ *verb* [I] *They've been feuding* ***with*** *their neighbours for years* ***over*** *a boundary issue.*

feudal /ˈfjuː.dᵊl/ *adj* relating to the social system of Western Europe in THE MIDDLE AGES or any society that is organised according to rank: *the feudal system* ○ *a feudal lord/kingdom/society* **feudalism** /ˈfjuː.dᵊl.ɪ.zᵊm/ *noun* [U]

fever [ILLNESS] /ˈfiː.vəʳ/ Ⓤⓢ /-vɚ/ *noun* [C or U] a medical condition in which the body temperature is higher than usual and the heart beats very fast: *He's got a headache and a slight fever.* **fevered** /ˈfiː.vəd/ Ⓤⓢ /-vɚd/ *adj* [usually before n] *The nurse wiped my fevered brow.*
feverish /ˈfiː.vᵊr.ɪʃ/ *adj* suffering from fever: *I'm feeling a bit feverish – I hope it's not the start of flu.*

fever [EXCITEMENT] /ˈfiː.vəʳ/ Ⓤⓢ /-vɚ/ *noun* [U] a state of great excitement: *The whole country seems to be in the grip of football fever.*
fevered /ˈfiː.vəd/ Ⓤⓢ /-vɚd/ *adj* [usually before n] DISAPPROVING unnaturally excited or active: *The film is clearly the product of a fevered* ***imagination.*** **feverish** /ˈfiː.vᵊr.ɪʃ/ *adj* [before n] *Have you seen the feverish* ***activity*** *in the kitchen?* **feverishly** /ˈfiː.vᵊr.ɪ.ʃli/ *adv*: *They* ***worked*** *feverishly to meet the deadline.*

ˈfever ˌpitch *noun* [U] a state of very strong emotion: *Excitement among the waiting crowd had* ***reached/was at*** *fever pitch.*

few [SOME] /fjuː/ *determiner, pronoun* **1 a few** some, or a small number of something: *I need to get a few things in town.* ○ *There are a few cakes left over from the party.* ○ *We've been having a few problems with the new computer.* ○ *If you can't fit all the cases in your car, I can take a few in mine.* ○ *"How many potatoes do you want?" "Oh, just a few, please."* * NOTE: **a few** is used with countable nouns. ⊃Compare **little** SMALL. **2** used in expressions such as 'quite a few' or 'a good few' to mean quite a large number: *I know quite a few people who've had the same problem.* ○ *Lots of people at the club are under twenty, but there are a good few who aren't.*
• **have a few (too many)** INFORMAL to drink quite a large number of, or too many, alcoholic drinks: *By the look of her, she'd had a few even before she arrived at the party.*

few [NOT MANY] /fjuː/ *determiner, pronoun, noun, adj* a small number, not many or not enough: *It was embarrassing how few people attended the party.* ○ *He is among the few people I can trust.* ○ *Very few people can afford to pay those prices.* ○ *We leave for France in a few days.* ○ *Few of the children can read or write yet.* ○ *Few things in this world give me more pleasure than a long bath.* ○ *Fewer people smoke these days than used to.* ○ *We get few complaints.* ○ *According to the survey,* ***as*** *few* ***as*** *10% of us are happy with our jobs.* ○ *The benefits of this scheme are few.* * NOTE: **few** is used with countable nouns. ⊃Compare **little** NOT ENOUGH.
• **few and far between** not happening or existing very often: *Flats which are both comfortable and reasonably priced are few and far between.*
• **a man/woman of few words** a man/woman who says very little: *My father was a man of few words, but when he spoke it was worth listening to.*
• **no fewer than** FORMAL used to show that you consider a number to be surprisingly large: *No fewer than five hundred delegates attended the conference.*

fey /feɪ/ *adj* LITERARY OFTEN DISAPPROVING mysterious and strange, or trying to appear like this: *He dismissed her later poems as fey and frivolous.*

fez /fez/ *noun* [C] *plural* **fezzes** a high, cone-shaped hat with a flat top and no brim, usually made of red material and with threads hanging from the top, especially as worn in the past by men in some Muslim countries ⊃See picture **Hairstyles and Hats** on page Centre 8

ff WRITTEN ABBREVIATION FOR and the following pages

fiancé /fiˈɑ̃ːn.seɪ/ Ⓤⓢ /ˌfiː.ɑːnˈseɪ/ *noun* [C] the man to whom a woman is ENGAGED to be married: *Have you met Christina's fiancé?*

fiancée /fiˈɑ̃ːn.seɪ/ Ⓤⓢ /ˌfiː.ɑːnˈseɪ/ *noun* [C] the woman to whom a man is ENGAGED to be married

fiasco /fiˈæs.kəʊ/ Ⓤⓢ /-koʊ/ *noun* [C] *plural* **fiascos** or MAINLY US **fiascoes** something planned that goes wrong and is a complete failure, usually in an embarrassing way: *The show was a fiasco – the lights wouldn't work, one actor forgot his lines and another fell off the stage.*

fiat /ˈfiː.æt/ *noun* [C or U] FORMAL an order given by a person in authority: *No company can set industry standards* ***by*** *fiat.*

fib /fɪb/ *verb* [I] **-bb-** INFORMAL to tell an unimportant and harmless lie, sometimes in a playful way: *I can tell he's fibbing because he's smiling!* **fib** /fɪb/ *noun* [C] *Don't believe him – he's* ***telling*** *fibs again.*
fibber /ˈfɪb.əʳ/ Ⓤⓢ /-ɚ/ *noun* [C] INFORMAL a person who tells fibs: *Fibber! You couldn't run 10km, let alone a marathon!*

fibre [THREAD] *UK, US* **fiber** /ˈfaɪ.bəʳ/ Ⓤⓢ /-bɚ/ *noun* **1** [C] any of the thread-like parts which form plant or artificial material and which can be made into cloth: *The fibres are woven into fabric.* **2** [C or U] threads when they are in a mass that can be used for making products such as cloth and rope: *Natural fibres such as cotton tend to be cooler.* ○ *artificial/man-made/natural fibre* **3** [C or U] one of various thread-like structures in the body, such as those found in muscle: *muscle fibre(s)*
fibrous /ˈfaɪ.brəs/ *adj* made of fibres, or like fibre

fibre [CHARACTER] *UK, US* **fiber** /ˈfaɪ.bəʳ/ Ⓤⓢ /-bɚ/ *noun* [U] strength of character: *He lacked the* ***moral*** *fibre to be leader.*
• **with every fibre of *your* being** If you want or believe something with every fibre of your being, you want or believe it very much: *She wanted to win the race with every fibre of her being.*

fibre [FOOD] *UK, US* **fiber** /ˈfaɪ.bəʳ/ Ⓤⓢ /-bɚ/ *noun* [U] a substance in foods such as fruit, vegetables and brown

bread, which travels through the body as waste and helps the contents of the bowels to pass through the body easily: *You should eat more* ***dietary*** *fibre to reduce the risk of bowel cancer.*
fibrous /ˈfaɪ.brəs/ *adj* Food which is fibrous contains fibre.

fibreglass *UK, US* **fiberglass** /ˈfaɪ.bəˌɡlɑːs/ [US] /-bɚˌɡlæs/ *noun* [U] a strong light material made by twisting together small fibres of glass and plastic, used especially for structures such as cars and boats: *a fibreglass hull/speedboat*

ˌfibre ˈoptics *plural noun SPECIALIZED* the use of very thin glass or plastic fibres through which light can travel to carry information, especially in telephone, television and computer systems

fibula /ˈfɪb.jʊ.lə/ *noun* [C] *plural* **fibulas** or **fibulae** *SPECIALIZED* the outer of the two bones in the lower part of the human leg ➲See picture **The Body** on page Centre 5

fickle /ˈfɪk.l̩/ *adj DISAPPROVING* **1** likely to change your opinion or your feelings suddenly and without a good reason: *She's so fickle – she's never been interested in the same man for more than a week!* ○ *The world of popular music is notoriously fickle.* **2** describes conditions that tend to change suddenly and without warning: *Fickle winds made sailing conditions difficult.* **fickleness** /ˈfɪk.l̩.nəs/ *noun* [U]

fiction /ˈfɪk.ʃᵊn/ *noun* **1** [U] the type of book or story which is written about imaginary characters and events and not based on real people and facts: *The book is a* ***work of*** *fiction and not intended as a historical account.* ○ *a writer of children's fiction* **2** [C or U] a false report or statement which you pretend is true: [+ that] *At work she kept up* ***the*** *fiction* ***that*** *she had a university degree.* ○ *When he's telling you something, you never know what's fact and what's fiction.*
fictional /ˈfɪk.ʃᵊn.ᵊl/ *adj* imaginary: *a fictional story* ○ *fictional characters*
fictionalize, *UK USUALLY* **-ise** /ˈfɪk.ʃᵊn.ᵊl.aɪz/ *verb* [T] to write about a real event or character, but adding imaginary details and changing the real facts: *a fictionalized* ***account*** *of the life of St Francis* **fictionalization**, *UK USUALLY* **-isation** /ˌfɪk.ʃᵊn.ᵊl.aɪˈzeɪ.ʃᵊn/ *noun* [C or U]

fictitious /fɪkˈtɪʃ.əs/ *adj* invented and not true or not existing: *He dismissed recent rumours about his private life as fictitious.* ○ *Characters in this film are entirely fictitious.*

fiddle [CHEAT] /ˈfɪd.l̩/ *verb* [T] *INFORMAL* to act dishonestly in order to get something for yourself, or to change something dishonestly, especially to your advantage: *She managed to fiddle a free trip to America.* ○ *He had been fiddling* ***the accounts/books/finances*** *for years.*
fiddle /ˈfɪd.l̩/ *noun* [C or U] *MAINLY UK INFORMAL* *a tax fiddle* ○ *Everyone suspected they were* ***on the*** *fiddle* (= cheating).

fiddle [MOVE ABOUT] /ˈfɪd.l̩/ *verb* [I] to move things about or touch things with no particular purpose: *Put your papers down and stop fiddling!*

PHRASAL VERBS WITH **fiddle**

▲ **fiddle about/around** *phrasal verb DISAPPROVING* to spend time doing small, unimportant or unnecessary things: *I was just fiddling around in the kitchen.*
▲ **fiddle (about/around) with** ***sth*** *phrasal verb* **1** to touch or move things with your fingers because you are nervous or bored: *He was just fiddling around with the things on his desk.* **2** to make small changes to something to try to make it work: *Stop fiddling about with your hair – it looks fine.* ○ *Someone's been fiddling around with my computer!*

fiddle [INSTRUMENT] /ˈfɪd.l̩/ *noun* [C] *INFORMAL* a violin: *to play the fiddle*
fiddle /ˈfɪd.l̩/ *verb* [I] *INFORMAL* to play the violin
fiddler /ˈfɪd.ləʳ/ [US] /-lɚ/ *noun* [C] *INFORMAL* a violin player

fiddle [DIFFICULTY] /ˈfɪd.l̩/ *noun* [S] *UK INFORMAL* something difficult to do, especially because the things involved are small or need careful use of the fingers: *I find threading a needle* ***a*** *terrible fiddle.* ○ [+ to infinitive] ***It's a*** *real fiddle* ***to*** *assemble because of all the small parts.*

fiddly /ˈfɪd.li/ *adj INFORMAL* difficult to do because the parts involved are small: *Repairing a watch is a very fiddly job.* ○ *I hate painting the fiddly* ***bits*** *in the corner.*

fiddlesticks /ˈfɪd.l̩.stɪks/ *exclamation* (*US ALSO* **fiddle-faddle**) *OLD-FASHIONED* used to express disagreement or to say that something is nonsense

fiddling /ˈfɪd.lɪŋ/ *adj* [before n] unimportant, or of no real interest: *fiddling little details* ○ *fiddling restrictions*

fidelity /fɪˈdel.ə.ti/ [US] /-t̬i/ *noun* [U] **1** *FORMAL* honest or lasting support, or loyalty, especially to a sexual partner: *Somerset Maugham's comedy of* ***marital*** *fidelity, 'The Constant Wife'* ○ *How important do you think* ***sexual*** *fidelity is in a marriage?* **2** *APPROVING* when you copy the detail and quality of an original, such as a picture, sound or story exactly: *The best ink-jet printers can reproduce photographs with amazing fidelity.*

fidget /ˈfɪdʒ.ɪt/ *verb* [I] to make continuous small movements which annoy other people: *Children can't sit still for long without fidgeting.* ○ *Stop fidgeting* ***about!***
fidget /ˈfɪdʒ.ɪt/ *noun* [C] a person who often fidgets: *Tim's a terrible fidget.*
the fidgets *plural noun UK INFORMAL* when you keep fidgeting: *I got the fidgets halfway through the lecture.*
fidgety /ˈfɪdʒ.ɪ.ti/ *adj*: *a fidgety child/audience*

fiduciary /fɪˈdjuː.ʃi.ə.ri/ [US] /-ˈduː.ʃi.er-/ *adj SPECIALIZED* relating to the responsiblility to look after someone else's money in a correct way: *a breach of fiduciary duty*

field [LAND] /fiːld/ *noun* [C] **1** an area of land, used for growing crops or keeping animals, usually surrounded by a fence: *We drove past fields of ripening wheat.* ○ *The cows were all standing in one corner of the field.* **2 the field** an area of land in which you are working or studying: *I spoke to an aid worker who had recently returned from the field.*
• ***sb's*** **field of vision** the whole area that someone can see
-field /-fiːld/ *suffix* an area of land containing a particular natural substance: *an oilfield* ○ *a coalfield*

field [SPORTS GROUND] /fiːld/ *noun* [C] an area, usually covered with grass, used for playing sport: *the school* ***playing/sports*** *field* ○ *a football/hockey/rugby field*
• **take the field** to go onto the field at the start of a game: *There were loud cheers as the Irish team took the field.*
field /fiːld/ *verb* [I or T] to catch or pick up the ball after it has been hit in a game such as cricket or baseball, and to try to prevent the other team from scoring: *He fielded the ball well.* ○ *Our team is fielding first.*
fielder /ˈfiːl.dəʳ/ [US] /-dɚ/ *noun* [C] any member of the team which is fielding in a game such as cricket or baseball and tries to prevent the opposition from scoring

field [COMPETITORS] /fiːld/ *group noun* [S] all the competitors taking part in a race or activity: *The race started with a field of eleven, but two horses fell.* ○ *We have a* ***strong*** *field this afternoon.* ○ *Once again, Jones finished ahead of* ***the*** *field.*
• **leave the field clear for** ***sb*** to stop competing with someone, making it possible for them to succeed: *John decided not to apply for the job, which left the field clear for Emma.*
field /fiːld/ *verb* [T] to have or produce a team of people to take part in an activity or event: *The company fielded a group of experts to take part in the conference.*

field [AREA OF INTEREST] /fiːld/ *noun* [C] an area of activity or interest: *the field* ***of*** *history/science/medicine* ○ *Are you still in the same field* (= Are you doing the same type of work)*?*
• **not be/be outside** ***your*** **field** to be something you do not know much about: *Programming really isn't my field – you'd better ask Phil.*

field [ANSWER] /fiːld/ *verb* [T] to answer something cleverly or to avoid answering something directly: *He fielded some awkward questions very skilfully.*

field [COMPUTER] /fiːld/ *noun* [C] *SPECIALIZED* a division of a DATABASE (= collection of similar information on a computer) which contains a particular type of information, such as names or numbers

ˈfield ˌday *noun* [C] *US* a special day of organized sports or other outside activities for students
• **have a field day** to enjoy yourself very much or take advantage of an opportunity: *The newspapers had a field*

day when the wedding was announced (= they wrote a lot about it and printed many photographs of it).

'field ,event *noun* [C] a sports event in which competitors take part one after the other rather than racing or competing together: *High jump and javelin throwing are field events.*

'field ,glasses *plural noun* **binoculars**

'field ,hockey *noun* [C] US FOR **hockey** ⊃See picture **Sports** on page Centre 10

'field ,marshal *noun* [C] a British army officer of the highest rank

'field ,trip *noun* [C] a visit made by students to study something away from their school or college: *a geography field trip*

fieldwork /'fiːld.wɜːk/ Ⓤ /-wɝːk/ *noun* [U] study which consists of practical activities that are done away from your school, college or place of work

fiend /fiːnd/ *noun* [C] **1** an evil and cruel person: *He was portrayed in the media as a complete fiend.* **2** someone who likes something very much or is very interested in something: *a health/sex/chocolate fiend* ○ *McCormack is a fiend for punctuality.*

fiendish /'fiːn.dɪʃ/ *adj* **1** evil and cruel: *a fiendish attack* **2** clever and difficult, sometimes in a bad way: *a fiendish crossword* ○ *a fiendish plot/scheme*
fiendishly /'fiːn.dɪʃ.li/ *adv* INFORMAL extremely: *fiendishly difficult* **fiendishness** /'fiːn.dɪʃ.nəs/ *noun* [U]

fierce /fɪəs/ Ⓤ /fɪrs/ *adj* **1** physically violent and frightening: *a fierce attack/battle* ○ *Two men were shot during fierce fighting last weekend.* **2** strong and powerful: *Fierce winds/seas prevented the race from taking place.* ○ *Fire fighters had to retreat from the fierce heat.* **3** showing strong feeling or energetic activity: *The expansion plans will face fierce opposition/resistance from environmentalists.* ○ *There is fierce competition to join the Special Branch.* **4** US INFORMAL difficult: *The chemistry exam was fierce!*
• **something fierce** US INFORMAL very much: *I need a cold drink something fierce.*
fiercely /'fɪə.sli/ Ⓤ /'fɪr.sli/ *adv* **1** in a frightening, violent or powerful way: *to growl/fight fiercely* ○ *to burn fiercely* **2** extremely: *She's fiercely competitive/ independent.* **fierceness** /'fɪə.snəs/ Ⓤ /'fɪr.snəs/ *noun* [U]

fiery /'faɪə.ri/ *adj* **1** bright red, like fire: *a fiery sky/sunset* **2** describes food which causes a strong burning feeling in the mouth: *a fiery chilli sauce* **3** showing very strong feeling: *A fiery debate ensued.* ○ *a fiery temperament/ temper* ○ *a fiery orator/speech*

fiesta /fi'es.tə/ *noun* [C] a public celebration in Spain or Latin America, especially one on a religious holiday, with entertainments and activities

fifteen /,fɪf'tiːn/ /'--/ *determiner, pronoun, noun* (the number) 15: *thirteen, fourteen, fifteen* ○ *a fifteen-storey building* ○ *"How many books were returned?" "Fifteen (books)."*
fifteenth /,fɪf'tiːnθ/ /'--/ *determiner, pronoun, adj, adv, noun* 15th written as a word

fifth /fɪfθ/ *determiner, pronoun, adj, adv, noun* [S] 5th written as a word: *the fifth floor of the building* ○ *Tomorrow is the fifth (of September).* ○ *She is fifth in the line of succession to the throne.* ○ *He came fifth.*
fifth /fɪfθ/ *noun* [C] one of five equal parts of something: *One fifth is the same as 20 percent.*

,fifth 'column *noun* [C] a group of people who support the enemies of the country they live in and secretly help them
,fifth 'columnist *noun* [C] a member of such a group

fifty /'fɪf.ti/ *determiner, pronoun, noun* (the number) 50: *forty, fifty, sixty* ○ *fifty pounds* ○ *The US flag has fifty stars on it.* ○ *"How fast were they driving?" "They were doing fifty (miles an hour)."*
fifties /'fɪf.tiz/ *plural noun* A person's fifties are the period in which they are aged between 50 and 59: *My dad's in his fifties.*
the 'fifties *plural noun* **1** the range of temperature between 50° and 59°: *It's been in the fifties all week.* **2** the period of years between 50 and 59 in any century: *Rock and roll first became popular in the fifties* (= between 1950 and 1959).

fiftieth /'fɪf.ti.əθ/ *determiner, pronoun, adj, adv, noun* 50th written as a word

fifty-fifty /,fɪf.ti'fɪf.ti/ *adv, adj* (into) equal halves: *They divided the prize fifty-fifty.* ○ *There's only a fifty-fifty chance that she'll survive the operation.*

fig FRUIT /fɪg/ *noun* [C] a sweet, soft, purple or green fruit with many edible seeds, or a tree on which these grow ⊃See picture **Fruit** on page Centre 1
• **not care/give a fig** OLD-FASHIONED to not be at all worried by or interested in something: *They can say what they like. I don't give a fig.*

fig. PICTURE *noun* WRITTEN ABBREVIATION FOR **figure** PICTURE

fig LANGUAGE *adj* WRITTEN ABBREVIATION FOR **figurative** LANGUAGE

fight /faɪt/ *verb* **fought, fought 1** [I or T] to use physical force to try to defeat another person or group of people: *There were children fighting in the playground.* ○ *The soldiers fought from house to house.* ○ *They fought with* (= on the side of) *the North against the South.* ○ *The birds were fighting over* (= competing for) *a scrap of food.* ○ *They fight like cats and dogs* (= fight or argue very angrily and violently). ○ *They fought to the bitter end/to the death* (= until everyone on one side was dead or completely defeated). **2** [I or T] to use a lot of effort to defeat or achieve something, or to stop something happening: *He fought the disease bravely for three years.* ○ *We need the public's help in fighting crime.* ○ *He fought against racism.* ○ *Vitamin C is thought to help fight colds and flu.* ○ *They had to fight hard for improvements to the road system.* ○ *I had to fight (back)* (= tried hard not to show or produce) *the tears when he said he was leaving.* ○ *The bank fought off* (= successfully prevented) *a takeover by another bank recently.* ○ *I was getting a cold at the start of the week but I seem to have fought it off* (= got rid of it). **3** [I] INFORMAL to argue: *I wish they wouldn't fight in front of the kids.* ○ *I could hear them fighting about money again.*
• **fight it out** INFORMAL to decide which of a group of people will get something good when there is only one or a few of that thing: *There's only one ticket so you'll have to fight it out between you.*
• **fight your corner** UK to defend something that you believe in by arguing: *You'll have to be prepared to fight your corner if you want them to extend the project.*
• **fight fire with fire** to use the same methods as someone else in order to defeat them
• **fight a losing battle** to try hard to do something when there is no chance that you will succeed
• **fight shy of** UK to try to avoid something: *Before this course I'd always fought shy of technology.*

fight /faɪt/ *noun* **1** [C] an argument or an occasion when someone uses physical force to try to defeat someone: *Jeff's always getting into/starting fights.* ○ *The older boys broke up* (= stopped) *the fight.* ○ UK *I had a stand-up fight with her* (= we argued strongly) *about the tele-phone bill.* ○ *Have you got tickets for the big fight* (= boxing competition)*?* ○ *He put up a fight when the police tried to arrest him.* **2** [C] when you use a lot of effort to defeat someone or achieve something, or to stop something happening: *We must continue the fight against homelessness.* ○ *He died last week after a long fight with cancer.* ○ *They put up a good fight* (= played well) *against a more experienced football team.* **3** [U] desire or ability to fight or act energetically: *The team came out on the field full of fight.*
• **a fight to the finish** when two groups or people intend to fight until one side has been defeated

fighting /'faɪ.tɪŋ/ Ⓤ /-t̬ɪŋ/ *noun* [U] when people fight, especially in a war: *Fierce fighting has continued all day on the outskirts of the town.*
▲ **fight back** *phrasal verb* to defend yourself when someone attacks you or causes problems for you

fighter PERSON /'faɪ.tə/ Ⓤ /-t̬ɚ/ *noun* [C] someone who fights: *She's a fighter* (= she tries hard and will not easily give up).

fighter AIRCRAFT /'faɪ.tə/ Ⓤ /'faɪ.t̬ɚ/ *noun* [C] a small fast military aircraft used for chasing and destroying enemy aircraft: *a fighter plane/aircraft* ○ *a fighter pilot* ⊃See picture **Planes, Ships and Boats** on page Centre 14

fighting 'chance noun [S] a small but real possibility that something can be done: *If we can raise enough money, there's a fighting chance **(that)** we can save the project.*

fighting 'fit adj [after v] UK extremely healthy: *At 73, she's still fighting fit, walking five miles a day.*

fighting 'spirit noun [U] the willingness to compete or to do things which are difficult: *Don't take no for an answer – where's your fighting spirit?*

'fighting ˌwords noun [U] (UK ALSO **fighting talk**) speech that shows you are willing to fight

'fig ˌleaf LEAF noun [C usually sing] the type of leaf sometimes used in paintings to cover a naked person's sex organs

'fig ˌleaf FALSE noun [C usually sing] UK something that hides something else, especially something that is dishonest or embarrassing: *The spokesperson said the information campaign was a fig leaf to hide the most regressive tax in history.*

figment /'fɪg.mənt/ noun **a figment of sb's imagination** something which seems real but is not: *Was it just a figment of my imagination or did I hear John's voice in the other room?*

figurative LANGUAGE /'fɪg.ᵊr.ə.tɪv/ ⑩ /-ɚ.ə.t̬ɪv/ adj (of words and phrases) used not with their basic meaning but with a more imaginative meaning: *Of course, she was using the term 'massacre' in the figurative sense.* ➔Compare **literal**.
figuratively /'fɪg.ᵊr.ə.tɪv.li/ ⑩ /-ɚ.ə.t̬ɪv-/ adv: *Christopher will come with you to hold your hand, figuratively speaking.*

figurative ART /'fɪg.ᵊr.ə.tɪv/ ⑩ /-ɚ.ə.t̬ɪv/ adj (of a painting, drawing, etc.) representing something as it really looks, rather than in an ABSTRACT way

figure SHAPE /'fɪg.ə'/ ⑩ /-jʊr/ noun [C] **1** the shape of the human body, or a person: *I could see two tall figures in the distance.* ○ *A strange bearded figure* (= person) *entered the room.* ○ FIGURATIVE *She was a **central/key/leading** figure in* (= was an important person in) *the movement for constitutional reform.* **2** a painting, drawing or model of a person: *There are several reclining figures in the painting.* **3** a woman's body shape: *She's got a lovely figure.* ○ *She **got** her **figure** **back*** (= returned to her usual shape) *a couple of months after having the baby.*
• **fine figure of a man/woman** OFTEN HUMOROUS a person who is tall, with a large physically attractive body

figure NUMBER /'fɪg.ə'/ ⑩ /-jʊr/ noun [C] the symbol for a number or an amount expressed in numbers: *Can you read this figure? Is it a three or an eight?* ○ *Write the amount in both words and figures.* ○ *I looked quickly down the **column of** figures.* ○ *He earns a six-figure salary* (= an amount of money with six figures).
• **in single/double figures** between 1 and 9/between 10 and 99: *The job vacancies are now in double figures.*
• **put a figure on it** to say exactly how much something is or costs: *I'm sure we'll make a good profit, but I couldn't put a figure on it.*
figure /'fɪg.ə'/ ⑩ /-jʊr/ verb [T] US to calculate an amount: *I'm still figuring my taxes.*

COMMON LEARNER ERROR

figure or figures?

When referring to a set of numbers always use the plural form.

This report shows the company's sales figures for Asia.
~~This report shows the company's sales figure for Asia.~~

figure PICTURE /'fɪg.ə'/ ⑩ /-jʊr/ noun [C] (WRITTEN ABBREVIATION **fig**) a picture or drawing, often numbered, in a book or other document: *Please see figures 8 and 9.*

figure APPEAR /'fɪg.ə'/ ⑩ /-jʊr/ verb [I usually + adv or prep] to be, appear, take part or be included in something: *Their names did not figure in the list of finalists.* ○ *They denied that violence and intimidation had figured prominently in achieving the decision.*

figure EXPECT /'fɪg.ə'/ ⑩ /-jʊr/ verb [I] MAINLY US to expect or think that something will happen: [+ (that)] *We figured (that) you'd want to rest after your journey.*

• **Go figure!** MAINLY US used when you tell someone a fact and you then want to say that the fact is surprising or strange or stupid: *It's a terrible movie and it made $200 million. Go figure!*
• **it figures** (ALSO **that figures**) INFORMAL used to say that you are not surprised by something unpleasant that has happened: *"Dad, Sadie spilled her milk all over the floor." "It figures."*
▲ **figure** *sth/sb* **out** phrasal verb INFORMAL to finally understand something or someone, or find the solution to a problem after a lot of thought: [+ question word] *I can't figure out **why** he did it.* ○ *I find him really odd – I can't figure him out at all.* ○ *Can you figure out the answer to question 5?*

figurehead PERSON /'fɪg.ə.hed/ ⑩ /-jɚ-/ noun [C] someone who has the position of leader in an organization but who has no real power: *The President of this company is just a figurehead – the Chief Executive has day-to-day control.*

figurehead MODEL /'fɪg.ə.hed/ ⑩ /-jɚ-/ noun [C] a painted model, usually of a person, which in the past was fixed to the front of a ship

ˌfigure of 'eight UK noun [C] (US **figure eight**) the shape made when drawing an 8: *She skated a perfect figure of eight.*

ˌfigure of 'fun noun [C usually sing] MAINLY UK someone who is laughed at unkindly

ˌfigure of 'speech noun [C] plural **figures of speech** an expression which uses words to mean something different from their ordinary meaning: *'Get up with the lark' is a figure of speech, meaning 'Get out of bed early'.*

'figure ˌskating noun [U] a type of SKATING which involves circular patterns and often includes jumps

figurine /ˌfɪg.ə'riːn/ ⑩ /-jɚ-/ noun [C] a small model of a human, usually made of clay or PORCELAIN

filament /'fɪl.ə.mənt/ noun [C] **1** a thin thread or fibre of natural or artificial material: *Toothbrushes should be replaced when the filaments become worn.* ○ *glass/silk filaments* **2** a thin wire, especially one which lights up inside an electric LIGHT BULB: *a tungsten filament*

filbert /'fɪl.bət/ ⑩ /-bɚt/ noun [C] MAINLY US a **hazelnut**

filch /fɪltʃ/ verb [T] INFORMAL to steal something of little value: *Who's filched my pencils?*

file CONTAINER /faɪl/ noun **1** [C or U] any of several different types of container used to store papers, letters and other documents in an ordered way, especially in an office: *a box/envelope file* ○ *secret/confidential/personnel files* ○ *You'll find it **in the** files under 'C'.* ○ *We keep your records **on** file for five years.* ➔See picture **In the Office** on page Centre 15 **2** [C] written records that are kept about a particular person or subject: *The police have **opened** a file **on** local burglaries.* **3** [C] information stored on a computer as one unit with one name: *What's the file name?* ○ *I'm going to copy/save this file.*
file /faɪl/ verb [T] **1** to store information in a careful and particular way: *We file these reports* (= put them in a file) ***under** country of origin.* **2** LEGAL to officially record something especially in a law court: *The police filed charges against the two suspects.* **3** News reporters file a story by sending it to their office, usually by telephone, email or other electronic method: *Our foreign correspondent filed this report earlier today.*
filing /'faɪ.lɪŋ/ noun **1** [U] the activity of putting documents, electronic information, etc. into files: *a filing cabinet* ○ *Her job involves filing and other general office work.* **2** [C] LEGAL an official record of something: *a bankruptcy filing*
▲ **file for** *sth* phrasal verb LEGAL to make an official request for something such as DIVORCE or BANKRUPTCY

file LINE /faɪl/ noun [C or U] a long line of people or animals, one behind another: *They were horrified to see files **of** ants marching through the kitchen.* ○ *They walked in (single) file* (= one behind another).
file /faɪl/ verb [I usually + adv or prep] to walk in a line, one behind another: *The visitors filed **through** the entrance to the ticket offices.*

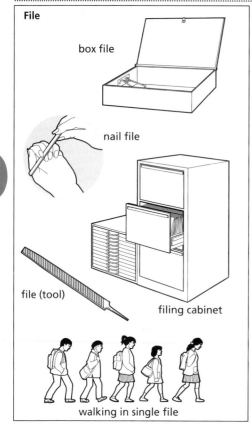

File

box file

nail file

file (tool)

filing cabinet

walking in single file

file TOOL /faɪl/ noun [C] a thin flat or rounded metal tool, which has rough surfaces for rubbing wooden or metal objects to make them smooth or to change their shape

file /faɪl/ verb [I + adv or prep; T] to use a file in order to make an object smooth or to change its shape: *File (down) the sharp edges.* ○ [+ obj + adj] *The surface had been filed smooth.* ○ *She filed her nails as she watched TV.*

filings /ˈfaɪ.lɪŋz/ plural noun small pieces of metal which are removed from a larger piece by filing: *iron filings*

filet /fɪˈleɪ/ noun [C], verb [T] US FOR **fillet**

filial /ˈfɪl.i.əl/ adj FORMAL of a son or daughter: *filial duty/respect/affection*

filibuster /ˈfɪl.ɪ.bʌs.tər/ US /-tɚ/ verb [I or T] MAINLY US to make a long speech in order to delay or prevent a new law being made: *Conceivably, supporters of the law could filibuster to prevent it from being revised.* **filibuster** /ˈfɪl.ɪ.bʌs.tər/ US /-tɚ/ noun [C]

filigree /ˈfɪl.ɪ.griː/ noun [U] delicate jewellery made from twisted, especially silver, wire: *a beautiful filigree brooch* ○ *filigree ironwork*

filing cabinet noun [C] a large piece of furniture in an office, used for holding documents ⊃See picture **In the Office** on page Centre 15

fill /fɪl/ verb **1** [I or T] to make or become full; to use empty space: *I filled the bucket with water.* ○ *I could hear the cistern filling.* ○ *I went to the library to fill (in) an hour* (= use that period of time) *until the meeting.* ○ FIGURATIVE *Happy sounds filled the room* (= could be heard everywhere in the room). ○ FIGURATIVE *The thought of it fills me with* (= makes me feel) *dread.* **2** [T] to give a job or position to someone: *I'm sorry, the job/post/vacancy has already been filled.* ○ *We would prefer to fill the post with* (= give it to) *a recent graduate.* **3** [I or T] to put a substance into an empty space: *Before pain-*

ting, fill **(in)** all the cracks in the plaster. ○ *These cakes are filled with cream.* ○ FIGURATIVE *The product clearly filled a need/gap in the market.* **4** [T] to put a substance into a hole in a tooth to repair it: *You should get that cavity filled.*

fill /fɪl/ noun [U] someone's fill is as much as they want or as much as they can deal with: *He took only a few minutes to eat/drink his fill.* ○ *I'd had my fill of his rude remarks.* **-filled** /-fɪld/ suffix: *a smoke-filled room* ○ *a fun-filled weekend*

filler /ˈfɪl.ər/ US /-ɚ/ noun **1** [C or U] a substance that is used to fill small holes and cracks, especially in wood and walls **2** [C] a short text or drawings used to fill extra space in a magazine or newspaper, or talk, music, etc. used to fill extra time in a radio or television broadcast

filling /ˈfɪl.ɪŋ/ noun **1** [U] any material used to fill something: *duvets with synthetic filling* **2** [C or U] the layer of food inside a sandwich, cake, etc: *pies with sweet or savoury fillings* ○ *sandwich fillings* **3** [C] the artificial substance put into holes in teeth to repair them

filling /ˈfɪl.ɪŋ/ adj If food is filling, you feel full after you have eaten only a little of it.

PHRASAL VERBS WITH **fill** ▼

▲ **fill** *sth* **in/out** WRITE phrasal verb [M] to write the necessary information on an official document: *to fill in a form/questionnaire*

▲ **fill** *sb* **in** GIVE INFORMATION phrasal verb [M] to give someone extra or missing information: *I filled her in on the latest gossip.*

▲ **fill in** REPLACE phrasal verb to do someone else's work for them because they cannot or will not do it themselves: *Volunteers would fill in for teachers in the event of a strike.* ○ *I'm not her regular secretary – I'm just filling in.*

▲ **fill out** phrasal verb If someone who is thin fills out, they become heavier and more rounded, often because they have grown older.

▲ **fill** *(sth)* **up** phrasal verb [M] to become full, or to make something become full: *The seats in the hall were filling up fast.* ○ *As she read the poem, their eyes filled up with tears.*

▲ **fill** *sb* **up** phrasal verb [M] If food fills you up, it makes you feel as if you have eaten enough: *That sandwich really filled me up.*

fillet UK /ˈfɪl.ɪt/ noun [C or U] (US **filet**) a piece of meat or fish without bones: *a piece of cod fillet* ○ *fillet of plaice* ○ *small trout fillets* ○ *fillet steak* ○ *fillet of beef*

fillet UK /ˈfɪl.ɪt/ verb [T] (US **filet**) to cut a piece of meat or fish from the bones

filling station noun [C] UK AND US FOR **petrol station**

fillip /ˈfɪl.ɪp/ noun [C usually sing] something which causes a sudden improvement: *The athletics win provided a much-needed fillip to/for national pride.* ○ *The news gave the stock market a big fillip.*

filly /ˈfɪl.i/ noun [C] a young female horse ⊃Compare **colt** HORSE.

film MOVING PICTURES /fɪlm/ noun [C or U] (US **movie**) a series of moving pictures, usually shown in a cinema or on television and often telling a story: *What's your favourite film?* ○ *We took the children to (see) a film.* ○ *She had a long career in films/film* (= the business of making films). ○ *a film star/critic* ○ *the film industry* ○ *a film-maker* ○ *Her last film was shot* (= made) *on location in South America.* ○ *I hate people talking while I'm watching a film.* ○ *Would you like to go and see a film tonight?*

film /fɪlm/ verb [I or T] to record moving pictures with a camera, usually to make a film for the cinema or television: *Most of the scenes were filmed in a studio.* ○ *They filmed for a week in Spain.*

filming /ˈfɪl.mɪŋ/ noun [U] the activity of making a film: *Filming was halted after the lead actor became ill.*

film MATERIAL /fɪlm/ noun [C or U] (a length of) dark plastic-like material which can record images as photographs or as a moving picture: *a roll of film* ○ *a 24 exposure/16mm/high-speed film* ○ *A passer-by recorded the incident on film.* ○ *I'm getting my film developed at the chemist's.*

film [LAYER] /fɪlm/ *noun* [C] a thin layer of something on a surface: *a film **of** dust/oil/grease* ○ *a film **of** smoke* **filmy** /ˈfɪl.mi/ *adj*: *filmy material* ○ *a filmy dress* **filminess** /ˈfɪl.mɪ.nəs/ *noun* [U]

▲ **film over** *phrasal verb* If something films over, it becomes lightly covered with a thin layer of something: *Her eyes suddenly filmed over **(with** tears).*

ˈfilm diˌrector *noun* [C] a person who is in charge of a film and tells the actors how to play their parts

filmgoer /ˈfɪlmˌɡəʊ.əʳ/ [US] /-ˌɡoʊ.ɚ/ *noun* [C] (*MAINLY US* **moviegoer**) a person who regularly goes to watch films at the cinema **filmgoing** *UK* /ˈfɪlmˌɡəʊ.ɪŋ/ [US] /ˌɡoʊ-/ *noun* [U], *adj* [before n] (*MAINLY US* **moviegoing**) *the filmgoing public*

ˈfilm ˌmaker *noun* [C] someone who is in charge of making a film

ˈfilm ˌstar *MAINLY UK noun* [C] (*MAINLY US* **movie star**) a famous cinema actor or actress

ˈfilm ˌstrip *noun* [C] *UK* a length of film with a set of pictures which are shown one at a time: *a health education film strip*

Filofax *TRADEMARK* /ˈfaɪ.lə.fæks/ *noun* [C] (*ALSO* **personal organizer**) a small book in which a record can be kept of telephone numbers, future plans and visits, business meetings, etc. ➲See picture **In the Office** on page Centre 15

filo (pastry) *UK, US* **phyllo (pastry)** /ˌfiː.ləʊˈpeɪ.stri/ [US] /-loʊ/ *noun* [U] a type of pastry made in thin, almost transparent layers

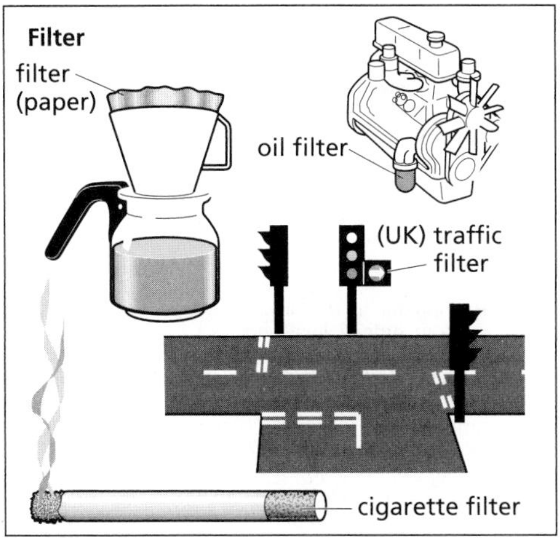

filter [REMOVE] /ˈfɪl.təʳ/ [US] /-t̬ɚ/ *noun* [C] any of several types of equipment or devices for removing solids from liquids or gases, or for removing particular types of light: *a water filter* ○ *a dust filter* ○ *I like to experiment with different light filters on my camera.* ○ *Ozone is the earth's primary filter for ultraviolet radiation.*

filter /ˈfɪl.təʳ/ [US] /-t̬ɚ/ *verb* [T] to remove solids from liquids or gases, or to remove particular types of light, using special equipment: *The water is filtered to remove any impurities.* ○ *Devices in the two chimneys would filter **(out)*** (= remove) *radioactive dust from smoke released into the air.*

filtration /fɪlˈtreɪ.ʃᵊn/ *noun* [U] the act of filtering: *a filtration unit/plant* ○ *The technology exists to remove all of these contaminants through filtration.*

filter [APPEAR GRADUALLY] /ˈfɪl.təʳ/ [US] /-t̬ɚ/ *verb* [I + adv or prep] to appear or happen gradually or to a limited degree: *News filtered **down** to us during the day.* ○ *Reports about an accident began to filter **in**.* ○ *Sunlight filtered **through** the branches.*

filter [TRAFFIC] /ˈfɪl.təʳ/ [US] /-t̬ɚ/ *noun* [C] *UK* a green arrow-shaped light which is part of a set of TRAFFIC LIGHTS and which tells drivers when they can turn left or right: *a traffic filter* ○ *a left/right filter*

▲ **filter in** *phrasal verb UK* to join a line of moving traffic without causing other vehicles to slow down

ˈfilter ˌbed *noun* [C] an area of stones and sand through which water flows to be cleaned

ˈfilter/ˈfiltered ˌcoffee *UK noun* [C or U] (*US* **drip coffee**) coffee made by slowly pouring hot water through crushed coffee beans in a coffee filter

ˈfilter ˌpaper *noun* **1** [U] thin paper which allows only liquid to flow through **2** [C] *UK* a paper cone which allows only water through and is used to make filter coffee

ˈfilter ˌtip *noun* [C] (*ALSO* **filter-tipped cigarette**) a cigarette with a filter on the end to remove TAR from the tobacco

filth [DIRT] /fɪlθ/ *noun* [U] thick, unpleasant dirt: *The floor was covered in filth.*

filthy /ˈfɪl.θi/ *adj* extremely or unpleasantly dirty: *Wash your hands – they're filthy!* ○ *Look at this cloth – it's filthy!* ○ *I've never smoked – it's a filthy **habit**.* ○ *FIGURATIVE That girl just gave me a filthy **look*** (= looked at me in very unpleasant, disapproving way). ○ *UK He was in a filthy* (= a very bad) ***temper/mood**.*

filthy /ˈfɪl.θi/ *adv* **filthy dirty** extremely dirty

• **filthy rich** *INFORMAL* extremely rich

filthiness /ˈfɪl.θɪ.nəs/ *noun* [U] the quality of being filthy

filth [OFFENSIVE MATERIAL] /fɪlθ/ *noun* [U] sexually offensive material: *People complain about the filth on TV and in the press.*

filthy /ˈfɪl.θi/ *adj* containing sexually offensive words or pictures: *filthy language* ○ *a filthy joke* ○ *HUMOROUS You've got a filthy mind!*

fin /fɪn/ *noun* [C] a thin vertical part sticking out of the body of especially a fish or an aircraft which helps balance and movement: *We could see the fin of a shark as it slowly circled our boat.* ○ *a fish's dorsal fin* ○ *The aircraft has a long tail fin.*

finagle /fɪˈneɪ.ɡl̩/ *verb* [I or T] *US* to use tricks and dishonest methods to get what you want: *He somehow finagled his way into the army as a lieutenant.*

final [LAST] /ˈfaɪ.nᵊl/ *adj* last: *a final warning/offer* ○ *the final chapters of a book* ○ *the final years* ○ *The game is **in** its final **stages**.*

• **in the final analysis** used when you are talking about what is most important or true in a situation: *In the final analysis, it is the drug companies that are going to profit from this policy.*

• **that's final** used to show that you are certain you will not change your decision about something: *It's no use begging me – I'm not coming and that's final.*

finality /faɪˈnæl.ə.ti/ [US] /-t̬i/ *noun* [U] *FORMAL* the quality of being finished and therefore not able to be changed: *the finality of death*

finalize, *UK USUALLY* **-ise** /ˈfaɪ.nə.laɪz/ *verb* [T] to make a final and certain decision about a plan, date, etc: *We'll finalize the details later.* **finalization**, *UK USUALLY* **-isation** /ˌfaɪ.nə.laɪˈzeɪ.ʃᵊn/ *noun* [U] *the finalization of negotiations*

finals /ˈfaɪ.nᵊlz/ *plural noun UK* the exams taken at the end of a university or college course: *I'm **taking** my finals in June.* ○ *The finals results have gone up on the noticeboard.*

final [COMPETITION] /ˈfaɪ.nᵊl/ *noun* [C] the last in a series of games, races or competitions, usually the one in which the winner is chosen: *Last year we got **through to** the final.* ○ *The men's basketball final will be on Sunday.*

finalist /ˈfaɪ.nə.lɪst/ *noun* [C] a person or group competing in a final

the finals *plural noun* the last set of games in a competition: *Do you think Scotland will qualify for the European Championship finals?*

ˌfinal deˈmand *noun* [C] the last request for the payment of money owed for goods or services before an action is taken against the person who owes that money

finale /fɪˈnɑː.li/ *noun* [C usually sing] the last part of especially a musical or theatrical performance, which is often very exciting or emotional: *All the dancers come on stage during the **grand** finale.* ○ *FIGURATIVE What better finale **to** her career than this extravagant gesture?*

ˌfinal (eˈxam) *noun* [C] *US* a test taken on a subject at the end of a school year or college course: *The final exam for this class will be on May 21st.* ○ *When is your chemistry/French/algebra final?*

F

finally [AFTER TIME] /ˈfaɪ.nə.li/ *adv* after a long time or some difficulty: *We finally got home at midnight.* ○ *After months of looking he finally found a job.*

finally [LAST] /ˈfaɪ.nə.li/ *adv* used especially at the beginning of a sentence to introduce the last point or idea: *Finally, I'd like to thank everyone for coming this evening.*

finally [CERTAINLY] /ˈfaɪ.nə.li/ *adv* in a way that will not be changed: *The plan hasn't been finally approved.*

finance /ˈfaɪ.nænts/ *noun* **[U]** (the management of) a supply of money: *corporate/personal/public finance* ○ *the minister of finance/the finance minister* ○ *You need to speak to someone in the finance* ***department.*** ○ *The finance* ***committee*** *controls the school's budget.*

finance /ˈfaɪ.nænts/ *verb* **[T]** to provide the money needed for something to happen: *The local authority has refused to finance the scheme.*

finances /ˈfaɪ.nænt.sɪz/ *plural noun* the money which a person or company has: *We keep a tight control on the organization's finances.* ○ UK INFORMAL *My finances won't* ***run to*** (= I do not have enough money to buy) *a new car this year.*

financial /faɪˈnæn.tʃəl/ /fɪ-/ *adj* relating to money or how money is managed: *financial difficulties/success* ○ *a financial adviser* ○ *financial affairs* ➲See Note **economic, economical or financial?** at **economy** SAVING MONEY.

financially /faɪˈnæn.t.ʃəl.i/ /fɪ-/ *adv*: *The project is not financially* ***viable*** (= will not produce enough money). ○ *He's still financially* ***dependent on*** (= regularly receives money to live from) *his parents.*

financier /fɪˈnænt.si.əʳ/ Ⓤⓢ /-ɚ/ *noun* **[C]** a person who has control of a large amount of money and can give or lend it to people or organizations

fiˌnancial ˈyear *noun* **[C]** a period of twelve months (not always January to December) for which a business, government, etc. plans its management of money

finch /fɪntʃ/ *noun* **[C]** any of various types of small singing bird with a short wide pointed beak ➲See also **bullfinch**; **chaffinch**.

find [DISCOVER] /faɪnd/ *verb* **[T] found, found 1** to discover, especially where a thing or person is, either unexpectedly or by searching, or to discover where to obtain or how to achieve something: *I've just found a ten-pound note in my pocket.* ○ *I couldn't find Andrew's telephone number.* ○ *You'll find the knives and forks in the left-hand drawer.* ○ *Researchers are hoping to find a cure for the disease.* ○ **[+ two objects]** *Has he found himself a place to live yet?* ○ **[+ obj + adj]** *She was found unconscious and bleeding.* ○ **[+ that]** *The study found* ***that*** *men who were married lived longer than those who were not.* ○ *Do you think they'll ever find a way of bringing peace to the region?* ○ *We're really struggling to find* (= obtain) *enough money to pay the rent at the moment.* ○ *After years of abuse from her husband, she eventually found the courage to leave him.* ○ *I wish I could find (the) time to do more reading.* **2** to think or feel a particular way about someone or something: **[+ obj + n or adj]** *Do you find Clive difficult to talk to?* ○ *I don't find him an easy person to get on with.* ○ *She doesn't find it easy to talk about her problems.* ○ **[+ v-ing]** *I find living in the city quite stressful.* **3** to become aware that something exists or has happened: **[+ (that)]** *We came home to find* ***(that)*** *the cat had had kittens.* ○ *I found* ***(that)*** *I could easily swim a mile.* **4 be found** to exist or be present somewhere: *Many plant and animal species are found only in the rainforests.* ○ *Vitamin C is found in oranges and other citrus fruit.*

find *yourself* *verb* **[R]** to become aware that you are in a particular situation or place, or doing a particular thing, unintentionally: *He'll find himself with no friends at all if he carries on behaving this way.* ○ *We fell asleep on the train and woke up to find ourselves* ***in*** *Calais.*

• **find *yourself*** OFTEN HUMOROUS If you go somewhere or do something to find yourself, you go there or do it to discover your true character: *Simon spent a year in an ashram in India to find himself.*

• **find *your* feet** to become familiar with and confident in a new situation: *Did it take you long to find your feet when you started your new job?*

• **find *your* way** to get somewhere you are trying to reach: *I had a map but I still couldn't find my way back to the hotel.*

• **find it in *your* heart to do *sth*** to be willing and able to do something unpleasant or difficult: *Could you find it in your heart to forgive her?*

• **find *your* tongue** (US ALSO **find *your* voice**) to become willing to talk: *Witnesses often find their tongues when they hear a reward has been offered.*

• **find fault with** to criticize someone or something: *She's always finding fault with the way he works.*

find /faɪnd/ *noun* **[C]** a good or valuable thing or a special person that has been discovered but was not known about before: *This café's quite a find – I had no idea there was anywhere like it around here.* ○ *A recent find* ***of*** *ancient artefacts is on display at the local museum.*

finder /ˈfaɪn.dəʳ/ Ⓤⓢ /-dɚ/ *noun* **[C]** someone who finds something

• **Finders keepers (losers weepers).** SAYING said by a child who has found an object to the child who has lost it to show that they intend to keep it

finding /ˈfaɪn.dɪŋ/ *noun* **[C]** a piece of information that is discovered during an official examination of a problem, situation or object: *The report's finding on the decrease in violent crime supports the police chief's claims.*

PHRASAL VERBS WITH **find**

▲ **find *(sth)* out** *phrasal verb* **[M]** to get information about something because you want to know more about it, or to learn a fact or piece of information for the first time: *How did you find out* ***about*** *the party?* ○ *The holiday was a complete surprise – I only found out* ***about*** *it the day before we left.* ○ **[+ question word]** *I'll just go and find out* ***what's*** *going on outside.* ○ **[+ that]** *Too late, she found out* ***that*** *the train had been cancelled.*

▲ **find *sb* out** *phrasal verb* **[M usually passive]** to discover that someone has done something wrong: *He lived in dread of being found out.*

find [JUDGE] /faɪnd/ *verb* **[I or T] found, found** LEGAL to make a judgment in a law court: **[+ obj + adj]** *In a unanimous verdict, the jury found him* ***guilty/not guilty*** *of the murder.*

finding /ˈfaɪn.dɪŋ/ *noun* **[C usually sing]** a judgment made at the end of an official legal INQUIRY (= a process to discover the answer to something)

fin-de-siècle /ˌfæn.də.siːˈek.lə/ *adj* **[before n]** relating to the end of the 19th century, especially the art, culture and morals of the period: *The novel begins with an evocative description of fin-de-siècle Paris.*

fine [SATISFACTORY] /faɪn/ *adj* **[after v]** good or good enough; healthy and well: *I felt terrible last night but I feel fine this morning.* ○ *The apartments are very small, which is fine for one person.* ○ *"Are you all right?" "Everything's just fine, thanks."* ○ *"I'll come round to your place at eight." "Fine. See you then."*

fine /faɪn/ *adv* in a satisfactory way: *"Will a loan of $500 be sufficient?" "That will* ***suit*** *me fine."* ○ *It was working fine yesterday.*

fine [EXCELLENT] /faɪn/ *adj* **1** excellent or much better than average: *purveyors of fine wines and gourmet food* ○ *The world's finest collection of Impressionist paintings is housed in the Musée d'Orsay in Paris.* ○ *This building is the finest example of its type.* **2** INFORMAL bad or inconvenient: *That's a fine* (= very unpleasant) *thing to say about your father after all he's done for you!* ○ *He picked a fine time to leave us.*

• **have *sth* down to a fine art** (UK ALSO **have *sth* off to a fine art**) to be able to do something very well or quickly, often because you have done it so many times

finest /ˈfaɪ.nɪst/ *noun* **[U] 1** the best example of its type: *This 100-year old restaurant is among London's finest.* **2** US INFORMAL A city's finest is its police force: *New York's finest*

finely /ˈfaɪn.li/ *adv* beautifully: *The painting depicts a finely-dressed couple.*

fine [THIN] /faɪn/ *adj* very thin or in very small pieces or drops: *The baby's head was covered in fine blond hair.* ○ *The eruption had covered the town with a fine layer of ash.* ○ *Apply a fine line of highlighter along the middle of* *your top lip.* ○ *She has inherited her mother's fine* (= delicate and beautiful) ***features.***

• **not to put too fine a point on** to be completely direct and honest: *I think she's wrong – not to put too fine a point on it.*

finely /ˈfaɪn.li/ *adv* into very thin or small pieces: *Chop the herbs very finely.* ○ *Make sure the spices are finely ground.* **fineness** /ˈfaɪn.nəs/ *noun* [U] *It's the fineness of the thread that makes the cloth so soft.*

fine [EXACT] /faɪn/ *adj* [usually before n] very exact and delicate, or needing to be done, treated or considered very carefully: *I understood in general what she was talking about, but some of the finer **details/points** were beyond me.* ○ *There's **a** fine **line** between love and hate.*

finely /ˈfaɪn.li/ *adv* to an exact degree: *a finely-tuned engine* ○ *a finely-executed manoeuvre* **fineness** /ˈfaɪn.nəs/ *noun* [U] *When I look at her paintings I'm always struck by the fineness of the details.*

fine [SUNNY] /faɪn/ *adj* MAINLY UK sunny and dry: *The weather forecast said it would be fine and dry today.*

fine [PUNISHMENT] /faɪn/ *noun* [C] an amount of money that has to be paid as a punishment for not obeying a rule or law: *The maximum penalty for the offence is a $1000 fine.* ○ *If found guilty, he faces six months in jail and a **heavy*** (= severe) *fine.* **fine** /faɪn/ *verb* [T] *Drivers who exceed the speed limit can expect to be fined heavily.* ○ [+ two objects] *They fined him $100 **for** using threatening behaviour.*

ˌfine ˈart *noun* [U] drawings, paintings and sculptures that are admired for their beauty and have no practical use

ˌfine ˈarts *plural noun* painting and sculpture: *a fine arts degree* ○ *The fine arts have suffered from a lack of government funding.*

ˌfine ˈprint *noun* [U] US FOR **small print**

finery /ˈfaɪ.nər.i/ [US] /-nɚ.i/ *noun* [U] beautiful clothing and jewellery worn on a special occasion: *There we all were **in our** finery, waiting for the bride and groom to arrive.*

fines herbes /ˌfiːnˈeəb/ [US] /ˌfiːnˈzerb/ *plural noun* a mixture of fresh or dried herbs that are used to flavour food

finesse /fɪˈnes/ *noun* [U] great skill or style: *It was a disappointing performance which lacked finesse.*

finesse /fɪˈnes/ *verb* [T] to deal with a situation or a person in a skilful and often slightly dishonest way: *She finessed the interview by playing down her lack of experience and talking about her long-standing interest in the field.*

fine-tooth comb /ˌfaɪn.tuːθˈkəʊm/ [US] /-ˈkoʊm/ *noun* **with a fine-tooth comb** If you go through something with a fine-tooth comb, you examine it in great detail and with great care: *We have gone through the evidence with a fine-tooth comb.*

fine-tune /ˌfaɪnˈtjuːn/ [US] /-ˈtuːn/ *verb* [T] to make very small changes to something in order to make it work as well as possible: *She spent hours fine-tuning her speech.*

finger /ˈfɪŋ.gəʳ/ [US] /-gɚ/ *noun* [C] **1** any of the long thin separate parts of the hand, especially those which are not thumbs: *He noticed her long delicate fingers.* ○ *I cut my finger chopping onions last night.* ➲See also **forefinger**; **index finger**; **ring finger**; **little finger**. **2** a part of a glove which covers a finger

• **be all fingers and thumbs** UK (US **be all thumbs**) to move your hands in an awkward or clumsy way: *I'm all fingers and thumbs today. That's the second plate I've dropped this morning.*

• **give *sb* the finger** US to show someone in an offensive way that you are angry with them by turning the back of your hand towards them and putting your middle finger up

• **have a finger in every pie** to be involved in and have influence over many different activities, often in a way that people do not approve of

• **have a finger in the pie** to be involved in something, often when your involvement is not wanted

• **have *your* fingers in the till** UK to steal money from the place where you work

• **cross *your* fingers** (ALSO **keep *your* fingers crossed**) to hope that things will happen in the way that you want them to: *It's her exam this morning so cross your fingers.* ○ *We're just hoping the weather stays nice and keeping our fingers crossed.*

• **not lift/raise a finger** to not make any effort to help: *He never lifts a finger to help with the housework.*

• **point the finger at *sb*** to accuse someone of being responsible for something bad that has happened: *Unhappy tourists have pointed the finger at unhelpful travel agents.*

finger-pointing accusations against someone: *There's the usual finger-pointing when mistakes are made.*

• **pull/get *your* finger out** UK INFORMAL to start working hard, especially after a period of low activity: *She's really going to have to pull her finger out if she wants to finish before Friday.*

• **put *your* finger on *sth*** to discover the exact reason why a situation is the way it is, especially when something is wrong: *There's something odd about him but I can't quite put my finger on it.*

finger /ˈfɪŋ.gəʳ/ [US] /-gɚ/ *verb* [T] **1** to touch or feel something with your fingers: *She fingered her necklace absent-mindedly as she talked.* **2** INFORMAL If you finger someone, you tell the police that they are guilty of a crime.

-fingered /-fɪŋ.gəd/ [US] /-gɚd/ *suffix* with or using the stated number of fingers: *two-fingered typing*

fingering /ˈfɪŋ.gər.ɪŋ/ [US] /-gɚ-/ *noun* [U] The fingering of a piece of music is the way that fingers are used to play particular notes, or the numbers on a sheet of music that show which fingers should play which notes.

fingerboard /ˈfɪŋ.gə.bɔːd/ [US] /-gɚ.bɔːrd/ *noun* [C] the long strip of wood on a stringed musical instrument against which the strings are pressed by the fingers in order to vary the note that is played: *Guitars and banjos have fingerboards.*

ˈfinger ˌbowl *noun* [C] a small bowl filled with water that a person can use to wash their fingers during a meal

ˈfinger ˌbuffet *noun* [C] a meal, often on a special occasion, in which the food is eaten with the fingers, often by guests who are standing

ˈfinger ˌfood *noun* [U] food that you can eat without using knives, forks or spoons

fingermark UK /ˈfɪŋ.gə.mɑːk/ [US] /-gɚ.mɑːrk/ *noun* [C] (US USUALLY **fingerprint**) a mark left by a dirty or oily finger on a clean surface: *He'd left sticky fingermarks all over the glass.*

fingernail /ˈfɪŋ.gə.neɪl/ [US] /-gɚ-/ *noun* [C] (ALSO **nail**) the hard slightly curved part that covers and protects the top of the end of a finger: *dirty fingernails* ○ *She had long red fingernails.* ➲See picture **The Body** on page Centre 5

fingerprint /ˈfɪŋ.gə.prɪnt/ [US] /-gɚ-/ *noun* [C] **1** (INFORMAL **print**) the pattern of curved lines on the end of a finger or thumb, which is different in every person, or a mark left by this pattern: *His fingerprints were all over the gun.* ○ *The police have **taken** fingerprints from every man in the neighbourhood.* **2** a **fingermark**

fingerprint /ˈfɪŋ.gə.prɪnt/ [US] /-gɚ-/ *verb* [T] *We would like to fingerprint* (= record the pattern of the fingerprints of) *every one of your employees.*

fingertip /ˈfɪŋ.gə.tɪp/ [US] /-gɚ-/ *noun* [C] the end of a finger: *Use your fingertips to gently flatten the pastry.*

• **at *your* fingertips** If you have something at your fingertips, you can get it and use it very easily: *He has all the latest statistics at his fingertips.*

• **be an *artist/professional, etc.* to *your* fingertips** UK to be a perfect or typical example of something: *Mark, a professional to his fingertips, insisted that we follow the correct procedures.*

finicky /ˈfɪn.ɪ.ki/ *adj* **1** DISAPPROVING difficult to please: *a finicky eater* ○ *He's terribly finicky **about** his food.* **2** needing a lot of attention to detail: *Repairing watches must be a very finicky job.*

finish [COMPLETE/END] /ˈfɪn.ɪʃ/ *verb* **1** [I or T] to complete something or come to the end of an activity: *I'll call you when I've finished my homework.* ○ *Please place your questionnaire in the box when you've finished.* ○ *She finished (the concert) **with** a song from her first album.* ○ *She finished second* (= in second place) *in the finals.*

F

○ [+ v-ing] *Have you finished reading that magazine?* ○ *They've already run out of money and the building isn't even* ***half****-finished* (= half of it has not been completed). **2** [I] to end: *The meeting should finish around four o'clock.* ○ *The play finishes with a song.* **3** [T] to eat, drink or use something completely so that none remains: *Make sure she finishes her dinner.* ○ *He finished his drink and left.* ○ *We finished* (= ate all of) *the pie last night.*
• **put the finishing touches to** *UK* (*US* **put the finishing touches on**) to add the final improvements to something so that you are satisfied with it or certain that it is complete
finish /ˈfɪn.ɪʃ/ *noun* [C] the end of a race, or the last part of something: *a close finish* ○ *They replayed the finish in slow motion.*
finished /ˈfɪn.ɪʃt/ *adj* completed: *How much does the finished product cost?* ○ *Are you finished* ***with*** *that drill?* ○ *When do you expect to be finished?* ○ *UK The rebels' ammunition is almost finished* (= completely used) *and it is only a matter of time before they surrender.* ○ *This financial crisis means that the government's economic policy is finished* (= destroyed).
finisher /ˈfɪn.ɪ.ʃəʳ/ [US] /-ʃɚ/ *noun* [C usually pl] a person or animal who completes a race or competiton

PHRASAL VERBS WITH **finish** ▼

▲ **finish *sth* off** [COMPLETE] *phrasal verb* [M] to complete the last part of something that you are doing: *I want to finish off this essay before I go to bed.*
▲ **finish *sth* off** [USE] *phrasal verb* [M] to eat, drink or use the last part of something: *We may as well finish off this pie – there's only a little bit left.*
▲ **finish *sb/sth* off** [KILL] *phrasal verb* [M] *INFORMAL* to kill someone or something, especially if they have already been injured: *A third heart attack finally finished off the old man.*
▲ **finish *sb* off** [TIRE] *phrasal verb* [M] *INFORMAL* to make someone extremely tired, weak or unhappy: *That game of football has really finished me off.*
▲ **finish up** [FINALLY BE] *phrasal verb* [I or L] *UK* If you finish up in a particular place or situation, that is the place or situation that you are in finally: *You'll finish up dead if you carry on drinking like that.* ○ *She married a Spaniard and finished up in Barcelona.*
▲ **finish (*sth*) up** [EAT/DRINK] *phrasal verb* [M] to eat or drink all of what you are eating or drinking: *Finish up your dinner and you can have dessert.*
▲ **finish with *sth*** *phrasal verb* to stop using or needing something: *Have you finished with that magazine?*
▲ **finish with *sb*** *phrasal verb UK* to stop having a romantic relationship with someone: *She finished with him when she discovered he was having an affair.*

finish [WOOD] /ˈfɪn.ɪʃ/ *verb* [T] If you finish something made of wood, you give it a last covering of paint, polish or varnish so that it is ready to be used.
finish /ˈfɪn.ɪʃ/ *noun* [C] **1** the condition of the surface of a material such as wood: *Look at the lovely shiny finish on that piano.* **2** the last covering of varnish, polish or paint, that is put onto something: *Even a clear finish will alter the colour of wood slightly.*
ˈfinishing ˌschool *noun* [C] a school or college where young women from rich families learn how to behave in high-class society
finite [LIMITED] /ˈfaɪ.naɪt/ *adj* having a limit or end: *The funds available for the health service are finite and we cannot afford to waste money.* ○ *We only have a finite* ***amount*** *of time to complete this task – we can't continue indefinitely.*
finite [GRAMMAR] /ˈfaɪ.naɪt/ *adj* in a form that shows the tense and subject of a verb, rather than the INFINITIVE form or a participle: *In the following sentence 'go' is finite: "I often go to the cinema."*
finito /fɪˈniː.təʊ/ [US] /-t̬oʊ/ *adj* [after v] *INFORMAL* finished: *As far as I am concerned the relationship is over – finito – and I can start living again.*
fink /fɪŋk/ *noun* [C] *US INFORMAL* someone who tells secret and damaging information about someone else; an unpleasant person: *Kelly's such a fink – she told Mom I was smoking again.*
fink /fɪŋk/ *verb*
▲ **fink on *sb*** *phrasal verb OLD-FASHIONED US SLANG* to tell other people secret and damaging information about someone
Finnish /ˈfɪn.ɪʃ/ *adj* from, belonging to or relating to Finland
Finnish /ˈfɪn.ɪʃ/ *noun* [U] the language of Finland
fiord /fjɔːd/ [US] /fjɔːrd/ *noun* [C] a **fjord**
fire [FLAMES] /faɪəʳ/ [US] /faɪr/ *noun* **1** [C or U] (material that is in) the state of burning that produces flames which send out heat and light, and might produce smoke: *Animals are usually afraid of fire.* ○ *The fire was* ***started*** *by children playing with matches.* ○ *Forty people helped to* ***put out*** (= stop) *the fire.* ○ *The library was badly damaged* ***in*** *the fire.* ○ *How many historic buildings are damaged* ***by*** *fire each year?* ○ *She had to be rescued by her neighbours when her house (UK)* ***caught****/(US)* ***caught on*** *fire* (= started to burn unintentionally). ➲See also **fiery**. **2** [C] a small controlled fire that is used for heating or cooking: *It's very cold in here – should I* ***light*** *a fire?* ○ *We* ***built*** *a fire on the beach.* ○ *We put up our tents and* ***made*** *a small fire.* **3 on fire** If something is on fire, it is burning when it should not be: *If your home was on fire and you could save only one thing, what would it be?* **4** [C] *UK* a gas or electric heater that is used to warm up a room: *a gas/electric fire* ○ *If you're cold just put the fire on.*
• **fire and brimstone** used to mean the threat of Hell or DAMNATION (= punishment which lasts forever) after death: *The preacher's sermon was full of fire and brimstone.*
• **play with fire** to act in a way that is very dangerous or risky
• **set *sth/sb* on fire** to cause something or someone to start burning: *A peace campaigner had set herself on fire in protest at the government's involvement in the war.*
• **set fire to *sth/sb*** *MAINLY UK* to cause something or someone to start burning: *Soldiers had chased the protesters into a warehouse and set fire to it.*
• **go through fire and water** *UK OLD-FASHIONED* to experience many difficulties or dangers in order to achieve something
fire /faɪəʳ/ [US] /faɪr/ *verb* [T] to heat objects made of clay in a KILN (= a special oven) so that they harden
-fired /-faɪəd/ [US] /-faɪrd/ *suffix*: ***Gas****-fired* (= using gas for fuel) *power stations are expected to produce cheaper electricity than* ***coal****-fired ones.*
fire [SHOOT] /faɪəʳ/ [US] /faɪr/ *verb* [I or T] **1** to cause a weapon to shoot bullets, arrows or missiles: *He fired his gun into the air.* ○ *Someone started firing* ***at*** *us.* ○ *Without warning he started firing* ***into*** *the crowd.* ○ *I just prayed that he would stop firing.* ○ *The ambassador denied that any missiles had been fired across the border.* **2** to direct a series of questions or criticisms at someone: *The journalists were firing questions at me for two whole hours.* ○ *"I'd like to ask you some questions about your childhood, if I may." "Fire* ***away****!* (= You can start asking them now)*"*.
• **in the firing line** (*US ALSO* **on the firing line**) likely to be criticized, attacked or got rid of: *He found himself in the firing line for his sexist remarks.*
fire /faɪəʳ/ [US] /faɪr/ *noun* [U] the shooting of guns or other weapons: *The police* ***opened*** *fire* ***on*** (= started shooting at) *the protesters.* ○ *The command was given to* ***cease*** *fire* (= stop shooting). ○ *The city* ***came under*** *fire* ***from*** *anti-government forces last night.*
• **come under fire** to be criticized: *The government has come under fire for its decision to close the mines.*
• **hang/hold fire** *UK* to delay making a decision: *Ideally we would settle the matter now, but I think we should hang fire until the general situation becomes clearer.*
fire [DISMISS] /faɪəʳ/ [US] /faɪr/ *verb* [T] to remove someone from their job, either because they have done something wrong or badly, or as a way of saving the cost of employing them: *She was fired after she was caught stealing from her employer.* ○ *He was fired* ***from*** *his $165 000 job* ***for*** *poor performance.* ○ *She has just been fired as editor of the newspaper.* ○ *The company is reducing its workforce by firing 500 employees.*
firing /ˈfaɪə.rɪŋ/ [US] /ˈfaɪ.rɪŋ/ *noun* [C] *MAINLY US* an act of removing someone from their job: ***hirings and*** *firings*

fire [EXCITE] /faɪəʳ/ [US] /faɪr/ *verb* [T] to cause a strong emotion in someone: *I had a brilliant English teacher who fired me* ***with*** *enthusiasm for literature at an early age.* ○ *Talk of treasure and lost cities had fired their* ***imaginations****.*
fire /faɪəʳ/ [US] /faɪr/ *noun* [U] *The fire* (= strong emotion) *in her speech inspired everyone.*

PHRASAL VERBS WITH **fire**

▲ **fire *sth* off** [SHOT] to fire a shot from a gun: *They fired off several shots to frighten us.*
▲ **fire *sth* off** [LETTER] *phrasal verb* [M] to write and send an angry letter to someone: *He fired off an angry letter to the editor.*
▲ **fire *sb* up** *phrasal verb* to make someone become excited or angry: *We had an argument about it and she got all fired up.*

ˈfire aˌlarm *noun* [C] (the switch connected to) a device such as a bell or SIREN that warns the people in a building that the building is on fire: *If the fire alarm* ***goes off*** (= starts making a sound)*, leave the building quickly and calmly.*
firearm /ˈfaɪə.rɑːm/ [US] /ˈfaɪr.ɑːrm/ *noun* [C] *SLIGHTLY FORMAL* a gun that can be carried easily: *He was found guilty of possessing an unlicensed firearm.*
fireball /ˈfaɪə.bɔːl/ [US] /ˈfaɪr.bɑːl/ *noun* [C] a large ball of fire, especially one caused by a very powerful explosion: *Witnesses reported seeing a huge orange fireball as the oil refinery exploded.*
ˈfire ˌblanket *noun* [C] a type of cover made of a material which does not burn very easily, which you throw over a fire to put it out or stop it from spreading
firebomb /ˈfaɪə.bɒm/ [US] /ˈfaɪr.bɑːm/ *noun* [C] a bomb that causes destruction by starting a fire rather than exploding: *Rioters armed with firebombs set light to police barricades.* **firebomb** /ˈfaɪə.bɒm/ [US] /ˈfaɪr.bɑːm/ *verb* [T] *Animal rights extremists have threatened to firebomb any department stores that continue to stock fur coats.*
firebrand /ˈfaɪə.brænd/ [US] /ˈfaɪr-/ *noun* [C] a person who causes political or social trouble by opposing authority and encouraging others to do so
firebreak /ˈfaɪə.breɪk/ [US] /ˈfaɪr-/ *noun* [C] (*AUS ALSO* **firetrail**) a strip of land in a wood or forest from which the trees have been removed to prevent an accidental fire from spreading
ˈfire briˌgade *UK noun* [C usually sing] (*US* **fire department**) an organization that is in charge of preventing and stopping unwanted fires
firecracker /ˈfaɪəˌkræk.əʳ/ [US] /ˈfaɪrˌkræk.ɚ/ *noun* [C] a firework that makes a loud noise when it explodes
ˈfire ˌdoor *noun* [C] a door made of material that cannot burn which is used to prevent a fire from spreading within a building
ˈfire ˌdrill *noun* [C] (the practising of) the set of actions that should be performed in order to leave a building such as an office, factory or school safely when it is on fire
fire-eater /ˈfaɪəˌiː.təʳ/ [US] /ˈfaɪrˌiː.t̬ɚ/ *noun* [C] a performer who entertains people by seeming to swallow the flames on sticks that are burning at one end
ˈfire ˌengine *noun* [C] (*US ALSO* **fire truck**) a large vehicle that carries FIREFIGHTERS and their equipment to a fire ➲See picture **Cars and Trucks** on page Centre 13
ˈfire esˌcape *noun* [C] a set of metal stairs, especially on the outside of a building, which allows people to escape from a burning building
ˈfire exˌtinguisher *noun* [C] a device which contains water or a special gas, powder or FOAM (= a mass of small bubbles) that is put onto a fire to stop it burning
firefight /ˈfaɪə.faɪt/ [US] /ˈfaɪr-/ *noun* [C] a fight, often unexpected, between opposing groups of soldiers in which they shoot at each other: *The opposing units opened fire simultaneously at close range and a 15-minute firefight ensued.*
firefighter /ˈfaɪəˌfaɪ.təʳ/ [US] /ˈfaɪrˌfaɪ.t̬ɚ/ /-mən/ *noun* [C] a person whose job is to stop fires from burning
firefighting /ˈfaɪəˌfaɪ.tɪŋ/ [US] /ˈfaɪrˌfaɪ.t̬ɪŋ/ *noun* [U] the activity of stopping fires burning
firefly /ˈfaɪə.flaɪ/ [US] /ˈfaɪr-/ *noun* [C] an insect which is active during the night and whose tail shines on and off in the dark
fireguard /ˈfaɪə.gɑːd/ [US] /ˈfaɪr.gɑːrd/ *noun* [C] (*US ALSO* **firescreen**) a metal frame that is put in front of a fireplace to prevent burning wood or coal from falling onto the floor, or prevent children or pets from burning themselves
ˈfire ˌhydrant *noun* [C] (*US ALSO* **fire plug**) a large pipe in the street that FIREFIGHTERS can get water from to use to stop fires burning
firelight /ˈfaɪə.laɪt/ [US] /ˈfaɪr-/ *noun* [U] the light produced by a fire, especially one in a fireplace
firelighter /ˈfaɪəˌlaɪ.təʳ/ [US] /ˈfaɪrˌlaɪ.t̬ɚ/ *noun* [C] (*US USUALLY* **fire starter**) (a small block of) material which burns very easily and is used for helping to start wood or coal fires
fireman /ˈfaɪə.mən/ [US] /ˈfaɪr-/ *noun* [C] a man whose job is to stop fires from burning
fireplace /ˈfaɪə.pleɪs/ [US] /ˈfaɪr-/ *noun* [C] a space in the wall of a room for a fire to burn in, or the decorated part which surrounds this space: *She swept the ashes from the fireplace.*
ˈfire ˌplug *noun* [C] *US INFORMAL FOR* **fire hydrant**
firepower /ˈfaɪə.paʊəʳ/ [US] /ˈfaɪr.paʊɚ/ *noun* [U] the number and size of guns that a military group has available: *Although badly out-numbered by the enemy, we had vastly superior firepower.*
fireproof /ˈfaɪə.pruːf/ [US] /ˈfaɪr-/ *adj* unable to be damaged by fire: *She keeps all her important papers in a fireproof safe.*
fire-raising /ˈfaɪəˌreɪ.zɪŋ/ [US] /ˈfaɪr-/ *noun* [U] *UK FOR* **arson**
fire-raiser /ˈfaɪəˌreɪ.zəʳ/ [US] /ˈfaɪrˌreɪ.zɚ/ *noun* [C] *UK FOR* **arsonist**
firescreen /ˈfaɪə.skriːn/ [US] /ˈfaɪr-/ *noun* [C] *US FOR* **fireguard**
fireside /ˈfaɪə.saɪd/ [US] /ˈfaɪr-/ *noun* [C usually sing] the part of a room which surrounds a fireplace: *She sat reading* ***by*** *the fireside.*
ˈfire ˌstation *noun* [C] (*US ALSO* **fire house**) a building where fire engines are kept and where FIREFIGHTERS work and stay in the hours they are working
firestorm /ˈfaɪə.stɔːm/ [US] /ˈfaɪr.stɔːrm/ *noun* [C] a very large uncontrollable fire, sometimes caused by heavy bombing from aircraft
firetrail /ˈfaɪə.treɪl/ [US] /ˈfaɪr-/ *noun* [C] *AUS FOR* **firebreak**
firetrap /ˈfaɪə.træp/ [US] /ˈfaɪr-/ *noun* [C] (a part of) a building that would burn easily if a fire started accidentally or would be difficult to escape from during a fire
ˈfire ˌtruck *noun* [C] *US* **fire engine**
firewall /ˈfaɪə.wɔːl/ *noun* [C] *SPECIALIZED* a device or program that stops people accessing a computer without permission while it is connected to the Internet
firewater /ˈfaɪəˌwɔː.təʳ/ [US] /ˈfaɪrˌwɑː.t̬ɚ/ *noun* [U] *INFORMAL HUMOROUS* a very strong alcoholic drink, especially whisky
firewood /ˈfaɪə.wʊd/ [US] /ˈfaɪr-/ *noun* [U] wood used as fuel for a fire: *We can use those old shelves as firewood.*
firework /ˈfaɪə.wɜːk/ [US] /ˈfaɪr.wɝːk/ *noun* [C] a small container filled with explosive chemicals which produce bright coloured patterns or loud noises when they explode: *a firework display* ○ *When it gets dark we'll (UK)* ***let off****/(US)* ***set off*** (= light) *the fireworks.* ○ *What time do the fireworks start?*
fireworks /ˈfaɪə.wɜːks/ [US] /ˈfaɪr.wɝːks/ *plural noun INFORMAL HUMOROUS* a lot of angry shouting: *I have to go home now – there'll be fireworks if I'm late!*
ˈfiring ˌsquad *noun* [C] a group of soldiers who are ordered to shoot and kill a prisoner
firm [HARD] /fɜːm/ [US] /fɝːm/ *adj* not soft but not completely hard: *I'd rather sleep on a firm mattress than a soft one.* ○ *These pears are still too firm to eat.*
firm /fɜːm/ [US] /fɝːm/ *verb* [T] to make soil harder by pressing on it: *Firm the soil around the cuttings and water them in.* **firmness** /fɜːm.nəs/ [US] /fɝːm-/ *noun* [U] *The bed's firmness suited him.*

F

firm

464

firm FIXED /fɜːm/ ⓤ /fɝːm/ *adj* **1** well fixed in place or position: *The bridge provided a firm platform for the bungee jumpers.* **2** fixed at the same level or opinion and not changing: *The government remains firm in its opposition to tax reform.*
● **hold/stand firm** to remain in the same place or at the same level: *The protesters stood firm as the police tried to disperse them.* ○ *The pound held firm against the Deutschmark today.*
firm /fɜːm/ ⓤ /fɝːm/ *verb* [I] to stop changing or to remain at the same level, amount, etc: *After a turbulent week on the markets, share prices firmed today.*
firmly /'fɜːm.li/ ⓤ /'fɝːm-/ *adv* strongly, in a way that will not become loose: *Make sure the rope is firmly attached before attempting to climb down it.*

firm STRONG /fɜːm/ ⓤ /fɝːm/ strong and tight: *a firm handshake* ○ *Keep a firm hold of the handrail as you go down.* ○ FIGURATIVE *No one seems to have a firm grip on the company at the moment.* ○ FIGURATIVE *You need a firm grasp of mathematics to become an astronaut.*
firmly /'fɜːm.li/ ⓤ /'fɝːm-/ *adv*: *He shook my hand firmly* (= strongly) *and climbed into the taxi.* **firmness** /'fɜːm.nəs/ ⓤ /'fɝːm-/ *noun* [U] *The firmness of his handshake reassured me.*

firm CERTAIN /fɜːm/ ⓤ /fɝːm/ *adj* certain and not likely to change; definite: *He is a firm believer in traditional family values.* ○ *Some people still claim that there is no firm evidence linking smoking with lung cancer.* **firmly** /'fɜːm.li/ ⓤ /'fɝːm-/ *adv*: *We are firmly committed to reducing unemployment.* **firmness** /'fɜːm.nəs/ ⓤ /'fɝːm-/ *noun* [U]

firm FORCEFUL /fɜːm/ ⓤ /fɝːm/ *adj* forceful and making people do what you want: *I was always very firm with my children – they knew the rules and I made sure they kept to them.*
● **a firm hand** strong control: *Reforming these young offenders will require a firm hand.*
firmly /'fɜːm.li/ ⓤ /'fɝːm-/ *adv* forcefully: *"You're not going to the party and that's that!" she said firmly.* **firmness** /'fɜːm.nəs/ ⓤ /'fɝːm-/ *noun* [U] *The new teacher has a reputation for firmness and is unlikely to tolerate misbehaviour.*

firm BUSINESS /fɜːm/ ⓤ /fɝːm/ *noun* [C] a company or business: *He works for a law firm called Neil and Vigliano.* ○ *He's just started working for an accountancy firm/a firm of accountants in Cambridge.*

PHRASAL VERBS WITH **firm** ▼

▲ **firm** *sth* **up** MAKE DEFINITE *phrasal verb* [M] to make something more definite or less likely to change: *Could we have a meeting so we can firm up the details of our agreement?*
▲ **firm** *(sth)* **up** MAKE HARDER *phrasal verb* [M] to make a part of your body have less fat and more muscle by doing exercise: *Cycling is one of the best ways to firm up your thighs.* ○ *My stomach has begun to firm up since I started exercising.*

the firmament /ðə'fɜː.mə.mənt/ ⓤ /-'fɝːr-/ *noun* [S] LITERARY the sky: FIGURATIVE *She is one of the rising stars in the political firmament.*

first /fɜːst/ ⓤ /fɝːst/ *adj, adv, noun, pronoun* (a person or thing) coming before all others in order, time, amount, quality or importance: *This is my first visit to New York.* ○ *I fell in love with him the first time I saw him.* ○ *I'm always nervous for the first few minutes of an exam.* ○ *Who finished first?* ○ *When did you first meet each other?* ○ *The company was still very small when I first joined.* ○ [+ to infinitive] *She was one of the first to arrive.* ○ *He is the first* (= very willing) *to admit that much of his success is due to his good looks.* ○ *This new surgical technique is a first for* (= has never been done before in) *Britain.* ○ *Tonight sees the first of three documentaries about cancer.* ○ *First (of all)* (UK ALSO *First off*) (= Before anything else), *I'd like to ask you a few questions about your childhood.*
● **at first** in or at the beginning: *At first I thought he was joking but then I realized he meant it.*

● **first come, first served** used to mean that people will receive something or be dealt with in the order in which they ask or arrive
● **first among equals** UK a member of a group who is officially on the same level as the other members but who in fact has slightly more responsibility or power: *The British Prime Minister is first among equals in the Cabinet.*
● **be in the first flush of** to be at the start of something: *He's no longer in the first flush of youth.*
● **first and foremost** more than anything else: *In spite of being elected to office, she remains first and foremost a writer.*
● **first and last** as the most important fact: *Don was, first and last, a good friend.*
● **from the (very) first** from the beginning: *I've opposed the proposal from the very first.*
● **in the first place** in or at the beginning (of a series of events): *The trousers shrank when I washed them, but they weren't really big enough in the first place.* ○ *Thankfully, he wasn't hurt, but he never should have been there in the first place.*
● **in the first instance** UK for the first attempt or effort: *Enquiries about the post should be addressed in the first instance to the personnel manager.*
● **first thing** at the earliest time in the day: *He said he'd phone back first thing tomorrow.*
● **first things first** used to tell someone that more important things should be done before less important things: *First things first, let's have something to eat.*
firstly /'fɜːst.li/ ⓤ /'fɝːst-/ *adv* (ALSO **first**) used to refer to the first thing in a list: *There are two very good reasons why we can't do it. Firstly, we don't have enough money, and secondly, we don't have enough time.*
first /fɜːst/ ⓤ /fɝːst/ *noun* [C] (ALSO **first class degree**) UK the best possible degree qualification you can obtain from a British university: *She has a first in English from Newcastle University.*

first 'aid *noun* [U] basic medical treatment which is given to someone as soon as possible after they have been hurt in an accident or suddenly become ill: *Did you learn any first aid at school?* ○ *first-aid equipment*
first-aider /ˌfɜːst'eɪ.dəʳ/ ⓤ /ˌfɝːst'eɪ.dɚ/ *noun* [C] UK someone who is qualified to give first aid: *How many first-aiders are there in your office?*

first 'base *noun* [C usually sing] in baseball, the first of four places you must run to after hitting the ball and before scoring a point, or the position of a player defending this place: *Mattingley played first base for the Yankees.*
● **get to/reach first base** US INFORMAL to have the first achievement or agreement which is needed for later success: *The proposal is so poorly designed, they won't even get to first base with the directors.*
● **get to first base** US INFORMAL HUMOROUS to kiss someone in a sexual way

first-born (child) /ˌfɜːst.bɔːn'tʃaɪld/ ⓤ /ˌfɝːst.bɔːrn-/ *noun* [C usually sing] the first child of a set of parents: *Olaf is my first-born.*

first 'class *noun* [U] **1** the best and most expensive seats on a plane or in a train: *Because of the delay, we were offered seats in first class.* **2** a mail service that delivers letters, etc. quickly.
first 'class *adj, adv* **1** relating to the highest quality service on a plane, train, or in a hotel: *a first-class ticket* ○ *first-class accommodation/travel* ○ *She always travels first class.* **2** relating to the fastest mail service: *first-class mail/postage* ○ *How much is a first-class stamp?* ○ *How much more would it cost to send it first class?*
first 'class *adj* **1** excellent: *She's made a first-class job of decorating the living room.* **2** A first class degree is the best possible degree qualification you can obtain from a British university.

first 'cousin *noun* [C] a child of your aunt or uncle

first-degree burn /ˌfɜːst.dɪ.griː'bɜːn/ ⓤ /ˌfɝːst.dɪ.griː-'bɝːn/ *noun* [C] the least serious type of burn that needs medical treatment ⊃Compare **second-degree burn**; **third-degree burn**.

first-degree murder /ˌfɜːst.dɪˌgriːˈmɜː.dər/ ⓤⓢ /ˌfɜːst-ˌdɪ.griːˈmɜːr.dɚ/ noun [C] US the most serious type of murder

the ˌFirst ˈFleet noun AUS the ships that brought the first Europeans to Australia

ˌfirst ˈfleeter noun [C] AUS someone who is related to a person who travelled in the First Fleet

the ˌfirst ˈfloor noun [S] in British English, the floor of a building that is directly above ground level, or in American English, the floor at ground level: *She works on the first floor.* **first-floor** /ˌfɜːstˈflɔːr/ ⓤⓢ /ˌfɜːstˈflɔːr/ adj *a first-floor flat/apartment/office*

ˈfirst ˈfruit noun [C usually pl] MAINLY UK the first result of someone's effort or work: *These improvements in quality are the first fruits of our investment.*

ˌfirst (ˈgear) noun [U] (in a vehicle) the gear used when starting to drive forward or when driving up a steep hill

first-hand, firsthand /ˌfɜːstˈhænd/ ⓤⓢ /ˌfɜːst-/ adv If you experience something first-hand, you experience it yourself: *Most of the older reporters have experienced war first-hand.* **first-hand** /ˌfɜːstˈhænd/ ⓤⓢ /ˈfɜːst-/ adj [before n] *Most of us have first-hand experience of teaching.*

ˌfirst ˈlady noun [C] a woman whose husband is the political leader of a country or a part of a country

ˌfirst ˈlanguage noun [C] the language that someone learns to speak first

ˌfirst ˈlight noun [U] the time when the sun first appears in the morning: *We'll leave at first light.*

ˌfirst ˈmate noun [C] the second most important officer on a ship which is not part of the navy

ˈfirst ˌname noun [C] the name that was given to you when you were born and that comes before your family name: *It can be rude to call someone by their first name if they are much older or more important than you.*
● **on first-name terms** UK (US **on a first-name basis**) friendly or familiar enough with someone to call them by their first name

ˌfirst ˈnight UK noun [C] (US **opening night**) the first public performance of a play

ˌfirst ofˈfender noun [C] someone who has been officially judged to be guilty of a crime for the first time

ˌfirst ˈofficer noun [C] **first mate**

first-past-the-post /ˌfɜːst.pɑːst.ðəˈpəʊst/ ⓤⓢ /ˌfɜːst.pæst.ðəˈpoʊst/ adj UK using a voting system in which a person is elected by obtaining more votes than anyone else in the area that they want to represent, whether or not their political party obtains more votes than any other party in the whole of the country

the ˌfirst ˈperson noun [S] the form of a verb or pronoun that is used when people are speaking or writing about themselves: *Autobiographies are written in the first person.* ○ *'I' and 'we' are first-person pronouns.*

ˌfirst ˈprinciples plural noun UK the basic and most important reasons for doing or believing something: *We seem to have forgotten why we're fighting this campaign – we really need to return to first principles.*

first-rate /ˌfɜːstˈreɪt/ ⓤⓢ /ˌfɜːst-/ adj extremely good: *a first-rate restaurant*

ˌfirst reˈfusal noun [U] the opportunity to buy something before it is offered to anyone else: *My sister's selling her car and she's offered me first refusal on it.*

ˌfirst ˈstrike noun [C] in a nuclear war, an attack intended to destroy the enemy's ability to fire before they have had an opportunity to do so

first-time buyer /ˌfɜːst.taɪmˈbaɪ.ər/ ⓤⓢ /ˌfɜːst.taɪmˈbaɪ.ɚ/ noun [C] UK someone who is buying their own house or apartment for the first time, especially by borrowing money from a bank or similar organization

the ˌFirst ˌWorld ˈWar noun [S] **World War One**

firth /fɜːθ/ ⓤⓢ /fɝːθ/ noun [C] SCOTTISH ENGLISH a long strip of sea reaching into the land: *the Firth of Forth*

fir (tree) /ˈfɜːˌtriː/ ⓤⓢ /ˈfɝː-/ noun [C] a tall evergreen tree that grows in cold countries and has needle-like leaves

fiscal /ˈfɪs.kəl/ adj SPECIALIZED connected with (public) money: *fiscal policy* **fiscally** /ˈfɪs.kəl.i/ adv: *The proposal is fiscally sound.*

ˌfiscal ˌyear noun [C] **financial year**

fish ANIMAL /fɪʃ/ noun [C or U] plural fish or fishes **1** an animal which lives in water, is covered with SCALES and which breathes by taking water in through its mouth, or the flesh of these animals eaten as food: *Several large fish live in the pond.* ○ *Sanjay caught the biggest fish I've ever seen.* ○ *I don't like fish* (= don't like to eat fish). **2** MAINLY UK OLD-FASHIONED **an odd/queer fish** a strange person
● **have bigger/other fish to fry** INFORMAL to have something more important to do
● **be like a fish out of water** to feel awkward because you are in an situation which you have not experienced before or because you are very different from the people around you
● **There are plenty more fish in the sea.** used to say that there are many other people or possibilities, especially when one person or thing has been unsuitable or unsuccessful: *Don't cry over Pierre – there are plenty more fish in the sea!*
● **be neither fish nor fowl** like one thing in some ways and like another thing in other ways
● **be a big fish in a small pond** to have a lot of influence only over a small area

fish /fɪʃ/ verb [I or T] to catch fish from a river, sea, lake, etc., or to try to do this: *They're fishing for tuna.* ○ *The sea here has been fished intensely over the last ten years.*
● **fished out** If an area of water has been fished out, all or most of the fish in it have been caught.
● **fish or cut bait** US INFORMAL used to tell someone to take action or to stop saying that they will: *He's been promising voters that he'll support gun control, now it's time to fish or cut bait.*
● **fish in troubled waters** UK to try to gain an advantage from a difficult situation or from someone else's problems

COMMON LEARNER ERROR

fish or **fishes**

Fish is the usual plural.

I caught six fish in the river.

~~I caught six fishes in the river.~~

Fishes is sometimes used to talk about different types of fish.

In the Pacific we saw exotic fishes that you never see in Europe.

fish SEARCH /fɪʃ/ verb [I usually + adv or prep] to search, especially in difficult conditions: *She fished in her tool box for the right spanner.* ○ *The director was fishing for information about our strategy.* ○ *He's always fishing for compliments* (= trying to make people say good things about him).
▲ **fish sth out** phrasal verb [M] INFORMAL to pull something out of water or take something out of a bag or pocket: *Police fished a body out of the river this morning.* ○ *He fished out a coin from his pocket.*

ˌfish and ˈchips noun [U] fish covered with BATTER (= mixture of flour, eggs and milk) and then fried and served with pieces of fried potato

fishbowl /ˈfɪʃ.bəʊl/ ⓤⓢ /-boʊl/ noun [C] US FOR **goldfish bowl**

fishcake /ˈfɪʃ.keɪk/ noun [C] a mixture of fish and potato which has been formed into small flat round shapes, covered with breadcrumbs and then cooked in oil

fisherman /ˈfɪʃ.ə.mən/ ⓤⓢ /-ɚ-/ noun [C] someone who catches fish, especially as their job

fishery /ˈfɪʃ.ər.i/ ⓤⓢ /-ɚ.i/ noun [C] an area of water where fish are caught so they can be sold: *an offshore fishery*

fish-eye lens /ˌfɪʃ.aɪˈlenz/ noun [C] SPECIALIZED a camera lens which curves out from the camera and gives a view of an extremely wide area, with the central objects appearing closer than those at the edge

ˈfish ˌfarm noun [C] an enclosed area of water used for breeding and growing fish

fish-finger UK /ˌfɪʃˈfɪŋ.gər/ ⓤⓢ /-gɚ/ noun [C] (US **fish stick**) a rectangular piece of fish covered in breadcrumbs and cooked

fishing /ˈfɪʃ.ɪŋ/ noun [U] the sport or job of catching fish: *My dad loves to go fishing.* ○ *a fishing (UK) rod/(US) pole* ○ *salmon/trout fishing* ○ *fishing tackle* (= equipment used for catching fish) ○ *Fishing is still their main source of income.*

ˈfish ˌkettle *noun* [C] a large metal pan for cooking fish

ˈfish ˌknife *noun* [C] a knife for eating fish, with a wide blade and a round edge

fishmonger /ˈfɪʃˌmʌŋ.gəʳ/ [US] /-gɚ/ *noun* [C] MAINLY UK someone who sells fish, especially from a shop

fishmonger's (*plural* **fishmongers**), **fishmongers** /ˈfɪʃˌmʌŋ.gəz/ [US] /-gɚz/ *noun* [C] UK a shop which sells fish: *I'll stop at the fishmonger's on my way home from work.*

fishnet /ˈfɪʃ.net/ *noun* [U] a type of material which looks like net: *She was wearing black fishnet* ***stockings.***

ˈfish ˌslice MAINLY UK *noun* [C] (US USUALLY **spatula**) a kitchen utensil which has a wide flat blade with long holes in it, used for lifting and turning food while cooking

F

ˈfish ˌtank *noun* [C] a glass container used for keeping fish in, especially pet tropical fish

fishwife /ˈfɪʃ.waɪf/ *noun* [C] *plural* **fishwives** UK OLD-FASHIONED a loud, unpleasant woman

fishy [DISHONEST] /ˈfɪʃ.i/ *adj* INFORMAL seeming dishonest or false: *There's something fishy going on here.*

• **smell fishy** INFORMAL If a situation or an explanation smells fishy, it causes you to think that someone is being dishonest.

fishy [LIKE FISH] /ˈfɪʃ.i/ *adj* tasting or smelling of fish

fission /ˈfɪʃ.ən/ *noun* [U] SPECIALIZED the splitting of the nucleus of an atom, which results in the release of a large amount of energy, or the division of a living cell as part of reproduction: ***nuclear** fission* ○ *The fission* ***of*** *the cell could be inhibited with certain chemicals.*

fissure /ˈfɪʃ.əʳ/ [US] /-ɚ/ *noun* [C] a deep narrow crack in rock or the earth

fist /fɪst/ *noun* [C] a hand with the fingers and thumb held tightly in: *She* ***clenched*** *her fists.* ○ *Protestors were* ***shaking*** *their fists at the soldiers.*

fist-fight /ˈfɪst.faɪt/ *noun* [C] a fight between people using their hands but no weapons

fistful /ˈfɪst.fʊl/ *group noun* [C] **1** an amount of something that you can hold in your fist: *He held out a fistful of crumpled notes.* **2** INFORMAL a large collection or number: *He won international acclaim for his King Lear and has a fistful of other acting awards.*

fisticuffs /ˈfɪs.tɪ.kʌfs/ *plural noun* OLD-FASHIONED OR HUMOROUS fighting in which people hit each other with their fists

fit [CORRECT SIZE] /fɪt/ *verb* [I or T] **-tt-** to be the right size or shape for someone or something: *That jacket fits you perfectly.* ○ *The dress fits* ***like a glove*** (= very well). ○ *Our new sofa doesn't fit* ***through*** *the door.* ○ *I don't think another desk will fit* ***into*** *this classroom.* ○ *My car's too big to fit* ***in*** *this space.*

• **If the cap fits, (wear it).** UK (US **If the shoe fits, (wear it).**) SAYING said to tell someone that if they are guilty of bad behaviour, they should accept criticism

fit /fɪt/ *noun* [S] the way that something fits: *These shoes are a perfect fit.* ○ *The trousers were a good fit but the jacket was too small.* ○ *Check the fit* ***of*** *the pieces before gluing them in place.*

fitted /ˈfɪt.ɪd/ [US] /ˈfɪt̬-/ *adj* [before n] made to fit the shape of someone or something: *a fitted jacket/shirt* ○ *fitted sheets*

fitting /ˈfɪt.ɪŋ/ [US] /ˈfɪt̬-/ *noun* [C] an occasion when someone who is having clothes made for them puts on the clothes before they are completed to make certain they will fit: *I'm having the final fitting of my wedding dress on Thursday.*

COMMON LEARNER ERROR

fit or **suit?**

Remember that the verb **fit** means to be the right shape or size.

This jacket doesn't fit me – it's too tight.

Use **suit** when you want to say that something is right for someone or makes them look more attractive.

You should wear more red – it suits you.

Life in the big city didn't suit him.

~~*Life in the big city didn't fit him.*~~

fit [SUIT] /fɪt/ *verb* [T] **-tt-** to be suitable for something: *With her qualifications, she should fit the job perfectly.* ○ *Let the punishment fit the crime.* ○ *I'm sure we'll have something to fit your requirements, Madam.*

• **fit the bill** to be suitable for a particular purpose: *This new software certainly fits the bill.*

fit /fɪt/ *adj* **fitter, fittest** suitable for a particular purpose or activity: *She's not fit* ***for*** *the level of responsibility she's been given.* ✻ NOTE: The opposite is **unfit**.

• **be in no fit state to do** ***sth*** to not be able to do something because you are upset, ill, drunk, etc: *He's very upset and is in no fit state to drive.*

• **see/think** ***sth*** **fit** to consider an action or decision to be correct for the situation: *Just do whatever you think fit – I'm sure you'll make the right decision.* ○ *Spend the money as you see fit.*

• **fit for human consumption** safe for people to eat

• **fit to drop** MAINLY UK extremely tired: *After the run they were fit to drop.*

• **fit to be tied** US INFORMAL extremely angry

fitness /ˈfɪt.nəs/ *noun* [U] suitability: *His fitness* ***for*** *the new position is not in question.* ○ [+ **to** infinitive] *Many people are concerned about her fitness* ***to*** *govern.*

fitting /ˈfɪt.ɪŋ/ [US] /ˈfɪt̬-/ *adj* [+ **that**] FORMAL suitable or right for a particular situation or occasion: *a fitting tribute* ○ ***It*** *is fitting* ***that*** *we should remember those who died.*

fit [POSITION] /fɪt/ *verb* [T] **-tt-** to provide something and put it in the correct position: *All the carpets we sell are fitted free.* ○ *She's been fitted with an artificial leg.*

fitted /ˈfɪt.ɪd/ [US] /ˈfɪt̬-/ *adj* [before n] MAINLY UK permanently fixed in position: *a fitted wardrobe/cupboard* ○ *We're having a new fitted kitchen put in.*

fitting /ˈfɪt.ɪŋ/ [US] /ˈfɪt̬-/ *noun* [C usually pl] **1** a small part or item: *plumbing fittings* ○ *electric light fittings* ➲Compare **fixture** FIXED OBJECT. **2** UK (US **furnishing**) an item, such as a cooker, washing machine or curtain pole, which is not permanently fixed in or part of the structure of a house and which a person might be expected to take with them when they move to a new home: *The house price, including* ***fixtures and*** *fittings, is £200 000.*

fit [HEALTHY] /fɪt/ *adj* **fitter, fittest 1** healthy and strong, especially as a result of exercise: *I jog to* ***keep*** *fit.* ○ *You need to be very fit to hike the Inca Trail.* ✻ NOTE: The opposite is **unfit**. **2** UK SLANG sexually attractive: *I met this really fit bloke in the pub last night.*

• **be (as) fit as a fiddle** (UK ALSO **be (as) fit as a flea**) to be very healthy and strong: *My grandmother's 89, but she's as fit as a fiddle.*

fitness /ˈfɪt.nəs/ *noun* [U] the condition of being physically strong and healthy: *I'm trying to improve my fitness by cycling to work.*

fit [ILLNESS] /fɪt/ *noun* [C] a sudden attack of illness when someone cannot control their movements and becomes unconscious: *an epileptic fit* ○ *He* ***had*** *a fit at work and collapsed.*

• **have/throw a fit** INFORMAL to become very angry or anxious, often shouting a lot: *She'll throw a fit when she sees the mess you've made.*

• **in fits (of laughter)** UK INFORMAL laughing a lot: *His stories had them in fits of laughter.*

fit /fɪt/ *verb* [I] **-tt-** UK SPECIALIZED to have a fit

fit [SHORT PERIOD] /fɪt/ *noun* [C] a sudden, uncontrolled period of doing something or feeling something: *a coughing/sneezing fit* ○ *She hit him* ***in a*** *fit* ***of*** *anger.*

• **in/by fits and starts** If something happens in fits and starts, it often stops and then starts again: *Replies to the advertisement are arriving in fits and starts.*

fitful /ˈfɪt.fəl/ *adj* often stopping and starting and not happening in a regular or continuous way: *fitful breathing* ○ *a fitful sleep*

fitfully /ˈfɪt.fəl.i/ *adv*: *She* ***slept*** *fitfully* (= only for short, irregular periods) *throughout the night and arose before dawn.*

PHRASAL VERBS WITH **fit** ▼

▲ **fit in** [BELONG] *phrasal verb* **1** to feel that you belong to a particular group and are accepted by them: *It's no surprise she's leaving – she never really fitted in.* **2** If one thing fits in with another thing, they look pleasant together or are suitable for each other: *It's a very nice sofa but it doesn't fit in **with** the rest of the room.*

▲ **fit sb/sth in** [FIND TIME] *phrasal verb* [M] to find time to do or deal with something or someone: *Dr Jones is very busy but I'm sure she'll be able to fit you in tomorrow.*

▲ **fit in with sth** *phrasal verb* If one activity or event fits in with another, they exist or happen together in a way that is convenient.

▲ **fit sth out** *phrasal verb* [M usually passive] to supply someone or something with all of the things which will be needed: *The ship will be in dock for eight months to be fitted out for its new duties.*

▲ **fit sth up** [ARRANGE FURNITURE] *phrasal verb* [M] *UK* to put furniture in a room or building: *We've fitted up the spare room **as** a nursery.*

▲ **fit sb up** [MAKE GUILTY] *phrasal verb* [M] *UK SLANG* to make someone appear guilty: *Of course she didn't do it – someone fitted her up.*

fitment /ˈfɪt.mənt/ *noun* [C usually pl] *MAINLY UK* a piece of furniture or equipment made especially for a particular room or space: *kitchen/bathroom fitments*

ˌfitted ˈcarpet *UK noun* [C or U] (*US* **wall-to-wall carpet**) carpet which is cut to cover the whole floor in a room

fitter /ˈfɪt.əʳ/ [US] /ˈfɪt̬.ɚ/ *noun* [C] **1** someone whose job is to repair or put together equipment or machines: *an engine fitter* ○ *a gas fitter* **2** someone whose job is to cut and fit especially clothes or carpets: *a carpet fitter*

ˈfitting ˌroom *noun* [C] a room or area in a shop where you can put on clothes to check that they fit before you buy them

five /faɪv/ *determiner, pronoun, noun* (the number) 5: *Five, four, three, two, one, blast-off!* ○ *I work five days a week.* ○ *Emily is five (years old).* ○ *Is that number a five or an eight?*

• **give sb (a) five** *INFORMAL* to hit someone's open hand with your own to celebrate doing something well or achieving something, especially in sports

• **take five** *US INFORMAL* used to tell someone to stop working and relax for a short period of time

five o'clock shadow /ˌfaɪv.ə.klɒkˈʃæd.əʊ/ [US] /-klɑːk-ˈʃæd.oʊ/ *noun* [S] the slight darkness on a man's face, especially his chin, caused by the growth of hair during the day

fiver /ˈfaɪ.vəʳ/ [US] /-vɚ/ *noun* [C] *UK INFORMAL* five pounds, or a note worth five pounds: *This CD only cost me a fiver.* ○ *Can you change a tenner for two fivers?* ➲See also **tenner**.

five-star /ˌfaɪvˈstɑːʳ/ [US] /-ˌstɑːr/ *adj* [before n] describes a hotel or service that is of the best possible quality: *a five-star hotel*

fix [REPAIR] /fɪks/ *verb* [T] **1** to repair something: *They couldn't fix my old computer, so I bought a new one.* **2** to make your hair, make-up, clothes, etc. look tidy: *Give me a couple of minutes while I fix my hair.*

fix [FASTEN] /fɪks/ *verb* [T + adv or prep] to fasten something in position so that it cannot move: *We fixed the bookcase **to** the wall.*

fixed /fɪkst/ *adj* fastened somewhere and not able to be moved

• **be of/have no fixed abode/address** *LEGAL* to not have a permanent home

fix [ARRANGE] /fɪks/ *verb* [I or T] *MAINLY UK* to arrange or agree a time, place, price, etc: *Shall we fix a time for our next meeting?* ○ *I understand the rent is fixed **at** £750 a month.*

fixed /fɪkst/ *adj* arranged or decided already and not able to be changed: *a fixed price* ○ *fixed interest rates* ○ *Is the date of the wedding fixed yet?*

• **How are you fixed for sth?** *INFORMAL* used to ask how much of something someone has, or to ask about someone's arrangements: *How are you fixed for cash?* ○ *How are you fixed for Saturday evening?*

fixer /ˈfɪk.səʳ/ [US] /-sɚ/ *noun* [C] *INFORMAL* someone who is skilled at arranging for things to happen, especially dishonestly

fix [PREPARE FOOD] /fɪks/ *verb* [T] *MAINLY US INFORMAL* to cook or prepare food or drink: *Whose turn is it to fix dinner?* ○ [+ two objects] *Can I fix you a drink?/Can I fix a drink for you?*

fix [AWKWARD SITUATION] /fɪks/ *noun* [C usually sing] *INFORMAL* an awkward or difficult situation: *I'm **in** a bit of a fix with the arrangements.*

fix [CHEAT] /fɪks/ *verb* [T often passive] to do something dishonest to make certain that a competition, race, or election is won by a particular person: *Several jockeys were arrested on suspicion of fixing the race.* ○ *It sounds like the election was fixed.* **fix** /fɪks/ *noun* [C usually sing] *The result was a fix!*

-fixing /ˈfɪk.sɪŋ/ *suffix* dishonest activity to make certain that a competition, race or election is won by a particular person: *Seven jockeys were arrested and charged with race-fixing.* ○ *After several days of questioning, he admitted to match-fixing.*

fix [PUNISH] /fɪks/ *verb* [T] *SLANG* to punish especially someone who has been unfair: *I'm gonna fix her if she doesn't stop telling lies about me!*

fix [DRUG] /fɪks/ *noun* [C] *SLANG* an amount of an illegal drug, or of another substance which has an effect on someone if they take it: *He was shaking badly and needed a fix.* ○ *HUMOROUS Ginny needs her daily fix of chocolate.*

fix /fɪks/ *verb* [I] *SLANG* to inject an illegal drug: *We saw kids as young as twelve fixing in doorways.*

fix [POSITION] /fɪks/ *noun* [C] (the calculation of) the position of a vehicle, usually in relation to the Earth: *Do we still have a fix **on** that jet?*

fix [PRESERVE COLOURS] /fɪks/ *verb* [T] *SPECIALIZED* to treat something, especially photographic material, with chemicals to prevent its colours from becoming paler

fix [SIGHT] /fɪks/ *verb* [T] to keep something or someone in sight: *His eyes were fixed **on** the distant yacht.* ○ *She fixed the child **with** a stare of such disapproval he did not dare move.*

fixedly /ˈfɪk.sɪd.li/ *adv* **gaze/look/stare fixedly** to look continuously at one thing: *Taylor was staring fixedly at her.*

fix [STOP REPRODUCTION] /fɪks/ *verb* [T] *US INFORMAL* to remove the reproductive organs of an animal

PHRASAL VERBS WITH **fix**

▲ **fix sth up** [ARRANGE] *phrasal verb* [M] to arrange a meeting, date, event, etc: *I'd like to fix up a meeting with you next week sometime.*

▲ **fix sth up** [REPAIR] *phrasal verb* [M] to repair or change something in order to improve it: *Nick loves fixing up old cars.*

▲ **fix sb up** [PROVIDE] *phrasal verb* [M] to provide someone with something that they need: *Can he fix us up **with** somewhere to stay?*

▲ **fix sb up** [PERSON] *phrasal verb* [M] *INFORMAL* to find a romantic partner for someone: *Jacques tried to fix me up **with** his older sister.*

fixated /fɪkˈseɪ.tɪd/ [US] /ˈfɪk.seɪ.t̬ɪd/ *adj* [after v] unable to stop thinking about something: *a nation fixated **on** the past* ○ *Back in London, he became fixated **with** his best friend's daughter.*

fixation /fɪkˈseɪ.ʃən/ *noun* [C] an inability to stop thinking about something or someone, or an unnaturally strong interest in them: *Liz has a fixation (UK) **with**/(US) **on** food.* ○ *Again Cagney was at his twisted best in White Heat, playing a psychopath with a mother fixation.*

fixative /ˈfɪk.sə.tɪv/ [US] /-t̬ɪv/ *noun* [C or U] **1** a substance which holds something in position: *a fixative for dentures* **2** a chemical used to treat photographic material in order to preserve its colour

ˌfixed ˈassets *plural noun* (in business) buildings, equipment and land owned by a company

fixity /ˈfɪk.sə.ti/ [US] /-t̬i/ *noun* [U] *FORMAL* the quality of not changing

fixture [FIXED OBJECT] /ˈfɪks.tʃəʳ/ [US] /-tʃɚ/ *noun* [C] *MAINLY UK* a permanently fixed item in a house, such as a bath, which would not be taken by someone when they move to a new home: *All fixtures **and fittings** are included in the house price.* ○ *FIGURATIVE They've been together so long he's become a permanent fixture in her life.* ➲Compare **fitting** at **fit** POSITION.

F

fixture SPORTS EVENT /ˈfɪks.tʃəʳ/ ⓤ /-tʃɚ/ *noun* [C] *UK* a day and usually a time agreed for a sports event: *Next season's fixtures will be published early next month.*

fizz /fɪz/ *verb* [I] If a liquid fizzes, it produces a lot of bubbles and makes a continuous 's' sound: *I could hear the champagne fizz as he poured it into my glass.*

fizz /fɪz/ *noun* [U] **1** bubbles of gas in a liquid **2** *UK INFORMAL* a fizzy drink, especially CHAMPAGNE: *Who'd like some fizz?*

fizzy /ˈfɪz.i/ *adj* having a lot of bubbles: *fizzy orange/mineral water* **fizziness** /ˈfɪz.ɪ.nəs/ *noun* [U]

fizzle /ˈfɪz.l̩/ *verb* [I] **1** *MAINLY US* to gradually end: *Interest in the project fizzled after the funding was withdrawn.* **2** *UK* to make a weak continuous 's' sound: *The fire fizzled miserably in the rain.*

▲ **fizzle out** *phrasal verb* to gradually end, often in a disappointing or weak way: *They went off to different universities and their relationship just fizzled out.*

fjord, **fiord** /fjɔːd/ ⓤ /fjɔːrd/ *noun* [C] a long strip of sea between steep hills, found especially in Norway

flab /flæb/ *noun* [U] *INFORMAL DISAPPROVING* soft loose flesh on someone's body: *I've got to lose this flab on my belly!*

flabbergast /ˈflæb.ə.gɑːst/ ⓤ /-ɚ.gæst/ *verb* [T often passive] *INFORMAL* to shock someone, usually by telling them something they were not expecting: *He was flabbergasted when we told him how cheap it was.* **flabbergasted** /ˈflæb.ə.gɑː.stɪd/ ⓤ /-ɚ.gæ-/ *adj*: *When they announced her name, the winner just sat there, flabbergasted.*

flabby /ˈflæb.i/ *adj* **1** *INFORMAL DISAPPROVING* soft and fat: *flabby arms/thighs* ○ *I was starting to get a bit flabby around my waist.* **2** weak and lacking force: *a flabby argument* **flabbiness** /ˈflæb.ɪ.nəs/ *noun* [U]

flaccid /ˈflæs.ɪd/ *adj* **1** *FORMAL* soft rather than firm; weak: *The penis is usually in a flaccid state.* **2** *DISAPPROVING* weak and ineffective: *The program included a lacklustre and flaccid account of Rossini's Overture to "La gazza ladra".*

flack /flæk/ *noun* **1** [U] flak **2** [C] *US INFORMAL* a person chosen by a group or organization which is in a difficult situation to speak officially for them to the public and answer questions and criticisms

flag SYMBOL /flæg/ *noun* [C] a piece of cloth, usually rectangular and fixed to a pole at one edge, that has a pattern which shows it represents a country or a group, or has a particular meaning: *Flags of all the participating countries are **flying** outside the stadium.* ○ *Flags were flapping/fluttering in the breeze.* ○ *The guard **waved** his flag and the train pulled away from the station.* ⊃See picture **Sports** on page Centre 10

• **wave/show/fly the flag** *UK* to show support for the country, group or organization that you belong to

• **Put the flags out!** *UK HUMOROUS* something that you say when you are pleased and surprised that something has happened: *Josh has cleaned the bathroom – put the flags out!*

• **keep the flag flying** *MAINLY UK* to act or speak for the country or group which a flag represents

flag MARK /flæg/ *verb* [T] **-gg-** to put a mark on something so it can be found easily among other similar things: *Flag any files which might be useful later.*

▲ **flag sth/sb down** *phrasal verb* [M] to cause a vehicle to stop by waving at its driver: *I managed to flag down a passing police car.*

flag BECOME TIRED /flæg/ *verb* [I] **-gg-** to become tired or less interested: *I was starting to flag after the ninth mile.* ○ *The conversation was flagging.*

flagging /ˈflæg/ *adj* becoming weaker: *flagging energy/enthusiasm*

flag STONE /flæg/ *noun* [C] a **flagstone**

flagged /flæg/ *adj* *MAINLY UK* made of or covered in FLAGSTONES: *a flagged path*

'flag ˌday *noun* [C] **1** *UK* (*AUS* **button day**) a day when money is collected in public places for a charity **2** Flag Day 14 June, a holiday in the US marking the day in 1777 when the US first officially used its flag

flagellate /ˈflædʒ.ə.leɪt/ *verb* [T] *FORMAL* to whip someone, especially as a religious act **flagellation** /ˌflædʒ.əˈleɪ.ʃn̩/ *noun* [U]

flagellant /ˈflædʒ.ɪ.lᵊnt/ *noun* [C] *FORMAL* someone who whips himself or someone else for religious reasons

flagon /ˈflæg.ən/ *noun* [C] *OLD USE* a large container for especially alcoholic drink, used in the past: *a flagon of wine*

flagpole /ˈflæg.pəʊl/ ⓤ /-poʊl/ *noun* [C] (*ALSO* **flagstaff**) a long pole which a flag is fastened to

flagrant /ˈfleɪ.grᵊnt/ *adj* (of a bad action, situation, person, etc.) shocking because of being so obvious: *a flagrant misuse of funds/privilege* ○ *a flagrant breach of trust* ○ *a flagrant disregard for the law* **flagrantly** /ˈfleɪ.grᵊnt.li/ *adv*: *The organization flagrantly promotes the use of violence.*

flagship BEST PRODUCT /ˈflæg.ʃɪp/ *noun* [C] the best or most important product, idea, building, etc. that an organization owns or produces: *This machine is the flagship in our new range of computers.* ○ *The company's flagship store is in New York.*

flagship SHIP /ˈflæg.ʃɪp/ *noun* [C] the ship within a group on which the most important officer sails

flagstaff /ˈflæg.stɑːf/ ⓤ /-stæf/ *noun* [C] a **flagpole**

flagstone /ˈflæg.stəʊn/ ⓤ /-stoʊn/ *noun* [C] (*ALSO* **flag**) a large flat piece of stone or concrete used for paths, floors, etc.

flag-waving /ˈflægˌweɪ.vɪŋ/ *noun* [U] *DISAPPROVING* the strong expression of support for a country or group, sometimes with military intention

flail WAVE /fleɪl/ *verb* [I or T] (*ALSO* **flail about/around**) (especially of arms and legs) to move energetically in an uncontrolled way: *A wasp came towards us and Howard started flailing his arms around.* ○ *She ran from the house in a terrible rage, her arms flailing in the air.*

flail TOOL /fleɪl/ *noun* [C] a tool consisting of a rod which swings from a long handle, used especially in the past for THRESHING grain

flair /fleəʳ/ ⓤ /fler/ *noun* **1** [S] natural ability to do something well: *He has a flair **for** languages.* **2** [U] when something is done in an exciting and interesting way: *He played with great imagination and flair.* ○ *It's a competent enough piece of writing but it lacks flair.*

flak CRITICISM, **flack** /flæk/ *noun* [U] *INFORMAL* strong criticism or opposition: *She **took/caught** some flak from her parents about her new dress.*

flak FIRING OF GUNS /flæk/ *noun* [U] (*ALSO* **flack**) the firing of guns from the ground at enemy aircraft, or the things that the guns fire: *They flew into heavy flak over the target area.*

flake SMALL PIECE /fleɪk/ *noun* [C] a small thin piece of something, especially if it has come from a layered surface: *flakes of snow* ○ *soap flakes* ○ *This room needs decorating – flakes of paint keep coming off the walls.* **flake** /fleɪk/ *verb* [I] *Patches of skin are starting to flake off.*

flaky /ˈfleɪ.ki/ *adj* coming off easily in small, flat, thin pieces: *dry, flaky skin* ○ *a flaky scalp*

flake PERSON /fleɪk/ *noun* [C] *MAINLY US INFORMAL* a person who you cannot trust to remember things or to do what they say they will do, or someone who behaves in a strange way

flaky /ˈfleɪ.ki/ *adj* *MAINLY US INFORMAL* behaving in a way that is not responsible or expected: *The central character of the play is a flaky neurotic.*

▲ **flake out** *phrasal verb* *INFORMAL* to suddenly fall asleep or feel weak because you are extremely tired: *I got home and flaked out on the sofa.*

'flak ˌjacket *noun* [C] a special piece of clothing worn by soldiers and police to protect them from bullets and weapons

flambé /ˈflɒm.beɪ/ ⓤ /flɑːmˈbeɪ/ *verb* [T] to pour alcohol over food and set fire to it during cooking: *flambéed pancakes* **flambé** /ˈflɒm.beɪ/ ⓤ /flɑːmˈbeɪ/ *adj* [after n] *steak flambé*

flamboyant /flæmˈbɔɪ.ənt/ *adj* very confident in behaviour, or intended to be noticed, especially by being brightly coloured: *a flamboyant gesture* ○ *The writer's flamboyant lifestyle was well known.* ○ *His clothes were rather flamboyant for such a serious occasion.* **flamboyance** /flæmˈbɔɪ.ənts/ *noun* [U] *Her flamboyance* annoys some people but delights others. **flamboyantly** /flæm'bɔɪ.ənt.li/ *adv*

flame [FIRE] /fleɪm/ *noun* [C or U] burning gas (from something on fire) which produces usually yellow light: *The flames grew larger as the fire spread.* ○ *The car flipped over and* ***burst into*** *flames* (= started burning immediately). ○ *When the fire engine arrived the house was already* ***in*** *flames* (= burning). ➲See also **old flame**.
• **go up in flames** to burn or be destroyed by fire: *The factory went up in flames.*
flame /fleɪm/ *verb* [I] *LITERARY* to burn (more) brightly: *The fire flamed cozily in the hearth.* ○ *The fire suddenly flamed* ***(up)***.

flame [EMOTION] /fleɪm/ *noun* [C] *LITERARY* a powerful feeling: *Flames* ***of*** *passion swept through both of them.*
flame /fleɪm/ *verb* [I] *LITERARY* **1** If an emotion flames, you feel it suddenly and strongly: *Seeing the damage made hatred flame* ***within*** *her.* **2** to suddenly become hot and red with emotion: *His face flamed* ***(red)*** *with anger.*
flaming /'fleɪ.mɪŋ/ *adj INFORMAL* **a flaming row** a very angry argument in which people shout at each other: *We had a flaming row over it last night.*

flame [COMPUTING] /fleɪm/ *noun* [C] *SLANG* an angry or offensive email: *flame wars*
flame /fleɪm/ *verb* [T] *SLANG* to send an insulting electronic message over the Internet about someone who you disagree with: *Please don't flame me if you disagree with this message.* **flamer** /'fleɪ.məʳ/ [US] /-mɚ/ *noun* [C]

flamenco /flə'meŋ.kəʊ/ [US] /-koʊ/ *noun* [C or U] *plural* **flamencos** a type of Spanish dance music, or the dance performed to this music: *flamenco music/dancers*

flameproof /'fleɪm.pruːf/ *adj* not likely to burn or be damaged by fire: *flameproof clothing*

'flame re,tardant *adj* If a substance is flame retardant, it will slow down the spread of fire.

flame-thrower /'fleɪm,θrəʊ.əʳ/ [US] /-,θroʊ.ɚ/ *noun* [C] a device which produces a stream of burning liquid and is used for military purposes or for removing plants from an area of wild land

flaming /'fleɪ.mɪŋ/ *adj* [before n] *UK SLANG* used to add force, especially anger, to something which is said: *Put that down you flaming idiot!*

flamingo /flə'mɪŋ.gəʊ/ [US] /-goʊ/ *noun* [C] *plural* **flamingos** or **flamingoes** a large bird with pink feathers, long thin legs, a long neck and a beak that curves down

flammable /'flæm.ə.bl̩/ *adj* describes something that burns easily: *Caution! This solvent is highly flammable.*
* NOTE: The opposite of **flammable** is **non-flammable**. ➲See usage note at **inflammable**.

flan /flæn/ *noun* [C] **1** *UK* a case of pastry or cake without a top, which contains fruit or something savoury such as cheese: *a cheese and onion flan* ○ *a pear flan* ○ *a flan dish* **2** *US* a sweet soft food made from milk, eggs and sugar

flange /flændʒ/ *noun* [C] a flat surface sticking out from an object, which is used to fix it to something or to make it stronger: *The flange around the wheels on railway trains helps to keep them on the rails.*

flank [SIDE] /flæŋk/ *verb* [T] to be at the side of someone or something: *The president was flanked by senior ministers.* **flank** /flæŋk/ *noun* [C] *right/left flank* ○ *A small group of houses clings to the eastern flank of the mountain.*

flank [BODY] /flæŋk/ *noun* [C] the area of the body between the ribs and the hips of an animal or a person

flannel [PIECE OF CLOTH] /'flæn.əl/ *noun* [C] *UK FOR* **facecloth** (= a small cloth used to wash the body, especially the face and hands)

flannel [TYPE OF CLOTH] /'flæn.əl/ *noun* [U] a light cloth usually made from wool, used especially for making clothes: *flannel trousers*
flannels /'flæn.əlz/ *plural noun UK* trousers made of flannel: *Traditionally, white flannels are worn when playing cricket.*

flannel [UNNECESSARY WORDS] /'flæn.əl/ *noun* [U] *UK INFORMAL* speech containing a lot of words which is used to avoid telling the truth or answering a question, and is frequently intended to deceive: *Leave out the flannel and answer the question!* **flannel** /'flæn.əl/ *verb* [I or T] -ll-

flannelette /,flæn.əl'et/ *noun* [U] a soft cloth made of cotton: *flannelette sheets/pyjamas* ○ *a flannelette nightdress*

flap [WAVE] /flæp/ *verb* [I or T] -pp- to wave something, especially wings when or as if flying: *A small bird flapped its wings furiously and flew upwards.* ○ *Flags flapped in the breeze above their tents.* **flap** /flæp/ *noun* [C] *A few flaps of its long wings and the bird was gone.*

flap [ADDITIONAL PIECE] /flæp/ *noun* [C] a piece of cloth or other material fixed along one edge, especially used for covering or closing something: *a pocket flap* ○ *a tent flap* (= a piece of cloth which acts like a door) ○ *A small flap of skin can be seen above the wound.*

flap [ANXIOUS STATE] /flæp/ *noun* [S] *INFORMAL* a state of anxious excitement: *She's* ***in a*** *flap because her parents are coming to visit.* **flap** /flæp/ *verb* [I] -pp- *Don't flap – there's plenty of time to cook before they arrive.* ○ *Stop flapping* ***about/around***!

flap [AIRCRAFT PART] /flæp/ *noun* [C] *SPECIALIZED* part of the back of an aircraft wing which can be moved up or down to help the aircraft go up or down

flapjack /'flæp.dʒæk/ *noun* [C] **1** *UK* a type of sweet chewy cake made from oats **2** *US* a PANCAKE (= a sweet thick cake eaten hot, usually for breakfast)

flapper /'flæp.əʳ/ [US] /-ɚ/ *noun* [C] in the 1920s, a fashionable young woman, especially one showing independent behaviour

flare [BURN BRIGHTLY] /fleəʳ/ [US] /fler/ *verb* [I] to burn brightly either for a short time or irregularly: *The flame above the oil well flared* ***(up)*** *into the dark sky.*
flare /fleəʳ/ [US] /fler/ *noun* [C] **1** a sudden increase in the brightness of a fire: *There was a sudden flare when she threw the petrol onto the fire.* **2** a very bright light or coloured smoke which can be used as a signal, or a device which produces this: *We set off a flare to help guide our rescuers.*

flare [GET WORSE] /fleəʳ/ [US] /fler/ *verb* [I] (*ALSO* **flare up**) When something bad such as violence, pain or anger flares (up), it suddenly starts or gets much worse: *Violence flared up again last night.* ○ ***Tempers*** *flared after a three-hour delay at Gatwick Airport yesterday.*
flare-up /'fleə.rʌp/ [US] /'fler.ʌp/ *noun* [C usually sing] *There was another flare-up* ***of*** *rioting later that day.*

flare [MAKE WIDER] /fleəʳ/ [US] /fler/ *verb* [I or T] to (cause to) become wider: *The horse's nostrils flared.* ○ *The skirt fits tightly over the hips and flares just below the knees.*
flare /fleəʳ/ [US] /fler/ *noun* [C usually sing] *This skirt has a definite flare.* **flared** /fleəd/ [US] /flerd/ *adj*: *flared trousers*
flares /fleəz/ [US] /flerz/ *plural noun UK* trousers that get a lot wider below the knee

flash [SHINE SUDDENLY] /flæʃ/ *verb* **1** [I or T] to shine brightly and suddenly, or to make something shine in this way: *Stop flashing that light* ***in*** *my eyes!* ○ *The lightning flashed and distant thunder rolled.* ○ *You'd better slow down, that car was flashing (its lights)* ***at*** *you.* **2** [I] *LITERARY* If someone's eyes flash, they look bright because of the anger or excitement the person is feeling.
flash /flæʃ/ *noun* [C] a sudden bright light that quickly disappears: *a flash of lightning* ○ *The bomb exploded in a flash* ***of*** *yellow light.*
• **in a flash** (*ALSO* **quick as a flash**) *INFORMAL* quickly or suddenly: *The ceremony was over in a flash.*
• **flash in the pan** something that happened only once or for a short time and was not repeated: *Sadly, their success was just a flash in the pan.*

flash [MOVE FAST] /flæʃ/ *verb* [I usually + adv or prep] to move very fast: *They flashed* ***past/by*** *on a motorcycle.*

flash [SHOW QUICKLY] /flæʃ/ *verb* **1** [T] to show something for a short time: *He flashed a smile and offered to buy me a drink.* **2** [I or T] *INFORMAL* If someone flashes, they show their sexual organs in public: *He came out of the bushes and flashed at me.*
flash /flæʃ/ *noun* [C] *HUMOROUS* a quick look at something: *She leant over and I caught a flash of pink underwear.*
flasher /'flæʃ.əʳ/ [US] /-ɚ/ *noun* [C] *INFORMAL* someone who shows their sexual organs in public

F

flash SUDDEN EXPERIENCE /flæʃ/ *noun* [C usually sing] a sudden, powerful emotional or mental experience: *The idea came to her in a flash of inspiration/genius.*

flash /flæʃ/ *verb* [I + adv or prep] If something flashes through/across your mind, you suddenly or briefly think of it: *The thought suddenly flashed through my mind that she didn't want to be here.*

flash SEEMING EXPENSIVE /flæʃ/ *adj UK* expensive-looking in a way that attracts attention: *That's a very flash suit he's wearing.*

flashy /ˈflæʃ.i/ *adj DISAPPROVING* looking too bright, big and expensive in a way that is intended to get attention and admiration: *flashy clothes* ○ *a flashy car* ○ *flashy gold jewellery* **flashily** /ˈflæʃ.ɪ.li/ *adv*: *flashily dressed* **flashiness** /ˈflæʃ.ɪ.nəs/ *noun* [U]

flash PHOTOGRAPHY /flæʃ/ *noun* [C or U] the device or system used to produce a bright light for a short time when taking a photograph: *Where's the flash for the camera?* ○ *It's quite dark in here, I'll have to use flash.*

flash COMMUNICATE /flæʃ/ *verb* [T usually + adv or prep] to communicate something quickly, especially using radio or light waves: *Within moments of an event happening, the news can be flashed around the world.*

flash MILITARY SIGN /flæʃ/ *noun* [C] *UK* a small object or piece of material worn on a military uniform as a sign of rank, or (on clothing) a strip or mark of colour different from the main colour

PHRASAL VERBS WITH **flash** ▼

▲ **flash** *sth* **around/about** *phrasal verb INFORMAL* to intentionally make people aware that you have something valuable, especially in order to make them feel unhappy because they do not have it: *She was flashing her engagement ring around.*

▲ **flash back** *phrasal verb* If your mind or thoughts flash back to something that happened in the past, you suddenly remember it: *Her mind flashed back to the day of their divorce.*

flashback /ˈflæʃ.bæk/ *noun* **1** [C or U] a short part of a film, story or play that goes back to events in the past: *The novel began with a flashback to the hero's experiences in the war.* **2** [C usually pl] a sudden, clear memory of a past event or time, usually one that was bad: *I kept having flashbacks of her lying there bleeding.*

flashbulb /ˈflæʃ.bʌlb/ *noun* [C] *SPECIALIZED* a small electric light that can be fixed to a camera and which makes a bright flash so that photographs can be taken inside or when it is dark

ˈflash ˌcard *noun* [C] a card with a word or picture on it which is used to help students learn

ˌflash ˈflood *noun* [C] a sudden and severe flood: *The unusually heavy rain caused flash floods in several mountain villages.*

flash-fry /ˌflæʃˈfraɪ/ *verb* [T] to fry something quickly on both sides in very hot oil

flashgun /ˈflæʃ.gʌn/ *noun* [C] *SPECIALIZED* a device usually held away from a camera which automatically makes a flash when a camera is taking a picture

flashlight /ˈflæʃ.laɪt/ *noun* [C] *US FOR* **torch** (= a small light that you can carry with you)

flashpoint VIOLENCE, *US ALSO* **flash point** /ˈflæʃ.pɔɪnt/ *noun* [C] a place or stage at which violence might be expected to begin: *Because of the army's presence, the city is seen to be the flashpoint of the area.*

flashpoint TEMPERATURE /ˈflæʃ.pɔɪnt/ *noun* [C usually sing] *SPECIALIZED* The flashpoint of a liquid is the lowest temperature at which the VAPOUR it produces will burn in air.

flask HOT DRINKS /flɑːsk/ *UK* /flæsk/ *noun* [C] (*US TRADEMARK* **Thermos**) a special container that keeps drinks hot or cold: *a flask of coffee/tea*

flask ALCOHOL /flɑːsk/ /flæsk/ *noun* [C] a flat bottle that is used to carry alcohol in your pocket: *a hip flask*

flask SCIENCE /flɑːsk/ /flæsk/ *noun* [C] a glass container for liquids which has a wide base and a narrow neck and which is used in a LABORATORY

flat LEVEL /flæt/ *adj* flatter, flattest level and smooth, with no curved, high, or hollow parts: *An ice rink needs to be* completely flat. ○ *Roll out the pastry on a flat surface.* ○ *Much of the countryside in East Anglia is very flat.*

• **be (as) flat as a pancake** *INFORMAL* to be very flat: *The countryside around Cambridge is as flat as a pancake.*

flat /flæt/ *noun* [C often pl] an area of low level ground, often near water: *The salt flats are used for motor racing.* ○ *The mud flats attract large numbers of birds.*

• **the flat of your hand** the palm and fingers when they are held straight and level: *He hit me with the flat of his hand.*

• **be on the flat** to be on a level surface, not on a slope or hill: *Most of the path is on the flat.*

flat /flæt/ *adv* flatter, flattest in a level position, often against another surface: *Lay the cloth flat across the table.*

flatness /ˈflæt.nəs/ *noun* [U] the quality of being level and without curved, high or hollow parts: *The flatness of the desert was broken only by a few large piles of rocks.*

flatten /ˈflæt.ən/ /ˈflæt̬-/ *verb* [I or T] to become level or cause something to become level: *Several trees were flattened* (= knocked down) *by the storm.* ○ *The path flattens (out)* (= does not go up so much) *as it reaches the top of the hill.*

flat NOT HIGH /flæt/ *adj* flatter, flattest **1** level but having little or no height: *flat shoes* (= shoes which do not have a raised heel) **2** describes bread which is made without yeast, and therefore does not rise: *Pitta and naan are two types of flat bread.* **3** *UK* **flat cap/hat** a hat which is not rounded on top and has little height

flats /flæts/ *plural noun* women's shoes without high heels: *I feel more comfortable in flats.*

flat /flæt/ *adv* flatter, flattest into a flat shape without height: *These garden chairs will fold flat for storage.*

flatten /ˈflæt.ən/ /ˈflæt̬-/ *verb* [I or T] to become level and thinner or to cause something to become level and thinner: *Flatten the pastry into a thin disc with your hands.* ○ *The biscuits will flatten out as they cook.*

flat NOT ACTIVE /flæt/ *adj* flatter, flattest **1** not active; not interesting or lacking emotion: *After the excitement of the party, life seems rather flat now.* ○ *I thought her performance a little flat.* ○ *I think the colours in this painting are rather flat* (= not varied or bright). ○ *UK I left my car lights on all night and now the battery is flat* (*US* **dead**) (= has no electrical power left in it). **2** describes a drink which has stopped being fizzy: *If you don't put the top back on that bottle of beer, it will go flat.* ⊃Compare **still** NOT MOVING.

flatly /ˈflæt.li/ *adv* in a way that lacks emotion or interest: *The witness responded flatly to the judge's questions.*

flatness /ˈflæt.nəs/ *noun* [U] when someone or something lacks emotion or interest: *All the critics remarked on the flatness of the performance.*

flat COMPLETE /flæt/ *adj* [before n] (*US ALSO* **flat-out**) complete or certain, and not likely to change: *His request for time off work was met with a flat refusal.* ○ *The minister has issued a flat denial of the accusations against her.*

flat /flæt/ *adv INFORMAL* completely or to the greatest degree possible: *She told him flat/*(*US ALSO*) **flat out** *that she would not go to the show.* ○ *Could you lend me some money, I'm flat broke* (= I have no money). ⊃See also **stony broke.**

• **three minutes/half an hour, etc. flat** exactly three minutes/half an hour, etc: *We managed to get to the station in five minutes flat.*

• **flat out** as fast or as hard as possible: *My car only does about 60 mph, even when it's going flat out.* ○ *We've been working flat out to get this done.*

flatly /ˈflæt.li/ *adv* If you flatly deny, refuse or disagree with something or someone, you do it completely or in a very clear and definite way.

flat WITHOUT AIR /flæt/ *adj* flatter, flattest If something such as a tyre or ball is flat, it does not contain enough air: *I got a flat* (*US*) **tyre**/(*US*) **tire** (= The air went out of it) *after driving over a nail.*

flat /flæt/ *noun* [C usually sing] *MAINLY US INFORMAL* a **flat tyre**: *We were late because we had to stop and fix a flat.*

flat FIXED /flæt/ *adj* [before n] (especially of an amount of money) fixed; not likely to vary: *We charge a flat fee/rate of $25 per hour.*

flat [MUSIC] /flæt/ *adj, adv* **flatter**, **flattest** (in music) lower than a particular note or the correct note: *The top string on your violin is flat.* ○ *She sang flat throughout the song* (= all the notes she sang were too low). ➲Compare **natural** MUSIC; **sharp** MUSIC.

flat /flæt/ *noun* [C] (a symbol for) a note that is a SEMITONE lower than a stated note

flat [HOME] *UK* /flæt/ *noun* [C] (*US* **apartment**) a set of rooms for living which are part of a larger building and are usually all on one floor: *a furnished/unfurnished flat* ○ *a block of flats* ○ *They have a house in the country and a flat in London.* ➲See also **flatmate**.

flatlet /ˈflæt.lət/ *noun* [C] *UK* a very small flat

flat-chested /ˌflætˈtʃes.tɪd/ *adj MAINLY DISAPPROVING* A woman who is flat-chested has small breasts.

ˌflat ˈfeet *plural noun* feet that are level across the bottom instead of curved

flatfish /ˈflæt.fɪʃ/ *noun* [C] *plural* **flatfish** any thin flat sea fish, such as a PLAICE or a SOLE

flat-footed /ˌflætˈfʊt.ɪd/ [US] /-ˈfʊt̬-/ *adj* [before n], *adv* having feet whose bottom part is flat against the ground and not curved up in an arch

flathead /ˈflæt.hed/ *noun* [C] *AUS* a thin flat sea fish which can be eaten

flatmate /ˈflæt.meɪt/ *noun* [C] *UK* a person who shares an apartment with another person

flatpack /ˈflæt.pæk/ *noun* [C] *UK* a piece of furniture that is sold in pieces inside a flat box, ready for the buyer to put them together

ˈflat ˌracing *noun* [U] a type of horse racing where the horses do not jump over fences

ˈflat ˌrate *noun* [C] *UK* a charge that is the same for everyone: *Clients are charged a flat rate of £15 monthly.* ○ *a flat-rate contribution*

flatter /ˈflæt.əʳ/ [US] /ˈflæt̬.ɚ/ *verb* [T] **1** to praise someone in order to make them feel attractive or important, sometimes in a way that is not sincere: *I knew he was only flattering me because he wanted to borrow some money.* **2** to make someone look more attractive than usual: *That new hairstyle really flatters her.* ○ *Short skirts don't flatter me at all.*

flatter *yourself* *verb* [R] to believe something good about yourself although it might not be true: [+ **that**] *Clive flatters himself* ***that*** *he's a excellent speaker.*

• **flatter to deceive** to give the appearance of being better than the true situation: *I suspect these statistics flatter to deceive.*

• **be/feel flattered** to feel very pleased and proud because someone has said good things about you or has made you feel important: *She was flattered by his attention.* ○ *They were flattered* ***to*** *be invited to dinner by the mayor.* ○ *We felt flattered* ***that*** *so many people came to our party.*

flatterer /ˈflæt.ᵊr.əʳ/ [US] /ˈflæt̬.ɚ.ɚ/ *noun* [C] *SLIGHTLY DISAPPROVING* someone who praises people without being sincere: *You can't believe a word Tony says, he's a real flatterer.*

flattering /ˈflæt.ᵊr.ɪŋ/ [US] /ˈflæt̬.ɚ-/ *adj* making someone look or seem better or more attractive than usual: *a flattering photograph* ○ *That suit is very flattering.* ○ *He's always making flattering* ***remarks****, but he doesn't really mean them.*

flattery /ˈflæt.ᵊr.i/ [US] /ˈflæt̬-/ *noun* [U] when you praise someone, often because you want something from them: *I was really pleased when he said how well I'd done, because he isn't known for flattery.*

• **Flattery will get you nowhere.** *HUMOROUS SAYING* used to tell someone that their praise will not persuade you to do anything you do not want to do

flatties /ˈflæt.iːz/ [US] /ˈflæt̬/ *plural noun UK INFORMAL* women's shoes without high heels

ˌflat ˈtyre *noun* [C usually sing] (*MAINLY US INFORMAL* **flat**) a tyre that does not have any or enough air in it ➲See also **puncture**.

flatulence /ˈflæt.jʊ.lᵊnts/ *noun* [U] *FORMAL* gas in the stomach and bowels: *Eating beans can cause flatulence.*

flatulent /ˈflæt.jʊ.lᵊnt/ *adj*

flatware /ˈflæt.weəʳ/ [US] /-wer/ *noun* [U] *US* **cutlery**

flatworm /ˈflæt.wɜːm/ [US] /-wɝːm/ *noun* [C] a worm with a flat body that can live inside the bodies of people and animals and often causes disease

flaunt /flɔːnt/ [US] /flɑːnt/ *verb* [T] *MAINLY DISAPPROVING* to show or make obvious something you are proud of in order to get admiration: *He's got a lot of money but he doesn't flaunt it.* ○ *Annabelle was flaunting her tan in a little white dress.*

flaunt *yourself* *verb* [R] *MAINLY DISAPPROVING* to show your body in a confident and sexual manner

flautist /ˈflɔː.tɪst/ [US] /ˈflɑː.t̬ɪst/ *noun* [C] (*US ALSO* **flutist**) a person who plays the FLUTE

flavour *UK, US* **flavor** /ˈfleɪ.vəʳ/ [US] /-vɚ/ *noun* **1** [C or U] how food or drink tastes, or a particular taste itself: *Add a little salt to bring out the flavour* ***of*** *the herbs.* ○ *My fish was delicious but Charles' beef had almost no flavour* (= did not taste of anything). ○ *This wine has a light, fruity flavour* (= the taste of fruit). ○ *We sell 32 different flavours* (= particular types of taste) *of ice cream.* **2** [S] a particular quality or character: *The resort has a nautical flavour.* **3** [S] an idea or quick experience of something: *To give you a flavour of what the book is like Jilly is going to read out a brief extract.*

• **flavour of the month** *UK INFORMAL* the most popular person at a particular time: *Andy is certainly flavour of the month with the boss.*

flavour *UK, US* **flavor** /ˈfleɪ.vəʳ/ [US] /-vɚ/ *verb* [T often passive] to give a particular taste to food or drink: *This sauce is flavoured with garlic and herbs.* ○ *You can use fresh herbs to flavour the soup.*

-flavoured *UK, US* **-flavored** /-fleɪ.vəd/ [US] /-vɚd/ *suffix* tasting of the thing stated: *orange-flavoured chocolate* ○ *mint-flavoured sweets*

flavourful *UK, US* **flavorful** /ˈfleɪ.və.fʊl/ [US] /-vɚ-/ *adj* full of flavour: *a flavourful sauce*

flavouring *UK, US* **flavoring** /ˈfleɪ.vᵊr.ɪŋ/ [US] /-vɚ-/ *noun* [C or U] something that is added to food or drink to give it a particular taste: *artificial/natural flavouring(s)*

flavourless *UK, US* **flavorless** /ˈfleɪ.və.ləs/ [US] /-vɚ-/ *adj* having little or no flavour: *These grapes are completely flavourless.*

flavoursome /ˈfleɪ.və.səm/ [US] /-vɚ-/ *adj UK* having good flavour or a lot of flavour: *flavoursome wine*

ˈflavour enˌhancer *noun* [C] *UK* a substance used to improve the taste of a food or drink

flaw /flɔː/ [US] /flɑː/ *noun* [C] a fault, mistake or weakness, especially one that happens while something is being planned or made, or which causes something not to be perfect: *I returned the material because it had a flaw* ***in*** *it.* ○ *There's a* ***fatal*** *flaw in your reasoning.* ○ *This report is full of flaws.* ○ *a character flaw*

flaw /flɔː/ [US] /flɑː/ *verb* [T] to cause something to be not perfect: *A tiny mark flawed the otherwise perfect silk shirt.*

flawed /flɔːd/ [US] /flɑːd/ *adj* not perfect, or containing mistakes: *Diamonds are still valuable, even when they are flawed.* ○ *His argument is deeply flawed.* ○ *flawed beauty*

flawless /ˈflɔː.ləs/ [US] /ˈflɑː-/ *adj* perfect or without mistakes: *a flawless complexion* ○ *a flawless performance*

flawlessly /ˈflɔː.ləs.li/ [US] /ˈflɑː-/ *adv*

flax /flæks/ *noun* [U] a plant with blue flowers grown for its stems or seeds, or the thread made from this plant

flaxen /ˈflæk.sᵊn/ *adj LITERARY* (of hair) pale yellow: *a flaxen-haired youth*

flay /fleɪ/ *verb* [T] **1** to remove the skin from a person's or animal's body **2** to whip a person or animal so hard that some of their skin comes off: *FIGURATIVE The critics really flayed* (= severely criticized) *his new book.*

• **flay *sb* alive** *INFORMAL* to punish or tell someone off severely: *I'll be flayed alive when she finds out!*

flea /fliː/ *noun* [C] a very small jumping insect which feeds on the blood of animals and humans

• **send *sb* away with a flea in *their* ear** *UK INFORMAL* to angrily tell someone to go away: *A young kid came asking for money but I sent him away with a flea in his ear.*

fleabag [PERSON OR ANIMAL] /ˈfliː.bæg/ *noun* [C] *UK INFORMAL* a dirty and/or unpleasant person or animal

fleabag [HOTEL] /ˈfliː.bæg/ *noun* [C] *US* a cheap dirty hotel

fleabite /ˈfliː.baɪt/ *noun* [C] the bite of a FLEA

fleabitten /ˈfliː.bɪt.ən/ [US] /-bɪt-/ *adj* INFORMAL dirty and in bad condition: *I'm not going to stay in that fleabitten old place.*

ˈflea ˌcollar *noun* [C] a collar for dogs and cats that has been treated with chemicals which kill FLEAS

ˈflea ˌmarket *noun* [C] a market, which usually takes place outside, where old or used goods are sold cheaply

fleapit /ˈfliː.pɪt/ *noun* [C] UK OLD-FASHIONED INFORMAL an old, dirty cinema or theatre

fleck /flek/ *noun* [C usually pl] a small mark or spot: *Blackbirds' eggs are pale blue with brown flecks on them.* ○ *I got a few flecks **of** paint on the window.*
flecked /flekt/ *adj* having small marks or spots: *It's a dark grey material but it's flecked **with** white.*

fled /fled/ *past simple and past participle of* **flee**

fledged /fledʒd/ *adj* (of young birds) able to fly ➲See **fully-fledged**.

fledgling [BIRD], **fledgeling** /ˈfledʒ.lɪŋ/ *noun* [C] a young bird that has grown feathers and is learning to fly

fledgling [NEW], **fledgeling** /ˈfledʒ.lɪŋ/ *adj* [before n] new and lacking experience: *The current economic climate is particularly difficult for fledgling businesses.*

flee /fliː/ *verb* [I or T; never passive] **fleeing**, **fled**, **fled** to escape by running away, especially because of danger or fear: *She fled **(from)** the room in tears.* ○ *In order to escape capture, he fled **to** the mountains.*
• **flee the country** to quickly go to another country in order to escape from something or someone: *It is likely that the suspects have fled the country by now.*

fleece [SHEEP] /fliːs/ *noun* [C or U] **1** the thick covering of wool on a sheep, or this covering used to make a piece of clothing: *My jacket is lined with fleece/is fleece-**lined**.* **2** a type of warm soft material, or a jacket made from this ➲See picture **Clothes** on page Centre 6
fleecy /ˈfliː.si/ *adj* soft and wooly, or looking like this: *fleecy clouds*

fleece [CHEAT] /fliːs/ *verb* [T] INFORMAL to take someone's money dishonestly, by charging too much money or by cheating them: *That restaurant really fleeced us!*

fleet [SHIPS] /fliːt/ *noun* [C] a group of ships, or all of the ships in a country's navy: *a fleet **of** 20 sailing ships* ○ *a fishing fleet* ○ *The British fleet sailed from Southampton early this morning.*

fleet [VEHICLES] /fliːt/ *noun* [C] a number of buses, aircraft, etc. under the control of one person or organization: *He owns a fleet of taxis.*

fleet [QUICK] /fliːt/ *adj* LITERARY able to run quickly: *She was slight and fleet **of foot**/fleet-**footed**.*
fleeting /ˈfliː.tɪŋ/ [US] /-t̬ɪŋ/ *adj* brief or quick: *a fleeting **glimpse*** ○ *This is just a fleeting visit.* **fleetingly** /ˈfliː.tɪŋ.li/ [US] /-t̬ɪŋ-/ *adv*: *I glimpsed her fleetingly through the window.* **fleetness** /ˈfliːt.nəs/ *noun* [U]

ˌfleet ˈadmiral *noun* [C] an officer of the highest rank in the US Navy

ˈFleet ˌStreet *noun* the road in London where most of Britain's national newspapers were produced in the past, often used to refer to British national newspapers in general: *He's a Fleet Street journalist* (= He works for a British national newspaper).

flesh /fleʃ/ *noun* [U] **1** the soft part of the body of a person or animal which is between the skin and the bones, or the soft inner part of a fruit or vegetable: *The thorn went deep into the flesh of my hand.* ○ *The flesh of the fruit is white.* ○ *Vegetarians don't eat animal flesh* (= meat). **2** LITERARY **the flesh** the physical body and not the mind or the SOUL: *This left him plenty of time to indulge in **the pleasures of** the flesh* (= physical pleasures, such as sex or eating). ➲See also **fleshpot**.
• **in the flesh** in real life, and not on TV, in a film, in a picture, etc: *I've seen her perform on television, but never in the flesh.*
• **be (only) flesh and blood** to have normal human limits, needs, etc: *Of course I find pretty young women attractive – I'm only flesh and blood.*
• **be *sb's* own flesh and blood** to be someone's relative: *I couldn't send him away – he's my own flesh and blood.*
• **make *your* flesh crawl/creep** to make someone very anxious or frightened: *I don't mind spiders but worms make my flesh crawl.*
• **put flesh on (the bones of) *sth*** to add more details to a plan, idea, argument, etc. to make it better or more complete
fleshy /ˈfleʃ.i/ *adj* having a lot of soft flesh **fleshiness** /ˈfleʃ.ɪ.nəs/ *noun* [U]

flesh /fleʃ/ *verb*
▲ **flesh *sth* out** *phrasal verb* [M] to add more details or information to something: *These plans need to be fleshed out **with** some more figures before the committee votes on them.*

flesh-coloured UK, US **flesh-colored** /ˈfleʃˌkʌl.əd/ [US] /-ˌkʌl.ɚd/ *adj* approximately the colour of white people's skin: *a pair of flesh-coloured tights*

fleshpot /ˈfleʃ.pɒt/ [US] /-pɑːt/ *noun* [C usually pl] HUMOROUS a place which supplies sexual entertainment and food and drink

ˈflesh ˌwound *noun* [C] a wound that does not damage the bones or inner organs

fleur-de-lis (*plural* **fleurs-de-lis**) /ˌflɜː.dəˈliː/ [US] /ˌflɝː-/ *noun* [C] (ALSO **fleur-de-lys**) a pattern representing a flower with three separate parts joined at the bottom, used in COATS OF ARMS

flew /fluː/ *past simple and past participle of* **fly**

flex [BEND] /fleks/ *verb* [T] to bend an arm, leg, etc. or tighten a muscle: *First, straighten your legs, then flex your feet.* ○ *He tried to impress me by flexing his huge muscles.*
• **flex *your* muscles** to try to worry an opponent with a public display of military, political or financial power: *The parade is the first sign of the new regime flexing its military muscles.* ➲See also **muscle-flexing**.

flex [WIRE] UK /fleks/ *noun* [C or U] (US **cord**) (a length of) wire with a plastic cover used for connecting a piece of electrical equipment to a supply of electricity: *The flex on this iron isn't long enough to reach the socket.*

flexible [ABLE TO BEND] /ˈflek.sɪ.bl̩/ *adj* able to bend or to be bent easily without breaking: *Rubber is a flexible substance.* ○ *Dancers and gymnasts need to be very flexible* (= able to bend their bodies easily). **flexibility** /ˌflek.sɪˈbɪl.ɪ.ti/ [US] /-ə.t̬i/ *noun* [U] *You can improve your flexibility by exercising.*

flexible [CHANGEABLE] /ˈflek.sɪ.bl̩/ *adj* able to change or be changed easily according to the situation: *My schedule is quite flexible – I could arrange to meet with you any day next week.* **flexibility** /ˌflek.sɪˈbɪl.ɪ.ti/ [US] /-ə.t̬i/ *noun* [U] *The advantage of this system is its flexibility.* **flexibly** /ˈflek.sɪ.bli/ *adv*: *Today's schedule of events is organized flexibly so that people can decide for themselves what they want to do.*

flexitime UK /ˈflek.si.taɪm/ *noun* [U] (US **flextime**) a system of working in which people work a set number of hours within a fixed period of time, but can vary the time they start or finish work

flibbertigibbet /ˌflɪb.ə.tiˈdʒɪb.ɪt/ [US] /-ɚ.t̬i-/ *noun* [C] UK OLD-FASHIONED a foolish person who talks too much

flick /flɪk/ *verb* [I + adv or prep; T] to move or hit something with a short sudden movement: *He carefully flicked the loose hairs **from** the shoulders of his jacket.* ○ *She quickly flicked the crumbs **off** the table.* ○ *Horses flick their tails to make flies go away.* ○ *Windscreen wipers flick from side to side.* ○ *The boys ran round the swimming pool, flicking each other with their towels.* ○ *The lizard flicked **out** its tongue at a fly.* ○ *His eyes flicked between her and the door.*
flick /flɪk/ *noun* [C] a sudden, quick movement: *With a flick **of** its tail, the cat was gone.* ○ *A flick **of a switch** turns the machine on.*
• **have a flick through *sth*** to quickly look at the pages of a book, magazine, etc: *I've had a flick through their brochure and it looks quite interesting.*

PHRASAL VERBS WITH **flick**

▲ **flick *sth* on/off** *phrasal verb* [M] to move a switch in order to make electrical equipment start/stop working: *Could you flick the light switch on for me, please.*
▲ **flick through *sth*** *phrasal verb* to look quickly at the pages of a magazine, book, etc.

flicker /ˈflɪk.əʳ/ ⓤ /-ɚ/ *verb* **1** [I] to shine with a light that is sometimes bright and sometimes weak: *I felt a cold draft and the candle started to flicker.* **2** [I or T] to appear for a short time or to make a sudden movement: *A smile flickered across her face.* ○ *He'd been in a coma for weeks, when all of a sudden he flickered an eyelid.*

flicker /ˈflɪk.əʳ/ ⓤ /-ɚ/ *noun* [C usually sing] **1** when a light is sometimes bright and sometimes weak: *the soft flicker of candlelight* **2** a brief feeling or expression of an emotion or quality: *There was a flicker of hope in his eyes.*

flickering /ˈflɪk.ʳr.ɪŋ/ ⓤ /-ɚ-/ *adj*: *a flickering candle/fire* ○ *a flickering hope*

ˈflick ˌknife UK *noun* [C] (US **switchblade**) a knife with a blade hidden inside its handle which springs out when a button is pressed

the flicks *plural noun* UK OLD-FASHIONED INFORMAL the cinema: *What's on at the flicks this week?*

flick /flɪk/ *noun* [C] OLD-FASHIONED INFORMAL a film ⊃See **skin flick**; **chick flick**.

flier TRAVELLER, **flyer** /ˈflaɪ.əʳ/ ⓤ /-ɚ/ *noun* [C] ⊃See at **fly** TRAVEL.

flier INFORMATION, US USUALLY **flyer** /ˈflaɪ.əʳ/ ⓤ /-ɚ/ *noun* [C] a small piece of paper with information on it about a product or event

flies /flaɪz/ *plural of* **fly** INSECT

flies /flaɪz/ *plural noun* UK FOR **fly** TROUSERS

flight JOURNEY /flaɪt/ *noun* [C] a journey in an aircraft: *I'll never forget my first flight.* ○ *How was your flight?* ○ *All flights to New York today are delayed because of bad weather.* ○ *My flight was cancelled.*

flight AIRCRAFT /flaɪt/ *noun* [C] an aircraft that is making a particular journey: *Flight 474 to Buenos Aires is now boarding at gate 9.*

flight MOVEMENT /flaɪt/ *noun* **1** [U] when something flies or moves through the air: *an eagle in flight* ○ *Suddenly the whole flock of geese took flight* (= started flying). ○ *Modern missiles are so accurate because their flight is controlled by computer.* **2** [C] a group of birds, aircraft, etc. flying together: *a flight of geese/swans*

• **flight of fancy** an idea which shows a lot of imagination but which is not practical: *He was talking about cycling across the US or was that just another flight of fancy?*

flightless /ˈflaɪt.ləs/ *adj* not able to fly: *The ostrich is a flightless bird.*

flight ESCAPE /flaɪt/ *noun* [U] (an act or example of) escape, running away or avoiding something: *They lost all their possessions during their flight from the invading army.*

• **put sb to flight** UK OLD-FASHIONED to defeat someone and force them to run away

• **take flight** to run away: *The burglars took flight when the alarm sounded.*

flight STAIRS /flaɪt/ *noun* [C] a set of steps or stairs, usually between two floors of a building: *We live up three flights of stairs.*

• **the top flight** UK the highest level in a job or sport: *The Sheffield Eagles move down to the second division after two seasons in the top flight.*

ˈflight atˌtendant *noun* [C] someone who serves passengers on an aircraft

ˈflight ˌdeck AIRCRAFT *noun* [C] the part of an aircraft where the pilot sits and where the controls are

ˈflight ˌdeck SHIP *noun* [C] a flat open surface on a ship from which aircraft take off

ˈflight lieuˈtenant *noun* [C] an officer in the British air force

ˈflight ˌpath *noun* [C] a route followed by an aircraft

ˈflight reˌcorder *noun* [C] a device which records information about an aircraft while it is flying ⊃See also **black box**.

ˈflight ˌsergeant *noun* [C] the next rank above SERGEANT in the British air force

flighty /ˈflaɪ.ti/ ⓤ /-t̬i/ *adj* DISAPPROVING (especially of a woman) not responsible and likely to change activities, jobs, lovers, etc. frequently: *a flighty young woman*

flightiness /ˈflaɪ.tɪ.nəs/ ⓤ /-t̬ɪ-/ *noun* [U]

flim flam /ˈflɪm.flæm/ *noun* [U] OLD-FASHIONED INFORMAL talk that is confusing and intended to deceive

flimsy THIN /ˈflɪm.zi/ *adj* very thin, or easily broken or destroyed: *You won't be warm enough in that flimsy dress.* ○ *We spent the night in a flimsy wooden hut.* ○ *a flimsy cardboard box* **flimsily** /ˈflɪm.zɪ.li/ *adv* **flimsiness** /ˈflɪm.zɪ.nəs/ *noun* [U]

flimsy DIFFICULT TO BELIEVE /ˈflɪm.zi/ A flimsy argument, excuse, etc. is weak and difficult to believe: *When I asked him why he was late, he gave me some flimsy excuse about having car trouble.* **flimsily** /ˈflɪm.zɪ.li/ *adv* **flimsiness** /ˈflɪm.zɪ.nəs/ *noun* [U]

flinch /flɪntʃ/ *verb* [I] to make a sudden small movement because of pain or fear: *He didn't even flinch when the nurse cleaned the wound.*

▲ **flinch from sth/doing sth** *phrasal verb* to avoid doing something that you consider unpleasant or painful: *We must not flinch from difficult decisions.*

fling THROW /flɪŋ/ *verb* [T usually + adv or prep] flung, flung to throw something or someone suddenly and with a lot of force: *He crumpled up the letter and flung it into the fire.* ○ *"And you can take your ring back too!" she cried, flinging it down on the table.* ○ INFORMAL *Could you fling the paper over here* (= give me the paper)?

fling MOVE/DO /flɪŋ/ *verb* [T usually + adv or prep] flung, flung to move or do something quickly and energetically: *She flung her arms around his neck.* ○ *The door was flung open by the wind.* ○ *Sergei flung himself down on the sofa.* ○ INFORMAL *Let me just fling* (= quickly put) *a few things into my bag, and I'll be right with you.* ○ INFORMAL *They were flung* (= quickly put) *in prison.*

• **fling up your hands** to show that you are very shocked or frightened: *They flung up their hands in horror at the cost of the trip.*

fling SAY ANGRILY /flɪŋ/ *verb* [I or T; usually + adv or prep] flung, flung to say something angrily: *They were flinging bitter accusations at each other.* ○ [+ speech] *"I don't care what you think", she flung (back) at him.*

fling PERIOD /flɪŋ/ *noun* [C usually sing] INFORMAL a short period of enjoyment: *The students are having a final/last fling before they leave university and start work.*

• **have a fling** to have a short sexual relationship with someone: *She's been having a fling with her boss.*

PHRASAL VERBS WITH **fling** ▼

▲ **fling yourself at sb** *phrasal verb* [R] INFORMAL DISAPPROVING to make it very obvious to someone that you want to have a sexual relationship with them

▲ **fling yourself into sth** *phrasal verb* [R] to do something with a lot of enthusiasm: *Tom has really flung himself into his work this year.*

▲ **fling sth on/off** *phrasal verb* [M] to quickly put on/ remove something, especially a piece of clothing: *We were so hot we flung off our clothes and dived into the swimming pool.*

▲ **fling sth/sb out** *phrasal verb* [M] MAINLY UK INFORMAL to get rid of something you do not want, or to make someone leave a place when they do not want to: *I think it's about time we flung out these old magazines.* ○ *They were flung out of the pub for fighting.*

flint /flɪnt/ *noun* [C or U] **1** (a piece of) shiny grey or black stone that is like glass **2** (a piece of) stone or metal used in a MUSKET to make it fire or in a cigarette LIGHTER to produce a flame

flinty /ˈflɪn.ti/ ⓤ /-t̬i/ *adj* **1** made of or like flint: *a flinty material* **2** severe and determined: *The head teacher has a rather flinty manner.*

flip TURN QUICKLY /flɪp/ *verb* [I or T; usually + adv or prep] -pp- If you flip something, you turn it over quickly one or more times, and if something flips, it turns over quickly: *When one side is done, flip the pancake (over) to cook the other side.* ○ *I lost my place in my book when the pages flipped over in the wind.* ○ *You turn the television on by flipping* (= operating) *the switch at the side.* ○ *The captains flipped a coin into the air* (= made it turn over in the air to see which side it landed on) *to decide which side would bat first.*

• **flip (your lid)** INFORMAL to become very angry: *She'll flip her lid if I'm late again.*

flip /flɪp/ *noun* [C] when something turns over quickly or repeatedly: *a flip of a coin* ○ *The acrobats were doing* *somersaults and flips* (= jumping and turning their bodies over in the air).

▲ **flip through** ***sth*** *phrasal verb* to look quickly at the pages of a magazine, book etc.

flip [NOT SERIOUS] /flɪp/ *adj* UK INFORMAL FOR **flippant**

ˈ**flip** ˌ**chart** *noun* [C] a board standing on legs with large pieces of paper fixed to the top which can be turned over

flip-flop /ˈflɪp.flɒp/ [US] /-flɑːp/ *noun* [C usually pl] (AUS AND US ALSO **thong**) a type of open shoe, often made of rubber, with a V-shaped strap which goes between the big toe and the toe next to it

flippant /ˈflɪp.ᵊnt/ *adj* (UK INFORMAL **flip**) not serious about a serious subject, in an attempt to be amusing or to appear clever: *a flippant remark/attitude* ○ *It's easy to be flippant, but we have a serious problem to deal with here.* ○ *I think she just thought I was being flippant.* **flippantly** /ˈflɪp.ᵊnt.li/ *adv* **flippancy** /ˈflɪp.ᵊnt.si/ *noun* [U]

flipper [PART OF CREATURE] /ˈflɪp.əʳ/ [US] /-ɚ/ *noun* [C] one of two arm-like parts of particular sea creatures, such as seals and PENGUINS, used for swimming

flipper [SHOE] /ˈflɪp.əʳ/ [US] /-ɚ/ *noun* [C] (US ALSO **fin**) a type of large flat rubber shoe, used for swimming, especially under water

flipping /ˈflɪp.ɪŋ/ *adj, adv* UK SLANG used to emphasize what is being said, or to express annoyance: *It's a flipping nuisance!* ○ *You'll do as you're flipping well told!*

ˈ**flip** ˌ**side** *noun* [S] **1** the opposite, less good, or less popular side of something: *We're now starting to see the flip side **of** the government's economic policy.* **2** OLD-FASHIONED the less popular side of a record

flirt /flɜːt/ [US] /flɝːt/ *verb* [I] to behave as if sexually attracted to someone, although not seriously: *Christina was flirting **with** just about every man in the room.*

flirt /flɜːt/ [US] /flɝːt/ *noun* [C] someone who behaves as if they are sexually attracted to a lot of people: *He's a compulsive flirt.*

flirtation /flɜːˈteɪ.ʃᵊn/ [US] /flɝː-/ *noun* [C or U] when someone behaves as if they are sexually attracted to another person, without being seriously interested: *It was a harmless flirtation and nothing more.* ⊃See also **flirtation** at **flirt with**.

flirtatious /flɜːˈteɪ.ʃəs/ [US] /flɝː-/ *adj* behaving as if you are sexually attracted to someone, usually not in a serious way: *She's very flirtatious.* ○ *a flirtatious relationship* **flirtatiously** /flɜːˈteɪ.ʃə.sli/ [US] /flɝː-/ *adv* **flirtatiousness** /flɜːˈteɪ.ʃə.snəs/ [US] /flɝː-/ *noun* [U]

PHRASAL VERBS WITH **flirt** ▼

▲ **flirt with** ***sth*** [ACTIVITY] *phrasal verb* to consider doing something, but not seriously, or to be interested in something for a short time: *I'm flirting with **the idea of** taking a year off and travelling round the world.*

flirtation /flɜːˈteɪ.ʃᵊn/ [US] /flɝː-/ *noun* [S] a brief period of being interested in something or doing something: *a brief flirtation with Communism*

▲ **flirt with** ***sth*** [DANGER] *phrasal verb* to intentionally put yourself in a dangerous, risky or difficult situation: *Like a lot of young men, he flirts with **danger**.*

flit /flɪt/ *verb* [I usually + adv or prep] **-tt-** **1** to fly or move quickly and lightly: *In the fading light we saw bats flitting **around/about** in the garden.* ○ FIGURATIVE *Sara finds it very difficult to settle – she's always flitting **from** one thing **to** another* (= changing her activities). **2** to appear or exist suddenly and briefly in someone's mind or on their face: *A ghost of a smile flitted across his face.*

flit /flɪt/ *noun* [C] UK ⊃See **do a moonlight flit** at **moonlight**.

float [NOT SINK] /fləʊt/ [US] /floʊt/ *verb* [I] to stay on the surface of a liquid and not sink: *An empty bottle will float.* ○ *You can float very easily **in/on** the Dead Sea because it's so salty.*

• **be floating on air** MAINLY UK to be very happy: *When he got his exam results he was floating on air.*

float /fləʊt/ [US] /floʊt/ *noun* [C] **1** a piece of wood or other light material that stays on the surface of water: *Fishing nets are often held in position by floats.* **2** a drink with ice cream on the top: *I'll have a root beer float, please.*

floatation /fləʊˈteɪ.ʃᵊn/ [US] /floʊ-/ *noun* [U] UK **flotation** FLOAT

float [MOVE] /fləʊt/ [US] /floʊt/ *verb* **1** [I or T; usually + adv or prep] to (cause to) move easily through, or along the surface of a liquid, or to (cause to) move easily through air: *We spent a lazy afternoon floating **down/along** the river.* ○ *He tossed the bottle into the waves and watched it float **out to** sea.* ○ *The children enjoy floating their boats **on** the pond in the park.* ○ *Fluffy white clouds were floating across the sky.* ○ FIGURATIVE *The sound of piano-playing floated out through the open window.* **2** [I usually + adv or prep] LITERARY to move gracefully: *She sort of floats around, like a ballet dancer.* **3** [I usually + adv or prep] to move or act without purpose: *Since he lost his job, he's just floated **around/about** doing nothing.*

floating /ˈfləʊ.tɪŋ/ [US] /ˈfloʊ.t̬ɪŋ/ *adj* [before n] **1** not fixed in one position, place or level: *The city has a large floating **population*** (= people who move around a lot). ○ *The bank has offered us a loan with a floating **interest rate**.* **2** SPECIALIZED describes a part of the body that is out of its usual position, or not connected to another part of the body: *a floating rib*

floaty /ˈfləʊ.ti/ [US] /ˈfloʊ.t̬i/ *adj* describes material which is very light and moves a lot in the air: *floaty dresses*

PHRASAL VERBS WITH **float** ▼

▲ **float around/about** [OBJECT] *phrasal verb* INFORMAL You say that an object is floating around when you think it is not far away but you cannot see exactly where: *I can't find my purse, but it must be floating around here somewhere.*

▲ **float around/about** [IDEA] *phrasal verb* INFORMAL If an idea or story floats around, it is discussed or repeated by a lot of people: *Have you heard the rumours floating around that the shop is going to close?*

float [CHANGE VALUE] /fləʊt/ [US] /floʊt/ *verb* [I or T] SPECIALIZED to allow the value of a country's money to vary according to the value of other countries' money: *The government has decided to float the pound.*

float [BUSINESS] /fləʊt/ [US] /floʊt/ *verb* [T] to start selling shares in a business or company for the first time

floatation /fləʊˈteɪ.ʃᵊn/ [US] /floʊ-/ *noun* UK **flotation** BUSINESS

float [SUGGEST] /fləʊt/ [US] /floʊt/ *verb* [T] to suggest a plan or an idea for consideration: *Ian has floated the **idea** that we should think about expanding into Europe next year.*

float [MONEY] /fləʊt/ [US] /floʊt/ *noun* [S] UK a small sum of money, available before any money is received for goods sold, which is used for giving customers CHANGE

float [VEHICLE] /fləʊt/ [US] /floʊt/ *noun* [C] a large vehicle with a flat surface which is decorated and used in festivals: *carnival floats*

ˌ**floating** ˈ**voter** *noun* [C] UK someone who does not always vote for the same political party

flock [GROUP] /flɒk/ [US] /flɑːk/ *group noun* [C] a group of sheep, goats or birds, or a group of people: *a flock **of** sheep/goats/geese* ○ *The shepherd is bringing his flock down from the hills.* ○ *A noisy flock **of** tourists came into the building.* ○ *The vicar invited all the members of his flock* (= all the people who go to his church) *to attend the special service.*

flock /flɒk/ [US] /flɑːk/ *verb* [I usually + adv or prep] to move or gather together in large numbers: *Hundreds of people flocked **to** the football match.* ○ [+ **to** infinitive] *Crowds of people flocked to see the Picasso exhibition.*

flock [MATERIAL] /flɒk/ [US] /flɑːk/ *noun* [U] (US ALSO **flocking**) soft material used for filling objects such as cushions, or soft material that forms a raised pattern on wallpaper or curtains

floe /fləʊ/ [US] /floʊ/ *noun* [C] (ALSO **ice floe**) a large area of ice floating in the sea

flog [PUNISH] /flɒg/ [US] /flɑːg/ *verb* [T] **-gg-** to beat someone very hard with a whip or a stick, as a punishment: *Soldiers used to be flogged for disobedience.*

• **flog a dead horse** UK INFORMAL to waste effort on something that there is no chance of succeeding at: *He keeps trying to get it published but I think he's flogging a dead horse.*

• **flog *yourself* to death** (*ALSO* **flog *yourself* into the ground**) *UK INFORMAL* to work too hard

• **flog *sth* to death** *UK INFORMAL* to use, do or say something so often that it is no longer interesting: *It's a theme that's been flogged to death.*

flogging /ˈflɒg.ɪŋ/ [US] /ˈflɑː.gɪŋ/ *noun* [C or U] a punishment in which someone is beaten severely with a whip or a stick

flog [SELL] /flɒg/ [US] /flɑːg/ *verb* [T] **-gg-** *UK INFORMAL* to sell, especially quickly or cheaply: *He tried to flog his old car, but no one would buy it.*

flood [COVER WITH WATER] /flʌd/ *verb* [I or T] to cause to fill or become covered with water, especially in a way that causes problems: *Our washing machine broke down yesterday and flooded the kitchen.* ○ *The whole town flooded when the river burst its banks.* ○ *Several families living by the river were flooded* ***out*** (= forced to leave their houses because they became covered with water).

flood /flʌd/ *noun* [C or U] a large amount of water covering an area that is usually dry: *After the flood it took weeks for the water level to go down.* ○ *The river is* ***in*** *flood* (= water has flowed over its banks) *again.*

• **in floods of tears** *UK* crying a lot: *I found her in floods of tears in the toilets.*

• **the Flood** (in the Bible) a flood sent by God that covered the whole earth as a punishment

• **before the Flood** *UK HUMOROUS* a very long time ago

flooded /ˈflʌd.ɪd/ *adj* covered with water: *For miles you could see nothing but flooded fields.*

flooding /ˈflʌd.ɪŋ/ *noun* [U] *Some roads have been closed because of flooding.*

flood [ARRIVE OR FILL] /flʌd/ *verb* [I usually + adv or prep; T] to fill or enter a place in large numbers or amounts: *Donations are flooding* ***into*** *the appeal office.* ○ *She drew back the curtains and the sunlight came flooding* ***in***. ○ *Japanese cars have flooded the* ***market*** (= a lot of them are on sale). ○ *He was flooded* ***with*** (= suddenly felt a lot of) *joy when his first child was born.* ○ *For Proust, the taste of a madeleine brought childhood memories flooding* ***back*** (= made him suddenly rememember a lot of things).

flood /flʌd/ *noun* [C] a large amount or number of something: *A flood* ***of*** *cheap imports has come into the country.*

flooded /ˈflʌd.ɪd/ *adj* containing a large amount or number of something: *The* ***market*** *is flooded* ***with*** *cheap imports.*

▲ **flood *sth* with *sth*** *phrasal verb* If you are flooded with letters, telephone calls, messages, etc., you receive so many that you cannot deal with them: *We were flooded with calls from worried parents.*

floodgate /ˈflʌd.geɪt/ *noun* [C usually pl] a gate which can be opened or closed to control a flow of water

• **open the floodgates** If an action or a decision opens the floodgates, it allows something to happen a lot or allows many people to do something that was not previously allowed: *Officials are worried that allowing these refugees into the country will open the floodgates* ***to*** *thousands more.*

floodlight /ˈflʌd.laɪt/ *noun* [C usually pl] a large powerful electric light used for lighting outside areas, such as sports grounds or buildings, in the dark: *This evening's match will be played* ***under*** *floodlights.*

floodlit /ˈflʌd.lɪt/ *adj* lit by floodlights: *a floodlit stadium*

ˈflood ˌplain *noun* [C] an area of flat land beside a river that is frequently flooded when the river becomes too full

ˈflood ˌtide *noun* [C] the regular movement of the sea in towards the coast ➲Compare **ebb tide**.

floor [SURFACE] /flɔːʳ/ [US] /flɔːr/ *noun* [C usually sing] the flat surface of a room on which you walk: *The floor was partly covered with a dirty old rug.* ○ *The bathroom floor needs cleaning.* ○ *The children sat playing* ***on*** *the floor.* ○ *There's barely enough floor* ***space*** *to fit a bed in this room.*

• **go through the floor** to fall to very low levels: *House prices have gone through the floor this year.*

floor [OPEN SPACE] /flɔːʳ/ [US] /flɔːr/ *noun* [C usually sing] a public space for activities such as dancing and having formal discussions: *a dance floor* ○ *The new proposal will be discussed* ***on the*** *floor* ***of*** *the House of Commons* (= in Parliament) *tomorrow.* ○ *He spent several years working on the* ***factory*** *floor* (= in the factory) *before becoming a manager.* ○ *The chairman said that he would now take questions* ***from the*** *floor* (= from the audience).

• **have the floor** to have the right to speak: *Silence, please, the Prime Minister has the floor.*

• **take (to) the floor** to stand and begin to dance: *The Prince and Princess were the first to take the floor.*

• **take the floor** start speaking: *The Chancellor of the Exchequer will take the floor for his Budget speech at 3.00 p.m.*

floor [LEVEL OF BUILDING] /flɔːʳ/ [US] /flɔːr/ *noun* [C] a level of a building: *This building has five floors.* ○ *Take the elevator to the 51st floor.* ○ *We live* ***on*** *the third floor.* ○ *a ground floor apartment* ∗ NOTE: In British English the first floor of a building is the level above ground level. In American English the first floor of a building is at ground level.

COMMON LEARNER ERROR

on the...floor

Remember to use the preposition 'on' when you are referring to something or someone on a particular **floor** of a building.

Their office is on the 12th floor.

~~*Their office is in the 12th floor.*~~

floor [BOTTOM] /flɔːʳ/ [US] /flɔːr/ *noun* **the floor** the bottom surface of the sea, a forest, a cave, etc: *the floor* ***of*** *the ocean/the ocean floor*

floor [CAUSE TO FALL] /flɔːʳ/ [US] /flɔːr/ *verb* **1** [T] to hit someone and cause them to fall: *He was floored with a single punch to the head.* **2** [T often passive] *INFORMAL* to surprise or confuse someone so much that they are unable to think what to say or do next: *I didn't know what to say – I was completely floored.*

floorboard /ˈflɔː.bɔːd/ [US] /ˈflɔːr.bɔːrd/ *noun* [C] one of the long straight pieces of wood used to make a floor

flooring /ˈflɔː.rɪŋ/ [US] /ˈflɔː-/ *noun* [U] the material that a floor is made of: *wooden/marble/vinyl flooring*

ˈfloor ˌlamp *noun* [C] *US FOR* **standard lamp**

ˈfloor ˌshow *noun* [C] a set of musical, dance, or comedy acts performed in a restaurant

floozie, floozy /ˈfluː.zi/ *noun* [C] *OLD-FASHIONED INFORMAL* a woman who has a lot of sexual relationships, or who wears clothes that attract sexual attention in a way that is too obvious

flop [FALL] /flɒp/ [US] /flɑːp/ *verb* [I usually + adv or prep] **-pp-** to fall or drop heavily: *Hugh's hair keeps flopping* ***over/into*** *his eyes.* ○ *When she gets home from school, she's so tired all she can do is flop* ***down*** *in front of the television.*

flop /flɒp/ [US] /flɑːp/ *noun* [S] *He fell with a flop* (= he dropped heavily) *on the bed.*

flop [FAILURE] /flɒp/ [US] /flɑːp/ *noun* [C usually sing] *INFORMAL* a failure: *The play was a* ***complete/total*** *flop.*

flop /flɒp/ [US] /flɑːp/ *verb* [I] **-pp-** If a book, play, film, etc. flops, it is not successful: *Her first book flopped, but her second became a bestseller.*

flophouse /ˈflɒp.haʊs/ [US] /ˈflɑːp-/ *noun* [C] *US FOR* **doss-house**

floppy /ˈflɒp.i/ [US] /ˈflɑː.pi/ *adj* soft and not able to maintain a firm shape or position: *a floppy* ***hat*** ○ *a dog with big floppy ears* ○ *He's got floppy blond hair that's always falling in his eyes.* **floppiness** /ˈflɒp.ɪ.nəs/ [US] /ˈflɑː.pɪ-/ *noun* [U]

ˌfloppy (ˈdisk) *noun* [C] a **diskette** (= a flat circular device, usually inside a square container, which has a magnetic covering and is used for storing computer information) ➲Compare **hard disk**.

flora /ˈflɔː.rə/ [US] /ˈflɔːr.ə/ *noun* [U] *SPECIALIZED* all the plants of a particular place or from a particular time in history: *the flora of the Balearic Islands* ○ *Stone Age flora*

ˌflora and ˈfauna *plural noun SPECIALIZED* The flora and fauna of a place are its plants and animals.

floral /ˈflɔː.rəl/ [US] /ˈflɔːr.əl/ *adj* made of flowers, or decorated with pictures of flowers: *floral curtains/print/wallpaper* ○ *a floral display/tribute*

floret /ˈflɒr.ət/ ⓤ /ˈflɔːr-/ *noun* [C] a small flower-like part of a vegetable: *broccoli/cauliflower florets*

florid DECORATED /ˈflɒr.ɪd/ ⓤ /ˈflɔːr-/ *adj* with too much decoration or detail: *a florid architectural style* ○ *florid prose/rhetoric* **floridly** /ˈflɒr.ɪd.li/ ⓤ /ˈflɔːr-/ *adv*

florid RED /ˈflɒr.ɪd/ ⓤ /ˈflɔːr-/ *adj* FORMAL (of a person's face) too red, especially in a way that is unhealthy: *a florid complexion*

florist /ˈflɒr.ɪst/ ⓤ /ˈflɔːr-/ *noun* [C] a person who works in a shop which sells cut flowers and plants for inside the house

florist's /ˈflɒr.ɪsts/ ⓤ /ˈflɔːr-/ *noun* [C] a shop which sells cut flowers and plants for inside the house

floss TEETH /flɒs/ ⓤ /flɑːs/ *noun* [U] **dental floss**

floss /flɒs/ ⓤ /flɑːs/ *verb* [I or T] to clean between your teeth using dental floss: *It's important to floss every day.*

floss THREAD /flɒs/ ⓤ /flɑːs/ *noun* [U] a mass of soft smooth threads especially produced by particular insects and plants ⊃See also **candyfloss**.

flotation FLOAT, *UK ALSO* **floatation** /fləʊˈteɪ.ʃən/ ⓤ /floʊ-/ *noun* [U] **1** the action of floating **2** **flotation chamber/compartment/tank** a container filled with water that you can float in for relaxation

flotation BUSINESS, *UK ALSO* **floatation** /fləʊˈteɪ.ʃən/ ⓤ /floʊ-/ *noun* [C or U] when a company's shares are sold to the public for the first time: *The Glasgow-based company is to launch a stock-market flotation this summer.* ⊃See also **float** BUSINESS.

flotilla /fləˈtɪl.ə/ *noun* [C] a large group of boats or small ships ⊃See also **fleet** SHIPS.

flotsam /ˈflɒt.səm/ ⓤ /ˈflɑːt-/ *noun* [U] (*ALSO* **flotsam and jetsam**) **1** pieces of broken wood and other waste materials found on the beach or floating on the sea: *We wandered along the shore, stepping over the flotsam that had washed up in the night.* **2** anything or anyone that is unwanted or worthless: *The homeless sleep in doorways and stations – we step over their bodies like so much human flotsam.*

flounce WALK /flaʊnts/ *verb* [I usually + adv or prep] to walk with large noticeable movements, especially to attract attention or show that you are angry: *"Right, don't expect any help from me in future!" he said and flounced out of the room.*

flounce DECORATION /flaʊnts/ *noun* [C] a wide strip of cloth sewn along the edge of especially a dress or skirt for decoration

flouncy /ˈflaʊnt.si/ *adj* (*ALSO* **flounced**) Flouncy clothes are loose-fitting and have a lot of material: *She was wearing a dreadful pink flouncy skirt.*

flounder HAVE DIFFICULTY /ˈflaʊn.dər/ ⓤ /-dɚ/ *verb* [I] to experience great difficulties or be completely unable to decide what to do or say next: *He lost the next page of his speech and floundered (about/around) for a few seconds.* ○ *Although his business was a success, his marriage was floundering.* ○ *In 1986 Richardson resigned as chairman, leaving the company floundering.*

flounder FISH /ˈflaʊn.dər/ ⓤ /-dɚ/ *noun* [C or U] *plural* **flounder** or **flounders** a flat fish that lives in the sea, or its flesh eaten as food

flour /flaʊər/ ⓤ /flaʊɚ/ *noun* [U] powder made from grain, especially wheat, used for making bread, cakes, pasta, pastry, etc. ⊃See also **cornflour**.

flour /flaʊər/ ⓤ /flaʊɚ/ *verb* [T] to put flour on a surface to prevent food from sticking: *Grease and flour* (= put a thin layer of flour on) *the tins thoroughly.*

floury /ˈflaʊə.ri/ ⓤ /ˈflaʊɚ.i/ *adj* **1** covered in flour, or tasting or feeling like flour: *She wiped her floury hands on a cloth.* **2** *UK* describes potatoes that are dry and break into small pieces when they are cooked

flourish SUCCEED /ˈflʌr.ɪʃ/ ⓤ /ˈflɝː-/ *verb* [I] to grow or develop successfully: *My tomatoes are flourishing this summer – it must be the warm weather.* ○ *Watercolour painting began to flourish in Britain around 1750.* **flourishing** /ˈflʌr.ɪ.ʃɪŋ/ ⓤ /ˈflɝː-/ *adj*: *There's a flourishing trade in second-hand video machines.*

flourish WAVE /ˈflʌr.ɪʃ/ ⓤ /ˈflɝː-/ *verb* [T] to move something in your hand in order to make people look at it: *She came in smiling, flourishing her exam results.*

flourish /ˈflʌr.ɪʃ/ ⓤ /ˈflɝː-/ *noun* **with a flourish** If you do something with a flourish, you do it with one big, noticeable movement: *The waiter handed me the menu with a flourish.* ○ *He took off his hat with a flourish.*

flout /flaʊt/ *verb* [T] to intentionally disobey a rule, law, or custom: *Many motorcyclists flout the law by not wearing helmets.* ○ *The orchestra decided to flout convention/tradition, and wear their everyday clothes for the concert.*

flow MOVE /fləʊ/ ⓤ /floʊ/ *verb* [I] (especially of liquids, gases or electricity) to move in one direction, especially continuously and easily: *Lava from the volcano was flowing down the hillside.* ○ *Many short rivers flow into the Pacific Ocean.* ○ *The river flows through three counties before flowing into the sea just south of here.* ○ *With fewer cars on the roads, traffic is flowing* (= moving forward) *more smoothly than usual.* **flow** /fləʊ/ ⓤ /floʊ/ *noun* [C usually sing] *the flow of a river* ○ *the flow of traffic* ○ *the flow of blood*

• **go with the flow** INFORMAL to do what other people are doing or to agree with other people because it is the easiest thing to do: *Just relax and go with the flow!*

• **go against the flow** to do or say the opposite of what most people are doing or saying: *With this new book, she is going against the flow.*

flowing /ˈfləʊ.ɪŋ/ ⓤ /ˈfloʊ-/ *adj* moving in one direction, especially continuously and easily: *a fast-flowing river*

flow CONTINUE /fləʊ/ ⓤ /floʊ/ *verb* [I] to continue to arrive or be produced: *Please keep the money flowing in!* ○ *Offers of help are flowing into the disaster area from all over the country.* ○ *My thoughts flow more easily if I work on a word processor.* ○ *By eleven o'clock, the wine was starting to flow.* ○ *After they'd all had a drink or two, the conversation began to flow.*

flow /fləʊ/ ⓤ /floʊ/ *noun* **1** [C usually sing] a regular and quite large number of something: *There's been a steady flow of visitors.* **2** [S] when something is produced or moved continuously: *the flow of ideas/information*

flowing /ˈfləʊ.ɪŋ/ ⓤ /ˈfloʊ-/ *adj* produced in a smooth, continuous or relaxed style: *flowing movements/lines* ○ *I thought I recognized your flowing script.*

flow HANG DOWN /fləʊ/ ⓤ /floʊ/ *verb* [I] to hang down loosely and often attractively: *Her long red hair flowed down over her shoulders.*

flowing /ˈfləʊ.ɪŋ/ ⓤ /ˈfloʊ-/ *adj* describes hair and clothes that are long and hang down loosely: *I remember her as a young girl with flowing black hair.* ○ *Everyone on stage was dressed in flowing white robes.*

flowchart /ˈfləʊ.tʃɑːt/ ⓤ /ˈfloʊ.tʃɑːrt/ *noun* [C] (*ALSO* **flow diagram**) a diagram which shows the stages of a process

flower PLANT /ˈflaʊ.ər/ ⓤ /ˈflaʊ.ɚ/ *noun* [C] the part of a plant which is often brightly coloured with a pleasant smell, or the type of plant that produces these: *wild flowers* ○ *to pick flowers* ○ *a bunch/bouquet of flowers* ○ *cut/dried flowers* ⊃See picture **Flowers and Plants** on page Centre 3

• **in flower** describes a plant that has open flowers: *Our roses are usually in flower from April to November.*

• **in the flower of sb's youth** LITERARY when someone was young and in the best and most active period of life: *He died in the very flower of his youth.*

• **the flower of sth** LITERARY the best of a particular group or type: *The flower of the nation's youth were killed in the war.*

flower /ˈflaʊ.ər/ ⓤ /ˈflaʊ.ɚ/ *verb* [I] to produce flowers: *When does this plant flower?*

flowery /ˈflaʊ.ə.ri/ ⓤ /ˈflaʊ.ɚ.i/ *adj* **1** (*ALSO* **flowered**) decorated with pictures of flowers: *a flowery material/dress* ○ *flowery curtains/wallpaper* **2** DISAPPROVING If a speech or writing style is flowery, it uses too many complicated words or phrases in an attempt to sound skilful: *a flowery description/speech*

flower DEVELOP /ˈflaʊ.ər/ ⓤ /ˈflaʊ.ɚ/ *verb* [I] LITERARY to develop completely and become obvious: *Her talent flowered during her later years.*

flower arranging *noun* [U] the skill or activity of arranging flowers in an attractive or artistic way: *flower-arranging classes*

flowerbed /ˈflaʊ.ə.bed/ [US] /-ɚ-/ *noun* [C] a part of a garden where flowers are planted

ˈ**flower ˌchild** *noun* [C] a **hippie**

flowerpot /ˈflaʊ.ə.pɒt/ [US] /-ɚ.pɑːt/ *noun* [C] a container usually made of clay or plastic in which a plant is grown

ˈ**flower ˌpower** *noun* [U] the ideas and beliefs of some young people in the 1960s and 1970s who opposed war and encouraged people to love each other

flown /fləʊn/ [US] /floʊn/ *past participle of* **fly**

fl oz *WRITTEN ABBREVIATION FOR* **fluid ounce**

flu /fluː/ *noun* [U] (*FORMAL* **influenza**) an infectious illness which is like a very bad cold, but which causes a fever: *a flu virus* ○ *to catch/get/have (the) flu*

fluctuate /ˈflʌk.tju.eɪt/ *verb* [I] to change or vary, especially continuously and between one level or thing and another: *Vegetable prices fluctuate* ***according to*** *the season.* ○ *Her wages fluctuate* ***between*** *£150 and £200 a week.* ○ *Her weight fluctuates* ***wildly***. ○ *fluctuating prices* **fluctuation** /ˌflʌk.tjuˈeɪ.ʃən/ *noun* [C or U] *fluctuations* ***in*** *share prices/the exchange rate/temperature*

flue /fluː/ *noun* [C] a pipe which leads from a fire or heater to the outside of a building, taking smoke, gases or hot air away

fluent /ˈfluː.ənt/ *adj* **1** When a person is fluent, they can speak a language easily, well and quickly: *She's fluent* ***in*** *French.* **2** When a language is fluent, it is spoken easily and without many pauses: *He speaks fluent Chinese.* ○ *He's a fluent Russian speaker.* **fluency** /ˈfluː.ənt.si/ *noun* [U] *One of the requirements of the job is fluency* ***in*** *two or more African languages.* **fluently** /ˈfluː.ənt.li/ *adv*: *I'd like to speak English fluently.*

fluff [SOFT MASS] /flʌf/ *noun* [U] small loose bits of wool or other soft material, or the DOWN (= soft new hairs) on a young animal: *He brushed the fluff off his coat.*
fluffy /ˈflʌf.i/ *adj* **1** soft and woolly or furry: *fluffy toys* **2** light and full of air: *Beat the eggs and sugar together until they are pale and fluffy.* **fluffiness** /ˈflʌf.ɪ.nəs/ *noun* [U]
▲ **fluff** ***sth*** **up** *phrasal verb* to make something appear bigger or full of air by hitting or shaking it: *I'll just fluff up your pillows for you.*

fluff [ENTERTAINMENT] /flʌf/ *noun* [U] *US* entertainment that is not serious or valuable

fluff [FAIL] /flʌf/ *verb* [T] (*US ALSO* **flub**) *INFORMAL* to fail something or do it badly: *I fluffed my driving test three times before I finally got it.* ○ *All the time I was acting with him, I never once heard him fluff* ***his lines*** (= say something wrong when acting).

fluid [LIQUID] /ˈfluː.ɪd/ *noun* [C or U] a substance which flows and is not solid: *If you have a fever you should drink plenty of fluid(s).* ○ *The virus is contracted through exchange of* ***bodily*** *fluids.* **fluidity** /fluˈɪd.ɪ.ti/ [US] /-ə.t̬i/ *noun* [U]

fluid [MOVEMENT] /ˈfluː.ɪd/ *adj* smooth and continuous: *fluid movements* **fluidity** /fluˈɪd.ɪ.ti/ [US] /-ə.t̬i/ *noun* [U] *FORMAL Durante dances with fluidity and grace.*

fluid [CHANGE] /ˈfluː.ɪd/ *adj* If situations, ideas or plans are fluid, they are not fixed and are likely to change, often repeatedly and unexpectedly: *The military situation is still very fluid.*
fluidity /fluˈɪd.ɪ.ti/ [US] /-ə.t̬i/ *noun* [U] the quality of being likely to change, repeatedly and unexpectedly: *the fluidity of the political situation*

ˌ**fluid ˈounce** *noun* [C] (*WRITTEN ABBREVIATION* **fl oz**) *OLD-FASHIONED* a measurement of liquid equal to *(UK)* 0.024 or *(US)* 0.030 of a litre

fluke /fluːk/ *noun* [C usually sing] *INFORMAL* something good that has happened that is the result of chance instead of skill or planning: *The first goal was just a fluke.* **flukey** (**flukier**, **flukiest**), **fluky** /ˈfluː.ki/ *adj*

flume /fluːm/ *noun* [C] **1** a narrow channel made for carrying water, for example to factories that produce electricity **2** a structure for people to slide down at a SWIMMING POOL or WATER PARK, which is shaped like a large tube and has water flowing through it

flummox /ˈflʌm.əks/ *verb* [T] *INFORMAL* to confuse someone so much that they do not know what to do: *I have to say that last question flummoxed me.* **flummoxed** /ˈflʌm.əkst/ *adj*: *He looked completely flummoxed.*

flung /flʌŋ/ *past simple and past participle of* **fling**

flunk /flʌŋk/ *verb* [T] *MAINLY US INFORMAL* to fail an exam or course of study: *I flunked my second year exams and was lucky not to be thrown out of college.*
▲ **flunk out** *phrasal verb US INFORMAL* to have to leave school or college because your work is not good enough: *Dan won't be in college next year – he flunked out.*

flunkey /ˈflʌŋ.ki/ *noun* [C] (*ALSO* **flunky**) *OLD-FASHIONED* a male servant wearing a uniform

fluorescent /flʊəˈres.ənt/ [US] /flʊ-/ *adj* **1** Fluorescent lights are very bright, tube-shaped electric lights, often used in offices: *fluorescent lighting* **2** Fluorescent colours are very bright and can be seen in the dark: *fluorescent green* **fluorescence** /flʊəˈres.ənts/ [US] /flʊ-/ *noun* [U]

fluoride /ˈflʊə.raɪd/ [US] /ˈflʊ-/ *noun* [U] a chemical substance sometimes added to water or TOOTHPASTE (= substance for cleaning teeth) in order to help keep teeth healthy
fluoridate /ˈflʊə.rɪ.deɪt/ [US] /ˈflʊ-/ *verb* [T] to add fluoride to water **fluoridation** /ˌflʊə.rɪˈdeɪ.ʃən/ [US] /ˌflʊ-/ *noun* [U]

fluorine /ˈflʊə.riːn/ [US] /ˈflʊ-/ *noun* [U] a poisonous pale yellow gas

fluorocarbon /ˌflʊə.rəˈkɑː.bən/ [US] /ˌflʊ.roʊˈkɑːr-/ *noun* [C] *SPECIALIZED* a chemical containing FLUORINE and carbon, with various industrial uses ➲See also **CFC**.

flurry [SNOW] /ˈflʌr.i/ [US] /ˈflɝː-/ *noun* [C] a sudden light fall of snow, blown in different directions by the wind: *There may be the odd flurry* ***of snow*** *over the hills tonight.*

flurry [ACTIVITY] /ˈflʌr.i/ [US] /ˈflɝː-/ *noun* [C usually sing] a sudden, short period of activity, excitement or interest: *The prince's words on marriage have prompted a flurry* ***of*** *speculation in the press this week.* ○ *a flurry of activity*

flush [EMPTY] /flʌʃ/ *verb* [I or T] **1** If you flush a toilet, or if a toilet flushes, its contents empty and it fills with water again: *My children never flush* ***the loo/toilet*** *after them.* ○ *I can't get the toilet to flush.* **2 flush** ***sth*** **down the toilet** to get rid of something by putting it in the toilet and operating the toilet: *I tend to flush old medicines down the toilet.* **flush** /flʌʃ/ *noun* [C]

PHRASAL VERBS WITH **flush**

▲ **flush** ***sb/sth*** **out** *phrasal verb* [M] to force a person or animal to leave a place where they are hiding: *Planes bombed the guerrilla positions yesterday in an attempt to flush out snipers from underground tunnels.* ○ *We used a dog to flush the rabbits out.*
▲ **flush** ***sb*** **out** *phrasal verb* [M] to do something in order to discover people who have been dishonest: *By cross-checking claims, we will flush out the fraudsters.*
▲ **flush** ***sth*** **out** *phrasal verb* [M] to remove something using a sudden flow of water: *Drink a lot of water to flush the toxins out of your system.*

flush [BECOME RED] /flʌʃ/ *verb* [I] When you flush, you become red in the face, especially as a result of strong emotions, heat or alcohol: *She flushed* ***with*** *pleasure as she accepted the prize.* ○ *The champagne had caused his face to flush.*
flush /flʌʃ/ *noun* **a flush of anger/excitement/pleasure** a sudden strong feeling of anger, excitement or pleasure
flushed /flʌʃt/ *adj* red in the face: *You look a bit flushed – are you hot?* ○ *flushed* ***cheeks*** ○ *flushed* ***with*** *anger*
• **flushed with success** feeling excited and confident after achieving something: *Flushed with success after their surprise win against Italy, Belgium are preparing for Saturday's game against Spain.*

flush [LEVEL] /flʌʃ/ *adj* at the same level as another surface: *I want the light fittings to be flush* ***with*** *the ceiling.*

flush [RICH] /flʌʃ/ *adj* [after v] *INFORMAL* having a lot of money: *I've just been paid so I'm feeling flush.*

flush [CARD GAMES] /flʌʃ/ *noun* [C] a number of playing cards held by one player which are all from the same suit

fluster /ˈflʌs.tər/ [US] /-tɚ/ *verb* [T] to make someone upset and confused, especially when they are trying to do something

F

fluster /ˈflʌs.təʳ/ [US] /-tɚ/ *noun* [U] *The important thing when you're cooking for a lot of people is not to get* ***in a*** *fluster* (= a nervous state).
flustered /ˈflʌs.təd/ [US] /-tɚd/ *adj* upset and confused: *She seemed a bit flustered.* ○ *If I look flustered it's because I'm trying to do about twenty things at once.*

flute /fluːt/ *noun* [C] a tube-shaped musical instrument with a hole that you blow across at one end while holding the tube out horizontally to one side of you
flutist /ˈfluː.tɪst/ [US] /-t̬ɪst/ *noun* [C] US FOR **flautist** (= flute player)

fluted /ˈfluː.tɪd/ [US] /ˈfluː.t̬ɪd/ *adj* If an object, especially a round object, is fluted, it is wavy around the edge: *a flan dish with fluted edges* ○ *fluted columns/pillars*

flutter [MOVE] /ˈflʌt.əʳ/ [US] /ˈflʌt̬.ɚ/ *verb* [I or T] to make a series of quick delicate movements up and down or from side to side, or to cause something to do this: *Brightly coloured flags were fluttering in the breeze.* ○ *Leaves fluttered* ***down*** *onto the path.* ○ *Butterflies fluttered* ***about*** *in the sunshine.* ○ *A white bird poised on a wire and fluttered its wings.*
• **flutter *your* eyelashes** HUMOROUS If a woman flutters her eyelashes at a man, she uses her charm and attractiveness to persuade him to do something for her: *Go and flutter your eyelashes* ***at*** *the barman, Janet, and see if you can get him to serve us.*
flutter /ˈflʌt.əʳ/ [US] /ˈflʌt̬.ɚ/ *noun* [S] a quick up-and-down movement

flutter [EXCITEMENT] /ˈflʌt.əʳ/ [US] /ˈflʌt̬.ɚ/ *noun* [C usually sing] a brief period of excited activity: *The publication of her first novel last autumn caused a flutter* ***of excitement.***
• **in a flutter** in a confused and excited state: *When economic statistics are first published they grab headlines and put markets in a flutter.*
• **all of a flutter** in a state of nervous excitement: *Peter was coming round for dinner and I was all of a flutter.*
flutter /ˈflʌt.əʳ/ [US] /ˈflʌt̬.ɚ/ *verb* [I] If your heart or stomach flutters, you feel slightly uncomfortable because you are excited or nervous: *Every time I think about my exams my stomach flutters!*
• **make *your* heart flutter** If someone makes your heart flutter, you find them very physically attractive and you feel excited when you see or talk to them: *James has been making hearts flutter ever since he joined the company.*

flutter [MONEY] /ˈflʌt.əʳ/ [US] /ˈflʌt̬.ɚ/ *noun* [C usually sing] UK INFORMAL a small bet, especially on a horse race: *Aunty Paula likes to* ***have*** *a bit of a flutter* ***on*** *the horses.*

fluvial /ˈfluː.vi.əl/ *adj* SPECIALIZED of a river: *a fluvial basin* ○ *fluvial ice*

flux [CHANGE] /flʌks/ *noun* [U] continuous change: *Our plans are* ***in a state of*** *flux at the moment.*

flux [CHEMICAL] /flʌks/ *noun* [U] SPECIALIZED a substance added to a metal to make it easier to SOLDER (= join by melting) to another metal

fly [TRAVEL] /flaɪ/ *verb* **flew, flown 1** [I] When a bird, insect or aircraft flies, it moves through the air: *The poor bird couldn't fly because it had a broken wing.* ○ *As soon as it saw us, the bird flew* ***away/off.*** **2** [I or T] to travel by aircraft, or to go somewhere or cross something in an aircraft: *We flew* ***to*** *Paris.* ○ *We fly* ***from/out from/out of*** *Heathrow, but fly* ***back (in)to*** *Gatwick.* ○ *We are flying* ***at*** *a height of 9 000 metres.* ○ *She has to fly thousands of miles every year for her job.* ○ *Who was the first person to fly* ***(across)*** *the Atlantic?* **3** [T] to use a particular company to travel by aircraft: *I usually fly Lufthansa/Japan Airlines/El Al.* **4** [T] to transport people or goods by aircraft: *The restaurant flies its fish* ***in*** *daily from Scotland.* ○ *We will be flying 100 badly wounded civilians* ***out*** *of the battle zone tonight.* **5** [T] to control an aircraft: *I learned to fly when I was in Australia.*
• **fly in the face of *sth*** not to obey something, or not to act in a way that agrees with something: *This is an argument that seems to fly in the face of* ***common sense.***
flier, flyer /ˈflaɪ.əʳ/ [US] /-ɚ/ *noun* [C] ***Frequent*** *fliers* (= people who travel by air frequently) *receive travel privileges.*
flying /ˈflaɪ.ɪŋ/ *noun* [U] *Annette's scared of flying* (= travelling by aircraft).

fly [MOVE QUICKLY] /flaɪ/ *verb* [I] **flew, flown** to move or go quickly: *With the explosion, glass flew* ***across*** *the room.* ○ *Cathy flew* ***by/past*** *me in the corridor.* ○ *My holiday seems to have flown* ***(by)*** (= passed very quickly) *this year.* ○ *The door/window suddenly flew* ***open.*** ○ INFORMAL *Anyway, I* ***must*** *fly* (= leave quickly) – *I didn't realize how late it was!*
• **go/send *sth/sb* flying** INFORMAL to fall, or to cause something or someone to fall or move through the air, suddenly and accidentally: *I tripped going up the stairs and I/my books went flying.*
• **fly into a rage** (UK ALSO **fly into a temper/fury**) to suddenly become very angry: *I asked to speak to her boss and she just flew into a rage.*
• **fly off the handle** to react in a very angry way to something that someone says or does: *He's extremely irritable – he flies off the handle at the slightest thing.*

fly [INSECT] /flaɪ/ *noun* [C] a small insect with two wings
• **drop like flies** INFORMAL **1** If people are dropping like flies they are dying or falling down in large numbers: *The heat was overwhelming and people were dropping like flies.* **2** to stop doing an activity in large numbers: *There used to be over twenty of us in our aerobics class but they're dropping like flies.*
• **fly in the ointment** INFORMAL a single thing or person that is spoiling a situation which could have been very positive or enjoyable: *I'm looking forward to Sunday, the only fly in the ointment being the fact that I shall have to sit next to my mother-in-law.*
• **fly on the wall** If you say that you would like to be a fly on the wall on an occasion, you mean that you would like to hear what will be said or see what will happen while not being noticed: *I'd love to be a fly on the wall when those two get home!* ➲See also **fly-on-the-wall.**
• **no flies on *sb*** If you say there are no flies on someone, you mean that they cannot easily be deceived.
• **wouldn't harm/hurt a fly** INFORMAL If you say that someone wouldn't harm/hurt a fly, you mean they are gentle and would not do anything to injure or offend anyone.

fly [FISHING] /flaɪ/ *noun* [C] a hook with coloured threads fastened to it, fixed to the end of a fishing line to attract fish

fly [TROUSERS] /flaɪz/ *noun* [C] (UK ALSO **flies**) the opening at the front of a pair of trousers: *Hey Chris, your fly's undone!*

fly [WAVE] /flaɪ/ *verb* [I or T] **flew, flown** to wave or move about in the air while being fixed at one end: *The ship was flying the Spanish flag.* ○ *The flag was flying* ***at half-mast*** (= lowered to a point half way down the pole) *to mark the death of the President.* ○ *There isn't really enough wind to fly a kite today.*
• **Go fly a kite!** MAINLY US INFORMAL used to tell someone who is being annoying to go away
• **with flying colours** If you do something such as pass an exam with flying colours, you do it very successfully.

fly [TENT] /flaɪ/ *noun* [C] MAINLY US FOR **flysheet**

PHRASAL VERBS WITH **fly** ▼

▲ **fly about/around** *phrasal verb* INFORMAL If ideas, remarks, or accusations are flying about/around, they are passed quickly from one person to another and cause excitement: *All kinds of rumours are flying around about the school closing.*
▲ **fly at *sb/sth*** *phrasal verb* to attack another person or animal suddenly: *He flew at his brother like a mad thing.*

flyaway /ˈflaɪ.ə.weɪ/ *adj* **flyaway hair** hair that is soft, light and difficult to keep in place

flyby /ˈflaɪ.baɪ/ *noun* [C] **1** a flight, especially in a spacecraft, past a particular place: *The pictures were taken during the spacecraft's 25-minute flyby of the asteroid.* **2** US FOR **flypast**

fly-by-night /ˈflaɪ.baɪ.naɪt/ *adj* [before n] INFORMAL DISAPPROVING Fly-by-night companies or business people cannot be trusted because they are likely to get into debt and close down the business to avoid paying the debts or fulfilling agreements: *a fly-by-night operator/organization*

flycatcher /ˈflaɪˌkætʃ.əʳ/ [US] /-ɚ/ *noun* [C] a small bird which catches insects in the air

F

fly-drive holiday UK /ˌflaɪ.draɪvˈhɒl.ɪ.deɪ/ US /-ˈhɑː.lɪ-/ noun [C] (US **fly-drive vacation**) an organized holiday which includes your air ticket and the use of a car

flyer /ˈflaɪ.əʳ/ US /-ɚ/ noun [C] See **flier** TRAVELLER and **flier** INFORMATION.

fly-fishing /ˈflaɪˌfɪʃ.ɪŋ/ noun [U] when you try to catch fish using a fly to attract the fish

flying 'buttress noun [C] SPECIALIZED an arch built against a wall, especially of a church, to support its weight

flying 'doctor noun [C] a doctor, usually in Australia, who travels by air to see ill people who live a long way from a city

flying 'fish noun [C] a tropical fish that can jump above the surface of the water using its very large FINS

flying 'fox noun [C] a large bat that eats fruit

flying 'picket noun [C] MAINLY UK a worker who travels to support workers who are on strike at another place of work

flying 'saucer noun [C] OLD-FASHIONED FOR **UFO**

flying 'squad noun [C] a small group of police officers which is trained to act quickly, especially when there is a serious crime

flying 'start noun [C] in a race, when one competitor starts more quickly than the others: FIGURATIVE *She's **got off to** a flying start* (= has begun very well) *in her new job.*

flying 'visit noun [C usually sing] a very short visit

flyleaf /ˈflaɪ.liːf/ noun [C] plural **flyleaves** an empty page at the beginning or end of a book next to the cover

fly-on-the-wall /ˌflaɪ.ɒn.ðəˈwɔːl/ US /-ɑːn.ðəˈwɑːl/ adj [before n] UK describes a television programme in which the people involved behave normally, as if they are not being filmed: *a fly-on-the-wall documentary*

flyover BRIDGE UK /ˈflaɪˌəʊ.vəʳ/ US /-ˌoʊ.vɚ/ noun [C] (US **overpass**) a bridge that carries a road or railway over another road

flyover AIRCRAFT /ˈflaɪˌəʊ.vəʳ/ US /-ˌoʊ.vɚ/ noun [C usually sing] US FOR **flypast**

flypaper /ˈflaɪˌpeɪ.pəʳ/ US /-pɚ/ noun [C or U] a long strip of sticky paper which you hang in a room to catch flies

flypast UK /ˈflaɪ.pɑːst/ US /-pæst/ noun [C usually sing] (US **flyby/flyover**) when a group of aircraft flies in a special pattern as a part of a ceremony

flyposting /ˈflaɪˌpəʊ.stɪŋ/ US /-ˌpoʊ-/ noun [U] UK illegally sticking a political or other POSTER (= notice) on a public wall, fence, etc.

flyposter /ˈflaɪˌpəʊ.stəʳ/ US /-ˌpoʊ.stɚ/ noun [C] UK a person who goes flyposting or the POSTER (= notice) they put up: *Flyposters will be prosecuted.*

flysheet UK /ˈflaɪ.ʃiːt/ noun [C] (MAINLY US **fly**) an extra sheet of CANVAS (= strong cloth) stretched over the outside of a tent to keep the rain out

flyweight /ˈflaɪ.weɪt/ noun [C] SPECIALIZED a boxer who is in the lightest weight group, weighing 51 kilograms or less

flywheel /ˈflaɪ.wiːl/ noun [C] SPECIALIZED a heavy wheel in a machine which helps the machine to work at a regular speed

FM /ˌefˈem/ noun [U] ABBREVIATION FOR frequency modulation: a radio system for broadcasting which produces a very clear sound

foal /fəʊl/ US /foʊl/ noun [C] a young horse
• **in foal** (of a female horse) pregnant: *Two of the mares are in foal.*

foal /fəʊl/ US /foʊl/ verb [I] If a MARE (= a female horse) foals, she gives birth to a baby horse.

foam /fəʊm/ US /foʊm/ noun [U] **1** a mass of very small bubbles formed on the surface of a liquid **2** a cream-like substance which is filled with bubbles of air: ***shaving foam*** **3** a soft material used to fill furniture and other objects

foam /fəʊm/ US /foʊm/ verb [I] to produce small bubbles
• **foam at the mouth** If a person or an animal foams at the mouth, they have bubbles coming out of their mouth as a result of a disease.

• **be foaming at the mouth** to be extremely angry: *The Almeida theatre's recent staging of the opera had critics foaming at the mouth.*

foamy /ˈfəʊ.mi/ US /ˈfoʊ-/ adj made of or producing a mass of very small bubbles: *foamy beer* ○ *foamy shampoo*

foam 'rubber noun [U] soft rubber with air bubbles in it

fob /fɒb/ US /fɑːb/ noun [C] a piece of leather or other material to which a group of keys is fastened, or a chain or piece of material used, especially in the past, to fasten a watch to a man's WAISTCOAT: *a key fob* ○ *a fob watch*

fob /fɒb/ US /fɑːb/ verb **-bb-**
▲ **fob sb off** phrasal verb [M] (ALSO **fob sth off on sb**) UK to persuade someone to accept something that is of a low quality or different to what he or she really wanted: *Well, he wants the report ready by tomorrow but I can always fob him off **with** some excuse.*

focal 'length noun [C usually sing] SPECIALIZED the distance between a point where waves of light meet and the centre of a lens

focal 'point INTEREST noun [C usually sing] the thing that everyone looks at or is interested in: *The television is usually the focal point of the living room.*

focal 'point SCIENCE noun [C] SPECIALIZED **focus** SCIENCE

focus CENTRE /ˈfəʊ.kəs/ US /ˈfoʊ-/ noun [C] plural **focuses** or FORMAL **foci** the main or central point of something, especially of attention or interest: *I think Dave likes to be the focus **of attention**.* ○ *The main focus **of interest** at the fashion show was Christian Lacroix's outrageous evening wear.* ○ *The media focus **on** politicians' private lives inevitably switches the attention away from the real issues.*

focal /ˈfəʊ.kəl/ US /ˈfoʊ-/ adj central and important: *The focal **figure** of the film is Annette Corley, a dancer who has boyfriend troubles.*

focus SCIENCE /ˈfəʊ.kəs/ US /ˈfoʊ-/ noun [C] plural **focuses** or FORMAL **foci** **1** (in physics) the point where waves of light or sound which are moving towards each other meet: *the focus of a lens* **2** be in/out of focus describes a photograph which is clear/not clear

focus /ˈfəʊ.kəs/ US /ˈfoʊ-/ verb **-s-** **1** [T] If you focus a device such as a camera or microscope, you move a device on the lens so that you can see a clear picture. **2** [I or T] If you focus your eyes, or if your eyes focus, you try to look directly at an object so that you can see it more clearly: *When they first took the bandages off, she/ her eyes couldn't focus properly* (= she couldn't see clearly).

focused, ALSO **focussed** /ˈfəʊ.kəst/ US /ˈfoʊ-/ adj: *a focused* (= clear) *image*
▲ **focus (sth) on/upon sb/sth** phrasal verb to give a lot of attention to one particular person, subject or thing: *Tonight's programme focuses on the way that homelessness affects the young.* ○ *When the kitchen is finished I'm going to focus **my attention** on the garden and get that sorted out.*

focus 'group group noun [C] a group of people who have been brought together to discuss a particular subject in order to solve a problem or suggest ideas

fodder /ˈfɒd.əʳ/ US /ˈfɑː.dɚ/ noun [U] **1** food that is given to cows, horses and other farm animals **2** people or things that are useful for the stated purpose: *Politicians are always good fodder **for** comedians* (= they make jokes about them). ⊃See **cannon fodder**.

foe /fəʊ/ US /foʊ/ noun [C] LITERARY an enemy: *The two countries have united against their common foe.* ○ *They were **bitter** foes for many years.* ○ *Foes **of** the government will be delighting in its current difficulties.*

FoE /ˌef.əʊˈiː/ US /-oʊ-/ group noun [U] ABBREVIATION FOR **Friends of the Earth**

foetid /ˈfet.ɪd/ US /ˈfet̬-/ adj **fetid**

foetus, US ALSO **fetus** /ˈfiː.təs/ US /-t̬əs/ noun [C] a young human being or animal before birth, after the organs have started to develop **foetal**, US ALSO **fetal** /ˈfiː.t̬əl/ US /-t̬əl/ adj: *foetal abnormalities*

fog /fɒg/ US /fɑːg/ noun **1** [C or U] a weather condition in which very small drops of water gather together to form a thick cloud close to the land or sea, making it difficult to see: *Thick/Heavy/Dense fog has made driving conditions dangerous.* ○ *Mists, freezing fogs and snow are common in this area.* ○ *It took several hours for the fog to lift.* **2** [S] INFORMAL a confused or unclear state, usually mentally or emotionally: *I went home in a fog of disbelief.*

fog /fɒg/ ⓤ /fɑːg/ *verb* [T] **-gg-** to make something or someone confused or unclear: *Alcohol fogs the brain.* ○ *The minister's speech had merely fogged the issue.*

foggy /'fɒg.i/ ⓤ /'fɑː.gi/ *adj* with fog: *a cold, foggy day*

● **not have the foggiest (idea)** INFORMAL to not know or understand something at all: *I hadn't the foggiest idea what he was talking about.*

▲ **fog up** *phrasal verb* If a glass surface fogs up, a thin layer of liquid develops on it so that it is difficult to see through: *I couldn't see a thing because my glasses had fogged up.*

fogbound /'fɒg.baʊnd/ ⓤ /'fɑːg-/ *adj* prevented from operating as usual because of fog: *Their flight was cancelled because the airport was fogbound.*

fogey, **fogy** /'fəʊ.gi/ ⓤ /'foʊ-/ *noun* [C] INFORMAL a person who is old-fashioned and likes tradition: *The party is run by a bunch of old fogies who resist progress.* ○ *When you're 16, anyone over 25 is an old fogey.*

foghorn /'fɒg.hɔːn/ ⓤ /'fɑːg.hɔːrn/ *noun* [C] a horn that makes a very loud sound to warn ships that they are close to land or other ships: *He has a voice like a foghorn* (= an unpleasantly loud voice).

foible /'fɔɪ.bl̩/ *noun* [C usually pl] a strange habit or characteristic that is seen as harmless and unimportant: *We all have our little foibles.*

foil METAL SHEET /fɔɪl/ *noun* [U] a very thin sheet of metal, especially used to wrap food in to keep it fresh: *tin/ silver foil* ○ (UK) *aluminium/*(US) *aluminum foil*

foil PREVENT /fɔɪl/ *verb* [T] to prevent someone or something from being successful: *The prisoners' attempt to escape was foiled at the last minute when police received a tip-off.*

foil COMPARISON /fɔɪl/ *noun* [C] something or someone that makes another's good or bad qualities more noticeable: *The older, cynical character in the play is the perfect foil for the innocent William.*

foil SWORD /fɔɪl/ *noun* [C] a thin light sword used in the sport of FENCING

foist /fɔɪst/ *verb*

▲ **foist** *sth* **on/upon** *sb phrasal verb* to force someone to have or experience something they do not want: *I try not to foist my values on the children but it's hard.*

fold BEND /fəʊld/ ⓤ /foʊld/ *verb* **1** [I or T] to bend something, especially paper or cloth, so that one part of it lies on the other part, or to be able to be bent in this way: *I folded the letter (in half) and put it in an envelope.* ○ *He had a neatly folded handkerchief in his jacket pocket.* ○ *Will you help me to fold (up) the sheets?* **2** [T] to wrap: *She folded her baby in a blanket.* ○ *He folded his arms around her.* **3 fold your arms** to bring your arms close to your chest and hold them together **4** [T] to move a part of your body into a position where it is close to your body: *She sat with her legs folded under her.*

fold /fəʊld/ ⓤ /foʊld/ *noun* [C] **1** a line or mark where paper, cloth, etc. was or is folded: *Make a fold across the centre of the card.* **2** SPECIALIZED a bend in a layer of rock under the earth's surface caused by movement there

▲ **fold** *sth* **in/fold** *sth* **into something** *phrasal verb* (in cooking) to mix a substance into another substance by turning it gently with a spoon: *Fold the egg whites into the cake mixture.* ○ *Fold in the flour.*

fold FAIL /fəʊld/ ⓤ /foʊld/ *verb* [I] (of a business) to close because of failure: *Many small businesses fold within the first year.*

fold SHELTER /fəʊld/ ⓤ /foʊld/ *noun* [C] a small area of a field surrounded by a fence where sheep can be put for shelter for the night

the fold *noun* [S] your home or an organization where you feel you belong: *Her children are all away at college now, but they always return to the fold in the holidays.*

-fold NUMBER /-fəʊld/ ⓤ /-foʊld/ *suffix* having the stated number of parts, or multiplied by the stated number: *threefold* ○ *fourfold* ○ *The problems are twofold – firstly, economic, and secondly, political.* ○ *In the last 50 years, there has been a 33-fold increase in the amount of pesticide used in farming.*

foldaway /'fəʊld.ə.weɪ/ ⓤ /'foʊld-/ *adj* able to be folded away out of sight: *a foldaway bed*

folder /'fəʊl.dəʳ/ ⓤ /'foʊl.dɚ/ *noun* [C] a piece of plastic or cardboard folded down the middle and used for keeping loose papers in

folding /'fəʊl.dɪŋ/ ⓤ /'foʊl-/ *adj* [before n] **1** describes a chair, bed, bicycle, etc. that can be folded into a smaller size to make it easier to store or carry **2** describes a door made of several parts joined together which can be folded against each other when the door is opened

foliage /'fəʊ.li.ɪdʒ/ ⓤ /'foʊ-/ *noun* [U] the leaves of a plant or tree, or leaves on the stems or branches on which they are growing: *The dense foliage overhead almost blocked out the sun.*

folic acid /ˌfəʊ.lɪkˈæs.ɪd/ ⓤ /ˌfoʊ-/ *noun* [C] a vitamin found in the leaves of plants and in liver, and which is needed by the body for the production of red blood cells

folio /'fəʊ.li.əʊ/ ⓤ /'foʊ.li.oʊ/ *noun* [C] *plural* **folios 1** a book made of paper of a large size, especially one of the earliest books printed in Europe **2** a single sheet of paper from a book

folk PEOPLE /fəʊk/ ⓤ /foʊk/ *plural noun* (MAINLY US **folks**) people, especially those of a particular group or type: *old folk* ○ *Ordinary folk can't afford cars like that.* ⊃See also **folksy**.

folks /fəʊks/ ⓤ /foʊks/ *plural noun* **1** [as form of address] INFORMAL used when speaking informally to a group of people: *All right, folks, dinner's ready!* **2** MAINLY US someone's parents: *I'm going home to see my folks.*

folk TRADITIONAL /fəʊk/ ⓤ /foʊk/ *adj* [before n] **1** traditional to or typical of a particular group or country, especially one where people mainly live in the countryside, and usually passed on from parents to their children over a long period of time: *folk culture* ⊃See also **folksy**. **2** describes art that expresses something about the lives and feelings of ordinary people in a particular group or country, especially those living in the countryside: *folk art* ○ *folk dancing*

folk /fəʊk/ ⓤ /foʊk/ *noun* [U] modern music and songs that are written in a style similar to that of traditional music: *I enjoy listening to folk (music/songs).* ○ *folk singers* ○ *a folk club/festival*

'folk ˌhero *noun* [C] someone who is popular with and respected by ordinary people: *The mayor is still a folk hero in Chicago's black community.*

folklore /'fəʊk.lɔːʳ/ ⓤ /'foʊk.lɔːr/ *noun* [U] the traditional stories and culture of a group of people: *Her books are often based on folklore and fairy-tales.* ○ *In Irish folklore, the leprechaun had a large piece of gold.* ○ *Arguments between directors and stars are part of the folklore of Hollywood.*

'folk ˌmemory *noun* [C usually sing] the knowledge that people have about something that happened in the past because parents have spoken to their children about it over many years

folksy /'fəʊk.si/ ⓤ /'foʊk-/ *adj* having a traditional artistic or musical style, or (pretending to be) simple and informal: *The book has a certain folksy charm.*

'folk ˌtale *noun* [C] a story that parents have passed on to their children through speech over many years

follicle /'fɒl.ɪ.kl̩/ ⓤ /'fɑː.lɪ-/ *noun* [C] any of the very small holes in the skin, especially one that a hair grows from

follow GO /'fɒl.əʊ/ ⓤ /'fɑː.loʊ/ *verb* [I or T] to move behind someone or something and go where they go: *A dog followed us home.* ○ *She followed me into the kitchen.* ○ *The book was delivered yesterday with a note saying the bill for it would follow in a day or two.* ○ *He had the feeling he was being followed* (= someone was going after him to catch him or see where he was going). ○ *I could feel them following me with their eyes* (= watching my movements closely). ○ *Follow* (= Go in the same direction as) *the road for two kilometres, then turn left.* ○ *Do your own thing, don't just follow the crowd* (= do what everyone else does.)

• **follow in** ***sb's*** **footsteps** to do the same thing as someone else did previously: *She followed in her mother's footsteps, starting her own business.*
• **follow** ***your*** **nose** *INFORMAL* **1** to trust your own feelings rather than obeying rules or allowing yourself to be influenced by other people's opinions: *Take a chance and follow your nose – you may be right!* **2** go in a straight line: *Turn left, then just follow your nose and you'll see the shop on your left.*
• **follow suit** to do the same thing as someone else: *When one airline cuts prices, the rest soon follow suit.*
following /ˈfɒl.əʊ.ɪŋ/ [US] /ˈfɑː.loʊ-/ *adj* **following wind** a wind which is blowing in the same direction as the one in which you are going

follow [HAPPEN] /ˈfɒl.əʊ/ [US] /ˈfɑː.loʊ/ *verb* **[I or T]** to happen or come after something: *We were not prepared for the events that followed* (= happened next). ○ *The meal consisted of smoked salmon, followed by guinea fowl* (= with this as the next part). ○ *She published a book of poems and followed it* ***(up) with*** (= next produced) *a novel.*
• **as follows** said to introduce a list of things: *The winners are as follows – Woods, Smith and Cassidy.*
following /ˈfɒl.əʊ.ɪŋ/ [US] /ˈfɑː.loʊ-/ *adj* **[before n]** The following day/morning etc., is the next one.
following /ˈfɒl.əʊ.ɪŋ/ [US] /ˈfɑː.loʊ-/ *prep* after: *The weeks following the riots were extremely tense.* ○ *Following the dinner, there will be a dance.*
the ˈfollowing *noun* (often used to introduce a list, report etc.) what comes next: *The following is an extract from her diary.*

follow [OBEY] /ˈfɒl.əʊ/ [US] /ˈfɑː.loʊ/ *verb* **[T]** to obey or to act as ordered by someone: *Follow the* ***instructions*** *on the back of the packet carefully.* ○ *I decided to follow her* ***advice*** *and go to bed early.* ○ *Muslims follow the* ***teachings*** *of the Koran.*
follower /ˈfɒl.əʊ.əʳ/ [US] /ˈfɑː.loʊ.ɚ/ *noun* **[C]** **1** a person who does what someone else does or tells them to do: *Be a leader, not a follower!* **2** someone who supports, admires or believes in a particular person, group or idea: *a follower of Jesus* ○ *followers* ***of*** *the Dalai Lama/Buddhism*
following /ˈfɒl.əʊ.ɪŋ/ [US] /ˈfɑː.loʊ-/ *noun* **[S]** a group of people who support, admire or believe in a particular person, group or idea

follow [UNDERSTAND] /ˈfɒl.əʊ/ [US] /ˈfɑː.loʊ/ *verb* **1** **[I or T]** to understand something as it is being said or done: *I'm sorry, I don't quite follow (you).* ○ *His lecture was complicated and difficult to follow.* **2** **[T]** To follow a piece of music or writing is to read the notes or words at the same time as they are being played or said.

follow [HAVE INTEREST IN] /ˈfɒl.əʊ/ [US] /ˈfɑː.loʊ/ *verb* **[T]** to have a great interest in something or watch something closely: *He follows most sports avidly.* ○ *They followed her academic progress closely.*
follower /ˈfɒl.əʊ.əʳ/ [US] /ˈfɑː.loʊ.ɚ/ *noun* **[C]** *They are keen followers* ***of*** (= have a great interest in) *their local football team.*
following /ˈfɒl.əʊ.ɪŋ/ [US] /ˈfɑː.loʊ-/ *noun* **[S]** a group of people who admire something or someone: *She has* ***attracted*** *a large following among the rich and famous.* ○ *The shop has a small but* ***loyal/devoted*** *following.*

follow [BE RESULT] /ˈfɒl.əʊ/ [US] /ˈfɑː.loʊ/ *verb* **[not continuous]** to happen as a result, or to be a likely result: **[+ *that*]** *Just because I agreed last time,* ***it*** *doesn't* ***necessarily*** *follow* ***that*** *I will do so again.*

PHRASAL VERBS WITH **follow**

▲ **follow on** *phrasal verb MAINLY UK* to happen or exist as the next part of something: *Following on* ***from*** *what I said earlier...*
▲ **follow** ***(sth)*** **through** *phrasal verb* **[M]** to do something as the next part of an activity or period of development: *The essay started interestingly, but failed to follow through (its argument).*
▲ **follow through** *phrasal verb* to complete the movement of hitting, kicking or throwing a ball by continuing to move your arm or leg in the same direction: *You need to follow through more on your backhand.*
▲ **follow** ***sth*** **up** *phrasal verb* (*US ALSO* **follow up on** ***sth***) to find out more about something, or take further action connected with it: *The idea sounded interesting and I decided to follow it up.* ○ *He decided to follow up on his initial research and write a book.*
follow-up /ˈfɒl.əʊ.ʌp/ [US] /ˈfɑː.loʊ-/ *noun* **[C]** *This meeting is a follow-up* ***to*** *the one we had last month.*

follow-my-leader *UK* /ˌfɒl.əʊ.məˈliː.dəʳ/ [US] /ˌfɑː.loʊ.məˈliː.dɚ/ *noun* **[U]** (*US* **follow-the-leader**) a children's game in which one child is followed by a line of other children, who have to copy everything the first child does

folly [STUPIDITY] /ˈfɒl.i/ [US] /ˈfɑː.li/ *noun* **[C or U]** *FORMAL* stupidity, or a stupid action, idea, etc: *She said that the idea was folly.* ○ **[+ to infinitive]** ***It*** *would be folly* ***for*** *the country* ***to*** *become involved in the war.*

folly [BUILDING] /ˈfɒl.i/ [US] /ˈfɑː.li/ *noun* **[C]** (especially in Britain) a building in the form of a small castle, TEMPLE, etc., that has been built as a decoration in a large garden or park: *a Gothic garden folly*

foment /fəʊˈment/ [US] /foʊ-/ *verb* **[T]** *FORMAL* to cause trouble to develop: *The song was banned on the grounds that it might foment racial tension.*

fond [LIKING] /fɒnd/ [US] /fɑːnd/ *adj* **[before n]** having a great liking for someone or something: *She was very fond* ***of*** *horses.* ○ *"I'm very fond* ***of*** *you, you know," he said.* ○ *My brother is fond* ***of*** *pointing out my mistakes.* ○ *Many of us have fond* ***memories*** *of our childhoods.* ○ *We said a fond* ***farewell*** *to each other* (= We said goodbye in a loving way) *and promised to write.*
fondly /ˈfɒnd.li/ [US] /ˈfɑːnd-/ *adv*: *He smiled fondly* (= in a loving way) *at the children.*
fondness /ˈfɒnd.nəs/ [US] /ˈfɑːnd-/ *noun* **[U]** *George's fondness* (= liking) ***for*** *pink gins was well known.*

fond [FOOLISH] /fɒnd/ [US] /fɑːnd/ *adj* **a fond belief/hope** something that you would like to be true but that is probably not: *I waited in all evening in the fond hope that he might call.*
fondly /ˈfɒnd.li/ [US] /ˈfɑːnd-/ *adv*: *She fondly* (= foolishly) *believed that he might come.*

fondant /ˈfɒn.dᵊnt/ [US] /ˈfɑːn-/ *noun* **[C or U]** a thick, soft, sweet food, made mainly of sugar and used to cover cakes, or a small soft sweet made mainly from sugar: *fondant icing*

fondle /ˈfɒn.dl/ [US] /ˈfɑːn-/ *verb* **[T]** to touch gently and in a loving way, or to touch in a sexual way: *She fondled the puppies.* ○ *He gently fondled the baby's feet.* ○ *She accused him of fondling her* (= touching her in a sexual way) *in the back of a taxi.*

fondue /fɒnˈduː/ [US] /fɑːn-/ *noun* **[C]** a hot dish prepared by keeping a container of either hot oil or melted cheese over a flame at the table and putting pieces of meat in the oil to be cooked or pieces of bread into the cheese: *a cheese fondue* ○ *a meat fondue*

fonˈdue ˌset *noun* **[C]** the equipment needed to make a fondue

font [CONTAINER] /fɒnt/ [US] /fɑːnt/ *noun* **[C]** a large, usually stone, container in a church, which holds the water used for BAPTISMS

font [LETTERS] /fɒnt/ [US] /fɑːnt/ *noun* **[C]** a set of letters and symbols in a particular design and size

food /fuːd/ *noun* **[C or U]** something that people and animals eat, or plants absorb, to keep them alive: *baby food* ○ *cat food* ○ *plant food* ○ *There was lots of food* ***and drink*** *at the party.* ○ *I'm allergic to certain foods.*
• **be off** ***your*** **food** to not want to eat, usually because you are ill
• **give** ***sb*** **food for thought** to make someone think seriously about something

ˈfood ˌadditive *noun* **[C]** an artificial substance added to food to give it taste or colour

the ˈfood ˌchain *noun* a series of living things which are connected because each group of things eats the group below it in the series

foodie /ˈfuː.di/ *noun* **[C]** *INFORMAL* a person who loves food and is very interested in different types of food

ˈfood ˌpoisoning *noun* **[U]** an illness usually caused by eating food that contains harmful bacteria

ˈfood ˌprocessor *noun* [C] an electric machine that cuts, slices and mixes food quickly

ˈfood ˌstamp *noun* [C] *US* a piece of paper which is given to poor people by the government and with which they can then buy food

foodstuff /ˈfuːd.stʌf/ *noun* [C] any substance that is used as food or to make food: *They lack basic foodstuffs, such as bread and milk.*

fool PERSON /fuːl/ *noun* [C] **1** a person who behaves in a silly way without thinking: [as form of address] *You fool, you've missed your chance!* ○ *He's a fool if he thinks she still loves him.* ○ [+ to infinitive] *He's a fool* ***to*** *think she still loves him.* ○ *He's fool* ***enough to*** *think she still loves him.* ○ *My fool* ***of a*** (= silly) *husband has gone out and taken my keys!* **2** in the past, a person who was employed in the court of a king or queen to make them laugh by telling jokes and doing amusing things

• **act/play the fool** to behave in a silly way, often intentionally to make people laugh: *Stop acting the fool, I'm trying to talk to you.*

• **any fool** anyone: *Any fool could tell that she was joking.*

• **make a fool of** ***sb*** to trick someone or make them appear stupid in some way

• **make a fool of** ***yourself*** to do something that makes other people think you are silly or not to be respected: *I got a bit drunk and made a fool of myself.*

• **more fool** ***sb*** *MAINLY UK* said to mean that you think someone is being unwise: *"I lent Rhoda $100 and she hasn't paid me back." "More fool you – you know what she's like!"*

• **be no fool** (*ALSO* **be nobody's fool**) to not be stupid or easily deceived: *I notice Ed didn't offer to pay for her – he's no fool.*

fool /fuːl/ *verb* [I or T] to trick someone: *Don't be fooled by his appearance.* ○ *She said she was doing it to help me but I wasn't fooled.* ○ *Tim was fooled* ***into*** *believing that he'd won a lot of money.*

• **You could have fooled me!** *INFORMAL* used to tell someone that you do not believe what they have just said: *"Really, I'm very happy." "You could have fooled me."*

fool /fuːl/ *adj* [before n] *MAINLY US INFORMAL* silly: *You've done some fool things in your time, but this beats everything.*

foolery /ˈfuː.lᵊr.i/ US /-lɚ.i/ *noun UK OLD-FASHIONED* silly behaviour

foolish /ˈfuː.lɪʃ/ *adj* unwise, ridiculous or lacking in judgment: *That was a rather foolish thing to do.* ○ *She was afraid that she would look foolish if she refused.* ○ ***It was foolish of*** *them* ***to*** *pay so much.* **foolishly** /ˈfuː.lɪʃ.li/ *adv*: *Foolishly, I didn't write the phone number down.* **foolishness** /ˈfuː.lɪʃ.nəs/ *noun* [U]

PHRASAL VERBS WITH **fool**

▲ **fool around/about** SILLY *phrasal verb* to behave in a silly way, especially in a way that might have dangerous results: *Don't fool around* ***with*** *matches.*

▲ **fool around/about** AMUSING *phrasal verb* to behave in an amusing way in order to make other people laugh: *He's always getting into trouble for fooling around in class.*

▲ **fool around** NOT USEFUL *phrasal verb* to spend your time doing nothing useful: *We spent the afternoon fooling around on the beach.*

▲ **fool around** SEXUAL *phrasal verb MAINLY US* If a married person fools around, they have a sexual relationship with someone who is not their husband or wife: *She'd been fooling around* ***with*** *someone at work.*

fool SWEET DISH /fuːl/ *noun* [C or U] a sweet soft food made of crushed fruit, cream and sugar: ***gooseberry*** *fool*

foolhardy /ˈfuːlˌhɑː.di/ US /-ˌhɑːr-/ *adj* foolishly brave, taking unnecessary risks: *a foolhardy decision* ○ *Sailing the Atlantic in such a tiny boat wasn't so much brave as foolhardy.* ○ ***It*** *would be foolhardy* ***to*** *try and predict the outcome of the talks at this stage.*

foolproof /ˈfuːl.pruːf/ *adj* (of a plan or machine) so simple and easy to understand that it is unable to go wrong or be used wrongly: *I don't believe there's any such thing as a foolproof scheme for making money.* ○ *This new video-recorder is supposed to be foolproof.*

foolscap /ˈfuːl.skæp/ *noun* [U] paper of a standard size, measuring 17.2 centimetres x 21.6 centimetres

fool's gold /ˌfuːlzˈgəʊld/ US /-ˈgoʊld/ *noun* [U] **1** a mineral that is found in rocks and looks like gold but is worthless **2** something that you think will be very pleasant or successful but is not

fool's paradise /ˌfuːlzˈpær.ə.daɪs/ US /-ˈper-/ *noun* **live in a fool's paradise** to be happy because you do not know or will not accept how bad a situation really is

foot BODY PART /fʊt/ *noun* [C] *plural* **feet** the part of the body at the bottom of the leg on which a person or animal stands: *I've got a blister on my left foot.* ○ *I've been* ***on*** *my feet* (= standing) *all day and I'm exhausted.* ○ *He* ***got to/rose to/jumped to*** *his feet* (= stood up) *when she walked in.* ○ *INFORMAL "You look tired. Why don't you* ***put*** *your feet* ***up*** (= sit or lie down with your feet resting on something)?*"* ○ *Please wipe your feet* (= clean the bottom of your shoes) *before you come into the house.* ➲See picture **The Body** on page Centre 5

• **on foot** walking: *Are you going by bicycle or on foot?*

• **be back on** ***your*** **feet** to be healthy again after a period of illness: *"We'll soon have you back on your feet again," said the nurse.*

• **get a/*your* foot in the door** to enter a business or organization at a low level, but with a chance of being more successful in the future: *Making contacts can help you get a foot in the door when it comes to getting a job.*

• **have a foot in both camps** to be connected to two groups with opposing interests

• **have/keep** ***your*** **feet on the ground** (*ALSO* **have both feet on the ground**) to be very practical and see things as they really are

• **have one foot in the grave** *HUMOROUS* to be very old and near death

• **fall/land on** ***your*** **feet** to be successful or lucky, especially after a period of not having success or luck: *She's really fallen on her feet with that new job.*

• **have feet of clay** to have a bad quality which you keep hidden: *Some of the greatest geniuses in history had feet of clay.*

• **my foot** *INFORMAL* used to mean that you do not believe what another person has just told you: *"He says his car isn't working." "Not working my foot. He's just too lazy to come."*

• **get off on the right/wrong foot** to make a successful/unsuccessful start in something

• **not put a foot wrong** to not make any mistakes

• **put** ***your*** **foot down** **1** to use your authority to stop something happening: *When she started borrowing my clothes without asking, I had to put my foot down.* **2** *UK* (*US* **floor it**) to increase your speed when you are driving: *The road ahead was clear, so I put my foot down.*

• **put** ***your*** **foot in it** (*MAINLY US* **put** ***your*** **foot in** ***your*** **mouth**) *INFORMAL* to say something by accident which embarrasses or upsets someone: *I really put my foot in it with Alison. I had no idea she was divorced.*

• **put one foot in front of the other** If you can hardly/barely put one foot in front of the other, you are having difficulty walking: *I was so tired that I could hardly put one foot in front of the other.*

• **rush/run** ***sb*** **off** ***their*** **feet** to cause someone to be very busy: *I've been rushed off my feet all morning.*

• **set foot in** ***somewhere*** to go to a place: *He refuses to set foot in an art gallery.*

• **under** ***your*** **feet** If someone is under your feet, their presence prevents you from doing what you want to be doing: *The children were under my feet all day so I couldn't get anything done.*

-footed /-fʊt.ɪd/ US /-fʊt̬-/ *suffix*: *our four-footed friends* (= animals having four feet) ○ *bare-footed children* (= children wearing no shoes)

foot MEASUREMENT (*plural* **feet** or **foot**) /fʊt/ *noun* [C] (*WRITTEN ABBREVIATION* **ft**) a unit of measurement, equal to twelve inches or 0.3048 metres, sometimes shown by the symbol ′: *The man was standing only a few feet away.* ○ *She is five feet/foot three inches tall.* ○ *She is 5′ 3″ tall.*

-footer /-fʊt.əʳ/ US /-fʊt̬.ɚ/ *suffix*: *Our boat's a forty-footer* (= is of this number of FEET in length).

foot BOTTOM /fʊt/ *noun* [S] the bottom or lower end of a space or object: *They built a house at the foot* ***of*** *a cliff.*

○ *She dreamed she saw someone standing at the foot of her bed.* ○ *There's a note to that effect at the foot of the page.*

foot PAY /fʊt/ *verb* [T] INFORMAL to pay an amount of money: *His parents footed the bill for his course fees.* ○ *They refused to foot the cost of the wedding.* ○ *The company will foot her expenses.*

foot POETRY /fʊt/ *noun* [C] *plural* **feet** SPECIALIZED a unit of division of a line of poetry containing one strong beat and one or two weaker ones

footage /'fʊt.ɪdʒ/ US /'fʊt̬-/ *noun* [U] (a piece of) film especially one showing an event: *early newsreel footage*

foot and 'mouth (di,sease) UK *noun* [U] (*US* **hoof and mouth (disease)**) a infectious illness of cattle, sheep, pigs and goats that causes painful areas in the mouth and on the feet

football /'fʊt.bɔːl/ US /-bɑːl/ *noun* **1** [U] UK (*UK AND US* **soccer**) a game played between two teams of eleven people, where each team tries to win by kicking a ball into the other team's goal: *a football player/team* ○ *He's playing football.* ○ *Are you coming to the football match?* ○ *I'm not a big football fan.* ⊃See picture **Sports** on page Centre 10 **2** [U] *US* (*UK* **American football**) a game for two teams of eleven players in which an oval ball is moved along the field by running with it or throwing it: *a football game* ⊃See picture **Sports** on page Centre 10 **3** [C] a large ball made of leather or plastic and filled with air, used in games of football

footballer /'fʊt.bɔː.lə^r/ US /-bɑː.lə-/ *noun* [C] UK someone who plays football, especially as their job: *professional footballers*

footballing /'fʊt.bɔː.lɪŋ/ *before n* relating to or playing football: *It was the high point of his footballing career.* ○ *a footballing country/hero*

'football ,pools *plural noun* UK **the pools**

footbridge /'fʊt.brɪdʒ/ *noun* [C] a narrow bridge that is only used by people who are walking

footfall /'fʊt.fɔːl/ US /-fɑːl/ *noun* [C] LITERARY the sound of a person's foot hitting the ground as they walk: *I heard echoing footfalls in the corridor.*

'foot ,fault *noun* [C] in tennis, when a player steps over the back line of the COURT while SERVING

foothill /'fʊt.hɪl/ *noun* [C usually pl] a low mountain or low hill at the bottom of a larger mountain or range of mountains: *the foothills of the Pyrenees*

foothold /'fʊt.həʊld/ US /-hoʊld/ *noun* [C] **1** a place such as a hole in a rock where you can put your foot safely when climbing **2** a strong first position from which further advances can be made: *We are still trying to get/gain a foothold in the Japanese market.*

footing FEET /'fʊt.ɪŋ/ US /'fʊt̬-/ *noun* [S] when you are standing firmly on a slope or other dangerous surface: *I lost/missed my footing and fell.* ○ *It was a struggle just to keep my footing.*

footing SITUATION /'fʊt.ɪŋ/ US /'fʊt̬-/ **1** the way in which something operates and the set of conditions that influences it: *The council wants to put the bus service on a commercial footing.* **2** **be on an equal/firm, etc. footing** to be in an equal, safe, etc. situation: *Men and women ought to be able to compete for jobs on an equal footing.*

footlights /'fʊt.laɪts/ *plural noun* a row of lights along the front of a stage at a theatre

footling /'fuː.tl.ɪŋ/ US /-t̬l-/ *adj* OLD-FASHIONED unimportant or silly: *He could always do something useful instead of wasting my time with footling queries.*

footloose /'fʊt.luːs/ *adj* free to do what you like and go where you like because you have no responsibilities: *My sister's married but I'm still footloose and fancy-free.*

footman /'fʊt.mən/ *noun* [C] a male servant whose job includes opening doors and serving food, and who often wears a uniform

footnote /'fʊt.nəʊt/ US /-noʊt/ *noun* **1** [C] a note printed at the bottom of a page which gives extra information about something that has been written on that page **2** [C usually sing] an unimportant event, subject or detail: *His tumultuous triumph 5 years ago now seems a mere footnote in history.*

footpath /'fʊt.pɑːθ/ US /-pæθ/ *noun* [C] a path, especially in the countryside, for walking on

footplate /'fʊt.pleɪt/ *noun* [C] the part of a steam railway engine on which the driver stands

footprint /'fʊt.prɪnt/ *noun* [C] the mark made by a person's or animal's foot

footsie FEET /'fʊt.si/ *noun* [U] **play footsie**, see at **play** GAME

Footsie SHARE PRICES /'fʊt.si/ *noun* INFORMAL FOR **the FTSE 100 (Index)**

footslogging /'fʊt.slɒg.ɪŋ/ US /-ˌslɑː.gɪŋ/ *noun* [U] UK INFORMAL when you walk over a long distance or from place to place so that you become tired

'foot ,soldier *noun* [C] an **infantryman** ⊃See at **infantry**.

footsore /'fʊt.sɔː^r/ US /-sɔːr/ *adj* having painful tired feet, especially after a lot of walking

footstep /'fʊt.step/ *noun* [C] the sound made by a person walking as their foot touches the ground, or a STEP (= foot movement): *Walking along the darkened street, he heard footsteps close behind him.*

footsteps /'fʊt.steps/ *plural noun* the route a person has taken in order to reach a place or to achieve something: *When he realized he'd lost his wallet, he retraced his footsteps (= went back the way he had come).*

footstool /'fʊt.stuːl/ *noun* [C] a low support on which a person who is sitting can place their feet

footwear /'fʊt.weə^r/ US /-wer/ *noun* [U] shoes, boots or any other outer covering for the human foot: *You'll need some fairly tough footwear to go walking up mountains.*

footwork /'fʊt.wɜːk/ US /-wɜːk/ *noun* [U] the way in which the feet are used in sports or dancing, especially when it is skilful: *And that's a marvellous bit of footwork there from Ponti as he takes the ball from Garcia.*

footy, **footie** /'fʊt.i/ US /'fʊt̬-/ *noun* [U] **1** UK INFORMAL football **2** AUS INFORMAL **rugby**

fop /fɒp/ US /fɑːp/ *noun* [C] (especially in the past) a man who is extremely interested in his appearance and who wears very decorative clothes **foppish** /'fɒp.ɪʃ/ US /'fɑː.pɪʃ/ *adj* OLD USE DISAPPROVING

for INTENDED FOR STRONG /fɔː^r/ US /fɔːr/, WEAK /fə^r/ US /fɚ/ *prep* intended to be given to: *There's a phone message for you.* ○ *I'd better buy something for the new baby.* ○ *There's a prize for the fastest three runners.*

● **that/there's ... for you** DISAPPROVING describes something that you think is a typical example: *You spend two hours cooking a meal and they say "it's disgusting" – that's children for you!*

for PURPOSE STRONG /fɔː^r/ US /fɔːr/, WEAK /fə^r/ US /fɚ/ *prep* having the purpose of: *There's a sign there saying 'boats for hire'.* ○ *This pool is for the use of hotel residents only.* ○ *I'm sorry, the books are not for sale.* ○ *They've invited us round for dinner on Saturday.* ○ *Everyone in the office is contributing money for his leaving present.* ○ *I need some money for tonight.* ○ *Which vitamins should you take for (= in order to cure) skin problems?* ○ *Put those clothes in a pile for washing (= so that they can be washed).*

● **what ... for?** why: *What did you do that for?* ○ *What are you emptying that cupboard for?*

for BECAUSE OF STRONG /fɔː^r/ US /fɔːr/, WEAK /fə^r/ US /fɚ/ *prep* because of or as a result of something: *I'm feeling all the better for my holiday.* ○ *"How are you?" "Fine, and all the better for seeing you!"* ○ *She did fifteen years in prison for murder.* ○ *I don't eat meat for various reasons.* ○ *I couldn't see for the tears in my eyes.* ○ *The things you do for love!* ○ *She couldn't talk for coughing (= she was coughing too much to talk).* ○ *Scotland is famous for its spectacular countryside.* ○ *He's best remembered for his novels.* ○ *I didn't dare say anything for fear of (= because I was frightened of) offending him.*

● **if it wasn't/weren't for** (ALSO **if it hadn't been for**) without: *If it wasn't for the life jacket, I would have drowned.*

for TIME/DISTANCE STRONG /fɔː^r/ US /fɔːr/, WEAK /fə^r/ US /fɚ/ *prep* used to show an amount of time or distance: *We walked for miles.* ○ *She's out of the office for a few days next week.* ○ *I'm just going to bed for an hour or so.* ○ *I haven't played tennis for years.* ⊃See Note **during or for?** at **during** AT SOME TIME IN.

for OCCASION *STRONG* /fɔːʳ/ ⓤ /fɔːr/, *WEAK* /fəʳ/ ⓤ /fɚ/ *prep* on the occasion of or at the time of: *What did you buy him for Christmas?* ○ *I'd like an appointment with the doctor for some time this week.* ○ *We're having a party for Jim's 60th birthday party.* ○ *I've booked a table at the restaurant for nine o'clock.*

for COMPARING *STRONG* /fɔːʳ/ ⓤ /fɔːr/, *WEAK* /fəʳ/ ⓤ /fɚ/ *prep* used for comparing one thing with others of the same type: *She's very mature for her age.* ○ *For every two people in favour of the law there are three against.* ○ *The summer has been quite hot for England.* ○ *It was a difficult decision, especially for a child.* ○ *For a man of his wealth he's not exactly generous.*

● **for all** *sb* **cares/knows** *INFORMAL* said to show that something is not important to someone: *You could be the Queen of England, for all I care – you're not coming in here without a ticket.*

for SUPPORT *STRONG* /fɔːʳ/ ⓤ /fɔːr/, *WEAK* /fəʳ/ ⓤ /fɚ/ *prep* in support of or in agreement with: *I voted for the Greens at the last election.* ○ *Those voting for the motion, 96, and those voting against, 54.* ○ *So let's hear some applause for these talented young performers.* ○ *Who's for* (= Who wants to play) *tennis?*

● **be all for** *sth* to approve of or support something very much: *I've got nothing against change – I'm all for it.* ○ *I'm all for sexual equality, but I don't want my wife earning more than I do.*

for IN RELATION TO *STRONG* /fɔːʳ/ ⓤ /fɔːr/, *WEAK* /fəʳ/ ⓤ /fɚ/ *prep* in relation to someone or something: *Her feelings for him had changed.* ○ *He felt nothing but contempt for her.* ○ *I've got a lot of admiration for people who do that sort of work.* ○ *He's quite good-looking but he's a bit too short for me.* ○ *The ice-cream was a little bit sweet for me.* ○ *That jacket looks a bit big for you.* ○ *Jackie's already left and,* **as** *for me, I'm going at the end of the month.* ○ *Luckily for me* (= I was lucky)*, I already had another job when the redundancies were announced.* ○ *How are you doing for money/time* (= have you got enough money/time)*?*

● **for all** despite: *For all her qualifications, she's still useless at the job.*

for PAYMENT *STRONG* /fɔːʳ/ ⓤ /fɔːr/, *WEAK* /fəʳ/ ⓤ /fɚ/ *prep* (getting) in exchange: *How much did you pay for your glasses?* ○ *I've sponsored her £1 for every mile that she runs.* ○ *She sold the house for quite a lot of money.* ○ *They've said they'll repair my car for £300.*

for REPRESENTING *STRONG* /fɔːʳ/ ⓤ /fɔːr/, *WEAK* /fəʳ/ ⓤ /fɚ/ *prep* being employed by or representing a company, country, etc: *She works for a charity.* ○ *He used to swim for his country when he was younger.*

for TOWARDS *STRONG* /fɔːʳ/ ⓤ /fɔːr/, *WEAK* /fəʳ/ ⓤ /fɚ/ *prep* towards; in the direction of: *They looked as if they were heading for the train station.* ○ *Just follow signs for the town centre.* ○ *This time tomorrow we'll be setting off for the States.* ○ *It says this train is for* (= going to stop at) *Birmingham and Coventry only.*

for MEANING *STRONG* /fɔːʳ/ ⓤ /fɔːr/, *WEAK* /fəʳ/ ⓤ /fɚ/ *prep* showing meaning: *What's the Spanish word for 'vegetarian'?* ○ *What does the 'M.J.' **stand** for? Maria Jose?*

for TO GET *STRONG* /fɔːʳ/ ⓤ /fɔːr/, *WEAK* /fəʳ/ ⓤ /fɚ/ *prep* in order to get or achieve: *I hate waiting for public transport.* ○ *I had to run for the bus.* ○ *Did you send off for details of the competition?* ○ *I've applied for a job with another computer company.*

for DUTY *STRONG* /fɔːʳ/ ⓤ /fɔːr/, *WEAK* /fəʳ/ ⓤ /fɚ/ *prep* the duty or responsibility of: *As to whether you should marry him – that's for you to decide.* ○ *It's not for me to tell her what she should do with her life.* ○ *As to how many she invites, it's not really for me to say.*

for BECAUSE *STRONG* /fɔːʳ/ ⓤ /fɔːr/, *WEAK* /fəʳ/ ⓤ /fɚ/ *conjunction* *OLD-FASHIONED OR LITERARY* because; as: *She remained silent, for her heart was heavy and her spirits low.*

COMMON LEARNER ERROR

for or **because**?

For is only used to mean 'because' or 'as a result of' in very old-fashioned, especially literary English.

Forgive them O Lord, for they know not what they do.

The common word is **because**.

Erik ate nothing because he was feeling sick.
~~Erik ate nothing for he was feeling sick.~~

for IN TROUBLE *STRONG* /fɔːʳ/ ⓤ /fɔːr/, *WEAK* /fəʳ/ ⓤ /fɚ/ *prep* *INFORMAL* **for it** in trouble: *You'll be for it when she finds out!*

forage /ˈfɒr.ɪdʒ/ ⓤ /ˈfɔːr-/ *verb* [I] to go from place to place searching, especially for food: *The children had been living on the streets, foraging **for** scraps and sleeping rough.* ○ *The pigs foraged in the woods for acorns.*

forage /ˈfɒr.ɪdʒ/ ⓤ /ˈfɔːr-/ *noun* [U] food grown for horses and farm animals: *winter forage* ○ *forage crops.*

foray ATTEMPT /ˈfɒr.eɪ/ ⓤ /ˈfɔːr-/ *noun* [C] a brief involvement in an activity which is different from and outside the range of a usual set of activities: *She **made** a brief foray **into** acting before becoming a teacher.*

foray VISIT /ˈfɒr.eɪ/ ⓤ /ˈfɔːr-/ *noun* [C] a short visit, especially with a known purpose: *I **made** a quick foray **into** town before lunch to get my sister a present.*

foray ATTACK /ˈfɒr.eɪ/ ⓤ /ˈfɔːr-/ *noun* [C] the act of an army suddenly and quickly entering the area belonging to the enemy in order to attack them or steal their supplies

forbear STOP YOURSELF /fɔːˈbeəʳ/ ⓤ /fɔːrˈber/ *verb* [I] **forbore, forborne** *FORMAL* to prevent yourself from saying or doing something, especially in a way that shows control, good judgment or kindness to others: *His plan was such a success that even his original critics could scarcely forbear **from** congratulating him.* ○ *The doctor said she was optimistic about the outcome of the operation but forbore **to** make any promises at this early stage.*

forbearance /fɔːˈbeə.rⁿnts/ ⓤ /fɔːr-/ *noun* [U] *FORMAL* the quality of patience, forgiveness and self-control shown in a difficult situation: [+ **(that)**] *He thanked his employees for the forbearance **(that)** they had shown during the company's difficult times.*

forbearing /fɔːˈbeə.rɪŋ/ ⓤ /fɔːrˈber.ɪŋ/ *adj* *FORMAL* patient and forgiving: *The vicar praised what he called her "kind and forbearing nature".*

forbear PERSON /ˈfɔː.beəʳ/ ⓤ /ˈfɔːr.ber/ *noun* [C usually pl] a **forebear**

forbid /fəˈbɪd/ ⓤ /fɚ-/ *verb* [T] **forbidding, forbade** or *OLD USE* **forbad, forbidden** to refuse to allow something, especially officially, or to prevent a particular plan of action by making it impossible: *The law forbids the sale of cigarettes to people under the age of 16.* ○ [+ **to** infinitive] *He's obviously quite embarrassed about it because he forbade me **to** tell anyone.* ○ *He is forbidden **from** leaving the country.*

● **heaven forbid** (*ALSO* **God forbid**) a way of saying that you hope something does not happen: *Heaven forbid **(that)** his parents should ever find out.*

forbidden /fəˈbɪd.ⁿn/ ⓤ /fɚ-/ *adj* not permitted, especially by law: *Smoking is forbidden in the cinema.*

● **forbidden fruit** *LITERARY* something, especially something sexual, which has a greater attraction because it is not allowed: *He was always drawn to other men's wives – the forbidden fruit.*

forbidding /fəˈbɪd.ɪŋ/ ⓤ /fɚ-/ *adj* unfriendly and likely to be unpleasant or harmful: *Concealed by a forbidding row of security guards, the pop-star left the building.* ○ *With storm clouds rushing over them, the mountains looked dark and forbidding.* **forbiddingly** /fəˈbɪd.ɪŋ.li/ ⓤ /fɚ-/ *adv*

forbore /fɔːˈbɔːʳ/ ⓤ /fɔːrˈbɔːr/ *past simple of* **forbear** STOP YOURSELF

forborne /fɔːˈbɔːn/ ⓤ /fɔːrˈbɔːrn/ *past participle of* **forbear** STOP YOURSELF

force PHYSICAL POWER /fɔːs/ ⓤ /fɔːrs/ *noun* **1** [U] physical, especially violent, strength or power: *The force of the wind had brought down a great many trees in the area.* ○ *She slapped his face with unexpected force.* ○ *Teachers aren't allowed to use force in controlling their pupils.* ○ *The police were able to control the crowd by sheer force **of** numbers* (= because there were more police than there were people in the crowd). **2 in force** in large numbers: *Photographers were out in force at the palace today* **3** [C or U] *SPECIALIZED* in scientific use, (a measure of) the influence which changes movement: *the force of gravity*

• **combine/join forces** to work with someone else in order to achieve something which you both want

force /fɔːs/ [US] /fɔːrs/ *verb* [T] **1** to use physical strength or effort to make something move or open: *Move your leg up gently when you're doing this exercise, but don't force it.* ○ *If you force the zip, it'll break.* ○ *She forced her way through the crowds.* **2** to break a lock, door, window, etc. in order to allow someone to get in: *I forgot my key, so I had to force a window.* ○ [+ adj] *The police had forced* ***open*** *the door because nobody had answered.* ○ *The burglar forced* ***an entry*** (= broke a window, door, etc. to get into the house).

forcible /ˈfɔː.sɪ.bl̩/ [US] /ˈfɔːr-/ *adj* describes actions that involve the use of physical power or of violence: *The police's forcible entry into the building has come under a lot of criticism.* **forcibly** /ˈfɔː.sɪ.bli/ [US] /ˈfɔːr-/ *adv*: *Several rioters were forcibly removed from the town square.*

force [INFLUENCE] /fɔːs/ [US] /fɔːrs/ *noun* [C or U] (a person or thing with a lot of) influence and energy: *He was a powerful force in British politics during the war years.* ○ *A united Europe, he said, would be a great force in world affairs.* ○ *LITERARY* *Fishermen are always at the mercy of* ***the forces of nature*** (= bad weather conditions).

• **a force to be reckoned with** If an organization or a person is described as a force to be reckoned with, it means that they are powerful and have a lot of influence: *The United Nations is now a force to be reckoned with.*

• **the forces of evil** things that have a very bad influence or effect: *Poverty and ignorance, the bishop said, were the forces of evil in our society today.*

• **force of habit** If you do something from force of habit, you do it without thinking because you have done it so often before.

forceful /ˈfɔːs.fəl/ [US] /ˈfɔːrs-/ *adj* expressing opinions strongly and demanding attention or action: *The opposition leader led a very forceful attack on the government in parliament this morning.* ○ *She has a very forceful personality which will serve her well in politics.* **forcefully** /ˈfɔːs.fəl.i/ [US] /ˈfɔːrs-/ *adv*: *He argued forcefully that stricter laws were necessary to deal with the problem.* **forcefulness** /ˈfɔːs.fəl.nəs/ [US] /ˈfɔːrs-/ *noun* [U]

force [GIVE NO CHOICE] /fɔːs/ [US] /fɔːrs/ *verb* [T] to make something happen or make someone do something difficult, unpleasant or unusual, especially by threatening or not offering the possibility of choice: [R + *to* infinitive] *I really have to force myself* ***to*** *be pleasant to him.* ○ [+ *to* infinitive] *You can't force her* ***to*** *make a decision.* ○ *Hospitals are being forced* ***to*** *close departments because of lack of money.* ○ *You could tell he was having to force* ***back*** *the tears* (= stop himself from crying). ○ *I didn't actually want any more dessert, but Julia forced it* ***on*** *me* (= made me accept it). ○ [R] *I couldn't stay at their flat – I'd feel as if I was forcing my****self on*** *them* (= making them allow me to stay). ○ *You never tell me how you're feeling – I have to force it* ***out of*** *you* (= make you tell me)*!*

• **force a laugh/smile** to manage, with difficulty, to laugh or smile: *I managed to force a smile as they were leaving.*

• **force an/the issue** to take action to make certain that an urgent problem or matter is dealt with now: *If the management wouldn't listen to their demands, they would have to force the issue by striking.*

• **force *sb's* hand** to make someone do something they do not want to do, or act sooner than they had intended

forcible /ˈfɔː.sɪ.bl̩/ [US] /ˈfɔːr-/ *adj* happening or done against someone's wishes, especially with the use of physical force: *There's a law to protect refugees from forcible return to countries where they face persecution.*

force [IN OPERATION] /fɔːs/ [US] /fɔːrs/ *noun* **in/into force** (of laws, rules or systems) existing and being used: *New driving regulations are going to* ***come*** *into force later this year.*

force [GROUP] /fɔːs/ [US] /fɔːrs/ *noun* [C] a group of people organized and trained, especially for military, police or a stated purpose: *the security forces* ○ *the work force* ○ *He joined the* ***police*** *force straight after school.*

the ˈforces *plural noun* the military organizations for air, land and sea

forced /fɔːst/ [US] /fɔːrst/ *adj* **1** done against your wishes: *forced repatriation* **2** describes an action which is done because it is suddenly made necessary by a new and usually unexpected situation: *The aeroplane had to make a forced* ***landing*** *because one of the engines cut out.* **3** describes laughter, a smile or an emotion which is produced with effort and is not sincerely felt: *She tried hard to smile but suspected that it looked forced.*

force-feed /ˌfɔːsˈfiːd/ [US] /-ˈfiːd/ *verb* [T] to make a person or animal eat and drink, often sending food to the stomach through a pipe in the mouth: *Eventually, the hunger strikers were force-fed.* ○ *FIGURATIVE* *The whole nation was force-fed government propaganda about how well the country was doing.*

forceps /ˈfɔː.seps/ [US] /ˈfɔːr-/ *plural noun* a metal instrument with two handles used in medical operations for picking up, pulling and holding things

ford /fɔːd/ [US] /fɔːrd/ *noun* [C] an area in a river or stream which is not deep and can be crossed on foot or in a vehicle

ford /fɔːd/ [US] /fɔːrd/ *verb* [T] to cross a river, where it is not deep, on foot or in a vehicle

fore /fɔːʳ/ [US] /fɔːr/ *adj* [before n], *adv* (especially on ships) towards or in the front **fore-** /fɔː-/ [US] /fɔːr-/ *prefix*: *the forelegs* (= front legs) *of a horse* ○ *the foreground* (= things that seem nearest to you) *of a picture*

the fore *noun* [S] public attention or a noticeable position: *Various ecological issues have* ***come to*** *the fore since the discovery of the hole in the Earth's ozone layer.* ○ *The prime minister has deliberately* ***brought to*** *the fore those ministers with a more caring image.* ➲See also **the forefront**.

forearm /ˈfɔː.rɑːm/ [US] /ˈfɔːr.ɑːrm/ *noun* [C] the lower part of the arm, between the wrist and the elbow ➲See picture **The Body** on page Centre 5

forearmed /fɔːˈrɑːmd/ [US] /fɔːrˈɑːrmd/ *adj* **Forewarned is forearmed**, see at **forewarn**

forebear, **forbear** /ˈfɔː.beəʳ/ [US] /ˈfɔːr.ber/ *noun* [C usually pl] *FORMAL* a relative who lived in the past; an **ancestor**

foreboding /fɔːˈbəʊ.dɪŋ/ [US] /fɔːrˈboʊ-/ *noun* [C or U] *LITERARY* a feeling that something very bad is going to happen soon: *There's a* ***sense of*** *foreboding in the capital, as if fighting might at any minute break out.* ○ *Her forebodings about the future were to prove justified.* ○ [+ (*that*)] *He had a strange foreboding* ***(that)*** *something would go wrong.*

forecast /ˈfɔː.kɑːst/ [US] /ˈfɔːr.kæst/ *noun* [C] a statement of what is judged likely to happen in the future, especially in connection with a particular situation, or the expected weather conditions: ***economic*** *forecasts* ○ *The* ***weather*** *forecast said it was going to rain later today.*

forecast /ˈfɔː.kɑːst/ [US] /ˈfɔːr.kæst/ *verb* [T] **forecast** or **forecasted**, **forecast** or **forecasted** to say what you expect to happen in the future: *They forecast a large drop in unemployment over the next two years.* ○ *Snow has been forecast* ***for*** *tonight.* ○ [+ *to* infinitive] *Oil prices are forecast* ***to*** *increase by less than 2% this year.*

forecaster /ˈfɔː.kɑː.stəʳ/ [US] /ˈfɔːr.kæs.tɚ/ *noun* [C] a person who tells you what particular conditions are expected to be like: *an economic forecaster* ○ *a weather forecaster*

foreclose [TAKE POSSESSION] /fɔːˈkləʊz/ [US] /fɔːrˈkloʊz/ *verb* [I or T] *SPECIALIZED* (especially of banks) to take back property that was bought with borrowed money because the money was not being paid back as formally agreed **foreclosure** /fɔːˈkləʊ.ʒəʳ/ [US] /fɔːrˈkloʊ.ʒɚ/ *noun* [U]

foreclose [PREVENT] /fɔːˈkləʊz/ [US] /fɔːrˈkloʊz/ *verb* [T] *FORMAL* to prevent something from being considered as a possibility in the future: *The leader's aggressive stance seems to have foreclosed any chance of diplomatic compromise.*

forecourt /ˈfɔː.kɔːt/ [US] /ˈfɔːr.kɔːrt/ *noun* [C] **1** a flat area in front of a large building: *the garage forecourt* **2** *SPECIALIZED* the area next to the net in sports such as tennis

foredoomed /fɔːˈduːmd/ [US] /fɔːr-/ *adj* LITERARY (especially of planned activities) going to fail; extremely unlucky from the beginning: *The whole project seemed foredoomed* ***to*** *failure from the start.*

forefathers /ˈfɔːˌfɑː.ðəz/ [US] /ˈfɔːrˌfɑː.ðɚz/ *plural noun* LITERARY relatives who lived in the past

forefinger /ˈfɔːˌfɪŋ.gəʳ/ [US] /ˈfɔːrˌfɪŋ.gɚ/ *noun* [C] (ALSO **index finger**) the finger next to the thumb

forefoot /ˈfɔː.fʊt/ [US] /ˈfɔːr-/ *noun* [C] *plural* **forefeet** one of the two front feet of a four-legged animal

the forefront /ðəˈfɔː.frʌnt/ [US] /-ˈfɔːr-/ *noun* [S] the most noticeable or important position: *She was one of the politicians* ***at/in*** *the forefront* ***of*** *the campaign to free the prisoners.* ○ *His team are* ***at*** *the forefront* ***of*** *scientific research into vaccines.*

F

forego /fɔːˈgəʊ/ [US] /fɔːrˈgoʊ/ *verb* [T] **foregoing, forewent, foregone** to **forgo**

the foregoing /ðəˈfɔː.gəʊ.ɪŋ/ [US] /-ˈfɔːr.goʊ-/ *noun* [S] FORMAL what has just been mentioned or described: *I can testify to the foregoing since I was actually present when it happened.* **foregoing** /ˈfɔː.gəʊ.ɪŋ/ [US] /ˈfɔːr.goʊ-/ *adj* [before n] *The foregoing account was written fifty years after the incident.*

foregone conclusion /ˌfɔː.gɒn.kənˈkluː.ʒən/ [US] /ˌfɔːr.gɑːn.-/ *noun* [C usually sing] a result that is obvious to everyone even before it happens: *The result of the election seems to be a foregone conclusion.*

the foreground /ðəˈfɔː.graʊnd/ [US] /-ˈfɔːr-/ *noun* [S] **1** the people, objects, countryside, etc. in a picture or photograph that seem nearest to you and form its main part: ***In*** *the foreground of the painting is a horse and cart.* ➲Compare **background** THINGS BEHIND. **2** the area of most importance and activity, or which people pay attention to: *Historically, issues of this kind have not occupied the foreground* ***of*** *political debate.*

forehand /ˈfɔː.hænd/ [US] /ˈfɔːr-/ *noun* [C] (in sports such as tennis) a hit in which the palm of the hand which is holding the RACKET faces the same direction as the hit itself, or the player's ability to perform this hit: *a forehand volley* ○ *His forehand is his weakest shot.* ○ *serve to her forehand* ➲Compare **backhand**.

forehead /ˈfɒr.ɪd/ /ˈfɔː.hed/ [US] /ˈfɑː.rɪd/ *noun* [C] the flat part of the face, above the eyes and below the hair: *She's got a* ***high*** *forehead.* ➲See picture **The Body** on page Centre 5

foreign /ˈfɒr.ən/ [US] /ˈfɔːr-/ *adj* **1** belonging or connected to a country which is not your own: *Spain was the first foreign country she had visited.* ○ *foreign languages* ○ *His work provided him with the opportunity for a lot of foreign travel.* **2** FORMAL **foreign to** Something can be described as foreign to a particular person if it is unknown to them or not within their experience: *The whole concept of democracy, she claimed, was utterly foreign to the present government.* **3** describes an object or substance which has entered something else, possibly by accident, and does not belong there: *a foreign object/substance* ○ *foreign matter*

foreigner /ˈfɒr.ə.nəʳ/ [US] /ˈfɔːr.ə.nɚ/ *noun* [C] a person who comes from another country

COMMON LEARNER ERROR

foreign (spelling)

Many learners make mistakes when spelling this word. The correct spelling of the last syllable is 'eign'.

The past is a foreign country.

ˌforeign afˈfairs *plural noun* matters that are connected with other countries

ˌforeign ˈaid *noun* [U] the help that is given by a richer country to a poorer one, usually in the form of money or food

ˌforeign exˈchange *noun* [C usually sing] the system by which the type of money used in one country is exchanged for another country's money, making international trade easier: *On the foreign-exchange markets the pound remained firm.*

the ˈForeign ˌOffice *noun* in Britain, the department of the government which deals with Britain's connections with other countries

foreknowledge /fɔːˈnɒl.ɪdʒ/ [US] /fɔːrˈnɑː.lɪdʒ/ *noun* [U] FORMAL knowledge of an event before it happens

foreleg /ˈfɔː.leg/ [US] /ˈfɔːr-/ *noun* [C] one of the two front legs of a four-legged animal

forelock /ˈfɔː.lɒk/ [US] /ˈfɔːr.lɑːk/ *noun* [C] a piece of hair which grows or falls over the forehead or the part of a horse's MANE that falls forward between its ears

• **tug at/touch *your* forelock** to show respect to someone in a higher position than you in a way that seems old-fashioned

foreman /ˈfɔː.mən/ [US] /ˈfɔːr-/ *noun* [C] **1** a skilled person with experience who is in charge of and watches over a group of workers **2** in a court of law, one member of the jury who is chosen to be in charge of their discussions and to speak officially for them

foremost /ˈfɔː.məʊst/ [US] /ˈfɔːr.moʊst/ *adj* most important or best; leading: *She's one of the foremost experts on child psychology.* ○ *This is one of the country's foremost arts centres.*

forename /ˈfɔː.neɪm/ [US] /ˈfɔːr-/ *noun* [C] FORMAL the name which is chosen for you at birth and goes before your family name

forensic /fəˈren.zɪk/ *adj* [before n] related to scientific methods of solving crimes, involving examining the objects or substances that are involved in the crime: *forensic evidence/medicine/science* ○ *Forensic examination revealed a large quantity of poison in the dead man's stomach.*

foreplay /ˈfɔː.pleɪ/ [US] /ˈfɔːr-/ *noun* [U] the sexual activity such as kissing and touching that people do before they have sex

forerunner /ˈfɔːˌrʌn.əʳ/ [US] /ˈfɔːrˌrʌn.ɚ/ *noun* [C] something or someone that acts as an early and less advanced model for what will appear in the future, or a warning or sign of what is to follow: *Germany's Green party was said to be the forerunner* ***of*** *environmental parties throughout Europe.* ○ *The drop in share prices in March was a forerunner* ***of*** *the financial crash that followed in June.*

foresee /fəˈsiː/ [US] /fɚ-/ *verb* [T] **foreseeing, foresaw, foreseen** to know about something before it happens: *I don't foresee any difficulties so long as we keep within budget.*

foreseeable /fɔːˈsiː.ə.bl̩/ [US] /fɔːr-/ *adj* A foreseeable event or situation is one that can be known about or guessed before it happens.

• **in/for the foreseeable future** as far into the future as you can imagine or plan for: *I'll certainly carry on living here for the foreseeable future.* ○ *He asked me if there was any point in the foreseeable future when I'd like to have children.*

foreshadow /fɔːˈʃæd.əʊ/ [US] /fɔːrˈʃæd.oʊ/ *verb* [T] FORMAL to act as a warning or sign of a future event: *The recent outbreak of violence was foreshadowed by isolated incidents in the city earlier this year.*

the foreshore /ðəˈfɔː.ʃɔːʳ/ [US] /-ˈfɔːr.ʃɔːr/ *noun* [S] SPECIALIZED the part of the land next to the sea which is between the limits reached by high and low tide, or any part of this land that does not have grass or buildings on it

foreshorten /fɔːˈʃɔː.tən/ [US] /fɔːrˈʃɔːr.t̬ən/ *verb* [T] **1** SPECIALIZED to draw, paint or photograph people or objects to make them seem smaller or closer together than they really are **2** to reduce or shorten: *Smoking was certainly one of the factors that foreshortened his life.* **foreshortened** /fɔːˈʃɔː.tənd/ [US] /fɔːrˈʃɔːr.t̬ənd/ *adj*

foresight /ˈfɔː.saɪt/ [US] /ˈfɔːr-/ *noun* [U] the ability to judge correctly what is going to happen in the future and plan your actions based on this knowledge: *She'd had the foresight to sell her apartment just before house prices came down.*

foreskin /ˈfɔː.skɪn/ [US] /ˈfɔːr-/ *noun* [C] the loose skin which covers the end of the penis

forest /ˈfɒr.ɪst/ [US] /ˈfɔːr-/ *noun* [C or U] a large area of land covered with trees and plants, usually larger than a wood, or the trees and plants themselves: *the Black Forest* ○ *The children got lost* ***in*** *the forest.*

forester /ˈfɒr.ɪ.stəʳ/ [US] /ˈfɔːr.ɪ.stɚ/ *noun* [C] a person who is in charge of taking care of a forest

forestry /ˈfɒr.ɪ.stri/ [US] /ˈfɔːr-/ *noun* [U] the science of planting and taking care of large areas of trees

forestall /fɔːˈstɔːl/ [US] /fɔːrˈstɑːl/ *verb* [T] to prevent something from happening by acting first: *The government forestalled criticism by holding a public enquiry into the matter.*

foretaste /ˈfɔː.teɪst/ [US] /ˈfɔːr-/ *noun* [S] something that gives you an idea of what something else is like by allowing you to experience a small example of it in advance: *a foretaste of spring* ○ *The recent factory closures and job losses are just a foretaste of the recession that is to come.*

foretell /fɔːˈtel/ [US] /fɔːr-/ *verb* [T] **foretold, foretold** *LITERARY* to state what is going to happen in the future: [+ question word] *He was a sixteenth-century prophet who foretold **how** the world would end.*

forethought /ˈfɔː.θɔːt/ [US] /ˈfɔːr.θɑːt/ *noun* [U] the good judgment to consider the near future in your present actions; planning in advance: *I'm glad I had the forethought to make a copy of the letter, as proof of what had been promised.*

forever, *UK ALSO* **for ever** /fəˈre.vəʳ/ [US] /fɔːˈrev.ɚ/ *adv* **1** for all time: *I like the house but I don't imagine I'll live there forever.* **2** *INFORMAL* continually, suggesting too often: *She's forever telling him she's going to leave him but she never actually does.* **3** for an extremely long time or too much time: *We'd better walk a bit quicker – it's going to **take** forever if we go at this pace.*

forewarn /fɔːˈwɔːn/ [US] /fɔːrˈwɔːrn/ *verb* [T] to tell someone that something unpleasant is going to happen: [+ (*that*)] *The employees had been forewarned **(that)** the end-of-year financial results would be poor.*

• **Forewarned is forearmed.** *SAYING* This means that if you know about something before it happens, you can be prepared for it.

forewoman /ˈfɔːˌwʊm.ən/ [US] /ˈfɔːr-/ *noun* [C] a female FOREMAN

foreword /ˈfɔː.wɜːd/ [US] /ˈfɔːr.wɝːd/ *noun* [C] a short piece of writing at the beginning of a book, sometimes praise by a famous person or someone who is not the writer

forfeit /ˈfɔː.fɪt/ [US] /ˈfɔːr-/ *verb* [T] to lose the right to do or have something because you have broken a rule: *If you cancel now I'm afraid you forfeit your deposit.* ○ *These people have forfeited the right to live in society.*

forfeit /ˈfɔː.fɪt/ [US] /ˈfɔːr-/ *noun* [C] **1** something that you have lost the right to do or have because you have broken a rule **2 pay a forfeit** to give up something, especially in a game

forfeit /ˈfɔː.fɪt/ [US] /ˈfɔːr-/ *adj* [after v] *FORMAL* taken away from someone as a punishment

forfeiture /ˈfɔː.fɪ.tʃəʳ/ [US] /ˈfɔːr.fɪ.tʃɚ/ *noun* [C or U] *LEGAL* the loss of rights, property or money, especially as a result of breaking a legal agreement: *He was deep in debt and faced with forfeiture of his property.*

forgave /fəˈgeɪv/ [US] /fɚ-/ *past simple of* **forgive**

forge [COPY] /fɔːdʒ/ [US] /fɔːrdʒ/ *verb* [T] to make an illegal copy of something in order to deceive: *a forged passport* ○ *a forged signature* ○ *A number of forged works of art have been sold as genuine.*

forger /ˈfɔː.dʒəʳ/ [US] /ˈfɔːr.dʒɚ/ *noun* [C] someone who makes forged copies: *an art forger*

forgery /ˈfɔː.dʒəʳr.i/ [US] /ˈfɔːr.dʒɚ.i/ *noun* [C or U] an illegal copy of a document, painting, etc. or the crime of making such illegal copies: *These banknotes are forgeries.* ○ *He increased his income by forgery.*

forge [WORK AREA] /fɔːdʒ/ [US] /fɔːrdʒ/ *noun* [C] a working area with a fire for heating metal until it is soft enough to be beaten into different shapes: *a blacksmith's forge*

forge [MAKE] /fɔːdʒ/ [US] /fɔːrdʒ/ *verb* [T] to make or produce, especially with some difficulty: *The accident forged a **close bond** between the two families.* ○ *She forged a new career for herself as a singer.*

forge [MOVE] /fɔːdʒ/ [US] /fɔːrdʒ/ *verb* [I + adv or prep] *FORMAL* to suddenly and quickly move forward: *Just 100 metres from the finishing line Jackson forged ahead.* ○ *She forged down the straight.*

▲ **forge ahead** *phrasal verb* to suddenly make a lot of progress with something: *The organizers are forging ahead with a programme of public events.*

forget [NOT REMEMBER] /fəˈget/ [US] /fɚ-/ *verb* [I or T] **forgetting, forgot, forgotten** to be unable to remember a fact, something that happened, or how to do something: *I'm sorry, I've forgotten your name.* ○ *Let me write down that date before I forget it.* ○ *I completely forgot **about** Gemma's party.* ○ [+ (*that*)] *We had forgotten **(that)** she doesn't come on Thursdays.* ○ *I'm sorry, I was forgetting* (= I had forgotten) ***(that)*** *you would be away in August.* ○ [+ v-*ing*] *She would never forget see**ing** the Himalayas for the first time.* ○ [+ question word] *I've forgotten **wh**at you do next/**how** to do it.* ○ *I never forget **a face*** (= I'm good at remembering people).

• **forget it** *INFORMAL* **1** used to tell someone that what they want is impossible: *"I'd like to take a week's holiday." "Forget it, we're way too busy."* **2** used to tell someone that something is not important and not to worry about it: *"I'm so sorry about that cup." "Oh, forget it – I've got plenty."*

• **and don't you forget it** used to tell someone that a particular fact is important and it should influence the way they behave: *I've been in the job longer than you and don't you forget it!*

• **not forgetting** including: *This is where we keep all the books, not forgetting the magazines and newspapers.*

forget [NOT DO] /fəˈget/ [US] /fɚ-/ *verb* [I + *to* infinitive; T] **forgetting, forgot, forgotten** to not remember to do something: *Don't forget to lock the door.* ○ *Dad's always forgetting (to take) his pills.*

forget [NOT BRING] /fəˈget/ [US] /fɚ-/ *verb* [T] **forgetting, forgot, forgotten** to not bring something with you because you did not remember it: *I've forgotten my keys.*

forget [STOP THINKING] /fəˈget/ [US] /fɚ-/ *verb* [I or T] **forgetting, forgot, forgotten** to stop thinking about someone or something: *He tried to forget her.* ○ *It seemed unlikely that the debt would ever be paid so we just forgot **(about)** it.*

forget *yourself* [BEHAVE BADLY] *verb* [R] to act in a socially unacceptable way because you have lost control of your emotions: *He was so angry he forgot himself and swore loudly.*

forgetful /fəˈget.fəl/ [US] /fɚ-/ *adj* often forgetting things: *She's getting very forgetful in her old age.* **forgetfully** /fəˈget.fəl.i/ [US] /fɚ-/ *adv* **forgetfulness** /fəˈget.fəl.nəs/ [US] /fɚ-/ *noun* [U]

forget-me-not /fəˈget.mi.nɒt/ [US] /fɚˈget.mi.nɑːt/ *noun* [C] a small garden plant with blue or pink flowers which grows from seed every year

forgettable /fəˈget.ə.bl/ [US] /fɚˈget̬-/ *adj* not important or good enough to be remembered: *a forgettable film/song* ○ *Dennis White scored the only goal in an otherwise forgettable match.*

forgive /fəˈgɪv/ [US] /fɚ-/ *verb* [I or T; not continuous] **forgave, forgiven** to stop blaming or being angry with someone for something they have done, or not punish them for something: *I don't think she's ever quite forgiven me **for** getting her name wrong that time.* ○ *I've never found it easy to forgive **and forget*** (= to behave as if something wrong had never happened). ○ [R] *I'd never forgive myself if anything happened to the kids.*

• **forgive me** *FORMAL* used before you ask or say something that might seem rude: *Forgive me for asking, but how much did you pay for your bag?*

forgivable /fəˈgɪv.ə.bl/ [US] /fɚ-/ *adj* describes something that you are able to forgive because you understand it: *a forgivable mistake*

forgiveness /fəˈgɪv.nəs/ [US] /fɚ-/ *noun* [U] the act of forgiving or the willingness to forgive: *to ask for/beg forgiveness*

forgiving /fəˈgɪv.ɪŋ/ [US] /fɚ-/ *adj* willing to forgive: *She's very forgiving.*

forgo (**forgoing, forwent, forgone**) /fɔːˈgəʊ/ [US] /fɔːrˈgoʊ/ *verb* [T] (*ALSO* **forego**) *FORMAL* to not have or do something enjoyable: *I shall have to forgo **the pleasure of** seeing you this week.*

F

Fork

pitchfork

forked lightning

fork (cutlery)

garden fork

tuning fork

fork in the road

fork FOOD /fɔːk/ ⓤ /fɔːrk/ *noun* [C] a small object with three or four points and a handle, that you use to pick up food and eat with: *a **knife** and fork*. **forkful** /'fɔːk.ful/ ⓤ /'fɔːrk-/ *noun* [C] *a forkful of baked beans*

fork GARDEN /fɔːk/ ⓤ /fɔːrk/ *noun* [C] a tool with a long handle and three or four points, used for digging and breaking soil into pieces: *a **garden** fork.*

fork /fɔːk/ ⓤ /fɔːrk/ *verb* [T] to move or dig something with a fork

fork DIVISION /fɔːk/ ⓤ /fɔːrk/ *noun* [C] a place where a road or river etc. divides into two parts, or either of those two parts: *When you reach a fork **in the road** take the right-hand path.*

fork /fɔːk/ ⓤ /fɔːrk/ *verb* **1** [I] If a road or river forks, it divides into two parts: *The pub is near where the road forks.* **2** [I + adv or prep] *UK* to turn in one of two different directions: *Fork **left/right** where the road divides.*

forked /fɔːkt/ ⓤ /fɔːrkt/ *adj* with one end divided into two parts: *a **forked** tail* ○ *a snake's forked tongue* ○ *forked lightning*

PHRASAL VERBS WITH fork ▼

▲ **fork** *(sth)* **out** *phrasal verb* [M] INFORMAL to pay, especially unwillingly: *I forked out ten quid **for/on** the ticket.* ○ *I couldn't persuade him to fork out **for** a new one.*

▲ **fork over/up** *sth phrasal verb* [M] *US INFORMAL* to give something, especially money to someone, especially when you do not want to: *We had to fork over ten bucks to park near the stadium.* ○ *Hey, that's mine. Fork it over!*

,**forked** '**tongue** *noun* **speak with a forked tongue** to tell lies or say one thing and mean something else

---

fork-lift (truck) /,fɔːk.lɪft'trʌk/ ⓤ /,fɔːrk-/ *noun* [C] a small vehicle which has two strong bars of metal fixed to the front used for lifting piles of goods ⊃See picture **Cars and Trucks** on page Centre 13

forlorn /fə'lɔːn/ ⓤ /fɚ'lɔːrn/ *adj* **1** LITERARY alone and unhappy; left alone and not cared for: *She looked a forlorn figure standing at the bus stop.* **2** [before n] very unlikely to be achieved or to succeed: *Their only hope now is that the outside world will intervene but it is an increasingly forlorn **hope**.* ○ *She appeared on daytime TV in a forlorn **attempt** to persuade the public of her innocence.*

forlornly /fə'lɔːn.li/ ⓤ /fɚ'lɔːrn.li/ *adv*: *She sat forlornly* (= alone and unhappy) *looking out to sea.*

form SHAPE /fɔːm/ ⓤ /fɔːrm/ *noun* [C] the shape or appearance of something: *I could just about make out his sleeping form on the bed.* ○ *The moon highlighted the shadowy forms of the hills.* ○ *The lawn was laid out **in the** form of the figure eight.*

● **take form** to gradually be seen or gradually develop: *Trees and hedges started to take form as the fog cleared.* ○ *As they chatted, the idea of a holiday together gradually took form.*

form /fɔːm/ ⓤ /fɔːrm/ *verb* **1** [I or T] to begin to exist or to make something begin to exist: *A crowd formed around the accident.* ○ *A solution began to form in her mind.* ○ *She formed the clay **into** a small bowl.* ○ *I formed **the impression** (= the way she behaved suggested to me) that she didn't really want to come.* **2** [I] (ALSO **form up**) SLIGHTLY FORMAL If separate things form, they come together to make a whole: *The children formed into lines.* ○ *The procession formed up and moved off slowly.* **3** [L only + n] to make or be something: *The lorries formed a barricade across the road.* ○ *Together they would form the next government.* ○ *This information formed the basis of the report.*

formation /fɔː'meɪ.ʃ°n/ ⓤ /fɔːr-/ *noun* **1** [C] the way something is naturally made or the way it has been arranged: *a rock formation* ○ *cloud formations* **2** [U] the development of something into a particular thing or shape: *the formation of a crystal* **3** [C] **in formation** Activities which are done in formation are done in a pattern by a number of people, vehicles, etc: *marching in close formation*

formative /'fɔː.mə.tɪv/ ⓤ /'fɔːr.mə.tɪv/ *adj* FORMAL relating to the time when someone or something is starting to develop in character: *She spent her formative **years** in Africa.* ○ *a formative experience/influence* ○ *a formative period*

formless /'fɔːm.ləs/ ⓤ /'fɔːrm-/ *adj* without clear shape or expression

form GRAMMAR /fɔːm/ ⓤ /fɔːrm/ *noun* [C] a part of a verb, or a different but related word: *The continuous form of 'stand' is 'standing'.* ○ *'Stood' is an inflected form of 'stand'.* ○ *'Hers' is the possessive form of 'her'.* ○ *'Isn't' is the short form of 'is not'.*

form DOCUMENT /fɔːm/ ⓤ /fɔːrm/ *noun* [C] a paper or set of papers printed with marked spaces in which answers to questions can be written or information can be recorded in an organized way: *an application form* (= document used for asking officially for something, for example a job) ○ *an entry form* (= document used to enter a competition) ○ *Please **fill in/out** the form with black ink.* ○ *When you have **completed** the form, hand it in at the desk.*

form TYPE /fɔːm/ ⓤ /fɔːrm/ *noun* [C] a type of something: *Swimming is the best form **of** exercise.*

form SCHOOL GROUP /fɔːm/ ⓤ /fɔːrm/ *noun* [C] in the UK, a class of school children or a group of classes of children of a similar age

-former /-fɔː.məʳ/ ⓤ /-fɔːr.mɚ/ *suffix*: *sixth-formers* (= students usually aged 16-18)

form BEHAVIOUR /fɔːm/ ⓤ /fɔːrm/ *noun* OLD-FASHIONED **bad form** rude behaviour: *Was that bad form then, leaving so early?*

form ABILITY /fɔːm/ ⓤ /fɔːrm/ *noun* [U] A competitor's form is their ability to be successful over a period of time: *Both horses have shown good form over the last season.* ○ *After a bad year, she has regained her form.*

● **be on good/great, etc. form** *UK* (*US* **be in good/great, etc. form**) to be feeling or performing well: *Paul was on good* *form at the wedding and kept everyone entertained.*

formal SERIOUS /ˈfɔː.məl/ ⓤ /ˈfɔːr-/ *adj* describes language, clothes and behaviour that are serious and correct: *a formal dinner party* **formally** /ˈfɔː.mə.li/ ⓤ /ˈfɔːr-/ *adv*: *He was formally dressed in a grey suit.* ○ *The headteacher greeted us very formally.*

formality /fɔːˈmæl.ə.ti/ ⓤ /- t̬i/ *noun* [U] *She found the formality* (= serious and not relaxed behaviour) *of the occasion rather daunting.* ○ *A note of formality in his voice alerted her to the fact that others were listening.*

formal OFFICIAL /ˈfɔː.məl/ ⓤ /ˈfɔːr-/ *adj* **1** public or official: *formal procedures* ○ *a formal announcement* **2** in appearance or by name only: *I am the formal leader of the project but the everyday management is in the hands of my assistant.*

formalize, *UK USUALLY* **-ise** /ˈfɔː.mə.laɪz/ ⓤ /ˈfɔːr-/ *verb* [T] to make something official or decide to arrange it according to a fixed structure: *They started as informal gatherings but they have become increasingly formalized in the last few years.* ○ *We need to formalize our initial thoughts about the way to proceed.*

formally /ˈfɔː.mə.li/ ⓤ /ˈfɔːr-/ *adv* officially: *The deal will be formally announced on Tuesday.*

formal EDUCATION /ˈfɔː.məl/ ⓤ /ˈfɔːr-/ *adj* describes education or training received in a school or college: *Tom had little in the way of a formal **education**.*

formal GARDEN /ˈfɔː.məl/ ⓤ /ˈfɔːr-/ *adj* A formal garden is carefully designed and kept according to a plan, and it is not allowed to grow naturally. **formally** /ˈfɔː.mə.li/ ⓤ /ˈfɔːr-/ *adv*

formality /fɔːˈmæl.ə.ti/ ⓤ /-t̬i/ *noun* [C] something which has to be done but which has no real importance: *You'll have to sign the visitors' book, but **it's just a** formality.*

formalities /fɔːˈmæl.ə.tiz/ ⓤ /-t̬iz/ *plural noun* something that the law or an official process says must be done: *We'll have to observe the formalities* (= do what is expected).

format /ˈfɔː.mæt/ ⓤ /ˈfɔːr-/ *noun* [C or U] **1** a pattern, plan or arrangement: *The meeting will have the usual format – introductory session, group work and then a time for reporting back.* **2** SPECIALIZED the way in which information is arranged and stored on a computer

format /ˈfɔː.mæt/ ⓤ /ˈfɔːr-/ *verb* [T] **-tt-** **1** to organize or arrange text, especially on a computer, according to a chosen pattern **2** to prepare a computer disk for use with a particular type of computer

former EARLIER /ˈfɔː.mə r/ ⓤ /ˈfɔːr.mə r/ *adj* [before n] of or in an earlier time; before the present time or in the past: *his former wife* ○ *a former employer* ○ *the former president of the United States* ○ *The house, a former barn, has been attractively converted.* ○ *The painting was then restored to its former **glory*** (= returned to its original good condition). ○ *It was a long time after the accident before he seemed like his former **self*** (= behaved in the way he had done before).

formerly /ˈfɔː.mə.li/ ⓤ /ˈfɔːr.mə-/ *adv* FORMAL in the past: *The European Union was formerly called the European Community.*

the ˈformer FIRST *noun* [S] the first of two people, things or groups previously mentioned: *Of the two suggestions, I prefer the former.* ⊃Compare **the latter** SECOND.

Formica /fɔːˈmaɪ.kə/ ⓤ /fɔːr-/ *noun* [U] TRADEMARK a type of hard plastic made into a thin sheet which is used to cover table tops and other pieces of especially kitchen furniture

formidable /fɔːˈmɪ.də.bl̩/ ⓤ /fɔːr-/ *adj* causing you to have fear or respect for something or someone because they are impressive, powerful or difficult: *a formidable obstacle/task* ○ *a formidable adversary/enemy/opponent* ○ *a formidable intellect* ○ DISAPPROVING *the director and his formidable wife* **formidably** /fɔːˈmɪd.ə.bli/ ⓤ /fɔːr-/ *adv*

formula /ˈfɔː.mjʊ.lə/ ⓤ /ˈfɔːr-/ *noun plural* **formulas** or **formulae** **1** [C] a standard or accepted way of doing or making something, the items needed for it, or a mathematical rule expressed in a set of numbers and letters: *We have changed the formula **of** the washing powder.* ○ *We had to learn chemical formulae at school,*

but I can only remember H_2O for water. ○ *There's no magic formula **for** success.* **2** [U] artificial milk which can be given to babies instead of milk from their mother

formulate /ˈfɔː.mjʊ.leɪt/ ⓤ /ˈfɔːr-/ *verb* [T] to develop all the details of a plan for doing something: *to formulate a new plan* ○ *to formulate legislation* **formulation** /ˌfɔː.mjʊˈleɪ.ʃ ə n/ ⓤ /ˌfɔːr-/ *noun* [C or U]

formulaic /ˌfɔː.mjʊˈleɪ.ɪk/ ⓤ /ˌfɔːr-/ *adj* FORMAL containing or consisting of fixed and repeated groups of words or ideas: *The text was dull and formulaic.*

fornicate /ˈfɔː.nɪ.keɪt/ ⓤ /ˈfɔːr-/ *verb* [I] FORMAL DISAPPROVING to have sex with someone who you are not married to **fornication** /ˌfɔː.nɪˈkeɪ.ʃ ə n/ ⓤ /ˌfɔːr-/ *noun* [U] **fornicator** /ˈfɔː.nɪ.keɪ.tə r/ ⓤ /ˈfɔːr.nɪ.keɪ.t̬ə-/ *noun* [C]

forsake LEAVE /fɔːˈseɪk/ ⓤ /fɔːr-/ *verb* [T] **forsook**, **forsaken** LITERARY to leave someone forever, especially when they need you: *Do not forsake me!*

forsake STOP /fɔːˈseɪk/ ⓤ /fɔːr-/ *verb* [T] **forsook**, **forsaken** FORMAL to stop doing or having something: *He decided to forsake politics for journalism.*

forswear /fɔːˈsweə r/ ⓤ /fɔːrˈswer/ *verb* [T] **forswore**, **forsworn** FORMAL to make a serious decision to stop doing something: *to forswear alcohol*

forsythia /fɔːˈsaɪ.θi.ə/ ⓤ /fɔːr-/ *noun* [C] a medium-sized bush grown in gardens, which has yellow flowers before the leaves appear

fort /fɔːt/ ⓤ /fɔːrt/ *noun* [C] a military building consisting of an area enclosed by a strong wall, in which soldiers live and which is designed to be defended from attack: *The remains of the Roman fort are well preserved.*

forte /ˈfɔː.teɪ/ ⓤ /ˈfɔːr-/ *noun* [C usually sing] a strong ability, something that a person can do well: *I'm afraid sewing isn't one of my fortes.*

forth /fɔːθ/ ⓤ /fɔːrθ/ *adv* FORMAL (from a place) out or away, or (from a point in time) forward: *They set forth on their travels in early June.* ○ *From that day forth he never drank again.* ⊃See also **back and forth** at **back** FURTHER AWAY; **hold forth**.

forthcoming SOON /ˌfɔːθˈkʌm.ɪŋ/ ⓤ /ˌfɔːrθ-/ *adj* [before n] happening soon: *We have just received the information about the forthcoming conference.*

forthcoming WILLING /ˌfɔːθˈkʌm.ɪŋ/ ⓤ /ˌfɔːrθ-/ *adj* friendly and helpful, willing to give information or to talk: *I had difficulty getting any details. He wasn't very forthcoming.*

forthcoming SUPPLIED /ˌfɔːθˈkʌm.ɪŋ/ ⓤ /ˌfɔːrθ-/ *adj* [after v] produced, supplied, given: *No explanation for his absence was forthcoming.* ○ *Will financial support for the theatre project be forthcoming?*

forthright /ˈfɔːθ.raɪt/ ⓤ /ˈfɔːrθ-/ *adj* (too) honest or direct in behaviour: *His forthright manner can be mistaken for rudeness.* ○ *I admire her forthright way of dealing with people.* **forthrightness** /ˈfɔːθ.raɪt.nəs/ ⓤ /ˈfɔːrθ-/ *noun* [U]

forthwith /ˌfɔːθˈwɪθ/ ⓤ /ˌfɔːrθ-/ *adv* FORMAL immediately: *We expect these practices to cease forthwith.*

fortified ˈwine *noun* [C] a wine that contains more alcohol than wines usually do: *Sherry and Martini are fortified wines.*

fortify /ˈfɔː.tɪ.faɪ/ ⓤ /ˈfɔːr.t̬ə-/ *verb* [T] to strengthen something, especially in order to protect it: *a fortified town* ○ *They hurriedly fortified the village **with** barricades of carts, tree trunks and whatever came to hand.* ○ *The argument had fortified her resolve to prove she was right.* ○ *He fortified himself **with** a drink and a sandwich before driving on.* ○ *a fruit drink fortified **with** vitamin C* (= with vitamin C added)

fortification /ˌfɔː.tɪ.fɪˈkeɪ.ʃ ə n/ ⓤ /ˌfɔːr.t̬ə-/ *noun* **1** [C usually pl] strong walls, towers, etc. that are built to protect a place: *The fortifications of the castle were massive and impenetrable.* **2** [U] the act of fortifying something

fortitude /ˈfɔː.tɪ.tjuːd/ ⓤ /ˈfɔːr.t̬ə.tuːd/ *noun* [U] FORMAL bravery over a long period: *I thought she showed remarkable fortitude during that period.*

Fort Knox /ˌfɔːtˈnɒks/ ⓤ /ˌfɔːrtˈnɑːks/ *noun* HUMOROUS **be like Fort Knox** If a building or an area is like Fort Knox, it is impossible to enter or leave it because it is so well protected.

fortnight /ˈfɔːt.naɪt/ [US] /ˈfɔːrt-/ *noun* [C usually sing] *UK* a period of two weeks: *a fortnight's holiday* ○ *once a fortnight* ○ *a fortnight ago* **fortnightly** /ˈfɔːt.naɪt.li/ [US] /ˈfɔːrt-/ *adj, adv*: *We make a fortnightly check on supplies.* ○ *The group meets fortnightly on Tuesdays.*

fortress /ˈfɔː.trəs/ [US] /ˈfɔːr-/ *noun* [C] a large strong building or group of buildings which can be defended from attack

fortuitous /fɔːˈtjuː.ɪ.təs/ [US] /fɔːrˈtuː.ə.t̬əs/ *adj FORMAL* (of something that is to your advantage) not planned, happening by chance: *The timing of the meeting is certainly fortuitous.* ○ *The collapse of its rivals brought fortuitous gains to the company.* **fortuitously** /fɔː-ˈtjuː.ɪ.tə.sli/ [US] /fɔːrˈtuː.ə.t̬ə.sli/ *adv* **fortuitousness** /fɔː-ˈtjuː.ɪ.tə.snəs/ [US] /fɔːrˈtuː.ə.t̬ə.snəs/ *noun* [U]

fortunate /ˈfɔː.tʃən.ət/ [US] /ˈfɔːr-/ *adj APPROVING* lucky: [+ **to** infinitive] *You're very fortunate **to** have found such a lovely house.* ○ *He was fortunate **in** his choice of assistant.* ○ [+ **that**] *It was fortunate **that** they had left in plenty of time.* * NOTE: The opposite is **unfortunate**.

fortunately /ˈfɔː.tʃən.ət.li/ [US] /ˈfɔːr-/ *adv* happening because of good luck: *Fortunately, we got home before it started to rain.* * NOTE: The opposite is **unfortunately**.

fortune [WEALTH] /ˈfɔː.tʃuːn/ [US] /ˈfɔːr-/ *noun* [C] a large amount of money, goods, property, etc: *She inherited a fortune from her grandmother.* ○ *He lost a fortune gambling.* ○ *You can **make** a fortune out of junk if you call it 'antiques'.* ○ *This dress **cost** a **(small)** fortune.* ○ *Any painting by Van Gogh is **worth** a fortune.*

fortune [CHANCE] /ˈfɔː.tʃuːn/ [US] /ˈfɔːr-/ *noun* [C or U] **1** chance and the way it affects your life: *He **had** the **(good)** fortune **to** train with some of the world's top athletes.* ○ *The family's fortunes changed overnight.* **2** **tell *sb's* fortune** to discover what will happen to someone in the future, for example by looking at the lines on their hands or using a special set of cards

• **fortune smiles on *sb*** If fortune smiles on you, you are lucky and good things happen to you.

ˈfortune ˌcookie *noun* [C] a biscuit containing a message, usually about your future, eaten especially after a Chinese meal

ˈfortune ˌhunter *noun* [C] *DISAPPROVING* someone who tries to marry a person who has a lot of money

ˈfortune ˌteller *noun* [C] a person who tells you what they think will happen to you in the future

forty /ˈfɔː.ti/ [US] /ˈfɔːr.t̬i/ *determiner, pronoun, noun* 40

forties /ˈfɔː.tiz/ [US] /ˈfɔːr.t̬iz/ *plural noun* A person's forties are the period in which they are aged between 40 and 49: *She's probably in her early forties.*

the forties *plural noun* **1** the range of temperature between 40° and 49°: *The temperature is expected to be **in** the forties tomorrow.* **2** the period of years between 40 and 49 in any century: *Our house was built some time **in** the forties.*

fortieth /ˈfɔː.ti.əθ/ [US] /ˈfɔːr.t̬i-/ *determiner, pronoun, adj, adv, noun* 40th written as a word

ˌforty ˈwinks *plural noun INFORMAL* a short sleep during the day: *He usually has forty winks going home on the train.*

forum /ˈfɔː.rəm/ [US] /ˈfɔːr.əm/ *noun* [C] **1** a situation or meeting in which people can talk about a problem or matter especially of public interest: *a forum for debate/discussion* **2** in ancient Rome, the area in the middle of the town used for public business **3** a place on the Internet where people can leave messages or discuss particular subjects with other people at the same time: ***Discussion** forums are a way of contacting people with similar interests from all over the world.*

forward [DIRECTION] /ˈfɔː.wəd/ [US] /ˈfɔːr.wɚd/ *adv* (*ALSO* **forwards**) towards the direction that is in front of you: *She leaned forward to whisper something in my ear.* **forward** /ˈfɔː.wəd/ [US] /ˈfɔːr.wɚd/ *adj*: *forward motion/movement*

forward [FUTURE] /ˈfɔː.wəd/ [US] /ˈfɔːr.wɚd/ *adv* (*ALSO* **forwards**) towards the future: *I always look forward, not back.* **forward** /ˈfɔː.wəd/ [US] /ˈfɔːr.wɚd/ *adj*: *forward planning/thinking*

• **from that day forward** *FORMAL* after that point: *From that day forward they never spoke to each other.*

forward [PROGRESS] /ˈfɔː.wəd/ [US] /ˈfɔːr.wɚd/ *adv* (*ALSO* **forwards**) used in expressions related to progress: *This is a big **step** forward for democracy.*

forward [CONFIDENT] /ˈfɔː.wəd/ [US] /ˈfɔːr.wɚd/ *adj DISAPPROVING* confident and honest in a way that ignores the usual social rules and might seem rude: *Do you think it was forward of me to invite her to dinner when we'd only just met?* **forwardness** /ˈfɔː.wəd.nəs/ [US] /ˈfɔːr.-wɚd-/ *noun* [U]

forward [SEND] /ˈfɔː.wəd/ [US] /ˈfɔːr.wɚd/ *verb* [T] to send a letter etc., especially from someone's old address to their new address, or to send a letter, email etc. that you have received to someone else: *I'll forward any mail **to** your new address.* ○ *I'll forward his email to you if you're interested.*

forward [SPORT] /ˈfɔː.wəd/ [US] /ˈfɔːr.wɚd/ *noun* [C] a player who is in an attacking position in a team

ˈforwarding adˌdress *noun* [C usually sing] where you want your post sent after you have left the address at which it will arrive

forward-looking /ˈfɔː.wədˌlʊk.ɪŋ/ [US] /ˈfɔːr.wɚd-/ *adj* Someone who is forward-looking always plans for the future.

forwards /ˈfɔː.wədz/ [US] /ˈfɔːr.wɚdz/ *adv* **forward** ➲Compare **backwards**.

forwent /fɔːˈwent/ [US] /fɔːr-/ *past participle of* **forgo**

fossil /ˈfɒs.əl/ [US] /ˈfɑː.səl/ *noun* [C] **1** a bone, a shell or the shape of a plant or animal which has been preserved in rock for a very long period **2** *INFORMAL HUMOROUS* an old person, especially one who will not accept new ideas

fossilize, *UK USUALLY* **-ise** /ˈfɒs.ɪ.laɪz/ [US] /ˈfɑː.səl.aɪz/ *verb* [I] to become a fossil: *The remains gradually fossilized.*

fossilized, *UK USUALLY* **-ised** /ˈfɒs.ɪ.laɪzd/ [US] /ˈfɑː.səl.aɪzd/ *adj* **1** having become a fossil: *fossilized bones* **2** old-fashioned and never changing **fossilization**, *UK USUALLY* **-isation** /ˌfɒs.ɪ.laɪˈzeɪ.ʃən/ [US] /ˌfɑː.səl.aɪ-/ *noun* [U]

ˈfossil ˌfuel *noun* [C or U] fuels such as gas, coal and oil, which were formed underground from plant and animal remains millions of years ago

foster [TAKE CARE OF] /ˈfɒs.təʳ/ [US] /ˈfɑː.stɚ/ *verb* [I or T] to take care of a child, usually for a limited time, without being the child's legal parent: *Would you consider fostering **(a child)**?* ➲Compare **adopt** TAKE CHILD. **foster** /ˈfɒs.-təʳ/ [US] /ˈfɑː.stɚ/ *adj* [before n] *a foster care/home/child/mother* ○ *She was taken into care by the local council and placed with a foster **family**.* ○ *As a child, he had lived with a succession of foster **parents**.*

foster [ENCOURAGE] /ˈfɒs.təʳ/ [US] /ˈfɑː.stɚ/ *verb* [T] to encourage the development or growth of ideas or feelings: *I'm trying to foster an interest in classical music **in** my children.* ○ *They were discussing the best way to foster democracy and prosperity in the former communist countries.*

fought /fɔːt/ [US] /fɑːt/ *past simple and past participle of* **fight**

foul [UNPLEASANT] /faʊl/ *adj* **1** extremely unpleasant: *Those toilets smell foul!* ○ *I've had a foul day at work.* ○ *Why are you in such a foul mood this morning?* ○ *What foul weather!* **2** describes speech or other language that is offensive, rude or shocking: *There's too much foul **language** on TV these days.*

foul [SPORT] /faʊl/ *noun* [C] an act which is against the rules of a sport, often causing injury to another player: *He was sent off for a foul **on** the French captain.* **foul** /faʊl/ *verb* [I or T]

foul [MAKE DIRTY] /faʊl/ *verb* [T] *FORMAL* to ruin or damage something by making it dirty: *Penalty for dogs fouling the pavement – £50.*

▲ **foul *(sth)* up** *phrasal verb* [M] *INFORMAL* to spoil something by making a mistake or doing something stupid: *I don't want David organizing this party after the way he fouled (things) up last year.*

foul-up /ˈfaʊl.ʌp/ *noun* [C] *This investigation has been mismanaged right from the start – I've never seen such a foul-up.*

foul-mouthed /ˌfaʊlˈmaʊðd/ *adj* If someone is foul-mouthed, they swear a lot and use offensive language.

ˌfoul ˈplay [CRIME] *noun* [U] a criminal act which results in serious damage or injury, especially murder: *It is not* *clear what caused the explosion, but the police do not* **suspect** *foul play.*

foul 'play SPORT *noun* [U] in sport, when someone plays unfairly or acts against the rules

found FIND /faʊnd/ *past simple and past participle of* **find**

found BEGIN /faʊnd/ *verb* [T] to bring something into existence: *York was founded by the Romans in the year 71 AD.* ○ *She left a large sum of money in her will to found a wildlife sanctuary.* ○ *We are planning a dinner to celebrate the fiftieth anniversary of the founding of the company.*

foundation /faʊnˈdeɪ.ʃ°n/ *noun* **1** [U] when an organization, state, etc. is established: *the foundation of a new state* **2** [C] an organization that has been established in order to provide money for a particular group of people in need of help or for a particular type of study: *the British Heart Foundation* ○ *the Environmental Research Foundation* **3** [U] *UK* the first year of INFANT school, previously known as **reception**: *a foundation class/teacher* ○ *Her youngest child starts (in) foundation in September.*

founder /ˈfaʊn.dəʳ/ US /-dɚ/ *noun* [C] someone who establishes an organization: *She is the founder and managing director of the company.*

found BUILD /faʊnd/ *verb* **1** [T usually + adv or prep] SPECIALIZED to build a support in the ground for a large structure such as a building or road **2** [T + adv or prep] to base a belief, claim, idea, etc. on something: *Her lawyer accused the prosecution of founding its case on insufficient evidence.* ○ *I'd like to see the research that these recommendations are founded on.* ○ *a society founded on egalitarian principles* **foundation** /faʊnˈdeɪ.ʃ°n/ *noun* [U]
● **be without foundation** (*ALSO* **have no foundation**) to be untrue: *These allegations are completely without foundation.*

foundations /faʊnˈdeɪ.ʃ°nz/ *plural noun* the structures below the surface of the ground which support a building: *The foundations will have to be reinforced to prevent the house from sinking further into the ground.*
● **shake/rock sth to its foundations** to seriously damage, upset or change an organization or someone's beliefs: *The scandal has shaken the Democratic Party to its foundations.*
● **lay the foundations of/for** to produce the basic ideas or structures from which something much larger develops: *The two leaders have laid the foundations of a new era in cooperation between their countries.* ○ *He helped to lay the foundations of English drama.*

foundation /faʊnˈdeɪ.ʃ°n/ *noun* [U] a type of make-up which is spread over the skin of the face, usually before other make-up is put on, giving it a better and more even colour and hiding unwanted marks

founˈdation ˌcourse *UK noun* [C] (*US* **introductory course**) a college or university course that introduces students to a subject and prepares them for studying it at a higher level

founˈdation ˌstone *noun* [C] a large block of stone that is put in position at the start of work on a public building, often with a ceremony

founder /ˈfaʊn.dəʳ/ US /-dɚ/ *verb* [I] **1** (especially of a boat) to fill with water and sink: *The ferry foundered in a heavy storm, taking many of the passengers and crew with it.* **2** to be unsuccessful: *Teaching computers to read and write has always foundered on the unpredictable human element in language.*

founder 'member *UK noun* [C] (*US USUALLY* **founding member**) one of the original members of an organization or rock group: *France is a founder member of the European Union.*

founding 'father *noun* [C] someone who establishes an important organization or idea: *John Reith was the founding father of the BBC.*

foundling /ˈfaʊnd.lɪŋ/ *noun* [C] *OLD-FASHIONED* a young child who is left by its unknown parents and then found and cared for by someone else

foundry /ˈfaʊn.dri/ *noun* [C] a factory where metal is melted and poured into specially shaped containers to produce objects such as wheels and bars

fount /faʊnt/ *noun* LITERARY OR HUMOROUS **the fount of all knowledge/gossip/wisdom, etc.** the person or place from which all information on a particular subject comes: *He's renowned as the fount of all knowledge on disease.*

fountain /ˈfaʊn.tɪn/ *noun* [C] a stream of water that is forced up into the air through a small hole, especially for decorative effect, or the structure in a lake or pool from which this flows

'fountain ˌpen *noun* [C] a pen whose NIB (= point at the end which you write with) is supplied with ink from a container inside it

four /fɔːʳ/ US /fɔːr/ *determiner, pronoun, noun* 4: *Most animals have four legs.*
● **on all fours** with your hands and knees on the ground: *You'll have to get down on all fours to clean behind the toilet.*

four /fɔːʳ/ US /fɔːr/ *group noun* [C] a team of four people in rowing, or the boat that they use

fourth /fɔːθ/ US /fɔːrθ/ *determiner, pronoun, adj, adv, noun* [S] 4th written as a number: *My birthday is on the fourth of December.* ○ *Daniel was/finished fourth in the race.*

four-eyes /ˈfɔː.raɪz/ US /ˈfɔː-/ *noun* [S] INFORMAL an offensive way of addressing someone who wears glasses

four-leaf clover /ˌfɔː.liːfˈkləʊ.vəʳ/ US /ˌfɔːr.liːfˈkloʊ.vɚ/ *noun* [C] (*ALSO* **four-leaved clover**) a CLOVER (= small plant) with a leaf which is divided into four parts rather than the usual three, which is thought to bring good luck to anyone who finds it

four-letter word /ˌfɔː.let.əˈwɜːd/ US /ˌfɔː.let̬.ɚˈwɜːd/ *noun* [C] a short swear word that is considered to be extremely rude or offensive: *Four-letter words are often edited out of films before they are shown on television.*

four-oh-four, 404 /ˌfɔː.rəʊˈfɔː/ US /ˌfɔːr.oʊˈfɔːr/ *adj* [after v] HUMOROUS DISAPPROVING describes someone stupid who does not know how to use email and computers: *Don't bother asking him. He's 404, man.*

four-poster (bed) /ˌfɔː.pəʊ.stəˈbed/ US /ˌfɔːr.poʊ.stɚ-/ *noun* [C] a large old-fashioned bed with tall posts at each corner which support a frame from which curtains hang

foursome /ˈfɔː.səm/ US /ˈfɔːr-/ *noun* [C] (*ALSO* **four**) a group of four people meeting for a social activity, such as playing a game or having a meal: *Why don't we invite Caroline and Mark and make up a foursome?*

four-square SOLID /ˈfɔː.skweəʳ/ US /ˈfɔːr.skwer/ *adj* square or wide and built strongly and firmly: *The architecture tends to be four-square and unimaginative.*

four-square DETERMINED /ˈfɔː.skweəʳ/ US /ˈfɔːr.skwer/ *adv* with determination: *Clarke said he stood four-square behind* (= believed strongly in) *the Prime minister's decision.*

four-star /ˌfɔːˈstɑːʳ/ US /ˌfɔːrˈstɑːr/ *adj* [before n] describes a restaurant or hotel of a very high standard

four-star ('petrol) *UK noun* [U] (*US* **premium (gas)**, *AUS* **super (petrol)**) the highest quality LEADED fuel that can be used in cars

fourteen /ˌfɔːˈtiːn/ US /ˌfɔːr-/ /ˈ--/ *determiner, pronoun, noun* 14

fourteenth /ˌfɔːˈtiːnθ/ US /ˌfɔːr-/ /ˈ--/ *determiner, pronoun, adj, adv, noun* 14th written as a word

the ˌfourth diˈmension *noun* [S] refers to time, especially in SCIENCE FICTION

the ˌFourth Esˈtate *noun* [S] newspapers, magazines, television and radio stations and the people who work for them who are thought to have a lot of political influence

the ˌFourth of Juˈly *noun* [S] (FORMAL **Independence Day**) a national holiday in the US that celebrates the country's independence from Great Britain in 1776

four-wheel drive /ˌfɔː.wiːlˈdraɪv/ US /ˌfɔːr-/ *noun* **1** [C or U] (*WRITTEN ABBREVIATION* **4WD**, *ALSO* **4x4**) If a vehicle has four-wheel drive, its engine supplies power to all four wheels instead of the usual two, so that the vehicle can travel easily over difficult ground. **2** [C] a vehicle that uses this system **four-wheel drive** /ˌfɔː.wiːlˈdraɪv/ US /ˌfɔːr-/ *adj*: *a four-wheel drive car*

fowl /faʊl/ *noun* [C or U] *plural* **fowl** or **fowls** **1** a bird of a type that is used to produce meat or eggs **2** OLD USE any bird ⊃See also **waterfowl**; **wildfowl**.

F

fox [ANIMAL] /fɒks/ [US] /fɑːks/ *noun* **1** [C] a wild mammal belonging to the dog family which has a pointed face and ears, a wide furry tail and often reddish-brown fur **2** [U] the skin of this animal used to make coats and hats **3** [C usually sing] someone who is clever and good at deceiving people: *He's a cunning/sly/wily old fox.*
foxy /ˈfɒk.si/ [US] /ˈfɑːk-/ *adj* **1** like a fox in appearance **2** good at deceiving people

fox [WOMAN] /fɒks/ [US] /fɑːks/ *noun* [C] *US INFORMAL* a sexually attractive woman
foxy /ˈfɒk.si/ [US] /ˈfɑːk-/ *adj INFORMAL* sexy: *a foxy chick*

fox [CONFUSE] /fɒks/ [US] /fɑːks/ *verb* [T] to confuse someone or be too difficult to be understood by someone: *This puzzle has well and truly foxed me!*

fox [DECEIVE] /fɒks/ [US] /fɑːks/ *verb* [T] to deceive someone in a clever way

foxglove /ˈfɒks.glʌv/ [US] /ˈfɑːks-/ *noun* [C] a tall thin plant with white, yellow, pink, red or purple bell-shaped flowers growing all the way up its stem ➲See picture **Flowers and Plants** on page Centre 3

foxhole /ˈfɒks.həʊl/ [US] /ˈfɑːks.hoʊl/ *noun* [C] a small hole dug in the ground during a war or military attack which is used by a small group of soldiers as a base for firing at the enemy and as a shelter from attack ➲Compare **trench**.

foxhound /ˈfɒks.haʊnd/ [US] /ˈfɑːks-/ *noun* [C] a type of small dog with ears that hang down and short smooth usually black, white and light brown fur

foxhunting /ˈfɒksˌhʌn.tɪŋ/ [US] /ˈfɑːksˌhʌn.t̬ɪŋ/ *noun* [U] the activity of hunting foxes for entertainment in which people on horses follow dogs which chase a fox and kill it when they catch it **foxhunt** /ˈfɒks.hʌnt/ [US] /ˈfɑːks-/ *noun* [C]

ˌfox ˈterrier *noun* [C] a small dog with smooth or rough fur that is white with black or pale brown marks

foxtrot /ˈfɒks.trɒt/ [US] /ˈfɑːks.trɑːt/ *noun* [C] (a piece of music for) a type of formal BALLROOM dance that combines short quick steps with longer ones in various patterns

foyer /ˈfɔɪ.eɪ/ *noun* [C] **1** a large open area just inside the entrance of a public building such as a theatre or a hotel, where people can wait and meet each other: *I'll see you downstairs **in** the foyer in half an hour.* **2** *US* (*UK* **hall**) the room in a house or apartment leading from the front door to other rooms, where items like coats and hats are kept

Fr *noun* [before n] *ABBREVIATION FOR* **Father** when used as a title of a Christian priest, especially a Roman Catholic or Orthodox priest: *Fr McDonald conducted the mass.*

fracas /ˈfræk.ɑː/ *noun* [S] a noisy argument or fight: *He was injured in a Saturday-night fracas outside a disco.* ○ *The Prime Minister has joined the fracas **over** the proposed changes to the health service.*

fraction /ˈfræk.ʃᵊn/ *noun* [C] a number that results from dividing one whole number by another, or a small part of something: *¼ and 0.25 are different ways of representing the same fraction.* ○ *Although sexual and violent crimes have increased by 10%, they remain **only a tiny/small** fraction **of** the total number of crimes committed each year.* ○ *They can produce it **at a** fraction **of** the cost of* (= much more cheaply than) *traditional methods.*
fractional /ˈfræk.ʃᵊn.ᵊl/ *adj* extremely small: *The fall in the value of the yen might result in a fractional increase in interest rates of perhaps a quarter of one per cent.*
fractionally /ˈfræk.ʃᵊn.ᵊl.i/ *adv*: *Despite substantial price cuts, sales have increased only fractionally* (= by a very small amount).

fractious /ˈfræk.ʃəs/ *adj* easily upset or annoyed, and tending to complain: *a fractious child* **fractiousness** /ˈfræk.ʃə.snəs/ *noun* [U]

fracture /ˈfræk.tʃəʳ/ [US] /-tʃɚ/ *verb* [I or T] **1** If something hard, such as a bone, fractures or is fractured, it cracks or breaks: *She fractured her **skull** in the accident.* ○ *Two of her ribs fractured when she was thrown from her horse.* ○ *A fractured pipe at a steelworks has leaked 20 tons of oil into the Severn estuary.* **2** *FORMAL* to divide an organization or society, or (of an organization or society) to be divided: *Intense disagreement over economic policy risks fracturing the coalition government.*
fracture /ˈfræk.tʃəʳ/ [US] /-tʃɚ/ *noun* [C] *He suffered/sustained **multiple** fractures in a motorcycle accident.* ○ *He has a **hairline** fracture* (= a thin crack in the bone) *of the wrist.*

fragile /ˈfrædʒ.aɪl/ [US] /ˈfrædʒ.ᵊl/ *adj* easily damaged, broken or harmed: *Be careful with that vase – it's very fragile.* ○ *The assassination could do serious damage to the fragile peace agreement that was signed last month.* ○ *I felt rather fragile* (= weak) *for a few days after the operation.* ○ *HUMOROUS No breakfast for me, thanks – I'm feeling rather fragile* (= ill, upset or tired) *after last night's party.* **fragility** /frəˈdʒɪl.ɪ.ti/ [US] /-t̬i/ *noun* [U] *The collapse of the bank is an ominous reminder of the fragility of the world's banking system.*

fragment /ˈfræg.mənt/ *noun* [C] a small piece or a part, especially when broken from something whole: *The road was covered with fragments **of** glass from the shattered window.* ○ *Literary scholars are piecing together her last unpublished novel from fragments **of** a recently discovered manuscript.*
fragment /frægˈment/ *verb* [I or T] to break something into small parts or to be broken up in this way: *The satellite will fragment and burn up as it falls through the Earth's atmosphere.* ○ *The government is planning to fragment the industry before privatizing it.*
fragmented /frægˈmen.tɪd/ [US] /-t̬ɪd/ *adj* consisting of several separate parts: *In this increasingly fragmented society, a sense of community is a thing of the past.* ○ *The President has only held onto power because the opposition is so fragmented.*
fragmentary /ˈfræg.mən.tᵊr.i/ [US] /ˈfræg.mən.ter-/ *adj FORMAL* existing only in small parts and not complete: *Reports are still fragmentary but it is already clear that the explosion has left many dead and injured.*
fragmentation /ˌfræg.menˈteɪ.ʃᵊn/ *noun* [U] *It was partly the fragmentation of the opposition which helped to get the Republicans re-elected.*

fragrance /ˈfreɪ.grᵊnts/ *noun* [C or U] **1** a sweet or pleasant smell: *the delicate fragrance of roses* **2** a liquid which people put on their bodies to make themselves smell pleasant: *a brand new fragrance for men*
fragrant /ˈfreɪ.grᵊnt/ *adj* with a pleasant smell: *fragrant flowers* ○ *The sauce itself was light, fragrant and slightly sweet.*

frail /freɪl/ *adj* weak or unhealthy, or easily damaged, broken or harmed: *a frail old lady* ○ *I last saw him just last week and thought how old and frail he looked.* ○ *the country's frail economy*
frailty /ˈfreɪl.ti/ [US] /-t̬i/ *noun* **1** [U] weakness and lack of health or strength: *Though ill for most of her life, physical frailty never stopped her from working.* **2** [C or U] moral weakness: *Most of the characters in the novel exhibit those common **human** frailties – ignorance and greed.* ○ *Tolerant of **human** frailty in whatever form, she almost never judged people.*

frame [BORDER] /freɪm/ *noun* [C] a border which encloses and supports a picture, door or window: *a picture frame*
frame /freɪm/ *verb* [T] **1** to fix a border around a picture etc. and often glass in front of it: *I keep meaning to get that photo framed.* **2** to form an edge to something in an attractive way: *Her new hairstyle frames her face in a much more flattering way.* **framed** /freɪmd/ *adj*: *a framed photograph* ○ *a pair of silver-framed spectacles*
frames /freɪmz/ *plural noun* the plastic or metal structure that holds together a pair of glasses

frame [STRUCTURE] /freɪm/ *noun* [C] **1** the basic structure of a building, vehicle or piece of furniture that other parts are added onto: *a bicycle frame* **2** *UK* (*US* **rack**) a wooden or plastic triangular object used to put the balls into position at the start of a game such as billiards or snooker **3** the size and shape of someone's body: *My sister has a much bigger frame than me.*
• **frame of mind** the way someone thinks or feels about something at a particular time: *The most important thing is to go into the exam **in** a positive frame of mind.*
• **frame of reference** a set of ideas or facts accepted by a person which explains their behaviour, opinions or decisions: *How can Christians and atheists ever come to understand each other when their frames of reference are so different?*

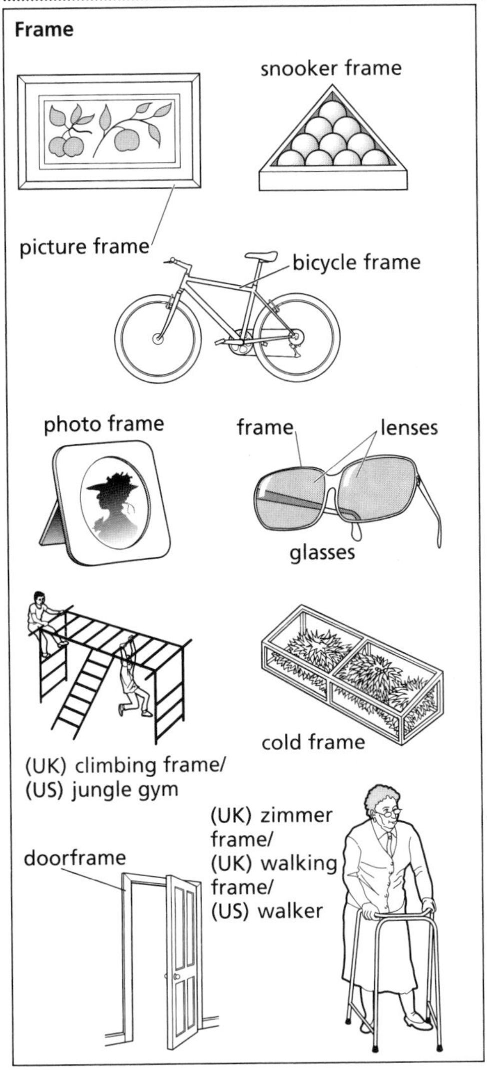
Frame
snooker frame
picture frame
bicycle frame
photo frame
frame
lenses
glasses
cold frame
(UK) climbing frame/
(US) jungle gym
(UK) zimmer
frame/
(UK) walking
frame/
(US) walker
doorframe

frame [GAME] /freɪm/ *noun* [C] a period of play in some games, such as snooker: *She lost the next two frames.*

frame [PHOTOGRAPH] /freɪm/ *noun* [C] SPECIALIZED one of the pictures on a strip of photographic film, or one of the single pictures which together form a television or cinema film

frame [EXPRESS] /freɪm/ *verb* [T] to express something choosing your words carefully: *The interview would have been more productive if the questions had been framed more precisely.*

frame [MAKE GUILTY] /freɪm/ *verb* [T often passive] INFORMAL to make a person seem to be guilty of a crime when they are not by producing facts or information which are not true: *He claimed he'd been framed by the police.*

frame-up /'freɪm.ʌp/ *noun* [C] INFORMAL a situation in which someone is made to seem guilty of a crime although they have not done it: *The organization protested that it was the victim of a politically motivated frame-up.*

framework /'freɪm.wɜːk/ [US] /-wɝːk/ *noun* **1** [C] a supporting structure around which something can be built **2** a system of rules, ideas or beliefs that is used to plan or decide something: *a legal framework for resolving disputes*

franc /fræŋk/ *noun* [C] (WRITTEN ABBREVIATION **Fr**) the standard unit of money used in France, Belgium and Luxembourg before they started using the Euro, and also used in many African countries that were ruled by France in the past

franchise [BUSINESS] /'fræn.tʃaɪz/ *noun* [C] a right to sell a company's products in a particular area using the company's name: *a fast-food franchise* ○ *a franchise holder*

franchise /'fræn.tʃaɪz/ *verb* [T] to give or sell a franchise to someone

franchisee /ˌfræn.tʃaɪ'ziː/ *noun* [C] someone who is given or sold a franchise **franchiser** /'fræn.tʃaɪ.zə^{r}/ [US] /-zɚ/ *noun* [C] **franchising** /'fræn.tʃaɪ.zɪŋ/ *noun* [U]

the franchise [VOTE] *noun* [S] the right to vote in an election, especially for representatives in a parliament or similar law-making organization: *In 1918 the suffragists* ***won the*** *franchise for UK women over the age of 29.*

Franciscan /fræn'sɪs.kən/ *noun* [C] a person belonging to a Christian group originally established by St Francis of Assisi in 1209 **Franciscan** /fræn'sɪs.kən/ *adj*

Franco- /fræŋ.kəʊ-/ [US] /-koʊ-/ *prefix* of or connected with France: *the Franco-German border* (= the border between France and Germany) ○ *a francophile* (= someone who loves France)

francophone /'fræŋ.kəʊ.fəʊn/ [US] /'fræŋ.koʊ.foʊn/ *adj* [before n] speaking French as the main or official language: *francophone Africa* **francophone** /'fræŋ.kəʊ.fəʊn/ [US] /'fræŋ.koʊ.foʊn/ *noun* [C] *Most of the Francophones live in these two provinces.*

frank [HONEST] /fræŋk/ *adj* honest, sincere and truthful, even when this might be awkward or make other people uncomfortable: *a full and frank discussion* ○ *There followed a frank exchange of views.* ○ *The magazine, which gives frank advice about sex and romance, is aimed at the teenage market.* ○ ***To be perfectly*** *frank with you, I don't think she's the woman for the job.*

frankly /'fræŋ.kli/ *adv* **1** in an honest and direct way: *She spoke very frankly about her experiences.* **2** used when giving an honest and direct opinion, often one that might upset someone: ***Quite*** *frankly, I think this whole situation is ridiculous.* ○ *That's a frankly absurd suggestion.*

frankness /'fræŋk.nəs/ *noun* [U] honesty: *A lot more frankness is needed in sex education if we are to reduce the number of teenage pregnancies.*

frank [PRINT] /fræŋk/ *verb* [T] to print a mark on a stamp so that the stamp cannot be used again, or to print a mark on an envelope to show that the cost of sending it has been paid

Frankenstein /'fræŋ.kən.staɪn/ *noun* [C] (ALSO **Frankenstein's monster**) something that destroys or harms the person or people who created it: *In arming the dictator, the US was creating a Frankenstein who would threaten their influence in the region.*

frankfurter /'fræŋk.fɜː.tə^{r}/ [US] /-fɝː.t̬ɚ/ *noun* [C] a thin red-brown sausage which is preserved using smoke or chemicals and often eaten with bread

frankincense /'fræŋ.kɪn.sents/ *noun* [U] a thick sticky liquid that produces a sweet smell when burned and is obtained from a tree that grows in eastern Africa and Asia

frantic [EMOTIONAL] /'fræn.tɪk/ [US] /-t̬ɪk/ *adj* almost out of control because of extreme emotion, such as anxiety: *Where on earth have you been? We've been frantic* ***with*** *worry.* **frantically** /'fræn.tɪ.kli/ [US] /-t̬ɪ-/ *adv*: *As the helicopter flew overhead, they waved frantically, trying to attract its attention.*

frantic [HURRIED] /'fræn.tɪk/ [US] /-t̬ɪk/ *adj* done or arranged in a hurry and a state of excitement or confusion: *Share prices have soared to a new all-time high in a day of frantic trading on the stock market.* ○ *Rescuers were engaged in a frantic all-night effort to reach the survivors before their supply of air ran out.* **frantically** /'fræn.tɪ.kli/ [US] /-t̬ɪ-/ *adv*: *I've been working frantically all week to get it finished on time.* ○ *I got home to find Lara frantically searching for her keys.*

frappé /'fræp.eɪ/ [US] /-'-/ *noun* [C] a partly frozen drink made of milk or fruit juice, or a strongly alcoholic drink served with ice: *a chocolate/strawberry/crème de menthe frappé*

frat /fræt/ *noun* [C] *US INFORMAL FOR* **fraternity** (= a social organization for male university students in the US)

fraternal /frəˈtɜː.nəl/ [US] /-ˈtɝː-/ *adj* **1** relating to brothers: *fraternal rivalry* **2** friendly, like brothers: *The President's official visit marks the start of a more fraternal relationship between the two countries.*
fraternally /frəˈtɜː.nə.li/ [US] /-ˈtɝː-/ *adv*
fraternity /frəˈtɜː.nə.ti/ [US] /-ˈtɝː.nə.t̬i/ *noun* [U] *He described sport as a symbol of peace and a means of promoting fraternity* (= friendship) *between nations.*

fraternity /frəˈtɜː.nə.ti/ [US] /-ˈtɝː.nə.t̬i/ *group noun* [C] **1** a group of people who have the same job or interest: *the legal fraternity* (= lawyers) ○ *the criminal fraternity* (= criminals) ○ *The racing world is a pretty* ***close-knit*** *fraternity.* ➲See also **fraternity** at **fraternal**. **2** (*INFORMAL* **frat**) *US* a social organization for male students at an American or Canadian college ➲Compare **sorority**.

fraternize, *UK USUALLY* **-ise** /ˈfræt.ə.naɪz/ [US] /-ɚ-/ *verb* [I] to meet someone socially, especially someone who belongs to an opposing army or team, or has a different social position: *Do the doctors fraternize much* ***with*** *the nurses here?* ○ *He accused the England team of fraternizing too much* ***with*** *the opposition.* **fraternization**, *UK USUALLY* **-isation** /ˌfræt.ən.aɪˈzeɪ.ʃən/ [US] /-ɚ.nɪ-/ *noun* [U]

fratricide /ˈfræt.rɪ.saɪd/ *noun* [U] *FORMAL* the crime of murdering your brother, or killing members of your own group or country **fratricidal** /ˌfræt.rɪˈsaɪ.dəl/ *adj*

fraud [CRIME] /frɔːd/ [US] /frɑːd/ *noun* [C or U] the crime of obtaining money by deceiving people: *credit card fraud* ○ *He is fighting extradition to Hong Kong to face trial on fraud* ***charges***.
fraudster /ˈfrɔːd.stər/ [US] /ˈfrɑːd.stɚ/ *noun* [C] someone who obtains money by deceiving people: *New measures are needed to prevent fraudsters opening bank accounts with stolen cheques.*
fraudulent /ˈfrɔː.djʊ.lənt/ [US] /ˈfrɑː-/ *adj* dishonest and illegal: *A worrying trend for insurers has been a rise in fraudulent* ***claims***. **fraudulently** /ˈfrɔː.djʊ.lənt.li/ [US] /ˈfrɑː-/ *adv*

fraud [FALSE] /frɔːd/ [US] /frɑːd/ *noun* [C] someone or something that deceives people by claiming to be someone or something that they are not: *She was a psychic who was later revealed to be a fraud.*
fraudulent /ˈfrɔː.djʊ.lənt/ [US] /ˈfrɑː-/ *adj* intended to deceive: *They claim that the fall in unemployment is based on a fraudulent manipulation of statistics.*
fraudulently /ˈfrɔː.djʊ.lənt.li/ [US] /ˈfrɑː-/ *adv*
fraudulence /ˈfrɔː.djʊ.lənts/ [US] /ˈfrɑː-/ *noun* [U]

the ˈFraud ˌSquad *noun* [S] a department in the British police force which discovers and takes action against business fraud

fraught [FULL OF] /frɔːt/ [US] /frɑːt/ *adj* **fraught with** full of unpleasant things such as problems or dangers: *The negotiations have been fraught with* ***difficulties/problems*** *right from the start.* ○ *From beginning to end, the airlift was fraught with* ***risks***.

fraught [ANXIOUS] /frɔːt/ [US] /frɑːt/ *adj* causing or having extreme worry or anxiety: *This is one of the most fraught weekends of the year for the security forces.* ○ *The atmosphere in the office is rather fraught.*

fray [CLOTH] /freɪ/ *verb* [I or T] to become or to cause the threads in cloth or rope to become slightly separated, forming loose threads at the edge or end: *Denim frays so easily.* ○ *I'd frayed the edges of my jeans as that was the fashion in those days.*
• **fray around/at the edges** to start to become less effective or successful: *Without the unifying forces of the army and the monarchy, it seems, the nation would begin to fray at the edges.*
frayed /freɪd/ *adj*: with the threads at the edge coming loose: *frayed cuffs*

fray [ANNOYED] /freɪ/ *verb* [I] If your temper frays or your nerves fray, you gradually become upset or annoyed: *Tempers frayed as thousands of motorists began the Christmas holiday with long waits in traffic jams.*
frayed /freɪd/ *adj*: *The whole experience left me with frayed* ***nerves*** (= feeling anxious).

the fray [ACTION] *noun* [S] an energetic and often not well organized effort, activity, fight or disagreement: *With a third country about to* ***enter*** (= take part in) *the fray, the fighting looks set to continue.* ○ *A good holiday should leave you feeling refreshed and* ***ready for*** *the fray* (= ready to work) *again.*

frazzled [TIRED] /ˈfræz.l̩d/ *adj INFORMAL* extremely tired in a nervous or slightly anxious way after a lot of mental or physical effort: *I've had a stressful day at work and it's left me feeling a bit frazzled.*
frazzle /ˈfræz.l̩/ *noun* [S] *INFORMAL She's* ***worn*** *herself* ***to a*** *frazzle* (= made herself very tired and nervous) *trying to meet the deadline.*

frazzled [BURNED] /ˈfræz.l̩d/ *adj UK INFORMAL* burned or dried out after being in the sun or cooking for too long: *I'd only been in the sun a couple of hours and my back was frazzled.* ○ *By the time I remembered about the meat it was frazzled.*
frazzle /ˈfræz.l̩/ *noun* [S] *UK INFORMAL I went to answer the phone and when I came back the eggs were* ***burned to a*** *frazzle* (= completely burned).

freak [STRANGE] /friːk/ *noun* [C] a thing, person, animal or event that is extremely unusual or unlikely and not like any other of its type: *I was born with black hair all over my back, like some sort of freak.* ○ *The pearl, valued at £75 000, is so big that it has been described as a freak* ***of nature***. ○ *HUMOROUS At my school you were regarded as a freak if you weren't interested in sport.*
freak /friːk/ *adj* [before n] very unusual or unexpected: *She was crushed in a freak* (= very unlikely) ***accident*** *in a cave in France.* ○ *A freak whirlwind has destroyed over 20 caravans in west Wales.*
freakish /ˈfriː.kɪʃ/ *adj* (*INFORMAL* **freaky**) very unusual or unexpected, especially in an unpleasant or strange way: *Freakish weather conditions have caused massive traffic hold-ups in the area.* ○ *When you're a child you always imagine that your own bodily imperfections are somehow freakish.* **freakishly** /ˈfriː.kɪʃ.li/ *adv* **freakishness** /ˈfriː.kɪʃ.nəs/ *noun* [U]

freak [ENTHUSIASTIC PERSON] /friːk/ *noun INFORMAL* **a health/computer/surf, etc. freak** someone who is extremely interested in a particular subject or activity

freak [GET EMOTIONAL] /friːk/ *verb* [I or T] *INFORMAL* to become or cause someone to become extremely emotional: *My parents freaked when I told them I was pregnant.* ○ *He freaked* ***out*** *when he heard he'd got the job.* ○ *This song just freaks me* ***out*** *whenever I hear it.*

ˈfreak ˌshow *noun* [C] in the past, an event at which the public came to look at people and animals that had not developed normally: *She felt like something out of a freak show.*

freckle /ˈfrek.l̩/ *noun* [C] a small pale brown spot on the skin, usually on the face, especially of a light-skinned person: *He has red hair and freckles.* ➲Compare **mole** SPOT. **freckled** /ˈfrek.l̩d/ *adj* (*ALSO* **freckly**) *a freckly complexion*

freckle-faced /ˈfrek.l̩.feɪst/ *adj* having a lot of FRECKLES (= small brown spots) on the face

free [NOT LIMITED] /friː/ *adj, adv* not limited or controlled: [+ to infinitive] *Am I free* (= Do I have permission) ***to*** *leave now?* ○ *I'll give you a key then you're free* ***to*** *come and go as you please.* ○ *Please* ***feel*** *free* ***to*** *interrupt me if you don't understand anything.* ○ *The agreement gives companies free* ***access*** *to the markets of member countries.* ○ *A great deal has been achieved, most notably free* ***elections*** (= elections in which people can vote as they wish).
• **ˌfree and ˈeasy** relaxed and informal: *The atmosphere in the office is fairly free and easy.*
free /friː/ *verb* [T + obj + to infinitive] *Her retirement from politics will free her* (= provide her with enough time) ***to*** *write her memoirs.*
freely /ˈfriː.li/ *adv* without being controlled or limited: *For the first time in months she could move freely.* ○ *Exotic foods are freely available in supermarkets.* ○ *She freely* (= willingly) ***admits*** *that she's not as fast a runner as she used to be.* ○ *We encourage the victims to talk freely* (= talk a lot and honestly) *about their experiences.*

free [NOT IN PRISON] /friː/ *adj, adv* not a prisoner any longer, or having unlimited movement: *She left the court a free woman after the case against her collapsed because of a legal technicality.* ○ *The new government has decided to* ***set*** *all political prisoners free.* ○ *She* ***went/walked*** *free after the charges against her were dropped.* ○ *I let the dogs run free in the park.*
free /friː/ *verb* [T] to allow someone to leave a prison or place where they have been kept: *After a ten-hour siege the gunman agreed to free the hostages.* ○ *Anti-vivisectionists last night freed a number of animals* ***from*** *a laboratory.*

free [NO CHARGE] /friː/ *adj, adv* costing nothing; not needing to be paid for: *I got some free cinema tickets.* ○ *Members all receive a free copy of the monthly newsletter.* ○ *The elderly travel free on public transport.* ○ *We will install your washing machine free* ***of charge/for*** *free* (= without charge).
• **There's no such thing as a free lunch.** *SAYING* said to emphasize that you cannot get something for nothing: *"I get to travel with my job but the downside is I have to give talks." "Well, there's no such thing as a free lunch."*
-free /-friː/ *suffix* used at the end of words to mean 'without having to pay': *They agreed to let us live there rent-free.* ○ *Many banks are now offering interest-free overdrafts to students.*

free [NOT BUSY] /friː/ *adj* not doing anything planned or important, or not being used: *I do a lot of reading in my free* ***time.*** ○ *She's in a meeting at the moment, but she should be free* ***to*** *see you in ten minutes.* ○ *I'm working in the café all this week, but I've got a free evening next Monday.* ○ *Excuse me, is this seat free* (= is anyone intending to sit in this seat)? ○ *We queued for half an hour waiting for a free space in the car park.* ○ *If you take these bags that will give me a free hand to open the door.*
free /friː/ *verb* [T] to make something available for someone to use: *They planned to extend the car park, freeing existing parking spaces for visitors.* ○ *Can you cancel my meetings – I need to free* ***(up)*** *the afternoon to write this report.*

free [LOOSE] /friː/ *adj, adv* not in a fixed position or not joined to anything: *Both bookcases stand free* ***of*** *the wall.* ○ *The bolts have worked themselves free because of the vibrations.* ○ *Rescuers took several hours to cut the survivors free* ***from*** *the wreckage.*
free /friː/ *verb* [T] to move or make loose someone or something that is trapped: *Both men were freed from the wreckage after a four-hour operation.* ○ *In vain he tried to free the rope around his hands.* **freely** /ˈfriː.li/ *adv: Remember to apply plenty of oil so that the wheel can rotate freely.*

free [WITHOUT] /friː/ *adj* [after v] not having something that is unwanted or unpleasant: *Because the organization is a charitable enterprise it is free* ***from*** *tax worldwide.* ○ *She'll never be completely free* ***of*** *the disease.* ○ *Ensure the wound is free* ***from/of*** *dirt before applying the bandage.*
-free /-friː/ *suffix* used at the end of words to mean 'without': *lead-free fuel* ○ *No working environment is entirely stress-free.* ○ *The journey was surprisingly hassle-free.*
▲ **free** ***sb*** **from/of** ***sth*** *phrasal verb* to help or make life better for someone by taking something unpleasant away from them: *He dedicated his life to freeing the world from famine and disease.* ○ [R] *I'd like to free myself of some of the responsibilities of this job.*

free [GIVING/USING OFTEN] /friː/ *adj* **free with** giving or using frequently or in large amounts: *He's rather free with his wife's money.* ○ *She's very free with advice but she never seems to act on it herself.* ○ *He's very free with his criticism!*
• **make free with** *DISAPPROVING* to use something that belongs to someone else a lot: *Don't her parents mind her making free with their house while they're on holiday?*

free [CHEMICAL] /friː/ *adj* In chemistry, if an element is free, it is not combined chemically with anything else: *free oxygen/nitrogen*

ˌfree ˈagent *noun* [C] someone whose actions are not limited or controlled by anyone else

ˌfree associˈation *noun* [U] a method of trying to see how the human mind works, in which a person says the first word that they think of after hearing a word that is spoken to them

freebasing /ˈfriː.beɪ.sɪŋ/ *noun* [U] *SLANG* the activity of smoking a specially prepared form of the drug COCAINE
freebase /ˈfriː.beɪs/ *verb* [I]

freebie /ˈfriː.bi/ *noun* [C] *INFORMAL* something which is given to you without you having to pay for it, especially as a way of attracting your support for or interest in something: *The company's marketing rep was giving out pens and mugs – the usual freebies.* ○ *The journalists were all given a freebie lunch.*

ˌFree ˈChurch *noun* [C usually sing] a Protestant Church that is not part of a country's officially accepted church

ˌfree collective ˈbargaining *noun* [U] *UK SPECIALIZED* formal discussions between workers and employers that are not limited by the law or government, about pay, working hours and conditions at work ⊃See also **collective bargaining**.

ˌfree ˈcountry *noun* [C] **1** a country where the government does not control what people say or do for political reasons and where people can express their opinions without punishment: *The transition from a totalitarian state to a free country will be long and slow.* ○ *I can say what I like – it's a free country!* **2** a country which is not controlled by another country

freedom /ˈfriː.dəm/ *noun* **1** [C or U] the condition or right of being able or allowed to do, say, think, etc. whatever you want to, without being controlled or limited: *I felt such a sense of freedom, up in the hills alone.* ○ *Children are allowed much more freedom these days.* ○ [+ to infinitive] *At university, you* ***have*** *the freedom* ***to*** *do what you want.* ○ *Everyone should be allowed freedom* ***of choice*** (= the ability to make their own choices). ○ *Freedom* ***of speech*** *and freedom* ***of thought*** (= The ability to say and think whatever you want) *were both denied under the dictatorship.* ○ *They are campaigning for freedom* ***of information*** (= for any information to be allowed to be given to anyone who wants it). ○ *We demand freedom* ***from*** *injustice/persecution* (= the condition of not having to suffer these things). ⊃Compare **liberty** FREEDOM. **2** [C] a right to act in the way you think you should: *Being able to vote as you want to is an important political/democratic freedom.* **3** [U] the state of not being in prison: *They regained their freedom after ten years of unjust imprisonment.*
• **give** ***sb*** **the freedom of** in Britain, to honour someone by giving them special rights in a particular city ⊃See also **freeman**.

ˈfreedom ˌfighter *noun* [C] a person who uses violent methods to try to remove a government from power: *It's often said that one person's freedom fighter is another person's terrorist.*

ˌfree ˈenterprise *noun* [U] an economic system in which private businesses compete with each other to sell goods and services in order to make a profit, and in which government control is limited to protecting the public and running the economy

ˌfree ˈfall *noun* [U] **1** when something or someone falls quickly under the influence of GRAVITY **2** *INFORMAL* the process of failing or losing value or strength quickly and continuously: *Only massive changes in government policies will prevent the peso* ***going into*** *free fall* (= falling quickly in value by a large amount).

free-floating /ˌfriːˈfləʊ.tɪŋ/ [US] /-ˈfloʊ.t̬ɪŋ/ *adj* not supporting any particular political party

Freefone /ˈfriː.fəʊn/ [US] /-foʊn/ *noun* [U] *UK TRADEMARK FOR* **Freephone**

free-for-all /ˌfriː.fəˈrɔːl/ [US] /-fəˈrɑːl/ *noun* [S] a situation without limits or controls in which people can have or do what they want they want: *The row between the Prime Minister and the opposition leader soon developed into a free-for-all between MPs from all parties.*

free-form /ˈfriː.fɔːm/ [US] /-fɔːrm/ *adj* not having or following a particular style or structure: *free-form skating*

ˌfree ˈgift *noun* [C] an item which is given to a customer free when they buy something in order to

F

encourage people to buy more of it: *You get a free gift if you spend more than £20.*

freehand DRAWING /ˈfriː.hænd/ *adj, adv* (of a drawing) done without the help of any special equipment for accurately creating circles, straight lines, symbols, etc: *a freehand sketch*

free 'hand AUTHORITY *noun* [S] the right or authority to do anything you consider necessary: *The company's given me a free hand to negotiate a deal with the Japanese.*

freehold /ˈfriː.həʊld/ ⓤ /-hoʊld/ *noun* [C] legal ownership and control of a building or piece of land for an unlimited time: *Who owns the freehold of/on the property?* ⊃Compare **leasehold**. **freehold** /ˈfriː.həʊld/ ⓤ /-hoʊld/ *adj: Are those flats freehold or leasehold?*
freeholder /ˈfriː.həʊl.dəʳ/ ⓤ /-hoʊl.dɚ/ *noun* [C] an owner of a particular building or piece of land

free 'house *noun* [C] UK a type of bar in the UK which is not owned and controlled by a BREWERY (= business which makes beer), so the range of beers and other drinks that it can sell is not limited ⊃Compare **tied house**.

free 'jazz *noun* [U] a type of modern music in which the players do not follow any written structure

free 'kick *noun* [C] in football, an opportunity to kick the ball without opposition from the other team, which is allowed when a player from the other team has not obeyed one of the rules

freelance /ˈfriː.lɑːnts/ ⓤ /-lænts/ *adj, adv* doing particular pieces of work for different organizations, rather than working all the time for a single organization: *Most of the journalists I know are/work freelance.* ○ *a freelance artist* **freelance** /ˈfriː.lɑːnts/ ⓤ /-lænts/ *noun* [C] (ALSO **freelancer**) *The firm employs several freelances.* **freelance** /ˈfriː.lɑːnts/ ⓤ /-lænts/ *verb* [I] *I prefer to freelance from home rather than to work in an office,*

freeloader /ˈfriː.ləʊ.dəʳ/ ⓤ /-ˌloʊ.dɚ/ *noun* [C] DISAPPROVING a person who uses money, food, a room in a house, etc. given by other people, but who gives nothing to them in exchange **freeloading** /ˈfriː.ləʊ.dɪŋ/ ⓤ /-ˌloʊ.dɪŋ/ *noun* [U]

free 'love *noun* [U] OLD-FASHIONED sexual activity with several partners which does not involve loyalty to any particular person

freely /ˈfriː.li/ *adv:* ⊃See at **free** NOT LIMITED, **free** LOOSE.

freeman /ˈfriː.mən/ ⓤ /-mæn/ *noun* [C] UK a person who has been given particular special rights in a city, as an honour: *Paul McCartney was made a freeman of the City of Liverpool.*

free 'market *noun* [S] an economic system with only a small amount of government control, in which prices and earnings are decided by the level of demand for, and production of goods and services: *In a free market, if demand for a product increases then so does its price.* ○ *the free-market economy*

Freemason /ˈfriːˌmeɪ.sⁿn/ *noun* [C] (ALSO **Mason**) a member of a large, old and powerful secret society for men in which all the members help each other and use secret signs to communicate with each other
Freemasonry /ˈfriːˌmeɪ.sⁿn.ri/ *noun* [U] (ALSO **Masonry**) Freemasons considered as a group, or their beliefs and activities

free 'pardon UK *noun* [C usually sing] (US **pardon**) LEGAL official forgiveness for a crime: *The new government is to grant a free pardon to all political prisoners.* ⊃Compare **royal pardon**.

Freephone, TRADEMARK **Freefone** /ˈfriː.fəʊn/ ⓤ /-foʊn/ *noun* [U] a system in the UK which allows you to telephone particular organizations without paying for the call, because the organizations will pay the cost: *a 24-hour freephone customer ordering service* ○ *For further details, call Freephone 0800 123456/call our Freephone number 0800 123456.*

free 'port *noun* [C] an area near a port or airport to which goods from foreign countries can be brought without tax being paid if they are sent to another country when they leave this area

Freepost /ˈfriː.pəʊst/ ⓤ /-poʊst/ *noun* [U] UK a system which allows you to send something by post to

particular organizations without payment, because the organizations will pay the cost

free 'radical *noun* [C often pl] SPECIALIZED a molecule that has an extra ELECTRON and therefore reacts very easily with other molecules: *Free radicals have been implicated in cancer and many other serious diseases.*

free-range /ˌfriː.ˈreɪndʒ/ *adj* relating to or produced by farm animals that are allowed to move around outside and are not kept in cages: *free-range eggs/chickens/turkeys*

freesheet /ˈfriː.ʃiːt/ *noun* [C] UK a free newspaper in which local shops or other businesses put advertisements telling people about their services, and which often gives details of local entertainment

freesia /ˈfriː.ʒə/ *noun* [C] a plant with pleasant smelling yellow, white, pink or purple flowers

free 'speech *noun* [U] the right to express your opinions publicly

free 'spirit *noun* [C usually sing] a person who does what they want with enjoyment and pleasure and does not feel limited by the usual rules of social behaviour

free-standing /ˌfriː.ˈstæn.dɪŋ/ *adj* standing alone and not fixed to a wall, etc: *a free-standing bookshelf* ○ FIGURATIVE *The electronics division was split off into a freestanding company.*

freestyle /ˈfriː.staɪl/ *noun* [S] a sports competition, especially a swimming race, in which each competitor can use any style or method they choose: *He won the 400 metres freestyle.*

freethinker /ˌfriː.ˈθɪŋ.kəʳ/ ⓤ /-kɚ/ *noun* [C] OLD-FASHIONED someone who forms their own opinions and beliefs, especially about religion or politics, rather than just accepting what is officially or commonly believed and taught **freethinking** /ˈfriːˌθɪŋ.kɪŋ/ /ˌ-ˈ--/ *adj*

free 'throw *noun* [C] in basketball, an opportunity to score extra points which is given to a member of one team if a player from the other team has not obeyed one of the rules

free 'trade *noun* [U] international buying and selling of goods, without limits on the amount of goods that one country can sell to another, and without special taxes on the goods bought from a foreign country: *a free-trade agreement*

free 'verse *noun* [U] poetry whose lines do not have a regular pattern

freeware /ˈfriː.weəʳ/ ⓤ /ˈfriː.wer/ *noun* [U] computer programs that you can often copy from the Internet and do not have to pay for

freeway /ˈfriː.weɪ/ *noun* [C] US FOR **motorway**

freewheel /ˈfriː.wiːl/ *verb* [I] (ALSO **coast**) UK to travel, especially down a hill, on a bicycle or in a vehicle without using the legs or engine to provide power
freewheeling /ˈfriː.wiː.lɪŋ/ *adj* INFORMAL not limited by rules or accepted ways of doing things: *a freewheeling lifestyle/society*

free 'will *noun* [U] the ability to decide what to do independently of any outside influence: *No one told me to do it – I did it of my own free will.*

freeze /friːz/ *verb* **froze**, **frozen 1** [I or T] If you freeze something, you lower its temperature below 0°C, causing it to become cold and often hard, and if something freezes, its temperature goes below 0°C: *Water freezes to ice at a temperature of 0°C.* ○ *The ground had frozen hard/solid.* ○ *When the lake freezes (over)* (= turns into ice on the surface), *we can go skating on it.* ○ *Our pipes froze (up)* (= the water in them turned to ice) *several times last winter.* ○ *The weather forecast says that it is going to freeze tonight* (= that the temperature will be at or below 0°C). ○ *Without a sleeping bag, you would freeze to death* (= become so cold that you die) *out there on the mountainside.* **2** [I] (ALSO **freeze up**) US If an engine or lock freezes, it stops working because its parts have become stuck and can no longer move: *My old bicycle was so rusty that the gears had frozen.* ○ *If the lock has frozen up, try lubricating it with oil.* **3** [I or T] to preserve food by storing it at a very low temperature so that it becomes hard: *I'll freeze any food that's left over.* ○ *Most soups freeze* (= can be preserved by being stored at a very low temperature) *well.* **4** [I] If a person or animal

F

that is moving freezes, it stops suddenly and becomes completely still, especially because of fear: *She saw someone outside the window and froze.* ○ *"Freeze* (= Don't move) *or I'll shoot", screamed the gunman.* **5** [T] To freeze something such as pay or prices is to fix them at a particular level and not allow any increases: *The Government has frozen pensions until the end of next year.* **6** [T] to officially and legally prevent money or property from being used or moved: *When it was obvious the company was going bankrupt, the government ordered all their assets to be frozen.*

• **be cold enough to freeze the balls off a brass monkey** *HUMOROUS* to be very cold

freeze /friːz/ *noun* **1** [S] a period of extremely cold weather **2** [C] a temporary stopping of something: *The Government has imposed a wage freeze/a freeze* **on** *wage increases.*

freezing /ˈfriː.zɪŋ/ *adj* turning to ice: *Freezing fog and icy patches are expected to cause problems for motorists tonight.*

freezing /ˈfriː.zɪŋ/ *adj, adv* extremely cold: ***It's freezing*** *in here – can I close the window?* ○ *They survived for four hours in the freezing water before they were finally rescued.* ○ *After walking through the snow, my feet were freezing.* ○ *I had to wait for hours on the freezing* ***cold*** *station platform.*

▲ **freeze *sb* out** *phrasal verb* [M] to make someone feel that they are not part of a group by being unfriendly towards them, or to stop someone from being included in an arrangement or activity: *I felt I was being frozen out* ***of/from*** *the discussions.* ○ *He believed that organizations like theirs were being frozen out.*

freeze-dry /ˌfriːzˈdraɪ/ *verb* [T] to preserve something, especially food, by freezing and then drying it: *freeze-dried coffee*

freeze-frame /ˈfriːzˌfreɪm/ *noun* [C] a single picture from a film, or the device on a VIDEO RECORDER that allows you to stop a film at a particular point and look at a single picture

freezer /ˈfriː.zəʳ/ [US] /-zɚ/ *noun* [C] (*ALSO* **deep freeze**) a container, operated by electricity, which preserves food at a very cold temperature so that it becomes solid and can be kept safely for a long time: *a chest/upright freezer* ➲See picture **In the Kitchen** on page Centre 16

ˈfreezer comˌpartment *noun* [C] a small, very cold part of a fridge used for preserving and keeping food at a very cold temperature for long periods

ˈfreezer ˌpack *noun* [C] a plastic container filled with water or other liquid which can be frozen and then put in a container holding food and drink, in order to keep the food and drink cold

ˈfreezing (ˌpoint) *noun* [U] the temperature (0°C) at which water becomes ice: *The temperature was below freezing for most of the day.*

freight /freɪt/ *noun* [U] **1** goods, but not passengers, that are carried from one place to another, by ship, aircraft, train or truck, or the system of transporting these goods: *The ship* ***carries*** *both freight and passengers.* ○ *a freight company* ○ *Will the goods be sent by* ***air*** *or* ***sea*** *freight?* ○ *freight* ***trains*** ○ *US The escaped prisoner made his getaway in a freight car/wagon on a train.* **2** the money paid for transporting goods

freight /freɪt/ *adv*: *It would be much cheaper to send the goods freight* (= as part of a large group).

freight /freɪt/ *verb* [T] to send goods by air, sea or train: *Grapes from this region are freighted all over the world.*

freighter /ˈfreɪ.təʳ/ [US] /-t̬ɚ/ *noun* [C] a large ship or aircraft for carrying goods

French /frentʃ/ *noun* [U] **1** the language that people speak in France, Belgium, parts of Canada and other countries **2 the French** the people of France

• **Excuse/Pardon my French.** *OLD-FASHIONED HUMOROUS* said when you are pretending to be sorry for saying a swear word: *That sod Wilkins, excuse my French, has taken my bloody parking space.*

French /frentʃ/ *adj* from, belonging to or relating to France: *French food/culture/music*

ˌFrench ˈbean *noun* [C] *UK FOR* **green bean**

ˌFrench ˈbread *noun* [U] a type of usually white bread in the form of a long thin loaf with a hard outer layer ➲See also **baguette**.

ˌFrench Caˈnadian *noun* [C], *adj* a person from Canada whose first language is French, or of or from that part of Canada where French is spoken

ˌFrench ˈdoors *plural noun MAINLY US FOR* **French windows**

ˌFrench ˈdressing *noun* [U] **1** *UK* a mixture of oil, vinegar and spices, used to flavour salad: *She tossed the lettuce in French dressing.* **2** *US* a mixture of oil, MAYONNAISE (= a thick cold white sauce) and KETCHUP (= a thick cold red sauce), used to flavour salad

ˌFrench ˈfries *plural noun* (*ALSO* **fries**) *MAINLY US* long thin pieces of fried potato

ˌFrench ˈhorn *noun* [C] a musical instrument which consists of a long metal tube bent into circles, with a wide opening at one end, played by blowing down the tube and moving the fingers on valves

ˌFrench ˈkiss *noun* [C] a kiss with the lips apart and the tongues touching

ˌFrench ˈletter *noun* [C] *UK OLD-FASHIONED INFORMAL FOR* **condom**

ˌFrench ˈloaf *noun* [C] a loaf of FRENCH BREAD

Frenchman /ˈfrentʃ.mən/ *noun* [C] a man who comes from France

ˌFrench ˈpolish *noun* [U] *UK* a very shiny varnish used on furniture **ˌFrench ˈpolish** *verb* [T]

ˌFrench ˈstick *noun* [C] *UK FOR* **baguette**

ˌFrench ˈtoast *noun* [U] bread which has been covered in egg and fried

ˌFrench ˈwindows *plural noun* a pair of glass doors, usually opening from the back of a house into its garden

Frenchwoman /ˈfrentʃˌwʊm.ən/ *noun* [C] a woman who comes from France

frenetic /frəˈnet.ɪk/ [US] /-ˈnet̬-/ *adj* involving a lot of movement or activity; extremely active, excited or uncontrolled: *After weeks of frenetic* ***activity***, *the job was finally finished.* ○ *There was frenetic trading on the Stock Exchange yesterday.* **frenetically** /frəˈnet.ɪ.kli/ [US] /-net̬-/ *adv*

frenzy /ˈfren.zi/ *noun* [C or U] (an example of) uncontrolled and excited behaviour or emotion, which is sometimes violent: *In a frenzy* ***of*** *rage she hit him.* ○ *the media frenzy over the Princess's death* ○ *The audience* ***worked/whipped themselves up into*** *a frenzy as they waited for her to come on stage.* ○ *There was a frenzy* ***of*** *activity on the financial markets yesterday.* ○ *In a moment of jealous frenzy, she cut the sleeves off all his shirts.* **frenzied** /ˈfren.ziːd/ *adj*: *The office was a scene of frenzied* ***activity*** *this morning.* ○ *As the evening wore on the* ***dancing*** *got more and more frenzied.*

frequency [HAPPENING] /ˈfriː.kwənt.si/ *noun* [C or U] the number of times something happens within a particular period, or the fact of something happening often or a large number or times: *Complaints about the frequency* ***of*** *trains rose by 201% in the last year.* ○ *the increasing frequency* ***of*** *terrorist attacks* ○ *It's not the duration of his absences from work so much as the frequency that worries me.*

frequency [WAVES] /ˈfriː.kwᵊnt.si/ *noun SPECIALIZED* **1** [U] the number of times that a wave, especially a sound or radio wave, is produced within a particular period, especially one second: *the frequency of light* ○ *low frequency radiation* ○ *The human ear cannot hear very high-frequency sounds.* **2** [C] a particular number of radio waves produced in a second at which a radio signal is broadcast: *Do you know what frequency the BBC World Service is* ***on****?*

frequent [COMMON] /ˈfriː.kwᵊnt/ *adj* happening often; common: *a frequent visitor to the US* ○ *A frequent criticism of the proposal has been its high cost.* ○ *The most frequent cause of death is heart attack.* ○ *The attacks were increasingly frequent and serious.*

frequently /ˈfriː.kwᵊnt.li/ *adv* often: *frequently asked questions* ○ *I see him quite frequently.* ○ *The buses run less frequently on Sundays.*

F

frequent [VISIT] /frɪˈkwent/ [US] /ˈfriː.kwənt/ *verb* [T] *FORMAL* to be in or visit a particular place often: *a bar frequented by criminals*

fresco /ˈfres.kəʊ/ [US] /-koʊ/ *noun* [C or U] *plural* **frescos** or **frescoes** (a picture made by) painting on wet PLASTER (= mixture of sand, LIME and water) on a wall or ceiling: *Michelangelo's famous frescoes are in the Sistine Chapel in Rome.*

fresh [NEW] /freʃ/ *adj* [before n] **1** new; different or another: *The original orders were cancelled and I was given fresh instructions.* ○ *Fresh evidence has emerged that casts doubts on the men's conviction.* ○ *We need to take a fresh look at the problem.* ○ *Your coffee is cold – let me make you a fresh cup.* ○ *There has been fresh fighting between police and demonstrators.* ○ *They decided to move abroad and* ***make a** fresh **start**.* **2** *APPROVING* new and therefore interesting or exciting: *His book offers some fresh insights into the events leading up to the war.* ○ *We have tried to come up with a fresh new approach.*

freshen /ˈfreʃ.ən/ *verb* [T] (*ALSO* **freshen up**) *MAINLY US* If you freshen someone's especially alcoholic drink, you add more to it: *Here, let me freshen your drink.*

freshness /ˈfreʃ.nəs/ *noun* [U] the quality of being fresh

fresh [RECENT] /freʃ/ *adj* recently made, done, arrived, etc., and especially not yet changed by time: *There was a fresh fall of snow during the night.* ○ *There's nothing better than fresh bread, straight from the oven.* ○ *The house, with its fresh coat of paint, looked lovely in the sunshine.* ○ *She's fresh* ***out of/from*** *university and very bright.* ○ *The events of last year are still fresh in people's minds* (= people can remember them easily).

• **be fresh out** *MAINLY US* If you are fresh out of something, you have just finished or sold all of it, so that there is no more left.

fresh- /freʃ-/ *prefix* recently done: *fresh-baked bread* ○ *fresh-cut flowers*

freshly /ˈfreʃ.li/ *adv* recently done: *freshly baked bread* ○ *freshly made sandwiches* ○ *freshly washed hair* **freshness** /ˈfreʃ.nəs/ *noun* [U]

fresh [NATURAL] /freʃ/ *adj* (of food or flowers) in a natural condition rather than artificially preserved by a process such as freezing: *fresh fruit and vegetables* ○ *fresh fish/meat* ○ *fresh coffee* **freshness** /ˈfreʃ.nəs/ *noun* [U]

fresh [AIR] /freʃ/ *adj* **1** (of air) clean and cool; found outside rather than in a room: *I opened the window to let some fresh air in.* ○ *fresh mountain air* ○ *I'm just going out for a breath of fresh air.* **2** describes weather that is cool and sometimes windy: *It was a lovely fresh spring morning.* ○ *There's quite a fresh breeze today.*

freshen /ˈfreʃ.ən/ *verb* **1** [T] (*ALSO* **freshen up**) to make something cleaner and/or cooler: *She opened a window to freshen up the room.* **2** [I] If a wind freshens, it becomes stronger and cooler: *The wind is expected to freshen as it moves in from the east.* **freshly** /ˈfreʃ.li/ *adv* **freshness** /ˈfreʃ.nəs/ *noun* [U]

PHRASAL VERBS WITH **freshen** ▼

▲ **freshen** *(sb/sth)* **up** [CLEAN] *phrasal verb* [M] to make someone or something clean and pleasant: *Would you like to freshen up after your journey?* ○ [R] *I'm just going to have a shower to freshen myself up.*

▲ **freshen** *sth* **up** [NEW] *phrasal verb* [M] to make something different and more interesting or attractive: *The Prime Minister has freshened up her Cabinet with a few new faces.*

fresh [CLEAN] /freʃ/ *adj* clean and pleasant: *I felt wonderfully clean and fresh after my shower.* ○ *I use a mouthwash to keep my breath fresh.* ○ *This wine has a light, fresh taste.* **freshness** /ˈfreʃ.nəs/ *noun* [U]

fresh [NOT TIRED] /freʃ/ *adj* [after v] energetic and enthusiastic; not tired: *I'll deal with this problem in the morning when I'm fresh.* ○ *Try and get some sleep on the plane, then you'll arrive feeling fresh.*

• **be as fresh as a daisy** to be full of energy and enthusiasm: *After a good night's sleep I'll be as fresh as a daisy.*

fresh [SKIN] /freʃ/ *adj* (of a face) natural, healthy and young looking: *She has a lovely fresh* (= clear and smooth) ***complexion***.

fresh [NOT SALTY] /freʃ/ *adj* [before n] (of water) not salty: *Trout are fresh water fish* (= live in water that is not salty). ○ *These plants are found in fresh water lakes and rivers* (= those containing water that is not salty).

freshness /ˈfreʃ.nəs/ *noun* [U]

fresh [TOO CONFIDENT] /freʃ/ *adj* *INFORMAL* being too confident and showing a lack of respect, or showing by your actions or words that you want to have sex with someone: *Don't you* ***get** fresh **with*** *me, young woman!* ○ *He started* ***getting*** *fresh* (= behaving in a sexual way) *in the cinema, so she slapped his face.*

fresher /ˈfreʃ.əʳ/ [US] /-ɚ/ *noun* [C] *UK INFORMAL* a student who has recently started studying at a college or university

fresh-faced /ˈfreʃ.feɪst/ *adj* looking young: *fresh-faced 18- and 19-year-old soldiers*

freshman /ˈfreʃ.mən/ *noun* [C] *US* **1** (*INFORMAL* **frosh**) a student in the first year of HIGH SCHOOL, college, or university: *He's a freshman at Harvard.* ○ *Greg and Jody met in their freshman year at college and married soon after they graduated.* **2** someone who has recently started any particular job or activity: *a freshman in Congress* ○ *a freshman football player*

freshwater /ˈfreʃˌwɔː.təʳ/ [US] /-ˌwɑː.t̬ɚ/ *adj* [before n] living in or containing water that is not salty: *freshwater fish* ○ *a freshwater lake/river* ➲Compare **salt water**.

fret [WORRY] /fret/ *verb* [I] **-tt-** to be anxious or worried: *Don't fret – I'm sure he's OK.* ○ *She spent the day fretting* ***about/over*** *what she'd said to Nicky.*

fretful /ˈfret.fəl/ *adj*: *By midnight the children were tired and fretful* (= complaining a lot because they were unhappy). **fretfully** /ˈfret.fəl.i/ *adv*

fret [MUSIC] /fret/ *noun* [C] any of the small raised metal bars across the long thin part of a stringed musical instrument such as a guitar, that show you where to put your fingers on the strings in order to produce different notes **fretted** /ˈfret.ɪd/ [US] /ˈfret̬-/ *adj*: *Guitars and lutes are fretted musical instruments.*

fretboard /ˈfret.bɔːd/ [US] /-bɔːrd/ *noun* [C] a FINGERBOARD (= long strip of wood on a stringed musical instrument against which the strings are pressed) with FRETS, such as on a guitar

fretsaw /ˈfret.sɔː/ [US] /-sɑː/ *noun* [C] a saw for cutting curves and inside corners in wood

fretwork /ˈfret.wɜːk/ [US] /-wɝːk/ *noun* [U] decorative open patterns especially cut out of wood or metal or made in EMBROIDERY

Freudian /ˈfrɔɪ.di.ən/ *adj* relating to the ideas or methods of Sigmund Freud, especially his ideas about the way in which people's hidden thoughts and feelings influence their behaviour

ˌFreudian ˈslip *noun* [C] something which you say accidentally which is different from what you intended to say, and which seems to show your true thoughts

FRG /ef.ɑːˈdʒiː/ [US] /-ɑːr-/ *noun* [U] *ABBREVIATION FOR* (the former) Federal Republic of Germany

Fri *noun WRITTEN ABBREVIATION FOR* Friday

friable /ˈfraɪ.ə.bl̩/ *adj SPECIALIZED* easily broken into small pieces

friar /fraɪəʳ/ [US] /fraɪr/ *noun* [C] a man belonging to one of several Roman Catholic religious groups, whose members often promise to stay poor

friary /ˈfraɪə.ri/ [US] /ˈfraɪɚ.i/ *noun* [C] a building in which friars live

fricassee /ˈfrɪk.ə.siː/ *noun* [C or U] a dish made of pieces of meat, especially chicken or VEAL (= meat from young cows), cooked and served in a white sauce

friction [FORCE] /ˈfrɪk.ʃən/ *noun* [U] the force which makes it difficult for one object to slide along the surface of another or to move through a liquid or gas: *When you rub your hands together the friction produces heat.* **frictional** /ˈfrɪk.ʃən.əl/ *adj*

friction [DISAGREEMENT] /ˈfrɪk.ʃən/ *noun* [U] disagreement or unfriendliness caused by people having different opinions: *There's a lot of friction* ***between*** *my wife and my mother.* ○ *Politics is a source of considerable friction in our family.* ○ *Border clashes have led to increased friction* ***between*** *the two countries.*

Friday /ˈfraɪ.deɪ/ noun [C or U] (WRITTEN ABBREVIATION Fri) the day of the week after Thursday and before Saturday: *Shall we go to the theatre on Friday?* ○ *I love Fridays because I leave work early.*

fridge /frɪdʒ/ noun [C] (ALSO **refrigerator**, US OLD-FASHIONED **ice-box**) a piece of kitchen equipment which uses electricity to preserve food at a cold temperature: *Don't forget to put the milk back in the fridge.* ⊃See picture **In the Kitchen** on page Centre 16

fridge-freezer /ˌfrɪdʒˈfriː.zəʳ/ ⓤ /-zɚ/ noun [C] (US USUALLY **refrigerator-freezer**) a piece of kitchen equipment divided into two parts for preserving food, one of which is a fridge and the other a freezer

fridge ˌmagnet noun [C] a small decorative magnet used for attaching messages and notes to a fridge

friend COMPANION /frend/ noun [C] **1** a person whom you know well and whom you like a lot, but who is usually not a member of your family: *She's my best/oldest/closest friend – we've known each other since we were five.* ○ *He's a family friend/friend of the family.* ○ *This restaurant was recommended to me by a friend of mine.* ○ *We've been friends for years.* ○ *José and Pilar are (good) friends of ours.* ○ *We're (good) friends with José and Pilar.* ○ *She said that she and Peter were just (good) friends* (= they were not having a sexual relationship). ○ *I've made a lot of friends in this job.* ○ *He finds it difficult to make friends.* ⊃See also **befriend**. **2** someone who is not an enemy and whom you can trust: *You don't have to pretend anymore – you're among friends now.* **3** someone who gives money to a theatre, other arts organization or charity in order to support it: *The Friends of the Royal Academy raised £10 000 towards the cost of the exhibition.*

• **have friends in high places** to know important people who can help you get what you want

• **A friend in need (is a friend indeed).** SAYING This means that a friend who helps you when you really need help is a true friend.

• **With friends like you, who needs enemies?** HUMOROUS SAYING said to or about someone who claims to be your friend but who is treating you very badly

• **What are friends for?** (ALSO **That's what friends are for.**) SAYING said to a friend who has thanked you for doing something special for them

friendless /ˈfrend.ləs/ adj without friends: *Friendless and jobless, he wondered how he would survive the year ahead.*

friendly /ˈfrend.li/ adj **1** behaving in a pleasant, kind way towards someone: *a friendly face/smile* ○ *Our neighbours have always been very friendly to/towards us.* ○ *I'm on quite friendly terms with my daughter's teacher.* ○ *Are you friendly with* (= a friend of) *Graham?* ✻ NOTE: The opposite is **unfriendly**. **2** describes a place that is pleasant and that makes you feel happy and comfortable: *It's a friendly little restaurant.* **3** A friendly game or argument is one which you play or have for pleasure and in order to practise your skills, rather than playing or arguing seriously with the aim of winning: *We were having a friendly argument about French politics.* ○ *The teams are playing a friendly match on Sunday.* **4** Friendly countries and friendly soldiers are ones who are not your enemies and who are working or fighting with you.

friendly /ˈfrend.li/ noun [C] a game which is played for enjoyment and in order to practise, not with the aim of winning points as part of a serious competition: *The rugby club has a friendly next week against the Giants.*

-friendly /-frend.li/ suffix **1** used at the end of words to mean 'not harmful': *environmentally-friendly detergent* ○ *ozone-friendly aerosols* ○ *dolphin-friendly tuna* (= fish caught without harming DOLPHINS). **2** used at the end of words to mean 'suitable for particular people to use': *a family-friendly restaurant* **friendliness** /ˈfrend.lɪ.nəs/ noun [U]

friendship /ˈfrend.ʃɪp/ noun [C or U] when two people are friends: *Their friendship goes back to when they were at school together.* ○ *Did you form any close/lasting friendships while you were at college?* ○ *I value her friendship above anything else.*

Friend RELIGION /frend/ noun [C] a **Quaker**

ˌfriendly ˈfire noun [U] during a war, shooting that is hitting you from your own side, not from the enemy: *Three soldiers were killed by friendly fire when a mortar bomb hit their truck.*

ˈfriendly soˌciety noun [C] in Britain, an organization to which members pay small amounts of money over a long period so that when they are ill or old they will receive money back

ˌFriends of the ˈEarth group noun (WRITTEN ABBREVIATION **FoE**) an international organization which aims to protect the environment

frier /ˈfraɪ.əʳ/ ⓤ /-ɚ/ noun [C] a **fryer**, see at **fry** COOK

fries /fraɪz/ plural noun **French fries**

Friesian MAINLY UK /ˈfriː.ʒən/ noun [C] (MAINLY US **Holstein**) a black and white cow that produces a large amount of milk

frieze /friːz/ noun [C] a narrow piece of decoration along a wall, either inside a room or on the outside of a building just under the roof

frig /frɪg/ verb **-gg-**

▲ **frig about/around** phrasal verb OFFENSIVE to behave stupidly: *Stop frigging about, will you!*

frigate /ˈfrɪg.ət/ noun [C] a small fast military ship

frigging /ˈfrɪg.ɪŋ/ adj [before n], adv OFFENSIVE used to give more force to an expression of annoyance or anger: *You frigging idiot!*

fright /fraɪt/ noun [S or U] the feeling of fear, especially if felt suddenly, or an experience of fear which happens suddenly: *I lay in bed shaking with fright.* ○ *You gave her such a fright turning the lights out like that.* ○ *You gave me the fright of my life* (= a very severe fright), *jumping out of the shadows like that!*

• **look a fright** OLD-FASHIONED INFORMAL to look ugly or stupid: *Didn't she look a fright in that dress?*

• **take fright** to feel fear: *Our dog took fright at the noise of the fireworks and ran indoors.*

frighten /ˈfraɪ.tən/ verb [T] **1** to make someone feel fear: *He frightens me when he drives so fast.* ○ *You'll frighten the baby wearing that mask.* ○ *The noise frightened me to death/out of my wits* (= gave me a severe fright). **2 frighten sb into sth** to make someone so frightened that they do something they did not want to do

frightened /ˈfraɪ.tənd/ adj feeling afraid or nervous: *She gets frightened when he shouts at her.* ○ *The policewoman found a frightened child in the hut.* ○ *Are you frightened of spiders?* ○ *I was frightened (that) you would fall.* ○ *Don't be frightened to complain if the service is bad.*

frightening /ˈfraɪ.tən.ɪŋ/ adj making you feel fear: *a frightening thought* ○ *a frightening film* ○ *It is frightening to think what might happen if she left him.* **frighteningly** /ˈfraɪ.tən.ɪŋ.li/ adv: *She looked frighteningly thin.*

▲ **frighten sb/sth away/off** phrasal verb to make a person or animal feel fear in order to make them go away: *Be quiet or you'll frighten the deer off.*

frighteners /ˈfraɪ.tən.əz/ ⓤ /-ɚz/ plural noun UK OLD-FASHIONED **put the frighteners on sb** to threaten someone: *He said he wouldn't pay up so I sent my brother round to put the frighteners on him.*

frightful /ˈfraɪt.fəl/ adj OLD-FASHIONED INFORMAL used to emphasize what you are saying, especially how bad something is: *He made a frightful mess in the kitchen.* ○ *Of course the cleaning is a frightful bore.*

frightfully /ˈfraɪt.fəl.i/ adv OLD-FASHIONED INFORMAL very: *I'm frightfully sorry about the noise last night.*

frigid DISLIKING SEX /ˈfrɪdʒ.ɪd/ adj (of a woman) having difficulty in becoming sexually excited **frigidity** /frɪˈdʒɪd.ɪ.ti/ ⓤ /-t̬i/ noun [U]

frigid UNFRIENDLY /ˈfrɪdʒ.ɪd/ adj unfriendly or very formal: *There's a rather frigid atmosphere in the school.* **frigidly** /ˈfrɪdʒ.ɪd.li/ adv: *Sarah shook his hand frigidly.* **frigidity** /frɪˈdʒɪd.ɪ.ti/ ⓤ /-t̬i/ noun [U]

frigid COLD /ˈfrɪdʒ.ɪd/ adj (of weather conditions or the conditions in a room) extremely cold: *Few plants can grow in such a frigid environment.*

ˈFrigid ˌZones plural noun SPECIALIZED the cold areas inside the ARCTIC and ANTARCTIC Circles which receive very little light from the sun

frill /frɪl/ *noun* [C] **1** a long, narrow strip of cloth with folds along one side which is sewn along the edge of a piece of clothing or material for decoration: *You could always sew a frill or two around the bottom of the skirt if you think it's too plain.* **2** INFORMAL **frills** extra things that are added to something to make it more pleasant or more attractive, but that are not necessary: *a cheap, no frills airline*

frilly /'frɪl.i/ *adj* (ALSO **frilled**) with a lot of frills: *a baby in a white frilly dress*

fringe EDGE /frɪndʒ/ *noun* [C] the outer or less important part of an area, group or activity: *the southern fringe of the city* ○ *the radical fringes of the party*

fringe /frɪndʒ/ *verb* **be fringed with** *sth* If a place is fringed with something, that thing forms a border along the edge: *The river is fringed with wild flowers.*

fringe DECORATION /frɪndʒ/ *noun* [C] a decorative edge of hanging narrow strips of material or threads on a piece of clothing or material: *a fringe around the edge of a tablecloth*

fringed /frɪndʒd/ *adj* with a fringe: *a fringed denim skirt* ○ *a robe fringed with fur*

fringe HAIR UK /frɪndʒ/ *noun* [C] (US **bangs**) an area of hair hanging over the forehead that is cut shorter than the rest of the hair: *a short fringe* ➔See picture **Hairstyles and Hats** on page Centre 8

'fringe ˌbenefit *noun* [C usually pl] something that you get because of your job which is additional to your pay but is not in the form of money: *Fringe benefits include a company car and free health insurance.*

frippery /'frɪp.ˀr.i/ /'-ɚ-/ *noun* [C or U] DISAPPROVING a silly decoration or other useless object: *fashion fripperies*

Frisbee /'frɪz.bi/ *noun* [C] TRADEMARK a circular piece of plastic with a curved edge which is thrown between people as a game

frisée, **frisé** /'friː.zeɪ/ *noun* [U] a plant which has green leaves with uneven edges which are eaten raw in salads

frisk /frɪsk/ *verb* [T] to use your hands to search someone's body when they are wearing clothes for hidden illegal objects or weapons: *We were all frisked at the airport.*

frisky /'frɪs.ki/ *adj* INFORMAL (of a person or an animal) playful or full of activity: *It's a beautiful horse but a bit too frisky for an inexperienced rider.* **friskily** /'frɪs.kɪ.li/ *adv* **friskiness** /'frɪs.kɪ.nəs/ *noun* [U]

frisk /frɪsk/ *verb* [I] to move around in a happy, energetic way: *a postcard with a picture of lambs frisking in the fields*

frisson /'friː.sõ/ /friː'soʊn/ *noun* [C usually sing] a sudden feeling of excitement or fear, especially when you think that something is about to happen: *As the music stopped, a frisson of excitement ran through the crowd.*

fritter /'frɪt.ər/ /'frɪt.ɚ/ *noun* [C] a slice of fruit, vegetable or meat covered with BATTER (= a mixture of flour, egg and milk) and then fried: *banana/apple fritters*

fritter /'frɪt.ər/ /'frɪt.ɚ/ *verb*

▲ **fritter** *sth* **away** *phrasal verb* [M] DISAPPROVING to waste money, time or an opportunity: *If I've got money in my pocket, I tend to fritter it away.* ○ *She fritters so much money away on expensive make-up.*

frivolous /'frɪv.ˀl.əs/ *adj* **1** behaving in a silly and foolish way when you should be serious: *I think he sees her as a frivolous young woman.* **2** describes an activity or object which is silly or unimportant rather than useful or serious: *I feel like doing something completely frivolous today.* **frivolously** /'frɪv.ˀl.ə.sli/ *adv* **frivolousness** /'frɪv.ˀl.ə.snəs/ *noun* [U]

frivolity /frɪ'vɒl.ə.ti/ /-'vɑː.lə.t̬i/ *noun* [C or U] You shouldn't treat such a serious subject with frivolity. ○ *I'm far too busy to waste time on frivolities* (= unimportant activities) *like going to the cinema.*

frizzled /'frɪz.ld/ *adj* (of food) fried for too long making it burnt and unpleasant to eat: *frizzled bacon*

frizzy /'frɪz.i/ *adj* DISAPPROVING (of hair) very curly and not smooth or shiny: *My hair goes all frizzy if it gets rained on.*

frizz /frɪz/ *verb* [T] INFORMAL *She's just had her hair frizzed* (= made curly), *and I didn't recognise her at first.*

frizz /frɪz/ *noun* [U] when hair is frizzy: *This mousse says it's designed to eliminate frizz and make hair glossy and easier to manage.*

fro /frəʊ/ /froʊ/ *adv* ➔See **to and fro**.

frock /frɒk/ /frɑːk/ *noun* [C] OLD-FASHIONED a dress: *a little girl in a pretty frock*

'frock ˌcoat *noun* [C] a short coat with a skirt which reaches the knees, worn by men, especially in the past

frog ANIMAL /frɒg/ /frɑːg/ *noun* [C] a small animal which has smooth skin, lives in water and on land, has long powerful back legs with which it jumps from place to place, has no tail, and is usually greenish-brown in colour: *Frogs make a low noise called a croak.* ➔See also **bullfrog**.

• **have a frog in** *your* **throat** to have difficulty in speaking because your throat feels dry and you want to cough

Frog PERSON /frɒg/ /frɑːg/ *noun* [C] UK OFFENSIVE a French person

frogman /'frɒg.mən/ /'frɑːg-/ *noun* [C] someone who swims or works under water for a long time wearing breathing equipment, FLIPPERS (= rubber or plastic shoes which are longer than the feet) and usually a rubber suit: *The body of the missing woman was recovered by police frogmen from a lake near her home.*

frogmarch /'frɒg.mɑːtʃ/ /'frɑːg.mɑːrtʃ/ *verb* [T usually + adv or prep] to force someone who is unwilling to move forward by holding the person's arms behind their back and then pushing them forward: *He was frogmarched off by two police officers.*

frogspawn /'frɒg.spɔːn/ /'frɑːg.spɑːn/ *noun* [U] a close group of frog's eggs, each egg being a small almost transparent ball with a black grain near its centre

frolic /'frɒl.ɪk/ /'frɑː.lɪk/ *verb* [I] **frolicking**, **frolicked**, **frolicked** to behave in a happy and playful way: *A group of suntanned children were frolicking on the beach.*

frolic /'frɒl.ɪk/ /'frɑː.lɪk/ *noun* [C or U] OLD-FASHIONED happy and playful behaviour: *a harmless frolic* ○ *It was all fun and frolics until it began to pour down with rain.*

frolicsome /'frɒl.ɪk.səm/ /'frɑː.lɪk-/ *adj* LITERARY lively and playful

from PLACE /frɒm/ STRONG /frɒm/ /frɑːm/, WEAK /frəm/ *prep* used to show the place where someone or something starts: *What time does the flight from Amsterdam arrive?* ○ *The wind is coming from the north.* ○ *She sent me a postcard from Majorca.* ○ *He took a handkerchief from his pocket.* ○ *She took her hairbrush from her handbag and began to brush her hair.* ○ *So did you really walk all the way from Bond Street?*

from TIME STRONG /frɒm/ /frɑːm/, WEAK /frəm/ *prep* used to show the time when something starts or the time when it was made or first existed: *Drinks will be served from seven o'clock.* ○ *The price of petrol will rise by 5p a gallon from tomorrow.* ○ *Most of the tapestries in this room date from the seventeenth century.* ○ *The museum is open from 9.30 to 6.00 Tuesday to Sunday.*

• **from that day/time on(wards)** LITERARY starting at that time and then continuing: *From that day on, she vowed never to trust him again.*

from DISTANCE STRONG /frɒm/ /frɑːm/, WEAK /frəm/ *prep* used to show the distance between two places: *It's about two kilometres from the airport to your hotel.* ○ *We're about a mile from home.*

from ORIGIN STRONG /frɒm/ /frɑːm/, WEAK /frəm/ *prep* used to show the origin of something or someone: *"Where are you from?" "I'm from Italy."* ○ *I wonder who this card is from.* ○ *Could I speak to someone from the sales department?* ○ *The sales executive from Unilever is here to see you.* ○ *What sort of reaction did you get from him?*

from MATERIAL STRONG /frɒm/ /frɑːm/, WEAK /frəm/ *prep* used to show the material of which something is made: *The desk is made from pine.* ○ *Meringues are made from sugar and egg whites.*

from LEVEL STRONG /frɒm/ /frɑːm/, WEAK /frəm/ *prep* used to show the level at which a range of things begins, such as numbers or prices: *Prices start from £2.99.* ○ *Tickets will cost from $10 to $45.* ○ *The number of people employed by the company has risen from 25 to 200 in three years.*

from [CHANGE] *STRONG* /frɒm/ [US] /frɑːm/, *WEAK* /frəm/ *prep* used to show a change in the state of someone or something: *Things went from bad* ***to*** *worse.* ○ *She has been promoted from deputy manager* ***to*** *senior manager.* ○ *Since the success of her first play, she has gone from strength* ***to*** *strength* (= her success has continued to increase).

from [CAUSE] *STRONG* /frɒm/ [US] /frɑːm/, *WEAK* /frəm/ *prep* used to show the cause of something or the reason why something happens: *He was rushed to hospital but died from his injuries.* ○ *She made her money from investing in property.* ○ *You could tell she wasn't lying from the fear in her voice.* ○ *Wearing the correct type of clothing will reduce the risk from radiation.*

from [CONSIDERING] *STRONG* /frɒm/ [US] /frɑːm/, *WEAK* /frəm/ *prep* used to show the facts or opinions you consider before making a judgment or decision: *Just from looking at the clouds, I would say it's going to rain.* ○ *It's difficult to guess what they will conclude from the evidence.*

from [REMOVE] *STRONG* /frɒm/ [US] /frɑːm/, *WEAK* /frəm/ *prep* **1** used to show that someone has left a place, or that something has been removed or taken away: *They were exiled from their homes during the war.* ○ *Her handbag was snatched from her in the street.* ○ *A refining process is used to extract usable fuel from crude oil.* **2** If you take a smaller amount from a larger amount, you reduce the larger amount by the smaller one: *Three from sixteen is thirteen.*

from [DIFFERENCE] *STRONG* /frɒm/ [US] /frɑːm/, *WEAK* /frəm/ *prep* used to show a difference between two people or things: *His opinion could hardly be more different from mine.* ○ *The two sisters are so similar that it's almost impossible to tell one from the other.*

from [POSITION] *STRONG* /frɒm/ [US] /frɑːm/, *WEAK* /frəm/ *prep* used to show the position of something in comparison with other things, or the point of view of someone when considering a matter or problem: *From the restaurant there is a beautiful view of Siena.* ○ *She was talking from her own experience of the problem.* ○ *From our point of view, we do not see how these changes will be beneficial to the company.*

from [PROTECTION] *STRONG* /frɒm/ [US] /frɑːm/, *WEAK* /frəm/ *prep* used to show what someone is being protected against: *They found shelter from the storm under a large oak tree.*

from [PREVENTING] *STRONG* /frɒm/ [US] /frɑːm/, *WEAK* /frəm/ *prep* used to show what someone is not allowed to do or know, or what has been stopped happening: *He's been banned from driving for six months.* ○ *For many years, the truth was kept from the public.* ○ *The bank loan saved her company from bankruptcy.*

fromage frais /ˌfrɒm.ɑːʒˈfreɪ/ [US] /frəˌmɑːʒ-/ *noun* **[C or U]** a type of soft, pale cheese which is low in fat, and which is often produced with fruit flavours and sugar added

frond /frɒnd/ [US] /frɑːnd/ *noun* **[C]** *SPECIALIZED* a long thin leaf of a plant: *Ferns and palms have fronds.*

front [PLACE] /frʌnt/ *noun* **[C usually sing] 1** the part of a building, object or person's body which faces forward or which is most often seen or used: *The front of the museum is very impressive.* ○ *He spilt soup all down his front.* ○ *He was lying on his front.* ○ *The* ***shop*** *front occupies a very prominent position on the main street.* **2** the part of a vehicle which is nearest to its direction of movement: *Do you want to sit* ***in the*** *front* (= next to the driver)*?* ○ *If we sit near the front of the bus, we'll have a better view.* **3** the outside part or cover of a book, newspaper, or magazine: *There was a picture of the Trevi fountain* ***on*** *the front of the book.* **4** one of the first pages in a book: *There's an inscription* ***in*** *the front of the book.*
• **in front 1** further forward than someone or something else: *The car in front suddenly stopped and I went into the back of it.* ○ *She started talking to the man in front* ***of*** *her.* **2** winning a game or competition: *By half time the Italians were well in front.*
• **in front of 1** close to the front part of something: *There's parking space in front of the hotel.* **2** where someone can see or hear you: *Please don't swear in front of the children.*
• **up front** If you give someone an amount of money up front, you pay them in advance: *He wants all the money up front or he won't do the job.*

front /frʌnt/ *adj* **[before n]** in or at the front of something: *One of his front teeth is missing.* ○ *I'd like seats on the front row of the stalls.* ○ *a dog's front paws*

front /frʌnt/ *verb* **1 [I or T]** (*ALSO* **front onto**) If a building or area fronts (onto) a particular place, it is near it and faces it: *All the apartments front onto the sea.* **2 [T]** to lead an organization or group of musicians: *She fronts a large IT company.* **3 be fronted with** If a building is fronted with something, its surface is covered with it: *a brick house fronted on three sides with timber*

frontal /ˈfrʌn.tᵊl/ [US] /-t̬ᵊl/ *adj* **[before n] 1** relating to the front of something: *the frontal lobes/regions of the brain* ➲See also **full-frontal**. **2 frontal assault/attack** very strong criticism of someone or something: *a frontal attack* ***on*** *the politician*

front [AREA OF ACTIVITY] /frʌnt/ *noun* **[C usually sing]** a particular area of activity: *How are things on the work front* (= Is the situation at work satisfactory)*?* ○ *She's very creative on the design front* (= She is very good at design).

Front [POLITICS] /frʌnt/ *noun* **[C usually sing]** a group of people sharing a political belief who perform actions in public to achieve their aims: *The National Front is an extremely right-wing political party in Britain.* ○ *The Animal Liberation Front has claimed responsibility for releasing the monkeys from the laboratory.*

front [APPEARANCE] /frʌnt/ *noun* **[C usually sing]** the character or qualities which a person or organization appears to have in public which is different from their real character, and whose purpose is often to deceive people or hide an illegal activity: *Don't be fooled by his kindness and sensitivity – it's just a front.* ○ *She presents such a cheerful front that you'd never guess she's ill.* ○ *The machinery company was a front operation for arms smuggling.* ○ *Several trading companies were set up in the early 1960s to act as fronts* ***for*** *money-laundering operations.*
▲ **front for** ***sth*** *phrasal verb* If a person fronts for an illegal organization, they help that organization by using their good reputation to hide its secret activities: *The police suspect him of fronting for a crime syndicate.*

front [WEATHER] /frʌnt/ *noun* **[C]** *SPECIALIZED* the place where two masses of air which have different temperatures meet: *A* ***cold/warm*** *front is approaching from the west.*

front [LAND] /frʌnt/ *noun* **[C usually sing]** land beside the sea or a lake, or the part of a coastal town next to the beach which often has a wide road or path along it: *Let's go for a stroll along the front.* ○ *The company specializes in building lake-front property.*

frontage /ˈfrʌn.tɪdʒ/ [US] /-t̬ɪdʒ/ *noun* **[C]** *FORMAL* the front part of a building which faces a road or river, or land beside a road or river: *These apartments all have a delightful dockside frontage.* ○ *The estate for sale includes two miles of river frontage.*

ˈfrontal ˌsystem *noun* **[C]** *SPECIALIZED* a combination of weather conditions in which one or more weather fronts can be identified: *With so many frontal systems so close together, we can expect the weather to be highly changeable over the next few days.*

frontbench /ˌfrʌntˈbentʃ/ *noun* **[C]** (one of the two rows of seats in the British parliament used by) leading members of the government and leading members of the main opposition party: *The Prime Minister's reply was met with howls of laughter from the opposition frontbench.* ○ *a former frontbench Treasury spokeswoman* ➲Compare **backbench**. **frontbencher** /ˌfrʌntˈben.tʃəʳ/ [US] /-tʃɚ/ *noun* **[C]** *He is the government's longest serving frontbencher.* ➲Compare **backbencher** at **backbench**.

ˌfront ˈdoor *noun* **[C]** the main entrance to a building, especially a house, which usually faces the road

frontier /frʌnˈtɪəʳ/ /ˈ--/ [US] /-ˈtɪr/ *noun* **[C]** a border between two countries, or (especially in the past in the United States) a border between cultivated land where people live and wild land: *Some of the frontier* ***between*** *Germany and Poland follows the course of the river Oder*

F

F

○ *Nepal has frontiers* **with** *both India and China.* ○ *They lived in a town close to* **the** *frontier.*

• **the frontiers of** *sth* the limits of what is known or what has been done before in an area of knowledge or an activity: *the frontiers of science and technology*

frontiersman /frʌnˈtɪəz.mən/ ⓤ /-ˈtɪrz-/ *noun* [C] a person who lives on the border between cultivated land and wild land, especially in the past in the United States: *The book portrays him as a heroic frontiersman of the Wild West.*

frontispiece /ˈfrʌn.tɪ.spiːs/ ⓤ /-ţɪ-/ *noun* [C] the picture which faces the page of a book with the title on: *A photograph of the author forms the frontispiece to the book.*

the ˌfront ˈline *noun* [S] a place where opposing armies face each other in war and where fighting happens: *Tens of thousands of soldiers died* **at the** *front line.* ○ *More front-line troops will be flown to the battle zone over the next few days.*

• **be in the front line** to be in an important position where you have influence, but where you are likely to be criticized or attacked: *Many social workers are in the front line of racial tension.*

ˈfront ˌman/woman *noun* [C] **1** a person who represents an organization when speaking to the public **2** someone who represents an illegal organization but whose behaviour makes people think that the organization is legal

front-of-house /ˌfrʌnt.əvˈhaʊs/ *noun* [U] SPECIALIZED the area in a theatre which is used by the public

front-page /ˌfrʌntˈpeɪdʒ/ *adj* [before n] describes information that is so important that it deserves to be printed on the front page of a newspaper: *The story made front-page news.*

ˌfront ˈroom *noun* [C] MAINLY UK OLD-FASHIONED a LIVING ROOM (= room in a house used for relaxing, but not for eating in) that faces the road

front-runner /ˌfrʌntˈrʌn.əʳ/ ⓤ /-ɚ/ *noun* [C] the person, animal or organization that is most likely to win something: *She is one of the front-runners in the contest.*

front-wheel drive /ˌfrʌnt.wiːlˈdraɪv/ *noun* [C] a vehicle in which the power from the engine is put directly to the front wheels rather than the back wheels

frosh /frɒʃ/ ⓤ /frɑːʃ/ *noun* [C] US INFORMAL FOR **freshman** (= a first-year student in high school, college or university)

frost COLD /frɒst/ ⓤ /frɑːst/ *noun* [C or U] (a period of time in which there is) an air temperature below the freezing point of water, or the white, powdery layer of ice which forms in these conditions, especially outside at night: *There was a frost last night.* ○ *When I woke up this morning the ground was covered with frost.* ○ *There were a lot of* **hard/heavy** (= severe) *frosts that winter.* **frost** /frɒst/ ⓤ /frɑːst/ *verb* [I or T] *Our bedroom window frosted* **up.** ○ *Our lawn is frosted* **over.**

frosty /ˈfrɒs.ti/ ⓤ /ˈfrɑː.sti/ *adj* **1** very cold, with a thin layer of white ice covering everything: *Be careful – the pavements are very frosty.* ○ *It was a cold and frosty morning.* **2** If someone or their behaviour is frosty, they are unfriendly and not welcoming: *He gave me a frosty look.* ○ *The chairperson's plan received a frosty* **reception** *from the committee.*

frostily /ˈfrɒs.tɪ.li/ ⓤ /ˈfrɑː.stə-/ *adv*: *"I didn't ask you to come," she said, frostily* (= in an unfriendly way). **frostiness** /ˈfrɒs.tɪ.nəs/ ⓤ /ˈfrɑː.stɪ-/ *noun* [U]

frost CAKE US /frɒst/ ⓤ /frɑːst/ *verb* [T] (UK **ice**) to cover a cake with FROSTING: *Leave the cake to cool before frosting it.*

frosting US /ˈfrɒs.tɪŋ/ ⓤ /ˈfrɑː.stɪŋ/ *noun* [U] (UK **icing**) a sweet food used to cover or fill cakes, made from sugar and water or sugar and butter

frost HAIR /frɒst/ ⓤ /frɑːst/ *verb* [T] US to make narrow strips of a person's hair paler in colour than the surrounding hair

frost GLASS /frɒst/ ⓤ /frɑːst/ *verb* [T] to intentionally make glass less smooth to stop it being transparent **frosted** /ˈfrɒs.tɪd/ ⓤ /ˈfrɑː.stɪd/ *adj*: *We had frosted glass put in the bathroom window.*

frostbite /ˈfrɒst.baɪt/ ⓤ /ˈfrɑːst-/ *noun* [U] injury to someone caused by severe cold, usually to their toes, fingers,

ears or nose **frostbitten** /ˈfrɒstˌbɪt.ᵊn/ ⓤ /ˈfrɑːstˌbɪt̬-/ *adj*: *frostbitten fingers/toes*

froth /frɒθ/ ⓤ /frɑːθ/ *verb* [I or T] to (cause a liquid to) have or produce a lot of small bubbles which often rise to the surface: *The waves frothed as they crashed onto the beach.* ○ *Shake the drink before serving it to froth it* **up.**

• **froth at the mouth 1** If a person or animal froths at the mouth, a mass of small bubbles appears from their mouth as the result of a disease. **2** INFORMAL to be extremely angry

froth /frɒθ/ ⓤ /frɑːθ/ *noun* [U] **1** small white bubbles on the surface of a liquid: *I like the froth on the top of the coffee.* **2** something which is not serious and has no real value but which is entertaining or attractive: *His books are just froth, but they're enjoyable enough.*

frothy /ˈfrɒθ.i/ ⓤ /ˈfrɑː.θi/ *adj* (of a liquid) with small white bubbles on the surface: *Beat the mixture until it becomes frothy.* ○ *frothy coffee*

frou-frou /ˈfruː.fruː/ *noun* [U] decorative pieces added to women's clothing: *a frou-frou gown/skirt*

frown /fraʊn/ *verb* [I] to bring your eyebrows together so that there are lines on your face above your eyes to show that you are annoyed or worried: *She frowned* **at** *me, clearly annoyed.* ○ *He frowned as he read the instructions, as if puzzled.* **frown** /fraʊn/ *noun* [C] *"Leave me alone," she said with a frown.*

▲ **frown on/upon** *sth phrasal verb* [often passive] to disapprove of something: *Smoking is frowned upon in many restaurants.*

frowsty /ˈfraʊ.sti/ *adj* MAINLY UK INFORMAL DISAPPROVING (of a room) having an unpleasant smell because of a lack of fresh air

froze /frəʊz/ ⓤ /froʊz/ *past simple of* **freeze**

frozen FREEZE /ˈfrəʊ.zᵊn/ ⓤ /ˈfroʊ-/ *past participle of* **freeze**

frozen TURNED INTO ICE /ˈfrəʊ.zᵊn/ ⓤ /ˈfroʊ-/ *adj* **1** (of water) turned into ice, or (of food) preserved by freezing: *They skated over the frozen lake.* ○ *We don't have any fresh vegetables, only frozen peas.* **2** If a person, or a part of their body is frozen, they are very cold: *I'm frozen – could you close the window?* ○ *After walking through the snow, my feet were frozen* **stiff.**

fructose /ˈfrʌk.təʊs/ ⓤ /-toʊs/ *noun* [U] a type of sugar found in honey and many fruits

frugal /ˈfruː.gᵊl/ *adj* careful when using money or food, or (of a meal) cheap or small in amount: *a frugal lifestyle* ○ *a frugal meal of bread and soup* **frugally** /ˈfruː.gᵊl.i/ *adv*: *We had very little money left, so we ate frugally in cheap cafés and bars.* **frugality** /fruːˈgæl.ə.ti/ ⓤ /-ţi/ *noun* [U]

fruit PLANT PART /fruːt/ *noun* **1** [C or U] the usually sweet-tasting part of a tree or bush which holds seeds and which can be eaten: *Apricots are the one fruit I don't like.* ○ *Oranges, apples, pears and bananas are all types of fruit.* ○ *Would you like some fruit for dessert?* ○ *The cherry tree in our garden is* **in** *fruit* (= it has fruit growing on it). ○ *I like* **exotic** *fruit, like mangoes and papayas.* ○ *How many pieces of* **fresh** *fruit do you eat in a day?* ○ *fruit trees* ○ *He runs a fruit* **and vegetable** *stall in the market.* ◆Compare **vegetable.** ◆See picture **Fruit** on page Centre 1 **2** [C] SPECIALIZED the part of any plant which holds the seeds

• **fruits of the earth** LITERARY types of food which have come from plants, such as vegetables or wheat

fruit /fruːt/ *verb* [I] SPECIALIZED *Over the last few years, our apple trees have been fruiting* (= producing fruit) *much earlier than usual.*

fruity /ˈfruː.ti/ ⓤ /-ţi/ *adj* smelling or tasting of fruit: *This wine has a delicious fruity flavour.* ◆See also **fruity** REMARK; **fruity** VOICE. **fruitfulness** /ˈfruːt.fᵊl.nəs/ *noun* [U] LITERARY *She loved the beauty and fruitfulness of the autumn, when the whole countryside was ablaze with rich golden colours.* **fruitiness** /ˈfruː.tɪ.nəs/ ⓤ /-ţɪ-/ *noun* [U] *a lively wine with a refreshing lemon fruitiness*

fruit RESULT /fruːt/ *noun* **the fruit/fruits of** *sth* the pleasant or successful result of work or actions: *This book is the fruit of 15 years' research.* ○ *It's been hard work, but now the business is running smoothly you can sit back and enjoy the fruits* **of your labours.**

fruitful /ˈfruːt.fəl/ *adj* **1** *FORMAL* producing good results: *It was a most fruitful discussion, with both sides agreeing to adopt a common policy.* * NOTE: The opposite is **fruitless**. **2** *OLD USE* If a person is fruitful, they produce a lot of children. **fruitfully** /ˈfruːt.fəl.i/ *adv* **fruitfulness** /ˈfruːt.fəl.nəs/ *noun* [U]

fruition /fruːˈɪʃ.ən/ *noun* [U] *FORMAL* when a plan or an idea begins to happen, exist or be successful: *None of his grand plans for a TV series ever **came to** fruition.*

fruitless /ˈfruːt.ləs/ *adj* If an action or attempt to do something is fruitless, it is unsuccessful or produces nothing of value: *All diplomatic attempts at a peaceful solution to the crisis have been fruitless.* * NOTE: The opposite is **fruitful**. **fruitlessly** /ˈfruːt.lə.sli/ *adv* **fruitlessness** /ˈfruːt.lə.snəs/ *noun* [U]

fruit [PERSON] /fruːt/ *noun* [C] *US SLANG* a male homosexual. Many people consider this word offensive.

ˈfruit ˌbat *noun* [C] (*ALSO* **flying fox**) a large flying mammal which eats fruit and lives in warm or hot countries

fruitcake [CAKE] /ˈfruːt.keɪk/ *noun* [C or U] a cake containing a lot of dried fruit, such as RAISINS

fruitcake [PERSON] /ˈfruːt.keɪk/ *noun* [C] *UK SLANG* a crazy person: *My teacher's a bit of a fruitcake.*

fruiterer /ˈfruː.tər.əʳ/ [US] /-t̬ɚ.ɚ/ *noun* [C] *MAINLY UK OLD-FASHIONED* a person who sells fruit in a shop or market

ˈfruit ˌfly *noun* [C] a small flying insect which feeds on plants and leaves its eggs on the leaves of plants

ˈfruit maˌchine *noun* [C] *UK* a **slot machine**

ˌfruit ˈsalad *noun* [C or U] a mixture of pieces of different types of fruit, which is usually served at the end of a meal

fruity [REMARK] /ˈfruː.ti/ [US] /-t̬i/ *adj* (of a remark) humorous in a slightly shocking way: *He was well known for his fruity jokes.* ➲See also **fruity** at **fruit** PLANT PART.

fruity [VOICE] /ˈfruː.ti/ [US] /-t̬i/ *adj INFORMAL APPROVING* (of a voice) deep and pleasant

frump /frʌmp/ *noun* [C] *DISAPPROVING* a woman who wears old-fashioned and unattractive clothes: *She looked a frump in her shapeless skirt and flat shoes.*

frumpy /ˈfrʌm.pi/ *adj* (*ALSO* **frumpish**) *DISAPPROVING* (of a person or their clothes) old-fashioned and unattractive: *I felt fat and frumpy.* ○ *a frumpy cardigan*

frustrate [DISCOURAGE] /frʌsˈtreɪt/ *verb* [T] to make someone feel annoyed or discouraged because they cannot achieve want they want: *It frustrates me that I'm not able to put any of my ideas into practice.* **frustrated** /frʌsˈtreɪ.tɪd/ [US] /-t̬ɪd/ *adj*: *Are you feeling frustrated in your present job?*

frustrating /frʌsˈtreɪ.tɪŋ/ [US] /-t̬ɪŋ/ *adj* making you feel frustrated: *He doesn't listen to what I say and it's so frustrating.*

frustration /frʌsˈtreɪ.ʃən/ *noun* [C or U] *I could sense his frustration **at** not being able to help.* ○ *This job has more than its fair share of frustrations* (= problems that make me feel frustrated).

frustrate [PREVENT] /frʌsˈtreɪt/ *verb* [T] to prevent the plans or efforts of someone or something from being achieved: *The continuing civil war is frustrating the efforts of relief agencies to feed thousands of famine victims.*

frustrated /frʌsˈtreɪ.tɪd/ [US] /-t̬ɪd/ *adj* **1** [before n] describes a person who has not succeeded in a particular type of job: *Frustrated writers often end up in publishing.* **2** A frustrated emotion is one that you are not able to express: *her frustrated love for him* **3** not fulfilled sexually **frustration** /frʌsˈtreɪ.ʃən/ *noun* [U]

fry [COOK] /fraɪ/ *verb* [I or T] to cook food in hot oil or fat: *Fry the mushrooms in a little butter.* ○ *INFORMAL FIGURATIVE You'll fry* (= burn) *if you lie in the sun all day.* ➲See picture **In the Kitchen** on page Centre 16

fried /fraɪd/ *adj* cooked in hot oil or fat: *a fried egg* ○ *fried onions*

fryer, frier /ˈfraɪ.əʳ/ [US] /-ɚ/ *noun* [C] **1** a large deep pan in which food is fried: *I've just bought a **deep-fat** fryer for cooking chips.* **2** *US* a chicken suitable for frying

fry [FISH] /fraɪ/ *plural noun* young, small fish

ˈfrying ˌpan *noun* [C] (*US ALSO* **skillet**) a flat metal pan with a long handle which is used for frying food
• **Out of the frying pan into the fire.** *SAYING* said when you move from a bad or difficult situation to one which is worse

fry-up /ˈfraɪ.ʌp/ *noun* [C] *UK INFORMAL* a meal consisting of fried meat, eggs and vegetables

ft *noun* [C] *plural* **ft** *WRITTEN ABBREVIATION FOR* **foot** MEASUREMENT: *The main bedroom measures 24ft by 18ft (24' x 18').*

the FTSE 100 (Index) *TRADEMARK* /ðəˌfʊt.si.wʌnˌhʌn.drədˈɪn.deks/ *noun* [S] (*INFORMAL* **the Footsie**) a number which expresses the value of the share prices of the one hundred most important British companies, which is published by the Financial Times (= a British newspaper for people interested in business and finance): *The FTSE 100 closed 31.6 points down at 2459.3 in today's trading.* ➲Compare **the Dow Jones (industrial) average**; **the Nikkei (index)**.

fuchsia /ˈfjuː.ʃə/ *noun* [C] a small plant, often grown in gardens, which has red, purple or white flowers that hang down ➲See picture **Flowers and Plants** on page Centre 3

fuchsia /ˈfjuː.ʃə/ *adj, noun* [U] a pinkish-purple colour

fuck [HAVE SEX] /fʌk/ *verb* [I or T] *OFFENSIVE* to have sex with someone

fuck /fʌk/ *noun* [C] *OFFENSIVE* **1** an act of having sex **2** a sexual partner

fuck [EXTREME ANGER] /fʌk/ *exclamation OFFENSIVE* used when expressing extreme anger or annoyance, or to add force to what is being said: *Fuck – the bloody car won't start!* ○ *Shut **the fuck** up!* ○ *Who the fuck does she think she is, telling me what to do?*

fucking /ˈfʌk.ɪŋ/ *adj, adv OFFENSIVE* used to emphasize a statement, especially an angry one: *What a fucking waste of time!* ○ *He's a fucking idiot.* ○ *He'd fucking well better do it.*

PHRASAL VERBS WITH **fuck** ▼

▲ **fuck about/around** [BEHAVE BADLY] *phrasal verb OFFENSIVE* to behave stupidly, or to waste time doing unimportant things: *Stop fucking around!*

▲ **fuck *sb* about** [TREAT BADLY] *phrasal verb OFFENSIVE* to treat someone badly by wasting their time or causing them problems: *I'm warning you, don't fuck me about!*

▲ **fuck off** [GO AWAY] *phrasal verb OFFENSIVE* to leave or go away, used especially as a rude way of telling someone to go away: *Just fuck off and leave me alone!* ○ *He's fucked off somewhere and left me to do all the work.*

▲ **fuck *sb* off** [ANNOY] *phrasal verb* [M] *OFFENSIVE* to annoy or upset someone greatly: *You speak to me as if I'm stupid and it really fucks me off.*

▲ **fuck *(sth)* up** *phrasal verb* [M] *OFFENSIVE* to damage, harm or upset someone or something, or to do something very badly: *Her parents' divorce really fucked her up.* ○ *I fucked up the interview.* ○ *The exam was a disaster – I really fucked up.*

fuck-up /ˈfʌk.ʌp/ *noun* [C] *OFFENSIVE* a serious problem: *It's been one fuck-up after another since she took charge.*

ˌfuck ˈall *noun* [U] *OFFENSIVE* nothing: *Don't blame me, mate – I had fuck all to do with it!* ○ *I've had fuck all to eat all day.*

ˌfuck ˈall *determiner OFFENSIVE Now that the wheel's broken, it's fuck all* (= no) *use to anyone.*

fucker /ˈfʌk.əʳ/ [US] /-ɚ/ *noun* [C] *OFFENSIVE* a stupid person: *You stupid fucker!*

fuckwit /ˈfʌk.wɪt/ *noun* [C] *OFFENSIVE* a stupid person: *Some fuckwit walked off with my bag.*

fuddle /ˈfʌd.l̩/ *verb* [T] *INFORMAL* to confuse someone and make them unable to think clearly: *The heat had fuddled my brain.*

fuddle /ˈfʌd.l̩/ *noun* [C usually sing] *INFORMAL Sometimes he gets in a fuddle* (= confused) *and then he can't find things.*

fuddy-duddy /ˈfʌd.iˌdʌd.i/ *noun* [C] *DISAPPROVING* a person who has old-fashioned ideas and opinions: *They think I'm an old fuddy-duddy because I don't approve of tattoos.*

fudge [SWEET] /fʌdʒ/ *noun* [U] a soft sweet made from sugar, butter and milk

F

fudge AVOID /fʌdʒ/ *verb* [T] MAINLY DISAPPROVING to avoid making a decision or giving a clear answer about something: *The government continues to fudge* **the issue** *by refusing to give exact figures.* **fudge** /fʌdʒ/ *noun* [C usually sing] *She suspects that this compromise deal will be nothing more than a fudge.* ○ *It's a bit of a fudge but we could put the cost through on next year's budget.*

fuel /fjʊəl/ *noun* **1** [C or U] a substance which is used to provide heat or power, usually by being burned: *Wood, coal, oil, petrol and gas are all different kinds of fuel.* ○ *Plutonium is a fuel used to produce nuclear energy.* ○ **nuclear** *fuel* ○ **unleaded** *fuel* ○ *The new exhaust system, it is claimed, will lower fuel* **consumption.** **2** [U] anything that keeps people's ideas or feelings active, or makes them stronger: *Reports in today's newspapers have* **added** *fuel to the controversy* (= made it worse).

• **add fuel to the fire/flames** to make an argument or bad situation worse: *The discovery that the government was aware of the cover-up has really added fuel to the fire.*

fuel /fjʊəl/ *verb* [T] -ll- or US USUALLY -l- **1** to supply a system with a substance which can be burnt to provide heat or power: *Our heating system is fuelled by gas.* ○ *We have a gas-fuelled heating system.* ○ *petrol/hydrogen-fuelled cars* **2** Something that fuels a feeling or a type of behaviour increases or strengthens it: *The rapid promotion of the director's son has itself fuelled resentment within the company.* ○ *The prime minister's speech fuelled* **speculation** *that she is about to resign.*

'fuel in,jection *noun* [U] a system in a vehicle which directs an exact amount of fuel into the engine as necessary **fuel-injected** /ˈfjʊəl.ɪnˌdʒek.tɪd/ US /-ˌtɪd/ *adj: a fuel-injected engine/car*

fug /fʌɡ/ *noun* [S] a condition which can exist in a small, crowded place when the air is not pure, especially because of smoke or heat: *We smiled at each other through a grey fug of cigarette smoke.* **fuggy** /ˈfʌɡ.i/ *adj*

fugitive PERSON /ˈfjuː.dʒɪ.tɪv/ US /-tɪv/ *noun* [C] a person who is running away or hiding from the police or a dangerous situation: *Thousands of fugitives are fleeing from the war-torn area.* ○ *Butch Cassidy and the Sundance Kid were fugitives* **from justice** (= they ran away to avoid being tried in court). **fugitive** /ˈfjuː.dʒɪ.tɪv/ US /-tɪv/ *adj* [before n] *Fugitive families who have fled* (= families who have run away from) *the fighting in the cities are now trying to survive in the mountains.*

fugitive TEMPORARY /ˈfjuː.dʒɪ.tɪv/ US /-tɪv/ *adj* FORMAL (especially of thoughts or feelings) lasting for only a short time; temporary: *a fugitive impression*

fugue /fjuːɡ/ *noun* [C] a piece of music consisting of three or more tunes played together: *a Bach organ fugue*

-ful HAVING /-fʊl/ /-fəl/ *suffix* having the stated quality to a high degree, or causing it: *colourful* ○ *powerful* ○ *painful* ○ *truthful* ○ *beautiful* **-fully** /-fˑl.i/ /-fʊ.li/ *suffix: powerfully* ○ *tearfully* ○ *truthfully*

-ful AMOUNT /-fˑl/ /-fʊl/ *suffix* the amount of something needed to fill the stated container or place: *a spoonful of sugar* ○ *a mouthful* **of** *tea* ○ *a houseful* **of** *people*

fulcrum /ˈfʊl.krəm/ *noun plural* **fulcrums** or SPECIALIZED **fulcra 1** [C] the point at which a bar, or something that is balancing, is supported or balances: *A see-saw balances at its fulcrum.* **2** [S] FORMAL the main thing or person needed to support something or to make it work or happen: *The fulcrum of the* **debate/argument** *is the individual's right to choose.*

fulfil MAKE HAPPEN /fʊlˈfɪl/ (-ll-), US USUALLY ALSO **fulfill** /fʊlˈfɪl/ *verb* [T] to do something that is expected, hoped for or promised or to cause it to happen: *A school fails if it does not fulfil the* **needs/requirements** *of its pupils.* ○ *At the age of 45, she finally fulfilled her* **ambition** *to run a marathon.* ○ *Zoos fulfil an important* **function** *in the protection of rare species.* ○ *He has failed to fulfil his* **duties** *as a father.* ○ *We're looking for a very specific sort of person and this woman seems to fulfil all of our* **criteria.** ○ *So did the course fulfil all your* **expectations?** ○ *We're suing our suppliers for failing to fulfil their contract.*

fulfilment, US USUALLY ALSO **fulfillment** /fʊlˈfɪl.mənt/ *noun* [U] when someone does something that is necessary or something that they have wanted or promised to do: *For many women, the fulfilment of family* **obligations** *prevents the furtherance of their career.* ○ *Being here is the fulfilment* **of** *a lifelong ambition.*

fulfil SATISFY (-ll-), US USUALLY ALSO **fulfill** /fʊlˈfɪl/ *verb* [T] to satisfy; to make happy: *I don't feel that my present way of life really fulfils me.* ○ [R] *I've finally found a job in which I can fulfil myself* (= completely develop my abilities and interests).

fulfilled /fʊlˈfɪld/ *adj* feeling happy because you are getting everything that you want from life: *For the first time in my life, I feel really fulfilled.*

fulfilling /fʊlˈfɪl.ɪŋ/ *adj*: *Nursing is hard work, but it can be very fulfilling* (= can make you feel happy and satisfied).

fulfilment, US USUALLY **fulfillment** /fʊlˈfɪl.mənt/ *noun* [U] a feeling of pleasure because you are getting what you want from life: *She finally* **found** *fulfilment in motherhood.* ○ *sexual fulfilment*

full CONTAINING A LOT /fʊl/ *adj* **1** (of a container or a space) holding or containing as much as possible or a lot; filled: *This cup is very full so be careful with it.* ○ *My plate was already full.* ○ *I tried to get in the cinema last night but it was full.* ○ *Don't talk with your* **mouth** *full!* ○ *The shelves were full* **of** *books.* ○ *When she looked at him her eyes were full of tears.* ○ *I tried to get on the 8.45 train but it was full* **(up).** ○ *Don't* **fill** *your glass too full or you'll spill it.* ○ *The theatre was only* **half** *full.* **2** containing a lot of things or people or a lot of something: *This sweater is full* **of** *holes.* ○ *His essay was full* **of** *spelling errors.* ○ *I'm full* **of** *admiration for you.* ○ *You're always so full* **of** *energy.* **3** involving a lot of activities: *I've got rather a full week next week – could we postpone our meeting?* ○ *She has a very full life.*

• **be full of beans** INFORMAL to have a lot of energy and enthusiasm: *I've never known anyone be so full of beans before breakfast.*

• **be full of** *sth* to be talking or thinking a lot about something that you have enjoyed or found exciting: *"Did the kids enjoy their trip to the zoo?" "Oh, yes, they were full of it when they got back this afternoon."*

• **be full of** *your* **own importance** DISAPPROVING to think and act as if you are very important: *Since he got his new job, he's been very full of his own importance.*

• **be full of** *yourself* DISAPPROVING to think that you are very important in a way that annoys other people: *I can't stand her – she's so full of herself.*

• **be full of the joys of spring** HUMOROUS to be very happy: *He bounced into the office, full of the joys of spring.*

fullness, fulness /ˈfʊl.nəs/ *noun* [U] when something is full

full FOOD /fʊl/ *adj* (ALSO **full up**) having eaten so much food that you cannot eat any more: *No more cake for me, thanks, I'm full.*

• **on a full stomach** having recently eaten: *Never go swimming on a full stomach.*

fullness, fulness /ˈfʊl.nəs/ *noun* [U] *I've always disliked that feeling of fullness* (= of having eaten a lot) *after a large meal.*

full COMPLETE /fʊl/ *adj* [before n] complete; whole; containing a lot of detail: *Please give your full name and address.* ○ *We do not yet have full details of the story.* ○ *Few journalists have managed to convey the full horror of the situation.* ○ *The full impact of the tax changes is yet to be felt.* ○ *Today's my last full day in Paris.* ○ *He unwound the rope to its full extent.* ○ *Are you a full* **member** (= do you have all the membership rights) *of the club?* ○ *Some plants need to be in full sun* (= to have the sun shining on them) *all the time.*

• **come/go/turn full circle** If something or someone has come full circle after changing a lot, they are now the same as they were in the beginning: *Things have come full circle now that long skirts are back in fashion.*

• **in full** completely: *The bill must be paid in full by the end of the month.*

• **in full flow** If an activity is in full flow, it is happening fast and with energy: *Preparations for the event are now in full flow.*

• **be in full swing** If an event is in full swing, it has already been happening for a period of time and there is

a lot of activity: *The party was in full swing by the time we arrived.*
• **in full view** able to be seen by other people: *Andy and Vicki had a furious row outside their house, in full view **of** the neighbours.*
full /fʊl/ *adv* **know full well** to be completely aware of something: *You know full well that you're not supposed to go there without asking me!*
fullness, fulness /'fʊl.nəs/ *noun* [U] *The fullness **of** the research report* (= how much detail it contains) *has been widely praised.* ○ *I envy him the fullness **of** his life* (= how busy and interesting his life is).
• **in the fullness of time** If you say something will happen in the fullness of time, you mean that it will happen if you wait long enough: *Everything will become clear in the fullness of time.*
fully /'fʊl.i/ *adv* completely: *Have you fully recovered from your illness?* ○ *I'd fully intended to call you last night.* ○ *I'm sorry, madam, the restaurant is fully booked.* ○ *a fully qualified teacher*

full [GREATEST POSSIBLE] /fʊl/ *adj* [before n] the greatest possible; MAXIMUM: *James is very bright, but he doesn't make full use of his abilities.* ○ *Nobody got full **marks*** (= all the answers right) *in the spelling test.* ○ *It doesn't seem likely that we will see a return to full employment* (= that all the people in the country will have a job) *in the near future.*
• **full marks to *sb*** something you say to praise someone for something clever or good that they have said or done: *Full marks to Jo for spotting the error in time.*
• **(at) full blast** as loud as possible: *He had the television on at full blast.*
• **(at) full speed/tilt/pelt** as fast as possible: *He was driving at full speed down the motorway when it happened.*
• **full steam ahead** with all your energy and enthusiasm: *Now that problem is out of the way, it's full steam ahead to get the job finished.*
• **(at) full stretch** *UK* when you are working as hard as possible and could not manage to do any more: *The emergency services are **working** at full stretch today to cope with the accident.*
• **be in full cry** to criticize someone or something in a noisy and eager way: *The opposition was in full cry over the changes to the education bill.*
full /fʊl/ *noun* **to the full** as much or as well as possible: *She certainly lives life to the full.*
fully /'fʊl.i/ *adv* as much as possible: *Kate has always participated fully in the life of the school.* ○ *Students are advised to answer all questions as fully as possible.*

full [LARGE] /fʊl/ *adj* **1** (of clothing) loose or containing a lot of material, or (of parts of the body) quite large and rounded: *a full skirt* ○ *Women often have full **faces**/become full **in the face** when they're pregnant.* ○ *She has wonderful full lips.* **2** used to avoid saying 'fat': *They advertise clothes 'for the fuller **figure**'.* **fullness, fulness** /'fʊl.nəs/ *noun* [U]

full [STRONG] /fʊl/ *adj* (of a flavour, sound, smell, etc.) strong or deep: *This wine has a full fruity flavour.* ○ *A cello has a fuller sound than a violin.*
fullness, fulness /'fʊl.nəs/ *noun* [U] *I like this cheese's for the fullness **of** its flavour* (= its strong flavour).

full [STRAIGHT] /fʊl/ *adv* straight; directly: *He was kicked full **in** the stomach.* ○ *The intruders turned and ran as the police shone their torches full **on** them.*

fullback /'fʊl.bæk/ *noun* [C] a defending player in games such as football and hockey who plays near the end of the field, or a player in American football whose team has control of the ball

full-blooded [RACE] /ˌfʊl'blʌd.ɪd/ *adj* [before n] having parents, grandparents and earlier relatives all belonging to the same race: *a full-blooded Maori*

full-blooded [ENTHUSIASTIC] /ˌfʊl'blʌd.ɪd/ *adj* [before n] enthusiastic and loyal: *a full-blooded Liverpool supporter*

full-blown /ˌfʊl'bləʊn/ [US] /-'bloʊn/ *adj* [before n] (*ALSO* **fully-blown**) fully developed: *full-blown AIDS*

ˌfull 'board *UK noun* [U] (*US* **American plan**) when all your meals are provided at the hotel or rooms that you are paying to stay in: *The price of the holiday includes flights, full board, and all extras.* ➲Compare **half board**.

full-bodied /ˌfʊl'bɒd.id/ [US] /-'bɑː.did/ *adj* describes wine with a strong, satisfying quality and taste: *a full-bodied red wine*

full-frontal [NO CLOTHES] /ˌfʊl'frʌn.tᵊl/ [US] /-ţᵊl/ *adj* [before n] showing someone's body naked and from the front: *full frontal nudity* ○ *full-frontal pictures*
ˌfull 'frontal *noun* [C] a full-frontal photograph or picture

full-frontal [STRONG] /ˌfʊl'frʌn.tᵊl/ [US] /-ţᵊl/ *adj* [before n] *INFORMAL* very strongly and clearly expressed: *Cash Junior made a full-frontal **assault/attack** on Hollywood's 'moral delinquency'.*

full-grown /ˌfʊl'grəʊn/ [US] /-'groʊn/ *adj* (*MAINLY UK* **fully-grown**) describes people and other living things that have completed their physical growth and will not grow taller: *A full-grown giraffe is 5.5m tall.*

ˌfull 'house [AUDIENCE] *noun* [C usually sing] when every seat in a cinema/theatre/concert, etc. is filled: *We're expecting a full house tonight.*

ˌfull 'house [CARD GAME] *noun* [C] when a card player has three cards of one type and two cards of another: *Steve won the poker game with a full house.*

full length [BODY] /ˌfʊl'leŋkθ/ *adv* describes the way a person moves or lies so that their whole body is flat on the floor: *He was lying full length on the grass.*

full-length [REACHING FLOOR] /ˌfʊl'leŋkθ/ *adj* describes a mirror, curtain or piece of clothing that reaches the floor: *Victoria wore a full-length evening gown to the ball.*

full-length [USUAL LENGTH] /ˌfʊl'leŋkθ/ *adj* of the usual length and not made shorter: *a full-length feature film*

the full monty /ðəˌfʊl'mɒn.ti/ [US] /-mɑːn.ţi/ *noun UK INFORMAL* the most or best that you can have, do, get or achieve, or all that you want or need: *When we bought the television, we decided to go for the full monty – a large screen, 38 channels and a video.*
• **do the full monty** *UK INFORMAL* to take off all your clothes in front of other people

ˌfull 'moon *noun* [S] the moon when it is shaped like a complete disc, or a time when it is: *There's a full moon tonight.*

full-page /ˌfʊl'peɪdʒ/ *adj* [before n] filling a complete page of a newspaper or book: *a full-page advertisement/feature*

full-scale [FULL SIZE] /ˌfʊl'skeɪl/ *adj* describes a model of the same size as the original thing: *full-scale models of dinosaurs*

full-scale [COMPLETE] /ˌfʊl'skeɪl/ *adj* [before n] complete or using all available methods, equipment, money, etc: *a full-scale investigation* ○ *a full-scale attack*

full-service /ˌfʊl'sɜː.vɪs/ [US] /-'sɝː-/ *adj* [before n] *US* describes a business that provides customers with a complete range of services: *I need to find a good full-service bank.*

ˌfull 'stop *UK noun* [C] (*US* **period**) the . punctuation mark that is put at the end of a sentence, or at the end of a word that has been shortened
• **come to a full stop** to end, especially because of problems: *It looks like negotiations between the two sides have come to a full stop.*
ˌfull 'stop *UK adv* (*US* **period**) used at the end of a sentence, usually when you are angry, to say you will not continue to discuss a subject: *Look, I'm not lending you my car, full stop!*

full-time [WORK/EDUCATION] /ˌfʊl'taɪm/ *adj, adv* **1** (of work or education) done for the whole of a working week: *a full-time **job*** ○ *Most children in the UK remain in full-time education until they are at least 16 years old.* ○ *She went back to work full-time when her youngest child went to school.* **2 full-time job/activity** an activity which uses a lot of your time: *Keeping a garden tidy is a full-time job.*

ˌfull 'time [SPORTS] /ˌfʊl'taɪm/ *noun* [U] *UK* the end of a sports match: *The score was 2-2 at full time.* ➲Compare **half-time**.

-fully /-fᵊl.i/ /-fʊ.li/ *suffix* ➲See at **-ful** HAVING

fully-fledged *UK* /ˌfʊ.li'fledʒd/ *adj* (*US* **full-fledged**) completely developed or trained: *What started as a small*

F

business is now a fully-fledged company. ○ *After years of study, Tim is now a fully-fledged architect.*

fulminate /ˈfʊl.mɪ.neɪt/ *verb* [I usually + adv or prep] FORMAL to criticize strongly: *I had to listen to Michael fulminating against the government.* **fulmination** /ˌfʊl.mɪˈneɪ.ʃᵊn/ *noun* [C or U]

fulsome /ˈfʊl.səm/ *adj* FORMAL expressing a lot of admiration for or appreciation of someone, often too much, in a way that does not sound sincere: *Her new book has received fulsome praise from the critics.* ○ *Our guests were fulsome in their compliments about the food.* **fulsomely** /ˈfʊl.səm.li/ *adv*: *He thanked her fulsomely for her help.* **fulsomeness** /ˈfʊl.səm.nəs/ *noun* [U]

fumble /ˈfʌm.bl̩/ *verb* **1** [I usually + adv or prep] to do something awkwardly, especially when using your hands: *I fumbled with the lock.* ○ *He fumbled in his pockets for some change.* ○ *She fumbled around/about in her handbag, looking for her key.* ○ *They fumbled around/about* (= moved awkwardly) *in the dark, trying to find their way out of the cinema.* **2** [T] in sport, to fail to catch a ball: *If Wilson hadn't fumbled that catch, we might have won the match.* **3** [I usually + adv or prep] to have difficulty saying or thinking of suitable words: *I was fumbling for the right word.*

fume /fjuːm/ *verb* [I] to be very angry, sometimes without expressing it: *I saw her a week after they'd had the argument and she was still fuming.* ○ *The whole episode left me fuming at the injustice of it all.*

fumes /fjuːmz/ *plural noun* strong, unpleasant and sometimes dangerous gas or smoke: *exhaust fumes* ○ *Petrol fumes always make me feel ill.* ○ *cigar fumes*

fumigate /ˈfjuː.mɪ.geɪt/ *verb* [T] to use poisonous gas to remove harmful insects, bacteria, disease, etc. from somewhere or something: *We had to fumigate the cellar to get rid of cockroaches.* **fumigation** /ˌfjuː.mɪˈgeɪ.ʃᵊn/ *noun* [U] *Two hospital wards have had to be closed for fumigation.*

fun PLEASURE /fʌn/ *noun* [U] pleasure, enjoyment, amusement: *Have fun!* (= Enjoy yourself)*!* ○ *Having fun?* (= Are you enjoying yourself)*?* ○ *I really enjoyed your party – it was such good fun.* ○ *She's great fun to be with.* ○ *Mark was ill for most of the holiday so that took all the fun out of it.* ○ *It's no fun/not much fun* (= not enjoyable) *having to work on Saturdays.* ○ *a fun-loving girl* ○ *"We're going on a picnic at the weekend." "What fun* (= how enjoyable)*!"* ○ *The relationship was never going to work, but it was fun while it lasted.* ⊃See Note **fun** or **funny?** at **funny** AMUSING.
- **for fun** (ALSO **for the fun of it**) for pleasure: *I ran but just for fun.*
- **make fun of sb/sth** to make a joke about someone or something in a way that is not kind: *The other children were always making fun of him because he was fat and wore glasses.*

fun /fʌn/ *adj* [before n] enjoyable: *There are lots of fun things to do here.*

fun PLAYFUL ACTIVITY /fʌn/ *noun* [U] playful and often energetic activity: *The children are always full of fun.* ○ *I didn't mean to upset her – it was just a bit of fun.* ○ *I didn't mean what I said, it was only in fun* (= a joke).
- **not be all fun and games** If an activity is not all fun and games, parts of it are difficult or unpleasant: *It's not all fun and games being a tour representative.*
- **have fun and games** HUMOROUS to have difficulty doing something: *We had real fun and games trying to bath the dog.*

function PURPOSE /ˈfʌŋk.ʃᵊn/ *noun* [C] the natural purpose (of something) or the duty (of a person): *The function of the veins is to carry blood to the heart.* ○ *I'm not quite sure what my function is within the company.* ○ *A thermostat performs the function of controlling temperature.*

functional /ˈfʌŋk.ʃᵊn.ᵊl/ *adj* designed to be practical and useful rather than attractive: *functional clothing/furniture*

functionalism /ˈfʌŋk.ʃᵊn.ᵊl.ɪ.zᵊm/ *noun* [U] the principle that the most important thing about an object such as a building is its use rather than what it looks like **functionalist** /ˈfʌŋk.ʃᵊn.ᵊl.ɪst/ *adj*

functionally /ˈfʌŋk.ʃᵊn.ᵊl.i/ *adv*: *The office is functionally designed* (= is planned to be easy to use rather than to look attractive).

function WORK /ˈfʌŋk.ʃᵊn/ *verb* [I] to work or operate: *You'll soon learn how the office functions.* ○ *The television was functioning normally until yesterday.* ○ *I'm so tired today, I can barely function.*
▲ **function as sth/sb** *phrasal verb* to perform the purpose of a particular thing or the duties of a particular person: *We have a spare bedroom which also functions as a study.* **function** /ˈfʌŋk.ʃᵊn/ *noun* [U] *It's a disease which affects the function of the nervous system* (= the way in which it works or operates). ○ *Studies suggest that regular intake of the vitamin significantly improves brain function.*

functional /ˈfʌŋk.ʃᵊn.ᵊl/ *adj* **1** (of a machine, system, etc.) working in the usual way: *Is the central heating functional yet?* **2** performing a particular operation: *a functional disorder* (= when an organ does not work as it should) **functionally** /ˈfʌŋk.ʃᵊn.ᵊl.i/ *adv*

function CEREMONY /ˈfʌŋk.ʃᵊn/ *noun* [C] an official ceremony or a formal social event, such as a party or a special meal, at which a lot of people are usually present: *As a mayor, he has a lot of official functions to attend.* ○ *I see her two or three times a year, usually at social functions.*

function RESULT /ˈfʌŋk.ʃᵊn/ *noun* FORMAL **a function of sth** something which results from something else, or which is as it is because of something else: *His success is a function of his having worked so hard.* ○ *The low temperatures here are a function of the terrain as much as of the climate.*

function VALUE /ˈfʌŋk.ʃᵊn/ *noun* [C] SPECIALIZED (in mathematics) a value which depends on and varies with another value: x is a function of y.

functional food *noun* [C] another phrase for NUTRACEUTICAL

functional illiterate *noun* [C] MAINLY US SPECIALIZED someone who is able to live and possibly work in society, but who cannot read and write **functional illiteracy** *noun* [U] *There's a high rate of functional illiteracy here.*

functionary /ˈfʌŋk.ʃᵊn.ᵊr.i/ ⓊⓈ /-er-/ *noun* [C] FORMAL a person who has official duties, especially in a government or political party: *The visitors were met by a functionary who escorted them to the director's office.* ○ *a government functionary*

function key *noun* [C] one of the keys at the top of the keyboard which make the computer perform particular operations

fund /fʌnd/ *noun* [C] a sum of money saved, collected or provided for a particular purpose: *a pension/trust fund* ○ *The hospital has set up a special fund to buy new equipment.* ○ *Contributions are being sought for the disaster fund.*
- **a fund of sth** a lot of something: *She has a fund of knowledge on the subject.*

fund /fʌnd/ *verb* [T] to provide the money to pay for an event, activity or organization: *The company has agreed to fund my trip to Australia.* ○ *The new college is being privately funded* (= money for it is not being provided from taxes).

funding /ˈfʌn.dɪŋ/ *noun* [U] money given by a government or organization for an event or activity: *Ian is trying to get funding for his research.* ○ *They received state funding for the project.*

funds /fʌndz/ *plural noun* money needed or available to spend on something: *Following the repairs to the roof, church funds are now seriously depleted.* ○ *The President has agreed to allocate further funds to develop the new submarine.* ○ INFORMAL *It's one of those people I'd love to come on holiday with you, but I'm a bit short of/low on funds* (= I have little money) *at the moment.*

fundamental /ˌfʌn.dəˈmen.tᵊl/ ⓊⓈ /-t̬ᵊl/ *adj* forming the base, from which everything else originates; more important than anything else: *We need to make fundamental changes to the way in which we treat our environment.* ○ *It's one of the fundamental differences between men and women.* ○ *The school is based on the fundamental principle that each child should develop its full* *potential.* ○ *Diversity is **of** fundamental **importance** to all ecosystems and all economies.* ○ *Some understanding of grammar is fundamental **to** learning a language.*

fundamentally /ˌfʌn.dəˈmen.tᵊl.i/ [US] /-t̬ᵊl-/ *adv*: *Our new managing director has reorganized the company a bit, but nothing has fundamentally **changed/altered*** (= its basic character has not changed). ○ *I still believe that people are fundamentally* (= in a basic and important way) *good.* ○ *I disagree fundamentally* (= in every way that is important) *with what you're saying.*

fundamentals /ˌfʌn.dəˈmen.tᵊlz/ [US] /-t̬ᵊlz/ *plural noun* the main or most important rules or parts: *It's important for children to be taught the fundamentals **of** science.*

fundamentalism /ˌfʌn.dəˈmen.tᵊl.ɪ.zᵊm/ [US] /-t̬ᵊl-/ *noun* [U] the belief in old and traditional forms of religion, or the belief that what is written in a holy book, such as the Christian Bible, is completely true: *Recent years have witnessed a growth in religious fundamentalism.*

fundamentalist /ˌfʌn.dəˈmen.tᵊl.ɪst/ [US] /-t̬ᵊl-/ *noun* [C]

fundamentalist /ˌfʌn.dəˈmen.tᵊl.ɪst/ [US] /-t̬ᵊl-/ *adj*

fundraising /ˈfʌndˌreɪ.zɪŋ/ *noun* [U] when you collect or produce money for a particular purpose, especially for a charity: *The summer fête will be the school's main fundraising **event** this year.*

fundraiser /ˈfʌndˌreɪ.zəʳ/ [US] /-zɚ/ *noun* [C] a person or event involved in collecting money for a particular purpose, especially a charity

funeral /ˈfjuː.nᵊr.ᵊl/ [US] /-nɚ.əl/ *noun* [C] a (usually religious) ceremony for burying or burning the body of a dead person: *The funeral will be **held** next Friday.* ○ *Over 300 mourners attended the funeral.* ○ *a funeral **procession***

• **That's/it's *your* funeral!** *INFORMAL* something that you say which means that if someone suffers bad results from their actions, it will be their fault

funereal /fjuːˈnɪə.ri.əl/ [US] /-ˈnɪr.i-/ *adj FORMAL* suitable for a funeral: *funereal music* ○ *dressed in funereal black*

ˈfuneral diˌrector *noun* [C] a person whose job it is to arrange for the bodies of dead people to be buried or burned

ˈfuneral ˌhome *noun* [C] *US FOR* **funeral parlour**

ˈfuneral ˌparlour *UK, US* **funeral parlor** *noun* [C] a place where the bodies of dead people are prepared to be buried or burned

funfair *UK* /ˈfʌn.feəʳ/ [US] /-fer/ *noun* [C] (*US* **amusement park**) a place of outside entertainment where there are machines for riding on and games that can be played for prizes

ˈfun ˌfur *noun* [C or U] artificial fur that is used in clothing, often brightly coloured in a way that is obviously not natural

fungicide /ˈfʌn.dʒɪ.saɪd/ /ˈfʌŋ.gɪ-/ *noun* [C or U] a chemical substance used to kill fungus or prevent it from growing

fungus /ˈfʌŋ.gəs/ *noun* [C or U] *plural* **fungi** or **funguses** any of various types of organism which obtain their food from decaying material or other living things: *Mushrooms and mould are funguses.* ○ *Fungus can be poisonous.*

fungal /ˈfʌŋ.gəl/ *adj* caused by a fungus: *a fungal infection*

fungoid /ˈfʌŋ.gɔɪd/ *adj SPECIALIZED* like a fungus

ˈfun ˌhouse *noun* [C] *US* a building at a fair containing frightening or amusing objects and devices

funicular (railway) /fjʊˌnɪk.jʊ.ləˈreɪl.weɪ/ [US] /-juː.lɚ-/ *noun* [C] a special type of railway which travels up and down steep slopes, with the carriages being pulled by a strong metal rope

funk /fʌŋk/ *noun* [U] a style of music, usually for dancing to, with a strong jazz-based rhythm and a tune that repeats itself: *James Brown is the master of funk.*

• **be in a funk** *US INFORMAL* to be very unhappy and without hope: *He's been in a real funk since she left him.*

funky [MUSIC] /ˈfʌŋ.ki/ *adj* describes a style of music, usually for dancing to, with a strong, jazz-based rhythm and a tune that repeats itself: *Have you heard their new record? It's really funky.*

funky [FASHIONABLE] /ˈfʌŋ.ki/ *adj SLANG* fashionable in an unusual and noticeable way: *She has some really funky clothes.* ○ *short funky haircuts*

funnel [TUBE] /ˈfʌn.ᵊl/ *noun* [C] an object which has a wide round opening at the top, sloping sides, and a narrow tube at the bottom, used for pouring liquids or powders into containers with narrow necks: *When you've ground the coffee, use a funnel to pour it into the jar.*

funnel /ˈfʌn.ᵊl/ *verb* [I or T; usually + adv or prep] **-ll-** or *US USUALLY* **-l-** to put something, or to travel, through a funnel or something that acts like a funnel: *The wind funnels **down** these narrow streets.* ○ *The children funnelled **along** the corridor into the school hall.* ○ *If you funnel the oil **into** the engine, you're less likely to spill it.*

funnel [PIPE] /ˈfʌn.ᵊl/ *noun* [C] (*US ALSO* **smokestack**) a vertical metal pipe on the top of a ship or steam train through which smoke comes out ➲See picture **Planes, Ships and Boats** on page Centre 14

funnel-web /ˈfʌn.ᵊl.web/ *noun* [C] *AUS* a large poisonous spider found in eastern Australia which makes a WEB (= sticky net), with a funnel-shaped entrance

funny [AMUSING] /ˈfʌn.i/ *adj* amusing; causing laughter: *Do you know any funny jokes?* ○ *I've never found Charlie Chaplin very funny.* ○ *It's a really funny film.* ○ *It's not funny – don't laugh!* ○ *Breaking your leg isn't funny* (= is serious), *I can assure you.* ○ *No matter how disastrous the situation there always seems to be a funny **side to it**.* ○ *Don't you try to be funny **with** me* (= Be serious and show respect), *young man!*

• **funny ha-ha or funny peculiar?** *UK* used when someone has described a person as 'funny' and you want to know whether they mean 'amusing', ('ha-ha'), or 'strange' ('peculiar'): *"She's a very funny woman." "Funny ha-ha or funny peculiar?"*

the funnies /ðəˈfʌn.iz/ *plural noun MAINLY US* the series of drawings in a newspaper that tell an amusing story ➲See also **comic strip**.

COMMON LEARNER ERROR

fun or funny?

If something is **fun**, you enjoy doing it.

I really liked the skating – it was such fun.

If something is **funny**, it makes you laugh.

It's a very funny film.

funny [STRANGE] /ˈfʌn.i/ *adj* strange, surprising, unexpected or difficult to explain or understand: *The washing machine is making a funny noise again.* ○ *He's got some funny ideas about how to bring up children.* ○ ***That's** funny – I'm sure I left my keys here.* ○ *A funny **thing** happened to me on the way to the crematorium.* ○ *Do you think this jacket looks **a bit** funny with these trousers?* ○ *It's funny **how** Alec always disappears whenever there's work to be done.* ○ *She's a funny girl* (= she is strange and difficult to understand). ○ *UK INFORMAL The television's **gone** funny* (= isn't working correctly).

• **It's a funny old world.** *UK SAYING* said when someone has told you something that is strange or surprising

funnily /ˈfʌn.ɪ.li/ *adv*: *If I'm talking a bit funnily* (= strangely) *it's because I've just had an injection in my mouth.*

• **funnily enough** strangely: *Funnily enough, I was just thinking about you when you called.*

funny [DISHONEST] /ˈfʌn.i/ *adj INFORMAL* dishonest; involving cheating: *I think there's something funny **going on** next door.*

funny [UNFRIENDLY] /ˈfʌn.i/ *adj* [after v] *UK INFORMAL* unfriendly or seeming to be offended: *I'm not being funny or anything but I think I'd rather go on my own.* ○ *She sounded a bit funny with me on the phone last night and I wondered if I'd offended her.*

funny [ILL] /ˈfʌn.i/ *adj* [after v] *INFORMAL* slightly ill: *I don't know if it was something I ate but I'm feeling a bit funny.*

funny [CRAZY] /ˈfʌn.i/ *adj UK INFORMAL* slightly crazy: *All the stress made him **go** a bit funny.*

ˈfunny ˌbone *noun* [C] *INFORMAL* the outer part of the ELBOW (= the middle part of the arm where it bends), which hurts a lot if it is knocked

ˈfunny ˌbusiness *noun* [U] dishonest actions or behaviour intended to trick someone: *If you try any*

funny business you'll be sorry.

the ˈfunny ˌfarm *noun* [S] *UK INFORMAL* sometimes used in a humorous or offensive way to refer to a hospital for mentally ill people: *If things get much worse, I'll soon be carted off to the funny farm.*

ˈfun ˌrun *noun* [C] an event in which people run a certain distance for amusement, usually to make money for charity

fur [HAIR] /fɜːʳ/ [US] /fɝː/ *noun* [C or U] the thick hair that covers the bodies of some animals, or the hair-covered skin(s) of animals, removed from their bodies: *She stroked the rabbit's soft fur.* ○ *"Is that real fur on your collar?" "Certainly not – I only wear **fake** fur."* ○ *a fur **coat*** ○ *Native Americans traded furs with early European settlers.*

• **the fur flies** If the fur flies, people have a bad argument: *The fur was really flying during that meeting.*

furry /ˈfɜː.ri/ [US] /ˈfɝː.i/ *adj* **1** covered with fur: *small furry animals* **2** describes items that are made from a soft material that looks like fur: *furry **slippers*** ○ *Rosie has a massive collection of furry toys.*

furrier /ˈfʌr.i.əʳ/ [US] /ˈfɝː.i.ɚ/ *noun* [C] a person who makes or sells clothes made from fur

fur [GREY SUBSTANCE] /fɜːʳ/ [US] /fɝː/ *noun* [U] a hard pale grey substance which can form on the inside of water pipes, KETTLES etc.

fur /fɜːʳ/ [US] /fɝː/ *verb* [I] **-rr-** *Over the years, the pipes in our house have slowly furred **(up)*** (= a hard grey substance has formed in them).

fur [TONGUE] /fɜːʳ/ [US] /fɝː/ *noun* [U] a greyish covering on the tongue, caused by illness or by smoking cigarettes

furred /fɜːd/ [US] /fɝːd/ *adj*: *He had the furred tongue of a sick man.*

furious [ANGRY] /ˈfjʊə.ri.əs/ [US] /ˈfjɝː.i-/ *adj* extremely angry: *I was late and he was furious **with** me.* ○ *He's furious **about/at** the way he's been treated.* ○ *We had a furious row last night.* ➲See also **fury**.

furiously /ˈfjʊə.ri.ə.sli/ [US] /ˈfjɝː.i-/ *adv*: *"Get out of here!" she shouted furiously* (= in a very angry way). **furiousness** /ˈfjʊə.ri.ə.snəs/ [US] /ˈfjɝː.i-/ *noun* [U] ➲See also **fury**.

furious [STRONG] /ˈfjʊə.ri.əs/ [US] /ˈfjɝː.i-/ *adj* using a lot of effort or strength: *There is a furious struggle going on between the two presidential candidates.* ○ *He set off running at a furious pace.*

furiously /ˈfjʊə.ri.ə.sli/ [US] /ˈfjɝː.i-/ *adv*: *I was pedalling furiously* (= with as much effort as possible) *to try to keep up with the other children.* **furiousness** /ˈfjʊə.ri.ə.snəs/ [US] /ˈfjɝː.i-/ *noun* [U] ➲See also **fury**.

furl /fɜːl/ [US] /fɝːl/ *verb* [T] to fold and roll something such as a flag, sail or UMBRELLA into a tight tube shape

furlong /ˈfɜː.lɒŋ/ [US] /ˈfɝː.lɑːŋ/ *noun* [C] a unit of length equal to 201 metres or 1/8 mile, used especially in horse racing: *a five-furlong race*

furlough /ˈfɜː.ləʊ/ [US] /ˈfɝː.loʊ/ *noun* [C] *US* a period of time that a worker or a soldier is allowed to be absent, especially to return temporarily to their own town or country

furlough /ˈfɜː.ləʊ/ [US] /ˈfɝː.loʊ/ *verb* [T] *US* to allow or force someone to be absent temporarily from work: *After safety concerns, the company furloughed all 4000 of it's employees.*

furnace /ˈfɜː.nɪs/ [US] /ˈfɝː-/ *noun* [C] **1** a container which is heated to a very high temperature, so that substances that are put inside it, such as metal, will melt or burn: *People who work with furnaces in a steel factory need to wear protective clothing.* ○ *This room's **like** a furnace* (= is very hot)*!* **2** *US* a piece of equipment for heating a building: *It's cold in here – should I turn on the furnace?*

furnish /ˈfɜː.nɪʃ/ [US] /ˈfɝː-/ *verb* [T] to provide with furniture; to put furniture in: *They've furnished the room very simply.*

furnished /ˈfɜː.nɪʃt/ [US] /ˈfɝː-/ *adj*: *She's looking for a furnished **flat/apartment*** (= one which already has furniture in it). ○ *Their house is expensively furnished* (= the furniture in it is expensive).

furnishings /ˈfɜː.nɪ.ʃɪŋz/ [US] /ˈfɝː-/ *plural noun* the furniture, curtains and other decorations in a room or building: *Bathroom furnishings are in the basement of the store, Sir.*

▲ **furnish *sb* with *sth*** *phrasal verb FORMAL* to provide someone with something: *Furnished with maps, a compass and sandwiches, they set off for a day's hiking.*

furniture /ˈfɜː.nɪ.tʃəʳ/ [US] /ˈfɝː.nɪ.tʃɚ/ *noun* [U] items such as chairs, tables, beds, cupboards, etc. which are put into a house or other building to make it suitable and comfortable for living or working in: *They have a lot of antique furniture.* ○ *The only **piece/item of** furniture he has in his bedroom is a bed.* ○ *We've just bought some new garden furniture* (= tables, chairs, etc. for use in the garden).

furore *UK*, *US* **furor** /ˈfjʊ.rɔːʳ/ [US] /-rɔːr/ *noun* [S] a sudden excited or angry reaction to something by a lot of people: *The government's decision to raise taxes has caused a great furore.* ○ *the furore **over** his latest film*

furphy /ˈfɜː.fi/ [US] /ˈfɝː-/ *noun* [C] *AUS SLANG* a RUMOUR (= unofficial interesting story or piece of news that might be true or invented)

furred /fɜːd/ [US] /fɝːd/ *adj* ➲See at **fur** TONGUE.

furrier /ˈfʌr.i.əʳ/ [US] /ˈfɝː.i.ɚ/ *noun* [C] ➲See at **fur** HAIR.

furrow /ˈfʌr.əʊ/ [US] /ˈfɝː.oʊ/ *noun* [C] a long line or hollow which is formed or cut into the surface of something: *A deep furrow has formed in the rock, where water has run over it for centuries.* ○ *Years of anxiety have lined her brow with deep furrows.*

furrow /ˈfʌr.əʊ/ [US] /ˈfɝː.oʊ/ *verb* [T] *The wheels of the heavy tractor furrowed* (= made long shallow holes in) *the soft ground.* ○ *The pain of the headache made him furrow his **brow*** (= make lines in the skin above his eyes).

furrowed /ˈfʌr.əʊd/ [US] /ˈfɝː.oʊd/ *adj* **a furrowed brow** a forehead that has lines in the skin, usually caused by worry

furry /ˈfɜː.ri/ [US] /ˈfɝː.i/ *adj* See at **fur** HAIR.

further [GREATER DISTANCE] /ˈfɜː.ðəʳ/ [US] /ˈfɝː.ðɚ/ *adv* **1** comparative of **far** DISTANCE; to a greater distance or degree; at a more advanced level: *I'm afraid I never got further than the first five pages of 'Ulysses'.* ○ *We discussed the problem but we didn't **get** much further in actually solving it.* ○ *The whole matter is further complicated by the fact that Amanda and Jo refuse to speak to each other.* ○ *Every day she sinks further and further into depression.* **2 go further/take *sth* further** If you go or take something further, you take it to a more advanced stage: *Before we go any further with the project I think we should check that there's enough money to fund it.* ○ *If you wish to take **the matter** further, you can file charges against him.*

further /ˈfɜː.ðəʳ/ [US] /ˈfɝː.ðɚ/ *adj* at a greater distance: *It was much further to the town centre than I remembered.* ○ *Fourteen miles is further than you'd think once you start to run it.* ○ *Is that her at the further* (= other) *end of the room?*

• **Nothing could have been further from my mind/thoughts.** used to say that you certainly did not intend something: *I certainly wasn't trying to get money off him – nothing could have been further from my mind!*

furthermost /ˈfɜː.ðə.məʊst/ [US] /ˈfɝː.ðɚ.moʊst/ *adj FORMAL* The furthermost place or places are those at the greatest distance away: *the furthermost ports of northern Europe*

USAGE

further or farther?

Further means the same as **farther** when you are talking about distance. In British English **farther** is slightly more formal and less common.

further/farther along the street

Only **further** is used to talk about something more or additional.

Are there any further questions?
Petrol prices have increased further.

further [EXTRA] /ˈfɜː.ðəʳ/ [US] /ˈfɝː.ðɚ/ *adj, adv* **1** more or additional: *Have you anything further to add?* ○ *If you have any further problems do let me know.* ○ *It cost me £50 a day and a further £60 for insurance.* ○ *This shop will be closed until further notice.* ○ *We need to talk* *further about this.* ➲See Note **further or farther?** at **further** GREATER DISTANCE. **2** *MAINLY UK FORMAL* **further to** used in business letters to state the subject that you are referring to or which conversation or letter you are answering: *Further to your letter of March 11th, I should like to inform you of a number of recent developments regarding the Saffron Hill site.*

further [ADVANCE] /ˈfɜː.ðəʳ/ [US] /ˈfɝː.ðɚ/ *verb* [T] to advance something: *He has probably done more to further **the cause** of interracial harmony than any other person.* ○ *Additional training is probably the best way to further your career these days.* **furtherance** /ˈfɜː.ðəʳ.ᵊnts/ [US] /ˈfɝː.ðɚ-/ *noun* [U] *FORMAL* *The charter states that the press shall be devoted to printing and publishing **in** the furtherance and dissemination **of** knowledge.*

ˌfurther eduˈcation *AUS FORMAL AND UK* *noun* [U] (*US* **adult education**) education below the level of a university degree for people who are older than school age: *She teaches at a college of further education.*

furthermore /ˌfɜː.ðəˈmɔːʳ/ /ˈ---/ [US] /ˈfɝː.ðɚ.mɔːr/ *adv* *FORMAL* in addition; more importantly: *I suggest we use Barkers as our main suppliers – they're good and furthermore they're cheap.*

furthest /ˈfɜː.ðɪst/ [US] /ˈfɝː-/ *adv, superlative of* **far** DISTANCE: *That's the furthest I can see without glasses.* ○ *I wanted to be an actress but the furthest I ever got was selling ice-creams in a theatre.* * NOTE: Both **furthest** and **farthest** are used to talk about distance. **Furthest** is used in all other situations. **furthest** /ˈfɜː.ðɪst/ [US] /ˈfɝː-/ *adj*: *The novel explores the furthest extremes of human experience.*

furtive /ˈfɜː.tɪv/ [US] /ˈfɝː.t̬ɪv/ *adj* (of people) behaving secretly so that other people do not notice them, or (of actions) done secretly and often quickly so that people do not notice: *I saw him cast a furtive **glance** at the woman at the table to his right.* ○ *He made one or two furtive phone calls.* ○ *There was something furtive **about** his behaviour and I immediately felt suspicious.* **furtively** /ˈfɜː.tɪv.li/ [US] /ˈfɝː.t̬ɪv-/ *adv*: *As she turned away I saw him sniff furtively under his arm.* **furtiveness** /ˈfɜː.tɪv.nəs/ [US] /ˈfɝː.t̬ɪv-/ *noun* [U]

fury /ˈfjʊə.ri/ [US] /ˈfjɝː.i/ *noun* [S or U] extreme anger: *He could hardly contain his fury.* ○ *She flew into a fury at the suggestion.* ➲See also **furious** ANGRY.

• **like fury** *OLD-FASHIONED* with great energy and determination: *I've been working like fury these past few days to catch up.*

fuse [SAFETY PART] /fjuːz/ *noun* [C] a small safety part in an electrical device or piece of machinery which causes it to stop working if the electric current is too high, and so prevents fires or other dangers: *My hairdrier's stopped working – I think the fuse has **blown/***(*UK ALSO*) ***gone*** (= broken). ○ *Have you tried **changing** the fuse?*

fuse /fjuːz/ *verb* [I or T] *UK* When an electrical device or piece of machinery fuses, or when someone or something fuses it, it stops working because the electric current is too high: *Either my headlights have fused or the bulbs have gone.* ○ *The kids were messing around with the switches and they fused the lights.*

fused /fjuːzd/ *adj* describes an electrical device or a piece of machinery that has a fuse in it

fuse [DEVICE ON EXPLOSIVE] /fjuːz/ *noun* [C] a string or piece of paper connected to a firework or other explosive item by which it is lit, or a device inside a bomb which causes it to explode after a fixed length of time or when it hits or is near something: *He **lit** the fuse and ran.*

• **have a short fuse** to get angry very easily

fuse [JOIN] /fjuːz/ *verb* [I or T] to join or become combined: *Genes determine how we develop from the moment the sperm fuses with the egg.* ○ *The bones of the skull are not properly fused at birth.* ○ *In Istanbul, East and West fuse together in a way that is fascinating to observe.*

fusion /ˈfjuː.ʒᵊn/ *noun* [U] when two or more things join or are combined: ***nuclear** fusion* ○ *Their music is described as 'an explosive fusion of Latin American and modern jazz rhythms'.*

fuse [MELT] /fjuːz/ *verb* [I or T] to (cause to) melt (together) especially at a high temperature: *The heat of the fire fused many of the machine's parts together.*

ˈfuse ˌbox *noun* [C] a container holding several fuses, such as all the fuses for the electrical system of a single house

fuselage /ˈfjuː.zᵊl.ɑːʒ/ *noun* [C] the main body of an aircraft: *A close inspection revealed minute cracks in the aircraft's fuselage and wings.* ➲See picture **Planes, Ships and Boats** on page Centre 14

fusilier /ˌfjuː.zɪˈlɪəʳ/ [US] /-ˈlɪr/ *noun* [C] *UK* a low-ranked British soldier who is in the INFANTRY

fusillade /ˌfjuː.zɪˈleɪd/ *noun* [C] a large number of bullets fired at the same time or one after another very quickly: *a fusillade **of** automatic fire* ○ *FORMAL FIGURATIVE* *A fusillade* (= sudden large amount) ***of** questions greeted the president at this afternoon's press conference.*

fuss [FEELING] /fʌs/ *noun* [S or U] a show of annoyance, anxiety, dissatisfaction or excitement, usually one which is greater than the situation deserves: *She **made such a** fuss when Richard spilt a drop of wine on her blouse!* ○ *It's all a fuss **about nothing**.* ○ *I don't see **what the** fuss **is about** – he seems like a fairly ordinary looking guy to me.* ○ *We tried to arrange a ceremony with as little fuss as possible.*

• **make a fuss of/over *sb*** to give someone a lot of attention and treat them well: *She doesn't see her grandchildren very often so she makes a real fuss of them when she does.*

fuss /fʌs/ *verb* [T] *US* to make someone nervous and angry by trying to get their attention when they are very busy: *Don't fuss me, honey, I've got a whole pile of work to do.*

fuss [GIVE ATTENTION TO] /fʌs/ *verb* [I] to give too much attention to small and unimportant matters, usually in a way which shows that you are anxious and not relaxed: *Please, stop fussing – the food's cooking and there's nothing more to do until the guests arrive.* ○ *It irritates me the way she's always fussing **with** her hair!*

fuss /fʌs/ *noun* [U] attention given to small and unimportant matters: *The article was entitled 'Making up with the minimum of fuss: a five-minute beauty routine that every busy woman should know'.*

▲ **fuss over *sb/sth*** *phrasal verb* to give someone or something too much attention because you want to show that you like them: *She's always fussing over that son of hers as if he were a little boy.*

fusspot /ˈfʌs.pɒt/ [US] /-pɑːt/ *noun* [C] (*US ALSO* **fussbudget**) *INFORMAL* a person who is often dissatisfied and complains about things that are not important: *"I can't eat this meat – it's too tough." "You old fusspot – give it here and I'll eat it!"*

fussy [NOT EASILY SATISFIED] /ˈfʌs.i/ *adj* *DISAPPROVING* not easily satisfied; having very high standards or very fixed standards about particular things: *All my children were fussy eaters.* ○ *He's so fussy **about** the house – everything has to be absolutely perfect.* ○ *"I haven't met a man I've fancied for ages!" "You're too fussy – that's your problem!"*

• **I'm not fussy/fussed** *UK INFORMAL* something that you say when you would be satisfied with either choice that is offered you: *"Red wine or white?" "I'm not fussy – either would be lovely."*

fussily /ˈfʌs.ɪ.li/ *adv* in a fussy way **fussiness** /ˈfʌs.ɪ.nəs/ *noun* [U]

fussy [TOO HIGHLY DECORATED] /ˈfʌs.i/ *adj* *DISAPPROVING* having too much decoration and too many small details, in a way that is not stylish: *They've got those curtains that tie up with big bows – they're a bit fussy for my taste.* **fussily** /ˈfʌs.ɪ.li/ *adv*: *fussily decorated* **fussiness** /ˈfʌs.ɪ.nəs/ *noun* [U]

fustian /ˈfʌs.ti.ən/ [US] /-tʃᵊn/ *noun* [U] a thick rough cotton cloth that lasts for a long time **fustian** /ˈfʌs.ti.ən/ [US] /-tʃᵊn/ *adj*

fusty /ˈfʌs.ti/ *adj* **1** *DISAPPROVING* not fresh and smelling unpleasant especially because of being left slightly wet: *This room smells a bit fusty – I think I'll just open a window.* **2** old-fashioned in ideas and beliefs: *Rupert's father belongs to some fusty old gentleman's club in London where they don't allow women in.*

futile /ˈfjuː.taɪl/ [US] /-t̬əl/ *adj* (of actions) having no effect or achieving nothing; unsuccessful: *Attempts to get supplies to the region are futile because troops will not*

F

allow the aid convoy to enter the city. ○ ***It's** quite futile trying to reason with him – he just won't listen.* ○ *All my attempts to cheer her up **proved** futile.* **futility** /fjuːˈtɪl.ɪ.ti/ Ⓤ /-t̬i/ *noun* [U] *"What's his latest book about?" "Oh, the usual – the transience of love and the futility of life."*

futon /ˈfuː.tɒn/ Ⓤ /-tɑːn/ *noun* [C] a mattress which is used on the floor or on a wooden frame

the ˈfuture *noun* [S] **1** a period of time that is to come: *Sometimes I worry about the future.* ○ *I wonder what the future **holds** for* (= what will happen to) *you and me.* ○ *I'm sure at some point **in** the future I'll want a baby.* ○ *We need to plan for the future.* ○ *Do you plan to leave London in the **distant** future or the **near** future?* ○ *I can see those two getting married in the **not too distant** future* (= quite soon). **2** in grammar, the form of a verb which you use when talking about something that will happen or exist: *In the sentence 'Who will look after the dog?' the verb phrase 'will look' is **in** the future.*

future /ˈfjuː.tʃəʳ/ Ⓤ /-tʃɚ/ *noun* **1** [C] what will happen to someone or something in the time that is to come: *Torn apart by war, its economy virtually destroyed, this country now faces a very **uncertain** future.* ○ *She's a very talented young singer, Mike and I personally think she's got a **great** future ahead of her!* ○ *The future isn't looking too rosy for these companies.* **2** [S or U] the chance of continuing success or existence for something: *With falling audiences, the future of this theatre is in doubt.*

• **in future** (*US USUALLY* **in the future**) *MAINLY UK* used at the beginning or end of a sentence in which there is a decision about a plan of action or a warning: *Could you be more careful in future?* ○ *In future I won't bother asking him out anywhere if he's just going to complain that he's bored!* ○ *In future I'm going to check every single piece of work that you do!*

future /ˈfjuː.tʃəʳ/ Ⓤ /-tʃɚ/ *adj* [before n] **1** happening or existing in the future: *Of course we'll keep you up to date with any future developments.* ○ *There's an old superstition that young girls going to bed on this night dream of their future husbands.* **2** In grammar, the future form of a verb is used when talking about something that will happen or exist: *How do you say that in the future **tense**?*

• **for future reference** used when you tell someone something so that it will be known about and can be used in the future: *For future reference, could you use the headed paper for any correspondence that leaves this office?*

futurism /ˈfjuː.tʃəʳr.ɪ.zəm/ Ⓤ /-tʃɚ-/ *noun* [U] a new way of thinking in the arts that started in the 1920s and 1930s which attempted to express through a range of art forms the characteristics and images of the modern age, such as machines, speed, movement and power **futurist** /ˈfjuː.tʃəʳr.ɪst/ Ⓤ /-tʃɚ-/ *adj, noun* [C] *a futurist painter*

futuristic /ˌfjuː.tʃəˈrɪs.tɪk/ *adj* strange and very modern, or intended or seeming to come from some imagined time in the future: *At the unspoiled North Bay, three white pyramids rise like futuristic sails from the sea.* ○ *Her latest novel is a futuristic thriller, set some time in the late twenty-first century.*

the ˌfuture ˈperfect *noun* [S] the tense which is used to show that an action will have been performed by a particular time. In English it is formed by 'will have' or 'shall have' and a past participle: *In the sentence 'By that time I will have finished,' the verb phrase 'will have finished' is **in** the future perfect.*

futures /ˈfjuː.tʃəz/ Ⓤ /-tʃɚz/ *plural noun* agreements for the buying and selling of goods, in which the price is agreed in advance of a particular future time at which the goods will be provided: *the futures market* ○ *She works in futures.*

fuzz /fʌz/ *noun* [U] **1** *INFORMAL* a covering of short thin soft hairs, or a mass of tightly curled and often untidy hair: *He's got that bit of adolescent fuzz on his upper lip.* ○ *I must buy a razor today and get rid of the fuzz on my legs!* **2** *UK AND US OLD-FASHIONED SLANG INFORMAL* the police: *Watch out! It's the fuzz.*

fuzzy /ˈfʌz.i/ *adj INFORMAL* **1** (of hair) in an untidy mass of tight curls: *Oh no, it's raining – my hair will go all fuzzy.* **2** describes a surface that feels like short fur: *the fuzzy skin of a peach*

fuzzy /ˈfʌz.i/ *adj* **1** (of an image) having shapes that do not have clear edges, or (of a sound, especially from a television, radio, etc.) not clear, usually because of other unwanted noises making it difficult to hear: *Is the picture always fuzzy on your TV?* ○ *You can pick up a lot of stations on the car radio but the sound is usually a bit fuzzy.* ⊃See also **fuzzy** at **fuzz**. **2** *INFORMAL* unclear: *The basic facts of the story are starting to emerge though the details are still fuzzy.* ○ *My head's a bit fuzzy* (= I cannot think clearly) *this morning after all that wine last night.* **fuzzily** /ˈfʌz.ɪ.li/ *adv* **fuzziness** /ˈfʌz.ɪ.nəs/ *noun* [U]

ˌfuzzy ˈlogic *noun* [C usually sing] a theoretical system used in mathematics, computing and philosophy to deal with statements which are neither true nor false

FWIW, fwiw *INTERNET ABBREVIATION FOR* for what it's worth: used when you are giving someone information and you do not know if it is useful or not

the f-word /ˈef,wɜːd/ Ⓤ /-ˌwɝːd/ *noun* [U] *POLITE WORD FOR* **fuck**: *Entertainment Research reports that there are 245 mentions of the f-word in this movie.*

-fy /-faɪ/ *suffix* ⊃See at **-ify**

FYA, fya *INTERNET ABBREVIATION FOR* for your amusement: used when you send someone a joke by email

FYI, fyi *INTERNET ABBREVIATION FOR* for your information: used when you send someone an announcement or tell them something that you think they should know

G

G [LETTER] (*plural* **G's** or **Gs**), **g** (*plural* **g's** or **gs**) /dʒiː/ *noun* [C] the 7th letter of the English alphabet

G [MUSIC] /dʒiː/ *noun* [C or U] *plural* **G's** or **Gs** a note in Western music

g [FORCE] /dʒiː/ *noun* [C] *plural* **g** SPECIALIZED a unit of measurement of the ACCELERATION (= rate of change of speed) of an object caused by GRAVITY

g [MASS] (ALSO **gm**) WRITTEN ABBREVIATION FOR gram

G [FILM] /dʒiː/ *noun* [C] *plural* **G's** or **Gs** or **G** in the US, a symbol that marks a film that is considered suitable for children of any age

G [MONEY] /dʒiː/ *noun* [C] *plural* **G's** or **Gs** or **G** US INFORMAL 1000 dollars: *You've got 6 G's worth of machinery here – you should get it insured.*

gab /gæb/ *verb* [I] **-bb-** INFORMAL DISAPPROVING to talk continuously and eagerly, especially about unimportant matters: *I got so bored listening to him gabbing* ***on*** *about nothing.*

gabardine, **gaberdine** /ˈgæb.ə.diːn/ [US] /-ɚ-/ *noun* [C or U] a thick cloth which is especially used for making coats, or a long coat made from this cloth

gabble /ˈgæb.l̩/ *verb* [I or T] to speak quickly and not clearly so that it is difficult to understand: *She started gabbling* ***away*** *at me in Spanish and I didn't understand a word.* ○ *Gina, as usual, was gabbling* ***away*** *on the telephone!*

gabble /ˈgæb.l̩/ *noun* [U] fast conversation or speech which is difficult to understand, often because many people are talking at the same time

gable /ˈgeɪ.bl̩/ *noun* [C] the triangular top end of the wall of a building where it meets the sloping parts of a roof

gabled /ˈgeɪ.bl̩d/ *adj* with gables: *With its narrow cobbled streets and gabled houses, Brugge must be one of the most beautiful cities in Europe.*

gad /gæd/ *verb* **-dd-**

▲ **gad about/around** ***(somewhere)*** *phrasal verb* OLD-FASHIONED to visit or travel to a lot of different places, enjoying yourself and having few worries or responsibilities: *We spent the weekend gadding about London and generally enjoying ourselves.*

gadabout /ˈgæd.ə.baʊt/ *noun* [C] OLD-FASHIONED HUMOROUS *Where have you been, you young gadabout!*

gadget /ˈgædʒ.ɪt/ *noun* [C] a small device or machine with a particular purpose: *kitchen gadgets* ○ *Have you seen this handy little gadget – it's for separating egg yolks from whites.* **gadgetry** /ˈgædʒ.ɪ.tri/ *noun* [U] *We've got a juicer, a blender, a coffee grinder – in fact all manner of kitchen gadgetry.*

Gaelic /ˈgeɪ.lɪk/ /ˈgæl.ɪk/ *noun* [U] a language spoken in parts of Ireland, Scotland and, in the past, the Isle of Man **Gaelic** /ˈgeɪ.lɪk/ /ˈgæl.ɪk/ *adj*

gaffe /gæf/ *noun* [C] a remark or action that is a social mistake and not considered polite; FAUX PAS: *I* ***made*** *a real gaffe – I called his new wife 'Judy' which is the name of his ex-wife.* ○ *Was that a bit of a gaffe then, starting to eat before everyone else had been served?*

gaffer [MAN IN CHARGE] /ˈgæf.əʳ/ [US] /-ɚ/ *noun* [C] UK INFORMAL a man who is in charge of other workers

gaffer [FILM] /ˈgæf.əʳ/ [US] /-ɚ/ *noun* [C] SPECIALIZED the person responsible for the lights and other electrical equipment used when making a film or television programme

gaffer [OLD MAN] /ˈgæf.əʳ/ [US] /-ɚ/ *noun* [C] INFORMAL an old man

gag [PIECE OF CLOTH] /gæg/ *noun* [C] a piece of cloth which is tied around a person's mouth or put inside it in order to stop them from speaking, shouting or calling for help: *Her hands and feet were tied and a gag placed over her mouth.*

gag /gæg/ *verb* **-gg-** **1** [T] to put a gag on someone's mouth: *He was* ***bound and*** *gagged and left in a cell for three days.* **2** [T often passive] to prevent a person or organization from talking or writing about a particular subject: *The media have obviously been gagged because nothing has been reported.*

gag [ALMOST VOMIT] /gæg/ *verb* [I] **-gg-** to experience the sudden uncomfortable feeling of tightness in the throat and stomach that makes you feel you are going to vomit: *Just the smell of liver cooking makes me gag.* ○ *I tried my best to eat it but the meat was so fatty I gagged* ***on*** *it.*

gag [JOKE] /gæg/ *noun* [C] **1** INFORMAL a joke or funny story, especially one told by a COMEDIAN (= person whose job is to make people laugh): *I did a few opening gags about the band that had been on before me.* **2** US a trick played on someone or an action performed to amuse other people

gag [EAGER] /gæg/ **1** UK SLANG **be gagging for/to do *sth*** to be very eager to do something: *I was gagging for a pint of cold lager.* **2** SLANG **be gagging for it** to be very eager to have sex; used especially by a man to say he thinks a woman wants very much to have sex with him

gaga [MENTALLY UNCLEAR] /ˈgɑː.gɑː/ *adj* INFORMAL unable to think clearly and make decisions because of old age; SENILE: *My granny's 94 and she's a bit gaga.* ○ *I know I'm seventy-three but I haven't* ***gone*** *gaga yet!*

gaga [IN LOVE] /ˈgɑː.gɑː/ *adj* [after v] INFORMAL having a strong but usually temporary love for someone: *She's totally gaga* ***about/over*** *him!* ○ *Just standing near her makes him* ***go*** *gaga!*

ˈgagging ˌorder UK *noun* [C] (US **gag order**) an official order not to discuss something, especially a legal case: *The judge* ***issued*** *a gagging order to prevent the witnesses from speaking to the press.*

gaggle /ˈgæg.l̩/ *group noun* [C] **1** a group of geese **2** DISAPPROVING a group of noisy or silly people: *There was the usual gaggle* ***of*** *journalists waiting for the princess when she got out of her car.*

gaiety /ˈgeɪ.ə.ti/ [US] /-t̬i/ *noun* [U] OLD-FASHIONED happiness and excitement: *I felt there was an air of forced gaiety about her manner.*

gaily /ˈgeɪ.li/ *adv* OLD-FASHIONED happily or brightly: *I could hear her gaily singing in her bedroom.* ○ *The tree lights twinkled gaily across the lake.*

gain [OBTAIN] /geɪn/ *verb* [I or T] to obtain something that is useful, that gives you an advantage, or that is in some way positive, especially over a period of time: *The Nationalist Party have gained a lot of support in the south of the country.* ○ *What do you hope to gain* ***from*** *the course?* ○ *Alternative medicine has only just started to gain respectability in our society.* ○ [+ two objects] *It was her performances in Aida which gained her an international reputation as a soprano.* ○ *After you've gained some experience teaching abroad you can come home and get a job.* ○ *From the late nineteenth century Britain and other European powers began to gain control of parts of the Ottoman Empire.* ○ *She's certainly gained* ***(in)*** *confidence over the last couple of years.* ○ *The data exists all right – the difficulty is in gaining access to it.* ○ *The thieves gained entrance through an upstairs window that was left open.*

• **gain ground** If a political party or an idea or belief gains ground, it becomes more popular or accepted: *The Republicans are gaining ground in the southern states.*

gain /geɪn/ *noun* [C or U] when you get something useful or positive: *Whatever the objections to this sort of treatment, the gains in terms of the number of lives saved are substantial.* ○ *The minister was sacked for abusing power for his* ***personal*** *gain.*

gain [INCREASE] /geɪn/ *verb* [I or T] **1** to increase in weight, speed, height or amount: *I gained a lot of weight while I was on holiday.* ○ *The car gained speed going down the hill.* ○ *Good economic indicators caused the share index to gain* ***(by)*** *ten points.* ○ *The campaign has been gaining momentum ever since the television appeal.* **2** If a clock or watch gains, it works too quickly and shows a time which is later than the real time: *My watch has gained* ***(by)*** *ten minutes over the last twenty-four hours.*

gain /geɪn/ *noun* [C or U] an increase in something such as size, weight or amount: *Side effects of the drugs may include tiredness, headaches or weight gain.* ○ *Having deducted costs we still made a net gain of five thousand* *pounds.* ○ *Oil prices rose again today after yesterday's gains.*

▲ **gain on *sb/sth*** *phrasal verb* to get nearer to someone or something that you are chasing: *Garcia was gaining on her opponent throughout the race, but only overtook her at the very end.*

gainful /ˈgeɪn.fəl/ *adj FORMAL* providing money or something else that is useful: *Many graduates tell of months spent in search of gainful **employment**.* **gainfully** /ˈgeɪn.fəl.i/ *adv*: *His estate continues to keep lawyers gainfully **employed** even seven years after his death.*

gainsay /ˌgeɪnˈseɪ/ *verb* [T often used in negatives] **gainsaid, gainsaid** *FORMAL* to refuse to accept something as the truth: *Certainly there's no gainsaying* (= It is not possible to doubt) *the technical brilliance of his performance.*

gait /geɪt/ *noun* [C] *FORMAL* a particular way of walking: *He walked **with** a slow stiff gait.*

gaiters /ˈgeɪ.təz/ [US] /-t̬ɚz/ *plural noun* a pair of coverings for the lower half of the legs, often worn in the past but worn now mainly by climbers and walkers in order to stop earth and water from entering their boots

G

gal [GIRL] /gæl/ *noun* [C] *plural* **gals** *INFORMAL OR HUMOROUS* a woman or girl: *You're just an old-fashioned gal, aren't you, honey!*

gal [UNIT OF MEASUREMENT] (*UK ALSO* **gall**) *WRITTEN ABBREVIATION FOR* **gallon**

gala [CELEBRATION] /ˈgɑː.lə/ [US] /ˈgeɪ-/ *noun* [C] a special public occasion at which there is a lot of entertainment, usually in the form of a variety of performances: *There will be many stars performing in the Royal Ballet's Gala Night, held in aid of children's charities.*

gala [SPORTS EVENT] /ˈgɑː.lə/ [US] /ˈgeɪ-/ *noun* [C] *UK* a sports competition, especially in swimming: *a **swimming** gala*

galah /gəˈlɑː/ *noun* [C] **1** a medium-sized COCKATOO (= type of bird) common in most parts of Australia, that has a grey upper part of its body and a pink lower part **2** *AUS INFORMAL* a stupid person

galaxy /ˈgæl.ək.si/ *noun* [C] **1** one of the independent groups of stars in the universe **2** a gathering of rich and famous people: *Present tonight at the long-awaited opening of this film are a whole galaxy **of** stars from the acting and musical professions.*

● **the Galaxy** the very large group of stars that contains the SOLAR SYSTEM (= the sun and all the planets, including Earth, that go round it)

galactic /gəˈlæk.tɪk/ *adj* relating to the Galaxy or other galaxies: *inter-galactic travel*

gale /geɪl/ *noun* [C] a very strong wind: *Hundreds of old trees were blown down in the gales.*

● **gales of laughter** a lot of loud laughter: *I could hear gales of laughter coming from downstairs.*

gall [RUDENESS] /gɔːl/ [US] /gɑːl/ *noun* [U] rudeness and inability to understand that your behaviour or what you say is not acceptable to other people: [+ *to* infinitive] *Considering that he never even bothers to visit my parents I'm amazed that Tim **has the** gall **to** ask them for money!*

gall [ANNOY] /gɔːl/ [US] /gɑːl/ *verb* [T] to make someone feel annoyed: *I think it galls him to take orders from a younger and less experienced colleague.*

galling /ˈgɔː.lɪŋ/ [US] /ˈgɑː-/ *adj* annoying: [+ *to* infinitive] *It was very galling **to** have a younger brother who did everything better than me.*

gallant [BRAVE] /ˈgæl.ənt/ [US] /gəˈlænt/ *adj FORMAL APPROVING* showing no fear of dangerous or difficult things: *Despite fierce competition she made a gallant effort to win the first medal of the championships.* **gallantly** /ˈgæl.ənt.li/ [US] /gəˈlænt-/ *adv* **gallantry** /ˈgæl.ən.tri/ *noun* [U] *The speech praised those who had displayed gallantry in the liberation of their country.*

gallant [POLITE] /ˈgæl.ənt/ [US] /gəˈlænt/ *adj FORMAL* (of a man) polite and kind towards women, especially when in public: *That wasn't very gallant of you, Paul, pushing a young lady out of the way like that!* **gallantly** /ˈgæl.ənt.li/ [US] /gəˈlænt-/ *adv* **gallantry** /ˈgæl.ən.tri/ *noun* [U] *FORMAL*

ˈgall ˌbladder *noun* [C] a small bag-like bodily organ connected to the liver which stores BILE (= a bitter liquid that helps to digest food): *She had an operation to remove a stone from her gall bladder.*

galleon /ˈgæl.i.ən/ *noun* [C] a large sailing ship with three or four masts, used both in trade and war from the 15th to the 18th centuries

gallery [BUILDING] /ˈgæl.ər.i/ [US] /-ɚ-/ *noun* [C] a room or building which is used for showing works of art, sometimes so that they can be sold: *the National Portrait Gallery* ○ *a contemporary **art** gallery*

gallery [RAISED AREA] /ˈgæl.ər.i/ [US] /-ɚ-/ *noun* [C] a raised area around the sides or at the back of a large room which provides extra space for people to sit or stand, or the highest floor in a theatre that contains the cheapest seats ➲Compare **the circle** UPPER FLOOR; **the stalls** THEATRE.

galley [KITCHEN] /ˈgæl.i/ *noun* [C] a kitchen in a ship or aircraft

galley [BOAT] /ˈgæl.i/ *noun* [C] (in the past) a long low ship which had sails and was usually rowed by prisoners and slaves: *a galley slave*

Gallic /ˈgæl.ɪk/ *adj* French or typically French: *Catherine Deneuve seemed to typify cool Gallic elegance.*

gallivant /ˈgæl.ɪ.vænt/ *verb* [I usually + adv or prep] *HUMOROUS* to visit or go to a lot of different places, enjoying yourself and having few worries or responsibilities: *Well you won't be able to go off gallivanting **around** like this when there's a baby to be taken care of.*

gallon /ˈgæl.ən/ *noun* [C] a unit for measuring volume: *An imperial gallon, used in Britain, is equal to 4546 cubic centimetres.* ○ *A US gallon is equal to 3785 cubic centimetres.* ○ *INFORMAL I love milk – I drink gallons* (= a great amount) *of the stuff.*

gallop /ˈgæl.əp/ *verb* **1** [I or T] (of a horse) to run fast so that all four feet come off the ground together in each act of forward movement, or (of a person) to ride a horse that is running in this way: *We galloped through the woods.* ➲Compare **canter**; **trot** RUN. **2** [I usually + adv or prep] *INFORMAL* to move or act quickly: *It is the height of folly and a tragic waste to gallop into war.*

gallop /ˈgæl.əp/ *noun* [S] *At the sound of gunfire the horse suddenly **broke into** a gallop.* ○ *We had to complete the work **at a** gallop* (= very quickly).

▲ **gallop through *sth*** *phrasal verb INFORMAL* to perform, read or do something very quickly and without enough care: *They often gallop through 10 news items in 20 minutes.*

galloping /ˈgæl.ə.pɪŋ/ *adj* [before n] increasing or developing at a very fast and often uncontrollable rate: *galloping **inflation***

gallows /ˈgæl.əʊz/ [US] /-oʊz/ *noun* [C] *plural* **gallows** a wooden structure used, especially in the past, to hang criminals from as a form of EXECUTION (= killing as a punishment): *New witnesses have cast doubt on some of the evidence that **sent** the 19 year old **to the** gallows.*

ˌgallows ˈhumour *noun* [U] jokes or humorous remarks that are made about unpleasant or worrying subjects such as death and illness

gallstone /ˈgɔːl.stəʊn/ [US] /ˈgɑːl.stoʊn/ *noun* [C] a small piece of hard material which sometimes forms in the GALL BLADDER (= a bodily organ) and can cause great pain

Gallup poll /ˈgæl.əp.pəʊl/ [US] /-ˌpoʊl/ *noun* [C] *TRADEMARK* a series of questions asked of a group of people in order to find out what they think about a particular subject or how they will vote in an election

galore /gəˈlɔːr/ [US] /-ˈlɔːr/ *adj* [after n] *OLD-FASHIONED INFORMAL* in great amounts or numbers: *And for the sweet-toothed, this café has desserts galore.*

galoshes /gəˈlɒʃ.ɪz/ [US] /-ˈlɑː.ʃɪz/ *plural noun US FOR* **overshoes**

galumphing /gəˈlʌmp.fɪŋ/ *adj UK INFORMAL* moving about or behaving in an awkward manner: *In his galumphing way he managed to wake the whole house on his return.* ○ *Her galumphing entry into the music business has annoyed many of the established stars.*

galvanize, *UK USUALLY* **-ise** /ˈgæl.və.naɪz/ *verb* [T] to cause someone to suddenly take action, especially by shocking or exciting them in some way: *Western charities were galvanized by TV pictures of starving people.* ○ *The prospect of his mother coming to stay galvanized him **into action** and he immediately set about cleaning the house.*

galvanized, UK USUALLY **-ised** /ˈɡæl.və.naɪzd/ adj describes metal, or something made of metal, that is covered with a thin protective layer of ZINC: *galvanized iron/steel* ○ *galvanized nails/rivets*

gambit CLEVER ACTION /ˈɡæm.bɪt/ noun [C] **1** a clever action in a game or other situation which is intended to achieve an advantage and usually involves taking a risk: *Her clever **opening** gambit gave her an early advantage.* ○ *Their promise to lower taxes is clearly an election-year gambit.* **2** SPECIALIZED a way of beginning a game of chess, in which you intentionally lose a PAWN (= game piece) in order to gain some other form of advantage later

gambit REMARK /ˈɡæm.bɪt/ noun [C] a remark that you make to someone in order to start a conversation: *"I hear you're a friend of Jamie's," was her **opening** gambit.*

gamble /ˈɡæm.bl̩/ verb **1** [I] to do something risky that might result in loss of money or failure, hoping to get money or achieve success: *Anyone who gambles **on** the stock exchange has to be prepared to lose money.* **2** [I or T] to bet money, for example in a game or on a horse race: *I like to gamble when I play cards – it makes it more interesting.* ○ *He gambles **on** the horses* (= horse races). ○ *He gambled **away** all of our savings.*

gamble /ˈɡæm.bl̩/ noun [C usually sing] a risk that might result in loss of money or failure: *Her publishers knew they were **taking** a gamble when they agreed to publish such an unusual novel.* ○ *It was a gamble using such an inexperienced director, but it **paid off*** (= was successful).

gambler /ˈɡæm.blər/ ⓤ /-blɚ/ noun [C] someone who often bets money, for example in a game or on a horse race: *a self-help group for **compulsive** gamblers*

gambling /ˈɡæm.blɪŋ/ noun [U] *He had to borrow money to pay off his gambling debts.*

▲ **gamble on sth** phrasal verb to take a risk that something will happen: *You're rather gambling on it being a nice day by holding the party in the garden, aren't you?*

gambol /ˈɡæm.bl̩/ verb [I] **-ll-** or US USUALLY **-l-** LITERARY to run and jump in a happy and playful way: *Lambs were gambolling (**about/around**) in the spring sunshine.*

game ENTERTAINING ACTIVITY /ɡeɪm/ noun **1** [C] an entertaining activity or sport, especially one played by children, or the equipment needed for such an activity: *a board game* ○ *indoor/computer games* ○ *The children played a game **of** cops and robbers.* ○ *I told the children to put their toys and games away.* **2** [C] a particular competition, match or occasion when people play a game: *a game **of** chess/tennis/baseball* **3** [C] one part of a competition in activities such as tennis: *I won the first game, and then lost the next two.* **4** [U] the way in which a person plays a particular sport: *Susan is playing golf every day to try to improve her game.* **5** [S] something that is not treated seriously: *Love is just a game to him.*

gaming /ˈɡeɪ.mɪŋ/ noun [U] the activity of playing VIDEO GAMES

gamer /ˈɡeɪ.mər/ ⓤ /-mɚ/ noun [C] a person who plays VIDEO GAMES

games /ɡeɪmz/ plural noun **1** UK organized sports activities that children do at school: *the games teacher* ○ *It's games this afternoon.* **2** an organized competition consisting of several different sports events: *the Olympic/Commonwealth Games*

game ACTIVITY /ɡeɪm/ noun [S] **1** INFORMAL an illegal or secret activity **2** OLD-FASHIONED INFORMAL a type of business activity: *I'm in the stocks and shares game.*

• **on the game** UK INFORMAL working as a prostitute: *She went on the game to pay for her drug habit.*

• **be new to this game** to be involved in an activity or situation that you have not experienced before

• **give the game away** INFORMAL to spoil a surprise or a joke by telling someone something that should have been kept secret: *It's a secret, so don't give the game away, will you?*

• **the game is up** used to tell someone that you know what their secret activities or plans are and they cannot continue: *Okay, you two, the game's up! Give me the cigarettes – this time I'm telling your parents.*

• **What's your game?** UK INFORMAL something you ask when you want to know what someone is doing or

secretly planning to do: *The porter saw me climbing over the wall and shouted "Hey you, what's your game?"*

game WILLING /ɡeɪm/ adj willing to do things that are new, risky or difficult: *It was a difficult challenge, but Roberta was game.* ○ *She's game **for** anything.*

gamely /ˈɡeɪm.li/ adv: *"I'll look after the baby," he said gamely* (= bravely).

game ANIMALS /ɡeɪm/ noun [U] wild animals and birds that are hunted for food or sport: *game **birds***

gamey /ˈɡeɪ.mi/ adj gamier, gamiest having the strong smell or taste of game

Gameboy /ˈɡeɪm.bɔɪ/ noun [C] TRADEMARK a small machine that you play computer games on and that you can carry with you

gamekeeper /ˈɡeɪmˌkiː.pər/ ⓤ /-pɚ/ noun [C] a person whose job is to take care of wild animals and birds that are kept especially for hunting

game plan noun [C] a plan for achieving success

game show noun [C] a television programme where people score points by answering questions or doing things: *a game show **host*** (= a person who introduces the programme and asks the questions)

gamesmanship /ˈɡeɪmz.mən.ʃɪp/ noun [U] INFORMAL the activity of trying to win a game by doing things that are not really breaking the rules but are intended to destroy the confidence of the other player

gamete /ˈɡæm.iːt/ noun [C] SPECIALIZED a cell connected with sexual reproduction, which is either a male sperm or a female egg

gamine /ˈɡæm.iːn/ adj APPROVING describes a girl or young woman who is thin, short-haired and attractively like a young boy in appearance: *Her newly cropped hair gives her a fashionably gamine look.* **gamine** /ˈɡæm.iːn/ noun [C]

gaming /ˈɡeɪ.mɪŋ/ noun [U] the risking of money in games of chance, especially at a CASINO: *gaming machines/tables*

gamma, γ /ˈɡæm.ə/ noun [C] the third letter of the Greek alphabet ⊃Compare **alpha; beta.**

gamma globulin /ˌɡæm.əˈɡlɒb.jʊ.lɪn/ ⓤ /-ˈɡlɑː.bjə-/ noun [U] a natural substance in the blood that gives protection against disease

gamma radiation noun [U] a type of radiation of very short wave length, often produced in radioactive decay, which goes through most solid objects

gamma ray noun [C usually pl] a beam of gamma radiation

gammon MAINLY UK /ˈɡæm.ən/ noun [U] (US USUALLY **ham**) meat taken from the back leg or side of a pig and preserved with smoke or salt

gammy /ˈɡæm.i/ adj UK INFORMAL A gammy leg or other body part is damaged or does not work correctly: *I've got a gammy knee.*

the gamut /ðəˈɡæm.ət/ noun [S] the whole range of things that can be included in something: *In her stories she expresses the **whole** gamut **of** emotions, from happiness to sorrow.*

• **run the gamut of sth** to experience or show the whole range of something: *Jonson has run the gamut of hotel work, from porter to owner of a large chain of hotels.*

gander BIRD /ˈɡæn.dər/ ⓤ /-dɚ/ noun [C] a male goose

gander LOOK /ˈɡæn.dər/ ⓤ /-dɚ/ noun INFORMAL **have/take a gander** to have a quick look: *Let's take a gander **at** your new car, then.*

gang /ɡæŋ/ group noun [C] **1** a group of young people, especially young men, who spend time together, often fighting with other groups and behaving badly: *Fights among rival gangs account for most murders in the city.* **2** a group of criminals who work together: *a gang of armed robbers* **3** INFORMAL a group of friends: *She was in our gang at school.* ○ *I went out with the usual gang from college on Friday night.* **4** a group of workers or prisoners who work together: *a gang of labourers*

gang /ɡæŋ/ verb

▲ **gang up** phrasal verb DISAPPROVING to unite as a group against someone: *They all ganged up to try and get him to change his decision.* ○ *The whole class ganged up **against/on** her because she was the teacher's pet.*

gang-bang /ˈgæŋ.bæŋ/ *noun* [C], *verb* [T] SLANG **gang rape**

gangbanger /ˈgæŋˌbæŋ.əʳ/ [US] /-ɚ/ *noun* [C] US SLANG a member of a violent group of young men, especially ones who use guns and commit crimes

gangland /ˈgæŋ.lænd/ *noun* [U] the people and places involved in violent crime: *a gangland feud/murder*

ganglion /ˈgæŋ.gli.ən/ *noun* [C] *plural* **ganglions** or **ganglia** SPECIALIZED **1** a swelling, often on the back of the hand **2** a mass of nerve cells, especially appearing outside the brain or spine

gangly /ˈgæŋ.glɪŋ/ *adj* (ALSO **gangling**) describes someone, usually a boy or young man, who is very tall and thin and moves awkwardly: *a gangly youth*

gangplank /ˈgæŋ.plæŋk/ *noun* [C] a board or similar object put between a boat or ship and the land, so that people can get on and off

ˈgang ˌrape *noun* [C] (SLANG **gang-bang**) when a group of men use violence or threatening behaviour to force a woman to have sex with all of them **gang rape** *verb* [T] (SLANG **gang-bang**)

gangrene /ˈgæŋ.griːn/ *noun* [U] the decay of a part of a person's body because the blood has stopped flowing there: *They had to amputate his leg because gangrene had* ***set in***. **gangrenous** /ˈgæŋ.grɪ.nəs/ *adj*: *His foot had become gangrenous.*

gangsta rap /ˈgæŋ*k*.stəˌræp/ [US] /-stɚ-/ *noun* [U] a type of RAP music which is about life in the poor parts of cities, especially violence and drugs

gangster /ˈgæŋ*k*.stəʳ/ [US] /-stɚ/ *noun* [C] a member of an organized group of violent criminals

gangway /ˈgæŋ.weɪ/ *noun* [C] **1** a passage between two rows of seats, for example in a cinema or bus: *His suitcase was blocking the gangway.* **2** a wide or big GANGPLANK

Gangway! /ˈgæŋ.weɪ/ *exclamation* something you shout when you want people to move so that you can get someone or something through a crowd quickly

ganja /ˈgæn.dʒə/ *noun* [U] SLANG **marijuana**

gannet /ˈgæn.ɪt/ *noun* [C] a large bird with mainly white feathers and a yellow beak that lives by the sea

gantry /ˈgæn.tri/ *noun* [C] a tall metal frame that supports heavy machines such as CRANES, railway signals or other equipment

gaol /dʒeɪl/ *noun, verb* UK OLD-FASHIONED FOR **jail**

gaoler /ˈdʒeɪ.ləʳ/ [US] /-lɚ/ *noun* [C] UK OLD-FASHIONED FOR **jailer**

gap [HOLE] /gæp/ *noun* [C] an empty space or opening in the middle of something or between two things: *The children squeezed through a gap* ***in*** *the wall.* ○ *She has a small gap* ***between*** *her front teeth.*

• **a gap in the market** an opportunity for a product or service that does not already exist: *There is a gap in the magazine market that needs to be filled.*

gap [DIFFERENCE] /gæp/ *noun* [C usually sing] **1** a difference between two things: *The gap* ***between*** *rich and poor is still widening* (= becoming greater). **2** a period of time spent doing something different: *After a gap* ***of*** *five years, Jennifer decided to go back to work full-time.*

• **bridge a/the gap** to connect two things or to make the difference between them smaller: *Mr Clinton singled out education as a vital tool in bridging the gap* ***between*** *rich and poor.* ○ *This collection of stories bridges the gap between history and fiction.*

gape [LOOK] /geɪp/ *verb* [I] to look in great surprise at someone or something, especially with an open mouth: *They stood gaping* ***at*** *the pig in the kitchen.*

gape [OPEN] /geɪp/ *verb* [I] to be or become wide open: *Peter's jacket gaped at the seams.* **gaping** /ˈgeɪ.pɪŋ/ *adj*: *The bomb had left gaping holes in the wall.*

gap-toothed /ˌgæpˈtuːθt/ *adj* having spaces between the front teeth

ˈgap ˌyear *noun* [C] UK a year between leaving school and starting university which is usually spent travelling or working: *I didn't* ***take*** *a gap year. Did you?*

garage [BUILDING] /ˈgær.ɑːʒ/ /-ɪdʒ/ [US] /gəˈrɑːʒ/ *noun* [C] **1** a building where a car is kept, which is built next to or as part of a house: *Did you put the car in the garage?* **2** a place where cars are repaired: *The car's still* ***at*** *the garage getting fixed.* **3** UK (US **gas station**) a place where fuel is sold for cars and other vehicles

garage /ˈgær.ɑːʒ/ /-ɪdʒ/ [US] /gəˈrɑːʒ/ *verb* [T] *If your car is garaged* (= kept in a garage), *you get much cheaper insurance.*

garage [MUSIC] /ˈgær.ɑːʒ/ /-ɪdʒ/ [US] /gəˈrɑːʒ/ *noun* [U] fast, electronic dance music with a strong beat, keyboards and singing

ˈgarage ˌsale *noun* [C] an occasion when people sell things, often in their garage or outside their house, that they no longer want

garb /gɑːb/ [US] /gɑːrb/ *noun* [U] LITERARY clothes that are in a particular style or are a uniform: *prison/clerical/military garb*

garbage /ˈgɑː.bɪdʒ/ [US] /ˈgɑːr-/ *noun* [U] **1** US (UK **rubbish**) waste material or unwanted things that you throw away **2** nonsense or worthless ideas or things: *He talks a lot of garbage about education.*

ˈgarbage ˌbag *noun* [C] US FOR **dustbin bag/liner**

ˈgarbage ˌcan *noun* [C] US FOR **dustbin**

ˈgarbage colˌlector *noun* [C] US FOR **dustman**

ˈgarbage disˌposal *noun* [C] US FOR **waste disposal**

ˈgarbage ˌman *noun* [C] US FOR **dustman**

ˈgarbage ˌtruck *noun* [C] US FOR **dustcart** ➲See picture **Cars and Trucks** on page Centre 13

garbanzo bean /gɑːˈbæn.zəʊˌbiːn/ [US] /gɑːrˈbɑːn.zoʊ-/ *noun* [C] US FOR **chickpea**

garbled /ˈgɑː.bl̩d/ [US] /ˈgɑːr-/ *adj* If words or messages are garbled, they are not clear and are very difficult to understand, often giving a false idea of the facts: *He left a rather garbled* ***message*** *on my answerphone.*

garçon /ˈgɑː.sɒn/ /-ˈ-/ [US] /gɑːrˈsoʊn/ *noun* [C] OLD-FASHIONED a WAITER in a French restaurant

garden /ˈgɑː.dᵊn/ [US] /ˈgɑːr-/ *noun* **1** [C] (US USUALLY **yard**) a piece of land next to and belonging to a house, where flowers and other plants are grown, and often containing an area of grass: *garden tools/furniture* ○ *a garden shed* ○ MAINLY UK *The house has a large* ***back*** *garden, and a small* ***front*** *garden.* **2** [C usually pl] a public park with flowers, plants and places to sit: *the Botanical Gardens*

gardener /ˈgɑː.dᵊn.əʳ/ [US] /ˈgɑːr.dᵊn.ɚ/ *noun* [C] someone who works in a garden, growing and taking care of plants: *I'm not much of a gardener* (= not very good at taking care of my garden).

gardening /ˈgɑː.dᵊn.ɪŋ/ [US] /ˈgɑːr-/ *noun* [U] *Many people in Britain are fond of gardening* (= working in and taking care of their gardens). ○ *gardening gloves*

ˈgarden ˌcentre *noun* [C] a place where you can buy things such as plants and equipment for your garden

ˌgarden ˈcity *noun* [C] UK a town that has been planned to include lots of trees, plants and open spaces

ˈgarden ˌflat *noun* [C] UK an apartment which is on the ground level of a building and has its own garden

gardenia /gɑːˈdiː.ni.ə/ [US] /gɑːr-/ *noun* [C] a large white or yellow flower with a pleasant smell, or the bush that produces this

the ˌgarden of ˈEden *noun* [U] LITERARY the beautiful garden, described in the Bible, made by God for Adam and Eve

ˈgarden ˌparty *noun* [C] (US ALSO **lawn party**) a formal party that happens outside in the afternoon, often in a large private garden

gargantuan /gɑːˈgæn.tju.ən/ [US] /gɑːr-/ *adj* very large: *a problem* ***of*** *gargantuan* ***proportions*** ○ *a gargantuan appetite*

gargle /ˈgɑː.gl̩/ [US] /ˈgɑːr-/ *verb* [I] to move a liquid around in your throat without swallowing, especially to clean it or stop it feeling painful **gargle** /ˈgɑː.gl̩/ [US] /ˈgɑːr-/ *noun* [S] *Have* ***a*** *gargle with this mouthwash.*

gargoyle /ˈgɑː.gɔɪl/ [US] /ˈgɑːr-/ *noun* [C] an ugly creature or head cut from stone and fixed to the roof of an old church, etc., often with an open mouth through which rain water flows away

garish /ˈgeə.rɪʃ/ [US] /ˈger.ɪʃ/ *adj* DISAPPROVING unpleasantly bright: *a pair of garish Bermuda shorts*

garland /ˈgɑː.lənd/ [US] /ˈgɑːr-/ *noun* [C] a circle made of flowers and leaves worn around the neck or head as a decoration: *a garland of white roses* **garland** /ˈgɑː.lənd/ [US] /ˈgɑːr-/ *verb* [T] *They garlanded the visitors* ***with*** *scented flowers.*

garlic /ˈgɑː.lɪk/ [US] /ˈgɑːr-/ *noun* [U] a plant of the onion family that has a strong taste and smell and is used in cooking to add flavour: *For this recipe you need four* ***cloves*** (= single pieces) *of garlic, crushed.* ○ *a garlic bulb* ➲See picture **Vegetables** on page Centre 2
garlicky /ˈgɑː.lɪ.ki/ [US] /ˈgɑːr-/ *adj* containing, tasting or smelling of garlic: *garlicky food/breath*

ˌ**garlic ˈbread** *noun* [U] bread that has been spread with a mixture of butter, garlic and herbs before being baked

garment /ˈgɑː.mənt/ [US] /ˈgɑːr-/ *noun* [C] *FORMAL* a piece of clothing

garner /ˈgɑː.nəʳ/ [US] /ˈgɑːr.nɚ/ *verb* [T] *LITERARY* to collect something, usually after much work or with difficulty: *Coppola garnered several Oscar awards for 'The Godfather'.*

garnet /ˈgɑː.nɪt/ [US] /ˈgɑːr-/ *noun* [C] a hard dark-red stone used in jewellery

garnish /ˈgɑː.nɪʃ/ [US] /ˈgɑːr-/ *verb* [T] to decorate food with a small amount of different food: *Garnish the dish* ***with*** *parsley before serving.* **garnish** /ˈgɑː.nɪʃ/ [US] /ˈgɑːr-/ *noun* [C or U] *a lemon and herb garnish*

garret /ˈgær.ɪt/ *noun* [C] *LITERARY* a very small uncomfortable room at the top of a house

garrison /ˈgær.ɪ.sᵊn/ [US] /ˈger-/ *group noun* [C] a group of soldiers living in or defending a town or building, or the buildings that the soldiers live in: *The 100-strong garrison has/have received no supplies for a week.* ○ *a garrison* ***town*** **garrison** /ˈgær.ɪ.sᵊn/ [US] /ˈger-/ *verb* [T usually + adv or prep] *British troops are garrisoned in the area.*

garrotte, **garotte**, *US ALSO* **garrote** /gəˈrɒt/ [US] /-ˈrɑːt/ *verb* [T] to kill someone by putting a metal wire or collar around their neck to break their neck or stop them breathing
garrotte, **garotte**, *US ALSO* **garrote** /gəˈrɒt/ [US] /-ˈrɑːt/ *noun* [C] a metal wire or collar used to kill someone

garrulous /ˈgær.ᵊl.əs/ [US] /ˈger-/ *adj* having the habit of talking a lot, especially about unimportant things **garrulously** /ˈgær.ᵊl.ə.sli/ [US] /ˈger-/ *adv* **garrulousness** /ˈgær.ᵊl.ə.snəs/ [US] /ˈger-/ *noun* [U]

garter /ˈgɑː.təʳ/ [US] /ˈgɑːr.t̬ɚ/ *noun* [C] a piece of elastic used, especially in the past, for holding up a stocking or sock
garters /ˈgɑː.təz/ [US] /ˈgɑːr.t̬ɚz/ *plural noun US FOR* **suspenders** ➲See also **garter belt** at **suspender belt**.

gas [MATTER] /gæs/ *noun plural* **gases** or **gasses** **1** [C or U] a substance in an air-like form that is neither solid nor liquid: *Oxygen, hydrogen and nitrogen are all gases.* **2** [C or U] a substance in air-like form that is used as a fuel for heating and cooking: *Do you prefer cooking with electricity or gas?* ○ *UK A leak in the gas* ***mains*** (= pipes) *caused a major explosion.* ○ *poisonous/inflammable/toxic gas* ○ *a gas-****fired*** *power station* **3** [U] *INFORMAL* a substance in an air-like form used for medical purposes to prevent people feeling pain or being conscious during an operation: *I had/was given gas when I got my wisdom teeth out.* **4** [U] *MAINLY US FOR* **wind** BOWELS: *Beer gives me gas.*
gas /gæs/ *verb* [T] **-ss-** to kill or injure a person by making them breathe poisonous gas: *Hundreds of thousands of soldiers were gassed in the First World War.*
gaseous /ˈgeɪ.si.əs/ *adj SPECIALIZED a gaseous mixture* (= a mixture of gases) ○ *Steam is water in its gaseous form.*
gassy /ˈgæs.i/ *adj* fizzy; containing a lot of gas

gas [LIQUID FUEL] /gæs/ *noun* [U] **1** *US FOR* **petrol**: *I'll stop and get some gas – we're running low.* ○ *a gas tank/pump* **2** *US* **the gas** the part of a car which you push with your foot to make it go faster: *Step on the gas* (= drive faster)*!*

gas [AMUSING SITUATION] /gæs/ *noun* [S] *MAINLY US INFORMAL* an amusing or enjoyable situation: *Some kids put on a show for the moms and dads, – it was* ***a*** *gas.*

gas [TALK] /gæs/ *verb* [I] **-ss-** *OLD-FASHIONED INFORMAL* to talk for a long time about unimportant things: *Susan came round and we sat gassing for hours.*
▲ **gas (sth) up** *phrasal verb* [M] *US* to fill a vehicle's fuel container with fuel: *I want to gas up when we get to the next town.* ○ *You should gas the car up before you head home.*

gasbag /ˈgæs.bæg/ *noun* [C] *INFORMAL* a person who always talks too much

ˈ**gas ˌchamber** *noun* [C] a room which can be filled with poisonous gas in order to kill the people or animals inside it

ˈ**gas ˌfire** *UK noun* [C] (*US* **gas heater**) a fire that uses gas as a fuel to heat a room

ˈ**gas ˌguzzler** *noun* [C] *MAINLY US INFORMAL* a car that uses a lot of fuel **gas-guzzling** /ˈgæsˌgʌz.lɪŋ/ *adj* [before n]

gash /gæʃ/ *noun* [C] a long deep cut, especially in the skin
gash /gæʃ/ *verb* [T] *She slipped on a rock and gashed her knee.*

gasket /ˈgæs.kɪt/ *noun* [C] a flat piece of soft material or rubber that is put between two joined metal surfaces to prevent gas, oil or steam from escaping: *The gasket has* ***blown*** (= allowed gas, oil or steam to escape). ➲See **blow a fuse/gasket** at **blow** DESTROY.

gaslight /ˈgæs.laɪt/ *noun* [C or U] *MAINLY OLD USE* a light that uses gas as fuel, or the light that is produced by this

gasman /ˈgæs.mæn/ *noun* [C] *UK INFORMAL* a man whose job is reading gas METERS and repairing gas systems

ˈ**gas ˌmark** *noun* [U] *UK* one of a set of numbers on a gas cooker that is used instead of the temperature to show how hot it is: *Preheat the oven to gas mark 4.*

ˈ**gas ˌmask** *noun* [C] a device worn over the face to prevent you from breathing in poisonous gases

gasoline /ˈgæs.ᵊl.iːn/ *noun* [U] *US FORMAL FOR* **gas** LIQUID FUEL

gasometer /gæsˈɒm.ɪ.təʳ/ [US] /-ˈɑː.mə.t̬ɚ/ *noun* [C] (*ALSO* **gasholder**) a large metal container where gas is stored before it is supplied to customers

gasp /gɑːsp/ [US] /gæsp/ *verb* [I] **1** to take a short quick breath through the mouth, especially because of surprise, pain or shock: *When she saw the money hidden in the box she gasped* ***in*** *surprise.* ○ [+ speech] *"Help me!" he gasped.* **2** *UK INFORMAL* **be gasping** to be very thirsty
• **be gasping for sth** *UK INFORMAL* to want or need something very much: *I'm absolutely gasping for a cigarette/drink.*
gasp /gɑːsp/ [US] /gæsp/ *noun* [C] when you gasp: *He gave a gasp* ***of*** *amazement.*

ˈ**gas ˌpedal** *noun* [C usually sing] *US* **accelerator**, see at **accelerate** MOVE FASTER

gasses /ˈgæs.ɪz/ *plural of* **gas** MATTER

ˈ**gas ˌstation** *noun* [C] *US FOR* **petrol station**

gassy /ˈgæs.i/ *adj*: ➲See at **gas** MATTER

gastric /ˈgæs.trɪk/ *adj SPECIALIZED* relating to the stomach: *gastric juices* ○ *a gastric ulcer*
gastritis /gæsˈtraɪ.tɪs/ [US] /-t̬əs/ *noun* [U] *SPECIALIZED* an illness in which the stomach walls become swollen and painful

gastroenteritis /ˌgæs.trəʊˌen.təˈraɪ.tɪs/ [US] /-troʊˌen.t̬əˈraɪ.t̬əs/ *noun* [U] *SPECIALIZED* an illness which causes the stomach and bowels to become swollen and painful

gastronomy /gæsˈtrɒn.ə.mi/ [US] /-ˈtrɑː.nə-/ *noun* [U] *FORMAL* the art and knowledge involved in preparing and eating good food
gastronome /ˈgæs.trə.nəʊm/ [US] /-noʊm/ *noun* [C] someone who enjoys and knows about high quality food and drink **gastronomic** /ˌgæs.trəˈnɒm.ɪk/ [US] /-ˈnɑː.mɪk/ *adj* (*ALSO* **gastronomical**) *This dish is a gastronomic delight.*

gastropub /ˈgæs.trəʊ.pʌb/ [US] /-troʊ-/ *noun* [C] a bar where high quality food is served: *an organic gastropub*

gasworks /ˈgæs.wɜːks/ [US] /-wɝːks/ *group noun* [C] *plural* **gasworks** a factory where coal is made into gas for use as fuel for heating and cooking

gate /geɪt/ *noun* [C] **1** a part of a fence or outside wall that is fixed at one side and opens and closes like a door, usually made of metal or wooden strips **2** a similar device that slides across an opening, often folding into a smaller space as it is opened: *The lift won't move if the safety gate isn't shut properly.* **3** a part of an airport where travellers are allowed to get on or off a particular aircraft: *All passengers for flight LH103 please proceed to gate 16.* **4** *UK INFORMAL* the number of people that go to see a sports event or other large event, or the amount of money people pay to see it: *Gates at football matches* *were lower than average last season.*

gateau /ˈgæt.əʊ/ [US] /gæt̬ˈoʊ/ *noun* [C or U] *plural* **gateaux** a large sweet cake, usually with cream or fruit in it: *a chocolate/raspberry gateau*

gatecrash /ˈgeɪt.kræʃ/ *verb* [I or T] *INFORMAL* to go to a party or other event when you have not been invited: *He decided to gatecrash the wedding.* **gatecrasher** /ˈgeɪtˌkræʃ.əʳ/ [US] /-ˌkræʃ.ɚ/ *noun* [C] *The party was ruined by a couple of rowdy gatecrashers.*

gatehouse /ˈgeɪt.haʊs/ *noun* [C] a small house at the gate into a castle, park or other large property, often lived in by someone employed to take care of that property

gatekeeper /ˈgeɪtˌkiː.pəʳ/ [US] /-pɚ/ *noun* [C] *OLD-FASHIONED* a person whose job is to open and close a gate and to prevent people entering without permission

gatepost /ˈgeɪt.pəʊst/ [US] /-poʊst/ *noun* [C] a post to which a gate is fixed, or to which it fastens when closed

• **between you, me and the gatepost** *INFORMAL* **between you and me** ➲See at **between** AMONG.

gateway /ˈgeɪt.weɪ/ *noun* [C] **1** an entrance through a wall, fence, etc. where there is a gate **2 gateway to *somewhere*** a place through which you have to go to get to a particular area: *Manchester is known as the gateway to the north.*

gather [COLLECT] /ˈgæð.əʳ/ [US] /-ɚ/ *verb* **1** [T] to collect or obtain several things, often from different places or people: *I went to several libraries to gather information about the scheme.* ○ *We gathered blackberries from the hedgerow.* ○ *She gathered **up** the newspapers that were scattered around the floor.* ○ *We gathered our things **together** and left quickly.* **2** [T + adv or prep] to put your arms around someone and hold or carry them in a protective or affectionate way: *He gathered her **in** his arms and kissed her.* ○ *She gathered the children up and hurried into the house.*

• **gather dust** to not be used for a long time: *My guitar has just been gathering dust since I injured my hand.*

• **gather speed/strength/momentum, etc.** to become faster or stronger, etc: *The bicycle gathered speed as it went down the hill.* ○ *Economic recovery is gathering pace.*

• **gather (up) strength/courage** to prepare to make a great effort to be strong or brave: *I spent a week gathering the courage to say no.*

gather [CLOTH] /ˈgæð.əʳ/ [US] /-ɚ/ *verb* [T] **1** to pull cloth into small folds by sewing a thread through it and then pulling the thread tight: *a gathered skirt* **2** If you gather a piece of clothing or loose cloth about/around yourself, you pull it close to your body: *She shivered, and gathered the blanket **around** her.*

gathers /ˈgæð.əz/ [US] /-ɚz/ *plural noun* small folds that have been sewn into cloth

gather [COME TOGETHER] /ˈgæð.əʳ/ [US] /-ɚ/ *verb* [I] **1** When people or animals gather, they come together in a group: *A crowd had gathered to hear her speak.* ○ *Gather **(a)round**, children, and I'll tell you a story.* **2** *LITERARY* to get thicker and closer: *Storm **clouds** were gathering.*

gathering /ˈgæð.ᵊr.ɪŋ/ [US] /-ɚ-/ *noun* [C] *There will be a gathering **of** world leaders in Vienna next month.* ○ *a **social** gathering* (= when people meet for pleasure not work)

gather [UNDERSTAND] /ˈgæð.əʳ/ [US] /-ɚ/ *verb* [T] to understand or believe something as a result of something that has been said or done: *Harry loves his new job, I gather.* ○ [+ (that)] *From the look on their faces, she gathered **(that)** they were annoyed with her.* ○ [+ question word] *I never really gathered **why** he left his job.* ○ *I didn't gather much from his lecture.*

GATT /gæt/ *group noun* [U] *ABBREVIATION FOR* General Agreement on Tariffs and Trade: an international agreement among more than 100 countries to end rules that limit trade between them

gauche /gəʊʃ/ [US] /goʊʃ/ *adj* awkward and uncomfortable with other people, especially because young and lacking in experience: *She had grown from a gauche teenager to a self-assured young woman.*

gaucho /ˈgaʊ.tʃəʊ/ [US] /-tʃoʊ/ *noun* [C] *plural* **gauchos** a South American COWBOY (= person who takes care of cattle)

gaudy /ˈgɔː.di/ [US] /ˈgɑː-/ *adj* unpleasantly bright in colour or decoration: *gaudy plastic flowers* **gaudily** /ˈgɔː.di.li/ [US] /ˈgɑː-/ *adv* **gaudiness** /ˈgɔː.dɪ.nəs/ [US] /ˈgɑː-/ *noun* [U]

gauge [MEASURE], *US ALSO* **gage** /geɪdʒ/ *verb* [T] to calculate an amount, especially by using a measuring device: *Use a thermometer to gauge the temperature.* ○ *I tried to gauge* (= guess) *the weight of the box.*

gauge, *US ALSO* **gage** /geɪdʒ/ *noun* [C] **1** a device for measuring the amount or size of something: *a fuel/rain/temperature gauge* **2** *SPECIALIZED* the distance between the RAILS (= the two long metal bars fixed to the ground) on a railway line: *a **narrow/standard** gauge railway* **3** *SPECIALIZED* the thickness of something, especially metal or wire

gauge [JUDGE], *US ALSO* **gage** /geɪdʒ/ *verb* [T] to make a judgment about something, usually people's feelings: *A poll was conducted to gauge consumers' attitudes.* ○ [+ question word] *It's difficult to gauge **how** they'll react.*

gauge /geɪdʒ/ *noun* [S] a way of judging or showing something, especially the success or popularity of something: *The fact that the play has transferred to New York is a gauge **of** its success.*

gaunt /gɔːnt/ [US] /gɑːnt/ *adj* **1** very thin, especially because of illness or hunger: *Her face was gaunt and grey.* **2** *LITERARY* bare and unattractive: *The house looked gaunt and unwelcoming.* **gauntness** /ˈgɔːnt.nəs/ [US] /ˈgɑːnt-/ *noun* [U]

gauntlet /ˈgɔːnt.lət/ [US] /ˈgɑːnt-/ *noun* [C] a long thick glove, worn for protection

• **run the gauntlet** to have to deal with a lot of people who are criticizing or attacking you: *Every day they had to run the gauntlet **of** hostile journalists on their way to school.*

• **throw down the gauntlet** to invite someone to fight or compete with you: *A price war looks likely now that a leading supermarket has thrown down the gauntlet to its competitors.*

• **take/pick up the gauntlet** to agree to fight or compete with someone

gauze /gɔːz/ [US] /gɑːz/ *noun* **1** [U] a very thin light cloth, used to make clothing, to cover cuts and to separate solids from liquids, etc: *a gauze skirt* ○ *a piece of sterile gauze* **2** [C or U] a net-like material formed by wires crossing over each other: ***wire** gauze* **gauzy** /ˈgɔː.zi/ [US] /ˈgɑː-/ *adj*

gave /geɪv/ *past simple of* **give**

gavel /ˈgæv.ᵊl/ *noun* [C] a small hammer which an official in charge of a meeting hits against a wooden block or table to get people to be quiet and listen

gavotte /gəˈvɒt/ [US] /-ˈvɑːt/ *noun* [C] a fast dance from France, popular in the past, or a piece of music for this

Gawd, **gawd** /gɔːd/ [US] /gɑːd/ *MAINLY HUMOROUS* GOD, when used in expressions of fear, surprise, etc: *"Gawd help us," she cried out.* ○ *Oh gawd! You don't believe that do you?*

gawk /gɔːk/ [US] /gɑːk/ *verb* [I] (*UK ALSO* **gawp**) *INFORMAL* to look at something or someone in a stupid or rude way: *Don't sit there gawking like that – give me a hand!* ○ *UK They just stood there gawping **at** me.*

gawky /ˈgɔː.ki/ [US] /ˈgɑː-/ *adj INFORMAL* tall and awkward: *a gawky teenager*

gawp /gɔːp/ [US] /gɑːp/ *verb* [I] *UK FOR* **gawk**

gay [HOMOSEXUAL] /geɪ/ *adj* homosexual: *gay rights* ○ *Mark knew he was gay by the time he was fourteen.* ○ *the lesbian and gay community*

gay /geɪ/ *noun* [C] a homosexual person, especially a man **gayness** /ˈgeɪ.nəs/ *noun* [U]

gay [HAPPY] /geɪ/ *adj OLD-FASHIONED* **1** happy: *We had a gay old time down at the dance hall.* **2** If a place is gay, it is bright and attractive: *The streets were gay and full of people.* ➲See also **gaiety**; **gaily**.

ˌgay liberˈation *noun* [U] the principle that homosexuals should be treated equally in society: *the gay liberation movement*

ˌgay ˈpride *noun* [U] the idea that homosexual people should not keep the fact of their sexuality secret and that they should be proud of it instead, or the social and political movement that is based on this idea: *a gay pride rally*

gaze /geɪz/ *verb* **[I usually + adv or prep]** to look at something or someone for a long time, especially in surprise, admiration or because you are thinking about something else: *Annette gazed admiringly* ***at*** *Warren as he spoke.* ○ *He spends hours gazing* ***out of*** *the window when he should be working.* **gaze** /geɪz/ *noun* **[U]** *a steady gaze* ○ *an innocent/admiring gaze*

gazebo /gəˈziː.bəʊ/ [US] /-boʊ/ *noun* **[C]** *plural* **gazebos** a small decorated building, usually in a garden, giving a good view of the surrounding countryside

gazelle /gəˈzel/ *noun* **[C]** an African or Asian deer-like animal that moves quickly and gracefully and has large eyes

gazette /gəˈzet/ *noun* **[C]** **1** *OLD-FASHIONED* a newspaper **2** used in the titles of some newspapers and magazines: *the Montreal Gazette*

gazetteer /ˌgæz.əˈtɪəʳ/ [US] /-ˈtɪr/ *noun* **[C]** a book or part of a book that contains a list of names of places, usually with some additional information: *the Cambridge Gazetteer of the United States and Canada*

gazpacho /gæsˈpætʃ.əʊ/ [US] /-pɑː.tʃoʊ/ *noun* **[U]** a spicy soup made from tomatoes and other raw vegetables and eaten cold

gazump /gəˈzʌmp/ *verb* **[T often passive]** *UK INFORMAL* to refuse to sell a house that you own to someone you have agreed to sell it to, and to sell it instead to someone who offers to pay more for it: *Sally's offer for the house has been accepted, but she's worried she might be gazumped.* **gazumping** /gəˈzʌm.pɪŋ/ *noun* **[U]** *During the 1980s, practices like gazumping gave the property business in England a bad name.*

gazunder /gəˈzʌn.dəʳ/ [US] /-dɚ/ *verb* **[T often passive]** *UK INFORMAL* to unfairly demand a reduction in the price you have agreed to pay for a house just before you buy it **gazundering** /gəˈzʌn.dᵊr.ɪŋ/ [US] /-dɚ-/ *noun* **[U]**

GB /ˌdʒiːˈbiː/ *noun* **[U]** *ABBREVIATION FOR* Great Britain

GBH /ˌdʒiː.biːˈeɪtʃ/ *noun* **[U]** *ABBREVIATION FOR* **grievous bodily harm**

GCE /ˌdʒiː.siːˈiː/ *noun* **[C]** *ABBREVIATION FOR* General Certificate of Education: before 1988, a British public exam taken in various subjects, especially one taken at the age of about 16

GCSE /ˌdʒiː.siː.esˈiː/ *noun* **[C or U]** General Certificate of Secondary Education: the British system of public examinations taken in various subjects from the age of about 16, or one of these exams, or a qualification obtained in this system: *I'm taking six subjects for GCSE.* ○ *Owen is retaking two of his GCSEs.* ○ *She's got nine GCSEs, all at grade A.*

g'day /gəˈdeɪ/ *exclamation AUS INFORMAL* used when meeting or greeting someone

GDP /ˌdʒiː.diːˈpiː/ *noun* **[U]** *SPECIALIZED ABBREVIATION FOR* Gross Domestic Product: the total value of goods and services produced by a country in a year: *If the GDP continues to shrink, the country will be in a recession.* ➲Compare **GNP**.

gear [ENGINE PART] /gɪəʳ/ [US] /gɪr/ *noun* **[C or U]** a device, often consisting of connecting sets of wheels with teeth around the edge, that controls how much power from an engine goes to the moving parts of a machine: *Does your car have four or five gears?* ○ *I couldn't find reverse gear.* ○ *The car should be* ***in*** *gear* (= with its gears in position, allowing the vehicle to move). ○ *When you start a car you need to be* ***in*** *first/(US ALSO)* ***low*** *gear.* ○ *FIGURATIVE After a slow start, the leadership campaign suddenly shifted into* ***top*** *gear* (= started to advance very quickly).

• **change gear** *UK* (*US ALSO* **shift gear**) to change the position of the gears to make a vehicle go faster or more slowly

• **step/move up a gear** *INFORMAL* to noticeably start to do something better, especially in sport: *After a disappointing first half, United moved up a gear and took control of the game.*

gear [EQUIPMENT] /gɪəʳ/ [US] /gɪr/ *noun* **[U]** **1** the equipment, clothes etc. that you use to do a particular activity: *fishing/camping gear* ○ *Police in* ***riot*** *gear* (= protective clothing) *arrived to control the protesters.* ➲See also **headgear**. **2** *INFORMAL* clothes: *She wears all the latest gear.*

gear /gɪəʳ/ [US] /gɪr/ *verb*

PHRASAL VERBS WITH ˌ**gear** ▼

▲ **gear *sth* to/towards *sb/sth*** *phrasal verb* to design or organize something so that it is suitable for a particular purpose, situation or group of people: *Most public places are simply not geared to the needs of people with disabilities.* ○ *The workshops are geared towards helping people to become more employable.* ○ *These advertisements are geared towards a younger audience.*

▲ **gear *(sb/sth)* up** *phrasal verb* **[M]** to prepare for something that you have to do, or to prepare someone else for something: *Politicians are already gearing up* ***for*** *the election.* ○ **[R + to infinitive]** *I'm gearing myself up* ***to*** *ask him to give me my money back.* ○ **[R]** *I'm trying to gear myself up* ***for*** *tomorrow's exam.*

gearbox /ˈgɪə.bɒks/ [US] /ˈgɪr.bɑːks/ *noun* **[C]** *SPECIALIZED* a metal box containing the gears in a vehicle

ˈgear ˌlever *noun* **[C]** (*ALSO* **gear stick**) *UK* a metal rod that you use to change gear in a car or other vehicle ➲See picture **Car** on page Centre 12

gearshift /ˈgɪə.ʃɪft/ [US] /ˈgɪr-/ *noun* **[C]** *US FOR* **gear lever**

gecko /ˈgek.əʊ/ [US] /-oʊ/ *noun* **[C]** *plural* **geckos** or **geckoes** a small lizard with wide feet, found especially in warm countries

GED /ˌdʒiː.iːˈdiː/ *noun* **[C]** *ABBREVIATION FOR* General Equivalency Diploma: an official document in the US that is given to someone who did not complete HIGH SCHOOL (= school for students aged 15 -18) but who has passed a government exam instead

geddit? /ˈged.ɪt/ *exclamation UK INFORMAL* used at the end of a statement to attract attention to an obvious joke that has been made with two meanings of a word: *'The new series of plays on Channel Four is called 4-Play. Geddit?'*

gee /dʒiː/ *exclamation MAINLY US INFORMAL* an expression of surprise or enthusiasm: *"Gee, honey, is that all your own hair?"*

gee /dʒiː/ *verb*

▲ **gee *sb* up** *phrasal verb* **[M]** *UK INFORMAL* to encourage someone to show more effort or enthusiasm

ˌ**gee ˈup** *exclamation UK INFORMAL* something that you say to a horse to make it move faster: *Gee up, Neddy!*

gee-gee /ˈdʒiː.dʒiː/ *noun* **[C]** *UK CHILD'S WORD* a horse

geek /giːk/ *noun* **[C]** *INFORMAL* a person, especially a man, who is boring and not fashionable: *He's such a geek.* **geeky** /ˈgiː.ki/ *adj INFORMAL* boring and not fashionable: *a geeky-looking guy in glasses*

geese /giːs/ *plural of* **goose** BIRD

gee-whiz /ˌdʒiːˈwɪz/ *exclamation OLD-FASHIONED* a childish expression of surprise and enthusiasm

geezer /ˈgiː.zəʳ/ [US] /-zɚ/ *noun* **[C]** *UK INFORMAL* a man, often old or unusual in some way: *a funny old geezer* ○ *She got talking to some geezer in the pub.*

Geiger counter /ˈgaɪ.gəˌkaʊn.təʳ/ [US] /-gɚˌkaʊn.t̬ɚ/ *noun* **[C]** an electronic device for measuring the level of RADIOACTIVITY

geisha (girl) /ˈgeɪ.ʃəˌgɜːl/ [US] /-ˌgɝːl/ *noun* **[C]** a Japanese woman trained in music and dancing whose job is entertaining men

gel [SUBSTANCE] /dʒel/ *noun* **[U]** a thick, clear, liquid substance, especially one used on the hair or body: *shower gel* ○ *hair gel*

gel /dʒel/ *verb* **[T] -ll-** to put gel on someone's hair: *He had spiky light brown hair, shaved at the sides and gelled on top.*

gel [BECOME FIRM] **(-ll-)**, **jell** /dʒel/ *verb* **[I]** **1** to change from a liquid into a thick soft solid **2** If two or more people gel, they form a good relationship or become friends: *The team really gelled during the first few games of the season.* **3** If an idea or situation gels, it starts to become more clear and fixed: *The race issue gelled in the 1960s.*

gelatine, *US USUALLY ALSO* **gelatin** /ˈdʒel.ə.tiːn/ *noun* **[U]** a clear substance, often sold in the form of a powder, made from animal bones and used especially to make jelly

gelatinous /dʒə'læt.ɪ.nəs/ [US] /-læt̬-/ *adj* thick and like jelly: *The liquid suddenly solidifies into a gelatinous mass.*

geld /geld/ *verb* [T] to remove the testicles of a male horse or similar animal

gelding /'gel.dɪŋ/ *noun* [C] a male horse that has been gelded

gelignite /'dʒel.ɪg.naɪt/ *noun* [U] a very powerful explosive substance, similar to DYNAMITE

gem [JEWEL] /dʒem/ *noun* [C] (*ALSO* **gemstone**) a jewel, especially when cut into a particular regular shape

gem [VERY GOOD] /dʒem/ *noun* [C] someone or something that is very good, pleasing or useful: *You've been an* ***absolute*** *gem – I couldn't have managed without your help.* ○ *He came out with a gem* (= clever or pleasing remark) *about the absurdity of the situation.*

Gemini /'dʒem.ɪ.naɪ/ *noun* [C or U] the third sign of the zodiac, relating to the period 23 May to 21 June, represented by TWINS (= two people born together), or a person born during this period

gen /dʒen/ *noun* [U] *UK OLD-FASHIONED INFORMAL* information about a particular subject: *So who's going to* ***give*** *me* ***the*** *gen* ***on*** *what's been happening while I've been away?*

gen /dʒen/ *verb*

▲ **gen up** *phrasal verb UK OLD-FASHIONED INFORMAL* to find out as much information as possible: *Derek genned up* ***on*** *the country's history before going there.*

genned up /ˌdʒend'ʌp/ *adj* [after v]

gender [SEX] /'dʒen.dəʳ/ [US] /-dɚ/ *noun* [U] *FORMAL* the physical and/or social condition of being male or female: *Does this test show the gender of the baby?* ○ *Discrimination on the basis of race, gender, age or disability is not allowed.*

gender /'dʒen.dəʳ/ [US] /-dɚ/ *group noun* [C] *FORMAL* all males, or all females, considered as one group: *I think both genders are equally capable of looking after children.*

gender [GRAMMAR] /'dʒen.dəʳ/ [US] /-dɚ/ *noun* [C] *SPECIALIZED* the grammatical arrangement of nouns, pronouns and adjectives into masculine, feminine and NEUTER types in some languages

gene /dʒiːn/ *noun* [C] a part of the DNA in a cell which contains information in a special pattern received by each animal or plant from its parents, and which controls its physical development, behaviour, etc: *The illness is believed to be caused by a defective gene.*

genealogy /ˌdʒiː.ni'æl.ə.dʒi/ *noun* **1** [U] (the study of) the history of the past and present members of a family: *I became interested in the genealogy* ***of*** *my family.* **2** [C] a drawing showing the history of a family with all past and present members joined together by lines **genealogical** /ˌdʒiː.ni.ə'lɒdʒ.ɪ.kᵊl/ [US] /'lɑː.dʒɪ-/ *adj* **genealogically** /ˌdʒiː.ni.ə'lɒdʒ.ɪ.kli/ [US] /'lɑː.dʒɪ-/ *adv* **genealogist** /ˌdʒiː.ni'æl.ə.dʒɪst/ *noun* [C]

'gene ˌpool *noun* [C] all the genes of a particular group of people or animals

genera /'dʒen.ᵊr.ə/ [US] /-ɚ-/ *plural of* **genus**

general [COMMON] /'dʒen.ᵊr.ᵊl/ [US] /-ɚ-/ *adj* **1** involving or relating to most or all people, things or places, especially when these are considered as a unit: *The general feeling at the meeting was that a vote should be taken.* ○ *There is general concern about rising crime rates.* ○ *My general impression of the place was good.* ○ *The talk is intended to be of general* ***interest*** (= of interest to most people). ○ *UK FORMAL Rain will become more general in the south-east during the afternoon.* **2** not detailed, but including the most basic or necessary information: *What he said was very general.* ○ *The school aims to give children a general background in a variety of subjects.* ○ *I'm not an expert, so I can only speak* ***in*** *general* ***terms*** *on this matter.* **3** including a lot of things or subjects and not limited to only one or a few: *general knowledge* **4** used as part of the title of a job of someone who is in charge of a whole organization or company: *the general* ***manager*** ○ *the General Secretary of the UN*

● **in general 1** (*ALSO* **as a general rule**) usually, or in most situations: *In general, men are taller than women.* ○ *As a general rule, we don't allow children in the bar.* **2** considering the whole of someone or something, and not just a particular part of them: *So, apart from the bad ankle, how are you in general?*

● **be in the general interest** *FORMAL* to be advantageous for the public: *The government will only say it is not in the general interest to reveal any more information.*

the general *noun* [S] things considered as a unit and without giving attention to details: *His book moves from the general to the particular.*

generalist /'dʒen.ᵊr.ᵊl.ɪst/ [US] /-ɚ-/ *adj, noun* [C] *FORMAL* (someone who is) not specialized: *Children of this age need specialist rather than generalist teachers.*

generality /ˌdʒen.ə'ræl.ɪ.ti/ [US] /-ə.t̬i/ *noun* [C usually pl; U] **1** when what someone says contains no details, and often very little meaning: *We need to get away from generalities and focus on the issues.* **2** *FORMAL* **the generality** most: *For the generality* ***of*** *young people, university is not an option.*

generalize, *UK USUALLY* **-ise** /'dʒen.ᵊr.ə.laɪz/ [US] /-ɚ-/ *verb* [I] to say something very basic, based on limited facts, that is partly or sometimes true, but not always: *You can't generalize* ***about*** *a continent as varied as Europe.*

generalized, *UK USUALLY* **-ised** /'dʒen.ᵊr.ə.laɪzd/ [US] /-ɚ-/ *adj* involving a lot of people, places or things: *He spoke of generalized corruption in the government.* ○ *Isolated showers will give way to more generalized rain later in the day.* * NOTE: The opposite is **localized**.

generalization, *UK USUALLY* **-isation** /ˌdʒen.ᵊr.ᵊl.aɪ'zeɪ.ʃᵊn/ [US] /-ɚ-/ *noun* [C or U] *MAINLY DISAPPROVING* when someone generalizes in what they say or write: *The report is full of errors and* ***sweeping*** (= extreme) *generalizations.*

general [RANK] /'dʒen.ᵊr.ᵊl/ [US] /-ɚ-/ *noun* [C] a very high-ranking officer, especially in the army

ˌgeneral anaes'thetic *noun* [C or U] a drug which is used to make you unconscious when you have an operation so that you do not feel any pain

ˌgeneral de'livery *noun* [U] *US FOR* **poste restante**

ˌgeneral e'lection *noun* [C] an election in which all the voters in a country elect the government

ˌgeneral 'knowledge *noun* [U] information on many different subjects that you collect gradually, from reading, television, etc., rather than detailed information on subjects that you have studied formally

generally /'dʒen.ᵊr.ᵊl.i/ [US] /-ɚ-/ *adv* **1** considering the whole of someone or something, and not just a particular part of them: *Your health is generally good, but you do have a few minor problems.* ○ *He wants more money to be given to the arts generally.* ○ *I shall now develop my previous point more generally* (= to say more about what it includes). **2** usually, or in most situations: *The baby generally wakes up three times during the night.* ○ *Well, generally* ***speaking*** (= in most situations), *it's quicker on public transport.* **3** by most people, or to most people: *It was generally believed at the time that both men were guilty.* ○ *The proposal has received a generally favourable reaction.*

ˌgeneral 'practice *noun* [C or U] *UK* the work of a GP (= doctor) who treats the people who live in the local area and treats injuries and diseases that do not need a hospital visit **ˌgeneral prac'titioner** *noun* [C]

the ˌgeneral 'public *group noun* [S] ordinary people, especially all the people who are not members of a particular organization or who do not have any special type of knowledge: *This is a matter of great concern to the general public.*

ˌgeneral 'staff *group noun* [C] the group of army officers who work for and give advice to a COMMANDING officer

ˌgeneral 'store *noun* [C] (*UK ALSO* **general stores**) a shop which sells food and a wide range of products, often the only shop in a village

ˌgeneral 'strike *noun* [C] a strike in which most people in a country refuse to work until they are given higher pay or something else that they want

generate /'dʒen.ᵊr.eɪt/ [US] /-ɚ-/ *verb* [T] **1** to cause something to exist: *Her latest film has generated a lot of* ***interest/excitement.*** ○ *The new development will generate 1500 new jobs.* ○ *These measures will increase the club's ability to generate* ***revenue/income.*** **2** to produce energy in a particular form: *The wind farm may be able to generate enough **electricity/power** for 2000 homes.* **generation** /ˌdʒen.ə'reɪ.ʃᵊn/ *noun* [U] *electricity generation from wind and wave power* ⊃See also **generation**.

generative /'dʒen.ᵊr.ə.tɪv/ ⓤ /-ɚ.ə.t̬ɪv/ *adj* SPECIALIZED able to produce or create something: *the generative power of the mind*

generator /'dʒen.ə.reɪ.tər/ ⓤ /-ɚ.eɪ.t̬ɚ/ *noun* [C] a machine which produces something, especially electricity

generation /ˌdʒen.ə'reɪ.ʃᵊn/ *group noun* [C] **1** all the people of about the same age within a society or within a particular family: *The **younger** generation smoke/ smokes less than their parents did.* ○ *There were at least three generations – grandparents, parents and children – at the wedding.* ○ *It's our duty to preserve the planet for **future** generations.* ○ *This painting has been in the family **for** generations.* ⊃See also **generation** at **generate**. **2** a group of products or machines which are all at the same stage of development: *a **new** generation of low-fat margarines* ○ *Scientists are working on developing the **next** generation of supercomputers.* **3** a period of about 23 to 30 years, in which most human babies become adults and have their own children: *A generation ago, home computers were virtually unknown.* **4** first/second/third, etc. generation describes the nationality of someone belonging to the first/second/third, etc. group of people of the same age in the family to have been born in that country: *She's a second generation American* (= her parents were American, although their parents were not).

the gene'ration ˌgap *noun* [S] when older and younger people do not understand each other because of their different experiences, opinions, habits and behaviour: *She's a young politician who manages to **bridge/cross** (= understand both groups in) the generation gap.*

generic /dʒə'ner.ɪk/ *adj* **1** FORMAL shared by, typical of or relating to a whole group of similar things, rather than to any particular thing: *The new range of engines all had a generic problem with their fan blades.* **2** MAINLY US describes a product that is not marked with the name of the company that produced it: *a generic drug*

ge,neric 'brand *noun* [U] MAINLY AUS FOR **own brand**

generous CHARACTER /'dʒen.ᵊr.əs/ ⓤ /-ɚ-/ *adj* willing to give money, help, kindness, etc., especially more than is usual or expected: *a very generous man* ○ [+ *to* infinitive] *It was most generous **of** you to lend me the money.* ○ *She's been very generous **with** her time.* ○ *There's a generous* (= kinder than deserved) *review of the book in today's newspaper.*

generosity /ˌdʒen.ə'rɒs.ɪ.ti/ ⓤ /-'rɑː.sə.t̬i/ *noun* [U] *Her friends take advantage of* (= benefit unfairly from) *her generosity.* **generously** /'dʒen.ᵊr.ə.sli/ ⓤ /-ɚ-/ *adv*: *Please **give** generously to Children in Need.*

generous SIZE /'dʒen.ᵊr.əs/ ⓤ /-ɚ-/ *adj* larger than usual or expected: *a generous slice of cake* ○ *a generous pay increase* **generosity** /ˌdʒen.ə'rɒs.ɪ.ti/ ⓤ /-'rɑː.sə.t̬i/ *noun* [U] **generously** /'dʒen.ᵊr.ə.sli/ ⓤ /-ɚ-/ *adv*: *The jacket is very generously cut.*

genesis /'dʒen.ə.sɪs/ *noun* [S] FORMAL **1** the origin of something, when it is begun or starts to exist: *In her autobiography, she describes the song's genesis late one night in a Dublin bar.* ○ *research into **the** genesis **of** cancer* **2 Genesis** the first book of the Bible, which describes how God made the world

'gene ˌtherapy *noun* [U] the science of changing genes in order to stop or prevent a disease

ge,netically 'modified *adj* (ALSO **genetically engineered**) describes a plant or animal that has had some of its genes changed scientifically: *genetically modified **food/crops***

ge,netic 'code *noun* [C] the arrangement of GENES which controls the development of characteristics and qualities in a living thing

ge,netic engin'eering *noun* [U] (the science of) changing the structure of the GENES of a living thing in order

to make it healthier or stronger or more useful to humans

ge,netic 'fingerprinting *noun* [U] the process of recording and/or examining a person's pattern of genes, which is different from that of anyone else, often to prove that they did or did not commit a crime

genetics /dʒə'net.ɪks/ ⓤ /-'net̬-/ *noun* [U] the study of how, in all living things, the characteristics and qualities of parents are given to their children by their genes **genetic** /dʒə'net.ɪk/ ⓤ /-'net̬-/ *adj*: *a genetic **defect/disease** genetically* /dʒə'net.ɪ.kli/ ⓤ /-'net̬-/ *adv* **geneticist** /dʒə'net.ɪ.sɪst/ ⓤ /-'net̬-/ *noun* [C] a person whose job is studying genetics

genial /'dʒiː.ni.əl/ *adj* friendly and pleasant: *The headteacher is very genial/has a genial manner.* **genially** /'dʒiː.ni.ᵊl.i/ *adv* **geniality** /ˌdʒiː.ni'æl.ɪ.ti/ ⓤ /-ə.t̬i/ *noun* [U] *His geniality, reliability and ability made him a popular figure.*

genie /'dʒiː.ni/ *noun* [C] *plural* **genies** or **genii** a magical spirit, originally in Arab traditional stories, who does or provides whatever the person who controls it asks

genitals /'dʒen.ɪ.t̬ᵊlz/ ⓤ /-t̬ᵊlz/ *plural noun* (ALSO **genitalia**) SPECIALIZED the outer sexual organs, especially the penis or vulva **genital** /'dʒen.ɪ.t̬ᵊl/ ⓤ /-t̬ᵊl/ *adj*: *the genital area/organs*

genitive /'dʒen.ɪ.tɪv/ ⓤ /-t̬ɪv/ *noun* [C] SPECIALIZED the form of a noun, pronoun, etc. in the grammar of some languages, which shows that the noun, pronoun, etc. possesses something **genitive** /'dʒen.ɪ.tɪv/ ⓤ /-t̬ɪv/ *adj*: *the genitive form of a noun*

genius /'dʒiː.ni.əs/ *noun* [C or U] *plural* **geniuses** very great and rare natural ability or skill, especially in a particular area such as science or art, or a person who has this: *(an) artistic/creative/musical genius* ○ *Einstein was a (mathematical) genius.* ○ *From the age of three, she showed signs of genius.* ○ *It was such a brilliant idea – a real **stroke of** genius.*

• **have a genius for sth** to be especially skilled at a particular activity: *She has a genius for raising money.*

genocide /'dʒen.ə.saɪd/ *noun* [U] the murder of a whole group of people, especially a whole nation, race or religious group: *victims of genocide* **genocidal** /'dʒen.ə.saɪ.dᵊl/ /ˌ--'--/ *adj*: *a genocidal war/regime*

genome /'dʒiː.nəʊm/ ⓤ /-noʊm/ *noun* [C] SPECIALIZED the complete set of genetic material of a human, animal, plant or other living thing

genotype /'dʒen.əʊ.taɪp/ ⓤ /-oʊ-/ *noun* [C] SPECIALIZED the particular type and arrangement of genes that each organism has ⊃Compare **phenotype**.

genre /'ʒɑ̃ː.rə/ /'ʒɒn-/ *noun* [C] FORMAL a style, especially in the arts, that involves a particular set of characteristics: *What genre does the book fall into – comedy or tragedy?* ○ *a literary/musical/film genre* **genre** /'ʒɑ̃ː.rə/ /'ʒɒn-/ *adj* produced according to a particular model or style: *a genre movie* ○ *genre fiction*

gent /dʒent/ *noun* [C] OLD-FASHIONED a GENTLEMAN (= polite man who behaves well towards other people, especially women)

the gents *group noun* [S] UK a public toilet for men

genteel /dʒen'tiːl/ ⓤ /-'tiːl/ *adj* **1** having or typical of a high social class: *a genteel old lady* ○ *The mansion had an atmosphere of genteel elegance and decay.* **2** being very polite, or trying too hard to seem of a higher social class than you really are: *He took elocution lessons to try to make his accent sound more genteel.* **3** calm and gentle: *The game seemed to be a more genteel version of American football.* **genteelly** /dʒen'tiə.li/ ⓤ /-'tiː-/ *adv*: *She tittered genteelly.*

gentility /dʒen'tɪl.ɪ.ti/ ⓤ /-ə.t̬i/ *noun* [U] when someone or something is genteel: *an air* (= manner) *of gentility*

gentile, Gentile /'dʒen.taɪl/ *noun* [C] a person who is not Jewish: *The war memorial was dedicated to both **Jews and** Gentiles.* **gentile** /'dʒen.taɪl/ *adj*

gentle /'dʒen.t̬l/ ⓤ /-t̬l/ *adj* **1** calm, kind or soft: *a gentle smile* ○ *He's very gentle with his kids.* **2** not violent, severe or strong: *gentle **exercise*** ○ *a gentle **breeze*** ○ *You can actually accomplish a lot more by gentle **persuasion**.* **3** not steep or sudden: *The path has a gentle **slope/gradient**.*

gently /ˈdʒent.li/ *adv*: *He lifted the baby gently out of its cot.* ○ *to smile/laugh/blow gently* ○ *gently* (= slightly) *rolling hills*

• **Gently does it!** (*US* **Easy does it!**) *UK* said when telling someone to be slow and careful

gentleness /ˈdʒen.tl̩.nəs/ [US] /-t̬l̩-/ *noun* [U] the quality of being gentle

COMMON LEARNER ERROR

gentle

Be careful when using the word **gentle** to describe people. It does not mean exactly the same as **kind** or **nice**. **Gentle** tells you that someone behaves in a calm, quiet way that does not upset or hurt people.

She has a very gentle, loving personality.

If you simply mean that someone is helpful and nice you should use the word **kind**.

His family were very kind to me when I lost my job and needed somewhere to stay.

~~*His family were very gentle to me when I lost my job and needed somewhere to stay.*~~

gentleman /ˈdʒen.tl̩.mən/ [US] /-t̬l̩-/ *noun* [C] **1** a polite way of addressing or referring to a man: ***Ladies and*** *gentlemen, the show is about to begin.* ○ *Excuse me, this gentleman has a question for you.* **2** *APPROVING* a man who is polite and behaves well towards other people, especially women: *He was a perfect gentleman.* ○ *Not holding a door for a lady? You're no gentleman, are you?* **3** *APPROVING* a man of a high social class: *a gentlemen's club*

gentlemanly /ˈdʒen.tl̩.mən.li/ [US] /-t̬l̩-/ *adj* typical of a polite gentleman: *a gentlemanly manner*

gentleman's agreement /ˌdʒen.tl̩.mənz.əˈgriː.mənt/ [US] /-t̬l̩-/ *noun* [C] an agreement which is based on trust and is not written down

gentlewoman /ˈdʒen.tl̩ˌwʊm.ən/ [US] /-t̬l̩-/ *noun* [C] *OLD-FASHIONED* a woman who belongs to a high social class, or who is kind, polite and honest

the gentry /ðəˈdʒen.tri/ *plural noun* people of high social class, especially in the past: *a member of the* ***landed*** *gentry* (= those who own a lot of land)

gentrify /ˈdʒen.trɪ.faɪ/ *verb* [T often passive] *DISAPPROVING* to change a place from being a poor area to a richer one, by people of a higher social class moving to live there: *The area where I grew up has been all modernized and gentrified, and has lost all its old character.*

gentrification /ˌdʒen.trɪ.fɪˈkeɪ.ʃən/ *noun* [U] when an area is gentrified

genuflect /ˈdʒen.jʊ.flekt/ *verb* [I] to bend one or both knees as a sign of respect to God, especially when entering or leaving a Catholic church: *People were genuflecting in front of the altar.*

genuflection /ˌdʒen.jʊˈflek.ʃən/ *noun* [C or U] when you genuflect

genuine /ˈdʒen.ju.ɪn/ *adj* **1** If something is genuine, it is real and exactly what it appears to be: *genuine leather* ○ *If it is a genuine Michelangelo drawing, it will sell for millions.* **2** If people or emotions are genuine, they are honest and sincere: *He's a very genuine person.* ○ *Machiko looked at me in genuine surprise – "Are you really going?" she said.*

• **the genuine article** *INFORMAL* a good and real example of a particular thing: *Those cowboy boots sure look like the genuine article.*

genuinely /ˈdʒen.ju.ɪn.li/ *adv* really: *I'm genuinely sorry for what I said, I really am.* **genuineness** /ˈdʒen.ju.ɪn.nəs/ *noun* [U]

genus /ˈdʒiː.nəs/ *noun* [C] *plural* **genera** *SPECIALIZED* a group of animals or plants, more closely related than a family, but less similar than a species

geo- /dʒiː.əʊ-/ [US] /-oʊ-/ *prefix* of or relating to the Earth: *geophysics* ○ *geology*

geocentric /ˌdʒiː.əʊˈsen.trɪk/ [US] /-oʊ-/ *adj SPECIALIZED* having the Earth as its centre

geography /dʒiˈɒg.rə.fi/ [US] /dʒiˈɑː.grə-/ *noun* [U] **1** the study of the systems and processes involved in the world's weather, mountains, seas, lakes, etc. and of the ways in which countries and people organize life within an area ⊃See also **physical geography**. **2 the geography of *somewhere*** the way all the parts of an area are arranged within it: *We learnt about the geography of Australia.* ○ *It's impossible to work out the geography of this hospital.*

geographer /dʒiˈɒg.rə.fəʳ/ [US] /dʒiˈɑː.grə.fɚ/ *noun* [C] a person who studies geography **geographical** /ˌdʒi.əˈgræf.ɪ.kəl/ *adj* (*MAINLY US* **geographic**) *a geographical region* **geographically** /ˌdʒi.əˈgræf.ɪ.kli/ *adv*

geology /dʒiˈɒl.ə.dʒi/ [US] /-ˈɑː.lə-/ *noun* [U] **1** the study of the rocks and similar substances that make up the Earth's surface: *a geology course/teacher* **2 the geology of *somewhere*** the particular rocks and similar substances that form an area of the Earth, and their arrangement **geological** /ˌdʒi.əˈlɒdʒ.ɪ.kəl/ [US] /-ˈlɑː.dʒɪ-/ *adj*: *a geological survey/map* **geologically** /ˌdʒi.əˈlɒdʒ.ɪ.kli/ [US] /-ˈlɑː.dʒɪ-/ *adv*

geologist /dʒiˈɒl.ə.dʒɪst/ [US] /-ˈɑː.lə-/ *noun* [C] a person who studies geology

geoˌmetric(al) proˈgression *noun* [C] an ordered set of numbers, where each number in turn is multiplied by a fixed amount to produce the next

geometry /dʒiˈɒm.ə.tri/ [US] /dʒiˈɑː.mə-/ *noun* [U] **1** the area of mathematics relating to the study of space and the relationships between points, lines, curves and surfaces: *the laws of geometry* ○ *a geometry lesson* **2 the geometry of *sth*** the way the parts of a particular object fit together: *the geometry of a DNA molecule*

geometric /ˌdʒiː.əˈmet.rɪk/ *adj* (*ALSO* **geometrical**) describes a pattern or arrangement that is made up of shapes such as squares, triangles or rectangles: *a geometric design of overlapping circles* **geometrically** /ˌdʒiː.əˈmet.rɪ.kli/ *adv*: *geometrically patterned*

geophysics /ˌdʒiː.əˈfɪz.ɪks/ *noun* [U] *SPECIALIZED* the study of the rocks and other substances that make up the Earth and the physical processes happening on, in and above the Earth **geophysical** /ˌdʒiː.əˈfɪz.ɪ.kəl/ *adj*: *geophysical and geological phenomena*

geophysicist /ˌdʒi.əˈfɪz.ɪ.sɪst/ *noun* [C] *SPECIALIZED* a person who studies geophysics

geopolitics /ˌdʒiː.əʊˈpɒl.ə.tɪks/ [US] /-oʊˈpɑː.lə.t̬ɪks/ *noun* [U] the study of the way a country's size, position, etc. influence its power and its relationships with other countries **geopolitical** /ˌdʒiː.əʊ.pəˈlɪt.ɪ.kəl/ [US] /-oʊ.pəˈlɪt̬-/ *adj*

Geordie /ˈdʒɔː.di/ [US] /ˈdʒɔːr-/ *noun* **1** [C] someone who comes from Tyneside in Northeast England **2** [U] the variety of English spoken by someone from Tyneside: *a Geordie accent*

Georgian /ˈdʒɔː.dʒən/ [US] /ˈdʒɔːr-/ *adj* belonging to the period when Kings George I, II and III ruled Britain, especially from 1714 to 1811: *Georgian furniture/architecture*

geothermal /ˌdʒiː.əʊˈθɜː.məl/ [US] /-oʊˈθɝː-/ *adj SPECIALIZED* of or connected with the heat inside the Earth: *a geothermal power station*

geranium /dʒəˈreɪ.ni.əm/ *noun* [C] a plant with red, pink or white flowers, often grown in containers and gardens ⊃See picture **Flowers and Plants** on page Centre 3

gerbil /ˈdʒɜː.bəl/ [US] /ˈdʒɝː-/ *noun* [C] a small mouse-like animal with long back legs that is often kept as a pet

geriatric /ˌdʒer.iˈæt.rɪk/ *adj* **1** for or relating to old people, especially those who are ill: *a geriatric hospital/ward/nurse* **2** *INFORMAL DISAPPROVING* old and weak: *Who's going to elect a geriatric President?* **geriatric** /ˌdʒer.iˈæt.rɪk/ *noun* [C] *a clinic for the care of geriatrics*

geriatrician /ˌdʒer.i.əˈtrɪʃ.ən/ *noun* [C] *SPECIALIZED* a doctor who specializes in the care and treatment of old people who are ill

geriatrics /ˌdʒer.iˈæt.rɪks/ *noun* [U] *SPECIALIZED* the care and treatment of old people who are ill

germ [ORGANISM] /dʒɜːm/ [US] /dʒɝːm/ *noun* [C usually pl] a very small organism that causes disease: *Wash your hands so you don't get germs on the food.* ○ *Rats and flies* ***spread*** *germs.*

germ [AMOUNT] /dʒɜːm/ [US] /dʒɝːm/ *noun* **germ of *sth*** a small amount, usually one which develops into something large or important: *He found the germ of* ***an idea*** *in an old newspaper.*

German /'dʒɜː.mən/ ⓤ /'dʒɜ˞-/ *noun* **1** [U] the language of Germany, Austria and parts of Switzerland **2** [C] a person from Germany: *We have a group of Germans staying at the hotel.*
German /'dʒɜː.mən/ ⓤ /'dʒɜː.r-/ *adj* of or relating to Germany

germane /dʒɜː'meɪn/ ⓤ /dʒɜː-/ *adj FORMAL* describes ideas or information connected with and important to a particular subject or situation: *Her remarks could not have been more germane to the discussion.*

Germanic /dʒɜː'mæn.ɪk/ ⓤ /dʒɜ˞-/ *adj* **1** typical of German people or things: *Germanic efficiency* **2** *SPECIALIZED* belonging or relating to the group of languages that includes German, English and Dutch: *a Germanic language*

,**German 'measles** *noun* [U] (*SPECIALIZED* **rubella**) an infectious disease which causes red spots on your skin, a cough and a sore throat

,**German 'shepherd** *noun* [C] *MAINLY US FOR* **Alsatian**

germicide /'dʒɜː.mɪ.saɪd/ ⓤ /'dʒɜː-/ *noun* [C or U] a substance that kills GERMS **germicidal** /dʒɜː.mɪ'saɪ.dᵊl/ ⓤ /dʒɜː-/ *adj*

germinate /'dʒɜː.mɪ.neɪt/ ⓤ /'dʒɜː-/ *verb* **1** [I or T] *SPECIALIZED* to (cause a seed to) start growing: *The beans will only germinate if the temperature is warm enough.* **2** [I] to start developing: *I felt an idea germinating in my head/mind.* **germination** /ˌdʒɜː.mɪ'neɪ.ʃᵊn/ ⓤ /ˌdʒɜː-/ *noun* [U]

,**germ 'warfare** *noun* [U] (*ALSO* **biological warfare**) the use of GERMS (= extremely small organisms) during periods of war to cause disease among enemy soldiers or among crops in enemy countries

gerontology /ˌdʒer.ən'tɒl.ə.dʒi/ ⓤ /-'tɑː.lə-/ *noun* [U] *SPECIALIZED* the study of old age and of the problems and diseases of old people **gerontological** /ˌdʒer.ən.tə-'lɒdʒ.ɪ.kᵊl/ ⓤ /-lɑː.dʒɪ-/ *adj*: *a centre for gerontological research*
gerontologist /ˌdʒer.ən'tɒl.ə.dʒɪst/ ⓤ /-'tɑː.lə-/ *noun* [C] *SPECIALIZED* a person who studies old age

gerrymandering /'dʒer.i,mæn.dᵊr.ɪŋ/ ⓤ /-dɚ-/ *noun* [U] when someone in authority changes the borders of an area in order to increase the number of people within that area who will vote for a particular party or person: *The boundary changes were denounced as blatant gerrymandering.* **gerrymander** /'dʒer.i,mæn.dər/ ⓤ /-dɚ/ *verb* [I or T]

gerund /'dʒer.ᵊnd/ *noun* [C] *SPECIALIZED* a word that ends in '-ing' which is made from a verb, and which is used like a noun: *In the sentence 'Everyone enjoyed Tyler's singing', the word 'singing' is a gerund.*

gestation /dʒes'teɪ.ʃᵊn/ *noun* [U] **1** *SPECIALIZED* (the period of) the development of a child or young animal while it is still inside its mother's body: *The baby was born prematurely at 28 weeks gestation.* ○ *The **period of** gestation **of** rats is 21 days.* **2** (the period of) the development of ideas, thoughts or plans: *The scheme had a very long gestation **period**.* **gestate** /dʒes'teɪt/ *verb* [I]

gesticulate /dʒes'tɪk.jʊ.leɪt/ *verb* [I] *FORMAL* to make movements with your hands or arms, to express something or to emphasize what you are saying: *There was a man outside the window gesticulating **wildly**.* **gesticulation** /dʒes,tɪk.jʊ'leɪ.ʃᵊn/ *noun* [C or U]

gesture [MOVEMENT] /'dʒes.tʃər/ ⓤ /-tʃɚ/ *noun* [C] a movement of the hands, arms or head, etc. to express an idea or feeling: *The prisoner raised his fist in a gesture **of** defiance as he was led out of the courtroom.* ○ *She **made** a rude gesture at the other driver.*
gesture /'dʒes.tʃər/ ⓤ /-tʃɚ/ *verb* [I] to use a gesture to express or emphasize something: *When he asked where the children were, she gestured vaguely in the direction of the beach.* ○ *He made no answer but walked on, gesturing **for** me to follow.*

gesture [SYMBOLIC ACT] /'dʒes.tʃər/ ⓤ /-tʃɚ/ *noun* [C] an action that you take which expresses your feelings or intentions, although it might have little practical effect: *The Government donated £500 000 as a gesture **of** goodwill.* ○ *Not having butter on his potatoes was his only gesture towards healthy eating.*

gesundheit /gə'zʊnt.haɪt/ *exclamation MAINLY US* said to someone after they have sneezed ⊃See also **bless you!** at **bless**.

get [OBTAIN] /get/ *verb* [T] getting, got, got or *US* gotten **1** to obtain, buy or earn something: *He's gone down to the corner shop to get some milk.* ○ *I think she gets about forty thousand pounds a year.* ○ *We stopped off on the motorway to get some breakfast.* ○ *I managed to get all three suitcases **for** under $200.* ○ *How much did he get **for** his car* (= How much money did he sell it for)*?* ○ *Where did you get your radio **from**?* ⊃See Note **become or get?** at **become** BE. **2** to receive or be given something: *I got quite a surprise when I saw her with short hair.* ○ *When did you get the news about Sam?* ○ *I got a (telephone) call **from** Phil last night.* ○ *What mark did he get in his exam?* ○ *I got the impression that they'd rather be alone.* ○ *What did you get for your birthday?* ○ *We don't get much snow* (= It does not often snow) *here.* ○ *I managed to get a glimpse of him* (= see him for a moment) *through the crowds.* ○ *If you get a moment* (= have time available)*, could you help me fill in that form?* ○ *She gets such pleasure **from** her garden.* ○ *If you can get some time **off** work, we could finish the decorating.* ○ *I can never get her **to** myself* (= be alone with her) *because she's always surrounded by people.* **3** to go somewhere and bring back someone or something: *I must just get the washing **in**.* ○ [+ two objects] *Can I get you a drink?* **4** to take someone or something into your possession by force: *Have the police got the man who did it yet?* ○ *Your cat got a bird this morning!* ✱ NOTE: The past participle of the verb **get** is **got** in British English and **gotten** in American English.

get [DEAL WITH] /get/ *verb* [T] getting, got, got or *US* gotten *INFORMAL* **1** to deal with or answer a ringing telephone, knock on the door, etc: *Hey, Ty, someone's at the door – would you get it, please?* **2** to pay for something: *Put your money away – I'll get these drinks.*

get [BECOME ILL WITH] /get/ *verb* [T] getting, got, got or *US* gotten *INFORMAL* to become ill with a disease, virus, etc: *I got food poisoning at that cheap little seafood restaurant.* ○ *Kids get all kinds of bugs at school.*

get [BECOME] /get/ *verb* [L] getting, got, got or *US* gotten to become or start to be: *He gets really upset if you mention his baldness.* ○ *Is your cold getting any better?* ○ *Your coffee's getting cold.* ○ *After a while you get used to all the noise.* ○ *You're getting quite a big boy now, aren't you!* ○ [+ to infinitive] *How did you get **to** be a belly dancer?* ⊃See Note **become** or **get** at **become** BE.
● **get going/moving** *INFORMAL* to start to go or move: *We'd better get moving or we'll be late.*

get [CAUSE] /get/ *verb* getting, got, got or *US* gotten **1** [T] to cause something to happen, or cause someone or something to do something: [+ adj] *She had to get the kids **ready** for school.* ○ [+ past participle] *I'm trying to get this article **finished** for Thursday.* ○ *We get our milk **delivered**.* ○ [+ v-ing] *Haven't you got the photocopier working yet?* ○ [+ to infinitive] *I can't get my computer **to** work!* **2** [T + obj + to infinitive] to persuade someone to do something: *Why don't you get Nicole **to** come to the party?* **3** [T + past participle] to do something to something or someone unintentionally or accidentally: *He got his bag caught in the train doors as they were closing.* ○ *I always get the two youngest sisters' names confused.*

get [BE] /get/ *verb* [L + past participle] getting, got, got or *US* gotten sometimes used instead of 'be' to form the passive: *I got shouted at by some idiot for walking past his house.* ○ *They're getting married later this year.* ○ *This window seems to have got broken.*

get [MOVE] /get/ *verb* [I usually + adv or prep] getting, got, got or *US* gotten to move to a different place or into a different position: *I hit my head as I was getting **into** the car.* ○ *Get out of here now or I'll call the police.* ○ *The bed is too wide – we'll never get it through the door.* ○ *Getting **up** the ladder was easy enough – it was coming down that was the problem.* ○ *He got **down** on his knees and asked me to marry him!*

get [TRAVEL] /get/ *verb* [T] getting, got, got or *US* gotten to travel somewhere in a train, bus or other vehicle: *Shall we get a taxi to the station?*

get [UNDERSTAND/HEAR] /get/ *verb* [T] getting, got, got or *US* gotten to understand or hear something: *I didn't get* what he said because the music was so loud. ○ I told that joke to Sophia, but she didn't get it. ➔See also **get the message** at **message** IDEA; **get the picture** at **picture** IDEA.

get PREPARE /get/ verb [T] getting, got, got or US gotten to prepare a meal: I'll put the kids to bed while you're getting the dinner.

get CONFUSE /get/ verb [T] getting, got, got or US gotten INFORMAL to confuse someone and make them completely unable to understand or explain: Give him a technical question – that'll really get him!

• **You've got me there!** INFORMAL something that you say when you do not know the answer to a question: 'How many miles is five kilometres?' 'You've got me there.'

get ANNOY /get/ verb [T] getting, got, got or US gotten INFORMAL to annoy someone: It really gets me the way we're expected to actually laugh at his pathetic jokes!

get EMOTION /get/ verb [T] getting, got, got or US gotten INFORMAL to make someone feel strongly emotional and often to cry: That bit in the film when he finds out that his daughter is alive – that always gets me!

get HIT /get/ verb [T] getting, got, got or US gotten to hit someone, especially with a bullet or something thrown: The bullet got her in the leg.

get REACH /get/ verb getting, got, got or US gotten **1** [I usually + adv or prep; T] to reach or arrive at a particular place: We hadn't even got as far as London when the car broke down. ○ What time does he normally get home (from work)? ○ If you get to the restaurant before us just wait at the bar. **2** [I usually + adv or prep] to reach a particular stage, condition or time: You earn loads if you get to the top in that profession. ○ It got to Thursday and she still hadn't heard any news. ○ INFORMAL I'm getting to the stage now where I just want to give up.

• **get far/somewhere/anywhere** to make progress or to improve: She's taking flute lessons, but she really doesn't seem to be getting anywhere with it. ○ It's been hard settling in, but I feel I'm getting somewhere at last.

• **getting on for** UK (US going on) almost: He must be getting on for 80 now. ○ It was getting on for midnight.

get HAVE CHANCE /get/ verb [I + to infinitive] getting, got, got or US gotten to have the chance to do something: I never get to see her now that she's left the company.

get LOOK AT /get/ verb [T not continuous] INFORMAL to look at or notice someone, and usually laugh at them: Get him in his new clothes! ✻ NOTE: This is usually used in the imperative form.

PHRASAL VERBS WITH get ▼

▲ **get about** TRAVEL UK phrasal verb (US **get around**) to travel to a lot of places: Spain last week and Germany this week – he gets about, doesn't he!

▲ **get about** MOVE UK phrasal verb (US **get around**) to be able to go to different places without difficulty, especially if you are old or ill: My gran is finding it harder to get about these days.

▲ **get sth across** phrasal verb [M] to manage to make someone understand or believe something: We tried to get our point across, but he just wouldn't listen. ○ This is the message that we want to get across to the public.

▲ **get ahead** phrasal verb to be successful in the work that you do: It's tough for a woman to get ahead in politics.

▲ **get along** BE FRIENDLY MAINLY US phrasal verb (MAINLY UK **get on**) If two or more people get along, they like each other and are friendly to each other: I don't really get along with my sister's husband.

▲ **get along** DEAL WITH MAINLY US phrasal verb (MAINLY UK **get on**) to deal with a situation, usually successfully: I wonder how Michael is getting on in his new job?

▲ **get around** phrasal verb MAINLY US FOR **get round**: News of Helen's pregnancy soon got around the office.

▲ **get at sth** SUGGEST phrasal verb INFORMAL When someone is getting at something, they mean it or are trying to express it: I'm not sure what you're getting at – don't you think I should come tonight? ○ What do you think the poet is getting at in these lines?

▲ **get at sb** CRITICIZE UK phrasal verb (US USUALLY **get on sb**) INFORMAL to criticize a person repeatedly in a way

that makes them unhappy: He keeps getting at me and I really don't know what I've done wrong.

▲ **get at sb** INFLUENCE phrasal verb INFORMAL to influence a person illegally, usually by offering them money or threatening them: The accused claimed that the witness had been got at.

▲ **get at sth** REACH phrasal verb to reach or obtain something, especially something that is difficult to get: I've put the cake on a high shelf where he can't get at it.

▲ **get away** phrasal verb **1** to leave or escape from a person or place, often when it is difficult to do this: We walked to the next beach to get away from the crowds. ○ I'll get away from work as soon as I can. **2** to go somewhere to have a holiday, often because you need to rest: I just need to get away for a few days. ○ We've decided to go to Scotland to get away **from it all**.

• **Get away (with you!)** OLD-FASHIONED INFORMAL said when you don't believe or agree with what someone is saying: "Ralph painted that, you know." "Get away!"

getaway /'get.ə‚weɪ/ US /'get-/ noun [C] INFORMAL when someone leaves a place quickly, usually after committing a crime: The two masked men **made** their getaway in a stolen van. ○ a getaway **car**

▲ **get away with sth** AVOID PUNISHMENT phrasal verb to succeed in avoiding punishment for something: If I thought I could get away with it, I wouldn't pay any tax at all.

• **get away with murder** INFORMAL to be allowed to do things that other people would be punished or criticised for: He's so charming that he really does get away with murder.

▲ **get away with sth** SUCCEED phrasal verb to do something successfully although it is not the best way of doing it: Do you think we could get away with just one coat of paint on that wall?

▲ **get back** RETURN phrasal verb to return to a place after you have been somewhere else: If you get back in time, you can come with us. ○ When we got back to the hotel, Ann had already left.

▲ **get sth back** BE GIVEN phrasal verb [M] to be given something again that you had before: He went next door to get his ball back. ○ Don't lend him money, you'll never get it back.

▲ **get sb back** ACT UNPLEASANTLY phrasal verb (ALSO **get back at sb**) INFORMAL to do something unpleasant to someone because they have done something unpleasant to you: I'll get you back for this, just you wait! ○ I think he's trying to get back at her **for** those remarks she made in the meeting.

▲ **get back to sth** phrasal verb to start doing or talking about something again: Anyway, I'd better get back to work.

▲ **get back to sb** phrasal verb to talk to someone again, usually on the telephone, in order to give them some information or because you were not able to speak to them before: I'll get back to you later with those figures.

▲ **get behind** phrasal verb to fail to do as much work or pay as much money as you should by a particular time: She got behind **with** her mortgage and the house was repossessed.

▲ **get by** phrasal verb to be able to live or deal with a situation with difficulty, usually by having just enough of something you need, such as money: How can he get by **on** so little money? ○ We can get by **with** four computers at the moment, but we'll need a couple more when the new staff arrive.

▲ **get sb down** MAKE UNHAPPY phrasal verb If something gets you down, it makes you feel unhappy and dissatisfied: The chaos in his house was starting to get him down. ○ I know it's frustrating, but don't let it get you down.

▲ **get sth down** WRITE phrasal verb [M] to write something, especially something that someone has said: I didn't manage to get down that last bit she said, about the meeting.

▲ **get sth down** (sb) SWALLOW phrasal verb [M] to succeed in swallowing something although it is difficult: Her throat was so swollen that she couldn't get the tablets down. ○ INFORMAL HUMOROUS Your dinner is on the table and you've got ten minutes to get it down (you).

▲ **get down to** *sth phrasal verb* to start to direct your efforts and attention towards something: *I've got a lot of work to do, but I can't seem to get down to it.* ○ [+ *v-ing*] *I must get down to booking our holiday.*

▲ **get in** ENTER *phrasal verb* to succeed in entering a place, especially by using force or a trick: *They must have got in through the bathroom window.*

▲ **get in** ARRIVE *phrasal verb* **1** to arrive at your home or the place where you work: *What time did you get in last night?* **2** If a train or other vehicle gets in at a particular time, that is when it arrives: *What time is the plane expected to get in?*

▲ **get in/get into** *sth* BE CHOSEN *phrasal verb* to succeed in being chosen or elected: *He wanted to go to Oxford, but he didn't get in.* ○ *The Republicans are bound to get in at the next elections.*

▲ **get** *sth* **in** FIND TIME *phrasal verb* [M] INFORMAL to manage to find time to do something or deal with someone: *I get in a bit of gardening most evenings.*

▲ **get** *sth* **in** SAY *phrasal verb* [M] to succeed in saying something, although it is difficult to do this because other people are talking too: *He couldn't get a word in because she was talking so much.* ○ *I'll try to get my suggestion in at the start of the meeting.*

▲ **get** *sth* **in** BUY *phrasal verb* [M] UK INFORMAL to buy a supply of something, usually food or drink, so that you will have enough of it when you need: *We'll have to get some food in for the weekend if we're having visitors.*

● **get the drinks in** UK INFORMAL to buy drinks for yourself and another person or a group of people in a pub or bar: *Who's getting the drinks in?*

▲ **get** *sth* **in** SEND *phrasal verb* [M] to send something so that it arrives by a particular time: *I have to get my application in by Thursday.*

▲ **get** *sb* **in** EMPLOY *phrasal verb* to ask a trained person to come to your home to do some paid work: *We'll have to get a plumber in to look at that water tank.*

▲ **get in on** *sth phrasal verb* to start to take part in an activity that is already happening because you will gain an advantage from it: *A Japanese company tried to get in on the deal.*

▲ **get into** *sth* ACTIVITY *phrasal verb* to become interested in an activity or subject, or start being involved in an activity: *She's been getting into yoga recently – she does three classes a week.*

▲ **get into** *sb* BEHAVIOUR *phrasal verb* If you do not know what has got into someone, you do not understand why they are behaving strangely: *I can't think what's got into him. He doesn't usually make such a fuss.*

▲ **get** *(sb)* **into** *sth* PROBLEM *phrasal verb* to (cause someone to) become involved in a difficult situation, often without intending to: *After he lost his job, he got into debt.* ○ *Are you trying to get me into trouble?*

▲ **get** *(sth)* **off** VEHICLE *phrasal verb* to leave a train, bus or aircraft: *Get off at Camden Town.* ○ *I tripped as I got off the bus.* ➡See picture **Phrasal Verbs** on page Centre 9

▲ **get off** PLACE *phrasal verb* **1** to leave a place, usually in order to start a journey: *If we can get off by seven o'clock, the roads will be clearer.* **2** INFORMAL to leave work with permission, usually at the end of the day: *How early can you get off this afternoon?*

▲ **get** *sth* **off** POST *phrasal verb* to send a letter or parcel to someone: *I got that letter off this morning.*

▲ **get** *(sb)* **off** SLEEP *phrasal verb* to start sleeping, or to help a baby to start sleeping: *It was so hot that I didn't get off (to sleep) till three o'clock.* ○ *I've been trying to get the baby off (to sleep) for an hour!*

▲ **get** *(sb)* **off** *(sth)* ESCAPE PUNISHMENT *phrasal verb* to avoid punishment, or to help another person to avoid punishment for something: *She was charged with fraud, but her lawyer managed to get her off.* ○ *"Was he found guilty?" "No, he got off."* ○ *She got off with* (= her only punishment was) *a small fine.*

● **get off lightly** to experience less serious punishment, injury or harm than you might have expected: *I think I got off quite lightly with one or two cuts, bearing in mind how damaged the car was.*

▲ **get** *sth* **off** *(sth)* REMOVE *phrasal verb* INFORMAL to remove a part of your body from a particular place: *Get*

your dirty feet off the settee! ○ *Get your hands off me!*

▲ **get** *(sb)* **off** PLEASURE *phrasal verb* MAINLY US SLANG to have or give someone an ORGASM: *They got off at the same time.*

▲ **get off on** *sth phrasal verb* INFORMAL to find something exciting, especially in a sexual way: *Dave likes power – he gets off on it.*

▲ **get off with** *sb phrasal verb* UK SLANG to begin a sexual relationship with someone: *She'd got off with some bloke at the party.*

▲ **get on** *(sth)* VEHICLE *phrasal verb* to go onto a bus, train, aircraft or boat: *I think we got on the wrong bus.* ➡See picture **Phrasal Verbs** on page 9

▲ **get on** RELATIONSHIP MAINLY UK *phrasal verb* (MAINLY US **get along**) to have a good relationship: *We're getting on much better now that we don't live together.* ○ *He doesn't get on with his daughter.*

● **get it on** SLANG to have sex: *Did you get it on with him?*

▲ **get on** MANAGE MAINLY UK *phrasal verb* (MAINLY US **get along**) to manage or deal with a situation, especially successfully: *How are you getting on in your new flat?* ○ *We're getting on quite well with the decorating.*

▲ **get on** CONTINUE *phrasal verb* to continue doing something, especially work: *I suppose I could get on with the ironing while I'm waiting.* ○ *I'll leave you to get on then, shall I?*

▲ **get on** OLD *phrasal verb* INFORMAL **be getting on** to be getting old: *He's getting on (a bit) – he'll be seventy-six next birthday.*

▲ **get on** LATE *phrasal verb* INFORMAL If you say it's getting on, or time is getting on, you mean it is becoming late: *It's getting on – we'd better be going.*

▲ **get on to/onto** *sth* SUBJECT *phrasal verb* to start talking about a different subject: *How did we get on to (the subject of) your grandmother's cat?*

▲ **get on to/onto** *sth* PERSON *phrasal verb* UK to speak or write to a person or organization because you want them to help you in some way: *Did you remember to get on to the plumber about the shower?*

▲ **get out** LEAVE *phrasal verb* to leave an enclosed vehicle, building, etc: *I'll get out when you stop at the traffic lights.*

▲ **get** *(sb/sth)* **out** *phrasal verb* to (help someone or something to) escape from or leave a place: *I left the door open and the cat got out.* ○ *A team of commandoes got the hostages out from the rebel base.*

▲ **get out** VISIT PLACES *phrasal verb* to go out to different places and socialize: *We don't get out much since we had the children.*

● **You should get out more.** HUMOROUS used to tell someone that they are spending too much time doing boring or unimportant things: *"I've ordered all my CD's alphabetically." "Mmm, I think you should get out more, Mike."*

▲ **get out** BECOME KNOWN *phrasal verb* If news or information gets out, people hear about it although someone is trying to keep it secret: *I don't want it to get out that I'm leaving before I've had a chance to tell Anthony.*

▲ **get out of** *sth* AVOID *phrasal verb* to avoid doing something that you do not want to do, especially by giving an excuse: *I reckon her backache was just a way of getting out of the housework.* ○ [+ *v-ing*] *If I can get out of going to the meeting tonight I will.*

▲ **get out of** *sth* STOP *phrasal verb* to give up or stop a habit or a regular activity: *I must get out of the habit of finishing off people's sentences for them.* ○ *If you get out of a routine, it's very hard to get back into it.*

▲ **get** *sth* **out of** *sth* ENJOY *phrasal verb* to enjoy something or think something is useful: *It was a really boring course and I don't think I got much out of it.*

▲ **get** *sth* **out of** *sb* PERSUADE *phrasal verb* to persuade or force someone to tell or give you something: *He was determined to get the truth out of her.*

▲ **get over** *sth/sb phrasal verb* to get better after an illness, or feel better after something or someone has made you unhappy: *She was only just getting over the flu when she got a stomach bug.* ○ *It took him years to get over the shock of his wife dying.* ○ *It took her months to get over Rupert when she finished the relationship.*

● **not get over** *sth* When you say that you can't get over something, you mean that you are very surprised by it:

G

I can't get over the way he behaved at your party – it was appalling!

▲ **get *sth* over with** *phrasal verb* to do or finish an unpleasant but necessary piece of work or duty so that you do not have to worry about it in the future: *I'll be glad to get these exams over with.*

▲ **get round *(somewhere)*** [NEWS] *UK phrasal verb* (*US* **get around *(somewhere)***) If news or information gets round, a lot of people hear about it: *News of her pregnancy soon got round (the office).*

▲ **get round *sb*** [PERSUADE] *phrasal verb UK* to persuade someone to allow you something by charming them: [+ to infinitive] *See if you can get round your father **to** give you a lift to the cinema.*

▲ **get round *sth*** [AVOID] *UK phrasal verb* (*US* **get around *sth***) to succeed in avoiding or solving a problem: *We can get round the problem of space by building an extension.*

▲ **get round to *sth*** *phrasal verb UK* to do something that you have intended to do for a long time: *I still haven't got round to fixing that tap.*

G

▲ **get through** [TELEPHONE] *phrasal verb* to succeed in talking to someone on the telephone: *I tried to phone her but couldn't get through.* ○ *I got through **to** the wrong department.*

▲ **get through *sth*** [EXAM] *phrasal verb* to succeed in an exam or competition: *She got through her exams without too much trouble.*

▲ **get through *sth*** [FINISH] *phrasal verb* to use up or finish something: *We're getting through a lot of coffee/toilet paper.* ○ *I can get through a lot more work when I'm on my own.*

▲ **get *(sb)* through *sth*** [DEAL WITH] *phrasal verb* to deal with a difficult or unpleasant experience, or to help someone do this: *I don't know how I got through the first couple of months after Andy's death.* ○ *We need to conserve our supplies so we can get through the winter.*

▲ **get (*sth*) through (to *sb*)** *phrasal verb* to succeed in making someone understand or believe something: [+ question word] *We can't get through to the government just **how** serious the problem is!* ○ *I don't seem to be able to get through to* (= communicate with) *him these days.*

▲ **get to *sb*** [SUFFER] *phrasal verb INFORMAL* If something gets to you, it makes you suffer: *The heat was beginning to get to me, so I went indoors.*

▲ **get to *sb*** [UPSET] *phrasal verb INFORMAL* If someone gets to you, they make you feel upset or angry: *I know he's annoying, but you shouldn't let him get to you.*

▲ **get to** [DISAPPEAR] *phrasal verb* You ask where people or things have got to when they do not arrive or are not where you expect them to be and you want to know where they are: *I wonder where my glasses have got to.* ○ *Where's Annabel got to? She should be here by now.*

▲ **get together** [MEET] *phrasal verb* If two or more people get together, they meet each other, having arranged it before: *Shall we get together on Friday and go for a drink or something?*

get-together /ˈget.tə,geð.əʳ/ [US] /-ɚ/ *noun* [C] an informal meeting or social gathering, often arranged for a particular purpose: *a family get-together*

▲ **get together** [START] *phrasal verb INFORMAL* to start a romantic relationship: *She got together with Paul two years ago.* ○ *They finally get **it** together right at the end of the film.*

• **get it together** *INFORMAL* to make a decision or take positive action in your life: *Brian has really got it together since I last saw him – he has started a teaching course and lost a lot of weight.*

▲ **get *(sb)* up** [WAKE] *phrasal verb* to wake up and get out of bed, or to tell or help someone to do this: *I got up at five o'clock this morning!* ○ *It's dreadful trying to get the kids up on school days.* ➲See picture **Phrasal Verbs** on page Centre 9

▲ **get up** [STAND] *phrasal verb* to stand up: *The whole audience got up and started clapping.*

▲ **get *sth* up** [ORGANIZE] *phrasal verb* [M] to organize a group of people to do something: *He's getting up a small group to go carol-singing for charity.*

▲ **get up** [GROW STRONG] *phrasal verb UK* If the wind gets up, it starts to grow stronger: *The wind is getting up.*

• **get your courage up** to force yourself to be brave: *He couldn't get up the courage to ask her for a date.*

▲ **get *sb* up** [DRESS] *phrasal verb INFORMAL* to dress someone in particular clothing, especially clothing which is strange and unusual and intended to achieve a particular effect: [R] *He'd got himself up **as** a Roman emperor for the fancy-dress party.*

get-up /ˈget.ʌp/ [US] /ˈget̬-/ *noun* [C] *He was in a sort of Mafia get-up, with a pin-striped suit and wide tie.*

▲ **get up to *sth*** *phrasal verb UK* to do something, often something that other people would disapprove of: *She's been getting up to all sorts of **mischief** lately.* ○ *I wonder what those two got up to yesterday?*

get-up-and-go /,get.ʌp.ənˈgəʊ/ [US] /,get̬.ʌp.ənˈgoʊ/ *noun* [U] *INFORMAL* the quality of being positive and having lots of new ideas, determination and energy: *This job needs someone with a bit of get-up-and-go.*

geyser /ˈgiː.zəʳ/ [US] /ˈgaɪ.zɚ/ *noun* [C] a hole in the ground from which hot water and steam are sent out

ghastly /ˈgɑːst.li/ [US] /ˈgæst-/ *adj* **1** *INFORMAL* unpleasant and shocking: *Today's newspaper gives all the ghastly details of the murder.* **2** *INFORMAL* extremely bad: *What ghastly **weather**!* ○ *It was all a ghastly **mistake**.* ○ *I thought her outfit was ghastly.* **3** *LITERARY* describes someone who looks very ill or very shocked, especially with a very pale face: *You look ghastly – are you okay?* **ghastliness** /ˈgɑːst.lɪ.nəs/ [US] /ˈgæst-/ *noun* [U]

ghee /giː/ *noun* [U] a type of clear butter used in Indian cookery

gherkin /ˈgɜː.kɪn/ [US] /ˈgɝː-/ *noun* [C] a small type of CUCUMBER (= long thin green vegetable) which is often PICKLED (= preserved in vinegar): *a pickled gherkin*

ghetto /ˈget.əʊ/ [US] /ˈget̬.oʊ/ *noun* [C] *plural* **ghettos** or **ghettoes** **1** an area of a city, especially a very poor area, where people of a particular race or religion live closely together and apart from other people: *As a child she lived in one of New York's poorest ghettos.* ○ *to live in ghetto conditions* **2** *OLD USE* in the past, an area of a city where Jews were made to live

ghetto blaster /ˈget.əʊ,blɑː.stəʳ/ [US] /ˈget̬.oʊ,blæs.t̬ɚ/ *noun* [C] (*US ALSO* **boom box**) *INFORMAL* a large long TAPE RECORDER that can be carried around by hand

ghost [SPIRIT] /gəʊst/ [US] /goʊst/ *noun* [C] the spirit of a dead person, sometimes represented as a pale, almost transparent image of that person, which some people believe appears to people who are alive: *Do you **believe in** ghosts?* ○ *The gardens are said to be **haunted** by the ghost **of** a child who drowned in the river.*

• **look like/as though *you've* seen a ghost** to look very shocked: *Whatever's the matter? You look as though you've just seen a ghost!*

• **not have a/the ghost of a chance** *INFORMAL* to have no chance at all: *They haven't got a ghost of a chance **of** winning.*

• **give up the ghost** **1** to die **2** *HUMOROUS* If a machine gives up the ghost, it stops working: *We've had the same TV for over ten years and it's just given up the ghost.*

ghostly /ˈgəʊst.li/ [US] /ˈgoʊst-/ *adj* **1** pale and transparent: *a ghostly figure/apparition* **2** not loud or clear: *a ghostly voice/echo* **ghostliness** /ˈgəʊst.lɪ.nəs/ [US] /ˈgoʊst-/ *noun* [U]

ghost [MEMORY] /gəʊst/ [US] /goʊst/ *noun* [S] *LITERARY* a memory, usually of something or someone bad: *The ghost **of** the old dictator still lingers on.*

ghost [WRITE] /gəʊst/ [US] /goʊst/ *verb* [T] (*ALSO* **ghost-write**) to write a book or article etc. for another person, so that they can pretend it is their own or use it themselves: *His autobiography was ghosted.* **ghost-writer** /ˈgəʊst,raɪ.təʳ/ [US] /ˈgoʊst,raɪ.t̬ɚ/ *noun* [C]

ˈ**ghost ˌstory** *noun* [C] a frightening story about ghosts and their activities

ˈ**ghost ˌtown** *noun* [C] a town where few or no people now live

ˈ**ghost ˌtrain** *noun* [C] an entertainment for adults and children, in which you travel in a vehicle through a set of exciting and frightening experiences

ghoul /guːl/ *noun* [C] **1** an evil spirit that eats dead bodies **2** *INFORMAL* someone who is very interested in death and unpleasant things

ghoulish /ˈguː.lɪʃ/ *adj* **1** ugly and unpleasant, or frightening: *ghoulish faces* **2** *DISAPPROVING* connected with death and unpleasant things: *He takes a ghoulish delight in reading about horrific murders.* **ghoulishly** /ˈguː.lɪʃ.li/ *adv*

GHQ /ˌdʒiː.eɪtʃˈkjuː/ *noun* [U] *ABBREVIATION FOR* General Headquarters: the main centre from which a military operation is controlled

GI /ˌdʒiːˈaɪ/ *noun* [C] *INFORMAL* a soldier in the US army, especially in World War Two

giant /ˈdʒaɪ.ənt/ *noun* [C] **1** an imaginary creature like a man but extremely tall, strong and usually very cruel, appearing especially in children's stories ➲See also **gigantic**. **2** someone who is unusually tall or large **3** a very successful and powerful person or organization: *He was one of the intellectual/political giants of this century.* ○ *The takeover battle is between two of America's industrial/retail giants* (= large companies).

giant /ˈdʒaɪ.ənt/ *adj* extremely large: *a giant earth-moving machine* ○ *to take giant steps*

ˌgiant ˈpanda *noun* [C] a **panda**

gibber /ˈdʒɪb.əʳ/ [US] /-ɚ/ *verb* [I] *MAINLY DISAPPROVING* to speak quickly in a way that cannot be understood, usually when you are very frightened or confused: *Stop gibbering, man, and tell us what you saw.* **gibbering** /ˈdʒɪb.ər.ɪŋ/ [US] /-ɚ-/ *adj*: *I stood there like a gibbering **idiot** – I didn't know what I was saying.*

gibberish /ˈdʒɪb.ər.ɪʃ/ [US] /-ɚ-/ *noun* [U] *DISAPPROVING* spoken or written words which are nonsense and have no meaning: *I was so nervous, I just started **talking** gibberish.*

gibbet /ˈdʒɪb.ɪt/ *noun* [C] a wooden structure from which criminals were hung, in the past, as a form of EXECUTION (= killing as a punishment) ➲Compare **gallows**.

gibbon /ˈgɪb.ən/ *noun* [C] a small long-armed ape which lives in trees in the forests of S Asia

gibe /dʒaɪb/ *noun* [C], *verb* [I] **jibe**

giblets /ˈdʒɪb.ləts/ *plural noun* the inside parts and neck of a bird, which are usually removed before it is cooked, but are often used to flavour sauces, etc.

giddy /ˈgɪd.i/ *adj* **dizzy**

gift [PRESENT] /gɪft/ *noun* [C] **1** a present or something which is given: *a birthday/wedding gift* ○ *The guests all arrived **bearing*** (= bringing) *gifts.* **2** *INFORMAL* something which is surprisingly easy or cheap: *That goal was a gift!* ○ *£100 for a good leather coat? It's a gift!*

• **a gift from the gods** an especially good or lucky thing or person that comes to you

gift [ABILITY] /gɪft/ *noun* [C] a special ability to do something: *He has a gift **for** languages.*

• **the gift of the gab** *UK* (*US* **the gift of gab**) *INFORMAL* the ability to speak easily and confidently in a way that makes people want to listen to you and believe you: *She's got the gift of the gab – she should work in sales and marketing.*

gifted /ˈgɪf.tɪd/ *adj* **1** having special ability in a particular subject or activity: *a gifted dancer/musician* **2** clever, or having a special ability: *Schools often fail to cater for the needs of gifted **children**.*

ˈgift ˌshop *noun* [C] a shop which sells goods which are suitable for giving as presents

ˈgift ˌtoken/ˌvoucher *UK noun* [C] (*US* **gift certificate**) a card or piece of paper which can be exchanged in a shop for goods of the value that is printed on it

gift-wrapped /ˈgɪft.ræpt/ *adj* A present which is gift-wrapped has been put in decorative paper ready for giving.

gig [PERFORMANCE] /gɪg/ *noun* [C] *INFORMAL* a single performance by a musician or group of musicians, especially playing modern or pop music: *This week the band **did** the last gig of their world-tour.* **gig** /gɪg/ *verb* [I] **-gg-** *Gigging around the London clubs helped the band develop their own sound.*

gig [CARRIAGE] /gɪg/ *noun* [C] a light two-wheeled carriage pulled by one horse, used especially in the past

giga- /gɪg.ə-/ *prefix* used to form words with the meaning 1 000 000 000: *gigavolt* ○ *gigahertz* ○ *gigawatt*

gigabyte /ˈgɪg.ə.baɪt/ *noun* [C] *SPECIALIZED* a unit of computer information, consisting of 1024 MEGABYTES

gigantic /ˌdʒaɪˈgæn.tɪk/ [US] /-t̬ɪk/ *adj* extremely large: *a gigantic statue* ○ *The cost has been gigantic.* **gigantically** /dʒaɪˈgæn.tɪ.kli/ [US] /-t̬ɪ-/ *adv*

giggle /ˈgɪg.l̩/ *verb* [I] to laugh repeatedly in a quiet but uncontrolled and childish way, often at something silly or rude or when you are nervous: *Stop that giggling at the back!*

giggle /ˈgɪg.l̩/ *noun* **1** [C] a nervous or silly laugh: *There were a few **nervous** giggles from people in the audience.* ○ *I caught Roz **having** a giggle over some of Janet's awful poetry.* **2** [S] *UK INFORMAL* something which is amusing, often when it involves laughing at someone else: *Just **for a** giggle, we hid his trousers while he was in the water.*

the giggles *plural noun INFORMAL* when you can't stop giggling: *I often used to **get/have** the giggles in lectures when I was at college.*

giggler /ˈgɪg.ləʳ/ [US] /-lɚ/ *noun* [C] a person who often giggles

giggly /ˈgɪg.l̩.i/ /-li/ *adj MAINLY DISAPPROVING* giggling a lot: *There were a load of giggly school-kids at the back of the bus.*

gigolo /ˈdʒɪg.ə.ləʊ/ [US] /-loʊ/ *noun* [C] *plural* **gigolos** *OLD-FASHIONED* a man who is paid by a woman to be her lover and companion

gild /gɪld/ *verb* [T] **1** to cover a surface with a thin layer of gold or a substance that looks like gold **2** *LITERARY* to cover the surface of something with bright golden light: *Sunlight gilded the children's faces.*

• **gild the lily** *DISAPPROVING* to improve or decorate something which is already perfect and therefore spoil it: *Should I add a scarf to this jacket or would it be gilding the lily?*

gilded /ˈgɪl.dɪd/ *adj* **1** [before n] covered with a thin layer of gold or a substance that looks like gold; GILT: *The gilded dome of the cathedral rises above the city.* **2** *LITERARY* rich or of a higher social class: *The story revolves around the gilded **youth** of the 1920s and their glittering lifestyles.*

gill [ORGAN] /gɪl/ *noun* [C usually pl] the organ through which fish and other water creatures breathe

• **be green/pale about the gills** *HUMOROUS* to look ill and pale: *Matt was out drinking last night and he's a bit green about the gills this morning!*

• **to the gills** *INFORMAL* used in expressions to mean completely full: *By the time the fourth course was served, I was **stuffed** to the gills.* ○ *The restaurant was **packed** to the gills.*

gill [MEASUREMENT] /dʒɪl/ *noun* [C] a measure of liquid that is equal to 0.142 litres or a quarter of a pint

gilt /gɪlt/ *adj* covered with a thin layer of gold or a substance which is intended to look like it: *a gilt picture frame* ○ *It's not solid gold – it's just gilt.* ➲See also **gild**.

gilt /gɪlt/ *noun* [U] when a very thin layer of gold, silver or a similar substance, is used to cover the surface of something: *a crucifix cast in **silver** gilt/a silver gilt crucifix* ○ *gilt lettering*

gilts /gɪlts/ *plural noun* (*ALSO* **gilt-edged securities**) *UK SPECIALIZED* a type of investment offered by the government which pays a fixed rate of interest and is considered low-risk

gimcrack /ˈdʒɪm.kræk/ *adj DISAPPROVING* attractive on the surface but badly made and of no real or permanent value

gimlet [TOOL] /ˈgɪm.lət/ *noun* [C] a small tool used for making holes in wood

• **have gimlet eyes** (*ALSO* **be gimlet-eyed**) *LITERARY* to look at things very carefully and not miss anything

gimlet [DRINK] /ˈgɪm.lət/ *noun* [C] *US* a drink made with GIN or VODKA and lime juice

gimme [GIVE] /ˈgɪm.i/ *NOT STANDARD FOR* give me: *Gimme that pen back!*

gimme [EASY] /ˈgɪm.i/ *noun* [C usually sing] *US SLANG* something which is extremely easy to do: *That first test question was a gimme, for sure.*

gimmick /ˈgɪm.ɪk/ *noun* [C] *MAINLY DISAPPROVING* something which is not serious or of real value that is used to

G

attract people's attention or interest temporarily, especially to make them buy something: *a* ***publicity*** *gimmick* ○ *They give away free gifts with children's meals as a* ***sales/marketing*** *gimmick.*

gimmickry /ˈgɪm.ɪ.kri/ *noun* [U] *MAINLY DISAPPROVING* when gimmicks are used, especially in order to make a product or activity more successful **gimmicky** /ˈgɪm.ɪ.ki/ *adj DISAPPROVING gimmicky foods/fashions*

gin /dʒɪn/ *noun* [C or U] a colourless strong alcoholic drink flavoured with JUNIPER BERRIES (= small fruits): *a bottle of gin* ○ *gin and tonic*

ginger /ˈdʒɪn.dʒəʳ/ [US] /-dʒɚ/ *noun* [U] **1** the spicy root of a tropical plant which is used in cooking or eaten preserved in sugar: ***ground*** (= powdered) *ginger* ○ ***crystallized*** *ginger* ➲See picture **Vegetables** on page Centre 2 **2** a red or orange-brown colour: *His nickname was Ginger because of his ginger* ***hair***. **gingery** /ˈdʒɪn.dʒᵊr.i/ [US] /-dʒɚ-/ *adj*: *a gingery taste/colour*

ginger /ˈdʒɪn.dʒəʳ/ [US] /-dʒɚ/ *verb*

▲ **ginger** ***sth*** **up** *phrasal verb* [M] to make something more exciting, interesting or active: *They've gingered up the book cover with a new design, but the contents are the same.*

ˌginger ˈale *noun* [C or U] (*UK ALSO* **ginger**, *UK* **dry ginger**) a fizzy drink containing ginger, which is sometimes mixed with an alcoholic drink

ˌginger ˈbeer *noun* [C or U] a British fizzy drink containing ginger and a small amount of alcohol

gingerbread /ˈdʒɪn.dʒə.bred/ [US] /-dʒɚ-/ *noun* [U] a type of cake, usually very dark brown and soft, which contains GINGER

ˈgingerbread ˌman *noun* [C] a hard ginger biscuit shaped like a person

gingerly /ˈdʒɪn.dʒə.li/ [US] /-dʒɚ-/ *adv* in a way that is careful or CAUTIOUS: *Holding her painful back, she sat down gingerly on the bench.*

ˌginger ˈnut/ˈbiscuit *UK noun* [C] (*US AND UK* **ginger snap**) a type of hard biscuit flavoured with ginger

gingham /ˈgɪŋ.ᵊm/ *noun* [U] a cotton cloth which has a pattern of coloured squares on a white background: *a gingham dress/tablecloth*

gingivitis /ˌdʒɪn.dʒɪˈvaɪ.tɪs/ [US] /-t̬əs/ *noun* [U] *SPECIALIZED* an infection of the GUMS (= the part of the mouth from which the teeth grow) which causes swelling, pain, and sometimes bleeding

ginormous /ˌdʒaɪˈnɔː.məs/ [US] /-ˈnɔːr-/ *adj UK INFORMAL* extremely large: *Even little Billie ate his way through a ginormous ice-cream sundae.*

ˌgin ˈrummy *noun* [U] a card game which is a type of RUMMY

ginseng /ˈdʒɪn.seŋ/ *noun* [U] the root of a tropical plant, especially from China, used as a medicine and to improve health

gipsy /ˈdʒɪp.si/ *noun* [C] *MAINLY UK* a **gypsy**

giraffe /dʒɪˈrɑːf/ [US] /-ˈræf/ *noun* [C] *plural* **giraffes** or **giraffe** a large African animal with a very long neck and long legs ➲See picture **Animals and Birds** on page Centre 4

gird /gɜːd/ [US] /gɝːd/ *verb* [T] **girded** or **girt**, **girded** or **girt** *OLD USE* to tie something around your body or part of your body: [R] *The knights girded themselves* ***for*** *battle* (= put on their swords and fighting clothes).

• **gird *your*self** (*ALSO* **gird (up) *your* loins**) *LITERARY OR HUMOROUS* to get ready to do something or deal with something: *We girded ourselves for* ***the fray*** (= prepared for action or trouble). ○ *Europe's finest golfers are girding their loins for the challenge of the Ryder Cup.*

girder /ˈgɜː.dəʳ/ [US] /ˈgɝː.dɚ/ *noun* [C] a long thick piece of steel or concrete, etc. which supports a roof, floor, bridge or other large structure: *steel roof girders*

girdle /ˈgɜː.dl̩/ [US] /ˈgɝː-/ *noun* [C] **1** *OLD-FASHIONED* an elastic piece of underwear for women worn around the waist and bottom to shape the body **2** *OLD USE* a long strip of cloth worn tied around the waist

girl /gɜːl/ [US] /gɝːl/ *noun* **1** [C] a female child or young woman, especially one still at school: *Two girls showed us round the classrooms.* **2** [C] a daughter: *We have two girls.* ○ *My little girl is five.* **3** [C usually pl] a woman worker, especially when seen as one of a group: *shop/office girls*

the girls *plural noun* a group of female friends: *I'm going out with the girls tonight.* ○ *The girls at work gave it to me.*

girlhood /ˈgɜːl.hʊd/ [US] /ˈgɝːl-/ *noun* [C or U] *OLD-FASHIONED* the period when a person is a girl, and not yet a woman, or the state of being a girl: *She lived in India during her girlhood.*

girlish /ˈgɜː.lɪʃ/ [US] /ˈgɝː-/ *adj USUALLY APPROVING* describes behaviour or characteristics that are typical of a girl: *a girlish laugh* ○ *His eyelashes were long and girlish.* **girlishly** /ˈgɜː.lɪʃ.li/ [US] /ˈgɝː-/ *adv*

ˌgirl ˈFriday *noun* [C] *OLD-FASHIONED* a female helper or office worker who is willing to do various different types of work

girlfriend /ˈgɜːl.frend/ [US] /ˈgɝːl-/ *noun* [C] the close female friend of a man, with whom he has a romantic or sexual relationship, or the female friend of a woman: *I've never met his girlfriend.* ○ *Susan was going out to lunch with her girlfriends.* ➲Compare **boyfriend**.

ˌGirl ˈGuide *noun* [C] *UK OLD-FASHIONED* a **Guide** ➲See at **the Guides**.

girlie, **girly** /ˈgɜː.li/ [US] /ˈgɝː-/ *adj* **1 girlie magazine/picture, etc.** a magazine etc. which shows women wearing few or no clothes **2** *INFORMAL* typically feminine in character, or suitable for girls rather than boys: *My sister has always been a very girlie girl, not like me.* ○ *We had a real girlie chat.* ○ *We do lots of girlie things together.* ○ *DISAPPROVING Sometimes she speaks in this silly, girly voice.*

ˈgirl ˌpower *noun* [U] the idea that women and girls should be confident, make decisions and achieve things independently of men, or the social and political movement that is based on this idea

ˌGirl ˈScout *noun* [C] *US* a girl or young woman who belongs to an organization similar to the Guides and Scouts

giro /ˈdʒaɪ.rəʊ/ [US] /-roʊ/ *noun* **1** [U] a system used between European banks and similar organizations, in which money can be moved from one account to another by a central computer: *The money was* ***transferred by*** *giro.* **2** [C] *UK* a cheque which provides money from the government, through the giro, to someone unemployed, ill, or with very little income: *a giro cheque* ○ *She didn't know how she would manage until (she got) her next giro.*

girth /gɜːθ/ [US] /gɝːθ/ *noun* **1** [C or U] the distance around the outside of a thick or fat object, like a tree or a body: *The oak was 2 metres* ***in*** *girth.* ○ *HUMOROUS His* ***ample*** *girth was evidence of his love of good food.* **2** [C] the strap which goes around the middle of a horse to keep the SADDLE (= rider's seat) or the load in the right position: *Loosen the girth a little.*

gismo /ˈgɪz.məʊ/ [US] /-moʊ/ *noun* [C] *plural* **gismos** *ANOTHER SPELLING OF* **gizmo**

the gist /ðəˈdʒɪst/ *noun* [S] the most important pieces of information about something, or general information without details: *That was the gist* ***of*** *what he said.* ○ *I think I* ***got*** (= understood) *the gist* ***of*** *what she was saying.*

git /gɪt/ *noun* [C] *UK INFORMAL* a person, especially a man, who is stupid or unpleasant: *You stupid/lying git!* ○ *He's a miserable old git.*

gite /ʒiːt/ *noun* [C] *UK* a holiday house for renting in France

give [PROVIDE] /gɪv/ *verb* **gave**, **given** **1** [I or T] to offer something to someone, or to provide them with it: [+ two objects] *She gave us a set of saucepans as a wedding present.* ○ *Can you give me a date for another appointment?* ○ *They never gave me a chance/choice.* ○ *Has the director given you permission to do that?* ○ [+ adv or prep] *We always try to give* ***to*** *charity.* ○ *We're collecting for the children's home – please give generously.* ○ *The police gave* ***(out)*** *road-safety booklets* ***to*** *the children* (= gave them to all the children). ○ *Please give* ***(up)*** *your* ***seat*** *to an elderly or disabled person if they require it.* **2** [T] to pay someone a particular amount: *I gave £40* ***for*** *this pump and it's broken already!* **3** [T] to tell someone something: *The winner's name was given* ***(out)****/They gave the* *winner's name (out)* on the news. ○ [+ two objects] *Can you give Jo a message for me?* **4** [T] to punish someone by making them go to prison for a particular period: [+ two objects] *If you're found guilty, they'll give you three years.* **5** [T] to allow a person or activity a particular amount of time: [+ two objects] *I'm nearly ready – just give me a couple of minutes.* **6** [T] INFORMAL to calculate that something will last a particular amount of time: [+ two objects] *Look at that old car she's bought – I give it two weeks before it breaks down.*

● **Don't give me that!** INFORMAL don't expect me to believe that, because I know it is untrue: *"But I was going to let you have it tomorrow." "Don't give me that!"*

● **give as good as *you* get** to be strong and confident enough to treat people in the same way that they treat you, especially in an argument or a fight: *There's a lot of teasing and fighting among the crew, and you have to be able to give as good as you get.*

● **Give me ... any day/every time!** INFORMAL used to say that you always like or prefer a particular thing: *This new stuff is all very well, but give me the old-style weather forecast any day!*

● **give or take** possibly a little more or less than the amount or time mentioned: *It'll be ready at six, give or take a few minutes.* ○ *It cost £200, give or take.*

● **give (sth) your all** (US ALSO **give (sth) your best**) OLD-FASHIONED to put a lot of effort into doing something: *We must be finished by tonight, so I want you to give it your all.*

● **give way 1** UK to allow other vehicles to go past before you move onto a road: *You have to give way **to** traffic coming from the right.* **2** to stop arguing or fighting against someone or something: *Neither of them will give way, so they could be arguing for a very long time.* ○ *Don't give way **to** your fears.* **3** to break, especially when under pressure from strong forces: *Because of an unusually strong current, the bridge's central support gave way, tipping a coach into the river.*

● **give sb what for** OLD-FASHIONED INFORMAL to tell off someone whose behaviour you strongly disapprove of

● **given the chance/choice** (ALSO **given half a chance**) if I were allowed to, or if I could choose: *Given the chance, I'd spend all day reading.*

● **I would give anything/a lot** (ALSO **I would give my** eye teeth/right arm) used to say that you would like to have or to do something very much: *I'd give anything to see the Taj Mahal.* ○ *Janice would give her eye teeth **for** a house like that.*

● **what I wouldn't give for sth** (ALSO **what wouldn't I give for sth**) used to say that you want something very much: *What I wouldn't give for a cold drink!*

give CAUSE /gɪv/ *verb* [T] gave, given to produce or cause something: [+ two objects] *The fresh air gave us an appetite* (= made us hungry). ○ *What you said has given me an idea.* ○ *The alarm gave (out) a high-pitched sound.*

● **give sb to understand sth** FORMAL to tell someone something or cause them to think that something is true: *I was given to understand she was staying at this hotel.*

give DO /gɪv/ *verb* gave, given **1** [T] to perform an action: [+ two objects] *She gave me a smile/strange look.* ○ *They had to give the car a **push** to start it.* ○ *Give me a **call/ring*** (= telephone me) *when you get back from holiday.* ○ *Who is giving the speech/lecture/concert?* **2** [T] to organize a party, meal, etc: *They're always giving parties.* ○ *The ambassador is giving a banquet for the visiting president.* **3** [T + two objects] FORMAL to state publicly that everyone present at a formal occasion, especially a meal, should drink a TOAST to someone (= have a drink in honour of someone): *Gentlemen, I give you the Queen.*

● **give sth a go** to attempt something: *Only a few people are successful as sports professionals, but it's worth giving it a go.*

give STRETCH /gɪv/ *verb* [I] gave, given If something gives, it stretches, bends or breaks, or becomes less firm or tight, under pressure: *The rope gave **under/with** the weight of the load.* ○ *The shoes will give a little after you've worn them once or twice.* ○ FIGURATIVE *You can't work so hard all the time – something will have to give* (= change). ○ FIGURATIVE *Suddenly her patience gave (out) and she*

shouted crossly at the children.

give /gɪv/ *noun* [U] *A sweater knitted in pure cotton hasn't much give* (= will not stretch much).

give DECIDE /gɪv/ *verb* [T + obj + adj] gave, given UK in some sports, to decide and state officially that a player or the ball is in a particular condition or place: *The umpire gave the batsman out.* ○ *The ball was clearly out, but the line judge gave it in.*

PHRASAL VERBS WITH **give** ▼

▲ **give sth away** FREE *phrasal verb* [M] to give something to someone without asking for payment: *The shop is giving away a sample pack to every customer.* ○ *Nobody wants this type of heater anymore – I can't even give it away!*

giveaway /'gɪv.ə.weɪ/ *noun* [C] something that is given free to a customer

giveaway /'gɪv.ə.weɪ/ *adj* [before n] describes a price that is very low: *The furniture shop's offering three-piece suites at giveaway **prices**.*

▲ **give sth away** SECRET *phrasal verb* [M] to tell people something secret, often without intending to: *The party was meant to be a surprise, but Sharon gave it away.* ○ *I won't give **the game*** (= the information or plan) *away.*

▲ **give sb away** *phrasal verb* to show someone's secret feelings: *I know she likes him because her face when I said he'd be there really gave her away!*

give-away /'gɪv.ə.weɪ/ *noun* [C usually sing] INFORMAL *He said he'd given up smoking, but the empty packets in the bin were **a dead** give-away* (= clearly showed the secret truth).

▲ **give sb away** MARRIAGE *phrasal verb* [M] FORMAL in a marriage ceremony, to formally bring a woman who is getting married to the front of the church so that she is standing beside her future husband, and then to give permission for her to marry: *The bride was given away by her father.*

▲ **give sth back** *phrasal verb* [M] to return something to the person who gave it to you: *Has she given you those books back yet?*

▲ **give in** AGREE *phrasal verb* to finally agree to what someone wants, after refusing for a period of time: *He nagged me so much for a new bike that eventually I gave in.* ○ *The government cannot be seen to give in to terrorists' demands.*

▲ **give in** ADMIT DEFEAT *phrasal verb* to accept that you have been defeated and agree to stop competing or fighting: *You'll never guess the answer – do you give in?* ○ *She wouldn't give in until she received a full apology.*

▲ **give sth in** OFFER FOR JUDGMENT *phrasal verb* [M] UK to give a piece of written work or a document to someone for them to read, judge or deal with: *Have you given that essay in yet?*

▲ **give sth off** *phrasal verb* to produce heat, light, a smell or a gas: *That tiny radiator doesn't give off much heat.*

▲ **give onto sth** *phrasal verb* SLIGHTLY FORMAL to open in the direction of something: *The patio doors give onto a small courtyard.*

▲ **give out** *phrasal verb* If a machine or part of your body gives out, it stops working: *At the end of the race his legs gave out and he collapsed on the ground.*

▲ **give over** *phrasal verb* UK OLD-FASHIONED INFORMAL to stop doing something, usually something annoying: *Oh (do) give over* (= stop complaining), *it's not my fault!* ○ [+ v-ing] *It's time you gave over pretending you were still a teenager.*

▲ **give sth over to sth/sb** PERSON *phrasal verb* [M] to give another person the use of something, or the responsibility for something or someone: *We've given the attic over to the children.*

▲ **give yourself over/up to sth** ACTIVITY *phrasal verb* [R] to spend all your time and energy doing or feeling something: *After her death he gave himself up to grief.*

▲ **give up** NOT TRY *phrasal verb* to stop trying to guess: *You'll never guess the answer – do you give up?* ○ *I give up – how many were there?*

▲ **give sth up** NOT DO *phrasal verb* [M] to stop doing a regular activity or job: [+ v-ing] *He's given up driving since his illness.* ○ *We're going to give up our sports club membership after this year.*

G

▲ **give up** ***(sth)*** *phrasal verb* to stop doing something before you have completed it, usually because it is too difficult: **[+ v-ing]** *I've given up* ***trying*** *to help her.*

▲ **give** ***(sth)*** **up** *phrasal verb* **[M]** If you give up a habit, such as smoking, or something such as alcohol, you stop doing it or using it: **[+ v-ing]** *I gave up smok****ing*** *two years ago.* ○ *Don't offer him a cigarette, he's trying to give up.*

▲ **give up** ***sth*** [NOT HAVE] *phrasal verb* to stop owning and using something: *They were forced to give up their home because they couldn't pay the mortgage.*

▲ ˌ**give** ***sb*** ˈ**up** *phrasal verb* **[M]** to stop having a friendship with someone: *She seems to have given up all her old friends.*

• **give up hope** to stop hoping that a particular thing will happen: *We still haven't given up hope* ***of*** *finding her alive.*

▲ **give** ***sb*** **up** [NOT EXPECT] *phrasal verb* (*ALSO* **give up on** ***sb***) to stop expecting that someone will arrive: *I've been waiting half-an-hour – I'd almost given you up.*

• **give** ***sb*** **up for dead** (*ALSO* **give up on** ***sb***) to think that someone is certain to die or to be dead: *The hospital had virtually given her up for dead, but she eventually recovered.* ○ *After a three-day search on the mountain, they gave him up for dead.*

▲ **give** ***yourself*** **up** [BECOME PRISONER] *phrasal verb* **[R]** to allow the police or an enemy to take you as a prisoner: *The gunman gave himself up to the police.*

give-and-take /ˌgɪv.ən.ˈteɪk/ *noun* **1** **[U]** willingness to accept suggestions from another person and give up some of your own: *In every friendship there has to be some give-and-take.* **2** **[S]** *US* an exchange of ideas or statements: *The candidates engaged in a* ***lively*** *give-and-take, witnessed by a huge television audience.*

given [CERTAIN] /ˈgɪv.^{ə}n/ *noun* **[C]** something which is certain to happen: *You can* ***take it as*** *a given that there will be champagne at the wedding.*

given [GIVE] /ˈgɪv.^{ə}n/ *past participle of* **give**

given [KNOWING] /ˈgɪv.^{ə}n/ *prep* knowing about or considering a particular thing: *Given his age, he's a remarkably fast runner.* ○ *Given* ***(the fact) that*** *a prospective student is bombarded by prospectuses, selecting a suitable course is not easy.*

given [ARRANGED] /ˈgɪv.^{ə}n/ *adj* already decided, arranged or agreed: *At the given signal, the group rushed forward to the barrier.* ○ *The bomb could go off at* ***any*** *given* (= any) *time and in* ***any*** *given* (= any) *place.*

given [HAVING HABIT] /ˈgɪv.^{ə}n/ *adj* **be given to** ***sth*** to do something regularly or as a habit: *She was given to staying in bed till lunchtime.*

ˈ**given** ˌ**name** *US noun* **[C]** (*UK* **first name**) the name which is chosen for you at birth and which is not your family name: *Her family name is Smith and her given names are Mary Elizabeth.*

gizmo (*plural* **gizmos**), **gismo** (*plural* **gismos**) /ˈgɪz.məʊ/ [US] /-moʊ/ *noun* **[C]** *INFORMAL* any small device with a particular purpose: *electronic gizmos*

glacé /ˈglæs.eɪ/ [US] /glæsˈeɪ/ *adj* **[before n]** (*US ALSO* **glacéed**) preserved in liquid sugar and then dried: *glacé fruit/cherries*

ˈ**glacial** ˌ**period** *noun* **[C]** (*ALSO* **ice age**) *SPECIALIZED* a time in the past when the temperature was very cold and GLACIERS (= large masses of ice) spread over large parts of the Earth

glacier /ˈglæs.i.ə^r/ [US] /ˈgleɪ.si.ɚ/ *noun* **[C]** a large mass of ice which moves slowly

glacial /ˈgleɪ.si.əl/ *adj* **1** made or left by a glacier: *glacial deposits* **2** extremely cold: *glacial temperatures* ○ *a glacial period* **3** extremely unfriendly: *She gave me a glacial smile/stare.*

glad /glæd/ *adj* **gladder, gladdest** pleased and happy: *We were glad* ***about*** *her success.* ○ *I'm glad* ***(that)*** *you came.* ○ *I'm glad* ***to*** *know the parcel arrived safely.* ○ *I'd be* ***(only too)*** *glad* ***to*** *help you.* ○ *We'd be glad* ***of*** *the chance to meet her.*

gladly /ˈglæd.li/ *adv* willingly or happily: *I'd gladly meet her, but I'm on holiday that week.* **gladness** /glæd.nəs/ *noun* **[U]**

gladden /ˈglæd.^{ə}n/ *verb* **[T]** *LITERARY* to make someone or something glad: *The news gladdened his* ***heart.***

glade /gleɪd/ *noun* **[C]** *LITERARY* a small area of grass without trees in a wood

glad-handing /ˈglædˌhænd.ɪŋ/ *noun* **[U]** *INFORMAL* being very friendly to people you have not met before, as a way of trying to get an advantage: *political glad-handing*

glad-hand /ˈglæd.hænd/ *verb* **[I or T]**

gladiator /ˈglæd.i.eɪ.tə^r/ [US] /-t̬ɚ/ *noun* **[C]** in ancient Rome, a man who fought another man or an animal, usually until one of them died, for public entertainment

gladiatorial /ˌglæd.i.əˈtɔː.ri.əl/ [US] /-ˈtɔːr.i-/ *adj LITERARY* relating to fierce fighting in which only one person or group can win: *gladiatorial combat*

gladiolus (*plural* **gladioli** or **gladioluses**) /ˌglæd.iˈəʊ.ləs/ [US] /-ˈoʊ-/ *noun* **[C]** (*US USUALLY* **gladiola**) a garden plant which has a long stem along which grow many brightly-coloured flowers

ˈ**glad** ˌ**rags** *plural noun HUMOROUS* Someone's glad rags are their best clothes: *Let's put on our glad rags and go out tonight!*

glam /glæm/ *adj INFORMAL SHORT FOR* glamorous: *You look dead glam in that dress!*

glam /glæm/ *verb*

▲ **glam** ***(yourself)*** **up** *phrasal verb* **[R]** *UK INFORMAL* to dress yourself attractively and put on make-up, etc: *Have I got time to glam (myself) up?*

glammed up /ˌglæmdˈʌp/ *adj*: *She* ***got/was*** *all glammed up for the party.*

glamour /ˈglæm.ə^r/ [US] /-ɚ/ *noun* **[U]** the special excitement and attractiveness of a person, place or activity: *Who can resist the glamour* ***of*** *Hollywood/a theatre première?*

glamorous, *UK ALSO* **glamourous** /ˈglæm.^{ə}r.əs/ [US] /-ə-/ *adj* (*MAINLY UK INFORMAL* **glam**) attractive in an exciting and special way: *a glamorous woman/outfit* ○ *a glamorous job* ○ *She was looking very glam.* **glamorously** /ˈglæm.^{ə}r.ə.sli/ [US] /-ɚ-/ *adv*

glamorize, *UK USUALLY* **-ise** /ˈglæm.ə.raɪz/ [US] /-ɚ.aɪz/ *verb* **[T]** to make something seem better than it is and therefore more attractive: *The ad glamorized life in the army, emphasizing travel and adventure.*

glance [LOOK] /glɑːnts/ [US] /glænts/ *verb* **[I usually + adv or prep]** to give a quick short look: *She glanced* ***around/round*** *the room to see who was there.* ○ *He glanced* ***up*** *from his book as I passed.* ○ *Could you glance* ***over/through*** *this letter and see if it's alright?* **glance** /glɑːnts/ [US] /glænts/ *noun* **[C]** *She* ***took/cast*** *a glance* ***at*** *her watch.*

• **at a glance** immediately: *He could* ***tell*** *at a glance that something was wrong.*

• **at first glance** when first looking: *At first glance I thought it was a dog (but I was mistaken).*

glance [SHINE] /glɑːnts/ [US] /glænts/ *verb* **[I + adv or prep]** to shine, reflect light or SPARKLE: *The sunlight glanced* ***on*** *the lake.*

▲ **glance off** ***(sth)*** *phrasal verb* to hit or touch something quickly and lightly at an angle and bounce away in another direction: *The bullets glanced off the car.*

glancing /ˈglɑːnt.sɪŋ/ [US] /ˈglænt-/ *adj* **[before n]** hitting quickly and lightly at an angle: *a glancing* ***blow*** *to the head*

gland /glænd/ *noun* **[C]** an organ of the body or of a plant which SECRETES (= produces) liquid chemicals that have various purposes: *The glands in my neck are a bit swollen.* **glandular** /ˈglæn.djʊ.lə^r/ [US] /-dʒə.lɚ/ *adj*: *glandular secretions* ○ *a glandular problem*

ˌ**glandular** ˈ**fever** *UK noun* **[U]** (*US* **mononucleosis**) an infectious disease which has an effect on particular GLANDS (= small organs in the body which produce chemicals), and makes you feel weak and ill for a long time

glare [LOOK] /gleə^r/ [US] /gler/ *noun* **[C]** a long angry look: *She gave me a fierce glare.* **glare** /gleə^r/ [US] /gler/ *verb* **[I]** *She glared angrily* ***at*** *everyone and stormed out of the room.*

glare [SHINE] /gleə^r/ [US] /gler/ *verb* **[I]** to shine too brightly: *The sun was glaring right in my eyes.* **glare** /gleə^r/ [US] /gler/ *noun* **[U]** *Tinted windows will cut down* ***the*** *glare/the sun's glare.* ○ *This screen* ***gives off*** *a lot of glare.*

• **the/a glare of** ***sth*** when something receives the largest amount of attention possible: *The actor's wedding took place* ***in the full*** *glare of* ***publicity/the media.***

glaring /ˈgleə.rɪŋ/ [US] /ˈgler.ɪŋ/ *adj* shining too brightly: *glaring light* ○ *glaring colours*

glaring /ˈgleə.rɪŋ/ [US] /ˈgler.ɪŋ/ *adj* describes something bad that is very obvious: *glaring errors* ○ *a glaring injustice* ➲See also **glaring** at **glare** SHINE. **glaringly** /ˈgleə.rɪŋ.li/ [US] /ˈgler.ɪŋ-/ *adv*: *glaringly obvious*

glass [SUBSTANCE] /glɑːs/ [US] /glæs/ *noun* [U] **1** a hard transparent material which is used to make windows, bottles and other objects: *coloured/broken glass* ○ *a glass jar/dish/ornament* ○ *It's a huge window made from a single* ***pane of*** *glass.* **2** objects made from glass when thought of as a group: *The museum has a fine collection of valuable glass.*

• **under glass** in a GLASSHOUSE: *In cool climates you have to grow tropical plants under glass.*

• **People who live in glass houses shouldn't throw stones.** *SAYING* This means that you should not criticize other people for bad qualities in their character that you have yourself.

glassy /ˈglɑː.si/ [US] /ˈglæs.i/ *adj* **1** *LITERARY* describes a surface which is smooth and shiny, like glass: *a glassy sea/lake* **2** describes a person's eyes when they have a fixed expression and seem unable to see anything: *Her eyes were glassy and her skin pale.*

glass [CONTAINER] /glɑːs/ [US] /glæs/ *noun* [C] **1** a small container for drinks made of glass or similar material, with a flat base and typically tube-shaped with no handle: *a* ***beer/wine*** *glass* ○ *She poured some milk into a glass.* **2** **a glass of *sth*** a type or amount of drink contained in a glass: *Would you like a glass of water?* ○ *Two glasses of lemonade, please.*

glassful /ˈglɑːs.fʊl/ [US] /ˈglæs-/ *noun* [C] an amount contained in a glass: *She drank two whole glassfuls* ***of*** *orange juice.*

the glass *noun* [S] *OLD-FASHIONED* a **barometer**: *The glass has been* ***falling/rising*** (= showing a change to bad/good weather) *all day.*

glass /glɑːs/ [US] /glæs/ *verb*

▲ **glass *sth* in/over** *phrasal verb* [M] to use glass to fill the open spaces in something or to cover something: *We glassed in the porch to make a small conservatory.* ○ *The manuscripts are now glassed over, to stop them being damaged.*

glassblower /ˈglɑːsˌbləʊ.əʳ/ [US] /ˈglæsˌbloʊ.ɚ/ *noun* [C] someone who blows air down a tube to form heated glass into objects **glass-blowing** /ˈglɑːsˌbləʊ.ɪŋ/ [US] /ˈglæsˌbloʊ-/ *noun* [U]

ˌglass ˈceiling *noun* [C usually sing] a point beyond which you cannot go, usually in improving your position at work: *Various reasons are given for the apparent glass ceiling women hit in many professions.*

glasses /ˈglɑː.sɪz/ [US] /ˈglæs.ɪz/ *plural noun* two small pieces of special glass or plastic in a frame worn in front of the eyes to improve sight: *a* ***pair of*** *glasses* ○ ***reading*** *glasses*

ˌglass ˈfibre *noun* [U] *UK* **fibreglass**

glasshouse /ˈglɑːs.haʊs/ [US] /ˈglæs-/ *noun* [C] (*US USUALLY* **greenhouse**) a large building with glass sides and roof for growing plants in

glassware /ˈglɑːs.weəʳ/ [US] /ˈglæs.wer/ *noun* [U] drinking glasses or other objects made of glass: *a display/collection of ornamental glassware*

Glaswegian /glæzˈwiː.dʒᵊn/ *noun* [C] a person from Glasgow, the largest city in Scotland **Glaswegian** /glæzˈwiː.dʒᵊn/ *adj*: *Steven has a Glaswegian accent.*

glaucoma /glaʊˈkəʊ.mə/ [US] /-ˈkoʊ-/ *noun* [U] a disease of the eye which can cause a person to gradually lose their sight

glaze [GLASS] /gleɪz/ *verb* [T] to put a piece of glass into a window or the windows of a building: *The house is nearly finished but it hasn't been glazed yet.* **glazed** /gleɪzd/ *adj*: *All the rooms have glazed doors.*

glazier /ˈgleɪ.zi.əʳ/ [US] /-ʒɚ/ *noun* [C] a person who sells glass or fits it into windows

glazing /ˈgleɪ.zɪŋ/ *noun* [U] the glass used for windows

glaze [SHINY] /gleɪz/ *verb* [T] to make a surface shiny by putting a liquid substance onto it and leaving it or heating it until it dries: *Glaze the pastry with beaten egg.* ○ *The pot had been badly glazed.*

glaze /gleɪz/ *noun* [C] a substance used to glaze something: *a cake with a redcurrant glaze*

glaze [BORED] /gleɪz/ *verb* [I] (*ALSO* **glaze over**) If your eyes glaze or glaze over, they stay still and stop showing any emotion because you are bored or tired or have stopped listening: *Among the audience, eyes glazed over and a few heads started to nod.* **glazed** /gleɪzd/ *adj*: *a glazed* ***expression/look***

gleam /gliːm/ *verb* [I] **1** to produce or reflect a small, bright light: *He polished the table until it gleamed.* **2** When eyes gleam, they shine in a way that expresses a particular emotion: *His eyes gleamed* ***with/in*** *triumph.*

gleam /gliːm/ *noun* [C usually sing] when something gleams

gleaming /ˈgliː.mɪŋ/ *adj* bright and shiny from being cleaned: *a gleaming kitchen* ○ *gleaming windows*

glean /gliːn/ *verb* [T] to collect information in small amounts and often with difficulty: *From what I was able to glean, the news isn't good.* ○ *They're leaving on Tuesday – I managed to glean that much* ***(from*** *them).*

glee /gliː/ *noun* [U] happiness, excitement or pleasure: *She opened her presents with glee.* **gleeful** /ˈgliː.fᵊl/ *adj*: *a gleeful smile/shout* **gleefully** /ˈgliː.fᵊl.i/ *adv*

glen /glen/ *noun* [C] a deep narrow valley, especially among mountains: *the glens of Scotland* ○ *Glen Maye*

glib /glɪb/ *adj* **glibber, glibbest** speaking or spoken in a confident and persuasive way but without honesty or careful consideration: *He's a glib, self-centred man.* ○ *No one was convinced by his glib* ***answers/explanations.*** **glibly** /ˈglɪb.li/ *adv*: *He spoke glibly about an economic recovery just around the corner.* **glibness** /ˈglɪb.nəs/ *noun* [U]

glide [MOVE] /glaɪd/ *verb* [I usually + adv or prep] **1** to move easily without stopping and without effort or noise: *She came gliding gracefully into the ballroom in a long flowing gown.* ○ *I love my new pen – it just glides across/over the paper.* **2** to move or progress without difficulty or effort: *Some people glide effortlessly through life with no real worries.* **glide** /glaɪd/ *noun* [C]

glide [FLY] /glaɪd/ *verb* [I] to fly by floating on air currents instead of using power from wings or an engine: *We saw a condor gliding high above the mountains.* ○ *Unlike other spacecraft, the shuttle can glide back* ***through*** *the atmosphere, land safely, and be reused.*

glider /ˈglaɪ.dəʳ/ [US] /-dɚ/ *noun* [C] an aircraft without an engine and with long fixed wings, which flies by gliding ➲See picture **Planes, Ships and Boats** on page Centre 14

gliding /ˈglaɪ.dɪŋ/ *noun* [U] the sport or activity of flying in a GLIDER

glimmer /ˈglɪm.əʳ/ [US] /-ɚ/ *verb* [I] to shine with a weak light or a light that is not continuous: *The lights of the village were glimmering in the distance.* ○ *The sky glimmered* ***with*** *stars.* ○ *a glimmering candle* ○ *FIGURATIVE The first faint signs of an agreement began to glimmer through* (= appear).

glimmer /ˈglɪm.əʳ/ [US] /-ɚ/ *noun* [C] (*ALSO* **glimmering**) **1** a light that glimmers weakly: *We saw a glimmer* ***of light*** *in the distance.* **2** a slight sign of something good or positive: *This month's sales figures offer a glimmer* ***of hope*** *for the depressed economy.* ○ *She's never shown a glimmer* ***of interest*** *in classical music.* ○ *The first glimmer* ***of light*** (= sign of development or understanding) *has appeared in the peace talks.*

glimpse /glɪmps/ *verb* [T] to see something or someone for a very short time or only partly: *We glimpsed the ruined abbey from the windows of the train.*

glimpse /glɪmps/ *noun* [C] **1** when you see something or someone for a very short time: *I only* ***caught*** (= had) *a* ***fleeting*** *glimpse* ***of*** *the driver of the getaway car, but I doubt I would recognize her if I saw her again.* **2** a brief idea or understanding of what something is like: *This biography offers a few glimpses* ***of*** *his life before he became famous.*

glint /glɪnt/ *verb* [I] **1** to produce small bright flashes of light reflected from a surface: *The stream glinted in the moonlight.* ○ *A large diamond glinted on her finger.* **2** When someone's eyes glint, they look bright, expressing a lively emotion: *She smiled at him, her eyes glinting* ***with*** *mischief.*

G

glint /glɪnt/ *noun* [C usually sing] when something glints: *the glint of a knife* ○ *There was a mischievous glint in his eye.*

glisten /ˈglɪs.ən/ *verb* [I] to shine by reflecting light from a wet, oily or smooth surface: *The grass glistened in the early-morning dew.* ○ *His eyes glistened with tears.*

glitch /glɪtʃ/ *noun* [C] a small problem or fault that prevents something from being successful or working as well as it should: *We'd expected a few glitches, but everything's gone remarkably smoothly.* ○ *The system has been plagued with glitches ever since its launch.*

glitter BRIGHT LIGHT /ˈglɪt.əʳ/ US /ˈglɪt̬.ɚ/ *verb* [I] **1** to produce a lot of small bright flashes of reflected light: *Her diamond necklace glittered brilliantly under the spotlights.* **2** LITERARY If someone's eyes glitter, they look bright and express strong feeling: *His dark eyes glittered with anger behind his spectacles.*

● **All that glitters is not gold.** SAYING said about something that seems to be good on the surface, but might not be when you look at it more closely
glitter /ˈglɪt.əʳ/ US /ˈglɪt̬.ɚ/ *noun* [U] **1** when something glitters: *the glitter of the fireworks* **2** very small pieces of shiny material used to decorate the skin or used by children to make pictures **glittering** /ˈglɪt.ə.rɪŋ/ US /ˈglɪt̬.ɚ-/ *adj: the glittering skyline of Manhattan* **glittery** /ˈglɪt.ər.i/ US /ˈglɪt̬.ɚ-/ *adj: glittery eye shadow* ○ *a glittery dress*

glitter EXCITEMENT /ˈglɪt.əʳ/ US /ˈglɪt̬.ɚ/ *noun* [U] excitement and attractiveness connected with rich and famous people: *He was attracted by the glitter of Hollywood.*
glittering /ˈglɪt.ə.rɪŋ/ US /ˈglɪt̬.ɚ-/ *adj* exciting or admirable, usually relating to rich and famous people: *a glittering career* ○ *The Cannes Film Festival is one of the most glittering occasions in the movie world.*

glitterati /ˌglɪt.əˈrɑː.ti/ US /ˌglɪt̬.əˈrɑː.t̬i/ *plural noun* rich, famous and fashionable people whose activities are of interest to the public and are written about in some newspapers and magazines: *The restaurant is popular with the glitterati of the music world.* ➔Compare **literati**.

glitzy /ˈglɪt.si/ *adj* having a fashionable appearance intended to attract attention: *He celebrated his birthday at a glitzy party in Beverly Hills.* **glitz** /glɪts/ *noun* [U] *The party's electoral message may be obscured by the glitz and glamour of its presentation.*

gloat /gləʊt/ US /gloʊt/ *verb* [I] to feel or express great pleasure or satisfaction because of your own success or good luck, or someone else's failure or bad luck: *She's continually gloating over/about her new job.* ○ *I know I shouldn't gloat, but it really serves him right.* ○ *His enemies were quick to gloat at his humiliation.* ○ [+ speech] *"This is our fourth victory in a row," he gloated.*
gloat /gləʊt/ US /gloʊt/ *noun* [C] when you gloat about something: *to have a gloat at/over/about something* **gloatingly** /ˈgləʊ.tɪŋ.li/ US /ˈgloʊ.t̬ɪŋ-/ *adv*

glob /glɒb/ US /glɑːb/ *noun* [C] INFORMAL a round mass of a thick liquid or a sticky substance: *a glob of ketchup/yoghurt*

global WORLD /ˈgləʊ.bəl/ US /ˈgloʊ-/ *adj* relating to the whole world: *a global catastrophe/problem*
globally /ˈgləʊ.bəl.i/ US /ˈgloʊ-/ *adv* relating to the whole world: *The company has to be able to compete globally.*

global SITUATION /ˈgləʊ.bəl/ US /ˈgloʊ-/ *adj* considering or relating to all parts of a situation or subject: *This report gives a global picture of the company's finances.* **globally** /ˈgləʊ.bəl.i/ US /ˈgloʊ-/ *adv: We need to look at this issue globally.*

globalism /ˈgləʊ.bəl.ɪ.zəm/ US /ˈgloʊ-/ *noun* [U] the idea that events in one country cannot be separated from those in another and that a government should therefore consider the effects of its actions in other countries as well as its own ➔Compare **isolationism** at **isolate**.

globalize, UK USUALLY -**ise** /ˈgləʊ.bəl.aɪz/ US /ˈgloʊ-/ *verb* [I or T] to (make a company or system) spread or operate internationally: *Satellite broadcasting is helping to globalize television.* ○ *As the economy develops, it will continue to globalize.*

globalization /ˌgləʊ.bəl.aɪˈzeɪ.ʃən/ US /ˌgloʊ-/ *noun* [U] **1** (UK USUALLY -**isation**) the increase of trade around the world, especially by large companies producing and trading goods in many different countries: *We must take advantage of the increased globalization of the commodity trading business.* **2** when available goods and services, or social and cultural influences, gradually become similar in all parts of the world: *the globalization of fashion/American youth culture*

global 'warming *noun* [U] a gradual increase in world temperatures caused by polluting gases such as CARBON DIOXIDE which are collecting in the air around the Earth and preventing heat escaping into space

the globe WORLD *noun* [S] the world: *His greatest ambition is to sail round the globe.* ○ *She is a superstar all around the globe.*

globe ROUND OBJECT /gləʊb/ US /gloʊb/ *noun* [C] **1** a map of the world in the shape of a ball, which is fixed to a support and can be turned round at the same angle as the Earth turns in space: *She spun the globe, and pointed to the Solomon Islands.* **2** any ball-shaped object **3** AUS a **light globe**

globe 'artichoke *noun* [C] a plant which has a round mass of pointed leaf-like parts, which are eaten as a vegetable, surrounding its flower ➔See picture **Vegetables** on page Centre 2

globetrotter /ˈgləʊbˌtrɒt.əʳ/ US /ˈgloʊbˌtrɑː.t̬ɚ/ *noun* [C] someone who travels frequently to a lot of different countries: *Japan last month, New York next month – you've become a regular globetrotter, haven't you?* **globetrotting** /ˈgləʊbˌtrɒt.ɪŋ/ US /ˈgloʊbˌtrɑː.t̬ɪŋ/ *noun* [U], *adj: The Prime Minister's globetrotting has led to accusations that he is ignoring domestic problems.* ○ *a globetrotting lifestyle*

globule /ˈglɒb.juːl/ US /ˈglɑːb-/ *noun* [C] a small ball of something, especially a drop of liquid: *The disease is caused by globules of fat blocking the blood vessels.* **globular** /ˈglɒb.jʊ.ləʳ/ US /ˈglɑːb.jə.lɚ/ *adj* shaped like a ball

glockenspiel /ˈglɒk.ən.ʃpiːl/ US /ˈglɑː.kən.spiːl/ *noun* [C] a musical instrument made of flat metal bars of different lengths which you hit with a pair of small hammers

glom /glɒm/ US /glɑːm/ *verb*

▲ **glom onto** *sth/sb phrasal verb* US INFORMAL **1** to become very interested in something such as a new idea or fashion or in someone: *Retailers are glomming onto a new fashion among teens for outsize clothes.* ○ *This guy glommed onto me at Tasha's party and wouldn't take no for an answer.* **2** to get or take something that you want: *He's glommed onto a couple of my tapes and I can't get them back off him.*

gloom WITHOUT HOPE /gluːm/ *noun* [U] feelings of great unhappiness and loss of hope: *Bergman's films are often full of gloom and despair.* ○ *There is widespread gloom and doom about the company's future.* **gloomy** /ˈgluː.mi/ *adj: a gloomy economic forecast* ○ *The vet is rather gloomy about my cat's chances of recovery.* ○ *The cemetery is a gloomy place.* **gloomily** /ˈgluː.mɪ.li/ *adv* **gloominess** /ˈgluː.mɪ.nəs/ *noun* [U]

gloom DARKNESS /gluːm/ *noun* [U] when it is nearly dark and difficult to see well: *She peered into the gloom, but she couldn't see where the noise was coming from.* ○ *A figure emerged from the gloom of the corridor.* **gloomy** /ˈgluː.mi/ *adj: What gloomy weather we're having!* ○ *We waited in a gloomy waiting-room.*

gloop /gluːp/ *noun* [U] UK INFORMAL any thick liquid or sticky substance

glop /glɒp/ US /glɑːp/ *noun* [U] INFORMAL any thick unpleasant liquid, especially food: *The soup was a greyish glop, with bits in it.*

glorify /ˈglɔː.rɪ.faɪ/ US /ˈglɔːr.ɪ-/ *verb* [T] **1** to make something seem splendid or excellent, often when it is really not: *I didn't like the way the film glorified war/violence.* ○ INFORMAL *My word processor's really just a glorified typewriter.* **2** to praise and honour God or a person: *There are 99 prayer beads – one for each way Allah can be glorified in the Koran.* ○ *A statue was erected to glorify the country's national heroes.* **glorification** /ˌglɔː.rɪ.fɪˈkeɪ.ʃən/ US /ˌglɔːr.ɪ-/ *noun* [U] *He criticized the entertain-*

ment industry for the glorification of violence. ○ *Cathedrals are built for the glorification of God.*

the ˌGlorious ˈTwelfth *noun UK* the start of the GROUSE (= a big bird) shooting season in Britain

glory [ADMIRATION] /ˈglɔː.ri/ [US] /ˈglɔːr.i/ *noun* **1** **[U]** great admiration, honour and praise which you earn by doing something successfully: *He revelled in the glory* ***of*** *scoring three goals in the final 8 minutes.* ○ *This was her final professional match, and she wanted to end her career in* ***a blaze of*** *glory.* **2** **[C]** an important achievement which earns someone great admiration, honour and praise: *The reunion is an opportunity for the soldiers to remember their past glories.* **3** **[U]** praise and thanks, especially as given to God: *Glory be to God!* ○ *He dedicated his poetry to the glory of God.*

• **cover *yourself* in/with glory** to be very successful and earn admiration: *He didn't exactly cover himself with glory in his last job.*

• **bask/bathe in reflected glory** to feel successful and admired for something, despite the fact that you did not achieve it yourself but were only connected to it in some way: *The government is bathing in the reflected glory of its victorious military forces.*

glorious /ˈglɔː.ri.əs/ [US] /ˈglɔːr.i-/ *adj* deserving great admiration, praise and honour: *a glorious victory* ○ *a memorial to the glorious dead of two world wars* **gloriously** /ˈglɔː.ri.ə.sli/ [US] /ˈglɔːr.i-/ *adv*

glory [BEAUTY] /ˈglɔː.ri/ [US] /ˈglɔːr.i/ *noun* **[C or U]** great beauty, or something splendid or extremely beautiful, which gives great pleasure: *They want to restore the castle to its former glory.* ○ *The garden* ***in all*** *its glory is now open to the public.*

• **crowning glory** the greatest or most beautiful thing: *The ballroom is the crowning glory* ***of*** *the palace.* ○ *Her hair is her crowning glory.*

glorious /ˈglɔː.ri.əs/ [US] /ˈglɔːr.i-/ *adj* **1** very beautiful: *The beetroot had turned the soup a glorious pink.* ○ *Your roses are glorious!* **2** describes weather that is very pleasant, especially weather that is hot and sunny: *They had glorious weather for their wedding.* ○ *It was a glorious winter day – crisp and clear.* **3** very enjoyable or giving great pleasure: *This wine is absolutely glorious.* ○ *We had a glorious time in the south of France last summer.* **gloriously** /ˈglɔː.ri.ə.sli/ [US] /ˈglɔːr.i-/ *adv*: *We've had gloriously sunny weather.* ○ *They looked gloriously happy.*

glory /ˈglɔː.ri/ [US] /ˈglɔːr.i/ *verb*

▲ **glory in *sth*** *phrasal verb* to feel or show great pride and happiness about something: *He is still glorying in the success of his first Hollywood film.* ○ *She glories in the fact that she's much better qualified than her sister.*

ˈglory ˌdays *plural noun* Someone's glory days are a period of time when they were very successful: *Her popularity as a singer has waned since the glory days of the 1980s.*

gloss [APPEARANCE] /glɒs/ [US] /glɑːs/ *noun* **[S or U]** a smooth shiny appearance on the surface of something, or paint or a similar substance which produces this appearance: *Marble can be polished to* ***a*** *high gloss.* ○ *This varnish provides a long-lasting and hard-wearing gloss* ***finish.*** ○ ***lip*** *gloss* ○ *We'll need a litre of gloss* ***(paint)*** *to cover the woodwork.*

• **put a gloss on *sth*** to emphasize the good parts of something that has been done, especially those which are to your advantage, and to avoid the bad parts: *Politics is all about putting a* ***good*** *gloss on unpleasant or difficult situations.*

• **take the gloss off *sth*** to make an event or occasion less special and enjoyable: *The bad weather really took the gloss off our trip to the zoo.*

glossy /ˈglɒs.i/ [US] /ˈglɑː.si/ *adj* **1** smooth and shiny: *She has wonderfully glossy hair.* ○ *a dog with a glossy coat* **2** describes a book or magazine which has been produced on shiny and expensive paper and contains many colour pictures: *a glossy coffee-table book* ○ *a pile of glossy magazines/car brochures*

glossy /ˈglɒs.i/ [US] /ˈglɑː.si/ *noun* **[C]** *US* a photograph printed on smooth shiny paper

glossiness /ˈglɒs.ɪ.nəs/ [US] /ˈglɑː.sɪ-/ *noun* **[U]** the quality of being glossy

gloss [EXPLANATION] /glɒs/ [US] /glɑːs/ *verb* **[T]** to provide an explanation for a word or phrase: *In the school edition of the book, the older and more rare words have been glossed.*

gloss /glɒs/ [US] /glɑːs/ *noun* **[C]** an explanation for a word or phrase: *Difficult expressions are explained in the glosses at the bottom of the page.*

▲ **gloss over *sth*** *phrasal verb* to avoid considering something, such as an embarrassing mistake, to make it seem unimportant, and to quickly continue talking about something else: *She glossed over the company's fall in profits, focusing instead on her plans for investment and modernization.* ○ *The film was well researched, but it glossed over the important issues.*

glossary /ˈglɒs.ᵊr.i/ [US] /ˈglɑː.sɚ-/ *noun* **[C]** an alphabetical list, with meanings, of the words or phrases in a text that are difficult to understand: *a glossary* ***of*** *technical terms*

ˌglossy magaˈzine *noun* **[C]** (*ALSO* **glossy**) a magazine printed on shiny high-quality paper which contains a lot of colour photographs and advertisements, usually about famous people, fashion and beauty

glottal stop /ˌglɒt.ᵊlˈstɒp/ [US] /ˌglɑː.t̬ᵊlˈstɑːp/ *noun* **[C]** *SPECIALIZED* a speech sound produced by closing the VOCAL CORDS and then opening them quickly so that the air from the lungs is released with force

glove /glʌv/ *noun* **[C]** a piece of clothing which is worn on the hand and wrist for warmth or protection, with separate parts for each finger: *leather/woollen/rubber gloves* ○ *a* ***pair of*** *gloves* ➲See picture **Sports** on page Centre 10

glove /glʌv/ *verb* **[T]** *US* **1** to put gloves on your hands: *She gloved her hands to protect them from the chemicals.* **2** to catch a ball when playing baseball: *He gloved the ball, turned and threw in one motion.*

gloved /glʌvd/ *adj* having a glove or gloves on: *She held out a gloved hand.*

ˈglove comˌpartment *noun* **[C]** (*ALSO* **glove box**) a small cupboard or shelf in the front of a car, used for storing small items ➲See picture **Car** on page Centre 12

ˈglove ˌpuppet *UK noun* **[C]** (*US* **hand puppet**) a toy person or animal which has a soft hollow body so that you can put your hand inside and move its head and arms with your fingers

glow /gləʊ/ [US] /gloʊ/ *verb* **[I]** **1** to produce a continuous light and sometimes heat: *A nightlight glowed dimly in the corner of the children's bedroom.* ○ *This substance is so radioactive that it glows in the dark.* **2** to look attractive because you are happy or healthy, especially with eyes that are shining: *The children's faces were glowing* ***with*** *excitement.* ○ *They came back from their week by the sea, glowing* ***with*** *health.*

glow /gləʊ/ [US] /gloʊ/ *noun* **[S]** **1** when something produces a continuous light and/or heat: *the glow* ***of*** *the fire* ○ *Neon emits a characteristic red glow.* **2** a positive feeling: *They felt a glow* ***of*** *pride as they watched their daughter collect the award.* ○ *She felt a* ***warm*** *glow* ***of*** *satisfaction.*

glower /ˈglaʊ.əʳ/ [US] /-ɚ/ *verb* **[I]** to look very angry, annoyed or threatening: *There's no point glowering* ***at*** *me like that – you know the rules.* ○ *FIGURATIVE Large black rain clouds glowered* (= looked likely to produce rain) *in the sky.* **glower** /ˈglaʊ.əʳ/ [US] /-ɚ/ *noun* **[C]** *an angry glower*

glowing /ˈgləʊ.ɪŋ/ [US] /ˈgloʊ-/ *adj* praising with enthusiasm: *In her speech, she paid a glowing* ***tribute*** *to her predecessor.* ○ *His latest book has received glowing* ***reviews.*** **glowingly** /ˈgləʊ.ɪŋ.li/ [US] /ˈgloʊ-/ *adv*

glow-worm /ˈgləʊ.wɜːm/ [US] /ˈgloʊ.wɝːm/ *noun* **[C]** a beetle, of which the females and young produce a green light from the tail

glucose /ˈgluː.kəʊs/ [US] /-koʊs/ *noun* **[U]** a type of sugar which is found in plants, especially fruit, and which supplies an important part of the energy animals need

glue /gluː/ *noun* **[U]** a sticky substance which is used for joining things together permanently, produced from animal bones and skins or by a chemical process **glue** /gluː/ *verb* **[T usually + adv or prep]** **glueing** or **gluing**, **glued**, **glued** *Is it worth trying to glue this plate back together?*

○ *I've nearly finished making my model aeroplane – I just have to glue the wings* **on**.

● **be glued to** *sth INFORMAL* to be unable to stop watching something: *We were glued to the television watching the election results come in*.

● **glued to the spot** *INFORMAL* unable to move because you are very frightened, nervous or interested: *I just stood there, glued to the spot*.

gluey /ˈɡluː.i/ *adj* **gluier**, **gluiest** covered with glue: *You'd better wash those gluey hands of yours*.

'glue ,sniffer *noun* [C] someone who breathes in the dangerous gases produced by some types of glue to achieve an excited mental condition **'glue ,sniffing** *noun* [U] *Drugs, glue sniffing and under-age drinking are prevalent amongst the older teenagers*.

glum /ɡlʌm/ *adj INFORMAL* disappointed or unhappy, and quiet: *You look glum. What's up?* ○ *He's very glum* **about** *the company's prospects*. **glumly** /ˈɡlʌm.li/ *adv*: *"I'll never find another job at my age," she said glumly*. **glumness** /ˈɡlʌm.nəs/ *noun* [U]

glut /ɡlʌt/ *noun* [C] a supply of something that is much greater than can be sold or is needed or wanted: *The fall in demand for coffee could cause a glut* **on/in the market**. ○ *The current glut* **of** *graduates means that many of them will not be able to find jobs*. **glut** /ɡlʌt/ *verb* [T often passive] -**tt**- *Higher mortgage rates and over-building left some markets glutted with unsold houses*.

gluten /ˈɡluː.tᵊn/ ⑩ /-t̬ᵊn/ *noun* [U] a protein which is contained in wheat and some other grains: *a gluten-free diet*

glutinous /ˈɡluː.tɪ.nəs/ ⑩ /-t̬ɪ-/ *adj* sticky: *Short-grain rice turns into a soft glutinous mass when cooked*.

glutton /ˈɡlʌt.ᵊn/ ⑩ /ˈɡlʌt̬-/ *noun* [C] *DISAPPROVING* a person who regularly eats and drinks more than is needed

● **be a glutton for** *sth* to like something very much: *Sophie is a glutton for books*.

● **be a glutton for punishment** to be someone who seems to enjoy doing something that you consider unpleasant: *He's a real glutton for punishment, taking on all that extra work without getting paid for it*.

gluttonous /ˈɡlʌt.ᵊn.əs/ ⑩ /ˈɡlʌt̬-/ *adj DISAPPROVING* eating and drinking more than you need **gluttonously** /ˈɡlʌt.ᵊn.ə.sli/ ⑩ /ˈɡlʌt̬-/ *adv*

gluttony /ˈɡlʌt.ᵊn.i/ ⑩ /ˈɡlʌt̬-/ *noun* [U] *DISAPPROVING* when people eat and drink more than they need to: *They treat Christmas as just another excuse for gluttony*.

glycerine, *US ALSO* **glycerin** /ˈɡlɪs.ᵊr.iːn/ /-ɪn/ ⑩ /-ɚ.rɪn/ *noun* [U] a colourless sweet thick liquid which is used in making explosives and medicines and for sweetening foods ⊃Compare **nitroglycerine**.

gm *noun WRITTEN ABBREVIATION FOR* **gram**

GM /ˌdʒiːˈem/ *adj* [before n] *ABBREVIATION FOR* **genetically modified**

,GM 'food *noun* [U] genetically modified food: food from crops whose genes have been scientifically changed: *Agricultural companies have failed to convince consumers that GM foods are safe*.

GMO /ˌdʒiː.emˈəʊ/ ⑩ /-ˈoʊ/ *noun* [U] *ABBREVIATION FOR* genetically modified organism: a plant or animal whose genes have been scientifically changed

GMT /ˌdʒiː.emˈtiː/ *noun* [U] *ABBREVIATION FOR* **Greenwich Mean Time**

gnarled /nɑːld/ ⑩ /nɑːrld/ *adj* rough and twisted, especially because of old age or a lack of protection from bad weather: *a gnarled tree trunk* ○ *The old man drew a long gnarled finger across his throat*.

gnash /næʃ/ *verb* **gnash** *your* **teeth** to bring your teeth forcefully together when you are angry: *The monster roared and gnashed its teeth*.

,gnashing of 'teeth *noun* [U] (*ALSO* **teeth-gnashing**) *HUMOROUS* angry noise and upset: *There has been much gnashing of teeth about the proposal to close the hospital*.

gnat /næt/ *noun* [C] a very small flying insect that bites animals and people

gnaw /nɔː/ ⑩ /nɑː/ *verb* [I + prep; T] to bite or chew something repeatedly, usually making a hole in it or gradually destroying it: *Babies like to gnaw hard objects when they're teething*. ○ *A dog lay under the table, gnawing on a bone*.

gnaw FEEL ANXIOUS /nɔː/ ⑩ /nɑː/ *verb* [I + prep; T] to make you feel anxious or uncomfortable: *I've been gnawed* **by** *guilt about not replying to her letter yet*. ○ *The feeling that I've forgotten something has been gnawing* **at** *me all day*.

gnawing /ˈnɔː.ɪŋ/ ⑩ /ˈnɑː-/ *adj* continuously uncomfortable, worrying or painful: *I've had gnawing doubts about this project for some time*. ○ *After three days, we felt an agonizing, gnawing hunger*.

▲ **gnaw away at** *sth phrasal verb* to gradually reduce or spoil something: *Bad debts are continuing to gnaw away at the bank's profits*.

gnocchi /ˈnjɒk-/ ⑩ /ˈnjɑː.ki/ *plural noun* small round balls made from potato or wheat flour mixed with water, served in soup or with sauce

gnome /nəʊm/ ⑩ /noʊm/ *noun* [C] **1** an imaginary, very small, old man with a beard and a pointed hat, in traditional children's stories **2** a model of a gnome used as a garden decoration: *I don't think* **garden** *gnomes are in very good taste*.

● **the gnomes of Zurich** *LITERARY* the powerful BANKERS (= people who own or control banks) from Switzerland who control a lot of money, much of it belonging to foreign governments

gnomic /ˈnəʊ.mɪk/ ⑩ /ˈnoʊ-/ *adj FORMAL* describes something spoken or written that is brief, mysterious and not easily understood, but often seems wise: *Peter is always coming out with gnomic utterances/pronouncements*.

GNP /ˌdʒiː.enˈpiː/ *noun* [U] *ABBREVIATION FOR* Gross National Product: the total value of goods and services produced by a country in one year, including profits made in foreign countries ⊃Compare **GDP**.

gnu /nuː/ *noun* [C] *plural* **gnu** or **gnus** a large African animal with a long tail and horns that curve to the sides, which lives in areas covered with grass

---

USAGE

Forms of the verb **to go**.

This is a table of all the usual forms of the irregular verb **to go**.

Present tense	past tense
I go	I went
you go	you went
he/she/it goes	he/she/it went
we go	we went
you go	you went
they go	they went

past participle

gone	They have gone to the cinema.

(NOTE: also look at the word **been**)

present participle

going	Where are you going, Brian?

---

go MOVE/TRAVEL /ɡəʊ/ ⑩ /ɡoʊ/ *verb* **going**, **went**, **gone** **1** [I usually + adv or prep] to travel or move to another place: *We went into the house*. ○ *I went to Paris last summer. Have you ever been there?* ○ *We don't go to the cinema very often these days*. ○ *Wouldn't it be quicker to go by train?* ○ *Does this train go to Newcastle?* ○ *Where do you think you're going? Shouldn't you be at school?* **2** [I usually + adv or prep] to be in the process of moving: *Can't we go any faster?* ○ *We were going* **along** *at about 50 miles an hour*. ○ *to go* **down** *the road* ○ *to go* **up/down** *stairs* ○ *to go* **over** *the bridge* ○ *to go* **through** *a tunnel* ○ *FIGURATIVE I've got a tune going* **around/round** *in my head (= I am continually hearing it) and I just can't remember the name of it*. **3** [I] to move or travel somewhere in order to do something: [+ v-ing] *I've never gone* **shopping** *every Friday night*. ○ *I've never gone* **skiing**. ○ *They've gone* **for** *a walk, but they should be back soon*. ○ [+ to infinitive] *She's gone* **to** *meet Brian at the station*. ○ *There's a good film on at the Odeon. Shall we go?* **4 where has/have** *sth*

gone? said when you cannot find something: *Where have my keys gone?*

• **go and...** *INFORMAL* used to express disapproval of something that is done: *He's gone and lost* (= He has lost) *that wallet I gave him for his birthday.* ○ *Mike's really gone and* ***done it*** *now – he'll be in terrible trouble for breaking that window.*

• **as *you* go along** as you are doing a job or activity: *We have a flexible approach to what we're doing that allows us to make any necessary changes as we go along.*

• **go it alone** to do something without other people: *He's decided to leave the band and go it alone as a singer.*

• **not go there** to not start to think about or discuss a subject: *"Then there's the guilt I feel about leaving her for seven hours every day." "Don't* ***even*** *go there!"*

-goer /-gəʊ.əʳ/ [US] /-goʊ.ɚ/ *suffix* a person who goes to the stated type of place: *Restaurant-goers ought to complain more about bad food and service.* ○ *regular filmgoers*

-going /-gəʊ.ɪŋ/ [US] /-goʊ-/ *suffix* refers to the activity of going to the stated place: *He grew up in a strict church-going family.*

USAGE

gone **or** been?

The past participle of 'go' is **gone**.

I'm sorry but she's gone abroad on business – she'll be back next week.

Sometimes, however, **been** is used to say that someone has gone somewhere and come back, or to say that someone has visited somewhere.

He's been abroad many times.

go [LEAVE] /gəʊ/ [US] /goʊ/ *verb* **[I] going, went, gone 1** to leave a place, especially in order to travel to somewhere else: *Is it midnight already? I really must go/must be going.* ○ *She wasn't feeling well, so she went* ***home*** *early.* ○ **[mainly UK]** *What time does the last train to Bath go?* ○ *I'm afraid he'll have to go* (= be dismissed from his job) *– he's far too inefficient to continue working for us.* ○ *This carpet's terribly old and worn – it really will have to go* (= be got rid of). **2** *POLITE WORD FOR* to die: *She went peacefully in her sleep.*

• **to go** *MAINLY US* If you ask for some food to go at a restaurant, you want it wrapped up so that you can take it away with you instead of eating it in the restaurant: *I'd like a cheeseburger and strawberry milk shake to go, please.* ➲See also **takeaway**.

gone /gɒn/ [US] /gɑːn/ *adj* **[after v] 1** dead: *Fortunately I'll be* ***dead and*** *gone long before the money runs out.* ○ *They did everything they could to save him, but he was already* ***too far*** *gone* (= too close to death) *when the ambulance arrived.* **2** If something is gone, there is none of it left: *All my money is gone and I have nothing to buy food with.*

• **be gone on *sb*** *INFORMAL* to like someone a lot: *Nicky's really gone on Marty.*

goner /ˈgɒn.əʳ/ [US] /ˈgɑː.nɚ/ *noun* **[C usually sing]** *INFORMAL* a person or thing that has no chance of continuing to live: *I thought I was a goner when I saw that car heading towards me.*

go [LEAD] /gəʊ/ [US] /goʊ/ *verb* **going, went, gone 1 [I + adv or prep]** If a road, path, etc. goes in a particular direction, it leads there: *This road goes* ***to*** *Birmingham.* ○ *A huge crack went* ***from*** *the top* ***to*** *the bottom of the wall.* **2 [I usually + adv or prep]** to continue for a particular length: *The tree's roots go* ***down*** *three metres.*

go [FUTURE TIME] /ˈgəʊ.ɪŋ/ [US] /ˈgoʊ-/ **1 be going to *do/be sth*** to intend to do or be something in the future: *Are you going to go to Claire's party?* ○ *He wants me to mend his shirt for him, but I'm not going to!* ○ *I'm going to be a famous pop star when I'm older.* **2 be going to *do/be sth*** to be certain or expected to happen in the future: *They're going to have a baby in the spring.* ○ *There's going to be trouble when Paul finds out about this.* ○ *The forecast said it was going to be hot and sunny tomorrow.*

go [BECOME] /gəʊ/ [US] /goʊ/ *verb* **[L only + adj] going, went, gone** to become: *The idea of going grey doesn't bother me, but I'd hate to go bald.* ○ *Her father's going senile/blind/deaf.* ○ *If anything goes* ***wrong****, you can call our emergency hotline free of charge.* ○ *After 12 years of Republican presidents, the US went Democratic in 1992.*

• ***sth* gone mad** a particular type of thing that has gone out of control: *He described the new regulations as bureaucracy gone mad.*

go [BE] /gəʊ/ [US] /goʊ/ *verb* **[L only + adj] going, went, gone** to be or stay in a particular, especially unpleasant, condition: *In spite of the relief effort, thousands of people continue to go hungry.* ○ *Why do so many rapes go unreported?*

• **as...go** in comparison with most other things of a particular type, especially when you do not think that type of thing is very good: *It was quite a good film, as horror films go.* ○ *I suppose the concert was OK, as* ***these things*** *go.*

• **go to prove/show** to prove that something is true: *Your daughter's attitude* ***only*** *goes to prove how much society has changed over the last 30 years.*

going /ˈgəʊ.ɪŋ/ [US] /ˈgoʊ-/ *adj* **[after n]** available or existing: *I wouldn't trust him if I were you – he's the biggest crook going* (= he's the most dishonest person that exists). ○ *I don't suppose there's any left-over pie going, is there?*

• **have *sth* going for *you*** If someone or something has something going for them, that thing causes them to have a lot of advantages and to be successful: *They've got a happy marriage, brilliant careers, wonderful kids – in fact they've got* ***everything*** *going for them.*

go [MOVE BODY] /gəʊ/ [US] /goʊ/ *verb* **[I usually + adv or prep] going, went, gone** to move a part of the body in a particular way or the way that is shown: *Go* ***like this with*** *your hand to show that you're turning left.*

go [START] /gəʊ/ [US] /goʊ/ *verb* **[I] going, went, gone** *INFORMAL* to start doing or using something: *I'll just connect up the printer to the computer and then we'll be ready to go.*

go [OPERATE] /gəʊ/ [US] /goʊ/ *verb* **[I] going, went, gone** to operate (in the right way): *Have you any idea why this watch won't go?* ○ *Can you help me get my car going?* ○ *Our company has been going* (= has been in business) *for twenty years.*

go [DIVIDE] /gəʊ/ [US] /goʊ/ *verb* **[I not continuous] went, gone** (of a number) to fit into another number especially resulting in a whole number: *5* ***into*** *11 won't go.* ○ *5 goes* ***into*** *11 twice with 1 left over.*

go [WEAKEN] /gəʊ/ [US] /goʊ/ *verb* **[I] going, went, gone** to become weak or damaged, especially from being used (too much), or to stop working: *After a gruelling six months singing on a world tour, it is hardly surprising that her voice is starting to go.* ○ *I really must get a new jacket – this one's starting to go at the elbows.* ○ *Her hearing is going, but otherwise she's remarkably fit for a 95-year-old.*

go [TIME] /gəʊ/ [US] /goʊ/ *verb* **[I] going, went, gone** If a period of time goes, it passes: *I had a wonderful weekend but it went awfully quickly.* ○ *Time seems to go faster as you get older.* ○ *There's only a week* ***to*** *go before* (= until) *my exam results come out.*

go [NOISE] /gəʊ/ [US] /goʊ/ *verb* **[I or T] going, went, gone** to produce a noise: *I think I heard the doorbell go* (= ring) *just now.* ○ *I wish my computer would stop going 'beep' whenever I do something wrong.*

go [BE EXPRESSED] /gəʊ/ [US] /goʊ/ *verb* **[I not continuous] went, gone** to be expressed, sung or played: *I can never remember* ***how*** *that song goes.* ○ *"Doesn't it go something* ***like*** *this?" said Joan, and played the first couple of bars on her guitar.* ○ **[+ (that)]** *The story goes* (= People say) ***(that)*** *he was sacked after he was caught stealing company property.* ○ *A headless ghost walks the castle at night – or* ***so*** *the story goes* (= so people say).

• **the same/that goes for *sb/sth*** what I have said about one person or thing is also true for or relates to another person or thing: *You really need to smarten up your appearance, Chris – and the same goes for the rest of you.*

go [SAY] /gəʊ/ [US] /goʊ/ *verb* **[+ speech] going, went, gone** *INFORMAL* to say, especially when a story is being told: *"I never want to see you ever again," he goes, and storms out the house.*

go [HAPPEN] /gəʊ/ [US] /goʊ/ *verb* **[I usually + adv or prep] going, went, gone** to happen or be found habitually or typically with each other or another: *Wisdom and maturity don't necessarily go* ***together***. ○ *She knows all about the health problems that go* ***with*** *smoking*. ○ *Great wealth often goes* ***hand in hand with*** *meanness.*

go [BE SOLD] /gəʊ/ [US] /goʊ/ *verb* [I] **going, went, gone** to be sold or be available: *The shop is having a closing-down sale – everything must go.* ○ *The painting will go* ***to*** *the highest bidder.* ○ *I bought some flowers that were going* ***cheap***. ○ *"Going... going... gone!* (= Sold!)*" said the auctioneer, banging down the hammer.*

go [BE ACCEPTABLE] /gəʊ/ [US] /goʊ/ *verb* [I not continuous] **went, gone** to look or be acceptable or suitable: *That picture would go* ***well*** *on the wall in the living room.* ○ *The TV would go nicely* ***in*** *that corner, wouldn't it?* ○ *If I wear the orange hat with the blue dress, do you think it will go?* ○ *Just remember that I'm the boss and what I say goes* (= you have to accept what I say). ○ *My parents don't worry too much about what I get up to, and most of the time* ***anything*** *goes* (= I can do what I want).

G

go [BE SITUATED] /gəʊ/ [US] /goʊ/ *verb* [I usually + adv or prep; not continuous] **went, gone** to be put in a particular place, especially as the usual place: *The sofa went* ***against*** *that wall before we had the radiator put in.* ○ *I'll put it all away if you tell me* ***where*** *everything goes.*

go [BE KNOWN] /gəʊ/ [US] /goʊ/ *verb* [I usually + adv or prep] **going, went, gone** to be known (by a particular name): *He had a scruffy old teddy bear which went* ***by the name of*** *Augustus.* ○ *In Britain, this flour usually goes* ***under the name of*** *maize meal.*

go [DEVELOP] /gəʊ/ [US] /goʊ/ *verb* [I usually + adv or prep] **going, went, gone** to develop or happen: *"****How*** *did the interview go?" "It went very well, thanks."* ○ *Things have gone badly* ***for*** *him since his business collapsed.*

go [OPPORTUNITY] (*plural* **goes**) /gəʊ/ [US] /goʊ/ *noun* [C] (*US USUALLY* **turn**) an opportunity to play in a game, or to do or use something: *Hey, it's Ken's go now! You've just had your go.* ○ *Please can I* ***have a*** *go* (= can I ride) *on your bike?* ○ *I'll* ***have a*** *go* ***at*** *driv****ing*** *for a while if you're tired.*

go /gəʊ/ [US] /goʊ/ *verb* [I] **going, went, gone** to use your opportunity to play in a game: *It's your turn to go now.*

go [ATTEMPT] (*plural* **goes**) /gəʊ/ [US] /goʊ/ *noun* [C] (*US USUALLY* **try**) an attempt to do something: *Georgina passed her driving test (****on*** *her) first go.* ○ *"This jar is impossible to open." "Here, let me* ***have*** *a go."* ○ *I want to* ***have a*** *go* ***at*** *finish****ing*** *my essay tonight.* ○ *We can't do the work* ***all in one*** *go* (= all at the same time).

• **be no go** *INFORMAL* to be impossible or ineffective, or to not happen: *They tried for hours to get her to come down from the roof, but it was no go.* ○ *The launch was no go due to the weather.*

• **make a go of *sth*** to try to make something succeed, usually by working hard: *She's really making a go of her new antique shop.* ○ *I can't see him ever making a go of accountancy.*

go [CRITICIZE] /gəʊ/ [US] /goʊ/ *noun UK* **have a go at *sb*** to criticize someone: *My Dad's always having a go at me about getting a proper job.*

go [ENERGY] /gəʊ/ [US] /goʊ/ *noun* [U] the condition of being energetic and active: *You're full of go this morning.* ○ *He doesn't have much go about him, does he?* ➲See also **get-up-and-go**.

PHRASAL VERBS WITH **go** ▼

▲ **go about *sth*** *phrasal verb* to begin to do something or deal with something: *What's the best way of going about this?* ○ [+ v-ing] *How can we go about solv****ing*** *this problem?*

• **go about *your* business** to continue doing what you usually do: *In spite of last night's terrorist attack, most people seem to be going about their business as if nothing had happened.*

▲ **go after *sb*** *phrasal verb* **1** to chase or follow someone in order to catch them: *The police went after him but he got away.* **2** *INFORMAL* to try to obtain something: *Are you planning to go after Paul's job when he leaves?*

▲ **go against *sth/sb*** *phrasal verb* to oppose or disagree with something or someone: *Public opinion is going against the government on this issue.* ○ *What you're asking me to do goes against everything I believe in.*

▲ **go against *sb*** *phrasal verb* If a decision or vote goes against someone, they do not get the result that they needed: *The judge's decision went against us.* ○ *The vote went against her* (= She lost the vote).

▲ **go ahead** *phrasal verb* **1** to start to do something: *We've received permission to go ahead* ***with*** *the music festival in spite of opposition from local residents.* ○ *I got so fed up with waiting for him to do it that I just went ahead and did it myself.* **2** *INFORMAL* said to someone in order to give them permission to start to do something: *"Could I ask you a rather personal question?" "Sure, go ahead."* **3** If an event goes ahead, it happens: *The festival is now going ahead as planned.* **go-ahead** /ˈgəʊ.ə.hed/ [US] /ˈgoʊ-/ *noun* [S] *The government has* ***given the*** *go-ahead* (= given permission) *for a multi-billion pound road-building project.* ○ *We're ready to start but we're still waiting to* ***get the*** *go-ahead from our head office.*

go-ahead /ˈgəʊ.ə.hed/ [US] /ˈgoʊ-/ *adj UK* enthusiastic about using new inventions and modern methods of doing things: *We have a flexitime system and crèche facilities and like to think of ourselves as a go-ahead employer.*

▲ **go along** [PLACE] *phrasal verb UK* to go to a place or event, usually without much planning: *I might go along* ***to*** *the party later.*

▲ **go along** [CONTINUE] *phrasal verb* to continue doing something: *I'll explain the rules as we go along.*

▲ **go along with *sth/sb*** *phrasal verb* to support an idea, or to agree with someone's opinion: *Kate's already agreed, but it's going to be harder persuading Mike to go along with it.*

▲ **go around** *phrasal verb US FOR* **go round**

▲ **go at *sth*** [DO] *phrasal verb INFORMAL* to start doing something with a lot of energy and enthusiasm: *He went at* (= ate eagerly) *his dinner as if he hadn't had anything to eat for weeks.*

▲ **go at *sb*** [ATTACK] *phrasal verb* to attack someone: *Suddenly, he went at me with a knife.*

▲ **go away** [LEAVE] *phrasal verb* **1** to leave a place: *Go away and leave me alone!* ✻ NOTE: This is usually used in the imperative form to tell someone to leave a place. **2** to leave your home in order to spend time somewhere else, usually for a holiday: *We usually go away for the summer.* ○ *He goes away on business a lot.*

▲ **go away** [DISAPPEAR] *phrasal verb* to disappear: *It was weeks before the bruises went away.*

▲ **go back** [ORIGIN] *phrasal verb* to have existed since a time in the past: *Their relationship goes back* ***to*** *when they were at university together.* ○ *Our house goes back* ***to*** (= has existed since) *the 18th century.*

▲ **go back** [RETURN] *phrasal verb* **1** to return: *That restaurant was terrible – I'm never going back there again.* ○ *I'll have to go back* ***for*** *my umbrella.* ○ *Do you think you'll ever go back* ***to*** *London?* ○ *When do you go back* ***to*** *school?* ○ *Let's go back* ***to*** *the beginning and start again.* ○ *We can always go back* ***to*** *the original plan if necessary.* **2** to be returned: *When are these library books due to go back ?* ○ *That TV will have to go back* ***to*** *the shop – it hasn't worked properly ever since I bought it.*

▲ **go back on *sth*** *phrasal verb* to fail to keep a promise, or to change a decision or agreement: *The government looks likely to go back on its decision to close the mines.* ○ *She's gone back on* ***her word*** *and decided not to give me the job after all.*

▲ **go back to *sb*** [RELATIONSHIP] *phrasal verb* to start a relationship again with a person you had a romantic relationship with in the past: *I hear he's ended the affair and gone back to his wife.*

▲ **go back to *sth*** [ACTIVITY] *phrasal verb* to start doing something again that you were doing before: *It's time to go back to work.*

▲ **go by** [MOVE PAST] *phrasal verb* to move past, in space or time: *You can watch the trains going by from this window.* ○ *You can't let an opportunity like that go by – it's too good to miss.* ○ *Hardly a day goes by when I don't think about her.*

• **in days gone by** in the past: *The house was a railway station in days gone by.*

▲ **go by** *sth* FOLLOW *phrasal verb* to follow something or be shown the way by something: *I'm sorry, madam, but we have to go by the rules.*

▲ **go by** *sth* BASE *phrasal verb* to base an opinion, decision or judgment on something: *What do you go by when you're deciding whether or not to employ someone?* ○ *Going by what she said yesterday, I would say she's about to resign.* ○ *If past experience* **is anything to** *go by, he'll completely ignore our suggestions and then change his mind at the last minute.*

▲ **go down** *(sth)* MOVE DOWN *phrasal verb* to move down to a lower level or place: *He went down on his knees and begged for forgiveness.* ○ *He first went down the mines when he was 17.* ○ *The plane went down (= fell to the ground because of an accident, bomb, etc.) ten minutes after take-off.* ○ *Everyone took to the lifeboats when the ship started to go down (= sink).* ○ *Could I have a glass of water to help these pills go down (= to help me swallow them)?*

▲ **go down** *(sth)* REACH *phrasal verb* to reach or go as far as: *Its roots can go down three metres.* ○ *This path goes down* **to** *the river.* ○ *Go down to (= Read as far as) the bottom of the page.*

▲ **go down** SUN *phrasal verb* When the sun goes down, it moves down in the sky until it cannot be seen any more: *On summer evenings we would sit on the verandah and watch the sun go down.*

▲ **go down** BE REDUCED *phrasal verb* to be reduced in price, value, amount, quality, level or size: *The temperature went down* **to** *minus ten last night.* ○ *The company's shares went down 7p* **to** *53p.* ○ *The swelling's gone down but there's still a lot of bruising.* ○ *He went down in my* **estimation** *when he started trying to be a singer as well as an actor.*

▲ **go down** BE REMEMBERED *phrasal verb* to be remembered or recorded in a particular way: *Hurricane Hugo will go down* **in** *the record books* **as** *the costliest storm ever faced by insurers.*

▲ **go down** BE RECEIVED *phrasal verb* to be received in a particular way: *I think my speech went down rather* **well,** *don't you?*

▲ **go down** LOSE *phrasal verb* to lose or be defeated: *England's unbeaten run of ten games ended last night when they went down 4-2 to France.* ○ *Dictators rarely go down without a fight.*

▲ **go down** PRISON *phrasal verb* UK SLANG to be put in prison: *She went down* **for** *three years for her part in the robbery.*

▲ **go down** COMPUTER *phrasal verb* If a computer system goes down, it stops working: *The battery should prevent the computer system from going down in the event of a power cut.*

▲ **go down** HAPPEN *phrasal verb* US SLANG If an event such as a crime or a DEAL goes down, it happens: *I tried to tell Tyrell what was going down, but he wouldn't listen.*

▲ **go down** LEAVE *phrasal verb* UK OLD-FASHIONED If you go down from a college or university, especially Oxford University or Cambridge University, you leave either permanently or for a holiday.

▲ **go down on** *sb phrasal verb* SLANG to use the tongue and lips to touch someone's sexual organs in order to give pleasure

▲ **go down with** *sth* UK *phrasal verb* (ALSO **come down with** *sth*) to start to suffer from an infectious disease: *Half of Martha's class has gone down with flu.*

▲ **go for** *sb* ATTACK *phrasal verb* to attack someone: *Their dog had to be put to sleep after it went for the postwoman.*

▲ **go for** *sth* TRY *phrasal verb* to try to have or achieve something: *She tripped me as I went for the ball.* ○ *Are you planning to go for that scholarship to Harvard University?* ○ *The Russian relay team will again be going for the gold medal at the Olympic Games.*

● **go for it** INFORMAL to do anything you have to in order to get something: *"I'm thinking of applying for that job." "Go for it!"* ✳ NOTE: Usually used in the imperative.

▲ **go for** *sth* CHOOSE *phrasal verb* to choose something: *Instead of butter, I always go for margarine or a low-fat spread.*

▲ **go for** *sth* LIKE *phrasal verb* to like or admire: *I don't go for war films in a big way (= very much).* ○ *What sort of men do you go for (= are you attracted to)?*

▲ **go for** *sth* MONEY *phrasal verb* If something goes for a certain amount of money, it is sold for that amount: *The painting is expected to go for at least a million dollars.*

▲ **go in** ENTER *phrasal verb* to enter a place: *I looked through the window, but I didn't actually go in.*

▲ **go in** BECOME HIDDEN *phrasal verb* If the sun goes in, it becomes hidden from view by clouds.

▲ **go in** BE UNDERSTOOD *phrasal verb* MAINLY UK INFORMAL If a fact or piece of information goes in, you understand it or remember it: *No matter how many times you tell him something, it never seems to go in.*

▲ **go in for** *sth* COMPETE *phrasal verb* to take part in a competition: *Are you planning to go in for the 100 metres race?*

▲ **go in for** *sth* ENJOY *phrasal verb* to do something regularly, or to enjoy something: *I've never really gone in for classical music, but I love jazz.* ✳ NOTE: This is usually used in negative sentences.

▲ **go into** *sth* START *phrasal verb* **1** to start doing a particular type of work: *My son's planning to go into journalism.* ○ *She's decided to go into business as a freelance computer programmer.* **2** to start an activity, or start to be in a particular state or condition: *The drug is still being tested and will not go into commercial* **production** *for at least two years.* ○ *How many companies have gone into* **liquidation/receivership** *during the current recession?* ○ *Repeated death threats have forced them to go into* **hiding.** ○ *Her baby was born three hours after she went into* **labour.** ○ *Some of the fans seemed to go into* **a trance** *when she appeared on stage.*

▲ **go into** *sth* DISCUSS *phrasal verb* to discuss, examine, describe or explain something in a detailed or careful way: *This is the first book to go into her personal life as well as her work.* ○ *I'd rather not go into that now. Can we discuss it later?* ○ *I'm unable to go into* **detail(s)** *at this stage because I still have very little information about how the accident happened.*

▲ **go into** *sth* HIT *phrasal verb* If a vehicle goes into something such as a tree or a wall, it hits it: *Their car was travelling at 50 miles an hour when it went into the tree.* ➔Compare **collide.**

▲ **go into** *sth* BE USED *phrasal verb* MAINLY UK If time, money or effort goes into a product or activity, it is used when producing or doing it: *A considerable amount of time and effort has gone into this exhibition.*

▲ **go off** STOP WORKING *phrasal verb* If a light or a machine goes off, it stops working: *The lights went off in several villages because of the storm.*

▲ **go off** EXPLODE *phrasal verb* **1** If a bomb goes off, it explodes: *The* **bomb** *went off at midday.* **2** If a gun goes off, it fires: *His gun went off accidentally as he was climbing over a fence.*

▲ **go off** HAPPEN *phrasal verb* to happen in a particular way: *The protest march went off peacefully with only two arrests.*

▲ **go off** FOOD *phrasal verb* UK If food or drink goes off, it is not good to eat or drink any more because it is too old: *This bacon smells a bit funny – do you think it's gone off?* ➔See also **off** BAD.

▲ **go off** NOISE *phrasal verb* If a warning device goes off, it starts to ring loudly or make a loud noise: *The* **alarm** *should go off automatically as soon as smoke is detected.* ○ *Didn't you hear your* **alarm clock** *going off this morning?*

▲ **go off** BECOME WORSE *phrasal verb* UK to become worse in quality: *That paper's really gone off since they got that new editor.*

▲ **go off** *sb/sth* STOP LIKING *phrasal verb* to stop liking or being interested in someone or something: *I went off beefburgers after I got food poisoning from a take-away.* ○ *I went off Peter when he said those dreadful things about Clare.*

▲ **go off with** *sth* TAKE *phrasal verb* to take something without obtaining permission from the owner first: *I do wish you'd stop going off with my car without asking me beforehand.*

▲ **go off with** *sb* LEAVE *phrasal verb* to leave a wife, husband or partner in order to have a sexual or romantic relationship with someone else: *Did you know that Hugh had gone off with his sister-in-law?*

▲ **go on** HAPPEN *phrasal verb* to happen: *I'm sure we never hear about a lot of what goes on in government.* ○ *This war has been going on for years.*

goings-on /ˌgəʊ.ɪŋzˈɒn/ US /ˌgoʊ.ɪŋzˈɑːn/ *plural noun* strange, unusual, amusing or unsuitable events or activities: *There've been a lot of **strange/odd** goings-on in that house recently.*

▲ **go on** OPERATE *phrasal verb* to start operating: *The spotlights go on automatically when an intruder is detected in the garden.* ○ *When does the heating go on?*

▲ **go on** CONTINUE *phrasal verb* to continue or move to the next thing: *Please go on **with** what you're doing and don't let us interrupt you.* ○ [+ v-ing] *We really can't go on living like this – we'll have to find a bigger house.* ○ [+ to infinitive] *She admitted her company's responsibility for the disaster and went on **to** explain how compensation would be paid to the victims.* ○ *What proportion of people who are HIV-positive go on **to** develop* (= later develop) *AIDS?* ○ *If you go on* (= continue behaving) *like this you won't have any friends left at all.*

▲ **go on** TALK *phrasal verb* UK to talk in an annoying way about something for a long time: *I just wish he'd stop going on **about** how brilliant his daughter is." "Yes, he does go on **(a bit)**, doesn't he?"* ○ *I wish you'd stop going on **at*** (= criticizing repeatedly) *me about my haircut.*

▲ **go on** TALK AGAIN *phrasal verb* **1** to start talking again after a pause: *She paused to light another cigarette and then went on **with** her account of the accident.* ○ [+ speech] *"What I want more than anything else," he went on, "is a house in the country with a large garden for the children to play in."* **2** INFORMAL something that you say to encourage someone to say or do something: *Go on, what happened next?*

▲ **Go on!** NOT BELIEVE *phrasal verb* MAINLY UK OLD-FASHIONED used when you do not believe someone

▲ **go on** TIME *phrasal verb* to continue or pass: *Tomorrow will start cold but it should get warmer as the day goes on.* ○ *As the evening went on it became clear that we should never have agreed to see each other again.*

▲ **go on** PLEASE DO *phrasal verb* used when encouraging or asking someone to do something: *Go on, have another drink.* ○ *"I don't really feel like seeing a film tonight." "Oh go on. We haven't been to the cinema for ages."*

▲ **go on** AGREE *phrasal verb* INFORMAL something that you say in order to agree to do or allow something that you did not want to do or to allow before: *"Are you sure you don't want another slice of cake?" "Oh go on **then**, but just a small one."*

▲ **go on** *sth* BASE *phrasal verb* to use a piece of information in order to help you discover or understand something: *I'm only going on what I overheard him saying to Chris, but I think he's planning to leave next month.* ○ *The investigation has only just started so the police **haven't got much** to go on at the moment.*

▲ **go out** LEAVE *phrasal verb* to leave a room or building, especially in order to do something for entertainment: *Please close the door as you go out.* ○ *Do you fancy going out **for** a meal after work?* ○ *It's terribly smoky in here – I'm just going out **for** a breath of fresh air.* ○ [+ v-ing] *I wish you'd spend more time at home instead of going out drinking with your friends every night.*

▲ **go out** SEA *phrasal verb* If the tide goes out, it moves back and covers less of the beach. ○Compare **come in** SEA.

▲ **go out** RELATIONSHIP *phrasal verb* to have a romantic and usually sexual relationship with someone: *How long have you been going out **with** him?* ○ *They'd been going out **(together/with each other)** for almost five years before he moved in with her.*

▲ **go out** SPORT *phrasal verb* UK to lose when you are playing in a sports competition, so that you must stop playing in the competition: *England went out **to** France in the second round of the championship.*

▲ **go out to** *sb* *phrasal verb* If your thoughts or sympathies go out to someone in a difficult or sad situation, you think of them and feel sorry for them: *Our*

deepest sympathies go out to her husband and children.

▲ **go over** *sth* EXAMINE *phrasal verb* to examine or look at something in a careful or detailed way: *Forensic scientists are going over the victim's flat in a search for clues about the murderer.* ○ *Remember to go over your essay checking for grammar and spelling mistakes before you hand it in to me.* ○ *I've gone over the problem several times, but I can't think of a solution.*

▲ **go over** *sth* STUDY *phrasal verb* to study or explain something: *I always go over my revision notes just before I go into an exam.* ○ *Could you go over the main points of your argument again, Professor?*

▲ **go over** BE RECEIVED *phrasal verb* US FOR **go down** BE RECEIVED

▲ **go over to** *sth* *phrasal verb* **1** to change to something new or to a new way of doing things: *Many motorists are going over **from** leaded **to** unleaded fuel.* ○ *She went over* (= changed her support) *to the Democrats at the last election.* **2** to change to another broadcaster or place of broadcast: *We're now going over to Kate Adie speaking live from Baghdad.* ○ *Later in this bulletin we'll be going over to our Westminster studio for an update on the situation.*

▲ **go round** BE ENOUGH UK *phrasal verb* (US **go around**) If there is enough of something to go round, there is enough for everyone in a group of people: *Are there enough pencils to go round?*

▲ **go round** BEHAVE BADLY UK *phrasal verb* (US **go around**) to spend your time behaving in the stated way: [+ v-ing] *You can't go round being rude to people.*

▲ **go round** SPIN UK *phrasal verb* (US **go around**) to spin like a wheel ○Compare **revolve**; **rotate**.

▲ **go round** VISIT UK *phrasal verb* (US **go around**) to visit someone in their home: *I'm just going round to Martha's for half an hour.* ○ *Why didn't you tell me Perry had been round?*

▲ **go round** *sth* SEE MAIN PARTS UK *phrasal verb* (US **go around**) to travel to all, or the main, parts of a place that you are visiting in order to find out what it is like or to learn about it: *For a few weeks in the summer, visitors are able to go round Buckingham Palace.*

▲ **go round (somewhere)** BE PASSED UK *phrasal verb* (US **go around (somewhere)**) to go or be given from one person to another, or to move from one place to another: *A nasty flu bug's going round (the school) at the moment.* ○ *There's a rumour going round (the village) that they're having an affair.*

▲ **go through** *sth* EXPERIENCE *phrasal verb* to experience a difficult or unpleasant situation: *I've been going through a bad patch recently.* ○ *You'd think his children would be more sympathetic towards him **after all** he's gone through* (= the many bad things he has experienced).

▲ **go through** *sth* EXAMINE *phrasal verb* to examine something which contains a collection of things carefully in order to organize them or find something: *I'm going through my wardrobe and throwing out all the clothes I don't wear any more.* ○ *Remember to go through the pockets before you put those trousers in the washing machine.*

▲ **go through** *sth* PRACTISE *phrasal verb* to do something in order to practise or as a test: *I'd like you to go through that manoeuvre again and then bring the car to a halt next to the kerb.*

▲ **go through** *sth* USE *phrasal verb* to use a lot of something: *Before I gave up smoking I was going through 40 cigarettes a day.* ○ *I went through a hundred quid on my last trip to London.*

▲ **go through** BE ACCEPTED *phrasal verb* to be officially accepted or approved: *A council spokeswoman said that the proposals for the new shopping centre were unlikely to go through.*

▲ **go through with** *sth* *phrasal verb* to do something unpleasant or difficult that has already been agreed or promised: *He'd threatened to divorce her but I never thought he'd go through with it.* ○ *The company has decided not to go through with the takeover of its smaller rival.*

▲ **go to** *sb* *phrasal verb* to be given or sold to someone: *Who did the award for Best Actress go to?* ○ *All the money raised will go to charity.* ○ *The painting went to the highest bidder.*

▲ **go together** [LOOK GOOD] *phrasal verb* to look good together: *Do you think the cream dress and the blue jacket go together?* ➲Compare **match** SUITABLE; **suit** LOOK ATTRACTIVE.

▲ **go together** [RELATIONSHIP] *phrasal verb* INFORMAL If two people are going together, they have a romantic or sexual relationship with each other.

▲ **go together** [BE FOUND] *phrasal verb* to happen or be found together: *Wisdom and maturity don't necessarily go together.* ○ *Researchers have discovered that short-sightedness and high IQs seem to go together in children.*

▲ **go under** [SINK] *phrasal verb* to sink: *The ship went under just minutes after the last passenger had been rescued.*

▲ **go under** [FAIL] *phrasal verb* If a company goes under, it fails financially: *The charity will go under unless a generous donor can be found within the next few months.*

▲ **go up** [RISE] *phrasal verb* to move higher, rise or increase: *The average cost of a new house has gone up **by** 5% **to** £76 500.*

▲ **go up** [EXPLODE] *phrasal verb* to suddenly explode: *There's a gas leak and the whole building could go up at any moment.*

▲ **go up** [BUILD] *phrasal verb* If a building goes up, it is built: *A new factory is going up on the old airport.*

▲ **go up** [BE FIXED] *phrasal verb* If a sign goes up, it is fixed into position: *The new 'No Parking' signs went up yesterday.*

▲ **go up** [UNIVERSITY] *phrasal verb* UK OLD-FASHIONED If you go up to a college or university, especially Oxford University or Cambridge University, you begin studying there, or continue studying after a holiday.

▲ **go up to *sth*** *phrasal verb* to reach as far as something: *The path going up to the back door is very muddy.* ○ *This edition's rather out-of-date and only goes up to 1989.*

▲ **go with *sth*** [SUIT] *phrasal verb* If one thing goes with another, they suit each other or they look or taste good together: *This wine goes particularly well with seafood.* ○ *I'm not sure that this hat really goes **with** this dress.* ➲Compare **match** SUITABLE; **suit** LOOK ATTRACTIVE.

▲ **go with *sth*** [RESULT] *phrasal verb* If a problem, activity or quality goes with another one, they often happen or exist together and the first thing is often caused by the second: **[+ v-ing]** *What are the main health problems that go with smok**ing**?*

▲ **go with *sb*** [RELATIONSHIP] *phrasal verb* INFORMAL to have a romantic or sexual relationship with someone: *Did he ever go with anyone else while they were living together?*

▲ **go with *sb/sth*** [AGREE] *phrasal verb* INFORMAL to accept an idea or agree with a person: *I think we can go with the advertising agency's suggestions, don't you?*

▲ **go without *(sth)*** *phrasal verb* to not have something or to manage to live despite not having something: *If you don't want fish for dinner, then you'll just have to go without!* ○ *I'd rather go without food than work for him.*

goad /gəʊd/ [US] /goʊd/ *verb* **[T]** to make a person or an animal react or do something by continuously annoying or upsetting them: *Will the pressure applied by environmentalists be enough to goad the industrialized nations **into** us**ing** less fossil fuels?* ○ *He refused to be goaded by their insults.* ○ *The team were goaded **on** by their desire to be first to complete the course.* ○ *A group of children were goading* (= laughing at or pushing) *another child in the school playground.* **goad** /gəʊd/ [US] /goʊd/ *noun* **[S]** *The thought of exams next week is a great goad to the students to work hard.*

goal [SPORT] /gəʊl/ [US] /goʊl/ *noun* **[C]** **1** an area on a playing field, usually marked by two posts with a net fixed behind them, where players try to send the ball in order to score in sports such as football and hockey: *Black kicked/headed the ball **into/towards** the goal.* **2** a point scored in some sports, such as football or hockey, when a player gets the ball into this area: *Brazil won by three goals to one.* ○ *Only one goal was **scored** in the entire match.* **3** UK **be/play in goal** to be the player who tries to prevent the other team from scoring goals: *Who is playing in goal for Milan this evening?*

goalless /ˈgəʊl.ləs/ [US] /ˈgoʊl-/ *adj* without any goals being scored: *The match ended in a goalless **draw**.*

goal [AIM] /gəʊl/ [US] /goʊl/ *noun* **[C]** an aim or purpose: *Our goal is for the country to be fully independent within two years.* ○ *They have **set** themselves a series of goals to achieve by the end of the month.* ○ *Do you think I'll be able to **achieve** my goal **of** los**ing** 5 kilos before the summer?*

goalkeeper UK /ˈgəʊlˌkiː.pəʳ/ [US] /ˈgoʊlˌkiː.pɚ/ *noun* **[C]** (INFORMAL **goalie**, US **goaltender**) the player who stands in the team's goal to try to stop the other team from scoring

ˈgoal ˌline *noun* **[C]** the line between the two posts that mark the goal, over which the ball must pass if a point is to be scored

goalmouth /ˈgəʊl.maʊθ/ [US] /ˈgoʊl-/ *noun* **[C]** the area exactly in front of the goal

goalpost /ˈgəʊl.pəʊst/ [US] /ˈgoʊl.poʊst/ *noun* **[C]** (ALSO **post**, UK ALSO **upright**) in some sports, one of the two vertical posts, often painted white, which are connected with a CROSSBAR to form a goal: *The shot rebounded off the goal post.*

• **move the goalposts** UK INFORMAL DISAPPROVING to change the rules while someone is trying to do something in order to make it more difficult for them: *We'd almost signed the contract when the other guys moved the goalposts and said they wanted more money.*

goalscorer /ˈgəʊlˌskɔː.rəʳ/ [US] /ˈgoʊlˌskɔːr.ɚ/ *noun* **[C]** MAINLY UK a person who scores goals for their team in games such as football: *Matthew Le Tissier was Southampton's **leading/top** goalscorer that season.* **goalscoring** /ˈgəʊlˌskɔː.rɪŋ/ [US] /ˈgoʊlˌskɔːr.ɪŋ/ *noun* **[U]** *a fine goalscoring record*

goaltender /ˈgəʊlˌten.dəʳ/ [US] /ˈgoʊlˌten.dɚ/ *noun* **[C]** **1** the person who stands in goal in ICE HOCKEY (= a game played by two teams on ice) and tries to stop the opposing team from scoring **2** US a **goalkeeper**

goanna /gəʊˈæn.ə/ [US] /goʊ-/ *noun* **[C]** a type of large lizard which is common in Australia

goat [ANIMAL] /gəʊt/ [US] /goʊt/ *noun* **[C]** an animal which is related to sheep, which usually has horns, and which lives wild on mountains or is kept on farms to provide milk, meat, wool, etc: *goat's milk/cheese*

• **act/play the goat** UK INFORMAL to behave in a silly way: *Stop acting the goat!*

• **get *sb's* goat** (AUS ALSO **get on *sb's* goat**) INFORMAL to greatly annoy someone: *That sort of attitude really gets my goat.*

goat [MAN] /gəʊt/ [US] /goʊt/ *noun* **[C]** INFORMAL DISAPPROVING a man who is very active sexually, or would like to be and makes it obvious: *an **old** goat*

goatee /ˈgəʊ.tiː/ [US] /ˈgoʊ-/ *noun* **[C]** a small usually pointed beard grown only on the chin, not the cheeks

goatherd /ˈgəʊt.hɜːd/ [US] /ˈgoʊt.hɝːd/ *noun* **[C]** a person who takes care of a FLOCK (= group) of goats

goatskin /ˈgəʊt.skɪn/ [US] /ˈgoʊt-/ *noun* **[C or U]** the skin of a single goat, or leather made from the skin

gob [MOUTH] /gɒb/ [US] /gɑːb/ *noun* **[C]** UK SLANG a mouth

• **keep *your* gob shut** UK to not say anything: *You'd better keep your gob shut about what happened.*

gob [FORCE OUT] /gɒb/ [US] /gɑːb/ *verb* **[I]** **-bb-** UK SLANG to force out the contents of the mouth, usually SALIVA; to **spit**

gobbet /ˈgɒb.ɪt/ [US] /ˈgɑː.bɪt/ *noun* **[C]** INFORMAL a small piece or lump of something, especially food

gobble [MAKE NOISE] /ˈgɒb.l̩/ [US] /ˈgɑː.bl̩/ *verb* **[I]** to make the sound of a male turkey

gobble [EAT] /ˈgɒb.l̩/ [US] /ˈgɑː.bl̩/ *verb* **[I or T]** INFORMAL to eat food too fast: *She gobbled her dinner **(down/up)**.*

▲ **gobble *sth* up** *phrasal verb* INFORMAL to use a lot of your supply of something, usually money: *The mounting legal costs quickly gobbled up their savings.*

gobbledegook, **gobbledygook** /ˈgɒb.l̩.di.guːk/ [US] /ˈgɑː.bl̩-/ *noun* **[U]** INFORMAL DISAPPROVING language, especially used in official letters, forms and statements, which seems difficult or meaningless because you do not understand it: *This computer manual is complete gobbledegook.*

go-between /ˈgəʊ.bɪˌtwiːn/ [US] /ˈgoʊ-/ *noun* **[C]** someone who delivers messages between people who are unable or unwilling to meet: *The ambassador has offered to **act***

G

as a go-between for the two countries involved in the conflict.

goblet /ˈɡɒb.lət/ [US] /ˈɡɑː.blət/ *noun* [C] *MAINLY OLD USE* a container from which drink, especially wine, is drunk, usually made of glass or metal, and with a stem and a base but no handles

goblin /ˈɡɒb.lɪn/ [US] /ˈɡɑː.blɪn/ *noun* [C] (in stories) a small, usually ugly, creature which is harmful to humans ➲See also **hobgoblin**.

gobsmacked /ˈɡɒb.smækt/ [US] /ˈɡɑːb-/ *adj UK INFORMAL* so shocked that you cannot speak: *He was gobsmacked when he heard of the redundancies.*

gobstopper *UK* /ˈɡɒbˌstɒp.əʳ/ [US] /ˈɡɑːbˌstɑː.pɚ/ *noun* [C] (*US* **jawbreaker**) a large round hard sweet which often has different coloured layers

go-cart, *UK ALSO* **go-kart** /ˈɡəʊ.kɑːt/ [US] /ˈɡoʊ.kɑːrt/ *noun* [C] a small low car used for racing, or a toy car which you operate with your feet

go-carting, *UK ALSO* **go-karting** /ˈɡəʊˌkɑː.tɪŋ/ [US] /ˈɡoʊˌkɑːr.t̬ɪŋ/ *noun* [U] racing in go-carts

god [SPIRIT] /ɡɒd/ [US] /ɡɑːd/ *noun* [C] **1** a spirit or being believed to control some part of the universe or life and often worshipped for doing so, or a representation of this spirit or being: *the ancient Greek gods and goddesses* ➲See also **the gods**. **2** someone who is very important to you, whom you admire very much, and who greatly influences you: *His most devoted fans think of Elvis Presley as a sort of god.*

God [MAKER] /ɡɒd/ [US] /ɡɑːd/ *noun* [S not after *the*] (in especially Christian, Jewish and Muslim belief) the being which made the universe, the Earth and its people and is believed to have an effect on all things: *Do you believe in God?*

• **(Oh my) God!** *INFORMAL* used to emphasize how surprised, angry, shocked, etc. you are: *My God, what a mess!* ○ *Oh my God, I've never seen anything like it!*
* NOTE: Some people consider informal expressions that use the word **God** to be offensive.

• **God knows** *INFORMAL* used to emphasize that you do not understand something at all or have absolutely no knowledge of something: *God knows **where** he's put the keys!* ○ *"What did he mean by that?" "God knows!"*

• **God willing** used to say you hope everything happens in the way you want: *We'll be there tomorrow, God willing!*

• **hope/wish/swear to God** *INFORMAL* used for emphasis: *I hope to God **(that)** he turns up.* ○ *I swear to God **(that)** I didn't know about it.*

• **thank God** *INFORMAL* something you say when you are happy because something bad did not happen: *Thank God nobody was hurt in the accident.* ○ *Oh, there's my wallet. Thank God.*

• **There is a God!** *HUMOROUS* said in a bad situation when something good happens unexpectedly

god-awful /ˈɡɒdˌɔː.fəl/ [US] /ˈɡɑːdˌɑː-/ *adj INFORMAL* very bad, difficult or unpleasant: *That was a god-awful meal.*

godchild /ˈɡɒd.tʃaɪld/ [US] /ˈɡɑːd-/ *noun* [C] *plural* **godchildren** in the Christian religion, a child whose moral and religious development is partly the responsibility of two or more GODPARENTS (= adults who promise to take this responsibility at a ceremony)

goddamn, **God damn**, **goddamned**, *US ALSO* **goddam** /ˈɡɒd.dæm/ [US] /ˌɡɑːdˈdæm/ *exclamation, adj, adv MAINLY US VERY INFORMAL* used to add emphasis to what is being said: *Goddamn **(it)**, how much longer will it take?* ○ *Don't drive so goddamn fast!* ➲See also **damn** EXPRESSION.
* NOTE: Some people consider this offensive.

goddaughter /ˈɡɒdˌdɔː.təʳ/ [US] /ˈɡɑːdˌdɑː.t̬ɚ/ *noun* [C] a female GODCHILD

goddess /ˈɡɒd.es/ [US] /ˈɡɑː.des/ *noun* [C] a female god: *Aphrodite was the ancient Greek goddess **of** love.*

godfather /ˈɡɒdˌfɑː.ðəʳ/ [US] /ˈɡɑːdˌfɑː.ðɚ/ *noun* [C] **1** a male GODPARENT **2** the leader of a criminal group, especially a MAFIA family

god-fearing /ˈɡɒdˌfɪə.rɪŋ/ [US] /ˈɡɑːdˌfɪr.ɪŋ/ *adj OLD USE* Someone who is God-fearing is religious and tries to live in the way they believe God would wish them to.

godforsaken /ˈɡɒd.fəˌseɪ.kən/ [US] /ˈɡɑːd.fɚ-/ *adj* [before n] *DISAPPROVING* describes a place that is unattractive and contains nothing interesting or pleasant: *The town is a godforsaken place at night.*

God-given /ˈɡɒdˌɡɪv.ən/ [US] /ˈɡɑːd-/ *adj* **1** If you say something is God-given, you mean that it has not been made by people: *She has a God-given talent as a painter.* **2** having to be obeyed: *She seems to think she has a God-given **right** to tell us all what to do.*

godless /ˈɡɒd.ləs/ [US] /ˈɡɑːd-/ *adj* **1** not having or believing in God or gods: *a godless society* **2** bad or evil **godlessly** /ˈɡɒd.ləs.li/ [US] /ˈɡɑːd-/ *adv* **godlessness** /ˈɡɒd.ləs.nəs/ [US] /ˈɡɑːd-/ *noun* [U]

godlike /ˈɡɒd.laɪk/ [US] /ˈɡɑːd-/ *adj* like God or a god in some way: *godlike powers*

godly /ˈɡɒd.li/ [US] /ˈɡɑːd-/ *adj* showing obedience to God: *a godly woman* **godliness** /ˈɡɒd.lɪ.nəs/ [US] /ˈɡɑːd-/ *noun* [U]

godmother /ˈɡɒdˌmʌð.əʳ/ [US] /ˈɡɑːdˌmʌð.ɚ/ *noun* [C] a female GODPARENT ➲See also **fairy godmother**.

godparent /ˈɡɒdˌpeə.rənt/ [US] /ˈɡɑːdˌper.ənt/ *noun* [C] (in the Christian religion) a person who, at a BAPTISM ceremony, promises to help a new member of the religion, usually a child, in religious and moral matters

the gods *plural noun UK INFORMAL* the seats in a theatre which are at the highest level and the furthest distance from the stage ➲See also **god**.

godsend /ˈɡɒd.send/ [US] /ˈɡɑːd-/ *noun* [S] *INFORMAL* something good which happens unexpectedly, especially at a time when it is needed: *The grant was a **real** godsend, especially considering the theatre was due to close next month.*

God's gift /ˌɡɒdzˈɡɪft/ [US] /ˌɡɑːdz-/ *noun* [U] *DISAPPROVING* If you say that someone thinks or behaves as if they are God's gift (to someone or something), you mean that they believe that they are better than anyone else: *He **thinks** he's God's gift **to women*** (= He thinks he is extremely attractive to women).

godson /ˈɡɒd.sʌn/ [US] /ˈɡɑːd-/ *noun* [C] a male GODCHILD

godsquad /ˈɡɒd.skwɒd/ [US] /ˈɡɑːd.skwɑːd/ *group noun* [C] *INFORMAL MAINLY DISAPPROVING* any group of EVANGELICAL Christians whose members are generally thought to be too forceful in trying to persuade other people to believe as they do

God's truth /ˌɡɒdzˈtruːθ/ [US] /ˌɡɑːdz-/ *exclamation* said to emphasise that something is the complete truth: *I didn't know she would be there – God's **honest** truth.*

goer /ˈɡəʊ.əʳ/ [US] /ˈɡoʊ.ɚ/ *noun* [C] *INFORMAL* a woman who is sexually active with a lot of people: *Apparently, she was a bit of a goer before she got married.* ➲See also **-goer** at **go** MOVE/TRAVEL.

goes /ɡəʊz/ [US] /ɡoʊz/ *he/she/it form of* **go**

gofer /ˈɡəʊ.fəʳ/ [US] /ˈɡoʊ.fɚ/ *noun* [C] *US INFORMAL* someone whose job is to be sent to get and carry things such as messages, drinks, etc. for other people in a company

go-getter /ˈɡəʊˌɡet.əʳ/ [US] /ˈɡoʊˌɡet̬.ɚ/ *noun* [C] someone who is very energetic, determined to be successful and able to deal with new or difficult situations easily: *We only recruit go-getters who will be actively involved in the company's development.* **go-getting** /ˈɡəʊˌɡet.ɪŋ/ [US] /ˈɡoʊˌɡet̬-/ *adj*: *He's a go-getting high-powered business manager.*

goggle /ˈɡɒɡ.l̩/ [US] /ˈɡɑː.ɡl̩/ *verb* [I] *INFORMAL* to look with the eyes wide open because you are surprised: *The cathedral was full of goggling tourists.*

goggle-box /ˈɡɒɡ.l̩.bɒks/ [US] /ˈɡɑː.ɡl̩.bɑːks/ *noun* [C usually sing] *UK OLD-FASHIONED INFORMAL FOR* television

goggle-eyed /ˌɡɒɡ.l̩ˈaɪd/ [US] /ˌɡɑː.ɡl̩-/ *adj INFORMAL* If someone is goggle-eyed, their eyes are very wide open, usually because of surprise.

goggles /ˈɡɒɡ.l̩z/ [US] /ˈɡɑː.ɡl̩z/ *plural noun* special glasses which fit close to the face to protect the eyes from chemicals, wind, water, etc: *ski goggles* ○ ***(a pair of)** safety goggles*

go-go dancer /ˌɡəʊ.ɡəʊˈdɑːnt.səʳ/ [US] /ˌɡoʊ.ɡoʊˈdænt.sɚ/ *noun* [C] (*ALSO* **go-go girl**) a dancer who performs in places such as bars, dancing energetically to modern music with a strong beat, often in a sexually exciting manner and while wearing very little clothing

going [SPEED] /ˈgəʊ.ɪŋ/ [US] /ˈgoʊ-/ *noun* [U] how quickly you do something: *Cambridge to Newcastle in four hours is* ***good*** *going – you must have been driving flat out all the way.*

going [DIFFICULTY] /ˈgəʊ.ɪŋ/ [US] /ˈgoʊ-/ *noun* [U] how easy or difficult something is: *She's obviously very intelligent, but her lectures are* ***heavy*** *going* (= they are difficult to understand). ○ *He found three 400 metre races in two days* ***hard*** *going* (= difficult).

going [GROUND] /ˈgəʊ.ɪŋ/ [US] /ˈgoʊ-/ *noun* [U] the condition of the ground for walking or riding etc: *After an inch of rain at the racecourse overnight, the going is described as good to soft.*
- **while the going is good** while an opportunity lasts: *Many people fear that the newly-elected government will be ousted in a military coup and are leaving their country while the going is good.*
- **When the going gets tough, the tough get going.** *SAYING* said to emphasize that when conditions become difficult, strong people take action

going [LEAVING] /ˈgəʊ.ɪŋ/ [US] /ˈgoʊ-/ *noun* [S] when someone leaves somewhere: *His going came as as shock.*

ˈgoing ˌon *adv, prep* **1** (*UK ALSO* **going on for**) *INFORMAL* nearly or almost (a particular number, age, time or amount): *It was going on midnight when we left the party.* ○ *There were/was going on two hundred people at their wedding.* **2** *HUMOROUS* You say someone is a particular age going on a much older age, if they behave like a much older person: *"How old is Brian?" "30 going on 50."*

going-over /ˈgəʊ.ɪŋˌəʊ.vəʳ/ [US] /ˈgoʊ.ɪŋˌoʊ.vɚ/ *noun* [S] **1** an activity such as cleaning that is done carefully and completely: *This carpet's filthy! It needs a really good going-over.* ○ *Detectives have* ***given*** *the flat a thorough going-over* (= examined it carefully). **2** *INFORMAL* when someone is hit repeatedly: *They said I'd get a real going-over if I didn't pay them by tomorrow.*

goings-on /ˌgəʊ.ɪŋzˈɒn/ [US] /ˌgoʊ.ɪŋzˈɑːn/ *plural noun* ➲See at **go on** HAPPEN.

goitre *UK* /ˈgɔɪ.təʳ/ [US] /-t̬ɚ/ *noun* [U] (*US* **goiter**) a swelling at the front of the neck caused by an increase in size of the THYROID GLAND

gold [METAL] /gəʊld/ [US] /goʊld/ *noun* [U] a valuable, shiny, yellow metal used to make coins and jewellery: *gold jewellery/bullion* ○ *a gold watch/necklace*
- **go gold** If a recording of a popular song, or of a collection of popular songs, goes gold, it sells a large number of copies.

gold [COLOUR] /gəʊld/ [US] /goʊld/ *adj, noun* [U] (of) a yellowish colour, like the colour of gold: *a gold dome* ○ *gold paint* ○ *I love the gold of the autumn leaves.*

goldish /ˈgəʊld.ɪʃ/ [US] /ˈgoʊld-/ *adj* slightly gold

ˈgold ˌcard *noun* [C] a credit card which you can get if you earn a lot of money

ˈgold ˌdigger *noun* [C] *DISAPPROVING* someone, usually a woman, who tries to sexually attract a rich person, usually a man, in order to obtain presents or money

ˌgold ˈdisc *noun* [C] a prize given to the performer(s) of a popular song, or a collection of popular songs, when a large number of copies of the recording of it have been sold

ˈgold ˌdust *noun* [U] gold in powder form
- **like gold dust** *MAINLY UK* said about something that is very difficult to obtain because a lot of people want it: *Tickets for the concert are like gold dust.*

golden /ˈgəʊl.dᵊn/ [US] /ˈgoʊl-/ *adj* **1** made of gold: *a golden necklace* **2** [before n] special, advantageous or successful: *the golden days of our youth* ○ *He's got a place at university which gives him a golden* ***opportunity*** *to do research in the subject which interests him.* ○ *I like listening to those radio stations that play all the golden* ***oldies*** (= old popular songs which people still like or which have become liked again.) **3** the colour of gold: *golden hair/skin* ○ *miles of golden beaches*

ˌgolden ˈage *noun* [C usually sing] a period of time, sometimes imaginary, when everyone was happy, or when a particular art, business, etc. was very successful: *Adults often look back on their childhood as a golden age.* ○ *She was an actress from the golden age* ***of*** *the cinema.*

ˈgolden ˌboy/ˌgirl *noun* [C] a person who is very successful and is much admired, although often only temporarily: *She's the current golden girl* ***of*** *American ice-skating.*

ˌgolden ˈeagle *noun* [C] a large flesh-eating bird with golden brown feathers on its back, which lives in northern parts of the world

ˌgolden ˈgoose *noun* [C usually sing] something which gives you an advantage, especially a financial advantage ➲See also **kill the goose that lays the golden egg** at **kill** DEATH.

ˌgolden ˈhandcuffs *plural noun SLANG* payments made to employees, especially those in a high position, as a way of persuading them not to leave their jobs and go and work somewhere else

ˌgolden ˈhandshake *noun* [C usually sing] *INFORMAL* a usually large payment made to someone when they leave their job, either when their employer has asked them to leave or when they are leaving at the end of their working life, as a reward for very long or good service in their job

ˌgolden ˈhello *noun* [C] *UK* an extra payment made to a new employee who is particularly valued

ˌgolden ˈjubilee *noun* [C usually sing] *MAINLY UK* the day exactly 50 years after an important occasion, or a special event to celebrate this: *The local hospital will be* ***celebrating*** *its golden jubilee on Thursday.*

ˌgolden ˈparachute *noun* [C] *MAINLY US INFORMAL* a large payment made to someone who has an important job with a company when they are forced to leave their job

ˌgolden reˈtriever *noun* [C] a large dog which has golden or cream-coloured fur

ˌgolden ˈrule *noun* [C usually sing] an important rule or principle, especially in a particular situation: *The golden rule for working in any factory is to observe its safety regulations.*

ˌgolden ˈsyrup *noun* [U] *UK* a thick sweet golden-coloured liquid used in cooking to sweeten food

ˌgolden ˈwedding (anniˌversary) *noun* [C] the day exactly 50 years after a marriage, often celebrated with a party

goldfield /ˈgəʊld.fiːld/ [US] /ˈgoʊld-/ *noun* [C] an area where gold is found in the ground

goldfish /ˈgəʊld.fɪʃ/ [US] /ˈgoʊld-/ *noun* [C] *plural* **goldfish** or **goldfishes** a small, shiny, gold or orange-coloured fish which is often kept as a pet in a bowl or garden pool

ˈgoldfish ˌbowl *noun* [C] (*US ALSO* **fishbowl**) a bowl which is usually round and made of glass and is used for keeping pet fish in, especially goldfish: *FIGURATIVE There are so many windows in the office, it's* ***like*** *being in* ***a*** *goldfish bowl* (= people can easily see what you are doing)*!*

ˌgold ˈleaf *noun* [U] gold in the form of very thin sheets which is often used to cover objects, such as decorative details in a building

ˌgold (ˈmedal) *noun* [C] a small disc of gold which is given to the person who wins a competition, especially in a sport: *He's running so well, surely he'll take the gold.*

goldmine /ˈgəʊld.maɪn/ [US] /goʊld-/ *noun* **1** [C] a place where gold is taken from the ground **2** [S] something which produces wealth or information: *The archive is a goldmine for historians.*

gold-plated /ˌgəʊldˈpleɪ.tɪd/ [US] /ˌgoʊldˈpleɪ.t̬ɪd/ *adj* covered with a very thin layer of gold: *gold-plated earrings*

ˈgold reˌserve *noun* [C] the amount of gold held by a national bank, which is used for dealing with the national banks of other countries

ˈgold ˌrush *noun* [S] a situation in which a lot of people move to a place to try to find gold because they have heard that gold has been found there

goldsmith /ˈgəʊld.smɪθ/ [US] /ˈgoʊld-/ *noun* [C] someone who makes objects from gold

ˈgold ˌstandard *noun* [S] a system of providing and controlling the exchange of money in a country, in which the value of money (relative to foreign money) is fixed against that of gold

G

G

golf /gɒlf/ [US] /gɑːlf/ *noun* **[U]** a game played outside on grass in which each player tries to hit a small ball into a series of nine or 18 small holes, using a long thin stick: *We often play a **round** (= game) of golf at the weekend.* ➲See picture **Sports** on page Centre 10 **golfer** /ˈgɒl.fəʳ/ [US] /ˈgɑːl.fɚ/ *noun* **[C]** *He's one of the highest-earning professional golfers in the world.* **golfing** /ˈgɒl.fɪŋ/ [US] /ˈgɑːl-/ *noun* **[U]** *a golfing **holiday***

ˈgolf ˌball [SPORT] *noun* **[C]** a small hard white ball used for playing golf

ˈgolf ˌball [PRINTING] *noun* **[C]** a small metal ball with raised letter shapes on it which is used in some types of computer printer and typewriter

ˈgolf ˌclub [STICK] *noun* **[C]** one of a set of specially shaped wooden or metal sticks used for hitting a golf ball

ˈgolf ˌclub [CLUB] *noun* **[C]** an organized group of golf players, or the building in which they meet and the area on which they play

ˈgolf ˌcourse *noun* **[C]** an area of land used for playing golf

goliath, Goliath /gəˈlaɪ.əθ/ *noun* **[C usually sing]** a very large and powerful person or organization: *The country is being seen as **the** Goliath (= the most powerful) **of** the region.*

Goliath /gəˈlaɪ.əθ/ *noun* **[S]** in the Bible, a GIANT (= extremely tall man) who was killed by the boy David throwing a stone at him

golliwog, gollywog /ˈgɒl.ɪ.wɒg/ [US] /ˈgɑː.lɪ.wɑːg/ *noun* **[C]** (*ALSO* **golly**) *UK OLD-FASHIONED* a child's toy made of soft material, in the form of a small man with a black face and stiff black hair ✻ NOTE: Such toys are considered offensive by many people and are not now common.

golly /ˈgɒl.i/ [US] /ˈgɑː.li/ *exclamation OLD-FASHIONED INFORMAL* used to show surprise: *Grandad might be 70 but he said he'd finish the marathon and, **by** golly, he did.*

gonad /ˈgəʊ.næd/ [US] /ˈgoʊ-/ *noun* **[C]** *SPECIALIZED* the sex organs in a male or female animal which make the cells needed to produce babies; an OVARY or a testicle

gondola /ˈgɒn.dəl.ə/ [US] /ˈgɑːn-/ *noun* **[C]** a narrow boat with a raised point at both ends, which is used on canals in Venice and is moved by a man with a pole

gondolier /ˌgɒn.dəˈlɪəʳ/ [US] /ˌgɑːn.dəˈlɪr/ *noun* **[C]** a man who takes people from one place to another in a gondola

gone [GO] /gɒn/ [US] /gɑːn/ *past participle of* **go**

gone [PAST] /gɒn/ [US] /gɑːn/ *prep UK* later or older than: *I said I'd be home by six and it's already gone seven.* ➲See also **gone** at **go** LEAVE.

gone [PREGNANT] /gɒn/ [US] /gɑːn/ *adj* **[after n]** *INFORMAL* pregnant: *How far gone is she* (= How long has she been pregnant)*?*

goner /ˈgɒn.əʳ/ [US] /ˈgɑː.nɚ/ *noun* **[C usually sing]** ➲See at **go** LEAVE.

gong /gɒŋ/ [US] /gɑːŋ/ *noun* **[C]** **1** a round piece of metal which is hung in a frame and hit with a stick to produce a sound, usually for musical purposes but sometimes as a signal **2** *UK INFORMAL* an honour that is given to someone for the public service they have done, or a for a particular acting or singing performance

gonna /ˈgə.nə/ [US] /ˈgɑː.nə/ *MAINLY US INFORMAL FOR* going to: *What are you gonna do?* ➲See **go** FUTURE TIME. ✻ NOTE: This is not usually used in written English.

gonorrhoea, *MAINLY US* **gonorrhea** /ˌgɒn.əˈriː.ə/ [US] /ˌgɑː.nəˈ-/ *noun* **[U]** (*SLANG* **clap**) a disease of the sexual organs which can be given from one person to another during sex

gonzo /ˈgɒn.zəʊ/ [US] /ˈgɑːn.zoʊ/ *adj US SLANG* (especially used of pieces of writing in newspapers) intended to shock and excite rather than to inform: *gonzo **journalism***

goo /guː/ *noun* **[U]** *INFORMAL* an unpleasantly sticky substance

good [PLEASANT] /gʊd/ *adj* **better, best** very satisfactory, enjoyable, pleasant or interesting: *a good book* ○ *Did you have a good time at the party?* ○ *The weather has been really good for the time of year.* ○ *I've just had some very good news.* ○ ***It's** so good **to** see you after all this time!*

• **as good as** almost: *The decorating is as good as finished – I just need to finish off the painting.*

• **be (as) good as new** to be in very good condition: *A coat of paint and it will be as good as new.*

• **get off to a good start** to begin an activity successfully: *I didn't get off to a very good start this morning – I'd been at work five minutes and my computer stopped working!*

• **good and ...** *INFORMAL* very: *Drink your coffee while it's good and hot.*

• **good and proper** *INFORMAL* completely: *The table is broken good and proper.*

• **be good for *sth*** *INFORMAL* to be able and willing to provide something: *Bette is **always** good for a laugh.* ○ *Dad will probably be good for a few pounds, if we ask him.*

• **good show** *UK OLD-FASHIONED* used as an expression of approval: *Good show chaps, you completed the course in the time allowed.*

• **in good time** *MAINLY UK* early: *We'll be at the airport in good time.*

• **it's a good job/thing** used to mean 'it is lucky': *It's a good job they didn't go camping last weekend – the weather was awful.*

• **make good** When someone makes good something, they either pay for it, or make it happen: *The shortfall in the budget will be made good by selling further shares.*

• **make good time** to complete a journey quickly

• **be no good** (*ALSO* **be not any/much good**) to be useless or of low quality: *Shoes are no good if they let in water.* ○ *Food aid isn't much good until the fighting stops.*

• **what good is** (*ALSO* **what's the good of**) a way of asking what the purpose of (doing) something is: *What good is sitting alone in your room?*

good [HIGH QUALITY] /gʊd/ *adj* **better, best** **1** of a high quality or level: *She speaks very good French.* ○ *I've heard it's a very good school.* ○ *The apple pie was **as** good **as** the one my grandmother used to make.* ○ *This restaurant has a good **reputation**.* **2** used to express praise: *Good man! Splendid catch.*

good [SUCCESSFUL] /gʊd/ *adj* **better, best** successful, or able to do something well: *Kate's a good cook.* ○ *She's very good **at** Geography.* ○ *They have a good relationship.* ○ *She's very good **with** children.*

• **Good for *you*!** (*AUS ALSO* **Good on *you*!**) used to show approval for someone's success or good luck: *You passed your exam – good for you!*

• **make good** to succeed and become rich: *a working-class boy made good*

good [KIND] /gʊd/ *adj* **better, best** kind or helpful: *a good friend* ○ ***It's** good **of** you to offer to help.* ○ *He's very good **to** his mother.*

• **be so good as to** (*ALSO* **be good enough to**) *FORMAL* used to make a polite request: *Be so good as to close the door when you leave.*

• **do (*sb*) a good turn** *OLD-FASHIONED* to do something kind which helps someone else

good /gʊd/ *noun* **[U]** something that is an advantage or help to a person or situation: *Even a small donation can do **a lot of** good.* ○ *I'm telling you **for** your **own** good.*

good [BEHAVIOUR] /gʊd/ *adj* **better, best** **1** A good child or animal behaves well: *If you're a good boy at the doctor's I'll take you swimming afterwards.* **2** able to be trusted: *Her credit is good* (= She can be trusted to pay her debts).

• **be (as) good as gold** (of a child) to behave very well: *She's been as good as gold all morning.*

• **Be good, and if you can't be good, be careful.** *HUMOROUS SAYING* said to someone to tell them to enjoy themselves at an event or during an activity, but to be sensible, too

good [MORAL RIGHT] /gʊd/ *adj* **better, best** morally right or based on religious principles; kind and helpful: *She led a good life.* ○ *Try to set a good example to the children.*

• **Good heavens/grief/gracious!** (*ALSO* **Good God/Lord!**) used to emphasize how surprised, angry, shocked, etc. you are

• **be as good as *your* word** to do everything that you promise someone you will: *He said he'd call every day and he was as good as his word.*

• **in good faith** If something is done in good faith, it is done sincerely and honestly: *She was* ***acting*** *in good faith for her client.*

good /gʊd/ *noun* [U] that which is morally right: *There is an eternal struggle between good* (= the force which produces morally right action) *and evil.* ○ *Ambition can sometimes be a force* ***for*** *good.*

• **no good** *INFORMAL OLD-FASHIONED* morally bad: *I'd keep away from him if I were you – he's no good.*

• **be up to no good** *INFORMAL* to be behaving in a dishonest or bad way: *He certainly looked as if he was up to no good.*

the good *plural noun* all the people who are good: *You can't buy your way into the ranks of the good.* **goodness** /ˈgʊd.nəs/ *noun* [U] *Mother Teresa's goodness is an example to us all.*

good [GREETING] /gʊd/ *adj* used in greetings: *good morning/afternoon/evening*

good [HEALTH] /gʊd/ *adj* **better, best** having a positive or useful effect, especially on the health: *Make sure you eat plenty of good fresh food.* ○ *Too much sugar in your diet isn't good* ***for*** *you.* ○ ***It's*** *good* ***for*** *old people* ***to*** *stay active if they can.*

good /gʊd/ *noun* [U] the state of being healthy or in a satisfactory condition; benefit: *You should stop smoking* ***for*** *your* ***own*** *good* (= the benefit of your health). ○ *He goes running every day* ***for the*** *good* ***of*** *his* ***health.*** ○ *Modernizing historic buildings can often* ***do more harm than*** *good.* ○ *The rally has been cancelled* ***for the*** *good* ***of*** *all concerned.*

• **do *you* good** to improve your health or life: *You can't work all the time – it does you good* ***to*** *go out and enjoy yourself sometimes.* ○ *Take the medicine – it will do you* ***(a power/world of)*** *good* (= improve your health a lot).

• **to the good** generally helpful: *Greater international stability can surely only be to the good.*

goodness /ˈgʊd.nəs/ *noun* [U] the part of something, especially of food, which is good for health: *Don't cook vegetables for too long – they'll lose all their goodness.*

good [LARGE AMOUNT] /gʊd/ *adj* [before n] used to emphasize the large number, amount or level of something: *We've walked a good distance today.* ○ *There was a good-sized crowd at the airport waiting for the plane to land.* ○ *Not all of his films have been successful – there were* ***a*** *good* ***few*** (= several) *failures in the early years.* ○ *Have a good think about it and let me know tomorrow.* ○ *You have a good cry and you'll feel better after.* ○ *There's a good chance the operation will be successful.*

• **a good deal of** much: *The new law met with a good deal of opposition at local level.*

• **a good ...** (*ALSO* **a good ...'s**) more than: *It's a good half hour's walk to the station from here.* ○ *The police said a good twenty kilos of explosive were found during the raid.* ○ *Driving through the deserted town we saw a good* ***many*** (= a lot of) *burnt-out houses.*

• **all in good time** *MAINLY UK* used to tell someone to be patient because the thing they are eager for will happen when the time is right: *Be patient, you'll hear the result all in good time.*

• **have a good innings** *UK INFORMAL* If you say that someone has had a good innings, you mean that they have had a long and successful life: *He was 86 when he died so I suppose he'd had a good innings.*

• **for good measure** in addition: *The concert was excellent – there were lots of well-known songs with some new ones* ***thrown in*** *for good measure.*

good /gʊd/ *noun* **for good** forever: *She's gone and this time it's for good.*

ˌgood ˌafterˈnoon *exclamation SLIGHTLY FORMAL* something you say to greet someone when you meet them in the afternoon

the ˌgood ˈbook *noun* [S] *OLD-FASHIONED* the Bible

goodbye /ˈgʊd.baɪ/ /ˈgʊb-/ /ˌ-ˈ-/ *exclamation, noun* [C] (*INFORMAL* **bye**) used when someone leaves or is left: *Goodbye Bill! See you next week.* ○ *Don't go without* ***saying*** *goodbye* ***to*** *me, will you?* ○ *She* ***kissed*** *her children goodbye before leaving for work.* ○ *We* ***said*** *our goodbyes, and left.* ○ *I hate long drawn-out goodbyes* (= acts of leaving). ○ *She only finished sixth – that surely means goodbye* ***to*** (= accepting that there is no possibility of) *a place in the final.*

ˌgood ˈday *exclamation OLD-FASHIONED* used as a greeting or when saying goodbye during the day ➲See also **g'day**.

ˌgood ˈevening *exclamation SLIGHTLY FORMAL* something you say to greet someone when you meet them in the evening

good-for-nothing /ˌgʊd.fəˈnʌθ.ɪŋ/ [US] /-fɚ-/ *noun* [C] *INFORMAL* a worthless person: *She told him he was a lazy good-for-nothing and should get a job.*

good-for-nothing /ˌgʊd.fəˈnʌθ.ɪŋ/ [US] /-fɚ-/ *adj* [before n] useless: *They're all good-for-nothing* ***layabouts.***

ˌGood ˈFriday *noun* [C or U] In the Christian religion, Good Friday is the day Jesus is believed to have died, the Friday before Easter Sunday.

good-hearted /ˌgʊdˈhɑː.tɪd/ [US] /-ˈhɑːr.t̬ɪd/ *adj* kind and generous

good-humoured /ˌgʊdˈhjuː.məd/ [US] /-mɚd/ *adj* friendly or cheerful: *a good-humoured remark* ○ *The walkers were good-humoured despite the bad weather.*

goodish /ˈgʊd.ɪʃ/ *adj* [before n] *UK INFORMAL* **1** good but not very good **2** quite large: *a goodish distance/number*

good-looking /ˌgʊdˈlʊk.ɪŋ/ *adj* describes a physically attractive man or woman: *He's very good-looking but not terribly bright.*

ˌgood ˈlooks *plural noun* an especially attractive appearance: *his boyish good looks*

goodly /ˈgʊd.li/ *adj* [before n] *OLD-FASHIONED* great or large: *The audience was of a goodly size.*

ˌgood ˈmoney *noun* [U] an amount of money that you think is large: *I paid good money for it.*

ˌgood ˈmorning *exclamation SLIGHTLY FORMAL* something you say to greet someone when you meet them in the morning

good-natured /ˌgʊdˈneɪ.tʃəd/ [US] /-tʃɚd/ *adj* pleasant or friendly: *a good-natured face/crowd*

ˌgoodness (ˈgracious) *exclamation* used to express any strong emotion, especially surprise: ***(My)*** *goodness! how many more times do I have to tell you!* ○ *Goodness gracious* ***(me)****, what a terrible thought!*

ˌgood ˈnight, goodnight *exclamation* said when people leave each other in the evening or before going to bed or to sleep: *Well, good night – sleep well.* ○ *Give the children a goodnight kiss.*

goodo /ˌgʊdˈəʊ/ [US] /-ˈoʊ/ *exclamation, adj* [after v], *adv AUS SLANG FOR* good

goods /gʊdz/ *plural noun* **1** items for sale, or the things that you own: *There is a 25% discount on all electrical goods until the end of the week.* ○ *The house insurance will not cover your personal goods.* **2** *UK* items, but not people, which are transported by railway or road: *a goods train*

• **come up with the goods** (*ALSO* **deliver the goods**) *INFORMAL* to produce what is wanted: *What they promise sounds impressive enough – let's see if they come up with the goods.*

ˌgoods and ˈchattels *plural noun LEGAL* the things that you own other than land and buildings

good-time girl /ˈgʊd.taɪm ˌgɜːl/ [US] /-ˌgɜːrl/ *noun* [C] *OLD-FASHIONED* a young woman who is only interested in having fun, not in serious activities, work, etc.

goodwill /gʊdˈwɪl/ *noun* [U] friendly and helpful feelings: *The school has to rely on the goodwill of the parents to help it raise money.* ○ *Releasing the hostages has been seen as a* ***gesture of*** *goodwill/a goodwill* ***gesture.***

a ˌgood ˈword *noun* [S] a statement of approval and support for someone or something: *If you see the captain could you* ***put in*** *a good word* ***for*** *me?* ○ *The critics didn't* ***have*** *a good word* ***(to say) for/to say about*** *the performance.*

goody [PLEASANT THING] /ˈgʊd.i/ *noun* [C usually pl] *INFORMAL* an object which is desirable or gives pleasure, often something nice to eat: *All the children were given a bag of goodies – mostly sweets and toys.*

goody [EXPRESSION] /ˈgʊd.i/ *exclamation* (*OLD-FASHIONED* **goody gumdrops**) *INFORMAL OR CHILD'S WORD* used to show pleasure: *Oh goody! Chocolate cake.*

goody [PERSON] /ˈɡʊd.i/ *noun* [C usually pl] INFORMAL someone, especially in a film or story, who is good: *It's one of those films where you don't know until the last moment who are the goodies and who are the baddies.*

goody-goody /ˈɡʊd.i,ɡʊd.i/ *noun* [C] INFORMAL DISAPPROVING someone who behaves in a way intended to please people in authority

gooey /ˈɡuː.i/ *adj* **gooier, gooiest** soft and sticky: *a gooey cake*

goof /ɡuːf/ *verb* [I or T] MAINLY US INFORMAL to make a silly mistake: *If Tom hadn't goofed and missed that shot, we'd have won the game.* ○ *She goofed her lines* (= said the words in the play wrong).
goof /ɡuːf/ *noun* [C] **1** MAINLY US INFORMAL a silly mistake: *I made a real goof by forgetting his name.* **2** US INFORMAL a silly or stupid person
goofy /ˈɡuː.fi/ *adj* MAINLY US INFORMAL silly: *That was a real goofy thing to do.* ○ *I like Jim, but he's a little goofy.*

PHRASAL VERBS WITH **goof** ▼

▲ **goof around** *phrasal verb* US INFORMAL to spend time doing nothing important or behaving in a silly way: *The boys spent the whole summer just goofing around.*
▲ **goof off** *phrasal verb* US INFORMAL to avoid doing any work: *They've goofed off and gone to the ball game.*

goon [SILLY PERSON] /ɡuːn/ *noun* [C] OLD-FASHIONED INFORMAL a silly or stupid person
goon [CRIMINAL] /ɡuːn/ *noun* [C] US INFORMAL a violent criminal who is paid to hurt or threaten people

goop /ɡuːp/ *noun* [U] INFORMAL any thick liquid or sticky substance

goose [BIRD] /ɡuːs/ *noun* [C or U] *plural* **geese** a large water bird similar to a duck but larger, or the meat from this bird * NOTE: The female bird is called a **goose** and the male bird is called a **gander**.
goose [PERSON] /ɡuːs/ *noun* [C] *plural* **geese** OLD-FASHIONED INFORMAL a silly person
goose [SQUEEZE] /ɡuːs/ *verb* [T] INFORMAL to squeeze or press someone's bottom
goose [MAKE ACTIVE] /ɡuːs/ *verb* [T] US INFORMAL to encourage or cause something or someone to be more active

gooseberry /ˈɡʊz.bᵊr.i/ *noun* [C] a small green fruit covered with short hairs, which grows on a bush and has a sour taste: *Gooseberries are used for making pies and jam.*
• **play gooseberry** (ALSO **feel like a gooseberry**) UK INFORMAL to be an unwanted third person who is present when two other people, especially two lovers, want to be alone

goosebumps /ˈɡuːs.bʌmps/ *plural noun* (UK ALSO **goose pimples**) small, raised lumps that appear on the skin because of cold, fear or excitement: *You're cold – look, you've got goosebumps!*

gooseflesh /ˈɡuːs.fleʃ/ *noun* [U] UK **goosebumps**

goosestep /ˈɡuːs.step/ *noun* [S] a special way of marching with the legs lifted high and straight: *Hitler's soldiers used to do (the) goosestep.* **goosestep** /ˈɡuːs.step/ *verb* [I] -pp-

the GOP /ðə,dʒiːˈəʊˈpiː/ *noun* [S] ABBREVIATION FOR the Grand Old Party: the Republican political party in the US

gopher /ˈɡəʊ.fər/ ⓤ /ˈɡoʊ.fɚ/ *noun* [C] a North American animal which lives in holes that it makes in the ground

Gordian knot /,ɡɔː.di.ən'nɒt/ ⓤ /,ɡɔːr.di.ən'nɑːt/ *noun* [S] a difficult problem or situation: *to cut the Gordian knot* (= to deal with problems by taking forceful action)

Gordon Bennett /,ɡɔː.dᵊn'ben.ɪt/ *exclamation* UK OLD-FASHIONED SLANG used to express great surprise or annoyance

gore [INJURE] /ɡɔːr/ ⓤ /ɡɔːr/ *verb* [T] (of an animal) to cause an injury with the horns or tusks: *gored by a bull*
gore [BLOOD] /ɡɔːr/ ⓤ /ɡɔːr/ *noun* [U] blood that has come from an injury and become thick: *It's a good film, but there's a lot of blood and gore in it* (= pictures of people being badly injured). ➔See also **gory**.

gorge [VALLEY] /ɡɔːdʒ/ ⓤ /ɡɔːrdʒ/ *noun* [C] a deep narrow valley with steep sides, usually formed by a river or stream cutting through hard rock

gorge [EAT] /ɡɔːdʒ/ ⓤ /ɡɔːrdʒ/ *verb* [I or R] to eat until you are unable to eat any more: [R] *If you gorge yourself on crisps like that, you won't eat your dinner.*

gorge [DISGUST] /ɡɔːdʒ/ ⓤ /ɡɔːrdʒ/ *noun* **make your gorge rise** to make you feel disgusted and angry

gorgeous /ˈɡɔː.dʒəs/ ⓤ /ˈɡɔːr-/ *adj* very beautiful or pleasant: *What a gorgeous room/dress/colour!* ○ *The bride looked gorgeous.* ○ *The weather was so gorgeous.*
gorgeously /ˈɡɔː.dʒə.sli/ ⓤ /ˈɡɔːr-/ *adv*: *She's always gorgeously dressed.* **gorgeousness** /ˈɡɔː.dʒə.snəs/ ⓤ /ˈɡɔːr-/ *noun* [U]

gorgon /ˈɡɔː.ɡən/ ⓤ /ˈɡɔːr-/ *noun* [C] INFORMAL a woman whose appearance and behaviour causes fear: *Our teacher is a real gorgon!*
Gorgon /ˈɡɔː.ɡən/ ⓤ /ˈɡɔːr-/ *noun* [C] one of three sisters in ancient Greek stories who had snakes on their heads instead of hair, and who turned anyone who looked at them into stone

gorilla /ɡəˈrɪl.ə/ *noun* [C] a large ape that comes from western Africa ➔See picture **Animals and Birds** on page Centre 4

gormless /ˈɡɔːm.ləs/ ⓤ /ˈɡɔːrm-/ *adj* UK INFORMAL stupid and slow to understand: *He looks really gormless.*

gorse /ɡɔːs/ ⓤ /ɡɔːrs/ *noun* [U] (ALSO **furze**) a bush with sharp thorns and small yellow flowers, which grows in the countryside

gory /ˈɡɔː.ri/ ⓤ /ˈɡɔːr.i/ *adj* involving violence and blood: *a very gory film* ○ *the gory details of the operation*
• **the gory details** the interesting and usually personal bits of information about a person or event: *Come on, I want to know all the gory details about your date with Jon.*

gosh /ɡɒʃ/ ⓤ /ɡɑːʃ/ *exclamation* INFORMAL SLIGHTLY OLD-FASHIONED used to express surprise or strength of feeling: *Gosh, I didn't expect to see you here!*

gosling /ˈɡɒz.lɪŋ/ ⓤ /ˈɡɑːz-/ *noun* [C] a young goose

go-slow UK /,ɡəʊˈsləʊ/ ⓤ /,ɡoʊˈsloʊ/ *noun* [C usually sing] (US **slowdown**) when employees work more slowly and with less effort than usual to try to persuade an employer to agree to higher pay or better working conditions or arrangements

gospel /ˈɡɒs.pᵊl/ ⓤ /ˈɡɑː.spᵊl/ *noun* [C] any of the four books of the Bible which contain details of the life of Jesus Christ: *St Mark's Gospel/the Gospel according to St Mark*
the gospel *noun* [S] the teachings of Jesus Christ: *to preach/spread the gospel*
gospel /ˈɡɒs.pᵊl/ ⓤ /ˈɡɑː.spᵊl/ *noun* [S] LITERARY a set of principles or ideas which someone believes in: *the gospel of hard work*
gospel (**music**) *noun* [U] a style of religious music originally performed by black Americans
gospel (**truth**) *noun* [U] the complete truth: *If Mary tells you something, you can take it as gospel.*

gossamer /ˈɡɒs.ə.mər/ ⓤ /ˈɡɑː.sə.mɚ/ *noun* [U] the very thin thread that spiders produce to make WEBS
gossamer /ˈɡɒs.ə.mər/ ⓤ /ˈɡɑː.sə.mɚ/ *adj* [before n] LITERARY very delicate and light: *gossamer wings* ○ *a gossamer veil*

gossip /ˈɡɒs.ɪp/ ⓤ /ˈɡɑː.səp/ *noun* **1** [S or U] (a) conversation or reports about other people's private lives which might be unkind, disapproving or not true: *Jane was full of gossip.* ○ *Jane and Lyn sat in the kitchen having a good gossip about their friends.* ○ *I don't like all this idle gossip.* ○ *I've got some juicy gossip for you.* ○ *Have you heard the (latest) gossip?* **2** [C] (MAINLY UK **gossipmonger**) DISAPPROVING someone who enjoys talking about other people and their private lives: *She's a terrible gossip.*
gossip /ˈɡɒs.ɪp/ ⓤ /ˈɡɑː.səp/ *verb* [I] to talk about other people's private lives: *Stop gossiping and get on with some work.* ○ *People have started to gossip about us.* **gossipy** /ˈɡɒs.ɪ.pi/ ⓤ /ˈɡɑː.sɪ-/ *adj*: *a gossipy letter* ○ *gossipy people*
gossip (**column**) *noun* [C] the part of a newspaper in which you find stories about the social and private lives of famous people

got /ɡɒt/ ⓤ /ɡɑːt/ *past simple and past participle of* **get** ➔See also **gotten**.

gotcha /ˈgɒtʃ.ə/ [US] /ˈgɑːtʃ-/ *exclamation* SLANG said to mean 'I have got you' in order to surprise or frighten someone you have caught, or to show that you have an advantage over them

Gothic [BUILDING] /ˈgɒθ.ɪk/ [US] /ˈgɑː.θɪk/ *adj* of or like a style of building which was common in Europe between the 12th and the 16th centuries, and which has pointed arches and windows, high ceilings and tall, thin columns

Gothic [STORIES] /ˈgɒθ.ɪk/ [US] /ˈgɑː.θɪk/ *adj* describes writing or films in which strange things happen in frightening places

gotta /ˈgɒt.ə/ [US] /ˈgɑː.t̬ə/ *verb* [I + infinitive without *to*; T] NOT STANDARD 'have got to' or 'have got a': *I gotta go now.* ○ *He's gotta be kidding.* ○ *Gotta* (= Have you got a) *cigarette?*

• **A man's gotta do what a man's gotta do.** MAINLY HUMOROUS SAYING said to mean that you will do whatever you have to do, even if it is difficult or dangerous

gotten /ˈgɒt.ᵊn/ [US] /ˈgɑː.t̬ᵊn/ US *past participle of* **get**: *They were so pleased that they'd finally gotten to visit* (= succeeded in visiting) *England.*

gouge /gaʊdʒ/ *verb* [T] to make a hole in something in a rough or violent way: *He drove into some railings and gouged a* ***hole*** *in the back of his car.*

gouge /gaʊdʒ/ *noun* [C] a hole that has been made roughly or violently

▲ **gouge** ***sth*** **out** *phrasal verb* [M] to remove something by digging or cutting it out of a surface: *In Shakespeare's play, 'King Lear', the Earl of Gloucester's eyes are gouged out.*

goulash /ˈguː.læʃ/ *noun* [U] a savoury dish, originally from Hungary, which consists of meat cooked in a sauce with PAPRIKA (= a hot-tasting spice)

gourd /gʊəd/ /gɔːd/ [US] /gɔːrd/ *noun* [C] a large fruit which has a hard shell and cannot be eaten, or the shell of this fruit used as a container

gourmand /gɔːˈmɑ̃ːd/ [US] /ˈgʊr.mɑːnd/ *noun* [C] a person who enjoys eating large amounts of food

gourmet /ˈgɔː.meɪ/ [US] /ˈgʊr.meɪ/ *noun* [C] a person who knows a lot about food and cooking, and who enjoys eating high-quality food: *a gourmet restaurant* (= restaurant that has high-quality food)

gout /gaʊt/ *noun* [U] a painful disease which makes the joints, especially the feet, knees and hands, swell **gouty** /ˈgaʊ.ti/ [US] /-t̬i/ *adj*

.gov /ˌdɒtˈgʌv/ [US] /ˌdɑːt-/ INTERNET ABBREVIATION FOR government: used to show that an Internet address belongs to a government organization: *www.nasa.gov*

govern [RULE] /ˈgʌv.ᵊn/ [US] /-ɚn/ *verb* [I or T] to control and direct the public business of a country, city, group of people, etc: *The country is now being governed by the Labour Party.* ○ *They accused the government of being unfit to govern.*

governing /ˈgʌv.ᵊn.ɪŋ/ [US] /-ɚ.nɪŋ/ *adj* [before n] having the power to govern a country or an organization: *a governing* ***body***

govern [INFLUENCE] /ˈgʌv.ᵊn/ [US] /-ɚn/ *verb* [T] to have a controlling influence on something: *Prices of goods are governed by the cost of the raw materials, as well as by the cost of production and distribution.*

governess /ˈgʌv.ᵊn.əs/ [US] /-ɚ.nəs/ *noun* [C] (especially in the past) a woman who lives with a family and teaches their children at home

government /ˈgʌv.ᵊn.mənt/ /-ᵊm-/ [US] /-ɚn-/ *group noun* [C] (WRITTEN ABBREVIATION **govt**) the group of people who officially control a country: *the government of Israel* ○ *The government is/are expected to announce its/their tax proposals today.* ○ *The minister has announced that there will be no change in government policy.* ○ *Senior government officials will be attending a meeting tomorrow.* ○ *Theatre companies are very concerned about cuts in government grants to the arts.* ○ *A government enquiry has been launched.*

government /ˈgʌv.ᵊn.mənt/ /-ᵊm-/ [US] /-ɚn-/ *noun* [U] **1** the system used for controlling a country, city, or group of people: *The 1990s have seen a shift to democratic government in Eastern Europe.* ○ *What this state needs is really strong government.* **2** the activities involved in controlling a country, city, group of people, etc: *The party that was elected to power has no experience of government.* ○ UK *The party was* ***in*** *government* (= controlled the country) *for four years in the 1960s.*

• **Her/His Majesty's Government** the group of people who control Britain

governmental /ˌgʌv.ᵊmˈmen.tᵊl/ [US] /-ɚnˈmen.t̬ᵊl/ *adj*: *We await a governmental decision* (= a decision made by the government) *about the future of the programme.*

governor /ˈgʌv.ᵊn.əʳ/ [US] /-ɚ.nɚ/ *noun* [C] (WRITTEN ABBREVIATION **Gov**) **1** a person in charge of a particular political unit: *the governor of Texas* ⊃See also **gubernatorial**; **guvnor**. **2** MAINLY UK a person in charge of a particular organization: *a prison/school governor*

governorship /ˈgʌv.ᵊn.ə.ʃɪp/ [US] /-ɚ.nɚ-/ *noun* [U] the period of time that someone is a governor: *His governorship was marked by fairness and prosperity.*

governor-general /ˌgʌv.ᵊn.əˈdʒen.rəl/ [US] /-ɚ-/ *noun* [C] *plural* **governor-generals** or **governors-general** the main representative of a country in another country which is controlled by the first country, especially the representative of the British king or queen in a country which is a member of the COMMONWEALTH

gown /gaʊn/ *noun* [C] a woman's dress, especially a long one worn on formal occasions, or a long loose piece of clothing worn over other clothes for a particular purpose: *a* ***ball*** *gown* ○ *a* ***hospital*** *gown*

GP /ˌdʒiːˈpiː/ *noun* [C] MAINLY UK ABBREVIATION FOR general practitioner: a doctor who provides general medical treatment for people who live in a particular area: *I went along to the* ***local*** *GP*

grab [TAKE WITH HAND] /græb/ *verb* [I or T] **-bb-** to take hold of something or someone suddenly and roughly: *A mugger grabbed her handbag as she was walking across the park.* ○ *He grabbed* ***(hold of)*** *his child's arm to stop her from running into the road.*

grab /græb/ *noun* [C] *The two children both* ***made*** *a grab* ***for*** (= made a sudden attempt to take) *the same cake.*

• **up for grabs** available and ready to be won or taken: *There are hundreds of prizes up for grabs in our competition.*

grab [OPPORTUNITY] /græb/ *verb* [T] **-bb-** INFORMAL to take the opportunity to get, use or enjoy something quickly: *If you don't grab this opportunity, you might not get another one.* ○ *We'd better get there early, or someone else will grab the best seats.* ○ *Let's just grab a quick bite.*

• **How does ... grab you?** INFORMAL used to ask if someone would like to do something or is interested in something: *We could have a picnic in the park. How does that grab you?*

-grabbing /-græb.ɪŋ/ *suffix*: *a* ***headline****-grabbing court case* (= one which is being written about a lot in newspapers)

▲ **grab at** ***sth/sb*** *phrasal verb* to try to get hold of someone or something quickly, with your hand: *I tried to grab at her arm as she went past.*

ˈgrab ˌbag *noun* [C] **1** US FOR **lucky dip 2** US any mixed collection of things

grace [MOVEMENT] /greɪs/ *noun* [U] a quality of moving in a smooth, relaxed and attractive way: *Joanna has natural grace and elegance.*

grace [MAKE ATTRACTIVE] /greɪs/ *verb* [T] When a person or thing graces a place or thing, they make it more attractive: *Her face has graced the covers of magazines across the world.*

• **grace** ***sb*** **with** ***your*** **presence** to honour people by taking part in something: *We are delighted that the mayor will be gracing us with his presence at our annual dinner.* ○ HUMOROUS *So you've finally decided to grace us with your presence, have you?* (= You are late.)

grace [POLITENESS] /greɪs/ *noun* [U] the quality of being pleasantly polite, or a willingness to be fair and honourable: *They accepted their defeat* ***with good*** *grace.*

graces /greɪsɪz/ *plural noun*: *Ken is sadly lacking in* ***social*** *graces* (= does not behave in a way considered polite).

grace [APPROVAL] /greɪs/ *noun* [U] FORMAL approval or kindness, especially (in the Christian religion) that is freely given by God to all human beings: *Betty believed that it*

G

was through ***divine*** *grace that her husband had recovered from his illness.*

• **by the grace of God** with the help of God: *By the grace of God, the pilot managed to land the damaged plane safely.*

• **There but for the grace of God (go I).** *SAYING* said when something bad that has happened to someone else could have happened to you

grace [TIME] /greɪs/ *noun* [U] a period of time left or allowed before something happens or before something must be done: *The exams have been postponed, so the students have a few days' grace before they start.*

grace [PRAYER] /greɪs/ *noun* [C or U] a prayer said by Christians before a meal to thank God for the food: *The children always* ***say*** *grace at school.*

Grace [TITLE] /greɪs/ *noun* **Your/His/Her Grace** used to address or refer to a DUKE, DUCHESS or ARCHBISHOP

graceful /ˈgreɪs.fəl/ *adj* **1** moving in a smooth, relaxed, attractive way, or having a smooth, attractive shape: *graceful movements* ○ *a graceful neck* **2** behaving in a polite and pleasant way: *She finally apologized, but she wasn't very graceful about it.* **gracefully** /ˈgreɪs.fəl.i/ *adv*

graceless /ˈgreɪ.sləs/ *adj* **1** without beauty: *graceless movements* **2** without politeness: *a graceless manner* **gracelessly** /ˈgreɪ.slə.sli/ *adv*

gracious [PLEASANT] /ˈgreɪ.ʃəs/ *adj* behaving in a pleasant, polite, calm way: *a gracious smile* ○ *He was gracious* ***enough*** *to thank me.* ○ *The losing team were gracious* ***in*** *defeat.* **graciously** /ˈgreɪ.ʃə.sli/ *adv*: *She graciously accepted the flowers that were presented to her.* **graciousness** /ˈgreɪ.ʃə.snəs/ *noun* [U]

gracious [COMFORTABLE] /ˈgreɪ.ʃəs/ *adj* having the qualities of great comfort, beauty and freedom made possible by wealth: *We can't afford gracious* ***living****.*

gracious [SURPRISE] /ˈgreɪ.ʃəs/ *exclamation OLD-FASHIONED* used to express surprise or to emphasize what is being said: *Gracious* ***(me)/Good*** *gracious* ***(me)****, I never thought he'd do that!*

grad /græd/ *noun* [C] *MAINLY US INFORMAL FOR* **graduate** PERSON

gradable /ˈgreɪ.də.bl̩/ *adj* A gradable adjective or adverb is one which can be used in the COMPARATIVE or SUPERLATIVE, or which can be qualified by words such as 'very' or 'quite'. **gradability** /greɪ.dəˈbɪl.ɪ.ti/ [US] /-ə.t̬i/ *noun* [U]

gradation /grəˈdeɪ.ʃən/ [US] /greɪ-/ *noun* [C or U] (a) gradual change, or a stage in the process of change: *The gradation* ***in/of*** *tempo in this piece of music is very subtle.* ○ *the gradations* (= marks showing units of measurement) *on a ruler*

grade [LEVEL] /greɪd/ *noun* [C] **1** a level of quality, size, importance etc: *He's suffering from some kind of* ***low****-grade* (= slight) *infection, which he can't seem to get rid of.* ○ *There's some really* ***high****-grade* (= high quality) *musicianship on this recording.* ○ *Bill has been (UK)* ***on****/ (US)* ***at*** *the same grade* (= his job has been of the same level of importance, or he has had the same level of pay) *for several years now.* **2** a number or letter that shows how good someone's work or performance is: *Steve never studies, but he always gets good grades.* ○ *UK Carla got a grade A in German.*

• **make the grade** to perform well enough to succeed in something: *Ian wanted to be an actor, but he didn't make the grade.*

grade /greɪd/ *verb* [T] **1** to separate people or things into different levels of quality, size, importance etc: *The fruit is washed and then graded* ***by*** *size.* ○ *The books are graded according to the difficulty of the language.* **2** *US* (*UK* **mark**) to give a score to a student's piece of work: *to grade work/papers*

grade [SCHOOL] /greɪd/ *noun* [C] *US* a school class or group of classes in which all the children are of a similar age or ability: *Jackie is in the sixth grade.*

-grader /-greɪ.dəʳ/ [US] /-greɪ.dɚ/ *suffix US an eighth-grader* (= a student in the eighth level of school)

grade [SLOPE] /greɪd/ *noun* [C] *US FOR* **gradient**: *The next hill has a real* ***steep*** *grade.*

ˈgrade ˌcrossing *noun* [C] *US FOR* **level crossing**

ˈgrade point ˌaverage *noun* [C] (*ABBREVIATION* **GPA**) *US* a number which is the average mark received for all the courses a student takes and shows how well the student is doing

ˈgrade ˌschool *noun* [C] *US* a school for children from the age of five to the age of ten or 14

gradient /ˈgreɪ.di.ənt/ *noun* [C] (*US ALSO* **grade**) how steep a slope is: *a* ***steep/gentle*** *gradient*

gradual /ˈgræd.ju.əl/ /ˈgrædʒ.u.əl/ *adj* happening or changing slowly over a long period of time or distance: *There has been a gradual* ***improvement*** *in our sales figures over the last two years.* ○ *As you go further south, you will notice a gradual* ***change*** *of climate.*

gradually /ˈgræd.ju.li/ /ˈgrædʒ.u.li/ *adv* slowly over a period of time or a distance: *Gradually, she realized that he wasn't telling her the truth.* ○ *The bank slopes gradually down to the river.*

graduate [PERSON] /ˈgrædʒ.u.ət/ *noun* [C] **1** *UK* a person who has a first degree from a university or college: *a Cambridge graduate* ○ *Chris is a physics graduate.* ➲See also **postgraduate**; **undergraduate**. **2** (*INFORMAL* **grad**) *US* a person who has completed their school, college or university education: *high-school graduates* ○ *a graduate* ***of*** *Yale*

graduate [QUALIFY] /ˈgrædʒ.u.eɪt/ *verb* **1** [I] *UK* to complete a first university degree successfully: *Lorna graduated* ***from*** *the University of London.* ○ *Tom has just graduated* ***with*** *first-class* ***honours in*** *psychology.* **2** [I or T] *US* to complete school, college or university correctly: *After he graduated high school, he joined the Army.*

graduate [ADVANCE] /ˈgrædʒ.u.eɪt/ *verb* [I] to advance or improve: *She graduated* ***from*** *being a secretary* ***to*** *running her own department.*

graduated /ˈgræd.ju.eɪ.tɪd/ [US] /-t̬ɪd/ *adj* divided into levels or stages: *The books that the children are using to learn to read are on a graduated* ***scale*** *of difficulty.*

ˈgraduate ˌschool *noun* [C] *US* a college or a college department where students who already have a first degree are taught

graduation /ˌgrædʒ.uˈeɪ.ʃən/ *noun* [C or U] when you receive your degree for completing your education or a course of study: *a graduation ceremony*

Graeco- /griː.kəʊ-/ /grek.əʊ-/ [US] /grek.oʊ-/ *prefix UK SPELLING OF* **Greco-**

graffiti /grəˈfiː.ti/ [US] /-t̬i/ *noun* [U], *plural noun* words or drawings, especially humorous, rude or political, on walls, doors, etc. in public places: *The subway walls are covered in graffiti.*

graft [PIECE] /grɑːft/ [US] /græft/ *noun* [C] a piece of healthy skin or bone cut from one part of a person's body and used to repair another damaged part, or a piece cut from one living plant and fixed to another plant so that it grows there: *He has had a* ***skin*** *graft on his badly burned arm.*

graft /grɑːft/ [US] /græft/ *verb* [T] **1** to take and attach a graft: *Skin was removed from her leg and grafted* ***on/ onto*** *her face.* **2** to join or add something new: *The management tried unsuccessfully to graft new working methods* ***onto*** *the existing ways of doing things.*

graft [WORK] /grɑːft/ [US] /græft/ *noun* [U] *UK INFORMAL* work: *I've never been afraid of* ***hard*** *graft.*

graft /grɑːft/ [US] /græft/ *verb* [I] *UK INFORMAL* to work hard: *It was very sad that after spending all those years grafting* ***(away)****, he died so soon after he retired.*

grafter /ˈgrɑːf.təʳ/ [US] /ˈgræf.t̬ɚ/ *noun* [C] *UK INFORMAL* a hard worker

graft [INFLUENCE] /grɑːft/ [US] /græft/ *noun* [U] *MAINLY US* the act of obtaining money or advantage through the dishonest use of political power and influence: *The whole government was riddled with graft, bribery, and corruption.*

the Grail /ðəˈgreɪl/ *noun* [S] **the Holy Grail**

grain [SEED] /greɪn/ *noun* [C or U] (a) seed from a plant, especially a grass-like plant such as rice or wheat: *grains of wheat/rice* ○ *Grain* (= the crop from grass-like food plants) *is one of the main exports of the American Midwest.* ➲See also **wholegrain**.

G

grain SMALL PIECE /greɪn/ *noun* **1** [C] a very small piece of a hard substance: *grains* **of** *sand* **2** [S] a very small amount of a particular quality: *There wasn't a grain of* ***truth*** *in anything she said.* ○ *Anyone with a grain of common sense would have known what to do.*

the grain PATTERN *noun* [S] the natural patterns of lines in the surface of wood, cloth, etc: *to cut something* ***along/against*** *the grain*
• **go against the grain** If something goes against the grain, you would not usually do it because it would be unusual or morally wrong: *These days it goes against the grain to show respect for authority.*

grain WEIGHT /greɪn/ *noun* [C] OLD-FASHIONED a unit of mass, equal to 0.0648 grams

grainy /ˈgreɪ.ni/ *adj* If photographs are grainy, they are unclear because the many black and white or coloured dots which make up the image can be seen.

gram, *UK ALSO* **gramme** /græm/ *noun* [C] (ALSO abbreviation **g** or **gm**) a unit of mass equal to 0.001 kilograms

grammar /ˈgræm.əʳ/ ⓤ /-ɚ/ *noun* **1** [U] (the study or use of) the rules about how words change their form and combine with other words to make sentences **2** [C] MAINLY UK a book of grammar rules: *a German grammar*

grammarian /grəˈmeə.ri.ən/ ⓤ /-ˈmer.i-/ *noun* [C] a person who studies grammar and usually writes books about it

'grammar ˌschool *noun* [C] a British school, especially in the past, for children aged 11-18 who are good at studying. In America, especially in the past, it is a school for children aged 5-12 or 5-14.

grammatical /grəˈmæt.ɪ.kʲl/ ⓤ /-ˈmæt̬-/ *adj* relating to grammar or obeying the rules of grammar: *a grammatical* (= grammatically correct) *sentence* **grammatically** /grəˈmæt.ɪ.kli/ ⓤ /-mæt̬-/ *adv*

gramme /græm/ *noun* [C] UK SPELLING OF **gram**

Grammy /ˈgræm.i/ *noun* [C] *plural* **Grammys** TRADEMARK in the US, one of a set of prizes given each year to people involved in different areas of the music industry: *She's won five Grammys.*

gramophone /ˈgræm.ə.fəʊn/ ⓤ /-foʊn/ *noun* [C] OLD-FASHIONED FOR **record player**

gran /græn/ *noun* [C] INFORMAL FOR **grandmother**

granary /ˈgræn.ərʲi/ ⓤ /-ɚ-/ *noun* **1** [C] a large building for storing wheat or other similar crops **2** [S] an area where a lot of wheat is grown: *Punjab, the granary of India*

'granary ˌbread UK *noun* [U] (US **whole wheat bread,** AUS **wholegrain bread**) a type of bread containing whole seeds of wheat

grand SPLENDID /grænd/ *adj* **1** splendid in style and appearance; attracting admiration and attention: *The Palace of Versailles is very grand.* ○ *They always entertain their guests in* ***grand style.*** **2** used in the name of a place or building to show that it is splendid or large: *the Grand Hotel* ○ *the Grand Canyon* ○ *the Grand Canal*
• **grand old age** If a person or animal lives to a grand old age, they live until they are very old: *He lived to the grand old age of 97.*
grandly /ˈgrænd.li/ *adv* in a grand way: *Their house is very grandly furnished.* **grandness** /ˈgrænd.nəs/ *noun* [U]

grand IMPORTANT /grænd/ *adj* important and large in degree: *She has all kinds of grand ideas.* ○ *His job has a grand title, but he's little more than a clerk.*
• **the grand old man of** *sth* HUMOROUS a man who has been involved in a particular activity for a long time and is known and respected by a lot of people: *He's been called the grand old man of cricket.*
grandly /ˈgrænd.li/ *adv* in a way suggesting that something or someone has great importance: *She announced grandly that she was spending Christmas in the Caribbean.* **grandness** /ˈgrænd.nəs/ *noun* [U]

grand EXCELLENT /grænd/ *adj* OLD-FASHIONED INFORMAL OR IRISH ENGLISH excellent; pleasing: *We had grand weather on our holiday.* ○ *My grandson is a grand little chap.* ○ *You've done a grand job.*

grand MONEY (*plural* **grand**) /grænd/ *noun* [C] (US **G**) INFORMAL £1000 or $1000: *John's new car cost him 20 grand!*

grand INSTRUMENT /grænd/ *noun* [C] *plural* **grand** INFORMAL FOR **grand piano**

grandad, granddad /ˈgræn.dæd/ *noun* [C] INFORMAL **1** grandfather **2** used rudely or humorously to address an old man: *Come on, grandad!*

grandaddy, granddaddy /ˈgræn.dæd.i/ *noun* [C] US INFORMAL FOR **grandfather**
• **the grandaddy of** *sth* MAINLY US INFORMAL the biggest, most important or most powerful event or person of their type: *'Modern Times' is a classic comedy starring Charlie Chaplin, the grandaddy of comic film actors.*

grandchild /ˈgrænd.tʃaɪld/ *noun* [C] *plural* **grandchildren** the child of a person's son or daughter

granddaughter /ˈgrænd.dɔː.təʳ/ ⓤ /-dɑː.t̬ɚ/ *noun* [C] the daughter of a person's son or daughter

grande dame /ˌgrɑːndˈdɑːm/ *noun* [C usually sing] a woman who is respected because of her experience and knowledge of a particular subject: *Vivienne Westwood is the grande dame of British fashion.*

grandee /grænˈdiː/ *noun* [C] an important person, especially in a particular job or area of public life

grandeur /ˈgræn.djəʳ/ ⓤ /-dʒɚ/ *noun* [U] the quality of being very large and special or beautiful: *We were struck by the silent grandeur* ***of*** *the desert.* ○ *the grandeur* ***of*** *Wagner's music*

grandfather /ˈgrænd.fɑː.ðəʳ/ ⓤ /-ðɚ/ *noun* [C] (INFORMAL **grandpa,** INFORMAL **grandad**) the father of a person's mother or father

'grandfather ˌclock *noun* [C] a tall clock in a wooden case which stands on the floor

grandiloquent /grænˈdɪl.ə.kwᵊnt/ *adj* FORMAL MAINLY DISAPPROVING describes a style or a way of using language that is complicated in order to attract admiration and attention, especially in order to make someone or something seem important: *Her speech was full of grandiloquent language, but it contained no new ideas.* **grandiloquence** /grænˈdɪl.ə.kwᵊnts/ *noun* [U] **grandiloquently** /grænˈdɪl.ə.kwᵊnt.li/ *adv*

grandiose /ˈgræn.di.əʊs/ ⓤ /-oʊs/ *adj* DISAPPROVING larger and containing more detail than necessary, or intended to seem important or splendid: *grandiose* ***plans/schemes/ideas*** *for making money*

ˌgrand 'jury *noun* [C] in the US, a group of people who decide whether a person who has been charged with a crime should be given a trial in a court of law

grandma /ˈgrænd.mɑː/ /ˈgræm-/ *noun* [C] INFORMAL FOR **grandmother**

grandmaster /ˈgrænd.mɑː.stəʳ/ ⓤ /-ˌmæs.t̬ɚ/ *noun* [C] (WRITTEN ABBREVIATION **GM**) (the rank of) a person who plays the game of chess with the highest level of skill

grandmother /ˈgrænd.mʌð.əʳ/ /ˈgræm-/ ⓤ /-ɚ/ *noun* [C] (INFORMAL **grandma,** INFORMAL **granny,** INFORMAL **gran**) the mother of a person's father or mother
• **teach your grandmother to suck eggs** UK DISAPPROVING to give advice to someone about a subject that they already know more about than you

ˌgrand 'opera *noun* [U] a type of serious opera

grandpa /ˈgrænd.pɑː/ /ˈgræm-/ *noun* [C] INFORMAL FOR **grandfather**

grandparent /ˈgrænd.peə.rᵊnt/ ⓤ /-per.ᵊnt/ *noun* [C] the father or mother of a person's father or mother

ˌgrand pi'ano *noun* [C] (INFORMAL **grand**) a large piano which has horizontal strings in a case supported on three legs

grand prix /ˌgrɑːˈpriː/ ⓤ /ˌgrɑːn-/ *noun* [C] *plural* **grands prix** one of a series of important international races for very fast and powerful cars: *the Italian Grand Prix*

ˌgrand 'slam WINNING EVERYTHING *noun* [C usually sing] when someone wins all of a set of important sports competitions

ˌgrand 'slam CARDS *noun* [C usually sing] when someone wins all the cards in a card game, especially BRIDGE

ˌgrand 'slam BASEBALL *noun* [C] in baseball, the hitting of a HOME RUN with runners at all three BASES, so that four points are scored

grandson /ˈgrænd.sʌn/ *noun* [C] the son of a person's son or daughter

grandstand /ˈgrænd.stænd/ *noun* [C] a set of seats arranged in rising rows, sometimes covered by a roof, from which people can easily watch sports or other events
• **have a grandstand view** *INFORMAL* to be in a position where you can see something very well: *From our hotel room window, we had a grandstand view* ***of*** *the parade.*

grandstanding /ˈgrænd,stæn.dɪŋ/ *noun* [U] *US INFORMAL* acting or speaking in a way intended to attract the good opinion of other people who are watching

ˌgrand ˈtotal *noun* [C] the complete number after everything has been added up: *The school bazaar raised a/the grand total of £550.*

ˌgrand ˈtour *noun* [C] **1** (*ALSO* **Grand Tour**) a visit to the most important countries and cities of Europe which rich young people made in the past as part of their education **2** *OFTEN HUMOROUS* when someone shows you round a house or other building: *Let me give you a grand tour* ***of*** *the house.*

G

grange /ˈgreɪndʒ/ *noun* [C] **1** (*ALSO* **Grange**) a large house in the countryside with farm buildings connected to it: *Chiltern Grange* **2** *US FOR* **farm**

granite /ˈgræn.ɪt/ *noun* [U] a very hard, grey, pink and black rock, which is used for building

granny, grannie /ˈgræn.i/ *noun* [C] *INFORMAL FOR* **grandmother**
granny, grannie /ˈgræn.i/ *adj UK INFORMAL* used of something that you wear, to mean having a style like those worn by old women: *granny glasses/shoes*

ˈgranny ˌflat *noun* [C] *UK* a set of rooms, often connected to or part of a relative's house, in which an old person lives

ˈgranny ˌknot *noun* [C] a simple knot that is not fully tied, so it can be easily unfastened

granola /grəˈnəʊ.lə/ [US] /-ˈnoʊ-/ *noun* [U] *US* a food made of baked grains, nuts and dried fruit which is usually eaten in the morning: *Granola is a lot like muesli, only crunchier.*

grant [MONEY] /grɑːnt/ [US] /grænt/ *noun* [C] a sum of money given especially by the government to a person or organization for a special purpose: *a student/research grant* ○ *a local authority/government grant* ○ [+ **to** infinitive] *They* ***gave/awarded*** *her a grant* ***to*** *study abroad for one year.*

grant [GIVE] /grɑːnt/ [US] /grænt/ *verb* [T] to give or allow someone something, usually in an official way: [+ two objects] *They granted her an entry visa.* ○ *He was granted asylum.* ○ *FORMAL She granted their request/wish.*

grant [ACCEPT] /grɑːnt/ [US] /grænt/ *verb* [T + (*that*) clause] to accept that something is true, often before expressing an opposite opinion: *I grant* ***that*** *it must have been upsetting but even so I think she made a bit of a fuss.* ○ ***I grant you*** (= It is true that), *it's a difficult situation but I feel sure he could have handled it more sensitively.*
• **take *sth* for granted** to believe something to be the truth without even thinking about it: *I didn't realize that Melanie hadn't been to college – I suppose I just took it for granted.*
• **take *sth or sb* for granted** If you take situations or people for granted, you do not appreciate or show that you are grateful for how much you benefit from them: *One of the problems with relationships is that after a while you just take each other for granted.*
granted /ˈgrɑːn.tɪd/ [US] /ˈgræn.t̬ɪd/ *conjunction* used to mean 'if you accept' something: *Granted* ***(that)*** *the story's true, what are you going to do about it?*

grant-maintained school /ˌgrɑːnt.meɪnˌteɪndˈskuːl/ [US] /ˌgrænt-/ *noun* [C] (*ALSO* **GM school**) a school in the UK that receives its money directly from central rather than local government

granulated /ˈgræn.jʊ.leɪ.tɪd/ [US] /-t̬ɪd/ *adj* in small grains: *granulated* ***sugar***

granule /ˈgræn.juːl/ *noun* [C] a small grain-like piece of something: *coffee granules*
granular /ˈgræn.jʊ.ləʳ/ [US] /-jə.lɚ/ *adj* made of, or seeming like, granules: *a granular texture*

grape /greɪp/ *noun* [C] a small round purple or pale green fruit that you can eat or make into wine: *black/white/red/green grapes* ○ *a bunch of grapes* ○ *seedless grapes* ○ *grape juice* ➲See picture **Fruit** on page Centre 1
• **the grape** *HUMOROUS* wine

grapefruit /ˈgreɪp.fruːt/ *noun* [C] *plural* **grapefruit** or **grapefruits** a fruit which is like a large orange, but has a yellow skin and tastes less sweet ➲See picture **Fruit** on page Centre 1

grapevine /ˈgreɪp.vaɪn/ *noun* [C] (*ALSO* **vine**) a type of climbing plant on which grapes grow
• **hear *(sth)* on/through the grapevine** to hear news from someone who heard the news from someone else: *I heard on the grapevine* ***that*** *he was leaving – is it true?*

graph /grɑːf/ /græf/ *noun* [C] a picture which shows how two sets of information or variable amounts are related, usually by lines or curves: *This graph shows how crime has varied in relationship to unemployment over the last 20 years.* **graphic** /ˈgræf.ɪk/ *adj* (*MAINLY UK* **graphical**) **graphically** /ˈgræf.ɪ.kli/ *adv*

graphic [CLEAR] /ˈgræf.ɪk/ *adj* very clear and powerful: *a graphic description/account* ○ *He insisted on describing his operation* ***in*** *graphic* ***detail*** *while we were eating lunch.*
graphically /ˈgræf.ɪ.kli/ *adv*: *The incident graphically* (= very clearly) *illustrates just how dangerous the situation in the war zone has become.*

COMMON LEARNER ERROR

graphic, graphical or **striking?**

Graphical is not a common word and is only used to describe information displayed in the form of a graph. To describe a very detailed and realistic image use **graphic**. To describe someone or something that is very impressive or unusual to look at use **striking**.
The film contains one very graphic scene of horrifying violence.
The huge white tower on the waterfront is very striking.
~~*The huge white tower on the waterfront is very graphical.*~~

graphic [DRAWING] /ˈgræf.ɪk/ *adj* [before n] related to drawing or printing: *a graphic artist*

ˌgraphical ˌuser ˈinterface *noun* [C] (*ABBREVIATION* **GUI**) a way of arranging information on a computer screen that is easy to understand and use because it uses ICONS, MENUS and a MOUSE rather than only text

ˌgraphic deˈsign *noun* [U] the art of designing pictures and text for books, magazines, advertising, etc.
ˌgraphic deˈsigner *noun* [C] someone who works in graphic design

graphics /ˈgræf.ɪks/ *plural noun* images and designs used in books, magazines, etc: ***computer*** *graphics*

ˈgraphics ˌcard *noun* [C] (*ALSO* **video card**) a CIRCUIT BOARD (= small piece of electronic equipment) inside a computer that enables it to receive and display pictures and video

graphite /ˈgræf.aɪt/ *noun* [U] a soft dark grey form of carbon, used in the middle of pencils, as a LUBRICANT in machines, and in some atomic REACTORS

graphology /grəˈfɒl.ə.dʒi/ [US] /-ˈfɑː.lə-/ *noun* [U] the study of the way people write letters and words, especially in order to discover things about their characters
graphologist /grəˈfɒl.ə.dʒɪst/ [US] /-ˈfɑː.lə-/ *noun* [C]

grapnel /ˈgræp.nəl/ *noun* [C] (*ALSO* **grappling iron/hook**) a device which consists of several hooks on the end of a rope, used especially in the past on ships

grappa /ˈgræp.ə/ [US] /ˈgrɑː.pə/ *noun* [U] a type of brandy made from grapes

grapple /ˈgræp.l̩/ *verb* [I] to fight, especially in order to gain something: *The children grappled* ***for*** *the ball.*

PHRASAL VERBS WITH **grapple** ▼

▲ **grapple with *sb*** [FIGHT] *phrasal verb* to hold onto someone and fight with them: *Two officers grappled with the gunman.*
▲ **grapple with *sth*** [PROBLEM] *phrasal verb* to try to deal with or understand a difficult problem or subject: *Today, many Americans are still grappling with the issue of race.*

ˈgrappling ˌiron/ˌhook *noun* [C] a **grapnel**

grasp [HOLD] /grɑːsp/ [US] /græsp/ *verb* [T] **1** to quickly take something in your hand(s) and hold it firmly: *Rosie* *suddenly grasped my hand.* **2** If you grasp an opportunity, you take it eagerly: *We must grasp every opportunity to strengthen economic ties with other countries.*

• **grasp the nettle** *UK* to force yourself to be brave and do something that is difficult or unpleasant: *You've been putting off making that phone call for days – I think it's about time you grasped the nettle!*

grasp /grɑːsp/ [US] /græsp/ *noun* **1** [S] when you hold onto someone or something: *He shook my hand with a very firm grasp.* **2** [U] the ability to get, achieve or keep something: *The presidency at last looked* ***within*** *her grasp* (= It looked possible that she might become president). ○ *Why is success always* ***beyond*** *my grasp* (= impossible to get)? ○ *The gold medal* ***slipped from*** *his grasp* (= He was unable to get it) *in the last moments of the race.* ○ *I sometimes think that he's* ***losing*** *his grasp* ***on*** *reality* (= his ability to judge what is real and what is not).

grasp [UNDERSTAND] /grɑːsp/ [US] /græsp/ *verb* [T] to understand something, especially something difficult: *I think I managed to grasp the main points of the lecture.* ○ *The Government has acknowledged that homelessness is a problem but it has failed to grasp the scale of the problem.*

grasp /grɑːsp/ [US] /græsp/ *noun* [S or U] understanding: *I'm afraid my grasp of economics is rather limited.*

PHRASAL VERBS WITH **grasp**

▲ **grasp at *sth*** [OPPORTUNITY] *phrasal verb* to try to take an opportunity: *Certainly if the job were offered me I'd grasp at the chance.*

▲ **grasp at *sth*** [OBJECT] *phrasal verb* to try to hold or touch something: *She grasped at his shirt as he ran past.*

grasping /ˈgrɑː.spɪŋ/ [US] /ˈgræs.pɪŋ/ *adj DISAPPROVING* (of people) always trying to get and keep more of something, especially money: *a grasping, greedy man*

grass /grɑːs/ [US] /græs/ *noun* **1** [C or U] a low green plant which grows naturally over a lot of the Earth's surface, having groups of very thin leaves which grow in large numbers very close together: *a blade of grass* ○ ***cut*** *the grass* ○ *a vase of dried flowers and grasses* (= different types of grass) **2** [U] *SLANG* **cannabis**

• **put *sb* out to grass** *INFORMAL* to make someone stop work permanently because they are too old

• **The grass is always greener on the other side (of the fence).** *SAYING* something that you say which means that other people always seem to be in a better situation than you, although they may not be: *I sometimes think I'd be happier teaching in Spain. Oh well, the grass is always greener on the other side!*

grassy /ˈgrɑː.si/ [US] /ˈgræs.i/ *adj* covered with grass: *a grassy slope/hillside*

grass /grɑːs/ [US] /græs/ *verb*

PHRASAL VERBS WITH **grass**

▲ **grass on *sb*** *phrasal verb UK SLANG* If a person grasses on somebody else, they tell the police or someone in authority about something bad that that person has done: *Dan grassed on them* ***to*** *the local police.*

grass /grɑːs/ [US] /græs/ *noun* [C] *UK SLANG* a person, usually a criminal, who informs the police of other criminals' activities ➲See also **supergrass**.

▲ **grass *sth* over** *verb* [T] to grow grass on an area of land

grasshopper /ˈgrɑːsˌhɒp.əʳ/ [US] /ˈgræsˌhɑː.pɚ/ *noun* [C] a plant-eating insect with long back legs that can jump very high and makes a sharp high noise using its back legs or wings

grassland /ˈgrɑːs.lænd/ /-lənd/ [US] /ˈgræs-/ *noun* [C or U] a large area of land covered with grass: *the grasslands of North America*

the ˌgrass'roots *plural noun* the ordinary people in a society or an organization, especially a political party: *The feeling among the grassroots of the party is that the leaders are not radical enough.* **grassroots** /ˈgrɑːs.ruːts/ [US] /ˈgræs-/ *adj* [before n] *grassroots support* ○ *a grassroots movement/campaign*

ˌgrass 'widow *noun* [C] *HUMOROUS* a woman who spends a lot of time apart from her husband, often because he is working in a different place

grate [FIRE] /greɪt/ *noun* [C] a metal structure which holds coal or wood in a fireplace

grate [RUB TOGETHER] /greɪt/ *verb* [I] When two hard objects grate, they rub together, sometimes making a sharp unpleasant sound.

grate [ANNOY] /greɪt/ *verb* [I] When a noise or behaviour grates, it annoys you: *After a while her voice really started to grate* ***on*** *me.* ○ *It's the way she's always talking about herself – it just grates* ***on*** *me.*

grate [COOKING] /greɪt/ *verb* [T] to rub food against a GRATER (= metal device with sharp holes in it), in order to cut it into a lot of small pieces: *grated cheese* ➲See picture **In the Kitchen** on page Centre 16

grateful /ˈgreɪt.fəl/ *adj* showing or expressing thanks, especially to another person: *I'm so grateful (to you)* ***for*** *all that you've done.* ○ *If you could get that report finished by Thursday I'd be very grateful.* ○ *After the earthquake we felt grateful* ***to*** *be alive.* ○ *I'm just grateful* ***that*** *I'm not still working for him.* ○ *FORMAL I would be* ***most*** *grateful if you would send me the book immediately.*
✻ NOTE: The opposite is **ungrateful**. **gratefully** /ˈgreɪt.fəl.i/ *adv*: *She smiled at me gratefully.*

grater /ˈgreɪ.təʳ/ [US] /-t̬ɚ/ *noun* [C] a metal device with holes surrounded by sharp edges used to cut food into small pieces ➲See picture **In the Kitchen** on page Centre 16

gratify /ˈgræt.ɪ.faɪ/ [US] /ˈgræt̬.ə-/ *verb* [T] to please someone, or to satisfy a wish or need: *We were gratified* ***by*** *the response to our appeal.* ○ [+ **to** infinitive] *He was gratified* ***to*** *see how well his students had done.*

gratification /ˌgræt.ɪ.fɪˈkeɪ.ʃən/ [US] /ˌgræt̬.ə-/ *noun* [U] *sexual gratification* ○ *Some people expect* ***instant*** *gratification* (= to get what they want immediately). **gratifying** /ˈgræt.ɪ.faɪ.ɪŋ/ [US] /ˈgræt̬-/ *adj* [+ **to** infinitive] *It must be very gratifying* ***to*** *see all your children grown up and happy.* **gratifyingly** /ˈgræt.ɪ.faɪ.ɪŋ.li/ [US] /ˈgræt̬-/ *adv*: *The success rate in the exam was gratifyingly high.*

gratin /ˈgræt.æ̃ŋ/ [US] /ˈgrɑː.t̬ən/ *noun* [C or U], *adj* [after n] in cookery, a dish which has a thin layer of cheese and often breadcrumbs on top: *aubergine and tomato gratin*

grating [SOUND] /ˈgreɪ.tɪŋ/ [US] /-t̬ɪŋ/ *adj* describes a sound which is unpleasant and annoying

grating [COVERING] /ˈgreɪ.tɪŋ/ [US] /-t̬ɪŋ/ *noun* [C] a structure made of metal bars which covers a hole, especially in the ground over a DRAIN

gratis /ˈgræ.tɪs/ *adv, adj* [after v] free: *I'll give it to you, gratis!*

gratitude /ˈgræt.ɪ.tjuːd/ [US] /ˈgræt̬.ə.tuːd/ *noun* [U] (*ALSO* **gratefulness**) the feeling or quality of being grateful: *deep/eternal gratitude* ○ *She sent them a present to* ***show/express*** *her gratitude.* ○ *Take this* ***as a token of*** *my gratitude for all your help.*

gratuitous /grəˈtjuː.ɪ.təs/ [US] /-ˈtuː.ə.t̬əs/ *adj DISAPPROVING* (of something such as bad behaviour) not necessary; with no cause: *A lot of viewers complained that there was too much gratuitous* ***sex*** *and* ***violence*** *in the film.* **gratuitously** /grəˈtjuː.ɪ.tə.sli/ [US] /-ˈtuː.ə-/ *adv*: *gratuitously violent* **gratuitousness** /grəˈtjuː.ɪ.tə.snəs/ [US] /-ˈtuː.ə-/ *noun* [U]

gratuity /grəˈtjuː.ə.ti/ [US] /-ˈtuː.ə.t̬i/ *noun* [C] a sum of money given as a reward for a service: *FORMAL The guides sometimes receive gratuities from the tourists which supplement their salaries.* ○ *UK After he was disabled in the accident, he left the army with a one-off gratuity of £5000.*

grave [DEATH] /greɪv/ *noun* [C] a place in the ground where a dead person is buried: *a mass grave* ○ *an unmarked grave* ○ *a grave digger* ○ *He visits his mother's grave every Sunday.*

• **beyond the grave** after death: *Do you think there's life beyond the grave?*

• **turn in *your* grave** *UK* (*US* **turn over/spin in your grave**) If you say that a dead person would turn in their grave, you mean that they would be very angry or upset about something if they knew about it: *She'd turn in her grave if she knew what he was spending his inheritance on.*

grave [SERIOUS] /greɪv/ *adj* seriously bad: *a grave situation* **gravely** /ˈgreɪv.li/ *adv*: *gravely ill*

G

gravity /ˈgræv.ɪ.ti/ [US] /-ə.t̬i/ *noun* [U] *I don't think you understand the gravity* (= seriousness) *of the situation.* ➲See also **gravity**.

ˌ**grave (ˈaccent)** *noun* [C] a symbol used over a letter in some languages, for example the letter 'è' in French, to show that it is pronounced in a particular way

gravel /ˈgræv.ᵊl/ *noun* [U] small rounded stones, often mixed with sand: *a gravel path* **gravelled**, *US USUALLY* **graveled** /ˈgræv.ᵊld/ *adj* **gravelly** /ˈgræv.ᵊl.i/ *adj*: *gravelly soil*

gravelly /ˈgræv.ᵊl.i/ *adj* If a voice, especially a man's voice, is gravelly, it is low and rough.

ˈ**gravel** ˌ**pit** *noun* [C] a place where gravel is dug out of the ground

graven image /ˌgreɪ.vᵊnˈɪm.ɪdʒ/ *noun* [C] *DISAPPROVING* an object made especially from wood, stone, etc. and used for religious worship

graveside /ˈgreɪv.saɪd/ *noun* [C usually sing] the area next to a GRAVE: *He made a short speech* ***at the*** *graveside, then the body was finally buried.*

gravestone /ˈgreɪv.stəʊn/ [US] /-stoʊn/ *noun* [C] a stone that shows where a dead person is buried and which usually has their name and the years of their birth and death written on it ➲Compare **headstone**.

graveyard /ˈgreɪv.jɑːd/ [US] /-jɑːrd/ *noun* [C] a place, often beside a church where dead people are buried

ˈ**graveyard** ˌ**shift** *noun* [C] *INFORMAL* a period of work, for example in a factory, which begins late at night and ends early in the morning: *to work* ***the*** *graveyard shift*

gravitas /ˈgræv.ɪ.tæs/ *noun* [U] *FORMAL* seriousness and importance of manner, causing feelings of respect and trust in others: *He's an effective enough politician but somehow he lacks the statesmanlike gravitas of a world leader.*

gravitate /ˈgræv.ɪ.teɪt/ *verb*

▲ **gravitate towards/to** ***sth/sb*** *UK phrasal verb* (*US* **gravitate toward** ***sth/sb***) to be attracted by or to move in the direction of something or someone: *Susie always gravitates towards the older children in her playgroup.*

gravitation /ˌgræv.ɪˈteɪ.ʃᵊn/ *noun* [S or U] *The gravitation of country people* ***to/towards*** *the capital began in the 1920s.*

gravity /ˈgræv.ɪ.ti/ [US] /-ə.t̬i/ *noun* [U] the force which attracts objects towards one another, especially the force that makes things fall to the ground: *the laws of gravity* **gravitational** /ˌgræv.ɪˈteɪ.ʃᵊn.ᵊl/ *adj*: *gravitational forces*

gravy /ˈgreɪ.vi/ *noun* [U] a sauce made from meat juices, liquid and flour, and served with meat and vegetables

ˈ**gravy** ˌ**boat** *noun* [C] a long low container with a handle, used for serving gravy at the table

ˈ**gravy** ˌ**train** *noun* [C usually sing] a way of making money quickly, easily, and often dishonestly

gray /greɪ/ *adj US SPELLING OF* grey

graze [SURFACE] /greɪz/ *verb* [T] **1** to break the surface of the skin by rubbing against something rough: *He fell down and grazed his* ***knee***. ○ *He was lucky, the bullet just grazed his leg.* **2** If an object grazes something, it touches its surface lightly when it passes it: *The aircraft's landing gear grazed the treetops as it landed.*

graze /greɪz/ *noun* [C] *Her legs were covered with cuts and grazes.*

graze [FOOD] /greɪz/ *verb* **1** [I or T] to (cause animals to) eat grass: *The cows were grazing.* ○ *The farmer grazes cattle on this land in the summer months.* **2** [I] *INFORMAL* to eat small amounts of food many times during the day instead of sitting down to eat meals at particular times: *No dinner for me, thanks – I've been grazing all day.*

ˈ**grazing (**ˌ**land)** *noun* [U] land where farm animals feed on grass

grease /griːs/ *noun* [U] animal or vegetable fat that is soft after melting, or more generally, any thick oily substance: *The dinner plates were thick with grease.* ○ *You'll have to put some grease on those ball bearings.*

grease /griːs/ *verb* [T] to put fat or oil on something: *Grease the tins well before adding the cake mixture.*

• **grease** ***sb's*** **palm** *DISAPPROVING* to secretly give someone money in order to persuade them to do something for you

• **like greased lightning** very fast: *As soon as I mentioned work, he was out of the door like greased lightning!*

ˈ**grease** ˌ**monkey** *noun* [C] *MAINLY US OLD-FASHIONED SLANG* someone whose job is repairing car or aircraft engines

greasepaint /ˈgriːs.peɪnt/ *noun* [U] make-up as used by actors in the theatre

greaseproof paper /ˌgriːs.pruːfˈpeɪ.pəʳ/ [US] /-pɚ/ *noun* [U] *UK* paper which does not allow oil through, used especially in cooking: *Line the tins with greaseproof paper.*

greasy /ˈgriː.si/ *adj* covered with or full of fat or oil: *greasy food/dishes/skin/hair* **greasiness** /ˈgriː.sɪ.nəs/ *noun* [U]

ˌ**greasy** ˈ**spoon** *noun* [C usually sing] *SLANG* a small, cheap restaurant, especially one which sells a lot of fried food

great [BIG] /greɪt/ *adj* **1** large in amount, size or degree: *an enormous great hole* ○ *A great crowd had gathered outside the President's palace.* ○ *The improvement in water standards over the last 50 years has been very great.* ○ *A great many people would agree.* ○ ***The*** *great* ***majority of*** (= Almost all) *people would agree.* ○ *FORMAL It gives us great* ***pleasure*** *to announce the engagement of our daughter Maria.* ○ *FORMAL It is with great* ***sorrow*** *that I inform you of the death of our director.* ○ *I have great* ***sympathy*** *for you.* ○ *I spent a great* ***deal of*** *time there.* **2** [before n] used in names, especially to mean large or important: *a Great Dane* (= large type of dog) ○ *Catherine the Great* ○ *the Great Wall of China* ○ *the Great Bear* (= group of stars)

• **go great guns** *OLD-FASHIONED INFORMAL* to go fast or successfully: *For the first 400 metres he was going great guns, but then he fell and that lost him the race.*

• **no great shakes** *INFORMAL* not very good: *I'm afraid I am no great shakes* ***as*** *a cook/****at*** *cook****ing****!*

Greater /ˈgreɪ.təʳ/ [US] /-t̬ɚ/ *adj* [before n] used before names of some cities to refer to both the city itself and the area around it: *Greater Manchester*

great [FAMOUS] /greɪt/ *adj APPROVING* famous, powerful, or important as one of a particular type: *a great politician/leader/artist/man/woman* ○ *This is one of Rembrandt's greatest paintings.* ○ *Who do you think is the greatest modern novelist?*

• **great minds think alike** *HUMOROUS* said to someone just after you have discovered that they have had the same idea as you

great /greɪt/ *noun* [C] a famous person in a particular area of activity: *former tennis great Arthur Ashe* ○ *Woody Allen, one of the* ***all-time*** *greats of the cinema*

• **the great and the good** *UK* important people: *The great and the good are calling on the Government to support the arts.*

greatness /ˈgreɪt.nəs/ *noun* [U] skill and importance: *Her greatness as a writer is unquestioned.*

great [GOOD] /greɪt/ *adj INFORMAL* **1** very good: *a great idea* ○ *We had a great time last night at the party.* ○ ***It's*** *great* ***to*** *see you after all this time!* ○ *"I'll lend you the car if you like." "Great! Thanks a lot!"* ○ *"What's your new teacher like?" "Oh, he's great."* ○ *"How are you feeling now?" "Great."* **2** used to mean that something is very bad: *Oh great ! That's all I need – more bills!*

• **be a great one for** ***sth*** to enjoy or do something a lot: *He's a great one for gett****ing*** *other people to do his work for him, old Peter!*

great [EXTREME] /greɪt/ *adj* extreme: *great success/difficulty*

greatly /ˈgreɪt.li/ *adv* very much, used especially to show how much you feel or experience something: *I greatly regret not having told the truth.* ○ *Her piano playing has greatly improved/has improved greatly.*

great [EMPHASIS] /greɪt/ *adv, adj* [before n] *INFORMAL* used to emphasize the meaning of another word: *a great big spider* ○ *a great long queue* ○ *You great idiot!* ○ *Pat's a great friend of mine.*

great- [FAMILIES] /greɪt-/ *prefix* used with a word for a family member to mean one GENERATION away from that member: *your great-grandmother* (= the grandmother of one of your parents) ○ *your great-grandson* (= the grandson of your child)

G

greatcoat /'greɪt.kəʊt/ ⓤ /-koʊt/ *noun* [C] a long heavy warm coat, worn especially by soldiers over their uniform

the ˌGreat 'War *noun* [S] *UK* **World War One**

grebe /griːb/ *noun* [C] any of a family of grey or brown water birds which swim on or under the water

Grecian /'griː.ʃᵊn/ *adj* (especially of building styles or a person's appearance) beautiful and simple, in the style of Ancient Greece: *a Grecian column*

Greco-, Graeco- /griː.kəʊ-/ /grek.oʊ-/ ⓤ /grek.oʊ-/ *prefix* of or connected with ancient Greece: *splendid Greco-Roman ruins*

greed /griːd/ *noun* [U] a very strong wish to continually get more of something, especially food or money: *I don't know why I'm eating more – it's not hunger, it's just greed!* ○ *He was unsympathetic with many house sellers, complaining that they were motivated by greed.*

greedy /'griː.di/ *adj* wanting a lot more food, money, etc. than you need: *greedy, selfish people* ○ *He's greedy for power/success.* **greedily** /'griː.dɪ.li/ *adv*: *He ate the bread greedily.* **greediness** /'griː.di.nəs/ *noun* [U]

greedy-guts /'griː.di.gʌts/ *noun* [S] *UK INFORMAL OR CHILD'S WORD* someone who eats too much

Greek /griːk/ *adj* from, belonging to or relating to Greece: *Greek history/culture* ○ *Greek food*
Greek /griːk/ *noun* **1** [U] the language of Greece: *modern/ancient Greek* **2** [C] a person from Greece ⊃See also **Grecian**.
● **It's all Greek to me.** a way of saying that you do not understand something that is said or written

ˌGreek 'cross *noun* [C] a cross with four arms which are all the same length

green [COLOUR] /griːn/ *adj* of a colour between blue and yellow; of the colour of grass: *green vegetables* **green** /griːn/ *noun* [C or U] *light/pale green* ○ *dark/bottle green*
● **give the green light to sth** (*INFORMAL* **green-light**) to give permission for someone to do something or for something to happen: *The council has given the green light to the new shopping development.*
● **go/turn green** to look pale and ill as if you are going to vomit
● **be green with envy** to be very unhappy because someone has something that you want: *Ben's heading off to Spain for the week and I'm green with envy.*
greenish /'griː.nɪʃ/ *adj* slightly green: *greenish blue eyes*

green [POLITICAL] /griːn/ *adj* relating to the protection of the environment: *green politics/issues* ○ *a green campaigner/activist* ○ *the Green Party*
Green /griːn/ *noun* [C] a member of the Green Party: *He used to be a Liberal, but now he's a Green.*
greening /'griː.nɪŋ/ *noun* [S] *The next ten years, he predicted, would see the greening of America* (= Americans starting to take more care of the environment).

green [NOT RIPE] /griːn/ *adj* (especially of fruit) not ripe enough to eat, or (of wood) not dry enough to use: *green bananas/tomatoes*

green [NOT EXPERIENCED] /griːn/ *adj* not experienced or trained: *I was very green when I started working there.*

green [PLANTS] /griːn/ *adj* covered with grass, trees and other plants: *the green hills of Ireland*
green /griːn/ *noun* [C] **1** an area planted with grass, especially for use by the public: *Children were playing on the village green.* **2** used as a part of a name: *Sheep's Green* **3** a flat area of grass surrounding the hole on a golf course
greenery /'griː.nᵊr.i/ *noun* [U] green plants or branches, especially when cut and used as decoration
greening /'griː.nɪŋ/ *noun* [S] *Concern about the ugly effects of industrialization has led to the greening of* (= the planting of grass, trees and plants in) *many of our cities.* **greenness** /'griː.nəs/ *noun* [U] *What first struck her when she arrived in England was the greenness of the countryside.*

ˈgreen ˌaudit *noun* [C] an official examination of the effects a company or other organization has on the environment, especially the damage that it causes: *Management refused to carry out/conduct a green audit.*

greenback /'griːn.bæk/ *noun* [C] *US OLD-FASHIONED SLANG* a US dollar

ˌgreen 'bean *noun* [C] (*UK ALSO* **French bean**) a type of long, green, edible bean ⊃See picture **Vegetables** on page Centre 2

ˈgreen ˌbelt *noun* [C usually sing] a strip of countryside round a city or town where building is not allowed

ˈgreen ˌcard [WORK] *noun* [C] a document giving a foreigner permission to live and work in the United States

ˈgreen ˌcard [CAR] *noun* [C] *UK* a document which INSURES your car against accidents (= protects you financially if you have a car accident) when travelling in other countries

greenfield /'griːn.fiːld/ *adj* [before n] *UK* describes land that has not yet been built on, or buildings built on land that had never been used before for building: *a greenfield site*

greenfinch /'griːn.fɪntʃ/ *noun* [C] a medium-sized greenish bird, common in Europe

ˌgreen 'fingers *UK plural noun* (*US* **green thumb**) the ability to make plants grow **green-fingered** *UK* /ˌgriːn-'fɪŋ.gəd/ ⓤ /-gɚd/ *adj* (*US* **green-thumbed**)

greenfly /'griːn.flaɪ/ *noun* [C] *plural* **greenfly** or **greenflies** a very small pale green insect that often harms plants

greengage /'griːn.geɪdʒ/ *noun* [C] a small greenish yellow PLUM (= soft, juicy fruit)

greengrocer /'griːn.grəʊ.sər/ ⓤ /-groʊ.sɚ/ *noun* [C] *MAINLY UK* **1** a person who owns or works in a shop that sells fresh vegetables and fruit **2** (*ALSO* **greengrocer's**) a shop in which fresh vegetables and fruit are sold

greenhorn /'griːn.hɔːn/ ⓤ /-hɔːrn/ *noun* [C] a person who is not experienced

greenhouse /'griːn.haʊs/ *noun* [C] a building with a roof and sides made of glass, used for growing plants that need warmth and protection: *Gladys grows a lot of tomatoes in her greenhouse.*

the 'greenhouse efˌfect *noun* [S] an increase in the amount of CARBON DIOXIDE and other gases in the atmosphere which is believed to be the cause of a gradual warming of the surface of the Earth

ˌgreenhouse 'gas *noun* [C] a gas which causes the greenhouse effect, especially CARBON DIOXIDE

greenish /'griː.nɪʃ/ *adj* ⊃See at **green** COLOUR

ˌgreen 'onion *noun* [C] *US FOR* a **spring onion** ⊃See picture **Vegetables** on page Centre 2

ˈgreen ˌpaper *noun* [C] a document prepared by the British Government for anyone interested to study and make suggestions about, especially before a law is changed or a new law is made ⊃Compare **white paper**.

ˌgreen 'pepper *noun* [C] a shiny green vegetable with a hollow centre which can be eaten raw or cooked

ˈgreen ˌroom *noun* [S] a room, for example in a theatre, where performers can relax

greens /griːnz/ *plural noun* the leaves of green vegetables such as SPINACH or cabbage when eaten as food

ˌgreen 'salad *noun* [C or U] *UK* a salad which consists of lettuce and other raw green vegetables

ˌgreen 'shoots *plural noun* (used especially in newspapers) the first signs of an improvement in an economy that is performing badly: *the green shoots of recovery*

ˌgreen 'tea *noun* [U] the light-coloured tea drunk especially in China and Japan

Greenwich Mean Time /ˌgren.ɪtʃ'miːn.taɪm/ *noun* [U] (*ABBREVIATION* **GMT**) the time at Greenwich, Greater London, that world TIME ZONES are based on ⊃See also **British Summer Time** and **standard time**.

greet /griːt/ *verb* **1** [T] to welcome someone with particular words or a particular action, or to react to something in the stated way: *He greeted me at the door.* ○ *The teacher greeted each child with a friendly 'Hello!'* ○ *The unions have greeted the decision with delight/anger.* **2** [T often passive] If you are greeted by a sight, sound or smell, you notice it immediately when you arrive somewhere: *As we walked into the house, we were greeted by a wonderful smell of baking.*

greeting /'griː.tɪŋ/ ⓤ /-t̬ɪŋ/ *noun* [C or U] something friendly or polite that you say or do when you meet or welcome someone: *They briskly **exchanged** greetings before starting the session.* ○ *He nodded his head **in** greeting.*

greetings /ˈgriː.tɪŋz/ (US) /-t̬ɪŋz/ *plural noun* a message that says you hope someone is well, happy, etc: *birthday/Christmas greetings* ○ FORMAL *My father **sends** his greetings.* ○ FORMAL *Greetings to you, my friends and colleagues.*

ˈgreetings ˌcard UK *noun* [C] (US **greeting card**) a piece of thick paper folded in half with a picture on the outside and a message inside, which you write in and send or give to someone, for example at Christmas or on their BIRTHDAY

gregarious /grɪˈgeə.ri.əs/ (US) /-ˈger.i-/ *adj* (of people) liking to be with other people, or (especially of animals) living in groups: *Emma's a gregarious, outgoing sort of person.* ➲See also **sociable** at **social**. **gregariously** /grɪˈgeə.ri.ə.sli/ (US) /-ˈger.i-/ *adv* **gregariousness** /grɪˈgeə.ri.ə.snəs/ (US) /-ˈger.i-/ *noun* [U]

G

the Gregorian calendar /ðə.grɪˌgɔː.ri.ənˈkæl.ɪn.dəʳ/ (US) /-ˌgɔːr.i.ənˈkæl.ɪn.dɚ/ *noun* [S] the system used in large parts of the world to divide the 365 days of the year into weeks and months, and to number the years

Gregorian chant /grɪˌgɔː.ri.ənˈtʃɑːnt/ (US) /-ˌgɔːr.i.ənˈtʃænt/ *noun* [C or U] a type of Christian church music for voices alone, used since the Middle Ages; PLAINSONG

gremlin /ˈgrem.lɪn/ *noun* [C] an imaginary little creature which gets inside things, especially machines, and makes them stop working: *We must have a gremlin in the engine – it isn't working properly.*

grenade /grəˈneɪd/ *noun* [C] a small bomb thrown by hand or shot from a gun: *a hand grenade*

grenadier /ˌgren.əˈdɪəʳ/ (US) /-ˈdɪr/ *noun* [C] a member of the GRENADIER GUARDS (= a special part of the British, Canadian or other army)

grenadine /ˈgren.ə.diːn/ *noun* [U] a sweet liquid made from the juice of the POMEGRANATE and used to colour and sweeten drinks

grew /gruː/ *past simple of* **grow**

grey, US USUALLY **gray** /greɪ/ *adj, noun* [C or U] (of) the colour that is a mixture of black and white, the colour of rain clouds: *a grey sky* ○ *She was dressed in grey.*

grey, US USUALLY **gray** /greɪ/ *adj* **1** having hair that has become grey or white, usually because of age: *He started to **go/turn** grey in his mid-forties.* **2** describes the weather when there are a lot of clouds and little light: *Night turned into morning, grey and cold.* **3** boring and sad: *He saw a grey future stretch ahead of him.*

greying, US USUALLY **graying** /ˈgreɪ.ɪŋ/ *adj* If a person or their hair is greying, their hair is becoming grey: *He is greying now but still elegant.*

greyish, US USUALLY **grayish** /ˈgreɪ.ɪʃ/ *adj* slightly grey

greyness, US USUALLY **grayness** /ˈgreɪ.nəs/ *noun* [U]

ˈgrey ˌarea *noun* [C usually sing] a situation which is not clear or where the rules are not known: *The difference between gross negligence and recklessness is a legal grey area.*

greyhound /ˈgreɪ.haʊnd/ *noun* [C] a type of dog that has a thin body and long thin legs and can run fast, especially in races

ˈgrey ˌmatter *noun* [U] INFORMAL a person's intelligence: *It's not the sort of movie that stimulates the old grey matter much.*

the ˌgrey ˈpound UK *noun* [S] (US **the gray dollar**) the money which all old people as a group have available to spend

grid /grɪd/ *noun* [C] **1** a pattern or structure made from horizontal and vertical lines crossing each other to form squares: *A metal grid had been placed across the hole to stop people falling in.* ○ *In Barcelona the streets are laid out in/on a grid **system**.* ➲See also **gridiron**. **2** a system of wires through which electricity is connected to different power stations across a region: *the national grid* **3** a pattern of squares with numbers or letters used to find places on a map

griddle /ˈgrɪd.l̩/ *noun* [C] a round, flat piece of metal used for cooking over a fire or cooker

gridiron /ˈgrɪd.aɪən/ (US) /-aɪrn/ *noun* [C] US a field marked with lines for American football

gridlock /ˈgrɪd.lɒk/ (US) /-lɑːk/ *noun* [U] **1** a situation where roads in a town become so blocked by cars that it is impossible for any traffic to move: *A car breaking down at rush hour could cause gridlock across half the city.* **2** a situation in which no progress can be made

ˈgrid ˌreference *noun* [C] a position on a map which has been marked into squares by numbered lines going from one side to the other and from top to bottom so that you can find places easily on it: *What's the grid reference of the village on this map?*

grief /griːf/ *noun* [C or U] very great sadness, especially at the death of someone: *Her grief at her son's death was terrible.* ○ *Newspapers should not intrude on people's private grief.* ○ *newspaper pictures of grief-**stricken** relatives*

• **come to grief** to suddenly fail in what you are doing, often because you have an accident: *The Italian champion was in second position when he came to grief on the third lap.*

• **give *sb* grief** INFORMAL to criticize someone angrily

• **get grief** INFORMAL to be criticized angrily: *I got a load of grief off Esther because I was ten minutes late.*

grievance /ˈgriː.vᵊnts/ *noun* [C or U] a complaint or a strong feeling that you have been treated unfairly: *A special committee has been appointed to handle prisoners' grievances.* ○ *Bill still **harbours/nurses** a grievance **against** his employers for not promoting him.* ○ *The small amount of compensation is a further source of grievance to the people forced to leave their homes.*

grieve /griːv/ *verb* **1** [I] to feel or express great sadness, especially when someone dies: *He is still grieving **for/over** his wife.* **2** [T] FORMAL to make you feel sad and angry: [+ obj + *to* infinitive] *It grieves me **to** see all this food going to waste.*

grieving /ˈgriː.vɪŋ/ *adj* feeling very sad because someone has died: *grieving relatives*

grievous /ˈgriː.vəs/ *adj* FORMAL having very serious effects or causing great pain: *Her death is a grievous loss to the whole of the community.* ○ *grievous wounds* **grievously** /ˈgriː.və.sli/ *adv*

ˌgrievous bodily ˈharm *noun* [U] (ABBREVIATION **GBH**) UK LEGAL a crime in which one person does serious physical injury to another

griffin /ˈgrɪf.ɪn/ *noun* [C] (ALSO **gryphon**) an imaginary creature with the head and wings of an eagle and the body of a lion

grill [COOK] /grɪl/ *verb* [T] (US ALSO **broil**) to cook something by direct heat, especially under a very hot surface in a cooker: *I grilled the sausages.* ➲See picture **In the Kitchen** on page Centre 16

grill /grɪl/ *noun* [C] **1** (US ALSO **broiler**) the surface in a cooker which can be heated to very high temperatures and under which you put food to be cooked ➲See picture **In the Kitchen** on page Centre 16 **2** a frame of metal bars over a fire on which food can be put to be cooked **3** MAINLY US an informal restaurant

grill [QUESTION] /grɪl/ *verb* [T] to ask someone a lot of questions for a long time: *After being grilled by the police for two days, Johnson signed a confession.* ○ *Her parents would grill her **about** where she'd been.*

grilling /ˈgrɪl.ɪŋ/ *noun* [C usually sing] INFORMAL *She faced a grilling* (= being asked lots of questions) *when she got home.*

grille /grɪl/ *noun* [C] a frame of metal bars used to cover something such as a window or a machine: *a security grille* ○ *A grille separated the prisoners from their visitors.*

ˈgrill ˌpan UK *noun* [C] (AUS **grill tray**, US **broiler pan**) an open rectangular metal container, often with a frame of metal bars inside, on which food is cooked under a grill

grim [WITHOUT HOPE] /grɪm/ *adj* **grimmer, grimmest** worried or worrying, without hope: *The future **looks** grim.* ○ *Her face was grim as she told them the bad news.* ○ *The expression on his face was one of grim **determination**.* ○ *Later Mr Ashby left the court, grim-faced and silent.*

• **hang/hold on like grim death** UK to hold on very tightly to something, despite great difficulty: *Darren always drives and I sit behind him, hanging on like grim death.*

grimly /'grɪm.li/ *adv* in a grim way **grimness** /'grɪm.-nəs/ *noun* [U]

grim UNPLEASANT /grɪm/ *adj* **grimmer**, **grimmest** INFORMAL very unpleasant or ugly: *a grim-looking block of flats* **grimness** /'grɪm.nəs/ *noun* [U]

grimace /'grɪ.məs/ *verb* [I] to make an expression of pain, strong dislike, etc. in which the face twists in an ugly way: *He tried to stand and grimaced **with** pain.* **grimace** /'grɪ.məs/ *noun* [C] *Helen made a grimace **of** disgust when she saw the raw meat.*

grime /graɪm/ *noun* [U] a layer of dirt on skin or on a building: *The walls were covered in grime.* **grimy** /'graɪ.mi/ *adj: The child's face was grimy (= dirty) and streaked with tears.*

the grim reaper /ðə,grɪm'riː.pər/ US /-pɚ/ *noun* LITERARY death thought of in the shape of a SKELETON with a large curved tool used for cutting crops

grin /grɪn/ *noun* [C] a wide smile: *I assumed things had gone well for him as he had a big grin on his face.* ○ *a broad/sheepish grin* **grin** /grɪn/ *verb* [I] **-nn-** *He grinned **at** me from the doorway.* ○ *What are you grinning about?*

• **grin and bear it** to accept something bad without complaining: *I really don't want to go but I guess I'll just have to grin and bear it.*

grind MAKE SMALLER /graɪnd/ *verb* [T] **ground**, **ground** to make something into small pieces or a powder by pressing between hard surfaces: *to grind coffee* ○ *Shall I grind a little black pepper over your pizza?* ○ *They grind the grain **into** flour (= make flour by crushing grain) between two large stones.* ➲See also **grounds**; **grounds at ground** LAND.

grinder /'graɪn.dər/ US /-dɚ/ *noun* [C] a machine used to rub or press something until it becomes a powder: *a coffee/pepper grinder*

grind RUB /graɪnd/ *verb* [T] **ground**, **ground 1** to rub something against a hard surface, in order to make it sharper or smoother: *She has a set of chef's knives which she grinds every week.* ○ *He ground **down** the sharp metal edges to make them smooth.* ○ *The car engine was making a strange grinding noise.* ➲See also **grindstone. 2 grind your teeth** to make a noise by rubbing your teeth together: *She grinds her teeth in her sleep.*

• **grind to a halt/standstill** to stop slowly: *The car juddered and ground to a halt right in the middle of the road.* ○ FIGURATIVE *If we don't do something soon, the whole theatre industry could grind to a halt (= stop operating).*

grinder /'graɪn.dər/ US /-dɚ/ *noun* **knife grinder** a device for making knives sharper, or a person whose job is to do this

grind ACTIVITY /graɪnd/ *noun* [S] INFORMAL a difficult or boring activity which needs a lot of effort: *Having to type up my handwritten work was a real grind.* ○ *The **daily** grind of looking after three children was wearing her down.*

PHRASAL VERBS WITH **grind** ▼

▲ **grind sb down** *phrasal verb* to treat someone so badly for such a long time that they are no longer able to fight back: *Ground down by years of abuse, she did not have the confidence to leave him.*

▲ **grind sth into sth** *phrasal verb* to press something hard into something else using a twisting movement: *Sara angrily ground her cigarette into the ashtray.*

▲ **grind sth out** *phrasal verb* [M] to produce the same thing, especially a boring thing, again and again: *The orchestra ground out the same tunes it has been playing for the last twenty years.*

grinding /'graɪn.dɪŋ/ *adj* LITERARY **grinding poverty** when people are extremely poor over a long period

grindstone /'graɪnd.stəʊn/ US /-stoʊn/ *noun* [C] a large round stone that is turned by a machine and is used to make tools sharper or sharp edges smooth

gringo /'grɪŋ.gəʊ/ US /-goʊ/ *noun* [C] *plural* **gringos** INFORMAL DISAPPROVING a foreigner in a Latin American country, especially one who speaks only English

grip HOLD /grɪp/ *verb* [I or T] **-pp-** to hold very tightly: *The baby gripped my finger with her tiny hand.* ○ *Old tyres won't grip (= stay on the surface of the road) in the rain very well.*

grip /grɪp/ *noun* [C usually sing] *She tightened her grip (= tight hold) **on** my arm.* ○ *She would not loosen her grip **on** my arm.*

• **get/keep a grip on yourself** to make an effort to control your emotions and behave more calmly: *I just think he ought to get a grip on himself – he's behaving like a child.*

grip INTEREST /grɪp/ *verb* [T] **-pp-** to keep someone's attention completely: *This trial has gripped the whole nation.* ○ *I was gripped throughout the entire two hours of the film.*

gripping /'grɪp.ɪŋ/ *adj* describes something that is so interesting or exciting that it holds your attention completely: *I found the book so gripping that I couldn't put it down.*

grip EMOTION /grɪp/ *verb* [T usually passive] **-pp-** When an emotion such as fear grips you, you feel it strongly: *Then he turned towards me and I was suddenly gripped by fear.*

grip CONTROL /grɪp/ *noun* [S] control over something or someone: *Rebels have tightened their grip **on** the city.*

• **be in the grip of sth** to be experiencing something unpleasant that you have no control over: *The country is currently in the grip of the worst recession for twenty years.*

• **come/get to grips with sth** to make an effort to understand and deal with a problem or situation: *The government have failed to come to grips with the two most important social issues of our time.* ○ *I can't seem to get to grips with this problem.*

grip BAG /grɪp/ *noun* [C] OLD-FASHIONED a bag for travelling that is smaller than a SUITCASE

gripe /graɪp/ *noun* [C] INFORMAL a strong complaint: *Her main gripe is that she's not being trained properly.* **gripe** /graɪp/ *verb* [I] *There's no point griping **about** the price of things.*

Gripe ˌWater *noun* [U] UK TRADEMARK a medicine given to babies to cure stomach pain

grisly /'grɪz.li/ *adj* extremely unpleasant, especially because death or blood is involved: *The 55-year-old Canadian had suffered a grisly death.* ○ *a grisly murder*

grist /grɪst/ *noun* UK **grist to the mill**/(US) **grist for someone's mill** anything that can be used to your advantage: *I might as well learn another language, it's all grist to the mill when it comes to getting a job.*

gristle /'grɪs.l̩/ *noun* [U] a solid white substance in meat that comes from near the bone and is hard to chew **gristly** /'grɪs.li/ *adj*

grit STONES /grɪt/ *noun* [U] very small pieces of stone or sand: *The road had been covered with grit.* **grit** /grɪt/ *verb* [T] **-tt-** to put small stones on a surface so that it is less smooth and therefore safer: *Council lorries had been out gritting the icy roads the night before.*

• **grit your teeth 1** to press your top and bottom teeth together, often in anger: *He gritted his teeth in silent fury.* **2** to accept a difficult situation and deal with it in a determined way: *We had to grit our teeth and agree with their conditions because we wanted the contract.*

gritter UK /'grɪt.ər/ US /'grɪt̬.ɚ/ *noun* [C] (US **sander**) a special vehicle that spreads grit on the roads when they are covered with ice **gritty** /'grɪt.i/ US /'grɪt̬.i/ *adj* containing grit

grit BRAVERY /grɪt/ *noun* [U] bravery and determination despite difficulty: *It takes **true** (= real) grit to stand up to a bully.*

gritty /'grɪt.i/ US /'grɪt̬.i/ *adj* **1** brave and determined: *He showed the gritty determination that we've come to expect from him.* **2** showing unpleasant details about a situation in a way that is realistic: *a gritty portrayal of inner-city poverty* ○ *a gritty documentary*

grits /grɪts/ *plural noun* US a dish of HOMINY grain eaten especially as a morning meal

grizzle /'grɪz.l̩/ *verb* [I] DISAPPROVING (especially of a young child) to cry continually but not very loudly, or to complain all the time: *The baby was cutting a tooth and grizzled all day long.* ○ *They're always grizzling (= complaining) **about** how nobody invites them anywhere.*

grizzled /ˈgrɪz.l̩d/ *adj* *LITERARY* having hair that is grey or becoming grey: *Grizzled veterans in uniform gathered at the war monument.*

grizzly (bear) /ˌgrɪz.liˈbeəʳ/ [US] /-ˈber/ *noun* **[C]** a very large greyish brown bear from North America and Canada

groan /grəʊn/ [US] /groʊn/ *noun* **[C]** a deep long sound showing great pain or unhappiness: *We could hear the groans of the wounded soldiers.* ○ *He looked at the piles of dirty dishes and gave a groan* ***of*** *dismay.*

groan /grəʊn/ [US] /groʊn/ *verb* **[I]** *He collapsed, groaning with pain.* ○ **[+ speech]** *"Not again," he groaned* (= said in a low unhappy voice). ○ *She's always* ***moaning and*** *groaning* (= complaining a lot) *about the weather.*

• **groan with/under (the weight of)** ***sth*** *HUMOROUS* to carry a very large quantity of something: *The tables were positively groaning with food.*

grocer /ˈgrəʊ.səʳ/ [US] /ˈgroʊ.sɚ/ *noun* **[C]** *OLD-FASHIONED* a person who owns or works in a shop selling food and small items for the home ➲See also **greengrocer**.

grocer's /ˈgrəʊ.səz/ [US] /ˈgroʊ.sɚz/ *noun* **[C]** *plural* **grocers** *OLD-FASHIONED* the shop where a grocer works: *I popped into the grocer's on the way home from work to get some cheese.*

groceries /ˈgrəʊ.sᵊr.iːz/ [US] /ˈgroʊ.sɚ-/ *plural noun* the food that you buy in a grocer's shop or SUPERMARKET

grog /grɒg/ [US] /grɑːg/ *noun* **[U]** **1** *OLD-FASHIONED* strong alcohol, such as RUM, that has been mixed with water **2** *MAINLY AUS* any alcoholic drink

groggy /ˈgrɒg.i/ [US] /ˈgrɑː.gi/ *adj* *INFORMAL* weak and unable to think clearly or walk correctly, usually because of tiredness or illness: *I felt a bit groggy for a couple of days after the operation.*

groin [BODY] /grɔɪn/ *noun* **[C]** **1** the place where your legs meet the front of your body: *He pulled a muscle in his groin.* ○ *a groin strain* ➲See picture **The Body** on page Centre 5 **2** the male sex organs: *He was kicked in the stomach and the groin.*

groin [SEA] /grɔɪn/ *noun* **[C]** a **groyne**

groom [CLEAN] /gruːm/ *verb* **[T]** to clean an animal, often by brushing its fur: *Polly spends hours in the stables grooming her pony.*

groom /gruːm/ *noun* **[C]** a person whose job is to take care of and clean horses

groom [PREPARE] /gruːm/ *verb* **[T]** to prepare someone for a special job or activity: *She was being groomed* ***for*** *leadership.* ○ **[+ to infinitive]** *My boss is grooming me* ***to*** *take over his job next year.*

groom [MAN] /gruːm/ *noun* **[C]** a **bridegroom**: *The* ***bride and*** *groom walked down the aisle together.*

groomed /gruːmd/ *adj* having a tidy and pleasant appearance that is produced with care: *His mother was always impeccably groomed.* ➲See also **well-groomed**.

grooming /ˈgruː.mɪŋ/ *noun* **[U]** the things that you do to make your appearance tidy and pleasant, for example brushing your hair, or the things that you do to keep an animal's hair or fur clean and tidy

groove /gruːv/ *noun* **[C]** a long narrow hollow space cut into a surface: *The window slides along a deep metal groove to open and close.*

• **be stuck in a groove** to be bored because you are doing the same things that you have done for a long time: *We never do anything exciting any more – we seem to be stuck in a groove.*

• **be in the groove** *INFORMAL* to be operating or performing successfully: *Alex Popov proved he was back in the groove by winning the 100 metres freestyle.*

grooved /gruːvd/ *adj* having a groove or grooves

groovy /ˈgruː.vi/ *adj* *OLD-FASHIONED SLANG* very fashionable and interesting: *That's a groovy hat you're wearing, did you knit it yourself?*

grope /grəʊp/ [US] /groʊp/ *verb* **1** **[I or T]** to feel with your hands, especially in order to find or move towards something when you cannot see easily: *She groped* ***for*** *her glasses on the bedside table.* ○ *I had to grope my* ***way*** *up the dark stairs.* **2** **[T]** *INFORMAL* to touch someone's body in order to get sexual pleasure, usually when the person does not want you to do this: *He groped me as I was going to the bar.*

grope /grəʊp/ [US] /groʊp/ *noun* **[C]** *INFORMAL* a sexual touch, usually an unwanted and unpleasant one

▲ **grope for** ***sth*** *phrasal verb* to try to think of something, especially the right words, the correct answer, etc: *I'm groping for the right words here.*

groper /ˈgrəʊ.pəʳ/ [US] /ˈgroʊ.pɚ/ *noun* **[C]** *AUS* a large fish with a very wide mouth

gross [UNACCEPTABLE] /grəʊs/ [US] /groʊs/ *adj* **[before n]** *FORMAL* (especially in law) unacceptable because clearly wrong: *gross misconduct/indecency* ○ *a gross violation of justice*

grossly /ˈgrəʊ.sli/ [US] /ˈgroʊ-/ *adv*: *It was grossly* (= extremely) *unfair to demand such a high interest rate on the loan.* ○ *He's grossly* (= extremely) *overweight.*

gross [FAT] /grəʊs/ [US] /groʊs/ *adj* extremely fat or large and ugly: *I'd put on ten kilos and felt gross in my bikini.*

gross [UNPLEASANT] /grəʊs/ [US] /groʊs/ *adj* *INFORMAL* extremely unpleasant: *"Oh, gross!" she said, looking at the flies buzzing above the piles of dirty plates.*

gross [TOTAL] /grəʊs/ [US] /groʊs/ *adj, adv* (in) total: *A person's gross* ***income*** *is the money they earn before tax is deducted from it.* ○ *Once wrapped, the gross* ***weight*** *of the package is 2kg.* ○ *She earns £30,000 a year gross.* ➲Compare **net** LEFT OVER.

gross /grəʊs/ [US] /groʊs/ *verb* **[T]** to earn a particular amount of money before tax is paid or costs are subtracted: *The film has grossed over $200 million this year.*

gross [NUMBER] /grəʊs/ [US] /groʊs/ *noun* **[C]** *plural* **gross** or **grosses** *OLD-FASHIONED* (a group of) 144

▲ **gross** ***sb*** **out** *phrasal verb* **[M]** *MAINLY US INFORMAL* If something grosses you out, you think it is very unpleasant or disgusting: *He smells and he's dirty – he really grosses me out.*

grotesque /grəʊˈtesk/ [US] /groʊ-/ *adj* strange and unpleasant, especially in a ridiculous or slightly frightening way: *By now she'd had so much cosmetic surgery that she looked quite grotesque.* ○ *Gothic churches are full of devils and grotesque figures.*

grotesque /grəʊˈtesk/ [US] /groʊ-/ *noun* **[C]** *Spencer's grotesques* (= paintings of ugly and unpleasant subjects) *are his best works.*

grotesquely /grəʊˈtes.kli/ [US] /groʊ-/ *adv*: *a grotesquely fat man* ○ *My views were grotesquely* (= extremely) *misrepresented.*

grotto /ˈgrɒt.əʊ/ [US] /ˈgrɑː.t̬oʊ/ *noun* **[C]** *plural* **grottoes** or **grottos** a small cave, especially one that is made to look attractive

grotty /ˈgrɒt.i/ [US] /ˈgrɑː.t̬i/ *adj* *INFORMAL* unpleasant or of bad quality: *a grotty little room*

grouch /graʊtʃ/ *verb* **[I]** *INFORMAL* to complain in an angry way: *Oh, stop grouching!*

grouch /graʊtʃ/ *noun* **[C]** *INFORMAL* a person who often complains

grouchy /ˈgraʊ.tʃi/ *adj* *INFORMAL* easily annoyed and complaining: *Don't be so grouchy!* **grouchiness** /ˈgraʊ.tʃɪ.nəs/ *noun* **[U]**

ground [LAND] /graʊnd/ *noun* **1 the ground** the surface of the Earth: *I sat down on the ground.* **2** **[U]** soil: *soft/stony ground* ○ *The ground was frozen hard and was impossible to dig.* **3** **[C]** an area of land used for a particular purpose or activity: *a football/training ground*

• **drive/work** ***yourself*** **into the ground** to make yourself tired or ill by working too hard

• **on the ground** among the general public: *Their political ideas have a lot of support on the ground.*

• **go/be run to ground** to hide in order to escape someone or something following you: *He found the media attention intolerable and went to ground abroad for several months.*

• **get (*sth*) off the ground** If a plan or activity gets off the ground or you get it off the ground, it starts or succeeds: *A lot more money will be required to get this project off the ground.*

ground /graʊnd/ *verb* **1** **[T always passive]** If a ship is grounded, it cannot move because it has hit solid ground: *The oil tanker was grounded* ***on*** *a sandbank.* **2** **[T often passive]** If aircraft are grounded, they are prevented from flying or forbidden to fly: *The snowstorm meant that all planes were grounded.*

G

grounds /graʊndz/ *plural noun* the gardens and land that surround a building and are often enclosed by a wall or fence: *We went for a walk around the hospital grounds.* ➲See also **grounds**.

ground [AREA OF KNOWLEDGE] /graʊnd/ *noun* [U] an area of knowledge or experience; a subject: *When the conversation turns to politics he's* ***on familiar*** *ground* (= he knows a lot about this subject). ○ *Once we'd found some* ***common*** *ground* (= things we both knew about) *we got on very well together.* ○ *The lectures* ***covered a lot of*** *ground* (= included information on many different subjects). ○ *I enjoyed her first novel, but I felt in the second she was* ***going over the same*** *ground* (= dealing with the same area of experience).

grounding /ˈgraʊn.dɪŋ/ *noun* [U] *This course is designed to give drivers a grounding* (= a knowledge of the basic facts) ***in*** *car maintenance.*

ground [CAUSE] /graʊnd/ *noun* [C usually pl] a reason, cause or argument: *She is suing the company* ***on*** *grounds* ***of*** *unfair dismissal.* ○ *Do you have any ground* ***for*** *suspecting them?* ○ [+ to infinitive] *We have grounds* ***to*** *believe that you have been lying to us.* ○ [+ that] *He refused to answer* ***on the*** *grounds* ***that*** *she was unfairly dismissed.*

ground /graʊnd/ *verb FORMAL* **be grounded in** ***sth*** to be based firmly on something: *Fiction should be grounded in reality.* ○ *Most phobias are grounded in childhood experiences.* ➲See also **well-grounded**.

groundless /ˈgraʊnd.ləs/ *adj* without cause: *My fears turned out to be groundless.*

ground [PUNISH] /graʊnd/ *verb* [T] to forbid a child or young person from going out as a punishment: *My parents have grounded me for a week.*

ground [WIRE] /graʊnd/ *noun* [C usually sing] *US FOR* **earth** WIRE

ground [GRIND] /graʊnd/ *past simple and past participle of* **grind**

ˈground ˌball *noun* [C] *US* a **grounder**

ˌground ˈbeef *noun* [U] *US FOR* **mince** MEAT

ground-breaking /ˈgraʊndˌbreɪ.kɪŋ/ *adj* If something is ground-breaking, it is very new and a big change from other things of its type: *His latest film is interesting, but not ground-breaking.*

groundcloth /ˈgraʊnd.klɒθ/ [US] /-klɑːθ/ *noun* [C] *US FOR* **groundsheet**

ˈground ˌcover *noun* [U] plants which grow thickly and close to the ground, sometimes used in gardens to prevent weeds from growing: *This plant grows quickly and provides excellent ground cover.*

ˈground ˌcrew *group noun* [C] the people at an airport who take care of the aircraft while it is on the ground

grounder /ˈgraʊn.dəʳ/ [US] /-dɚ/ *noun* [C] (*ALSO* **ground ball**) *US* a ball which moves along the ground rather than through the air when it has been hit in a game of baseball

the ˌground ˈfloor *UK noun* [S] (*US USUALLY ALSO* **first floor**) the floor of a building that is at the same level as the ground outside: *My flat is on the ground floor.*

ground-floor /ˌgraʊndˈflɔːʳ/ [US] /-ˈflɔːr/ *adj* [before n] *a ground-floor office*

ˈground ˌfrost *noun* [C usually sing] a temperature at or below freezing point on and near the ground during the night which can damage plants

groundhog /ˈgraʊnd.hɒg/ [US] /-hɑːg/ *noun* [C] *US* a **woodchuck**

ˈground ˌlevel *noun* [S] the same level as the surface of the ground

groundnut /ˈgraʊnd.nʌt/ *noun* [C] a PEANUT, especially as a crop or when used in particular products: *groundnut oil*

groundout /ˈgraʊnd.aʊt/ *noun* [C] *US* in baseball, the act of hitting a ball along the ground so that it is caught by someone on the other team who then causes the BATTER (= person who hits the ball) to be out

ˈground ˌplan [BUILDING] *noun* [C usually sing] the plan that has been drawn of a building

ˈground ˌplan [ACTION] *noun* [C usually sing] *MAINLY US* the basic plan of action for something: *He doesn't have a ground plan, he just makes decisions as the need arises.*

ˈground ˌrent *noun* [C usually sing] money paid by the owner of a building or apartment to the person who owns the land on which it has been built

ˈground ˌrules *plural noun* the principles on which future behaviour is based: *In all relationships a few ground rules have to be established.*

grounds /graʊndz/ *plural noun* the small bits of coffee left at the bottom of a cup or other container that has had coffee in it ➲See also **grind** MAKE SMALLER; **grounds** at **ground** LAND.

groundsheet /ˈgraʊnd.ʃiːt/ *noun* [C] (*US ALSO* **groundcloth**) a piece of waterproof material which you put on the ground to sleep on when camping

groundsman *UK* /ˈgraʊndz.mən/ *noun* [C] (*US* **groundskeeper**) a man whose job is to take care of a sports ground or park

ˈground ˌspeed *noun* [C usually sing] *SPECIALIZED* An aircraft's ground speed is its speed when measured against the ground rather than the air through which it moves.

ˈground ˌstaff *plural noun* the people whose job is to take care of a sports ground and its equipment

ˈground ˌstroke *noun* [C] in tennis and similar games, when you hit the ball after it has hit the ground

groundswell /ˈgraʊnd.swel/ *noun* [S] a growth of strong feeling among a large group of people: *There is a groundswell* ***of*** *opinion against the new rules.*

ˈground ˌwater *noun* [U] underground water that is held in the soil and rocks

groundwork /ˈgraʊnd.wɜːk/ [US] /-wɝːk/ *noun* [U] work that is done as a preparation for work that will be done later: *The committee will meet today to* ***lay*** *the groundwork* ***for*** *inter-party talks next month.*

ˌground ˈzero *noun* **1** [C usually sing] the exact place where a nuclear bomb explodes: *The blast was felt as far as 30 miles from ground zero.* **2** [U] the site of the former World Trade Center in New York City, which was destroyed in an attack on September 11, 2002

group [SET] /gruːp/ *noun* [C] a number of people or things that are put together or considered as a unit: *I'm meeting a group* ***of*** *friends for dinner tonight.* ○ *The car was parked near a small group* ***of*** *trees.* ○ *She showed me another group* ***of*** *pictures, this time of children playing.*

group /gruːp/ *verb* [I or T; + adv or prep] to form a group or put people or things into a group: *We all grouped together round the bride for a family photograph.* ○ *I grouped the children according to age.* ○ *The books were grouped by size.*

grouping /ˈgruː.pɪŋ/ *noun* [C] several people or things when they have been arranged into a group or are being considered as a group: *There exist two clearly defined political groupings in the country – the establishment and the dissidents.*

group [MUSIC] /gruːp/ *group noun* [C] a number of people who play music together, especially pop music: *What's your favourite group?* ○ *a pop/rock group*

ˌgroup ˈcaptain *noun* [C] an officer in the British air force

groupie /ˈgruː.pi/ *noun* [C] a person who likes a particular popular singer or other famous person and follows them to try to meet them, especially in order to have sex with them

ˌGroup of ˈEight *group noun* [S] (*ABBREVIATION* **G8**) the eight countries of Canada, France, Germany, Italy, Japan, Russia, the UK, and the US, whose leaders meet every year to discuss international problems

ˌgroup ˈpractice *noun* [C] several doctors who work together in the same place

ˌgroup ˈtherapy *noun* [U] treatment in which people meet in a group to talk about their emotional problems, with a trained leader or doctor present

grouse [BIRD] /graʊs/ *noun* [C] *plural* **grouse** a small fat bird, shot for sport and food

grouse [COMPLAIN] /graʊs/ *verb* [I] *INFORMAL* to complain angrily: *She's always grousing* ***about*** *how she's been treated by the management.*

grouse /graʊs/ *noun* [C] *plural* **grouses** *INFORMAL* an angry complaint

grout /graʊt/ *verb* [T] to put a thin line of MORTAR in the spaces between TILES: *We spent the weekend grouting the bathroom.* **grout** /graʊt/ *noun* [U] (*ALSO* **grouting**)

grove /grəʊv/ [US] /groʊv/ *noun* [C] **1** a group of trees planted close together: *Orange groves grow around the village.* **2 Grove** used in some road and place names: *Ladbroke/Camberwell Grove*

• **the groves of academe** universities considered as a whole: *It's yet another novel set in the groves of academe.*

grovel [TRY TO PLEASE] /ˈgrɒv.əl/ [US] /ˈgrɑː.vəl/ *verb* [I] **-ll-** or *US USUALLY* **-l-** to behave with too much respect towards someone to show them that you are very eager to please them: *He sent a grovelling note of apology.*

grovel [MOVE] /ˈgrɒv.əl/ [US] /ˈgrɑː.vəl/ *verb* [I] **-ll-** or *US USUALLY* **-l-** to move close to or on the ground: *I was grovelling under the sofa, trying to find my contact lens.*

grow [INCREASE] /grəʊ/ [US] /groʊ/ *verb* **grew, grown 1** [I or L or T] to increase in size or amount, or to become more advanced or developed: *Children grow so quickly.* ○ *This plant grows best in the shade.* ○ *She's grown three centimetres this year.* ○ *Football's popularity continues to grow.* ○ *The labour force is expected to grow by 2% next year.* ○ *The male deer grows large branching horns called antlers.* **2** [I or T] If your hair or nails grow, or if you grow them, they become longer: *Lottie wants to grow her hair long.* ○ *Are you growing a beard?* ○ *Golly, your hair's grown!* **3** [I] If a plant grows in a particular place, it exists and develops there: *There were roses growing up against the wall of the cottage.* **4** [T] If you grow a plant, you put it in the ground and take care of it, usually in order to sell it: *The villagers grow coffee and maize to sell in the market.*

grower /ˈgrəʊ.əʳ/ [US] /ˈgroʊ.ɚ/ *noun* [C] **1** a person who grows large amounts of a particular plant or crop in order to sell them **2** a plant that grows in a particular way: *The new varieties of wheat are good growers even in poor soil.*

growing /ˈgrəʊ.ɪŋ/ [US] /ˈgroʊ-/ *adj* increasing in size or quantity: *There is a growing awareness of the seriousness of this disease.* ○ *A growing boy needs his food.*

grown /grəʊn/ [US] /groʊn/ *adj* **a grown man/woman** an adult: *I don't like to see a grown man in tears.*

growth /grəʊθ/ [US] /groʊθ/ *noun* **1** [U] The growth of a person, animal or plant is its process of increasing in size: *A balanced diet is essential for healthy growth.* ○ *Plant growth is most noticeable in spring and early summer.* **2** [U] an increase in the size or the importance of something: *The government is trying to limit population growth.* ○ *The rapid growth of opposition to the plan has surprised the council.* ○ *Electronic publishing is a growth* ***area*** (= an area of activity that is increasing in size and developing quickly). **3** [C] a lump growing on the outside or inside of a person, animal or plant which is caused by a disease: *a cancerous growth on the liver* **4** [C or U] something which has grown: *Graham came back from holiday with a week's growth of beard on his chin.*

grow [BECOME] /grəʊ/ [US] /groʊ/ *verb* **1 grow tired/old/calm, etc.** to gradually become tired/old/calm, etc: *He grew bored of the countryside.* ○ *Growing old is so awful.* **2 grow to do *sth*** to gradually start to do something: *I've grown to like her over the months.*

PHRASAL VERBS WITH **grow** ▼

▲ **grow apart** *phrasal verb* (*ALSO* **grow away from *sb***) If two people in a close relationship grow apart or if they grow away from each other, they gradually begin to have a less close relationship, usually because they no longer have the same interests and desires: *There was nobody else involved, we just grew apart.*

▲ **grow into *sb/sth*** [DEVELOP] *phrasal verb* to develop into a particular type of person or thing: *He's grown into a fine, responsible young man.*

▲ **grow into *sth*** [CLOTHES] *phrasal verb* If children grow into clothes, they gradually become big enough to wear them.

▲ **grow on *sb*** *phrasal verb* If someone or something grows on you, you like them more and more although you did not like them at first: *I wasn't sure about this album when I bought it but it's really grown on me.*

▲ **grow out of *sth*** [CLOTHES] *phrasal verb* If children grow out of clothes, they become too big to fit into them.

▲ **grow out of *sth*** [INTEREST] *phrasal verb* If you grow out of an interest or way of behaving, you stop having or doing it as you become older: *He wants to join the army when he leaves school, but I hope he'll grow out of the idea.*

▲ **grow out of *sth*** [IDEA] *phrasal verb* If an idea grows out of another one, it develops from it: *The idea for the story grew out of a strange experience I had last year.*

▲ **grow up** [PERSON] *phrasal verb* to gradually become an adult: *I grew up in Scotland* (= I lived in Scotland when I was young). ○ *Taking responsibility for yourself is part of the process of growing up.*

▲ **grow up** [CITY] *phrasal verb* If a town or city grows up in a particular place or way, it develops there or in that way: *The city grew up originally as a crossing point on the river.*

ˈgrowing ˌpains [PHYSICAL PAIN] *plural noun* pains felt by young people in the bones or joints of their legs

ˈgrowing ˌpains [DIFFICULTIES] *plural noun* the problems of a new organization or activity

growl /graʊl/ *verb* [I] to make a low rough sound, usually in anger: *The dog growled* ***at*** *her and snapped at her ankles.* ○ [+ speech] *"Not now, I'm busy," he growled.* **growl** /graʊl/ *noun* [C] *The dog eyed me suspiciously and gave a low growl.*

grown-up /ˈgrəʊn.ʌp/ [US] /ˈgroʊn-/ *noun* [C] an adult, used especially when talking to children: *Ask a grown-up to cut the shape out for you.*

grown-up /ˌgrəʊnˈʌp/ [US] /ˌgroʊn-/ *adj* If you say that someone is grown-up, you mean that they are an adult or that they behave in a responsible way: *She has two grown-up children who work in the family business.* ○ *He seems very grown-up for a ten-year-old.* ○ *This book is a bit too grown-up for you* (= you are too young to understand this book).

groyne /grɔɪn/ *noun* [C] (*ALSO* **groin**) a low wall built out from the coast into the sea, to prevent the continual movement of the waves from removing parts of the land

grub [INSECT] /grʌb/ *noun* [C] an insect in the stage when it has just come out of its egg: *A grub looks like a short fat worm.*

grub [FOOD] /grʌb/ *noun* [U] *INFORMAL* food: *They do really good grub in our local pub.*

grub [DIG] /grʌb/ *verb* **-bb- 1** [I usually + adv or prep] to search for something by digging or turning over earth: *The dog was grubbing* ***around/about*** *in the mud for a bone.* **2** [T usually + adv or prep] *US SLANG* to ask someone for something without intending to pay for it: *Could I grub a cigarette* ***off*** *you?*

▲ **grub *sth* up/out** *phrasal verb* [M] to dig something out of the ground to get rid of it: *She spent the morning in the garden, grubbing up weeds.*

grubby /ˈgrʌb.i/ *adj* **1** *INFORMAL* dirty: *He was wearing some old shorts and a grubby T-shirt.* ○ *Don't wipe your grubby hands on my clean towel!* **2** *DISAPPROVING* If you describe an activity or someone's behaviour as grubby, you do not think that it is honourable or acceptable: *She sees the business of making money as just grubby opportunism.* ○ *He doesn't want this story to get into the grubby hands of the tabloid press* (= to be obtained by newspapers who are not honourable).

grudge /grʌdʒ/ *noun* [C] a strong feeling of anger and dislike for a person who you feel has treated you badly, which often lasts for a long time: *I don't* ***bear*** *any grudge* ***against*** *you.* ○ *Philippa still* ***has/holds*** *a grudge against me for refusing to lend her that money.*

grudge /grʌdʒ/ *verb* [T] **1** to not want to spend time or money on someone or something, or to not want to give something to someone: *She grudged every hour she spent helping him.* **2** to think that someone does not deserve something good that they have: [+ two objects] *I don't grudge you your holiday, it's just that you've chosen a bad time to go.*

grudging /ˈgrʌdʒ.ɪŋ/ *adj* A grudging action or feeling is one which you do or have unwillingly: *She won the grudging respect of her boss.*

grudgingly /ˈgrʌdʒ.ɪŋ.li/ adv: She grudgingly (= unwillingly) admitted that she had been wrong to criticize him.

gruel /ˈgruː.əl/ noun [U] a cheap simple food made especially in the past by boiling oats with water or milk

gruelling, US USUALLY **grueling** /ˈgruː.ə.lɪŋ/ adj extremely tiring and difficult, and demanding great effort and determination: Junior doctors often have to work a gruelling 100-hour week. ○ He eventually won the match after five gruelling sets. **gruellingly**, US **gruelingly** /ˈgruː.ə.lɪŋ.li/ adv

gruesome /ˈgruː.səm/ adj extremely unpleasant and shocking, and usually dealing with death or injury: The newspaper article included a gruesome description of the murder. **gruesomely** /ˈgruː.səm.li/ adv

gruff /grʌf/ adj (of a person's voice) low and unfriendly, or (of a person's behaviour) unfriendly or lacking patience: "If you must," came the gruff reply. ○ He's quite a sweet man beneath the gruff exterior. **gruffly** /ˈgrʌf.li/ adv **gruffness** /ˈgrʌf.nəs/ noun [U]

grumble /ˈgrʌm.bl̩/ verb [I] **1** to complain about someone or something in an annoyed way: She spent the evening grumbling to me about her job. ○ [+ speech] "You never hang your coat up," she grumbled. **2** If your stomach grumbles, it makes a low continuous noise, usually because you are hungry.
• **mustn't grumble** UK HUMOROUS something you say to mean that your life is not bad and that you should not complain about it: "How's it going then, Mike?" "Oh, all right. Mustn't grumble."
grumble /ˈgrʌm.bl̩/ noun [C usually pl] a complaint: If I hear any more grumbles about the food, you can do the cooking yourself!
grumbler /ˈgrʌm.blər/ US /-blɚ/ noun [C] a person who complains a lot

grumbling ap'pendix noun [C usually sing] UK a medical condition in which the APPENDIX (= tube-shaped part that is joined to the intestines) causes you slight pain over a period of time

grumpy /ˈgrʌm.pi/ adj INFORMAL easily annoyed and complaining: I hadn't had enough sleep and was feeling a bit grumpy. ○ a grumpy old man
grump /grʌmp/ noun [C] INFORMAL someone who is easily annoyed and complains a lot: He's only an old grump – don't listen to him. **grumpily** /ˈgrʌm.pɪ.li/ adv **grumpiness** /ˈgrʌm.pɪ.nəs/ noun [U]

grunge /grʌndʒ/ noun [U] a type of rock music, and a fashion for untidy clothes which was popular in the early 1990s: Nirvana was one of the most famous grunge bands.

grungy /ˈgrʌn.dʒi/ adj MAINLY US SLANG (of a person) feeling tired and dirty, or (of a thing) dirty: He showed up for the interview wearing some grungy old sweatshirt and jeans.

grunt /grʌnt/ verb [I] (of a pig) to make a low rough noise, or (of a person) to make a short low sound instead of speaking, usually because of anger or pain: The pigs were grunting contentedly as they ate their food. ○ He hauled himself over the wall, grunting with the effort. ○ [+ speech] "Too tired," he grunted and sat down. **grunt** /grʌnt/ noun [C] Loud grunts were coming from the pig sty.

Gruyère /ˈgruː.jeər/ US /gruˈjer/ noun [U] a hard, pale yellow, strong-tasting cheese which was originally made in Switzerland

GSOH noun [U] ABBREVIATION FOR good sense of humour: used in newspapers and magazine advertisements by people looking for a new friend or sexual partner: Male non-smoker, 36, GSOH, would like to meet interesting female.

G-spot /ˈdʒiː.spɒt/ US /-spɑːt/ noun [C usually sing] a small area that is believed to be inside the vagina which increases sexual pleasure when rubbed

G-string /ˈdʒiː.strɪŋ/ noun [C] a narrow piece of cloth worn between a person's legs to cover their sexual organs that is held in place by a piece of string around their waist

GTG, **gtg** INTERNET ABBREVIATION FOR got to go

GTi /ˌdʒiː.tiːˈaɪ/ noun [C] ABBREVIATION FOR Gran Turismo injection: a version of a car which is comfortable, expensive and very powerful: She drives a white Golf GTi.

guacamole /ˌgwæk.əˈməʊ.li/ US /-ˈmoʊ-/ noun [U] a thick mixture of AVOCADO (= a savoury green tropical fruit), tomato, onion and spices, which is usually eaten cold

guano /ˈgwɑː.nəʊ/ US /-noʊ/ noun [U] the excrement of sea birds: Guano is often used as a fertilizer.

guarantee /ˌgær.ənˈtiː/ noun **1** [C or U] a promise that something will be done or will happen, especially a written promise by a company to repair or change a product that develops a fault within a particular period of time: The system costs £99.95 including postage, packing and a 12-month guarantee. ○ The video recorder **comes with/has** a two-year guarantee. ○ a money-back guarantee ○ [+ that] The United Nations has demanded a guarantee from the army **that** food convoys will not be attacked. ○ [+ (that)] There is no guarantee **(that)** the discussions will lead to a deal. ○ A product as good as this is a guarantee **of** commercial success (= It is certain to be successful). ○ The shop said they would replace the television as it was still **under** guarantee. **2** [C] a formal acceptance of responsibility for something, such as the payment of someone else's debt **3** [C] SPECIALIZED something valuable which you give to someone temporarily while you do what you promised to do for them, and which they will keep if you fail to do it

guarantee /ˌgær.ənˈtiː/ verb [T] **1** If a product is guaranteed, the company that made it promises to repair or change it if a fault develops within a particular period of time: The fridge is guaranteed **for** three years. **2** to promise that something will happen or exist: [+ two objects] European Airlines guarantees its customers top-quality service. ○ The label on this bread says it is guaranteed free of/from preservatives (= it contains no preservatives). **3** If something guarantees something else, it makes certain that it will happen: [+ (that)] The £50 deposit guarantees **(that)** people return the boats after their hour has finished. **4** If something is guaranteed to happen or have a particular result, it is certain that it will happen or have that result: [+ to infinitive] Just looking at a picture of the sea is guaranteed **to** make me feel sick. **5** If you guarantee someone's debt, you formally promise to accept the responsibility for that debt if the person fails to pay it.

guarantor /ˌgær.ənˈtɔːr/ US /-ˈtɔːr/ noun [C] **1** FORMAL a person who makes certain that something happens or that something is protected: The armed forces see themselves as the guarantors of free elections in the country. **2** LEGAL someone who formally accepts responsibility for you or for something that belongs to you: You must have a guarantor in order to get a visa to enter the country.

guard /gɑːd/ US /gɑːrd/ noun [C] **1** a person or group of people whose job is to protect a person, place or thing from danger or attack, or to prevent a person such as a criminal from escaping: prison guards ○ security guards ○ There are guards **posted** (= standing and watching) at every entrance. ○ **Armed** guards are posted around the site. ○ The frontier is patrolled by **border** guards. **2** UK (US **conductor**) a railway official who travels on and is responsible for a train **3** a device that protects a dangerous part of something or that protects something from getting damaged: a fire guard ○ a trigger guard ○ The helmet has a face guard attached.
• **be under guard** to be kept in a place by a group of people who have weapons: The ex-President was under **armed** guard in the Palace.
• **stand/keep guard** (ALSO **be on guard**) to be responsible for protecting someone or something, or for preventing someone from escaping: Two of the soldiers kept guard **over** the captured guns. ○ Armed police stand guard outside the house.
• **be on *your* guard** to be careful to avoid being tricked or getting into a dangerous situation: You always have to be on your guard **against** pickpockets.
• **catch *sb* off guard** to surprise someone by doing something which they are not expecting and are not ready for
• **the changing of the guard** a ceremony held outside Buckingham Palace in London when one set of soldiers

replaces the soldiers who have finished their time on duty standing outside the palace

Guards /gɑːdz/ ⓤ /gɑːrdz/ *plural noun* used in the name of several important REGIMENTS (= units) in an army: *the Grenadier Guards* ○ *a Guards officer* ➲See also **guardsman**.

guard /gɑːd/ ⓤ /gɑːrd/ *verb* [T] **1** to protect someone or something from being attacked or stolen: *Soldiers guard the main doors of the embassy.* **2** to watch someone and make certain they do not escape from a place: *Five prison officers guarded the prisoners.* **3** to keep information secret: *Journalists jealously* (= carefully) *guard their sources of information.*

▲ **guard against sth** *phrasal verb* to take careful action in order to try to prevent something from happening: *Regular exercise helps guard against heart disease.*

guard dog *noun* [C] a dog trained to protect a place

guarded /ˈgɑː.dɪd/ ⓤ /ˈgɑːr-/ *adj* careful not to give too much information or show how you really feel: *a guarded response* **guardedly** /ˈgɑː.dɪd.li/ ⓤ /ˈgɑːr-/ *adv*

guardhouse /ˈgɑːd.haʊs/ ⓤ /ˈgɑːrd-/ *noun* [C] a building for the soldiers who are protecting a place

guardian /ˈgɑː.di.ən/ ⓤ /ˈgɑːr-/ *noun* [C] **1** a person who has the legal right and responsibility of taking care of someone who cannot take care of themselves, such as a child whose parents have died: *The child's parents or guardians must give their consent before she has the operation.* **2** FORMAL someone who protects something: *These three official bodies are the guardians of the nation's countryside.* ○ *a self-appointed guardian of public morals*

guardianship /ˈgɑː.di.ən.ʃɪp/ ⓤ /ˈgɑːr-/ *noun* [U] the state or duty of being a guardian

guardian 'angel *noun* [C] a spirit who is believed to protect and help a particular person

guard of 'honour *noun* [C usually sing] a group of people, usually soldiers, who are arranged in a row at a special occasion such as a marriage ceremony or an official visit, to honour someone very important

guard post *noun* [C] a small building for the soldiers who are protecting a place

guard rail *noun* [C] a bar along the edge of something steep, such as stairs or a cliff, to prevent people from falling off

guardroom /ˈgɑːd.rʊm/ /-ruːm/ ⓤ /ˈgɑːrd-/ *noun* [C] a room for soldiers who are protecting a place

guardsman /ˈgɑːdz.mən/ ⓤ /ˈgɑːrdz-/ *noun* [C] a soldier who is a member of the Guards (= a particular army unit)

guard's van UK /ˈgɑːdz.væn/ ⓤ /ˈgɑːrdz-/ *noun* [C] (*US* **caboose**) a small train carriage, usually at the back of a train, in which the guard travels

guava /ˈgwɑː.və/ *noun* [C] a round yellow tropical fruit with pink or white flesh and hard seeds, or the small tropical tree on which it grows

gubbins /ˈgʌb.ɪnz/ *noun* [U] UK INFORMAL a collection of unimportant objects: *I've just got to clear all this gubbins off my desk before I start working.*

gubernatorial /ˌguː.bᵊn.əˈtɔː.ri.əl/ ⓤ /-bɚ.nəˈtɔːr.i-/ *adj* US SPECIALIZED relating to a GOVERNOR (= the official leader of a state in the United States)

guerrilla, **guerilla** /gəˈrɪl.ə/ *noun* [C] a member of an unofficial military group that is trying to change the government by making sudden, unexpected attacks on the official army forces: *A small band of guerrillas has blown up a train in the mountains.* ○ *guerrilla warfare*

guess /ges/ *verb* [I or T] **1** to give an answer to a particular question when you do not have all the facts and so cannot be certain if you are correct: *I didn't know the answer, so I had to guess.* ○ *On the last question, she guessed right/wrong.* ○ [+ question word] *Guess when this was built.* ○ [+ (that)] *I guessed (that) she was your sister.* ○ *She asked me to guess her age.* ○ *I guessed the total amount to be about £50,000.* **2** to give the correct answer or make the correct judgment: [+ question word] *I bet you can't guess how old he is.* ○ *She guessed the answer first time.* ○ *"You've got a new job, haven't you?" "Yes, how did you guess?"* **3** INFORMAL **I guess** used when you believe something is true or likely but are not

certain: [+ (that)] *I guess (that) things are pretty hard for you now.*

● **Guess what?** INFORMAL used before telling someone something interesting or surprising: *Guess what? We won the match 4-0.*

● **keep sb guessing** to not tell someone what you are going to do next

▲ **guess at sth** *phrasal verb* to try to imagine something when you have little knowledge or experience of it: *There are no photographs of him so we can only guess at what he looked like.*

guess /ges/ *noun* [C] **1** an attempt to give the right answer when you are not certain if you are correct: *Go on – have/make/*(US) *take a guess.* ○ *Both teams made some wild guesses* (= ones which were made without much thought), *none of which were right.* ○ *"What's the time?" "It's about 5 o'clock, at a guess"* (= without knowing exactly).*"* **2** someone's opinion about something which is formed without any knowledge of the situation: *"I wonder why she's not here." "My guess is that her car has broken down."*

● **be anyone's guess** If a piece of information is anyone's guess, no one knows it: *"So what's going to happen now?" "That's anyone's guess."*

● **Your guess is as good as mine.** INFORMAL something you say when you do not know the answer to a question: *"What's he doing?" "Your guess is as good as mine."*

guesstimate, **guestimate** /ˈges.tə.mət/ *noun* [C] INFORMAL an approximate calculation of the size or amount of something when you do not know all the facts: *Current guesstimates are that the company's turnover will increase by 7% this year.*

guesswork /ˈges.wɜːk/ ⓤ /-wɝːk/ *noun* [U] the process of making a guess when you do not know all the facts: *The projected sales figures are pure guesswork on our part.*

guest /gest/ *noun* [C] **1** a person who is staying with you, or a person whom you have invited to a social occasion, such as a party or a meal: *150 guests were invited to the wedding.* ○ *We have guests* (US **houseguests**) *staying this weekend.* ○ *Is he on the guest list?* ○ *He is a paying guest* (= He pays for the use of a room in someone's home). **2** a person who is staying in a hotel: *We would like to remind all our guests to leave their keys at reception before they depart.* **3** a person, such as an entertainer, who has been invited to appear on a television or radio programme or in a performance: *Our special guest on the programme tonight is Robert De Niro.* ○ *Madonna made a guest appearance at the concert.* ○ *Simon Rattle will be the guest conductor with the London Symphony Orchestra.*

● **Be my guest.** something you say when you give someone permission to do or use something: *"Can I try out your new bicycle?" "Be my guest."*

guest /gest/ *verb* [I] If a person, especially an entertainer, guests on a programme or show, they are invited to appear or perform on it: *He guests on their latest video.*

guest book *noun* [C] a book in which people write their names and addresses when they have been staying at a hotel

guesthouse /ˈgest.haʊs/ *noun* [C] a small cheap hotel

guest of 'honour UK *noun* [C] (US **guest of honor**) the most important person at a social occasion: *The Prime Minister was guest of honour at the dinner.*

guestroom /ˈgest.rʊm/ ⓤ /-ruːm/ *noun* [C] a bedroom in a house for visitors to sleep in

guest worker *noun* [C] a person who lives and works in a foreign country for a limited period of time, doing low paid and usually unskilled work

guff /gʌf/ *noun* [U] INFORMAL speech or writing that is nonsense

guffaw /gʌfˈɔː/ ⓤ /-ˈɑː/ *verb* [I] to laugh loudly, especially at something stupid that someone has said or done: *He guffawed with delight when he heard the news.* **guffaw** /gʌfˈɔː/ ⓤ /-ˈɑː/ *noun* [C] *She let out a loud guffaw.*

GUI /ˈguː.i/ *noun* ABBREVIATION FOR **graphical user interface**

ˈguidance ˌcounselor *noun* [C] *US* someone whose job is to help people choose a job or CAREER

guide [SHOW WAY] /gaɪd/ *noun* [C] a person whose job is showing a place or a particular route to visitors: *We hired a guide to take us up into the mountains.* ○ *a* ***tour*** *guide*

guide /gaɪd/ *verb* **1** [T] to show people round a place: *The curator guided us* ***round*** *the gallery, pointing out the most famous paintings in the collection.* ○ *a guided* ***tour*** *of the city* **2** [T] to take someone somewhere or show them how to get there: *The shop assistant guided me* ***to*** *the shelf where the gardening books were displayed.* ○ *The runway lights guide the plane in to land.* **3** [T usually + adv or prep] to take hold of part of someone's body, especially their arm, and take them somewhere: *He took my arm and guided me to the bar.*

guide [MAKE MOVE] /gaɪd/ *verb* [T usually + adv or prep] to make something move in the direction in which you want it to go: *The pilot guided the plane onto the runway.* ○ *She guided the child's head and arms into the T-shirt.*

guide [BOOK] /gaɪd/ *noun* [C] **1** a book which gives you the most important information about a particular subject: *a hotel/wine guide* ○ *a guide* ***to*** *the birds of North America* **2** a **guidebook**: *a guide* ***to*** *the British Isles* ○ ***tourist*** *guides*

guide [HELP] /gaɪd/ *noun* [C] something that helps you form an opinion or make a decision about something else: *I never follow recipes exactly when I cook – I just use them as* ***rough*** *guides.*

guide /gaɪd/ *verb* [T] to show someone how to do something difficult: *Our lawyer guided us* ***through*** *the more complicated questions on the form.*

guidance /ˈgaɪ.dᵊnts/ *noun* [U] **1** help and advice about how to do something or about how to deal with problems connected with your work, education, or personal relationships: *I've always looked to my father for guidance in these matters.* ○ *careers guidance* **2** the process of directing the flight of a missile or rocket: *a missile guidance system*

guide [INFLUENCE] /gaɪd/ *verb* [T] to influence someone's behaviour: *Trust your own judgment and don't be guided by what anyone else thinks.*

guide /gaɪd/ *noun* [C] a person or thing that influences what you do or think: *Let your conscience be your guide.*

guidebook /ˈgaɪd.bʊk/ *noun* [C] (*ALSO* **guide**) a book which gives information for visitors about a place, such as a city or country: *a guidebook* ***to*** *Montreal*

ˌguided ˈmissile *noun* [C] an explosive weapon whose direction is controlled electronically during its flight

ˈguide ˌdog *noun* [C] a dog that has been specially trained to help a blind person travel around safely: *guide dogs for the blind*

guidelines /ˈgaɪd.laɪnz/ *plural noun* information intended to advise people on how something should be done or what something should be: *The EU has* ***issued*** *guidelines on appropriate levels of pay for part-time manual workers.*

the Guides *plural noun* an international organization for young women which encourages them to take part in different activities and to become responsible and independent ➲Compare **the Scouts**.

Guide /gaɪd/ *noun* [C] (*OLD-FASHIONED* **girl guide**) a girl between 10 and 14 years old who is a member of the Guides

ˈguide ˌword *noun* [C] In this dictionary, guide words help you find the explanation you are looking for when a word has more than one main meaning. They are printed in capital letters at the start of an entry inside a box.

ˌguiding ˈprinciple *noun* [C] an idea which influences you greatly when making a decision or considering a matter: *Equality of opportunity has been the government's guiding principle in its education reforms.*

ˌguiding ˈspirit *noun* [C usually sing] (*ALSO* **guiding light**) a person who influences a person or group and shows them how to do something successfully: *She was the founder of the company, and for forty years its guiding spirit.*

guild /gɪld/ *noun* [C] an organization of people who do the same job or have the same interests: *the Writers' Guild* ○ *the Fashion Designers' Guild*

guilder /ˈgɪl.dəʳ/ [US] /-dɚ/ *noun* [C] the standard unit of money used in the Netherlands before they started using the euro, and also used in Suriname

guildhall /ˈgɪld.hɔːl/ [US] /-hɑːl/ *noun* [C usually sing] (in Britain) a building in the centre of a town in which members of a GUILD met in the past, which is now often used as a place for meetings or performances or as local government offices

guile /gaɪl/ *noun* [U] *FORMAL* clever but sometimes dishonest behaviour that you use to deceive someone: *The President will need to use all her political guile to stay in power.* ○ *He is a simple, honest man, totally lacking in guile.*

guileless /ˈgaɪl.ləs/ *adj FORMAL* honest, not able to deceive: *She regarded him with wide, guileless blue eyes.*

guillemot /ˈgɪl.ɪ.mɒt/ [US] /-ə.mɑːt/ *noun* [C] a black and white sea bird with a long narrow beak that lives in northern parts of the world

G

guillotine [DEVICE] /ˈgɪl.ə.tiːn/ *noun* **1** [C or S] a device, invented in France, consisting of a sharp blade in a tall frame which was used in the past for killing criminals by cutting off their heads: *King Louis XVI and Marie Antoinette* ***went to*** *the guillotine* (= were killed by the guillotine) *during the French Revolution.* **2** [C] *UK* a device with a long sharp blade which is used for cutting large quantities of paper

guillotine /ˈgɪl.ə.tiːn/ *verb* [T] to cut someone's head off using a guillotine: *During the French Revolution, thousands of people were guillotined.*

guillotine [LIMIT] /ˈgɪl.ə.tiːn/ *noun* [C] *UK SPECIALIZED* a limit on the amount of discussion allowed about a particular law in Parliament, which is made by setting a fixed time before a final vote must be taken

guillotine /ˈgɪl.ə.tiːn/ *verb* [T] *The bill was guillotined by 318 votes to 236.*

guilt [FEELING] /gɪlt/ *noun* [U] a feeling of anxiety or unhappiness that you have because you have done something wrong, such as causing harm to another person: *He suffered such feelings of guilt over leaving his children.* ○ *She remembered with* ***a pang of*** *guilt that she hadn't called her mother.*

guilty /ˈgɪl.ti/ [US] /-t̬i/ *adj* feeling guilt: *I feel so guilty* ***about*** *forgetting her birthday.* ○ *She must have done something wrong, because she's looking so guilty.* ○ *You've got a guilty* ***conscience*** *– that's why you can't sleep.* **guiltily** /ˈgɪl.tɪ.li/ [US] /-t̬ɪ-/ *adv* **guiltiness** /ˈgɪl.ti.nəs/ [US] /-t̬i-/ *noun* [U]

guilt [RESPONSIBILITY] /gɪlt/ *noun* [U] the fact of having done something wrong or committed a crime: *Both suspects* ***admitted*** *their guilt to the police.* ○ *The prosecution's task in a case is to* ***establish*** *a person's guilt beyond any reasonable doubt.* ➲Compare **innocence** at **innocent**.

guilty /ˈgɪl.ti/ [US] /-t̬i/ *adj* **1** responsible for breaking a law: *The jury has to decide whether a person is guilty or innocent* ***of*** *a crime.* ○ *A person accused of a crime is presumed innocent until* ***proven*** *guilty.* ○ *The company* ***pleaded*** *guilty* (= They formally admitted their guilt in court) ***to*** *the charge of manslaughter.* ➲Compare **innocent**. **2 guilty party** the person who has done something wrong or who has committed a crime

guiltless /ˈgɪlt.ləs/ *adj* not responsible for doing something wrong or committing a crime

ˈguilt ˌcomplex *noun* [C] a very strong feeling of guilt which you cannot get rid of: *She has a guilt complex about inheriting so much money.*

guilt-ridden /ˈgɪltˌrɪd.ᵊn/ *adj* feeling very guilty

ˈguilt ˌtrip *noun* [C] *INFORMAL* a strong feeling of guilt because of something you have done wrong or forgotten to do: *I never call her and every time she calls me I have a guilt trip.*

guilt-trip /ˈgɪlt.trɪp/ *verb* [T] **-pp-** *INFORMAL* to make someone feel guilty, usually in order to make them do something: *He's just trying to guilt-trip you* ***into*** *paying him more.*

guinea /ˈgɪn.i/ *noun* [C] an old British gold coin worth £1.05

'guinea ˌfowl *noun* [C] *plural* **guinea fowl** a large grey and white African bird, kept for its eggs and meat

'guinea ˌpig [ANIMAL] *noun* [C] a small furry animal with rounded ears, short legs and no tail, which is often kept as a pet by children

'guinea ˌpig [TEST] *noun* [C] a person used in a scientific test, usually to discover the effect of a drug on humans: *They're asking for students to be guinea pigs in their research into the common cold.*

guise /gaɪz/ *noun* [U] the appearance of someone or something, especially when intended to deceive: *The men who arrived* ***in the*** *guise* ***of*** *drug dealers were actually undercover police officers.* ○ *The company has been accused of trying to sell their products* ***under the*** *guise* ***of*** *market research.*

guitar /gɪ'tɑːʳ/ Ⓤⓢ /-'tɑːr/ *noun* [C] a musical instrument with six strings and a long neck which is usually made of wood, and which is played by pulling or hitting the strings with the fingers: *He sat on the grass, strumming his guitar.* ○ *an acoustic guitar* ○ *an electric guitar*
guitarist /gɪ'tɑː.rɪst/ Ⓤⓢ /-'tɑːr.ɪst/ *noun* [C] a person who plays the guitar: *a classical/folk/rock guitarist*

G

the gulag /ðə'guː.læg/ *noun* [S] severe work prisons for people found guilty of crimes against their country

gulch /gʌltʃ/ *noun* [C] *US FOR* **gully**

gulf [AREA] /gʌlf/ *noun* [C] **1** a very large area of sea surrounded on three sides by a coast: *the Gulf of Mexico* **2 the Gulf** the Persian Gulf and the countries around it: *The Gulf states include Iran, Iraq, Saudi Arabia, Kuwait, Bahrain, Oman, Qatar, and the United Arab Emirates.* **3** *FORMAL* a very large deep hole in the ground

gulf [DIFFERENCE] /gʌlf/ *noun* [C] an important difference between the ideas, opinions, or situations of two groups of people: *There is a widening gulf* ***between*** *the middle classes and the poorest sections of society.* ○ *It is hoped that the peace plan will* ***bridge*** *the gulf* (= reduce the very large difference) ***between*** *the government and the rebels.*

the 'Gulf ˌStream *noun* the current of warm water which flows across the Atlantic Ocean from the Gulf of Mexico towards Europe

gull /gʌl/ *noun* [C] (*ALSO* **seagull**) a sea bird with black and white or grey and white feathers ➲See picture **Animals and Birds** on page Centre 4

gullet /'gʌl.ət/ *noun* [C] *OLD-FASHIONED* the tube which food travels down from the mouth to the stomach

gullible /'gʌl.ə.bl/ *adj* easily deceived or tricked, and too willing to believe everything that other people say: *There are any number of miracle cures on the market for people gullible enough to buy them.*

gully, gulley /'gʌl.i/ *noun* [C] (*US ALSO* **gulch**) a narrow, rocky valley or channel with steep sides, made by a fast flowing stream

gulp /gʌlp/ *verb* **1** [I or T] to eat or drink food or liquid quickly by swallowing it in large amounts, or to make a swallowing movement because of fear, surprise or excitement: *She gulped* ***down*** *her drink and made a hasty exit.* ○ *When it was his turn to dive, he gulped and stepped up onto the diving board.* **2** [T] to breathe in a large amount of air very quickly **gulp** /gʌlp/ *noun* [C] *He swallowed his drink in one gulp.* ○ *She rose to the surface of the water once every minute to get/take a gulp of air.*
▲ **gulp *sth* back** *phrasal verb* [M] to try not to show that you are upset, usually by swallowing hard: *She gulped back* ***the tears.***

gum [MOUTH] /gʌm/ *noun* [C] either of the two areas of firm pink flesh inside the mouth which cover the bones into which the teeth are fixed: *sore gums* ➲See picture **The Body** on page Centre 5
gummy /'gʌm.i/ *adj* showing the gums: *The baby gave her a gummy smile.*

gum [STICKY SUBSTANCE] /gʌm/ *noun* **1** [U] a sticky substance obtained from the stems of some trees and plants, or a type of glue used for sticking together pieces of paper **2** [U] **chewing gum** or **bubble gum** (= a soft sweet that you chew but do not swallow) **3** [C] *UK* used in the names of some chewy, fruit-flavoured sweets: *fruit/wine gums*
• **By gum!** *UK OLD-FASHIONED INFORMAL* used to express surprise: *By gum, he's a big lad!*
gum /gʌm/ *verb* [T] **-mm-** *SLIGHTLY OLD-FASHIONED* If you gum one piece of paper to another, you stick them together using glue: *The labels were already gummed to the envelopes.*
gummed /gʌmd/ *adj* (*ALSO* **gummy**) sticky or with glue on the surface: *gummed labels/envelopes*
▲ **gum *sth* up** *phrasal verb* [M often passive] to prevent something from working or opening in the usual way by covering it with a sticky substance: *When I woke up this morning my eyes were all gummed up.*

gumbo /'gʌm.bəʊ/ Ⓤⓢ /-boʊ/ *noun plural* **gumbos 1** [C or U] a thick soup made with OKRA (= a small green vegetable) and meat or fish, which comes from America **2** [U] *US FOR* **okra**

gumboot /'gʌm.buːt/ *noun* [C] *AUS AND UK OLD-FASHIONED FOR* **wellington (boot)**

gumdrop /'gʌm.drɒp/ Ⓤⓢ /-drɑːp/ *noun* [C] (*ALSO* **gum**) a chewy sweet that is usually fruit-flavoured

gumption /'gʌmp.ʃᵊn/ *noun* [U] *INFORMAL* the ability to decide what is the best thing to do in a particular situation, and to do it with energy and determination: *She* ***had the*** *gumption* ***to*** *write directly to the company manager and persuade him to give her a job.*

'gum ˌshield *noun* [C] *UK* a device which boxers put inside their mouths in order to protect their teeth and gums during fights

gumshoe /'gʌm.ʃuː/ *noun* [C] *US OLD-FASHIONED INFORMAL FOR* **detective** (= someone whose job is to discover facts about a crime)

'gum ˌtree *noun* [C] a **eucalyptus (tree)**

gun /gʌn/ *noun* [C] **1** a weapon from which bullets or SHELLS (= explosive containers) are fired: *The British police do not* ***carry*** *guns.* ○ *You could hear the noise of guns* ***firing*** *in the distance.* **2** in sport, a device which makes a very loud sudden noise as a signal to start a race: ***At the*** *gun, the runners sprinted away down the track.* **3** a device which you hold in your hand and use for sending out a liquid or object: *a spray gun* ○ *a staple gun* ➲See also **staple-gun**.
• **hired gun** *MAINLY US INFORMAL* a person who is paid to shoot and kill someone
• **with guns blazing** (*ALSO* **all guns blazing**) If you do something, especially argue, with guns blazing, you do it with a lot of force and energy: *I went into the meeting with guns blazing, determined not to let him win.*
gun /gʌn/ *verb* [T] **-nn-** *MAINLY US OLD-FASHIONED INFORMAL* to make an engine operate at a higher speed: *You must have been really gunning the engine to get here on time.*
• **be gunning for *sb*** *INFORMAL* to often criticize someone or be trying to cause trouble for them: *She's been gunning for me ever since I got the promotion she wanted.*
gunner /'gʌn.əʳ/ Ⓤⓢ /-ɚ/ *noun* [C] a member of the armed forces who is trained to use ARTILLERY (= very large guns)
gunnery /'gʌn.ᵊr.i/ Ⓤⓢ /-ɚ-/ *noun* [U] the skill or activity of shooting with ARTILLERY (= very large guns)
▲ **gun *sb* down** *phrasal verb* [M] to shoot someone and kill or seriously injure them, often when they cannot defend themselves: *The police officer was gunned down as he took his children to school.*

gunboat /'gʌn.bəʊt/ Ⓤⓢ /-boʊt/ *noun* [C] a small military ship with large guns, used especially in coastal areas

ˌgunboat di'plomacy *noun* [U] *DISAPPROVING* the use of military threats by a strong country against a weaker country in order to make that country obey it

'gun ˌcarriage *noun* [C] a frame on wheels for a CANNON (= a large powerful gun)

'gun ˌdog *noun* [C] (*US ALSO* **bird dog**) a dog used by hunters to find and gather birds they have shot

gunfight /'gʌn.faɪt/ *noun* [C] a fight using guns between two or more people, especially cowboys **gunfighter** /'gʌnˌfaɪ.təʳ/ Ⓤⓢ /-t̬ɚ/ *noun* [C]

gunfire /'gʌn.faɪəʳ/ Ⓤⓢ /-faɪr/ *noun* [U] the usually repeated firing of one or more guns: *The sound of gunfire echoed into the night.*

gunge /gʌndʒ/ *noun* [U] (*ALSO* **gunk**) any unpleasant soft dirty substance, often one which you can not recognize:

It was amazing how much gunge had accumulated in the pipe.

gung-ho /ˌgʌŋˈhəʊ/ [US] /-ˈhoʊ/ *adj* INFORMAL extremely enthusiastic about doing something, especially going to war: *The film stars Mark Burgess-Ashton as the gung-ho young fighter pilot.* ○ *Mrs Parsons had organized the village fête with her customary gung-ho zeal.*

gunman /ˈgʌn.mən/ *noun* [C] a man, usually a criminal, who is armed with a gun: *The three men were held hostage for two days by masked gunmen.*

gunmetal grey /ˌgʌnˌmet.əlˈgreɪ/ [US] /-ˌmet̬-/ *adj* dark grey

gunnel /ˈgʌn.əl/ *noun* [C] a **gunwale**

gunner /ˈgʌn.əʳ/ [US] /-ɚ/ *noun* ➲See at **gun**.

gunnery /ˈgʌn.əʳr.i/ [US] /-ɚ-/ *noun* ➲See at **gun**.

gunpoint /ˈgʌn.pɔɪnt/ *noun* **at gunpoint** experiencing or using a threat of killing with a gun: *The family were held at gunpoint for an hour while the men raided their house.*

gunpowder /ˈgʌnˌpaʊ.dəʳ/ [US] /-dɚ/ *noun* [U] an explosive mixture of substances in the form of a powder, used for making explosive devices and fireworks

gun-running /ˈgʌnˌrʌn.ɪŋ/ *noun* [U] the activity of bringing guns and other weapons into a country illegally, especially for use against the government

gun-runner /ˈgʌnˌrʌn.əʳ/ [US] /-ɚ/ *noun* [C] a person who illegally brings guns into a country

gunshot /ˈgʌn.ʃɒt/ [US] /-ʃɑːt/ *noun* [C] (the sound of) the firing of a gun: *I then heard what sounded like a gunshot in the hall.* ○ *gunshot* ***wounds***

gunslinger /ˈgʌnˌslɪŋ.əʳ/ [US] /-ɚ/ *noun* [C] especially in the past in North America, someone who is good at shooting guns and is employed for protection or to kill people

gunsmith /ˈgʌn.smɪθ/ *noun* [C] a person who makes and repairs guns, especially small guns

gunwale /ˈgʌn.əl/ *noun* [C] (ALSO **gunnel**) the upper edge of the side of a boat or ship

• **to the gunwales** OLD-FASHIONED If something is filled to the gunwales, it is extremely full: *A crowd of fifty thousand packed the stadium almost to the gunwales.*

gurgle /ˈgɜː.gl̩/ [US] /ˈgɝː-/ *verb* [I] (of babies) to make a happy sound with the back of the throat, or (of water, especially small streams) to flow with a low, uneven and pleasant noise: *The baby lay gurgling in her cot.* ○ *Outside of her window the stream gurgled over the rocks.* **gurgle** /ˈgɜː.gl̩/ [US] /ˈgɝː-/ *noun* [C] *The water went down the plughole with a loud gurgle.*

gurgler /ˈgɜː.gləʳ/ [US] /ˈgɝː.glɚ/ *noun* [C] AUS INFORMAL a **plughole**

• **go down the gurgler** AUS If work or money goes down the gurgler, it is wasted: *So say he gives up his training, that's four thousand pounds down the gurgler.*

gurney /ˈgɜː.ni/ [US] /ˈgɝː-/ *noun* [C] US a light bed on wheels, used to move patients in a hospital

guru /ˈgʊr.uː/ *noun* [C] a religious leader or teacher in the Hindu or Sikh religion or, more generally, a person who is respected for their knowledge of a particular subject and who gives advice: *For the last decade she has acted as the president's economics guru.*

gush [FLOW] /gʌʃ/ *verb* [I usually + adv or prep; T] to flow or send out quickly and in large amounts: *Oil gushed* ***(out) from*** *the hole in the tanker.* ○ *Blood was gushing* ***from*** *his nose.* ○ *Her arm gushed blood where the knife had gone in.*

gush /gʌʃ/ *noun* [S] a large amount of liquid or gas that flows quickly: *Showers with pumps are more expensive, but they deliver* ***a*** *really powerful gush* ***of*** *water.*

gusher /ˈgʌʃ.əʳ/ [US] /-ɚ/ *noun* [C] an OIL WELL from which oil flows without the use of a PUMP DEVICE

gush [EXPRESS] /gʌʃ/ *verb* [I or T] to express a positive feeling, especially praise, in such a strong way that it does not sound sincere: [+ speech] *"You're just so talented!" she gushed.* **gush** /gʌʃ/ *noun* [S]

gushing /ˈgʌʃ.ɪŋ/ *adj* (ALSO **gushy**) expressing a positive feeling, especially praise, in such a strong way that it does not sound sincere: *One of the more gushing newspapers described the occasion as 'a fairy-tale wedding'.*

gushingly /ˈgʌʃ.ɪŋ.li/ *adv* (ALSO **gushily**)

gusset /ˈgʌs.ɪt/ *noun* [C] a second layer of cloth which is sewn into a piece of clothing to make it larger, stronger or more comfortable: *silk panties with a cotton gusset*

gust /gʌst/ *noun* [C] a sudden strong wind: *A sudden gust* ***of*** *wind blew his umbrella inside out.* ○ FIGURATIVE *She could hear gusts* ***of*** *laughter* (= sudden, loud laughter) *from within the room.*

gust /gʌst/ *verb* [I] to blow strongly: *Winds gusting* ***to*** *50 mph brought down power cables.*

gusty /ˈgʌs.ti/ *adj* with sudden, strong winds: *The forecast was for gusty winds and rain.*

gustatory /ˈgʌs.tə.tər.i/ [US] /-tɔː.ri/ *adj* SPECIALIZED connected with taste: *gustatory pleasures*

gusto /ˈgʌs.təʊ/ [US] /-toʊ/ *noun* [U] great energy, enthusiasm and enjoyment that is experienced by someone taking part in an activity, especially a performance: *Everyone joined in the singing* ***with*** *great gusto.*

gut [BOWEL] /gʌt/ *noun* **1** [U] the long tube in the body of a person or animal through which food moves during digestion: *Meat stays in the gut longer than vegetable matter.* **2** [C] INFORMAL a person's stomach when it is extremely large: *He's got a huge* ***beer*** *gut* (= large stomach caused by drinking beer). **3** [U] a strong thread made from an animal's bowel used, especially in the past, for making musical instruments and sports RACKETS

• **gut feeling/reaction** INFORMAL a strong belief about someone or something which cannot completely be explained and is not necessarily decided by reasoning: *I have a gut feeling that the relationship won't last.*

gut /gʌt/ *verb* [T] **-tt-** to remove the inner organs of an animal, especially in preparation for eating it: *She gutted the fish and cut off their heads.*

guts /gʌts/ *plural noun* bowels: *My guts hurt.* ➲See also **guts**.

• **have *sb's* guts for garters** UK INFORMAL If you say you will have someone's guts for garters, you mean that you will punish them severely: *If that boy has taken my bike again, I'll have his guts for garters!*

• **slog/sweat/work *your* guts out** INFORMAL to work extremely hard: *I've been slogging my guts out these past few weeks and all he can do is criticize.*

gut [DESTROY] /gʌt/ *verb* [T] **-tt- 1** to destroy the inside of a building completely, usually by fire: *A fire gutted the bookshop last week.* **2** to remove the inside parts and contents of a building, usually so that it can be decorated in a completely new way **3** UK INFORMAL to clean very thoroughly the inside of a house or room

guts /gʌts/ *plural noun* INFORMAL bravery; the ability to control fear and to deal with danger and uncertainty: [+ to infinitive] ***It takes*** *a lot of guts* ***to*** *admit to so many people that you've made a mistake.*

gutsy /ˈgʌt.si/ *adj* INFORMAL brave and determined: *a gutsy performance*

gutless /ˈgʌt.ləs/ *adj* INFORMAL lacking bravery: *This government is too gutless to take on the big long-term problems such as pollution.*

gutted /ˈgʌt.ɪd/ [US] /ˈgʌt̬-/ *adj* UK SLANG extremely disappointed and unhappy: *He was gutted when she finished the relationship.*

gutter [CHANNEL] /ˈgʌt.əʳ/ [US] /ˈgʌt̬.ɚ/ *noun* [C] **1** the edge of a road where rain flows away **2** an open pipe at the lower edge of a roof which collects and carries away rain

the gutter *noun* [S] the lowest level, especially of society: *Born to a poverty-stricken family, she dragged herself out of the gutter to become one of the wealthiest people in Britain today.*

guttering /ˈgʌt.ər.ɪŋ/ [US] /ˈgʌt̬.ɚ-/ *noun* [U] UK the system of open pipes on a building which collects and carries away rain

gutter [BURN WEAKLY] /ˈgʌt.əʳ/ [US] /ˈgʌt̬.ɚ/ *verb* [I] LITERARY (of a flame or candle) to burn unevenly and weakly, especially before completely stopping burning: *a guttering candle*

the ˌgutter ˈpress *noun* [S] UK DISAPPROVING the type of newspapers which pay more attention to shocking stories about crime and sex than to serious matters

guttersnipe /ˈgʌt.ə.snaɪp/ [US] /ˈgʌt̬.ɚ-/ *noun* [C] OLD-FASHIONED a child from a poor area of a town who is dirty and dressed badly: *a Victorian guttersnipe*

G

guttural /ˈgʌt.ᵊr.ᵊl/ [US] /ˈgʌt̬.ɚ-/ *adj* (of speech sounds) produced at the back of the throat and therefore deep: *Two Egyptians were arguing outside the room, their voices loud and guttural.*

gut-wrenching /ˈgʌtˌrentʃ.ɪŋ/ *adj* INFORMAL making you want to vomit: *gut-wrenching scenes of bloodshed*

guv /gʌv/ *noun* UK OLD-FASHIONED SLANG used to address a man: *Excuse me, guv, could you spare an old man the price of a cup of tea?*

guvnor /ˈgʌv.nəʳ/ [US] /-nɚ/ *noun* [C] (ALSO **guv**) UK OLD-FASHIONED SLANG a man who is in a position of authority over you: *If you want any time off work you'll have to ask the guvnor.*

guy /gaɪ/ *noun* [C] **1** INFORMAL a man: *He's a really nice guy.* ○ *Do you mean the guy with the blonde hair and glasses?* **2** MAINLY US **guys** used to address a group of people of either sex: *Come on, you guys, let's go.* **3** in the UK, a model of a man that is burnt on a large fire on GUY FAWKES NIGHT

G

Guy Fawkes Night /ˈgaɪ.fɔːksˌnaɪt/ [US] /-fɔːrks-/ *noun* [C or U] (ALSO **Bonfire Night**) UK in Britain, the evening of November 5th when models of men, called **guys**, are burned on large fires outside and there are firework displays. This is in memory of the failed attempt by Guy Fawkes to destroy the Houses of Parliament in London in 1605 with explosives.

ˈguy (ˌrope) *noun* [C] (US ALSO **guyline**) a rope which at one end is connected to a tent or pole and at the other end is fastened to the ground by a PEG, keeping the tent or pole in position

guzzle /ˈgʌz.l̩/ *verb* [I or T] INFORMAL to eat or drink quickly, eagerly and usually in large amounts: *I'm not surprised you feel sick after guzzling three ice-creams!* ○ *You're bound to get indigestion if you guzzle like that!* **guzzler** /ˈgʌz.l̩əʳ/ /-ləʳ/ [US] /-l̩ɚ/ *noun* [C] *She's a real guzzler!*

gym /dʒɪm/ *noun* **1** [U] GYMNASTICS, especially when done as a subject at school: *a gym skirt* ○ *gym shoes* ○ *Class 3 do gym on a Wednesday afternoon.* **2** [C] a large room with weights for lifting, horizontal bars and other equipment for exercising the body and increasing strength: *I go to the gym twice a week.* **3** [U] US FOR **physical education**

gymkhana /dʒɪmˈkɑː.nə/ *noun* [C] MAINLY UK an event at which people ride horses, taking part in various competitions involving horse racing and jumping over special fences

gymnasium /dʒɪmˈneɪ.zi.əm/ *noun* [C] (ALSO **gym**) FORMAL a large room with weights for lifting, horizontal bars and other equipment for exercising the body and increasing strength

gymnastics /dʒɪmˈnæs.tɪks/ *noun* [U] physical exercises and activities performed inside, often using equipment such as bars and ropes which are intended to increase the body's strength and the ability to move and bend easily: *the U.S. women's gymnastics team* ○ FIGURATIVE *Legal arguments require incredible* ***mental/verbal*** *gymnastics* (= the ability to think/speak cleverly and quickly). ➲See picture **Sports** on page Centre 10 **gymnastic** /dʒɪmˈnæs.tɪk/ *adj* [before n] *a gymnastic display*
gymnast /ˈdʒɪm.næst/ *noun* [C] a person who is skilled in gymnastics, often someone who competes in gymnastic competitions: *a great Russian gymnast*

gymslip /ˈdʒɪm.slɪp/ *noun* [C] UK a plain dress without sleeves usually worn over a shirt, especially in the past, by girls as a part of their school uniform

gynaecology UK, US **gynecology** /ˌgaɪ.nəˈkɒl.ə.dʒi/ [US] /-ˈkɑː.lə-/ *noun* [U] the area of medicine which involves the treatment of women's diseases, especially those of the reproductive organs **gynaecological** UK, US **gynecological** /ˌgaɪ.nə.kəˈlɒdʒ.ɪ.kᵊl/ [US] /-ˈlɑː.dʒɪ-/ *adj*: *gynaecological problems*
gynaecologist UK, US **gynecologist** /ˌgaɪ.nəˈkɒl.ə.dʒɪst/ [US] /-ˈkɑː.lə-/ *noun* [C] a doctor who specializes in the treatment of women's diseases, especially those of the reproductive organs

gyp /dʒɪp/ *noun* [U] UK INFORMAL pain or trouble: *My knee has been* ***giving*** *me gyp since I started running.*

gypsum /ˈdʒɪp.səm/ *noun* [U] a hard white substance that is used in making PLASTER OF PARIS

gypsy, **gipsy** /ˈdʒɪp.si/ *noun* [C] (UK ALSO **Romany**) a member of a race of people originally from northern India who typically used to travel from place to place, and now live especially in Europe and North America: *a gypsy caravan/encampment*

gyrate /dʒaɪˈreɪt/ [US] /ˈ--/ *verb* [I] **1** to turn around and around on a fixed point, usually quickly **2** to dance, especially in a sexual way: *A line of male dancers gyrated to the music while the audience screamed their appreciation.* **gyration** /ˌdʒaɪˈreɪ.ʃᵊn/ *noun* [C or U]

gyro [DEVICE] /ˈdʒaɪ.rəʊ/ [US] /-roʊ/ *noun* [C] *plural* **gyros** a GYROSCOPE

gyro [FOOD] /ˈjɪə.rəʊ/ /ˈdʒɪə-/ [US] /ˈjɪr.oʊ/ *noun* [C] *plural* **gyros** US a food consisting of PITTA bread filled with lamb and vegetables

gyroscope /ˈdʒaɪ.rə.skəʊp/ [US] /-skoʊp/ *noun* [C] (ALSO **gyro**) a device containing a wheel which spins freely within a frame, used on aircraft and ships to help keep them horizontal, and as a children's toy

H

H (*plural* **H's** or **Hs**), **h** (*plural* **h's** or **hs**) /eɪtʃ/ *noun* [C] the 8th letter of the English alphabet

ha, hah /hɑː/ /hæ/ *exclamation* MAINLY HUMOROUS used to express satisfaction that something bad has happened to someone who deserved it, or to express a feeling of victory: *He's left her has he? Ha! That'll teach her to go chasing other women's husbands!* ○ *Ha! So I am right after all!*

habeas corpus /ˌheɪ.bi.əsˈkɔː.pəs/ [US] /-ˈkɔːr-/ *noun* [U] LEGAL a legal order which states that a person in prison must appear before and be judged by a court of law before he or she can be forced by law to stay in prison

haberdashery [CLOTH] UK /ˌhæb.əˈdæʃ.ər.i/ [US] /-ɚˈdæʃ.ɚ-/ *noun* [C or U] (US **notions**) cloth, pins, thread, etc. used for sewing, or a shop or a department of a large shop which sells these

haberdashery [MEN'S CLOTHES] /ˌhæb.əˈdæʃ.ər.i/ [US] /-ɚˈdæʃ.ɚ-/ *noun* [C or U] US OLD-FASHIONED clothing for men, or a shop or department in a large shop which sells this

habit [REPEATED ACTION] /ˈhæb.ɪt/ *noun* **1** [C or U] something which you do often and regularly, sometimes without knowing that you are doing it: *I always buy the same brand of toothpaste just* ***out of*** (= because of) *habit.* ○ *I'm trying not to* ***get into*** (= start) *the habit of always having biscuits with my coffee.* ○ *I used to swim twice a week, but I seem to have* ***got out of*** (= ended) *the habit recently.* ○ *I was taught to drive by my boyfriend and I'm afraid I've* ***picked up*** (= caught) *some of his bad habits.* ○ *His eating habits are extraordinary.* ○ *I'm trying to get him to* ***break*** (= end intentionally) *the habit of switching on the TV when he comes home at night.* ○ *I don't mind being woken up once or twice in the middle of the night by my flatmate so long as she doesn't* ***make a habit of it*** (= do it frequently). ○ *I'm not really* ***in the*** *habit* ***of*** *looking at* (= I don't usually look at) *other people's clothes, but even I noticed that awful suit!* **2** [C] something annoying that someone often does: *She* ***has a*** *habit* ***of*** *finishing off other people's sentences.* **3** [C] a strong physical need to keep having a particular drug: *a cocaine habit* ○ FIGURATIVE HUMOROUS *I'm afraid I've got a chocloate habit.*

habit [CLOTHING] /ˈhæb.ɪt/ *noun* [C] a special piece of long clothing worn by monks and nuns

habitable /ˈhæb.ɪ.tə.bl̩/ [US] /-t̬ə-/ *adj* (ALSO **inhabitable**) providing conditions which are good enough to live in or on: *A lot of improvements would have to be made before the building was habitable.* ○ *Some areas of the country are just too cold to be habitable.* * NOTE: The opposite is **uninhabitable**.

habitat /ˈhæb.ɪ.tæt/ *noun* [C or U] the natural surroundings in which an animal or plant usually lives: *With so many areas of woodland being cut down, a lot of wildlife is losing its natural habitat.*

habitation /ˌhæb.ɪˈteɪ.ʃən/ *noun* [U] FORMAL **1** the act of living in a building **2 unfit for human habitation** describes a house that is too dirty or dangerous for people to be allowed to live in it

habit-forming /ˈhæb.ɪtˌfɔː.mɪŋ/ [US] /-ˌfɔːr-/ *adj* A habit-forming activity or drug makes you want to do or have it repeatedly.

habitual /həˈbɪtʃ.u.əl/ *adj* SLIGHTLY FORMAL usual or repeated: *a habitual thief* ○ *habitual drug use* ○ *dressed in his habitual black* ○ *her habitual meanness* **habitually** /həˈbɪtʃ.ʊ.ə.li/ *adv*: *There is something wrong with anyone who is so habitually rude.*

habituated /həˈbɪtʃ.u.eɪ.tɪd/ [US] /-t̬ɪd/ *adj* FORMAL used to something, especially something unpleasant: *We find children's emotional needs difficult to respond to because we are habituated* ***to*** *disregarding our own.*

habitué /hæˈbɪt.juː.eɪ/ *noun* [C] LITERARY a person who regularly visits a particular place: *Habitués* ***of*** *this gentlemen's club are generally middle-aged, grey-haired and overweight.*

hack [CUT] /hæk/ *verb* **1** [I or T; + adv or prep] to cut into pieces in a rough and violent way, often without aiming exactly: *Three villagers were hacked* ***to death*** *in a savage attack.* ○ *Don't just hack* ***(away) at*** *the bread – cut it properly!* ○ *The butcher hacked* ***off*** *a large chunk of meat.* ○ FIGURATIVE *The article had been hacked* ***about*** (= carelessly changed) *so much it was scarcely recognizable.* **2** [T usually + adv or prep] UK in football and rugby, to kick the ball away or to FOUL (= act against the rules) by kicking another player in the leg: *Platt was twice hacked* ***down*** *in the second half by the other team's sweeper.*

hack [WRITER] /hæk/ *noun* [C] DISAPPROVING a JOURNALIST (= writer for newspapers or magazines) whose work is low in quality or lacks imagination: *Fleet Street hacks*

hack [POLITICIAN] /hæk/ *noun* [C] DISAPPROVING a politician, especially an unimportant one: *tired old* ***party*** *hacks*

hack [COMPUTING] /hæk/ *verb* [I usually + adv or prep] to get into someone else's computer system without permission in order to find out information or do something illegal: ***Computer*** *hacking has become very widespread over the last decade.* ○ *A programmer had managed to hack* ***into*** *some top-secret government data.*

hacker /ˈhæk.əʳ/ [US] /-ɚ/ *noun* [C] (ALSO **computer hacker**) someone who hacks into other people's computer systems

hack [HORSE] /hæk/ *noun* [C] a ride on a horse in the countryside

hack /hæk/ *verb* [I usually + adv or prep] (ALSO **go hacking**) to ride a horse in the countryside

hack [DRIVER/CAR] /hæk/ *noun* [C] US INFORMAL (the driver of) a car which is available for rent, especially a taxi

hack [MANAGE] /hæk/ *verb* [T usually in negatives] INFORMAL to manage to deal successfully with something: *I tried working on the night shift for a while, but I just* ***couldn't*** *hack it.*

▲ **hack *sb* off** *phrasal verb* MAINLY UK INFORMAL to make someone feel annoyed: *He leaves all the difficult stuff for me to do and it really hacks me off.*

ˌhacked ˈoff *adj* [after v] INFORMAL unhappy, dissatisfied or annoyed, especially because of the situation you are in: *She's getting a bit hacked off* ***with*** *all the travelling she has to do.*

ˌhacking ˈcough *noun* [C usually sing] a loud cough that sounds painful

hackles /ˈhæk.l̩z/ *plural noun* the hairs on the back of some animals or the feathers on the back of the neck of some birds which rise when the animal or bird is frightened or about to fight

• **make (*sb's*) hackles rise** (ALSO **raise (*sb's*) hackles**) to annoy someone: *The prime minister's speech has raised hackles among the opposition.*

hackney carriage /ˌhæk.niˈkær.ɪdʒ/ [US] /-ˈker-/ *noun* [C] UK **1** (ALSO **hackney cab**) FORMAL a taxi **2** a carriage pulled by a horse that can be rented with a driver for making short journeys, used especially in the past

hackneyed /ˈhæk.nid/ *adj* DISAPPROVING describes a phrase or an idea which has been said or used so often that it has become meaningless or boring: *The plot of the film is just a hackneyed boy-meets-girl scenario.*

hacksaw /ˈhæk.sɔː/ [US] /-sɑː/ *noun* [C] a small saw used especially for cutting metal

had [HAVE] STRONG /hæd/, WEAK /həd, əd/ (SHORT FORM **'d**) *past simple and past participle of* have, also used with the past participle of other verbs to form the past perfect: *When I was a child I had a dog.* ○ *No more food please – I've had enough.* ○ *I had heard/I'd heard they were planning to move to Boston.* ○ FORMAL *Had I known* (= If I had known), *I would have come home sooner.*

• **had better/best do *sth*** If you had better/best do something, you should do it or it would be good to do it: *I'd better leave a note so they'll know I'll be late.*

had [TRICKED] /hæd/ *adj* INFORMAL **be had** to be tricked and given less than you agreed or paid for: *"I paid £2000 for this car." "You've been had, mate. It's not worth more than £1000."*

had [FINISHED] /hæd/ *verb* INFORMAL **have had it** (of a machine, etc.) to be in such a bad condition that it is useless or (of a person, team, etc.) to be doing so badly that they are certain to fail: *I think this kettle's had it.* ○ *Liverpool have had it for this season.*

• **have had it (up to here) with** *INFORMAL* to have suffered because of someone or something and to be no longer able to bear them: *I've had it up to here with you – get out!* ○ *I've had it with foreign holidays.*

haddock /'hæd.ək/ *noun* [C or U] *plural* **haddock** a fish that can be eaten, which is found in the North Atlantic

Hades /'heɪ.diːz/ *noun* (in stories about Ancient Greece) a place under the earth where the SPIRITS (= forms of dead people that cannot be seen) of the dead go; the **underworld**

hadj /hædʒ/ *noun* [C] *plural* **hadjes** a **hajj**

hadn't /'hæd.ənt/ *short form of* had not: *If you hadn't told him he would never have known.*

haematology *UK*, *US* **hematology** /ˌhiː.mə'tɒl.ə.dʒi/ *US* /-'tɑː.lə-/ *noun* [U] *SPECIALIZED* the scientific study of blood and the body tissues which make it **haematological** *UK*, *US* **hematological** /ˌhiː.mə.tə'lɒdʒ.ɪ.kᵊl/ *US* /-'lɑː.dʒɪ-/ *adj* **haematologist** *UK*, *US* **hematologist** /ˌhiː.mə-'tɒl.ə.dʒɪst/ *US* /-'tɑː.lə-/ *noun* [C]

haemoglobin *UK*, *US* **hemoglobin** /ˌhiː.mə'gləʊ.bɪn/ *US* /-gloʊ-/ *noun* [U] a substance in red blood cells which combines with and carries oxygen around the body, and gives blood its red colour

haemophilia *UK*, *US* **hemophilia** /ˌhiː.mə'fɪl.i.ə/ *noun* [U] a rare blood disease in which blood continues to flow after a cut or other injury because one of the substances which causes it to thicken does not work correctly **haemophiliac** *UK*, *US* **hemophiliac** /ˌhiː.mə'fɪl.i.æk/ *noun* [C] a person who suffers from haemophilia

haemorrhage *UK*, *US* **hemorrhage** /'hem.ᵊr.ɪdʒ/ *US* /-ɚ-/ *noun* [C] **1** a large flow of blood from a damaged BLOOD VESSEL (= tube carrying blood around the body): *a brain haemorrhage* **2** a sudden or serious loss: *The higher salaries paid overseas have caused a haemorrhage of talent from this country.*
haemorrhage /'hem.ᵊr.ɪdʒ/ *US* /-ɚ-/ *verb* **1** [I] *UK* (*US* **hemorrhage**) to lose a large amount of blood in a short time: *She started haemorrhaging while giving birth to the baby.* **2** [I or T] to lose large amounts of something such as money over a period of time and be unable to stop this happening: *The business has been haemorrhaging money for several months.*

haemorrhoids *UK*, *US* **hemorrhoids** /'hem.ᵊr.ɔɪdz/ *US* /-ɚ-/ *plural noun* *SPECIALIZED* a medical condition in which the veins at the anus become swollen and painful and sometimes bleed; PILES

hag /hæg/ *noun* [C] *DISAPPROVING* an ugly old woman

haggard /'hæg.əd/ *US* /-ɚd/ *adj* looking ill or tired, often with dark skin under the eyes: *He'd been drinking the night before and was looking a bit haggard.*

haggis /'hæg.ɪs/ *noun* [U] a dish which comes from Scotland consisting of various sheep's organs cut up with onions and spices and cooked inside a sheep's stomach

haggle /'hæg.l̩/ *verb* [I or T] to attempt to decide on a price or conditions which are acceptable to the person selling the goods and the person buying them, usually by arguing: *It's traditional that you haggle over/about the price of things in the market.*

hagiography /ˌhæg.i'ɒg.rə.fi/ *US* /-'ɑː.grə-/ *noun* **1** [C or U] a BIOGRAPHY in which the writer represents the person as perfect or much better than they really are, or the tendency to write so many admiring things about a person that it is not realistic **2** [U] *SPECIALIZED* writings about the lives of holy people such as saints

hah /hɑː/ /hæ/ *exclamation* **ha**

ha-ha, ha ha, ha ha /'hɑ'hɑː/ /'hɑː.hɑː/ *exclamation* used in writing to represent a shout of laughter, or said by children or by adults childishly as a way of making someone look foolish

haiku /'haɪ.kuː/ *noun* [C] *plural* **haiku** a short Japanese poem in 17 syllables

hail ICE /heɪl/ *noun* [U] **1** small hard balls of ice which fall from the sky like rain **2 a hail of** *sth* a lot of similar things or remarks, thrown or shouted at someone at the same time: *a hail of bullets* ○ *The Prime Minister was*

greeted with a hail of insults as she arrived at the students' union.

hail /heɪl/ *verb* [I] If it hails, small hard balls of ice fall from the sky like rain.

hail CALL /heɪl/ *verb* [T] *SLIGHTLY FORMAL* to call someone in order to attract their attention: *Shall we hail a taxi?* ○ *I tried to hail her from across the room.*

• **be within hailing distance of** *somewhere* *OLD-FASHIONED* to be near somewhere

PHRASAL VERBS WITH **hail** ▼

▲ **hail** *sb/sth* **as** *sth* *phrasal verb* [often passive] to praise a person or an achievement by saying that they are similar to someone or something very good: *She's being hailed as one of the best up-and-coming young dancers today.* ○ *The film was hailed as a masterpiece in its day.*

▲ **hail from** *somewhere* *phrasal verb* *FORMAL* to come from or to have been born in a particular place: *Joe originally hails from Toronto.*

hail-fellow-well-met /ˌheɪl.fel.əʊ.wel'met/ *US* /-oʊ-/ *OLD-FASHIONED* If a man or his actions are described as hail-fellow-well-met, they are very friendly and enthusiastic, sometimes in a way that is not sincere: *He was greeted with the usual hail-fellow-well-met slap on the back and handshake.*

Hail Mary /ˌheɪl'meə.ri/ *US* /-'mer.i/ *noun* [C] a Catholic prayer to Mary, the mother of Jesus Christ

hailstone /'heɪl.stəʊn/ *US* /-stoʊn/ *noun* [C] a small hard ball of ice which falls from the sky like rain; a piece of HAIL

hailstorm /'heɪl.stɔːm/ *US* /-stɔːrm/ *noun* [C] a sudden heavy fall of HAIL

hair /heəʳ/ *US* /her/ *noun* [C or U] the mass of thin thread-like structures on the head of a person, or any of these structures that grow out of the skin of a person or animal: *He's got short dark hair.* ○ *I'm going to have/get my hair cut.* ○ *She brushed her long red hair.* ○ *He had lost his hair by the time he was twenty-five.* ○ *He's starting to get a few grey hairs now.* ○ *I found a hair in my soup.*

• **That'll put hairs on** *your* **chest!** *HUMOROUS* something that is said to someone who is going to drink something that is very strongly alcoholic or eat something satisfying that will make their stomach feel full

• **get in** *sb's* **hair** *INFORMAL* to annoy someone, usually by being present all the time: *My flatmate has been getting in my hair a bit recently.*

• **keep** *your* **hair on** ⊃See **keep** *your* **shirt on** at **shirt**.

• **make** *sb's* **hair stand on end** *INFORMAL* to make someone very frightened: *To be honest, the thought of jumping out of a moving aeroplane makes my hair stand on end.*

• **the hair of the dog (that bit you)** *HUMOROUS* an alcoholic drink taken as a cure the morning after an occasion when you have drunk too much alcohol

-haired /-heəd/ *US* /-herd/ *suffix* with the hair described: *dark-haired* ○ *short-haired*

hairless /'heə.ləs/ *US* /'her-/ *adj* without hair: *To my mind, a hairless armpit looks unnatural.*

hairband /'heə.bænd/ *US* /'her-/ *noun* [C] (*UK ALSO* **Alice band**) a curved plastic strip worn in the hair, which fits closely over the top of the head and behind the ears ⊃See picture **Hairstyles and Hats** on page Centre 8

hairbrush /'heə.brʌʃ/ *US* /'her-/ *noun* [C] a brush used for making the hair on your head tidy and smooth

haircut /'heə.kʌt/ *US* /'her-/ *noun* [C] the style in which someone's hair is cut, or an occasion of cutting or styling the hair: *I've had a really awful haircut.* ○ *I wish he'd get/have a haircut.*

hairdo /'heə.duː/ *US* /'her-/ *noun* [C] *plural* **hairdos** *OLD-FASHIONED* the style in which a person, especially a woman, has had their hair cut and arranged, especially if it is unusual or done for a particular occasion: *She had a most elaborate hairdo, all piled up on top of her head.*

hairdresser /'heə.dres.əʳ/ *US* /'her.dres.ɚ/ *noun* [C] a person who cuts people's hair and puts it into a style, usually working in a special shop, called a hairdresser's: *I'm going to change my hairdresser.* ○ *I've got a four o'clock appointment at the hairdresser's.* **hair-**

dressing /ˈheəˌdres.ɪŋ/ [US] /ˈher-/ *noun* [U] *a hairdressing salon*

hairdryer /ˈheəˌdraɪ.əʳ/ [US] /ˈherˌdraɪ.ɚ/ *noun* [C] (*ALSO* **hair-drier**) an electrical device, usually held in the hand, which blows out hot air and is used for drying and sometimes styling a person's hair

ˈhair ˌextension *noun* [C usually pl] a long piece of hair that is added to a person's own hair in order to make the hair longer

ˈhair ˌgel *noun* [C or U] a thick liquid substance which is put in the hair to help the hair keep a particular shape or style

hairgrip *UK* /ˈheə.grɪp/ [US] /ˈher-/ *noun* [C] (*US* **bobby pin**) a metal U-shaped pin which is tightly bent and slides into the hair in order to keep it back off the face or to keep part of the hair in the desired position

ˈhair ˌlacquer *noun* [U] *UK* **hair spray**

hairless /ˈheə.ləs/ [US] /ˈher-/ *adj* ➲See at **hair**.

hairline [HEAD] /ˈheə.laɪn/ [US] /ˈher-/ *noun* [C] the edge of a person's hair, especially along the top of the forehead: *He's got a **receding** hairline* (= He's losing his hair at the front of the head).

hairline [NARROW] /ˈheə.laɪn/ [US] /ˈher-/ *adj* [before n] (of cracks or lines) very narrow: *a hairline **fracture***

ˈhair ˌmousse *noun* [C or U] a light creamy substance which is put in the hair to help the hair keep a particular shape or style

hairnet /ˈheə.net/ [US] /ˈher-/ *noun* [C] a light net that some women wear over their hair to keep it in place

hairpiece /ˈheə.piːs/ [US] /ˈher-/ *noun* [C] an artificial covering of hair used to hide an area of the head where there is no hair: *Do you think he **wears** a hairpiece?*

hairpin /ˈheə.pɪn/ [US] /ˈher-/ *noun* [C] a thin metal U-shaped pin which is used to hold part of the hair in the desired position

ˌhairpin ˈbend *UK noun* [C] (*US* **hairpin turn**) a bend in the road which curves so sharply that it almost turns back to go in the opposite direction

hair-raising /ˈheəˌreɪ.zɪŋ/ [US] /ˈher-/ *adj* very frightening: *She gave a hair-raising account of her escape through the desert.*

ˈhair ˌsalon *noun* [C] a shop where people go to have their hair cut and put into a particular style

a hair's breadth /əˈheəzˌbretθ/ [US] /-ˈherz-/ *noun* [S] a very small distance or amount: *His finger was **within** a hair's breadth **of** touching the alarm.* ○ *FIGURATIVE She came **within** a hair's breadth **of** losing her life* (= She very nearly died).

ˈhair ˌslide *UK noun* [C] (*US* **barrette**) a small decorative fastener that a woman or girl wears in her hair, often to stop it falling in front of her face ➲See picture **Hairstyles and Hats** on page Centre 8

ˈhair ˌspray *noun* [C or U] (*UK ALSO* **hair lacquer**) a sticky liquid which is sprayed onto someone's hair to keep it in a particular shape

hairstyle /ˈheə.staɪl/ [US] /ˈher-/ *noun* [C] the style in which someone's hair is cut and arranged ➲See picture **Hairstyles and Hats** on page Centre 8

hair-trigger /ˌheəˈtrɪg.əʳ/ [US] /ˌherˈtrɪg.ɚ/ *adj INFORMAL* **a hair-trigger temper** a tendency to become very angry very easily

hairy [WITH HAIR] /ˈheə.ri/ [US] /ˈher.i/ *adj* having a lot of hair, especially on parts of the body other than the head: *hairy armpits/legs* ○ *a hairy chest* ○ *She's very hairy for a woman.* **hairiness** /ˈheə.rɪ.nəs/ [US] /ˈher.ɪ.-/ *noun* [U]

hairy [FRIGHTENING] /ˈheə.ri/ [US] /ˈher.i/ *adj INFORMAL* frightening or dangerous, especially in a way that is exciting: *I like going on the back of Laurent's motorbike, though it can get a bit hairy.*

hajj (*plural* **hajjes**), **hadj** (*plural* **hadjes**) /hædʒ/ *noun* [C] the religious journey to Mecca which all Muslims try to make at least once in their life

haka /ˈhæ.kə/ *noun* [C] a traditional war dance of the Maori people of New Zealand, or a similar performance before a sports event which is intended to give support to one team while discouraging the opposing team

hake /heɪk/ *noun* [C or U] *plural* **hake** or **hakes** a big sea fish which can be eaten

halal /hæˈlæl/ *adj* [before n] describes meat from an animal that has been killed in the way that is demanded by Islamic law, or someone who sells this meat: *halal meat* ○ *a halal butcher*

halcyon days /ˌhæl.si.ənˈdeɪz/ *plural noun LITERARY* a very happy or successful period in the past: *She recalled the halcyon days of her youth.*

hale and hearty /ˌheɪl.ənˈhɑː.ti/ [US] /-ˈhɑːr.t̬i/ *adj OLD-FASHIONED* (especially of old people) healthy and strong: *She found her grandfather hale and hearty, walking five miles each day before breakfast.*

half /hɑːf/ [US] /hæf/ *noun, pronoun, predeterminer, adj, adv* **1** either of the two equal or nearly equal parts that together make up a whole: *"What's half **of** ninety-six?" "Forty-eight."* ○ *Roughly half **(of)** the class are Spanish and the others are a mixture of nationalities.* ○ *Cut the apple **in** half/**into** halves* (= into two equal parts). ○ *My little brother is half **as** tall as me/half my height.* ○ *half **a dozen*** (= six) *eggs* ○ *Half **of** me would just like to give it all up and travel around the world* (= partly I would like to, but partly I would not). ○ *She was born in the latter half of the eighteenth century.* ○ *The recipe tells you to use a pound and a half of butter.* **2** *INFORMAL* a lot: *She invited a lot of people to the party but half of them didn't turn up.* ○ *I don't even know where she is half **(of) the time**.* **3** only partly: *He answered the door half naked.* ○ *I was half expecting to see her at the party.* ○ *I'm half inclined to take the job just because it's in London.* ○ *He was being funny but I think he was half serious.* ○ *The bottle's half empty.* **4 half past** Half past a particular hour is 30 minutes later than that hour: *I'll meet you at half past nine* (= 09.30 or 21.30). ○ *UK INFORMAL I'll meet you at half seven* (= half past seven).

half /hɑːf/ [US] /hæf/ *noun* [C] *plural* **halves 1** *UK INFORMAL* half a pint of a drink, especially beer: *A pint of lager and two halves, please.* **2** *UK* a ticket which is cheaper because it is for a child: *Two adults and three halves to Manchester, please.* **3 first/second half** either of two periods of time into which a game is divided

• **not know the half of it** (*ALSO* **have not heard the half of it**) *INFORMAL* If someone does not know the half of it, they know that a situation is bad but they do not know how serious it is: *"I hear things aren't going too well at work." "You don't know the half of it!"*

• **That was a game/meal/walk, etc. and a half!** *INFORMAL* something that you say about something that was very surprising, very good, or took a lot of time

• **be half the battle** to be the most difficult part of a process so that once you have completed this part, you have almost succeeded: *For a lot of jobs, getting an interview is half the battle.*

• **given half a/the chance** *INFORMAL* If someone would do something given half a chance, they would certainly do it if they had the opportunity: *I'd give up work given half a chance.*

• **go halves** *INFORMAL* to divide the cost of something with someone: *Shall we go halves **on** a bottle of champagne?* ○ *I'll go halves **with** you on a bottle of champagne.*

• **how the other half lives** *HUMOROUS* how people who are much richer than you live their lives

• **not do things by halves** *HUMOROUS* If someone does not do things by halves, they put a lot of effort and enthusiasm into doing things, often more than is necessary: *"I didn't realize you were decorating the whole house." "Oh, we don't do things by halves round here."*

• **half and half** equal amounts of two different things: *"Do you use milk or cream in the recipe?" "Half and half."*

• **half as much again** (*US ALSO* **half again as much**) 50% more of the existing number or amount

• **not half** *UK INFORMAL* used in spoken English to express a positive statement more strongly: *It wasn't half crowded in the club last night* (= It was very crowded). ○ *She didn't half shout at him* (= She shouted a lot at him)*!* ○ *"You enjoyed yourself last night, didn't you?" "Not half* (= Very much)*!"*

• **not half as** (*ALSO* **not half such a**) *INFORMAL* not nearly as: *It wasn't half as good as that other restaurant we went to.*

• **be half the dancer/writer, etc. you used to be** to be much less good at doing something than you used to be: *She's half the tennis player she used to be.*

halve /hɑːv/ [US] /hæv/ *verb* **1** [T] to reduce something by half or divide something into two equal pieces: *In the past eight years, the elephant population in Africa has been halved.* ○ *The potatoes will cook more quickly if you halve them before you put them in the oven.* **2** [I] If something halves, it is reduced by half: *Their profits have halved in the last six months.*

half-assed, *UK ALSO* **half-arsed** /ˈhɑːf.æst/ [US] /ˈhæf-/ *adj SLANG DISAPPROVING* A half-assed idea or plan is stupid or has not been considered carefully enough: *It's another one of her half-assed ideas for getting rich.*

halfback /ˈhɑːf.bæk/ [US] /ˈhæf-/ *noun* [C] (*ALSO* **half**) (in football and other sports) a player who plays in the middle of the field, in front of the FULLBACKS and behind the FORWARDS

half-baked /ˌhɑːfˈbeɪkt/ [US] /ˌhæf-/ *adj INFORMAL DISAPPROVING* An idea or plan which is half-baked has not been considered carefully enough: *The government has set up some half-baked scheme for training teachers on the job.*

ˌhalf ˈboard *UK noun* [U] (*US* **modified American plan**) a hotel room combined with breakfast and either lunch or dinner: *Expect to pay about £350 for a week's half board in a three-star hotel.* ○ *half-board* ***accommodation*** ➲Compare **full board**.

half-brother /ˈhɑːfˌbrʌð.əʳ/ [US] /ˈhæfˌbrʌð.ɚ/ *noun* [C] a brother who is the son of only one of your parents

half-caste /ˈhɑːf.kɑːst/ [US] /ˈhæf.kæst/ *noun* [C] a person whose parents are from different races. This is usually considered offensive. **half-caste** /ˈhɑːf.kɑːst/ [US] /ˈhæf.kæst/ *adj*

half-cock /ˌhɑːfˈkɒk/ [US] /ˌhæfˈkɑːk/ *OLD-FASHIONED (UK)* ***go off at half-cock/****(US)* ***go off half-cocked*** to start before arrangements are complete, failing as a result

half-cut /ˌhɑːfˈkʌt/ [US] /ˌhæf-/ *adj* [after v] *UK INFORMAL* drunk: *He looked half-cut to me.*

half-dead /ˌhɑːfˈded/ [US] /ˌhæf-/ *adj* [after v] *INFORMAL* extremely tired

half-decent /ˌhɑːfˈdiː.sᵊnt/ [US] /ˌhæf-/ *adj* [before n] *INFORMAL* quite good or skilled: *Any half-decent sprinter can run 100m in 11 seconds.*

half-hearted /ˌhɑːfˈhɑː.tɪd/ [US] /ˌhæfˈhɑːr.t̬ɪd/ *adj* showing a lack of enthusiasm and interest: *He made a rather half-hearted* ***attempt*** *to clear up the rubbish.* **half-heartedly** /ˌhɑːfˈhɑː.tɪd.li/ [US] /ˌhæfˈhɑːr.t̬ɪd-/ *adv*: *The audience applauded half-heartedly.*

ˌhalf ˈhour *noun* [C] (*ALSO* **half an hour**) a period of 30 minutes: *The dollar surged against the yen in the final half hour of trading.* ○ *Half an hour later, she was smiling and chatting as if nothing had happened.* ○ *She is to host a new half-hour show which will be broadcast every weekday evening.* ○ *Trains for Washington depart* ***on the/every*** *half hour* (= at 10.30, 11.30, etc.).

half-hourly /ˌhɑːfˈaʊə.li/ [US] /ˌhæfˈaʊr-/ *adj* [before n], *adv* happening twice every hour: *There's a half-hourly train service to London from here.*

half-life /ˈhɑːf.laɪf/ [US] /ˈhæf-/ *noun* [C] *SPECIALIZED* the length of time needed for the RADIOACTIVITY of a radioactive substance to be reduced by half

half-light /ˈhɑːf.laɪt/ [US] /ˈhæf-/ *noun* [U] a low light in which you cannot see things well: *In the dim half-light of evening, I was unable to tell whether it was Mary or her sister.*

half-marathon /ˌhɑːfˈmær.ə.θᵊn/ [US] /ˌhæfˈmær.ə.θɑːn/ *noun* [C] a running race over a distance of about 21 kilometres

half-mast /ˌhɑːfˈmɑːst/ [US] /ˌhæfˈmæst/ *noun* (*US ALSO* **half-staff**) **at half-mast** describes a flag that has been lowered to a point half the way down the pole as an expression of sadness at someone's death: *The palace flags were all* ***flying at*** *half-mast.*

half-measures /ˌhɑːfˈmeʒ.əz/ [US] /ˌhæfˈmeʒ.ɚz/ *plural noun DISAPPROVING* actions which only achieve part of what they are intended to achieve: *I'm not interested in half-measures.*

half-moon /ˌhɑːfˈmuːn/ [US] /ˌhæf-/ *noun* [C usually sing] (something shaped like) the moon when only half of the surface facing the Earth is lit by light from the sun

ˈhalf ˌnote *noun* [C] *MAINLY US FOR* **minim**

ˈhalf ˌpipe *noun* [C] a U-shaped structure used in SKATEBOARDING, SNOWBOARDING, etc.

half-price /ˌhɑːfˈpraɪs/ [US] /ˌhæf-/ *adj, adv* costing half the usual price: *I got some half-price pizzas at the supermarket.* ○ *The railcard allows students and young people to travel half-price on most trains.*

half-sister /ˈhɑːfˌsɪs.təʳ/ [US] /ˈhæfˌsɪs.tɚ/ *noun* [C] a sister who is the daughter of only one of your parents

half-size /ˈhɑːf.saɪz/ [US] /ˈhæf-/ *noun* [C] a size of clothing which is half of the way between two usual sizes

ˈhalf ˌstep *noun* [C] *US FOR* **semitone**

ˌhalf ˈterm *noun* [C usually sing] in the UK, a short holiday in the middle of each of the three periods into which the school year is divided

half-timbered /ˌhɑːfˈtɪm.bəd/ [US] /ˌhæfˈtɪm.bɚd/ *adj* A half-timbered building has a wooden frame whose spaces are filled with brick or stone to form the walls, so that the wood still shows on the surface.

half-time /ˌhɑːfˈtaɪm/ [US] /ˈhæf-/ *noun* [U] a short rest period between the two parts of a sports game: *Italy had a comfortable three-goal lead over France by half-time.* ○ *What was the half-time score?* ➲Compare **full time**.

halftone [PRINTING] /ˌhɑːfˈtəʊn/ [US] /ˈhæf.toʊn/ *noun* [C or U] (a method of printing) a picture built up from a pattern of very small black spots

halftone [MUSIC] /ˌhɑːfˈtəʊn/ [US] /ˈhæf.toʊn/ *noun* [C] (*ALSO* **half step**) *US FOR* **semitone**

half-truth /ˈhɑːf.truːθ/ [US] /ˈhæf-/ *noun* [C] a statement which is intended to deceive by being only partly true

ˌhalf ˈvolley *noun* [C] a shot in a game such as tennis in which the ball is hit just after it has bounced

halfway [IN THE MIDDLE] /ˌhɑːfˈweɪ/ [US] /ˌhæf-/ *adj, adv* in the middle of something, or at a place which is equally distant from two other places: *York is halfway* ***between*** *Edinburgh and London.* ○ *I'd like you to look at the diagram which is halfway* ***down*** *page 27.* ○ *She started feeling sick halfway* ***through*** *dinner.* ○ *The management's proposals don't even* ***go*** *halfway* ***towards*** *meeting our demands.*

halfway [QUITE] /ˌhɑːfˈweɪ/ [US] /ˌhæf-/ *adv* not very, but satisfactorily: *Any halfway* ***decent*** *teacher should be able to explain the difference between transitive and intransitive verbs.*

ˌhalfway ˈhouse *noun* **1** [C usually sing] something which combines particular features of two other things, especially in order to try to please people who do not like the two things on their own: *The new proposals are a halfway house* ***between*** *the original treaty and the British government's revised version.* **2** [C] a place where prisoners or people with mental health problems stay after they leave prison or hospital and before they start to live on their own

half-wit /ˈhɑːf.wɪt/ [US] /ˈhæf-/ *noun* [C] *DISAPPROVING* a stupid person

half-witted /ˌhɑːfˈwɪ.tɪd/ [US] /ˌhæfˈwɪ.t̬ɪd/ *adj DISAPPROVING* stupid: *a half-witted remark*

halibut /ˈhæl.ɪ.bət/ *noun* [C] *plural* **halibut** or **halibuts** a big, flat sea fish which can be eaten

halitosis /ˌhæl.ɪˈtəʊ.sɪs/ [US] /-ˈtoʊ-/ *noun* [U] (*ALSO* **bad breath**) breath which smells unpleasant when it comes out of the mouth

hall [ENTRANCE] /hɔːl/ [US] /hɑːl/ *noun* [C] (*ALSO* **hallway**) the room just inside the main entrance of a house, apartment or other building which leads to other rooms and usually to the stairs: *I've left my bags* ***in*** *the hall.*

hall [BUILDING] /hɔːl/ [US] /hɑːl/ *noun* [C] a building or large room used for events involving a lot of people: *the Royal Albert Hall* ○ *a* ***concert*** *hall* ○ *the school* ***sports*** *hall* ○ *I'm playing in a concert at the* ***village/church*** *hall next weekend.*

hallelujah, **alleluia** /ˌhæl.ɪˈluː.jə/ *exclamation, noun* [C] **1** (an emotional expression of) praise and thanks to God **2** *INFORMAL HUMOROUS* said to express surprise and pleasure that something positive that you were certain would not happen has happened: *At last, Richard's found himself a girlfriend – hallelujah!*

hallmark [MARK] /ˈhɔːl.mɑːk/ ⓤ /ˈhɑːl.mɑːrk/ *noun* [C] in the UK, an official mark put on objects made of gold or silver which shows their place and year of origin and the purity of the metal used to make them
hallmark /ˈhɔːl.mɑːk/ ⓤ /ˈhɑːl.mɑːrk/ *verb* [T] to put an official mark on an object made of gold or silver
hallmark [CHARACTERISTIC] /ˈhɔːl.mɑːk/ ⓤ /ˈhɑːl.mɑːrk/ *noun* [C] a typical characteristic or feature of a person or thing: *Simplicity is a hallmark of this design.* ○ *This explosion bears/has all the hallmarks of* (= is extremely likely to have been) *a terrorist attack.*

hallo /hælˈəʊ/ ⓤ /-ˈoʊ/ *noun* [C], *exclamation plural* **hallos** MAINLY UK FOR **hello**

,**hall of ˈfame** , Hall of Fame *noun* [C usually sing] MAINLY US a building which contains images of famous people and interesting things that are connected with them: *You really know you've made it when they enshrine you in the Rock 'n' Roll Hall of Fame.*

,**hall of ˈresidence** UK (*plural* **halls of residence**) *noun* [C] (US **dormitory**) a college building where students live

hallowed /ˈhæl.əʊd/ ⓤ /-oʊd/ *adj* **1** very respected and praised because of great importance or great age: *hallowed icons such as Marilyn Monroe and James Dean* **2** holy: *Can atheists be buried in hallowed ground?*

Halloween, Hallowe'en /ˌhæl.əʊˈiːn/ ⓤ /-oʊ-/ *noun* [C or U] the night of 31 October when children dress in special clothes and people try to frighten each other

hallucinate /həˈluː.sɪ.neɪt/ *verb* [I] to seem to see, hear, feel or smell something which does not exist, usually because you are ill or have taken a drug: *Mental disorders, drug use and hypnosis can all cause people to hallucinate.*
hallucination /həˌluː.sɪˈneɪ.ʃ³n/ *noun* [C or U] when you see, hear, feel or smell something which does not exist, usually because you are ill or have taken a drug: *A high temperature can cause hallucinations.* ○ *auditory/olfactory hallucinations*
hallucinatory /həˈluː.sɪ.nə.tri/ ⓤ /-tɔːr.i/ *adj* relating to or causing hallucinations: *In some patients the drug has been found to have hallucinatory side-effects.*

hallucinogen /ˌhæl.uːˈsɪn.ə.dʒ³n/ ⓤ /həˈluː.sɪ.nə.dʒen/ *noun* [C] a drug which makes people hallucinate: *hallucinogens such as acid and ecstasy*
hallucinogenic /həˌluː.sɪ.nəˈdʒen.ɪk/ *adj* causing hallucinations: *LSD is a hallucinogenic drug.*

hallway /ˈhɔːl.weɪ/ ⓤ /ˈhɑːl-/ *noun* [C] a **hall** ENTRANCE

halo /ˈheɪ.ləʊ/ ⓤ /-loʊ/ *noun plural* **halos** or **haloes** **1** [C] a ring of light around the head of a holy person in a religious drawing or painting **2** [C usually sing] a bright circle of light around something, or something that looks like this: *the halo around the moon* ○ *a halo of blonde curls*

halogen /ˈhæl.ə.dʒen/ *noun* [C] a member of a group of five particular chemical elements: *Chlorine and iodine are halogens.*

halt /hɒlt/ ⓤ /hɑːlt/ *verb* [I or T] to (cause to) stop moving or doing something or happening: *"Halt!" called the guard. "You can't go any further without a permit."* ○ *Production has halted at all of the company's factories because of the pay dispute.* ○ *Security forces halted the demonstrators by blocking the road.*
halt /hɒlt/ ⓤ /hɑːlt/ *noun* [S] when something stops moving or happening: *the recent halt in production* ○ *Severe flooding has brought trains to a halt* (= prevented them from moving) *on several lines in Scotland.* ○ *The bus came to a halt* (= stopped) *just in time to avoid hitting the wall.* ○ *If traffic increases beyond a certain level, the city grinds to a halt* (= stops completely). ○ *The car screeched to a halt* (= suddenly and noisily stopped) *just as the lights turned red.*
● **call a halt to** *sth* to prevent something from continuing: *How many more people will have to die before they call a halt to the fighting?*

halter [ROPE] /ˈhɒl.tə/ ⓤ /ˈhɑːl.tə/ *noun* [C] a piece of rope or a leather strap which is tied round an animal's head so that it can be led by someone or tied to something

halter [CLOTHING] /ˈhɒl.tə/ ⓤ /ˈhɑːl.tə/ *noun* US FOR **halterneck**

halterneck UK /ˈhɒl.tə.nek/ ⓤ /ˈhɑːl.tə-/ ⓤ /ˈhɑːl.tə-/ *noun* (US **halter (top)**) a piece of women's clothing which is held in position by a strap which goes behind the neck, leaving the upper back and shoulders bare: *a halterneck dress/swimsuit*

halting /ˈhɒl.tɪŋ/ ⓤ /ˈhɑːl.tɪŋ/ *adj* stopping often while you are saying or doing something, especially because you are nervous: *He spoke quietly, in halting English.*
haltingly /ˈhɒl.tɪŋ.li/ ⓤ /ˈhɑːl.tɪŋ-/ *adv*: *He spoke haltingly* (= often stopping) *about his experiences as a hostage.*

halva /ˈhæl.və/ *noun* [U] (ALSO **halvah**) a sweet food made of crushed SESAME seeds and honey

halve /hɑːv/ ⓤ /hæv/ *verb* ⊃See at **half**.
halves /hɑːvz/ ⓤ /hævz/ *plural of* **half**

ham [MEAT] /hæm/ *noun* [C or U] pig's meat from the leg or shoulder, preserved with salt or smoke

ham [ACTOR] /hæm/ *noun* [C] INFORMAL an actor whose style of acting is artificial and old-fashioned, tending to use movements and emotions that are too obvious: *They were some dreadful old ham in the main part.* ○ *a ham actor*
hammy /ˈhæm.i/ *adj* INFORMAL describes an actor or acting that is unnatural and uses too much emotion: *a hammy performance*

ham [RADIO] /hæm/ *noun* [C] a person who operates a radio station as a hobby rather than as a job: *He's a radio ham.*

ham /hæm/ *verb* -mm-
▲ **ham it up** *phrasal verb* INFORMAL to perform or behave in a false way, especially in a way that is too obvious or that makes people laugh

hamburger /ˈhæm.bɜː.gə/ ⓤ /-,bɜː-.gə/ *noun* **1** [C] (INFORMAL **burger**, UK ALSO **beefburger**) a round flat shape made of beef, which is fried and eaten between two halves of a bread roll **2** [U] US (UK **mince**) beef that is cut into very small pieces, used to make hamburgers

ham-fisted MAINLY UK /ˌhæmˈfɪs.tɪd/ ⓤ /-tɪd/ *adj* (US **ham-handed**) doing things in an awkward or unskilled way when using the hands or dealing with people: *The report criticizes the ham-fisted way in which complaints were dealt with.*

hamlet /ˈhæm.lət/ *noun* [C] a small village, usually without a church

hammer [TOOL] /ˈhæm.ə/ ⓤ /-ə/ *noun* [C] a tool consisting of a piece of metal with a flattened end which is fixed onto the end of a long thin usually wooden handle, used for hitting things
● **be/go at it hammer and tongs** INFORMAL to do something, especially to argue, with a lot of energy or violence
● **come/go under the hammer** to be sold at an AUCTION (= public sale where objects are bought by the people who offer the most money): *A private collection of her early paintings is expected to go under the hammer early next year.*
hammer /ˈhæm.ə/ ⓤ /-ə/ *verb* [I or T; usually + adv or prep] to hit something with a hammer: *Can you hold this nail in position while I hammer it into the door? ○ I could hear you hammering upstairs. ○ My car's got a dent, and I was hoping they'd be able to hammer it out* (= remove it by hammering).

hammer [FORCE] /ˈhæm.ə/ ⓤ /-ə/ *verb* [I or T; usually + adv or prep] to hit or kick something with a lot of force: *I was woken up suddenly by the sound of someone hammering on/at the front door. ○ He hammered the ball into the net, giving France a 3-2 win over Italy.*
● **hammer home** *sth* to make certain that something is understood by expressing it clearly and forcefully: *The advertising campaign will try to hammer home the message that excessive drinking is a health risk.*

hammer [DEFEAT] /ˈhæm.ə/ ⓤ /-ə/ *verb* [T] INFORMAL to defeat someone completely in a game or a fight: *We were hammered in both games.*
hammering /ˈhæm.ə.rɪŋ/ ⓤ /-ə-/ *noun* [S] when someone is defeated completely: *You should have seen the hammering I gave her in the second game.* ○ *Both countries took a tremendous hammering in the war.*

hammer [CRITICIZE] /ˈhæm.ə/ ⓤ /-ə/ *verb* [T] INFORMAL to criticize someone or something strongly: *Her latest film has been hammered by the critics.*

hammering /ˈhæm.ᵊr.ɪŋ/ [US] /-ɚ-/ *noun* [S] strong criticism: *Store cards have* ***taken*** *a hammering in recent years because of their high interest rates.*

PHRASAL VERBS WITH **hammer**

▲ **hammer away at** ***sth*** *phrasal verb* INFORMAL to work without stopping and with a lot of effort
▲ **hammer** ***sth*** **into** ***sb*** *phrasal verb* (ALSO **hammer** ***sth*** **in**) to force someone to understand something by repeating it a lot: *I always had it hammered into me that I mustn't lie.*
▲ **hammer** ***sth*** **out** *phrasal verb* [M] to reach an agreement or solution after a lot of argument or discussion: *Three years after the accident the lawyers finally managed to hammer out a settlement with the insurance company.*

ˌhammer and ˈsickle *noun* [S] a symbol of COMMUNISM, which was based on tools used by workers in factories and on farms
hammered /ˈhæm.əd/ [US] /-ɚd/ *adj* [after v] INFORMAL very drunk
hammer-throwing /ˈhæm.əˌθrəʊ.ɪŋ/ [US] /-ɚˌθroʊ-/ *noun* [U] a sport in which a heavy metal ball joined by a wire to a handle is thrown as far as possible
hammock /ˈhæm.ək/ *noun* [C] a type of bed used especially outside, consisting of a net or long piece of strong cloth which you tie between two trees or poles so that it swings
hammy /ˈhæm.i/ *adj* ➲See at **ham** ACTOR.
hamper [CAUSE DIFFICULTY] /ˈhæm.pəʳ/ [US] /-pɚ/ *verb* [T] to prevent someone doing something easily: *Fierce storms have been hampering rescue efforts and there is now little chance of finding more survivors.*
hamper [CONTAINER] /ˈhæm.pəʳ/ [US] /-pɚ/ *noun* [C] **1** a large rectangular container with a lid: *a* ***picnic*** *hamper* **2** UK a box containing food and drink, usually given as a present, for example at Christmas **3** US OLD-FASHIONED a container used for carrying dirty clothes and bed sheets and for storing them while they are waiting to be washed
hamster /ˈhæmp.stəʳ/ [US] /-stɚ/ *noun* [C] a small furry animal with a short tail and large spaces in each side of its mouth which are used for storing food. It is often kept as a pet.
hamstring [LIMIT] /ˈhæm.strɪŋ/ *verb* [T often passive] **hamstrung, hamstrung** to limit the amount of something that can be done or the ability or power of someone to do something: *The company was hamstrung by traditional but inefficient ways of conducting business.*
hamstring [BACK OF KNEE] /ˈhæm.strɪŋ/ *noun* [C] any of five TENDONS (= cords of tissue connecting muscles to bones) at the back of the knee: *He* ***pulled*** (= injured) *a hamstring while playing rugby.*
hand [BODY PART] /hænd/ *noun* **1** [C] the part of the body at the end of the arm which is used for holding, moving, touching and feeling things: *All their toys are made* ***by*** *hand.* ○ *I delivered her invitation* ***by*** *hand* (= not using the postal service). ○ INFORMAL ***Get*** *your hands* ***off*** (= Stop touching) *my bike!* ○ *He can mend anything – he's so* ***good with*** *his hands.* ○ *You have to* ***hold*** *my hand when we cross the road.* ○ *They walked by,* ***holding*** *hands.* ○ *Hold your fork* ***in*** *your left hand and your knife* ***in*** *your right hand.* ○ *She sat, pen* ***in*** *hand* (= with a pen in her hand)*, searching for the right words.* ○ *They can't* ***keep*** *their hands* ***off*** *each other – they never stop kissing and cuddling.* ○ *"Congratulations!" she said and* ***shook*** *me* ***by the*** *hand/****shook*** *my hand/****shook*** *hands* ***with*** *me.* ○ *She* ***took*** *me* ***by the*** *hand and led me into the cave.* ○ *a hand* ***towel*** ➲See picture **The Body** on page Centre 5 **2** [S] OLD USE a person's writing: *an untidy hand*
• **at hand** near in time or position: *We want to ensure that* ***help*** *is at hand* (= easily available) *for all children suffering abuse.*
• **at the hands of** ***sb*** If you suffer at the hands of someone, they hurt you or treat you badly: *How many people have died at the hands of terrorist organizations since the violence began?*
• **get/lay/put** ***your*** **hands on** ***sb*** INFORMAL to catch someone: *I'll kill him if I ever get my hands on him.*

Hand

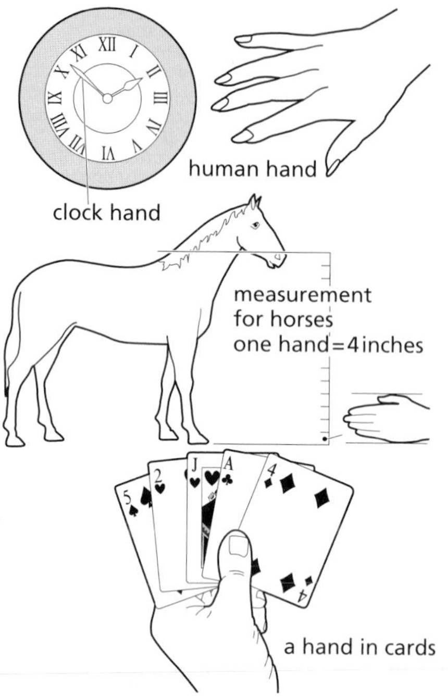
human hand
clock hand
measurement
for horses
one hand=4inches
a hand in cards

• **get/lay/put** ***your*** **hands on** ***sth*** INFORMAL to obtain something: *I can never lay my hands on a stapler in this office.*
• **go hand in hand with** ***sth*** If something goes hand in hand with something else, it is closely related to it and happens at the same time as it or as a result of it: *Prosperity goes hand in hand with investment.*
• **have** ***your*** **hands full** to be so busy that you do not have time to do anything else: *I'd love to help but I've got my hands full organizing the school play.*
• **have** ***sth*** **on** ***your*** **hands** If you have a difficult situation on your hands, you have to deal with it: *If the police carry on like this they'll have a riot on their hands.*
• **hand in glove** (US ALSO **hand and glove**) working together, often to do something dishonest: *It was rumoured at the time that some of the gangs were working hand in glove with the police.*
• **hand in hand** holding each other's hand: *I saw them walking hand in hand through town the other day.*
• **hand over fist** If you make or lose money hand over fist, you make or lose a lot of money very quickly: *Business was good and we were making money hand over fist.*
• **have** ***sth*** **in hand** MAINLY UK If you have something in hand, you have not yet used it and it is still available: *I've got enough money in hand to buy a new car.* ○ *Italy are three points behind France in the championship, but they have one game in hand* (= one game more than France still to play).
• **in hand** being worked on or dealt with now: *They've had plenty of time to prepare, so the arrangements should be* ***well*** *in hand* (= almost ready).
• **the job/matter in hand** UK (US **the job/matter at hand**) the job or matter that is important at the present moment: *Could you just concentrate on the job in hand?* ○ *If we could return to the matter in hand, we can discuss other issues later.*
• **live (from) hand to mouth** to have just enough money to live on and nothing extra: *My father earned very little and there were four kids so we lived from hand to mouth.*
• **hand-to-mouth** /ˌhænd.təˈmaʊθ/ *adj*: *Low wages mean a hand-to-mouth* ***existence*** *for many people.*
• **on hand** (UK ALSO **to hand**) near to someone or something, and ready to help or be used if necessary: *A 1200-strong military force will be on hand to monitor the cease-*

fire. ○ *For those of you who don't have an atlas to hand, Newcastle is a city in the north-east of England.*

• **on the one hand ... on the other hand** used when you are comparing two different facts or two opposite ways of thinking about a situation: *On the one hand I'd like a job which pays more, but on the other hand I enjoy the work I'm doing at the moment.*

• **out of hand** If you refuse something out of hand, you refuse it completely without thinking about or discussing it: *Moving to London is certainly a possibility – I wouldn't dismiss it out of hand.*

• **put *your* hand in *your* pocket** to give money to someone or to charity (= organizations that collect money to give to poor people, ill people, etc.): *People are more inclined to put their hands in their pockets to help children.*

• **win (*sth*) hands down** (*ALSO* **beat *sb* hands down**) to win something/beat someone very easily: *She won the debate hands down.* ○ *The last time we played squash he beat me hands down.*

hand /hænd/ *verb* [T] to put something into someone's hand from your own hand: [+ two objects] *The waiter smiled politely as he handed me my bill/handed my bill **to** me.* ○ *Please read this memo carefully and hand it **on** (to your colleagues).*

• **have (got) to hand it to *sb*** If you say you have (got) to hand it to someone you mean that they have been very successful or skilful: *I mean you've got to hand it to her, she's brought up those three children all on her own.*

hand [CLOCK/WATCH] /hænd/ *noun* [C] one of the long, thin pieces that point to the numbers on a clock or watch: *Does anyone have a watch with a **second** hand?*

hand [CARDS] /hænd/ *noun* [C] a (single part of a) game of cards, or the set of cards which a player has in a game: *Who's for a hand **of** poker?* ○ *You **dealt** me an appalling hand in that game.*

hand [PERSON] /hænd/ *noun* [C] **1** a person who does physical work or is skilled or experienced in something: *How many extra hands will we need to help with the harvest?* ○ *I joined the firm as a **factory** hand and gradually worked my way up to the top.* ➲See also **farmhand**. **2** a sailor: *All hands on deck!*

hand [HELP] /hænd/ *noun* [S] help with doing something that needs a lot of effort: [+ v-ing] *Would you like **a** hand carry**ing** those bags?* ○ *Could you **give/lend** me **a** hand **with*** (= help me to move) *the table, please?* ○ *I think Matthew might **need a** hand **with** his maths homework.* ○ *I could really **use a** hand **with** these accounts if you could spare a moment.*

hand [INVOLVEMENT] /hænd/ *noun* [S] involvement in or influence over an event: *It is not thought that terrorists **had a** hand **in** the explosion.*

• **keep *your* hand in** to practise a skill often enough so that you do not lose the skill: *I do a bit of teaching now and then just to keep my hand in.*

hand [CONTROL] /hænd/ *noun* [U] control or responsibility: *Things **got** a little **out of** hand* (= the situation stopped being controlled) *at the party and three windows were broken.* ○ *The police have the situation **in** hand* (= under control). ○ *How come there's a problem? I thought you had everything **in** hand* (= arranged and organized). ○ *Their youngest child needs **taking in** hand* (= they should start to control her) *if you ask me.*

• **keep a firm hand on *sth*** to control something or someone carefully: *Susan keeps a firm hand on everything that goes on in the office.*

hands /hændz/ *plural noun* control or responsibility: *I'm worried about confidential information **falling into the wrong** hands* (= being received by people who could use it against us). ○ *Are you sure your money's **in safe** hands?* ○ *You're **in** excellent hands with her – she's a very good doctor.* ○ *Unless I receive a satisfactory response from you within a month I shall put this matter **in(to) the** hands **of*** (= make it the responsibility of) *my solicitor.* ○ *They're trying to **get** old stock **off** their hands by cutting prices.* ○ *We **get** Daryl **off** our hands one evening a week when my mother looks after him.* ○ *The problem's **out of** my hands* (= is not mine) *now that Colin's taken over responsibility for the department.* ○ *He's got a real problem **on his** hands* (= he has something difficult to deal with). ○ *I don't **have** enough **time on my** hands* (= I do not have enough time) *to work and look after the children.*

• **a safe pair of hands** someone who you can trust to do an important job well, without making mistakes

hand [CLAP] /hænd/ *noun* [U] clapping for a performer: *So please **give a big** hand **to*** (= welcome with clapping) *your host for the evening, Bill Cronshaw!*

hand [MEASUREMENT] /hænd/ *noun* [C] a unit for measuring the height of a horse up to its shoulder: *One hand equals 4 inches* (= 10.16 centimetres).

PHRASAL VERBS WITH **hand** ▼

▲ **hand *sth* around** *phrasal verb* [M] (*UK ALSO* **hand round**) to pass or offer something to all the people in a group: *Ben, could you hand round the biscuits?*

▲ **hand *sth* back** *phrasal verb* [M] to return something to the person who gave it to you: [+ two objects] *"No, I've never seen him before," I said, handing her back the photograph.*

▲ **hand *sth* down** [OBJECT] *phrasal verb* [M] to give something to someone younger than you in the family because you want them to have it or because you no longer need it: *This necklace was handed down to my mother by my grandmother.*

▲ **hand *sth* down** [TRADITION] *phrasal verb* [M] to pass traditions from older people to younger ones: *a custom handed down through the generations*

▲ **hand *sth* down** [DECISION] *phrasal verb* [M] *FORMAL* to announce an official decision, often a decision about how someone should be punished: *Although it was only his first offence, the court handed down an eight-year sentence.*

▲ **hand *sth* in** *phrasal verb* to give something to someone in a position of authority: *Have you handed in your history essay yet?* ○ *I've decided to hand in my resignation* (= tell my employer I am leaving my job).

▲ **hand *sth* out** *phrasal verb* [M] to give something to each person in a group or place: *The teacher asked her to hand out the worksheets.* ○ *They stood on the street corner handing out leaflets.*

▲ **hand *sth* over** [GIVE SOMETHING] *phrasal verb* [M] to give something to someone else: *We were ordered to hand over our passports.* ➲See also **handover**.

▲ **hand *sth/sb* over** [GIVE RESPONSIBILITY] *phrasal verb* [M] to give another person control of someone or something, or responsibility for dealing with them: *The hijacker was handed over **to** the French police.* ○ *If you'll hold the line a moment I'll hand you over to someone who might be able to help.* ➲See also **handover**.

handbag /ˈhænd.bæg/ *noun* [C] (*US ALSO* **purse**) a small bag for money, keys, make-up, etc. carried especially by women

ˈhand ˌluggage *noun* [U] the small cases or bags that a passenger carries with them onto an aircraft or bus: *How many items of hand luggage am I allowed to take onto the plane?*

handball /ˈhænd.bɔːl/ [US] /-bɑːl/ *noun* **1** [U] in the US, a game in which players hit a small hard rubber ball against a wall with their hands **2** [C or U] in football, when a player intentionally touches the ball with their hand or arm **3** [U] a game similar to football, played by hitting a ball with your hands instead of your feet

handbill /ˈhænd.bɪl/ *noun* [C] a small printed advertisement or notice that is given to people by hand

handbook /ˈhænd.bʊk/ *noun* [C] a book which contains instructions or advice about how to do something or the most important and useful information about a subject: *The student handbook gives details of all courses.*

handbrake *UK* /ˈhænd.breɪk/ *noun* [C] (*US* **emergency brake**, *US ALSO* **parking brake**) a device operated by hand which locks into position and prevents a vehicle from moving: *You're supposed to **put** the handbrake **on** whenever you stop on a hill.* ➲See picture **Car** on page Centre 12

handcart /ˈhænd.kɑːt/ [US] /-kɑːrt/ *noun* [C] a small vehicle with two wheels and two long handles which is used for carrying goods, and is pushed or pulled with your hands

handclap /ˈhænd.klæp/ *noun* [C] ➲See **slow handclap**.

H

handcraft /ˈhænd.krɑːfts/ ⓤ /-kræfts/ *noun* AUS FOR **handicraft**

handcuffs /ˈhænd.kʌfs/ *plural noun* (INFORMAL **cuffs**) two metal rings joined by a short chain which lock around a prisoner's wrists: *a pair of handcuffs* ○ *She was taken to the police station in handcuffs.*

handcuff /ˈhænd.kʌf/ *verb* [T often passive] (INFORMAL **cuff**) to put handcuffs on someone: *He arrived in court handcuffed to two police officers.*

handful AMOUNT /ˈhænd.fʊl/ *noun* [C] an amount of something that can be held in one hand: *He pulled out a handful of coins from his pocket.*

handful A FEW /ˈhænd.fʊl/ *noun* [S] a small number of people or things: *She invited loads of friends to her party, but only a handful of them turned up.*

handful DIFFICULT PERSON /ˈhænd.fʊl/ *noun* [S] a person, often a child, who is difficult to control: *Her older son is fine but the little one is a bit of a handful.*

hand gre‚nade *noun* [C] a small bomb consisting of explosive material in a metal or plastic container that can be thrown easily

handgun /ˈhænd.gʌn/ *noun* [C] a gun which can be held in one hand and which does not need to be supported against the shoulder when it is fired

hand-held /ˌhænd'held/ *adj* [before n] describes something that has been designed so that it can be held and used easily with one or two hands: *a hand-held computer/device*

handhold /ˈhænd.həʊld/ ⓤ /-hoʊld/ *noun* [C] a thing you can hold on to with your hand as a support

handicap CONDITION /ˈhæn.dɪ.kæp/ *noun* [C or U] SLIGHTLY OLD-FASHIONED something that is wrong with your mind or body permanently: *a **physical** handicap* ○ *In cases of severe **mental** handicap, constant supervision is recommended.*

handicapped /ˈhæn.dɪ.kæpt/ *adj, plural noun* OLD-FASHIONED **1** not able to use part of your body or your mind because it has been damaged in some way: *What's the best way of improving theatre access for people who are physically handicapped?* **2 the handicapped** people who cannot use part of their body or mind because it has been damaged in some way

handicap DIFFICULTY /ˈhæn.dɪ.kæp/ *noun* [C] something which makes it difficult for you to do something: *I found not having a car quite a handicap in the country.*

handicap /ˈhæn.dɪ.kæp/ *verb* [T] **-pp-** *Rescue efforts have been handicapped* (= made difficult) *by rough seas and hurricane-force winds.*

handicap COMPETITION /ˈhæn.dɪ.kæp/ *noun* [C] a disadvantage given to a person taking part in a game or competition in order to reduce their chances of winning, or a sports event in which such disadvantages are given: *Handicaps give people with different abilities an equal chance of winning.* ○ *My current golf handicap is nine.*

handicraft /ˈhæn.dɪ.krɑːfts/ ⓤ /-kræfts/ *noun* [C usually plural] a skilled activity in which something is made in a traditional way with the hands rather than being produced by machines in a factory, or an object made by such an activity

handily /ˈhænd.ɪ.li/ *adv* ➭See at **handy** USEFUL.

handiwork /ˈhæn.dɪ.wɜːk/ ⓤ /-wɝːk/ *noun* [U] **1** work done skilfully with the hands: *Susannah put down the paintbrush and stood back to admire her handiwork.* **2** something that you have done or caused, usually something bad: *"Is this your handiwork?" he asked, pointing at the graffiti on the wall.*

handkerchief (*plural* **handkerchiefs** or UK ALSO **handkerchieves**) /ˈhæŋ.kə.tʃiːf/ ⓤ /-kɚ-/ *noun* [C] (INFORMAL **hankie/hanky**) a square piece of cloth used for cleaning the nose or drying the eyes when they are wet with tears: *She took out her handkerchief and blew her nose loudly.* ➭Compare **tissue** PAPER.

handle PART /ˈhæn.dl/ *noun* [C] a part of an object designed for holding, moving or carrying the object easily: *a door handle* ○ *the handle on a suitcase* ○ *I can't pick the kettle up – the handle's too hot.* ○ *She **turned** the handle and slowly opened the door.* ➭See picture **Car** on page Centre 12

handle TOUCH /ˈhæn.dl/ *verb* [T] to pick something up and touch, hold or move it with your hands: *Always wash your hands before handling food.* ○ *Please don't handle the vases – they're very fragile.*

handler /ˈhænd.lər/ ⓤ /-lɚ/ *noun* [C] someone who carries or moves things as part of their job: *airport baggage handlers*

handle DEAL WITH /ˈhæn.dl/ *verb* [T] to deal with, have responsibility for, or be in charge of: *I thought he handled the situation very well.* ○ *Some people are brilliant with computers, but have no idea how to handle* (= behave with) *other people.* ○ *If you can't handle the job I'll get someone else to do it.* ○ *Who handles the marketing in your company?*

handler /ˈhænd.lər/ ⓤ /-lɚ/ *noun* [C] **1** a person who trains and is in charge of animals, especially dogs: *police dog handlers* **2** US someone who advises someone important: *The president's handlers are telling him to pull out of the talks.*

handling /ˈhænd.lɪŋ/ *noun* [U] the way that someone deals with a situation or person: *President Kennedy made his reputation with his handling **of** the Cuban missile crisis.*

handle OPERATE /ˈhæn.dl/ *verb* **1** [T] to operate or control something which could be difficult or dangerous: *Have you ever handled a gun before?* **2** [I usually + adv or prep] If a car handles well, it is easy and pleasant to drive.

handling /ˈhænd.lɪŋ/ *noun* [U] how easy a vehicle is to control: *Power steering can dramatically improve a car's handling.*

handle SELL /ˈhæn.dl/ *verb* [T] to buy and sell goods: *We only handle cosmetics which have not been tested on animals.* ○ MAINLY UK *He's been arrested for handling stolen goods.*

handle NAME /ˈhæn.dl/ *noun* [C] INFORMAL a name of a person or place, especially a strange one: *That's some handle to go through life with!*

handlebar moustache /ˌhæn.dl.bɑː.mʊˈstɑːʃ/ ⓤ /-bɑːrˈmʌs.tæʃ/ *noun* [C] a thick wide moustache with curled ends in the shape of handlebars

handlebars /ˈhæn.dl.bɑːz/ ⓤ /-bɑːrz/ *plural noun* a bar with curved ends forming handles which turns the front wheel of a bicycle or motorcycle so that it points in a different direction

handmade /ˌhænd'meɪd/ *adj* made using the hands rather than a machine: *handmade chocolates/paper/shoes*

handmaiden /ˈhænd.meɪ.dᵊn/ *noun* [C] **1** (ALSO **handmaid**) OLD USE a female servant **2** FORMAL something, such as an idea, which helps and supports something else: *Technique is the handmaiden of art.*

hand-me-down /ˈhænd.mɪ.daʊn/ *noun* [C] a piece of clothing which someone has given to a younger relative or friend because they no longer want it: *I got fed up with having to wear my sister's hand-me-downs.*

handout PRESENT /ˈhænd.aʊt/ *noun* [C] OFTEN DISAPPROVING something such as food, clothing or money that is given free to someone who has a great need for it: *I'm not interested in **state/government** handouts – all I want is a job.*

handout INFORMATION /ˈhænd.aʊt/ *noun* [C] a document given to students or reporters which contains information about a particular subject: *On page two of your handout you will find a list of the books that I have referred to during the lecture.*

handover /ˈhæn.dəʊ.vər/ ⓤ /-doʊ.vɚ/ *noun* [U] the giving of control of or responsibility for something to someone else: *The United Nations is to supervise the handover of the prisoners of war.* ➭See also **hand over**.

hand-picked /ˌhænd'pɪkt/ *adj* Someone who is hand-picked has been carefully chosen for a special job or purpose: *a hand-picked audience*

handrail /ˈhænd.reɪl/ *noun* [C] a long narrow bar of wood or metal which people can hold on to for support, especially when going up or down stairs

handset /ˈhænd.set/ *noun* [C] **1** the outer part of a MOBILE PHONE (= a telephone that you can carry with you) which does not include the battery or the SIM CARD **2** the part of a telephone that you hold in front of your mouth and against your ear

ˌhands ˈfree *adj* describes a piece of equipment, especially a telephone, that you can use without needing to hold it in your hand: *a hands free car phone* ○ *a hands-free tap*

ˌhands ˈfree *noun* **[C]** a piece of equipment, especially a telephone, that you can use without needing to hold it in your hand ➲See picture **In the Office** on page Centre 15

handshake /ˈhænd.ʃeɪk/ *noun* **[C]** a greeting, or an act showing that you have made an agreement, in which two people who are facing each other take hold of and shake each other's right hand: *He welcomed me with a wide smile and a warm handshake.*

hands-off /ˈhænd.zɒf/ [US] /-zɑːf/ *adj* **[before n]** Someone who has a hands-off way of organizing or dealing with something allows other people to make decisions about how things should be done and avoids becoming directly involved: *Paul has a hands-off style of management.*

handsome [ATTRACTIVE] /ˈhæn.səm/ *adj* **1** describes a man who is physically attractive in a traditional, masculine way: *She's dreaming she'll be whisked off her feet by a* ***tall, dark*** *handsome stranger.* **2** describes a woman who is attractive but in a strong way: *a handsome woman in her fifties*

handsome [LARGE AMOUNT] /ˈhæn.səm/ *adj* **[before n]** in a large amount: *They made a handsome profit on their house.* **handsomely** /ˈhæn.səm.li/ *adv*: *He said if his results were good, he would* ***reward*** *him handsomely.*

hands-on [INVOLVED] /ˈhænd.zɒn/ [US] /-zɑːn/ *adj* **[before n]** Someone with a hands-on way of doing things becomes closely involved in managing and organizing things and in making decisions: *She's very much a hands-on manager.*

hands-on [PRACTICAL EXPERIENCE] /ˈhænd.zɒn/ [US] /-zɑːn/ *adj* **[before n]** Someone who has hands-on experience of something has done or used it rather than just read or learned about it: *Many employers consider hands-on experience to be as useful as academic qualifications.*

handstand /ˈhænd.stænd/ *noun* **[C]** an action in which you balance vertically on your hands with your legs pointing straight up in the air

hand-to-hand /ˌhænd.təˈhænd/ *adj* **[before n]**, *adv* If people fight hand-to-hand, they are very near or touching each other while they are fighting rather than firing guns at each other from a long way away: *hand-to-hand* ***combat***

handwriting /ˈhænd,raɪ.tɪŋ/ [US] /-t̬ɪŋ/ *noun* **[U]** **1** writing with a pen or pencil: *We need to ensure that handwriting is properly taught in our primary schools.* **2** the particular way in which someone forms letters with a pen or pencil: *His handwriting is illegible.*

handwritten /ˌhændˈrɪt.ᵊn/ [US] /-ˈrɪt̬-/ *adj* written using your hand rather than printed by a machine

handy [USEFUL] /ˈhæn.di/ *adj* useful or convenient: *a handy container/tool* ○ *First-time visitors to France will find this guide particularly handy.* ○ *It's a nice house and it's handy* ***for*** (= near) *the station.* ○ *INFORMAL Don't throw those bottles away – they'll* ***come in*** *handy* (= be useful) ***for*** *the picnic next Sunday.*

handily /ˈhæn.dɪ.li/ *adv*: *An additional power switch for the radio is handily located next to the steering wheel.* ○ *US The Yankees handily* (= easily) ***defeated*** *the Boston Red Sox.*

handy [SKILFUL] /ˈhæn.di/ *adj* **[after v]** able to use something skilfully: *Jonathan's good at wallpapering but he's not so handy* ***with*** *a paintbrush.* ○ *Susannah's very handy* (= good at doing things which need skilled use of the hands) ***about*** *the house.*

handyman /ˈhæn.di.mæn/ *noun* **[C]** a man who is skilled at repairing and making things inside or outside the house and who does this in his own home or as a job

hang [FIX AT TOP] /hæŋ/ *verb* **hung, hung 1** **[I or T; + adv or prep]** to fasten or support something at the top leaving the other parts free to move, or to be held in this way: *A heavy gold necklace hung* ***around*** *her neck.* ○ *Long creepers hung* ***(down) from*** *the trees.* ○ *The curtains hung* ***in*** *thick folds.* ○ *Hang your coat and hat* ***(up)*** *on the rack over there.* ○ *Many of his finest pictures hang/are hung* (= are fixed to the wall so that they can be seen) *in the National Gallery.* ○ *Hang the pheasant/Let the pheasant hang for a few days for the flavour to improve before you cook it.* **2** **[T]** If you hang wallpaper, you fix it to the wall.

• **hang by a thread** If a serious situation hangs by a thread, it means that even a slight change can decide what will happen and that a bad result such as death, failure, etc. is likely: *The mayor's political future has been hanging by a thread since the fraud scandal.*

• **hang on in there** (*ALSO* **hang in there**) said as a way of telling someone to not give up, despite difficulties: *Work can get tough in the middle of a term but hang on in there and it'll be OK.*

• **have *sb/sth* hanging round *your* neck** *INFORMAL DISAPPROVING* to be limited in what you can do by someone or something: *The last thing I want is a couple of kids hanging round my neck!*

the hang *noun* **[S]** the way something made of cloth looks when it is hanging: *That coat fits you so well – the hang is perfect.*

• **get the hang of *sth*** *INFORMAL* to learn how to do something, especially if it is not obvious or simple: *"I've never used a word processor before." "Don't worry – you'll soon get the hang of* ***it****."*

hang [KILL] /hæŋ/ *verb* **[I or T]** **hanged** or **hung**, **hanged** or **hung** to kill someone, especially as punishment for a serious crime, by dropping them with a rope tied around their neck, or to die in this way: *He was found guilty and hanged later that year.* ○ *With so little evidence to prove her guilt, few people thought she should hang.* ○ **[R]** *The woman tried to hang herself with a sheet.* ➲See also **hangman**. * NOTE: The standard past form of the verb is **hanged**, but **hung** is quite commonly used too.

• **hung, drawn and quartered** In the past, if someone was hung, drawn and quartered, they were hanged by the neck and their body was cut into pieces.

• **go hang (*yourself*)** *INFORMAL* You say that someone can go hang (themselves) if you do not care what they say or do about something: *If she's expecting the report by tomorrow she can go hang herself.*

• **I'll be hanged if...** *UK OLD-FASHIONED* used to express your determination not to do something or not to permit someone else to do something: *I'll be hanged if I'm going to clean up after him!*

• **hang the cost/expense** the cost is not important: *Just buy it and hang the expense!*

• **I'll be hanged if I know** (*ALSO* **I'm hanged if I know**) *UK OLD-FASHIONED INFORMAL* used to say that you definitely do not know

• **You might as well be hung for a sheep as for a lamb.** *UK SAYING* said to mean that because the punishment for a bad action and an even worse one will be the same, you have no reason not to do the worse one

hanging /ˈhæŋ.ɪŋ/ *noun* **[C or U]** the practice of killing someone, especially as a punishment for a serious crime, by dropping them with a rope tied around their neck

hang [STAY] /hæŋ/ *verb* **[I]** **hung, hung** to stay in the air: *The falcon seemed to hang* ***in the air*** *for a moment before diving onto its prey.* ○ *Smoke from the houses hung* ***above*** *the village.* ○ *LITERARY The sound of the bells hung in the midnight air.*

hang [BEND DOWN] /hæŋ/ *verb* **[I or T]** **hung, hung** to curve down: *The branches hung heavy with snow.* ○ *He knew he'd done something wrong and hung his head in shame.*

PHRASAL VERBS WITH **hang** ▼

▲ **hang around** [MOVE SLOWLY] *phrasal verb* (*UK ALSO* **hang about**) *INFORMAL* to move or do things slowly: *Go and pack but don't hang around – we have to go in an hour.*

▲ **hang around *(somewhere)*** [SPEND TIME] *phrasal verb* (*UK ALSO* **hang about**) to wait or spend time somewhere, usually for no particular reason: *I spent most of my youth hanging around the bars of Dublin.* ○ *I thought I'd hang around for a while and see if she comes.*

▲ **hang around with *sb*** *phrasal verb* (*UK ALSO* **hang about with *sb***) to spend time with someone: *I got into drugs because I was hanging around with the wrong people.*

H

▲ **hang back** *phrasal verb* to be slow to do something, often because of fear or lack of confidence: *There's no need to hang back – you can sing as well as anyone.*

▲ **hang on** [WAIT] *phrasal verb* INFORMAL to wait for a short time: *Sally's on the other phone – would you like to hang on?* ○ *Do you need the toilet right now or can you hang on for a while?* ○ *Hang on a minute – I'll be with you in a moment!*

▲ **hang on** [HOLD] *phrasal verb* to hold or continue holding onto something: *Hang on **tight** – it's going to be a very bumpy ride.* ➲See also **hanger-on**.

▲ **hang *sth* on *sb*** [BLAME] *phrasal verb* INFORMAL to blame someone for something, especially something they did not do: *I wasn't anywhere near the house when the window was broken so you can't hang that on me!*

▲ **hang on/upon *sth*** [GIVE ATTENTION] *phrasal verb* to give careful attention to something, especially something that someone says: *He hangs on her **every word** as if she were some sort of goddess.*

▲ **hang on/upon *sth*** [DEPEND ON] *phrasal verb* to depend on something: *The safety of air travel hangs partly on the thoroughness of baggage checking.*

H

▲ **hang onto *sth*** *phrasal verb* to keep something: *You should hang onto that painting – it might be valuable one day.*

▲ **hang out** *phrasal verb* INFORMAL to spend a lot of time in a place or with someone: *You still hang out **at** the pool hall?* ○ *I've been hanging out backstage **with** the band.*

▲ **hang over *sth*** *phrasal verb* If a threat or doubt hangs over a place or a situation, it exists: *Uncertainty again hangs over the project.*

▲ **hang together** [STAY TOGETHER] *phrasal verb* If people hang together, they help each other and work together to achieve something: *If the opposition party can hang together over the next six months, they might just stand a chance of being elected.*

▲ **hang together** [SEEM TRUE] *phrasal verb* If the parts of something hang together, they are well organized or they seem to be true or correct: *Somehow her story doesn't quite hang together.* * NOTE: This is often used in the negative form.

▲ **hang up** [TELEPHONE] *phrasal verb* to end a telephone conversation: *He started shouting so I hung up (**on** him).* ○ *Let me speak to Melanie before you hang up.* ➲See picture **Phrasal Verbs** on page Centre 9

▲ **hang *sth* up** [STOP USING] *phrasal verb* [M] to stop using and needing something because you have given up the sport or activity it is used for: *So when did you hang up your boxing gloves/golf clubs/ballet shoes?*

hangar /ˈhæŋ.əʳ/ [US] /-ɚ/ *noun* [C] a large building in which aircraft are kept

hangdog /ˈhæŋ.dɒg/ [US] /-dɑːg/ *adj* [before n] (of an expression on a face) unhappy or ashamed, especially because of feeling guilty: *a hangdog look/expression*

hanger /ˈhæŋ.əʳ/ [US] /-ɚ/ *noun* [C] (ALSO **clothes hanger,** ALSO **coat hanger**) a curved piece of wire, wood or plastic on which clothes are hung while they are being stored

hanger-on /ˌhæŋ.ərˈɒn/ [US] /-ɚˈɑːn/ *noun* [C] *plural* **hangers-on** DISAPPROVING a person who tries to be friendly and spend time with rich and important people, especially to get an advantage: *Wherever there is royalty, there are always hangers-on.*

hang-glider /ˈhæŋˌglaɪ.dəʳ/ [US] /-dɚ/ *noun* [C] a very small aircraft without an engine. It consists of a frame covered in cloth, which forms a wing, and the pilot hangs from this frame. **hang-gliding** /ˈhæŋˌglaɪ.dɪŋ/ *noun* [U] *She's taken up hang-gliding.*

hanging /ˈhæŋ.ɪŋ/ *noun* [C usually pl] a large piece of cloth, often with a picture on it, that is hung on a wall for decoration: *The castle's great hall was decorated with sumptuous **wall** hangings.* ➲See also **hanging** at **hang** KILL.

ˌhanging ˈbasket *noun* [C] a light, open container, often in the shape of a half sphere, which holds a variety of flowering plants and hangs above the ground in a garden or outside a building

hangman /ˈhæŋ.mən/ /-mæn/ *noun* [C] a person whose job is to operate the device which kills criminals by hanging them from a rope by their necks ➲See also **hang** KILL.

hangout /ˈhæŋ.aʊt/ *noun* [C] INFORMAL a place where someone spends a lot of time or where they live: *The café is a favourite hangout of artists.*

hangover [ILLNESS] /ˈhæŋˌəʊ.vəʳ/ [US] /-ˌoʊ.vɚ/ *noun* [C] a feeling of illness after drinking too much alcohol: *I **had** a terrible hangover the next morning.* ○ *a hangover cure* ➲See also **hung-over**.

hangover [CONTINUING] /ˈhæŋˌəʊ.vəʳ/ [US] /-ˌoʊ.vɚ/ *noun* [C] something that continues from an earlier time: *The present political system is a hangover **from** the nineteenth century colonial era.*

hang-up /ˈhæŋ.ʌp/ *noun* [C] INFORMAL a permanent and unreasonable feeling of anxiety about a particular feature of yourself: ***sexual** hang-ups* ○ *He's one of these men who went bald very young and has a terrible hang-up **about** it.* ➲See also **hang up**.

hung-up /ˌhʌŋˈʌp/ *adj* [after v] INFORMAL having a hang-up: *Why are so many women so hung-up **about** food?*

• **be hung-up on *sth*** INFORMAL to be extremely interested in or worried by a particular subject and spend an unreasonably large amount of time thinking about it: *Why are the British so hung-up on class?*

hanker /ˈhæŋ.kəʳ/ [US] /-kɚ/ *verb*

▲ **hanker after/for *sth*** *phrasal verb* to have a strong desire for something, especially if you cannot or should not have it: *What did you hanker after most when you were in prison?* ○ *Even after all these years, I still hanker for a motorbike.*

hankering /ˈhæŋ.kᵊr.ɪŋ/ [US] /-kɚ-/ *noun* [C] *Don't you ever **have** a hankering* (= strong desire) ***for** a different lifestyle?*

hanky /ˈhæŋ.ki/ *noun* [C] (ALSO **hankie**) INFORMAL a HANDKERCHIEF (= square piece of cloth used for cleaning the nose and drying the eyes)

hanky-panky /ˌhæŋ.kɪˈpæŋ.ki/ *noun* [U] OLD-FASHIONED INFORMAL dishonest behaviour, especially involving sexual activity or money: *There was a bit of hanky-panky going on at the Christmas party.*

Hansard /ˈhæn.sɑːd/ [US] /-sɚd/ *noun* [S] the official record of what is said and done in the British, Australian, New Zealand and Canadian parliaments

hansom (cab) /ˈhæn.səmˌkæb/ *noun* [C] a two-wheeled carriage pulled by a horse, used like a taxi in the past

Hanukkah /ˈhɑː.nə.kə/ *noun* [C or U] (ALSO **Chanukah**) a Jewish religious holiday lasting for eight days in December

haphazard /ˌhæpˈhæz.əd/ [US] /-ɚd/ *adj* not having an obvious order or plan: *He tackled the problem in a typically haphazard manner.* **haphazardly** /ˌhæpˈhæz.əd.li/ [US] /-ɚd-/ *adv* DISAPPROVING

hapless /ˈhæp.ləs/ *adj* [before n] FORMAL unlucky and usually unhappy: *Many children are hapless **victims** of this war.* **haplessly** /ˈhæp.lə.sli/ *adv* LITERARY

ha'porth /ˈheɪ.pəθ/ *noun* UK OLD-FASHIONED INFORMAL **(not) a ha'porth of difference** (not) any difference: *You can shout as much as you like but it won't make a ha'porth of difference – you're not going.*

happen [HAVE EXISTENCE] /ˈhæp.ᵊn/ *verb* [I] **1** (of a situation or an event) to have existence or come into existence: *No one knows exactly what happened but several people have been hurt.* ○ *Anything could happen in the next half hour.* ○ *A funny thing happened in the office today.* ○ *I don't like to think what might have happened if he'd been driving any faster.* **2 happen to *sb*** If something happens to someone or something, it has an effect on them and changes them in some way: *I don't know what I'd do if anything happened to him* (= if he was hurt, became ill, or died). ○ *What happened to your jacket? There's a big rip in the sleeve.* ○ *What's happened to my pen* (= Where is it)*? I put it down there a few moments ago.*

happening /ˈhæp.ᵊn.ɪŋ/ *noun* [C usually pl] **1** something that has happened: *Recent happenings on the money markets can be interpreted in various ways.* **2** a performance or similar event that happens without preparation

happening /ˈhæp.ᵊn.ɪŋ/ *adj* INFORMAL describes a place that is extremely fashionable and exciting: *Ask Caroline – she knows all the happening clubs in town.*

happen [CHANCE] /ˈhæp.ᵊn/ *verb* [I] to do or be by chance: [+ to infinitive] *They happened **to** look* (= looked by chance) *in the right place almost immediately.* ○ [+ (that)] *Fortunately **it** happened **(that)** there was no one in the house at the time of the explosion.* ○ [+ that] ***It just so** happens **that** I have her phone number right here.* ○ *She happens **to** like cleaning* (= She likes cleaning, although that is surprising). ○ *I happen **to** think he's right* (= I do think so, although you do not). ○ ***As it** happened* (= Although it was not planned), *I had a few minutes to spare.*

happen [POSSIBLY] /ˈhæp.ᵊn/ *adv* NORTHERN ENGLISH possibly; I expect that: *Happen it'll rain later on.*

PHRASAL VERBS WITH **happen**

▲ **happen along/by *(somewhere)*** *phrasal verb* MAINLY US to go to a place by chance or without planning to: *I'd have drowned if he hadn't happened along and pulled me out of the river.*

▲ **happen on/upon *sth/sb*** *phrasal verb* LITERARY to find or meet something or someone by chance: *Eventually they happened on a road leading across the desert.*

happenstance /ˈhæp.ᵊn.stɑːnts/ [US] /-stænts/ *noun* [C or U] MAINLY US chance or a chance situation, especially one producing a good result: *By (a strange) happenstance they were both in Paris at the same time.*

happy [PLEASED] /ˈhæp.i/ *adj* feeling, showing or causing pleasure or satisfaction: *a happy marriage/childhood* ○ *She looks so happy.* ○ *School days are said to be the happiest days of your life.* ○ *Nicky seems a lot happier since she met Steve.* ○ *You'll be happy **to** know that Jean is coming with us.* ○ *I'm perfectly happy **to*** (= I will willingly) *help out.* ○ *I'm so happy **(that)** everything is working out for you.* ○ *Barry seems happy enough work**ing** for himself.* ○ *Are you happy **about/with*** (= satisfied with) *your new working arrangements?* ○ *Your mother's not going to be very happy when she sees the mess you've made!* ○ FORMAL *The manager will be happy* (= is willing) ***to** see you this afternoon.*

● **the happy day** HUMOROUS a marriage: *So when's the happy day then?*

● **the happy event** (US ALSO **the blessed event**) HUMOROUS the birth of a child

happily /ˈhæp.ɪ.li/ *adv* **1** in a happy way: *He was happily married with two young children.* ○ *She munched happily on her chocolate bar.* **2** willingly: *I'd happily offer to help him if I thought it would make any difference.*

happiness /ˈhæp.ɪ.nəs/ *noun* [U] the feeling of being happy: *It was only later in life that she found happiness and peace of mind.* ○ FORMAL *Will you join me in wishing the bride and groom **every** happiness?*

happy [LUCKY] /ˈhæp.i/ *adj* [before n] (of a condition or situation) lucky: *We hadn't planned to be in France at the same time as Ann and Charles – it was just a happy **coincidence**.*

happily /ˈhæp.ɪ.li/ *adv* having a good or lucky result: *Happily, the weather remained fine throughout the afternoon.*

happy [SUITABLE] /ˈhæp.i/ *adj* LITERARY (of words or behaviour) suitable: *It wasn't a happy choice of phrase given the circumstances.*

happy [GREETING] /ˈhæp.i/ *adj* [before n] (used in greetings for special occasions) full of enjoyment and pleasure: *Happy Birthday!* ○ *Happy Anniversary!* ○ *Happy New Year!*

ˌhappy ˈcamper *noun* [C] HUMOROUS someone who is happy with the situation they are in: *She's just found out about the pay cut and she's not a happy camper.*

happy clappy /ˌhæp.iˈklæp.i/ *adj* UK INFORMAL OFTEN DISAPPROVING describes Christians who sing, talk and shout enthusiastically during their religious ceremonies and who try to persuade other people to join them

happy-go-lucky /ˌhæp.i.gəʊˈlʌk.i/ [US] /-goʊ-/ *adj* describes someone who does not plan much and accepts what happens without being made anxious by it

ˈhappy ˌhour *noun* [C usually sing] a period of time, usually in the early evening, when drinks are sold cheaply in a bar or a pub

ˌhappy ˈmedium *noun* [S] APPROVING a state or way of doing something which avoids being extreme, often combining the best of two opposite states or ways of doing something: *I try to **strike a*** (= achieve a) *happy medium when I'm on holiday, and spend half my time doing things and the other half just relaxing.*

hara-kiri /ˌhær.əˈkiː.ri/ *noun* [U] (in Japan, especially in the past) a ceremonial way of killing yourself by cutting open your stomach with a sword

harangue /həˈræŋ/ *verb* [T] DISAPPROVING to speak to someone or a group of people, often for a long time, in a forceful and sometimes angry way, especially to persuade them: *A drunk in the station was haranguing passers-by.* **harangue** /həˈræŋ/ *noun* [C] *The team were given the usual half-time harangue by their manager.*

harass /ˈhær.əs/ *verb* [T] to continue to annoy or upset someone over a period of time: *Stop harassing me!*

harassed /ˈhær.əst/ *adj* anxious, annoyed and tired, especially because you have too many things to deal with: *The supermarket was full of harassed-looking mothers with young children.*

harassment /ˈhær.ə.smənt/ *noun* [U] behaviour that annoys or upsets someone: ***sexual** harassment*

harbinger /ˈhɑː.bɪn.dʒəʳ/ [US] /ˈhɑːr.bɪn.dʒɚ/ *noun* [C] LITERARY someone or a thing that shows that something is going to happen soon, especially something bad: *a harbinger **of doom***

harbour [WATER] UK, US **harbor** /ˈhɑː.bəʳ/ [US] /ˈhɑːr.bɚ/ *noun* [C or U] an area of water next to the coast, often protected from the sea by a thick wall, where ships and boats can shelter: *Our hotel room overlooked a pretty little fishing harbour.* ➲Compare **dock** FOR SHIPS.

harbour [HAVE IN MIND] UK, US **harbor** /ˈhɑː.bəʳ/ [US] /ˈhɑːr.bɚ/ *verb* [T] to have in mind a thought or feeling, usually over a long period: *He's been harbouring a **grudge** against her ever since his promotion was refused.* ○ *There are those who harbour suspicions about his motives.* ○ *Powell remains non-committal about any political ambitions he may harbour.*

harbour [HIDE] UK, US **harbor** /ˈhɑː.bəʳ/ [US] /ˈhɑːr.bɚ/ *verb* [T] to protect someone or something bad, especially by hiding them when the police are looking for them: *to harbour a criminal*

harbour-master /ˈhɑː.bəˌmɑː.stəʳ/ [US] /ˈhɑːr.bɚˌmæs.tɚ/ *noun* [C] the official who is in charge of a harbour

hard [SOLID] /hɑːd/ [US] /hɑːrd/ *adj* firm and stiff; not easy to bend, cut or break: *a hard surface* ○ *There was a heavy frost last night and the ground is still hard.* ○ *Heating the clay makes it hard.* ✱ NOTE: The opposite is **soft**.

● **be no hard and fast rules** If there are no hard and fast rules, there are no clear rules for you to follow.

harden /ˈhɑː.dᵊn/ [US] /ˈhɑːr-/ *verb* [I or T] to become or make hard: *The mixture hardens as it cools.* ○ *It is thought that high cholesterol levels in the blood can harden the arteries* (= make them thicker and stiffer, causing disease). **hardness** /ˈhɑːd.nəs/ [US] /ˈhɑːrd-/ *noun* [U] *These alloys are characterized by their extreme hardness.*

hard [DIFFICULT] /hɑːd/ [US] /hɑːrd/ *adj* difficult to understand, do, experience or deal with: *There were some really hard questions in the exam.* ○ ***It's** hard **to say** which of them is lying.* ○ ***It's** hard be**ing** a single mother.* ○ *Her handwriting is very hard **to** read.* ○ *He's a hard man **to please**.* ○ *The topics **get** harder later in the course.* ○ *I feel sorry for the kids, too – they've had a hard **time**.* ✱ NOTE: The opposite is **easy**.

● **the hard way** a way of doing something which is unnecessarily difficult: *She always does things the hard way.* ➲See also **the hard way** at **hard** SEVERE.

● **hard to swallow** difficult to believe: *I found her story rather hard to swallow.*

hard [USING EFFORT] /hɑːd/ [US] /hɑːrd/ *adj* needing or using a lot of physical or mental effort: *Go on – give it a good hard push!* ○ *It was hard **work** on the farm but satisfying.*

● **hard at it** UK INFORMAL putting a lot of effort into what you are doing: *That's what I like to see – everybody hard at it!*

hard /hɑːd/ [US] /hɑːrd/ *adv* with a lot of physical or mental effort: *Work hard and play hard, that's my motto.*

○ *I'm not surprised he failed his exam – he didn't exactly try very hard!*

hard [SEVERE] /hɑːd/ [US] /hɑːrd/ *adj* **1** not pleasant or gentle; severe: *You have to be quite hard to succeed in the property business.* ○ *Ooh, you're a hard woman, Elaine!* ○ *Our boss has been giving us all a hard **time** at work* (= making our time at work difficult). **2 be hard on *sb*** to criticize someone severely, or to treat them unfairly: *Don't be too hard on him – he's new to the job.*

• **feel hard done-by** (*ALSO* **feel hard done-to**) *UK* to feel that you have been treated unfairly: *I'm feeling hard done-by because I've been looking after the kids all week and Steve's been out every night.*

• **Hard luck!** *MAINLY UK* used to express sympathy to someone because something slightly bad has happened: *"We lost again." "Oh, hard luck!"*

• **(that's) *your* hard luck** *UK INFORMAL* said if you think that it is someone's own fault that something bad has happened to them: *Well, if you missed the presentation because you couldn't be bothered to turn up on time, that's your hard luck!*

• **take a hard line on *sb/sth*** to be very severe in the way that you deal with someone or something

• **hard feelings** anger towards someone that you have argued with: *So we're friends again, are we? **No** hard feelings?*

• **the hard way** If you learn something the hard way, you learn from unpleasant experiences rather than by being taught: *If she won't listen, she'll have to **learn/find out** the hard way.* ➲See also **the hard way** at **hard** DIFFICULT.

harden /ˈhɑː.dᵊn/ [US] /ˈhɑːr-/ *verb* **[I or T]** *Living rough in the desert hardened the recruits a lot* (= made them stronger). ○ *As the war progressed, attitudes on both sides hardened* (= became more severe and determined).

• **harden *your* heart** to make yourself stop feeling kind or friendly towards someone: *You've just got to harden your heart and tell him to leave.*

hardened /ˈhɑː.dᵊnd/ [US] /ˈhɑːr-/ *adj* **1 a hardened criminal/detective, etc.** someone who has had a lot of bad experiences and as a result does not get upset or shocked **2 be/become hardened to *sth*** to develop a way of dealing with a sad situation so that it no longer upsets you: *You see all sorts of terrible things when you're a nurse so you become hardened to it.* **hardening** /ˈhɑː.dnɪŋ/ [US] /ˈhɑːrd-/ *noun* **[U]** *There has been a hardening of government policy since the invasion.* **hardness** /hɑːd.nəs/ [US] /hɑːrd-/ *noun* **[U]**

hard [ALCOHOL] /hɑːd/ [US] /hɑːrd/ *adj* **[before n]** describes a drink that contains a high level of alcohol: *hard **liquor***

hard [WEATHER] /hɑːd/ [US] /hɑːrd/ *adv* If it rains or snows hard, it rains or snows a lot: *It had been raining hard most of the afternoon.*

hard /hɑːd/ [US] /hɑːrd/ *adj*: *We had a very hard **winter*** (= with very bad weather) *last year and some of the plants died.*

hard [WATER] /hɑːd/ [US] /hɑːrd/ *adj* describes water which contains a lot of LIME which prevents soap from cleaning

hardness /hɑːd.nəs/ [US] /hɑːrd-/ *noun* **[U]**

hard [CLEAR] /hɑːd/ [US] /hɑːrd/ *adj* **[before n]** able to be proven: *hard facts/evidence*

hardback /ˈhɑːd.bæk/ [US] /ˈhɑːrd-/ *noun* **[C or U]** (*US ALSO* **hardcover**) a book which has a stiff cover: *His latest novel will be published **in** hardback later this month.* ➲Compare **paperback**; **softback**.

hardball /ˈhɑːd.bɔːl/ [US] /ˈhɑːrd.bɑːl/ *noun* **[U]** *US FOR* **baseball** ➲Compare **softball**.

hard-bitten /ˌhɑːdˈbɪt.ᵊn/ [US] /ˌhɑːrdˈbɪt̬-/ *adj* If someone is hard-bitten, their character has been made stronger as a result of difficult experiences in the past and they control and do not show their emotions: *This particular murder case was so horrific that it shocked even the most hard-bitten of New York police officers.*

hardboard /ˈhɑːd.bɔːd/ [US] /ˈhɑːrd.bɔːrd/ *noun* **[U]** a substance made of wood fibres mixed with glue and pressed into large thin flat pieces

hard-boiled [EGG] /ˌhɑːdˈbɔɪld/ [US] /ˌhɑːrd-/ *adj* describes an egg which has been heated in its shell in boiling water until both the white and yellow parts are solid

hard-boiled [STRONG] /ˌhɑːdˈbɔɪld/ [US] /ˌhɑːrd-/ *adj INFORMAL* describes a strong and determined person who shows little emotion: *The film stars Kathleen Turner as the hard-boiled detective of Sarah Paretsky's novel.*

ˌhard ˈby *adv, prep LITERARY OR OLD USE* very near: *The house where he lived as a child is hard by the main plaza.*

ˈhard ˌcase *noun* **[C usually sing]** (*ALSO* **hard nut**) *MAINLY UK INFORMAL* someone who is difficult to deal with and possibly angry and violent ➲See also **a hard/tough nut to crack** at **nut** FOOD.

ˌhard ˈcash *noun* **[U]** money in the form of coins or notes but not cheques or a credit card

ˌhard ˈcider *noun* **[U]** *US FOR* **cider**

ˌhard ˈcopy *noun* **[C or U]** information from a computer which has been printed on paper

ˈhard ˌcore [STONE/BRICK] *noun* **[U]** *MAINLY UK* the pieces of broken stone, brick, etc. used to make the base under a floor, path or road

ˌhard ˈcore [BELIEF] *group noun* **[S]** a small group of people within a larger group, who strongly believe in the group's principles and usually have a lot of power in it: *The hard core of the party has not lost sight of the original ideals.* **hard-core** /ˌhɑːdˈkɔːʳ/ [US] /ˌhɑːrdˈkɔːr/ *adj*: *hard-core party members*

hard-core [SEX] /ˌhɑːdˈkɔːʳ/ [US] /ˌhɑːrdˈkɔːr/ *adj* showing sexual acts clearly and in detail: *hard-core pornography*

hardcover /ˈhɑːdˌkʌv.əʳ/ [US] /ˈhɑːrdˌkʌv.ɚ/ *noun* **[C or U]** *US FOR* **hardback**: *The novel was originally published **in** hardcover.*

ˌhard ˈcurrency *noun* **[U]** money that is valuable and can be exchanged easily because it comes from a powerful country

ˌhard ˈdisk *noun* **[C]** a magnetic device that is fixed inside a computer and stores a very large amount of information ➲Compare **floppy (disk)**.

ˌhard ˈdrinker *noun* **[C]** someone who often drinks a lot of alcohol

ˌhard ˈdrug *noun* **[C usually pl]** a very strong, illegal drug

hard-earned /ˌhɑːdˈɜːnd/ [US] /ˌhɑːrdˈɝːnd/ *adj* If something such as a holiday is hard-earned, you deserve it because you have been working very hard.

hard-fought /ˌhɑːdˈfɔːt/ [US] /ˌhɑːrdˈfɑːt/ *adj* achieved after a lot of difficulty or fighting: *a hard-fought victory*

ˌhard ˈgoing *adj* **[after v]** *INFORMAL* difficult and tiring to do, deal with, or make progress with: *I find her books a bit hard going.*

ˈhard ˌhat *noun* **[C]** a hat made of a strong substance which is worn by builders and other workers to protect their head

hard-headed /ˌhɑːdˈhed.ɪd/ [US] /ˌhɑːrd-/ *adj* not influenced by emotions: *a hard-headed approach to problems*

hard-hearted /ˌhɑːdˈhɑː.tɪd/ [US] /ˌhɑːrdˈhɑːr.t̬ɪd/ *adj DISAPPROVING* If someone is hard-hearted, they are not kind or sympathetic. ➲Compare **kind-hearted**; **soft-hearted**.

hard-hitting /ˌhɑːdˈhɪt.ɪŋ/ [US] /ˌhɑːrdˈhɪt̬.ɪŋ/ *adj* A speech or piece of writing that is hard-hitting is extremely critical of something: *The committee published a hard-hitting report on the bank's management.*

hardiness /ˈhɑː.dɪ.nəs/ [US] /ˈhɑːr-/ *noun* **[U]** ➲See at **hardy**.

ˌhard ˈlabour *UK, US* **hard labor** *noun* **[U]** a punishment for criminals, especially used in the past, which involves a lot of tiring, physical work

hard line /ˌhɑːdˈlaɪn/ [US] /ˌhɑːrd-/ *noun* **[S]** when someone is very strict and severe: *The government wants to **take** a hard line against the strikers.*

hard-line /ˌhɑːdˈlaɪn/ [US] /ˌhɑːrd-/ *adj* extreme and severe and not likely to change: *a hard-line manifesto* ○ *a hard-line politician* **hard-liner** /ˌhɑːdˈlaɪ.nəʳ/ [US] /ˌhɑːrdˈlaɪ.nɚ/ *noun* **[C]** *He needs to persuade the hard-liners in the cabinet.*

hard-luck story /ˌhɑːdˈlʌkˌstɔː.ri/ [US] /ˌhɑːrdˈlʌkˌstɔːr.i/ *noun* **[C]** *INFORMAL DISAPPROVING* a story or piece of information that someone tells you or writes about themselves which is intended to make you feel sad and sympathetic towards them: *She came out with some* *hard-luck story about never having been loved by her mother.*

hardly ONLY JUST /ˈhɑːd.li/ ⑥ /ˈhɑːrd-/ *adv* only just; almost not: *I could hardly hear her at the back.* ○ *The party had hardly started when she left.* ○ *He hardly ate anything/He ate hardly anything.* ○ *We hardly ever* (= almost never) *go to concerts.* ○ *Hardly had a moment passed before the door creaked open.* ✳ NOTE: **hardly** cannot be used with 'not' or other negative words.

hardly CERTAINLY NOT /ˈhɑːd.li/ ⑥ /ˈhɑːrd-/ *adv* certainly not: *You **can** hardly expect a pay rise when you've only been working for the company for two weeks!* ○ *Well don't be angry with me – it's hardly my fault that it's raining!*

hard-nosed /ˌhɑːdˈnəʊzd/ ⑥ /ˌhɑːrdˈnoʊzd/ *adj* practical and determined: *His hard-nosed business approach is combined with a very real concern for the less fortunate in society.*

hard of 'hearing *adj* [after v] not able to hear well: *My father is quite old now and he's increasingly hard of hearing.*

hard-on /ˈhɑːd.ɒn/ ⑥ /ˈhɑːrd.ɑːn/ *noun* [C] OFFENSIVE an ERECTION (= condition of the penis when it is stiff): *to have a hard-on*

hard 'porn *noun* [U] PORNOGRAPHY (= books, films, etc. showing sexual acts) which shows sex in a very detailed way ⊃Compare **soft porn.**

hard-pressed /ˌhɑːdˈprest/ ⑥ /ˌhɑːrd-/ *adj* having a lot of difficulties doing something, especially because there is not enough time or money: *The latest education reforms have put extra pressure on teachers who are already hard-pressed.* ○ *Because of shortages, the emergency services were hard-pressed to deal with the accident.* ○ *Most people would be hard-pressed* (= would find it difficult) *to name more than half a dozen members of the government.*

hard 'rock *noun* [U] a type of rock music with a strong beat in which drums and electric guitars are played very loudly

hard 'science *noun* [C or U] (a) science in which facts and theories can be firmly and exactly measured, tested or proved

hard 'sell *noun* [S] a method of selling in which the seller tries very hard to persuade the customer to buy something

hardship /ˈhɑːd.ʃɪp/ ⑥ /ˈhɑːrd-/ *noun* [C or U] (something which causes) difficult or unpleasant conditions of life, or an example of this: *The 1930s was a time of high unemployment and economic hardship in much of the United Kingdom.*

hard 'shoulder UK *noun* [C usually sing] (US **shoulder,** IRISH ENGLISH **hard margin**) a hard area beside a main road, especially a motorway, where a driver can stop if there is a serious problem

the 'hard ˌstuff *noun* [S] INFORMAL HUMOROUS strong alcohol: *Would you like **a drop** of the hard stuff?*

hardtop /ˈhɑːd.tɒp/ ⑥ /ˈhɑːrd.tɑːp/ *noun* [C] a car with a metal roof

hard 'up *adj* [after v] INFORMAL having very little money: *We're a bit hard up at the moment so we're not thinking in terms of holidays.*

hardware COMPUTER /ˈhɑːd.weəʳ/ ⑥ /ˈhɑːrd.wer/ *noun* [U] the physical and electronic parts of a computer, rather than the instructions it follows ⊃Compare **software.**

hardware TOOLS /ˈhɑːd.weəʳ/ ⑥ /ˈhɑːrd.wer/ *noun* [U] metal tools, materials and equipment used in a house or a garden, such as hammers, nails and screws

hardware MILITARY /ˈhɑːd.weəʳ/ ⑥ /ˈhɑːrd.wer/ *noun* [U] INFORMAL equipment, especially if it is for military use or if it is heavy

hard-wearing /ˌhɑːdˈweə.rɪŋ/ ⑥ /ˌhɑːrdˈwer-/ *adj* If something, especially clothing or material, is hard-wearing it lasts for a long time and looks good even if it is used a lot.

hard-won /ˌhɑːdˈwʌn/ ⑥ /ˌhɑːrdˈwɑːn/ *adj* If something is hard-won, it was only achieved after a lot of effort: *a hard-won battle*

hardwood /ˈhɑːd.wʊd/ ⑥ /ˈhɑːrd-/ *noun* [C or U] strong heavy wood or the tree it comes from ⊃Compare **softwood.**

hard-working /ˌhɑːdˈwɜː.kɪŋ/ ⑥ /ˌhɑːrdˈwɜː-/ *adj* continually doing a lot of work: *She was always very hard-working at school.*

hardy /ˈhɑː.di/ ⑥ /ˈhɑːr-/ *adj* **1** strong enough to bear extreme conditions or difficult situations: *A few hardy souls continue to swim in the sea even in the middle of winter.* **2** describes a plant that can live through the winter without protection from the weather: *a hardy perennial* **hardiness** /ˈhɑː.dɪ.nəs/ ⑥ /ˈhɑːr-/ *noun* [U]

hare ANIMAL /heəʳ/ ⑥ /her/ *noun* [C] *plural* **hares** or **hare** an animal like a large rabbit that can run very fast and has long ears

hare RUN /heəʳ/ ⑥ /her/ *verb* [I + adv or prep] MAINLY UK to run or go very quickly, usually in an uncontrolled way: *I saw her haring off down the road after Molly.*

harebell /ˈheə.bel/ ⑥ /ˈher-/ *noun* [C] a wild plant found in northern parts of the world which has blue cup-shaped flowers

harebrained /ˈheə.breɪnd/ ⑥ /ˈher-/ *adj* (of plans or people) not practical; foolish: *That sounds like another of his harebrained **schemes**.*

'hare ˌcoursing *noun* [U] MAINLY UK the activity of chasing a hare using dogs

Hare 'Krishna *noun* **1** [U] a modern type of Hinduism in which the god KRISHNA is especially worshipped **2** [C] INFORMAL a member of this religion

harelip /ˌheəˈlɪp/ ⑥ /ˌher-/ *noun* [C] OLD-FASHIONED a **cleft lip**

harem /ˈhɑː.riːm/ ⑥ /ˌ-ˈ-/ *noun* [C] especially in the past in some Muslim societies, the wives or other female sexual partners of a man, or the part of a house in which they live

haricot (bean) /ˌhær.ɪ.kəʊˈbiːn/ ⑥ /-koʊ-/ *noun* [C] a small, usually white bean

hark /hɑːk/ ⑥ /hɑːrk/ *verb* [I] (ALSO **hearken**) OLD USE used to tell someone to listen: *Hark, I hear a distant trumpet!*
● **Hark at sb!** HUMOROUS said to someone who has just accused you of something that you think they are guilty of themselves: *Hark at him calling me lazy when he never walks anywhere if he can drive!*

PHRASAL VERBS WITH **hark** ▼

▲ **hark back to sth** REPEAT *phrasal verb* If someone harks back to something in the past, they talk about it again and again, often in a way which annoys other people: *He's always harking back to his childhood and saying how things were better then.*

▲ **hark back to sth** BE SIMILAR *phrasal verb* If something harks back to something in the past, it is similar to it: *The director's latest film harks back to the early years of cinema.*

harlequin /ˈhɑː.lɪ.kwɪn/ ⑥ /ˈhɑːr-/ *noun* [C] a humorous character in plays at the theatre, especially in the past, who wears brightly-coloured clothes with a diamond pattern

Harley-'Davidson *noun* [C] TRADEMARK a type of large, powerful motorcycle

'Harley ˌStreet *noun* [S] (the area around) a road in central London where many respected and well-known doctors treat their patients

harlot /ˈhɑː.lət/ ⑥ /ˈhɑːr-/ *noun* [C] OLD USE DISAPPROVING a female prostitute

harm /hɑːm/ ⑥ /hɑːrm/ *noun* [U] physical or other injury or damage: *Both deny conspiring to cause actual bodily harm.* ○ *A mistake like that will **do** his credibility a lot of harm.* ○ *Missing a meal once in a while never **did** anyone any harm.* ○ *You could always ask Jim if they need any more staff in his office – **(there's) no harm in** asking* (= no one will be annoyed and you might benefit). ○ *She **meant no harm*** (= did not intend to offend), *she was joking.* ○ *She was frightened by the experience but she **came to** no harm* (= was not hurt).
● **do more harm than good** to be damaging and not helpful: *Getting involved at this stage would do more harm than good.*

• **out of harm's way** in a position which is safe from harm or from which harm cannot be done: *The children will be here soon – you'd better put that plate out of harm's way.*

harm /hɑːm/ [US] /hɑːrm/ *verb* [T] to hurt someone or damage something: *Thankfully no one was harmed in the accident.* ○ *The government's reputation has already been harmed by a series of scandals.*

• **harm a hair on sb's head** to hurt someone: *If he so much as harms a hair on her head I won't be responsible for my actions.*

harmful /ˈhɑːm.fᵊl/ [US] /ˈhɑːrm-/ *adj* causing harm: *This group of chemicals is known to be harmful **to** people with asthma.* **harmfully** /ˈhɑːm.fᵊl.i/ [US] /ˈhɑːrm-/ *adv* **harmfulness** /ˈhɑːm.fᵊl.nəs/ [US] /ˈhɑːrm-/ *noun* [U]

harmless /ˈhɑːm.ləs/ [US] /ˈhɑːrm-/ *adj* not able or not likely to cause harm: *Peter might look a bit fierce, but actually he's fairly harmless.* ○ *There were those who found the joke offensive, but Johnson insisted it was just a bit of harmless **fun**.* **harmlessly** /ˈhɑːm.lə.sli/ [US] /ˈhɑːrm-/ *adv* **harmlessness** /ˈhɑːm.lə.snəs/ [US] /ˈhɑːrm-/ *noun* [U]

harmonica /hɑːˈmɒn.ɪ.kə/ [US] /hɑːrˈmɑː.nɪ-/ *noun* [C] (*ALSO* **mouth organ**) a small rectangular musical instrument which is played by blowing or sucking air through one of the long sides at different places to make different notes

harmony [MUSIC] /ˈhɑː.mə.ni/ [US] /ˈhɑːr-/ *noun* [C or U] a pleasant musical sound made by different notes being played or sung at the same time: *singing **in** harmony* ○ *It is a simple melody with complex harmonies.* **harmonic** /hɑːˈmɒn.ɪk/ [US] /hɑːrˈmɑː.nɪk/ *adj SPECIALIZED* *harmonic complexity*

harmonic /hɑːˈmɒn.ɪk/ [US] /hɑːrˈmɑː.nɪk/ *noun* [C] *SPECIALIZED* a special note that a musical instrument can play which sounds different from the usual notes

harmonious /hɑːˈməʊ.ni.əs/ [US] /hɑːrˈmoʊ-/ *adj* having a pleasant tune or harmony **harmoniously** /hɑːˈməʊ.ni.ə.sli/ [US] /hɑːrˈmoʊ-/ *adv*

harmonize, *UK USUALLY* **-ise** /ˈhɑː.mə.naɪz/ [US] /ˈhɑːr-/ *verb* [I or T] to add harmonies to a tune

harmony [MATCH] /ˈhɑː.mə.ni/ [US] /ˈhɑːr-/ *noun* [U] when people are peaceful and agree with each other, or when things seem right or suitable together: *racial harmony* (= good feelings between different races) ○ *domestic harmony* (= good feelings in the family or home) ○ *Imagine a society in which everyone lived together **in (perfect)** harmony.* ○ *We must ensure that tourism develops **in** harmony **with** the environment.*

harmonious /hɑːˈməʊ.ni.əs/ [US] /hɑːrˈmoʊ-/ *adj* friendly and peaceful: *The government is understandably reluctant to do anything which might spoil the harmonious relations between the country's ethnic groups.* **harmoniously** /hɑːˈməʊ.ni.ə.sli/ [US] /hɑːrˈmoʊ-/ *adv*

harmonize, *UK USUALLY* **-ise** /ˈhɑː.mə.naɪz/ [US] /ˈhɑːr-/ *verb* [I or T] to be suitable together, or to make different people, plans, situations, etc. suitable for each other: *The garden has been designed to harmonize **with** the natural landscape.* ○ *The plan is to harmonize* (= make similar) *safety standards across all the countries involved.* **harmonization**, *UK USUALLY* **-isation** /ˌhɑː.mə.naɪˈzeɪ.ʃᵊn/ [US] /ˌhɑːr-/ *noun* [U]

harness /ˈhɑː.nəs/ [US] /ˈhɑːr-/ *noun* [C] a piece of equipment, with straps and fastenings, used to control or hold in place a person, animal or object: *a safety harness* ○ *a baby harness* ○ *a parachute harness*

• **in harness with sb** working together with someone to achieve something

• **be back in harness** to have returned to work after a period of absence

harness /ˈhɑː.nəs/ [US] /ˈhɑːr-/ *verb* [T] **1** to put a harness on a horse, or to connect a horse to a vehicle using a harness **2** to control something, usually in order to use its power: *There is a great deal of interest in harnessing wind and waves as new sources of power.*

harp /hɑːp/ [US] /hɑːrp/ *noun* [C] a large, wooden musical instrument with many strings that you play with the fingers

harpist /ˈhɑː.pɪst/ [US] /ˈhɑːr-/ *noun* [C] a person who plays the harp

harp /hɑːp/ [US] /hɑːrp/ *verb*

▲ **harp on** *phrasal verb INFORMAL DISAPPROVING* to talk or complain about something many times: *He's always harping on **about** lack of discipline.* ○ *I know you want to go to Paris. Don't keep harping on (**about** it)!*

harpoon /hɑːˈpuːn/ [US] /hɑːr-/ *noun* [C] a long heavy SPEAR (= long sharp weapon) fixed to a rope, used for killing whales

harpoon /hɑːˈpuːn/ [US] /hɑːr-/ *verb* [T] to use a harpoon, usually to kill a whale

harpsichord /ˈhɑːp.sɪ.kɔːd/ [US] /ˈhɑːrp.sɪ.kɔːrd/ *noun* [C] a large musical instrument similar to a piano. It was played especially in the 17th and 18th centuries.

harpy /ˈhɑː.pi/ [US] /ˈhɑːr-/ *noun* [C] **1** in Greek mythology, a creature with the head of a woman and the body of a bird **2** *LITERARY* a cruel, unpleasant woman who shouts a lot

harridan /ˈhær.ɪ.dᵊn/ [US] /ˈher-/ *noun* [C] *OLD-FASHIONED DISAPPROVING* an unpleasant, especially older woman, who shouts a lot

harrow /ˈhær.əʊ/ [US] /ˈher.oʊ/ *noun* [C] a large piece of equipment which is pulled behind a TRACTOR (= farm vehicle) to break the earth into small pieces ready for planting **harrow** /ˈhær.əʊ/ [US] /ˈher.oʊ/ *verb* [I or T]

harrowing /ˈhær.əʊ.ɪŋ/ [US] /ˈher.oʊ-/ *adj* extremely upsetting because connected with suffering: *a harrowing story* ○ *For many women, the harrowing prospect of giving evidence in a rape case can be too much to bear.*

harrowed /ˈhær.əʊd/ [US] /ˈher.oʊd/ *adj* looking as if you have suffered: *His face was harrowed.*

harry /ˈhær.i/ *verb* [T] *FORMAL* to repeatedly demand something from someone, often causing them to feel anxious or angry: *She harried the authorities, writing letters and getting up petitions.* **harried** /ˈhær.id/ *adj*: *a harried-looking mother with two small children*

harsh /hɑːʃ/ [US] /hɑːrʃ/ *adj* **1** unpleasant, unkind, cruel or unnecessarily severe: *harsh criticism* ○ *The children had had a harsh upbringing.* ○ *We thought the punishment was rather harsh for such a minor offence.* ○ *"There is no alternative," she said in a harsh voice.* ○ *He said some harsh **words*** (= spoke unkindly) *about his brother.* **2** too strong, bright, loud, etc: *harsh chemicals/lighting* **harshly** /ˈhɑːʃ.li/ [US] /ˈhɑːrʃ-/ *adv*: *I thought she'd been treated rather harshly.* **harshness** /ˈhɑːʃ.nəs/ [US] /ˈhɑːrʃ-/ *noun* [C]

harum-scarum /ˌheə.rəmˈskeə.rəm/ [US] /ˌher.əmˈsker.əm/ *adv OLD-FASHIONED* uncontrolled, in all directions or without thinking

harvest /ˈhɑː.vɪst/ [US] /ˈhɑːr-/ *noun* [C or U] the time of year when crops are cut and collected from the fields, or the activity of cutting and collecting them, or the crops which are cut and collected: *the grain/potato/grape harvest* ○ *We had a good harvest this year.* ○ *Farmers are reporting a **bumper*** (= very big) *harvest this year.* ○ *It won't be long now till harvest (time).* **harvest** /ˈhɑː.vɪst/ [US] /ˈhɑːr-/ *verb* [I or T] *In the US, winter wheat is harvested in the early summer.*

harvester /ˈhɑː.vɪ.stəʳ/ [US] /ˈhɑːr.vɪ.stɚ/ *noun* [C] **1** a machine for harvesting crops **2** *OLD USE* a person who harvests crops

ˌharvest ˈfestival *noun* [C usually sing] a celebration which is held in churches and schools in the autumn, which gives thanks for crops and food

has *STRONG* /hæz/, *WEAK* /həz/ /əz/ *he/she/it form of* **have**

has-been /ˈhæz.biːn/ *noun* [C] *INFORMAL DISAPPROVING* a person who in the past was famous, important, admired or good at something, but is no longer any of these

hash [FAILURE] /hæʃ/ *noun UK INFORMAL* **make a hash of *sth*** to do something very badly: *He made a complete hash of the last question.*

hash [FOOD] /hæʃ/ *noun* [U] a mixture of meat, potatoes and vegetables cut into small pieces and baked or fried: *corned beef hash* ○ *US eggs and hash*

hash [DRUGS] /hæʃ/ *noun* [U] *INFORMAL FOR* **hashish**

hash /hæʃ/ *verb*

▲ **hash *sth* up** *phrasal verb* [M] *UK INFORMAL* to spoil something by doing it badly: *The first interview was all right but I rather think I hashed up the second one.*

ˌhash ˈbrowns *plural noun* small pieces of potato pressed into flat shapes and fried

hashish /hæʃˈiːʃ/ *noun* [U] a drug, illegal in many countries, made from the CANNABIS plant and usually smoked

hasn't /ˈhæz.ᵊnt/ *short form of* has not: *Hasn't he grown!*

hasp /hɑːsp/ [US] /hæsp/ *noun* [C] a fastener for a box or door, used with a PADLOCK (= removable lock)

hassle /ˈhæs.l̩/ *noun* [C or U] *INFORMAL* (a situation causing) difficulty or trouble: *I can't face the hassle of moving house again.* ○ *My boss has been **giving** me a lot of hassle this week.* ○ *It's one of the few bars that women can go to and not **get** any hassle from men.* ○ *It was such a hassle trying to get my bank account changed that I nearly gave up.* ○ *I should have taken it back to the shop but I just didn't think it was worth **(all)** the hassle.*
hassle /ˈhæs.l̩/ *verb* [T] *INFORMAL* to annoy someone, especially by repeatedly asking them something: *I'll do it in my own time – just stop hassling me!* ○ [+ **to** infinitive] *The children keep hassling me **to** take them to Disneyland.*

haste /heɪst/ *noun* [U] *DISAPPROVING* (too much) speed: *Unfortunately the report was prepared **in** haste and contained several inaccuracies.* ○ [+ **to** infinitive] ***In** her haste **to** get up from the table, she knocked over a cup.* ○ *His father had just died and he didn't want to marry with indecent haste.*
• **More haste less speed.** *UK SAYING* said to mean that if you try to do things too quickly, it will take you longer in the end
• **make haste** *OLD USE* hurry up: *Make haste!*
hasten /ˈheɪ.sᵊn/ *verb FORMAL* **1** [T] You hasten something by acting in order to make it happen sooner: *I was grateful for his letter which hastened the course of the enquiry.* ○ *There is little doubt that poor medical treatment hastened her death.* **2** [+ **to** infinitive] If you hasten to do something, you quickly do it: *The president hastened to reassure his people that he was in perfect health.* **3** [+ **to** infinitive] If you hasten to say something, you want to make it clear: *It was an unfortunate decision and I hasten **to** say it had nothing to do with me.* ○ *"People round here dress so badly – except you, Justin," she hastened **to** add.*

hasty /ˈheɪ.sti/ *adj* describes something that is done in a hurry, sometimes without the necessary care or consideration: *He warned against making hasty decisions.* ○ *Now let's not leap to any hasty conclusions.* ○ *We saw the rain and made a hasty retreat into the bar.* ○ *I think perhaps we were a little hasty **in** judg**ing** him.* **hastily** /ˈheɪ.stɪ.li/ *adv*: *"He's looks good for his age. Not that 55 is old," she hastily added.* **hastiness** /ˈheɪ.stɪ.nəs/ *noun* [U]

hat /hæt/ *noun* [C] **1** a covering for the head that is not part of a piece of clothing: *a straw hat* ○ *a woolly hat* ○ *a wide-brimmed hat* ➲See pictures **Clothes** on page Centre 6, **Hairstyles and Hats** on page Centre 8 **2** used to refer to one of the various jobs or responsibilities that someone has: *A couple of the kitchen staff are on holiday so I'm **wearing my** chef's hat tonight.* ○ *This is me **with my** manager's hat **on** talking.*
• **take *your* hat off to *sb*** If you say that you take your hat off to someone, you mean that you admire them for an achievement: *So Emma actually manages to juggle two small children and a full-time job, does she? Well, I take my hat off to her.*
• **throw *your* hat into the ring** to announce your intention of entering a competition or election

hatband /ˈhæt.bænd/ *noun* [C] a strip of material which is fixed around the outside of a hat

hatbox /ˈhæt.bɒks/ [US] /-bɑːks/ *noun* [C] a round container for storing or carrying hats

hatch [EGG] /hætʃ/ *verb* [I or T] to (cause an egg to) break in order to allow a young animal to come out
hatchery /ˈhætʃ.ᵊr.i/ [US] /-ɚ-/ *noun* [C] a place where large numbers of eggs, especially fish eggs, are hatched and the young are taken care of

hatch [PLAN] /hætʃ/ *verb* [T] to make a plan, especially a secret plan: *It was in August of 1978 that the Bolton brothers hatched their plot to kill their parents.*

hatch [OPENING] /hætʃ/ *noun* [C] (*ALSO* **hatchway**) an opening through a wall, floor, etc., or the cover for it: *an escape hatch* ○ *a serving hatch*
• **Down the hatch!** *INFORMAL SAYING* said before swallowing a drink, especially an alcoholic one

hatchback /ˈhætʃ.bæk/ *noun* [C] a car which has an extra door at the back which can be lifted up to allow things to be loaded in

hatchet /ˈhætʃ.ɪt/ *noun* [C] a small AXE (= tool with a blade which cuts when you hit things with it)

hatchet-faced /ˈhætʃ.ɪtˌfeɪst/ *adj* Someone who is hatchet-faced has a thin, hard and unpleasant face.

ˈhatchet ˌjob *noun* [C usually sing] *INFORMAL* a cruel written or spoken attack on someone or something: *Fleck was certainly not the only critic to **do** a hatchet job **on** his latest novel.*

ˈhatchet ˌman *noun* [C usually sing] *INFORMAL* someone who is used for unpleasant and difficult or violent jobs

hate /heɪt/ *verb* [I or T; not continuous] to dislike someone or something very much: *Kelly hates her teacher.* ○ *She hated the cold dark days of winter.* ○ *I hate it when you do that.* ○ [+ v-ing] *I have always hated speak**ing** in public.* ○ *I hate him tell**ing** me what do to all the time.* ○ [+ **to** infinitive] *I hate* (= do not want) ***to** interrupt, but it's time we left.* ○ *I'd hate* (= would not like) *you **to** think I didn't appreciate what you'd done.*
• **hate *sb's* guts** *INFORMAL* to dislike someone very much
hate /heɪt/ *noun* [C or U] an extremely strong dislike: *She gave him a look of pure hate.* ○ *The feelings of hate grew stronger every day.* *UK* *One of my **pet** hates* (= one of the main things I dislike) *is people who use your name all the while when they're speaking to you.* ➲See also **hatred**.
hated /ˈheɪ.tɪd/ [US] /-t̬ɪd/ *adj*: *He was the most hated teacher in the school.*
-hater /-heɪ.təʳ/ [US] /-t̬ɚ/ *suffix* someone who dislikes the stated thing: *He thinks I'm a real **man**-hater.*

hateful /ˈheɪt.fᵊl/ *adj OLD-FASHIONED* very unpleasant: *I never wear grey because it reminds me of my hateful school uniform.*

ˈhate ˌmail *noun* [U] unpleasant or cruel letters from someone who dislikes you

hatpin /ˈhæt.pɪn/ *noun* [C] a long metal pin, often with a decorated end, which is pushed through a woman's hat and hair to keep the hat on the head

hatred /ˈheɪ.trɪd/ *noun* [U] an extremely strong feeling of dislike: *What is very clear in these letters is Clark's passionate hatred **of** his father.* ○ *The motive for this shocking attack seems to be racial hatred.*

hatstand /ˈhæt.stænd/ *noun* [C] a vertical pole with hooks at the top for hanging hats and coats on

hatter /ˈhæt.əʳ/ [US] /ˈhæt̬.ɚ/ *noun* [C] *OLD-FASHIONED* someone who makes hats ➲See **(as) mad as a hatter/March hare** at **mad** FOOLISH.

ˈhat ˌtrick *noun* [C] when a player scores three times in the same game, especially in football, or when someone is successful at achieving something three times: *Goal! Fowler makes it a hat trick!* ○ *After two election victories the government clearly has hopes of a hat trick.*

haughty /ˈhɔː.ti/ [US] /ˈhɑː.t̬i/ *adj DISAPPROVING* unfriendly and seeming to consider yourself better than other people: *She has a rather haughty manner.* **haughtily** /ˈhɔː.tɪ.li/ [US] /ˈhɑː.t̬ɪ-/ *adv* **haughtiness** /ˈhɔː.tɪ.nəs/ [US] /ˈhɑː.t̬ɪ-/ *noun* [U]

haul [PULL] /hɔːl/ [US] /hɑːl/ *verb* [T] to pull something heavy slowly and with difficulty: *They hauled the boat out of the water.* ○ *She hauled herself **up** into the tree.*
• **haul ass** *US OFFENSIVE* to move very quickly to a different place: *When the shooting started we hauled ass out of there.*

haul [AMOUNT] /hɔːl/ [US] /hɑːl/ *noun* [C] **1** a usually large amount of something that has been stolen or is illegal: *a haul of arms/drugs* **2** the amount of fish caught: *Fishermen have been complaining of poor hauls all year.*

haul [PERIOD OF TIME] /hɔːl/ [US] /hɑːl/ *noun* [C] **1** a journey, often a difficult one: *From there it was a **long** haul/only a **short** haul* (= long and difficult/short and easy journey) *back to our camp.* ○ *It was a long haul* (= It took a long time and was difficult), *but the alterations to the house are finished at last.* **2** **long-haul flight/short-**

H

haul flight a long/short journey by air

▲ **haul** *sb* **up** *phrasal verb* [M often passive] INFORMAL to force someone to go somewhere or see someone in order to be punished or to answer questions about their behaviour: *He was hauled up in court/in front of a magistrate.*

haulage /ˈhɔː.lɪdʒ/ ⓊⓈ /ˈhɑː-/ *noun* [U] UK the business of moving things by road or railway: *a road haulage firm*

haulier UK /ˈhɔː.li.əʳ/ ⓊⓈ /ˈhɑː.li.ɚ/ *noun* [C] (US **hauler**) a business or a person involved in a business which transports goods by road

haunch /hɔːntʃ/ ⓊⓈ /hɑːntʃ/ *noun* [C] **1** one of the back legs of an animal with four legs that is used for meat: *a haunch of venison* **2 haunches** the top of a person's legs and their bottom: *She was sitting/squatting on her haunches.*

haunt ⟨SPIRIT⟩ /hɔːnt/ ⓊⓈ /hɑːnt/ *verb* [T] (of a ghost) to appear in a place repeatedly: *A ghostly lady is said to haunt the stairway looking for her children.* **haunted** /ˈhɔːn.tɪd/ ⓊⓈ /ˈhɑːn.t̬ɪd/ *adj: a haunted* **house** ○ *This room is said to be haunted.*

haunt ⟨REPEATEDLY TROUBLE⟩ /hɔːnt/ ⓊⓈ /hɑːnt/ *verb* [T] to cause repeated suffering or anxiety: *Fighting in Vietnam was an experience that would haunt him for the rest of his life.* ○ *Thirty years after the fire he is still haunted by images of death and destruction.* **haunted** /ˈhɔːn.tɪd/ ⓊⓈ /ˈhɑːn.t̬ɪd/ *adj*: showing signs of suffering or severe anxiety: *He had a haunted* **look** *about him.*

haunt ⟨PLACE⟩ /hɔːnt/ ⓊⓈ /hɑːnt/ *noun* [C] a place often visited: *This pub used to be one of your* **old** *haunts, didn't it Jim?*

haunting /ˈhɔːn.tɪŋ/ ⓊⓈ /ˈhɑːn.t̬ɪŋ/ *adj* beautiful, but in a sad way and often in a way which cannot be forgotten: *a haunting melody* ○ *the haunting beauty of Africa*

haute couˈture *noun* [U] (the business of making) expensive clothes of original design and high quality

haute cuiˈsine *noun* [U] cooking of a high standard, typically French cooking

hauteur /əʊˈtɜːʳ/ ⓊⓈ /hoʊˈtɝː/ *noun* [U] LITERARY a formal and unfriendly way of behaving which suggests that the person thinks they are better than other people

---

USAGE

Forms of the verb **to have**.

This is a table of all the usual forms of the irregular verb **to have**. Short forms are given in brackets.

present tense	past tense
I have (I've)	I had (I'd)
you have (you've)	you had (you'd)
he/she/it has (he's/she's/it's)	he/she/it had (he'd/she'd/it'd)
we have (we've)	we had (we'd)
you have (you've)	you had (you'd)
they have (they've)	they had (they'd)

past participle	
had	He has had a bad car accident.

present participle	
having	She is having some problems at school.

short negative forms		
haven't	hasn't	hadn't

I haven't got any money with me.

---

have ⟨PERFECT TENSE⟩ STRONG /hæv/, WEAK /həv/ /əv/ *auxiliary verb* [+ past participle] had, had ALSO **'ve/'s** used with the past participle of other verbs to form the present and past perfect tenses: *I've heard that story before.* ○ *Diane's already gone.* ○ *John hasn't phoned.* ○ *I haven't visited*

London before. ○ *Have you seen Roz?* ○ *Has she been invited?* ○ *They still hadn't had any news when I spoke to them yesterday.* ○ FORMAL *Had I known* (= if I had known) *you were coming, I'd have booked a larger room.*

have ⟨POSSESS⟩ (had, had) /hæv/ *verb* [T not continuous] **1** (ALSO **'ve/'s**, MAINLY UK **have got**) to own or possess: *They have a beautiful home.* ○ *He has plenty of money but no style.* ○ *I've got two brothers.* ○ *Have you got time to finish the report today?* ○ *I've got a suggestion/an idea.* ✻ NOTE: **got** is only used in the present tense. **2** SLANG to have sex with someone: *He asked me how many men I'd had.* **3 have the decency/good sense, etc. to do sth** to do one good thing, although you do other bad or silly things: **At least** *he had the good sense to turn the gas off.* ○ **At least** *she had the decency to apologize.*

• **have it in you** to possess a particular quality or ability: *His speech was really funny – we didn't know he had it in him.*

• **have nothing on sb or sth** INFORMAL to not be as good as someone or something: *He's a good player, but he's got nothing on his brother.*

• **have it in for sb** INFORMAL to be determined to harm or criticize someone: *She's always had it in for me.*

• **have it off** (ALSO **have it away**) UK SLANG to have sex: *He was having it off* **with** *his friend's wife.*

• **have it out with sb** to talk to someone about something they have done which makes you angry, in order to try to solve the problem: *She'd been late for work every morning that week and I thought I'd better have it out with her.*

haves /hævz/ **the haves and have-nots** the people who are not poor and the people who are poor: *The government's change of policy is intended to reduce the gap between the haves and have-nots in our society.*

have ⟨BABY⟩ /hæv/ *verb* [T] had, had to give birth to a baby: *Elaine had a baby girl yesterday.* ○ *My mother had me at home.*

have /hæv/ *verb* **be having a baby/twins, etc.** to be pregnant/pregnant with twins (= two babies), etc: *I hear his wife's having a baby.*

have ⟨BE ILL⟩ (had, had) /hæv/ *verb* [T] (MAINLY UK **have got**) If you have a particular illness, you suffer from it: *Have you ever had measles?* ○ *I've got a cold.*

have ⟨DO⟩ /hæv/ *verb* [T] had, had to perform the action mentioned: *have a wash/bath/shower* ○ *I had a swim.* ○ *We had a short walk after lunch.* ○ *I've never done it before but I'd like to have a try* (= to try). ○ *Why don't you have a rest?*

have ⟨EAT/DRINK⟩ /hæv/ *verb* [T] had, had to eat or drink something: *I had prawns and rice for lunch.* ○ *Can I have a drink of water?* ○ *When are we having dinner?*

have ⟨RECEIVE⟩ /hæv/ *verb* [T] had, had to receive, accept or allow something to happen: *Here, have some more coffee.* ○ [+ **to** infinitive] *My mother's having visitors* (**to** stay) *next week.* ○ *Let me have the book* **back** *next week.* ○ *In the end they solved their problems and she had him* **back** (= allowed him to come and live with her again). ○ *I looked in all the shops for string but there was* **none to be** *had* (= none that anyone could obtain). ○ *I kept telling him that you were French but he* **wouldn't** *have* **it** (= would not accept that it was true). ○ [+ v-ing] *I* **won't** *have those kids* **running** *all over my flowerbeds* (= I refuse to allow them to do this).

• **not have any of it** INFORMAL to be completely unwilling or to refuse: *I asked him to help out, but he wasn't having any of it.*

have ⟨CAUSE⟩ /hæv/ *verb* had, had **1** [T] to cause something to happen or someone to do something: [+ past participle] *We're having the house painted next month.* ○ [+ infinitive without to] *If you wait, I'll have someone collect it for you.* ○ [+ obj + v-ing] *The film soon had us crying.* ○ *Guy'll have it working in no time.* ○ *She had her parents* **down** (= invited them to stay) *for a week in the summer.* ○ *We had the boat* **out** (= went out in the boat) *for the first time this week.* ○ *We often have friends* **over/round** (= invite them to come) *on a Saturday night.* **2** [T + past participle] to suffer something that someone does to you: *She had her car stolen* (= it was stolen) *last week.*

• **and have done with it** (ALSO **and be done with it**) to deal with and finish the whole matter: *Why don't you just* *pull up all the plants and have done with the idea of having a garden.*

have [EXPERIENCE] /hæv/ *verb* [T] **had, had** to experience something: *We're having a wonderful time here in Venice.* ○ *We didn't have any difficulty/problem finding the house.* ○ *He hasn't been having much luck recently.*

• **A good time was had by all.** *SAYING* said to mean that everyone enjoyed themselves

have [MUST] /hæv/ *modal verb* **have (got) to do *sth*** to need to or be forced: *I have to go to Manchester tomorrow on business.* ○ *What time have you got to be there?* ○ *Do we have to finish this today?* ○ *We'll have to start keeping detailed records.* ○ *Jackie's ill so they've had to change their plans.*

PHRASAL VERBS WITH **have**

▲ **have *sb* on** [TRICK] *UK phrasal verb* (*US* **put *sb* on**) *INFORMAL* to persuade someone that something is true when it is not, usually as a joke: *That's your new car? You're having me on!* * NOTE: This is usually used in the continuous form.

▲ **have (got) *sth* on** [WEAR] *phrasal verb* [M] If you have clothes or shoes on, you are wearing them: *I loved that dress you had on last night.* * NOTE: This is not used in the continuous or passive form.

▲ **have (got) *sth* on** [PLAN] *phrasal verb* If you have something on, you have planned to do it: *Have you got anything on this week?* ○ *I've got something on this Tuesday, but I'm free on Wednesday.* * NOTE: This is not used in the continuous or passive form.

▲ **have *sth* out** [BODY PART] *phrasal verb* to have something removed from your body: *You'll have to have that tooth out.* ○ *He had his appendix out last week.*

▲ **have *sb* up** *phrasal verb* [usually passive] *UK INFORMAL* to take someone to court for a trial: *He was had up **for** burglary.*

haven /ˈheɪ.vᵊn/ *noun* [C] a safe or peaceful place: *The garden was a haven **from** the noise and bustle of the city.* ○ *They wanted to provide **safe** havens for the refugees.*

haven't /ˈhæv.ᵊnt/ *short form of* have not: *I haven't been to Australia.*

haversack /ˈhæv.ə.sæk/ [US] /-ɚ-/ *noun* [C] *OLD-FASHIONED* a bag, often made from strong rough cloth, with one or two shoulder straps

havoc /ˈhæv.ək/ *noun* [U] confusion and lack of order, especially causing damage or trouble: *The storm **wreaked*** (= caused) *havoc in the garden, uprooting trees and blowing a fence down.* ○ *The delay **played*** (= caused) *havoc **with** their travel arrangements.*

haw /hɔː/ [US] /hɑː/ *verb* **hum and haw** ➲See at **hum**.

hawk [BIRD] /hɔːk/ [US] /hɑːk/ *noun* [C] a type of large bird which catches small birds and animals for food: *She was watching me like a hawk.*

hawk [PERSON] /hɔːk/ [US] /hɑːk/ *noun* [C] a person who strongly supports the use of force in political relationships rather than discussion or other more peaceful solutions ➲Compare **dove** PERSON. **hawkish** /ˈhɔː.kɪʃ/ [US] /ˈhɑː-/ *adj*: *The president is hawkish on foreign policy.*

hawk [SELL] /hɔːk/ [US] /hɑːk/ *verb* [T] to sell goods informally in public places: *On every street corner there were traders hawking their wares.*

hawker /ˈhɔː.kəʳ/ [US] /ˈhɑː.kɚ/ *noun* [C] someone who makes money from hawking goods

hawk-eyed /ˌhɔːkˈaɪd/ [US] /ˌhɑːk-/ *adj* Someone who is hawk-eyed watches and notices everything that happens: *Hawk-eyed store detectives stood by the doors.*

hawser /ˈhɔː.zəʳ/ [US] /ˈhɑː.zɚ/ *noun* [C] a strong thick rope, often made of steel

hawthorn /ˈhɔː.θɔːn/ [US] /ˈhɑː.θɔːrn/ *noun* [U] a type of small wild tree with thorns, white or pink flowers in spring and small red fruits in the autumn

hay /heɪ/ *noun* [U] grass which is cut, dried and used as animal food or as covering material

• **Make hay while the sun shines.** *SAYING* said to mean that you should make good use of an opportunity while it lasts

ˈhay ˌfever *noun* [U] an illness like a cold, caused by POLLEN: *She gets really bad hay fever.* ○ *hay fever sufferers*

haystack /ˈheɪ.stæk/ *noun* [C] a large tall pile of hay in a field

haywire /ˈheɪ.waɪəʳ/ [US] /-waɪr/ *adj INFORMAL* **go haywire** to stop working properly, often in a way that is very sudden and noticeable: *The television's gone haywire.*

hazard [DANGER] /ˈhæz.əd/ [US] /-ɚd/ *noun* [C] something that is dangerous and likely to cause damage: *a health/fire hazard* ○ *The busy traffic entrance was a hazard **to** pedestrians.*

hazardous /ˈhæz.ə.dəs/ [US] /-ɚ-/ *adj* dangerous: *a hazardous journey/occupation*

hazard [RISK] /ˈhæz.əd/ [US] /-ɚd/ *verb* [T] to risk doing something, especially making a guess, suggestion, etc: *I wouldn't like to hazard a **guess**.*

ˌhazard (ˈwarning) ˌlight *noun* [C] one of the orange lights at the front and back of a car which turn on and off repeatedly to warn other drivers of danger

haze /heɪz/ *noun* [C or U] when the air is not very clear because of something such as heat or smoke, making it difficult to see well: *The road through the desert shimmered in the haze.* ○ *I saw her through a haze of cigarette smoke.* **hazy** /ˈheɪ.zi/ *adj* **1** *hazy sunshine* ○ *the hazy days of summer* **2** not remembering things clearly: *hazy memories of childhood*

hazily /ˈheɪ.zɪ.li/ *adv*: *She only hazily* (= unclearly) *remembered her last visit twenty years ago.*

haze /heɪz/ *verb*

▲ **haze over** *phrasal verb* If the sky hazes over, the air becomes less clear because of something such as heat or smoke: *The sky began to haze over during the afternoon.*

hazel [TREE] /ˈheɪ.zᵊl/ *noun* [C] a small tree that produces nuts that can be eaten

hazel [COLOUR] /ˈheɪ.zᵊl/ *adj* (especially of eyes) greenish brown or yellowish brown in colour

hazelnut /ˈheɪ.zᵊl.nʌt/ *noun* [C] the nut of the HAZEL tree which has a hard brown shell

H-bomb /ˈeɪtʃ.bɒm/ [US] /-bɑːm/ *noun* [C] a **hydrogen bomb**

he *STRONG* /hiː/, *WEAK* /hi/ /i/ *pronoun* **1** used to refer to a man, boy or male animal that has already been mentioned: *Don't ask Andrew, he won't know.* ○ *There's no need to be frightened – he's a very friendly dog.* **2** used to refer to a person whose sex is not known: *The modern traveller can go where he likes.* ○ *As soon as the baby is born he'll start to take an interest in the world around him.*

he /hiː/ *noun* [C] a male: *How can you tell whether the fish is a he or a she?*

USAGE

he (avoiding sexist language)

Many people do not like the use of **he** to refer to a person whose sex is not known, as it seems unfair to women. Instead, they prefer to use **they**.

"Someone's on the phone." "What do they want?"

He or she can be used, but this can be repetitive in normal conversation. **He/she** and **s/he** are sometimes used in writing, but **they** is also correct, even in formal writing. The same is true of **his/their** and **him/them**.

Somebody called and left their number.
If anybody needs to speak to me, tell them I'll be in the office this afternoon.

head [BODY PART] /hed/ *noun* **1** [C] the part of the body above the neck that contains the eyes, nose, mouth and ears and the brain: *Put this hat on to keep your head warm.* ○ *He banged his head on the car as he was getting in.* ○ *She **nodded/shook** her head* (= showed her agreement/disagreement). ➲See picture **The Body** on page Centre 5 **2** a person or animal when considered as a unit: *Dinner will cost £20 a/per head* (= for each person). ○ *I did a quick head **count*** (= calculated how many people there were). ○ *They own a hundred head of* (= 100) *cattle.* **3** [S] a measure of length or height equal to the size of a head: *Her horse won **by a** head.* ○ *Paul is **a** head taller than Andrew.*

H

• **an old/a wise head on young shoulders** a child or young person who thinks and talks like an older person who has more experience of life
• **be banging, etc. *your* head against a brick wall** INFORMAL to try to do something that is very difficult or impossible to achieve and therefore causes you to feel annoyed: *I keep asking her not to park there but it's like banging your head against a brick wall.*
• **bite/snap *sb's* head off** INFORMAL to speak to someone angrily: *I asked what was wrong, but he just bit my head off.*
• **bury/have *your* head in the sand** to refuse to think about unpleasant facts, although they will have an influence on your situation: *You've got to face facts here – you can't just bury your head in the sand.*
• **come to a head** (ALSO **bring *sth* to a head**) If something comes to a head or someone brings something to a head, a situation reaches a point where something must be done about it: *Things hadn't been good between us for a while and this incident just brought it to a head.*
• **from head to foot/toe** completely covering your body: *The dog was covered in mud from head to foot.*
• **get *your* head down** UK INFORMAL to direct all your efforts into the particular task you are involved in: *I'm going to get my head down and try and finish this report before I go home today.*
• **get/put *your* head down** INFORMAL to sleep: *I'm just going to put my head down for a couple of hours.*
• **give head** OFFENSIVE to perform FELLATIO or CUNNILINGUS
• **give *sb their* head** OLD-FASHIONED to allow someone to do what they want to do without trying to help them or give them advice
• **have your head (buried/stuck) in a book** to be reading: *Rose always has her head buried in a book.*
• **have your head in the clouds** to not be aware of the facts of a situation
• **laugh/shout/scream, etc. *your* head off** INFORMAL to laugh, shout, scream, etc. very noisily and for a long time: *There I was lying face down on the pavement and you two were laughing your heads off!*
• **a full/good/thick, etc. head of hair** a lot of hair: *Even as a tiny baby, she had a thick head of hair.*
• **head over heels (in love)** completely in love
• **have your head screwed on (the right way)** INFORMAL to be practical and wise: *Ask Lois to help – she's got her head screwed on the right way.*
• **head and shoulders above** If someone or something is head and shoulders above other people or things, they are a lot better than them: *There's no competition – they're head and shoulders above the rest.*
• **Heads will roll!** something that is said to mean that people will be punished for something bad that has happened
• **be in over *your* head** INFORMAL to be involved in a difficult situation that you cannot get out of: *Sean tried to pay back his gambling debts, but he was in over his head.*
• **keep *your* head above water** to just be able to manage, especially when you have financial difficulties: *The business is in trouble, but we are just about keeping our heads above water.*
• **keep *your* head down** to avoid trouble: *He's in a bad mood today – I'm just keeping my head down.*
• **go over *sb's* head** to speak to or ask permission from someone who has more authority than the person who you would normally go to in that situation: *Amanda was refusing to give me the week off so I went over her head and spoke to the boss.*

-headed /-hed.ɪd/ *suffix* having the number or type of heads mentioned: *a many-headed monster*

head /hed/ *verb* [T] to hit a ball with your head: *Owen headed the ball into the back of the net.*

header /ˈhed.əʳ/ [US] /-ɚ/ *noun* [C] the act of hitting the ball with your head in football: *A fine header!*

headless /ˈhed.ləs/ *adj* without a head: *a headless corpse*
• **run round like a headless chicken** to be very busy doing lots of things, but in a way that is not very effective

head [MIND] /hed/ *noun* [C] the mind and mental abilities: *You need a **clear** head to be able to drive safely.* ○ *What put that **(idea) into** your head* (= What made you think that)? ○ *I can't get that tune/that man **out of** my head* (= I cannot stop hearing the tune in my mind/thinking about that man). ○ ***Use** your head* (= Think more carefully)! ○ *Harriet has **a (good)** head **for** figures* (= She is very clever at calculating numbers). ○ UK *Do you have **a** head **for heights*** (= Are you able to be in high places without fear)?
• **can't get *your* head around** INFORMAL If you say that you can't get your head around something, you mean that you cannot understand it: *I just can't get my head around these tax forms.*
• **get *sth* into *your* head** to start to believe something: *When will you get it into your head that he's not coming back?* ○ *One day, she got it into her head* (= decided for no reason) *that we all hated her.*
• **go to *sb's* head** **1** If something goes to someone's head, it makes them think that they are very important and makes them a less pleasant person: *Don't let fame/success go to your head.* **2** If alcohol goes to your head, it makes you feel slightly drunk: *Champagne always goes straight to my head.*
• **keep *your* head** (ALSO **keep a cool head**) to stay calm despite great difficulties: *She kept her head under pressure and went on to win the race.*
• **be off *your* head** INFORMAL **1** to be crazy: *You must be off your head going out in this weather!* **2** to not be in control of your behaviour because you have drunk too much alcohol or taken drugs: *Hannah was off her head as usual.*
• **over *your* head** too difficult or strange for you to understand: *I tried to take in what he was saying about nuclear fusion, but most of it **went** over my head.*
• **put *their* heads together** If two or more people put their heads together, they plan something together: *I'm sure that if we put our heads together, we can think of a solution to the problem.*
• **take it into *your* head to do *sth*** to suddenly decide to do something, often something silly or surprising: *Anyway, they took it into their heads to get married.*

-head /-hed/ *suffix*: *a crack-head* (= someone who depends on the drug CRACK)

head [TOP PART] /hed/ *noun* **1** [S] the top part or beginning of something: *the head of the queue* ○ *the head of the page* ○ *Diana, the guest of honour, sat at the head of the table* (= the most important end of it). **2** [C] the larger end of a nail, hammer, etc. **3** [C] the top part of a plant where a flower or leaves grow: *a head of lettuce* **4** [C] the layer of white bubbles on top of beer after it has been poured **5** [C] the upper part of a river, where it begins **6** [C] the top part of a spot when it contains PUS (= yellow liquid) **7** **head of steam** the force produced by a large amount of steam in an enclosed space
• **heads or tails?** asked before you throw a coin into the air and want someone else to guess which side it will land on
• **can't make head nor tail of *sth*** to not be able to understand something: *I can't make head nor tail of these instructions on the packet.*
• **Heads I win, tails you lose.** HUMOROUS SAYING said about a situation in which you will benefit whatever happens

head /hed/ *verb* [T] to be at the front or top of something: *The Queen's carriage headed the procession.* ○ *Jo's name headed the list of candidates.*

head [LEADER] /hed/ *noun* [C] **1** someone in charge of or leading an organization, group, etc: *the head of the History department* ○ *the head chef* **2** MAINLY UK a **headteacher** **3** MAINLY UK **head boy/girl** a boy or girl who is the leader of the other PREFECTS and often represents his or her school on formal occasions

head /hed/ *verb* [T] to be in charge of a group or organization: *She heads one of Britain's leading travel firms.* ○ *Judge Hawthorne was chosen to head the team investigating the allegations of abuse.*

headship /ˈhed.ʃɪp/ *noun* MAINLY UK **1** [C] the position of being in charge of an organization or, especially in Britain, in charge of a school: *Dozens of well-qualified teachers applied for the headship.* **2** [C usually sing] the period during which a particular person is in charge of a school or other organization: *A lot of changes have taken place during her headship.*

head [DEVICE] /hed/ *noun* [C] the part of a tape or video RECORDER (= machine for recording sound or pictures) which touches the tape to record and play music, speech, etc.

head [GO] /hed/ *verb* [I + adv or prep] to go in a particular direction: *I was heading* ***out of*** *the room when she called me back.* ○ *We were heading* ***towards*** *Kumasi when our truck broke down.* ○ *He headed straight* ***for*** (= went towards) *the fridge.* ○ *I think we ought to head* ***back/home*** (= return to where we started) *now, before it gets too dark.*

headed /ˈhed.ɪd/ *adj* [after v] *Which way are you headed* (= In which direction are you going)?

PHRASAL VERBS WITH **head**

▲ **head for** ***sth*** *phrasal verb* to be likely to experience a bad situation soon, because of your own actions or behaviour: *They're heading for disaster if they're not careful.* ○ *The country is heading for recession.*

▲ **head off** [JOURNEY] *phrasal verb* to start a journey or leave a place: *What time are you heading off?*

▲ **head** ***sb/sth*** **off** [DIRECTION] *phrasal verb* [M] to force someone or something to change direction: *I tried to head the dog off by running towards it.*

▲ **head** ***sth*** **off** [PREVENT] *phrasal verb* [M] to prevent a difficult or unpleasant situation from happening: *The company is putting up wages in an attempt to head off a strike.*

headache /ˈhed.eɪk/ *noun* [C] **1** a pain you feel inside your head: *I've* ***got*** *a* ***splitting*** (= severe) *headache.* **2** something that causes you great difficulty and worry: *Finding a babysitter for Saturday evening will be a major headache.*

headachy /ˈhed,eɪ.ki/ *adj*: *I knew I was getting a cold when I started feeling tired and headachy* (= having headaches).

headband /ˈhed.bænd/ *noun* [C] a narrow strip of material worn around the head, usually to keep your hair or sweat out of your eyes

headbanging /ˈhed,bæŋ.ɪŋ/ *noun* [U] the activity of shaking your head up and down with great force to the beat of rock music

headbanger /ˈhed,bæŋ.əʳ/ [US] /-ɚ/ *noun* [C] **1** someone, especially a boy or young man, who enjoys listening to loud, energetic rock music **2** *UK* a stupid or foolish person

headboard /ˈhed.bɔːd/ [US] /-bɔːrd/ *noun* [C] a vertical board at the end of a bed behind where your head rests

head-butt /ˈhed.bʌt/ *verb* [T] to hit someone violently on the head or in the face using the front of your head

head-butt /ˈhed.bʌt/ *noun* [C]

headcase /ˈhed.keɪs/ *noun* [C] *INFORMAL* a person who behaves strangely or who is very foolish or violent

headcheese /ˈhed.tʃiːz/ *noun* [U] *US FOR* **brawn** FOOD

ˈhead ˌcold *noun* [C] a cold when your nose feels very blocked

headdress /ˈhed.dres/ *noun* [C] a decorative covering for the head

ˌheaded ˈnotepaper *noun* [U] writing paper with a person's or organization's name and address printed at the top of it

headfirst /ˌhedˈfɜːst/ [US] /-ˈfɝːst/ *adj, adv* **1** [before n] (*US ALSO* **headlong**) with the head going first: *She* ***dived*** *head-first* ***into*** *the pool.* **2** without thinking or preparation: *You shouldn't rush headfirst* ***into*** *starting your own business without proper advice.*

headgear /ˈhed.gɪəʳ/ [US] /-gɪr/ *noun* [U] a hat or other covering that is worn on the head: *When riding a bicycle, you should wear the proper headgear.*

headhunter [FIGHTER] /ˈhed,hʌn.təʳ/ [US] /-t̬ɚ/ *noun* [C] a member of a tribe that keeps the heads of the enemies that it has killed

headhunter [PERSUADE] /ˈhed,hʌn.təʳ/ [US] /-t̬ɚ/ *noun* [C] *INFORMAL* a person who tries to persuade someone to leave their job by offering them another job with more pay and a higher position

headhunt /ˈhed.hʌnt/ *verb* [T] to persuade someone to leave their job by offering them another job with more pay and a higher position: *She was headhunted by a rival firm.*

heading /ˈhed.ɪŋ/ *noun* [C] words written or printed at the top of a text as a title

headland /ˈhed.lənd/ /-lænd/ *noun* [C] a piece of land that sticks out from the coast into the sea

headless /ˈhed.ləs/ *adj* ➲See at **head** BODY PART.

headlight /ˈhed.laɪt/ *noun* [C usually pl] (*UK ALSO* **headlamp**) a large powerful light at the front of a vehicle, usually one of two: *I could see a car's headlights coming towards me.* ○ *It was foggy, and all the cars had their headlights* ***on***. ○ ***Dip*** *your headlights* (= Make them shine downwards) *when you see another car coming towards you.* ➲Compare **sidelight**. ➲See picture **Car** on page Centre 12

headline /ˈhed.laɪn/ *noun* [C] a line of words printed in large letters as the title of a story in a newspaper, or the main points of the news that are broadcast on television or radio: *The news of his death was splashed in headlines across all the newspapers.* ○ *the eight o'clock headlines* ➲Compare **by-line** and **dateline**.

headline /ˈhed.laɪn/ *verb* [T + obj + n] *The story was headlined* (= had as its headline) *'Killer dogs on the loose'*.

headlong /ˈhed.lɒŋ/ [US] /-lɑːŋ/ *adv, adj* **1** [before n] with great speed or without thinking: *The car skidded and* ***plunged*** *headlong over the cliff.* ○ *In the headlong* ***rush*** *to buy houses, many people got into debt.* **2** *US FOR* **headfirst**

headman /ˈhed.mæn/ *noun* [C] the CHIEF (= leader) of a village or tribe

headmaster /ˌhedˈmɑː.stəʳ/ [US] /ˈhed,mæs.t̬ɚ/ *noun* [C] *MAINLY UK* a male HEADTEACHER

headmistress /ˌhedˈmɪs.trəs/ [US] /ˈ-ˌ--/ *noun* [C] *MAINLY UK* a female HEADTEACHER

ˌhead ˈoffice *group noun* [C usually sing] the most important office of an organization or company, or the people working there: *Last year Paul was transferred to our head office in London.* ○ *Head office have asked for a report.*

ˌhead of ˈstate *noun* [C] the official leader of a country, often someone who has few or no real political powers

head-on /ˈhed.ɒn/ [US] /-ɑːn/ *adj* [before n], *adv* describes an accident in which the fronts of two vehicles hit each other: *The car crossed the road and hit a truck head-on.* ○ *a head-on collision*

headphones /ˈhed.fəʊnz/ [US] /-foʊnz/ *plural noun* a device with a part to cover each ear through which you can listen to music, radio broadcasts, etc. without other people hearing

headquarters (*plural* **headquarters**) /ˌhedˈkwɔː.təz/ [US] /-ˌkwɔːr.t̬ɚz/ *group noun* [C] (*ABBREVIATION* **HQ**) the main offices of an organization such as the army, police or a business company: *The company's headquarters is/are in Amsterdam.*

headrest /ˈhed.rest/ *noun* [C] the part of a chair that supports the head, especially a support fixed to the back of the seat of a car

headroom /ˈhed.ruːm/ /-rʊm/ *noun* [U] the amount of space below a roof or bridge: *It's a small car but there's lots of headroom.*

headscarf /ˈhed.skɑːf/ [US] /-skɑːrf/ *noun* [C] *plural* **headscarves** a square piece of material worn on the head by women, often folded into a triangle and tied under the chin: *a silk headscarf* ➲See picture **Hairstyles and Hats** on page Centre 8

headset /ˈhed.set/ *noun* [C] a set of HEADPHONES, especially one with a MICROPHONE fixed to it

headship /ˈhed.ʃɪp/ *noun* [C] ➲See at **head** LEADER.

headstand /ˈhed.stænd/ *noun* [C] when you balance upside down on your head, using your hands to support you

ˌhead ˈstart *noun* [C usually sing] an advantage that someone has over other people in something such as a competition or race: *You've got a head start* ***over/on*** *others trying to get the job because you've got relevant work experience.*

headstone /ˈhed.stəʊn/ [US] /-stoʊn/ *noun* [C] a large stone that is put at one end of a GRAVE with the name of the

H

person who has died and other details such as the year they died

headstrong /ˈhed.strɒŋ/ [US] /-strɑːŋ/ *adj* very determined to do what you want without listening to others: *She was a headstrong child, always getting into trouble.*

headteacher *MAINLY UK* /ˌhedˈtiː.tʃəʳ/ [US] /ˈhedˌtiː.tʃɚ/ *noun* [C] (*US USUALLY* **principal,** *UK ALSO* **head**) someone who is in charge of a school

head-to-head /ˌhed.təˈhed/ *noun* [C] a direct competition between two people or teams: *a head-to-head contest*

headway /ˈhed.weɪ/ *noun* **make headway** to advance or get closer to achieving something: *I'm trying to learn to drive, but I'm not making much headway* ***(with** it).* ○ *Little headway has been made so far* ***in*** *the negotiations.*

headwind /ˈhed.wɪnd/ *noun* [C] a wind blowing in the opposite direction to the one you are moving in: *The runners had to battle against a* ***stiff/strong*** *headwind.*

heady /ˈhed.i/ *adj* having a powerful effect, making you feel slightly drunk or excited: *a heady wine/perfume* ○ *In the heady* ***days*** *of their youth, they thought anything was possible.*

heal /hɪəl/ *verb* [I or T] **1** to make or become well again, especially after a cut or other injury: *The wounds were gradually healing* ***(up).*** ○ *The plaster cast helps to heal the broken bone.* **2** If a bad situation or painful emotion heals, it ends or improves, and if something heals it, it makes it end or improve: *Peace talks were held to try to heal the growing rift between the two sides.* ○ *A broken heart takes a long time to heal.* **healing** /ˈhɪə.lɪŋ/ *noun* [U] *the healing properties of plants*

healer /ˈhɪə.ləʳ/ [US] /-lɚ/ *noun* [C] a person who has the power to heal people without using ordinary medicines: *a spiritual healer*

health /helθ/ *noun* [U] **1** the condition of the body and the degree to which it is free from illness, or the state of being well: *to be in good/poor health* ○ *Regular exercise is good for your health.* ○ *I had to give up drinking for health reasons.* ○ *He gave up work because of* ***ill****-health.* **2** the condition of something that changes or develops, such as an organization or system: *the financial health of the business*

ˈhealth auˌthority *noun* [C usually sing] in Britain, an organization that is responsible for hospitals and medical services in a particular area

healthcare /ˈhelθ.keəʳ/ [US] /-ker/ *noun* [U] the set of services provided by a country or an organization for the treatment of the physically and the mentally ill: *Healthcare workers are some of the lowest paid people in the country.*

ˈhealth ˌcentre *noun* [C] a building in which several doctors have offices and where people go to visit them

ˈhealth ˌfarm *noun* [C] (*US USUALLY* **health spa**) a place where you go for a holiday and eat healthy food, take exercise, etc.

ˈhealth ˌfood *noun* [C or U] food that is believed to be good for you because it does not contain artificial chemicals or much sugar or fat ➲Compare **junk food**.

ˈhealth inˌsurance *noun* [U] when you make regular payments to an insurance company in exchange for that company paying most or all of your medical expenses

ˈhealth ˌvisitor *noun* [C] *UK* a person employed to give advice to people, especially older people and the parents of very young children, about health care, sometimes by visiting them in their own homes

healthy /ˈhel.θi/ *adj* **1** strong and well: *She's a normal healthy child.* ○ *He looks healthy enough.* **2** showing that you are strong and well: *The walk had given her a healthy glow.* ○ *a healthy appetite* **3** good for your health: *a healthy diet* ○ *a good healthy walk* **4** successful and strong: *a healthy economy* **5** normal and showing good judgement: *a healthy disrespect for authority*

healthily /ˈhel.θɪ.li/ *adv*: *Eat healthily* (= Eat foods that are good for you) *and take plenty of exercise.*

healthful /ˈhelθ.fəl/ *adj US* helping to produce good health: *A healthful diet includes lots of green vegetables.*

heap /hiːp/ *noun* [C] an untidy pile or mass of things: *a heap of clothes/rubbish*

• **a (whole) heap of** ***sth*** *INFORMAL* a lot of something: *I've got a whole heap of work to do.*

• **the bottom of the heap** People who are at the bottom of the heap are poor and unsuccessful and have the lowest position in society.

• **collapse/fall in a heap** to fall down heavily and lie on the ground without moving: *The woman staggered and collapsed in a heap.*

heap /hiːp/ *verb* [T + adv or prep] to put things into a large untidy pile: *He heaped more food* ***onto*** *his plate.*

heaped /hiːpt/ *adj* (of a spoon or plate) containing as much as possible: *Add a heaped teaspoonful of sugar.*

heaps /hiːps/ *plural noun, adv INFORMAL* a lot: *Let Sarah pay for dinner, she's got heaps* ***of*** *money.* ○ *Our new house is heaps bigger than our last one.*

▲ **heap** ***sth*** **on** ***sb*** *phrasal verb* to give someone a lot of praise/criticism, etc: *He deals well with all the criticism heaped on him.*

hear [RECEIVE SOUND] /hɪəʳ/ [US] /hɪr/ *verb* [I or T] **heard, heard** to receive or become aware of a sound using your ears: *She heard a noise outside.* ○ *My grandfather is getting old and can't hear very well.* ○ *You'll have to speak up, I can't hear you.* ○ [+ obj + v-*ing*] *I heard/I could hear someone calling my name.* ○ [+ obj + infinitive without *to*] *At eight o'clock Jane heard him go out.* ➲See Note **listen, listen to or hear?** at **listen**.

• **hear wedding bells** *INFORMAL* to think that someone is going to get married: *She knew that if she brought her boyfriend home her mother would start hearing wedding bells.*

• **I must be hearing things.** *HUMOROUS* said when you cannot believe something because it is so unlikely: *He's offered to wash the dishes – I must be hearing things.*

• **can't hear** ***yourself*** **think** If you can not hear yourself think, you cannot give your attention to anything because there is so much noise: *There was so much noise in the classroom that I could hardly hear myself think.*

hearer /ˈhɪə.rəʳ/ [US] /ˈhɪr.ɚ/ *noun* [C] a person who hears something

hear [BE TOLD] /hɪəʳ/ [US] /hɪr/ *verb* [I or T] **heard, heard** to be told or informed (of); receive news: *Have you heard the news?* ○ *If you haven't heard by Friday, assume I'm not coming.* ○ [+ question word] *Have you heard* ***what's*** *happened?* ○ [+ (*that*)] *I hear* ***(that)*** *you're leaving.*

• **do you hear?** a way of emphasizing that you want people to give their attention to what you are saying: *I won't stand for this rudeness, do you hear?*

• **Hear, hear!** said to strongly agree with what someone else has just said

• **hear tell (of)** *OLD-FASHIONED* If you hear tell (of) something, someone tells you about it.

• **will never hear the end of it** *INFORMAL* If you say you will never hear the end of it, you mean that someone is continually going to speak proudly, critically, etc. about something: *If Linda gets that promotion, we'll never hear the end of it.*

COMMON LEARNER ERROR

hear from someone

Remember to use the preposition 'from' when you use **hear** to mean receive a letter, telephone call, etc. from someone.

I look forward to hearing from you.
~~*I look forward to hearing you.*~~

hear [LISTEN] /hɪəʳ/ [US] /hɪr/ *verb* [T] **heard, heard** to listen to someone or something attentively or officially: *I heard a really interesting programme on the radio this morning.* ○ [+ infinitive without *to*] *I heard the orchestra play at Carnegie Hall last summer.* ○ *An audience gathered to hear him speak.* ○ *FORMAL Lord, hear our prayers.* ○ *The case will be heard* (= officially listened to) *by the High Court.* **hearer** /ˈhɪə.rəʳ/ [US] /ˈhɪr.ɚ/ *noun* [C] *Jokes establish an intimacy between the teller and the hearer.*

PHRASAL VERBS WITH **hear**

▲ **hear from** ***sb*** *phrasal verb* If you hear from someone, you get a letter or telephone call from them, or they tell you something: *We haven't heard from her for ages.*

○ *You'll be hearing from my solicitors* (= They will write to you about my complaint).
▲ **hear of *sth*** [NOT ALLOW] *phrasal verb* If someone says they will not hear of something, they mean they will not allow it, usually when you want to do something good for them: *I wanted to pay but she wouldn't hear of it.*
▲ **hear of *sb/sth*** [KNOW] *phrasal verb* If you have heard of someone or something, you know that that person or thing exists: *I'd never heard of him before he won the prize.* ○ *It's a tiny country that most people have never heard of.* ✻ NOTE: This is usually used in the negative form.
▲ **hear *sth* of *sb*** [RECEIVE NEWS] *phrasal verb* to receive news about someone: *We haven't heard anything of Jan for months.*
▲ **hear *sb* out** *phrasal verb* to listen to someone until they have said everything they want to say: *At least hear me out before making up your mind.*

hearing [ABILITY] /ˈhɪə.rɪŋ/ [US] /ˈhɪr.ɪŋ/ *noun* [U] the ability to hear: *He's getting old and his hearing isn't very good.*

hearing [MEETING] /ˈhɪə.rɪŋ/ [US] /ˈhɪr.ɪŋ/ *noun* [C] an official meeting that is held to gather the facts about an event or problem: *A disciplinary hearing will examine charges of serious professional misconduct against three surgeons.* ○ *I think we should give him a* ***(fair)*** *hearing* (= we should listen to what he wants to say).

ˈhearing ˌaid *noun* [C] a device worn inside or next to the ear by people who cannot hear well in order to help them to hear better

hearken /ˈhɑː.kᵊn/ [US] /ˈhɑːr-/ *verb* [I] *LITERARY* to listen

hearsay /ˈhɪə.seɪ/ [US] /ˈhɪr-/ *noun* [U] information you have heard, although you do not know whether it is true or not: *The evidence against them is all hearsay.*

hearse /hɜːs/ [US] /hɝːs/ *noun* [C] a vehicle used to carry a body in a coffin to a funeral ➲See picture **Cars and Trucks** on page Centre 13

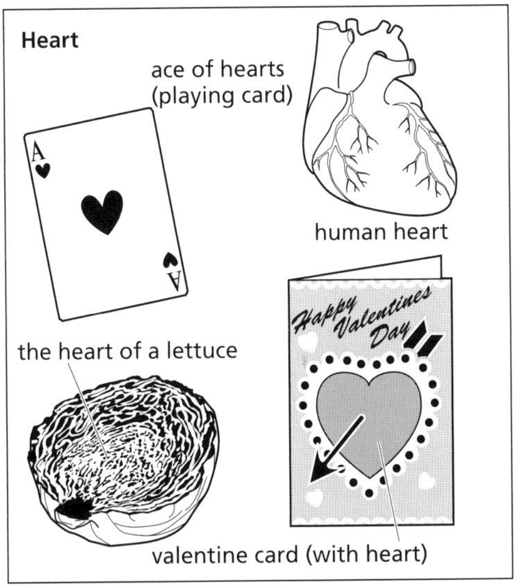
Heart
ace of hearts
(playing card)
human heart
the heart of a lettuce
Happy Valentines Day
valentine card (with heart)

heart [ORGAN] /hɑːt/ [US] /hɑːrt/ *noun* [C] the organ in your chest that sends the blood around your body: *heart disease/failure* ○ *He's got a weak/bad heart* (= His heart is not healthy). ○ *Isabel's heart was beating fast with fright.*
• **(off) by heart** learnt in such a way that you can say it from memory: *My father can still recite the poems he learned off by heart at school.*
• **my heart bleeds for *sb*** used to say that you feel great sadness for someone. This phrase is often used humorously to mean the opposite: *HUMOROUS John complains he only has two cars – my heart bleeds for him* (= I certainly do not feel sadness about that)*!*

heart [EMOTIONS] /hɑːt/ [US] /hɑːrt/ *noun* [C or U] used to refer to a person's character, or the place within a person where their feelings or emotions are considered to come from: *She has a good heart* (= She is a kind person). ○ *I love you, and I mean it* ***from the bottom of*** *my heart* (= very sincerely). ○ *I love you* ***with all*** *my heart* (= very much). ○ *He said he'd never marry but he had a* ***change of*** *heart* (= his feelings changed) *when he met her.* ○ *Homelessness is a subject very* ***close/dear to*** *her heart* (= is very important to her and she has strong feelings about it). ○ *He* ***broke*** *her heart* (= made her very sad) *when he left her for another woman.* ○ *It* ***breaks*** *my heart* (= makes me feel very sad) *to see him so unhappy.* ○ *They say he died of a* ***broken*** *heart* (= because he was so sad). ○ *OLD-FASHIONED It* ***does*** *my heart* ***good*** (= makes me very happy) *to see those children so happy.* ○ *She has a good heart* (= She is a kind person). ○ *His heart* ***leapt*** (= He suddenly felt very excited and happy) *when the phone rang.* ○ *My heart* ***sank*** (= I felt sad and disappointed) *when I heard the news.*
• ***your*** **heart skips/misses a beat** When your heart skips/misses a beat, you feel very excited or nervous: *Every time he looks at me my heart skips a beat.*
• ***your*** **heart aches** If your heart aches, you feel sad or feel a sense of sympathy and sadness for the suffering of other people: *His heart ached with pity for her.*
• **after *your* own heart** having the same opinions or interests as you: *She's a woman after my own heart.*
• **be all heart** to be very kind and generous. This phrase is often used humorously to mean the opposite: *She's all heart.* ○ *HUMOROUS "He deserves all he gets." "Oh, you're all heart* (= you are not kind)*!"*
• **Have a heart!** used to ask someone to be kinder to you: *Don't make me write it again! Have a heart!*
• ***your*** **heart's desire** *LITERARY* the thing or person you most want
• ***your*** **heart isn't in it** If your heart isn't in it, you do not feel interested or enthusiastic about something: *I tried to look interested, but my heart wasn't in it.*
• ***your*** **heart in *your* mouth** If your heart is in your mouth, you are feeling extremely nervous: *My heart was in my mouth when I opened the letter.*
• **heart and soul** *LITERARY* completely: *She loves those children heart and soul.*
• ***her/his*** **heart is in the right place** said about someone who you think has good intentions: *He's an odd man but his heart is in the right place.*
• **have a heart of gold** to be very kind and generous: *She has a heart of gold.*
• **have a heart of stone** to be unkind or cruel
• **in *your* heart of hearts** in your most secret and true thoughts: *I didn't want to believe it, but in my heart of hearts I knew that it was true.*
• **set *your* heart on *sth/doing sth*** to want to get or achieve something very much: *She's set her heart on having a pony.*
• **to *your* heart's content** If you do something to your heart's content, you do something enjoyable for as long as you want to do it: *You've got a whole week to yourself and you can read to your heart's content.*
• **put *your* heart and soul into *sth*** to make a lot of effort to do something: *She's one of those people who puts their heart and soul into their work.*
• **not have the heart to *do sth*** to feel unable to do something because you feel it would unkind: *She asked me to go with her and I didn't have the heart to refuse.*

-hearted /-hɑː.tɪd/ [US] /-hɑːr.t̬ɪd/ *suffix* having a character or feelings of the stated type: *a light-hearted play*-**heartedly** /-hɑː.tɪd.li/ [US] /-hɑːr.t̬ɪd-/ *suffix*-**heartedness** /-hɑː.tɪd.nəs/ [US] /-hɑːr.t̬ɪd-/ *suffix*

heart [BRAVERY] /hɑːt/ [US] /hɑːrt/ *noun* [U] bravery or determination or hope: *You're doing really well – don't* ***lose*** *heart now.* ○ ***Take*** *heart – things can only get better.*
• **heart in *your* boots** *UK INFORMAL* feeling very sad, disappointed, worried, etc: *Their hearts were in their boots when they realized that they would have to do the work all over again.*

heart [CENTRE] /hɑːt/ [US] /hɑːrt/ *noun* **1** [S] the central or most important part: *The demonstrators will march through* ***the*** *heart* ***of*** *the capital.* ○ *A disagreement about boundaries is* ***at the*** *heart* ***of*** *the dispute.* ○ *Let's get to the heart* ***of the matter.*** **2** [C] the firm central part of a vegetable, especially a leafy one: *artichoke hearts* ○ *the heart of a lettuce*

heart SHAPE /hɑːt/ ⓤ /hɑːrt/ *noun* [C] **1** a shape, consisting of two half-circles next to each other at the top and a v-shape at the bottom, which is often coloured pink or red, and which represents love **2** a card, with a red heart shape on it, which belongs to one of the four suits in a set of playing cards

heartache /'hɑːt.eɪk/ ⓤ /'hɑːrt-/ *noun* [C or U] LITERARY feelings of great sadness: *You've caused me nothing but heartache.* ○ *She writes about the joys and heartaches of bringing up children.*

'heart at,tack *noun* [C] a serious medical condition in which the heart does not get enough blood, causing great pain and often leading to death: *John **had** a heart attack three years ago.*

● **nearly/almost have a heart attack** INFORMAL to be extremely surprised or shocked: *I almost had a heart attack when I found out how much the meal cost.*

heartbeat /'hɑːt.biːt/ ⓤ /'hɑːrt-/ *noun* [C or U] the regular movement or sound that the heart makes as it sends blood around your body: *a steady heartbeat*

heartbreak /'hɑːt.breɪk/ ⓤ /'hɑːrt-/ *noun* [U] feelings of great sadness or disappointment: *The kidnap has caused the family months of heartbreak and suffering.*

heartbreaking /'hɑːt.breɪ.kɪŋ/ ⓤ /'hɑːrt-/ *adj* causing extreme sadness: *a heartbreaking story* ○ *It is heartbreaking (for him) that he cannot see his children.* ⊃See also **heartrending**.

heartbroken /'hɑːt.brəʊ.kən/ ⓤ /'hɑːrt,broʊ-/ *adj* extremely sad: *If she ever left him he would be heartbroken.*

heartburn /'hɑːt.bɜːn/ ⓤ /'hɑːrt.bɜːn/ *noun* [U] a painful burning feeling in the lower chest caused by the stomach not digesting food correctly

hearten /'hɑː.tən/ ⓤ /'hɑːr.tən/ *verb* [T] to make someone feel happier and more positive about a situation: *Anti-government protesters have been heartened by recent government promises of free and fair elections.* ✳ NOTE: The opposite is **dishearten**.

heartened /'hɑː.tənd/ ⓤ /'hɑːr.tənd/ *adj* [after v] feeling happier and more positive about something: *We all felt heartened by the news.*

heartening /'hɑː.tən.ɪŋ/ ⓤ /'hɑːr.tən-/ *adj* making you feel happier and more positive: *It was heartening to see so many people at the rally.*

'heart ,failure *noun* [U] when the heart stops working correctly or stops completely

heartfelt /'hɑːt.felt/ ⓤ /'hɑːrt-/ *adj* strongly felt and sincere: *heartfelt relief* ○ *FORMAL Please accept my heartfelt apologies/thanks.*

hearth /hɑːθ/ ⓤ /hɑːrθ/ *noun* [C] **1** the area around a fireplace or the area of floor in front of it: *A bright fire was burning in the hearth.* **2** LITERARY a home, especially when seen as a place of comfort and love: *They were reluctant to leave hearth **and home**.*

heartily /'hɑː.tɪ.li/ ⓤ /'hɑːr.tɪ-/ *adv* ⊃See at **hearty**.

heartland /'hɑːt.lænd/ ⓤ /'hɑːrt-/ *noun* [C] the central or most important area: *the Labour/Tory heartlands*

heartless /'hɑːt.ləs/ ⓤ /'hɑːrt-/ *adj* cruel and not caring about other people: *Don't be so heartless!*

'heart ,murmur *noun* [C usually sing] a condition in which unusual sounds can be heard in the heart, sometimes as a result of a fault in its structure

heartrending /'hɑːt.ren.dɪŋ/ ⓤ /'hɑːrt-/ *adj* causing great sympathy or sadness: *a heartrending story* ⊃See also **heartbreaking** at **heartbreak**.

heart-searching /'hɑːt.sɜː.tʃɪŋ/ ⓤ /'hɑːrt,sɜː-/ *noun* [U] when you think very seriously about your feelings, usually before making an important decision: *After a lot of heart-searching, we decided to split up.*

heartsick /'hɑːt.sɪk/ ⓤ /'hɑːrt-/ *adj* LITERARY very sad or disappointed

heartstrings /'hɑːt.strɪŋz/ ⓤ /'hɑːrt-/ *plural noun* **pull/tug, etc. at the heartstrings** to cause strong feelings of love or sympathy: *It's the story of a lost child – guaranteed to tug at the heartstrings.*

heartthrob, **heart-throb** /'hɑːt.θrɒb/ ⓤ /'hɑːrt.θrɑːb/ *noun* [C] INFORMAL a famous man, often a singer or an actor, who is attractive to many women

heart-to-heart /,hɑːt.tə'hɑːt/ ⓤ /,hɑːrt.tə'hɑːrt/ *noun* [C usually sing] a serious conversation between two people, usually close friends, in which they talk honestly about their feelings: *We **had** a heart-to-heart over a bottle of wine.* ○ *a heart-to-heart talk/chat*

heartwarming /'hɑːt.wɔː.mɪŋ/ ⓤ /'hɑːrt.wɔːr-/ *adj* (especially of an event, action or story) seeming to be something positive and good and therefore causing feelings of pleasure and happiness: *a heartwarming tale of triumph over adversity*

hearty ENTHUSIASTIC /'hɑː.ti/ ⓤ /'hɑːr.ti/ *adj* enthusiastic, energetic, and often loudly expressed: *a hearty welcome* ○ *a hearty laugh*

heartily /'hɑː.tɪ.li/ ⓤ /'hɑːr.tɪ-/ *adv*: *She laughed heartily* (= enthusiastically and loudly) *at the joke.*

hearty LARGE /'hɑː.ti/ ⓤ /'hɑːr.ti/ *adj* **1** large or (especially of food) in large amounts: *We ate a hearty breakfast before we set off.* ○ *She's got a hearty **appetite*** (= she eats a lot). **2** OLD-FASHIONED very great: *She has a hearty dislike of any sort of office work.*

heartily /'hɑː.tɪ.li/ ⓤ /'hɑːr.tɪ-/ *adv* completely or very much: *I am heartily sick of the whole situation.*

heat TEMPERATURE /hiːt/ *noun* [S or U] the quality of being hot or warm, or the temperature of something: *the heat of the sun/fire* ○ *How do you manage to work in this heat without air conditioning?* ○ *She always wore a coat, even in the heat of summer.* ○ *Cook the meat on a **high/low** heat* (= at a high/low temperature).

● **put the heat on sb** INFORMAL to try to persuade or force someone to do something

● **take the heat off sb** INFORMAL If someone or something takes the heat off you, they reduce the amount of criticism you have to deal with: *The deputy's resignation over the scandal has taken some of the heat off his superior.*

● **the heat is on** SLANG If you say the heat is on, you mean that a time of great activity and/or pressure has begun: *With only three months to go before the deadline, the heat is on.*

● **If you can't stand the heat, get out of the kitchen.** SAYING used as a way to tell someone that they should either stop complaining about a difficult or unpleasant activity, or stop doing it

heat /hiːt/ *verb* [I or T] to make something hot or warm, or to become hot or warm: *A large house like this must be expensive to heat.* ○ *Shall I heat **up** some soup for lunch?* **heated** /'hiː.tɪd/ ⓤ /-tɪd/ *adj*: *a heated towel rail* ○ *a heated swimming pool*

heat EMOTION /hiːt/ *noun* **in the heat of the moment** If you say or do something in the heat of the moment, you say or do it without thinking because you are very angry or excited: *He didn't mean it – he said it in the heat of the moment.*

heated /'hiː.tɪd/ ⓤ /-tɪd/ *adj*: excited or angry: *a heated debate* **heatedly** /'hiː.tɪd.li/ ⓤ /-tɪd-/ *adv*

heat RACE /hiːt/ *noun* [C] a less important race or competition in which it is decided who will compete in the final event

heat ANIMAL /hiːt/ *noun* (UK) **on**/(US) **in heat** describes an animal that is in a state of sexual excitement and ready to breed

heater /'hiː.tər/ ⓤ /-tɚ/ *noun* [C] a device which produces heat: *a gas/electric heater*

'heat ex,haustion *noun* [U] (US ALSO **heat prostration**) a condition in which you feel very weak and ill after being in a very hot place for too long

heath /hiːθ/ *noun* [C] an area of land that is not farmed, where grass and other small plants grow, but where there are few trees or bushes

'heat ,haze UK *noun* [U] (US **haze**) an effect of very hot sun, making it difficult to see objects clearly: *When the heat haze lifted, the island could be seen clearly.*

heathen /'hiː.ðən/ *adj* OLD USE DISAPPROVING (of people or their way of life, activities and ideas) having no religion, or belonging to a religion that is not Christianity, Judaism or Islam **heathen** /'hiː.ðən/ *noun* [C]

the heathen *plural noun* OLD-FASHIONED heathen people: *Those who attempted to **convert** the heathen were put to death.*

heather /ˈheð.əʳ/ ⓤ /-ɚ/ *noun* [C or U] a low spreading bush with small pink, purple or white flowers, which grows wild, especially on hills

heathland /ˈhiːθ.lənd/ *noun* [C or U] an area of HEATH

Heath Robinson /ˌhiːθˈrɒb.ɪn.sᵊn/ ⓤ /-ˈrɑː.bɪn-/ *adj* UK HUMOROUS OLD-FASHIONED describes a machine which is very cleverly made and is complicated in a ridiculous and amusing way, but which is not practical or effective enough for general use: *a Heath Robinson contraption*

heating /ˈhiː.tɪŋ/ ⓤ /-t̬ɪŋ/ *noun* [U] (*US* **heat**) the system that keeps a building warm: *Is the heating on?* ➔See also **central heating**.

heat ˌrash *noun* [C or U] (ALSO **prickly heat**) a condition in which the skin feels uncomfortable and is covered by red spots

heat-seeking /ˈhiːtˌsiː.kɪŋ/ *adj* [before n] describes a weapon that can direct itself towards something hot, especially the hot engine of an aircraft: *heat-seeking missiles*

heat ˌshield *noun* [C] the part of a spacecraft's structure which prevents it from getting too hot as it returns to Earth

heat ˌstroke *noun* [U] a condition which can lead to death, caused by being too long in a very hot place

heat ˌtreatment *noun* [C usually sing] when a part of the body is heated with an electrical device, usually in order to relax it

heat ˌwave *noun* [C usually sing] a period of time such as a few weeks when the weather is much hotter than usual

heave MOVE /hiːv/ *verb* **1** [I or T; usually + adv or prep] to move something heavy using a lot of effort: *He heaved the bag onto his shoulder* ○ *He cleared a space, heaving boxes out of the way.* **2** [T usually + adv or prep] INFORMAL to throw something forcefully, especially something large and heavy: *She picked up a great book and heaved it at him.* **3** [I] If something heaves, it makes one or more large movements up and down: *As the wind increased, the deck of the ship began to heave beneath his feet.*
• **heave a sigh of relief** to suddenly feel very happy because something unpleasant has not happened or has ended: *We both heaved a sigh of relief when she left.*
heave /hiːv/ *noun* [C] when you throw, push or pull something with a lot of effort: *They gave a great heave and rolled the boulder out of the way.* **heaving** /ˈhiː.vɪŋ/ *adj*: *He stood on the heaving deck.*

heave VOMIT /hiːv/ *verb* [I] to feel as if you are going to vomit: *The smell of the fish made me/my stomach heave.*

heave ˈho SHOUT *exclamation* OLD-FASHIONED a phrase which you say or shout when you are making a big effort to pull or lift something

the ˌheave ˈho DISMISS *noun* INFORMAL HUMOROUS **give sb the heave-ho 1** to take someone's job away from them, usually because they have done something wrong: *The newspaper's foreign editor was given the heave-ho yesterday.* **2** to end a romantic relationship with someone

heaven /ˈhev.ᵊn/ *noun* [U] **1** in some religions, the place, sometimes imagined to be in the sky, where God or the gods live and where good people are believed to go after they die, so that they can enjoy perfect happiness **2** INFORMAL a situation that gives you great pleasure: *I just lay in the sun for a week and did nothing – it was heaven.*
heavenly /ˈhev.ᵊn.li/ *adj* **1** of heaven: *heavenly music* ○ *heavenly light* **2** giving great pleasure: *It was a good party and the food was heavenly.*
the heavens /ðəˈhev.ᵊnz/ *plural noun* the sky: *We stared up at the heavens trying to see the comet.*
• **the heavens open** If the heavens open, it suddenly starts to rain a lot: *Just as we got to the park, the heavens opened.*

heavenly ˈbody *noun* [C] any object existing in space, especially a planet, star, or the moon

heavenly ˈhost *noun* [C] LITERARY a group of ANGELS

Heavens (above)! /ˌhev.ᵊnz.əˈbʌv/ *exclamation* (ALSO **Good Heavens!**) OLD-FASHIONED used to express surprise or anger

heaven-sent /ˌhev.ᵊnˈsent/ *adj* If someone or something is heaven-sent, they arrive or happen, usually unexpectedly, at the time when they are most useful.

heavenward /ˈhev.ᵊn.wəd/ ⓤ /-wɚd/ *adv* (ALSO **heavenwards**) LITERARY upwards: *She raised her eyes heavenward.*

heavy WEIGHING A LOT /ˈhev.i/ *adj* weighing a lot; needing effort to move or lift: *heavy equipment* ○ *heavy work/lifting* ○ ***How** heavy is that box* (= How much does it weigh)?
heavily /ˈhev.ɪ.li/ *adv*: *The news she had received weighed heavily **on** her* (= worried her). **heaviness** /ˈhev.ɪ.nəs/ *noun* [U]

heavy SOLID /ˈhev.i/ *adj* **1** thick, strong, solid or strongly made: *a heavy winter coat* ○ *a heavy meal* (= a large amount of solid food) ○ *a big man with heavy features* **2** describes soil which is thick and difficult to dig or walk through **3** describes machines or vehicles that are very large and powerful: *heavy artillery/machinery* **4** thick, solid-looking and not delicate: *The sun disappeared behind heavy clouds.*
heavily /ˈhev.ɪ.li/ *adv*: *He's a heavily **built** (= large and strong) man.*

heavy MAN /ˈhev.i/ *noun* [C] SLANG a large strong man employed to protect someone else or to frighten other people: *Frank always took a couple of heavies along with him when he went collecting his debts.*

heavy TO A GREAT DEGREE /ˈhev.i/ *adj* **1** (especially of something unpleasant) of very or unusually great force, amount or degree: *a heavy blow to the head* ○ *heavy fighting* ○ *heavy traffic* ○ *heavy rain/snow* ○ *a heavy smoker/drinker* ○ *a heavy sleeper* **2 heavy seas** sea which is rough with large waves **3** OLD-FASHIONED SLANG describes something such as a situation that is dangerous or unpleasant: *Then the police arrived and things got really heavy.*
• **be heavy on sb** to treat or punish someone severely: *I think his parents are being a bit heavy on him.*
• **be/go heavy on sth** to use a lot of something: *The engine is heavy on fuel.*
• **heavy with** If something is heavy with something else, it has a lot of it or is full of it: *The trees were heavy with fruit.* ○ *The atmosphere was heavy with menace.*
• **make heavy weather of sth** UK DISAPPROVING to find something hard to do and spend a lot of time on it, although it is not difficult: *She's making such heavy weather of that report she's writing.*
• **a heavy heart** a feeling of unhappiness: ***With** a heavy heart, she turned to wave goodbye.*
heavily /ˈhev.ɪ.li/ *adv*: to a great degree: *The terrorists are heavily armed.* ○ *The compound is heavily guarded.* ○ *She's heavily involved in the project.*
• **be heavily into sth** INFORMAL to be very interested in and involved with something: *When I was younger I was heavily into politics.*
heaviness /ˈhev.ɪ.nəs/ *noun* [U] when something happens or is done to a great degree

heavy ˈbreather *noun* [C] a man who gets sexual pleasure from making telephone calls, saying nothing, and breathing noisily

heavy-duty /ˌhev.iˈdjuː.ti/ ⓤ /-ˈduː.t̬i/ *adj* [before n] describes clothing, machinery or equipment that is stronger than usual so that it can be used a lot, especially in difficult conditions: *heavy-duty tools/shoes*

heavy ˈgoing *adj* difficult to read or understand: *I liked the film but the book was rather heavy going.* ○ *I'm **finding** the advanced physics a bit heavy going.*

heavy ˈgoods vehicle *noun* [C] (ABBREVIATION **HGV**) UK a large truck used for transporting goods

heavy-handed /ˌhev.iˈhæn.dɪd/ *adj* DISAPPROVING using too much force in dealing with someone: *The protestors accused the police of using heavy-handed **tactics**.*

heavy ˈindustry *noun* [C usually sing] industry that uses large machines to produce either materials such as steel or large goods such as ships and trains

ˌheavy ˈmetal [METAL] *noun* [C] SPECIALIZED a dense and usually poisonous metal, such as lead

ˌheavy ˈmetal [MUSIC] *noun* [U] a style of rock music with a strong beat, played very loudly using electrical instruments

ˌheavy ˈpetting *noun* [U] when two people kiss, hold and touch each other in a sexual way, but do not have sex

heavy-set /ˌhev.iˈset/ *adj* Someone who is heavy-set has a large, wide, strong body.

heavyweight /ˈhev.ɪ.weɪt/ *noun* [C] **1** a boxer who weighs more than 175 pounds (79.5 kilograms) and is therefore in the heaviest group: *Mike Tyson was heavyweight champion of the world.* ➲Compare **lightweight**. **2** a person or thing that is important or serious and that other people notice: *Her extraordinary intelligence and speaking ability made her a political heavyweight.*

Hebrew /ˈhiː.bruː/ *noun* **1** [U] the ancient language of the Jewish people and the official language of modern Israel **2** [C] a Jewish person, used especially about the Jews of ancient Israel **Hebrew** /ˈhiː.bruː/ *adj* **Hebraic** /hɪˈbreɪ.ɪk/ *adj*: *Hebraic studies*

H

heck /hek/ *exclamation, noun* INFORMAL an expression of usually slight annoyance or surprise, or a way of adding force to a statement, question, etc: *Oh heck! It's later than I thought.* ○ *Where the heck have you been?*

• **a heck of a** INFORMAL used for emphasis; a very: *It's a heck of a long way to the nearest shop from here.*

• **what the heck** INFORMAL used to say that you will do something although you know you should not do it: *The doctor said I shouldn't drink, but what the heck.*

heckle /ˈhek.l̩/ *verb* [I or T] to interrupt a public speech or performance with loud unfriendly statements or questions: *A few angry locals started heckling (the speaker).* **heckler** /ˈhek.ləʳ/ [US] /-lɚ/ *noun* [C] *The heckler was ejected from the hall by a couple of police officers.*

hectare /ˈhek.teəʳ/ [US] /-ter/ *noun* [C] a unit of measurement of an area of land (10,000 m^2)

hectic /ˈhek.tɪk/ *adj* full of activity; very busy and fast: *a hectic schedule* ○ *The area has become a haven for people tired of the hectic **pace** of city life.*

hector /ˈhek.təʳ/ [US] /-tɚ/ *verb* [T] DISAPPROVING to talk and behave towards someone in a loud and unpleasantly forceful way, especially in order to get them to act or think as you want them to **hectoring** /ˈhek.tᵊr.ɪŋ/ [US] /-tɚ-/ *adj*: *He had a loud, hectoring manner.*

he'd /hiːd/ *short form of* **1** he had: *He'd already spent all his money by the second day of the trip.* **2** he would: *He'd be able to do it, if anyone could.*

hedge [BUSHES] /hedʒ/ *noun* [C] a line of bushes or small trees planted very close together, especially along the edge of a garden, field or road: *a privet hedge*

hedge [PROTECTION] /hedʒ/ *noun* [C] a way of protecting, controlling or limiting something: *She'd made some overseas investments as a hedge **against** rising inflation in this country.*

hedge /hedʒ/ *verb* **1** [T + adv or prep; usually passive] to limit something severely: *We've got permission, but it's hedged **about/around with** strict conditions.* **2** [I] to try to avoid giving an answer or taking any action: *Stop hedging and tell me what you really think.*

• **hedge *your* bets** to protect yourself against loss by supporting more than one possible result or both sides in a competition: *They're hedging their bets and keeping up contacts with both companies.*

hedgehog /ˈhedʒ.hɒg/ [US] /-hɑːg/ *noun* [C] a small brown mammal with a protective covering of spines on its back

hedgerow /ˈhedʒ.rəʊ/ [US] /-roʊ/ *noun* [C] a line of different types of bushes and small trees growing very close together, especially between fields or along the sides of roads in the countryside

hedge-trimmers /ˈhedʒˌtrɪm.əz/ [US] /-ɚz/ *plural noun* a tool with which you cut a garden hedge to keep it tidy

hedonism /ˈhed.ᵊn.ɪ.zᵊm/ *noun* [U] living and behaving in ways that mean you get as much pleasure out of life as possible, according to the belief that the most important thing in life is to enjoy yourself **hedonist** /ˈhed.ᵊn.ɪst/ *noun* [C] **hedonistic** /ˌhed.ᵊnˈɪs.tɪk/ *adj*

the heebie-jeebies /ðəˌhiː.bɪˈjiː.biz/ *plural noun* INFORMAL strong feelings of fear or anxiety: *Don't start talking about ghosts – they **give** me the heebie-jeebies.*

heed /hiːd/ *verb* [T] FORMAL to pay attention to something, especially advice or a warning: *The airline has been criticized for failing to heed **advice/warnings** about lack of safety routines.*

heed /hiːd/ *noun* [U] FORMAL *The company **took** no heed **of*** (= did not consider) *public opposition to the plans.*

heedless /ˈhiːd.ləs/ *adj* FORMAL not giving attention to a risk or possible difficulty: *Heedless destruction of the rainforests is contributing to global warming.* ○ *Journalists insisted on getting to the front line of the battle, heedless **of** the risks.* **heedlessly** /ˈhiːd.lə.sli/ *adv*

hee-haw /ˈhiː.hɔː/ [US] /-hɑː/ *noun* [C] the sound that a donkey makes

heel [BODY PART] /hɪəl/ *noun* [C] **1** the rounded back part of the foot ➲See also **well-heeled**. ➲See picture **The Body** on page Centre 5 **2** the part of a sock or shoe which covers the heel of the foot **3** the raised part at the back of a shoe, under your heel **4** the raised part of the palm of your hand nearest the wrist **5** the end part of something, especially of a loaf of bread, that is usually left after the rest has been eaten or used

• **bring/call *sth/sb* to heel 1** to order a dog to come close to you **2** to force someone to obey you

• **come to heel** If a person or organization comes to heel, they agree to obey, usually because they have been forcefully persuaded to do so.

• **under the heel of *sth or sb*** DISAPPROVING completely controlled by something or someone: *This country would never submit to living under the heel of a foreign power.*

• **hard/hot on *sb's* heels** following someone very closely: *She ran down the steps with a group of journalists hard on her heels.*

• **come/follow hard/hot on the heels of *sth*** to happen very soon after something: *For Walter, disaster followed hard on the heels of his initial success.*

• **take to *your* heels** to quickly run away: *When they saw the soldiers coming, they took to their heels.*

heel /hɪəl/ *exclamation* said to a dog to order it to come and stand next to you or to walk close beside you as you walk

heel /hɪəl/ *verb* [T] **1** to repair the heel of a shoe **2** SPECIALIZED In rugby, to heel the ball is to kick it backwards with the heel.

heel [PERSON] /hɪəl/ *noun* [C] OLD-FASHIONED INFORMAL a person who treats other people badly and unfairly: *I felt like a real heel when I saw how I'd upset her.*

heel-bar /ˈhɪəl.bɑːʳ/ [US] /-bɑːr/ *noun* [C] UK a small shop which repairs shoes, especially while a customer waits

heft /heft/ *verb* [T usually + adv or prep] to lift, hold or carry something heavy using your hands: *I watched him heft the heavy sack onto his shoulder.*

hefty /ˈhef.ti/ *adj* large in amount, size, force, etc: *a hefty bill/fine* ○ *Her salary will go up by a hefty 10%.* ○ *a hefty woman with dyed blond hair*

hegemony /hɪˈgem.ə.ni/ /-ˈdʒem-/ [US] /hɪˈdʒem.ə-/ /ˈhedʒ.ə.moʊ-/ *noun* [U] FORMAL (especially of countries) the position of being the strongest and most powerful and therefore able to control others: *The three nations competed for regional hegemony.* **hegemonic** /ˌheg.ɪˈmɒn.ɪk/ /ˌhedʒ-/ [US] /ˌhedʒɪˈmɑː.nɪk/ *adj*

heifer /ˈhef.əʳ/ [US] /-ɚ/ *noun* [C] a young cow, especially one that has not yet given birth to a CALF (= baby cow)

heigh-ho /ˈheɪ.həʊ/ [US] /-hoʊ/ *exclamation* an expression of tiredness or of acceptance of something

height /haɪt/ *noun* [C or U] **1** the distance from the top to the bottom of something, or the quality of being tall: *The sheer height of New York's skyscrapers is so impressive.* ○ *She's about average height* (= neither short nor tall). **2** the particular distance that something is above a surface: *The bullet entered the body at chest height.*

• **the height of *sth* 1** the time when a situation or event is strongest or most full of activity: *August is the height of the tourist season.* ○ *At the height of the violence/crisis we were left without any help.* **2** an extreme example of something: *the height of fashion* **3** the time when you are most successful in what you do: *She was **at** the* *height of her career when he first met her.*

heights /haɪts/ *plural noun* **1** high places, or the top of hills: *Don't go up the tower if you're* ***afraid of*** *heights.* ○ *Machine guns were mounted along the heights behind the town.* **2** a high level of success: *He* ***reached*** *the heights* ***of*** *his profession at the age of 35.* ○ *Share prices* ***scaled*** *new heights yesterday.* ○ *Her husband* ***rose to*** *the* ***dizzy/lofty*** *heights of transport minister.*

heighten /ˈhaɪ.tᵊn/ [US] /-ṱᵊn/ *verb* [I or T] to increase or make something increase, especially an emotion or effect: *The strong police presence only heightened the tension among the crowd.*

heinous /ˈhiː.nəs/ *adj* FORMAL very bad and shocking: *a heinous* ***crime***

heir /eəʳ/ [US] /er/ *noun* **1** [C] a person who will legally receive money, property or a title from another person, especially an older member of the same family, when that other person dies: *The guest of honour was the Romanoff heir* ***to*** *the throne of all Russia.* ○ *Despite having a large family, they still had no* ***son and*** *heir.* ➲See also **heiress**. **2** [C usually sing] someone who now has responsibility for dealing with a problem or situation that existed or was created earlier: *The French finance minister is heir* ***to*** *a tradition of central control that goes back to Louis XIV's minister, Colbert.* **3** [C usually sing] someone who continues to do the work of someone important who has died or who has the same symbolic position as they had: *Imam Ali, the prophet's son-in-law, is regarded by Shia Muslims as the heir* ***to*** *Mohammed's spiritual authority.*

ˌheir apˈparent *noun* [C usually sing] **1** the person with the automatic right to legally receive all or most of the money, property, titles, etc. from another person when they die: *The Prince of Wales is the heir apparent* ***to*** *the throne.* **2** a person who seems certain to take the place of someone in power when they stop working

heiress /ˈeə.res/ [US] /ˈer.es/ *noun* [C] a woman or girl who will receive or already has received a lot of money, property or a title from another person, especially an older member of the same family, when that person dies: *the heiress* ***to*** *the throne* ○ *a Texan oil heiress* ➲See also **heir**.

heirloom /ˈeə.luːm/ [US] /ˈer-/ *noun* [C] a valuable object that has been given by older members of a family to younger members of the same family over many years: *This ring is a family heirloom.*

heist /haɪst/ *noun* [C] INFORMAL a crime in which valuable items are taken illegally and often violently from a place or person: *a $2 million jewellery heist*

held [HOLD] /held/ *past simple and past participle of* **hold**

held [KEPT] /held/ *adj* kept or maintained: *firmly held beliefs* ○ *widely held opinions*

helicopter /ˈhel.ɪˌkɒp.təʳ/ [US] /-ˌkɑːp.tɚ/ *noun* [C] a type of aircraft without wings, that has one or two sets of large blades which go round very fast on top. It can land and take off vertically and can stay in one place in the air: *The injured were ferried to hospital* ***by*** *helicopter.* ○ *a helicopter pilot* ➲See picture **Planes, Ships and Boats** on page Centre 14

helipad /ˈhel.ɪ.pæd/ *noun* [C] a place where a single helicopter can take off and land

heliport /ˈhel.ɪ.pɔːt/ [US] /-pɔːrt/ *noun* [C] an airport for helicopters

helium /ˈhiː.li.əm/ *noun* [U] a gas that is lighter than air, will not burn, is an element and is used in BALLOONS, AIRSHIPS and some types of lights

helix /ˈhiː.lɪks/ *noun* [C] *plural* **helices** SPECIALIZED a curve that goes around a central tube or cone shape in the form of a SPIRAL **helical** /ˈhiː.lɪ.kᵊl/ *adj*: *helical molecules* ○ *a helical structure*

hell [PLACE] /hel/ *noun* **1** [S or U] an extremely unpleasant or difficult place, situation or experience: *Work is* ***sheer*** *hell at the moment.* ○ *The last few months have been absolute hell.* ➲See also **hellhole**; **infernal**. **2** [S] (ALSO **Hell**) in some religions, the place where some people are believed to go after death to be punished forever for the bad things they have done during their lives: *I'll* ***go to*** *Hell for this*

• **hell on Earth** INFORMAL an extremely unpleasant place or situation: *Soldiers who survived the war described it as hell on Earth.*

• **all hell breaks loose** INFORMAL If all hell breaks loose, a situation suddenly becomes violent and noisy, especially with people arguing or fighting: *One policeman drew his gun and then suddenly all hell broke loose.*

• **go to hell and back** INFORMAL to live through an extremely unpleasant, difficult or painful experience: *I've been to hell and back over this court case.*

• **come hell or high water** INFORMAL If you say that you will do something come hell or high water, you mean that you are determined to do it, despite any difficulties that there might be: *I'll get you to the airport by noon, come hell or high water!*

• **for the hell of it** INFORMAL If you do something for the hell of it, you do it without having any particular purpose or desire, but usually for amusement: *I didn't know what I wanted to do, so I drove my van round Europe, just for the hell of it.*

• **from hell** INFORMAL used to say that someone or something is extremely bad: *Now Miranda – she was the housemate from hell.* ○ *Poor Ann has the mother-in-law from hell.*

• **give** ***sb*** **hell** INFORMAL **1** If someone gives you hell, they criticize you severely: *She gave me hell for being twenty minutes late.* **2** If something gives you hell, it causes you a lot of pain: *These new shoes are giving me hell.*

• **go to hell** INFORMAL used to angrily tell someone to stop talking and go away: *"Anyway, it's your own fault." "Oh, go to hell!"*

• **hell for leather** OLD-FASHIONED INFORMAL If you go, run, ride, etc. hell for leather, you go as fast as you can.

• **when hell freezes over** OLD-FASHIONED INFORMAL If you say that something will happen when hell freezes over, you mean that it will never happen.

• **there'll be hell to pay** INFORMAL something you say which means someone will be very angry if something happens: *There'll be hell to pay if she doesn't get the money in time.*

• **make** ***sb's*** **life hell** (ALSO **make life hell for** ***sb***) INFORMAL to cause a lot of problems for someone and make them very unhappy: *I worked for her for two years and she made my life hell.*

hell [EXPRESSION] /hel/ *exclamation, noun* [U] used to express anger or to add emphasis: *Oh hell, I've forgotten my key!* ○ ***What the*** *hell was that noise?* ○ *We haven't got a* ***hope in*** *hell* (= we have no hope) *of meeting such a tight deadline.*

• **hell of a, helluva** INFORMAL extremely, or extremely big: *It's a/one hell of a big decision to take.* ○ *The house was in a/one hell of a mess.*

• **(as) ... as hell** INFORMAL used to emphasize a description of an unpleasant characteristic: *She's really quite unpleasant about other people and she's as mean as hell.*

• **get the hell out of** ***somewhere*** INFORMAL to leave a place quickly: *Let's get the hell out of here, before any shooting starts.*

• **like hell** INFORMAL **1** very much: *We ran like hell.* ○ *We worked like hell to finish the job.* ○ *It hurt like hell.* **2** certainly not: *"Try to be polite to him." "Like hell I will!"*

• **annoy/frighten/scare, etc. the hell out of** ***sb*** INFORMAL to make someone extremely annoyed/frightened, etc: *He jumped out from behind a wall and scared the hell out of her.*

• **beat the hell out of** ***sb*** INFORMAL to hit someone repeatedly with great force

• **the hell** ***you*** **do** US INFORMAL used to tell someone that you do not believe what they have said or that you will not allow them to do what they want: *"I don't need your advice, Gene, I know what's good for me." "The hell you do!"*

• **to hell** INFORMAL If you wish or hope to hell that something is true or that it will happen, you are saying how strongly you want it to be true or to happen: *I hope to hell she hasn't missed that plane.*

• **what the hell** INFORMAL said when you suddenly realize that your plan is not important to you and that you will do something else: *I was supposed to be working this* *evening but what the hell – I'll see you in the pub in half an hour.*

• **be hell-bent on sth** INFORMAL to be extremely determined to do something, without caring about risks or possible dangerous results: *He was hell-bent on revenge.*

he'll /hiːl/ *short form of* he will: *He'll be there, don't worry.*

Hellenic /həˈlen.ɪk/ *adj* of or relating to the ancient or modern Greeks, and their history, art, etc.

hellhole /ˈhel.həʊl/ [US] /-hoʊl/ *noun* [C] INFORMAL an extremely unpleasant place

hellish /ˈhel.ɪʃ/ *adj* very bad or unpleasant: *a hellish experience*

hellishly /ˈhel.ɪʃ.li/ *adv*: *a hellishly* (= very unpleasantly) *busy week*

hello /helˈəʊ/ [US] /-ˈoʊ/ *exclamation, noun* **1** (UK ALSO **hallo, hullo**) used when meeting or greeting someone: *Hello, Paul. I haven't seen you for ages.* ○ *I know her vaguely – we've exchanged hellos a few times.* ○ *I just thought I'd call by and **say** hello.* ○ *And **a big** hello* (= welcome) *to all the parents who've come to see the show.* **2** something that is said at the beginning of a telephone conversation: *"Hello, I'd like some information about your flights to the USA, please."* **3** something that is said to attract someone's attention: *The front door was open so she walked inside and called out, "Hello! Is there anybody in?"* **4** INFORMAL said to someone who has just said or done something stupid, especially something that shows they are not noticing what is happening around them: *She asked me if I'd just arrived and I was like 'hello, I've been here for an hour.'* **5** OLD-FASHIONED an expression of surprise: *Hello, this is very strange – I know that man.*

hell's bells /ˌhelzˈbelz/ *exclamation* (UK ALSO **hell's teeth**) OLD-FASHIONED INFORMAL used to express anger or surprise: *Hell's bells, can't you do anything right?*

helluva /ˈhel.ə.və/ *adj, adv* (ALSO **hell of a**) INFORMAL extremely, or extremely big: *It's a helluva nice place.* ○ *We're going to have a helluva problem.*

helm /helm/ *noun* [C] the handle or wheel which controls the direction in which a ship or boat travels: *Who was **at** the helm when the collision occurred?*

• **at the helm** officially controlling an organization or company: *With Steve Lewis at the helm, we are certain of success.*

ˌ**take the** ˈ**helm** to start to officially control an organization or company

helmet /ˈhel.mət/ *noun* [C] a strong hard hat that covers and protects the head: *a crash helmet* ○ *a cycle helmet* ➲See picture **Hairstyles and Hats** on page Centre 8

helmeted /ˈhel.mə.tɪd/ [US] /-t̬ɪd/ *adj* wearing a helmet: *Helmeted, baton-wielding police forced back the crowd.*

helmsman /ˈhelmz.mən/ *noun* [C] a person who directs a ship or boat, using a handle or wheel

help [MAKE EASIER] /help/ *verb* **1** [I or T] to make it possible or easier for someone to do something, by doing part of the work yourself or by providing advice, money, support, etc: *How can I help you?* ○ *I wonder if you could help me – I'd like some information about flights to New Zealand.* ○ *My dad said he would help **with** the costs of* (= give part of the cost of) *buying a house.* ○ [+ obj + (*to*) infinitive] *The £10,000 loan from the bank helped her **(to)** start her own business.* ○ *I feel that learning English will help* (= improve) *my chances of promotion at work.* ○ *Nothing can help her now* (= Her situation is too bad for anyone to be able to improve it). ➲See also **helpline**. **2** [I or T] If something helps a difficult or painful situation, it improves it or makes it easier or less painful: *The morphine didn't seem to help (the pain).* **3** [+ (*to*) infinitive] If something or someone helps to do something, they are one of several reasons for it happening: *The drought has helped **(to)** make this a disastrous year for Somalia.*

• **can't/couldn't help** If you can't/couldn't help something, such as acting in a particular way or making a particular remark, you are/were not able to control or stop it: *It was awful, but I couldn't help laugh**ing**.* ○ *"Stop giggling!" "I can't help it!"* ○ *I can't help think**ing*** (= My true feeling is that) *she'd be better off without him.*

• **give/lend sb a helping hand** to help someone: *These tax cuts will give industry a helping hand.*

• **it can't be helped** used to say that an unpleasant or painful situation, or an unwanted duty cannot be avoided and must be accepted: *I really didn't want to go away this weekend but, oh well, it can't be helped.*

• **God help sb** (ALSO **heaven help sb**) used to give force to a statement of the danger or seriousness of a situation or action: *God help us if they attack now while we're still unprepared.*

• **so help me (God)** FORMAL used to make a promise in a very formal and serious way: *Everything I have said is true, so help me God.*

Help! /help/ *exclamation* shouted by a person who is asking for someone to come and save them from a dangerous situation

help /help/ *noun* **1** [U] when someone helps another person: *Do you need any help with those boxes?* ○ *Her parents gave her some help **with** her bank loan* (= paid some of it). **2** [S] something or someone that helps: *Having a word processor would be a help.* ○ *He was a great help **(to me)** while my husband was away.* **3** [C] someone, usually a woman, who is employed to clean your house and do other small jobs: *a home help*

• **there's no help for it** MAINLY UK there is no other choice in this situation: *If you catch them stealing again, there'll be no help for it **but*** (= except) ***to** call the police.*

helper /ˈhel.pəʳ/ [US] /-pɚ/ *noun* [C] someone who helps with an activity: *The teachers make great use of volunteer helpers.*

COMMON LEARNER ERROR

help someone **with** something

When you are are talking about **helping** someone **with** a problem, task, etc. remember to use the preposition 'with'.

I try to help my mother with the housework and the shopping.

~~*I try to help my mother the housework and the shopping.*~~

help [GIVE/TAKE] /help/ *verb* [T] to give something to someone or to take something for yourself: *"Might I have some more bread?" "Please, help **yourself**!"* ○ SLIGHTLY FORMAL *Shall I help you **to** some more soup?*

▲ **help (sb) out** *phrasal verb* [M] If you help out, you do a part of someone's work or give someone money: *Her parents helped (her) out with a £500 loan.*

ˈ**help** ˌ**desk** *noun* [C] a service which provides information and help to people using a computer NETWORK

helpful /ˈhelp.fᵊl/ *adj* willing to help, or useful: *She's such a pleasant, helpful child!* ○ *I'm sorry, I was only trying to be helpful.* ○ *He made several helpful suggestions.*

helpfully /ˈhelp.fᵊl.i/ *adv*: *The manufacturers helpfully provide an instruction manual.* **helpfulness** /ˈhelp.fᵊl.nəs/ *noun* [U]

helping /ˈhel.pɪŋ/ *noun* [C] an amount of food given to one person at one time: *a small/large helping **of** pasta*

helpless /ˈhel.pləs/ *adj* unable to do anything to help yourself or anyone else: *a helpless two-day-old baby* ○ *You feel so helpless because there's nothing you can do to make the child better.* ○ *The government is helpless **(to act) against** these crooks.* **helplessly** /ˈhel.plə.sli/ *adv*: *Unable to swim, he watched helplessly as the child struggled desperately in the water.* **helplessness** /ˈhel.plə.snəs/ *noun* [U] *I was overwhelmed by a feeling of helplessness as I watched her being wheeled into the operating theatre.*

helpline /ˈhelp.laɪn/ *noun* [C] a telephone service providing advice and comfort to worried or unhappy people: *A new helpline is now available for people trying to stop smoking.*

ˈ**help** ˌ**screen** *noun* [C] information or instructions which you can ask the computer to show you if you are having difficulty using the computer

helter-skelter [QUICKLY] /ˌhel.təˈskel.təʳ/ [US] /-t̬ɚˈskel.t̬ɚ/ *adv* quickly and in all directions: *People were screaming and running helter-skelter down the steps to escape the flames.*

helter-skelter [STRUCTURE] /ˌhel.təˈskel.təʳ/ [US] /-t̬ɚˈskel.t̬ɚ/ *noun* [C] UK a tall structure at a fair which you slide down and around for enjoyment

hem /hem/ *noun* [C] the edge of a piece of cloth, such as the bottom edge of a skirt or dress, which is folded over and sewn so that it does not develop loose threads: *I **took the** hem **up/let the** hem **down**.*

hem /hem/ *verb* [T] **-mm-** to sew a hem on a piece of clothing or cloth: *I need to hem those curtains.*

▲ **hem *sb* in** *phrasal verb* [M] to surround someone and prevent them from moving or doing what they want to do: *When they reached Oxford Circus, the demonstrators were hemmed in by the police.*

he-man /ˈhiː.mæn/ *noun* [C usually sing] *INFORMAL* a man who is very strong and who likes to show everyone how strong he is

hematology /ˌhiː.məˈtɒl.ə.dʒi/ [US] /-ˈtɑː.lə-/ *noun* [U] *MAINLY US FOR* **haematology**

hemisphere /ˈhem.ɪ.sfɪəʳ/ [US] /-sfɪr/ *noun* [C] half of a sphere, especially the Earth: *the northern hemisphere*

hemline /ˈhem.laɪn/ *noun* [C] the length of a skirt or dress, or the lower edge of a skirt or dress: *In the 1960s hemlines suddenly shot up with the introduction of the miniskirt.*

hemlock /ˈhem.lɒk/ [US] /-lɑːk/ *noun* [U] a type of poison made from a plant which has small white flowers and divided leaves

hemoglobin /ˌhiː.məˈgləʊ.bɪn/ [US] /-gloʊ-/ *noun* [U] *MAINLY US FOR* **haemoglobin**

hemophilia /ˌhiː.məˈfɪl.i.ə/ *noun* [U] *MAINLY US FOR* **haemophilia**

hemorrhage /ˈhem.ᵊr.ɪdʒ/ [US] /-ɚ-/ *noun* [C], *verb* [I] *US FOR* **haemorrhage**

hemorrhoids /ˈhem.ᵊr.ɔɪdz/ [US] /-ɚ-/ *plural noun MAINLY US FOR* **haemorrhoids**

hemp /hemp/ *noun* [U] a family of plants, some of which are used to make rope and strong rough cloth and others of which are used to obtain the drug CANNABIS

hen /hen/ *noun* [C] **1** an adult female chicken which is often kept for its eggs, or the female of any bird ➲See picture **Animals and Birds** on page Centre 4 **2** *SCOTTISH ENGLISH INFORMAL* used as a way of addressing a woman or girl, especially someone that you like: *"Are you not feeling too good, hen?"*

hence [THEREFORE] /hents/ *adv FORMAL* that is the reason or explanation for; therefore: *His mother was Italian, hence his name – Luca.*

hence [FROM NOW] /hents/ *adv FORMAL* from this time: *The project will be completed at the end of the decade, two years hence.*

henceforth /ˌhentsˈfɔːθ/ [US] /-ˈfɔːrθ/ *adv* (*ALSO* **henceforward**) *FORMAL OR LEGAL* starting from this time: *Henceforth, the said building shall be the property of Brendan Duggan.*

henchman /ˈhentʃ.mən/ *noun* [C] *DISAPPROVING* someone who does unpleasant or illegal things for a powerful person: *Like other dictators, he tried to distance himself from the dirty deeds carried out by his henchmen.*

henna /ˈhen.ə/ *noun* [U] a reddish brown DYE, used mainly for colouring the hair and skin

henna /ˈhen.ə/ *verb* [T] **hennaing, hennaed, hennaed** to put henna on the hair or skin in order to change its colour: *Is her hair hennaed or is that a natural red?*

ˈhen ˌnight *noun* [C] (*ALSO* **hen party**) *UK* a party for women only, usually one held for a woman before she is married ➲Compare **stag night/party**.

henpecked /ˈhen.pekt/ *adj DISAPPROVING* A henpecked man is controlled by and a little frightened of a woman, especially his wife.

hepatic /hepˈæt.ɪk/ [US] /-ˈæt̬-/ *adj SPECIALIZED* relating to the liver

hepatitis /ˌhep.əˈtaɪ.tɪs/ [US] /-t̬ɪs/ *noun* [U] a serious disease of the liver. There are three main types of hepatitis: hepatitis A, B and C.

heptagon /ˈhep.tə.gᵊn/ [US] /-gɑːn/ *noun* [C] a shape which has seven straight sides**heptagonal** /hepˈtæg.ᵊn.ᵊl/ *adj*

heptathlon /hepˈtæθ.lɒn/ [US] /-lɑːn/ *noun* [C] a competition in which women athletes compete in seven sports events ➲Compare **biathlon**; **decathlon**; **pentathlon**.

heptathlete /hepˈtæθ.liːt/ *noun* [C]

her *STRONG* /hɜːʳ/ [US] /hɝː/, *WEAK* /həʳ/ /əʳ/ [US] /hɚ/ /ɚ/ *pronoun, determiner* **1** (belonging to or connected with) a woman, girl or female animal that has just been mentioned or is known about: *If your sister's around, bring her too.* ○ *I'll see if Louisa will bring her guitar to the party.* ○ *I gave her the letter.* ○ *I don't know why she quit her job.* ➲See also **hers**. **2** *SLIGHTLY OLD-FASHIONED* used to refer to a country, a boat or a car: *The boat sank with all her crew.* ✻ NOTE: Many people now prefer to use 'it' or 'its' instead of 'her' in this sense. **3 her own** used to emphasize that something belongs to or is connected with a particular woman or girl and not anyone else: *She got her **very** own pony as a birthday present when she was eleven.*

herself /hɜːˈself/ [US] /hɝː-/ *pronoun* **1** the reflexive form of the pronoun *her*: *She kept telling herself that nothing was wrong.* ○ *My mother would worry herself to death if she knew what I was doing.* **2** used to give special attention to a female noun or to make clear which female person or animal is being referred to: *She decorated the cake herself.* ○ *She herself admitted that it was wrong.* **3 (all) by herself** If a woman or girl does something by herself, she does it alone or without help from anyone else: *She lives by herself in an enormous house.* ○ *Holly's only three but she wrote her name all by herself.* **4 (all) to herself** for her use only: *Mum's got the house to herself this weekend.* **5 not be/seem herself** If a woman or girl is not/does not seem herself, she does not seem as happy as usual: *Is Michelle all right? She doesn't seem quite herself at the moment.*

• **in herself** *UK INFORMAL* used when describing or asking about a woman's state of mind, when she is physically ill: *I know she's got back trouble but how is she in herself?*

herald /ˈher.ᵊld/ *verb* [T] *FORMAL* to be a sign that something important, and often good, is starting to happen, or to make something publicly known, especially by celebrating or praising it: *The president's speech heralds a new era in foreign policy.* ○ *This drug has been heralded **as** a major breakthrough in the fight against breast cancer.*

herald /ˈher.ᵊld/ *noun* [C] **1** *FORMAL* a sign that something will happen, change, etc: *If this first opera of the season is a herald* (= sign) ***of** what is to come, we can expect great things.* **2** in the past, a person who delivered important messages and made announcements

heraldry /ˈher.ᵊl.dri/ *noun* [U] the study of COATS OF ARMS and the history of the families which they belong to

heraldic /herˈæl.dɪk/ *adj*: *a heraldic banner*

herb /hɜːb/ [US] /ɝːb/ *noun* [C] a type of plant whose leaves are used in cooking to give flavour to particular dishes, or which are used in making medicine: *dried/fresh herbs* ○ *Basil, oregano, thyme and rosemary are all herbs.* ○ *A large range of herbs **and spices** are used in Indian cookery.*

herbal /ˈhɜː.bᵊl/ [US] /ˈɝː-/ *adj* relating to or made from herbs: *herbal tea* ○ *herbal cigarettes/remedies*

herbalist /ˈhɜː.bᵊl.ɪst/ [US] /ˈɝː-/ *noun* [C] a person who grows or sells herbs for use as medicine

herby /ˈhɜː.bi/ [US] /ˈɝː-/ *adj INFORMAL* tasting or smelling of herbs: *This salad dressing is nice and herby.*

herbaceous /hɜːˈbeɪ.ʃəs/ [US] /hɚ-/ *adj SPECIALIZED* (of plants) soft and not woody

herˌbaceous ˈborder *noun* [C] a narrow strip of land in a garden which is planted with different types of flowering plants that mainly live for more than two years

herbicide /ˈhɜː.bɪ.saɪd/ [US] /ˈhɝː-/ *noun* [C or U] a chemical which is used to destroy plants, especially weeds ➲Compare **insecticide**; **pesticide**.

herbivore /ˈhɜː.bɪ.vɔːʳ/ [US] /ˈhɝː.bə.vɔːr/ *noun* [C] an animal that eats only plants: *Cows and sheep are herbivores.* ➲Compare **carnivore**. **herbivorous** /hɜːˈbɪv.ᵊr.əs/ [US] /hɝːˈbɪv.ɚ-/ *adj*

herculean /ˌhɜː.kjʊˈliː.ən/ [US] /ˌhɝː-/ *adj* needing great strength and determination: *a herculean **effort*** ○ *She faces the herculean **task** of bringing up four children single-handedly.*

herd /hɜːd/ [US] /hɝːd/ *group noun* [C] **1** a large group of animals of the same type that live and feed together: *a*

H

herd of cattle/elephants/goats **2** MAINLY DISAPPROVING a large group of people that is considered together as a group and not separately: *Poor Janine – she just follows the herd* (= does what all the other people are doing).

herd /hɜːd/ US /hɜːd/ *verb* **1** [I or T; + adv or prep] to make animals move together as a group: *A old woman was herding the goats up the mountainside.* **2** [T + adv or prep] MAINLY DISAPPROVING to make people move somewhere as a group, often with force or against their wishes: *The football fans complained that they had been herded into a small alley.*

herd instinct *noun* [S] DISAPPROVING the tendency to act like everyone else without considering the reason why

herdsman /ˈhɜːdz.mən/ US /ˈhɜːdz-/ *noun* [C] a man who takes care of a large group of animals of the same type

here /hɪəʳ/ US /hɪr/ *adv* **1** in, at, or to this place: *I've lived here for about two years.* ○ *I like it here.* ○ *London is only 50 miles from here.* ○ **Come** here – *I've got something to show you.* ○ *How long are you over here* (= in this country)? **2** used at the beginning of a statement to introduce someone or something: *Here's Fiona – let me introduce you to her.* ○ *Here's the book I said I'd lend you.* **3** used to show that someone has arrived or that something has started: *Here they are! We thought you'd never come!* ○ *Here we are* (= We have arrived) – *I said it wouldn't take more than half an hour by car.* ○ *Now that Christmas is here* (= has begun), *I might as well give up my diet.* **4** describes someone or something that is near you: *I don't know anything about this, but I'm sure my colleague here can help you.* ○ *It says here* (= in this piece of writing) *that she was born in 1943.* **5** now: *Shall we break here and have a coffee?* ○ *Where do we go/Where do we take it from here?* (= What should we do next?)

• **here (you are)** used when giving something to someone: *"Could you pass the sugar, please?" "Here you are."* ○ *Here, try some of this – it's delicious!*

• **the here and now** the present time: *Most people can't be bothered thinking about their retirement – they're too busy concentrating on the here and now.*

• **here and there** in different places: *There were a few books here and there, but apart from that the room was quite bare.*

• **Here goes!** (US ALSO **Here goes nothing!**) INFORMAL said just before you do something brave or something that you have never done before: *Well, I've never ridden a motorbike before, so here goes!*

• **here we go** INFORMAL a phrase often sung repeatedly by British football crowds when their team is successful

• **here we go (again)** INFORMAL said when something bad starts happening again: *Oh, here we go again! Claude's just asked to borrow some more money from me.* ○ *Here we go again – moan, moan, moan!*

• **here's to ...** said when asking a group of people to hold up their glasses and then drink as an expression of good wishes to someone: *Here's to the happy couple!*

• **Here today, gone tomorrow.** SAYING said about something which lasts only a short time: *A lot of new Internet companies are here today and gone tomorrow.*

hereabouts UK /ˌhɪə.rəˈbaʊts/ US /ˌhɪr.ə-/ *adv* (US **hereabout**) in this area; near this place: *Any trouble hereabouts is swiftly dealt with by the police.*

hereafter IN THE FUTURE /ˌhɪəˈrɑːf.təʳ/ US /ˌhɪrˈæf.tə-/ *adv* (ALSO **hereinafter**) FORMAL OR LEGAL starting from this time; in the future: *Elizabeth Gaskell's novel 'Ruth' will hereafter be cited within the text as EG.*

the hereafter AFTER DEATH *noun* [S] FORMAL life after death: *She had a firm conviction that they would meet again in the hereafter.*

hereby /ˌhɪəˈbaɪ/ US /ˌhɪr-/ *adv* FORMAL OR LEGAL with these words or with this action: *I hereby pronounce you man and wife.*

hereditary /həˈred.ɪ.tri/ *adj* (of characteristics or diseases) passed from the genes of a parent to a child, or (of titles and positions in society) passed from parent to a child as a right: *a hereditary disease* ○ *Depression is often hereditary.* ○ *It is a hereditary title, so Mark Howard will become Sir Mark Howard on his father's death.*

hereditary peer *noun* [C] a person who has received a particular title and who can give it to their child

heredity /həˈred.ə.ti/ *noun* [U] the process by which characteristics are passed from a parent to their child through the genes: *Diet and exercise can influence a person's weight, but heredity is also a factor.*

herein /ˌhɪəˈrɪn/ US /ˌhɪr.ɪn/ *adv* FORMAL OR LEGAL in this: *The people have no faith in their government, and herein lies the root of the problem.*

hereinafter /ˌhɪə.rɪnˈɑːf.təʳ/ US /ˌhɪr.ɪnˈæf.tə-/ *adv* FORMAL OR LEGAL **hereafter**

heresy /ˈher.ə.si/ *noun* **1** [C or U] (the act of having) an opinion or belief that is the opposite of or against what is the official or popular opinion, or an action which shows that you have no respect for the official opinion: *Radical remarks like this amount to heresy for most members of the Republican party.* ○ *She committed the heresy of playing a Madonna song on a classical music station.* **2** [U] a belief which is against the principles of a particular religion: *He was burned at the stake in the fifteenth century for heresy.*

heretic /ˈher.ə.tɪk/ *noun* [C] a person who is guilty of heresy **heretical** /həˈret.ɪ.kəl/ US /-ˈret̬-/ *adj*: *Her belief that a split would be good for the party was regarded as heretical.*

hereto /ˌhɪəˈtuː/ US /ˌhɪr-/ *adv* FORMAL OR LEGAL to this matter or document: *You will find attached hereto the text of the Treaty on European Union.*

heretofore /ˌhɪə.tʊˈfɔːʳ/ US /ˌhɪr.tʊˈfɔːr/ *adv* FORMAL OR LEGAL before this point in time; previously

hereupon /ˌhɪə.rəˈpɒn/ US /ˌhɪr.əˈpɑːn/ *adv* FORMAL at this point in time

herewith /ˌhɪəˈwɪð/ /-ˈwɪθ/ US /ˌhɪr-/ *adv* FORMAL OR LEGAL together with this letter or other official written material: *I enclose three documents herewith.*

heritage /ˈher.ɪ.tɪdʒ/ US /-t̬ɪdʒ/ *noun* [U] features belonging to the culture of a particular society, such as traditions, languages or buildings, which still exist from the past and which have a historical importance: *These monuments are a vital part of the **cultural** heritage of South America.*

heritage-listed building /ˌher.ɪ.tɪdʒˌlɪs.tɪdˈbɪl.dɪŋ/ US /-t̬ɪdʒ-/ *noun* [C] AUS FOR **listed building**

hermaphrodite /hɜːˈmæf.rə.daɪt/ US /hɜː-/ *noun* [C] a plant, animal or person with both male and female sex organs

hermetic /hɜːˈmet.ɪk/ US /hɚˈmet̬-/ *adj* **1** SPECIALIZED (of a container) so tightly closed that no air can leave or enter: *a hermetic seal* **2** FORMAL If a particular group is hermetic, the people who live within it rarely communicate with those who live outside it: *He entered the hermetic world of the monastery at a young age.*

hermetically sealed /hɜːˌmet.ɪ.kli'siːld/ US /hɚˌmet̬-/ *adj* **1** SPECIALIZED describes a container or space which is so tightly closed that no air can leave or enter it **2** DISAPPROVING separated and protected from very different conditions outside, in an unnatural way: *We drove past a row of squalid shacks on the way to our hotel, where we slept in air-conditioned, hermetically sealed rooms.*

hermit /ˈhɜː.mɪt/ US /ˈhɜː-/ *noun* [C] a person who lives alone and apart from the rest of society, especially for religious reasons

hermitage /ˈhɜː.mɪ.tɪdʒ/ US /ˈhɜː.mɪ.t̬ɪdʒ/ *noun* [C] a place where a religious person lives on their own, apart from the rest of society

hernia /ˈhɜː.ni.ə/ US /ˈhɜː-/ *noun* [C] a medical condition in which an organ pushes through the muscle which surrounds it

hero PERSON (*plural* **heroes**) /ˈhɪə.rəʊ/ US /ˈhɪr.oʊ/ *noun* [C] **1** (FEMALE **heroine**) a person who is admired for having done something very brave or having achieved something great: *a war hero* ○ *He became a national hero for his part in the revolution.* ○ HUMOROUS *Graham says he'll take my parents to the airport at four o'clock in the morning – what a hero!* ⊃See also **anti-hero**. **2** (FEMALE **heroine**) the main male character in a book or film who is usually good: *the hero of her latest novel* **3** someone who you admire greatly: *Humphrey Bogart's my hero – I've seen every one of his films.*

heroic /hɪˈrəʊ.ɪk/ US /-ˈroʊ-/ adj **1** very brave or great: *a heroic act/deed* **2** INFORMAL If you make a heroic attempt or effort to do something, you try very hard to do it: *Despite Roz's heroic efforts to liven it up, the party was a disaster.*

heroically /hɪˈrəʊ.ɪ.kli/ US /-ˈroʊ/ adv bravely or with a lot of effort: *She fought heroically against the disease.*

heroics /hɪˈrəʊ.ɪks/ US /-ˈroʊ-/ plural noun MAINLY DISAPPROVING risky or foolish actions which are only done to make other people admire you: *I was in no mood for heroics after my fall and skied very slowly down the mountainside.*

heroism /ˈher.əʊ.ɪ.zᵊm/ US /-oʊ-/ noun [U] great bravery: *an act of heroism*

hero FOOD /ˈhɪə.rəʊ/ US /ˈhɪr.oʊ/ noun [C] plural **heroes** US a long thin sandwich filled with cold meat, cheese, salad, etc.

heroin /ˈher.əʊ.ɪn/ US /-oʊ-/ noun [U] a powerful illegal drug: *Heroin is obtained from morphine and is extremely addictive.* ○ *a heroin addict* ○ *She died from a heroin overdose.*

heroine /ˈher.əʊ.ɪn/ US /-oʊ-/ noun [C] ⊃See at **hero** PERSON.

heron /ˈher.ᵊn/ noun [C] plural **herons** or **heron** a large bird with long legs, a long neck and grey or white feathers that lives near water

ˈhero ˌworship noun [U] a feeling of extreme admiration for someone, imagining that they have qualities or abilities that are better than anyone else's **hero-worship** /ˈhɪə.rəʊˌwɜː.ʃɪp/ US /ˈhɪr.oʊˌwɜːˈ-/ verb [T] **-pp-** *She hero-worshipped her elder brother, and she was devastated when he died.*

herpes /ˈhɜː.piːz/ US /ˈhɜː-/ noun [U] an infectious disease which causes painful red spots to appear on the skin, especially on the lips or sexual organs

herring /ˈher.ɪŋ/ noun [C or U] plural **herrings** or **herring** a long silvery coloured fish which swims in large groups in the sea, or its flesh eaten as food

herringbone /ˈher.ɪŋ.bəʊn/ US /-boʊn/ noun [U] a pattern, used especially in cloth, which consists of rows of V shapes: *herringbone tweed*

hers /hɜːz/ US /hɜːz/ pronoun used to show that something belongs to or is connected with a woman, girl or female animal that has just been mentioned: *Nicky and I both have red hair but hers is lighter than mine.*

herself /hɜːˈself/ US /hɜː-/ pronoun ⊃See at **her**.

hertz (plural **hertz**) /hɜːts/ US /hɜːts/ noun [C] (WRITTEN ABBREVIATION **Hz**) a unit for measuring the number of CYCLES (= events that are repeated) which happen every second, used especially in ELECTRONICS ⊃See also **kilohertz**; **megahertz**.

he's /hiːz/ short form **1** he is: *He's a great guy.* **2** he has: *He's just bought a new digital camera.*

hesitate /ˈhez.ɪ.teɪt/ verb [I] to pause before you do or say something, often because you are uncertain or nervous about it: *She hesitated slightly before answering the inspector's question.* ○ *"Do you love me?" she asked. He hesitated and then said, "I'm not sure".* ○ [+ to infinitive] *If you need anything, don't hesitate to call me.*

hesitation /ˌhez.ɪˈteɪ.ʃᵊn/ noun [C or U] when you pause before doing something, especially because you are nervous or not certain: *After a slight hesitation, she began to speak.* ○ *Any hesitation on the part of the government will be seen as weakness.* ○ FORMAL *I have no hesitation in recommending Ms Shapur for the job.*

hesitant /ˈhez.ɪ.tᵊnt/ adj If you are hesitant, you do not do something immediately or quickly because you are nervous or not certain: *You seemed a bit hesitant about recommending that restaurant – is something wrong with it?* ○ *She gave me a hesitant smile.* **hesitantly** /ˈhez.ɪ.tᵊnt.li/ adv: *She approached the teacher hesitantly.* **hesitancy** /ˈhez.ɪ.tᵊnt.si/ noun [U] *The president is not known for his hesitancy in such matters.*

hessian UK /ˈhes.i.ən/ noun [U] (US **burlap**) a type of thick rough cloth used for items and coverings which must be strong

hetero /ˈhet.ᵊr.əʊ/ US /ˈhet̬.ɚ.oʊ/ noun [C] plural **heteros** INFORMAL FOR **heterosexual**

heterodox /ˈhet.ᵊr.ə.dɒks/ US /ˈhet̬.ɚ.ə.dɑːks/ adj FORMAL (of beliefs, ideas or activities) different and in opposition to generally accepted beliefs or standards: *His opinions have always been distinctly heterodox.* ⊃Compare **orthodox**. **heterodoxy** /ˈhet.ᵊr.ə.dɒk.si/ US /ˈhet̬.ɚ.ə.dɑːk-/ noun [U]

heterogeneous /ˌhet.ᵊr.əˈdʒiː.ni.əs/ US /ˌhet̬.ə.roʊ-/ adj FORMAL consisting of parts or things that are very different from each other: *Switzerland is a heterogeneous confederation of 26 self-governing cantons.* ⊃Compare **homogeneous**. **heterogeneity** /ˌhet.ᵊr.əʊ.dʒəˈneɪ.ɪ.ti/ US /ˌhet̬.ə.roʊ.dʒəˈneɪ.ə.ti/ noun [U] *Archaeological studies of the tombs have shown the heterogeneity of religious practices in the region.*

heterosexual /ˌhet.ᵊr.əʊˈsek.sju.ᵊl/ US /ˌhet̬.ə.roʊ-/ noun [C] (INFORMAL **hetero**) a person who is sexually attracted to people of the opposite sex ⊃Compare **bisexual**; **homosexual**. **heterosexual** /ˌhet.ᵊr.əʊˈsek.sju.ᵊl/ US /ˌhet̬.ə.roʊ-/ adj: *heterosexual sex/relationships* **heterosexually** /ˌhet.ᵊr.əʊˈsek.sju.ᵊl.i/ US /ˌhet̬.ə.roʊ-/ adv: *I don't think he's heterosexually inclined.* **heterosexuality** /ˌhet.ᵊr.əʊˌsek.sjuˈæl.ə.ti/ US /ˌhet̬.ə.roʊˌsek.ʃu-ˈæl.ə.ti/ noun [U]

het up /ˌhetˈʌp/ US /ˌhet̬-/ adj [after v] UK INFORMAL anxious or angry and not calm: *There's no need to get so het up about a few dirty dishes in the sink!*

heuristic /hjʊəˈrɪs.tɪk/ adj SPECIALIZED (of a method of teaching) allowing students to learn by discovering things themselves and learning from their own experiences rather than by telling them things

hew /hjuː/ verb [T] **hewed**, **hewed** or **hewn** to cut a large piece out of rock, stone or another hard material in a rough way: *The monument was hewn out of the side of a mountain.*

hex /heks/ noun [C] US INFORMAL an evil spell, bringing bad luck and trouble: *Someone's put a hex on my computer this morning – it keeps on crashing.*

hexagon /ˈhek.sə.gən/ US /-gɑːn/ noun [C] a shape which has six straight sides **hexagonal** /hekˈsæg.ᵊn.ᵊl/ adj: *a hexagonal building/object*

hey /heɪ/ exclamation INFORMAL used as a way of attracting someone's attention, sometimes in a way which is not very polite: *Hey! What are you doing with my car?* ○ *Hey, are you guys coming to Angela's party?*

heyday /ˈheɪ.deɪ/ noun [C usually sing] the most successful or popular period of someone or something: *In their heyday, they sold as many records as all the other groups in the country put together.*

hey presto UK /ˌheɪˈpres.təʊ/ US /-toʊ/ exclamation (US **presto**) INFORMAL said when something appears or happens so quickly or easily that it seems to be magic: *You put your money in the machine and, hey presto, the coffee comes out!*

HHOK, **hhok** INTERNET ABBREVIATION FOR ha ha only kidding: used in an e-mail or in a discussion in a CHAT ROOM to show that you have written something that is not true and is a joke

hi /haɪ/ exclamation INFORMAL used as an informal greeting, usually to people who you know: *Hi, there!* ○ *Hi, how're you doing?*

hiatus /haɪˈeɪ.təs/ US /-t̬əs/ noun [C usually sing] FORMAL a short pause in which nothing happens or is said, or a space where something is missing: *The company expects to resume production of the vehicle again after a two-month hiatus.*

hibernate /ˈhaɪ.bə.neɪt/ US /-bɚ-/ verb [I] (of some animals) to spend the winter sleeping: *The turtle hibernates in a shallow burrow for six months of the year.* **hibernation** /ˌhaɪ.bəˈneɪ.ʃᵊn/ US /-bɚ-/ noun [U] *Bears go into hibernation in the autumn.*

hibiscus /hɪˈbɪs.kəs/ noun [C] a tropical plant or bush with large brightly coloured flowers

hiccup NOISE, **hiccough** /ˈhɪk.ʌp/ noun [C usually pl] a loud noise made in the throat caused by a sudden uncontrollable tightening of a muscle just below the chest, usually happening repeatedly over a short period
the hiccups, the hiccoughs plural noun a series of hiccups: *I've got the hiccups.* ○ *an attack of the hiccups* **hiccup** /ˈhɪk.ʌp/ verb [I] **-p-** or **-pp-** *I can't stop hiccuping – does anyone know a good cure?*

hiccup PROBLEM, **hiccough** /ˈhɪk.ʌp/ *noun* [C] a problem which delays or interrupts something for a while, but which does not usually cause serious difficulties: *We've had one or two slight hiccups, but progress has generally been quite steady.*

hick /hɪk/ *noun* [C] *US INFORMAL DISAPPROVING* a person from the countryside who is considered to be stupid and lacking experience: *a hick town* (= a small town which is a long way from a city)

hickey /ˈhɪk.i/ *US noun* [C] (*UK* **love bite**) a temporary red mark on someone's skin, often their neck, where someone has sucked or bitten it as a sexual act

hickory /ˈhɪk.ər.i/ ⓤ /-ɚ-/ *noun* [C or U] a small tree from North America or East Asia which has edible nuts, or the hard wood from this tree

'hickory ,chips *plural noun* small pieces of hickory wood used as a fuel for a BARBECUE (= a method of cooking outside) which give food a special taste

hicksville /ˈhɪks.vɪl/ *noun* [U] *US INFORMAL DISAPPROVING* a small town or village which is not interesting and not modern

,hidden a'genda *noun* [C] a secret reason for doing something: [+ *to* infinitive] *The prime minister denied that the new visa requirements were part of a hidden agenda to reduce immigration.*

hide OUT OF VIEW /haɪd/ *verb* **hid**, **hidden** [I or T] **1** to put something or someone in a place where they cannot be seen or found, or to put yourself somewhere where you cannot be seen or found: *She used to hide her diary under her pillow.* ○ *A kilo of heroin was found hidden inside the lining of the suitcase.* ○ *I like wearing sunglasses – I feel I can hide behind them.* **2** [T] to prevent something from being seen: *He tries to hide his bald patch by sweeping his hair over to one side.* **3** [T] to not show an emotion: *She tried to hide her disappointment at not getting the promotion.* **4** [T] If you hide information from someone, you do not permit that person to know it: *I feel sure there's something about her past that she's trying to hide from me.*
• **Don't hide your light under a bushel.** *SAYING* said to advise someone not to keep their good qualities and abilities secret from other people

hide *UK* /haɪd/ *noun* [C] (*US* **blind**) a place where people can watch wild animals or birds without being noticed by them

hiding /ˈhaɪ.dɪŋ/ *noun* [U] **1** the state of being hidden: *a hiding place* (= a place to hide someone or something) ⊃See also **hiding**. **2** be in hiding/go into hiding to be/go somewhere where you cannot be found

hide SKIN /haɪd/ *noun* [C or U] the strong thick skin of an animal which is used for making leather

hide-and-seek /ˌhaɪd.ənˈsiːk/ *noun* [U] a children's game in which a group of children hide in secret places and then one child has to go to look for them

hideaway /ˈhaɪd.ə.weɪ/ *noun* [C] *INFORMAL* a place where someone goes when they want to relax away from other people

hidebound /ˈhaɪd.baʊnd/ *adj DISAPPROVING* having fixed opinions and ways of doing things and not willing to change or be influenced, especially by new or modern ideas

hideous /ˈhɪd.i.əs/ *adj* extremely ugly or bad: *They've just built some hideous new apartment blocks on the seafront.* ○ *She wears the most hideous colour combinations you could ever imagine.*
hideously /ˈhɪd.i.ə.sli/ *adv* **1** extremely ugly: *hideously fat/ugly* ○ *a hideously misshapen body* **2** *INFORMAL* used to emphasize the great degree of something: *a hideously expensive restaurant* **hideousness** /ˈhɪd.i.ə.snəs/ *noun* [U]

hideout /ˈhaɪd.aʊt/ *noun* [C] a secret place where someone can go when they do not want to be found by other people

hidey-hole /ˈhaɪd.i.həʊl/ ⓤ /-hoʊl/ *noun* [C] (*ALSO* **hidy-hole**) *UK INFORMAL* a small place for hiding things in

hiding /ˈhaɪ.dɪŋ/ *noun* [C usually sing] **1** *OLD-FASHIONED* a punishment by being beaten repeatedly ⊃See also **hiding** at **hide** OUT OF VIEW. **2** *UK INFORMAL* a total defeat: *"How did the French team get on in their match against*

Italy?" "They got a real hiding!"
• **be on a hiding to nothing** *UK INFORMAL* to be trying to do something when there is no chance that you will succeed

hie /haɪ/ *verb* [I or T] **hying**, **hied**, **hied** *OLD USE OR HUMOROUS* to go quickly or to hurry yourself: *I must hie me to the sales before all the bargains are gone.*

hierarchy /ˈhaɪə.rɑː.ki/ ⓤ /ˈhaɪr.ɑːr-/ *noun* [C] **1** a system in which people or things are arranged according to their importance: *Some monkeys have a very complex social hierarchy.* ○ *He rose quickly through the political hierarchy to become party leader.* **2** the people in the upper levels of an organization who control it
hierarchical /ˌhaɪəˈrɑː.kɪ.kəl/ ⓤ /ˌhaɪrˈɑːr-/ *adj*: *It's a very hierarchical organization in which everyone's status is clearly defined.* **hierarchically** /ˌhaɪəˈrɑː.kɪ.kli/ ⓤ /ˌhaɪrˈɑːr-/ *adv*: *The company is hierarchically structured.*

hieroglyph /ˌhaɪə.rəˈɡlɪf/ ⓤ /-roʊ-/ *noun* [C] a picture or symbol which represents a word, and which is used in some writing systems, such as that used in ancient Egypt

hieroglyphics /ˌhaɪə.rəˈɡlɪf.ɪks/ ⓤ /-roʊ-/ *plural noun* a system of writing which uses pictures instead of words, especially as used in ancient Egypt

hifalutin /ˌhaɪ.fəˈluː.tɪn/ ⓤ /-t̬ɪn/ *adj* **highfalutin**

hi-fi /ˈhaɪ.faɪ/ *noun* [C] a set of electronic equipment which is used to play recorded sound, especially music: *I've just bought a new hi-fi.* ○ *hi-fi equipment*
hi-fi /ˈhaɪ.faɪ/ *noun* [U] *ABBREVIATION FOR* **high fidelity**

higgledy-piggledy /ˌhɪɡ.l̩.diˈpɪɡ.l̩.di/ *adj, adv INFORMAL* mixed up and in no particular order: *My clothes are all higgledy-piggledy in my drawers.*

high DISTANCE /haɪ/ *adj* (especially of things that are not living) being a large distance from top to bottom or a long way above the ground, or having the stated distance from top to bottom: *a high building/mountain* ○ *high ceilings* ○ *It's two and a half metres high and one metre wide.* ○ *The corn grew waist-high* (= as high as a person's waist) *in the fields.*
• **leave sb high and dry** *INFORMAL* to do something which is very inconvenient for someone and put them in a very difficult situation: *They pulled out of the deal at the last minute leaving us high and dry.*
• **on high** *OLD USE* in heaven: *God looked down from on high.* ⊃See also **on high** at **high** IMPORTANT.
high /haɪ/ *adv* at or to a large distance from the ground: *You'll have to hit the ball quite high to get it over that net.* ○ *Concorde flies much higher than most aeroplanes.*
• **hunt/search high and low** to search everywhere for something: *I've been hunting high and low for that certificate and I still can't find it!*

high ABOVE AVERAGE /haɪ/ *adj* **1** greater than the usual level or amount: *The job demands a high level of concentration.* ○ *He suffers from high blood pressure.* ○ *Antique furniture fetches very high prices these days.* ○ *She got very high marks in her geography exam.* ○ *It's very dangerous to drive at high speed when the roads are wet.* ○ *He's in a high-security prison.* **2** high standards/principles very good or very moral standards: *She was a woman of high principles.* ○ *She demands very high standards from the people who work for her.*
high /haɪ/ *noun* [C] a higher level than has ever been reached previously: *Interest rates have reached an all-time/record high.*
highly /ˈhaɪ.li/ *adv* **1** very, to a large degree, or at a high level: *a highly paid job* ○ *a highly profitable line of products* ○ *For our country to remain competitive, we need a highly-skilled, highly-educated workforce.* **2** think/speak highly of sb to admire/say admiring things about someone: *He's very highly thought of within the company.*

high IMPORTANT /haɪ/ *adj* having power, an important position, or great influence: *an officer of high rank*
• **have friends in high places** to know important people who can help you get what you want
• **high and mighty** *DISAPPROVING* Someone who is high and mighty behaves as if they are more important than other people.

- **on high** *MAINLY HUMOROUS* If an order comes from on high, it comes from someone in a position of authority: *Instructions came from on high to reduce our travel expenses.* ➲See also **on high** at **high** DISTANCE.
- **get on *your* high horse** to start talking angrily about something bad that someone else has done as if you feel you are better or more clever than they are
- **come/get (down) off *your* high horse** to stop talking as if you were better or more clever than other people: *It's time you came down off your high horse and admitted you were wrong.*
- **live high on/off the hog** *US INFORMAL OFTEN DISAPPROVING* to live in great comfort with a lot of money

highly /ˈhaɪ.li/ *adv* in an important or influential position: *According to one highly-**placed** source, the Prime Minister had threatened to resign over this issue.*

high [MENTAL STATE] /haɪ/ *noun* **[C usually sing]** a period of extreme excitement or happiness when you feel full of energy, often caused by a feeling of success, or by drugs or alcohol or a religious experience: *Exercise gives you a high.* ○ *She's been **on** a high ever since she got her article published.* ○ *There are lots of highs **and lows** in this job.*

high /haɪ/ *adj* not thinking or behaving normally because of taking drugs: *He was high **on** heroin at the time.*

- **be as high as a kite 1** *INFORMAL* to behave in a silly or excited way because you have taken drugs or drunk a lot of alcohol: *I tried to talk to her after the party, but she was as high as a kite.* **2** to feel very happy and excited: *I was a high as a kite when I'd heard I'd got the job.*

high [SOUND] /haɪ/ *adj* near or at the top of the range of sounds: *I can't reach the high notes.*

high [EDUCATION] /haɪ/ *noun* **[S]** *US INFORMAL FOR* **high school** when used in the name of a school: *I go to Santa Ana High.*

higher /ˈhaɪ.əʳ/ [US] /-ɚ/ *adj* **[before n]** describes an advanced level of education: *A greater proportion of people with first degrees are now going on to study for higher degrees.*

higher /ˈhaɪ.əʳ/ [US] /-ɚ/ *noun* **[C]** *SCOTTISH ENGLISH* (in Scotland) an official exam that is taken in schools, especially by students who want to study at college or university

high [BAD] /haɪ/ *adj UK* (of food) smelling bad and no longer good to eat: *This meat is rather high – shall I throw it out?*

highball /ˈhaɪ.bɔːl/ [US] /-bɑːl/ *noun* **[C]** *MAINLY US* an alcoholic drink made with whisky and water or SODA (= fizzy water)

ˈhigh ˌbeams *plural noun US* car HEADLIGHTS which are on as brightly as possible

highbrow /ˈhaɪ.braʊ/ *adj MAINLY DISAPPROVING* (of books, plays, etc.) involving serious and complicated or artistic ideas, or (of people) interested in serious and complicated subjects ➲Compare **lowbrow**; **middlebrow**. **highbrow** /ˈhaɪ.braʊ/ *noun* **[C]**

ˈhigh ˌchair *noun* **[C]** a long-legged chair for a baby or a small child, usually with a small table connected to it for the child to eat from

ˌhigh ˈchurch *adj* related to the part of the Church of England that is closest to the Roman Catholic Church and contains a lot of ceremonies ➲Compare **low church**.

high-class /ˌhaɪˈklɑːs/ [US] /-ˈklæs/ *adj* of very good quality, or of high social rank

ˌHigh Comˈmission *noun* **[C usually sing] 1** the EMBASSY of one COMMONWEALTH country in another Commonwealth country **2** an international organization that has been established for a particular purpose: *According to the United Nations High Commission for Refugees, at least 24,000 people have fled the country.*

ˌHigh Comˈmissioner *noun* **[C]** the main representative of one COMMONWEALTH country in another Commonwealth country, or a person in charge of a High Commission

ˌHigh ˈCourt *noun* **[C usually sing] 1** *UK* a law court in England and Wales for trials of CIVIL rather than criminal cases and where decisions made in regional courts can be considered again **2 high court** *US* **the Supreme Court**

High Court of Australia /ˌhaɪ.kɔːt.əv.ɒsˈtreɪ.li.ə/ [US] /-kɔːrt.əv.ɑːˈstreɪl.jə/ *noun* **[S]** the law court in Australia where decisions that are made in the Supreme Court of each state can be considered again

ˌhigh defiˈnition ˌtelevision *noun* **[U]** a system which produces very good quality television images in greater detail than ordinary systems

ˌhigher eduˈcation *noun* **[U]** education at a college or university where subjects are studied at an advanced level

higher-up /ˌhaɪ.ərˈʌp/ [US] /-ɚ-/ *noun* **[C]** *INFORMAL* someone with a more important position than you in an organization: *They're still waiting for a decision about the extra money from the higher-ups.*

ˌhigh exˈplosive *noun* **[C or U]** a very powerful explosive that can damage a large area

highfalutin /ˌhaɪ.fəˈluː.tɪn/ [US] /-t̬ɪn/ *adj* (*ALSO* **hifalutin**) *INFORMAL* trying to seem very important or serious, but without having a good reason for doing so and looking foolish as a result

ˌhigh fiˈdelity *noun* **[U]** (*ABBREVIATION* **hi-fi**) the production by electrical equipment of very good quality sound that is as similar as possible to the original sound: *a major manufacturer of high fidelity audio equipment*

high-five /ˌhaɪˈfaɪv/ *noun* **[C]** a greeting or an expression of admiration in which two people each raise a hand above their shoulder and bring the fronts of their hands together with force

high-flier /ˌhaɪˈflaɪ.əʳ/ [US] /-ɚ/ *noun* **[C]** ➲See **high-flyer**.

high-flown /haɪˈfləʊn/ [US] /-ˈfloʊn/ *adj SLIGHTLY DISAPPROVING* describes language, ideas, or behaviour that is meant to be impressive

high-flyer, **high-flier** /ˌhaɪˈflaɪ.əʳ/ [US] /-ɚ/ *noun* **[C]** someone who has a lot of ability and a strong desire to be successful and is therefore expected to achieve a lot: *High-flyers in the industry typically earn 25% more than their colleagues.*

high-flyer /ˌhaɪˈflaɪ.əʳ/ [US] /-ɚ/ *group noun* **[C]** (*ALSO* **high-flier**) *MAINLY UK* an extremely successful organization, business or team

high-flying /ˌhaɪˈflaɪ.ɪŋ/ *adj* **[before n]** extremely successful: *a high-flying investment banker*

high-grade /ˌhaɪˈgreɪd/ *adj* **[before n]** of very good quality or of better quality than usual: *high-grade petrol*

high-handed /ˌhaɪˈhæn.dɪd/ *adj DISAPPROVING* Someone who is high-handed uses their power or authority more forcefully than is needed without thinking about the feelings or wishes of other people. **high-handedness** /ˌhaɪˈhæn.dɪd.nəs/ *noun* **[U]**

ˌhigh ˈheels *plural noun* women's shoes in which the heels are raised high off the ground **high-heeled** /ˌhaɪˈhɪəld/ *adj* **[before n]** *high-heeled shoes*

high jinks, *US ALSO* **hijinks** /ˌhaɪˈdʒɪŋks/ *plural noun INFORMAL* energetic and excited behaviour in which people do amusing things or play tricks on someone

the ˈhigh ˌjump *noun* **[S]** a sport in which competitors try to jump over a bar supported on two poles. The height of the bar is gradually raised and the winner is the person who jumps highest without knocking the bar off the poles.

- **be for the high jump** *UK* to be going to be punished for something you have done wrong

ˈhigh ˌjumper *noun* **[C]** someone who competes in the high jump

ˌHighland ˈfling *noun* **[C usually sing]** an energetic Scottish dance

ˌHighland ˈGames *plural noun* an event which involves traditional Scottish dancing, music and sports competitions

highlands /ˈhaɪ.ləndz/ *plural noun* a mountainous area of a country: *Most villages in the highlands are now connected by roads.*

the Highlands *plural noun* a mountainous area in northern Scotland: *the Scottish Highlands*

Highlander /ˈhaɪ.lən.dəʳ/ [US] /-dɚ/ *noun* **[C]** a person who comes from the Scottish Highlands

Highland /ˈhaɪ.lənd/ *adj* **[before n]** related to or connected with the Scottish Highlands: *a Highland reel*

H

highland /ˈhaɪ.lənd/ *adj* [before n] in or relating to an area with mountains or hills: *highland springs*

high-level /ˌhaɪˈlev.əl/ *adj* If discussions are high-level, very important people are involved in them: *high-level* ***meetings/talks*** *between the two sides*

ˌhigh-level ˈlanguage *noun* [C] SPECIALIZED a language for writing computer programs which looks more like human language than computer language and is therefore easier to understand

the ˈhigh ˌlife *noun* [S] an exciting way of living in which rich and successful people enjoy themselves by spending a lot of time and money in fashionable places

highlight [BEST PART] /ˈhaɪ.laɪt/ *noun* [C] the best or most exciting, entertaining or interesting part of something: *Highlights* ***of*** *the match will be shown after the news.*

highlight [HAIR] /ˈhaɪ.laɪt/ *noun* [C usually pl] a narrow strip of hair on a person's head which has been made paler in colour than the surrounding hair

highlight [EMPHASIZE] /ˈhaɪ.laɪt/ *verb* [T] to attract attention to or emphasize something important: *The report highlights the need for improved safety.* ○ *The spelling mistakes in the text had been highlighted* ***in*** *green.*

highlighter /ˈhaɪˌlaɪ.təʳ/ [US] /-t̬ɚ/ *noun* [C] a special pen containing bright ink which is used to mark words in a book, magazine, etc.

highly-strung /ˌhaɪ.liˈstrʌŋ/ *adj* (*US* **high-strung**) very nervous and easily upset: *a highly-strung young woman* ○ *a highly-strung racehorse*

high-minded /ˌhaɪˈmaɪn.dɪd/ *adj* having very high moral standards of behaviour

Highness /ˈhaɪ.nəs/ *noun* FORMAL **Her/His/Your Highness** used when you are speaking to or about a royal person: [as form of address] *Will that be all, Your Highness?*

ˌhigh ˈnoon *noun* [U] exactly twelve o'clock, when the sun should be at its highest point in the sky

high-octane /ˌhaɪˈɒk.teɪn/ [US] /-ˈɑːk-/ *adj* [before n] **1** describes fuel that is of very good quality: *high-octane fuel* ○ *high-octane (UK) petrol/(US) gas* **2** full of energy or very powerful: *a high-octane performance*

high-pitched [VOICE] /ˌhaɪˈpɪtʃt/ *adj* A voice that is high-pitched is higher than usual.

high-pitched [NOISE] /ˌhaɪˈpɪtʃt/ *adj* describes a noise that is high and sometimes also loud or unpleasant: *I was almost deafened by the high-pitched scream of the fire alarm.*

ˈhigh ˌpoint *noun* [S] the best part of an experience: *The high point of the trip for me was visiting the Pyramids.*

high-powered [POWERFUL] /ˌhaɪˈpaʊəd/ [US] /-ˈpaʊɚd/ *adj* (of machines) very powerful: *a high-powered motorbike* ○ *a high-powered computer*

high-powered [IMPORTANT JOB] /ˌhaɪˈpaʊəd/ [US] /-ˈpaʊɚd/ *adj* (of people) very successful or having a very important job: *a high-powered attorney*

high-pressure [PRESSURE] /ˌhaɪˈpreʃ.əʳ/ [US] /-ɚ/ *adj* [before n] involving pressure which is greater than usual: *They used special high-pressure hoses to help them put out the fires.*

high-pressure [SELLING] /ˌhaɪˈpreʃ.əʳ/ [US] /-ɚ/ *adj* [before n] describes methods of selling that involve persuading people in a forceful way to buy something that often they do not want: *I refuse to be intimidated by high-pressure sales techniques.*

high-pressure [WORRY] /ˌhaɪˈpreʃ.əʳ/ [US] /-ɚ/ *adj* [before n] involving a lot of responsibility or worry: *a high-pressure job in advertising*

ˌhigh ˈpriest *noun* [C] (*FEMALE* **high priestess**) **1** a very important priest or priestess in a religious or spiritual organization **2** the most important or famous person in a particular area of interest: *She is widely regarded as the high priestess* ***of*** *contemporary dance.*

high-profile /ˌhaɪˈprəʊ.faɪl/ [US] /-ˈproʊ-/ *adj* [before n] attracting a lot of attention and interest from the public and newpapers, television, etc: *high-profile politicians* ○ *He resigned from a high-profile job as economic adviser to the Prime Minister.*

high-ranking /ˌhaɪˈræŋ.kɪŋ/ *adj* having an important position in an organization

ˈhigh ˌrise *noun* [C] a tall modern building with a lot of floors: *She lives in a high rise overlooking the river.*
high-rise /ˈhaɪ.raɪz/ *adj*: *a high-rise office building*

high-risk /ˌhaɪˈrɪsk/ *adj* [before n] involving a greater than usual amount of risk: *Only people who can afford to lose their money should make high-risk investments.*

ˌhigh ˈroller *noun* [C] someone who spends a lot of money or who gambles with large amounts of money

ˈhigh ˌschool *noun* [C] **1** (*INFORMAL* **high**) a school in the US for children aged from 14 to 18, or from 16 to 18 if there is also a JUNIOR HIGH SCHOOL: *Diane goes to Santa Ana High.* **2** in the UK and Australia, sometimes used in the names of schools for children aged from 11 to 18

the ˌhigh ˈseas *plural noun* the seas which are not controlled by any country

ˌhigh ˈseason *noun* [U] the time of year when the greatest number of people visit a place and when the prices are at their highest level: *People on limited budgets should avoid travelling* ***in/during/****(UK)* ***at*** *high season if they can.* ➲Compare **low season**.

high-speed /ˌhaɪˈspiːd/ *adj* [before n] describes something that moves or operates very quickly: *a high-speed train/ferry* ○ *a high-speed computer* ○ *high-speed data transmission*

high-spirited [PERSON] /ˌhaɪˈspɪr.ɪ.tɪd/ [US] /-t̬ɪd/ *adj* Someone who is high-spirited is energetic and happy and likes doing exciting and enjoyable things.

high-spirited [ANIMAL] /ˌhaɪˈspɪr.ɪ.tɪd/ [US] /-t̬ɪd/ *adj* describes a very active horse that is difficult to control

ˌhigh ˈspirits *plural noun* If someone is in high spirits, they are extremely happy and enjoying themselves: *They'd had a couple of drinks and were* ***in*** *high spirits.*

ˈhigh ˌstreet *noun* [C] *UK* **1** a street where the most important shops and businesses in a town are: *There's a new Italian restaurant opening* ***on*** *the high street.* **2 the high street** business done in shops: *There are signs of economic recovery in the high street.*
high-street /ˈhaɪ.striːt/ *adj* **1** relating to business done in shops: *There was a modest rise in high-street spending last month.* **2** describes products, especially clothes, which are intended for the ordinary public and not for rich people: *high-street fashions*

ˌhigh ˈtable *noun* [C or U] *UK* a table at a formal dinner where the most important guests sit

hightail /ˈhaɪ.teɪl/ *verb* MAINLY US INFORMAL **hightail it** to leave or go somewhere in a great hurry: *As soon as I heard he was coming I hightailed it* ***out*** *of there.*

ˌhigh ˈtea *noun* [C or U] *UK* a light meal eaten in the late afternoon or early evening which usually includes cooked food, cakes and tea to drink

high-tech /ˌhaɪˈtek/ *adj* **1** (*ALSO* **hi-tech**) using the most advanced and developed machines and methods: *This weapons system is an affordable, hi-tech solution.* ➲Compare **low-tech**. **2** very modern looking or made with modern materials: *high-tech architecture*

ˌhigh ˈtechnology *noun* [U] the most advanced and developed machines and methods: *a thriving economy built on high technology*

ˌhigh ˈtension *adj* [before n] OLD-FASHIONED **high-voltage**: *a high-tension cable*

ˌhigh ˈtide *noun* **1** [C or U] the time when the sea or a river reaches its highest level and comes furthest up the beach or the bank **2** [S] *UK* Something's high tide is its most successful point: *The signing of the peace treaty was the high tide* ***of*** *her presidency.*

ˌhigh ˈtreason *noun* [U] the committing of a crime which seriously threatens the safety of your country

ˌhigh ˈup *adj* [after v] Someone who is high up in an organization has an important position in it.

high-voltage /ˌhaɪˈvɒl.tɪdʒ/ [US] /-ˈvoʊl.t̬ɪdʒ/ *adj* **1** relating to or containing large amounts of electricity **2** INFORMAL very exciting and full of energy: *Sara Hughes gives a high-voltage performance in one of the most exciting plays to hit London this year.*

ˌhigh ˈwater *noun* [U] *UK FOR* **high tide**

ˌhigh ˈwater ˌmark *noun* [C usually sing] **1** a mark which shows the highest level that the sea or river reaches at a particular place **2** the most successful point of something: *His 1991 election victory was probably the high water mark* ***of*** *his popularity.*

highway /ˈhaɪ.weɪ/ *noun* [C] *US OR UK FORMAL* a public road, especially an important road that joins cities or towns together: *a coastal/interstate highway* ➲See also **superhighway**.

the ˌHighway ˈCode *noun* [S] *UK* the set of official rules, published in a small book, which have to be obeyed by drivers in the UK

highwayman /ˈhaɪ.weɪ.mən/ *noun* [C] in the past, a man on a horse and carrying a gun who stopped people travelling on public roads and stole from them

hijack /ˈhaɪ.dʒæk/ *verb* [T] **1** to take control of an aircraft or other vehicle during a journey, especially using violence: *Two men hijacked a jet travelling to Paris and demanded $125 000.* **2** *DISAPPROVING* to take control of or use something that does not belong to you for your own advantage: *He resents the way his ideas have been hijacked by others in the department.*

hijack /ˈhaɪ.dʒæk/ *noun* [C or U] (*ALSO* **hijacking**) when someone uses force to take control of an aircraft or other vehicle: *The hijack ended with the release of all the plane's passengers unharmed.* **hijacker** /ˈhaɪˌdʒæk.əʳ/ [US] /-ɚ/ *noun* [C]

hike [WALK] /haɪk/ *noun* [C] a long walk, especially in the countryside

• **Take a hike!** *US INFORMAL* a rude way of telling someone to leave

hike /haɪk/ *verb* [I] to go for a long walk in the countryside **hiking** /ˈhaɪ.kɪŋ/ *noun* [U] *We're* ***going*** *hiking in the Lake District next weekend.* **hiker** /ˈhaɪ.kəʳ/ [US] /-kɚ/ *noun* [C] *On sunny days the trails are full of hikers.*

hike [INCREASE] /haɪk/ *noun* [C] an increase in the cost of something, especially a large or unwanted increase: *The recent hike* ***in*** *train fares came as a shock to commuters.*

hike /haɪk/ *verb* [I or T] *The Chancellor has hiked* ***(up)*** *interest rates again.*

▲ **hike *sth* up** *phrasal verb* [M] *INFORMAL* to lift or raise something with a quick movement: *She hiked up her skirt and climbed onto the bicycle.*

hilarious /hɪˈleə.ri.əs/ [US] /-ˈler.i-/ *adj* extremely amusing and causing a lot of laughter: *He didn't like the film at all – I thought it was hilarious.* **hilariously** /hɪˈleə.ri.ə.sli/ [US] /-ˈler.i-/ *adv*: *Her new book's hilariously funny.*

hilarity /hɪˈlær.ə.ti/ [US] /-ˈler.ə.t̬i/ *noun* [U] when people laugh very loudly and think something is very funny: *What was all the hilarity about?*

hill /hɪl/ *noun* [C] **1** an area of land that is higher than the surrounding land: *Hills are not as high as mountains.* ○ *Their house is on the top of a hill.* ○ *In the summer, the shepherds move their sheep up into* ***the*** *hills* (= an area where there are hills). **2** a slope in a road: *That hill's far too steep to cycle up.*

• **be over the hill** *INFORMAL DISAPPROVING* to be too old, especially to do a particular job

hilly /ˈhɪl.i/ *adj* having a lot of hills: *hilly countryside* ○ *a hilly area*

hillbilly /ˈhɪlˌbɪl.i/ *noun* [C] *US OLD-FASHIONED DISAPPROVING* a person from a mountainous area of the US who has a simple way of life and is considered to be slightly stupid by people living in towns and cities

hillock /ˈhɪl.ək/ *noun* [C] a small hill

hillside /ˈhɪl.saɪd/ *noun* [C] the sloping surface of a hill, rather than the level surface at the top of it

ˈhill ˌstation *noun* [C] *UK* a village or town high up in the hills, especially in India, where people go in the summer to escape from the heat

hilltop /ˈhɪl.tɒp/ [US] /-tɑːp/ *noun* [C] the top part of a hill, rather than its sloping sides

hilt /hɪlt/ *noun* [C] the handle of a sharp pointed weapon such as a sword

• **(up) to the hilt** Something that is done (up) to the hilt is done completely and without any limitation: *The government is already borrowing up to the hilt, so it can't afford to spend any more.*

him [MALE] *STRONG* /hɪm/, *WEAK* /ɪm/ *pronoun* used, usually after a verb or preposition, to refer to a man, boy or male animal that has just been mentioned or is just about to be mentioned: *If you see Kevin give him my love.* ○ *What's Terry up to – I haven't seen him for ages.* ○ *Why don't you give him his present?* ○ *We've just got a new cat, but we haven't named him yet.*

himself /hɪmˈself/ *pronoun* **1** used to refer to a male object of a verb that is the same person or animal as the subject of the verb: *He'd cut himself shaving.* ○ *Most nights he would cry himself to sleep.* **2** used to give special attention to a male noun or to make clear which male person or animal is being referred to: *Did you want to talk to the chairman himself, or could his personal assistant help you?* ○ *Guy was going to buy a bookcase, but in the end he made one himself.* **3 (all) to himself** for his use only: *Johnny's got the apartment to himself next week.* **4 (all) by himself** If a man or boy does something by himself, he does it alone or without help from anyone else: *Little Timmy made that snowman all by himself.* **5 not be/not seem himself** not being or seeming as happy or as healthy as usual: *Is Tom all right? He doesn't seem quite himself this morning.*

• **in himself** *UK INFORMAL* used when describing or asking about a man's state of mind when he is physically ill: *He's well enough in himself – he just can't shake this cold off.*

him [FEMALE OR MALE] /hɪm/, *WEAK* /ɪm/ *pronoun* used, especially in formal situations, usually after a verb or preposition, to refer to a person or animal that has just been mentioned or is just about to be mentioned and whose sex is not known or not considered to be important: *Man's ability to talk makes him unlike any other animal.*
* NOTE: Many people prefer to use **them**, and this can sometimes mean changing other words in the sentence: *Human beings' ability to talk makes them unlike any other animal.* **It** can be used for animals. ➲See Note **he (avoiding sexist language)** at **he**.

himself /hɪmˈself/ *pronoun*: *Any fool can teach himself to type.*

hind [BACK] /haɪnd/ *adj* [before n] at the back of an animal's body: *a hind leg*

hind [ANIMAL] /haɪnd/ *noun* [C] *plural* **hinds** or **hind** *MAINLY UK* a female deer, especially a red deer

hinder /ˈhɪn.dəʳ/ [US] /-dɚ/ *verb* [T] to limit the ability of someone to do something, or to limit the development of something: *High winds have hindered firefighters* ***in*** *their efforts to put out the blaze.* ○ *Her progress certainly hasn't been hindered by her lack of experience.*

Hindi /ˈhɪn.di/ *noun* [U] one of the official languages of India, spoken especially in northern India

hindquarters /ˌhaɪndˈkwɔː.təz/ [US] /-ˈkwɔːr.t̬ɚz/ *plural noun* the back part of a four-legged animal

hindrance /ˈhɪn.drənts/ *noun* [C usually sing; U] something which makes it more difficult for you to do something or for something to develop: *I've never considered my disability a hindrance, but other people have.*

hindsight /ˈhaɪnd.saɪt/ *noun* [U] the ability to understand an event or situation only after it has happened: ***With (the benefit/wisdom of)*** *hindsight, I should have taken the job.* ○ ***In*** *hindsight, it would have been better to wait.*

Hindu /ˈhɪn.duː/ *noun* [C] someone who believes in Hinduism

Hinduism /ˈhɪn.duː.ɪ.zᵊm/ *noun* [U] an ancient religion with Indian origins whose characteristics include the worship of many gods and goddesses and the belief that when a person or creature dies, their spirit returns to life in another body

hinge /hɪndʒ/ *noun* [C] a metal fastening that joins the edge of a door, window, lid, etc. to something else and allows it to swing open or closed: *We had to take the front door off its hinges to get our new sofa into the house.*

hinged /ˈhɪndʒd/ *adj*: *a hinged lid*

hinge /hɪndʒ/ *verb*

▲ **hinge on/upon *sth*** *phrasal verb* **1** If one thing hinges on another, the first thing depends on the second thing or is very influenced by it: *The prosecution's case hinged on the evidence of a witness who died before the trial.* **2** If a story or situation hinges on an idea or subject, it develops from that idea or that is the most important subject in it: *The film's plot hinges on a case of mistaken identity.*

H

hint [INDIRECT STATEMENT] /hɪnt/ *noun* [C] something that you say or do that shows in an indirect way what you think or want: [+ *that*] *He's* ***dropped*** (= given) *several hints to the boss* ***that*** *he'll quit if he doesn't get a promotion.* ○ *Did she* ***give*** *you any hints about where she was going?* ○ *You can't* ***take*** (= understand) *a hint, can you? Just go away and leave me alone!* **hint** /hɪnt/ *verb* [I] [+ (*that*)] *Mum's hinted* ***(that)*** *she might pay for my trip to Mexico if I pass all my exams.* ○ *He's hinted* ***at*** *the possibility of moving to America.*

hint [ADVICE] /hɪnt/ *noun* [C] a piece of advice which helps you to do something: *Could you* ***give*** *us a hint* ***about*** *how to do this exercise, please?* ○ *This recipe book is full of* ***handy*** (= useful) *hints.*

hint [SMALL AMOUNT] /hɪnt/ *noun* [C usually sing] a very small amount of something: *There's just a hint* ***of*** *brandy in the sauce.* ○ *I detected a hint* ***of*** *doubt in his voice.*

hinterland /ˈhɪn.tə.lænd/ ⓤ /-t̬ɚ-/ *noun* [C usually sing] the land behind the coast or beyond the banks of a river, or an area of a country that is far away from cities

hinterlands /ˈhɪn.tə.lændz/ ⓤ /-t̬ɚ-/ *plural noun* us a part of the country that is far away from the big city areas

hip [BODY PART] /hɪp/ *noun* [C] the area below the waist and above the legs at either side of the body, or the joint which connects the leg to the upper part of the body: *This exercise is designed to trim your hips and stomach.* ○ *The skirt was a bit tight across the hips.* ➭See picture **The Body** on page Centre 5

hip [FRUIT] /hɪp/ *noun* [C] MAINLY UK FOR **rose hip**

hip [FASHIONABLE] /hɪp/ *adj* **hipper**, **hippest** INFORMAL fashionable: *The bars and cafés in the old part of the town are frequented by hip young students.*

hip [APPROVAL] /hɪp/ *exclamation* **Hip, hip hooray/ hurray!** an expression that is called out, often by a group of people at the same time, to express approval of someone: *Three cheers for the bride and groom! Hip, hip, hooray!*

hipbath /ˈhɪp.bɑːθ/ ⓤ /-bæθ/ *noun* [C] UK a small bath with a seat built into it which is designed for sitting rather than lying in

'hip ˌflask *noun* [C] a small flat bottle that is used to carry alcohol in your pocket

hip-hop /ˈhɪp.hɒp/ ⓤ /-hɑːp/ *noun* [U] a type of popular music in which the subject of the songs is often politics or society and the words are spoken rather than sung

hippie ˌ**hippy** /ˈhɪp.i/ *noun* [C] a person, typically young, especially in the late 1960s and early 1970s, who believed in peace, was opposed to many of the accepted ideas about how to live, had long hair, and often lived in groups and took drugs

the Hippocratic oath /ðəˌhɪp.ə.kræt.ɪkˈəʊθ/ ⓤ /-kræt̬.-ɪkˈoʊθ/ *noun* [S] a promise made by people when they become doctors to do everything possible to preserve human life and to maintain high working standards

hippopotamus (*plural* **hippopotamuses** or **hippopotami**) /ˌhɪp.əˈpɒt.ə.məs/ ⓤ /-ˈpɑː.t̬ə-/ *noun* [C] (INFORMAL **hippo**) a very large animal with short legs and thick, dark grey skin which lives near water in Africa ➭See picture **Animals and Birds** on page Centre 4

hipsters UK /ˈhɪp.stəz/ ⓤ /-stɚz/ *plural noun* (us **hiphuggers**) trousers which do not reach as high as the waist

hire /haɪəʳ/ ⓤ /haɪr/ *verb* [T] **1** UK (US **rent**) to pay to use something for a short period: *How much would it cost to hire a car for a fortnight?* ○ *You could always hire a dress for the ball if you can't afford to buy one.* ➭See Note **rent or hire?** at **rent** PAYMENT. **2** to employ someone or pay them to do a particular job: *I was hired by the first company I applied to.* ○ [+ *to* infinitive] *We ought to hire a public relations consultant to help improve our image.*

hire /haɪəʳ/ ⓤ /haɪr/ *noun* [U] UK when you arrange to use something by paying for it: *The price includes flights and* ***car hire***. ○ *There's a camping shop in town that has tents* ***for hire*** (= available to be hired) *at £10 a week.*

hired /haɪəd/ ⓤ /haɪrd/ *adj*: *a hired car* ○ *The police believe he was killed by a hired assassin.*

hiring /ˈhaɪə.rɪŋ/ ⓤ /ˈhaɪr.ɪŋ/ *noun* [C usually pl] the act of starting to employ someone: *The office has completely*

changed in the past few weeks because there have been so many hirings ***and firings*** (= a lot of new people have been employed and a lot of others have lost their jobs).

▲ **hire** *sth/sb* **out** *phrasal verb* [M] UK to allow someone to use something or someone temporarily in exchange for money: *How much do you charge for hiring out a bicycle for a week?* ○ [R] *He's decided to go freelance and hire himself out as a technical writer.*

hireling /ˈhaɪə.lɪŋ/ ⓤ /ˈhaɪr-/ *noun* [C] UK DISAPPROVING someone who has been persuaded by an offer of money to do an unpleasant or unpopular job: *He's not the boss, he's just a hireling employed to do the dirty work.*

ˌ**hire ˈpurchase** UK *noun* [U] (ABBREVIATION **HP**, US **installment plan**) a method of paying for something in which the buyer pays part of the cost immediately and then makes small regular payments until the debt is completely paid

hirsute /ˈhɜː.sjuːt/ ⓤ /ˈhɝː.suːt/ *adj* LITERARY OR HUMOROUS having a lot of hair, especially on the face or body

his [MALE] /hɪz/ *determiner, pronoun* **1** (something) belonging to or connected with a man, boy or male animal that has just been mentioned: *"She's got a new boyfriend." "Oh really? What's his name?"* ○ *Mark just phoned to say he'd left his coat behind. Do you know if this is his?* ○ FORMAL *Did Chris tell you about his winning some money in the lottery?* **2 his own** used to emphasize that something belongs to or is connected with a particular man or boy and no one else: *He got his* ***very*** *own computer for Christmas.*

his [FEMALE OR MALE] /hɪz/ *determiner, pronoun* (something) belonging to or connected with a person or animal that has just been mentioned and whose sex is not known or not considered to be important: *Anyone who drives his car at 100 miles an hour is asking for trouble.* ○ *What a lovely dog! What's his name?* ✳ NOTE: Many people prefer to use **their**, and this can sometimes mean changing other words in the sentence. **Its** can be used for animals. ➭See Note **he (avoiding sexist language)** at **he**.

ˌ**his and ˈhers** *adj* [before n] describes a pair of similar items designed for a man and woman in a romantic relationship to use: *My mum gave us his and hers matching dressing gowns for Christmas.*

Hispanic /hɪˈspæn.ɪk/ *adj* connected with Spain or Spanish-speaking countries, especially those countries in Latin America **Hispanic** /hɪˈspæn.ɪk/ *noun* [C] *Hispanics make up a large proportion of the population of Miami.*

hiss /hɪs/ *verb* **1** [I] to make a noise which is like the first sound in the word 'sing' but which lasts a longer: *Why do snakes hiss?* ○ *The iron was hissing and spluttering.* ○ *People in the audience were hissing their disapproval.* **2** [T] to say something in a quiet angry way: *"Shut up, Tom!" she hissed.*

hiss /hɪs/ *noun* [C or U] a sound like the letter 's': *I heard a hiss and a pop as the cork came out of the bottle.*

hissy (fit) /ˈhɪs.i.fɪt/ *noun* [C] INFORMAL a sudden period of uncontrolled and childish anger: *Sue, of course,* ***threw*** *a hissy when she found out.*

histamine /ˈhɪs.tə.miːn/ *noun* [U] SPECIALIZED a chemical in the body which is released after an injury or during an ALLERGIC reaction

histogram /ˈhɪs.tə.græm/ *noun* [C] SPECIALIZED a **bar chart/graph**

histology /hɪˈstɒl.ə.dʒi/ ⓤ /-ˈstɑː.lə-/ *noun* [U] SPECIALIZED the scientific study of the structure of tissue from plants, animals and other living things

histˌoric ˈpresent *noun* [C usually sing] SPECIALIZED the present tense when it is used to describe past events, either informally, or to produce a special effect

history [PAST EVENTS] /ˈhɪs.tʳr.i/ ⓤ /-t̬ɚ-/ *noun* **1** [C or U] (the study of or a record of) past events considered together, especially events of a particular period, country or subject: *I studied modern European history at college.* ○ *American history* ○ *Annie's decided to write a history of electronic music.* ○ *I only asked him for a cigarette, but two hours later he'd told me his whole* ***life history***. **2** [U] INFORMAL something that happened or ended a long time ago and is not important now, or a person who is not

important now, although they were in the past: *Last year's report is **ancient** history and totally irrelevant to the current situation.* ○ *"What about Dan – are you still seeing him?" "Oh, he's history."*
• **make history** to do something important which has not been done before and which will be recorded publicly and remembered for a long time: *Margaret Thatcher made history when she became the first British woman Prime Minister.*

historian /hɪˈstɔː.ri.ən/ ⓤ /-ˈstɔːr.i-/ *noun* [C] someone who writes about or studies history

historic /hɪˈstɒr.ɪk/ ⓤ /-ˈstɔːr-/ *adj* important or likely to be important in history: *historic buildings* ○ *a historic day/moment* ○ *In a historic vote, the Church of England decided to allow women to become priests.*

historical /hɪˈstɒr.ɪ.kºl/ ⓤ /-ˈstɔːr-/ *adj* connected with the study or representation of things from the past: *Many important historical documents were destroyed when the library was bombed.* ○ *She specializes in historical novels set in eighteenth-century England.*

historically /hɪˈstɒr.ɪ.kli/ ⓤ /-ˈstɔːr-/ *adv*: *The film makes no attempt to be historically accurate.* ○ *Historically (= Over a long period in the past), there have always been close links between France and Scotland.*

COMMON LEARNER ERROR

history or **story**?

History means all the events that happened in the past.

He's studying medieval history at university.

A **story** is a description of real or imaginary events, often told to entertain people.

The story is about two friends travelling across India.
~~The history is about two friends travelling across India.~~

---

history PARTICULAR RECORD /ˈhɪs.tºr.i/ ⓤ /-tɚ-/ *noun* [C usually sing] something that has been done or experienced by a particular person or thing repeatedly over a long period: *Her family **has** a history **of** heart problems.* ○ *There's a long history **of** industrial disputes at the factory.* ○ *He has a good **credit** history (= a good record of paying money that he owes).*

histrionic /ˌhɪs.triˈɒn.ɪk/ ⓤ /-ˈɑː.nɪk/ *adj* DISAPPROVING very emotional and energetic, but lacking sincerity or real meaning: *a histrionic outburst* ○ *She put on a histrionic display of grief at her ex-husband's funeral.*
histrionically /ˌhɪs.triˈɒn.ɪ.kli/ ⓤ /-ˈɑː.nɪ-/ *adv*
histrionics /ˌhɪs.triˈɒn.ɪks/ ⓤ /-ˈɑː.nɪks/ *plural noun* DISAPPROVING very emotional and energetic behaviour that lacks sincerity and real meaning: *I'd had enough of Lydia's histrionics.*

hit TOUCH /hɪt/ *verb* [T] hitting, hit, hit **1** to swing your hand or an object onto the surface of something so that it touches it, usually with force: *Teachers are not allowed to hit their pupils.* ○ *This type of glass won't shatter no matter how hard you hit it.* ○ *She hit her thumb **with** the hammer.* **2** to touch something with sudden force: *They were going at about 60 kilometres an hour when their car hit the tree.* ○ *One journalist was hit **in** the leg by a stray bullet.* ○ *That new shelf in the bathroom is too low – I just hit my head **on** it.*
• **not know what hit you** to feel shocked or confused because something bad has happened to you suddenly when you were not expecting it
• **hit the jackpot** to suddenly get or win a lot of money
• **hit the nail on the head** to describe exactly what is causing a situation or problem: *I think Mick hit the nail on the head when he said that what's lacking from this company is a feeling of confidence.*

hit /hɪt/ *noun* [C] **1** when you hit something or someone, or when something or someone hits you: *She gave him a hit **on** the head which knocked him flying.* **2** in baseball, when the BATTER (= person trying to hit the ball) safely reaches FIRST BASE after hitting the ball

hit EFFECT /hɪt/ *verb* [T] hitting, hit, hit to have an unpleasant or negative effect on a person or thing: *Production has been badly hit by the strike.* ○ *Demand for transatlantic flights has been hit by fears of terrorist attacks.*

• **hit sb where it hurts** to do or say something to someone that will upset them as much as possible: *He's always worrying about his weight, so if you want to hit him where it hurts, tell him he's looking a bit fat.*
• **hit sb between the eyes** to shock someone or have a sudden strong effect on them
• **hit home** to cause you to fully realize how unpleasant or difficult something is: *The full horror of the war only hit home when we started seeing the television pictures of it in our living rooms.*

hit REACH /hɪt/ *verb* [T] hitting, hit, hit **1** to arrive at a place or position: *If we turn left at the next junction, we should hit the main road after five miles or so.* **2** to succeed in reaching or achieving something: *Our profits hit an all-time high of £20 million last year.* ○ *I just can't hit (= sing) those high notes like I used to.*
• **hit the bottle** to start to drink too much alcohol
• **hit the ceiling/roof** to become extremely angry: *Dad'll hit the ceiling when he finds out I've left school.*
• **hit the deck** to lie down quickly and suddenly so that you are hidden from view or sheltered from something dangerous
• **hit the ground running** to immediately work hard and successfully at a new activity
• **hit the hay/sack** INFORMAL to go to bed in order to sleep: *I've got a busy day tomorrow, so I think I'll hit the sack.*
• **hit the headlines** to appear in the news suddenly or receive a lot of attention in news reports: *He hit the headlines two years ago when he was arrested for selling drugs to the Prime Minister's nephew.*
• **hit the road** to leave a place or begin a journey: *I'd love to stay longer but I must be hitting the road.*
• **hit the spot** to be exactly what is needed: *That bacon sandwich really hit the spot!*

hit SHOOT /hɪt/ *verb* [T often passive] hitting, hit, hit to shoot at or bomb a place or person, causing damage or injury: *Two schools were hit during the air raid.* ○ *He was hit in the neck by a bullet from a sniper.* ○ *Try to hit the middle of the target.*
hit /hɪt/ *noun* [C] when something that has been thrown, dropped, shot, etc. at a place or object reaches that place or object: *The rebel headquarters took a **direct** hit from a bomb during the attack.* ○ *I scored a hit on my second shot.*

hit ATTACK /hɪt/ *verb* [T] hitting, hit, hit MAINLY US SLANG to kill someone: *Three drug dealers were hit in the city over the weekend.*
hit /hɪt/ *noun* [C] MAINLY US SLANG an act of murder: *He was the victim of a mafia hit.*

hit SUCCESS /hɪt/ *noun* [C] a thing or person that is very popular or successful: *The Beatles had a string of number-one hits in the 1960s.* ○ *Your cake was a real hit at the party – everyone commented.* ○ *They've just released a CD of their **greatest** hits (= their most successful songs).*
• **are/make a hit with** INFORMAL If you are/make a hit with someone, they like you a lot from the time that they first meet you: *You've made a big hit with my dad – he hasn't stopped talking about you.*
hit /hɪt/ *verb* INFORMAL **hit it off** to like someone and become friendly immediately: *I didn't really hit it off **with** his friends.* ○ *Jake and Sue hit it off immediately.*

hit COMPUTING /hɪt/ *noun* [C] a request to access a WEB PAGE on the Internet that is then counted to calculate the number of people looking at the page: *Our web page had 243 hits this week.*

PHRASAL VERBS WITH **hit** ▼

▲ **hit back** *phrasal verb* to attack or criticize someone who has attacked or criticized you: *In tonight's speech, the minister is expected to hit back **at** critics who have attacked her handling of the crisis.*

▲ **hit on sb** SHOW INTEREST *phrasal verb* US SLANG to show someone that you are sexually attracted to them: *Some guy hit on me while I was standing at the bar.*

▲ **hit on/upon sth** DISCOVER *phrasal verb* to think of an idea unexpectedly or unintentionally, especially one that solves a problem: *When we first hit on the idea, everyone told us it would never work.*

H

▲ **hit out** *phrasal verb* to criticise something or someone strongly: *The Medical Association yesterday hit out **at** government cuts in healthcare services.*

▲ **hit** *sb* **up** *phrasal verb* [M] *US INFORMAL* to ask someone for something: *She hit me up **for** $20.*

hit-and-miss /ˌhɪt.ənˈmɪs/ *adj* (*ALSO* **hit-or-miss**) If something is hit-and-miss you cannot depend on it to be of good quality, on time, accurate, etc: *The trains are often late, so getting to work on time is a fairly hit-and-miss affair.*

hit-and-run ACCIDENT /ˌhɪt.ənˈrʌn/ *adj* [before n] describes a road accident in which the driver who caused the accident drives away without helping the other people involved and without telling the police: *a hit-and-run driver/accident*

hit-and-run MILITARY /ˌhɪt.ənˈrʌn/ *adj* [before n] describes a military attack that needs to happen unexpectedly and quickly in order to be successful: *hit-and-run warfare*

hitch DIFFICULTY /hɪtʃ/ *noun* [C] a temporary difficulty which causes a short delay: *Due to a slight **technical** hitch the concert will be starting approximately half an hour late.*

● **go (off) without a hitch** to happen successfully without any problems: *To the bride's relief, the wedding ceremony went off without a hitch.*

hitch RIDE /hɪtʃ/ *verb INFORMAL* **hitch a lift/ride** to get a free ride in someone else's vehicle as a way of travelling: *They hitched a lift to Edinburgh from a passing car.*

hitch FASTEN /hɪtʃ/ *verb* [T usually + adv or prep] to fasten something to another thing by tying it with a rope or using a metal hook: *The horses were hitched **to** a shiny black carriage.* ○ *We just need to hitch the trailer **(on)to** the car and then we can go.*

▲ **hitch** *sth* **up** *phrasal verb* [M] **1** to pull something, especially trousers or a skirt, upwards to a slightly higher position: *She hitched her skirt up before wading across the stream.* **2** If you hitch up a vehicle, you attach it so that it can be pulled, and if you hitch up an animal to a vehicle, you attach it so that it can pull the vehicle: *We watched as the farmer hitched up a team of oxen.*

hitched /hɪtʃt/ *adj SLANG* **get hitched** to get married: *Is Tracy really getting hitched then?*

hitchhike /ˈhɪtʃ.haɪk/ *verb* [I] to travel by getting free rides in someone else's vehicle: *Women should never hitchhike on their own.* ⊃See also **hitch** RIDE.**hitchhiker** /ˈhɪtʃ.haɪ.kəʳ/ ⓤ /-kɚ/ *noun* [C] *Jack often **picks up** hitchhikers.*

hither /ˈhɪð.əʳ/ ⓤ /-ɚ/ *adv OLD USE OR FORMAL* to or towards this place: *Come hither, young sir!*

● **hither and thither** (*LITERARY* **hither and yon**) in many directions: *In clearer water, one encounters shoals of tiny fish, which dart hither and thither like flights of arrows.*

hitherto /ˌhɪð.əˈtuː/ ⓤ /-ɚ-/ *adv FORMAL* until now or until a particular time: *Mira revealed hitherto **unsuspected** talents on the cricket pitch.*

'hit ˌlist *noun* [C usually sing] a list of people that someone intends to murder or take unpleasant action against: *The newspapers were sent a hit list of 100 military and political targets.*

'hit ˌman *noun* [C usually sing] a man who is paid to murder someone

'hit paˌrade *noun* [C] *OLD-FASHIONED* a list which shows which pop songs have sold the most copies in a particular week

HIV /ˌeɪtʃ.aɪˈviː/ *noun* [U] *ABBREVIATION FOR* human immunodeficiency virus: the virus that causes AIDS (= a serious disease that destroys the body's ability to fight infection)

hive /haɪv/ *group noun* [C] a structure where bees live, especially a BEEHIVE (= box-like container), or the group of bees living there

● **a hive of activity/industry** a place where a lot of people are working very hard: *The whole house was a hive of activity on the day before the wedding.*

hive /haɪv/ *verb*

▲ **hive** *sth* **off** *phrasal verb* [M] *UK* to separate one part of a company, usually by selling it: *The plan is to hive off individual companies as soon as they are profitable.*

hives /haɪvz/ *noun* [U] a condition in which a person's skin develops red raised areas: *She **broke out in** hives after eating strawberries.*

HIV-positive /ˌeɪtʃ.aɪ.viːˈpɒz.ə.tɪv/ ⓤ /-ˈpɑː.zə.t̬ɪv/ *adj* If a person is HIV-positive, they are infected with HIV although they might not have AIDS or develop it for a long time.

hiya /ˈhaɪ.jə/ *exclamation INFORMAL* an expression said when people who know each other well meet: *Hiya, Pete, how're you doing?*

hm ,hmm /həm/ *exclamation* something you say when you pause while talking or when you are uncertain: *"Which one do you like best?" "Hm. I'm not sure."* ○ *"He says he's doing it for our benefit." "Hmm, I'm still not convinced."*

HMS /ˌeɪtʃ.emˈes/ *ABBREVIATION FOR* Her or His Majesty's Ship: used before the names of ships in the British navy: *HMS Illustrious*

HNC /ˌeɪtʃ.enˈsiː/ *noun* [C] *ABBREVIATION FOR* Higher National Certificate: a qualification, especially in a scientific or technical subject, that is studied for at a British college

HND /ˌeɪtʃ.enˈdiː/ *noun* [C] *ABBREVIATION FOR* Higher National Diploma: a qualification, especially in a scientific or technical subject, that is studied for at a British college

hoagie /ˈhəʊ.gi/ ⓤ /ˈhoʊ-/ *noun* [C] *US* a long thin loaf of bread filled with salad and cold meat or cheese

hoard /hɔːd/ ⓤ /hɔːrd/ *verb* [T] to collect large amounts of something and keep it in a safe, often secret, place: *During the siege people began hoarding food and supplies.* ○ *There would be enough food on a daily basis if people were not hoarding it.***hoard** /hɔːd/ ⓤ /hɔːrd/ *noun* [C] *We found a huge hoard **of** tinned food in the basement.* **hoarder** /ˈhɔː.dəʳ/ ⓤ /ˈhɔːr.dɚ/ *noun* [C]

hoarding ADVERTISEMENT /ˈhɔː.dɪŋ/ ⓤ /ˈhɔːr-/ *noun* [C] (*US* **billboard**) a very large board on which advertisements are shown, especially at the side of a road: *an advertising hoarding*

hoarding FENCE /ˈhɔː.dɪŋ/ ⓤ /ˈhɔːr-/ *noun* [C] *UK* a temporary fence, usually made of boards, put around an area, especially one where people are building

hoar frost /ˈhɔː.frɒst/ ⓤ /ˈhɔːr.frɑːst/ *noun* [U] a white layer of needle-like pieces of ice which forms on objects outside when it is very cold

hoarse /hɔːs/ ⓤ /hɔːrs/ *adj* (of a voice or a person) having a rough voice, often because of a sore throat or a cold: *a hoarse **voice*** ○ *She **sounded** a bit hoarse.* ○ *You'll **make** yourself hoarse if you keep shouting like that!* ⊃See also **husky** VOICE.**hoarsely** /ˈhɔː.sli/ ⓤ /ˈhɔːr.sli/ *adv* **hoarseness** /ˈhɔː.snəs/ ⓤ /ˈhɔːr.snəs/ *noun* [U]

hoary /ˈhɔː.ri/ ⓤ /ˈhɔːr.i/ *adj* **1** *OLD-FASHIONED* very old and familiar and therefore not interesting or amusing: *He told a few hoary **old** jokes and nobody laughed.* **2** *LITERARY* (of a person) very old and white- or grey-haired

hoax /həʊks/ ⓤ /hoʊks/ *noun* [C] a plan to deceive someone, such as telling the police there is a bomb somewhere when there is not one, or a trick: *The bomb threat turned out to be a hoax.*

hoax /həʊks/ ⓤ /hoʊks/ *verb* [T] to deceive, especially by playing a trick on someone **hoaxer** /ˈhəʊk.səʳ/ ⓤ /ˈhoʊk.sɚ/ *noun* [C]

hob /hɒb/ ⓤ /hɑːb/ *noun* [C] **1** *UK* (*US* **stove, stovetop**) the top part or surface of a cooker on which pans can be heated: *Most domestic hobs have four gas or electric rings.* ⊃See picture **In the Kitchen** on page Centre 16 **2** *UK OLD-FASHIONED* in the past, a metal shelf next to a fireplace where pans were heated

hobble WALK /ˈhɒb.l̩/ ⓤ /ˈhɑː.bl̩/ *verb* [I usually + adv or prep] to walk in an awkward way, usually because the feet or legs are injured: *The last time I saw Rachel she was hobbling around with a stick.* ○ *Some of the runners could only manage to hobble over the finishing line.*

hobble LIMIT /ˈhɒb.l̩/ ⓤ /ˈhɑː.bl̩/ *verb* [T] **1** to limit something or control the freedom of someone: *A long list of amendments have hobbled the new legislation.* **2** *LITERARY* If you hobble an animal, especially a horse, you tie two of its legs together so that it cannot run away.

hobby /ˈhɒb.i/ ⓤ /ˈhɑː.bi/ *noun* [C] an activity which someone does for pleasure when they are not working: *Ben's hobby is restoring vintage motorcycles.*

hobbyist /ˈhɒb.i.ɪst/ ⓤ /ˈhɑː.bi-/ *noun* [C] MAINLY US someone who does something as a hobby: *a computer hobbyist*

ˈhobby ˌhorse SUBJECT *noun* [C] a subject that someone talks about frequently, usually for a long time: *Don't mention tax or Bernard'll* **get on** *his hobby horse again.*

ˈhobby ˌhorse TOY *noun* [C] a toy made from a long stick with a shape like a horse's head at one end, which a child can pretend to ride

hobgoblin /ˌhɒbˈɡɒb.lɪn/ ⓤ /ˈhɑːbˌɡɑː.blɪn/ *noun* [C] (in stories) a small ugly creature which causes trouble

hobnail (boot) /ˌhɒb.neɪlˈbuːts/ ⓤ /ˌhɑːb-/ *noun* [C] (ALSO **hobnailed boot**) a heavy boot or shoe that has nails hammered into the bottom to make it last longer

hobnob /ˈhɒb.nɒb/ ⓤ /ˈhɑːb.nɑːb/ *verb* [I] **-bb-** INFORMAL DISAPPROVING to spend time being friendly with someone who is important or famous: *She often has her picture in the papers, hobnobbing* **with** *the rich and famous.*

hobo /ˈhəʊ.bəʊ/ ⓤ /ˈhoʊ.boʊ/ *noun* [C] *plural* **hobos** or **hoboes** US someone who does not have a job or a house and who moves from one place to another

Hobson's choice /ˌhɒb.sᵊnzˈtʃɔɪs/ ⓤ /ˌhɑːb-/ *noun* [U] a situation in which it seems that you can choose between different things or actions, but there is really only one thing that you can take or do: *It's* **a case of Hobson's choice***, because if I don't agree to their terms, I'll lose my job.*

hock WINE /hɒk/ ⓤ /hɑːk/ *noun* [U] MAINLY UK a type of white wine from Germany

hock MONEY /hɒk/ ⓤ /hɑːk/ *noun* INFORMAL **in hock 1** in debt; owing or owed: *The company's entire assets are now in hock* **to** *the banks.* **2** Possessions which are in hock are PAWNED (= left temporarily with a person in exchange for an amount of money which must be paid back after a limited time to prevent the item from being sold): *Most of her jewellery is in hock.*

hock /hɒk/ ⓤ /hɑːk/ *verb* [T] INFORMAL to sell something which you hope to buy back later because you need money now: *She had to hock her wedding ring.*

hock JOINT /hɒk/ ⓤ /hɑːk/ *noun* [C] **1** the middle joint in the back leg of an animal such as a horse **2** MAINLY US the meat on the lower leg of an animal: *ham hocks*

hockey /ˈhɒk.i/ ⓤ /ˈhɑː.ki/ *noun* [U] **1** UK (US **field hockey**) a game played on a sports field between two teams of eleven players who each have a curved stick with which they try to put a small hard ball into the other team's goal ➔See picture **Sports** on page Centre 10 **2** US FOR **ice hockey** ➔See picture **Sports** on page Centre 10

hocus-pocus /ˌhəʊ.kəsˈpəʊ.kəs/ ⓤ /ˌhoʊ.kəsˈpoʊ-/ *noun* [U] tricks used to deceive, or words used to hide what is happening or make it unclear: *So much of what politicians say is just hocus-pocus.*

hod /hɒd/ ⓤ /hɑːd/ *noun* [C] a container for carrying bricks made of an open box on a pole which is held against the shoulder

hodgepodge /ˈhɒdʒ.pɒdʒ/ ⓤ /ˈhɑːdʒ.pɑːdʒ/ *noun* [C] a **hotchpotch**

hoe /həʊ/ ⓤ /hoʊ/ *noun* [C] a garden tool with a long handle and a short blade used to remove weeds and break up the surface of the ground **hoe** /həʊ/ ⓤ /hoʊ/ *verb* [I or T] **hoeing, hoed, hoed** *They spent the afternoon hoeing (the vegetable patch).*

hoedown /ˈhəʊ.daʊn/ ⓤ /ˈhoʊ-/ *noun* [C] in the US, a party, usually in the countryside, where there is traditional music and dancing

hog ANIMAL /hɒɡ/ ⓤ /hɑːɡ/ *noun* [C] **1** US a pig, especially one which is allowed to grow large so that it can be eaten **2** UK a male pig with its sexual organs removed which is kept for its meat ➔Compare **boar; sow** ANIMAL.

hog PERSON /hɒɡ/ ⓤ /hɑːɡ/ *noun* [C] INFORMAL DISAPPROVING someone who takes much more than a fair share of something, especially by eating too much: *You've eaten it all? You hog!*

hog /hɒɡ/ ⓤ /hɑːɡ/ *verb* [T] **-gg-** INFORMAL to take or use more than your share of something: *He's always*

hogging the bathroom (= spending too much time in the bathroom, so that no one else can use it).

● **hog the road** DISAPPROVING to drive so that other vehicles cannot go past

Hogmanay /ˈhɒɡ.mə.neɪ/ ⓤ /ˈhɑːɡ.mə.neɪ/ *noun* [C or U] UK in Scotland, the last day of the year and the parties to celebrate it which start in the evening and continue until the next day ➔See also **New Year's Eve**.

hogwash /ˈhɒɡ.wɒʃ/ ⓤ /ˈhɑːɡ.wɑːʃ/ *noun* [U] INFORMAL nonsense, or words which are intended to deceive: *His answer was pure hogwash.*

ho-ho(-ho) /ˌhəʊˈhəʊ/ ⓤ /ˌhoʊˈhoʊ/ *exclamation* used in writing or sometimes spoken to represent the sound of laughter

ho-hum /ˌhəʊˈhʌm/ ⓤ /ˌhoʊ-/ *exclamation* an expression used when someone is bored, or when they accept that something unpleasant cannot be stopped from happening: *So I've got to do it all again. Ho-hum.*

ho-hum /ˌhəʊˈhʌm/ ⓤ /ˌhoʊ-/ *adj* boring or ordinary

hoick /hɔɪk/ *verb* [T + adv or prep] UK INFORMAL to raise or pull something, usually with a quick movement and with effort: *They hoicked the box onto the table.* ○ *He hoicked* **up** *his trousers.*

the hoi polloi /ðəˌhɔɪ.pəˈlɔɪ/ *plural noun* DISAPPROVING OR HUMOROUS ordinary people: *Anthony will be in the VIP lounge where he doesn't have to mix with the hoi polloi.*

hoist /hɔɪst/ *verb* [T] **1** to lift something heavy, sometimes using ropes or a machine: *A helicopter hoisted the final section of the bridge into place.* ○ *With some difficulty he hoisted her onto his shoulders.* ○ [R] *I scrabbled for a handhold and hoisted myself up.* **2 hoist a flag** to raise a flag to the top of a pole using a rope

● **be hoist(ed) with/by** *your* **own petard** FORMAL to suffer harm from a plan by which you had intended to harm someone else

hoist /hɔɪst/ *noun* [C] a device used for lifting heavy things

hoity-toity /ˌhɔɪ.tiˈtɔɪ.ti/ ⓤ /-t̬iˈtɔɪ.t̬i/ *adj* INFORMAL DISAPPROVING behaving as if you are better or more important than other people

hokey /ˈhəʊ.ki/ ⓤ /ˈhoʊ-/ *adj* US INFORMAL too emotional or artificial and therefore difficult to believe: *The ending of the movie was awful hokey.*

hokum /ˈhəʊ.kəm/ ⓤ /ˈhoʊ-/ *noun* [U] MAINLY US INFORMAL a film, play or television programme which is not realistic: *As a whole the series was never less than watchable – hokum, perhaps, but entertaining.*

hold SUPPORT /həʊld/ ⓤ /hoʊld/ *verb* [T] **held, held 1** to take and keep something in your hand or arms: *Can you hold the bag while I open the door?* ○ *He was holding a gun.* ○ *The little girl held her mother's* **hand***. He held her in his arms.* ○ [+ obj + adj] *Could you hold the door* **open***, please?* ○ *Rosie held* **out** *an apple for the horse.* ○ *All those who agree please hold* **up** *their hand* (= raise their arm). **2** to support something: *Will the rope be strong enough to hold my weight?* ○ *Each wheel is held* **on** *with four bolts.* ○ *The parts are held* **together** *with glue.* **3 hold** *your* **nose** to press your nose tightly between your thumb and finger in order to close it: *I have to hold my nose when I jump into water.*

● **hold hands** When two people hold hands, one person holds the other person's hand in their hand, especially to show that they love each other: *They walked along holding hands.* ➔See also **hand in hand** at hand BODY PART.

● **hold** *your* **head (up) high** to be very confident and proud: *If you know that you did your best, you can hold your head high.*

● **can't hold a candle to** to not be as good as the person or thing mentioned: *Her latest book is readable enough, but it can't hold a candle to her earlier work.*

hold /həʊld/ ⓤ /hoʊld/ *noun* **1** [S or U] when you hold something or someone, or the way you do this: *Keep a tight hold* **on** *your tickets.* ○ *Don't worry if you* **lose hold** *of the reins – the horse won't wander off.* ➔See also **foothold; handhold; toehold**. **2 catch/get/grab/take hold of** *sth/sb* to start holding something or someone: *He took hold of one end of the carpet and tugged.* ○ *I just managed to grab hold of Lucy before she fell in the pool.*

3 [C] in fighting sports, a position in which one person holds another person so that they cannot move part of their body **4** [C] a place to put the hands and feet, especially when climbing

• **get hold of 1** UK (US **get ahold of**) INFORMAL to find someone or obtain something: *Where can I get hold of some stamps?* ○ *How can I get ahold of Chris?* **2** MAINLY UK to understand something: *This is a very difficult concept to get hold of.*

• **no holds barred** without limits or controls: *This is comedy with no holds barred.*

holder /ˈhəʊl.dər/ ⓤ /ˈhoʊl.dɚ/ *noun* [C] a device for putting objects in or for keeping them in place: *a toothbrush holder* ○ *a cigarette holder*

hold [KEEP] /həʊld/ ⓤ /hoʊld/ *verb* [T] **held**, **held 1** to keep something, especially when it might have been lost: *I asked the shop to hold the dress for me until this afternoon.* ○ *You have to be a fairly good speaker to hold an audience's **attention/interest**.* **2** to keep someone in a place so that they cannot leave: *The police are holding several people **in custody** (= at the police station) for questioning.* ○ [+ obj + n] *The terrorists held him **hostage** for 18 months.* ○ *I was held **prisoner** in a tiny attic room.*

• **can't hold *your*** drink (US USUALLY **can't hold *your*** liquor) DISAPPROVING If you can't hold your drink, you feel ill quickly when you drink alcohol.

hold [CONTINUE] /həʊld/ ⓤ /hoʊld/ *verb* [I or T] **held**, **held** to cause to stay or continue in the same way as before: *Let's hope our good luck holds.* ○ *I hope the repair holds until we get the car to a garage.* ○ *The old adage that 'money talks' still holds **true** (= is still true).* ○ *The government is committed to holding exports at their present level.* ○ *The ship/aircraft held its course.*

• **hold good** to continue to be true: *Their arguments were valid a hundred years ago and they still hold good today.*

• **hold on/tight** to make yourself continue to do what you are doing or stay where you are although it is difficult or unpleasant: *If you can just hold on I'll go and get some help.* ➶See also **hold** SUPPORT.

• **hold *your*** own (ALSO **hold *your*** (own) ground) to be as successful as other people or things in a situation: *Josie can hold her own in any argument.*

• **hold *your*** own to not become more ill or more weak: *He's still ill but holding his own.*

• **hold the road** If a vehicle holds the road, its wheels stay firmly on the road and do not slide while moving. ➶See also **roadholding**.

hold [DELAY] /həʊld/ ⓤ /hoʊld/ *verb* **held**, **held 1** [I or T] to wait, or to stop something temporarily: *They've decided to hold all future deliveries until the invoice has been paid.* ○ *How long can you hold your **breath** (= stop breathing)?* ○ *Will you hold my calls for the next half hour please?* ○ *She's on the phone at the moment – will you hold **(the line)** (= wait on the telephone until she can speak to you)?* **2** [T] US If you ask someone to hold something, you do not want them to include it: *I'd like a ham sandwich on rye, hold the lettuce.*

• **don't hold *your*** breath INFORMAL do not expect a stated thing to happen for a very long time: *She said she'd get back to us, but don't hold your breath!*

• **there is no holding *sb*** (back) If there is no holding someone (back), they do what they want to do eagerly and cannot be stopped.

• **Hold everything!** INFORMAL used to tell someone to stop what they are doing: *Hold everything! He's changed his mind again.*

• **Hold it!** INFORMAL used to tell someone to wait or stop doing something: *Hold it! I haven't got my coat on yet.* ○ *Hold it! What are you saying?*

• **hold still** used to tell someone to stop moving: *Hold still, this won't hurt.*

• **hold *your*** tongue to not speak: *Hold your tongue, young man!* ○ *I'm going to have to learn to hold my tongue (= not say things that upset people).*

• **hold *your*** horses OLD-FASHIONED INFORMAL used to tell someone to stop and consider carefully their decision or opinion about something: *Just hold your horses, Bill! Let's think about this for a moment.*

hold /həʊld/ ⓤ /hoʊld/ *noun* **on hold 1** If you are on hold when using the telephone, you are waiting to speak

to someone: *Mr Briggs is on hold.* ○ *His phone is engaged – can I **put** you on hold?* **2** If an activity is on hold, it has been intentionally delayed: *Everything's on hold again because of the bad weather.* ○ *The film's been **put** on hold until the financial situation improves.*

hold [CONTAIN] /həʊld/ ⓤ /hoʊld/ *verb* [T not continuous] **held**, **held 1** to contain or be able to contain something: *This jug holds exactly one pint.* ○ *One bag won't hold all of the shopping – we'd better take two.* ○ *Modern computers can hold huge amounts of information.* **2** to have or contain something which you will experience: *Who can tell what the future holds?* ○ *She's very religious, so death holds no fear for her.*

• **hold water** If a reason, argument or explanation holds water, it is true: *Her alibi just didn't hold water.*

hold [CONTROL] /həʊld/ ⓤ /hoʊld/ *verb* [T] **held**, **held** to have something, especially a position or money, or to control something: *He currently holds the position of technical manager.* ○ *The bank holds large reserves of gold.* ○ *Despite incurring heavy losses, the rebels now hold the town and the surrounding hills.*

• **hold all the cards** to be in a strong position when you are competing with someone else, because you have all the advantages: *Management holds all the cards when it comes to the negotiations over job cuts.*

• **hold court** MAINLY HUMOROUS to receive a lot of attention from other people who gather round to listen, especially on a social occasion: *Patrick is holding court at the end table.*

• **hold the floor** to speak to a group of people, often for a long time, without allowing anyone else to speak

• **hold (down) the fort** HUMOROUS to have responsibility for something while someone is absent: *I'll be out of the office for a few hours – will you hold the fort until I get back?*

• **hold the key** to have control of something: *Because the two main parties have won almost the same number of votes, the minority group holds the key **to** the result.*

• **hold the reins** to be in control: *She's the boss but her secretary often seems to hold the reins.*

• **hold sway** to have power or a very strong influence: *Fundamentalist beliefs hold sway **over** whole districts, ensuring the popularity of religious leaders.*

hold /həʊld/ ⓤ /hoʊld/ *noun* [S] power or control over something or someone: *Their company has a **strong** hold **on/over** the computer market.*

holder /ˈhəʊl.dər/ ⓤ /ˈhoʊl.dɚ/ *noun* [C] someone who officially owns something: *an account/licence/passport holder* ○ *Holders of shares in the company receive various benefits.* ➶See also **shareholder**.

hold [MAKE HAPPEN] /həʊld/ ⓤ /hoʊld/ *verb* [T] **held**, **held** to make something, especially a meeting or an election happen: *Could we hold a meeting to discuss this tomorrow afternoon?* ○ *The election will be held on 8th of August.* ○ *I find it's almost impossible to hold a sensible conversation with her.*

hold [BELIEVE] /həʊld/ ⓤ /hoʊld/ *verb* [T not continuous] **held**, **held** to believe an idea or opinion: [+ *to* infinitive] *Small amounts of alcohol are held to be good for the heart.* ○ *You sold it to me, so if it breaks I'll hold you **responsible** (= make you take responsibility).*

hold [SPACE] /həʊld/ ⓤ /hoʊld/ *noun* [C] the space in a ship or aircraft in which goods are carried

---

PHRASAL VERBS WITH **hold** ▼

▲ **hold it/that against *sb*** *phrasal verb* to like someone less because they have done something wrong or behaved badly in the past: *He made a mistake but I don't hold it against him – we all make mistakes.*

▲ **hold *sth*** back [INFORMATION] *phrasal verb* [M] to keep information secret from someone on purpose

▲ **hold *sb/sth*** back [DELAY] *phrasal verb* [M] to delay the development of something: *She felt that having children would hold her back.*

▲ **hold *sb/sth*** back [STOP] *phrasal verb* [M] If you hold something back, you stop it coming or advancing: *Sandbags will hold the flood waters back for a while.*

▲ **hold back** [NOT DO] *phrasal verb* to not do something, often because of fear or because you do not want to make a bad situation worse: *He held back, terrified of going into the dark room.*

▲ **hold** *sb/sth* **down** STOP FROM MOVING *phrasal verb* [M] to keep someone or something in a particular place or position and to stop them from moving: *He was struggling so much that it took three police officers to hold him down.*

▲ **hold** *sth* **down** KEEP LOW *phrasal verb* [M] to keep something, especially costs, at a low level: *to hold down prices/wages*

● **hold down a job** to manage to keep a job for a period of time * NOTE: This is not used in the passive.

▲ **hold forth** *phrasal verb* USUALLY DISAPPROVING to talk about a particular subject for a long time, often in a way that other people find boring: *She held forth all afternoon **about/on** government incompetence.*

▲ **hold off** WAIT *phrasal verb* **1** to not do something immediately: [+ v-ing] *Let's hold off **making** a decision until next week.* ○ US *They've decided to hold off **on** buying a car until they're both working.* **2** If rain or a storm holds off, it does not start immediately: *If the rain holds off we could walk there.*

▲ **,hold** *sb* **'off** PREVENT DEFEAT *phrasal verb* [M] to stop someone from attacking or defeating you: *How much longer will the resistance fighters be able to hold off the enemy?*

▲ **hold on** WAIT *phrasal verb* INFORMAL to wait for a short time: *Hold on, I'll check in my diary.* * NOTE: This is often used in the imperative form.

▲ **hold on** HOLD FIRMLY *phrasal verb* to hold something or someone firmly with your hands or arms: *She held on tightly to his waist.*

▲ **hold onto** *sth* HOLD FIRMLY *phrasal verb* to hold something or someone firmly with your hands or your arms: *Hold onto the rope and don't let go.* ○ *She held onto me so tightly it was quite painful.*

▲ **hold onto/on to** *sth* KEEP *phrasal verb* to keep something you have: *Hold on to your ticket – you'll need it later.* ○ *Lewis held onto the lead until the final lap.*

▲ **hold** *sth* **out** OFFER *phrasal verb* to offer a possibility, solution, hope etc: *Few people hold out any **hope** of finding more survivors.*

▲ **hold out** CONTINUE *phrasal verb* to continue to demand, do or believe something, despite other people trying to force you not to: *The other side are holding out **for** a higher price.*

▲ **hold out** DEFEND *phrasal verb* to continue to defend yourself against an enemy or attack without being defeated: *They won't be able to hold out much longer under this sort of bombardment.*

▲ **hold out** LAST *phrasal verb* If a supply of something such as food or money holds out, there is enough of it to last for a particular period of time.

▲ **hold out for** *sth* *phrasal verb* to wait until you get what you want: *The workers are holding out for a 10% pay rise.*

▲ **hold out on** *sb* *phrasal verb* **1** INFORMAL to refuse to give help or information to someone: *Don't hold out on me – I need to know who did it.* **2** MAINLY US INFORMAL to refuse to give money to someone

▲ **hold** *sth* **over** *phrasal verb* US If a film, play, etc. is held over, it is shown or performed more times than was originally planned, usually because it is very popular with the public.

▲ **hold** *sb* **to** *sth* *phrasal verb* to cause someone to act on a promise or agreement: *We'll hold him to the exact terms of the contract.*

▲ **hold** *sb/sth* **up** STEAL *phrasal verb* [M] to steal from someone using violence or the threat of violence: *They held the same bank up twice in one week.* ○ *He was held up at gunpoint by a gang of masked youths.*

▲ **hold** *sb/sth* **up** DELAY *phrasal verb* [M] to delay someone or something: *Traffic was held up for several hours by the accident.*

▲ **hold up** REMAIN STRONG *phrasal verb* to remain strong or successful: *Will his alibi hold up* (= continue to seem true) *in court?* ○ *I hope the repairs hold up until we can get to a garage.*

▲ **hold** *sth* **up as** *sth* *phrasal verb* (ALSO **hold up** *sth* **as** *sth*) to use something or someone as an example of something, especially something very good: *Sweden is often held up as an example of a successful social democracy.*

▲ **not hold with** *sth* *phrasal verb* FORMAL to not approve of an idea or activity

holdall MAINLY UK /'həʊld.ɔːl/ US /'hoʊld.ɑːl/ noun [C] (US USUALLY **carryall**) a small case used for carrying clothes and personal items when travelling

holding /'həʊl.dɪŋ/ US /'hoʊl-/ noun [C] something that you own such as shares in a company or buildings, or land which you rent and farm: *To ensure security the investment fund has holdings in many companies.*

'holding ,company noun [C] a company whose main purpose is to control another company or companies through owning shares in it or them

'holding ,ope'ration noun [C usually sing] UK a temporary way of dealing with a situation until a new and better way can be introduced: *This is just a holding operation until we get the new management structure sorted out.*

holdout /'həʊld.aʊt/ US /'hoʊld-/ noun [C] a person, organization or country that continues to do something, despite other people trying to force them not to: *It's time to shame holdouts like the USA into signing the treaty.*

hold-up DELAY /'həʊld.ʌp/ US /'hoʊld-/ noun [C] a delay: *Come on, let's go. What's the hold-up?*

hold-up STEALING /'həʊld.ʌp/ US /'hoʊld-/ noun [C] when someone steals from someone else using violence or the threat of violence: *In the hold-up, a masked youth threatened the bank staff with a gun.*

hold-ups /'həʊld.ʌps/ US /'hoʊld-/ plural noun STOCKINGS (= light coverings for the legs and feet) which are elasticated or have a piece of sticky material at the top and can hold themselves up

hole SPACE /həʊl/ US /hoʊl/ noun [C] **1** an empty space in an object, usually with an opening to the object's surface, or an opening which goes completely through an object: *We **dug** a hole and planted the tree.* ○ *My jumper's got a hole **in** it.* ○ *Drill a hole through the back of the cupboard and pass the wires through.* **2** in golf, one of the small circular spaces in the ground into which the ball is hit **3** in golf, one of the usually 18 areas of play: *the famous 18-hole Old Course at St. Andrews*

● **be in a hole** UK INFORMAL to be in a difficult or an embarrassing situation: *We've lost the order and we're in a bit of a hole.*

● **a hole in one** in golf, when someone's ball goes into the hole the first time they hit it, which is rare

● **be in the hole** US INFORMAL to be in debt: *After selling all its assets, the bank was still half a million dollars in the hole.*

● **make a hole in** *sth* UK to reduce an amount of money by a lot: *The holiday made a big hole in our savings but I'm glad we went.*

● **need** *sth* **like you need a hole in the head** HUMOROUS to not need or want something at all: *Extra work? I need that like I need a hole in the head.*

hole /həʊl/ US /hoʊl/ verb [T] SPECIALIZED to make a hole in something, especially a ship or boat: *A torpedo holed the ship below the water and it quickly sank.*

hole PLACE /həʊl/ US /hoʊl/ noun [C] **1** a place in the ground where a small animal lives: *a mouse/rabbit/fox hole* **2** INFORMAL a small unpleasant place where someone lives: *What a hole that house was – I'm so pleased we moved.* ⊃See also **hole in the wall** BUILDING.

hole FAULT /həʊl/ US /hoʊl/ noun [C] a mistake or problem in the reasoning of an argument, discussion, plan, etc: *The new proposal has several holes in it.*

▲ **hole up (somewhere)** *phrasal verb* INFORMAL to stay in a safe place, often as a way of escape: *We'd better find some shelter and hole up until the storm passes.*

● **be holed up** to be hiding in a safe place: *The robbers were holed up in a deserted warehouse.*

,hole in the 'heart noun [C] a medical condition in which there is an additional opening between the main parts of the heart

,hole in the 'wall MONEY noun [C usually sing] UK INFORMAL FOR **cash machine**

,hole in the 'wall BUILDING noun [C usually sing] US a small, often unpleasant, shop, house or restaurant: *It's*

just a hole in the wall but the food is good.

hole punch(er) /'həʊl̩pʌn.tʃəʳ/ [US] /'hoʊl̩pʌn.tʃɚ/ *noun* [C] a device used for making holes in pieces of paper so that they can be fastened together

holiday /'hɒl.ɪ.deɪ/ [US] /'hɑː.lɪ-/ *noun* **1** [C or U] *UK* (*US* **vacation**) a time, often one or two weeks, when someone does not go to work or school but is free to do what they want, such as travel or relax: *a camping/skiing holiday* ○ *Have you decided where you're going **for** your holiday this year?* ○ *Patricia is **on** holiday next week.* ○ *How many days' holiday do you get with your new job?* ○ *We thought we'd go to France for our **summer** holiday.* **2** [C] an official day when you do not have to go to work or school: *a public holiday* ○ *St Patrick's Day is a holiday in Ireland.*

holidays /'hɒl.ɪ.deɪz/ [US] /'hɑː.lɪ-/ *plural noun* (*INFORMAL* **hols**) *UK Have you decided where you're going **for** your holidays* (= holiday) *this year?* ○ *Surely the **school** holidays start soon.*

holiday *UK* /'hɒl.ɪ.deɪ/ [US] /'hɑː.lɪ-/ *verb* [I usually + adv or prep] (*US* **vacation**) to take a holiday: *My parents are holidaying in Spain this year.*

'holiday ˌcamp *noun* [C] *UK* a place where people on holiday can stay and entertainments are provided for them

holidaymaker *UK* /'hɒl.ə.diˌmeɪ.kəʳ/ [US] /'hɑː.lə.deɪ-ˌmeɪ.kɚ/ *noun* [C] (*US* **vacationer**) a person who is on holiday away from where they usually live

the 'holiday ˌseason *noun* [S] *MAINLY US* the period around Christmas and New Year

holier-than-thou /ˌhəʊ.li.ə.ðən'ðaʊ/ [US] /ˌhoʊl.i.ɚ-/ *adj DISAPPROVING* If a person is holier-than-thou, they think that they are morally better than anyone else.

holistic /həʊ'lɪs.tɪk/ [US] /hoʊ'lɪs-/ *adj* dealing with or treating the whole of something or someone and not just a part: *My doctor takes a holistic **approach** to disease.* ○ *Ecological problems usually require holistic solutions.*

holistically /həʊ'lɪs.tɪ.kli/ [US] /hoʊl.ɪs-/ *adv*

holism /'həʊ.lɪ.zᵊm/ [US] /'hoʊl.ɪ-/ *noun* [U] the belief that each thing is a whole which is more important than the parts that make it up

hoˌlistic 'medicine *noun* [U] treatment which deals with the whole person, not just the injury or disease

holler /'hɒl.əʳ/ [US] /'hɑː.lɚ/ *verb* [I or T] *MAINLY US INFORMAL* to shout loudly: *He was hollering something about seeing a snake.* **holler** /'hɒl.əʳ/ [US] /'hɑː.lɚ/ *noun* [C] *He **let out a** holler as he fell.*

hollow [EMPTY] /'hɒl.əʊ/ [US] /'hɑː.loʊ/ *adj* **1** having a hole or empty space inside: *a hollow tube* ○ *Hollow blocks are used because they are lighter.* ○ *a hollow log* **2 hollow cheeks/eyes** If someone has hollow cheeks or eyes, their cheeks curve in or their eyes look deep in their head because they are old, tired, or ill.

hollow /'hɒl.əʊ/ [US] /'hɑː.loʊ/ *noun* [C] **1** a hole or empty space in something, or a low area in a surface: *The dog found a hollow in the ground to hide in from the wind.* **2** (*ALSO* **Hollow**) *US* a valley: *We used to go for long walks in the hollow.* ○ *Sleepy Hollow* **hollowness** /'hɒl.əʊ.nəs/ [US] /'hɑː.loʊ-/ *noun* [U]

hollow [WITHOUT VALUE] /'hɒl.əʊ/ [US] /'hɑː.loʊ/ *adj* (of situations, feelings or words) lacking value; not true or sincere: *It was something of **a** hollow **victory** – she won the case but lost all her savings in legal fees.* ○ *Even sex had become a hollow pleasure.* ○ *Will their good intentions become realities or are they just hollow promises?*

• **ring/sound hollow** If something someone says rings hollow, it does not sound true or sincere.

hollowly /'hɒl.əʊ.li/ [US] /'hɑː.loʊ.li/ *adv* in a way that does not sound true or sincere **hollowness** /'hɒl.əʊ.nəs/ [US] /'hɑː.loʊ-/ *noun* [U] *the hollowness of fame/success*

hollow [SOUND] /'hɒl.əʊ/ [US] /'hɑː.loʊ/ *adj* (of sound) as if made by hitting an empty container: *a hollow sound* ○ *This tree trunk **sounds** hollow.* **hollowly** /'hɒl.əʊ.li/ [US] /'hɑː.loʊ.li/ *adv*: *Her footsteps echoed hollowly in the quiet streets.*

hollow /'hɒl.əʊ/ [US] /'hɑː.loʊ/ *verb*

▲ **ˌhollow *sth* 'out** *phrasal verb* [M] to make an empty space inside something: *Sand carried by the wind has hollowed out the base of the cliff.*

hollow-cheeked /ˌhɒl.əʊ'tʃiːkt/ [US] /ˌhɑː.loʊ-/ *adj* describes a person whose face is too thin

hollow-eyed /ˌhɒl.əʊ'aɪd/ [US] /ˌhɑː.loʊ-/ *adj* describes a person whose eyes seem to have sunk into their face because of illness or tiredness

holly /'hɒl.i/ [US] /'hɑː.li/ *noun* [C or U] a small evergreen tree with shiny sharp leaves and small round red fruit

hollyhock /'hɒl.i.hɒk/ [US] /'hɑː.li.hɑːk/ *noun* [C] a garden plant which has very tall stems covered with brightly coloured flowers ➲See picture **Flowers and Plants** on page Centre 3

Hollywood /'hɒl.i.wʊd/ [US] /'hɑː.li-/ *noun* the centre of the US film industry

holocaust /'hɒl.ə.kɔːst/ [US] /'hɑː.lə.kɑːst/ *noun* [C] **1** a very large amount of destruction, especially by fire or heat, or the killing of very large numbers of people: *A **nuclear** holocaust* (= destruction caused by nuclear weapons) *would leave few survivors.* **2 the Holocaust** the killing of millions of Jews and others by the NAZIS before and during the Second World War

hologram /'hɒl.ə.græm/ [US] /'hɑː.lə-/ *noun* [C] a special type of photograph or image made with a LASER in which the objects shown look solid, as if they are real, rather than flat

holography /hɒl'ɒg.rə.fi/ [US] /hoʊ'lɑː.grə-/ *noun* [U] the making of holograms **holographic** /ˌhɒl.ə'græf.ɪk/ [US] /ˌhɑː.lə-/ *adj*: *a holographic picture/image/projection*

hols /hɒlz/ [US] /hɑːlz/ *plural noun UK INFORMAL FOR* **holidays**

Holstein /'hɒl.staɪn/ /'həʊl-/ [US] /'hoʊl.stiːn/ *noun* [C] *US FOR* **Friesian**

holster /'həʊl.stəʳ/ [US] /'hoʊl.stɚ/ *noun* [C] a small case usually made of leather and fixed on a belt or a strap, used for carrying a gun

holy [GOOD] /'həʊ.li/ [US] /'hoʊ-/ *adj* **1** related to a religion or a god: *holy scriptures/rites* **2** very religious or pure: *a holy person*

holiness /'həʊ.lɪ.nəs/ [US] /'hoʊ-/ *noun* [U] the quality of being holy: *This temple is a place of great holiness for the religion's followers.*

Holiness /'həʊ.lɪ.nəs/ [US] /'hoʊ-/ *noun* **His/Your Holiness** a title used when talking to or about the Pope: *Yes, Your Holiness.*

holy [EMPHASIS] /'həʊ.li/ [US] /'hoʊ-/ *adj MAINLY US INFORMAL* **Holy cow/mackerel/shit, etc!** used to show surprise, fear, etc: *Holy cow! How did you get that black eye?*

ˌHoly Com'munion *noun* [U] *FORMAL* **Communion** ➲See also **communicant**.

the Holy Grail /ðəˌhəʊ.li'greɪl/ [US] /-ˌhoʊ-/ *noun* [S] **1** a cup believed to have been used by Jesus Christ at the meal before his death **2** something that is extremely difficult to find or obtain: *Sustained nuclear fusion is the holy grail of the power industry.*

the ˌholy of 'holies [RELIGIOUS PLACE] *noun* [S] **1** the holiest part of a religious building, especially the Jewish TEMPLE **2** *UK HUMOROUS* any place which is very special: *This football stadium is the holy of holies to many fans.*

ˌholy 'orders *plural noun* the ceremony by which someone becomes a priest in some parts of the Christian Church: *Will you be **taking** holy orders?*

the Holy See /ðəˌhəʊ.li'siː/ [US] /-ˌhoʊ-/ *noun* [S] the government of the Roman Catholic Church, under the pope

ˌHoly 'Spirit *noun* [S] (*ALSO* **Holy Ghost**) in the Christian Church, God in the form of a spirit

ˌholy 'war *noun* [C] a war fought to defend religious beliefs or to force others to follow a different religion ➲See also **crusade**; **jihad**.

'Holy ˌWeek *noun* [S] the week before Easter Sunday

homage /'hɒm.ɪdʒ/ [US] /'hɑː.mɪdʒ/ *noun* [U] deep respect and often praise shown for a person or god: *On this occasion we **pay** homage **to** him for his achievements.*

homburg /'hɒm.bɜːg/ [US] /'hɑːm.bɝːg/ *noun* [C] a man's hat with a wide curled brim and a fold in the middle of the top

home [HOUSE/APARTMENT] /həʊm/ [US] /hoʊm/ *noun* **1** [C or U] the house, apartment, etc. where you live, especially with your family: *The senator has two homes – an apartment in Washington and a house in Colorado.* ○ *He was living on the streets for three months, and his home was a cardboard box.* ○ *Phone me* ***at*** *home after four o'clock.* ○ *I* ***took*** *home a couple of books to read.* ○ *He* ***left*** *home* (= stopped living with his parents) *when he was 23.* ○ *More and more couples are* ***setting up*** *home together without getting married.* **2** [C] a house, apartment, etc. when it is considered as property which you can buy or sell: *luxury/starter homes* **3** [C] the type of family you come from: *We had a happy home.* ○ *children from a* ***broken*** *home* (= from a family in which the parents had separated) **4** [C] a place where people or animals live and are cared for by people who are not their relatives or owners: *a children's home/an old people's home/a dogs' home* ○ *He spent his early years* ***in a*** *home.*

• **be/feel at home** to feel comfortable and relaxed: *By the end of the week she was beginning to feel at home* ***in*** *her new job.*

• **make *yourself* at home** to relax and make yourself comfortable in someone else's home

• **home from home** *UK* (*US* **home away from home**) a place where you feel as comfortable as you do in your own home: *The hotel was a real home from home.*

home /həʊm/ [US] /hoʊm/ *adj* done at home, or intended to be used at home: *home cooking* ○ *home-brewed beer* ○ *a home computer*

homeless /ˈhəʊm.ləs/ [US] /ˈhoʊm-/ *adj* without a home: *Accommodation needs to be found for thousands of homeless families.*

the homeless *plural noun* people who do not have a home, usually because they are poor **homelessness** /ˈhəʊm.lə.snəs/ [US] /ˈhoʊm-/ *noun* [U] *One common cause of homelessness is separation or divorce.*

COMMON LEARNER ERROR

home

When you use verbs of movement with **home**, for example 'go' or 'come', you do not need to use a preposition.

What time did you go home?
I'll call you as soon as I get home.
~~*What time did you go at home?*~~

When you use the verbs 'be' or 'stay' with **home**, you should use the preposition 'at', although it is possible, especially in US English, to use no preposition.

I was at home all afternoon.
I'll stay at home to look after the children.
Let's stay home tonight and watch a movie on TV.

home [ORIGIN] /həʊm/ [US] /hoʊm/ *noun* [C or U] someone's or something's place of origin, or the place where a person feels they belong: *I live in London, but my home* (= where I was born) *is in Yorkshire.* ○ *I was actually born in New Zealand, but I've lived in England for so long that it* ***feels like*** *home now.*

• **be home and dry** (*AUS* **be home and hosed**) to have successfully completed something: *We just have to finish this section, then we're home and dry.*

• **be home free** *US INFORMAL* to be certain to succeed at something because you have done the most difficult part of it: *Once you leave the main road and cross the bridge, you're home free – we live just three houses further on.*

• **bring *sth* home (to *sb*)** to make someone understand something much more clearly than they did before, especially something unpleasant: *When I saw for myself the damage that had been caused, that really brought home to me the scale of the disaster.*

• **come home to *sb*** If something comes home to someone, they understand it clearly: *The danger really came home to me when I saw the pictures on TV.*

• **drive/hammer *sth* home** to say something clearly and with a lot of force so that you are certain people understand it: *She really drove home the message that we need to economize.*

home [COUNTRY] /həʊm/ [US] /hoʊm/ *noun* [C or U] **1** your own country or your own area: *I wonder what they're doing* ***back*** *home.* **2 be/play at home** If a sports team are/play at home, they play on their own sports field.

home /həʊm/ [US] /hoʊm/ *adj* **1** [before n] connected with or done in your own country: *His books were a success in his home* ***market****, but failed to find an audience abroad.* **2** relating to the place where a sports event happens: *the home team/side*

home /həʊm/ [US] /hoʊm/ *verb*

▲ **home in on *sth/sb*** *phrasal verb INFORMAL* **1** to aim for: *The missile homed in on the ship.* **2** to find and give a lot of attention to something or someone: *The report homed in on the weaknesses in the management structure.*

ˌhome adˈdress *noun* [C usually sing] the address of the house or apartment you live in

ˌhome ˈbase [BASEBALL] *noun* [U] **home plate**

ˌhome ˈbase [PLACE] *noun* [C usually sing] a place where someone or something usually lives, works, or operates from

homeboy /ˈhəʊm.bɔɪ/ [US] /hoʊm-/ *noun* [C] (*ALSO* **homey**) *US SLANG* a boy or man from your own town, or someone who is a close friend or a member of your GANG

ˈhome ˌbuyer *noun* [C] a person who is buying a house or an apartment

homecoming /ˈhəʊmˌkʌm.ɪŋ/ [US] /ˈhoʊm-/ *noun* **1** [C] a person's arrival home after being away for a long time: *They planned a special celebration for her homecoming.* **2** [C or U] *US* a celebration at a school or a college to honour people who were students there earlier

the ˌHome ˈCounties *plural noun* the counties around London in southeast England, considered to be a place where wealthy people live

ˌhome ecoˈnomics *noun* [U] at school, the study of cooking, sewing and all matters relating to the management of a home

the ˌhome ˈfront *US* /- ˈ- ˌ-/ *noun* [S] the people who stay in their own country during a foreign war

home-grown /ˌhəʊmˈgrəʊn/ [US] /ˌhoʊmˈgroʊn/ *adj* **1** from your own garden: *home-grown vegetables* **2** If someone or something is home-grown, they belong to or were developed in your own country: *She's a home-grown talent.*

ˌhome ˈhelp *noun* [C] *UK* someone who is paid to help someone else with the cleaning of their home

homeland /ˈhəʊm.lænd/ [US] /ˈhoʊm-/ *noun* [C] **1** the country you were born in **2** (in the past) one of the areas in South Africa in which black people were separated from whites under the political system of APARTHEID

ˈhome ˌloan *noun* [C] money borrowed from a bank or similar organization in order to buy a house or apartment

homely [PLAIN] *UK* /ˈhəʊm.li/ [US] /ˈhoʊm-/ *adj* (*US* **homey**) plain or ordinary, but pleasant: *The hotel was homely and comfortable.* **homeliness** /ˈhəʊm.lɪ.nəs/ [US] /ˈhoʊm-/ *noun* [U] *MAINLY UK*

homely [UGLY] /ˈhəʊm.li/ [US] /ˈhoʊm-/ *adj US DISAPPROVING* describes a person who is unattractive **homeliness** /ˈhəʊm.lɪ.nəs/ [US] /ˈhoʊm-/ *noun* [U]

homemade, home-made /ˌhəʊmˈmeɪd/ [US] /ˌhoʊm-/ *adj* made at home and not bought from a shop: *homemade bread/cakes* ○ *homemade wine*

homemaker /ˈhəʊmˌmeɪ.kəʳ/ [US] /ˈhoʊmˌmeɪ.kɚ/ *noun* [C] *MAINLY US* a woman who manages a home and often raises children instead of earning money from employment ⊃Compare **house husband**.

ˌhome ˈmovie *noun* [C] a film that you make yourself using a VIDEO CAMERA, especially one of family or holiday activities

ˌhome (ˈphone) ˌnumber *noun* [C usually sing] the telephone number at the house or apartment where you live

ˈHome ˌOffice *noun* [S] the British government department which deals with matters inside Britain that are not the responsibility of other departments, for example justice and the rules for people from other countries entering Britain

homeopathy, *UK ALSO* **homoeopathy** /ˌhəʊ.miˈɒp.ə.θi/ [US] /ˌhoʊ.miˈɑː.pə-/ *noun* [U] a system of treating diseases in which ill people are given very small amounts of natural substances which, in healthy people, would produce the same effects as the diseases produce

homeopath, UK ALSO **homoeopath** /ˈhəʊ.mi.əʊ.pæθ/ /ˈhoʊ.mi.oʊ-/ *noun* [C] a person who treats ill people by homeopathy **homeopathic**, UK ALSO **homoeopathic** /ˌhəʊ.mi.əʊ'pæθ.ɪk/ /ˌhoʊ.mi.oʊ-/ *adj*: *homeopathic medicine/remedies*

homeowner /ˈhəʊmˌəʊ.nəʳ/ /ˈhoʊmˌoʊ.nɚ/ *noun* [C] a person who owns their house or apartment: *The new law will benefit mainly homeowners.*

'home ˌpage *noun* [C] **1** the first page that you see when you look at a WEBSITE on the Internet, usually containing LINKS to other pages **2** a personal WEBSITE on the Internet, containing personal information, photographs, etc.

'home ˌplate *noun* [S] (US INFORMAL **the plate**) in baseball, the place that the player has to stand next to in order to hit the ball, and the last place they have to touch to score a point

homer /ˈhəʊ.məʳ/ /ˈhoʊ.mɚ/ *noun* [C] US INFORMAL a **home run**

home ˈrule *noun* [U] a political arrangement in which a part of a country governs itself independently of the central government of the country

ˌhome ˈrun *noun* [C] (INFORMAL **homer**) US a point scored in baseball by hitting the ball so far that you have time to run all the way round the four corners of the playing field before it is returned

ˌhome ˈschooling *noun* [U] the teaching of children at home, usually by parents

Home ˈSecretary *noun* [U] the British government politician who controls the HOME OFFICE

homesick /ˈhəʊm.sɪk/ /ˈhoʊm-/ *adj* unhappy because of being away from home for a long period: *As I read my mother's letter, I began to feel more and more homesick.* **homesickness** /ˈhəʊm.sɪk.nəs/ /ˈhoʊm-/ *noun* [U]

homespun /ˈhəʊm.spʌn/ /ˈhoʊm-/ *adj* (of beliefs, theories, etc.) simple and ordinary: *homespun philosophy/wisdom*

homestead /ˈhəʊm.sted/ /ˈhoʊm-/ *noun* [C] **1** MAINLY US a house and the surrounding area of land usually used as a farm **2** US in the past, land given by the government for farming

homestead /ˈhəʊm.sted/ /ˈhoʊm-/ *verb* [I or T] US in the past, to build a house and grow crops on land given by the government

homesteader /ˈhəʊmˌsted.əʳ/ /ˈhoʊmˌsted.ɚ/ *noun* [C] US someone who goes to live and grow crops on land given by the government, especially in the past: *In the 1800s, thousands of homesteaders settled on the prairies of the western US.*

ˌhome ˈstraight *noun* [S] UK (US **homestretch**) **1** the last part of something which is being done: *It's taken three months so far, but we're on the home straight now.* **2** the last part of a race

ˌhome ˈtown *noun* [C] (US USUALLY **hometown**) the town or city that a person is from, especially the one in which they were born and lived while they were young: *He was born in Bristol, but he considers London his home town since he's lived there most of his life.*

ˌhome ˈtruth *noun* [C] MAINLY UK a piece of information which is not pleasant or wanted, but is true: *He decided it was time to tell her a few home truths.*

homewards /ˈhəʊm.wədz/ /ˈhoʊm.wɚdz/ *adv* (ALSO **homeward**) towards home: *After three hours cycling we decided to turn homewards.* **homeward** /ˈhəʊm.wəd/ /ˈhoʊm.wɚd/ *adj*: *It was a long homeward journey.*

homework /ˈhəʊm.wɜːk/ /ˈhoʊm.wɜːk/ *noun* [U] work which teachers give their students to do at home: *You can't watch TV until you've done your homework.* ○ *history/geography homework* ✳ NOTE: Do not confuse with **housework**, which is work you do in the house to keep it clean.

● **do your homework** to study a subject or situation carefully so that you know a lot about it and can deal with it successfully: *It was obvious that she had done her homework and thoroughly prepared for her interview.*

homey PERSON /ˈhəʊ.mi/ /ˈhoʊ-/ *noun* [C] US SLANG HOMEBOY

homey PLAIN /ˈhəʊ.mi/ /ˈhoʊ-/ *adj* US FOR **homely** PLAIN

homicide /ˈhɒm.ɪ.saɪd/ /ˈhɑː.mə-/ *noun* [C or U] US FORMAL OR LEGAL (an act of) murder: *He was convicted of homicide.* ○ *The number of homicides in the city has risen sharply.*

homicidal /ˌhɒm.ɪ'saɪ.dᵊl/ /ˌhɑː.mə-/ *adj* likely to murder: *a homicidal maniac*

homily /ˈhɒm.ɪ.li/ /ˈhɑː.mə-/ *noun* [C] DISAPPROVING a piece of spoken or written advice about how someone should behave: *He launched into a homily on family relationships.*

homing /ˈhəʊ.mɪŋ/ /ˈhoʊ-/ *adj* [before n] relating to the ability of some animals to find their way home, or (of an electronic device) producing a special signal so that it can be found using electronic equipment: *Migrating birds and fish have a strong homing instinct.* ○ *The president's car is equipped with a homing device as a security measure.*

ˈhoming ˌpigeon *noun* [C] a PIGEON (= a type of bird) that is trained to return to its home from any place that it starts its journey ✦See also **carrier pigeon**; **racing pigeon**.

hominy /ˈhɒm.ə.ni/ /ˈhɑː.mə-/ *noun* [U] US dried maize which is boiled and eaten

homoerotic /ˌhəʊ.məʊ.ɪ'rɒt.ɪk/ /ˌhoʊ.moʊ.ɪ'rɑː.t̬ɪk/ *adj* (of art, literature, etc.) connected to or causing homosexual desire or pleasure: *homoerotic photographs/literature*

homogeneous /ˌhɒm.ə'dʒiː.ni.əs/ /ˌhəʊ.mə-/ /ˌhoʊ.moʊ'dʒiː-/ *adj* (ALSO **homogenous**) consisting of parts or people which are similar to each other or are of the same type: *a homogeneous group/society* ○ *The population of the village has remained remarkably homogeneous.* ✦Compare **heterogeneous**. **homogeneity** /ˌhɒm.ə.dʒə'neɪ.ɪ.ti/ /ˌhɑː.mə.dʒə'neɪ.ə.t̬i/ *noun* [U] *cultural/racial homogeneity*

homogenized, UK USUALLY **-ised** /həˈmɒdʒ.ɪ.naɪzd/ /həˈmɑː.dʒə-/ *adj* SPECIALIZED describes milk which has been treated so that the cream is mixed into the other parts of the liquid

homogenous /ˌhɒm.ə'dʒiː.ni.əs/ /ˌhəʊ.mə-/ /ˌhoʊ.moʊ-'dʒiː-/ *adj* **homogeneous**

homograph /ˈhɒm.əʊ.grɑːf/ /ˈhɑː.mə.græf/ *noun* [C] SPECIALIZED a word which is spelled the same as another word and might be pronounced the same or differently, but which has a different meaning: *'Bow' meaning the front of a ship, 'bow' meaning a loop made in a string or ribbon and 'bow' meaning a device used to shoot arrows are all homographs.*

homonym /ˈhɒm.ə.nɪm/ /ˈhɑː.mə-/ *noun* [C] a word that sounds the same or is spelled the same as another word but has a different meaning: *'No' and 'know' are homonyms.* ○ *'Bow' (= bend at the waist) and 'bow' (= weapon) are also homonyms.*

homophobia /ˌhəʊ.mə'fəʊ.bi.ə/ /ˌhoʊ.mə'foʊ-/ *noun* [U] a fear or dislike of homosexuals **homophobic** /ˌhəʊ.mə'fəʊ.bɪk/ /ˌhoʊ.mə'foʊ-/ *adj*: *a homophobic attitude*

homophone /ˈhɒm.ə.fəʊn/ /ˈhɑː.mə.foʊn/ *noun* [C] SPECIALIZED a word which is pronounced the same as another word but has a different meaning or a different spelling or both: *The words 'so' and 'sew' are homophones.*

Homo sapiens /ˌhəʊ.məʊ'sæp.i.enz/ /ˌhoʊ.moʊ-/ *noun* [U] SPECIALIZED human beings considered together as a type of animal

homosexual /ˌhəʊ.məʊ'sek.sju.ᵊl/ /ˌhɒm.əʊ'-/ /ˌhoʊ.moʊ'sek.ʃu.ᵊl/ *noun* [C] a person, especially a man, who is sexually attracted to people of the same sex and not to people of the opposite sex **homosexual** /ˌhəʊ.məʊ-'sek.sju.ᵊl/ /ˌhɒm.əʊ-/ /ˌhoʊ.moʊ'sek.ʃu.ᵊl/ *adj*: *homosexual sex/relationships* **homosexuality** /ˌhəʊ.məʊˌsek.sju'æl.ə.ti/ /ˌhɒm.əʊ-/ /ˌhoʊ.moʊˌsek.ʃu'æl.ə.t̬i/ *noun* [U] *I've never been ashamed of my homosexuality.*

hon /hɒn/ /ɑːn/ *adj* [before n] UK ABBREVIATION FOR **honorary**, when used as part of a title: *the hon treasurer*

Hon /hɒn/ /ɑːn/ *adj* [before n] ABBREVIATION FOR **Honourable**, when used as a title: *The report was written by a recently appointed judge, the Hon Mr Justice Carlton.*

honcho /ˈhɒn.tʃəʊ/ [US] /ˈhɑːn.tʃoʊ/ *noun* [C] *MAINLY US INFORMAL* the person in charge: *Who's the* ***head*** *honcho round here?*

hone /həʊn/ [US] /hoʊn/ *verb* [T] **1** to sharpen an object: *The bone had been honed* ***to a point.*** **2** to make something perfect or completely suitable for its purpose: *His physique was honed* ***to perfection.*** ○ *Her debating skills were honed in the students' union.*

honest /ˈɒn.ɪst/ [US] /ˈɑː.nɪst/ *adj* truthful or able to be trusted and not likely to steal, cheat or lie: *She's completely honest.* ○ *I'd like you to give me an honest answer/your honest opinion.* ○ *He had an honest face* (= He looked like he could be trusted). ○ *To be honest* ***(with*** *you), I don't think it will be possible.* ✻ NOTE: The opposite is **dishonest**.

• **honest (to God/goodness)** *INFORMAL* used to emphasize that what you are saying is true: *I tried to be nice to him, honest to God I did!*

honest-to-goodness /ˌɒn.ɪst.təˈgʊd.nəs/ [US] /ˌɑː.nɪst-/ *adj* [before n] real or true: *The book is an honest-to-goodness account of her early life.*

• **make an honest woman (out) of sb** *INFORMAL HUMOROUS* to marry a woman you are having a sexual relationship with

• **make an honest living** *HUMOROUS* earn money by working hard at a job

honestly /ˈɒn.ɪst.li/ [US] /ˈɑː.nɪst-/ *adv* in a way that is truthful: *They have always dealt honestly and fairly with their customers.* ○ *I can't honestly say what time I'll be home.* ○ *I'll do it tomorrow, honestly* (= I promise that I will do it).

honestly /ˈɒn.ɪst.li/ [US] /ˈɑː.nɪst-/ *adv, exclamation* used to emphasize disapproval: *Honestly, you'd think she'd have asked you first!* ○ *Honestly, some people!*

honesty /ˈɒn.ə.sti/ [US] /ˈɑː.nə-/ *noun* [U] the quality of being honest: *I appreciate your honesty.* ○ *I must tell you* ***in all*** *honesty* (= truthfully and hiding nothing) *that there is little chance of the scheme being approved.*

• **Honesty is the best policy.** *SAYING* said to advise someone that it is better to tell the truth than to lie

ˌhonest ˈbroker *noun* [C] someone who speaks to both sides involved in an argument or disagreement and tries to help them to agree

honey [SWEET SUBSTANCE] /ˈhʌn.i/ *noun* [U] a sweet sticky yellow substance made by bees and used as food: *UK set honey/runny honey* ○ *clover honey*

honey [PERSON] /ˈhʌn.i/ *noun* [C] *MAINLY US* a name that you call someone you love or like very much: *Hi, honey, I'm home!*

honeybee /ˈhʌn.i.biː/ *noun* [C] a type of bee which lives with others in a HIVE and makes honey

honeycomb /ˈhʌn.i.kəʊm/ [US] /-koʊm/ *noun* **1** [C or U] a wax structure containing many small holes which is made by bees to store their honey **2** [C] something with a similar structure: *The hotel complex was a honeycomb* ***of*** *rooms and courtyards* (= there were many small rooms and passages). **honeycombed** /ˈhʌn.i.kəʊmd/ [US] /-koʊmd/ *adj* [after v] *The tomb was honeycombed* ***with*** *passages and chambers.*

honeydew /ˈhʌn.i.djuː/ [US] /-duː/ *noun* [U] a sticky substance left on leaves by some types of insect

ˌhoneydew (ˈmelon) *noun* [C or U] a type of MELON (= large fruit with a thick skin) that has white, green or yellow skin and sweet juicy flesh

honeyed /ˈhʌn.id/ *adj* **honeyed tones/words/voice** describes speech or a person's voice when it is gentle and pleasant to listen to, sometimes in a way that is not sincere

honeymoon /ˈhʌn.i.muːn/ *noun* [C or U] a holiday taken by a man and a woman immediately after their marriage: *Where are you going* ***on*** *your honeymoon?* **honeymoon** /ˈhʌn.i.muːn/ *verb* [I usually + adv or prep] *They are honeymooning* ***in*** *the Bahamas.* **honeymooners** /ˈhʌn.iˌmuː.nəz/ [US] /-nɚz/ *plural noun*

ˈhoneymoon (ˌperiod) *noun* [C usually sing] a short period at the beginning of a new job, government, etc. when the relationship is good

honeysuckle /ˈhʌn.iˌsʌk.l̩/ *noun* [C or U] a climbing plant with flowers that smell sweet ➲See picture **Flowers and Plants** on page Centre 3

ˈhoney ˌtrap *noun* [C usually sing] *UK* a big attraction: *The Tower of London is a honey trap* ***for*** *tourists.*

honk [SOUND] /hɒŋk/ [US] /hɑːŋk/ *verb* [I or T] If a goose or a car horn honks, it makes a short, loud sound. **honk** /hɒŋk/ [US] /hɑːŋk/ *noun* [C] *He gave us a honk on his horn as he drove off.*

honk [VOMIT] /hɒŋk/ [US] /hɑːŋk/ *verb* [I or T] *UK SLANG* to vomit: *He honked* ***(up)*** *all over the floor.*

honky /ˈhɒŋ.ki/ [US] /ˈhɑːŋ-/ *noun* [C] *US SLANG DISAPPROVING* a word sometimes used by black people to refer to a white person

honky-tonk /ˈhɒŋ.ki.tɒŋk/ [US] /ˈhɑːŋ.ki.tɑːŋk/ *adj* [before n] connected with an informal type of jazz piano playing: *a honky-tonk piano* ○ *honky-tonk music*

honky-tonk /ˈhɒŋ.ki.tɒŋk/ [US] /ˈhɑːŋ.ki.tɑːŋk/ *noun* [C] *US* a noisy, cheap bar with loud jazz or COUNTRY (= traditional) music

honor /ˈɒn.əʳ/ [US] /ˈɑː.nɚ/ *noun US FOR* **honour**

honorable *adj US FOR* **honourable** ➲See at HONOUR

honorably *adv US FOR* **honourably** ➲See at **honour** RESPECT

honorarium /ˌɒn.əˈreə.ri.əm/ [US] /ˌɑː.nəˈrer.i-/ *noun* [C] *plural* **honorariums** or **honoraria** *FORMAL* a usually small sum of money paid to someone for a service for which no official charge is made: *We usually offer our visiting lecturers an honorarium of £50.*

honorary /ˈɒn.ᵊr.ə.ri/ [US] /ˈɑː.nə.rer.i/ *adj* **1** (especially of a degree) given as an honour to someone who has not completed a course of study: *She received an honorary doctorate from Oxford University in recognition of her work for the homeless.* **2** An honorary position in an organization is one for which no payment is made: *Charities often have a well-known person as their honorary treasurer.*

honorific /ˌɒn.ᵊrˈɪf.ɪk/ [US] /ˌɑː.nəˈrɪf-/ *adj* [before n] *FORMAL* showing or giving honour or respect: *an honorific post/title*

honors /ˈɒn.əz/ [US] /ˈɑː.nɚz/ *plural noun US FOR* **honours** ➲See at **honour** REWARD

ˈhonors deˌgree *noun* [C] (*FORMAL* **degree with honors**) in the US, a degree from a school, college or university which shows that a student has done work of a very high standard ➲Compare **honours degree**.

honour [RESPECT] *UK, US* **honor** /ˈɒn.əʳ/ [US] /ˈɑː.nɚ/ *noun* [U] **1** a quality that combines respect, pride and honesty: *a man of honour* ○ *We fought for the honour of our country.* **2 in honour of *sb/sth*** in order to celebrate or show great respect for someone or something: *a banquet in honour of the president*

• **be/feel honour bound to do *sth*** to feel you must do something because it is morally right, even if you do not want to do it: *I felt honour bound to tell him the truth.*

• **be on your honour** *OLD-FASHIONED* If you are on your honour to do something, you have made a promise to act as you have said you will.

• **do *sb* the honour of *doing sth*** *FORMAL* to make someone proud and happy by doing or being something: *Would you do me the honour of accompanying me to the New Year Ball?*

• **Your Honour** *FORMAL* the way to address a judge

honour *UK, US* **honor** /ˈɒn.əʳ/ [US] /ˈɑː.nɚ/ *verb* [T] **1** to show great respect for someone or something, especially in public: *He was honoured* ***for*** *his bravery.* ○ *FORMAL We are honoured* (= proud and happy) *to have you here tonight.* **2** To honour a promise or agreement is to do what you said you would: *They decided not to honour an existing order for aircraft.*

honourable *UK, US* **honorable** /ˈɒn.ᵊr.ə.bl̩/ [US] /ˈɑː.nɚ-/ *adj* honest and fair, or deserving praise and respect: *an honourable person* **honourably** *UK, US* **honorably** /ˈɒn.ᵊr.ə.bli/ [US] /ˈɑː.nɚ-/ *adv*: *They acted honourably and returned the wallet.*

honour [REWARD] *UK, US* **honor** /ˈɒn.əʳ/ [US] /ˈɑː.nɚ/ *noun* [C] a reward, prize or title that publicly expresses admiration or respect: *She received an honour for her services to the community.* ○ *He was buried with* ***full military***

honours (= with a special celebration to show respect).

honour *UK, US* **honor** /ˈɒn.əʳ/ ⓤ /ˈɑː.nɚ/ *verb* [T] to give someone public praise or a reward: *He was honoured* **with** *a knighthood.*

honours *UK, US* **honors** /ˈɒn.əz/ ⓤ /ˈɑː.nɚz/ *plural noun* **with honours/honors** If you complete a school or university qualification with honours, you achieve a high standard.

• **do the honours** *HUMOROUS* to pour drinks or serve food: *John, will you do the honours?*

Honourable *UK, US* **Honorable** /ˈɒn.ˀr.ə.bl̩/ ⓤ /ˈɑː.nɚ-/ *adj* (*WRITTEN ABBREVIATION* **Hon**) **the Honourable** a title used before the name of some government officials, and in the UK before the names of certain people of high social rank: *the Honourable Andrew Robinson* ○ *the Honorable Daniel P. Moynihan of New York*

ˌhonourable ˈmention *noun* [C] a prize given in a competition for work of high quality which did not receive first, second or third prize

ˈhonours deˌgree *noun* [C] (*FORMAL* **degree with honours**) in the UK, a first university degree, based especially on one subject ⊃Compare **honors degree**.

ˈhonours ˌlist *noun* [S] in the UK, the list of people who receive a title and public praise as a reward for things they have done

hooch, **hootch** /huːtʃ/ *noun* [U] *US SLANG* strong alcohol, especially whisky

hood ⌈CLOTHING⌉ /hʊd/ *noun* [C] **1** part of a piece of clothing which can be pulled up to cover the top and back of the head: *The coat has a detachable hood.* **2** a bag placed over someone's head so that they cannot see or be recognized: *The prisoners had been tortured and made to wear hoods.*

hooded /ˈhʊd.ɪd/ *adj* **1** having a hood: *a hooded jacket* ○ *armed and hooded intruders* **2** describes eyes which are partly covered by the eyelids because the eyelids are big: *He watched her from under hooded eyelids.*

hood ⌈COVER⌉ /hʊd/ *noun* [C] a part which covers or shelters a piece of equipment: *The hood over the air vent is loose.*

hood ⌈CAR⌉ /hʊd/ *noun* [C] *US FOR* **bonnet** METAL COVER ⊃See picture **Car** on page Centre 12

hood ⌈PLACE⌉, ˈhood /hʊd/ *noun* [C] *US SLANG* a poor **neighbourhood**: *When he started he was just a poor boy from the hood – now he's a multimillionaire.*

-hood /-hʊd/ *suffix* used to form nouns describing the state of being a particular thing: *priesthood* ○ *childhood/manhood* ○ *nationhood*

hoodlum /ˈhuːd.ləm/ *noun* [C] (*ALSO* **hood**) *OLD-FASHIONED* a violent person, especially one who is member of a group of criminals

hoodwink /ˈhʊd.wɪŋk/ *verb* [T] to deceive or trick someone: *He hoodwinked us* **into** *agreeing.*

hoof /huːf/ *noun* [C] *plural* **hooves** or **hoofs** the hard part on the bottom of the feet of animals such as horses, sheep and deer ⊃Compare **paw**.

• **on the hoof** *UK INFORMAL* If you do something on the hoof, you do it while you are moving about or doing something else, often without giving it the attention it deserves: *I've got a meeting downtown in 20 minutes so I'll have lunch on the hoof.*

hoof /huːf/ *verb* [T] *INFORMAL* to kick a ball: *The defender hoofed the ball up the field.*

• **hoof it** *INFORMAL* to walk somewhere, or to walk somewhere quickly: *We missed the bus and had to hoof it.*

ˌhoof and ˈmouth (diˌsease) *noun* [U] *US FOR* **foot and mouth (disease)**

hoo-ha /ˈhuː.hɑː/ *noun* [S or U] *INFORMAL* when there is too much interest in or discussion of something unimportant: *One of the tabloids published the pictures and they caused a great hoo-ha.*

hook ⌈DEVICE⌉ /hʊk/ *noun* [C] a curved device used for catching or holding things, especially one fixed to a surface for hanging things on: *a coat/picture hook* ○ *a boat hook* ○ *a fish hook* ⊃See picture **In the Office** on page Centre 15

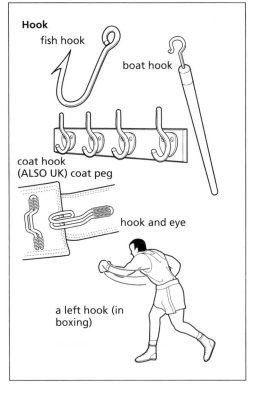

Hook

fish hook

boat hook

coat hook
(ALSO UK) coat peg

hook and eye

a left hook (in boxing)

• **off the hook 1** If you leave the telephone off the hook, you do not put the part of it that you talk with back correctly and it will not ring. **2** If you are off the hook, you have escaped from a difficult situation: *John's agreed to go to the meeting in my place so that gets/lets me off the hook.*

• **fall for** *sth* **hook, line and sinker** to completely believe something that someone tells you which is not true: *She told him she needed the money for her baby and he fell for it hook, line and sinker.*

• **by hook or by crook** by any method possible: *I decided I was going to get that job by hook or by crook.*

• **get** *your* **hooks into** *sb/sth* to get control or influence over someone or something: *This product has really got its hooks into the American market.*

hook /hʊk/ *verb* [T] to fasten something with a hook, hang something on a hook, or catch something with a hook: *He hooked the trailer* (= joined it with a hook) *to his car.* ○ *How many salmon did you hook* (= catch) *this afternoon?* ○ *She hooked the shoe* (= lifted it with a hook) *out of the water.*

hook ⌈HIT⌉ /hʊk/ *noun* [C] a way of hitting something in boxing, cricket or golf: *a right/left hook* ○ *a hook shot*

▲ **hook** (*sb/sth*) **up to** *sth phrasal verb* to connect a machine to a power supply or to another machine, or to connect a person to a piece of medical equipment: *Can we hook up to the electricity supply at the campsite?* ○ *Helen was unconscious and hooked up to a life support machine.*

hookah /ˈhʊk.ə/ *noun* [C] a type of pipe which brings smoke through a container of water before it is breathed in

ˌhook and ˈeye *noun* [C usually sing] a device for fastening clothes consisting of a small bent piece of metal into which a hook fits

hooked ⌈CAN'T STOP⌉ /hʊkt/ *adj* [after v] *INFORMAL* **1** unable to stop taking a drug: *to be hooked on cocaine* **2** enjoying something so much that you are unable to stop having, watching, doing, etc. it: *I was hooked after two episodes.*

hooked [NOSE] /hʊkt/ *adj* describes a nose which is large and curved

hooker [SEX] /ˈhʊk.əʳ/ [US] /-ɚ/ *noun* [C] *INFORMAL* a PROSTITUTE (= woman who has sex for money)

hook /hʊk/ *verb* [I] *US INFORMAL* to have sex for money

hooker [SPORT] /ˈhʊk.əʳ/ [US] /-ɚ/ *noun* [C] a rugby player who pulls the ball out of the SCRUM with his foot

hook-nosed /ˈhʊkˌnəʊzd/ [US] /-ˌnoʊzd/ *adj* Someone who is hook-nosed has a large nose which curves out from the face.

hook-up /ˈhʊk.ʌp/ *noun* [C] a connection between two or more things, places or people using electronic equipment: *We hope to bring you a live report from Ouagadougou via our **satellite** hook-up.*

hooky /ˈhʊk.i/ *noun MAINLY US INFORMAL* **play hooky** to stay away from school without permission

hooligan /ˈhuː.lɪ.gᵊn/ *noun* [C] a person who acts in a violent way without thinking and causes damage: *Hooligans had sprayed paint all over the car.* **hooliganism** /ˈhuː.lɪ.gᵊn.ɪ.zᵊm/ *noun* [U] *football/soccer hooliganism*

hoop /huːp/ *noun* [C] a ring of wood, metal or plastic, or sometimes a half ring: *The dogs had been trained to jump through hoops.*

• **go/jump through hoops** to do a lot of difficult things before you are allowed to have or do something you want

ˌ**hoop (ˈearring)** *noun* [C] a ring-shaped EARRING (= a piece of jewellery which hangs from the ear): *She was wearing large gold hoops in her ears.*

hoopla [GAME] *UK* /ˈhuːp.lɑː/ *noun* [U] (*US* **ring toss**) a game in which a ring is thrown so that it falls over an object: *a game of hoopla*

hoopla [EXCITEMENT] /ˈhuːp.lɑː/ *noun* [S or U] *MAINLY US* exciting noise and activity in celebration of an event: *The usual hoopla surrounded the arrival of the pop star.*

hooray /hʊˈreɪ/ /hə-/ *exclamation, noun* **hurray**

hooroo /hʊˈruː/ *exclamation AUS INFORMAL FOR* **goodbye**

hoot /huːt/ *noun* [C] **1** a short loud high sound: *She gave three short hoots on the car horn.* ○ *He gave a hoot **of** laughter/derision.* **2** the sound an OWL makes

• **be a hoot** *INFORMAL* to be very amusing: *He's an absolute hoot.*

• **not care/give two hoots** (*ALSO* **not care/give a hoot**) *INFORMAL* to not care about something or someone: *I don't give two hoots what she thinks.*

hoot /huːt/ *verb* **1** [I or T] to make a short loud high sound: *She hooted her horn **at** the dog in the road.* ○ *He hooted **with** laughter.* **2** [I] to make the sound that an OWL makes

hooter /ˈhuː.təʳ/ [US] /-t̬ɚ/ *noun* [C] *OLD-FASHIONED* an electrical device which makes a loud noise, often to mark the start or end of work at a factory

hooter /ˈhuː.təʳ/ [US] /-t̬ɚ/ *noun* [C] *UK OLD-FASHIONED INFORMAL* a nose

hooters /ˈhuː.təʳ/ [US] /-t̬ɚ/ *plural noun US SLANG* a woman's breasts. This word is considered offensive.

Hoover /ˈhuː.vəʳ/ [US] /-vɚ/ *noun* [C] *UK TRADEMARK* a **vacuum (cleaner)** **hoover** /ˈhuː.vəʳ/ [US] /-vɚ/ *verb* [I or T] *UK He was busy hoovering the bedroom carpet when I got home.* **hoovering** /ˈhuː.və.rɪŋ/ [US] /-vɚ.ɪŋ/ *noun* [U] *Could you **do** the hoovering?*

hooves /huːvz/ *plural of* **hoof**

hop /hɒp/ [US] /hɑːp/ *verb* **-pp- 1** [I] to jump on one foot or to move about in this way: *I tried to hop on my good foot while holding onto Jim.* **2** [I + adv or prep] *INFORMAL* to go somewhere quickly or to get into or out of a vehicle quickly: *We hopped over to Bruges for the weekend.* ○ *I hopped on the bus at the traffic lights.* **3** [I] If a small animal, bird or insect hops, it moves by jumping on all or two of its feet at the same time: *The rabbit/bird hopped across the grass.*

• **hop it** *UK OLD-FASHIONED INFORMAL* used to tell someone to go away

• **hopping mad** *OLD-FASHIONED* very angry

hop /hɒp/ [US] /hɑːp/ *noun* [C] a short jump by a person on one foot, or by a small animal, bird or insect on all or two of its feet at the same time: *With his feet tied together he could only move in little hops.*

• **be a short hop** *INFORMAL* to be a short journey or distance, especially in an aircraft: *London to Edinburgh is just a short hop by plane.*

• **catch *sb* on the hop** *UK INFORMAL* to do something when someone is not ready for it and is not able to deal with it: *I'm afraid you've caught me on the hop – I wasn't expecting you till next week.*

hope /həʊp/ [US] /hoʊp/ *noun* [C or U] something good that you want to happen in the future, or a confident feeling about what will happen in the future: *What are your hopes and dreams **for** the future?* ○ *Is there any hope **of** getting financial support for the project?* ○ [+ that] *Is there any hope **that** they will be home in time?* ○ *Young people are growing up in our cities without any hope **of finding** a job.* ○ *His reply **dashed*** (= destroyed) *our hopes.* ○ *They have **pinned (all)** their hopes **on*** (= They are depending for success on) *their new player.* ○ *She's very ill, but there's still hope/we **live in** hope* (= we think she might be cured). ○ *The situation is now **beyond/past** hope* (= unlikely to produce the desired result). ○ *We never **gave up** hope* (= stopped hoping) *that she would be found alive.* ○ *The letter offered us **a glimmer/ray of*** (= a little) *hope.* ○ *I didn't phone till four o'clock **in the** hope **that** you'd be finished.* ○ *I **don't hold out much** hope **of** getting* (= I don't expect to be able to get) *a ticket.*

• **not have a hope in hell** *INFORMAL* to have no possibility of doing or achieving something: *We were so outclassed – we didn't have a hope in hell of winning.*

hope /həʊp/ [US] /hoʊp/ *verb* [I or T] to want something to happen or to be true, and usually have a good reason to think that it might: *I'm hoping **for** an interview next week.* ○ [+ (that)] *She's hoping **(that)** she won't be away too long.* ○ *I hope **(that)** she'll win.* ○ *We have to hope **and pray (that)** the operation will go well.* ○ [+ to infinitive] *They hope **to** visit us next year.* ○ *It's good news, I hope.* ○ *"Will you be at the meeting tomorrow?" "I hope **not/so**".* ➲Compare **wish** HOPE.

• **hope for the best** to hope that something will be successful or happen in the way you want, even if it seems unlikely: *I've repaired it as well as I can – we'll just have to hope for the best.*

• **hope against hope** to hope very strongly that something will happen, although you know it is not likely: *They're just hoping against hope that she's still alive.*

hopeful /ˈhəʊp.fᵊl/ [US] /ˈhoʊp-/ *adj* **1** having hope: *He was hopeful **about** the outcome of the meeting.* ○ *They were hopeful **of** a successful agreement.* ○ *I'm hopeful **(that)** we can reach a compromise.* **2** giving hope: *The green shoots were hopeful signs of spring.*

hopeful /ˈhəʊp.fᵊl/ [US] /ˈhoʊp-/ *noun* [C usually pl] a person who is trying to get a part in a film, play for a famous football team, etc: *Over a thousand **young** hopefuls went to the Theatre Royal today to audition for a part in the new musical.* **hopefulness** /ˈhəʊp.fᵊl.nəs/ [US] /ˈhoʊp-/ *noun* [U]

hopefully /ˈhəʊp.fᵊl.i/ [US] /ˈhoʊp-/ *adv* **1** used, often at the start of a sentence, to express what you would like to happen: *Hopefully it won't rain.* ○ *Hopefully we'll be in Norwich by early evening.* **2** in a hopeful way: *"Do you have a cigarette?" he asked hopefully.*

hopeless /ˈhəʊ.pləs/ [US] /ˈhoʊ-/ *adj* **1** without hope: *a hopeless situation* ○ *They searched for survivors but it was hopeless.* ○ *She was depressed and felt totally hopeless about the future.* **2** completely without skill at a particular activity: *I'm hopeless **at** sports.* ○ *He's a hopeless cook.*

hopelessly /ˈhəʊ.plə.sli/ [US] /ˈhoʊ-/ *adv* extremely, or in a way that makes you lose hope: *They met at university and fell hopelessly in love.* ○ *We were hopelessly lost.*

hopelessness /ˈhəʊ.plə.snəs/ [US] /ˈhoʊ-/ *noun* [U] *I find the hopelessness of the situation very depressing.*

ˈ**hope** ˌ**chest** *noun* [C usually sing] *US FOR* **bottom drawer**

hopper /ˈhɒp.əʳ/ [US] /ˈhɑː.pɚ/ *noun* [C] *SPECIALIZED* a large tube, wide at one end, through which large amounts of small separate items, for example seeds, can be moved from one container to another

hops /hɒps/ [US] /hɑːps/ *plural noun* the dried fruits of a climbing plant which are used to give a bitter flavour to beer **hop** /hɒp/ [US] /hɑːp/ *adj* [before n] *a hop plant*

H

hopscotch /ˈhɒp.skɒtʃ/ ⓤ /ˈhɑːp.skɑːtʃ/ *noun* [U] a game played by children, who throw a stone onto a set of joined squares drawn on the ground and jump on one leg and then on two legs into each square in turn to get the stone

horde /hɔːd/ ⓤ /hɔːrd/ *noun* [C] *OFTEN DISAPPROVING* a large group of people: *Hordes **of** students on bikes made crossing the road difficult.*
● **in their hordes** *INFORMAL* in very great numbers: *When they heard the concert was free, they came in their hordes.*

horizon /həˈraɪ.zⁿn/ *noun* [S] the line at the most distant place which you can see, where the sky seems to touch the land or sea: *The moon rose slowly above the horizon.* ○ *We could see a row of camels silhouetted **on** the horizon.*
● **on the horizon** likely to happen or exist soon: *There is no new drug on the horizon that will make this disease easier to treat.*
● **broaden/expand/widen** *sb's* **horizons** to increase the range of things that someone knows about or has experienced: *Travelling certainly broadens your horizons.*

horizontal /ˌhɒr.ɪˈzɒn.tⁿl/ ⓤ /ˌhɔːr.ɪˈzɑːn.tⁿl/ *adj* flat or level; parallel to the ground or to the bottom or top edge of something: *Draw a horizontal line across the bottom of the page.* ○ *Keep the patient horizontal with the feet slightly raised.* ⊃Compare **vertical**.
horizontal /ˌhɒr.ɪˈzɒn.tⁿl/ ⓤ /ˌhɔːr.ɪˈzɑːn.tⁿl/ *noun* [C usually sing] a horizontal line, surface or position: *Rotate it slowly from **the** horizontal into a vertical position.* **horizontally** /ˌhɒr.ɪˈzɒn.tⁿl.i/ ⓤ /ˌhɔːr.ɪˈzɑːn.tⁿl-/ *adv*

hormone /ˈhɔː.məʊn/ ⓤ /ˈhɔːr.moʊn/ *noun* [C] any of various chemicals made by living cells which influence the development, growth, sex, etc. of an animal and are carried around the body in the blood: *male and female hormones* ○ *growth hormones* **hormonal** /hɔːˈməʊ.nəl/ ⓤ /hɔːr.moʊ-/ *adj*: *a hormonal imbalance*

hormone reˈplacement ˌtherapy *noun* [U] (*ABBREVIATION* **HRT**) a treatment for women whose level of female hormones is low because they have reached the MENOPAUSE

horn [ANIMAL] /hɔːn/ ⓤ /hɔːrn/ *noun* [C or U] a hard, pointed, often curved part that grows from the top of the head of some animals, or the hard substance of which a horn is made
● **draw/pull in** *your* **horns** to act in a more careful way than you did before, especially by spending less money: *He'll have to draw in his horns now he's lost his job.*
● **be on the horns of a dilemma** to be unable to decide which of two things to do because either could have bad results
horned /hɔːnd/ ⓤ /hɔːrnd/ *adj* with horns: *horned cattle*
horny /ˈhɔː.ni/ ⓤ /ˈhɔːr-/ *adj* **1** made of a hard substance, like horn: *Birds have horny beaks.* **2** (especially of skin) hard and rough ⊃See also **horny**.

horn [MUSIC] /hɔːn/ ⓤ /hɔːrn/ *noun* [C] a curved musical instrument made of metal, which is narrow at the end you blow down to make a sound, and wider towards the other end

horn [VEHICLE] /hɔːn/ ⓤ /hɔːrn/ *noun* [C] a device on a vehicle that is used to make a loud noise as a warning or signal to other people: *The driver **blew/sounded/** (INFORMAL) **honked** her horn.* ⊃See also **foghorn**. ⊃See picture **Car** on page Centre 12

horn /hɔːn/ ⓤ /hɔːrn/ *verb*
▲ **horn in** *phrasal verb US INFORMAL* to try to become involved in a discussion or activity where you are not wanted: *She's always horning in **on** our conversations.*

hornet /ˈhɔː.nɪt/ ⓤ /ˈhɔːr-/ *noun* [C] a large WASP (= type of flying insect) which can give you a bad sting

hornet's nest /ˌhɔː.nɪts'nest/ ⓤ /ˌhɔːr-/ *noun* [C usually sing] a very difficult or unpleasant situation, especially in which lots of people get very angry and complain: *His remarks about the lack of good women tennis players **stirred up a (real)** hornet's nest.*

horn-rimmed /ˈhɔːn.rɪmd/ ⓤ /ˈhɔːrn-/ *adj* [before n] describes glasses with frames that are coloured with a mixture of dark and light brown

horny /ˈhɔː.ni/ ⓤ /ˈhɔːr-/ *adj INFORMAL* **1** sexually excited: *She'd had a couple of drinks and was **feeling** horny.* **2** *UK* sexually attractive: *You look horny in that skirt.* ⊃See also **horny** at **horn** *ANIMAL.* **horniness** /ˈhɔː.nɪ.nəs/ ⓤ /ˈhɔːr-/ *noun* [U]

horoscope /ˈhɒr.ə.skəʊp/ ⓤ /ˈhɔːr.ə.skoʊp/ *noun* [C] a description of what is going to happen to you, based on the position of the stars and planets at the time of your birth: *I **read** my horoscope most days.* ○ *My horoscope said I was going to be lucky in love this month.*

horrendous /həˈren.dəs/ *adj* extremely unpleasant or bad: *a horrendous accident/tragedy/crime* ○ *horrendous suffering/damage* ○ *Conditions in the refugee camps were horrendous.* ○ *The firm made horrendous (= very big)* **losses** *last year.* **horrendously** /həˈren.də.sli/ *adv:* *horrendously **expensive** clothes* ○ *It was horrendously hot in the room.* **horrendousness** /həˈren.də.snəs/ *noun* [U]

horrible /ˈhɒr.ɪ.bl̩/ ⓤ /ˈhɔːr-/ *adj* **1** very unpleasant or bad: *He's got a horrible cold.* ○ *What's that horrible smell?* ○ *That was a horrible thing to say!* **2** very shocking and frightening: *a horrible crime*
horribly /ˈhɒr.ɪ.bli/ ⓤ /ˈhɔːr-/ *adv* extremely, especially in a very bad or unpleasant way: *His face was horribly scarred.* ○ *Their plans went horribly wrong.*

horrid /ˈhɒr.ɪd/ ⓤ /ˈhɔːr-/ *adj OLD-FASHIONED INFORMAL* unpleasant or unkind; NASTY: *Don't be so horrid!* ○ *The medicine tasted horrid.* **horridly** /ˈhɒr.ɪd.li/ ⓤ /ˈhɔːr-/ *adv INFORMAL* **horridness** /ˈhɒr.ɪd.nəs/ ⓤ /ˈhɔːr-/ *noun* [U]

horrific /həˈrɪf.ɪk/ *adj* very bad and shocking: *a horrific accident/crime* ○ *horrific injuries* **horrifically** /həˈrɪf.ɪ.kli/ *adv*

horrify /ˈhɒr.ɪ.faɪ/ ⓤ /ˈhɔːr-/ *verb* [T] to shock someone very greatly: *This news will horrify my parents.*
horrified /ˈhɒr.ɪ.faɪd/ ⓤ /ˈhɔːr-/ *adj* very shocked: *He looked horrified when I told him.* ○ *We were horrified **at/by** the size of the bill.* ○ *I was horrified **to** hear of his death.* ○ *I was horrified **that** they hadn't included you.*
horrifying /ˈhɒr.ɪ.faɪ.ɪŋ/ ⓤ /ˈhɔːr-/ *adj* very shocking: *horrifying injuries/conditions/news* **horrifyingly** /ˈhɒr.ɪ.faɪ.ɪŋ.li/ ⓤ /ˈhɔːr-/ *adv:* *The prediction of 4 million unemployed now looks horrifyingly realistic.*

horror /ˈhɒr.əʳ/ ⓤ /ˈhɔːr.ɚ/ *noun* **1** [U] an extremely strong feeling of fear and shock, or the frightening and shocking character of something: *The crowd cried out **in** horror as the car burst into flames.* ○ *The thought of speaking in front of so many people **fills** me **with** horror.* ○ *I then realized **to my** absolute horror, that I had forgotten the present.* ○ *What the book does convey very successfully is the horror **of** war.* **2** [C] *UK INFORMAL* a child who behaves very badly: *Her youngest boy is a **little** horror.*
● **have a horror of** *sth* to hate something very much or be very frightened of something: *It may be childish but I have a horror of worms.*
● **horror of horrors** *UK HUMOROUS* said when you are telling someone about a very bad or embarrassing situation: *Then I went to the toilets and, horror of horrors, discovered that my zip had been undone.*
horrors /ˈhɒr.əz/ ⓤ /ˈhɔːr.ɚz/ *plural noun* things that are very shocking or frightening: *The population now faces the horrors of starvation.* ○ *Nuclear war is one of the horrors that face the modern world.*

ˈhorror ˌfilm *MAINLY UK noun* [C] (*MAINLY US* **horror movie**) a film in which very frightening and especially unnatural things happen, for example dead people coming to life and people being murdered

ˈhorror ˌstory *noun* [C] **1** a story in which very frightening and unnatural things happen **2** a report of real events in which things have gone very wrong: *the usual travel horror stories about delays at the airport and flight cancellations*

horror-struck /ˈhɒr.ə.strʌk/ ⓤ /ˈhɔːr.ɚ-/ *adj* [after v] (*ALSO* **horror-stricken**) extremely shocked and frightened: *They watched, horror-struck, as the car came off the road.*

hors d'oeuvre /ˌɔːˈdɜːv/ ⓤ /ˌɔːrˈdɝːv/ *noun* [C] *plural* **hors d'oeuvre** *or* **hors d'oeuvres** **1** *UK* a small savoury dish eaten at the start of a meal **2** *US* small pieces of food eaten at a party

horse ANIMAL /hɔːs/ ⓤ /hɔːrs/ *noun* [C] a large animal with four legs which people ride on or use for carrying things or pulling vehicles: *to ride a horse ○ a horse and cart*

• **horses for courses** *UK* something that you say which means that it is important to choose suitable people for particular activities because everyone has different skills

• **(straight) from the horse's mouth** If you hear something (straight) from the horse's mouth, you hear it from the person who has direct personal knowledge of the matter.

• **You can lead a horse to water, but you can't make him drink.** *SAYING* said to emphasize that you can make it easy for someone to do something, but you cannot force them to do it

 the horses *plural noun INFORMAL* horse races where you try to win money by correctly guessing which horse will win: *He spends all his money on the horses.*

 horsey (**horsier, horsiest**), **horsy** /ˈhɔːsi/ ⓤ /ˈhɔːr-/ *adj* **1** *INFORMAL* liking horses and being involved with them **2** *DISAPPROVING* looking like a horse, usually in an unattractive way

horse WOODEN STRUCTURE /hɔːs/ ⓤ /hɔːrs/ *noun* [C] (*ALSO* **vaulting horse**) a wooden structure which you jump over for exercise

horse DRUG /hɔːs/ ⓤ /hɔːrs/ *noun* [U] *SLANG* heroin

horse /hɔːs/ ⓤ /hɔːrs/ *verb*

▲ **horse around/about** *phrasal verb INFORMAL* to behave in a silly and noisy way: *He was horsing around in the kitchen and broke my favourite bowl.*

horseback /ˈhɔːs.bæk/ ⓤ /ˈhɔːrs-/ *adj* [before n] on a horse: *horseback riding ○ a horseback rider*

 horseback /ˈhɔːs.bæk/ ⓤ /ˈhɔːrs-/ *noun* **on horseback** riding a horse: *police on horseback*

horsebox *UK* /ˈhɔːs.bɒks/ ⓤ /ˈhɔːrs.bɑːks/ *noun* [C] (*AUS ALSO* **horse float**) a vehicle for transporting horses, sometimes pulled by another vehicle

horse chestnut *noun* [C] (the poisonous shiny brown nut from) a large tree with pink or white flowers ⊃See also **conker**.

horse-drawn /ˈhɔːs.drɔːn/ ⓤ /ˈhɔːrs.drɑːn/ *adj* [before n] describes a vehicle pulled by a horse

horsefly /ˈhɔːs.flaɪ/ ⓤ /ˈhɔːrs-/ *noun* [C] any of various large flying insects that bite horses, cattle and sometimes people

horsehair /ˈhɔːs.heəʳ/ ⓤ /ˈhɔːrs.her/ *noun* [U] hairs from a horse's tail and MANE, used especially in the past as a soft filling for furniture

horseman /ˈhɔːs.mən/ ⓤ /ˈhɔːrs-/ *noun* [C] a person who rides a horse, especially someone who rides well

horsemanship /ˈhɔːs.mən.ʃɪp/ ⓤ /ˈhɔːrs-/ *noun* [U] skill at riding horses

horseplay /ˈhɔːs.pleɪ/ ⓤ /ˈhɔːrs-/ *noun* [U] *SLIGHTLY OLD-FASHIONED* rough noisy behaviour, especially when people push each other as a joke

horsepower (*plural* **horsepower**) /ˈhɔːs.paʊəʳ/ ⓤ /ˈhɔːrs.paʊr/ *noun* [C or U] (*ABBREVIATION* **hp**) a unit for measuring the power of an engine: *a 100-horsepower engine*

 horse racing *noun* [U] a sport in which people race on horses, usually to win money for the horses's owners ⊃See picture **Sports** on page Centre 10

horseradish /ˈhɔːs.ræd.ɪʃ/ ⓤ /ˈhɔːrs-/ *noun* [U] a plant with large green leaves and a long white root with a strong sharp taste: *roast beef and horseradish sauce*

 horse riding *UK noun* [U] (*US* **horseback riding**) the sport or activity of riding a horse ⊃See picture **Sports** on page Centre 10

horse's ass /ˈhɔː.sɪzˈæs/ ⓤ /ˌhɔːr-/ *noun* [C usually sing] *US OFFENSIVE* a stupid and annoying person: *You may think you're being funny, but everyone else thinks you're being a real horse's ass.*

 horse sense *noun* [U] *OLD-FASHIONED* practical knowledge and good judgment about ordinary life; **common sense**

horseshit /ˈhɔːs.ʃɪt/ ⓤ /ˈhɔːrs-/ *noun* [U] *US OFFENSIVE* nonsense; BULLSHIT: *He described the film as 'middle-class, bourgeois horseshit'.*

horseshoe /ˈhɔːs.ʃuː/ ⓤ /ˈhɔːrs-/ *noun* [C] a U-shaped piece of metal which is fixed to the bottom of a horse's HOOF to protect it: *For many people the horseshoe is a symbol of good luck.*

 horseshoes /ˈhɔːs.ʃuːz/ ⓤ /ˈhɔːrs-/ *noun* [U] *US* a game in which horseshoes are thrown at a wooden or metal rod in the ground

horsetrading /ˈhɔːs.treɪ.dɪŋ/ ⓤ /ˈhɔːrs-/ *noun* [U] *OFTEN DISAPPROVING* unofficial discussion in which people make agreements that provide both sides with advantages: *There's been a lot of political horsetrading while the parties try to form a government.* **horsetrade** /ˈhɔːs.treɪd/ ⓤ /ˈhɔːrs-/ *verb* [I] *DISAPPROVING*

 horse trailer *US noun* [C] (*UK* **horsebox**, *AUS* **horse float**) a vehicle for transporting horses that is pulled behind another vehicle

horsewhip /ˈhɔːs.wɪp/ ⓤ /ˈhɔːrs-/ *verb* [T] **-pp-** to hit someone with a whip

horsewoman /ˈhɔːs.wʊm.ən/ ⓤ /ˈhɔːrs-/ *noun* [C] a female HORSEMAN: *She's a keen horsewoman.*

horticulture /ˈhɔː.tɪ.kʌl.tʃəʳ/ ⓤ /ˈhɔːr.tə.kʌl.tʃɚ/ *noun* [U] the study or activity of cultivating gardens **horticultural** /ˌhɔː.tɪˈkʌl.tʃʳr.ᵊl/ ⓤ /ˌhɔːr.təˈkʌl.tʃɚ.əl/ *adj*: *a horticultural show* **horticulturalist** /ˌhɔː.tɪˈkʌl.tʃʳr.ᵊl.ɪst/ ⓤ /ˌhɔːr.təˈkʌl.tʃɚ-/ *noun* [C] (*ALSO* **horticulturist**)

hosanna /həʊˈzæn.ə/ ⓤ /hoʊ-/ *exclamation* a shout of praise to God

hose PIPE /həʊz/ ⓤ /hoʊz/ *noun* [C] (*UK ALSO* **hosepipe**) a long plastic or rubber pipe, used to direct water onto fires, gardens, etc: *The severe drought has led to a hosepipe ban in eastern England.*

 hose /həʊz/ ⓤ /hoʊz/ *verb* [T] *He was covered in mud so we hosed him down (= cleaned him with water from a hose).*

hose CLOTHING /həʊz/ ⓤ /hoʊz/ *noun* [U] *SPECIALIZED* **hosiery** ⊃See also **pantyhose**.

hoser /ˈhəʊ.zəʳ/ ⓤ /ˈhoʊ.zɚ/ *noun* [C] *US AND CANADIAN SLANG* a stupid or rude person

hosiery /ˈhəʊz.jə.ri/ ⓤ /ˈhoʊʒ.ɚ.i/ *noun* [U] (*ALSO* **hose**) *FORMAL* a word used especially in shops for items such as socks, tights and stockings: *Women's hosiery you'll find on the second floor, Madam.*

hospice /ˈhɒs.pɪs/ ⓤ /ˈhɑː.spɪs/ *noun* [C] a hospital for people who are dying, especially from cancer

hospitable /hɒsˈpɪt.ə.bl̩/ ⓤ /hɑːˈspɪt-/ *adj* **1** friendly and welcoming to guests and visitors: *The villagers were very hospitable to/towards anyone who passed through.* ✳ NOTE: The opposite is **inhospitable**. **2** providing good conditions for living or growing: *It's difficult to think of a less hospitable environment than the surface of the Moon.* **hospitably** /hɒsˈpɪt.ə.bli/ ⓤ /hɑːˈspɪt-/ *adv*

hospitality /ˌhɒs.pɪˈtæl.ə.ti/ ⓤ /ˌhɑː.spɪˈtæl.ə.ţi/ *noun* [U] **1** when people are friendly and welcoming to guests and visitors: *The local people showed me great hospitality.* **2** the food, drink, etc. that an organization provides in order to keep its guests happy: *The company's guests at Ascot are entertained in the corporate hospitality area.*

hospital /ˈhɒs.pɪ.tᵊl/ ⓤ /ˈhɑː.spɪ.ţᵊl/ *noun* [C or U] a place where people who are ill or injured are treated and taken care of by doctors and nurses: *a general/children's/maternity hospital ○ hospital patients/staff ○ UK I've got to go (in)to hospital (= to the hospital) for three weeks to have an operation. ○ UK She spent a week in hospital (US in the hospital) last year.*

hospitalize, *UK USUALLY* **-ise** /ˈhɒs.pɪ.tᵊl.aɪz/ ⓤ /ˈhɑː.spɪ.ţᵊl-/ *verb* [T often passive] to take someone to hospital and keep them there for treatment: *His wife's been hospitalized for depression.* **hospitalization** *UK USUALLY* **-isation** /ˌhɒs.pɪ.tᵊl.aɪˈzeɪ.ʃᵊn/ ⓤ /ˌhɑː.spɪ.ţᵊl-/ *noun* [U]

host ENTERTAIN /həʊst/ ⓤ /hoʊst/ *noun* [C] (*FEMALE ALSO* **hostess**) someone who has guests: *We thanked our hosts for the lovely evening. ○ The local language school is advertising for host families (= families with whom people stay when they are visiting another country).*

host TELEVISION /həʊst/ ⓤ /hoʊst/ *noun* [C] (*FEMALE ALSO* **hostess**) a person who introduces guests and performers, especially on television or radio: *Our host for tonight's show is Terry Wogan.* **host** /həʊst/ ⓤ /hoʊst/ *verb* [T] to *host a show/programme*

host EVENT /həʊst/ ⓤ /hoʊst/ *noun* [C] a place or organization that provides the space and other necessary things for a special event: *Japan is **playing** host to the next international conference.* ○ *the host **nation** for the next World Cup* **host** /həʊst/ ⓤ /hoʊst/ *verb* [T] *Which country is hosting the next Olympic Games?*

host INTERNET /həʊst/ ⓤ /hoʊst/ *verb* [T] to provide the computer HARDWARE and SOFTWARE which enables a WEBSITE to exist on the Internet: *I've written my website, now I just need to find a company to host it.*

host /həʊst/ ⓤ /hoʊst/ *noun* [C] a company which hosts WEBSITES on the Internet

host ANIMAL /həʊst/ ⓤ /hoʊst/ *noun* [C] *SPECIALIZED* a plant or animal that another plant or animal lives on as a PARASITE

host A LOT /həʊst/ ⓤ /hoʊst/ *noun* **a host of** a large number of something: *There's a **whole** host of reasons why he didn't get the job.*

the host CHURCH *noun* [S] *SPECIALIZED* the holy bread which is eaten at COMMUNION (= a Christian religious ceremony)

hostage /ˈhɒs.tɪdʒ/ ⓤ /ˈhɑː.stɪdʒ/ *noun* [C] someone who is taken as a prisoner by an enemy in order to force the other people involved to do what the enemy wants: *She was **taken/held** hostage by the gunmen.* ○ *The terrorists have **seized** 20 hostages and are threatening to kill one a day unless their demands are met.*
● **hostage to fortune** an action or statement that is risky because it could cause you trouble later: *The Prime Minister was extremely cautious, saying nothing inflammatory and **giving** no hostages to fortune.*

hostel /ˈhɒs.təl/ ⓤ /ˈhɑː.stəl/ *noun* [C] **1** a large house where people can stay free or cheaply: *a student hostel* ⊃Compare **hotel**. **2** *UK* (*US* **shelter**) a building where people with no home can live for a short time: *a hostel **for** the homeless* ○ *a Salvation Army hostel*

hostelry /ˈhɒs.təl.ri/ ⓤ /ˈhɑː.stəl-/ *noun* [C] *OLD USE OR HUMOROUS* a bar or pub

hostess /ˈhəʊ.stes/ ⓤ /ˈhoʊ.stɪs/ *noun* [C] **1** a woman who has guests **2** a woman who entertains customers, especially men, at a nightclub

hostile UNFRIENDLY /ˈhɒs.taɪl/ ⓤ /ˈhɑː.stəl/ *adj* unfriendly and not liking or agreeing with something: *a hostile crowd* ○ *The President had a hostile **reception** in Ohio this morning.* ○ *I'm not hostile **to** (= against) the idea of change as such.*
hostility /hɒsˈtɪl.ɪ.ti/ ⓤ /hɑːˈstɪl.ə.ţi/ *noun* [U] *They showed **open** (= obvious) hostility **to/towards** their new neighbours.*

hostile DIFFICULT /ˈhɒs.taɪl/ ⓤ /ˈhɑː.stəl/ *adj* difficult or not suitable for living or growing: *hostile weather conditions* ○ *a hostile climate/environment*

hostile ENEMY /ˈhɒs.taɪl/ ⓤ /ˈhɑː.stəl/ *adj* [before n] connected with the enemy in a war: *hostile aircraft/ships/forces*
hostilities /hɒsˈtɪl.ɪ.tiz/ ⓤ /hɑːˈstɪl.ə.ţiz/ *plural noun FORMAL* fighting in a war: *Hostilities **began/broke out** just after midnight.* ○ *Hostilities were **suspended** (= fighting stopped temporarily) during the talks.*

hot VERY WARM /hɒt/ ⓤ /hɑːt/ *adj* **hotter**, **hottest** having a high temperature: *a hot sunny day* ○ *hot weather* ○ *a hot drink/meal* ○ *It's too hot in here, can we turn down the heating?* ○ *Bake the cake in a hot oven, about 220°C, for 30 minutes.* ○ *The food was **piping** hot (= very hot).*
● (all) hot and bothered *INFORMAL* worried or angry, and sometimes physically hot
● in the hot seat in a position where you are responsible for important or difficult things
● hot off the press News that is hot off the press has just been printed and often contains the most recent information about something.
● hot under the collar *INFORMAL* embarrassed or angry about something: *When I suggested he was mistaken he got rather hot under the collar.*

● be in hot water (*ALSO* get into hot water) to be in or get into a difficult situation in which you are in danger of being criticized or punished: *He found himself in hot water over his comments about immigration.*
● go/sell like hot cakes *INFORMAL* to be bought quickly and in large numbers: *His new video game is apparently selling like hot cakes.*
● hot air *INFORMAL* If something that someone says is hot air, it is not sincere and will have no practical results: *His promises turned out to be so much hot air.*
● Hot dog! *US INFORMAL* something that you say when you are very pleased about something: *You won your race? Hot dog!*
● be hot on *sb's* track/trail to be very close to catching or finding someone
● in hot pursuit following someone closely, trying hard to catch them: *The gang drove off, with the police in hot pursuit.*

hot SPICY /hɒt/ ⓤ /hɑːt/ *adj* **hotter**, **hottest** describes food which causes a burning feeling in the mouth: *a hot curry* ○ *hot spicy food* ✳ NOTE: The opposite is **mild**.

hot SKILFUL /hɒt/ ⓤ /hɑːt/ *adj* [after v] **hotter**, **hottest** *INFORMAL* knowing a lot or skilful: *I'm **not too** hot **on** Russian history.*
● be hot stuff *INFORMAL* to be very skilful: *She's really hot stuff **at** baseball.* ⊃See also be hot stuff at hot SEXY.

hot CAUSING DISAGREEMENT /hɒt/ ⓤ /hɑːt/ *adj* **hotter**, **hottest** describes a subject which causes a lot of disagreement or discussion: *Global warming has become a very hot issue.*
● be too hot to handle *INFORMAL* to be too difficult to deal with or talk about: *For many politicians, abortion is an issue that's too hot to handle.*

hot NEW/EXCITING /hɒt/ ⓤ /hɑːt/ *adj* **hotter**, **hottest** new and exciting: *Hollywood's hottest new actress* ○ *hot gossip* ○ *This 21-year old actor has become Hollywood's hottest **property**.*

hot MOST LIKELY /hɒt/ ⓤ /hɑːt/ *adj* **1** *INFORMAL* **hot tip** an accurate piece of advice about who will win a race: *Have you got any hot tips for this afternoon's race?* **2** **hot favourite** the person or animal that is most likely to win a race, competition, election, etc: *He's the hot favourite **to** win the election.*

hot DEMANDING /hɒt/ ⓤ /hɑːt/ *adj* *INFORMAL* **be hot on** *sth* to think that a particular thing is very important and to demand that it is done well or correctly: *They're very hot on dress at work so she always looks very smart for the office.*

hot STOLEN /hɒt/ ⓤ /hɑːt/ *adj* **hotter**, **hottest** *SLANG* describes goods that have been recently stolen and are therefore difficult to sell or dangerous to deal with because the police are still looking for them

hot SEXY /hɒt/ ⓤ /hɑːt/ *adj* **hotter**, **hottest** *INFORMAL* sexually attractive, or feeling sexually excited: *She's hot alright.* ○ *I'm hot for you, baby.* ○ *I've got a hot **date** tonight.*
● be hot stuff *INFORMAL* to be very sexually attractive: *Man, she's hot stuff.*
● hot to trot *US INFORMAL* sexually excited and wanting to find someone to have sex with
● have (got) the hots for *sb* *INFORMAL* to be very sexually attracted to someone: *She's got the hots for this guy in her office.*

hot ANGRY /hɒt/ ⓤ /hɑːt/ *adj* **hot temper** If someone has a hot temper, they are easily made angry.

hot /hɒt/ ⓤ /hɑːt/ *verb*
▲ hot up *phrasal verb* *UK INFORMAL* If an event or situation hots up, it becomes more exciting and more things start to happen: *A few days before the elections, the pace began to hot up.* ○ *The competition is really hotting up now.*

hot-ˈair balˌloon *noun* [C] an aircraft consisting of a very large bag filled with heated air or other gas, with a BASKET (= container) hanging under it in which people can ride

hot-ˈair ˌgun *noun* [C] an electrical tool which blows out hot air and is used to soften paint on surfaces so that it can be removed more easily

hotbed /ˈhɒt.bed/ ⓤ /ˈhɑːt-/ *noun* **a hotbed of sth** a place or situation where a lot of a particular activity, especially an unwanted or unpleasant activity, is happening or might happen: *The police department was a hotbed of corruption.* ○ *In the 60's the city was a hotbed of crime.*

hot-blooded [SHOWING FEELINGS] /ˌhɒtˈblʌd.ɪd/ ⓤ /ˌhɑːt-/ *adj* showing strong feelings very easily and quickly, especially anger or love

hot-blooded [SEXUAL] /ˌhɒtˈblʌd.ɪd/ ⓤ /ˌhɑːt-/ *adj* describes a person with strong sexual feelings and energy: *He's just your average 25-year-old hot-blooded **male**.*

hot ˌbutton *noun* [C] *US SLANG* a subject that is important to people and which they feel strongly about: *Gender issues have become something of a hot button.* ○ *Abortion has become a hot button **issue**.*

hot ˈchocolate *noun* [C or U] a hot drink made from milk and/or water, powdered chocolate and sugar

hotchpotch /ˈhɒtʃ.pɒtʃ/ ⓤ /ˈhɑːtʃ.pɑːtʃ/ *noun* [C] (*US USUALLY* **hodgepodge**) a confused mixture of different things: *New Age thinking seems to be a hotchpotch **of** old and new ideas.*

hot cross ˈbun *noun* [C] a round sweet bread-like cake with a cross marked on the top, which is eaten in some Christian countries at EASTER

hotdesk /ˌhɒtˈdesk/ ⓤ /ˌhɑːt-/ *verb* [I] to work at whatever desk and computer is available in an office
   hotdesk /ˌhɒtˈdesk/ ⓤ /ˌhɑːt-/ *noun* [C] a desk and computer in an office which are available to be used by any worker who needs them
   hotdesking /ˌhɒtˈdes.kɪŋ/ ⓤ /ˌhɑːt-/ *noun* [U] (*US ALSO* **hoteling**) a way of saving office space in which workers do not have their own desk and are only given a desk when they need it: *Hotdesking allows a company to have significantly smaller premises.*

hot ˌdog [FOOD] *noun* [C] a cooked sausage eaten in a long soft roll, often with fried onions: *a hot dog stand*

hot ˌdog [SPORT] *noun* [C] *MAINLY US INFORMAL* a person who makes fast skilful movements in particular sports, especially skiing, in order to make people notice them
   hotdog /ˈhɒt.dɒg/ ⓤ /ˈhɑːt.dɑːg/ *verb* [I]

hotel /həʊˈtel/ ⓤ /hoʊ-/ *noun* [C] a building where you pay to have a room to sleep in, and where you can eat meals: *a 4-star hotel* ○ *the Clarendon Hotel* ○ *We stayed **in/at** a hotel on the seafront.* ○ *hotel guests* ⊃Compare **hostel**.
   hotelier /həʊˈtel.i.əʳ/ ⓤ /ˌhoʊ.təˈljeɪ/ *noun* [C] a person who manages or owns a hotel

hoteling /həʊˈtel.ɪŋ/ ⓤ /hoʊ-/ *noun* [U] *US FOR* **hotdesking**

hot ˈflush *noun* [C] (*US USUALLY* **hot flash**) a sudden hot uncomfortable feeling experienced by some women during the MENOPAUSE

hotfoot /ˌhɒtˈfʊt/ ⓤ /ˈhɑːt.fʊt/ *adv INFORMAL* very quickly and without delay: *She'd come hotfoot from the palace with the latest news.*
   hotfoot /ˈhɒt.fʊt/ ⓤ /ˈhɑːt.fʊt/ *verb INFORMAL* **hotfoot it** to run or walk somewhere as quickly as possible: *He walked in and I hotfooted it out the back door.*

hothead /ˈhɒt.hed/ ⓤ /ˈhɑːt-/ *noun* [C] someone who does things or reacts to things quickly and without thinking carefully first **hotheaded** /ˌhɒtˈhed.ɪd/ ⓤ /ˈhɑːt.hed.ɪd/ *adj*: *She's a bit hotheaded and rash.*

hothouse /ˈhɒt.haʊs/ ⓤ /ˈhɑːt-/ *noun* **1** [C] a heated glass building in which plants are grown: *hothouse tomatoes* **2** [C usually sing] *OFTEN DISAPPROVING* a place or surroundings in which people, especially children, are taught to develop skills and knowledge unusually quickly: *He was attracted by the hothouse **atmosphere** of Britain's top schools.* **3** [C] a place where there is a lot of a particular activity: *a literary/political hothouse*

hotline /ˈhɒt.laɪn/ ⓤ /ˈhɑːt-/ *noun* [C] a special direct telephone connection for emergencies: *A national telephone hotline has been set up for students suffering from stress.*

hotly /ˈhɒt.li/ ⓤ /ˈhɑːt.li/ *adv* **1** in an angry or excited way: *She hotly **denied** having taken the money.* **2** closely and with determination: *He ran down the street, hotly **pursued** by two police officers.* ○ *a hotly contested election*

hotplate /ˈhɒt.pleɪt/ ⓤ /ˈhɑːt-/ *noun* [C] **1** a small cooker that can be moved, on which pans of food are heated **2** *UK* a round flat metal surface on an electric cooker, on which pans of food are heated

hotpot /ˈhɒt.pɒt/ ⓤ /ˈhɑːt.pɑːt/ *noun* [C or U] a mixture of meat and vegetables, usually including sliced potatoes, cooked slowly in a covered dish inside a cooker: *Lancashire hotpot*

hot poˈtato *noun* [C] a problem, situation, etc. that is difficult to deal with and causes a lot of disagreement: *The abortion issue is a **political** hot potato in the United States.*

hotrod /ˈhɒt.rɒd/ ⓤ /ˈhɑːt.rɑːd/ *noun* [C] *OLD-FASHIONED SLANG* a car which is specially built or changed so that it will go very fast ⊃See picture **Cars and Trucks** on page Centre 13

hot ˈshit *noun* [U] *US OFFENSIVE* someone or something that is very good

hotshot /ˈhɒt.ʃɒt/ ⓤ /ˈhɑːt.ʃɑːt/ *noun* [C] *MAINLY US INFORMAL* someone who is skilful and successful at something: *Now he's a lecturer, he thinks he's a **real** hotshot!* ○ *She's quite a hotshot **at** chess.*

hot ˌspot [FIGHTING] *noun* [C] a place where war or other fighting is likely to happen: *The border has become a major hot spot.*

hot ˌspot [POPULAR PLACE] *noun* [C] *INFORMAL* a popular and exciting place: *The Manhattan Club is one of the best hot spots in town.*

hot ˌtub *noun* [C] a large, usually wooden, container full of hot water in which more than one person can sit

hot-water ˌbottle /ˌhɒtˈwɔː.tə.bɒt.l/ ⓤ /ˌhɑːtˈwɑː.t̬ɚˌbɑː.t̬l/ *noun* [C] a rubber container which you fill with very hot water and use to warm a bed or a part of your body

hot ˈwater ˌcylinder *UK noun* [C] (*US AND UK ALSO* **hot water tank**) a metal container usually found in or near the bathroom, which holds and heats the water for a house

hot-wire ʊʃ /ˈhɒt.waɪəʳ/ ⓤ /ˈhɑːt.waɪr/ *verb* [T] *INFORMAL* to start a car engine without using the key, especially in order to steal the car

houmous, **hummus** /ˈhʊm.əs/ *noun* [U] a soft smooth savoury food made from crushed CHICKPEAS, oil and lemon juice

hound [ANIMAL] /haʊnd/ *noun* [C] a dog used for hunting, especially a FOXHOUND

hound [CHASE] /haʊnd/ *verb* [T] to chase someone or refuse to leave them alone, especially because you want to get something from them; HARASS: *The reporters wouldn't stop hounding her.*
▲ **hound sb out** *phrasal verb* to force someone to leave a job or a place: *He claims he was hounded out **of** his job by a group of students who disapproved of his views.*

hour /aʊəʳ/ ⓤ /aʊr/ *noun* **1** [C] a period of 60 minutes: *The exam lasted an hour and a half.* ○ *There are 24 hours in a day.* ○ *How many hours' sleep do you need?* ○ *I'll be back in an hour's/two hours' **time** (= after one/two hours).* ○ *The village is an hour from Doncaster/an hour away (= It takes an hour to travel there).* ○ *He gets paid **by the** hour (= gets a particular amount of money for each hour he works).* ○ *Trains leave **every** hour **on the** hour (= at exactly one o'clock, two o'clock, etc.).* ○ *Buses leave at ten minutes past/to **the** hour (= at ten past/to one o'clock, two o'clock, etc.).* ○ *War was declared at eighteen hundred/18.00 hours (= at six o'clock in the evening).* **2** [C usually pl] the period of time when a particular activity happens or when a shop or public building is open: *I did it in my lunch hour.* ○ *office/working hours* ○ *Our opening hours are from 8 to 6.* **3** [C] a particular time during the day or night: *Who could be phoning us at this **unearthly/ungodly** hour (= so late at night)?* ○ *He returned in **the** early/small hours (= at night, after midnight).* **4 work long/regular/unsocial, etc. hours** used to describe how many hours in the day you work or what part of the day you work: *She's a nurse so she often works unsocial hours.* ○ *He's paid well but he works long hours.*
● **(from) hour to hour** If something changes from hour to hour, it is different every hour.

• **after hours** after the usual hours of work: *I often do some of my own work after hours.*

• **out of hours** MAINLY UK (US **after hours**) If you drink in a bar out of hours, you drink alcohol at a time when it is not allowed by law: *The police are trying to stop out-of-hours drinking.*

• **for hours (and hours)** INFORMAL for a very long time: *I waited for him for hours.*

• **at all hours (of the day and night)** DISAPPROVING continually during the day and the night: *They keep ringing me up at all hours (of the day and night).*

• **till all hours** DISAPPROVING very late: *He stays up drinking till all hours.*

• **hour after hour** for many hours without stopping: *I sat by her bedside for hour after hour.*

• **in sb's hour of need** LITERARY when someone urgently needs help: *She helped me in my hour of need.*

• **your hour has come** LITERARY If you think your hour has come, you think you are going to die: *I thought my hour had come when he pointed his gun at me.*

hourly /'aʊə.li/ ⓤ /'aʊr-/ *adj* **1** done or happening every hour: *There's an hourly bus service into town.* ○ *Take two tablets at hourly intervals.* **2 hourly fee/rate, etc.** the amount that is charged or earned every hour
hourly /'aʊə.li/ ⓤ /'aʊr-/ *adv*: *Trains call here hourly* (= once every hour).

COMMON LEARNER ERROR

hour or **time**?

An **hour** is a period of 60 minutes.

The journey takes about three hours.
We went for a 2-hour walk.

Time is measured in hours and minutes. We use **time** to refer to a particular point during the day or night, or to say when something happens.

What time do you get up in the morning?
There's only one bus at that time of night.

Remember to use **time** not **hour** when you are talking about what time it is.

"What time is it?" "It's 2 o'clock."
~~*"What hour is it?" "It's 2 o'clock."*~~

hourglass /'aʊə.glɑːs/ ⓤ /'aʊr.glæs/ *noun* [C] a glass container filled with sand that takes one hour to move from an upper to a lower part through a narrow opening in the middle, used especially in the past to measure time
hourglass 'figure *noun* [C usually sing] If a woman has an hourglass figure, she has a very small waist.
hour ,hand *noun* [C usually sing] the part on a clock or watch which points to the hours. It is shorter than the MINUTE HAND.
house HOME /haʊs/ *noun plural* **houses** /'haʊzɪz/ **1** [C] a building which people, usually one family, live in: *a detached/semi-detached house* ○ *to buy/rent a house* ○ *house prices* ○ *She lives in a little house* (UK) *in*/(US) *on Cross Street.* ⊃See also **farmhouse** HOUSE; **roadhouse**. **2** [C usually sing] all the people living in a house: *Try not to wake the **whole** house when you come in!* **3** [C] a building where animals are kept: *the monkey/lion house at the zoo* ○ *a hen house* **4** [C] a building or part of a building which is used for a special purpose: *the Sydney Opera House* ○ *Broadcasting House*

• **go (all) round the houses** UK to waste time doing or asking something in a very complicated way

• **get/put *your* own house in order** to solve your own problems: *You should put your own house in order before you start telling me what to do!*

• **house of cards** a complicated organization or plan that is very weak and can easily be destroyed or easily go wrong

house /haʊz/ *verb* [T] to give a person or animal a place to live, or to provide space for something: *It will be difficult to house all the refugees.* ○ *The museum houses the biggest collection of antique toys in Europe.*

houseful /'haʊs.fʊl/ *noun* a lot of people or things in your house: *We've got a houseful of visitors at the moment.*

housing /'haʊ.zɪŋ/ *noun* [U] buildings for people to live in: *There's a shortage of cheap housing in the region.*
house BUSINESS /haʊs/ *noun* [C] *plural* **houses** /'haʊzɪz/ a business or organization of the stated type, especially one that produces books or designs clothes: *a publishing house* ○ *a fashion house* ○ UK *a curry house* (= Indian restaurant)

• **on the house** If you have something on the house, it is given to you free by a business: *All the drinks were on the house.*

house SCHOOL GROUP /haʊs/ *noun* [C] *plural* **houses** /'haʊzɪz/ UK any of a small number of groups which the children in a school are put in for sports and other competitions: *an inter-house football match*
house FAMILY /haʊs/ *noun* [C] *plural* **houses** /'haʊzɪz/ an important family, especially a royal one: *The British Royal Family belong to the House of Windsor.*
house POLITICS /haʊs/ *noun plural* **houses** /'haʊzɪz/ **1** [C] an organization which makes laws, or its meeting place **2 the House** the members of the organization which makes laws: *The House began sitting at 3 p.m./rose at 2 a.m.* **3** [S] the group of people who suggest a subject for a DEBATE: *The motion for tonight's debate is, "This house believes that capital punishment should be abolished."*
house THEATRE /haʊs/ *noun* [C] *plural* **houses** /'haʊzɪz/ the people watching a performance, especially in a theatre: *The opera played to a **full/packed** house.*
'house ar,rest *noun* **under house arrest** legally forced to stay in your house as if it were a prison: *The opposition leader has just been **put/placed** under house arrest.*
houseboat /'haʊs.bəʊt/ ⓤ /-boʊt/ *noun* [C] a boat which people use as their home, often kept in one place on a river or canal
housebound /'haʊs.baʊnd/ *adj* unable to leave your home, especially because you are ill: *She's been housebound since the accident.*
housebreaker /'haʊs.breɪ.kər/ ⓤ /-kɚ/ *noun* [C] a person who illegally enters a house in order to steal something
housebreaking /'haʊs.breɪ.kɪŋ/ *noun* [U]
housebroken /'haʊs.brəʊ.kən/ ⓤ /-.broʊ-/ *adj* US FOR **house-trained**
housebuyer /'haʊs.baɪ.ər/ ⓤ /-ɚ/ *noun* [C usually pl] a person who wishes to buy, or is buying a house or other form of place to live in
'house ,call *noun* [C] when a doctor or other health worker comes to your home, usually to give treatment
'House Com,mittee *noun* [C] in the US, a group of people chosen by the House of Representatives to consider a particular matter: *He appeared before the House Committee on Space, Science and Technology.*
housefly /'haʊs.flaɪ/ *noun* [C] a small common fly often found in houses
houseful /'haʊs.fʊl/ *noun* ⊃See at **house** HOME.
houseguest /'haʊs.gest/ *noun* [C] MAINLY US a person who stays at someone else's house for one or more nights
household /'haʊs.həʊld/ ⓤ /-hoʊld/ *group noun* [C] a group of people, often a family, who live together: *By the 1960s, most households had a TV.* ○ *household chores* ○ *household expenses*
householder /'haʊs.həʊl.dər/ ⓤ /-.hoʊl.dɚ/ *noun* [C] the person who owns or is in charge of a house

COMMON LEARNER ERROR

household or **housework**?

In English **household** is not used to mean the work that you do to keep your house clean. The name for this work is **housework**.

Traditionally women stayed at home to do the housework and raise the children.
~~*Traditionally women stayed at home to do the household and raise the children.*~~

,household 'name *noun* [C] a famous person that most people know of: *He was a household name in the 1950s.*

ˌ**household ˈword** *noun* **[C usually sing]** a word or name that everyone knows: *'McDonalds' quickly became a household word.*

house-hunting /ˈhaʊsˌhʌn.tɪŋ/ [US] /-t̬ɪŋ/ *noun* **[U]** the activity of looking for a house to live in: *We've been house-hunting for months.* ○ *I'm* ***going*** *house-hunting later today.*

ˈ**house ˌhusband** *noun* **[C]** a man who stays at home and cleans the house, takes care of the children, etc. while his wife goes out to work

ˈ**house ˌjournal** *UK noun* **[C]** (*US* **house organ**) a newspaper produced by a company to tell workers what is happening in the company

housekeeper /ˈhaʊsˌkiː.pəʳ/ [US] /-pɚ/ *noun* **[C]** a person, especially a woman, whose job is to organize another person's house and deal with cooking, cleaning, etc.

housekeeping (money) /ˌhaʊsˈkiː.pɪŋˌmʌn.i/ *noun* **[U]** the money used for buying food and other things necessary for living in a house

ˈ**house ˌlights** *plural noun* the lights in the place where the public sit in a theatre, cinema, etc.

housemaid /ˈhaʊs.meɪd/ *noun* **[C]** *OLD-FASHIONED* a woman servant whose job is to clean a particular usually large house and who often lives there

houseman *UK* /ˈhaʊs.mən/ /-mæn/ *noun* **[C]** (*US* **intern,** *AUS* **resident**) a male or female doctor who is still training, and who works in a hospital

ˈ**house ˌmartin** *noun* **[C]** a small bird that makes its nest under the edge of the roof of a house

housemaster /ˈhaʊsˌmɑː.stəʳ/ [US] /-ˌmæs.tɚ/ *noun* **[C]** a male teacher who is in charge of the children who live in one of several separate buildings in a school

housemate /ˈhaʊs.meɪt/ *noun* **[C]** someone you live with in a house but are not related to and do not have a romantic or sexual relationship with

housemistress /ˈhaʊsˌmɪs.trəs/ *noun* **[C]** a female HOUSEMASTER

ˈ**house (ˌmusic)** *noun* **[U]** popular music with a fast regular beat, usually produced on electronic equipment: *House music first appeared in the late 1980s.*

the ˌHouse of ˈCommons *noun* **[S]** (*ALSO* **the Commons**) one of the two parts of parliament in Britain and Canada, whose members are each elected to represent a particular official area of the country, or its members or the place where it meets: *The mood was sombre as the Commons sat down on Wednesday to debate the crisis.*

ˌ**house of corˈrection** *noun* **[C]** *US* a building where people who have committed crimes that are not serious are sent to improve their behaviour

ˌ**house of ˈGod** *noun* **[S]** *LITERARY* a church

the ˌHouse of ˈLords *noun* **[S]** (*ALSO* **the Lords**) one of the two parts of the British parliament, whose members are not elected but have a high social position, or its members or the place where it meets

the ˌHouse of Repreˈsentatives *noun* **[S]** the lower house of the parliaments of the United States, Australia and New Zealand

houseplant /ˈhaʊs.plɑːnt/ [US] /-plænt/ *noun* **[C]** (*UK ALSO* **pot plant**) a plant which is grown in a container inside a house or other building

houseproud /ˈhaʊs.praʊd/ *adj MAINLY UK* very anxious about your house being completely clean and tidy, and spending a lot of time making it so

house-room /ˈhaʊs.ruːm/ *noun* **wouldn't give** ***sth*** **house-room** something that you say about something that you would not like to have in your house: *Most of the furniture is so ugly, you wouldn't give it house-room.*

house-sit /ˈhaʊs.sɪt/ *verb* **[I]** to stay in someone's house while they are away in order to keep it safe **house-sitter** /ˈhaʊsˌsɪt.əʳ/ [US] /-ˌsɪt̬.ɚ/ *noun* **[C]** **house-sitting** *noun* **[U]**

the ˌHouses of ˈParliament *plural noun UK* the HOUSE OF COMMONS and the HOUSE OF LORDS

ˈ**house ˌsparrow** *noun* **[C]** a common small grey and brown bird

house-to-house /ˌhaʊs.təˈhaʊs/ *adj* **[before n]**, *adv* going to every house, or from one house to the next, in a particular area or road: *to make house-to-house enquiries*

house-trained *MAINLY UK* /ˈhaʊs.treɪnd/ *adj* (*US USUALLY* **housebroken**) describes a pet that has learned not to urinate or empty its bowels in your home

housewares *US* /ˈhaʊs.weəz/ [US] /-werz/ *plural noun* (*UK* **household goods**) equipment, utensils, tools and machines used in a house, especially in the kitchen: *the housewares department of a supermarket*

housewarming (party) /ˈhaʊs.wɔː.mɪŋˌpɑː.ti/ [US] /-wɔːr.mɪŋˌpɑːr.t̬i/ *noun* **[C]** a party which you give when you move into a new house: *We're* ***having*** *a housewarming on Friday if you'd like to come.*

housewife /ˈhaʊs.waɪf/ *noun* **[C]** *plural* **housewives** a woman whose work is inside the home doing the cleaning, cooking, etc., and who usually does not have any other job **housewifely** /ˈhaʊsˌwaɪf.li/ *adj*

housework /ˈhaʊs.wɜːk/ [US] /-wɝːk/ *noun* **[U]** the work of keeping a house clean and tidy: *I hate* ***doing*** *housework.* ➲See usage note at **homework.**

ˈ**housing asˌsociation** *group noun* **[C]** *UK* a group of people who join together so that they can build or buy houses or apartments at low cost

ˈ**housing ˌbenefit** *noun* **[U]** in the UK, money paid by the government to help people who are poor pay for a place to live in

ˈ**housing esˌtate** *UK noun* **[C]** (*US* **housing development, subdivision**) an area containing a large number of houses or apartments built close together at the same time: *They live* ***on/in*** *a housing estate.*

ˈ**housing ˌproject** *noun* **[C]** *US* (*ALSO* **project,** *UK* **council estate**) a group of houses or apartments, usually provided by the government for families who have low incomes

hove /həʊv/ [US] /hoʊv/ *verb LITERARY* **hove in(to) sight/view** appeared: *After 30 minutes, a large ship hove into sight on the horizon.*

hovel /ˈhɒv.əl/ [US] /ˈhɑː.vəl/ *noun* **[C]** a small home which is dirty and in bad condition

hover /ˈhɒv.əʳ/ [US] /ˈhɑː.vɚ/ *verb* **1 [I usually + adv or prep]** to stay in one place in the air, usually by moving the wings quickly: *A hawk hovered in the sky, waiting to swoop down on its prey.* ○ *I heard the noise of a helicopter hovering overhead.* **2 [I usually + adv or prep]** to stand somewhere, especially near another person, eagerly or nervously waiting for their attention: *A waiter hovered at the table, ready to take our order.* ○ *I could sense him behind me, hovering and building up the courage to ask me a question.* **3 [I + adv or prep]** to stay at or near a particular level: *Inflation is hovering* ***at*** *3%.*

hovercraft /ˈhɒv.ə.krɑːft/ [US] /ˈhɑː.vɚ.kræft/ *noun* **[C]** *plural* **hovercrafts** or **hovercraft** a vehicle which flies over land or water by keeping close to the surface and producing a current of air under it to support it ➲See picture **Planes, Ships and Boats** on page Centre 14

ˈ**hover (ˌmower)** *noun* **[C]** *UK* a LAWNMOWER which cuts grass with blades that spin round in a circle and which is held slightly above the ground by a current of air below it

hoverport /ˈhɒv.ə.pɔːt/ [US] /ˈhɑː.vɚ.pɔːrt/ *noun* **[C]** a place where people get on or off HOVERCRAFT

how /haʊ/ *adv* **1** in what way; by what methods: *How do we get to the town from here?* ○ *How did you hear about the concert?* ○ *How does this machine work?* ○ *How do you plan to spend your holiday?* ○ *Roz doesn't know how* ***to*** *ride a bicycle.* ○ *It all depends on how you look at it.* ○ *I don't care about fashion, I dress how I please.* ○ *I was horrified to hear about how* (= the way) *she had been treated.* ○ *How* ***can/could*** *he be so stupid?* ○ *I don't know how anyone* ***could*** *think that way.* **2** used to mean in what condition, especially of physical or emotional health: *How is your mother?* ○ *How are you feeling this morning?* **3** used in questions which ask what an experience or event was like: *How was your flight?* ○ *How did you* ***find*** *the lecture?* (= did you think it was good)? ○ *How* ***did*** *you* ***like*** *the concert* (= did you enjoy it)? ○ *She didn't say how* ***far*** *it is* (= what the distance is) *to her house.* ○ *How* ***long*** *are you going to be* (= what amount of time are you going to spend) *in the bathroom?* ○ *Do you know how* ***many*** (= what number of) *people are* *coming?* ○ *How* **much** *does this cost* (= what is its price)? ○ *How* **old** *is his daughter* (= what age is she)? ○ *"Can you lift this case?" "It depends on how heavy it is."* ○ *Do you remember how* (= the fact that) *we used to see every new film as soon as it came out?* **4** used for emphasis: *I can't tell you how pleased I am* (= I am very pleased) *that you came.* ○ *SLIGHTLY FORMAL How* (= It is very) *nice to see you!* ○ *"She paid for everything." "How* (= that was very) *generous."*

• **How about...?** **1** *INFORMAL* used to make a suggestion: *How about the cinema tonight?* ○ *How about* **going** *to the cimena?* **2** used when asking someone about a different thing: *You don't eat meat, do you? How about fish?*

• **How strange/stupid/weird, etc. is that?** *INFORMAL* used to emphasize that something is strange/stupid, etc.

• **How about that?** *INFORMAL* used to emphasize that something is surprising: *Sales are up by thirty-six percent. How about that?*

• **How are you?** used to ask someone if they are well and happy: *"Hi, Lucy, how are you?" "Fine, thanks, how are you?"*

• **How are things?** (*ALSO* **How's everything?**, *ALSO* **How's it going?**) *INFORMAL* used as greetings

• **How come?** *INFORMAL* used to ask about the reason for something: *So how come you got an invitation and not me?* ○ *"I don't think I'll be able to go swimming tomorrow." "How come?"*

• **How do you mean?** used when you want someone to explain what they have just said: *"I think we need to reconsider our position." "How do you mean?"*

• **How do you do?** *FORMAL* a formal greeting for someone that you have not met before: *"I'm Jack Stewart." "How do you do? I'm Angela Black."*

• **How's that?** used when asking if something you have done for someone is satisfactory: *Let me put a cushion behind your back. How's that?*

• **And how!** *INFORMAL* used to show that you feel the same way as someone: *"I'll be so glad when this project is finished." "And how!"*

COMMON LEARNER ERROR

how or what?

Many learners wrongly use **how** when they are talking about **what** something is called or **what** something or someone looks like. In these expressions remember to use **what**.

I don't know what it's called in English.
~~I don't know how it's called in English.~~
I'd like to see what it looks like before I buy it.
~~I'd like to see how it looks like before I buy it.~~

howdy /ˈhaʊ.di/ *exclamation US INFORMAL* hello

however [DEGREE] /ˌhaʊˈev.əʳ/ [US] /-ɚ/ *adv* despite whatever amount or degree: *However hungry I am, I never seem to be able to finish off a whole pizza.* ○ *If Emma likes something she'll buy it however much it costs.* ○ *I'll see you after the show and give you £20 for the tickets, or however much* (= whatever) *they cost.*

however [WAY] /ˌhaʊˈev.əʳ/ [US] /-ɚ/ *adv* **1** in whatever way: *However you look at it, it's still a mess.* ○ *You can do it however you like, it really doesn't matter.* **2** used to express surprise: *However did you manage to get him to agree to that?*

however [DESPITE] /ˌhaʊˈev.əʳ/ [US] /-ɚ/ *adv* despite this: *This is one possible solution to the problem. However, there are others.* ○ *There may, however, be other reasons that we don't know about.*

howitzer /ˈhaʊ.ɪt.səʳ/ [US] /-sɚ/ *noun* **[C]** a large gun which fires SHELLS (= very large bullets) high into the air so that they drop onto the place at which they are aimed

howl /haʊl/ *verb* **1** **[I]** If a dog or wolf howls, it makes a long, sad sound: *In the silence of the night, a lone* **wolf** *howled.* **2** **[I or T]** to make a loud sound, usually to express pain, sadness or another strong emotion: *An injured dog lay in the middle of the road, howling* **with/in** *pain.* ○ *We were howling* **with laughter**. ○ *FIGURATIVE The opposition howled* **down** *the government's proposal* (= shouted loudly to express disapproval). **3** **[I]** If the wind howls, it blows hard and makes a lot of noise: *Is there someone outside, or is it just the* **wind** *howling in the trees?*

howl /haʊl/ *noun* **1** **[C]** a long, loud, sad sound: *the howl of the wind in the trees* ○ *He leaves his dog shut up in the house all day, and we can hear its howls.* ○ *She let out a howl* **of** *pain.* **2** **[C usually pl]** a strong expression of emotion, such as anger or dissatisfaction: *Plans to build a new supermarket have been greeted with howls* **of** *protest from local residents.*

howler /ˈhaʊ.ləʳ/ [US] /-lɚ/ *noun* **[C]** a stupid and obvious mistake, especially in something that someone says or writes: *I called her by the name of his first wife, which was a bit of a howler.*

howling /ˈhaʊ.lɪŋ/ *adj* **be a howling success** to be very successful: *Neither film was a howling success.*

howsoever /ˌhaʊ.səʊˈev.əʳ/ [US] /-soʊˈev.ɚ/ *adv LITERARY FOR* **however** DEGREE *or* **however** WAY

how-to /ˌhaʊˈtuː/ *adj* **[before n]** describes a book, video or other product that provides advice on a particular activity: *How-to books on dieting are often at the top of the bestseller lists.*

hp [POWER] /ˌeɪtʃˈpiː/ *WRITTEN ABBREVIATION FOR* **horsepower**

HP [PAYMENT] /ˌeɪtʃˈpiː/ *noun* **[U]** *UK ABBREVIATION FOR* **hire purchase**: *We bought our television* **on** *HP.*

HQ /ˌeɪtʃˈkjuː/ *group noun* **[C]** *ABBREVIATION FOR* **headquarters**: *We've just received instructions from HQ.*

hr *noun* **[C]** *plural* **hrs** *WRITTEN ABBREVIATION FOR* **hour**: *He ran the marathon in 2 hrs 48 mins.* ○ *The plane departs at 15.00 hrs.*

HRH /ˌeɪtʃ.ɑːˈreɪtʃ/ [US] /-ɑːr-/ *ABBREVIATION FOR* His or Her Royal Highness: a title of some members of a royal family: *HRH the Prince of Wales*

HRT /ˌeɪtʃ.ɑːˈtiː/ [US] /-ɑːr-/ *noun* **[U]** *ABBREVIATION FOR* **hormone replacement therapy**

HSC /ˌeɪtʃ.esˈsiː/ *noun* **[C]** *ABBREVIATION FOR* Higher School Certificate: an Australian exam taken in the last two years of school education

ht *noun* **[U]** *ABBREVIATION FOR* **height**: *Ht of bridge 1.8 m.*

HTH, hth *INTERNET ABBREVIATION FOR* hope this helps: used when you send somebody information that you think is useful, often when answering a question

HTML /ˌeɪtʃ.tiː.emˈel/ *noun* **[U]** *TRADEMARK ABBREVIATION FOR* hypertext markup language: a way of marking text so that it can be seen on the Internet

http /ˌeɪtʃ.tiː.tiːˈpiː/ *noun* **[U]** *TRADEMARK ABBREVIATION FOR* hypertext transfer protocol: a set of instructions made by a computer program that enables your computer to connect to an Internet document: *http://www.cambridge.org*

hub /hʌb/ *noun* **[C]** **1** the central or main part of something where there is most activity: *The City of London is the hub* **of** *Britain's financial world.* ○ *The computer department is* **at the** *hub* **of** *the company's operations.* **2** the central part of a wheel into which the SPOKES (= bars connecting the central part to the outer edge of the wheel) are fixed

hubbub /ˈhʌb.ʌb/ *noun* **[U]** **1** a loud noise, especially caused by a lot of people all talking at the same time: *I could hardly hear myself speak above all the hubbub in the theatre bar.* **2** general excitement and activity: *Once the hubbub* **of** *the election had died down, it was back to normal for the President.*

hubby /ˈhʌb.i/ *noun* **[C]** *INFORMAL FOR* husband: *She speaks fondly of Richard Moreland, hubby No.1, whom she still sees regularly.*

hubcap /ˈhʌb.kæp/ *noun* **[C]** the circular metal covering over the HUB (= central part) of the wheel of a car or other motor vehicle ➲See picture **Car** on page Centre 12

hubris /ˈhjuː.brɪs/ *noun* **[U]** *LITERARY* very great pride and belief in your own importance: *He was punished for his hubris.*

huckleberry /ˈhʌk.l̩ˌber.i/ *noun* **[C]** a small round dark blue fruit, or the low North American bush on which it grows

huckster /ˈhʌk.stəʳ/ [US] /-stɚ/ *noun* **[C]** *US OFTEN DISAPPROVING* a person who writes advertisements, especially for radio and television, or who sells things or brings ideas

H

or people to the public's attention in a noisy annoying way

huddle /ˈhʌd.l̩/ *verb* **[I usually + adv or prep]** to come close together in a group, or to hold your arms and legs close to your body, especially because of cold or fear: *Everyone huddled **round** the fire to keep warm.* ○ *It was so cold that we huddled **together** for warmth.* ○ *Sophie was so frightened by the noise of the fireworks that she huddled **(up)** in a corner of the room.*

huddle /ˈhʌd.l̩/ *noun* **[C]** **1** a small group of people or things that are close together: *A small group of people stood **in a** huddle at the bus stop.* **2** *US* a group formed by the members of a team in American football before they separate and continue to play

• **go into a huddle** get into a group in order to talk secretly: *The judges went into a huddle to decide the winner.*

huddled /ˈhʌd.l̩d/ *adj* gathered close together: *We stood huddled **together** for warmth.*

hue [COLOUR] /hjuː/ *noun* **[C]** (a degree of lightness, darkness, strength, etc. of) a colour: *In the Caribbean waters there are fish of every hue.*

hue [TYPE] /hjuː/ *noun* **[C]** *LITERARY* a different type or group: *Politicians **of all** hues wish to get sleaze off the agenda so that they can discuss the real issues.*

• **hue and cry** a noisy expression of public anger or disapproval: *There has been a **great** hue and cry about the council's plans to close the school.*

huff /hʌf/ *noun* **[C]** *INFORMAL* an angry and offended mood: *Ted's **gone into** one of his huffs again.*

• **in a huff** angry and offended: *She's in a real huff because I forgot her birthday.* ○ *Julia criticized some aspect of his work and he **left/went off** in a huff.*

huff /hʌf/ *verb* **[I]** *"Well if that's how you feel, I'll go," she huffed* (= said in an annoyed or offended way).

• **huff and puff 1** *INFORMAL* to breathe loudly, usually after physical exercise: *We were huffing and puffing by the time we'd climbed to the top of the hill.* **2** *INFORMAL DISAPPROVING* to complain loudly and express disapproval: *They huffed and puffed about the price but eventually they paid up.*

huffy /ˈhʌf.i/ *adj* angry and offended: *I told her she'd made a mistake and she **got** huffy **with** me.* **huffily** /ˈhʌf.ɪ.li/ *adv*

hug /hʌg/ *verb* **[T]** **-gg- 1** to hold someone or something close to your body with your arms, usually to show that you like, love or value them: *Have you hugged your child today?* ○ *They hugged each other when they met at the station.* ○ *Emily hugged her teddy bear **tightly** to her chest.* ○ *She sat on the floor hugging her **knees*** (= with her knees bent up against her chest and her arms around them). ○ *Whenever I travel in the city I make sure I hug my handbag tightly **to** me.* **2** to stay very close to something or someone: *The road hugs the coast for several miles, then turns inland.* ○ *This type of car will hug* (= not slide on) *the road, even in the wettest conditions.* ○ *a figure-hugging dress* **3** *LITERARY* to keep something that comforts or pleases you private or secret: *I hugged the idea **to myself** all through dinner.* **hug** /hʌg/ *noun* **[C]** *Come here and **give** me a **big** hug.* ○ *We always exchange hugs **and kisses** when we meet.*

huggable /ˈhʌg.ə.bl̩/ *adj INFORMAL He's so huggable* (= he makes me want to hug him)*!*

huge /hjuːdʒ/ *adj* extremely large in size or amount: *They live in a huge house.* ○ *The costs involved in building a spacecraft are huge.* ○ *A huge number of people attended.* ○ *His last three films have all been huge successes.* **hugely** /ˈhjuːdʒ.li/ *adv*: *He gave her a hugely expensive diamond ring.* ○ *Their business has been hugely successful.*

huh /hə/ *exclamation* **1** *INFORMAL* used to show that you have not heard or understood something: *"So what do you want to do tonight?" "Huh? What did you say?"* ○ *Huh? These instructions don't make sense!* **2** *HUMOROUS* used to express disapproval: *Huh, I don't think much of that idea!* **3** *MAINLY US* used at the end of a question or statement, especially when you want someone to agree with what you have said: *I'll bet you wish you hadn't done that, huh?* ○ *Pretty cool, huh?*

hula hoop /ˈhuː.lə.huːp/ *noun* **[C]** *TRADEMARK* a large ring, usually made of plastic, which children play with by putting it around their waist and moving their body so that it spins

hulk [SHIP] /hʌlk/ *noun* **[C]** the body of an old ship, car or very large piece of equipment, which is broken and no longer used: *Here and there the rusted hulk of an abandoned car dots the landscape.*

hulk [AWKWARD] /hʌlk/ *noun* **[C]** a large, heavy, awkward person or thing: *Henry's a real hulk of a man.* ○ *The Incredible Hulk is a character in a comic who turns from a scientist into a two-metre tall monster.*

hulking /ˈhʌl.kɪŋ/ *adj* large and heavy: *We were stopped by two hulking security guards.* ○ *How do you expect me to lift that hulking **great** box?*

hull [SHIP] /hʌl/ *noun* **[C]** the body or frame of a ship, most of which goes under the water

hull [REMOVE COVER] /hʌl/ *verb* **[T]** (*US ALSO* **shuck**) to remove the covering or the stem and leaves from some fruits, vegetables and seeds: *We sat in the garden hulling strawberries.*

hullabaloo /ˌhʌl.ə.bəˈluː/ *noun* **[S]** *OLD-FASHIONED* a loud noise made by people who are angry or annoyed: *There's a crowd of angry demonstrators **making** a real hullabaloo outside the Houses of Parliament.* ○ *The minister resigned after all the hullabaloo* (= public disapproval) *over his affair with an actress.*

hullo /həˈləʊ/ [US] /-ˈloʊ/ *exclamation, noun* **[C]** *plural* **hullos** *UK* **hello**

hum /hʌm/ *verb* **-mm- 1** **[I]** to make a continuous low sound: *The computers were humming in the background.* ○ *What's that strange humming sound?* **2** **[I or T]** to sing without opening your mouth: *She hummed to herself as she walked to school.* ○ *I've forgotten how that tune goes – could you hum it for me?* **3** **[I]** *INFORMAL* to be busy and full of activity, excitement, sounds or voices: *The pub was really humming last night.*

• **hum and haw** *UK* (*US* **hem and haw**) to be uncertain and take a long time: *We hummed and hawed for months before actually deciding to buy the house.*

hum /hʌm/ *noun* **[C usually sing]** *Our house is on a main road, so we can hear the constant hum* (= continuous low noise) ***of** traffic.* ○ *There's an annoying hum on this computer.*

human /ˈhjuː.mən/ *adj* of or typical of people: *The human **body** is composed of about 60% water.* ○ *Early human **remains** were found in the Dordogne region of France.* ○ *Victory in the war was achieved at the cost of great human **suffering**.* ○ *The inspector declared the meat **fit for** human **consumption*** (= in good enough condition for people to eat). ○ *Of course I make mistakes, I'm **only** human* (= I am not perfect). ○ *The fault was due to human **error*** (= a person making a mistake).

ˌhuman (ˈbeing) *noun* **[C]** a man, woman or child: *The greatest damage being done to our planet today is that being done by humans.*

humanity /hjuːˈmæn.ə.ti/ [US] /-t̬i/ *noun* **[U]** people in general: *The massacre was a crime against humanity.* ➲See also **humanity** at **humane**; **(the) humanities**.

humanize, *UK USUALLY* **-ise** /ˈhjuː.mə.naɪz/ *verb* **[T]** *Steps are being taken to humanize the prison* (= to make it less unpleasant and more suitable for people). **humanization**, *UK USUALLY* **-isation** /ˌhjuː.mə.naɪˈzeɪ.ʃən/ *noun* **[U]**

humanly /ˈhjuː.mən.li/ *adv* **humanly possible** able to be done by people: *Rescuers are doing everything that is humanly possible to free the trapped people.*

humane /hjuːˈmeɪn/ *adj* showing kindness, care and sympathy towards others, especially those who are suffering: *The humane way of dealing with a suffering animal* (= the way that causes the least pain) *is to kill it quickly.* ✱ NOTE: The opposite is **inhumane**. **humanely** /hjuː-ˈmeɪn.li/ *adv*: *I don't support the death penalty, but if people are to be executed, it should be done humanely.*

humanity /hjuːˈmæn.ə.ti/ [US] /-t̬i/ *noun* **[U]** *If only he would **show/display** a little humanity* (= understanding and kindness towards other people) *for once.* ➲See also **humanity** at **human**.

ˌHuman ˈGenome ˌProject *noun* **[S]** an attempt to discover all the genetic information in the human body

ˌhuman ˈinterest *noun* [U] details about people's experiences and feelings: *I like newspapers with lots of human interest **stories** in them.*

humanism /ˈhjuː.mə.nɪ.zᵊm/ *noun* [U] a belief system based on the principle that people's spiritual and emotional needs can be fulfilled without following a god or religion

humanist /ˈhjuː.mə.nɪst/ *noun* [C] a person who believes in humanism **humanist** /ˈhjuː.mə.nɪst/ *adj*: *humanist beliefs/writers/ideas* **humanistic** /ˌhjuː.məˈnɪs.tɪk/ *adj*: *humanistic principles*

humanitarian /hjuːˌmæn.ɪˈteə.ri.ən/ [US] /-ˈter.i-/ *adj, noun* [C] (a person who is) involved in or connected with improving people's lives and reducing suffering: *The prisoner has been released for humanitarian reasons.* ○ *The United Nations is sending humanitarian **aid*** (= food and supplies to help people) *to the areas worst affected by the conflict.* ○ *The well-known humanitarian, Joseph Rowntree, was concerned with the welfare of his employees.* **humanitarianism** /hjuːˌmæn.ɪˈteə.ri.ə.nɪ.zᵊm/ [US] /-ˈter.i-/ *noun* [U]

H

(the) humanities /hjuːˈmæn.ɪ.tiz/ [US] /-ə.t̬iz/ *plural noun* the study of subjects such as literature, language, history and philosophy: *I've always been more interested in the humanities than the sciences.*

humankind /ˌhjuː.mənˈkaɪnd/ *noun* [U] the whole of the human race, including both men and women * NOTE: This is now often used in preference to **mankind**.

humanly /ˈhjuː.mən.li/ *adv* ➲See at **human**.

ˌhuman ˈnature *noun* [U] the natural ways of behaving that most people share: *You can't change human nature.* ○ *It's **only** human nature* (= It is natural) *to want the best for your children.*

humanoid /ˈhjuː.mə.nɔɪd/ *noun* [C] a machine or creature with the appearance and qualities of a human **humanoid** /ˈhjuː.mə.nɔɪd/ *adj*

the ˌhuman ˈrace *noun* [S] all people, considered as a species

ˌhuman reˈlations *plural noun* relationships between groups of people, especially between workers in a place of work, or the study of these relationships

ˌhuman reˈsources *plural noun* the department of an organization that deals with finding new employees, keeping records about all the organization's employees, and helping them with any problems

ˌhuman ˈrights *plural noun* the basic rights which it is generally considered all people should have, such as justice and the freedom to say what you think: *She's claiming that her detention by the police was a violation of her human rights.*

ˌhuman ˈshield *noun* [C] a person or group of people kept in a particular place in order to stop an enemy from attacking that place: *Military bases were protected by captured enemy soldiers who were housed there as a human shield.*

the ˌhuman ˈtouch *noun* [S] a friendly and pleasant way of treating other people which makes them feel relaxed: *He is certainly an effective lawyer but colleagues say that he lacks the human touch.*

humble /ˈhʌm.bl̩/ *adj* **1** not proud or not believing that you are important: *He's very humble about his success.* ○ FORMAL *Please accept our humble **apologies** for the error.* ○ *In my humble **opinion*** (= I want to emphasize that I think that) *we should never have bought the car in the first place.* **2** poor or of a low social rank: *Even when she became rich and famous, she never forgot her humble background.* **3** ordinary; not special or very important: *At that time she was just a humble mechanic.* ○ HUMOROUS *Welcome to our humble **abode*** (= our home).

humble /ˈhʌm.bl̩/ *verb* [T] to make someone understand that they are not as important or special as they thought they were: *He was humbled by the child's generosity.* ○ *The world champion was humbled* (= unexpectedly defeated) *by an unknown outsider in last night's race.* **humbling** /ˈhʌm.blɪŋ/ *adj*: *It's a humbling **experience** to see people being so positive about life when they have so little.*

humbly /ˈhʌm.bli/ *adv*: *He very humbly* (= showing that he does not think himself important) *ascribes his success to his wife.*

humbug [DISHONESTY] /ˈhʌm.bʌg/ *noun* [U] dishonest talk, writing or behaviour that is intended to deceive people: *the usual political humbug*

humbug [SWEET] /ˈhʌm.bʌg/ *noun* [C] UK a hard sweet, usually with a mint taste and strips of two different colours on the outside: *mint humbugs*

humdinger /ˌhʌmˈdɪŋ.əʳ/ [US] /-ɚ/ *noun* [S] HUMOROUS something or someone that is noticeable because it is a very good example of its type: *Annabel's party was a real humdinger.* ○ *My brother and sister had a humdinger **of** a row last night.*

humdrum /ˈhʌm.drʌm/ *adj* lacking excitement, interest or new and different events; ordinary: *We lead such a humdrum **life/existence**.* ○ *Most of the work is fairly humdrum.*

humerus /ˈhjuː.mə.rəs/ *noun* [C] *plural* **humeri** SPECIALIZED the long bone in the upper half of your arm, between your shoulder and your ELBOW (= the middle part of the arm where it bends) ➲See picture **The Body** on page Centre 5

humid /ˈhjuː.mɪd/ *adj* (of air and weather conditions) containing extremely small drops of water in the air: *New York is very hot and humid in the summer.* ○ *a hot and humid climate*

humidify /hjuːˈmɪd.ɪ.faɪ/ *verb* [T] *If the air in a room is too dry, you can put a bowl of water near the radiator to humidify it* (= make the air wetter).

humidifier /hjuːˈmɪd.ɪ.faɪ.əʳ/ [US] /-ɚ/ *noun* [C] a machine which makes dry air in a room wetter

humidity /hjuːˈmɪd.ɪ.ti/ [US] /-ə.t̬i/ *noun* [U] **1** the quality of being humid: *I don't like the humidity of this climate.* **2** a measurement of how much water there is in the air: *The temperature is almost eighty degrees, the humidity in the low thirties.*

humiliate /hjuːˈmɪl.i.eɪt/ *verb* [T] to make someone feel ashamed or lose their respect for themselves: *How could you humiliate me by questioning my judgment in front of everyone like that?* ○ *England were humiliated* (= completely defeated) *in last night's match.* **humiliation** /hjuːˌmɪl.iˈeɪ.ʃᵊn/ *noun* [C or U] *After the humiliation **of** last week's defeat, the Mets were back on form.* ○ *Imagine the humilation of having to apologize.*

humiliated /hjuːˈmɪl.i.eɪ.tɪd/ [US] /-t̬ɪd/ *adj*: *I've never felt so humiliated* (= been made to feel so ashamed) *in my life.*

humiliating /hjuːˈmɪl.i.eɪ.tɪŋ/ [US] /-t̬ɪŋ/ *adj* making you feel ashamed or stupid: *Losing my job was the most humiliating thing that ever happened to me.* ○ *The government suffered a humiliating **defeat** in yesterday's debate.* ○ *He found it humiliating **to** have to ask for money.*

humility /hjuːˈmɪl.ɪ.ti/ [US] /-ə.t̬i/ *noun* [U] the quality of not being proud because you are aware of your bad qualities: *He doesn't have the humility to admit when he's wrong.* ○ *They might be very rich, but it wouldn't hurt them to show a little humility.*

hummingbird /ˈhʌm.ɪŋ.bɜːd/ [US] /-bɝːd/ *noun* [C] a very small brightly coloured bird with a long thin beak whose wings move very fast and make a HUMMING noise

hummock /ˈhʌm.ək/ *noun* [C] LITERARY a very small hill or raised part of the ground: *a grassy hummock*

hummus /ˈhʊm.əs/ *noun* [U] **houmous**

humour [AMUSEMENT] UK, US **humor** /ˈhjuː.məʳ/ [US] /-mɚ/ *noun* [U] the ability to be amused by things, the way in which people see that some things are amusing or the quality of being amusing: *He's got a great **sense of** humour* (= he is very able to see things as amusing). ○ *I must say I find his **schoolboy*** (= childish) *humour rather tiresome.*

humorist /ˈhjuː.mə.rɪst/ *noun* [C] a person who writes or tells amusing stories

humorous /ˈhjuː.mə.rəs/ *adj* funny, or making you laugh: *Her latest book is a humorous look at teenage life.*

humorously /ˈhjuː.mə.rə.sli/ *adv*

humourless *UK* /'hjuː.mə.ləs/ *US* /-mɚ-/ *adj* (*US* **humorless**) lacking humour

humour [MOOD] *UK, US* humor /'hjuː.mər/ *US* /-mɚ/ *noun* [C or U] *FORMAL* the state of your feelings; mood: *You seem in a very good humour today.*

humour *UK, US* humor /'hjuː.mər/ *US* /-mɚ/ *verb* [T] to do what someone wants so that they do not become annoyed or upset: *I applied for the job just to humour my parents.* **-humoured** *UK* /-hjuː.məd/ *US* /-mɚd/ *suffix* (*US* **-humored**) *The election campaign has been remarkably peaceful, even good-humoured.*

humungous *UK, US* humongous /hjuː'mʌŋ.gəs/ *adj* *INFORMAL* extremely large: *Zesto's restaurant serves humungous burgers.* ○ *This minor glitch has turned into a humungous problem for the airline.*

hump [LUMP] /hʌmp/ *noun* [C] **1** a large round raised lump or part: *The car hit a hump in the road and swerved.* ○ *UK Local residents are asking for speed humps* (= raised areas across the road which make people drive slowly) *to be installed in their street.* **2** a round raised part on a person's or animal's back: *Some types of camel have two humps and others have one.* ⮕See also **humpbacked**. ⮕See picture **Animals and Birds** on page Centre 4
● **be over the hump** *INFORMAL* to be past the most difficult or dangerous part of an activity or period of time: *It's been hard work but I think we're over the hump now.*

hump [CARRY] /hʌmp/ *verb* [T usually + adv or prep] *INFORMAL* to carry or lift something heavy with difficulty: *My back really aches after humping those heavy boxes around all day.*

hump [HAVE SEX] /hʌmp/ *verb* [I or T] *OFFENSIVE* to have sex (with someone)

the hump [ANGER] *noun UK INFORMAL* **get the hump** to get upset and annoyed with someone because you think they have done something bad to you: *She got the hump because I didn't invite her to the party.*

humpback bridge /ˌhʌmp.bækt'brɪdʒ/ *noun* [C] (*ALSO* **humpbacked bridge**) *UK* a small steep road bridge

humpbacked /'hʌmp.bækt/ *adj* (of an animal) having a round raised part on its back: *a humpbacked whale*

humph /hʌmpf/ *exclamation OFTEN HUMOROUS* a short deep sound made with the lips closed, expressing annoyance or doubt, or pretended annoyance: *Humph, I see you've got yourself some lunch and you haven't made any for the rest of us!*

humus /'hjuː.məs/ *noun* [U] dark earth made of ORGANIC material such as decayed leaves and plants

Hun /hʌn/ *noun* [C] a member of a group of people from Asia who attacked Europe in the 300s and 400s A.D.

hunch [IDEA] /hʌntʃ/ *noun* [C] an idea which is based on feeling and for which there is no proof: [+ that] *I had a hunch that you'd be here.* ○ *Sometimes you have to be prepared to act on/follow a hunch.*

hunch [BEND] /hʌntʃ/ *verb* [I or T] to lean forward with your shoulders raised or to bend your back and shoulders into a rounded shape: *We hunched round the fire to keep warm.* ○ *Stand up straight and don't hunch your back.* **hunched** /hʌntʃt/ *adj*: *Sitting hunched over a computer all day can cause problems.*

hunchback /'hʌntʃ.bæk/ *noun* [C] *OLD-FASHIONED* (a person who has) a back with a large round lump on it, either because of illness or age **hunchbacked** /'hʌntʃ.-bækt/ *adj*

hundred /'hʌn.drəd/ *determiner, noun, pronoun* **1** (the number) 100: *We've driven a/one hundred miles in the last two hours.* ○ *"How many children are there in the school?" "About three hundred."* ○ *That dress costs hundreds of pounds.* **2** *INFORMAL* a large number: *There were hundreds of people at the pool today.*
● **a/one hundred per cent** completely: *I agree with you one hundred per cent.* ○ *I'm better than I was last week but I'm still not (feeling) a hundred per cent* (= I'm not completely well).

hundredth /'hʌn.drətθ/ *determiner, pronoun, adj, adv, noun* 100th written as a word: *He is now ranked one* (*UK ALSO* **a**) *hundredth in world tennis.* ○ *1991 was the two hundredth anniversary of Mozart's death.*

hundredth /'hʌn.drətθ/ *noun* [C] one of a hundred equal parts of something: *She has knocked one/a hundredth of a second off the world record.*

COMMON LEARNER ERROR

hundred or **hundreds**?

If you are using **hundred** to describe a particular number, use the singular form. Only use it in the plural form to refer to a large number that is not exact.

There are three hundred people employed here.
~~There are over three hundreds people employed here.~~
Hundreds of fans were waiting outside the theatre.

hundredweight (*plural* **hundredweight**) /'hʌn.drəd.weɪt/ *noun* [C] (*WRITTEN ABBREVIATION* **cwt**) a measure of weight equal to 50.80 kilograms in Britain or 45.36 kilograms in the US: *We ordered a hundredweight of coal.*

hung [HANG] /hʌŋ/ *past simple and past participle of* **hang**

hung [EQUAL] /hʌŋ/ *adj* having an equal or nearly equal number of members with opposing opinions, so that no decisions can be made: *The general election in Britain was expected to result in a hung parliament.* ○ *a hung jury*

Hungarian /hʌŋ'geə.ri.ən/ *US* /-'ger.i-/ *adj* from, belonging to or relating to Hungary: *Hungarian goulash*
Hungarian /hʌŋ'geə.ri.ən/ *US* /-'ger.i-/ *noun* **1** [C] a person from Hungary **2** [U] the language of Hungary

hunger [NEED FOR FOOD] /'hʌŋ.gər/ *US* /-gɚ/ *noun* [U] **1** the feeling you have when you need to eat: *I can't believe that that enormous meal wasn't enough to satisfy your hunger.* ○ *By about 9 o'clock she started to feel faint from/with hunger.* ○ *I often suffer from hunger pangs* (= strong feelings of needing something to eat) *in the middle of the afternoon.* **2** when the body does not have enough food: *All over the world, people die of hunger every day.*

hunger [DESIRE] /'hʌŋ.gər/ *US* /-gɚ/ *noun* [U] a strong wish or desire: *a hunger for adventure/knowledge/success*
hunger /'hʌŋ.gər/ *US* /-gɚ/ *verb*
▲ **hunger after/for** *sth phrasal verb LITERARY* to want something very much: *I hunger for your touch.* ○ *I've never hungered after power.*

hunger strike *noun* [C or U] a refusal to eat in order to make a protest: *The prisoners have gone on (a) hunger strike to protest about prison conditions.* **hunger striker** *noun* [C]

hung-over /ˌhʌŋ'əʊ.vər/ *US* /-'oʊ.vɚ/ *adj* [after v] feeling ill with a bad pain in the head and often wanting to vomit after having drunk too much alcohol: *That was a great party last night, but I'm (feeling) really hung-over this morning.* ⮕See also **hangover** ILLNESS.

hungry [NEEDING FOOD] /'hʌŋ.gri/ *adj* wanting or needing food: *By four o'clock I felt/was really hungry.* ○ *Digging the garden is hungry work* (= makes you feel hunger). ○ *The children are always hungry* (= want something to eat) *when they get home from school.* ○ *There are too many hungry people* (= people without enough to eat) *in the world.* ○ *She often goes hungry herself* (= does not eat) *so that her children can have enough to eat.* **hungrily** /'hʌŋ.grɪ.li/ *adv*: *They sat down and ate hungrily.*

hungry [WANTING] /'hʌŋ.gri/ *adj* having a strong wish or desire for something: *She was so hungry for success that she'd do anything to achieve it.* ○ *Journalists were hungry for details.*
-hungry /-hʌŋ.gri/ *suffix* having a strong wish or desire for the stated thing: *power-hungry politicians*
hungrily /'hʌŋ.grɪ.li/ *adv*: *He looked at her hungrily* (= showing desire for her).

hunk [PIECE] /hʌŋk/ *noun* [C] a large thick piece, especially of food: *a hunk of bread/cheese/meat*

hunk [MAN] /hʌŋk/ *noun* [C] *INFORMAL APPROVING* a tall strong attractive man: *Who was that hunk in the red shirt last night?*

hunky /'hʌŋ.ki/ *adj INFORMAL APPROVING* describes a man who is sexually attractive and usually big and strong: *I think he's quite hunky.*

hunker /'hʌŋ.kə^r/ ⓤ /-kɚ/ *verb*

▲ **hunker down** *phrasal verb US* **1** to sit down on your heels: *We hunkered down round the campfire, toasting marshmallows.* **2** to make yourself comfortable in a place or situation, or to prepare to stay in a place or position for a long time, usually in order to achieve something or for protection: *The press have hunkered down for the night outside the palace, waiting for news.*

hunky dory *adj* [after v] OLD-FASHIONED INFORMAL describes events or situations that are very satisfactory and pleasant: *You can't lose your temper with everyone like that one minute, and then expect **everything** to be hunky dory again the next.*

hunt CHASE /hʌnt/ *verb* [I or T] **1** to chase and try to catch and kill an animal or bird for food, sport or profit: *Some animals hunt at night.* ○ *When lion cubs are young, the mother stays with them while the father hunts **for** food.* ○ *Jack and Charlie like to hunt/**go** hunting (= chase and kill animals for sport) at weekends.* ○ *Cats like to hunt mice and birds.* ○ *Elephants used to be hunted **for** the ivory from their tusks.* **2** in Britain, to chase and kill animals, especially foxes, using dogs and riding on horses

hunt /hʌnt/ *noun* [C] **1** when people chase wild animals in order to kill them: *to **go on** a fox/deer hunt* **2** in Britain, a group of people who meet regularly in order to chase and kill animals, especially foxes: *They are members of the local hunt.*

hunter /'hʌn.tə^r/ ⓤ /-tɚ/ *noun* [C] **1** a person or an animal that hunts animals for food or for sport: *Animals in the cat family are hunters.* **2** a type of horse, especially one used in hunting animals

-hunter /-hʌn.tə^r/ ⓤ /-tɚ/ *suffix* someone who hunts the stated animal: *a fox-hunter*

hunting /'hʌn.tɪŋ/ ⓤ /-tɪŋ/ *noun* [U] **1** chasing and killing an animal or bird for food, sport or profit: *deer hunting* ○ *a hunting dog/rifle* **2** in Britain, the chasing and killing of animals, especially foxes, for sport, using dogs and riding horses

huntsman /'hʌnts.mən/ *noun* [C] **1** someone who hunts animals with a gun or other weapons **2** in Britain, someone who uses dogs and rides a horse to hunt animals, especially foxes, for sport

hunt SEARCH /hʌnt/ *verb* [I or T] to search for something or someone; to try to find something or someone: *I've hunted all over the place, but I can't find that book.* ○ *They are still hunting **for** the missing child.* ○ *I've hunted **high** and **low** (= looked everywhere) **for** my gloves.* ○ *Police are hunting the terrorists who planted the bomb.* ○ *I'll try and hunt **out** (= find) those old photographs for you.* ○ *They have spent months **house-/job**-hunting (= looking for a house/a job).*

hunt /hʌnt/ *noun* [C usually sing] a search for something or someone: *After a long hunt we finally found a house we liked.* ○ *The hunt **for** the injured climber continued throughout the night.* ○ *Police are **on the** hunt (= searching) **for** the kidnappers.* ○ *The hunt **is on** (= the search has started) **for** a successor to Sir James Gordon.*

-hunter /-hʌn.tə^r/ ⓤ /-tɚ/ *suffix* someone who is trying to find or get the stated thing: *a job-hunter* ○ *a house-hunter* ○ *bargain-hunters*

▲ **hunt** *sb/sth* **down** *phrasal verb* [M] to search everywhere for someone or something until you find them: *The terrorists must be hunted down and brought to justice.*

hunted /hʌn.tɪd/ ⓤ /-tɪd/ *adj* **1** appearing or looking frightened and anxious: *Carla always has such a hunted **look**.* **2** [before n] A hunted animal or person is being chased by someone.

hunting ground *noun* [C] a place where you can find lots of what you are looking for: *Flea markets are **happy** hunting grounds for people looking for antiques at good prices.*

hunt saboteur *noun* [C] a person who tries to stop a hunt, especially a fox hunt, because they think it is cruel to animals

hurdle FENCE /'hɜː.dl/ ⓤ /'hɜː-/ *noun* [C] a frame or fence for jumping over in a race: *He fell at the last hurdle.* ○ *She **cleared** (= jumped over) all the hurdles easily and raced to the finishing line.*

hurdle /'hɜː.dl/ ⓤ /'hɜː-/ *verb* [I or T] to run in a race in which there are hurdles to be jumped over, or to jump over something while running: *He hurdled the gate and scrambled up the hill.*

hurdler /'hɜː.dlə^r/ ⓤ /'hɜː.dlɚ/ *noun* [C] a person or horse that runs in races where there are hurdles

hurdles /'hɜː.dlz/ ⓤ /'hɜː-/ *plural noun* a race in which people or horses jump over hurdles: *the 400-metres hurdles* ⊃See picture **Sports** on page Centre 10

hurdle PROBLEM /'hɜː.dl/ ⓤ /'hɜː-/ *noun* [C] a problem that you have to deal with before you can make progress: *Getting a work permit was the first hurdle to **overcome**.* ○ *The cost of this exercise is proving a major hurdle.*

hurdy gurdy /'hɜː.di.gɜː.di/ ⓤ /'hɜː.di.gɜːr.di/ *noun* [C] a musical instrument which is played by turning a handle, causing a small wheel to be rubbed against a set of strings

hurl /hɜːl/ ⓤ /hɜːl/ *verb* [T] **1** to throw something with a lot of force, usually in an angry or violent way: *In a fit of temper he hurled the book **across** the room.* ○ *Youths hurled stones **at** the soldiers.* **2** **hurl abuse/insults, etc. at** *sb* to shout insults or rude language at someone angrily: *I wasn't going to stand there while he hurled abuse at me!*

hurly-burly /'hɜː.li.bɜː.li/ ⓤ /'hɜː.li.bɜːr-/ *noun* [U] noisy activity: *We got tired of the hurly-burly **of** city life, so we moved to the country.*

hurray /hə'reɪ/ /hʊ-/ *exclamation* (ALSO **hooray**, ALSO **hurrah**) used to express excitement, pleasure or approval: *You won? Hurray!* ○ *Hurray! It's time to go home.* ⊃See also **hip** APPROVAL.

hurricane /'hʌr.ɪ.kən/ /-keɪn/ ⓤ /'hɜː-/ *noun* [C] a violent wind which has a circular movement, especially found in the West Atlantic Ocean: *The state of Florida was **hit** by a hurricane that did serious damage.* ○ *Hurricane force* (= Very strong) *winds are expected tonight.*

hurricane lamp *noun* [C] a light fuelled by PARAFFIN which has a strong glass cover to protect the flame from wind

hurry /'hʌr.i/ ⓤ /'hɜː-/ *verb* [I or T] to move or do things more quickly than normal or to make someone do this: *Hurry or you'll be late.* ○ [+ to infinitive] *She hurried to answer the telephone.* ○ *I hate to hurry you, but I have to leave in a few minutes.* ○ *Don't hurry your food (= Don't eat it too quickly).* ○ *I refuse to be hurried **into** a decision (= to be forced to make a decision too quickly).* ○ *After spending her lunch hour shopping, she hurried **back** (= returned quickly) to work.*

hurry /'hʌr.i/ ⓤ /'hɜː-/ *noun* [S] the need to move or do things more quickly than normal: *We left in such a hurry that we forgot our tickets.* ○ *"Can you wait a few minutes?" "Yes, I'm not in any hurry/I'm in no hurry (= I can wait)."* ○ *Are you **in a** hurry (= wanting) **to** leave?* ○ *What's (all) the hurry (for)/Why (all) the hurry (= Why are you acting or moving so quickly) – we've got plenty of time.* ○ *"I'll let you have this back next week." "That's all right, there's no (great) hurry/there isn't any (great) hurry (= no need to do it quickly)."*

hurried /'hʌr.id/ ⓤ /'hɜː-/ *adj* done very or too quickly: *We left early, after a hurried breakfast.* ○ *I'm sorry this is such a hurried note.*

hurriedly /'hʌr.id.li/ ⓤ /'hɜː-/ *adv*: *The party was a rather hurriedly (= quickly) arranged affair.*

▲ **hurry (sb/sth) up** *phrasal verb* [M] to move or do things more quickly than normal or to make someone do this: *Hurry up or we'll miss the train.* ○ *Could you hurry the children up, or their dinner will get cold.*

hurt /hɜːt/ ⓤ /hɜːt/ *verb* [I or T] **hurt**, **hurt 1** to feel pain in a part of your body, or to injure someone or cause them pain: *Tell me where it hurts.* ○ *My head hurts.* ○ *She says that her ear hurts her.* ○ *Emma hurt her back when she fell off her horse.* ○ *Several people were **seriously/badly** hurt in the explosion.* **2** to cause emotional pain to someone: *She criticized my writing quite severely and that hurt.* ○ *He was badly hurt by the end of his marriage.* **3** to cause harm or difficulty: *A lot of businesses are being hurt by the current high interest rates.* ○ *These allegations have **seriously** hurt her reputation.* ○ *Hard work **never** hurt anyone (= does no one any harm).* ○ INFORMAL

One more drink won't hurt (= won't cause any harm).

• **it wouldn't hurt** *you* **to do** *sth* INFORMAL something that you say which means you think someone should do something because they rarely do it: *It wouldn't hurt you to do the ironing for once.*

• **it never hurts to do** *sth* it is wise: *It never hurts to check the flight departure time before you leave for the airport.*

hurt /hɜːt/ US /hɝːt/ adj **1** [after v] injured or in pain: *Let me help you up. Are you hurt?* ○ *Put that knife away before someone* **gets** *hurt.* **2** upset or unhappy: *I feel very hurt by what you said.* ○ *"That was very unkind," he said in a hurt voice.*

hurt /hɜːt/ US /hɝːt/ noun [S or U] emotional pain: *The hurt after a relationship breaks up can be awful.* ○ *Her brave smile concealed a* **deep** *hurt.*

hurtful /ˈhɜːt.fəl/ US /ˈhɝːt-/ adj causing emotional pain: *That was a very hurtful remark!* ○ *How can you be so hurtful?* **hurtfully** /ˈhɜːt.fəl.i/ US /ˈhɝːt-/ adv **hurtfulness** /ˈhɜːt.fəl.nəs/ US /ˈhɝːt-/ noun [U]

hurtle /ˈhɜː.tl̩/ US /ˈhɝː.tl̩/ verb [I usually + adv or prep] to move very fast, especially in what seems a dangerous way: *The truck came hurtling towards us.* ○ *The explosion sent pieces of metal and glass hurtling through the air.*

husband MAN /ˈhʌz.bənd/ noun [C] the man to whom a woman is married: *I've never met Fiona's husband.*

• **as husband and wife** in the same way as two people who are married: *Although never married, they lived together as husband and wife for fifty years.*

husband SAVE /ˈhʌz.bənd/ verb [T] FORMAL to use something carefully so that you do not use all of it

husbandry /ˈhʌz.bən.dri/ noun [U] OLD USE the careful use of money, food, supplies, etc.

husbandry /ˈhʌz.bən.dri/ noun [U] SPECIALIZED farming: *He gave a lecture on crop and animal husbandry.*

hush /hʌʃ/ noun [S or U] a sudden calm silence: *There was a* **deathly** *hush after she made the announcement.* ○ *A hush* **fell** *over the room.* ○ INFORMAL *Let's have some hush, please!* (= Be quiet, please!)
hush /hʌʃ/ exclamation used to tell someone to be quiet: *Hush! You'll wake the baby!*
hushed /hʌʃt/ adj quiet: *She stood up to address a hushed courtroom.* ○ *People still speak in hushed* **tones** (= very quietly) *of the murders.*
hush /hʌʃ/ verb
▲ **hush** *sth* **up** phrasal verb [M usually passive] DISAPPROVING to try to prevent people from discovering particular facts: *There was some financial scandal involving one of the ministers but it was all hushed up.*

hush-hush /ˌhʌʃˈhʌʃ/ adj INFORMAL kept secret from people: *In the end he was forced to resign but it was all very hush-hush.*

'hush ˌmoney noun [U] INFORMAL money that is given to someone to make them keep something they know secret: *She claimed that the minister had offered her hush money to keep their child a secret.*

husk /hʌsk/ noun [C] the dry outer covering of some seeds

husky VOICE /ˈhʌs.ki/ adj (of a person's voice) low and rough, often in an attractive way, or because of illness: *She's got a nice husky voice – very sexy.* ○ *You sound husky – do you have a cold?*

husky STRONG /ˈhʌs.ki/ adj US A husky man or boy is big and strong.

husky DOG /ˈhʌs.ki/ noun [C] a large, furry dog which is used for pulling SLEDGES over the snow

hussy /ˈhʌs.i/ noun [C] HUMOROUS a woman or girl who is sexually immoral: *"You asked him out? Oh, you* **brazen/ shameless** *hussy, you!"*

the hustings /ðəˈhʌs.tɪŋz/ plural noun UK the political activities and speeches that happen before an election and are intended to win votes: *Three weeks before the election the candidates are all out* **on/at** *the hustings.*

hustle PUSH /ˈhʌs.l̩/ verb [T usually + adv or prep] to make someone move quickly by pushing or pulling them along: *After giving his speech, Johnson was hustled out of the hall by bodyguards.*

hustle PERSUADE /ˈhʌs.l̩/ verb [I or T] MAINLY US INFORMAL to try to persuade someone, especially to buy something,

often illegally: *to hustle for business/customers* ○ *They made a living hustling stolen goods on the streets.*

hustler /ˈhʌs.lər/ US /-lɚ/ noun [C] MAINLY US INFORMAL **1** someone who tries to deceive people into giving them money **2** a PROSTITUTE (= person who has sex for money): *The street was full of hustlers, drug addicts and pimps.*

hustle NOISE /ˈhʌs.l̩/ noun **hustle and bustle** all the noise and activity: *I love the hustle and bustle of the marketplace.*

hut /hʌt/ noun [C] a small, simple building, usually consisting of one room: *a mountain hut* ○ *a row of beach huts*

hutch /hʌtʃ/ noun [C] a box made of wood with a wire front where small animals such as rabbits are kept

hyacinth /ˈhaɪ.ə.sɪntθ/ noun [C] a pleasant-smelling plant with a lot of small flowers that grow close together around one thick stem ᐅSee picture **Flowers and Plants** on page Centre 3

hybrid /ˈhaɪ.brɪd/ noun [C] a plant or animal that has been produced from two different types of plant or animal, especially to get better characteristics, or anything that is a mixture of two very different things: *The garden strawberry is a large-fruited hybrid.* **hybrid** /ˈhaɪ.brɪd/ adj FIGURATIVE *His choreography is described as 'a hybrid* **mix** *of mime and circus tricks'.*

Hyde /haɪd/ noun ᐅSee **Jekyll and Hyde**.

hydra /ˈhaɪ.drə/ noun [C] in ancient Greek stories, a creature with many heads that grew again when cut off, or, more generally, a difficult problem that keeps returning

hydrangea /haɪˈdreɪn.dʒə/ noun [C] a bush on which grow round groups of pink, white or blue flowers

hydrant /ˈhaɪ.drənt/ noun [C] a vertical pipe, usually at the side of the road, that is connected to the main water system of a town and from which water can be obtained especially for dealing with fires: *a fire hydrant*

hydrate /ˈhaɪ.dreɪt/ noun [C] SPECIALIZED a chemical that contains water

hydraulic /haɪˈdrɒl.ɪk/ US /-ˈdrɑː.lɪk/ adj operated by or involving the pressure of water or some other liquid: *a hydraulic lift/platform/pump*
hydraulics /haɪˈdrɒl.ɪks/ US /-ˈdrɑː.lɪks/ plural noun a system of using water to produce power: *The hydraulics failed and the digger stopped.*

hydro- WATER /haɪ.drəʊ-/ US /-droʊ-/ prefix connected with or using the power of water

hydro- GAS /haɪ.drəʊ-/ US /-droʊ-/ prefix showing the presence of hydrogen

hydrocarbon /ˌhaɪ.drəʊˈkɑː.bən/ US /-droʊˈkɑːr-/ noun [C] a chemical combination of hydrogen and carbon, such as in oil or petrol: *hydrocarbon emissions*

hydrochloric acid /ˌhaɪd.rə.klɒr.ɪkˈæs.ɪd/ US /-ˈklɔːr-/ noun [U] an acid containing hydrogen and CHLORINE

hydroelectric /ˌhaɪ.drəʊ.ɪˈlek.trɪk/ US /-droʊ-/ adj relating to or producing electricity by the force of fast moving water such as rivers or waterfalls: *a hydroelectric power station* **hydroelectricity** /ˌhaɪ.drəʊ.ɪ.lekˈtrɪs.ɪ.ti/ US /-droʊ.ɪ.lekˈtrɪs.ə.t̬i/ noun [U]

hydrofoil /ˈhaɪ.drəʊ.fɔɪl/ US /-droʊ-/ noun [C] a large boat which is able to travel quickly above the surface of the water on wing-like structures

hydrogen /ˈhaɪ.drɪ.dʒən/ noun [U] the lightest gas, with no colour, taste or smell, that combines with oxygen to form water

'hydrogen ˌbomb noun [C usually sing] (ABBREVIATION **H-bomb**) a nuclear bomb which explodes when the central parts of its hydrogen atoms join together

hydrolysis /haɪˈdrɒl.ə.sɪs/ US /-ˈdrɑː.lə-/ noun [U] SPECIALIZED a chemical reaction in which one substance reacts with water to produce another

hydrophobia /ˌhaɪ.drəʊˈfəʊ.bi.ə/ US /-droʊˈfoʊ-/ noun [U] **1** SPECIALIZED a great fear of drinking and water, often a sign of RABIES **2** OLD-FASHIONED the disease of RABIES itself

hydroplane /ˈhaɪ.drəʊ.pleɪn/ US /-droʊ-/ verb [I] US FOR **aquaplane**

hydroponics /ˌhaɪ.drəʊˈpɒn.ɪks/ US /-droʊˈpɑː.nɪks/ noun [U] SPECIALIZED the method of growing plants in water to which special chemicals are added, rather than growing them in earth

hydropower /ˈhaɪd.rəʊ.paʊər/ ⓤ /-roʊ.paʊr/ *noun* [U] the production of electricity by the force of fast moving water; HYDROELECTRIC power

hydrotherapy /ˌhaɪ.drəʊˈθer.ə.pi/ ⓤ /-droʊ-/ *noun* [U] a method of treating people with particular diseases or injuries by making them exercise in water

hyena /haɪˈiː.nə/ *noun* [C] a wild animal from Africa and Asia that looks like a dog, hunts in groups and makes a sound similar to an unpleasant human laugh

hygiene /ˈhaɪ.dʒiːn/ *noun* [U] the degree to which people keep themselves or their surroundings clean, especially to prevent disease: *Poor standards of hygiene mean that the disease spreads fast.* ○ *health and hygiene regulations* ○ *dental/personal hygiene*
hygienic /haɪˈdʒiː.nɪk/ ⓤ /-ˈdʒen-/ *adj*: *It isn't hygienic* (= clean) *to let the cat sit on the dining table.*
hygienist /haɪˈdʒiː.nɪst/ ⓤ /-ˈdʒen.ɪst/ *noun* [C] (*ALSO* **dental hygienist**) a person who works with a dentist and cleans people's teeth to keep them healthy

hying /ˈhaɪ.ɪŋ/ *present participle of* **hie**

hymen /ˈhaɪ.mən/ *noun* [C] a thin piece of skin that partly covers the opening to a girl's or woman's vagina and breaks when she has sex for the first time

hymn /hɪm/ *noun* [C] a song of praise that Christians sing to God: *a hymn book*
hymnal /ˈhɪm.nəl/ *noun* [C] *FORMAL OR OLD-FASHIONED* a book containing HYMNS

hype /haɪp/ *noun* [U] *INFORMAL* when something is continually advertised and discussed in newspapers, on television, etc. in order to attract everyone's interest: *media hype* ○ *There's been a lot of hype **around**/**surrounding** his latest film.* ○ *I've been put off reading the book by all the hype.*
hype /haɪp/ *verb* [T often passive] (*ALSO* **hype up**) *INFORMAL* to continually advertise and discuss something in newspapers, on television, etc. in order to attract everyone's interest: *It's being hyped **as** the musical event of the year.*
▲ **hype** *sb* **up** *phrasal verb* to make someone feel very excited: *She took pills to keep her awake, to help her sleep, to calm her down and to hype her up.*
hyped 'up *adj* [after v] *INFORMAL* too excited or nervous and unable to rest or be calm: *He gets really hyped up when he's playing video games.*

hyper- TOO MUCH /ˈhaɪ.pər/ ⓤ /-pɚ-/ *prefix* having too much of the stated quality: *hyperactive* ○ *hypercritical* ○ *hypersensitive*

hyper EXCITED /ˈhaɪ.pər/ ⓤ /-pɚ/ *adj INFORMAL* too excited and energetic: *I don't let him have sweet fizzy drinks because they tend to make him hyper.* ⊃See also **hyperactive.**

hyperactive /ˌhaɪ.pərˈæk.tɪv/ ⓤ /-pɚˈæk.tɪv/ *adj* Someone who is hyperactive has more energy than is normal, gets excited easily and cannot still or think about their work: *Hyperactive children often have poor concentration and require very little sleep.* ⊃See also **hyper** EXCITED. **hyperactivity** /ˌhaɪ.pə.ræk'tɪv.ɪ.ti/ ⓤ /-pɚ.æk'tɪv.ə.t̬i/ *noun* [U]

hyperbola /haɪˈpɜː.bəl.ə/ ⓤ /-ˈpɝː-/ *noun* [C] *SPECIALIZED* a curve whose ends continue to move apart from each other

hyperbole /haɪˈpɜː.bəl.i/ ⓤ /-ˈpɝː-/ *noun* [U] *FORMAL* a way of speaking or writing that makes someone or something sound bigger, better, more, etc. than they are: *The blurb on the back of the book was full of the usual hyperbole – 'enthralling', 'fascinating' and so on.* **hyperbolic** /ˌhaɪ.pəˈbɒl.ɪk/ ⓤ /-pɚˈbɑː.lɪk/ *adj*: *hyperbolic rhetoric*

hypercritical /ˌhaɪ.pəˈkrɪt.ɪ.kəl/ ⓤ /-pɚˈkrɪt̬-/ *adj* too eager to find mistakes in everything; extremely critical

hyperinflation /ˌhaɪ.pə.rɪnˈfleɪʃ.ən/ ⓤ /-pɚ.ɪn-/ *noun* [U] a condition where the price of everything in a national economy goes out of control and increases very quickly

hyperlink /ˈhaɪ.pə.lɪŋk/ ⓤ /ˈhaɪ.pɚ.lɪŋk/ *noun* [C] a connection that allows you to move easily between two computer documents or two pages on the Internet

hypermarket /ˈhaɪ.pəˌmɑː.kɪt/ ⓤ /-pɚˌmɑːr-/ *noun* [C] a very large shop, usually outside the centre of town

hypersensitive /ˌhaɪ.pəˈsen.sɪ.tɪv/ ⓤ /-pɚˈsen.sə.t̬ɪv/ *adj* **1** too easily upset by criticism: *He's hypersensitive **about** his height.* **2** very easily influenced, changed or damaged, especially by a physical activity or effect: *hypersensitive skin*

hypertension /ˌhaɪ.pəˈten.tʃən/ ⓤ /-pɚ-/ *noun* [U] *SPECIALIZED* a medical condition in which your blood pressure is extremely high

hypertext /ˈhaɪ.pə.tekst/ ⓤ /-pɚ-/ *noun* [U] *SPECIALIZED* a way of joining a word or image to another page, document, etc. on the Internet or in another computer program so that you can move from one to the other easily: *The Web is based on hypertext **links** that allow people to easily move from document to document.*

hyperventilation /ˌhaɪ.pəˌven.tɪˈleɪ.ʃən/ ⓤ /-pɚˌven.t̬əlˈeɪ-/ *noun* [U] *SPECIALIZED* breathing too quickly and so causing too much oxygen to enter the blood: *Hyperventilation can be caused by fear or panic.* **hyperventilate** /ˌhaɪ.pəˈven.tɪ.leɪt/ ⓤ /-pɚˈven.t̬əl.eɪt/ *verb* [I]

hyphen /ˈhaɪ.fən/ *noun* [C] the – punctuation mark that joins two words together, or shows that a word has been divided into two parts at the end of one line and the beginning of the next: *There should be a hyphen in 'short-sighted'.* ⊃Compare **dash** PUNCTUATION. **hyphenation** /ˌhaɪ.fənˈeɪ.ʃən/ *noun* [U] *the rules of hyphenation* **hyphenate** /ˈhaɪ.fən.eɪt/ *verb* [T]
hyphenated /ˈhaɪ.fən.eɪ.tɪd/ ⓤ /-t̬ɪd/ *adj* written with a hyphen: *hyphenated compounds*

hypnosis /hɪpˈnəʊ.sɪs/ ⓤ /-ˈnoʊ-/ *noun* [U] a mental state like sleep, in which a person's thoughts can be easily influenced by someone else: *Under deep hypnosis she remembered the traumatic events of that night.*
hypnotic /hɪpˈnɒt.ɪk/ ⓤ /-ˈnɑː.t̬ɪk/ *adj* **1** caused by hypnosis: *She went into a hypnotic trance.* **2** describes sounds or movements that are very regular and make you feel as if you want to sleep: *The beat of the music was strangely hypnotic.*
hypnotize, *UK USUALLY* **-ise** /ˈhɪp.nə.taɪz/ *verb* **1** [T] to put someone in a state of hypnosis: *She agreed to be hypnotized to try to remember what had happened.* **2** [T usually passive] to keep your attention so strongly that you feel unable to move or look away: *I was hypnotized by his steely grey eyes.* **hypnotism** /ˈhɪp.nə.tɪ.zəm/ ⓤ /-t̬ɪ-/ *noun* [U] *Some people try hypnotism to cure themselves of addictions.*
hypnotist /ˈhɪp.nə.tɪst/ ⓤ /-t̬ɪst/ *noun* [C] a person who uses hypnosis as a form of treatment, or sometimes entertainment: *I went to a hypnotist to try to give up smoking.*

hypnotherapy /ˌhɪp.nəʊˈθer.ə.pi/ ⓤ /-noʊ-/ *noun* [U] the use of HYPNOSIS to treat emotional problems

hypochondria /ˌhaɪ.pəʊˈkɒn.dri.ə/ ⓤ /-poʊˈkɑːn-/ *noun* [U] a state in which a person continually worries about their health without having any reason to do so: *I thought the doctor was going to accuse me of hypochondria.* **hypochondriac** /ˌhaɪ.pəʊˈkɒn.dri.æk/ ⓤ /-poʊˈkɑːn-/ *noun* [C] *She's a terrible hypochondriac – she's always at the doctor's.* **hypochondriac** /ˌhaɪ.pəʊˈkɒn.dri.æk/ ⓤ /-poʊˈkɑːn-/ *adj*

hypocrisy /hɪˈpɒk.rɪ.si/ ⓤ /-ˈpɑː.krə-/ *noun* [U] when someone pretends to believe something that they do not really believe or that is the opposite of what they do or say at another time: *There's one rule for her and another rule for everyone else and it's sheer hypocrisy.* **hypocrite** /ˈhɪp.ə.krɪt/ *noun* [C] *He's a hypocrite – he's always lecturing other people on the environment but he drives around in a huge great car.* **hypocritical** /ˌhɪp.əʊˈkrɪt.ɪ.kəl/ ⓤ /-əˈkrɪt̬-/ *adj*: *Their accusations of corruption are hypocritical – they have been just as corrupt themselves.* **hypocritically** /ˌhɪp.əˈkrɪt.ɪ.kli/ ⓤ /-ˈkrɪt̬-/ *adv*

hypodermic /ˌhaɪ.pəʊˈdɜː.mɪk/ ⓤ /-poʊˈdɝː-/ *adj* *SPECIALIZED* (of medical tools) used to inject drugs under a person's skin: *a hypodermic needle*

hypoglycaemia, *MAINLY US* **hypoglycemia** /ˌhaɪ.pəʊ.glaɪˈsiː.mi.ə/ ⓤ /-poʊ-/ *noun* [U] *SPECIALIZED* a medical condition resulting from dangerously low levels of sugar in the blood **hypoglycaemic**, MAINLY US **hypoglycemic** /ˌhaɪ.pəʊ.glaɪˈsiː.mɪk/ US /-poʊ-/ adj: As a diabetic she was accustomed to the occasional hypoglycaemic **attack**.

hypotenuse /haɪˈpɒt.ᵊn.juːz/ US /-ˈpɑː.t̬ə.nuːz/ noun [C] SPECIALIZED the longest side of any triangle which has one angle of 90°

hypothermia /ˌhaɪ.pəʊˈθɜː.mi.ə/ US /-poʊˈθɜ-/ noun [U] a serious medical condition in which a person's body temperature falls below the usual level as a result of being in severe cold for a long time: In this current cold spell, many old people are dying needlessly of hypothermia.

hypothesis /haɪˈpɒθ.ə.sɪs/ US /-ˈpɑː.θə-/ noun [C] plural **hypotheses** an idea or explanation for something that is based on known facts but has not yet been proved: Several hypotheses for global warming have been suggested.

hypothesize /haɪˈpɒθ.ə.saɪz/ US /-ˈpɑː.θə-/ verb [I or T] FORMAL to give a possible but not yet proved explanation for something: There's no point hypothesizing **about** how the accident happened, since we'll never really know.

hypothetical /ˌhaɪ.pəˈθet.ɪ.kᵊl/ US /-ˈθet̬-/ adj imagined or suggested but not necessarily real or true: a hypothetical example/situation ○ This is all very hypothetical but supposing Jackie got the job, how would that affect you?

hysterectomy /ˌhɪs.tᵊrˈek.tə.mi/ US /-təˈrek-/ noun [C] a medical operation to remove part or all of a woman's womb

hysteria /hɪˈstɪə.ri.ə/ US /-ˈstɪr.i-/ noun [U] extreme fear, excitement, anger, etc. which cannot be controlled: One woman, close to hysteria, grabbed my arm. ○ Tabloid hysteria about the murders has increased public fears. ○ mass hysteria

hysterical /hɪˈster.ɪ.kᵊl/ adj **1** unable to control your feelings or behaviour because you are extremely frightened, angry, excited, etc: Calm down, you're getting hysterical. ○ The police were accused of hysterical over-reaction. ○ hysterical laughter (= uncontrolled laughter) **2** INFORMAL extremely funny: His last film was hysterical. **hysterically** /hɪˈster.ɪ.kli/ adv: She started laughing/crying hysterically (= without control).

hysterics /hɪˈster.ɪks/ plural noun **1** uncontrolled behaviour or crying, usually caused by extreme fear or sadness: Convinced the plane was about to crash, many people were sobbing and **in** hysterics. **2** INFORMAL uncontrolled laughter: He was hilarious – he had us all **in** hysterics.
• **have hysterics** INFORMAL to get extremely angry or upset: She'll have hysterics when she finds out how much money is missing.

Hz WRITTEN ABBREVIATION FOR **hertz**

I LETTER (*plural* **I's**), **i** (*plural* **i's**) /aɪ/ *noun* [C] the 9th letter of the English alphabet

I NUMBER, **i** /aɪ/ *noun* [C] the sign used in the Roman system for the number 1 and as part of the numbers 2 (ii), 3 (iii), 4 (iv), 6 (vi), 7 (vii), 8 (viii), and 9 (ix)

I PERSON SPEAKING /aɪ/ *pronoun* (used as the subject of a verb) the person speaking: *I love you.* ○ *Am I invited?* ○ *I'm not mistaken, am I?* ○ *I'd like a coffee, please.* ⊃See Note **me or I?** at **me** PERSON.

:-I INTERNET SYMBOL FOR bored or not interested

Iberian /aɪˈbɪə.ri.ən/ ⓤ /-ˈbɪr.i-/ *adj* of Spain and Portugal: *the Iberian Peninsula*

ibid /ˈɪb.ɪd/ *adv* SPECIALIZED used in formal writing to refer to a book or article that has already been mentioned

-ibility /-ɪ.bɪl.ɪ.ti/ ⓤ /-ə.ti/ *suffix* ⊃See at **-ability** QUALITY: *accessibility* ○ *responsibility*

-ible /-ɪ.bl̩/ /-ə.bl̩/ *suffix* (ALSO **-able**) ⊃See at **-able** CAN BE and **-able** WORTH BEING: *convertible* ○ *accessible* ○ *permissible*

IBS /ˌaɪ.biːˈes/ *noun* [U] ABBREVIATION FOR **irritable bowel syndrome**

-ic /-ɪk/ *suffix* (ALSO **-ical**) used to form adjectives: *scenic* ○ *economic*

ICBM /ˌaɪ.siː.biːˈem/ *noun* [C] ABBREVIATION FOR intercontinental ballistic missile: a flying bomb that can travel a long distance to its target

ice FROZEN WATER /aɪs/ *noun* **1** [U] water which has frozen and become solid, or pieces of this: *The pond was covered in ice all winter.* ○ *Would you like ice in your juice?* ○ *He skidded on a patch of ice.* ○ *I've put a couple of bottles of champagne on ice (= in a container of ice to get cold).* **2** [C] UK OLD-FASHIONED an ice cream, especially one bought in a shop: *The shop sign said 'Drinks, Cakes, Ices.'*

• **be on ice** If a plan is on ice, a decision has been made to delay it for a period of time: *Both projects are on ice until the question of funding is resolved.*

iced /aɪst/ *adj* An iced drink has been made very cold, usually by having ice added to it: *iced tea* ○ *iced water*

icy /ˈaɪ.si/ *adj* **1** covered in ice: *icy roads* ○ *an icy pavement* ⊃See also **icy**. **2** extremely cold: *She opened the window and I was hit by an icy blast of air.* ○ *He fell into the icy waters of the Moscow river.* ○ *Her skin was icy to the touch.*

ice COVER CAKES UK /aɪs/ *verb* [T] (US **frost**) to cover a cake with ICING (= a food made mainly with sugar): *I've made her a chocolate cake – now I just need to ice it.*

icing /ˈaɪ.sɪŋ/ *noun* [U] (US ALSO **frosting**) a sweet food used to cover or fill cakes, made from sugar and water or sugar and butter: *chocolate butter icing*

• **the icing on the cake** UK (US **the frosting on the cake**) something which makes a good situation even better: *I was just content to see my daughter in such a stable relationship but a grandchild, that really was the icing on the cake.*

ice KILL /aɪs/ *verb* [T] US SLANG to murder someone

PHRASAL VERBS WITH **ice** ▼

▲ **ice over** *phrasal verb* If an area of water ices over, it becomes covered with a layer of ice: *The lake has iced over.*

▲ **ice up** *phrasal verb* to become covered in ice and often stop working: *The plane was delayed because the engine had iced up.*

ˈice ˌage *noun* [C] (SPECIALIZED **glacial period**) a time in the past when the temperature was very cold and GLACIERS (= large masses of ice) spread over large parts of the Earth

iceberg /ˈaɪs.bɜːɡ/ ⓤ /-bɜːːɡ/ *noun* [C] a very large mass of ice that floats in the sea

iceblock /ˈaɪs.blɒk/ ⓤ /-blɑːk/ *noun* [C] AUS FOR **ice lolly**

icebox /ˈaɪs.bɒks/ ⓤ /-bɑːks/ *noun* [C] US OLD-FASHIONED a FRIDGE (= container which uses electricity to keep food cold)

ˈice-ˌbreaker SHIP *noun* [C] a strong ship that can break a passage through ice

ice-breaker FUN ACTIVITY /ˈaɪsˌbreɪ.kər/ ⓤ /-kɚ/ *noun* [C] a game or joke that makes people who do not know each other feel more relaxed together

ˈice ˌbucket *noun* [C] a container in which pieces of ice for cooling drinks or bottles of wine are kept

ˈice ˌcap *noun* [C] (ALSO **ice sheet**) a thick layer of ice that permanently covers an area of land: *polar ice caps*

ice-cold /ˌaɪsˈkəʊld/ ⓤ /-ˈkoʊld/ *adj* extremely cold: *I felt her hand and it was ice-cold.* ○ *I'd love an ice-cold beer.*

ˈice ˌcream *noun* [C or U] a very cold sweet food made from frozen milk or cream, sugar and flavourings: *a tub of ice cream* ○ *chocolate chip/vanilla ice cream*

ice-cream soda /ˌaɪs.kriːmˈsəʊ.də/ ⓤ /-ˈsoʊ-/ *noun* [C] a sweet dish made from ice cream, thick fruit juice and SODA (= fizzy water), usually served in a tall glass

ˈice ˌcube *noun* [C] a small block of ice that you put into drinks to make them cold

ˈice ˌfloe *noun* [C] a large area of ice floating in the sea

ˈice ˌhockey *noun* [U] (US ALSO **hockey**) a game played on ice between two teams of players who each have a curved stick with which they try to put a PUCK (= a small hard disc) into the other team's goal ⊃See picture **Sports** on page Centre 10

ˌice ˈlolly UK *noun* [C] (AUS **iceblock**, US TRADEMARK **Popsicle**) a sweet, fruit-flavoured piece of ice on a small stick

icemaker /ˈaɪsˌmeɪ.kər/ ⓤ /-kɚ/ *noun* [C] a device that makes small pieces of ice to put in drinks, etc.

ˈice ˌpack *noun* [C] a bag containing ice which is put on a part of a person's body to make it cool and reduce swelling

ˈice ˌpick *noun* [C] a sharp tool for breaking large blocks of ice

ˈice ˌrink *noun* [C] a level area of ice, often inside a building, that is kept frozen for people to SKATE on

ˈice ˌskate *noun* [C] a special shoe with a thin metal bar fixed to the bottom that you wear to move quickly on ice **ˈice ˌskate** *verb* [I] to move across ice using ice skates **ˈice ˌskating** *noun* [U] *Would you like to go ice skating?*

ˈice ˌwater *noun* [U] MAINLY US water that has been made extremely cold

icicle /ˈaɪ.sɪ.kl̩/ *noun* [C] a long pointed stick of ice that is formed when drops of water freeze: *Icicles hung from the roof.*

ˈicing ˌsugar UK *noun* [U] (US **powdered sugar, confectioners' sugar**) soft powdery sugar used to make icing for cakes

ick /ɪk/ *exclamation* US INFORMAL used to express disgust: *Then he kissed her! Ick!*

icky /ˈɪk.i/ *adj* US INFORMAL unpleasant, especially to look at: *an icky shade of green*

icon COMPUTER SYMBOL /ˈaɪ.kɒn/ ⓤ /-kɑːn/ *noun* [C] a small picture or symbol on a computer screen that you point to and CLICK on (= press) with a MOUSE (= small control device) to give the computer an instruction

icon REPRESENTATION /ˈaɪ.kɒn/ ⓤ /-kɑːn/ *noun* [C] a very famous person or thing considered as representing a set of beliefs or a way of life: *Marilyn Monroe and James Dean are still icons for many young people.* **iconic** /aɪˈkɒn.ɪk/ ⓤ /-ˈkɑː.nɪk/ *adj*: FORMAL *John Lennon gained iconic status following his death.*

iconography /ˌaɪ.kəˈnɒɡ.rə.fi/ ⓤ /-ˈnɑː.ɡrə-/ *noun* [U] the use of images and symbols to represent ideas, or the particular images and symbols used in this way by a religious or political group, etc: *religious/political iconography* ○ *The iconography of this picture is fascinating.* ○ *I am studying the iconography of Islamic texts, with special reference to the representation of women.*

icon HOLY PAINTING, **ikon** /ˈaɪ.kɒn/ ⓤ /-kɑːn/ *noun* [C] a painting, usually on wood, of Jesus Christ, or of a person considered holy by some Christians, especially in Russia, Greece and other countries

iconoclast /aɪˈkɒn.ə.klæst/ [US] /-ˈkɑː.nə-/ *noun* [C] *FORMAL* a person who strongly opposes generally accepted beliefs and traditions: *Rogers, an iconoclast in architecture, is sometimes described as putting the insides of buildings on the outside.* **iconoclastic** /aɪˌkɒn.əˈklæs.tɪk/ [US] /-kɑː.nə-/ *adj*: *His plays were fairly iconoclastic in their day.* ○ *iconoclastic views* **iconoclasm** /aɪˈkɒn.əˌklæz.ᵊm/ [US] /-ˈkɑː.nə-/ *noun* [U]

-ics /-ɪks/ *suffix* used to form nouns which refer to an area of work or study: *the world of politics* ○ *the study of economics/physics/ethics*

icy /ˈaɪ.si/ *adj* unfriendly and showing no emotion: *an icy stare* ➲See also **icy** at **ice** FROZEN WATER. **icily** /ˈaɪ.sɪ.li/ *adv*

ID /ˌaɪˈdiː/ *noun* [U] *INFORMAL* any official card or document with your name and photograph or other information on it that you use to prove who you are: *Have you got any ID? A driving licence or cheque card will do.*

ID /ˌaɪˈdiː/ *verb* [T] *US INFORMAL* to look at a person or a body and say who they are to someone in authority: *He had to go to the morgue to ID the body.*

id /ɪd/ *noun* [C] *SPECIALIZED* in PSYCHOANALYSIS the deepest part of the unconscious mind that represents the most basic natural human needs and emotions such as hunger, anger and the wish for pleasure

I'd /aɪd/ *short form of* **1** I had: *I'd just got in the bath when the phone rang.* **2** I would: *Of course I'd love to see you.*

I.D. card /ˌaɪˈdiːˌkɑːd/ [US] /-ˌkɑːrd/ *noun* [C] an **identity card**

idea [SUGGESTION] /aɪˈdɪə/ *noun* [C] a suggestion or plan for doing something: *I've* ***had an*** *idea – why don't we go to the coast?* ○ *"Let's go swimming." "That's a* ***good*** *idea!"* ○ *If you have any ideas* ***for*** *what I could buy Jack, let me know.* ○ *That's when I first had* ***the*** *idea* ***of*** *starting* (= planned to start) *my own business.* ○ *I like the idea* ***of*** *living in the countryside but I'm not sure I'd like the reality.* ○ *She's full of* ***bright*** (= good) *ideas.* ○ [+ to infinitive] *It was Kate's idea* ***to*** *hire bikes.* ○ ***It's*** *not a good idea* ***to*** *drive for hours without a rest.*

• ***your*** **idea of** ***sth*** what you consider to be something: *Playing card games is not my idea of fun.* ○ *Is this your idea of* ***a joke*** (= Do you think that this is amusing)*?*

• **put ideas into** ***sb's*** **head** to make someone want to do something they had not thought about before, especially something stupid: *Don't go putting ideas into his head. We can't afford a new car.*

• **What an idea!** (*ALSO* **The idea of it!**) *OLD-FASHIONED* something you say to show that you think a suggestion is stupid: *I can't turn up at a funeral in a pink jacket. What an idea!*

idea [KNOWLEDGE] /aɪˈdɪə/ *noun* [S or U] an understanding, thought or picture in your mind: *Do you* ***have any*** *idea* ***of*** *what he looks like?* ○ *Can you* ***give*** *me an idea* ***of*** *the cost* (= Can you tell me approximately how much the cost is)*?* ○ *I don't like the idea* ***of*** *living so far away from my family.* ○ [+ question word] *I haven't* ***the slightest/faintest*** *idea* ***where*** *they've gone.* ○ *I've got a* ***pretty good*** *idea* ***why*** *they left early.* ○ *"Where's Serge?" "I've* ***no*** *idea* (= I do not know)*."*

• **you have no idea** said for emphasis when you are describing how good or bad an experience is: *Flying a plane is wonderful, you have no idea.* ○ *You have no idea* ***how*** *embarrassed I was.*

idea [BELIEF] /aɪˈdɪə/ *noun* [C] a belief or opinion: *We have very different ideas* ***about*** *disciplining children.* ○ [+ that] *Leach puts forward the idea* ***that*** *it is impossible to spoil a child.* ○ *I'm not married – where did you get that idea* (= what made you believe that)*?*

idea [PURPOSE] /aɪˈdɪə/ *noun* [S] a purpose or reason for doing something: *The idea* ***of*** *the game is to get rid of all your cards as soon as you can.* ○ *The* ***whole*** *idea* (= only purpose) ***of*** *advertising is to make people buy things.* ○ *The idea* ***behind*** *the national lottery is to raise money for good causes.*

ideal [PERFECT] /aɪˈdɪəl/ *adj* without fault; perfect, or the best possible: *the ideal employer* ○ *She's the ideal person* (= exactly the right type of person) ***for*** *the job.* ○ *The television also comes in a compact 36 cm screen size, ideal* ***for*** *bedroom or kitchen use.* ○ *It's the ideal* ***opportunity*** *to meet people.* ○ ***In an*** *ideal* ***world*** *no one would go hungry.*

ideal /aɪˈdɪəl/ *noun* [S] a perfect thing or situation: *The ideal would be to have a place in the town and one in the country.*

ideally /aɪˈdɪə.li/ *adv* used when describing the perfect situation: *Ideally, I'd like to work at home but it's just not practical.* ○ *She's ideally* (= perfectly) ***suited*** *to the job.*

idealize, *UK USUALLY* **-ise** /aɪˈdɪə.laɪz/ *verb* [T] to think of or represent someone or something as better than they are: *Why do people idealize their school days?*

idealized, *UK USUALLY* **-ised** /aɪˈdɪə.laɪzd/ *adj*: *The film presents a very idealized view of 19th-century Ireland* (= making it seem more pleasant than it was). **idealization**, *UK USUALLY* **-isation** /aɪˌdɪə.laɪˈzeɪ.ʃᵊn/ *noun* [U]

ideal [PRINCIPLE] /aɪˈdɪəl/ *noun* [C] a principle or a way of behaving that is of a very high standard: *democratic ideals* ○ *We are committed to the ideal of equality.* ○ *They share the same high ideals.*

idealism /aɪˈdɪə.lɪ.zᵊm/ *noun* [U] **1** the belief that your ideals can be achieved, often when this does not seem likely to others: *She never lost her youthful idealism and campaigned for just causes all her life.* ➲Compare **realism** at **real** NOT IMAGINARY. **2** *SPECIALIZED* the belief in philosophy that objects in the world are ideas which only exist in the mind of God or people who see them

idealist /aɪˈdɪə.lɪst/ *noun* [C] someone who believes that ideals can be achieved, often when this does not seem likely to others **idealistic** /ˌaɪ.dɪəˈlɪs.tɪk/ *adj*: *When I was young and idealistic I believed it was possible to change the world.* **idealistically** /ˌaɪ.dɪəˈlɪs.tɪ.kli/ *adv*

identical /aɪˈden.tɪ.kᵊl/ [US] /-t̬ə-/ *adj* exactly the same, or very similar: *I've got three identical blue suits.* ○ *The two rooms were virtually identical.* ○ *The interests of both parties may not be identical, but they do overlap considerably.* ○ *The tests are identical* ***to*** *those carried out last year.*

identically /aɪˈden.tɪ.kli/ [US] /-t̬ə-/ *adv*: *The two sisters were always dressed identically* (= in the same clothes).

iˌdentical ˈtwin *noun* [C usually pl] one of two babies of the same sex who were born at the same time, developed from the same egg, and look very similar

identify /aɪˈden.tɪ.faɪ/ [US] /-t̬ə-/ *verb* [T] **1** to recognize someone or something and say or prove who or what they are: *Even the smallest baby can identify its mother by her voice.* ○ *The gunman in Wednesday's attack has been identified as Lee Giggs, an unemployed truck driver.* ○ [R] *The police officer identified himself* (= gave his name or proved who he was) *and asked for our help.* **2** to recognize a problem, need, fact, etc. and to show that it exists: *The research will be used to identify training needs.* ○ *You need to identify your priorities.*

identifiable /aɪˈden.tɪ.faɪ.ə.bl̩/ [US] /aɪˌden.t̬əˈ-/ *adj* able to be recognized: *In her bright yellow coat, she was easily identifiable in the crowd.*

identification /aɪˌden.tɪ.fɪˈkeɪ.ʃᵊn/ [US] /-t̬ə-/ *noun* [U] **1** when you recognize and can name someone or something: *Most of the bodies were badly burned, making identification almost impossible.* **2** (*ALSO* **ID**) an official document that shows or proves who you are: *We were asked to show some identification before the security guards would let us in.*

PHRASAL VERBS WITH **identify** ▼

▲ **identify with** ***sb*** [BE SIMILAR] *phrasal verb* to feel that you are similar to someone in some way and that you can understand them or their situation because of this: *Many women of normal weight feel unable to identify with the super-thin models in glossy magazines.*

▲ **identify** ***sb/sth*** **with** ***sth*** [CONNECT] *phrasal verb* [usually passive] to believe that someone or something is closely connected or involved with something: *Many football fans are unfairly identified with violent behaviour.*

Identikit /aɪˈden.tɪ.kɪt/ [US] /-t̬ə-/ *noun* [C] *UK TRADEMARK* a picture of the face of someone whom the police want to question, usually because that person is thought to have been involved in a crime. The picture is made from a collection of drawings of noses, eyes, ears, etc. and is based on the descriptions of WITNESSES to the crime: *an*

Identikit picture ○ *Police have issued an Identikit of the man they want to question.* ⊃See also **Photofit (picture)**.
identikit /aɪˈden.tɪ.kɪt/ [US] /-t̬ə-/ *adj* [before n] very similar in appearance, in a way that is boring and lacks character: *He's been seen out at nightclubs and restaurants with a series of identikit blondes.*

identity /aɪˈden.tɪ.ti/ [US] /-t̬ə.t̬i/ *noun* [C or U] who a person is, or the qualities of a person or group which make them different from others: *The man's identity was being kept secret while he was helping police with enquiries.* ○ *I cannot reveal the identity of my source.* ○ *The informant was given a new identity* (= a different name and new official documents) *for protection.* ○ *The newspaper photo apparently showed him in Rome but it was a case of* ***mistaken*** *identity* (= it was the wrong person). ○ *In prison people often suffer from* ***a loss of*** *identity.* ○ *I think my job gives me* ***a sense of*** *identity.*

iˈdentity ˌcard *noun* [C] an official document or plastic card with your name, date of birth, photograph or other information on it which proves who you are

iˈdentity ˌcrisis *noun* [C usually sing] a feeling of being uncertain about who or what you are: *For some people, becoming a parent can bring on an identity crisis.*

iˈdentity paˌrade *UK noun* [C] (*US* **lineup**) a row of people, including a person who is believed to have committed a crime, who are shown to a WITNESS (= person who saw the crime) to find out whether the witness recognises that person

ideogram /ˈɪd.i.ə.græm/ *noun* [C] (*ALSO* **ideograph**) a written sign or symbol used in some writing systems such as Chinese, which represents an idea or object

ideology /ˌaɪ.diˈɒl.ə.dʒi/ [US] /-ˈɑː.lə-/ *noun* [C or U] a theory, or set of beliefs or principles, especially one on which a political system, party or organization is based: *socialist/capitalist ideology* ○ *The people are caught between two opposing ideologies.*
ideologue /ˈaɪ.di.ə.lɒg/ [US] /-lɑːg/ *noun* [C] *FORMAL* a person who believes very strongly in particular principles and tries to follow them carefully
ideological /ˌaɪ.di.əˈlɒdʒ.ɪ.kəl/ [US] /-ˈlɑː.dʒɪ-/ *adj* based on or relating to a particular set of ideas or beliefs: *ideological differences* ○ *There are some fairly profound ideological disagreements within the movement.*
ideologically /ˌaɪ.di.əˈlɒdʒ.ɪ.kli/ [US] /-ˈlɑː.dʒɪ-/ *adv*: *The government is ideologically opposed to spending more on the arts* (= this is in opposition to its political beliefs). ○ *Little separates the two women ideologically* (= they believe in similar things).

idiom /ˈɪd.i.əm/ *noun* **1** [C] a group of words in a fixed order that have a particular meaning, that is different from the meanings of each word understood on its own: *To "have bitten off more than you can chew" is an idiom that means you have tried to do something which is too difficult for you.* **2** [C or U] *FORMAL* the style of expression in writing, speech or music that is typical of a particular period, person or group: *Both operas are very much* ***in the modern*** *idiom.*
idiomatic /ˌɪd.i.əˈmæt.ɪk/ [US] /-ˈmæt̬-/ *adj*: *"Bite the bullet" is an idiomatic expression that means to accept something unpleasant without complaining.* ○ *She was born in Italy but her English is fluent and idiomatic* (= completely natural and correct in grammar and style).

idiosyncrasy /ˌɪd.i.əˈsɪŋ.krə.si/ *noun* [C usually pl] a strange or unusual habit, way of behaving or feature that someone or something has: *She often cracks her knuckles when she's speaking – it's one of her* ***little*** *idiosyncrasies.* ○ *One of the idiosyncrasies of this printer is that you can't stop it once it has started to print.*
idiosyncratic /ˌɪd.i.ə.sɪŋˈkræt.ɪk/ [US] /-ˈkræt̬-/ *adj*: *The film, 3 hours long, is directed in his usual idiosyncratic style.*

idiot /ˈɪd.i.ət/ *noun* [C] a stupid person or someone who is behaving in a stupid way: *Some idiot left the tap running in the bathroom and there's water everywhere.* ○ [as form of address] *You stupid idiot – that's a month's work you've lost!*
idiotic /ˌɪd.iˈɒt.ɪk/ [US] /-ˈɑː.t̬ɪk/ *adj* stupid **idiotically** /ˌɪd.iˈɒt.ɪ.kli/ [US] /-ˈɑː.t̬ɪ-/ *adv*
idiocy /ˈɪd.i.ə.si/ *noun* [C or U] a stupid action, or stupidity: *the idiocies of war* ○ *the idiocy of the whole scheme*

idle /ˈaɪ.dl̩/ *adj* **1** not working or being used: *Half these factories now* ***stand*** *idle.* ○ *It's crazy to have £7000* ***sitting*** *idle in the bank.* **2** [before n] without any particular purpose: *idle chatter/gossip/speculation* ○ *an idle glance* ○ *This is no idle threat.* **3** lazy and not willing to work: *He's a very able student, he's just* ***bone*** *idle* (= very lazy). **4** An idle moment or period of time is one in which there is no work or activity: *If you have an idle moment, call me.* **5** without work; unemployed: *Almost half of the workforce are now idle.* **idleness** /ˈaɪ.dl̩.nəs/ *noun* [U]
idle /ˈaɪ.dl̩/ *verb* [I] (*UK ALSO* **tick over**) If an engine or machine idles, it runs slowly but does not move or do any work: *He left the engine idling and ran into the shop.*
idly /ˈaɪd.li/ *adv*: *I was just glancing idly* (= without any particular purpose) *through a magazine.* ○ *We cannot* ***stand*** *idly* ***by*** (= do nothing) *while these people suffer.*
▲ **idle *sth* away** *phrasal verb* [M] to spend a period of time relaxing and doing very little: *We idled away the hours drinking and playing cards.*

idol /ˈaɪ.dəl/ *noun* [C] **1** someone who is admired and respected very much: *a pop/sporting idol* ○ *The Hollywood film idols of the 1940s were glamorous figures, adored by millions.* **2** a picture or object that people pray to as part of their religion: *The ancient people of this area worshipped a huge bronze idol in the shape of an elephant.*
idolize, *UK USUALLY* **-ise** /ˈaɪ.dəl.aɪz/ *verb* [T] to admire and respect someone very much, often too much: *She idolized her father.*

idyll, idyl /ˈɪd.əl/ *noun* [C] a very happy, peaceful and simple situation or period of time, especially in the countryside, or a piece of music, literature, etc. that describes this: *Every year thousands of people flee the big cities in search of the* ***pastoral/rural*** *idyll.*
idyllic /ɪˈdɪl.ɪk/ *adj* An idyllic place or experience is extremely pleasant, beautiful or peaceful: *an idyllic childhood/summer* ○ *an idyllic village in the Yorkshire Dales* **idyllically** /ɪˈdɪl.ɪ.kli/ *adv*: *They seem idyllically happy in their cottage.*

i.e. /ˌaɪˈiː/ used especially in writing before a piece of information that makes the meaning of something clearer or shows its true meaning: *The hotel is closed during low season, i.e. from October to March.* ○ *The price must be more realistic, i.e. lower.*

if [IN THAT SITUATION] /ɪf/ *conjunction* **1** used to say that a particular thing can or will happen only after something else happens or becomes true: *I'll pay you double if you get the work finished by Friday.* ○ *We'll have the party in the garden if the weather's good. If* ***not*** (= If the weather is not good), *it'll have to be inside.* ○ *If anyone rings for me, please tell them I'll be back in the office at 4 o'clock.* ○ *If she hadn't called, I wouldn't have known.* ○ *I wouldn't work for them* ***(even)*** *if they paid me twice my current salary.* ○ *We'll deal with that problem if* ***and when*** *it arises.* ○ *If disturbed, the bird may abandon the nest, leaving the chicks to die.* ⊃See Note **when or if?** at **when** AT WHAT TIME. **2** although: *She's a lovely woman,* ***even*** *if she can be a bit tiring at times.* ○ *LITERARY It was a hot, if windy day.* **3** every time: *If water is heated to 100°C it turns to steam.* ○ *If I don't get enough sleep I get a headache.* **4** used to mean 'if it is true that': *I'm very sorry if I've offended you.* **5** used when you want to make a polite request or remark: *If you'd like to take a seat, Mr Chang will be with you in a moment.* ○ *Would you mind if I open/opened* (= Can I open) *the window?* ○ *There are, if you don't mind me saying so, one or two problems with this plan.*
• **if I were you** used when you give someone advice: *If I were you, I'd probably go.* ○ *I think I'd take the money if I were you.*
if /ɪf/ *noun* [C usually sing] *INFORMAL* something which is not certain or not yet decided: *There's* ***a big*** *if hanging over the project still* (= it is uncertain whether the project will happen).
• **no ifs and buts** *UK* (*US* **no ifs, ands or buts**) something that you say to a child to stop them arguing with you

when you want them to do something: *I want no ifs and buts – just get on and tidy your room now.*

if WHETHER /ɪf/ *conjunction* (used to introduce a clause, often in indirect speech) whether: *Mrs Kramer rang half an hour ago to ask if her cake was ready.* ○ *I don't care if he likes it or not – I'm coming!* ○ *I was wondering if you'd like to come to the cinema with me this evening?*

iffy /ˈɪf.i/ *adj* **1** INFORMAL not certain or decided: *Simon's still kind of iffy about going to Columbia.* **2** not completely good, honest or suitable: *The milk smells a bit iffy.* ○ *I was hoping to go to the park but the weather's looking a bit iffy.*

-ify, -fy /-ɪ.faɪ/ *suffix* used to form verbs meaning to cause an increase in the stated quality; to become: *simplify* ○ *beautify*

igloo /ˈɪg.luː/ *noun* [C] *plural* **igloos** a circular house made of blocks of hard snow, especially as built by the Inuit people of northern North America

igneous /ˈɪg.ni.əs/ *adj* SPECIALIZED (of rocks) formed from MAGMA (= very hot liquid rock that has cooled)

ignite /ɪgˈnaɪt/ *verb* **1** [I or T] FORMAL to (cause to) start burning or explode: *The fuel spontaneously ignites because of the high temperature and pressure.* **2** [T] to cause a dangerous, excited or angry situation to begin: *The proposed restrictions have ignited a storm of protest from human rights groups.*

ignition /ɪgˈnɪʃ.ən/ *noun* **1** [C usually sing] the electrical system in an engine that causes the fuel to burn or explode in order to start the engine: *Switch/Turn the ignition on.* ○ *an ignition key* ⊃See picture **Car** on page Centre 12 **2** [U] FORMAL the act or process of something starting to burn

ignoble /ɪgˈnəʊ.bl̩/ *adj* FORMAL morally bad and making you feel ashamed: *an ignoble action/idea* **ignobly** /ɪgˈnəʊ.bli/ ⓤ /-ˈnoʊ-/ *adv* LITERARY

ignominious /ˌɪg.nəˈmɪn.i.əs/ *adj* LITERARY (especially of events or behaviour) embarrassing because so completely a failure: *an ignominious defeat/failure/ retreat* **ignominiously** /ˌɪg.nəˈmɪn.i.ə.sli/ *adv* **ignominy** /ˈɪg.nə.mɪ.ni/ *noun* [U] LITERARY public embarrassment: *The Workers' Coalition experienced the ignominy of total defeat in the last election.*

ignoramus /ˌɪg.nəˈreɪ.məs/ *noun* [C] a person who knows nothing: *I'm a complete ignoramus where computers are concerned.*

ignorant /ˈɪg.nə.ʳr.ənt/ ⓤ /-nɚ-/ *adj* **1** not having enough knowledge, understanding or information about something: *Many teenagers are surprisingly ignorant about current politics.* ○ *We remained blissfully ignorant of the troubles that lay ahead.* **2** UK INFORMAL not polite or respectful: *Ignorant lout!* **ignorance** /ˈɪg.nə.ʳr.ənts/ ⓤ /-nɚ-/ *noun* [U] lack of knowledge, understanding or information about something: *Public ignorance about the disease is still a cause for concern.* ○ *Patients, it is claimed, were kept/left in ignorance of what was wrong with them.*
● **Ignorance is bliss.** SAYING said to emphasize that sometimes it is better for you if you do not know all the facts about a situation

ignore /ɪgˈnɔːʳ/ ⓤ /-ˈnɔːr/ *verb* [T] to intentionally not listen or give attention to: *She can be really irritating but I try to ignore her.* ○ *Safety regulations are being ignored by company managers in the drive to increase profits.* ○ *How can the government ignore the wishes of the majority?* ○ *I smiled at her but she just ignored me.*

iguana /ɪˈgwɑː.nə/ *noun* [C] a large greyish green lizard of tropical America

IIRC, iirc INTERNET ABBREVIATION FOR if I remember correctly

ikon /ˈaɪ.kɒn/ ⓤ /-kɑːn/ *noun* [C] an **icon**

il- /ɪl-/ *prefix* ⊃See at **in-**.

ilk /ɪlk/ *noun* [S] MAINLY DISAPPROVING a particular type: *The worst of her criticism was reserved for journalists, photographers and others of their ilk.*

ill NOT WELL /ɪl/ *adj* not feeling well, or suffering from a disease: *I felt ill so I went home.* ○ *He's been ill with meningitis.* ○ *Sophia fell ill/was taken ill* (= became ill) *while on holiday.* ○ *He is critically* (= very badly) *ill in hospital.* ⊃See Note **sick, ill and be sick** at **sick** ILL.

illness /ˈɪl.nəs/ *noun* **1** [C] a disease of the body or mind: *He died at home after a long illness.* **2** [U] when you are ill: *She had five days off work due to illness.*

ill BAD /ɪl/ *adv* **1** FORMAL badly: *Hospital staff, it is claimed, were ill-prepared to deal with the severity of the injuries.* ○ *We certainly weren't ill-treated.* **2** FORMAL OR OLD-FASHIONED **speak ill of sb** to say unkind things about someone: *I realize one shouldn't speak ill of the dead.* **3** FORMAL OR OLD-FASHIONED **augur/bode ill** to be a sign of bad things in the future: *This weather bodes ill for the garden party tonight.* **4** FORMAL OR OLD-FASHIONED **can ill afford (to do sth)** If you can ill afford to do something, it will cause problems for you if you do it: *We can ill afford to lose another member of staff.*

ill /ɪl/ *adj* [before n] FORMAL OR OLD-FASHIONED bad: *ill health* ○ *Did you experience any ill effects from the treatment?*
● **be ill at ease** to be anxious and not relaxed: *He seemed ill at ease and not his usual self.*
● **It's an ill wind (that blows nobody any good).** SAYING said to show that even a very bad situation must have some good results

ill /ɪl/ *noun* **1** [U] FORMAL OR OLD-FASHIONED harm: *I wish her no ill.* **2** [C usually pl] a problem: *There seems to be no cure for Britain's economic/social ills.*

ill-advised /ˌɪl.ədˈvaɪzd/ *adj* not wise, and likely to cause problems in the future: *an ill-advised career move*

ill-assorted /ˌɪl.əˈsɔː.tɪd/ ⓤ /-ˈsɔːr.t̬ɪd/ *adj* MAINLY UK looking strange together and not seeming to be a good match: *ill-assorted furniture* ○ *an ill-assorted couple*

ill-bred /ˌɪlˈbred/ *adj* OLD-FASHIONED rude and behaving badly: *an ill-bred young man*

ill-conceived /ˌɪl.kənˈsiːvd/ *adj* badly planned and unwise: *The whole project was ill-conceived.*

ill-disposed /ˌɪl.dɪˈspəʊzd/ ⓤ /-ˈspoʊzd/ *adj* FORMAL **be ill-disposed towards sb** to not be friendly to someone or not support them: *Most of the audience seemed ill-disposed towards the speaker.*

illegal /ɪˈliː.gʲl̩/ *adj* against the law; not allowed by law: *a campaign to stop the illegal sale of cigarettes to children under 16* ○ *Prostitution is illegal in some countries.* ○ *It is illegal to drive a car that is not taxed and insured.* ○ *Cocaine, LSD and heroin are all illegal drugs/ substances.* **illegally** /ɪˈliː.gʲl̩.i/ *adv*: *They entered the country illegally.* ○ *an illegally parked car*

il,legal im'migrant *noun* [C] (US ALSO **illegal alien**) someone who goes to live or work in another country when they do not have the legal right to do this

illegality /ˌɪl.iːˈgæl.ɪ.ti/ ⓤ /-ə.t̬i/ *noun* [C or U] the state of being illegal, or an illegal action

illegible /ɪˈledʒ.ə.bl̩/ *adj* (of writing or print) impossible or almost impossible to read because of being very unclear or untidy: *His writing is almost illegible.* **illegibly** /ɪˈledʒ.ə.bli/ *adv*

illegitimate /ˌɪl.ɪˈdʒɪt.ə.mət/ ⓤ /-ˈdʒɪt̬-/ *adj* **1** born of parents not married to each other **2** FORMAL not legal or fair: *The rebels regard the official parliament as illegitimate.* **illegitimacy** /ˌɪl.ɪˈdʒɪt.ə.mə.si/ ⓤ /-ˈdʒɪt̬-/ *noun* [U]

ill-equipped /ˌɪl.ɪˈkwɪpt/ *adj* lacking the ability, qualities or equipment to do something: [+ to infinitive] *He seems to me ill-equipped to cope with the responsibility.* ○ *school leavers ill-equipped for adult life*

ill-fated /ˌɪlˈfeɪ.tɪd/ ⓤ /-t̬ɪd/ *adj* [before n] unlucky and unsuccessful, often resulting in death: *The ill-fated aircraft later crashed into the hillside.*

ill-fitting /ˌɪlˈfɪt.ɪŋ/ ⓤ /-ˈfɪt̬-/ *adj* Ill-fitting clothes do not fit well.

ill-gotten /ˌɪlˈgɒt.ən/ ⓤ /-ˈgɑː.t̬ən/ *adj* [before n] MAINLY HUMOROUS dishonestly obtained: *He deposited his ill-gotten gains in foreign bank accounts.*

illiberal /ɪˈlɪb.ə.ʳr.əl/ ⓤ /-ɚ-/ *adj* FORMAL limiting freedom of expression, thought, behaviour, etc: *illiberal policies/ legislation*

illicit /ɪˈlɪs.ɪt/ *adj* illegal or disapproved of by society: *illicit drugs such as cocaine and cannabis* ○ *the illicit trade in stolen vehicles* ○ *an illicit love affair* **illicitly** /ɪˈlɪs.ɪt.li/ *adv*

ill-informed /ˌɪl.ɪnˈfɔːmd/ ⓤ /-ˈfɔːrmd/ *adj* knowing less than you should about a particular subject

illiterate /ɪˈlɪt.ᵊr.ət/ (US) /-ˈlɪt̬.ɚ-/ *adj* **1** unable to read and write: *A surprising percentage of the population are illiterate.* ➲Compare **innumerate**. **2** knowing little or nothing about a particular subject: *computer illiterate* ○ *financially/technologically illiterate*
illiterate /ɪˈlɪt.ᵊr.ət/ (US) /-ˈlɪt̬.ɚ-/ *noun* [C] someone who is illiterate **illiteracy** /ɪˈlɪt.ᵊr.ə.si/ (US) /-ˈlɪt̬.ɚ-/ *noun* [U] *In the rural areas, illiteracy is widespread.*

ill-mannered /ˌɪlˈmæn.əd/ (US) /-ɚd/ *adj* rude and unpleasant

illness /ˈɪl.nəs/ *noun* ➲See at **ill** NOT WELL

illogical /ɪˈlɒdʒ.ɪ.kᵊl/ (US) /-ˈlɑː.dʒɪ-/ *adj* not reasonable, wise or practical, usually because directed by the emotions rather than by careful thought: *It is an illogical statement, because if one part is true, then the other must be false.* **illogicality** /ɪˌlɒdʒ.ɪˈkæl.ɪ.ti/ (US) /-ˌlɑː.dʒɪˈkæl.ə.t̬i/ *noun* [U] **illogically** /ɪˈlɒdʒ.ɪ.kli/ (US) /-ˈlɑː.dʒɪ-/ *adv*

ill-starred /ˌɪlˈstɑːd/ (US) /-ˈstɑːrd/ *adj* [before n] (ALSO **ill-omened**) LITERARY **ill-fated**

ill-tempered /ˌɪlˈtem.pəd/ (US) /-pɚd/ *adj* **1** FORMAL easily annoyed **2** If an occasion, such as a game, is ill-tempered, people get angry during it: *An increasingly ill-tempered match saw three players sent off before half-time.*

ill-timed /ˌɪlˈtaɪmd/ *adj* done or made at a wrong or unsuitable time: *an ill-timed comment*

ill-treat /ˌɪlˈtriːt/ *verb* [T] to treat someone badly, especially by being violent or by not taking care of them: *The court heard how the child had been severely ill-treated by his parents.*

illuminate /ɪˈluː.mɪ.neɪt/ *verb* [T] FORMAL **1** to light something and make it brighter: *The streets were illuminated with strings of coloured lights.* **2** to explain and show more clearly something that is difficult to understand: *an article which illuminates the issues at stake*
illuminating /ɪˈluː.mɪ.neɪ.tɪŋ/ (US) /-t̬ɪŋ/ *adj* FORMAL giving you new information about a subject or making it easier to understand: *The book is full of illuminating detail on the causes of the war.* ○ *a most illuminating discussion*
illumination /ɪˌluː.mɪˈneɪ.ʃᵊn/ *noun* [C or U] FORMAL light: *The only illumination was from a skylight.*
illuminations /ɪˌluː.mɪˈneɪ.ʃᵊnz/ *plural noun* MAINLY UK coloured decorative lights outside which make a town look bright and exciting at night: *the Blackpool illuminations*

illuminated /ɪˈluː.mɪ.neɪ.tɪd/ (US) /-t̬ɪd/ *adj* An illuminated book or other piece of writing is one decorated with added colour, gold paint and small pictures: *an illuminated* ***manuscript***

illusion /ɪˈluː.ʒᵊn/ *noun* **1** [C or U] an idea or belief which is not true: *He* ***had no*** *illusions* ***about*** *his talents as a singer.* ○ *I'm* ***under no*** *illusions* (= I understand the truth) *about the man I married.* ○ *My boss is* ***labouring under the*** *illusion* ***that*** (= wrongly believes that) *the project will be completed on time.* **2** [C] something that is not really what it seems to be: *A large mirror in a room can* ***create the*** *illusion* ***of*** *space.* ○ *The impression of calm in the office is just an illusion.*
illusionist /ɪˈluː.ʒᵊn.ɪst/ *noun* [C] an entertainer who performs tricks where objects seem to appear and then disappear
illusory /ɪˈluː.sᵊr.i/ (US) /-sɚ-/ *adj* (ALSO **illusive**) FORMAL not real; based on illusion: *Their hopes of a peaceful solution turned out to be illusory.*

illustrate EXPLAIN /ˈɪl.ə.streɪt/ *verb* [T] to show the meaning or truth of something more clearly, especially by giving examples: *The lecturer illustrated his point* ***with*** *a diagram on the blackboard.* ○ *This latest conflict further illustrates the weakness of the UN.* ○ [+ question word] *The exhibition will illustrate* ***how*** *life evolved from water.*
illustration /ˌɪl.əˈstreɪ.ʃᵊn/ *noun* [C or U] an example that explains or proves something: *This delay is a perfect illustration* ***of*** *why we need a new computer system.* ○ *A couple of examples are included,* ***by way of*** *illustration* (= to show the meaning more clearly).
illustrative /ˈɪl.ə.strə.tɪv/ (US) /ɪˈlʌs.trə.t̬ɪv/ *adj* FORMAL helping to explain or prove something: *Falling house prices are illustrative* ***of*** *the crisis facing the construction industry.*

illustrate PICTURES /ˈɪl.ə.streɪt/ *verb* [T] to draw pictures for a book, magazine, etc: *a beautifully illustrated book/old manuscript*
illustration /ˌɪl.əˈstreɪ.ʃᵊn/ *noun* [C or U] a picture in a book, magazine, etc. or the process of illustrating something: *a full-page illustration* ○ *colour/black and white illustrations*
illustrator /ˈɪl.ə.streɪ.təʳ/ (US) /-t̬ɚ/ *noun* [C] a person who draws pictures, especially for books

illustrious /ɪˈlʌs.tri.əs/ *adj* FORMAL famous, well respected and admired: *She comes from an illustrious political family which includes two former Cabinet ministers.*

ˌill ˈwill *noun* [U] bad feelings between people because of things that happened in the past
• **bear *sb* ill will** FORMAL to feel angry with someone because of something they have done: *I bear him no ill will.*

im- /ɪm-/ *prefix* ➲See at **in-**.

I'm /aɪm/ *short form* I am: *I'm so happy for you!*

image MENTAL PICTURE /ˈɪm.ɪdʒ/ *noun* **1** [C] a picture in your mind or an idea of how someone or something is: *I have an image in my mind of how I want the garden to be.* ○ *He doesn't* ***fit*** (= he is different to) *my image of how an actor should look.* **2** [C or U] the way that something or someone is thought of by other people: *The aim is to improve the* ***public*** *image of the police.* ○ *The company has made strenuous attempts to improve its image in recent years.* ○ *He's terribly image-****conscious*** (= tries to dress and behave in a way that other people will admire). **3** [C] SPECIALIZED a mental picture or idea which forms in a reader's or listener's mind from the words that they read or hear: *The poem is full of images of birth and new life.*

image PICTURE /ˈɪm.ɪdʒ/ *noun* [C] any picture, especially one formed by a mirror or a lens: *television images of starving children* ○ *The image you see in the mirror seems to be reversed.*
• **be the (living/spitting) image of *sb*** to look very similar to someone: *She's the spitting image of her mother.*

imagery /ˈɪm.ɪ.dʒᵊr.i/ (US) /-dʒɚ-/ *noun* [U] the use of words or pictures in books, films, paintings, etc. to describe ideas or situations: *The imagery in the poem is mostly to do with death.*

imagination /ɪˌmædʒ.ɪˈneɪ.ʃᵊn/ *noun* **1** [C or U] the ability to form pictures in the mind: *My younger son has a very* ***vivid*** (= active) *imagination.* ○ *I can never make up stories – I have absolutely no imagination.* ○ *For some reason the story* ***captured/caught the*** *imagination* ***of*** *the public* (= made them very interested). ○ *It couldn't* ***by any stretch of the*** *imagination be described as a* (= it is certainly not a) *beautiful city.* ○ *There's a sex scene in the film which apparently* ***leaves nothing to the*** *imagination* (= shows sexual parts of the body very clearly). **2** [U] something that you think exists or is true, although in fact it is not real or true: *Was she paying him a lot of attention or was it just my imagination?* ○ *Is it my imagination or is David behaving strangely at the moment?* **3** [U] the ability to think of new ideas: *It's a job that needs someone with a bit of imagination.*

imagine /ɪˈmædʒ.ɪn/ *verb* [T] **1** to form or have a mental picture or idea of something: *Imagine Robert Redford when he was young – that's what John looks like.* ○ [+ (that)] *Imagine* ***(that)*** *you're eating an ice cream – try to feel how cold it is.* ○ [+ question word] *Can you imagine* ***how*** *it feels to be blind?* ○ [+ v-ing] *She imagined herself* ***sitting*** *in her favourite armchair back home.* ○ *They hadn't imagined* (= expected) ***(that)*** *it would be so difficult.* ○ *I can't imagine* (= I really don't know) *what he wants from us.* **2** to believe that something is probably true: [+ (that)] *I imagine* ***(that)*** *he's under a lot of pressure at the moment.* ○ *I don't imagine* ***(that)*** *they have much money.* ○ *"Will they change it?" "I imagine* ***so****."* **3** to think that something exists or is true, although in fact it is not real or true: *"Did you hear a noise?" "No, you're imagining* ***things****/No, you must have imagined it."* ○ *I've never heard her criticize you – I think you imagine it.* **4** UK **you can't imagine** used to emphasize a statement: *You can't imagine what a mess the house was in after the party.* **5**

used to express shock or surprise, often at someone else's behaviour: *She got married at 16! Imagine that!* ○ [+ *v-ing*] *Imagine spending all that money on a coat!*

imaginable /ɪˈmædʒ.ɪ.nə.bl̩/ *adj* possible to think of: *The school offers courses in every subject imaginable.* ○ *ice cream of every imaginable flavour*

imaginary /ɪˈmædʒ.ɪ.nᵊr.i/ ⓤ /-ə.ner-/ *adj* describes something that is created by and exists only in the mind; that is not real: *As a child I had an imaginary friend called Polly.* ○ *The story is set in an imaginary world.* ○ *imaginary fears*

imaginative /ɪˈmædʒ.ɪ.nə.tɪv/ ⓤ /-t̬ɪv/ *adj* APPROVING **1** new, original and clever: *an imaginative new approach/ policy* ○ *The architects have made imaginative use of glass and transparent plastic.* **2** good at producing ideas or things that are unusual, clever or showing skill in inventing: *an imaginative designer* **imaginatively** /ɪˈmædʒ.ɪ.nə.tɪv.li/ ⓤ /-t̬ɪv-/ *adv*

imaging /ˈɪm.ɪ.dʒɪŋ/ *noun* [U] SPECIALIZED the process of producing an exact picture of something, especially on a computer screen: *computer/digital imaging*

imam /ɪˈmɑːm/ *noun* [C] a leader in the Islamic religion

IMAX /ˈaɪ.mæks/ *noun* [U] TRADEMARK a system for making and showing specially photographed films on an extremely large screen: *an IMAX cinema/theatre*

imbalance /ˌɪmˈbæl.ᵊnts/ *noun* [C] when two things which should be equal or are normally equal are not: *There is huge economic imbalance between the two countries.*

imbecile /ˈɪm.bə.siːl/ ⓤ /-sɪl/ *noun* [C] a person who behaves in a stupid way: *What an imbecile that boy is!* **imbecilic** /ˌɪm.bəˈsɪl.ɪk/ *adj* (ALSO **imbecile**) *That was an imbecilic thing to do!* ○ *She looked at me with an imbecile grin.*

imbed /ɪmˈbed/ *verb* **-dd-** US **embed**

imbibe /ɪmˈbaɪb/ *verb* [I or T] FORMAL OR HUMOROUS to drink, especially alcohol: *Have you been imbibing again?*

imbroglio /ɪmˈbrəʊ.li.əʊ/ ⓤ /-ˈbroʊ.li.oʊ/ *noun* [C] plural **imbroglios** FORMAL an unwanted, difficult and confusing situation, full of trouble and problems: *The Soviet Union became anxious to withdraw its soldiers from the Afghan imbroglio.*

imbue /ɪmˈbjuː/ *verb*

▲ **imbue** *sth/sb* **with** *sth* phrasal verb FORMAL to fill something or someone with a particular feeling, quality or idea: *His poetry is imbued with deep, religious feeling.*

the IMF /ˌðiː.aɪ.emˈef/ *noun* [S] ABBREVIATION FOR the International Monetary Fund: a part of the United Nations which encourages international trade and gives financial help to poor countries

IMHO, imho INTERNET ABBREVIATION FOR in my humble opinion: used when you build up somebody your opinion

imitate /ˈɪm.ɪ.teɪt/ *verb* [T] to behave in a similar way to someone or something else, or to copy the speech or behaviour, etc. of someone or something: *Some of the younger pop bands try to imitate their musical heroes from the past.* ○ *They produce artificial chemicals which exactly imitate particular natural ones.*

imitation /ˌɪm.ɪˈteɪ.ʃᵊn/ *noun* **1** [C or U] when someone or something imitates another person or thing: *Ten-year-olds have started wearing lipstick and make-up in imitation of the older girls.* ○ *She can do a wonderful imitation of a blackbird's song.* **2** [C] a copy: *His songs are just cheap* (= low quality) *imitations of Beatles tunes.*

imitation /ˌɪm.ɪˈteɪ.ʃᵊn/ *adj* made to look like something else: *an imitation leather watch-strap* ○ *It's not real silk – it's just imitation.*

imitative /ˈɪm.ɪ.tə.tɪv/ ⓤ /-teɪ.t̬ɪv/ *adj* MAINLY DISAPPROVING *All these magazines are imitative of* (= copy) *each other.* ○ *He's an imitative artist, with very little originality in his work.* **imitator** /ˈɪm.ɪ.teɪ.tər/ ⓤ /-t̬ɚ/ *noun* [C usually pl] *The difference between Ms McArthur and her countless imitators is the elegance of her writing.*

immaculate /ɪˈmæk.jʊ.lət/ *adj* APPROVING **1** perfectly clean or tidy: *dressed in an immaculate white suit* ○ *an immaculate garden* **2** perfect and without any mistakes: *He gave an immaculate performance as the aging hero.* **immaculately** /ɪˈmæk.jʊ.lət.li/ *adv*: *immaculately dressed*

the Im·maculate Con·ception *noun* [S] the Christian belief that Jesus Christ's mother Mary, or, more generally, Jesus Christ himself, was born free from SIN (= immorality)

immaterial /ˌɪm.əˈtɪə.ri.əl/ ⓤ /-ˈtɪr.i-/ *adj* not important, or not relating to the matter you are interested in: *Whether the book is well or badly written is immaterial (to me) – it has an important message.*

immature /ˌɪm.əˈtʃʊər/ ⓤ /-ˈtʊr/ *adj* **1** DISAPPROVING not behaving in a way which is as calm and wise as people expect from someone of your age: *Stop being so silly and immature, Ben!* ○ *She's rather immature for her age, don't you think?* **2** DISAPPROVING not experienced in a particular matter: *politically immature* **3** SPECIALIZED not yet completely grown or developed: *While the animals are still immature, they do not breed.* **immaturity** /ˌɪm.əˈtʃʊə.rɪ.ti/ ⓤ /-ˈtʊr.ə.t̬i/ *noun* [U]

immeasurable /ɪˈmeʒ.ᵊr.ə.bl̩/ ⓤ /-ɚ-/ *adj* so large or great that it cannot be measured or known exactly: *Her films had an immeasurable effect on a generation of Americans.* **immeasurably** /ɪˈmeʒ.ᵊr.ə.bli/ ⓤ /-ɚ-/ *adv*: *The damage from the 1956 hurricane was immeasurably greater.*

immediate /ɪˈmiː.di.ət/ *adj* **1** happening or done without delay or very soon after something else: *We must make an immediate response.* ○ *Dioxin is a poison that takes immediate effect.* **2** describes something or someone that is close to, or is a cause of or an effect of, something or someone else: *There are few facilities in the immediate area.* ○ *An immediate result/effect of the war was a breakdown of law and order.* **3** in the present or as soon as possible: *We have no immediate plans.* ○ *MPs have demanded his immediate resignation.* **4 the immediate future** the period of time that is coming next **5 your immediate family** your closest relatives, such as your parents, children, husband or wife

immediately /ɪˈmiː.di.ət.li/ *adv, conjunction* **1** now or without waiting or thinking: *We really ought to leave immediately.* ○ *Immediately after/* (UK ALSO) *Immediately* (= As soon as) *she'd gone, the boys started to mess about.* **2** close to something or someone in distance or time: *Milton Street is on the left, immediately after the bank.* ○ *The people most immediately affected by the drought are the farmers themselves.*

immediacy /ɪˈmiː.di.ə.si/ *noun* [U] when something seems real and important, so that you feel involved with it: *Pre-recorded TV programmes have so much less immediacy and warmth than live theatre.*

immemorial /ˌɪm.əˈmɔː.ri.əl/ ⓤ /-ˈmɔːr.i-/ *adj* LITERARY **from/since time immemorial** for a very long time: *Her family had farmed that land since time immemorial.*

immense /ɪˈments/ *adj* extremely large in size or degree: *immense wealth/value* ○ *They spent an immense amount of time getting the engine into perfect condition.* **immensely** /ɪˈment.sli/ *adv* extremely: *He was immensely popular in his day.* ○ *She's an immensely talented young athlete.*

immensity /ɪˈment.sə.ti/ ⓤ /-t̬i/ *noun* [U] FORMAL extremely great size: *The immensity of the task is daunting.*

immensities /ɪˈment.sə.tiz/ ⓤ /-t̬iz/ plural noun LITERARY the immensities (= immensity) **of space**

immerse /ɪˈmɜːs/ ⓤ /-ˈmɜːs/ *verb* **1** [R] to become completely involved in something: *She got some books out of the library and immersed herself in Jewish history and culture.* **2** [T] FORMAL to put something or someone completely under the surface of a liquid: *The shells should be immersed in boiling water for two minutes.* **immersion** /ɪˈmɜː.ʃᵊn/ ⓤ /-ˈmɜːr-/ *noun* [C or U]

im·mersion (·heater) *noun* [C] a type of electric heater used for heating water

immigrant /ˈɪm.ɪ.grənt/ *noun* [C] (AUS ALSO **migrant**) a person who has come to a different country in order to live there permanently: *a large immigrant population* ○ *Illegal immigrants are sent back across the border if they are caught.*

immigration /ˌɪm.ɪˈgreɪ.ʃᵊn/ *noun* [U] **1** when someone comes to live in a different country: *There are strict limits on immigration (into the country).* **2** the process of examining your PASSPORT and other documents to make certain that you can be allowed to enter the country, or the place where this is done: *After you've been through immigration **(control)**, you can go and get your luggage.* ○ *immigration policy* ○ *immigration officers* **immigrate** /ˈɪm.ɪ.greɪt/ *verb* [I] *He immigrated with his parents in 1895, and grew up in Long Island.*

imminent /ˈɪm.ɪ.nᵊnt/ *adj* coming or likely to happen very soon: *imminent disaster/danger* ○ *A strike is imminent.*

imminence /ˈɪm.ɪ.nᵊnts/ *noun* [U] when something is imminent

immobile /ɪˈməʊ.baɪl/ [US] /-ˈmoʊ.bᵊl/ *adj* not moving or not able to move: *She sat immobile, wondering what to do next.* **immobility** /ˌɪm.əʊˈbɪl.ə.ti/ [US] /-oʊˈbɪl.ə.t̬i/ *noun* [U] **immobilize**, *UK USUALLY* **-ise** /ɪˈməʊ.bᵊl.aɪz/ [US] /-ˈmoʊ-/ *verb* [T] *You can immobilize the car by removing the spark plugs.* **immobilization**, *UK USUALLY* **-isation** /ɪˌməʊ.bᵊl.aɪˈzeɪ.ʃᵊn/ [US] /-ˌmoʊ.bə.lɪ-/ *noun* [U]

immobilizer, *UK USUALLY* **-iser** /ɪˈməʊ.bᵊl.aɪ.zəʳ/ [US] /-zɚ/ *noun* [C] a device fitted to a car which stops it from moving so that it cannot be stolen

immoderate /ɪˈmɒd.ᵊr.ət/ [US] /-ˈmɑː.dɚ-/ *adj FORMAL* too much or many, or more than is usual or reasonable: *immoderate drinking* ○ *immoderate demands* **immoderately** /ɪˈmɒd.ᵊr.ət.li/ [US] /-ˈmɑː.dɚ-/ *adv*

immodest /ɪˈmɒd.ɪst/ [US] /-ˈmɑː.dɪst/ *adj FORMAL DISAPPROVING* **1** showing too much self-confidence: *He makes these immodest statements of his own brilliance.* **2** showing too much of the body: *showing an immodest amount of leg* **immodesty** /ɪˈmɒd.ə.sti/ [US] /-ˈmɑː.də-/ *noun* [U] *FORMAL*

immolate /ˈɪm.ə.leɪt/ *verb* [T] *FORMAL* to kill yourself or someone else, or to destroy something, usually by burning, in a ceremonial way **immolation** /ˌɪm.əˈleɪ.ʃᵊn/ *noun* [U]

immoral /ɪˈmɒr.ᵊl/ [US] /-ˈmɑːr-/ *adj* not within society's standards of acceptable, honest and moral behaviour; morally wrong: *an immoral act* ○ *immoral behaviour* ○ *It's an immoral tax, because the poor will pay relatively more.* ➲Compare **amoral**; **moral**. **immorally** /ɪˈmɒr.ᵊl.i/ [US] /-ˈmɑːr-/ *adv*

immorality /ˌɪm.əˈræl.ə.ti/ [US] /-ɑːˈræl.ə.t̬i/ *noun* [U] when someone or something is immoral

imˌmoral ˈearnings *plural noun* money earned from PROSTITUTION (= having sex in exchange for money): *If convicted, she could be jailed for five years for **living off** immoral earnings.*

immortal /ɪˈmɔː.tᵊl/ [US] /-ˈmɔːr.t̬ᵊl/ *adj* **1** living or lasting forever: *immortal God* ○ *The priest said he was endangering his immortal soul.* **2** very special and famous and therefore likely to be remembered for a long time: *In the immortal **words** of Samuel Goldwyn, "Include me out".*

the immortals *plural noun LITERARY* the Greek or Roman gods

immortal /ɪˈmɔː.tᵊl/ [US] /-ˈmɔːr.t̬ᵊl/ *noun* [C] *LITERARY* someone who is so famous that they are remembered for a long time after they are dead: *She is one of the immortals of classical opera.* **immortality** /ˌɪm.ɔːˈtæl.ə.ti/ [US] /-ɔːrˈtæl.ə.t̬i/ *noun* [U] *FIGURATIVE The Wright brothers achieved immortality with the first powered flight in 1903.*

immortalize, *UK USUALLY* **-ise** /ɪˈmɔː.tᵊl.aɪz/ [US] /-ˈmɔːr.t̬ᵊl-/ *verb* [T often passive] to make someone or something so famous that they are remembered for a very long time: *Marlene Dietrich was immortalized through her roles **in** films like 'The Blue Angel'.*

immovable /ɪˈmuː.və.bl̩/ *adj* **1** fixed and impossible to move: *The rock weighed over a ton and was completely immovable.* **2** describes a firm opinion that is impossible to change, or someone with such an opinion

immune /ɪˈmjuːn/ *adj* **1** protected against a particular disease by particular substances in the blood: *Most people who've had chicken pox once are immune **to** it for the rest of their lives.* ○ *He seems to be immune **to** colds – he just never gets them.* **2** [after v] not affected or upset by a particular type of behaviour or emotion: *The press had criticised her so often that in the end she had become immune **(to** it).* **3** [after v] not able to be punished or damaged by something: *Journalists, he insisted, must be immune* (= protected) ***from** prosecution.*

immunity /ɪˈmjuː.nɪ.ti/ [US] /-ə.t̬i/ *noun* [U] when you are immune, especially to disease or from legal action: *The vaccination gives you immunity **against** the disease for up to six months.* ○ *He was granted immunity **from** prosecution because he confessed the names of the other spies.*

immunize, *UK USUALLY* **-ise** /ˈɪm.jʊ.naɪz/ *verb* [T] to give a person or animal protection against a particular disease by introducing a special substance into their body, usually by injection: *Children are routinely immunized **against** polio.* **immunization**, *UK USUALLY* **-isation** /ˌɪm.jʊ.naɪˈzeɪ.ʃᵊn/ *noun* [C or U] *mass/routine immunization*

imˈmune ˌsystem *noun* [C usually sing] the various cells and tissues in the body which make it able to protect itself against infection

immunodeficiency /ˌɪm.jʊ.nəʊ.dɪˈfɪʃ.ᵊnt.si/ [US] /-noʊ-/ *noun* [U] *SPECIALIZED* when a body in unable to produce enough ANTIBODIES to fight bacteria and viruses, often resulting in infection and disease

immunology /ˌɪm.jəˈnɒl.ə.dʒi/ [US] /-ˈnɑː.lə-/ *noun* [U] *SPECIALIZED* the study of IMMUNITY (= the ability of the body to fight disease and infection) and its causes and effects

immured /ɪˈmjʊəd/ [US] /-ˈmjʊrd/ *adj LITERARY* kept as a prisoner or closed away and out of sight: *Immured **in** a dark airless cell, the hostages waited six months for their release.*

immutable /ɪˈmjuː.tə.bl̩/ [US] /-t̬ə-/ *adj FORMAL* not changing, or unable to be changed: *an immutable law* ○ *Some people regard grammar as an immutable set of rules.* **immutability** /ɪˌmjuː.təˈbɪl.ɪ.ti/ [US] /-t̬əˈbɪl.ə.t̬i/ *noun* [U]

IMO, **imo** *INTERNET ABBREVIATION FOR* in my opinion

imp /ɪmp/ *noun* [C] **1** a small evil spirit **2** *OFTEN HUMOROUS* a badly behaved but playful child: *Come here, you little imp!*

impish /ˈɪm.pɪʃ/ *adj* showing a child-like pleasure in being playful and making trouble: *At seventy, he still retains his impish grin.* **impishly** /ˈɪm.pɪʃ.li/ *adv* **impishness** /ˈɪm.pɪʃ.nəs/ *noun* [U]

impact /ˈɪm.pækt/ *noun* [C usually sing; U] **1** the force or action of one object hitting another: *The impact of the crash reduced the car to a third of its original length.* ○ *The bullet explodes **on** impact* (= when it hits another object). **2** a powerful effect that something, especially something new, has on a situation or person: *The anti-smoking campaign had **had/made** quite an impact **on** young people.* ○ *The new proposals were intended to **soften** the impact of the reformed tax system.*

impact /ɪmˈpækt/ *verb* [I or T] *MAINLY US* to have an influence on something: *Falling export rates have impacted **(on)** the country's economy quite considerably.*

impacted /ɪmˈpæk.tɪd/ *adj* describes a tooth that cannot grow in the right way, usually because it is growing against another tooth below the GUM

impair /ɪmˈpeəʳ/ [US] /-ˈper/ *verb* [T] to spoil or weaken something so that it is less effective: *A recurring knee injury may have impaired his chances of winning the tournament.* **impaired** /ɪmˈpeəd/ [US] /-ˈperd/ *adj*: *She suffers from impaired vision/hearing.* **impairment** /ɪmˈpeə.mənt/ [US] /-ˈper-/ *noun* [U] *physical/mental impairment*

impale /ɪmˈpeɪl/ *verb* [T often passive] to push a sharp object through something, especially the body of an animal or person: *The dead deer was impaled **on** a spear.*

impalpable /ɪmˈpæl.pə.bl̩/ *adj LITERARY* difficult to feel or understand: *an impalpable beauty/quality*

impanel /ɪmˈpæn.ᵊl/ *verb* [T] to **empanel**

impart /ɪmˈpɑːt/ [US] /-ˈpɑːrt/ *verb* [T] *FORMAL* **1** to communicate information to someone: *to impart the bad news* ○ *I was rather quiet as I didn't feel I had much wisdom to impart on the subject.* **2** to give something a particular feeling, quality or taste: *Preservatives can impart colour and flavour **to** a product.*

impartial /ɪmˈpɑː.ʃᵊl/ [US] /-ˈpɑːr-/ *adj* not supporting any of the sides involved in an argument: *impartial advice* ○ *A trial must be fair and impartial.* **impartially** /ɪmˈpɑː.ʃᵊl.i/ [US] /-ˈpɑːr-/ *adv* **impartiality** /ɪmˌpɑː.ʃiˈæl.ɪ.ti/ [US]

/-ˌpɑːr.ʃiˈæl.ə.ti/ *noun* [U] *The state must ensure the independence and impartiality of the justice system.*

impassable /ɪmˈpɑː.sə.bl̩/ [US] /-ˈpæs.ə-/ *adj* describes a road or path that cannot be travelled on because of bad weather conditions or because it is blocked: *Many roads were flooded and impassable following the storm.*

impasse /æmˈpæs/ [US] /ˈɪm.pæs/ *noun* [U] a situation in which further development is impossible: *The dispute had **reached** an impasse, as neither side would compromise.*

impassioned /ɪmˈpæʃ.ənd/ *adj* describes speech or writing that is full of strongly felt and strongly expressed emotion: *Relatives of the dead made an impassioned **plea** for the bodies to be flown back to this country.*

impassive /ɪmˈpæs.ɪv/ *adj* describes a person's face when it expresses no emotion, because they seem not to be affected by the situation they are experiencing **impassively** /ɪmˈpæs.ɪv.li/ *adv*: *The defendant sat impassively in the dock while evidence was given against him.* **impassivity** /ˌɪm.pæsˈɪv.ɪ.ti/ [US] /-ə.ti/ *noun* [U]

impatience /ɪmˈpeɪ.ʃənts/ *noun* [U] **1** when you are annoyed by someone's mistakes or because you have to wait: *"Well, I have shown you how to do this before," she said, unable to disguise her impatience.* ○ *There's a growing impatience among the electorate **with** the old two-party system.* **2** when you want something to happen as soon as possible: [+ *to* infinitive] *He was already half an hour late which explains his impatience **to** leave.*

impatient /ɪmˈpeɪ.ʃənt/ *adj* **1** easily annoyed by someone's mistakes or because you have to wait: *He's a good teacher, but inclined to be a bit impatient **with** slow learners.* ○ *You'd be hopeless looking after children – you're far too impatient!* **2** wanting something to happen as soon as possible: *He's got a lot of exciting ideas and he's impatient **to** get started.* ○ *People are increasingly impatient **for** change in this country.*

impatiently /ɪmˈpeɪ.ʃənt.li/ *adv*: *"Yes, you said that before," she said, impatiently.* ○ *We were waiting impatiently for the show to begin* (= wanting it to start).

impeach /ɪmˈpiːtʃ/ *verb* [T] to make a formal statement saying that a public official is guilty of a serious offence in connection with their job, especially in the US: *The governor was impeached for wrongful use of state money.*

impeachable /ɪmˈpiː.tʃə.bl̩/ *adj*: *an impeachable offence*

impeachment /ɪmˈpiːtʃ.mənt/ *noun* [C or U]

impeccable /ɪmˈpek.ə.bl̩/ *adj* perfect, with no problems or bad parts: *impeccable taste/manners/credentials* ○ *His English is impeccable.* **impeccably** /ɪmˈpek.ə.bli/ *adv*: *She was impeccably dressed.*

impecunious /ˌɪm.pəˈkjuː.ni.əs/ *adj* FORMAL having very little money; poor: *I first knew him as an impecunious **student** living in a tiny bedsit.*

impede /ɪmˈpiːd/ *verb* [T] FORMAL to slow down or cause problems for the advancement or completion of something: *Although he's shy, it certainly hasn't impeded his career in any way.*

impediment /ɪmˈped.ɪ.mənt/ *noun* [C] FORMAL something that makes progress, movement, or completing something difficult or impossible: *In a number of developing countries, war has been an additional impediment **to** progress.* ➲See also **speech impediment**.

impedimenta /ɪmˌped.ɪˈmen.tə/ *plural noun* MAINLY HUMOROUS the inconvenient or unnecessary objects which you need for a particular activity: *We were weighed down with sleeping bags, gas cookers and pans – all the impedimenta of camping.*

impel /ɪmˈpel/ *verb* [T] **-ll-** to make someone feel that they must do something: [+ *to* infinitive] *She was in such a mess I **felt** impelled **to*** (= felt I had to) *offer your services.* ○ *I wonder what it is that impels him **to** exercise all the time.*

impending /ɪmˈpen.dɪŋ/ *adj* [before n] describes an event, usually something unpleasant or unwanted, that is going to happen soon: *impending disaster/doom* ○ *Lineker announced his impending retirement from international football before the 1992 European Championships.*

impenetrable /ɪmˈpen.ɪ.trə.bl̩/ *adj* **1** impossible to see through or go through: *Outside, the fog was thick and impenetrable.* ○ *an impenetrable barrier* **2** impossible to understand: *Some of the lyrics on their latest album are completely impenetrable.* **impenetrably** /ɪmˈpen.ɪ.trə.bli/ *adv*

imperative [URGENT] /ɪmˈper.ə.tɪv/ [US] /-t̬ɪv/ *adj* extremely important or urgent; needing to be done or given attention immediately: [+ *that*] *The president said it was imperative **that** the release of all hostages be secured.* ○ [+ *to* infinitive] *It's imperative **to** act now before the problem gets really serious.* **imperative** /ɪmˈper.ə.tɪv/ [US] /-t̬ɪv/ *noun* [C] *Getting the unemployed back to work, said the minister, is a **moral** imperative.*

imperative [GRAMMAR] /ɪmˈper.ə.tɪv/ [US] /-t̬ɪv/ *noun* [S] SPECIALIZED the form of a verb which is usually used for giving orders: *In the phrase 'Leave him alone!', the verb 'leave' is an imperative/is **in the** imperative.* **imperative** /ɪmˈper.ə.tɪv/ [US] /-t̬ɪv/ *adj*: *the imperative form of the verb*

imperceptible /ˌɪm.pəˈsep.tɪ.bl̩/ [US] /-pɚˈsep.tə-/ *adj* unable to be noticed or felt because of being very slight: *She heard a faint, almost imperceptible cry.* **imperceptibly** /ˌɪm.pəˈsep.tɪ.bli/ [US] /-pɚˈsep.tə-/ *adv*: *Gradually, almost imperceptibly, her condition had worsened.*

imperfect [NOT PERFECT] /ɪmˈpɜː.fekt/ [US] /-ˈpɝː-/ *adj* damaged, containing problems or lacking something: *We're living in an imperfect world.* ○ *I explained as well as I was able, given my own imperfect understanding of the situation.* **imperfection** /ˌɪm.pəˈfek.ʃən/ [US] /-pɚ-/ *noun* [C or U] *Gradually she began to notice one or two little imperfections in his character.* ○ *She won't tolerate imperfection in her own or anyone else's work.* **imperfectly** /ɪmˈpɜː.fekt.li/ [US] /-ˈpɝː-/ *adv*

the imˈperfect (ˌtense) [GRAMMAR] *noun* [S] SPECIALIZED the tense of a verb which describes an action which has not been completed in the past, used, for example, to refer to an action which was happening when it was suddenly interrupted, or to describe an existing situation at the beginning of a story: *In the sentence 'He was hit by a car as he was crossing the road', the verb 'cross' is **in** the imperfect.*

imperial [EMPIRE] /ɪmˈpɪə.ri.əl/ [US] /-ˈpɪr.i-/ *adj* belonging or relating to an empire or the person or country that rules it: *Imperial China* ○ *Britain's imperial past* ○ *the Imperial palace* ○ *imperial grandeur*

imperialism /ɪmˈpɪə.ri.ə.lɪ.zəm/ [US] /-ˈpɪr.i-/ *noun* [U] OFTEN DISAPPROVING **1** a system in which a country rules other countries, sometimes having used force to obtain power over them: *the age of imperialism* **2** when one country has a lot of power or influence over others, especially in political and economic matters: *She accused the United States of **economic** imperialism.* **imperialist** /ɪmˈpɪə.ri.ə.lɪst/ [US] /-ˈpɪr.i-/ *adj* (ALSO **imperialistic**) *an imperialist power*

imperialist /ɪmˈpɪə.ri.ə.lɪst/ [US] /-ˈpɪr.i-/ *noun* [C] OFTEN DISAPPROVING someone who supports imperialism

imperial [MEASUREMENT] /ɪmˈpɪə.ri.əl/ [US] /-ˈpɪr-/ *adj* describes a system of measurement that uses units such as inches, miles and pints: *Imperial units have in many cases been replaced by metric ones in Britain.* ➲Compare **metric**.

imperil /ɪmˈper.əl/ *verb* [T] **-ll-** or US USUALLY **-l-** SLIGHTLY FORMAL to put something or someone at risk or in danger of being harmed or destroyed: *A police raid would imperil the lives of the hostages.*

imperious /ɪmˈpɪə.ri.əs/ [US] /-ˈpɪr.i-/ *adj* unpleasantly proud and expecting obedience: *an imperious manner/voice* ○ *She sent them away with an imperious wave of the hand.* **imperiously** /ɪmˈpɪə.ri.ə.sli/ [US] /-ˈpɪr.i-/ *adv* **imperiousness** /ɪmˈpɪə.ri.ə.snəs/ [US] /-ˈpɪr.i-/ *noun* [U]

imperishable /ɪmˈper.ɪ.ʃə.bl̩/ *adj* LITERARY lasting forever, or never weakening with age

impermanence /ɪmˈpɜː.mə.nənts/ [US] /-ˈpɝː-/ *noun* [U] FORMAL the quality of not lasting forever or not lasting for a long time: *the impermanence and fragility of life* **impermanent** /ɪmˈpɜː.mə.nənt/ [US] /-ˈpɝː-/ *adj*: *Acrylic paint is quick-drying but impermanent.*

impermeable /ɪm'pɜː.mi.ə.bl̩/ [US] /-'pɝː-/ *adj* not allowing liquid or gas to go through: *an impermeable membrane*

impermissible /ˌɪm.pə'mɪs.ə.bl̩/ [US] /-pɚ-/ *adj* SLIGHTLY FORMAL not allowed or permitted: *There are certain topics of conversation that are impermissible in polite society.*

impersonal /ɪm'pɜː.sən.əl/ [US] /-'pɝː-/ *adj* DISAPPROVING lacking human warmth and interest: *Hospitals always seem such impersonal places – rows of identical beds in dull grey rooms.* ○ *She has a very cold and impersonal manner.*

impersonate /ɪm'pɜː.sən.eɪt/ [US] /-'pɝː-/ *verb* [T] **1** to intentionally copy another person's characteristics, such as their behaviour, speech, appearance or facial expressions, especially to make people laugh: *She's the woman who impersonates the Queen on TV.* **2** to attempt to deceive someone by pretending that you are another person: *He was fined for impersonating a police officer.* **impersonation** /ɪmˌpɜː.sən'eɪ.ʃən/ [US] /-ˌpɝː-/ *noun* [C or U] *He* ***does*** *a brilliant impersonation of Charles.*
impersonator /ɪm'pɜː.sən.eɪ.təʳ/ [US] /-'pɝː.sən.eɪ.t̬ɚ/ *noun* [C] someone who impersonates another person: *an Elvis impersonator*

impertinent /ɪm'pɜː.tɪ.nənt/ [US] /-'pɝː.t̬ən.ənt/ *adj* rude and not respectful, especially towards someone older or in a higher position than you: *I hope he didn't think me impertinent when I asked him about his private life.* ○ *an impertinent remark/question* **impertinently** /ɪm'pɜː.tɪ.nənt.li/ [US] /-'pɝː.t̬ən.ənt-/ *adv* **impertinence** /ɪm'pɜː.tɪ.nənts/ [US] /-'pɝː.t̬ən.ənts/ *noun* [C or U] *She even* ***had*** *the impertinence* ***to*** *lecture Loretta on how to be the wife of an eminent clergyman.*

imperturbable /ˌɪm.pə'tɜː.bə.bl̩/ [US] /-pɚ'tɝː-/ *adj* always staying calm and controlled, even in difficult situations that would cause anxiety to others **imperturbably** /ˌɪm.pə'tɜː.bə.bli/ [US] /-pɚ'tɝː-/ *adv* FORMAL

impervious [SUBSTANCE] /ɪm'pɜː.vi.əs/ [US] /-'pɝː-/ *adj* not allowing liquid to go through: *How does glue bond with impervious substances like glass and metal?*

impervious [PERSON] /ɪm'pɜː.vi.əs/ [US] /-'pɝː-/ *adj* describes a person who is not influenced or affected by something: *He is impervious* ***to*** *criticism and rational argument.*

impetigo /ˌɪm.pə'taɪ.gəʊ/ [US] /-goʊ/ *noun* [U] an infectious skin disease in which yellowish areas appear on the body

impetuous /ɪm'pet.ju.əs/ *adj* **1** tending to act on a sudden idea or wish, without considering the results of your actions: *He's so impetuous – why can't he think things over before he rushes into them?* **2** An impetuous word or action is said or done suddenly, without considering the likely results: *The Prime Minister may now be regretting her impetuous promise to reduce unemployment by half.* **impetuously** /ɪm'pet.ju.ə.sli/ *adv* **impetuousness** /ɪm'pet.ju.ə.snəs/ *noun* [U] (FORMAL **impetuosity**)

impetus /'ɪm.pɪ.təs/ [US] /-pə.t̬əs/ *noun* [S or U] something which encourages a particular activity or makes that activity more energetic or effective: *The recent publicity surrounding homelessness has given* ***(a) fresh*** *impetus to the cause.*

impinge /ɪm'pɪndʒ/ *verb*
▲ **impinge on/upon *sb/sth*** *phrasal verb* to have an effect on something, often causing problems by limiting it in some way: *The government's spending limits will seriously impinge on the education budget.*

impish /'ɪm.pɪʃ/ *adj* ➲See at **imp**.

implacable /ɪm'plæk.ə.bl̩/ *adj* SLIGHTLY FORMAL describes (someone who has) strong opinions or feelings which are impossible to change: *an implacable enemy* ○ *implacable opposition/hostility* **implacably** /ɪm'plæk.ə.bli/ *adv*

implant [OBJECT] /ɪm'plɑːnt/ [US] /-'plænt/ *verb* [T] to put an organ, group of cells, or device into the body in a medical operation: *The owner's name and address is stored on a microchip and implanted in the dog's body.* ➲Compare **transplant**. **implant** /'ɪm.plɑːnt/ [US] /-plænt/ *noun* [C] *breast/heart valve implants*

implant [IDEA] /ɪm'plɑːnt/ [US] /-'plænt/ *verb* [T] to fix ideas, feelings or opinions in someone else's mind: *He implanted some very strange attitudes* ***in*** *his children.* ○ *There is much debate on the issue of "therapists" implanting false memories of sexual abuse* ***in*** *adults.*

implausible /ɪm'plɔː.zɪ.bl̩/ [US] /-'plɑː.zə-/ *adj* difficult to believe, or unlikely: *The whole plot of the film is ridiculously implausible.* **implausibly** /ɪm'plɔː.zɪ.bli/ [US] /-'plɑː.zə-/ *adv* **implausibility** /ɪmˌplɔː.zɪ'bɪl.ɪ.ti/ [US] /-ˌplɑː.zə'bɪl.ə.t̬i/ *noun* [U]

implement [TOOL] /'ɪm.plɪ.mənt/ *noun* [C] a tool which works by being moved by hand or by being pulled across a surface, but which is not powered directly by electricity or fuel: *garden/household/agricultural implements* ○ *Shopkeepers are not supposed to sell knives and other sharp implements to children.*

implement [USE] /'ɪm.plɪ.ment/ *verb* [T] to put a plan or system into operation: *The changes to the national health system will be implemented next year.* **implementation** /ˌɪm.plɪ.men'teɪ.ʃən/ *noun* [U] *implementation of the law/agreement*

implicate /'ɪm.plɪ.keɪt/ *verb* [T] to show that someone is involved in a crime or partly responsible for something bad that has happened: *Have they any evidence to implicate him* ***in*** *the robbery?* **implication** /ˌɪm.plɪ'keɪ.ʃən/ *noun* [U] *The case depended upon his implication of his co-workers in the fraud.* ➲See also **implication** at **imply**.

implicit [SUGGESTED] /ɪm'plɪs.ɪt/ *adj* suggested but not communicated directly: *He interpreted her comments as an implicit* ***criticism*** *of the government.* ○ *Implicit* ***in*** *the poem's closing lines are the poet's own religious doubts.* ➲Compare **explicit**. **implicitly** /ɪm'plɪs.ɪt.li/ *adv*

implicit [COMPLETE] /ɪm'plɪs.ɪt/ *adj* complete and without any doubts: *implicit* ***trust*** ○ *All her life she had implicit* ***faith*** *in socialism.* **implicitly** /ɪm'plɪs.ɪt.li/ *adv*: *He trusts her implicitly.*

implode /ɪm'pləʊd/ [US] /-'ploʊd/ *verb* [I] **1** SPECIALIZED to fall inward with force: *The vacuum inside the tube caused it to implode when the external air pressure was increased.* ➲Compare **explode** BURST. **2** to fail suddenly and completely and be unable to operate: *Their economy is in danger of imploding.* **implosion** /ɪm'pləʊ.ʒən/ [US] /-'ploʊ-/ *noun* [C or U] SPECIALIZED

implore /ɪm'plɔːʳ/ [US] /-'plɔːr/ *verb* **1** [T + *to* infinitive] to ask someone to do or not do something in a very sincere, emotional and determined way: *She implored her parents not* ***to*** *send her away to school.* **2** [T] LITERARY to ask for something in this way: *She clasped her hands, and glancing upward, seemed to implore divine assistance.* **imploring** /ɪm'plɔː.rɪŋ/ [US] /-'plɔːr.ɪŋ/ *adj*: *He had an imploring look in his eyes.* **imploringly** /ɪm'plɔː.rɪŋ.li/ [US] /-'plɔːr.ɪŋ.li/ *adv*

imply /ɪm'plaɪ/ *verb* [T] **1** to communicate an idea or feeling without saying it directly: [+ (*that*)] *Are you implying* ***(that)*** *I'm fat?* ○ *I'm not implying anything about your cooking, but could we eat out tonight?* **2** FORMAL to involve something or make it necessary: *Socialism implies equality.* **implied** /ɪm'plaɪd/ *adj*: *Her threat to resign was implied rather than stated explicitly.* ○ *I detected an implied* ***criticism*** *of the way he was treated.*
implication /ˌɪm.plɪ'keɪ.ʃən/ *noun* **1** [C or U] when you seem to suggest something without saying it directly: [+ *that*] *From what she said, the implication was* ***that*** *they were splitting up.* ○ *She accused the party and,* ***by*** *implication, its leader too.* ➲See also **implication** at **implicate**. **2** [C usually pl] the effect that an action or decision will have on something else in the future: *The company is cutting back its spending and I wonder what the implications will be* ***for*** *our department.* ○ *What are the implications* ***of*** *the new law?*

impolite /ˌɪm.pəl'aɪt/ *adj* SLIGHTLY FORMAL rude: *impolite language/behaviour* ○ *It is impolite* ***to*** *point at people.* **impolitely** /ˌɪm.pəl'aɪt.li/ *adv*

impolitic /ɪm'pɒl.ɪ.tɪk/ [US] /-'pɑː.lə.t̬ɪk/ *adj* FORMAL describes unwise words or actions which are likely to cause offence or problems, especially in social situations: *I thought it impolitic to ask any questions about her ex-husband.*

imponderable /ɪmˈpɒn.d^{ə}r.ə.bl̩/ [US] /-ˈpɑːn-/ *adj* FORMAL If an effect or result, etc. is imponderable, it cannot be guessed or calculated because it is completely unknown. **imponderable** /ɪmˈpɒn.d^{ə}r.ə.bl̩/ [US] /-ˈpɑːn-/ *noun* [C] *There are too many imponderables to make an accurate forecast.*

import [BRING IN] /ɪmˈpɔːt/ [US] /ˈɪm.pɔːrt/ *verb* [T] **1** to buy or bring in products from another country: *We import a large number of cars* ***from*** *Japan.* ➲Compare **export**. **2** to introduce new goods, customs or ideas to one country from another: *The fashion for wearing baseball hats was imported directly* ***from*** *the States.* **3** SPECIALIZED to copy information from one computer or computer program to another: *I need to import data from the database into my word processor.* ○ *imported files*

import /ˈɪm.pɔːt/ [US] /-pɔːrt/ *noun* **1** [C usually pl] goods bought by one country from another: *restrictions on foreign imports* **2** [U] (ALSO **importation**) the action of bringing goods or fashions into a country: *the illegal importation of drugs* ○ *an import licence* ○ *import duties* **importer** /ɪmˈpɔː.tə^{r}/ [US] /-ˈpɔːr.t̬ɚ/ *noun* [C] *After the USA, Japan is the second biggest importer of oil.* ○ *He is an importer of African foodstuffs.*

import [IMPORTANCE] /ˈɪm.pɔːt/ [US] /-pɔːrt/ *noun* [U] FORMAL importance or meaning: *Whether it is to be a 'working' visit or an 'official' visit is of* ***little/no*** *import.*

important /ɪmˈpɔː.t^{ə}nt/ [US] /-ˈpɔːr.t̬^{ə}nt/ *adj* **1** necessary or of great value: *I think his career is more important* ***to*** *him than I am.* ○ ***It's*** *important* ***for*** *children* ***to*** *learn to get on with each other.* ○ ***The*** *important* ***thing*** *is to keep the heat low or the sugar will burn.* ○ *He's not amazingly handsome, but he's nice and that's more important.* ⁎ NOTE: The opposite is **unimportant**. **2** having great effect or influence: *He was one of the most important writers of that period.* ○ *an important person/decision* **importantly** /ɪmˈpɔː.t^{ə}nt.li/ [US] /-ˈpɔːr.t̬^{ə}nt-/ *adv*: *If we served more soft drinks, there would be fewer hangovers and,* ***more*** *importantly, fewer drink-driving incidents.* **importance** /ɪmˈpɔː.t^{ə}nts/ [US] /-ˈpɔːr.t̬^{ə}nts/ *noun* [U] *The health report stresses the importance* ***of*** *fresh food in a diet.* ○ *She* ***attaches*** *a lot of importance* ***to*** *personal possessions.*

importunate /ɪmˈpɔː.tjʊ.nət/ [US] /-ˈpɔːr.tʃə.nɪt/ *adj* FORMAL **1** continually asking for something, in a forceful and annoying way: *an importunate beggar/crowd* **2** An importunate request or question is repeated and forceful in an annoying way: *importunate demands*

importune /ˌɪm.pɔːˈtjuːn/ [US] /ˌɪm.pɔːrˈtuːn/ *verb* [T] FORMAL to make repeated forceful requests for something, usually in a way that is annoying or inconvenient: *As a tourist, you are importuned* ***for*** *money the moment you step outside your hotel.*

impose [FORCE] /ɪmˈpəʊz/ [US] /-ˈpoʊz/ *verb* [T] **1** to officially force a rule, tax, punishment, etc. to be obeyed or received: *Very high taxes have recently been imposed* ***on*** *cigarettes.* ○ *Judges are imposing increasingly heavy fines for minor driving offences.* ○ *The council has imposed a ban* ***on*** *alcohol in the city parks.* **2** to force someone to accept something, especially a belief or way of living: *I don't want them to impose their religious beliefs* ***on*** *my children.* ○ *We must impose some kind of order* ***on*** *the way this office is run.* **imposition** /ˌɪm.pəˈzɪʃ.^{ə}n/ *noun* [U] *the imposition* ***of*** *the death penalty/martial law/sanctions*

impose [EXPECT] /ɪmˈpəʊz/ [US] /-ˈpoʊz/ *verb* [I] to expect someone to do something for you or spend time with you when they do not want to or when it is inconvenient for them: *Are you sure it's all right for me to come tonight? I don't want to impose.* ○ *She's always imposing* ***on*** *people – asking favours and getting everyone to do things for her.*

imposition /ˌɪm.pəˈzɪʃ.^{ə}n/ *noun* [S] when someone imposes on another person: *Would it be too much of an imposition to ask you to pick my parents up from the airport?*

imposing /ɪmˈpəʊ.zɪŋ/ [US] /-ˈpoʊ-/ *adj* having an appearance which looks important or causes admiration: *an imposing mansion* ○ *He was an imposing figure on stage.*

impossible /ɪmˈpɒs.ɪ.bl̩/ [US] /-ˈpɑː.sə-/ *adj* **1** If an action or event is impossible, it cannot happen or be achieved: *It was impossible* ***to*** *sleep because of the noise.* ○ *It seems impossible* ***that*** *I could have walked by without noticing her.* ○ *He made it impossible for me to say no.* ○ *She ate three plates of spaghetti and a dessert? That's impossible. I don't believe it!* **2** describes a situation which is extremely difficult to deal with or solve: *It's an impossible situation – she's got to leave him but she can't bear losing her children.* **3** describes a person who behaves very badly or is extremely difficult to deal with: *I had to leave the job because my boss was impossible.* ○ *My niece is impossible when she's tired – you can't do anything to please her.*

the impossible *noun* [S] something which cannot be expected to happen or exist: *She wants a man who is bright, attractive and funny as well, which is* ***asking*** *the impossible in my opinion.* **impossibility** /ɪmˌpɒs.ɪˈbɪl.ɪ.ti/ [US] /-ˌpɑː.səˈbɪl.ə.t̬i/ *noun* [C or U] *What you're asking just can't be done – it's an impossibility.*

impossibly /ɪmˈpɒs.ɪ.bli/ [US] /-ˈpɑː.sə-/ *adv* extremely or unusually: *Doctors are being forced to work impossibly long hours.* ○ *She has an impossibly thin waist.*

impostor, imposter /ɪmˈpɒs.tə^{r}/ [US] /-ˈpɑː.stɚ/ *noun* [C] a person who pretends to be someone else in order to deceive others: *He felt like an impostor among all those intelligent people, as if he had no right to be there.*

imposture /ɪmˈpɒs.tjə^{r}/ [US] /-ˈpɑː.stjɚ/ *noun* [C or U] FORMAL the act of pretending to be someone else in order to deceive others

impotent [LACKING POWER] /ˈɪm.pə.t^{ə}nt/ [US] /-t̬^{ə}nt/ *adj* lacking the power or ability to change or improve a situation: *You feel so impotent when your child is ill and you cannot help them.* **impotence** /ˈɪm.pə.t^{ə}nts/ [US] /-t̬^{ə}nts/ *noun* [U] *political impotence* ○ *a sense of impotence*

impotent [SEXUAL PROBLEM] /ˈɪm.pə.t^{ə}nt/ [US] /-t̬^{ə}nt/ *adj* If a man is impotent, he cannot have sex because his penis cannot harden or stay hard. **impotence** /ˈɪm.pə.t^{ə}nts/ [US] /-t̬^{ə}nts/ *noun* [U] *Men sometimes suffer from impotence after a serious illness.*

impound /ɪmˈpaʊnd/ *verb* [T] If the police or someone in authority impounds something that belongs to you, they take it away because you have broken the law: *The police impounded cars and other personal property belonging to the drug dealers.* ○ *The vehicle was impounded by customs.*

impoverished /ɪmˈpɒv.^{ə}r.ɪʃt/ [US] /-ˈpɑː.vɚ-/ *adj* FORMAL **1** very poor: *She's going out with an impoverished young actor.* **2** weakened or made worse in quality: *He warned that the breakdown of the family unit would lead to an impoverished society.* **impoverish** /ɪmˈpɒv.^{ə}r.ɪʃ/ [US] /-ˈpɑː.vɚ-/ *verb* [T] *Excessive farming had impoverished the soil.*

impoverishment /ɪmˈpɒv.^{ə}r.ɪʃ.mənt/ [US] /-ˈpɑː.vɚ-/ *noun* [U] FORMAL when something is impoverished: *cultural/economic/spiritual impoverishment*

impracticable /ɪmˈpræk.tɪ.kə.bl̩/ *adj* If a course of action, plan, etc. is impracticable, it is impossible to do in an effective way: *The changes to the tax system proved impracticable as they were impossible to enforce.*

impractical /ɪmˈpræk.tɪ.k^{ə}l/ *adj* **1** Impractical people are not naturally good at doing useful jobs such as making or repairing things. **2** Impractical arrangements, ideas or methods cannot be done or used easily or effectively: *It's impractical to have so many people all trying to use this equipment at the same time.* **3** Impractical clothes, devices, etc. cause problems when used in normal situations: *I love high heels but they're rather impractical.*

imprecation /ˌɪm.prəˈkeɪ.ʃ^{ə}n/ *noun* [C] FORMAL a swear word: *The old woman walked along the street muttering imprecations.*

imprecise /ˌɪm.prɪˈsaɪs/ *adj* not accurate or exact: *The figures are imprecise because they're based on a prediction of next year's sales.* **imprecision** /ˌɪm.prɪˈsɪʒ.^{ə}n/ *noun* [U]

impregnable /ɪmˈpreg.nə.bl̩/ adj **1** A building or other place that is impregnable is so strongly built and/or defended that it cannot be entered by force: *Despite burglar alarms and window locks, homes are never impregnable against determined thieves.* **2** MAINLY UK powerful and impossible to beat, especially in sport: *Surrey have been building up an impregnable lead in this season's County Championship.*

impregnate CAUSE TO ABSORB /ˈɪm.preg.neɪt/ US /-ˈ--/ verb [T] FORMAL to cause something, usually a solid substance, to absorb something, usually a liquid: *This cloth has been impregnated with special chemicals for cleaning computer screens.*

impregnate MAKE PREGNANT /ˈɪm.preg.neɪt/ US /-ˈ--/ verb [T] SPECIALIZED to make a woman or female animal pregnant

impresario /ˌɪm.prəˈsɑː.ri.əʊ/ US /-ˈsɑːr.i.oʊ/ noun [C] plural **impresarios** a person who arranges public entertainments, such as theatre, musical and dance events: *London's leading theatrical impresario*

impress /ɪmˈpres/ verb [I or T; not continuous] to cause someone to admire or respect you because of something that you have done or said: *I remember when I was a child being very impressed with how many toys she had.* ○ *Your mother was clearly not impressed by our behaviour in the restaurant.* ○ *He tried to impress me with his extensive knowledge of wine.* ○ FORMAL *I'm afraid the new theatre fails to impress.*

impressive /ɪmˈpres.ɪv/ adj **1** If an object or achievement is impressive, you admire or respect it, usually because it is special, important or very large: *That was an impressive performance from such a young tennis player.* ○ *an impressive collection of modern paintings* ○ *There are some very impressive buildings in the town.* ＊ NOTE: The opposite is **unimpressive**. **2** An impressive person causes you to admire or respect them for their special skills or abilities: *She's a very impressive public speaker.*
impressively /ɪmˈpres.ɪv.li/ adv

▲ **impress sth on/upon sb** phrasal verb to make someone understand or be aware of the importance or value of something: *Mr Simmons tried to impress on me how much easier my life would be if I were better organized.*

impression OPINION /ɪmˈpreʃ.ən/ noun [C] an idea or opinion of what something is like: *I didn't get much of an impression of the place because it was dark when we drove through it.* ○ *What was your impression of Charlotte's husband?* ○ *I don't tend to trust first impressions* (= the opinion you form when you meet someone or see something for the first time). ○ [+ that] *When I first met him I got/had the impression that he was a shy sort of a bloke.*

• **be under the impression** to think or understand a particular stated thing: *I was under the impression (that) you didn't get on too well.* ○ *He was under the mistaken* (= false) *impression (that) you were married.*

impression EFFECT /ɪmˈpreʃ.ən/ noun [S] the way that something seems, looks or feels to a particular person: *It makes/gives/creates a very bad impression if you're late for an interview.* ○ [+ (that)] *He likes to give the impression (that) he's terribly popular and has loads of friends.*

• **make an impression on sb** to cause someone to notice and admire you: *He made quite an impression on the girls at the tennis club.*

impressionable /ɪmˈpreʃ.ən.ə.bl̩/ adj OFTEN DISAPPROVING describes someone, usually a young person, who is very easily influenced by the people around them and by what they are told, and who sometimes copies other people's behaviour: *He's at that impressionable age when he's very easily led by other children.*

impressionistic /ɪmˌpreʃ.ənˈɪs.tɪk/ adj giving a general view or representation of something instead of particular details or facts: *The new play at the Youth Theatre is an impressionistic view of life in the fifties.*

impression COPY /ɪmˈpreʃ.ən/ noun [C] an attempt at copying another person's manner and speech, etc. or an animal's behaviour, especially in order to make people laugh: *She does a really good impression of the president.*
impressionist /ɪmˈpreʃ.ən.ɪst/ noun [C] a person who copies other people's manner and speech in order to en-

tertain other people and make them laugh

impression MARK /ɪmˈpreʃ.ən/ noun [C] a mark made on the surface of something by pressing an object onto it: *There were impressions round her ankles made by the tops of her socks.*

impression BOOKS /ɪmˈpreʃ.ən/ noun [C usually sing] (US ALSO **printing**) all the copies of a book that have been printed at the same time without any changes being made: *This is the second impression of the encyclopedia.*

Impressionism /ɪmˈpreʃ.ən.ɪ.z²m/ noun [U] a style of painting, originating in France in the 1860s, in which the artist tries to represent the effects of light on an object, person, area of countryside, etc. **Impressionist** /ɪmˈpreʃ.ən.ɪst/ noun [C] **Impressionist** /ɪmˈpreʃ.ən.ɪst/ adj: *Impressionist paintings* ○ *an Impressionist painter/style*

imprimatur /ˌɪm.prɪˈmeɪ.tər/ US /-ˈt̬ɚ/ noun [S] FORMAL official permission to do something that is given by a person or group in a position of power: *When he suspended the constitution and dissolved Congress, he had the imprimatur of the armed forces.*

imprint MARK /ɪmˈprɪnt/ verb [T] **1** to mark a surface by pressing something hard into it **2** to fix an event or experience so firmly in the memory that it cannot be forgotten although you do not try to remember it: *That look of pure grief would be imprinted on her mind forever.*
imprint /ˈɪm.prɪnt/ noun **1** [C usually sing] when an object presses on something and leaves a mark: *The button had left an imprint on my arm.* **2** [S] when an event or experience becomes fixed in someone's memory or marked in some way on their appearance: *War has left its imprint on the strained faces of these people.*

imprint BOOK /ˈɪm.prɪnt/ noun [C] the name of a PUBLISHER (= a company that produces books) as it appears on a particular set of books

imprison /ɪmˈprɪz.ən/ verb [T usually passive] to put someone in prison: *He was imprisoned in 1965 for attempted murder.* ○ FIGURATIVE *Unable to go out because of the deep snow, she felt imprisoned in her own house.* **imprisonment** /ɪmˈprɪz.ən.mənt/ noun [C or U] *She was sentenced to five years' imprisonment.*

improbable /ɪmˈprɒb.ə.bl̩/ US /-ˈprɑː.bə-/ adj not likely to happen or be true: *It's highly improbable that Norris will agree.* ○ *an improbable-sounding excuse* **improbably** /ɪmˈprɒb.ə.bli/ US /-ˈprɑː.bə-/ adv: *improbably cheap prices* ○ *improbably large/long* **improbability** /ɪmˌprɒb.əˈbɪl.ɪ.ti/ US /ˌɪm.prɑː.bəˈbɪl.ə.t̬i/ noun [C or U]

impromptu /ɪmˈprɒmp.tʃuː/ US /-tuː/ adj done or said without earlier planning or preparation: *an impromptu party/performance*

improper DISHONEST /ɪmˈprɒp.ər/ US /-ˈprɑː.pɚ/ adj FORMAL dishonest and against a law or a rule: *The governor has denied making improper use of state money.* **improperly** /ɪmˈprɒp.ə.li/ US /-ˈprɑː.pɚ-/ adv **impropriety** /ˌɪm.prəˈpraɪ.ə.ti/ US /-t̬i/ noun [C or U] *financial/legal impropriety*

improper WRONG /ɪmˈprɒp.ər/ US /-ˈprɑː.pɚ/ adj SLIGHTLY FORMAL unsuitable or not correct for a particular use or occasion: *improper prescription of medicines* ○ *Is it considered improper to wear such a short skirt to a formal occasion?* **improperly** /ɪmˈprɒp.ə.li/ US /-ˈprɑː.pɚ-/ adv **impropriety** /ˌɪm.prəˈpraɪ.ə.ti/ US /-t̬i/ noun [U]

improper RUDE /ɪmˈprɒp.ər/ US /-ˈprɑː.pɚ/ adj related to sex in a way that is rude or socially unacceptable: *I trust you're not making improper suggestions to my husband!* **impropriety** /ˌɪm.prəˈpraɪ.ə.ti/ US /-t̬i/ noun [C or U] SLIGHTLY FORMAL *allegations of sexual impropriety*

im‚proper 'fraction noun [C] SPECIALIZED a fraction in which the number below the line is smaller than the number above it: *3/2 is an improper fraction.*

improve /ɪmˈpruːv/ verb [I or T] to (cause something to) get better: *He did a lot to improve conditions for factory workers.* ○ *I thought the best way to improve my French was to live in France.* ○ *Her health has improved dramatically since she started on this new diet.* **improvement** /ɪmˈpruːv.mənt/ noun [C or U] when something gets better or when you make it better: *a slight* *improvement* ***in*** *the economy* ○ *home improvements* ○ *These white walls are a big improvement* ***on*** *that disgusting old wallpaper.* ○ *He's been having treatment for two months now without any improvement.*

▲ **improve on/upon *sth*** *phrasal verb* to do something in a better way or with better results than before: *Last time she ran the race in twenty minutes, so she's hoping to improve on that.*

improvident /ɪmˈprɒv.ɪ.dᵊnt/ [US] /-ˈprɑː.və-/ *adj* FORMAL spending money in a way that is not sensible, and/or not planning carefully for the future **improvidence** /ɪmˈprɒv.ɪ.dᵊnts/ [US] /-ˈprɑː.və-/ *noun* [U]

improvise /ˈɪm.prə.vaɪz/ *verb* [I or T] **1** to invent or make something, such as a speech or a device, at the time when it is needed without already having planned it: *I hadn't prepared a speech so I suddenly had to improvise.* ○ *To sleep on, we improvised a mattress* ***from*** *a pile of blankets.* **2** When actors or musicians improvise, they perform without fixed speech or music, making it up as they perform it: *During certain scenes of the play there isn't any script and the actors just improvise (the dialogue).* **improvisation** /ˌɪm.prə.vaɪˈzeɪ.ʃᵊn/ [US] /ɪm-ˌprɑː.vɪˈ-/ *noun* [C or U] *a blues/jazz improvisation* ○ *There are classes in movement, dance, acting and improvisation.*

imprudent /ɪmˈpruː.dᵊnt/ *adj* FORMAL unwise, by failing to consider the likely results of your actions: *The report criticizes the banks for being imprudent in their lending.* **imprudence** /ɪmˈpruː.dᵊnts/ *noun* [U] SLIGHTLY FORMAL

impudent /ˈɪm.pjʊ.dᵊnt/ *adj* rude and not respectful, especially towards someone who is older or in a more important position: *an impudent remark/child* **impudence** /ˈɪm.pjʊ.dᵊnts/ *noun* [U]

impugn /ɪmˈpjuːn/ *verb* [T] FORMAL to cause people to doubt someone's character, qualities or reputation by criticizing them: *Are you impugning my competence as a professional designer?*

impulse [DESIRE] /ˈɪm.pʌls/ *noun* [C + **to** infinitive] a sudden strong desire to do something: *I had this sudden impulse* ***to*** *shout out "Rubbish!" in the middle of her speech.*

• **on (an) impulse** because you suddenly want to, although you haven't planned to: *"I didn't know you were looking for some new shoes." "Oh, I wasn't – I just bought them on impulse."*

impulsive /ɪmˈpʌl.sɪv/ *adj* showing behaviour in which you do things suddenly without any planning and without considering the effects they may have: *Don't be so impulsive – think before you act.* ○ *an impulsive man/decision/gesture* **impulsively** /ɪmˈpʌl.sɪv.li/ *adv*

impulse [SIGNAL] /ˈɪm.pʌls/ *noun* [C] a short electrical, radio or light signal which carries information or instructions between the parts of a system: *an electrical/nerve impulse*

impulse [REASON] /ˈɪm.pʌls/ *noun* [C usually sing] FORMAL something that is the force behind or reason for something else: *a creative/commercial impulse*

ˈimpulse ˌbuying *noun* [U] when you buy something that you had not planned to buy, because you suddenly want it when you see it: *They display chocolates next to supermarket checkouts to encourage impulse buying.* **ˈimpulse, buy** *noun* [C] *I hadn't intended to get one - it was an impulse buy.*

impunity /ɪmˈpjuː.nɪ.ti/ [US] /-ə.t̬i/ *noun* [U] freedom from punishment or from the unpleasant results of something that has been done: *Criminal gangs are terrorizing the city* ***with*** *apparent impunity.*

impure [MIXED] /ɪmˈpjʊəʳ/ [US] /-ˈpjʊr/ *adj* mixed with other substances and therefore lower in quality: *impure heroin/gold* **impurity** /ɪmˈpjʊə.rɪ.ti/ [US] /-ˈpjʊr.ə.t̬i/ *noun* [C or U] *Impurities are removed from the blood by the kidneys.* ○ *The impurity of the water is a serious health risk.*

impure [IMMORAL] /ɪmˈpjʊəʳ/ [US] /-ˈpjʊr/ *adj* LITERARY OR HUMOROUS involving immoral sexual thoughts or behaviour: *She was accused of having impure* ***thoughts*** *about her male students.* **impurity** /ɪmˈpjʊə.rɪ.ti/ [US] /-ˈpjʊr.ə.t̬i/ *noun* [U]

impute /ɪmˈpjuːt/ *verb*

PHRASAL VERBS WITH **impute** ▼

▲ **impute *sth* to *sb*** [ACCUSE] *phrasal verb* FORMAL to say that someone is responsible for something that has happened, or that something is the cause of something else: *They imputed the error to the lawyer who was handling her case.* **imputation** /ˌɪm.pjʊˈteɪ.ʃᵊn/ *noun* [C or U] *imputations of dishonesty*

▲ **impute *sth* to *sb*** [BELIEVE] *phrasal verb* FORMAL to believe that someone or something has a particular characteristic, quality or meaning: *He arrogantly imputed stupidity to anyone who disagreed with him.*

in [INSIDE] /ɪn/ *prep, adv* **1** inside or towards the inside of a container, place or area, or surrounded or enclosed by something: *Put the milk back in the fridge when you've finished with it.* ○ *Is Mark still in bed?* ○ *I got stuck in a traffic jam for half an hour.* ○ *Come on, we're late – get in the car.* ○ *They live in a charming old cottage.* ○ *How much is that coat on display in the window* (= in the space behind the window of the shop)? ○ *I've got a pain in my back.* ○ *What's that in your hand?* ○ *I've got something in* (= on the surface of) *my eye.* ○ *They used to live in Paris, but now they're somewhere in Austria.* ○ *He's always looking at himself in the mirror* (= at the image of his face produced by the mirror). ○ *When did you get home? I never heard you come in.* ○ *What time is Roz's flight due in?* ○ *Why are you never in* (= at home) *when I phone?* ○ *I never know what's going on in her head* (= what she's thinking about). ○ *Is the boss in* (= at work) *yet?* ○ *My daughter's* (UK) *in hospital/*(US) *in the hospital having her tonsils out.* ○ US *Is Erika still in school* (= does she still go to school)? **2** If the ball is in during a game of tennis or a similar sport, it has not gone outside the edges of the area on which the game is played: *I won that point, I'm telling you! The ball was definitely in!*

• **be in and out of *somewhere*** INFORMAL to be frequently staying in and receiving treatment in a particular place: *She's been in and out of hospitals ever since the accident.*

COMMON LEARNER ERROR

in or at?

The preposition 'in' emphasises 'inside a place'.

Mum doesn't like people wearing their shoes in the house.

The preposition 'at' is used to talk about time spent at a place.

We had a really good time at your house last weekend.

~~*We had a really good time in your house last weekend.*~~

in [PART] /ɪn/ *prep* forming a part of something: *He used to be the lead singer in a rock 'n' roll band.* ○ *There are too many spelling mistakes in this essay.* ○ *I've been waiting in this queue for ages.* ○ *What do you look for in a relationship?* ○ *I can see a future champion in Joely* (= I think that Joely might become a champion). ○ *Talent like hers is rare in someone so young.*

in [INVOLVED] /ɪn/ *prep* involved or connected with a particular subject or activity: *I never knew you were in publishing.* ○ *a degree in philosophy* ○ *advances in medical science*

in [WEARING] /ɪn/ *prep* wearing: *Do you recognize that man in the grey suit?* ○ *Pat can't resist men in uniform.* ○ *You look nice in green* (= green clothes).

in [EXPRESSED] /ɪn/ *prep* expressed or written in a particular way: *Cheques should be written in ink.* ○ *She usually paints in watercolour.* ○ *They spoke in Russian the whole time.* ○ *He always talks in a whisper.*

• **in all honesty/seriousness/truthfulness** said when expressing your opinion honestly, seriously or truthfully: *In all honesty, I do have some criticisms to make.*

in [DURING] /ɪn/ *prep* during part or all of a period of time: *We're going to Italy in April.* ○ *Some trees lose their leaves in (the) autumn.* ○ *I started working here in 1991.* ○ *Life in the 19th century was very different from what it is now.* ○ *Bye, see you in the morning* (= tomorrow morning). ○ *She was a brilliant gymnast in her youth* (= when she was young). ○ *How many civilians died in the Vietnam War?* ○ *This is the first cigarette I've had in three years.* ○ *I haven't had a decent night's sleep in* *years/ages* (= for a long time).

• **in between** between the two times mentioned: *I have breakfast at 7.30, lunch at 1 o'clock and sometimes a snack in between.*

in NO MORE THAN /ɪn/ *prep* needing or using no more time than a particular amount of time: *Can you finish the job in two weeks?* ○ *She could get that essay done in a couple of hours if she really tried.* ○ *They completed the journey in record time* (= faster than ever done before).

in BEFORE THE END /ɪn/ *prep* before or at the end of a particular period: *Dinner will be ready in ten minutes.* ○ *We'll all be dead in a hundred years so there's no point worrying about it.* ○ *I'm just setting off, so I should be with you in half an hour.*

in EXPERIENCING /ɪn/ *prep, adv* experiencing a situation or condition, or feeling an emotion: *We watched in horror as they pulled the bodies from the wreckage.* ○ *He's living in luxury in the south of France.* ○ *She left in a bit of a hurry.* ○ *You're in great danger.* ○ *Could I have a word with you in private?* ○ *Have you ever been in love?* ○ *Your car's in very good condition, considering how old it is.*

• **in on** *sth* involved with or knowing about a particular activity or plan: *He seems to be in on everything that happens at work.* ○ *She's trying to get in on a research project organised by the university.*

• **be well in there** *UK INFORMAL* to be likely to experience something good because of a situation you are in: *She's well in there now that she's married her boss's son.*

in RESULT /ɪn/ *prep* used when referring to something that is done as a result of something else: *I'd like to do something for you in return/exchange for everything you've done for me.* ○ *The changes are in response to demand from our customers.* ○ *He refused to say anything in reply to the journalists' questions.*

in ARRANGEMENT /ɪn/ *prep* used to show how things or people are arranged or divided: *We all sat down in a circle.* ○ *The desks were arranged in rows of ten.* ○ *Discounts are available to people travelling in large groups.* ○ *Sometimes customers buy books in twos and threes, but rarely in larger quantities than that.* ○ *Cut the potatoes in two.* ○ *People are dying in their thousands from typhoid, cold and starvation.*

• **in all** with everything added together to make a total: *The bill came to £25 in all.*

in COMPARING AMOUNTS /ɪn/ *prep* used to compare one part of an amount of something with the total amount of it: *Apparently one in ten people/one person in ten has problems with reading.* ○ *UK The basic rate of income tax is 25 pence in (US on) the pound.*

• **be nothing/not much/very little in it** *INFORMAL* said when two things that are being compared are the same or very similar: *One house has a slightly bigger garden, but there's really not much in it.*

in CHARACTERISTIC /ɪn/ *prep* used to show which characteristic or part of a person or thing is being described: *The new version is worse in every respect – I much preferred the original.* ○ *Are the two bags equal in weight?* ○ *She's deaf in her left ear.*

in CAUSE /ɪn/ *prep* [+ v-ing] used to show when doing one thing is the cause of another thing happening: *In refusing* (= Because she refused) *to work abroad, she missed an excellent job opportunity.* ○ *The government banned tobacco advertising and, in doing so* (= because of this), *contributed greatly to the nation's health.*

• **in that** *FORMAL* because: *This research is important in that it confirms the link between aggression and alcohol.*

in FROM OUTSIDE /ɪn/ *adv* from outside, or towards the centre: *Could you bring the clothes in for me?* ○ *The roof of their house caved in during a hurricane.* ○ *Cut the pastry into a square and turn in the corners.*

in SENT /ɪn/ *adv* given or sent to someone official in order to be read: *When does your essay have to be in?* ○ *Remember to get your application in by the end of the week.*

in COAST /ɪn/ *adv* towards the coast, beach or harbour: *The tide comes in very quickly here and you can soon find yourself stranded.* ○ *We stood watching the ship come in.*

in COMPLETION /ɪn/ *adv* used to refer to an activity which makes something complete: *Just pencil in the answer unless you're sure it's correct.* ○ *The text is finished, but*

the pictures will have to be pasted in later. ○ *UK Would you mind filling in a questionnaire about what you watch on television?*

in SPORT /ɪn/ *adv* taking your turn to play, especially taking your turn to hit the ball: *Who's in next for our team?* ○ *It started to rain just as our team was going in to bat.*

in FASHIONABLE /ɪn/ *adj INFORMAL* fashionable or popular: *High heels are in this season.* ○ *The new jazz club seems to be the in place to go at the moment.*

• **be/get in with** *sb INFORMAL* to be or become popular or friendly with someone: *He's always trying to get in with the teachers.*

in AGE/TEMPERATURE /ɪn/ *prep* used when referring approximately to someone's age or the weather temperature: *Nowadays many women are in their late thirties when they have their first child.* ○ *Temperatures will be in the mid-twenties* (= about 25 degrees).

in- LACKING, *BEFORE L* il-, *BEFORE B, M OR P* im-, *BEFORE R* ir- *prefix* used to add the meaning 'not', 'lacking', or 'the opposite of' to adjectives and to words formed from adjectives: *incomplete/incompletely* ○ *illegal/illegally* ○ *impossible/impossibly* ○ *irregular/irregularly* ⊃Compare **dis-**; **non-**; **un-**.

inability /ˌɪn.əˈbɪl.ɪ.ti/ ⓤ /-t̬i/ *noun* [S or U] lack of ability to do something: [+ *to* infinitive] *Inability to use a computer is a serious disadvantage when you are applying for jobs.* ⊃Compare **disability**.

in absentia /ˌɪn.æbˈsen.ti.ə/ /-ʃi.ə/ *adv FORMAL* while the person involved is not present: *An Italian court convicted him in absentia for his terrorist activities.*

inaccessible PLACE /ˌɪn.əkˈses.ɪ.bl̩/ *adj* very difficult or impossible to travel to: *one of the most inaccessible places in the world* ○ *Some of the houses on the hillside are inaccessible to cars.* **inaccessibility** /ˌɪn.ək͵ses.ɪˈbɪl.ɪ.ti/ ⓤ /-ə.t̬i/ *noun* [U]

inaccessible MEANING /ˌɪn.əkˈses.ɪ.bl̩/ *adj* difficult to understand or appreciate: *Why is opera so inaccessible to so many people?* ○ *I found his lecture completely inaccessible.*

inaccurate /ɪˈnæk.jʊ.rət/ ⓤ /-jɚ.ət/ *adj* not completely correct or exact, or not able to do something correctly or exactly: *Their estimate of the cost of the project was wildly* (= extremely) *inaccurate.* ○ *an inaccurate device/ weapon* **inaccurately** /ɪˈnæk.jʊ.rət.li/ ⓤ /-jɚ.ət-/ *adv* **inaccuracy** /ɪˈnæk.jʊ.rə.si/ ⓤ /-jɚ.ə-/ *noun* [C or U] *The film is full of historical inaccuracies.* ○ *The inaccuracy of the missiles greatly diminishes their effectiveness.*

inaction /ɪˈnæk.ʃ⁰n/ *noun* [U] *FORMAL* failure to do anything which might provide a solution to a problem: *The West's inaction has put millions of people at risk of starvation.* ○ *This announcement follows months of inaction and delay.*

inactive /ɪˈnæk.tɪv/ *adj* doing nothing: *It's bad for your health to be physically inactive.* ○ *The property market remains largely inactive.* **inactivity** /ˌɪn.ækˈtɪv.ɪ.ti/ ⓤ /-ə.t̬i/ *noun* [U] *a period of inactivity* ○ *economic/physical inactivity*

inadequate /ɪˈnæd.ɪ.kwət/ *adj* **1** not good enough or too low in quality: *This work is woefully* (= extremely) *inadequate – you'll have to do it again.* ○ *Maddie's a real expert on art, so I feel completely inadequate whenever I talk to her about it.* **2** too small in amount: *She rejected the $2 million offer as totally inadequate.* **inadequately** /ɪˈnæd.ɪ.kwət.li/ *adv: Our scientific research is inadequately funded.* **inadequacy** /ɪˈnæd.ɪ.kwə.si/ *noun* [C or U] *Economic growth is hindered by the inadequacies of the public transport system.* ○ *I always suffer from feelings of inadequacy when I'm with him.*

inadmissible /ˌɪn.ədˈmɪs.ə.bl̩/ *adj FORMAL* unable to be accepted in a law court: *Her confession was ruled inadmissible as evidence because it was given under pressure from the police.*

inadvertent /ˌɪn.ədˈvɜː.t⁰nt/ ⓤ /-ˈvɝː.t̬⁰nt/ *adj* done unintentionally: *All authors need to be wary of inadvertent copying of other people's ideas.* **inadvertently** /ˌɪn.ədˈvɜː.t⁰nt.li/ ⓤ /-ˈvɝː.t̬⁰nt-/ *adv* **inadvertence** /ˌɪn.-ədˈvɜː.t⁰nts/ ⓤ /-ˈvɝː.t̬⁰nts/ *noun* [U]

inadvisable /ˌɪn.ədˈvaɪ.zə.bl̩/ *adj* unwise and likely to have unwanted results and therefore worth avoiding:

Skiing is inadvisable if you have a weak heart. ○ *It is inadvisable* ***to*** *generalize from the results of a single experiment.*

inalienable /ɪˈneɪ.li.ə.nə.bl̩/ *adj* FORMAL unable to be removed: *an inalienable* ***right*** ○ *He maintains that Taiwan has always been an inalienable part of China.*

inane /ɪˈneɪn/ *adj* extremely silly or lacking real meaning or importance: *There are too many inane quiz shows on television these days.* **inanely** /ɪˈneɪn.li/ *adv*: *He grinned inanely.* **inanity** /ɪˈnæn.ə.ti/ [US] /-t̬i/ *noun* [C or U] *His speech was full of inanities that were meant to be funny.* ○ *I was amazed at the inanity of some of her comments.*

inanimate /ɪˈnæn.ɪ.mət/ *adj* possessing none of the characteristics of life that an animal or plant has: *He looks at me as if I'm an inanimate* ***object***.

inapplicable /ˌɪn.əˈplɪk.ə.bl̩/ *adj* not directed at, intended for or suitable for someone or something: *These regulations are inapplicable* ***to*** *visitors from outside the European Community.*

inappropriate /ˌɪn.əˈprəʊ.pri.ət/ [US] /-ˈproʊ-/ *adj* unsuitable: *His casual behaviour was wholly inappropriate* ***for*** *such a formal occasion.* ○ *I think it would be inappropriate* ***(for*** *you)* ***to*** *invite her to a party so soon after her husband's death.* **inappropriately** /ˌɪn.əˈprəʊ.pri.ət.li/ [US] /-ˈproʊ-/ *adv* **inappropriateness** /ˌɪn.əˈprəʊ.pri.ət.nəs/ [US] /-ˈproʊ-/ *noun* [U]

inarticulate /ˌɪn.ɑːˈtɪk.jʊ.lət/ [US] /-ɑːr-/ *adj* unable to express feelings or ideas clearly, or expressed in a way that is difficult to understand: *When it comes to expressing their emotions, most men are hopelessly inarticulate.* ○ *His speech was inarticulate and it was obvious he had been drinking.* **inarticulately** /ˌɪn.ɑːˈtɪk.jʊ.lət.li/ [US] /-ɑːr-/ *adv* **inarticulacy** /ˌɪn.ɑːˈtɪk.ʊ.lə.si/ [US] /-ɑːr-/ *noun* [U] (ALSO **inarticulateness**)

inasmuch as /ɪ.nəˈsmʌtʃ.əz/ *conjunction* FORMAL used to introduce a phrase which explains why or how much something described in another part of the sentence is true: *Inasmuch as you are their commanding officer, you are responsible for the behaviour of these men.*

inattention /ˌɪn.əˈten.tʃən/ *noun* [U] failure to give attention: *Her disappointing exam results are entirely due to her inattention in class.* **inattentive** /ˌɪn.əˈten.tɪv/ [US] /-t̬ɪv/ *adj* DISAPPROVING *He was wholly inattentive* ***to*** *the needs of his children.* **inattentively** /ˌɪn.əˈten.tɪv.li/ [US] /-t̬ɪv-/ *adv*

inaudible /ɪˈnɔː.dɪ.bl̩/ [US] /-ˈnɑː-/ *adj* unable to be heard: *The noise of the machinery made her voice inaudible.* **inaudibly** /ɪˈnɔː.dɪ.bli/ [US] /-ˈnɑː-/ *adv* **inaudibility** /ɪˌnɔː.dəˈbɪl.ɪ.ti/ [US] /-ˌnɑː.dəˈbɪl.ə.t̬i/ *noun* [U]

inaugurate /ɪˈnɔː.gjʊ.reɪt/ [US] /-ˈnɑː-/ *verb* [T] **1** to put someone into an official position with a ceremony: *American presidents are always inaugurated on January 20th.* **2** to put something into use or action officially: *The European Community inaugurated the Single European Market in 1993.* **3** to mark the beginning of a new period, style or activity: *The change of government inaugurated a new era of economic prosperity.* **inauguration** /ɪˌnɔː.gjʊˈreɪ.ʃən/ [US] /-ˌnɑː-/ *noun* [C or U] *an inauguration ceremony* **inaugural** /ɪˈnɔː.gjʊ.rəl/ [US] /-ˈnɑː.gjɚ-/ *adj* [before n] *the President's inaugural address to the nation*

inauspicious /ˌɪn.ɔːˈspɪʃ.əs/ [US] /-ɑː-/ *adj* FORMAL showing signs that something will not be successful or positive: *After an inauspicious* ***start****, Scotland went on to win the match.* **inauspiciously** /ˌɪn.ɔːˈspɪʃ.ə.sli/ [US] /-ɑː-/ *adv*

in-between /ˌɪn.bɪˈtwiːn/ *adj* [before n] between two definite or accepted stages or states, and therefore difficult to describe or know exactly: *He knows quite a lot of French, but he's at an in-between* ***stage*** *and not fluent yet.*

inborn /ˈɪn.bɔːn/ /ˌ-ˈ-/ [US] /ˈɪn.bɔːrn/ *adj* describes a mental or physical characteristic that is possessed from birth: *Apparently some people have an inborn tendency to develop certain kinds of tumour.* ○ *She seems to have an inborn talent for physics.*

inbound /ˈɪn.baʊnd/ *adj* travelling towards a particular point: *We expect delays to both inbound and outbound trains.*

in-box /ˈɪn.bɒks/ [US] /-bɑːks/ *noun* [C] **1** US FOR **in-tray 2** a place on a computer where email messages which are sent to you are kept

inbred [ESTABLISHED] /ˌɪnˈbred/ [US] /ˈ--/ *adj* describes a quality or characteristic firmly established in a person: *an inbred sense of right and wrong* ○ *inbred racism*

inbred [RELATED] /ˌɪnˈbred/ [US] /ˈ--/ *adj* produced by breeding between closely related plants, animals or people: *an inbred population/family/strain*

inbreeding /ˌɪnˈbriː.dɪŋ/ [US] /ˈ-ˌ--/ *noun* [U] when plants, animals or people are inbred: *the dangers/effects of inbreeding*

in-built MAINLY UK /ˈɪn.bɪlt/ *adj* (US USUALLY **built-in**) describes something that is an original part of something or someone which cannot be separated from them: *an in-built advantage/problem*

Inc. /ɪŋk/ *adj* [after n] ABBREVIATION FOR incorporated: used in the names of US companies that are legally established: *Bishop Computer Services, Inc.*

incalculable /ɪnˈkæl.kjʊ.lə.bl̩/ *adj* extremely large and therefore unable to be measured: *The ecological consequences of a nuclear war are incalculable.* **incalculably** /ɪnˈkæl.kjʊ.lə.bli/ *adv*

incandescent [LIGHT] /ˌɪn.kænˈdes.ənt/ *adj* **1** producing a bright light from a heated FILAMENT or other part: *an incandescent lamp* **2** LITERARY extremely bright: *The mountain's snow-white peak was incandescent against the blue sky.* **incandescence** /ˌɪn.kænˈdes.ənts/ *noun* [U]

incandescent [QUALITY] /ˌɪn.kænˈdes.ənt/ *adj* **1** showing extreme anger or happiness: *He was incandescent* ***with rage****.* ○ *Her beauty had an incandescent quality to it.* **2** extremely good, special or skilled: *an incandescent performance/career*

incantation /ˌɪn.kænˈteɪ.ʃən/ *noun* [C or U] (the performance of) words that are believed to have a magical effect when spoken or sung: *Around the fire, tribal elders* ***chanted*** *incantations.*

incapable /ɪnˈkeɪ.pə.bl̩/ *adj* unable to do something: *He seems incapable* ***of*** *walk****ing*** *past a music shop without going in and buying another CD.* ○ *I think she's incapable* ***of*** *love.*

incapacitate /ˌɪn.kəˈpæs.ɪ.teɪt/ *verb* [T often passive] to make someone unable to work or do things normally, or unable to do what they intended to do: *The accident left me incapacitated for seven months.* ○ *Rubber bullets are designed to incapacitate people rather than kill them.* **incapacitating** /ˌɪŋ.kəˈpæs.ɪ.teɪ.tɪŋ/ [US] /-t̬ɪŋ/ *adj*: *Extreme shyness can be very incapacitating.*

incapacity /ˌɪn.kəˈpæs.ə.ti/ [US] /-t̬i/ *noun* [U] when you are unable to do something because you do not have the ability or you are too weak: [+ **to** infinitive] *the incapacity of the police* ***to*** *limit the rise in crime*

incarcerate /ɪnˈkɑː.sər.eɪt/ [US] /-ˈkɑːr.sə.reɪt/ *verb* [T] **1** FORMAL to put or keep someone in prison or in a place used as a prison: *Thousands of dissidents have been interrogated or incarcerated.* **2** to keep someone in an enclosed place and prevent them from leaving it: *We were incarcerated* ***in*** *that broken elevator for four hours.* **incarceration** /ɪnˌkɑː.sərˈeɪ.ʃən/ [US] /-ˌkɑːr.səˈreɪ-/ *noun* [U]

incarnate /ɪnˈkɑː.nət/ [US] /-ˈkɑːr-/ *adj* [after n] in human form: *One survivor described his torturers as* ***devils*** *incarnate.*

incarnation /ˌɪn.kɑːˈneɪ.ʃən/ [US] /-kɑːr-/ *noun* **1** [C] a particular life, in religions that believe that we have many lives: *He believes that he was a Roman warrior in a* ***previous*** *incarnation.* ➲Compare **reincarnation**. **2** [C] a particular physical form or condition of something or someone that is changing or developing: *This film is the latest incarnation of a fairy tale that dates back to the Middle Ages.* **3 the incarnation of** ***sth*** an extreme example, in human form, of a particular characteristic or type of behaviour: *He was* ***the*** *incarnation* ***of*** *evil* (= was extremely evil). ○ *She's* ***the*** *incarnation* ***of*** *everything I hate about politics.* **4** [U] the appearance of a god as a human

incautious /ɪnˈkɔː.ʃəs/ [US] /-ˈkɑː-/ *adj* FORMAL not showing or giving careful thought to the possible results: *Bill and Sandra haven't spoken to each other since he made an incautious* ***remark*** *about her husband's drinking* *problem.* **incautiously** /ɪnˈkɔː.ʃəs.li/ [US] /-ˈkɑː-/ *adv*

incendiary [FIRE] /ɪnˈsen.di.ᵊr.i/ [US] /-er.i/ *adj* **[before n]** designed to cause fires: *an incendiary bomb/device*

incendiary [CAUSING ANGER] /ɪnˈsen.di.ᵊr.i/ [US] /-er.i/ *adj* likely to cause violence or strong feelings of anger: *incendiary remarks*

incense [SUBSTANCE] /ˈɪn.sents/ *noun* **[U]** a substance that is burnt to produce a sweet smell, especially as part of a religious ceremony: *an incense burner/stick*

incense [ANGER] /ɪnˈsents/ *verb* **[T usually passive]** to cause someone to be extremely angry: *The editor said a lot of readers would be incensed by my article on abortion.* ○ *I was so incensed by what he was saying I had to walk out.* **incensed** /ɪnˈsentst/ *adj*: *The villagers are incensed* ***at*** *the decision to close the railway station.*

incentive /ɪnˈsen.tɪv/ [US] /-t̬ɪv/ *noun* **[C or U]** something which encourages a person to do something: ***Tax*** *incentives have been very effective in encouraging people to save and invest more of their income.* ○ **[+ to infinitive]** *There is little incentive* ***for*** *people* ***to*** *leave their cars at home when public transport remains so expensive.* ○ *Bonus payments provide an incentive* ***to*** *work harder.*
incentivize, *UK USUALLY* **-ise** /ɪnˈsen.tɪ.vaɪz/ [US] /-t̬ə-/ *verb* to make someone want to do something: *We need to incentivize our sales managers to achieve these targets.*

inception /ɪnˈsep.ʃᵊn/ *noun* **[S]** the establishment of an organization or official activity: ***Since its*** *inception in 1968, the company has been at the forefront of computer development.*

incessant /ɪnˈses.ᵊnt/ *adj* never stopping, especially in an annoying or unpleasant way: *incessant rain/noise/complaints* **incessantly** /ɪnˈses.ᵊnt.li/ *adv*

incest /ˈɪn.sest/ *noun* **[U]** sexual activity involving people who are closely related and not legally permitted to marry: *a victim of incest*
incestuous /ɪnˈses.tju.əs/ *adj* **1** involving incest: *The film is about Auteil's incestuous love for his sister.* **2** *DISAPPROVING* involving only a close or limited group of people, who do not communicate or do business with people outside the group: *Journalists and politicians often have a rather incestuous* ***relationship***.
incestuously /ɪnˈses.tju.ə.sli/ *adv* **incestuousness** /ɪnˈses.tju.ə.snəs/ *noun* **[U]**

inch [MEASUREMENT] /ɪntʃ/ *noun* **[C]** a unit used for measuring length, which is approximately equal to 2.54 centimetres, sometimes shown by the symbol ″: *Twelve inches are equal to one foot.* ○ *He had a cut an inch long above his left eye.* ○ *The snow was six inches deep in some places.* ○ *a piece of wood 2″ by 2″*
• **by inches** very closely or only just: *The car skidded and I avoided the dog by inches* (= I very nearly hit the dog).
• **come within an inch of *sth*** to very nearly do something, especially something dangerous or exciting: *I came within an inch of losing my life on the rocks below.*
• **every inch** exactly like: *She looked every inch a vampire in her costume.*
• **every inch of *sth/somewhere*** all of a thing or place: *Every inch of her bedroom wall is covered with photos of pop stars.*
• **inch by inch** in great detail and in many very small stages: *Detectives searched the area around the murder scene inch by inch.*
• **not give/budge/move an inch** to not change your opinion: *She's definite that she wants to do it, and she'll not give an inch, however hard you try to persuade her.*
• **Give someone an inch and they'll take a mile.** *SAYING* said about someone who has been given a small amount of power or freedom to do something, and then has tried to obtain a lot more

inch [MOVE] /ɪntʃ/ *verb* **[I or T; + adv or prep]** to move very slowly or in a lot of short stages: *We are inching* ***towards*** *an agreement.* ○ *Share prices inched* ***up/higher*** *during the day.* ○ *Residents watched the flames inch* ***closer*** *and closer.*

inchoate /ɪnˈkəʊ.eɪt/ [US] /-ˈkoʊ-/ *adj LITERARY* only recently or partly formed, or not completely developed or clear: *She had a child's inchoate awareness of language.*

incidence /ˈɪnt.sɪ.dᵊnts/ *noun* **[C usually sing]** *FORMAL* an event, or the rate at which something happens: *There have been quite a few incidences of bullying in the school this year.* ○ *an increased incidence* ***of*** *cancer near nuclear power stations*

incident /ˈɪnt.sɪ.dᵊnt/ *noun* **[C]** an event which is either unpleasant or unusual: *an isolated/serious/unfortunate incident* ○ *A youth was seriously injured in a shooting incident on Saturday night.*
• **without incident** with nothing unpleasant or unusual happening: *Despite fears of violence, the demonstration passed off without incident.*

incidental /ˌɪnt.sɪˈden.tᵊl/ [US] /-t̬ᵊl/ *adj* less important than the thing something is connected with or part of: *Try not to be distracted by incidental details.* ○ *The points you make are true, but they're incidental* ***to*** *the main problem.*
incidentals /ɪn.sɪˈden.tᵊlz/ [US] /-t̬ᵊlz/ *plural noun* incidental details or expenses: *Take some foreign currency to cover incidentals like the taxi fare to your hotel.*

incidentally /ˌɪnt.sɪˈden.tᵊl.i/ [US] /-t̬ᵊl-/ *adv* **1** used before saying something that is not as important as the main subject of conversation, but is connected to it in some way: *We had a marvellous meal at that restaurant you recommended – incidentally, I must give you the number of a similar one I know.* **2** used when mentioning a subject that has not been discussed before, often making it seem less important than it really is: *Incidentally, I wanted to have a word with you about your expenses claim.*

ˌincidental ˈmusic *noun* **[U]** music that is played in the background during a film, broadcast or play to create or strengthen a particular mood

incinerate /ɪnˈsɪn.ᵊr.eɪt/ [US] /-ə.reɪt/ *verb* **[T]** to burn something completely: *to incinerate waste* ○ *The spacecraft and its crew were incinerated by the billion-degree temperatures generated by the fireball.* **incineration** /ɪnˌsɪn.ᵊrˈeɪ.ʃᵊn/ [US] /-əˈreɪ-/ *noun* **[U]**
incinerator /ɪnˈsɪn.ᵊr.eɪ.təʳ/ [US] /-ə.reɪ.t̬ɚ/ *noun* **[C]** a device for burning things which are no longer wanted: *a garbage/hazardous-waste incinerator* ○ *a hospital incinerator*

incipient /ɪnˈsɪp.i.ᵊnt/ *adj FORMAL* just beginning: *signs of incipient public frustration*

incise /ɪnˈsaɪz/ *verb* **[T usually passive]** *FORMAL* to cut the surface of something carefully with a sharp tool: *The design is incised* ***into*** *a metal plate.* ○ *a shield incised* ***with*** *Celtic symbols*
incision /ɪnˈsɪʒ.ᵊn/ *noun* **[C or U]** an opening that is made in something with a sharp tool, especially in someone's body during an operation: *The surgeon* ***makes*** *a small incision into which a tube is inserted.*

incisive /ɪnˈsaɪ.sɪv/ *adj* expressing an idea or opinion in a clear and persuasive way: *incisive questions/comments* **incisively** /ɪnˈsaɪ.sɪv.li/ *adv* **incisiveness** /ɪnˈsaɪ.sɪv.nəs/ *noun* **[U]**

incisor /ɪnˈsaɪ.zəʳ/ [US] /-zɚ/ *noun* **[C]** one of the sharp teeth at the front of the mouth which cut food when you bite into it ➲Compare **canine (tooth)** at **canine**; **molar**.

incite /ɪnˈsaɪt/ *verb* **[T]** to encourage someone to do or feel something unpleasant or violent: *She incited racial hatred by distributing anti-Semitic leaflets.* ○ **[+ to infinitive]** *She was expelled for inciting her classmates* ***to*** *rebel against their teachers.* ○ *They denied inciting the crowd* ***to*** *violence.* **incitement** /ɪnˈsaɪt.mənt/ *noun* **[U]** **[+ to infinitive]** *They were imprisoned for incitement* ***to*** *commit grievous bodily harm.*

incivility /ˌɪn.sɪˈvɪl.ɪ.ti/ [US] /-ə.t̬i/ *noun* **[U]** *FORMAL* rudeness ➲See also **uncivil**.

incl *ABBREVIATION FOR* **including** or **inclusive**: *$449 incl delivery* ○ *car hire £35 per day incl* * NOTE: This abbreviation is used mainly in advertisements.

inclement /ɪnˈklem.ᵊnt/ *adj FORMAL* describes weather which is unpleasant, especially cold or stormy

incline [FEEL] /ɪnˈklaɪn/ *verb* **[I or T; usually + adv or prep]** *FORMAL* to (make someone) tend to feel something or want to do something: *The Prime Minister is believed to be inclining* ***towards*** *an April election.*

inclination /ˌɪn.klɪˈneɪ.ʃⁿn/ noun [C or U] a preference or tendency, or a feeling that makes a person want to do something: [+ to infinitive] My own inclination would be to look for another job. ○ We should be basing our decisions on solid facts, not inclinations and hunches.

inclined /ɪnˈklaɪnd/ adj [after v; + to infinitive] **1** tending or wanting to do something: Tom is inclined to be lazy. ○ No one seemed inclined to help. **2** artistically/technically, etc. inclined having natural artistic/technical, etc. ability: She's very bright, but she's not academically inclined.

incline MOVE /ɪnˈklaɪn/ verb [T] FORMAL **1** to (cause to) slope at a particular angle: The ground inclined steeply towards the ridge in the distance. **2** incline your head to bend your head slightly forward and down: He inclined his head and said nothing.

inclination /ˌɪn.klɪˈneɪ.ʃⁿn/ noun **1** [C] FORMAL a small downwards movement: a solemn inclination of the head **2** [C usually sing; U] SPECIALIZED the angle at which something slopes

incline /ˈɪn.klaɪn/ noun [C] FORMAL a slope: a steep/gentle incline

▲ **incline to/towards** sth phrasal verb FORMAL to think that a belief or opinion is probably correct: I incline to the view that peace can be achieved.

include /ɪnˈkluːd/ verb [T] to contain something as a part of something else, or to make something part of something else: The bill includes tax and service. ○ Tax and service are included in the bill. ○ [+ v-ing] Your responsibilities will include making appointments on her behalf. ⊃Compare **exclude**. See Note **contain or include?** at **contain** HOLD. **including** /ɪnˈkluː.dɪŋ/ prep: Eight people, including two children, were injured in the explosion. **inclusion** /ɪnˈkluː.ʒⁿn/ noun [C or U] She is being considered for inclusion in the England team. ○ Two last-minute inclusions in the team are the Dunstable twins from Bristol.

inclusive /ɪnˈkluː.sɪv/ adj **1** An inclusive price or amount includes everything: My rent is $700 a month inclusive (of bills). **2** [after n] including the first and last date or number stated: I'll be away from the 20th to the 31st of May inclusive. **3** describes a group or organization which tries to include many different types of people and treat them all fairly and equally: Our aim is to create a fairer, more inclusive society.

incognito /ˌɪn.kɒgˈniː.təʊ/ US /-kɑːgˈniː.t̬oʊ/ adv avoiding being recognized, by changing your name or appearance: The prince often travelled abroad incognito.

incoherent /ˌɪn.kəʊˈhɪə.rənt/ US /-koʊˈhɪr.ⁿnt/ adj **1** expressing yourself unclearly: He was confused and incoherent and I didn't get much sense out of him. **2** expressed unclearly, especially with words or ideas that are joined together badly: The talk she gave was incoherent and badly prepared. **incoherently** /ˌɪn.kəʊˈhɪə.rənt.li/ US /-koʊˈhɪr.ⁿnt-/ adv: to mutter incoherently **incoherence** /ˌɪn.kəʊˈhɪə.rⁿnts/ US /-koʊˈhɪr.ⁿnts/ noun [U]

income /ˈɪn.kʌm/ noun [C or U] money that is earned from doing work or received from investments: Average incomes have risen by 4.5% over the past year. ○ More help is needed for people on **low** incomes. ○ I haven't had much income from my stocks and shares this year.

income sup'port noun [U] in the United Kingdom, money that is paid by the government to people who have no income or a very low income: Many single mothers are **on** income support.

income ,tax noun [C or U] a tax that you have to pay on your income, which is usually higher for people with larger incomes

incoming /ˈɪn.kʌm.ɪŋ/ adj [before n] **1** arriving at or coming towards a place: incoming mail/telephone calls ○ an incoming flight **2** soon to start something such as a job because recently chosen or elected: the incoming government ○ What are the biggest problems faced by the incoming president? ○ US Incoming freshmen (= students in the first year at college) start a week before everyone else.

incommunicado /ˌɪn.kəˌmjuː.nɪˈkɑː.dəʊ/ US /-doʊ/ [after v], adv FORMAL not communicating with anyone else because you do not want to or are not allowed to: His secretary says he will be incommunicado for the rest of the day. ○ He was **held** incommunicado for the first 48 hours after he was arrested.

incomparable /ɪnˈkɒm.pⁿr.ə.bl̩/ US /-ˈkɑːm.pɚ-/ adj so good or great that nothing or no one else could achieve the same standard: incomparable beauty/skill ○ the incomparable Mohammed Ali **incomparably** /ɪnˈkɒm.pⁿr.ə.bli/ US /-ˈkɑːm.pɚ-/ adv: His second novel was incomparably better than his first.

incompatible /ˌɪn.kəmˈpæt.ɪ.bl̩/ US /-ˈpæt̬.ə-/ adj not able to exist or work with another person or thing because of basic differences: When we started living together we realized how incompatible we were – our interests were so different. ○ Maintaining quality is incompatible **with** increasing output. ○ Any new video system that is incompatible **with** existing ones has little chance of success. **incompatibility** /ˌɪn.kəmˌpæt.ɪˈbɪl.ɪ.ti/ US /-ˌpæt̬.əˈbɪl.ə.t̬i/ noun [U] An incompatibility problem prevents the two pieces of software from being used together.

incompetence /ɪnˈkɒm.pɪ.tⁿnts/ US /-ˈkɑːm.pə.t̬ənts/ noun [U] lack of ability or skill to do something successfully or as it should be done: Management have demonstrated almost unbelievable incompetence in their handling of the dispute. ○ allegations/accusations of incompetence **incompetent** /ɪnˈkɒm.pɪ.tⁿnt/ US /-ˈkɑːm.pə.t̬ənt/ adj: an incompetent teacher/doctor ○ He has described the government as corrupt and incompetent. **incompetent** /ɪnˈkɒm.pɪ.tⁿnt/ US /-ˈkɑːm.pə.t̬ənt/ noun [C] The country's being governed by a **bunch of** incompetents. **incompetently** /ɪnˈkɒm.pɪ.tⁿnt.li/ US /-ˈkɑːm.pə.t̬ənt-/ adv

incomplete /ˌɪn.kəmˈpliːt/ adj lacking some parts, or not finished: The decision was based on incomplete or inaccurate information. ○ The building is still incomplete. **incompletely** /ˌɪn.kəmˈpliːt.li/ adv: The chemical properties of coal are still incompletely understood. **incompleteness** /ˌɪn.kəmˈpliːt.nəs/ noun [U]

incomprehensible /ɪnˌkɒm.prɪˈhent.sɪ.bl̩/ US /-kɑːm-/ adj impossible or extremely difficult to understand: These accounts are utterly incomprehensible. Can you explain them to me? ○ It's incomprehensible **to** me why he would want to kill himself. **incomprehensibly** /ɪnˌkɒm.prɪˈhent.sɪ.bli/ US /ˌɪn.kɑːm-/ adv **incomprehensibility** /ɪnˌkɒm.prɪˌhent.sɪˈbɪl.ɪ.ti/ US /ˌɪn.kɑːm.prɪ.hent.səˈbɪl.ə.t̬i/ noun [U]

incomprehension /ɪnˌkɒm.prɪˈhen.tʃⁿn/ US /ˌɪn.kɑːm-/ noun [U] FORMAL a person's failure or inability to understand something: She stared at him in total incomprehension. ○ a look of blank incomprehension

inconceivable /ˌɪn.kənˈsiː.və.bl̩/ adj **1** impossible to imagine or think of: The idea that they might not win was inconceivable **to** them. ○ It would be inconceivable **for** her to change her mind. **2** extremely unlikely: Another nuclear accident in the same place is **virtually/almost** inconceivable. ○ It is not inconceivable (= It is possible) **that** she could be lying. **inconceivably** /ˌɪn.kənˈsiː.və.bli/ adv

inconclusive /ˌɪn.kənˈkluː.sɪv/ adj not giving or having a result or decision: The evidence is inconclusive. ○ The medical tests were inconclusive, and will need to be repeated. **inconclusively** /ˌɪn.kənˈkluː.sɪv.li/ adv

incongruous /ɪnˈkɒŋ.gru.əs/ US /-ˈkɑːŋ-/ adj unusual or different from the surroundings or from what is generally happening: The new computer looked incongruous in the dark book-filled library. ○ It **seems** incongruous to have a woman as the editor of a men's magazine. **incongruity** /ˌɪn.kənˈgruː.ə.ti/ US /-kənˈgruː.ə.t̬i/ noun [C or U] FORMAL when something is incongruous

inconsequential /ɪnˌkɒnt.sɪˈkwen.tʃⁿl/ US /-ˌkɑːnt-/ adj not important: an inconsequential matter/remark ○ Most of what she said was pretty inconsequential. **inconsequentially** /ɪnˌkɒnt.sɪˈkwen.tʃⁿl.i/ US /-ˌkɑːnt-/ adv

inconsiderable /ˌɪn.kənˈsɪd.ⁿr.ə.bl̩/ US /-ɚ-/ adj [usually in negatives] very small and therefore unimportant or not worth considering: He inherited a **not** inconsiderable (= a large) **sum/amount**.

inconsiderate /ˌɪn.kənˈsɪd.ⁿr.ət/ US /-ɚ-/ adj DISAPPROVING not caring about other people or their feelings; selfish: Our neighbours are very inconsiderate – they're *always playing loud music late at night.* **inconsiderately** /ˌɪn.kənˈsɪd.ər.ət.li/ [US] /-ɚ-/ *adv*

inconsistent [NOT AGREEING] /ˌɪn.kənˈsɪs.tənt/ *adj* If a reason, idea, opinion, etc. is inconsistent, different parts of it do not agree, or it does not agree with something else: *These findings are inconsistent* ***with*** *those of previous studies.* **inconsistency** /ˌɪn.kənˈsɪs.tənt.si/ *noun* [C or U] *There are a few inconsistencies in what you've written.*

inconsistent [CHANGEABLE] /ˌɪn.kənˈsɪs.tənt/ *adj* not staying the same in behaviour or quality: *The teacher said that Alex's schoolwork was very inconsistent.* ○ *Problems arise if the parents' approach to discipline is inconsistent.* **inconsistency** /ˌɪn.kənˈsɪs.tənt.si/ *noun* [U] *Logan showed his inconsistency in missing half his kicks.* **inconsistently** /ˌɪn.kənˈsɪs.tənt.li/ *adv*

inconsolable /ˌɪn.kənˈsəʊ.lə.bl̩/ [US] /-ˈsoʊ-/ *adj* impossible to comfort because of great sadness or unhappiness: *They were inconsolable after the death of their young son.* **inconsolably** /ˌɪn.kənˈsəʊ.lə.bli/ [US] /-ˈsoʊ-/ *adv*: *The child was crying inconsolably.*

inconspicuous /ˌɪn.kənˈspɪk.ju.əs/ *adj* not easily or quickly noticed or seen; not attracting attention: *This type of bird is very inconspicuous because of its dull feathers.* ○ *At parties, he always stands in a corner and tries to look inconspicuous.* **inconspicuously** /ˌɪn.kənˈspɪk.ju.ə.sli/ *adv*

inconstant /ɪnˈkɒnt.stənt/ [US] /-ˈkɑːnt-/ *adj* LITERARY OR FORMAL not staying the same, especially in emotion, behaviour or choice of sexual partner: *an inconstant lover* **inconstancy** /ɪnˈkɒnt.stənt.si/ [US] /-ˈkɑːnt-/ *noun* [U]

incontestable /ˌɪn.kənˈtes.tə.bl̩/ *adj* FORMAL impossible to question because of being obviously true: *There is now incontestable* ***evidence*** *that the killings did take place.* **incontestably** /ˌɪn.kənˈtes.tə.bli/ *adv*

incontinent /ɪnˈkɒn.tɪ.nənt/ [US] /-ˈkɑːn.tə-/ *adj* unable to control the excretion of urine or the contents of the bowels: *Many of our elderly patients are incontinent.* ○ *As the illness progressed, she became* ***doubly*** *incontinent* (= unable to control the excretion both of urine and the contents of the bowels). **incontinence** /ɪnˈkɒn.tɪ.nənts/ [US] /-ˈkɑːn.tə-/ *noun* [U]

incontrovertible /ɪnˌkɒn.trəˈvɜː.tɪ.bl̩/ [US] /-ˌkɑːn.trəˈvɝː.t̬ə-/ *adj* FORMAL impossible to doubt because of being obviously true: *incontrovertible* ***proof/evidence*** ○ *Her logic is utterly incontrovertible.* **incontrovertibly** /ɪnˌkɒn.trəˈvɜː.tɪ.bli/ [US] /-ˌkɑːn.trəˈvɝː.t̬ə-/ *adv*: *Your assertion is incontrovertibly true.*

inconvenience /ˌɪn.kənˈviː.ni.ənts/ *noun* [C or U] a state or an example of problems or trouble, which often causes a delay or loss of comfort: *We apologize for any inconvenience caused by the late arrival of the train.* ○ *We had the inconvenience of being unable to use the kitchen for several weeks.* ○ *Having to wait for ten minutes was a minor inconvenience.* **inconvenience** /ˌɪn.kənˈviː.ni.ənts/ *verb* [T] *The strike inconvenienced many people.* **inconvenient** /ˌɪn.kənˈviː.ni.ənt/ *adj*: *an inconvenient time/place* ○ ***It*** *will be very inconvenient* ***for*** *me* ***to*** *have no car.* **inconveniently** /ˌɪn.kənˈviː.ni.ənt.li/ *adv*

incorporate /ɪnˈkɔː.pər.eɪt/ [US] /-ˈkɔːr.pɚ-/ *verb* [T] to include something as part of something larger: *Suggestions from the survey have been incorporated* ***into/in*** *the final design.* ○ *This aircraft incorporates several new safety features.* **incorporation** /ɪnˌkɔː.pərˈeɪ.ʃən/ [US] /-ˌkɔːr.pəˈreɪ-/ *noun* [U] *the regular incorporation* ***of*** *organic material into garden soil*

Incorporated /ɪnˈkɔː.pər.eɪ.tɪd/ [US] /-ˈkɔːr.pə.reɪ.t̬ɪd/ *adj* [after n] (ABBREVIATION **Inc.**) used after the name of a company organized as a legal CORPORATION (= a group of people acting as one), especially in business: *Bishop Computer Services Incorporated*

incorporeal /ˌɪn.kɔːˈpɔː.ri.əl/ [US] /ˌɪn.kɔːrˈpɔːr.i-/ *adj* FORMAL not having a physical body but a spiritual form: *In the film, the house was visited by a strange incorporeal being.*

incorrect /ˌɪn.kərˈekt/ [US] /-kəˈrekt/ *adj* **1** not correct or not true: *an incorrect answer/diagnosis* ○ *The assumptions made about the economy's rate of growth* ***proved*** *to be incorrect.* **2** not acceptable or not as it should be: *It's incorrect* ***to*** *address people by their first names at these formal events.* ○ *incorrect grammar* **incorrectly** /ˌɪn.kərˈekt.li/ [US] /-kəˈrekt-/ *adv*: *For many years the sculpture was incorrectly thought to be by Donatello.*

incorrigible /ɪnˈkɒr.ɪ.dʒə.bl̩/ [US] /-ˈkɔːr-/ *adj* MAINLY HUMOROUS An incorrigible person or behaviour is bad and impossible to change or improve: *an incorrigible* ***liar/rogue*** **incorrigibly** /ɪnˈkɒr.ɪ.dʒə.bli/ [US] /-ˈkɔːr-/ *adv*

incorruptible /ˌɪn.kəˈrʌp.tɪ.bl̩/ *adj* **1** morally strong enough not to be persuaded into doing something wrong: *Most politicians genuinely believe they are incorruptible.* **2** FORMAL If something is incorruptible, it will not decay or be destroyed: *Some people think the soul, unlike the body, is incorruptible.* **incorruptibly** /ˌɪn.kəˈrʌp.tɪ.bli/ *adv* **incorruptibility** /ˌɪn.kə.rʌp.tɪˈbɪl.ɪ.ti/ [US] /-ə.t̬i/ *noun* [U]

increase /ɪnˈkriːs/ *verb* [I or T] to (make something) become larger in amount or size: *Incidents of armed robbery have increased over the last few years.* ○ *The cost of the project has increased* ***dramatically/significantly*** *since it began.* ○ *Gradually increase the temperature* ***to*** *boiling point.* ○ *Increased/Increasing efforts are being made to end the dispute.* ➲Compare **decrease**. **increase** /ˈɪn.kriːs/ *noun* [C or U] ***price/tax*** *increases* ○ *There were 39,000 new cases last year – an increase* ***of*** *7 per cent.* ○ *Any increase* ***in*** *production would be helpful.*

• **on the increase** increasing: *Homelessness is on the increase in many cities.*

increasingly /ɪnˈkriː.sɪŋ.li/ *adv* more and more: *to be increasingly important/common* ○ *Increasingly, there is pressure on the council to reverse its decision.*

USAGE

an increase in or an increase of?

The preposition 'in' is used before something that is **increasing**.

an increase in profits/sales

The preposition 'of' is used before the size of the **increase**.

an increase of 10%

incredible [DIFFICULT TO BELIEVE] /ɪnˈkred.ɪ.bl̩/ *adj* impossible, or very difficult, to believe: *an incredible story* ○ *The latest missiles can be fired with incredible accuracy.* ○ ***It*** *seems incredible* ***that*** *no one foresaw the crisis.* **incredibly** /ɪnˈkred.ɪ.bli/ *adv*: *Incredibly, no one was hurt in the accident.*

incredible [EXTREME] /ɪnˈkred.ɪ.bl̩/ *adj* INFORMAL extremely good: *Yeah, it was an incredible performance.* ○ *What an incredible motorbike!*

incredibly /ɪnˈkred.ɪ.bli/ *adv* extremely: *He was incredibly rich/angry/quick.* ○ *An incredibly loud bang followed the flash.*

incredulous /ɪnˈkred.jʊ.ləs/ *adj* not wanting or not able to believe something, and usually showing this: *A few incredulous spectators watched as Paterson, ranked 23rd in the world, beat the champion.* **incredulity** /ˌɪn.krəˈdjuː.lɪ.ti/ [US] /-ˈduː.lə.t̬i/ *noun* [U] *He felt a sense of incredulity, anger and pain at the accusation made against him.* **incredulously** /ɪnˈkred.jʊ.lə.sli/ *adv*: *"Did you see that?" she asked incredulously.*

increment /ˈɪŋ.krə.mənt/ *noun* [C] one of a series of increases: *You will receive annual* ***salary/pay*** *increments every September.*

incremental /ˌɪŋ.krəˈmen.təl/ [US] /-t̬əl/ *adj* in a series of amounts: *Most research proceeds by small incremental advances.* **incrementally** /ˌɪŋ.krəˈmen.təl.i/ [US] /-t̬əl-/ *adv*

incriminate /ɪnˈkrɪm.ɪ.neɪt/ *verb* [T] to make someone seem guilty, especially of a crime: *A secret report incriminating the company was leaked last week.* ○ [R] *He refused to say anything on the grounds that he might incriminate himself.* **incriminating** /ɪnˈkrɪm.ɪ.neɪ.tɪŋ/ [US] /-t̬ɪŋ/ *adj*: *incriminating remarks/statements* **incrimination** /ɪnˌkrɪm.ɪˈneɪ.ʃən/ *noun* [U] ➲See **self-incrimination**.

incrustation /ˌɪn.krʌsˈteɪ.ʃən/ *noun* [C] (US ALSO **encrustation**) a layer of material, such as dirt or a chemical, which forms on something, especially slowly

incubate [EGG] /ˈɪŋ.kjʊ.beɪt/ *verb* [I or T] When a bird, etc. incubates its eggs, it keeps them warm until the young come out, and when eggs incubate, they develop to the stage at which the young come out: *The female bird incubates the eggs for about sixteen days while the male brings food.* **incubation** /ˌɪŋ.kjʊˈbeɪ.ʃᵊn/ *noun* [U] *The incubation **period** varies depending on the time of year when the eggs were laid.*

incubator /ˈɪŋ.kjʊ.beɪ.təʳ/ [US] /-t̬ɚ/ *noun* [C] **1** a container that has controlled air and temperature conditions in which a weak or PREMATURE baby (= one which was born too early) can be kept alive **2** a device for keeping birds' eggs at the correct temperature to enable young birds to develop until they break out of the shell

incubate [DISEASE] /ˈɪŋ.kjʊ.beɪt/ *verb* [I or T] When harmful bacteria or viruses incubate, they grow and reproduce in a human or an animal but do not yet produce the effects of disease, and when the body of a person or animal incubates bacteria or viruses, it has them growing and reproducing inside, but does not yet show the effects of disease. **incubation** /ˌɪŋ.kjʊˈbeɪ.ʃᵊn/ *noun* [U] *In smallpox, there is an incubation **period** of 8-18 days between initial infection and first symptoms.*

inculcate /ˈɪŋ.kʌl.keɪt/ *verb* [T] *FORMAL* to fix beliefs or ideas in someone's mind, especially by repeating them often: *Our football coach has worked hard to inculcate a team spirit **in/into** the players.* **inculcation** /ˌɪŋ.kʌlˈkeɪ.ʃᵊn/ *noun* [U]

incumbent [PERSON] /ɪnˈkʌm.bᵊnt/ *adj* [before n] officially having the named position: *The incumbent president faces problems which began many years before he took office.*

incumbent /ɪnˈkʌm.bᵊnt/ *noun* [C] the person who has or had a particular official position: *the first/last/previous incumbent* ○ *The **present** incumbent **(of** the post) is due to retire next month.*

incumbency /ɪnˈkʌm.bᵊnt.si/ *noun* [C] the period during which someone held a particular position: *During her incumbency (**as** commissioner), several changes were introduced.*

incumbent [NECESSARY] /ɪnˈkʌm.bᵊnt/ *adj FORMAL* **be incumbent on/upon *sb*** to be necessary for someone: *She felt it incumbent upon/on her **to** raise the subject at their meeting.*

incur /ɪnˈkɜːʳ/ [US] /-ˈkɝː/ *verb* [T] **-rr-** *SLIGHTLY FORMAL* to experience something, usually something unpleasant, as a result of actions you have taken: *to incur debts/fines/bills* ○ *The play has incurred **the wrath/anger** of both audiences and critics.* ○ *Please detail any **costs/expenses** incurred by you in attending the interview.*

incurable [DISEASE] /ɪnˈkjʊə.rə.bl̩/ [US] /-ˈkjʊr.ə-/ *adj* not able to be healed or cured: *Parkinson's disease is a debilitating and incurable **disease** of the nervous system.* **incurably** /ɪnˈkjʊə.rə.bli/ [US] /-ˈkjʊr.ə-/ *adv*: *She was told that she was incurably **ill**.*

incurable [PERSONALITY] /ɪnˈkjʊə.rə.bl̩/ [US] /-ˈkjʊr.ə-/ *adj* [usually before n] describes someone whose personality type does not change or cannot be changed: *an incurable romantic/optimist/pessimist* **incurably** /ɪnˈkjʊə.rə.bli/ [US] /-ˈkjʊr.ə-/ *adv*: *He's incurably cheerful.*

incurious /ɪnˈkjʊə.ri.əs/ [US] /-ˈkjʊr.i-/ *adj FORMAL* not interested in knowing what is happening, or not wanting to discover anything new: *He's strangely incurious **about** what goes on around him.*

incursion /ɪnˈkɜː.ʒᵊn/ [US] /-ˈkɝː-/ *noun* [C] **1** a sudden attack on or entry into a place, especially across a border: *incursions **into** enemy territory* **2** *FORMAL* when people suddenly involve themselves in another person's private situation

indebted [GRATEFUL] /ɪnˈdet.ɪd/ [US] /-ˈdet̬-/ *adj* [after v] grateful because of help given: *We're **deeply** indebted **to** you **for** your help.* **indebtedness** /ɪnˈdet.ɪd.nəs/ [US] /-ˈdet̬-/ *noun* [U]

indebted [OWING] /ɪnˈdet.ɪd/ [US] /-ˈdet̬-/ *adj* owing money: *indebted countries* ○ *The company is **heavily** indebted.* **indebtedness** /ɪnˈdet.ɪd.nəs/ [US] /-ˈdet̬-/ *noun* [U]

indecent [IMMORAL] /ɪnˈdiː.sᵊnt/ *adj* morally offensive, especially in a sexual way: *an indecent act/photograph* ○ *She accused him of making indecent suggestions to her.*

indecently /ɪnˈdiː.sᵊnt.li/ *adv*

indecency /ɪnˈdiː.sᵊnt.si/ *noun* [U] indecent behaviour, or when something is indecent: *acts of gross indecency*

indecent [NOT SUITABLE] /ɪnˈdiː.sᵊnt/ *adj* not suitable or correct for a situation: *The premier left his residence with almost indecent **haste** following his resignation.*

inˌdecent asˈsault *noun* [C or U] *UK LEGAL* an attack on someone which usually involves sexual actions but not RAPE (= forced sex)

inˌdecent exˈposure *noun* [U] *LEGAL* when someone shows their sexual organs in public in a way which is intended to upset people

indecipherable /ˌɪn.dɪˈsaɪ.fᵊr.ə.bl̩/ [US] /-fɚ-/ *adj* unable to be read or understood: *Her handwriting is virtually indecipherable.*

indecision /ˌɪn.dɪˈsɪʒ.ᵊn/ *noun* [U] (*ALSO* **indecisiveness**) inability to make a choice: *A moment's indecision when you've got the ball and you could lose the game.* ○ *There is a great deal of indecision **about/over** how to tackle the problem.*

indecisive /ˌɪn.dɪˈsaɪ.sɪv/ *adj* **1** not good at making decisions: *He is widely thought to be an indecisive leader.* **2** not having a clear meaning or producing a decision **indecisively** /ˌɪn.dɪˈsaɪ.sɪv.li/ *adv*

indecorous /ɪnˈdek.ᵊr.əs/ [US] /-ɚ-/ *adj FORMAL* behaving badly or rudely **indecorously** /ɪnˈdek.ᵊr.əs.li/ [US] /-ɚ-/ *adv*

indeed [CERTAINLY] /ɪnˈdiːd/ *adv* **1** really or certainly, often used to emphasize something: *Indeed, it could be the worst environmental disaster in Western Europe this century.* ○ *Evidence suggests that errors may indeed be occurring.* ○ *We live in strange times indeed.* ○ *MAINLY UK Many people are **very** poor indeed.* **2** used to express that something is correct: *"Is this your dog?" "It is indeed."/ "Indeed it is."* ○ *Yes, I did indeed say that.* **3** used to add some extra information which develops or supports something you have just said: *For such creatures, speed is not important – indeed it is counterproductive.* ○ *I am happy, indeed proud, to be associated with this project.*

indeed [EXPRESSION] /ɪnˈdiːd/ *exclamation* used to express surprise, annoyance, or lack of belief or interest: *"She said she won't come back until Monday." "Won't she, indeed?"* ○ *"When will we get a pay rise?" "When indeed?"*

indefatigable /ˌɪn.dɪˈfæt.ɪ.gə.bl̩/ [US] /-ˈfæt̬-/ *adj FORMAL* always determined and energetic in attempting to achieve something and never willing to admit defeat: *Annie was an indefatigable campaigner for better community services.* **indefatigably** /ˌɪn.dɪˈfæt.ɪ.gə.bli/ [US] /-ˈfæt̬-/ *adv*

indefensible /ˌɪn.dɪˈfent.sɪ.bl̩/ *adj* **1** too bad to be protected from criticism: *The war is **morally** indefensible.* ○ *His opinions/attitudes are completely indefensible.* **2** not able to be protected against attack: *indefensible borders* **indefensibly** /ˌɪn.dɪˈfent.sɪ.bli/ *adv*

indefinable, *US ALSO* **undefinable** /ˌɪn.dɪˈfaɪ.nə.bl̩/ /ˌʌn-/ *adj* impossible to clearly describe or explain: *She had that indefinable something that went beyond mere sex appeal.* **indefinably**, *US ALSO* **undefinably** /ˌɪn.dɪˈfaɪ.nə.bli/ /ˌʌn-/ *adv*: *The two versions are indefinably different.*

indefinite /ɪnˈdef.ɪ.nət/ *adj* not exact, not clear, or without clear limits: *The project has been postponed for an indefinite **period**.* ○ *an indefinite **number** of people* **indefinitely** /ɪnˈdef.ɪ.nət.li/ *adv*: *The negotiations have been **put off/postponed** indefinitely.*

inˌdefinite ˈarticle *noun* [C] *SPECIALIZED* the grammatical name for the words "a" and "an" in English or words in other languages which have a similar use ➲Compare **definite article**.

indelible /ɪnˈdel.ɪ.bl̩/ *adj* **1** describes a mark or substance that is impossible to remove by washing or in any other way: *indelible ink* ○ *The blood had left an indelible **mark** on her shirt.* **2** [usually before n] Indelible memories or actions are impossible to forget, or have a permanent influence or effect: *I have an indelible **memory** of that meeting with Anastasia.* ○ *In his twenty years working for the company, Joe Pearson made an indelible **impression** on it.* **indelibly** /ɪnˈdel.ɪ.bli/ *adv*

indelicate /ɪnˈdel.ɪ.kət/ *adj* describes words or actions that are not suitable for a situation and likely to be offensive: *an indelicate comment* ○ *Would **it** be indelicate*

I

to mention the fee at this point? **indelicacy** /ɪnˈdel.ɪ.kə.si/ *noun* [U]

indemnity /ɪnˈdem.nə.ti/ [US] /-t̬i/ *noun* [C or U] FORMAL OR SPECIALIZED protection against possible damage or loss, especially a promise of payment, or the money paid if there is such damage or loss

indemnify /ɪnˈdem.nɪ.faɪ/ *verb* [T] to protect someone or something against possible damage or loss by paying an indemnity to cover the costs: *The insurance also indemnifies the house **against** flooding.*

indent [SPACE] /ɪnˈdent/ *verb* [T] to make a space in the edge or on the surface of something: *Each new paragraph should be indented about two centimetres **from** the margin.* **indentation** /ˌɪn.denˈteɪ.ʃᵊn/ *noun* [C]

indent [REQUEST] /ɪnˈdent/ *verb* [I] UK SPECIALIZED to make an official request for goods: *We indented **for** the engine spares last month.* **indent** /ˈɪn.dent/ *noun* [C] *We **made** an indent **for** the engine spares last week.*

indenture /ɪnˈden.tʃəʳ/ [US] /-tʃɚ/ *verb* [T] MAINLY OLD USE to officially agree that someone, often a young person, will work for someone else, especially in order to learn a job: *He was indentured **to** a carpenter.* ○ *The land was worked on by indentured labourers.*

Indeˈpendence ˌDay [US] *noun* [C] in the US, the official name for the **Fourth of July** holiday

Indeˈpendence ˌDay [OTHER COUNTRIES] *noun* [C] a day on which a country celebrates its independence from foreign rule

independent [NOT INFLUENCED] /ˌɪn.dɪˈpen.dᵊnt/ *adj* **1** not influenced or controlled in any way by other people, events or things: *an independent **enquiry/organization*** ○ *They all made the same comment, quite independent **of** each other* (= without deciding together to do so). **2** describes a politician who does not agree or vote with any particular political party **3** SPECIALIZED describes a grammatical clause which forms part of a sentence but can also form a separate sentence **independently** /ˌɪn.dɪˈpen.dᵊnt.li/ *adv*: *The two scientists both made the same discovery independently, at roughly the same time.* ○ *Each part of the organization operates independently **of** the others.*

independent [NOT RULED] /ˌɪn.dɪˈpen.dᵊnt/ *adj* An independent country is not governed or ruled by another country: *Belize became fully independent **from** Britain in 1981.* ○ *Tibet, once an independent country, is now part of China.* **independence** /ˌɪn.dɪˈpen.dᵊnts/ *noun* [U] *Mexico **gained** its independence **from** Spain in 1821.*

independent [NOT HELPED] /ˌɪn.dɪˈpen.dᵊnt/ *adj* not taking help or money from other people: *Grandma's very independent and does all her own shopping and cooking.* ○ *I've always been **financially** independent.* **independence** /ˌɪn.dɪˈpen.dᵊnts/ *noun* [U] *It's important that parents should allow their children some independence.*

ˌindependent ˈmeans *plural noun* income which you have from investments, etc. rather than from a job: *As a woman **of** independent means, she spent most of her life in voluntary work.* ○ *He **has** independent means.*

ˌindependent ˈschool *noun* [C] in Britain, a school which does not receive money from the government ➲Compare **public school**.

in-depth /ˈɪn.depθ/ *adj* [before n] done carefully and in great detail, or discovering the real reasons which cause something: *an in-depth report/interview/analysis*

indescribable /ˌɪn.dɪˈskraɪ.bə.bl̩/ *adj* impossible to describe, especially because of being extremely good or bad: *a scene of indescribable beauty* ○ *The pain was indescribable.* **indescribably** /ˌɪn.dɪˈskraɪ.bə.bli/ *adv*: *indescribably awful*

indestructible /ˌɪn.dɪˈstrʌk.tɪ.bl̩/ *adj* impossible to destroy or break: *These plastic cups are **virtually** indestructible.* ○ *Whatever the degradation, the human spirit can be indestructible.* **indestructibility** /ˌɪn.dɪ.strʌk.tɪˈbɪl.ɪ.ti/ [US] /-ə.t̬i/ *noun* [U]

indeterminate /ˌɪn.dɪˈtɜː.mɪ.nət/ [US] /-ˈtɝː-/ *adj* not measured, counted or clearly described: *An indeterminate **number** of workers have already been exposed to the danger.* ○ *a man of indeterminate **age*** **indeterminacy** /ˌɪn.dɪˈtɜː.mɪ.nə.si/ [US] /-ˈtɝː-/ *noun* [U]

index [LIST] /ˈɪn.deks/ *noun* [C] *plural* **indices** or **indexes** **1** an alphabetical list, such as one printed at the back of a book showing which page a subject, name, etc. is found on: *Try looking up 'heart disease' **in** the index.* **2** a collection of information stored on a computer or on a set of cards, in alphabetical order: *He has all his friends' names and addresses **on a card** index.*

index /ˈɪn.deks/ *verb* [T] to prepare an index for a book or collection, or arrange it in an index: *Our computer indexes several thousand new records every second.* ○ *The book contains a lot of information, but it's not very well indexed.*

index [COMPARISON] /ˈɪn.deks/ *noun plural* **indices** or **indexes** **1** [C] a system of numbers used for comparing values of things which vary against each other or against a fixed standard: *the FTSE 100 Index* ○ *the Dow Jones Index* ○ *a wage/price index* **2** [C usually sing] something which shows how strong or common a condition or feeling is: *Consumer spending is often a good index **of** public confidence in the economy.*

index /ˈɪn.deks/ *verb* [T] to vary a system of numbers against each other or against a fixed standard: *Living expenses will be indexed **to/in line with** inflation* (= to take inflation into consideration).

indexation /ˌɪn.dekˈseɪ.ʃᵊn/ *noun* [U] when you index a system of numbers: *Indexation of pay rises **to** productivity will give people an incentive to work harder.*

ˈindex ˌfinger *noun* [C] the finger next to the thumb ➲See picture **The Body** on page Centre 5

index-linked UK /ˌɪn.deksˈlɪŋkt/ *adj* (US **indexed**) describes an investment or government payment that changes by the same amount as the general level of prices: *an index-linked pension/benefit*

ˌindex of ˌleading ecoˈnomic ˌindicators *plural noun* the US government's system for describing how active the national economy will be

Indian [INDIA] /ˈɪn.di.ən/ *noun* [C] someone from India

Indian /ˈɪn.di.ən/ *adj* from, belonging to or relating to India: *an Indian family* ○ *the Indian ambassador*

Indian [AMERICA] /ˈɪn.di.ən/ *noun* [C] OFFENSIVE OLD-FASHIONED a **Native American**: *playing cowboys and Indians*

Indian /ˈɪn.di.ən/ *adj* OFFENSIVE OLD-FASHIONED belonging or relating to NATIVE AMERICANS: *an Indian chief*

ˌIndian ˈclub *noun* [C] an object shaped like a bottle, used especially by JUGGLERS (= entertainers who throw objects into the air and catch them)

ˌIndian ˈink UK *noun* [U] (US **India ink**) a thick black ink used especially for drawing

ˌIndian ˈsummer *noun* [C] **1** a period of calm warm weather which sometimes happens in the early autumn **2** a pleasant or successful time nearly at the end of someone's life, job or other period: *A star of the 1960s, she's enjoying an Indian summer with her second highly acclaimed film this year.*

indicate [SHOW] /ˈɪn.dɪ.keɪt/ *verb* [T] to show, point or make clear in another way: *Exploratory investigations have indicated large amounts of oil below the sea bed.* ○ [+ question word] *Please indicate **which** free gift you would like to receive.* ○ [+ (that)] *She indicated **to me (that)** she didn't want me to say anything.* **indication** /ˌɪn.dɪˈkeɪ.ʃᵊn/ *noun* [C or U] *There are few indications **(that)** the economy is on an upswing.* ○ *Helen's face gave no indication **of** what she was thinking.*

indicative /ɪnˈdɪk.ə.tɪv/ [US] /-t̬ɪv/ *adj* being or relating to a sign that something exists, is true, or is likely to happen: *Resumption of the talks is indicative **of** an improving relationship between the countries.* **indicator** /ˈɪn.dɪ.keɪ.təʳ/ [US] /-t̬ɚ/ *noun* [C] *Commodity prices can be a useful indicator **of** inflation, he claimed.* ○ *an economic indicator*

indicate [SIGNAL] /ˈɪn.dɪ.keɪt/ *verb* **1** [I or T] UK to show other road users that you intend to turn left or right when you are driving a vehicle **2** [T] When a device indicates a value or change, it signals it: *The gauge indicates a temperature below freezing point.*

indicator /ˈɪn.dɪ.keɪ.təʳ/ [US] /ˈɪn.dɪ.keɪ.t̬ɚ/ *noun* [C] **1** UK (US **turn signal**) one of the lights at the front and back of a road vehicle which flash to show which way the vehicle is turning ⊃See picture **Car** on page Centre 12 **2** a device which indicates a value or a change in level, speed, etc: *The car has an overhead console with a compass and outside temperature indicator.*

indicate [SUGGEST] /ˈɪn.dɪ.keɪt/ *verb* [T] to suggest something as being suitable: *SPECIALIZED Antihistamine is indicated for this patient as a treatment for her allergies.* ○ *HUMOROUS I'm so hot and tired – I think a long cool drink is indicated!*
indication /ˌɪn.dɪˈkeɪ.ʃən/ *noun* [C] a suitable action that is suggested by something: *The indication from the trade figures is to reduce stock by at least 30%.*

indices /ˈɪn.dɪ.siːz/ *plural of* **index**

indict /ɪnˈdaɪt/ *verb* [T] LEGAL If a law court or a GRAND JURY indicts someone, it accuses them officially of a crime: *UK He was indicted on drug charges at Snaresbrook Crown Court.* ○ *US Five people were indicted for making and selling counterfeit currency.* **indictable** /ɪnˈdaɪ.tə.bl̩/ US /-t̬ə-/ *adj: Robbery is an indictable offence.*
indictment /ɪnˈdaɪt.mənt/ *noun* **1** [C usually sing] a reason for giving blame: *This seems to me to be a damning indictment of education policy.* **2** [C] LEGAL a formal statement of accusation: *The charges on the indictment include murder and attempted murder.*

indie /ˈɪn.di/ *adj* describes music or films made by small companies which are not owned by larger companies: *an indie movie/film/record label* ○ *The popularity of indie bands has soared in recent years.*
indie /ˈɪn.di/ *noun* [C] **1** a small music, film or television company that is not owned by a larger company: *She made five records with indies in the early 90s.* **2** a film or recording made by a small company which is not owned by a larger company

indifferent [NOT INTERESTED] /ɪnˈdɪf.ᵊr.ᵊnt/ /-rənt/ US /-ɚ-/ *adj* not caring about or interested in someone or something: *Why don't you vote – how can you be so indifferent (to what is going on)!* ○ *He found it very hard teaching a class full of indifferent teenagers.* **indifference** /ɪnˈdɪf.ᵊr.ᵊnts/ /-rənts/ US /-ɚ-/ *noun* [U] *Many native speakers of a language show indifference to/towards grammatical points.* ○ *His attitude was one of bored indifference.* **indifferently** /ɪnˈdɪf.ᵊr.ᵊnt.li/ /-rənt-/ US /-ɚ-/ *adv: She shrugged indifferently.*
indifferent [NOT GOOD] /ɪnˈdɪf.ᵊr.ᵊnt/ /-rənt/ US /-ɚ-/ *adj* not good, but not very bad: *We didn't like the restaurant much – the food was indifferent and the service rather slow.* **indifferently** /ɪnˈdɪf.ᵊr.ᵊnt.li/ /-rənt-/ US /-ɚ-/ *adv*

indigenous /ɪnˈdɪdʒ.ɪ.nəs/ *adj* naturally existing in a place or country rather than arriving from another place: *Are there any species of frog indigenous to the area?* ○ *The Maori are the indigenous people of New Zealand.*

indigent /ˈɪn.dɪ.dʒᵊnt/ *adj* FORMAL very poor **indigence** /ˈɪn.dɪ.dʒᵊnts/ *noun* [U]

indigestible [FOOD] /ˌɪn.dɪˈdʒes.tɪ.bl̩/ *adj* describes food that is difficult or impossible for the stomach to break down: *a tough and indigestible piece of steak* **indigestibility** /ˌɪn.dɪ.dʒes.tɪˈbɪl.ɪ.ti/ US /-ə.t̬i/ *noun* [U]
indigestible [INFORMATION] /ˌɪn.dɪˈdʒes.tɪ.bl̩/ *adj* DISAPPROVING describes information that is difficult or impossible to understand: *The statistics are virtually indigestible presented in this form.* **indigestibility** /ˌɪn.dɪ.dʒes.tɪˈbɪl.ɪ.ti/ US /-ə.t̬i/ *noun* [U]

indigestion /ˌɪn.dɪˈdʒes.tʃᵊn/ *noun* [U] pain caused in the region of the stomach by the stomach not correctly breaking down food so that it can be used by the body: *Do you suffer from indigestion after you have eaten?* ○ *You'll give yourself indigestion if you swallow your dinner so quickly.*

indignant /ɪnˈdɪg.nənt/ *adj* angry because of something which is wrong or not fair: *She wrote an indignant letter to the paper complaining about the council's action.* ○ *He became very indignant when it was suggested he had made a mistake.* **indignantly** /ɪnˈdɪg.nənt.li/ *adv: "I said no such thing!" she cried indignantly.* **indignation** /ˌɪn.dɪgˈneɪ.ʃᵊn/ *noun* [U]

indignity /ɪnˈdɪg.nɪ.ti/ US /-nə.t̬i/ *noun* [C or U] a loss of respect or self-respect, or something which causes this: *They were subjected to various indignities and dis-*

comforts, including having to get dressed and undressed in public. ○ *Clint suffered the indignity of being called 'Puppy' in front of his girlfriend.*

indigo /ˈɪn.dɪ.gəʊ/ US /-goʊ/ *adj, noun* [C or U] (having) a bluish purple colour

indirect [NOT OBVIOUS] /ˌɪn.daɪˈrekt/ *adj* **1** happening in addition to an intended result, often in a way that is complicated or not obvious: *The benefits from pure research are often indirect.* ○ *Indirect effects of the fighting include disease and food shortages.* **2** avoiding clearly mentioning or saying something: *indirect criticism* **indirectly** /ˌɪn.daɪˈrekt.li/ *adv: She still controls the company indirectly through her son, who is the managing director.*
indirect [NOT STRAIGHT] /ˌɪn.daɪˈrekt/ *adj* not following a straight line, or not directly or simply connected: *to take an indirect route/flight* **indirectly** *adv*

indirect ˈcost *noun* [C] an amount of money spent by a business on things other than the products they make

indirect ˈobject *noun* [C] SPECIALIZED the person or thing which receives the effect of the action of a verb with two objects: *In the sentence 'Give Val some cake', 'Val' is the indirect object.* ⊃See also **object** GRAMMAR. Compare **direct object**.

indirect ˈspeech *noun* [U] (*UK ALSO* **reported speech**, *US ALSO* **indirect discourse**) SPECIALIZED the act of reporting something that was said, but not using exactly the same words ⊃Compare **direct speech**.

indirect ˈtax *noun* [C] **1** *UK* a tax charged on goods and services rather than on the money that people earn ⊃Compare **direct tax**. **2** *US* a tax charged on goods before they reach their final buyer **indirect taxˈation** *noun* [U]

indiscernible /ˌɪn.dɪˈsɜː.nɪ.bl̩/ US /-ˈsɜːː-/ *adj*: impossible to see, see clearly, or understand: *an indiscernible change/shape/reason*

indiscipline /ɪnˈdɪs.ə.plɪn/ *noun* [U] FORMAL a lack of control or obedience: *The school was given three months to sort out the problem of indiscipline.*

indiscreet /ˌɪn.dɪˈskriːt/ *adj* saying or doing things which let people know things that should be secret or which embarrass people: *In an indiscreet moment, the president let his genuine opinions be known.* ○ *They have been rather indiscreet about their affair.* **indiscreetly** /ˌɪn.dɪˈskriːt.li/ *adv*

indiscretion /ˌɪn.dɪˈskreʃ.ᵊn/ *noun* **1** [U] when a person or their behaviour is indiscreet: *Jones was censured for indiscretion in leaking a secret report to the press.* **2** [C] something, especially a sexual relationship, that is considered embarrassing or morally wrong: *We should forgive him a few youthful indiscretions.*

indiscriminate /ˌɪn.dɪˈskrɪm.ɪ.nət/ *adj* not showing careful thought or planning, especially so that harm results: *an indiscriminate terrorist attack on civilians* ○ *The indiscriminate use of fertilizers can cause longterm problems.* **indiscriminately** /ˌɪn.dɪˈskrɪm.ɪ.nət.li/ *adv: They fired indiscriminately into the crowd.*

indispensable /ˌɪn.dɪˈspent.sə.bl̩/ *adj* Something or someone that is indispensable is so good or important that you consider them to be essential: *This book is an indispensable resource for researchers.* ○ *His long experience at the United Nations makes him indispensable to the talks.* **indispensability** /ˌɪn.dɪ.spent.sɪˈbɪl.ɪ.ti/ US /-ə.t̬i/ *noun* [U]

indisposed [ILL] /ˌɪn.dɪˈspəʊzd/ US /-ˈspoʊzd/ *adj* FORMAL ill, especially in a way that makes you unable to do something: *Sheila Jones is indisposed, so the part of the Countess will be sung tonight by Della Drake.* **indisposition** /ˌɪn.dɪs.pəˈzɪʃ.ᵊn/ *noun* [C or U] FORMAL when someone is indisposed

indisposed [NOT WILLING] /ˌɪn.dɪˈspəʊzd/ US /-ˈspoʊzd/ *adj* [after v; + to infinitive] FORMAL not willing: *After their rude attitude in the past, we feel distinctly indisposed to help them now.* **indisposition** /ˌɪn.dɪs.pəˈzɪʃ.ᵊn/ *noun* [U + to infinitive] *an indisposition to cooperate*

indisputable /ˌɪn.dɪˈspjuː.tə.bl̩/ US /-t̬ə-/ *adj* true, and impossible to doubt: *an artist of indisputable skill* ○ *One fact is indisputable – this must never be allowed to happen again.* **indisputably** /ˌɪn.dɪˈspjuː.tə.bli/ US /-t̬ə-/

adv: Segovia, she said, was indisputably the finest guitar player of the twentieth century.

indissoluble /ˌɪn.dɪˈsɒl.jʊ.bl̩/ [US] /-ˈsɑːl.jə-/ *adj* impossible to take apart or bring to an end; existing for a very long time: *an indissoluble bond of friendship* ○ *The links between the two nations are indissoluble.* **indissolubly** /ˌɪn.dɪˈsɒl.jʊ.bli/ [US] /-ˈsɑːl.jə-/ *adv* **indissolubility** /ˌɪn.dɪ.sɒl.jʊˈbɪl.ɪ.ti/ [US] /-ˌsɑːl.jəˈbɪl.ə.t̬i/ *noun* [U]

indistinct /ˌɪn.dɪˈstɪŋkt/ *adj* not clear: *an indistinct shape/sound/recollection* ⊃Compare **distinct** DIFFERENT; **distinct** NOTICEABLE. **indistinctly** /ˌɪn.dɪˈstɪŋkt.li/ *adv*

indistinguishable /ˌɪn.dɪˈstɪŋ.gwɪ.ʃə.bl̩/ *adj* impossible to judge as being different when compared to another similar thing: *These forgeries are so good that they are more or less indistinguishable* ***from*** *the originals.*

individual [SINGLE] /ˌɪn.dɪˈvɪd.ju.əl/ *noun* [C] a single person or thing, especially when compared to the group or set to which they belong: *Every individual has rights which must never be taken away.* ○ *Like many creative individuals, she can be very bad-tempered.* ○ *We try to treat our students as individuals.*

individual /ˌɪn.dɪˈvɪd.ju.əl/ *adj* [before n] **1** existing and considered separately from the other things or people in a group: *Each individual table is finished by hand.* **2** given to or relating to a single, separate person or thing: *We deal with each case on an individual basis.*

individualized, *UK USUALLY* **-ised** /ˌɪn.dɪˈvɪd.ju.ə.laɪzd/ *adj MAINLY US* prepared or suitable for individual people: *The hospital gives individualized care/attention/treatment to all its patients.*

individually /ˌɪn.dɪˈvɪd.ju.ə.li/ *adv* separately: *The children will first sing individually and then together as a group.*

individual [DIFFERENT] /ˌɪn.dɪˈvɪd.ju.əl/ *adj* belonging or relating to, or suitable for, people or things that are different or particular in some way: *children with individual needs* ○ *Marion has a very individual writing style.*

individual /ˈɪn.dɪˌvɪd.ju.əl/ *noun* [C] a person who thinks or behaves in their own original way: *If nothing else, the school will turn her into an individual.*

individually /ˌɪn.dɪˈvɪd.ju.ə.li/ *adv* in a different and usually original way

individualism /ˌɪn.dɪˈvɪd.ju.ə.lɪ.zᵊm/ *noun* [U] the quality of being different or original

individualist /ˌɪn.dɪˈvɪd.ju.ə.lɪst/ *noun* [C] someone who is different or original **individualistic** /ˌɪn.dɪˌvɪd.ju.əˈlɪs.tɪk/ [US] /-t̬ɪk/ *adj* **individualistically** /ˌɪn.dɪ.vɪd.ju.əˈlɪs.tɪ.kli/ [US] /-t̬ɪ-/ *adv* **individuality** /ˌɪn.dɪ.vɪd.juˈæl.ə.ti/ [US] /-t̬i/ *noun* [U] *It's a competent essay but it* ***lacks*** *individuality.*

indivisible /ˌɪn.dɪˈvɪz.ɪ.bl̩/ *adj* not able to be separated from something else or into different parts: *He regards e-commerce as an indivisible* ***part*** *of modern retail.* ○ *A country's language is indivisible* ***from*** *its culture.* **indivisibly** /ˌɪn.dɪˈvɪz.ɪ.bli/ *adv* **indivisibility** /ˌɪn.dɪ.vɪz.ɪˈbɪl.ɪ.ti/ [US] /-ə.t̬i/ *noun* [U]

Indo- /ɪn.dəʊ-/ *prefix* of or connected with India: *Indo-European languages* ○ *the Indo-Chinese border*

indoctrinate /ɪnˈdɒk.trɪ.neɪt/ [US] /-ˈdɑːk-/ *verb* [T] *DISAPPROVING* to repeat an idea or belief frequently to someone in order to persuade them to accept it: *Some parents were critical of attempts to indoctrinate children* ***in*** *green ideology.* ○ *They have been indoctrinated by television to believe that violence is normal.* **indoctrination** /ɪnˌdɒk.trɪˈneɪ.ʃᵊn/ [US] /-ˌdɑːk-/ *noun* [U] *religious/political/ideological indoctrination*

indolent /ˈɪn.dᵊl.ᵊnt/ *adj LITERARY* lazy; showing no real interest or effort: *an indolent wave of the hand* ○ *an indolent reply* **indolently** /ˈɪn.dᵊl.ᵊnt.li/ *adv* **indolence** /ˈɪn.dᵊl.ᵊnts/ *noun* [U] *After a sudden burst of activity, the team lapsed back into indolence.*

indomitable /ɪnˈdɒm.ɪ.tə.bl̩/ [US] /-ˈdɑː.mə.t̬ə-/ *adj* describes someone strong, brave, determined and difficult to defeat or frighten: *The indomitable Mrs Furlong said she would continue to fight for justice.* **indomitably** /ɪnˈdɒm.ɪ.tə.bli/ [US] /-ˈdɑː.mə.t̬ə-/ *adv*: *indomitably cheerful* ○ *to fight indomitably*

indoor /ˌɪnˈdɔːʳ/ [US] /-ˈdɔːr/ *adj* [before n] happening, used or situated inside a building: *indoor sports/activities* ○ *an indoor racetrack/swimming pool* ✻ NOTE: The opposite is **outdoor**. **indoors** /ˌɪnˈdɔːz/ [US] /-ˈdɔːrz/ *adv*: *Come indoors, it's cold outside.*

indubitable /ɪnˈdjuː.bɪ.tə.bl̩/ [US] /-ˈduː.bɪ.t̬ə-/ *adj FORMAL* that cannot be doubted: *an indubitable fact* **indubitably** /ɪnˈdjuː.bɪ.tə.bli/ [US] /-ˈduː.bɪ.t̬ə-/ *adv*: *He looked different, but it was indubitably John.*

induce /ɪnˈdjuːs/ [US] /-ˈduːs/ *verb FORMAL* **1** [T + obj + *to* infinitive] to persuade someone to do something: *They induced her* ***to*** *take the job by promising editorial freedom.* ○ ***Nothing could*** *induce me* (= I definitely cannot be persuaded) ***to*** *climb a mountain/ride a bike.* **2** [T] to cause something to happen: *Pills for seasickness often induce drowsiness.* **3** [T] to cause a pregnant woman to give birth to her baby earlier than she would naturally, or cause a baby to be born earlier than it would be naturally: *In this hospital, twins are often induced.*

-induced /-ɪn.djuːst/ [US] /-duːst/ *suffix* caused by the stated person or activity: *a self-induced illness* ○ *work-induced stress*

inducement /ɪnˈdjuːs.mᵊnt/ [US] /-ˈduːs-/ *noun* [C or U] an act or thing that is intended to persuade someone or something: ***financial/cash*** *inducements* ○ *Those tenants are not going to swap life-time security for shorter-term leases without some inducement.* ○ [+ *to* infinitive] *They offered voters a massive inducement* ***to*** *oust the president by announcing that sanctions would be lifted if there was 'democratic change'.*

induction /ɪnˈdʌk.ʃᵊn/ *noun* [U] *FORMAL* when an event or process is induced: *the induction* ***of labour***

induct /ɪnˈdʌkt/ *verb* [T] *FORMAL* to introduce someone formally or with a special ceremony to an organization or group, or to beliefs or ideas: *Li Xiannian was inducted* ***into*** *the Politburo in 1956.* **induction** /ɪnˈdʌk.ʃᵊn/ *noun* [C or U] *Their induction* ***into*** *the church took place in June.* ○ *Her induction* ***as*** *councillor took place in the town hall.* ○ *an induction course/program/ceremony*

induction [ELECTRICITY] /ɪnˈdʌk.ʃᵊn/ *noun* [U] *SPECIALIZED* when electrical power goes from one object to another without the objects touching: *an induction coil/motor*

induction [THINKING] /ɪnˈdʌk.ʃᵊn/ *noun* [U] *SPECIALIZED* the process of discovering a general principle from a set of facts **inductive** /ɪnˈdʌk.tɪv/ *adj*: *inductive reasoning* **inductively** /ɪnˈdʌk.tɪv.li/ *adv*

indulge /ɪnˈdʌldʒ/ *verb* **1** [I or T] to allow yourself or another person to have something enjoyable, especially more than is good for you: *The soccer fans indulged their patriotism, waving flags and singing songs.* ○ [R] *I love champagne but I don't often indulge myself.* ○ *We took a deliberate decision to indulge* ***in*** *a little nostalgia.* **2** [T] to give someone anything they want and not to mind if they behave badly: *My aunt indulges the children dreadfully.*

indulgence /ɪnˈdʌl.dʒᵊnts/ *noun* **1** [C or U] when you indulge someone or yourself: *Chocolate is my only indulgence.* ○ *All the pleasures and indulgences of the weekend are over, and I must get down to some serious hard work.* ○ *His health suffered from* ***over****-indulgence* ***in*** (= too much) *rich food and drink.* ⊃See also **self-indulgence**. **2** [U] when you allow or do not mind someone's failure or bad behaviour: *My inability to do needlework was treated with surprising indulgence by my teacher.* **indulgent** /ɪnˈdʌl.dʒᵊnt/ *adj*: *indulgent relatives* ○ *an indulgent smile* ○ *He had been a strict father but was indulgent* ***to/towards*** *his grandchildren.* **indulgently** /ɪnˈdʌl.dʒᵊnt.li/ *adv*

inˌdustrial ˈaction *noun* [U] when workers act in a way that is intended to force an employer to agree to something, especially by stopping work

inˌdustrial ˈespionage *noun* [U] when one company steals secrets from another company with which it is competing

inˈdustrial esˌtate *UK noun* [C] (*US* **industrial park**) a special area on the edge of a town where there are a lot of factories and businesses

inˌdustrial reˈlations *plural noun* the relationships between companies and their workers

the in,dustrial revo'lution *noun* [S] the period of time during which work began to be done more by machines in factories than by hand at home

in'dustrial ,strength *adj* **1** If a product is industrial strength, it is much stronger or more powerful than the product normally available to use: *an industrial-strength cleaner* **2** HUMOROUS extremely strong, or greater than necessary: *She arrived in a cloud of industrial-strength perfume.*

in,dustrial tri'bunal *noun* [C] a type of law court which decides on disagreements between companies and their workers

industrious /ɪnˈdʌs.tri.əs/ *adj* having the characteristic of regularly working hard: *an industrious worker* ○ *She's extremely competent and industrious.* **industriously** /ɪnˈdʌs.tri.ə.sli/ *adv*: *Marco was working industriously at his desk.* **industriousness** /ɪnˈdʌs.tri.ə.snəs/ *noun* [U]

industry /ˈɪn.də.stri/ *noun* [U] FORMAL the quality of regularly working hard ➔See also **industry** PRODUCTION.

industry PRODUCTION /ˈɪn.də.stri/ *noun* [U] the companies and activities involved in the process of producing goods for sale, especially in a factory or special area: *trade and industry* ○ *industry and commerce* ○ *The city needs to attract more industry.* ○ *The strike seriously reduced coal deliveries to industry.* ➔See also **industry** at **industrious**.

industrial /ɪnˈdʌs.tri.əl/ *adj* in or related to industry, or having a lot of industry and factories, etc: *industrial output* ○ *industrial expansion* ○ *an industrial city/country/landscape/nation* ○ *He has an industrial background (= He has worked in industry).* **industrially** /ɪnˈdʌs.tri.ə.li/ *adv*

industrialism /ɪnˈdʌs.tri.ə.lɪ.z²m/ *noun* [U] the idea or state of having a country's economy, society or political system based on industry

industrialist /ɪnˈdʌs.tri.ə.lɪst/ *noun* [C] an owner or an employee in a high position in industry

industrialize, UK USUALLY **-ise** /ɪnˈdʌs.tri.ə.laɪz/ *verb* [I or T] to develop industry: *It was the first country to industrialize.*

industrialized, UK USUALLY **-ised** /ɪnˈdʌs.tri.ə.laɪzd/ *adj* having developed a lot of industry: *industrialized nations/countries*

industrialization, UK USUALLY **-isation** /ɪnˌdʌs.tri.ə.laɪˈzeɪ.ʃ²n/ *noun* [U] the process of developing industries in a country

industry TYPE OF WORK /ˈɪn.də.stri/ *noun* [C] **1** the people and activities involved in one type of business: *the gas/electricity industry* ○ *the tourist industry* ○ *manufacturing industries* ○ *The computer industry has been booming.* **2** DISAPPROVING something which is produced or available in large quantities and which makes a lot of money: *the heritage industry*

inebriated /ɪˈniː.bri.eɪ.tɪd/ ⓤ /-t̬ɪd/ *adj* FORMAL having drunk too much alcohol: *In her inebriated state, she was ready to agree to anything.* **inebriation** /ɪˌniː.briˈeɪ.ʃ²n/ *noun* [U] *He was in an advanced state of inebriation.*

inedible /ɪˈned.ɪ.bl̩/ *adj* not suitable as food: *The meat was inedible.*

ineffable /ɪˈnef.ə.bl̩/ *adj* FORMAL causing so much emotion, especially pleasure, that it cannot be described: *ineffable joy/beauty*

ineffective /ˌɪn.ɪˈfek.tɪv/ *adj* not producing the effects or results that are wanted: *They made an ineffective attempt to get the rules changed.* ○ *The army has **proved** ineffective in protecting the civilian population.* **ineffectively** /ˌɪn.ɪˈfek.tɪv.li/ *adv*

ineffectual /ˌɪn.ɪˈfek.tju.²l/ *adj* FORMAL not skilled at achieving, or not able to produce, good results: *an ineffectual leader* ○ *Several of the teachers were ineffectual **at** maintaining discipline.* **ineffectually** /ˌɪn.ɪˈfek.tju.²l.i/ *adv*

inefficient /ˌɪn.ɪˈfɪʃ.²nt/ *adj* not organized, skilled or able to work satisfactorily: *Existing methods of production are expensive and inefficient.* ○ *I'm hopelessly inefficient **at** mending things.* **inefficiently** /ˌɪn.ɪˈfɪʃ.²nt.li/ *adv*: *The hotel is inefficiently run.* **inefficiency** /ˌɪn.ɪ-*

*ˈfɪʃ.²nt.si/ *noun* [U] *They were accused of **gross** inefficiency in their handling of the case.*

inelegant /ɪˈnel.ɪ.g²nt/ *adj* not pleasing or attractive: *an inelegant posture* ○ *inelegant surroundings*

ineligible /ɪˈnel.ɪ.dʒə.bl̩/ *adj* not allowed to do or have something, according to particular rules: *He was **declared** ineligible **for** the competition because he worked for the company that ran it.* ○ *Many people became ineligible **to** receive state aid because their earnings were above the new limit.* **ineligibility** /ɪˌnel.ɪ.dʒə-ˈbɪl.ɪ.ti/ ⓤ /-t̬i/ *noun* [U]

inept /ɪˈnept/ *adj* not skilled or effective: *an inept **comment/remark*** ○ *He was always rather inept **at** sport.* ○ *He was criticized for his inept **handling** of the situation.* ○ *Dick was **socially** inept and uncomfortable in the presence of women.* **ineptitude** /ɪˈnep.tɪ.tjuːd/ ⓤ /-t̬ɪ.tuːd/ *noun* [U] *political/social/economic ineptitude*

inequality /ˌɪn.ɪˈkwɒl.ə.ti/ ⓤ /-ˈkwɑː.lə.t̬i/ *noun* [C or U] a lack of equality or fair treatment in the sharing of wealth or opportunities between different groups in society: *The law has done little to prevent racial discrimination and inequality.* ○ ***sexual** inequality* ○ *There remain major inequalities of opportunity in the workplace.*

inequitable /ɪˈnek.wɪ.tə.bl̩/ ⓤ /-wə.t̬ə-/ *adj* FORMAL not fair; good for some and bad for others: *The current health care system is inequitable and unjust, with huge disparities between rich and poor.* **inequity** /ɪˈnek.wɪ.ti/ ⓤ /-t̬i/ *noun* [C or U] *inequities in the health care system*

ineradicable /ˌɪn.ɪˈræd.ɪ.kə.bl̩/ *adj* FORMAL not able to be removed: *Some experiences in early life have ineradicable effects.*

inert NOT MOVING /ɪˈnɜːt/ ⓤ /-ˈnɜːt/ *adj* not moving or not able to move: *The inert figure of a man could be seen lying in the front of the car.* **inertly** /ɪˈnɜːt.li/ ⓤ /-ˈnɜːt-/ *adv*

inert CHEMICAL CHARACTERISTIC /ɪˈnɜːt/ ⓤ /-ˈnɜːt/ *adj* SPECIALIZED not reacting chemically with other substances: *inert **gases***

inertia LACK OF ACTIVITY /ɪˈnɜː.ʃə/ ⓤ /-ˈnɜː-/ *noun* [U] lack of activity or interest, or unwillingness to make an effort to do anything: *The organization is stifled by bureaucratic inertia.*

inertia FORCE /ɪˈnɜː.ʃə/ ⓤ /-ˈnɜː-/ *noun* [U] SPECIALIZED the physical force that keeps something in the same position or moving in the same direction

i'nertia ,selling *noun* [U] UK the practice of sending products to people who have not asked for them, and then demanding payment

inescapable /ˌɪn.ɪˈskeɪ.pə.bl̩/ *adj* If a fact or a situation is inescapable, it cannot be ignored or avoided. **inescapably** /ˌɪn.ɪˈskeɪ.pə.bli/ *adv*: *We are inescapably conditioned by our upbringing.*

inessential /ˌɪn.ɪˈsen.tʃ²l/ *adj* not necessary: *make-up and other inessential items* **inessential** /ˌɪn.ɪˈsen.tʃ²l/ *noun* [C]

inestimable /ɪˈnes.tɪ.mə.bl̩/ *adj* FORMAL extremely great, or too great to be described or expressed exactly: *The medical importance of this discovery is **of** inestimable value.* **inestimably** /ɪˈnes.tɪ.mə.bli/ *adv*

inevitable /ɪˈnev.ɪ.tə.bl̩/ ⓤ /-t̬ə-/ *adj* certain to happen and unable to be avoided or prevented: *The accident was the inevitable **consequence/result/outcome** of carelessness.*

● **the inevitable** something that is certain to happen and cannot be prevented: *Eventually the inevitable happened and he had a heart attack.*

inevitably /ɪˈnev.ɪ.tə.bli/ ⓤ /-t̬ə-/ *adv* in a way that cannot be avoided: *Their arguments inevitably end in tears.* **inevitability** /ɪˌnev.ɪ.təˈbɪl.ɪ.ti/ ⓤ /-t̬əˈbɪl.ə.t̬i/ *noun* [U] *the inevitability of change*

inexact /ˌɪn.ɪgˈzækt/ *adj* not exact or not known in detail: *Estimates of the numbers involved remain inexact.*

inexcusable /ˌɪn.ɪkˈskjuː.zə.bl̩/ *adj* (of behaviour) too bad to be accepted: *His drunken outbursts during the mayor's speech were inexcusable.* ○ *It's inexcusable **that** such young children were left in the house alone.*

inexhaustible /ˌɪn.ɪgˈzɔː.stɪ.bl̩/ ⓤ /-ˈzɑː-/ *adj* existing in very great amounts that will never be finished: *There* *seemed to be an inexhaustible* **supply** *of champagne at the wedding.*

inexorable /ɪˈnek.s³r.ə.bl̩/ ⓊⓈ /-sɚ-/ *adj FORMAL* continuing without any possibility of being stopped: *the inexorable progress of science* **inexorably** /ɪˈnek.s³r.ə.bli/ ⓊⓈ /-sɚ-/ *adv: These events led inexorably to war.* **inexorability** /ɪˌnek.s³r.əˈbɪl.ɪ.ti/ ⓊⓈ /-sɚ.əˈbɪl.ə.t̬i/ *noun* [U]

inexpedient /ˌɪn.ɪkˈspiː.di.ənt/ *adj* [+ *to* infinitive] *FORMAL* not suitable or convenient: *It was inexpedient for him to be seen to approve of the decision.*

inexpensive /ˌɪn.ɪkˈspent.sɪv/ *adj* not costing a lot of money: *It's an inexpensive perfume.* ✳ NOTE: This is often used to avoid saying **cheap**, which can sound negative.

inexperience /ˌɪn.ɪkˈspɪə.ri.ənts/ ⓊⓈ /-ˈspɪr.i-/ *noun* [U] lack of knowledge or experience: *As a leader, he's been criticized for his inexperience in foreign affairs.* **inexperienced** /ˌɪn.ɪkˈspɪə.ri.əntst/ ⓊⓈ /-ˈspɪr.i-/ *adj: They are young inexperienced parents and need support.*

inexpert /ɪˈnek.spɜːt/ ⓊⓈ /-spɝːt/ *adj* lacking in skill: *She had made an inexpert attempt to repair the car.* **inexpertly** /ɪˈnek.spɜːt.li/ ⓊⓈ /-spɝːt-/ *adv*

inexplicable /ˌɪn.ɪkˈsplɪk.ə.bl̩/ *adj* unable to be explained or understood: *For some inexplicable reason, he's decided to cancel the project.* **inexplicably** /ˌɪn.ɪkˈsplɪk.ə.bli/ *adv: Inexplicably, the men were never questioned about where the explosives came from.*

inexpressible /ˌɪn.ɪkˈspres.ɪ.bl̩/ *adj* describes a feeling that is too strong to be described: *The news filled him with inexpressible delight/joy/horror/pain.* **inexpressibly** /ˌɪn.ɪkˈspres.ɪ.bli/ *adv: The jokes were inexpressibly awful.*

inexpressive /ˌɪn.ɪkˈspres.ɪv/ *adj* showing no feelings: *Although the shock must have been great, her face remained inexpressive.*

inextinguishable /ˌɪn.ɪkˈstɪŋ.gwɪ.ʃə.bl̩/ *adj* unable to be stopped from burning or existing

in extremis /ˌɪn.ɪkˈstriː.mɪs/ /-ekˈstreɪ-/ *adv* **1** *FORMAL* in an extremely difficult situation: *I'll only ask the bank for a loan in extremis.* **2** *SPECIALIZED* at the point of death

inextricable /ˌɪn.ɪkˈstrɪk.ə.bl̩/ *adj* unable to be separated, freed or escaped from: *In the case of King Arthur, legend and truth are often inextricable.* **inextricably** /ˌɪn.ɪkˈstrɪk.ə.bli/ *adv: His name was inextricably* **linked** *with the environmental movement.*

infallible /ɪnˈfæl.ɪ.bl̩/ *adj* never wrong, failing or making a mistake: *Even the experts are not infallible.* **infallibly** /ɪnˈfæl.ɪ.bli/ *adv* always: *He's infallibly cheerful, despite his difficulties.* **infallibility** /ɪnˌfæl.əˈbɪl.ɪ.ti/ ⓊⓈ /-ə.t̬i/ *noun* [U]

infamous /ˈɪn.fə.məs/ *adj* famous for something considered bad: *The list included the infamous George Drake, a double murderer.* ○ *He's infamous for his bigoted sense of humour.*

infamy /ˈɪn.fə.mi/ *noun FORMAL* **1** [U] when someone or something is famous for something considered bad: *Franklin D. Roosevelt described the bombing of Pearl Harbor in 1947 as 'a day that will live in infamy'.* **2** [C] a bad and shocking act or event: *For the relatives of those who had died in the war, the final infamy was the pardoning of the draft-dodgers.*

infant [YOUNG CHILD] /ˈɪn.fənt/ *noun* [C] a baby or a very young child: *a* **newborn** *infant*

infanticide /ɪnˈfæn.tɪ.saɪd/ ⓊⓈ /-t̬ə-/ *noun* [U] *FORMAL* the crime of killing a child

infantile /ˈɪn.fən.taɪl/ ⓊⓈ /-t̬ᵊl/ *adj DISAPPROVING* typical of a child and therefore unsuitable for an adult: *infantile behaviour*

infancy /ˈɪn.fənt.si/ *noun* [U] the time when someone is a baby or a very young child: *Her youngest child died in infancy.*

● **be in** *its* **infancy** to be very new and still developing: *The system is still in its infancy.*

infant [SCHOOL] /ˈɪn.fənt/ *adj UK* related to or connected with the first stage of school in the UK, for children aged 4 to 7 years: *an infant teacher/class* ➲See also **junior school**.

infant /ˈɪn.fənt/ *noun* [C] *UK* a student at an **infant school**: *Jenny is a top-year infant now.*

the infants *plural noun UK* **infant school**: *Andrew's still in the infants.*

'infant ˌformula *noun* [U] *US FOR* **baby milk**

infantry /ˈɪn.fən.tri/ *group noun* [U] the part of an army that fights on foot: *The infantry was/were sent into battle.* ○ *It's a* **light/heavy** *infantry unit.* ➲Compare **cavalry. infantryman** /ˈɪn.fən.tri.mən/ /-mæn/ *noun* [C]

'infant ˌschool *noun* [C] (*ALSO* **the infants**) in the UK, a school or part of a school for children who are 4 to 7 years old: *Erik starts infant school in September.*

infatuated /ɪnˈfæt.ju.eɪ.tɪd/ ⓊⓈ /-t̬ɪd/ *adj* having a very strong but not usually lasting feeling of love or attraction for someone or something: *She was infatuated* **with** *her boss.* **infatuation** /ɪnˌfæt.juˈeɪ.ʃᵊn/ *noun* [C or U] *It's just an infatuation. She'll get over it.* ○ *No one expected their infatuation* **with** *each other to last.*

infeasible /ɪnˈfiː.zɪ.bl̩/ *adj US for* **unfeasible**

infect /ɪnˈfekt/ *verb* [T] **1** to pass a disease to a person, animal or plant: *The ward was full of children infected* **with** *TB.* ○ *All the tomato plants are infected with a virus.* **2** to make someone have the same feeling or emotion as you: *Her optimism seemed to infect all those around her.* **3** to pass harmful programs from one computer to another, or within files in the same computer: *A computer virus may lurk unseen in a computer's memory, calling up and infecting each of the machine's data files in turn.*

infected /ɪnˈfek.tɪd/ *adj* **1** containing bacteria, dirt or other things that can cause disease: *an infected wound/cut* ○ *After the operation the wound became infected.* **2** An infected computer file contains a computer VIRUS (= a program that can harm computers and their files).

infectious /ɪnˈfek.ʃəs/ *adj* **1** able to infect: *an infectious disease/patient* **2** describes something that has an effect on everyone who is present and makes them want to join in: *an infectious laugh* ○ *infectious enthusiasm*

infection /ɪnˈfek.ʃᵊn/ *noun* [C or U] a disease in a part of your body that is caused by bacteria or a virus: *a serious infection* ○ *a throat infection* ○ *Bandage the wound to reduce the* **risk** *of infection.*

infelicitous /ˌɪn.fəˈlɪs.ɪ.təs/ ⓊⓈ /-t̬əs/ *adj FORMAL* not suitable; not fitting the occasion: *an infelicitous remark* **infelicity** /ˌɪn.fəˈlɪs.ɪ.ti/ ⓊⓈ /-ə.t̬i/ *noun* [C usually pl] *FORMAL His article was full of mistakes and verbal infelicities (= unsuitable expressions).*

infer /ɪnˈfɜːr/ ⓊⓈ /-ˈfɝː/ *verb* [T] *-rr- FORMAL* to form an opinion or guess that something is true because of the information that you have: *What do you infer* **from** *her refusal?* ○ [+ *that*] *I inferred from her expression* **that** *she wanted to leave.* **inference** /ˈɪn.fᵊr.ᵊnts/ ⓊⓈ /-fɚ-/ *noun* [C or U] *They were warned to expect a heavy air attack and* **by inference** *many casualties.* ○ *His change of mind was recent and sudden, the inference being that someone had persuaded him.*

inferior /ɪnˈfɪə.ri.ər/ ⓊⓈ /-ˈfɪr.i.ɚ/ *adj* **1** not good, or not as good as someone or something else: *These products are inferior* **to** *those we bought last year.* ○ *She cited cases in which women had received inferior health care.* ○ *It was clear the group were regarded as* **intellectually/ morally/socially** *inferior.* ➲Compare **superior** BETTER. **2** *SPECIALIZED* lower, or of lower rank: *an inferior officer* ➲Compare **superior** BETTER. **inferiority** /ɪnˌfɪə.riˈɒr.ə.ti/ ⓊⓈ /-ˌfɪr.iˈɔːr.ə.t̬i/ *noun* [U] *His ill treatment as a child had given him a strong* **sense** *of inferiority.* ➲Compare **superiority** at **superior** BETTER.

inferiˈority ˌcomplex *noun* [C] a feeling that you are not as good, as intelligent, as attractive, etc. as other people: *He's always had an inferiority complex* **about** *his height.*

infernal /ɪnˈfɜː.nᵊl/ ⓊⓈ /-ˈfɝː-/ *adj* **1** [before n] *OLD-FASHIONED* very bad or unpleasant: *What an infernal noise!* **2** having the qualities of HELL (= place to which bad people go after death): *He described a journey through the infernal world.*

inferno /ɪnˈfɜː.nəʊ/ ⓊⓈ /-ˈfɝː.noʊ/ *noun* [C] *plural* **infernos** a very large uncontrolled fire: *a raging inferno* ○ *The building was an inferno by the time the fire service arrived.*

infertile /ɪn'fɜː.taɪl/ ⑩ /-'fɝː.t̬əl/ *adj* **1** An infertile person, animal or plant cannot reproduce: *It has been estimated that one in eight couples is infertile.* **2** Infertile land or soil is not good enough for plants or crops to grow well there: *Poor farmers have little option but to try to grow food on these infertile **soils**.* **infertility** /ˌɪn.fə-'tɪl.ɪ.ti/ ⑩ /-fɝː'tɪl.ə.t̬i/ *noun* [U] *male/female infertility*

infer'tility ˌclinic *noun* [C] a special building or part of a hospital where people go to get medical treatment or advice when they are unable to produce children

infest /ɪn'fest/ *verb* [T] (of animals and insects which carry disease) to cause a problem by being present in large numbers: *The barn was infested **with** rats.* **infestation** /ˌɪn.fes'teɪ.ʃən/ *noun* [C or U] *a flea infestation* ○ *an infestation **of** cockroaches/head lice*

infidel /'ɪn.fɪ.dəl/ ⑩ /-fə.del/ *noun* [C or U] *OLD USE DISAPPROVING* (used especially between Christians and Muslims) someone who does not have the same religious beliefs as the person speaking: *He lived among infidels/**the** infidel.* ○ *infidel armies*

infidelity /ˌɪn.fɪ'del.ə.ti/ ⑩ /-fə'del.ə.t̬i/ *noun* [C or U] (an act of) having sex with someone who is not your husband, wife or regular sexual partner, or (an example of) not being loyal or *FAITHFUL*: ***marital/sexual** infidelity* ○ *She could not forgive his many infidelities.*

the infield /ðiː'ɪn.fiːld/ *noun* [S] the part of a cricket or baseball field that is closest to the player who hits the ball, or the group of players there **○**Compare **the outfield**.

infielder /'ɪn.fiːl.dər/ ⑩ /-dɚ/ *noun* [C] (in baseball) an infielder is any of the four players who regularly play between the positions of *FIRST BASE* and third *BASE*

infighting /'ɪn.faɪ.tɪŋ/ ⑩ /-t̬ɪŋ/ *noun* [U] competition between people within a group, especially to improve their own position or to get agreement for their ideas: *political infighting* ○ *Years of infighting **among** the leaders have destroyed the party.*

infiltrate /'ɪn.fɪl.treɪt/ *verb* [I + adv or prep; T] **1** to secretly become part of a group in order to get information or to influence the way that group thinks or behaves: *A journalist managed to infiltrate the powerful drug cartel.* **2** to move slowly into a substance, place, system or organization: *At about this time the new ideas about 'corporate management' had begun to infiltrate **(into)** local government.* **infiltration** /ˌɪn.fɪl'treɪ.ʃən/ *noun* [U] **infiltrator** /'ɪn.fɪl.treɪ.tər/ ⑩ /-t̬ɚ/ *noun* [C] *The infiltrator was identified and killed.*

infinite /'ɪn.fɪ.nət/ *adj* without limits; extremely large or great: *an infinite number/variety* ○ *The universe is theoretically infinite.* ○ *With infinite **patience**, she explained the complex procedure to us.*
● **in *sb's* infinite wisdom** *DISAPPROVING* used to show that you do not understand why someone has done something and that you think it was a stupid action: *The authorities, in their infinite wisdom, decided to close the advice centre.*
● **the Infinite** God
infinitely /'ɪn.fɪ.nət.li/ *adv* very or very much: *Travel is infinitely more comfortable now than it used to be.*

infinitesimal /ˌɪn.fɪ.nɪ'tes.ɪ.məl/ *adj FORMAL* extremely small: *The amounts of radioactivity present were infinitesimal.* **infinitesimally** /ˌɪn.fɪ.nɪ'tes.ɪ.mə.li/ *adv*: *infinitesimally small*

infinitive /ɪn'fɪn.ɪ.tɪv/ ⑩ /-ə.t̬ɪv/ *noun* [C] *SPECIALIZED* the basic form of a verb that usually follows 'to': *In the sentences 'I had to go' and 'I must go', 'go' is an infinitive.* ○ *'Go' is the infinitive **form**.*

infinity /ɪn'fɪn.ɪ.ti/ ⑩ /-ə.t̬i/ *noun* **1** [U] time or space that has no end: *the infinity of the universe* ○ *the concept of infinity* **2** [U] a point which is so far away that it cannot be reached: *FIGURATIVE The mountain range stretched away **into** infinity.* **3** [U] a number that is larger than all other numbers **4** [S] an extremely large number of something: *an infinity of stars in the galaxy*

infirm /ɪn'fɜːm/ ⑩ /-'fɝːm/ *adj FORMAL* ill or needing care, especially for long periods and often because of old age: *She was too elderly and infirm to remain at home.*
the infirm *plural noun* people who are ill for long periods: *The old and the infirm are the most susceptible to this disease.* **infirmity** /ɪn'fɜː.mə.ti/ ⑩ /-'fɝː.mə.t̬i/ *noun* [C or U] *FORMAL* an advanced state of infirmity ○ *She suffered from a long list of infirmities.*

infirmary /ɪn'fɜː.mə.ri/ ⑩ /-'fɝː.mɚ-/ *noun* [C] **1** *UK OLD USE* (especially in names) a hospital: *Leeds General Infirmary* ○ *the Royal Infirmary* **2** *US* In the US, an infirmary is a room in a school, college or university where students who are injured or feeling ill can go to a nurse for treatment.

inflame /ɪn'fleɪm/ *verb* [T] to cause or increase very strong feelings such as anger or excitement: *Reducing the number of staff is certain to inflame the already angry medical profession.* ○ *Pictures of the bombed and burning city inflamed **feelings/passions** further.* **○**See also **inflammatory**.

inflamed /ɪn'fleɪmd/ *adj* (of a part of the body) red, painful and swollen, especially because of infection: *an inflamed eye/toe* ○ *You should call the doctor if the area around the wound becomes inflamed.*

inflammatory /ɪn'flæm.ə.tri/ ⑩ /-tɔːr.i/ *adj SPECIALIZED* causing or related to swelling and pain in the body **○**See also **inflammatory**.

inflammable /ɪn'flæm.ə.bl̩/ *adj* **1** describes something that burns very easily: *a highly inflammable liquid such as petrol* ✲ NOTE: **inflammable** is sometimes wrongly thought to mean 'not easily burned' because of the prefix **in**. However, the opposite of **inflammable** is **non-flammable**. To avoid confusion, **flammable** is often preferred on labels and official notices. **2** likely to become violent or angry very quickly and in an uncontrolled way: *an inflammable situation/region* ○ *a highly inflammable **mix** of intellectual outrage and personal bitterness*

inflammation /ˌɪn.flə'meɪ.ʃən/ *noun* [C or U] a red, painful and often swollen area in or on a part of your body: *Aspirin reduces pain and inflammation.* ○ *an inflammation of the eye/toe/ear*

inflammatory /ɪn'flæm.ə.t̬r.i/ /-tri/ ⑩ /-tɔːr-/ *adj* intended or likely to cause anger or hate: *The men were using inflammatory **language**/making inflammatory **remarks** about the other team's supporters.*

inflate FILL WITH AIR /ɪn'fleɪt/ *verb* [I or T] to cause to increase in size by filling with air: *He inflated the balloons with helium.* ○ *We watch the hot-air balloon slowly inflate.*

inflatable /ɪn'fleɪ.tə.bl̩/ ⑩ /-t̬ə-/ *adj* able to be inflated: *inflatable pillows/mattresses*

inflatable /ɪn'fleɪ.tə.bl̩/ ⑩ /-t̬ə-/ *noun* [C] a boat or something similar which must be filled with air in order to float on the water

inflate MAKE LARGER /ɪn'fleɪt/ *verb* [T] to make something larger or more important: *They inflated their part in the rescue every time they told the story.*

inflated /ɪn'fleɪ.tɪd/ ⑩ /-t̬ɪd/ *adj* Inflated prices, costs, numbers, etc. are higher than they should be, or higher than people think is reasonable.

inflation /ɪn'fleɪ.ʃən/ *noun* [U] a general, continuous increase in prices: *high/low inflation* ○ *the rate of inflation* ○ *Your salary will be increased in line with the 3% inflation expected this autumn.* **○**Compare **deflation** at **deflate** REDUCE MONEY SUPPLY.

inflationary /ɪn'fleɪ.ʃən.ər.i/ ⑩ /-er.i/ *adj* causing price increases and inflation: *inflationary policies/pressures/trends*

in,flationary 'spiral *noun* [C] a situation in which prices increase, then people are paid more in their jobs, which then causes the price of goods and services to increase again, and so on

in,flected 'language *noun* [C] one which changes the form or ending of some words when the way in which they are used in sentences changes: *Latin, Polish and Finnish are all highly inflected languages.*

inflection GRAMMAR, *UK ALSO* **inflexion** /ɪn'flek.ʃən/ *noun* [C] a change in or addition to the form of a word which shows a change in the way it is used in sentences: *If you add the plural inflection '-s' to 'dog' you get 'dogs'.* **inflected** /ɪn'flek.tɪd/ *adj*: *'Finds' and 'found' are inflected forms of 'find'.*

inflection SPEECH, *UK ALSO* **inflexion** /ɪn'flek.ʃən/ *noun* [C or U] the way in which the sound of your voice changes during speech, for example when you emphasize particular words: *His voice was low and flat, with almost no inflection.*

inflexible /ɪnˈflek.sɪ.bl/ *adj* USUALLY DISAPPROVING (especially of opinions and rules) fixed and unable or unwilling to change: *The prime minister has adopted an inflexible position on immigration.* ○ *This type of computer is too slow and inflexible to meet many business needs.* **inflexibility** /ɪnˌflek.sɪˈbɪl.ɪ.ti/ [US] /-ə.t̬i/ *noun* [U]

inflict /ɪnˈflɪkt/ *verb* [T] to force someone to experience something very unpleasant: *These new bullets are capable of inflicting massive injuries.* ○ *The suffering inflicted **on** these children was unimaginable.* **infliction** /ɪnˈflɪk.ʃᵊn/ *noun* [U]

in-flight /ˈɪn.flaɪt/ *adj* [before n] happening or available during a flight: *in-flight **entertainment*** ○ *I always read the in-flight **magazine**.*

inflow /ˈɪn.fləʊ/ [US] /-floʊ/ *noun* [U] the action of people or things arriving somewhere: *The government wanted an inflow **of** foreign investment.*

influence /ˈɪn.flu.ənts/ *noun* [C or U] the power to have an effect on people or things, or a person or thing that is able to do this: *Helen's a **bad/good** influence **on** him.* ○ *He **has** a huge amount of influence **over** the city council.* ○ *Christopher hoped to **exert** his influence to make them change their minds.* ○ *At the time she was **under the** influence **of** her father.*

• **under the influence** drunk: *Driving under the influence is a very serious offence.*

influence /ˈɪn.flu.ənts/ *verb* [T] to affect or change how someone or something develops, behaves or thinks: *She's very good at making friends and influencing people.* ○ [+ obj + *to* infinitive] *What influenced you **to** choose a career in nursing?*

influential /ˌɪn.fluˈen.tʃᵊl/ *adj*: *She wanted to work for a bigger and more influential* (= powerful) *newspaper.* ○ *Johnson was influential* (= important) ***in** persuad**ing** the producers to put money into the film.*

influenza /ˌɪn.fluˈen.zə/ *noun* [U] FORMAL FOR **flu**

influx /ˈɪn.flʌks/ *noun* [U] the arrival of a large number of people or things at the same time: *Turkey is expecting an influx **of** several thousand refugees over the next few days.*

info /ˈɪn.fəʊ/ [US] /-foʊ/ *noun* [U] INFORMAL FOR **information**, see at **inform**

infomercial /ˌɪn.fəʊˈmɜː.ʃᵊl/ [US] /ˈɪn.foʊ.mɝː-/ *noun* [C] MAINLY US an unusually long television advertisement, which contains a lot of information and seems like a normal programme

inform /ɪnˈfɔːm/ [US] /-ˈfɔːrm/ *verb* [T] to tell someone about particular facts: *The name of the dead man will not be released until his relatives have been informed.* ○ *Why wasn't I informed **about** this earlier?* ○ *Walters was not properly informed **of** the reasons for her arrest.* ○ [+ obj + that] *I informed my boss **that** I was going to be away next week.*

informant /ɪnˈfɔː.mənt/ [US] /-ˈfɔːr-/ *noun* [C] someone who gives information to another person or organization: *a police/secret informant* ○ *Our survey is based on information from over 200 informants.*

information /ˌɪn.fəˈmeɪ.ʃᵊn/ [US] /-fɚ-/ *noun* [U] (INFORMAL **info**) facts about a situation, person, event, etc: *Do you have any information **about/on** train times?* ○ *I read an interesting **bit/piece** of information in the newspaper.* ○ ***For further** information* (= if you want to know more), *please contact your local library.* ○ [+ that] *We have reliable information **that** a strike is planned next month.*

informational /ɪn.fəˈmeɪ.ʃᵊn.ᵊl/ [US] /-fɚ-/ *adj* containing information

informative /ɪnˈfɔː.mə.tɪv/ [US] /-ˈfɔːr.mə.t̬ɪv/ *adj* providing a lot of useful information: *This is an interesting and highly informative book.*

informed /ɪnˈfɔːmd/ [US] /-ˈfɔːrmd/ *adj* having a lot of knowledge or information about something: *an informed choice/opinion* ○ *The school promised to **keep** parents informed **about** the situation.* ○ *Elizabeth is remarkably **well**-informed.*

informer /ɪnˈfɔː.məʳ/ [US] /-ˈfɔːr.mɚ/ *noun* [C] a person who gives information in secret, especially to the police: *Most police informers receive a reward for their information.*

COMMON LEARNER ERROR

information

Remember you cannot make **information** plural. Do not say 'informations'.

Could you send me some information about your courses?
For more information please contact our office.
We've been able to find out several pieces of information.
~~*For more informations please contact our office.*~~

▲ **inform against/on *sb*** *phrasal verb* If you inform on/against someone, you give the police information, usually secretly, about that person, showing that he or she has done something wrong: *The terrorists said that anyone caught informing on them would be killed.*

informal /ɪnˈfɔː.məl/ [US] /-ˈfɔːr-/ *adj* (of situations) not formal or official, or (of clothing, behaviour, speech) suitable when you are with friends and family but not for official occasions: *The two groups agreed to hold an informal meeting.* ○ *He's the ideal sort of teacher – direct, friendly and informal.* ○ *'Hi' is an informal way of greeting people.* **informally** /ɪnˈfɔː.məl.i/ [US] /-ˈfɔːr-/ *adv*: *It's an outdoor party, so dress informally.* ○ *They've agreed informally to separate.* **informality** /ˌɪn.fɔːˈmæl.ə.ti/ [US] /-fɔːrˈmæl.ə.t̬i/ *noun* [U]

inforˌmation ˈoverload *noun* [U] when you receive too much information at one time and cannot think about it in a clear way: *Spread your visit to the museum over two days if you want to avoid information overload.*

inforˌmation reˈtrieval *noun* [U] the process of finding stored information on a computer

inforˌmation superˈhighway *noun* [S] all the systems of storing and sending information using computers and other electronic equipment considered as a whole

inforˌmation techˈnology *noun* [U] (ABBREVIATION **IT**) the science and activity of using computers and other electronic equipment to store and send information

informed /ɪnˈfɔːmd/ [US] /-ˈfɔːrmd/ *adj* ➲See at **inform**.

informer /ɪnˈfɔː.məʳ/ [US] /-ˈfɔːr.mɚ/ *noun* [C] ➲See at **inform**.

infotainment /ɪn.fəʊˈteɪn.mənt/ [US] /-foʊ-/ *noun* [U] MAINLY DISAPPROVING (in television) the reporting of news and facts in an entertaining and amusing way rather than providing real information: *It wasn't a real documentary – it was more what you'd call infotainment.*

infraction /ɪnˈfræk.ʃᵊn/ *noun* [C or U] FORMAL when someone breaks a rule or law: *Any attempt to influence the judges will be seen as an infraction **of** the rules.*

infra dig /ˌɪn.frəˈdɪg/ *adj* [after v] UK OLD-FASHIONED below what you consider to be socially acceptable: [+ *to* infinitive] *Diane thinks it's a bit infra dig **to** do her own housework.*

infrared /ˌɪn.frəˈred/ *adj* a type of light that feels warm but cannot be seen: *Their pilots are guided by an infrared optical system that shows images clearly even at night.*

infrastructure /ˈɪn.frəˌstrʌk.tʃəʳ/ [US] /-tʃɚ/ *noun* [C usually sing] the basic systems and services, such as transport and power supplies, that a country or organization uses in order to work effectively: *The war has badly damaged the country's infrastructure.*

infrequent /ɪnˈfriː.kwənt/ *adj* not happening very often: *His letters became infrequent, then stopped completely.* **infrequently** /ɪnˈfriː.kwənt.li/ *adv*

infringe /ɪnˈfrɪndʒ/ *verb* [T] FORMAL to break a rule, law, etc: *They infringed building regulations.* **infringement** /ɪnˈfrɪndʒ.mənt/ *noun* [C or U] *copyright infringement* ○ *Even minor infringements **of** the law will be severely punished.*

▲ **infringe on/upon *sth*** *phrasal verb* FORMAL If something infringes on/upon someone's rights or freedom, it takes away some of their rights or limits their freedom: *These restrictions infringe upon basic human rights.*

infuriate /ɪnˈfjʊə.ri.eɪt/ [US] /-ˈfjʊr.i-/ *verb* [T] to make someone extremely angry: *His sexist attitude infuriates me.* **infuriating** /ɪnˈfjʊə.ri.eɪ.tɪŋ/ [US] /-ˈfjʊr.i.eɪ.t̬ɪŋ/ *adj*:

It's infuriating when people keep spelling your name wrong, isn't it?

infuse /ɪn'fjuːz/ *verb* **1** [T + obj + prep] to fill someone or something with an emotion or quality: *The pulling down of the Berlin Wall infused the world* ***with*** *optimism.* ○ *The arrival of a group of friends on Saturday infused new life* ***into*** *the weekend.* **2** [I or T] If you infuse a drink or it infuses, you leave substances such as tea leaves or herbs in hot water so that their flavour goes into the liquid: *Allow the tea to infuse for five minutes.*

infusion /ɪn'fjuː.ʒən/ *noun* [C or U] when one thing is added to another to make it stronger or better: *An infusion of $100 000* ***into*** *the company is required.* ○ *She drinks an infusion of herbs* (= a drink made by leaving herbs in hot water).

-ing /-ɪŋ/ *suffix* used to form the present participle of regular verbs: *calling* ○ *asking*

ingenious /ɪn'dʒiː.ni.əs/ *adj* (of a person) very clever and skilful, or (of a thing) cleverly made or planned and involving new ideas and methods: *an ingenious idea/method/solution* ○ *Johnny is so ingenious – he can make the most remarkable sculptures from the most ordinary materials.* **ingeniously** /ɪn'dʒiː.ni.ə.sli/ *adv*: *The umbrella was ingeniously devised to fold up into your pocket.*

ingenuity /ˌɪn.dʒə'njuː.ɪ.ti/ [US] /-ə.t̬i/ *noun* [U] someone's ability to think of clever new ways of doing something: *Drug smugglers constantly use their ingenuity to find new ways of getting drugs into a country.*

ingenue /'æn.ʒeɪ.nuː/ [US] /'æn.ʒə-/ *noun* [C] FORMAL a young woman who lacks experience and is very trusting, especially as played in films and plays

ingenuous /ɪn'dʒen.ju.əs/ *adj* FORMAL honest, sincere and trusting, sometimes in a way that seems foolish: *It has to be said it was rather ingenuous of him to ask a complete stranger to look after his luggage.* **ingenuously** /ɪn'dʒen.ju.ə.sli/ *adv*

ingest /ɪn'dʒest/ *verb* [T] SPECIALIZED to eat or drink something: *The chemicals can be poisonous if ingested.* **ingestion** /ɪn'dʒes.tʃən/ *noun* [U]

inglenook /'ɪŋ.gl̩.nʊk/ *noun* [C] a partly enclosed space by a large open fireplace built so that you can sit close to the fire

inglorious /ɪn'glɔː.ri.əs/ [US] /-'glɔːr.i-/ *adj* not honourable or not to be proud of: *That country has a long, inglorious record of dealing harshly with political prisoners.*

ingot /'ɪŋ.gət/ *noun* [C] a piece of metal, usually in the shape of a narrow brick: *a gold/silver ingot*

ingrained /ɪn'greɪnd/ *adj* **1** (of beliefs) so firmly held that they are not likely to change: *Such ingrained prejudices cannot be corrected easily.* ○ *The belief that you should own your house is* ***deeply*** *ingrained* ***in*** *British society.* **2** Ingrained dirt has got under the surface of something and is difficult to remove: *The oil had become ingrained* ***in*** *his skin.*

ingrate /'ɪŋ.greɪt/ *noun* [C] LITERARY a person who is not grateful

ingratiate *yourself* /ɪŋ'greɪ.ʃiː.eɪt/ *verb* [R] DISAPPROVING to make someone like you by praising or trying to please them: *He's always trying to ingratiate himself* ***with*** *his boss.*

ingratiating /ɪn'greɪ.ʃiː.eɪ.tɪŋ/ [US] /-t̬ɪŋ/ *adj* DISAPPROVING describes behaviour that is intended to make people like you: *an ingratiating smile/manner*

ingratitude /ɪn'græt.ɪ.tjuːd/ [US] /-'græt̬.ə.tuːd/ *noun* [U] when someone is not grateful for something

ingredient /ɪn'griː.di.ənt/ *noun* [C] **1** a food that is used with other foods in the preparation of a particular dish: *The* ***list of*** *ingredients included 250g of almonds.* **2** one of the parts of something successful: *Trust is a vital ingredient in a successful marriage.*

in-group /'ɪn.gruːp/ *noun* [C] MAINLY DISAPPROVING a social group whose members are very loyal to each other and share a lot of interests, and who usually try to keep other people out of the group

ingrowing /'ɪŋˌgrəʊ.ɪŋ/ [US] /-groʊ-/ *adj* (US USUALLY **ingrown**) growing into the flesh: *She's having an operation on an ingrowing* ***toenail.*** ○ *an ingrowing hair*

inhabit /ɪn'hæb.ɪt/ *verb* [T often passive] to live in a place: *These remote islands are inhabited only by birds and small animals.*

inhabitant /ɪn'hæb.ɪ.tənt/ *noun* [C] a person or animal that lives in a particular place: *a city of 5 million inhabitants*

inhabitable /ɪn'hæb.ɪ.tə.bl̩/ [US] /-t̬ə-/ *adj* able to be lived in or on * NOTE: The opposite is **uninhabitable**.

inhale /ɪn'heɪl/ *verb* [I or T] to breathe air, smoke, or gas into your lungs: *She flung open the window and inhaled deeply.* ○ *She became ill shortly after inhaling the fumes.* ⊃Compare **exhale**. **inhalation** /ˌɪn.hə'leɪ.ʃən/ *noun* [U] *Two firefighters were treated for* ***smoke*** *inhalation.*

inhaler /ɪn'heɪ.lər/ [US] /-lɚ/ *noun* [C] a small device you use to breathe in particular medicines

inherent /ɪn'her.ənt/ /-'hɪə.rənt/ [US] /-'hɪr.ənt/ *adj* existing as a natural or basic part of something: *There are* ***dangers/risks*** *inherent* ***in*** *almost every sport.* ○ *I have an inherent distrust of lawyers.* **inherently** /ɪn'her.ənt.li/ *adv*: *There's nothing inherently wrong with his ideas.*

inherit [FROM DEAD PERSON] /ɪn'her.ɪt/ *verb* [I or T] to receive money, a house, etc. from someone after they have died: *Who will inherit the house when he dies?* ○ *All her children will inherit equally.*

inheritance /ɪn'her.ɪ.tənts/ *noun* [C usually sing; U] money or objects that someone gives you when they die: *The large inheritance* ***from*** *his aunt meant that he could buy his own boat.* ○ *At twenty-one she* ***came into*** *her inheritance* (= it was given to her).

inheritor /ɪn'her.ɪ.tər/ [US] /-t̬ɚ/ *noun* [C] a person who has been given something by someone who is dead: FIGURATIVE *We are the inheritors* ***of*** *Greek and Roman culture.*

inherit [QUALITY] /ɪn'her.ɪt/ *verb* [T] to be born with the same physical or mental characteristics as one of your parents or grandparents: *Rosie inherited her red hair* ***from*** *her mother.*

inheritance /ɪn'her.ɪ.tənts/ *noun* [C usually sing; U] a physical or mental characteristic inherited from your parents, or the process by which this happens: *genetic inheritance* ○ *A particular gene is responsible for the inheritance of eye colour.*

inherit [PROBLEM] /ɪn'her.ɪt/ *verb* [T] to begin to have responsibility for a problem or situation that previously existed or belonged to another person: *When I took on the job of manager, I inherited certain financial problems.*

in'heritance ˌtax *noun* [C or U] a tax paid on money or property you have received from someone who has died

inhibit /ɪn'hɪb.ɪt/ *verb* [T] to prevent someone from doing something, or to slow down a process or the growth of something: *Some workers were inhibited* ***(from*** *speaking) by the presence of their managers.* ○ *This drug inhibits the growth of tumours.*

inhibited /ɪn'hɪb.ɪ.tɪd/ [US] /-t̬ɪd/ *adj* not confident enough to say or do what you want: *The presence of strangers made her feel inhibited.*

inhibition /ˌɪn.hɪ'bɪʃ.ən/ *noun* [C or U] a feeling of embarrassment or worry that prevents you from saying or doing what you want: *After a couple of drinks he* ***lost*** *his inhibition and started talking and laughing loudly.* ○ *She was determined to shed her inhibitions and have a good time.*

in-home /ˌɪn'həʊm/ [US] /-'hoʊm/ *adj* [before n] US provided at someone's home: *in-home care for the disabled*

inhospitable /ˌɪn.hɒs'pɪt.ə.bl̩/ /ˌɪn.hɑː'spɪt̬-/ *adj* **1** not welcoming or generous to people who visit you: *I'll have to cook them a meal or they'll think I'm inhospitable.* **2** describes an area which is not suitable for humans to live in: *They had to trek for miles through inhospitable countryside.*

in-house /ˌɪn'haʊs/ *adj, adv* Something that is done in-house is done within an organization or business by its employees rather than by other people: *an in-house training scheme* ○ *All our advertising material is designed in-house.*

inhuman /ɪn'hjuː.mən/ *adj* extremely cruel, or not human in an unusual or frightening way: *Prisoners of war were subjected to inhuman and degrading treatment.*

○ *Most people feel that there is something almost inhuman about perfection.*

inhumanity /ˌɪn.hjʊˈmæn.ə.ti/ [US] /-ə.t̬i/ *noun* [U] extremely cruel behaviour: *They were accused of inhumanity in their treatment of the hostages.*

inhumane /ˌɪn.hjʊˈmeɪn/ *adj* cruel and not caring about the suffering of people or animals: *Conditions for prisoners were described as inhumane.* ○ *Many people believe factory farming is inhumane.* **inhumanely** /ˌɪn.hjʊˈmeɪn.li/ *adv*

inimical /ɪˈnɪm.ɪ.kəl/ *adj* FORMAL harmful or limiting: *Excessive managerial control is inimical **to** creative expression.*

inimitable /ɪˈnɪm.ɪ.tə.bl̩/ [US] /-t̬ə-/ *adj* very unusual or of very high quality and therefore impossible to copy: *He was describing, in his **own** inimitable **style/way**, how to write a best-selling novel.* ○ *She appeared at the Oscar's wearing one of Versace's inimitable creations.*

iniquitous /ɪˈnɪk.wɪ.təs/ [US] /-t̬əs/ *adj* FORMAL very wrong and unfair: *It is an iniquitous **system** that allows a person to die because they have no money to pay for medicine.* **iniquity** /ɪˈnɪk.wə.ti/ [US] /-t̬i/ *noun* [C or U] *They fought long and hard against the iniquities of apartheid.* ○ *The writer reflects on human injustice and iniquity.*

initial [BEGINNING] /ɪˈnɪʃ.əl/ *adj* [before n] of or at the beginning: *My initial surprise was soon replaced by delight.* ○ *Initial reports say that seven people have died, though this has not yet been confirmed.*

initially /ɪˈnɪʃ.əl.i/ *adv* at the beginning: *Initially, most people approved of the new scheme.* ○ *The damage was far more serious than initially believed.*

initial [FIRST LETTER] /ɪˈnɪʃ.əl/ *noun* [C usually pl] the first letter of a name, especially when used to represent a name: *He wrote his initials, P.M.R., at the bottom of the page.* ○ *Paul M. Reynolds refused to say what the initial "M" **stood for**.* ○ *They carved their initials into a tree.*

initial /ɪˈnɪʃ.əl/ *verb* [T] **-ll-** or US USUALLY **-l-** to write your initials on something: *I initialled the documents and returned them to personnel.*

initialize /ɪˈnɪʃ.əl.aɪz/ *verb* [T] SPECIALIZED to set the numbers, amounts etc. in a computer program so that it is ready to start working

initiate [START] /ɪˈnɪʃ.i.eɪt/ *verb* [T] SLIGHTLY FORMAL to cause something to begin: *Who initiated the violence?*

initiation /ɪˌnɪʃ.iˈeɪ.ʃən/ *noun* [U] FORMAL when something starts: *Lawyers for the couple have announced the initiation of divorce proceedings.*

initiate [TEACH] /ɪˈnɪʃ.i.eɪt/ *verb* [T] to teach someone about an area of knowledge, or to allow someone into a group by a special ceremony: *At the age of eleven, Harry was initiated **into** the art of golf by his father.* ○ *Each culture had a special ritual to initiate boys **into** manhood.*

initiate /ɪˈnɪʃ.i.ət/ *noun* [C] FORMAL a person who has recently joined a group and has been taught its secrets

initiation /ɪˌnɪʃ.iˈeɪ.ʃən/ *noun* [C or U] when someone is first introduced to an activity or skill: *My initiation **into** the mysteries of home brewing was not a success.*

initiˈation ˌceremony *noun* [C] a process or event that a person takes part in to become an official member of a group

initiative [JUDGMENT] /ɪˈnɪʃ.ə.tɪv/ [US] /-t̬ɪv/ *noun* [U] **1** the ability to use your judgment to make decisions and do things without needing to be told what to do: *Although she was quite young, she **showed** a lot of initiative and was promoted to manager after a year.* ○ *I shouldn't always have to tell you what to do, **use** your initiative* (= use your own judgment to decide what to do)*!* **2 on your own initiative** If you do something on your own initiative, you plan it and decide to do it yourself without anyone telling you what to do.

initiative [NEW ACTION] /ɪˈnɪʃ.ə.tɪv/ [US] /-t̬ɪv/ *noun* [C] a new action or movement, often intended to solve a problem: *The **peace** initiative was welcomed by both sides.*

the initiative [ADVANTAGE] *noun* [S] the power or opportunity to gain an advantage: *to **seize/take/lose** the initiative*

inject [DRUG] /ɪnˈdʒekt/ *verb* [T] to use a needle and SYRINGE (= small tube) to put a liquid such as a drug into a person's body: *Phil's a diabetic and has to inject himself **with** insulin every day.*

injection /ɪnˈdʒek.ʃən/ *noun* [C or U] when someone puts a liquid, especially a drug, into a person's body using a needle and a SYRINGE (= small tube): *Daily insulin injections are necessary for some diabetics.* ○ *This steroid is sometimes given **by** injection.*

inject [SOMETHING NEW] /ɪnˈdʒekt/ *verb* [T] to introduce something new that is necessary or helpful to a situation or process: *A large amount of money will have to be injected **into** the company if it is to survive.* ○ *I tried to inject a little humour **into** the meeting.* **injection** /ɪnˈdʒek.ʃən/ *noun* [C or U] *A cash injection of £20 million will be used to improve the health service.* ○ *an injection of humour/excitement*

in-joke /ˈɪn.dʒəʊk/ [US] /-dʒoʊk/ *noun* [C] a private joke which can only be understood by a limited group of people who have a special knowledge of something that is referred to in the joke

injudicious /ˌɪn.dʒuːˈdɪʃ.əs/ *adj* FORMAL unwise; showing bad judgment: *an injudicious remark*

injunction /ɪnˈdʒʌŋk.ʃən/ *noun* [C] an official order given by a court of law, usually to stop someone from doing something: [+ *to* infinitive] *The court has **issued** an injunction **to** prevent the airline from increasing its prices.* ○ [+ *v-ing*] *She is **seeking** an injunction bann**ing** the newspaper from publishing the photographs.*

injure /ˈɪn.dʒər/ [US] /-dʒɚ/ *verb* [T] to hurt or cause physical harm to a person or animal: *A bomb exploded at the embassy, injuring several people.* ○ *She fell and injured her shoulder.* ○ *He was badly injured in the crash.* ○ *He claimed that working too hard was injuring his health.*

injured /ˈɪn.dʒəd/ [US] /-dʒɚd/ *adj* hurt or physically harmed: *She was told to stay in bed to rest her injured back.*

the injured *plural noun* people who are injured, considered as a group: *The injured were taken to several nearby hospitals.*

injured /ˈɪn.dʒəd/ [US] /-dʒɚd/ *adj* If your feelings are injured, someone has offended or upset you.

injury /ˈɪn.dʒər.i/ [US] /-dʒɚ-/ *noun* [C or U] physical harm or damage to someone's body caused by an accident or an attack: *a head/back/knee injury* ○ *Several train passengers **received/sustained** serious injuries in the crash.* ○ *Injuries **to** the spine are common amongst these workers.* ○ *They were lucky to **escape** (without) injury.*

• **do *yourself* an injury** UK INFORMAL to hurt yourself: *Don't even think about lifting me up, Ted, you might do yourself an injury.*

injurious /ɪnˈdʒʊə.ri.əs/ [US] /-ˈdʒʊr.i-/ *adj* FORMAL harmful: *Too much alcohol is injurious **to** your health.*

ˈinjury ˌtime *noun* [U] UK a period of time added to the end of a sports game because play was stopped during the game to take care of players who were hurt

injustice /ɪnˈdʒʌs.tɪs/ *noun* [C or U] (an example of) lack of fairness and lack of justice: *The sight of people suffering arouses a deep **sense of** injustice in her.* ○ *They were aware of the injustices of the system.* ➲See also **unjust**.

ink /ɪŋk/ *noun* [C or U] coloured liquid used for writing, printing and drawing: *a bottle of ink* ○ *blue/black/red ink* ○ *Please write **in** ink, not in pencil.* ○ *The book is printed in three different coloured inks.*

ink /ɪŋk/ *verb* [T] SPECIALIZED to put ink on something: *The printing plates have to be inked before they will print on the paper.*

inky /ˈɪŋ.ki/ *adj* **1** covered with ink: *inky stains/fingers* **2** LITERARY very dark: *It was night and the water looked cold and inky **black**.*

ink-jet printer /ˈɪŋk.dʒetˌprɪn.tər/ [US] /-ˌprɪn.t̬ɚ/ *noun* [C] SPECIALIZED an electronic printer which blows ink onto paper using very small JETS (= small openings which push out liquid)

inkling /ˈɪŋ.klɪŋ/ *noun* [C usually sing; U] when you think that something is true or likely to happen, although you are not certain: [+ *that*] *I didn't **have** the slightest inkling **that** she was unhappy.* ○ *He must have had some inkling **of** what was happening.*

inkstand /ˈɪŋk.stænd/ *noun* [C] a container for bottles of ink, pens and pencils, etc.

inkwell /ˈɪŋk.wel/ *noun* [C] a container for ink, used in the past, which fitted into a hole in a table

inland /ˈɪn.lənd/ /-lænd/ /ˌ-ˈ-/ *adj* [before n], *adv* towards or in the middle of a country, away from the sea: *Seabirds often come inland to find food.* ○ *The Black Sea is a large inland sea.*

the ˌInland ˈRevenue *group noun* [S] in the UK, the government office which collects the main taxes

in-laws /ˈɪn.lɔːz/ [US] /-lɑːz/ *plural noun* INFORMAL the parents of your husband or wife and other members of their family

inlay /ˈɪn.leɪ/ *noun* [C or U] a decorative pattern put into the surface of an object: *The walls of the palace are marble with silver inlay.* **inlaid** /ɪnˈleɪd/ *adj*: *The top of the wooden chest was inlaid* ***with*** *ivory.*

inlet [CHANNEL] /ˈɪn.let/ *noun* [C] a narrow strip of water that goes from a sea or lake into the land or between islands

inlet [MACHINE PART] /ˈɪn.let/ *noun* [C] UK SPECIALIZED the part of a machine through which liquid or gas enters: *an inlet pipe/manifold/valve*

ˌin-line ˈskate *noun* [C] US a **Rollerblade**

in loco parentis /ɪnˌləʊ.kəʊ.pəˈren.tɪs/ [US] /-ˌloʊ.koʊ.pəˈren.t̬ɪs/ *adj* [after v], *adv* FORMAL being responsible for a child while the child's parents are absent: *While children are in school, teachers are legally in loco parentis.*

inmate /ˈɪn.meɪt/ *noun* [C] a person who is kept in a prison or a hospital for people who are mentally ill

inn /ɪn/ *noun* [C] **1** UK a pub where you can stay for the night, usually in the countryside **2** US a small hotel, usually in the countryside **3 Inn** used in the names of some hotels and restaurants

innards /ˈɪn.ədz/ [US] /-ɚdz/ *plural noun* INFORMAL the inner organs of a person or animal, or the inside parts of a machine

innate /ɪˈneɪt/ *adj* An innate quality or ability is one that you were born with, not one you have learned: *Cyril's most impressive quality was his innate goodness.* **innately** /ɪˈneɪt.li/ *adv*: *I don't believe that human beings are innately evil.*

inner /ˈɪn.əʳ/ [US] /-ɚ/ *adj* [before n] **1** inside or contained within something else: *Leading off the main hall is a series of small inner rooms.* ○ HUMOROUS *Few people ever managed to penetrate the director's* ***inner sanctum*** (= very private room). **2** Inner feelings or thoughts are ones that you do not show or tell other people: *Sarah seemed to have a profound sense of inner peace.*

ˌinner ˈchild *noun* [C usually sing] Your inner child is the part of your personality that still reacts and feels like a child: *Many therapists think it's important for adults to get in touch with their inner child.*

ˌinner ˈcircle *noun* [C] the small group of people who control an organization, political party, etc: *Dr Simpson was a member of the inner circle* ***of*** *government officials.*

ˌinner ˈcity *noun* [C] the central part of a city where people live and where there are often problems because people are poor and there are few jobs and bad houses: *a child from the inner city* ○ *an inner-city area*

innermost /ˈɪn.ə.məʊst/ [US] /-ɚ.moʊst/ *adj* [before n] (OLD USE OR LITERARY **inmost**) most secret and hidden, or nearest to the centre: *This was the diary in which Gina recorded her innermost thoughts and secrets.* ○ *The spacecraft will fly through the innermost rings of Saturn.*

ˈinner ˌtube *noun* [C] a tube filled with air that fits inside a car or bicycle tyre

inning /ˈɪn.ɪŋ/ *noun* [C] one of the nine playing periods in a game of baseball

innings /ˈɪn.ɪŋz/ *noun* [C] *plural* **innings** the period in a game of cricket in which a team or a player bats

innit /ˈɪn.ɪt/ *short form* UK SLANG isn't it. Used in a non-standard way at the end of a statement for emphasis: *"It's wrong, innit?"* ○ *"They're such a wicked band, innit."*

innkeeper /ˈɪnˌkiː.pəʳ/ [US] /-pɚ/ *noun* [C] MAINLY OLD USE a person, especially in the past, who owns or looks after an INN

innocent /ˈɪn.ə.sᵊnt/ *adj* **1** (of a person) not guilty of a particular crime, or having no knowledge of the unpleasant and evil things in life, or (of a thing) harmlessly intended: *He firmly believes that she is innocent* ***of*** *the crime.* ○ *She has such an innocent face that I find it hard to believe anything bad of her.* ○ *It was an innocent remark, I didn't mean to hurt his feelings.* ➲Compare **guilty**. **2** An innocent person is someone who is not involved with any military group or war: *Several innocent* ***bystanders*** *were injured in the explosion.*

innocence /ˈɪn.ə.sᵊnts/ *noun* [U] when someone is not guilty of a crime, or does not have much experience of life and does not know about the bad things that happen in life: *She* ***pleaded*** *her innocence, but no one believed her.* ○ *He was led away,* ***protesting*** *his innocence* (= saying he was not guilty). ○ *She has a child-like innocence which I find very appealing.*

innocent /ˈɪn.ə.sᵊnt/ *noun* [C] a person who has very little experience and does not know about the bad things that happen in life

innocently /ˈɪn.ə.sᵊnt.li/ *adv*: *"Have I done something wrong?", she asked innocently* (= seeming not to have done anything wrong). ○ *He said he had obtained the television innocently, not knowing it had been stolen.*

innocuous /ɪˈnɒk.ju.əs/ [US] /-ˈnɑː.kju-/ *adj* completely harmless: *Some mushrooms look innocuous but are in fact poisonous.* **innocuously** /ɪˈnɒk.ju.ə.sli/ [US] /-ˈnɑːk-/ *adv* **innocuousness** /ɪˈnɒk.ju.ə.snəs/ [US] /-ˈnɑːk-/ *noun* [U]

innovate /ˈɪn.əʊ.veɪt/ *verb* [I] to introduce changes and new ideas: *The fashion industry is always desperate to innovate.*

innovative /ˈɪn.ə.və.tɪv/ [US] /-veɪ.t̬ɪv/ *adj* (UK ALSO **innovatory**) using new methods or ideas: *innovative ideas/methods* ○ *She was an imaginative and innovative manager.*

innovation /ˌɪn.əʊˈveɪ.ʃᵊn/ *noun* [C or U] (the use of) a new idea or method: *the latest innovations in computer technology* **innovator** /ˈɪn.əʊ.veɪ.təʳ/ [US] /-t̬ɚ/ *noun* [C]

innuendo /ˌɪn.juˈen.dəʊ/ [US] /-doʊ/ *noun* [C or U] *plural* **innuendoes** or **innuendos** (the making of) a remark or remarks that suggest something sexual or something unpleasant but do not refer to it directly: *There's always an element of* ***sexual*** *innuendo in our conversations.*

innumerable /ɪˈnjuː.mər.ə.bl̩/ [US] /ɪˈnuː.mɚ-/ *adj* too many to be counted: *The project has been delayed by innumerable problems.*

innumerate /ɪˈnjuː.mə.rət/ [US] /ɪˈnuː.mɚ.ət-/ *adj* unable to understand and use numbers in calculations ➲Compare **illiterate**. **innumeracy** /ɪˈnjuː.mᵊr.ə.si/ [US] /-ˈnuː.mɚ-/ *noun* [U]

inoculate /ɪˈnɒk.jʊ.leɪt/ [US] /-ˈnɑː.kjə-/ *verb* [T] to give a weak form of a disease to a person or animal, usually by injection, as a protection against that disease: *My children have been inoculated* ***against*** *polio.* **inoculation** /ɪˌnɒk.jʊˈleɪ.ʃᵊn/ [US] /-ˌnɑː.kjə-/ *noun* [C or U]

inoffensive /ˌɪn.əˈfent.sɪv/ *adj* (especially of a person or their behaviour) not causing any harm or offence: *an inoffensive article* ○ *He seemed like a quiet, inoffensive sort of a guy.*

inoperable [DISEASE] /ɪˈnɒp.ᵊr.ə.bl̩/ [US] /ˌɪnˈɑː.pɚ-/ *adj* If a TUMOUR (= a diseased growth) or other medical condition is inoperable, doctors are unable to remove or treat it with an operation.

inoperable [NOT WORKING] /ɪˈnɒp.ᵊr.ə.bl̩/ [US] /ˌɪnˈɑː.pɚ-/ *adj* If a system, plan, machine, etc. is inoperable, it cannot be done or made to work.

inoperative /ɪˈnɒp.ᵊr.ə.tɪv/ [US] /-ˈnɑː.pɚ.ə.t̬ɪv/ *adj* FORMAL (of a law, rule, etc.) not having effect or power, or (of a machine, system, etc.) not working or not able to work as usual: *The old regulations became inoperative when the new ones were issued.*

inopportune /ɪˈnɒp.ə.tjuːn/ [US] /ɪˈnɑː.pɚ.tuːn/ *adj* FORMAL happening or done at a time which is not suitable or convenient: *I'm sorry, you've called at an inopportune* ***moment.*** **inopportunely** /ɪˈnɒp.ə.tjuːn.li/ [US] /ɪˈnɑː.pɚ.tuːn-/ *adv*

inordinate /ɪˈnɔː.dɪ.nət/ [US] /ˌɪnˈɔːr-/ *adj* FORMAL unreasonably or unusually large in size or degree: *Margot has always spent an inordinate* ***amount*** *of time on her* *appearance.* **inordinately** /ɪˈnɔː.dɪ.nət.li/ ⓊⓈ /ɪnˈɔːr-/ *adv: She was inordinately fond of her pets.*

inorganic /ˌɪn.ɔːˈgæn.ɪk/ ⓊⓈ /-ɔːr-/ *adj* SPECIALIZED not being or consisting of living material, or (of chemical substances) containing no carbon or only small amounts of carbon: *Salt is an inorganic chemical.* ○ *The meteorites contained only inorganic material.* ➔Compare **organic**.

inorganic 'chemistry *noun* [U] the scientific study of chemical substances which do not contain carbon

inpatient /ˈɪn.peɪ.ʃ³nt/ *noun* [C] a person who goes into hospital to receive medical care, and stays there one or more nights while they are being treated ➔Compare **outpatient**.

input /ˈɪn.pʊt/ *noun* **1** [C or U] something such as energy, money or information that is put into a system, organization or machine so that it can operate: *I didn't have much input into the project* (= The help I gave or work I did on it was small). ○ *The power input will come largely from hydroelectricity.* **2** [C] SPECIALIZED the part that carries information to a machine, or the place where this is connected: *The inputs for the CD-ROM are at the back of the computer.* ○ *an input device*
input /ˈɪn.pʊt/ *verb* [T] inputting or inputted or **input**, **inputted** or **input** *I've spent the morning inputting data **into** the computer* (= adding information using a keyboard).

inquest /ˈɪn.kwest/ *noun* [C] **1** an official process to discover the cause of someone's death: *An inquest is always held if murder is suspected.* **2** an examination of or discussion about the reasons for someone's or something's failure: *a inquest into the department's poor performance*

inquire, UK ALSO **enquire** /ɪnˈkwaɪəʳ/ ⓊⓈ /-ˈkwaɪr/ *verb* [I or T] to ask for information: *Shall I inquire **about** the price of tickets?* ○ [+ question word] *She rang up to inquire **when** her car would be ready.* ○ [+ speech] *"Where are we going?" he inquired politely.*
• **inquire within** MAINLY UK written on a notice on a building, meaning that information can be found inside: *Saturday staff needed – Inquire within.*
inquirer, UK ALSO **enquirer** /ɪnˈkwaɪə.rəʳ/ ⓊⓈ /-ˈkwaɪr.əʳ/ *noun* [C] FORMAL someone who asks about something
inquiring, UK ALSO **enquiring** /ɪnˈkwaɪə.rɪŋ/ ⓊⓈ /-ˈkwaɪr.-ɪŋ/ *adj* (of someone's behaviour) always wanting to learn new things, or (of someone's expression) wanting to know something: *You have a very inquiring **mind**, don't you.* ○ *He gave her an inquiring look.* **inquiringly**, UK ALSO **enquiringly** /ɪnˈkwaɪə.rɪŋ.li/ ⓊⓈ /-ˈkwaɪr.ɪŋ-/ *adv: She looked at her mother inquiringly.*

PHRASAL VERBS WITH **inquire** ▼

▲ **inquire after** *sb*, UK ALSO **enquire after** *sb phrasal verb* MAINLY UK to ask for information about someone, especially about their health, in order to be polite: *She inquired after his grandfather's health.*

▲ **inquire into** *sth*, UK ALSO **enquire into** *sth phrasal verb* FORMAL to try to discover the facts about something: *When the authorities inquired into his background, they found he had a criminal record.*

inquiry, UK ALSO **enquiry** /ɪnˈkwaɪə.ri/ ⓊⓈ /ˈɪŋ.kwə.i/ *noun* **1** [C or U] (the process of asking) a question: *I've been making inquiries **about/into** the cost of a round-the-world ticket.* ○ FORMAL *Inquiry **into** the matter is pointless – no one will tell you anything.* **2** [C] an official process to discover the facts about something bad that has happened: *a judicial inquiry* ○ *Citizens have demanded a full inquiry **into** the government's handling of the epidemic.*

inquisition /ˌɪn.kwɪˈzɪʃ.³n/ *noun* [C] FORMAL DISAPPROVING a period of detailed and unfriendly questioning: *The police subjected him to an inquisition that lasted 12 hours.*
the Inquisition *noun* [S] in the past, an official organization in the Roman Catholic Church whose purpose was to find and punish people who opposed its beliefs
inquisitor /ɪnˈkwɪz.ɪ.təʳ/ ⓊⓈ /-t̬əʳ/ *noun* [C] FORMAL DISAPPROVING someone who asks a lot of questions: *The prime minister found himself arraigned before the media inquisitors.*

inquisitorial /ɪnˌkwɪz.ɪˈtɔː.ri.əl/ ⓊⓈ /-ˈtɔːr.i-/ *adj* FORMAL DISAPPROVING asking a lot of questions, especially in a way that makes you feel annoyed: *an inquisitorial manner*

inquisitive /ɪnˈkwɪz.ɪ.tɪv/ ⓊⓈ /-t̬ɪv/ *adj* wanting to discover as much as you can about things, sometimes in a way that annoys people: *an inquisitive child* ○ *an inquisitive mind* ○ *She could see inquisitive faces looking out from the windows next door.* **inquisitively** /ɪnˈkwɪz.ɪ.tɪv.li/ ⓊⓈ /-t̬ɪv.li/ *adv: The mouse looked around the room inquisitively.* **inquisitiveness** /ɪnˈkwɪz.ɪ.tɪv.nəs/ ⓊⓈ /-t̬ɪv-/ *noun* [U]

inquorate /ɪnˈkwɔː.reɪt/ ⓊⓈ /-kwɔːr.eɪt/ *adj* MAINLY UK FORMAL (of a meeting) not having enough people present and so unable to make any official decisions

in-residence /ɪnˈrez.ɪ.d³nts/ *adj* [after n] A painter, poet, etc. in-residence works with an organization, usually for a limited period.

inroads /ˈɪn.rəʊdz/ ⓊⓈ /-roʊdz/ *plural noun* **make inroads** to start to have a direct and noticeable effect (on something): *The government is definitely making inroads **into** the problem of unemployment.*

insalubrious /ˌɪn.səˈluː.bri.əs/ *adj* FORMAL unpleasant, dirty or likely to cause disease

the ˌins and 'outs *plural noun* the detailed or complicated facts of something: *I know how to use computers, but I don't really understand the ins and outs of how they work.*

insane /ɪnˈseɪn/ *adj* **1** mentally ill: *For the last ten years of his life he was clinically insane.* ○ INFORMAL *I sometimes think I'm going insane* (= I feel very confused). **2** INFORMAL extremely unreasonable: *In a fit of insane jealousy he tried to stab her.*
the insane *plural noun* mentally ill people: *a hospital for the criminally insane*
insanely /ɪnˈseɪn.li/ *adv* extremely and unreasonably: *She gets insanely jealous if he so much as looks at another woman.*
insanity /ɪnˈsæn.ə.ti/ ⓊⓈ /-t̬i/ *noun* [U] **1** when someone is seriously mentally ill: *He was found not guilty of murder by reason of insanity.* ○ *He suffered from periodic bouts of insanity.* **2** when something is not sensible and is likely to have extremely bad results: *It would be insanity to expand the business now.*

insanitary /ɪnˈsæn.ə.tri/ ⓊⓈ /-ter.i/ *adj* UK FOR **unsanitary**

insatiable /ɪnˈseɪ.ʃə.bl̩/ *adj* (especially of a desire or need) too great to be satisfied: *Like so many politicians, he had an insatiable appetite/desire/hunger for power.* ○ *Nothing, it seemed, would satisfy his insatiable curiosity.* **insatiably** /ɪnˈseɪ.ʃə.bli/ *adv*

inscribe /ɪnˈskraɪb/ *verb* [T] FORMAL to write words in a book or CARVE (= cut) them on an object: *The prize winners each receive a book with their names inscribed on the first page.* ○ *The wall of the church was inscribed with the names of the dead from the Great War.*

inscription /ɪnˈskrɪp.ʃ³n/ *noun* [C] words that are written or cut in something: *The inscription read 'To darling Molly. Christmas 1904.'* ○ *The inscriptions on the gravestones were worn away.*

inscrutable /ɪnˈskruː.tɪ.bl̩/ ⓊⓈ /-t̬ə-/ *adj* (especially of a person or their expression) not showing emotions or thoughts and therefore very difficult to understand or get to know: *an inscrutable face/expression/smile* **inscrutably** /ɪnˈskruː.tɪ.bli/ ⓊⓈ /-t̬ə-/ *adv: She smiled inscrutably.* **inscrutability** /ɪnˌskruː.tɪˈbɪl.ɪ.ti/ ⓊⓈ /-t̬əˈbɪl.ə.-t̬i/ *noun* [U]

inseam /ˈɪn.siːm/ *noun* [C] US FOR **inside leg**

insect /ˈɪn.sekt/ *noun* [C] a type of very small, air-breathing animal with six legs, a body divided into three parts and usually two pairs of wings, or, more generally, any similar very small animal: *Ants, beetles, butterflies and flies are all insects.* ○ *I've got some sort of insect bite on my leg.*

insecticide /ɪnˈsek.tɪ.saɪd/ *noun* [C or U] a chemical substance made and used for killing insects, especially those which eat plants ➔Compare **herbicide**; **pesticide**.

insectivore /ɪnˈsek.tɪ.vɔːʳ/ ⓊⓈ /-vɔːr/ *noun* [C] SPECIALIZED an animal which eats only insects **insectivorous** /ˌɪn.sekˈtɪv.³r.əs/ ⓊⓈ /-ɚ-/ *adj*

insecure NOT CONFIDENT /ˌɪn.sɪˈkjʊəʳ/ ⓤ /-ˈkjʊr/ adj Insecure people lack confidence and are uncertain about their own abilities and about whether other people really like them: *I wonder what it was about her upbringing that made her so insecure.* ○ *He still feels insecure about his ability to do the job.* **insecurity** /ˌɪn.sɪˈkjʊə.rɪ.ti/ ⓤ /-ˈkjʊr.ə.t̬i/ noun [C or U] *a sense/feeling of insecurity* ○ *She had developed an outgoing personality to mask her deep insecurities.*

insecure NOT SAFE /ˌɪn.sɪˈkjʊəʳ/ ⓤ /-ˈkjʊr/ adj (of objects or situations) not safe or not protected: *The situation is still insecure, with many of the rebels roaming the streets.* ○ *Nations which are not self-sufficient in energy will face an insecure future.* ○ *We've gone through a few financially insecure years.* **insecurely** /ˌɪn.sɪˈkjʊə.li/ ⓤ /-ˈkjʊr-/ adv: *The shelves were insecurely fastened and fell to the floor.* **insecurity** /ˌɪn.sɪˈkjʊə.rɪ.ti/ ⓤ /-ˈkjʊr.ə.t̬i/ noun [U]

inseminate /ɪnˈsem.ɪ.neɪt/ verb [T] to put a male animal's sperm into a female animal, either by the sexual act or by an artificial method **insemination** /ɪn-ˌsem.ɪˈneɪ.ʃᵊn/ noun [U] *artificial insemination*

insensible /ɪnˈsent.sɪ.bl̩/ adj FORMAL **1** unconscious: *We found her lying on the floor, drunk and insensible.* **2 be insensible of/to sth** to not care about something or be unwilling to react to it: *I think he's largely insensible to other people's distress.* **insensibility** /ɪnˌsent.sɪˈbɪl.ɪ.ti/ ⓤ /-ə.t̬i/ noun [C or U]

insensitive /ɪnˈsent.sɪ.tɪv/ ⓤ /-sə.t̬ɪv/ adj **1** DISAPPROVING (of a person or their behaviour) not aware of or showing sympathy for other people's feelings, or refusing to give importance to something: *It was a bit insensitive of Fiona to go on so much about fat people when she knows Mandy is desperate to lose weight.* ○ *The police have been criticized for being insensitive to complaints from the public.* **2** SPECIALIZED not showing the effect of something as a reaction to it, or unable to feel something: *The protective covering must be insensitive to light and heat.* ○ *His feet seem to be insensitive to pain.* **insensitivity** /ɪnˌsent.sɪˈtɪv.ɪ.ti/ ⓤ /-ə.t̬i/ noun [U] *His insensitivity towards the feelings of others is remarkable.* ○ *an insensitivity to pain/light/noise* **insensitively** /ɪn-ˈsent.sɪ.tɪv.li/ ⓤ /-sə.t̬ɪv-/ adv

inseparable /ɪnˈsep.rə.bl̩/ adj describes two or more people who are such good friends that they spend most of their time together, or two or more things that are so closely connected that they cannot be considered separately: *When we were kids Zoe and I were inseparable.* ○ *Unemployment and inner city decay are inseparable issues which must be tackled together.* **inseparably** /ɪnˈsep.rə.bli/ adv: *These two causes are inseparably linked.*

insert /ɪnˈsɜːt/ ⓤ /-ˈsɜːt/ verb [T] to put something inside something else, or to add something, especially words, to something else: *Insert the key in/into the lock.* ○ *I've filled in the form, but you still need to insert (= add) your bank details and date of birth.*
insert /ˈɪn.sɜːt/ ⓤ /-ˈsɜːt/ noun [C] something that is made to go inside or into something else: *These magazines have too many annoying inserts (= extra loose pages) advertising various products.* **insertion** /ɪnˈsɜː.ʃᵊn/ /-ˈsɜːr-/ noun [U] *Scientists hope that the insertion of normal genes into the diseased cells will provide a cure.*

in-service /ˌɪn.sɜː.vɪs/ ⓤ /-ˈsɜːr-/ adj [before n] happening during your time at work: *Instead of sending employees away on courses, the company relies on in-service training.*

inset /ˈɪn.set/ noun [C] SPECIALIZED something positioned within a larger object: *The map has an inset (= small extra map) in the top corner, that shows the city centre in more detail.* **inset** /ɪnˈset/ adj [after v] *He bought her a gold necklace inset with rubies.*

inshore adj /ˈɪn.ʃɔːʳ/ ⓤ /-ʃɔːr/, adv /-ˈ-/ near or towards the coast: *an inshore fishing zone* ○ *an inshore lifeboat* ○ *The ships moved slowly inshore.*

inside INNER PART /ɪnˈsaɪd/ noun [C usually sing] **1** the inner part, space or side of something: *Did you clean the inside of the car?* ○ *The hotel looked shabby from the street, but it was fine on the inside.* ○ *the insides of people's houses* ⊃Compare **outside** OUTER PART. **2** The inside of a part of

the body such as the arm or leg is the part facing in towards the rest of the body: *She dabbed perfume on the inside of her wrist.*
● **on the inside** INFORMAL If someone is on the inside, they have a job or position in which they have special or secret information: *Who do we know on the inside who can help us?*

insides /ɪnˈsaɪdz/ plural noun INFORMAL a person's or animal's internal organs, especially their stomach or bowels: *The dead seal's insides were spread all over the snow.*

inside /ɪnˈsaɪd/ adv, prep, adj in or into a room, building, container, or something similar: *"Is Anna in the garden?" "No, she's inside (= in the house)."* ○ *What's inside the box?* ○ *Luckily, no one was inside the building when it collapsed.* ○ FIGURATIVE *She couldn't cope with the grief she felt inside.* ○ FIGURATIVE *Who can tell what goes on inside his head?* ○ *He put the documents carefully in his inside pocket (= pocket on the inner side of a jacket or coat).*

inside /ɪnˈsaɪd/ adv INFORMAL in prison: *Her husband's inside for armed robbery.*
● **inside out** If something is inside out, it has the usual inside part on the outside and the usual outside part on the inside: *She had her jumper on inside out.*
● **know sth inside out** INFORMAL to know everything about a subject: *He knows the system inside out.*
● **turn a place inside out** UK INFORMAL to search a place very thoroughly: *I've turned the house inside out but I still can't find my keys.*
● **have the inside track** to have a special position within an organization, or a special relationship with a person that gives you advantages that other people do not have

inside SPECIAL KNOWLEDGE /ˈɪn.saɪd/ /ˌ-ˈ-/ adj [before n] (of information) obtained by someone in a group, organization or company and therefore involving special or secret knowledge: *inside information/knowledge* ○ *I'll call up Clare and get the inside story (= a true report of the facts).*

insider /ɪnˈsaɪ.dəʳ/ ⓤ /-dɚ/ noun [C] someone who is an accepted member of a group and who therefore has special or secret knowledge or influence: *According to insiders, the committee is having difficulty making up its mind.*

inside TIME /ˌɪnˈsaɪd/ preposition (ALSO **inside of**) If you do something or if something happens inside (of) a particular time or limit, you do it or it happens in less than that amount of time or under the limit: *The new faster trains can do the journey inside two hours.* ○ *He finished it inside of two hours.*

ˈinside ˌjob noun [C] a crime, especially stealing, committed by someone in the place where they work

ˌinside ˈlane ROAD noun [C] **1** UK the part of the road nearest the edge, used especially by slower vehicles **2** US the part of the road nearest the vehicles going in the opposite direction

ˌinside ˈlane RUNNING noun [C] the part of a RACETRACK nearest the middle

ˌinside ˈleg UK noun [C usually sing] (US **inseam**) the measurement from the top of your inner leg to your ankle

inˌsider ˈdealing noun [U] (ALSO **insider trading**) the illegal buying and selling of company SHARES (= a financial part of the ownership of a company) by people who have special information because they are involved with the company

insidious /ɪnˈsɪd.i.əs/ adj (of something unpleasant or dangerous) gradually and secretly causing harm: *High blood pressure is an insidious condition which has few symptoms.* **insidiously** /ɪnˈsɪd.i.ə.sli/ adv **insidiousness** /ɪnˈsɪd.i.əs.nəs/ noun [U]

insight /ˈɪn.saɪt/ noun [C or U] (the ability to have) a clear, deep and sometimes sudden understanding of a complicated problem or situation: *It was an interesting book, full of fascinating insights into human relationships.* **insightful** /ˈɪn.saɪt.fᵊl/ adj APPROVING

insignia /ɪnˈsɪg.ni.ə/ noun [C] plural **insignia** an object or mark which shows that a person belongs to a particular organization or group, or has a particular rank: *the royal insignia*

insignificant /ˌɪn.sɪɡˈnɪf.ɪ.kᵊnt/ *adj* not important or thought to be valuable, especially because of being small: *Why bother arguing about such an insignificant amount of money?* ○ *The difference between the two results was insignificant.*
insignificance /ˌɪn.sɪɡˈnɪf.ɪ.kᵊnts/ *noun* [U] *The traumas of my own upbringing **pale/fade into** insignificance* (= seem very unimportant) *when I hear stories about the way Peter's parents treated him.* **insignificantly** /ˌɪn.sɪɡˈnɪf.ɪ.kᵊnt.li/ *adv*

insincere /ˌɪn.sɪnˈsɪəʳ/ [US] /-ˈsɪr/ *adj* DISAPPROVING pretending to feel something that you do not really feel, or not meaning what you say: *an insincere apology* ○ *And all this praise just because the poor man has died – doesn't it strike you as a bit insincere?* **insincerely** /ˌɪn.sɪnˈsɪə.li/ [US] /-ˈsɪr-/ *adv* **insincerity** /ˌɪn.sɪnˈser.ə.ti/ [US] /-t̬i/ *noun* [U]

insinuate /ɪnˈsɪn.ju.eɪt/ *verb* [T] to suggest, without being direct, that something unpleasant is true: [+ (*that*)] *Are you insinuating **(that)** I'm losing my nerve?* ○ *What are you insinuating, Daniel?*
insinuating /ɪnˈsɪn.ju.eɪ.tɪŋ/ [US] /-t̬ɪŋ/ *adj* suggesting ideas without stating them directly: *She didn't reply – she merely smiled that insinuating smile.* ○ *Both songs are in danger of being banned for their sexy, insinuating lyrics.* **insinuation** /ɪnˌsɪn.juˈeɪ.ʃᵊn/ *noun* [C or U] [+ *that*] *We resent these insinuations **that** we are not capable of leading the company forward.*
▲ **insinuate *yourself* into *sth*** *phrasal verb* [R] FORMAL DISAPPROVING to use clever, secret and often unpleasant methods to gradually become part of something: *Over the years she insinuated herself into the great man's life.*

insipid /ɪnˈsɪp.ɪd/ *adj* DISAPPROVING lacking a strong taste or character, or lacking interest or energy: *a pale insipid wine* ○ *He's an insipid old bore.* ○ *Why anyone buys music with such insipid lyrics is a mystery.* **insipidly** /ɪnˈsɪp.ɪd.li/ *adv* **insipidness** /ɪnˈsɪp.ɪd.nəs/ *noun* [U] (ALSO **insipidity**)

insist /ɪnˈsɪst/ *verb* [I] to state or demand forcefully, especially despite opposition: [+ (*that*)] *Greg still insists **(that)** he did nothing wrong.* ○ *Please go first – I insist!* ○ *She insisted **on** seeing her lawyer.*
insistence /ɪnˈsɪs.tᵊnts/ *noun* [U] when you demand something and refuse to accept opposition, or when you say firmly that something is true: *Insistence **on** better working conditions by the union has resulted in fewer employee absences.* ○ ***At** her father**'s** insistence, Amelia's been moved into a new class.* ○ [+ *that*] *Her insistence **that** she should have the best room annoyed everyone.*
insistent /ɪnˈsɪs.tᵊnt/ *adj* firmly saying that something must be true or done: *insistent demands/appeals/signals* ○ *The teacher is insistent **that** the school is not to blame for the situation.* **insistently** /ɪnˈsɪs.tᵊnt.li/ *adv*

in situ /ˌɪnˈsɪt.juː/ *adj, adv* FORMAL in the original place instead of being moved to another place

insofar as /ˌɪn.səˈfɑːr.əz/ *conjunction* FORMAL to the degree that

insole /ˈɪn.səʊl/ [US] /-soʊl/ *noun* [C] (ALSO **inner sole**) a piece of material inside a shoe on which your foot rests, or a piece of material that you put in a shoe to make it warmer or more comfortable

insolent /ˈɪnt.sᵊl.ənt/ *adj* rude and not showing respect: *an insolent child/young man* ○ *an insolent gesture/remark* **insolently** /ˈɪnt.sᵊl.ənt.li/ *adv* **insolence** /ˈɪnt.sᵊl.ənts/ *noun* [U]

insoluble [DIFFICULT TO SOLVE] /ɪnˈsɒl.jʊ.bl̩/ [US] /-ˈsɑːl.jə-/ *adj* (US ALSO **insolvable**) (of a problem) so difficult that it is impossible to solve: *Traffic congestion in large cities seems to be an insoluble problem.* **insolubility** /ɪnˌsɒl.jʊˈbɪl.ɪ.ti/ [US] /-ˌsɑːl.jəˈbɪl.ə.t̬i/ *noun* [U]

insoluble [IMPOSSIBLE TO MIX] /ɪnˈsɒl.jʊ.bl̩/ [US] /-ˈsɑːl.jə-/ *adj* (of a substance) impossible to dissolve: *These minerals are all insoluble in water.* **insolubility** /ɪnˌsɒl.jʊˈbɪl.ɪ.ti/ [US] /-ˌsɑːl.jəˈbɪl.ə.t̬i/ *noun* [U]

insolvent /ɪnˈsɒl.vᵊnt/ [US] /-ˈsɑːl-/ *adj* SPECIALIZED (especially of a company) not having enough money to pay debts, buy goods, etc. **insolvency** /ɪnˈsɒl.vᵊnt.si/ [US] /-ˈsɑːl-/ *noun* [U]

insomnia /ɪnˈsɒm.ni.ə/ [US] /-ˈsɑːm-/ *noun* [U] inability to sleep, over a period of time: *Holly **suffered from** insomnia for months after her daughter was born.*
insomniac /ɪnˈsɒm.ni.æk/ [US] /-ˈsɑːm-/ *noun* [C] someone who often finds it difficult to sleep

insouciance /ɪnˈsuː.si.ənts/ *noun* [U] LITERARY a relaxed and happy way of acting without worry or guilt: *I admired his youthful insouciance.* **insouciant** /ɪnˈsuː.si.ənt/ *adj*

inspect /ɪnˈspekt/ *verb* [T] **1** to look at something or someone carefully in order to discover information, especially about their quality or condition: *After the crash both drivers got out and inspected their cars for damage.* ○ *She held the bank note up to the light and inspected it **carefully**.* **2** to officially visit a place or a group of people in order to check that everything is correct and legal: *An official from the Department of Health will be inspecting the restaurant this afternoon.* ○ *The King inspected the troops.*
inspection /ɪnˈspek.ʃᵊn/ *noun* [C or U] when you look at something carefully, or an official visit to a building or organization to check that everything is correct and legal: *Her passport seemed legitimate, but **on closer** inspection, it was found to have been altered.* ○ *She arrived to **carry out/make** a health and safety inspection of the building.*
inspector /ɪnˈspek.təʳ/ *noun* [C] **1** someone whose job is to officially inspect something: *a tax inspector* ○ *a school inspector/an inspector of schools* **2** UK a police officer of middle rank, above a SERGEANT and below a SUPERINTENDENT
inspectorate /ɪnˈspek.tᵊr.ət/ *noun* [C] MAINLY UK an official organization which sends inspectors to visit places and organizations in order to make certain they are in good condition and that the rules are being obeyed: *the education/pollution/schools inspectorate*

inspire /ɪnˈspaɪəʳ/ [US] /-ˈspaɪr/ *verb* [T] **1** to make someone feel that they want to do something and can do it: *His confident leadership inspired his followers.* ○ [+ **to** infinitive] *After her trip to Venezuela, she felt inspired **to** learn Spanish.* **2** to make someone have a particular strong feeling or reaction: *She inspires great loyalty among her followers.* ○ *The captain's heroic effort inspired them **with** determination.* **3** to give someone an idea for a book, film, product, etc: *a piece of music inspired by dolphin sounds* ○ *The design of the car has inspired many imitations.*
inspiration /ˌɪn.spɪˈreɪ.ʃᵊn/ *noun* **1** [C or U] someone or something that gives you ideas for doing something: *The golden autumn light provided the inspiration **for** the painting.* ○ *He went to church, perhaps seeking **divine** inspiration.* **2** [C] a sudden good idea: *He **had** an inspiration – why not apply for some government money?* **3** [S] an example which people admire: *She has been **an** inspiration **to** us all.*
inspirational /ˌɪn.spɪˈreɪ.ʃᵊn.əl/ *adj* making you feel hopeful or encouraged: *He gave an inspirational reading of his own poems.*
inspired /ɪnˈspaɪəd/ [US] /-ˈspaɪrd/ *adj* excellent, or resulting from inspiration: *an inspired performance/choice* ○ *an inspired suggestion/guess*
inspiring /ɪnˈspaɪə.rɪŋ/ [US] /-ˈspaɪr.ɪŋ/ *adj* encouraging, or making you feel you want to do something: *She was an inspiring example to her followers.*

instability /ˌɪn.stəˈbɪl.ɪ.ti/ [US] /-ə.t̬i/ *noun* [U] uncertainty caused by the possibility of a sudden change in the present situation: *political/economic instability* ○ *The instability of the euro continues.* ○ *The building's instability makes it extremely dangerous.*

install [PUT IN], UK ALSO **instal** /ɪnˈstɔːl/ [US] /-ˈstɑːl/ *verb* [T] **1** to put furniture, a machine or a piece of equipment into position and make it ready to use: *The plumber is coming tomorrow to install the new washing machine.* **2** SPECIALIZED to put a computer program onto a computer so that the computer can use it: *Andrew, can you help me install this software?*
installation /ˌɪn.stəˈleɪ.ʃᵊn/ *noun* **1** [U] when equipment or furniture is put into position: *Do you have to pay extra for installation?* **2** [C] a nearly permanent place with people, buildings and equipment which have a

particular, especially military, purpose: *a nuclear installation* ○ *The Americans still have several military bases and installations on the island.* **3** [C] a form of modern sculpture where the artist uses sound, movement or space as well as objects in order to make an often temporary work of art

install [PLACE], *UK ALSO* **instal** /ɪnˈstɔːl/ [US] /-ˈstɑːl/ *verb* [T] **1** to place someone in an official position: *She has installed a couple of young academics* ***as*** *her advisers.* **2** *UK* **install *sb/yourself* in/at *somewhere*** to put someone/yourself in a comfortable position where you want to stay: *He seems to have installed himself in your spare room for good!* **installation** /ˌɪn.stəˈleɪ.ʃᵊn/ *noun* [U] *The installation of the new archbishop will take place in January.*

inˈstallment ˌplan *noun* [C] *US FOR* **hire purchase**

instalment *UK*, *US* **installment** /ɪnˈstɔːl.mənt/ [US] /-ˈstɑːl-/ *noun* [C] one of a number of parts into which a story, plan or amount of money owed has been divided, so that each part happens or is paid at different times until the end or total is reached: *The novel has been serialized for radio* ***in*** *five instalments.* ○ *We agreed to* ***pay for*** *the car* ***by/in*** *instalments.*

instance /ˈɪn.stənts/ *noun* [C] a particular situation, event or fact, especially an example of something that happens generally: *There have been several instances* ***of*** *violence at the school.* ○ *I don't usually side with the management, but* ***in this*** *instance I agree with what they're saying.*

• **for instance** for example: *In the electronics industry, for instance, 5000 jobs are being lost.*

instance /ˈɪn.stənts/ *verb* [T] *UK FORMAL* *She argued the need for legal reform and instanced* (= gave as examples) *several recent cases with grossly unfair verdicts.*

instant /ˈɪn.stənt/ *noun* [S] an extremely short period of time; a moment: ***In*** *an instant her mood had changed.* ○ *The startled boy froze* ***for*** *an instant, then fled.* ○ *"Stop that noise* ***this*** *instant* (= now)*!"* ○ *I'll call you* ***the*** *instant* (= as soon as) *I get home.*

instant /ˈɪn.stənt/ *adj* **1** happening immediately, without any delay: *This type of account offers you instant* ***access*** *to your money.* ○ *Contrary to expectations, the film was an instant* ***success.*** **2** Instant food or drink is dried, usually in the form of a powder, and can be prepared very quickly by adding hot water: *instant coffee/soup*

instantly /ˈɪn.stənt.li/ *adv* immediately: *Both drivers were killed instantly.*

instantaneous /ˌɪn.stənˈteɪ.ni.əs/ *adj* happening immediately, without any delay: *an instantaneous response/reply/reaction* **instantaneously** /ˌɪn.stənˈteɪ.ni.ə.sli/ *adv*

ˌinstant ˈmessaging *noun* [U] a type of service available on the Internet that allows you to exchange written messages with someone else who is using the service at the same time

ˌinstant ˈreplay *noun* [C] *US FOR* **action replay**

instead /ɪnˈsted/ *adv* in place of someone or something else: *There's no coffee – would you like a cup of tea instead?* ○ *You can go instead* ***of*** *me, if you want.*

instep /ˈɪn.step/ *noun* [C] the curved upper part of the foot between the toes and the heel, or the part of a shoe or sock which fits around this ➲See picture **The Body** on page Centre 5

instigate /ˈɪn.stɪ.geɪt/ *verb* [T] *FORMAL* to cause an event or situation to happen by making a set of actions or a formal process begin: *The government will instigate new measures to combat terrorism.* ○ *The revolt in the north is believed to have been instigated by a high-ranking general.* **instigation** /ˌɪn.stɪˈgeɪ.ʃᵊn/ *noun* [U] *The inquiry was begun* ***at the*** *instigation* ***of*** *a local MP.* **instigator** /ˈɪn.stɪ.geɪ.təʳ/ [US] /-tɚ/ *noun* [C]

instil *UK* (-ll-), *US* **instill** /ɪnˈstɪl/ *verb* [T] to put a feeling, idea or principle gradually into someone's mind, so that it has a strong influence on the way they think or behave: *It is part of a teacher's job to instil* ***confidence in/into*** *his or her students.*

instinct /ˈɪn.stɪŋkt/ *noun* [C or U] the way people or animals naturally react or behave, without having to think or learn about it: *All his instincts told him to stay near the car and wait for help.* ○ [+ **to** infinitive] *Her* ***first*** *instinct was* ***to*** *run.* ○ *It is instinct that tells the birds when to begin their migration.* ○ *FIGURATIVE* *Bob seems to* ***have*** *an instinct* ***for*** (= is naturally good at) *knowing which products will sell.*

instinctive /ɪnˈstɪŋk.tɪv/ *adj* Instinctive behaviour or reactions are not thought about, planned or developed by training: *an instinctive reaction* **instinctively** /ɪnˈstɪŋk.tɪv.li/ *adv*: *She knew instinctively that he was dangerous.*

institute [ORGANIZATION] /ˈɪnt.stɪ.tjuːt/ [US] /-tuːt/ *noun* [C] an organization where people do a particular kind of scientific, educational or social work, or the buildings which it uses: *the Massachusetts Institute of Technology*

institute [START] /ˈɪnt.stɪ.tjuːt/ [US] /-tuːt/ *verb* [T] *FORMAL* to start or cause a system, rule, legal action, etc. to exist: *She is threatening to institute legal proceedings against the hospital.*

institution [ORGANIZATION] /ˌɪnt.stɪˈtjuː.ʃᵊn/ [US] /-ˈtuː-/ *noun* [C] a large and important organization, such as a university or bank: *a medical/educational/financial institution* ○ *Oxford and Cambridge universities are internationally respected institutions.*

institution [PLACE] /ˌɪnt.stɪˈtjuː.ʃᵊn/ [US] /-ˈtuː-/ *noun* [C] *MAINLY DISAPPROVING* a place or building where people are sent to be cared for, especially a hospital or prison **institutional** /ˌɪnt.stɪˈtjuː.ʃᵊn.ᵊl/ [US] /-ˈtuː-/ *adj* *MAINLY DISAPPROVING* relating to an institution: *The hospital provides typically awful institutional food.*

institutionalize, *UK USUALLY* **-ise** /ˌɪnt.stɪˈtjuː.ʃᵊn.ə.laɪz/ [US] /-ˈtuː-/ *verb* [T] *MAINLY DISAPPROVING* to send someone to live in an institution

institutionalized, *UK USUALLY* **-ised** /ˌɪnt.stɪˈtjuː.ʃᵊn.ə.laɪzd/ [US] /-ˈtuː-/ *adj* *MAINLY DISAPPROVING* If someone becomes institutionalized, they gradually become less able to think and act independently, because they have lived for a long time under the rules of an institution: *We need to avoid long-stay patients in the hospital becoming institutionalized.*

institution [CUSTOM] /ˌɪnt.stɪˈtjuː.ʃᵊn/ [US] /-ˈtuː-/ *noun* [C] a custom or tradition that has existed for a long time and is accepted as an important part of a particular society: *the venerable institution of marriage* ○ *FIGURATIVE* *Mrs Daly is an institution – she's been with the company 40 years and knows absolutely everyone.* **institutionalize**, *UK USUALLY* **-ise** /ˌɪnt.stɪˈtjuː.ʃᵊn.ə.laɪz/ [US] /-ˈtuː-/ *verb* [T] *What was once an informal event has now become institutionalized.* ➲See also **institutionalize** at **institution** PLACE.

institution [START] /ˌɪnt.stɪˈtjuː.ʃᵊn/ [US] /-ˈtuː-/ *noun* [U] when a law, system, etc. begins or is introduced: *The institution of a Freedom of Information Act has had a significant effect.*

instiˌtutionalized ˈracism *noun* [U] *MAINLY UK* RACISM (= when someone is treated unfairly because of their race) that has become part of the normal behaviour of people within an organization: *The police had to fend off allegations of institutional racism after a black suspect was beaten by four white police officers.*

in-store /ˌɪnˈstɔːʳ/ [US] /-ˈstɔːr/ *adj* [before n] happening or established inside a large shop, or available for customers to use or obtain inside a large shop: *an in-store bakery/cafe* ○ *in-store banking*

instruct [ORDER] /ɪnˈstrʌkt/ *verb* **1** [T + **to** infinitive] to order or tell someone to do something, especially in a formal way: *The police have been instructed* ***to*** *patrol the building and surrounding area.* **2** [T] *UK* to employ a lawyer to represent you in court **3** [T] When a judge instructs a JURY, they tell it what the law means and how to use it. **instruction** /ɪnˈstrʌk.ʃᵊn/ *noun* [C usually pl] *The police who broke into the house were only acting* ***on/under*** *instructions.* ○ [+ **to** infinitive] *He* ***gave*** *me strict instructions* ***to*** *get there by eight o'clock.*

instruct [TEACH] /ɪnˈstrʌkt/ *verb* [T] to teach someone how to do something: *He works in a sports centre instructing people* ***in*** *the use of the gym equipment.* **instruction** /ɪnˈstrʌk.ʃᵊn/ *noun* [U] *The video provides instruction* ***on*** *how to operate the computer.* ○ *The course gives you* ***basic*** *instruction* ***in*** *car maintenance.* ○ *Have you seen the in-*

struction **manual** for the washing machine?

instructions /ɪnˈstrʌk.ʃᵊnz/ *plural noun* advice and information about how to do or use something, often written in a small book or on the side of a container: *The cooking instructions say bake it for half an hour.* ○ *You obviously didn't read the instructions properly.* ○ *They need clear instructions on what to do next.*

instructive /ɪnˈstrʌk.tɪv/ *adj APPROVING* giving useful or interesting information **instructively** /ɪnˈstrʌk.tɪv.li/ ⓤ /-tɪv-/ *adv*

instructor /ɪnˈstrʌk.tər/ ⓤ /-tɚ/ *noun* [C] **1** a person whose job is to teach people a practical skill: *an aerobics instructor* ○ *a driving/ski/swimming instructor* **2** *US* a teacher of a college or university subject, who usually teaches a limited number of classes: *a history/science/sociology instructor.*

instrument MUSIC /ˈɪn.strə.mənt/ *noun* [C] (*ALSO* **musical instrument**) an object, such as a piano, guitar or drum, which is played to produce musical sounds: *Which instrument do you **play**?*

instrumental /ˌɪn.strəˈmen.tᵊl/ ⓤ /-t̬ᵊl/ *adj* involving only musical instruments, and no singing: *instrumental music* ○ *an instrumental piece/arrangement*

instrumental /ˌɪn.strəˈmen.tᵊl/ ⓤ /-t̬ᵊl/ *noun* [C] a piece of music without singing

instrumentalist /ˌɪn.strəˈmen.tᵊl.ɪst/ ⓤ /-t̬ᵊl-/ *noun* [C] a person who plays a musical instrument, especially as a job: *He was one of the finest instrumentalists of his day.*

instrumentation /ˌɪn.strə.menˈteɪ.ʃᵊn/ *noun* [U] *SPECIALIZED* the particular combination of musical instruments that are used to play a piece of music

instrument TOOL /ˈɪn.strə.mənt/ *noun* [C] **1** a tool or other device, especially one without electrical power, used for performing a particular piece of work: *surgical instruments* ○ *instruments of torture* ○ *The man's injuries had obviously been caused by a blunt instrument.* **2** *FORMAL* a way of achieving or causing something: *He saw the theatre as an instrument of change – a way of forcing people to consider social and political issues.* **3** Instruments are also the various devices used for measuring speed, height, etc. that are found in vehicles, especially aircraft: *the instrument panel* ○ *The lightning had damaged the plane's instruments, and they weren't giving any readings.*

instrumental /ˌɪn.strəˈmen.tᵊl/ ⓤ /-t̬ᵊl/ *adj* [after v] *FORMAL* If someone or something is instrumental in a process, plan or system, they are one of the most important influences in causing it to happen: *She was instrumental in bringing about the prison reform act.*

instrumentation /ˌɪn.strə.menˈteɪ.ʃᵊn/ *noun* [U] *SPECIALIZED* the set of instruments that are used to operate a machine

insubordinate /ˌɪn.səˈbɔː.dɪ.nət/ ⓤ /-ˈbɔːr-/ *adj DISAPPROVING* (of a person) not willing to obey orders from people in authority, or (of actions and speech etc.) showing that you are not willing to obey orders: *an insubordinate child* **insubordination** /ˌɪn.sə.bɔː.dɪˈneɪ.ʃᵊn/ ⓤ /-ˌbɔːr-/ *noun* [U] *an act of insubordination* ○ *Several officers were arrested for insubordination.*

insubstantial NOT ENOUGH /ˌɪn.səbˈstænt.ʃᵊl/ /-ˈstɑːn-/ *adj* not enough or not strong enough: *an insubstantial meal* ○ *insubstantial evidence*

insubstantial IMAGINARY /ˌɪn.səbˈstænt.ʃᵊl/ /-ˈstɑːn-/ *adj LITERARY* not existing as a physical person or thing; imaginary: *She seemed somehow insubstantial – a shadow of a woman.*

insufferable /ɪnˈsʌf.ᵊr.ə.bl̩/ ⓤ /-ɚ-/ *adj* very annoying, unpleasant or uncomfortable, and therefore extremely difficult to bear: *She disliked the president, whom she once described as an 'insufferable bore'.* ○ *The metro is insufferable in this heat.* **insufferably** /ɪnˈsʌf.ᵊr.ə.bli/ ⓤ /-ɚ-/ *adv*

insufficient /ˌɪn.səˈfɪʃ.ᵊnt/ *adj* not enough: *insufficient information/time* ○ [+ to infinitive] *There was insufficient money to fund the project.* **insufficiently** /ˌɪn.səˈfɪʃ.ᵊnt.li/ *adv*: *I felt that the whole project was insufficiently researched.* **insufficiency** /ˌɪn.səˈfɪʃ.ᵊnt.si/ *noun* [C or U]

insular /ˈɪn.sjʊ.lər/ ⓤ /-lɚ/ *adj DISAPPROVING* interested only in your own country or group and not willing to

accept different or foreign ideas **insularity** /ˌɪn.sjʊˈlær.ə.ti/ ⓤ /-t̬i/ *noun* [U]

insulate COVER /ˈɪn.sjʊ.leɪt/ *verb* [T] to cover and surround something with a material or substance in order to stop heat, sound or electricity from escaping or entering: *You can insulate a house **against** heat loss by having the windows double-glazed.*

insulation /ˌɪn.sjʊˈleɪ.ʃᵊn/ *noun* [U] **1** when you insulate something, or when something is insulated: *The animal's thick fur provides very good insulation **against** the arctic cold.* **2** material which is used to insulate something: *Glass fibre is often used as roof insulation.*

insulator /ˈɪn.sjʊ.leɪ.tər/ ⓤ /-t̬ɚ/ *noun* [C] a material or covering which electricity, heat or sound cannot go through: *Generally, plastics tend to be good insulators.*

insulate PROTECT /ˈɪn.sjʊ.leɪt/ *verb* [T] to protect someone or something from outside influences: *Children should be insulated **from** the horrors of war.* ○ *Until recently the country's economy has been insulated **from** recession by its reserves of raw materials.* **insulation** /ˌɪn.sjʊˈleɪ.ʃᵊn/ *noun* [U]

insulating tape *noun* [U] a strip of sticky material which is put around a bare piece of electrical wire in order to stop someone or something from being harmed by the electricity

insulin /ˈɪn.sjʊ.lɪn/ ⓤ /-sə-/ *noun* [U] a hormone in the body which controls the amount of sugar in the blood: *She has to have insulin injections for her diabetes.*

insult /ˈɪn.sʌlt/ *noun* [C] an offensive remark or action: *She made several insults about my appearance.* ○ *The steelworkers' leader rejected the 2% pay-rise saying it was an insult **to** the profession.* ○ *The instructions are so easy they are an insult **to** your intelligence* (= they seem to suggest you are not clever if you need to use them).

insult /ɪnˈsʌlt/ *verb* [T] to say or do something to someone that is rude or offensive: *First he drank all my wine and then he insulted all my friends.* **insulting** /ɪnˈsʌl.tɪŋ/ ⓤ /-t̬ɪŋ/ *adj*: *You can't offer such a low salary to someone who is so highly skilled – it's insulting.* **insultingly** /ɪnˈsʌl.tɪŋ.li/ ⓤ /-t̬ɪŋ-/ *adv*: *The questions were insultingly easy.*

insuperable /ɪnˈsjuː.pᵊr.ə.bl̩/ ⓤ /-ˈsuː.pɚ-/ *adj FORMAL* (especially of a problem) so great or severe that it cannot be defeated or dealt with successfully **insuperably** /ɪnˈsjuː.pᵊr.ə.bli/ ⓤ /-ˈsuː.pɚ-/ *adv*

insupportable /ˌɪn.səˈpɔː.tə.bl̩/ ⓤ /-ˈpɔːr.t̬ə-/ *adj FORMAL* difficult or impossible to bear: *The war had put an insupportable financial burden on the country.*

insurance policy *noun* [C] a written agreement between an insurance company and a person who wants insurance which states the rules of the agreement: *I **took out** a travel insurance policy before I boarded the plane.* ○ *FIGURATIVE There's one particular job I'm after but I'm applying for several others as an insurance policy* (= because I might not get the job I want).

insure /ɪnˈʃɔːr/ ⓤ /-ˈʃɔːr/ *verb* **1** [I or T; usually + adv or prep] to protect yourself against risk by regularly paying a special company that will provide a fixed amount of money if you are killed or injured or if your home or possessions are damaged, destroyed or stolen: *The house is insured for two million pounds.* ○ *All our household goods are insured **against** accidental damage.* ○ [+ obj + to infinitive] *I'm not insured to drive his car.* **2** [T] to provide INSURANCE for someone or something: *They refused to insure us because they said we're too old.* ○ *Many companies won't insure new or young drivers.*

insurance /ɪnˈʃɔː.rᵊnts/ ⓤ /-ˈʃɔːr.ᵊnts/ *noun* [U] an agreement in which you pay a company money and they pay your costs if you have an accident, injury, etc: *life/health/car/travel insurance* ○ *I'll need to **take out** extra car insurance for another driver.* ○ *The insurance doesn't cover you for* (= include) *household items.* ⊃Compare **assurance** at **assure** PROTECT.

insured /ɪnˈʃɔːd/ ⓤ /-ˈʃɔːrd/ *noun SPECIALIZED* **the insured** the person, group of people or organization who is insured in a particular agreement

insurer /ɪnˈʃɔː.rər/ ⓤ /-ˈʃɔːr.ɚ/ *noun* [C] a person or company that provides insurance: *Please contact your insurer if you have any inquiries.*

▲ **insure against** ***sth*** *phrasal verb* to do something in order to prevent something unpleasant from happening or from affecting you: *We thought we'd insure against rain by putting a tent up where people could take shelter.*

insurgent /ɪn'sɜː.dʒᵊnt/ [US] /-'sɝː-/ *noun* **1** [C usually pl] *FORMAL* someone who is fighting against the government in their own country: *All approaches to the capital are now under the control of the insurgents.* **2** [C] *US* someone who opposes especially political authority **insurgency** /ɪn'sɜː.dʒᵊnt.si/ [US] /-'sɝː-/ *noun* [U] *The government is reported to be concerned about the growing insurgency in the South.* ⊃Compare **counterinsurgency**.

insurmountable /ˌɪn.sə'maʊn.tə.bl̩/ [US] /-sɚ'maʊn.t̬ə-/ *adj FORMAL* (especially of a problem or a difficulty) so great that it cannot be dealt with successfully: *insurmountable difficulties* ○ *This small country is faced with an insurmountable debt.*

insurrection /ˌɪn.sᵊr'ek.ʃᵊn/ [US] /-sɚ-/ *noun* [C or U] an organized attempt by a group of people to defeat their government and take control of their country, usually by violence: *armed insurrection*

intact /ɪn'tækt/ *adj* **1** complete and in the original state: *The church was destroyed in the bombing but the altar survived intact.* **2** not damaged: *It's difficult to emerge from such a scandal with your reputation still intact.*

intake [BREATH] /'ɪn.teɪk/ *noun* [C] an act of taking in something, especially breath: *I heard a* ***sharp*** *intake* ***of breath*** *behind me.*

intake [AMOUNT] /'ɪn.teɪk/ *noun* [U] the amount of a particular substance which is eaten or drunk during a particular time: *It says on the packet that four slices of this bread contains one half of your recommended* ***daily*** *intake of fibre.*

intake [NUMBER OF PEOPLE] /'ɪn.teɪk/ *noun* [U] the number of people that are accepted at a particular time by an organization, especially a college or university: *The teacher-training college has increased its intake of students by 50% this year.*

intake [OPENING] /'ɪn.teɪk/ *noun* [C] an opening through which air, liquid or gas is taken in: *The Tornado jet fighter-bomber has two* ***air*** *intakes, one at the base of each wing.*

intangible /ɪn'tæn.dʒɪ.bl̩/ *adj* An intangible feeling or quality exists but you cannot describe it exactly or prove it: *She has that intangible quality which you might call charisma.* **intangible** /ɪn'tæn.dʒɪ.bl̩/ *noun* [C] *Common sense and creativity are some of the intangibles we're looking for in an employee.* **intangibly** /ɪn'tæn.dʒɪ.bli/ *adv*

inˌtangible 'asset *noun* [C] something valuable which a company possesses which is not material, such as a good reputation

integer /'ɪn.tɪ.dʒəʳ/ [US] /-dʒɚ/ *noun* [C] *SPECIALIZED* a whole number and not a fraction: *The numbers -5, 0 and 3 are integers.*

integral /'ɪn.tɪ.grəl/ [US] /-t̬ə-/ *adj* necessary and important as a part of, or contained within, a whole: *He's an integral* ***part*** *of the team and we can't do without him.* ○ *Bars and terrace cafés are integral* ***to*** *the social life of the city.*

integrate /'ɪn.tɪ.greɪt/ [US] /-t̬ə-/ *verb* **1** [I or T] to mix with and join society or a group of people, often changing to suit their way of life, habits and customs: *He seems to find it difficult to integrate socially.* ○ [R] *It's very difficult to integrate yourself* ***into*** *a society whose culture is so different from your own.* ○ *Children are often very good at integrating* ***into*** *a new culture.* **2** [T] to combine two or more things in order to become more effective: *The aim, said the minister, was to integrate Britain both politically and economically* ***into*** *the European Community.* ○ *The idea with young children is to integrate learning* ***with*** *play.* **integrated** /'ɪn.tɪ.greɪ.tɪd/ [US] /-t̬ə.greɪ.t̬ɪd/ *adj*: *The town's modern architecture is very well integrated* ***with*** *the old.* **integration** /ˌɪn.tɪ'greɪ.ʃᵊn/ [US] /-t̬ə-/ *noun* [U] *racial/cultural integration*

ˌintegrated 'circuit *noun* [C] (*ABBREVIATION* **IC**) *SPECIALIZED* a very small electronic circuit which consists of a lot of small parts made on a piece of SEMICONDUCTING material

integrity [HONESTY] /ɪn'teg.rə.ti/ [US] /-t̬i/ *noun* [U] *APPROVING* the quality of being honest and having strong moral principles that you refuse to change: *No one doubted that the president was a man of the highest integrity.*

• ***sb's*** **artistic/professional, etc. integrity** *APPROVING* someone's high artistic standards or standards of doing their job and their determination not to lower those standards: *Keen to preserve his artistic integrity, he refused several lucrative Hollywood offers.*

integrity [UNITY] /ɪn'teg.rə.ti/ [US] /-t̬i/ *noun* [U] *FORMAL* the quality of being whole and complete: *A modern extension on the old building would ruin its architectural integrity.*

intellect /'ɪn.tᵊl.ekt/ [US] /-t̬ə-/ *noun* **1** [U] the ability to understand and to think in an intelligent way, or the ability to do these things to a high level: *Her energy and intellect are respected all over the world.* ○ *He is a man more noted for his intellect than his charm.* **2** [C] *FORMAL* a highly educated person whose interests are studying and other activities that involve careful thinking

intellectual /ˌɪn.tᵊl'ek.tju.əl/ [US] /-t̬ᵊl'ek.tʃu-/ *adj* relating to your ability to think and understand things, esp complicated ideas: *Looking after a baby at home all day is nice but it doesn't provide much intellectual* ***stimulation.*** ○ *I like detective stories and romances – nothing too intellectual.*

intellectual /ˌɪn.tᵊl'ek.tju.əl/ [US] /-t̬ᵊl'ek.tʃu-/ *noun* [C] a highly educated person whose interests are studying and other activities that involve careful thinking and mental effort: *She was too much of an intellectual to find popular films interesting.* **intellectually** /ˌɪn.tᵊl'ek.tju.ə.li/ [US] /-t̬ᵊl'ek.tʃu-/ *adv*: *She's hoping to find a job which is more demanding intellectually.*

intellectualize, *UK USUALLY* **-ise** /ˌɪn.tᵊl'ek.tju.ə.laɪz/ [US] /-t̬ᵊl'ek.tʃu-/ *verb* [I or T] to think about or discuss a subject in a detailed and intellectual way, without involving your emotions or feelings: *She couldn't stand all that pointless intellectualizing about subjects that just didn't matter.* **intellectualism** /ˌɪn.tᵊl'ek.tju.ə.lɪ.zᵊm/ [US] /-t̬ᵊl'ek.tʃu-/ *noun* [U] *USUALLY DISAPPROVING*

intelˌlectual 'property *noun* [U] *LEGAL* someone's idea, invention, creation, etc., which can be protected by law from being copied by someone else

intelligence [ABILITY] /ɪn'tel.ɪ.dʒᵊnts/ *noun* [U] the ability to learn, understand and make judgments or have opinions that are based on reason: *an intelligence test* ○ *a child of high/average/low intelligence* ○ *It's the intelligence of her writing that impresses me.*

intelligent /ɪn'tel.ɪ.dʒᵊnt/ *adj* showing intelligence, or able to learn and understand things easily: *a highly intelligent young man* ○ *an intelligent remark* ○ *Helen had a few intelligent things to say on the subject.* **intelligently** /ɪn'tel.ɪ.dʒᵊnt.li/ *adv*

intelligence [SECRET INFORMATION] /ɪn'tel.ɪ.dʒᵊnts/ *group noun* [U] secret information about the governments of other countries, especially enemy governments, or a group of people who gather and deal with this information: *the Central Intelligence Agency* ○ *military intelligence* ○ *They received intelligence (reports)* ***that*** *the factory was a target for the bombing.*

the intelligentsia /ðiˌɪnˌtel.ɪ'dʒent.si.ə/ *group noun* [S] highly educated people in a society, especially those interested in the arts and in politics

intelligible /ɪn'tel.ɪ.dʒɪ.bl̩/ *adj* (of speech and writing) clear enough to be understood: *She was so upset when she spoke that she was hardly intelligible.* ✱ NOTE: The opposite is **unintelligible**. **intelligibly** /ɪn'tel.ɪ.dʒɪ.bli/ *adv* **intelligibility** /ɪnˌtel.ɪ.dʒə'bɪl.ɪ.ti/ [US] /-ə.t̬i/ *noun* [U]

intemperate /ɪn'tem.pᵊr.ət/ [US] /-pɚ-/ *adj FORMAL* (of a person or their behaviour or speech) not controlled and too extreme or violent: *an intemperate outburst* ○ *intemperate language* ○ *The governor said he would not be provoked into intemperate action.* **intemperately** /ɪn'tem.pᵊr.ət.li/ [US] /-pɚ-/ *adv* **intemperance** /ɪn'tem.pᵊr.ᵊnts/ [US] /-pɚ-/ *noun* [U]

intend /ɪn'tend/ *verb* [T] to have as a plan or purpose: [+ *to* infinitive] *We intend* ***to*** *go to Australia next year.* ○ *Somehow I offended him, which wasn't what I'd intended.* ○ [+ obj + *to* infinitive] *I don't think she intended me*

***to** hear the remark.* ○ *The course is intended **for** intermediate-level students.* ○ *It was intended **as** a compliment, honestly!*

intent /ɪnˈtent/ *noun* [U] *FORMAL* when you want and plan to do something: *I spent half the morning on the phone, which wasn't really my intent.* ○ [+ *to* infinitive] *It was not his intent **to** hurt anyone.* ○ *LEGAL She was charged with possessing weapons **with** intent **to** endanger life.*

• **to/for all intents and purposes** in all the most important ways: *For all intents and purposes, the project is completed.*

intention /ɪnˈten.ʃᵊn/ *noun* [C or U] something that you want and plan to do: [+ *to* infinitive] *It wasn't my intention **to** exclude her from the list – I just forgot her.* ○ *I've no intention **of** changing my plans just to fit in with his.* ○ *He's full of **good** intentions, but he never does anything about them!*

intentional /ɪnˈten.ʃᵊn.əl/ *adj* planned or intended: *Did you leave his name out by accident or was it intentional?* **intentionally** /ɪnˈten.ʃᵊn.ᵊl.i/ *adv*: *I didn't ignore her intentionally – I just didn't recognize her.* **-intentioned** /-ɪn.ten.ʃᵊnd/ *suffix*: *I'm sure he's **well**-intentioned – he wouldn't mean any harm.*

intended /ɪnˈten.dɪd/ *noun* [C usually sing] *OLD-FASHIONED OR HUMOROUS* the person that you are going to marry: *I shall be there with my intended.*

intense /ɪnˈtents/ *adj* **1** extreme and forceful or (of a feeling) very strong: *intense cold/heat/hatred* ○ *an intense flavour/colour* ○ *He suddenly felt an intense pain in his back.* **2** Intense people are very serious, and usually have strong emotions or opinions: *an intense young man*

intensely /ɪnˈtent.sli/ *adv*: *His strongest criticism is reserved for his father, whom he disliked intensely.* **intensity** /ɪnˈtent.sɪ.ti/ [US] /-sə.t̬i/ *noun* [U] *The explosion was of such intensity that it was heard five miles away.*

intensifier /ɪnˈtent.sɪ.faɪ.əʳ/ [US] /-ɚ/ *noun* [C] (*ALSO* **intensive**) *SPECIALIZED* In English grammar, an intensifier is a word, especially an adverb or adjective, which has little meaning itself but is used to add force to another adjective, verb or adverb: *In the phrases 'an extremely large man' and 'I strongly object', 'extremely' and 'strongly' are both intensifiers.*

intensify /ɪnˈtent.sɪ.faɪ/ *verb* [I or T] to become greater, more serious or more extreme, or to make something do this: *Fighting around the capital has intensified in the last few hours.* **intensification** /ɪnˌtent.sɪ.fɪˈkeɪ.ʃᵊn/ *noun* [U]

intensive /ɪnˈtent.sɪv/ *adj* **1** involving a lot of effort or activity in a short period of time: *two weeks of intensive training* ○ *an intensive course in English* ○ *Intensive bombing had reduced the city to rubble.* **2** Intensive farming methods are intended to produce as much food as possible from an area of land: *intensive farming/agriculture* **intensively** /ɪnˈtent.sɪv.li/ *adv*

inˌtensive ˈcare *noun* [U] **1** (in a hospital) continuous treatment for patients who are seriously ill, very badly injured or have just had an operation: *She needed intensive care for three weeks.* **2** (*ALSO* **the intensive care unit**) the part of a hospital which provides intensive care: *He nearly died in the accident and was **in** intensive care for over a month.*

intent [CONCENTRATING] /ɪnˈtent/ *adj* giving all your attention to something: *an intent stare* ○ *She had an intent look on her face.* ➲See also **intent** at **intend**. **intently** /ɪnˈtent.li/ *adv*: *The child stared intently at her.*

intent [DETERMINED] /ɪnˈtent/ *adj* **be intent on *sth*/doing *sth*** to be determined to do or achieve something: *I've tried persuading her not to go but she's intent on it.* ○ *He seems intent on upsetting everyone in the room!* ➲See also **intent** at **intend**.

inter [BURY] /ɪnˈtɜːʳ/ [US] /-ˈtɝː/ *verb* [T] **-rr-** *FORMAL* to bury a dead body: *Many of the soldiers were interred **in** unmarked graves.*

interment /ɪnˈtɜː.mənt/ [US] /-ˈtɝː-/ *noun* [C or U] *FORMAL* the act of burying a dead body

inter- [BETWEEN] /ɪn.təʳ-/ [US] /-t̬ɚ-/ *prefix* used to form adjectives meaning 'between or among the stated people, things or places': *interactive television* ○ *intergovernmental meetings* ○ *intercontinental missiles* ➲Compare **intra-**.

interact /ˌɪn.təˈrækt/ [US] /-t̬ɚˈækt/ *verb* [I] to communicate with or react to: *Dominique's teacher says that she interacts well **with** the other children.* ○ *It's interesting at parties to see how people interact socially.* ○ *We are studying how these two chemicals interact.*

interaction /ˌɪn.təˈræk.ʃᵊn/ [US] /-t̬ɚ-/ *noun* [C or U] when two or more people or things interact: *There's not enough interaction **between** the management and the workers.* ○ *Language games are usually intended to encourage student interaction.* ○ *The play follows the interactions of three very different characters.*

interactive /ˌɪn.təˈræk.tɪv/ [US] /-t̬ɚ-/ *adj* **1** describes a system or computer program which is designed to involve the user in the exchange of information: *an interactive game/video* ○ *This is an interactive museum where children can actively manipulate the exhibits.* **2** involving communication between people: *interactive teaching methods* **interactively** /ˌɪn.təˈræk.tɪv.li/ [US] /-t̬ɚ-/ *adv*: *The program lets you work through a text interactively, correcting as you go along.*

inter alia /ˌɪn.təˈreɪ.li.ə/ [US] /-t̬ɚˈeɪ-/ *adv FORMAL* among other things

interbreed /ˌɪn.təˈbriːd/ [US] /-t̬ɚ-/ *verb* [I or T] **interbred, interbred** to breed or cause to breed with members of another breed or group: *Some of the wolves had interbred **with** domestic dogs.* **interbreeding** /ˌɪn.təˈbriː.dɪŋ/ [US] /-t̬ɚ-/ *noun* [U]

intercede /ˌɪn.təˈsiːd/ [US] /-t̬ɚ-/ *verb* [I] to use your influence to persuade someone in authority to save someone else from punishment or to obtain forgiveness for this person: *Several religious leaders have interceded **with** the authorities on behalf of the condemned prisoner.*

intercession /ˌɪn.təˈseʃ.ᵊn/ [US] /-t̬ɚ-/ *noun* **1** [U] when you use your influence to make someone in authority forgive someone else or save them from punishment: *Several political prisoners have been released through the intercession of Amnesty International.* **2** [C or U] a prayer which asks God or a god to help or cure other people

intercept /ˌɪn.təˈsept/ [US] /-t̬ɚ-/ *verb* [T] to stop and catch something or someone before they are able to reach a particular place: *Law enforcement agents intercepted a shipment of drugs from Latin America.* ○ *Batistuta intercepted Neville's pass and scored the third goal.* **interception** /ˌɪn.təˈsep.ʃᵊn/ [US] /-t̬ɚ-/ *noun* [C or U] *the interception of enemy messages* ○ *a pass interception*

interceptor /ˌɪn.təˈsep.təʳ/ [US] /-t̬ɚˈsep.tɚ/ *noun* [C] a fast aircraft which attacks enemy aircraft

interchange [EXCHANGE] /ˈɪn.tə.tʃeɪndʒ/ [US] /-t̬ɚ-/ *noun* [C or U] *FORMAL* an exchange, especially of ideas or information, between different people or groups: *An international medical conference was established for the interchange of new ideas and approaches.* **interchange** /ˌɪn.təˈtʃeɪndʒ/ [US] /-t̬ɚ-/ *verb* [I or T]

interchange [ROAD] /ˈɪn.tə.tʃeɪndʒ/ [US] /-t̬ɚ-/ *noun* [C] *UK* a JUNCTION at which smaller roads meet a larger road, especially a motorway

interchangeable /ˌɪn.təˈtʃeɪn.dʒə.bl̩/ [US] /-t̬ɚ-/ *adj* able to be exchanged with each other without making any difference or without being noticed: *interchangeable parts* ○ *The terms 'drinking problem' and 'alcohol abuse' are often interchangeable.* **interchangeably** /ˌɪn.təˈtʃeɪn.dʒə.bli/ [US] /-t̬ɚ-/ *adv*

intercity /ˌɪn.təˈsɪt.i/ [US] /-t̬ɚˈsɪt̬-/ *adj* [before n] travelling from one city to another, or happening between cities: *intercity bus/train/rail service*

intercom /ˈɪn.tə.kɒm/ [US] /-t̬ɚ.kɑːm/ *noun* [C] a device which people speak into when they want to communicate with, for example, someone who is inside a building or in a different room

interconnect /ˌɪn.tə.kəˈnekt/ [US] /-t̬ɚ-/ *verb* [I or T] (of two or more things) to connect with or be related to each other: *The problems of poverty, homelessness and unemployment are all interconnected.* **interconnection** /ˌɪn.tə.kəˈnek.ʃᵊn/ [US] /-t̬ɚ-/ *noun* [C or U]

intercontinental /ˌɪn.təˌkɒn.tɪˈnen.tᵊl/ [US] /-t̬ɚˌkɑːn.t̬əˈnen.t̬ᵊl/ *adj* between continents: *intercontinental flights*

intercourse [SEX] /ˈɪn.tə.kɔːs/ [US] /-t̬ɚ.kɔːrs/ *noun* [U] (*ALSO* **sexual intercourse**) *FORMAL* the act of having sex:

vaginal/anal intercourse ○ *Our survey reveals that most couples* **have** *intercourse once a week.*

intercourse CONVERSATION /ˈɪn.tə.kɔːs/ US /-tɚ.kɔːrs/ *noun* [U] OLD-FASHIONED FORMAL conversation and social activity between people

interdenominational /ˌɪn.tə.dɪˌnɒm.ɪˈneɪ.ʃᵊn.ᵊl/ US /-tɚˌdɪˌnɑːˈmə-/ *adj* shared by different groups of the Christian church: *an interdenominational church service*

interdepartmental /ˌɪn.tə.diːˌpɑːtˈmen.tᵊl/ US /-tɚˌdiːˌpɑːrtˈmen.t̬ᵊl/ *adj* between or involving different departments of a school, university, business, etc: *an interdepartmental committee/project*

interdependent /ˌɪn.tə.dɪˈpen.dᵊnt/ US /-tɚ-/ *adj* dependent on each other: *All living things are interdependent.* **interdependence** /ˌɪn.tə.dɪˈpen.dᵊnts/ US /-tɚ-/ *noun* [U]

interdisciplinary /ˌɪn.tə.ˈdɪs.ə.plɪ.nᵊr.i/ US /-tɚˈdɪs.ə.plɪ.ner-/ *adj* involving two or more different subjects or areas of knowledge: *interdisciplinary courses* ○ *an interdisciplinary approach to the problem*

interest INVOLVEMENT /ˈɪn.t̬ᵊr.est/ US /-tɚ-/ *noun* **1** [S or U] the feeling of wanting to give your attention to something or of wanting to be involved with and to discover more about something: *I've always* **had** *an interest* **in** *astronomy.* ○ *He never seems to* **show** *any interest* **in** *his children.* ○ *Unfortunately, I* **lost** *interest half way through the film.* ○ *She* **takes** *more of* **an** *interest in politics these days.* ○ INFORMAL *Just* **out** *of interest, how old is your wife?* **2** [C] Your interests are the activities that you enjoy doing and the subjects that you like to spend time learning about: *On his form he lists his interests as cycling, the cinema and cooking.* **3** [U] the quality that makes you think that something is interesting: *Would this book* **be** *of any interest* **to** *you?*

interest /ˈɪn.t̬ᵊr.est/ US /-tɚ-/ *verb* [T] If someone or something interests you, you want to give them your attention and discover more about them: *Sport has never really interested me.*

interested /ˈɪn.t̬ᵊr.es.tɪd/ US /-tɚ-/ *adj* wanting to give your attention to something and discover more about it: *He didn't seem very interested* **in** *what I was saying.* ○ *She's at that age where she's starting to get interested* **in** *boys.* ○ *I'd be interested* **to** *hear more about your work.* ○ *"Really?" he said, with an interested look on his face.* ○ *Yes, I'd be very interested* **in** *knowing more about the services your firm offers.* ✲ NOTE: The opposite is **uninterested**.

interesting /ˈɪn.t̬ᵊr.es.tɪŋ/ US /-tɚ-/ *adj* **1** Someone or something that is interesting keeps your attention because they are unusual, exciting, or have lots of ideas: *She's quite an interesting woman.* ○ *She's got some very interesting things to say on the subject.* ○ *It is always interesting* **to** *hear other people's point of view.* ○ *Oh, I didn't know they were married – that's interesting.* **2** HUMOROUS strange or different: *That's an interesting looking hat you're wearing, Neil!*

interestingly /ˈɪn.t̬ᵊr.es.tɪŋ.li/ US /-tɚ-/ *adv* sometimes used to introduce a piece of information that the speaker finds strange and interesting: *Interestingly* **(enough)**, *he never actually said that he was innocent.*

COMMON LEARNER ERROR

interested in

Many learners wrongly use different prepositions such as 'to/about/for/on' after **interested**, but the only correct preposition is 'in'.

Ben is very interested in his family history.

~~Ben is very interested on his family history.~~

COMMON LEARNER ERROR

interesting

If something is **interesting** it is usually something that you will like or enjoy. Do not use **interesting** to describe something that will help you in a practical way. For that meaning you should use a word such as **profitable** or **worthwhile**.

~~This kind of experience could be very interesting for their future careers.~~

This kind of experience could be very **profitable/worthwhile** *for their future careers.*

interest ADVANTAGE /ˈɪn.t̬ᵊr.est/ US /-tɚ-/ *noun* [C usually plural; U] something that bring advantages to or affects someone or something: *A union looks after the interests of its members.* ○ *It's* **in** *his interests to keep careful records.* ○ **In the** *interests* **of** *safety, please do not smoke.* ○ *Despite what you think, I'm only acting in your* **best** *interests* (= doing what is best for you). ➲See also **vested interest**.

interest MONEY /ˈɪn.t̬ᵊr.est/ US /-tɚ-/ *noun* [U] **1** money which is charged by a bank or other financial organization for borrowing money: *I got a loan with an interest* **rate** *of 10%.* ○ *Interest* **charges** *on an overdraft are usually quite high.* **2** money that you earn from keeping your money in an account in a bank or other financial organization: *You should put the money in a savings account where it will* **earn** *interest.*

interest LEGAL RIGHT /ˈɪn.t̬ᵊr.est/ US /-tɚ-/ *noun* [C] an involvement or a legal right, usually relating to a business or possessions: *He is a multi-millionaire with business interests around the world.* ○ SPECIALIZED *When they divorced she retained a legal interest in the property.*

interested /ˈɪn.t̬ᵊr.es.tɪd/ US /-tɚ-/ *adj* relating to a person or group who have a connection with a particular situation, event, business, etc: *All interested* **parties** (= people who are involved) *are advised to contact this office.*

▲ **interest sb in sth** *phrasal verb* Someone might ask if they can interest you in something when they are trying to persuade you to buy something or when they are offering you something: *Can I interest you in our new range of kitchen fittings, madam?* ○ *I don't suppose I can interest you in a quick drink after work, can I?*

ˈinterest ˌgroup *noun* [C] a group or organization with particular aims and ideas which tries to influence the government: *There's too much lobbying of MPs by special interest groups.*

interface /ˈɪn.tə.feɪs/ US /-tɚ-/ *noun* [C] **1** a connection between two pieces of electronic equipment, or between a person and a computer: *My computer has a network interface, which allows me to get to other computers.* ○ *The new version of the program comes with a much better* **user** *interface* (= way of showing information to a user) *than the original.* **2** a situation, way or place where two things come together and affect each other: *the interface* **between** *technology and tradition* ○ *We need a clearer interface* **between** *management and the workforce.*

interface /ˈɪn.tə.feɪs/ US /-tɚ-/ *verb* **1** [T] SPECIALIZED to connect two or more pieces of equipment, such as computers: *The computers must be properly interfaced.* **2** [I] to communicate with someone, especially in a work-related situation: *We use email to interface* **with** *our customers.*

interfaith /ˌɪn.tə.ˈfeɪθ/ US /-tɚ-/ *adj* relating to activities involving members of different religions: *interfaith prayers/services/relations*

interfere /ˌɪn.tə.ˈfɪə/ US /-tɚ.ˈfɪr/ *verb* [I] to involve yourself in a situation when your involvement is not wanted or is not helpful: *It's their problem and I'm not going to interfere.* ○ *I'd never interfere* (UK) **between** *a husband and wife/*(US) **with** *a husband and wife.* ○ *Interfering* **in** *other people's relationships is always a mistake.*

interference /ˌɪn.tə.ˈfɪə.rᵊnts/ US /-tɚ.ˈfɪr.ᵊnts/ *noun* [U] **1** when someone tries to interfere in a situation: *She seems to regard any advice or help from me as interference.* ○ *The government's interference* **in** *the strike has been widely criticized.* **2** noise or other electronic signals that stop you from getting good pictures or sound on a television or radio

interfering /ˌɪn.tə.ˈfɪə.rɪŋ/ US /-tɚ.ˈfɪr.ɪŋ/ *adj* [before n] describes someone who gets involved in other people's lives in an unwanted and annoying way: *He's an interfering* **old busybody** *– who I go out with is none of his business!*

I

PHRASAL VERBS WITH interfere   ▼

▲ **interfere with** *sth* ⟨SPOIL⟩ *phrasal verb* **1** to prevent something from working effectively or from developing successfully: *Even a low level of noise interferes with my concentration.* **2** If something interferes with radio or television signals, it stops you from getting good sound or pictures.

▲ **interfere with** *sb* ⟨TOUCH⟩ *phrasal verb* UK DISAPPROVING to touch a child in a sexual manner: *He was sent to prison for interfering with little boys.*

interferon /ˌɪn.təˈfɪə.rɒn/ ⓊⓈ /-t̬ɚˈfɪr.ɑːn/ *noun* [C or U] SPECIALIZED any of various proteins in the body which are produced by cells as a reaction to infection by a virus

intergalactic /ˌɪn.tə.gəˈlæk.tɪk/ ⓊⓈ /-t̬ɚ-/ *adj* [before n] between GALAXIES (= large groups of stars and other matter): *intergalactic space*

interim /ˈɪn.t̬ᵊr.ɪm/ ⓊⓈ /-t̬ɚ-/ *adj* [before n] temporary and intended to be used or accepted until something permanent exists: *an interim solution* ○ *An interim **government** was set up for the period before the country's first free election.*

interim /ˈɪn.t̬ᵊr.ɪm/ ⓊⓈ /-t̬ɚ-/ *noun* **in the interim** in the time between two particular periods or events: *The new secretary starts in June, but in the interim we're having to type our own letters.*

interior /ɪnˈtɪə.ri.əʳ/ ⓊⓈ /-ˈtɪr.i.ɚ/ *noun* **1** [C] the inside part of something: *The estate agent had pictures of the house from the outside but none of its interior.* ○ *The car's interior is very impressive – wonderful leather seats and a wooden dashboard.* ⊃Compare **exterior**. **2** [S] the land which is furthest away from the outside or coast of a country or continent: *the African interior* **3** the **interior** in some countries, the government department which deals with events and matters which are of importance to the country itself instead of events in other countries: *the Ministry of the Interior* ○ *officials of the U.S. Interior Department* ○ *France's interior minister*

interior /ɪnˈtɪə.ri.əʳ/ ⓊⓈ /-ˈtɪr.i.ɚ/ *adj* [before n] inside: *The interior walls have patches of damp on them.* ○ *The paintwork on the interior doors (= those not in the outside wall of a building) is in good condition.*

in,terior deˈcorator *noun* [C] a person whose job is either planning the decoration of the inside of a building such as a house or office or doing the decoration themselves

in,terior deˈsign *noun* [U] the art of planning the decoration of the inside of a building such as a house or office **in,terior deˈsigner** *noun* [C]

interject /ˌɪn.təˈdʒekt/ ⓊⓈ /-t̬ɚ-/ *verb* [I or T] FORMAL to say something while another person is speaking; to interrupt: [+ speech] *"That's absolutely ridiculous!" Mary interjected.*

interjection /ˌɪn.təˈdʒek.ʃᵊn/ ⓊⓈ /-t̬ɚ-/ *noun* FORMAL **1** [C or U] when someone interrupts someone else, or the interruptions themselves: *Her controversial speech was punctuated with noisy interjections from the audience.* **2** [C] In grammar, an interjection is a word which is used to show a short sudden expression of emotion: *"Hey!"* is an interjection.

interlace /ˌɪn.təˈleɪs/ ⓊⓈ /-t̬ɚ-/ *verb* [T] to join different parts together to make a whole, especially by crossing one thing over another or fitting one part into another: *In her latest book, she interlaces historical events **with** her own childhood memories.*

interlink /ˌɪn.təˈlɪŋk/ ⓊⓈ /-t̬ɚ-/ *verb* [I or T] to cause to join or connect together, with the parts joined often having an effect on each other: *Police forces across Europe have begun to interlink their databases on stolen cars.* **interlinked** /ˌɪn.təˈlɪŋkt/ ⓊⓈ /-t̬ɚ-/ *adj*: *The circuits are interlinked **with** each other and the main power supply.* ○ *It's clear that unemployment, housing problems and crime are all interlinked.* **interlinking** /ˌɪn.təˈlɪŋ.kɪŋ/ ⓊⓈ /-t̬ɚ-/ *adj*

interlocking /ˌɪn.təˈlɒk.ɪŋ/ ⓊⓈ /-t̬ɚˈlɑː.kɪŋ/ *adj* firmly joined together, especially by one part fitting into another: *This jigsaw puzzle has 1000 interlocking pieces.* ○ *The fish has strong jaws and sharp interlocking teeth.*

interlock /ˌɪn.təˈlɒk/ ⓊⓈ /-t̬ɚˈlɑːk/ *verb* [I or T] to fit together firmly: *The edges interlock to form a tight seal.*

interlocutor /ˌɪn.təˈlɒk.jʊ.təʳ/ ⓊⓈ /-t̬ɚˈlɑː.kjə.t̬ɚ/ *noun* [C] FORMAL **1** someone who is involved in a conversation **2** someone who is involved in a conversation and who is representing someone else: *Abraham was able to act as interpreter and interlocutor for our group.*

interloper /ˈɪn.tə.ləʊ.pəʳ/ ⓊⓈ /-t̬ɚ.loʊ.pɚ/ *noun* [C] DISAPPROVING someone who becomes involved in an activity or a social group without being asked, or enters a place without permission: *Security did not prevent an interloper from getting onto the stage at the opening ceremony.*

interlude /ˈɪn.tə.luːd/ ⓊⓈ /-t̬ɚ-/ *noun* [C] a brief period when a situation or activity is different from what comes before and after it: *Except for a brief Christian interlude at the beginning of the 11th century, Istanbul has been a Muslim city for almost 1300 years.* ○ *The musical interludes don't really fit in with the rest of the play.*

intermarriage /ˌɪn.təˈmær.ɪdʒ/ ⓊⓈ /-t̬ɚˈmer-/ *noun* [U] marriage between people who are from different social groups, races or religions, or who are from the same family: *Have ethnic tensions in the area been reduced by intermarriage?* ○ *Intermarriage **between** close relatives is prohibited in most societies.* **intermarry** /ˌɪn.təˈmær.i/ ⓊⓈ /-t̬ɚˈmer-/ *verb* [I] *Many of the immigrants have intermarried **with** the island's original inhabitants.*

intermediary /ˌɪn.təˈmiː.di.ə.ri/ ⓊⓈ /-t̬ɚ-/ *noun* [C] someone who carries messages between people who are unwilling or unable to meet: *The police negotiated with the gunman **through** an intermediary.* ○ *The former president has agreed to act as an intermediary **between** the government and the rebels.*

intermediate /ˌɪn.təˈmiː.di.ət/ ⓊⓈ /-t̬ɚ-/ *adj* being between two other related things, levels or points: *There are three levels of difficulty in this game: low, intermediate and high.* ○ *This novel is too difficult for intermediate students of English.*

interˈmediate ˌschool *noun* [C] in the US, a school for students who are 12 to 14 years old, or 10 to 12 years old

interment /ɪnˈtɜː.mənt/ ⓊⓈ /-ˈtɜː-/ *noun* See at **inter**.

intermezzo /ˌɪn.təˈmet.səʊ/ ⓊⓈ /-t̬ɚˈmet.soʊ/ *noun* [C] *plural* **intermezzos** or **intermezzi** a short piece of music written to be played on its own or as part of a longer piece

interminable /ɪnˈtɜː.mɪ.nə.bl̩/ ⓊⓈ /-ˈtɜː-/ *adj* continuing for too long and therefore boring or annoying: *an interminable delay* ○ *We had to listen to another of his interminable stories of his days as a soldier.* **interminably** /ɪnˈtɜː.mɪ.nə.bli/ ⓊⓈ /-ˈtɜː-/ *adv*

intermingle /ˌɪn.təˈmɪŋ.gl̩/ ⓊⓈ /-t̬ɚ-/ *verb* [I] to become mixed together: *The flavours intermingle to produce a very unusual taste.* ○ *Fact is intermingled **with** fiction throughout the book.*

intermission ⓊⓈ /ˌɪn.təˈmɪʃ.ᵊn/ ⓊⓈ /-t̬ɚ-/ *noun* [C or U] (UK **interval**) **1** a brief period between the parts of a play, film, concert, etc. **2** a period between parts of a game when the players rest and people watching can leave their seats: *The Sonics led by only 2 points at intermission.*

intermittent /ˌɪn.təˈmɪt.ᵊnt/ ⓊⓈ /-t̬ɚ-/ *adj* not happening regularly or continuously; stopping and starting repeatedly or with periods in between: *intermittent rain* ○ *an intermittent noise* ○ *Although she made intermittent movie appearances, she was essentially a stage actress.* **intermittently** /ˌɪn.təˈmɪt.ᵊnt.li/ ⓊⓈ /-t̬ɚ-/ *adv*: *We've discussed this problem intermittently, but so far we've failed to come up with a solution.*

intern ⟨PUNISH⟩ /ɪnˈtɜːn/ ⓊⓈ /-ˈtɜːn/ *verb* [T often passive] to put someone in prison for political or military reasons, especially during a war: *Many foreigners were interned for the duration of the war.*

internee /ˌɪn.tɜːˈniː/ ⓊⓈ /-t̬ɚ-/ *noun* [C] a person who has been put in prison for political or military reasons, especially during a war **internment** /ɪnˈtɜːn.mənt/ ⓊⓈ /-ˈtɜːn-/ *noun* [U] *an internment **camp***

intern ⟨MEDICAL⟩ /ˈɪn.tɜːn/ ⓊⓈ /-tɜːn/ *noun* [C] US a **houseman**

interpret

internist /ˈɪn.tɜː.nɪst/ ⓊⓈ /-ˈtɜːː-/ *noun* [C] ⓊⓈ a doctor who specializes in identifying and treating diseases which do not need SURGERY (= cutting into the body)

internship /ˈɪn.tɜːn.ʃɪp/ ⓊⓈ /-tɜːn-/ *noun* [C] ⓊⓈ a period of training spent in a hospital by a young doctor in order to finish their medical qualification: *He served his internship at Garfield Hospital.*

intern STUDENT /ˈɪn.tɜːn/ ⓊⓈ /-tɜːn/ *noun* [C] MAINLY US someone who is finishing their training for a skilled job especially by obtaining practical experience of the work involved: *She worked in the White House as an intern.* **intern** /ɪnˈtɜːn/ ⓊⓈ /-ˈtɜːn/ *verb* [I] US *After graduation he'll intern for six months with a San Francisco firm.*

internship /ˈɪn.tɜːn.ʃɪp/ ⓊⓈ /-tɜːn-/ *noun* [C] ⓊⓈ a period of time spent doing a job as part of becoming qualified to do it: *She has a **summer** internship at a local TV station.*

internal /ɪnˈtɜː.nəl/ ⓊⓈ /-ˈtɜːː-/ *adj* existing or happening inside a person, object, organization, place or country: *He sustained injuries to his arms, legs and several internal **organs**.* ○ *The bank conducted its own internal investigation into the robbery.* ○ *The government warned its neighbours not to interfere in its internal **affairs**.* ⊃See also **interior**. Compare **external**. **internally** /ɪnˈtɜː.nəl.i/ ⓊⓈ /-ˈtɜːː-/ *adv*: *This medicine is for external use only and should not be taken internally.*

in,ternal com'bustion ,engine *noun* [C] an engine which produces energy by burning fuel within itself

internalize, UK USUALLY -**ise** /ɪnˈtɜː.nəl.aɪz/ ⓊⓈ /-ˈtɜːː-/ *verb* [T] FORMAL **1** to accept or absorb an idea, attitude, belief, etc. so that it becomes part of your character: *He had not expected the people so readily to internalize the values of democracy.* **2** If you internalize your emotions or feelings, you do not allow them to show although you think about them: *Women tend to internalize all their anxiety and distress – men hit out.* **internalization** UK USUALLY -**isation** /ɪnˌtɜː.nəl.aɪˈzeɪ.ʃən/ ⓊⓈ /-ˌtɜːː-/ *noun* [U]

in,ternal 'medicine *noun* [U] US the part of medical science that is involved in the discovery of diseases inside the body and the treatment of them without cutting the body open

the In,ternal 'Revenue ,Service *noun* [S] (ABBREVIATION **the IRS**) US the government department that collects most national taxes in the United States

international /ˌɪn.təˈnæʃ.ən.ᵊl/ ⓊⓈ /-tɚ-/ *adj* involving more than one country: *international politics* ○ *an international team of scientists*

international /ˌɪn.təˈnæʃ.ən.ᵊl/ ⓊⓈ /-tɚ-/ *noun* [C] UK a sports event involving more than one country, or a person who competes in it: *a one-day international* ○ *Six rugby internationals* (= players) *were charged with taking drugs to improve their performance.* **internationally** /ˌɪn.təˈnæʃ.ən.ᵊl.i/ ⓊⓈ /-tɚ-/ *adv*: *Her internationally acclaimed novel has won several literary prizes.*

internationalize, UK USUALLY -**ise** /ˌɪn.təˈnæʃ.ən.ᵊl.aɪz/ ⓊⓈ /-tɚ-/ *verb* [T] to make something become international: *Bob Marley internationalized reggae, making it known throughout the world.* **internationalization** UK USUALLY -**isation** /ˌɪn.tə,næʃ.ən.ᵊl.aɪˈzeɪ.ʃən/ ⓊⓈ /-tɚ-/ *noun* [U]

internationalism /ˌɪn.təˈnæʃ.ən.ᵊl.ɪ.zᵊm/ ⓊⓈ /-tɚ-/ *noun* [U] **1** the state of being international, or happening in and between many countries: *the increasing internationalism of criminals* **2** the belief that countries can benefit more by working together and trying to understand each other than by arguing and fighting wars **internationalist** /ˌɪn.təˈnæʃ.ən.ᵊl.ɪst/ ⓊⓈ /-tɚ-/ *noun* [C]

the inter,national com'munity *noun* [S] countries of the world considered or acting together as a group: *Any taking of hostages is unacceptable and must be firmly opposed by the international community.*

Inter,national 'Date Line *noun* [S] The International Date Line is an imaginary line between the most northern and southern points on the Earth which goes through the Pacific Ocean. The date on the west side of the line is one day earlier than the date on the east side of the line.

the Internationale /ˌðɪˌɪn.təˌnæʃ.əˈnɑːl/ ⓊⓈ /-tɚ-/ *noun* [S] a song which is sung by people who believe in COMMUNISM

inter,national 'law *noun* [U] the set of rules that most countries obey when dealing with other countries

Inter,national 'Monetary ,Fund *noun* [S] ⊃See **the IMF**.

Inter,national Pho,netic 'Alphabet *noun* [U] ⊃See **IPA**.

internecine /ˌɪn.təˈniː.saɪn/ ⓊⓈ /-tɚˈniː.sɪn/ *adj* FORMAL Internecine war or fighting happens between members of the same group, religion or country: *internecine war/warfare*

internee /ˌɪn.tɜːˈniː/ ⓊⓈ /-tɜː-/ *noun* [C] ⊃See at **intern** PUNISH.

the Internet /ðɪˈɪn.tə.net/ ⓊⓈ /-tɚ-/ *noun* [S] (INFORMAL **the Net**) the large system of connected computers around the world which allow people to share information and communicate with each other using EMAIL (= electronic mail): *I found out about the bombings **from/on** the Internet.*

internet banking /ˌɪn.tə.netˈbæŋ.kɪŋ/ ⓊⓈ /-tɚ-/ *noun* [U] the system that allows you to put in or take out money from a bank account by using the Internet

,internet 'café *noun* [C] a small informal restaurant where you can pay to use the Internet

internment /ɪnˈtɜːn.mənt/ ⓊⓈ /-ˈtɜːn-/ *noun* [U] ⊃See at **intern** PUNISH.

internship /ˈɪn.tɜːn.ʃɪp/ ⓊⓈ /-tɜːn-/ *noun* [C] See at **intern** STUDENT.

interpersonal /ˌɪn.təˈpɜː.sᵊn.ᵊl/ ⓊⓈ /-tɚˈpɜːː-/ *adj* connected with relationships between people: *The successful applicant will have excellent interpersonal **skills**.*

interplanetary /ˌɪn.təˈplæn.ɪ.tri/ ⓊⓈ /-ter.i/ *adj* [before n] between planets: *interplanetary space*

interplay /ˈɪn.tə.pleɪ/ ⓊⓈ /-tɚ-/ *noun* [U] the effect that two or more things have on each other: *Our personalities result from the complex interplay **between** our genes and our environment.*

Interpol /ˈɪn.tə.pɒl/ ⓊⓈ /-tɚ.pɑːl/ *group noun* [U not after **the**] an international police organization which helps national police forces to work together to catch criminals

interpolate /ɪnˈtɜː.pə.leɪt/ ⓊⓈ /-ˈtɜːː-/ *verb* [T] FORMAL **1** to add words to a text **2** to interrupt someone by saying something **interpolation** /ɪnˌtɜː.pəˈleɪ.ʃən/ ⓊⓈ /-ˌtɜːː-/ *noun* [C or U]

interpose PUT BETWEEN /ˌɪn.təˈpəʊz/ ⓊⓈ /-tɚˈpoʊz/ *verb* [T] FORMAL to put yourself or something between two things, people or groups, especially in order to stop them doing something: [R] *The teacher interposed herself **between** the two snarling boys.*

interpose INTERRUPT /ˌɪn.təˈpəʊz/ ⓊⓈ /-tɚˈpoʊz/ *verb* [T] FORMAL to interrupt someone: [+ speech] *"I can't agree with you, Mr Heathcliff," he interposed.* **interposition** /ˌɪn.tə.pəˈzɪʃ.ᵊn/ ⓊⓈ /-tɚ-/ *noun* [C or U]

interpret FIND MEANING /ɪnˈtɜː.prɪt/ ⓊⓈ /-ˈtɜːː-/ *verb* [T] to decide what the intended meaning of something is: *It's difficult to interpret these statistics without knowing how they were obtained.* ○ *A jury should not interpret the silence of a defendant **as** a sign of guilt.* **interpretation** /ɪnˌtɜː.prɪˈteɪ.ʃᵊn/ ⓊⓈ /-ˈtɜːː-/ *noun* [C or U] an explanation or opinion of what something means: *The dispute is based on two widely differing interpretations of the law.* ○ *The rules are vague and **open to** interpretation.* ○ *It is difficult for many people to accept a **literal** interpretation of the Bible.* **interpretive** /ɪnˈtɜː.prɪ.tə.tɪv/ ⓊⓈ /-ˈtɜːː.prə.tə.tɪv/ *adj* (ALSO **interpretative**) FORMAL related to explaining or understanding the meaning of something: *an interpretive display/centre*

interpret EXPRESS /ɪnˈtɜː.prɪt/ ⓊⓈ /-ˈtɜːː-/ *verb* [T] to express your own ideas about the intended meaning of a play or a piece of music when performing it: *If Shakespeare's plays are to reach a large audience they need to be interpreted in a modern style.* **interpreter** /ɪnˈtɜː.prɪ.tər/ ⓊⓈ /-ˈtɜːː.prɪ.tɚ/ *noun* [C] *He's a noted interpreter of traditional Irish music.* **interpretation** /ɪnˌtɜː.prɪˈteɪ.ʃᵊn/ ⓊⓈ /-ˌtɜːː.prɪˈteɪ-/ *noun* [C or U] *Her interpretation of Juliet was one of the best performances I have ever seen.*

interpret BETWEEN LANGUAGES /ɪnˈtɜː.prɪt/ ⓤ /-ˈtɝː-/ *verb* [I or T] to change what someone is saying into another language: *We had to ask our guide to interpret for us.* ⊃Compare **translate**.

interpreter /ɪnˈtɜː.prɪ.təʳ/ ⓤ /-ˈtɝː.prɪ.t̬ɚ/ *noun* [C] **1** someone whose job is to change what someone else is saying into another language: *She works as an interpreter in Brussels.* ○ *Speaking through an interpreter, the president said the terms of the ceasefire were completely unacceptable.* **2** SPECIALIZED a computer program that changes the instructions in another program into a form that can be easily understood by a computer

interracial /ˌɪn.təˈreɪ.ʃʳl/ ⓤ /-t̬ɚ-/ *adj* involving different human races: *an interracial marriage/relationship* ○ *The government must act to stamp out interracial hatred and violence.*

interregnum /ˌɪn.təˈreg.nəm/ ⓤ /-t̬ɚ-/ *noun* [S] FORMAL a period when a country or organization lacks a leader

interrelate /ˌɪn.tə.rɪˈleɪt/ ⓤ /-t̬ɚ-/ *verb* [I] to be connected in such a way that each thing has an effect on or depends on the other: *Children need to be educated about the way that diet and health interrelate.* **interrelated** /ˌɪn.tə.rɪˈleɪ.tɪd/ ⓤ /-t̬ɚ.rɪˈleɪ.t̬ɪd/ *adj: interrelated problems/issues/activities*

interrelationship /ˌɪn.tə.rɪˈleɪ.ʃʳn.ʃɪp/ ⓤ /-t̬ɚ-/ *noun* [C or U] (ALSO **interrelation**) the way in which two or more things or people are connected and affect one another: *the interrelationship between smoking and respiratory disease*

interrogate /ɪnˈter.ə.geɪt/ *verb* [T] **1** to ask someone a lot of questions for a long time in order to obtain information, sometimes using threats or violence: *Thousands of dissidents have been interrogated or imprisoned in recent weeks.* **2** SPECIALIZED to obtain information from a computer **interrogation** /ɪnˌter.əˈgeɪ.ʃʳn/ *noun* [C or U] *One by one they were taken for interrogation.* ○ *She was subjected to a long and lengthy interrogations.* **interrogator** /ɪnˈter.ə.geɪ.təʳ/ ⓤ /-t̬ɚ/ *noun* [C]

interrogative /ˌɪn.təˈrɒg.ə.tɪv/ ⓤ /-t̬əˈrɑː.gə.t̬ɪv/ *noun* [C] SPECIALIZED a word or sentence used when asking a question: *'Who' and 'why' are interrogatives.*

the interrogative *noun* [S] the form of a sentence that is used for asking questions

interrogative /ˌɪn.təˈrɒg.ə.tɪv/ ⓤ /-t̬əˈrɑː.gə.t̬ɪv/ *adj* in the form of a question, or used in questions: *an interrogative adverb*

interrupt /ˌɪn.təˈrʌpt/ ⓤ /-t̬ə-/ *verb* [I or T] to stop a person from speaking for a short period by something you say or do, or to stop something from happening for a short period: *She tried to explain what had happened but he kept interrupting her.* ○ *I wish you'd stop interrupting.* ○ *We had to interrupt our trip when we heard John's mother was ill.* **interruption** /ˌɪn.təˈrʌp.ʃʳn/ ⓤ /-t̬ə-/ *noun* [C or U] *a brief interruption* ○ *I worked all morning without interruption.*

interscholastic /ˌɪn.tə.skəˈlæs.tɪk/ ⓤ /-t̬ɚ.skə-/ *adj* [before n] US involving two or more schools: *an interscholastic competition/debate*

intersect /ˌɪn.təˈsekt/ ⓤ /-t̬ɚ-/ *verb* **1** [I or T] (of lines, roads, etc.) to cross one another: *The roads intersect near the bridge.* **2** [T] to divide an area into smaller parts by crossing it with straight lines: *The gardens are intersected by gravel paths.*

intersection /ˌɪn.təˈsek.ʃʳn/ ⓤ /-t̬ɚ-/ *noun* **1** [C or U] when two lines cross, or the point where this happens: *The intersection of the lines on the graph marks the point where we start to make a profit.* **2** [C] MAINLY US the place where two or more roads join or cross each other: *a busy intersection* ○ *Turn right at the next intersection.*

intersperse /ˌɪn.təˈspɜːs/ ⓤ /-t̬ɚˈspɝːs/ *verb* [T] to mix one thing in with another in an irregular way: *The documentary intersperses graphical animations with film clips of the actual event.* ○ *Her handwritten notes were interspersed throughout the text.*

interspersed /ˌɪn.təˈspɜːst/ ⓤ /-t̬ɚˈspɝːst/ *adj* **interspersed with sth** having something in several places among something else: *forests interspersed with meadows and lakes*

interstate /ˌɪn.təˈsteɪt/ ⓤ /ˈɪn.t̬ɚ.steɪt/ *adj* [before n] involving two or more of the states into which some countries such as the US are divided: *the interstate highway system* ○ *interstate banking legislation* ○ *interstate road transport costs*

interstate /ˈɪn.tə.steɪt/ ⓤ /ˈɪn.t̬ɚ.steɪt/ *noun* [C] a fast wide road which goes between states and connects important cities in the United States

interstellar /ˌɪn.təˈstel.əʳ/ ⓤ /-t̬ɚˈstel.ɚ/ *adj* [before n] between the stars: *interstellar space*

interstice /ɪnˈtɜː.stɪs/ ⓤ /-ˈtɝː-/ *noun* [C usually pl] FORMAL a very small crack or space: *The wall was old and crumbling with plants growing in the interstices between/in/of the bricks.*

intertwine /ˌɪn.təˈtwaɪn/ ⓤ /-t̬ɚ-/ *verb* [I or T] to twist or be twisted together, or to be connected so as to be difficult to separate: *The town's prosperity is inextricably intertwined with the fortunes of the factory.* ○ *The trees' branches intertwined to form a dark roof over the path.*

interval SPACE /ˈɪn.tə.vʳl/ ⓤ /-t̬ɚ-/ *noun* [C] **1** a period between two events or times, or the space between two points: *We see each other at regular intervals – usually about once a month.* ○ *There's often a long interval between an author completing a book and it appearing in the shops.* **2** UK (US **intermission**) a brief period between the parts of a performance or a sports event: *There will be two twenty-minute intervals during the opera.* ○ *He scored his first goal of the match three minutes after the interval.* **3** **at intervals** repeated after a particular period of time or a particular distance: *In the event of fire, the alarm will sound at 15-second intervals/at intervals of 15 seconds.*

interval MUSIC /ˈɪn.tə.vʳl/ ⓤ /-t̬ɚ-/ *noun* [C] SPECIALIZED the amount by which one note is higher or lower than another: *an interval of a 5th* (= the top note four notes higher than the bottom one)

intervene GET INVOLVED /ˌɪn.təˈviːn/ ⓤ /-t̬ɚ-/ *verb* [I] to intentionally become involved in a difficult situation in order to improve it or prevent it from getting worse: *The Central Bank intervened in the currency markets today to try to stabilize the exchange rate.* ○ [+ to infinitive] *The Minister intervened personally to stop the museum being closed.* **intervention** /ˌɪn.təˈven.ʃʳn/ ⓤ /-t̬ɚ-/ *noun* [C or U] *Half the people questioned said they were opposed to military intervention (in the civil war).* ○ *Repeated interventions on the currency markets have failed to prevent the value of the currency falling.*

interventionist /ˌɪn.təˈven.ʃʳn.ɪst/ ⓤ /-t̬ɚ-/ *adj* (of a government or their actions) tending to become involved, either in the problems of another country, or in the economy of one's own country: *an interventionist role* ○ *interventionist economic policy* **interventionism** /ˌɪn.təˈven.ʃʳn.ɪ.zʳm/ ⓤ /-t̬ɚ-/ *noun* [U] *UN interventionism*

intervene COME BETWEEN /ˌɪn.təˈviːn/ ⓤ /-t̬ɚ-/ *verb* [I] to happen between two times or between other events or activities: *Two decades intervened between the completion of the design and the opening of the theatre.* **intervening** /ˌɪn.təˈviː.nɪŋ/ ⓤ /-t̬ɚ-/ *adj* [before n] *It was a long time since my last visit to Berlin, and it had changed dramatically in the intervening period/years.*

interview /ˈɪn.tə.vjuː/ ⓤ /-t̬ɚ-/ *noun* [C] **1** a meeting in which someone asks you questions to see if you are suitable for a job or course: *a job interview* ○ *I had an interview for a job with a publishing firm.* **2** a meeting in which someone is asked questions about themselves for a newspaper article, television show, etc: *an exclusive interview with Paul Simon* ○ *In a television interview last night she denied she had any intention of resigning.* **3** a meeting in which the police ask someone questions to see if they have committed a crime

interview /ˈɪn.tə.vjuː/ ⓤ /-t̬ɚ-/ *verb* [T] to ask someone questions in an interview: *We've had 200 applicants for the job, but we only plan to interview about 20 of them.* ○ *Who's the most famous person you've ever interviewed on TV?* ○ *Police are interviewing a 43-year-old man in connection with the murder.*

interviewee /ˌɪn.tə.vjuˈiː/ ⓤ /-t̬ɚ-/ *noun* [C] the person who answers the questions during an interview

interviewer /ˈɪn.tə.vjuː.əʳ/ [US] /-t̬ɚ.vjuː.ɚ/ *noun* [C] the person who asks the questions during an interview

interweave /ˌɪn.təˈwiːv/ [US] /-t̬ɚ-/ *verb* [T] **interwove, interwoven** to weave together or combine two or more things so that they cannot be separated easily: *She has created an intriguing story by skillfully interweaving fictional and historical events.*

intestate /ɪnˈtes.teɪt/ *adj* [after v] SPECIALIZED describes someone who has died without leaving instructions about who should be given their property: *Many people* ***die*** *intestate because they thought they were too young to make a will.*

intesˌtinal ˈfortitude *noun* [U] US bravery and determination: *The fact that he's still trying for the championship is a tribute to his intestinal fortitude.*

intestine /ɪnˈtes.tɪn/ *noun* [C usually pl] (either of the two parts of) a long tube through which food travels from the stomach and out of the body while it is being digested: *Antibodies from the mother's milk line the baby's intestines and prevent infection.* **intestinal** /ɪnˈtes.tɪ.nəl/ /ˌɪn.tesˈtaɪ-/ *adj*: *intestinal surgery*

intimate [PERSONAL] /ˈɪn.tɪ.mət/ [US] /-t̬ə-/ *adj* having, or being likely to cause, a very close friendship or personal or sexual relationship: *intimate relationships* ○ *The restaurant has a very intimate* ***atmosphere****.* ○ *He's become very intimate* ***with*** *an actress.*

intimate /ˈɪn.tɪ.mət/ [US] /-t̬ə-/ *noun* [C] FORMAL a close friend: *Intimates of the star say that he has been upset by the personal attacks on him that have appeared in the press recently.*

intimacy /ˈɪn.tɪ.mə.si/ [US] /-t̬ə-/ *noun* **1** [U] when you have a close friendship or sexual relationship with someone: *Intimacy between teachers and students is not recommended.* **2** [C usually pl] things which are said or done only by people who have a close relationship with each other: *It was obvious from their witty intimacies that they had been good friends for many years.*

intimately /ˈɪn.tɪ.mət.li/ [US] /-t̬ə-/ *adv*: *Well, I know who she is although I'm not intimately* (= closely) ***acquainted*** *with her.*

intimate [EXPERT] /ˈɪn.tɪ.mət/ [US] /-t̬ə-/ *adj* expert, detailed and obtained from a lot of studying or experience: *She has an intimate* ***knowledge*** *of Tuscany, where she has lived for twenty years.* **intimately** /ˈɪn.tɪ.mət.li/ [US] /-t̬ə-/ *adv*: *She's been intimately* ***involved*** *in the project since it began.*

intimate [SUGGEST] /ˈɪn.tɪ.meɪt/ [US] /-t̬ə-/ *verb* [T] FORMAL to make clear what you think or want without stating it directly: [+ (that)] *She has intimated* ***that*** *she will resign if she loses the vote.* **intimation** /ˌɪn.tɪˈmeɪ.ʃᵊn/ [US] /-t̬ə-/ *noun* [C] *His suicide attempt was the first intimation* ***that*** *he was seriously depressed.*

intimidate /ɪnˈtɪm.ɪ.deɪt/ *verb* [T] to frighten or threaten someone, usually in order to persuade them to do something that you want them to do: *They were intimidated* ***into*** *accepting a pay cut by the threat of losing their jobs.*

intimidated /ɪnˈtɪm.ɪ.deɪ.tɪd/ [US] /-t̬ɪd/ *adj* frightened or nervous because you are not confident in a situation: *Older people can feel very intimidated by computers* **intimidation** /ɪnˌtɪm.ɪˈdeɪ.ʃᵊn/ *noun* [U] *The campaign of violence and intimidation* ***against*** *them intensifies daily.*

intimidating /ɪnˈtɪm.ɪ.deɪ.tɪŋ/ [US] /-t̬ɪŋ/ *adj* making you feel frightened or nervous: *an intimidating array of weapons* ○ *an intimidating manner* ○ *She can be very intimidating when she's angry.*

into [INSIDE] /ˈɪn.tuː/ *prep* towards the inside or middle of something and about to be contained, surrounded or enclosed by it: *Would you put the jar back into the cupboard for me, please?* ○ *Shall we go into the garden?* ○ *Stop running around and get into bed!* ○ *I can't get into these trousers anymore. They're far too small for me.*

into [CHANGE] /ˈɪn.tuː/ *prep* used to show when a person or thing is changing from one form or condition to another: *Peel the cucumber and chop it into small cubes.* ○ *There was a series of explosions and the van burst into flames* (= started to burn violently). ○ *Her novels have been translated into nineteen languages.* ○ *We're planning to turn the smallest bedroom into an office.*

into [ABOUT] /ˈɪn.tuː/ *prep* involving or about something: *an inquiry into the cause of the accident*

into [TOWARDS] /ˈɪn.tuː/ *prep* in the direction of something or someone: *She was looking straight into his eyes.*

into [TOUCHING FORCEFULLY] /ˈɪn.tuː/ *prep* used to show movement which involves something touching something else with a lot of force but without moving inside it: *He's always walking into things when he hasn't got his glasses on.*

into [DIVISION] /ˈɪn.tuː/ *prep* used when referring to the division of one number by another number: *What's 5 into 125?*

into [INTERESTED] /ˈɪn.tuː/ *prep* enthusiastic about or interested in: *Jackie's really into classical music.*

intolerable /ɪnˈtɒl.ᵊr.ə.bl̩/ [US] /-ˈtɑː.lɚ-/ *adj* too bad or unpleasant to deal with or accept: *The situation has become intolerable.* ○ *The constant fighting made life at home intolerable.* ○ *Three-quarters of the world's population live in conditions that people in the West would find intolerable.* **intolerably** /ɪnˈtɒl.ᵊr.ə.bli/ [US] /-ˈtɑː.lɚ-/ *adv*

intolerant /ɪnˈtɒl.ᵊr.ᵊnt/ [US] /-ˈtɑː.lɚ-/ *adj* DISAPPROVING disapproving of or refusing to accept ideas or ways of behaving that are different from your own: *She can be very intolerant* ***of*** *students who don't understand what she's talking about.* **intolerantly** /ɪnˈtɒl.ᵊr.ᵊnt.li/ [US] /-ˈtɑː.lɚ-/ *adv*

intolerance /ɪnˈtɒl.ᵊr.ᵊnts/ [US] /-ˈtɑː.lɚ-/ *noun* **1** [U] when you refuse to accept ideas, beliefs or behaviour that are different from your own: *racial/religious intolerance* ○ *One side-effect of the drug is intolerance* ***of*** (= being unable to bear) *bright light.* **2** [C or U] If you have a food intolerance, you cannot digest a particular food properly and may feel ill if you eat it: *(a)* ***food*** *intolerance* ○ *a wheat/lactose intolerance* ○ *Amy has an intolerance* ***to*** *dairy products.*

intonation /ˌɪn.təˈneɪ.ʃᵊn/ *noun* **1** [C or U] the sound changes produced by the rise and fall of the voice when speaking, especially when this has an effect on the meaning of what is said: *The end of a sentence that is not a question is usually marked by falling intonation.* **2** [U] the degree to which the notes of a piece of music are played or sung correctly: *The violinist had good intonation, and a wonderful pure tone.*

intone /ɪnˈtəʊn/ [US] /-ˈtoʊn/ *verb* [T] FORMAL to say something slowly and seriously in a voice which does not rise or fall much: [+ speech] *"Let us pray," the priest intoned to his congregation.*

ˌin ˈtoto *adv* FORMAL as a total or whole: *The available information amounts to very little in toto.*

intoxicated /ɪnˈtɒk.sɪ.keɪ.tɪd/ [US] /-ˈtɑːk.sɪ.keɪ.t̬ɪd/ *adj* **1** FORMAL drunk: *She was charged with driving while intoxicated.* **2** excited, happy and slightly out of control because of an experience such as love, success, etc: *She was understandably intoxicated by her success in the national competition.*

intoxicating /ɪnˈtɒk.sɪ.keɪ.tɪŋ/ [US] /-ˈtɑːk.sɪ.keɪ.t̬ɪŋ/ *adj* **1** If a drink is intoxicating, it makes you drunk if you have too much: *intoxicating* ***liquor*** **2** An intoxicating experience or idea makes you feel excited and emotional: *an intoxicating thought*

intoxication /ɪnˌtɒk.sɪˈkeɪ.ʃᵊn/ [US] /-ˌtɑːk-/ *noun* [U] *He used to claim that he had his best ideas after several days of intoxication* (= being drunk). ○ *The feeling of intoxication* (= excitement) *that followed her victory was cut short by her father's sudden death.*

intoxicant /ɪnˈtɒk.sɪ.kᵊnt/ [US] /-ˈtɑːk-/ *noun* [C] SPECIALIZED a substance such as alcohol that produces feelings of pleasure or happiness in a person artificially

intra- /ɪn.trə-/ *prefix* used to form adjectives meaning 'within' (the stated place or group): *intra-EU trade* ○ *intrafamily disputes* ➲Compare **inter-** BETWEEN.

intractable /ɪnˈtræk.tə.bl̩/ *adj* FORMAL very difficult and seeming to be impossible to control, manage or solve: *We are facing an intractable* ***problem****.* **intractably** /ɪnˈtræk.tə.bli/ [US] /-t̬ə-/ *adv*: *an intractably violent relationship* **intractability** /ɪnˌtræk.təˈbɪl.ɪ.ti/ [US] /-ə.t̬i/ *noun* [U]

intramural /ˌɪn.trəˈmjʊə.rəl/ [US] /-ˈmjʊr.ᵊl/ *adj* happening within or involving the members of one school, college or university: *an intramural basketball competition*

intranet /'ɪn.trə.net/ *noun* [C] a system of connected computers which works like the Internet and which enables people within an organization to communicate with each other and share information: *I'll post the agenda for next week's meeting on the intranet.*

intransigent /ɪn'træn.zɪ.dʒ³nt/ /-'trɑː.n-/ *adj* FORMAL refusing to be persuaded, especially refusing to change opinions that are strongly believed in: *Unions claim that the management continues to maintain an intransigent position.* **intransigently** /ɪn'træn.zɪ.dʒ³nt.li/ /-'trɑː.n-/ *adv* **intransigence** /ɪn'træn.zɪ.dʒ³nts/ /-'trɑː.n-/ *noun* [U]

intransitive /ɪn'træn.zɪ.tɪv/ Ⓤ /-t̬ɪv/ *adj* SPECIALIZED (of a verb) having or needing no object: *In the sentence 'I tried to persuade him, but he wouldn't come', 'come' is an intransitive verb.* ○ *In this dictionary, verbs which are intransitive are marked [I].* ⊃Compare **ditransitive**; **transitive**. **intransitive** /ɪn'træn.zɪ.tɪv/ Ⓤ /-t̬ɪv/ *noun* [C] **intransitively** /ɪn'træn.zɪ.tɪv.li/ Ⓤ /-t̬ɪv/ *adv*

intravenous /ˌɪn.trə'viː.nəs/ *adj* (ABBREVIATION **IV**) into or connected to a vein: *intravenous feeding/fluids* ○ *an intravenous drip/injection.* ○ *Intravenous drug users are at particular risk of contracting the disease.* **intravenously** /ˌɪn.trə'viː.nə.sli/ *adv*

in-tray UK /'ɪn.treɪ/ *noun* [C] (US **in-box**) a flat open container where letters and other documents are put when they arrive in a person's office and where they are kept until the person has time to deal with them: *Just put it in my in-tray and I'll look at it later.*

intrepid /ɪn'trep.ɪd/ *adj* extremely brave and showing no fear of dangerous situations: *a team of intrepid explorers* **intrepidly** /ɪn'trep.ɪd.li/ *adv*

intricate /'ɪn.trɪ.kət/ *adj* having a lot of small parts or details that are arranged in a complicated way and are therefore sometimes difficult to understand, solve or produce: *The watch mechanism is extremely intricate and very difficult to repair.* ○ *Police officers uncovered an intricate web of deceit.* **intricately** /'ɪn.trɪ.kət.li/ *adv: an intricately engraved pendant* **intricacy** /'ɪn.trɪ.kə.si/ *noun* [U] *the intricacy of the needlework*

intricacies /'ɪn.trɪ.kə.siz/ *plural noun* complicated details: *I enjoyed the film, but I couldn't follow all the intricacies of the plot.*

intrigue INTEREST /ɪn'triːg/ *verb* [T] to interest someone a lot, especially by being strange, unusual or mysterious: *Throughout history, people have been intrigued by the question of whether there is intelligent life elsewhere in the universe.* **intriguing** /ɪn'triː.ɡɪŋ/ *adj: an intriguing possibility/question* ○ *She has a really intriguing personality.* **intriguingly** /ɪn'triː.ɡɪŋ.li/ *adv*

intrigue SECRET /'ɪn.triːg/ *noun* [C or U] (the making of) a secret plan to do something, especially something that will harm another person: *a tale of political intrigue*

intrinsic /ɪn'trɪn.zɪk/ *adj* being an extremely important and basic characteristic of a person or thing: *works of little intrinsic value/interest* ○ *Maths is an intrinsic part of the school curriculum.* **intrinsically** /ɪn'trɪn.zɪ.kli/ *adv*

intro /'ɪn.trəʊ/ Ⓤ /-troʊ/ *noun* [C] *plural* **intros** INFORMAL an **introduction**, see at **introduce** MAKE KNOWN, **introduce** BEGIN: *This song has a brilliant piano intro.* ○ *Would you mind doing the intros, Martha, while I pour some drinks?*

introduce MAKE KNOWN /ˌɪn.trə'djuːs/ Ⓤ /-'duːs/ *verb* [T] to tell someone another person's name the first time that they meet: *I'd like to introduce my younger son, Mark.* ○ *Have you two been introduced (to each other)?* **introduction** /ˌɪn.trə'dʌk.ʃ³n/ *noun* [C or U] *You'll have to do/make the introductions – I don't know everyone's name.* ○ *My next guest needs no introduction* (= is already known to everyone).

introduce PUT INTO USE /ˌɪn.trə'djuːs/ Ⓤ /-'duːs/ *verb* [T] to put something into use, operation or a place for the first time: *The smaller 10 pence coin was introduced in 1992.* ○ *Such unpopular legislation is unlikely to be introduced before the next election.* ○ SPECIALIZED *The tube which carries the laser is introduced into the abdomen through a small cut in the skin.* **introduction** /ˌɪn.trə'dʌk.ʃ³n/ *noun* [U] *The introduction of new working practices has dramatically improved productivity.* ○ *Within a few years of their introduction, CDs were outselling vinyl records.*

○ SPECIALIZED *The introduction of the tube into the artery is a very delicate procedure.*

introductory /ˌɪn.trə'dʌk.t³r.i/ *adj: an introductory price/offer* ○ *an introductory course in word processing* (= a course for people who have not done word processing before)

introduce BEGIN /ˌɪn.trə'djuːs/ Ⓤ /-'duːs/ *verb* [T] **1** to be the beginning of something: *A haunting oboe solo introduces the third movement of the concerto.* **2** to speak or write before the beginning of a programme or book and give information about its contents: *The director will introduce the film personally at its world première.* ○ *This is the first official biography of her and it is introduced by her daughter.* **introduction** /ˌɪn.trə'dʌk.ʃ³n/ *noun* [C] *Have you read the introduction to the third edition?* ○ *The song's great, but the introduction's a bit too long.* **introductory** /ˌɪn.trə'dʌk.t³r.i/ *adj: an introductory chapter* ○ *I'd like to make some introductory remarks before beginning the lecture properly.*

▲ **introduce** *sb* **to** *sth phrasal verb* to help someone experience something for the first time: *When were you first introduced to sailing?*

introspection /ˌɪn.trə'spek.ʃ³n/ *noun* [U] examination and consideration of your own ideas, thoughts and feelings: *His defeat in the world championship led to a long period of gloomy introspection.* **introspective** /ˌɪn.trə-'spek.tɪv/ *adj: She is famous for her introspective songs about failed relationships.* **introspectively** /ˌɪn.trə-'spek.tɪv.li/ *adv*

introvert /'ɪn.trə.vɜːt/ Ⓤ /-vɝːt/ *noun* [C] someone who is shy, quiet and unable to make friends easily ⊃Compare **extrovert**. **introverted** /ˌɪn.trə'vɜː.tɪd/ Ⓤ /-'vɝː.t̬ɪd/ *adj* (ALSO **introvert**) *an introverted child* **introversion** /ˌɪn.trə'vɜː.ʃ³n/ Ⓤ /-'vɝː-/ *noun* [U]

intrude /ɪn'truːd/ *verb* [I] to go into a place or situation in which you are not wanted or not expected to be: *I didn't realise your husband was here, Dr Jones – I hope I'm not intruding.* ○ *Newspaper editors are being urged not to intrude on/into the grief of the families of missing servicemen.*

intruder /ɪn'truː.dəʳ/ Ⓤ /-dɚ/ *noun* [C] **1** someone who is in a place or situation where they are not wanted: *I feel like an intruder when I visit their home.* **2** someone who enters a place without permission in order to commit a crime: *Intruders had entered the house through a back window.* **intrusion** /ɪn'truː.ʒ³n/ *noun* [C or U] *They complained about excessive government intrusion* (= unwanted involvement) *into their legitimate activities.* ○ *His phone call was a welcome intrusion into an otherwise tedious morning.* **intrusive** /ɪn'truː.sɪv/ *adj: intrusive questioning*

intuition /ˌɪn.tju:'ɪʃ.³n/ Ⓤ /-tuː-/ *noun* [C or U] (knowledge obtained from) an ability to understand or know something immediately without needing to think about it, learn it or discover it by using reason: *Often there's no clear evidence one way or the other and you just have to base your judgement on intuition.* ○ *I can't explain how I knew – I just had an intuition that you'd been involved in an accident.* **intuit** /ɪn'tju:.ɪt/ Ⓤ /-tuː-/ *verb* [T] FORMAL [+ that] *He intuited that I was worried about the situation.* **intuitive** /ɪn'tju:.ɪ.tɪv/ Ⓤ /-'tuː.ɪ.t̬ɪv/ *adj: Men are often regarded as less intuitive than women.* ○ *an intuitive approach/judgement* ○ *Most people have an intuitive sense of right and wrong.* **intuitively** /ɪn'tju:.ɪ.tɪv.li/ Ⓤ /-'tuː.ɪ.t̬ɪv-/ *adv: I knew intuitively that something dreadful had happened to him.*

Inuit /'ɪn.ju.ɪt/ *noun* [C] *plural* **Inuit** or **Inuits** a member of a Native American tribe who live in the cold northern areas of North America and Greenland ⊃See usage note at ESKIMO.

inundate TOO MUCH /'ɪn.ʌn.deɪt/ *verb* [T] to give someone so much work or so many things that they cannot deal with them all: *We have been inundated with requests for help.* ○ *They were inundated with gifts and flowers when the baby was born.* **inundation** /ˌɪn.ʌn'deɪ.ʃ³n/ *noun* [U]

inundate FLOOD /'ɪn.ʌn.deɪt/ *verb* [T] FORMAL to flood an area with water: *If the dam breaks it will inundate large parts of the town.* **inundation** /ˌɪn.ʌn'deɪ.ʃ³n/ *noun* [C or U]

inure /ɪnˈjʊəʳ/ ⑥ /-ˈjʊr/ *verb*
▲ **inure** *sb* **to** *sth phrasal verb* FORMAL If you become inured to something unpleasant, you become familiar with it and able to accept and bear it: *After spending some time on the island they became inured to the hardships.*

invade /ɪnˈveɪd/ *verb* **1** [I or T] to enter a country by force with large numbers of soldiers in order to take possession of it: *Concentrations of troops near the border look set to invade within the next few days.* **2** [I or T] to enter a place in large numbers, usually when unwanted and in order to take possession or do damage: *Hundreds of squatters have invaded waste land in the hope that they will be allowed to stay.* **3** [T] to enter an area of activity in a forceful and noticeable way: *Maria looks set to invade the music scene with her style and image.* **4** [T] to spoil a situation or quality that another person values with very noticeable and selfish behaviour: *Famous people often find their **privacy** is invaded by the press.* **invader** /ɪnˈveɪdəʳ/ ⑥ /-dəˈ/ *noun* [C] *The **foreign** invaders were finally defeated by allied forces.* ○ *Any new company is seen as an invader in an already competitive market.* **invasion** /ɪnˈveɪʒᵊn/ *noun* [C or U] *They were planning to mount an invasion **of** the north of the country.* ○ *an invasion **of** privacy*
invasive /ɪnˈveɪsɪv/ *adj* moving into all areas of something and difficult to stop: *an invasive disease* ○ *They treated the cancer with **non**-invasive methods/surgery* (= not cutting into the body).

invalid NOT CORRECT /ɪnˈvæl.ɪd/ *adj* **1** An invalid document, ticket, law, etc. is not legally or officially acceptable: *I'm afraid your driving licence is invalid in Eastern Europe.* **2** An invalid opinion, argument, etc. is not correct, usually because it is not logical or not based on correct information: *an invalid argument*
invalidate /ɪnˈvæl.ɪ.deɪt/ *verb* [T] **1** to officially stop a document, ticket, law, etc. being legally or officially acceptable **2** to prove that an opinion, argument, etc. is wrong **invalidation** /ɪnˌvæl.ɪˈdeɪ.ʃᵊn/ *noun* [U] *Premature disclosure of the test sites might lead to invalidation of the experiment.* **invalidity** /ˌɪn.vəˈlɪd.ɪ.ti/ ⑥ /-ə.t̬i/ *noun* [U]
invalidly /ɪnˈvæl.ɪd.li/ *adv*

invalid PERSON /ˈɪn.və.lɪd/ *noun* [C] OLD-FASHIONED someone who is ill, usually for a long time and often needing to be cared for by another person: *Is the invalid in bed?* **invalidity** /ˌɪn.vəˈlɪd.ɪ.ti/ ⑥ /-ə.t̬i/ *noun* [U]

invalid /ˈɪn.və.lɪd/ *verb*
▲ **invalid** *sb* **out** *phrasal verb* If you are invalided out of a job, especially a military job, you are forced to leave because of injury or illness: *She was invalided out **of** the service because of injuries she received in a fire.*

invaluable /ɪnˈvæl.jʊ.bl̩/ *adj* extremely useful: *The new job will provide you with invaluable experience.* ○ *Such data will prove invaluable **to/for** researchers.*

invariable /ɪnˈveə.ri.ə.bl̩/ *adj* FORMAL never changing; staying the same: *The menu is invariable but the food is always good.*
invariably /ɪnˈveə.ri.ə.bli/ *adv* always: *The train is invariably late.*

invasion /ɪnˈveɪʒᵊn/ *noun* ⊃See at **invade**.
invasive /ɪnˈveɪsɪv/ *adj* ⊃See at **invade**.

invective /ɪnˈvek.tɪv/ *noun* [U] FORMAL criticism that is very forceful, unkind and often rude: *A **stream of** invective from some sectors of the press continues to assail the government.*

inveigh /ɪnˈveɪ/ *verb*
▲ **inveigh against** *sb/sth phrasal verb* FORMAL to strongly criticize something or someone: *There were politicians who inveighed against immigrants to get votes.*

inveigle /ɪnˈveɪ.gl̩/ *verb* [T] FORMAL to persuade someone to do something in a clever and dishonest way, when they do not want to do it: *Her son tried to inveigle her **into** giving him the money for a car.*

invent /ɪnˈvent/ *verb* [T] **1** to design and/or create something which has never been made before: *The first safety razor was invented by company founder King C. Gillette in 1903.* **2** to create a reason, excuse, story etc. which is not true, usually to deceive someone: *But I didn't invent the story – everything I told you is true.*

invention /ɪnˈvent.ʃᵊn/ *noun* [C or U] *The world changed rapidly after the invention of the telephone.* ○ *a most amazing invention* ○ *Be careful what you believe – her **powers of** invention* (= ability to think of excuses etc.) *are well known.* **inventive** /ɪnˈven.tɪv/ ⑥ /-t̬ɪv/ *adj* APPROVING *He is very inventive, always dreaming up new gadgets for the home.* **inventively** /ɪnˈven.tɪv.li/ ⑥ /-t̬ɪv-/ *adv* **inventiveness** /ɪnˈven.tɪv.nəs/ ⑥ /-t̬ɪv-/ *noun* [U] **inventor** /ɪnˈven.təʳ/ ⑥ /-t̬əˈ/ *noun* [C]

inventory /ˈɪn.vᵊn.tri/ ⑥ /-tɔːr.i/ *noun* [C] **1** a detailed list of all the items in a place: *A set of twenty-four carved and gilded chairs appear on the inventory of the house for 1736.* **2** US the amount of goods a shop has, or the value of them: *Our inventory of used cars is the best in town.* **3** US FOR **stocktaking**

invert /ɪnˈvɜːt/ ⑥ /-ˈvɜːt/ *verb* [T] FORMAL to turn something upside down or change the order of two things: *In some languages, the word order in questions is inverted* (= the verb comes before the subject of the sentence). **inverted** /ɪnˈvɜː.tɪd/ ⑥ /-ˈvɜːr.t̬ɪd/ *adj*: *Cover the bowl with an inverted plate.*
inverse /ɪnˈvɜːs/ ⑥ /-ˈvɜːrs/ *adj* [before n] opposite in relation to something else: *Their generosity was **in** inverse **proportion/relation** to their income* (= the more money they had the less generous they were).
the inverse *noun* [S] FORMAL the opposite: *Dividing by two is the inverse of multiplying by two.*
inversely /ɪnˈvɜː.sli/ ⑥ /-ˈvɜːr-/ *adv*: *Sometimes it seems that press coverage of an event is inversely **proportional** to its true importance* (= the more important the event, the less attention is paid to it).
inversion /ɪnˈvɜː.ʒᵊn/ ⑥ /-ˈvɜːr-/ *noun* [U] *Her account of the case was an inversion **of** the facts* (= said the opposite of what really happened).

invertebrate /ɪnˈvɜː.tɪ.brət/ ⑥ /-ˈvɜːr.t̬ə-/ *noun* [C] SPECIALIZED an animal with no spine: *Invertebrates, such as worms, are the main diet of these water birds.* ⊃Compare **vertebrate**. **invertebrate** /ɪnˈvɜː.tɪ.brət/ ⑥ /-ˈvɜːr.t̬ə-/ *adj*

in,verted 'commas *plural noun* UK the " " punctuation marks that are put around a word or phrase to show that someone else has written or said it
● **in inverted commas** UK used in spoken English after a word or phrase to show that it has not been used accurately or that the opposite meaning is intended: *Sick prisoners in the camp were 'cared for', in inverted commas, by guards, not nurses.*

in,verted 'snob *noun* [C] UK DISAPPROVING a person who makes it known that they do not like things which suggest high social position but approve of things related to low social position **in,verted 'snobbery** *noun* [U]

invest /ɪnˈvest/ *verb* [I or T] to put money, effort, time etc. into something to make a profit or get an advantage: *The institute will invest 5 million **in** the project.* ○ *He's not certain whether to invest **in** the property market.* ○ *You have all invested significant amounts of time and energy **in** mak**ing** this project the success that it is.* **investment** /ɪnˈvest.mənt/ *noun* [C or U] *Stocks are regarded as good long-term investments.* ○ *an investment **banker***
investor /ɪnˈves.təʳ/ ⑥ /-t̬əˈ/ *noun* [C] *A New York investor offered to acquire the company's shares for $13 each.* ○ *Small investors* (= people who invest only a small amount of money) *are hoping that the markets will improve.*

PHRASAL VERBS WITH **invest** ▼

▲ **invest in** *sth phrasal verb* to buy something because you think it will be useful, even if you think it is expensive: *We've decided it's time to invest in a new computer.*
▲ **invest** *sb* **with** *sth* POWER *phrasal verb* FORMAL to give authority or power to someone: *Our government has invested the minister for trade with all the necessary powers to resolve the dispute.*
▲ **invest** *sb/sth* **with** *sth* CHARACTERISTIC *phrasal verb* LITERARY to make someone or something seem to have a particular characteristic: *In his poems everyday reality is invested with a sense of wonder and delight.*

investigate /ɪnˈves.tɪ.geɪt/ *verb* [T] to examine a crime, problem, statement, etc. carefully, especially to discover the truth: *Police are investigating allegations of corruption involving senior executives.* ○ [+ question word] *We are of course investigating* ***how*** *an error like this could have occurred.* **investigation** /ɪnˌves.tɪˈgeɪ.ʃᵊn/ *noun* [C or U] *An investigation has been under way for several days* ***into*** *the disappearance of a thirteen-year-old boy.* ○ *a* ***full/thorough*** *investigation of the incident* ○ *Currently, the individuals who might have caused the accident are* ***subject to/under*** *investigation.* **investigative** /ɪnˈves.tɪ.gə.tɪv/ [US] /-t̬ɪv/ *adj* (*FORMAL* **investigatory**) *Children are encouraged to take an investigative approach to learning.* ○ *the investigatory panel* **investigator** [US] /ɪnˈves.tɪ.geɪ.tə/ [US] /-t̬ɚ/ *noun* [C] *Investigators have studied the possible effects of contamination.* ○ *a private investigator*

inˌvestigative ˈjournalism *noun* [U] the activity of news reporters trying to discover information which is of public interest but which someone might be keeping hidden: *Conspiracy is a popular subject for investigative journalism.* **inˌvestigative ˈjournalist** *noun* [C]

investiture /ɪnˈves.tɪ.tʃəʳ/ [US] /-tʃɚ/ *noun* [C] *FORMAL* a ceremony in which someone is given an official rank, authority, power, etc: *The investiture of the new president will take place this evening.*

inveterate /ɪnˈvet.ᵊr.ət/ [US] /-ˈvet̬.ɚ-/ *adj USUALLY DISAPPROVING* **an inveterate liar/gambler, etc.** someone who does something very often and cannot stop doing it: *I never trust anything he says – the man's an inveterate liar.*

invidious /ɪnˈvɪd.i.əs/ *adj FORMAL* likely to cause unhappiness or be unpleasant, especially because unfair: *Such a difficult choice placed her in an invidious* ***position.*** **invidiously** /ɪnˈvɪd.i.ə.sli/ *adv* **invidiousness** /ɪnˈvɪd.i.ə.snəs/ *noun* [U]

invigilate *UK* /ɪnˈvɪdʒ.ɪ.leɪt/ *verb* [I or T] (*US* **proctor**) to watch people taking an exam in order to check that they do not cheat: *Miss Jekyll will be invigilating (your chemistry exam) today.* **invigilator** *UK* /ɪnˈvɪdʒ.ɪ.leɪ.təʳ/ [US] /-t̬ɚ/ *noun* [C] (*US* **proctor**) *If you need more paper, please ask the invigilator.*

invigorate /ɪnˈvɪg.ᵊr.eɪt/ [US] /-ɚ-/ *verb* [T] to make someone feel fresher, healthier and more energetic: *We were invigorated by our walk.* **invigorating** /ɪnˈvɪg.ə.reɪ.tɪŋ/ [US] /-t̬ɪŋ/ *adj*: *an invigorating swim/run*

invincible /ɪnˈvɪn.sɪ.bḷ/ *adj* impossible to defeat or prevent from doing what is intended: *Last year the company* ***seemed/looked*** *invincible but in recent weeks has begun to have problems.* **invincibility** /ɪnˌvɪn.sɪˈbɪl.ɪ.ti/ [US] /-ə.t̬i/ *noun* [U] **invincibly** /ɪnˈvɪn.sɪ.bli/ *adv*

inviolable /ɪnˈvaɪə.lə.bḷ/ *adj FORMAL* which must not or cannot be broken, damaged or doubted: *Everyone has an inviolable* ***right*** *to protection by a fair legal system.* **inviolability** /ɪnˌvaɪə.ləˈbɪl.ɪ.ti/ [US] /-ə.t̬i/ *noun* [U]
inviolate /ɪnˈvaɪə.lət/ *adj* [after v] *FORMAL For centuries the tomb lay inviolate* (= not harmed or damaged) *until, by chance, it was discovered by two miners.*

invisible /ɪnˈvɪz.ɪ.bḷ/ *adj* **1** impossible to see: *The aircraft is designed to be invisible* ***to*** *radar.* ○ *These bacteria are invisible unless viewed with a microscope.* **2** [before n] *SPECIALIZED* describes money that is added to a country's economy by activities such as the service and financial industries rather than the production of goods in factories: *an increase in invisible* ***exports*** ○ *Tourism brings in 40% of the island's invisible* ***earnings.***
invisibility /ɪnˌvɪz.əˈbɪl.ɪ.ti/ [US] /-ə.t̬i/ *noun* [U] *The bits of gold in the sand were small* ***to the point of*** *invisibility* (= so small that they almost could not be seen). **invisibly** /ɪnˈvɪz.ə.bli/ *adv*

inˌvisible ˈink *noun* [U] ink which cannot be seen until it is treated with chemicals or heat: *It's a secret message written in invisible ink.*

invite [ASK TO AN EVENT] /ɪnˈvaɪt/ *verb* [T] to ask or request someone to go to an event: *We're invited* ***to*** *Lola's party.* ○ *Candidates who are successful in the written test will be invited* ***for*** *an interview.* ○ [+ obj + *to* infinitive] *Her family invited me* ***to*** *stay with them for a few weeks.*

invitation /ˌɪn.vɪˈteɪ.ʃᵊn/ *noun* [C or U] *Thanks for the invitation* ***to*** *your birthday party.* ○ *I'm happy to* ***accept*** *your invitation.* ○ *The first day of the exhibition will be* ***by*** *invitation* ***(only)*** (= only those who have been invited can come).
invitational /ˌɪn.vɪˈteɪ.ʃᵊn.ᵊl/ *noun* [C] *US* a sports event that people can only go to if they have been invited: *an invitational basketball tournament*

COMMON LEARNER ERROR

invite someone **to** something

Remember that the usual preposition with the verb **invite** is 'to'.

She invited me to her party.
~~*She invited me at her party.*~~
~~*She invited me for her party.*~~

invite [REQUEST FORMALLY] /ɪnˈvaɪt/ *verb* [T] to request something, especially formally or politely: *Offers in the region of £1 000 000 are invited* ***for*** *the property.* ○ [+ obj + *to* infinitive] *The newspaper invited readers* ***to*** *write in with their views.* **invitation** /ˌɪn.vɪˈteɪ.ʃᵊn/ *noun* [C or U] [+ *to* infinitive] *This is a once in a lifetime invitation* ***to*** *invest in your dream home in the sun.*

invite [ENCOURAGE] /ɪnˈvaɪt/ *verb* [T] to act in a way which causes or encourages something to happen or someone to believe or feel something: *Behaving provocatively in class is just inviting* ***trouble.*** ○ *Such a badly presented exhibition invites* ***criticism.***
inviting /ɪnˈvaɪ.tɪŋ/ [US] /-t̬ɪŋ/ *adj* If someone or something is inviting, they encourage you to feel welcome or attracted: *The room looked cosy and inviting.* ○ *an inviting smile* **invitingly** /ɪnˈvaɪ.tɪŋ.li/ [US] /-t̬ɪŋ-/ *adv*
invitation /ˌɪn.vɪˈteɪ.ʃᵊn/ *noun* [C or U] *Leaving your house unlocked is an* ***open*** (= clear) *invitation* ***to*** *burglars.*

PHRASAL VERBS WITH **invite** ▼

▲ **invite** ***sb*** **in** *phrasal verb* to ask someone to come into your house: *The neighbours invited us in for coffee.*
▲ **invite** ***sb*** **over** *phrasal verb* (*UK ALSO* **invite** ***sb*** **round**) to invite someone to come to your house: *Let's invite some people over.*

ˌin ˈvitro *adj* [before n], *adv* (of biological processes or reactions) happening outside the body in artificial conditions, often in a TEST TUBE: *Scientists are studying these cells in vitro.* ○ *in vitro experiments*

in ˌvitro fertiliˈzation *noun* [U] (*ABBREVIATION* **IVF**) a treatment for a woman who cannot become pregnant with her partner naturally in which an egg is FERTILIZED outside her body and the resulting EMBRYO is put into her womb to develop into a baby

invoice /ˈɪn.vɔɪs/ *noun* [C] a list of items provided or work done together with their cost, for payment at a later time: *Invoices must be* ***submitted*** *by the 24th of every month.*
invoice /ˈɪn.vɔɪs/ *verb* [T] to supply an invoice: *We'll invoice you* ***for*** *parts and labour.*

invoke /ɪnˈvəʊk/ [US] /-ˈvoʊk/ *verb* [T] *FORMAL* **1** to request or use a power outside yourself, especially a law or a god, to help you when you want to improve a situation: *Police can invoke the law of trespass to regulate access to these places.* ○ *Their sacred dance is performed to invoke ancient gods.* **2** to make someone have a particular feeling or remember something **invocation** /ˌɪn.vəˈkeɪ.ʃᵊn/ *noun* [C or U]

involuntary /ɪnˈvɒl.ən.tri/ [US] /-ˈvɑː.lən.ter.i/ *adj* not done by choice; done unwillingly, or without the decision or intention of the person involved: *A sharp tap on the knee usually causes an involuntary movement of the lower leg.* **involuntarily** /ɪnˌvɒl.ənˈter.ᵊl.i/ [US] /-ˈvɑː.lən-/ *adv*: *Arthur shivered involuntarily as he came out of the building.*

involve /ɪnˈvɒlv/ [US] /-ˈvɑːlv/ *verb* [T not continuous] to include someone or something in something, or to make them take part in or feel part of it: *The second accident involved two cars and a lorry.* ○ *I prefer teaching methods that actively involve students* ***in*** *learning.* ○ [+ v-ing] *The operation involves putting a small tube into your heart.* ○ *Research involving the use of biological warfare* *agents will be used for defensive purposes.* ○ *She's been involved **with** animal rights for many years.* ○ *It would be difficult not to involve the child's father in the arrangements.* **involvement** /ɪnˈvɒlv.mənt/ ⓤ /-ˈvɑːlv-/ *noun* [C or U] *The team's continued involvement **in** the competition is uncertain.* ○ *Being on the committee is one involvement I could do without.*

involved DIFFICULT /ɪnˈvɒlvd/ ⓤ /-ˈvɑːlvd/ *adj* complicated; not simple and therefore difficult to understand: *an involved reason/excuse/argument* ○ *The plot of the film was too involved – I couldn't understand it.*

involved EMOTIONAL /ɪnˈvɒlvd/ ⓤ /-ˈvɑːlvd/ *adj* being in a close relationship with someone: *emotionally/ romantically involved* ○ *Try not to become too emotionally involved **with** the children in your care.*

invulnerable /ɪnˈvʌl.n³r.ə.bl̩/ ⓤ /-nɚ-/ *adj* impossible to damage or hurt in any way: *The command bunker is virtually invulnerable, even to a nuclear attack.* **invulnerability** /ɪnˌvʌl.n³r.əˈbɪl.ɪ.ti/ ⓤ /-nɚ.əˈbɪl.ə.t̬i/ *noun* [U]

-in-waiting /-ɪn.weɪ.tɪŋ/ ⓤ /-t̬ɪŋ/ *suffix* (of a person) waiting or expecting to be given the authority, job or power named: *The press has identified several government ministers-in-waiting, saying that they are likely to be appointed in the autumn.*

inward /ˈɪn.wəd/ ⓤ /-wɚd/ *adj* **1** on or towards the inside ⊃Compare **outward**. **2** inside your mind and not expressed to other people: *inward feelings*
inwardly /ˈɪn.wəd.li/ ⓤ /-wɚd-/ *adv*: inside your mind and not expressed to other people: *He was inwardly relieved that the test was cancelled.*
inward /ˈɪn.wəd/ ⓤ /-wɚd/ *adv* (ALSO **inwards**) *After the accident, her thoughts began to turn inward* (= to her own interests or problems). ○ *Fold the outside edges inward* (= towards the inside).

the IOC /ˌðiˌaɪ.əʊˈsiː/ ⓤ /-oʊ-/ *noun* [S] ABBREVIATION FOR the International Olympic Committee

iodine /ˈaɪ.ə.diːn/ ⓤ /-daɪn/ *noun* [U] an element found in small amounts in sea water and used to prevent infection

iodized salt /ˌaɪ.ə.daɪzdˈsɒlt/ ⓤ /-ˈsɑːlt/ *noun* [U] salt to which IODINE has been added

ion ATOM /ˈaɪ.ɒn/ ⓤ /-ɑːn/ *noun* [C] SPECIALIZED an atom or small group of atoms which has an electrical charge because it has gained or lost one or more electrons ⊃See also **the ionosphere**.
ionize, *UK USUALLY* **-ise** /ˈaɪ.ə.naɪz/ *verb* [I or T] SPECIALIZED to (cause to) form an ion **ionized**, *UK USUALLY* **-ised** /ˈaɪ.ə.naɪzd/ *adj*: *Nebulae contain very large amounts of ionized gas.* **ionization**, *UK USUALLY* **-isation** /ˌaɪ.ə.naɪˈzeɪ.ʃ³n/ *noun* [U] *Widespread ionization occurs readily in the Earth's upper atmosphere.*
ionizer, *UK USUALLY* **-iser** /ˈaɪ.ə.naɪ.zə/ ⓤ /-zɚ/ *noun* [C] an electrical device which puts negative ions into the air in a room in order to make the air fresher and healthier

-ion ACTION /-³n/ *suffix* (ALSO **-ation**, ALSO **-ition**) added to verbs to form nouns showing action or condition: *obsession* ○ *restoration* ○ *repetition*

Ionic /aɪˈɒn.ɪk/ ⓤ /-ˈɑː.nɪk/ *adj* of or copying a style of ancient Greek building which has only a small amount of decoration: *an Ionic column* ⊃Compare **Corinthian**; **Doric**.

the ionosphere /ðiˌaɪˈɒn.ə.sfɪə/ ⓤ /-ˈɑː.nə.sfɪr/ *noun* [S] part of the Earth's atmosphere, from about 60 kilometres to about 1000 kilometres above the surface, in which there are always IONS ⊃Compare **the stratosphere**. **ionospheric** /ˌaɪ.ɒ.nəˈsfer.ɪk/ *adj*

iota /aɪˈəʊ.tə/ ⓤ /-ˈoʊ.t̬ə/ *noun* [S] an extremely small amount: *I haven't seen **one** iota **of** evidence to support his claim.*

IOU /ˌaɪ.əʊˈjuː/ ⓤ /-oʊ-/ *noun* [C] ABBREVIATION FOR I owe you: a written promise to pay back a debt: *Here's an IOU for the fiver you lent me. I'll pay you back on Monday.*

IOW, iow INTERNET ABBREVIATION FOR in other words: used to introduce an explanation that is simpler than the one given earlier

IPA /ˌaɪ.piːˈeɪ/ *noun* [S] ABBREVIATION FOR the International Phonetic Alphabet: a system of symbols for showing how words are pronounced

IPO /ˌaɪ.piːˈəʊ/ ⓤ /-ˈoʊ/ *noun* [C usually sing] ABBREVIATION FOR initial public offering: the first sale of a company's shares to the public

ipso facto /ˌɪp.səʊˈfæk.təʊ/ ⓤ /-soʊˈfæk.toʊ/ *adv* FORMAL by reasoning from previously known facts: *You admit you fired the gun and we now know that the shot killed the victim so you are, ipso facto, responsible for his death.*

IQ /aɪˈkjuː/ *noun* [C or U] ABBREVIATION FOR intelligence quotient: a measure of someone's intelligence found from special tests which are adjusted for age: *Children with very **low/high** IQs often have problems at school.* ○ *IQ is just one measure of intelligence.*

ir- /ɪr-/ *prefix* ⊃See at **in-** LACKING.

the IRA /ˌðiˌaɪ.ɑːˈreɪ/ ⓤ /-ɑːrˈeɪ/ *noun* [S] ABBREVIATION FOR the Irish Republican Army: an illegal organization which wants Northern Ireland to be politically independent of the UK and united with the Republic of Ireland

irascible /ɪˈræs.ə.bl̩/ *adj* FORMAL made angry easily: *She's becoming more and more irascible as she grows older.* **irascibility** /ɪˌræs.əˈbɪl.ɪ.ti/ ⓤ /-ə.t̬i/ *noun* [U] **irascibly** /ɪˈræs.ə.bli/ *adv*

irate /aɪˈreɪt/ *adj* very angry: *We have received some irate phone calls from customers.*

IRC /ˌaɪ.ɑːˈsiː/ ⓤ /ˌaɪ.ɑːrˈsiː/ *noun* [U] ABBREVIATION FOR Internet Relay Chat: a computer program that connects computers to a central computer and enables people in different places to discuss subjects at the same time by using their computers

ire /aɪə/ ⓤ /aɪr/ *noun* [U] FORMAL anger: *Petty restrictions easily **raised/aroused** the ire of such a creative artist.*

iridescent /ˌɪr.ɪˈdes.³nt/ *adj* showing many bright colours which change with movement: *Her latest fashion collection features shimmering iridescent materials.* **iridescence** /ˌɪr.ɪˈdes.³nts/ *noun* [U]

iridium /ɪˈrɪd.i.əm/ *noun* [U] a very hard yellowish-white metal

iris FLOWER /ˈaɪ.rɪs/ *noun* [C] a type of plant which grows especially in wet places and which has blue, yellow or white flowers and long narrow leaves

iris EYE /ˈaɪ.rɪs/ *noun* [C] the coloured circular part of an eye surrounding the black PUPIL (= central part)

Irish /ˈaɪə.rɪʃ/ ⓤ /ˈaɪ-/ *adj* **1** coming from Ireland, or relating to Ireland or its language: *Irish whiskey* ○ *The Irish contingent sang loudest at the show.* **2 the Irish** the people of Ireland
Irishman /ˈaɪə.rɪʃ.mən/ *noun* [C] a man who comes from Ireland
Irishwoman /ˈaɪə.rɪʃˌwʊm.ən/ *noun* [C] a woman who comes from Ireland

Irish-American /ˌaɪə.rɪʃ.əˈmer.ɪ.kən/ *noun* [C] a person who lives in the US but whose family originally came from Ireland

Irish 'coffee *noun* [U] hot coffee mixed with whisky and with thick cream on the top, usually served in a glass

Irish 'stew *noun* [U] meat, often MUTTON (= meat from a sheep), cooked in water with onions, potatoes, etc.

irk /ɜːk/ ⓤ /ɜːk/ *verb* [T] SLIGHTLY FORMAL to annoy someone: *The negative reply to my complaint really irked me.* **irksome** /ˈɜːk.səm/ ⓤ /ˈɜːk-/ *adj* SLIGHTLY FORMAL *The vibration can become irksome* (= annoying) *after a while.*

iron METAL /aɪən/ ⓤ /aɪrn/ *noun* [U] a common silver-coloured metal element which is magnetic. It is strong, used in making steel and found in very small amounts, in a chemically combined form, in blood: *Iron rusts easily.* ○ *Liver is a particularly rich source of dietary iron.* ○ *iron ore* ○ *an iron deficiency*
● **have *a few/several, etc.* irons in the fire** to be involved with many activities or jobs at the same time or to make certain that there are always several possibilities available: *If that job application doesn't work out I've got a couple more irons in the fire.*

• **rule** *sth* **with an iron hand/fist** *US* to control a group of people very firmly, having complete power over everything they do

• **an iron hand/fist in a velvet glove** used to describe someone who seems to be gentle but is in fact severe and firm

iron /aɪən/ ⓤ /aɪrn/ *adj* [before n] very strong physically, mentally or emotionally: *I think you have to have an iron* **will** *to make some of these decisions.*

iron DEVICE /aɪən/ ⓤ /aɪrn/ *noun* [C] a device for making clothes flat and smooth, especially after they have been washed, which has a handle and a flat base and is usually electrically heated: *a steam iron* ○ *a travel iron*

iron /aɪən/ ⓤ /aɪrn/ *verb* [I or T] to make clothes flat and smooth using an iron: *It takes about five minutes to iron a shirt properly.*

ironing /ˈaɪə.nɪŋ/ ⓤ /ˈaɪr-/ *noun* [U] **1** the activity of making clothes flat and smooth, using an iron: *I must* **do** *some/the ironing tonight.* **2** clothes which are waiting to be ironed or have just been ironed: *a basket full of ironing*

iron GOLF /aɪən/ ⓤ /aɪrn/ *noun* [C] a stick which has an iron or steel part at the end that is used to hit the ball in golf: *He'll probably use a 2 or 3 iron for the shot.*

▲ **iron** *sth* **out** *phrasal verb* [M] to remove problems or find solutions: *We're still trying to iron out some problems with the computer system.* ○ *We hope they can iron out their* **differences** *and get on with working together.*

the ˈ**Iron** ˌ**Age** *noun* [S] the period in early history starting about 1100 BC when iron was used for tools: *an Iron-Age settlement* ⊃Compare **the Bronze Age**; **the Stone Age**.

ironbark /ˈaɪən.bɑːk/ ⓤ /ˈaɪrn.bɑːrk/ *noun* [C] *AUS* a type of eucalyptus tree which has deep lines on the stem

iron-clad /ˈaɪən.klæd/ ⓤ /ˈaɪrn-/ *adj* [usually before n] very certain and unlikely to be changed: *iron-clad rules*

the ˌ**Iron** ˈ**Curtain** *noun* [S] From 1946-1989 the Iron Curtain was the name of the border between Western Europe and the communist countries of Eastern Europe, which made it very difficult to travel into or out of Eastern Europe.

ˈ**ironing** ˌ**board** *noun* [C] a narrow table, usually covered with cloth and having folding legs, on which clothes can be put flat to iron them

ˌ**iron** ˈ**lung** *noun* [C] a machine with a large metal tube which pushes air in and out of someone's lungs to help them when they find it difficult to breathe because of an illness

ˈ**iron** ˌ**man** *noun* [C] *US* a person of great physical strength and with the ability to continue doing something difficult for a long time

ironmonger /ˈaɪən,mʌŋ.gəʳ/ ⓤ /ˈaɪrn,mʌŋ.gɚ/ *noun* [C] *UK OLD-FASHIONED* someone who sells tools for use in homes and gardens

ironmonger's /ˈaɪən,mʌŋ.gəz/ ⓤ /ˈaɪrn,mʌŋ.gɚz/ *noun* [C] *UK OLD-FASHIONED* a shop where tools for homes and gardens are sold **ironmongery** /ˈaɪən,mʌŋ.gʳr.i/ ⓤ /ˈaɪrn,mʌŋ.gɚ-/ *noun* [U]

ˌ**iron** ˈ**rations** *plural noun OLD-FASHIONED* a basic amount of food for a person to live on: *The hotel food was dreadful, so for three days our iron rations were fruit, cheese and bread.*

irons /aɪənz/ ⓤ /aɪrnz/ *plural noun LITERARY* chains tied around someone to prevent them from escaping or moving: *It was common practice for the prisoners to be* **clapped in** *irons* (= tied with chains).

ironwork /ˈaɪən.wɜːk/ ⓤ /ˈaɪrn.wɝːk/ *noun* [U] items made of iron such as gates, especially if made in a decorated way

ironworks /ˈaɪən.wɜːks/ ⓤ /ˈaɪrn.wɝːks/ *group noun* [C] *plural* **ironworks** a factory where iron is produced or iron objects are made

irony FIGURATIVE SPEECH /ˈaɪə.rə.ni/ ⓤ /ˈaɪ-/ *noun* [U] a means of expression which suggests a different, usually humorous or angry, meaning for the words used: *Her voice* **heavy with** *irony, Simone said, "We're so pleased you were able to stay so long."* (= Her voice made it obvious they were not pleased). ⊃Compare **sarcasm**.

ironic /aɪəˈrɒn.ɪk/ ⓤ /aɪˈrɑː.nɪk/ *adj* (ALSO **ironical**) an

ironic comment/reply **ironically** /aɪəˈrɒn.ɪ.kli/ ⓤ /aɪˈrɑː.nɪ-/ *adv*

irony WRONG RESULT /ˈaɪə.rə.ni/ ⓤ /ˈaɪ-/ *noun* [U] a situation in which something which was intended to have a particular result has the opposite or a very different result: *The irony* (**of it**) *is that the new tax system will burden those it was intended to help.* **ironic** /aɪəˈrɒn.ɪk/ ⓤ /aɪˈrɑː.nɪk/ *adj* (ALSO **ironical**) [+ that] *It is ironic* **that** *although many items are now cheaper to make, fewer people can afford to buy them.* **ironically** /aɪəˈrɒn.ɪ.kli/ ⓤ /aɪˈrɑː.nɪ-/ *adv*

irradiate /ɪˈreɪ.di.eɪt/ *verb* [T] *SPECIALIZED* to treat with light or other types of radiation: *The cells are irradiated so that they cannot reproduce.* **irradiated** /ɪˈreɪ.di.eɪ.tɪd/ ⓤ /-t̬ɪd/ *adj: irradiated fuel* ○ *irradiated food* **irradiation** /ɪˌreɪ.diˈeɪ.ʃʰn/ *noun* [U]

irrational /ɪˈræʃ.ʰn.ʰl/ *adj* not using reason or clear thinking: *It's totally irrational, but I'm frightened of mice.* ○ *His parents were worried by his increasingly irrational behaviour.* **irrationality** /ɪˌræʃ.ʰnˈæl.ə.ti/ ⓤ /-t̬i/ *noun* [U] **irrationally** /ɪˈræʃ.ʰn.ʰl.i/ *adv: People often behave irrationally when they are under stress.*

irreconcilable /ˌɪr.ek.ʰnˈsaɪ.lə.bl̩/ *adj* impossible to find agreement between or with; impossible to deal with: *irreconcilable* **differences** *of opinion* ○ *They have become irreconcilable, with both sides refusing to compromise any further.* **irreconcilably** /ˌɪr.ek.ʰnˈsaɪ.lə.bli/ *adv*

irrecoverable /ˌɪr.ɪˈkʌv.ʰr.ə.bl̩/ *adj* impossible to get back: *irrecoverable financial losses* **irrecoverably** /ˌɪr.ɪ-ˈkʌv.ʰr.ə.bli/ *adv*

irredeemable /ˌɪr.ɪˈdiː.mə.bl̩/ *adj FORMAL* impossible to correct, improve or change: *There are irredeemable flaws in the logic of the argument.* **irredeemably** /ˌɪr.ɪ-ˈdiː.mə.bli/ *adv: The writing itself was irredeemably bad.*

irreducible /ˌɪr.ɪˈdjuː.sə.bl̩/ ⓤ /-ˈduː-/ *adj FORMAL* impossible to make smaller or simpler: *A few simple shapes are the irreducible forms from which all of the patterns are generated.* **irreducibly** /ˌɪr.ɪˈdjuː.sə.bli/ ⓤ /-ˈduː-/ *adv*

irrefutable /ˌɪr.ɪˈfjuː.tə.bl̩/ ⓤ /-t̬ə-/ *adj FORMAL* impossible to prove wrong: *an irrefutable* **argument** ○ *irrefutable* **evidence** *of health risks* **irrefutably** /ˌɪr.ɪ-ˈfjuː.tə.bli/ ⓤ /-t̬ə-/ *adv*

irregardless /ˌɪr.ɪˈgɑːd.ləs/ ⓤ /-ˈgɑːrd-/ *adv US NOT STANDARD* despite; not being affected by something: *I don't think children should be hit, irregardless* **of** *what they've done wrong.*

irregular SHAPE /ɪˈreg.jʊ.ləʳ/ ⓤ /-lɚ/ *adj* not regular in shape or form; having parts of different shapes or sizes: *an irregular coastline* ○ *irregular teeth* **irregularity** /ɪ-ˌreg.jʊˈlær.ə.ti/ ⓤ /-jə'ler.ə.t̬i/ *noun* [C or U] *The pictures showed cracks and other irregularities in otherwise perfectly regular crystals.* ○ *The west of the island is famous for the irregularity of its coastline.* **irregularly** /ɪˈreg.jʊ.lə.li/ ⓤ /-lɚ-/ *adv: irregularly shaped*

irregular TIME/SPACE /ɪˈreg.jʊ.ləʳ/ ⓤ /-lɚ/ *adj* **1** not happening at regular times or not with regular spaces in between: *an irregular heartbeat* ○ *They met at irregular intervals.* **2** *US INFORMAL* not emptying your bowels as frequently as you would usually **irregularity** /ɪˌreg.jʊˈlær.ə.ti/ ⓤ /-jə'ler.ə.t̬i/ *noun* [U] **irregularly** /ɪ-ˈreg.jʊ.lə.li/ ⓤ /-lɚ-/ *adv*

irregular RULE /ɪˈreg.jʊ.ləʳ/ ⓤ /-lɚ/ *adj FORMAL* **1** (of behaviour or actions) not according to usual rules or what is expected: *Releasing the goods without an invoice is* **most** *irregular.* **2** In grammar, an irregular verb, noun, adjective etc. does not obey the usual rules for words in the language. **irregularity** /ɪˌreg.jʊ'lær.ə.ti/ ⓤ /-jə'ler.ə.t̬i/ *noun* [C or U] something which is not correct or acceptable: *The inspectors found several irregularities* **in** *the business accounts.* ○ *The irregularity* **of** (= The lack of rules for) *English spelling means that it is easy to make mistakes.* **irregularly** /ɪˈreg.jʊ.lə.li/ ⓤ /-lɚ-/ *adv: The verb acts irregularly.*

irregular SOLDIER /ɪˈreg.jʊ.ləʳ/ ⓤ /-lɚ/ *adj* (of a soldier) fighting for a country but not as a member of its official army

irregular /ɪˈreg.jʊ.ləʳ/ [US] /-lɚ/ *noun* [C] a soldier who is not a member of the official army of a country

irrelevant /ɪˈrel.ɪ.vᵊnt/ *adj* not related to what is being discussed or considered and therefore of no importance: *These documents are* ***largely*** *irrelevant* ***to*** *the present investigation.* ○ *Making a large profit is irrelevant* ***to*** *us – the important thing is to make the book available to the largest possible audience.* **irrelevance** /ɪˈrel.ɪ.vᵊnts/ *noun* [C or U] (FORMAL **irrelevancy**) *Sympathy is an irrelevance – we need practical help.* ○ *Many of these problems may simply fade into irrelevance when the new rules come into force.* **irrelevantly** /ɪˈrel.ɪ.vᵊnt.li/ *adv*

irreligious /ˌɪr.ɪˈlɪdʒ.əs/ *adj* FORMAL DISAPPROVING having no interest in religion, or generally opposed to religion

irremediable /ˌɪr.ɪˈmiː.di.ə.bl̩/ *adj* FORMAL impossible to correct or cure: *The merits of this plan outweighed several obvious flaws in it, which were irremediable.*

irreparable /ɪˈrep.rə.bl̩/ *adj* impossible to repair or make right again: *Unless the oil spill is contained, irreparable* ***damage*** *will be done to the coastline.* **irreparably** /ɪˈrep.rə.bli/ *adv*: *The ship has been irreparably damaged.*

irreplaceable /ˌɪr.ɪˈpleɪ.sə.bl̩/ *adj* too special, unusual or valuable to replace with something or someone else: *Most of the porcelain you see in the display cabinets is irreplaceable.* ○ *No-one's irreplaceable in the workplace.*

irrepressible /ˌɪr.ɪˈpres.ə.bl̩/ *adj* full of energy and enthusiasm; impossible to stop: *Even the rain failed to dampen his irrepressible* ***spirits***. **irrepressibly** /ˌɪr.ɪˈpres.ə.bli/ *adv*

irreproachable /ˌɪr.ɪˈprəʊ.tʃə.bl̩/ [US] /-ˈproʊ-/ *adj* FORMAL APPROVING without fault and therefore impossible to criticize: *Her conduct throughout was irreproachable.* **irreproachably** /ˌɪr.ɪˈprəʊ.tʃə.bli/ [US] /-ˈproʊ-/ *adv*

irresistible /ˌɪr.ɪˈzɪs.tə.bl̩/ *adj* impossible to refuse, oppose or avoid because too pleasant, attractive or strong: *an irresistible offer* ○ *She gave me one of those irresistible smiles and I just had to agree.* **irresistibly** /ˌɪr.ɪˈzɪs.tə.bli/ *adv*

irresolute /ɪˈrez.ᵊl.uːt/ *adj* FORMAL DISAPPROVING not able or willing to take decisions or actions: *an irresolute reply* **irresolution** /ɪˌrez.ᵊlˈuː.ʃᵊn/ *noun* [U] **irresolutely** /ɪˈrez.ᵊl.uːt.li/ *adv*

irrespective /ˌɪr.ɪˈspek.tɪv/ *adv* without considering; not needing to allow for: *The legislation must be applied irrespective* ***of*** *someone's ethnic origins.*

irresponsible /ˌɪr.ɪˈspɒnt.sɪ.bl̩/ [US] /-ˈspɑːnt-/ *adj* DISAPPROVING not thinking carefully enough or not caring about what might result from actions taken: [+ to infinitive] *It would be irresponsible* ***to*** *ignore these warnings.* **irresponsibility** /ˌɪr.ɪˌspɒnt.səˈbɪl.ɪ.ti/ [US] /-ˌspɑːnt.səˈbɪl.ə.t̬i/ *noun* [U] *It was an act of gross irresponsibility to leave someone who wasn't properly trained in charge of the machine.* **irresponsibly** /ˌɪr.ɪˈspɒnt.sə.bli/ [US] /-ˈspɑːnt-/ *adv*

irretrievable /ˌɪr.ɪˈtriː.və.bl̩/ *adj* impossible to correct or return to a previously existing situation or condition: *I agree things look difficult, but the situation is far from irretrievable.* ○ *The couple separated on the grounds of irretrievable* ***breakdown*** *(of their marriage).* **irretrievably** /ˌɪr.ɪˈtriː.və.bli/ *adv*: *irretrievably damaged/lost*

irreverent /ɪˈrev.ᵊr.ᵊnt/ [US] /-ɚ-/ *adj* lacking the expected respect for official, important or holy things: *an irreverent comment/approach/attitude* ○ *irreverent thoughts* **irreverence** /ɪˈrev.ᵊr.ᵊnts/ [US] /-ɚ-/ *noun* [U] **irreverently** /ɪˈrev.ᵊr.ᵊnt.li/ [US] /ˈ-ɚ-/ *adv*

irreversible /ˌɪr.ɪˈvɜː.sɪ.bl̩/ [US] /-ˈvɜː/ *adj* not possible to change; impossible to return to a previous condition: *Smoking has caused irreversible damage to his lungs.* **irreversibly** /ˌɪr.ɪˈvɜː.sə.bli/ [US] /-ˈvɜː/ *adv*

irrevocable /ɪˈrev.ə.kə.bl̩/ *adj* impossible to change: *an irrevocable decision* **irrevocably** /ɪˈrev.ə.kə.bli/ *adv*: *Closing the factory would irrevocably alter the character of the local community for the worse.*

irrigate [SUPPLY WATER] /ˈɪr.ɪ.geɪt/ *verb* [T] to supply land with water so that crops and plants will grow: *irrigated land/fields* **irrigation** /ˌɪr.ɪˈgeɪ.ʃᵊn/ *noun* [U]

irrigate [WASH] /ˈɪr.ɪ.geɪt/ *verb* [T] SPECIALIZED to wash an injured part of a person's body, especially a cut, with a flow of liquid

irritable /ˈɪr.ɪ.tə.bl̩/ [US] /-t̬ə-/ *adj* becoming annoyed very easily: *Be careful what you say – he's rather irritable today.* ○ *"Don't disturb me again," she said in an irritable* (= angry) *voice.* **irritably** /ˈɪr.ɪ.tə.bli/ [US] /-t̬ə-/ *adv* **irritability** /ˌɪr.ɪ.təˈbɪl.ɪ.ti/ [US] /-t̬əˈbɪl.ə.t̬i/ *noun* [U]

ˌirritable ˈbowel ˌsyndrome *noun* [U] a condition that affects the bowels and causes stomach pain, and is often caused by worry or anxiety

irritate [MAKE ANGRY] /ˈɪr.ɪ.teɪt/ *verb* [T] to make angry or annoyed: *After a while her behaviour really began to irritate me.*

irritated /ˈɪr.ɪ.teɪ.tɪd/ [US] /-t̬ɪd/ *adj* annoyed: *Ben began to get increasingly irritated* ***by/at*** *her questions.*

irritant /ˈɪr.ɪ.tᵊnt/ [US] /-t̬ənt/ *noun* [C] something that causes trouble or makes you annoyed: *The report is bound to add a new irritant to international relations.*

irritating /ˈɪr.ɪ.teɪ.tɪŋ/ [US] /-t̬ɪŋ/ *adj*: making you feel annoyed: *an irritating habit* **irritatingly** /ˈɪr.ɪ.teɪ.tɪŋ.li/ [US] /-t̬ɪŋ-/ *adv*: *I can't bear working with him – he's so irritatingly slow.*

irritation /ˌɪr.ɪˈteɪ.ʃᵊn/ *noun* [C or U] *That kind of behaviour is sure to cause irritation.* ○ *Traffic noise is just one of several* ***minor*** *irritations* (= small problems).

irritate [MAKE SORE] /ˈɪr.ɪ.teɪt/ *verb* [T] to make sore or painful: *At first my contact lenses irritated my eyes.*

irritant /ˈɪr.ɪ.tᵊnt/ [US] /-t̬ənt/ *noun* [C] *Pollen is an irritant* (= cause of pain), *causing red and sore eyes in sensitive people.* **irritation** /ˌɪr.ɪˈteɪ.ʃᵊn/ *noun* [C or U] *It is an antiseptic cream suitable for minor* ***skin*** *irritations.* ○ *The strap had rubbed against his skin and caused irritation.*

is STRONG /ɪz/, WEAK /z/ /s/ *he/she/it form of* **be**

ISA /ˈaɪ.sə/ *noun* [C] ABBREVIATION FOR Individual Savings Account: a British investment account in which the tax on income is lower than usual, and there is no tax on profits made from an increase in the value of shares

ISBN /ˌaɪ.es.biːˈen/ *noun* [C] ABBREVIATION FOR International Standard Book Number: a set of numbers used to identify a particular book and show that it is different from other books

ISDN /ˌaɪ.es.diːˈen/ *noun* ABBREVIATION FOR Integrated Services Digital Network: a system for sending voice, video and information over telephone wires very quickly

-ise /-aɪz/ *suffix* UK ➲See at **-ize**.

-ish [PLACE] /-ɪʃ/ *suffix* used to form adjectives and nouns which say what country or area a person, thing or language comes from: *Spanish dancing* (= dancing from Spain) ○ *Are you English* (= someone from England)*?* ○ *I've always liked the Irish* (= people from Ireland). ○ *Do you speak Swedish* (= the language of Sweden)*?*

-ish [LIKE] /-ɪʃ/ *suffix* used to form adjectives which say what a person, thing or action is like: *foolish* ○ *childish*

-ish [QUITE] /-ɪʃ/ *suffix* used to form adjectives to give the meaning to some degree; partly; quite: *He had a sort of reddish beard.* ○ *She was oldish – about 60, I'd say.* ○ *We'll start at sevenish* (= about 7 o'clock).

Islam /ˈɪz.lɑːm/ /-læm/ *noun* [U] the Muslim religion, and the people and countries who believe in it **Islamic** /ɪzˈlæm.ɪk/ /-ˈlɑː.mɪk/ *adj*: *Islamic culture/beliefs/art/law*

island /ˈaɪ.lənd/ *noun* [C] **1** a piece of land completely surrounded by water: *a desert island* ○ *a Pacific island* ○ *They live* ***on*** *the large Japanese island of Hokkaido.* **2** UK **traffic island**

islander /ˈaɪ.lən.dəʳ/ [US] /-dɚ/ *noun* [C] someone who lives on an island: *Scottish islanders*

COMMON LEARNER ERROR

on an island

Remember to use the preposition 'on' before **island**.

They grew up on an island in the Pacific.

~~*They grew up in an island in the Pacific.*~~

isle /aɪl/ *noun* [C] LITERARY (used especially in place names) an island: *Explore the more remote Caribbean isles.* ○ *the Isle of Skye*

-ism /-ɪ.zᵊm/ *suffix* used to form nouns which describe social, political or religious beliefs, studies or ways of behaving: *sexism* ○ *feminism* ○ *Buddhism*
-ism /-ɪ.zᵊm/ *noun* [C] an example of typical behaviour: *That expression was a real Taylor-ism* (= an example of behaving or speaking like Taylor).
ism /ˈɪz.ᵊm/ *noun* [C] *INFORMAL MAINLY HUMOROUS* a set of beliefs, especially ones that you disapprove of: *Thatcher is unique among her predecessors in having given the English language a brand new ism, created from her own name.*

isn't /ˈɪz.ᵊnt/ *short form of* is not: *He isn't coming until tomorrow.*

isobar /ˈaɪ.səʊ.bɑːʳ/ [US] /-soʊ.bɑːr/ *noun* [C] *SPECIALIZED* a line drawn on a weather map joining all the places which have the same air pressure

isolate /ˈaɪ.sə.leɪt/ *verb* [T] to separate something or someone from other things or people with which they are joined or mixed, or to keep them separate: *He was isolated **from** all the other prisoners.* ○ *A high wall isolated the house **from** the rest of the village.* ○ *They tried to isolate* (= find) *the cause of the problem.* ○ *SPECIALIZED Virus particles were eventually isolated **from** the tissue.*
isolated /ˈaɪ.sə.leɪ.tɪd/ [US] /-t̬ɪd/ *adj*: *an isolated farm/village* (= not near other farms/villages) ○ *There were only a few isolated* (= not connected with each other, separate) *cases of violent behaviour.*
isolation /ˌaɪ.sᵊl.eɪ.ʃᵊn/ *noun* [U] *I can't think about it **in** isolation* (= separately) – *I need some examples of the problem.* ○ *The prisoner had been kept **in** isolation* (= alone without other people) *for three days.* ○ *After all the visitors had left, she experienced a feeling of complete isolation* (= being completely alone).
isolationism /ˌaɪ.sᵊlˈeɪ.ʃᵊn.ɪ.zᵊm/ *noun* [U] *DISAPPROVING* the political principle or practice of showing interest only in your own country and not being involved in international activities ➲Compare **globalism**.
isolationist /ˌaɪ.sᵊlˈeɪ.ʃᵊn.ɪst/ *adj*: *an isolationist policy/nation/attitude*

isomer /ˈaɪ.sə.məʳ/ [US] /-soʊ.mɚ/ *noun* [C] *SPECIALIZED* any one of a group of chemical substances which all have the same number and type of atoms but in which the arrangement of the atoms is slightly different between each substance: *structural/geometrical/optical isomers*

isosceles triangle /aɪˌsɒs.ᵊl.iːzˈtraɪ.æŋ.gl/ [US] /-ˌsɑː.sᵊl-/ *noun* [C] a triangle with two sides of equal length

isotherm /ˈaɪ.səʊ.θɜːm/ [US] /-soʊ.θɝːm/ *noun* [C] *SPECIALIZED* a line drawn on a weather map joining all the places which have the same temperature

isotonic /aɪ.səʊˈtɒn.ɪk/ [US] /-ˈtɑː.nɪk/ *adj* describes a drink containing the liquid and minerals your body needs after physical exercise

isotope /ˈaɪ.sə.təʊp/ [US] /-toʊp/ *noun* [C] *SPECIALIZED* a form of an atom which has a different atomic weight from other forms of the same atom but the same chemical structure: *a radioactive isotope of hydrogen*

ISP /ˌaɪ.esˈpiː/ *noun* [C] *ABBREVIATION FOR* Internet service provider: a company that provides access to the Internet, enables you to use email, and gives you space on the Internet to display documents: *Some ISPs are free and give you as many email addresses as you want.*

Israeli /ɪzˈreɪ.li/ *adj* from, belonging to or relating to Israel: *Israeli exports* ○ *an Israeli newspaper*
Israeli /ɪzˈreɪ.li/ *noun* [C] *plural* **Israelis** a person from Israel

Israelite /ˈɪz.rə.laɪt/ *noun* [C] one of a race of people who lived in Israel in ancient times

issue [SUBJECT] /ˈɪʃ.uː/ /ˈɪs.juː/ *noun* [C] a subject or problem which people are thinking and talking about: *environmental/ethical/personal issues* ○ *As employers we need to be seen to be **addressing*** (= dealing with) *these issues sympathetically.* ○ *Don't worry about who will do it – that's just a **side** issue* (= not the main problem).
• **at issue** most important in what is being discussed: *The point at issue is what is best for the child.*
• **make an issue of *sth*** *DISAPPROVING* to make something seem more important than it should be, or to argue about it: *Of course I'll help you, there's no need to make an issue of it.*
• **take issue with *sth*** *FORMAL* to disagree strongly: *I took issue with him **over** his interpretation of the instructions.*
issues /ˈɪʃ.uːz/ /ˈɪs.juːz/ *plural noun* **have issues (with *sb/sth*)** to have difficulty or disagreement with someone or something: *All the people in the study had low self-esteem and had issues with their bodies.* ○ *Anna has major issues with her employer.*

issue [PRODUCE] /ˈɪʃ.uː/ /ˈɪs.juː/ *verb* [T] to produce or provide something official: *The office will be issuing permits on Tuesday and Thursday mornings.* ○ *The school issued a statement about its plans **to** the press./The school issued the press **with** a statement about its plans.*
issue /ˈɪʃ.uː/ /ˈɪs.juː/ *noun* [C] **1** a set of newspapers or magazines published at the same time or a single copy of a newspaper or magazine: *There's an article on motorbikes in the latest/next issue.* ○ *An old issue of 'Homes and Gardens' lay on the table.* **2** An issue of shares is when a company gives people the chance to buy part of it or gives extra shares to people who already own some.
• **without issue** *OLD USE* If someone dies without issue, they have no children.
▲ **issue from *sth*** *phrasal verb LITERARY* If something issues from a place, it comes out of that place: *A terrible scream issued **from** the room.*

-ist /-ɪst/ *suffix* used to form adjectives and nouns which describe (a person with) a particular set of beliefs or way of behaving: *Marxist philosophy* ○ *a feminist* ○ *a sexist* ➲Compare **-ite**.

isthmus /ˈɪsθ.məs/ /ˈɪs-/ *noun* [C] a narrow piece of land with water on each side which joins two larger areas of land: *the Isthmus of Panama*

IT /ˌaɪˈtiː/ *noun* [U] *ABBREVIATION FOR* **information technology**

it /ɪt/ *pronoun* (as subject or object) the thing, animal or situation which has already been mentioned: *"Where's my pen? It was on my desk a minute ago." "You left it by the phone."* ○ *The company was losing money and it had to make people redundant.* ○ *The argument was upsetting for us all – I don't want to talk about it.* ○ *Children who stay away from school do it for different reasons.*
its /ɪts/ *determiner* belonging to or relating to something that has already been mentioned: *The dog hurt its paw.* ○ *Their house has its own swimming pool.* ○ *The company increased its profits.* ○ *I prefer the second option – its advantages are simplicity and cheapness.* * NOTE: Do not confuse with **it's**, the contraction of **it is**.
itself /ɪtˈself/ *pronoun* **1** the reflexive form of the pronoun 'it': *The cat licked itself all over.* **2** used to put emphasis on a word: *The shop itself* (= only the shop and nothing else) *started 15 years ago but the mail order side of the business is new.* ○ *The dog managed to drag the box into the room **by** itself* (= without help). ○ *The animal had been left in the house **by** itself* (= alone) *for a week.* ○ *The plan wasn't illegal **in** itself* (= there was nothing in the plan that was illegal) *but it would lead to some doubtful practices.* ○ *The committee **kept** the results of the survey **to** itself* (= did not tell anyone), *fearing a bad public reaction.*

Italian /ɪˈtæl.jən/ /-i.ən/ *noun* **1** [C] a person from Italy: *We met three Italians.* **2** [U] the language of Italy: *I'm learning Italian.*
Italian /ɪˈtæl.jən/ /-i.ən/ *adj* from, belonging to or relating to Italy: *Italian food/art/wine*

italics /ɪˈtæl.ɪks/ *plural noun* a style of writing or printing in which the letters lean to the right: *This sentence is printed **in** italics.* **italic** /ɪˈtæl.ɪk/ *adj*: *italic type/print/script* **italicize**, *UK ALSO* **-ise** /ɪˈtæl.ɪ.saɪz/ *verb* [T] *Words are sometimes italicized for emphasis.*

Italo- /ɪˈtæl.əʊ-/ [US] /-oʊ-/ *prefix* of or connected with Italy: *an Italo-German production*

itch /ɪtʃ/ *verb* [I] to have or cause an uncomfortable feeling on the skin which makes you want to rub it with your nails: *I can't wear wool – it makes me itch.*
• **itch to do *sth*** (*ALSO* **itch for *sth***) *INFORMAL* to want to do something very much and as soon as possible: *He was*

I

itching to hear the results. ○ By four o'clock I was itching for the meeting to end.

itch /ɪtʃ/ noun [C] an uncomfortable feeling on the skin which makes you want to rub it with your nails: I've got an itch on the back of my neck. **itchiness** /'ɪtʃ.ɪ.nəs/ noun [U] **itching** /'ɪtʃ.ɪŋ/ noun [U] This cream will reduce the itching.

itchy /'ɪtʃ.i/ adj: The sweater was itchy (= made me itch). ○ The dust made me **feel** itchy all over.

• **get itchy feet** UK INFORMAL to start to want to travel or do something different: After three years in the job she began to get itchy feet.

it'd /'ɪt.əd/ ⓤ /'ɪt̬-/ short form of **1** it would: It'd be better if we finished it off today. **2** it had: I found the radio – it'd been left in the shed all weekend.

-ite /-aɪt/ suffix used for a person who supports particular beliefs, actions or ideas, especially when added to the name of the person who is the origin of the ideas: a Thatcherite ○ a Reaganite

item /'aɪ.təm/ ⓤ /-t̬əm/ noun [C] **1** something which is part of a list or group of things: the last item on the list ○ The restaurant has a long menu of about 50 items. ○ Several items **of clothing** (= clothes) lay on the floor. **2** one of several subjects to be considered: There are three items on the agenda.

• **item by item** one thing at a time: Buyers from stores are given the opportunity to go through fashion collections item by item and place orders.

• **be an item** INFORMAL If two people are said to be an item, they are having a romantic relationship: I saw Darren and Emma there. Are they an item?

itemize, UK USUALLY **-ise** /'aɪ.tə.maɪz/ ⓤ /-t̬ə-/ verb [T] to list things separately, often including details about each thing: We asked for an itemized **bill**, listing all our phone calls and how long they were.

itinerant /aɪ'tɪn.ər.ənt/ ⓤ /-ɚ-/ adj [before n] travelling from one place to another, usually to work for a short period: an itinerant journalist/labourer/preacher **itinerant** /aɪ'tɪn.ər.ənt/ ⓤ /-ɚ-/ noun [C]

itinerary /aɪ'tɪn.ər.ər.i/ ⓤ /-ə.rer-/ noun [C] a detailed plan or route of a journey: The tour operator will arrange transport and plan your itinerary.

-ition /-ɪʃ.ən/ suffix ⊃See at **-ion** ACTION.

it'll /'ɪt.əl/ ⓤ /'ɪt̬-/ short form of it will: It'll be hard to find someone to help.

it's /ɪts/ short form of **1** it is: It's my turn to do it. **2** it has: It's been a wonderful day – thank you.

its /ɪts/ determiner ⊃See at **it**.

itself /ɪt'self/ pronoun ⊃See at **it**.

itsy-bitsy /ˌɪt.si'bɪt.si/ adj [before n] (US ALSO **itty-bitty**) HUMOROUS extremely small: She has these itsy-bitsy little

hands and feet.

ITV /ˌaɪ.tiː'viː/ group noun [U] ABBREVIATION FOR Independent Television: a group of British television companies which earn most of their income from advertising: There's a good film **on** ITV tonight. ⊃Compare **the BBC**.

-ity /-ɪ.ti/ ⓤ /-ə.t̬i/ suffix added to adjectives to form nouns referring to a state or quality: brutality ○ legality

IUD /ˌaɪ.juː'diː/ noun [C] ABBREVIATION FOR intra-uterine device: a small object put by a doctor into the womb of a woman who wants to avoid becoming pregnant

IV /ˌaɪ'viː/ adj ABBREVIATION FOR **intravenous**: IV drug users

I've /aɪv/ short form of I have: I've been waiting an hour already.

-ive /-ɪv/ suffix (ALSO **-ative**, ALSO **-itive**, ALSO **-tive**) added to verbs to form adjectives meaning showing the ability to perform the activity represented by the verb: imaginative ○ descriptive

IVF /ˌaɪ.viː'ef/ noun [U] ABBREVIATION FOR in vitro fertilization

ivory /'aɪ.vər.i/ ⓤ /-vɚ-/ noun [U] the hard yellowish-white substance that forms the tusks of some animals such as elephants, used especially in the past to make decorative objects: intricately carved ivory earrings ○ a ban on ivory trading

ivories /'aɪ.vər.iz/ ⓤ /-vɚ-/ noun [C usually pl] an object made from ivory: a collection of Japanese ivories

• **tickle the ivories** OLD-FASHIONED HUMOROUS to play the piano

ivory 'tower noun [C] DISAPPROVING To live or be in an ivory tower is not to know about or to want to avoid the ordinary and unpleasant things that happen in people's lives: Academics sitting **in** ivory towers have no understanding of what is important for ordinary people.

ivy /'aɪ.vi/ noun [C or U] an evergreen plant which often grows up trees or buildings: Ivy covered the broken walls. ○ Variegated ivies (= types of ivy) are a popular choice for covering fences.

ivied /'aɪ.vid/ adj LITERARY covered with ivy: these ancient ivied walls

Ivy 'League noun [S] a group of old colleges in the northeastern US with a good reputation: an Ivy League education

-ization, UK USUALLY **-isation** /-aɪ'zeɪ.ʃən/ suffix used to form nouns: the modernization of the office

-ize, UK USUALLY **-ise** /-aɪz/ suffix added to adjectives to form verbs meaning to cause to become: to modernize (= to make modern) ○ to centralize

J

J, j /dʒeɪ/ *noun* the 10th letter of the English alphabet

jab /dʒæb/ *verb* **-bb- 1** [I or T; usually + adv or prep] to push or hit something forcefully and quickly, often with a thin or sharp object: *The doctor jabbed the needle **into** the dog's leg.* ○ *Watch out! You nearly jabbed me **in** the eye **with** your umbrella!* ○ *He was jabbing a finger **at** (= towards) them and shouting angrily.* **2** [I] to make quick forceful hits with your fist when boxing **3** [T] to kick a ball hard and quickly: *He jabbed the ball into the net in the final minute of the game.*

jab /dʒæb/ *noun* [C] **1** a quick hard push or hit: *She gave me a sharp jab **in** the ribs with her elbow to stop me from saying any more.* ○ *The boxer was floored by a punishing left jab.* **2** *UK INFORMAL* an injection: *a flu jab* ○ *You'll need some jabs if you're going to Egypt.*

jabber /'dʒæb.əʳ/ ⓤ /-ɚ/ *verb* [I or T] *MAINLY DISAPPROVING* to speak or say something quickly in a way that is difficult to understand: *The train was full of people jabbering **(away)** into their mobile phones.* ○ *He jabbered **(out)** something about an accident further down the road.*

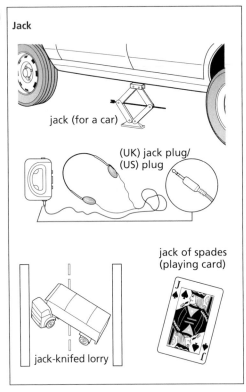

Jack

jack (for a car)

(UK) jack plug/
(US) plug

jack of spades
(playing card)

jack-knifed lorry

jack EQUIPMENT /dʒæk/ *noun* [C] a piece of equipment which can be opened slowly under a heavy object such as a car in order to raise it off the ground: *You need a car jack in order to change a wheel.*

jack CARD /dʒæk/ *noun* [C] (*ALSO* **knave**) a playing card with a picture of a man on it. It has a lower value than the cards showing a king or queen: *the jack of clubs*

jack BALL /dʒæk/ *noun* [C] a small ball towards which other balls are rolled or thrown in the games of BOWLS or BOULES

jack ELECTRICAL /dʒæk/ *noun* [C] a connection between two pieces of electrical equipment

jack /dʒæk/ *verb*

PHRASAL VERBS WITH jack ▼

▲ **jack** *sth* **in** *phrasal verb* [M] *UK INFORMAL* to stop doing something, often a job or something that you are not enjoying: *He's jacked in his job.*

▲ **jack** *sth* **up** LIFT *phrasal verb* [M] to raise a heavy object such as a car off the ground with a jack

▲ **jack** *sth* **up** INCREASE *phrasal verb* [M] *INFORMAL DISAPPROVING* to increase the price of something suddenly and by a large amount: *Once the tourists arrive, the restaurants jack up their prices.*

jackal /'dʒæk.ᵊl/ *noun* [C] a wild dog-like animal that lives in Africa and southern Asia and eats animals which have died or been killed by others

jackaroo /dʒæk.ə'ruː/ *noun* [C] *plural* **jackaroos** *AUS* a man who is learning to work on a sheep or cattle farm ↪Compare **jillaroo**

jackass /'dʒæk.æs/ *noun* [C] **1** *OLD-FASHIONED INFORMAL* a person who behaves foolishly **2** *AUS OLD-FASHIONED* a **kookaburra**

jackboot /'dʒæk.buːt/ *noun* [C] a long boot which covers the leg up to the knee, especially as worn by NAZIS **jackbooted** /'dʒæk.buː.tɪd/ ⓤ /-t̬ɪd/ *adj* wearing jackboots: *a jackbooted thug*

jackdaw /'dʒæk.dɔː/ ⓤ /-dɑː/ *noun* [C] a black and grey bird of the crow family, which is known for liking to take bright objects back to its nest

jacket /'dʒæk.ɪt/ *noun* [C] **1** a short coat: *a leather/ denim/tweed jacket* ○ *The keys are in my jacket pocket.* ↪See picture **Clothes** on page Centre 6 **2** dust jacket

jacket po'tato *noun* [C] *plural* **jacket potatoes** *UK FOR* **baked potato**

Jack 'Frost *noun* *OLD-FASHIONED CHILD'S WORD* very cold weather, when it is thought of as a person

jackhammer /'dʒæk.hæm.əʳ/ ⓤ /-ɚ/ *noun* [C] *US FOR* **pneumatic drill**

jack-in-the-box /'dʒæk.ɪn.ðə.bɒks/ ⓤ /-bɑːks/ *noun* [C] a children's toy consisting of a box with a model of a person inside it which jumps out and gives you a surprise when the top of the box is raised

jack-knife BEND /'dʒæk.naɪf/ *verb* [I] If a truck which has two parts jack-knifes, one part swings round so far towards the other part that it cannot be driven: *The oil tanker jack-knifed after skidding on the ice.*

jack-knife KNIFE /'dʒæk.naɪf/ *noun* [C] *plural* **jack-knives** a large knife with a blade which folds into the handle

jack-of-all-trades /dʒæk.əv.ɔːl'treɪdz/ ⓤ /-ɑːl-/ *noun* [C] someone who can do many different jobs

• **Jack-of-all-trades, master of none.** *SAYING* said about someone who is able to do many things, but is not an expert in any of them

jack-o'-lantern /dʒæk.ə'læn.tən/ ⓤ /-t̬ɚn/ *noun* [C] *US* a light made from a hollow PUMPKIN with holes cut into the sides like the eyes and mouth of a person's face, inside of which there is a candle

'jack .plug *UK noun* [C] (*US* **plug**) a metal pin at the end of a long wire attached to a piece of electrical equipment and used to connect it to another piece of electrical equipment

jackpot /'dʒæk.pɒt/ ⓤ /-pɑːt/ *noun* [C] the largest prize offered in a competition: *We **won** the jackpot.*

jackrabbit /'dʒæk.ræb.ɪt/ *noun* [C] a large type of North American rabbit

Jack Robinson /dʒæk'rɒb.ɪn.sᵊn/ ⓤ /-'rɑː.bɪn-/ *noun* *OLD-FASHIONED* **before you can/could say Jack Robinson** done or happening very quickly: *I put the plate of food on the floor, and before you could say Jack Robinson, the dog had eaten it.*

jacks /dʒæks/ *noun* [U] a children's game in which you throw a ball into the air and try to pick up a number of small metal or plastic objects with the same hand before catching the ball again

Jack the 'Lad *noun* [C usually sing] *UK OLD-FASHIONED* a young man who behaves in a very confident way

Jacobean /dʒæk.ə'biː.ᵊn/ *adj* relating to the period from 1603 to 1625 when James I was king of England: *Jacobean furniture* ○ *a Jacobean mansion*

Jacuzzi /dʒəˈkuː.zi/ *noun* [C] TRADEMARK a bath or pool into which warm water flows through small holes, producing a pleasant bubbling effect

jade /dʒeɪd/ *noun* [U] a precious green stone from which jewellery and small models are made, particularly in China and Japan: *jade earrings*

jaded /ˈdʒeɪ.dɪd/ *adj* lacking or losing interest because something has been experienced too many times: *Flying is exciting the first time you do it, but you soon become jaded.* ○ *Perhaps some caviar can tempt your jaded* ***palate.***

jagged /ˈdʒæg.ɪd/ *adj* rough and uneven, with sharp points: *a jagged cut/tear* ○ *jagged rocks* ○ *a jagged line/edge* **jaggedly** /ˈdʒæg.ɪd.li/ *adv*

jaguar /ˈdʒæg.ju.əʳ/ [US] /-juː.ɑːr/ *noun* [C] a large wild animal of the cat family which lives in Central and South America

jail, UK OLD-FASHIONED **gaol** /dʒeɪl/ *noun* [C or U] a place where criminals are kept to punish them for their crimes, or where people accused of crimes are kept while waiting for their trials: *the country's overcrowded jails* ○ *a 13-year jail* ***sentence/term*** ○ *The financier was* ***released from*** *jail last week.* ○ *They spent ten years* ***in*** *jail* ***for*** *fraud.* **jail**, UK OLD-FASHIONED **gaol** /dʒeɪl/ *verb* [T often passive] *He was jailed* ***for*** *three years.*

jailer, UK OLD-FASHIONED **gaoler** /ˈdʒeɪ.ləʳ/ [US] /-lɚ/ *noun* [C] a prison guard

jailbird, UK OLD-FASHIONED **gaolbird** /ˈdʒeɪl.bɜːd/ [US] /-bɝːd/ *noun* [C] INFORMAL a person who has been in prison

jailbreak, UK OLD-FASHIONED **gaolbreak** /ˈdʒeɪl.breɪk/ *noun* [C] an escape from prison: *Three prisoners were involved in a dawn jailbreak today.*

jalopy /dʒəˈlɒp.i/ [US] /-ˈlɑː.pi/ *noun* [C] INFORMAL HUMOROUS an old car: *I've sold my old jalopy to my neighbour's son.*

jam [FOOD] /dʒæm/ *noun* [C or U] (US ALSO **jelly**) a sweet soft food made by cooking fruit with sugar to preserve it. It is eaten on bread or cakes: *strawberry/raspberry jam* ○ *jam sandwiches*

• **jam tomorrow** UK something good that is promised but never happens: *As children we were always being promised jam tomorrow, if only we would be patient.*

jammy /ˈdʒæm.i/ *adj* containing or consisting of jam: *She left jammy fingermarks on the tablecloth.* ➲See also **jammy** EASY; **jammy** LUCKY.

jam [STICK] /dʒæm/ *verb* -mm- **1** [I or T] to be unable to move: *The door jammed behind me and I couldn't get out* ○ [+ obj + adj] *He jammed the window open with a piece of wood.* ○ *The motorway was jammed* ***solid*** (= the traffic could not move) *all morning.* **2** [T] to stop radio signals from reaching the people who want to receive them: *Foreign radio broadcasts were regularly jammed.*

jam /dʒæm/ *noun* **1** [C] **traffic jam**: *We were stuck in a jam for two hours.* **2** [S] INFORMAL a difficult situation: *I'm in a bit of a jam – could you lend me some money till next week?* ○ *How are we going to get ourselves out of this jam?* **jammed** /dʒæmd/ *adj*: *This drawer is jammed.*

jam [MUSIC] /dʒæm/ *verb* [I] -mm- to play jazz or rock music with other people informally without planning it or practising together

jam [PUSH] /dʒæm/ *verb* [T + adv or prep] -mm- to push something forcefully or with difficulty into something else: *He jammed the boxes* ***into*** *the back of the car.*

• **jam on the brakes** to use the brakes of a road vehicle suddenly and forcefully: *A motorbike appeared from nowhere and I had to jam on the brakes.*

jam /dʒæm/ *noun* [S] a situation in which a lot of people are in a small space: *It's a real jam inside – it took me ten minutes to get to the bar.*

jamboree /ˌdʒæm.bəˈriː/ *noun* [C] a large organized event which many people go to, or a busy, noisy occasion or period: *The beer festival was a huge open-air jamboree with music, stalls and everyone enjoying themselves.*

jammy [LUCKY] /ˈdʒæm.i/ *adj* INFORMAL unfairly lucky: *He wasn't even trying to score – the ball just bounced off the jammy* ***beggar's/bastard's*** *head into the goal.* ➲See also **jammy** at **jam** FOOD.

jammy [EASY] /ˈdʒæm.i/ *adj* INFORMAL very easy: *It was a jammy assignment – more of a holiday really.*

jam-packed /ˌdʒæmˈpækt/ *adj* full of people or things that are pushed closely together: *The streets were jam-packed* ***with*** *tourists.*

ˌjam ˈsandwich *noun* [C] two pieces of bread with jam between them, or a type of cake made in two parts with jam spread between

ˈjam ˌsession *noun* [C] an informal performance of jazz or rock music which the musicians have not planned or practised

Jane Doe /ˌdʒeɪnˈdəʊ/ [US] /-ˈdoʊ/ *noun* US a female JOHN DOE

jangle /ˈdʒæŋ.gl/ *verb* [I or T] to make a noise like metal hitting metal: *He jangled his keys in his pocket.* ○ *The wind-chimes jangled gently in the tree above us.*

• **jangle** ***sb's*** **nerves** to make someone feel annoyed or nervous: *The constant whine of the machinery jangled his nerves.*

jangling /ˈdʒæŋ.glɪŋ/ *noun* [U] the noise of metal hitting metal: *the jangling of sleigh bells* ○ *a loud jangling noise*

janitor /ˈdʒæn.ɪ.təʳ/ [US] /-t̬ɚ/ *noun* [C] US AND SCOTTISH ENGLISH FOR **caretaker** BUILDING WORKER

January /ˈdʒæn.jʊə.ri/ [US] /-juː.er.i/ *noun* [C or U] (WRITTEN ABBREVIATION **Jan**) the first month of the year, after December and before February

Japanese /ˌdʒæp.ənˈiːz/ *adj* from, belonging to or relating to Japan: *the Japanese stock market* ○ *Japanese art*

Japanese /ˌdʒæp.ənˈiːz/ *noun* [U] **1** the language of Japan: *Do you speak Japanese?* **2 the Japanese** the people of Japan: *The Japanese make excellent cars.*

jape /dʒeɪp/ *noun* [C] OLD-FASHIONED OR HUMOROUS an activity done to cause amusement or to trick someone

jar [CONTAINER] /dʒɑːʳ/ [US] /dʒɑːr/ *noun* [C] **1** a glass or clay container, with a wide opening at the top and sometimes a fitted lid, which is usually used for storing food: *a jar of coffee/pickled onions* ○ *a jam jar* **2** UK INFORMAL a drink of beer: *We often* ***have*** *a jar or two at the pub after work.*

jarful /ˈdʒɑː.fʊl/ [US] /ˈdʒɑːr-/ *noun* [C] the amount that a jar can hold: *The recipe uses a whole jarful/two jarfuls of jam.*

jar [SHAKE] /dʒɑːʳ/ [US] /dʒɑːr/ *verb* [I or T] -rr- to shake or move someone or something unpleasantly or violently: *The sudden movement jarred his injured ribs.*

jar /dʒɑːʳ/ [US] /dʒɑːr/ *noun* [C] a sudden forceful or unpleasant shake or movement: *With every jar of the carriage, the children shrieked with excitement.* **jarring** /ˈdʒɑː.rɪŋ/ [US] /ˈdʒɑːr.ɪŋ/ *adj*: *a jarring tackle/collision*

jar [NOT PLEASANT] /dʒɑːʳ/ [US] /dʒɑːr/ *verb* [I or T] -rr- If a sight, sound or experience jars, it is so different or unexpected that it has a strong and unpleasant effect on something or someone: *The harsh colours jarred the eye.* ○ *A screech of brakes jarred the silence.* **jarring** /ˈdʒɑː.rɪŋ/ [US] /ˈdʒɑːr.ɪŋ/ *adj*: *a jarring cry/chord* ○ *jarring colours*

jar [NOT RIGHT] /dʒɑːʳ/ [US] /dʒɑːr/ *verb* [I] -rr- to disagree or seem wrong or unsuitable: *This comment jars* ***with*** *the opinions we have heard expressed elsewhere.* **jarring** /ˈdʒɑː.rɪŋ/ [US] /ˈdʒɑːr.ɪŋ/ *adj*: *a jarring contrast*

▲ **jar on** ***sb phrasal verb*** If something, especially a noise, jars on you, it annoys you: *His rather superior manner jars on me.* ○ *That squeaky voice is beginning to jar on me.*

jarring /ˈdʒɑː.rɪŋ/ [US] /ˈdʒɑːr.ɪŋ/ *adj*: annoying or upsetting: *a jarring experience*

jargon /ˈdʒɑː.gən/ [US] /ˈdʒɑːr-/ *noun* [U] USUALLY DISAPPROVING special words and phrases which are used by particular groups of people, especially in their work: *military/legal/computer jargon* ➲Compare **terminology**.

jasmine /ˈdʒæz.mɪn/ *noun* [C or U] a climbing plant. One type has white sweet-smelling flowers in summer and another type has yellow flowers in winter.

jaundice /ˈdʒɔːn.dɪs/ [US] /ˈdʒɑːn-/ *noun* [U] a serious disease in which substances not usually in the blood cause your skin and the white part of your eyes to turn yellow

jaundiced /ˈdʒɔːn.dɪst/ [US] /ˈdʒɑːn-/ *adj* FORMAL judging everything as bad because bad things have happened to you in the past: *He seems to* ***have/take*** *a very jaundiced* ***view*** *of life.* ○ *I'm afraid I look on all travel companies' claims with a rather jaundiced* ***eye,*** *having been dis-*

J

appointed by them so often in the past.

jaunt /dʒɔːnt/ [US] /dʒɑːnt/ *noun* [C] a short journey for pleasure, sometimes including a stay: *a Sunday jaunt into the hills*
jaunt /dʒɔːnt/ [US] /dʒɑːnt/ *verb* [I usually + adv or prep] to go on a jaunt: DISAPPROVING *He's always jaunting* ***off*** *around the world on business trips, leaving his wife to cope with the babies by herself.*

jaunty /ˈdʒɔːn.ti/ [US] /ˈdʒɑːn.t̬i/ *adj* showing that you are happy and confident: *a jaunty grin/step.* ○ *When he came back his hat was at a jaunty angle and he was smiling.* **jauntily** /ˈdʒɔːn.tɪ.li/ [US] /ˈdʒɑːn.t̬ɪ-/ *adv* **jauntiness** /ˈdʒɔːn.tɪ.nəs/ [US] /ˈdʒɑːn.t̬ɪ-/ *noun* [U]

Java /ˈdʒɑː.və/ *noun* [U] TRADEMARK a computer programming language frequently used on the Internet

javelin /ˈdʒæv.lɪn/ *noun* [C] a long stick with a pointed end which is thrown in sports competitions
the javelin *noun* [S] a competition in which javelins are thrown: *She was first in the javelin.*

jaw [BODY PART] /dʒɔː/ [US] /dʒɑː/ *noun* [C] **1** the lower part of your face which moves when you open your mouth: *a broken jaw* ○ *a punch* (UK) ***on***/(US) ***in*** *the jaw* ○ *He has a strong/square jaw.* **2** either of the two bones in your mouth which hold your teeth: *upper/lower jaw*
• **jaw drops (open)** If someone's jaw drops (open), they look very surprised: *My jaw dropped open when she told me how old she was.*
jaws /dʒɔːz/ [US] /dʒɑːz/ *plural noun* **1** the mouth of a person or animal, especially a large and fierce animal: *The lion opened its jaws and roared.* ➲See picture **Animals and Birds** on page Centre 4 **2** something which opens and closes like the upper and lower parts of a mouth: *His foot was caught in the jaws of the trap.* **3** something dangerous: *The rescuers snatched the children from the jaws* ***of death***.

jaw [TALK] /dʒɔː/ [US] /dʒɑː/ *verb* [I] INFORMAL to talk for a long time: *He was jawing* ***away to*** *his girlfriend for hours on the phone.* **jaw** /dʒɔː/ [US] /dʒɑː/ *noun* [S] *I met Jane and we had a good jaw over lunch.*

ˈjaw ˌbone *noun* [C] the bone which forms the shape of the lower part of the face
jawbone /ˈdʒɔː.bəʊn/ [US] /ˈdʒɑː.boʊn/ *verb* [I or T] US INFORMAL to talk to someone, especially to try to persuade them to do something: *Congresswoman Weintrob jawboned local officials* ***about*** *their responsibilities toward the immigrant community.*

jawbreaker [SWEET] /ˈdʒɔːˌbreɪ.kəʳ/ [US] /ˈdʒɑːˌbreɪ.kɚ/ *noun* [C] US a large, hard, round sweet

jawbreaker [LANGUAGE] /ˈdʒɔːˌbreɪ.kəʳ/ [US] /ˈdʒɑːˌbreɪ.kɚ/ *noun* [C] **1** UK INFORMAL a **tongue twister** **2** US INFORMAL a word that is difficult to pronounce

ˌJaws of ˈLife *plural noun* US TRADEMARK a piece of equipment which can cut through metal and which is used to get people out from their vehicles after an accident: *Fire fighters used the Jaws of Life to free the trapped victims.*

jay /dʒeɪ/ *noun* [C] a noisy, brightly coloured bird

jaywalk /ˈdʒeɪ.wɔːk/ [US] /-wɑːk/ *verb* [I] MAINLY US to walk across a road at a place where it is not allowed or without taking care to avoid the traffic **jaywalker** /ˈdʒeɪ.wɔː.kəʳ/ [US] /-wɑː.kɚ/ *noun* [C] *We nearly ran over a couple of jaywalkers who walked out in front of the car.*

jazz /dʒæz/ *noun* [U] a type of modern music with a rhythm in which the strong notes are usually not on the beat and which is usually IMPROVISED (= invented as it is played)
• **and all that jazz** INFORMAL used when speaking to mean 'and other similar things': *They sell televisions and radios and all that jazz.*
jazzy /ˈdʒæz.i/ *adj* in the style of jazz music

jazz /dʒæz/ *verb*
▲ **jazz *sth* up** *phrasal verb* [M] INFORMAL to make something more attractive or interesting: *Jazz the dress up* ***with*** *some bright accessories.* ○ *He jazzed up the food* ***with*** *a spicy sauce.*

jazzy /ˈdʒæz.i/ *adj* INFORMAL very bright and colourful: *a jazzy tie/dress*

JCB /ˌdʒeɪ.siːˈbiː/ *noun* [C] UK TRADEMARK a machine used for digging and moving earth

J-cloth, **Jeye cloth** /ˈdʒeɪ.klɒθ/ [US] /-klɑːθ/ *noun* [C] UK TRADEMARK a cloth used for cleaning the home

jealous [UNHAPPY] /ˈdʒel.əs/ *adj* unhappy and angry because someone has something or someone you want, or because you think they might take something or someone that you love away from you: *He had always been very jealous* ***of*** *his brother's good looks.* ○ *Anna says she* ***feels*** *jealous every time another woman looks at her boyfriend.* ➲Compare **envious** at **envy**. **jealously** /ˈdʒel.ə.sli/ *adv*
jealousy /ˈdʒel.ə.si/ *noun* [C or U] a feeling of unhappiness and anger because someone has something or someone that you want: *He broke his brother's new bike* ***in a fit of*** *jealousy.* ○ *She was* ***consumed by/eaten up with*** *jealousy* (= She was very jealous) *when she heard that he had been given a promotion.* ○ *The team has performed very badly this season due to* ***petty*** *jealousies* (= feelings of jealousy about unimportant things) *among the players.* ➲Compare **envy**.

jealous [CAREFUL] /ˈdʒel.əs/ *adj* extremely careful in protecting someone or something: *She is very jealous* ***of*** *her independence, and doesn't want to get married.* ○ *Her parents used to keep a jealous* ***watch*** *over her when she was young.*
jealously /ˈdʒel.ə.sli/ *adv*: *The exact location of the hotel where the royal couple is staying is a jealously* (= carefully) ***guarded*** *secret.*

jeans /dʒiːnz/ *plural noun* trousers made of denim which are worn informally: *jeans and a T-shirt* ○ *I never wear jeans for work.* ➲See picture **Clothes** on page Centre 6

Jeep /dʒiːp/ *noun* [C] TRADEMARK a small strong vehicle used for travelling over rough ground, especially by the army ➲See picture **Cars and Trucks** on page Centre 13

jeepers (creepers) /ˌdʒiː.pəzˈkriː.pəz/ [US] /-pɚzˈkriː.pɚz/ *exclamation* US OLD-FASHIONED an expression of surprise: *Jeepers, just look at the time! I'm going to be late!*

jeer /dʒɪəʳ/ [US] /dʒɪr/ *verb* [I or T] to laugh or shout insults at someone to show you have no respect for them: *The people at the back of the hall jeered* ***(at)*** *the speaker.* **jeer** /dʒɪəʳ/ [US] /dʒɪr/ *noun* [C] *The news that the performance was being cancelled was greeted by* ***boos and*** *jeers from the audience.* **jeering** /ˈdʒɪə.rɪŋ/ [US] /ˈdʒɪr.ɪŋ/ *noun* [U] *There was loud jeering from the opposition parties when the prime minister stood up to speak.*

jeez /dʒiːz/ *exclamation* US SLANG an expression of surprise or strong emotion: *Jeez, don't yell at me – I'm just telling you what she said!*

Jehovah /dʒɪˈhəʊ.və/ [US] /-ˈhoʊ-/ *noun* the name of God used in the OLD TESTAMENT of the Bible

Jehovah's Witness /dʒɪˌhəʊ.vəzˈwɪt.nə.sɪz/ [US] /-ˈhoʊ-/ *noun* [C] a member of a religious organization which believes that the world will end soon and that only its members will be saved

jejune /dʒɪˈdʒuːn/ *adj* FORMAL DISAPPROVING very simple or childish: *He made jejune generalizations about how all students were lazy and never did any work.*

Jekyll and Hyde /ˌdʒek.l̩.ᵊndˈhaɪd/ *noun* [S] DISAPPROVING a person with two very different sides to their personality, one good and the other evil: *The professor was a real Jekyll and Hyde – sometimes kind and charming, and at other times rude and obnoxious.*

jell /dʒel/ *verb* [I] to **gel**

jellied /ˈdʒel.id/ *adj* If meat or fish is jellied, it is cooked and then served in its own juices which become firm when cold: *jellied beef/eels*

Jell-O, **jello** /ˈdʒel.əʊ/ [US] /-oʊ/ *noun* [U] US TRADEMARK FOR **jelly**

jelly /ˈdʒel.i/ *noun* **1** [C or U] UK (US TRADEMARK **Jell-O**) a soft, coloured sweet food made from sugar, GELATINE and fruit flavours, that shakes slightly when it is moved: *I've made a strawberry jelly for the children's tea.* ○ *jelly and ice cream* **2** US (UK **jam**) a sweet soft food made by cooking fruit with sugar to preserve it. It is eaten on bread or cakes: *a peanut butter and jelly sandwich* **3** [C or U] jam that is transparent and does not contain pieces of fruit: *apple jelly* **4** [U] any soft, slightly wet substance that shakes slightly when it is moved: *Frogs' eggs are covered in a sort of transparent jelly.*

• **turn to jelly** to suddenly feel weak because you are frightened, nervous or ill: *As she knocked on the director's door, **her legs** turned to jelly.*

'jelly ˌbaby *noun* [C] *UK* a small soft fruit-flavoured sweet in the shape of a baby

'jelly ˌbean *noun* [C] a small sweet in the shape of a bean which is soft in the middle and covered with hard sugar

jellyfish /'dʒel.i.fɪʃ/ *noun* [C] *plural* **jellyfish** a sea animal with a soft oval almost transparent body

'jelly ˌroll *noun* [C] *US FOR* **Swiss roll**

jemmy *UK* /'dʒem.i/ *noun* [C] (*US* **jimmy**) a short, strong metal bar with a curved end, often used by thieves to force open windows or doors

jemmy *UK* /'dʒem.i/ *verb* [T] (*US* **jimmy**) to force a window or lock open with a jemmy

je ne sais quoi /ˌʒə.nə.seɪ'kwɑː/ *noun* [S] a pleasing quality which cannot be exactly named or described: *Although he's not conventionally attractive, he has **a certain** je ne sais quoi which makes him popular with the ladies.*

jeopardize, *UK USUALLY* **-ise** /'dʒep.ə.daɪz/ [US] /-ɚ-/ *verb* [T] to put something such as a plan or system in danger of being harmed or damaged: *She knew that by failing her exams she could jeopardize her whole future.*

jeopardy /'dʒep.ə.di/ [US] /-ɚ-/ *noun* **in jeopardy** in danger of being damaged or destroyed: *The lives of thousands of birds are in jeopardy as a result of the oil spillage.*

jerk [MOVE] /dʒɜːk/ [US] /dʒɝːk/ *verb* [I or T; usually + adv or prep] **1** to make a short sudden movement, or to cause someone or something to do this: *The car made a strange noise and then jerked **to a halt**.* ○ *"What's wrong?" she asked, jerking her head up.* **2** to (force or cause someone or something to) suddenly behave differently, usually by becoming aware or active again: *The shock of losing his job jerked him **out of** his settled lifestyle.*

jerk /dʒɜːk/ [US] /dʒɝːk/ *noun* [C] a quick sudden movement: *She pulled the bush out of the ground **with** a sharp jerk.* ○ *The alarm went off and he woke up **with** a jerk.*

jerky /'dʒɜː.ki/ [US] /'dʒɝː-/ *adj* quick and sudden: *The disease causes sudden jerky **movements** of the hands and legs.* **jerkily** /'dʒɜː.kɪ.li/ [US] /'dʒɝː-/ *adv* **jerkiness** /'dʒɜː.kɪ.nəs/ [US] /'dʒɝː-/ *noun* [U]

jerk [PERSON] /dʒɜːk/ [US] /dʒɝːk/ *noun* [C] (*US ALSO* **jerk-off**) *SLANG* a stupid person, usually a man: *You stupid jerk! You've just spilled beer all down my new shirt!*

▲ **jerk off** *phrasal verb OFFENSIVE* (of a man) to **masturbate**

jerkin /'dʒɜː.kɪn/ [US] /'dʒɝː-/ *noun* [C] a jacket with no sleeves or collar

jerkwater /'dʒɜːkˌwɔː.təʳ/ [US] /'dʒɝːkˌwɑː.t̬ɚ/ *adj* [before n] *US INFORMAL* describes a place that is small, unimportant and a long way from other places: *I grew up in a jerkwater **town** in the middle of nowhere.* ➲Compare **backwater**.

jerky /'dʒɜː.ki/ [US] /'dʒɝː-/ *noun* [U] *US* meat that has been cut into long thin strips and dried in the sun: *beef jerky*

jeroboam /ˌdʒer.ə'bəʊ.əm/ [US] /-'boʊ-/ *noun* [C] a very large wine bottle which contains four or six times the usual amount: *a jeroboam of champagne*

jerry-built /'dʒer.i.bɪlt/ *adj INFORMAL DISAPPROVING* built quickly and badly using cheap materials

'jerry ˌcan *noun* [C] a large metal container with flat sides used for storing or carrying liquids such as fuel or water

jersey [CLOTHING] /'dʒɜː.zi/ [US] /'dʒɝː-/ *noun* [C] **1** a piece of woollen or cotton clothing with sleeves which is worn on the upper part of the body and which does not open at the front **2** a shirt which is worn by a member of a sports team

jersey [CLOTH] /'dʒɜː.zi/ [US] /'dʒɝː-/ *noun* [U] soft thin cloth, usually made from wool, cotton or silk, which is used for making clothes: *100% cotton jersey*

Jersey [COW] /'dʒɜː.zi/ [US] /'dʒɝː-/ *noun* [C] a type of pale brown cow which produces very creamy milk

Jerusalem artichoke /dʒəˌruː.sə.ləm'ɑː.tɪ.tʃəʊk/ [US] /-ˌ'ɑːr.t̬ɪ.tʃoʊk/ *noun* [C] a root vegetable that looks like a potato

jest /dʒest/ *noun* [C] *FORMAL* something which is said or done in order to amuse: *His proposal was no jest – he was completely sincere.*

• **in jest** intended as a joke and not said seriously: *I only said it in jest – you're obviously not fat.*

• **Many a true word is spoken in jest.** *SAYING* said about humorous remarks which contain serious or truthful statements

jest /dʒest/ *verb* [I] to say something intended to amuse: *Would I jest **about** something so important?*

jester /'dʒes.təʳ/ [US] /-tɚ/ *noun* [C] a man in the past whose job was to tell jokes and make people laugh: *a court jester*

Jesuit /'dʒez.ju:.ɪt/ *noun* [C] a Roman Catholic priest who is a member of the Society of Jesus, a religious group begun in 1540: *He spent three years training to be a Jesuit **priest**.*

Jesus (Christ) /ˌdʒiː.zəs'kraɪst/ *noun* (*ALSO* **Christ**) (the title given to) the man who his religious followers believe is the son of God and on whose teachings and life Christianity is based

Jesus (Christ) /ˌdʒiː.zəs'kraɪst/ *exclamation* (*ALSO* **Christ**) *INFORMAL* an expression of surprise, shock or annoyance. Some people might consider this offensive: *Jesus, just look what a mess they've made!*

jet [STREAM] /dʒet/ *noun* [C] **1** a thin stream of something, such as water or gas, which is forced out of a small hole: *She turned on the hose and a jet **of** water sprayed across the garden.* **2** a small hole in a piece of equipment through which gas or another fuel is forced before it is burned: *I think the **gas** jet must be blocked, because the oven won't light.*

jet [AIRCRAFT] /dʒet/ *noun* [C] an aircraft with a JET ENGINE, which is able to fly very fast: *a jet plane* ○ *a private jet* ○ *We flew to New York **by** jet.* ➲See also **jetliner**.

jet /dʒet/ *verb* [I + adv or prep] **-tt-** *INFORMAL* to travel somewhere by plane: *I'm jetting **off** to New Zealand next week.*

jet [STONE] /dʒet/ *noun* [U] a hard black stone which shines when it is rubbed and is used to make jewellery and other decorative objects

jet-black /ˌdʒet'blæk/ *adj* completely black: *I was born with jet-black **hair**.*

'jet ˌengine *noun* [C] a very powerful engine. When fuel is burned inside the engine, hot air and gases are produced and then pushed out of the back of the engine at high speed and this forces the engine forward.

jetfoil /'dʒet.fɔɪl/ *noun* [C] a HYDROFOIL that is powered by water being sucked in from the sea and forced out at the back at great pressure

'jet ˌlag *noun* [U] the feeling of tiredness and confusion which people experience after making a long journey in an aircraft to a place where the time is different from the place they left: *Every time I fly to the States, I **get** really bad jet lag.* **jet-lagged** /'dʒet.lægd/ *adj*

jetliner /'dʒetˌlaɪ.nəʳ/ [US] /-nɚ/ *noun* [C] a large JET aircraft that can carry a lot of passengers

ˌjet pro'pulsion *noun* [U] powerful forward movement produced by forcing gases backwards, as in a jet engine

jetsam /'dʒet.səm/ *noun* [U] things that are thrown away from ships and float onto the land beside the sea ➲See also **flotsam**.

the 'jet ˌset *noun* [S] rich fashionable people who travel around the world enjoying themselves **jet-set** /'dʒet.set/ *verb* [I] *She spends the summer jet-setting around the fashionable European resorts.*

jet-setter /'dʒetˌset.əʳ/ [US] /-ˌset̬.ɚ/ *noun* [C] *INFORMAL* a member of the jet set **jet-setting** /'dʒetˌset.ɪŋ/ [US] /-ˌset̬-/ *adj* [before n] *a jet-setting millionaire*

'jet ˌski *noun* [C] *TRADEMARK* a small vehicle for one or two people to ride on water which is moved forward by a fast stream of water being pushed out behind it **jet-ski** /'dʒet.skiː/ *verb* [I] **jet-skiing** /'dʒetˌskiː.ɪŋ/ *noun* [U]

'jet ˌstream *noun* [C usually sing] a narrow current of strong winds high above the Earth which move from west to east

jettison /ˈdʒet.ɪ.sᵊn/ ⓤⓈ /ˈdʒeṯ-/ verb [T] **1** to get rid of something or someone that is not wanted or needed: *The station has jettisoned educational broadcasts.* **2** to decide not to use an idea or plan: *We've had to jettison our holiday plans because of David's accident.* **3** to throw goods, fuel or equipment from a ship or aircraft to make it lighter: *The captain was forced to jettison the cargo and make an emergency landing.*

jetty /ˈdʒet.i/ ⓤⓈ /ˈdʒeṯ-/ noun [C] a wooden or stone structure which is built in the water at the edge of a sea or lake and is used by people getting on and off boats

jetway /ˈdʒet.weɪ/ noun [C] a raised enclosed passage through which passengers walk from an airport building to an aircraft

Jew /dʒuː/ noun [C] a member of a race of people whose traditional religion is Judaism: *Although my family is Jewish, we're not practising Jews* (= actively involved in the religion). **Jewish** /ˈdʒuː.ɪʃ/ adj: *New York has one of the largest Jewish communities in the world.* **Jewishness** /ˈdʒuː.ɪʃ.nəs/ noun [U]

Jewry /ˈdʒʊə.ri/ ⓤⓈ /ˈdʒuː-/ noun [U] FORMAL all the Jews

jewel /ˈdʒuː.ᵊl/ noun [C] **1** a precious stone which is used to decorate valuable objects: *She was wearing a large gold necklace set with jewels.* **2** SPECIALIZED a small precious stone or a piece of specially cut glass which is used in the machinery of a watch **3** something that is very beautiful or valuable: *Many visitors consider the Sistine Chapel to be the jewel of the Vatican.* **4** OLD-FASHIONED a very kind or helpful person
  • **the jewel in the crown** the best or most valuable part of something

jewels /ˈdʒuː.ᵊlz/ plural noun **jewellery**

jewelled, US USUALLY **jeweled** /ˈdʒuː.ᵊld/ adj decorated with jewels

jewel case noun [C] a transparent plastic case in which COMPACT DISC is kept

jeweller, US USUALLY **jeweler** /ˈdʒuː.ə.ləʳ/ ⓤⓈ /-lɚ/ noun [C] a person who sells and sometimes repairs jewellery and watches

jewellery UK, US **jewelry** /ˈdʒuː.ᵊl.ri/ noun [U] decorative objects worn on your clothes or body which are usually made from valuable metals, such as gold and silver, and precious stones: *a jewellery box* ○ *a piece of gold/silver jewellery*

jewellery box noun [C] a special box for keeping jewellery, often decorated and containing several sections

jewfish /ˈdʒuː.fɪʃ/ noun [C or U] plural **jewfish** a large fish which lives in warm or tropical seas

Jew's harp /ˌdʒuːzˈhɑːp/ ⓤⓈ /-ˈhɑːrp/ noun [C] a small musical instrument which is held between the teeth and played by hitting a metal strip with the finger

Jeye cloth noun [C] UK TRADEMARK a **J-cloth**

Jezebel /ˈdʒez.ə.bel/ noun [C] OLD-FASHIONED DISAPPROVING an immoral woman who deceives people in order to get what she wants

jib BOAT /dʒɪb/ noun [C] SPECIALIZED a small triangular sail on a boat, in front of the main sail

jib LIFTING DEVICE /dʒɪb/ noun [C] SPECIALIZED a long horizontal frame that sticks out from a CRANE and from which the hook hangs

jib /dʒɪb/ verb **-bb-**

PHRASAL VERBS WITH **jib** ▼

▲ **jib at sth** PERSON phrasal verb OLD-FASHIONED to be unwilling to do or continue with something: [+ v-ing] *Although the tax is unpopular, the government has jibbed at abolishing it completely.*

▲ **jib at sth** HORSE phrasal verb OLD-FASHIONED If a horse jibs at something, it stops suddenly in front of it and refuses to move forward.

jibe, US USUALLY **gibe** /dʒaɪb/ noun [C] an insulting remark that is intended to make someone look stupid: *Unlike many other politicians, he refuses to indulge in cheap jibes at other people's expense.* **jibe**, US USUALLY **gibe** /dʒaɪb/ verb [I] *She jibed constantly at the way he ran his business.*

▲ **jibe with sth** phrasal verb (ALSO **jive with sth**) US INFORMAL If one statement or opinion jibes with another, it is similar to it and matches it: *Her account of the accident jibes with mine.*

jiffy /ˈdʒɪf.i/ noun [S] INFORMAL a very short time: *I'll be with you in a jiffy.* ○ *I've just got to fetch some books from upstairs – I won't be a jiffy* (= I'll be very quick).

Jiffy bag noun [C] TRADEMARK a thick protective envelope for sending objects that are easily damaged through the post

jig DANCE /dʒɪg/ noun [C] an energetic traditional dance of Great Britain and Ireland, or the music that is played for such a dance

jig MOVE /dʒɪg/ verb [I or T; usually + adv or prep] **-gg-** to move quickly up and down or from side to side, or to make someone or something do this: *Stop jigging about, Billy, and just stand still for a moment!*

jig DEVICE /dʒɪg/ noun [C] SPECIALIZED a device for holding a tool or piece of wood, etc. firmly in position while you work with it

jigger ALCOHOL /ˈdʒɪg.əʳ/ ⓤⓈ /-ɚ/ noun [C] US a small round metal container which is used for measuring strong alcoholic drinks, or the amount of alcohol which this container holds

jigger CHANGE /ˈdʒɪg.əʳ/ ⓤⓈ /-ɚ/ verb [T] US to change something, especially unfairly or illegally: *The ruling party jiggered the election results to be sure they would stay in power.*

jiggery-pokery /ˌdʒɪg.ᵊrˈiˈpoʊ.kᵊr.i/ ⓤⓈ /-ɚ.iˈpoʊ.kɚ-/ noun [U] OLD-FASHIONED INFORMAL secret or dishonest behaviour

jiggle /ˈdʒɪg.l̩/ verb [I or T] to move from side to side or up and down with quick short movements, or to make something do this: *If the door won't open, try jiggling the key in the lock.*

jigsaw /ˈdʒɪg.sɔː/ ⓤⓈ /-sɑː/ noun [C] a tool with an electric motor and a thin steel blade which is used for cutting curves in flat materials, such as wood or metal

jigsaw (puzzle) noun **1** [C] a picture stuck onto wood or cardboard and cut into irregular pieces which must be joined together correctly to form the picture again: *We spent all evening doing a 1000-piece jigsaw.* **2** [S] a complicated or mysterious problem which can only be solved or explained by connecting several pieces of information: *The police are trying to piece together the jigsaw of how the dead man spent his last hours.*

jihad /dʒɪˈhæd/ noun [C or U] a holy war which is fought by Muslims against people who are a threat to the Islamic religion or who oppose its teachings

jillaroo /ˌdʒɪl.əˈruː/ noun [C] plural **jillaroos** AUS a woman who is learning to work on a sheep or cattle farm ⊃Compare **jackaroo**.

jilt /dʒɪlt/ verb [T] to finish a romantic relationship with someone suddenly and unkindly: *He jilted her for his best friend's sister.*

Jim Crow noun [U] US OLD-FASHIONED DISAPPROVING the laws and policies formerly used in the US to treat black people unfairly and to keep them apart from white people

jim-dandy /ˌdʒɪmˈdæn.di/ noun [C] plural **jim-dandies** US OLD-FASHIONED INFORMAL something which is very pleasing or of excellent quality: *That new car you bought is a real jim-dandy.* **jim-dandy** /ˌdʒɪmˈdæn.di/ adj [before n]

jimjams /ˈdʒɪm.dʒæmz/ plural noun UK CHILD'S WORD FOR **pyjamas** (= trousers and a shirt worn in bed)

jimmy /ˈdʒɪ.mi/ noun [C], verb [T] US FOR **jemmy**

jingle RING /ˈdʒɪŋ.gl̩/ verb [I or T] to make a repeated gentle ringing sound, or to make things do this: *She waited for him by the car, jingling the keys in her hand.* ○ *The coins jingled in her pocket as she walked along.* **jingle** /ˈdʒɪŋ.gl̩/ noun [U] *the jingle of sleigh bells*

jingle TUNE /ˈdʒɪŋ.gl̩/ noun [C] a short simple tune, often with words, which is easy to remember and is used to advertise a product on the radio or television

jingoism /ˈdʒɪŋ.gəʊ.ɪ.zᵊm/ ⓤⓈ /-goʊ-/ noun [U] DISAPPROVING the extreme belief that your own country is always best, which is often shown in enthusiastic support for a war against another country: *Patriotism can turn into* *jingoism and intolerance very quickly.* **jingoistic** /ˌdʒɪŋ.-ɡəʊˈɪs.tɪk/ ⓤ /-ɡoʊ-/ *adj*

jinx /dʒɪŋks/ *noun* [S] bad luck, or a person or thing that is believed to bring bad luck: *There's a jinx on this computer – it's gone wrong three times this morning!* **jinxed** /dʒɪŋkst/ *adj*: *I must be jinxed – whenever I wash a wine glass, it breaks.*

JIT /ˌdʒeɪ.aɪˈtiː/ *adj* [before n] ABBREVIATION FOR **just-in-time**

jitney /ˈdʒɪt.ni/ *noun* [C] US a small bus that follows a regular route

jitters /ˈdʒɪt.əz/ ⓤ /ˈdʒɪt.ɚz/ *plural noun* INFORMAL a feeling of nervousness which you experience before something important happens: *I always get the jitters the morning before an exam.* ○ FIGURATIVE *The collapse of the company has caused jitters in the financial markets.*
• **give sb the jitters** INFORMAL to make someone nervous or frightened: *Come away from that cliff edge! You're giving me the jitters!*

jittery /ˈdʒɪt.ər.i/ ⓤ /ˈdʒɪt.ɚ-/ *adj* INFORMAL **1** nervous: *He felt all jittery before the interview.* **2** shaky and slightly uncontrolled: *I get really jittery if I drink too much coffee.*

jiujitsu /ˌdʒuːˈdʒɪt.suː/ *noun* [U] AUS FOR **ju-jitsu**

jive DANCE /dʒaɪv/ *noun* [S or U] a fast dance which was very popular with young people in the 1940s and 1950s: *My father taught me how to do the jive.* **jive** /dʒaɪv/ *verb* [I]

jive TALK /dʒaɪv/ *noun* [U] US SLANG talk which is meaningless or dishonest: *Don't believe a word he says, it's just a bunch of* (= a lot of) *jive!*
jive /dʒaɪv/ *verb* [T] US SLANG to try to make someone believe something that is untrue: *Quit jiving me and just tell me where you were!*

Jnr UK *adj* [after n] (MAINLY US **Jr**) ABBREVIATION FOR **junior** YOUNGER: used after a man's name to refer to the younger of two men in the same family who have the same name

job EMPLOYMENT /dʒɒb/ ⓤ /dʒɑːb/ *noun* [C] the regular work which a person does to earn money: *a temporary/permanent job* ○ *When she left college, she got a job as an editor in a publishing company.* ○ *It's very difficult trying to bring up two children while doing a full-time job.* ○ *He's never managed to hold down* (= keep) *a steady* (= permanent) *job.* ○ *She's applied for a job with an insurance company.* ○ *Are you going to give up your job when you have your baby?* ○ *How long have you been out of a job* (= unemployed)? ○ *After a disastrous first month in office, many people are beginning to wonder if the new president is up to* (= able to do) *the job.* ○ *Hundreds of workers could lose their jobs.* ⊃See Note **work or job?** at **work** ACTIVITY.
• **on-the-job** happening while you are working: *No formal qualifications are required for the work – you'll get on-the-job training.*
• **jobs for the boys** UK INFORMAL DISAPPROVING work that someone in an important position gives to their friends or relatives
• **It's more than my job's worth.** something that you say in order to tell someone that you cannot do what they want you to do because you would lose your job
jobless /ˈdʒɒb.ləs/ ⓤ /ˈdʒɑː.bləs/ *adj* unemployed: *He's been jobless for the past six months.*
the jobless *plural noun* MAINLY UK unemployed people: *The council has been running training schemes for the jobless.* ○ *The jobless total* (= The number of people unemployed) *reached four million this week.* **joblessness** /ˈdʒɒb.lə.snəs/ ⓤ /ˈdʒɑː.blə-/ *noun* [U]

job PIECE OF WORK /dʒɒb/ ⓤ /dʒɑːb/ *noun* [C] a particular piece of work: *The builders are aiming to get the job done by the end of the month.* ○ *He spent the afternoon doing jobs around the house.* ○ INFORMAL *Will you be able to carry all the shopping back home on your bike, or will it have to be a car job* (= will you need the car)?
• **do the job** INFORMAL If something does the job, it performs the piece of work you want to be done and achieves the result you want: *Here, this knife should do the job.*
• **do a good/bad job** to do something well/badly: *You've done a great job – thank you Sam.*

• **do/make a good/bad job of** *sth* to do something well/badly: *I'm not going to let him repair my bike again because he made a really bad job of it last time.* ○ *The dry cleaner's did a good job of removing that oil stain from my shirt.*
• **just the man/woman for the job** a man/woman who has all the skills for a particular piece of work: *We need someone who has experience in marketing and teaching, and I think Alex is just the woman for the job.*
jobbing /ˈdʒɒb.ɪŋ/ ⓤ /ˈdʒɑː.bɪŋ/ *adj* **a jobbing actor/builder/gardener**, etc. someone who does not work regularly for one person or organization but does small pieces of work for different people

job RESPONSIBILITY /dʒɒb/ ⓤ /dʒɑːb/ *noun* [S] something that is your responsibility: [+ to infinitive] *She believed her job as a politician was to represent the views of her party and the people who voted for her.* ○ *I know it's not my job to tell you how to run your life, but I do think you've made a mistake.*

job PROBLEM /dʒɒb/ ⓤ /dʒɑːb/ *noun* [S] INFORMAL a problem or an activity which is difficult: [+ v-ing] *It was a real job getting the wheel off the bike.* ○ *We were only given an hour to do the exam, and I had a job finishing it.*

job EXAMPLE /dʒɒb/ ⓤ /dʒɑːb/ *noun* [C] INFORMAL an example of a particular type: *It's an original, not one of those imitation jobs.*
• **be just the job** INFORMAL to be exactly what you want or need: *I've been looking for a new stereo system for my car, and this is just the job.*

job CRIME /dʒɒb/ ⓤ /dʒɑːb/ *noun* [C] SLANG a crime in which money or goods are stolen, or an action or activity which is dishonest or unpleasant: *He was put in prison for five years for doing a bank job.* ○ US *He really did a job on her, telling her that he would love her for ever and then moving to Fiji with someone else.* ⊃See also **hatchet job**.

job ˌaction *noun* [C usually sing] US a temporary show of lack of satisfaction by a group of workers, often by doing their work more slowly, in order to make managers pay attention to their demands

job ˌcentre *noun* [C] UK a government office where unemployed people can go for advice and information about jobs which are available

job desˌcription *noun* [C] a list of the responsibilities which you have and the duties which you are expected to perform in your work

job evaluˌation *noun* [C] UK the process of comparing a job with other jobs in an organization and deciding how much the person who is doing the job should be paid

job ˈlot *noun* [C] UK INFORMAL a collection of various objects which are bought or sold as a group, usually at a cheap price: *I bought a job lot of second-hand children's books.*

job satisˈfaction *noun* [U] the feeling of pleasure and achievement which you experience in your job when you know that your work is worth doing, or the degree to which your work gives you this feeling: *Many people are more interested in job satisfaction than in earning large amounts of money.*

job seˈcurity *noun* [U] If you have job security, your job is likely to be permanent.

jobseeker /ˈdʒɒb.siː.kəʳ/ ⓤ /ˈdʒɑː.bˌsiː.kɚ/ *noun* [C] UK someone who is trying to find a job

Jobseeker's ˈAllowance /ˈdʒɒb.siː.kəz.əˈlaʊ.ⁿnts/ ⓤ /ˌdʒɑː.bˌsiː.kɚz-/ *noun* [U] (ABBREVIATION **JSA**) in the UK, money that the government pays to unemployed people who are looking for a job

jobshare /ˈdʒɒb.ʃeəʳ/ ⓤ /ˈdʒɑː.bʃer/ *verb* [I] UK to divide the duties and the pay of one job between two people who work at different times during the day or week **jobshare** /ˈdʒɒb.ʃeəʳ/ ⓤ /ˈdʒɑː.bʃer/ *noun* [C] **jobsharing** /ˈdʒɒb.ʃeə.rɪŋ/ ⓤ /ˈdʒɑː.bʃer.ɪŋ/ *noun* [U] *The city council is encouraging jobsharing to make it easier for parents of young children to work.*

Jock MAN /dʒɒk/ ⓤ /dʒɑːk/ *noun* [C] UK SLANG a man who comes from Scotland. This term is considered offensive by some people.

jock [SPORT] /dʒɒk/ [US] /dʒɑːk/ *noun* [C] *US INFORMAL DISAPPROVING* a person who is extremely enthusiastic about sport

jockey [RIDER] /ˈdʒɒk.i/ [US] /ˈdʒɑː.ki/ *noun* [C] a person whose job is riding horses in races: *a champion jockey* ➲See picture **Sports** on page Centre 10

jockey [GET ADVANTAGE] /ˈdʒɒk.i/ [US] /ˈdʒɑː.ki/ *verb* [I] to attempt to obtain power or get into a more advantageous position than other people using any methods you can: *Since the death of the president, opposition parties and the army have been jockeying **for** power.* ○ *As the singer came on stage, the photographers jockeyed **for position** at the front of the hall.*

▲ **jockey *sb* into *sth*** *phrasal verb* to persuade someone to do what you want, often by deceiving them in a clever way: [+ v-ing] *The bosses were eventually jockeyed into sign**ing** the union agreement.*

jocks /dʒɒks/ [US] /dʒɑːks/ *plural noun AUS INFORMAL* a piece of underwear worn by men and boys which covers the area between the waist and the tops of the legs

jockstrap /ˈdʒɒk.stræp/ [US] /ˈdʒɑːk-/ *noun* [C] (*FORMAL* **athletic support**) a tight piece of underwear worn by men to support and protect their sexual organs when playing sport

jocose /dʒəˈkəʊs/ [US] /dʒoʊˈkoʊs/ *adj LITERARY* amusing or playful: *His jocose manner was unsuitable for such a solemn occasion.* **jocosely** /dʒəˈkəʊ.sli/ [US] /dʒoʊˈkoʊ-/ *adv*

jocular /ˈdʒɒk.jʊ.ləʳ/ [US] /ˈdʒɑː.kjə.lɚ/ *adj FORMAL* **1** amusing or intended to cause amusement: *a jocular comment* **2** describes someone who is happy and likes to make jokes: *Michael was in a very jocular **mood** at the party.* **jocularly** /ˈdʒɒk.jʊ.lə.li/ [US] /ˈdʒɑː.kjə.lɚ-/ *adv* **jocularity** /ˌdʒɒk.jʊˈlær.ə.ti/ [US] /ˌdʒɑː.kjəˈler.ə.t̬i/ *noun* [U] *SLIGHTLY FORMAL*

jodhpurs /ˈdʒɒd.pəz/ [US] /ˈdʒɑːd.pɚz/ *plural noun* trousers which are loose above the knees and tight below them and which are designed to be worn when riding a horse: *a new **pair of** jodhpurs*

Joe Bloggs *UK* /ˌdʒəʊˈblɒgz/ [US] /ˌdʒoʊˈblɑːgz/ *noun* [S] (*US* **Joe Blow**) *INFORMAL* an average or typical man: *This stereo system is the most expensive in the range and is not the sort of thing that Joe Bloggs would buy.*

Joe Public *UK INFORMAL* /ˌdʒəʊˈpʌb.lɪk/ [US] /ˌdʒoʊ-/ *noun* [S] (*US INFORMAL* **John Q Public**) the general public: *The government's decision to tax gas and electricity has not been popular with Joe Public.*

joey /ˈdʒəʊ.i/ [US] /ˈdʒoʊ.i/ *noun* [C] a young KANGAROO

jog [RUN] /dʒɒg/ [US] /dʒɑːg/ *verb* [I] **-gg-** to run at a slow regular speed, especially as a form of exercise: *"What do you do to keep fit?" "I jog and go swimming."* ○ *He was walking at a very quick pace and I had to jog to keep up with him.* **jog** /dʒɒg/ [US] /dʒɑːg/ *noun* [S] *I haven't done much exercise all week, so I think I'll **go for a** jog this morning.* **jogger** /ˈdʒɒg.əʳ/ [US] /ˈdʒɑː.gɚ/ *noun* [C] **jogging** /ˈdʒɒg.ɪŋ/ [US] /ˈdʒɑː.gɪŋ/ *noun* [U] *He usually **goes** jogging for half an hour before breakfast.*

jog [PUSH] /dʒɒg/ [US] /dʒɑːg/ *verb* [T] **-gg-** to push or knock someone or something slightly, especially with your arm: *A man rushed past and jogged her **elbow**, making her drop the bag.*

• **jog *sb's* memory** to make someone remember something: *The police showed him a photo to try to jog his memory about what had happened on the night of the robbery.*

▲ **jog along** *phrasal verb INFORMAL* If something, such as your work, jogs along, it advances at a slow but regular speed: *"How's your research going?" "Oh, it's jogging along."*

ˈjogging ˌsuit *noun* [C] a loose shirt and loose trousers, often made of thick cotton, which are worn informally or for running

joggle /ˈdʒɒg.l̩/ [US] /ˈdʒɑː.gl̩/ *verb* [T] to shake or move someone or something up and down in a gentle way

jog-trot /ˈdʒɒg.trɒt/ [US] /ˈdʒɑːg.trɑːt/ *noun* [S] If you move at a jog-trot, you run at a slow regular speed.

john [TOILET] /ˈdʒɒn/ [US] /ˈdʒɑːn/ *noun* [C] *US INFORMAL* a toilet: *I'm just **going to** the john – can you wait for me?*

john [PERSON] /ˈdʒɒn/ [US] /ˈdʒɑːn/ *noun* [C] *US SLANG* a man who is the customer of a prostitute

ˌJohn ˈBull *noun OLD-FASHIONED INFORMAL* a character who represents a typical Englishman or the English people in general: *John Bull is traditionally depicted as a short fat man wearing a waistcoat with the British flag on it.*

ˌJohn ˈDoe *noun US* **1** *LEGAL* a name used in a law court for a person whose real name is kept secret or is not known **2** an average or typical person

ˌJohn ˈDory *noun* [C or U] *plural* **John Dory** or **John Dories** a thin edible fish

John Hancock /ˌdʒɒnˈhæŋ.kɒk/ [US] /ˌdʒɑːnˈhæn.kɑːk/ *noun* [C] (*ALSO* **John Henry**) *US INFORMAL* a person's signature: *Put your John Hancock at the bottom of the page.* ✻ NOTE: John Hancock was the first person to sign the American Declaration of Independence.

johnny /ˈdʒɒn.i/ [US] /ˈdʒɑː.ni/ *noun* [C] *UK SLANG* a condom

johnny-come-lately /ˌdʒɒn.i.kʌmˈleɪt.li/ [US] /ˌdʒɑː.ni-/ *noun* [C] *plural* **johnny-come-latelies** or **johnnies-come-lately** *DISAPPROVING* someone who has only recently started a job or activity and has suddenly become very successful

joie de vivre /ˌʒwɑː.dəˈviː.vrə/ *noun* [U] *FORMAL* a feeling of great happiness and enjoyment of life

join [CONNECT] /dʒɔɪn/ *verb* **1** [T] to connect or fasten things together: *A long suspension bridge joins the two islands.* ○ *Join the two pieces **together** using strong glue.* ○ *The island is joined **to** the mainland by a road bridge.* ○ *If you join **(up)** the dots on the paper, you'll get a picture.* **2** [I or T] If roads or rivers join, they meet at a particular point: *The A11 joins the M11 south of Cambridge.* ○ *The River Murray and the River Darling join east of Adelaide.*

• **be joined in marriage/matrimony** *FORMAL* to become husband and wife in an official ceremony

• **join hands** If two or more people join hands, they hold each other's hands, especially in order to do something: *The teacher asked us to form a circle and join hands.*

• **join battle** *FORMAL* If armies join battle, they start to fight.

join /dʒɔɪn/ *noun* [C] a place where two things meet or are fastened together: *She'd stitched the two pieces together really carefully so that you couldn't see the join.*

join [DO TOGETHER] /dʒɔɪn/ *verb* [I or T] to get involved in an activity or journey with another person or group: *I don't have time for a drink now, but I'll join you later.* ○ *Why don't you ask your sister if she would like to join us **for** supper?* ○ *We took the ferry across the Channel and then joined* (= got on) *the Paris train at Calais.* ○ *If you've come to buy tickets for tonight's performance, please join the (UK) **queue**/(US) **line*** (= stand at the end of it). ○ *I'm sure everyone will join me **in** wish**ing** you a very happy retirement* (= everyone else will do this too). ○ *The police have joined **with*** (= They have begun to work with) *the drugs squad **in** try**ing** to catch major drug traffickers.* ○ *The design company is planning to join **up with** a shoe manufacturer and create a new range of footwear.*

join [BECOME A MEMBER] /dʒɔɪn/ *verb* [I or T] to become a member of an organization: *I felt so unfit after Christmas that I decided to join a gym.* ○ *It's a great club. Why don't you join?*

• **join the ranks** to become one of a particular large group of people: *When I leave school at the end of this month, I'll probably have to join the ranks **of** the unemployed.*

• **Join the club!** *INFORMAL* said in answer to something that someone has said, meaning that you are in the same bad situation as them: *"I've got no money till the end of this week." "Join the club!"*

PHRASAL VERBS WITH ˌ**join** ▼

▲ **join in *(sth)*** *phrasal verb* to become involved in an activity with other people: *We only need one more player for this game – can you persuade your sister to join in?* ○ *At the end of this verse, we'd like everyone to join in **with** the chorus.*

▲ **join up** *phrasal verb UK* If you join up, you become a member of one of the armed forces: *"Have you been in the army for a long time?" "I joined up as soon as I'd left school."*

joined-up /ˌdʒɔɪnd'ʌp/ *adj* **1** *MAINLY UK* If writing is joined-up, each letter in a word is connected to the next one: *My daughter is just starting to learn how to do joined-up* ***writing*** *at school.* **2** *UK* If ideas, systems or parts are joined-up, they are combined in a useful and effective way.

ˌjoined-up 'thinking *noun* [U] thinking about a complicated problem in an intelligent way that includes all the important facts: *This complex issue needs some joined-up thinking from ministers.*

joiner /'dʒɔɪ.nəʳ/ [US] /-nɚ/ *noun* [C] a skilled worker who makes the wooden structures inside buildings, such as doors and window frames

joinery /'dʒɔɪ.nᵊr.i/ [US] /-nɚ-/ *noun* [U] the work of a joiner or the things made by a joiner

joint [SHARED] /dʒɔɪnt/ *adj* belonging to or shared between two or more people: *a joint bank account* ○ *The project was a joint effort/venture between the two schools* (= they worked on it together). ○ *The two Russian ice-skaters came joint second* (= They were both given second prize) *in the world championship.* ○ *In court, the parents were awarded joint* ***custody*** *of their son* (= the right to care for him was shared between them). ○ *UK Adrian has a joint* ***honours*** *(AUS* ***double honours****) degree in English and philosophy* (= He studied both subjects to the same standard). **jointly** /dʒɔɪnt.li/ *adv*: *The Channel Tunnel was jointly funded by the French and British.*

joint [BODY] /dʒɔɪnt/ *noun* [C] a place in your body where two bones are connected: *an elbow/hip/knee joint* ○ *As you become older, your joints get stiffer.*

• **put *sth* out of joint** to accidentally force a joint in the body out of its correct position: *I put my shoulder out of joint last weekend lifting heavy boxes.*

jointed /'dʒɔɪn.tɪd/ [US] /-t̬ɪd/ *adj* having joints and able to bend

joint [CONNECTION] /dʒɔɪnt/ *noun* [C] a place where two things are fixed together: *Damp has penetrated the joints in the wood panelling.*

• **put *sth* out of joint** to prevent a plan from working correctly: *Our whole schedule was put out of joint by the designs arriving a week late.*

jointed /'dʒɔɪn.tɪd/ [US] /-t̬ɪd/ *adj* having a place or places where two things are fixed together: *A flute is made of wood or metal in three jointed sections.*

joint [MEAT] /dʒɔɪnt/ *noun* [C] **1** a large piece of meat which is cooked in one piece: *a joint of beef/pork* **2** a piece of meat for cooking, usually containing a bone: *Fry four chicken joints in a pan with some mushrooms and garlic.*

joint /dʒɔɪnt/ *verb* [T] to cut meat into large pieces ready for cooking

joint [PLACE] /dʒɔɪnt/ *noun* [C] *INFORMAL* a bar or restaurant which serves cheap food and drink: *We had lunch at a* ***hamburger*** *joint and then went to see a movie.*

joint [DRUG] /dʒɔɪnt/ *noun* [C] *SLANG* a cigarette containing the drug CANNABIS

the ˌJoint ˌChiefs of 'Staff *plural noun* the leaders of the United States armed forces, who give military advice to the president

ˌjoint reso'lution *noun* [C usually sing] *US* a decision which is approved by both houses of the US Congress and becomes law when approved by the President

joint-stock company /ˌdʒɔɪnt.stɒk'kʌm.pə.ni/ [US] /-stɑːk-/ *noun* [C] *SPECIALIZED* a business which is owned by the group of people who have shares in the company

joist /dʒɔɪst/ *noun* [C] a long thick piece of wood, steel or concrete which is used in buildings to support a floor or ceiling

jojoba /hə'həʊ.bə/ [US] /-'hoʊ-/ *noun* [U] a large American plant with sharp leaves whose seeds contain a valuable oil which is used in beauty products: *jojoba oil*

joke [AMUSING] /dʒəʊk/ [US] /dʒoʊk/ *noun* [C] something, such as an amusing story or trick, that is said or done in order to make people laugh: *Did I* ***tell*** *you the joke about the chicken crossing the road?* ○ *She spent the evening* ***cracking*** (= telling) *jokes and telling funny stories.* ○ *She tied his shoelaces together* ***for a*** *joke.* ○ *I hope Rob doesn't tell any of his* ***dirty*** *jokes* (= jokes about sex) *when my mother's here.* ○ *He tried to do a comedy routine, but all his jokes* ***fell flat*** (= no one laughed at them). ○ *Don't you* ***get*** (= understand) *the joke?*

• **take a joke** to laugh when someone says something amusing about you and not be offended: *What's the matter? Can't you take a joke or something?*

• **get/go beyond a joke** to start to become annoying or worrying: *I don't mind helping her out occasionally, but this is getting beyond a joke.*

• **make a joke of *sth*** to laugh at something although it is serious or important: *He tried to make a joke of the fact that he hadn't passed the exam.*

• **be no joke** *INFORMAL* to be serious or difficult: *It's no joke driving on icy roads.*

• **the joke is on *sb*** *INFORMAL* If you say that the joke is on a particular person, you mean that they have tried to make someone else look foolish but have made themselves look foolish instead.

joke /dʒəʊk/ [US] /dʒoʊk/ *verb* [I] **1** to say amusing things: *They joked and laughed as they looked at the photos.* ○ *It's more serious than you think, so please don't joke* ***about*** *it.* ○ [+ speech] *"I didn't expect to be out so soon", he joked, after spending nine months in hospital.* **2** If you think that someone is joking when they say something, you think that they do not really mean it: *I thought he was joking when he said Helen was pregnant, but she really is.* ○ *She wasn't joking* (= She was serious) *when she said she was going to move out of the house by the end of the week.*

• **Only joking!** said when you mean that something you said was not intended to be serious: *Think I'll leave you with the kids while I go for a beer – only joking!*

• **joking apart/aside** said when you want to start speaking seriously about something after making jokes and laughing about it: *Joking apart, will you be able to manage on your own?*

• **You're joking!** something you say to show that you are surprised by what someone has said, or do not believe it is true: *"Hey, Maria's leaving." "You're joking!"*

• **you must be joking** (*ALSO* **you've got to be joking**) said in answer to something that someone has said, meaning that you do not believe they said it seriously, or you think it is a ridiculous thing to say: *You've got to be joking if you think I'm going to stand in the rain watching you play rugby!*

joker /'dʒəʊ.kəʳ/ [US] /'dʒoʊ.kɚ/ *noun* [C] someone who likes telling amusing stories or doing stupid things in order to make people laugh: *He's always been a bit of a joker and can't resist playing tricks on people.* ⊃See also **joker**; **joker** at **joke** RIDICULOUS.

jokey /'dʒəʊ.ki/ [US] /'dʒoʊ-/ *adj INFORMAL* amusing

jokingly /'dʒəʊ.kɪŋ.li/ [US] /'dʒoʊ-/ *adv*: *She suggested* ***half****-jokingly* (= in a way which was intended to be both amusing and slightly serious) *that they should sell the family car and all buy bikes instead.*

joke [RIDICULOUS] /dʒəʊk/ [US] /dʒoʊk/ *noun* [S] *INFORMAL* a person or thing that is ridiculous and does not deserve respect: *Our new teacher's a bit of a joke – he can't even control the class.* ○ *The new software is a* ***complete*** *joke – it keeps going wrong.* ○ *The exam was a joke* (= was very easy) *– everyone finished in less than an hour.*

joker /'dʒəʊ.kəʳ/ [US] /'dʒoʊ.kɚ/ *noun* [C] *INFORMAL* a person who has done something which annoys you: *Some joker keeps setting off the fire alarm.* ⊃See also **joker**; **joker** at **joke** AMUSING.

joker /'dʒəʊ.kəʳ/ [US] /'dʒoʊ.kɚ/ *noun* [C] a special playing card which can be given any value and is used in some card games instead of any other card ⊃See also **joker** at **joke** AMUSING, **joke** RIDICULOUS.

• **joker in the pack** the person or thing that could change the situation in an unexpected way

jollies /'dʒɒl.iz/ [US] /'dʒɑː.liz/ *noun MAINLY US INFORMAL* **get your jollies** to get enjoyment from something, especially something unpleasant

jollification /ˌdʒɒl.ɪ.fɪ'keɪ.ʃᵊn/ [US] /ˌdʒɑː.lə.fə-/ *noun* [C or U] *OLD-FASHIONED* an enjoyable activity or celebration

jolly [HAPPY] /'dʒɒl.i/ [US] /'dʒɑː.li/ *adj* happy and cheerful: *a jolly smile/manner/mood* ○ *She's a very jolly, upbeat sort of a person.*

J

• **jolly hockey sticks** *UK HUMOROUS* describes a woman or girl of a high social class who is enthusiastic in a way that annoys most people

jolly [ENJOYABLE] /ˈdʒɒl.i/ [US] /ˈdʒɑː.li/ *adj OLD-FASHIONED* enjoyable and lively: *a jolly occasion* ○ *We spent a very jolly evening together, chatting and drinking.*

jolly [ATTRACTIVE] /ˈdʒɒl.i/ [US] /ˈdʒɑː.li/ *adj* bright and attractive: *I love the bright yellow you've painted the children's room – it makes it look really jolly.*

jolly [VERY] /ˈdʒɒl.i/ [US] /ˈdʒɑː.li/ *adv UK OLD-FASHIONED INFORMAL* very: *That's a jolly nice scarf you're wearing.*

• **jolly good** *OLD-FASHIONED* used to express approval of something that someone has said or done, or to show that you have heard or understood what someone has said: *"I've left all the papers you need on your desk." "Oh, jolly good."*

• **Jolly good show!** *OLD USE* used to express admiration for what someone has said or done: *"We won!" "Oh, jolly good show!"*

jolly [ENCOURAGE] /ˈdʒɒl.i/ [US] /ˈdʒɑː.li/ *verb* [T + adv or prep] *INFORMAL* to encourage someone to do something by putting them in a good mood and using gentle persuasion: *I'll try to jolly my parents **into** letting me borrow the car this weekend.* ○ *She didn't really want to go to the party, so we had to jolly her **along** a bit.*

▲ **jolly *sth* up** *phrasal verb* [M] *UK INFORMAL* to make something brighter and more attractive: *I thought I'd jolly the room up **with** some colourful curtains.*

the ˌJolly ˈRoger *noun* [S] the black flag with a picture of bones on it which was traditionally used on a ship belonging to PIRATES

ˈjolly ˌwell *adv UK OLD-FASHIONED* used to emphasize something you are saying, especially when you are angry or annoyed: *I'm going to jolly well tell her what I think of her!* ○ *"Is she ready to leave yet?" "I jolly well hope so!"*

jolt /dʒəʊlt/ [US] /dʒoʊlt/ *verb* **1** [I or T; usually + adv or prep] to (cause something or someone to) move suddenly and violently: *The train stopped unexpectedly and we were jolted forwards.* ○ *The truck jolted **along** the rough track through the field.* **2** [T] to shock someone in order to change their behaviour or way of thinking: *The charity used photos of starving children in an attempt to jolt the public conscience* (= make them feel guilty and take action).

• **jolted *sb* into/out of *sth*** to give someone a sudden shock which forces them to act: *The news about Sam's illness jolted her into **action**.*

jolt /dʒəʊlt/ [US] /dʒoʊlt/ *noun* [C] **1** a sudden violent movement: *As the plane touched the ground, there was a massive jolt and we were thrown forwards.* ○ *I woke up **with a** jolt as I thought I heard my bedroom door being pushed open.* **2** an unpleasant shock or surprise: *His self-confidence **took** a sudden jolt with the news that he had not been selected.*

jones /dʒəʊnz/ [US] /dʒoʊnz/ *verb MAINLY US INFORMAL* **be jonesing for *sth*** to want something very much: *I'm jonesing for a coffee – can we take a break?*

josh /dʒɒʃ/ [US] /dʒɑːʃ/ *verb* [I or T] *INFORMAL* to joke, often with the intention of annoying someone in a playful way: *They were always joshing him **about** his bald head.*

joss stick /ˈdʒɒsˌstɪk/ [US] /ˈdʒɑːs-/ *noun* [C] a thin wooden stick covered with a substance which burns slowly and produces a pleasant smell that fills the air

jostle /ˈdʒɒs.l̩/ [US] /ˈdʒɑː.sl̩/ *verb* [I or T] to knock or push roughly against someone in order to move past them or get more space when you are in a crowd of people: *As we came into the arena, we were jostled by fans pushing their way towards the stage.* ○ *Photographers jostled and shoved to get a better view of the royal couple.* **jostling** /ˈdʒɒs.lɪŋ/ [US] /ˈdʒɑː.slɪŋ/ *noun* [U] **jostling** /ˈdʒɒs.lɪŋ/ [US] /ˈdʒɑː.slɪŋ/ *adj*: *a crowd of jostling reporters*

▲ **jostle for *sth*** *phrasal verb* If people jostle for something, they compete with each other in order to get what they want: *Since the fall of the government, the two opposition parties have been jostling for **position**.*

jot [WRITE] /dʒɒt/ [US] /dʒɑːt/ *verb* [T usually + adv or prep] **-tt-** to make a quick short note of something: *Could you jot your address and phone number **in** my address book?*

jottings /ˈdʒɒt.ɪŋz/ [US] /ˈdʒɑː.t̬ɪŋz/ *plural noun* quickly written brief notes: *She **made** some jottings in the margin of the book she was reading.*

jotter (pad) /ˈdʒɒt.əˌpæd/ [US] /ˈdʒɑː.t̬ɚ-/ *noun* [C] *UK* a small book which is used for writing brief notes in

jot [AMOUNT] /dʒɒt/ [US] /dʒɑːt/ *noun INFORMAL* **not a/one jot** not at all or not even a small amount: *Don't listen to her! There's not a jot of truth* (= There is no truth) *in what she's saying.* ○ *None of the committee's proposals will matter a jot* (= They will not matter) *if no-one reads their report.*

▲ **jot *sth* down** *phrasal verb* [M] to write something quickly on a piece of paper so that you remember it: *I carry a notebook so that I can jot down any ideas.*

joule /dʒuːl/ *noun* [C] (*WRITTEN ABBREVIATION* **J**) *SPECIALIZED* a unit of energy or work done

journal [MAGAZINE] /ˈdʒɜː.nəl/ [US] /ˈdʒɝː-/ *noun* [C] a serious magazine or newspaper which is published regularly, usually about a specialist subject: *a medical/trade journal*

journal [RECORD] /ˈdʒɜː.nəl/ [US] /ˈdʒɝː-/ *noun* [C] a written record of what you have done each day; a **diary**: *She **kept** a travel journal during her trip to South America.*

journalese /ˌdʒɜː.nəˈliːz/ [US] /ˌdʒɝː-/ *noun* [U] *DISAPPROVING* a style of language considered typical of newspapers, which is full of expressions that have been used so often that they have become almost meaningless

journalism /ˈdʒɜː.nə.lɪ.zᵊm/ [US] /ˈdʒɝː-/ *noun* [U] the work of collecting, writing and publishing news stories and articles in newspapers and magazines or broadcasting them on the radio and television

journalist /ˈdʒɜː.nə.lɪst/ [US] /ˈdʒɝː-/ *noun* [C] a person who writes news stories or articles for a newspaper or magazine or broadcasts them on radio or television: *a freelance political journalist* **journalistic** /ˌdʒɜː.nəˈlɪs.tɪk/ [US] /ˌdʒɝː-/ *adj*: *the decline of journalistic **standards** in the popular press*

journey /ˈdʒɜː.ni/ [US] /ˈdʒɝː-/ *noun* [C] the act of travelling from one place to another, especially in a vehicle: *It's a two-hour train journey **from** York **to** London.* ○ *I love **going on** long journeys.* ○ *We **broke** our journey* (= stopped for a short time) *in Edinburgh before travelling on to Inverness the next day.* ○ *Did you have a **good** journey?* ○ *Have a **safe** journey!* ○ *FIGURATIVE He views his life as a **spiritual** journey towards a greater understanding of his faith.* ➲See Note **way or journey?** at **way** ROUTE. See Note **travel, journey or trip?** at **travel**.

journey /ˈdʒɜː.ni/ [US] /ˈdʒɝː-/ *verb* [I usually + adv or prep] *LITERARY* to travel somewhere: *As we journeyed south, the landscape became drier and rockier.*

journeyman /ˈdʒɜː.ni.mən/ [US] /ˈdʒɝː-/ *noun* [C] **1** *OLD-FASHIONED* a skilled worker who is qualified to work at their particular job and who usually works for someone else **2** any worker who produces good, but not excellent work

journo /ˈdʒɜː.nəʊ/ [US] /ˈdʒɜːr.noʊ/ *noun* [C] *INFORMAL FOR* **journalist**

joust /dʒaʊst/ *verb* [I] **1** (in the past) to fight with a LANCE (= a long pointed weapon) while riding on a horse, especially as a sport **2** to compete, especially for power or control: *Manchester United and Liverpool are jousting **for** position at the top of the football league.*

by Jove /baɪˈdʒəʊv/ [US] /-ˈdʒoʊv/ *exclamation OLD-FASHIONED* used to express surprise or to emphasize a statement: *By Jove, I think he's won!*

jovial /ˈdʒəʊ.vi.əl/ [US] /ˈdʒoʊ-/ *adj* (of a person) friendly and in a good mood, or (of a situation) enjoyable because of being friendly and pleasant: *He seemed a very jovial chap.* ○ *a jovial time/evening/chat* **jovially** /ˈdʒəʊ.vi.ə.li/ [US] /ˈdʒoʊ-/ *adv* **joviality** /ˌdʒəʊ.viˈæl.ə.ti/ [US] /ˌdʒoʊ.viˈæl.ə.t̬i/ *noun* [U]

jowl /dʒaʊl/ *noun* [C usually pl] the loose skin and flesh under the jaw: *a bloodhound with **heavy** jowls* (= loose folds of skin and flesh on the lower parts of its face) **jowly** /ˈdʒaʊ.li/ *adj*: *She's become increasingly jowly* (= the skin and flesh on the lower part of her face has become looser) *as she's got older.*

joy [HAPPINESS] /dʒɔɪ/ *noun* **1** [U] great happiness: *They were **filled with** joy when their first child was born.* ○ *She*

***wept for** joy when she was told that her husband was still alive.* **2** [C] a person or thing which causes happiness: *Listening to music is one of his greatest joys.* ○ *the joys of parenthood* ○ [+ **to** infinitive] *Her singing is **a** joy **to** listen to.*

joyful /ˈdʒɔɪ.fᵊl/ *adj* very happy: *Christmas is such a joyful time of year.* ○ *I don't have very much to feel joyful **about/over** at the moment.* **joyfully** /ˈdʒɔɪ.fᵊl.i/ *adv* **joyfulness** /ˈdʒɔɪ.fᵊl.nəs/ *noun* [U]

joyless /ˈdʒɔɪ.ləs/ *adj* unhappy: *Jane is trapped in a joyless marriage.* **joylessly** /ˈdʒɔɪ.lə.sli/ *adv* **joylessness** /ˈdʒɔɪ.lə.snəs/ *noun* [U]

joyous /ˈdʒɔɪ.əs/ *adj* LITERARY full of joy; very happy: *a joyous hymn/event/voice* **joyously** /ˈdʒɔɪ.ə.sli/ *adv* **joyousness** /ˈdʒɔɪ.ə.snəs/ *noun* [U]

joy [SUCCESS] /dʒɔɪ/ *noun* [U] UK INFORMAL success, action or help: [+ v-ing] *Did you **have** any joy find**ing** that book you wanted?* ○ *We tried asking local libraries for information, but **got no** joy **from** any of them.*

joyriding /ˈdʒɔɪˌraɪ.dɪŋ/ *noun* [U] UK the crime of stealing a vehicle and driving fast and dangerously for fun **joyrider** /ˈdʒɔɪˌraɪ.dəʳ/ [US] /-dɚ/ *noun* [C] UK *He was knocked down by a car that was being driven by joyriders* (= people who have stolen a car in order to drive it for enjoyment). **joyride** /ˈdʒɔɪ.raɪd/ *noun* [C]

joystick /ˈdʒɔɪ.stɪk/ *noun* [C] a vertical handle which can be moved forwards, backwards and sideways to control the direction or height of an aircraft or to control a machine or computer game

JP /ˌdʒeɪˈpiː/ *noun* [C] ABBREVIATION FOR **Justice of the Peace**

JPEG /ˈdʒeɪ.peg/ *noun* **1** [U] ABBREVIATION FOR joint photographic experts group: a system for reducing the size of electronic image files: *JPEG can reduce files to 5% of their original size.* **2** [C] a type of computer file that contains pictures or photographs: *a JPEG file* ○ *Sam sent me a JPEG of her family having Christmas dinner, but I can't open it.*

Jr *adj* [after n] MAINLY US ABBREVIATION FOR **junior** YOUNGER

JSA /ˌdʒeɪ.esˈeɪ/ *noun* [U] ABBREVIATION FOR **Jobseeker's Allowance**

jubilant /ˈdʒuː.bɪ.lənt/ *adj* feeling or expressing great happiness, especially because of a success: *The fans were jubilant **at/about/over** England's victory.* **jubilantly** /ˈdʒuː.bɪ.lənt.li/ *adv* **jubilation** /ˌdʒuː.bɪˈleɪ.ʃᵊn/ *noun* [U] *There was jubilation in the crowd as the winning goal was scored.*

jubilee /ˈdʒuː.bɪ.liː/ /ˌ--ˈ-/ *noun* [C] (the celebration of) the day on which an important event happened many years ago: *the Queen's silver jubilee*

Judaeo-Christian UK, US **Judeo-Christian** /dʒuːˈdeɪ.əʊˌkrɪs.tʃən/ [US] /-oʊ-/ *adj* belonging to, shared by, or including both the Jewish and the Christian religion, or both Jewish and Christian people: *Judaeo-Christian tradition/values/fellowship*

Judaism /ˈdʒuː.deɪ.ɪ.zᵊm/ *noun* [U] the religion of the Jewish people, based on belief in one God and on the laws contained in the Torah and Talmud **Judaic** /dʒuːˈdeɪ.ɪk/ *adj* belonging or relating to Judaism: *Judaic tradition*

Judas /ˈdʒuː.dəs/ *noun* [C] a person who is not loyal to a friend and helps the friend's enemies; a **traitor**

judder UK /ˈdʒʌd.əʳ/ [US] /-ɚ/ *verb* [I] (US **shudder**) (especially of a vehicle) to shake violently: *The train juddered **to a halt**.* **judder** UK /ˈdʒʌd.əʳ/ [US] /-ɚ/ *noun* [C] (US **shudder**) *The car gave **a** sudden judder, then stopped dead.*

judge [PERSON] /dʒʌdʒ/ *noun* [C] a person who is in charge of a trial in a court and decides how a person who is guilty of a crime should be punished, or who makes decisions on legal matters: *a British high-court judge* ○ *a US Supreme Court judge* **judgment, judgement** /ˈdʒʌdʒ.mənt/ *noun* [C or U] an official legal decision: *It is the judgment **of** this court that you are guilty of murder.* ○ *We are still waiting for the court to **pass/pronounce** judgment* (= give a decision) ***on** the case.*

judge [DECIDE] /dʒʌdʒ/ *verb* [I or T] **1** to form, give or have as an opinion, or to decide about something or someone, especially after thinking carefully: *So far, he seems to be handling the job well, but it's really too soon to judge.* ○ [+ question word] *It's difficult to judge **wh**ether the new system really is an improvement.* ○ *The meeting was judged (**to** have been) a success.* ○ *You shouldn't judge **by/on** appearances alone.* ○ *I'm hopeless at judging **distance(s)*** (= guessing how far it is between places). **2** to officially decide who will be the winner of a competition: *I've been asked to judge the fancy-dress competition.*

• **judging by/from** (ALSO **to judge by/from**) used to express the reasons why you have a particular opinion: *Judging by what he said, I think it's very unlikely that he'll be able to support your application.*

• **You can't judge a book by its cover.** SAYING said to show that you cannot know what something or someone is like by looking only at their appearance

judge /dʒʌdʒ/ *noun* [C] **1** the person who officially decides who is the winner of a competition: *a panel of judges* **2** a person who has the knowledge to give an opinion about something or is able to decide whether someone or something is good or bad: *She's such a bad judge **of** character.* ○ *"I really don't think you should have another drink." "I'll be/Let me be the judge **of** that* (= I am able to make my own decision about that)."

judgment, judgement /ˈdʒʌdʒ.mənt/ *noun* **1** [U] the ability to form valuable opinions and make good decisions: *to show **good/sound/poor** judgment* ○ *I don't think you have the right to **pass** judgment (**on** others)* (= to say whether you think other people are good or bad). ○ *I'm going to **reserve** judgment (**on** the decision)* (= not say whether I think it is good or bad) *for the time being.* **2** [C] a decision or opinion about someone or something that you form after thinking carefully: *It proved difficult to **come to/form/make** a judgment about how well the school was performing.*

• **in *sb's* judgment** according to someone's opinion: *In my judgment, we should let the solicitor deal with this.*

judgmental /dʒʌdʒˈmen.tᵊl/ [US] /-t̬ᵊl/ *adj* DISAPPROVING too quick to criticize people: *You must try not to be so judgmental **about** people.* **judgmentally** /dʒʌdʒˈmen.tᵊl.i/ [US] /-t̬ᵊl-/ *adv*

ˈJudgment ˌDay *noun* [U] (ALSO **the Day of Judgment**) the time when some people believe the world will end and all the dead people will come back to life so that God can judge how everyone behaved when they were alive

judicature /ˈdʒuː.dɪ.kə.tʃəʳ/ [US] /-tʃɚ/ *noun* [U] SPECIALIZED the giving of justice in a court of law

judiciary /dʒuːˈdɪʃ.ᵊr.i/ [US] /-ɚ-/ *group noun* [C] the part of a country's government which is responsible for its legal system and which consists of all the judges in the country's courts of law: *a member of the judiciary* **judicial** /dʒuːˈdɪʃ.ᵊl/ *adj* involving a court of law: *the judicial system* ○ *judicial **enquiry/review*** * NOTE: Do not confuse with **judicious**. **judicially** /dʒuːˈdɪʃ.ᵊl.i/ *adv*

judicious /dʒuːˈdɪʃ.əs/ *adj* having or showing reason and good judgment in making decisions: *We should make judicious use of the resources available to us.* * NOTE: Do not confuse with **judicial**. **judiciously** /dʒuːˈdɪʃ.ə.sli/ *adv*: *a judiciously worded statement*

judo /ˈdʒuː.dəʊ/ [US] /-doʊ/ *noun* [U] a sport in which two people fight using their arms and legs and hands and feet, and try to throw each other to the ground: *He's a black belt* (= has the highest level of skill) ***in/at** judo.* ➲See picture **Sports** on page Centre 10

jug [CONTAINER] /dʒʌg/ *noun* [C] **1** UK (US **pitcher**) a container for holding liquids which has a handle and a shaped opening at the top for pouring: *a glass/plastic jug* ○ *a milk/water jug* **2** US a large round container for liquids which has a flat base, a handle and a very narrow raised opening at the top for pouring: *a whiskey jug* **3** the amount of liquid that a jug holds: *a jug **of** milk* **jugful** /ˈdʒʌg.fʊl/ *noun* [C] *There was a jugful of water on each table.*

jug [PRISON] /dʒʌg/ *noun* [U] UK OLD-FASHIONED SLANG prison: *I always knew he'd end up **in (the)** jug.*

juggernaut [VEHICLE] UK /ˈdʒʌg.ə.nɔːt/ [US] /-ɚ.nɑːt/ *noun* [C] (US **semi(-trailer)**, US **tractor-trailer**) a very large heavy truck: *The peace of the village has been shattered by juggernauts thundering through it.*

juggernaut POWERFUL FORCE /'dʒʌg.ə.nɔːt/ US /-ɚ.nɑːt/ *noun* [C] *DISAPPROVING* a large powerful force or organization that cannot be stopped

juggle ENTERTAIN /'dʒʌg.l/ *verb* [I or T] to throw several objects up into the air, and then catch and throw them up repeatedly so that one or more stays in the air, usually in order to entertain people: *We all watched in amazement as he juggled with three flaming torches.*
juggler /'dʒʌg.lɚ/ US /-lɚ/ *noun* [C] a person who juggles objects in order to entertain people **juggling** /'dʒʌg.lɪŋ/ *noun* [U]

juggle MANAGE /'dʒʌg.l/ *verb* [T] *INFORMAL* to succeed in arranging your life so that you have time to involve yourself in two or more different activities or groups of people: *Many parents find it hard to juggle children and a career.*

juggle CHANGE /'dʒʌg.l/ *verb* [T] *INFORMAL* to change results or information recorded as numbers so that a situation seems to be better that it really is: *It won't matter if we juggle the figures – no one will know.*

juggling act *noun* [S] a difficult task or situation that involves dealing with several different things at the same time: *Her life is a constant juggling act, coping with career, family, and home life single-handed.*

jugular (vein) /'dʒʌg.ju.lə.ˌveɪn/ US /-lɚ-/ *noun* [C] any of several large veins in the neck that carry blood from the head to the heart
● **go for the jugular** to make serious effort to defeat someone, usually by criticizing them or harming them in a cruel way: *Cunningham went straight for the jugular, telling him that his work was a complete disaster.*

juice LIQUID /dʒuːs/ *noun* [U] the liquid that comes from fruit or vegetables: *orange/lemon/grapefruit/carrot juice* ○ *a carton of apple juice*
juicer /'dʒuː.sɚ/ US /-sɚ/ *noun* [C] a machine for removing juice from fruit or vegetables
juices /'dʒuː.sɪz/ *plural noun* **1** the liquid in meat: *Fry the meat first to seal in the juices.* **2** the liquid in the stomach that helps the body to digest food: *digestive/gastric juices*
juicy /'dʒuː.si/ *adj* Juicy foods contain a lot of juice, which makes them very enjoyable to eat: *a nice juicy orange/steak* **juiciness** /'dʒuː.sɪ.nəs/ *noun* [U]

juice POWER /dʒuːs/ *noun* [U] *US SLANG* power or influence: *My cousin Gianni's got all the juice* (= influence) *in this neighborhood.*
juices /'dʒuː.sɪz/ *plural noun* *INFORMAL* energy: *This early in the morning it's hard to get the creative juices flowing* (= to start thinking of good ideas).
juicy /'dʒuː.si/ *adj* [before n] *INFORMAL* **1** big, important, or of a high quality: *If sales continue like this, we should be showing a nice juicy profit at the end of the year.* **2** describes information that is especially interesting because it is shocking or personal: *I've got some really juicy gossip for you.*

ju-jitsu, *MAINLY US* **jiujitsu** /ˌdʒuːˈdʒɪt.suː/ *noun* [U] a type of self-defence from Japan which does not involve weapons and which is done as a sport, and on which other similar sports such as JUDO and KARATE are based

jukebox /'dʒuːk.bɒks/ US /-bɑːks/ *noun* [C] a machine in bars etc. which plays recorded music when a coin is put into it

julep /'dʒuː.lɪp/ *noun* [C] ⊃See **mint julep**.

July /dʒʊˈlaɪ/ *noun* [C or U] (*WRITTEN ABBREVIATION* **Jul**) the seventh month of the year, after June and before August: *22(nd) July/July 22(nd)* ○ *Clea's birthday is on the eleventh of July/July the eleventh/(MAINLY US) July eleventh.* ○ *next/last July* ○ *The film festival is in/during July.*

jumble /'dʒʌm.bl/ *noun* **1** [S] an untidy and confused mixture of things, feelings or ideas: *He rummaged through the jumble of papers on his desk.* ○ *a jumble of thoughts/ideas* **2** [U] UK things you no longer want that are sold at a JUMBLE SALE
jumble /'dʒʌm.bl/ *verb* [T] to mix things together untidily: *Her clothes were all jumbled up/together in the suitcase.*

jumble sale UK *noun* [C] (*US* **rummage sale**) a sale of a mixed collection of things that people no longer want,

especially in order to make money for an organization

jumbo /'dʒʌm.bəʊ/ US /-boʊ/ *adj* [before n] extremely large: *a jumbo bag of sweets* ○ *a jumbo-sized packet*

jumbo 'jet *noun* [C] (*INFORMAL* **jumbo**) a very large aircraft which can carry a lot of people ⊃See picture **Planes, Ships and Boats** on page Centre 14

jump IN THE AIR /dʒʌmp/ *verb* **1** [I] to push yourself suddenly off the ground and into the air using your legs: *The children were jumping up and down with excitement.* ○ *She ran across the grass and jumped into the water.* ○ *He had to jump out of an upstairs window to escape.* ○ *Our cat is always jumping up on/onto the furniture.* **2** [I or T] to push yourself suddenly off the ground in order to go over something: *Can you jump over/across this stream?* ○ *All the horses are finding it difficult to jump the last fence.*
● **be jumping up and down** UK *INFORMAL* to be angry or annoyed: *Bill's jumping up and down because Mark didn't get his report finished in time.*
● **jump for joy** to be extremely happy: *"So how did Robert take the news?" "He didn't exactly jump for joy."*
● **go (and) jump in the lake** *INFORMAL* a rude way of telling someone to go away and stop annoying you: *He just wouldn't leave me alone, so finally I told him to go jump in the lake.*
jump /dʒʌmp/ *noun* [C] *He won with a jump of 8.5 metres.* ○ *a parachute jump* ○ *Several horses fell at the last jump* (= fence or other thing to be jumped over).
● **be/stay/keep one jump ahead** to do something before other people do it: *The way to be successful in business is always to stay one jump ahead of your competitors.*
● **get a jump on sb/sth** *MAINLY US INFORMAL* to start doing something before other people start, or before something happens, in order to gain an advantage for yourself: *I like to leave work early on Fridays so I can get a jump on the traffic.*
jumper /'dʒʌm.pɚ/ US /-pɚ/ *noun* [C] a person or animal that jumps

jump MOVE/ACT SUDDENLY /dʒʌmp/ *verb* **1** [I usually + adv or prep] to move or act suddenly or quickly: *He suddenly jumped to his feet/jumped up and left.* ○ *She jumped in/into a taxi and rushed to the station.* **2** [I] If a noise or action causes you to jump, your body makes a sudden sharp movement because of surprise or fear: *The loud explosion made everyone jump.* ○ *I almost jumped out of my skin when I heard a loud crash downstairs.*
● **jump down sb's throat** *INFORMAL* to react angrily to something that someone says or does: *I made the mildest of criticisms and he jumped down my throat.*
● **jump in with both feet** *INFORMAL* to become involved in a situation too quickly without thinking about it first: *That's just like Julie – always jumping in with both feet before she knows the facts.*
● **jump to it** *INFORMAL* used to tell someone to do something quickly: *I told you to tidy this room – now jump to it!*
● **jump to conclusions** to guess the facts about a situation without having enough information: *Don't jump to conclusions! Perhaps it was his daughter he was dancing with.*
● **jump to sb's defence** to quickly defend someone: *Whenever anyone criticizes her husband, she immediately jumps to his defence.*
● **jump the gun** to do something too soon, especially without thinking carefully about it: *They've only just met – isn't it jumping the gun to be talking about marriage already?*

jump SEQUENCE /dʒʌmp/ *verb* [I usually + adv or prep] If a story, film, play, etc. jumps, it moves suddenly between different parts of it: *The film is about his adult life, but it keeps jumping (back) to when he was a child.* ○ *His talk was hard to follow because he kept jumping from one subject to another.*

jump AVOID /dʒʌmp/ *verb* [T] to avoid or leave out a point or stage from the correct order in a series: *You have to follow the instructions exactly, you can't just jump a few steps ahead.*

jump INCREASE /dʒʌmp/ *verb* [I] to increase suddenly by a large amount: *House prices have jumped dramatically.* ○ *The cost of building the road has jumped by 70%.*

jump [BE BUSY] /dʒʌmp/ *verb OLD-FASHIONED INFORMAL* **be jumping** If a place is jumping, it is lively and crowded: *This joint* (= place of entertainment) *is really jumping tonight.*

jump [ATTACK] /dʒʌmp/ *verb* [T] *INFORMAL* to attack someone suddenly: *They were just walking home when a bunch of guys jumped **(on)** them.*

jump [MOVE ILLEGALLY] /dʒʌmp/ *verb* [T] **1** to go past or away from something illegally or wrongly: *The police video showed that she had jumped the **(traffic) lights.*** ○ *Several sailors jumped **ship*** (= left their ship without permission) *in New York.* **2 jump bail** to fail to appear for a court trial after being released until the trial in exchange for payment: *I'd never have thought Hugh would jump bail.*

PHRASAL VERBS WITH **jump** ▼

▲ **jump at** ***sth*** *phrasal verb* to accept something eagerly: *She jumped at the **chance** of a trip to Paris.*
▲ **jump in** *phrasal verb* to interrupt when someone else is speaking: *I wish you'd stop jumping in and finishing my sentences for me all the time.*
▲ **jump on** ***sb*** *phrasal verb* to criticise someone as soon as they have done something wrong or said something that you disagree with: *She jumps on her children instantly if they're disobedient.*
▲ **jump out at** ***sb*** If something jumps out at you, you notice it immediately: *That's a very effective advertisement – it really jumps out at you.*

jumped-up /ˌdʒʌmptˈʌp/ *adj* [before n] *UK INFORMAL DISAPPROVING* describes someone who behaves as if they are very important in their job or position, especially because they used to be in a much lower position: *He's just a jumped-up office boy* (= he was once only an office boy).

jumper /ˈdʒʌm.pəʳ/ [US] /-pɚ/ *noun* [C] **1** *UK* (*US* **sweater**) a woollen item of clothing which covers the upper part of the body and the arms, and which does not open at the front: *a red woolly jumper* ➲See picture **Clothes** on page Centre 6 **2** *US* a dress which does not cover the arms and is usually worn over another item of clothing which does cover the arms

jumping-off point /ˌdʒʌm.pɪŋˈɒfˌpɔɪnt/ [US] /-ˈɑːf-/ *noun* [C usually sing] a point from which to start a journey or activity

ˈ**jump** ˌ**leads** *UK plural noun* (*US* **jumper cables**, *AUS* **jumper leads**) a pair of thick wires for starting the engine of one vehicle with electricity from the battery of another vehicle

ˈ**jump** ˌ**rope** *noun* [C] *US* a **skipping rope**
ˌ**jump** ˈ**rope** *verb* [I] *US* to **skip** JUMP

jump-start /ˈdʒʌmp.stɑːt/ [US] /-stɑːrt/ *verb* [T] To jump-start a car is to start its engine by pushing the car, or by using jump leads. ➲Compare **push-start**. **jump-start** /ˈdʒʌmp.stɑːt/ [US] /-stɑːrt/ *noun* [C usually sing]

jumpsuit /ˈdʒʌmp.sjuːt/ [US] /-suːt/ *noun* [C] a single item of clothing which covers both the upper body and the legs

jumpy /ˈdʒʌm.pi/ *adj INFORMAL* nervous and anxious, especially because of fear or guilt: *My mother gets very jumpy when she's alone in the house.*

junction /ˈdʒʌŋk.ʃən/ *noun* [C] (*US USUALLY* **intersection**) a place where things, especially roads or railways, come together: *You should slow down as you approach the junction.* ○ *UK There's a service station at the next **motorway** junction* (= point from which you can leave the motorway).

ˈ**junction** ˌ**box** *noun* [C] a box in which electrical wires can be safely joined together

juncture /ˈdʒʌŋk.tʃəʳ/ [US] /-tʃɚ/ *noun* [U] *FORMAL* a particular point in time: ***At** this juncture, it is impossible to say whether she will make a full recovery.*

June /dʒuːn/ *noun* [C or U] (*WRITTEN ABBREVIATION* **Jun**) the sixth month of the year, after May and before July: *24(th) June/June 24(th)* ○ *He arrived **on** the fifth of June/June the fifth/(MAINLY US) June fifth* ○ *last/next June* ○ *I went to visit my father **in/during** June.*

jungle [PLACE] /ˈdʒʌŋ.gl̩/ *noun* **1** [C or U] a tropical forest in which trees and plants grow very closely together: *The Yanomami people live in the South American jungle.* ○ *Either side of the river is dense, impenetrable jungle.* **2** [S] an uncontrolled or confusing mass of things: *Our garden is a real jungle.* ○ *a jungle **of regulations/laws***

jungle [SITUATION] /ˈdʒʌŋ.gl̩/ *noun* [S] *INFORMAL* a situation in which it is difficult to succeed because a lot of people are competing against each other: *You've got to be determined in this life – it's a jungle out there, kid.*

jungle [MUSIC] /ˈdʒʌŋ.gl̩/ *noun* [U] a type of popular dance music with an extremely fast rhythm and a low range of musical notes

ˈ**jungle** ˌ**gym** *noun* [C] *US FOR* **climbing frame**

ˌ**jungle** ˈ**warfare** *noun* [U] war fought in a tropical forest where it is difficult to see the enemy and they can attack unexpectedly

junior [YOUNGER] /ˈdʒuː.ni.əʳ/ [US] /-njɚ/ *noun, adj* **1** (someone) younger: *My brother is my junior **by** three years./ My brother is three years my junior* (= He is three years younger than me). ➲Compare **senior** OLDER. **2** (*US WRITTEN ABBREVIATION* **Jr**, *MAINLY UK WRITTEN ABBREVIATION* **Jnr**) used after a man's name to refer to the younger of two men in the same family who have the same name: *Sammy Davis, Jr* **3** *MAINLY US* used to refer to your son: *Come on, Junior, time for bed.*

junior [LOW RANK] /ˈdʒuː.ni.əʳ/ [US] /-njɚ/ *adj* low or lower in rank: *I object to being told what to do by someone junior **to** me.* ○ *a junior doctor/partner* ➲Compare **senior** HIGH RANK.
junior /ˈdʒuː.ni.əʳ/ [US] /-njɚ/ *noun* [C] someone who has a job at a low level within an organization: *an office junior*

junior [STUDENT] /ˈdʒuː.ni.əʳ/ [US] /-njɚ/ *noun* [C] **1** *UK* a student at a JUNIOR SCHOOL **2** *US* a student in the third year of a course that lasts for four years at a school or college
the juniors *plural noun UK* **junior school**: *Lewis has just moved up to the juniors.*

ˌ**junior** ˈ**college** *noun* [C or U] *US* a college in the US where students study for two years

ˌ**junior** ˈ**high (school)** *noun* [C] *US* a school in the US for children who are 12 to 15 years old

ˈ**junior** ˌ**school** *noun* [C] a school in the UK for children who are 7 to 11 years old: *My son goes to the local junior school.*

juniper /ˈdʒuː.nɪ.pəʳ/ [US] /-pɚ/ *noun* [C or U] a small evergreen bush which has sharp leaves and small purple fruits which are used in medicine and in making GIN (= a type of strong alcoholic drink): *juniper berries*

junk [RUBBISH] /dʒʌŋk/ *noun* [U] things that are considered to be of no use or value, or of low quality: *We ought to clear out this cupboard – it's full of junk.* ○ *I can't stand watching the junk that's on TV these days.*
junk /dʒʌŋk/ *verb* [T] *INFORMAL* to get rid of something because it is of no use or value

junk [DRUG] /dʒʌŋk/ *noun* [U] *MAINLY US SLANG* a dangerous drug, especially heroin
junkie /ˈdʒʌŋ.ki/ *noun* [C] *INFORMAL* **1** (*ALSO* **junky**) someone who cannot stop taking illegal drugs **2** someone who wants to have or do something all the time: *a computer/TV junkie* ○ *a publicity junkie*

junk [SHIP] /dʒʌŋk/ *noun* [C] a Chinese ship with a flat bottom and square sails

junket /ˈdʒʌŋ.kɪt/ *noun* [C] *DISAPPROVING* a journey or visit made for pleasure by an official, which is paid for by someone else or is paid for with public money

ˈ**junk** ˌ**food** *noun* [C or U] food that is unhealthy but is quick and easy to eat ➲Compare **health food**.

ˈ**junk** ˌ**mail** *noun* [U] post, usually advertising products or services, which is sent to people although they have not asked for it

ˈ**junk** ˌ**shop** *noun* [C] a shop which sells old furniture and other items of little value

junkyard /ˈdʒʌŋk.jɑːd/ [US] /-jɑːrd/ *noun* [C] *MAINLY US* a place to which people take large things such as old furniture or machines that they no longer want

junta /ˈdʒʌn.tə/ /ˈhʊn-/ *group noun* [C] a government, especially a military one, that has taken power in a country by force and not by election: *The* ***military*** *junta has/have today broadcast an appeal for calm.*

Jupiter /ˈdʒuː.pɪ.təʳ/ [US] /-t̬ɚ/ *noun* [S] the planet fifth in order of distance from the Sun, after Mars and before Saturn

jurisdiction /ˌdʒʊə.rɪsˈdɪk.ʃᵊn/ [US] /ˌdʒʊr.ɪs-/ *noun* [U] the authority of an official organization to make and deal with especially legal decisions: *The court* ***has*** *no jurisdiction* ***in/over*** *cases of this kind.* ○ *School admissions are not* ***under/within*** *our jurisdiction.*

jurisprudence /ˌdʒʊə.rɪˈspruː.dᵊnts/ [US] /ˌdʒʊr.ɪ-/ *noun* [U] *SPECIALIZED* the study of law and the principles on which law is based

jurist /ˈdʒʊə.rɪst/ [US] /ˈdʒʊr.ɪst/ *noun* [C] *SPECIALIZED* an expert in law, especially a judge

jury /ˈdʒʊə.ri/ [US] /ˈdʒʊr.i/ *group noun* [C] **1** a group of people who have been chosen to listen to all the facts in a trial in a law court and to decide whether a person is guilty or not guilty, or whether a claim has been proved: *members of the jury* ○ *The jury has/have been unable to return a verdict* (= reach a decision). ○ *Police officers aren't usually allowed to* ***be/sit/serve on*** *a jury.* **2** a group of people chosen to decide the winner of a competition

• **the jury is (still) out** If the jury is (still) out on a subject, people do not yet know the answer or have a definite opinion about it: *The jury's still out* ***on*** *the safety of irradiated food.*

juror, *OLD USE* **juryman** /ˈdʒʊə.rəʳ/ [US] /ˈdʒʊr.ɚ/ *noun* [C] a member of a jury

J

ˈ**jury** ˌ**box** *noun* [C usually sing] the place in a court where the jury sits

ˈ**jury** ˌ**service** *UK noun* [U] (*US* **jury duty**) a period of time when a person is a member of a jury: *I'm* ***on/doing*** *jury service next week.*

jus /ʒuː/ *noun* [C] a sauce: *pan-fried beef in a balsamic jus*

just [NOW] /dʒʌst/ *adv* now, very soon, or very recently: *"Where are you, Jim?" "I'm just coming."* ○ *I'll just finish this, then we can go.* ○ *He'd just got into the bath when the phone rang.* ○ *The children arrived at school just* ***as*** (= at the same moment as) *the bell was ringing.* ○ *The doctor will be with you in just* ***a minute/moment/second*** (= very soon). ○ *It's just after/past/(UK ALSO) gone* (= has recently become) *ten (o'clock).*

• **just a minute/moment/second 1** used to ask someone to wait for a short period of time: *Just a second – I've nearly finished.* **2** *MAINLY UK* used to interrupt someone in order to ask them to explain something, to calm them, or to express disagreement: *Just a minute – can you tell me how to do that again?*

• **just now 1** a very short time ago: *Who was that at the door just now?* **2** at the present time: *John's in the bath just now – can he call you back?*

just [EXACTLY] /dʒʌst/ *adv* exactly or equally: *This carpet would be just right for the dining room.* ○ *The twins look just like each other.* ○ *Things turned out just* ***as*** *I expected.* ○ *You've got just* ***as*** *many toys* ***as*** *your brother.* ○ *Thank you, it's just what I've always wanted.* ○ *I can't help you just* ***now/yet.*** ○ *Just* ***then***, *the lights went out.* ○ *I can just imagine Sophie as a police officer.* ○ *INFORMAL APPROVING That dress is just you* (= suits you very well).

• **might just as well** If you might just as well do something, there are no reasons not to do it: *For the little extra it'll cost, we might just as well stay for another night.*

• **(it's) just as well (that)** it is a good thing: *It's beginning to rain – it's just as well that we brought our umbrellas.*

• **Just my luck!** something that you say when something bad happens to you: *They sold the last ticket five minutes before I got there – just my luck!*

just [ONLY] /dʒʌst/ *adv* **1** only; simply: *"Would you like another drink?" "OK, just one more."* ○ *It was just a joke.* ○ *His daughter's just a baby/just a few weeks old.* ○ *We'll just have to* (= The only thing we can do is) *wait and see what happens.* ○ *She lives just down the road* (= very near). ○ *Just* ***because*** *you're older than me doesn't mean you can tell me what to do.* **2** used to make a statement or order stronger: *He just won't do as he's told.* ○ *It's just too expensive.* **3** used to reduce the force of a statement and to suggest that it is not very important: *Can I just borrow the scissors for a second?* ○ *I just wanted to ask you if you're free this afternoon.*

• **just like that** *DISAPPROVING* suddenly and unexpectedly: *Their son went off and got married last week, just like that.*

• **It's just one of those things.** *SAYING* said about an event or situation that you cannot explain, or do not like but cannot change

just [ALMOST] /dʒʌst/ *adv* **1** almost not or almost: *We arrived at the airport just in time to catch the plane.* ○ *This dress* ***(only)*** *just fits.* ○ *"Can you see the stage?" "Yes,* ***only*** *just/just* ***about***.*"* ○ *I've just* ***about*** *finished painting the living room.* **2 be just possible** If something is just possible, there is a slight chance that it will happen: *It's just possible that we might be going away that weekend.*

just [VERY] /dʒʌst/ *adv* very; completely: *It's just dreadful what happened to her.*

• **isn't *it*/aren't *they* just** *INFORMAL* used to strongly agree with what someone has said about someone or something: *"This is rather expensive." "Isn't it just?"*

just [FAIR] /dʒʌst/ *adj* fair; morally correct: *The judge's sentence was perfectly just in the circumstances.* ○ *I don't really think he had just* ***cause*** *to complain.*

• **get *your* just deserts** If you get your just deserts, something bad happens to you that you deserve because of something bad you have done.

the just *plural noun OLD USE* people who behave in a morally correct way **justly** /ˈdʒʌst.li/ *adv* **justness** /ˈdʒʌst.nəs/ *noun* [U]

justice [FAIRNESS] /ˈdʒʌs.tɪs/ *noun* [U] fairness in the way people are dealt with: *There's no justice in the world when people can be made to suffer like that.* ○ *The winner has been disqualified for cheating, so justice has been* ***done*** (= a fair situation has been achieved). * NOTE: The opposite is **injustice**.

• **do justice to *sb/sth*** (*ALSO* **do *sb/sth* justice**) to treat someone or something in a way that is fair and shows their true qualities: *This postcard doesn't do justice to the wonderful scenery.*

• **do justice to *yourself*** (*ALSO* **do *yourself* justice**) to do something as well as you can in order to show your true qualities and ability: *She didn't really do justice to herself in the interview.*

justice [LAW] /ˈdʒʌs.tɪs/ *noun* [U] the system of laws in a country which judges and punishes people: *the justice system in this country consists of a series of law courts at different levels.* ○ *The police are doing all they can to* ***bring*** *those responsible for the bombing* ***to*** *justice.* ○ *They are victims of a* ***miscarriage of*** *justice* (= when the law has been carried out wrongly). ○ *He has been accused of* ***obstructing the course of*** *justice* (= preventing the law being put into action).

justice [JUDGE] /ˈdʒʌs.tɪs/ *noun* [C] **1** *US* a judge in a court of law: *The President is expected to name a new Supreme Court justice within the next few days.* ○ *Justice Ben Overton* **2** *UK* used before the name of a judge in the HIGH COURT: *Mr Justice Ellis*

ˌ**Justice of the** ˈ**Peace** *noun* [C] (*WRITTEN ABBREVIATION* **JP**) a person who is not a lawyer but who acts as a judge in local law courts and, in the US, can marry people

justiˌfiable ˈ**homicide** *noun* [U] *US* an act of killing someone, especially in self-defence, which the law allows because it considers that there is a good reason for it

justify /ˈdʒʌs.tɪ.faɪ/ *verb* [T] to give or to be a good reason for: [+ v-ing] *I can't really justify tak**ing** another day off work* ○ *Are you sure that these measures are justified?*

justify *yourself* *verb* [R] If you justify yourself, you give a good reason for what you have done: *It was the only thing that I could do – I don't have to justify myself* ***to*** *anyone.*

justifiable /ˈdʒʌs.tɪ.faɪ.ə.bl̩/ /ˌ--ˈ---/ *adj*: *Her actions were quite justifiable* (= there was a good reason for them) *in the circumstances.* **justifiably** /ˈdʒʌs.tɪ.faɪ.ə.bli/ /ˌ--ˈ---/ *adv*: *He was justifiably proud of his achievements.*

justification /ˌdʒʌs.tɪ.fɪˈkeɪ.ʃᵊn/ *noun* [C or U] a good reason or explanation for something: *There is no* *justification* ***for*** *treating people so badly.* ○ *It can be said,* ***with*** *some justification, that she is one of the greatest actresses on the English stage today.*

justified /ˈdʒʌs.tɪ.faɪd/ *adj* having a good reason for something: *I accept that the criticism is completely justified.* ○ *I think you were quite justified* ***in*** *complaining.*

just-in-time /ˌdʒʌst.ɪnˈtaɪm/ *adj* (*ALSO* **JIT**) A just-in-time system of MANUFACTURING (= producing goods) is based on preventing waste by producing only the amount of goods needed at a particular time, and not paying to produce and store more goods than are needed.

jut /dʒʌt/ *verb* [I or T; usually + adv or prep] **-tt-** to (cause to) stick out, especially above or beyond the edge or surface of something: *The pier juts* ***(out) into*** *the sea.* ○ *He jutted his* ***chin/jaw*** *(out) defiantly.* **jutting** /ˈdʒʌt.ɪŋ/ [US] /ˈdʒʌt̬-/ *adj* [before n] *jutting rocks*

jute /dʒuːt/ *noun* [U] a substance which comes from a Southeast Asian plant and which is used for making rope and cloth

juvenile /ˈdʒuː.vᵊn.aɪl/ [US] /-nᵊl/ *adj* **1** *FORMAL OR LEGAL* relating to a young person who is not yet old enough to be considered an adult: *juvenile crime/offenders* **2** *DISAPPROVING* silly and typical of a child: *juvenile behaviour* ○ *a juvenile sense of humour*

juvenile /ˈdʒuː.vᵊn.aɪl/ [US] /-nᵊl/ *noun* [C] a young person

ˌjuvenile deˈlinquent *noun* [C] a young person who commits crimes **ˌjuvenile deˈlinquency** *noun* [U]

juxtapose /ˌdʒʌk.stəˈpəʊz/ [US] /-ˈpoʊz/ *verb* [T] to put things which are not similar next to each other: *The exhibition juxtaposes Picasso's early drawings* ***with*** *some of his later works.* **juxtaposition** /ˌdʒʌk.stə.pəˈzɪʃ.ᵊn/ *noun* [U] *the juxtaposition* ***of*** *two very different cultures*

J

K LETTER (*plural* **K's** or **Ks**), **k** (*plural* **k's** or **ks**) /keɪ/ *noun* [C] the 11th letter of the English alphabet

K COMPUTER /keɪ/ *noun* [C] *plural* **K** ABBREVIATION FOR **kilobyte**: *a computer with 256K of memory*

K MONEY /keɪ/ *noun* [C] *plural* **K** INFORMAL FOR 1000 pounds, dollars, etc: *His car cost him £20K.*

K TEMPERATURE /keɪ/ *noun* [after n] ABBREVIATION FOR **kelvin**: *273°K*

kabuki /kəˈbuː.ki/ *noun* [U] a type of Japanese theatre which only uses male actors, who perform in a traditional and artificial manner

kaftan /ˈkæf.tæn/ *noun* [C] a **caftan**

Kalashnikov /kəˈlæʃ.nɪ.kɒf/ ⑩ /-kɑːf/ *noun* [C] a Russian-made rifle which can fire bullets continuously

kale /keɪl/ *noun* [U] a type of cabbage with green or purple tightly curled leaves

kaleidoscope /kəˈlaɪ.də.skəʊp/ ⑩ /-skoʊp/ *noun* **1** [C] a tube-like toy that you look through to see different patterns of light made by pieces of coloured glass and mirrors **2** [S] a changing and enjoyable mixture or pattern: *The street bazaar was a kaleidoscope of colours, smells and sounds.*
kaleidoscopic /kəˌlaɪ.dəˈskɒp.ɪk/ ⑩ /-ˈskɑː.pɪk/ *adj* quickly changing from one thing to another
kaleidoscopically /kəˌlaɪ.dəˈskɒp.ɪ.kli/ ⑩ /-ˈskɑː.pɪ-/ *adv*

kalif /ˈkeɪ.lɪf/ *noun* [C] another spelling of CALIPH

kamikaze /ˌkæm.iˈkɑː.zi/ *adj* **1** [before n] describes a sudden violent attack on an enemy, especially one in which the person or people attacking know that they will be killed: *a kamikaze attack/mission* **2** being willing to take risks and not worrying about safety: *kamikaze taxi drivers* ○ *a kamikaze attitude*

kangaroo /ˌkæŋ.ɡəˈruː/ ⑩ /-ɡəˈruː/ *noun* [C] *plural* **kangaroos** or SPECIALIZED **kangaroo** a large Australian mammal with a long stiff tail, short front legs and long powerful back legs on which it moves by jumping

kangaroo 'court *noun* [C] an unofficial court of law set up by a group of people, especially in a prison, TRADE UNION or other organization, to deal with a disagreement or with a member of the group who is considered to have broken the rules

kanji /ˈkæn.dʒi/ *noun* [U] a Japanese writing system which uses Chinese symbols

kaolin /ˈkeɪə.lɪn/ *noun* [U] a white clay which is used in making PORCELAIN and some medicines

kapok /ˈkeɪ.pɒk/ ⑩ /-pɑːk/ *noun* [U] a soft white material that is used as the filling in soft toys and cushions or for making a thick warm layer in clothes

kaput /kəˈpʊt/ *adj* [after v] INFORMAL broken; not working correctly: *The radio's kaput.*

karaoke /ˌkær.iˈəʊ.ki/ ⑩ /ˌker.iˈoʊ.ki/ *noun* [U] a form of entertainment, originally from Japan, in which recordings of the music but not the words of popular songs are played, so that people can sing the words themselves: *a karaoke bar/machine/night*

karat /ˈkær.ət/ ⑩ /ˈker-/ *noun* [C] US FOR **carat**

karate /kəˈrɑː.ti/ ⑩ /- t̬i/ *noun* [U] a sport originally from Japan in which people fight using their arms, legs, hands and feet. The level of skill a person has is shown by what colour belt they wear. ⮑See picture **Sports** on page Centre 10

karma /ˈkɑː.mə/ ⑩ /ˈkɑːr-/ *noun* [U] (in the Buddhist and Hindu religions) the force produced by a person's actions in one of their lives which influences what happens to them in their future lives

kayak /ˈkaɪ.æk/ *noun* [C] a light narrow CANOE with a covering over the top
kayaking /ˈkaɪ.æk.ɪŋ/ *noun* [U] the activity of travelling in a kayak

kazoo /kəˈzuː/ *noun* [C] *plural* **kazoos** a small musical instrument consisting of a plastic or metal tube with a small piece of paper inside which shakes when the player HUMS (= sings with closed mouth) into it, making a high sound

KC /ˌkeɪˈsiː/ *noun* [C] ABBREVIATION FOR King's Counsel: a high-ranking British lawyer who is allowed to represent a person in court, or the title given to such a lawyer when a king is ruling: *Sir William Garner, KC.* ⮑Compare **QC**.

kebab /kɪˈbæb/ ⑩ /-ˈbɑːb/ *noun* [C] (ALSO **shish kebab**) a dish consisting of small pieces of meat and vegetables that have been put on a long thin stick or metal rod and cooked together

kedgeree /ˈkedʒ.ə.riː/ ⑩ /-ə-/ *noun* [U] a dish consisting of rice, fish and eggs mixed together

keel /kiːl/ *noun* [C] the long piece of wood or steel along the bottom of a boat that forms part of its structure and helps to keep the boat balanced in the water

keel /kiːl/ *verb*

PHRASAL VERBS WITH **keel** ▼

▲ **keel over** PERSON *phrasal verb* to fall over suddenly: *He finished the bottle of whiskey, stood up to leave and keeled over.*

▲ **keel over** BOAT *phrasal verb* If a boat keels over, it turns upside down in the water: *The storm raged and they struggled to stop the boat from keeling over.*

keelhaul /ˈkiːl.hɔːl/ ⑩ /-hɑːl/ *verb* [T] OLD-FASHIONED INFORMAL to tell someone off severely

keen EAGER /kiːn/ *adj* very interested, eager or wanting (to do) something very much: *They were very keen to start work as soon as possible.* ○ *Joan wanted to go to a movie but I wasn't keen* (= I didn't want to go). ○ *She's a keen tennis player* ○ *She's keen on (playing) tennis.* ○ UK *My son's mad keen on cycling.* ○ *He's rather keen on a girl in his school* (= he is very attracted to her).
● **(as) keen as mustard** UK OLD-FASHIONED very eager and interested in everything
keenness /ˈkiːn.nəs/ *noun* [U] the quality of being keen

keen STRONG /kiːn/ *adj* **1** extreme or very strong: *Many people are taking a keen interest* (= a very great interest) *in the result of the vote.* **2** very good or well developed: *a keen sense of smell*
keenly /ˈkiːn.li/ *adv*: *They are keenly* (= extremely) *aware that this will be their last chance to succeed.*

keen SHARP /kiːn/ *adj* LITERARY very sharp: *a keen north wind*

keen CRY /kiːn/ *verb* [I] LITERARY to make a loud, long, sad sound, especially because someone has died

keep POSSESS /kiːp/ *verb* [T] kept, kept **1** to have or continue to have in your possession: *Do you want this photograph back or can I keep it?* ○ *Keep medicines in a locked cupboard* (= Store them there). ⮑See also **well-kept** HIDDEN. **2** to own and manage a small shop: *My uncle kept a little tobacconist's in Gloucester.* **3** If you keep animals, you own and take care of them, but not in your home as pets: *to keep pigs/goats/chickens* US to watch and care for someone's children while their parents are away: *Jody will keep the children while I shop.* **5 keep your promise/word; keep an appointment** to do what you have told someone that you would do: *I made a promise to you and I intend to keep it.* ○ *She phoned to say she couldn't keep her appointment.* **6 keep a diary/an account/a record, etc.** to make a regular record of events or other information so that you can refer to it later: *I've kept a diary for twelve years now.* ○ *Keep an account of how much you're spending.* **7 keep a secret** to not tell anyone a secret that you know **8 keep goal** to be the player who defends your team's goal by trying to prevent balls from the other team scoring goals
keeper /ˈkiː.pər/ ⑩ /-pɚ/ *noun* [C] **1** a person who takes care of animals or is in charge of valuable objects, a building, etc: *a zoo keeper* ○ *a lighthouse-keeper* **2** UK INFORMAL a **goalkeeper**
keeping /ˈkiː.pɪŋ/ *noun* **1 in your keeping** If something is in your keeping, you are taking care of it: *I left my word processor in her keeping when I went abroad.* **2 in safe keeping** being carefully looked after: *I left my son in safe keeping with my mother.*

• **in/out of keeping (with** *sth***)** suitable or not suitable for a particular situation: *In keeping with tradition, they always have turkey on Christmas Day.* ○ *The modern furniture was out of keeping with the old house.*

keep STAY /kiːp/ *verb* [L only + adj; T] **kept, kept** to (cause to) stay in a particular place or condition: *I wish you'd keep quiet.* ○ *I like to keep busy.* ○ *Keep left* (= Stay on the road to the left) *at the traffic lights.* ○ *Can you keep the dog outside, please?* ○ [+ obj + adj] *Close the door to keep the room warm.* ○ *The noise from their party kept me awake half the night.*

• **How are you keeping?** MAINLY UK OLD-FASHIONED used to ask if someone is well: *How's your mother keeping?*

• **keep up with the Joneses** DISAPPROVING to always want to own the same expensive objects and do the same things as your friends or NEIGHBOURS because you are worried about seeming less important socially than they are

keep DELAY /kiːp/ *verb* [T] **kept, kept** to delay someone or prevent them from doing something: *He's very late, what's keeping him?* ○ [+ v-ing] *I'm so sorry to keep you* ***waiting***. ○ *She kept me talking on the phone for half an hour.* ○ *I hope I'm not keeping you* ***up*** (= preventing you from going to bed).

keep CONTINUE DOING (**kept, kept**) /kiːp/ *verb* [I + v-ing] (*ALSO* **keep on**) to continue doing something without stopping, or to do it repeatedly: *He keeps trying to distract me.* ○ *I keep on thinking I've seen her before somewhere.* ○ *I kept hoping that he'd phone me.*

• **keep (***sb***) at it** to continue working hard at something difficult, or to make someone continue to work hard: *I kept at it and finally finished at 3 o'clock in the morning.* ○ *We need to keep her at it if she's going to pass the exam.*

keep STAY FRESH /kiːp/ *verb* [I] **kept, kept** (of food) to stay fresh and in good condition: *Milk keeps much longer in a fridge.*

keep PROVIDE /kiːp/ *verb* [T] **kept, kept** to provide yourself or another person with food, clothing, a home and other things necessary for basic living: *He wanted a job that would allow him to keep his family in comfort.*

keep /kiːp/ *noun* [U] the cost of providing food, heating and other necessary things for someone: *He's old enough now to* ***earn*** *his keep and stop living off his parents.*

• **for keeps** INFORMAL forever: *"Do you want it back?" "No it's yours, for keeps."*

kept /kept/ *adj* USUALLY HUMOROUS **kept woman/man** someone who does not work but is instead given money and a place to live by a person with whom she or he is having a sexual relationship

keep TOWER /kiːp/ *noun* [C] SPECIALIZED the strong main tower of a castle

PHRASAL VERBS WITH **keep** ▼

▲ **keep (***sb/sth***) away** *phrasal verb* [M] to not go somewhere or near something, or to prevent someone from going somewhere or near something: *Keep away from the edge of the cliff.*

▲ **keep (***sth/sb***) back** STOP *phrasal verb* [M] to not go near something, or to prevent someone or something from going past a particular place: *Barriers were built to keep back the flood water.*

▲ **keep** *sth* **back** AMOUNT *phrasal verb* [M] to not use the whole amount of something so that there is a small amount remaining for later

▲ **keep** *sth* **back** NOT TELL *phrasal verb* to not tell someone everything you know about a situation or an event that has happened: *I suspect she's keeping something back.*

▲ **keep** *sth* **down** FOOD *phrasal verb* to be able to eat or drink something without vomiting: *On the day after her operation she couldn't keep anything down.*

▲ **keep** *sth* **down** SIZE *phrasal verb* [M] to control the size or number of something and prevent it from increasing: *We need to work hard to keep our prices down.*

▲ **keep** *sb* **down** POWER *phrasal verb* to prevent a person or group of people from having any power or freedom: *It's all part of a conspiracy to keep women down.*

▲ **keep from doing** *sth* NOT DO *phrasal verb* to manage to prevent yourself from doing something: *I'm afraid I couldn't keep from smiling when she told me what she'd done.*

▲ **keep** *sb/sth* **from** *sth* PREVENT *phrasal verb* to prevent someone or something from doing something: [+ v-ing] *Try to keep the children from throwing food all over the floor.* ○ *Am I keeping you from your work?*

▲ **keep** *sth* **from** *sb* NOT TELL *phrasal verb* to not tell someone about something: *He says it's alright but I think he's keeping something from me.*

▲ **keep** *sb* **in** *phrasal verb* to make a child stay inside as a punishment, or to make someone stay in hospital: *They kept her in overnight for observation.*

▲ **keep in with** *sb* *phrasal verb* to continue to try to be friendly with someone, especially because they can help you: *I like to keep in with my ex-employer, you never know when you might need a reference.*

▲ **keep (***sb/sth***) off** *sth* NOT GO *phrasal verb* to not go onto an area, or to stop someone or something going onto an area: *There was a notice saying 'Keep off the grass'.*

▲ **keep** *sth* **off** (*sb/sth*) STOP *phrasal verb* to stop something touching or harming someone or something: *Put a cloth over the salad to keep the flies off.* ○ *Wear a hat to keep the sun off* (= to prevent it harming your skin).

▲ **keep (***sb***) off** *sth* NOT EAT *phrasal verb* to not eat, drink or use something that can harm you, or to stop someone else from doing this: *The doctor told me to keep off fatty foods.*

▲ **keep off** *sth* NOT DISCUSS *phrasal verb* MAINLY UK If you keep off a particular subject, you avoid talking about it.

▲ **keep on doing** *sth* CONTINUE *phrasal verb* to continue to do something, or to do something again and again: *She kept on asking me questions the whole time.*

▲ **keep on** *sth* TALK *phrasal verb* UK INFORMAL to continue to talk in an annoying way about something: *Don't keep on, I'll sort it out in a minute.* ○ *He kept on* ***at*** *me about the money, even though I told him I hadn't got it.*

▲ **keep (***sb/sth***) out** *phrasal verb* to not go in a place, or to stop someone or something from going into a place: *Building work in progress. Keep out!*

▲ **keep (***sb/sth***) out of** *sth* *phrasal verb* to avoid becoming involved in something, or to stop someone or something becoming involved in something: *I prefer to keep* ***out of*** *arguments about money.* ○ *Keep me out of this!*

▲ **keep to** *somewhere* PLACE *phrasal verb* to stay in one particular area: *Please keep to the footpaths.*

▲ **keep to** *sth* PLAN *phrasal verb* to do what you have promised or planned to do: *I think we should keep to our original plan.*

▲ **keep** *sth* **to** *sth* AMOUNT *phrasal verb* If you keep something to a particular number or amount, you make certain it does not become larger than that.

▲ **keep** *sth* **to** *yourself* SECRET *phrasal verb* [R] to keep something secret: *I don't want everyone to know, so if you could keep it to yourself I'd appreciate it.*

▲ **keep** *yourself* **to** *yourself* NOT TALK *phrasal verb* to not talk to other people very much: *He's a very private person – he keeps himself to himself.*

▲ **keep to** *sth* SUBJECT *phrasal verb* If you keep to a particular subject, you only talk about that subject: *For heaven's sake let's keep to* ***the point*** *or we'll never reach any decisions.*

▲ **keep** *sth* **up** STOP FROM FALLING *phrasal verb* [M] to not allow something that is at a high level to fall to a lower level: *You must eat to keep your strength up.*

▲ **keep (***sth***) up** CONTINUE *phrasal verb* [M] to continue without stopping or changing, or to continue something without allowing it to stop or change: *Keep up the good work!*

• **keep it up** used to encourage someone to continue doing something: *You're doing very well everybody. Keep it up!*

▲ **keep up (with** *sb/sth***)** STAY LEVEL *phrasal verb* If someone or something keeps up with someone or something else, they do whatever is necessary to stay level or equal with that person or thing: *He started to walk faster and the children had to run to keep up.* ○ *Wages are failing to keep up with inflation.*

• **keep up appearances** to pretend to be happier, less poor, etc. than you really are, because you do not want people to know how bad your situation is: *They were*

K

very unhappily married but kept up appearances for the sake of their children.

▲ **keep up** [UNDERSTAND] phrasal verb to be able to understand or deal with something that is happening or changing very fast: *I read the papers to keep up **with** what's happening in the outside world.*

keep-fit /ˌkiːpˈfɪt/ noun [U] UK physical exercises to keep your body healthy, often done regularly with other people: *a keep-fit class*

keepnet /ˈkiːp.net/ noun [C] a cone-shaped net which is used by people who catch fish for sport to keep live fish at the edge of a river after they have been caught

keepsake /ˈkiːp.seɪk/ noun [C] a small present, usually not expensive, that is given to you by someone so that you will remember that person

keg /keg/ noun [C] a small barrel usually used for storing beer or other alcoholic drinks

'keg ˌparty noun [C] US in the US, a party in which people drink beer which is poured from kegs rather than bottles or other containers

kelp /kelp/ noun [U] a large brown plant that grows in the sea, used in some foods and medicines

kelvin /ˈkel.vɪn/ noun [C or U] (WRITTEN ABBREVIATION **K**) SPECIALIZED a standard unit of temperature. One degree kelvin is equal to one degree CELSIUS.

ken /ken/ noun OLD-FASHIONED **beyond your ken** not in your area of knowledge: *Financial matters are beyond my ken, I'm afraid.*

ken /ken/ verb [I or T: not continuous] -nn- SCOTTISH ENGLISH to know someone or something

kennel /ˈken.ᵊl/ noun [C] **1** (US USUALLY **doghouse**) a small, usually wooden shelter for a dog to sleep in outside **2** US (UK **kennels**) a place where people leave their dogs to be taken care of while they are away, or a place where dogs are bred: *We left our dog **in** kennels when we went away on holiday.*

kept /kept/ past simple and past participle of **keep**

kerb UK /kɜːb/ US /kɝːb/ noun [C] (US **curb**) the edge of a raised path nearest the road

'kerb ˌcrawling noun [U] UK the activity of driving slowly along a road close to the path at the side in order to ask prostitutes for sex

kerbside UK /ˈkɜːb.saɪd/ US /ˈkɝːb-/ noun [C usually sing] (US **curbside**) the area near where a road and the raised path next to it join

kerchief /ˈkɜː.tʃɪf/ US /ˈkɝː-/ noun [C] OLD USE a square piece of cloth worn around the neck or on the head

kerfuffle /kəˈfʌf.l̩/ US /kɝ-/ noun [S] UK INFORMAL noise, excitement and argument: *Her glasses were broken in the kerfuffle.*

kernel /ˈkɜː.nᵊl/ US /ˈkɝː-/ noun [C] **1** the edible part of a nut that is inside the shell **2** the whole seed of the maize plant **3** the most important part of something, although it might not always be easy to find: *There is often a kernel **of truth** in what they say.*

kerosene /ˈker.ə.siːn/ noun [U] (AUS INFORMAL **kero**) MAINLY US FOR **paraffin**, especially when used as fuel for heaters and oil lamps

kestrel /ˈkes.trᵊl/ noun [C] a type of small FALCON (= a meat-eating bird)

ketchup /ˈketʃ.ʌp/ noun [U] (UK **tomato ketchup**, US ALSO **catsup**) a thick cold red sauce made from tomatoes: *Do you want some ketchup with your burger?*

kettle /ˈket.l̩/ US /ˈket̬-/ noun [C] a covered metal or plastic container with a handle and a shaped opening for pouring, used for boiling water ⊃See picture **In the Kitchen** on page Centre 16

• **put the kettle on** to start to boil water in a kettle

• **be another/a different kettle of fish** to be completely different from something or someone else that has been talked about: *Having knowledge is one thing but being able to communicate it to others is another kettle of fish.*

• **a pretty/fine kettle of fish** OLD-FASHIONED a very difficult and annoying situation

kettledrum /ˈket.l̩.drʌm/ US /ˈket̬-/ noun [C] a very large drum with a round bottom which is played especially in an orchestra ⊃See also **timpani**.

Key

key signature

door key

clarinet key

piano key

computer key

typewriter key

map key

key [LOCK] /kiː/ noun [C] a piece of metal that has been cut into a special shape and is used for fastening or unfastening a lock, starting a car engine, etc: *car/door keys*
• **the key to sth** the best or only way to achieve something: *Hard work is the key to success.*

key /kiː/ noun [C] any of the set of moving parts that you press with your fingers on a computer, typewriter or musical instrument to produce letters, numbers, symbols or musical notes

key [IMPORTANT] /kiː/ adj very important and having a lot of influence on other people or things: *She was a key figure in the international art world.* ○ *a key factor in tackling the problem*

key [MUSICAL NOTES] /kiː/ noun [C] a set of musical notes based on one particular note: *The song changes key halfway through.* ○ *the key of C minor*

key [LIST] /kiː/ noun [C] a list of the symbols used in a map or book with explanations of what they mean

key /kiː/ verb

PHRASAL VERBS WITH **key** ▼

▲ **key sth in** phrasal verb [M] to put information into a computer or a machine using a keyboard ⊃See also **keyboard**.

▲ **key sth to sb** phrasal verb [usually passive] to arrange or plan something so that it is suitable for a particular person or situation: *The books are keyed to the interests of very young children.*

keyboard /ˈkiː.bɔːd/ ⓤ /-bɔːrd/ *noun* [C] **1** the set of keys on a computer or typewriter that you press in order to make it work, or the row of keys on a musical instrument such as a piano ⊃See picture **In the Office** on page Centre 15 **2** an electronic musical instrument similar to a piano

keyboard /ˈkiː.bɔːd/ ⓤ /-bɔːrd/ *verb* [I or T] to put information into a computer using a keyboard

keyboarder /ˈkiː.bɔː.dər/ ⓤ /-ˌbɔːr.dər/ *noun* [C] someone whose job is to put information into a computer using a keyboard

keyboardist /ˈkiː.bɔː.dɪst/ ⓤ /-ˌbɔːr-/ *noun* [C] a person who plays an electronic musical instrument that has a keyboard

keycard /ˈkiː.kɑːd/ ⓤ /-kɑːrd/ *noun* [C] an electronic device in the form of a small plastic card which is used to open a door

keyed up /ˌkiːd ˈʌp/ *adj* [after v] very excited or nervous, usually before an important event: *He always gets keyed up about exams.*

keyhole /ˈkiː.həʊl/ ⓤ /-hoʊl/ *noun* [C] a hole in a lock that you put a key into
• **keyhole surgery** *UK* a medical operation in which a very small hole is made in a person's body to reach the organ or tissue inside

ˈkey ˌmoney *noun* [U] a payment demanded by the owner of a house, apartment or shop from the person who is going to rent it

keynote /ˈkiː.nəʊt/ ⓤ /-noʊt/ *noun* [C] the most important or most emphasized part of something: *This issue has become the keynote of the election campaign.* ○ *a keynote address/speech/speaker* (= an important talk/ speaker at a formal meeting) ⊃See also **key** IMPORTANT.

keypad /ˈkiː.pæd/ *noun* [C] a small set of keys with numbers on them used to operate a television, telephone, CALCULATOR, etc., or the keys with numbers on them usually found on the right side of a computer keyboard

ˈkey ˌring *noun* [C] a metal or plastic ring used for keeping your keys together

ˈkey ˌsignature *noun* [C] the symbols on a printed piece of music that show the KEY in which that music is to be played

keystone /ˈkiː.stəʊn/ ⓤ /-stoʊn/ *noun* [C] **1** the middle stone in the top of an arch which has a special shape and holds all the other stones in position **2** the most important part of a plan, idea, etc. on which everything else depends ⊃See also **key** IMPORTANT.

kg WRITTEN ABBREVIATION FOR **kilogram**

khaki /ˈkɑː.ki/ *noun* [U], *adj* (of) a dark yellowish-green colour, often worn by soldiers

khaki /ˈkɑː.ki/ *noun* [U] dark yellowish-green cloth, often worn by soldiers

khalif /ˈkeɪ.lɪf/ *noun* [C] another spelling of CALIPH

kHz WRITTEN ABBREVIATION FOR **kilohertz**

kibbutz /kɪˈbʊts/ *noun* [C] *plural* **kibbutzim** or **kibbutzes** a farm or factory in Israel where profits and duties are shared and all work is valued equally: *to work on a kibbutz*

kibosh /ˈkaɪ.bɒʃ/ ⓤ /-bɑːʃ/ *noun* INFORMAL **put the kibosh on sth** to spoil or destroy an idea or plan: *The rain certainly put the kibosh on our plans for a picnic.*

kick HIT /kɪk/ *verb* **1** [I or T] to hit someone or something with the foot, or to move the feet and legs suddenly and violently: *I kicked the ball as hard as I could.* ○ *He was accused of kicking a man in the face.* ○ *She felt the baby kicking inside her.* **2** [I] If a gun kicks, it jumps back suddenly and with force when the gun is fired. **3** be **kicking yourself/could have kicked yourself** used to say that you are very annoyed with yourself because you have done something stupid or missed a chance: *When I realized what I'd done I could have kicked myself.* ○ *They must be kicking themselves for selling their shares too early.*
• **kick against the pricks** INFORMAL to argue and fight against people in authority
• **kick (some) ass** MAINLY US OFFENSIVE to punish someone or to defeat someone with a lot of force: *We're gonna go in there and kick ass.*

• **kick the bucket** (*US* **kick off**) INFORMAL to die
• **kick the habit** INFORMAL to give up something harmful that you have done for a long time: *She used to be a heavy smoker but she kicked the habit last year.*
• **kick your heels** *UK* INFORMAL to be forced to wait for a period of time
• **kick up your heels** *US* INFORMAL to do things that you enjoy: *After the exams we kicked up our heels and had a really good party.*
• **kick sth into touch** *UK* INFORMAL to decide not to do what you had planned to do: *Our plans to buy a new car have had to be kicked into touch now Kev's lost his job.*
• **kick over the traces** OLD-FASHIONED INFORMAL to behave badly and show no respect for authority
• **kick up a fuss/row/stink** INFORMAL to show great annoyance about something, especially when this does not seem necessary: *He kicked up a tremendous fuss about having to wait.*
• **kick sb upstairs** to give someone a new job which seems more powerful but is really less powerful, usually in order to stop them causing trouble for you

kick /kɪk/ *noun* **1** [C] the action of kicking something: *She gave the cat a kick when no-one was looking.* **2** [C usually sing] INFORMAL the strong effect of an alcoholic drink: *Watch out for the fruit punch, it's got a real kick.*
• **kick in the teeth** INFORMAL If you describe the way someone treats you as a kick in the teeth, you mean that they treat you badly and unfairly, especially at a time when you need their support: *She was dismissed from her job, which was a real kick in the teeth after all the work she'd done.*
• **a kick up the arse/backside** *UK* (*US* **a kick in the butt/pants**) OFFENSIVE If you give someone a kick up the arse, you do or say something to try to stop them being lazy.

kick EXCITEMENT /kɪk/ *noun* [C] a strong feeling of excitement and pleasure: *I get a real kick out of owning my own car.* ○ *He decided to steal something from the shop, just for kicks* (= because he thought it would be exciting).

kick INTEREST /kɪk/ *noun* [C usually sing] INFORMAL a new interest, especially one that does not last long: *He's on an exercise kick* (= He exercises a lot) *at the moment.*

PHRASAL VERBS WITH **kick**   ▼

▲ **kick about/around** *phrasal verb* INFORMAL If something is kicking around a place, it is somewhere in that place, not being used: *There must be a copy of it kicking around the office somewhere.*

▲ **kick against sth** *phrasal verb* *UK* INFORMAL to refuse to accept something and react strongly against it: *As a boy he always kicked against his father's authority.*

▲ **kick sth around** *phrasal verb* [M] INFORMAL If you kick ideas around, you talk about them informally in a group: *We need to get everyone together and kick a few ideas around.*

▲ **kick in** *phrasal verb* INFORMAL to start to have an effect or to happen: *It takes half an hour for the tablets to kick in.*

▲ **kick off** FOOTBALL *phrasal verb* If a game of football kicks off, it starts: *What time does the match kick off?* ⊃See also **kick-off**.

▲ **kick (sth) off** ACTIVITY *phrasal verb* [M] If you kick off a discussion or an activity, you start it: *I'd like to kick off the discussion with a few statistics.* ○ *Right, any suggestions? Jim, you kick off.*

▲ **kick sb out** *phrasal verb* [M] INFORMAL to force someone to leave a place or organization: *His wife kicked him out.* ○ *She was kicked out of the squad.*

kickabout /ˈkɪk.ə.baʊt/ *noun* [C usually sing] *UK* INFORMAL when a group of people kick a ball to each other for pleasure

kickback /ˈkɪk.bæk/ *noun* [C] an amount of money that is paid to someone illegally in exchange for secret help or work

kick-off /ˈkɪk.ɒf/ ⓤ /-ɑːf/ *noun* [C or U] **1** *UK* (*US* **kickoff**) the time when a game of football starts, or when it begins again after it has stopped because of a goal, etc. ⊃See also **kick off**. **2** INFORMAL the time when an activity starts

kick-start [MOTORCYCLE] /ˈkɪk.stɑːt/ [US] /-stɑːrt/ *verb* [T] to make the engine of a motorcycle start by forcefully pushing down a metal bar with your foot
kick-start /ˈkɪk.stɑːt/ [US] /-stɑːrt/ *noun* [C] a metal bar that you push down forcefully with your foot to make the engine of a motorcycle start

kick-start [HELP] /ˈkɪk.stɑːt/ [US] /-stɑːrt/ *verb* [T] to make something start to happen: *Taxes were drastically cut in an attempt to kick-start the economy.*

kid [CHILD] /kɪd/ *noun* [C] **1** INFORMAL a child: *He took the kids to the park while I was working.* **2** INFORMAL a young person: *He was only 16, just a kid really.* **3** MAINLY US INFORMAL **sb's kid sister/brother** someone's younger sister or brother

kid [ANIMAL] /kɪd/ *noun* **1** [C] a young goat **2** [U] very soft leather made from the skin of a young goat: *kid gloves*
• **handle/treat *sb* with kid gloves** to be very polite or kind to someone because you do not want to make them angry or upset

kid [JOKE] /kɪd/ *verb* [I or T] **-dd-** INFORMAL **1** to say something as a joke, often making someone believe something that is not true: *Oh no, I've forgotten your birthday! Hey,* ***just/only*** *kidding!* ○ *You won first prize? You're kidding!* (= I'm really surprised.) ○ *I'm just kidding you!* **2 kid *yourself*** to believe something that is not true, usually because you want it to be true: *He says there's a good chance she'll come back to him but I think he's kidding himself.*
• **no kidding** (ALSO **I kid you not**) INFORMAL used when you are surprised by what someone has just said: *Dean was there? No kidding!*
▲ **kid around** *phrasal verb* US INFORMAL to be silly or not serious: *Stop kidding around and listen to me!*

kiddie, kiddy /ˈkɪd.i/ *noun* [C] INFORMAL a young child: *a kiddie pool*

kidnap /ˈkɪd.næp/ *verb* [T] **-pp-** or US ALSO **-p-** to take a person away illegally by force, usually in order to demand money in exchange for releasing them: *The wife of a businessman has been kidnapped from her home in Surrey.*
kidnap /ˈkɪd.næp/ *noun* [C or U] the crime of taking someone away by force and demanding money in exchange for releasing them **kidnapper**, US ALSO **kidnaper** /ˈkɪd.næp.əʳ/ [US] /-ɚ/ *noun* [C]
kidnapping /ˈkɪd.næp.ɪŋ/ *noun* [C or U] when someone is kidnapped

kidney /ˈkɪd.ni/ *noun* **1** [C] either of a pair of small organs in the body which take away waste matter from the blood to produce urine: *kidney failure* **2** [C or U] these organs from an animal, used as food: *steak and kidney pie*

ˈkidney ˌbean *noun* [C usually pl] a small dark-red edible bean which has a curved shape like a kidney

ˈkidney ˌmachine *noun* [C] a machine used to do the work of a human kidney for people whose kidneys have stopped working or have been removed ➲See also **dialysis**.

ˈkidney ˌstone *noun* [C] a lump of hard material that can form in the kidney and cause pain

kids' stuff UK /ˈkɪdz.stʌf/ *noun* [U] (US **kid stuff**) DISAPPROVING an activity or piece of work that is very easy: *A five-mile bike ride? That's kids' stuff.*

kike /kaɪk/ *noun* [C] US OFFENSIVE a Jew

kill [DEATH] /kɪl/ *verb* [I or T] to cause someone or something to die: *Her parents were killed in a plane crash.* ○ *Smoking can kill.* ○ *Food must be heated to a high temperature to kill harmful bacteria.*
• **kill or cure** UK a way of solving a problem that will either fail completely or be very successful: *Having a baby can be kill or cure for a troubled marriage.*
• **kill *sb* with kindness** to be too kind to someone, harming them because you are helping or giving them too much
• **kill the fatted calf** to have a special celebration for someone who has been away for a long time
• **kill the goose that lays the golden egg** to destroy something that makes a lot of money for you
• **kill time/an hour, etc.** to do something that keeps you busy while you are waiting for something else to happen: *The train was late, so I killed an hour or so window-shopping.*
• **kill two birds with one stone** to succeed in achieving two things in a single action: *I killed two birds with one stone and picked the kids up on the way to the station.*
kill /kɪl/ *noun* [C usually sing] an animal or bird which has been hunted and killed, or the action of killing: *The leopard seizes its kill and begins to eat.* ○ *Like other birds of prey, it quickly* ***moves in for the*** *kill.*
• **be in at the kill** to be present at the end of an unpleasant process
• **move/go in for the kill** to prepare to defeat someone in an argument or competition when they are already in a weak position: *He asked her a couple of difficult questions and then went in for the kill.*
killer /ˈkɪl.əʳ/ [US] /-ɚ/ *noun* [C] **1** someone who kills another person: *Police are still hoping to find the dead woman's killer.* **2** something that kills people, especially a disease or other illness: *Cancer and heart disease are the UK's biggest killers.* **3** something that destroys something: *This chemical is found in most weed killers.*
killing /ˈkɪl.ɪŋ/ *noun* [C] when a person is murdered: *a series of brutal killings*
• **make a killing** INFORMAL to earn a lot of money in a short time and with little effort: *They made a killing with the sale of their London house.*

kill [STOP] /kɪl/ *verb* [T] **1** to stop or destroy a relationship, activity or experience: *Lack of romance can kill a marriage.* ○ *They've given her some tablets to kill the pain.* ○ *Kill your speed.* **2** (ALSO **kill off**) MAINLY US INFORMAL to drink all of something: *We killed off two six-packs watching the game.*

kill [EFFORT] /kɪl/ *verb* [T] INFORMAL to cause someone a lot of effort or difficulty: *It wouldn't kill you to apologize.* ○ *He didn't exactly kill him****self*** *trying to get the work finished.*
killer /ˈkɪl.əʳ/ [US] /-ɚ/ *noun* [S] INFORMAL something that is very difficult: *The last question was a real killer.* **killer** /ˈkɪl.əʳ/ [US] /-ɚ/ *adj*
killing /ˈkɪl.ɪŋ/ *adj* INFORMAL extremely tiring: *We had to do some killing stomach exercises last night.*

kill [PAIN] /kɪl/ *verb* [T] INFORMAL to cause someone a lot of pain: *I must sit down, my feet are killing me!*

kill [ANGER] /kɪl/ *verb* [T] INFORMAL If you say that someone will kill you, you mean that they will be very angry with you: *My sister would kill me if she heard me say that.*

kill [AMUSEMENT] /kɪl/ *verb* [T] **1** MAINLY US INFORMAL to amuse someone very much: *That comedian kills me.* **2** INFORMAL **kill *yourself*** to laugh very much: *We were killing ourselves* ***laughing***.
killer /ˈkɪl.əʳ/ [US] /-ɚ/ *noun* [C] US INFORMAL a very entertaining or skilful person, story or performance: *Dizzy was a* ***real*** *killer on the trumpet.*
killing /ˈkɪl.ɪŋ/ *adj* OLD-FASHIONED extremely amusing: *She told us a killing story about her driving test.*
▲ **kill *sth* off** *phrasal verb* [M] to destroy something completely, usually over a period of time: *The use of pesticides is killing off birds, fish and wildlife.* ○ FIGURATIVE *Lack of funding is killing off small theatres.*

killer app /ˌkɪl.əˈræp/ [US] /-ɚˈæp/ *noun* [C] (ALSO **killer application**) INFORMAL **1** a computer program that is much better than all others of its type **2** a use for a particular technology that becomes extremely popular: *Many software companies and internet providers believe that e-learning is the next killer app.*

ˈkiller ˌinstinct *noun* [C usually sing] the desire to act for your own advantage without caring whether it hurts other people

ˈkiller ˌwhale *noun* [C] a small black-and-white WHALE that eats large fish and other sea animals

killjoy /ˈkɪl.dʒɔɪ/ *noun* [C] DISAPPROVING a person who does not like other people enjoying themselves

kiln /kɪln/ *noun* [C] a type of large oven used for making bricks and clay objects hard after they have been shaped

kilo /ˈkiː.ləʊ/ [US] /-loʊ/ *noun* [C] *plural* **kilos** a kilogram: *a 200 kilo block of concrete*
kilo- /kɪl.ə-/ *prefix* Kilo- means 1000 times the stated unit: *kilowatt* ○ *kilohertz*

K

kilobyte /ˈkɪl.ə.baɪt/ *noun* [C] (*ABBREVIATION* **k**) *SPECIALIZED* a unit of measurement of computer memory consisting of 1024 BYTES: *a 20-kilobyte file*

kilogram /ˈkɪl.ə.græm/ *noun* [C] (*WRITTEN ABBREVIATION* **kg**) a unit of mass equal to 1000 grams, or 2.2 pounds

kilohertz (*plural* **kilohertz**) /ˈkɪl.ə.hɜːts/ ⑩ /-hɝːts/ *noun* [C] (*WRITTEN ABBREVIATION* **kHz**) a unit of measurement of radio waves which is equal to 1000 HERTZ

kilometre *UK*, *US* **kilometer** /ˈkɪl.ə.miː.tər/ ⑩ /kɪ-ˈlɑː.mə.t̬ə/ *noun* [C] (*WRITTEN ABBREVIATION* **km**) a unit of measurement equal to 1000 metres

kilowatt /ˈkɪl.ə.wɒt/ ⑩ /-wɑːt/ *noun* [C] (*WRITTEN ABBREVIATION* **kW**) a unit of power equal to 1000 WATTS

kilt /kɪlt/ *noun* [C] a skirt with many folds, made from TARTAN cloth and traditionally worn by Scottish men and boys

kilter /ˈkɪl.tər/ ⑩ /-t̬ə/ *noun* *INFORMAL* **out of kilter** in a state of not working well: *Missing more than one night's sleep can throw your body out of kilter.*

kimono /kɪˈməʊ.nəʊ/ ⑩ /-ˈmoʊ.noʊ/ *noun* [C] *plural* **kimonos** a long loose piece of outer clothing with very wide sleeves, traditionally worn by the Japanese

kin /kɪn/ *plural noun* *OLD-FASHIONED* family and relatives
● **next of kin** *FORMAL* your closest relatives: *We can't release his name until we have informed his next of kin.*

kind GOOD /kaɪnd/ *adj* **1** generous, helpful and caring about other people's feelings: *She's a very kind and thoughtful person.* ○ *It's really kind of you to help us.* ○ *Please be kind to your sister!* ○ *FORMAL Would you be kind **enough** to/**so** kind **as** to close the door?* (= please would you do this) **2** not causing harm or damage: *kind to the environment* ○ *This soap is kinder to the skin.*

kindly /ˈkaɪnd.li/ *adv* **1** in a kind way: *Stella has very kindly offered to help out with the food for the party.* **2** *OLD-FASHIONED FORMAL* used when asking someone to do something, especially when you are annoyed with them but still want to be polite: *You are kindly requested to leave the building.*
● **not take kindly to** *sth* to not like something: *After years of being looked after by his mother, he didn't take kindly to being told to cook for himself.*

kindly /ˈkaɪnd.li/ *adj* *OLD-FASHIONED* A kindly person or action is a kind one: *a kindly old lady*

kindness /ˈkaɪnd.nəs/ *noun* **1** [U] the quality of being kind: *love and kindness* **2** [C] a kind action: *I wanted to thank them for all their kindnesses.*

kind TYPE /kaɪnd/ *noun* [C] a group with similar characteristics, or a particular type: *Today's vehicles use two kinds **of** fuel – petrol and diesel.* ○ *What kind **of** (a) job are you looking for?* ○ *I just don't have that kind **of** money* (= I haven't got so much money). ○ *The cupboard contained **all** kinds of strange things.* ○ *Her travel company was the first **of its** kind* (= of others that are similar).
● **in kind 1** (of payment) given in the form of goods or services and not money: *She wouldn't take any money but said I could pay her in kind by lending her the car.* **2** *FORMAL* If you do something in kind, you do the same thing to someone that they have just done to you.
● **of the kind** like or similar to what has been said: *"You said I was fat." "I didn't say anything of the kind!"*
● **kind of** *INFORMAL* used when you are trying to explain or describe something, but you cannot be exact: *It was kind of strange to see him again.* ⊃See also **kinda**.
● **of a kind** used to describe something that exists but is not very good: *The school had a swimming pool of a kind, but it was too small for most classes to use.*

kinda /ˈkaɪ.ndə/ *adv* *NOT STANDARD* used in writing to represent an informal way of saying "kind of": *I was kinda sorry to see him go.*

kindergarten /ˈkɪn.də.ɡɑː.t³n/ ⑩ /-dɚ.ɡɑːr-/ *noun* [C or U] **1** *MAINLY US* the first year of school, for children aged 5 **2** *UK FOR* **nursery school**

kind-hearted /ˌkaɪndˈhɑː.tɪd/ ⑩ /-ˈhɑːr.t̬ɪd/ *adj* A kind-hearted person is one who cares a lot about other people and always wants to help them. ⊃Compare **hard-hearted**.

kindle /ˈkɪn.dl̩/ *verb* **1** [T] to cause a fire to start burning by lighting paper, wood etc. **2** [T often passive] *LITERARY* to

cause strong feelings or ideas in someone: *Her imagination was kindled by the exciting stories her grandmother told her.*

kindling /ˈkɪnd.lɪŋ/ *noun* [U] small dry sticks or other materials used to start a fire

kindred spirit /ˌkɪn.drədˈspɪr.ɪt/ *noun* [C] *OLD-FASHIONED* a person who has the same opinions, feelings and interests as you

kinetic /kɪˈnet.ɪk/ ⑩ /-ˈnet̬-/ *adj* *SPECIALIZED* involving or producing movement: *kinetic energy*

kinetics /kɪˈnet.ɪks/ ⑩ /-ˈnet̬-/ *noun* [U] *SPECIALIZED* the scientific study of forces on things that are moving

kinfolk /ˈkɪn.fəʊk/ ⑩ /-foʊk/ *plural noun* (*UK ALSO* **kinsfolk**) *OLD-FASHIONED* members of the same family

king RULER /kɪŋ/ *noun* [C] **1** (the title of) a male ruler of a country, who holds this position because of his royal birth: *King Richard II* ○ *the kings and queens of England* **2** the most important, best or most impressive member of a group of animals, things or people: *The lion is often called the king of the jungle.* ○ *He's the new king of pop music.* **3** In the game of chess, the king is the most important piece on the board. It can move one square in any direction. **4** a card with a picture of a king on it, used in games: *the king of hearts*
● **a king's ransom** a large amount of money: *That diamond necklace must have cost a king's ransom.*

kingship /ˈkɪŋ.ʃɪp/ *noun* [U] *FORMAL* being a king: *the duties of kingship*

king LARGE /kɪŋ/ *adj* [before n] used as part of the name of something that is larger than the ordinary type: *king prawns* ○ *a king penguin*

kingdom /ˈkɪŋ.dəm/ *noun* [C] **1** a country ruled by a king or queen: *the United Kingdom of Great Britain and Northern Ireland* **2** an area which is controlled by a particular person or where a particular quality is important: *the kingdom of God/Heaven* ○ *the kingdom of love* **3** one of the groups into which natural things can be divided, depending on their type: *the animal/plant kingdom*
● **till/until kingdom come** forever: *I don't want to have to wait till kingdom come for you to make up your mind.*
● **blast/blow** *sb/sth* **to kingdom come** to destroy someone or something completely using a gun or bomb: *The bombs are capable of blasting a whole city to kingdom come.*

kingfisher /ˈkɪŋ.fɪʃ.ər/ ⑩ /-ɚ/ *noun* [C] a small brightly-coloured bird with a long pointed beak, which lives near rivers and lakes and eats fish

kingmaker /ˈkɪŋ.meɪ.kər/ ⑩ /-kɚ/ *noun* [C] a person who influences the choice of people for powerful positions within an organization

kingpin /ˈkɪŋ.pɪn/ *noun* [C] the most important person within a particular organization

King's evidence /ˌkɪŋzˈev.ɪ.d³nts/ *noun* [U] *UK* the term used for QUEEN'S EVIDENCE when a king is ruling the United Kingdom

kingside /ˈkɪŋ.saɪd/ *noun* [U] *SPECIALIZED* (in the game of chess) the side of the board where your king is at the start of the game **kingside** /ˈkɪŋ.saɪd/ *adj*

king-size /ˈkɪŋ.saɪz/ *adj* (*ALSO* **king-sized**) If something is king-size or king-sized, it is larger than the ordinary size: *a king-size bed/hamburger*

kink /kɪŋk/ *noun* [C] **1** an unwanted twist or bend in a wire, rope, pipe, etc. that is usually straight: *There must be a kink **in** the pipe.* ⊃See also **kink** at **kinky**. **2** *US* a sore muscle, especially in the neck or back **3** something that is wrong: *Pete still needs to **iron out** a few kinks in his game.*

kinky /ˈkɪŋ.ki/ *adj* *INFORMAL* unusual, strange and possibly exciting, especially in ways involving unusual sexual acts: *kinky ideas/behaviour*
kink /kɪŋk/ *noun* [C] a strange habit

kinship /ˈkɪn.ʃɪp/ *noun* [U] the relationship between members of the same family, or a feeling of being close or similar to other people or things: *Different ethnic groups have different systems of kinship.* ○ *He felt a real sense of kinship **with** his fellow soldiers.*

kinsman /ˈkɪnz.mən/ *noun* [C] *FORMAL OR OLD USE* someone who belongs to the same family

kinswoman /ˈkɪnzˌwʊm.ən/ *noun* [C] a female kinsman

kiosk /ˈkiː.ɒsk/ [US] /-ɑːsk/ *noun* [C] **1** a small building where things such as sweets, drinks or newspapers are sold through an open window: *a station kiosk* **2** (*ALSO* **telephone kiosk**) *UK FORMAL* a **telephone box**

kip /kɪp/ *verb* [I usually + adv or prep] **-pp-** *UK INFORMAL* to sleep, especially in a place which is not your home: *You can have my bed and I'll kip* ***(down)*** *on the sofa.*

kip /kɪp/ *noun* [S or U] *UK INFORMAL* sleep: *I must* ***get*** *some kip.* ○ *I* ***had a*** *quick kip after lunch.*

kipper /ˈkɪp.əʳ/ [US] /-ɚ/ *noun* [C] a HERRING that has been preserved by being treated with salt and then with smoke

kir /kɪəʳ/ [US] /kɪr/ *noun* [C or U] a drink consisting of a mixture of white wine and an alcoholic BLACKCURRANT drink

kirk /kɜːk/ [US] /kɝːk/ *noun* [C] **1** *SCOTTISH ENGLISH* a church **2 the Kirk** the Church of Scotland

kirsch /kɪəʃ/ [US] /kɪrʃ/ *noun* [C or U] a strong alcoholic drink made from CHERRIES

kiss /kɪs/ *verb* **1** [I or T] to touch with your lips, especially as a greeting, or to press your mouth onto another person's mouth in a sexual way: *There was a young couple on the sofa, kissing passionately.* ○ *She kissed him* ***on*** *the mouth.* ○ [+ two objects] *He kissed the children* ***good night/goodbye*** (= kissed them as a part of saying good night/goodbye). **2** [T] *LITERARY* to gently touch something: *The breeze/sun kissed her bare shoulders.*

• **kiss *sth* better** If you tell a child you will kiss a part of the body that hurts better, you mean you will make it feel better by kissing it: *"Mummy, I hurt my knee." "Come here, darling, and let me kiss it better."*

• **kiss *sth* goodbye** (*ALSO* **kiss goodbye to *sth***) *INFORMAL* to accept that you have lost something or that you will not be able to have something: *If France lose this game, they can kiss their chances of winning the cup goodbye.*

• **kiss and tell** to talk on television, in a newspaper, etc. about a sexual relationship you have had with a famous person, especially in order to get a lot of money

kiss-and-tell /ˌkɪs.ᵊndˈtel/ *adj* [before n] *She did a kiss-and-tell interview for a local newspaper.*

• **kiss *sb's* arse** *UK* (*US* **kiss *sb's* ass**) *OFFENSIVE* to be too respectful and obedient towards someone, in order to get an advantage

kiss ass *MAINLY US OFFENSIVE* to be too respectful and obedient towards someone in authority

• **Kiss my arse!** *UK* (*US* **Kiss my ass!**) *OFFENSIVE* used to tell someone that you will not do what they want you to do

kiss /kɪs/ *noun* [C] an act of kissing someone: ***Give*** *your granny a kiss.* ○ *a kiss* ***on*** *the lips*

kiss of death *INFORMAL* If you describe something as the kiss of death, you mean that it is certain to cause something else to fail: *Rain is the kiss of death* ***for*** *a barbecue.*

• **the kiss of life** *MAINLY UK INFORMAL* **artificial respiration**

kissagram, **kissogram** /ˈkɪs.ə.græm/ *noun* [C] a message delivered by someone who kisses the person who is receiving it, especially one which other people have arranged to be sent as a surprise to that person on a day when they are celebrating something

ˈkiss ˌcurl *UK noun* [C] (*US* **spit curl**) a curved piece of hair that hangs flat against the face on the cheek or forehead

kit /kɪt/ *noun* **1** [C] a set of things, such as tools or clothes, used for a particular purpose or activity: *a first-aid/tool kit* ○ *a pregnancy-testing kit* **2** [C] a set of parts sold ready to be put together: *He's making a model car from a kit.* **3** [U] *MAINLY UK* the particular clothing worn by a sports team, or the particular clothing and small pieces of equipment worn and used by people such as soldiers and sailors: *football kit*

• **get *your* kit off** *MAINLY UK SLANG HUMOROUS* to take off your clothes: *Come on, get your kit off!*

kit /kɪt/ *verb*

▲ **kit *sb/sth* out** *phrasal verb* [M] *MAINLY UK* to supply someone or something with the clothes or equipment that are needed for a particular purpose: *They went shopping to get kitted out* ***for*** *the trip.*

ˈkit ˌbag *noun* [C] a long narrow bag used by soldiers, sailors, etc. for carrying their clothes and small pieces of equipment

kitchen /ˈkɪtʃ.ᵊn/ *noun* [C] a room where food is kept, prepared and cooked and where the dishes are washed: *We usually eat breakfast in the kitchen.* ○ *the kitchen table* ○ *a new* ***fitted*** *kitchen* (= cupboards that look the same fixed to the walls and floor in the kitchen) ➲See picture **In the Kitchen** on page Centre 16

kitchenette /ˌkɪtʃ.ɪˈnet/ *noun* [C] a small room or area used as a kitchen

COMMON LEARNER ERROR

kitchen or **cuisine?**

A **kitchen** is a room in the house.

Chris is in the kitchen cooking dinner.

Cuisine is used to talk about a style of cooking.

Italian/Greek cuisine

The restaurant is famous for its French cuisine.

~~*The restaurant is famous for its French kitchen.*~~

ˌkitchen ˈcabinet *noun* [C] a small unofficial group of people who give advice to a political leader

ˌkitchen ˈcounter *noun* [C] *US FOR* **worktop**

ˌkitchen ˈgarden *noun* [C] an area, especially a part of a large garden, where fruit, vegetables and herbs are grown

ˈkitchen ˌpaper *noun* [U] *UK* **kitchen roll**

ˈkitchen ˌroll *noun* [U] (*UK ALSO* **kitchen towel**) soft, thick paper on a roll, from which square pieces are torn and used in the kitchen or other places, especially for removing liquid

kitchen-sink /ˌkɪtʃ.ᵊnˈsɪŋk/ *adj* [before n] *UK* describes plays, films and novels that are about ordinary people's lives: *a kitchen-sink drama*

ˈkitchen ˌtowel *noun* [C] *US FOR* **tea towel** ➲See also **kitchen roll**.

kitchenware /ˈkɪtʃ.ᵊn.weəʳ/ [US] /-wer/ *noun* [U] plates, bowls, knives, forks, spoons, etc. used in the kitchen

kite [FLYING OBJECT] /kaɪt/ *noun* [C] an object consisting of a frame covered with plastic, paper or cloth that is flown in the air at the end of a long string, especially for amusement: *to fly a kite*

kite [BIRD] /kaɪt/ *noun* [C] a large bird that kills and eats small animals

kite-flying /ˈkaɪtˌflaɪ.ɪŋ/ *noun* [U] the act of trying to find out what people's opinion about something new will be by informally spreading news of it: *These rumours of a new political party are obviously a kite-flying exercise.* ➲See also **go fly a kite** at **fly** WAVE.

ˈKite ˌmark *noun* [S] in Britain, a mark on goods that have been officially said to be of high quality

kith and kin /ˌkɪθ.ᵊndˈkɪn/ *plural noun MAINLY OLD USE* people with whom you are connected, especially by family relationships

kitsch /kɪtʃ/ *noun* [U] art, decorative objects or design considered by many people to be ugly, lacking in style, or false but enjoyed by other people, often because they are funny: *His home's full of 1950's kitsch.* **kitschy** /ˈkɪtʃ.i/ *adj*: *a kitschy gilt-framed mirror*

kitten /ˈkɪt.ᵊn/ [US] /ˈkɪt̬-/ *noun* [C] a very young cat

• **have kittens** (*US* **have a cow**) *INFORMAL* to be very worried, upset or angry about something: *My mother nearly had kittens when I said I was going to buy a motorbike.*

kittenish /ˈkɪt.ᵊn.ɪʃ/ [US] /ˈkɪt̬-/ *adj OLD-FASHIONED* describes a woman who behaves in a playful, silly way, especially as a way of attracting sexual attention **kittenishly** /ˈkɪt.ᵊn.ɪʃ.li/ [US] /ˈkɪt̬-/ *adv*

kitty [MONEY] /ˈkɪ.ti/ [US] /-t̬i/ *noun* [C usually sing] an amount of money which consists of small amounts given by different people and which is used by them for an agreed purpose: *We all put £20 in/into the kitty to cover the cost of food.*

kitty [CAT] /ˈkɪ.ti/ [US] /-t̬i/ *noun* [C] *INFORMAL* a cat or KITTEN: *Here kitty, kitty, kitty!*

kiwi [BIRD] /ˈkiː.wiː/ *noun* [C] a New Zealand bird, with a long beak and hair-like feathers, which cannot fly and is the national symbol of New Zealand

kiwi [PERSON] /ˈkiː.wiː/ *noun* [C] INFORMAL a person from New Zealand

ˈkiwi (ˌfruit) *noun* [C] (ALSO **Chinese gooseberry**) an oval fruit with brown hairy skin and bright green flesh ➲See picture **Fruit** on page Centre 1

the KKK /ðəˌkeɪ.keɪˈkeɪ/ *noun* [S] ABBREVIATION FOR **the Ku Klux Klan**

klaxon /ˈklæk.sᵊn/ *noun* [C] TRADEMARK a very loud horn used (especially in the past on motor vehicles in emergencies) as a way of warning other people

Kleenex /ˈkliː.neks/ *noun* [C or U] TRADEMARK (a piece of) thin soft paper used especially for cleaning the nose

kleptomania /ˌklep.təʊˈmeɪ.ni.ə/ [US] /-toʊ-/ *noun* [U] a very strong and uncontrollable desire to steal, especially without any need or purpose, usually considered to be a type of mental illness **kleptomaniac** /ˌklep.təʊˈmeɪ.ni.æk/ [US] /-toʊ-/ *noun* [C]

klutz /klʌts/ *noun* [C] MAINLY US SLANG a very foolish or stupid person, or a person who moves awkwardly **klutzy** *adj* /ˈklʌt.si/

km WRITTEN ABBREVIATION FOR **kilometre**

knack /næk/ *noun* [S] a skill or an ability to do something easily and well: *a knack **for** remembering faces* ○ *She **has** the knack **of** making people feel comfortable.* ○ *There's **a** knack **to** using this corkscrew.*

knacker /ˈnæk.əʳ/ [US] /-ɚ/ *verb* [T] UK SLANG **1** to break something: *Careful or you'll knacker the gears!* **2** to make someone very tired: *Don't go too fast or you'll knacker yourself in the first hour.*

knackered /ˈnæk.əd/ [US] /-ɚd/ *adj* UK SLANG **1** broken or too old to use: *My bike's knackered.* **2** [after v] very tired: *I'm too knackered to go out this evening.*

knackering /ˈnæk.ᵊr.ɪŋ/ [US] /-ɚ-/ *adj* UK SLANG tiring: *What a knackering day it's been!*

knacker's yard /ˈnæk.əzˌjɑːd/ [US] /-ɚzˌjɑːrd/ *noun* [C usually sing] a place where old or useless horses are killed: INFORMAL FIGURATIVE *The state of the economy has led to many small businesses ending up in the knacker's yard* (= failing completely).

knapsack /ˈnæp.sæk/ *noun* [C] UK OLD-FASHIONED OR US a bag carried on the back or over the shoulder, usually quite small and made of cloth and leather, used especially by walkers or climbers for carrying food, clothes, etc.

knave /neɪv/ *noun* [C] OLD USE **1** a dishonest man **2** a **jack** CARD

knead /niːd/ *verb* [T] to press something, especially a mixture for making bread, firmly and repeatedly with the hands and fingers: *Knead the dough until smooth.*

knee /niː/ *noun* [C] **1** the middle joint of the leg, which allows it to bend: *The baby was crawling around on its **hands and** knees.* ○ *He got/went **down on** his knees* (= got into a position where his knees were on the ground) *in front of the altar.* ○ *She took the child and sat it on her knee* (= on the part of the leg above the knee when sitting down). ➲See picture **The Body** on page Centre 5 **2** the part of a piece of clothing that covers the knee: *She was wearing an old pair of trousers with rips at the knees.*

• **bring *sb/sth* to *their* knees** to destroy or defeat someone or something: *The strikes had brought the economy to its knees.*

knee /niː/ *verb* [T] to hit someone with your knee: *She kneed him **in** the groin.*

kneecap /ˈniː.kæp/ *noun* [C] (SPECIALIZED **patella**) the bone at the front of the knee joint ➲See picture **The Body** on page Centre 5

kneecap /ˈniː.kæp/ *verb* [T] **-pp-** to injure someone in the knee as a punishment, especially by shooting

knee-deep /ˌniːˈdiːp/ *adj* **1** If you are knee-deep in a substance, it reaches up to your knees: *We walked through the field, knee-deep **in** mud.* **2** INFORMAL very involved in a difficult situation or large task: *I'm knee-deep **in** paperwork.*

knee-high /ˌniːˈhaɪ/ *adj* tall enough to reach your knees: *knee-high grass/boots*

• **be knee-high to a grasshopper** INFORMAL HUMOROUS to be very small or young

knee-jerk /ˈniː.dʒɜːk/ [US] /-dʒɝːk/ *adj* DISAPPROVING **knee-jerk reaction/response, etc.** an immediate reaction that does not allow you time to consider something carefully

kneel /niːl/ *verb* [I] **knelt** or **kneeled**, **knelt** or **kneeled** to go down into, or stay in, a position where one or both knees are on the ground: *She knelt **(down)** beside the child.* ○ *He knelt in front of the altar and prayed.*

knee-length /ˈniː.leŋkθ/ *adj* Something that is knee-length is long enough to reach the knee: *knee-length socks* ○ *a knee-length skirt*

knees-up /ˈniːz.ʌp/ *noun* [C usually sing] UK INFORMAL an energetic noisy party where people dance

knell /nel/ *noun* **death knell**, see at **death**

knew /njuː/ [US] /nuː/ *past simple of* **know**

knickerbocker glory /ˌnɪk.əˌbɒk.əˈglɔː.ri/ [US] /ˌnɪk.ɚˌbɑː.kɚˈglɔːr.i/ *noun* [C] UK a sweet food consisting of layers of ice cream, fruit, jelly and cream, served in a tall glass

knickerbockers /ˈnɪk.əˌbɒk.əz/ [US] /-ɚˌbɑː.kɚz/ *plural noun* (US ALSO **knickers**) short loose trousers that fit tightly below the knee, worn especially in the past or for ceremonies

knickers /ˈnɪk.əz/ [US] /-ɚz/ *plural noun* **1** UK (US **panties**) a piece of underwear worn by women and girls covering the area between the waist and the tops of the legs: *a pair of black cotton knickers* **2** US FOR **knickerbockers**

Knickers! /ˈnɪk.əz/ [US] /-ɚz/ *exclamation* UK SLANG HUMOROUS used to express disagreement with something someone has said

• **get *your* knickers in a twist** UK INFORMAL HUMOROUS to become confused, worried or annoyed about something

knick-knack, nick-nack /ˈnɪk.næk/ *noun* [C usually pl] a small decorative object, especially in a house: *The shelves were covered with ornaments and useless knick-knacks.*

knife /naɪf/ *noun* [C] *plural* **knives** a tool, usually with a metal blade and a handle, used for cutting and spreading food or other substances, or as a weapon: *a fish/butter/steak knife* ○ *I prefer to use a knife **and fork**.* ○ *He **drew/pulled** a knife and stabbed her.*

• **put/stick the knife into *sb*** (ALSO **put/stick the knife in**) to be unpleasant about someone or try to harm them: *The reviewer in the magazine that I read really put the knife in.*

• **have *your* knife into *sb*** UK to try to upset or harm someone because you dislike them

• **the knives are out** UK something you say which means that people are being unpleasant about someone, or trying to harm them: *The knives are out **for** the former president.*

• **twist/turn the knife (in the wound)** to make someone who is annoyed, anxious or upset feel even worse: *Just to turn the knife a little, he told me he'd seen my old girlfriend with her new man.*

• **go under the knife** to have a medical operation: *More and more women are choosing to go under the knife to improve their appearance.*

• **under the knife** while having a medical operation

knife /naɪf/ *verb* [T] to attack someone using a knife: *He knifed her **in** the back.*

knife-edge [UNCERTAIN] /ˈnaɪf.edʒ/ *noun* **on a knife-edge** in a difficult or worrying situation of which the result is very uncertain: *At the moment the election seems **balanced** on a knife-edge.* **knife-edge** /ˈnaɪf.edʒ/ *adj* [before n] *a knife-edge vote*

knife-edge [SHARP] /ˈnaɪf.edʒ/ *adj* [before n] narrow and sharp: *We had to climb over a knife-edge mountain ridge.*

knight /naɪt/ *noun* [C] **1** a man given a rank of honour by a British king or queen because of his special achievements, and who has the right to be called 'Sir', or (in the past) a man of high social position trained to fight as a soldier on a horse: *He hopes to be made a knight for his work at the Bank of England.* ○ *knights in black armour* **2** in the game of chess, a piece in the

K

shape of a horse's head that moves two squares in one direction and then one square at an angle of 90°

• **a knight in shining armour** someone who saves you from a difficult or dangerous situation

knight /naɪt/ *verb* [T] to give someone the rank of knight: *He was knighted by the Queen* ***for*** *his work with famine victims.*

knighthood /ˈnaɪt.hʊd/ *noun* [C or U] the rank of knight

knightly /ˈnaɪt.li/ *adj* LITERARY of or suitable for a knight in the past, especially involving bravery, honour, etc: *knightly virtue*

knight-errant /ˌnaɪtˈer.ənt/ *noun* [C] *plural* **knights-errant** LITERARY a MEDIEVAL knight who travelled around doing brave things and helping people who were in trouble

knit [MAKE CLOTHES] /nɪt/ *verb* **knitting, knitted** or **knit, knitted** or **knit 1** [I or T] to make clothes, etc. by using two long needles to connect wool or another type of thread into joined rows: *She's forever knitting.* ○ *She's busy knitting baby clothes.* ○ [+ two objects] *My granny knitted me some gloves/knitted some gloves* ***for*** *me.* ➲See also **knitwear**. **2** [T] SPECIALIZED to do the most basic type of stitch, when knitting something: *Knit one, purl one.* **knitted** /ˈnɪt.ɪd/ [US] /ˈnɪt̬-/ *adj* (ALSO **knit**) *a knitted jumper* ○ *hand-knitted gloves*

knitter /ˈnɪt.əʳ/ [US] /ˈnɪt̬.ɚ/ *noun* [C] a person who knits

knitting /ˈnɪt.ɪŋ/ [US] /ˈnɪt̬-/ *noun* [U] the activity of knitting something, or a thing that is being knitted: *I'm hopeless at knitting.* ○ *She takes her knitting with her everywhere.*

knit [JOIN] /nɪt/ *verb* [I or T] **knitting, knit, knit** to join together: *The broken bone should begin to knit* ***(together)*** *in a few days.* ○ *The two communities are closely knit by a common faith.*

• **knit *your* brow/brows** LITERARY to FROWN (= move your eyebrows down and together) because you are thinking carefully, or because you are angry or worried: *He knitted his brow in concentration.*

• **closely/tightly knit** (ALSO **close/tight-knit**) closely connected: *a very close-knit family* ○ *a tightly knit community*

knitwear /ˈnɪt.weəʳ/ [US] /-wer/ *noun* [U] clothes made by connecting wool or another type of thread into joined rows

knob /nɒb/ [US] /nɑːb/ *noun* [C] **1** a round handle, or a small round device for controlling a machine or electrical equipment: *a brass door knob* ○ *Turn/Twiddle the little knob to adjust the volume.* **2** a round lump on the surface or end of something **3** a small amount of something solid, especially butter: *Put a knob of butter in the frying pan.* **4** UK OFFENSIVE a penis

• **and the same to you with (brass) knobs on** UK OLD-FASHIONED HUMOROUS used to return an insult forcefully to someone who has insulted you

• **with (brass) knobs on** UK If you describe something as a particular thing with knobs on, you mean it has similar qualities to that thing but they are more extreme: *Disney World was like an ordinary amusement park with knobs on.*

knobbly /ˈnɒb.l̩.i/ /-bli/ [US] /ˈnɑː.bli/ *adj* (US **knobby**) having lumps on the surface: *knobbly knees/elbows*

knock [MAKE NOISE] /nɒk/ [US] /nɑːk/ *verb* [I] **1** to repeatedly hit something, producing a noise: *She knocked* ***on*** *the window to attract his attention.* ○ *There's someone knocking* ***on/at*** *the door.* ○ *Please knock before entering.* **2** SPECIALIZED If an engine is knocking, it is producing a repeated high sound either because the fuel is not burning correctly or because a small part is damaged and is therefore allowing another part to move in ways that it should not. **3** If something such as a pipe knocks, it makes a repeated high sound.

• **knock (on) wood** US FOR **touch wood** ➲See at **touch** MOVE HAND.

knock /nɒk/ [US] /nɑːk/ *noun* [C] a sudden short noise made when someone or something hits a surface: *There was a knock* ***at/on*** *the door.*

knock [HIT] /nɒk/ [US] /nɑːk/ *verb* [I + adv or prep; T] **1** to hit, especially forcefully, and cause to move or fall: *He accidentally knocked the vase* ***off*** *the table.* ○ *She knocked her head* ***against*** *the wall as she fell.* ○ *Who knocked* ***over*** *that mug of coffee?* ○ [+ obj + adj] *Some thug knocked him* ***unconscious/senseless.*** ○ *She took a hammer and knocked* ***a hole in*** *the wall.* **2 knock into each other/knock through** If you knock two rooms into each other or knock two rooms through, you remove the wall between them so that they form one room.

• **be knocking (on) 60/70, etc.** INFORMAL to have almost reached a particular, usually old, age: *She was knocking on 80 when she died.*

• **knock it off** INFORMAL used to tell someone to stop doing something which annoys you: *Oh, knock it off Alex, I'm really not in the mood for your jokes.*

• **knock *sb's* block off** INFORMAL If you say that you will knock someone's block off, you are threatening to hit them very hard, especially on the head: *I'll knock his block off if he tries anything with me!*

• **Knock 'em dead!** INFORMAL used to tell someone to perform or play as well as they can

• **knock *sb* off *their* pedestal** to show people that someone is not as perfect as they seem to be: *This recent scandal has really knocked the President off his pedestal.* ➲Compare **put** sb **on a pedestal** at **pedestal**.

• **knock *sth* on the head** UK INFORMAL to prevent something from happening, or to finally finish something: *It's nearly done – another couple of hours should knock it on the head.*

• **knock (some) sense into *sb*** INFORMAL to forcefully teach someone not to be foolish: *A couple of years in the army will knock some sense into him.*

• **knock spots off *sth*** UK INFORMAL to be much better than something or someone else: *It knocks spots off that restaurant in Cotswold Street.*

• **knock *sb* sideways/for six** UK INFORMAL to shock or upset someone very much, or to make someone very ill: *That flu really knocked me sideways.* ○ *The news of his death knocked me for six.*

• **knock the bottom out of *sth*** to damage something severely, especially by destroying its support: *The rise in mortgage rates really knocked the bottom out of the housing market.*

• **You could have knocked me down/over with a feather.** SAYING said when you are extremely surprised

knock /nɒk/ [US] /nɑːk/ *noun* [C] when something hard hits a person or thing: *He received a nasty knock* ***on*** *the head from a falling slate.*

• **take/have a knock** to be damaged because of a bad experience: *Her confidence took a* ***hard*** *knock when her application was rejected.*

knock [CRITICIZE] /nɒk/ [US] /nɑːk/ *verb* [T] UK INFORMAL to criticize, especially unfairly: *Don't knock him – he's doing his best.*

knocker /ˈnɒk.əʳ/ [US] /ˈnɑː.kɚ/ *noun* [C] UK INFORMAL DISAPPROVING a person who is always criticizing someone or something

PHRASAL VERBS WITH **knock**

▲ **knock *sb* about/around** *phrasal verb* INFORMAL to behave violently towards someone and hit them: *Her husband used to knock her about.*

▲ **knock about/around (sth)** [BE SOMEWHERE] *phrasal verb* INFORMAL to be in a place which is not exactly known or in various places especially over a long period of time: *I'm sure I've got a copy of 'Time's Arrow' knocking about somewhere.* ○ *He spent years knocking around the Far East before World War One.*

▲ **knock around/about** [RELAX] *phrasal verb* INFORMAL to spend time relaxing and doing very little: *I spent the weekend just knocking about the house.*

▲ **knock around/about** [BE WITH SOMEONE] *phrasal verb* INFORMAL to spend a lot of time with someone: *I used to knock around with him at school.*

▲ **knock *sb* back (*sth*)** [COST] *phrasal verb* UK INFORMAL to cost someone a large amount of money: *I bet that computer knocked you back a few thousand.*

▲ **knock back (*sth*)** [DRINK] *phrasal verb* [M] UK INFORMAL to quickly drink something, especially a lot of alcohol: *She was knocking back the champagne at Maria's party.*

▲ **knock *sb* down** [HIT WITH A VEHICLE] *phrasal verb* [M often passive] UK to hit someone with a vehicle and injure or kill them: *She was knocked down by a bus.*

▲ **knock *sb/sth* down** [MAKE FALL] *phrasal verb* [M] to cause someone or something to fall to the ground by hitting them ➲See picture **Phrasal Verbs** on page Centre 9

▲ **knock *sth* down** [DESTROY] *phrasal verb* [M] to destroy a building or part of a building: *The Council plans to knock the library down and replace it with a hotel complex.* ○ FIGURATIVE *She easily knocked down every argument he put up.*

▲ **knock *sth/sb* down** [REDUCE] *phrasal verb* [M] INFORMAL to reduce a price, or to persuade someone to reduce the price of something they are selling: *She wanted £200 but I knocked her down **to** £175.* ➲See also **knockdown**.

▲ **knock off (*sth*)** [STOP WORK] *phrasal verb* INFORMAL to stop working, usually at the end of the day: *I don't knock off until six.* ○ *What time do you knock off work?*

▲ **knock *sth* off (*sth*)** [REDUCE] *phrasal verb* [M] INFORMAL to take a particular amount away from a price: *The manager knocked £5 off because it was damaged.*

▲ **knock *sth* off** [STEAL] *phrasal verb* [M] SLANG to steal something: *He has a stack of computer equipment he's knocked off **from** various shops.* ○ *Terrorist groups are knocking off (*US ALSO **knocking over**) *banks to get money.* ○ *He was caught selling knocked-off car radios in the pub.*

▲ **knock *sth* off** [PRODUCE] *phrasal verb* [M] INFORMAL to produce something quickly and easily: *She can knock off* (= write) *a novel in a couple of weeks.* ➲See also **knock out** PRODUCE.

▲ **knock *sb* off** [MURDER] *phrasal verb* [M] SLANG to murder someone: *He hired a hit-man to knock off a business rival.*

▲ **knock *sb* off** [HAVE SEX] *phrasal verb* [M] OFFENSIVE OLD-FASHIONED to have sex with someone

▲ **knock *sb* out** [MAKE UNCONSCIOUS] *phrasal verb* [M] to hit someone so that they become unconscious: [R] *She hit her head on the ceiling and knocked herself out.* ➲See also **knockout** UNCONSCIOUS.

▲ **knock *sb* out** [MAKE SLEEP] *phrasal verb* If a drug or alcohol knocks you out, it makes you go to sleep: *The sleeping tablets knocked him out for 18 hours.*

▲ **knock *yourself* out** [MAKE TIRED] *phrasal verb* [R] INFORMAL to make yourself ill with tiredness: *If you carry on working like this, you'll knock yourself out.*

▲ **knock *sb* out** [DEFEAT] *phrasal verb* [M] to defeat a person or a team in a competition so that they can no longer take part in it: *The champion was unexpectedly knocked out (**of** the tournament) in the first round.*

▲ **knock *sb* out** [CAUSE ADMIRATION] *phrasal verb* [M] OLD-FASHIONED SLANG to cause enjoyment or admiration in someone: *We were all really knocked out by the film, especially the photography.*

▲ **knock *sth* out** [PRODUCE] *phrasal verb* [M] INFORMAL to produce something quickly without spending time thinking about the details: *I've knocked out a first draft of the report which we can amend at a later date.* ➲See also **knock off** PRODUCE.

▲ **knock *sth* out** [DESTROY] *phrasal verb* [M] If something such as a piece of equipment is knocked out by something else, it is made useless, damaged or destroyed: *The surge in the power supply knocked out all the computers.* ○ *Enemy aircraft have knocked out 25 tanks.*

▲ **knock *sth* out of *sb*** *phrasal verb* If a quality is knocked out of someone, they lose that quality because the situation they are in does not allow it to exist: *Any creativity I had was soon knocked out of me at school.*

▲ **knock *sth* over** [STEAL] *phrasal verb* [M] US FOR **knock off** STEAL

▲ **knock *sb* over** [HIT] *phrasal verb* [M usually passive] to hit someone with a vehicle and injure or kill them: *She got knocked over by a taxi as she ran for the bus.*

▲ **knock *sth* together/up** *phrasal verb* [M] INFORMAL to make something quickly and without much care: *I could knock together a quick lunch if you like.*

▲ **knock up** [PRACTISE] *phrasal verb* Players knock up before beginning a game of tennis or similar sport by hitting the ball to each other: *The players have a couple of minutes to knock up before the match starts.*
knock-up /ˈnɒk.ʌp/ [US] /ˈnɑːk-/ *noun* [C usually sing] *Shall we have a quick knock-up before the game?*

▲ **knock *sb* up** [WAKE UP] *phrasal verb* [M] UK INFORMAL to wake someone up by knocking on the door of their house or bedroom: *I'm sorry to have to knock you up in the middle of the night.*

▲ **knock *sb* up** [MAKE PREGNANT] *phrasal verb* [M] SLANG to make a woman pregnant: *You don't want to get knocked up by some guy you hardly know.*

knockabout /ˈnɒk.ə.baʊt/ [US] /ˈnɑːk-/ *adj* [before n] (especially of a theatre performance) causing laughter by very silly behaviour; SLAPSTICK

knockdown /ˈnɒk.daʊn/ [US] /ˈnɑːk-/ *adj* [before n] (of a price) extremely cheap: *They're selling jeans for ridiculous knockdown **prices**.* ➲See also **knock down** REDUCE.

knocker /ˈnɒk.əʳ/ [US] /ˈnɑː.kɚ/ *noun* [C] (ALSO **doorknocker**) a metal object fixed to a door which visitors use to hit the door in order to attract attention

knockers /ˈnɒk.əz/ [US] /ˈnɑː.kɚz/ *plural noun* SLANG a woman's breasts. Some people consider this offensive.

knocking-shop /ˈnɒk.ɪŋ.ʃɒp/ [US] /ˈnɑː.kɪŋ.ʃɑːp/ *noun* [C usually sing] UK HUMOROUS FOR **brothel**

knock-kneed /ˌnɒkˈniːd/ [US] /ˌnɑːk-/ *adj* If someone is knock-kneed, their knees bend towards each other.

knockoff /ˈnɒk.ɒf/ [US] /ˈnɑːk.ɑːf/ *noun* [C] MAINLY US INFORMAL a cheap copy of a popular product: *Is that the real thing or a knockoff?*

knock-on effect /ˈnɒk.ɒn.ɪˌfekt/ [US] /ˈnɑːk.ɑːn-/ *noun* [C usually sing] MAINLY UK When an event or situation has a knock-on effect, it indirectly causes other events or situations: *If one or two trains run late, it **has** a knock-on effect on the entire rail service.*

knockout [UNCONSCIOUS] /ˈnɒk.aʊt/ [US] /ˈnɑːk-/ *noun* [C] in boxing, the act of hitting the other fighter so that they fall to the ground and are unable to get up again within ten seconds: *a knockout punch/blow* ➲See also **knock out** MAKE UNCONSCIOUS.
• **a knockout blow** an event or action that causes someone or something to fail: *Already out of training, the latest illness has dealt her hopes of a gold medal a knockout blow.*

knockout [COMPETITION] /ˈnɒk.aʊt/ [US] /ˈnɑːk-/ *noun* [C] (US **elimination tournament**) a competition in which only the winners of each stage play in the next stage, until one competitor or team is the final winner: *The tournament is a straight knockout.* ○ *a knockout competition/championship/match*

knockout [ATTRACTIVE] /ˈnɒk.aʊt/ [US] /ˈnɑːk-/ *noun* [C] INFORMAL a person or thing that looks, sounds, etc. extremely attractive: *Your sister's a real knockout!* **knockout** /ˈnɒk.aʊt/ *adj*

ˈknockout ˌdrops *plural noun* OLD-FASHIONED INFORMAL a drug, usually put secretly into your drink, that makes you sleep

knoll /nəʊl/ [US] /noʊl/ *noun* [C] a small low hill with a rounded top: *a grassy knoll*

knot [FASTENING] /nɒt/ [US] /nɑːt/ *noun* [C] a fastening made by tying together the ends of a piece or pieces of string, rope, cloth, etc: *to **tie** a knot*
knot /nɒt/ [US] /nɑːt/ *verb* [T] **-tt-** *He caught the rope and knotted it **around*** (= fastened it to) *a post.* **knotted** /ˈnɒt.ɪd/ [US] /ˈnɑː.t̬ɪd/ *adj*: *a knotted rope*
• **Get knotted!** UK OLD-FASHIONED SLANG a rude way of telling someone who is annoying you to go away

knot [MASS] /nɒt/ [US] /nɑːt/ *noun* [C] a tight mass, for example of hair or string: *Alice's hair is always full of knots and tangles.*
• **in knots** INFORMAL If your stomach is in knots, it feels tight and uncomfortable because you are nervous or excited.
knot /nɒt/ [US] /nɑːt/ *verb* [I] **-tt-** to form a tight, hard, rounded mass: *His muscles knotted* (= swelled) *with the strain.*

knot [GROUP] /nɒt/ [US] /nɑːt/ *noun* [C] a small group of people standing close together: *Knots **of** anxious people stood waiting in the hall.*

knot [WOOD] /nɒt/ [US] /nɑːt/ *noun* [C] a small hard area on a tree or piece of wood where a branch was joined to the tree **knotty** /ˈnɒt.i/ [US] /ˈnɑː.t̬i/ *adj*: *a knotty piece of wood* ➲See also **knotty**.

K

knot [MEASUREMENT] /nɒt/ ⓤ /nɑːt/ *noun* [C] SPECIALIZED a measure of the speed of ships, aircraft or movements of water and air. One knot is approximately 1.85 kilometres per hour: *a top speed of about 20 knots.*

knotty /ˈnɒt.i/ ⓤ /ˈnɑː. t̬i/ *adj* INFORMAL (of a problem or difficulty) complicated and difficult to solve: *That's rather a knotty question.* ⊃See also **knotty** at **knot** WOOD.

know [HAVE INFORMATION] /nəʊ/ ⓤ /noʊ/ *verb* knew, known **1** [I or T; not continuous] to have information in your mind: *"Where did he go?" "I don't know."* ○ *"What does it cost?" "Ask Kate. She'll know."* ○ *She knows the name of every kid in the school.* ○ *I don't know anything about this.* ○ [+ question word] *We don't know when he's arriving.* ○ *I don't know (= understand) what all the fuss is about.* ○ [+ (that)] *I just knew (that) it was going to be a disaster.* ○ *She knew (= was aware) (that) something was wrong.* ○ [+ obj + to infinitive] *Even small amounts of these substances are known to cause skin problems.* ○ FORMAL *The authorities know him to be* (= know that he is) *a cocaine dealer.* **2** [T not continuous] used to ask someone to tell you a piece of information: *Do you know the time?* ○ [+ question word] *Do you know where the Post Office is?* **3** [I or T; not continuous] to be certain: [+ (that)] *I know (that) she'll be really pleased to hear the news.* ○ [+ question word] *I don't know whether I should tell her or not.* ○ *The party is at Sarah's house as/so far as I know* (= I think but I am not certain).

• **Goodness/God/Heaven/Christ knows** INFORMAL used to mean 'I don't know' or to emphasize a statement. Some people may find this offensive: *God only knows what'll happen next!* ○ *Take your shirt off – Heaven knows it's hot enough today!*

• **How was I to know?** INFORMAL used to say that something you did wrong was not your fault because you did not have enough information to have acted differently: *I just wanted to give her a surprise, how was I to know you'd already bought tickets?*

• **I don't know** INFORMAL used to express your lack of understanding or annoyance at something that someone has done: *I don't know, however many notices I put up, people still park in my space.*

• **I don't know how/what/why, etc.** INFORMAL used to add force to criticisms, expressions of surprise, etc: *I don't know how you can eat that revolting stuff!* ○ *I don't know why you bother.*

• **I know 1** said when you suddenly think of a good idea, an answer or a solution: *I know – let's go to the beach!* **2** said to show you agree with something someone has just said: *"But he's so awful." "I know – he's dreadful."*

• **know sth back to front** (ALSO **know sth backwards**) INFORMAL to have very good and detailed knowledge of something: *She knows her part in the play back to front.*

• **know better (than to do sth)** to be wise or moral enough not to do something: *Sure, she's only six, but she's old enough to know better than to run off without us.* ○ *I'm surprised at you behaving so badly – you ought to/ should know better.*

• **know better (than sb)** to know more than someone else because you have more experience and more skill: *They thought the painting was a fake, but Shackleton knew better.*

• **know best** to be the most suitable person to have responsibility and make important decisions: *When it comes to dealing with my own son, I think I know best.*

• **know sth like the back of your hand** INFORMAL to have very good and detailed knowledge of something: *I know this area like the back of my hand.*

• **know your own mind** to be certain about what you believe or want

• **know your place** to accept your position within society, an organization, your family, etc. and to not want to improve it: *I just get on with my job and do as I'm told – I know my place.*

• **know the score** INFORMAL to know all the important facts in a situation, especially the unpleasant ones: *You know the score – no payment till after the article is published.*

• **know what you are talking about** to understand a subject because of your experience: *He doesn't know what he's talking about – he's never even been to Africa.*

• **know your stuff** (OLD-FASHIONED **know your onions**) INFORMAL to have good practical skills and knowledge in a particular activity or subject

• **know what's what** INFORMAL If you know what's what, you have a lot of experience and can judge people and situations well: *Linda's been in the business for thirty years – she knows what's what.*

• **know which side your bread is buttered (on)** INFORMAL to be careful not to act in ways that would lose you other people's approval, or lose you an advantage

• **not know the first thing about sth** to know nothing about a subject: *I'm afraid I don't know the first thing about car engines.*

• **not know what has hit you** INFORMAL to be shocked and surprised because something unpleasant suddenly and unexpectedly happens to you: *You wait till he starts working for Michael – he won't know what's hit him!*

• **not know where to put yourself** INFORMAL to feel very embarrassed: *And then he started to sing. Well, I didn't know where to put myself.*

• **not know whether to laugh or cry** to not know how to react in a particular situation: *When she told me they were getting married I didn't know whether to laugh or cry.*

• **not know where/which way to turn** to not know what to do or who to ask for help: *When both her parents died, she didn't know which way to turn.*

• **not that I know of** used when answering a question to mean that, judging from the information you have, the answer is no: *"Is she especially unhappy at school?" "Not that I know of."*

• **there's no knowing** If you say there's no knowing, you mean it is impossible to be certain about something: *There's no knowing what she'll do if she finds out about this.*

• **(Well) what do you know!** INFORMAL something you say when you are surprised by a piece of information. This phrase is often used humorously to mean the opposite: *So they're getting married, are they? Well, what do you know!* ○ *Well, what do you know! The Raiders lost again!*

• **You know something?** (ALSO **You know what?**) INFORMAL said before giving an opinion or a piece of information: *You know something? I don't think I like that man.* ○ *You know what? I think it's time to go home.*

• **you know** INFORMAL **1** a phrase with little meaning, which you use while you are trying to think of what to say next: *Well I just thought, you know, I'd better agree to it.* ○ *I'm not happy with the situation but, you know, there isn't much I can do about it.* **2** used when trying to help someone remember something or when trying to explain something: *What's the name of that guy on TV – you know, the American one with the silly voice?*

• **(you) know what I mean** INFORMAL used when you think that the person listening understands and so you do not need to say any more: *You've got to give him a chance, you know what I mean?*

• **you never know** INFORMAL said to mean there is a possiblity that something good might happen, even though it is slight: *You never know, she might change her mind.*

know /nəʊ/ ⓤ /noʊ/ *noun* INFORMAL **be in the know** to have knowledge about something which most people do not have: *This resort is considered by those who are in the know to have the best downhill skiing in Europe.*

knowable /ˈnəʊ.ə.bl̩/ ⓤ /ˈnoʊ-/ *adj* able to be known

knowing /ˈnəʊ.ɪŋ/ ⓤ /ˈnoʊ-/ *adj* showing that you know about something, even when it has not been talked about: *a knowing look/glance/smile*

knowingly /ˈnəʊ.ɪŋ.li/ ⓤ /ˈnoʊ-/ *adv* **1** in a way that shows you know about something: *She smiled knowingly at him.* **2** If you do something knowingly, you do it with awareness, especially of its likely effect: *I've never knowingly offended him.*

COMMON LEARNER ERROR

know or **find out**

If you **know** something, you already have the information.

Andy knows what time the train leaves.

Her parents already know about the problem.

If you **find** something **out**, you learn new information for the first time.

I'll ring the station to find out what time the train leaves.
~~I'll ring the station to know what time the train leaves.~~

---

know [BE FAMILIAR WITH] /nəʊ/ ⓤ /noʊ/ *verb* knew, known **1** [T not continuous] to be familiar with or have experience and understanding of: *I've known Daniel since we were at school together.* ○ *She grew up in Paris so she knows it well.* ○ *I've seen the film 'Casablanca' so many times that I know a lot of it by heart* (= I know it in my memory). ○ *Knowing Sarah* (= from my experience of her in the past), *she'll have done a good job.* ○ FORMAL *I have known* (= experienced) *great happiness in my life.* ⊃See Note **meet, see, visit or get to know?** at **meet** BECOME FAMILIAR WITH. **2** [I or T; not continuous] (*ALSO* **know about**) If you know a subject, you are familiar with it and understand it: *Do you know about computers?* ○ *She knows her subject inside out/*(UK ALSO) ***backwards*** (= very well). **3** [T not continuous] If you know a language, you can speak and understand it: *Do you know any French?* **4** [T not continuous] to recognize someone or something: *That's Peter alright – I'd know him anywhere!* ○ *I know a bargain when I see one.* **5 know how to do** *sth* to be able to do something because you have the necessary knowledge: *Do you know how to print on this computer?*
● **get to know** *sb/sth* to spend time with someone or something so that you gradually learn more about them: *The first couple of meetings are for the doctor and patient to get to know each other.* ○ *I'll need a few weeks to get to know the system.*
● **know** *sb* **by name** to have heard the name of a person but not seen or talked to them
● **know** *sb* **by sight** If you know someone by sight, their face is familiar to you, but they are not a friend of yours.
● *sth* **knows no bounds** FORMAL If someone has a quality that knows no bounds, it is extreme: *Her generosity knows no bounds.*
● **know** *your* **way around** *sth* (*ALSO* **know the ropes**) to be familiar with a place or organization and able to act effectively within it
● **not know** *sb* **from Adam** INFORMAL to have never met someone and not know anything about them: *Why should she lend me money? She doesn't know me from Adam.*
● **wouldn't know** *sth* **if** *you* **fell over one/it** (*ALSO* **wouldn't know** *sth* **if it hit** *you* **in the face**) INFORMAL used to say that someone would not recognize something even if it was obvious: *She wouldn't know a bargain if she fell over one!*

known /nəʊn/ ⓤ /noʊn/ *adj* describes something or someone that is familiar to or understood by people: *These people are known criminals.* ○ *There is no known reason for the accident.* ○ *He is known to the police because of his previous criminal record.* ⊃See also **well known**.
● **known as** *sth* If someone or something is known as a particular name, they are called by that name: *And this is Terry, otherwise known as 'Muscleman'.*
● **make** *sth* **known** to tell people about something so that it becomes publicly known: *Local residents have made known their objections to the proposals.* ○ *I made it known that I was not happy with the decision.*
● **make** *yourself* **known** to tell someone who you are: *Just go to the hotel reception and make yourself known (to the receptionist).*

COMMON LEARNER ERROR

meet, get to know and **know**

When you **meet** someone, you see or speak to them for the first time.
When you **get to know** someone, you learn more about them and after this you can say that you **know** them.

I met Nick on holiday.
~~I knew Nick on holiday.~~
We got to know each other and became good friends.
~~We knew each other and became friends.~~
How long have you known Nick?
~~How long have you got to know Nick?~~

PHRASAL VERBS WITH **know** ▼

▲ **know** *sth* **from** *sth phrasal verb* to know the difference between two things and therefore be able to recognise either, used especially to mean that you have a good knowledge and understanding of a particular subject: *Computer expert? He doesn't know a mouse from a modem* (= He knows nothing about computers)*!*
▲ **know of** *sb/sth phrasal verb* MAINLY UK to have heard of someone or something and be able to give a small amount of information about them: *Do you know of a good doctor?*

know-all UK /ˈnəʊ.ɔːl/ ⓤ /ˈnoʊ.ɑːl/ *noun* [C] (US **know-it-all**) INFORMAL DISAPPROVING a person who thinks that they know much more than other people

know-how /ˈnəʊ.haʊ/ ⓤ /ˈnoʊ-/ *noun* [U] INFORMAL practical knowledge and ability: *technical know-how*

knowledge /ˈnɒl.ɪdʒ/ ⓤ /ˈnɑː.lɪdʒ/ *noun* **1** [S or U] understanding of or information about a subject which has been obtained by experience or study, and which is either in a person's mind or possessed by people generally: *Her knowledge of English grammar is very extensive.* ○ *He has a limited knowledge of French.* ○ *The details of the scandal are now common knowledge* (= familiar to most people). ○ *She started to photograph the documents, safe in the knowledge that* (= knowing that) *she wouldn't be disturbed for at least an hour.* ○ *In this town there are only a couple of restaurants that to my knowledge* (= judging from my personal experience and information) *serve good food.* **2** [U] awareness: *The Government deny all knowledge of the affair.* ○ *It has come/been brought to our knowledge* (= We have discovered) *that several computers have gone missing.*

knowledgeable /ˈnɒl.ɪ.dʒə.bl̩/ ⓤ /ˈnɑː.lɪ-/ *adj* knowing a lot: *He's very knowledgeable about German literature.*
knowledgeably /ˈnɒl.ɪ.dʒə.bli/ ⓤ /ˈnɑː.lɪ-/ *adv*

knuckle /ˈnʌk.l̩/ *noun* [C] one of the joints in the hand where your fingers bend, especially where your fingers join on to the main part of your hand ⊃See picture **The Body** on page Centre 5
● **near the knuckle** UK INFORMAL about sex and so likely to offend people: *Some of his jokes were a bit near the knuckle.*

knuckle /ˈnʌk.l̩/ *verb*

PHRASAL VERBS WITH **knuckle** ▼

▲ **knuckle down** *phrasal verb* INFORMAL to start working or studying hard: *You're going to have to really knuckle down (to your work) if you want to pass your exams.*
▲ **knuckle under** *phrasal verb* INFORMAL to accept someone's power over you and do what they tell you to do

knuckle-duster /ˈnʌk.l̩ˌdʌs.tər/ ⓤ /-tɚ/ *noun* [C] **1** UK (US **brass knuckles**) a metal weapon which is worn over the knuckles and is intended to increase the injuries caused when hitting a person **2** INFORMAL a large and noticeable ring

knucklehead /ˈnʌk.l̩.hed/ *noun* [C] MAINLY US INFORMAL a stupid person; IDIOT

KO /ˌkeɪˈəʊ/ ⓤ /-ˈoʊ/ *verb* [T] KO'ing, KO'd, KO'd INFORMAL to KNOCK OUT (= make unconscious), especially in boxing
KO /ˌkeɪˈəʊ/ ⓤ /-ˈoʊ/ *noun* [C] plural **KOs** ⊃See also **knockout** UNCONSCIOUS.

koala /kəʊˈɑː.lə/ ⓤ /koʊ-/ *noun* [C] (*ALSO* **koala bear**) an Australian animal which lives in trees and looks like a small bear with grey fur

kohl /kəʊl/ ⓤ /koʊl/ *noun* [U] a dark substance which people put around their eyes, especially the edge of their eyelids, to make them more attractive: *a kohl pencil*

kookaburra /ˈkʊk.ə.bʌr.ə/ *noun* [C] a large Australian bird which lives in trees and makes a strange sound like laughter

kooky /ˈkuː.ki/ *adj* MAINLY US INFORMAL (especially of a person) strange in their appearance or behaviour, especially in a way that is interesting: *She's got this kooky, high-pitched voice.*

K

kook /kuːk/ *noun* [C] *US INFORMAL* a strange person
kookiness /ˈkuː.kɪ.nəs/ *noun* [U] *MAINLY US INFORMAL*

Koori, **Koorie** /ˈkʊə.ri/ *noun* [C], *adj* (an) **Aborigine**

the Koran, **Qur'an** /ðə.kɒrˈɑːn/ [US] /-kəˈrɑːn/ *noun* [S] the holy book of the Islamic religion

korma /ˈkɔː.mə/ [US] /ˈkɔːr-/ *noun* [U] an Indian dish which consists of meat, fish or vegetables in a creamy sauce: *chicken/vegetable korma*

koruna /kɒrˈuː.nə/ [US] /ˈkɔːr.uː-/ *noun* [C] the standard unit of money used in the Czech Republic and in Slovakia

kosher /ˈkəʊ.ʃəʳ/ [US] /ˈkoʊ.ʃɚ/ *adj* **1** (of food or places where food is sold etc.) prepared or kept in conditions that follow the rules of Jewish law: *kosher food/meat* ○ *a kosher restaurant/butcher/shop* **2** *INFORMAL HUMOROUS* legal, able to be trusted and therefore good: *Their business activities aren't quite kosher.*

kowtow /ˌkaʊˈtaʊ/ *verb* [I] *DISAPPROVING* to show too much respect to someone in authority, always obeying them and changing what you do in order to please them

kph *ABBREVIATION FOR* kilometres per hour

the Kremlin /ðəˈkrem.lɪn/ *noun* [S] a group of buildings in Moscow which is now the centre of government of Russia, or the government itself. In the past the Kremlin also meant the government of the Soviet Union.

krill /krɪl/ *group noun* [U] very small animals with a hard outer shell which live in the sea and are eaten in large numbers by some types of whale

Krishna /ˈkrɪʃ.nə/ *noun* one of the most important of the Hindu gods, considered to be one of the many ways that Vishnu appears

Kris Kringle /ˌkrɪsˈkrɪŋ.gl/ *noun US FOR* **Santa Claus**

krona /ˈkrəʊ.nə/ [US] /ˈkroʊ-/ *noun* [C] the standard unit of money used in Sweden and Iceland

krone /ˈkrəʊ.nə/ [US] /ˈkroʊ-/ *noun* [C] the standard unit of money used in Denmark and Norway

krypton /ˈkrɪp.tɒn/ [US] /-tɑːn/ *noun* [U] a gas which is used in particular types of lights and LASERS

kudos /ˈkjuː.dɒs/ [US] /ˈkuː.dɑːs/ *noun* [U] the fame and public admiration that a person receives as a result of a particular achievement or position in society: *Being an actor has a certain amount of kudos attached to it.*

the Ku Klux Klan /ðəˌkuː.klʌksˈklæn/ *noun* [S] (*ABBREVIATION* **the KKK**) a secret US organization of white PROTESTANT Americans, especially in the south of the country, who oppose people of other races or religions

kumquat, *AUS USUALLY* **cumquat** /ˈkʌm.kwɒt/ [US] /-kwɑːt/ *noun* [C] a small oval orange-like fruit, with a sweet skin which can be eaten

kung fu /ˌkʌŋˈfuː/ *noun* [U] a Chinese method of fighting which involves using your hands and feet and not using weapons

Kurd /kɜːd/ [US] /kɝːd/ *noun* [C] a member of a NOMADIC (= moving from place to place) race who live mainly in eastern Turkey, western Iran and northern Iraq
Kurdish /ˈkɜː.dɪʃ/ [US] /ˈkɝː-/ *adj*

kW *WRITTEN ABBREVIATION FOR* **kilowatt**

Kwanzaa, **Kwanza** /ˈkwæn.zə/ [US] /ˈkwɑːn.zɑː/ *noun* [U] *US* an African-American cultural celebration lasting from December 26 to January 1

K-Y jelly /ˌkeɪ.waɪˈdʒel.i/ *noun* [U] *TRADEMARK* a transparent cream-like substance that can be put on part of the body in order to make the skin less dry and which is used especially during sexual activity

L

L |LETTER| (*plural* **L's** or **Ls**), **l** (*plural* **l's** or **ls**) /el/ *noun* [C] the 12th letter of the English alphabet

L |NUMBER| (*plural* **Ls**), **l** /el/ *noun* [C] the sign used in the Roman system for the number 50

L |LAKE| *noun* WRITTEN ABBREVIATION FOR lake: *L. Ontario*

l |LINE OF PRINTING| *noun* [C] *plural* **ll** WRITTEN ABBREVIATION FOR line

l |LITRE| WRITTEN ABBREVIATION FOR **litre**

<L> INTERNET ABBREVIATION FOR laughing

L8R, **l8r** INTERNET ABBREVIATION FOR later

lab |SCIENCE| /læb/ *noun* [C] INFORMAL a **laboratory**: *a science lab* ○ *a lab technician*

Lab |POLITICS| /læb/ WRITTEN ABBREVIATION FOR **Labour** POLITICAL PARTY

label |SIGN| /'leɪ.bᵊl/ *noun* [C] **1** a piece of paper or other material which gives you information about the object it is fixed to: *Remember to put some address labels on the suitcases.* ○ *Washing instructions should be on the label.* **2** a word or a phrase which is used to describe the characteristics or qualities of people, activities or things, often in a way that is unfair: *He seems to be stuck with the label of 'troublemaker'.* **label** /'leɪ.bᵊl/ *verb* [T] -ll- or US USUALLY -l- [+ adj] *The parcel was clearly labelled 'Fragile'.* ○ *If you spend any time in prison, you're labelled as a criminal for the rest of your life.*

label |COMPANY| /'leɪ.bᵊl/ *noun* [C] a company which produces goods for sale, the goods themselves, or the company's name or symbol: *Her favourite designer label* (= maker of expensive clothes) *is Armani.* ○ *Their own-label vegetarian products have been a huge success.* ○ *The group have just signed* (= arranged to record) *with a new record label.*

labia /'leɪ.bi.ə/ *plural noun* SPECIALIZED folds on the outside of the female sex organs

Labor /'leɪ.bɚ/ ⓤⓢ /-bɚ/ *group noun* [S] (ABBREVIATION **ALP**) the Labor Party, an Australian political party that believes in social equality and the rights of workers ⊃See also **Labour** POLITICAL PARTY.

labor /'leɪ.bɚ/ ⓤⓢ /-bɚ/ ⊃See at **labour**. **laborer** /'leɪ.bᵊr.-ə/ⓤⓢ /-bɚ.ɚ/ *noun*

laboratory /lə'bɒr.ə.tri/ ⓤⓢ /'læb.rə.tɔːr.i/ *noun* [C] (INFORMAL **lab**) a room or building with scientific equipment for doing scientific tests or for teaching science, or a place where chemicals or medicines are produced: *research laboratories* ○ *a computer laboratory* ○ *Laboratory tests suggest that the new drug may be used to treat cancer.*

laborious /lə'bɔː.ri.əs/ ⓤⓢ /-'bɔːr.i-/ *adj* needing a lot of time and effort: *a laborious task* **laboriously** /lə-'bɔː.ri.ə.sli/ ⓤⓢ /-'bɔːr.i-/ *adv*: *He wrote out the list laboriously by hand.*

'labor ˌunion *noun* [C] US FOR **trade union**

labour |WORK| UK, US **labor** /'leɪ.bɚ/ ⓤⓢ /-bɚ/ *noun* **1** practical work, especially that which involves physical effort: *The car parts themselves are not expensive, it's the labour that costs the money.* ○ *manual labour* (= hard work using the hands) **2** workers, especially people who do practical work with their hands: *skilled/unskilled labour*

● **ˌlabour of 'love** a piece of hard work which you do because you enjoy it and not because you will receive money or praise for it, or because you need to do it: *He's always working on his car – it's a labour of love.*

labourer UK, US **laborer** /'leɪ.bᵊr.ə/ ⓤⓢ /-bɚ.ɚ/ *noun* [C] a person who does unskilled physical work, especially outside: *a farm labourer*

labour UK, US **labor** /'leɪ.bɚ/ ⓤⓢ /-bɚ/ *verb* **1** [I] to do hard physical work: *He travelled around Europe labouring to pay his way.* ○ [+ **to** infinitive] *Three hours after the explosion, rescue teams were still labouring to free those trapped.* **2** [I + adv or prep] to do something slowly with great physical or mental effort: *He laboured up the hill*

with his heavy load. ○ *She's been labouring over the same article for days.*

● **labour the point** to try too hard to express an idea, feeling or opinion, repeating it unnecessarily: *Look, there's no need to labour the point – I made a mistake – I admit it!*

● **labour under the delusion/illusion/misapprehension, etc.** to wrongly believe that something is true: *At the time I was still labouring under the delusion that the project might be a success.*

Labour |POLITICAL PARTY| /'leɪ.bɚ/ ⓤⓢ /-bɚ/ *group noun* [S] the Labour Party, the political party in Britain that believes in social equality, a more equal sharing out of wealth, and the rights of workers: *Labour are sure to get in at the next election.* ○ *I voted Labour in the last election.* **Labour** /'leɪ.bɚ/ ⓤⓢ /-bɚ/ *adj*: *the Labour Party* ○ *Labour voters* ○ *the Labour candidate for Coventry North*

labour |BIRTH| UK, US **labor** /'leɪ.bɚ/ ⓤⓢ /-bɚ/ *noun* [C or U] the last stage of pregnancy from the time when the muscles of the womb start to push the baby out of the body until the baby appears: *labour pains* ○ *She went into* (= started) *labour at twelve o'clock last night.* ○ *I was in labour for twelve hours with my first baby.* ○ *No two labours are ever the same.*

'labour ˌcamp UK, US **labor camp** *noun* [C] a place in which people are kept as prisoners and forced to do hard physical work in bad conditions

'labour ˌday UK, US **labor day** *noun* [C usually sing] a public holiday which celebrates the worker: *May 1st is labour day in a lot of countries.*

laboured UK, US **labored** /'leɪ.bəd/ ⓤⓢ /-bɚd/ *adj* done with difficulty, either because of tiredness or because of a lack of ability: *Her breathing was heavy and laboured.* ○ *a laboured joke*

'labour ˌforce UK, US **labor force** *noun* [U] all the people in a particular country who are of the right age to work or all the people who work for a particular company

labour-intensive UK, US **labor-intensive** /ˌleɪ.bər.ɪn-'tent.sɪv/ ⓤⓢ /-bɚ-/ *adj* Industries and methods which are labour-intensive need a lot of workers: *A lot of farming techniques have been abandoned because they were too labour-intensive.*

'labour ˌmarket UK, US **labor market** *noun* [C] the supply of people in a particular country or area who are able and willing to work: *More women are being encouraged into the labour market these days.*

'labour reˌlations UK, US **labor relations** *plural noun* the relationships between employees and employers: *The firm prided itself on its good labour relations.*

labour-saving UK, US **labor-saving** /'leɪ.bə.seɪ.vɪŋ/ ⓤⓢ /-bɚ-/ *adj* describes a device or method which saves a lot of effort and time

Labrador /'læb.rə.dɔːr/ ⓤⓢ /-dɔːr/ *noun* [C] a big yellow or black dog with short hair: *Labradors are used as guide-dogs for blind people.*

laburnum /lə'bɜː.nəm/ ⓤⓢ /-'bɜː:-/ *noun* [C or U] a small tree with groups of yellow flowers hanging down

labyrinth /'læb.ə.rɪnθ/ *noun* [C] LITERARY **1** a confusing set of connecting passages or paths in which it is easy to get lost: *Finally, through a labyrinth of corridors she found his office.* **2** something which is very confusing: *He was no stranger to the labyrinth of love.* **labyrinthine** /ˌlæb.ə'rɪn.θaɪn/ *adj* LITERARY describes something that has lots of parts and is therefore confusing: *Beneath the city lies a labyrinthine network of tunnels.* ○ *It takes a fair amount of concentration to follow the film's labyrinthine plot.*

lace |MATERIAL| /leɪs/ *noun* [U] a decorative cloth which is made by weaving thin thread in delicate patterns with holes in them: *lace curtains* **lacy** /'leɪ.si/ *adj*: *lacy underwear*

lace |STRING| /leɪs/ *noun* [C usually pl] a string which you use to fasten openings, especially in shoes, by putting it through two lines of small holes and tying the ends together: *Your shoe laces are undone.*

lace /leɪs/ verb [T] to put the lace of a shoe or boot through its holes, or to fasten a shoe or boot by tying a lace

lace ADD ALCOHOL /leɪs/ verb [T] to add alcohol or drugs to food or drink, often secretly: *coffee laced **with** brandy*

▲ **lace** *sth* **up** phrasal verb [M] to fasten shoes, boots or a piece of clothing by tying the laces: *She can lace up her shoes and she's only five!* ○ *lace-up shoes*

lace-ups /ˈleɪs.ʌps/ plural noun shoes or boots which are fastened using laces: *a pair of lace-ups*

lacerate /ˈlæs.ər.eɪt/ ⑩ /-ə.reɪt/ verb [T] FORMAL to cut or tear something, especially flesh: *The man's face was severely lacerated in the accident.*

laceration /ˌlæs.əˈreɪ.ʃən/ ⑩ /-əˈreɪ-/ noun [C or U] FORMAL a cut: *The boy had received horrific injuries in the attack, including lacerations **to** both arms.* ○ *The body showed signs of laceration and bruising.*

lachrymose /ˈlæk.rɪ.məʊs/ ⑩ /-moʊs/ adj LITERARY sad or tending to cry often and easily: *He is better known for his lachrymose ballads than hard rock numbers.*

lack /læk/ verb [T] to not have or not have enough of something that is needed or wanted: *He just lacks a little confidence.* ○ *What we lack in this house is space to store things.* ○ *We are lacking three members of staff due to illness.* ➲See Note **miss or lack?** at **miss** NOT DO.

lack /læk/ noun **lack of** *sth* the absence of something or when there is not enough of it: *Her only problem is lack of confidence.* ○ *Lack of sleep had made him irritable.* ○ *If he fails it won't be **for/through** lack of effort* (= he has certainly tried). ○ *We won't be going on holiday this year – lack of funds, I'm afraid.*

lacking /ˈlæk.ɪŋ/ adj **1 be lacking** If something that you need is lacking, you do not have enough of it: *Enthusiasm has been **sadly** lacking these past months at work.* **2 be lacking in** *sth* to not have a quality: *He's totally lacking in charm.*

lackadaisical /ˌlæk.əˈdeɪ.zɪ.kəl/ adj FORMAL lacking enthusiasm and effort: *The food was nice enough but the service was rather lackadaisical.* **lackadaisically** /ˌlæk.əˈdeɪ.zɪ.kli/ adv

lackey /ˈlæk.i/ noun [C] DISAPPROVING a servant or someone who behaves like one by obeying someone else's orders without questioning them or by doing all their unpleasant work for them: *He treats us all like his lackeys.*

lacklustre UK, US **lackluster** /ˈlæk.lʌs.tər/ ⑩ /-tɚ/ adj lacking energy and effort: *Britain's number-one tennis player gave a disappointingly lacklustre performance.*

laconic /ləˈkɒn.ɪk/ ⑩ /-ˈkɑː.nɪk/ adj FORMAL using very few words to express what you mean: *She had a laconic wit.* **laconically** /ləˈkɒn.ɪ.kli/ ⑩ /-ˈkɑː.nɪ-/ adv

lacquer WOOD/METAL /ˈlæk.ər/ ⑩ /-ɚ/ noun [U] a liquid which is painted on wood or metal and forms a hard, shiny, protective surface when it dries **lacquer** /ˈlæk.ər/ ⑩ /-ɚ/ verb [T]

lacquer HAIR /ˈlæk.ər/ ⑩ /-ɚ/ noun [U] (ALSO **hair lacquer**) UK FOR **hair spray**

lacrosse /ləˈkrɒs/ ⑩ /-ˈkrɑːs/ noun [U] a game played by two teams in which the players each use a long stick with a net at the end to catch, carry and throw a small ball, and try to get the ball in the other team's goal

lactate /lækˈteɪt/ verb [I] SPECIALIZED (of a woman or female mammal) to produce milk **lactation** /lækˈteɪ.ʃən/ noun [U]

lactic /ˈlæk.tɪk/ adj SPECIALIZED relating to milk

lactic ˈacid noun [U] an acid that exists in sour milk and is produced in muscles after a lot of exercise

lactose /ˈlæk.təʊs/ ⑩ /-toʊs/ noun [U] SPECIALIZED a type of sugar which is found in milk

lactose inˌtolerant adj unable to digest LACTOSE (= a substance in milk) **lactose inˌtolerance** noun [U]

lacuna /ləˈkjuː.nə/ ⑩ /-ˈkuː-/ noun [C] plural **lacunas** or **lacunae** FORMAL an absent part, especially in a book or other piece of writing

lacy /ˈleɪ.si/ adj ➲See at **lace** MATERIAL.

lad /læd/ noun [C] a boy or young man: *A group of young lads were standing outside the shop.* ○ *He's a nice lad.*

○ *The Prime Minister's a **local** lad* (= he was born and lived in this area). ○ OLD-FASHIONED OR NORTHERN ENGLISH *lads **and lasses*** (= boys and girls) ○ [as form of address] *Come on, lads, let's get this job finished, shall we!*

● **the lads** UK INFORMAL used to refer to the group of men that a young man spends time with socially, especially those who he drinks alcohol with or plays sport with: *I'm having a night out with the lads.*

● **a bit of a lad** UK INFORMAL a young man who has sex with a lot of different women

laddish /ˈlæd.ɪʃ/ adj UK DISAPPROVING describes the noisy, energetic and sometimes rude behaviour that some young men show in social groups **laddishness** /ˈlæd.ɪʃ.nəs/ noun [U]

ladder EQUIPMENT /ˈlæd.ər/ ⑩ /-ɚ/ noun [C] a piece of equipment used for climbing up and down, which consists of two vertical bars or lengths of rope joined to each other by a set of horizontal steps: *She was **up** a ladder, cleaning the window.*

ladder SERIES OF STAGES /ˈlæd.ər/ ⑩ /-ɚ/ noun [S] a series of increasingly important jobs or stages in a particular type of work or process: *Once he started at Paramount in 1967, he moved rapidly up the corporate ladder.* ○ *a first **rung/step on** the employment ladder*

ladder HOLE /ˈlæd.ər/ ⑩ /-ɚ/ noun [C] (US **run**) a long vertical hole in a pair of tights or a stocking **ladder** /ˈlæd.ər/ ⑩ /-ɚ/ verb [I or T] UK *Damn! That's the second pair of tights I've laddered today!*

ˈladder (ˌtournament) noun [C] MAINLY UK (in particular sports) a system in which all the players who play regularly are given a position in a list and can improve their position by beating other players in that list: *a squash ladder*

laddie /ˈlæd.i/ noun [as form of address] SCOTTISH ENGLISH INFORMAL FOR **lad**

laden /ˈleɪ.dən/ adj carrying or holding a lot of something: *He always comes back from France laden **with** presents for everyone.* ○ *The table, as always, was laden **with** food.*

la-di-da, **lah-di-dah** /ˌlɑː.dɪˈdɑː/ adj OLD-FASHIONED INFORMAL describes speech or behaviour which is not sincere because the person, usually a woman, is pretending to belong to a higher social class

ladies UK /ˈleɪ.diz/ group noun [S] (US **ladies' room**) a women's toilet in a public place or building such as a hotel or restaurant: *I'm just going to the ladies.* ○ *Is there a ladies on this floor?*

ladies' fingers /ˌleɪ.dizˈfɪŋ.gəz/ ⑩ /-gɚz/ plural noun UK OLD-FASHIONED **okra**

ladies' man /ˈleɪ.dizˌmæn/ noun [C usually sing] OLD-FASHIONED a man who gives women a lot of attention and likes to be with them: *John was always **a bit of a** ladies' man.*

ladies' room US /ˈleɪ.dizˌruːm/ noun [S] (UK **ladies**) a women's toilet in a public building such as a hotel or restaurant

ladle /ˈleɪ.dl/ noun [C] a very big spoon with a long handle and a deep cup-shaped part, used especially for serving soup: *a soup ladle*

ladle /ˈleɪ.dl/ verb [T] (ALSO **ladle out**) to put soup or other liquid food into bowls to give to people, using a ladle

▲ **ladle** *sth* **out** phrasal verb [M] INFORMAL to give money or goods in a (too) generous way to a lot of people: *In those days doctors ladled out antibiotics to patients.*

lady WOMAN /ˈleɪ.di/ noun **1** [C] a polite or old fashioned way of referring to or addressing a woman: *There's a young lady here to see you.* ○ *Mind your language – there are ladies present!* ○ *Say "thank you" to the lady, children.* ○ OLD-FASHIONED *Is the lady **of the house*** (= the most important or only woman who lives in the house) *at home?* **2** [C] OLD-FASHIONED a woman who behaves in a way that is traditionally considered to be suitable for a woman: *Of course I remember Mrs Connor – she was a real lady.* **3** [C] OLD-FASHIONED sometimes used before the name of a job done by a woman: *a lady doctor* ✳ NOTE: Most people consider this sexist. **4** [as form of address] US used to address a woman in a way that is not polite and is considered offensive by many women: *Hey, lady, what's the rush?*

• **ladies and gentlemen** used to address the members of the audience when you are making a speech: *Good evening, ladies and gentlemen, and welcome to the Theatre Royal.*

Lady TITLE /'leɪ.di/ *noun* [C] a title given in Britain to a woman or girl who has the social rank of a PEER, or to the wife of a PEER or KNIGHT: *Before she married Charles, her title was Lady Diana Spencer.* ○ *Sir Charles and Lady Finlater* ⊃Compare **Lord** TITLE.

ladybird UK /'leɪ.di.bɜːd/ US /-bɝːd/ *noun* [C] (*US* **ladybug**) a small red beetle which is round and has black spots

Lady 'Bountiful *noun* [S] DISAPPROVING a woman who enjoys showing people how rich and kind she is by giving things to poor people

lady-in-waiting /ˌleɪ.di.ɪn'weɪ.tɪŋ/ US /-t̬ɪŋ/ *noun* [C] *plural* **ladies-in-waiting** a woman whose job is to help a queen or other woman of high social position

lady-killer /'leɪ.di.kɪl.əʳ/ US /-ɚ/ *noun* [C] OLD-FASHIONED a sexually attractive man who has sexual relationships with many women

ladylike /'leɪ.di.laɪk/ *adj* OLD-FASHIONED graceful, controlled and behaving in a way that is socially acceptable for a woman: *Well, it might not be ladylike but I'm going to pull my skirt up to get over this fence.*

Lady 'Muck *noun* [S] UK INFORMAL DISAPPROVING a woman who thinks she is very important and should be treated better than everyone else: *Look at Lady Muck over there, expecting everyone to wait on her!*

ladyship /'leɪ.di.ʃɪp/ *noun* FORMAL **her/your ladyship** a respectful way of referring to or addressing a woman or girl who has the rank of a PEER or KNIGHT without using her title: *We are honoured to welcome your ladyship* (= you) *here tonight.* ⊃Compare **lordship**.

lag MOVE SLOWLY /læg/ *verb* [I] **-gg-** to move or advance so slowly that you are behind other people or things: *He's lagging **behind** a bit – I think we'd better wait for him to catch us up.* ○ *Sales are lagging at the moment.*

lag /læg/ *noun* [C] a delay between two things happening: *You have to allow for a time lag **between** order and delivery.*

lag COVER /læg/ *verb* [T] **-gg-** to cover something with a thick layer of material in order to stop heat from escaping or to stop water from freezing: *to lag pipes*

lag PRISON /læg/ *verb* [T] **-gg-** AUS INFORMAL to send someone to prison or to arrest someone

lag /læg/ *noun* [C] UK OLD-FASHIONED INFORMAL a prisoner or a person who has often been a prisoner in the past: *an **old** lag*

lager /'lɑː.gəʳ/ US /-gɚ/ *noun* [C or U] a type of beer which is pale in colour and usually contains a lot of bubbles: *Two pints of lager and a packet of crisps, please.*

'lager ˌlout *noun* [C usually pl] UK INFORMAL a young man whose behaviour is noisy, offensive and often violent after drinking too much alcohol

laggard /'læg.əd/ US /-ɚd/ *noun* [C] OLD-FASHIONED someone or something that is very slow

lagging /'læg.ɪŋ/ *noun* [U] a thick layer of material used to cover pipes, water TANKS (= large containers) and other surfaces in order to stop heat from escaping or water from freezing

lagoon /lə'guːn/ *noun* [C] an area of sea water separated from the sea by a REEF (= a line of rocks and sand): *a tropical lagoon*

lah-di-dah /ˌlɑː.di'dɑː/ *adj* **la-di-da**

laid /leɪd/ *past simple and past participle of* **lay**
• **be laid up** to be forced to stay in bed because of an illness or accident: *She's been laid up in bed **with** flu for a week.*

laid-back /ˌleɪd'bæk/ *adj* INFORMAL relaxed in manner and character; not tending to get anxious about other people's behaviour or things that need to be done: *I've never seen her worried or anxious in any way – she's so laid-back.*

lain /leɪn/ *past participle of* **lie** POSITION

lair /leəʳ/ US /ler/ *noun* [C usually sing] a place where a wild animal lives, often hidden and underground, or a place where a person hides: *a fox's lair* ○ *the thieves' lair*

laird /leəd/ US /lerd/ *noun* [C] a Scottish man who owns a large area of land

lairy /'leə.ri/ US /'ler.i/ *adj* UK SLANG behaving in a loud, excited manner, especially when you are enjoying yourself or drinking alcohol: *The bar was full of lairy, pint-swilling lads in football shirts.*

laissez-faire /ˌleɪ.seɪ'feəʳ/ US /-'fer/ *noun* [U] (*ALSO* **laisser-faire**) **1** unwillingness to get involved in or influence other people's activities: *The problems began long before he became headteacher, but they worsened with his laissez-faire **approach/attitude**.* **2** If a government is laissez-faire, it does not have many laws and rules which control the buying and selling of goods and services.

the laity /ðə'leɪ.ə.ti/ US /-t̬i/ *group noun* [S] all the people who are involved with a church but who are not priests

lake /leɪk/ *noun* [C] **1** a large area of water surrounded by land and not connected to the sea except by rivers or streams: *We used to go boating on that lake.* ○ *Lake Windermere* **2** DISAPPROVING **milk/oil/wine, etc. lake** when too much of a liquid product is produced, making it necessary to store it or waste it: *Overproduction caused butter mountains and wine lakes.*

lakeside /'leɪk.saɪd/ *noun* [S] the area at the edge of a lake: *a walk by the lakeside* ○ *a lakeside chalet*

lakh /lɑːk/ US /læk/ *determiner, noun* [C] INDIAN ENGLISH one hundred thousand: *The total cost of the project is around Rs 50 lakh.*

la-la land /'lɑː.lɑːˌlænd/ *noun* INFORMAL **be/live in la-la land** to not be realistic but to think that things which are completely impossible might happen

lam /læm/ *noun* US **on the lam** to be escaping, especially from the police: *The robbers were on the lam for several days before they were caught.*

lama /'lɑː.mə/ *noun* [C] a title given to a Tibetan Buddhist spiritual teacher ⊃See also **the Dalai Lama**.
Lamaism /'lɑː.mə.ɪ.zᵊm/ *noun* [U] Tibetan Buddhism

lamb /læm/ *noun* [C or U] a young sheep, or the flesh of a young sheep eaten as meat: *lambs gambolling about in the fields* ○ *lamb chops* ○ *roast lamb* ⊃See also **mutton**.
• **like a lamb to the slaughter** If a person does something or goes somewhere like a lamb to the slaughter, they do it without knowing that something bad is going to happen and therefore act calmly and without fighting against the situation.
• **Lamb of God** in the Christian religion, a name for Christ

lamb /læm/ *verb* [I] When sheep lamb, they give birth to lambs.

lambada /læm'bɑː.də/ *noun* [C] a dance, originally from Brazil, in which two people hold each other closely and move their hips at the same time

lambaste, lambast /læm'bæst/ *verb* [T] to criticize someone or something severely: *His first novel was well and truly lambasted by the critics.*

lambent /'læm.bᵊnt/ *adj* LITERARY **1** shining gently: *a lambent glow* **2** **lambent wit** the ability to use words in a clever and humorous way without being unkind

'lambing ˌseason *noun* [C usually sing] the time in the year when sheep give birth to lambs

lambskin /'læm.skɪn/ *noun* [U] leather made from the skin of a lamb with the wool still joined to it

lambswool /'læmz.wʊl/ *noun* [U] the soft wool which is obtained from a young sheep, used especially to make clothes: *a lambswool sweater*

lame UNABLE TO WALK /leɪm/ *adj* (especially of animals) not able to walk correctly because of physical injury to or weakness in the legs or feet **lameness** /'leɪm.nəs/ *noun* [U]

lame NOT SATISFACTORY /leɪm/ *adj* (especially of an excuse or argument) weak and unsatisfactory: *a lame **excuse*** **lamely** /'leɪm.li/ *adv*

lamé /'lɑː.meɪ/ *noun* [U] a type of cloth with threads of gold or silver in it: *gold/silver lamé*

ˌlame 'duck UNSUCCESSFUL *noun* [C] an unsuccessful person or thing

ˌlame 'duck AMERICAN POLITICS *noun* [C] US in American politics, an elected official whose power is reduced because the person who will replace them has already been elected

lament /ləˈment/ *verb* [I or T] to express sadness and regret about: *The poem opens by lamenting (over) the death of a young man.* ○ *My grandmother, as usual, lamented the decline in moral standards in today's society.* ○ *The late lamented* (= dead and remembered with affection) *Frank Giotto used to live here.*

lament /ləˈment/ *noun* [C] FORMAL a song, poem or other piece of writing which expresses sadness about someone's death: *The whole play can be interpreted as a lament for lost youth.*

lamentation /ˌlæm.enˈteɪ.ʃᵊn/ *noun* [C or U] FORMAL sadness and regret, or something that expresses these feelings: *For all the lamentations that schools do not teach the game, it is still played in some areas.*

lamentable /ləˈmen.tə.bl̩/ /ˈlæm.ən-/ US /-t̬ə-/ *adj* FORMAL deserving severe criticism; very bad: *the lamentable state of the economy* **lamentably** /ləˈmen.tə.bli/ US /-t̬ə-/ *adv: The government, says the report, have carried out lamentably few of their promises.*

laminated /ˈlæm.ɪ.neɪ.tɪd/ US /-t̬ɪd/ *adj* consisting of several thin layers of wood, plastic, glass, etc. stuck together, or (of surfaces) covered with a thin protective layer of plastic: *The recipe cards are laminated so they can be wiped clean.*

laminate /ˈlæm.ɪ.nət/ *noun* [C or U] any material which is made by sticking several layers of the same material together: *a laminate finish*

lamington /ˈlæm.ɪŋ.tən/ *noun* [C or U] AUS a cake covered with a chocolate layer and COCONUT

lamp /læmp/ *noun* [C] **1** a device for giving light, especially one that has a covering or is contained within something: *an electric/oil/gas lamp* ○ *a street lamp* ○ *a table/bedside lamp* ➷See also **sunlamp**. **2** any of various devices that produce particular types of light: *an infrared lamp*

lamplight /ˈlæmp.laɪt/ *noun* [U] LITERARY light from a lamp, especially light which is not very bright and only shines over a small area: *She studied the pale skin of his face in the dim lamplight.*

lampoon /læmˈpuːn/ *noun* [C] a piece of writing, a drawing, etc. which criticizes in an amusing way a famous person or a public organization, allowing their bad qualities to be seen and making them seem stupid: *The magazine is famed for its merciless political lampoons.* **lampoon** /læmˈpuːn/ *verb* [T]

lamppost /ˈlæmp.pəʊst/ US /-poʊst/ *noun* [C] a tall post which holds a light at the side of roads and in other public places

lamprey /ˈlæm.pri/ *noun* [C] a long snake-like fish which uses its sucking mouth to feed off the blood of other animals

lampshade /ˈlæmp.ʃeɪd/ *noun* [C] a decorative covering around an electric light which reduces its brightness or controls where it shines

lampstand /ˈlæmp.stænd/ *noun* [C] a heavy, often decorative, base for an electric light which stands on a table or the floor

lance WEAPON /lɑːnts/ US /lænts/ *noun* [C] a long thin pole with a sharp point which soldiers used in the past as a weapon when riding horses
lancer /ˈlɑːnt.sə/ US /ˈlænt.sɚ/ *noun* [C] a soldier who belongs to the part of an army that used lances in the past: *the Queen's Royal Lancers*

lance CUT /lɑːnts/ US /lænts/ *verb* [T] to cut the skin with a sharp tool in order to release infected matter that has collected under it: *She had a boil lanced at the doctor's this morning.*

lance corporal *noun* [C] a soldier who has the second lowest rank in the British, Australian or other army

lancet /ˈlɑːnt.sɪt/ US /ˈlænt-/ *noun* [C] a small knife with two cutting edges and a sharp point that a doctor uses when cutting the skin

land DRY SURFACE /lænd/ *noun* [U] **1** the surface of the Earth that is not covered by water: *It is cheaper to drill for oil on land than at sea.* ○ *The treaty has led to a dramatic reduction in the number of land-based missiles in Europe.* ○ *The military commanders won't deploy their*

land *forces* until they're satisfied that the air attacks have done their job. **2** an area of ground, especially when used for a particular purpose such as farming or building: *This sort of land is no good for growing potatoes.* ○ *I always prosecute people who trespass on my land.* ○ *We want to buy a plot of land to build a house.*
• **find out/see how the land lies** to wait until you have all the available information about a situation before you take any action

the land *noun* [S] farms, farming and the countryside: *Most of the families lived off the land* (= grew their own food etc.). ○ *My parents worked (on) the land all their lives.*

landed /ˈlæn.dɪd/ *adj* [before n] describes people whose families have owned a lot of land for many generations: *the landed gentry*

landless /ˈlænd.ləs/ *adj* describes people who do not have any land for farming or who are prevented from owning the land that they farm by the economic system or by rich people who own a lot of land: *landless labourers/peasants*

land COUNTRY /lænd/ *noun* [C] LITERARY a country: *a land of ice and snow* ○ *The group want to promote their ideas in schools throughout the land.* ➷See also **fatherland; homeland; motherland**. See Note **country, land, nation, or state?** at **country** POLITICAL UNIT.
• **the land of the midnight sun** the part of Norway, Sweden and Finland inside the Arctic Circle where the sun is in the sky very late at night in the summer
• **the Land of the Rising Sun** Japan
• **be in the land of the living** HUMOROUS to be awake or to be alive: *She was partying till the early hours, so I don't imagine she'll be in the land of the living before lunchtime.*
• **be in the land of nod** OLD-FASHIONED INFORMAL to be sleeping: *Jamie's in the land of nod at last.*
• **land of milk and honey** a country where living conditions are good and people have the opportunity to make a lot of money: *Many Mexicans regard the United States as a land of milk and honey.*

land ARRIVE /lænd/ *verb* **1** [I or T] to (cause to) arrive at a place after moving down through the air: *We should land in Madrid at 7am.* ○ *You can land a plane on water in an emergency.* ○ FIGURATIVE *The report first landed on my desk this morning.* **2** [I] to arrive in a boat: *We landed at Port Said in the early evening.*
• **land on your feet** to return to a good situation after experiencing problems, especially because of good luck rather than skill or hard work: *She's really landed on her feet with this new job.*

land UNLOAD /lænd/ *verb* [T] to unload people or things from a ship or aircraft onto the ground: *The general's plan involved landing undercover troops behind enemy lines.*

land CATCH /lænd/ *verb* [T] to catch a fish with a hook or net and remove it from the water: *He landed a huge salmon.*

land ACHIEVE /lænd/ *verb* [T] to get or achieve something good, especially in a way which seems easy or unexpected: *He's just landed a senior editorial job with a men's magazine.*

PHRASAL VERBS WITH **land** ▼

▲ **land sb in sth** *phrasal verb* to cause someone to be in a difficult situation: *Revealing confidential information to a rival company could land you in serious trouble with your boss.* ○ *The demonstration outside the embassy landed some of the protesters in jail overnight.* ○ *He landed himself in deep/hot water* (= in a very difficult or unpleasant situation) *by lying to the tax office about his earnings.*

▲ **land up** *phrasal verb* INFORMAL to finally be in a particular place, state or situation, especially without having planned it: *When we accepted that lift in Paris, we never expected to land up in Athens.* ○ *He'll land up in hospital if he carries on drinking like that.*

▲ **land sb with sth** *phrasal verb* If someone or something lands you with something, they cause problems for you: *I hope you don't mind me landing you with the children at such short notice.* ○ *Alan's gone off on holiday and I've* *been landed with the job of sorting out his mistakes.*

landfall /'lænd.fɔːl/ [US] /-fɑːl/ *noun* [C or U] (an arrival on) the first land that is reached or seen at the end of a journey across the sea or through the air: *Shannon Airport in Ireland was the first European landfall for airplanes flying from North America.*

landfill /'lænd.fɪl/ *noun* [C or U] getting rid of large amounts of rubbish by burying it, or a place where rubbish is buried: *Ninety per cent of American rubbish is dumped in landfill* ***sites****.*

landholding /'lænd,həʊl.dɪŋ/ [US] /-,hoʊl-/ *noun* [C] an area of land that someone owns or rents **landholder** /'lænd,həʊl.dəʳ/ [US] /-,hoʊl.dɚ/ *noun* [C]

landing [PLANE] /'læn.dɪŋ/ *noun* [C] an arrival on the ground of an aircraft or boat: *One person has died after the pilot of a light aircraft was forced to make a* ***crash/emergency*** *landing in a field.*

landing [FLOOR] /'læn.dɪŋ/ *noun* [C] an area of floor joining two sets of stairs, or an area of floor or a passage at the top of a set of stairs which leads to bedrooms and other rooms

'landing ,craft *noun* [C] a small boat with a flat bottom that opens at one end and is used to take soldiers and their equipment from a ship onto land that is controlled by enemy forces

'landing ,gear *noun* [U] (*UK ALSO* **undercarriage**) the set of wheels and other parts which support a plane when it is on the ground and make it possible to take off and land ➲See picture **Planes, Ships and Boats** on page Centre 14

'landing ,stage *noun* [C] a flat structure, often wooden and floating, that acts as a bridge with the land when loading and unloading boats or ships

'landing ,strip *noun* [C] a long flat area of ground that is used by aircraft with wings when taking off and landing

landlady [OWNER] /'lænd,leɪ.di/ *noun* [C] a woman who is paid rent by people for the use of a room, building, or piece of land which she owns

landlady [BAR MANAGER] /'lænd,leɪ.di/ *noun* [C] a woman who is in charge of a pub or bar

landlocked /'lænd.lɒkt/ [US] /-lɑːkt/ *adj* enclosed by the land of other countries and having no sea coast

landlord [OWNER] /'lænd.lɔːd/ [US] /-lɔːrd/ *noun* [C] a person or organization that owns a building or an area of land and is paid by other people for the use of it: *The landlord had promised to redecorate the bedrooms before we moved in.* ○ *Housing associations are the biggest landlords in this area.*

landlord [BAR MANAGER] *UK* /'lænd.lɔːd/ [US] /-lɔːrd/ *noun* [C] (*MAINLY AUS* **publican**) a man who is in charge of a pub or bar

landlubber /'lænd,lʌb.əʳ/ [US] /-ɚ/ *noun* [C] *OLD-FASHIONED* a person who has little knowledge or experience of ships and travelling by sea

landmark [OBJECT] /'lænd.mɑːk/ [US] /-mɑːrk/ *noun* [C] a building or place that is easily recognized, especially one which you can use to judge where you are: *The Rock of Gibraltar is one of Europe's most* ***famous*** *landmarks.*

landmark [STAGE] /'lænd.mɑːk/ [US] /-mɑːrk/ *noun* [C] an important stage in something's development: *The invention of the silicon chip was a landmark* ***in the history of*** *the computer.* ○ *In a landmark* ***case/decision****, the Governor pardoned a woman convicted of killing her husband, who had physically abused her.*

landmarked building /,lænd.mɑːkt'bɪl.dɪŋ/ [US] /-mɑːrkt-/ *noun* [C] *US FOR* **listed building**

landmass /'lænd.mæs/ *noun* [C] *SPECIALIZED* a large area of land that is in one piece and not broken up by seas

landmine /'lænd.maɪn/ *noun* [C] (*ALSO* **mine**) a bomb placed on or under the ground that explodes when a person steps on it or a vehicle drives over it

landowner /'lænd,əʊ.nəʳ/ [US] /-,oʊ.nɚ/ *noun* [C] someone who owns land, often a lot of land **landowning** /'lænd,əʊ.nɪŋ/ [US] /-,oʊ-/ *adj* [before n] *She was born into a wealthy landowning* ***family****.*

Land Rover /'lænd,rəʊ.vəʳ/ [US] /-,roʊ.vɚ/ *noun* [C] *TRADEMARK* a strong, powerful vehicle designed for travelling over rough or steep ground and used especially by people who work in the countryside

landscape [COUNTRYSIDE] /'lænd.skeɪp/ *noun* **1** [C] a large area of countryside, especially in relation to its appearance: *a rural/barren landscape* ○ *The landscape is dotted with the tents of campers and hikers.* ○ *The cathedral dominates the landscape for miles around.* **2** [C or U] a view or picture of the countryside, or the art of making such pictures: *a watercolour landscape.* ○ *J.M.W. Turner is one of Britain's best-known landscape* ***painters****.*

landscape [CHANGE APPEARANCE] /'lænd.skeɪp/ *verb* [T] to change the appearance of an area of land, especially next to a building or road so that it looks more like natural countryside

,landscape 'gardening *noun* [U] the art of making gardens, parks and areas around buildings look more natural and attractive

,landscape 'gardener *noun* [C] (*US ALSO* **landscaper**) someone whose job is doing this

landslide [FALLING EARTH] /'lænd.slaɪd/ *noun* [C] (*ALSO* **landslip**) a mass of rock and earth moving suddenly and quickly down a steep slope

landslide [VICTORY] /'lænd.slaɪd/ *noun* [C] the winning of an election with an extremely large number of votes: *The opinion polls are predicting a Liberal landslide in next week's election.* ○ *a landslide* ***victory***

'land ,tenure *noun* [U] *SPECIALIZED* the rules and arrangements connected with the ownership of land, especially land that is used for farming

lane [ROAD] /leɪn/ *noun* [C] a narrow road in the countryside or in a town: *He drives so fast along those narrow country lanes.* ○ *I live at the end of Church Lane.*

lane [STRIP] /leɪn/ *noun* [C] **1** a specially marked strip of a road, sports track or swimming pool that is used to keep vehicles or competitors separate: *a bus/cycle lane* ○ *The northbound lane is closed because of an accident.* ○ *I find driving in the* ***fast*** *lane rather stressful.* ○ *The British runners/swimmers are in lanes 4 and 6.* **2** a route through the sea or the air which ships or aircraft regularly sail or fly along: *The English Channel is the busiest* ***shipping*** *lane in the world.*

language /'læŋ.gwɪdʒ/ *noun* [C or U] a system of communication consisting of sounds, words and grammar, or the system of communication used by the people of a particular country or profession: *She does research into how children acquire language.* ○ *Do you* ***speak*** *any foreign languages?"* ○ *I'm hopeless at learning languages.* ○ *the English language* ○ *legal/technical language* ○ *the language of business* ○ *Java and Perl are both important computer programming languages* (= systems of writing instructions for computers).

• **speak/talk the same language** to have similar ideas and similar ways of expressing them: *We come from similar backgrounds, so we speak the same language.*

'language la,boratory *noun* [C] (*ALSO* **language lab**) a room in a school or college in which students can use equipment to help them practise listening to and speaking a foreign language

languid /'læŋ.gwɪd/ *adj LITERARY* moving or speaking slowly with little energy, often in an attractive way: *a languid manner/voice* **languidly** /'læŋ.gwɪd.li/ *adv*

languish /'læŋ.gwɪʃ/ *verb* [I] to exist in an unpleasant or unwanted situation, often for a long time: *After languishing* ***in obscurity*** *for many years, her early novels have recently been rediscovered.* ○ *He has been languishing* ***in jail*** *for the past twenty years.* ○ *The ruling party is languishing* ***in*** *third place in the opinion polls.*

languor /'læŋ.gəʳ/ [US] /-gɚ/ *noun* [U] *LITERARY* pleasant mental or physical tiredness or lack of activity: *She missed Spain and the languor of a siesta on a hot summer afternoon.* **languorous** /'læŋ.gə.rəs/ [US] /-gɚ.əs/ *adj* **languorously** /'læŋ.gə.rə.sli/ [US] /-gɚ.ə.sli/ *adv*

lank /læŋk/ *adj* Lank hair is unattractive because it is completely straight and thin: *His hair was lank and greasy and looked like it hadn't been washed for a month.* **lankly** /læŋk/ *adv* **lankness** /'læŋk.nəs/ *noun* [U]

L

lanky /ˈlæŋ.ki/ *adj* tall and thin and tending to move awkwardly as a result: *I was your typical lanky teenager.*

lanolin /ˈlæn.ə.lɪn/ *noun* [U] (*ALSO* **lanoline**) a fatty substance that is obtained from wool and used in skin creams to soften the skin

lantern /ˈlæn.tən/ [US] /-tɚn/ *noun* [C] a light enclosed in a container which has a handle for holding it or hanging it up, or the container itself

lap [LEGS] /læp/ *noun* [C usually sing] the top surface of the upper part of the legs of a person who is sitting down: *Come and sit* ***on*** *my lap and I'll read you a story.*
• **in the lap of luxury** living in very comfortable conditions because you have a lot of money
• **in the lap of the gods** *UK* describes a situation that cannot be controlled and which depends only on good luck: *The doctors have done everything possible for him, so his recovery now is in the lap of the gods.*

lap [DRINK] /læp/ *verb* [T] **-pp-** (of an animal) to drink a liquid by taking it in small amounts into the mouth with a lot of short quick movements of the tongue

lap [HIT GENTLY] /læp/ *verb* [I or T] **-pp-** (of waves) to hit something gently, producing quiet sounds: *The water lapped* ***against*** *the side of the pool.* ○ *The waves gently lapped the shore.*

lap [RACING] /læp/ *noun* [C] a complete journey around a race track that is repeated several times during a competition: *He recorded the fastest lap in last weekend's Hungarian Grand Prix.* ○ *After a strong start, she was passed by several runners* ***in/on*** *the final/last lap and finished ninth.*
• **lap of honour** *UK* (*US* **victory lap**) a journey around a track or sports field that is made by a winner of a race or a team that has won a game
lap /læp/ *verb* **-pp- 1** [T] to go past someone in a race who has been round the track one less time than you: *He finished last after being lapped twice by the leading runners.* **2** [I] to make one complete journey around a track
▲ **lap** ***sth*** **up** *phrasal verb* [M] to enjoy something very much: *We walked around the city, lapping up the atmosphere.* ○ *Everyone clapped and cheered and you could see he was lapping it up.*

ˈlap ˌdancing *noun* [U] an activity in a bar or nightclub in which a woman wearing very little clothing dances very close to a customer in exchange for money

lapdog [DOG] /ˈlæp.dɒg/ [US] /-dɑːg/ *noun* [C] a small pet dog that is given a lot of attention by its owner

lapdog [PERSON] /ˈlæp.dɒg/ [US] /-dɑːg/ *noun* [C] *DISAPPROVING* someone who is willing to do anything that a more important person tells them to do: *Opposition parties accuse the newspaper's editor of being a government lapdog.*

lapel /ləˈpel/ *noun* [C] a strip of cloth which is part of the front of a jacket or coat. It is joined to the collar and folded back onto the chest: *A flower was pinned* ***to/in*** *her lapel.*

lapse [FAILURE] /læps/ *noun* [C] a temporary failure: *a lapse* ***of*** *concentration* ○ *The management's decision to ignore the safety warnings demonstrated a remarkable lapse* ***of*** *judgment.* ○ *a* ***memory*** *lapse*

lapse [PERIOD] /læps/ *noun* [C usually sing] a period of time passing between two things happening: *a time lapse/a lapse of time* ○ *He turned up again after a lapse of two years.*

lapse [END] /læps/ *verb* [I] to end legally or officially by not being continued or made effective for a longer period: *The association needs to win back former members who have allowed their subscriptions to lapse.*
lapsed /læpst/ *adj* [before n] **1** no longer involved in an activity or organization: *a lapsed Catholic* **2** no longer being continued or paid: *a lapsed subscription*

PHRASAL VERBS WITH **lapse**

▲ **lapse into** ***sth*** [LESS ACTIVE] *phrasal verb* to start speaking or behaving in a less active or acceptable way: *No one could think of anything more to say, and the meeting lapsed into* ***silence.***

▲ **lapse into** ***sth*** [WORSE] *phrasal verb* to gradually get into a worse state or condition: *He lapsed into* ***a coma*** *and died four days later.*

laptop (computer) /ˌlæp.tɒp.kəmˈpjuː.təʳ/ [US] /-tɑːp.-kəmˈpjuː.t̬ɚ/ *noun* [C] a computer which is small enough to be carried around easily and is designed for use outside an office: *A laptop would be really useful for when I'm working on the train.* ➲See picture **In the Office** on page Centre 15

lapwing /ˈlæp.wɪŋ/ *noun* [C] (*ALSO* **peewit**) a small dark bird with a white chest and raised feathers on its head

larceny /ˈlɑː.sᵊn.i/ [US] /ˈlɑːr-/ *noun* [C or U] *LEGAL* stealing, especially (in the US) the crime of taking something that does not belong to you, without getting illegally into a building to do so **larcenous** /ˈlɑː.sᵊn.əs/ [US] /ˈlɑːr-/ *adj US LEGAL*

larch /lɑːtʃ/ [US] /lɑːrtʃ/ *noun* [C] a tall tree which grows in cold northern countries and loses its needle-shaped leaves in winter

lard /lɑːd/ [US] /lɑːrd/ *noun* [U] a white substance made from pig fat and used in cooking

lard /lɑːd/ [US] /lɑːrd/ *verb*
▲ **lard** ***sth*** **with** ***sth*** *phrasal verb* If speech or a piece of writing is larded with a particular type of language, it has a lot of that type of language: *Her speech was larded with literary quotations.*

larder /ˈlɑː.dəʳ/ [US] /ˈlɑːr.dɚ/ *noun* [C] a cupboard or small room used, especially in the past, for storing food in a person's home: *a well-stocked* (= full of food) *larder*

large /lɑːdʒ/ [US] /lɑːrdʒ/ *adj* big in size or amount: *a large house* ○ *the world's largest computer manufacturer* ○ *We need a larger car.* ○ *We didn't expect such a large number of people to attend the concert.* ○ *We've made good progress, but there's still a large amount of work to be done.* ○ *There was a larger-than-expected fall in unemployment last month.* ○ *Researchers have just completed the largest-ever survey of criminal behaviour in the UK.* ○ *The population faces starvation this winter without large-scale emergency food aid.*
• **(as) large as life** used as a way of describing a person you see, and are surprised to see, in a particular place: *I looked up from my newspaper and there he was, as large as life, Tim Trotter!*
• **at large** generally: *This group is not representative of the population at large.*
• **be at large** If someone dangerous is at large, they are free when they should not be: *Twelve prisoners are at large following a series of escapes.*
• **by and large** when everything about a situation is considered together: *There are a few small things that I don't like about my job, but by and large it's very enjoyable.*
• **larger than life** If someone is larger than life, they attract a lot of attention because they are more exciting or interesting than most people: *Most characters in his films are somewhat larger than life.*

ˌlarge inˈtestine *noun* [C usually sing] *SPECIALIZED* the lower part of the bowels in which water is removed from digested food before it is excreted as solid waste

largely /ˈlɑːdʒ.li/ [US] /ˈlɑːrdʒ-/ *adv* almost completely: *a largely male company* ○ *Their complaints have been largely ignored.* ○ *Until recently the civil war had been largely unreported in the press.*

largesse, largess /lɑːˈʒes/ [US] /lɑːr-/ *noun* [U] *FORMAL* willingness to give money, or money given to poor people by rich people: *The national theatre will be the main beneficiary of the millionaire's largesse.*

largish /ˈlɑː.dʒɪʃ/ [US] /ˈlɑːr-/ *adj* quite large, although not very large: *Their new house is largish, but it's not as big as their old one.*

lark [BIRD] /lɑːk/ [US] /lɑːrk/ *noun* [C] (*ALSO* **skylark**) a small brown bird which is known for its beautiful singing
• **be up with the lark** *MAINLY UK* to get out of bed very early in the morning

lark [ACTIVITY] /lɑːk/ [US] /lɑːrk/ *noun* [C] *INFORMAL* **1** an activity done for amusement, which is slightly bad but is not intended to cause serious harm or damage: *The kids hid their teacher's bike* ***for*** *a lark.* **2 this ... lark** a way of referring to an activity or a situation that you

are not enjoying: *I don't really think I'm suited to this marriage lark.* ○ *I've had enough of this commuting lark.*
• **Bugger/Sod, etc. this for a lark!** *UK OFFENSIVE* used to show that you are extremely annoyed or bored with an activity and that you will not continue doing it: *I'd been waiting for him for an hour and I thought, sod this for a lark – I'm going home!*

lark /lɑːk/ [US] /lɑːrk/ *verb*
▲ **lark about/around** *phrasal verb INFORMAL* to behave in a silly or playful way: *I was woken up by a couple of drunks larking around with a dustbin in the street.* ○ *We were just larking about – we didn't mean to do any damage.*

larva /ˈlɑː.və/ [US] /ˈlɑːr-/ *noun* [C] *plural* **larvae** a form of an insect or an animal such as a frog that has left its egg but is not yet completely developed **larval** /ˈlɑː.vᵊl/ [US] /ˈlɑːr-/ *adj*

laryngitis /ˌlær.ɪnˈdʒaɪ.tɪs/ [US] /-t̬ɪs/ *noun* [U] a painful swelling of the LARYNX that is usually caused by an infection

larynx (*plural* **larynxes** or *SPECIALIZED* **larynges**) /ˈlær.ɪŋks/ *noun* [C] (*INFORMAL* **voice box**) a muscular hollow organ between the nose and the lungs which contains the tissue that moves very quickly to create the human voice and many animal sounds

lasagne, *US USUALLY ALSO* **lasagna** /ləˈzæn.jə/ [US] /-ˈzɑː.njə/ *noun* [U] thin wide sheets of pasta, or savoury food consisting of layers of this combined with cheese and meat or vegetables

lascivious /ləˈsɪv.i.əs/ *adj FORMAL DISAPPROVING* expressing a strong desire for sexual activity: *a lascivious smile* **lasciviously** /ləˈsɪv.i.ə.sli/ *adv* **lasciviousness** /ləˈsɪv.i.ə.snəs/ *noun* [U]

laser /ˈleɪ.zəʳ/ [US] /-zɚ/ *noun* [C] (a device which produces) a powerful narrow beam of light that can be used as a tool to cut metal, to perform medical operations, or to create patterns of light for entertainment: *laser beam* ○ *laser surgery*

ˈlaser ˌdisc *noun* [C] a disc which stores information in a form that can be obtained using a laser

ˈlaser ˌprinter *noun* [C] a computer printer that produces very clear text and pictures by means of a laser beam **ˈlaser ˌprinting** *noun* [U]

lash [HIT] /læʃ/ *verb* **1** [I or T] to hit with a lot of force: *The prisoners were regularly lashed with electric cable.* ○ *The sound of the rain lashing* ***against*** *the windows was deafening.* ➲See also **lash out**. **2** [T] to criticize someone severely

lash /læʃ/ *noun* **1** [C or S] a thin strip of leather at the end of a whip, or a hit with this, especially as a form of punishment: *He received 30 lashes for the crime.* ○ *The punishment for disobedience was* ***the*** *lash.* ➲See also **whiplash**. **2** [C] a sudden violent movement of something that can bend: *With a powerful lash of its tail, the fish jumped out of the net and back into the river.*
• **come/suffer under the lash** to be severely criticized: *The sales team came under the lash for poor results.*

lashing /ˈlæʃ.ɪŋ/ *noun* [C usually sing] when someone is hit with a whip as a punishment: *FIGURATIVE He was given a* ***tongue*** *lashing* (= criticized severely) *after the game.*

lash [TIE] /læʃ/ *verb* [T usually + adv or prep] to tie together tightly and firmly: *I've lashed your case* ***to*** *the roof rack.* ○ *These poles will be easier to carry if we lash them* ***together*** *with a rope.*

lash [HAIR] /læʃ/ *noun* [C usually pl] an **eyelash**

PHRASAL VERBS WITH **lash** ▼

▲ **lash out** ***(sth)*** [SPEND MONEY] *phrasal verb UK INFORMAL* to spend a large amount of money in an unnecessary or wasteful way: *He lashed out £5000* ***on*** *his daughter's wedding.*

▲ **lash out** [ATTACK] *phrasal verb* to suddenly attack someone or something physically or criticise them in an angry way: *I was only teasing him and suddenly he lashed out (****at*** *me) and hit me in the face.* ○ *Why's Tina in such a bad mood? She really lashed out* ***at*** *me when I was late for work.*

lashings /ˈlæʃ.ɪŋz/ *plural noun UK OLD-FASHIONED OR HUMOROUS* a lot of food or drink: *scones with lashings* ***of*** *cream* ○ *lashings* ***of*** *ginger beer*

lass /læs/ *noun* [C] (*ALSO* **lassie**) *MAINLY SCOTTISH AND NORTHERN ENGLISH* a girl or young woman

lassitude /ˈlæs.ɪ.tjuːd/ [US] /-tuːd/ *noun* [U] *FORMAL* physical or mental tiredness: *Shareholders are blaming the company's problems on the lassitude of the managing director.*

lasso /læsˈuː/ *noun* [C] *plural* **lassos** or *US ALSO* **lassoes** a rope which is shaped in a ring at one end, which can be tightened by pulling the other end: *Lassos are used particularly by cowboys to catch cattle and horses.*

lasso /læsˈuː/ *verb* [T] **lassoing, lassoed, lassoed** to catch an animal by throwing the ring of a lasso over its head and then tightening it around its neck

last [FINAL] /lɑːst/ [US] /læst/ *adj, adv, pronoun, noun* (the person or thing) after everyone or everything else: [+ to infinitive] *I hate being* ***the*** *last one* ***to*** *arrive at a meeting.* ○ *Our house is the last one on the left before the traffic lights.* ○ *The Mets will surely finish the season in last* ***place*** (= at the lowest rank of their division). ○ *I know Johnson finished last in the race, but who was* ***second to*** *last* (= the one before the one at the end)*?* ○ *I don't know why he bothers to bet – his horses always come in last.* ○ ***At*** *the last* ***moment*** (= as late as possible) *he changed his mind.* ○ *He always leaves important decisions* ***to*** *the last (possible)* ***moment*** (= as late as possible).
• **at (long) last** finally: *I've finished my essay at last!* ○ *At long last the government is starting to listen to our problems.*
• **(down) to the last ...** including all of the thing mentioned: used to emphasize what you are saying: *The model of the village is accurate down to the last detail.* ○ *He has calculated the costs down to the last penny.*
• **have the last laugh** to finally benefit from an argument or disagreement, when it seemed that you would not
• **last but not least** importantly, despite being mentioned after everyone else: *I would like to thank my publisher, my editor and, last but not least, my husband.*
• **last thing (at night)** at the latest time in the day: *I'll switch on the washing machine last thing so it'll be finished when I get up in the morning.*
• **the last but one** (*US ALSO* **the next to last**) the one before the final one: *I'm almost finished – this is the last but one box to empty.*
• **the last time** If you say that it is the last time you will do something, you mean that you will never do it again: *He never even thanked me, so that's the last time I do him a favour.*
• **to the last** *FORMAL* **1** until something is complete or has been achieved: *I think my position is right, and I'll defend it to the last.* **2** until the end of someone's life: *She was a true patriot to the last.*
• **to the last (man)** until every person is dead: *Both sides have declared themselves ready to fight to the last man.*

last [NO MORE] /lɑːst/ [US] /læst/ *adj* [before n], *noun* [U], *pronoun* (being) the only one or part that is left: *Do you mind if I have the last chocolate?* ○ *I'm down to my last 50p – could I borrow some money for lunch?* ○ *I'm afraid Martha's eaten* ***the*** *last* ***of*** *the ice cream.* ○ *She was* ***the*** *last* ***of*** *the great educational reformers.*
• **as a last resort** (*UK ALSO* **in the last resort**) if all other methods fail: *British police are supposed to use guns only as a last resort.*
• **hear/see the last of *sth*** *INFORMAL* If you hear/see the last of something or someone unpleasant or difficult, they do not cause you trouble again: *I paid them £100 for the damage and I hope that's the last I'll hear of it.* ○ *You haven't heard the last of this! – I'll see you in court.* ○ *He's horrible – I really hope we've seen the last of him.*
• **not hear the end/last of *sth*** to be told continually about something: *We'll never hear the last of it if they win that competition.*
• **on its last legs** *INFORMAL* Something that is on its last legs is in such bad condition that it will soon be unable to work as it should: *I've had the same TV for fifteen years now and it's really on its last legs.*
• **on *your* last legs** *INFORMAL* A person who is on their last legs is very tired or near to death: *We'd been out walking*

all day and I was on my last legs when we reached the hotel. ○ *It looks as though her grandfather's on his last legs.*

last [MOST RECENT] /lɑːst/ [US] /læst/ *adj, adv, pronoun* (being) the most recent or the one before the present one: *Did you hear the storm last night* (= during the previous night)? ○ *Did you see the news on TV last night* (= yesterday evening)? ○ *They got married last November.* ○ *When was the last time you had a cigarette?* ○ *When did you last have a cigarette?* ○ *She's been working there for the last month* (= for the four weeks until now). ○ FORMAL *Could you account for your whereabouts on Sunday last?* ○ *The/These last five years have been very difficult for him.* ○ ***The** last we heard of her, she was working as an English teacher in France.* ○ *Each of her paintings has been better than **the** last.*

• **the week/month/year before last** during the week/month/year before the previous one: *We had lunch together the week before last.*

last [UNSUITABLE] /lɑːst/ [US] /læst/ *adj* **the last person/thing, etc.** the least expected or wanted person or thing: *Three extra people to feed – that's the last thing I need!* ○ *The last thing I wanted was to make you unhappy.* ○ *Matthew is the last person I'd expect to be interested in dance.* ○ *He's the last person I'd trust with my keys.*

last [CONTINUE] /lɑːst/ [US] /læst/ *verb* [I; L only + n] **1** to continue to exist: *The meeting lasted two hours.* ○ *The drought lasted **for** several months.* ○ *They say the snow will last **until** the end of next week.* ○ *I can't see the cease-fire lasting.* ○ *They haven't had an argument for two weeks, but it's **too good to** last* (= they'll have an argument soon). ○ *I doubt their enthusiasm will last.* ○ *He's working very efficiently at the moment, but it won't last.* **2** to continue being good or suitable: *There's no point buying something that isn't going to last.* ○ *The cheaper washing machines should last about five years.* ○ *This pen should last (you) a lifetime if you look after it.* ○ *Her previous secretary only lasted a month* (= left after this period).

• **not last long** (UK ALSO **not last five minutes**) to fail or be unsuccessful very soon: *You won't last long in your job if you carry on being so rude to the customers.* ○ *He wouldn't last five minutes in the police force – it's far too tough for him.*

▲ **last out** *phrasal verb* [L] to manage to stay alive: *How long can they last out without food?* ○ *He won't last out the night.*

last-ditch /ˌlɑːstˈdɪtʃ/ [US] /ˌlæst-/ *adj* (ALSO **last-gasp**) **last-ditch attempt/effort** an effort or attempt which is made at the end of a series of failures to solve a problem, and is not expected to succeed: *In a last-ditch attempt to save his party from electoral defeat, he resigned from the leadership.*

ˌlast hurˈrah *noun* [C usually sing] MAINLY US **1** Someone's last hurrah is their final effort after a long period of work: *Petersen has said that this season will be his last hurrah **as** a player.* **2** Someone or something's last hurrah is their last period of influence or power: *This huge, unfinished building represents the last hurrah of the former regime.*

lasting /ˈlɑː.stɪŋ/ [US] /ˈlæs.tɪŋ/ *adj* continuing to exist for a long time or forever: *Few observers believe that the treaty will bring a lasting **peace** to the region.* ○ *Did any of your teachers make a lasting **impression** on you?* ○ *The tablets make you feel better for a while but the effect isn't **(long-)**lasting.*

the ˌlast ˈjudgment *noun* [U] **Judgment Day**

lastly /ˈlɑːst.li/ [US] /ˈlæst-/ *adv* (ALSO **last**) used to show when something comes after all the other items in a list: *In accepting this award, I would like to thank the producer, the director, the scriptwriter and, lastly, the film crew.*

the ˌlast ˈminute *noun* [S] the latest possible opportunity for doing something: *They only told me **at** the last minute that they couldn't come.* ○ *Why do you always **leave** everything **till** the last minute?* **last-minute** /ˌlɑːstˈmɪn.ɪt/ [US] /ˌlæst-/ *adj*: *a last-minute cancellation*

ˈlast ˌname *noun* [C] MAINLY US your family name, that you use in formal situations or with people whom you do not know well

ˌlast ˈorders *plural noun* in a British pub, the last drinks that customers are allowed to buy just before the bar closes: *Last orders, please!*

the ˌlast ˈpost *noun* [S] a tune that is played on a BUGLE at military funerals or when it is time for soldiers to go to bed

the ˌlast ˈrites *plural noun* a religious ceremony performed by a priest for a person who is dying

ˌlast will and ˈtestament *noun* [S] your written instructions about what should happen to your body and the things that you own after your death

ˌlast ˈword *noun* [S] the final remark in an argument or discussion: *You're not going, Helena, and that's my last word **on** the matter.* ○ *She always has to **have the** last word* (= win the argument).

lat /læt/ *noun* [U] WRITTEN ABBREVIATION FOR **latitude** POSITION

latch /lætʃ/ *noun* [C] a device for keeping a door or gate closed that consists of a metal bar which fits into a hole and which is lifted by pushing down on another bar

• **on the latch** UK closed but not fastened: *Don't forget to **leave** the front door on the latch if you go to bed before I get back.*

latch /lætʃ/ *verb* [I or T] to close a door etc. with a latch

PHRASAL VERBS WITH **latch**

▲ **latch on** *phrasal verb* UK INFORMAL to begin to understand something: *It took me ages to latch on **to** what she was talking about.*

▲ **latch onto *sth*** [BECOME CONNECTED] *phrasal verb* to become connected to something: *The antibodies work by latching onto proteins on the surfaces of the viruses and bacteria.*

▲ **latch onto *sth*** [USE] *phrasal verb* INFORMAL to become interested in an idea, story or activity, and to start to use it: *Unfortunately the press have already latched onto the story.*

▲ **latch onto *sb*** [STAY CLOSE] *phrasal verb* INFORMAL to stay close to someone or spend a lot of time with them, usually when they do not want you with them: *She latched onto me as soon as she arrived, and I had to spend the rest of the evening talking to her.*

latchkey kid /ˈlætʃ.kiːˌkɪd/ *noun* [C] OLD-FASHIONED INFORMAL a child who has a key to his or her home and is often alone at home after school has finished for the day because his or her parents are out at work

late [NEAR THE END] /leɪt/ *adj, adv* (happening or being) near the end of a period of time: *It was late at night.* ○ *We talked late into the night.* ○ *Is that the time? I'd no idea it was so late.* ○ *It was late summer when it happened.* ○ *It was built in the late nineteenth century.* ○ *We could always go later in the season.* ○ *I prefer her earlier paintings to her later work.* ○ *He's probably in his late twenties.* ○ *As late* (= As recently) *as the 1980s they were still using horses on this farm.* ○ *This software is for computers running on Windows 95 or later* (= more recent). ➲See also **latest**.

• **of late** FORMAL recently: *We haven't spoken of late.*

lateness /ˈleɪt.nəs/ *noun* [U] FORMAL the fact of being late: *It was no great surprise that you were tired given the lateness **of the hour**.*

late [AFTER] /leɪt/ *adj, adv* (happening or arriving) after the planned, expected, usual or necessary time: *This train is always late.* ○ *You'll be late **for** your flight if you don't hurry up.* ○ *Sorry I'm late. I was held up in the traffic.* ○ *It's too late to start complaining now.* ○ *We always have a late breakfast on Sunday mornings.* ○ *Some late **news*** (= news of something which happened after the news programme started) *has just come in – a bomb has exploded in central London.* ○ *Our ferry was two hours late because of the strike.* ○ *Kathryn's just phoned to say she's working late this evening.* ○ *She said she'd prefer us to arrive **no** later **than*** (= not after) *nine o'clock.* ➲See also **latecomer**.

• **at the (very) latest** used to emphasize that something must happen or be done before a stated time or day: *I have to get this finished by Friday at the latest.*

• **late in the day** too late to be useful: *It's rather late in the day to start studying – your exams are next week.*
• **later on** later: *What are you doing later on this evening?*
• **See/Catch you later.** *INFORMAL* goodbye: *"Bye." "See you later."*
• **too little, too late** not enough of something which should have been provided earlier: *A spokeswoman for the charity described the aid for the refugees as too little, too late.*
lateness /ˈleɪt.nəs/ *noun* **[U]** the fact of being late

late [DEAD] /leɪt/ *adj* **[before n]** describes someone who has died, especially recently: *She gave her late husband's clothes to charity.*

latecomer /ˈleɪtˌkʌm.əʳ/ [US] /-ɚ/ *noun* **[C]** a person who arrives late: *We regret that latecomers cannot be admitted until a suitable break in the performance.*

ˌlate deˈveloper *UK noun* **[C]** (*US* **late bloomer**) someone who becomes good at something after people usually become good at it: *At school she was a late developer, and it wasn't until she went to university that her talents became apparent.*

lately /ˈleɪt.li/ *adv* recently: *I haven't been feeling so well lately.* ○ *Have you been doing anything interesting lately?*

latent /ˈleɪ.tᵊnt/ *adj* present but needing particular conditions to become active, obvious or completely developed: *Recent developments in the area have brought latent ethnic tension out into the open.* ○ *We're trying to bring out the latent artistic talents that many people possess without realising it.* **latency** /ˈleɪ.tᵊnt.si/ *noun* **[U]** *FORMAL*

lateral /ˈlæt.rᵊl/ [US] /ˈlæt̬.ɚ.ᵊl/ *adj* **[before n]** *SPECIALIZED* relating to the sides of an object or to sideways movement: *lateral movement* ○ *Trim the lateral shoots of the flower* (= the ones which grow sideways from the main stem of a plant). **laterally** /ˈlæt.rᵊl.i/ [US] /ˈlæt̬.ɚ.ᵊl.i/ *adv*

ˌlateral ˈthinking *noun* **[U]** a way of solving a problem by thinking about it imaginatively and originally and not using traditional or expected methods

latest /ˈleɪ.tɪst/ [US] /-t̬ɪst/ *adj* **[before n]** being the newest or most recent or modern: *Have you seen her latest movie?* ○ *the latest fashions*
the latest *noun* **[S]** the most recent news or technical development: *Have you heard the latest* (= the most recent news) ***about*** *Jilly and Patrick – they're getting a divorce.* ○ *This machine is the latest* ***in*** *video recorder technology.*

latex /ˈleɪ.teks/ *noun* **[U]** a white liquid produced by many plants, especially rubber trees, or a rubber-like substance made from this or from plastic, which is used in making clothes, paint, glue, etc: *a latex mask* ○ *a pair of latex surgical gloves*

lath /lɑːθ/ [US] /læθ/ *noun* **[C]** a long thin flat strip of wood, used to make a structure to support plaster on walls or TILES on the roof of a building

lathe /leɪð/ *noun* **[C]** a machine for changing the shape of a piece of wood, metal, etc. which works by turning the material while a sharp tool is pressed against it

lather /ˈlɑː.ðəʳ/ [US] /ˈlæð.ɚ/ *noun* **1** **[S]** a pale, usually white, mass of small bubbles produced especially when soap is mixed with water: *Wet the hair, apply shampoo and massage into a rich lather.* **2** **[U]** small bubbles of sweat on a horse's skin, produced by physical effort
• **be in a lather** *INFORMAL* to be very anxious about something: *She was in a lather when I left because she couldn't find her ticket.* **get into a lather** *It's not worth getting into a lather over.*
lather /ˈlɑː.ðəʳ/ [US] /ˈlæð.ɚ/ *verb* **[I or T]** to produce a lather from soap, or to cover something or someone in lather: **[R]** *He stood under the shower lathering himself with the soap.* **lathery** /ˈlɑː.ðᵊr.i/ [US] /ˈlæð.ɚ-/ *adj*

Latin /ˈlæt.ɪn/ [US] /ˈlæt̬-/ *noun* **[U]** the language used by ancient Romans and as the language of educated people in many European countries in the past
Latin /ˈlæt.ɪn/ [US] /ˈlæt̬-/ *adj* **1** written in Latin: *a Latin poem* **2** relating to (people or things in) countries which use a language which developed from Latin: *his Latin good looks*

ˌLatin Aˈmerican *adj* from or relating to South America or Central America

Latino /ˌlætˈiː.nəʊ/ [US] /-noʊ/ *noun* **[C]** *plural* **Latinos** *MAINLY US* someone who lives in the US and who comes from or whose family comes from Latin America

latitude [POSITION] /ˈlæt.ɪ.tjuːd/ [US] /ˈlæt̬.ɪ.tuːd/ *noun* **[C or U]** the position north or south of the equator measured from 0° to 90° ➲Compare **longitude**.
latitudes /ˈlæt.ɪ.tjuːdz/ [US] /ˈlæt̬.ɪ.tuːdz/ *plural noun* an area near to a particular latitude: *At these latitudes the sun does not rise at all on winter days.* **latitudinal** /ˌlæt.ɪˈtjuː.dɪ.nəl/ [US] /ˌlæt̬.ɪˈtuː-/ *adj SPECIALIZED*

latitude [FREEDOM] /ˈlæt.ɪ.tjuːd/ [US] /ˈlæt̬.ɪ.tuːd/ *noun* **[U]** *FORMAL* freedom to behave, act or think in the way you want to: *Courts can show a considerable degree of latitude when it comes to applying the law.*

latrine /ləˈtriːn/ *noun* **[C]** a toilet, especially a simple one such as a hole in the ground, used in a military area or when camping

latte /ˈlæt.eɪ/ [US] /ˈlɑː.t̬eɪ/ *noun* **[C or U]** (*ALSO* **cafe latte**) a hot drink made from ESPRESSO (= strong coffee) and milk

latter [END] /ˈlæt.əʳ/ [US] /ˈlæt̬.ɚ/ *adj* **[before n]** near or towards the end of something: *Building of the new library should begin in the latter* ***part*** *of next year.* ○ *In the latter stages of the fight he began to tire.*

the latter [SECOND] *noun* **[S]** **1** the second of two people, things or groups previously mentioned: *She offered me more money or a car and I chose the latter.* ➲Compare **the former** FIRST. **2** *NOT STANDARD* the last of more than two people, things or groups previously mentioned

latter-day /ˈlæt.ə.deɪ/ [US] /ˈlæt̬.ɚ-/ *adj* **[before n]** describes a person or thing that is similar to someone or something that existed in the past: *the evil actions of a latter-day Caligula*

latterly /ˈlæt.ə.li/ [US] /ˈlæt̬.ɚ-/ *adv FORMAL* recently: *Latterly, her concentration hasn't been so good.*

lattice /ˈlæt.ɪs/ [US] /ˈlæt̬-/ *noun* **[C]** (*ALSO* **latticework**) a structure made from strips of wood or other material which cross over each other with spaces between

ˌlattice ˈwindow *noun* **[C]** a window made from small pieces of glass which are held in place by metal strips

laud /lɔːd/ [US] /lɑːd/ *verb* **[T]** *FORMAL* to praise: *The German leadership lauded the Russian initiative.*

laudable /ˈlɔː.də.bl̩/ [US] /ˈlɑː-/ *adj FORMAL* (of actions and behaviour) deserving praise, even if there is little or no success: *a laudable aim/ambition* ○ *The recycling programme is laudable, but does it save much money?*
laudably /ˈlɔː.də.bli/ [US] /ˈlɑː-/ *adv*
laudatory /ˈlɔː.də.tri/ [US] /ˈlɑː-/ *adj FORMAL* expressing praise

laugh /lɑːf/ [US] /læf/ *verb* **[I]** to smile while making sounds with your voice that show you think something is funny or you are happy: *They laughed* ***at*** *her jokes.* ○ *I couldn't stop laughing.* ○ *I said he'd have to give a talk and he laughed nervously.* ○ *She's so funny – she really* ***makes*** *me laugh.* ○ *It's very rare that a book is so good you actually laugh* ***out loud****.* ○ *It was so funny, I* ***burst out*** *laughing* (= laughed suddenly and loudly). ○ *I laughed* ***till I cried****.*
• **Don't make me laugh!** *INFORMAL* said to someone to show that you cannot take their suggestion seriously: *You'll pay? Don't make me laugh!*
• **be laughing all the way to the bank** *INFORMAL* to be earning lots of money easily: *We'll be laughing all the way to the bank if this deal works out.*
• **be laughing** (*ALSO* **will be laughing**) *UK INFORMAL* used to tell someone that they should not be worried by a particular situation, because they will get a benefit from it: *If the loan's approved you're laughing.*
• **laugh *your* head off** (*ALSO* **laugh *yourself* silly**) *INFORMAL* to laugh a lot, loudly: *You laughed your head off when I fell!*
• **laugh in *sb's* face** to show someone an obvious lack of respect: *They'd laugh in your face if you suggested me for the post.*
• **laugh like a drain** *UK INFORMAL* to laugh a lot, very loudly
• **be laughing on the other side of *your* face** *UK* (*US* **laugh out of the other side of *your* mouth**) used to tell someone that although they are pleased now, they will not be pleased later when things do not happen as they

L

expected or planned: *She's pleased with her promotion but she'll be laughing on the other side of her face when she sees the extra work.*

• **be laughed out of court** to be considered as too silly or impossible to take seriously, especially in a court of law: *The proposal will be laughed out of court.*

• **laugh up *your* sleeve** to be secretly amused: *They're very polite in your presence, but you get the feeling they're laughing up their sleeves.*

• **be no laughing matter** to be very serious: *It might seem funny but I tell you what, getting stuck up a tree is no laughing matter.*

• **you've got to laugh** (*ALSO* **you have to laugh**) *INFORMAL* said when you can see something funny in a difficult situation

• **He who laughs last, laughs longest/best.** *SAYING* said to emphasize that the person who has control of a situation in the end is most successful, even if other people had seemed originally to have an advantage

laugh /lɑːf/ ⓤ /læf/ *noun* [C] **1** the act or sound of laughing: *a loud/nervous laugh* ○ *I was embarrassed at the time, but I **had a good** laugh about it later.* **2** *INFORMAL* an enjoyable or amusing activity: *"How was the party?" "Oh, it was a laugh."* **3** *MAINLY UK INFORMAL* someone who is amusing: *You'd like Sharon – she's **a good** laugh.*

• **for a laugh** *INFORMAL* If you do something for a laugh, you do it for amusement: *Just for a laugh, I pretended that I'd forgotten it was his birthday.*

PHRASAL VERBS WITH **laugh** ▼

▲ **laugh at** *sb/sth phrasal verb* **1** to show that you think someone or something is stupid: *I can't go into work looking like this – everyone will laugh at me.* **2** to treat someone or something as if they are not important or do not deserve serious attention: *If you say that, people will just laugh at you.*

▲ **laugh** *sth* **off** *phrasal verb* [M] to make yourself laugh about something unpleasant in order to make it seem less important or serious: *She tried to laugh off their remarks, but I could see she was hurt.*

laughable /ˈlɑː.fə.bl̩/ ⓤ /ˈlæf.ə-/ *adj* foolish and not deserving serious consideration: *Privately they thought the idea laughable.*

laughing ˌgas *noun* [U] *INFORMAL* a type of gas which is used as an *ANAESTHETIC* (= substance which stops pain)

laughingly /ˈlɑː.fɪŋ.li/ ⓤ /ˈlæf.ɪŋ-/ *adv* **1** If you do something laughingly, you are laughing while you are doing it: *He laughingly pointed out our mistakes.* **2** *DISAPPROVING* If you say something is laughingly described in a particular way, you think this thing is so bad that it does not deserve the description: *It is only one of the absurd rules in the system of law laughingly known as British justice.*

laughing ˌstock *noun* [S] someone or something which seems stupid or ridiculous, especially by trying to be serious or important and not succeeding: *Another performance like that and this team will be **the** laughing stock **of** the league.*

laughter /ˈlɑːf.təʳ/ ⓤ /ˈlæf.tɚ/ *noun* [U] the act or sound of laughing: *She **roared with** laughter* (= laughed very loudly). ○ *As we approached the hall we could hear the sound of laughter.*

• **Laughter is the best medicine.** *SAYING* said to mean that trying to be happy is a good way to stop worrying

launch SEND /lɔːntʃ/ ⓤ /lɑːntʃ/ *verb* [T] to send something out, such as a new ship into water or a rocket into space: *A spokesman for the dockyard said they hoped to launch the first submarine within two years.* ○ *to launch a missile* **launch** /lɔːntʃ/ ⓤ /lɑːntʃ/ *noun* [C] *The launch of the space shuttle was delayed for 24 hours because of bad weather.* **launcher** /ˈlɔːn.tʃəʳ/ ⓤ /ˈlɑːn.tʃɚ/ *noun* [C] *a mobile **rocket** launcher*

launch *yourself* *verb* [R + adv or prep] *MAINLY UK* to jump with great force: *The defender launched himself **at** the attacking player, bringing him to the ground.*

launch BEGIN /lɔːntʃ/ ⓤ /lɑːntʃ/ *verb* [I or T] to begin something such as a plan or introduce something new such as a product: *The scheme was launched a year ago.* ○ *The airline will launch its new transatlantic service next*

month. ○ *A devastating attack was launched **on** the rebel stronghold.* ○ [+ adv or prep] *UK After working for the company for several years she decided to launch **out** on her own and set up in business.*

launch /lɔːntʃ/ ⓤ /lɑːntʃ/ *noun* [C] an event to celebrate or introduce something new: *How much champagne will we need for the launch?* ○ *Illness prevented her attending the launch **party** for her latest novel.*

launch BOAT /lɔːntʃ/ ⓤ /lɑːntʃ/ *noun* [C] a boat which has an engine and carries passengers for short distances, especially on a lake or a river, or from the land to a larger boat

▲ **launch into** *sth phrasal verb* to start saying something or criticizing something with a lot of energy or anger: *He launched into a verbal attack on her handling of the finances.*

launch ˌpad *noun* [C] (*UK ALSO* **launching pad**) a special area from which rockets or missiles are sent into the sky: *The rocket blew up on the launch pad.* ○ *FIGURATIVE Soap operas have long been a launch pad for film actors.*

launder CLOTHES /ˈlɔːn.dəʳ/ ⓤ /ˈlɑːn.dɚ/ *verb* [T] to wash, dry and iron clothes, sheets etc: *freshly laundered sheets*

launder MONEY /ˈlɔːn.dəʳ/ ⓤ /ˈlɑːn.dɚ/ *verb* [T] to move money which has been obtained illegally through banks and other businesses to make it seem to have been obtained legally: *Officials were accused of laundering the stolen funds overseas before returning them to the US.*

launderette *MAINLY UK*, **laundrette** /ˌlɔːnˈdret/ ⓤ /ˌlɑːnˈdret/ *noun* [C] (*US TRADEMARK* **laundromat**) a shop where you pay to use the machines there which will wash and dry clothes

laundromat /ˈlɔːn.drəʊ.mæt/ ⓤ /ˈlɑːn.droʊ-/ *noun* [C] *US TRADEMARK* a **launderette**

laundry /ˈlɔːn.dri/ ⓤ /ˈlɑːn-/ *noun* **1** [U] the dirty clothes and sheets which need to be, are being or have been washed: *I've got to **do** (= wash) my laundry.* **2** [C] a business which washes clothes, sheets, etc. for customers

laundry ˌbasket *noun* [C] (*US ALSO* **hamper**) a large container in which dirty clothes are kept until they are washed

laureate /ˈlɒr.i.ət/ ⓤ /ˈlɑːr-/ *noun* [C] a person who has been given a very high honour because of their ability in a subject of study: *a Nobel laureate*

laurel /ˈlɒr.ᵊl/ ⓤ /ˈlɑːr-/ *noun* [C or U] a small evergreen tree which has shiny leaves and small black fruit

laurels /ˈlɒr.ᵊlz/ ⓤ /ˈlɑːr-/ *plural noun FORMAL* praise for a person because of something which they have done, usually in sport, the arts or politics: *The actors are very good, but when all is considered the laurels must surely go to the director of the play.*

laurel ˌwreath *noun* [C] a circle of leaves which, in the past, was worn on the head by an important person or the winner of a competition

lav /læv/ *noun* [C] *INFORMAL FOR* **lavatory** (= toilet)

lava /ˈlɑː.və/ *noun* [U] hot liquid rock which comes out of the earth through a volcano, or the solid rock formed when it cools: *molten lava*

lava ˌlamp *noun* [C] a decorative electric lamp in which a brightly-coloured amount of wax moves up and down a container full of transparent liquid, forming new shapes as it does so

lavatory /ˈlæv.ə.tri/ *noun* [C] *MAINLY UK FORMAL* a toilet

lavatorial /ˌlæv.əˈtɔː.ri.ᵊl/ ⓤ /-ˈtɔːr.i-/ *adj UK DISAPPROVING* describes jokes that refer to toilets or excretion: *lavatorial humour*

lavender PLANT /ˈlæv.ɪn.dəʳ/ ⓤ /-dɚ/ *noun* [U] a plant which has grey-green needle-like leaves and small, pale purple flowers with a strong smell, or its dried flowers and stems which have a pleasant smell: *a lavender bush*

lavender COLOUR /ˈlæv.ɪn.dəʳ/ ⓤ /-dɚ/ *adj, noun* [U] (of) a pale purple colour

lavish /ˈlæv.ɪʃ/ *adj* more than enough, especially if expensive; very generous: *lavish gifts/promises/praise* ○ *lavish spending* ○ *lavish banquets* ○ *The evening was a lavish affair with glorious food and an endless supply of champagne.* ○ *The lavish production makes this musical truly memorable.* **lavishly** /ˈlæv.ɪʃ.li/ *adv: The dining* *room was lavishly decorated.* **lavishness** /ˈlæv.ɪʃ.nəs/ *noun* [U]

lavish /ˈlæv.ɪʃ/ *verb*

▲ **lavish *sth* on *sb/sth*** *phrasal verb* to give someone a lot, or too much, of something such as money, presents or attention: *She lavishes money on her grandchildren.* ○ *The committee lavished praise on the project.*

law [RULE] /lɔː/ [US] /lɑː/ *noun* [C or U] a rule, usually made by a government, that is used to order the way in which a society behaves, or the whole system of such rules: *There are laws* ***against*** *drinking in the street.* ○ *The laws* ***governing*** *the possession of firearms are being reviewed.* ○ *They led the fight to impose laws* ***on*** *smoking.* ○ *They have to provide a contract* ***by*** *law.* ○ *She's going to study law at university.* ○ [+ v-*ing* or + **to** infinitive] *Many doctors want to see a law bann****ing/to*** *ban all tobacco advertising.* ➲See also **bylaw**; **lawsuit**; **lawyer**.

the law *noun* [S] the system of rules of a particular country: *What does the law say about having alcohol in the blood while driving?* ○ *Of course robbery is* ***against*** *the law!* ○ *The judge ruled that the directors had knowingly* ***broken*** *the law.* ○ *You can't take that course of action and remain* ***within*** *the law.*

the law *group noun* [S] INFORMAL the police: *The law was/were out in force at the demonstration.*

• **the law of the jungle** the idea that people who care only about themselves will be most likely to succeed in a society or organization: *We hope for a world where the rule of law, not the law of the jungle, governs the conduct of nations.*

• **be a law unto *yourself*** DISAPPROVING to behave in a way which is independent and does not follow the usual rules for a situation: *Charlie, of course, never fills in the record forms but then he's a law unto himself.*

• **go to law** When someone goes to law about something, they ask a court to decide if it was done legally.

• **take the law into *your* own hands** to do something illegal and often violent in order to punish someone because you know the law will not punish that person: *One day, after years of violent abuse from her husband, she took the law into her own hands.*

• **There's one law for the rich and another for the poor.** SAYING said when a rich person has not been punished for something that a poor person would be punished for

law [PRINCIPLE] /lɔː/ [US] /lɑː/ *noun* [C] a general rule which states what always happens when the same conditions exist: *Newton's laws* ***of*** *motion* ○ *the laws of nature/physics* ○ HUMOROUS *The* ***first*** *law* ***of*** (= the most important principle in) *politics is – if you're going to lie, don't get found out!* ➲See also **Murphy's law**; **Parkinson's law**.

• **the law of averages** the belief that if something happens often then it will also happen regularly

law-abiding /ˈlɔː.əˌbaɪ.dɪŋ/ [US] /ˈlɑː-/ *adj* Someone who is law-abiding obeys the law: *Such actions against law-abiding* ***citizens*** *will not be tolerated.*

ˌlaw and ˈorder *noun* [U] when the laws of a country are being obeyed, especially when the police or army are used to make certain of this: *a complete* ***breakdown in*** *law and order*

law-breaker /ˈlɔːˌbreɪ.kəʳ/ [US] /ˈlɑːˌbreɪ.kɚ/ *noun* [C] a person who does not obey the law, especially intentionally and often

ˌlaw enˈforcement *noun* [U] MAINLY US the activity of making certain that the laws of an area are obeyed: *a law-enforcement officer*

lawful /ˈlɔː.fəl/ [US] /ˈlɑː-/ *adj* FORMAL allowed by the law: *Judge Keenan concluded that the surveillance had been lawful.* ○ *He said he was going about his lawful business as a journalist.* **lawfully** /ˈlɔː.fəl.i/ [US] /ˈlɑː-/ *adv*

lawless /ˈlɔː.ləs/ [US] /ˈlɑː-/ *adj* not controlled by laws, or illegal: *The film is set in a lawless city sometime in the future.* **lawlessly** /ˈlɔː.lə.sli/ [US] /ˈlɑː-/ *adv* **lawlessness** /ˈlɔː.lə.snəs/ [US] /ˈlɑː-/ *noun* [U]

lawmaker /ˈlɔːˌmeɪ.kəʳ/ [US] /ˈlɑːˌmeɪ.kɚ/ *noun* [C] someone, such as a politician, who is responsible for making and changing laws

lawn /lɔːn/ [US] /lɑːn/ *noun* [C or U] an area of grass, especially near to a house or in a park, which is cut regularly to keep it short: *Will you* ***mow*** *the lawn at the weekend?*

ˈlawn ˌbowling *noun* [U] US FOR **bowls**. ➲See at **bowl** ROLL.

lawnmower /ˈlɔːnˌməʊ.əʳ/ [US] /ˈlɑːnˌmoʊ.ɚ/ *noun* [C] a machine used for cutting grass

ˈlawn ˌparty *noun* [C] US FOR **garden party**

ˌlawn ˈtennis *noun* [U] FORMAL OR SPECIALIZED **tennis**

lawsuit /ˈlɔː.sjuːt/ [US] /ˈlɑː.suːt/ *noun* [C] (ALSO **suit**) a problem taken to a court of law, by an ordinary person or an organization rather than the police, for a legal decision: *Two of the directors have* ***brought/*** (MAINLY US) ***filed*** *a lawsuit against their former employer.*

lawyer /ˈlɔɪ.əʳ/ [US] /ˈlɑː.jɚ/ *noun* [C] (US ALSO **attorney**) someone whose job is to give advice to people about the law and speak for them in court: *I want to see my lawyer before I say anything.*

USAGE

lawyer, solicitor, barrister and **attorney**

In Britain, **lawyers** are divided into two types, **solicitors** and **barristers**. **Solicitors** give you advice on legal subjects and discuss your case with you. They can also represent you and argue your case in the lower courts. **Barristers** give specialist legal advice and can represent you in both higher and lower courts. In America, there is only one type of lawyer, who is sometimes called an **attorney**.

lax /læks/ *adj* lacking care, attention or control; not severe or strong enough: *He took a gun through baggage control to highlight the lax security.* ○ *The subcommittee contends that the authorities were lax* ***in*** *investigating most of the cases.* **laxity** /ˈlæk.sə.ti/ [US] /-t̬i/ *noun* [U] (ALSO **laxness**) **laxly** /ˈlæk.sli/ *adv*

laxative /ˈlæk.sə.tɪv/ [US] /-t̬ɪv/ *noun* [C] a substance that helps a person excrete the contents of their bowels

lay [PUT DOWN] /leɪ/ *verb* **laid, laid 1** [T usually + adv or prep] to put something in especially a flat or horizontal position, usually carefully or for a particular purpose: *She laid the baby on the bed.* ○ *He laid the tray down on the table.* ○ *She laid* ***aside*** *her book and went to answer the phone.* ○ *We're having a new carpet laid in the hall next week.* ○ *The plan is to lay* (= build) *the foundations for the new apartments in October.* **2** [T] to prepare a plan or a method of doing something: *Even the* ***best*** *laid plans go wrong sometimes.*

• **lay the basis/foundations for *sth*** to prepare for or start an activity or task: *The initial negotiations are seen as laying the basis for more detailed talks.*

• **lay down *your* life for *sth*** to die for something you believe in strongly: *Today we remember those who laid down their lives for their country.*

• **lay a finger on *sb*** to harm someone even slightly: *Don't you dare lay a finger on me.*

• **lay a hand on *sb*** to harm someone: *I never laid a hand on her!*

• **lay *sth* at *sb's* door** MAINLY UK to blame someone for something: *Blame for the accident has been laid at the government's door.*

• **lay *sb* to rest** to bury a dead person: *She was laid to rest next to her husband.*

• **lay *sth* to rest** to end a worry or fear: *I hope what he said has laid your fears to rest.*

• **lay the ghost of *sth* (to rest)** to finally stop being worried or upset about something that has worried or upset you for a long time: *With one stunning performance, Chelsea have laid to rest the ghost of their humiliating defeat at Old Trafford last season.*

• **lay *yourself* open to attack/criticism/ridicule, etc.** to make it easy for people to attack/criticise/ridicule you: *She lays herself open to criticism with such unashamedly extreme views.*

• **lay bare *sth*** to make something known: *It's been promoted as the biography that lays bare the truth behind the legend.*

• **lay *sb* low** to cause someone to be unable to do what they usually do: *A kidney infection laid her low for a couple of months.*

• **lay *sth* to waste** (ALSO **lay waste**) to completely destroy something: *The bomb laid the city centre to waste.*

• **lay up trouble for *yourself*** to do something that will cause you trouble in the future: *You're laying up trouble* *for yourself if you ignore health problems now.*

COMMON LEARNER ERROR

lay or **lie**?

Be careful not to confuse these verbs.

Lay means 'put down carefully' or 'put down flat'. This verb is always followed by an object. **Laying** is the present participle. **Laid** is the past simple and the past participle.

She laid the papers on the desk.

Lie means 'be in a horizontal position' or 'be in a particular place'. This verb is irregular and is never followed by an object. **Lying** is the present participle. **Lay** is the past simple and **lain** is the past participle.

The papers were lying on the desk.

~~The papers were laying on the desk.~~

I lay down and went to sleep.

~~I laid down and went to sleep.~~

The regular verb **lie** means 'not say the truth'. **Lying** is the present participle. **Lied** is the past simple and the past participle.

He lied to me about his age.

---

lay [NOT TRAINED] /leɪ/ *adj* [before n] not trained in or not having a detailed knowledge of a particular subject: *From a lay viewpoint the questionnaire is virtually incomprehensible.* ➔See also **layperson** at **layman** NOT TRAINED.

lay [CHURCH] /leɪ/ *adj* [before n] having a position in an organization, especially a religious one, that is not a full-time job and is not paid: *a lay preacher* ➔See also **layperson** at **layman** CHURCH.

lay [PRODUCE EGGS] /leɪ/ *verb* [I or T] laid, laid (of an animal or bird) to produce eggs from out of the body: *Thousands of turtles drag themselves onto the beach and lay their eggs in the sand.*

lay [HAVE SEX] /leɪ/ *verb* [T] laid, laid SLANG to have sex with someone: *So did you get laid* (= find someone to have sex with)?

lay /leɪ/ *noun* [C] SLANG *She's a good lay* (= Sex with her is enjoyable).

lay [BET] /leɪ/ *verb* [T] laid, laid to bet something, usually money, on the result of an event: *She won't get the job – I'd lay money on it!*

• **lay sth on the line** to risk harm to something: *I'd be laying my career/life on the line by giving you that information.* ➔See also **lay sth on the line** at **lay** EXPRESS.

lay [EXPRESS] /leɪ/ *verb* [T] laid, laid to express a claim, legal statement, etc. in a serious or official way: *She can't accept she made a mistake and now she's trying to lay the blame on* (= accuse) *her assistant.* ○ SPECIALIZED *Do you understand the seriousness of the charge* (= legal accusation) *which has been laid against you?*

• **lay claim to sth** to say that you own something: *Two companies have laid claim to the design.*

• **lay down the law** INFORMAL to forcefully make known what you think should happen: *She can't just come into this office and start laying down the law.*

• **lay sth on the line** INFORMAL to say very clearly that something is the case: *You're just going to have to lay it on the line and tell her that her work's not good enough.* ➔See also **lay sth on the line** at **lay** BET.

• **lay it on a bit thick** (ALSO **lay it on with a trowel**) INFORMAL to praise someone too much: *She went on and on about how she admired his work – laid it on a bit thick, if you ask me.*

lay [LIE] /leɪ/ *past simple of* **lie** POSITION

PHRASAL VERBS WITH lay ▼

▲ **lay sth aside** [STOP] *phrasal verb* [M] to stop doing or thinking about something, usually for a short period of time: *He's temporarily laid aside some quite interesting projects to write the script.*

▲ **lay sth aside** [MONEY] *phrasal verb* [M] to keep something, usually money, for use in the future: *She's trying to lay something aside* (= save some money) *for her retirement.*

▲ **lay sth down** [WINE] *phrasal verb* [M] SPECIALIZED to store wine for drinking in the future

▲ **lay sth down** [WEAPONS] *phrasal verb* [M] If someone lays down their weapons, they stop fighting: *They laid down their **weapons** and surrendered.* ○ *Mediators have persuaded both sides to lay down their **arms**.*

▲ **lay sth down** [RULES] *phrasal verb* [M] to officially establish a rule, or to officially state the way in which something should be done: *This is in line with the policy laid down by the management.*

▲ **lay sth in** *phrasal verb* [M] to obtain a supply of something because you will probably need it in the future: *We'd better lay in plenty of food in case we're cut off when it snows.*

▲ **lay into sb** *phrasal verb* INFORMAL to attack someone physically or to criticise them in an angry way: *In the middle of the meeting she suddenly laid into him.*

▲ **lay sb off** [NOT EMPLOY] *phrasal verb* [M often passive] to stop employing someone, usually because there is no work for them to do: *Because of falling orders, the company has been forced to lay off several hundred workers.*

▲ **lay off** (sth/sb) [STOP] *phrasal verb* INFORMAL to stop using or doing something: *You'd better lay off alcohol for a while.* ○ *Why can't you lay off* (= stop criticising or hurting) *the kid for once!*

▲ **lay sth on** [PROVIDE] *phrasal verb* [M] to provide something for a group of people: *They lay on free entertainment at the club every day.* ○ *They laid on a wonderful buffet after the wedding.*

▲ **lay sth on** [TELL] *phrasal verb* MAINLY US SLANG to tell someone something they were not aware of: *I hate to be the one to lay this on you, but your girlfriend has just left with another guy.*

▲ **lay sth out** [ARRANGE] *phrasal verb* [M] to arrange something on a flat surface: *Most of Manhattan is laid out in/on a grid pattern with avenues going north-south and streets east-west.* ○ *We laid the pieces of the dress pattern out on the floor.*

▲ **lay sth out** [SPEND] *phrasal verb* [M] INFORMAL to spend money, especially a large amount: *It's not every day you lay out £2000 on a holiday.* ➔See also **outlay**.

▲ **lay sb out** [DEAD BODY] *phrasal verb* [M] to prepare a dead person's body to be buried

▲ **lay sb out** [HIT] *phrasal verb* [M] INFORMAL to hit someone so hard that they fall down and become unconscious: *Tyson was laid out for several minutes by a blow to the head.*

layabout /ˈleɪ.əˌbaʊt/ *noun* [C] INFORMAL a person who is unwilling to work

layaway US /ˈleɪ.əˌweɪ/ *noun* [U] (AUS **lay-by**) a system of paying for goods in small amounts and receiving the goods after the full amount has been paid, or goods bought in this way: *Could I buy/put the dress on layaway?*

lay ˌbrother/ˌsister *noun* [C] someone who belongs to a religious group, especially a group living together in a monastery or convent, and who does simple work for the group, such as preparing food

lay-by [ROAD] /ˈleɪ.baɪ/ *noun* [C] *plural* **lay-bys** UK a place beside a road where a vehicle can stop for a short time without interrupting other traffic: *We pulled into a lay-by to look at the map.* ➔See also **rest stop**.

lay-by [PAYMENT] /ˈleɪ.baɪ/ *noun* [U] AUS FOR **layaway**

layer /ˈleɪ.əʳ/ ⓤⓢ /-ɚ/ *noun* [C] a level of material, such as a type of rock or gas, which is different from the material above or below it, or a thin sheet of a substance: *the ozone layer* ○ *A thick layer of clay lies over the sandstone.* ○ *There was a thin layer of oil on the surface of the water.* ○ *We stripped several layers of paint off the door.*

layer /ˈleɪ.əʳ/ ⓤⓢ /-ɚ/ *verb* [T] to arrange something in layers: *Layer the pasta with slices of tomato.* ○ *potatoes layered with onions* **layered** /ˈleɪ.əd/ ⓤⓢ /-ɚd/ *adj*

lay ˌcake *noun* [C] US two or more soft cakes put on top of each other with ICING (= a sweet creamy mixture) between the cakes and covering the top and sides

layette /leɪˈet/ *noun* [C] OLD-FASHIONED a complete set of clothes, sheets, bed covers and the other items needed for a baby who has recently been born

layman [CHURCH] /ˈleɪ.mən/ *noun* [C] (ALSO **layperson**) someone who is part of a religious organization but who is not paid or specially trained

layman [NOT TRAINED] /ˈleɪ.mən/ *noun* **[C]** (*ALSO* **layperson**) someone who is not trained in or does not have a detailed knowledge of a particular subject

layoff, lay-off /ˈleɪ.ɒf/ [US] /-ɑːf/ *noun* **1 [C often pl]** when someone stops employing someone, sometimes temporarily, because there is no money to pay them or because there is no work for them: *The recent economic crisis has led to massive layoffs.* **2 [C usually sing]** a period when someone is not working: *Foster is playing again after a six-week layoff due to injury.*

layout /ˈleɪ.aʊt/ *noun* **[C]** the way that something is arranged: *I like the the layout of the house.* ○ *Application forms vary greatly in layout and length.*

layover /ˈleɪˌəʊ.vəʳ/ [US] /-ˌoʊ.vɚ/ *noun* **[C]** *US FOR* **stopover** (= a short stay between parts of a journey, especially a plane journey): *We had a four-hour layover in Chicago.*

laywoman /ˈleɪˌwʊm.ən/ *noun* **[C]** a female layman

lazy /ˈleɪ.zi/ *adj* **1** *DISAPPROVING* not willing to work or use any effort: *Managers had complained that the workers were lazy and unreliable.* ○ *Get out of bed you lazy thing!* ○ *He's too lazy to walk to work.* **2** *APPROVING* slow and relaxed: *We spent a lazy day on the beach sunbathing.* **lazily** /ˈleɪ.zɪ.li/ *adv*: *Palm trees swayed lazily in the soft breeze.* **laziness** /ˈleɪ.zɪ.nəs/ *noun* **[U]** *I could go to the gym – it's just laziness that stops me.*

laze /leɪz/ *verb* **[I + adv or prep]** to relax and enjoy yourself, doing very little: *We spent the day lazing* ***around*** *in the garden.*

lazybones /ˈleɪ.zi.bəʊnz/ [US] /-boʊnz/ *noun* **[C]** *plural* **lazybones** *INFORMAL DISAPPROVING* someone who is lazy: **[as form of address]** *Hey lazybones, get up from the sofa and help me with the dishes!*

lb *noun* **[C]** *plural* **lb** or **lbs** *WRITTEN ABBREVIATION FOR* pound: *a 3lb bag of flour* ○ *I weighed 10lbs at birth.*

lbw /ˌel.biːˈdʌb.l̩.juː/ *adj, adv ABBREVIATION FOR* leg before wicket: (in cricket) describes a way of dismissing the BATSMAN (= person who is trying to hit the ball) by hitting his legs with the ball

LCD /ˌel.siːˈdiː/ *noun* **[C]** *ABBREVIATION FOR* **liquid-crystal display**

leach /liːtʃ/ *verb* **[T]** *SPECIALIZED* to remove a substance from a material, especially from earth, by the process of water moving through the material, or to remove parts of a material using water: *The soil has been so heavily leached through intensive farming that it is no longer fertile.*

lead [CONTROL] /liːd/ *verb* **[I or T] led, led** to control a group of people, a country, or a situation: *I think we've chosen the right person to lead the expedition.* ○ *I've asked Gemma to lead the discussion.* ○ *Who will be leading the inquiry into the accident?*

• **lead sb by the nose** *INFORMAL* to control someone and make them do exactly what you want them to do

lead [SHOW WAY] /liːd/ *verb* **led, led 1 [I]** to show the way to a group of people, animals, vehicles, etc. by going in front of them: *I don't know the way, so you'd better lead.* ○ *If you lead in the jeep, we'll follow behind on the horses.* **2 [T]** To lead a group of moving people or vehicles is to walk or drive in front of them: *The local youth band will lead the parade this weekend.* ○ *A large black hearse led the funeral procession.* **3 [T usually + adv or prep]** to take someone somewhere, by going with them: *She led them down the hall.* ○ *The waiter led us to our table.* ○ *Our guide led us through the mountains.* **4 [T usually + adv or prep]** to take hold of a person or an animal, or of something attached to them, and take them somewhere: *She took the child by the hand and led him upstairs to bed.* ○ *He led the horse out of the stable.*

• **lead the way 1** to show the way by going in front: *You've been there before – why don't you lead the way?* **2** to make more progress than other people in the development of something: *The company has been leading the way* ***in*** *network applications for several years.*

• **lead sb a (merry) dance** *INFORMAL* to cause someone a lot of trouble, especially by getting them to do a lot of things that are not necessary

• **lead sb up the garden path** *INFORMAL* to deceive someone: *It seems as if we've been led up the garden path about the position of our hotel – it's miles from the beach!*

lead /liːd/ *noun* **[C usually sing]** when you show a person or group of people what to do: *We'll go through the dance routine again –* ***follow*** *my lead* (= do what I do).

lead [INFORMATION] /liːd/ *noun* **[C]** a piece of information which allows a discovery to be made or a solution to be found: *A lead from an informer enabled the police to make several arrests.*

lead [DIRECTION] /liːd/ *verb* **[I or T; usually + adv or prep] led, led** (especially of roads, paths, doors, signs, information, etc.) to go in a particular direction or have a particular result, or to allow or cause this: *There's a track that leads directly* ***to*** *the reservoir.* ○ *The French windows lead* ***out onto*** *a wide shady terrace.* ○ *A narrow trail of blood led directly* ***into*** *the cave.* ○ *This information led the police* ***to*** *a house near the harbour.*

lead [BE WINNING] /liːd/ *verb* **[I or T] led, led** (especially in sport or other competitions) to be in front, to be first or to be winning: *After thirty minutes the challengers were leading* ***by*** *two goals.* ○ *With two laps to go Ngomo led* ***by*** *less than two seconds.* ○ *The Lions lead the Hawks 28 – 9.*

• **lead the field/pack/world** to be better than all other people or things: *Their scientists lead the world* ***in*** *nutrition research.*

lead /liːd/ *noun* **[S]** a winning position during a race or other situation where people are competing: *For the first time in the race Harrison is* ***in*** *the lead.* ○ *With a final burst of speed she* ***went/moved into*** *the lead.* ○ *After last night's win Johnson has* ***taken (over)*** *the lead in the championship table.* ○ *By the end of the day's play Davies had a lead* ***of*** *three points.*

lead [INFLUENCE] /liːd/ *verb* **[T] led, led** to cause someone to do something, especially something bad: **[+ *to* infinitive]** *The brochure led me* ***to believe*** *that the price included home delivery.* ○ *It's worrying that such a prominent politician is so* ***easily*** *led.* ○ *He was a weak man, led* ***astray*** *by ambition.*

lead [METAL] /led/ *noun* **[U]** a very dense, soft, dark-grey, poisonous metal, used especially in the past on roofs and for pipes and also for protection against radiation: *lead pipes*

• **go down like a lead balloon** *HUMOROUS* If something that you say or show to people goes down like a lead balloon, they do not like it at all: *My joke about the alcoholic went down like a lead balloon.*

leaded /ˈled.ɪd/ *adj* describes petrol (= fuel) with small amounts of lead in it ➲See also **unleaded**.

lead [PENCIL] /led/ *noun* **[C or U]** (the narrow strip of) coloured material, usually black and made of GRAPHITE, in the centre of a pencil

the lead [ACTOR] *noun* **[C]** the main actor in a film or play

lead [LIVE] /liːd/ *verb* **lead a busy/normal/quiet, etc. life** to live a particular type of life: *He was able to lead a normal life, despite the illness.* ○ *We certainly don't lead a life of luxury but we're not poor either.*

lead [ANIMAL] *MAINLY UK* /liːd/ *noun* **[C]** (*MAINLY US* **leash**) a piece of rope, chain, etc. tied to an animal, especially to a dog at its collar when taking it for a walk: *Please keep your dog* ***on*** *a lead when on the beach.*

lead [ELECTRICAL] /liːd/ *noun* **[C]** (*UK ALSO* **flex,** *US ALSO* **cord,** *US ALSO* **wire**) a wire covered in plastic and used to connect electrical equipment to the electricity supply

PHRASAL VERBS WITH **lead** ▼

▲ **lead sb on** *phrasal verb DISAPPROVING* to persuade someone to believe something that is untrue: *All that time she'd been leading him on* (= pretending she liked him)*, but she was only interested in his money.*

▲ **ˈlead ˌto sth** *phrasal verb* If an action or event leads to something, it causes that thing to happen or exist: *Reducing speed limits should lead to fewer deaths on the roads.*

▲ **lead up to sth** [HAPPEN] *phrasal verb* If a period of time or series of events leads up to an event or activity, it happens until that event or activity begins: *The pilot had no recollection of the events leading up to the crash.*

▲ **lead up to sth** [TALK] *phrasal verb* to prepare to talk about something by gradually mentioning the subject you want to talk about: *He started telling me about a wonderful new restaurant he'd been to and I wondered what he was leading up to.*

ˌleaded ˈwindow *noun* [C] a window made from small pieces of glass fixed together with lead strips

leaden /ˈled.ᵊn/ *adj* **1** LITERARY dark grey: *leaden skies* **2** DISAPPROVING without energy or feeling: *a leaden expression/performance*

leader [CONTROLLING] /ˈliː.dəʳ/ [US] /-dɚ/ *noun* [C] a person in control of a group, country or situation: *a religious leader* ○ *The Russian leader wants to introduce further changes.* ○ *He's a natural leader.* ○ *She was elected as leader **of** the campaign group.*

leader [WINNING] /ˈliː.dəʳ/ [US] /-dɚ/ *noun* [C] someone or something that is winning during a race or other situation where people are competing: *He's fallen two laps behind the leaders.* ○ *Microsoft is a world leader in software design.*

leader [NEWSPAPER] /ˈliː.dəʳ/ [US] /-dɚ/ *noun* [C] UK **editorial** ➲See at **edit**.

leader [MUSIC] UK /ˈliː.dəʳ/ [US] /-dɚ/ *noun* [C] (US **concertmaster**) the most important violin player in an orchestra

leadership /ˈliː.də.ʃɪp/ [US] /-dɚ-/ *noun* [U] **1** the set of characteristics that make a good leader: *What the company lacks is leadership.* ○ *He lacks leadership qualities/skills.* **2** the position or fact of being the leader: *The group flourished **under** her firm leadership.* ○ *R&M gained **market** leadership* (= sold more goods than other companies) *by selling products that were of superior quality.* **3 the leadership** the person or people in charge of an organization: *There is growing discontent with the leadership.* ○ *The election for the leadership **of** the council will take place on Tuesday.*

lead-in /ˈliːd.ɪn/ *noun* [C] something that introduces something else, such as the words and music that are used to introduce a television programme

leading [IMPORTANT] /ˈliː.dɪŋ/ *adj* [before n] very important or most important: *a leading **expert** on the country's ecology* ○ *the world's leading manufacturer of audio equipment*

leading [METAL] /ˈled.ɪŋ/ *noun* [U] UK the lead used to cover (parts of) a roof

ˌleading ˈarticle *noun* [C] UK **editorial** ➲See at **edit**.

ˌleading ˈedge *noun* [S] the most advanced position in an area of activity: *scientists **at** the leading edge of cancer research* **leading-edge** /ˌliː.dɪŋˈedʒ/ *adj* [before n] *leading-edge technology*

ˌleading ˈhand *noun* [C usually sing] AUS the most experienced person in a factory etc.

ˌleading ˈlady *noun* [C] the actress who has the most important part in a play or a film

ˌleading ˈlight *noun* [C] an important and respected person in a group or organization: *A leading light **in/of** the art and ballet world, he was a close friend of the Princess.*

ˌleading ˈman *noun* [C] the actor who has the most important part in a play or a film

ˌleading ˈquestion *noun* [C] a question that tricks someone into answering in a particular way

leaf [PLANT] /liːf/ *noun* [C] *plural* **leaves** **1** one of the flat, usually green parts of a plant which are joined at one end to the stem or branch: *a palm leaf* ○ *autumn leaves* ○ *He was sweeping up leaves in his garden.* **2 be in leaf/come into leaf** When a plant is in leaf or when it comes into leaf, it has or gets leaves on it: *The trees are in leaf early this year.* ○ *The bushes are just coming into leaf.*

leaf [PAPER] /liːf/ *noun* [C] *plural* **leaves** a thin sheet of paper
• **take a leaf out of *sb's* book** to copy something that someone else does because it will bring you advantages: *Maybe I should take a leaf out of Rick's book and start coming in at ten every morning.*

leaf [TABLE] /liːf/ *noun* [C] *plural* **leaves** an extra part of a table that can be folded away when not being used

leaf /liːf/ *verb*
▲ **leaf through *sth*** *phrasal verb* to quickly turn the pages of a book or a magazine, reading only a little of it: *The waiting room was full of people leafing through magazines.*

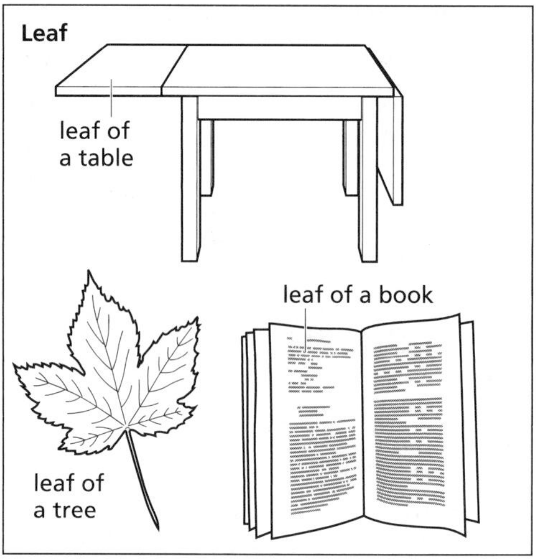

leaflet /ˈliː.flət/ *noun* [C] a piece of paper which gives you information or advertises something: *Demonstrators handed out leaflets to passers-by.* ○ *A leaflet about the new bus services came through the door today.*

leaflet /ˈliː.flət/ *verb* [I or T] **-t-** or UK ALSO **-tt-** to give out leaflets to people: *They leafleted the area two weeks before the event.*

ˈleaf ˌmould *noun* [U] a type of FERTILIZER (= substance that makes plants grow) made from leaves which fall from trees in the autumn

leafy /ˈliː.fi/ *adj* A leafy place is pleasant and has a lot of trees: *a leafy lane/suburb*

league [SPORT] /liːg/ *noun* [C] a group of teams playing a sport who take part in competitions between each other: *Who do you think will **win** the league championship this year?* ○ *Liverpool were **top of** the Football League that year.* ○ *They are currently **bottom of** the league.*
• **be in a different league** to be much better than something or someone else: *Our last hotel was quite good but this was in a different league.*
• **not be in the same league** to be not as good as someone or something else: *Her latest film is quite watchable but it's not in the same league **as** her first two epics.*
• **be out of *your* league** to be too good or too expensive for you: *He was so good-looking and so popular that I felt he was out of my league.*

league [ORGANIZATION] /liːg/ *noun* [C] a group of people or countries who join together because they have the same interest: *the League of Nations*
• **be in league with *sb*** to be secretly working or planning something with someone, usually to do something bad

leak /liːk/ *verb* [I or T] **1** (of a liquid or gas) to escape from a hole or crack in a pipe or container or (of a container) to allow liquid or gas to escape: *Water was leaking **from** the pipe.* ○ *Oil leaked **out** of the car.* ○ *The tin was leaking.* ○ *The car leaked oil all over the drive.* **2** to allow secret information to become generally known: *He leaked the names **to** the press.* ○ *News of the pay cuts had somehow leaked **out**.*
• **leak like a sieve** INFORMAL to leak a lot

leak /liːk/ *noun* [C] **1** a hole or space through which a liquid or gas can flow out of a container, or the liquid or gas that comes out: *There's water on the floor – we must have a leak.* ○ *If you suspect a **gas** leak, phone the emergency number.* **2** the origin of secret information which becomes known, or the act of making it known: *There have been several **security** leaks recently.* ○ *They traced the leak to a secretary in the finance department.*
• **take a leak/have a leak** SLANG to urinate

leakage /ˈliː.kɪdʒ/ *noun* [C or U] **1** the act of leaking or the leak itself: *The leakage was traced to an oil pipe in the cellar.* ○ *A lot of water is wasted through leakage.* **2** making known secret information

leaky /ˈliː.ki/ *adj* Something that is leaky has a hole in it and liquid or gas can get through: *leaky pipes* ○ *a leaky valve*

lean [SLOPE] /liːn/ *verb* [I or T; usually + adv or prep] **leaned** or *UK ALSO* **leant**, **leaned** or *UK ALSO* **leant** to (cause to) slope in one direction, or to move the top part of the body in a particular direction: *She leaned forward and whispered something in my ear.* ○ *I sat down next to Bernard, who leaned over to me and said "You're late."* ○ *Lean your head back a bit.* ○ *That fence is leaning to the right.*

lean [LITTLE FAT] /liːn/ *adj* **1** describes meat that has little fat **2** thin and healthy: *lean and fit* **3** If a period of time is lean, there is not enough of something, especially money or food, at that time: *It has been a particularly lean year for the education department.* **4** *APPROVING* A lean company or organization uses only a small number of people and a small amount of money etc. so that there is no waste: *Nowadays even efficient, lean, well-run industries are failing.*
• **lean and hungry** showing a very strong and determined desire to get something: *He's got that lean and hungry look.*

PHRASAL VERBS WITH **lean**

▲ **lean (*sth*) against/on *sth*** *phrasal verb* to sit or stand with part of your body touching something as a support: *He leaned against the wall.* ○ *She leaned her head on his shoulder.*
▲ **lean *sth* against/on *sth*** *phrasal verb* to put something against a wall or other surface so that it is supported: *She leant the brush against the wall.*
▲ **lean on *sb/sth*** [GET HELP] *phrasal verb* to use someone or something to help you, especially in a difficult situation: *He's always had his big brother to lean on.*
▲ **lean on *sb*** [PERSUADE] *phrasal verb INFORMAL* to try to make someone do what you want by threatening or persuading them: *We may have to lean on them a bit if we want our money.*

leaning /ˈliː.nɪŋ/ *noun* [C usually pl] a preference for a particular set of beliefs, opinions, etc: *I don't know what his political leanings are.*

lean-to /ˈliːn.tuː/ *noun* [C] **1** a building joined to one of the sides of a larger building with which it shares one wall: *a cottage with a lean-to garage* **2** *US* a shelter or simple building with a roof that slopes in one direction, which is slept in when camping

leap [MOVEMENT] /liːp/ *verb* [I + adv or prep] **leapt** or **leaped**, **leapt** or **leaped** to make a large jump or sudden movement, usually from one place to another: *He leapt out of his car and ran towards the house.* ○ *I leaped up to answer the phone* ○ *The dog leapt over the gate into the field.* **leap** /liːp/ *noun* [C] *With one leap he crossed the stream.*
• **by/in leaps and bounds** If someone or something gets better by/in leaps and bounds, they improve very quickly: *Her Spanish has* ***come on*** (= improved) *in leaps and bounds this year.*
• **a leap in the dark** something you do without being certain what will happen as a result: *I had very little information about the company, so writing to them was a bit of a leap in the dark.*

leap [SUDDEN CHANGE] /liːp/ *verb* **leapt** or **leaped**, **leapt** or **leaped** **1** [I + adv or prep] to provide help, protection etc. very quickly: *He leapt* ***to*** *his friend's defence.* ○ *Scott leapt* ***to*** *the rescue when he spotted the youngster in difficulty.* ○ *Mr Davies leapt* ***in*** *to explain.* **2** [I + adv or prep] to achieve something, usually fame, power or importance, suddenly: *Rufus Sewell leapt* ***to*** *fame after his lead performance as Will Ladislaw in the BBC's production of Middlemarch.* **3** [I + adv or prep] to increase, improve or grow very quickly: *Shares in the company leapt 250%.*
leap /liːp/ *noun* [C] a big change, increase or improvement: *a leap in profits* ○ *It takes quite a leap* ***of the imagination*** *to believe that it's the same person.*

PHRASAL VERBS WITH **leap**

▲ **leap at *sth*** *phrasal verb* to eagerly accept the chance to do or have something: *When I offered her the job, she leapt at it.*
▲ **leap out at *sb*** *phrasal verb* If something leaps out at you, you notice it immediately: *As I turned the page his picture leapt out at me.*

leapfrog /ˈliːp.frɒg/ [US] /-frɑːg/ *noun* [U] a children's game in which a number of children bend down and another child jumps over them one at a time
leapfrog /ˈliːp.frɒg/ [US] /-frɑːg/ *verb* [I or T; usually + adv or prep] **-gg-** to improve your position by going past other people quickly or by missing out some stages: *They've leapfrogged from third to first place.* ○ *She leapfrogged several older colleagues to get the manager's post.*

ˈleap ˌyear *noun* [C] a year that happens every four years and has an extra day on 29 February

learn /lɜːn/ [US] /lɝːn/ *verb* **learned** or *UK ALSO* **learnt**, **learned** or *UK ALSO* **learnt** **1** [I or T] to get knowledge or skill in a new subject or activity: *They learn Russian at school.* ○ *"Can you drive?" "I'm learning."* ○ *I've learned a lot* ***about*** *computers since I started work here.* ○ [+ *to* infinitive] *I'm learning* ***to*** *play the piano.* ○ [+ question word + *to* infinitive] *First you'll learn* ***(how) to*** *use this machine.* **2** [T] to make yourself remember a piece of writing by reading it or repeating it many times: *I don't know how actors manage to learn all those lines.* ○ *We were told to learn Portia's speech* ***by heart*** (= be able to say it from memory) *for homework.* **3** [I or T] to start to understand that you must change the way you behave: *She'll have to learn that she can't have everything she wants.* ○ *She soon learnt not* ***to*** *contradict him.* ○ *He's not afraid to learn* ***from his mistakes.*** **4** [I or T] to be told facts or information that you did not know: *We were all shocked to learn* ***of*** *his death.* ○ [+ (that)] *I later learnt* ***(that)*** *the message had never arrived.* ○ *I only learnt* ***about*** *the accident later.*
• **learn *your* lesson** to suffer a bad experience and know not to do it again: *I got horribly drunk once at college and that was enough – I learnt my lesson.*
• **learn to live with *sth*** to accept a new but unpleasant situation that you cannot change: *It's hard not having him around but I've learned to live with it.*
learned /lɜːnd/ [US] /lɜːrnd/ *adj SPECIALIZED* describes behaviour which has been copied from others: *This sort of aggression is learned behaviour – people aren't born that way.*
learner /ˈlɜː.nəʳ/ [US] /ˈlɝː.nɚ/ *noun* [C] a person who is still learning something: *He's a quick learner.* ○ *MAINLY UK a learner driver*
learning /ˈlɜː.nɪŋ/ [US] /ˈlɝː-/ *noun* [U] **1** the activity of obtaining knowledge: *This technique makes learning fun.* ○ *For the first month in her new job she was on a steep learning* ***curve*** (= she learnt a lot quickly). **2** knowledge obtained by study: *His friends praised his generosity, wit and learning.*

COMMON LEARNER ERROR

learn from

Remember to use the preposition 'from' when you are talking about **learning** something from someone or something.

I think I learnt a lot from my three years in the Navy.
~~*I think I learnt a lot with my three years in the Navy.*~~

COMMON LEARNER ERROR

learn, teach or study?

To **learn** is to get new knowledge or skills.

I want to learn how to drive.

When you **teach** someone, you give them new knowledge or skills.

My dad taught me how to drive.
~~*My dad learnt me how to drive.*~~

When you study, you go to classes, read books, etc. to try to understand new ideas and facts.

He is studying biology at university.

L

learned /'lɜː.nɪd/ ⓤ /'lɜːʳ-/ *adj FORMAL* describes someone who has studied for a long time and has a lot of knowledge: *a learned professor*

'learning ˌcurve *noun* [C] the rate of someone's progress in learning a new skill: *It's a pretty **steep** learning curve when you're thrown into a job with no prior experience.*

'learning ˌdifficulties *plural noun* mental problems which affect a person's ability to learn things: *Some of the children have specific learning difficulties.*

lease /liːs/ *verb* [T] to make a legal agreement by which money is paid in order to use land, a building, a vehicle or a piece of equipment for an agreed period of time: *The estate contains 300 new homes, about a third of which are leased **to** the council.* ○ [+ two objects] *It was agreed they would lease the flat **to** him/lease him the flat.*
lease /liːs/ *noun* [C] a legal agreement in which you pay money in order to use a building, piece of land, vehicle, etc. for a period: *He has the flat **on** a long lease.* ○ *The lease runs out/expires in two years' time.* ○ *We **signed** a three-year lease when we moved into the house.*

leaseback /'liːs.bæk/ *noun* [U] *SPECIALIZED* a legal agreement by which the owner of an item allows the previous owner to continue to use it for a regular amount of money

leasehold /'liːs.həʊld/ ⓤ /-hoʊld/ *noun* [C or U] the legal right to live in or use a building, piece of land, etc. for an agreed period of time: *His family **held** the leasehold/**had** the property **on** leasehold.* ⊃Compare **freehold**.
leasehold /'liːs.həʊld/ ⓤ /-hoʊld/ *adj: leasehold offices and shops*
leaseholder /'liːs.həʊl.dəʳ/ ⓤ /-hoʊl.dɚ/ *noun* [C] the person who pays the owner of a piece of land, a building, etc. in order to be able to use it

leash /liːʃ/ *noun* [C] *MAINLY US FOR* **lead** ANIMAL
'leash ˌlaw *noun* [C] a law in many US cities and towns that says people must keep their dogs on a LEASH when they are outside their home

least /liːst/ *adv, determiner, pronoun* less than anything or anyone else; the smallest amount or number: *This group is the least likely of the four to win.* ○ *Disaster struck when we least expected it.* ○ *It was the answer she least wanted to hear.* ○ *I like the green one least of all.* ○ *He's the relative I like **(the)** least.* ○ *No one believed her, least **of all** (= especially not) the police.* ○ *They refused to admit her, **not** least because (= there were several reasons but this was an important one) she hadn't got her membership card with her.*
● **at least 1** as much as, or more than, a number or amount: *It will cost at least $100.* ○ *It will be £200 at **the very** least.* ○ *You'll have to wait at least an hour.* **2** used to reduce the effect of a statement: *I've met the President – at least, he shook my hand once.* ⊃See also **leastways**. **3** used to emphasize that something is good in a bad situation: *It's a small house but at least there's a garden.* **4** used to say that someone should give a small amount of help although they do not intend to give a lot: *Even if she didn't want to send a present, she could at least have sent a card.*
● **it's the least I can do** a polite answer to someone who thanks you, usually when you feel you should do more to help: *"Thanks for cleaning up" "It's the least I can do, seeing as I'm staying here rent-free."*
● **not in the least** not in any way: *"Are you dissatisfied with the results?" "Not in the least."*
● **not the least** used for emphasis with nouns: *I haven't the least idea (= I do not know) who he was.* ○ *She hasn't the least interest (= She has no interest) in the project.*
● **Least said soonest mended.** *UK SAYING* This means a bad situation can be quickly forgotten if people stop talking about it.

leastways /'liːst.weɪz/ *adv US* used to reduce the effect of a statement: *He said he'd be back later – leastways, I think he did.* ⊃See also **at least** at **least**.

leather /'leð.əʳ/ ⓤ /-ɚ/ *noun* [U] animal skin treated in order to preserve it, and used to make shoes, bags, clothes, equipment, etc: *a leather coat/belt/handbag*

leatherette /ˌleð.ə'ret/ *noun* [U] *TRADEMARK* an artificial material which is made to look like leather

leathery /'leð.ᵊr.i/ ⓤ /-ɚ-/ *adj* with the look and feel of leather: *leathery skin/hands*

leave GO AWAY /liːv/ *verb* [I or T] **left, left** to go away from someone or something, for a short time or permanently: *I'll be leaving at five o'clock tomorrow.* ○ *He left the house by the back door.* ○ *She left the group of people she was with and came over to speak to us.* ○ *The bus leaves in five minutes.*

leave NOT TAKE /liːv/ *verb* **left, left 1** [T] to not take something or someone with you when you go, either intentionally or by accident: *Hey, you've left your keys on the table.* ○ *Can I leave a message **for** Sue?* ○ *Why don't you leave the kids **with** me on Friday?* **2** If something leaves something else, a part or effect of it stays after it has gone or been used: *His shoes left muddy marks on the floor.* ○ *There's some food left **over** from the party.* ○ [+ two objects] *If I give you £10 that won't leave me enough cash to pay the bill.* ○ [+ obj + adj] *Far from improving things the new law has left many people worse off* (= they are now in a worse situation) *than before.* **3** [T] To leave a wife, husband or other close family member is to die while these family members are still alive: *He left a wife and two children.* **4** [T] If you leave something in a particular condition, you do not touch it, move it or act to change it in any way, so that it stays in the same condition: *Leave that chair where it is.* ○ *He left most of his dinner* (= did not eat much of it). ○ [+ obj + adj] *The family were left* (= became and continued to be) *homeless.* ○ *I'll have to go back – I think I've left the iron on.* ○ *You can leave the window open.* ○ *Leave your sister alone* (= Stop annoying her). **5** [T + obj + v-ing] If you leave something or someone doing something, when you go away they are still doing it: *I left the children watching television.* ○ *He left the engine running.* **6** [T] If you leave (doing) something, you wait before you do it: *I'll leave these letters till Monday* (= write them on Monday). ○ *Don't leave it too late* (= Don't wait too long to do it). ○ [+ v-ing] *They left **booking** their holiday **till/to** the last minute.* **7** [+ two objects] If you leave money or things that you own to someone, you say they should receive it or them when you die: *He left his nieces all his money./He left all his money **to** his nieces.*
● **leave *sb* be** to not worry someone, or to allow them to continue what they are doing: *She's only having a bit of fun – leave her be.*
● **Leave it out!** *UK SLANG* **1** stop doing or saying that: *Hey, leave it out! That hurt.* **2** I don't believe you: *"I tell you, he was driving a sports car." "Leave it out!"*
● **leave a bad taste in *your* mouth** If an experience leaves a bad taste in your mouth, it leaves an unpleasant memory of it: *I think we all felt he'd been treated very unfairly and it left a bad taste in our mouths.*
● **leave a lot to be desired** to be much worse than you would like: *Apparently, Meg's cooking leaves a lot to be desired.*
● **leave *sb* cold** to not make you feel interested or excited: *I'm afraid opera leaves me cold.*
● **leave *sb* out in the cold** to not allow someone to become part of a group or an activity
● **be left holding the bag** (*US* **be left holding the bag**) to suddenly have to deal with a difficult situation because others have decided that they do not want the responsibility: *The other investors pulled out of the project and we were left holding the baby.*
● **leave *sb* in the lurch** to leave someone at a time when they need you to stay and help them
● **leave no stone unturned** to do everything you can to achieve a good result, especially when looking for something: *He left no stone unturned in his search for his natural mother.*
● **leave *sb* standing** (*ALSO* **leave *sb* on the sidelines**) to be much better than other people or things of the same type: *Her voice is excellent – it leaves the others standing.*
● **leave *sb* to *their* own devices** to allow someone to make their own decisions about what to do: *He seemed to be a responsible person, so I left him to his own devices.*
● **leave well alone** to allow something to stay as it is because doing more might make things worse: *It's going to get in a muddle if you carry on. I should just leave well alone if I were you.*

leave [STOP] /liːv/ *verb* [T] **left, left** to stop doing something, or to leave a place because you have finished an activity: *Many children leave school at sixteen.* ○ *He left work in June for health reasons.* ○ *She left **home*** (= stopped living with her parents) *at 18.* ○ *She's left her husband* (= stopped living with him) *and gone to live with another man.* ○ *Could we leave that subject* (= stop discussing that subject) *for the moment and go on to the next item on the agenda?*
- **leave go/hold of *sth*** INFORMAL to stop holding on to something: *Leave go of my arm!*
- **leave it at that** to agree that there has been enough discussion, study, etc. and that it is time to stop: *Let's leave it at that for today and meet again tomorrow.*

leave [GIVE RESPONSIBILITY] /liːv/ *verb* [T] **left, left** to allow someone to make a choice or decision about something, or to make someone responsible for something: *I left the decision **(up) to** her.* ○ [+ to infinitive] *I left it to her **to** make the decision.* ○ *Leave it* (= the problem) ***with** me, I'll see what I can do.* ○ *I'll leave it **to chance*** (= wait and see what happens without planning).

leave [PERMISSION] /liːv/ *noun* [U] FORMAL permission or agreement: *He did it **without** (my) leave.* ○ [+ to infinitive] *Did you **get** leave **to** do that?*
- **without so much as a by-your-leave** OLD-FASHIONED DISAPPROVING without asking for permission: *That's twice now he's just walked in here without so much as a by-your-leave and picked a book off the shelf!*

leave [HOLIDAY] /liːv/ *noun* [U] time permitted away from work for holiday or illness: *How much **annual/paid** leave do you get?* ○ *She's **(gone) on** leave* (= holiday). ○ *I've asked if I can take a week's **unpaid** leave.*
- **leave of absence** formal permission to be away from work or studies

leave [GOODBYE] /liːv/ *noun* **take leave** to say goodbye: *He decided the time had come to take leave **of** his home town.*
- **take leave of *your* senses** to lose your good judgment: *You can't take the children out sailing in this weather! Have you completely taken leave of your senses?*

PHRASAL VERBS WITH **leave** ▼

▲ **leave *sth* aside** *phrasal verb* [M] to not discuss one subject so that you can discuss a different subject: *Leaving aside the question of cost, how many people do we need on the job?*

▲ **leave *sth/sb* behind** [NOT TAKE] *phrasal verb* [M] to leave a place without taking someone or something with you: *We left in a hurry and I must have left my keys behind.* ○ *He was forced to leave the country, leaving behind his wife and children.*

▲ **leave *sth* behind** [CAUSE TO EXIST] *phrasal verb* [M] to cause a situation to exist after you have left a place: *The army left a trail of destruction behind them.*

▲ **leave *sth* for/to *sb*** *phrasal verb* to give someone responsibility for dealing with something: *I've left the paperwork for you.* ○ *Leave it to me – I'll sort it out tomorrow.*

▲ **leave *sth/sb* off *sth*** [NOT INCLUDE] *phrasal verb* to not include something or someone on a list: *He left three people off the list by mistake.*

▲ **leave off (*sth/doing sth*)** [STOP] *phrasal verb* to stop, or to stop doing something: *This film begins where the other one leaves off.* ○ *I've decided to leave off eating meat for a while.*

Leave off! /ˌliːvˈɒf/ (US) /-ˈɑːf/ OLD-FASHIONED INFORMAL used to tell someone to stop being annoying: *Hey, leave off! I hate people touching my hair.*

▲ **leave *sb/sth* out** *phrasal verb* [M] to not include someone or something: *You can leave the butter out of this recipe if you're on a low-fat diet.* ○ *I've made a list of names – I hope I haven't left anyone out.* ○ *None of the other children play with her, and I think she feels rather left out* (= feels that no one wants to be her friend).

leaven /ˈlev.ᵊn/ *verb* [T] **1** to add a substance to bread or another food made with flour to make it get bigger when it is cooked **2** FORMAL to make something less boring: *Even a speech on a serious subject should be leavened with a little humour.*

leaves /liːvz/ *plural of* **leaf**

leave-taking /ˈliːvˌteɪ.kɪŋ/ *noun* [C] FORMAL an act of saying goodbye

lech /letʃ/ *noun* [C] INFORMAL FOR **lecher**

lech /letʃ/ *verb*

▲ **lech after *sb*** *phrasal verb* INFORMAL DISAPPROVING to show too much sexual interest in someone, in an unpleasant way: *He's always leching after younger women.*

lecherous /ˈletʃ.ᵊr.əs/ (US) /-ɚ-/ *adj* DISAPPROVING (especially of men) showing a strong sexual interest in people: *He gave her a lecherous look.*
lecher /ˈletʃ.əʳ/ (US) /-ɚ/ *noun* [C] (INFORMAL **lech,** ALSO **letch**) DISAPPROVING a lecherous person **lechery** /ˈletʃ.ᵊr.i/ (US) /-ɚ-/ *noun* [U] FORMAL DISAPPROVING

lecithin /ˈles.ɪ.θɪn/ *noun* [U] a substance found in plant and animal tissue which is often used in food products to help the different parts mix together well

lectern /ˈlek.tən/ (US) /-tɝːn/ *noun* [C] a piece of furniture with a sloping part on which a book or paper is put to be read from

lecture /ˈlek.tʃəʳ/ (US) /-tʃɚ/ *noun* [C] **1** a formal talk on a serious or specialist subject given to a group of people, especially students: *We went to a lecture **on** Italian art.* ○ *Who's **giving** the lecture this afternoon?* ➲Compare **seminar**. **2** an angry or serious talk given to someone in order to criticize their behaviour: *My dad **gave** me a lecture **on** the evils of alcohol last night.*
lecture /ˈlek.tʃəʳ/ (US) /-tʃɚ/ *verb* **1** [I] to give a formal talk to a group of people, often at a university: *For ten years she lectured **in** law.* ○ *She travelled widely in North America, lecturing **on** women's rights.* **2** [T] to talk angrily to someone in order to criticize their behaviour: *His parents used to lecture him **on** his table manners.*

lecturer /ˈlek.tʃᵊr.əʳ/ (US) /-tʃɚ.ɚ/ *noun* [C] MAINLY UK someone who teaches at a college or university: *a senior lecturer* ○ *a lecturer in psychology*

USAGE

lecturer or teacher?

In American English, **lecturer** is formal. **Teacher** or **professor** is usually used instead.

lectureship /ˈlek.tʃə.ʃɪp/ (US) /-tʃɚ-/ *noun* [C] a post in a British university at the lowest rank: *a lectureship in linguistics*

led [LEAD] /led/ *past simple and past participle of* **lead**

-led [PLANNED] /-led/ *suffix* planned or controlled by a particular person or thing: *child-led activities* (= children deciding what to do)

LED [LIGHT] /ˌel.iːˈdiː/ *noun* [C] SPECIALIZED ABBREVIATION FOR light-emitting diode: a device which produces a light especially on electronic equipment

ˌLEˌD disˈplay *noun* [C] the letters or numbers shown in lights on a piece of electronic equipment

ledge /ledʒ/ *noun* [C] a narrow shelf which sticks out from a vertical surface

ledger /ˈledʒ.əʳ/ (US) /-ɚ/ *noun* [C] a book in which items are regularly recorded, especially business activities and money received or paid

lee /liː/ *noun* [S] the side of hill, wall, etc. that provides shelter from the wind

leech /liːtʃ/ *noun* [C] **1** a fat worm which lives in wet places and fastens itself onto the bodies of humans and animals to take their blood **2** DISAPPROVING a person who gives attention to someone over a long period in order to get their money or support

leek /liːk/ *noun* [C] a vegetable which looks like a white stick with long green leaves on top and which tastes and smells like an onion ➲See picture **Vegetables** on page Centre 2

leer /lɪəʳ/ (US) /lɪr/ *verb* [I] (especially of men) to look at someone in an unpleasant and sexually interested way: *He was always leering **at** female members of staff.* **leer** /lɪəʳ/ (US) /lɪr/ *noun* [C] *He gave the women at the bar a drunken leer.*

leery /ˈlɪə.ri/ (US) /ˈlɪr.i/ *adj* [after v] INFORMAL not trusting of someone or something and tending to avoid them if possible; WARY: *I've always been a bit leery **of** authority figures.*

L

the lees /ðəˈliːz/ *plural noun* the substance which is left at the bottom of a container of liquid, especially in a bottle of wine

leeward /ˈliː.wəd/ [US] /-wɚd/ *adj SPECIALIZED* (on the side of a ship, etc.) facing away from the wind

leeway [FREEDOM] /ˈliː.weɪ/ *noun* [U] freedom to act within particular limits: *Local councils will be* ***given*** *some leeway as to how they implement the legislation.*

leeway [PERIOD OF TIME] /ˈliː.weɪ/ *noun* [U] *UK* an amount or period of time, which might be additional or wasted: *There is a lot of leeway to* ***make up*** *after the holiday period.*

left [DIRECTION] /left/ *adj, adv* on or towards the side of your body that is to the west when you are facing north: *His left eye was heavily bandaged.* ○ ***Turn*** *left at the lights.* ➲Compare **right** DIRECTION.

left /left/ *noun* [S] the left side: *First I'll introduce the speaker sitting* ***on*** *my left.* ○ *Take the first/second/third* ***on the*** *left.* ○ *It's the shop to the left of the pub.* ○ *US After the grocery store I* ***made/took/*** *(INFORMAL)* ***hung*** *a left* (= turned into the next road on the left side).

the left [POLITICS], **the Left** *group noun* [S] the political groups that believe wealth and power should be shared between all parts of society: *The war is generally opposed* ***on*** *the left.* ➲Compare **the right** POLITICS. **left** /left/ *adj*: *The left* ***wing*** *of the party is unhappy with the legislation.*

leftie /ˈlef.ti/ *noun* [C] (*ALSO* **lefty**) *INFORMAL DISAPPROVING* a supporter of the political left

leftist /ˈlef.tɪst/ *noun* [C] a supporter of the political left

leftist /ˈlef.tɪst/ *adj* supporting the political left **leftism** /ˈlef.tɪ.zᵊm/ *noun* [U]

leftwards /ˈleft.wədz/ [US] /-wɚdz/ *adv* (*MAINLY US* **leftward**) towards the left in politics: *He accused the party leadership of moving leftwards.*

left [LEAVE] /left/ *past simple and past participle of* **leave**

ˌleft ˈfield *noun* [S] the left part of the field in baseball

• **be out in left field** *US INFORMAL* **1** to be completely wrong **2** to be very strange or very different from other people or things: *She's kind of out in left field but she's fun.*

• **come out of/in left field** *US INFORMAL* to be completely unexpected and often strange: *Her comments came out of left field.*

left-hand /ˈleft.hænd/ *adj* [before n] on or to the left: *the left-hand side*

ˌleft-hand ˈdrive *adj* describes a vehicle which has the STEERING WHEEL on the left-hand side **ˌleft-hand ˈdrive** *noun* [S]

left-handed /ˌleftˈhæn.dɪd/ *adj* **1** using your left hand to write and do most things: *Are you left-handed?* ○ *a left-handed bowler* **2** designed to be used by a left-handed person: *left-handed scissors* **3** done using the left hand: *a left-handed stroke* **left-handed** /ˌleftˈhæn.dɪd/ *adv* **left-handedness** /ˌleftˈhæn.dɪd.nəs/ *noun* [U]

ˌleft-handed ˈcompliment *US noun* [C] (*UK* **back-handed compliment**) a remark that seems to say something pleasant about a person but could also be an insult

left-hander /ˌleftˈhæn.dəʳ/ [US] /-dɚ/ *noun* [C] **1** someone who uses their left hand to write and do most things **2** (*ALSO* **left**) *INFORMAL* a hit with the left hand: *a powerful left-hander*

left-luggage office *UK* /ˌleftˈlʌg.ɪdʒ,ɒf.ɪs/ [US] /-ˌɑː.fɪs/ *noun* [C] (*US* **baggage room**) a place at a station, airport, hotel, etc. where you can put your bags for a short time until you need them ➲Compare **cloakroom**.

ˌleft of ˈcentre *UK, US* **left of center** *adj* describes a political belief that is accepted by most people and contains some SOCIALIST ideas

leftover /ˈleftˌəʊ.vəʳ/ [US] /ˈleftˌoʊ.vɚ/ *adj* [before n] describes part of something that has not been used or eaten when the other parts have been: *some leftover curry from last night's meal*

leftovers /ˈleftˌəʊ.vəz/ [US] /ˈleftˌoʊ.vɚz/ *plural noun* food remaining after a meal: *This recipe can serve four easily, and the leftovers are just as good eaten cold.*

left-wing /ˌleftˈwɪŋ/ *adj* relating to the belief that wealth and power should be shared equally: *Her views are fairly left-wing.* **left-winger** /ˌleftˈwɪŋ.əʳ/ [US] /-ɚ/ *noun* [C]

leg [BODY PART] /leg/ *noun* [C] **1** one of the parts of the body of a human or animal that is used for standing or walking, or one of the thin vertical parts of an object on which it stands: *My legs were tired after so much walking.* ○ *He broke his leg skiing.* ○ *The horse broke its front leg in the fall.* ○ *a chair/table leg* ➲See picture **The Body** on page Centre 5 **2** the part of a piece of clothing that you put your leg in: *He rolled up his trouser legs and waded into the water.*

• **not have a leg to stand on** to be in a situation where you cannot prove something: *If you haven't got a witness, you haven't got a leg to stand on.*

• **get *your* leg over** *UK SLANG* (of a man) to have sex

• **give *sb* a leg up** *INFORMAL* **1** to help someone to climb over something **2** to help someone to improve their situation, especially at work

• **have a leg up on *sb*** *US INFORMAL* to have an advantage over someone

• **pull *sb's* leg** *INFORMAL* to try to persuade someone to believe something which is not true as a joke: *Is it really your car or are you pulling my leg?*

• **leg before wicket** (*ABBREVIATION* **lbw**) in the game of cricket, when your time as the person trying to hit the ball is ended because the ball has hit your leg when it should not have

-legged /-leg.ɪd/ *suffix* having the number or type or legs mentioned: *a three-legged stool* ○ *a six-legged creature*

leg /leg/ *verb UK INFORMAL* **leg it** to run away in order to escape from something: *They legged it round the corner when they saw the police coming.*

leg [STAGE] /leg/ *noun* [C] a particular stage of a journey, competition or activity: *He has tickets for the* ***first*** *leg* ***of*** *the UEFA Cup tie.* ○ *The* ***last*** *leg* ***of*** *the race was Paris to London.*

legacy /ˈleg.ə.si/ *noun* [C] **1** money or property that you receive from someone after they die: *An elderly cousin had* ***left*** *her a small legacy.* **2** something that is a part of your history or which stays from an earlier time: *The Greeks have a rich legacy* ***of*** *literature.* ○ *The war has left a legacy* ***of*** *hatred.*

legal /ˈliː.gᵊl/ *adj* connected with the law: *legal advice* ○ *a legal obligation/requirement* ○ *legal status* ○ *your legal rights* ○ *legal action/proceedings* ○ *my legal representatives* (= my lawyers)

• **make legal history** If you make legal history, the case you win in court or take to court is the first of its type and changes the way future cases will be dealt with.

legal /ˈliː.gᵊl/ *adj* allowed by the law: *Is abortion legal in your country?* * NOTE: The opposite is **illegal**.

legally /ˈliː.gᵊl.i/ *adv* as stated by the law: *Children under sixteen are not legally allowed to buy cigarettes.*

ˌlegal ˈaid *noun* [U] a system of providing free advice about the law and practical help with legal matters for people who are too poor to pay for it: *Will we qualify for legal aid?*

legalese /ˌliː.gᵊlˈiːz/ *noun* [U] *DISAPPROVING* language used by lawyers and in legal documents, which is difficult for ordinary people to understand

legalistic /ˌliː.gᵊlˈɪs.tɪk/ *adj DISAPPROVING* giving too much attention to legal rules and details **legalistically** /ˌliː.gᵊlˈɪs.tɪ.kli/ *adv*

legality /liːˈgæl.ə.ti/ [US] /-t̬i/ *noun* [U] the fact that something is allowed by the law: *Six journalists sought to challenge in court the legality* ***of*** *the ban on broadcasting.*

legalities /liːˈgæl.ə.tiz/ [US] /-t̬iz/ *plural noun* the things which are demanded by law: *I'm not sure about the legalities, but I suggest we go ahead with the plan and see what happens.*

legalize, *UK USUALLY* **-ise** /ˈliː.gᵊl.aɪz/ *verb* [T] to allow something by law: *The Irish government announced it was to legalize homosexuality.* **legalization**, *UK USUALLY* **-isation** /ˌliː.gᵊl.aɪˈzeɪ.ʃᵊn/ *noun* [U] *the legalization of drugs*

ˌlegal ˈtender *noun* [U] the money which can be officially used in a country

legation /lɪˈgeɪ.ʃᵊn/ *noun* [C] *SPECIALIZED* **1** a group of officials who represent their government in a foreign country but who have less importance than an EMBASSY:

Britain has sent a legation to discuss trade and tariffs. **2** the office in which these officials work

legato /lɪˈgɑː.təʊ/ [US] /-toʊ/ *adj, adv* SPECIALIZED describes music that is played in a smooth continuous way, or this way of playing music: *smooth legato phrasing*

legend [STORY] /ˈledʒ.ᵊnd/ *noun* [C or U] a very old story or set of stories from ancient times, or the stories, not always true, that people tell about a famous event or person: *The dance was based on several Hindu legends.* ○ *She is writing a thesis on Irish legend and mythology.* ○ *Legend* ***has it*** (= People say) *that he always wore his boots in bed.* ○ *This match will go into tennis legend* (= it will always be remembered).

legendary /ˈledʒ.ᵊn.dri/ [US] /-der.i/ *adj* from a legend: *a legendary Greek hero* ○ *Was King Arthur a real or a legendary character?*

legend [FAME] /ˈledʒ.ᵊnd/ *noun* [C] someone or something very famous and admired, usually because of their ability in a particular area: *Jazz legend, Ella Fitzgerald, once sang in this bar.*

legendary /ˈledʒ.ᵊn.dri/ [US] /-der.i/ *adj* very famous and admired or spoken about: *He became editor of the legendary Irish journal 'The Bell'.* ○ *The British are legendary* (= well known) ***for*** *their incompetence with languages.*

legend [EXPLANATION] /ˈledʒ.ᵊnd/ *noun* [C] FORMAL the words written on or next to a picture, map, coin, etc. that explain what it is about or what the symbols on it mean

leggings /ˈleg.ɪŋz/ *plural noun* a pair of very tight trousers made from a material that stretches easily, usually worn by women ➲See picture **Clothes** on page Centre 6

leggy /ˈleg.i/ *adj* A leggy woman or girl has long legs: *She was a tall leggy blonde.*

legible /ˈledʒ.ɪ.bl̩/ *adj* describes writing or print that can be read easily: *Her handwriting is barely legible.* * NOTE: The opposite is **illegible**. **legibly** /ˈledʒ.ɪ.bli/ *adv*

legion [SOLDIERS] /ˈliː.dʒᵊn/ *noun* [C] a large group of soldiers who form a part of an army, especially the ancient Roman army: *Caesar's legions marched through France and crossed into Britain.*

legion [MANY] /ˈliː.dʒᵊn/ *adj* [after v] FORMAL very large in number: *The difficulties surrounding the court case are legion.*

legions /ˈliː.dʒᵊnz/ *plural noun* **legions of sb** large numbers of people: *He failed to turn up for the concert, disappointing the legions of fans waiting outside.*

Legionnaire's disease /liː.dʒᵊnˈeəz.dɪˌziːz/ [US] /-erz-/ *noun* [U] a serious and infectious disease of the lungs caused by bacteria in the air

legislate /ˈledʒ.ɪ.sleɪt/ *verb* [I] FORMAL If a government legislates, it makes a new law: *They promised to legislate* ***against*** *cigarette advertising.* ○ *It's hard to legislate* ***for*** (= make a law that will protect) *the ownership of an idea.*

legislative /ˈledʒ.ɪ.slə.tɪv/ [US] /-t̬ɪv/ *adj* FORMAL relating to laws or the making of laws: *The European Parliament will have greater legislative powers* (= ability to make laws).

legislation /ˌledʒ.ɪˈsleɪ.ʃᵊn/ *noun* [U] a law or set of laws suggested by a government and made official by a parliament: [+ *to* infinitive] *The government has promised to introduce legislation* ***to*** *limit fuel emissions from cars.*

ˌlegislative asˈsembly *noun* [C usually sing] (US USUALLY **assembly**) one of the two parts of the organization that makes laws in some American and Australian states, most Canadian PROVINCES and some countries

ˌlegislative ˈcouncil *noun* [C usually sing] one of the two parts of the organization which makes laws in some Australian and Indian states

legislator /ˈledʒ.ɪ.sleɪ.təʳ/ [US] /-t̬ɚ/ *noun* [C] FORMAL a member of a group of people who together have the power to make laws

legislature /ˈledʒ.ɪ.slə.tʃʊəʳ/ [US] /-tʃɚ/ *group noun* [C] FORMAL the group of people in a country or part of a country who have the power to make and change laws

legit /ləˈdʒɪt/ *adj* [after v] INFORMAL **legitimate**: *I'm not getting involved in this fund-raising scheme if it isn't legit.*

legitimate /ləˈdʒɪt.ɪ.mət/ [US] /-ˈdʒɪt̬-/ *adj* **1** allowed by law: *The army must give power back to the legitimate government.* **2** reasonable and acceptable: *He claimed that the restaurant bill was a legitimate business expense.* **3** A legitimate child is one whose parents are legally married at the time of his or her birth.

legitimately /ləˈdʒɪt.ɪ.mət.li/ [US] /-ˈdʒɪt̬-/ *adv*: *Most foreign visitors to Britain enter the country legitimately* (= legally).

legitimacy /ləˈdʒɪt.ɪ.mə.si/ [US] /-ˈdʒɪt̬-/ *noun* [U] *The government expressed serious doubts about the legitimacy of military action* (= about whether it is allowed by law).

legitimize, UK USUALLY **-ise** /ləˈdʒɪt.ɪ.maɪz/ [US] /-ˈdʒɪt̬-/ *verb* [T] (US **legitimate**) FORMAL *The government fears that talking to terrorists might legitimize* (= make acceptable) *their violent actions.*

legless /ˈleg.ləs/ *adj* [after v] UK SLANG extremely drunk

Lego /ˈleg.əʊ/ [US] /-oʊ/ *noun* [U] TRADEMARK a toy for children consisting of small plastic bricks and other pieces such as wheels and windows, which can be joined together to make models of many different objects

legroom /ˈleg.ruːm/ *noun* [U] the amount of space available for your legs when you are sitting behind another seat: *a car with plenty of legroom*

legume /ˈleg.juːm/ *noun* [C] SPECIALIZED a plant that has its seeds in a pod, such as the bean or pea **leguminous** /ˌlegˈjuː.mɪ.nəs/ *adj*: *leguminous plants*

legwarmers /ˈlegˌwɔː.məz/ [US] /-ˌwɔːr.mɚz/ *plural noun* long knitted leg-coverings, similar to socks but without feet, worn mainly by dancers to keep the lower leg muscles warm

legwork /ˈleg.wɜːk/ [US] /-wɝːk/ *noun* [U] INFORMAL the practical or boring work that needs to be done

leisure /ˈleʒ.əʳ/ [US] /-ɚ/ *noun* [U] the time when you are not working or doing other duties: *leisure activities* ○ *Most people only have a limited amount of leisure* ***time***. ○ *The town lacks leisure* ***facilities*** *such as a swimming pool or squash courts.*

• **at (your) leisure** when you want to and when you have time to: *You can take the documents home and study them at (your) leisure.*

leisurely /ˈleʒ.ə.li/ [US] /-ɚ-/ *adj* describes an action that is done in a relaxed way, without hurrying: *We enjoyed a leisurely picnic lunch on the lawn.*

ˈleisure ˌcentre *noun* [C] UK a building containing a swimming pool and other places where you can play sports

ˈleisure ˌwear *noun* [U] clothes that are worn for relaxing in

leitmotiv /ˈlaɪt.məʊ.tiːf/ [US] /-moʊ.t̬iːf/ *noun* [C] (ALSO **leitmotif**) SPECIALIZED a phrase or other feature that is repeated frequently in a work of art, literature or especially music and that tells you something important about it: *Death and renewal are leitmotivs running through the whole novel.*

lemming /ˈlem.ɪŋ/ *noun* [C] an animal that looks like a large mouse and lives in cold northern areas. Lemmings MIGRATE (= move from one place to another) in large groups and are often, but wrongly, thought to jump off cliffs together.

• **like lemmings** foolishly, without thinking, and in large numbers: *People rushed like lemmings to invest in the company.*

lemon /ˈlem.ən/ *noun* **1** [C or U] an oval fruit which has a thick yellow skin and sour juice: *For this recipe you need the juice of two lemons.* ○ *Would you like* ***a slice of*** *lemon in your tea?* ○ *lemon juice* ➲See picture **Fruit** on page Centre 1 **2** [U] the juice of a lemon or a drink made from this juice **3** [U] a pale yellow colour **4** [C] UK INFORMAL a very foolish person: *I felt such a lemon when I discovered I'd missed my appointment.* **5** [C] MAINLY US INFORMAL something that does not work: *Only one of his inventions turned out to be a lemon.*

lemonade /ˌlem.əˈneɪd/ *noun* [U] **1** UK a cold sweet fizzy drink with a lemon flavour **2** MAINLY US a drink made with the juice of lemons, water and sugar

ˌlemon ˈcurd MAINLY UK *noun* [U] (AUS **lemon butter**) a thick sweet substance made from lemons, sugar, eggs and butter that you can spread on bread or cakes

ˈlemon ˌgrass *noun* [U] a tropical grass with a lemon-like flavour, used especially in South East Asian cooking

ˌlemon ˈsole *noun* [C usually sing] a flat fish that can be cooked and eaten

lemur /ˈliː.məʳ/ [US] /-mɚ/ *noun* [C] a small monkey-like animal from Madagascar with thick fur and a long tail, which lives in trees and is active at night

lend /lend/ *verb* **lent, lent 1** [T] to give something to someone for a short period of time, expecting it to be given back: *She doesn't like lending her books.* ○ [+ two objects] *If you need a coat I can lend you one/lend one **to** you.* **2** [I or T] If a bank or other organization lends money, it gives money to someone who agrees that they will pay the money back in the future, usually with additional money added to the original amount: *The bank refuses to lend **to** students.* ○ [+ two objects] *The bank agreed to lend him $5000.* **3** [T] If something lends a particular quality to something else, it adds that quality to it: [+ two objects] *Vases of flowers all around the room lent the place a cheerful look/lent a cheerful look **to** the place.* ○ FORMAL *These events lend support to the view that the law is inadequate.*

• **lend itself to *sth*** FORMAL If something lends itself to something else, it is suitable for that thing or can be considered in that way: *The novel's complex, imaginative style does not lend itself to translation.*

• **lend an ear** OLD-FASHIONED to listen to someone with sympathy: *Claire's always one to lend a sympathetic ear if you have problems.*

• **lend *your* name to *sth*** to give something your support: *Some of the world's top dancers have lent their names to the project.*

COMMON LEARNER ERROR

lend or **borrow?**

Lend means to give something to someone for a period of time.

It was raining so she lent me an umbrella.

Borrow means to receive something which belongs to someone else and to use it for a period of time.

Can I borrow your umbrella?

~~Can I lend your umbrella?~~

lender /ˈlen.dəʳ/ [US] /-dɚ/ *noun* [C] someone or something that lends money, especially a large financial organization such as a bank: *The smaller local lenders charge high interest rates.*

ˈlending ˌlibrary *noun* [C] OLD-FASHIONED FOR **public library**

ˈlending ˌrate MAINLY UK *noun* [C] (ALSO **interest rate**) the amount that a bank charges on money that it lends: *Banks have raised their lending rates by 2%.*

length [DISTANCE] /leŋkθ/ *noun* **1** [C or U] the measurement of something from end to end or along its longest side: *The boat is ten metres **in** length.* ○ *The length of the bay is approximately 200 miles.* ○ *She planted rose bushes **(along) the** length **of** the garden* (= the whole distance along it). **2** [C] a piece of something such as string or pipe: *a length of rope* **3** [C] a unit used in describing the distance by which a horse or boat wins a race, which is equal to the measurement from one end of the horse or boat to the other: *We won by two lengths.* **4** [C] the distance from one end of a swimming pool to the other: *She swims forty lengths a day.*

• **the length and breadth of *somewhere*** If you travel the length and breadth of a place, you go to every part of it: *She travelled the length and breadth of Ireland looking for her missing brother.*

-length /-leŋkθ/ *suffix* Something which is a particular -length is long enough to reach the stated place: *a knee-length skirt* ○ *shoulder-length hair*

length [TIME] /leŋkθ/ *noun* **1** [C] the amount of time something takes: *the length of a film/speech/play* ○ *He is unable to concentrate on his work for any length **of time*** (= for anything more than a short time). **2** [C or U] the amount of writing in a book or document: *He's written books of various lengths on the subject.* ○ *All of your essays will be about the same length.*

• **at length 1** for a long time: *George went on at **great** length about his various illnesses.* **2** FORMAL If something happens at length, it happens after a long period of time: *At length, the authorities allowed her to go home.*

• **go to great lengths** (ALSO **go to any lengths**) to try very hard to achieve something: *Some people go to great lengths to make their homes attractive.* ○ *He'll go to any lengths to get what he wants.*

-length /-leŋkθ/ *suffix* of the stated amount of time: *a full-length movie* (= one which has not been shortened)

lengthen /ˈleŋk.θən/ *verb* [I or T] **1** to make something longer, or to become longer: *I'll have to lengthen this skirt.* ○ *lengthening waiting lists* ∗ NOTE: The opposite is **shorten**. **2** If you lengthen something, or it lengthens, it takes longer to happen: *There is a plan to lengthen the three-year course to four years.*

lengthways /ˈleŋkθ.weɪz/ *adv* (ALSO **lengthwise**) in the direction of the longest side: *Cut the beans in half lengthways.*

lengthy /ˈleŋk.θi/ *adj* continuing for a long time: *a lengthy discussion/process* ○ *Many airline passengers face lengthy delays because of the strike.*

lenient /ˈliː.ni.ənt/ *adj* not as severe or strong in punishment or judgment as would be expected: *They believe that judges are too lenient **with** terrorist suspects.* ○ *In view of the quantity of drugs involved, 16 years was the most lenient **sentence*** (= punishment) *the judge could impose.* **leniently** /ˈliː.ni.ənt.li/ *adv* **leniency** /ˈliː.ni.ənt.si/ *noun* [U] *The defending lawyer asked for leniency on the grounds of her client's youth.*

Leninism /ˈlen.ɪ.nɪ.zᵊm/ *noun* [U] the social, political and economic principles and theories developed from MARXISM by the Russian politician V.I. Lenin, supporting direct rule by workers **Leninist** /ˈlen.ɪ.nɪst/ *noun* [C]

lens [GLASS] /lenz/ *noun* [C] **1** a curved piece of glass, plastic or other transparent material used in cameras, glasses and scientific equipment, which makes objects seem closer, larger, smaller, etc: *a camera with a zoom lens* **2 contact lens**

lens [EYE] /lenz/ *noun* [C] the part of the eye behind the PUPIL (= the black hole at the front of the eye) that helps you to see clearly by FOCUSING (= collecting) light onto the RETINA

lent [LEND] /lent/ *past simple and past participle of* **lend**

Lent [RELIGION] /lent/ *noun* [U] in the Christian religion, the 40 days before EASTER, a period during which, for religious reasons, some people stop doing particular things that they enjoy: *The children have promised to **give up** sweets **for** Lent.*

lentil /ˈlen.tᵊl/ [US] /-t̬ᵊl/ *noun* [C] a very small dried bean that is cooked and eaten: *lentil soup* ○ *red/green/brown lentils*

Leo /ˈliː.əʊ/ [US] /-oʊ/ *noun* [C or U] *plural* **Leos** the fifth sign of the zodiac, relating to the period 23 July to August 22, represented by a lion, or a person born during this period, or a particular group of stars

leonine /ˈliː.ə.naɪn/ *adj* FORMAL (often of a person's head or hair) like a lion

leopard /ˈlep.əd/ [US] /-ɚd/ *noun* [C] a large wild cat that has yellow fur with black spots on it and lives in Africa and southern Asia

• **A leopard can't/doesn't change its spots.** SAYING something you say which means a person's character, especially if it is bad, will not change, even if they pretend it does

leotard /ˈliː.ə.tɑːd/ [US] /-tɑːrd/ *noun* [C] a tight piece of clothing that covers the body but not the legs, usually worn by female dancers or women doing physical exercise

leprechaun /ˈlep.rɪ.kɔːn/ [US] /-kɑːn/ *noun* [C] (in old Irish stories) a magical creature in the shape of a little old man who likes to cause trouble

leprosy /ˈlep.rə.si/ *noun* [U] an infectious disease that damages a person's nerves and skin

leper /ˈlep.əʳ/ [US] /-ɚ/ *noun* [C] **1** a person who has leprosy **2** a person who is strongly disliked and avoided by other people because of something bad that he or she has done: *She claimed that the rumours had made her a **social** leper.*

lesbian /ˈlez.bi.ən/ *noun* [C] a woman who is sexually attracted to other women: *gays and lesbians* **lesbian** /ˈlez.bi.ən/ *adj*

lesbianism /ˈlez.bi.ə.nɪ.zᵊm/ *noun* [U] the condition of being a lesbian

lesion /ˈliː.ʒᵊn/ *noun* [C] *SPECIALIZED* an injury to a person's body or to an organ inside their body: *skin/brain lesions*

less [SMALLER AMOUNT] /les/ *determiner, pronoun, adv* a smaller amount (of); not so much, or to a smaller degree: *We must try to spend less money.* ○ *Exercise more and eat less.* ○ *I eat less chocolate and fewer biscuits* ***than*** *I used to.* ○ *Getting out of bed in summer is less difficult* ***than*** *in winter.*

• **less than ...** describes behaviour which lacks a stated characteristic that is good or desirable: *I think he was less than honest with me.*

• **less and less** If something happens less and less, it becomes gradually not so frequent or smaller in amount: *He's less and less able to look after himself.*

• **much/still less** *FORMAL* used to make a negative statement stronger: *At the age of fourteen I had never even been on a train, much less an aircraft.*

• **no less than** used to show your surprise at a large number: *There were no less than a thousand people there buying tickets.*

• **no less** *HUMOROUS* used to show the importance of someone or something: *Who should arrive at the party but the Prime Minister, no less!*

lessen /ˈles.ᵊn/ *verb* [I or T] If something lessens or is lessened, it becomes less strong: *A healthy diet can lessen the risk of heart disease.*

lesser /ˈles.əʳ/ [US] /-ɚ/ *adj* [before n] used to describe something that is not as great in size, amount or importance as something else: *A lesser* ***man*** (= a man who was not as strong or brave) *might have given up at that point.* ○ *The charge of murder was altered to the lesser* (= less serious) *charge of manslaughter.* ○ *Ethiopia and,* ***to a*** *lesser* ***extent/degree***, *Kenya will be badly affected by the drought.*

• **the lesser of two evils** the less unpleasant of two choices, neither of which are good: *But allowing a criminal to go free is perhaps the lesser of two evils if the alternative is imprisoning an innocent person.*

USAGE

less or fewer?

It is quite common for English speakers to use **less** before countable nouns, meaning 'not so many'.

The trees have produced less apples this year

However, this is traditionally considered bad English. The standard word for 'not so many' is **fewer**.

The trees have produced fewer apples this year.

The standard use of **less** is before uncountable nouns, meaning 'not so much'.

less money/time/food

-less [WITHOUT] /-ləs/ /-lɪs/ *suffix* used to form adjectives meaning 'without (the thing mentioned)': *meaningless* ○ *friendless*

less [SUBTRACT] /les/ *prep* **minus** SUBTRACTION: *The total is thirty pounds, less the five pounds deposit that you've paid.*

lesser-known /ˌles.əˈnəʊn/ [US] /-ɚˈnoʊn/ *adj* not as popular or famous as something else: *We stayed on one of the lesser-known Greek islands.*

lesson /ˈles.ᵊn/ *noun* [C] **1** a period of time in which a person is taught about a subject or how to do something: *How can we make science lessons more interesting?* ○ *She has never* ***had/taken*** *any acting lessons.* ○ *He* ***gives*** *French lessons.* **2** an experience which teaches you how to behave better in a similar situation in the future: *There is a lesson for all parents* ***in*** *this tragic accident.* ○ *My parents made me pay back all the money and it was a lesson I never forgot.* ○ *We can* ***learn*** *important lessons* (= gain new understanding) ***from*** *this disaster.*

lest /lest/ *conjunction LITERARY* in order to prevent any possibility that something will happen: *They were afraid to complain about the noise lest they annoyed the neighbours.*

let [ALLOW] /let/ *verb* **letting, let, let 1** [T + infinitive without *to*] to allow something to happen or someone to do something by not doing anything to stop an action or by giving your permission: *She wanted to go but her parents wouldn't let her.* ○ *He decided to let his hair grow long.* ○ *Let your shoes dry completely before putting them on.* ○ *I'm letting you stay up late, just this once.* ○ *Don't let it worry you.* ○ *If he needs money, let him* (= he should) *earn it!* ⮊See Note **allow or let?** at **allow** PERMIT. **2** [T + obj + infinitive without *to*; not in past tenses] used to show that you accept what is going to happen, although you do not like it: *Let it rain – it won't spoil our afternoon.* ⮊See Note **allow** or **let?** at **allow** PERMIT.

• **let *sb* be** to stop criticizing or annoying someone

• **let *sb* in on a secret** to allow someone to know something that you have not told anyone else: *Shall I let you in on a little secret?*

• **let *sth* go/pass** to not correct or argue with something that a person says or does that is wrong: *I know what he said wasn't strictly accurate but I let it pass anyway.*

• **let *yourself* go 1** *INFORMAL* to allow yourself to become less attractive or healthy: *It's easy to let yourself go when you've got small kids.* **2** to relax completely and enjoy yourself: *It's a party – let yourself go!*

• **let *your* hair down** *OLD-FASHIONED INFORMAL* to allow yourself to behave much more freely than usual and enjoy yourself: *Oh let your hair down for once!*

• **let it all hang out** *OLD-FASHIONED SLANG* to behave freely without being shy or feeling worried about what other people will think of you

• **let it lie** (*ALSO* **let things lie**) to take no action about something: *Instead of going to the police they let things lie for a couple of months.*

• **let *sth* slip** to tell people about something unintentionally: *He let* ***it*** *slip* ***that*** *he hadn't actually read the report.*

• **let go** to stop holding something: *Hold on tight and don't let go!* ○ *Let go* ***of*** *my hand, you're hurting me!*

• **let *sb* have it** *SLANG* to attack someone with words or physically

• **let *sb* know** to tell someone something: *Let us know* ***when*** *you get there.* ○ *Let me know if you need any help.* ○ *Thank you for coming to the interview – we'll let you know* (= tell you whether we are going to offer you a job) *in the next week.*

• **let it be known** *FORMAL* to make certain that people are aware of something: *I let it be known* ***that*** *I was not happy about the decision that had been made.*

• **let rip/fly** *INFORMAL* to behave in an angry and emotional way: *She let rip about the state of the kitchen.*

let [SUGGEST] /let/ *verb* **let's**/*(FORMAL)* ***let us*** used to express a suggestion or request which includes you and the other person or people: *Let's go out to dinner.* ○ *Let us consider all the possibilities.* ○ *Let's not argue/(UK ALSO)* ***Don't*** *let's argue.*

• **let's face it** said before stating something that is unpleasant but true: *Let's face it, we're not going to win.*

• **let's see** (*ALSO* **let me see/think**) used when you want to think carefully about something or are trying to remember: *Next Saturday, let's see, that's when we're going to the theatre.* ○ *The last time I spoke to her was, now let me think, three weeks ago.*

let [CERTAINLY NOT] /let/ *adv* **let alone** used after a negative statement to emphasize how unlikely a situation is because something much more likely has never happened: *Some people never even read a newspaper, let alone a book.*

let [RENT] *MAINLY UK* (**letting, let, let**) /let/ *verb* [T] (*MAINLY US* **rent**) to allow your house or land to be lived in or used by someone else in exchange for a regular payment: *They are letting their house* ***(out)*** *for the summer.* ○ *He's let his flat* ***to*** *a young couple.* ○ *She has a room* ***to*** *let in her house.*

let /let/ *noun* [C] *UK* the act of allowing someone to use your house, land, etc. in exchange for regular payments: *a five-year let* ***on*** *a flat*

letting /ˈlet.ɪŋ/ [US] /ˈlet̬-/ *noun* [C] *UK The town offers several holiday lettings* (= buildings that can be rented).

[L]

let [SPORT] /let/ *noun* [C] (in tennis or similar games) a situation in which the ball touches the net as it crosses it, so that you have to play the point again

let [LAW] /let/ *noun* SPECIALIZED **without let or hindrance** without being prevented from doing something: *People will be able to travel from country to country without let or hindrance.*

PHRASAL VERBS WITH **let**

▲ **let *sb* down** [DISAPPOINT] *phrasal verb* [M] to disappoint someone by failing to do what you agreed to do or were expected to do: *You will be there tomorrow – you won't let me down, will you?* ○ *When I was sent to prison, I really felt I had let my parents down.*
• **let the side down** MAINLY UK INFORMAL to behave in a way that embarrasses or causes problems for a group of people that you are part of

▲ **let *sth* down** [CLOTHES] *phrasal verb* [M] If you let down a piece of clothing, you make it longer: *My trousers shrank in the wash so I let them down.*

▲ **let *sth* down** [AIR] *phrasal verb* [M] UK If you let down something filled with air, you cause the air to go out of it: *Someone let my tyres down while I was at the gym.*

▲ **let *sb/sth* in** *phrasal verb* [M] to allow someone or something to enter: *She opened the door and let me in.* ○ *These shoes are starting to let water in.*

▲ **let *yourself* in for *sth*** *phrasal verb* to become involved in a difficult or unpleasant situation without intending to: *Do you realize how much extra work you're letting yourself in for?*

▲ **let *sb* in on *sth*** *phrasal verb* to tell someone about something that is secret, or to allow someone to become involved in something which only very few people are involved in: *Debbie agreed to let me in on her plans.*

▲ **let *sb* off** [NOT PUNISH] *phrasal verb* [M] to not punish someone who has committed a crime or done something wrong, or to not punish them severely: *Instead of a prison sentence they were let off **with** a fine.* ○ *You won't be let off so **lightly*** (= you will be punished more severely) *the next time.*

▲ **let *sth* off** [EXPLODE] *phrasal verb* [M] to fire a gun or make something such as a bomb or fireworks explode: *Don't let off fireworks near the house.*

▲ **let on** *phrasal verb* INFORMAL to tell other people about something that you know, especially when it is a secret: *I suspect he knows more this than he's letting on.*

▲ **let *sb/sth* out** [ALLOW TO LEAVE] *phrasal verb* [M] to allow someone or something to leave a place, especially by opening a closed or fastened door: *I heard a voice from the cupboard shouting "Let me out!"*

▲ **let *sth* out** *phrasal verb* [M] to cause something to come out: *He let the air out of the balloon.* ○ *She let out a scream* (= She made this noise).

▲ **let out** [END] *phrasal verb* US When something that people go to, such as school or a show, lets out, it ends and everyone leaves: *When does school let out for the summer?*

▲ **let *sth* out** [CLOTHES] *phrasal verb* [M] to make a piece of clothing wider by removing the sewing from the sides and sewing closer to the edge of the material: *These trousers are too tight – I'm going to have to let them out.*

▲ **let up** [IMPROVE] *phrasal verb* INFORMAL If bad weather or an unpleasant situation lets up, it stops or improves: *When the rain lets up we'll go for a walk.*
let-up /ˈlet.ʌp/ Ⓤⓢ /ˈlet̬-/ *noun* [C usually sing] INFORMAL *The airline authorities are not expecting a let-up **in** delays* (= are not expecting delays to stop) *for the rest of the summer.*

▲ **let up** [STOP] *phrasal verb* INFORMAL to stop doing something that you have been doing continuously or in a determined way: *Neil spent the entire evening moaning about his job – he just wouldn't let up.* ○ *The police insist that they are not letting up **on** their campaign against drugs.* * NOTE: This is usually used in negative sentences.

letch /letʃ/ *noun* [C] INFORMAL FOR **lecher**

letdown /ˈlet.daʊn/ *noun* [S] INFORMAL a disappointment: *After all I'd heard about the film, it turned out to be a bit of a letdown.*

lethal /ˈliː.θəl/ *adj* able to cause or causing death; extremely dangerous: *Three minutes after the fire started, the house was full of lethal fumes.* ○ *In the car the police found guns, knives and other lethal **weapons*** (= weapons which can kill). ○ *A 59-year-old man was executed by lethal **injection*** (= by having a poisonous substance put into his body) *this morning.* ○ INFORMAL *That combination of tiredness and alcohol is lethal* (= has a very bad effect). **lethally** /ˈliː.θəl.i/ *adv*

lethargic /ləˈθɑː.dʒɪk/ Ⓤⓢ /-ˈθɑːr-/ *adj* lacking in energy; feeling unwilling and unable to do anything: *I was feeling tired and lethargic.* **lethargy** /ˈleθ.ə.dʒi/ Ⓤⓢ /-ɚ-/ *noun* [U]

letter [MESSAGE] /ˈlet.əʳ/ Ⓤⓢ /ˈlet̬.ɚ/ *noun* [C] a written message from one person to another, usually put in an envelope and sent by the post: *I **got** a letter **from** the bank this morning.*

letter [SYMBOL] /ˈlet.əʳ/ Ⓤⓢ /ˈlet̬.ɚ/ *noun* [C] any of the set of symbols used to write a language, representing a sound in the language: *the letter D*
• **the letter of the law** FORMAL the exact words of the law and not its more important general meaning
• **to the letter** If you obey instructions or rules to the letter, you do exactly what you have been told to do, giving great attention to every detail: *I followed the instructions to the letter and it still went wrong.*

ˈletter ˌbomb *noun* [C] a small bomb that is put in an envelope or parcel and sent to someone by post

letterbox UK /ˈlet.ə.bɒks/ Ⓤⓢ /ˈlet̬.ɚ.bɑːks/ *noun* [C] **1** (US **mail slot**) a rectangular hole in the door or in a wall near the entrance of a house or other building, through which letters, etc. are delivered **2** (US **mailbox**) a large, metal container in a public place where you can post letters

ˈletter ˌcarrier *noun* [C] US FOR **postman**

letterhead /ˈlet.ə.hed/ Ⓤⓢ /ˈlet̬.ɚ-/ *noun* [C] the top part of a piece of writing paper where the name and address of a person or business is printed

lettering /ˈlet.ər.ɪŋ/ Ⓤⓢ /ˈlet̬.ɚ-/ *noun* [U] writing in a particular colour, style etc: *a black box with gold lettering*

ˌletter of ˈcredit *noun* [C] a letter from a bank allowing the person who has it to take a particular amount of money from a bank in another country

ˌletter ˈperfect *adj* US FOR **word perfect**

lettuce /ˈlet.ɪs/ Ⓤⓢ /ˈlet̬-/ *noun* [C or U] a plant with large green leaves, eaten raw in salads ➲See picture **Vegetables** on page Centre 2

let-up /ˈlet.ʌp/ Ⓤⓢ /ˈlet̬-/ *noun* [C] ➲See at **let up** IMPROVE.

leucotomy /luːˈkɒt.ə.mi/ Ⓤⓢ /-ˈkɑː.t̬ə-/ *noun* [C] UK FOR **lobotomy**

leukaemia, MAINLY US **leukemia** /luːˈkiː.mi.ə/ *noun* [U] a serious disease in which the body produces too many white blood cells

the Levant /ðə.ləˈvænt/ *noun* [S] the countries and islands of the eastern Mediterranean

level [HEIGHT] /ˈlev.əl/ *noun* [C] **1** the height of something: *The water level in the lake is much higher after heavy rain.* **2** the amount or number of something: *Inflation is going to rise 2% from its present level.* ○ *Chess requires a very **high** level of concentration.* ○ *There is some danger of **low** level* (= a continuing small amount of) *radiation.*
• **on one level...on another level** something that you say when you are speaking about two opposite ways of thinking about or responding to a situation: *On one level I quite like the attention but on another level, I suppose I find it a bit disturbing.*
• **be on the level** to be acting or speaking honestly: *It seems too good to be true. Are you sure this guy's on the level?*

level [ABILITY] /ˈlev.əl/ *noun* [C] someone's ability compared to other people: *a course for advanced level students* ○ *Students at this level require a lot of help.* ○ *The exam can be taken at three levels.*
• **find *your* own level** to find out how much ability you have and find a position which is therefore suitable

level [FLOOR] /ˈlev.əl/ *noun* [C] a floor in a large building: *The library has three levels, with a conference centre **at***

L

ground level. ○ *The exhibition is on level three of the building.*

level RANK /'lev.ºl/ *noun* [C] **1** a position within a system in which people are arranged according to their importance: *These are subjects for discussion at management level.* **2** **at local/national level** relating to a particular area of the country/the whole of the country: *These sorts of policies are made at local level.*

level AT SAME HEIGHT /'lev.ºl/ *adj* [after v] at the same height: *The top of the tree is level with his bedroom window.*

• **do your level best** to try as hard as you can: *Tickets are hard to come by but I'll do my level best to get you one.*

level FLAT /'lev.ºl/ *adj* **1** flat or horizontal: *Make sure the camera is level before you take the picture.* ○ *Before I bang the nails in, would you say this picture was level?* **2** **level spoonful/cupful** an amount of a liquid or substance which fills a spoon/cup but does not go above the edges, used as a measure in cooking

level /'lev.ºl/ *verb* [T] **-ll-** or *US USUALLY* **-l- 1** to make a surface flat: *Level the wet cement before it sets.* **2** to completely destroy a building or area: *The bombing levelled the village.*

level EQUAL /'lev.ºl/ *adj* having the same value, amount, number of points, etc: *The unions are fighting to keep wages level* (*US USUALLY* **even**) *with inflation.* ○ *Chiappucci would have to win the next three stages in order to draw level with* (= reach the same position as) *Indurain in the Tour de France.*

• **level pegging** *UK* in an equal position in a competition or game: *Both teams are level pegging.*

• **a level playing field** a situation in which everyone has the same chance of succeeding: *If the tax systems are different in each European country, how can industries start on a level playing field?*

level CONTROLLED /'lev.ºl/ *adj* [before n] If you speak in a level voice or give someone a level look, you do it in a calm and controlled way: *In a level voice, he ordered the soldiers to aim and fire.*

levelly /'lev.ºl.i/ *adv*: *He looked levelly* (= calmly and without excitement) *across at me.*

PHRASAL VERBS WITH **level** ▼

▲ **level** *sth* **against/at** *sb* phrasal verb to accuse someone in public of doing something wrong: *Criticism has been levelled at senior figures in the industry.* ○ *Charges of corruption have been levelled against him.*

▲ **level** *sth* **at** *sb* phrasal verb to aim something such as a weapon at someone: *She picked up the gun and levelled it at me.*

▲ **level off/out** AIRCRAFT phrasal verb If an aircraft levels off/out, it starts to travel horizontally rather than going up or down: *The jet levelled off at 10,000 feet.*

▲ **level off** AMOUNT phrasal verb If a rate or amount levels off, it stops rising or falling and stays at the same level: *House prices now seem to be levelling off after the steep rises of the last few years.* ○ *Unemployment rose to 10% and then levelled off.*

▲ **level with** *sb* phrasal verb INFORMAL to tell someone the truth about something: *I'll level with you – the salary's not particularly good, and there's little chance of promotion.*

---

level 'crossing *UK noun* [C] (*US* **grade crossing**) a place where a railway and a road cross each other, usually with gates that stop the traffic while a train goes past

level-headed /,lev.ºl'hed.ɪd/ *adj* calm and able to deal easily with difficult situations

leveller, *US USUALLY* **leveler** /'lev.ºl.əʳ/ ⓤ /-ɚ/ *noun* [C usually sing] something, typically death, that affects people of every class and rank in the same way, making everyone seem equal: *death, the great leveller*

lever BAR/HANDLE /'liː.vəʳ/ ⓤ /'lev.ɚ/ *noun* [C] a bar or handle which moves around a fixed point, so that one end of it can be pushed or pulled in order to control the operation of a machine or move a heavy or stiff object **lever** /'liː.vəʳ/ ⓤ /'lev.ɚ/ *verb* [T usually + adv or prep] *She levered up the drain cover.*

lever ADVANTAGE /'liː.vəʳ/ ⓤ /'lev.ɚ/ *noun* [C] something you use, often unfairly, to try to persuade someone to do what you want

leverage ACTION /'liː.vᵊr.ɪdʒ/ ⓤ /'lev.ɚ.ɪdʒ/ *noun* [U] the action or advantage of using a lever

leverage POWER /'liː.vᵊr.ɪdʒ/ ⓤ /'lev.ɚ.ɪdʒ/ *noun* [U] power to influence people and get the results you want: *If the United Nations had more troops in the area, it would have greater leverage.*

leverage VALUE *US* /'liː.vᵊr.ɪdʒ/ ⓤ /'lev.ɚ.ɪdʒ/ *noun* [U] (*UK* **gearing**) SPECIALIZED the ratio between the amount of money that a company owes to banks and the value of the company

leverage BORROWING /'liː.vᵊr.ɪdʒ/ ⓤ /'lev.ɚ.ɪdʒ/ *verb* [T] SPECIALIZED to use borrowed money to buy a company **leveraged** /'liː.vᵊr.ɪdʒd/ ⓤ /'lev.ɚ.ɪdʒd/ *adj*: *The company is highly leveraged and struggling with interest payments.*

leveraged 'buyout *noun* [C] SPECIALIZED when a small company buys a larger one using money borrowed against the value of the equipment, buildings, etc. of both companies

lever 'arch ,file *noun* [C] a type of large container used to hold paper, in which paper is held on two big curved pieces of metal which are opened or closed using a metal bar

leviathan, **Leviathan** /lə'vaɪə.θᵊn/ *noun* [C] LITERARY something or someone that is extremely large and powerful: *The US is seen as an economic leviathan.*

Levi's /'liː.vaɪz/ *plural noun* TRADEMARK a type of JEANS

levitate /'lev.ɪ.teɪt/ *verb* [I or T] to (cause to) rise and float in the air without any physical support **levitation** /,lev.ɪ'teɪ.ʃᵊn/ *noun* [U]

levity /'lev.ɪ.ti/ ⓤ /-ţi/ *noun* [U] FORMAL amusement or lack of seriousness, especially during a serious occasion: *a brief moment of levity amid the solemn proceedings*

levy /'lev.i/ *noun* [C] an amount of money, such as a tax, that you have to pay to a government or organization: *They imposed a 5% levy on alcohol.* **levy** /'lev.i/ *verb* [T] *A new tax was levied on consumers of luxury goods.*

lewd /luːd/ *adj* DISAPPROVING (of behaviour, speech, dress, etc.) sexual in an obvious and rude way: *Ignore him – he's being lewd.* ○ *a lewd suggestion* **lewdly** /'luːd.li/ *adv* **lewdness** /'luːd.nəs/ *noun* [U]

lexical /'lek.sɪ.kᵊl/ *adj* SPECIALIZED relating to words

lexicography /,lek.sɪ'kɒg.rə.fi/ ⓤ /-'kɑː.grə-/ *noun* [U] SPECIALIZED the activity or job of writing dictionaries **lexicographer** /,lek.sɪ'kɒg.rə.fəʳ/ ⓤ /-'kɑː.grə.fɚ/ *noun* [C] a person whose job is to write dictionaries

lexicon /'lek.sɪ.kən/ *noun* [C] SPECIALIZED (a list of) all the words used in a particular language or subject, or a dictionary

lexis /'lek.sɪs/ *noun* [U] SPECIALIZED all the words of a language

ley line /'leɪ.laɪn/ *noun* [C] an imaginary line between some important places such as hills or very old churches in Britain, believed to be where there were very old paths

liable RESPONSIBLE /'laɪ.ə.bl̩/ *adj* [after v] SPECIALIZED having (legal) responsibility for something or someone: *The law holds parents liable if a child does not attend school.* ○ *If we lose the case we may be liable for* (= have to pay) *the costs of the whole trial.*
liability /,laɪ.ə'bɪl.ɪ.ti/ ⓤ /-ə.ţi/ *noun* **1** [U] when you are legally responsible for something: *He denies any liability for the damage caused.* **2** [S] something or someone that causes you a lot of trouble, often when they should be helping you: *After a certain age, a car's just a liability.* ○ *Sue always manages to upset somebody when we go out – she's a real liability.*
liabilities /,laɪ.ə'bɪl.ɪ.tiz/ ⓤ /-ə.ţiz/ *plural noun* SPECIALIZED debts: *The business has liabilities of £2 million.* ⊃Compare **asset**.

liable LIKELY /'laɪ.ə.bl̩/ *adj* [after v] very likely to happen: *The areas of town near the river are liable to flooding* (= are often flooded). ○ [+ to infinitive] *He's liable to make a fuss if you wake him.*

liaise /li'eɪz/ *verb* [I] to speak to people in other organizations in order to exchange information with them: *Our head office will liaise **with** the suppliers to ensure delivery.*

liaison /li'eɪ.zɒn/ ⓤ /-zɑːn/ *noun* **1** [S or U] communication between people or groups who work with each other: *He blamed the lack of liaison **between** the various government departments.* ○ *The police have appointed a liaison **officer** to work with the local community.* **2** [C] MAINLY US someone who helps groups to work effectively with each other: *She served as a liaison between the different groups.* **3** [C] FORMAL a sexual relationship, especially between two people not married to each other: *He's had a number of liaisons, even with people in the same office.*

liar /'laɪ.əʳ/ ⓤ /-ɚ/ *noun* [C] someone who tells lies: *He's such a liar – you can't trust a word he says.* ○ [as form of address] *You liar – I never touched it!*

lib FREEDOM /lɪb/ *noun* [U] (especially in informal names of organizations which try to remove the disadvantages experienced by particular groups within society) **liberation: *women's* lib** /'lɪb.əʳ/ ⓤ /-ɚ/ *noun* [C] INFORMAL *She's a **women's** libber.*

Lib POLITICS /lɪb/ *adj* UK ABBREVIATION FOR **liberal** POLITICS

libation /laɪ'beɪ.ʃən/ *noun* [C] FORMAL an amount of alcoholic drink poured out or drunk in honour of a god or a dead relative

Lib 'Dem *noun* [C] UK INFORMAL a member of the LIBERAL DEMOCRATS

libel /'laɪ.bəl/ *noun* [C or U] a piece of writing which contains bad and false things about a person: *She threatened to sue the magazine for libel.* ⊃Compare **slander**. **libel** /'laɪ.bəl/ *verb* [T] -ll- or US USUALLY -l- **libellous**, US USUALLY **libelous** /'laɪ.bəl.əs/ *adj: libellous accusations*

liberal SOCIETY /'lɪb.əʳr.əl/ /-rəl/ ⓤ /-ɚ-/ *adj* respecting and allowing many different types of beliefs or behaviour: *a liberal society/attitude* ○ *Her parents were far more liberal than mine.* ✳ NOTE: The opposite is **illiberal** or **intolerant**. **liberal** /'lɪb.əʳr.əl/ /-rəl/ ⓤ /-ɚ-/ *noun* [C] someone who is liberal: *He's a good old-fashioned liberal.* **liberalism** /'lɪb.əʳr.əl.ɪ.zəm/ /-rəl-/ ⓤ /-ɚ-/ *noun* [U]

liberal POLITICS /'lɪb.əʳr.əl/ /-rəl/ ⓤ /-ɚ-/ *adj* (of a political party or a country) believing in or allowing more personal freedom and a development towards a fairer sharing of wealth and power within society **liberalism**, **Liberalism** /'lɪb.əʳr.əl.ɪ.z²m/ /-rəl-/ ⓤ /-ɚ-/ *noun* [U]

liberal GENEROUS /'lɪb.əʳr.əl/ /-rəl/ ⓤ /-ɚ-/ *adj* FORMAL giving or given in a generous way: *He was very liberal with the wine.* **liberally** /'lɪb.əʳr.əl.i/ /-rəl.i/ ⓤ /-ɚ-/ *adv*: *Apply the cream liberally to the affected area.* **liberality** /ˌlɪb.ə'ræl.ə.ti/ ⓤ /-t̬i/ *noun* [U]

liberal NOT EXACT /'lɪb.əʳr.əl/ /-rəl/ ⓤ /-ɚ-/ *adj* not exact; without attention to or interest in detail: *a liberal interpretation of the law*

liberal 'arts *plural noun* MAINLY US college or university subjects such as history, languages and literature

Liberal 'Democrats *plural noun* in Britain, a political party that believes in more power for local government, more personal freedom and a gradual development towards a fairer sharing of wealth and power within society

liberalize, UK USUALLY **-ise** /'lɪb.əʳr.əl.aɪz/ /-rəl-/ ⓤ /-ɚ-/ *verb* [T] to make laws, systems or attitudes less severe: *They have plans to liberalize the prison system.* **liberalization**, UK USUALLY **-isation** /ˌlɪb.əʳr.əl.aɪ'zeɪ.ʃən/ /-rəl-/ ⓤ /-ɚ-/ *noun* [U] MAINLY US *Political reform and economic liberalization don't always go together.*

the 'Liberal ˌParty *group noun* [S] in Britain, a political party that joined with the SOCIAL DEMOCRATIC PARTY to become the 'Liberal Democrats'

liberate /'lɪb.əʳr.eɪt/ *verb* [T] **1** to help someone or something to be free: *They said they sent troops in to liberate the people/the country **from** a dictator.* **2** HUMOROUS to steal something: *She liberated those spoons from a restaurant last week.*

liberating /'lɪb.əʳr.eɪ.tɪŋ/ ⓤ /-ɚ.eɪ.t̬ɪŋ/ *adj* making you feel free and able to behave as you like: *Taking all your clothes off can be a very liberating experience.*

liberation /ˌlɪb.ə'reɪ.ʃən/ *noun* [U] **1** when something or someone is freed: *the liberation of France **from** Nazi occupation* ○ *Leaving school was such a liberation for me.* **2** used to refer to activities connected with removing the disadvantages experienced by particular groups within society: *the women's liberation (INFORMAL **lib**) movement* ○ *animal liberation organizations* **liberator** /'lɪb.əʳr.eɪ.təʳ/ ⓤ /-ɚ.eɪ.t̬ɚ/ *noun* [C] *People came out into the streets to welcome the liberators.*

liberated /'lɪb.əʳr.eɪ.tɪd/ ⓤ /-ɚ.eɪ.t̬ɪd/ *adj* not following traditional ways of behaving or old ideas: *She's chosen career advancement instead of having children – does that make her a liberated woman?*

libertarian /ˌlɪb.ə'teə.ri.ən/ ⓤ /-ɚ'ter.i-/ *noun* [C] a person who believes that people should be free to think and behave as they want and should not have limits put on them by governments: *Civil libertarians are worried about what they see as government censorship.* **libertarian** /ˌlɪb.ə'teə.ri.ən/ ⓤ /-ɚ'ter.i-/ *adj*

libertine /'lɪb.ə.tiːn/ ⓤ /-ɚ-/ *noun* [C] FORMAL DISAPPROVING a person, usually a man, who lives immorally, having sexual relationships with many people

liberty FREEDOM /'lɪb.ə.ti/ ⓤ /-ɚ.t̬i/ *noun* [U] FORMAL the freedom to live as you wish or go where you wish: *For most citizens, liberty means the freedom to practise their religious or political beliefs.* ○ *Hundreds of political prisoners are to be **given** their liberty (= released from prison).* ○ *Of the ten men who escaped this morning from Dartmoor Prison, only two are still **at** liberty (= free or not yet caught).*

● **be at liberty to do** *sth* FORMAL to be allowed to do something: *I'm not at liberty to reveal any names.*

liberties /'lɪb.ə.tiz/ ⓤ /-ɚ.t̬iz/ *plural noun* FORMAL liberty: *These laws will restrict our ancient rights and liberties.*

liberty BAD BEHAVIOUR /'lɪb.ə.ti/ ⓤ /-ɚ.t̬i/ *noun* [C] an example of speech or behaviour that upsets other people because it lacks respect or does not follow what is thought to be polite or acceptable: *What a liberty, to refuse the invitation on your behalf, without even asking you!*

● **take the liberty of doing** *sth* FORMAL to do something that will have an effect on someone else, without asking their permission: *I took the liberty of booking theatre seats for us.*

● **take liberties (with** *sth***)** to change something, especially a piece of writing, in a way that people disagree with

● **take liberties (with** *sb***)** OLD-FASHIONED to be too friendly with someone, usually in a sexual way: *Some of the younger women complained that he'd been taking liberties with them.*

libidinous /lɪ'bɪd.ɪ.nəs/ *adj* FORMAL having or showing strong sexual desires

libido /lɪ'biː.dəʊ/ ⓤ /-doʊ/ *noun* [C] *plural* **libidos** a person's sexual energy: *Symptoms include weight gain, sleep disorders and loss of libido.*

Libra /'liː.brə/ *noun* [C or U] the seventh sign of the zodiac, relating to the period 23 September to 22 October, represented by a pair of measuring SCALES, or a person born during this period **Libran** /'liː.brən/ *noun* [C] a Libra

librarian /laɪ'breə.ri.ən/ ⓤ /-'brer.i-/ *noun* [C] a person who works in a library

library /'laɪ.brər.i/ ⓤ /-bri/ *noun* [C] **1** a building, room or organization which has a collection, especially of books, for people to read or borrow usually without payment: *a public/university library* ○ *a record library* ○ *a library book* **2** a collection or set of books, records or other items, all produced in the same style or about the same subject: *the Penguin Shakespeare Library*

libretto /lɪ'bret.əʊ/ ⓤ /-'bret̬.oʊ/ *noun* [C] *plural* **librettos** SPECIALIZED the words that are sung or spoken in an opera or a musical

librettist /lɪ'bret.ɪst/ ⓤ /-'bret̬-/ *noun* [C] SPECIALIZED a person who writes the words for an opera or a musical

lice /laɪs/ *plural of* **louse**

licence UK, US **license** /'laɪ.s²nts/ *noun* **1** [C] an official document which gives you permission to own, do or use something, usually after you have paid money and/or taken a test: *a dog licence* ○ *a (UK) driving licence/(US) driver's license* ○ *a TV licence* **2** [S or U] *FORMAL* permission or freedom to do what you want: *As parents, they* **allowed** *their children very little licence.* ○ [+ *to* infinitive] *He was* **given** *licence* **to** *reform the organization.* **3** *artistic/poetic licence* the freedom of artists, writers etc. to change the facts of the real world when producing art

• **be a licence to print money** If a company or activity is a licence to print money, it causes people to become very rich without having to make any effort.

• **under licence** with special permission from the maker of a product: *It's a German product, made under licence in British factories.*

license /'laɪ.sᵊnts/ *verb* [T] to give someone official permission to do or have something: [+ *to* infinitive] *Several companies have been licensed* **to** *sell these products.*

licensed /'laɪ.sᵊntst/ *adj*: *a licensed pilot* ○ *a licensed* (= allowed to sell alcohol) *restaurant*

licensee /ˌlaɪ.sᵊnt'siː/ *noun* [C] *FORMAL* a person who has official permission to do something, especially to sell alcoholic drinks

ˌ**licensed** ˌ**practical** ˈ**nurse** *noun* [C] a nurse in the US who has been trained to do practical nursing but who is not allowed to give medicines without permission

ˈ**license** ˌ**plate** *noun* [C] *US FOR* **number plate** ⊃See picture **Car** on page Centre 12

ˈ**licensing** ˌ**laws** *plural noun* in Britain, the laws which control when and where alcoholic drinks can be sold

licentious /laɪ'sen.tʃəs/ *adj FORMAL DISAPPROVING* (especially of a person or their behaviour) sexual in an uncontrolled and socially unacceptable way **licentiously** /laɪ'sen.tʃə.sli/ *adv* **licentiousness** /laɪ'sen.tʃə.snəs/ *noun* [U]

lichen /'laɪ.kən/ /'lɪtʃ.ən/ *noun* [C or U] a grey, green or yellow plant-like organism that grows especially on rocks, walls and trees

lick MOVE TONGUE /lɪk/ *verb* **1** [T] to move the tongue across the surface of something: *He licked the chocolate off his fingers.* ○ *She licked the stamps and stuck them on the parcel.* **2** [T; I + *prep*] If flames or waves lick something, they pass over it quickly or touch it lightly like a tongue: *Within a few seconds flames were licking* **at** *the curtains.*

• **lick** *your* **lips 1** to move your tongue along your lips: *She took a bite of doughnut and licked her lips.* **2** to feel pleasure at the thought of something: *He licked his lips at the thought of all that money.*

• **lick** *sb's* **boots** *INFORMAL* (*OFFENSIVE* **lick** *sb's* **arse/ass**) to be extremely obedient to someone, usually in order to get an advantage: *He needn't expect me to go licking his boots!*

• **lick** *your* **wounds** to spend time getting back your strength or happiness after a defeat or bad experience

lick /lɪk/ *noun* [C] the action of licking something: *Can I* **have** *a lick of your ice cream?*

• **a lick and a promise** *OLD-FASHIONED INFORMAL* a quick and careless cleaning or wash

lick DEFEAT /lɪk/ *verb* [T] *INFORMAL* to defeat easily in a competition, fight, etc: *We'll lick the other teams.*

• **have (got)** *sth* **licked** *INFORMAL* to have solved a problem

lick HIT /lɪk/ *noun* [C] *OLD-FASHIONED INFORMAL* when you hit someone with something such as a whip

lick SPEED /lɪk/ *noun UK INFORMAL* **at a hell of lick** at a fast speed: *The trains go by at a hell of a lick.*

lick SMALL AMOUNT /lɪk/ *noun* [C] *INFORMAL* a small amount or thin layer: *The living room could do with a lick* **of** **paint***.*

lick MUSIC /lɪk/ *noun* [C] *SPECIALIZED* in jazz or rock music, a short series of notes played by one musician

lickety-split /ˌlɪk.ə.ti'splɪt/ ⓤ /-t̬i-/ *adv OLD-FASHIONED INFORMAL* very quickly

licking /'lɪk.ɪŋ/ *noun* [S] **1** *INFORMAL* a defeat in a competition: *The home team were* **given** *a good licking.* **2** *OLD-FASHIONED INFORMAL* when someone is hit as a punishment

licorice /'lɪk.ᵊr.ɪs/ /-ɪʃ/ ⓤ /-ɚ-/ *noun* [U] *MAINLY US FOR* **liquorice**

lid /lɪd/ *noun* [C] **1** a cover on a container, which can be lifted up or removed: *Can you get the lid off this jar?* ○ *Put a lid on the saucepan.* **2** an EYELID (= either of the two pieces of skin which can close over each eye): *She looked at him from under half-closed lids.*

• **keep the lid on** *sth INFORMAL* to control the level of something in order to stop it increasing: *The government have intervened to keep a lid on inflation.*

• **put the lid on** *sth UK OLD-FASHIONED* If something that happens puts the lid on a plan, it causes the plan to fail: *Well, James' resignation just about puts the lid on it/the project.*

• **blow/take the lid off** *sth* (*ALSO* **lift the lid on** *sth*) *INFORMAL* to cause something bad that was previously kept secret to be known by the public: *In 1989 they started an investigation that was to blow the lid off corruption in the police force.*

lido /'liː.dəʊ/ /'laɪ-/ ⓤ /'liː.doʊ/ *noun* [C] *plural* **lidos** *MAINLY UK OLD-FASHIONED* a public swimming pool which is outside, or part of a beach where people can swim, lie in the sun or do water sports

lie POSITION /laɪ/ *verb* lying, lay, lain **1** [I + *adv or prep*; L] to be in or move into a horizontal position on a surface: *to lie in bed* ○ *to lie on a beach* ○ *to lie on your side* ○ *A cat lay in front of the fire.* ○ *He lies* **awake** *at night, worrying.* ○ *A pen lay on the desk.* ⊃See Note **lay or lie?** at **lay** PUT DOWN. **2** [I + *adv or prep*; L] If something lies in a particular place, position or direction, it is in that place, position or direction: *There's an old pair of shoes of yours lying at/in the bottom of the wardrobe.* ○ *The river lies 30km to the south.* ○ *Cambridge United are lying third in the league.* ○ *Here lies the body of Mary Taylor* (= This is where Mary Taylor is buried). ○ *There are several houses lying empty in the town.* ○ *The town lay in ruins.* ○ *The ship lies* **off** (= is positioned near) *the coast of Spain.* **3** [I + *adv or prep*] to exist: *The hardest part of the competition still lies ahead of us.* **4** [I usually + *adv or prep*] If responsibility, blame, a decision, a choice, etc. lies with someone, they have responsibility, must make the decision, etc.: *Responsibility for the disaster must ultimately lie* **with** *the government.* ○ *Where does the blame lie?*

• **lie down on the job** *MAINLY US DISAPPROVING* to fail to work as hard or as well as you should

• **lie in state** When the dead body of an important person lies in state, it is arranged so that the public can see and honour it before it is buried.

• **lie low** *INFORMAL* to try not to be noticed: *I'd lie low if I were you till the trouble passes.*

• **not take** *sth* **lying down** to refuse to be treated badly by someone: *He can't treat you like that! Surely you're not going to take that lying down!*

• **the lie of the land** *UK* (*US* **the lay of the land**) the shape or height of the land ⊃See also **find out/see how the land lies** at **land** DRY SURFACE.

lie SPEAK FALSELY /laɪ/ *verb* [I] lying, lied, lied to say or write something which is not true in order to deceive someone: *Are you lying to me?* ○ *Don't trust her – she's lying.* ○ *I suspect he lies* **about** *his age.* ⊃See also **liar**. See Note **lay or lie?** at **lay** PUT DOWN.

• **lie through** *your* **teeth** *INFORMAL* to tell someone something which you know is completely false: *He asked me how old I was and, lying through my teeth, I said '29'.*

lie /laɪ/ *noun* [C] something that you say which you know is not true: *I* **told** *a lie when I said I liked her haircut.*

• **be a pack of lies** (*FORMAL* **be a tissue of lies**) to be completely untrue: *The whole report is a pack of lies.*

• **give the lie to** *sth* to prove that something is not true: *The fact that the number of deaths from cancer in the area has doubled surely gives the lie to official assurances of the safety of nuclear power.*

• **I tell a lie** *MAINLY UK* something you say when you have just said something wrong and want to correct it: *Her name is Paula, no, I tell a lie* (= I'm wrong) *– it's Pauline.*

PHRASAL VERBS WITH **lie** ▼

▲ **lie about/around** *phrasal verb* If things are lying about/around, they are left in places where they should not be: *Has anyone seen my keys lying about?* ○ *I*

L

wouldn't leave any money lying around the office if I were you.
▲ **lie around** *phrasal verb* to spend time lying down and doing very little: *I spent a week in Spain, lying around on the beach.*
▲ **lie back** *phrasal verb* to move the top half of your body from a sitting to a lying position: *She lay back in the dentist's chair and tried to relax.*
▲ **lie behind *sth*** *phrasal verb* If something lies behind something else, it is the hidden cause of it: *Do you know what lies behind their decision?*
▲ **lie down** *phrasal verb* to move into a position in which your body is flat, usually in order to sleep or rest: *He lay down on the bed and tried to relax.*
lie down *noun* [S] *MAINLY UK INFORMAL* a short rest, usually in bed: *I usually **have** a bit of a lie down after lunch.* ○ *She said she was going for a lie down.*
▲ **lie in** [SLEEP] *phrasal verb UK* to stay in bed later than usual in the morning: *It was a Sunday, so she could lie in till almost lunch time.* **lie-in** /ˌlaɪˈɪn/ *noun* [C usually sing] *I'm not working tomorrow so I can **have** a bit of a lie-in.*
▲ **lie in *sth*** [BE FOUND IN] *phrasal verb UK* to exist or be found in something: *His skill lies in his ability to communicate quite complex ideas very simply.* ○ *The play's interest lies in the questions it raises about sexuality.*

ˈlie deˌtector *noun* [C] (*SPECIALIZED* **polygraph**) a piece of equipment used to try to discover if someone is telling lies: *Both men refused to take a lie detector test.*

lieu /ljuː/ [US] /luː/ *noun FORMAL* **in lieu (of)** instead (of): *The paintings were left to the nation by the Duke of Norfolk in lieu of inheritance taxes.*

Lieut *noun* [before n] *WRITTEN ABBREVIATION FOR* **lieutenant**

lieutenant /lefˈten.ᵊnt/ [US] /luː-/ *noun* [C] (the title of) an officer of middle rank in the armed forces: *first/second lieutenant*

life /laɪf/ *noun plural* **lives 1** [C or U] the period between birth and death; the experience or state of being alive: *Life's too short to worry about money!* ○ *I'm not sure I want to **spend** the rest of my life with him.* ○ *Unfortunately, accidents are **part of** life.* ○ *He went mad towards the end of his life.* ○ *Cats are supposed to have nine lives.* ○ *He doesn't know what he really wants in/out of life.* ○ *The accident changed my whole outlook on life.* ○ *He **lost** his life* (= died suddenly because of a violent event or accident) *in the Great War.* ○ *A simple mixture of glucose and water can **save** lives in many parts of the world.* ○ *He ran off with her life **savings*** (= all the money she had saved). ➲See also **afterlife**; **pro-life**. **2** [C or U] way of living or a particular part of someone's life: *her family/private/sex life* ○ *my working life* ○ *We interviewed senior politicians, famous writers and others in **public** life.* ○ *Drugs and violence are deeply rooted in American life.* ○ *I left home at 16 to **see** life* (= have different experiences with a lot of people in lots of places). ○ *Teaching has been her life* (= the most important and enjoyable thing in her life). **3** [C usually sing] the period for which a machine or organization lasts: *The newer batteries have a much longer life.* ○ *Careful use will prolong the life of your machine.* ○ *The legislation won't be passed during the life of the present parliament.* **4** [U] the quality which makes people, animals and plants different from objects, substances, and things which are dead: *The doctor could find no **sign of** life in the old man's body.* ○ *FIGURATIVE I looked through the window but I couldn't see any **signs of** life* (= people moving). **5** [U] energy or enthusiasm: *She's so **full of** life.* **6** [U] everything which is alive: *human/marine/plant life* **7** [U] *SPECIALIZED* In art, if you work from life, you paint, draw, etc. real people or objects usually while they are in front of you rather than from memory: *life drawing classes* ➲See also **still life**. **8** [C] *INFORMAL* especially in children's games, one of the limited number of times that you can lose, but still continue playing: *Every time the little man gets hit, you **lose** a life.*
• **bring *sth* to life/come to life** to make something more real or exciting, or to become more real or exciting: *It's always been an interesting period in history and this film really brought it to life.*
• **for life** for the whole of a person's life: *I believe marriage is for life.*
• **for the life of *you*** *INFORMAL* although you are trying very hard: *I can't **remember** her name for the life of me.*
• **Get a life!** *INFORMAL* something you say to a boring person when you want them to do more exciting things: *Don't tell me you're cleaning the house on a Saturday night? Get a life, Hannah!*
• **give *your* life** (*ALSO* **lay down *your* life**) to die willingly while defending or supporting someone or something: *They were ready to give their lives **for** their country.*
• **give *your* life to *sth*** to continue to have a close involvement in a particular thing for the whole of your life: *She gave her life to cancer research.*
• **How's life (treating you)?** said as an informal greeting
• **life after death** If you believe in life after death, you believe that people continue to exist in some form after they die.
• **life and soul of the party** someone who is energetic and amusing and at the centre of activity during social occasions
• **be one/another of life's great mysteries** to be something which is very difficult to understand: *The market for those dreadful compilation records you see advertised on TV is just another of life's great mysteries.*
• **be (all) part of life's rich tapestry/pageant** to be one of the difficult or bad experiences that is part of a full and varied life
• **start a new life** (*ALSO* **make a new life for *yourself***) to completely change how or where you live: *She decided to start a new life in Australia.*
• **the man/woman in *sb's* life** *INFORMAL* your romantic/sexual partner: *Who's the new man in your life now then, eh?*
• **lead/live the life of Riley** *OLD-FASHIONED INFORMAL* to live an easy and comfortable life, without any need to work hard
• **Not on your life!** *INFORMAL* said as a way of strongly refusing someone's suggestion or request: *"So you're going to bring Kev, are you?" "Not on your life!"*
• **take *sb's* life** *FORMAL* to kill someone
• **take *your* (own) life** *FORMAL* to kill yourself
• **take *your* life in *your* hands** to do something that is very dangerous, especially where you risk death: *Every time you go parachuting you're taking your life in your hands.*
• **that's life** *INFORMAL* said after something bad or unlucky has happened, to express your feeling that such events will sometimes happen and have to be accepted: *No, I didn't get the job but that's life, isn't it?*
• **This is the life!** *INFORMAL* said to mean that you are very much enjoying the situation you are in
• **scare/frighten the life out of *sb*** to frighten someone very much

life-affirming /ˈlaɪf.əˌfɜː.mɪŋ/ [US] /-ˌfɝː-/ *adj* If you describe something as life-affirming, you mean that it makes you feel positive about life: *Such a warm, life-affirming film!*

ˈlife ˌbelt *noun* [C] (*ALSO* **life buoy**) a piece of equipment, usually a ring filled with air or light material that floats, which is designed to help someone float if they fall into water

lifeblood /ˈlaɪf.blʌd/ *noun* [U] the thing which is most important to the continuing success and existence of something else: *Tourism is the lifeblood of Hawaii's economy.*

lifeboat /ˈlaɪf.bəʊt/ [US] /-boʊt/ *noun* [C] a large boat which is kept ready to go out to sea and save people who are in danger, or a smaller boat kept on a ship for people to leave in if the ship is not safe or might sink ➲See picture **Planes, Ships and Boats** on page Centre 14

ˈlife ˌcycle *noun* [C usually sing] (*ALSO* **life history**) the series of changes that a living thing goes through from the beginning of its life until death

ˈlife exˌpectancy *noun* [C usually sing] the length of time that a living thing, especially a human being, is likely to live: *Life expectancy in Europe has increased greatly in the 20th century.*

ˈlife ˌform *noun* [C] any living thing: *They are searching for **intelligent** life forms in other solar systems.*

life-giving /ˈlaɪfˌgɪv.ɪŋ/ adj necessary for life or giving energy

lifeguard /ˈlaɪf.gɑːd/ ⓤ /-gɑːrd/ noun [C] (AUS **lifesaver**) a person on a beach or at a swimming pool whose job is to make certain that the swimmers are safe and save them if they are in danger

,**life 'history** noun [C] all the things that happen during the life of a living thing ⮞See also **life story**.

,**life im'prisonment** noun [U] (INFORMAL **life**) the punishment of being put in prison for a very long time without an arranged time for release or, in the US, until death ⮞See also **life sentence**.

'**life in,surance** noun [U] (UK USUALLY **life assurance**) a system in which you make regular payments to an insurance company in exchange for a fixed amount of money which will be paid to someone you have named, usually a member of your family, when you die

'**life ,jacket** noun [C] a piece of equipment, like a jacket without sleeves, that is filled with air or light material and is designed to help someone float if they fall into water

lifeless /ˈlaɪ.fləs/ adj **1** dead: *His lifeless body lay on the floor.* **2** lacking energy or interest: *a lifeless performance* **3** not filled with or used by people: *The offices are still empty and lifeless.* **lifelessly** /ˈlaɪ.fləs.li/ adv **lifelessness** /ˈlaɪ.fləs.nəs/ noun [U]

lifelike /ˈlaɪf.laɪk/ adj describes something that appears real or very similar to reality: *a lifelike portrait of the queen* ○ *The mask was so lifelike it was quite frightening.*

lifeline /ˈlaɪf.laɪn/ noun [C] **1** something, especially a way of getting help, on which you depend to lead your life in a satisfactory way: *For many old people living on their own the telephone is their lifeline **to** the outside world.* **2** a rope which is thrown to someone who is in the water, especially the sea, and is in danger

lifelong /ˈlaɪf.lɒŋ/ ⓤ /-lɑːŋ/ adj [before n] lasting for the whole of a person's life: *She was a lifelong member of the Labour party.* ○ *It's so hard to stop smoking when it's been a lifelong habit.*

,**life 'peer** noun [C] in Britain, a person who is given the honour of a title such as 'Lord' and a place in the House of Lords as a reward for the good things they have done for the country

,**life 'peerage** noun [C] the honour and position of being a life peer

life preserver /ˈlaɪf.prɪˌzɜː.vər/ ⓤ /-ˌzɝː.vɚ/ noun [C] US FOR **life belt** or **life jacket**

lifer /ˈlaɪ.fər/ ⓤ /-fɚ/ noun [C] INFORMAL someone who has been punished by being put in prison for a very long time or, in the US, until they die

'**life ,raft** noun [C] a type of boat which is carried on a large ship and is used in emergencies, for example when the ship is sinking, to take people to safety

life-saver WATER /ˈlaɪfˌseɪ.vər/ ⓤ /-vɚ/ noun [C] AUS FOR **lifeguard**

life-saver HELP /ˈlaɪfˌseɪ.vər/ ⓤ /-vɚ/ noun [C] someone or something that gives you a lot of help when you are in a very difficult situation: *When you're stuck in traffic, a mobile phone's an absolute life-saver.*

life-saving /ˈlaɪfˌseɪ.vɪŋ/ noun [U] when you learn how to save someone's life when they have fallen into water: *a certificate in life-saving*

'**life ,science** noun [C usually pl] one of the sections of science dealing with the structure and behaviour of living things, such as BOTANY, ZOOLOGY, BIOCHEMISTRY and ANTHROPOLOGY

,**life 'sentence** noun [C] (INFORMAL **life**) the punishment of being put in prison for a very long time, or, in the US, until death ⮞See also **life imprisonment**; **lifer**.

life-size(d) /ˈlaɪf.saɪzd/ adj describes a work of art or model that is the same size as the person or thing that it represents: *a life-size statue of the Prime Minister*

lifespan /ˈlaɪf.spæn/ noun [C] the length of time for which a person, animal or thing exists: *The **average** human lifespan in the developed countries has increased over the last hundred years.* ○ *The project's lifespan is estimated at about five years.*

'**life ,story** noun [C] everything that has happened to someone during their life: *The last time you sat me next to Alberto I had to hear his whole life story!*

lifestyle /ˈlaɪf.staɪl/ noun [C] someone's way of living; the things that a person or particular group of people usually do: *He doesn't have a very healthy lifestyle.* ○ *She needs a pretty high income to support her lifestyle.* ○ *an alternative lifestyle*

life-support system /ˈlaɪf.səˌpɔːt.sɪs.təm/ ⓤ /-ˌsɔːrt-/ noun [C] **1** the equipment used to keep a person alive when they are very ill or injured: *He's been on a life-support system since the crash.* **2** the natural structures and systems that are necessary for living things, especially human beings, to be able to live: *The lack of rain is threatening all the region's life-support systems (= the earth, trees and rivers).*

life's work UK /ˌlaɪfsˈwɜːk/ ⓤ /-ˈwɝːk/ noun [U] (US **life work**) A person's life's work is the work which is most important to them and to which they give a lot of time and effort: *Her garden was her life's work.*

life-threatening /ˈlaɪfˌθret.ᵊn.ɪŋ/ adj A life-threatening disease is a very serious one that can cause death: *life-threatening diseases such as cancer*

lifetime /ˈlaɪf.taɪm/ noun [C usually sing] the period of time during which someone lives or something exists: *We'll see a tremendous lot of technological changes **during/in** our lifetime.* ○ *Winners of the competition will receive the holiday **of a** lifetime (= the best holiday they will ever have).* ○ *I've only been working here two days, but it seems like a lifetime.* ○ *A watch of this quality should **last a** lifetime.* ○ *Enter our competition and this **once-in-a-lifetime** experience could be yours!* ○ *Marriage is no longer always seen as a lifetime commitment.* ○ *You could win a lifetime's supply of toothpaste.*

lift RAISE /lɪft/ verb [T] **1** to move something from a lower to a higher position: *Could you help me lift this table, please?* ○ *Could you lift your chair a bit – I've got my bag caught under it.* ○ *She lifted the cigarette **(up) to** her lips.* ○ *He lifted his eyes (= looked up) from the paper and glared.* **2** SPECIALIZED to dig underground vegetables or plants out of the ground: *They're lifting potatoes.*

lift /lɪft/ noun **1** [C or U] an act of lifting or raising something: *Give it one more lift and we'll have it at the top of the stairs.* **2** [U] SPECIALIZED the force on the wing of a bird or aircraft that keeps it in the air as it moves forward

lift TAKE HOLD /lɪft/ verb [I or T; usually + adv or prep] to take hold of and raise in order to remove, carry or move to a different position: *She lifted the baby out of her chair.* ○ *He lifted the box carefully down from the shelf.*

lift MAKE LOUD /lɪft/ verb [T] LITERARY to make your voice louder, especially when performing

lift MAKE INTERESTING /lɪft/ verb [T] INFORMAL to make something more interesting or enjoyable: *The article is informative enough, but it's a bit dull – we need something to lift it.*

lift MAKE HAPPY /lɪft/ verb INFORMAL **lift sb's spirits** to make someone happier: *Nothing – not even the prospect of dinner – could lift his spirits.*

lift /lɪft/ noun **give sb a lift** to make someone happier: *She'd been feeling a bit low but hearing that she'd got the job gave her a lift.*

lift GO AWAY /lɪft/ verb [I] (of mist or fog) to go away until none is left: *The morning mist had lifted and the sun was starting to come through.*

lift END /lɪft/ verb [T] to end a rule or law: *The restrictions on water usage have been lifted now that the river levels are normal.* ○ *At last they've lifted the ban on jeans at the club.*

lift STEAL /lɪft/ verb [T] INFORMAL **1** to steal something **2** to use someone else's writing, music or idea, pretending that it is your own: *He'd lifted whole passages from a journal.*

lift CARRYING DEVICE UK /lɪft/ noun [C] (US **elevator**) a box-like device which moves up and down, carrying people or goods from one floor of a building to another or raising and lowering people underground in a mine: *Take the lift to the sixth floor.*

lift [JOURNEY] /lɪft/ *noun* [C usually sing] a free journey in another person's vehicle, especially a car: *I'll **give** you a lift **to** the station if you like.* ○ *He **hitched** a lift* (= stood by the road and made a signal asking a car to stop and take him) ***to** Birmingham.*

lift-off /ˈlɪft.ɒf/ [US] /-ɑːf/ *noun* [C or U] when a spacecraft or rocket leaves the ground: *We **have** lift-off.*

ligament /ˈlɪg.ə.mənt/ *noun* [C] any of the strong strips of tissue in the body that connect bones together, limiting movements in joints and supporting muscles and other tissue

ligature /ˈlɪg.ə.tʃəʳ/ [US] /-tʃɚ/ *noun* [C] SPECIALIZED a thread or wire used for tying something, especially a BLOOD VESSEL: *Ligatures are used in surgery to stop the flow of a bleeding artery.*

light [BRIGHTNESS] /laɪt/ *noun* **1** [U] the brightness that comes from the sun, fire, etc. and from electrical devices, and that allows things to be seen: *a bright light* ○ *fluorescent/ultraviolet light* ○ *a beam/ray of light* ○ *Light was streaming in through the open door.* ○ *It's a north-facing room so it doesn't get much light* (= brightness from the sun). **2** [C] a device which produces light, such as a LAMP or a LIGHT BULB: *Could you switch/turn the light **on/off**, please?* ○ *She could see the city lights in the distance.* ○ *As the lights went down, the audience grew quiet.* ○ *My front bike light isn't working.*

• **light at the end of the tunnel** signs of improvement in a situation which has been bad for a long time, or signs that a long and difficult piece of work is almost completed: *As the exams approached, she felt that at last she could see the light at the end of the tunnel.*

• **the light of *your* life** HUMOROUS the person whom you love most

• **come to light** (*ALSO* **bring *sth* to light**) If facts come to light or are brought to light, they become known: *Fresh evidence has recently come to light which suggests that he didn't in fact commit the murder.*

• **cast/shed/throw light on *sth*** Something or someone that casts/sheds/throws light on a situation provides an explanation for it or information which makes it easier to understand: *As an economist, he was able to shed some light on the problem.*

• **go out like a light** INFORMAL to go to sleep very quickly or to become unconscious very quickly

• **show someone in a bad light** to make someone seem to be a bad person: *He was concerned that the film had shown him in a bad light.*

• **in the light of *sth*** (*US USUALLY* **in light of**) because of: *In the light of recent incidents, we are asking our customers to take particular care of their personal belongings.*

light /laɪt/ *verb* [T] **lit** or **lighted**, **lit** or **lighted** to produce light which makes an object or area bright or easy to see: *The stage had been lit with candles.* ○ *Fireworks lit **up** the sky* (= made the sky bright).

light /laɪt/ *adj* lit by the natural light of the day: *The big windows make the room feel wonderfully light and airy.* ○ *It gets light very early these summer mornings.* ○ *Summer is coming and the evenings are getting lighter* (= getting dark later).

lighten /ˈlaɪ.tᵊn/ [US] /-t̬ᵊn/ *verb* [I] to become less dark: *The sky had lightened and there were breaks in the clouds.*
* NOTE: The opposite is **darken**.

lighting /ˈlaɪ.tɪŋ/ [US] /-t̬ɪŋ/ *noun* [U] the arrangement of lights used in a room, house, theatre, etc.

light [FLAME] /laɪt/ *noun* **a light** something which will produce a flame and cause burning, such as a match or a cigarette LIGHTER: *Have you got a light, please?*

• **set light to *sth*** UK to cause something to start burning: *The lamp caught fire and set light to the curtains.*

light /laɪt/ *verb* [I or T] **lit** or **lighted**, **lit** or **lighted** to start to burn or to make something start to burn: *to light a fire* ○ *I can't get the cooker to light.* ○ *He lit his fifth cigarette in half an hour.*

lighted /ˈlaɪ.tɪd/ [US] /-t̬ɪd/ *adj* [before n] burning or starting to burn: *a lighted candle/match* ○ *a lighted fuse*

light [NOT HEAVY] /laɪt/ *adj* **1** not heavy: *Here, take this bag – it's quite light.* ○ *He's a few pounds lighter than he used to be.* ○ *How do you get your cakes so wonderfully light, Felicity?* ○ *He has a very light* (= gentle) ***touch**, which is what is required in massage.* ○ *She's very light **on her feet*** (= she moves gracefully). **2** describes clothes that are made of thin material which allows you to be cool: *a light summer dress* **3** A light meal is small and easy to digest: *I don't eat much for lunch – just a light snack.*

• **(as) light as a feather** very light

lighten /ˈlaɪ.tᵊn/ [US] /-t̬ᵊn/ *verb* **lighten *sb's* burden/load, etc.** to make a difficult situation or responsibility easier: *Getting a new assistant will lighten* (= reduce) *the workload considerably.*

lightness /ˈlaɪt.nəs/ *noun* [U] the state of being light

light [NOT SERIOUS] /laɪt/ *adj* entertaining and easily understood, but not serious and not intended to make you think: *I want some light **reading** for the summer holidays – a romance or something.*

• **make light of *sth*** to behave as if a situation, especially a problem, is not serious or important: *It is easy to make light of other people's problems.*

lighten /ˈlaɪ.tᵊn/ [US] /-t̬ᵊn/ *verb* [I or T] to (cause to) become happier and less anxious: *His **mood** lightened after the phone call.* ○ *He tried to lighten the atmosphere by telling a joke.*

lightly /ˈlaɪt.li/ *adv* **1** If you say something lightly, you are not serious when you say it: *"Anyway, it won't affect me because I'm leaving," she said lightly.* **2 not do *sth* lightly** If something is not said or treated lightly, it is said or treated in a serious way, after great consideration: *Accusations like these from a top minister are not **made** lightly.*

light [NOT STRONG] /laɪt/ *adj* **1** not great in strength or amount: *A light wind was blowing.* ○ *The traffic was quite light so we got through London quickly.* ○ *It's only light rain – you don't need an umbrella.* **2** describes alcoholic drinks that are not strong in flavour: *It's described on the label as 'light, fruity wine'.* **3 light eater/drinker/smoker** someone who eats/drinks/smokes only a little **4 light sleeper** someone who is easily woken up by noise, etc.

lightly /ˈlaɪt.li/ *adv* **1** gently or using very little of something: *She patted him lightly on the shoulder.* ○ *Dust the cake lightly with icing sugar.* **2** If food is lightly cooked, it is cooked for only a short time: *lightly cooked vegetables*

light [NOT SEVERE] /laɪt/ *adj* **1** needing only a very small amount of effort: *light exercise, such as walking* ○ *a bit of light housework* **2** A light sentence in prison is a short one: *He got off with a fairly light sentence because it was his first conviction.*

lightly /ˈlaɪt.li/ *adv* **get off lightly; let *sb* off lightly** to be punished or punish someone less severely than might have been expected: *I think he got off quite lightly considering it's his third driving offence.*

PHRASAL VERBS WITH **light**

▲ **light on/upon *sth*** *phrasal verb* FORMAL to find or think of something unexpectedly: *We lighted upon the solution entirely by accident.*

▲ **light *(sth)* up** [EXPRESSION] *phrasal verb* [M] If your face or eyes light up, or if a smile lights up your face, you suddenly look happy: *Rosie's whole face lit up **with** excitement when she saw the presents.*

▲ **light *(sth)* up** [CIGARETTE] *phrasal verb* [M] to light a cigarette: *I was lighting up when I noticed a 'no smoking' sign.*

light [PALE] /laɪt/ *adj* (of colours) pale: *light blue/green*
* NOTE: The opposite is **dark**.

lighten /ˈlaɪ.tᵊn/ [US] /-t̬ᵊn/ *verb* [T] to make something lighter: *The sun always lightens my hair.*

PHRASAL VERBS WITH **lighten**

▲ **lighten *sth* up** *phrasal verb* [M] to make a speech or piece of writing less serious: *I thought I'd slip in a few jokes to lighten up the talk.*

▲ **lighten up** *phrasal verb* INFORMAL to become more relaxed and less serious: *Oh, lighten up! I was only joking!* ○ *I wish she'd lighten up a bit.*

ˌlight ˈaircraft *noun* [C or U] a small plane suitable for carrying small loads

ˈlight ˌbulb *noun* [C] (*ALSO* **bulb**) a rounded glass container with a thin thread of metal inside which produces light when an electric current goes through it

lighter /ˈlaɪ.təʳ/ [US] /-t̬ɚ/ *noun* [C] a small device for providing a flame for a cigarette etc: *a cigarette lighter*

light-fingered /ˌlaɪtˈfɪŋ.gəd/ [US] /-gɚd/ *adj INFORMAL* If you describe someone as light-fingered you mean that they have a habit of stealing things.

ˈlight ˌglobe *noun* [C] (*ALSO* **globe**) *AUS FOR* **light bulb**

light-headed /ˌlaɪtˈhed.ɪd/ *adj* If you feel light-headed you feel weak and as if you are going to lose your balance: *She'd had a couple of glasses of champagne and was starting to feel light-headed.*

light-hearted /ˌlaɪtˈhɑː.tɪd/ [US] /-ˈhɑːr.t̬ɪd/ *adj* happy and not serious: *It was a fairly light-hearted discussion.*

ˌlight ˈheavyweight *noun* [C] a BOXER whose weight is between MIDDLEWEIGHT and HEAVYWEIGHT

lighthouse /ˈlaɪt.haʊs/ *noun* [C] a tall building by the sea with a flashing light at the top to warn ships of dangerous rocks

ˌlight ˈindustry *noun* [C or U] industry which makes small items and does not need to use large heavy machinery

lighting-up time /ˌlaɪ.tɪŋˈʌp.taɪm/ [US] /-t̬ɪŋ-/ *noun* [C usually sing] *UK* the time in the afternoon or evening when the law states that vehicles must have their lights switched on

ˈlight ˌmeter *noun* [C] a device for measuring how much light there is, especially to show how much light should be allowed to reach a film when taking a photograph

lightning /ˈlaɪt.nɪŋ/ *noun* [U] a flash of bright light in the sky which is produced by electricity moving between clouds or from clouds to the ground: ***thunder and** lightning* ○ *a **flash of** lightning* ○ *That tree was **struck by** lightning.* ○ *She changed her clothes **with** lightning **speed*** (= extremely quickly).

• **like lightning** extremely quickly

• **Lightning never strikes twice (in the same place).** *SAYING* said to show that it is unlikely that something bad or unusual will happen to the same person twice

ˈlightning conˌductor *UK noun* [C] (*US* **lightning rod**) a strip of metal going from the highest point of a building to the ground, which prevents lightning from damaging the building by taking the electricity to the ground before it can reach a dangerous level

ˈlightning ˌrod *noun* [C] *US* someone or something that takes all the blame for a situation, although other people or things are responsible too: *In a harsh economic climate, raises for teachers have become a lightning rod for criticism.*

ˈlightning ˌstrike *noun* [C] *US FOR* **wildcat strike**

light-pen /ˈlaɪt.pen/ *noun* [C] a pen-shaped device which is used for reading BAR CODES

ˌlight ˈrailway *noun* [C] a railway system for transporting people around a city

lights-out /ˈlaɪts.aʊt/ /ˌ-ˈ-/ *noun* [U] (at a school where children live or in the army) the time in the evening when the lights are switched off in the room where people sleep: *No talking after lights-out!*

lightweight /ˈlaɪt.weɪt/ *adj* **1** weighing only a little or less than average: *I need a lightweight jacket for the summer evenings.* **2** *DISAPPROVING* not showing deep understanding or knowledge of any subject: *She's the author of some fairly lightweight historical novels.*

lightweight /ˈlaɪt.weɪt/ *noun* [C] **1** in some sports, including boxing, a person whose weight is between FEATHERWEIGHT and WELTERWEIGHT ➲Compare **heavyweight. 2** *DISAPPROVING* a person whose work in a particular area of activity does not show a deep understanding or knowledge of that subject: *In certain circles he has been dismissed as a literary lightweight.*

ˈlight ˌyear *noun* [C] the distance that light travels in one year (about 9 500 000 000 000 kilometres)

• **light years away** an extremely long time from now in the past or future: *It all happened when I was at college, which seems light years away now that I'm over fifty.*

like [ENJOY] /laɪk/ *verb* [T] **1** to enjoy or approve of something or someone: *I like your new haircut.* ○ *Do you like fish?* ○ *I like it when a book is so good that you can't put it down.* ○ *I quite like wine but I could live without it.* ○ *He's very **well**-liked* (= popular) *at work.* ○ [+ v-ing] *I don't like upsetting people.* ○ [+ to infinitive] *He likes **to** spend his evenings in front of the television.* ○ [+ obj + past participle] *He likes his steak well-done.* **2** to be annoyed by something: *I like **the way** he just assumes we'll listen to him when he doesn't take in a word anyone else says!*

• **How do you like...? 1** used when asking someone how they like their drinks made: *"How do you like your tea?" "Milk and one sugar, please."* **2** used when asking someone for an opinion: *How do you like my new shoes?*

• **I'd like to see...** *INFORMAL* said to mean that you do not believe someone can do something: *He said women have an easier life than men, did he? – I'd like to see him bring up children and go to work at the same time.*

• **How would *you* like...?** *INFORMAL* said to suggest that someone would not like to be in a situation experienced by someone else: *I'm not surprised he shouted at you! How would you like to be pushed into a wall?*

• **we like cheap/tall/young, etc.** *HUMOROUS* used to say that you like or approve of something: *Cheap is good – we like cheap.* ○ *"He's blond and he's very tall." "We like tall."*

likes /laɪks/ *plural noun* the things that someone enjoys: *The pop-star lists his likes as 'my new Porsche, my girlfriend and staying up all night'.* ○ *They can't expect me to accommodate all their silly little likes **and dislikes**.*

like [WANT] /laɪk/ *verb* **1 would/**(*FORMAL*)***should* like...** used to say that you want or desire something: *I think I'd like the soup for my starter.* ○ [+ to infinitive] *I'd like **to** go to Moscow.* ○ *I would like **to** say a big thankyou to everyone who's helped to make our wedding such a special occasion!* **2** used in requests: *I'd like one of the round loaves, please.* ○ [+ to infinitive] *I'd like **to** book a seat for tonight's performance.* ○ [+ obj + to infinitive] *I'd like you **to** send this for me first class, please.* ○ [+ obj + past participle] *I would like the whole lot finish**ed** by the weekend.*

• **Would you like...?** used when offering something or inviting someone: *Would you like a drink?* ○ *Would you like **to** join us for dinner tonight?* ○ *Would you like me **to** take you in the car?*

• **if you like** used for asking if someone agrees with a suggestion: *We can leave now if you like.* ○ *I'm not sure if I have the confidence, the nerve if you like* (= if this phrase is suitable), *to apply for the job.*

like [SIMILAR TO] /laɪk/ *prep, conjunction* similar to; in the same way or manner as: *He **looks** like his brother.* ○ *She's very much like her mother* (= She is similar in appearance or character). ○ *Is Japanese food like Chinese?* ○ *I've got a sweater **just** like that.* ○ *Her hair was so soft it was like silk.* ○ *You're acting like a complete idiot!* ○ *She sings like an angel!* ○ *Like I said* (= As I have already said), *I don't wear perfume.* ○ *Like most people* (= As most people would), *I'd prefer to have enough money not to work* ○ *It **feels/seems** like* (= It seems to me) *ages since we last spoke.* ○ *There's **nothing** like a good cup of coffee* (= it's better than anything)*!*

• **be of like mind** *FORMAL* When people are of like mind, they agree.

• **like two peas in a pod** very similar, especially in appearance: *The twins are like two peas in a pod.*

• **What is *sb/sth* like?** something you say to ask someone to describe someone or something: *You've met Ben's new girlfriend, haven't you? What's she like?* ○ *I've never been to Bruges – what's it like?* ○ *So what's it like, then, not having to work?*

• **What are you like?** (*ALSO* **What is she/he like?**) *UK INFORMAL* used when someone has said or done something silly: *"Of course Emma's only worry was whether her lipstick had smudged." "Emma! What is she like?"*

like /laɪk/ *noun* **the like of *sb/sth*; *sb's/sth's* like** a person, thing or group similar in character or quality to the one mentioned: *He was a very great actor – we won't **see** his like again.* ○ *He described a superlative meal, the like of which he'd never eaten.*

• **and such like** (*ALSO* **and the like**) *INFORMAL* and similar things: *There's a big sports hall for tennis and badminton and such like.*

-like /-laɪk/ *suffix* like the thing mentioned: *The paper criticized what it described as the animal-like behaviour* *of the football fans.* ○ *There was a large, ball-like structure on top of the building.*

likes /laɪks/ *plural noun* (ALSO **like**) INFORMAL **not for the likes of sb** not for the type of people mentioned: *First-class travel is for posh people – it's not for the likes of us.*

like FEELINGS/SPEECH /laɪk/ *adv* INFORMAL used before you describe how you were feeling or what you said when something happened to you: *Then I saw how late it was and I'm like, so upset.* ○ *He started shouting at me and I'm like, "What's your problem? I'm on your side!"*

like TYPICAL OF /laɪk/ *prep* typical or characteristic of: *That's just like Maisie to turn up half an hour late to her own party!* ○ *It's not like you to be so quiet – are you all right, my love?*

like SUCH AS /laɪk/ *prep* such as: *She looks best in bright, vibrant colours, like red and pink.*

like AS IF /laɪk/ *prep, conjunction* in a way that suggests: *It looks like I'm going to be in the office until late tonight.* ○ *It looks like rain* (= I think it is going to rain). ○ *It sounds to me like you ought to change jobs.* ○ *You look like you've just got out of bed!* ○ NOT STANDARD *She acts like she's stupid!*

like PAUSE /laɪk/ *adv* INFORMAL used in conversation as a pause or to emphasize an adjective: *He's, like, really friendly – someone you can talk to.* ○ *If there's nothing you can do to change the situation, it's like – why bother?*

likeable, US **likable** /ˈlaɪ.kə.bl̩/ *adj* describes a person who is pleasant and easy to like: *He's a very likeable sort of bloke.*

likelihood /ˈlaɪ.kli.hʊd/ *noun* [U] the chance that something will happen: *This latest dispute greatly increases the likelihood of a strike.* ○ [+ that] *There is every likelihood that more jobs will be lost later this year.* ○ *There is little likelihood now that interest rates will come down further.*

likely /ˈlaɪ.kli/ *adj* describes something that will probably happen or is expected: *Do remind me because I'm likely to forget.* ○ *What's the likely outcome of this whole business?* ○ *I suppose that might happen but it's not very likely.* ○ [+ that] *It's quite likely that we'll be in Spain this time next year.* ○ INFORMAL *"Do you want to join me on a ten-mile run?" "Not likely* (= certainly not)*!"*
✻ NOTE: The opposite is **unlikely**.
● **as likely/like as not** probably: *As likely as not, she'll end up in court over this problem.*
● **(That's) a likely story!** INFORMAL said when you do not believe something: *"He said he bought them all very cheaply from some bloke he knows." "That's a likely story!"*

like /laɪk/ *adj* OLD USE **be like to do sth** to be likely to do something

like-minded /ˌlaɪkˈmaɪn.dɪd/ *adj* People who are described as like-minded share the same opinions, ideas or interests: *A dedicated football-fan herself, she started the magazine for like-minded women.*

liken /ˈlaɪ.kən/ *verb*
▲ **liken sb/sth to sb/sth** *phrasal verb* [often passive] to say that someone is similar to or has the same qualities as someone else: *She's been likened to a young Elizabeth Taylor.*

likeness /ˈlaɪk.nəs/ *noun* [C or U] **1** being similar in appearance: *There's a definite family likeness around the eyes.* **2 a good/remarkable, etc. likeness** a painting or other representation of a person that looks very like them

likewise /ˈlaɪk.waɪz/ *adv* in the same way: *Just water these plants twice a week, and likewise the ones in the bedroom.* ○ *I haven't got time to spend hours preparing one dish!" "Likewise* (= It's the same for me)*."*

liking /ˈlaɪ.kɪŋ/ *noun* [S] a feeling that you like someone or something: *She has a liking for fine wines.* ○ *I'm developing quite a liking for jazz.* ○ FORMAL *Is the room to your liking, Sir* (= are you satisfied with it)*?* ○ *The dessert was a bit sweet for my liking* (= I like it less sweet)*.*

lilac PLANT /ˈlaɪ.lək/ *noun* [C or U] a bush or small tree with sweet-smelling purple or white flowers: *The lilacs are in bloom.*

lilac COLOUR /ˈlaɪ.lək/ *adj, noun* [U] (having) a pale pinkish-purple colour

lilliputian /ˌlɪl.ɪˈpjuː.ʃᵊn/ *adj* MAINLY HUMOROUS extremely small

Lilo UK TRADEMARK (*plural* **Lilos**), **lilo** (*plural* **lilos**) /ˈlaɪ.ləʊ/ US /-loʊ/ *noun* [C] (US **air mattress**) a type of plastic or rubber mattress which you fill with air and use to lie on or to float on water

lilt /lɪlt/ *noun* [S] a gentle and pleasant rising and falling sound in a person's voice: *He's got that lovely Irish lilt in his voice.*

lilting /ˈlɪl.tɪŋ/ US /-t̬ɪŋ/ *adj* A lilting voice or tune gently rises and falls in a way that is pleasant to listen to.

lily /ˈlɪl.i/ *noun* [C] any of various plants with a large, bell-shaped flower on a long stem ⊃See picture **Flowers and Plants** on page Centre 3

lily-livered /ˌlɪl.iˈlɪv.əd/ US /-ɚd/ *adj* LITERARY cowardly

lily of the ˈvalley *noun* [C] a small plant with large oval leaves and small bell-shaped white flowers which smell sweet

'lily ˌpad *noun* [C] the large round-shaped leaf of the water lily which floats on the surface of water

lily-white COLOUR /ˌlɪl.iˈwaɪt/ *adj* OLD-FASHIONED pure white

lily-white RACE /ˌlɪl.iˈwaɪt/ *adj* US SLANG DISAPPROVING Caucasian: *a lily-white suburb*

lily-white CHARACTER /ˌlɪl.iˈwaɪt/ *adj* having a perfect character with no bad qualities

lima bean US /ˌlaɪ.məˈbiːn/ US /ˈliː-/ *noun* [C usually pl] (UK **butter bean**) a large, flat, creamy-yellow or pale green bean

limb /lɪm/ *noun* [C] an arm or leg of a person or animal, or a large branch of a tree: *The accident victims mostly had injuries to their lower limbs* (= legs)*.* ○ *an artificial limb*
● **out on a limb** having an opinion which is different from most people's and is unpopular: *She's going out on a limb in criticizing her own party leadership.*

limber /ˈlɪm.bəʳ/ US /-bɚ/ *adj* (of a person) able to bend and move easily and gracefully

limber /ˈlɪm.bəʳ/ US /-bɚ/ *verb*
▲ **limber up** *phrasal verb* to do gentle exercises to stretch the muscles in order to prepare the body for more active physical exercise: *The substitutes are beginning to limber up on the sidelines.*

limbo UNCERTAINTY /ˈlɪm.bəʊ/ US /-boʊ/ *noun* [U] an uncertain situation that you cannot control and in which there is no advancement or improvement: *Until we've got official permission to go ahead with the plans we're in limbo.*

the limbo DANCE *noun* a dance from the West Indies in which the dancer bends backwards to go under a low bar which is made lower each time he or she goes under it

lime FRUIT /laɪm/ *noun* [C or U] a juicy round fruit which is sour like a lemon but smaller and green, or the small Asian tree on which this fruit grows ⊃See picture **Fruit** on page Centre 1

lime CHEMICAL /laɪm/ *noun* [U] **1** (ALSO **quicklime**) a white powdery substance which is used especially to spread on the land to improve the quality of earth so that crops grow better **2** (ALSO **limescale**) white material that collects inside water pipes, KETTLES, etc. in areas where the water is HARD (= contains a lot of natural chemicals) ⊃See also **scale** COVERING.

lime /laɪm/ *verb* [T] to spread lime on a piece of land

limy /ˈlaɪ.mi/ *adj* describes land that has been covered with lime or contains it naturally

lime ˈgreen *noun* [U], *adj* (of) a light, bright, greenish-yellow colour

the limelight /ðəˈlaɪm.laɪt/ *noun* [S] public attention and interest: *She's been in the limelight* (= receiving a lot of public attention and interest) *recently, following the release of her controversial new film.*

limerick /ˈlɪm.ᵊr.ɪk/ US /-ɚ-/ *noun* [C] a humorous poem with five lines

limestone /ˈlaɪm.stəʊn/ [US] /-stoʊn/ *noun* [U] a white or light grey rock which is used as a building material and in the making of cement

ˈlime (ˌtree) *noun* [C] (*US USUALLY* **linden**) a large tree with leaves shaped like a heart and pale yellow flowers

limey /ˈlaɪ.mi/ *noun* [C] *US OLD-FASHIONED* a British person

limit /ˈlɪm.ɪt/ *noun* **1** [C] the greatest amount, number or level of something that is either possible or allowed: *Is there a limit* ***on*** *the amount of money you can claim?* ○ *I think we ought to* ***put*** *a strict limit* ***on*** *the amount of time we can spend on the project.* ○ *There's a limit* ***to*** *the number of times I can stop what I'm doing just so I can help him!* ○ *We* ***set*** *a* ***time*** *limit* ***of*** *thirty minutes for the test.* **2** [U] *INFORMAL* the amount of something that is enough and not too much: *Three martini cocktails are my limit.* ○ *I won't have any more – I* ***know*** *my limit!*
the limit *noun* [S] **1** *OLD-FASHIONED INFORMAL* something that is very annoying or inconvenient: *And now you're cutting your toenails in bed! – That really is the limit!* **2** the largest amount of alcohol that is legally allowed to be present in the blood while a person is driving a vehicle: *She was definitely driving* ***over*** *the limit.*
limits /ˈlɪm.ɪts/ *plural noun* limit: *I'd like to play squash, but I'm sixty and I* ***know*** *my limits.* ○ *His genius* ***knows no*** *limits.* ○ *The pay rise was in excess of* ***spending*** *limits* ***imposed/set*** *by the government.*
• **off limits 1** *MAINLY US* If a place is off limits, you are not allowed to go there: *The playing fields were off limits* ***to*** *the school-children during the winter months.* **2** not allowed: *An article on this topic would once have been considered off limits.*
• **within limits** avoiding behaviour which is extreme or silly: *You can wear what you like, within limits.*
limit /ˈlɪm.ɪt/ *verb* [T] to control something so that it is not greater than a particular amount, number or level: *I've been asked to limit my speech* ***to*** *ten minutes maximum.* ○ *Having so little money to spend on an apartment does limit you in your choice.*

limitation /ˌlɪm.ɪˈteɪ.ʃən/ *noun* [U] the act of controlling and especially reducing something: *the limitation of nuclear weapons*
limitations /ˌlɪm.ɪˈteɪ.ʃənz/ *plural noun DISAPPROVING* If someone or something has limitations, they are not as good as they could be: *Living in a flat is all right, but it* ***has its*** *limitations – for example, you don't have your own garden.* ○ *Despite her limitations as an actress, she was a great entertainer.*

limited /ˈlɪm.ɪ.tɪd/ [US] /-t̬ɪd/ *adj* **1** small in amount or number: *a limited choice* ○ *limited resources* **2** kept within a particular size, range, time, etc: *Places on the bus are limited* ***to*** *fifty – so book early!* ○ *The problem of stress is certainly not limited* ***to*** *people who work* (= it exists for others too). **3** (*WRITTEN ABBREVIATION* **Ltd**) used in the name of a LIMITED COMPANY

ˌlimited ˈcompany *noun* [C] a company, especially one in the UK, whose owners only have to pay part of the money they owe if the company fails financially

ˌlimited eˈdition *noun* [C] one of a small set of books or pictures that were printed: *She's got some very valuable limited editions on her shelves.*

limiting /ˈlɪm.ɪ.tɪŋ/ [US] /-t̬ɪŋ/ *adj* preventing you from having much choice: *Not eating meat or fish can be very limiting when you go to a restaurant.*

limitless /ˈlɪm.ɪt.ləs/ *adj* without limit: *the limitless sky* ○ *The minister said that the days of limitless spending were over.*

limousine /ˌlɪm.əˈziːn/ *noun* [C] (*INFORMAL* **limo**) **1** a large luxurious car, often driven by a CHAUFFEUR (= a person employed to drive a car for someone else) ➲See picture **Cars and Trucks** on page Centre 13 **2** *US* a small bus to take people to and from an airport

limp [PERSON/ANIMAL] /lɪmp/ *verb* [I] to walk unevenly and slowly because of having an injured or painful leg or foot: *Three minutes into the match, Jackson limped off the pitch with a serious ankle injury.* **limp** /lɪmp/ *noun* [S] *She* ***has*** *a slight limp.* ○ *He* ***walks with*** *a limp.*

limp [PROCESS] /lɪmp/ *verb* [I + adv or prep] *INFORMAL* to develop or grow slowly, unevenly or irregularly: *After limping* ***along*** *for almost two years, the economy is starting to show signs of recovery.*

limp [SOFT] /lɪmp/ *adj* soft and neither firm nor stiff: *a limp lettuce leaf/salad* ○ *a limp* ***handshake*** **limply** /ˈlɪm.pli/ *adv*: *She lay limply in his arms.* **limpness** /ˈlɪmp.nəs/ *noun* [U]

limpet /ˈlɪm.pɪt/ *noun* [C] a small sea animal with a cone-shaped shell which fixes itself to rocks

limpid /ˈlɪm.pɪd/ *adj* **1** *LITERARY* clear and transparent: *a limpid pool* **2** clearly expressed and easily understood: *limpid prose* **limpidly** /ˈlɪm.pɪd.li/ *adv*

limp wristed /ˌlɪmpˈrɪs.tɪd/ *adj* **1** describes a man who does not behave in the strong and determined way traditionally expected in men **2** *OFFENSIVE* describes a man who seems, by his manner, to be homosexual

limy /ˈlaɪ.mi/ *adj* ➲See at **lime** CHEMICAL.

linchpin, lynchpin /ˈlɪntʃ.pɪn/ *noun* **the linchpin of** the most important member of a group or part of a system, that holds together the other members or parts or makes it possible for them to operate as intended: *Woodford is the linchpin of the British athletics team.*

linctus /ˈlɪŋk.təs/ *noun* [U] *UK* a thick sweet liquid medicine that is used to treat coughs and sore throats

linden /ˈlɪn.dən/ *noun* [C] *US* a **lime (tree)**

line [LONG MARK] /laɪn/ *noun* [C] a long thin mark on the surface of something: *a straight line* ○ *Sign your name on the dotted line.* ○ *She was very old and her face was covered with lines.* ○ *My legs felt all wobbly when I stood up and I couldn't walk* ***in a straight*** *line* (= walk without moving to the side while moving forward).
lined /laɪnd/ *adj* (of paper) having lines printed across, or (of the skin on the face) having lines because of age: *lined paper* ○ *His face was heavily lined.*

line [EDGE] /laɪn/ *noun* [C] a long thin and sometimes imaginary mark that forms the edge, border or limit of something: *That ball was definitely in! It was nowhere near the line!* ○ *The police couldn't arrest him because he'd fled across the* ***state*** *line.* ○ *For many television viewers the* ***dividing*** *line between fact and fiction is becoming increasingly blurred.*
• **put/lay** ***sth*** **on the line** to risk something: *Firefighters put their lives on the line every working day.*
• **be on the line** to be at risk: *Almost 3 000 jobs have been lost recently, and a further 3 000 are on the line.*

line [SHAPE] /laɪn/ *noun* [C] the shape of something that has been designed or created: *They have a reputation for designing cars with elegant aerodynamic lines.*

line [SUPPORT] /laɪn/ *noun* [C] a long strong thin piece of material, such as string, rope or wire, that is used to support something: *I'd hung the washing out on the* ***clothes*** *line.* ○ *Can you feel the fish tugging on the line?*

line [ROW] /laɪn/ *noun* [C] **1** a group of people or things arranged in a row: *a line of trees* ○ *The prisoners formed a line against the wall.* **2** *US* (*UK* **queue**) a group of people standing one behind the other who are waiting for something: *Just* ***get in*** *line and wait your turn like everyone else.* ○ *I had to* ***wait/stand in*** *line for three hours to get tickets.* **3 a long line of** a series of people or things that follow each other in time: *She is the latest in a long line of controversial leaders.* ○ *He comes from a long line of doctors* (= A lot of his relatives were doctors before him).
• **along the lines of** ***sth*** (*ALSO* **along those lines**) similar in type: *I was thinking of doing a meal along the lines of that dinner I did for Annie and Dave.* ○ *They're campaigning for the electoral system to be reformed along the lines of* (= so that it becomes similar to) *the one in Germany.*
• **be in line with** ***sth*** to be similar to, or at the same level as something: *The company's results are in line with stock market expectations.* ○ *We're seeking a pay rise that's in line with inflation.* ○ *The salaries of temporary employees ought to be* ***brought into*** *line with those of permanent staff.*
• **step/be out of line** to behave in an unsuitable way: *It was made quite clear to me that if I stepped out of line again I'd be out of a job.*

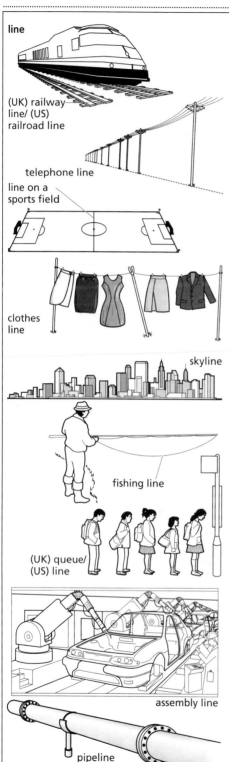

line

(UK) railway line/ (US) railroad line

telephone line

line on a sports field

clothes line

skyline

fishing line

(UK) queue/ (US) line

assembly line

pipeline

• **be out of line with** *sth* to be different from something: *Their predictions were hopelessly out of line with the actual results.*

• **be in line to the throne** to be the person who will become king or queen after the present ruler: *Prince Charles is first in line to the British throne.*

• **be in line to do** *sth* to have a very good chance of doing something: *Kim Bailey is next in line to replace Chris Finlay as managing director.*

• **be in line for** *sth* to be likely to get something, especially something good: *If anyone's in line for promotion, I should think it's Helen.*

line /laɪn/ *verb* [T] to form a row along the side of something: *Thousands of people lined the streets to watch the presidential procession pass by.* ○ *Police lined the route of the demonstration.* ○ *country lanes lined with trees*

line COVER /laɪn/ *verb* [T] to cover the inner surface of something: *I lined the drawers with old wallpaper.* ○ *How much would it cost to have this jacket lined?* ○ *Full-length mirrors lined each wall of the bathroom.*

• **line your pocket(s)** to earn money using dishonest or illegal methods: *Staff at the bank have apparently been lining their pockets with money from investors' accounts.*

line MILITARY /laɪn/ *noun* [C] a row of positions used to defend against enemy attack, particularly the ones closest to enemy positions: *They were taken prisoner while on a reconnaissance mission behind enemy lines.* ○ FIGURATIVE *In a game of football, the goalkeeper is the last line of defence.*

line TELEPHONE /laɪn/ *noun* [C] a connection to a telephone system: *I'm afraid your line's been disconnected because your last bill hasn't been paid.* ○ *If you want to air your opinions live on the radio, the lines will be open* (= you can telephone) *from eight o'clock.* ○ *I've got Chris Foster on the line for you. Do you want to take it now or call her back later?* ○ FORMAL *Please hold the line* (= wait). *I'll see if she's available.*

line RAILWAY /laɪn/ *noun* [C] (the route followed by) a railway track: *The train was delayed, apparently due to leaves on the line.* ○ *The Northern Line is the worst on the London Underground.* ○ **Main** *line services can be very quick, but travelling on the **branch** lines is much slower.*

• **somewhere along the line** at an unknown moment during a relationship or process: *I don't know what went wrong with our relationship, but somewhere along the line we just stopped loving each other.*

• **all along the line** ever since the beginning of a relationship or process: *The project's been plagued with financial problems all along the line.*

line COMPANY /laɪn/ *noun* [C] a company that transports people or goods: *a shipping line*

line WORDS /laɪn/ *noun* **1** [C] a row of words that form part of a text: *We could get more lines on the page if we reduced the type size.* ○ *The computer screen displays eighty characters per line.* **2** [C] a short series of musical notes **3** [C usually pl] the words that an actor or actress speaks when performing in a film, play etc: *I only had two lines in the whole play.* ○ *She hasn't **learned** her lines yet, and we've got our first rehearsal tomorrow.* ○ *I'm terrified of **forgetting** my lines.*

lines /laɪnz/ *plural noun* [C] UK a punishment for school students in which a sentence has to be written repeatedly: *She got 200 lines for swearing at her teacher.*

line REMARK /laɪn/ *noun* [C] a remark that is intended to amuse, persuade or deceive: *a speech full of memorable lines* ○ *He keeps giving me that line about not being able to do any work because his computer isn't working properly.* ○ *Who was it who came up with that famous line about "lies, damned lies and statistics"?*

line APPROACH TO SUBJECT /laɪn/ *noun* [C] a way of dealing with or thinking about something or someone: *The government's **official** line has always been to refuse to negotiate with terrorists.* ○ *The courts should **take** a tougher line **with** (= punish more severely) sex offenders.* ○ *Several Labour MPs disagree with their party's line **on** taxation.* ○ *What sort of line (= method of arguing) do you think we should **take** in the pay negotiations?* ○ *The police are confident that this new line of **inquiry** will lead them to the murderer.* ○ *It seems inevitable that the country will be **divided along** ethnic lines.*

• **get a line on** *sb* MAINLY US to find out information about someone that you do not know: *I've been trying to get a line on the guy they've nominated with no luck.*

line JOB /laɪn/ *noun* [C usually sing] the kind of job someone does: *"What line of work are you in?" "I'm a teacher."* ○ *You meet some very interesting people in my line of business.*

• **in the line of duty** Something which happens to you in the line of duty happens when you are doing your job: *This year alone eight police officers have been killed in the line of duty.*

line GOODS /laɪn/ *noun* [C] a range of similar things that are for sale: *There are discounts on many items from our older lines.* ○ *I was shown all their new lines.*

• **have a nice/good etc. line in** *sth* UK INFORMAL to do something skilfully and successfully: *He has a good line in anecdotes.*

PHRASAL VERBS WITH **line** ▼

▲ **line** *(sb)* **up** MOVE *phrasal verb* [M] to arrange people or things in a row or to stand in a row: *A fight broke out behind me as we lined up to receive our food rations.* ○ *The soldiers lined us up against a wall and I thought they were going to shoot us.*

▲ **line** *sth* **up** ORGANISE *phrasal verb* [M] to prepare, organize or arrange something: *Have you got anything exciting lined up for the weekend?* ○ *I've lined up a meeting with them for tomorrow morning.* ○ [+ to infinitive] *Have you got anyone lined up to do the catering at the Christmas party?*

lineage /ˈlɪn.i.ɪdʒ/ *noun* [C or U] FORMAL the members of a person's family who are directly related to that person and who lived a long time before him or her: *She's very proud of her ancient royal lineage.* **lineal** /ˈlɪn.i.əl/ *adj*: *She claims lineal descent from Henry VIII.* **lineally** /ˈlɪn.i.ə.li/ *adv*

linear LINES /ˈlɪn.i.əʳ/ US /-ɚ/ *adj* consisting of or to do with lines: *a linear diagram*

linear LENGTH /ˈlɪn.i.əʳ/ US /-ɚ/ *adj* [before n] relating to length, rather than area or volume: *linear measurement*

linear CONNECTION /ˈlɪn.i.əʳ/ US /-ɚ/ *adj* FORMAL **1** involving a series of events or thoughts in which one follows another one directly: *These mental exercises are designed to break linear thinking habits and encourage the creativity that is needed for innovation.* **2** describes a relationship between two things that is direct or clear: *Is there a linear relationship between salaries and productivity?*

linebacker /ˈlaɪnˌbæk.əʳ/ US /-ɚ/ *noun* [C] US a player in American football who tries to stop players from the other team from moving the ball along the field

line drawing *noun* [C] a pen or pencil drawing that consists only of lines

line item *noun* [C] US SPECIALIZED a single part of a financial statement, especially one giving details of the accounts of a company or government

line manager *noun* **1** MAINLY UK *sb's* **line manager** someone who is responsible for managing someone else in a company or business **2** one of the managers who are responsible for the most important activities of a large company, such as production

linen /ˈlɪn.ɪn/ *noun* [U] **1** strong cloth that is woven from the fibres of the FLAX plant: *a linen jacket* ○ *the crumpled charm of linen* **2** sheets, TABLECLOTHS, etc. which are made from linen or a similar material: *bed linen* ○ *table linen*

linen basket *noun* [C] a container for clothes and sheets etc. that need washing

line of scrimmage *noun* [C usually sing] US in American football, the line on which the ball is positioned at the beginning of PLAY (= a period of action)

lineout /ˈlaɪn.aʊt/ *noun* [C] UK a way of continuing a game of rugby after the ball has gone off the field, in which the attacking players from both teams form two parallel lines at the edge of the field and jump to catch the ball when it is thrown between the two lines

liner /ˈlaɪ.nəʳ/ US /-nɚ/ *noun* [C] a large ship for carrying passengers in great comfort on long journeys

liner note *noun* [C] US information about a performer or a performance that is supplied with a sound recording

linesman /ˈlaɪnz.mən/ *noun* [C] an official in some sports who is responsible for deciding when the ball has crossed the line that marks the edge of the playing area

line-up /ˈlaɪn.ʌp/ *noun* [C] **1** UK (US **lineup**) a group of people that has been brought together to form a team or take part in an event: *Several important changes are expected in the line-up for Thursday's match against Scotland.* ○ *We've got a star-studded line-up of guests on tonight's show.* **2** US FOR **identity parade 3** US the order in which the players in a baseball team hit the ball

linger /ˈlɪŋ.gəʳ/ US /-gɚ/ *verb* [I] to take a long time to leave or disappear: *After the play had finished, we lingered for a while in the bar hoping to catch sight of the actors.* ○ *The smell from the fire still lingered days later.* ○ *It's impossible to forget such horrific events – they linger (on) in the memory forever.* **lingerer** /ˈlɪŋ.gəʳ.əʳ/ US /-gɚ.ɚ/ *noun* [C]

lingering /ˈlɪŋ.gəʳ.ɪŋ/ US /-gɚ.ɪŋ/ *adj* [before n] lasting a long time: *She gave him a long, lingering kiss.* ○ *She's says she's stopped seeing him, but I still have lingering doubts.* ○ *The defeat ends any lingering hopes she might have had of winning the championship.* **lingeringly** /ˈlɪŋ.gəʳ.ɪŋ.li/ US /-gɚ.ɪŋ.li/ *adv*

lingerie /ˈlæn.ʒəʳ.i/ US /ˌlɑːn.ʒə'reɪ/ *noun* [U] women's underwear

lingo /ˈlɪŋ.gəʊ/ US /-goʊ/ *noun* [C usually sing] *plural* **lingoes** INFORMAL **1** a foreign language: *In Italy, of course, Stef can speak the lingo.* **2** a type of language that contains a lot of unusual or technical expressions: *Internet lingo*

lingua franca /ˌlɪŋ.gwəˈfræŋ.kə/ *noun* [C usually sing] a language which is used for communication between groups of people who speak different languages but which is not used between members of the same group: *The international business community sees English as a lingua franca.*

linguist /ˈlɪŋ.gwɪst/ *noun* [C] someone who studies foreign languages or can speak them very well, or someone who teaches or studies linguistics

linguistic /lɪŋˈgwɪs.tɪk/ *adj* connected with language or the study of language: *I'm particularly interested in the linguistic development of young children.* **linguistically** /lɪŋˈgwɪs.tɪ.kli/ *adv*

linguistics /lɪŋˈgwɪs.tɪks/ *noun* [U] (ALSO **linguistic science**) the systematic study of the structure and development of language in general or of particular languages

liniment /ˈlɪn.ə.mənt/ *noun* [U] OLD-FASHIONED an oily liquid, usually containing alcohol, that is rubbed into the skin to reduce pain or stiffness in a joint

lining /ˈlaɪ.nɪŋ/ *noun* [C] a material or substance that covers the inside surface of something: *a coat/jacket lining* ○ *the lining of the stomach*

link CHAIN /lɪŋk/ *noun* [C] one of the rings in a chain

link CONNECTION /lɪŋk/ *noun* [C] **1** a connection between two people, things or ideas: *There's a direct link between diet and heart disease.* ○ *Their links with Britain are still strong.* ○ *diplomatic links between the two countries* **2** a connection between documents on the Internet: *Click on this link to visit our online bookstore.*

link /lɪŋk/ *verb* [T] to make a connection between two or more people, things or ideas: *The explosions are not thought to be linked in any way.* ○ *The use of CFCs has been linked to the depletion of the ozone layer.*

linkage /ˈlɪŋ.kɪdʒ/ *noun* [C or U] the existence or establishment of connections between two things so that one thing happening or changing depends on the other thing happening or changing

▲ **link** *(sth)* **up** *phrasal verb* [M] to form a connection, especially in order to work or operate together: *The organization's aim is to link up people from all over the country who are suffering from the disease.* ○ *We offer advice to Polish companies who want to link up with Western businesses.*

link-up /ˈlɪŋk.ʌp/ *noun* [C]

linking verb *noun* [C] SPECIALIZED a verb which connects the qualities of an object or person to that object or person: *In the sentence 'My bags weigh 45kg', 'weigh' is a linking verb.*

links (*plural* **links**) /lɪŋks/ *group noun* [C] (*ALSO* **golf links**) **1** a large area of hills covered with sand beside the sea which is used for playing golf **2** *US* any area of land which is used for playing golf

linoleum /lɪˈnəʊ.li.əm/ ⓤ /-ˈnoʊ-/ *noun* [U] (*UK ALSO* **lino**) a stiff smooth material that is used for covering floors

linseed /ˈlɪn.siːd/ *noun* [U] a type of FLAX plant grown for its seeds from which oil is made

linseed 'oil *noun* [U] oil obtained from linseed which is used for making LINOLEUM, paint and ink, and for protecting wood

lint FIBRES /lɪnt/ *noun* [U] *UK* soft material made from loosely woven cloth fibres, used for protecting injuries

lint LOOSE MATERIAL /lɪnt/ *noun* [U] *MAINLY US FOR* **fluff** (= small loose bits of wool or other soft material)

lintel /ˈlɪn.tᵊl/ ⓤ /-t̬ᵊl/ *noun* [C] a long piece of stone or wood at the top of a door or window frame which supports the wall above

lion /ˈlaɪ.ən/ *noun* [C] **1** (*FEMALE* **lioness**) a large wild animal of the cat family with yellowish brown fur which lives in Africa and southern Asia: *a pride* (= group) *of lions* ⊃See picture **Animals and Birds** on page Centre 4 **2** someone who is important, successful or powerful: *a literary lion*

• **the lion's share** the largest part or most of something: *Reputable charities spend the lion's share of donations on aid and a tiny fraction on administration.*

• **the lion's den** a dangerous or threatening place or situation

lion-hearted /ˌlaɪ.ənˈhɑː.tɪd/ ⓤ /-ˈhɑːr.t̬ɪd/ *adj LITERARY* very brave

lionize, *UK USUALLY* **-ise** /ˈlaɪ.ə.naɪz/ *verb* [T] to make someone famous, or to treat someone as if they were famous **lionization**, *UK USUALLY* **-isation** /ˌlaɪ.ə.naɪˈzeɪ.ʃᵊn/ *noun* [U]

lip BODY PART /lɪp/ *noun* [C] one of the two soft, red edges of the mouth: *She kissed me on the lips.* ○ *He licked his lips.* ⊃See picture **The Body** on page Centre 5

• **my lips are sealed** said when you are promising to keep a secret: *"Oh and please don't tell him you saw me here." "Don't worry. My lips are sealed."*

• **on everyone's lips** being talked about by a lot of people: *The question now on everyone's lips is "Will the Prime Minister resign?"*

lip EDGE /lɪp/ *noun* [C] a part of an edge of a container that is shaped to allow liquid to be poured easily from the container

lip SPEECH /lɪp/ *noun* [U] *INFORMAL* when someone argues in a rude way or in a way the shows a lack of respect: *That's enough of your lip, young lady!*

lip 'gloss *noun* [C or U] a type of make-up that is put on the lips to make them look shiny ⊃Compare **lipstick**.

lipid /ˈlɪp.ɪd/ *noun* [C] *SPECIALIZED* a substance such as a fat, oil or wax that dissolves in alcohol but not in water and is an important part of living cells

liposuction /ˈlaɪp.əʊˌsʌk.ʃᵊn/ ⓤ /ˈlaɪ.poʊ-/ *noun* [U] an operation in which fat is sucked out from under skin

lippy TALK /ˈlɪp.i/ *adj INFORMAL* showing disrespect in the way that you talk to someone: *She can get a bit lippy with her parents.*

lippy MAKE-UP /ˈlɪp.i/ *noun* [U] *UK INFORMAL* **lipstick**: *You've got a bit of lippy on your tooth.*

lip-read /ˈlɪp.riːd/ *verb* [I or T] **lip-read, lip-read** to understand what someone is saying by watching the movements of their mouth ⊃See also **read** sb's **lips** at read UNDERSTAND. **lip-reading** /ˈlɪpˌriː.dɪŋ/ *noun* [U]

lip 'salve *noun* [U] a type of cream which is used to keep the lips soft or to help sore lips heal

lip 'service *noun* **pay lip service to sth** to say that you agree with something but do nothing to support it: *She claims to be in favour of training, but so far she's only paid lip service to the idea.*

lipstick /ˈlɪp.stɪk/ *noun* [C or U] a coloured substance that women put on their lips to make them more attractive

lip-synch /ˈlɪp.sɪŋk/ *verb* [I] Performers who lip-synch songs pretend to be singing them when in fact they are just moving their lips.

liquefy, **liquify** /ˈlɪk.wɪ.faɪ/ *verb* [I or T] to (cause a gas or a solid to) change into a liquid form: *Gases liquefy under pressure.*

liqueur /lɪˈkjʊəʳ/ ⓤ /-ˈkjɜː/ *noun* [C] a strong, sweet alcoholic drink which is usually drunk in small amounts at the end of a meal

liquid SUBSTANCE /ˈlɪk.wɪd/ *noun* [C or U] a substance, such as water, that is not solid or a gas and that can be poured easily: *Mercury is a liquid at room temperature.* **liquid** /ˈlɪk.wɪd/ *adj*: *liquid hydrogen* **liquidity** /lɪˈkwɪd.ɪ.ti/ ⓤ /-ə.t̬i/ *noun* [U]

liquid MONEY /ˈlɪk.wɪd/ *adj* in the form of money, rather than investments or property, or able to be changed into money easily: *She has very few liquid assets as most of her wealth is tied up in stocks and shares.* **liquidity** /lɪˈkwɪd.ɪ.ti/ ⓤ /-ə.t̬i/ *noun* [U]

liquidate CLOSE /ˈlɪk.wɪ.deɪt/ *verb* [I or T] to cause a business to close, so that its ASSETS can be sold to pay its debts **liquidation** /ˌlɪk.wɪˈdeɪ.ʃᵊn/ *noun* [C or U] *After three years of heavy losses the company went into liquidation with debts totalling £100 million.* **liquidator** /ˈlɪk.wɪ.deɪ.təʳ/ ⓤ /-t̬ɚ/ *noun* [C] one of the people in charge of closing a company

liquidate KILL /ˈlɪk.wɪ.deɪt/ *verb* [T] to kill someone who threatens a government or political organization

liquid 'courage *US noun* [U] (*UK* **Dutch courage**) the confidence some people get from drinking alcohol before they do something frightening

liquid-crystal display /ˌlɪk.wɪdˌkrɪs.tᵊl.dɪˈspleɪ/ *noun* [C] (*ABBREVIATION* **LCD**) a screen for showing text or pictures which uses a liquid that darkens when an electric current flows across it

liquidiser, **-izer** /ˈlɪk.wɪ.daɪ.zəʳ/ ⓤ /-zɚ/ *noun* [C] *UK FOR* **blender** (= electric machine that changes food into a thick liquid)

liquidize, *UK USUALLY* **-ise** /ˈlɪk.wɪ.daɪz/ *verb* [T] to change food into a thick liquid using a BLENDER (= electric machine with blades that turn very quickly) ⊃Compare **liquefy**.

Liquid 'Paper *noun* [U] *TRADEMARK* a white liquid for covering mistakes in a text or drawing so that they can be corrected

liquify /ˈlɪk.wɪ.faɪ/ *verb* to **liquefy**

liquor /ˈlɪk.əʳ/ ⓤ /-ɚ/ *noun* [U] *US* strong alcoholic drink

liquorice *UK*, *US* **licorice** /ˈlɪk.ᵊr.ɪs/ /-ɪʃ/ ⓤ /-ɚ-ɪs/ *noun* [U] **1** the dried root of a Mediterranean plant which is used in medicines and for flavouring food, particularly sweets **2** a black sweet made from liquorice

'liquor ˌstore *noun* [C] *US FOR* **off-licence**

lira /ˈlɪə.rə/ ⓤ /ˈlɪr.ə/ *noun* [C] *plural* **lire** or **liras** the standard unit of money used in Italy before they started using the Euro, and also used in Malta and Turkey

lisp SPEECH /lɪsp/ *verb* [I] to pronounce 's' and 'z' sounds like 'th' **lisp** /lɪsp/ *noun* [C] *I was teased a lot at school because I spoke with a lisp.*

lissom, **lissome** /ˈlɪs.ᵊm/ *adj LITERARY* attractively thin and able to move quickly and gracefully

list RECORD /lɪst/ *noun* [C] **1** a record of short pieces of information, such as people's names, usually written or printed with a single item on each line and often ordered in a way that makes a particular item easy to find: *a shopping list* ○ *Is your name on the list?* ○ *I've made a list of places I'd like to visit while we're in Paris.* **2** **A/B list** used to describe the group of people considered extremely/quite popular and famous at the present time: *He landed a part in a multi-million pound action thriller and made the Hollywood A list.* ○ *a B-list celebrity*

• **a list as long as your arm** *INFORMAL* a very long list: *I've got a list as long as my arm of the things we need to do before we go on holiday.*

list /lɪst/ *verb* [T] to make a list, or to include something in a list: *I've listed some useful reading material on the handout.*

list [LEAN] /lɪst/ *verb* **[I]** (of a ship) to lean to one side, particularly as a result of damage: *The tanker is listing badly and liable to sink at any moment.* **list** /lɪst/ *noun* **[S]**

ˌlisted 'building *UK noun* **[C]** (*US* **landmarked building,** *AUS* **heritage-listed building**) a building of great historical or artistic value which has official protection to prevent it from being changed or destroyed

ˌlisted 'company *noun* **[C]** a company whose shares can be traded on a country's main STOCK MARKET

listen /ˈlɪs.ᵊn/ *verb* **[I]** to give attention to someone or something in order to hear them: *What kind of music do you listen **to**?* ○ *She does all the talking – I just sit and listen.* ○ *You haven't listened to a word I've said!* ○ *We listened in silence as the names of the dead were read out.* ○ *Listen, we really need to sort out our insurance claim this weekend.* ○ *Listen **to this**! You can win a holiday for two in the south of France just by answering three simple questions.* **listen** /ˈlɪs.ᵊn/ *noun* **[S]** ***Have a** listen **to** this! I've never heard anything like it before.*

USAGE

listen, listen to or **hear?**

Use **hear** when you want to say that sounds, music, etc. come to your ears. You can **hear** something without wanting to.

I could hear his music through the wall.

Use **listen** to say that you pay attention to sounds or try to hear something.

The audience listened carefully.
Ssh! I'm listening!

Use **listen to** when you want to say what it is that you are trying to hear.

The audience listened to the speaker.
Ssh! I'm listening to the radio!

PHRASAL VERBS WITH **listen**

▲ **listen in on *sth*** *phrasal verb* If you listen in on a conversation, you listen to it, especially secretly, without saying anything: *I wish Dad would stop listening in on my phone conversations.*

▲ **listen out for *sth*** *phrasal verb* to make an effort to hear a noise that you are expecting: *Would you listen out for the phone while I'm in the garden?*

▲ **listen up** *phrasal verb MAINLY US INFORMAL* something you say to make people listen to you: *Okay everyone – listen up! I have an announcement to make.*

listener /ˈlɪs.ᵊn.əʳ/ /-nəʳ/ [US] /ˈlɪs.ᵊn.ɚ/ *noun* **[C]** someone who listens: *We've received a lot of complaints about the changes from regular listeners **to** the programme.*
• **a good listener** someone who gives you a lot of attention when you are talking about your problems or worries and tries to understand and support you

listeria /lɪˈstɪə.ri.ə/ [US] /-ˈstɪr.i-/ *noun* **[U]** a bacteria which causes food poisoning, found especially in cheese and other products made from milk

listeriosis /lɪˌstɪə.riˈəʊ.sɪs/ [US] /-ˈoʊ-/ *noun* **[U]** a serious type of food poisoning, caused by listeria, which is particularly harmful to babies before they are born

listings /ˈlɪs.tɪŋz/ *plural noun* **[C]** information about entertainments and activities that is published in newspapers and magazines

listless /ˈlɪst.ləs/ *adj* lacking energy and enthusiasm and unwilling to do anything needing effort: *He's been listless and a bit depressed ever since he got his exam results.* **listlessly** /ˈlɪst.lə.sli/ *adv* **listlessness** /ˈlɪst.lə.snəs/ *noun* **[U]**

'list ˌprice *noun* **[C]** *SPECIALIZED* the price at which the maker of something suggests it should be sold

lit [LIGHT] /lɪt/ *past simple and past participle of* **light** BRIGHTNESS *or* **light** FLAME

lit [LITERATURE] /lɪt/ *noun* **[U]** *ABBREVIATION FOR* literature: *a degree in English Lit*

litany /ˈlɪt.ᵊn.i/ *noun* **[C]** **1** a long Christian prayer in which the priest speaks some parts and the other people at the ceremony speak other parts **2 a litany of *sth*** a long list of unpleasant things, particularly things that are repeated: *The manufacturers are reported to have received a litany of complaints from dissatisfied customers.*

litchi /ˈlaɪ.tʃiː/ *noun* **[C]** **lychee**

lit crit /ˌlɪtˈkrɪt/ *noun* **[U]** *ABBREVIATION FOR* **literary criticism**

liter /ˈliː.təʳ/ [US] /-t̬ɚ/ *noun* **[C]** *US FOR* **litre**

literacy /ˈlɪt.ᵊr.ə.si/ [US] /ˈlɪt̬.ɚ-/ *noun* **[U]** **1** the ability to read and write: *Far more resources are needed to improve adult literacy.* **2** knowledge of a particular subject, or a particular type of knowledge: ***Computer** literacy is becoming as essential as the ability to drive a car.*

literal /ˈlɪt.ᵊr.ᵊl/ [US] /ˈlɪt̬.ɚ-/ *adj* The literal meaning of a word is its original, basic meaning: *The literal meaning of 'television' is 'seeing from a distance'.* ○ *You need to demonstrate to the examiners that you have more than a literal understanding of the text.* ○ *Her translation is too literal* (= done one word at a time), *resulting in heavy, unnatural prose.* ➲Compare **figurative** LANGUAGE.

literally /ˈlɪt.ᵊr.ᵊl.i/ /-rə.li/ [US] /ˈlɪt̬.ɚ-/ *adv* having the real or original meaning of a word or phrase: *They were responsible for literally millions of deaths.* ○ *We live literally just round the corner from her.* ○ *You'll lose marks if you translate too literally* (= one word at a time).

literally /ˈlɪt.ᵊr.ᵊl.i/ /-rə.li/ [US] /ˈlɪt̬.ɚ.ᵊl.i/ *adv INFORMAL* **1** used to emphasize what you are saying: *He missed that kick literally by miles.* ○ *I was literally bowled over by the news.* **2** simply or just: *Then you literally cut the sausage down the middle.*

literary /ˈlɪt.ᵊr.ᵊr.i/ [US] /ˈlɪt̬.ə.rer-/ *adj* connected with literature: *a literary critic* ○ *literary prizes* ○ *a literary style*

'literary ˌagent *noun* **[C]** someone who deals with a writer's business matters

ˌliterary 'criticism *noun* **[U]** the formal study and discussion of works of literature, which involves judging and explaining their importance and meaning

literate /ˈlɪt.ᵊr.ət/ [US] /ˈlɪt̬.ɚ-/ *adj* **1** able to read and write **2** having knowledge of a particular subject, or a particular type of knowledge: ***computer** literate*

literati /ˌlɪt.ᵊrˈɑː.tiː/ [US] /ˌlɪt̬.əˈrɑː.t̬iː/ *plural noun* people with a good education who know a lot about literature: *Her novels are popular with university literati, but they have failed to attract a wider audience.* ➲Compare **glitterati**.

literature [WRITING] /ˈlɪt.ᵊr.ɪ.tʃəʳ/ [US] /ˈlɪt̬.ɚ.ɪ.tʃɚ/ *noun* **[U]** written artistic works, particularly those with a high and lasting artistic value: *classical/modern literature* ○ *'Wuthering Heights' is a classic of English literature.*

literature [SPECIALIST TEXTS] /ˈlɪt.ᵊr.ɪ.tʃəʳ/ [US] /ˈlɪt̬.ɚ.ɪ.tʃɚ/ *noun* **[U]** all the information relating to a subject, particularly information written by specialists: *It's important to keep up-to-date with the literature in your field.* ○ *There is very little literature **on** the disease.*

literature [INFORMATION] /ˈlɪt.ᵊr.ɪ.tʃəʳ/ [US] /ˈlɪt̬.ɚ.ɪ.tʃɚ/ *noun* **[U]** **1** printed material published by a company which is intended to encourage people to buy that company's products or services: *Could you send me your literature **on/about** car insurance policies, please?* **2** material that an organization publishes in order to persuade people to agree with its opinions: *The Republicans were quick to highlight the Democrats' proposed tax increases in their **campaign** literature.*

lithe /laɪð/ *adj* young, healthy, attractive and able to move and bend gracefully: *He had the lithe, athletic body of a ballet dancer.* **lithely** /ˈlaɪð.li/ *adv*

lithium /ˈlɪθ.i.əm/ *noun* **[U]** a soft, silver metal

lithograph /ˈlɪθ.əʊ.grɑːf/ [US] /-oʊ.græf/ *noun* **[C]** a picture printed using a stone or metal block on which an image has been drawn with a thick oily substance that attracts ink **lithographic** /ˌlɪθ.əʊˈgræf.ɪk/ [US] /-oʊ-/ *adj* **lithography** /lɪˈθɒg.rə.fi/ [US] /-ˈθɑː.grə-/ *noun* **[U]**

litigate /ˈlɪt.ɪ.geɪt/ [US] /ˈlɪt̬-/ *verb* **[I or T]** *LEGAL* to cause an argument to be discussed in a law court so that a judgment can be made which must be accepted by both sides **litigation** /ˌlɪt.ɪˈgeɪ.ʃᵊn/ [US] /ˌlɪt̬-/ *noun* **[U]** *LEGAL* the process of taking a case to a law court so that an official decision can be made: *The company has consistently denied responsibility, but it agreed to the settlement to avoid the expense of lengthy litigation.*

litigant /ˈlɪt.ɪ.gᵊnt/ [US] /ˈlɪt̬-/ *noun* [C] *LEGAL* a person who is fighting a legal case

litigator /ˈlɪt.ɪ.geɪ.təʳ/ [US] /ˈlɪt̬.ɪ.geɪ.t̬ɚ/ *noun* [C] *US LEGAL* a lawyer who specializes in taking legal action against people and organizations: *a leading civil rights litigator*

litigious /lɪˈtɪdʒ.əs/ *adj FORMAL DISAPPROVING* too often taking arguments to a law court for a decision: *The United States is the most litigious society in the world.* **litigiousness** /lɪˈtɪdʒ.ə.snəs/ *noun* [U]

litmus /ˈlɪt.məs/ *noun* [U] a powder which is turned red by ACID and blue by ALKALI: *litmus paper* ○ *a litmus test*

ˈlitmus ˌtest *noun* [C usually sing] someone's decision or opinion about something which suggests what they think about a wider range of related things: *The President's policy on abortion is regarded as a litmus test **of** his views on women's rights.*

litre *UK, US USUALLY* **liter** /ˈliː.təʳ/ [US] /-t̬ɚ/ *noun* [C] (*WRITTEN ABBREVIATION* **l**) a unit for measuring the volume of a liquid or a gas: *The tax increase will add 4p to a litre of petrol.*

litter [RUBBISH] /ˈlɪt.əʳ/ [US] /ˈlɪt̬.ɚ/ *noun* [U] small pieces of rubbish that have been left lying on the ground in public places: *About 2% of fast-food packaging ends up as litter.*

litter [SPREAD] /ˈlɪt.əʳ/ [US] /ˈlɪt̬.ɚ/ *verb* [T] **1** to spread across an area or place untidily: *The park was littered **with** bottles and cans after the concert.* ○ *Dirty clothes littered the floor of her bedroom.* **2 be littered with *sth*** A place, document or other object that is littered with something, has or contains a lot of that thing: *The newspaper has a reputation for being littered with spelling mistakes.*

litter [BABY ANIMALS] /ˈlɪt.əʳ/ [US] /ˈlɪt̬.ɚ/ *group noun* [C] a group of animals that are born at the same time and have the same mother: *a litter of kittens*

litter [BED] /ˈlɪt.əʳ/ [US] /ˈlɪt̬.ɚ/ *noun* [U] dried grass or plant stems used by animals as a bed

litter [ANIMAL TOILET] /ˈlɪt.əʳ/ [US] /ˈlɪt̬.ɚ/ *noun* [U] a substance that is put in a container to be used as a toilet by pets: *cat/pet litter*

ˈlitter ˌbug *noun* [C] (*UK ALSO* **litter lout**) *INFORMAL DISAPPROVING* someone who drops rubbish on the ground in public places

little [SMALL] /ˈlɪt.l̩/ [US] /ˈlɪt̬-/ *adj* small in size or amount: *It came in a little box.* ○ *a little dog/nose/room* ○ *A little old man came into the shop.* ○ *He gave a little smile.* ○ *It'll only take a little while to clear up the kitchen.* ➲See Note **small or little?** at **small** LIMITED.

• **a little bird told me** said if you know who gave you the information being discussed but will not say who it was: *"How did you know he was leaving?" "Oh, let's just say a little bird told me."*

little /ˈlɪt.l̩/ [US] /ˈlɪt̬-/ *pronoun, noun* [S] a small amount: *I could only hear a little of what they were saying.* ○ *He does as little as possible at work.* ○ *There's not much flour left but you're welcome to the/what little there is.*

little /ˈlɪt.l̩/ [US] /ˈlɪt̬-/ *determiner* **a little** a small amount of something: *This sauce needs a little salt.* ○ *With a little training she could do very well.* ○ *Can I give you a little advice?*

little /ˈlɪt.l̩/ [US] /ˈlɪt̬-/ *adv* **a little (bit)** slightly: *I was little bit worried by what she said.* ○ *We'll wait a little longer and then I'll phone them.* ○ *There's only a little further to go.*

• **a little something 1** a small amount of food or drink: *I always like to have a little something around 11 o'clock in the morning.* **2** a present that is not of great value: *I want to buy a little something to give to Val when I visit her in hospital.*

• **little by little** slowly or gradually: *Little by little she came to understand why he had behaved the way he did.*

COMMON LEARNER ERROR

little

When little is used before a noun to show how much of the noun there is, remember that it can only be used with uncountable nouns.

There's very little sugar left.

~~There's very little sausages left.~~

For countable nouns, use a phrase like **not many** instead.

There aren't many sausages left.

little [YOUNG] /ˈlɪt.l̩/ [US] /ˈlɪt̬-/ *adj* young: *When you were little your hair was really curly.* ○ *She was my little* (= younger) *sister and I looked after her.* ○ *Her little boy* (= Her young son) *isn't well.*

little [NOT ENOUGH] /ˈlɪt.l̩/ [US] /ˈlɪt̬-/ *determiner* not much or enough: *There seems little hope of a ceasefire.* ○ *They have very little money.* ○ *There's so little choice.* **little** /ˈlɪt.l̩/ [US] /ˈlɪt̬-/ *pronoun, noun*: *We did **very** little on sunday.* ○ *Very little of what he said made any sense to me.* ○ *Unfortunately, little **of** the artist's work has survived.* ○ *The government has **done** little or nothing to help the poorest people in this country.* ○ *The little we do know about the people who lived here suggests they had a very sophisticated society.*

little /ˈlɪt.l̩/ [US] /ˈlɪt̬-/ *adv* not much or not enough: *She ate very little at dinner.* ○ *a little-known fact* ○ *Little **did he know** what lay in store for him.*

little [EMPHASIZE] /ˈlɪt.l̩/ [US] /ˈlɪt̬-/ *adj* [before n] used to emphasize an opinion which is being given about something or someone: *That was a nice little suit she was wearing.* ○ *It's not a bad little restaurant, this, is it?* ○ *He's a nasty little man.*

little [UNIMPORTANT] /ˈlɪt.l̩/ [US] /ˈlɪt̬-/ *adj* [before n] not very important or serious: *I had a little problem with my car, but it's been fixed now.* ○ *It's often the little things that count the most.* ○ *Can I have a little word* (= a short discussion about something not very important) *with you?*

• **make little of *sth*** to not consider something to be very important: *He made little of his ordeal.*

ˌlittle ˈfinger *noun* [C] the smallest finger on each hand ➲See picture **The Body** on page Centre 5

ˈlittle ˌone *noun* [C] *INFORMAL* a young child: *The little ones can play in the garden while we get lunch ready.*

ˈlittle ˌpeople *plural noun* [C] (*ALSO* **little folk**) *MAINLY IRISH ENGLISH* small imaginary creatures, such as LEPRECHAUNS, which look like small humans

ˌlittle ˈtoe *noun* [C] the smallest toe on each foot ➲See picture **The Body** on page Centre 5

liturgy /ˈlɪt.ə.dʒi/ [US] /ˈlɪt̬.ɚ-/ *noun* [C or U] (a particular set of) the words, music and actions used in ceremonies in some religions, especially Christianity **liturgical** /lɪˈtɜː.dʒɪ.kᵊl/ [US] /-ˈtɝː-/ *adj*

livable [PLACE], **liveable** /ˈlɪv.ə.bl̩/ *adj* (*UK* **livable in**) If a building or place is livable, it is suitable or good for living in: *It's not a luxurious apartment by any means but it's livable in.* ○ *It was rated the most livable city in the States.*

livable [LIFE], **liveable** *adj* able to be lived: *These are the basic requirements that make life livable.*

live [HAVE LIFE] /lɪv/ *verb* [I] (to continue) to be alive or have life: *He only lived a few days after the accident.* ○ *I hope I live to see my grandchildren.* ○ [+ to infinitive] *Her granny lived **to** the ripe old age of 94.* ○ *Can the right to live ever be denied to any human?* ○ *She lived **on** well into her nineties.*

• **you live and learn** said when you hear or discover something which is surprising: *I had no idea they were related. Oh well, you live and learn.*

• **live to fight another day** to have another chance to fight in a competition: *We didn't win this time, but we live to fight another day.*

• **live to tell the tale** to successfully deal with or continue to live despite a difficult situation or experience: *We had a horrific journey, but we lived to tell the tale.*

live /laɪv/ *adj* [before n] having life: *Millions of live animals are shipped around the world each year.* ○ *There was a tank of live lobsters in the restaurant.*

living /ˈlɪv.ɪŋ/ *adj* alive now: *living organisms* ○ *He is probably the best known living architect.*

• **within living memory** If something has happened within living memory, it can be remembered by some people who are still alive: *There is possibly less chance of another World War while the last one is within living memory.*

the living *plural noun* people who are still alive: *On this anniversary of the tragedy we remember the living as well as the dead.*

live [HAVE A HOME] /lɪv/ *verb* **1 live in/at, etc.** to have your home somewhere: *Where do you live?* ○ *We live in London.* ○ *Some students live on the University campus.* ○ *He lives with four other people in a shared house.* **2** [I] *INFORMAL* to be kept usually in a particular place: *Where do the knives live in your kitchen?* ○ *I'm not sure where this bowl lives.*

• **lived in** regularly used and comfortable: *I like a room to look lived in.*

live [STAY ALIVE] /lɪv/ *verb* [I] to stay alive, especially by getting enough money to pay for food, a place in which to stay, clothing, etc: *For several years she lived* ***by*** *begging.* ○ *She has an inheritance to live* ***off*** *(US ALSO live* ***off of****) so she doesn't need to work.* ○ *He only agreed to marry her so he could live* ***off*** *her (money).*

living /ˈlɪv.ɪŋ/ *noun* [C] **1** the money that you earn from your job: *What do you* ***do for a*** *living* (= What is your job)? ○ *I mean, I don't like my job but at least it's a living* (= a way of earning money). ○ *You can make a* ***good*** *living* (= earn a lot of money) *in sales if you have the right attitude.* ➲See also **livelihood**. **2** *OLD-FASHIONED* in the Church of England, the job, given to a priest, of being in charge of a particular area

live [SPEND LIFE] /lɪv/ *verb* [I usually + adv or prep; T] to spend your life in a particular way: *After a while you get used to living alone.* ○ *When you retire, you want to live a comfortable life.* ○ *So the prince and princess got married, and lived* ***happily ever after****.* ○ *He simply wants to live* ***(out)*** (= experience) *the rest of his days in peace.* ○ *The TV's broken – we'll just have to live* ***without*** (= not have) *it for a while.* ○ *She certainly lived her life* ***to the full*** (= was always doing something interesting). ○ *FIGURATIVE The US is living* ***beyond*** *its* ***means*** (= spending more than it earns).

• **live a lie** to live in a way that is dishonest because you are pretending to be something that you are not, to yourself or to other people: *She doesn't know you're married? You have to stop living a lie and tell her.*

• **live and breathe** ***sth*** When a person lives and breathes something, it is extremely important to them: *He lives and breathes music.*

• **live and let live** said to mean that people should accept the way other people live and behave, especially if they do things in a different way

• **live like a king/lord** to have a luxurious way of life

• **live by** ***your*** **wits** to make money in a clever and usually dishonest way

• **never live** ***sth*** **down** to be unable to stop feeling embarrassed about something you have done: *I wish I'd never opened my mouth in the meeting – I'm never going to live it down!*

living /ˈlɪv.ɪŋ/ *noun* [U] the way in which you live your life: *country/healthy living* ➲See also **cost of living** and **standard of living**.

live [AS IT HAPPENS] /laɪv/ *adj* (of a performance) broadcast, recorded or seen while it is happening: *This evening there will be a live broadcast of the debate.* ○ *a live recording* **live** /laɪv/ *adv*: *I've got two tickets to see them* ***(perform)*** *live.*

live [CONTINUE] /lɪv/ *verb* [I] (of things which can not be alive) to exist or continue to exist: *The memory of those terrible days lives* ***on****.*

• **live (on) in the memory** If something lives (on) in the memory, it has such an effect that it is remembered for a long time. ➲See also **within living memory** at **live** HAVE LIFE.

living /ˈlɪv.ɪŋ/ *adj* still existing: *The pyramids are a living monument to the skill of their builders.*

live [ELECTRICITY] /laɪv/ *adj* (of a wire) carrying or charged with electricity: *a live wire*

live [ABLE TO EXPLODE] /laɪv/ *adj* able to explode: *live rounds of ammunition* ○ *live shells*

live [BURNING] /laɪv/ *adj* (of a fire, coals or a match) still burning or able to burn: *There are live coals in the fireplace.*

live [INTERESTING LIFE] /lɪv/ *verb* [I] to have an interesting life: *I want to live* ***a bit*** *before I settle down.* ○ *If you haven't seen Venice, you haven't lived.*

• **live it up** *INFORMAL* to have an exciting and very enjoyable time with parties, good food and drink: *He's alive and well and living it up in the Bahamas.*

PHRASAL VERBS WITH **live** ▼

▲ **live for** ***sth/sb*** *phrasal verb* to have something or someone as the most important thing in your life: *She just lives for music.*

▲ **live on** ***sth*** [MONEY] *phrasal verb* If you live on an amount of money, that is the money that you use to buy the things that you need: *We lived on very little when we first got married.*

▲ **live on** ***sth*** [FOOD] *phrasal verb* to only eat a particular type of food: *I more or less live on pasta.*

▲ **live together** *phrasal verb* If two people live together, they share a house and have a sexual relationship but are not married: *Nowadays many young people live together before they get married.*

▲ **live up to** ***sth*** *phrasal verb* to be as good as something: *The concert was brilliant – it lived up to all our expectations.*

▲ **live with** ***sb*** [HAVE RELATIONSHIP] *phrasal verb* to share a home with someone and have a sexual relationship with them although you are not married

▲ **live with** ***sth*** [ACCEPT] *phrasal verb* to accept a difficult or unpleasant situation: *I can't change the situation so I'm going to have to learn to live with it.*

liveable /ˈlɪv.ə.bl̩/ *adj* **livable**

live-in [RELATIONSHIP] /ˈlɪv.ɪn/ *adj* [before n] describes someone's sexual partner who lives in their home but is not married to them: *a live-in lover*

live-in [WORK] /ˈlɪv.ɪn/ *adj* [before n] describes a person who lives in the home where they work: *a live-in housekeeper/nanny*

livelihood /ˈlaɪv.li.hʊd/ *noun* [C or U] (the way someone earns) the money people need to pay for food, a place to live, clothing, etc: *Many ship workers could* ***lose*** *their livelihoods because of falling orders for new ships.* ○ *That farm is his livelihood.* ➲See also **living** at **live** STAY ALIVE.

lively /ˈlaɪv.li/ *adj* **1** having or showing a lot of energy and enthusiasm, or showing interesting and exciting thought: *It's hard work teaching a class of lively children.* ○ *a lively city* ○ *They take a lively interest in their grandchildren.* ○ *There was some lively discussion at the meeting.* **2** describes colours that are bright and strong: *The room was painted a lively electric blue.* **liveliness** /ˈlaɪv.lɪ.nəs/ *noun* [U]

liven /ˈlaɪ.vᵊn/ *verb*

PHRASAL VERBS WITH **liven** ▼

▲ **liven** ***(sth)*** **up** [INTERESTING] *phrasal verb* [M] to become more interesting and exciting, or to make something become like this: *A new coat of paint would liven the kitchen up.* ○ *Liven up your meals with fresh herbs and spices.* ○ *The party livened up as soon as Sally arrived.*

▲ **liven** ***(sb)*** **up** [ENERGETIC] *phrasal verb* to become more energetic or cheerful, or to make someone feel this way: *She was a bit subdued to start with, but after a while she livened up.* ○ [R] *I'm going to liven myself up a bit by going for a run.*

liver /ˈlɪv.əʳ/ [US] /-ɚ/ *noun* [C or U] a large organ in the body which cleans the blood and produces BILE, or this organ from an animal used as meat

liverish /ˈlɪv.ᵊr.ɪʃ/ [US] /-ɚ-/ *adj UK OLD USE* feeling ill, usually because of having drunk or eaten too much

Liverpudlian /ˌlɪv.əˈpʌd.li.ən/ [US] /-ɚ-/ *noun* [C] a person from Liverpool, a city in northwest England **Liverpudlian** /ˌlɪv.əˈpʌd.li.ən/ [US] /-ɚ-/ *adj*: *a Liverpudlian accent*

ˈliver ˌsausage *noun* [C or U] (*US USUALLY* **liverwurst**) a type of cooked sausage which contains liver and is usually eaten cold on bread

livery /ˈlɪv.ᵊr.i/ [US] /-ɚ-/ *noun* **1** [C or U] a special uniform worn by servants or particular officials **2** [U] *UK* a special pattern or design which is put on the things that a company owns and sells

lives /laɪvz/ *plural of* **life**

L

livestock /ˈlaɪv.stɒk/ ⓤ /-stɑːk/ *plural noun* animals, such as cows and sheep, and birds, such as chickens, kept on a farm

live wire *noun* [C] someone who is very quick and active, both mentally and physically

livid ANGRY /ˈlɪv.ɪd/ *adj* extremely angry: *He was livid when he found out.*

livid COLOUR /ˈlɪv.ɪd/ *adj* (especially of marks on the skin) of an unpleasant purple or dark blue colour: *He had a long livid scar across his cheek.*

living 'death *noun* [S] a life that is so full of suffering that it would be better to be dead: *She can't walk or feed herself and she can barely speak – it's a living death.*

living room *noun* [C] (*UK ALSO* **sitting room**, *AUS ALSO* **lounge room**) the room in a house or apartment that is used for relaxing, and entertaining guests, but not usually for eating

living room suite *noun* [C] *US FOR* **three-piece suite**

living 'wage *noun* [S] enough money to buy the things that are necessary in order to live, such as food and clothes: *He does make a living wage but only by working 72 hours a week.*

living 'will *noun* [C usually sing] a written document in which a person says what type of medical treatment they would like if they become so ill that they are certain to die and are unable to communicate their wishes about their treatment

lizard /ˈlɪz.əd/ ⓤ /-ɚd/ *noun* [C] a small reptile that has a long body, four short legs, a long tail and thick skin

'll /ʲl/ *short form of* will: *I'll see you next week.*

llama /ˈlɑː.mə/ *noun* [C] a large South American animal with a long neck and long hair, and which is often kept for its meat, milk, fur and to carry heavy loads

LLB /ˌel.elˈbiː/ *noun* [C] (*US ALSO* **BL**) *ABBREVIATION FOR* Bachelor of Laws: a degree in law, or a person who has this degree

lo /ləʊ/ ⓤ /loʊ/ *exclamation OLD USE* look
• **lo and behold** *HUMOROUS* something that you say when you tell someone about something surprising that happened: *I was in Vienna sitting quietly in a café when, lo and behold, my cousin walked in.*

load AMOUNT CARRIED /ləʊd/ ⓤ /loʊd/ *noun* [C] **1** the amount of weight carried, especially by a vehicle, a structure such as a bridge, or an animal: *The maximum load for this elevator is eight persons.* ○ *One truck involved in the accident was **carrying** a heavy load **of** coal.* **2** *SPECIALIZED* in an electrical system, an electrical device which takes power, or the electrical power put into the system
• **a load/loads** *INFORMAL* a lot: *I've got a load **of** work to get through before tomorrow.* ○ *There were a load **of** people there.* ○ *Have some more food – there's loads.* ○ *She looks loads better with her new haircut.*
• **a load of crap/nonsense/rubbish, etc.** *UK INFORMAL* something that is not true, or something of very bad quality: *Who said they were cheaper – what a load of rubbish!* ○ *He liked the second series and I thought it was a load of crap.*
• **Get a load of that!** *SLANG* used to tell someone to pay attention to a person or thing that is interesting, surprising or attractive: *Get a load of that, lads! Very nice.*

-load /-ləʊd/ ⓤ /-loʊd/ *suffix* all the people or goods in the stated type of vehicle or container: *a coachload of football fans* ○ *Busloads **of** tourists pour into this place in the summer.* ○ *Truckloads of food and medical supplies arrived in the refugee camp.*

load /ləʊd/ ⓤ /loʊd/ *verb* [I or T] to put a lot of things into a vehicle or machine: *How long will it take to load this sand **onto** the lorry?* ○ *Let's load **up** the car and then we can go.* ○ *to load the dishwasher/washing machine* ⇒See also **overload**. ✳ NOTE: The opposite is **unload**.
• **be loaded down with sth** to have too much to carry, or too much work to do: *I was loaded down with shopping.*
• **be loaded with sth** to contain a lot of something: *Most fast foods are loaded with fat.*

load AMOUNT TO DO /ləʊd/ ⓤ /loʊd/ *noun* **1** [C] the amount of work to be done by a person: *If we share the organization of the party, that will help spread the load a bit.*

○ *I've got a **heavy/light** teaching load this term.* ⇒See also **caseload**; **workload**. **2** [S] a painful, difficult or tiring situation to deal with: *I wish I could do something to **lighten** your load* (= make your situation easier).

load PUT INTO /ləʊd/ ⓤ /loʊd/ *verb* [T] to put film in a camera or bullets in a gun: *Do not load the film* (= put it into the camera) *in bright light.*

loaded /ˈləʊ.dɪd/ ⓤ /ˈloʊ-/ *adj*: *It's dangerous to leave a loaded gun* (= one with bullets in it) *lying around.*

loaded NOT FAIR /ˈləʊ.dɪd/ ⓤ /ˈloʊ-/ *adj* **1** not fair, especially by being helpful to one person instead of another: *It seems that the report is loaded in favour of the developers.* **2** **loaded question** a question that has particular words chosen to suggest the answer that is wanted: *A survey should avoid asking loaded questions.* ⇒See also **leading question**.

loaded RICH /ˈləʊ.dɪd/ ⓤ /ˈloʊ-/ *adj* [after v] *INFORMAL* rich: *He inherited the family business – he must be loaded!*

loaded DRUNK /ˈləʊ.dɪd/ ⓤ /ˈloʊ-/ *adj* [after v] *MAINLY US SLANG* drunk: *What a party – everyone was loaded!*

'loading bay *UK noun* [C] (*US* **loading dock**) a space at the back of a shop where goods are delivered or taken away

loaf BREAD /ləʊf/ ⓤ /loʊf/ *noun* [C] *plural* **loaves** bread which is shaped and baked in a single piece and can be sliced for eating: *two loaves of white bread*
• **Half a loaf is better than none.** *OLD-FASHIONED SAYING* said about a situation in which you must accept less than you wanted
• **Use your loaf.** *UK OLD-FASHIONED* used to tell someone in a slightly angry way that they should think more carefully about what they are doing

loaf FOOD /ləʊf/ ⓤ /loʊf/ *noun* [C or U] *plural* **loaves** savoury food cut into small pieces then pressed together and cooked in a single solid piece: *meat/nut loaf*

loaf AVOID WORK /ləʊf/ ⓤ /loʊf/ *verb* [I] *INFORMAL* to avoid activity, especially work: *Stop loafing (**about/around**) and get on with cleaning the windows!* **loafer** /ˈləʊ.fəʳ/ ⓤ /ˈloʊ.fɚ/ *noun* [C] *an idle loafer*

loafer /ˈləʊ.fəʳ/ ⓤ /ˈloʊ.fɚ/ *noun* [C] *MAINLY US TRADEMARK* a type of leather shoe with a wide strip across the top, which a person's foot slides into, without any fastening ⇒See also **loafer** at **loaf** AVOID WORK.

loam /ləʊm/ ⓤ /loʊm/ *noun* [U] high-quality earth which is a mixture of sand, clay and decaying plant material **loamy** /ˈləʊ.mi/ ⓤ /ˈloʊ.mi/ *adj*

loan SUM /ləʊn/ ⓤ /loʊn/ *noun* [C] a sum of money which is borrowed, often from a bank, and has to be paid back, usually together with an additional amount of money that you have to pay as a charge for borrowing: *She's trying to **get** a $50 000 loan to start her own business.* ○ *We could **apply for/take out** a loan to buy a car.*

loan /ləʊn/ ⓤ /loʊn/ *verb* [T + two objects] to lend: *I'd loan you the money if I could./I'd loan the money **to** you if I could.*

loan BORROW /ləʊn/ ⓤ /loʊn/ *noun* [C or U] an act of borrowing or lending something: *Thank you very much for the loan **of** your bike.* ○ *This exhibit is **on** loan* (= being borrowed/lent) *from/to another museum.*

loan /ləʊn/ ⓤ /loʊn/ *verb* [T] *MAINLY US* to lend: *This library loans books, CDs and videotapes.*

'loan shark *noun* [C] *INFORMAL DISAPPROVING* a person who charges very large amounts of money for lending money to someone

loanword /ˈləʊn.wɜːd/ ⓤ /ˈloʊn.wɜːd/ *noun* [C] a word taken from one language and used in another

loath, loth /ləʊθ/ ⓤ /loʊθ/ *verb FORMAL* **be loath to do sth** to be unwilling to do something: *I'm loath to spend it all at once.*

loathe /ləʊð/ ⓤ /loʊð/ *verb* [T] to hate someone or something: *From an early age the brothers have loathed each other.* ○ *"Do you like fish?" "No, I loathe it."* ○ [+ v-ing] *I loathe doing housework.*

loathing /ˈləʊ.ðɪŋ/ ⓤ /ˈloʊ.ðɪŋ/ *noun* [S or U] *FORMAL* strong hatred: *The thought of him touching her filled her with deep loathing.* ○ *He approached his rival with **fear and** loathing.*

loathsome /ˈləʊð.səm/ [US] /ˈloʊð-/ *adj* extremely unpleasant: *He's a loathsome man.* **loathsomeness** /ˈləʊð.səm.nəs/ [US] /ˈloʊð-/ *noun* [U]

loaves /ləʊvz/ [US] /loʊvz/ *plural of* **loaf** BREAD

lob /lɒb/ [US] /lɑːb/ *verb* [T] **-bb-** to kick, hit or throw something, especially a ball in a game, in a high curve: *Police started lobbing* (= throwing) *tear gas canisters* ***into*** *the crowd.*

lob /lɒb/ [US] /lɑːb/ *noun* [C] *Jones hit a beautiful lob* (= high, curving hit) *over his opponent's head.*

lobby [ROOM] /ˈlɒb.i/ [US] /ˈlɑː.bi/ *noun* [C] the (large) room into which the main entrance door opens in a hotel or other large building

lobby [PARLIAMENT] /ˈlɒb.i/ [US] /ˈlɑː.bi/ *noun* [C] in the British parliament, a room where someone meets a member of parliament whom they have arranged to talk to, or one of the two passages which members of parliament walk through as a way of voting

lobby [PERSUADE] /ˈlɒb.i/ [US] /ˈlɑː.bi/ *verb* [I or T] to try to persuade a politician, the government or an official group that a particular thing should or should not happen, or that a law should be changed: *Small businesses have lobbied hard* ***for/against*** *changes in the tax laws.* ○ [+ to infinitive] *Local residents lobbied* ***to*** *have the factory shut down.* ○ [+ obj + to infinitive] *They have been lobbying Congress* ***to*** *change the legislation concerning guns.*

lobby /ˈlɒb.i/ [US] /ˈlɑː.bi/ *noun* [C] a group of people who try to persuade the government or an official group to do something: *the anti-smoking lobby*

lobbyist /ˈlɒb.i.ɪst/ [US] /ˈlɑː.bi-/ *noun* [C] someone who tries to persuade a politician or official group to do something: *Lobbyists for the tobacco industry have expressed concerns about the restriction of smoking in public places.*

lobe [ORGAN] /ləʊb/ [US] /loʊb/ *noun* [C] *SPECIALIZED* any part of an organ which seems to be separate in some way from the rest, especially one of the parts of the brain, lung or liver: *the frontal lobe of the brain* **lobed** /ləʊbd/ [US] /loʊbd/ *adj*

lobe [EAR] /ləʊb/ [US] /loʊb/ *noun* [C] **earlobe**

lobotomy /ləˈbɒt.ə.mi/ [US] /-ˈbɑː.t̬ə-/ *noun* [C] (*UK ALSO* **leucotomy**) a medical operation in which cuts are made in or near the front part of the brain, and which was used in the past for the treatment of severe mental problems

lobster /ˈlɒb.stəʳ/ [US] /ˈlɑːb.stɚ/ *noun* [C or U] an animal which lives in the sea and has a long body covered with a hard shell, two large claws and eight legs, or its flesh when used as food

ˈlobster ˌpot *noun* [C] a type of cage used for catching LOBSTERS

local [AREA] /ˈləʊ.kəl/ [US] /ˈloʊ-/ *adj* **1** from, existing in, serving, or responsible for a small area, especially of a country: *a local accent* ○ *local issues* ○ *a local newspaper/radio station* ○ *Most of the local population depend on fishing for their income.* ○ *Our children all go to the local school.* ○ *Many local shops will be forced to close if the new supermarket is built.* **2** limited to a particular part of the body: *a local anaesthetic* ○ *local swelling*

local /ˈləʊ.kəl/ [US] /ˈloʊ-/ *noun* [C] a person who lives in the particular small area which you are talking about: *The café is popular with both locals and visitors.*

localize, *UK USUALLY* **-ise** /ˈləʊ.kəl.aɪz/ [US] /ˈloʊ-/ *verb* [T] **1** to limit something to a particular area: *SPECIALIZED Gravity has localized the swelling to the foot and ankle.* **2** *FORMAL* to find the position of something: *Electricians worked through the night to localize the faulty switches.*

localized, *UK USUALLY* **-ised** /ˈləʊ.kəl.aɪzd/ [US] /ˈloʊ-/ *adj* happening or limited to a particular area: *localized flooding*

local [PUB] /ˈləʊ.kəl/ [US] /ˈloʊ-/ *noun* [C] *UK* a pub near to where a person lives, especially if they often go there to drink: *The George is my local.*

local [VEHICLE] /ˈləʊ.kəl/ [US] /ˈloʊ-/ *noun* [C] *US* a train or bus which stops at all or most of the places on its route where passengers can get on or off: *the 12.24 local to Poughkeepsie*

local [ORGANIZATION] /ˈləʊ.kəl/ [US] /ˈloʊ-/ *noun* [C] *US* a division within an organization, especially a national workers' organization, representing people from a particular area

ˌlocal auˈthority *group noun* [C] *UK* the group of people who govern an area, especially a city

ˌlocal ˈcolour *noun* [U] the special or unusual features of a place, especially as described or shown in a story, picture or film to make it seem more real

ˌlocal ˈderby *noun* [C] (*ALSO* **derby**) *UK* a sports competition, especially a game of football, between two teams from the same city or area

locale /ləʊˈkɑːl/ *noun* [C] *FORMAL* an area or place, especially one where something special happens, such as the action in a book or a film: *The book's locale is a seaside town in the summer of 1958.*

ˌlocal ˈgovernment *noun* [U] the control and organization of towns and small areas by people who are elected from them

locality /ləˈkæl.ə.ti/ [US] /loʊˈkæl.ə.t̬i/ *noun* [C] a particular area: *In 19th-century Britain, industries became concentrated in particular localities.*

locally /ˈləʊ.kəl.i/ [US] /ˈloʊ-/ *adv* in the particular small area which you are talking about: *The shopkeeper said all his fruit and vegetables are grown locally.* ○ *Do they live locally?*

ˈlocal ˌtime *noun* [U] the official time in a country or an area

locate [BE SITUATED] /ləʊˈkeɪt/ [US] /loʊ-/ *verb SLIGHTLY FORMAL* **be located in/near/on/etc.** to be in a particular place: *Our office is located in the city centre.*

locate [MOVE] /ləʊˈkeɪt/ [US] /loʊ-/ *verb* [I + adv or prep] *US* to move to a place to do business: *The company hopes to locate* ***in*** *its new offices by June.*

locate [FIND] /ləʊˈkeɪt/ [US] /loʊ-/ *verb* [T] *SLIGHTLY FORMAL* to find or discover the exact position of something: *Police are still trying to locate the suspect.* **location** /ləʊˈkeɪ.ʃən/ [US] /loʊ-/ *noun* [U] *The latest navigational aids make the location of the airfield quite easy.*

location [POSITION] /ləʊˈkeɪ.ʃən/ [US] /loʊ-/ *noun* [C] *SLIGHTLY FORMAL* a place or position: *The hotel is* ***in*** *a lovely location overlooking the lake.* ○ *A map showing the location* ***of*** *the property will be sent to you.*

location [OUTSIDE] /ləʊˈkeɪ.ʃən/ [US] /loʊ-/ *noun* [C or U] a place away from a STUDIO where all or part of a film or a television show is recorded: *The documentary was made* ***on*** *location in the Gobi desert.*

loch /lɒk/ [US] /lɑːk/ *noun* [C] *SCOTTISH ENGLISH* a **lake**: *Loch Lomond*

loci /ˈləʊ.saɪ/ [US] /ˈloʊ-/ *plural of* **locus**

lock [FASTEN] /lɒk/ [US] /lɑːk/ *noun* [C] a device which prevents something such as a door being opened and which you can only open with a key: *I heard someone turn a key* ***in*** *the lock.* ○ *safety locks* ○ *Thieves got in by smashing the lock off the door.* ➲See also **padlock**.

• **lock, stock and barrel** including all or every part of something: *We had to move our things lock, stock and barrel to the other side of the country.*

• **under lock and key 1** locked away safely: *Her jewellery is securely under lock and key at the bank.* **2** If a person, especially a criminal, is under lock and key, they are being kept in a place from which they cannot escape, usually a prison.

lock /lɒk/ [US] /lɑːk/ *verb* [I or T] to fasten something with a key, or be fastened with a key: *Don't forget to lock the door when you go out.* ○ *If you shut the door it will lock automatically.*

lockable /ˈlɒk.ə.bl/ [US] /lɑː.kə-/ *adj*: *All our suitcases are lockable* (= can be locked).

lock [MAKE SAFE] /lɒk/ [US] /lɑːk/ *verb* [T usually + adv or prep] to put something in a safe place and fasten the lock: *He locked the confidential documents* ***in*** *his filing cabinet.* ○ *You really should lock your car* ***(up)*** *or it'll get stolen.*

lock [WATER] /lɒk/ [US] /lɑːk/ *noun* [C] a length of water with gates at each end where the level of water can be changed to allow boats to move between parts of a canal or river which are at different heights

L

lock FIXED /lɒk/ US /lɑːk/ *verb* [I] to be fixed in one position: *I tried to move forwards but the wheels had locked.*
• **be locked together** If people or animals are locked together, they are holding each other tightly so that neither one can move: *Sometimes, fighting stags become locked together by their antlers.*
• **lock horns** to begin to argue or fight: *The mayor and her deputy locked horns over plans for the new road.*

lock /lɒk/ US /lɑːk/ *noun* [C] a way of holding someone that you are fighting against so that they cannot move: *The smaller wrestler held his opponent in a full body lock.*

lock DEFINITE EVENT /lɒk/ US /lɑːk/ *noun* [C] US INFORMAL something that is certain to happen: *She's a lock for promotion this year.*

lock HAIR /lɒk/ US /lɑːk/ *noun* [C] a small group of hairs, especially a curl: *There is a lock of Napoleon's hair in the display cabinet.*
locks /lɒks/ US /lɑːks/ *plural noun* LITERARY the hair on someone's head: *curly locks* ○ *flowing golden locks*

lock CAR /lɒk/ US /lɑːk/ *noun* [U] UK the amount a road vehicle's front wheels can be turned from one side to the other by turning its STEERING WHEEL: *You need it on full lock* (= with the wheel turned as much as possible).

PHRASAL VERBS WITH **lock** ▼

▲ **lock** *sth* **away** *phrasal verb* [M] to put something in a safe place and lock the door in order that someone else cannot get it: *If you keep valuables in your house, lock them away somewhere safe.*

▲ **lock** *sb* **in** *phrasal verb* [M] to prevent someone from leaving a room or building by locking the door: [R] *She stormed off to her bedroom and locked herself in.* ○ *He was locked in his bedroom as a punishment.*

▲ **be 'locked ,in** *sth phrasal verb* **1** to be prevented from moving by something: *We were locked in traffic for over two hours on the way home.* **2** If you are locked in a situation or process, it is impossible for you to advance from it: *Both parties wish to avoid being locked in discussions which will resolve nothing.*

▲ **lock** *sb* **out** PREVENT FROM ENTERING *phrasal verb* [M] to prevent someone from entering a building or room by locking the door: *He had to break into the house because his girlfriend had locked him out.*

▲ **lock** *sb* **out** PREVENT FROM WORKING *phrasal verb* [M] USUALLY DISAPPROVING to prevent workers from entering their place of work until they agree to particular conditions given by the employer: *Management has threatened to lock out the workforce if they do not accept the proposed changes in working methods.*
lockout /'lɒk.aʊt/ US /'lɑːk-/ *noun* [C or U] *The General Strike in Britain in 1926 was caused by the lockout of coal miners.*

▲ **lock** (*sth*) **up** BUILDING *phrasal verb* [M] to lock all the doors and windows of a building when you leave it: *Sandra, will you lock up tonight when you go?*

▲ **lock** *sb* **up** PUT IN PRISON *phrasal verb* [M] to put someone in a prison or a hospital for people who are mentally ill: *Murderers should be locked up for life.* ○ *After what she did, they should lock her up and throw away the key* (= lock her up until she dies).

locker /'lɒk.əʳ/ US /'lɑː.kɚ/ *noun* [C] a cupboard, often tall and made of metal, in which someone can keep their possessions, and leave them for a period of time: *We had several hours to wait for our train, so we left our bags in a (luggage) locker, and went to look around the town.*

'locker ,room *noun* [C usually sing] a room with lockers where people can keep clothes and other things, especially while doing sport

locker-room /'lɒk.ə.ruːm/ US /'lɑː.kɚ-/ *adj* [before n] describes the type of rude, sexual jokes and remarks that men are thought to enjoy when they are with each other: *locker-room talk/jokes*

locket /'lɒk.ɪt/ US /'lɑː.kɪt/ *noun* [C] a small item of jewellery which opens to show a small picture or piece of hair, usually worn on a chain around a person's neck

lock-in /'lɒk.ɪn/ US /'lɑːk-/ *noun* [C] UK INFORMAL when a pub locks its doors and allows people to continue drinking illegally after the time when it should have closed: *There was a lock-in at my local last night.*

lockjaw /'lɒk.dʒɔː/ US /'lɑːk.dʒɑː/ *noun* [U] INFORMAL FOR **tetanus**

'lock ,keeper *noun* [C] a person who is in control of a LOCK (= a body of water with gates), especially by opening or closing its gates

locksmith /'lɒk.smɪθ/ US /'lɑːk-/ *noun* [C] a person who repairs and/or makes locks and supplies keys

lockup PRISON /'lɒk.ʌp/ US /'lɑː.kʌp/ *noun* [C] a small room, used as a prison, usually in a small town, in which criminals can be kept for a short time

lock-up BUILDING /'lɒk.ʌp/ US /'lɑː.kʌp/ *noun* [C] MAINLY UK a building where objects, especially a car, can be safely kept

loco PERSON /'ləʊ.kəʊ/ US /'loʊ.koʊ/ *adj* [after v] MAINLY US SLANG crazy: *Man, he just went loco and smashed the place up.*

loco ENGINE /'ləʊ.kəʊ/ US /'loʊ.koʊ/ *noun* [C] *plural* **locos** UK INFORMAL FOR **locomotive**

locomotion /,ləʊ.kə'məʊ.ʃ°n/ US /,loʊ.kə'moʊ-/ *noun* [U] SPECIALIZED the ability to move; movement **locomotive** /,ləʊ.kə'məʊ.tɪv/ US /,loʊ.kə'moʊ.t̬ɪv/ *adj*

locomotive /,ləʊ.kə'məʊ.tɪv/ US /,loʊ.kə'moʊ.t̬ɪv/ *noun* [C] (UK INFORMAL **loco**) the engine of a train

locum /'ləʊ.kəm/ US /'loʊ-/ *noun* [C] MAINLY UK a doctor who does the job of another doctor who is ill or on holiday

locus /'ləʊ.kəs/ US /'loʊ.kəs/ *noun* [C] *plural* **loci** FORMAL the place where something happens or the central area of interest in something being discussed: *The locus of decision-making is sometimes far from the government's offices.*

locust /'ləʊ.kəst/ US /'loʊ-/ *noun* [C] a large insect with wings found in hot areas which flies in large groups and destroys plants and crops: *a swarm of locusts*

lode /ləʊd/ US /loʊd/ *noun* [C] an amount of metal in its natural form

lodestar /'ləʊd.stɑːʳ/ US /'loʊd.stɑːr/ *noun* [S] **1** a star, especially THE POLE STAR, used to help find direction **2** LITERARY an example or principle that people want to follow: *The party manifesto is no longer the lodestar it used to be.*

lodestone /'ləʊd.stəʊn/ US /'loʊd.stoʊn/ *noun* [C or U] (a piece of) rock which contains a lot of iron and can therefore be used as a MAGNET (= an object that pulls metal objects towards it)

lodge STAY /lɒdʒ/ US /lɑːdʒ/ *verb* [I usually + adv or prep] FORMAL to pay rent to stay somewhere: *She lodged with Mrs Higgins when she first came to Cambridge.*
lodging /'lɒdʒ.ɪŋ/ US /'lɑː.dʒɪŋ/ *noun* [U] *The price includes board and lodging* (= meals and a room to sleep in).

lodge SMALL BUILDING /lɒdʒ/ US /lɑːdʒ/ *noun* [C] **1** a small house in the country used especially by people on holiday or taking part in sports, or one on the land owned by a large house: *a ski/hunting lodge* **2** the place where a BEAVER lives **3** US a **wigwam**

lodge FIX /lɒdʒ/ US /lɑːdʒ/ *verb* [I or T; usually + adv or prep] to (cause to) become fixed in a place or position: *A fish bone had lodged in her throat.*

lodge COMPLAIN /lɒdʒ/ US /lɑːdʒ/ *verb* **lodge a claim/complaint/protest, etc.** to make an official complaint about something: *The US lodged a formal protest against the arrest of the foreign reporters.* ○ *Lee's solicitor said last night that they would be lodging an appeal against the sentence.*

lodge STORE /lɒdʒ/ US /lɑːdʒ/ *verb* [T usually + adv or prep] MAINLY UK FORMAL to put something in a safe place: *You should lodge a copy of the letter with your solicitor.*

lodge GROUP /lɒdʒ/ US /lɑːdʒ/ *group noun* [C] a local group of an organization such as the FREEMASONS: *a Masonic Lodge*

lodge ROOM /lɒdʒ/ US /lɑːdʒ/ *noun* [C] UK the room used by a person whose job is to be at the entrance to a large building such as a hotel or college in order to help people: *the porter's lodge*

lodger /'lɒdʒ.əʳ/ US /'lɑː.dʒɚ/ *noun* [C] (US ALSO **roomer**) someone who pays for a place to sleep, and usually for meals, in someone else's house: *She **takes in** lodgers to make a bit of extra money.*

ˈlodging ˌhouse *noun* [C] (*US ALSO* **rooming house**) a house which has rooms that people can rent

lodgings /ˈlɒdʒ.ɪŋz/ [US] /ˈlɑː.dʒɪŋz/ *plural noun* (*UK INFORMAL ALSO* **digs**) a room in someone's house that you pay money to live in

loft [ROOF SPACE] /lɒft/ [US] /lɑːft/ *noun* [C] **1** a space at the top of a building under the roof used for storage and usually entered by a LADDER, or sometimes made into a room: *The firm specializes in loft **conversions*** (= making lofts into rooms). **2** *US* an upper floor or room **3** an apartment in a large building that was previously used for industry

loft [HIT] /lɒft/ [US] /lɑːft/ *verb* [T] to hit a ball high

lofty /ˈlɒf.ti/ [US] /ˈlɑːf-/ *adj* **1** *FORMAL* high: *a lofty ceiling/mountain/wall* **2** *FORMAL* Lofty ideas etc. are of a high moral standard: *lofty sentiments/ideals* **3** *DISAPPROVING* If you have a lofty attitude etc., you act as if you think you are better than other people: *a lofty attitude/air/tone* **loftily** /ˈlɒf.tɪ.li/ [US] /ˈlɑːf-/ *adv DISAPPROVING* **loftiness** /ˈlɒf.tɪ.nəs/ [US] /ˈlɑːf-/ *noun* [U]

log [WOOD] /lɒg/ [US] /lɑːg/ *noun* [C] a thick piece of tree trunk or branch, especially one cut for burning on a fire

log /lɒg/ [US] /lɑːg/ *verb* [I or T] **-gg-** to cut down trees so that you can use their wood: *The forest has been so heavily logged that it is in danger of disappearing.*

logger /ˈlɒg.əʳ/ [US] /ˈlɑː.gɚ/ *noun* [C] a person who cuts down trees for wood

logging /ˈlɒg.ɪŋ/ [US] /ˈlɑː.gɪŋ/ *noun* [U] the activity of cutting down trees for wood: *logging companies.*

log [RECORD] /lɒg/ [US] /lɑːg/ *noun* [C] a full written record of a journey, a period of time, or an event: *the ship's log*

log /lɒg/ [US] /lɑːg/ *verb* [T] **-gg-** **1** to officially record something: *The Police Complaints Authority has logged more than 90 complaints.* **2** (*UK ALSO* **log up**) to travel and record a particular distance

log [NUMBER] /lɒg/ [US] /lɑːg/ *noun* [C] *INFORMAL FOR* **logarithm**

PHRASAL VERBS WITH **log**

▲ **log in/on** *phrasal verb* to connect a computer to a computer system by typing your name, so that you can start working: *Log on using your name and password.*

▲ **log off/out** *phrasal verb* to stop a computer being connected to a computer system, usually when you want to stop working: *Could you all log off for a few minutes, please?*

loganberry /ˈləʊ.gᵊn,bᵊr.i/ [US] /ˈloʊ.gən,ber-/ *noun* [C] a small red fruit, similar to a RASPBERRY, or the tall plant on which it grows

logarithm /ˈlɒg.ə.rɪ.ðᵊm/ [US] /ˈlɑː.gə-/ *noun* [C] (*INFORMAL* **log**) the number which shows how many times a number, called the BASE, has to be multiplied by itself to produce another number. Adding or subtracting logarithms can replace multiplying or dividing large numbers. **logarithmic** /ˌlɒg.ᵊrˈɪð.mɪk/ [US] /ˌlɑː.gəˈrɪð-/ *adj* **logarithmically** /ˌlɒg.ᵊrˈɪð.mɪ.kli/ [US] /ˌlɑː.gəˈrɪð-/ *adv*

ˈlog ˌbook *noun* [C] (*ALSO* **registration book**) *UK* an official document which records information about a car and the people who have owned it

ˌlog ˈcabin *noun* [C] a small house made from tree trunks

loggerheads /ˈlɒg.ə.hedz/ [US] /ˈlɑː.gɚ-/ *plural noun* **be at loggerheads (with *sb*)** to strongly disagree (with someone): *The Chancellor is at loggerheads with the Prime Minister **over** public spending.*

logic [REASONABLE THINKING] /ˈlɒdʒ.ɪk/ [US] /ˈlɑː.dʒɪk/ *noun* [U] a particular way of thinking, especially one which is reasonable and based on good judgment: *I fail to see the logic behind his argument.* ○ *If prices go up, wages will go up too – that's just logic.* ○ *There's no logic in the decision to reduce staff when orders are the highest for years.* ○ *The **internal** logic of her argument is undeniable.*

logic [FORMAL THINKING] /ˈlɒdʒ.ɪk/ [US] /ˈlɑː.dʒɪk/ *noun* [U] a formal scientific method of examining or thinking about ideas: *a treatise on formal logic*

logician /ləˈdʒɪʃ.ᵊn/ [US] /loʊˈdʒɪ-/ *noun* [C] someone who studies or is skilled in logic

logical /ˈlɒdʒ.ɪ.kᵊl/ [US] /ˈlɑː.dʒɪ-/ *adj* using reason: *a logical choice/conclusion* ○ *Students need the ability to construct a logical argument.* ○ *It was the logical thing to do* (= the decision was a reasonable one when all the facts were considered). ＊ NOTE: The opposite is **illogical**. **logically** /ˈlɒdʒ.ɪ.kli/ [US] /ˈlɑː.dʒɪ-/ *adv*: *Her ideas were clear and logically presented.*

logistics /ləˈdʒɪs.tɪks/ *plural noun* the careful organization of a complicated activity so that it happens in a successful and effective way: *We need to look at the logistics **of** the whole aid operation.* **logistic** /ləˈdʒɪs.tɪk/ *adj* (*ALSO* **logistical**) *logistic support/problems* **logistically** /ləˈdʒɪs.tɪ.kli/ *adv*

logjam, **log-jam** /ˈlɒg.dʒæm/ [US] /ˈlɑːg-/ *noun* **1** [C usually sing] a situation in which neither group involved in an argument can win or get an advantage and no action can be taken: *This is the latest attempt to **break** the logjam in the peace process.* **2** [C] a mass of floating logs that block a river

logo /ˈləʊ.gəʊ/ [US] /ˈloʊ.goʊ/ *noun* [C] *plural* **logos** a design or symbol used by a company to advertise its products: *a corporate logo* ○ *The players wore shirts with the sponsor's logo.*

loincloth /ˈlɔɪn.klɒθ/ [US] /-klɑːθ/ *noun* [C] a piece of cloth that hangs down from around the waist, sometimes worn by men in hot countries

loins /lɔɪnz/ *plural noun LITERARY OR HUMOROUS* the part of the body which is above the legs and below the waist, especially the sexual organs: ***the fruit of** your **loins*** (= your child/children)

loin /lɔɪn/ *noun* [C or U] (a piece of) meat from the back of an animal near the tail or from the top part of the back legs ➲See also **sirloin (steak)**.

loiter /ˈlɔɪ.təʳ/ [US] /-t̬ɚ/ *verb* [I] **1** to move slowly around or stand especially in a public place without an obvious reason: *A gang of youths were loitering outside the cinema.* **2** to go slowly, stopping often: *Come straight home and don't loiter, Alan.* **loiterer** /ˈlɔɪ.tᵊr.əʳ/ [US] /-t̬ɚ.ɚ/ *noun* [C]

loitering /ˈlɔɪ.tᵊr.ɪŋ/ [US] /-t̬ɚ-/ *noun* [U] (*US* **loitering with intent**) *LEGAL* the offence of waiting in a place, looking as if you are going to do something illegal

LOL, **lol** *INTERNET ABBREVIATION FOR* laughing out loud: used when you think something is very funny

Lolita /lɒlˈiː.tə/ /ləˈliː-/ [US] /loʊˈliː.t̬ə/ *noun* [C] a young girl who has a very sexual appearance or behaves in a very sexual way

loll /lɒl/ [US] /lɑːl/ *verb* [I usually + adv or prep] to lie, sit or hang down in a relaxed informal or uncontrolled way: *I spent most of the weekend lolling **about/around** on the beach.* ○ *a dog with its tongue lolling **out***

lollipop /ˈlɒl.i.pɒp/ [US] /ˈlɑː.li.pɑːp/ *noun* [C] a hard sweet on a stick

ˈlollipop ˌman/ˌlady *noun* [C] *UK INFORMAL* a person who helps children to cross the road near a school by standing in the middle of the road and holding up a stick with a sign on it which means that the traffic must stop

lollop /ˈlɒl.əp/ [US] /ˈlɑː.ləp/ *verb* [I usually + adv or prep] *INFORMAL* (of a person or especially a large animal) to move in an awkward, rolling way: *The dog lolloped along the beach.*

lolly [SWEET] /ˈlɒl.i/ [US] /ˈlɑː.li/ *noun* [C] **1** *UK* **ice lolly** or **lollipop** **2** *AUS* a wrapped sweet for sucking or chewing

lolly [MONEY] /ˈlɒl.i/ [US] /ˈlɑː.li/ *noun* [U] *UK OLD-FASHIONED SLANG FOR* money

lone /ləʊn/ [US] /loʊn/ *adj* [before n] **1** alone: *a lone survivor* ○ *He was a lone **voice*** (= the only person) *arguing against a reduction in resources.* **2** **lone parent/mother/father** someone who has children but no partner living with them

lonely /ˈləʊn.li/ [US] /ˈloʊn-/ *adj* **1** unhappy because you are not with other people: *She gets lonely now that all the kids have left home.* ○ *the lonely life of a farmer* ➲See Note **alone or lonely?** at **alone** WITHOUT PEOPLE. **2** A lonely place is a long way from where people live: *a lonely stretch of Arizona highway*

[L]

• **lonely hearts** (*ALSO* **lonely hearts club/column, etc.**) a place or section of a magazine etc. for people who would like to make new friends or meet a sexual partner

loneliness /ˈləʊn.lɪ.nəs/ [US] /ˈloʊn-/ *noun* [U] the state of being lonely

loner /ˈləʊ.nər/ [US] /ˈloʊ.nɚ/ *noun* [C] a person who likes to do things on their own without other people: *He was always a bit of a loner at school.*

lonesome /ˈləʊn.səm/ [US] /ˈloʊn-/ *adj US* **1** lonely **2** **by/on your lonesome** alone: *I was just sitting here all by my lonesome.*

ˌlone ˈwolf *noun* [C usually sing] a **loner**

long [TIME] /lɒŋ/ [US] /lɑːŋ/ *adj* continuing for a large amount of time: *a long film/meeting* ○ *I've been waiting a long time.* ○ *It's a long while since I worked there.* ○ *How long is the film?* ○ *The sessions are an hour long.*

• **(as) long as *your* arm** *INFORMAL* very long: *There was a list of complaints as long as your arm.*

• **the long arm of the law** *LITERARY* the police: *You can't escape the long arm of the law* (= The police will catch you if you have done something illegal).

• **a long way to go** a lot of work to do or improvements to make: *He has a long way to go before he can present the scheme to the public.*

• **have come a long way** to have advanced to an improved or more developed state: *Information technology has come a long way in the last twenty years.*

• **go a long way** If you say that someone will go a long way, you mean that they will be very successful. ➲See also **far** DISTANCE.

• **go a long way towards doing *sth*** to be very helpful: *The money raised will go a long way towards providing essential food and medicine.*

• **go back a long way** If people go back a long way, they have known each other for a long time.

• **be long in the tooth** *INFORMAL* to be old, often too old to do something: *He's a bit long in the tooth to be wearing jeans, don't you think?*

• **not by a long chalk/shot** *INFORMAL* not in any way: *It wasn't as good as his first book – not by a long chalk.*

• **so long** *INFORMAL* goodbye

• **before (very/too) long** (*ALSO* **before much longer**) soon: *They'll be home before very long.*

• **no longer** (*ALSO* **not any longer**) in the past but not now: *The cinema is no longer used.* ○ *She doesn't work here any longer.*

• **the long and the short of it** *INFORMAL* said when you want to explain the general situation without giving details: *The long and the short of it is that they are willing to start the work in January.*

• **Long time no see.** *SAYING* said when you meet someone who you haven't seen for a long period of time

• **not long for this world** *OLD-FASHIONED* If someone is not long for this world, they will die soon.

long /lɒŋ/ [US] /lɑːŋ/ *adv* **1** used to mean '(for) a long time', especially in questions and negative sentences: *Have you been waiting **(for)** long?* ○ *I'm just writing a letter but it won't take long.* ○ *How long have you been in England?* ○ *Don't rush – take as long as you like.* ○ *I've known her longer than you have.* ○ *I won't be staying much longer.* **2** used with the *past participle* or the *-ing* form of the verb to mean that a state or activity has continued for a long time: *long-serving employees*

• **long live *sb/sth*** said to show support for the person or thing mentioned: *Long live the President!*

long [DISTANCE] /lɒŋ/ [US] /lɑːŋ/ *adj* being a distance between two points which is more than average or usual: *long hair* ○ *long legs* ○ *a long dress* ○ *There was a long queue at the post office.* ○ *We're still a long way from the station.*

long [MANY WORDS] *adj* describes a piece of writing which has a lot of pages or words: *a long letter/book/report*

long [WANT] /lɒŋ/ [US] /lɑːŋ/ *verb FORMAL* **long for *sth*; long to do *sth*** to want something very much: *She longed to see him again.* ○ *I'm longing for news of him.*

longing /ˈlɒŋ.ɪŋ/ [US] /ˈlɑːŋ-/ *noun* [S or U] a feeling of wanting something or someone very much: *He gazed at her, his eyes full of longing.* ○ *a longing look* ○ *a longing **for** his homeland* **longingly** /ˈlɒŋ.ɪŋ.li/ [US] /ˈlɑːŋ-/ *adv*: *She gazed longingly at the cakes in the shop window.*

long [IF] /lɒŋ/ [US] /lɑːŋ/ *adv* **as/so long as** used to say that something must happen before something else can happen: *I can come as long as I can leave by 4.00.* ○ *Bring your friends by all means – just so long as I know how many are coming.*

long [MAP] /lɒŋ/ [US] /lɑːŋ/ *noun* [U] *WRITTEN ABBREVIATION FOR* **longitude**

long-awaited /ˌlɒŋ.əˈweɪ.tɪd/ *adj* having been expected for a long time: *Last week the commission published it's long-awaited report on the problem of teenage pregnancies.*

long-distance /ˌlɒŋˈdɪs.tənts/ [US] /ˌlɑːŋ-/ *adj* [before n], *adv* travelling a long way, or separated by a long distance: *a long-distance runner* ○ *long-distance lorry drivers* ○ *a long-distance phone call*

ˌlong diˈvision *noun* [C usually sing] in mathematics, a method of dividing one, usually large number by another, which makes it necessary to write down each stage of the work

long-drawn-out /ˌlɒŋ.drɔːnˈaʊt/ [US] /ˌlɑːŋ.drɑːn-/ *adj* taking more time than is necessary: *a long-drawn-out process*

longevity /lɒnˈdʒev.ə.ti/ [US] /lɑːnˈdʒev.ə.t̬i/ *noun* [U] *FORMAL* living for a long time: *To what to you attribute your longevity?*

longhand /ˈlɒŋ.hænd/ [US] /ˈlɑːŋ-/ *noun* [U] ordinary writing by hand

long-haul /ˈlɒŋ.hɔːl/ [US] /ˈlɑːŋ.hɑːl/ *adj* [before n] travelling a long distance: *a long-haul **flight***

longish /ˈlɒŋ.ɪʃ/ [US] /ˈlɑːŋ-/ *adj* quite long

longitude /ˈlɒn.dʒɪ.tjuːd/ /ˈlɒŋ.gɪ-/ [US] /ˈlɑːn.dʒə.tuːd/ *noun* [C or U] (*WRITTEN ABBREVIATION* **long**) the distance of a place east or west of an imaginary line from the top to the bottom of the Earth, measured in degrees ➲Compare **latitude** POSITION. **longitudinal** /ˌlɒn.dʒɪˈtjuː.dɪ.nəl/ /ˌlɒŋ.gɪ-/ /ˌlɒŋ.ɪ-/ [US] /ˌlɑːn.dʒəˈtuː-/ *adj*

ˈlong ˌjohns *plural noun* underwear with long legs, worn under your outer clothes to keep you warm

the ˈlong ˌjump *noun* [S] (*US ALSO* **the broad jump**) a sports event in which a person runs up to a mark and then jumps as far forward as they can ➲See picture **Sports** on page Centre 10

long-lasting /ˌlɒŋˈlɑː.stɪŋ/ [US] /ˌlɑːŋˈlæs.tɪŋ/ *adj* continuing for a long period of time: *a long-lasting friendship*

long-life /ˌlɒŋˈlaɪf/ [US] /ˌlɑːŋ-/ *adj* [before n] describes products which have been made or treated in such a way that they last for a long time: *long-life milk*

long-lost /ˈlɒŋ.lɒst/ [US] /ˈlɑːŋ.lɑːst/ *adj* [before n] describes a relative, friend or object that you have not seen for a long time: *my long-lost cousin*

long-range /ˈlɒŋ.reɪndʒ/ [US] /ˈlɑːŋ-/ *adj* [before n] for a long time into the future, or across a long distance: *a long-range weather forecast* ○ *long-range missiles/bombs*

long-running /ˈlɒŋ.rʌn.ɪŋ/ [US] /ˈlɑːŋ-/ *adj* [before n] continuing for a long time: *a long-running musical* ○ *their long-running dispute*

longshoreman /ˈlɒŋ.ʃɔː.mən/ [US] /ˈlɑːŋ.ʃɔːr-/ *noun* [C] *US FOR* **docker**, see at **dock** FOR SHIPS

ˈlong ˌshot *noun* [C usually sing] something you try although it is unlikely to be successful: *It's a long shot, but you could try phoning him at home.*

long-sighted /ˌlɒŋˈsaɪ.tɪd/ [US] /ˌlɑːŋˈsaɪ.t̬ɪd/ *adj* (*US* **far-sighted**) able to see things which are far away but not things which are near you

long-standing /ˌlɒŋˈstæn.dɪŋ/ [US] /ˌlɑːŋ-/ *adj* having existed for a long time: *a long-standing agreement*

long-suffering /ˌlɒŋˈsʌf.ər.ɪŋ/ [US] /ˌlɑːŋˈsʌf.ɚ-/ *adj* A long-suffering person is patient despite being annoyed or insulted regularly over a period of time: *Bill and his long-suffering wife*

long-term /ˌlɒŋˈtɜːm/ [US] /ˌlɑːŋˈtɝːm/ *adj* continuing a long time into the future: *long-term unemployment* ○ *long-term care for the seriously ill* ○ *the long-term effects of the drug*

long-time /ˈlɒŋ.taɪm/ [US] /ˈlɑːŋ-/ *adj* [before n] describes someone who has been in a particular position for a long period: *A long-time **friend** of the chairman said she had expected the resignation.*

L

longueur /lɔ̃ŋˈgɜːʳ/ (US) /-ˈgɝː/ *noun* **[C usually pl]** *LITERARY* a boring part of something, especially a book, film, etc: *Despite the occasional longueurs, this is an impressive first novel.*

ˌlong vaˈcation *noun* **[C]** (*INFORMAL* **long vac**) *UK* the three months in the summer when college and university students do not have classes

ˈlong ˌwave *noun* **[U]** (*WRITTEN ABBREVIATION* **LW**) a range of radio waves used for broadcasting and receiving which are of 1000 metres or more in length

longways /ˈlɒŋ.weɪz/ (US) /ˈlɑːŋ-/ *adv* (*US ALSO* **longwise**) along the length: *Fold the paper longways.* ➲See also **lengthways**.

ˌlong weekˈend *noun* **[C]** Saturday and Sunday with at least one additional day of holiday added, either Friday or Monday: *We spent a long weekend with my parents.*

long-winded /ˌlɒŋˈwɪn.dɪd/ (US) /ˌlɑːŋ-/ *adj* A long-winded speech, letter, article, etc. is too long, or uses too many words.

loo /luː/ *noun* **[C]** *plural* **loos** *UK INFORMAL FOR* toilet: *I'll just go to the loo.* ○ *loo roll*

loofah /ˈluː.fə/ *noun* **[C]** a piece of a rough plant, which is used to rub the body when washing

look [SEE] /lʊk/ *verb* **[I]** to direct your eyes in order to see: *Look! There's grandma.* ○ *They looked **at** the picture and laughed.* ○ *Look **at** all this rubbish on the floor.* ○ *She looked **up** from her book and smiled at me.* ○ *I looked out (of) the window.* ○ *Look over there – there's a rainbow!*

• **I'm just looking** said to a person working in a shop when they offer to help you but you want to continue looking at the goods on your own

• **never look back** to continue to be successful after doing something with a good result: *She never looked back after that first exhibition.*

• **look daggers at *sb*** *INFORMAL* to look angrily at someone

• **not look *sb* in the eye/face** If you cannot look someone in the eye/face, you are too ashamed to look at them directly and speak truthfully to them.

• **look kindly on *sb/sth*** to have a good opinion of someone or something: *She had hoped the critics would look kindly on her first novel.*

• **look on the bright side** to find good things in a bad situation: *Look on the bright side – no one was badly hurt.*

• **look straight/right through *sb*** *UK* to look at someone as if you cannot see them, either intentionally or because you are thinking about something else: *I said hello but she looked straight through me.*

• **be not much to look at** *INFORMAL* to not be attractive: *The house isn't much to look at but it's spacious.*

• **look to *your* laurels** to make an extra effort to succeed because there is more competition: *Nowadays there are a number of rival products on the market and the older, established companies are having to look to their laurels.*

• **Never look a gift horse in the mouth.** *SAYING* said to advise someone not to refuse something good that is being offered

look /lʊk/ *noun* **[C]** when you look at someone or something: *She gave him a look **of** real dislike.* ○ ***Take a (good)** look **at** this picture and see if you recognize anyone.* ○ *Can I **have a** look **at** your dictionary?*

• **If looks could kill.** *SAYING* said when you see someone look very angrily at someone else

COMMON LEARNER ERROR

look, see or **watch?**

See means to notice people and things with your eyes.

She saw a big spider and screamed.
Did you see anyone you knew at the party?

Look (at) is used when you are trying to see something or someone. If **look** is followed by an object, you must use a preposition. The usual preposition is 'at'.

I've looked everywhere, but can't find my keys.
He looked at the map to find the road.
~~*He looked the photographs.*~~

Watch means to look at something for a period of time, usually something which moves or changes.

He watched television all evening.
I watched them playing football.
~~*I looked them playing football.*~~

look [SEARCH] /lʊk/ *verb* **[I]** to try to find something or someone: *I'm looking **for** my keys.* ○ *I've looked everywhere but I can't find my glasses.* ○ *Have you looked in the dictionary?* ○ *I looked down the list but couldn't see his name.*

• **be looking for trouble** to be acting in a way that will certainly cause problems for you: *Parking outside the police station on double yellow lines is just looking for trouble.*

look /lʊk/ *noun* **[C usually sing]** when you look for someone or something: *I **had** another look **for** the watch, but couldn't find it.*

look [SEEM] /lʊk/ *verb* **[L; I usually + adv or prep]** to appear or seem: *You look well!* ○ *The roads look very icy.* ○ *That dress looks nice on you.* ○ *He has started to look his age* (= appear as old as he really is). ○ ***It's** looking good* (= Things are going well). ○ *He looked **(like)** a friendly sort of person.* ○ *The twins look just **like** their mother.* ○ *She looked **as if/though** she hadn't slept all night.* ○ ***It** looks **like** rain* (= as if it is going to rain).

• **Look lively/sharp!** *UK OLD-FASHIONED* used to tell someone to do something quickly: *Look lively – we haven't got all day!*

• **make *sb* look small** to show that someone is wrong in a way that makes them appear foolish

look /lʊk/ *noun* **[C]** **1** an expression on someone's face: *She had a worried look about her.* ○ *She **gave** me a questioning look.* **2 the look of *sb/sth*** the appearance of someone or something: *They liked the look of the hotel, but it was too expensive.* ○ *I don't like the look of that fence* (= It appears to have something wrong with it).

• **by the look(s) of things** (*ALSO* **by the look of it**) judging by the information we have now: *By the look of things, we won't be able to take our holiday till the autumn.*

look [WARNING] /lʊk/ *verb* **[I]** used when you are telling someone to be careful or to pay attention: **[+ question word]** *Look **where** you're going!* ○ *Look at the time – we're late!*

look [DIRECTION] /lʊk/ *verb* **[I usually + adv or prep]** to face a particular direction: *The garden looks south.* ○ *This window looks out onto the lake.*

look [HOPE] /lʊk/ *verb* **be looking to do *sth*** to plan to do something: *I'm looking to start my own business.*

look [EXPRESSION] /lʊk/ *exclamation* used to express annoyance: *Look, I've already told you it's not possible.* ○ *OLD-FASHIONED* *Look **here**, I've had enough of this.*

PHRASAL VERBS WITH **look** ▼

▲ **look after *sb/sth*** *phrasal verb* to take care of or be in charge of someone or something: *We look after the neighbours' cat while they're away.* ○ *If you look after your clothes they last a lot longer.* ○ **[R]** *Don't worry about Mia – she can look after herself.*

▲ **look ahead** *phrasal verb* to think about what will happen in the future and plan for these events: *We are trying to look ahead and see what our options are.*

▲ **look at *sth*** [THINK] *phrasal verb* to think about a subject carefully so that you can make a decision about it: *Management is looking at ways of cutting costs.*

▲ **look at *sth*** [READ] *phrasal verb* to read something in order to check it or form an opinion about it: *Can you look at my essay sometime?*

▲ **look at *sth*** [EXAMINE] *phrasal verb* If someone, usually an expert, looks at something, they examine it: *Did you get the doctor to look at your knee?*

▲ **look at *sth*** [OPINION] *phrasal verb* to consider something in a particular way: *If I'd had children I might have looked at things differently.*

▲ **look back** *phrasal verb* to think about something that happened in the past: *When I look back I can see where we went wrong.* ○ *It wasn't such a bad experience when I look back **on** it.*

▲ **look down on *sb*** *phrasal verb* (*ALSO* **look down *your* nose at *sb***) to think that someone is less important than you: *She thinks they look down on her because she didn't go to university.*

L

▲ **look forward to** ***sth*** *phrasal verb* **1** to feel pleased and excited about something that is going to happen: *I'm really looking forward to my holiday.* ○ [+ v-ing] *She was looking forward to seeing the grandchildren again.* ○ *I'm not looking forward to Christmas this year.* **2** [+ v-ing] *FORMAL* used at the end of a formal letter to say you hope to hear from or see someone soon, or that you expect something from them: *I look forward to* ***hearing from you.*** ○ *In the circumstances, I look forward to* ***receiving*** *your client's cheque for the sum of £570 within the next seven days.*

▲ **look in** *phrasal verb INFORMAL* to visit a person for a short time, usually when you are on your way somewhere else: *I thought I might look in* ***on*** *Bob on my way to the shops.* ○ *Can you look in on the kids before you go to bed?*

▲ **look into** ***sth*** *phrasal verb* to examine the facts about a problem or situation: *We're looking into the possibility of merging the two departments.*

▲ **look on** *phrasal verb SLIGHTLY FORMAL* to watch something happen but not become involved in it: *A large crowd looked on as the band played.* ➲See also **onlooker**.

▲ **look on/upon** ***sb*** **as** ***sth*** *phrasal verb* to consider or think of someone or something as something: *We looked on her as a daughter.* ○ *I've lived there so long I look on the town as my home.*

▲ **look out** [BE CAREFUL] *phrasal verb* **1** to watch what is happening and be careful: *The police have warned shopkeepers to look out* ***for*** *forged notes.* **2** said or shouted in order to tell someone that they are in danger: *Look out! There's a car coming!*

• **look out for number one** *INFORMAL* to do what you think is best for yourself and not care about other people

▲ **look** ***sth*** **out** [FIND] *phrasal verb* [M] *UK* to search for and find something: *I'll look out that recipe I told you about and send it to you.*

▲ **look out for** ***sb/sth*** *phrasal verb* to try to notice someone or something: *Look out for Anna while you're there.*

▲ **look over** ***sth*** *phrasal verb* [M] to quickly examine something or someone: *I had a few minutes before the meeting to look over what he'd written.* ○ *Would you quickly look over these figures for me and see if there are any obvious mistakes?*

▲ **look round** ***(somewhere/sth)*** *phrasal verb* to visit a place and look at the things in it: *She spent the afternoon looking round the shops.* ○ *When we went to Stratford, we only had a couple of hours to look round.*

▲ **look through** ***sth*** *phrasal verb* to read something quickly: *I've looked through some catalogues.*

▲ **look to** ***sb*** **to do** ***sth*** *phrasal verb* to hope that someone will do something for you: *We're looking to you to advise us on how to proceed.*

▲ **look to** ***sb*** **for** ***sth*** to hope that someone will provide something for you: *They looked to the government for additional support.*

▲ **look up** [IMPROVE] *phrasal verb INFORMAL* to become better: *I hope things will start to look up in the new year.* ○ *Our financial situation is looking up at last.*

▲ **look** ***sth*** **up** [INFORMATION] *phrasal verb* [M] to try to find a piece of information by looking in a book or on a computer: *If you don't know what the word means, look it up* ***in*** *a dictionary.*

▲ **look** ***sb*** **up** [VISIT] *phrasal verb* [M] *INFORMAL* to visit someone who you have not seen for a long time when you are visiting the place where they live: *Look me up next time you're in Los Angeles.*

▲ **look up to** ***sb*** *phrasal verb* to admire and respect someone: *He'd always looked up to his uncle.*

look-alike /ˈlʊk.ə.laɪk/ *noun* [C] someone or something that is similar in appearance to someone or something else: *an Elvis Presley look-alike*

looker /ˈlʊk.əʳ/ [US] /ˈlʊk.ɚ/ *noun* [C] *OLD-FASHIONED INFORMAL* a physically attractive person, usually a woman: *Have you seen Karl's new girlfriend? She's a real looker!*

look-in /ˈlʊk.ɪn/ *noun UK INFORMAL* **not get a look-in** to not have a chance to do something or to succeed: *There were so many children wanting a ride John didn't get a look-in.* ○ *Our opponents were so good – we didn't get a look-in.*

ˈlooking ˌglass *noun* [C] *OLD USE* a mirror

lookout /ˈlʊk.aʊt/ *noun* [C] **1** a person who watches for danger **2** a high place where a person can look at what is happening in the area around them, especially in order to watch for any danger

• **be on the lookout for** ***sth/sb*** to search for something or someone: *I'm always on the lookout for interesting new recipes.*

• **it's** ***your*** **own lookout** *UK INFORMAL* said to someone in order to tell them that they are responsible for their own problems: *It's your own lookout if you're not properly insured.*

• **keep a lookout for** ***sth/sb*** to continue to watch carefully for something or someone, especially in order to avoid danger: *Keep a lookout for small objects that a baby might swallow.*

looks /lʊks/ *plural noun* ***sb's*** **looks** a person's appearance, especially how attractive they are: *I like her looks.* ○ *Her looks improved as she grew older.* ○ *He put on weight and started to* ***lose*** *his looks.*

look-see /ˌlʊkˈsiː/ *noun* [S] *US INFORMAL* a quick look: *"Have they arrived yet?" "I'll* ***take/have*** *a look-see".*

loom [APPEAR] /luːm/ *verb* [I] to appear as a large, often frightening or unclear shape or object: *Dark storm clouds loomed* ***on the horizon.***

loom [WORRY] /luːm/ *verb* [I] If an unwanted or unpleasant event looms, it seems likely to happen soon and causes worry: *Her exams are looming.* ○ *Here, too, the threat of unemployment has been looming* ***on the horizon.*** ○ *The threat of closure looms* ***over*** *the workforce.*

• **loom large** If something looms large, it becomes very important and often causes worry: *The issue of pay will loom large at this Easter's teacher conference.*

looming /ˈluː.mɪŋ/ *adj* (of something unwanted or unpleasant) happening soon and causing worry: *the looming crisis*

loom [DEVICE] /luːm/ *noun* [C] a piece of equipment on which thread is woven into cloth

loony /ˈluː.ni/ *adj INFORMAL* foolish or stupid: *He had lots of loony ideas about education.*

ˈloony ˌbin *noun* [C] *OFFENSIVE OR HUMOROUS* a **psychiatric hospital**

loop /luːp/ *noun* [C] the curved shape made when something long and thin, such as a piece of string, bends until one part of it nearly touches or crosses another part of it: *belt loops* ○ *a loop* ***of*** *string* ○ *the loop* ***of*** *the river* ○ *The tape ran in a continuous loop, repeating the same songs over and over.*

loop /luːp/ *verb* [I or T; usually + adv or prep] *Loop* (= Make a loop with) *the rope over the bar.* ○ *Turn left where the road loops* (= curves) *round the farm buildings.*

• **loop the loop** to fly in the shape of a loop in the sky

loophole /ˈluːp.həʊl/ [US] /-hoʊl/ *noun* [C] a small mistake in an agreement or law which gives someone the chance to avoid having to do something: *tax loopholes* ○ *The company employed lawyers to find loopholes* ***in*** *environmental protection laws.*

loopy /ˈluː.pi/ *adj INFORMAL* strange, unusual or silly: *He must have* ***gone*** *completely loopy to give up a job like that.*

loose [NOT FIXED] /luːs/ *adj* **1** not firmly fixed in place: *There were some loose wires hanging out of the wall.* ○ *The nails in the bridge had* ***worked themselves*** *loose.* ○ *The prisoners were so thin that their skin* ***hung*** *loose.* **2** describes hair that is not tied back: *Her hair was* ***hanging*** *loose about her shoulders.* **3** describes items which are not fixed or held together or to anything else: *A few loose sheets of paper were lying around.*

• **let/set** ***sth*** **loose** to allow an animal to run around freely after it has been tied up: *She let her horse loose in the field.*

• **let** ***sb*** **loose** to allow someone to do what they want in a place: *You don't want to let Oliver loose in the kitchen.*

• **let loose** ***sth*** **1** If you let loose something such as bullets or bombs, you release a lot of them all together: *The allies let loose an intensive artillery bombardment over the border.* **2** to suddenly make a sound or speak in an uncontrolled way: *He turned round and let loose a torrent of abuse.*

• **be at a loose end** *INFORMAL* to have nothing to do: *If you find yourself at a loose end, you could always clean the bathroom.*
• **on the loose** If a dangerous person is on the loose, they are free to move around a place and harm people: *Brewer escaped from prison last year and has been on the loose ever since.*
• **hang/stay loose** *US INFORMAL* to be calm and relaxed
loosely /ˈluː.sli/ *adv* in a way that is not firmly fixed: *The parcel had only been loosely wrapped, and the paper had come off.*
loosen /ˈluː.sᵊn/ *verb* **[I or T]** to (cause to) become loose: *The screws holding the bed together had loosened.*
• **loosen *your* grip** If you loosen your grip on an object, or your grip loosens, you hold something less tightly: *He held my hand very tightly at first but gradually his grip loosened.*
• **loosen *your* grip/hold** If you loosen your grip/hold on a situation, or your grip/hold loosens, you decide to control it less: *The dictator's grip on the country has not loosened.*
• **loosen *your* tongue** to make you speak more freely: *A couple of glasses of champagne had loosened my tongue and I said things that perhaps I shouldn't have.*
looseness /ˈluː.snəs/ *noun* **[U]** when something is loose

COMMON LEARNER ERROR

loose or **lose**?

Be careful, these two words look and sound similar but have completely different meanings.

Loose is an adjective, meaning not fixed or not tight.

These trousers are a bit loose.

Lose is a verb, meaning 'to not be able to find something' or 'to have something taken away from you'. Be careful not to use **loose** when you really mean **lose**.

I hope he doesn't lose his job.
~~*I hope he doesn't loose his job.*~~

loose [NOT TIGHT] /luːs/ *adj* (of clothes) not fitting closely to the body: *Wear comfortable, loose clothing to your exercise class.* **loosely** /ˈluː.sli/ *adv*: *The jacket hung loosely on his thin body.*
loosen /ˈluː.sᵊn/ *verb* **[T]** to make something less tight: *He loosened his tie.* **looseness** /ˈluː.snəs/ *noun* **[U]**

loose [NOT EXACT] /luːs/ *adj* not tightly controlled or not exact: *It's a fairly loose adaptation of the novel.* ○ *It's only a loose translation of the poem.*
loosely /ˈluː.sli/ *adv* not exactly: *This phrase can be loosely translated as 'Go away'.* ○ *The film is loosely based on the novel by Kundera.*

loose [IMMORAL] /luːs/ *adj OLD-FASHIONED DISAPPROVING* lacking in morals; sexually free: *a loose **woman***

loose [EXPRESS FREELY] /luːs/ *verb* **[T]** to speak or express emotions very freely, especially in an uncontrolled way: *The minister loosed an angry tirade against the leader of the opposition.*

ˌloose ˈcannon *noun* **[C]** *DISAPPROVING* someone who behaves in an uncontrolled or unexpected way and is likely to cause problems for other people: *He's seen as something of a loose cannon by other team members.*

ˌloose ˈchange *noun* **[U]** the coins that you have in your pocket or PURSE

ˌloose ˈends *plural noun* things that still need to be done or explained: *At the end of the film all the loose ends are neatly **tied up**.*

loose-fitting /ˌluːsˈfɪt.ɪŋ/ [US] /-ˈfɪt̬-/ *adj* describes a piece of clothing that is quite large and does not fit tightly: *a loose-fitting shirt*

loose-leaf /ˌluːsˈliːf/ *adj* **[before n]** having pages that can easily be taken out and put back again: *a loose-leaf folder*

PHRASAL VERBS WITH **loosen**

▲ **loosen *(sth)* up** [STRETCH] *phrasal verb* **[M]** to prepare your muscles for a physical activity by stretching and doing simple exercises: *I do a few stretches to loosen up before I run.*

▲ **loosen *(sb)* up** [RELAX] *phrasal verb* to start to feel less embarrassed and to become more relaxed when you are with other people, or to make someone feel like this: *He seemed quite nervous at the beginning of the meeting, but he soon loosened up.* ○ *A gin and tonic will loosen you up.*

loot /luːt/ *verb* **[I or T]** (usually of large numbers of people during a violent event) to steal from shops and houses: *During the riot shops were looted and cars damaged or set on fire.*
looting /ˈluː.tɪŋ/ [US] /-t̬ɪŋ/ *noun* **[U]** the activity of stealing from shops during a violent event: *There were reports of **widespread** looting as football hooligans stampeded through the city centre.*
loot /luːt/ *noun* **[U]** money and valuable objects that have been stolen, especially by an army from a defeated enemy **looter** /ˈluː.təʳ/ [US] /-t̬ɚ/ *noun* **[C]**

lop /lɒp/ [US] /lɑːp/ *verb* **-pp-**

PHRASAL VERBS WITH **lop**

▲ **lop *sth* off** [CUT] *phrasal verb* **[M]** to cut something off in one quick movement: *I'll need to lop off the lower branches of the tree.*
▲ **lop *sth* off** [REDUCE] *phrasal verb* **[M]** *INFORMAL* to reduce a price or the amount of time taken to do something by a particular amount: *He lopped eight seconds off the record.*

lope /ləʊp/ [US] /loʊp/ *verb* **[I]** (of a person or animal) to run taking long relaxed steps: *The lion loped across the grass.* **lope** /ləʊp/ [US] /loʊp/ *noun* **[S]**

lopsided /ˌlɒpˈsaɪd.ɪd/ [US] /ˌlɑːp-/ *adj* with one side bigger, higher, etc. than the other; not equally balanced: *a charming, lopsided grin*

loquacious /ləʊˈkweɪ.ʃəs/ [US] /loʊˈkweɪ-/ *adj FORMAL* describes someone who talks a lot **loquaciously** /ləʊˈkweɪ.ʃə.sli/ [US] /loʊˈkweɪ-/ *adv*

lord [MAN] /lɔːd/ [US] /lɔːrd/ *noun* **[C]** **1** a male PEER **2** *INFORMAL* a man who has a lot of power in a particular area of activity: *Several alleged **drug** lords are to be put on trial.*
• ***your* lord and master** *HUMOROUS* a person who has authority over you, or your husband
lord /lɔːd/ [US] /lɔːrd/ *verb INFORMAL* **lord it over *sb*** to behave as if you are better than someone and have the right to tell them what to do: *He likes to lord it over his little sister.*

Lord [TITLE] /lɔːd/ [US] /lɔːrd/ *noun* **[U]** **1** a title used in front of the names of male PEERS and officials of very high rank: *Lord Longford* ○ *the Lord Chancellor* ➲Compare **Lady** TITLE. **2 my Lord** in Britain, used to address a judge or PEER

Lord [GOD] /lɔːd/ [US] /lɔːrd/ *noun* (in the Christian religion) God or Jesus Christ: *Praise **the** Lord!* ○ **[as form of address]** *Lord, hear our prayer.*
• **(Oh) Lord** (*ALSO* **Good Lord**) *INFORMAL* used to express surprise, shock or worry: *Oh Lord! I've forgotten the tickets!* ○ *Good lord! Is that the time?*
• **Lord knows** *INFORMAL* used to say that you do not know: *Lord knows where we're going to get the money from.*

lordly /ˈlɔːd.li/ [US] /ˈlɔːrd-/ *adj* describes someone who behaves as if they are better than other people: *a lordly air*

the Lords *group noun* **[S]** **the House of Lords**

lordship /ˈlɔːd.ʃɪp/ [US] /ˈlɔːrd-/ *noun FORMAL* **your/his lordship** a respectful way of referring to or addressing a male PEER without using his title: *It is a great pleasure to welcome your lordship this evening.* ➲Compare **ladyship**.

the Lord's Prayer /ðəˌlɔːdzˈpreəʳ/ [US] /-ˌlɔːrdzˈprer/ *noun* **[S]** in the Christian religion, the prayer taught by Jesus Christ to his DISCIPLES (= followers)

the Lord's Supper /ðeˌlɔːdzˈsʌp.əʳ/ [US] /-ˌlɔːrdzˈsʌp.ɚ/ *noun* **[U]** **Communion**

lore /lɔːʳ/ [US] /lɔːr/ *noun* **[U]** traditional knowledge and stories about a subject: *According to local lore, the water has healing properties.* ➲See also **folklore**.

lorgnette /lɔːˈnjet/ [US] /lɔːr-/ *noun* **[C]** a very old-fashioned pair of glasses with a long handle that you hold in front of your eyes

L

lorikeet /ˌlɒrɪˈkiːt/ ⓤ /ˌlɔːrɪ-/ *noun* [C] a small brightly coloured parrot found in Australia and Southeast Asia

lorn /lɔːn/ ⓤ /lɔːrn/ *adj* LITERARY alone and unhappy; left alone and not cared for

lorry UK /ˈlɒr.i/ ⓤ /ˈlɔːr-/ *noun* [C] (US **truck**) a large vehicle used for transporting goods: *an articulated lorry* ○ *a long-distance lorry driver* ⊃See picture **Cars and Trucks** on page Centre 13

lose NOT HAVE /luːz/ *verb* [T] lost, lost **1** to no longer possess something because you do not know where it is, or because it has been taken away from you: *I've lost my ticket.* ○ *He's always losing his car keys.* ○ *At least 600 staff will lose their jobs if the firm closes.* ○ *He lost his leg in a car accident.* ○ *She lost her mother* (= Her mother died) *last year.* ⊃See **loose or lose?** at **loose** NOT FIXED. **2** to stop feeling something: *to lose confidence/faith* ○ *I lost interest halfway through the book.* ○ *He kept on crying and I lost my patience.* **3** to have less of something than you had before: *I'm trying to lose weight.* ○ *He's losing his hair.* ○ *She lost a lot of blood in the accident.* ○ *to lose your memory/sight* **4** If you lose time, you waste it: *Four million hours were lost last year through stress-related illnesses.* ○ *We lost valuable time stuck in traffic.* **5** If a clock loses time, it goes more slowly than it should: *My watch loses ten minutes every day.* **6 lose money/pounds/dollars, etc.** A business that is losing money is spending more money than it is receiving: *Banks will lose millions of pounds because of new legislation.*

• **lose heart** to stop believing that you can succeed: *Don't lose heart, there'll be plenty more chances for promotion.*

• **be losing it** INFORMAL to start to become crazy: *That's the third time this week I've lost my keys – I think I must be losing it.*

• **lose it** INFORMAL to stop being able to control your emotions and suddenly start to shout, cry or laugh: *I'd been trying so hard to stay calm but in the end I just lost it.*

• **lose your life** to die suddenly because of an accident or violent event: *Many people lost their lives in the floods.*

• **You've got nothing to lose.** (*ALSO* **What have you got to lose?**) INFORMAL used to tell someone that they cannot cause any disadvantages for themselves by doing a particular thing: *Why don't you take the job? You've got nothing to lose.*

• **lose your heart to sb** LITERARY to fall in love with someone

• **lose your head** INFORMAL to lose control and not act in a calm way: *He usually stays quite calm in meetings but this time he just lost his head.*

• **lose your marbles** INFORMAL HUMOROUS to become crazy

• **lose your mind** INFORMAL to become mentally ill, or to start behaving in a foolish or strange way: *You spent all that money on a pair of shoes? Have you completely lost your mind?*

• **lose the plot** INFORMAL to behave strangely or foolishly: *I can't believe Stuart did that – he must be losing the plot.*

• **lose your rag** INFORMAL to suddenly become very angry: *He said one too many stupid things and I just lost my rag.*

• **lose your shirt** US INFORMAL to lose a lot of money, especially as a result of a bet

• **lose your way** to become lost

• **lose sight of sth** to forget about an important idea or fact because you are thinking too much about other things: *I'm worried that we're losing sight of our original objectives.*

• **lose sleep over/about sth** to worry about something: *I wouldn't lose any sleep over what happened.*

• **lose track** to no longer know what is happening, or not to remember something: *What he was saying was so complicated that I lost track after the first couple of sentences.* ○ *I've lost track of the number of times he's asked me to lend him money.*

COMMON LEARNER ERROR

lose or **miss**?

Usually you **miss** something which happens, such as an event, a train leaving, or an opportunity.

I'm sorry I'm late, I missed the bus.

~~I'm sorry I'm late, I lost the bus.~~

Usually you **lose** a thing.

I've lost my umbrella.

---

lose BE DEFEATED /luːz/ *verb* [I or T] lost, lost to fail to succeed in a game, competition, etc: *If we lose this game, we're out of the championship.* ○ *They're losing 3-1.* ○ *They lost to Arsenal.* ○ *Everyone hates losing an argument.* ○ *They hadn't lost an election in fifteen years.*

• **lose ground** to become less popular or to be given less support: *Do you agree that left-wing politics are losing ground among the working classes?*

▲ **lose out** *phrasal verb* to not have an advantage that other people have: *The new tax means that the vast majority of pensioners will lose out.*

loser /ˈluː.zəʳ/ ⓤ /-zɚ/ *noun* [C] **1** a person or team that does not win a game or competition: *The losers of both games will play each other for third place.* ○ *He's a **good/bad** loser* (= He behaves well/badly when he is defeated). **2** INFORMAL a person who is always unsuccessful at everything they do: *He's a **born** loser.* **3** someone who is at a disadvantage as a result of something that has happened: *The latest price rises mean that the real loser, as usual, is the consumer.*

loss /lɒs/ ⓤ /lɑːs/ *noun* **1** [C or U] when you no longer have something or have less of something: *Many parents feel a sense of loss when their children leave home.* ○ *He suffered a gradual loss of memory.* ○ *There will be substantial **job** losses if the factory closes down.* ○ *blood/hair/weight loss* **2** [S] a disadvantage caused by someone leaving an organization: *It would be a great loss **to** the department if you left.* **3** [C or U] the death of a person: *They never got over the loss of their son.* **4** [C] when a business spends more money than it earns: *The company announced a pre-tax loss of three million pounds.*

• **loss of life** when a number of people die: *The plane crashed with serious loss of life.*

• **be at a loss** to not know what to do or say: *I'm at a loss to know how I can help you.*

• **One man's loss is another man's gain.** SAYING said when someone gets an advantage from someone else's bad luck

loss adjuster /ˌlɒs.əˈdʒʌs.təʳ/ ⓤ /ˌlɑːs.əˈdʒʌs.tɚ/ *noun* [C] a person who works for an INSURANCE company and decides how much money should be paid out in each case of something having been damaged or lost

loss ˌleader *noun* [C] an article that is sold cheaply in order to attract the public and make them buy other, more expensive things

loss making /ˈlɒsˌmeɪkɪŋ/ *adj* not making a profit: *loss-making companies/businesses*

lost /lɒst/ ⓤ /lɑːst/ *adj* **1** not knowing where you are and how to get to a place: *I got lost in the London Underground.* ○ *You look lost – can I help you?* **2** If something is lost, no one knows where it is: *Things tend to **get** lost when you move house.* ○ *Lost: black cat with white paws.* ○ *Mikey turned up with the lost book.* **3** not knowing what to do in a new situation: *It was his first day in the office and he seemed a bit lost.* **4** giving so much attention to what you are doing that you are not aware of anything else that is happening around you: *Ann was completely lost **in** her book.*

• **be lost on sb** If a joke or remark is lost on someone, they do not understand it.

• **be lost without sb/sth** to be unable to live or work without someone or something: *I'm lost without my computer.* ○ *I'd be lost without you.*

• **Get lost!** INFORMAL used to tell someone forcefully and quite rudely to go away: *Tell him to get lost!*

ˌlost ˈcause *noun* [C usually sing] someone or something that has no chance of succeeding: *I used to try to get him to do some exercise but then decided he was a lost cause.*

ˌlost ˈproperty *noun* [U] UK personal objects that have been left accidentally in public places

ˌlost ˈproperty ˌoffice UK *noun* [C usually sing] (US **lost-and-found**) a place in a public building where lost things are stored

lot LARGE AMOUNT /lɒt/ ⓤ /lɑːt/ *noun* **1 a lot (of)**/(*INFOR-MAL*) **lots (of)** a large amount or number of people or things: *She eats lots of fruit.* ○ *There were a lot of people* there. ○ *He does a lot of travelling in his job.* ○ *I've got a lot to do today.* ○ *He earns lots of money.* ○ *There's lots of food.* ➲See Note **many, much or a lot of?** at **many. 2 a lot** very much or very often: *Your sister looks a lot like you.* ○ *I'm feeling a lot better today.* ○ *He looks a lot older than his wife.* ○ *We used to go there a lot.*

• **the lot** UK INFORMAL everything: *I made enough curry for three people and he ate the lot.* ○ *Have I got everything? Is that the lot?* ○ *I'll sell you the whole lot for only £50.* ○ *I'm sick of the lot of them.*

• **there's a lot of it about** HUMOROUS said to mean that the stated thing is very common

COMMON LEARNER ERROR

a lot

When you use a noun phrase after **a lot** or **lots**, remember to use the preposition 'of' before the noun phrase.

There have been a lot of changes in recent years.
~~There have been a lot changes in recent years.~~
Lots of people hate the new computer system.
~~Lots people hate the new computer system.~~

lot GROUP /lɒt/ ⓤ /lɑːt/ *noun* [C] UK an amount or set of things, especially when there are several of these amounts: *I've already done one lot of washing.* ○ *Another lot of visitors will be here this afternoon.*

lot /lɒt/ ⓤ /lɑːt/ *plural noun* UK INFORMAL a group of people: *You're an ignorant lot!* ○ *Are you lot coming to lunch?* ○ *My lot* (= children and family generally) *won't eat spinach.*

lot SALE /lɒt/ ⓤ /lɑːt/ *noun* [C] in an auction, an object or set of objects that are being sold: *Lot number 134 is a fine old walnut bureau.* ➲See also **job lot**.

lot LAND /lɒt/ ⓤ /lɑːt/ *noun* [C] **1** MAINLY US an area of land: *an empty lot* ○ *a parking lot* ○ *They're planning to build a house on a vacant lot on 35th Street.* **2** US a film STUDIO and the land around it

lot LIFE /lɒt/ ⓤ /lɑːt/ *noun* **sb's lot/the lot of sb** the quality of someone's life and the experiences that they have: *They should do something to improve the lot of the lowest-paid workers.* ○ *Do you think he's happy with his lot?*

lot CHANCE /lɒt/ ⓤ /lɑːt/ *noun* **draw lots** to make a decision by choosing from a set of objects such as pieces of paper or sticks that are all the same except for one

loth /ləʊθ/ ⓤ /loʊθ/ *adj* [after v; + *to* infinitive] **loath**

lotion /ˈləʊ.ʃən/ ⓤ /ˈloʊ-/ *noun* [C or U] a liquid that you put on your skin in order to protect it, improve its condition or make it smell pleasant: *suntan lotion*

lottery /ˈlɒt.ºr.i/ ⓤ /ˈlɑː.t̬ɚ-/ *noun* **1** [C] a game, often organized by the state or a charity in order to make money, in which numbered tickets are sold to people who then have a chance of winning a prize if their number is chosen **2** [S] DISAPPROVING something that depends only on luck and is not fair: *Education in England is something of a lottery.*

lotus /ˈləʊ.təs/ ⓤ /ˈloʊ.t̬əs/ *noun* [C] a type of tropical WATER LILY (= a plant with large flat leaves which float on the surface of lakes and pools)

lotus ˌeater *noun* [C] someone who has a very comfortable, lazy life and does not worry about anything

lotus poˌsition *noun* [S] a way of sitting with your legs crossed and your feet resting on your THIGHS (= part of the leg above the knee), especially used in YOGA (= a method of relaxation)

loud NOISY /laʊd/ *adj, adv* making a lot of noise: *a loud explosion/noise/voice* ○ *I heard a loud bang and then saw black smoke.* ○ *Could you speak a little louder, please?*

• **loud and clear** very clear and easy to understand: *I can hear you loud and clear.* ○ *The message from management came through loud and clear: things would have to change.*

loudly /ˈlaʊd.li/ *adv* making a lot of noise: *She spoke very loudly.* **loudness** /ˈlaʊd.nəs/ *noun* [U]

loud UNPLEASANT /laʊd/ *adj* DISAPPROVING (of clothes) having unpleasantly bright colours or too strong patterns, or (of a person) demanding attention and talking and

laughing loudly: *You shouldn't wear anything too loud to a job interview.* ○ *The men at the bar were loud and obnoxious.*

loudhailer /ˌlaʊdˈheɪ.ləʳ/ ⓤ /-lɚ/ *noun* [C] UK FOR **megaphone**

loudmouth /ˈlaʊd.maʊθ/ *noun* [C] INFORMAL a person who talks a lot, especially in an offensive or stupid way

loudspeaker /ˌlaʊdˈspiː.kəʳ/ ⓤ /ˈlaʊdˌspiː.kɚ/ *noun* [C] a piece of equipment that changes electrical signals into sounds, especially used in public places so that large numbers of people can hear someone speaking or music playing: *Music blared from loudspeakers.* ➲See also **speaker**.

lough /lɒk/ ⓤ /lɑːk/ *noun* [C] IRISH ENGLISH a lake, or a part of the sea that goes a long way into the land

lounge /laʊndʒ/ *noun* [C] **1** UK the room in a house or apartment that is used for relaxing, and entertaining guests, but not usually for eating: *All the family were sitting in the lounge watching television.* **2** a room in a hotel, airport, theatre, etc. where people can relax or wait: *an airport lounge* ○ *a cocktail lounge*

lounge /laʊndʒ/ *verb*

▲ **lounge about/around (sth)** *phrasal verb* to spend your time in a relaxed way, sitting or lying somewhere and doing very little: *We spent our days lounging around the pool.*

lounge ˌbar *noun* [C] UK a room in a pub that is more comfortable than the other rooms in the pub

lounger /ˈlaʊn.dʒəʳ/ ⓤ /-dʒɚ/ *noun* [C] a comfortable chair on which people can sit or lie in order to relax, especially outside in hot weather: *a sun lounger*

lounge ˌsuit *noun* [C] UK OLD-FASHIONED a man's suit worn for work or on quite formal occasions during the day

louse /laʊs/ *noun* [C] *plural* **lice** a very small insect that lives on the bodies or in the hair of people and animals

louse /laʊs/ *verb*

▲ **louse (sth) up** *phrasal verb* [M] MAINLY US INFORMAL to spoil something or cause it to fail: *This is a great opportunity, so don't louse it up.*

lousy /ˈlaʊ.zi/ *adj* INFORMAL very bad: *lousy food/service* ○ *a lousy film* ○ *I had a lousy weekend.* ○ *I feel lousy* (= very ill) – *I'm going home.* ○ *All he offered me was a lousy £20* (= a small amount of money)*!*

lout /laʊt/ *noun* [C] a young man who behaves in a very rude, offensive and sometimes violent way: *Teenage louts roam the streets at night.* **loutish** /ˈlaʊ.tɪʃ/ ⓤ /-t̬ɪʃ/ *adj* INFORMAL *loutish behaviour*

loutishness /ˈlaʊ.tɪʃ.nəs/ ⓤ /-t̬ɪʃ-/ *noun* [U] rude, offensive behaviour

louvre UK /ˈluː.vəʳ/ /-vrə/ ⓤ /-vɚ/ (*US USUALLY* **louver**) *noun* [C] a door or window with flat sloping pieces of wood, metal or glass across it to allow light and air to come in while keeping rain out **louvred** /ˈluː.vrəd/ *adj*: *a louvred door/window*

lovable, **loveable** /ˈlʌv.ə.bl̩/ *adj* having qualities which make a person or animal easy to love: *a lovable child* ○ *a lovable rogue*

love LIKE SOMEONE /lʌv/ *verb* [T] to have strong feelings of affection for another adult and to be romantically and sexually attracted to them, or to feel great affection for a friend or person in your family: *I love you.* ○ *Last night he told me he loved me.* ○ *I've only ever loved one man.* ○ *I'm sure he loves his kids.*

• **love sb to bits** UK INFORMAL to love someone very much: *He's my old man and I love him to bits but I can spend too much time with him.*

• **Love me, love my dog.** HUMOROUS SAYING said to warn someone that if they want to be in a relationship with you, they must be willing to accept everything about you

love /lʌv/ *noun* **1** [U] strong feelings of attraction towards and affection for, another adult, or great affection for a friend or family member: *"I've been seeing him over a year now." "Is it love?"* ○ *Children need to be shown lots of love.* ○ *"Oh, please give her my love"* (= tell her I am thinking about her with affection). ○ INFORMAL *How's your love life* (= your romantic and/or sexual relationships) *these days?* **2** [C] a person that you love and feel attracted to: *He was the love of my life.* ○ *She was my first love.* **3** [as form of address] *UK INFORMAL* used as a friendly form of address: *You look tired, love.* ○ *That'll be four pounds exactly, love.* ✱ NOTE: This is not generally used between men. **4** [U] (*ALSO* **love from,** *ALSO* **all my love**) *INFORMAL* used before your name at the end of letters, cards etc. to friends or family: *See you at Christmas. Love, Kate.*

• **be in love** to love someone in a romantic and sexual way: *I'm in love for the first time and it's wonderful.* ○ *They're still madly in love (with each other).*

• **fall in love (with sb)** to start to love someone romantically and sexually: *I was 20 when I first fell in love.*

• **make love** to have sex: *That night they made love for the first time.*

• **make love to sb** *OLD USE* to speak romantically and give attention to someone, especially in order to make them love you: *Mr Jackson, I do believe you are making love to me.*

• **be no/little love lost between** If there is no/little love lost between two people, they do not like each other.

• **for love nor money** If you cannot get something, or if someone will not do something, for love nor money, it is impossible to obtain it or to persuade them to do it: *You can't get hold of those tickets for love nor money these days.*

love LIKE SOMETHING /lʌv/ *verb* [T] **1** to like something very much: *She loves animals.* ○ *I absolutely love chocolate.* ○ *He really loves his job.* ○ [+ *v-ing*] *I love skiing.* ○ *Love it or hate it, reality TV is here to stay.* **2** **would love** used, often in requests, to say that you would very much like something: *I'd love a cup of coffee if you're making one.* ○ [+ *to infinitive*] *She would dearly love to start her own business.* ○ *I'd love you to come to dinner some night.* ○ *US I'd love for you to come to dinner tonight.*

love /lʌv/ *noun* **1** [U] strong liking for: *I don't share my boyfriend's love of sport.* **2** [C] something that you like very much: *Music is one of her greatest loves.*

love TENNIS /lʌv/ *noun* [U] (in tennis) the state of having no points: *The score now stands at forty-love.*

love af‚fair *noun* **1** [C] a romantic and sexual relationship between two people who are not married to each other **2** [S] a strong liking for a particular activity or place: *Her love affair with ballet began when she was ten.*

lovebirds /ˈlʌv.bɜːdz/ ⓤ /-bɝːdz/ *plural noun HUMOROUS* two people who are obviously very much in love with each other: *Look at those two lovebirds holding hands and gazing into each other's eyes.*

'love ‚bite *UK noun* [C] (*US* **hickey**) a temporary red mark on someone's skin, often their neck, where someone has sucked or bitten it as a sexual act

'love ‚child *noun* [C] *OLD-FASHIONED* a child whose parents are not married to each other

'loved ‚one *noun* [C usually pl] a person that you love, usually a member of your family: *People, naturally enough, want to know that their loved ones are out of danger.*

'love ‚handles *plural noun HUMOROUS* the layer of fat around the middle of a person's body

loveless /ˈlʌv.ləs/ *adj* without love: *She was trapped in a loveless marriage.*

'love ‚letter *noun* [C] a letter that you write to someone that you are having a romantic relationship with

lovelorn /ˈlʌv.lɔːn/ ⓤ /-lɔːrn/ *adj LITERARY* sad because the person you love does not love you

lovely BEAUTIFUL /ˈlʌv.li/ *adj MAINLY UK* beautiful: *She has lovely eyes.* ○ *You look lovely in that dress.* ○ *Thank you for the lovely present.* **loveliness** /ˈlʌv.lɪ.nəs/ *noun* [U] *She was a vision of loveliness in her wedding dress.*

lovely ENJOYABLE /ˈlʌv.li/ *MAINLY UK* pleasant or enjoyable: *a lovely meal/evening* ○ *We had a lovely time with them.* **loveliness** *noun* [U]

lovely KIND /ˈlʌv.li/ *adj MAINLY UK* describes a person who is kind, friendly and pleasant to be with: *He's a lovely bloke.* **loveliness** *noun* [U]

lovely ATTRACTIVE WOMAN /ˈlʌv.li/ *noun* [C] *OLD-FASHIONED* a sexually attractive woman: *Simon was there with the usual bevy of lovelies.*

love-making /ˈlʌv.meɪ.kɪŋ/ *noun* [U] sexual activity

lover /ˈlʌv.əʳ/ ⓤ /-ɚ/ *noun* [C] **1** the person with whom you are having a sexual relationship, but are not married to: *They were friends before they became lovers.* ○ *She had a string of lovers before her marriage finally broke up.* **2** someone with a strong liking for something: *an opera lover* ○ *nature lovers*

love-rat /ˈlʌv.ræt/ *noun* [C] *UK INFORMAL* a man who has had a secret sexual relationship with someone who is not his wife or GIRLFRIEND. This word is usually used in popular newspapers.

lovesick /ˈlʌv.sɪk/ *adj* sad because the person you love does not love you: *He was moping around like a lovesick teenager.*

love-struck /lʌv-/ *adj* so in love with someone that it is difficult to behave as usual or even think of anything else except the person you love: *Look at me, I'm behaving like a love-struck teenager!*

lovey-dovey /ˌlʌv.iˈdʌv.i/ *adj INFORMAL DISAPPROVING* If two people in a romantic relationship are lovey-dovey, they too often show their affection for each other in public by touching each other and saying loving things to each other.

loving /ˈlʌv.ɪŋ/ *adj* showing a lot of affection towards someone: *a loving relationship* ○ *He's a very loving child.* ○ *She's very loving.* **lovingly** /ˈlʌv.ɪŋ.li/ *adv: The table had been lovingly (= with great pleasure and care) restored.*

low DISTANCE /ləʊ/ ⓤ /loʊ/ *adj, adv* not measuring much from the base to the top, or close to the ground or the bottom of something: *a low fence* ○ *a low ceiling.* ○ *When we went skiing, I only went on the lower slopes.* ○ *The planes fly low across enemy territory.*

low LEVEL /ləʊ/ ⓤ /loʊ/ *adj* **1** below the usual level: *Temperatures are very low for the time of year.* ○ *The big supermarket offers the lowest prices in town.* ○ *These people are living on relatively low incomes.* ○ *There is a tremendous need for more low-cost housing.* ○ *a low-fat diet* ○ *low-alcohol beer* ○ *Vegetables are generally low in (= do not contain many) calories.* **2** producing only a small amount of sound, heat or light: *They spoke in low voices so I would not hear what they were saying.* ○ *Turn the oven to a low heat.* ○ *Soft music was playing and the lights were low.* **3** of bad quality, especially when referring to something that is not as good as it should be: *low standards* ○ *I have rather a low opinion of him.* ○ *She has very low self-esteem.*

• **be/get/run low (on sth)** to have nearly finished a supply of something: *We're running low on milk – could you buy some more?* ○ *The radio batteries are running low.*

low /ləʊ/ ⓤ /loʊ/ *adv* at or to a low level: *low-paid workers* ○ *Turn the oven on low.*

low /ləʊ/ ⓤ /loʊ/ *noun* **1** a new/record/all-time low the lowest level: *The dollar has hit an all-time low against the Japanese yen.* **2** a bad time in someone's life: *the highs and lows of an acting career*

low NOT IMPORTANT /ləʊ/ ⓤ /loʊ/ *adj* not important because of being at or near the bottom of a range of things, especially jobs or social positions: *low status jobs* ○ *a low priority task*

low NOT HONEST /ləʊ/ ⓤ /loʊ/ *adj* not honest or fair: *How low can you get?* ○ *That was a pretty low trick to play.*

• **the lowest of the low** people who have no moral standards and lack any personal qualities

low SOUND /ləʊ/ ⓤ /loʊ/ *adj* (of a sound or voice) near or at the bottom of the range of sounds: *He has a very low voice.* ○ *Those low notes are played by the double bass.*

low SAD /ləʊ/ ⓤ /loʊ/ *adj* unhappy: *Illness of any sort can leave you feeling low.* ○ *He seemed in low spirits.*

low COW NOISE /ləʊ/ ⓤ /loʊ/ *verb* [I] *LITERARY* to make the deep, long sound of a cow

lowbrow /ˈləʊ.braʊ/ ⓤ /ˈloʊ-/ *adj MAINLY DISAPPROVING* (of entertainment) not complicated or demanding much intelligence to be understood: *He regards the sort of books I read as very lowbrow.* ○ *I like a lowbrow action movie once in a while.* ➲Compare **highbrow**; **middlebrow**.

low ˈchurch *adj* related to the part of the Church of England that does not consider ceremonies and RITUALS to be an important part of the religion ⊃Compare **high church**.

low-cost /ˌləʊˈkɒst/ ⓤ /-ˈkɑːst/ *adj* cheap: *The 1990s saw a huge increase in the numbers of low-cost airlines.*

low-cut /ˌləʊˈkʌt/ *adj* describes a piece of clothing that does not cover a woman's neck and the top part of her chest: *a low-cut dress*

the lowdown INFORMATION /ˈləʊ.daʊn/ ⓤ /ˈloʊ-/ *noun* the most important facts and information about something: *Our fashion editor gives you the lowdown on winter coats for this season.*

low-down DISHONEST /ˈləʊ.daʊn/ ⓤ /ˈloʊ-/ *adj* [before n] INFORMAL describes a person or action that is very dishonest and unfair: *That was a pretty low-down thing to do.*

lower MOVE /ˈləʊ.əʳ/ ⓤ /ˈloʊ.ɚ/ *verb* [T] to move something into a low position: *They lowered the coffin into the grave.* ○ [R] *Heavily pregnant by now, she lowered herself carefully into the chair.* ○ *He lowered his eyes* (= looked down) *in embarrassment when he saw me.*

lower REDUCE /ˈləʊ.əʳ/ ⓤ /ˈloʊ.ɚ/ *verb* [T] **1** to reduce something: *Interest rates have been lowered again.* ○ *Boil for 5 minutes, then lower the heat and simmer for half an hour.* ○ *Please lower your voice* (= speak more quietly). **2** to make something worse than it was before: *a lowering of standards* ○ HUMOROUS *Dale lowered **the tone of** the evening* (= made it less socially acceptable) *by telling a dirty joke.*

lower BOTTOM PART /ˈləʊ.əʳ/ ⓤ /ˈloʊ.ɚ/ *adj* positioned below one or more similar things, or of the bottom part of something: *the lower deck of a ship* ○ *Her lower lip trembled as if she was about to cry.* ○ *I've got a pain in my lower* (= the bottom part of my) *back.* ✳ NOTE: The opposite is **upper**.

ˈlower yourself BEHAVE BADLY *verb* [R] to behave in a way that makes people lose respect for you: [+ *to* infinitive] *I wouldn't lower myself **to** respond to his insults if I were you.*

lower ˈcase *noun* [U] letters of the alphabet which are not written as capital letters, for example a, b, c ⊃Compare **upper case**. **ˈlower ˌcase** *adj*: *lower case letters*

lower ˈclass *adj* OLD-FASHIONED describes people who belong to the social class that has the lowest position in society and the least money ⊃Compare **upper class**; **middle class**; **working class**. **the ˌlower ˈclasses** *plural noun*

lower ˈhouse *noun* [C usually sing] (*ALSO* **lower chamber**) one of the two parts that some parliaments are divided into, usually the one with more political power ⊃Compare **upper house**.

lowering /ˈlaʊə.rɪŋ/ ⓤ /ˈlaʊɚ.ɪŋ/ *adj* LITERARY describes the sky when it is very dark and it looks as if it is about to rain: *The village fête took place under lowering skies.*

lowest common deˈnominator NUMBER *noun* [U] SPECIALIZED the smallest number that can be exactly divided by all the bottom numbers in a group of fractions

the ˌlowest common deˈnominator BAD QUALITY *noun* [S] the large number of people in society who will accept low-quality products and entertainment: *The problem with so much television is that it is aimed at the lowest common denominator.*

low-fat /ˌləʊˈfæt/ *adj* containing only a small amount of fat: *a low-fat diet* ○ *low-fat yoghurt/cheese/spreads*

low-key /ˌləʊˈkiː/ *adj* describes an event that is quiet and without a great show of excitement: *The wedding was a low-key affair, with fewer than thirty people attending.*

lowland /ˈləʊ.lənd/ ⓤ /ˈloʊ-/ *noun* [C usually pl] flat land that is at the same level as the sea: *From the lowlands of the south to the rugged peaks in the north, Derbyshire has something for everyone.* ○ *These plants are mainly found in lowland areas/regions.*

ˈlow ˌlife *noun* [U] people who exist by criminal activities or have a way of life most people disapprove

of: *He started mixing with drug-dealers, pimps and other low life.*

lowly /ˈləʊ.li/ ⓤ /ˈloʊ-/ *adj* low in position and importance, or not respected: *He took a lowly job in an insurance firm.* ○ *His first job in the hotel was as a lowly porter.*

low-lying /ˌləʊˈlaɪ.ɪŋ/ ⓤ /ˌloʊ-/ *adj* describes land that is at or near the level of the sea: *People living in low-lying areas were evacuated because of the floods.*

low-pitched /ˌləʊˈpɪtʃt/ ⓤ /ˌloʊ-/ *adj* describes a sound which is at the bottom of the range of sounds: *He gave a low-pitched whistle.*

low-rent /ˌləʊˈrent/ *adj* MAINLY US DISAPPROVING cheap and not of good quality

low-rise /ˈləʊ.raɪz/ ⓤ /ˈloʊ-/ *adj* A low-rise building is one with only one or two floors.

ˈlow ˌseason *noun* [U] the period in the year when the fewest number of people visit a place and when the prices are at their lowest level ⊃Compare **high season**.

low-spirited /ˌləʊˈspɪr.ɪ.tɪd/ ⓤ /ˌloʊˈspɪr.ɪ.t̬ɪd/ *adj* unhappy and having little hope

low-tech /ˌləʊˈtek/ ⓤ /ˌloʊ-/ *adj* not using the most recent equipment or methods: *a low-tech economy* ⊃Compare **high-tech**.

ˌlow ˈtide *noun* [C usually sing] the time when the sea has reached its lowest level

ˌlow ˈwater ˌmark *noun* [C usually sing] a mark which shows the lowest point on a beach that is reached by the sea

lox /lɒks/ ⓤ /lɑːks/ *noun* [U] US SALMON (= a type of fish) which has been preserved with smoke: *a bagel with lox and cream cheese*

loyal /ˈlɔɪ.əl/ *adj* firm and not changing in your friendship with or support for a person or an organization, or in your belief in your principles: *Jack has been a loyal worker in this company for almost 50 years.* ○ *When all her other friends deserted her, Steve remained loyal.* ○ *She's very loyal **to** her friends.* ✳ NOTE: The opposite is **disloyal**. **loyally** /ˈlɔɪ.ə.li/ *adv*

loyalty /ˈlɔɪ.əl.ti/ ⓤ /-t̬i/ *noun* [U] the quality of being loyal: *His loyalty was never in question.* ○ *Her loyalty **to** the cause is impressive.*

loyalties /ˈlɔɪ.əl.tiz/ ⓤ /-t̬iz/ *plural noun* your feelings of support or duty towards someone or something: *My loyalties **to** my family come before anything else.* ○ **divided** *loyalties* (= feelings of support for two different and opposing people or things)

loyalist /ˈlɔɪ.ə.lɪst/ *noun* [C] a person or group that strongly supports the government or ruler in power: *The rebel forces have been repeatedly attacked by loyalist troops.*

Loyalist /ˈlɔɪ.ə.lɪst/ *noun* [C] in Northern Ireland, a person who believes that Northern Ireland should continue to be part of the UK

ˈloyalty ˌcard *noun* [C] UK a plastic card which is given to a customer by a business and which is used to record information about what the customer buys and to reward them for buying goods or services from the business

lozenge /ˈlɒz.ɪndʒ/ ⓤ /ˈlɑː.zəndʒ/ *noun* [C] a small flat sweet which you suck to make your throat feel better: *a cough lozenge*

LP /ˌelˈpiː/ *noun* [C] ABBREVIATION FOR long-playing record: a record which is played at 33 ½ RPM, continuing to produce music for about 25 minutes

LPG /ˌel.piːˈdʒiː/ *noun* [U] ABBREVIATION FOR liquefied petroleum gas: a type of fuel used for heating, cooking and in some vehicles

L-plate /ˈel.pleɪt/ *noun* [C usually pl] UK a square white sign with a red letter L on it, which is fixed to the back and the front of a vehicle driven by a person who is learning to drive

LPN /ˌel.piːˈen/ *noun* [C] US ABBREVIATION FOR licensed practical nurse: a nurse who is trained to provide medical care by following the instructions of a nurse who has more training or a doctor

LSD /ˌel.esˈdiː/ *noun* [U] (*SLANG* **acid**) an illegal drug which causes people who use it to see the world differently from the way it really is or to see things that do not really exist

Lt /lef'ten.ᵊnt/ [US] /luː-/ *noun* [before n] *WRITTEN ABBREVIATION FOR* **lieutenant**

Ltd /'lɪm.ɪ.tɪd/ *adj* [after n] *UK WRITTEN ABBREVIATION FOR* limited liability company: used in the name of a company whose owners have limited responsibility for the money that it owes: *Smith and Jones Ltd*

.ltd.uk /dɒt.el.tiː,diː.dɒt.juː'keɪ/ [US] /dɑːt.el.tiː,diː.dɑːt-/ *INTERNET ABBREVIATION* the last part of an Internet address for a British company whose shares can be bought by members of the public

luau /'luː.aʊ/ *noun* [C] *AUS* a Hawaiian party or celebration

'lube ,job *noun* [C] *US* when the moving parts of a car are treated with oil or other substances in order to make them move more easily

lubricant /'luː.brɪ.kənt/ *noun* [C or U] (*US INFORMAL* **lube**) a liquid such as oil which is used to make the parts of an engine move easily together, or a substance put on any surface to help it move more easily against another one

lubricate /'luː.brɪ.keɪt/ *verb* [T] to use a substance such as oil to make a machine operate more easily, or to prevent something sticking or rubbing: *A car engine needs to be well lubricated with oil.* **lubrication** /,luː.brɪ'keɪ.ʃᵊn/ *noun* [U] (*US INFORMAL* **lube**)

lubricious /luː'brɪʃ.əs/ *adj FORMAL* having or showing too great an interest in sex, especially in an unpleasant way **lubriciously** /luː'brɪʃ.ə.sli/ *adv* **lubriciousness** /luː'brɪʃ.ə.snəs/ *noun* [U]

lucid /'luː.sɪd/ *adj* clearly expressed and easy to understand or (of a person) thinking or speaking clearly: *She gave a clear and lucid account of her plans for the company's future.* ○ *The drugs she's taking make her drowsy and confused, but there are times when she's quite lucid.* **lucidity** /luː'sɪd.ɪ.ti/ [US] /-ə.t̬i/ *noun* [U] (*ALSO* **lucidness**) **lucidly** /'luː.sɪd.li/ *adv*

L

Lucifer /'luː.sɪ.fəʳ/ [US] /-fɚ/ *noun* another name for SATAN (= a powerful evil force and the enemy of God)

Lucite /'luː.saɪt/ *noun* [U] *US TRADEMARK* a type of transparent plastic used to make paints and decorative objects such as picture frames

luck /lʌk/ *noun* [U] **1** the force that causes things, especially good things, to happen to you by chance and not as a result of your own efforts or abilities: *It was just luck that I asked for a job at the right time.* ○ *Then I met this gorgeous woman and I couldn't believe my luck.* ○ *She wears a charm that she thinks brings her* ***good*** *luck.* ○ *He seems to have had a lot of* ***bad*** *luck in his life.* ○ *So your interview's tomorrow? Good luck!* ○ *The best of luck* ***in/with*** *your exams!* **2** success: *Have you* ***had*** *any luck* ***with*** (= Have you been successful in) *booking your flight?* ○ *He tried to get into teacher training college but with no luck* (= no success).

• **Bad/Hard/Tough luck!** said to express sympathy with someone when something bad has happened to them: *"They've just run out of tickets." "Oh, bad luck!"*

• **as luck would have it** by chance: *We ran out of petrol on the way home, but as luck would have it, we were very near a garage.*

• **be bad luck on** ***sb*** *MAINLY UK* to be a bad thing that happened to someone by chance: *It was bad luck on Alex that he was ill on his birthday.*

• **be down on** ***your*** **luck** to be experiencing a bad situation or to have very little money: *He's been a bit down on his luck recently.*

• **for (good) luck** to bring good luck: *We have a horseshoe hanging on our wall for good luck.*

• **for luck** *USUALLY HUMOROUS* used to describe something extra which you take, especially in order to bring you good luck: *There's two spoonsful of sugar, and* ***one*** *for luck.*

• **be in/out of luck** *INFORMAL* to be able/unable to have or do what you want: *"Do you have any tuna sandwiches?" "You're in luck – there's one left."*

• **Your luck's in!** *UK HUMOROUS* something that you say in order to tell someone that you think another person would like a sexual relationship with them: *He's been looking at you all evening – I think your luck's in, Cath.*

• **be the luck of the draw** to be the result of chance and something that you have no control over: *You can't choose who you play against – it's just the luck of the draw.*

• **more by luck than judgment** *UK* by chance and not because of any special skill: *"You did amazingly well to get the ball in." "Oh, it was more by luck than judgment."*

• **no such luck** *INFORMAL* said after a desirable event or result has been suggested, to show disappointment that it cannot or did not happen: *I was rather hoping it would rain today and I wouldn't have to go on the walk, but no such luck.*

• **with any luck** (*ALSO* **with a bit of luck**) *INFORMAL* used before describing an event or a result that you are hoping for: *With any luck* (= I hope that) *we should get to Newcastle by early evening.*

luck /lʌk/ *verb*

PHRASAL VERBS WITH **luck** ▼

▲ **luck into** ***sth*** *phrasal verb US INFORMAL* to get something that you want by chance: *We lucked into tickets for the World Cup finals.*

▲ **luck out** *phrasal verb US INFORMAL* to be very lucky: *The Giants really lucked out in last night's game.*

luckily /'lʌk.ᵊl.i/ *adv* because of good luck: *Luckily, I had some money with me.*

luckless /'lʌk.ləs/ *adj LITERARY* describes someone who has a lot of bad luck: *The luckless defender, Mark Emery, sustained his third injury of the season.*

lucky /'lʌk.i/ *adj* having good things happen to you by chance: *"I'm going on holiday." "Lucky you!"* ○ *The lucky winner will be able to choose from three different holidays.* ○ [+ **to** infinitive] *They're lucky* ***to*** *have such a nice office to work in.* ○ *He's lucky* ***that*** *he wasn't fired.* ○ *It sounds as if you had a lucky* ***escape*** (= by good chance you were able to avoid something dangerous or unpleasant). ○ *We'll be lucky if we get there by midnight at this rate* (= We might get there by midnight or it might be later).

• **get lucky** *INFORMAL* to meet someone you can have a sexual or romantic relationship with: *Why don't you come to the party? You never know, you might get lucky.*

• ***You'll*** **be lucky!** (*ALSO* ***You*** **should be so lucky!**) *UK INFORMAL* said in order to tell someone that it is very unlikely that they will get what they want: *"She's going to ask for a salary increase." "She'll be lucky!"*

,lucky 'dip *noun* [C] *UK* a game in which you pay to pick a wrapped object out of a container which is filled with wrapped objects of various different values, hoping to get something of higher value than the amount you have paid ➲Compare **grab bag**.

lucrative /'luː.krə.tɪv/ [US] /-t̬ɪv/ *adj* (especially of a business, job or activity) producing a lot of money: *The merger proved to be very lucrative for both companies.* **lucratively** /'luː.krə.tɪv.li/ [US] /-t̬ɪv-/ *adv* **lucrativeness** /'luː.krə.tɪv.nəs/ [US] /-t̬ɪv-/ *noun* [U]

lucre /'luː.kəʳ/ [US] /-kɚ/ *noun* [U] *OLD-FASHIONED DISAPPROVING OR HUMOROUS* money or profit: ***filthy*** *lucre*

Luddite /'lʌd.aɪt/ *noun* [C] *USUALLY DISAPPROVING* a person who is opposed to the introduction of new working methods, especially new machines

ludicrous /'luː.dɪ.krəs/ *adj* stupid or unreasonable and deserving to be laughed at; ridiculous: *a ludicrous idea/suggestion* ○ *He looked ludicrous in that suit!* **ludicrously** /'luː.dɪ.krə.sli/ *adv*: *It's a beautiful dress, but it's ludicrously* (= unreasonably) *expensive.* **ludicrousness** /'luː.dɪ.krə.snəs/ *noun* [U]

lug [CARRY] /lʌg/ *verb* [T usually + adv or prep] **-gg-** *INFORMAL* to carry or pull something with effort or difficulty because it is heavy: *I'm exhausted after lugging these suitcases all the way across London.* ○ *I don't want to lug these shopping bags* ***around*** *with me all day.*

lug [EAR] /lʌg/ *noun* [C] *UK SLANG* a LUGHOLE (= ear)

lug [PERSON] /lʌg/ *noun* [C] *US SLANG* **1** an awkward or stupid man **2** an affectionate word for a man: *Come over here and give me a kiss, you* ***big*** *lug.*

luggage /'lʌg.ɪdʒ/ *noun* [U] (*MAINLY US* **baggage**) the bags, cases, etc. which contain your possessions and that you take with you when you are travelling: *Never leave your luggage unattended.* ○ ***hand** luggage* (= small bags and cases that you take with you onto the plane)

ˈluggage ˌlabel *UK noun* [C] (*US* **luggage tag**) a small piece of card or plastic with your name and address written on it, which you fasten to a bag or case to show that it belongs to you

ˈluggage ˌrack *noun* [C] *MAINLY UK* a shelf on a train or a bus on which you can put your bags and cases

ˈluggage ˌvan *UK noun* [C] (*US* **baggage car**) a train carriage in which large bags are transported

lughole /ˈlʌg.həʊl/ [US] /-hoʊl/ *noun* [C] (*ALSO* **lug**) *UK SLANG HUMOROUS* an ear: *You'll get a clip round the lughole if you're not careful.*

lugubrious /luːˈguː.bri.əs/ *adj LITERARY* sad, especially in a slow or serious way: *a lugubrious face* **lugubriously** /luːˈguː.bri.ə.sli/ *adv* **lugubriousness** /luːˈguː.bri.ə.snəs/ *noun* [U]

lukewarm [TEMPERATURE] /ˌluːkˈwɔːm/ /ˈ--/ [US] /ˈluːk.wɔːrm/ *adj MAINLY DISAPPROVING* (especially of a liquid) only slightly warm: *This coffee's lukewarm.*

lukewarm [REACTION] /ˌluːkˈwɔːm/ [US] /ˈluːk.wɔːrm/ *adj DISAPPROVING* not enthusiastic or interested: *Her proposals got a lukewarm **response**.*

lull /lʌl/ *verb* [T] to cause someone to feel calm or to feel as if they want to sleep: *The motion of the car almost lulled her **to sleep**.*

lull /lʌl/ *noun* [C] a short period of calm in which little happens: *There has been a lull **in** the fighting.* ○ *a lull in the conversation/traffic*

• **the lull before the storm** a time which seems quiet but which will very soon be followed by something unpleasant happening: *Things seem quiet in the office right now, but this is just the lull before the storm.*

▲ **lull *sb* into *sth*** *phrasal verb* to make someone feel safe in order to trick them: *Most exercise classes start gently, lulling you into thinking that you're fit.* ○ *Their promises lulled us **into a false sense of security*** (= made us feel safe, when in fact we were not).

lullaby /ˈlʌl.ə.baɪ/ *noun* [C] a quiet song which is sung to children to help them go to sleep

lulu /ˈluː.luː/ *noun* [C] *US OLD-FASHIONED SLANG* something which is extremely good or extremely bad: *I've seen a few black eyes in my time but that's a lulu!*

lumbago /lʌmˈbeɪ.gəʊ/ [US] /-goʊ/ *noun* [U] general pain in the lower part of the back

lumbar /ˈlʌm.bəʳ/ [US] /-bɚ/ *adj* [before n] *SPECIALIZED* in or of the lower part of the back

lumber [MOVE] /ˈlʌm.bəʳ/ [US] /-bɚ/ *verb* [I usually + adv or prep] to move slowly and awkwardly: *In the distance, we could see a herd of elephants lumbering across the plain.*

▲ **lumber *sb* with *sth*** *phrasal verb MAINLY UK INFORMAL* If you are/get lumbered with something, you have to deal with something or someone that you do not want to: *I always seem to get lumbered with the job of clearing up after a party.*

lumber [WOOD] /ˈlʌm.bəʳ/ [US] /-bɚ/ *noun* [U] *MAINLY US* wood that has been prepared for building

lumberjack /ˈlʌm.bə.dʒæk/ [US] /-bɚ-/ *noun* [C] (*ALSO* **lumberman**) (especially in the USA and Canada) a person whose job is to cut down trees which will be used for building etc. or to transport trees which have been cut down

ˈlumber ˌjacket *noun* [C] a warm short coat, often with a brightly-coloured pattern of squares on it

lumberman /ˈlʌm.bə.mæn/ [US] /-bɚ-/ *noun* [C] (especially in the US or Canada) a LUMBERJACK or a man whose business is the selling of wood

lumberyard /ˈlʌm.bə.jɑːd/ [US] /ˈlʌm.bɚ.jɑːrd/ *noun* [C] an outside area where wood for building is stored and sold

luminary /ˈluː.mɪ.nə.ri/ [US] /ˈluː.mə.ner.i/ *noun* [C] *FORMAL* a person who is famous and important in a particular area of activity: *Luminaries **of** stage and screen* (= famous actors) *assembled for last night's awards ceremony.*

luminescent /ˌluː.mɪˈnes.ᵊnt/ *adj LITERARY OR SPECIALIZED* producing a soft light **luminescence** /ˌluː.mɪˈnes.ᵊnts/ *noun* [U]

luminous /ˈluː.mɪ.nəs/ *adj* producing or reflecting bright light (especially in the dark): *luminous clothing* **luminosity** /ˌluː.mɪˈnɒs.ə.ti/ [US] /-ˈnɑː.sə.t̬i/ *noun* [U] **luminously** /ˈluː.mɪ.nə.sli/ *adv*

lummox /ˈlʌm.əks/ *noun* [C] *MAINLY US INFORMAL* a stupid or awkward person: *Be careful, you big lummox, you just stamped on my foot!*

lump [PIECE] /lʌmp/ *noun* [C] **1** a piece of a solid substance, usually with no particular shape: *a lump **of** coal* ○ *a sugar lump* ○ *You don't want lumps in the sauce.* **2** *INFORMAL* a separate large amount: *I'll be getting the insurance money in two lumps.* **3** a hard swelling found in or on the body, especially because of illness or injury: *She found a lump in her breast.*

• **bring a lump to *your* throat** to give you a tight feeling in your throat because you want to cry: *It was quite a moving speech – it almost brought a lump to my throat.*

• **take *your* lumps** *US OLD-FASHIONED INFORMAL* to be criticised or beaten as a punishment

lump [PERSON] /lʌmp/ *noun* [C] *INFORMAL* a heavy, awkward, stupid person: *Come on, you **great** lump, get up from in front of that television and do some work.*

lumpish /ˈlʌm.pɪʃ/ *adj* awkward and stupid

lump [ACCEPT] /lʌmp/ *verb INFORMAL* **lump it** to accept a situation or decision although you do not like it: *The decision has been made, so if Tom doesn't like it, he **can** lump it.*

▲ **lump *sb/sth* together** *phrasal verb* to put different groups together and think about them or deal with them in the same way: *All the children are lumped together in one class, regardless of their ability.*

lumpectomy /lʌmˈpek.tə.mi/ *noun* [C] a medical operation to remove a lump from the breast

lumpen [PERSON] /ˈlʌm.pən/ *adj INFORMAL DISAPPROVING* describes people who are not clever or well-educated, and who are not interested in changing or improving their situation: *the lumpen **proletariat*** (= unskilled working people)

lumpen [OBJECT] /ˈlʌm.pən/ *adj DISAPPROVING* lumpy and heavy

ˌlump ˈsum *noun* [C usually sing] a sum of money that is paid in one large amount on one occasion: *Her divorce settlement included a lump sum **of** $2 million.*

lumpy /ˈlʌm.pi/ *adj* covered with or containing lumps: *a lumpy bed/pillow* ○ *a lumpy sauce*

lunacy /ˈluː.nə.si/ *noun* [U] **1** stupid behaviour that will have bad results: *It would be lunacy to try to climb the mountain in this weather.* ○ *It was sheer lunacy spending all that money.* **2** *OLD-FASHIONED* mental illness

lunar /ˈluː.nəʳ/ [US] /-nɚ/ *adj* of or relating to the moon: *the lunar surface*

ˌlunar ˈmonth *noun* [C] the period of time (about 29.5 days) which the moon takes to go round the Earth ➲Compare **calendar month**.

lunatic /ˈluː.nə.tɪk/ [US] /-t̬ɪk/ *noun* [C] **1** someone who behaves in a foolish or dangerous way: *He drives like a lunatic.* **2** *OFFENSIVE OLD-FASHIONED* a person who is mentally ill **lunatic** /ˈluː.nə.tɪk/ [US] /-t̬ɪk/ *adj*

• **the lunatic fringe** *DISAPPROVING OR HUMOROUS* people who have very strong opinions that are outside the usual range

ˈlunatic aˌsylum *noun* [C] *OLD USE* a hospital for mentally ill people

lunch /lʌntʃ/ *noun* [C or U] a meal that is eaten in the middle of the day: *What's for lunch?* ○ *UK We had a **pub** lunch.* ○ *I'm sorry, Joanna isn't here at the moment, she's **(gone) out to/gone to** lunch.* ○ *We must **do** lunch sometime* (= have lunch together).

• **be out to lunch** *INFORMAL* to be crazy: *So do I take this guy seriously or is he out to lunch?*

lunch /lʌntʃ/ *verb* [I] to eat lunch: *I'm lunching **with** Giles.*

lunchbox /ˈlʌntʃ.bɒks/ [US] /-bɑːks/ *noun* [C] a box in which your lunch can be carried to work, school etc.

luncheon /ˈlʌn*t*.ʃən/ *noun* [C or U] *FORMAL FOR* **lunch**

luncheonette /ˌlʌn*t*.ʃəˈnet/ *noun* [C] *US* a small restaurant serving simple, light meals

L

ˈluncheon ˌvoucher *UK noun* [C] (*US* **meal ticket**) a type of ticket which people are given by their employer and which they can use instead of money for buying meals in some restaurants

ˈlunch ˌhour *noun* [C] (*ALSO* **lunch break**) the period in the middle of the day when people stop work to have lunch

ˈlunch ˌroom *US noun* [C usually sing] (*UK* **dining hall**) a large room in a school where children can sit down to eat

lunchtime /ˈlʌntʃ.taɪm/ *noun* [C or U] the time in the middle of the day when most people eat a meal: *What are you doing **at** lunchtime?*

lung /lʌŋ/ *noun* [C] either of the two organs in the chest with which people and some animals breathe: *lung cancer*

• **have a good/healthy pair of lungs** You say that a baby has a good/healthy pair of lungs when it cries loudly.

lunge /lʌndʒ/ *verb* [I usually + adv or prep] to move forward suddenly and with force, especially in order to attack someone: *He suddenly lunged **at** her **with** a broken bottle.* **lunge** /lʌndʒ/ *noun* [C]

lupin, *US USUALLY* **lupine** /ˈluː.pɪn/ *noun* [C] a garden plant which has a long pointed flower of various colours and which is sometimes used to feed animals ➲See picture **Flowers and Plants** on page Centre 3

lupus /ˈluː.pəs/ *noun* [U] *SPECIALIZED* a general name for various serious skin diseases which also affect the internal organs and bones

lurch /lɜːtʃ/ [US] /lɝːtʃ/ *verb* **1** [I] to move in an irregular way, especially making sudden movements backwards or forwards or from side to side: *The train lurched **forward** and some of the people standing fell over.* **2** [I + adv or prep] to act or continue in an irregular and uncontrolled way, often with sudden changes: *We seem to lurch **from** crisis **to** crisis.* ○ *She just lurches **from** one bad relationship **to** another.*

lurch /lɜːtʃ/ [US] /lɝːtʃ/ *noun* [C] *The truck gave a sudden lurch as it was hit by a strong gust of wind.* ○ *The party's lurch* (= sudden change) ***to** the left will lose it a lot of support.*

lure /ljʊəʳ/ [US] /lʊr/ *noun* **1** [C usually sing] the quality or power that something or someone has that makes them attractive: *the lure of fame/power/money* **2** [C] an artificial insect or other small animal which is put on the end of a fishing line to attract fish

lure /ljʊəʳ/ [US] /lʊr/ *verb* [T] to persuade someone to do something or go somewhere by offering them something exciting: *She was lured **into** the job by the offer of a high salary.* ○ *He had lured his victim **to** a deserted house.* ○ *Supermarket chains try to lure customers with price discounts.*

Lurex /ˈlʊə.reks/ [US] /ˈlʊr.eks/ *noun* [U] *TRADEMARK* (cloth made from) a type of thread that looks metallic: *a gold/silver Lurex top*

lurgy /ˈlɜː.gi/ [US] /ˈlɝː-/ *noun* [S] *UK HUMOROUS* an illness or disease, especially one that is not serious: *He's got **the dreaded** lurgy.*

lurid [SHOCKING] /ˈljʊə.rɪd/ [US] /ˈlʊr.ɪd/ *adj DISAPPROVING* (especially of a description) shocking because involving violence, sex or immoral activity: *You can read all the lurid **details** of the affair in today's paper.* **luridly** /ˈljʊə.rɪd.li/ [US] /ˈlʊr.ɪd-/ *adv* **luridness** /ˈljʊə.rɪd.nəs/ [US] /ˈlʊr.ɪd-/ *noun* [U]

lurid [COLOUR] /ˈljʊə.rɪd/ [US] /lʊr.ɪd/ *adj DISAPPROVING* too brightly coloured: *That's a very lurid shade of lipstick she's wearing.* **luridly** /ˈljʊə.rɪd.li/ [US] /ˈlʊr.ɪd-/ *adv* **luridness** /ˈljʊə.rɪd.nəs/ [US] /ˈlʊr.ɪd-/ *noun* [U]

lurk /lɜːk/ [US] /lɝːk/ *verb* **1** [I usually + adv or prep] to wait or move in a secret way so that you cannot be seen, especially because you are about to attack someone or do something wrong: *Someone was lurking **in** the shadows.* ○ *Why are you lurking **about** in the corridor?* **2** [I usually + adv or prep] (of an unpleasant feeling or quality) to exist although it is not always noticeable: ***Danger** lurks around every corner.* ○ *It seems that old prejudices are still lurking **beneath** the surface.* **3** [I] *INFORMAL* to enter a CHAT ROOM (= an address on the Internet where people can talk to each other using email) and read other people's messages without allowing them to know you are present

lurking /ˈlɜː.kɪŋ/ [US] /ˈlɝː-/ *adj*: *I have some lurking **doubts*** (= doubts which will not go completely away) *about whether Simon is really capable of doing this job.* ○ *She said she had a lurking **suspicion*** (= she had a very slight feeling) *that he wasn't telling the truth.*

lurve /lɜːv/ [US] /lɜːrv/ *noun* [U] *UK NOT STANDARD HUMOROUS* love: *They spend every evening together – I think it might be lurve.* **lurve** /lɜːv/ [US] /lɜːrv/ *verb* [T]

luscious /ˈlʌʃ.əs/ *adj* **1** having a pleasant sweet taste or containing a lot of juice: *luscious ripe figs* **2** *INFORMAL* (of a woman) very sexually attractive: *a luscious blonde* **3** (of an area of countryside) very green and attractive: *luscious landscapes* **lusciously** /ˈlʌʃ.ə.sli/ *adv* **lusciousness** /ˈlʌʃ.ə.snəs/ *noun* [U]

lush [PLANTS] /lʌʃ/ *adj* A lush area has a lot of green, healthy plants, grass and trees: *lush green valleys* **lushness** /ˈlʌʃ.nəs/ *noun* [U]

lush [LUXURIOUS] /lʌʃ/ *adj* (of places, furniture, decoration, etc.) expensive and luxurious: *a lush carpet* **lushly** /ˈlʌʃ.li/ *adv* **lushness** /ˈlʌʃ.nəs/ *noun* [U]

lush [PERSON] /lʌʃ/ *noun* [C] *SLANG* a person who regularly drinks too much alcohol: *She's a bit of a lush by all accounts.*

lust [SEX] /lʌst/ *noun* [U] a very strong sexual desire: *I don't think it's love so much as lust.* **lustful** /ˈlʌst.fᵊl/ *adj*: *lustful thoughts* **lustfully** /ˈlʌst.fᵊl.i/ *adv* **lustfulness** /ˈlʌst.fᵊl.nəs/ *noun* [U]

lust [WISH] /lʌst/ *noun* [C or U] a very powerful feeling of wanting something: *her lust **for** power* ○ *It's wonderful to see the children's lust **for** life* (= how enthusiastic they are about life).

lust /lʌst/ *verb*

PHRASAL VERBS WITH **lust** ▼

▲ **lust after *sb*** [SEXUAL] *phrasal verb* to feel sexual desire for someone you are not having a sexual relationship with: *She's been lusting after Dave for months.*

▲ **lust after/for *sth*** [WANT] *phrasal verb* to want something very much: *I've been lusting after one of their silk shirts for ages.*

lustre *UK*, *US* **luster** /ˈlʌs.təʳ/ [US] /-tɚ/ *noun* **1** [S or U] the brightness that a shiny surface has: *a treatment for restoring the lustre to dull hair* ○ *the rich lustre of well-polished furniture* **2** [U] a very special, admirable and attractive quality: *The dancing of the principal ballerina **added** lustre **to** an otherwise unimpressive production of 'Giselle'.*

lustrous /ˈlʌs.trəs/ *adj* very shiny: *long lustrous hair* **lustrously** /ˈlʌs.trə.sli/ *adv*

lusty /ˈlʌs.ti/ *adj* healthy; energetic; full of strength and power: *a baby's lusty cry* ○ *We could hear the lusty singing of the church choir.*

lustily /ˈlʌs.tɪ.li/ *adv*: *The baby cried lustily* (= loudly, showing good health) *the moment he was born.* **lustiness** /ˈlʌs.tɪ.nəs/ *noun* [U]

lute /luːt/ *noun* [C] a musical instrument which has a body with a round back and a flat top, a long neck and strings which are played with the fingers

Lutheran /ˈluː.θᵊr.ᵊn/ [US] /-θɚ-/ *adj* of or relating to the part of Protestant Christianity that is based on the ideas of the German religious leader Martin Luther: *the Lutheran church* **Lutheran** /ˈluː.θᵊr.ᵊn/ [US] /-θɚ-/ *noun* [C]

luv /lʌv/ *noun* [as form of address] *UK NOT STANDARD FOR* love: *Can I get you a drink, luv?*

luvvy /ˈlʌv.i/ *noun* [C] (*ALSO* **luvvie**) *HUMOROUS* an actor or actress who speaks and acts in a very artificial and noticeable way

lux /lʌks/ *noun* [C] *plural* **lux** *SPECIALIZED* a measure of the amount of light produced by something

luxuriant /lʌgˈʒʊə.ri.ənt/ [US] /-ˈʒʊr.i-/ *adj* **1** growing thickly, strongly and well: *Tall, luxuriant plants grew along the river bank.* ○ *This stretch of land was once covered with luxuriant forest, but is now bare.* ○ *Her luxuriant hair fell around her shoulders.* **2** pleasantly dense or full: *We've bought a wonderfully luxuriant carpet for our bedroom.* ○ *a luxuriant style of writing*

luxuriance /lʌgˈʒʊə.ri.ənts/ ⓤⓢ /-ˈʒʊr.i-/ *noun* [U]
luxuriantly /lʌgˈʒʊə.ri.ənt.li/ ⓤⓢ /-ˈʒʊr.i-/ *adv*

luxuriate /lʌgˈʒʊə.ri.eɪt/ ⓤⓢ /-ˈʒʊr.i-/ *verb*
▲ **luxuriate in** *sth phrasal verb FORMAL* to get great pleasure from something, especially because it provides physical comfort: *There's nothing better after a hard day's work than to luxuriate in a hot bath.*

luxury /ˈlʌk.ʃᵊr.i/ ⓤⓢ /-ʃɚ-/ *noun* **1** [U] great comfort, especially as provided by expensive and beautiful things: *to live in luxury* ○ *a luxury cruise* ○ *a luxury hotel* **2** [C] something expensive which is pleasant to have but is not necessary: *luxuries, such as champagne and chocolate* ○ *I like to buy myself **little** luxuries from time to time.* **3** [S or U] something which gives you a lot of pleasure but which you cannot often do: *A day off work is such a luxury.*

luxurious /lʌgˈʒʊə.ri.əs/ ⓤⓢ /-ˈʒʊr.i-/ *adj* **1** very comfortable and expensive: *They have a very luxurious house.* ○ *We spent a luxurious weekend at a country hotel.* **2** giving great pleasure: *The cat gave a long, luxurious stretch.* **luxuriously** /lʌgˈʒʊə.ri.ə.sli/ ⓤⓢ /-ˈʒʊr.i-/ *adv*

,**luxury 'goods** *plural noun* expensive items, such as jewellery and perfume, which are pleasant to have but are not essential: *The government will pay for the new schools by increasing the tax on luxury goods.*

LW *noun* [U] *ABBREVIATION FOR* **long wave**

-ly ADVERB /-li/ *suffix* **1** in the stated way: *quickly* ○ *carefully* ○ *angrily* ○ *loudly* **2** when considered in the stated way: *Personally* (= in my opinion)*, I don't think animals should be killed for their fur.* ○ *This is an environmentally* (= in relation to the environment) *disastrous proposal.* **3** regularly after the stated period of time: *a weekly/monthly meeting*

-ly ADJECTIVE /-li/ *suffix* **1** like the stated person or thing: *fatherly advice* ○ *priestly duties* ○ *cowardly behaviour* **2** describes one of a series of events which happen with the stated regular period of time between each: *a daily shower* ○ *a weekly meeting* ○ *a yearly check-up*

lycée /ˈliː.seɪ/ *noun* [C] a French school for older children, either in France or for French children living in other countries

lychee, **litchi** /ˈlaɪt.ʃiː/ *noun* [C] a fruit with a rough brown shell and sweet white flesh around a large shiny brown seed, or the evergreen tree on which this fruit grows ➋See picture **Fruit** on page Centre 1

lychgate /ˈlɪtʃ.geɪt/ *noun* [C] a small gate with a small sloping roof over it which leads into the grounds of a church

Lycra /ˈlaɪ.krə/ *noun* [U] *TRADEMARK* a stretchy material used especially for making clothes which fit very

tightly: *a Lycra swimsuit* ○ *Lycra leggings* ○ *These jeans have added Lycra for comfort and fit.*

lying /ˈlaɪ.ɪŋ/ *present participle of* **lie**

lymph /lɪmpf/ *noun* [U] a colourless liquid which takes useful substances around the body, and takes waste matter, such as unwanted bacteria, away from body tissue in order to prevent infection **lymphatic** /lɪmpˈfæt.ɪk/ ⓤⓢ /-ˈfæt̬-/ *adj: the lymphatic system*

'**lymph ,gland** *noun* [C] (*ALSO* **lymph node**) one of many small organs in the body which produce the white blood cells needed for the body to fight infection

lynch /lɪntʃ/ *verb* [T] If a crowd of people lynch someone who they believe is guilty of a crime, they kill them without a legal trial, usually by HANGING (= killing using a rope round the neck). **lynching** /ˈlɪn.tʃɪŋ/ *noun* [C or U]

'**lynch ,mob** *noun* [C] a group of people who want to attack someone whom they think has committed a serious crime

lynchpin /ˈlɪntʃ.pɪn/ *noun* [C] a **linchpin**

lynx /lɪŋks/ *noun* [C] *plural* **lynxes** or **lynx** a wild animal of the cat family which has brown hair, sometimes with dark spots on it, pointed ears and a short tail

lyre /laɪəʳ/ ⓤⓢ /laɪr/ *noun* [C] an ancient musical instrument consisting of a U-shaped frame with strings fixed to it

lyrebird /ˈlaɪə.bɜːd/ ⓤⓢ /ˈlaɪr.bɝːd/ *noun* [C] a long-legged Australian bird. The male has a tail which it can spread out into the shape of a LYRE.

lyric /ˈlɪr.ɪk/ *adj* (especially of poetry and songs) expressing personal thoughts and feelings: *William Wordsworth wrote lyric poetry/was a lyric poet.*

lyric /ˈlɪr.ɪk/ *noun* [C] a short poem which expresses the personal thoughts and feelings of the person who wrote it

lyrical /ˈlɪr.ɪ.kᵊl/ *adj* **1** expressing personal thoughts and feelings in a beautiful way: *The book contains lyrical descriptions of the author's childhood.* **2** **wax lyrical** to talk about something with a lot of interest or excitement: *I recall Rosie waxing lyrical about the flatness of his stomach.* **lyrically** /ˈlɪr.ɪ.kli/ *adv*

lyricism /ˈlɪr.ɪ.sɪ.zᵊm/ *noun* [U] the beautiful expression of personal thoughts and feelings in writing or music: *The harshness of the book's subject is softened by a certain lyricism in the writing.*

lyricist /ˈlɪr.ɪ.sɪst/ *noun* [C] someone who writes words for songs, especially pop songs

lyrics /ˈlɪr.ɪks/ *plural noun* the words of a song, especially a pop song: *Paul Simon writes the lyrics **for** most of his songs.*

L

M

M [LETTER] (*plural* **M's**), **m** (*plural* **m's**) /em/ *noun* [C] the 13th letter of the English alphabet

M [NUMBER], **m** /em/ *noun* [C] the sign used in the Roman system for the number 1000

M [ROAD] /em/ *noun* [U] *UK ABBREVIATION FOR* **motorway**: *The M4 goes from London to Bristol.*

M [SIZE] *adj ABBREVIATION FOR* **medium** VALUE: used on clothes to show that they are of medium size

m [AMOUNT] *noun* [C] *plural* **m** *WRITTEN ABBREVIATION FOR* **million**: *The new library cost £5m to build.*

m [LENGTH] *noun* [C] *plural* **m** *WRITTEN ABBREVIATION FOR* **metre** MEASUREMENT: *Jeff is 1.8 m tall.* ○ *She's the women's 1500 m champion* (= the winner of a race run over that distance).

m [DISTANCE] *noun WRITTEN ABBREVIATION FOR* **mile**

m [MALE] *adj WRITTEN ABBREVIATION FOR* **male** SEX (especially on forms)

'm /ᵊm/ *short form of* am, used in spoken and informal written English: *I'm sorry I'm late.*

ma [MOTHER] /mɑː/ *noun* [C] **1** *INFORMAL OLD-FASHIONED* a mother: *As my old ma used to say, you can't spend what you ain't got.* **2** *MAINLY US* a title for an old woman: *Ma Johnson always used to bake the best cookies.*

MA [DEGREE] /ˌemˈeɪ/ *noun* [C] *ABBREVIATION FOR* **Master of Arts**: *Julia Richards, MA* ○ *My brother has an MA* ***in*** *linguistics.* ○ *She's studying for/doing an MA* ***in*** *French literature.*

ma'am /mɑːm/ *noun* **[as form of address]** **1** **madam** WOMAN **2** in some parts of the US, used as a polite way of addressing a woman: *How can I help you, ma'am?* **3** in Britain, used to address the Queen, or a woman of high rank in particular organizations, such as the army or the police **4** in the past, used to address a woman of high social class

mac [COAT], **mack** /mæk/ *noun* [C] *UK* a waterproof coat: *a plastic mac*

Mac [COMPUTER] /mæk/ *noun* [C] (*ALSO* **(Apple) Macintosh**) *TRADEMARK* a type of computer designed for people who want to use computers without needing technical knowledge about how they work: *You can write up your report* ***on*** *the Mac.*

Mac [MAN] /mæk/ *noun* **[as form of address]** *US INFORMAL* used when speaking to a man whose name you do not know: *Hey, Mac, watch where you're going!*

macabre /məˈkɑː.brə/ *adj* describes something that is very strange and unpleasant because it is connected with death or violence: *Even the police were horrified at the macabre nature of the killings.* ○ *She has a rather macabre sense of humour.*

macaroni /ˌmæk.ᵊrˈəʊ.ni/ [US] /-əˈroʊ-/ *noun* [U] a type of pasta in the shape of small tubes

macaˌroni ˈcheese *UK noun* [U] (*US* **macaroni and cheese**) a dish made from macaroni and cheese sauce

macaroon /ˌmæk.ᵊrˈuːn/ [US] /-əˈruːn/ *noun* [C] a small light biscuit made from eggs and sugar and flavoured with ALMONDS or COCONUT

macaw /məˈkɔː/ [US] /-ˈkɑː/ *noun* [C] a brightly coloured bird of the PARROT family found in Central and South America

mace [SPICE] /meɪs/ *noun* [U] a spice made from the dried shell of NUTMEG

mace [ROD] /meɪs/ *noun* [C] a decorated rod that is carried by or put in front of particular public officials as a symbol of their authority

Mace [LIQUID] /meɪs/ *noun* [U] *TRADEMARK* a chemical in a container which, when sprayed into a person's face, causes their eyes to sting and become full of tears

macerate /ˈmæs.ə.reɪt/ *verb* [I or T] *SPECIALIZED* to leave food in a liquid so that it absorbs the liquid and becomes soft, or to become soft in this way: *Mix together all the ingredients and leave them to macerate in the fridge overnight.*

Mach /mɑːk/ /mæk/ *noun* [U] a measurement of speed which is calculated by dividing the speed of an object, often an aircraft, by the speed of sound

machete /məˈʃet.i/ [US] /-ˈʃet̬-/ *noun* [C] a large knife with a wide blade, used for cutting trees and plants or as a weapon

Machiavellian /ˌmæk.i.əˈvel.i.ən/ *adj* using clever but often dishonest methods which deceive people so that you can gain power or control

machinations /ˌmæʃ.ɪˈneɪ.ʃᵊnz/ /ˌmæk-/ *plural noun* complicated and secret plans to obtain power or control: *Despite a commitment to more open government, the public are still being kept in the dark about the inner machinations* ***of*** *the Cabinet.*

machinate /ˈmæʃ.ɪ.neɪt/ /ˈmæk-/ *verb* [I or T] to make secret plans in order to get an advantage

machine /məˈʃiːn/ *noun* [C] **1** a device with several moving parts which uses power to do a particular type of work: *Eggs are sorted into different sizes by a machine.* ○ *If I'm not home when you call, leave a message on the machine* (= answering machine). ○ *Don't forget to put the towels in the machine* (= washing machine) *before you go out.* ○ *I got some chocolate from a* ***vending*** *machine.* **2** *SPECIALIZED* a computer: *You'll need a powerful machine for editing videos.* **3** *INFORMAL* a vehicle, often a motorcycle: *APPROVING That's a* ***mean*** (= powerful) *machine you've got there, Bill.* **4** a group of people who control and organize something: *Churchill's* ***war*** *machine* ○ *The* ***party*** *machine has swung into action with its preparation for the election.* ○ *It's now up to the government's* ***propaganda*** *machine to restore the prime minister's image.*

machine /məˈʃiːn/ *verb* [T] to stitch cloth with a sewing machine: *I've almost finished making the curtains – I just have to machine the hem.*

machinery /məˈʃiː.nə.ri/ [US] /-nɚ.i/ *noun* [U] **1** a group of large machines or the parts of a machine which make it work: *industrial/farm machinery* ○ *His hand was injured when he got it caught in the machinery.* **2** the structure and systems of an organization or process: *bureaucratic/political/decision-making machinery* ○ *the machinery of government*

machinist /məˈʃiː.nɪst/ *noun* [C] a person whose job is operating a machine: *She works as a machinist in a clothing factory.*

maˈchine ˌcode *noun* [U] *SPECIALIZED* a set of numbers that gives instructions to a computer

maˈchine ˌgun *noun* [C] an automatic gun which can fire a lot of bullets one after the other very quickly: *Several journalists were caught in machine-gun* ***fire***.

machine-gun /məˈʃiːn.gʌn/ *verb* [T] to shoot someone with a machine gun: *The raiders machine-gunned everyone in the bank before escaping in a van.*

machine-readable /məˌʃiːnˈriː.də.bl̩/ *adj SPECIALIZED* able to be understood by a computer: *a machine-readable book/dictionary*

maˈchine ˌtool *noun* [C] a tool which uses power to cut and shape metal or other strong materials: *The car industry uses machine tools for cutting car body parts.*

maˌchine transˈlation *noun* [U] *SPECIALIZED* the process of changing text from one language into another language using a computer

machismo /məˈkɪz.məʊ/ [US] /-moʊ/ *noun* [U] *OFTEN DISAPPROVING* male behaviour which is characterized by being strong and forceful and having very traditional ideas about how men and women should behave

macho /ˈmætʃ.əʊ/ [US] /ˈmɑː.tʃoʊ/ *adj INFORMAL MAINLY DISAPPROVING* behaving forcefully or showing no emotion in a way traditionally thought to be typical of a man: *He's too macho to admit he was hurt when his girlfriend left him.* ○ *I can't stand macho men.*

Macintosh /ˈmæk.ɪn.tɒʃ/ [US] /-tɑːʃ/ *noun* [C] a MAC COMPUTER

mackerel /ˈmæk.rəl/ *noun* [C or U] *plural* **mackerel** or **mackerels** an edible sea fish which has a strong taste: ***smoked*** *mackerel*

mackintosh /ˈmæk.ɪn.tɒʃ/ [US] /-tɑːʃ/ *noun* [C] *UK OLD-FASHIONED* a MAC (= waterproof coat)

macramé /mə'krɑː.meɪ/ *noun* [U] the art of weaving pieces of string together in knots to form a decorative pattern, or something made this way: *a macramé wall-hanging*

macro- [LARGE] /mæk.rəʊ-/ [US] /-roʊ-/ *prefix* large; relating to the whole of something, rather than its parts: *macroscopic* (= large enough to be seen by the human eye) ➲Compare **micro-** SMALL.

macro [COMPUTING] /'mæk.rəʊ/ [US] /-roʊ/ *noun* [C] *plural* **macros** *SPECIALIZED* a single instruction given to a computer which produces a set of instructions for the computer to perform a particular piece of work: *I've created a macro to spell check all the files at the same time.*

macrobiotic /ˌmæk.rəʊ.baɪ'ɒt.ɪk/ [US] /-roʊ.baɪ'ɑː.t̬ɪk/ *adj* describes food that is arranged into groups according to special principles, grown without chemicals, and is thought to be very healthy: *A macrobiotic diet consists mainly of whole grains and certain kinds of vegetables.*

macrocosm /'mæk.rəʊˌkɒz.ᵊm/ [US] /-roʊˌkɑː.zᵊm/ *noun* [C] any large organized system considered as a whole, rather than as a group of smaller systems ➲Compare **microcosm**.

macroeconomics /'mæk.rəʊ-/ [US] /-roʊ-/ *noun* [U] the study of financial systems at a national level

mad [MENTALLY ILL] /mæd/ *adj* **madder** or **maddest** *OFFENSIVE* mentally ill, or unable to behave in a reasonable way; INSANE: *I think I must be **going** mad.* ○ *Do I look like some mad old woman in this hat?* ➲See also **madhouse**; **madman** ILL. ✽ NOTE: It is more polite to use the term **mentally ill** to describe someone with mental health problems. **maddened** /'mæd.ᵊnd/ *adj LITERARY* *Maddened by grief, she refused to let go of his dead body.* **madness** /'mæd.nəs/ *noun* [U] *She felt as if she were sliding into madness.*

mad [FOOLISH] /mæd/ *adj* **madder** or **maddest** *MAINLY UK INFORMAL* extremely foolish or stupid; crazy: [+ *to* infinitive] *You're mad **to** walk home alone at this time of night.* ○ *He must be mad spending all that money on a coat.* ○ *Some of the things she does are **completely** mad.* ➲See also **madcap**.
• **(as) mad as a hatter/March hare** extremely mad
madness /'mæd.nəs/ *noun* [U] stupid or dangerous behaviour: *To begin a war would be sheer madness.*

mad [HURRYING] /mæd/ *adj* [before n] hurrying or excited and not having time to think or plan: *We made a mad **dash** for the train.* ○ *I was in a mad **panic/rush** trying to get everything ready.*
madly /'mæd.li/ *adv* If you do something madly, you do it very quickly because you have little time: *I was rushing around madly tidying up the flat before they arrived.*

mad [ANGRY] /mæd/ *adj* [after v] **madder** or **maddest** *INFORMAL* very angry or annoyed: *He's always complaining and it **makes** me so mad.* ○ *MAINLY US* *Are you still mad **at** me?* ○ *MAINLY UK* *Kerry got really mad **with** Richard for not doing the washing up.* ○ *Bill's untidiness **drives** me mad.*
madden /'mæd.ᵊn/ *verb* [T] to make someone very angry or annoyed: *It maddens me to see how unfairly Jon has been treated.*
maddening /'mæd.ᵊn.ɪŋ/ *adj* making you angry: *She has a maddening habit of interrupting me when I'm talking to her.* **maddeningly** /'mæd.ᵊn.ɪŋ.li/ *adv*

mad [ENTHUSIASTIC] /mæd/ *adj INFORMAL* **be mad about *sb/sth*** to love someone or something: *He's the first real boyfriend she's had and she's mad about him.* ○ *He's mad about football.*
• **be mad for *sb/sth*** *UK INFORMAL* to want someone or something very much, or to be very interested in them: *Everyone's mad for him and I just don't see the attraction.*
• **like mad** *INFORMAL* If you do something like mad, you do it very enthusiastically, quickly or a lot: *She's been saving like mad because she wants to buy a car.*
-mad /-mæd/ *suffix UK* **car-/clothes-/sex-, etc. mad** extremely interested in cars/clothes/sex, etc: *She's sixteen and clothes-mad.*
madly /'mæd.li/ *adv* with a lot of energy and enthusiasm: *We cheered madly as the team came out onto the field.* ○ *She's madly* (= extremely) ***in love** with David.*

madam [WOMAN] /'mæd.əm/ *noun* **1** [U] a formal and polite way of speaking to a woman: [as form of address] *May I carry your cases for you, Madam?* **2 Dear Madam** the usual way of beginning a formal letter to a woman whose name you do not know **3** [S] *DISAPPROVING* a young girl who behaves like an older woman, expecting others to obey her: *She's turning into **a proper little** madam.*

madam [SEX] /'mæd.əm/ *noun* [C] a woman who is in charge of a group of prostitutes who live or work in the same house

madcap /'mæd.kæp/ *adj* [before n] *OLD-FASHIONED* describes crazy behaviour or a plan which is very foolish and unlikely to succeed: *the madcap antics of the clowns*

ˌmad 'cow disˌease *noun* [U] *UK INFORMAL* another name for BSE

made /meɪd/ *past simple and past participle of* **make**: *He was wearing a suit made **from** pure silk.* ○ *The house was made **of** wood with an iron roof.* ✽ NOTE: Do not confuse **made of** and **made from**. **Made of X** implies that the X is present in an unchanged form, so wine is made **from** grapes, not **of** grapes.
-made /-meɪd/ *suffix*: *On the bottom of the watch it said 'Swiss-made'.*
• **have (got) it made** *INFORMAL* to be certain to be successful and have a good life, often without much effort: *With his father at the head of the firm, he's got it made.*

made-to-measure /ˌmeɪd.tə'meʒ.əʳ/ [US] /-ɚ/ *adj* describes a piece of clothing that has been made specially for the person who will wear it so that it fits exactly

made-up [APPEARANCE] /ˌmeɪd'ʌp/ *adj* [after v] wearing make-up: *She's always very **heavily** made-up* (= wearing a lot of make-up). ➲See **make-up** FOR FACE.

made-up [INVENTED] /ˌmeɪd'ʌp/ *adj* [before n] describes a story or report that has been invented and is untrue: *made-up stories*

madhouse /'mæd.haʊs/ *noun* **1** [S] *INFORMAL DISAPPROVING* a place where there is a complete lack of order and control: *With four small children running around, the place is a madhouse.* ○ *He called the government's policy 'the economics of the madhouse'.* **2** [C] *OLD USE* a **mental hospital**

madman [WILD] /'mæd.mən/ /-mæn/ *noun* [C] *DISAPPROVING* a man who behaves in a very strange and uncontrolled or dangerous way: *I drove **like a** madman to get there in time.*

madman [ILL] /'mæd.mən/ /-mæn/ *noun* [C] *OLD USE OR OFFENSIVE* a man who is mentally ill

the Ma'donna *noun* Mary, the mother of Jesus Christ: *a picture of the Madonna*
Madonna /mə'dɒn.ə/ [US] /-'dɑː-/ *noun* [C] a picture or statue that represents her: *The painting depicts a Madonna and Child* (= Mary and Jesus).

madrigal /'mæd.rɪ.gᵊl/ *noun* [C] a song performed without musical instruments in which several singers sing different notes at the same time

madwoman [WILD] /'mædˌwʊm.ən/ *noun* [C] *DISAPPROVING* a woman who behaves in a very strange and uncontrolled or dangerous way

madwoman [ILL] /'mædˌwʊm.ən/ *noun* [C] *OLD USE OR OFFENSIVE* a woman who is mentally ill

maelstrom /'meɪl.strɒm/ [US] /-strəm/ *noun* **1** [C usually sing] a situation in which there is great confusion, violence and destruction: *The country is gradually being sucked into the maelstrom **of** civil war.* **2** [C] an area of water which moves with a very strong circular movement and sucks in anything that goes past

maestro /'maɪ.strəʊ/ [US] /-stroʊ/ *noun* [C] *plural* **maestros** or **maestri** a man who is very skilled at playing or CONDUCTING (= directing the performance of) music

mafia /'mæf.i.ə/ [US] /'mɑː.fi.ə/ *group noun* **1 the Mafia** a criminal organization which began in Sicily and is active in Italy and the US **2** [C] a close group of people who are involved in similar activities and who help and protect each other, sometimes to the disadvantage of others
mafioso /ˌmæf.i'əʊ.səʊ/ [US] /ˌmɑː.fi'oʊ.soʊ/ *noun* [C] *plural* **mafiosi** a member of the Mafia

magazine [BOOK] /ˌmæg.ə'ziːn/ *noun* [C] (*INFORMAL* **mag**) a type of thin book with large pages and a paper cover which contains articles and photographs and is published every week or month: *She has written articles for* *several women's magazines.* ○ *a* ***glossy*** *magazine* ○ *men's mags* ○ *a magazine rack*

magazine [GUN PART] /ˌmæg.əˈziːn/ *noun* **[C]** a part of a gun in which CARTRIDGES are stored, or a building in which explosives, weapons and supplies are kept

magenta /məˈdʒen.tə/ *adj* of a dark reddish purple colour

maggot /ˈmæg.ət/ *noun* **[C]** a creature like a very small worm which later develops into a fly and is found in decaying meat and other foods

the Magi /ðəˈmeɪ.dʒaɪ/ *plural noun* in the Bible, the three men, thought to be kings or ASTROLOGERS, who followed a star to visit Jesus Christ when he was a baby and give him presents. They are also called the Three Kings or the Three Wise Men.

magic [IMAGINARY POWER] /ˈmædʒ.ɪk/ *noun* **[U]** **1** the use of special powers to make things happen which would usually be impossible, such as in stories for children: *The group are known for their belief in witchcraft and magic.* ○ ***As if by*** *magic/****Like*** *magic, the car changes into a boat when it hits the water.* **2** the skill of performing tricks to entertain people, such as making things appear and disappear and pretending to cut someone in half: *He's a comedian who also does magic.*

magic /ˈmædʒ.ɪk/ *adj* **1** with special powers: *The witch put a magic* ***spell*** *on the prince and turned him into a frog.* ○ *I'll show you a magic* ***trick***. **2** happening in an unusual or unexpected way, or easily or quickly: *There's no magic* ***solution*** *to the problem.* ○ *There's no magic* ***formula*** *for winning – just lots of hard work.*

magical /ˈmædʒ.ɪ.kəl/ *adj* produced by or using magic: *Diamonds were once thought to have magical* ***powers***.

magically /ˈmædʒ.ɪ.kli/ *adv*

magic [SPECIAL QUALITY] /ˈmædʒ.ɪk/ *noun* **[U]** a special and exciting quality that makes something seem different from ordinary things: *Although the film was made fifty years ago, it has lost none of its magic.* ○ *No one could fail to be charmed by the magic* ***of*** *this beautiful city.*

magical /ˈmædʒ.ɪ.kəl/ *adj*: *We walked home arm-in-arm in the magical moonlight.* **magically** /ˈmædʒ.ɪ.kli/ *adv*

magic [GOOD] /ˈmædʒ.ɪk/ *exclamation* UK OLD-FASHIONED INFORMAL used when you think something is very good and you like it a lot: *"Kate's having a party on Saturday night." "Magic!"*

ˌmagic ˈcarpet *noun* **[C]** in children's stories, a special carpet that you can sit on as it flies through the air

magician /məˈdʒɪʃ.ən/ *noun* **[C]** a person who has magic powers in stories, or who performs tricks for entertainment: *Merlin was the magician in the stories of King Arthur and the Knights of the Round Table.* ○ *There'll be a magician at the kids' Christmas party.*

ˌmagic ˈwand *noun* **[C]** **1** a small stick used by people who perform tricks for entertainment: *He* ***waved*** *his magic wand and a rabbit appeared.* **2** a quick and easy solution: *She warned that she had no magic wand to solve the problem.*

ˌmagic ˈword *noun* **[C usually sing]** a word said by someone performing a trick to help it work successfully: *I'll just say the magic word and the rabbit will disappear – Abracadabra!*

• **What's the magic word?** said to a child who has not said 'please' when asking for something: *"Can I have another chocolate?" "What's the magic word?" "Please."*

magisterial /ˌmædʒ.ɪˈstɪə.ri.əl/ [US] /-ˈstɪr.i-/ *adj* FORMAL having or seeming to have complete authority: *his magisterial presence* ○ *Jenkins's magisterial biography of Gladstone*

magistrate /ˈmædʒ.ɪ.streɪt/ /-strət/ *noun* **[C]** a person who acts as a judge in a law court that deals with crimes that are not serious: *He will* ***appear before*** *the magistrates tomorrow.* ○ *Greenway appeared at Bow Street Magistrates'* ***Court*** *to face seven charges of accepting bribes.*

magistracy /ˈmædʒ.ɪ.strə.si/ *noun* **[U]** SPECIALIZED the position of being a magistrate

the magistracy *group noun* **[S]** SPECIALIZED magistrates considered as a group

magma /ˈmæg.mə/ *noun* **[U]** hot liquid rock found just below the surface of the Earth

magnanimous /mægˈnæn.ɪ.məs/ *adj* FORMAL very kind and generous towards an enemy or someone you have defeated: *Arsenal's manager was magnanimous in victory, and praised the losing team.* **magnanimously** /mægˈnæn.ɪ.mə.sli/ *adv*: *"The best man won," he said, magnanimously conceding defeat.* **magnanimity** /ˌmæg.nəˈnɪm.ɪ.ti/ [US] /-ə.t̬i/ *noun* **[U]**

magnate /ˈmæg.nət/ *noun* **[C]** a person who is very rich and successful in business or industry: *a well-known* ***shipping*** *magnate*

magnesia /mægˈniː.ʒə/ *noun* **[U]** a white substance used in stomach medicines

magnesium /mægˈniː.zi.əm/ *noun* **[U]** a silver-white metal element that burns very brightly and is used in making fireworks

magnet [OBJECT] /ˈmæg.nət/ *noun* **[C]** an object that is able both to attract iron and steel objects and also push them away

magnetic /mægˈnet.ɪk/ [US] /-ˈnet̬-/ *adj* with the power of a magnet **magnetism** /ˈmæg.nə.tɪ.zəm/ [US] /-t̬ɪ-/ *noun* **[U]**

magnetize, UK USUALLY **-ise** /ˈmæg.nə.taɪz/ *verb* **[T]** to make an object magnetic: *Each worker has to carry a magnetized plastic entry card.*

magnet [ATTRACTION] /ˈmæg.nət/ *noun* **[C]** a person, place or thing that other people feel strongly attracted to: *The United States has always acted as a magnet* ***for*** *people seeking fame and fortune.*

magnetic /mægˈnet.ɪk/ [US] /-ˈnet̬-/ *adj* describes someone whose personality attracts a lot of people

magnetism /ˈmæg.nə.tɪ.zəm/ [US] /-t̬ɪ-/ *noun* **[U]** a quality that makes someone very attractive to other people: *The actress has a personal magnetism that is rare in someone so young.*

magˌnetic ˈfield *noun* **[C]** an area around a MAGNET or something magnetic, in which its power to attract objects to itself can be felt

magˌnetic ˈhead *noun* **[C]** a **head** DEVICE

magˌnetic ˈnorth/ˈsouth *noun* **[U]** the direction towards north/south which the pointer of a COMPASS shows

magˌnetic ˈpole *noun* **[C]** a point on the Earth near **the North pole** or **the South pole** which the pointer of a COMPASS shows as north or south

magˌnetic ˈresonance ˌimaging *noun* **[U]** SPECIALIZED **MRI**

magˌnetic ˈtape *noun* **[U]** a plastic strip covered with a magnetic substance on which sound, images or computer information can be recorded

magnificent /mægˈnɪf.ɪ.sənt/ *adj* very good, beautiful or deserving to be admired: *a magnificent view* ○ *a magnificent piece of writing* ○ *They live in a magnificent Tudor house.* **magnificently** /mægˈnɪf.ɪ.sənt.li/ *adv*: *I thought she coped magnificently.* **magnificence** /mægˈnɪf.ɪ.sənts/ *noun* **[U]** *the splendour and magnificence of the pyramids*

magnify /ˈmæg.nɪ.faɪ/ *verb* **[T]** **1** to make something look larger than it is, especially by looking at it through a specially cut piece of glass: *Although our skin looks smooth, when magnified it is full of bumps and holes.* **2** DISAPPROVING to make a problem bigger and more important than it really is: *The hot summer magnified the racial tensions in the community.*

magnification /ˌmæg.nɪ.fɪˈkeɪ.ʃən/ *noun* **[U]** the process of making something look bigger than it is, for example by using a magnifying glass: *Magnification of the leaf allows us to see it in detail.* ○ *These binoculars have x10 magnification* (= they magnify 10 times).

ˈmagnifying ˌglass *noun* **[C]** a piece of curved glass which makes objects look larger than they are: *He uses a magnifying glass to read tiny print.*

magnitude /ˈmæg.nɪ.tjuːd/ [US] /-tuːd/ *noun* **[U]** the large size or importance of something: *They don't seem to grasp the magnitude* ***of the problem***.

magnolia /mægˈnəʊ.li.ə/ [US] /-ˈnoʊ-/ *noun* **[C]** a type of tree with large, usually white or pink flowers

magnum [WINE] /ˈmæg.nəm/ *noun* **[C]** 1.5 litres of wine, or a bottle containing this: *She won a magnum* ***of champagne***.

M

magnum [GUN] /ˈmæg.nəm/ *noun* [C] *TRADEMARK* a type of gun with bullets which are fired with more power than is usual for a gun of that size

ˌmagnum ˈopus *noun* [S] *FORMAL* the most important piece of work done by a writer or artist: *Picasso's Guernica is considered by many to be his magnum opus.*

magpie /ˈmæg.paɪ/ *noun* [C] **1** a bird with black and white feathers and a long tail: *Magpies are attracted to small shiny objects which they carry away to their nests.* **2** someone who likes to collect many different types of objects, or use many different styles

maharaja /ˌmɑː.həˈrɑː.dʒə/ *noun* [C] (*ALSO* **maharajah**) in the past, the male ruler of an Indian state

maharani /ˌmɑː.həˈrɑː.ni/ *noun* [C] a female MAHARAJA or the wife of a MAHARAJA

mah-jong /ˌmɑːˈdʒɒŋ/ [US] /-ˈdʒɑːŋ/ *noun* [U] (*ALSO* **mah-jongg**) a Chinese game in which players pick up and put down small painted pieces of wood or other material until they have the combination they want in order to win

mahogany /məˈhɒg.ən.i/ [US] /-ˈhɑː.gən-/ *noun* [U] a dark red-brown wood used to make furniture: *a handsome mahogany desk.*

maid [SERVANT] /meɪd/ *noun* [C] a woman who works as a servant in a hotel or in someone's home: *In the beach resort, the apartments and villas have daily maid* ***service****.* ○ *In California many illegal immigrants work as maids, nannies and gardeners.*

maid [GIRL] /meɪd/ *noun* [C] *OLD USE* a girl or young woman who is not married, or has not had sex

maiden [WOMAN] /ˈmeɪ.dən/ *noun* [C] *LITERARY* a girl or young woman: *In the story, the prince woos and wins the* ***fair*** *maiden.*

maiden [FIRST] /ˈmeɪ.dən/ *adj* [before n] of or about the first of its type: *The Titanic sank on her maiden* ***voyage****.*

ˌmaiden ˈaunt *noun* [C] *OLD-FASHIONED* an aunt who is not married and is no longer young

maidenhead /ˈmeɪ.dən.hed/ *noun* [U] *OLD USE OR LITERARY* a woman's virginity

ˈmaiden ˌname *noun* [C] A woman's maiden name is the family name she has before she gets married.

ˌmaiden (ˈover) *noun* [C] an OVER in cricket in which no runs are scored

ˌmaiden ˈspeech *noun* [C] the first formal speech made by a British Member of Parliament in the House of Commons or by a member of the House of Lords

ˌmaid of ˈhonour *noun* [C] *MAINLY US* the most important BRIDESMAID at a marriage ceremony

mail [POST] /meɪl/ *noun* [S or U] **1** (*MAINLY UK* **post**) the letters and parcels which are transported and delivered by post, or the postal system itself: *She spent the morning reading and answering her mail.* ○ *All of our customers will be contacted* ***by*** *mail.* ○ *The book came* ***in*** *yesterday's mail.* ○ *Some strange things get sent* ***through the*** *mail.* **2** **Mail** used in the name of some newspapers: *the Daily Mail* ○ *the Hull Mail*

mail *MAINLY US* /meɪl/ *verb* [T] (*MAINLY UK* **post**) to send a letter or parcel or email something: *She mailed it last week but it still hasn't arrived.* ○ [+ two objects] *I promised to mail him the article/mail the article* ***to*** *him.*

mail [COVERING] /meɪl/ *noun* [U] ➲See **chain mail**.

mailbag /ˈmeɪl.bæg/ *noun* **1** [C] (*UK ALSO* **postbag**) a large strong bag used by the post office for transporting and carrying letters and parcels **2** [C usually sing] the number of letters received at one time or on one subject: *Since the controversial programme was broadcast, the BBC's mailbag has been bulging.*

mailbox /ˈmeɪl.bɒks/ [US] /-bɑːks/ *noun* [C] in the US, a box outside a person's house where letters are delivered, or a POSTBOX

ˈmail ˌcarrier *noun* [C] (*ALSO* **letter carrier**) *US FOR* **postman**

Mailgram /ˈmeɪl.græm/ *noun* [C] *US TRADEMARK FOR* **Telemessage**

ˈmailing ˌlist *noun* [C usually sing] a list of names and addresses kept by an organization so that it can send information and advertisements to the people on the list: *I asked to be* ***put on*** *their mailing list.*

mailman /ˈmeɪl.mæn/ *noun* [C] (*ALSO* **mail carrier**) *US FOR* **postman**

ˈmail ˌorder *noun* [U] a way of buying goods in which you choose what you want, usually from a CATALOGUE, and it is sent to you: *I often buy clothes* ***by*** *mail order.* ○ *a mail-order catalogue/company*

mailshot *MAINLY UK* /ˈmeɪl.ʃɒt/ [US] /-ʃɑːt/ *noun* [C] (*US USUALLY* **mass mailing**) the posting of advertising or similar material to a lot of people at one time

ˈmail ˌslot *US noun* [C] (*UK* **letterbox**) a rectangular hole in the door or in a wall near the entrance of a house or other building, through which letters, etc. are delivered

maim /meɪm/ *verb* [I or T] to injure a person so severely that a part of their body will no longer work as it should: *Many children have been maimed for life by these bombs.*

main [MOST IMPORTANT] /meɪn/ *adj* [before n] larger, more important or more influential than others of the same type: *The main* ***thing*** *is not to worry.* ○ *One of the main* ***reasons*** *I came to England was to study the language.* ○ *You'll find the main* ***points*** *of my proposal in the report.* ○ *Our main* ***aim/objective*** *is to improve the company's productivity.* ○ *The main* ***problem*** *in the health service is lack of resources.* ○ *My main* ***concern*** *about moving to London is the cost of housing.*

main [PIPE] /meɪn/ *noun* [C] a large pipe which carries water or gas, or a wire carrying electricity, from one place to another, to which a house can be connected: *a* ***gas*** *main* ○ *The severe cold caused a* ***water*** *main to burst and flood the street.*

mains /meɪnz/ *plural noun UK* **1** the system of pipes or wires which carry water or electricity into a house, or the pipes which carry SEWAGE away from a house: *The house isn't* ***on*** *the mains.* ○ *They bought a house with no mains supply.* ○ *mains electricity* **2 the mains** the place at which outside pipes or wires carrying water, electricity, etc. connect with the system inside a house or building: *Switch off the electricity at the mains before starting work.*

main [MOSTLY] /meɪn/ *noun* **in the main** generally or mostly: *Her friends are teachers in the main.*

ˈmain ˌcourse *noun* [C] the largest or most important part of a meal in which there are different parts served separately: *I had salmon for my main course.*

ˌmain ˈdrag *noun* [C usually sing] *US INFORMAL* the largest or most important road in a town: *There's a great little restaurant just off the main drag.*

mainframe /ˈmeɪn.freɪm/ *noun* [C] *SPECIALIZED* a very large powerful computer with a lot of memory which many people can use at the same time

the mainland /ˈmeɪn.lænd/ *noun* [S] the main part of a country or continent, not including the islands around it: *He lives on an island off Scotland, but travels to the mainland once a month.* ○ *mainland Europe*

mainline [DRUGS] /ˈmeɪn.laɪn/ *verb* [I or T] *INFORMAL* to inject drugs directly into the blood: *Several of her friends were mainlining heroin.* ○ *By now she was mainlining.*

ˌmain ˈline [RAILWAY] *noun* [C] an important railway route between large towns or cities: *the main line between Belfast and Dublin* ○ *Three main line railway stations were closed because of bomb threats.*

mainly /ˈmeɪn.li/ *adv* usually or to a large degree: *I mainly go to bed around midnight.* ○ *The group is made up of mainly young people.* ○ *They argued that the tax will mainly benefit the rich.*

ˌmain ˈroad *noun* [C] a large road which goes from one town to another: *Stick to the main roads and you won't get lost.* ○ *They live on the main road out of town.*

mainspring /ˈmeɪn.sprɪŋ/ *noun* [C usually sing] *FORMAL* the most important reason for something; the thing that makes something else happen: *Work was* ***the*** *mainspring* ***of*** *his life.*

mainstay /ˈmeɪn.steɪ/ *noun* **the mainstay of sth** the most important part of something, providing support for everything else: *Cattle farming is the mainstay of the country's ecomony.* ○ *The white blouse will be the mainstay of your wardrobe this summer.*

the mainstream *noun* [S] the way of life or set of beliefs accepted by most people: *The new law should*

M

allow more disabled people to enter the mainstream **of American life. mainstream** /'meɪn.striːm/ adj: This is the director's first mainstream Hollywood film.

'main ˌstreet noun [C] US FOR **high street**

maintain CONTINUE TO HAVE /meɪnˈteɪn/ verb [T] to continue to have; to keep in existence, or not allow to become less: *The army has been brought in to maintain order in the region.* ○ *We have standards to maintain.* ○ *Despite living in different countries, the two families have maintained close links.* ○ *The film has maintained its position as the critics' favourite for another year.* **maintenance** /'meɪn.tɪ.nənts/ noun [U] the maintenance of living standards

maintain PRESERVE /meɪnˈteɪn/ verb [T] to keep a road, machine, building, etc. in good condition: *A large house costs a lot to maintain.* ○ *The roads around the town have been very poorly maintained.* **maintenance** /'meɪn.tɪ.nənts/ noun [U] *Old houses need a lot of maintenance.* ○ *There are thorough maintenance checks on each plane before take-off.* ○ *The magazine offers tips on cutting your house maintenance costs.*

maintain PROVIDE /meɪnˈteɪn/ verb [T] to provide someone with food and whatever is necessary for them to live on: *They barely earn enough to maintain themselves and their four children.* **maintenance** /'meɪn.tɪ.nənts/ noun [U] money that a person must pay regularly by law in order to support their child or former marriage partner after a DIVORCE (= official end to a marriage): *He refused to **pay** maintenance for his three children.*

maintain EXPRESS /meɪnˈteɪn/ verb [T] to express firmly your belief that something is true: *Throughout his prison sentence Dunn has always maintained his innocence.* ○ [+ that] *He maintains **that** he has never seen the woman before.*

ˌmaintenance ˌorder noun [C] UK an order made by a court of law that a person must pay maintenance

ˌmain 'verb noun [C] in a clause, the verb that contains the meaning, compared with any AUXILIARY VERBS that go with it: *In 'I should have been studying', 'studying' is the main verb.*

maisonette /ˌmeɪ.zəˈnet/ noun [C] UK a small apartment on two levels which is part of a larger building but has its own entrance

maitre d' (hotel) /ˌmet.rəˈdiː/ US /ˌmeɪ.tʃ ə-/ noun [C] FORMAL the person in charge of a restaurant or of the people who bring food to your table in a restaurant

maize UK /meɪz/ noun [U] (US **corn**) a tall plant grown in many parts of the world for its yellow seeds which are eaten as food, made into flour or fed to animals

majestic /məˈdʒes.tɪk/ adj beautiful, powerful or causing great admiration and respect: *The majestic Montana scenery will leave you breathless.* **majestically** /məˈdʒes.tɪ.kli/ adv: *The white cliffs rise majestically from the sea.*

majesty /'mædʒ.ə.sti/ noun [U] If something has majesty, it causes admiration and respect for its beauty: *This music has majesty, power and passion.* ○ *The photograph captures the sunset in all its majesty.*

Majesty /'mædʒ.ə.sti/ noun [C] the title used to speak to or about a king or queen: *I was invited to tea with **Her Majesty** the Queen.* ○ **their** *Majesties, the King and Queen of Spain* ○ [as form of address] *The performance begins at 8.30, **(Your)** Majesty.* ⊃See also **majesty** at **majestic**.

major IMPORTANT /'meɪ.dʒəʳ/ US /-dʒɚ/ adj [before n] more important, bigger or more serious than others of the same type: *All of her major plays have been translated into English.* ○ *Sugar is a major cause of tooth decay.* ○ *There are two problems with this situation, one major, one minor.* ○ *Citrus fruits are a major source of vitamin C.* ○ *There has been a major change in attitudes recently.* ○ *The United States is a major influence in the United Nations.* ⊃Compare **minor** UNIMPORTANT.

majorly /'meɪ.dʒə.li/ US /-dʒɚ-/ adv MAINLY US SLANG very or extremely: *Have you seen Chrissie's new leather jacket? It's majorly cool.*

major OFFICER /'meɪ.dʒəʳ/ US /-dʒɚ/ noun [C] **1** an officer of middle rank in the British, US and many other armed forces such as the US Air Force: *Her father was a major*

in the Scots Guards. ○ *I met Major Jones last year.* ○ [as form of address] *Thank you, Major Jones.* **2** the rank between CAPTAIN and LIEUTENANT COLONEL

major SPECIAL SUBJECT /'meɪ.dʒəʳ/ US /-dʒɚ/ noun [C] US the most important subject that a college or university student is studying, or the student himself or herself: *What is your major, English or French?* ○ *She was a philosophy major at an Ivy League college.*

major in *sth* verb US to study something as your main subject at university: *She majored in philosophy at Harvard.*

major MUSIC /'meɪ.dʒəʳ/ US /-dʒɚ/ adj [after n] SPECIALIZED (of music) based on a scale in which there is a whole tone between the second and third notes and a half tone between the third and fourth notes: *the key of C major* ○ *a concerto in A major* ⊃Compare **minor** MUSIC.

majordomo /ˌmeɪ.dʒəˈdəʊ.məʊ/ US /-dʒɚˈdoʊ.moʊ/ noun [C] plural **majordomos 1** OLD USE the most important servant in a house, in charge of the other servants **2** US a person whose job is to make arrangements or organize things for other people: *Can you ask the majordomo in the hotel to get tickets for the tennis match?*

majorette /ˌmeɪ.dʒəˈret/ US /-dʒɚˈret/ noun [C] (ALSO **drum majorette**) a young woman or girl who wears a uniform and makes a pattern of movements with a BATON (= stick) by spinning it and throwing it into the air, as part of a group of girls who do this or as the leader of a musical group

major-general /ˌmeɪ.dʒəˈdʒen.ʳr.ʳl/ US /-dʒɚˈdʒen.ɚ-/ noun [C] an officer of high rank in the British Army, US Army and many other armed forces such as the US Air Force

majority NUMBER /məˈdʒɒr.ə.ti/ US /-ˈdʒɑː.rə.ti/ noun **1** [S] the larger number or part of something: *The majority **of** the employees have university degrees.* ○ *A large majority **of** people approve of the death sentence.* ○ *In Britain women are **in the/a** majority.* ⊃Compare **minority** SMALL PART. **2** [C] in an election, the difference in the number of votes between the winning person or group and the one that comes second: *The Socialists won by a **narrow/large** majority.*

majority AGE /məˈdʒɒr.ə.ti/ US /-ˈdʒɑː.rə.ti/ noun [U] SPECIALIZED the age when you legally become an adult: *the **age of** majority* ○ *She will inherit her father's estate when she **reaches** her majority.*

maˌjority 'rule noun [U] the system of giving the largest group in a particular place or area the power to make decisions for everyone: *Government by majority rule can be a threat to minority rights.*

make PRODUCE /meɪk/ verb [T] made, made **1** to produce something, often using a particular substance or material: *Shall I make some coffee?* ○ *He'd made a chocolate cake.* ○ *She makes all her own clothes.* ○ [+ two objects] *He made us some coffee./He made some coffee **for** us.* ○ *The pot is made **to** withstand high temperatures.* ○ *He works for a company that makes garden furniture.* ○ *The label on the box said 'made in Taiwan'.* ○ *Butter is made **out of/from** milk.* ○ *earrings made **of** gold* ○ *Her new trainer has promised to make an Olympic athlete of her.* ⊃See Note **do or make?** at **do** PERFORM. **2** To make a film or television programme is to DIRECT, PRODUCE it, or act in it: *John Huston made some great films.* ○ *The film was made by Goldcrest Productions.* ○ *So why didn't Garbo make any films after 1941?*

● **make a day/night/evening/weekend of it** to lengthen an activity or combine a series of activities so that they last for the whole of that particular period of time: *Let's make an evening of it and catch the last train home.* ○ *We don't get out often so we thought we'd make a day of it.*

● **make do** to manage to live without things that you would like to have or with things of a worse quality than you would like: *We didn't have cupboards so we made do **with** boxes.*

● **make or break** *sth* to make something a success or a failure: *Recognition by this organization can make or break a career.*

make-or-break /ˌmeɪk.ɔːˈbreɪk/ US /-ɔːr-/ adj describes a situation that will bring great success or complete failure

• **make time** to make certain you have some time when you are not busy in order to do something you think you should do: *It's important to make time to read to your children.* ○ *In a relationship you have to make time for each other.*

• **make it with sb** *US INFORMAL* to have sex with someone

• **what sb is (really) made of** how strong, clever or brave someone is: *The 1500 metres race next week will be a chance for her to show what she's made of.*

• **be made of money** to be rich: *No you can't have another bike – I'm not made of money!*

make /meɪk/ *noun* [C] a type of product or the name of the company which made it: *There's a new make of shampoo on the market.* ○ *What make is your stereo?*

• **be on the make** *DISAPPROVING* to be trying very hard to obtain more money and power

maker /'meɪ.kəʳ/ ⓤⓢ /-kɚ/ *noun* [C] **1** the people or company that make something: *They're the biggest maker of fast-food products in the UK.* ○ *The makers of the film will want to see a decent return on their investment.* ⊃See also **bookmaker**; **holidaymaker**; **home-maker**; **icemaker**; **kingmaker**; **matchmaker**; **pace-maker** RUNNER; **pacemaker** DEVICE; **peacemaker**; **trouble-maker**. **2** your **Maker** God: *HUMOROUS He's gone to meet his Maker* (= He has died).

-maker /-meɪ.kəʳ/ ⓤⓢ /-kɚ/ *suffix* a person or machine which makes the stated thing: *a film-maker* ○ *a dress-maker* ○ *a watchmaker* ○ *car-makers* ○ *policy-makers* ○ *a coffee/tea-maker* ○ *an ice-maker*

making /'meɪ.kɪŋ/ *noun* [U] the activity or process of producing something: *the art of film making* ○ *There's an article on the making of the series.*

• **of your own making** your own fault: *Any problems she has with that child are of her own making.*

• **be an actor/athlete/chef, etc. in the making** to have the ability and interest to become an actor/athlete, etc. in the future

• **be the making of sb** If something is the making of someone, it develops in them good qualities and characteristics which might not have developed without it: *Five years in the army – that'll be the making of him!*

• **in the making** If something was a period of time in the making, it took that amount of time to make: *The film was several years in the making.*

• **have (all) the makings of sth** to seem likely to develop into something: *She has the makings of a great violinist.*

make CAUSE /meɪk/ *verb* [T] **made, made** to cause something: *The kids made such a mess in the kitchen.* ○ *The bullet made a hole right through his chest.* ○ *The wind is making my eyes water.* ○ *[+ infinitive without to] What made you change your mind?* ○ *Just seeing Woody Allen's face is enough to make me laugh.* ○ *The photograph makes me look horribly fat and about sixty years old!*

make CAUSE TO BE /meɪk/ *verb* [T] **made, made** to cause to be, to become or to appear as: *[+ n] It's the good weather that makes Spain such a popular tourist destination.* ○ *[R + past participle] She had to shout to make herself heard above the sound of the music.* ○ *I can make myself understood in French, but I'm not fluent.* ○ *They went up to the Ambassador and made themselves known (to her).* ○ *[+ adj] The company accounts have not yet been made public.* ○ *The book's advertised as "navigation made easy".* ○ *The President has made Lloyd Bentsen his Secretary of the Treasury.* ○ *I'll have a steak – no, make that chicken.*

• **make certain/sure** to take action so that you are certain that something happens, is true, etc: *I'll just make sure I've turned the oven off.* ○ *Make certain (that) we have enough drink for the party.* ○ *Make sure you're home by midnight.* ○ *Jones made sure of his place in the side with three goals.* ○ *I think I locked the door but I'll go back and check just to make sure.*

make PERFORM /meɪk/ *verb* [T] **made, made 1** to perform an action: *I must make a telephone call.* ○ *Somebody has made a donation of £1 million to Oxfam.* ○ *I need to make a trip to the shops.* ○ *On foot they could only make about 20 miles a day.* ○ *We must make a decision by tomorrow.* ○ *You're not making any effort.* ○ *Someone has made a mistake/an error.* ○ *We're making good progress.* ○ *She has made a request for a new car.* ○ *We made an offer of £150 000 for the house.* ○ *She made a short*

speech. ○ *Shall we make a start on the work?* ○ *Can I make a suggestion?* ○ *We made good time getting across town.* ○ *There's a drunk at the door making trouble.* **2 make room/space/way** If you make room/space/way for something or someone, you move or move other things, so that there is space for them.

• **make to do sth** *FORMAL* If you make to do something, you are just going to do it when something interrupts you: *I made to leave but she called me back.*

• **make as if to do sth** If you make as if to do something, you seem as if that is what you are going to do: *He made as if to speak.*

• **make like** *US* to pretend: *She made like she was about to leave, but then stayed for hours.* ○ *Stop making like you know everything, OK?*

make FORCE /meɪk/ *verb* **1 make sb do sth** to force someone or something to do something: *You can't make him go if he doesn't want to.* ○ *The vet put something down the dog's throat to make it vomit.* **2 be made to do sth** to be forced to do something: *The prisoners are made to dig holes and fill them in again.*

COMMON LEARNER ERROR

make

Remember that if you use **make** with the meaning 'cause something' or 'force someone to do something' then you need to use the pattern: 'make + object + infinitive without 'to''.

They made him clean the house.
~~They made him to clean the house.~~

The exception to this rule is when **make** is in the passive, when you must use 'to' with the infinitive.

The prisoners were made to clean out their cells.

---

make BE OR BECOME /meɪk/ *verb* [L only + n] **made, made 1** to be or become something, usually by having the necessary characteristics: *I don't think he will ever make a (good) lawyer.* ○ *He's a competent enough officer, but I doubt he'll ever make general.* ○ *It's a story that would make a great film.* ○ *She decided the back room would make a good study.* ○ *Champagne and caviar make a wonderful combination.* ○ *The story makes fascinating reading.* **2** If people or things make a particular pattern, they are arranged in that way: *Let's make a circle.* ○ *Those seven bright stars make the shape of a saucepan.*

make TOTAL /meɪk/ *verb* [L only + n; T] **made, made** to produce a total when added together: *12 and 12 make 24.* ○ *Today's earthquake makes five since the beginning of the year.* ○ *[+ obj + n] I've got 29 different teapots in my collection – if I buy this one that'll make it 30.*

make CALCULATE /meɪk/ *verb* [T + obj + n] **made, made** to calculate as: *How much do you make the total?* ○ *I make the answer (to be) 105.6.* ○ *What do you make the time?/ What time do you make it?*

make EARN/GET /meɪk/ *verb* [T] **made, made** to earn or get: *She makes $100 000 a year as a doctor.* ○ *How do you make a living as a painter?* ○ *The company has made huge profits/losses.* ○ *He's very good at making new friends.*

make ARRIVE /meɪk/ *verb* [T] **made, made** *INFORMAL* to arrive at or reach, especially successfully: *She made it to the airport just in time to catch her plane.* ○ *He made it to the bed and then collapsed.* ○ *Could you make a meeting at 8 am?/Could you make 8 am for the meeting?*

• **make it (to the top)** to be very successful: *She's very ambitious but I doubt she'll ever make it to the top.*

make PERFECT /meɪk/ *verb* [T] **made, made** *INFORMAL* to cause to be perfect: *Those little bows round the neck really make the dress!*

PHRASAL VERBS WITH make   ▼

▲ **make for somewhere/sth** GO TOWARDS *phrasal verb* to go in the direction of a place or thing: *They made for the centre of town.* ⊃See also **make towards**.

▲ **make for sth** MAKE POSSIBLE *phrasal verb* to result in or make possible: *Having faster computers would make for a more efficient system.*

▲ **make** *sth* **into** *sth* *phrasal verb* to change something into something else: *They've made the spare room into an office.*

▲ **make of** *sth/sb* OPINION *phrasal verb* If you ask someone what they make of someone or something, you want to know their opinion about that person or thing, often because there is something strange about them: *Can you make anything of this information?* ○ *What do you make of the new boss?* ○ *I don't know what to make of it. Even the police seem baffled.*

▲ **make** *sth* **of** *sth* VALUE *phrasal verb* **make enough/ much/more, etc. of** *sth* to give a particular level of value or importance to something: *You should make more of your IT skills on the application form.* ○ *I think we make too much of the benefits of Western society.* ⊃See also **make light of** at **light** NOT SERIOUS.

▲ **make much/a lot of** *sb* INFORMAL to treat someone very well: *His mother used to make much of him when he went home for holidays.*

● **Do you want to make something/anything of it?** INFORMAL something that you say to someone as a way of threatening or offering to fight them when they disagree with you

▲ **make off** *phrasal verb* INFORMAL to leave quickly, usually in order to escape: *The burglars made off before the police arrived.*

▲ **make off with** *sth* *phrasal verb* INFORMAL to steal something: *Somebody broke into the shop and made off with several TVs and videos.*

▲ **make** *sth/sb* **out** UNDERSTAND *phrasal verb* [M] to see, hear or understand something or someone with difficulty: *The numbers are too small – I can't make them out at all.* ○ *I can't make out your writing.* ○ *She's a strange person – I can't make her out at all.* ○ [+ question word] *Nobody can make out why you should have been attacked.*

▲ **make** *sth* **out** WRITE *phrasal verb* [M] to write all the necessary information on an official document: *I made a cheque out for £20 to 'Henry's Supermarket'.*

▲ **make out** *sth* CLAIM *phrasal verb* INFORMAL to claim, usually falsely, that something is true: [R + to infinitive] *He made himself out to be a millionaire.* ○ [(+ to infinitive)] *The British weather is not always as bad as it is made out (to be).* ○ [+ (that)] *He made out (that) he had been living in Paris all year.*

▲ **make out** SUCCEED *phrasal verb* US INFORMAL to deal with a situation, usually in a successful way: *How is Frances making out in her new job?* ○ *The business made out better than expected in 1992 and profits were slightly up.*

▲ **make out** HAVE SEX *phrasal verb* US INFORMAL to kiss and touch in a sexual way, or to succeed in having sex with someone: *Boys at that age are only interested in making out with girls.*

▲ **make** *sth* **over to** *sb* *phrasal verb* [M] to give something, such as money or land, to someone so that they legally own it: *Just before her death, she had made over $100 000 to her new husband.*

▲ **make towards** *sth/sb* *phrasal verb* MAINLY UK to go in the direction of something or someone: *He made towards the door, but stopped and turned to face me.* ⊃See also **make for** GO TOWARDS.

▲ **make** *sth* **up** INVENT *phrasal verb* [M] to invent something, such as an excuse or a story, often in order to deceive: *I made up an excuse about having to look after the kids.* ○ *My dad was always really good at making up stories.*

● **make** *sth* **up as you go along** to invent a story or a tune without having thought before about how it will end

▲ **make** *sth* **up** PREPARE *phrasal verb* [M] **1** to prepare or arrange something by putting different things together: *Could you make up a list of all the things that need to be done?* ○ *He asked the man behind the counter to make up a box with a mixed selection of chocolates.* ○ *The maid will make up your room later.* **2** SPECIALIZED to produce or prepare something from cloth: *We could use the rest of the material to make up some curtains.* **3** SPECIALIZED If you make up a page, book or newspaper, you arrange the text and pictures in the form in which they will be printed. **4** If you make up a bed for someone, you put

sheets and covers on a bed so that they have a place to sleep in your home. **5** UK If you make up a fire, you prepare it or put more wood or coal on it when it is burning.

▲ **make** *sth* **up** COMPLETE *phrasal verb* [M] to make an amount of something complete or correct: *I have £20 000 and I need £25 000 but my parents have promised to make up the difference.* ○ UK *I suspect we were only invited to make up numbers* (= to provide enough people).

▲ **make** *sth* **up** REPLACE *phrasal verb* [M] to reduce or replace something, usually an amount of time or work, that has been lost: *We're hoping to make up time on the return journey by not stopping at night.* ○ *You'll have to make up the work you've missed while you were away.*

● **make up for lost time** to enjoy an experience as much as possible because you did not have the opportunity to do it earlier in life: *I didn't travel much in my twenties but I'm certainly making up for lost time now.*

▲ **make** *(sb/sth)* **up** USE MAKE-UP *phrasal verb* [M] to put make-up on your face, or on another person's face, to improve or change its appearance: *She takes ages to make up in the mornings.* ○ *For the film, they made him up as an Indian.*

▲ **make up** *sth* FORM *phrasal verb* to form a particular thing, amount or number as a whole: *Road accident victims make up almost a quarter of the hospital's patients.* ○ *The book is made up of a number of different articles.*

▲ **make up** BE FRIENDLY *phrasal verb* (ALSO **make it up**) to forgive someone and be friendly with them again after an argument or disagreement: *They kissed and made up, as usual.* ○ *We often quarrel but we always make it up soon after.*

● **make it up to** *sb* to do something good for someone you have upset, in order to become friends with them again: *I'm sorry we can't take you with us, but I promise I'll make it up to you somehow.*

▲ **make up for** *sth* *phrasal verb* to take the place of something lost or damaged or to COMPENSATE for something bad with something good: *No amount of money can make up for the death of a child.* ○ *This year's good harvest will make up for last year's bad one.* ○ [+ v-ing] *He bought me dinner to make up for being so late the day before.*

▲ **make up to** *sb* *phrasal verb* UK DISAPPROVING to be too friendly to someone or to praise them in order to get advantages: *Have you seen the disgusting way she makes up to the boss?*

▲ **make with** *sth* *phrasal verb* US OLD-FASHIONED SLANG to give, bring or do something: *He pointed a gun and said "Make with the money bags, baby!"*

make-believe /ˈmeɪk.bɪˌliːv/ *noun* [U] DISAPPROVING believing in things that you want to believe because they are easy or exciting, but which are not real: *The ideal of a perfectly fair society is just make-believe.* ○ *He lives in a world of make-believe/make-believe world.*

makeover /ˈmeɪkˌəʊ.vəʳ/ US /-ˌoʊ.vɚ/ *noun* [C] a set of changes that are intended to make a person or place more attractive: *One of the prizes was a makeover at a top beauty salon.*

makeshift /ˈmeɪk.ʃɪft/ *adj* temporary and of low quality, but used because of a sudden need: *Thousands of refugees are living in makeshift camps.*

make-up FOR FACE /ˈmeɪk.ʌp/ *noun* [U] coloured substances used on your face to improve or change your appearance: *I put on a little eye make-up.* ○ *She wears a lot of make-up.*

make-up PARTS /ˈmeɪk.ʌp/ *noun* [U] The make-up of something or someone is the combination of things that form it: *They argue that the membership of the Council does not reflect the racial make-up of the city.* ○ *Organizational ability is not one of the most obvious parts of his make-up.*

makeweight /ˈmeɪk.weɪt/ *noun* [C] something or someone, without much value of its own, that is added so that there is the correct amount or number: *She may be the youngest member of the team, but she's no makeweight.*

mal- /mæl-/ *prefix* FORMAL badly or wrongly: *The disease rubella can cause pregnant women to have malformed babies.*

malachite /ˈmæl.ə.kaɪt/ *noun* [U] a green stone used in jewellery and decoration

maladjusted /ˌmæl.əˈdʒʌs.tɪd/ *adj* describes a person, usually a child, who has been raised in a way that does not prepare them well for the demands of life, which often leads to problems with behaviour in the future: *a residential school for disturbed and maladjusted children* **maladjustment** /ˌmæl.əˈdʒʌst.mənt/ *noun* [U] *anti-social behaviour and other signs of maladjustment*

maladministration /ˌmæl.ədˌmɪn.ɪˈstreɪ.ʃən/ *noun* [U] *FORMAL* lack of care, judgment or honesty in the management of something: *Thousands of refugees are dying because of the incompetence and maladministration of local officials.*

maladroit /ˌmæl.əˈdrɔɪt/ *adj FORMAL* awkward in movement or unskilled in behaviour or action: *She can be a little maladroit in social situations.* **maladroitly** /ˌmæl.əˈdrɔɪt.li/ *adv* **maladroitness** /ˌmæl.əˈdrɔɪt.nəs/ *noun* [U]

malady /ˈmæl.ə.di/ *noun* [C] *FORMAL* **1** a disease: *All the rose bushes seem to be suffering from the same mysterious malady.* **2** a problem within a system or organization: *Apathy is one of the maladies of modern society.*

malaise /mælˈeɪz/ *noun* [S or U] *FORMAL* a general feeling of bad health or lack of energy, or an uncomfortable feeling that something is wrong, especially with society, and a lack of ability to change the situation: *They claim it is a symptom of a deeper and more general malaise in society.* ○ *We were discussing the roots of the current* ***economic*** *malaise.*

malapropism /ˈmæl.ə.prɒp.ɪ.zəm/ [US] /-prɑː.pɪ-/ *noun* [C] the wrong use of one word instead of another word because they sound similar to each other, and which is amusing as a result

malaria /məˈleə.ri.ə/ [US] /-ˈler.i-/ *noun* [U] a disease that you can get from the bite of a particular type of MOSQUITO (= a small flying insect), which causes periods of fever and makes you feel very cold and shake. It is common in many hotter parts of the world.

malarkey /məˈlɑː.ki/ [US] /-ˈlɑːr-/ *noun* [U] *INFORMAL* silly behaviour or nonsense: *I like the socializing but I can't be bothered with the dressing up and* ***all that*** *malarkey.*

malcontent /ˈmæl.kən.tent/ *noun* [C] *LITERARY* a person who is not satisfied with the way things are, and who complains a lot and is unreasonable and difficult to deal with

male [SEX] /meɪl/ *adj* describes men or boys, or the sex that FERTILIZES eggs, and does not produce babies or eggs itself: *male students* ○ *a male giraffe* ○ *IT is very much a male-dominated industry.* ○ *What percentage of the adult male population is unemployed?* ○ *The male parts of the flower are the stamens and the anthers.* ➲See also **masculine** MALE. Compare **female** SEX. **male** /meɪl/ *noun* [C] *The male of the species is less aggressive.* ○ *Among the bodies are two unidentified British males.* **maleness** /ˈmeɪl.nəs/ *noun* [U]

male [CONNECTING PART] /meɪl/ *adj SPECIALIZED* describes a piece of equipment that has a part which sticks out and can be fitted into a hollow part in another piece of equipment: *a male plug* ➲Compare **female** CONNECTING PART.

ˌmale ˈbonding *noun* [U] the forming of close friendships between men

ˌmale ˌchauvinist (ˈpig) *noun* [C] *DISAPPROVING* a man who believes that women are naturally less important, intelligent or able than men, and so does not treat men and women equally **ˌmale ˈchauvinism** *noun* [U] *a bastion of male chauvinism*

malefactor /ˈmæl.ɪ.fæk.təʳ/ [US] /-tɚ/ *noun* [C] *FORMAL* a person who does bad or illegal things

ˌmale ˈmenopause *noun* [U] *MAINLY HUMOROUS* a state of mind experienced by some men about 40 or 50 years old in which they start to worry that they are not successful enough, and start to want suddenly to find a new job or a new partner

ˌmale ˈorgan *noun* [C] *POLITE PHRASE FOR* **penis**

malevolent /məˈlev.əl.ənt/ *adj LITERARY* causing or wanting to cause harm or evil: *The central character is a malevolent witch out for revenge.* ○ *I could feel his malevolent gaze as I walked away.* **malevolently** /məˈlev.əl.ənt.li/ *adv* **malevolence** /məˈlev.əl.ənts/ *noun* [U] *It was an act of great malevolence.*

malfeasance /mælˈfiː.zənts/ *noun* [U] *LEGAL* an example of dishonest and illegal behaviour, especially by a person in authority: *Several cases of malpractice and malfeasance in the financial world are currently being investigated.*

malformation /ˌmæl.fəˈmeɪ.ʃən/ [US] /-fɚ-/ *noun* [C or U] the condition of being wrongly formed, or a part of something, such as part of the body, that is wrongly formed: *Exposure to radiation can lead to malformation of the embryo.* ○ *She was born critically ill with a severe malformation of the heart.* **malformed** /ˌmælˈfɔːmd/ [US] /-fɔːrmd/ *adj*

malfunction /ˌmælˈfʌŋk.ʃən/ *verb* [I] *SLIGHTLY FORMAL* to fail to work or operate correctly **malfunction** /ˌmælˈfʌŋk.ʃən/ *noun* [C] *Shortly before the crash the pilot had reported a malfunction of the aircraft's navigation system.*

malice /ˈmæl.ɪs/ *noun* [U] the wish to harm or upset other people: *There certainly wasn't any malice in her comments.* ○ *FORMAL I* ***bear*** *him no malice* (= do not want to harm or upset him).

• **with malice aforethought** *LEGAL* To illegally harm someone with malice aforethought is to have thought about it and planned it before acting.

malicious /məˈlɪʃ.əs/ *adj* intended to harm or upset other people: *malicious gossip* ○ *a malicious look in his eyes* ○ *He complained that he'd been receiving malicious telephone calls.* ○ *LEGAL He was charged with malicious* ***wounding****.* **maliciously** /məˈlɪʃ.ə.sli/ *adv*

malign /məˈlaɪn/ *adj FORMAL* causing or intending to cause harm or evil: *Foreign domination had a malign* ***influence*** *on local politics.* ○ *She describes pornography as 'a malign industry'.* **malignity** /məˈlɪg.nə.ti/ [US] /-t̬i/ *noun* [U]

malign /məˈlaɪn/ *verb* [T often passive] to say false and unpleasant things about someone or to unfairly criticize them: *She has recently been maligned in the gossip columns of several newspapers.* ○ ***Much****-maligned for their derivative style, the band are nevertheless enduringly popular.*

malignant /məˈlɪg.nənt/ *adj* **1** describes a disease or a diseased growth that is likely to get uncontrollably worse and lead to death: *The process by which malignant cancer cells multiply isn't fully understood.* ○ *Is the tumour malignant or benign?* ➲Compare **benign**. **2** *FORMAL* evil: having a strong desire to do harm: *He developed a malignant hatred for the land of his birth.* **malignantly** /məˈlɪg.nənt.li/ *adv* **malignancy** /məˈlɪg.nənt.si/ *noun* [C or U] *SPECIALIZED The malignancy of these tumours makes them difficult to treat.* ○ *Tests revealed a malignancy that had to be removed.*

malinger /məˈlɪŋ.gəʳ/ [US] /-gɚ/ *verb* [I] *DISAPPROVING* to pretend to be ill in order to avoid having to work: *And is he really ill or just malingering?* **malingerer** /məˈlɪŋ.gər.əʳ/ [US] /-gɚ.ɚ/ *noun* [C] *I'm sure she thinks I'm a malingerer.*

mall /mɔːl/ [US] /mɑːl/ *noun* [C] (*ALSO* **shopping mall**) a large, usually enclosed, shopping area where cars are not allowed: *There are plans to build a new mall in the middle of town.*

mallard /ˈmæl.ɑːd/ [US] /-ɑːrd/ *noun* [C] *plural* **mallard** or **mallards** a wild duck that is common in Europe and North America: *The male mallard has a green head and reddish-brown chest.*

malleable /ˈmæl.i.ə.bl̩/ *adj* **1** describes a substance that is easily changed into a new shape: *Lead and tin are malleable metals.* **2** easily influenced, trained or controlled: *He had an actor's typically malleable features.* ○ *Europe saw its colonies as a source of raw material and a malleable workforce.* **malleability** /ˌmæl.i.əˈbɪl.ɪ.ti/ [US] /-ə.t̬i/ *noun* [U]

mallee /ˈmæl.i/ *noun* [C] a tree of the eucalyptus group which does not grow tall and is found in desert areas of Australia

mallet /ˈmæl.ɪt/ *noun* [C] a tool like a hammer with a large flattened end made of wood or rubber, or a wooden hammer with a long handle used in sports such as

M

CROQUET and POLO ⮕See also **hammer** TOOL.

mall ,rat noun [C] US SLANG a young person who goes to shopping MALLS (= large enclosed shopping areas) to spend time with their friends

malnourished /,mæl'nʌr.ɪʃt/ ⓤ /-'nɝː-/ adj weak and in bad health because of a lack of food or because of a lack of the types of food necessary for good health

malnutrition /,mæl.nju:'trɪ.ʃən/ ⓤ /-nuː-/ noun [U] physical weakness and bad health caused by a lack of food, or by a lack of the types of food necessary for good health: Many of the refugees are suffering from severe malnutrition.

malodorous /,mæl'əʊ.d²r.əs/ ⓤ /-'oʊ.dɚ-/ adj FORMAL having an unpleasant smell: The town is built on a malodorous swamp.

malpractice /,mæl'præk.tɪs/ noun [U] SPECIALIZED failure to act correctly or legally when doing your job, often causing injury or loss: They are accused of medical/financial/electoral malpractice.

malt /mɒlt/ ⓤ /mɑːlt/ noun [U] grain, usually barley, that has been left in water until it starts to grow and is then dried. It is used in the making of alcoholic drinks such as beer and whisky **malt** /mɒlt/ ⓤ /mɑːlt/ verb [T]

malted 'milk noun [U] a drink made from milk and malt

Maltese cross /,mɒl.tiːz'krɒs/ ⓤ /-'krɑːs/ noun [C] a cross with four equal parts that get wider further from the centre

malt 'extract noun [U] a sweet dark sticky substance made from malt and used in food

maltreat /,mæl'triːt/ verb [T] FORMAL to treat someone cruelly or violently: He had been badly maltreated as a child. **maltreatment** /,mæl'triːt.mənt/ noun [U] They complained about the physical and psychological maltreatment of prisoners.

malt 'whisky noun [C or U] (ALSO **malt**) whisky made using malt rather than ordinary grain: a fine Highland malt

mam /mæm/ noun [C] NORTHERN ENGLISH INFORMAL FOR **mum** MOTHER

mama /mə'mɑː/ ⓤ /'mɑː.mə/ noun [C] **1** UK OLD USE or US INFORMAL another word for **mother 2** US SLANG a woman, especially an attractive one: There's a good-looking mama sitting at the bar.

mama's boy /'mæm.əz,bɔɪ/ ⓤ /'mɑː.məz-/ noun [C] US FOR **mummy's boy**

mamba /'mæm.bə/ noun [C] a very poisonous snake that lives mainly in caves or trees in parts of Africa

mammal /'mæm.²l/ noun [C] any animal of which the female gives birth to babies, not eggs, and feeds them on milk from her own body: Humans, dogs, elephants and dolphins are all mammals, but birds, fish and crocodiles are not. **mammalian** /mə'meɪ.li.ən/ adj SPECIALIZED mammalian evolution ○ mammalian species

mammary /'mæm.²r.i/ ⓤ /-ɚ-/ adj SPECIALIZED relating to the breasts or milk organs

mammary ,gland noun [C] SPECIALIZED an organ in a woman's breast that produces milk to feed a baby, or a similar organ in a female animal

mammography /mə'mɒg.rə.fi/ ⓤ /-'mɑː.grə-/ noun [U] the use of X-ray photographs of the breasts to help discover possible cancers **mammogram** /'mæm.ə.græm/ noun [C] (ALSO **mammograph**) an X-ray photograph of the breasts

Mammon /'mæm.ən/ noun [U] LITERARY the force which makes people try to become as rich as possible and the belief that this is the most important thing in life

mammoth /'mæm.əθ/ adj extremely large: Cleaning up the city-wide mess is going to be a mammoth **task**. ○ It's a mammoth **undertaking** – are you sure you have the resources to cope?

mammoth /'mæm.əθ/ noun [C] a type of large hairy elephant with tusks which no longer exists

mammy /'mæm.i/ noun [C] **1** MAINLY US OR IRISH ENG., CHILD'S WORD mother **2** US OFFENSIVE OLD-FASHIONED a black woman whose job is to take care of white children

man MALE /mæn/ noun plural **men 1** [C] an adult male human being: a young/tall man ○ men and women ○ the man in the green jacket ○ the men's 400 metres champion ○ Steve can solve anything – the man's a genius. **2** [C] a male employee, without particular rank or title: The gas company said they would send some men to fix the heating system. ○ The man **from** the BBC wrote some positive things about the film. ○ The military expedition was made up of 100 officers and men. ○ Our man in Washington sent us the news by fax yesterday. ○ OLD USE My man (= male servant) will show you to the door. **3 a marketing/advertising, etc. man** a man typical of or involved in marketing/advertising, etc. **4** [C] INFORMAL a woman's husband or male partner: I hear she's got a new man. ○ Is there a man in her life? **5** MAINLY US INFORMAL used when addressing someone, especially a man: Hey, man, how are you doing?

man /mæn/ exclamation OLD-FASHIONED INFORMAL used as an exclamation, especially when you are expressing a strong emotion: Man, we had a good time – we drank all through the night!

• **the man** US SLANG the police

• **You the man!** US NOT STANDARD used to praise a man who has done something well

• **make a man (out) of sb** to cause a young man or boy to act like an adult and take responsibility: A couple of years in the army should make a man of him.

• **man and boy** UK OLD-FASHIONED all a man's life: From 1910 to 1970 he worked in that factory, man and boy.

• **man and wife** OLD-FASHIONED If a man and a woman are man and wife, they are married to each other.

• **the man in the moon** (in children's stories) the human face that you can imagine you see when you look at the moon

• **a man's man** a man who enjoys men's activities and being with other men: Terry's what you'd call a man's man – I don't expect you'd find him at the ballet too many nights a week.

• **(as) man to man** If two men talk (as) man to man, they talk seriously and honestly together as equals.

man PERSON /mæn/ noun **1** [U] the human race: Man is still far more intelligent than the cleverest robot. ○ Man is rapidly destroying the Earth. ○ This is one of the most dangerous substances **known** to man. ○ Try to imagine what life must have been like for Neolithic man 10 000 years ago. ＊ NOTE: Many people consider this use sexist and prefer to use terms such as 'people', 'humans' or 'the human race'. **2** LITERARY OR OLD-FASHIONED a person of either sex: All men are equal in the sight of the law. ＊ NOTE: Many people consider this use sexist and prefer to use 'person'.

• **as one man** FORMAL If a group of people do something as one man they do it together at exactly the same time: As one man, the delegates made for the exit.

• **to a man** every person in a group: There were 400 people at the meeting and they all, to a man, voted in favour.

• **man's best friend** a dog

• **man's inhumanity to man** the cruelty which people show to each other: Man's inhumanity to man never fails to shock me.

-man /-mæn/ /-mən/ suffix having the nationality or job mentioned, or (of a group or vehicle) containing the number of people mentioned: an Irishman ○ a policeman ○ businessmen ○ a five-man team ○ a two-man helicopter ＊ NOTE: Many people consider this use sexist and prefer to use terms such as 'police officer', 'business executives', or a 'five-person team'.

man /mæn/ verb [T] **-nn-** To man something such as a machine or vehicle is to be present in order to operate it: The phones are manned 24 hours a day. ○ Barricades were erected against the advancing government troops and they were manned throughout the night. ○ Man the pumps! ⮕See also **overmanned**; **undermanned**; **unmanned**. ＊ NOTE: Many people find this use sexist and prefer to use other verbs such as 'operate' or 'staff'.

man OBJECT /mæn/ noun [C] plural **men** any of the objects that are moved or played with in games such as chess

man-about-town /,mæn.ə.baʊt'taʊn/ /,wɒ.mən-/ noun [S] a man who spends a lot of time in fashionable places, doing fashionable things

manacles /'mæn.ə.k‌lz/ plural noun two metal rings joined by a chain, used to prevent a prisoner from escaping by fastening the legs or arms **manacle**

/ˈmæn.ə.kl̩/ *verb* [T] *They had manacled her legs* ***together****.* ○ *His arm was manacled* ***to*** *a ring on the wall.*

manage [SUCCEED] /ˈmæn.ɪdʒ/ *verb* **1** [I or T] to succeed in doing something, especially something difficult: [+ *to* infinitive] *Did you manage* ***to*** *get any bread?* ○ *I* ***only just*** *managed* ***to*** *finish on time.* ○ *A small dog had* ***somehow*** *managed* ***to*** *survive the fire.* ○ *I can't manage all this work on my own.* ○ *Don't worry about us – we'll manage!* ○ *Can you manage dinner on Saturday* (= Will you be able to come to dinner)*?* ○ *MAINLY UK I'm afraid I can't manage the time* (= I'm too busy) *to see you at the moment.* **2** [I] to succeed in living on a small amount of money: *After she lost her job, they had to manage* ***on*** *his salary.*

manageable /ˈmæn.ɪ.dʒə.bl̩/ *adj* easy or possible to deal with: *The work has been divided into smaller, more manageable sections.* ○ *Government targets for increased productivity are described as "tough but manageable".*

manage [CONTROL] /ˈmæn.ɪdʒ/ *verb* [T] to be responsible for controlling or organizing someone or something especially a business: *Has she had any experience of managing large projects?* ○ *He's not very good at managing people.* ○ *His job involved managing large investment funds.* ○ *When you have a job as well as children to look after, you have to learn how to manage your time.* ➲See also **mismanage**.

management /ˈmæn.ɪdʒ.mənt/ *noun* [U] the control and organization of something: *The company has suffered from several years of bad management.* ○ *There is a need for stricter financial management.* ○ *a management training scheme*

management /ˈmæn.ɪdʒ.mənt/ *group noun* [C] the group of people responsible for controlling and organizing a company: *Management has/have offered staff a 3% pay increase.*

manager /ˈmæn.ɪ.dʒəʳ/ Ⓤⓢ /-dʒɚ/ *noun* [C] **1** the person who is responsible for managing an organization: *a bank manager* ○ *a station manager* ○ *the production manager* ○ *I wish to speak to the manager.* **2** the person whose job is to organize and sometimes train a sports team: *a football manager* **3** The manager of a singer, actor or other entertainer is a person whose job is to arrange the business part of their work.

manageress /ˌmæn.ɪ.dʒəˈres/ Ⓤⓢ /-dʒə.res/ *noun* [C] *OLD-FASHIONED* a female manager ✱ NOTE: **manager** is generally used for both men and women.

managerial /ˌmæn.əˈdʒɪə.ri.əl/ Ⓤⓢ /-ˈdʒɪr.i-/ *adj* relating to a manager or management: *managerial responsibilities/decisions/skills*

ˌmanaging diˈrector *noun* [C] (*ABBREVIATION* **MD**) *UK* the person in charge of the way a company operates: *There's a board of five directors, but she is the Managing Director.*

mañana /mænˈjɑː.nə/ *adv* some time in the future; later: *"When will you do it?" "Oh, mañana!"*

Mancunian /mæŋˈkjuː.ni.ən/ *noun* [C] a person from Manchester, a city in the north of England **Mancunian** /mæŋˈkjuː.ni.ən/ *adj*

mandarin /ˈmæn.dər.ɪn/ Ⓤⓢ /-dɚ-/ *noun* [C] *MAINLY DISAPPROVING* a person who has a very important job in the government, and who is sometimes considered to be too powerful: *It often seems that true power lies with the Civil Service mandarins, rather than MPs and cabinet ministers.*

Mandarin (Chinese) /ˌmæn.dər.ɪn.tʃaɪˈniːz/ *noun* [U] one of the two main types of the Chinese language and the official language in China and Taiwan

ˌmandarin (ˈorange) *noun* [C] a small sweet type of orange but with a thinner, looser skin

mandate /ˈmæn.deɪt/ *noun* [C usually sing] **1** the authority given to an elected group of people, such as a government, to perform an action or govern a country: *At the forthcoming elections, the government will be seeking a fresh mandate* ***from*** *the people.* ○ [+ *to* infinitive] *The president secured the Congressional mandate* ***to*** *go to war by three votes.* **2** *SPECIALIZED* the name of an area of land which has been given to a country by the UN, following or as part of a peace agreement

mandate /ˈmæn.deɪt/ *verb* [T] **1** to give official permission for something to happen: *The UN rush to mandate war totally ruled out any alternatives.* **2** *MAINLY US* to order someone to do something: [+ *to* infinitive] *Our delegates have been mandated* ***to*** *vote against the proposal at the conference.*

mandatory /ˈmæn.də.tri/ Ⓤⓢ /-tɔːr.i/ *adj FORMAL* describes something which must be done, or which is demanded by law: *The minister is calling for mandatory prison sentences for people who assault police officers.* ○ *Athletes must undergo a mandatory drugs test before competing in the championship.* ○ *In 1991, the British government made it mandatory to wear rear seat belts in cars.*

mandolin, **mandoline** /ˌmæn.dəˈlɪn/ *noun* [C] a musical instrument with four pairs of metal strings and a round back

mandrake /ˈmæn.dreɪk/ *noun* [C] a plant with purple flowers and a root which is divided into two parts

mandrill /ˈmæn.drɪl/ *noun* [C] a large West African monkey which has a red and blue face and a very short tail

mane /meɪn/ *noun* [C] **1** the long thick hair that grows along the top of a horse's neck or around the face and neck of a lion ➲See picture **Animals and Birds** on page Centre 4 **2** thick long hair on a person's head: *The painting depicts a beautiful young man with a flowing mane* ***of*** *red hair.*

man-eater [WOMAN] /ˈmænˌiː.təʳ/ Ⓤⓢ /-t̬ɚ/ *noun* [C] *HUMOROUS* a woman who uses men to have a series of sexual relationships without loving them

man-eater [ANIMAL] /ˈmænˌiː.təʳ/ Ⓤⓢ /-t̬ɚ/ *noun* [C] an animal that can kill and eat a person **man-eating** /ˈmænˌiː.tɪŋ/ Ⓤⓢ /-t̬ɪŋ/ *adj* [before n] *a man-eating tiger*

maneuver /məˈnuː.vəʳ/ Ⓤⓢ /-vɚ/ *noun* [C], *verb* [I or T] *US FOR* **manoeuvre**

ˌman ˈFriday *noun* [C usually sing] a male helper who is loyal and can be trusted

manfully /ˈmæn.fəl.i/ *adv* with determination and bravery, despite great problems: *The actors struggled manfully with some of the worst lines of dialogue ever written.*

manga /ˈmæŋ.gə/ *noun* [C or U] COMIC books or ANIMATION from Japan which often include sex or violence

manganese /ˈmæŋ.gə.niːz/ *noun* [U] a grey-white metallic element, used in the process of making steel

mange /meɪndʒ/ *noun* [U] an infectious disease in hairy animals, such as dogs and cats, which makes hair fall out and causes areas of rough skin

mangy /ˈmeɪn.dʒi/ *adj* **1** suffering from mange: *a thin mangy dog* **2** *INFORMAL* describes something that is old and dirty and has been used a lot: *We need to get rid of that mangy old carpet in the bedroom.*

manger /ˈmeɪn.dʒəʳ/ Ⓤⓢ /-dʒɚ/ *noun* [C] *OLD USE* an open box from which cattle and horses feed

mangetout *UK* /ˌmɑ̃ːnʒˈtuː/ *noun* [C usually pl] (*US* **snow pea**) the sweet flat pods of a particular type of pea which are picked and eaten whole

mangle [DESTROY] /ˈmæŋ.gl̩/ *verb* **1** [T often passive] to destroy something by twisting it with force or tearing it into pieces so that its original form is completely changed: *My sweater got mangled in the washing machine.* ○ *His arm was mangled in the machine.* **2** [T] If you mangle a speech or a piece of written work, you make so many mistakes that you completely spoil it: *As he read the poem out loud, he mangled the rhythm so badly that it scarcely made any sense.* **mangled** /ˈmæŋ.gl̩d/ *adj*: *All that remains of yesterday's car crash is a pile of mangled metal.*

mangle [MACHINE] /ˈmæŋ.gl̩/ *noun* [C] (*ALSO* **wringer**) a machine used for pressing water out of clothes by putting the clothes between two heavy smooth round bars

mango /ˈmæŋ.gəʊ/ Ⓤⓢ /-goʊ/ *noun* [C or U] *plural* **mangoes** or **mangos** an oval tropical fruit with a smooth skin, juicy orange-yellow flesh and a large hard seed in the middle ➲See picture **Fruit** on page Centre 1

M

ˌ**mango ˈchutney** *noun* [U] a sweet PICKLE eaten with Indian food

mangrove /ˈmæŋ.grəʊv/ [US] /-groʊv/ *noun* [C] a tropical tree, found near water, whose twisted roots grow partly above ground: *a mangrove* ***swamp***

mangy /ˈmeɪn.dʒi/ *adj* ➲See at **mange**.

manhandle [HANDLE ROUGHLY] /ˌmænˈhæn.dl̩/ *verb* [T] to touch or hold someone roughly and with force, often when taking them somewhere: *There were complaints that the police had manhandled some of the demonstrators.*

manhandle [MOVE] /ˌmænˈhæn.dl̩/ *verb* [T] to move something using the physical strength of the body: *Several pieces of heavy equipment had to be manhandled into the lorry.*

manhattan /mænˈhæt.ən/ [US] /-ˈhæt̬-/ *noun* [C] a type of alcoholic drink: *A manhattan contains whisky and vermouth.*

manhole /ˈmæn.həʊl/ [US] /-hoʊl/ *noun* [C] a covered opening in a road which a worker can enter in order to reach underground pipes, wires or DRAINS which need to be examined or repaired: *a manhole cover*

manhood /ˈmæn.hʊd/ *noun* **1** [U] the state of being a man: *The story is seen through the eyes of a boy on the verge of manhood.* ○ *A celebration is held for the boy at the age when he is considered to have reached manhood.* **2** [U] the qualities that are considered typical of a man: *Tall, square-jawed and handsome, this young actor is Hollywood's ideal of manhood.* **3** [U] *LITERARY* men, especially all the men of a particular country: *The* ***flower of the nation's*** *manhood* (= the best young men in the country) *was killed in the war.* **4** [U] *MAINLY HUMOROUS* a man's ability to express or experience sexual feelings: *Why do you think he needs to have so many women around him – is it just a way of* ***proving*** *his manhood?* **5** [S] *HUMOROUS* penis: *Careful you don't trap your manhood in your zip!*

M

manhour /ˈmæn.aʊəʳ/ [US] /-aʊr/ *noun* [C] (*ALSO* **person hour**) the amount of work done by one person in one hour: *Just think how many manhours we could save if we computerized the system.*

manhunt /ˈmæn.hʌnt/ *noun* [C] an organized search for a person, especially a criminal: *The police have* ***launched*** *a manhunt after the body of a six-year-old boy was found last night.*

mania [STRONG INTEREST] /ˈmeɪ.ni.ə/ *noun* [C or U] *DISAPPROVING* a very strong interest in something which fills a person's mind or uses up all their time: *So why your sudden mania* ***for*** *exercise?* ○ *The article describes the* ***religious*** *mania which is sweeping the US.* **-mania** /-meɪ.ni.ə/ *suffix*: *Beatle-mania swept Britain in the 1960s.* ➲See also **kleptomania**; **nymphomania** at **nymphomaniac**; **pyromania**.

maniac /ˈmeɪ.ni.æk/ *noun* [C] *INFORMAL* a person who has a very strong interest in a particular activity: *a football/sex maniac*

• **like a maniac** If someone works or exercises like a maniac, they work or exercise extremely hard.

mania [MENTAL ILLNESS] /ˈmeɪ.ni.ə/ *noun* [C or U] **1** a state in which someone directs all their attention to one particular thing: *Van Gogh suffered from acute persecution mania.* ○ *She's always cleaning – it's like a mania with her.* **2** *SPECIALIZED* a state of extreme physical and mental activity, often characterized by a loss of judgment and periods of EUPHORIA

maniac /ˈmeɪ.ni.æk/ *noun* [C] a person who behaves in an uncontrolled way, not caring about risks or danger: *Some maniac was running down the street waving a massive metal bar.* ○ *INFORMAL I won't get in the car with Richard – he drives* ***like a*** *maniac!*

maniacal /məˈnaɪə.kəl/ *adj* describes a cry or laugh that is loud and wild: *He suddenly exploded into maniacal* ***laughter***.

manic /ˈmæn.ɪk/ *adj* very excited or anxious in a way that causes you to be very physically active: *He's a bit manic – I wish he'd calm down.*

ˌ**manic deˈpression** *noun* [U] a mental illness causing someone to change from being extremely happy and excited to being extremely sad: *He* ***suffers from*** *manic depression.*

ˌ**manic deˈpressive** *noun* [C] a person who has manic depression

manicure /ˈmæn.ɪ.kjʊəʳ/ [US] /-kjʊr/ *noun* [C or U] (a) treatment for the hands which involves softening the skin and making the nails look better by cutting, smoothing and possibly painting them ➲Compare **pedicure**.

manicure /ˈmæn.ɪ.kjʊəʳ/ [US] /-kjʊr/ *verb* [T]

manicured /ˈmæn.ɪ.kjʊəd/ [US] /-kjʊrd/ *adj* **1** having had a manicure: *He has very* ***well-****manicured hands.* **2** If something, such as a garden, is manicured, it is well cared for and looks very tidy: *The hotel is surrounded by perfectly manicured gardens.*

manicurist /ˈmæn.ɪ.kjʊə.rɪst/ [US] /-kjʊ.rɪst/ *noun* [C] a person whose job it is to give people manicures

ˈ**manicure ˌset** *noun* [C] a set of small tools which are used for cutting and smoothing the nails

manifest /ˈmæn.ɪ.fest/ *verb* [T] *FORMAL* to show something clearly, through signs or actions: *The workers chose to manifest their dissatisfaction* ***in*** *a series of strikes.* ○ *The illness first manifested* ***itself in/as*** *severe stomach pains.* ○ *Lack of confidence in the company manifested* ***itself in*** *a fall in the share price.*

manifest /ˈmæn.ɪ.fest/ *adj* *FORMAL* easily noticed or obvious: *There was manifest relief among the workers yesterday at the decision not to close the factory.* ○ *Her manifest lack of interest in the project has provoked severe criticism.*

manifestly /ˈmæn.ɪ.fest.li/ *adv* *FORMAL* very obviously: *He claims that he is completely committed to the project and yet this is manifestly untrue.* ○ *The government has manifestly failed to raise educational standards, despite its commitment to do so.*

manifestation /ˌmæn.ɪ.fesˈteɪ.ʃən/ *noun* *FORMAL* **1** [C] a sign of something existing or happening: *She claimed that the rise in unemployment was just a further manifestation* ***of*** *the government's incompetence.* **2** [U] appearance: *Unlike acid rain or deforestation, global warming has no visible manifestation .*

manifesto /ˌmæn.ɪˈfes.təʊ/ [US] /-toʊ/ *noun* [C] *plural* **manifestos** or **manifestoes** a written statement of the beliefs, aims and POLICIES of an organization, especially a political party: *In their election manifesto, the Liberal Democrats proposed increasing taxes to pay for improvements in education.*

manifold [MANY] /ˈmæn.ɪ.fəʊld/ [US] /-foʊld/ *adj* *FORMAL* many and of several different types: *Despite her manifold faults, she was a strong leader.*

manifold [PIPE] /ˈmæn.ɪ.fəʊld/ [US] /-foʊld/ *noun* [C] *SPECIALIZED* a pipe or enclosed space in a machine which has several openings, allowing liquids and gases to enter and leave

manikin [MODEL], **mannikin**, *US ALSO* **mannequin** /ˈmæn.ə.kɪn/ *noun* [C] a model of the human body, used for teaching medical or art students

manikin [MAN], **mannikin** /ˈmæn.ə.kɪn/ *noun* [C] *OLD-FASHIONED* a very short man: *Manikins often appear in children's stories.*

manila, **manilla** /məˈnɪl.ə/ *adj* made of strong brown paper: *manila envelopes*

manipulate [INFLUENCE] /məˈnɪp.jʊ.leɪt/ *verb* [T] *MAINLY DISAPPROVING* to control something or someone to your advantage, often unfairly or dishonestly: *Throughout her career she has very successfully manipulated the media.* ○ *The opposition leader accused government ministers of manipulating the statistics to suit themselves.*

manipulative /məˈnɪp.jʊ.lə.tɪv/ [US] /-t̬ɪv/ *adj* *MAINLY DISAPPROVING* describes someone who tries to control people to their advantage: *Even as a child she was manipulative and knew how to get her own way.* **manipulation** /məˌnɪp.jʊˈleɪ.ʃən/ *noun* [C or U] *They have been accused of fraud and stock market manipulations.* ○ *There's been so much* ***media*** *manipulation of the facts that nobody knows the truth of the matter.* ○ *The opposition party claims the president returned to power through* ***political*** *manipulation.* **manipulator** /məˈnɪp.jʊ.leɪ.təʳ/ [US] /-t̬ɚ/ *noun* [C] *She was, said the judge, a ruthless and scheming manipulator.*

manipulate [CONTROL] /mə'nɪp.jʊ.leɪt/ *verb* [T] **1** to control something using the hands: *The wheelchair is designed so that it is easy to manipulate.* **2** to treat a part of the body, using the hands to push back bones into the correct position and put pressure on muscles: *The doctor manipulated the base of my spine and the pain disappeared completely.* **manipulation** /mə,nɪp.jʊ'leɪ.ʃən/ *noun* [C or U] *Osteopathy involves massage and manipulation of the bones and joints.*

mankind /mæn'kaɪnd/ *noun* [U] (*ALSO* **humankind**) the whole of the human race, including both men and women: *Mankind has always been obsessed by power.* ➲Compare **womankind**.

manky /'mæŋ.ki/ *adj UK INFORMAL* describes an object that is unpleasantly dirty, usually because it is old or has been used a lot: *a manky tissue* ○ *manky old carpets*

manly /'mæn.li/ *adj APPROVING* having the qualities which people think a man should have: *He has such a manly voice.* ○ *My mother used to tell me it wasn't manly for little boys to cry.* **manliness** /'mæn.lɪ.nəs/ *noun* [U]

man-made /,mæn'meɪd/ *adj* artificial rather than natural: *man-made fibres* ○ *It's a man-made lake.*

manna /'mæn.ə/ *noun* [U] (in the Bible) a food which dropped from heaven and prevented Moses and his people from dying of hunger in the desert
• **manna from heaven** help that you get when you need it but are not expecting it

mannequin /'mæn.ə.kɪn/ *noun* [C] **1** a large model of a human being, used to show clothes in the window of a shop **2** *OLD-FASHIONED FOR* **model** PERSON **3** *US FOR* **manikin** MODEL

manner [WAY] /'mæn.əʳ/ [US] /-ɚ/ *noun* [S] the way in which something is done: *She stared at me* ***in*** *an accusing manner.* ○ *He was elected* ***in*** *the normal manner.* ○ *It was the manner* ***of*** *her death that stuck in the public's mind.*
• **in the manner of *sth*** in the style of something: *Her latest film is a suspense thriller very much in the manner of Hitchcock.*
• **as (if) to the manner born** *FORMAL* If you do something as (if) to the manner born, you do it very well and very naturally as if it is usual and easy for you.
• **in a manner of speaking** *FORMAL* used for saying that something is partly true: *She's his partner, in a manner of speaking.*
• **not by any manner of means** *UK OLD-FASHIONED* not in any way: *I'm not satisfied with his excuse – not by any manner of means.*

manner [BEHAVIOUR] /'mæn.əʳ/ [US] /-ɚ/ *noun* [S] the usual way in which you behave towards other people, or the way you behave on a particular occasion: *She has a rather cold, unfriendly manner.* ○ *As soon as he realized that we weren't going to buy anything, his whole manner changed.*

manner [TYPE] /'mæn.əʳ/ [US] /-ɚ/ *noun* [U] *FORMAL* a type: *Very little is known about the new candidate – what manner* ***of*** *man is he?*
• **all manner of *sth*** a lot of different types: *There are all manner of architectural styles in the capital.*

mannered /'mæn.əd/ [US] /-ɚd/ *adj DISAPPROVING* describes a style of speech or behaviour that is artificial, or intended to achieve a particular effect: *His performance as Hamlet was criticized for being very mannered.*

mannerism /'mæn.ər.ɪ.zəm/ [US] /-ɚ-/ *noun* [C] something that a person does repeatedly with their face, hands or voice, and which they may not be aware of: *He's got some very strange mannerisms.* ○ *We've spent so much time together that we've picked up each other's mannerisms.*

manners /'mæn.əz/ [US] /-ɚz/ *plural noun* polite ways of treating other people and behaving in public: *He needs to be* ***taught*** *some manners.* ○ *It's* ***bad*** *manners to eat with your mouth open.* ○ *It's considered* ***good*** *manners in some societies to leave a little food on your plate.*
-mannered /-mæn.əd/ [US] /-ɚd/ *suffix*: *an* ***ill/bad****-mannered boy* ○ *He was a* ***mild****-mannered* (= gentle and calm) *young man.* ○ *I noticed how* ***well****-mannered her children were.*

mannikin /'mæn.ɪ.kɪn/ *noun* [C] a **manikin**

mannish /'mæn.ɪʃ/ *adj DISAPPROVING* If you describe a woman as mannish, you mean that her appearance or behaviour are too much like a man's: *her mannish voice* ○ *She wondered if short hair made her look a bit mannish.*

manoeuvre [MOVEMENT] *UK, US* **maneuver** /mə'nuː.vəʳ/ [US] /-vɚ/ *noun* [C] a movement or set of movements needing skill and care: *Reversing round a corner is one of the manoeuvres you are required to perform in a driving test.*
manoeuvre *UK, US* **maneuver** /mə'nuː.vəʳ/ [US] /-vɚ/ *verb* [I or T] to turn and direct an object: *Loaded supermarket trolleys are often difficult to manoeuvre.* ○ *This car manoeuvres well at high speed.*
manoeuvrable *UK, US* **maneuverable** /mə'nuː.vrə.bl̩/ *adj* easy to direct: *The new missile is faster and more manoeuvrable than previous models.* **manoeuvrability** *UK, US* **maneuverability** /mə,nuː.vrə'bɪl.ɪ.ti/ [US] /-ə.ṭi/ *noun* [U] *Power-assisted steering improves a car's manoeuvrability.* **manoeuvring** *UK, US* **maneuvering** /mə'nuː.vər.ɪŋ/ [US] /-vɚ-/ *noun* [U] *With some careful manoeuvring, I was able to get the car into the narrow space.*

manoeuvre [MILITARY OPERATION] *UK, US* **maneuver** /mə'nuː.vəʳ/ [US] /-vɚ/ *noun* [C usually pl] a planned and controlled movement or operation by the armed forces for training purposes and in war: *military/naval manoeuvres* ○ *We saw the army* ***on*** *manoeuvres in the mountains.*

manoeuvre [CLEVER ACTION] *UK, US* **maneuver** /mə'nuː.vəʳ/ [US] /-vɚ/ *noun* [C] a cleverly planned action which is intended to obtain an advantage: *A series of impressive manoeuvres by the chairman had secured a lucrative contract for the company.*
• **room for manoeuvre** the opportunity to change your plans or choose between different ways of doing something: *The law in this area is very strict and doesn't allow us much room for manoeuvre.*
manoeuvre *UK, US* **maneuver** /mə'nuː.vəʳ/ [US] /-vɚ/ *verb* [T] to try to make someone act in a particular way: *The other directors are trying to manoeuvre her* ***into*** *resigning.* **manoeuvring** *UK, US* **maneuvering** /mə'nuː.vər.ɪŋ/ [US] /-vɚ-/ *noun* [C or U] *The directors managed to secure a good deal for the company with a bit of subtle manoeuvring.* ○ *He claimed he knew nothing about the political manoeuvrings which had got him into power.*

,man of 'God *noun* [C] (*ALSO* **man of the cloth**) *MAINLY HUMOROUS* a priest

,man of 'letters *noun* [C] *FORMAL* a man, usually a writer, who knows a lot about literature

manometer /mæn'ɒm.ɪ.təʳ/ [US] /mə'nɑː.mə.ṭɚ/ *noun* [C] a device for measuring the pressure of gases and liquids

manor /'mæn.əʳ/ [US] /-ɚ/ *noun* [C usually sing] *UK SLANG* the area in which a person works or which they are responsible for

'manor (,house) *noun* [C] a large old house in the country with land belonging to it

manpower /'mæn.paʊəʳ/ [US] /-paʊr/ *noun* [U] the supply of people who are able to work: *The industry has suffered from a lack of manpower.* ○ *manpower shortages*

manqué /mɒŋ'keɪ/ *adj FORMAL* **an artist/poet/writer, etc. manqué** someone who has not had the opportunity to do a particular job, despite having the ability to do it

manservant /'mæn,sɜː.vənt/ [US] /-,sɝː-/ *noun* [C] *OLD USE* a male servant with responsibility for the personal needs of his employer, such as preparing his food and clothes

mansion /'mæn.tʃən/ *noun* [C] a very large expensive house: *The street is lined with enormous mansions where the rich and famous live.*

Mansions /'mæn.tʃənz/ *plural noun UK* used in the name of some buildings that contain apartments: *Her new address is 12 Warwickshire Mansions.*

man-sized /'mæn.saɪzd/ *adj* [before n] *OLD-FASHIONED* big: *man-sized tissues*

manslaughter /'mæn,slɔː.təʳ/ [US] /-,slɑː.ṭɚ/ *noun* [U] *LEGAL* the crime of killing a person by someone who did not intend to do it or who cannot be responsible for their actions: *She was sentenced to five years imprisonment for manslaughter.* ○ *He denies murder but admits manslaughter on the grounds of diminished respons-*

M

ibility. ⊃Compare **murder**; **suicide** DEATH.

manta ray /ˈmæn.tə.reɪ/ *noun* [C] a very large flat sea fish with triangular fins, the largest type of RAY

mantelpiece /ˈmæn.tᵊl.piːs/ US /-t̬ᵊl-/ *noun* [C] (*US ALSO* **mantel**) a shelf above a fireplace, usually part of a frame which surrounds the fireplace: *She's got photographs of all her grandchildren on the mantelpiece.*

mantis /ˈmæn.tɪs/ US /-t̬ɪs/ *noun* [C] (*ALSO* **praying mantis**) a large green insect that holds its front legs in a way that makes it look as if it is praying when it is waiting to catch another insect

mantle RESPONSIBILITY /ˈmæn.tl̩/ US /-t̬l̩/ *noun* [S] FORMAL the responsibilities of an important position or job, especially as given from the person who had the job to the person who replaces them: *She unsuccessfully attempted to **assume** the mantle of presidency.* ○ *He has been asked to **take on** the mantle of managing director in the New York office.*

mantle LAYER /ˈmæn.tl̩/ US /-t̬l̩/ *noun* [C] **1** LITERARY a layer of something which covers a surface: *A thick mantle **of** snow lay on the ground.* ○ *We watched the building vanish under a mantle of thick grey smoke as the fire swiftly moved through it.* **2** SPECIALIZED the part of the Earth that surrounds the central CORE **3** in the past, a piece of clothing without sleeves which was worn over other clothes

man-to-man /ˌmæn.təˈmæn/ *adj* [before n], *adv* describes an honest and direct conversation between two men: *a man-to-man discussion* ○ *We talked man-to-man.*

mantra /ˈmæn.trə/ *noun* [C] **1** (especially in Hinduism and Buddhism) a word or sound which is believed to possess a special spiritual power: *A personal mantra is sometimes repeated as an aid to meditation or prayer.* **2** a word or phrase which is often repeated and which sometimes expresses a belief: *The crowds chanted that familiar football mantra: "Here we go, here we go, here we go..."*

manual BY HAND /ˈmæn.ju.əl/ *adj* **1** done with the hands: *the manual sorting of letters* ○ *She tried to cure the pain in my knee by putting manual pressure on the joint.* **2** describes a machine that is operated with the hands rather than by electricity or a motor: *He still works on an old manual typewriter.* **3** involving physical work rather than mental work: *unskilled manual **labour*** ○ *750 manual **workers** will lose their jobs as a result of company cutbacks.* ○ *Computer-controlled robots are taking over manual jobs in many industries.*

manually /ˈmæn.ju.ə.li/ *adv* by hand: *Few of the machines are operated manually.*

manual BOOK /ˈmæn.ju.əl/ *noun* [C] a book which gives you practical instructions on how to do something or how to use something, such as a machine: *a DIY manual* ○ *The computer comes with a 600-page **instruction** manual.*

manual dexˈterity *noun* [U] someone's ability to perform a difficult action with the hands skilfully and quickly so that it looks easy

manual transˈmission *noun* [U] If a car has manual transmission, the gears are changed by the driver. ⊃Compare **automatic transmission**.

manufacture PRODUCE /ˌmæn.juˈfæk.tʃər/ US /-tʃɚ/ *verb* [T] to produce goods in large numbers, usually in a factory using machines: *He works for a company that manufactures car parts.* ○ *The report notes a rapid decline in manufactured **goods**.* **manufacture** /ˌmæn.juˈfæk.tʃər/ US /-tʃɚ/ *noun* [U] *Oil is used in the manufacture of a number of fabrics.* ○ *The amount of recycled glass used in manufacture doubled in five years.* **manufacturer** /ˌmæn.juˈfæk.tʃᵊr.ər/ US /-tʃɚ.ɚ/ *noun* [C] *Germany is a major manufacturer of motor cars.* **manufacturers** /ˌmæn.juˈfæk.tʃᵊr.əz/ US /-tʃɚ.ɚz/ *plural noun* companies that produce manufactured goods: *Our kettle was leaking, so we had to send it back to the manufacturers.*

manufacture INVENT /ˌmæn.juˈfæk.tʃər/ US /-tʃɚ/ *verb* [T] to invent something, such as an excuse or story, in order to deceive someone: *She insisted that every scandalous detail of the story had been manufactured.*

manure /məˈnjʊər/ US /-ˈnʊr/ *noun* [U] excrement from animals, especially horses, which is spread on the land in order to make plants grow well

manuscript /ˈmæn.ju.skrɪpt/ *noun* [C] **1** the original copy of a book or article before it is printed: *He sent the 400-page manuscript to his publisher.* **2** an old document or book written by hand in the times before printing was invented: *It is thought that the manuscript is the work of a monk and dates from the twelfth century.*

Manx /mæŋks/ *adj* of the Isle of Man, the people who live there or their language

Manx ˈcat *noun* [C] a type of cat with no tail

many /ˈmen.i/ *determiner, pronoun* used mainly in negative sentences and questions to mean 'a large number of': *I don't have many clothes.* ○ ***Not** many people have heard of him.* ○ *There aren't very many weekends between now and Christmas.* ○ *Were there many cars on the road?* ○ ***How** many students are there in each class?* ○ *Many people would disagree with your ideas.* ○ *Rachel was at the party with her many admirers.* ○ *I've met him so many times and I still can't remember his name!* ○ *There are **too** many people chasing too few jobs. If there are only five of us going to the concert, then I've booked one too many seats.* ○ *If there were **as** many women as there are men in parliament, the situation would be very different.* ○ ***As** many **as** (= The surprisingly large number of) 6 000 people may have been infected with the disease.* ○ *There are already twelve bottles of wine, so if I buy **as** many **again** (= another twelve bottles) we'll have enough.* ○ *A **good/great** many people who voted for her in the last election will not be doing so this time.* ○ *She'd had five children **in as** many (= in the same number of) years and decided it was enough.*

• **many a time** many times: *I've told you many a time not to ride your bike on the pavement.*

• **many's the** used to show something has happened many times or for long periods of time: *Many's the hour I've spent by the telephone just waiting in case he should call.*

• **in so many words** directly, or in a way that makes it very clear what you mean: *"Did he say he was unhappy with Anna?" "Well, not in so many words but that was certainly the impression I got."* ○ *I told her, in so many words, to stop interfering.*

• **many happy returns (of the day)** said to mean 'Happy Birthday'

• **one too many** INFORMAL If you have had one too many, you have drunk too much alcohol.

USAGE

many, much or a lot of?

Many is used with countable nouns. It is more common in negative sentences and questions.

I haven't seen many films this year.

Much is used with uncountable nouns. It is more common in negative sentences and questions.

We haven't got much time left.

Many and much are both also used in formal positive sentences.

There is still much to do, if we are to be ready for the inspection.

In less formal positive sentences a lot of is generally used because many and much sound too formal. A lot of can be used with both countable and uncountable nouns.

a lot of people
There was a lot of enthusiasm for the project.
There was much enthusiasm for the project.

many-sided /ˌmen.iˈsaɪ.dɪd/ *adj* [before n] having many sides or a lot of different features or characteristics: *a many-sided object* ○ *A many-sided character, he wrote poetry and was a keen cricketer and cook.*

Maoism /ˈmaʊ.ɪ.zᵊm/ *noun* [U] the type of COMMUNISM introduced in China by Mao Zedong **Maoist** /ˈmaʊ.ɪst/ *noun* [C], *adj*

Maori /ˈmaʊ.ri/ *noun* [C] one of the original people of New Zealand and the Cook Islands: *The Maoris arrived in New Zealand from Polynesia over 1 000 years before the Europeans.* **Maori** /ˈmaʊ.ri/ *adj*: *The Maori language is now officially encouraged.* ○ *Before a rugby match, the*

New Zealand team perform a Maori war dance.

map /mæp/ *noun* [C] **1** a drawing of the Earth's surface, or part of that surface, showing the shape and position of different countries, political borders, natural features such as rivers and mountains, and artificial features such as roads and buildings: *a map of the world* ○ *a map of Paris* ○ *a road map* ○ *We need a large-scale map showing all the footpaths that we can walk along.* ○ *I'm hopeless at map* **reading** (= understanding maps). **2** something which shows the position of stars in the sky or the features on the surface of planets: *a celestial map* ○ *a map of Mars* **3** a very simple plan which shows a direction of travel between one place and another: *I'll draw you a quick map if you're worried about finding the hotel.*

● **put sth/sb on the map** to make a thing, person or place famous: *The governor has managed to put this sleepy southern state in America on the map.*

● **blow/bomb/wipe, etc. sth off the map** to destroy a place or thing completely, especially with bombs: *A nuclear bomb could wipe the whole country off the map.*

map /mæp/ *verb* [T] **-pp-** to represent an area of land in the form of a map: *Parts of the mountainous region in the north of the country have still not been mapped.*

▲ **map sth out** *phrasal verb* [M] to plan the future or a plan in detail: *The government has issued a new document mapping out its policies on education.* ○ *His future is all mapped out ahead of him.*

maple /ˈmeɪ.pl̩/ *noun* [C or U] a type of large tree which grows in northern areas of the world, or the wood of this tree: *a maple leaf* ○ *maple trees*

maple ˈsyrup *noun* [U] a thick sweet liquid produced from the maple tree which is eaten with or used in making food: *pancakes with maple syrup*

mar /mɑːʳ/ ⓊⓈ /mɑːr/ *verb* [T] **-rr-** SLIGHTLY FORMAL to spoil something, making it less perfect or less enjoyable: *Sadly, the text is marred by careless errors.* ○ *It was a really nice day, marred only by a little argument in the car on the way home.* ○ *I hope the fact that Louise isn't coming won't mar* **your enjoyment** *of the evening.*

maracas /məˈræk.əz/ *plural noun* a musical instrument consisting of two hollow containers filled with beans or small stones, which are shaken to provide the rhythm for some types of music

maraschino /ˌmær.əˈskiː.nəʊ/ /-ˈʃiː-/ ⓊⓈ /-nəʊ/ *noun* [U] slightly bitter LIQUEUR made from a particular type of CHERRY

maraˌschino ˈcherry *noun* [C usually pl] a cherry which is preserved in maraschino or a similar drink and used to decorate drinks and food

marathon /ˈmær.ə.θ⁽ᵊ⁾n/ /-θə.n/ *noun* [C] **1** a running race of slightly over 26 miles (42.195 kilometres): *the London/New York marathon* ○ *She did/ran her first marathon in just under three hours.* **2** an activity which takes a long time and makes you very tired: *The election broadcast, a nine-hour marathon, lasts until seven o'clock in the morning.* **marathon** /ˈmær.ə.θ⁽ᵊ⁾n/ ⓊⓈ /-θə.n/ *adj* [before n] *a marathon runner* ○ *I had a marathon session marking 55 exam papers yesterday.*

marauding /məˈrɔː.dɪŋ/ ⓊⓈ /-ˈrɑː-/ *adj* [before n] going from one place to another killing or using violence, stealing and destroying: *Witnesses reported gangs of marauding soldiers breaking into people's houses and setting fire to them.* **marauder** /məˈrɔː.dəʳ/ ⓊⓈ /-ˈrɑː.dɚ/ *noun* [C] a person or animal that goes from one place to another looking for something to kill or steal

marble Ⓡ ROCK /ˈmɑː.bl̩/ ⓊⓈ /ˈmɑːr-/ *noun* [U] a type of very hard rock which has a pattern of lines going through it, feels cold and becomes smooth and shiny when cut and polished: *a marble floor/statue* **marbled** /ˈmɑː.bl̩d/ ⓊⓈ /ˈmɑːr-/ *adj* decorated with a delicate pattern consisting of irregular lines and areas of colour: *The church has an ornate black and white marbled interior.* ○ *The plant has oval green leaves marbled with brownish-purple.* ○ *The steak was just how he liked – pink, juicy and marbled with fat.*

marble Ⓖ GLASS BALL /ˈmɑː.bl̩/ ⓊⓈ /ˈmɑːr-/ *noun* [C] a small ball usually made of coloured or transparent glass which is used in children's games

marbles /ˈmɑː.bl̩z/ ⓊⓈ /ˈmɑːr-/ *noun* [U] a children's game in which small round glass balls are rolled along the floor

marcasite /ˈmɑː.kə.saɪt/ ⓊⓈ /ˈmɑːr-/ *noun* [U] a mineral that can be cut and polished to look like precious stones and is used to make cheap jewellery

March Ⓜ MONTH /mɑːtʃ/ ⓊⓈ /mɑːrtʃ/ *noun* [C or U] (WRITTEN ABBREVIATION **Mar**) the third month of the year, after February and before April: *26(th) March/March 26(th)/ 26(th) Mar/Mar 26(th)* ○ *My birthday is* **on** *the eleventh of March/March the eleventh/*(MAINLY US) *March eleventh.* ○ *He retired* **last** *March/is retiring* **next** *March.* ○ *The meeting will be one day* **in/during** *March.* ○ *It has been one of the windiest Marches for several years.*

march Ⓦ WALK /mɑːtʃ/ ⓊⓈ /mɑːrtʃ/ *verb* **1** [I or T] to walk with regular steps keeping the body stiff, usually in a formal group of people who are all walking in the same way: *The band marched through the streets.* ○ *The soldiers marched 90 miles in three days.* **2** [I] to walk somewhere quickly and in a determined way, often because you are angry: *She marched into my office demanding to know why I hadn't written my report.* **march** /mɑːtʃ/ ⓊⓈ /mɑːrtʃ/ *noun* **1** [C or U] a walk, especially by a group of soldiers all walking with the same movement and speed: *It had been a long march and the soldiers were weary.* ○ *The border was within a day's march* (= distance measured in time taken to walk it). **2** [S] the determined advance of a state, activity or idea: *It is impossible to stop the forward march of progress/time.* ○ *The island is being destroyed by the relentless march of tourism.*

● **on the march** If soldiers are on the march, they have started marching to a place.

● **Quick march!** an order given to soldiers to make them start marching

march Ⓣ TAKE FORCEFULLY /mɑːtʃ/ ⓊⓈ /mɑːrtʃ/ *verb* [T + adv or prep] to forcefully make someone go somewhere by taking hold of them and pulling them there or going there with them: *Without saying a word, she took hold of my arm and marched me* **off** *to the headmaster's office.* ○ *The police marched a gang of youths* **out of** *the building.* ⊃See also **frogmarch**.

march Ⓜ MUSIC /mɑːtʃ/ ⓊⓈ /mɑːrtʃ/ *noun* [C] a piece of music with a strong regular rhythm which is written for marching to: *a funeral march* ○ *Mendelssohn's Wedding March*

march Ⓟ PUBLIC EVENT /mɑːtʃ/ ⓊⓈ /mɑːrtʃ/ *noun* [C] an event in which a large number of people walk through a public place to express their support for something, or their disagreement with or disapproval of something: *She's going on a march on Saturday in protest over the closure of the hospital.* **march** /mɑːtʃ/ ⓊⓈ /mɑːrtʃ/ *verb* [I] *Over four thousand people marched through London today to protest against the proposed new law.* **marcher** /ˈmɑː.tʃəʳ/ ⓊⓈ /ˈmɑːr.tʃɚ/ *noun* [C] a person marching: *The marchers stopped outside the American embassy, chanting slogans and waving banners.*

ˈmarching ˌorders *plural noun* (US USUALLY **walking papers**) INFORMAL If you give someone their marching orders, you ask them to leave a place or a job because they have done something wrong: *Three players* **got** *their marching orders last week.* ○ *She was called into the boss's office and* **given** *her marching orders*

march-past /ˈmɑːtʃ.pɑːst/ ⓊⓈ /ˈmɑːrtʃ.pæst/ *noun* [C usually sing] a march of the armed forces past an officer of high rank or a king or queen

Mardi Gras /ˌmɑː.diˈgrɑː/ ⓊⓈ /ˌmɑːr-/ *noun* [C usually sing] **1** the day before the beginning of LENT, which is celebrated in some countries with lots of music, colourful COSTUMES and dancing in the streets **2** another name for **Shrove Tuesday**

mare /meəʳ/ ⓊⓈ /mer/ *noun* [C] an adult female horse ⊃Compare **stallion**.

margarine /ˌmɑː.dʒəˈriːn/ ⓊⓈ /ˈmɑːr.dʒɚ-/ *noun* [U] (UK INFORMAL **marge**) a food used for cooking and spreading on bread, which is similar to butter but softer and usually made from vegetable fat

margarita /ˌmɑː.gəˈriː.tə/ ⓊⓈ /-gəˈriː.t̬ə/ *noun* [C] a type of alcoholic drink: *A margarita is made with tequila, an* *orange liqueur and lime or lemon juice.*

margin OUTER PART /ˈmɑː.dʒɪn/ ⓤ /ˈmɑːr-/ *noun* [C] **1** the outer edge of an area: *The plant tends to grow in the lighter margins of woodland areas.* **2** the empty space to the side of the text on a page, sometimes separated from the rest of the page by a vertical line: *If I have any comments to make, I'll write them in the margin.*

• **on the margins of** *sth* If someone is on the margins of a group of people, they are part of that group, but they are different in important ways, and if someone is on the margins of an activity, they are only slightly involved: *He spent the 1980s on the margins of British politics.* ○ *The government needs to reach out to those on the margins of society.*

margin DIFFERENCE /ˈmɑː.dʒɪn/ ⓤ /ˈmɑːr-/ *noun* [C] the amount by which one thing is different from another: *The Senate approved the use of military force by a margin of 52 votes to 47.* ○ *The poll shows that the government is leading by the* **narrowest** *of margins.*

marginal SMALL /ˈmɑː.dʒɪ.nəl/ ⓤ /ˈmɑːr-/ *adj* **1** very small in amount or effect: *The report suggests that there has only been a marginal improvement in women's pay over the past few years.* **2 of marginal interest** of interest to only a few people: *programmes about subjects of marginal interest*

marginally /ˈmɑː.dʒɪ.nə.li/ ⓤ /ˈmɑːr-/ *adv* slightly: *marginally more expensive*

marginalize, UK USUALLY **-ise** /ˈmɑː.dʒɪ.nə.laɪz/ ⓤ /ˈmɑːr-/ *verb* [T often passive] to treat someone or something as if they are not important: *Now that English has taken over as the main language, the country's native language has been marginalized.* UK USUALLY **marginalization**, UK USUALLY **-isation** /ˌmɑː.dʒɪ.nə.laɪˈzeɪ.ʃ³n/ ⓤ /ˌmɑːr.dʒɪ.nə.lɪ-/ *noun* [U] *The marginalization* **of** *certain groups within the community may lead to social unrest.*

marginal POLITICS /ˈmɑː.dʒɪ.nəl/ ⓤ /ˈmɑːr-/ *noun* [C] UK a political area or position in parliament which can be won by only a small number of votes because support for the main political parties is equally divided among the people voting: *Labour lost two of the key marginals in London.* ○ *The minister's own seat is a Tory marginal.* **marginal** /ˈmɑː.dʒɪ.nəl/ ⓤ /ˈmɑːr-/ *adj: The marginal* Tory **constituency** *was held by 2,200 votes in 1992.*

marginal land *noun* [U] land which is found on the edge of cultivated areas and is often difficult to grow crops on

margin of error *noun* [C] an additional amount of something, such as time or money, which you allow because there might be a mistake in your calculations: *When archaeologists date objects that are thousands of years old, they allow a margin of error of several hundred years.* ○ *The government estimates that its borrowing requirement this year could reach £150 billion, subject to a* **wide** *margin of error.*

marigold /ˈmær.ɪ.gəʊld/ ⓤ /-goʊld/ *noun* [C] a plant with bright yellow or orange flowers

marijuana, **marihuana** /ˌmær.əˈwɑː.nə/ *noun* [U] a usually illegal drug made from the dried leaves and flowers of the HEMP plant, which produces a feeling of pleasant relaxation if smoked or eaten

marina /məˈriː.nə/ *noun* [C] a small port that is used for pleasure rather than trade, often with hotels, restaurants and bars

marinade /ˌmær.ɪˈneɪd/ *noun* [C] a mixture, usually containing oil, wine or vinegar, and herbs and spices, which you pour over fish or meat before it is cooked, in order to add flavour to it or make it TENDER: *Pour the marinade over the beef and leave it for 24 hours.* **marinate** /ˈmær.ɪ.neɪt/ *verb* [T] *Marinate the chicken in white wine for a couple of hours before frying.*

marine SEA /məˈriːn/ *adj* [before n] related to the sea or sea transport: *The oil slick seriously threatens marine* **life** *around the islands.* ○ *Marine* **biologists** *are concerned about the effects of untreated sewage that is flowing into coastal waters.* ○ *One plane, a marine F18, was lost in the raid.* ○ *The Central harbour area will be closed to all marine traffic from 3.45 pm to 4.30 pm.* ⊃See also **maritime**.

marine SOLDIER /məˈriːn/ *noun* [C] a soldier who works closely with the navy and is trained especially for military operations on land which begin from the sea **Marines** /məˈriːnz/ *plural noun* a part of a country's military forces which takes part especially in operations on land which begin from the sea: *He's in* **the** *Royal Marines.*

• **Tell that/it to the Marines!** US SAYING said when you do not believe something

the Marine Corps *group noun* [S] a part of the United States military forces that consists of soldiers who operate on land and at sea

mariner /ˈmær.ɪ.nər/ ⓤ /-nə-/ *noun* [C] LITERARY OR OLD USE a sailor: *Many a mariner lost his life on these rocks.*

marionette /ˌmær.i.əˈnet/ *noun* [C] (ALSO **puppet**) a small model of a person or animal with parts of the body that are moved with strings

marital /ˈmær.ɪ.t³l/ ⓤ /-t̬³l/ *adj* FORMAL connected with marriage: *They've been having marital problems, apparently.* ○ HUMOROUS *You can't expect to live in a state of marital* **bliss**. ○ *marital breakdown*

marital aid *noun* [C] OLD-FASHIONED FOR **sex toy**

marital status *noun* [U] whether or not someone is married: *Could I ask you about your marital status?*

maritime /ˈmær.ɪ.taɪm/ *adj* FORMAL **1** connected with human activity at sea: *Amalfi and Venice were important maritime powers.* ○ *Make sure you visit the maritime museum if you're interested in anything to do with ships or seafaring.* **2** near the sea or coast: *The temperature change in winter is less pronounced in maritime areas.*

marjoram /ˈmɑː.dʒ³r.əm/ ⓤ /ˈmɑːr.dʒɚ-/ *noun* [U] a sweet Mediterranean herb used to flavour food

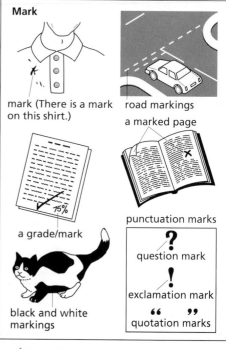

Mark

mark (There is a mark on this shirt.)

road markings

a marked page

a grade/mark

black and white markings

punctuation marks

question mark

exclamation mark

quotation marks

mark DIFFERENT AREA /mɑːk/ ⓤ /mɑːrk/ *noun* [C] **1** a small area on the surface of something which is damaged, dirty or different in some way: *There were dirty marks on her trousers where she had wiped her hands.* ○ *His fingers had left marks on the table's polished surface.* ○ *She had a red mark on her arm where she'd burnt herself.* **2** a typical feature or one which allows you to recognize someone or something: *Did your attacker have any distinguishing marks, such as a scar or a birthmark?* ○ *You can tell which puppy is which from the marks* (ALSO **markings**) *on their fur.*

• **leave *your*/its mark on *sb/sth*** to have an effect that changes someone or something, usually in a bad way: *The experience had left its mark on her.*
• **make a/*your* mark (on *sth*)** to have an important effect on something: *Daniel didn't work here for very long, but he definitely made his mark on the place.*
• **On your marks, get set, go!** (*US ALSO* **on your mark... get set... go**) something called out to competitors at the beginning of a running race
• **be quick/slow off the mark** to be quick/slow to act or react to an event or a situation: *The police were certainly quick off the mark reaching the scene of the accident.*
mark /mɑːk/ [US] /mɑːrk/ *verb* [I or T] to make a mark on something or someone: *Make sure you don't mark the paintwork while you're moving the furniture around.* ○ *A dark carpet won't mark as easily as a light one.*
marking /ˈmɑː.kɪŋ/ [US] /ˈmɑːr-/ *noun* [C usually pl] a mark which makes it possible to recognize something: *There are a couple of fish with blue markings, and a few more with gold stripes down the side.* ○ *The army said the relief flight would be too dangerous as none of its helicopters had Red Cross markings.*

mark [SYMBOL] /mɑːk/ [US] /mɑːrk/ *noun* [C] **1** a symbol which is used for giving information: *I've put a mark on the map where I think we should go for a picnic.* ○ *What do those marks in the middle of the road mean?* **2** a written or printed symbol: *a question mark* ○ *an exclamation mark* ○ *punctuation marks*
mark /mɑːk/ [US] /mɑːrk/ *verb* [T] to show where something is by drawing or putting something somewhere: *I've marked the route around the one-way system on the town plan.* ○ *I'd like everyone to mark their progress on the chart every week.* ○ *X marks the spot where the treasure is buried.*
• **(You) mark my words!** *OLD-FASHIONED* something that you say when you tell someone about something that you are certain will happen in the future: *He'll cause trouble – you mark my words!*
• **be marked out as *sth*** *UK* (*US* **be marked as *sth***) to be shown to be different because of a certain characteristic: *I can't speak a word of French so I'm marked out as a foreigner as soon as I arrive in France.*
marker /ˈmɑː.kəʳ/ [US] /ˈmɑːr.kɚ/ *noun* [C] a sign which shows where something is: *I've put in some markers where I planted the seeds.* ○ *She reached the 500-metre marker in record time.*

mark [REPRESENTATION] /mɑːk/ [US] /mɑːrk/ *noun* [C] an action which is understood to represent or show a characteristic of a person or thing or feeling: *He took off his hat as a mark **of respect** for her dead husband.* ○ *It's the mark **of** a gentleman to stand up when someone enters the room.* ○ *I'd like to give this bottle of wine as a mark **of** appreciation for all the work you've done for us.*
mark /mɑːk/ [US] /mɑːrk/ *verb* [T] **1** to represent or show a characteristic of a person or thing or feeling: *The band's songs have always been marked by controversial lyrics.* ○ *The signing of the treaty marked a major milestone on the road to European union.* **2** to show respect for or COMMEMORATE: *Tomorrow's parade will mark the fiftieth anniversary of the battle.*

mark [JUDGMENT] /mɑːk/ [US] /mɑːrk/ *noun* [C] *MAINLY UK* a judgment, expressed as a number or letter, about the quality of a piece of work done at school, college or university: *What mark did you **get** in the biology exam?* ○ *Matilda's had very good marks in/for English throughout the year.* ○ *UK You scored **full** marks in the test – ten out of ten!*
mark /mɑːk/ [US] /mɑːrk/ *verb* [T] to correct mistakes in and give points for a piece of work: *I was up half the night marking exam papers.* ○ *UK You'll be marked **down*** (= given a lower mark) *for poor spelling and punctuation.*

mark [LEVEL] /mɑːk/ [US] /mɑːrk/ *noun* [S] the intended or desired level: *Sales have already passed the million mark.*
• **be up to the mark** to be good enough: *Her latest batch of work just isn't up to the mark.*

mark [MACHINE] /mɑːk/ [US] /mɑːrk/ *noun* **Mark** used before a number to describe a variation of a machine, particularly one that is an improvement on the original machine: *The car has enjoyed modest success since its launch, but the Mark 2 version is expected to be far more popular.*

mark [SPORT] *UK* /mɑːk/ [US] /mɑːrk/ *verb* [T] (*US* **cover**) to prevent a member of the opposing team from taking control of the ball by staying close to them all the time

mark [MARCH] /mɑːk/ [US] /mɑːrk/ *verb* **1 mark time** to march in one place without moving forward **2 mark time** to do little while waiting for something that is going to happen: *She's just marking time until she goes off to university.*

PHRASAL VERBS WITH **mark** ▼

▲ **mark *sth* down** [REDUCE] *phrasal verb* [M] to reduce the price of something, usually in order to encourage people to buy it: *Low consumer demand has forced us to mark down a wide range of goods, sometimes **by** as much as 30%.* ○ *Shares in the electricity companies were marked down following the announcement of the new energy tax.*
▲ **mark *sth* down** [RECORD] *phrasal verb* [M] to write something on a piece of paper in order to make a record of it: *I've marked down the number of each item sold.* ○ *Look carefully at these questions and mark your answers down in the right-hand column.*
▲ **mark *sb* down as *sth*** *phrasal verb* to consider someone as a particular type of person: *I'd marked her down **as** a Labour Party supporter, but I was completely wrong.*
▲ **mark *sth/sb* off** [ON A LIST] *phrasal verb* [M] If you mark off items or people that are on a list, you record that you have dealt with them: *As I complete each task I mark it off.*
▲ **mark *sth* off** [SEPARATE] *phrasal verb* to separate an area by putting something around it: *Police had marked off the area where the body was found.*
▲ **mark *sth* out** *phrasal verb* to show the shape or position of something by drawing a line around it: *He'd marked out a volleyball court on the beach with a stick.*
▲ **mark *sth* up** *phrasal verb* [M] to increase the price of something: *They buy paintings at auctions, mark them up and then resell them at a vast profit to collectors.* ○ *In the days of hyperinflation, we would rush to the market as soon as we were paid and buy our weekly groceries before they were marked up.* ○ *Shares in retail businesses were marked up on the news that consumer spending rose last month.*

markdown /ˈmɑːk.daʊn/ [US] /ˈmɑːrk-/ *noun* [C] a reduction in the price of something: *We're offering a 10% markdown on selected items.*

marked /mɑːkt/ [US] /mɑːrkt/ *adj* describes a change or difference in behaviour or a situation that is very obvious or noticeable: *There was a marked improvement in my health when I gave up smoking.* ○ *Unemployment has fallen again, although the change is less marked than last month.* ○ *The president spoke with passion for an hour, **in** marked **contrast** to his subdued address to the parliament yesterday.* **markedly** /ˈmɑː.kɪd.li/ [US] /ˈmɑːr-/ *adv*: *Eye-witness accounts of the fighting differ markedly from police reports of what happened.*

ˌmarked ˈman/ˈwoman *noun* [C usually sing] someone who is at risk of unpleasant action being taken against them: *He is still free to travel the world, but he knows that he is a marked man.*

ˈmarker (ˌpen) *noun* [C] a thick pen for writing or drawing

market [PLACE] /ˈmɑː.kɪt/ [US] /ˈmɑːr-/ *noun* [C] a place or event at which people gather in order to buy and sell things: *Fruit and vegetables are much cheaper from/in/on the market than in the supermarket.* ○ *She runs a stall in/on the market.* ○ *The indoor flower market is a big tourist attraction.* ○ *a craft market* ○ *The town's always busy on market **day**.* ➲See also **marketplace**.

market [BUYING AND SELLING] /ˈmɑː.kɪt/ [US] /ˈmɑːr-/ *noun* [C] **1** the people who might want to buy something, or a part of the world where something is sold: *Are you sure there's a market **for** the product?* ○ *We estimate the potential market **for** the new phones to be around one million people in this country alone.* ○ *The domestic market is still depressed, but demand abroad is picking up.* ○ *They've increased their **share of** the market by 10%*

over the past year. **2** the business or trade in a particular product, including financial products: *the coffee market* ○ *the economic market* ○ *the commodities market* ○ *the stock market* ○ *the job market* ○ *the housing market*

• **in the market for *sth*** interested in buying something: *Thanks for the offer, but I'm not in the market for another car at the moment.*

• **on the market** available for sale: *We **put** our house on the market as soon as house prices started to rise.* ○ *This is one of the best televisions on the market.* ○ *The pictures would sell for half a million on the **open** market* (= if offered for sale without a fixed price).

marketeer /ˌmɑː.kɪˈtɪəʳ/ [US] /ˌmɑːr.kəˈtɪr/ *noun* [C] someone who works in or supports a particular market system: *Under the old regime **black** marketeers would buy almost anything from Western tourists and resell it at an enormous profit.* ○ ***Free** marketeers are vehemently opposed to the new safety regulations which they say will increase employers' costs.*

market [MAKE AVAILABLE] /ˈmɑː.kɪt/ [US] /ˈmɑːr-/ *verb* [T] to make goods available to buyers in a planned way which encourages people to buy more of them, for example by advertising: *Their products are very cleverly marketed.*

marketing /ˈmɑː.kɪ.tɪŋ/ [US] /ˈmɑːr.kɪ.t̬ɪŋ/ *noun* [U] a job that involves encouraging people to buy a product or service: *a career in marketing* ○ *Our marketing people have come up with a great idea for the launch of the new model.*

marketable /ˈmɑː.kɪ.tə.bl̩/ [US] /ˈmɑːr.kɪ.t̬ə-/ *adj* Marketable products or skills are easy to sell because a lot of people want them: *This is a highly marketable product.* **marketability** /ˌmɑː.kɪ.təˈbɪl.ɪ.ti/ [US] /ˌmɑːr.kɪ.t̬əˈbɪl.ə.t̬i/ *noun* [U] **marketer** /ˈmɑː.kɪ.təʳ/ [US] /ˈmɑːr.kɪ.t̬ɚ/ *noun* [C]

market [SHOP] /ˈmɑː.kɪt/ [US] /ˈmɑːr-/ *noun* [C] *US* a shop that sells mainly food ➲See also **hypermarket**; **supermarket**. **marketing** /ˈmɑː.kɪ.tɪŋ/ [US] /ˈmɑːr.kɪ.t̬ɪŋ/ *noun* [U] *We like to get the marketing done on Thursdays so we can have the weekend free.*

ˌmarket ˈforces *plural noun* the forces that decide price levels in an economy or trading system whose activities are not influenced or limited by government: *The action of market forces means that the cost of something rises if demand for it rises and the amount available remains constant.*

ˌmarket ˈgarden *UK noun* [C] (*US* **truck farm**) a small farm where fruit and vegetables are grown for selling to the public **ˌmarket ˈgardener** *UK noun* [C] (*US* **truck farmer**) *Farmers and market gardeners have been badly affected by the drought.* **ˌmarket ˈgardening** *UK noun* [U] (*US* **truck farming**)

marketplace /ˈmɑː.kɪt.pleɪs/ [US] /ˈmɑːr-/ *noun* [C] **1** a small outside area in a town where there is a market: *I'll meet you in the marketplace next to the fountain.* **2** a set of trading conditions or the business environment: *To remain competitive the company has to be able to adapt to the changing marketplace.* ○ *It's essential that we maintain our position in the marketplace* (= keep our share of business activity).

ˌmarket ˈprice *noun* [S] a price which is likely to be paid for something: *They're asking £60 000 for their flat, but the market price is nearer £55 000.*

ˌmarket reˈsearch *noun* [U] the collection and examination of information about things that people buy or might buy and their feelings about things that they have bought: *Market research shows that demand for small cars will continue to grow.*

ˌmarket reˈsearcher *noun* [C]

ˈmarket ˌtown *noun* [C] a small town in the countryside which has a regular market and acts as a business centre for surrounding farms and villages: *a quiet market town in Northumberland*

markka /ˈmɑː.kɑː/ [US] /ˈmɑːr-/ *noun* [C] the standard unit of money used in Finland before they started using the euro

marksman /ˈmɑːks.mən/ [US] /ˈmɑːrks-/ *noun* [C] someone who can shoot a gun very accurately: ***Police** marksmen were called to the scene.*

marksmanship /ˈmɑːks.mən.ʃɪp/ [US] /ˈmɑːrks-/ *noun* [U] skill in shooting

mark-up /ˈmɑːk.ʌp/ [US] /ˈmɑːrk-/ *noun* [C] the amount by which the price of something is increased before it is sold again: *The usual mark-up **on** clothes is about 20 percent.*

marmalade /ˈmɑː.mə.leɪd/ [US] /ˈmɑːr-/ *noun* [U] a soft substance with a sweet but slightly bitter taste, made by cooking fruit such as oranges with sugar to preserve it. It is eaten on bread, usually for breakfast.

marmoset /ˈmɑː.mə.set/ [US] /ˈmɑːr-/ *noun* [C] a very small monkey from the tropical forests of South and Central America which has large eyes, thick fur, a long hairy tail and long curved and pointed nails

maroon /məˈruːn/ *noun* [C or U], *adj* (of) a dark reddish purple colour

marooned /məˈruːnd/ *adj* left in a place from which you cannot escape: *What would you miss most if you found yourself marooned on a desert island?* ○ *The police are advising motorists marooned by the blizzards to stay in their cars until the rescue services can reach them.*

maroon /məˈruːn/ *verb* [T]

marque /mɑːk/ [US] /mɑːrk/ *noun* [C] a name of a range of cars, which is sometimes different from the name of the company that produces them

marquee [TENT] /mɑːˈkiː/ [US] /mɑːr-/ *noun* [C] *UK* a large tent used for eating and drinking in at events held mainly outside that involve a lot of people: *We're planning to hold the wedding reception in a marquee in the garden.*

marquee [ROOF] /mɑːˈkiː/ [US] /mɑːr-/ *noun* [C] *US* a roof-like structure which sticks out over the entrance to a public building, especially a theatre, and on which there is usually a sign

marquee [MAIN PERFORMER] /mɑːˈkiː/ [US] /mɑːr-/ *adj* [before n] *US* being the main performer or sports person in a show, film, sports event, etc. or being the performer, etc. whose name will attract most people to the show, film, etc: *The studio chiefs wanted a marquee name in the lead role, not some unknown.*

marquetry /ˈmɑː.kɪ.tri/ [US] /ˈmɑːr-/ *noun* [U] a decorative pattern on a piece of furniture which consists of thin sheets of very shiny wood of different colours fixed on the surface of the furniture

marquis, marquess /ˈmɑː.kwɪs/ [US] /ˈmɑːr-/ *noun* [C] (the title of) a British man of high social rank, between a DUKE and an EARL: ***the** Marquis **of** Blandford*

marriage /ˈmær.ɪdʒ/ [US] /ˈmer-/ *noun* [C or U] a legally accepted relationship between a woman and a man in which they live as husband and wife, or the official ceremony which results in this: *They had a long and **happy** marriage.* ○ *She went to live abroad after the break-up of her marriage.* ○ *She has two daughters by her first marriage.* ➲See also **marital**; **marry**.

• **marriage of convenience** a marriage in which the partners have married, not because they love each other, but in order to obtain a benefit, such as the right to live in the other partner's country

marriageable /ˈmær.ɪ.dʒə.bl̩/ [US] /ˈmer-/ *adj OLD-FASHIONED* suitable for marriage: *a wealthy man of marriageable age*

ˈmarriage ˌbureau *noun* [C] *UK OLD-FASHIONED* an organization for people who want to get married or find a partner, which people join in order to be introduced to each other

ˈmarriage cerˌtificate *noun* [C] the document that shows two people are legally married

ˌmarriage ˈguidance *UK noun* [U] (*US* **marriage counseling**) advice given by a trained person to people who are trying to find solutions to problems with their marriage: *a marriage guidance **counsellor***

ˈmarried ˌname *noun* [C usually sing] A woman's married name is the family name of her husband: *She used to be Rachel Elliot – I think her married name is Cartwright.*

marrow [TISSUE] /ˈmær.əʊ/ [US] /-oʊ/ *noun* [U] (*ALSO* **bone marrow**) soft fatty tissue in the centre of a bone

• **be chilled/frozen to the marrow** *MAINLY UK* to be extremely cold

M

marrow VEGETABLE *UK* /ˈmær.əʊ/ *US* /-oʊ/ *noun* [C or U] (*MAINLY US* **squash**) a long round vegetable with a thick green or yellow skin, white flesh and a lot of seeds at its centre ➲See picture **Vegetables** on page Centre 2

marrow bone *noun* [C] a bone that contains a lot of edible marrow and is used in cooking, often to flavour soups

marrowfat (pea) /ˌmær.əʊ.fætˈpiː/ *US* /-oʊ-/ *noun* [C] a large green pea

marry /ˈmær.i/ *US* /ˈmer-/ *verb* **1** [I or T] to become the legally accepted husband or wife of someone in an official or religious ceremony: *Men tend to marry later than women.* ○ *Paul married Lucy four years ago.* ○ *They don't have any plans to marry at present.* ➲See also **marriage**. **2** [T] to perform the ceremony of marriage as a priest or official: *The couple were married by the Archbishop of Canterbury* .

• **marry beneath** *you* to marry someone people think is not good enough for you because he or she is from a lower social class

• **not be the marrying kind** *HUMOROUS* If a man is not the marrying kind, he does not want to be married. People sometimes use this phrase to mean that the man is homosexual.

• **Marry in haste, repent at leisure.** *SAYING* This means that if you marry someone without knowing them well, you will regret it later.

married /ˈmær.id/ *US* /ˈmer-/ *adj* **1** having a wife or husband: *a married couple* ○ *We've been **happily** married for five years.* ○ *Please state whether you are single, cohabiting, married, separated, divorced or widowed.* ○ *PC Smith was married with two children.* ○ *So how are you enjoying married **life**?* ○ *She had an affair with a married **man**.* ○ *The survey reveals that two-thirds of married **women** earn less than their husbands.* ○ *So how long have you been married **to** Nicky?* ○ *FIGURATIVE Rachel seems to be married **to** (= very involved with) her new job at the moment, so we hardly ever see her.* **2 get married** to begin a legal relationship with someone as their husband or wife: *When are you getting married?* ○ *Chris and Debbie got married last summer.* ○ *Jamie's getting married to Laura.*

PHRASAL VERBS WITH **marry**   ▼

▲ **marry** *sb* **off** *phrasal verb* [M] to make certain that someone, especially a female member of your family, gets married, or that they marry the person you have chosen: *She was married off **to** the local doctor by the age of sixteen.*

▲ **marry up** (*sth*) *phrasal verb* [M] If two things marry up or if you marry them up, they match or join together: *We need to marry up the names on your list with those on my list and see what the overlap is.*

Mars /mɑːz/ *US* /mɑːrz/ *noun* [S] the planet fourth in order of distance from the Sun, after the Earth and before Jupiter: *Mars is sometimes called the Red Planet because of its distinctive colour.* ○ *So is there **life on** Mars?* **Martian** /ˈmɑː.ʃ⁰n/ *US* /ˈmɑːr-/ *adj*

Martian /ˈmɑː.ʃ⁰n/ *US* /ˈmɑːr-/ *noun* [C] a creature, usually appearing in films and books, who is believed to come from Mars

marsala /mɑːˈsɑː.lə/ *US* /mɑːrˈsɑː.lɑː/ *noun* [U] a strong dark wine which is drunk when eating sweet dishes and is used in cooking

marsh /mɑːʃ/ *US* /mɑːrʃ/ *noun* [C or U] ground near a lake, river or the sea, that tends to flood and is always wet: *At the mouth of the river is a large area of marsh.* ○ *Rain had been falling steadily all day and the ground had become a marsh.*

marshes /ˈmɑː.ʃɪz/ *US* /ˈmɑːr-/ *plural noun* a large area of marsh: *At low tide in the estuary, cows graze on the marshes.* **marshy** /ˈmɑː.ʃi/ *US* /ˈmɑːr-/ *adj*: *This area was very marshy before the drainage system was installed.*

marshal ORGANIZE /ˈmɑː.ʃ⁰l/ *US* /ˈmɑːr-/ *verb* [T] **-ll-** or *US USUALLY* **-l-** to gather or organize people or things in order to achieve a particular aim: *The fighting in the city followed reports of the rebels marshalling their **forces** in the countryside.* ○ *The company is marshalling its **forces/resources** for a long court case.* ○ *They had*

---

marshalled an armada of 1000 boats and a squadron of 70 aircraft to help clear up the oil. ○ *It is unlikely that the rebels will be able to marshal as much firepower as the government troops.*

marshal OFFICIAL /ˈmɑː.ʃ⁰l/ *US* /ˈmɑːr-/ *noun* [C] an official who is involved in the organization of a public event: *Marshals struggled in vain to prevent spectators rushing onto the racetrack.* ○ *US The parade's **grand** marshal* (= the person leading it) *carried an elaborately carved staff.*

marshal LAW /ˈmɑː.ʃ⁰l/ *US* /ˈmɑːr-/ *noun* [C] *US* a government official who is responsible for putting the decisions of a law court into action: *US marshals specialize in finding fugitives and escapees.*

marshal OFFICER /ˈmɑː.ʃ⁰l/ *US* /ˈmɑːr-/ *noun* [C] **1** a title used for important officers in the armed forces of some countries: *a **field** marshal/**air vice** marshal* **2** *US* a title used for police or fire officers in some parts of the United States: *The deputy state fire marshal led the arson investigation.*

Marshal of the Royal Air Force *noun* [C] the highest rank in the British air force

marsh gas *noun* [U] a gas produced in a MARSH (= an area of very wet ground) by decaying plants that are covered by water

marshland /ˈmɑː.ʃ.lænd/ *US* /ˈmɑːrʃ-/ *noun* [C or U] an area of marsh

marshmallow SWEET /ˈmɑː.ʃ.mæl.əʊ/ *US* /ˈmɑːrʃ.mæl.oʊ/ *noun* [C or U] a soft, sweet pink or white food: *Why don't we toast some marshmallows over the fire?*

marshmallow COWARD /ˈmɑː.ʃ.mæl.əʊ/ *US* /ˈmɑːrʃ.mæl.oʊ/ *noun* [C] *INFORMAL HUMOROUS* a person who is not strong, brave or confident: *The situation called for someone tough, and I was a complete marshmallow.*

marshy /ˈmɑː.ʃi/ *US* /ˈmɑːr-/ *adj* ➲See at **marsh**.

marsupial /mɑːˈsuː.pi.əl/ *US* /mɑːr-/ *noun* [C] a type of mammal from Australasia or South or Central America which is not completely developed when it is born and is carried around in a pocket on the mother's body where it is fed and protected until it is completely developed: *Marsupials include koalas, possums and kangaroos.*

mart /mɑːt/ *US* /mɑːrt/ *noun* [C] *MAINLY US AND IRISH ENGLISH* a market or shopping centre: *Remember to get some bananas at the mart.* ○ *discount marts*

martial /ˈmɑː.ʃ⁰l/ *US* /ˈmɑːr-/ *adj* relating to soldiers, war or life in the armed forces

martial art *noun* [C usually pl] a sport that is a traditional Japanese or Chinese form of fighting or defending yourself: *Kung fu and karate are martial arts.*

martial law *noun* [U] the control of a city, country, etc. by an army instead of by its usual leaders: *Renegade forces captured the capital and **declared/imposed** martial law.*

martin /ˈmɑː.tɪn/ *US* /ˈmɑːr.t⁰n/ *noun* [C] a small bird like a SWALLOW but with a shorter tail

martinet /ˌmɑː.tɪˈnet/ *US* /ˌmɑːr.t̬ɪ-/ *noun* [C] *FORMAL DISAPPROVING* someone who demands that rules and orders always be obeyed, even when it is unnecessary or unreasonable to do so

martini /mɑːˈtiː.ni/ *US* /mɑːr-/ *noun* [C] **1** an alcoholic drink which combines GIN and VERMOUTH **2** *TRADEMARK* **Martini** a type of VERMOUTH

martyr /ˈmɑː.tə⁰/ *US* /ˈmɑːr.t̬ə/ *noun* [C] **1** a person who suffers greatly or is killed because of their political or religious beliefs, and is often admired because of it: *a Christian/Islamic/religious martyr* ○ *She fought against racism all her life and died a martyr **to the cause**.* **2** *DISAPPROVING* someone who tries to get sympathy from others when they have a problem or too much work, usually having caused the problem or chosen to do the work themselves: *She offers to do extra work, then **plays the** martyr!*

• **be a martyr to** *sth HUMOROUS* to often suffer from an illness: *She's a martyr to migraine!*

martyr /ˈmɑː.tə⁰/ *US* /ˈmɑːr.t̬ə/ *verb* [T often passive] to kill someone because of their religious or political beliefs

martyred /ˈmɑː.təd/ *US* /ˈmɑːr.t̬ə·d/ *adj* **1** A martyred person has been killed because of their religious or political beliefs: *a martyred saint* ○ *a martyred civil rights activist* **2** DISAPPROVING showing that you are suffering so that people will have sympathy for you: *She was wearing a martyred expression.*

martyrdom /ˈmɑː.tə.dəm/ ⑩ /ˈmɑːr.tə-/ *noun* [U] when someone suffers or is killed for their beliefs

marvel /ˈmɑː.vəl/ ⑩ /ˈmɑːr-/ *verb* [I] -ll- or *US USUALLY* -l- to show or experience great surprise or admiration: *We paused to marvel **at** the view.* ○ [+ that] *'I often marvel **that** humans can treat each other so badly.'* ○ [+ speech] *"Just look at that waterfall! Isn't it amazing?" she marvelled.*

marvel /ˈmɑː.vəl/ ⑩ /ˈmɑːr-/ *noun* [C] a thing or person that is very surprising or causes a lot of admiration: *This miniature TV is the latest technological marvel from Japan.* ○ *It's a marvel **(to me) how** they've managed to build the tunnel so quickly.*

marvellous *UK, US* **marvelous** /ˈmɑː.vəl.əs/ ⑩ /ˈmɑːr-/ *adj* extremely good: *He's done a marvellous job of the decorating.* ○ *It took me ages to get it right, but it was a marvellous feeling when I did.* ○ *It's marvellous how everyone's tried to help.* ○ *He was a truly marvellous storyteller.* ○ *We've achieved some marvellous results with this new drug.* **marvellously** *UK, US* **marvelously** /ˈmɑː.vəl.ə.sli/ ⑩ /ˈmɑːr-/ *adv: We've had a few arguments over the years, but in general we get on marvellously.*

Marxism /ˈmɑːk.sɪ.zəm/ ⑩ /ˈmɑːrk-/ *noun* [U] a social, political and economic theory which is based on the writings of Karl Marx **Marxist** /ˈmɑːk.sɪst/ ⑩ /ˈmɑːrk-/ *noun* [C], *adj: a Marxist government*

Marxist-Leninist /ˌmɑːk.sɪstˈlen.ɪ.nɪst/ ⑩ /ˌmɑːrk-/ *adj* [before n], *noun* [C] relating to the variation of Marxism that was developed by Lenin before the political changes in Russia in 1917, or someone who follows this **Marxism-Leninism** /ˌmɑːk.sɪ.zəmˈlen.ɪ.nɪ.zəm/ ⑩ /ˌmɑːrk-/ *noun* [U]

marzipan /ˈmɑː.zɪ.pæn/ ⑩ /ˈmɑːr-/ *noun* [U] a soft yellow or white food made from ALMONDS, sugar and eggs that is used for decorating cakes and making sweets

masc *adj* ABBREVIATION FOR **masculine** GRAMMAR

mascara /mæsˈkɑː.rə/ ⑩ /-ˈkær.ə/ *noun* [C or U] a thick dark liquid make-up that is used for colouring EYELASHES and making them appear thicker and longer **mascaraed** /mæsˈkɑː.rəd/ ⑩ /-ˈkær.əd/ *adj: long mascaraed lashes*

mascot /ˈmæs.kɒt/ ⑩ /-kɑːt/ *noun* [C] a person, animal or object which is believed to bring good luck, or which represents an organization: *a team mascot* ○ *The Olympic Games always has an official mascot.*

masculine MALE /ˈmæs.kjʊ.lɪn/ *adj* having characteristics that are traditionally thought to be typical of or suitable for men: *a masculine appearance/voice* ⊃Compare **feminine** FEMALE.
masculinity /ˌmæs.kjʊˈlɪn.ɪ.ti/ ⑩ /-ə.ţi/ *noun* [U] the characteristics that are traditionally thought to be typical of or suitable for men: *I don't think his masculinity is in question.*

masculine GRAMMAR /ˈmæs.kjʊ.lɪn/ *adj* (WRITTEN ABBREVIATION **masc, m**) belonging to the group of nouns, pronouns, etc. which are not FEMININE or NEUTER: *The French word for 'sun' is masculine – 'le soleil', but the German word is feminine – 'die Sonne'.*

mash /mæʃ/ *verb* [T] **1** to crush food, usually after cooking it, so that it forms a soft mass: *Mash the potatoes and then mix in the butter and herbs.* ⊃See picture **In the Kitchen** on page Centre 16 **2** MAINLY US INFORMAL to violently crush part of a body or an object: *His face was badly mashed **up** in the accident.*
mashed /mæʃt/ *adj* crushed: *UK mashed potato/ US AND UK mashed potatoes*
mash /mæʃ/ *noun* [U] *UK INFORMAL* **mashed potatoes**: *sausage and mash*
masher /ˈmæʃ.əʳ/ ⑩ /-ɚ/ *noun* [C] a kitchen utensil for mashing potatoes and other vegetables: *a potato masher*
▲ **mash up** *sth phrasal verb* [M] to crush something, especially food: *He always mashes up his peas before he eats them.*

mashed po'tatoes *noun* [U] (*UK ALSO* **mashed potato**) potatoes that have been boiled and crushed until they are smooth

mask COVER /mɑːsk/ ⑩ /mæsk/ *noun* [C] **1** a covering for all or part of the face which protects, hides or decorates the person wearing it: *a gas mask* ○ *a surgical mask* ○ *The bank robbers wore masks throughout the raid.* **2** appearance or behaviour that hides the reality: *The newspaper revealed the sordid truth behind his mask **of** respectability.*
● *sb's* **mask slips** If someone's mask slips, they do something which suddenly shows their real character, when they have been pretending to be a different, usually nicer, type of person.
masked /mɑːskt/ ⑩ /mæskt/ *adj* wearing a mask: *Suddenly two masked gunmen burst into the shop and demanded all the cash in the till.*

mask HIDE /mɑːsk/ ⑩ /mæsk/ *verb* [T] to prevent something from being seen or noticed: *I've put some flowers in there to mask the smell.*

masked 'ball *noun* [C] a formal dance where masks are worn

masking ,tape *noun* [U] sticky paper tape that is used especially when painting to protect the edges of an area you do not intend to paint

masochism /ˈmæs.ə.kɪ.zəm/ *noun* [U] **1** the obtaining of especially sexual pleasure from being hurt or controlled by another person ⊃Compare **sadism**. **2** INFORMAL the enjoyment of an activity or situation that most people would find very unpleasant: *I reckon you need to be into masochism to run marathons.* ⊃Compare **sadism**.
masochist /ˈmæs.ə.kɪst/ *noun* [C] **masochistic** /ˌmæs.əˈkɪs.tɪk/ *adj: masochistic behaviour/pleasure/fantasies*

Mason SOCIETY MEMBER /ˈmeɪ.sən/ *noun* [C] a **Freemason**
Masonic /məˈsɒn.ɪk/ ⑩ /-ˈsɑː.nɪk/ *adj*
Masonry /ˈmeɪ.sən.ri/ *noun* [U] ⊃See **Freemasonry** at **Freemason**.

mason SKILLED WORKER /ˈmeɪ.sən/ *noun* [C] **1** a STONEMASON (= person who cuts stone) **2** US a **bricklayer**

the Mason-Dixon Line /ðəˌmeɪ.sənˈdɪk.sən̩laɪn/ *noun* [S] the border between the states of Maryland and Pennsylvania in the US, traditionally considered to mark the division between the north and south of the US

masonry /ˈmeɪ.sən.ri/ *noun* [U] **1** the bricks and pieces of stone that are used to make a building: *Several of the firefighters were injured by falling masonry.* **2** the skill of building with brick and stone

masque /mɑːsk/ ⑩ /mæsk/ *noun* [C] a theatrical entertainment including poetry, singing and dancing which was performed in England in the 16th and 17th centuries, especially at a royal COURT (= official home of a king or queen)

masquerade /ˌmæs.kəʳˈeɪd/ ⑩ /-kəˈreɪd/ *noun* [C or U] behaviour that is intended to prevent the truth about something unpleasant or not desirable from becoming known: *They kept up the masquerade of being happily married for over thirty years.*
masquerade /ˌmæs.kəʳˈeɪd/ ⑩ /-kəˈreɪd/ *verb*
▲ **masquerade as** *sb/sth phrasal verb* to pretend or appear to be someone or something: *Hooligans masquerading as football fans have once again caused disturbances.*

mass LARGE AMOUNT /mæs/ *noun* [S] a large amount of something that has no particular shape or arrangement: *The explosion reduced the church to **a** mass **of** rubble.* ○ *The forest is **a** mass **of** colour in autumn.*
● **the mass of** *sth* most of something: *The mass of the people support the government's reforms.*
masses /ˈmæs.ɪz/ *plural noun* MAINLY UK INFORMAL a lot: [+ to infinitive] *I've got masses **to** do at the weekend.* ○ *There were masses **of** people in town today.*

mass SOLID LUMP /mæs/ *noun* [C] a solid lump with no clear shape: *The sauce was now a sticky mass at the bottom of the pan.*

mass INVOLVING MANY /mæs/ *adj* [before n] having an effect on or involving a large number of people or forming a large amount: *weapons of mass destruction* ○ *a mass murderer* ○ *mass starvation* ○ *Opposition groups plan to*

stage mass demonstrations all over the country.
mass /mæs/ *verb* [I] to come together in large numbers: *Thousands of troops have massed along the border in preparation for an invasion.*
massed /mæst/ *adj* [before n] brought together in large numbers: *Every day, massed ranks of tourists pass slowly through the rooms of the palace.*
the ˈmasses *plural noun* the ordinary people who form the largest group in a society: *He was popular with the aristocracy but failed to win the support of the masses.*

mass [MATTER] /mæs/ *noun* [C] *SPECIALIZED* (in physics) the amount of matter in any solid object or in any volume of liquid or gas: *The acceleration of a body equals the force exerted on it divided by its mass.*

Mass [CEREMONY], **mass** /mæs/ *noun* [C or U] a religious ceremony in some Christian churches based on Christ's last meal with his DISCIPLES, or music written for the parts of this ceremony: *to go to Mass* ➲See also **Communion**.

massacre /ˈmæs.ə.kəʳ/ [US] /-kɚ/ *noun* [C] **1** an act of killing a lot of people: *He ordered the massacre of 2,000 women and children.* **2** *INFORMAL* a bad defeat, especially in sport: *The changes to the team come after their 7-2 massacre in the final.*
massacre /ˈmæs.ə.kəʳ/ [US] /-kɚ/ *verb* [T] **1** to kill many people in a short period of time: *Hundreds of civilians were massacred in the raid.* **2** *INFORMAL* to defeat an opponent very badly in a competition or election: *England was massacred 5-0 by France in the semi-final.*

massage [RUB BODY] /ˈmæs.ɑːdʒ/ [US] /məˈsɑːdʒ/ *verb* [T] to rub and press someone's body with regular repeated movements, in order to relax them or to reduce stiffness or pain in their joints or muscles: *Would you massage my shoulders?*
• **massage *sb's* ego** to praise someone in order to make them think they are better than they are
massage /ˈmæs.ɑːdʒ/ [US] /məˈsɑːdʒ/ *noun* [C or U] the activity of rubbing or pressing parts of someone's body in order to make them relax or to stop their muscles hurting: *a back/foot/head massage* ○ *a qualified massage therapist* ○ *She gave me a massage.*

massage [LIE] /ˈmæs.ɑːdʒ/ [US] /məˈsɑːdʒ/ *verb* [T] to try to make facts or numbers appear better than they really are in order to deceive somebody: *Television companies have been massaging their viewing figures in order to attract more advertising revenue.*

ˈmassage ˌparlour [TREATMENT] *UK, US* **masˈsage ˌparlor** *noun* [C] a place where you can pay someone to give you a massage

ˈmassage ˌparlour [SEX] *UK, US* **masˈsage ˌparlor** *noun* [C] a place where a person can pay to have sex

masseur /mæsˈɜːʳ/ [US] /-ˈsɝː/ *noun* [C] a person whose job it is to give MASSAGES to people

masseuse /mæˈsɜːz/ [US] /-ˈsɝːz/ *noun* [C] a female masseur

massif /mæsˈiːf/ *noun* [C] *SPECIALIZED* a group or area of mountains

massive /ˈmæs.ɪv/ *adj* very large in size, amount or number: *They've got a massive house.* ○ *She died after taking a massive overdose of drugs.* ○ *If the drought continues, deaths will occur on a massive scale.*
massively /ˈmæs.ɪv.li/ *adv*: *The film is a massively (= very) ambitious project.* **massiveness** /ˈmæs.ɪv.nəs/ *noun* [U]

ˌmass ˈmailing *noun* [C] *US FOR* **mailshot**

ˌmass ˈmarket *noun* [C usually sing] A product that is designed for the mass market is intended to be bought by as many people as possible, not just by people with a lot of money or a special interest: *Advances in microchip technology have made these cameras smaller and cheaper and affordable to the mass market.*

the ˌmass ˈmedia *group noun* newspapers, television and radio: *The mass media has become one of the main instruments of political change.*

mass-produce /ˌmæs.prəˈdjuːs/ [US] /-ˈduːs/ *verb* [T] to produce a lot of goods cheaply using machines in a factory **mass-produced** /ˌmæs.prəˈdjuːst/ [US] /-ˈduːst/ *adj*: *mass-produced souvenirs* **ˌmass proˈduction** *noun* [U]

ˌmass ˈtransit *noun* [U] *US FOR* **public transport**

mast /mɑːst/ [US] /mæst/ *noun* [C] **1** a tall pole on a boat or ship that supports its sails ➲See picture **Planes, Ships and Boats** on page Centre 14 **2** a tall metal pole used to support an AERIAL for radio or television signals: *a television/radio mast* **3** a pole that holds a flag

mastectomy /mæsˈtek.tə.mi/ *noun* [C] a medical operation to remove a woman's breast: *a partial mastectomy* (= when part of the breast is removed) ○ *a double mastectomy* (= when both breasts are removed)

master [CONTROL] /ˈmɑː.stəʳ/ [US] /ˈmæs.tɚ/ *noun* [C] **1** a person who has control over or responsibility for someone or something, or who is the most important or influential person in a situation or organization: *OLD-FASHIONED a slave and his master* ○ *With careful training, a dog will obey its master completely.* ○ *UK The Master of St. John's College will be launching the appeal.* **2** *UK OLD-FASHIONED* a male school teacher: *Mr Wells was my Latin master at school.* ➲See also **headmaster**.
• **be *your* own master** to be independent and able to make your own decisions
master /ˈmɑː.stəʳ/ [US] /ˈmæs.tɚ/ *verb* [T] to learn to control an emotion or feeling: *I finally mastered my fear of flying.*
masterful /ˈmɑː.stə.fəl/ [US] /ˈmæs.tɚ-/ *adj* able to control people and situations: *Once she became a prosecutor, she quickly established herself as a masterful trial lawyer.* ○ *He has a deep, masterful voice.*
mastery /ˈmɑː.stər.i/ [US] /ˈmæs.tɚ-/ *noun* [U] complete control of something: *her mastery **of** the situation*

master [SKILLED PERSON] /ˈmɑː.stəʳ/ [US] /ˈmæs.tɚ/ *noun* [C] **1** a person who is very skilled in a particular job or activity: *He was **a** master **of** disguise.* **2** a famous and very skilled painter: *This painting is clearly the work of a master.*
master /ˈmɑː.stəʳ/ [US] /ˈmæs.tɚ/ *adj* [before n] extremely skilled: *a master craftsman* ○ *a master chef*
master /ˈmɑː.stəʳ/ [US] /ˈmæs.tɚ/ *verb* [T] to learn how to do something well: *to master a technique* ○ *She lived in Italy for several years but never quite mastered the language.* ○ *He quickly mastered **the art of** interviewing people.*
masterful /ˈmɑː.stə.fəl/ [US] /ˈmæs.tɚ-/ *adj* If an action is masterful, it is very skilful: *a masterful performance*
masterfully /ˈmɑː.stə.fəl.i/ [US] /ˈmæs.tɚ-/ *adv*
masterly /ˈmɑː.stə.li/ [US] /ˈmæs.tɚ-/ *adj* done extremely well: *She gave a masterly performance as Kate in 'The Taming of the Shrew'.*
mastery /ˈmɑː.stər.i/ [US] /ˈmæs.tɚ-/ *noun* [U] If someone has a mastery of something, they are extremely skilled at it: *her mastery **of** the violin*

master [COPY] /ˈmɑː.stəʳ/ [US] /ˈmæs.tɚ/ *noun* [C] an original version of something from which copies can be made: *I've sent her a copy and have kept the master.* ○ *You should keep the master **copy*** (= the original) *in a safe place.*

ˌmaster ˈbedroom *noun* [C] the largest bedroom in a house

ˈmaster ˌclass *noun* [C] a class taught by someone who has an expert knowledge or skill in a particular area, especially in music

ˈmaster ˌkey *noun* [C] a key which can be used to open any of several different locks

mastermind /ˈmɑː.stə.maɪnd/ [US] /ˈmæs.tɚ-/ *verb* [T] to plan a difficult activity, often a crime, in detail and make certain that it happens successfully: *He's believed to have masterminded the attacks.* **mastermind** /ˈmɑː.stə.maɪnd/ [US] /ˈmæs.tɚ-/ *noun* [C] *a criminal mastermind*

ˌMaster of ˈArts *noun* [C] (*ABBREVIATION* **MA**) an advanced college or university degree in a subject such as literature, language, history or social science, or a person who has this degree

ˌmaster of ˈceremonies *noun* [C] (*ABBREVIATION* **MC**) a person who makes certain that official events happen correctly, for example by introducing performers at the right time

M

ˌMaster of Phiˈlosophy *noun* [C] (*ABBREVIATION* **MPhil**) in the UK, an advanced college or university degree in any subject, or a person who has this degree

ˌMaster of ˈScience *noun* [C] (*UK ABBREVIATION* **MSc**, *US ABBREVIATION* **MS**) an advanced college or university degree in a scientific subject, or a person who has this degree

masterpiece /ˈmɑː.stə.piːs/ [US] /ˈmæs.tɚ-/ *noun* [C] **1** (*ALSO* **masterwork**) a work of art such as a painting, film or book which is done or made with great skill, and is often a person's greatest work: *'The Last Supper' is widely regarded as Leonardo da Vinci's masterpiece.* ➲See also **chef d'oeuvre**. **2** a skilful or clever example of something: *Her press conference was a masterpiece **of** media manipulation.*

ˈmaster ˌplan *noun* [C] an organized set of decisions made by one person or a team of people about how to do something in the future

Master's degree /ˌmɑː.stəz.dɪˈgriː/ [US] /ˌmæs.tɚz-/ *noun* [C] (*INFORMAL* **Master's**) an advanced college or university degree: *An MA and a MSc are both Master's degrees.*

masterstroke /ˈmɑː.stə.strəʊk/ [US] /ˈmæs.tɚ.stroʊk/ *noun* [C usually sing] *MAINLY UK* an action which is very clever and produces success: *His decision to change the team's formation for the final match was a masterstroke.*

ˈmaster ˌswitch *noun* [C] a switch that can be used to turn on or off power to all the lights or machines in a building

mastery /ˈmɑː.stᵊr.i/ [US] /ˈmæs.tɚ-/ *noun* [U] ➲See at **master** CONTROL, **master** SKILLED PERSON.

masthead /ˈmɑːst.hed/ [US] /ˈmæst-/ *noun* [C] the title of a newspaper or magazine which is printed at the top of the front page

masticate /ˈmæs.tɪ.keɪt/ *verb* [I or T] *FORMAL* to chew food **mastication** /ˌmæs.tɪˈkeɪ.ʃᵊn/ *noun* [U]

mastiff /ˈmæs.tɪf/ *noun* [C] a large strong short-haired dog

mastitis /mæsˈtaɪ.tɪs/ [US] /-t̬ɪs/ *noun* [U] *SPECIALIZED* painful swelling of the breast or the UDDER (= the part of a cow which produces milk), usually because of an infection

masturbate /ˈmæs.tə.beɪt/ [US] /-tɚ-/ *verb* **1** [I] to touch or rub your sexual organs in order to give yourself sexual pleasure **2** [T] to touch or rub someone's sexual organs in order to give them sexual pleasure **masturbation** /ˌmæs.təˈbeɪ.ʃᵊn/ [US] /-tɚ-/ *noun* [U] **masturbatory** /ˌmæs.təˈbeɪ.tᵊr.i/ [US] /-tɚˈbeɪ.tɔːr.i/ *adj*: *masturbatory fantasies*

mat [FLOOR] /mæt/ *noun* [C] a small piece of strong material which covers and protects part of a floor: *Wipe your feet on the mat before you come inside.* ➲See also **doormat**.

mat [TABLE] /mæt/ *noun* [C] a small piece of cloth, cardboard or plastic which is put on a surface such as a table to protect it: *a beer mat* ○ *a place mat*

mat [SPORT] /mæt/ *noun* [C] a piece of thick rubber or other soft material used in some sports for people to lie or fall on: *Please remember to bring a mat and a towel with you to the next aerobics class.*

mat [LAYER] /mæt/ *noun* [C] a thick layer of something, such as grass or hair, which is twisted together untidily: *The top few buttons on his shirt were open, revealing a mat **of** dark hair on his chest.*

matted /ˈmæt.ɪd/ [US] /ˈmæt̬-/ *adj* twisted into a firm, untidy mass: *Her hair was matted **with** mud and rain.*

matador /ˈmæt.ə.dɔːʳ/ [US] /ˈmæt̬.ə.dɔːr/ *noun* [C] a man who fights and kills bulls at a BULLFIGHT ➲Compare **picador**; **toreador**.

match [COMPETITION] *MAINLY UK* /mætʃ/ *noun* [C] (*US USUALLY* **game**) a sports competition or event in which two people or teams compete against each other: *a football/cricket/tennis match* ○ *We won/lost the match.* ○ *Liverpool have a match **with** (= against) Blackburn next week.*

• **the man/woman of the match** *UK* the person who has scored the most points or played the best in a match

match [STICK] /mætʃ/ *noun* [C] a short thin stick made of wood or cardboard and covered with a special chemical at one end which burns when rubbed firmly against a rough surface: *a **box** of matches* ○ *You should always **strike** a match away from you.*

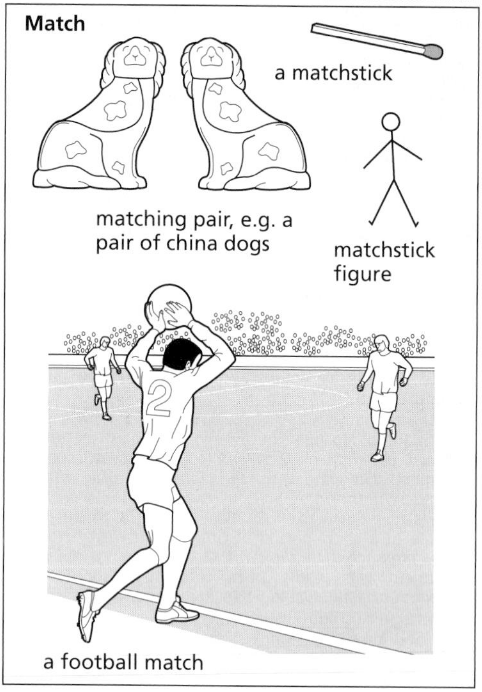
Match
a matchstick
matching pair, e.g. a pair of china dogs
matchstick figure
2
a football match

• **put a match to *sth*** *UK* to make something burn

match [SUITABLE] /mætʃ/ *noun* [S] **1** something which is similar to or combines well with something else: *The curtains look great – they're **a** perfect match **for** the sofa.* **2** *OLD-FASHIONED* If two people who are having a relationship are a good match, they are very suitable for each other: *Theirs is a match **made in heaven*** (= a very good relationship).

match /mætʃ/ *verb* [I or T] If two colours, designs or objects match, they are similar or look attractive together: *Do you think these two colours match?* ○ *Does this shirt match these trousers?* ○ *a sofa with curtains **to** match*

-matched /-mætʃt/ *suffix* **well-matched/ill-matched** similar and suitable for each other/different and not suitable for each other: *an ill-matched couple*

matching /ˈmætʃ.ɪŋ/ *adj* [before n] having the same colour or pattern as something else: *a green dress with matching green handbag*

match [EQUAL] /mætʃ/ *noun* [S] a person or thing which is equal to another person or thing in strength, speed or quality

• **be no match for *sth/sb*** to be less powerful or effective than someone or something else: *Gibson ran well but was no match for the young Italian.*

match /mætʃ/ *verb* [T] to be as good as someone or something else: *It would be difficult to match the service this airline gives its customers.*

PHRASAL VERBS WITH **match** ▼

▲ **match *sb* against *sb*** *phrasal verb* If one team or player is matched against another team or player, they are made to compete against each other: *Germany has been matched against Holland in the semi-final.*

▲ **match up** [SAME] *phrasal verb* If two pieces of information match up, they are the same: *Their accounts of what happened that evening don't match up.*

▲ **match up** [SIMILAR] *phrasal verb* If two things match up, they are similar and are designed to connect or to work together: *If the teeth on the cogs don't match up properly* (= If they are not in the correct place), *the mechanism will jam.*

▲ **match *sth* up** *phrasal verb* [M] If you match up a design or material, you look for something that would look good with it and be similar to it: *I'm trying to match up this wallpaper* **with** *some suitable curtain material.*

▲ **match** *sth/sb* **up** *phrasal verb* [M] to find a similarity or connection between two things or people: *Can you match up these songs* **with** *the bands who sang them?*

▲ **match up** [EQUALLY GOOD] *phrasal verb* UK to be as good as another thing, person or experience: *There was so much hype beforehand that it would have been difficult for the film to match up* **to/with** *our expectations of it.*

matchbox /'mætʃ.bɒks/ ⓤ /-bɑːks/ *noun* [C] a small box containing matches

match-fixing /'mætʃ.fɪk.sɪŋ/ *noun* [U] dishonest activity to make sure that one team wins a particular sports match

matchless /'mætʃ.ləs/ *adj* of a very high standard or quality and better than everything else: *her matchless beauty* ○ *matchless prose* **matchlessly** /'mætʃ.lə.sli/ *adv*

matchmaker /'mætʃ,meɪ.kər/ ⓤ /-kɚ/ *noun* [C] a person who tries to arrange marriages or romantic relationships between people **matchmaking** /'mætʃ,meɪ.kɪŋ/ *noun* [U]

,match 'point *noun* [C] a situation in a game such as tennis when the player who is winning will win the match if they get the next point

matchstick /'mætʃ.stɪk/ *noun* [C] the short wooden stick of a match, or the match itself

'matchstick ,figure *noun* [C] a **stick figure**

matchwood /'mætʃ.wʊd/ *noun* [U] UK the very small pieces of wood that are left after something wooden has been destroyed

mate [FRIEND] /meɪt/ *noun* [C] UK INFORMAL **1** a friend: *We've been mates since our school days.* ○ *I usually play football with some of my mates from the office on Saturdays.* ○ *She's my* **best** *mate.* **2** used as a friendly way of addressing someone, especially a man: *Have you got a light, mate?*

matey /'meɪ.ti/ ⓤ /-t̬i/ *adj* **matier, matiest** UK INFORMAL friendly: *They've been very matey since they started working together.*

matey /'meɪ.ti/ ⓤ /-t̬i/ *noun* [C] UK INFORMAL used an informal form of address: *Are you all right, matey?* **mateyness** /'meɪ.ti.nəs/ ⓤ /-t̬i-/ *noun* [U]

mate [REPRODUCE] /meɪt/ *verb* [I or T] to have sex and produce young, or to make animals do this: *Tigers mate repeatedly over a period of several days.*

● **mate for life** If animals mate for life, they keep the same sexual partner for their whole life.

mate /meɪt/ *noun* [C] an animal's sexual partner: *Peacocks use their beautiful tails to attract mates.*

mate [HELPER] /meɪt/ *noun* [C] UK a person who is employed to help a skilled worker: *a carpenter's/plumber's mate*

mate [SHIP] /meɪt/ *noun* [C] a type of officer on a trading ship rather than a military ship: *a ship's mate*

-mate [SHARING] /-meɪt/ *suffix* used to show two people share a space or are involved in the same activity: *flat mate* ○ *team-mate* ○ *workmate*

mater /'meɪ.tər/ ⓤ /-t̬ɚ/ *noun* [C] UK OLD-FASHIONED OR HUMOROUS mother

material [PHYSICAL SUBSTANCE] /mə'tɪə.ri.əl/ ⓤ /-'tɪr.i-/ *noun* [C] a physical substance which things can be made from: *building materials, such as stone* ○ *Crude oil is used as the* **raw** (= basic) *material for making plastics.*

material /mə'tɪə.ri.əl/ ⓤ /-'tɪr.i-/ *adj* relating to physical objects or money rather than emotions or the spiritual world: *the material world* ○ *Material wealth never interested her.*

materially /mə'tɪə.ri.ə.li/ ⓤ /-'tɪr.i-/ *adv*: *Materially, of course, we're better off* (= We have more money or possessions). ➭See also **materially** at **material** IMPORTANT.

materialize, UK USUALLY **-ise** /mə'tɪə.ri.ə.laɪz/ ⓤ /-'tɪr.i-/ *verb* [I] **1** If an object materializes, it appears suddenly: *Suddenly a lorry appeared in front of her – it seemed to materialize out of nowhere.* **2** If an idea or hope materializes, it becomes real: *She was promised a promotion but it never materialized.* ○ *Her hopes of becoming a painter never materialized.* **materialization,** UK USUALLY **-isation** /mə,tɪə.ri.ə.l.aɪ'zeɪ.ʃən/ ⓤ /-,tɪr.-i-/ *noun* [C or U]

material [CLOTH] /mə'tɪə.ri.əl/ ⓤ /-'tɪr.i-/ *noun* [C or U] cloth which can be used to make things such as clothes: *How much material will you need to make the skirt?*

material [INFORMATION] /mə'tɪə.ri.əl/ ⓤ /-'tɪr.i-/ *noun* [C or U] information used when writing something such as a book, or information produced in various forms to help people or to advertise products: *I'm in the process of collecting material for an article that I'm writing.*

material [IMPORTANT] /mə'tɪə.ri.əl/ ⓤ /-'tɪr.i-/ *adj* FORMAL important or having an important effect: *If you have any information that is material* **to** *the investigation, you should state it now.*

materially /mə'tɪə.ri.ə.li/ ⓤ /-'tɪr.i-/ *adv* FORMAL *Even if mistakes were made in the counting, they wouldn't have materially affected the results* (= affected them in an important way). ➭See also **materially** at **material** PHYSICAL SUBSTANCE.

materialism [MONEY] /mə'tɪə.ri.ə.lɪ.zᵊm/ ⓤ /-'tɪr.i-/ *noun* [U] the belief that having money and possessions is the most important thing in life: *So have we become a self-centred society, preoccupied with materialism?* **materialist** /mə'tɪə.ri.ə.lɪst/ ⓤ /-'tɪr.i-/ *noun* [C] **materialistic** /mə,tɪə.ri.ə'lɪs.tɪk/ ⓤ /-,tɪr.i-/ *adj*

materialism [PHYSICAL] /mə'tɪə.ri.ə.lɪ.zᵊm/ ⓤ /-'tɪr.i-/ *noun* [U] SPECIALIZED the belief that only physical matter exists and the spiritual world does not **materialist** /mə'tɪə.ri.ə.lɪst/ ⓤ /-'tɪr.i-/ *noun* [C] **materialist** /mə-'tɪə.ri.ə.lɪst/ ⓤ /-'tɪr.i-/ *adj*

materialize, UK USUALLY **-ise** /mə'tɪə.ri.ə.laɪz/ ⓤ /-'tɪr.i-/ *verb* [I] ➭See at **material** PHYSICAL SUBSTANCE.

materials /mə'tɪə.ri.əlz/ ⓤ /-'tɪr.i-/ *plural noun* equipment that you need for a particular activity: *"Do we need any writing materials?" "Only a pen and a pencil."* ○ *teaching materials*

maternal /mə'tɜː.nᵊl/ ⓤ /-'tɝː-/ *adj* **1** behaving or feeling in the way that a mother does towards her child, especially in a kind, caring way: *maternal* **instincts** ○ *She is very maternal* **towards** *her staff.* ➭Compare **paternal**. **2** related to a mother's side of the family: *Her maternal grandmother* (= mother's mother) *is still alive.* **maternally** /mə'tɜː.nᵊl.i/ ⓤ /-'tɝː-/ *adv*

maternity /mə'tɜː.nə.ti/ ⓤ /-'tɝː.nə.t̬i/ *noun* [U] FORMAL the state of being a mother

maternity /mə'tɜː.nə.ti/ ⓤ /-'tɝː.nə.t̬i/ *adj* [before n] related to pregnancy and birth: *maternity clothes*

ma'ternity ,leave *noun* [U] a period in which a woman is legally allowed to be absent from work in the weeks before and after she gives birth

ma'ternity ,ward *noun* [C] the part of a hospital in which women give birth and where they are taken care of after giving birth

matey /'meɪ.ti/ ⓤ /-t̬i/ *noun* [C], *adj* **matier, matiest** INFORMAL ➭See at **mate** FRIEND.

mathematics FORMAL /,mæθ'mæt.ɪks/ ⓤ /-'mæt̬-/ *noun* [U] (UK **maths,** US **math**) the study of numbers, shapes and space using reason and usually a special system of symbols and rules for organizing them ➭See also **algebra**; **arithmetic**; **geometry**. **mathematical** /,mæθ'mæt.ɪ.kᵊl/ ⓤ /-'mæt̬-/ *adj*: *a mathematical formula* **mathematically** /,mæθ'mæt.ɪ.kli/ ⓤ /-'mæt̬-/ *adv* **mathematician** /,mæθ.mə'tɪʃ.ᵊn/ *noun* [C] someone who studies, teaches or is an expert in mathematics

matinée /'mæt.ɪ.neɪ/ ⓤ /,mæt̬.ᵊn'eɪ/ *noun* [C] a film shown or a play performed during the day, especially in the afternoon

'matinée ,idol US matin'ée ,idol *noun* [C] OLD-FASHIONED a male actor, especially in films of the 1930s and 1940s, who was very attractive to women

matins /'mæt.ɪnz/ ⓤ /'mæt̬-/ *noun* [U] the morning ceremony in some Christian churches

matriarch /'meɪ.tri.ɑːk/ ⓤ /-ɑːrk/ *noun* [C] an old and powerful woman in a family, or the female leader of a society in which power passes from mother to daughter ➭Compare **patriarch** at **patriarchy**. **matriarchal** /,meɪ.tri'ɑː.kᵊl/ ⓤ /-'ɑːr-/ *adj*: *a matriarchal society* ➭Compare **patriarchal** at **patriarchy**.

matriarchy /'meɪ.tri.ɑː.ki/ ⓤ /-'ɑːr-/ *noun* [C or U] a type of society in which women have most of the authority and power, or a society in which property belongs to women

M

and is given to children by women rather than men ➲Compare **patriarchy**.

matricide /ˈmæt.rɪ.saɪd/ /ˈmeɪ.trɪ-/ *noun* [U] a crime in which a person kills their mother ➲Compare **parricide**; **patricide**.

matriculate /məˈtrɪk.jʊ.leɪt/ *verb* [I] FORMAL to be formally admitted to study at a university or college **matriculation** /məˌtrɪk.jʊˈleɪ.ʃən/ *noun* [C or U]

matrimony /ˈmæt.rɪ.mə.ni/ *noun* [U] FORMAL the state of being married

matrimonial /ˌmæt.rɪˈməʊ.ni.əl/ [US] /-ˈmoʊ-/ *adj* FORMAL related to marriage or people who are married

matrix [DEVELOPMENT] /ˈmeɪ.trɪks/ *noun* [C] *plural* **matrices** or **matrixes** FORMAL the set of conditions which provides a background in which something grows or develops: *Europe is remaking itself politically within the matrix of the European Community.*

matrix [MATHEMATICS] /ˈmeɪ.trɪks/ *noun* [C] *plural* **matrices** or **matrixes** SPECIALIZED a group of numbers or other symbols arranged in a rectangle which can be used together as a single unit to solve particular mathematical problems

matrix [SUBSTANCE] /ˈmeɪ.trɪks/ *noun* [C or U] *plural* **matrices** or **matrixes** SPECIALIZED a substance in which other things are fixed, buried, etc: *The fossils lie embedded in a matrix of shale and sandstone.*

matron [SCHOOL] /ˈmeɪ.trən/ *noun* [C] UK OLD-FASHIONED a female nurse in a school

matron [HOSPITAL] /ˈmeɪ.trən/ *noun* [C] UK OLD-FASHIONED FOR **senior nursing officer**

matron [PRISON] /ˈmeɪ.trən/ *noun* [C] US a woman who is in charge of female prisoners

matron [MARRIED WOMAN] /ˈmeɪ.trən/ *noun* [C] US a married woman, especially one who is old or a WIDOW (= a woman whose husband has died)

M

matronly /ˈmeɪ.trən.li/ *adj* OFTEN DISAPPROVING describes a woman, usually one who is not young, who is fat and does not dress in a fashionable way

matt UK, US **matte** /mæt/ *adj* describes a surface or colour or paint that is not shiny: *The paint is available in matt or gloss finish.* ➲Compare **emulsion**; **gloss** APPEARANCE.

matted /ˈmæt.ɪd/ [US] /ˈmæt̬-/ *adj* ➲See at **mat** LAYER.

matter [SITUATION] /ˈmæt.əʳ/ [US] /ˈmæt̬.ɚ/ *noun* [C] a situation or subject which is being dealt with or considered: *Could I talk to you about a personal matter?* ○ *Alois denied any knowledge of the matter.* ○ *Will you phone me back – it's a matter **of** some importance.* ○ *Talking about the world's problems is one thing, but solving them is **another** matter **altogether*** (= is completely different).

• **be a matter of confidence/luck/waiting, etc.** If something is a matter of confidence/luck/waiting, etc. that is all you need for it to happen: *Baking a cake isn't difficult – it's just a matter of following the recipe.*

• **for that matter** used to show that a statement is true in another situation: *Ming's never been to Spain, or to any European country for that matter.*

• **the matter in hand** UK (US **the matter at hand**) the subject or situation being considered: *Do these figures have any bearing on the matter in hand?*

• **as a matter of course** If something is done as a matter of course, it is a usual part of the way in which things are done and is not special: *Safety precautions are observed as a matter of course.*

• **be a matter of life and/or death** to be very serious: *And if you miss the bus, well, it's not a matter of life and death.*

• **be a matter of opinion** If something is a matter of opinion, different people have different opinions about it: *Both performances were excellent, it's simply a matter of opinion as to whose was better.*

• **That's a matter of opinion.** said to show that you do not agree with something that has just been said: *"Anyway, she's a wonderful mother." "That's a matter of opinion."*

• **be a matter of record** If a fact is a matter of record, it is generally known to be true.

• **be (only) a matter of time** If it is (only) a matter of time until something happens, it is certain to happen but you do not know when it will happen: *It's only a matter of time before he's forced to resign.*

• **be no laughing matter** to be very serious and not a situation that people should joke about: *Being arrested by the police is no laughing matter.*

• **no matter** MAINLY UK it is not a problem: *"I haven't got that form with me." "No matter – here's another."*

• **no matter what/when/why, etc.** used to emphasize that something cannot be changed: *I never seem to lose any weight, no matter how hard I try.* ○ *Anyway, we've got to get to the airport on time, no matter what.*

matters /ˈmæt.əz/ [US] /ˈmæt̬.ɚz/ *plural noun* the situation being dealt with or being discussed: *Her resignation is not going to **help** matters.*

• **to make matters worse** used to say that something has made a bad or difficult situation worse: *Three of our players were ill, and to make matters worse, our main scorer had broken his ankle.*

• **take matters into *your* own hands** to deal with a problem yourself because the people who should have dealt with it have failed to do so: *When the police failed to catch her son's murderer, she decided to take matters into her own hands.*

matter [BE IMPORTANT] /ˈmæt.əʳ/ [US] /ˈmæt̬.ɚ/ *verb* [I] to be important, or to affect what happens: *We were late but it didn't seem to matter.* ○ *"What did you say?" "Oh, **it** doesn't matter."* ○ [+ question word] ***It** doesn't matter **what** you wear – just as long as you come.* ○ [+ that] ***It** didn't matter **that** our best player was injured after 10 minutes – we still won.* ○ *I know Charles doesn't think this project is important, but it matters **to** me.*

the matter [PROBLEM] *noun* [S] the reason for pain, worry or a problem: ***What's** the matter? Why are you crying?* ○ *What's the matter **with** your hand? It's bleeding.* ○ *Is anything the matter?* ○ *I don't know what the matter is **with** the car, but it won't start.*

matter [SUBSTANCE] /ˈmæt.əʳ/ [US] /ˈmæt̬.ɚ/ *noun* [U] physical substance in the universe: *Some scientists believe that there is about ten times as much matter in the universe as astronomers have observed.*

matter [TYPE] /ˈmæt.əʳ/ [US] /ˈmæt̬.ɚ/ *noun* [U] a substance or things of a particular type: *advertising/printed matter* ○ *Do you find the **subject** matter of the book* (= the subject that the book deals with) *interesting?*

matter [SMALL AMOUNT] /ˈmæt.əʳ/ [US] /ˈmæt̬.ɚ/ *noun* [S] used in expressions describing how small an amount or period of time is: *The interview was over **in a** matter **of** minutes.* ○ *She complained he had short-changed her, but it was only **a** matter **of** a few pence.*

matter-of-fact /ˌmæt.ə.rəvˈfækt/ [US] /ˌmæt̬.ɚ.əv-/ *adj* not showing feelings or emotion, especially in a situation when emotion would be expected: *He spoke in a very matter-of-fact way about the accident.* ➲See also **as a matter of fact** at **fact**. **matter-of-factly** /ˌmæt.ə.rəvˈfækt.li/ [US] /ˌmæt̬.ɚ.əv-/ *adv* **matter-of-factness** /ˌmæt.ə.rəvˈfækt.nəs/ [US] /ˌmæt̬.ɚ.əv-/ *noun* [U]

matting /ˈmæt.ɪŋ/ [US] /ˈmæt̬-/ *noun* [U] strong rough material, often woven, which is used to cover floors: *straw/coconut matting*

mattress /ˈmæt.rəs/ *noun* [C] the part of a bed, made of a strong cloth cover filled with firm material, which makes the bed comfortable to lie on

mature [GROW PHYSICALLY] /məˈtjʊəʳ/ [US] /-ˈtʊr/ *verb* [I] to become completely grown physically: *Humans take longer to mature than most other animals.*

mature /məˈtjʊəʳ/ [US] /-tjʊr/ *adj* completely grown physically: *a mature adult* ○ *sexually mature* ○ *Mature male gorillas have silver-grey hairs on their backs.* ○ *mature oak trees*

maturity /məˈtjʊə.rɪ.ti/ [US] /-ˈtʊr.ə.t̬i/ *noun* [U] the state of being completely grown physically: *How long does it take for the chicks to grow to maturity?*

maturation /ˌmæt.jʊˈreɪ.ʃən/ *noun* [U] the process of becoming completely grown physically

mature [DEVELOP MENTALLY] /məˈtjʊəʳ/ [US] /-ˈtʊr/ *verb* MAINLY APPROVING **1** [I or T] to become more developed mentally and emotionally and behave in a responsible way: *Girls are said to mature faster than boys.* ○ *He matured a lot while he was at college.* **2** [I] If ideas, opinions, etc. mature, they reach an advanced or developed state: *It*

took several years for her ideas to mature.
mature /mə'tjʊəʳ/ [US] /-'tʊr/ *adj* **1** MAINLY APPROVING Mature people behave like adults in a way that shows they are well developed emotionally: *He's very mature for his age.* **2** FORMAL A mature decision is one which is made after a lot of careful thought: *Upon mature reflection, we find the accused guilty.*
maturely /mə'tjʊə.li/ [US] /-'tʊr-/ *adv* MAINLY APPROVING in a mature way
maturity /mə'tjʊə.rɪ.ti/ [US] /-'tʊr.ə.ṭi/ *noun* [U] MAINLY APPROVING **1** the quality of behaving mentally and emotionally like an adult **2** a very advanced or developed form or state
maturation /ˌmæt.jʊə'reɪ.ʃᵊn/ [US] /-jʊ-/ *noun* [U] MAINLY APPROVING the process of becoming completely developed mentally or emotionally

mature [FOOD] /mə'tjʊəʳ/ [US] /-'tʊr/ *verb* [I or T] to make food and wine old enough for the flavour to have developed completely: *The wine has been matured in oak vats.* ○ *The cheese is left to mature for two years.*
mature /mə'tjʊəʳ/ [US] /-'tjʊr/ *adj* having a flavour that is completely developed: *Do you prefer mild or mature cheddar?*

mature [FINANCE] /mə'tjʊəʳ/ [US] /-'tʊr/ *verb* [I] SPECIALIZED If an insurance agreement or an investment matures, it becomes ready to be paid: *The policy matures after fifteen years.*
mature /mə'tjʊəʳ/ [US] /-'tʊr/ *adj* SPECIALIZED A mature investment is ready to be paid.
maturity /mə'tjʊə.rɪ.ti/ [US] /-'tjʊr.ə.ṭi/ *noun* [U] SPECIALIZED *The investment* ***reaches*** *maturity* (= becomes mature) *after ten years.*

maˌture 'student UK *noun* [C] (US **older student,** AUS **mature age student**) a student at a college or university who is older than the usual age

maudlin /'mɔː.d.lɪn/ [US] /'mɑː.d-/ *adj* feeling sad and having a lot of pity for yourself, especially after you have drunk a lot of alcohol

maul /mɔːl/ [US] /mɑːl/ *verb* [T often passive] **1** If an animal mauls someone, it attacks them and injures them with its teeth or claws: *A small boy had been mauled by the neighbour's dog.* **2** to criticize something or someone severely: *Both films were mauled by the critics.*
mauling /'mɔː.lɪŋ/ [US] /'mɑː-/ *noun* [S or U] severe criticism of someone or something: *Her latest novel got a real mauling in the review that I read.*

mausoleum /ˌmɔː.zə'liː.əm/ [US] /ˌmɑː-/ *noun* [C] a building in which the bodies of dead people are buried

mauve /məʊv/ [US] /moʊv/ *adj, noun* [U] (having) a pale purple colour

maven /'meɪ.vᵊn/ *noun* [C] US INFORMAL a person with good knowledge or understanding of a subject

maverick /'mæv.ᵊr.ɪk/ [US] /-ɚ-/ *noun* [C] a person who thinks and acts in an independent way, often behaving differently from the expected or usual way: *a political maverick* ○ *He was considered as something of a maverick in the publishing world.*

maw /mɔː/ [US] /mɑː/ *noun* [C] LITERARY **1** the mouth of a fierce animal: *the lion's maw* **2** something that seems to surround and absorb everything near it: *She fears that the matter will simply be swallowed up by the maw of bureaucracy.*

mawkish /'mɔː.kɪʃ/ [US] /'mɑː-/ *adj* showing emotion or love in an awkward or foolish way: *The film lapses into mawkish sentimentality near the end.* **mawkishly** /'mɔː.kɪʃ.li/ [US] /'mɑː-/ *adv* **mawkishness** /'mɔː.kɪʃ.nəs/ [US] /'mɑː-/ *noun* [U]

max /mæks/ *adj* INFORMAL FOR **maximum**, often used after an amount: *"How much will the trip cost?" "Forty pounds max."*
• **to the max** US INFORMAL as much as possible: *These athletes push their bodies to the max.*

maxim /'mæk.sɪm/ *noun* [C] a brief statement of a general truth, principle or rule for behaviour

maximum /'mæk.sɪ.məm/ *adj* being the largest amount or number allowed or possible: *maximum speed/effort/temperature* ○ *The bomb was designed to cause the maximum* ***amount*** *of damage.* ➲Compare **minimum**.
maximum /'mæk.sɪ.məm/ *noun* [C usually sing] *plural* **maxima** or **maximums** the largest amount allowed or possible: *The temperature will reach* ***a*** *maximum* ***of*** *27°C today.*
maximal /'mæk.sɪ.məl/ *adj* SPECIALIZED largest or greatest: *Forty degrees centigrade is the maximal temperature at which this chemical reaction will occur.* ➲Compare **minimal** at **minimum**.
maximize, UK USUALLY **-ise** /'mæk.sɪ.maɪz/ *verb* [T] to make something as great in amount, size or importance as possible: *Some airlines have cancelled less popular routes in an effort to maximize profits.* ➲Compare **minimize** at **minimum**. **maximization**, UK USUALLY **-isation** /ˌmæk.sɪ.maɪ'zeɪ.ʃᵊn/ *noun* [U]

may [POSSIBILITY] /meɪ/ *modal verb* used to express possibility: *There may be other problems that we don't know about.* ○ *I may see you tomorrow before I leave.* ○ *The cause of the accident may never be discovered.* ○ *The explosion may have been caused by a faulty electrical connection.* ○ *We'd better not interfere – she may not like it.* ○ *There may be some evidence to suggest she's guilty,* ***but*** *it's hardly conclusive.* ➲Compare **might** POSSIBILITY.
• **be that as it may** SLIGHTLY FORMAL used to mean that you accept that a piece of information is true but it does not change your opinion of the subject you are discussing: *Building a new children's home will cost a lot of money but, be that as it may, there is an urgent need for the facility.*
• **may well** If you say that something may well happen, you mean that it is likely to happen: *She may well not want to travel alone.*

COMMON LEARNER ERROR

may be or **maybe?**

May be is written as two separate words when **may** is used as a modal verb and **be** is used as a verb.

I may be late this evening.
~~*I maybe late this evening.*~~

Maybe is an adverb, and is written as one word.

Maybe we should do it tomorrow.
~~*May be we should do it tomorrow.*~~

may [PERMISSION] /meɪ/ *modal verb* SLIGHTLY FORMAL used to ask or give permission: *A reader may borrow up to six books at any one time.* ○ *"May I help myself to some more food?" "Yes, of course."* ○ *Hi, my name's Tiffany. How may I help you?* ➲See Note **can, could or may?** at **can** PERMISSION. Compare **might** PERMISSION. ✻ NOTE: This use of **may** is slightly more formal and less common than **can**.
• **may I ask** used in questions to show disapproval: *What, may I ask, was the point of repeating the tests?*

may [WISH] /meɪ/ *modal verb* FORMAL used to introduce a wish or a hope: *May you have a long and fruitful marriage.*

may [TREE] /meɪ/ *noun* [U] (ALSO **may blossom**) the flowers of the HAWTHORN tree

May [MONTH] /meɪ/ *noun* [C or U] the fifth month of the year, after April and before June: *30(th) May/May 30(th)* ○ *My mother's birthday is* ***in*** *May.*

maybe /'meɪ.bi/ /ˌ-'-/ *adv* **1** used to show that something is possible or that something might be true: *Maybe they'll come tomorrow.* ○ *Maybe you were right after all.* ➲See Note **may be or maybe?** at **may** POSSIBILITY. **2** INFORMAL used to show that a number or amount is approximate: *There were 200, maybe 300, refugees on the boat.* **3** used to politely suggest or ask for something: *Maybe Ted would like to go.* ○ *Maybe we should start again.* **4** used to avoid giving a clear or certain answer to a question: *"Are you coming to Kelly's party?" "Maybe."* **5** used to mean that something is a possible explanation why something else happened: *"Why were you chosen for the team and not me?" "Maybe it's because I've been to more practice sessions than you."*

mayday /'meɪ.deɪ/ *noun* [S], *exclamation* a special radio signal sent from a ship or an aircraft when it needs help

'May ˌDay *noun* [C usually sing] the first day of May, which is a holiday in many countries. It traditionally celebrates spring but now it is often used to honour workers.

mayfly /ˈmeɪ.flaɪ/ *noun* [C] an insect which lives near water and only lives for a very short time as an adult

mayhem /ˈmeɪ.hem/ *noun* [U] a situation in which there is little or no order or control: *With twenty kids running round and only two adults to supervise, it was complete mayhem.*

mayonnaise /ˌmeɪ.əˈneɪz/ /ˈ---/ *noun* [U] (INFORMAL **mayo**) a thick creamy sauce made from oil, vinegar and the yellow part of eggs, which is usually eaten cold

mayor /meəʳ/ [US] /meɪr/ *noun* [C] a person who is elected or chosen to be the leader of the group who governs a town or city

mayoress /ˌmeəˈres/ [US] /ˈmeɪr.ɪs/ *noun* [C] a female mayor, or the wife of a mayor **mayoral** /ˈmeə.rəl/ [US] /ˈmeɪ.ɔːr.əl/ *adj*: *mayoral duties*

mayoralty /ˈmeə.rəl.ti/ [US] /ˈmeɪ.ɔːr.əl-/ *noun* [U] US the office of being a mayor, or the period of time for which someone is a mayor

maypole /ˈmeɪ.pəʊl/ [US] /-poʊl/ *noun* [C] a tall pole with long RIBBONS (= narrow strips of cloth) fixed to the top of it, the ends of which people hold as they dance around the pole on the first of May

may've /ˈmeɪ.əv/ INFORMAL *short form of* may have

maze /meɪz/ *noun* [C] **1** a complicated system of paths or passages which people try to find their way through for amusement **2** an area in which you can get easily lost because there are so many similar streets or passages: *The old part of the town was a maze of narrow passages.* **3** a complicated set of rules, ideas or subjects which you find difficult to deal with or understand: *It's almost impossible to get through the maze* ***of*** *bureaucracy.*

MB UK /ˌemˈbiː/ *noun* [C] (US **BM**) ABBREVIATION FOR Bachelor of Medicine: a degree in medicine, or a person who has this degree

MBA /ˌem.biːˈeɪ/ *noun* [C] ABBREVIATION FOR Master of Business Administration: an advanced degree in business, or a person who has this

MBE /ˌem.biːˈiː/ *noun* [C] ABBREVIATION FOR Member of the Order of the British Empire: a British honour given to a person by the Queen for a particular achievement

MC /ˌemˈsiː/ *noun* [C] ABBREVIATION FOR **master of ceremonies**

McCoy /məˈkɔɪ/ ➲See **the real McCoy**.

MD [DOCTOR] /ˌemˈdiː/ *noun* [C] US ABBREVIATION FOR Doctor of Medicine: a degree which someone must have to work as a doctor: *Steven Tay, MD*

MD [MANAGER] /ˌemˈdiː/ *noun* [C] UK ABBREVIATION FOR **managing director**: *You should talk to the MD about your proposal.*

MD [RECORDING] /ˌemˈdiː/ *noun* [C] ABBREVIATION FOR **Mini-Disc**

me [PERSON] /miː/ /mɪ/ *pronoun* used, usually after a verb or preposition, to refer to the person speaking or writing: *Is there one for me?* ○ *She gave me some money.* ○ *Could you pass me that book?* ○ *It wasn't me who offered to go, it was Charlotte.* ➲See also **I** PERSON SPEAKING.

USAGE

me or I?

Me is used after 'than', 'as', or 'to be'. It would be wrong or would sound very formal if you used **I**.

She's taller than me.
David is not as tall as me.
"Who's there?" "It's me."
"Who's there?" "It is I." (formal)

Sometimes **me** is used with another noun as the subject of a sentence, especially in informal English.

Jane and me went to the cinema yesterday. (informal)
Jane and I went to the cinema yesterday.

ME [ILLNESS] /ˌemˈiː/ *noun* [U] UK ABBREVIATION FOR myalgic encephalomyelitis: an illness, sometimes lasting for several years, in which a person's muscles and joints hurt and they are generally very tired ➲See also **chronic fatigue syndrome**.

mea culpa /ˌmeɪ.əˈkʊl.pə/ *exclamation* HUMOROUS used to admit that something was your fault

mead /miːd/ *noun* [U] an alcoholic drink made from honey which was drunk in the past

meadow /ˈmed.əʊ/ [US] /-oʊ/ *noun* [C or U] a field with grass and often wild flowers in it: *There was a path through the meadow to the village.*

meagre UK, US **meager** /ˈmiː.gəʳ/ [US] /-gɚ/ *adj* (of amounts or numbers) very small or not enough: *a meagre salary* ○ *The prisoners existed on a meagre diet of rice and fish.*

meal [FOOD] /mɪəl/ *noun* [C] an occasion when food is eaten, or the food which is eaten on such an occasion: *a hot meal* ○ *a three-course meal* ○ *a heavy* (= large) *meal* ○ *a light* (= small) *meal* ○ *I have my* ***main*** *meal at midday.* ○ *You must come round for a meal sometime.*

• **make a meal (out) of *sth*** UK DISAPPROVING to spend more time or energy doing something than is necessary: *I only asked for a summary of the main points but she's making a real meal out of it.*

meal [POWDER] /mɪəl/ *noun* [U] a substance which has been crushed to make a rough powder, especially plant seeds crushed to make flour or for animal food: *bone meal* ○ *soya meal*

mealy /ˈmɪə.li/ *adj* dry and powdery: *mealy potatoes* ○ *a mealy apple*

ˌmeals on ˈwheels *noun* [U] a service which takes hot meals to the homes of old and ill people, either for free or for a small payment

ˈmeal ˌticket [FOOD] *noun* [C] US FOR **luncheon voucher**

ˈmeal ˌticket [MONEY] *noun* [C usually sing] someone or something that you use as a way of getting regular amounts of money: *Gone are the days when a university degree was a meal ticket for life.*

mealtime /ˈmɪəl.taɪm/ *noun* [C usually pl] a time at which a meal is eaten: *The only time our family gets together is at mealtimes.*

mealy-mouthed /ˌmɪə.liˈmaʊðd/ *adj* DISAPPROVING not brave enough to say what you mean directly and honestly: *mealy-mouthed excuses* ○ *a mealy-mouthed spokesperson*

mean [EXPRESS] /miːn/ *verb* [T] **meant, meant 1** to express or represent something such as an idea, thought, or fact: *What does this word mean?* ○ [+ **that**] *These figures mean* ***that*** *almost 7% of the working population is unemployed.* ○ *What do you mean* ***by*** *that remark?* ○ *She's quite odd though. Do you know what I mean?* **2** used to add emphasis to what you are saying: *I want you home by midnight. And I mean midnight.* ○ *Give it back now! I mean* ***it****.*

• **I mean 1** used to correct what you have just said or to add more information: *I really do love him – as a friend, I mean.* **2** something that people often say before they start or continue their sentence: *I mean, I think he's a good teacher, but I just don't like him.*

• **What do you mean?** used to show that you are annoyed or that you disagree: *What do you mean, it was my fault?*

meaning /ˈmiː.nɪŋ/ *noun* [C or U] The meaning of something is what it expresses or represents: *The word 'flight' has two different meanings : a plane journey, and the act of running away.* ○ *The meaning of his gesture was clear.* ○ *His novels often have (a)* ***hidden*** *meaning.*

meaningless /ˈmiː.nɪŋ.ləs/ *adj* having no meaning: *a meaningless phrase*

mean [HAVE RESULT] /miːn/ *verb* [T] **meant, meant** to have a particular result: *Lower costs mean lower prices.* ○ [+ **that**] *Advances in electronics mean* ***that*** *the technology is already available.* ○ [+ **v-ing**] *If we want to catch the 7.30 train, that will mean leav****ing*** *the house at 6.00.*

mean [HAVE IMPORTANCE] /miːn/ *verb* [T] **meant, meant** to have an important emotional effect on someone: *It wasn't a valuable picture but it meant a lot* ***to*** *me.* ○ *Possessions mean nothing* ***to*** *him.*

meaning /ˈmiː.nɪŋ/ *noun* [U] importance or value: *The birth of her first grandchild gave new meaning to her life.* ○ *Education had no great meaning* ***for*** *him until much later in his life.*

meaningful /ˈmiː.nɪŋ.fəl/ *adj* useful, serious or important: *She seems to find it difficult to form meaningful relationships.* ○ *Having the opportunity to work would make retirement more meaningful* ***for*** *many* *pensioners.* **meaningfully** /ˈmiː.nɪŋ.fəl.i/ *adv* **meaningfulness** /ˈmiː.nɪŋ.fəl.nəs/ *noun* [U] **meaningless** /ˈmiː.nɪŋ.ləs/ *adj*: *a meaningless gesture* **meaninglessly** /ˈmiː.nɪŋ.lə.sli/ *adv* **meaninglessness** /ˈmiː.nɪŋ.lə.snəs/ *noun* [U]

mean [INTEND] /miːn/ *verb* [I or T] **meant, meant** to intend: *I'm sorry if I offended you – I didn't mean* ***any harm.*** ○ *The books with large print are meant* ***for*** *our partially sighted readers.* ○ [+ **to** infinitive] *I've been meaning* ***to*** *phone you all week.* ○ *Do you think she meant* ***to*** *say 9 a.m. instead of 9 p.m.?* ○ [+ obj + **to** infinitive] *This exercise isn't meant to be difficult.* ○ *They didn't mean* ***for*** *her* ***to*** *read the letter.*

• **be meant for each other** If you say two people are meant for each other, you think they suit each other as romantic partners.

• **mean business** *INFORMAL* to want very much to achieve something, even if other people disagree with you

• **mean well** to do what you think will be helpful, although you might unintentionally cause problems by doing it: *I know he means well, but he just gets in the way.* ➲See also **well-meaning**.

meaningful /ˈmiː.nɪŋ.fəl/ *adj* intended to show meaning, often secretly: *a meaningful look* ○ *He raised one eyebrow in a meaningful way.*

mean [NOT GENEROUS] /miːn/ *adj MAINLY UK* not willing to give or share things, especially money: *He's too mean to buy her a ring.* ○ *My landlord's very mean* ***with*** *the heating – it's only on for two hours each day.* **meanly** /ˈmiːn.li/ *adv* **meanness** /ˈmiːn.nəs/ *noun* [U]

mean [NOT KIND] /miːn/ *adj* unkind or unpleasant: *Stop being so mean* ***to*** *me!* ○ *She just said it to be mean.*

meanie, meany /ˈmiː.ni/ *noun* [C] *CHILD'S WORD* someone who is unkind: *Don't be such a meanie!*

mean [VIOLENT] /miːn/ *adj MAINLY US* frightening and likely to become violent: *a mean and angry mob* ○ *a mean-looking youth*

mean [GOOD] /miːn/ *adj* [before n] *INFORMAL* very good: *She's a mean piano player.* ○ *She plays a mean piano* (= She plays very well).

• **no mean** used to say a person is very good at a certain activity: *He's no mean cook.*

• **no mean achievement/feat** a great achievement: *Getting the job finished on time was no mean achievement.*

mean [VALUE] /miːn/ *noun* [S] **1** (*ALSO* **the arithmetic mean**) *SPECIALIZED* (in mathematics) the result obtained by adding two or more amounts together and dividing the total by the number of amounts; the AVERAGE: ***The*** *mean* ***of*** *5, 4, 10 and 15 is 8.5.* **2** *FORMAL* a quality or way of doing something which is in the middle of two completely different qualities or ways of doing something: *We need to find* ***a*** *mean* ***between*** *exam questions which are too difficult and those which are too easy.*

mean /miːn/ *adj* [before n] *SPECIALIZED* (in mathematics) a mean number is an average number: *a mean value* ○ *Their mean weight was 76.4 kilos.*

meander /miˈæn.dəʳ/ [US] /-dɚ/ *verb* **1** [I] If a river, stream or road meanders, it follows a route which is not straight or direct. **2** [I usually + adv or prep] to walk slowly without any clear direction: *We spent the afternoon meandering* ***around*** *the streets of the old town.* **3** [I] If a text, process or activity meanders, it has no clear direction: *The film meanders* ***along*** *with no particular story line.*

meander /miˈæn.dəʳ/ [US] /-dɚ/ *noun* [C] **1** a curve of a river or stream **2** a journey which has no particular direction: *The TV series continues its haphazard meander* ***around*** *the globe – this week it will be in Portugal.*

meandering /miˈæn.dər.ɪŋ/ [US] /-dɚ-/ *adj* moving slowly in no particular direction or with no clear purpose: *a meandering river* ○ *a long meandering speech*

meanderings /miˈæn.dər.ɪŋz/ [US] /-dɚ-/ *plural noun* talk which continues for a longer time than is necessary and which is often not interesting

means [METHOD] /miːnz/ *plural noun* a method or way of doing something: *They had no means* ***of*** *communication.* ○ *We need to find some other means* ***of*** *transportation.* ○ *We must use every means at our disposal.* ○ *She tried to explain* ***by*** *means* ***of*** *sign language.* ○ *There is no means of tracing the debt at all.* ○ *The family* ***had*** *no means* ***of*** *support* (= way of getting money). ➲See Note **way or method/means of?** at **way** METHOD.

• **a means to an end** something that you do because it will help you to achieve something else: *I didn't particularly like the job – it was just a means to an end.*

• **by all means** used to give permission: *"May I borrow this book?" "By all means."*

• **by no means** (*ALSO* **not by any means**) not at all: *It is by no means certain that we'll finish the project by June.* ○ *This isn't the last we'll hear of it by any means.*

means [MONEY] /miːnz/ *plural noun* money, for example from an income, that allows you to buy things: [+ **to** infinitive] *He* ***has*** *the means* ***to*** *buy half the houses in the street if he wanted to.*

• **live beyond *your* means** to spend more money than you receive as income

• **live within *your* means** to spend less money than you receive as income

• **a man/woman of means** a rich man/woman

means-testing /ˈmiːnzˌtes.tɪŋ/ *noun* [U] *UK* the official process of measuring how much income a person has in order to decide whether they should receive money from the government **ˈmeans ˌtest** *noun* [C] **means-test** /ˈmiːnz.test/ *verb* [T] *People who apply for housing benefit must be means-tested.* **means-tested** /ˈmiːnzˌtes.tɪd/ *adj*: *means-tested benefits*

meantime /ˈmiːn.taɪm/ *noun* **in the meantime** until something expected happens, or while something else is happening: *Your computer won't be arriving till Thursday. In the meantime, you can use Jude's.*

meanwhile /ˈmiːn.waɪl/ *adv* until something expected happens, or while something else is happening: *Carl's starting college in September. Meanwhile, he's travelling around Europe.*

meany /ˈmiː.ni/ *noun* [C] a **meanie**. ➲See at **mean** NOT KIND.

measles /ˈmiː.zl̩z/ *noun* [U] an infectious disease which produces small red spots all over the body

measly /ˈmiːz.li/ *adj INFORMAL* too small in size or amount, or not enough: *a measly amount of money* ○ *a measly little present* **measliness** /ˈmiːz.lɪ.nəs/ *noun* [U]

measure [SIZE] /ˈmeʒ.əʳ/ [US] /-ɚ/ *verb* [L only + n; T] to discover the exact size or amount of something, or to be of a particular size: *"Will the table fit in here?" "I don't know – let's measure it."* ○ *This machine measures your heart rate.* ○ *He measured the flour into the bowl.* ○ *The area, measuring/which measures 5 kilometres by 3 kilometres, has been purchased by the army.*

measure /ˈmeʒ.əʳ/ [US] /-ɚ/ *noun* **1** [C or U] a unit used for stating the size, weight, etc. of something, or a way of measuring: *weights and measures* ○ *The sample's density is a measure of its purity.* **2** [C or U] *FORMAL* amount: *There was* ***a*** *large measure* ***of*** *agreement between the candidates.* ○ *His success was* ***in*** *some measure due to his being in the right place at the right time.* **3** [C] an exact amount, especially of alcohol: *One unit of alcohol is equal to half a pint of beer or a standard measure of spirits.* **4** [C] *US FOR* **bar** MUSIC

• **have the measure of *sb/sth*** *SLIGHTLY FORMAL* to understand what someone or something is like and to know how to deal with them: *I don't think she's under any illusions about her husband – she's got the measure of him.*

measurable /ˈmeʒ.ər.ə.bl̩/ [US] /-ɚ-/ *adj* able to be measured, or large enough to be noticed: *The service produces clear, measurable benefits to people's health.*

measurably /ˈmeʒ.ər.ə.bli/ [US] /-ɚ-/ *adv*

measurement /ˈmeʒ.ə.mənt/ [US] /-ɚ-/ *noun* **1** [C or U] the act or process of measuring: *The test is based on the measurement of blood levels.* ○ *The machine makes thousands of measurements every day.* **2** [C] the size, shape, quality, etc. of something, which you discover by measuring it: *The measurements* ***of*** *both rooms were identical.* ○ *What is your inside leg measurement?*

measurements /ˈmeʒ.ə.mənts/ [US] /-ɚ-/ *plural noun* Your measurements are the sizes of various parts of your body, especially your chest, waist and hips, which you refer to when you want to buy clothes.

measure [JUDGE] /ˈmeʒ.əʳ/ [US] /-ɚ/ *verb* [T] to judge the quality, effect, importance, or value of something: *There* *is no way of measuring the damage done to morale.*

measure /ˈmeʒ.ər/ ⓤ /-ɚ/ *noun* [C] a way of judging something: *Record sales are not always **a** measure **of** a singer's popularity.* ○ *We have no accurate measure **of** the damage.*

measure METHOD /ˈmeʒ.ər/ ⓤ /-ɚ/ *noun* [C usually pl] a way of achieving something, or a method for dealing with a situation: *What further measures can we **take** to avoid terrorism?* ○ *These measures were designed to improve car safety.* ○ [+ *to* infinitive] *Emergency measures **to** help the refugees are badly needed.*

PHRASAL VERBS WITH measure ▼

▲ **measure** *sb/sth* **against** *sb/sth phrasal verb* to judge someone or something by comparing them against someone or something else: *She measured the shoe **against** the footprint, but it was smaller.*

▲ **measure** *sth* **out** *phrasal verb* [M] to weigh or measure a small amount of something from a larger amount of something: *Measure out 250 grams of flour and sift it into a large mixing bowl.*

▲ **measure up** GOOD ENOUGH *phrasal verb* to be good enough, or as good as someone or something else: *She could never measure up **to** her mother's expectations.*

▲ **measure** *sth/sb* **up** FIND SIZE *phrasal verb* [M] to discover what size something or someone is by measuring them

measured /ˈmeʒ.əd/ ⓤ /-ɚd/ *adj* careful and controlled, or not fast: *Her response to their criticism was calm and measured.*

measuring jug *UK noun* [C] (*US* **measuring cup**) a container used for measuring liquids which have lines marked on the side of it showing how much it contains

meat FOOD /miːt/ *noun* **1** [U] the flesh of an animal when it is used for food: *I don't eat meat.* ○ *raw meat* ○ *red/white meat* **2** [C] a type of meat: *a buffet of cold meats and cheeses*

● **be meat and drink to** *sb* If a difficult or unpleasant activity is meat and drink to someone, they enjoy doing it very much and find it easy.

● **One man's meat is another man's poison.** SAYING said to emphasize that people like different things

meaty /ˈmiː.ti/ ⓤ /-ṭi/ *adj* **1** full of meat or tasting a lot of meat: *a good meaty stew* **2** large and having a lot of flesh: *meaty tomatoes*

meat INTEREST /miːt/ *noun* [U] important, valuable or interesting ideas or information: *It was a nicely written article and quite amusing but there wasn't much meat to it.*

meaty /ˈmiː.ti/ ⓤ /-ṭi/ *adj* having a lot of important or interesting ideas: *a meaty book/letter/report* ○ *She has written some wonderfully meaty parts for older actresses.* **meatiness** /ˈmiː.tɪ.nəs/ ⓤ /-ṭɪ-/ *noun* [U]

meat-and-potatoes /ˌmiːt.ən.pəˈteɪ.təʊz/ ⓤ /-ˈtoʊz/ *adj* [before n] *US* more basic or important than other things: *For many unions, the meat-and-potatoes issue is no longer pay increases but job security.*

meatball /ˈmiːt.bɔːl/ ⓤ /-bɑːl/ *noun* [C] one of several small balls of meat that are eaten hot with a sauce: *spaghetti and meatballs*

meat loaf *noun* [C or U] meat cut into extremely small pieces, mixed with other things, cooked in a container and then cut into slices to be eaten

mecca /ˈmek.ə/ *noun* [C usually sing] a place to which many people are attracted: *His Indiana bookstore became a mecca **for** writers and artists.* ○ *The scheme would transform the park into a tourist mecca.*

mechanic /məˈkæn.ɪk/ *noun* [C] someone whose job is repairing the engines of vehicles and other machines: *a car/garage/motor mechanic*

mechanical MACHINES /məˈkæn.ɪ.kəl/ *adj* describes machines or their parts: *a mechanical device* ○ *The company produces mechanical parts for airplane engines.* ○ *The plane appeared to have crashed because of a mechanical problem.*
mechanically /məˈkæn.ɪ.kli/ *adv*: *Most crops are harvested mechanically* (= by a machine). ○ *I'm not very mechanically minded* (= do not understand how machines work).

mechanical WITHOUT THOUGHT /məˈkæn.ɪ.kəl/ *adj* (ALSO **mechanistic**) DISAPPROVING without thinking about what you are doing, especially because you do something often: *I was taught to read in a mechanical way.* **mechanically** /məˈkæn.ɪ.kli/ *adv* (ALSO **mechanistically**) "*Thank you,*" *replied the ticket collector mechanically as he took each ticket.*

mechanical engiˈneering *noun* [U] the study of the design and production of machines

mechanics STUDY /məˈkæn.ɪks/ *noun* [U] the study of the effect of physical forces on objects and their movement

the mechanics WAY OF WORKING *plural noun* INFORMAL the way something works or happens: *He knows a lot about the mechanics **of** running a school.*

mechanism MACHINE PART /ˈmek.ə.nɪ.zəm/ *noun* [C] a part of a machine, or a set of parts that work together: *These automatic cameras have a special focusing mechanism.*

mechanism SYSTEM /ˈmek.ə.nɪ.zəm/ *noun* [C] **1** a way of doing something which is planned or part of a system: *The mechanism **for** collecting taxes needs revising.* **2** a part of your behaviour which helps you to deal with a difficult situation: *She's actually rather insecure, and her rudeness is just a **defence** mechanism.*

mechanistic /ˌmek.əˈnɪs.tɪk/ *adj* thinking of living things as if they were machines: *According to mechanistic views of behaviour, human action can be explained in terms of cause and effect.*

mechanize, *UK USUALLY* **-ise** /ˈmek.ə.naɪz/ *verb* [T] to use a machine to do something that used to be done by hand: *Farming has been mechanized, reducing the need for labour.* **mechanization**, *UK USUALLY* **-isation** /ˌmek.ə.naɪˈzeɪ.ʃən/ *noun* [U] **mechanized**, *UK USUALLY* **-ised** /ˈmek.ə.naɪzd/ *adj*

the Med /ðəˈmed/ *noun* [S] *UK INFORMAL* the Mediterranean sea or the countries beside it: *They're going on a cruise round the Med.*

med /med/ *adj* MAINLY US INFORMAL **medical**: *med school* ○ *a med student*

medal /ˈmed.əl/ *noun* [C] a small metal disc, with words or a picture on it, which is given as a reward for a brave action, for winning in a competition, or to remember a special event: *He was **awarded** a medal **for** bravery.* ○ *She **won** three Olympic gold medals.*

medal /ˈmed.əl/ *verb* [I] to win a medal in a sports competition: *She's medalled in both the heptathlon and the long jump.*

medallist *UK*, *US* **medalist** /ˈmed.əl.ɪst/ *noun* [C] a person who has won a medal in sport: *She's a bronze medallist **in** judo.*

medallion /məˈdæl.jən/ *noun* [C] **1** a metal disc which is worn for decoration on a chain or string around the neck **2** a flat circular piece of meat without bones: *medallions of pork*

meddle /ˈmed.əl/ *verb* [I] DISAPPROVING to try to change or have an influence on things which are not your responsibility, especially in a critical, damaging or annoying way: *My sister's always meddling **in** other people's **affairs**.* ○ *People shouldn't meddle **with** things they don't understand.* **meddler** /ˈmed.əl.ər/ ⓤ /-ɚ/ *noun* [C] **meddling** /ˈmed.əl.ɪŋ/ /-lɪŋ/ *noun* [U]

meddlesome /ˈmed.əl.səm/ *adj* DISAPPROVING tending to get involved in situations where you are not wanted, especially in a critical, damaging or annoying way

the media NEWSPAPERS *group noun* [S] newspapers, magazines, radio and television considered as a group: *the local/national media* ○ *media attention/coverage/hype/reports* ○ *The issue has been much discussed **in** the media.* ◗See also **multimedia**.

media MEDIUM /ˈmiː.di.ə/ *plural of* **medium** METHOD

mediaeval /ˌmed.iˈiː.vəl/ *adj* **medieval**

media event *noun* [C] an event or activity planned to attract the attention of the media

median /ˈmiː.di.ən/ *adj* SPECIALIZED describes the value which is the middle one in a set of values arranged in order of size: *Median household income fell last year.*
median /ˈmiː.di.ən/ *noun* [C]

median strip *noun* [C usually sing] *US FOR* **central reservation**

mediate /ˈmiː.di.eɪt/ *verb* [I or T] to talk to two separate people or groups involved in a disagreement to try to help them to agree or find a solution to their problems: *Negotiators were called in to mediate* **between** *the two sides.* ○ *The two envoys have succeeded in mediating an end to the war.* **mediation** /ˌmiː.diˈeɪ.ʃən/ *noun* [U] *Last-minute attempts at mediation failed.* **mediator** /ˈmiː.di.eɪ.təʳ/ ⓤ /-t̬ɚ/ *noun* [C]

medic /ˈmed.ɪk/ *noun* [C] **1** *UK INFORMAL* a medical student or doctor **2** *US* someone who does medical work in the military

Medicaid /ˈmed.ɪ.keɪd/ *noun* [U] a government service in the US which allows poor people to receive medical treatment both in and out of hospitals ⊃Compare **Medicare**.

medical /ˈmed.ɪ.kəl/ *adj* related to the treatment of illness and injuries: *medical advice* ○ *medical books* ○ *a medical team* ○ *medical workers*

medical *MAINLY UK* /ˈmed.ɪ.kəl/ *noun* [C] (*MAINLY US* **physical**) an examination of your body by a doctor to find out if you are healthy: *The insurance company wanted me to have a medical.*

medically /ˈmed.ɪ.kli/ *adv*: *The doctor declared her medically fit* (= she had no illness or injury).

Medicare /ˈmed.ɪ.keəʳ/ ⓤ /-ker/ *noun* [U] **1** a government service in the US which allows people aged 65 and over to receive medical treatment both in and out of hospitals ⊃Compare **Medicaid**. **2** a government service in Australia which allows people to receive medical treatment, and which is paid for through taxation

medicated /ˈmed.ɪ.keɪ.tɪd/ ⓤ /-t̬ɪd/ *adj* containing a medical substance: *medicated lotion/shampoo/tissues*

medication /ˌmed.ɪˈkeɪ.ʃən/ *noun* [C or U] a medicine, or a set of medicines or drugs used to improve a particular condition or illness: *He is currently* **on/taking** *medication* **for** *his heart.* ○ *In the study, patients were taken off their usual medications.*

medicine *TREATMENT* /ˈmed.ɪ.sən/ *noun* [U] treatment for illness or injury, or the study of this: *paediatric/ preventative medicine* ○ *orthodox/Western medicine* ○ *a career in medicine* ○ *She is a doctor, but is unable to* **practise** *medicine* (= work as a doctor) *in her own country.*

medicine *SUBSTANCE* /ˈmed.ɪ.sən/ *noun* [C or U] a substance, especially in the form of a liquid or a pill, which is a treatment for illness or injury: *cough medicine* ○ *Take two spoonfuls of medicine at mealtimes.* ○ *She knows quite a lot about herbal medicines.*

• **give** *sb* **a dose/taste of** *their* **own medicine** to treat someone as badly as they have treated you

medicinal /məˈdɪs.ɪ.nəl/ *adj* Medicinal substances are used to cure illnesses: *I keep a bottle of brandy purely* **for** *medicinal* **purposes.** ○ *It is said that the spring water has medicinal properties.* **medicinally** /məˈdɪs.ɪ.nə.li/ *adv*

medico /ˈmed.ɪ.kəʊ/ ⓤ /-koʊ/ *noun* [C] *plural* **medicos** *UK INFORMAL* a doctor

medieval, **mediaeval** /ˌmed.iˈiː.vəl/ *adj* related to the MIDDLE AGES (= the period in European history from about 600 AD to 1500 AD): *a medieval building/ painting/town* ○ *a medieval manuscript*

mediocre /ˌmiː.diˈəʊ.kəʳ/ ⓤ /-ˈoʊ.kɚ/ *adj DISAPPROVING* not very good: *The film's plot is predictable and the acting is mediocre.* ○ *Parents don't want their children going to mediocre schools.*

mediocrity /ˌmiː.diˈɒk.rə.ti/ ⓤ /-ˈɑː.krə.t̬i/ *noun* [C or U] *A goal just before half-time rescued the match from mediocrity.* ○ *These people are just mediocrities* (= people who do not have much skill or ability at anything).

meditate /ˈmed.ɪ.teɪt/ *verb* [I] **1** to think calm thoughts in order to relax or as a religious activity: *Sophie meditates for 20 minutes every day.* **2** to think seriously about something for a long time: *He meditated* **on** *the consequences of his decision.*

meditation /ˌmed.ɪˈteɪ.ʃən/ *noun* **1** [U] the act of giving your attention to only one thing, either as a religious activity or as a way of becoming calm and relaxed: *prayer and meditation* ○ *She practises meditation.* **2** [C or U] serious thought or study, or the product of this

activity: *Let us spend a few moments* **in** *quiet meditation.* ○ *I left him deep in meditation.* ○ *The book is a meditation* **on** *the morality of art.* **meditative** /ˈmed.ɪ.tə.tɪv/ ⓤ /-t̬ɪv/ *adj FORMAL*

the Mediterranean *noun* [S] **1** (*ALSO* **the Mediterranean Sea,** *INFORMAL* **the Med**) the sea surrounded by southern Europe, northern Africa and the Middle East **2** the countries beside the Mediterranean Sea **Mediterranean** /ˌmed.ɪ.t̬ə³rˈeɪ.ni.ən/ ⓤ /-t̬əˈreɪ-/ *adj*: *a Mediterranean climate*

medium *VALUE* /ˈmiː.di.əm/ *adj* **1** being in the middle between an upper and lower amount, size, degree or value: *a girl of medium height* ○ *a medium-sized book* **2** (of meat) cooked so that it is no longer red in the middle: *Would you like your steak rare, medium, or well-done?*

medium *METHOD* /ˈmiː.di.əm/ *noun* [C] *plural* **media** or **mediums** a method or way of expressing something: *the broadcasting/print medium* ○ *They told the story* **through** *the medium* **of** *dance.*

medium *PERSON* /ˈmiː.di.əm/ *noun* [C] *plural* **mediums** a person who says that they can receive messages from people who are dead

'medium ˌwave *noun* [U] (*WRITTEN ABBREVIATION* **MW**) refers to radio waves which have a length of between about 150 and 550 metres

medley /ˈmed.li/ *noun* [C] **1** a mixture of different items, especially tunes put together to form a longer piece of music: *a medley of popular tunes* ○ *The menu described the dessert as 'a medley of exotic fruits'.* **2** a swimming competition in which each of four swimmers in a team uses a different method of swimming

meek /miːk/ *adj* quiet, gentle and not willing to argue or state your opinions in a forceful way: *She seemed so very meek and mild.* **meekly** /ˈmiː.kli/ *adv* **meekness** /ˈmiːk.nəs/ *noun* [U]

meet *BECOME FAMILIAR WITH* /miːt/ *verb* [I or T] met, met to see and speak to someone for the first time: *They met at work.* ○ *I met her in Hawaii.* ○ *Would you like to meet my sister?* ○ *Come and meet* (= be introduced to) *my friend Laura.* ⊃See also Note **know, get to know** and **meet** at **know** *HAVE INFORMATION*.

COMMON LEARNER ERROR

meet, see, visit, or **get to know?**

Meet is only used about people. It is not used to mean 'visit a place or thing'. For this meaning use **see** or **visit**.

Annie and Paul met on holiday.
People love to travel and see different places.
~~People love to travel and meet different places.~~

When you **get to know** someone, you gradually learn more about them.

It's too soon to think about marriage, we're still getting to know each other.

meet *COME TOGETHER* /miːt/ *verb* [I or T] met, met **1** to come together with someone intentionally: *Lorraine and I meet for lunch once a month.* ○ *We agreed to meet on Tuesday to discuss the project.* ○ *The children's club meets every Thursday afternoon.* ○ *They're meeting* **with** *their advisers to work out a new plan.* **2** to come together with someone unintentionally: *It's always awkward when you meet someone you know, but you can't remember their name.* ○ *We met our old neighbours at an auction last Saturday.*

• **meet** *sb* **halfway** to do some of the things that someone wants you to do, in order to show that you want to reach an agreement or improve your relationship with them

• **meet** *your* **maker** *HUMOROUS* to die

• **meet** *your* **match** to compete unsuccessfully with someone: *He was a good player, but he met his match* **in** *Peter.*

• **meet** *your* **Waterloo** to be defeated by someone who is too strong for you or by a problem which is too difficult for you

meet /miːt/ *noun* [C] **1** *US* a sports event: *a track/swim meet* ○ *the first meet of the season* **2** *UK* an occasion when people go FOXHUNTING

meeting /ˈmiː.tɪŋ/ ⓤ /-t̬ɪŋ/ *noun* [C] **1** an occasion when people come together intentionally or unintentionally:

We're having a meeting on Thursday to discuss the problem. ○ *I'm afraid she's in a meeting – I'll ask her to call you back later.* ○ *A* ***chance*** (= unintentional) *meeting with a publisher on an airplane had launched his career.* ○ *I liked him from our first meeting.* **2** UK a sports competition **3** a group of people who have met for a particular purpose: *The meeting wants to look at the proposal again.*

• **a meeting of minds** a situation when two or more people have the same opinions about something

meet [TOUCH] /miːt/ *verb* [I or T] **met, met** to touch or join something: *There's a large crack where the ceiling meets the wall.* ○ *The curtains don't quite meet.* ○ *Turn left where the lane meets the main road.*

• **eyes meet** If people's eyes meet, they look at each other at the same time: *Their eyes met across a crowded room.*

• **meet** ***sb's*** **eye** to look at someone directly while they are looking at you: *I tried to avoid meeting his eye.*

• **be more to this than meets the eye** If there is more to something than meets the eye, it is more difficult to understand or involves more things than you thought at the beginning.

meet [PLACE] /miːt/ *verb* [T] **met, met** to wait at a place for someone or something to arrive: *Will you meet me at the airport* (= be there when the aircraft arrives)*?*

meet [FULFIL] /miːt/ *verb* [T] **met, met 1** to fulfil, satisfy, or achieve: *The workers' demands for higher pay were not met by the management.* ○ *We haven't yet been able to find a house that meets our* ***needs/requirements.*** ○ *They will only agree to sign the contract if certain* ***conditions*** *are met.* ○ *Do you think we will be able to meet our* ***deadline/target?*** **2** to pay: *The company has agreed to meet all our expenses.*

meet [EXPERIENCE] /miːt/ *verb* [T] **met, met** to experience something: *I've never met that kind of problem/system before.* ○ *He met his death* (= he died) *in the icy waters of the South Atlantic.*

PHRASAL VERBS WITH **meet**

▲ **meet up** [PEOPLE] *phrasal verb* to meet another person in order to do something together: *They suggested we meet up at Mustafa's.*

▲ **meet up** [ROADS] *phrasal verb* If roads or paths meet up, they join at a particular place.

▲ **meet with** ***sth*** [EXPERIENCE] *phrasal verb* FORMAL to experience something, usually something unpleasant: *I heard she'd met with* ***an accident.*** ○ *If you meet with any difficulties, just let me know.*

▲ **meet with** ***sth*** [REACTION] *phrasal verb* to cause a particular reaction or result: *At the time the decision was met with a barrage of criticism.* ○ *I trust the arrangements meet with* ***your approval.***

'meeting ˌhouse *noun* [C usually sing] a building used by Quakers (= a Christian group) as their place of worship: *The Friends'* (= Quakers') *Meeting House*

'meeting ˌpoint *noun* [C] an area in a large public place, such as an airport or station, where people can arrange in advance to meet

mega [BIG/GOOD] /ˈme.gə/ *adj* SLANG very good or very big: *She's got a mega voice.*

mega- /meg.ə-/ *prefix* INFORMAL large in amount or size: *He's mega-rich.* ○ *They're earning megabucks* (= a lot of money).

mega- [NUMBER] /meg.ə-/ *prefix* 1 000 000 times the stated unit: *a megawatt* ○ *a megabyte*

megabyte /ˈmeg.ə.baɪt/ *noun* [C] (*WRITTEN ABBREVIATION* **MB**) SPECIALIZED a unit used in measuring the amount of information a computer can store, which has the value 1 048 576 BYTES

megahertz (*plural* **megahertz**) /ˈmeg.ə.hɜːts/ [US] /-hɝːts/ *noun* [C] (*WRITTEN ABBREVIATION* **MHz**) a million HERTZ

megalith /ˈmeg.ə.lɪθ/ *noun* [C] a large stone, sometimes forming part of a group or circle, which is thought to have been important to people in the distant past for social or religious reasons

megalithic /ˌmeg.əˈlɪθ.ɪk/ *adj*: *megalithic monuments* ○ *megalithic times* (= the period when megaliths were important)

megalomania /ˌmeg.əl.əˈmeɪ.ni.ə/ *noun* [U] an unnaturally great desire for power and control, or the belief that you are very much more important and powerful than you really are

megalomaniac /ˌmeg.əl.əˈmeɪ.ni.æk/ *noun* [C] a person with megalomania **megalomaniac** /ˌmeg.əl.əˈmeɪ.ni.æk/ *adj* [before n] (ALSO **megalomaniacal**)

megaphone /ˈmeg.ə.fəʊn/ [US] /-foʊn/ *noun* [C] a cone-shaped device which makes your voice louder when you speak into it, so that people can hear you although they are not near to you

megaplex /ˈme.gə.pleks/ *noun* [C] a very large cinema where a lot of films are shown at the same time: *a 12-screen megaplex*

megastar /ˈmeg.ə.stɑːʳ/ [US] /-stɑːr/ *noun* [C] a very famous person, especially an actor or pop star

megastore /ˈmeg.ə.stɔːʳ/ [US] /-stɔːr/ *noun* [C] a very large shop: *a furniture megastore*

megaton /ˈmeg.ə.tʌn/ *noun* [C] a unit which has the same value as the force produced by 1 000 000 TONS of TNT (= an explosive), and which is used for measuring the power of explosions, especially nuclear explosions

megawatt /ˈmeg.ə.wɒt/ [US] /-wɑːt/ *noun* [C] a unit for measuring electric power, which has the value of 1 000 000 WATTS

-meister /-maɪ.stəʳ/ [US] /-stɚ/ *suffix* INFORMAL used in a description showing what someone is famous for doing or what someone does very well: *funk-meister* ○ *the horror-meister, Stephen King*

melancholy /ˈmel.əŋ.kɒl.i/ [US] /-kɑː.li/ *adj* sad: *melancholy autumn days* ○ *a melancholy piece of music*

melancholic /ˌmel.əŋˈkɒl.ɪk/ [US] /-ˈkɑː.lɪk/ *adj* FORMAL *a melancholic expression* ○ *melancholic songs*

melancholy /ˈmel.əŋ.kɒl.i/ [US] /-kɑː.li/ *noun* [U] FORMAL sadness which lasts for a long period of time, often without any obvious reason

melancholia /ˌmel.əŋˈkəʊ.li.ə/ [US] /-ˈkoʊ-/ *noun* [U] OLD USE the condition of feeling unhappy or sad for no obvious reason

mélange /meɪˈlɑ̃ːʒ/ *noun* [C usually sing] FORMAL a mixture, or a group of different things or people: *Her book presents an interesting mélange* ***of*** *ideas.* ○ *The dessert was described as 'a mélange* ***of*** *summer fruits in a light syrup'.*

melanin /ˈmel.ə.nɪn/ *noun* [U] a dark brown PIGMENT (= substance which gives colour) which is found in eyes, skin, hair, feathers, etc., and which helps to protect the skin against harmful light from the sun

melanoma /ˌmel.əˈnəʊ.mə/ [US] /-ˈnoʊ-/ *noun* [C] SPECIALIZED a type of skin cancer that appears as a coloured mark or growth on the skin

melee /ˈmel.eɪ/ *noun* [C usually sing] LITERARY a large noisy uncontrolled crowd, in which people are moving in different directions and sometimes fighting with each other: *We lost sight of each other* ***in*** *the melee.*

mellifluous /melˈɪf.lu.əs/ *adj* FORMAL having a pleasant and flowing sound: *a deep mellifluous voice* ○ *the mellifluous sound of the cello*

mellow [SMOOTH] /ˈmel.əʊ/ [US] /-oʊ/ *adj* smooth, soft or developed; not too sharp, bright, new or rough: *mellow flavours* ○ *mellow sounds* ○ *mellow autumn sunlight*

mellow /ˈmel.əʊ/ [US] /-oʊ/ *verb* [I] to become softer and more developed in a pleasing way: *The brickwork will mellow over the years so that it blends with the surroundings.*

mellow [RELAXED] /ˈmel.əʊ/ [US] /-oʊ/ *adj* relaxed and pleasant or not severe: *a mellow mood/atmosphere* ○ *After a few drinks, he became very mellow.*

mellow /ˈmel.əʊ/ [US] /-oʊ/ *verb* [I or T] *She used to be very impatient, but she's mellowed over time.* ○ *The years have mellowed her.* ○ US INFORMAL *Oh don't be so tough on yourself, Bill – mellow* ***out*** (= become more relaxed and less severe).

melodrama /ˈmel.əˌdrɑː.mə/ [US] /-ˌdræm.ə/ *noun* [C or U] a story, play, or film in which the characters show stronger emotions than real people usually do: *a television melodrama* ○ MAINLY UK *The car's hardly damaged – there's no need to* ***make*** *a melodrama* ***out of*** *it* (= make the situation more important than it is).

M

melodramatic /ˌmel.ə.drəˈmæt.ɪk/ [US] /-ˈmæṭ-/ *adj* showing much stronger emotions than are necessary or usual for a situation: *a melodramatic speech* **melodramatically** /ˌmel.ə.drəˈmæt.ɪ.kli/ [US] /-ˈmæṭ-/ *adv*: *"Life is not worth living," she declared melodramatically.*

melody /ˈmel.ə.di/ *noun* [C or U] a tune, often forming part of a larger piece of music: *He played a few well-known melodies.* ○ *His songs are always strong on melody.*

melodic /məˈlɒd.ɪk/ [US] /-ˈlɑː.dɪk/ *adj* **1** very pleasant to listen to **2** relating to the melody in a piece of music

melodious /məˈləʊ.di.əs/ [US] /-ˈloʊ-/ *adj FORMAL* very pleasant to listen to

melon /ˈmel.ən/ *noun* [C or U] a large round fruit with hard yellow or green skin, sweet juicy flesh and a lot of seeds ➲See picture **Fruit** on page Centre 1

melt [BECOME LIQUID] /melt/ *verb* **1** [I or T] to turn from something solid into something soft or liquid, or to cause something to do this: *The snow usually melts by mid March.* ○ *Melt the chocolate slowly so that it doesn't burn.* ○ *The meat's beautifully cooked – it melts **in your mouth*** (= is so pleasantly soft that you do not need to chew it). **2** [I] to start to feel love or sympathy, especially after feeling angry: *He only has to look at her, and she melts.* ○ *He'd been going to refuse but his **heart** melted when he saw the children's faces.*

melted /ˈmel.tɪd/ [US] /-ṭɪd/ *adj* having turned soft or into a liquid: *melted butter/chocolate/cheese*

melting /ˈmel.tɪŋ/ [US] /-ṭɪŋ/ *adj* describes a look or voice which makes you feel sympathy or love

melt [SANDWICH] /melt/ *noun* [C] *MAINLY US* a sandwich containing melted cheese: *a tuna melt*

PHRASAL VERBS WITH **melt**

▲ **melt away** *phrasal verb* **1** to disappear slowly: *As the police sirens were heard, the crowd started to melt away.* **2** If a strong feeling melts away, you feel it less strongly and it disappears: *Her anger melted away when she read the letter.*

▲ **melt *sth* down** *phrasal verb* [M] to heat a metal object until it turns to liquid, because you want to use the metal rather than the object: *They melted down the gold rings and bracelets.*

▲ **melt (away) into *sth*** *phrasal verb* to look so similar to something else all around you, or to be so much a part of it, that people do not see or notice you: *The security men just melted into the background until they were needed.*

meltdown /ˈmelt.daʊn/ *noun* **1** [C or U] an extremely dangerous situation in a nuclear power station in which the nuclear fuel becomes very hot and melts through its container and escapes into the environment **2** [U] *INFORMAL* a complete failure, especially in financial matters: *financial/economic/market meltdown* ○ *The last few months have seen the progressive meltdown **of** the country's political system.*

ˈmelting ˌpoint *noun* [C usually sing] the temperature at which a substance melts

ˈmelting ˌpot *noun* [C usually sing] a place where many different people and ideas exist together, often mixing and producing something new: *a cultural melting pot* ○ *New Orleans is one of the great melting pots of America.*

member [PERSON] /ˈmem.bəʳ/ [US] /-bɚ/ *noun* [C] **1** a person, animal or thing which is part of a group: *a family member* ○ *a member of the older generation* ○ *male and female members of the group* ○ *The lion is a member **of** the cat family.* ○ *Representatives of the member states will be meeting next week.* **2** a person who joins a group to take part in a particular activity: *a new club member* ○ *Car parking facilities are for members only.* ○ *Michael is a member **of** the Royal Society for the Protection of Birds.*

membership /ˈmem.bə.ʃɪp/ [US] /-bɚ-/ *noun* [U] the state of belonging to an organization: *You have to **apply for** membership (UK) **of**/(US) **in** the sports club.* ○ *a membership fee/card* ○ *Annual membership* (= the amount you have to pay to join a particular organization for one year) *is £25.*

membership /ˈmem.bə.ʃɪp/ [US] /-bɚ-/ *group noun* [C] all the people who belong to an organization: *Our membership is/are divided on the issue.* ○ *The society has **a** very large membership* (= number of members).

member [BODY PART] /ˈmem.bəʳ/ [US] /-bɚ/ *noun* [C] *FORMAL* **1** a leg or arm **2** a penis: *the **male** member*

ˌMember of ˈParliament (*plural* **Members of Parliament**) *noun* [C] (*ABBREVIATION* **MP**) a person who has been elected to the parliament of a country

membrane /ˈmem.breɪn/ *noun* [C or U] *SPECIALIZED* **1** a thin piece of skin that covers or connects parts of a person's or animal's body: *The cornea is the transparent membrane that covers the front of the eye.* **2** a very thin piece of material that covers an opening **3** the outer covering of a cell: *a cell membrane*

memento /məˈmen.təʊ/ [US] /-toʊ/ *noun* [C] *plural* **mementos** or **mementoes** an object that you keep to remember a person, place or event: *I keep a stone as a memento **of** our holiday.*

memo (*plural* **memos**) /ˈmem.əʊ/ [US] /-oʊ/ *noun* [C] (*FORMAL* **memorandum**) a message or other information in writing sent by one person or department to another in the same business organization: *Did you get my memo about the meeting?*

memoirs /ˈmem.wɑːz/ [US] /-wɑːrz/ *plural noun* (*US ALSO* **memoir**) a written record of a usually famous person's own life and experiences: *She plans to write her memoirs.* ○ *Waugh's first volume of memoirs dealt with his childhood and youth.*

memoir /ˈmem.wɑːʳ/ [US] /-wɑːr/ *noun* [C] **1** a book or other piece of writing based on the writer's personal knowledge of famous people, places or events: *She has written a memoir of her encounters with W.H. Auden over the years.* **2** *US FOR* **memoirs**

memorabilia /ˌmem.ᵊr.əˈbɪl.i.ə/ *plural noun* objects that are collected because they are connected with a person or event which is thought to be very interesting: *an auction of pop memorabilia* ○ *Elvis memorabilia*

memorable /ˈmem.ᵊr.ə.bl̩/ *adj* likely to be remembered or worth remembering: *a memorable performance* ○ *a memorable tune* ○ *I haven't seen them since that memorable evening when the boat capsized.* **memorably** /ˈmem.ᵊr.ə.bli/ *adv*: *The book includes a range of memorably eccentric characters.*

memorandum [DOCUMENT] /ˌmem.əˈræn.dəm/ *noun* [C] *plural* **memoranda** or **memorandums** **1** *SPECIALIZED* a short written report prepared specially for a person or group of people which contains information about a particular matter: *Michael Davis has prepared a memorandum outlining our need for an additional warehouse.* **2** *LEGAL* an informal legal agreement: *The three countries have signed a memorandum pledging to work together.*

memorandum [MESSAGE] /ˌmem.əˈræn.dəm/ *noun* [C] *plural* **memoranda** or **memorandums** *FORMAL* a **memo**

memorial /məˈmɔː.ri.əl/ [US] /-ˈmɔːr.i-/ *noun* [C] an object, often large and made of stone, which has been built to honour a famous person or event: *a war memorial* ○ *The statue was erected as a memorial **to** those who died in the war.*

memorial /məˈmɔː.ri.əl/ [US] /-ˈmɔːr.i-/ *adj* [before n] A memorial event or object is a way of remembering a person or people who have died: *Hundreds of people came to Professor Conner's memorial **service**.* ○ *A memorial garden was created for the Princess in a London park.*

memorize, *UK USUALLY* **-ise** /ˈmem.ə.raɪz/ *verb* [T] to learn something so that you will remember it exactly: *When I was at school, we were required to memorize a poem every week.*

memory [ABILITY TO REMEMBER] /ˈmem.ᵊr.i/ [US] /-ɚ-/ *noun* **1** [C or U] the ability to remember information, experiences and people: *a good/bad memory* ○ *After the accident he suffered from **loss of** memory/memory **loss**.* ○ *She has **an** excellent memory **for** names* (= She can remember names easily). ➲See Note **remember or memory?** at **remember**. **2** [C usually sing; U] the part of a computer in which information or programs are stored either permanently or temporarily, or the amount of space available on it for storing information: *My computer has a gigabyte of memory.*

[M]

- **from memory** If you say something, such as a poem, or sing a song from memory, you speak or sing without looking at any words or music.

- **in memory of** *sb* as a way of remembering someone who has died: *A service was held in memory of those who had died in the fighting.*

- **have a memory like an elephant** to be able to remember things easily and for a long period of time

- **take a stroll/trip/walk down memory lane** to remember happy times in the past

- **within** *your* **memory** at a time that you are able to remember: *Women had gained the vote within my grandmother's memory.*

memory EVENT REMEMBERED /'mem.ªr.i/ ⓤ /-ɚ-/ noun [C] something that you remember from the past: *I have vivid memories of that evening.* ○ *That tune really **brings back** memories* (= makes me remember past events). ○ *School is just a **dim/distant** memory for me now* (= something I cannot remember very well).

men /men/ *plural of* **man** MALE

menace /'men.ɪs/ noun **1** [C usually sing] something that is likely to cause harm: *Drunk drivers are a menace **to** everyone.* ○ *Dogs running loose are a **public** menace.* ○ *the menace of industrial pollution* **2** [U] a dangerous quality that makes you think someone is going to do something bad: *He had a slight air of menace which I found unsettling.* ○ *He spoke with a hint of menace.* **3** [C] a person, especially a child, who is very annoying

- **demand money with menaces** UK LEGAL to demand money using threats: *He was accused of unlawfully demanding money with menaces.*

menace /'men.ɪs/ *verb* [T] SLIGHTLY FORMAL If someone or something menaces a person or thing, they threaten seriously to harm it: *Hurricane Hugo menaced the US coast for a week.*

menacing /'men.ɪ.sɪŋ/ adj making you think that someone is going to do something bad: *a menacing look/gesture* **menacingly** /'men.ɪ.sɪŋ.li/ adv

menage, **ménage** /mən'ɑːʒ/ *group noun* [S] FORMAL a group of people living together in the same house

ménage à trois /mən,ɑːʒ.ɑː'trwɑː/ noun [C] an arrangement in which three people live together and have sexual relationships with each other

menagerie /mə'nædʒ.ªr.i/ ⓤ /-ɚ-/ noun [C] a collection of wild animals which are kept privately or to show to the public

mend /mend/ *verb* [T] MAINLY UK to repair something that is broken or damaged: *Could you mend this hole in my shirt?* ○ *I've left my watch at the jeweller's to be mended.* ○ *The plumber came to mend the burst pipe.* ○ *The country's president is seeking to mend relations with the United States.* ✻ NOTE: In American English it is more usual to mend things that are torn, such as clothes or sheets, and to **repair** things that are broken, such as watches or furniture.

- **mend** *your* **fences** to try to be friendly again with someone after an argument

- **mend** *your* **ways** to begin to behave well having until now behaved badly

mend /mend/ *noun* [C] MAINLY UK a place in a piece of clothing where a repair has been made

- **be on the mend** INFORMAL to be getting better after an illness or injury: *She's been ill with flu but she's on the mend now.*

mending /'men.dɪŋ/ noun [U] OLD-FASHIONED clothes that need to be mended: *I have a pile of mending to do.*

mendacious /men'deɪ.ʃəs/ adj FORMAL not truthful: *Some of these statements are misleading and some downright mendacious.*

mendacity /men'dæs.ə.ti/ ⓤ /-ţi/ noun [U] FORMAL the act of not telling the truth: *Politicians are often accused of mendacity.*

mendicant /'men.dɪ.kªnt/ noun [C] FORMAL someone who lives by asking people they do not know for money, especially for religious reasons **mendicant** /'men.dɪ.kªnt/ adj

menfolk /'men.fəʊk/ ⓤ /-foʊk/ *plural noun* OLD-FASHIONED the men in a family or society

menial /'miː.ni.əl/ adj DISAPPROVING describes work that is boring, tiring and given a low social value: *It's fairly*

menial work, such as washing dishes and cleaning floors. ○ *a menial job/task*

meningitis /,men.ɪn'dʒaɪ.tɪs/ ⓤ /-ţɪs/ noun [U] a serious infectious disease that causes the tissues around the brain and SPINAL CORD to swell

menopause /'men.ə.pɔːz/ ⓤ /-pɑːz/ noun [U] (INFORMAL **the change (of life)**) the time in a woman's life when she gradually stops having periods: *Most women **go through** (UK) the menopause/*(US) menopause between the ages of 40 and 50.* **menopausal** /,men.ə'pɔː.zªl/ ⓤ /-pɑː-/ adj: *menopausal women/symptoms*

menorah /mə'nɔː.rə/ noun [C or S] in the Jewish religion, a special candle holder with places for 7-9 candles, which is used in religious celebrations

men's room US /'menz.ruːm/ noun [C usually sing] (UK **the gents**) a toilet for men in a public building such as a hotel or restaurant

menstrual 'period noun [C] FORMAL FOR **period** (= the bleeding from a woman's womb that happens every month)

menstruate /'ment.stru.eɪt/ *verb* [I] SLIGHTLY FORMAL When a woman menstruates, blood flows from her womb for a few days every month.

menstrual /'men.strəl/ adj SLIGHTLY FORMAL connected with the time when a woman menstruates: *menstrual pain* ○ *the menstrual cycle* ✺See also **premenstrual**.

menstruation /,men.stru'eɪ.ʃªn/ noun [U] SLIGHTLY FORMAL when a woman menstruates: *the onset of menstruation*

menswear /'menz.weəʳ/ ⓤ /-wer/ noun [U] **1** clothing for men **2** the part of a large shop where you find men's clothing

-ment /-mənt/ *suffix* used to form nouns which refer to an action or process or its result: *a great achievement* ○ *successful management* ○ *a disappointment*

mental /'men.tªl/ ⓤ /-ţªl/ adj **1** [before n] relating to the mind, or involving the process of thinking: *His physical and mental health had got worse.* ○ *Many people suffer from some form of mental illness during their lives.* ○ *She had a mental picture* (= a picture in her mind) *of how they finished decorating it.* ✺Compare **physical** BODY. **2** UK SLANG crazy

mentally /'men.tªl.i/ ⓤ /-ţªl-/ adv connected with or related to the mind: *mentally ill* ○ *It's going to be a tough competition but I'm mentally prepared for it.*

mentality /men'tæl.ə.ti/ ⓤ /-ţi/ noun [C usually sing] a person's particular way of thinking about things: *I can't understand the mentality of people who hurt defenceless animals.* ○ *He hopes that closer links between Britain and the rest of Europe will change the British mentality towards foreigners.*

mental 'age noun [C usually sing] A person's mental age is a measurement of their ability to think when compared to the average person's ability at that age: *Although Andrew is twenty-five, he has a mental age of six.*

mental a'rithmetic noun [U] calculations that you do in your mind, without writing down any numbers

mental 'block noun [C] If you have a mental block about something, you cannot understand it or do it because something in your mind prevents you: *He's got a mental block **about** names – he just can't remember them.*

mental 'cruelty noun [U] behaviour that causes extreme unhappiness to another person but which does not involve physical violence: *She divorced her husband on the grounds of mental cruelty.*

mental 'handicap noun [C usually sing] OLD-FASHIONED FOR **learning difficulties**

mental 'hospital noun [C] OLD-FASHIONED FOR **psychiatric hospital**

mentally de'fective adj OLD-FASHIONED If you say that someone is mentally defective, you mean that their brain is damaged because of an accident or illness or has been damaged since birth and that they have low mental abilities.

mental 'note noun **make a mental note of** *sth* to make an effort to remember something: *I made a mental note of her address.*

menthol /'men.θəl/ 🇺🇸 /-θɑːl/ *noun* [U] a solid white natural substance that smells and tastes like mint: *Menthol can help to clear your nose when you have a cold.* ○ *menthol cigarettes*
mentholated /'men.θəl.eɪ.tɪd/ 🇺🇸 /-t̬ɪd/ *adj* containing menthol as a flavouring

mention /'men.tʃən/ *verb* [T] **1** to speak about something briefly, giving little detail or using few words: *I'll mention your ideas to Jacinta.* ○ [+ (that)] *He casually mentioned (that) he was leaving his job.* ○ [+ v-ing] *My wife mentioned seeing you the other day.* ○ [+ question word] *Did she happen to mention whether she would be coming?* **2** to refer to something or someone: *I promised never to mention the incident again.* ○ *Did she mention me in her letter?*
● **not to mention** used when you want to emphasize something that you are adding to a list: *He's one of the kindest and most intelligent, not to mention handsome, men I know.*
● **Don't mention it.** said to be polite after someone has thanked you: *"Thanks for your help." "Don't mention it."*
mention /'men.tʃən/ *noun* **1** [C] a brief remark or written statement: *The story didn't even get a mention in the newspaper.* ○ *When I ordered the catalogue, there was no mention of any payment.* **2** [S] when something or someone is mentioned: *Even the mention of her name makes him blush.* **3** [C] when a person is publicly praised for having done something, such as their job, particularly well: *At the awards ceremony, Chrissie Scott got/received a special mention for her reporting of the conflict.*

COMMON LEARNER ERROR

mention

No preposition is normally needed after the verb **mention**.

He didn't mention the price.
He didn't mention about the price.

---

mentor /'men.tɔːʳ/ 🇺🇸 /-tɔːr/ *noun* [C] *FORMAL* a person who gives another person help and advice over a period of time and often also teaches them how to do their job ➔Compare **protégé**.

menu FOOD /'men.juː/ *noun* [C] a list of the food that you can eat in a restaurant: *The waiter brought the menu and the wine list.* ○ *What's on the menu today?*

menu COMPUTING /'men.juː/ *noun* [C] a list of choices that can be made to appear on a computer screen: *Select the 'Edit' menu and then choose 'Copy'.*

menu bar *noun* [C] a long, narrow area usually at the top of a computer screen that contains lists of instructions to the computer. These lists are kept out of view until you choose to see them: *Click 'File' in the menu bar, then click 'Exit'.*

menu-driven /'men.juː.drɪv.ən/ *adj* *SPECIALIZED* A computer that is menu-driven is operated by making choices from different menus rather than by giving separate instructions on a keyboard.

menu option *noun* [C] one of the choices available in a computer MENU (= a list of choices which appear on a computer screen)

meow /ˌmiːˈaʊ/ *noun* [C], *verb* [I] *US FOR* **miaow**

MEP /ˌem.iːˈpiː/ *noun* [C] *ABBREVIATION FOR* Member of the European Parliament: a person who represents an area of a European country in the European Parliament

Mephistopheles /ˌmef.ɪˈstɒf.əl.iːz/ 🇺🇸 /-ˈstɑː.fə.liːz/ *noun LITERARY* **the Devil**, see at **devil**

mercantile /'mɜː.kən.taɪl/ 🇺🇸 /'mɜː-/ *adj* *FORMAL* related to trade or business

mercenary SOLDIER /'mɜː.sən.ri/ 🇺🇸 /'mɜː-/ *noun* [C] a soldier who fights for any country or group that pays them

mercenary WANTING MONEY /'mɜː.sən.ri/ 🇺🇸 /'mɜː-/ *adj* *DISAPPROVING* interested only in the amount of money that can be obtained from a situation: *He had some mercenary scheme to marry a wealthy widow.*

merchandise /'mɜː.tʃən.daɪs/ 🇺🇸 /'mɜː-/ *noun* [U] *FORMAL* goods that are bought and sold: *Shoppers complained about poor quality merchandise and high prices.* ○ *Japan*

exported $117 billion in merchandise to the US in 1999.
merchandise /'mɜː.tʃən.daɪz/ 🇺🇸 /'mɜː-/ *verb* [T] *US SPECIALIZED* to encourage the sale of goods by advertising them or by making certain that they are noticed: *She had to merchandise the new product line.*
merchandising /'mɜː.tʃən.daɪ.zɪŋ/ 🇺🇸 /'mɜː-/ *noun* [U] products connected with a popular film, singer, event, etc., or the selling of these products

merchant /'mɜː.tʃənt/ 🇺🇸 /'mɜː-/ *noun* [C] **1** *FORMAL* a person whose job is to buy and sell products in large amounts, especially by trading with other countries: *a wine/grain merchant* **2** *UK INFORMAL DISAPPROVING* someone who is involved in or enjoys something which is unpleasant or annoying to others: *a gossip merchant* (= someone who enjoys talking about people's private lives) ○ *a speed merchant* (= someone who drives too fast)
● **merchant of doom/gloom** *UK DISAPPROVING* someone who is always saying that bad things are going to happen: *With exports rising and unemployment falling, the merchants of gloom are having to revise their opinions of the economy.*

merchant bank *noun* [C] a bank which does business with companies rather than with people **merchant banker** *noun* [C]

the merchant navy *UK noun* [U] (*US* **the merchant marine**) the ships of a country that are used for trading and not for fighting

merchant seaman *noun* [C] a sailor who works on a trading ship

mercurial /mɜːˈkjʊə.ri.əl/ 🇺🇸 /mɜːˈkjʊr.i-/ *adj LITERARY* **1** changing suddenly and often: *a mercurial temperament* ○ *She was entertaining but unpredictable, with mercurial mood swings.* **2** lively and quick: *a mercurial mind/wit*

mercury METAL /'mɜː.kjʊ.ri/ 🇺🇸 /'mɜː-/ *noun* [U] (*OLD USE* **quicksilver**) a heavy silver-coloured metal which is liquid at ordinary temperatures: *Mercury is used in batteries, pesticides and thermometers.*
● **the mercury** *OLD-FASHIONED INFORMAL* the temperature: *With the mercury climbing to 40 degrees, beaches and pools will be crowded this afternoon.*

Mercury PLANET /'mɜː.kjʊ.ri/ 🇺🇸 /'mɜː-/ *noun* [S] the planet closest in distance to the Sun, before Venus

mercy KINDNESS /'mɜː.si/ 🇺🇸 /'mɜː-/ *noun* [U] kindness and forgiveness shown to someone whom you have authority over: *She appealed to the judge to have mercy on her husband.* ○ *The prisoners pleaded for mercy.* ○ *The gunmen showed no mercy, killing innocent men and women.*
● **be at the mercy of sb/sth** to be in a situation where someone or something has complete power over you: *Poor people are increasingly at the mercy of money-lenders.*
merciful /'mɜː.sɪ.fəl/ 🇺🇸 /'mɜː-/ *adj APPROVING* describes someone who shows kindness and forgiveness to people who are in their power: *"God is merciful," said the priest.* ○ *a merciful ruler* **mercifully** /'mɜː.sɪ.fəl.i/ 🇺🇸 /'mɜː-/
merciless /'mɜː.sɪ.ləs/ 🇺🇸 /'mɜː-/ *adj DISAPPROVING* having or showing no mercy: *There are reports of merciless attacks on innocent civilians.* ○ *There was no shelter from the merciless* (= very strong) *heat.* **mercilessly** /'mɜː.sɪ.lə.sli/ 🇺🇸 /'mɜː-/ *adv: Louis was teased mercilessly by his schoolmates.*

mercy STOP /'mɜː.si/ 🇺🇸 /'mɜː-/ *noun* [S] an event or situation which you are grateful for because it stops something unpleasant: *After months of suffering, his death was a mercy.* ○ *They were on a mercy mission to take food to the refugees when they were attacked.* **merciful** /'mɜː.sɪ.fəl/ 🇺🇸 /'mɜː-/ *adj APPROVING After such a long illness, her death came as a merciful release.* **mercifully** /'mɜː.sɪ.fəl.i/ 🇺🇸 /'mɜː-/ *adv: His illness was mercifully brief.*

mercy killing *noun* [C or U] the act of killing someone who is very ill or very old so that they do not suffer any more

mere /mɪəʳ/ 🇺🇸 /mɪr/ *adj* [before n] used to emphasize that something is not large or important: *The plane crashed mere minutes after take-off.* ○ *It cost a mere twenty*

M

dollars. ○ *The mere thought of it makes me feel ill.*

merely /ˈmɪə.li/ [US] /ˈmɪr-/ *adv* used to emphasize that you mean exactly what you are saying and nothing more: *I wasn't complaining, I merely said that I was tired.* ○ *The medicine won't cure her – it merely stops the pain.*

merest /ˈmɪə.rɪst/ [US] /ˈmɪr.ɪst/ *adj* **the merest** used to emphasize the surprising or strong effect of a very small action or event: *The merest **mention** of seafood makes her feel sick.* ○ *The merest **hint** of criticism makes him defensive.*

meretricious /ˌmer.ɪˈtrɪʃ.əs/ *adj* FORMAL seeming attractive but really false or of little value: *He claims that a lot of journalism is meretricious and superficial.*

merge /mɜːdʒ/ [US] /mɝːdʒ/ *verb* **1** [I or T] to combine or join together, or to cause things to do this: *They decided to merge the two companies into one.* ○ *The country's two biggest banks are planning to merge.* ○ *After a while the narrow track merges **with** a wider path.* **2** [I] US FOR **filter in**

merger /ˈmɜː.dʒəʳ/ [US] /ˈmɝː.dʒɚ/ *noun* [C] when two or more companies join together: *She's an attorney who advises companies about mergers and takeovers.* ○ *The merger of these two companies would create the world's biggest accounting firm.*

meridian /məˈrɪd.i.ən/ *noun* [C] an imaginary line from the North Pole to the South Pole, drawn on maps to help to show the position of a place: *The prime meridian of longitude is in Greenwich, South London.*

meringue /məˈræŋ/ *noun* [C or U] a very light sweet cake made by mixing sugar with the colourless part of an egg and baking it: *lemon meringue pie*

merino /məˈriː.nəʊ/ [US] /-noʊ/ *noun* [C] a breed of sheep which produces soft good-quality wool: *merino **wool***

M

merit /ˈmer.ɪt/ *noun* [C or U] **1** FORMAL the quality of being good and deserving praise: *an entertaining film with little artistic merit* ○ *Her ideas have merit.* ○ *Brierley's book has the merit of being both informative and readable.* **2 the merits of sth** the advantages something has compared to something else: *We discussed the merits of herbal tea.*

• **on *your* (own) merits** according to the qualities you possess or have shown, without considering any other information or comparing you to someone else: *The committee say they will **consider/judge** each applicant on his or her own merits.*

merit /ˈmer.ɪt/ *verb* [T] FORMAL If something merits a particular treatment, it deserves or is considered important enough to be treated in that way: *This plan merits careful attention.* ○ *The accident merited only a small paragraph in the local paper.*

meritorious /ˌmer.ɪˈtɔː.ri.əs/ [US] /-ˈtɔːr.i-/ *adj* FORMAL deserving great praise: *an award for meritorious service*

meritocracy /ˌmer.ɪˈtɒk.rə.si/ [US] /-ˈtɑː.krə-/ *noun* [C or U] a social system or society in which people have power because of their abilities, not because of their wealth or social position: *The prime minister claims he wants to create a classless meritocracy in Britain.*

mermaid /ˈmɜː.meɪd/ [US] /ˈmɝː-/ *noun* [C] an imaginary creature described in stories, with the upper body of a woman and the tail of a fish

merry [HAPPY] /ˈmer.i/ *adj* OLD-FASHIONED happy or showing enjoyment: *the merry sound of laughter* ○ *She's a merry little soul.*

• **Merry Christmas!** said at Christmas to wish people a pleasant Christmas period: *Hello, Phoebe. Merry Christmas!* ○ *The shop assistant **wished** me a Merry Christmas.*

merrily /ˈmer.ɪ.li/ *adv* **1** showing happiness or enjoyment: *Her eyes sparkled merrily.* **2** INFORMAL without thinking about the result of what you are doing or about the problems it might cause: *The factory has been merrily pumping chemical waste into the river for the past ten years.*

merrymaking /ˈmer.iˌmeɪ.kɪŋ/ *noun* [U] LITERARY when people are celebrating and having an enjoyable time: *The eating, drinking and merrymaking went on late into the night.*

merriment /ˈmer.i.mənt/ *noun* [U] when people laugh or have an enjoyable time together: *Sounds of merriment came from the kitchen.* ○ *His unusual name has long been a source of merriment among his friends.*

merry [DRUNK] /ˈmer.i/ *adj* POLITE WORD FOR slightly drunk: *You **got** a bit merry last night, didn't you Cath?*

merry-go-round /ˈmer.i.gəʊˌraʊnd/ [US] /-goʊ-/ *noun* [C] **1** (UK ALSO **roundabout**, US ALSO **carousel**) a large machine at a fair which turns round and has wooden or plastic animals or vehicles on which children ride: *The girls wanted the merry-go-round to go faster.* **2** a series of similar activities, which can often seem boring: *With his first book came the endless merry-go-round **of** publicity and interviews.*

mescalin /ˈmes.kəl.ɪn/ *noun* [U] (ALSO **mescaline**) a drug obtained from PEYOTE (= a type of desert plant) that makes you HALLUCINATE (= see things which do not exist)

mesh [NET] /meʃ/ *noun* [C or U] (a piece of) net-like material with spaces in it, made from wire, plastic or thread: *a sieve with a fine/large mesh* ○ *a wire mesh fence*

mesh [SUIT] /meʃ/ *verb* [I] When different things or people mesh, they suit each other or work well together: *The members of the team just didn't mesh.* ○ *Whether the new personal pension works will depend much on how well it meshes **with** employers' schemes.*

mesh [JOIN] /meʃ/ *verb* [I] SPECIALIZED to join together in the correct position: *The car's gears aren't meshing properly.*

mesmerize, UK USUALLY **-ise** /ˈmez.mə.raɪz/ *verb* **1** [T often passive] to have someone's attention completely so that they cannot think of anything else: *I was completely mesmerized by the performance.* **2** [T] OLD-FASHIONED FOR **hypnotize**, see at **hypnosis**

mesmerizing, UK USUALLY **-ising** /ˈmez.mə.raɪ.zɪŋ/ *adj* very attractive, in a mysterious way, making you want to keep looking: *He had the most mesmerizing blue eyes.*

mesmeric /mezˈmer.ɪk/ *adj* LITERARY making you give your attention completely so that you cannot think of anything else: *music with a repetitive, slightly mesmeric quality*

mess [UNTIDINESS] /mes/ *noun* **1** [S or U] Something or someone that is a mess or is in a mess, looks dirty or untidy: *He **makes a** terrible mess when he's cooking.* ○ *Jem's house is always **in a** mess.* ○ *Go and **clear up** that mess in the kitchen.* ○ *Ian can't stand mess.* ○ *I **look a** mess – I can't go out like this!* ○ *My hair's such a mess today!* **2** [S] a situation that is full of problems: *She said that her life was a mess.* ○ *I **got** myself **into a** mess by telling a lie.* ○ *The company's finances are **in a** mess.* **3** [S] a person whose life is full of problems they cannot deal with: *After the divorce he was a real mess and drinking too much.* **4** [C] an animal's excrement: *Fido left another mess on the carpet.*

• **make a mess of *sth*** (ALSO **mess *sth* up**) to do something badly or spoil something: *I've made a real mess of my exams.*

mess /mes/ *verb* **1** [T] MAINLY US (UK **mess up**) INFORMAL to make something untidy: *Don't you dare mess my hair!* **2** [I] to leave excrement somewhere: *Next door's dog has messed on our steps again!*

• **(and) no messing** UK INFORMAL said to emphasize that you want something to be done: *I want you both in bed by 9 o'clock, no messing!*

messy /ˈmes.i/ *adj* **1** untidy: *a messy kitchen* ○ *messy hands/hair* ○ *His bedroom's always messy.* **2** producing or causing dirt and untidiness: *Eating spaghetti can be a messy business.* ○ *Vicky cooks really well but she's rather messy.* **3** describes a situation that is confused and unpleasant: *A war will be a long and messy business.* ○ *They had a bitter, messy divorce.* **messily** /ˈmes.ɪ.li/ *adv*

mess [ROOM] /mes/ *noun* [C] (US ALSO **mess hall**) a room or building in which members of the armed forces have their meals or spend their free time: *The group captain was having breakfast in the mess hall.* ○ *They spent their evenings in the **officers'** mess, drinking and playing cards.*

PHRASAL VERBS WITH **mess**

▲ **mess *sb* about/around** *phrasal verb UK* to treat someone badly: *I'm tired of being messed around by my bank.* ○ *Don't mess me about!*

▲ **mess about** *phrasal verb UK* **mess around**

▲ **mess around** SPEND TIME *phrasal verb* (*UK ALSO* **mess about**) *INFORMAL* to spend time doing unimportant or various things, without any particular purpose or plan: *They spend their weekends messing around on their boat.* ○ *My brother likes messing around **with** computers.* ○ *He spent the day with friends, just messing about.*

▲ **mess around** ACT STUPIDLY *phrasal verb* (*UK ALSO* **mess about**) to behave in a stupid or annoying way: *Stop messing about and listen to me!.*

▲ **mess around with *sth*** USE *phrasal verb* (*UK ALSO* **mess about with *sth***) *INFORMAL* to use or treat something in a careless or harmful way: *I don't want him coming in here and messing around with our computers.* ○ *Never mess around **with** scissors.*

▲ **mess around with *sb*** HAVE RELATIONSHIP *phrasal verb MAINLY US INFORMAL* If a married man or woman messes around with someone, they have a sexual relationship with someone who is not their wife or husband: *She found out that her husband was messing around with his secretary.*

▲ **mess *sth* up** UNTIDY *phrasal verb* **[M]** to make something untidy or dirty: *Who's messed up the bookshelf?*

▲ **mess *(sth)* up** SPOIL *phrasal verb* **[M]** *INFORMAL* to spoil or damage something, or to do something wrong or badly: *I feel I've messed up my chances of becoming a great singer.* ○ *He says that his divorce has really messed his life up.* ○ *You've really messed up this time.*

▲ **mess *sb* up** *phrasal verb* to cause someone to suffer emotional and mental problems: *Drugs can really mess you up.*

messed-up /ˌmestˈʌp/ *adj SLANG* unhappy and emotionally confused: *She was really messed-up as a teenager.*

▲ **mess *sb* up** INJURE *phrasal verb US SLANG* to hit someone repeatedly so that they are badly injured

▲ **mess with *sth/sb*** USE *phrasal verb INFORMAL* to use or become involved with something or someone dangerous: *You shouldn't mess with drugs.*

▲ **mess with *sth*** TAKE NO CARE *phrasal verb MAINLY US* to try to change or repair something, but not carefully and usually without success: *He was messing with his bike and then he couldn't fit the parts back together.*

▲ **mess with *sb*** TREAT BADLY *phrasal verb INFORMAL* to treat someone in a bad, rude or annoying way, or to start an argument with them: *I've warned you already, don't mess with me!*

message INFORMATION /ˈmes.ɪdʒ/ *noun* **[C]** a short piece of information that you give to a person when you cannot speak to them directly: *If I'm not there when you phone, leave a message.* ○ **[+ that]** *I **got** a message **that** she'll be late.*

message /ˈmes.ɪdʒ/ *verb* **[T]** to send someone an electronic message

messenger /ˈmes.ɪn.dʒəʳ/ (US) /-dʒɚ/ *noun* **[C]** someone who takes a message or documents from one person to another: *The documents were delivered by special messenger.* ○ *a messenger boy*

• **Don't shoot the messenger.** *SAYING* said to warn someone not to be angry with the person who tells them something bad

message IDEA /ˈmes.ɪdʒ/ *noun* **[C]** the most important idea in a book, film or play: *The film's message is that rich and poor are alike.*

• **get the message** *INFORMAL* to understand what someone is trying to tell you, even if they are not expressing themselves directly: *I never answer his calls and I ignore him every time I see him, so you'd think he'd get the message.*

• **get the message across** to make someone understand: *We need to get the message across **that** too much sun is dangerous.*

messiah /məˈsaɪ.ə/ *noun* **[S]** a leader who is believed to have the power to solve the world's problems: *An ordinary priest, he was hailed by thousands as the new messiah.*

the Messiah *noun* **[S]** **1** in the Christian religion, Jesus Christ **2** in the Jewish religion, the King of the Jews who will be sent by God

messianic /ˌmes.iˈæn.ɪk/ *adj* **1** *FORMAL* relating or belonging to a messiah: *He announced the imminent arrival of a messianic **leader**.* **2** describes a religious group which believes that a leader will or has come who has the power to change the world and bring peace: *a messianic cult/movement/sect* **3** describes a speech or style which is very persuasive and full of emotion: *She talks about her work with a messianic zeal.*

Messrs /ˈmes.əz/ (US) /-ɚz/ *FORMAL plural of* **Mr** (= title used before a man's name), used before the names of two or more people, usually in the title of a company: *Messrs Wood and Laurence, solicitors*

met MEET /met/ *past simple and past participle of* **meet**

met WEATHER /met/ *adj* **[before n]** *MAINLY UK INFORMAL FOR* **meteorological**: *the Met Office* ➲See at **meteorology**.

the Met POLICE /ðəˈmet/ *group noun* **[S]** *ABBREVIATION FOR* **the Metropolitan Police**

metabolism /məˈtæb.əl.ɪ.zəm/ *noun* **[C]** *SPECIALIZED* all the chemical processes in your body, especially those that cause food to be used for energy and growth: *Exercise is supposed to speed up your metabolism.*

metabolic /ˌmet.əˈbɒl.ɪk/ (US) /ˌmeţ.əˈbɑː.lɪk/ *adj SPECIALIZED The athletes had taken pills to stimulate their metabolic **rate*** (= the speed at which their bodies used energy).

metal /ˈmet.əl/ (US) /ˈmeţ-/ *noun* **[C or U]** a chemical element, such as iron or gold, or a mixture of such elements, such as steel, which electricity and heat can travel through and which is generally hard and strong: *Metal, paper and glass can be recycled.* ○ *Silver, gold and platinum are **precious** metals.* ○ *The wooden beam is reinforced with a metal plate.*

metallic /məˈtæl.ɪk/ *adj* **1** describes a sound, appearance or taste which is like metal: *a dull, metallic sound* ○ *Beer from a can often has a metallic taste.* ○ *Our new car is metallic blue.* **2** *SPECIALIZED* consisting of, or partly consisting of, metal: *Brass is a metallic alloy of copper and zinc.*

metalanguage /ˈmet.əˌlæŋ.gwɪdʒ/ (US) /ˈmeţ-/ *noun* **[C]** *SPECIALIZED* a specialized form of language or set of symbols used when discussing or describing the structure of a language

ˈmetal deˌtector *noun* **[C]** a machine that you move over the ground or a surface to discover if there is metal there: *He goes round fields and beaches with his metal detector, hoping to find buried treasure.*

ˈmetal faˌtigue *noun* **[U]** a weakness which develops in metal structures which are used repeatedly

metalled /ˈmet.əld/ (US) /ˈmeţ-/ *adj UK* describes a road covered with small or crushed stones

metallurgy /məˈtæl.ə.dʒi/ (US) /ˈmeţ.əl.ɜːr-/ *noun* **[U]** the scientific study of the structures and uses of metals: *She has a doctorate in metallurgy from the University of Utah.* **metallurgical** /ˌmet.əlˈɜː.dʒɪ.kəl/ (US) /ˌmeţ.əlˈɜːr-/ *adj*: *a metallurgical process* ○ *the metallurgical industry*

metallurgist /məˈtæl.ə.dʒɪst/ (US) /ˈmeţ.əl.ɜːr-/ *noun* **[C]** a person who studies or knows about metals

metalwork /ˈmet.əl.wɜːk/ (US) /ˈmeţ.əl.wɜːrk/ *noun* **[U]** **1** the activity of making metal objects: *Her favourite subject at school is metalwork.* **2** the metal part of something: *Rust has damaged the metalwork of the bicycle.*

metamorphose /ˌmet.əˈmɔː.fəʊz/ (US) /ˌmeţ.əˈmɔːr.foʊz/ *verb* **[I]** *FORMAL* to change into a completely different form or type: *The awkward boy I knew had metamorphosed **into** a tall, confident man.*

metamorphosis /ˌmet.əˈmɔː.fə.sɪs/ (US) /ˌmeţ.əˈmɔːr-/ *noun plural* **metamorphoses** **1** **[C]** a complete change: *Under the new editor, the magazine has undergone a metamorphosis.* **2** **[U]** *SPECIALIZED* the process by which the young form of insects and some animals, such as frogs, develops into the adult form

metaphor /ˈmet.ə.fɔːʳ/ (US) /ˈmeţ.ə.fɔːr/ *noun* **[C or U]** an expression which describes a person or object in a literary way by referring to something that is considered to possess similar characteristics to the person or object you are trying to describe: *'The mind is an*

M

ocean' and 'the city is a jungle' are both metaphors. ○ Metaphor and simile are the most commonly used figures of speech in everyday language.
• **a metaphor for sth** a symbol which represents a particular thing: *The author uses disease as a metaphor for the corruption in society.* ○ *In the film, the city is a metaphor for confusion and loneliness.*
metaphorical /ˌmet.əˈfɒr.ɪ.kəl/ [US] /ˌmet̬.əˈfɔːr-/ *adj* (*ALSO* **metaphoric**) **1** describes language which contains metaphors: *Her second novel is written in a very metaphorical style.* **2** not having real existence but symbolic and showing some truth about a situation or other subject: *A metaphorical ocean* (= extremely large area of disagreement) *lies between the two groups.* ○ *There is a danger that America's metaphoric 'war on drugs' may turn into a bloody reality.*
metaphorically /ˌmet.əˈfɒr.ɪ.kli/ [US] /ˌmet̬.əˈfɔːr-/ *adv*: *The phrase 'born again' is used metaphorically to mean that someone has suddenly become very religious.* ○ *By leaving school without any qualifications, she has, metaphorically* ***speaking****, shot herself in the foot* (= harmed her chances of success).

metaphysics /ˌmet.əˈfɪz.ɪks/ [US] /ˌmet̬-/ *noun* [U] the part of philosophy that is about understanding existence and knowledge **metaphysical** /ˌmet.əˈfɪz.ɪ.kəl/ [US] /ˌmet̬-/ *adj*: *Most teenagers ask themselves metaphysical questions such as "What is love?" and "What is death?"*

mete /miːt/ *verb*
▲ **mete sth out** *phrasal verb* [M often passive] *FORMAL* to give or order a punishment or make someone receive cruel or unfair treatment: *Victorian schoolteachers regularly meted out physical punishment to their pupils.*

meteor /ˈmiː.ti.ɔːr/ [US] /-t̬i.ɔːr/ *noun* [C] *SPECIALIZED* a piece of rock or other matter from space that produces a bright light as it travels through the Earth's atmosphere ⇒See also **shooting star**; **falling star**.
meteoric /ˌmiː.tiˈɒr.ɪk/ [US] /-t̬iˈɑːr-/ *adj* **1** relating to or caused by a meteor: *The sudden flash of light in the night sky was caused by a meteoric fireball.* **2** describes something which develops very fast and attracts a lot of attention: *The group had a meteoric* ***rise*** *to fame in the 70s.* ○ *Her parliamentary* ***career*** *has been meteoric.*

meteorite /ˈmiː.ti.ər.aɪt/ [US] /-t̬i.ə.raɪt/ *noun* [C] a piece of rock or other matter from space that has landed on Earth

meteorology /ˌmiː.ti.əˈrɒl.ə.dʒi/ [US] /-t̬i.əˈrɑː.lə-/ *noun* [U] the scientific study of the processes that cause particular weather conditions
meteorological /ˌmiː.ti.ər.əˈlɒdʒ.ɪ.kəl/ [US] /-t̬i.ɚ.əˈlɑː.dʒɪ-/ *adj* (*INFORMAL* **met**) relating to weather conditions: *Accurate meteorological records began 100 years ago.*
meteorologist /ˌmiː.ti.əˈrɒl.ə.dʒɪst/ [US] /-t̬i.əˈrɑːl-/ *noun* [C] someone who studies meteorology

meter [DEVICE] /ˈmiː.tər/ [US] /-t̬ɚ/ *noun* [C] **1** a device that measures the amount of something that is used: *The* ***electricity*** *meter is under the stairs.* ○ *You'll need some change for the* ***parking*** *meter.* ○ *The man from the gas board came to* ***read*** *the meter* (= see how much gas had been used). **2** the device in a taxi that measures the distance and the amount of time spent travelling and shows how much you have to pay: *The taxi driver left the meter* ***running*** *while I helped Mum to her front door.*
meter /ˈmiː.tər/ [US] /-t̬ɚ/ *verb* [T] to use meters to measure how much gas, electricity or water is used: *Britain's water companies are planning to meter water consumption.*

meter [MEASUREMENT] /ˈmiː.tər/ [US] /-t̬ɚ/ *noun* [C] *US FOR* **metre**

methadone /ˈmeθ.ə.dəʊn/ [US] /-doʊn/ *noun* [U] a drug which is often given to people who are trying to stop using HEROIN

methane /ˈmiː.θeɪn/ *noun* [U] a colourless gas without a smell, which is often used as a fuel: *Methane is the main constituent of natural gas.*

methanol /ˈmeθ.ə.nɒl/ [US] /-nɑːl/ *noun* [U] a poisonous chemical substance which is the simplest type of alcohol

methinks /mɪˈθɪŋks/ *OLD USE OR HUMOROUS FOR* I think: *There's more to this than meets the eye, methinks.*

metho /ˈmeθ.əʊ/ [US] /-oʊ/ *noun* [U] *AUS INFORMAL FOR* **methylated spirits**

method /ˈmeθ.əd/ *noun* [C] a particular way of doing something: *Travelling by train is still one of the safest methods of transport.* ○ *The new teaching methods encourage children to think for themselves.* ⇒See Note **way or method/means of?** at **way** METHOD.
• **have method in *your* madness** (*US USUALLY* **have a method to *your* madness**) to have a good reason for what you are doing, although you seem to be behaving strangely
methodical /məˈθɒd.ɪ.kəl/ [US] /-ˈθɑː.dɪ-/ *adj* describes people who do things in a very ordered, careful way: *Tom is a very methodical person and writes lists for everything.* **methodically** /məˈθɒd.ɪ.kli/ [US] /-ˈθɑː.dɪ-/ *adv*

Methodism /ˈmeθ.ə.dɪ.zəm/ *noun* [U] the beliefs and activities of a Christian group which follows the teachings of John Wesley **Methodist** /ˈmeθ.ə.dɪst/ *noun* [C], *adj*: *Her parents were staunch Methodists.* ○ *the Methodist church* ○ *a Methodist minister*

methodology /ˌmeθ.əˈdɒl.ə.dʒi/ [US] /-ˈdɑː.lə-/ *noun* [C or U] a system of ways of doing, teaching or studying something: *The methodology and findings of the research team have been criticized.* **methodological** /ˌmeθ.ə.dəlˈɒdʒ.ɪ.kəl/ [US] /-ˈɑː.dʒɪ-/ *adj*

meths /meθs/ *noun* [U] *UK INFORMAL FOR* **methylated spirits**

Methuselah /məˈθjuː.zəl.ə/ *noun* in the Bible, a man who was said to have lived for 969 years
• **as old as Methuselah** *HUMOROUS* describes an extremely old person

methylated spirits /ˌmeθ.ɪ.leɪ.tɪdˈspɪr.ɪts/ [US] /-t̬ɪd-/ *noun* [U] (*INFORMAL* **meths**) *UK* a liquid made from alcohol and other chemicals, used to remove dirty marks and as a fuel in small heaters and lights

meticulous /məˈtɪk.jʊ.ləs/ *adj APPROVING* very careful and with great attention to every detail: *Many hours of meticulous preparation have gone into writing the book.* **meticulously** /məˈtɪk.jʊ.lə.sli/ *adv*: *The entire project was meticulously planned.* **meticulousness** /məˈtɪk.jʊ.lə.snəs/ *noun* [U]

metier /ˈmet.ɪ.eɪ/ [US] /ˈmet̬-/ *noun* [C] (*ALSO* **métier**) *FORMAL* the type of work that you have a natural ability to do well: *Rose tried painting but found her metier in music.*

the 'Met ˌOffice *noun* [S] the British government department that studies weather conditions and says what is expected to happen with the weather: *The Met Office says that the heat wave will continue for most of the week.* ○ *a Met Office forecast/spokesman*

metonymy /metˈɒn.ə.mi/ [US] /məˈtɑː.nə-/ *noun* [U] *SPECIALIZED* when something is referred to by a word which describes a quality or feature of that thing **metonymic** /ˌmetˈɒn.ə.mɪk/ [US] /ˌməˈtɑː.nə-/ *adj* **metonym** /ˈmet.ə.nɪm/ [US] /ˈmet̬-/ *noun*

me-too /ˌmiːˈtuː/ *adj* [before n] *INFORMAL* a company's me-too product is one that is designed to be similar to a very popular product made by another company

metre [MEASUREMENT] *UK, US* **meter** /ˈmiː.tər/ [US] /-t̬ɚ/ *noun* [C] (*WRITTEN ABBREVIATION* **m**) a unit of measurement equal to 100 centimetres: *The bomb shelter has concrete walls that are three metres thick.* ○ *a 15-metre yacht* ○ *She won the 100 metres* (= a race run over this distance) *at the Olympics.* ○ *He is 1m 75 tall.* ○ *The price of water rose to 48p per* ***cubic*** *metre* (= a unit of volume equal to 1000 litres). ○ *The room is six metres square.*

metre [POETRY] *UK, US* **meter** /ˈmiː.tər/ [US] /-t̬ɚ/ *noun* [C or U] *SPECIALIZED* the regular arrangement of syllables in poetry according to the number and type of beats in a line: *He composes poems in a classical style and in strict metre.* ○ *Many hymns have a firm, regular metre.*

metric /ˈmet.rɪk/ *adj* using or relating to a system of measurement that uses metres, centimetres, litres etc: *The recipe is given in both metric and imperial measures.* ○ *Most high-tech industry has been metric for decades.*
metrication /ˌmet.rɪˈkeɪ.ʃən/ *noun* [U] when you change from measuring things in IMPERIAL units and start to use metric units

ˌmetric 'ton *noun* [C] a unit of weight equal to 1000 kilograms

M

metro RAILWAY /'met.rəʊ/ US /-roʊ/ noun [U] an underground electric railway system in some cities, especially in France: *Let's go by Metro.* ○ *a metro station* ○ *the Paris metro*

USAGE

metro, subway or **underground**?

All these words mean an underground railway system in a large city. **Underground** is the usual word in British English. **Subway** is the usual word in American English.

the Paris metro
the London underground
the New York subway

metro CITY /'met.rəʊ/ US /'met.roʊ/ adj [before n] US relating to a large city and the area surrounding it: *This guidebook includes a map of the Phoenix metro area.*

metronome /'met.rə.nəʊm/ US /-noʊm/ noun [C] a device that produces a regular repeated sound like a clock, to help musicians play music at a particular speed

metropolis /mə'trɒp.əl.ɪs/ US /-'trɑː.pəl-/ noun [C] FORMAL a very large city, often the most important city in a large area or country: *Soon afterwards he left to begin his career in the metropolis.* ○ *a sprawling/bustling/ modern metropolis* **metropolitan** /,met.rə'pɒl.ɪ.tⁿn/ US /-'pɑː.lɪ-/ adj: *the Metropolitan Museum of Art in New York* ○ *He was drawn to the metropolitan glamour and excitement of Paris.* ○ *a metropolitan area/council*

the Metro,politan Po'lice plural noun (INFORMAL **the Met**) UK the police responsible for London

mettle /'met.l̩/ US /'met̬-/ noun [U] ability and determination when competing or doing something difficult: *The German athletes showed/proved their mettle in the final round.* ○ *The real test of her political mettle came in the May elections.*
• **on your mettle** ready to do something as well as you can in a difficult situation: *Both players were on their mettle in the final round.* ○ *Cooking for such important people really puts you on your mettle.*

mew /mjuː/ noun [C] the soft crying sound that a cat makes ⊃Compare **miaow**; **purr**. **mew** /mjuː/ verb [I]

mews /mjuːz/ noun [C] plural **mews** MAINLY UK **1** a building which was used in the past for keeping horses and is now used as a house: *They bought a converted mews.* ○ *a tiny mews house* **2** a short narrow road where these buildings are found: *Their address is 6 Gloucester Mews.*

Mexican /'mek.sɪ.kⁿn/ adj from, belonging to or relating to Mexico

Mexican /'mek.sɪ.kⁿn/ noun [C] a person from Mexico

Mexican 'wave UK noun [C usually sing] (US **the Wave**) a wave-like movement made by a crowd watching a sports game, when everyone stands and lifts up their arms and then sits down again one after another

mezzanine /'met.sə.niːn/ US /'mez.ə-/ noun [C] **1** a small additional floor between one floor of a building and the next floor up: *You can look down from the mezzanine into the ground floor.* ○ *The shoe department is on the mezzanine floor.* **2** US the front few rows of seats of the level above ground, or all of the level above ground, in a place such as a theatre or sports STADIUM

mezzo-soprano (plural **mezzo sopranos**) /,met.səʊ.sə-'prɑː.nəʊ/ US /-soʊ.sə'præn.oʊ/ noun [C or U] (INFORMAL **mezzo**) a voice or musical part lower than SOPRANO but higher than CONTRALTO, or a singer with this type of voice: *She's the country's leading mezzo-soprano.*

mg WRITTEN ABBREVIATION FOR **milligram**

MHz WRITTEN ABBREVIATION FOR **megahertz**

mi noun WRITTEN ABBREVIATION FOR **mile(s)**: *a radius of 5 mi*

MI5 /,em.aɪ'faɪv/ group noun [U] the official British organization that is responsible for protecting military and political secrets

MI6 /,em.aɪ'sɪks/ group noun [U] the official British organization that is responsible for discovering foreign military and political secrets

miaow, US USUALLY **meow** /miː'aʊ/ noun [C] the high crying sound of a cat ⊃Compare **mew**; **purr**. **miaow** /,miː-'aʊ/ verb [I] *A cat was miaowing pitifully outside the door.*

miasma /mi'æz.mə/ noun [C] LITERARY **1** an unpleasant and bad-smelling fog: *A miasma of pollution hung in the air above Mexico City.* **2** a very unpleasant general feeling or character of a situation or place: *After he lost his job, he sank into a miasma of poverty and despair.*

mic /maɪk/ noun US INFORMAL FOR **microphone**

mica /'maɪ.kə/ noun [U] a natural glass-like substance that breaks easily into thin layers and is not damaged by heat, often used in electrical equipment

mice /maɪs/ plural of **mouse**

mickey /'mɪk.i/ noun UK INFORMAL **take the mickey/ mick (out of someone)** to laugh at someone and make them seem silly, by copying their behaviour or tricking them in an amusing or unkind way: *A group of other boys were taking the mickey out of him.* ○ *She's always taking the mick – she's got no respect for the managers at all.*

mickey (finn) /,mɪk.i'fɪn/ noun [C] SLANG a drug added to a drink, especially an alcoholic drink, in order to make the person who drinks it unconscious: *He must have slipped the guard a mickey finn.*

Mickey 'Mouse adj [before n] INFORMAL DISAPPROVING describes something such as an organization, machine or course of study that you think is not as good or serious as it should be: *He works for some Mickey Mouse outfit* (= company) *in Oklahoma.*

micro COMPUTER /'maɪ.krəʊ/ US /-kroʊ/ noun [C] plural **micros** INFORMAL FOR **microcomputer**

micro- SMALL /maɪ.krəʊ-/ US /-kroʊ-/ prefix very small: *a microorganism* ○ *microbiology* ⊃Compare **macro-** LARGE.

micro- MEASUREMENT /maɪ.krəʊ-/ US /-kroʊ-/ prefix 1 000 000th of the stated unit: *a micrometre* ○ *a microgram*

microbe /'maɪ.krəʊb/ US /-kroʊb/ noun [C] a very small living thing, especially one which causes disease, and which is too small to see without a microscope

microbiology /,maɪ.krəʊ.baɪ'ɒl.ə.dʒi/ US /-kroʊ.baɪ'ɑː.lə-/ noun [U] the study of very small living things, such as bacteria **microbiological** /,maɪ.krəʊ.baɪ.ə'lɒdʒ.ɪ.kⁿl/ US /-kroʊ.baɪ.ə'lɑː.dʒɪ-/ adj **microbiologist** /,maɪ.krəʊ.baɪ-'ɒl.ə.dʒɪst/ US /-kroʊ.baɪ'ɑː.lə-/ noun [C]

microbrewery /'maɪ.krəʊ,bruː.ⁿr.i/ US /-kroʊ,bruː.ɚ.i/ noun [C] MAINLY US a small company which makes beer, usually using traditional methods, and which often has a restaurant where its beer is served: *Redhook was one of the first microbreweries in Seattle, Washington.*

microchip /'maɪ.krəʊ.tʃɪp/ US /-kroʊ-/ noun [C] a chip COMPUTER PART

microcircuit /'maɪ.krəʊ,sɜː.kɪt/ US /-kroʊ,sɜː-/ noun an integrated circuit

microcomputer /'maɪ.krəʊ.kəm,pjuː.tⁿr/ US /-kroʊ.kəm-,pjuː.t̬ɚ/ noun [C] (INFORMAL **micro**) a small computer or PERSONAL COMPUTER containing a MICROPROCESSOR (= part which controls operations)

microcosm /'maɪ.krəʊ,kɒz.ⁿm/ US /-kroʊ,kɑː.zⁿm/ noun [C or U] a small place, society or situation which has the same characteristics as something much larger: *The audience was selected to create a microcosm of American society.* ⊃Compare **macrocosm**.

microelectronics /,maɪ.krəʊ,ɪl.ek'trɒn.ɪks/ US /-kroʊ.-,lek'trɑː.nɪks/ noun [U] the science and technology involved in the creation and use of very small electronic parts

microfiche /'maɪ.krəʊ.fiːʃ/ US /-kroʊ-/ noun [C or U] (ALSO **fiche**) a small rectangular sheet of film on which information is photographed in a reduced size: *The information is now available on microfiche.*

microfilm /'maɪ.krəʊ.fɪlm/ US /-kroʊ-/ noun [C or U] film which is used for photographing information in a reduced size, or a piece of this film **microfilm** /'maɪ.krəʊ.fɪlm/ US /-kroʊ-/ verb [T] *The paper records were microfilmed to save storage space.*

microgram /'maɪ.krəʊ.græm/ US /-kroʊ-/ noun [C] 0.000 001 of a gram

microlight /'maɪ.krəʊ.laɪt/ US /-kroʊ-/ noun [C] (ALSO **microlite**) an extremely light and small aircraft with a very small engine, which carries only one or two people ⊃See picture **Planes, Ships and Boats** on page Centre 14

micrometer /maɪˈkrɒm.ɪ.tə^r/ ⓤ /ˈkrɑː.mɪ.t̬ə/ *noun* [C] a device used for making very exact measurements or for measuring very small things

micrometre *UK, US* **micrometer** /ˈmaɪ.krəʊˌmiː.tə^r/ /-kroʊˌmiː.t̬ə/ *noun* [C] a **micron**

micron /ˈmaɪ.krɒn/ ⓤ /-krɑːn/ *noun* [C] 0.000 001 of a metre

microorganism /ˌmaɪ.krəʊˈɔː.g^ən.ɪ.z^əm/ ⓤ /-kroʊˈɔːr-/ *noun* [C] a living thing which on its own is too small to be seen without a microscope

microphone /ˈmaɪ.krə.fəʊn/ ⓤ /-foʊn/ *noun* [C] (*INFORMAL* **mike/mic**) a piece of equipment that you speak into to make your voice louder, or to record your voice or other sounds: *The interviewer asked her to* **speak into/ use** *the microphone.* ○ *My laptop has a* **built-in** *micro-phone.*

microprocessor /ˌmaɪ.krəʊˈprəʊ.ses.ə^r/ ⓤ /-kroʊˈprɑː.ses.ɚ/ *noun* [C] a part of a computer that controls its main operations

microscope /ˈmaɪ.krə.skəʊp/ ⓤ /-skoʊp/ *noun* [C] a device that uses lenses to make very small objects look larger, so that they can be scientifically examined and studied: *They looked at the blood samples* **under** *the microscope.*

• **put** *sth* **under the microscope** to examine or think about a situation very carefully: *The investigation put the company's financial accounts under the microscope*

microscopic /ˌmaɪ.krəˈskɒp.ɪk/ ⓤ /-ˈskɑː.pɪk/ *adj SPECIALIZED* very small and only able to be seen with a microscope: *microscopic algae*

microscopic /ˌmaɪ.krəˈskɒp.ɪk/ ⓤ /-ˈskɑː.pɪk/ *adj INFORMAL HUMOROUS* extremely small: *The helpings you get in the office canteen are microscopic!* **microscopically** /ˌmaɪ.krəˈskɒp.ɪ.kli/ ⓤ /-ˈskɑː.pɪ-/ *adv INFORMAL OR SPECIALIZED microscopically small*

microsecond /ˈmaɪ.krəʊˌsek.^ənd/ ⓤ /-kroʊ-/ *noun* [C] 0.000 001 of a second

microsurgery /ˌmaɪ.krəʊˈsɜː.dʒ^ər.i/ ⓤ /-kroʊˈsɜː.dʒɚ-/ *noun* [U] operations on very small areas of a body, for example nerve fibres or the small tubes that carry blood: *She underwent microsurgery to re-attach her severed fingers.*

microwave /ˈmaɪ.krəʊ.weɪv/ ⓤ /-kroʊ-/ *noun* [C] **1** a very short ELECTROMAGNETIC wave used for cooking food or for sending information by radio or RADAR **2** (*ALSO* **microwave oven**) an electric oven that uses waves of energy to cook or heat food quickly: *Put the fish* **in** *the microwave and it'll only take 5 minutes.* **microwave** /ˈmaɪ.krəʊ.weɪv/ ⓤ /-kroʊ-/ *verb* [T] *Shall I microwave something for dinner?* **microwaveable**, *US* **microwavable** /ˈmaɪ.krəʊ.weɪ.və.b^əl/ ⓤ /-kroʊ-/ *adj: microwaveable frozen chips*

mid [AMONG] /mɪd/ *prep OLD-FASHIONED LITERARY* among or in the middle of

mid- [MIDDLE] /mɪd-/ *prefix* the middle of: *mid-March* ○ *mid-afternoon* ○ *US the Mideast* ○ *He's in his mid-thirties.* ○ *He stopped (in) mid-sentence.*

mid-air /ˌmɪdˈeə^r/ ⓤ /ˌmɪdˈer/ *noun* [U] a point in the air, not on the ground: *She caught the ball* **in** *mid-air.* **mid-air** /ˌmɪdˈeə^r/ ⓤ /ˌmɪdˈer/ *adj: a mid-air collision*

Midas /ˈmaɪ.dəs/ *noun* **the Midas touch** If someone has the Midas touch, they are financially successful in everything they do.

midday /ˌmɪdˈdeɪ/ *noun* [U] 12 o'clock in the middle of the day: *I just have a sandwich* **at** *midday/for my midday meal.*

middle /ˈmɪd.l̩/ *noun* **1** [S] the central point, position or part: *This is my class photo – I'm the one* **in the middle.** ○ *He was standing in* **the middle of** *the road.* ○ *The noise woke us up* **in the middle of** *the night.* **2** [C usually sing] *INFORMAL* waist: *Those trousers look a bit tight around your middle.*

• **be in the middle of** *sth* to be busy with an activity: *Someone phoned when I was in the middle of bathing the baby.*

• **(in) the middle of nowhere** *INFORMAL DISAPPROVING* describes a place far away from any towns and cities and where few people live: *He lives in a tiny cottage in the middle of nowhere.*

• **divide/split** *(sth)* **down the middle** to separate, or to divide something, into two equal parts: *Let's split the cost right down the middle.* ○ *The family is split down the middle on this issue.*

middle /ˈmɪd.l̩/ *adj* [before n] **1** in a central position: *In the sequence a, b, c, d, e, the middle letter is c.* ○ *Jane sits at the middle desk, between Sue and Karen.* **2** neither high nor low in importance, amount or size: *middle* **in-come** *families* ○ *a middle-sized* (= average-sized) *sheepdog* **3** describes a child who has the same number of older brothers and sisters as younger brothers and sisters: *She's the middle child of three.* **4** describes a form of a particular language which existed between its origin and its present form: *14th century Middle English* ○ *Middle French*

• **follow/steer/take the middle course/way/path** to act in a way that is not extreme and that you consider will cause least harm: *Most parents try to steer a middle course between imposing very strict discipline and letting their kids run wild.*

middle ˈage *noun* [U] the period of your life, usually considered to be from about 40 to 60 years old, when you are no longer young, but are not yet old: *Once you reach middle age, you have to be sensible with your health.*

middle-aged /ˌmɪd.l̩ˈeɪdʒd/ *adj* **1** in middle age: *They're a middle-aged couple, with grown-up children.* **2** *DIS-APPROVING* too careful and not showing the enthusiasm, energy or style of someone young: *What a conventional, middle-aged attitude he has to life!*

the ˌMiddle ˈAges *plural noun* a period in European history, between about 1000 AD and 1500 AD, when the power of kings, people of high rank and the Christian Church was strong

middle-age spread /ˌmɪd.l̩.eɪdʒˈspred/ *noun* [U] *HUMOROUS* fat around the waist that some people get as they grow older

ˌMiddle Aˈmerica/ˈEngland *noun* [U] the part of American/English society that is neither rich nor poor and does not have extreme political or religious opinions

middlebrow /ˈmɪd.l̩.braʊ/ *adj MAINLY DISAPPROVING* describes music, literature, art or film which is of good quality, interesting and often popular, but can be under-stood easily ⊃Compare **highbrow; lowbrow.**

ˌmiddle ˈC *noun* [C usually sing] *SPECIALIZED* the musical note C near the middle of the keyboard on a piano

ˌmiddle ˈclass *group noun* [S] (*ALSO* **the middle classes**) a social group that consists of well-educated people, such as doctors, lawyers, and teachers, who have good jobs and are neither very rich nor very poor: *The* **upper** *middle class tend to go into business or the professions, becoming, for example, lawyers, doctors or accountants.* ⊃Compare **lower class; upper class; working class. middle-class** /ˌmɪd.l̩ˈklɑːs/ ⓤ /-ˈklæs/ *adj: a middle-class suburb of New York*

middle-distance [SPORTS] /ˈmɪd.l̩.dɪs.t^ənts/ *adj* [before n] describes a race which is run over a medium distance, especially 800 or 1500 metres: *a middle-distance event/ runner*

ˌmiddle ˈdistance [POSITION] *noun* [U] the part of a picture or a view that is neither very near nor very far away: *From the top of the hill we could see the ocean far away and, in the middle distance, the village.* ⊃Compare **the background** THINGS BEHIND; **the foreground.**

ˌmiddle ˈear *noun* [S] the central part of the ear, behind the EARDRUM, through which sound travels

the ˌMiddle ˈEast *noun* [S] (*US ALSO* **the Mideast**) the area from the eastern Mediterranean to Iran, including Syria, Jordan, Israel, Lebanon, Saudi Arabia, Iran and Iraq, and sometimes also Egypt: *He worked in the Middle East for ten years.* ⊃Compare **the Far East.** **ˌMiddle ˈEastern** *adj: Middle Eastern capitals include Baghdad and Tel Aviv.*

ˌmiddle ˈfinger *noun* [C] the longest finger on the hand ⊃See picture **The Body** on page Centre 5

ˌmiddle ˈground *noun* [U] a position between two opposite opinions in an argument, or between two descriptions: *The UN peace envoy has failed to find any middle ground between the government and the opposi-*

*tion parties. ○ He can be magical, he can be comical, but only rarely does he **occupy** the middle ground.*

middleman /ˈmɪd.l̩.mæn/ *noun* [C] **1** a person who buys goods from a producer and makes a profit by selling them to a shop or a user: *You can lower the price by **cutting out*** (= avoiding the use of) *the middleman and buying directly from the factory.* **2** someone who communicates or makes arrangements between two people or groups who are unwilling or unable to meet or deal directly with each other

ˌmiddle ˈmanagement *group noun* [U] the people within a company who are in charge of departments or groups, but who are below those in charge of the whole company: *He cut hundreds of jobs in middle management.* **ˌmiddle ˈmanager** *noun* [C]

ˌmiddle ˈname *noun* [C] the name some people have between their first name and their last name
• **be *sb's* middle name** *INFORMAL* to be a quality that is an important part of someone's character: *Don't worry, I won't tell anyone. Discretion is my middle name.*

middle-of-the-road /ˌmɪd.l̩.əv.ðəˈrəʊd/ [US] /-ˈroʊd/ *adj* describes a person, organization, opinion or type of entertainment that is not extreme and is acceptable to or liked by most people: *middle-of-the-road pop music* ○ *They adopted a sensible, middle-of-the-road policy on defence spending.*

ˈmiddle ˌschool *noun* [C] in parts of the UK and the US, a school for children between the ages of about 9 and 14

middleweight /ˈmɪd.l̩.weɪt/ *noun* [C] a boxer whose weight is between LIGHT HEAVYWEIGHT and WELTERWEIGHT

the ˌMiddle ˈWest *noun* [S] **the Midwest**

middling /ˈmɪd.l̩.ɪŋ/ /-lɪŋ/ *adj INFORMAL* medium or average; neither very good nor very bad: *a man of about middling height* ○ *a middling performance of 'Anthony and Cleopatra'*

middy /ˈmɪd.i/ *noun* [C] *AUS* a beer glass of medium size, which contains 285 ml

midfield /ˈmɪd.fiːld/ *noun* [C or U] the central area of a sports field, or a central structure of a sports team: *Simon's a defender, but I always play **in** midfield.* ○ *Arsenal's defence were strong, but their midfield fell apart in the first five minutes of the match.* ○ *a midfield player* **midfielder** /ˈmɪdˌfiːl.dəʳ/ [US] /-dɚ/ *noun* [C] *Inter Milan have signed two new midfielders.*

midge /mɪdʒ/ *noun* [C] a small fly which flies in groups, and often bites

midget /ˈmɪdʒ.ɪt/ *noun* [C] *OFFENSIVE* a very small person
midget /ˈmɪdʒ.ɪt/ *adj* [before n] describes an object that is much smaller than usual: *a midget submarine/car*

MIDI /ˈmɪd.i/ *noun SPECIALIZED ABBREVIATION FOR* Musical Instrument Digital Interface: a system for allowing electronic musical instruments to communicate with each other

ˈMIDI ˌsystem *noun* [C] a piece of high-quality electronic equipment for playing music, usually including a CD player, a TAPE DECK and a radio ➲Compare **mini-system**.

the ˈMidlands *group noun* [S] the central part of England, including the cities of Birmingham, Coventry, Nottingham and Derby: *There is a lot of manufacturing industry in the Midlands.* **midlands** /ˈmɪd.ləndz/ *adj* (*ALSO* **midland**) *He's got a real midlands accent.*

mid-life crisis /ˌmɪd.laɪfˈkraɪ.sɪs/ *noun* [C] *plural* **mid-life crises** feelings of unhappiness, anxiety and disappointment that some people experience at about 40 years old and that can sometimes lead them to make important changes in their life ➲See also **menopause**; **male menopause**.

midmorning /ˌmɪdˈmɔː.nɪŋ/ [US] /-ˈmɔːr-/ *adj* [before n] in the middle of the morning: *a midmorning coffee break*

midnight /ˈmɪd.naɪt/ *noun* [U] 12 o'clock in the middle of the night: *There's a great film on TV **at** midnight.*

ˌmidnight ˈfeast *noun* [C] *UK* a meal eaten late at night, often in secret: *The children raided the fridge for a midnight feast.*

the ˌmidnight ˈsun *noun* [S] the sun when seen in the middle of the night in summer in the ARCTIC or ANTARCTIC (= the parts of the world furthest to the north and the south)

midpoint /ˈmɪd.pɔɪnt/ *noun* [C usually sing] **1** a point half the distance along something such as a line: *The driveway is 20m long, so the midpoint must be at 10m.* **2** a point in the middle of a period of time: *the midpoint of the football season*

midriff /ˈmɪd.rɪf/ *noun* [C] (*US ALSO* **midsection**) the part of the human body between the chest and the waist: *She wore a short T-shirt that revealed her midriff.*

midshipman /ˈmɪdˌʃɪp.mən/ *noun* [C] a person training to become an officer in a navy

midsized /ˈmɪd.saɪzd/ *adj* (*ALSO* **mid-size**) *MAINLY US* describes something such as an organization or vehicle that is neither large nor small: *a midsized family car*

midst /mɪdst/ /mɪtst/ *noun* [U] *FORMAL* the middle of a group of people or things: *She caught sight of Johnny **in** their midst* (= among them), *laughing and talking.*
• **in the midst of *sth*** in the middle of an event, situation or activity: *I'm afraid I'm too busy – I'm in the midst of writing up a report.* ○ *The country is in the midst of an economic crisis.*
midst /mɪdst/ /mɪtst/ *prep LITERARY The summit of the mountain appeared midst* (= among) *the clouds.*

midstream /ˌmɪdˈstriːm/ *noun* [U] the middle of a river where the water flows fastest: *They slowly paddled the boat into midstream.*
• **(in) midstream** in the middle of an activity, often one that is interrupted: *She interrupted him in midstream to ask a question.*

midsummer /ˌmɪdˈsʌm.əʳ/ [US] /-ɚ/ *noun* [U] **1** the period in the middle of summer: *I don't normally take my holiday in midsummer.* ○ *a midsummer evening* **2** the summer SOLSTICE, the day of the year on which it is light for the longest length of time (21 June in northern parts of the world, 22 December in southern parts of the world): *It's midsummer sometime this week, isn't it?*

Midsummer('s) Day /ˌmɪd.sʌm.əzˈdeɪ/ [US] /-ɚ-/ *noun* [U] *UK* June 24th

midterm /ˈmɪd.tɜːm/ [US] /-tɝːm/ *adj* in the middle of the period when a government is in office: *The governing party usually does badly in midterm by-elections.*
midterm /ˈmɪd.tɜːm/ [US] /-tɝːm/ *noun* [U] *US FOR* **half term**

midway /ˌmɪdˈweɪ/ *adv* **1** half the distance between two places: *Leeds is midway **between** London and Edinburgh.* **2** in the middle of a process or period of time: *She stopped working midway **through** her pregnancy.*

midweek /ˌmɪdˈwiːk/ *noun* [U] the middle of the week, usually from Tuesday to Thursday: *By midweek, the situation had become worrying.* **midweek** /ˌmɪdˈwiːk/ *adj* **midweek** /ˌmɪdˈwiːk/ *adv*: *The magazine comes out midweek.*

the Midwest /ðəˌmɪdˈwest/ *noun* [S] an area in the US which includes Ohio, Indiana, Michigan, Illinois, Wisconsin, Iowa, Minnesota, Nebraska, Missouri and Kansas: *A tornado destroyed grain crops across much of the Midwest.*
Midwestern /ˌmɪdˈwes.tən/ [US] /-tɚn/ *adj* relating to the Midwest: *a Midwestern city/state*

midwife /ˈmɪd.waɪf/ *noun* [C] *plural* **midwives** a person, usually a woman, who is trained to help women when they are giving birth **midwifery** /mɪdˈwɪf.ᵊr.i/ [US] /-ɚ-/ *noun* [U] *At nursing college, she specialized in midwifery.*

midwinter /ˌmɪdˈwɪn.təʳ/ [US] /-t̬ɚ/ *noun* [U] **1** the middle of the winter: *Temperatures can drop well below freezing in midwinter.* **2** the winter SOLSTICE, the particular day of the year on which it is light for the shortest period of time (22 December in northern parts of the world, 21 June in southern parts of the world): *They celebrate midwinter by lighting candles.*

mien /miːn/ *noun* [C] *LITERARY* a person's appearance, especially the typical expression on their face: *His aristocratic mien and smart clothes singled him out.*

miffed /mɪft/ *adj INFORMAL* annoyed at someone's behaviour towards you: *She hadn't phoned for a week and I was getting quite miffed.*

M

might [MAY] /maɪt/ *past simple of* the verb 'may', used especially when reporting what someone has said, thought, asked, etc: *I brought him some sandwiches because I thought he might be hungry.* ○ *Very politely the little boy asked if he might have another piece of cake* (= he said "May I have another piece of cake, please?").

might [POSSIBILITY] /maɪt/ *modal verb* used to express the possibility that something will happen or be done, or that something is true although not very likely: *I might come and visit you in America next year, if I can save enough money.* ○ *Don't go any closer – it might be dangerous/it mightn't be safe.* ○ *Driving so fast, he might* ***have*** *had a nasty accident* (= it could have happened but it did not). ○ *The rain might* ***have*** *stopped by now.*

might [PERMISSION] /maɪt/ *modal verb* UK FORMAL used as a more polite form of *may* when asking for permission: *Might I ask a question?* ○ *I wonder if I might have a quick look at your newspaper?*

• **might I ask/inquire/know** UK FORMAL used in questions to show disapproval by being more polite than is expected: *And what are you doing in there, might I ask?*

might [SUGGESTION] /maɪt/ *modal verb* used to make a suggestion or suggest a possibility in a polite way: *You might like to try a little more basil in the sauce next time.* ○ *I thought you might like to join me for dinner.*

might [SHOULD] /maɪt/ *modal verb* used to suggest, especially angrily, what someone should do to be pleasant, correct, polite, etc: *You might at least try to look like you're enjoying yourself!* ○ *"I've asked the boss to dinner tonight." "Well, you might* ***have*** *warned me!"*

• **I might have known** SLIGHTLY DISAPPROVING said when you are not surprised at a situation or someone's behaviour, because you expected it: *I might have known* ***(that)*** *he'd still be in bed at noon.*

might [INTRODUCE] /maɪt/ *modal verb* (ALSO **may**) used to introduce a statement which is very different from the statement you really want to make, in order to compare the two: *Leeds might be an excellent team,* ***but*** *today they played appallingly.*

might [POWER] /maɪt/ *noun* [U] power, strength or force: *Pizarro defeated the might of the Inca Empire with only a few hundred men.* ○ *She struggled* ***with all*** *her might to get free.*

mighty /ˈmaɪ.ti/ (US) /-t̬i/ *adj* LITERARY very large, powerful or important: *In the next game they will face the mighty Redskins.* ○ *Through the fields flows the mighty River Po.*

mighty /ˈmaɪ.ti/ (US) /-t̬i/ *adv* MAINLY US INFORMAL very: *They offered to raise salaries by 12% – that's a mighty generous deal.*

mightily /ˈmaɪ.tɪ.li/ (US) /-t̬ɪ-/ *adv* FORMAL with great effort: *He spent ten years struggling mightily with the bureaucracy.*

mightn't /ˈmaɪ.tᵊnt/ *short form of* might not: *Don't panic – it mightn't be true.*

might've /ˈmaɪ.təv/ (US) /-t̬əv/ *short form of* might have: *She might've taken it with her to read on the train.*

migraine /ˈmiː.greɪn/ /ˈmaɪ-/ (US) /ˈmaɪ-/ *noun* [C or U] severe continuous pain in the head, often with vomiting and difficulty in seeing: *Do you suffer from migraine?* ○ *Considering the amount of stress she's under, it's not surprising she keeps getting migraines.* ○ *a migraine headache*

migrate /maɪˈgreɪt/ *verb* [I] **1** When an animal migrates, it travels to a different place, usually when the season changes: *These animals migrate annually in search of food.* ○ *In September, these birds migrate 2000 miles south* ***to*** *a warmer climate.* **2** If people migrate, they travel in large numbers to a new place to live temporarily: *Mexican farm workers migrate* ***into*** *the US each year to find work at harvest time.* **3** to move from one place to another: *Trade is migrating* ***from*** *local shops* ***to*** *the larger out-of-town stores.* **migrant** /ˈmaɪ.grᵊnt/ *noun* [C] *These birds are winter migrants from Scandinavia.* ○ *The cities are full of migrants looking for work.* ○ *migrant* ***workers*** ○ *a migrant population* **migration** /maɪˈgreɪ.ʃᵊn/ *noun* [C or U] *There was a mass migration of poverty-struck farmers* ***into*** *the cities.* ➲Compare **immigration**; **emigration**. **migratory** /ˈmaɪ.grə.tri/ /maɪˈgreɪ.tᵊr.i/ (US) /-tɔːr-/ *adj*: *migratory birds*

mike /maɪk/ *noun* [C] (US ALSO **mic**) INFORMAL FOR **microphone**

mild [SLIGHT] /maɪld/ *adj* **1** not violent, severe or extreme: *She can't accept even mild criticism of her work.* ○ *He has suffered a mild heart attack – nothing too serious.* **2** describes food or a food flavour that is not very strong: *He doesn't like a hot curry – he prefers a mild one.* ○ *a mild chilli sauce* **3** describes weather that is not very cold or not as cold as usual: *We've had a mild winter this year.* **mildly** /ˈmaɪld.li/ *adv*: *We were mildly surprised to see him again so soon.* **mildness** /ˈmaɪld.nəs/ *noun* [U]

mild [BEER] /maɪld/ *noun* [U] a dark-coloured beer, drunk in some parts of Britain, that does not have a very strong or bitter taste ➲Compare **bitter** BEER.

mild [GENTLE] /maɪld/ *adj* gentle and calm: *a shy, mild sort of guy* **mildly** /ˈmaɪld.li/ *adv*: *"I think you've made a mistake," he said mildly.* **mildness** /ˈmaɪld.nəs/ *noun* [U] *mildness of manner*

mildew /ˈmɪl.djuː/ (US) /-duː/ *noun* [U] a black, green or whitish area caused by a fungus that grows on things such as plants, paper, cloth or buildings, usually if the conditions are warm and wet: *There are patches of mildew on the walls.* **mildewed** /ˈmɪl.djuːd/ (US) /-duːd/ *adj*: *mildewed rose bushes*

mild-mannered /ˌmaɪldˈmæn.əd/ (US) /-ɚd/ *adj* describes a person who is gentle and does not show extreme emotions: *a mild-mannered philosophy professor*

mile /maɪl/ *noun* [C] a unit of distance equal to 1760 yards or 1.6 kilometres: *a ten-mile drive* ○ *The nearest town is ten miles away.* ○ *The speed limit is 30 miles* ***an/per*** *hour.*

• **a mile off** If you can see or realize something a mile off, you notice it easily and quickly: *She's lying – you can tell it a mile off.*

• **stand/stick out a mile** to be very obvious or easy to see: *His lack of experience sticks out a mile.*

miles /maɪlz/ *plural noun* a very long way: *From the top, we could see for miles in every direction.* ○ *He lives miles* ***away*** *on the other side of town.*

• **be miles away** MAINLY UK to not be aware of what is happening around you because you are thinking about something else: *You could tell by the expression on her face that she was miles away, thinking about home.*

• **(by) miles** INFORMAL used to say something is much greater or better than something else: *British restaurant food is* ***better*** *by miles/miles* ***better*** *than it used to be 20 years ago.*

• **miles from anywhere/nowhere** a long distance from other houses or a town: *They live miles from nowhere, in the middle of the countryside.*

• **miles too big/small/expensive, etc.** INFORMAL very much bigger/smaller/more expensive, etc. than you would like: *This tea is miles too sweet!*

mileage /ˈmaɪ.lɪdʒ/ *noun* [U] **1** the distance that a vehicle has travelled or the distance that it can travel using a particular amount of fuel: *'What's the mileage on your car?' 'Oh, about 40 000'.* ○ *Smaller cars have better mileage and so cost less to run.* **2** (ALSO **mileage allowance**) the amount of money that you are paid or that you must pay for each mile you travel: *The car costs £30 a day to rent, but you* ***get*** *unlimited mileage* (= no charge for the miles travelled). **3** INFORMAL the advantage that you can obtain from a situation: *There's no mileage* ***in*** *complaining to the Director – she'll just ignore you.* ○ *political mileage*

mileometer UK, UK ALSO **milometer** /maɪˈlɒm.ɪ.təʳ/ (US) /-ˈlɑː.mɪ.t̬ɚ/ *noun* [C] (US **odometer**) a device in a vehicle that measures and shows the distance it travels

milestone /ˈmaɪl.stəʊn/ (US) /-stoʊn/ *noun* [C] (UK ALSO **milepost**) **1** a stone or post at the side of the road on which is marked the distance to various places, especially to the nearest large town **2** an important event in the development or history of something or in someone's life: *He felt that moving out from his parents' home was a real milestone in his life.*

milieu /mɪˈljɜː/ (US) /miːlˈjɜː/ *noun* [C] *plural* **milieus** or **milieux** FORMAL the people, physical and social conditions and events which provide a background in which someone acts or lives: *It is a study of the social and cultural* *milieu in which Michelangelo lived and worked.*

militant /ˈmɪl.ɪ.tᵊnt/ *adj* active, determined and often willing to use force: *militant union extremists* ○ *The group has taken a militant position on the abortion issue and is refusing to compromise.* **militant** /ˈmɪl.ɪ.tᵊnt/ *noun* [C] *Militants within the party are demanding radical reforms.* **militantly** /ˈmɪl.ɪ.tᵊnt.li/ *adv* **militancy** /ˈmɪl.ɪ.tᵊnt.si/ *noun* [U] *The group has always been characterised by an uncompromising militancy.*

military /ˈmɪl.ɪ.tri/ [US] /-ter.i/ *adj* **1** relating to or belonging to the armed forces: *foreign military intervention* ○ *military targets/forces* ○ *military uniform* **2** describes a characteristic that is typical of the armed forces: *military precision* **militarily** /ˌmɪl.ɪˈter.ɪ.li/ *adv*

the military *group noun* [S] the armed forces: *The military has opposed any cuts in defence spending.*

militarism /ˈmɪl.ɪ.tᵊr.ɪ.zᵊm/ [US] /-t̬ɚ-/ *noun* [U] *DISAPPROVING* the belief that it is necessary to have strong armed forces and that they should be used in order to win political or economic advantages

militarist /ˈmɪl.ɪ.tᵊr.ɪst/ [US] /-t̬ə.rɪst/ *noun* [C] *DISAPPROVING* a person who wants more powerful armed forces in their country **militaristic** /ˌmɪl.ɪ.tᵊrˈɪs.tɪk/ [US] /-t̬əˈrɪs-/ *adj*: *a militaristic policy/government*

militarized, *UK USUALLY* **-ised** /ˈmɪl.ɪ.tᵊr.aɪzd/ [US] /-t̬ə.raɪzd/ *adj* describes an area, country or organization that has a large strong army and other armed forces and many weapons: *North Korea is said to be the world's most heavily militarized country, with over 1 million men in the armed forces.*

ˌmilitary aˈcademy *noun* [C] **1** a place where soldiers are trained to become officers **2** a private school in the US that expects obedience to rules, has uniforms and is generally run like the armed forces

ˌmilitary ˈband *noun* [C] a group of musicians within the armed forces who play marching and military music

ˌmilitary ˈhonours *plural noun* ceremonies performed by soldiers to honour a king, queen or other important person, or to honour someone important who has died: *The Colonel was buried with **full** military honours.*

the ˌMilitary Poˈlice *plural noun* the police force within the armed forces, responsible for dealing with members of the armed forces who break the law

ˌmilitary poˈliceman *noun* [C] (*ABBREVIATION* **MP**)

ˌmilitary ˈservice *noun* [U] army training that young people must do in some countries: *He has to **do** his military service before going to university.*

militate /ˈmɪl.ɪ.teɪt/ *verb*

▲ **militate against *sth*** *phrasal verb FORMAL* to make something less likely to happen or succeed: *The complexity and costliness of the judicial system militate against justice for the individual.*

militia /mɪˈlɪʃ.ə/ *group noun* [C] a military force which only operates for some of the time and whose members often have other jobs: *A UN force was sent in to stop fighting between three rival militias.* ○ *The government **called out** the militia to help cope with the rioting.*

militiaman /mɪˈlɪʃ.ə.mən/ /-mæn/ *noun* [C] a member of a militia

milk /mɪlk/ *noun* [U] **1** the white liquid produced by cows, goats, and sheep and used by humans as a drink or for making butter, cheese, etc: *a glass/carton of milk* ○ *cow's/goat's milk* ○ ***skimmed/pasteurized** milk* ○ *a milk bottle* **2** the white liquid produced by women and other female mammals as food for their young: ***Breast/Mother's** milk is the best nourishment for a baby.* **3** the white liquid obtained from some plants and trees: *coconut milk*

• **the milk of human kindness** good, kind qualities: *She's **full of** the milk of human kindness.*

milk /mɪlk/ *verb* **1** [I or T] to obtain milk from an animal: *Milking a cow by hand is a skilled process.* ○ *Some goats seem to milk* (= produce milk) *better than others.* **2** [T] *DISAPPROVING* to obtain as much money or information out of someone or something as possible, often in a selfish or dishonest way: [+ obj + adj] *The newspapers milked the story **dry**.* ○ *The directors milked the company **of** several million pounds.*

milky /ˈmɪl.ki/ *adj* **1** describes a liquid containing milk or made with a lot of milk: *a cup of milky coffee* ○ *Having a milky **drink** before bed helps me sleep.* **2** white, pale or cloudy: *milky skin* ○ *a milky white/blue*

ˈmilk ˌbar *noun* [C] *MAINLY AUS* a shop which sells milk products, bread and sweets

ˌmilk ˈchocolate *noun* [C or U] sweet, light brown chocolate made with milk: *biscuits coated with thick milk chocolate*

ˈmilk ˌfloat *noun* [C] *UK* a vehicle, usually electric-powered, used to deliver milk to people's houses in the UK

ˈmilking maˌchine *noun* [C] a machine used to take milk from cows

milkman /ˈmɪlk.mən/ *noun* [C] someone who delivers milk to your home in the early morning: *Britain is one of the few countries where milk is delivered daily to the doorstep by milkmen.*

ˌmilk of magˈnesia *noun* [U] a white liquid medicine containing MAGNESIUM, taken to cure slight stomach problems

the ˈmilk ˌround *noun* [S] *UK INFORMAL* the series of visits made at a particular time of the year by large companies to colleges to discuss giving jobs to students after they have finished their education

ˈmilk ˌrun *noun* [C usually sing] a journey that you make often, especially one including several stops

milkshake /ˈmɪlk.ʃeɪk/ *noun* [C or U] a drink made of milk and usually ice cream and flavouring such as fruit or chocolate, mixed quickly together until it is full of bubbles: *a chocolate milkshake*

ˈmilk ˌtooth *noun* [C] a **baby tooth**

the ˌMilky ˈWay *noun* [S] the pale strip across the sky which you can see at night, and which is part of the GALAXY (= star system) that includes the Earth

mill /mɪl/ *noun* [C] **1** a building where grain is crushed into flour **2** a small machine for crushing things into powder: *a pepper/coffee mill* **3** a factory where a particular substance is produced: *a cotton/paper/steel mill*

• **put *sb* through the mill** *INFORMAL* to cause someone to have a difficult and unpleasant experience, especially by asking them a lot of difficult questions: *I had the interview this morning – they really put me through the mill.*

mill /mɪl/ *verb* [T] **1** to crush grain into flour or another substance into powder: *The grain is still milled locally.* **2** *SPECIALIZED* to shape metal by removing parts from it using a special machine

miller /ˈmɪl.əʳ/ [US] /-ɚ/ *noun* [C] a person, especially in the past, who owned or was in charge of a mill

▲ **mill around** *phrasal verb* (*UK ALSO* **mill about**) If a group of people mill around, they move about with no particular purpose or in no fixed direction, sometimes while waiting for someone: *In the village square, people were milling about in the sunshine.*

millennium (*plural* **millennia** or **millenniums**) /mɪˈlen.i.əm/ *noun* [C] a period of 1000 years, or the time when a period of 1000 years ends: *The corpse had lain preserved in the soil for almost two millennia.* ○ *How did you celebrate the Millennium?* ➲Compare **century**. **millennial** /mɪˈlen.i.ᵊl/ *adj*

the Milˈlennium ˌBug *noun* [U] a problem with older computers whose clocks were unable to recognise dates after 31 December 1999, which was expected to result in computer programs and systems failing to work properly after 01 January 2000

millepede /ˈmɪl.ɪ.piːd/ *noun* [C] a **millipede**

millet /ˈmɪl.ɪt/ *noun* [U] a grass-like plant, or the small edible seeds from this plant

milli- /mɪl.ɪ-/ *prefix* 0.001 of the stated unit: *milliamp* ○ *millijoule*

millibar /ˈmɪl.ɪ.bɑːʳ/ [US] /-bɑːr/ *noun* [C] (*WRITTEN ABBREVIATION* **mb**) a unit of air pressure: *an anticyclone of 1030 millibars*

milligram, *UK ALSO* **milligramme** /ˈmɪl.ɪ.græm/ *noun* [C] (*WRITTEN ABBREVIATION* **mg**) a unit of mass which is equal to 0.001 grams

M

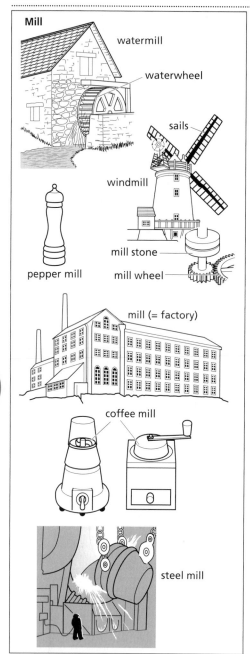

Mill

watermill

waterwheel

sails

windmill

mill stone

pepper mill

mill wheel

mill (= factory)

coffee mill

steel mill

millilitre *UK, US* **milliliter** /ˈmɪl.ɪˌliː.tər/ ⑩ /-t̬ər/ *noun* [C] (*WRITTEN ABBREVIATION* **ml**) a unit of volume which is equal to 0.001 litres

millimetre *UK, US* **millimeter** /ˈmɪl.ɪˌmiː.tər/ ⑩ /-t̬ər/ *noun* [C] (*WRITTEN ABBREVIATION* **mm**) a unit of length which is equal to 0.001 metres

milliner /ˈmɪl.ɪ.nər/ ⑩ /-nɚ/ *noun* [C] a person who makes or sells women's hats

millinery /ˈmɪl.ɪ.nᵊr.i/ ⑩ /-ner-/ *noun* [U] the hats and other goods that are sold by a milliner

million /ˈmɪl.jən/ *determiner, noun, pronoun plural* **million** or **millions 1** [C] (the number) 1 000 000: *She got eight million dollars for appearing in that film.* **2** [C] a lot

(of): *I've heard that joke a million times.*
● **thanks a million** *INFORMAL* thank you very much: *"I've done what you asked." "Thanks a million!"*
● **look/feel (like) a million dollars** (*US* **look/feel (like) a million bucks**) *INFORMAL* to look or feel extremely good, often because you are experiencing something luxurious: *"You look a million dollars in that dress, honey!"*
● **be one in a million** *APPROVING* to be a very special person: *Thanks again – you're one in a million!*
● **one-in-a-million** describes a chance that is extremely unlikely: *Don't worry – the chances of anything going wrong are one-in-a-million.*

millionth /ˈmɪl.jəntθ/ *noun* [C] one of a million equal parts of something: *Miraculously, the whole process only takes a millionth of a second.*

millionth /ˈmɪl.jəntθ/ *determiner, pronoun, adv, adj, noun*: *Coventry City football club counted their millionth supporter through the gates last Saturday.* ○ *INFORMAL They're showing 'High Noon' on TV, for the millionth time* (= having already shown it a lot of times).

COMMON LEARNER ERROR

million or **millions**?

If you are using **million** to describe a particular number, use the singular form.

The film cost $10 million to make.
~~The film cost $10 millions to make.~~

Only use **million** in the plural form to refer to a large number that is not exact.

You must know him – he's been on TV millions of times.

millionaire /ˌmɪl.jəˈneər/ ⑩ /-ˈner/ *noun* [C] (*FEMALE ALSO* **millionairess**) a person whose wealth is at least 1 000 000 in their country's money: *You want me to buy you a new car – do you think I'm a millionaire or something?*

millipede, **millepede** /ˈmɪl.ɪ.piːd/ *noun* [C] a small creature with a long cylindrical body consisting of many parts, each part having two pairs of legs

millisecond /ˈmɪl.ɪˌsek.ənd/ *noun* [C] (*WRITTEN ABBREVIATION* **ms, msec**) a unit of time which is equal to 0.001 seconds

millpond /ˈmɪl.pɒnd/ ⑩ /-pɑːnd/ *noun* [C] a pool of water which provides the power to make the wheel of a MILL turn: *The sea that day was like a millpond* (= very calm and not moving).

millstone /ˈmɪl.stəʊn/ ⑩ /-stoʊn/ *noun* [C] one of a pair of large circular flat stones used, especially in the past, to crush grain to make flour
● **be (like) a millstone around/round your neck** to be a responsibility that is difficult to bear and causes you trouble: *The mortgage on his house had become a millstone around his neck.*

mime /maɪm/ *noun* **1** [U] when you use movements of your hands and body, and expressions on your face, without speech, to communicate emotions and actions or to tell a story: *The first scene was performed in mime.* **2** [C] a short play without speech

mime /maɪm/ *verb* [I or T] **1** to act or tell a story in mime: *The whole of the banquet scene is mimed.* **2** to pretend to sing, play or say something without making any sound: *Most of the bands that appear on the show just mime **to** a recording of their songs.* ○ *He was miming something at me across the pub.*

'mime ,artist *noun* [C] a person who performs mime in a theatre or film

mimetic /mɪˈmet.ɪk/ ⑩ /-ˈmet̬-/ *adj SPECIALIZED* using mime: *The actors have to rely on their mimetic skills.*
mimetically /mɪˈmet.ɪ.kli/ ⑩ /-ˈmet̬-/ *adv*

mimic /ˈmɪm.ɪk/ *verb* [T] **mimicking, mimicked, mimicked** to copy the way in which a particular person usually speaks and moves, usually in order to amuse people: *She was mimicking the various people in our office.*

mimic /ˈmɪm.ɪk/ *noun* [C] a person who can copy the sounds or movements of other people: *She's a brilliant mimic.* **mimicry** /ˈmɪm.ɪ.kri/ *noun* [U]

mimosa /mɪˈməʊ.sə/ ⑩ /-ˈmoʊ-/ *noun* [C] *US FOR* **buck's fizz**

min. SMALLEST *noun* [C usually sing] *WRITTEN ABBREVIATION FOR* **minimum**, used in notices, advertisements, etc: *Holiday cottage: min. stay 3 days.*

min. TIME *noun* [C] *WRITTEN ABBREVIATION FOR* **minute** TIME: *Cooking time required: 30-35 mins.*

minaret /ˌmɪn.əˈret/ *noun* [C] a tall thin tower on or near a MOSQUE (= Muslim holy building) from which Muslims are called to pray

mince MEAT *UK* /mɪnts/ *noun* [U] (*US* **ground beef**) meat, usually beef, which has been cut up into very small pieces

mince /mɪnts/ *verb* [T] to cut meat, or other food, into very small pieces, sometimes using a special machine: *Mince two pounds of chicken finely.*

• **not mince (your) words** to say what you mean clearly and directly, even if you upset people by doing this: *The report does not mince words, describing the situation as 'ludicrous'.*

minced /mɪntst/ *adj* (*US USUALLY* **ground**) (especially of meat) having been cut up into very small pieces: *minced beef/lamb/onions*

mincer *UK* /ˈmɪn.səʳ/ *US* /-sɚ/ *noun* [C] (*US USUALLY* **meat grinder**) a machine for cutting food, especially meat, into small pieces

mince WALK /mɪnts/ *verb* [I] to walk in an artificial way, with small delicate steps: *He minced across the room in a pair of tight pink trousers.* **mincing** /ˈmɪnt.sɪŋ/ *adj*: *She took short mincing steps.*

mincemeat /ˈmɪnts.miːt/ *noun* [U] a sweet, spicy mixture of small pieces of apple, dried fruit and nuts which is often eaten at Christmas in MINCE PIES

• **make mincemeat of sb** *INFORMAL* to defeat someone very easily in an argument, competition or fight: *A decent lawyer would have made mincemeat of them in court.*

mince 'pie *noun* [C] a covered pastry case filled with MINCEMEAT

mind THOUGHTS /maɪnd/ *noun* [C] **1** the part of a person that enables a person to think, feel emotions and be aware of things: *Her mind was full of what had happened the night before, and she just wasn't concentrating.* ○ *Of course I'm telling the truth – you've got such a suspicious mind!* ○ *I just said the first thing that came into my mind.* ○ *I'm not quite clear in my mind about what I'm doing.* **2** a very clever person: *She was one of the most brilliant minds of last century.*

• **all in the/your mind** describes a problem that does not exist and is only imagined: *His doctor tried to convince him that he wasn't really ill and that it was all in the mind.*

• **a load/weight off your mind** when a problem which has been worrying you stops or is dealt with: *I'm so relieved that I don't have to do the after-dinner speech – it's such a weight off my mind!*

• **bear/keep sth in mind** to remember a piece of information when you are making a decision or thinking about a matter: *Bearing in mind how young she is, I thought she did really well.* ○ *Of course, repair work is expensive and you have to keep that in mind.*

• **bring/call sth to mind** to remember something: *I can see his face, but I just can't bring his name to mind.*

• **get your mind round something** to succeed in understanding something difficult or strange: *I find it hard to get my mind round such complex issues.*

• **get sth out of your mind** to make yourself stop thinking about something: *I can't get that dreadful moment/image out of my mind.*

• **go over sth in your mind** (*ALSO* **turn sth over in your mind**) to think repeatedly about an event that has happened: *She would go over the accident again and again in her mind, wishing that she could somehow have prevented it.*

• **have a mind of its own** *MAINLY HUMOROUS* A machine or other object can be said to have a mind of its own if it seems to be controlling the way it behaves or moves, independently of the person using it: *This shopping trolley has a mind of its own.*

• **have half a mind/a good mind to do sth** to think that you might do something, often because something has annoyed you: *I've a good mind to go without him if he's going to be such a bore!*

• **have sth on your mind** to be worrying about something: *Paul's got a lot on his mind at the moment.*

• **have something in mind** to have a plan or intention: *Did you have anything in mind for Helen's present?*

• **in your mind's eye** in your imagination or memory: *In my mind's eye, she remains a little girl of six although she's actually a grown woman.*

• **make up your mind** (*ALSO* **make your mind up**) to decide: *I haven't made up my mind where to go yet.*

• **your mind is on sth** When your mind is on something, you think about it or give attention to it: *I couldn't concentrate on my work – my mind was on other things.* ○ *My mind wasn't on what he was saying, so I'm afraid I missed half of it.*

• **your mind is a blank/goes blank** When your mind is a blank/goes blank, you cannot remember a particular thing, or you cannot remember anything: *I tried to remember her name, but my mind went a complete blank.*

• **be of sound/unsound mind** *LEGAL* to not be mentally ill/ to be mentally ill

• **be of the same mind** (*ALSO* **be of one mind**) to have the same opinion: *We're of the same mind on most political issues.*

• **be bored/drunk, etc. out of your mind** *INFORMAL* to be extremely bored/drunk, etc.

• **out of your mind 1** unable to behave or deal with things normally because something has made you very worried, unhappy or angry: *She was out of her mind with grief.* ○ *I'd go out of my mind if I had to do her job all day!* **2** *INFORMAL* extremely stupid or mentally ill: *You must be out of your mind paying £200 for one night in a hotel!*

• **mind over matter** the power of the mind to control and influence the body and the physical world generally: *He announced what he called 'the ultimate test of mind over matter' – a woman walking over hot coals.*

• **put you in mind of sth** to cause you to remember something: *The mention of skiing holidays put me in mind of a travelogue that I saw last week.*

• **put sth out of your mind** to force yourself not to think about something: *It's over, put it out of your mind.*

• **set/put your mind to sth** to decide you are going to do something and to put a lot of effort into doing it: *If you'd just put your mind to it, I'm sure you could do it.*

• **set/put sb's mind at rest/ease** to stop someone from worrying about something: *Chris phoned to say they'd arrived safely, so that really put my mind at rest.*

• **sb's state/frame of mind** the way someone feels about their life or situation at the moment: *He's in a much more positive state/frame of mind these days.*

• **take sb's mind off sth** to stop you from worrying or thinking about a problem or pain, often by forcing you to think about other things: *The good thing about running is that it takes my mind off any problems I've got.*

• **to my mind** in my opinion: *He's got pink walls and a green carpet, which to my mind looks all wrong.*

-minded /-maɪn.dɪd/ *suffix* having a particular character, interest or way of thinking about things: *She's very strong/independent-minded (= She has a very strong/independent character).* ○ *I don't imagine that he's very politically-minded (= interested in politics).*

mind BE CAREFUL /maɪnd/ *verb* [T] *MAINLY UK* **1** to be careful of, or give attention to something: *Mind that box – the bottom isn't very strong.* ○ *Mind (that) you don't bang your head on the shelf when you stand up.* ○ *Mind (= Make certain that) you take enough money with you.* ○ *OLD-FASHIONED Mind your language (= Don't use swear words), young lady!* **2 Mind (out)!** used to tell someone to move or to be careful, or to warn them of danger: *Mind out! We're coming through with the stretcher.* ○ *'Hey, mind!' he said when she trod on his foot.* ○ *Mind out for falling rocks on this part of the trail.*

• **mind how you go** *UK INFORMAL* said when you say goodbye to someone, meaning 'take care'

• **mind (you)** used when you want to make what you have just said sound less strong: *He's very untidy about the house; mind you, I'm not much better.* ○ *I know I'm lazy – I did go swimming yesterday, mind.*

M

• **don't mind me** said to tell someone who is in the same room as you not to pay any attention to you, because you do not want to interrupt what they are doing: *Don't mind me – I'm just sorting out some files here.*

• **mind** *your* **p's and q's** to make an effort to be especially polite in a particular situation: *I have to mind my p's and q's when I'm with my grandmother.*

mindful /'maɪnd.fəl/ *adj FORMAL* careful not to forget about something: *Mindful of the poor road conditions, she reduced her speed to 30 mph.* ○ *Politicians are increasingly mindful* **that** *young voters are turning away from traditional parties.*

mind TAKE CARE OF /maɪnd/ *verb* [T] to take care of someone or something: *She asked me if I'd mind the children for an hour while she went shopping.* ○ *Could you mind my bag for a moment while I go to the toilet?*

• **mind** *your* **own business** (*ABBREVIATION* **MYOB**) *INFORMAL MAINLY HUMOROUS* used to tell someone in a rude way that you do not want them to ask about something private: *"Where have you been?" "Mind your own business!"*

mind OPPOSE /maɪnd/ *verb* [I or T] (used in questions and negatives) to be annoyed or worried by something: *Do you think he'd mind if I borrowed his book?* ○ [+ *v-ing*] *I don't mind having a dog in the house so long as it's clean.* ○ *INFORMAL I wouldn't mind* (= I would like) *something to eat, actually.* ○ *Would you mind turning* (= Please would you turn) *your radio down a little please?* ○ *Do you mind if* (= May) *I put the television on?* ○ [+ *obj* + *v-ing*] *Do you mind me smoking?* ○ [+ *question word*] *I don't mind what you wear so long as it's not that awful pink shirt.* ○ *I'd prefer to stay in tonight, if you don't mind.* ○ *MAINLY UK "Would you like tea or coffee?" "I don't mind – either."*

• **Do you mind?** said to someone when you feel annoyed with them for what they have just done or said: *Do you mind? That's my seat you're sitting on!*

• **I don't mind if I do** said to politely accept an offer of food or drink: *"There's plenty more cake if you'd like another piece." "I don't mind if I do."*

• **if you don't mind me saying** used as a polite way to begin a criticism: *If you don't mind me saying (so), I think the curry could be a little hotter next time.*

mind-altering /'maɪnd.ɒl.tə.rɪŋ/ ⓤ /-ˌɑːl.t̬ɚ-/ *adj* describes a drug that has a strong influence on a person's mental state, causing feelings of extreme happiness and making people consider things in an unusual way

mind-blowing /'maɪnd.bləʊ.ɪŋ/ ⓤ /-ˌbloʊ-/ *adj SLANG* extremely impressive or surprising: *The special effects in this film are pretty mind-blowing.*

mind-boggling /'maɪnd.bɒɡ.l̩.ɪŋ/ ⓤ /-ˌbɑː.ɡl̩.ɪŋ/ *adj INFORMAL* extremely surprising and difficult to understand or imagine: *She was paid the mind-boggling sum of ten million pounds for that film.* **mindlessly** /'maɪnd.lə.sli/ *adv*: *Some children started mindlessly hurling stones at passing vehicles.* **mindlessness** /'maɪnd.lə.snəs/ *noun* [U]

minder /'maɪn.dəʳ/ ⓤ /-dɚ/ *noun* [C] someone who protects another person, often a famous person, from danger and unwanted public attention: *The President arrived surrounded by his minders.*

mindless /'maɪnd.ləs/ *adj DISAPPROVING* **1** stupid and meaningless: *The film is full of mindless* **violence**. ○ *pop songs with mindless lyrics* **2** not needing much mental effort: *I'm afraid it's fairly mindless work – opening mail and keying data into a computer.*

mind-numbing /'maɪnd.nʌm.ɪŋ/ *adj* extremely boring: *a mind-numbing task* **mind-numbingly** /'maɪnd.nʌm.ɪŋ.li/ *adv*: *mind-numbingly boring*

'mind ˌreader *noun* [C] *MAINLY HUMOROUS* a person who knows another person's thoughts without being told them: *Why didn't you tell me you weren't happy with the situation? – I'm not a mind reader, you know!*

mindset /'maɪnd.set/ *noun* [U] a person's way of thinking and their opinions: *to have a different/the same mindset* ○ *It's extraordinary how hard it is to change the mindset of the public and the press.*

mine BELONGING TO ME /maɪn/ *pronoun* the one(s) belonging to or connected with me: *"Whose bag is this?" "It's*

mine." ○ *Your son is the same age as mine.* ○ *She's an old friend of mine.*

mine HOLE /maɪn/ *noun* [C] a hole or system of holes in the ground made for the removal of substances such as coal, metal, and salt by digging: *a coal/salt/gold mine* ○ *a mine shaft* ○ *My grandfather used to work in/(UK) down the mines.*

• **a mine of information** someone who has a lot of knowledge and is willing to give this knowledge to other people

mine /maɪn/ *verb* [I or T] to dig coal or another substance out of the ground: *They're mining for salt.* ○ *They mine a lot of copper around these parts.*

miner /'maɪ.nəʳ/ ⓤ /-nɚ/ *noun* [C] a person who works in a mine: *a coal miner*

mining /'maɪ.nɪŋ/ *noun* [U] the industry or activity of removing substances such as coal or metal from the ground by digging: *coal/salt mining*

mine BOMB /maɪn/ *noun* [C] a type of bomb put below the earth or in the sea which explodes when vehicles, ships or people go over it: *He was killed when his tank ran over a mine.* ○ *The US forces were clearing the surrounding area of mines.* ➔See also **landmine**.

mine /maɪn/ *verb* [T often passive] to place or hide mines in an area of land or sea: *The desert was heavily mined.*

'mine deˌtector *noun* [C] a device which is used to discover whether there are MINES (= bombs) in a particular area

minefield BOMBS /'maɪn.fiːld/ *noun* [C] an area of land or water which contains MINES (= bombs)

minefield PROBLEMS /'maɪn.fiːld/ *noun* [C] a situation or subject which is very complicated and full of hidden problems and dangers: *a legal minefield* ○ *a minefield of ethical problems*

mineral /'mɪn.ªr.ªl/ *noun* [C] **1** a valuable or useful chemical substance which is formed naturally in the ground **2** a chemical that your body needs to stay healthy: *A healthy diet should supply all necessary vitamins and minerals.* ○ *a mineral supplement*

mineral /'mɪn.ªr.ªl/ *adj* being or consisting of a mineral or minerals: *a mineral deposit* (= substance or layer that is left) ○ *The speaker emphasized that much of South Africa's importance lay in its mineral wealth.*

mineralogy /ˌmɪn.ə'ræl.ə.dʒi/ *noun* [U] the scientific study of minerals

mineralogist /ˌmɪn.ə'ræl.ə.dʒɪst/ *noun* [C] someone who studies minerals

'mineral ˌwater *noun* [U] (*US ALSO* **bottled water**) natural water from underground, containing dissolved minerals which are believed to be good for your health: *still/carbonated mineral water*

minestrone (soup) /ˌmɪn.ɪˌstrəʊ.ni'suːp/ ⓤ /-ˌstroʊ-/ *noun* [C or U] a type of Italian soup containing a mixture of vegetables and pasta

minesweeper /'maɪnˌswiː.pəʳ/ ⓤ /-pɚ/ *noun* [C] a ship that is used to discover if MINES (= bombs) are present and to remove them from the sea

minging SMELL /'mɪŋ.ɪŋ/ *adj UK SLANG* smelling bad: *You're minging, mate! Go and take a shower.*

minging UGLY /'mɪŋ.ɪŋ/ *adj UK SLANG* ugly: *Man, she was minging!*

mingle MIX /'mɪŋ.ɡl̩/ *verb* [I or T] to mix or combine, or be mixed or combined: *The excitement of starting a new job is always mingled with a certain apprehension.* ○ *The two flavours mingle well.*

mingle BE WITH /'mɪŋ.ɡl̩/ *verb* [I] to move around and talk to other people at a social event: *You've been talking to Roger all evening – you really ought to be mingling with the other guests.*

mingy /'mɪn.dʒi/ *adj INFORMAL* **1** not generous and unwilling to give money: *I only gave five dollars towards his present – do you think that was a bit mingy?* **2** describes an amount that is smaller than you would like: *I hate that restaurant – they give you really mingy portions.*

mini- SMALL /mɪn.i-/ *prefix* smaller or less important than a normal example of the same thing: *There's a mini-library in each classroom, as well as the central library.* ○ *We took the kids to play mini-golf.*

mini SKIRT /'mɪn.i/ *noun* [C] a **miniskirt**

Mini CAR /'mɪn.i/ *noun* [C] *TRADEMARK* a type of small British car especially popular in the 1960s

miniature /'mɪn.ɪ.tʃəʳ/ ⓤ /-tʃɚ/ *adj* [before n] describes something which is a very small copy of an object: *I bought some miniature furniture for my niece's dolls' house.*

• **in miniature** smaller than usual: *He's made a model of our village, with all the buildings and roads in miniature.*

miniature /'mɪn.ɪ.tʃəʳ/ ⓤ /-tʃɚ/ *noun* [C] **1** a very small painting, usually of a person **2** a very small bottle of alcoholic drink

miniaturization, *UK USUALLY* -**isation** /ˌmɪn.ɪ.tʃəʳr.aɪ-'zeɪ.ʃən/ ⓤ /-tʃɚ-/ *noun* [U] the process of making something very small using modern technology: *The silicon chip is a classic example of the benefits of miniaturization.* **miniaturized**, *UK USUALLY* -**ised** /'mɪn.ɪ.tʃəʳr.aɪzd/ ⓤ /-tʃɚ-/ *adj: a miniaturized electronic circuit*

minibus /'mɪn.ɪ.bʌs/ *noun* [C] a small bus in which there are seats for about ten people

minicab /'mɪn.ɪ.kæb/ *noun* [C] *UK* a taxi which can only be called by telephone and which does not stop to collect passengers in the street

minicam /'mɪn.ɪ.kæm/ *noun* [C] *MAINLY US* a type of small VIDEO CAMERA often used by television news reporters

minicomputer /'mɪn.ɪ.kəmˌpjuː.təʳ/ ⓤ /-t̬ɚ/ *noun* [C] a computer of medium power which is often used by businesses

MiniDisc /'mɪn.ɪ.dɪsk/ *noun* [C] *TRADEMARK* a very small plastic disc on which high-quality sound, especially music, is recorded

minim *UK* /'mɪn.ɪm/ *noun* [C] (*US USUALLY* **half note**) *SPECIALIZED* a musical note with a time value equal to two CROCHETS or half a SEMIBREVE

minimalist SIMPLE /'mɪn.ɪ.mə.lɪst/ *adj* belonging or relating to a style in art, design and theatre that uses the smallest range of materials and colours possible, and only very simple shapes or forms: *minimalist painting* ○ *The set for the ballet is minimalist – three white walls and a chair.* **minimalist** /'mɪn.ɪ.mə.lɪst/ *noun* [C] an artist or DESIGNER who uses a minimalist style **minimalism** /'mɪn.ɪ.mə.lɪ-zᵊm/ *noun* [U]

minimalist NOT ACTING /'mɪn.ɪ.mə.lɪst/ *adj* taking or showing as little action and involvement in a situation as possible: *the party's minimalist* **approach** *to economic policy*

minimum (*plural* **minimums** or *SPECIALIZED* **minima**) /'mɪn.ɪ.məm/ *noun* [C usually sing] (*WRITTEN ABBREVIATION* **min**) the smallest amount or number allowed or possible: *Wage increases are being* **kept to a** *minimum because of the recession.* ○ *She hoped that her fiftieth birthday would pass with the minimum* **of** *fuss.* ○ *We need a minimum of ten people to play this game.* ✻ NOTE: The opposite is **maximum**. **minimum** /'mɪn.ɪ.məm/ *adj* (*WRITTEN ABBREVIATION* **min**) *The preparatory certificate is the minimum qualification required to teach English in most language schools.* ○ *Eighteen is the minimum* **age** *for entering most nightclubs.* **minimum** /'mɪn.ɪ.məm/ *adv: He reckons that you should do three exercise classes a week minimum to get any of the benefits.*

minimal /'mɪn.ɪ.məl/ *adj* very small in amount: *There were no injuries and damage to the building was minimal.* **minimally** /'mɪn.ɪ.mə.li/ *adv: minimally affected/involved/successful*

minimize, *UK USUALLY* -**ise** /'mɪn.ɪ.maɪz/ *verb* [T] **1** to reduce something to the least possible level or amount: *We must minimize the risk of infection.* ○ *Environmentalists are doing everything within their power to minimize the impact of the oil spill.* ✻ NOTE: The opposite is **maximize**. **2** to make something seem less important or smaller than it really is: *She accused the government of minimizing the suffering of thousands of people.* ○ *It's important to focus on your strengths and to minimize your weaknesses.* **minimization** /ˌmɪn.ɪ.maɪˈzeɪ.ʃən/ *noun* [U]

the ˌ**minimum** ˈ**wage** *noun* [S] the smallest amount of money that an employer is legally allowed to pay someone who works for them

mining /'maɪ.nɪŋ/ *noun* [U] ➔See at **mine** HOLE.

minion /'mɪn.jən/ *noun* [C] *USUALLY DISAPPROVING* a person who only exists in order to do what another person orders them to do: *He sent one of his minions to do something about it.*

minipill /'mɪn.ɪ.pɪl/ *noun* [C] a type of pill containing only PROGESTERONE which women can take every day to prevent them from becoming pregnant when they have sex

miniscule /'mɪn.ɪ.skjuːl/ *adj* a common spelling of MINUSCULE that is not correct

mini-series /'mɪn.ɪ.sɪə.riːz/ ⓤ /-sɪr.iːz/ *plural noun* a programme or play divided into several different parts which is broadcast on television over a short period of time

miniskirt /'mɪn.ɪˌskɜːt/ ⓤ /-skɝːt/ *noun* [C] (*ALSO* **mini**) a very short skirt ➔See picture **Clothes** on page Centre 6

minister POLITICIAN /'mɪn.ɪ.stəʳ/ ⓤ /-stɚ/ *noun* [C] a member of the government in Britain and many other countries who is in charge of a particular department or has an important position in it: *the foreign/health minister* ○ *the Minister of/for Education* **ministerial** /ˌmɪn.ɪ-'stɪə.ri.əl/ ⓤ /-'stɪr.i-/ *adj: ministerial responsibilities* ○ *a high-level ministerial meeting*

ministry /'mɪn.ɪ.stri/ *noun* [C] a department of the government led by a minister: *the Ministry of Defence/ Agriculture*

minister COUNTRY'S REPRESENTATIVE /'mɪn.ɪ.stəʳ/ ⓤ /-stɚ/ *noun* [C] *SPECIALIZED* a person below the rank of AMBASSADOR whose job is to represent his or her country in a foreign country: *the Belgian minister in Madrid* **ministerial** /ˌmɪn.ɪˈstɪə.ri.əl/ ⓤ /-'stɪr.i-/ *adj: He reached ministerial level in the Diplomatic Service.*

minister PRIEST /'mɪn.ɪ.stəʳ/ ⓤ /-stɚ/ *noun* [C] a priest in particular parts of the Christian church: *a minister at the local Baptist church*

ministry /'mɪn.ɪ.stri/ *noun* [U] **1** work as a minister: *He practised a preaching and teaching ministry there for over 40 years.* **2** **the ministry** the job of being a priest, in some parts of the Christian Church: *In 1985 he decided to* **go into/leave** *the ministry.*

minister /'mɪn.ɪ.stəʳ/ ⓤ /-stɚ/ *verb*

▲ **minister to** *sb phrasal verb* to give help to or care for people, for example people who are ill: *FORMAL The priest ministers to his flock* (= the people who go to his church). ○ *HUMOROUS I spent most of the morning ministering to my sick husband.*

ministering angel /ˌmɪn.ɪ.stə.rɪŋˈeɪn.dʒəl/ ⓤ /-stɚ.ɪŋ-/ *noun* [C] *UK HUMOROUS* a very kind woman who takes care of people who are ill

ministrations /ˌmɪn.ɪˈstreɪ.ʃənz/ *plural noun* acts of helping or caring for people or providing for the needs of people: *FORMAL In her last difficult years, she relied on* **the** *careful* **ministrations** *of her beloved husband.* ○ *HUMOROUS That plant seems to be dying in spite of all my ministrations.*

mini-system /'mɪn.ɪ.ˌsɪs.təm/ *noun* [C] a very small set of electronic equipment for playing recorded sound, usually including a CD player and a TAPE DECK

mink /mɪŋk/ *noun* [C or U] a small animal with valuable fur which is used to make expensive coats, or the fur from this animal: *a mink coat*

minnow /'mɪn.əʊ/ ⓤ /-oʊ/ *noun* [C] **1** a very small fish found in lakes and rivers **2** *LITERARY* an unimportant organization or person with little influence or power

minor UNIMPORTANT /'maɪ.nəʳ/ ⓤ /-nɚ/ *adj* having little importance, influence or effect, especially when compared with other things of the same type: *a minor operation* ○ *It's only a minor problem.* ○ *There's been an increase in minor offences, such as traffic violations and petty theft.* ○ *She suffered only minor* **injuries**. ○ *It requires a few minor adjustments.* ○ *a minor poet of the 16th-century* ➔Compare **major** IMPORTANT.

minor YOUNG PERSON /'maɪ.nəʳ/ ⓤ /-nɚ/ *noun* [C] someone who is too young to have the legal responsibilities of an adult: *He was accused of having sex with a minor.*

minor MUSIC /'maɪ.nəʳ/ ⓤ /-nɚ/ *adj* belonging or relating to a type of musical scale that generally has a sad sound, typically having a half tone between the second and third and between the fifth and sixth notes, and a whole tone between each of the others: *The piece is written in a minor key.* ○ *Mozart's Piano Concerto No. 20 in D minor.* ⊃Compare **major** MUSIC.

minority SMALL PART /maɪˈnɒr.ɪ.ti/ US /-nɑːr.ə.t̬i/ *noun* [S] a smaller number or part: *It's only a tiny minority of people who are causing the problem.* ○ *Children with single parents at my school were very much in the minority* (= there were very few). ○ *This section of the bookstore caters for minority interests* (= subjects that interest only a few people). ✳ NOTE: The opposite is **majority**.

minority PEOPLE /maɪˈnɒr.ɪ.ti/ US /-nɑːr.ə.t̬i/ *noun* [C] any small group in society that is different from the rest because of their race, religion or political beliefs, or a person who belongs to such a group: *ethnic/religious minorities* ○ *The plan was designed to help women and minorities overcome discrimination in the workplace.*
• **be in a minority of one** to be the only person who has your opinion

minster /ˈmɪn.stəʳ/ US /-stɚ/ *noun* [C] used in Britain in the name of a large or important church: *York Minster*

minstrel /ˈmɪn.strəl/ *noun* [C] a travelling musician and singer common between the 11th and 15th centuries: *a wandering minstrel*

mint PLANT /mɪnt/ *noun* **1** [U] a herb whose leaves have a strong fresh smell and taste and are used for giving flavour to food: *a sprig of mint* ○ *mint-flavoured gum/ toothpaste* **2** [C] a sweet with a mint flavour: *a packet of extra-strong mints* ○ *after-dinner chocolate mints*

mint COIN FACTORY /mɪnt/ *noun* **1** [C] a place where the new coins of a country are made **2** [S] INFORMAL an extremely large amount of money: *If his books sell in the States, he'll make a mint.*
mint /mɪnt/ *adj* [before n] describes stamps and coins, etc. which have not been used: *A collector would pay $500 for a mint copy.*
• **in mint condition** perfect, as if new: *CD player, in mint condition – £50.*
mint /mɪnt/ *verb* [T] **1** to produce a coin for the government **2** to produce something new, especially to invent a new phrase or word: *a freshly minted slogan/phrase* ○ *newly minted college graduates*

mint sauce MAINLY UK *noun* [U] (US USUALLY **mint jelly**) a sauce which is often served with lamb, made of vinegar, sugar and mint cut into very small pieces

minus SUBTRACTION /ˈmaɪ.nəs/ *prep* **1** reduced by a stated number: *What is 57 minus 39?* ○ *That will be £1500, minus the deposit of £150 that you have already paid.* ⊃Compare **plus** ADDITION. **2** INFORMAL lacking: *We're minus a chair for Ian – could you get one from the other room?*
minus /ˈmaɪ.nəs/ *adj* **1** [before n] A minus number or amount is less than zero. ⊃See also **negative** BELOW ZERO. **2** [before n] used to show that temperatures are less than zero: *Temperatures could fall to minus eight tonight.* **3** [after n] used after a mark given to written work to mean that it is of a slightly lower standard than that mark: *I got A minus for my English homework.*

minus DISADVANTAGE /ˈmaɪ.nəs/ *noun* [C] *plural* **minuses** a disadvantage or a bad feature: *Having to travel such a long way to work is a definite minus.* ⊃See also **minus** SUBTRACTION. **minus** /ˈmaɪ.nəs/ *adj* [before n] *One of the minus points of working at home is not having social contact with colleagues.*

minuscule /ˈmɪn.ɪ.skjuːl/ *adj* extremely small: *All she gave him to eat was two minuscule pieces of toast.*

minus (sign) *noun* [C] the – sign, written between two numbers to show that the second number should be subtracted from the first, or in front of one number to show that it has a value of less than 0 ⊃See also **minus** DISADVANTAGE.

minute TIME /ˈmɪn.ɪt/ *noun* [C] **1** (WRITTEN ABBREVIATION **min**) any of the 60 parts into which an hour is divided into, consisting of 60 seconds: *a twenty-minute bus ride* ○ *It takes me twenty minutes to get to work.* ○ *The train leaves at three minutes to eight, so we'd better get there a few minutes before then.* **2** used in spoken English to mean a very short time: *Hang on/Wait a minute – I'll just get my bag.* ○ *Just a minute – I'll be with you when I've*

finished this. ○ *I won't be a minute* (= I will be ready soon). ○ *When you've got a minute, I'd like a brief word with you.*
• **not for a minute** certainly not: *I'm not suggesting for a minute that she meant to cause a lot of trouble.*
• **the minute (that)** at the exact or first moment when: *The minute I saw him, I knew something was wrong.*
• **this minute** now or a very short time ago: *It doesn't have to be done this minute, but at some point this week please.* ○ *She's just this minute left the office.*
• **up-to-the-minute 1** modern: *up-to-the-minute fashion* **2** containing all the most recent information: *up-to-the-minute news*

minute SMALL /maɪˈnjuːt/ US /-ˈnuːt/ *adj* extremely small: *a minute amount/quantity* ○ *I've never seen a man with such tiny hands – they're minute!* ○ *The documentary showed an eye operation in minute detail* (= showing every small detail).
minutely /maɪˈnjuːt.li/ US /-ˈnuːt-/ *adv* very carefully, or looking at every small detail: *to examine something minutely*

minute ANGLE /ˈmɪn.ɪt/ *noun* [C] SPECIALIZED any of the 60 parts that the degrees of any angle are divided into

minute MESSAGE /ˈmɪn.ɪt/ *noun* [C] MAINLY UK FORMAL an official message from one person to another in an organization: *I've just received a minute from Jeremy authorizing the purchase of six more computers.* ⊃See also **the minutes**.

minute hand *noun* [C usually sing] the part on a clock or watch which points to the minutes and is longer than the HOUR HAND and thicker than the SECOND HAND

the minutes *plural noun* the written record of what was said at a meeting: *Could you take/do* (= write) *the minutes, Daniel?* ○ *The minutes of the last meeting were approved unanimously* (= everyone agreed that they were correct).
minute /ˈmɪn.ɪt/ *verb* [T] *The chairman is minuted* (= recorded in the minutes) *as having said that profits had fallen to an all-time low.*

minute steak *noun* [C or U] a thin slice of STEAK (= a type of meat especially from cattle) that can be cooked very quickly

the minutiae /ðə.mɪˈnuː.ʃi.aɪ/ *plural noun* small and often unimportant details: *The committee studied the minutiae of the report for hours.* ○ *Comedy is so often based in the minutiae of everyday life.*

minx /mɪŋks/ *noun* [C] SLIGHTLY OLD-FASHIONED USUALLY HUMOROUS a girl or young woman who knows how to control other people to her advantage

miracle /ˈmɪr.ɪ.kl̩/ *noun* [C] an unusual and mysterious event that is thought to have been caused by a god, or any very surprising and unexpected event: *[+ (that)] Looking at the state of his car, it's a miracle (that) he wasn't killed!* ○ *I can't promise a miracle cure, but I think we can improve things.*
• **perform/work miracles/a miracle** INFORMAL to be extremely effective in improving a situation: *You've performed a miracle on this kitchen – I've never seen it so clean!*
miraculous /mɪˈræk.jʊ.ləs/ *adj* very effective or surprising or difficult to believe: *The diet promised miraculous weight-loss.* ○ *Well, you've made a miraculous recovery since last night!* **miraculously** /mɪˈræk.jʊ.lə.sli/ *adv*

mirage /mɪˈrɑːʒ/ *noun* [C] **1** an image, produced by very hot air, of something which seems to be far away but does not really exist **2** LITERARY a hope or desire that has no chance of being achieved: *Electoral victory is just a distant mirage.*

mire /maɪəʳ/ US /maɪr/ *noun* **1** [C usually sing] an area of deep wet sticky earth **2** [S] LITERARY an unpleasant situation which is difficult to escape: *We must not be drawn into the mire of civil war.*
mired /maɪəd/ US /maɪrd/ *adj* **be/become mired (down) in something** to be involved in a difficult situation, especially for a long period of time: *The peace talks are mired in bureaucracy.*

mirror GLASS /ˈmɪr.əʳ/ US /-ɚ/ *noun* [C] a piece of glass with a shiny metallic back which reflects light, producing an image of whatever is in front of it: *the bathroom* *mirror* ○ *She was looking at her reflection* ***in*** *the mirror.*

mirror [REPRESENT] /ˈmɪr.əʳ/ [US] /-ɚ/ *verb* [T] **1** to represent something truthfully: *Our newspaper aims to mirror the opinions of ordinary people.* **2** to be very similar to something: *Her on-screen romances seem to mirror her experiences in her private life.*

mirror /ˈmɪr.əʳ/ [US] /-ɚ/ *noun* **be a mirror of *sth*** to be a truthful representation of something: *The movie is a mirror* ***of*** *daily life in wartime Britain.*

ˌmirror ˈimage *noun* [C] **1** something that looks exactly the same as another thing but with its left and right sides in opposite positions: *His home is two terraced houses knocked together, each the mirror image of the other.* **2** a person or object that is very similar to another: *The current economic situation is a mirror image of the situation in France a few years ago.*

mirth /mɜːθ/ [US] /mɝːθ/ *noun* [U] *LITERARY* laughter, amusement or happiness: *Her impersonations of our teachers were a source of considerable mirth.*

mirthless /ˈmɜːθ.ləs/ [US] /ˈmɝːθ-/ *adj LITERARY* not showing real amusement or happiness: *a mirthless laugh/smile* **mirthlessly** /ˈmɜːθ.ləs.li/ [US] /ˈmɝːθ-/ *adv*

mis- /mɪs-/ *prefix* added to the beginning of a verb or word formed from a verb, to show that the action referred to by the verb has been done wrongly or badly: *I never said that! You must have misheard me.* ○ *His misbehaviour eventually led to him being expelled from school.*

misadventure /ˌmɪs.ədˈven.tʃəʳ/ [US] /-tʃɚ/ *noun* [C] *LITERARY* an accident or bad luck

• **death by misadventure** *UK LEGAL* the official term used in court for an accidental death: *The coroner recorded a verdict of death by misadventure.*

misalign /ˌmɪs.əˈlaɪn/ *verb* [T] to arrange parts of a system badly, with the result that they do not work well together: *If the wheels are misaligned, it can cause excessive wear on your tyres.* **misalignment** /ˌmɪs.əˈlaɪn.mənt/ *noun* [U]

misandry /mɪˈsæn.dri/ /ˈmɪs.ən-/ [US] /ˈmɪs.æn-/ *noun* [U] hatred of men ⊃Compare **misogyny** **misandrist** /ˈmɪs.ən.drɪst/ *noun* [C] *Being a feminist doesn't necessarily make you a misandrist.*

misanthrope /ˈmɪs.ən.θrəʊp/ [US] /-θroʊp/ *noun* [C] (*ALSO* **misanthropist**) someone who dislikes other people and avoids involvement with society

misanthropic /ˌmɪs.ənˈθrɒp.ɪk/ [US] /-ˈθrɑː.pɪk/ *adj* not liking other people **misanthropy** /mɪˈsæn.θrə.pi/ *noun* [U]

misapply /ˌmɪs.əˈplaɪ/ *verb* [T] to use something badly, wrongly or in a way that was not intended: *It will be impossible to recover all the misapplied charity money.* **misapplication** /ˌmɪs.æp.lɪˈkeɪ.ʃən/ *noun* [C or U] *The inquiry found evidence of serious misapplication* ***of*** *funds.*

misapprehension /ˌmɪs.æp.rɪˈhen.tʃən/ *noun* [C or U] a failure to understand something, or an understanding or belief about something that is not correct: [+ *that*] *Most industrialists* ***labour under*** *a misapprehension* (= wrongly believe) ***that*** *unrestrained economic growth can be achieved without damaging the environment.*

misappropriate /ˌmɪs.əˈprəʊ.pri.eɪt/ [US] /-ˈproʊ-/ *verb* [T] *FORMAL* to steal something that you have been trusted to take care of and use it for your own benefit: *He is accused of misappropriating $30 000 to pay off gambling debts.* **misappropriation** /ˌmɪs.əˌprəʊ.priˈeɪ.ʃən/ [US] /-ˌproʊ-/ *noun* [U] *He was charged with forgery, embezzlement and misappropriation* ***of*** *union funds.*

misbegotten [BADLY PLANNED] /ˌmɪs.bɪˈgɒt.ən/ [US] /-ˈgɑː.t̬ən/ *adj FORMAL* badly or foolishly planned or designed: *a misbegotten belief/idea* ○ *misbegotten social and economic policies*

misbegotten [NOT RESPECTED] /ˌmɪs.bɪˈgɒt.ən/ [US] /-ˈgɑː.t̬ən/ *adj* [before n] *OLD-FASHIONED FORMAL* not deserving to be respected or thought valuable: *Her misbegotten father spent most of his adult life in prison.*

misbehave /ˌmɪs.bɪˈheɪv/ *verb* [I] to behave badly: *I was always getting in trouble for misbehaving at school.* **misbehaviour** *UK, US* **misbehavior** /ˌmɪs.bɪˈheɪ.vjəʳ/ [US] /-vjɚ/ *noun* [U] *The school expelled him for persistent misbehaviour.*

misc *WRITTEN ABBREVIATION FOR* **miscellaneous**

miscalculate /mɪˈskæl.kjʊ.leɪt/ *verb* [I or T] **1** to calculate an amount wrongly: [+ question word] *We had a lot of food left over from the party because I'd miscalculated* ***how*** *much people would eat.* **2** to judge a situation badly: *He miscalculated badly when he underestimated the response of the international community to the invasion.* **miscalculation** /ˌmɪs.kæl.kjʊˈleɪ.ʃən/ *noun* [C] *The project went over budget because of a miscalculation at the planning stage.* ○ *The conspirators' plot failed because they* ***made*** *two fatal miscalculations.*

miscarriage /ˈmɪsˌkær.ɪdʒ/ [US] /-ˌker-/ *noun* [C or U] an early unintentional end to a pregnancy when the baby is born too early and dies because it has not developed enough: *The amniocentesis test carries a significant risk of miscarriage.* ○ *I had two miscarriages before I gave birth to my daughter Heather.* ⊃Compare **abortion**; **stillbirth**. **miscarry** /ˌmɪsˈkær.i/ [US] /-ˈker-/ *verb* [I] *Sadly, she miscarried eight weeks into the pregnancy.*

misˌcarriage of ˈjustice *noun* [C] a situation in which someone is punished by the law courts for a crime that they have not committed: *Many people oppose the death penalty because of the possibility of miscarriages of justice.*

miscast /ˌmɪsˈkɑːst/ [US] /-ˈkæst/ *verb* [T] **miscast, miscast** to choose someone who is unsuitable to act in a film or play: *Tom Hanks was miscast as an arrogant city high-flier.*

miscellaneous /ˌmɪs.əlˈeɪ.ni.əs/ *adj* consisting of a mixture of various things which are not usually connected with each other: *miscellaneous household items*

miscellany /mɪˈsel.ə.ni/ *noun* [S] a mixture of different things: *The museum houses a fascinating miscellany of nautical treasures.*

mischance /ˌmɪsˈtʃɑːnts/ [US] /-ˈtʃænts/ *noun* [C or U] *FORMAL* bad luck or an unlucky event: ***By*** *an unfortunate mischance, the hospital had been placed immediately beside a large ammunition dump.*

mischief /ˈmɪs.tʃɪf/ *noun* **1** [U] behaviour, especially a child's, which is slightly bad but is not intended to cause serious harm or damage: *He needs a hobby to keep him busy and stop him from* ***getting into*** *mischief.* ○ *Perhaps a new bike would* ***keep*** *him* ***out of*** *mischief.* ○ *I hope you haven't been* ***up to*** *any mischief while I was away.* **2** [C] a MISCHIEVOUS child **3** [U] *INFORMAL* damage or harm: *criminal mischief*

• **do *sb/yourself* a mischief** *UK INFORMAL* to hurt someone or yourself: *You'll do yourself a mischief if you're not careful with that knife.*

• **make mischief** *OLD-FASHIONED* to say something which causes other people to be upset or annoyed with each other: *My children often try to make mischief* ***between*** *me and my new husband.*

mischief-making /ˈmɪs.tʃɪfˌmeɪ.kɪŋ/ *noun* [U] acting to intentionally cause problems for people: *He accused Mr James of mischief-making by raising allegations against Mr Aitken.*

mischievous /ˈmɪs.tʃɪ.vəs/ *adj* **1** behaving in a way, or describing behaviour, which is slightly bad but is not intended to cause serious harm or damage: *She has a mischievous sense of humour.* ○ *a book about the mischievous antics of his ten-year-old daughter* **2** expressing or suggesting mischief: *a mischievous grin* **3** describes behaviour or words that are intended to cause harm or trouble: *I think these rumours are mischievous.* **mischievously** /ˈmɪs.tʃɪ.və.sli/ *adv*: *to grin mischievously* **mischievousness** /ˈmɪs.tʃɪ.və.snəs/ *noun* [U]

misconceived /ˌmɪs.kənˈsiːvd/ *adj* badly planned because of a failure to understand a situation and therefore unsuitable or unlikely to succeed: *The plan to build the road through the forest is wholly misconceived.*

misconception /ˌmɪs.kənˈsep.ʃən/ *noun* [C] an idea which is wrong because it has been based on a failure to understand a situation: *We hope our work will help to change* ***popular*** *misconceptions* ***about*** *disabled people.* ○ [+ that] *I'd like to clear up the* ***common*** *misconception* ***that*** *American society is based on money.*

misconduct [BEHAVIOUR] /ˌmɪsˈkɒn.dʌkt/ [US] /-ˈkɑːn-/ *noun* [U] unacceptable or immoral behaviour by someone in a position of authority or responsibility: *The psychiatrist*

[M]

was found guilty of gross (= unacceptable) ***professional*** *misconduct.* ○ *The former priest denied allegations of **sexual** misconduct.*

misconduct [MANAGE] /ˌmɪs.kənˈdʌkt/ *verb* [T] to manage the activities of an organization badly: *The aid programme was misconducted, resulting in large quantities of food failing to reach the famine victims.* **misconduct** /ˌmɪsˈkɒn.dʌkt/ Ⓤⓢ /-ˈkɑːn-/ *noun* [U] *financial misconduct*

misconstrue /ˌmɪs.kənˈstruː/ *verb* [T] FORMAL to form a false understanding of the meaning or intention of something that someone does or says: *She said Harris had misconstrued her comments.* ○ *Their caution was misconstrued **as** cowardice.*

miscount /ˌmɪsˈkaʊnt/ *verb* [I or T] to reach a total, when counting, which is not correct: *I thought we had enough plates for the party, but perhaps I miscounted.* **miscount** /ˈmɪsˌkaʊnt/ *noun* [C]

miscreant /ˈmɪs.kri.ənt/ *noun* [C] FORMAL someone who behaves badly or does not obey rules: *We need tougher penalties to discourage miscreants.*

misdeed /ˌmɪsˈdiːd/ *noun* [C] FORMAL an act that is criminal or bad: *She's been making up for her past misdeeds by doing a lot of voluntary work.*

misdemeanor /ˌmɪs.dɪˈmiː.nəʳ/ Ⓤⓢ /-nɚ/ *noun* [C] US LEGAL a crime considered to be one of the less serious types of crime

misdemeanour UK, US **misdemeanor** /ˌmɪs.dɪˈmiː.nəʳ/ Ⓤⓢ /-nɚ/ *noun* [C] an action which is slightly bad or breaks a rule but is not a crime: *sexual/youthful misdemeanours* ○ *Every week, as children, we were beaten for some **minor** misdemeanour.*

misdirect /ˌmɪs.daɪˈrekt/ *verb* [T] **1** to send something to the wrong place or aim something in the wrong direction: *My luggage was misdirected **to** a different airport.* ○ *Vilas misdirected the shot, and the ball went over the net.* **2** to use something in a way which is not appropriate: *The report accuses the charity of misdirecting large quantities of aid.* **3** to be wrong in how you feel or act in a situation: *The public's admiration is misdirected, as he has done nothing to deserve it.* **misdirection** /ˌmɪs.daɪˈrek.ʃᵊn/ *noun* [U] *the misdirection **of** financial resources*

miser /ˈmaɪ.zəʳ/ Ⓤⓢ /-zɚ/ *noun* [C] DISAPPROVING someone who has a great desire to possess money and hates to spend it

miserly /ˈmaɪ.zᵊl.i/ Ⓤⓢ /-zɚ.li/ *adj* DISAPPROVING **1** like or typical of a miser: *a miserly person* **2** describes an amount that is extremely small: *a miserly 75p a week rise in the state pension* **miserliness** /ˈmaɪ.zᵊl.ɪ.nəs/ Ⓤⓢ /-zɚ.lɪ-/ *noun* [U]

miserable [UNHAPPY] /ˈmɪz.ᵊr.ə.bl̩/ Ⓤⓢ /-ɚ-/ *adj* **1** very unhappy: *She's miserable living on her own.* **2** unpleasant and causing unhappiness: *miserable weather* ○ *What a miserable existence! How could anyone live in such dreadful conditions?*

miserably /ˈmɪz.ᵊr.ə.bli/ Ⓤⓢ /-ɚ-/ *adv*: *"I'm so unhappy," sobbed Chris, miserably.* ○ *It's been miserably wet* (= raining a lot) *all week.* **misery** /ˈmɪz.ᵊr.i/ Ⓤⓢ /-ɚ-/ *noun* [C or U] *We have witnessed the most appalling scenes of **human** misery.* ○ *Ten years of marriage to him have made her life a misery.*

• **put *sth* out of *its* misery** to kill an animal because it is in great pain, so that it does not have to suffer any more

• **put *sb* out of *their* misery** INFORMAL to stop someone worrying, usually by giving them information that they have been waiting for: *We try to put our students out of their misery and give them their exam results as early as possible.*

miserable [LOW VALUE] /ˈmɪz.ᵊr.ə.bl̩/ Ⓤⓢ /ˈ-ɚ-/ *adj* [before n] having little value or quality: INFORMAL *She only offered me a miserable £20 for my old computer.* ○ SLANG *Some miserable bastard went and vandalised my car.*

miserably /ˈmɪz.ᵊr.ə.bli/ Ⓤⓢ /-ɚ-/ *adv*: *to **fail** miserably* (= completely fail) ○ *miserably low wages*

ˈ**misery (ˌguts)** *noun* [S] UK INFORMAL DISAPPROVING someone who is often very unhappy and is always complaining about things: *Stop being such an old misery guts!*

misfire /ˌmɪsˈfaɪəʳ/ Ⓤⓢ /-ˈfaɪr/ *verb* [I] **1** If a gun misfires, the bullet fails to come out. **2** When an engine misfires, the fuel inside it starts to burn at the wrong moment: *There was a loud bang, like the sound of an engine misfiring.* **3** If a plan misfires, it does not have the result that was intended: *The boy's death was the result of a practical joke that misfired.*

misfit /ˈmɪs.fɪt/ *noun* [C] someone who is not suited to a situation or who is not accepted by other people because their behaviour is strange or unusual: *I didn't really know anyone at the party, so I felt a bit of a misfit.* ○ *I was a bit of a **social** misfit at college because I didn't like going out in the evenings.*

misfortune /ˌmɪsˈfɔː.tʃuːn/ Ⓤⓢ /-ˈfɔːr.tʃən/ *noun* [C or U] bad luck, or an unlucky event: [+ to infinitive] *That was the worst film I've ever had the misfortune **to** see.* ○ *She's suffered a good deal of misfortune over the years.* ○ *It's unfair to take advantage of other people's misfortunes.*

misgiving /ˌmɪsˈgɪv.ɪŋ/ *noun* [C or U] a feeling of doubt or worry about a future event: *Many teachers expressed serious misgivings **about** the new exams.* ○ *My only misgiving is that we might not have enough time to do the job properly.*

misguided /ˌmɪsˈgaɪ.dɪd/ *adj* unreasonable or unsuitable because of being based on bad judgment or on wrong information or beliefs: *He was shot as he made a misguided attempt to stop the robbers single-handed.* ○ *The company blamed its disappointing performance on a misguided business plan.* **misguidedly** /ˌmɪsˈgaɪ.dɪd.li/ *adv*

mishandle /ˌmɪsˈhæn.dl̩/ *verb* [T] to deal with something without the necessary care or skill: *The police were accused of mishandling the investigation.* **mishandling** /ˌmɪsˈhæn.dl̩ɪŋ/ *noun* [U] *Who do you blame for the mishandling **of** the economy?*

mishap /ˈmɪs.hæp/ *noun* [C or U] bad luck, or an unlucky event or accident: *The parade was very well organised and passed without mishap.* ○ *A series of mishaps led to the nuclear power plant blowing up.*

mishear /ˌmɪsˈhɪəʳ/ Ⓤⓢ /-ˈhɪr/ *verb* [I or T] **misheard, misheard** to fail to hear someone's words correctly or in the way that was intended and to think that something different was said: *I'm sure I never said that! You must have misheard (me).*

mishmash /ˈmɪʃ.mæʃ/ *noun* [S] a badly organized mixture: *The new housing development is **a** mishmash **of** different architectural styles.*

misinform /ˌmɪs.ɪnˈfɔːm/ Ⓤⓢ /-ˈfɔːrm/ *verb* [T] to tell someone information that is not correct: *I was told she would be at the meeting, but clearly I was misinformed.*

misinformation /ˌmɪs.ɪn.fəˈmeɪ.ʃᵊn/ Ⓤⓢ /-fɚ-/ *noun* [U] **1** when people are misinformed: *There's a lot of misinformation **about** AIDS that needs to be corrected.* **2** information intended to deceive: *His election campaign was based on misinformation **about** the rival candidates.*

misinterpret /ˌmɪs.ɪnˈtɜː.prɪt/ Ⓤⓢ /-ˈtɝː-/ *verb* [T] to form an understanding that is not correct of something that is said or done: *My speech has been misinterpreted by the press.* ○ *When we re-examined the regulations, we realised that we had misinterpreted them.*

misinterpretation /ˌmɪs.ɪnˌtɜː.prɪˈteɪ.ʃᵊn/ Ⓤⓢ /-ˌtɝː-/ *noun* [C or U] *The minister's statement is unclear and **open to** misinterpretation* (= could easily be misinterpreted).

misjudge /ˌmɪsˈdʒʌdʒ/ *verb* [T] **1** to form an opinion or idea about someone or something which is unfair or wrong: *I thought he wasn't going to support me, but I misjudged him.* ○ *Chris totally misjudged the situation and behaved quite inappropriately.* **2** to guess an amount or distance wrongly **misjudgment, misjudgement** /ˌmɪsˈdʒʌdʒ.mənt/ *noun* [C or U] *Their decision to sell the house was a disastrous misjudgement.*

mislay /ˌmɪsˈleɪ/ *verb* [T] **mislaid, mislaid** to lose something temporarily by forgetting where you have put it: *Could I borrow a pen? I seem to have mislaid mine.*

mislead /ˌmɪsˈliːd/ *verb* [T] **misled, misled** to cause someone to believe something that is not true: *He has admitted misleading the police **about** his movements on* *the night of the murder.* **misleading** /ˌmɪsˈliː.dɪŋ/ *adj: misleading information/statements* ○ *Adverts must not create a misleading* ***impression***. **misleadingly** /ˌmɪsˈliː.dɪŋ.li/ *adv: A large sign misleadingly states: 'Escalator Works.'*

mismanage /ˌmɪsˈmæn.ɪdʒ/ *verb* [T] to organize or control something badly: *The restaurant was hopelessly mismanaged by a former rock musician with no business experience.* **mismanagement** /ˌmɪsˈmæn.ɪdʒ.mənt/ *noun* [U] *mismanagement* ***of*** *the economy/economic mismanagement* ○ *allegations of fraud and mismanagement*

mismatch /ˌmɪsˈmætʃ/ *verb* [T] to put together people or things that are unsuitable for each other: *I always thought Chris and Monique were mismatched, so I wasn't surprised when they got divorced.* **mismatch** /ˈmɪs.mætʃ/ *noun* [C] *There is a mismatch* ***between*** *the capacity of the airport and the large number of people wanting to fly from it.*

misnomer /ˌmɪsˈnəʊ.məʳ/ [US] /-ˈnoʊ.mɚ/ *noun* [C] a name that does not suit what it refers to, or the use of such a name: *It was the scruffiest place I've ever stayed in, so 'Hotel Royal' was* ***a bit of a*** *misnomer.* ○ *It's* ***something of a*** *misnomer to refer to these inexperienced boys as soldiers.*

misogynist /mɪˈsɒdʒ.ɪ.nɪst/ [US] /-ˈsɑː.dʒɪ-/ *noun* [C] a man who hates women or believes that men are much better than women **misogynist** /mɪˈsɒdʒ.ɪ.nɪst/ [US] /-ˈsɑː.dʒɪ-/ *adj* (ALSO **misogynistic**) *She left the Church because of its misogynist teachings on women and their position in society.* ○ *a misogynistic attitude/writer*

misogyny /mɪˈsɒdʒ.ɪ.ni/ [US] /-ˈsɑː.dʒɪ-/ *noun* [U] the hatred of women

misplace /ˌmɪsˈpleɪs/ *verb* [T] to lose something temporarily by forgetting where you have put it: *She misplaced her keys so often that her secretary used to carry spare ones for her.*

misplaced /ˌmɪsˈpleɪst/ *adj* directed towards someone or something wrongly or in a way that does not show good judgment: *misplaced* ***loyalty/trust*** ○ *I'm afraid your confidence in my abilities is misplaced.*

misprint /ˈmɪs.prɪnt/ *noun* [C] a mistake, such as a word that is spelled wrong, in a printed text: *We can't publish the newsletter like this – it's full of misprints.*

mispronounce /ˌmɪs.prəˈnaʊnts/ *verb* [T] to pronounce a word or sound wrongly: *French learners of English often mispronounce "ch"* ***as*** *"sh".* **mispronunciation** /ˌmɪs.prəˌnʌnt.siˈeɪ.ʃən/ *noun* [C or U] *Mispronunciation can be a serious obstacle to making yourself understood in a foreign language.*

misquote /ˌmɪsˈkwəʊt/ [US] /-ˈkwoʊt/ *verb* [T] to repeat something someone has said in a way that is not accurate: *Her promise was deliberately misquoted by her opponents, who then used it against her.* ○ *I never said that at all – the press misquoted me.* **misquotation** /ˌmɪs.kwəʊˈteɪ.ʃən/ [US] /-kwoʊ-/ *noun* [C or U] *That was a deliberate misquotation of what I said.*

misread /ˌmɪsˈriːd/ *verb* [T] **misread, misread 1** to make a mistake in the way that you read something: *I was given the wrong tablets when the chemist misread my prescription.* **2** to judge a situation incorrectly: *I thought he fancied me, but I'd completely misread the signals.* **misreading** /ˌmɪsˈriː.dɪŋ/ *noun* [C] *His misreading* ***of*** *the situation could have serious consequences.*

misreport /ˌmɪs.rɪˈpɔːt/ [US] /-ˈpɔːrt/ *verb* [T] to make known information that is not completely true or correct: *The magazine misreported its sales figures in order to boost advertising revenue.*

misrepresent /ˌmɪs.rep.rɪˈzent/ *verb* [T] to describe falsely an idea, opinion or situation or the opinions of someone, often in order to obtain an advantage: *She accused her opponents of deliberately misrepresenting her* ***as*** *an extremist.* ○ *I've grown used to my* ***views*** *being misrepresented in the press.* **misrepresentation** /ˌmɪs.rep.rɪ.zenˈteɪ.ʃən/ *noun* [C or U] *The documentary was a misrepresentation* ***of*** *the truth and bore little resemblance to actual events.* ○ *The MP laughed off the remarks as media misrepresentation.*

misrule /ˌmɪsˈruːl/ *noun* [U] bad government that lacks justice or fairness: *She blames her country's economic collapse on forty years of communist misrule.*

Miss [TITLE] /mɪs/ *noun* **1** a title or form of address for a girl or a woman who has never been married: *Dr White will see you now, Miss Carter.* ○ *Miss Helena Lewis* ➲Compare **Ms**; **Mrs.** ✻ NOTE: Some women use the title **Ms** rather than **Miss** to show that their position in life does not depend on a man, as **Ms** does not show whether they are married or not. **2** *OLD-FASHIONED* used as a form of address for a girl or young woman who does not appear to be married: *Excuse me, Miss, could you tell me the way to the station?* **3** *MAINLY UK* sometimes used by children to address teachers who are women: *Can I go to the toilet, Miss?* **4** When a woman wins a beauty competition, she is often given the title Miss and the name of the place that she represents: *Miss India/UK* ○ *the Miss World contest* **5** *UK OLD-FASHIONED* **miss** a girl or young woman, especially one who behaves rudely or shows no respect: *You're a cheeky little miss! Apologize at once.*

miss [NOT HIT] /mɪs/ *verb* [I or T] to fail to hit something or to avoid hitting something: *The bullet missed his heart by a couple of centimetres.* ○ *I swerved to avoid the other car and only just missed a tree.* ○ *He threw a book at me, but he/it missed.* **miss** /mɪs/ *noun* [C] *Well done! You scored eight hits and only two misses.* ➲See also **near miss**.

miss [NOT DO] /mɪs/ *verb* [T] **1** to fail to do or experience something, often something planned or expected, or to avoid doing or experiencing something: *I missed the start of the exam because my bus was late.* ○ *Often I miss* (= do not eat) *breakfast and have an early lunch instead.* ○ *You should leave early if you want to miss the rush hour.* ○ [+ v-ing] *I only just missed be****ing*** *run over by a bus this morning.* ➲See Note **lose** or **miss?** at **lose** NOT HAVE. **2** to arrive too late to get on a bus, train or aircraft: *You'll miss your train if you don't hurry up.* **3** to not go to something: *You'll fall behind in your studies if you keep missing school.* ○ *I'm trying to find an excuse for missing the office party.* **4** to not see or hear something or someone: *I missed the beginning of the film.* ○ *Her latest movie is* ***too good to*** *miss* (= It certainly should be seen). ○ *I was sorry I missed you at Pat's party – I must have arrived after you left.* **5** to not notice someone or something: *You don't miss much, do you? Nobody else noticed that mistake.* ○ *My office is first on the right with a bright red door. You* ***can't*** *miss* ***it*** (= It is very easy to find).

• **miss the boat** to lose an opportunity to do something by being slow to act: *There were tickets available last week, but he missed the boat by waiting till today to try to buy some.*

• **miss a chance/opportunity** to not use an opportunity to do something: *She missed the chance of promotion when she turned down the job of assistant manager.*

• **miss the mark** to fail to achieve the result that was intended: *Her speech missed the mark and failed to generate the public support she had been hoping for.*

• **miss the point** to not understand something correctly or what is important about it: *What you say is true, but you've missed the point* ***of*** *my argument.*

• **not miss a trick** said about someone who never fails to notice and take advantage of a good opportunity: *Jonathan doesn't miss a trick! If there's a bargain to be had at the market, he'll find it.*

• **not miss much** *INFORMAL* said when something you failed to see or experience was not important or special: *"I didn't manage to see that programme." "Don't worry, you didn't miss much."*

miss /mɪs/ *noun UK INFORMAL* **give *sth* a miss** to avoid or not do something: *We usually go to France in the summer, but we've decided to give it a miss this year.* ○ *The restaurant's very good for fish, but I'd give their vegetarian options a miss.*

COMMON LEARNER ERROR

miss or **lack?**

Be careful not to confuse the verb **lack** with **miss**. **Lack** means to not have something, or to not have enough of something.

Our town lacks a cinema.

~~*Our town misses a cinema.*~~

M

miss [REGRET] /mɪs/ *verb* [T] to regret that a person or thing is not present: *I really missed her when she went away.* ○ *She will be sadly missed by all who knew her.* ○ *I still miss my old car.* ○ *What did you miss most* ***about*** *England when you were living in France?* ○ [+ v-ing] *I haven't missed smok****ing*** *like I'd expected to.*

miss [NOTICE] /mɪs/ *verb* [T] to notice that something is lost or absent: *He didn't miss his wallet until the waiter brought the bill.*

PHRASAL VERBS WITH **miss**

▲ **miss *sb/sth* out** [NOT INCLUDE] *phrasal verb* [M] *UK* to fail to include someone or something that should be included: *You've missed out your address on the form.* ○ *Oh I'm sorry, Tina, I've missed you out. What would you like to drink?*

▲ **miss out** [NOT USE] *phrasal verb* to fail to use an opportunity to enjoy or benefit from something: *Don't miss out* ***on*** *the fantastic bargains in our summer sale.* ○ *We didn't have a TV at home when I was young, and I felt as though I missed out.*

misshapen /mɪsˈʃeɪ.pᵊn/ /mɪʃ-/ *adj* having an unusual shape or a shape which is not natural: *The drug caused some babies to be born with misshapen limbs.*

missile /ˈmɪs.aɪl/ [US] /-ᵊl/ *noun* [C] **1** a flying weapon which has its own engine so that it can travel a long distance before exploding at the place that it has been aimed at: *a missile* ***launcher*** ○ *Missile* ***attacks*** *on the capital resumed at dawn.* **2** *FORMAL* any object that is thrown with the intention of causing injury or damage: *Stones, bottles and other missiles were thrown at the police.*

missing /ˈmɪs.ɪŋ/ *adj* **1** Someone who is missing has disappeared: *Her father has been missing since September 1992.* ○ *UK The girl* ***went*** *missing during a family outing to Mount Snowdon.* **2** describes soldiers or military vehicles that have not returned from fighting in a war but are not known with total certainty to be dead or destroyed: *He was* ***listed as*** *missing* ***in action***. **3** describes something that cannot be found because it is not where it should be: *The burglars have been arrested but the jewellery is still missing.* ○ *When did you realise that the money was missing from your account?*

ˌmissing ˈlink *noun* [S] **1** something that is necessary to complete a series or solve a problem: *Those documents provided the missing link, and the police were able to make an arrest soon after they discovered them.* **2 the missing link** an animal which no longer exists or might never have existed and is thought to explain how humans developed from animals similar to monkeys

ˌmissing ˈperson *noun* [C] someone who has disappeared and is no longer in communication with their family and friends: *They reported his disappearance to the missing persons bureau.*

mission [JOB] /ˈmɪʃ.ᵊn/ *noun* [C] **1** an important job, especially a military one, that someone is sent somewhere to do: *Your mission is to isolate the enemy by destroying all the bridges across the river.* ○ *a* ***peace/rescue/fact-finding*** *mission* **2** any work that someone believes it is their duty to do: *My mission* ***in life*** *is to educate the rich about the suffering of the poor.* ○ *She's a woman* ***with a*** *mission and she's absolutely determined to finish the project.*

mission [PEOPLE] /ˈmɪʃ.ᵊn/ *group noun* [C] a group of people whose job is to increase what is known about their country, organization or religion in another country or area, or the place where such people are based: *More funds are needed to establish* ***trade*** *missions in eastern Europe.* ○ *The Methodist mission is situated in one of the poorest parts of the city.*

missionary /ˈmɪʃ.ᵊn.ri/ [US] /-er.i/ *noun* [C] a person who has been sent to a foreign country to teach their religion to the people who live there: *He did missionary work for the Presbyterian Church in Alaska.*

ˈmissionary poˌsition *noun* [S] a position for having sex in which a woman lies on her back and her partner is above and facing her

ˌmissionary ˈzeal *noun* [U] extreme enthusiasm

ˌmission conˈtrol *noun* [U] the place on Earth from which a journey into space is controlled: *For a few tense minutes, the astronauts lost radio contact with mission control.*

ˈmission ˌstatement *noun* [C] a short written description of the aims of a business, charity, government department or public organization

missive /ˈmɪs.ɪv/ *noun* [C] an official, formal or long letter: *She sent a ten-page missive to the council, detailing her objections.*

misspell /ˌmɪsˈspel/ *verb* [T] **misspelled** or *UK* **misspelt, misspelled** or *UK* **misspelt** to fail to spell a word correctly **misspelling** /ˌmɪsˈspel.ɪŋ/ *noun* [C or U] *This essay is full of misspellings.*

misspend /ˌmɪsˈspend/ *verb* [T] **misspent, misspent** to use time or money in a manner that is wasteful or unwise: *We must stop public money being misspent in this way.* ○ *Being a good pool player is usually a sign of a misspent* ***youth***.

missus /ˈmɪs.ɪz/ *noun* [S] *INFORMAL* wife: *Me and* ***the*** *missus* (= my wife) *are going to our daughter's for Christmas.* ○ *Have you met Jack's new missus?*

mist /mɪst/ *noun* [C or U] **1** thin fog produced by very small drops of water gathering in the air just above an area of ground or water: *The mountain villages seem to be permanently* ***shrouded in*** *mist.* ○ *The early-morning mist soon* ***lifted/cleared***. **2** a thin layer of liquid on the surface of something which makes it difficult to see: *UK There's always a mist on the bathroom mirror/windows when I've had a shower.* ○ *Through a mist* ***of*** *tears, I watched his train pull out of the station.*

• **the mists of time** used to show that something happened a very long time ago and is difficult to remember clearly: *The precise details of what happened have been lost in the mists of time.*

misty /ˈmɪs.ti/ *adj* **1** In misty weather, there is mist in the air which makes it difficult to see into the distance: *The morning will start off misty.* **2** describes a glass or similar surface that is covered with a mist which makes it difficult to see through: *The windscreen is all misty.* ➲See also **misty-eyed**. **mistily** /ˈmɪs.tɪ.li/ *adv* **mistiness** /ˈmɪs.tɪ.nəs/ *noun* [U]

mist /mɪst/ *verb*

▲ **mist over/up** *phrasal verb* **1** *MAINLY UK* If something that you can see through mists over/up, it becomes covered with a thin layer of liquid so that it is more difficult to see through: *Open the window when you have a shower to stop the mirror misting over.* ○ *The steam from the kettle misted up her glasses.* ➲See also **steam up** and **fog up**. **2** If your eyes mist over/up, they fill with tears.

mistake [NOT RECOGNIZE] /mɪˈsteɪk/ *verb* [T] **mistook, mistaken** to be wrong about or to fail to recognize something or someone: *You can't mistake their house – it's got a bright yellow front door.* ○ *FORMAL I mistook your signature and thought the letter was from someone else.*

• **be no mistaking *sth*** When there's no mistaking something, it is impossible not to recognize it: *There's no mistaking a painting by Picasso.*

mistaken /mɪˈsteɪ.kᵊn/ *adj* wrong in what you believe, or based on a belief that is wrong: *If you think you can carry on drinking so much without damaging your health, then you're mistaken.* ○ *I'm afraid I was mistaken* ***about*** *how much it would cost.* ○ *The negotiations continued* ***in the*** *mistaken* ***belief*** *that a peaceful agreement could be reached.* ○ *a case of mistaken* ***identity*** **mistakenly** /mɪˈsteɪ.kᵊn.li/ *adv*: *She mistakenly* ***believed*** *that she could get away with not paying her taxes.* **mistakable**, *UK ALSO* **mistakeable** /mɪˈsteɪ.kə.bl̩/ *adj*: *She's* ***easily*** *mistakeable* ***for*** *a man when she wears that suit and hat.*

mistake [WRONG ACTION] /mɪˈsteɪk/ *noun* [C] an action, decision or judgment which produces an unwanted or unintentional result: *I'm not blaming you – we all* ***make*** *mistakes.* ○ [+ to infinitive] *It was a mistake for us* ***to*** *come here tonight.* ○ *This letter's full of* ***spelling*** *mistakes.* ○ *I've discovered a few mistakes* ***in*** *your calculations.* ○ *Why am I under arrest? There must be* ***some*** *mistake.* ➲See Note **fault or mistake/error?** at **fault** MISTAKE.

• **by mistake** accidentally: *I've paid this bill twice by mistake.*
• **and no mistake** MAINLY UK OLD-FASHIONED added to the end of something you say to emphasize it: *He's a strange bloke and no mistake.*
• **make no mistake about it** used to show that you are certain about something: *Make no mistake about it, this decision is going to cause you a lot of problems.*

COMMON LEARNER ERROR

to make a mistake

Many learners wrongly use the verb 'do' with the noun **mistake**. The correct verb is 'make'.

I never make mistakes in my essays.
~~*I never do mistakes in my essays.*~~

▲ **mistake *sb/sth* for *sb/sth*** *phrasal verb* to confuse someone or something with a different person or thing: *I often mistake her **for** her mother on the phone.*

Mister /ˈmɪs.təʳ/ [US] /-tɚ/ *noun* **1** the complete form of the title **Mr 2** an informal and often rude form of address for a man whose name you do not know: *Listen to me, Mister, I don't ever wanna see you in this bar again.*

mistime /ˌmɪsˈtaɪm/ *verb* [T] to do something at the wrong moment with the result that it is unsuccessful or has an unwanted effect: *She mistimed her stroke and the ball went into the net.*

mistletoe /ˈmɪs.l̩.təʊ/ [US] /-toʊ/ *noun* [U] an evergreen plant with small white fruits and pale yellow flowers which grows on trees, often used as a Christmas decoration: *Chris and Pat were kissing **under** the mistletoe at the office party.*

the mistral /ðə.mɪˈstrɑːl/ *noun* [S] a strong cold dry wind that blows south through France to the Mediterranean

mistreat /ˌmɪsˈtriːt/ *verb* [T] to treat a person or animal badly, cruelly or unfairly: *Both parents have denied charges of mistreating their children.* ○ *I think people who mistreat their pets should be banned from keeping them.* **mistreatment** /mɪˈstriːt.mənt/ *noun* [U] *She suffered years of mistreatment from her violent husband.*

mistress [CONTROL] /ˈmɪs.trəs/ *noun* **1** [S or U] OLD-FASHIONED a woman who has control over or responsibility for someone or something: *I'll inform **the** mistress **(of** the house) of your arrival, madam.* ○ *She intends to remain mistress **of** (= in charge of) her own life when she gets married.* **2** [C] UK OLD-FASHIONED a female school teacher: *She got a good report from her German mistress.* **3** [C] OLD-FASHIONED a female owner of a dog

mistress [SEXUAL PARTNER] /ˈmɪs.trəs/ *noun* [C] a woman who is having a sexual relationship with a married man: *Edward VII and his mistress, Lillie Langtry*

mistrial /ˈmɪs.traɪəl/ *noun* [C] **1** a trial during which a mistake has been made, causing the judgment to have no legal value **2** US a trial in which no decision can be reached about whether a person is guilty or not

mistrust /ˌmɪsˈtrʌst/ *verb* [T] to have doubts about the honesty or abilities of someone: *I've always mistrusted politicians.* **mistrust** /ˌmɪsˈtrʌst/ *noun* [U] *There is still considerable mistrust **between** the management and the workforce.* **mistrustful** /ˌmɪsˈtrʌst.fəl/ *adj*: *Voters are bound to be mistrustful **of** a government that has broken so many promises.* **mistrustfully** /ˌmɪsˈtrʌst.fəl.i/ *adv*

misty /ˈmɪs.ti/ *adj* ➲See at **mist**.

misty-eyed /ˌmɪs.tiˈaɪd/ *adj* looking as if you are going to cry because you feel emotional about something: *He goes all misty-eyed whenever he hears that song.*

misunderstand /ˌmɪs.ʌn.dəˈstænd/ [US] /-dɚ-/ *verb* [I or T] **misunderstood, misunderstood** to think you have understood someone or something when you have not: *If you think that these transport problems can be solved by building more roads, you completely misunderstand the nature of the problem.* ○ *I told him I'd meet him here, but perhaps he misunderstood and went straight to the pub.* **misunderstanding** /ˌmɪs.ʌn.dəˈstæn.dɪŋ/ [US] /-dɚ-/ *noun* **1** [C or U] when someone does not understand something correctly: *There must be some misunderstanding. I never asked for these chairs to be delivered.* ○ *His ridiculous comments showed a complete misunderstanding **of** the situation.* **2** [C] INFORMAL a disagreement, argument or fight: OFTEN HUMOROUS *"How did you get your black eye?" "Oh, I had a little misunderstanding **with** someone at the football match."*

misuse /ˌmɪsˈjuːz/ *verb* [T] to use something in an unsuitable way or in a way that was not intended: *She was accused of misusing company funds.* **misuse** /ˌmɪsˈjuːs/ *noun* [C or U] *This new computer system is completely unnecessary and a misuse **of** taxpayers' money.* ○ *the misuse of power/drugs*

mite [ANIMAL] /maɪt/ *noun* [C] a very small animal similar to a spider: *a red spider mite*

mite [CHILD] /maɪt/ *noun* [C] MAINLY UK INFORMAL a young child, especially one deserving sympathy because they are ill or hungry: *Poor little mite, he looks so tired.*

mite [SMALL AMOUNT] /maɪt/ *noun* [U] OLD-FASHIONED a very small amount: *I couldn't eat another mite.*
• **a mite** INFORMAL slightly: *He seemed a mite embarrassed.*

mitigate /ˈmɪt.ɪ.geɪt/ [US] /ˈmɪt̬-/ *verb* [T] FORMAL to make something less harmful, unpleasant or bad: *It is unclear how to mitigate **the effects** of tourism on the island.* **mitigating** /ˈmɪt.ɪ.geɪ.tɪŋ/ [US] /ˈmɪt̬.ɪ.geɪ.t̬ɪŋ/ *adj* **1** FORMAL making something less harmful, unpleasant or bad: *Are there any mitigating **circumstances/factors** which might help explain her appalling behaviour?* ➲Compare **unmitigated**. **2** LEGAL causing you to judge a crime to be less serious or to make the punishment less severe: *The jury must take into account any mitigating **circumstances** presented by the defense, such as previous good character.* **mitigation** /ˌmɪt.ɪˈgeɪ.ʃən/ [US] /ˌmɪt̬-/ *noun* [U] FORMAL *'I was very young at the time,' he said **in** mitigation.*

mitre /ˈmaɪ.təʳ/ [US] /-t̬ɚ/ *noun* [C] (US ALSO **miter**) a tall pointed hat worn by bishops on ceremonial occasions

ˈ**mitre (ˌjoint)** *noun* [C] (US ALSO **miter (joint)**) a joint made by two pieces of wood which have both been cut at an angle of 45° at the joining ends

mitt /mɪt/ *noun* **1** [C] a special type of glove for protecting a person's hand, especially a thick leather glove used for catching a baseball: *a catcher's mitt* ○ *oven mitts* **2** [C usually pl] a **mitten**: *baby/woollen mitts* **3** [C usually pl] SLANG a person's hand: *Get your filthy mitts off my sandwich!*

mitten /ˈmɪt.ən/ [US] /ˈmɪt̬-/ *noun* [C] (ALSO **mitt**) a type of glove, either with a single part for all the fingers and a separate part for the thumb: *sheepskin mittens* ○ *woollen mittens* ➲Compare **glove**.

mix [COMBINE] /mɪks/ *verb* **1** [I or T] to (cause different substances to) combine, so that the result cannot easily be separated into its parts: *Oil and water don't mix. Even if you shake them together they separate into two layers.* ○ *Radioactive material was mixed **in/up** (with) the effluent.* ○ *Mix the eggs **into** the flour.* ○ *In a large bowl, mix **together** the flour, sugar and raisins in a bowl.* ○ [+ two objects] *Shall I mix (= make) you a cocktail?* **2** [T] to have or do two or more things, such as activities or qualities, at the same time: *Some people are happy to mix business **with/and** pleasure, but I'm not one of them.*
• **be mixed up with/in *sth*** USUALLY DISAPPROVING to be connected with a bad or unpleasant person or thing: *Please don't get mixed up with him. You'll regret it if you do.* ○ *I knew someone who was mixed up in that corruption scandal.*
• **mix it** (US **mix it up**) INFORMAL to fight or argue with people: *Don't take any notice of Sally – she just likes to mix it.*

mix /mɪks/ *noun* **1** [C usually sing] a combination: *There was an odd mix **of** people at Patrick's party.* ○ *"She's studying physics and philosophy." "That's an interesting mix."* **2** [C or U] something which is sold in the form of a powder and to which a liquid, such as water, can be added later: *cake/cement mix*

mixed /mɪkst/ *adj* **1** showing a mixture of different feelings or opinions: *There has been a mixed **reaction** to the changes.* **2** for both sexes: *Our children go to a mixed **school**.* ○ *Some of his jokes were too rude for mixed **company** (= a group where both males and females are*

M

present). **3** combining people of a different religion or race: *a mixed marriage/relationship* ○ *people of mixed race*

mix SOCIALIZE /mɪks/ *verb* [I] to be with or communicate well with other people: *I suppose you mix **with** a wide variety of people in your job.* ○ *She mixes very well – perhaps that's why she's so popular.*

mixer /'mɪk.sə^r/ US /-sɚ/ *noun* **a good/bad mixer** someone who is good/bad at socializing: *You get to know lots of people at college if you're a good mixer.*

mix RECORD MUSIC /mɪks/ *verb* [T] SPECIALIZED to control the amounts of various sounds which are combined on a recording **mix** /mɪks/ *noun* [C] *A new mix of their hit single is due to be released early next month.*

PHRASAL VERBS WITH **mix** ▼

▲ **mix** *sb/sth* **up** CONFUSE *phrasal verb* [M] to fail to identify two people or things correctly by thinking that one person or thing is the other person or thing: *People often mix us up because we look so similar.* ○ *I think you're mixing me up **with** my sister.*

▲ **mix** *sb* **up** *phrasal verb* [M] to confuse, worry or upset someone: *The roadworks mixed me up and I went the wrong way.*

mixed-up /ˌmɪkst'ʌp/ *adj* upset, worried and confused, especially because of personal problems: *He's just a mixed-up kid.*

mix-up /'mɪks.ʌp/ *noun* [C] a mistake that causes confusion: *There was a mix-up at the office and we all received the wrong forms.*

▲ **mix** *sth* **up** UNTIDY *phrasal verb* [M] to make a group of things untidy or badly organized, or to move them into the wrong order: *Don't mix up the bottles – you'll have to repeat the experiment if you do.* ○ *Your jigsaw puzzles and games are all mixed up **together** in that box. Shall we sort them out?*

mixed-ability /ˌmɪkst.ə'bɪl.ɪ.ti/ US /-ə.t̬i/ *adj* involving students of different levels of ability: *mixed-ability teaching/classes*

mixed 'bag *noun* [S] a range of different things or people: *There's a real mixed bag **of** people on the course.*

mixed 'blessing *noun* [S] something that has advantages and disadvantages: *Getting into the team is a mixed blessing – it's good to have the place, but I'll have to spend a lot of time training.*

mixed 'doubles *noun* [U] a game, for example a tennis game, in which each team consists of one female and one male player

mixed e'conomy *noun* [C] an economic system in which some industries are controlled privately and some by the government

mixed 'farming *noun* [U] a method of farming in which crops are grown and animals are kept on the same farm

mixed 'feelings *plural noun* If you have mixed feelings about something, you feel both pleased and not pleased about it at the same time: *I had mixed feelings about leaving home. I was excited but at the same time, I knew I would miss my family.*

mixed 'grill *noun* [C] a meal in which several types of meat are served together which have been cooked under a GRILL (= a hot surface which you cook food under)

mixer MACHINE /'mɪk.sə^r/ US /-sɚ/ *noun* [C] a machine which mixes substances: *a cement mixer* ○ *an electric (food) mixer*

mixer DRINK /'mɪk.sə^r/ US /-sɚ/ *noun* [C] a drink which does not contain alcohol and which can be mixed with an alcoholic drink, especially a SPIRIT (= strong alcoholic drink): *We have ginger ale, tonic water and various other mixers.*

'mixer ˌtap UK *noun* [C] (US **mixer faucet**) a device for controlling the flow of water, so that hot and cold water come out of the same pipe, but the flow of each is controlled separately so that the temperature of the water coming out can be adjusted

mixture /'mɪks.tʃə^r/ US /-tʃɚ/ *noun* **1** [C] a substance made from a combination of different substances, or any combination of different things: *The mixture **of** flour,*

water and yeast is then left in a warm place for four hours.* ○ *Their latest CD is a mixture **of** new and old songs.* **2** [U] the process of mixing **3** [U] a type of medicine which has to be shaken before being used: *cough mixture*

Mk *ABBREVIATION FOR* **mark** MACHINE: *She was driving a bright yellow Mk XI Lotus two-seater.*

ml *noun* [C] *plural* **ml** or **mls** WRITTEN ABBREVIATION FOR **millilitre**: *a 7 ml bottle of the perfume*

mm *noun* [C] *plural* **mm** WRITTEN ABBREVIATION FOR **millimetre**: *a 6mm (diameter) drill*

MMR /ˌem.emˈɑː^r/ US /-ˈɑːr/ *noun* [S] an injection given to young children to protect them against MEASLES, MUMPS and RUBELLA

mnemonic /nɪˈmɒn.ɪk/ US /-ˈmɑː.nɪk/ *noun* [C] something such as a very short poem or a special word used to help a person remember something: *The musical notes on the lines go EGBDF – use the mnemonic 'every good boy deserves fun'.* **mnemonic** /nɪˈmɒn.ɪk/ US /-ˈmɑː.nɪk/ *adj*

mo /məʊ/ US /moʊ/ *noun* [S] INFORMAL a short period of time; a moment: *"Come on! We're going to be late." "Hang on **a** mo! I'll just get my wallet."* ○ *I'll be with you **in a** mo* (= very soon). ✳ NOTE: This is mainly used in spoken English.

MO /ˌemˈəʊ/ US /-ˈoʊ/ *noun* [C] *plural* **MOs** ABBREVIATION FOR medical officer

moan SOUND /məʊn/ US /moʊn/ *verb* [I] to make a long low sound of pain, suffering or another strong emotion: *He moaned **with** pain before losing consciousness.* ○ *"Let me die," he moaned.* **moan** /məʊn/ US /moʊn/ *noun* [C] *We could hear the moans of someone trapped under the rubble.* ○ *moans of ecstasy/agony*

moan COMPLAIN /məʊn/ US /moʊn/ *verb* [I] INFORMAL DISAPPROVING to make a complaint in an unhappy voice, usually about something which does not seem important to other people: *Thelma's always moaning (**about** something), and forgets how lucky she actually is.* ○ [+ speech] *"I don't like potatoes," he moaned.* ○ [+ (that)] *First she moans (**that**) she's too hot, and then that she's too cold.* **moan** /məʊn/ US /moʊn/ *noun* [C] *Apart from a slight moan about the waiter, he seemed to enjoy the meal.* **moaner** /'məʊ.nə^r/ US /moʊ.nɚ/ *noun* [C]

moaning minnie /ˌməʊ.nɪŋˈmɪn.i/ US /ˌmoʊ-/ *noun* [C] UK INFORMAL someone who annoys other people by complaining all the time: *Oh stop being such a moaning minnie!*

moat /məʊt/ US /moʊt/ *noun* [C] a long wide channel which is dug all the way around a place such as a castle, and usually filled with water, to make it more difficult to attack

moated /'məʊ.tɪd/ US /'moʊ.t̬ɪd/ *adj* surrounded by a moat: *a moated house/castle*

mob CROWD /mɒb/ US /mɑːb/ *group noun* **1** [C] USUALLY DISAPPROVING a large angry crowd, especially one which could easily become violent: *The **angry** mob outside the jail was/were ready to riot.* ○ *a lynch mob* ○ *Fifty people were killed in three days of mob **violence**.* **2** [C] INFORMAL a group of people who are friends or who are similar in some way: *The usual mob were/was hanging out at the bar.* **3** [S] INFORMAL an organization of criminals: *a New York mob leader* ➡See also **mobster**.

mob GATHER /mɒb/ US /mɑːb/ *verb* [T usually passive] **-bb-** to gather around someone in a crowd to express admiration, interest or anger: *They were mobbed **by** fans when they arrived at the theatre.* ○ *Let's not go to the Old Town tonight – it's always mobbed* (= there are always a lot of people there) *on Fridays.*

mob /mɒb/ US /mɑːb/ *verb* [I or T] **-bb-** When a group of birds or small animals mob a fierce bird or animal that is hunting them, they attack it together and force it to go away.

mobile ABLE TO MOVE /'məʊ.baɪl/ US /'moʊ.b^əl/ *adj* able to move freely or be easily moved: *You've broken your ankle but you'll be mobile* (= able to walk as usual) *within a couple of months.* **mobility** /məʊˈbɪl.ɪ.ti/ US /moʊˈbɪl.ə.t̬i/ *noun* [U] SLIGHTLY FORMAL *Some neck injuries cause total loss of mobility below the point of injury.* ○ *I prefer the mobility of a hand-held camera.* ➡See also **upward mobility** at **upwardly mobile**.

mobile [DECORATION] /ˈməʊ.baɪl/ [US] /ˈmoʊ.bəl/ *noun* [C] a decoration or work of art which has many parts that move freely in the air, for example hanging from threads

ˌmobile ˈhome *noun* [C] a type of building which people live in and which usually stays in one place, but which can be moved using a vehicle or sometimes its own engine

ˌmobile ˈlibrary *UK noun* [C] (*US* **bookmobile**) a large road vehicle which travels around, especially in the countryside, carrying books for people to borrow

ˌmobile (ˈphone) *MAINLY UK noun* [C] (*US USUALLY* **cellphone**) a telephone which is connected to the telephone system by radio, rather than by a wire, and can therefore be used anywhere where its signals can be received ➲See picture **In the Office** on page Centre 15

mobilize, *UK ALSO* **-ise** /ˈməʊ.bɪ.laɪz/ [US] /ˈmoʊ-/ *verb* **1** [T] to organize or prepare something, such as a group of people, for a purpose: *Representatives for all the main candidates are trying to mobilize voter **support**.* **2** [I or T] to prepare to fight, especially in a war: *The government has mobilized several of the army's top combat units.* ○ *Troops have been mobilising for the past three weeks.*
mobilization, *UK ALSO* **-isation** /ˌməʊ.bɪ.laɪˈzeɪ.ʃən/ [US] /ˌmoʊ.bɪ.lɪ-/ *noun* [U]

mobster /ˈmɒb.stəʳ/ [US] /ˈmɑːb.stɚ/ *noun* [C] *MAINLY US FOR* **gangster**

moccasin /ˈmɒk.ə.sɪn/ [US] /ˈmɑː.kə-/ *noun* [C] a shoe which the wearer's foot slides into and which is made from soft leather with stitches around the top at the front

mocha /ˈmɒk.ə/ [US] /ˈmoʊ.kə/ *noun* [U] **1** a type of coffee of good quality, or a flavouring which tastes of this **2** a mixture of coffee and chocolate

mock [LAUGH AT] /mɒk/ [US] /mɑːk/ *verb* [T] **1** *SLIGHTLY FORMAL* to laugh at someone, often by copying them in an amusing but unkind way: *They were mocking him because he kept falling off his bike.* ○ *She made fun of him by mocking his limp.* **2** to make something appear stupid or useless: *The wind mocked their attempts to reach the shore by pushing the boat further and further out to sea.*
mockery /ˈmɒk.ər.i/ [US] /ˈmɑː.kɚ-/ *noun* **1** [U] when you mock someone or something: *Bill's mockery of his dad's twitch was a bit cruel, but it made us laugh.* **2** [S] an action or event which is a failure and makes the people involved in or affected by it appear foolish: *The trial was **a** mockery – the judge had decided the verdict before it began.*
• **make a mockery of *sth*** to make something seem stupid or without value: *The fact that he sent his children to private school makes a mockery of his socialist principles.*
mocking /ˈmɒk.ɪŋ/ [US] /ˈmɑː.kɪŋ/ *adj* when you laugh at someone or something in an unkind way: *a mocking voice* ○ *mocking humour/laughter* **mockingly** /ˈmɒk.ɪŋ.li/ [US] /ˈmɑː.kɪŋ-/ *adv*

mock [ARTIFICIAL] /mɒk/ [US] /mɑːk/ *adj* [before n] not real but appearing or pretending to be exactly like something: *mock cream* ○ *mock leather* ○ *mock surprise*

mock [EXAM] /mɒk/ [US] /mɑːk/ *noun* [C] *UK* an exam taken at school for practice before a real exam: *You will have your mocks during the first two weeks of March.*
▲ **mock *sth* up** *phrasal verb* [M] to make a model of something in order to show people what it will look like or how it will work
mock-up /ˈmɒk.ʌp/ [US] /ˈmɑːk-/ *noun* [C] a full-size model of something large that has not yet been built, which shows how it will look or operate, or which is used when the real thing is not needed: *She showed us a mock-up of what the car will look like when it goes into production.* ○ *Mock-up aircraft are used when we train staff for dealing with emergencies.*

mockers /ˈmɒk.əz/ [US] /ˈmɑː.kɚz/ *plural noun UK INFORMAL* **put the mockers on *sth*** to spoil something or stop it from happening: *It rained, so that rather put the mockers on the barbecue.*

mockingbird /ˈmɒk.ɪŋ.bɜːd/ [US] /ˈmɑː.kɪŋ.bɝːd/ *noun* [C] any of the types of North American or Australian birds which copy the sounds made by other birds

mockney /ˈmɒk.ni/ [US] /ˈmɑːk.ni/ *noun* [U] *INFORMAL DISAPPROVING* pronunciation of English by someone who pretends to speak like a COCKNEY, in order to seem as if they are from a lower social class

ˌmock ˈturtleneck *noun* [C] *US FOR* a **turtleneck**

Mod /mɒd/ [US] /mɑːd/ *noun* [C] a member of a group of young people, especially in Britain in the 1960s, who wore stylish clothes and rode SCOOTERS (= small motorcycles): *Mods and Rockers*

the ˌMoˈD *noun* [S] *ABBREVIATION FOR* the Ministry of Defence: the British government department that is responsible for defence, military activities, and the armed forces

modal (verb) /ˌməʊ.dəlˈvɜːb/ [US] /ˌmoʊ.dəlˈvɝːb/ *noun* [C] *SPECIALIZED* a verb, such as 'can', 'might' and 'must', that is used with another verb to express an idea such as possibility that is not expressed by the main verb of a sentence: *The first verb in the following sentence is a modal: We ought to pay the gas bill.*

ˌmod ˈcons *plural noun UK INFORMAL* the machines and devices, such as washing machines and fridges, which make the ordinary jobs in a home easier: *The kitchen of this delightful cottage is fully equipped with all mod cons including a dishwasher.*

mode [WAY] /məʊd/ [US] /moʊd/ *noun* [C] *SLIGHTLY FORMAL* a way of operating, living or behaving: *Each department in the company has its own mode **of** operation and none of them are compatible.* ○ *Railways are the most important mode **of** transport for the economy.*

mode [MATHS] /məʊd/ [US] /moʊd/ *noun* [C] *SPECIALIZED* the number or value which appears most frequently in a particular set

mode [FASHION] /məʊd/ [US] /moʊd/ *noun SLIGHTLY FORMAL* **be the mode** (especially of clothes) to be fashionable at a particular time: *Miniskirts were very much the mode in the 60s.* ➲See also **a la mode** MODERN.
modish /ˈməʊ.dɪʃ/ [US] /ˈmoʊ-/ *adj SLIGHTLY FORMAL* fashionable **modishly** /ˈməʊ.dɪʃ.li/ [US] /ˈmoʊ-/ *adv*

model [REPRESENTATION] /ˈmɒd.əl/ [US] /ˈmɑː.dəl/ *noun* [C] a representation of something, either as a physical object which is usually smaller than the real object, or as a simple description of the object which might be used in calculations: *a plastic model aircraft* ○ *By looking at this model you can get a better idea of how the bridge will look.* ○ *to construct a statistical/theoretical/mathematical model* ○ *No computer model **of** the economy can predict when the next recession will be.* **model** /ˈmɒd.əl/ [US] /ˈmɑː.dəl/ *verb* [T] **-ll-** or *US USUALLY* **-l-** *to model animals out of clay* ○ *to model clay into animal shapes* ○ *The whole car can be modelled on a computer before a single component is made.*

model [COPY] /ˈmɒd.əl/ [US] /ˈmɑː.dəl/ *noun* [C] something which a copy can be based on because it is an extremely good example of its type: *The educational system was a model for those of many other countries.* ○ *The council plans to build a model town on the site.* ○ *Some groups want to set up an Islamic state **on the** Iranian model.* ○ *Even Chris, **the very** model **of** calmness* (= someone who is usually extremely calm), *was angered by having to work such long hours.* ○ *She really is a model* (= perfect) *student.*

model [PERSON] /ˈmɒd.əl/ [US] /ˈmɑː.dəl/ *noun* [C] a person who wears clothes so that they can be photographed or shown to possible buyers, or a person who is employed to be photographed or painted: *a fashion/nude model* ○ *She's going out with a **male** model.* ○ *I worked as an artist's model when I was a student.* ➲See also **supermodel**.
model /ˈmɒd.əl/ [US] /ˈmɑː.dəl/ *verb* [I or T] **-ll-** or *US USUALLY* **-l-** to wear fashionable clothes, jewellery, etc. in order to advertise them: *Tatjana is modelling a Versace design.* ○ *I used to model when I was younger.*
modelling *UK*, *US* **modeling** /ˈmɒd.əl.ɪŋ/ [US] /ˈmɑː.dəl-/ *noun* [U] the job of wearing clothes, jewellery, etc. in order to advertise them: *Ashley's always wanted to go into modelling.* ○ *a modelling contract*

model [MACHINE] /ˈmɒd.əl/ [US] /ˈmɑː.dəl/ *noun* [C] a particular type of machine, especially a car, which is slightly different from machines of the same type: *a luxury/new model* ○ *the latest model*

▲ **model** *yourself* **on** *sb* phrasal verb to try to make yourself very similar to someone else: *Many of the younger generation of singers modelled themselves on Madonna.*

modem /ˈməʊ.dem/ US /ˈmoʊ.dəm/ noun [C] SPECIALIZED an electronic device which allows one computer to send information to another through standard telephone wires and therefore over long distances

moderate MEDIUM-SIZED /ˈmɒd.ə.rət/ US /ˈmɑː.də-/ adj neither small nor large but between the two; clearly within the limits of a range of possibilities: *moderate growth/inflation* ○ *He's a moderate drinker.* ○ *The cabin is of moderate size – just right for a small family.* ○ *Imposing sanctions is a moderate action when you consider that the alternative is military intervention.* **moderately** /ˈmɒd.ə.rət.li/ US /ˈmɑː.də-/ adv: *There's very little moderately priced housing in this area.* **moderation** /ˌmɒd.ə.reɪ.ʃən/ US /ˌmɑː.də.reɪ-/ noun [U] *You can eat whatever you like as long as it's in moderation.* ○ *All parties will have to show great moderation during these very difficult negotiations.*

• **Moderation in all things.** SAYING said to advise someone that it is best not to have or do too much or too little of anything

moderator /ˈmɒd.ə.reɪ.tər/ US /ˈmɑː.də.reɪ.t̬ə/ noun [C] **1** (US USUALLY **mediator**) FORMAL someone who tries to help other people come to an agreement: *An independent moderator should be appointed to oversee the negotiations.* **2** US someone who makes certain that a formal discussion happens without problems and follows the rules: *He challenged the president to a series of TV debates. Just the two of them, with no moderator.* **3** UK SPECIALIZED someone who makes certain that all the people marking an exam use the same standards: *The final marks awarded for coursework will depend upon the moderator.*

moderate OPINIONS /ˈmɒd.ə.rət/ US /ˈmɑː.də-/ noun [C] describes a person whose opinions, especially their political ones, are not extreme and are therefore acceptable to a large number of people: *He is well-known as a moderate in the party.* **moderate** /ˈmɒd.ə.rət/ US /ˈmɑː.də-/ adj: *The party leader is an extreme left-winger, but her deputy is more moderate in her views.*

moderate SLIGHT /ˈmɒd.ə.rət/ US /ˈmɑː.də-/ adj slight or limited; not as great as desired: *There has been a moderate improvement in her health since she began the treatment.* ○ *We have had moderate success in changing people's attitudes.* **moderately** /ˈmɒd.ə.rət.li/ US /ˈmɑː.də-/ adv: *The company remains moderately profitable, but it is not making as much money as it should.*

moderate REDUCE /ˈmɒd.ə.reɪt/ US /ˈmɑː.də.reɪt/ verb [I or T] to (cause to) become less in size, strength, or force; to reduce something: *There have been repeated calls for the president to moderate his stance on contraception.* ○ *Weather conditions have moderated, making a rescue attempt possible.* **moderation** /ˌmɒd.ə.reɪ.ʃən/ US /ˌmɑː.də.reɪ-/ noun [U] SLIGHTLY FORMAL *We can't sail until there is some moderation of the storm.*

modern MOST RECENT /ˈmɒd.ən/ US /ˈmɑː.də.n/ adj designed and made using the most recent ideas and methods: *modern technology/architecture/medicine/art* ○ *We're in the very modern-looking building opposite the station.* ○ APPROVING *My grandpa's attitudes are very modern, considering his age.* **modernistic** /ˌmɒd.ən.ˈɪs.tɪk/ US /ˌmɑː.də.ˈnɪs-/ adj designed in a way that is obviously modern: *The new airport has a very modernistic appearance.* **modernity** /mɒd.ˈɜː.nə.ti/ US /mɑː.ˈdɜː.nə.t̬i/ noun [U] the condition that results from being modern: *There is a stark contrast between tradition and modernity on the streets of the city.* **modernize**, UK USUALLY **-ise** /ˈmɒd.ə.naɪz/ US /ˈmɑː.də.naɪz/ verb [I or T] *Much of the house has been modernized.* ○ *There has been a lot of opposition to modernizing working practices.* ○ *If they want to increase output from the factory, they'll have to modernize.* **modernization**, UK USUALLY **-isation** /ˌmɒd.ə.naɪˈzeɪ.ʃən/ US /ˌmɑː.də.naɪ-/ noun [U] *The modernization of the 100-year-old sewage and water systems will cost millions of pounds.*

modern PRESENT /ˈmɒd.ən/ US /ˈmɑː.də.n/ adj of the present or recent times, especially the period of history since THE MIDDLE AGES (= the period from about 1000 AD to 1500 AD): *What do you think is the role of religion in the modern world?*

modern 'dance noun [U] a style of dance usually performed in a theatre, which expresses the dancer's feelings and does not have many rules about the dancer's movements

modern-day /ˈmɒd.ən.deɪ/ US /ˈmɑː.də.n-/ adj relating to people or things from modern times and not from some time in the past: *Modern-day engines are so much more efficient.*

modernism /ˈmɒd.ən.ɪ.z²m/ US /ˈmɑː.də.nɪ-/ noun [U] **1** modern thinking or methods: *Modernism seeks to find new forms of expression and rejects traditional or accepted ideas.* **2** SPECIALIZED the ideas and methods of modern art, especially in the simple design of buildings in the 1940s, 50s and 60s which were made from modern materials **modernist** /ˈmɒd.ən.ɪst/ US /ˈmɑː.də.nɪst/ adj, noun [C]

modern 'jazz noun [U] a type of jazz which began in the 1940s and 1950s

modern 'languages plural noun MAINLY UK languages that are spoken at the present time, especially European languages such as French, German and Spanish

modest NOT LARGE /ˈmɒd.ɪst/ US /ˈmɑː.dɪst/ adj not large in size or amount, or not expensive: *They live in a fairly modest house, considering their wealth.* ○ *There has been a modest improvement/recovery in housing conditions for the poor.* ○ *The party made modest gains in the elections, but nothing like the huge gains that were predicted.* ○ *Just a modest portion for me, please.* **modestly** /ˈmɒd.ɪst.li/ US /ˈmɑː.dɪst-/ adv: *At just £9, the training video is very modestly priced.*

modest QUIETLY SUCCESSFUL /ˈmɒd.ɪst/ US /ˈmɑː.dɪst/ adj APPROVING tending not to talk about or make obvious your own abilities and achievements: *He's very modest about his achievements.* **modestly** /ˈmɒd.ɪst.li/ US /ˈmɑː.dɪst-/ adv

modesty /ˈmɒd.ɪ.sti/ US /ˈmɑː.dɪ-/ noun [U] APPROVING when someone tends not to talk about or make obvious their abilities and achievements: *She does a lot of work for charities, but her modesty forbids her from talking about it.*

• **in all modesty** said when you want to say something good about yourself, but do not want to seem to think you are too important: *Quite frankly, and in all modesty, we'd probably have lost the game if I hadn't been playing.*

modest CLOTHES/BEHAVIOUR /ˈmɒd.ɪst/ US /ˈmɑː.dɪst/ adj OLD-FASHIONED describes something such as a woman's clothes or behaviour, which is intended to avoid attracting sexual interest: *a modest walk/manner* **modestly** /ˈmɒd.ɪst.li/ US /ˈmɑː.dɪst-/ adv: *She was dressed modestly.* **modesty** /ˈmɒd.ɪ.sti/ US /ˈmɑː.dɪ-/ noun [U]

modicum /ˈmɒd.ɪ.kəm/ US /ˈmɑː.dɪ-/ noun [S] FORMAL a small amount of something good such as truth or honesty: *There's not even a modicum of truth in her statement.* ○ *Anyone with a modicum of common sense could have seen that the plan wouldn't work.*

modified A'merican 'plan noun [U] (ABBREVIATION MAP) US FOR **half board**

modify CHANGE /ˈmɒd.ɪ.faɪ/ US /ˈmɑː.dɪ-/ verb [T] to change something such as a plan, opinion, law or way of behaviour slightly, usually to improve it or make it more acceptable: *Instead of simply punishing them, the system encourages offenders to modify their behaviour.* ○ *The proposals were unpopular and were only accepted in a modified form.* **modification** /ˌmɒd.ɪ.fɪˈkeɪ.ʃən/ US /ˌmɑː.dɪ-/ noun [C or U] *Modification of the engine to run on lead-free fuel is fairly simple.* ○ *A couple of modifications and the speech will be perfect.*

modify LIMIT /ˈmɒd.ɪ.faɪ/ US /ˈmɑː.dɪ-/ verb [T] SPECIALIZED If a word or phrase modifies another word or phrase used with it, it limits or adds to its meaning: *In the sentence 'She ran quickly', the adverb 'quickly' modifies the verb 'ran'.* **modification** /ˌmɒd.ɪ.fɪˈkeɪ.ʃən/ US /ˌmɑː.dɪ-/ noun [U] **modifier** /ˈmɒd.ɪ.faɪ.ə/ US /ˈmɑː.dɪ.faɪ.ə/

noun [C] *In 'safety barrier', the noun 'safety' is being used as a modifier.*

modish /ˈməʊ.dɪʃ/ ⓊⓈ /ˈmoʊ-/ *adj* ⊃See at **mode** FASHION.

modulate [VOICE] /ˈmɒd.jʊ.leɪt/ ⓊⓈ /ˈmɑː.dʒə-/ *verb* [T] to change the style, loudness, etc. of something such as your voice in order to achieve an effect or express an emotion: *His gentle introductory tone modulates into a football coach's pre-game pep talk.* **modulation** /ˌmɒd.-jʊˈleɪ.ʃᵊn/ ⓊⓈ /ˌmɑː.dʒə-/ *noun* [C or U]

modulate [CHANGE] /ˈmɒd.jʊ.leɪt/ ⓊⓈ /ˈmɑː.dʒə-/ *verb* [T] FORMAL to change something, such as an action or a process, to make it more suitable for its situation: *An elected committee will meet monthly to modulate the council's energy policy.* **modulation** /ˌmɒd.jʊˈleɪ.ʃᵊn/ ⓊⓈ /ˌmɑː.dʒə-/ *noun* [C or U]

modulate [BROADCASTING] /ˈmɒd.jʊ.leɪt/ ⓊⓈ /ˈmɑː.dʒə-/ *verb* [T] SPECIALIZED to mix an electrical signal which represents sounds or pictures with a radio signal so that it can be broadcast **modulation** /ˌmɒd.jʊˈleɪ.ʃᵊn/ ⓊⓈ /ˌmɑː.dʒə-/ *noun* [C or U] *frequency/amplitude modulation* ⊃See also **AM** RADIO; **FM**.

module /ˈmɒd.juːl/ ⓊⓈ /ˈmɑː.dʒuːl/ *noun* [C] **1** one of a set of separate parts which, when combined, form a complete whole: *The emergency building is transported in individual modules, such as bedrooms and a kitchen, which are put together on site.* ○ *The full computer program is made up of several modules (= small programs) which should be individually tested before being integrated.* **2** one of the units which together make a complete course taught especially at a college or university **3** a part of a spacecraft which can operate independently of the other parts, especially when separate from them: *a lunar landing module* **modular** /ˈmɒd.jʊ.lə/ ⓊⓈ /ˈmɑː.dʒə.lɚ/ *adj*: *Many colleges and universities now offer modular degree courses.*

modus operandi /ˌməʊ.dəs.ɒp.əˈræn.diː/ ⓊⓈ /ˌmoʊ.dəs-ˌoʊ.pəˈrɑːn.di/ *noun* [S] SPECIALIZED a particular way of doing something

modus vivendi /ˌməʊ.dəs.vɪˈven.diː/ ⓊⓈ /ˌmoʊ.dəs.viː-ˈven.di/ *noun* [S] FORMAL an arrangement allowing people or groups of people who have different opinions or beliefs to work or live together: *Our two countries must put aside the memory of war and seek a modus vivendi.*

moggy /ˈmɒg.i/ ⓊⓈ /ˈmɑː.gi/ *noun* [C] (ALSO **moggie**) UK INFORMAL a cat, especially one which is ordinary or has an untidy appearance

mogul [PERSON] /ˈməʊ.gᵊl/ ⓊⓈ /ˈmoʊ-/ *noun* [C] an important person who has great wealth or power: *movie/media/industry moguls*

mogul [SNOW] /ˈməʊ.gᵊl/ ⓊⓈ /ˈmoʊ-/ *noun* [C] SPECIALIZED a small pile of hard snow on the side of a hill or mountain used for skiing, created to add interest and difficulty to the sport

mohair /ˈməʊ.heə/ ⓊⓈ /ˈmoʊ.her/ *noun* [U] a soft wool or cloth made from the outer hair of ANGORA goats (= goats with long soft hair): *a mohair jumper*

Mohammed /məʊˈhæm.ɪd/ ⓊⓈ /moʊ-/ *noun* the Arab holy man on whose life and teaching Islam is based

Mohican UK /məʊˈhiː.kᵊn/ ⓊⓈ /moʊ-/ *noun* [C] (US **Mohawk**) a sometimes brightly coloured hairstyle, often worn in PUNK fashion, in which the hair is removed from the sides of the head and a central strip is made to point out from the head ⊃See picture **Hairstyles and Hats** on page Centre 8

moi /mwɑː/ *pronoun* HUMOROUS used instead of 'me', to express false surprise about something that you have been accused of: *Extravagant, moi?*

moist /mɔɪst/ *adj* slightly wet, especially in a good way: *Keep the soil in the pot moist, but not too wet.* ○ APPROVING *This cake is lovely and moist!* ⊃See also **damp**. **moisten** /ˈmɔɪ.sᵊn/ *verb* [I or T] to make something slightly wet or to become slightly wet: *Moisten the cloth before using it to clean glass.* **moistness** /ˈmɔɪst.nəs/ *noun* [U]

moisture /ˈmɔɪs.tʃə/ ⓊⓈ /-tʃɚ/ *noun* [U] a liquid such as water in the form of very small drops, either in the air, in a substance, or on a surface: *These plants need a rich soil which retains moisture.*

moisturizer, UK USUALLY **-iser** /ˈmɔɪs.tʃᵊr.aɪ.zə/ ⓊⓈ /-tʃɚ.aɪ.zɚ/ *noun* [C or U] a cream that you put on your skin to stop it from becoming dry: *I use (a) moisturizer every night.* **moisturize**, UK USUALLY **-ise** /ˈmɔɪs.tʃᵊr.aɪz/ ⓊⓈ /-tʃɚ-/ *verb* [I or T] *You should cleanse, tone and moisturize (your skin) every day.*

molar /ˈməʊ.lə/ ⓊⓈ /ˈmoʊ.lɚ/ *noun* [C] one of the large teeth at the back of the mouth in humans and some other animals used for crushing and chewing food ⊃Compare **canine (tooth)** at canine; **incisor**.

molasses /məˈlæs.ɪz/ *noun* [U] a thick dark brown liquid made from sugar plants which is used in cooking

mold /məʊld/ ⓊⓈ /moʊld/ *noun, verb* US FOR **mould**

molder /ˈməʊl.də/ ⓊⓈ /ˈmoʊl.dɚ/ *verb* [I] US FOR **moulder**

mole [ANIMAL] /məʊl/ ⓊⓈ /moʊl/ *noun* [C] a small mammal which is nearly blind, has dark fur and lives in passages that it digs under the ground

mole [SPOT] /məʊl/ ⓊⓈ /moʊl/ *noun* [C] a small dark spot or lump on a person's skin ⊃Compare **freckle**.

mole [PERSON] /məʊl/ ⓊⓈ /moʊl/ *noun* [C] a person who works for an organization or government and secretly gives information to its competitor or enemy: *A mole inside the Department of Transport had leaked secret proposals to the press.* ⊃Compare **spy** SECRET PERSON.

molecular biology *noun* [U] SPECIALIZED the study of the structure and action of important molecules which are found in living things

molecule /ˈmɒl.ɪ.kjuːl/ ⓊⓈ /ˈmɑː.lɪ-/ *noun* [C] SPECIALIZED the simplest unit of a chemical substance, usually a group of two or more atoms **molecular** /məˈlek.jʊ.lə/ ⓊⓈ /-lɚ/ *adj*

molehill /ˈməʊl.hɪl/ ⓊⓈ /ˈmoʊl-/ *noun* [C] a small pile of earth pushed up to the surface of the ground by the digging of a MOLE (= a mammal that lives underground)

moleskin /ˈməʊl.skɪn/ ⓊⓈ /ˈmoʊl-/ *noun* [U] a type of strong cotton cloth which is slightly furry on one side: *moleskin trousers*

molest [ATTACK SEXUALLY] /məˈlest/ *verb* [T] to touch or attack someone in a sexual way against their wishes: *The girl had been molested frequently by her stepfather from the age of eight.* ○ *The man had previously been arrested several times for molesting young boys.* **molestation** /ˌmɒl.esˈteɪ.ʃᵊn/ ⓊⓈ /ˌmɑː.les-/ *noun* [U] *sexual molestation* **molester** /məˈles.tə/ ⓊⓈ /-tɚ/ *noun* [C] *a child molester*

molest [ATTACK] /məˈlest/ *verb* [T] FORMAL to touch, push, etc. someone violently: *United Nations premises were looted and personnel were molested by demonstrators.* **molestation** /ˌmɒl.esˈteɪ.ʃᵊn/ ⓊⓈ /ˌmɑː.les-/ *noun* [U]

moll /mɒl/ ⓊⓈ /mɑːl/ *noun* [C] **1** US SLANG a female companion of a GANGSTER (= violent criminal) **2** AUS a female companion of a member of a group of people who ride motorcycles or SURF together

mollify /ˈmɒl.ɪ.faɪ/ ⓊⓈ /ˈmɑː.lɪ-/ *verb* [T] to make someone less angry or upset: *I tried to mollify her by giving her flowers.*

mollusc /ˈmɒl.əsk/ ⓊⓈ /ˈmɑː.ləsk/ *noun* [C] (US ALSO **mollusk**) any animal which has a soft body, no spine and is often covered with a shell. Many molluscs live in water: *Oysters are molluscs, as are snails and cuttlefish.*

mollycoddle /ˈmɒl.iˌkɒd.l̩/ ⓊⓈ /ˈmɑː.liˌkɑː.dl̩/ *verb* [T] INFORMAL MAINLY DISAPPROVING to give someone too much care or protection: *You're not helping the children by mollycoddling them – they have to grow up sometime.*

Molotov cocktail /ˌmɒl.ə.tɒfˈkɒk.teɪl/ ⓊⓈ /ˌmɑː.lə.tɑːf-ˈkɑːk-/ *noun* [C] OLD-FASHIONED a type of **petrol bomb**

molt /məʊlt/ ⓊⓈ /moʊlt/ *noun, verb* US FOR **moult**

molten /ˈməʊl.tᵊn/ ⓊⓈ /ˈmoʊl-/ *adj* describes metal or rock that is in a liquid state because of great heat: *molten glass/lava/lead*

molybdenum /mɒlˈɪb.dɪ.nəm/ ⓊⓈ /mɑːˈlɪb-/ *noun* [U] a very hard silver-coloured metallic element used especially to make steel stronger

mom /mɒm/ ⓊⓈ /mɑːm/ *noun* [C] US FOR **mum** MOTHER: *I miss my mom and dad a lot.* ○ [as form of address] *Aw, Mom, why can't I go?*

moment [SHORT TIME] /ˈməʊ.mənt/ ⓊⓈ /ˈmoʊ-/ *noun* [C] a very short period of time: *Can you wait a moment?* ○ *I'll*

M

be ready ***in*** *just* ***a*** *moment.* ○ *A car drew up outside and* ***a few*** *moments later the doorbell rang.* ○ *I'm expecting her to come* ***at any*** *moment* (= very soon). ○ *Have you* ***got a*** *moment* (= Are you busy or have you got time to speak to me)*?*

• **not a moment too soon** used to say that something happened when it was almost too late: *Help arrived – and not a moment too soon.*

• **not for a moment** used to say that you do not think or do something at all: *I don't believe that story for a moment.*

• **the moment of truth** an occasion when something important happens which tests someone or something and which will have an effect on the future: *Lift-off is always the moment of truth for a new rocket.*

momentary /ˈməʊ.mən.tri/ [US] /ˈmoʊ-/ *adj* lasting for a very short time: *a momentary hesitation*

momentarily /ˌməʊ.mənˈter.ɪ.li/ [US] /ˌmoʊ-/ *adv* **1** for a very short time: *She was momentarily confused by the foreign road signs.* **2** US very soon: *I'll be ready to leave momentarily.*

moment [OCCASION] /ˈməʊ.mənt/ [US] /ˈmoʊ-/ *noun* **[C]** a particular time or occasion: *When would be* ***the*** *best moment to tell the family?* ○ *Don't leave it to/till* ***the last*** *moment* (= the latest time possible). ○ *If you want a private conversation with her you'll have to* ***choose*** *your moment* (= find a suitable time). ○ ***The*** *moment* ***(that)*** (= As soon as) *I get the money I'll send the ticket.*

• **at the moment** now: *I'm afraid she's not here at the moment.*

• **at this moment in time** FORMAL now: *I can give no information at this precise moment in time.*

• **for the moment** If you do something for the moment, you are doing it now, but might do something different in the future: *Let's carry on with what we agreed for the moment.*

• **have *your*/its moments** to be sometimes very successful: *This album may not be as good as their last one but it has its moments.*

COMMON LEARNER ERROR

at that moment

Remember to use the preposition 'at' in the phrase **at that moment**.

At that moment all the lights went out.

~~*In that moment all the lights went out.*~~

moment [IMPORTANCE] /ˈməʊ.mənt/ [US] /ˈmoʊ-/ *noun* FORMAL **of (great) moment** very important: *a decision of great moment* ➲See also **momentous**.

momentous /məˈmen.təs/ [US] /-t̬əs/ *adj* very important because of effects on future events: *the momentous news of the President's death* ○ *Whether or not to move overseas was a momentous* ***decision*** *for the family.* **momentously** /məˈmen.tə.sli/ [US] /-t̬ə-/ *adv* **momentousness** /məˈmen.tə.snəs/ [US] /-t̬ə-/ *noun* **[U]**

momentum /məˈmen.təm/ [US] /-t̬əm/ *noun* **[U]** the force that keeps an object moving or keeps an event developing after it has started: *Once you push it, it keeps going* ***under*** *its own momentum.* ○ *The spacecraft will fly round the Earth to* ***gain/gather*** *momentum for its trip to Jupiter.* ○ *The play* ***loses*** *momentum* (= becomes less interesting, energetic, etc.) *by its half-way stage.* ○ *In an attempt to* ***give*** *new momentum to their plans, the committee set a date for starting detailed discussions.*

momma /ˈmɒm.ə/ [US] /ˈmɑː.mə/ *noun* **[C]** US INFORMAL FOR **mother** PARENT

mommy /ˈmɒm.i/ [US] /ˈmɑː.mi/ *noun* **[C]** US INFORMAL FOR **mummy** MOTHER

Mon WRITTEN ABBREVIATION FOR Monday

monarch /ˈmɒn.ək/ [US] /ˈmɑː.nɚk/ *noun* **[C]** a king or queen: *a* ***hereditary*** *monarch* ○ *Britain's head of state is a* ***constitutional*** *monarch* (= only has very limited powers). **monarchic** /məˈnɑː.kɪk/ [US] /-ˈnɑːr-/ *adj* (ALSO **monarchical**) FORMAL

monarchist /ˈmɒn.ə.kɪst/ [US] /ˈmɑː.nɚ-/ *noun* **[C]** a person who supports the system of having a king or queen

monarchy /ˈmɒn.ə.ki/ [US] /ˈmɑː.nɚ-/ *noun* **1 [C]** a country which has a king or queen **2 [U]** the system of having a king or queen: *Is monarchy relevant in the modern world or should it be abolished?*

monastery /ˈmɒn.ə.stri/ [US] /ˈmɑː.nə.ster.i/ *noun* **[C]** a building in which monks live and worship ➲Compare **convent**; **nunnery** at **nun**.

monastic /məˈnæs.tɪk/ *adj* **1** connected with monks or monasteries **2** describes a simple way of living with few possessions and no people near you: *a monastic life* **monasticism** /məˈnæs.tɪ.sɪ.zᵊm/ *noun* **[U]** the way monks live

Monday /ˈmʌn.deɪ/ *noun* **[C or U]** (WRITTEN ABBREVIATION **Mon**) the day of the week after Sunday and before Tuesday: *I start my new job* ***on*** *Monday.* ○ UK INFORMAL OR US *They'll be arriving Monday.* ○ ***last*** *Monday* ○ ***next*** *Monday* ○ *Term doesn't start* ***this*** *Monday* (= the first one from now), *it starts (on) Monday* ***week*** (= the second one from now). ○ *Don't you hate going back to school* ***on*** *Mondays?* ○ *The baby was born* ***on*** *a Monday.* ○ *She went home on* ***the*** *Monday* (= on the Monday of that particular week).

• **Monday morning feeling** (AUS **Mondayitis**) INFORMAL the way people feel after the WEEKEND (= Saturday and Sunday) when they do not want to go to work or school: *I've got* ***that*** *Monday morning feeling.*

• **Monday-morning quarterback** US someone who says how an event or problem should have been dealt with by others after it has already been dealt with

monetarism /ˈmʌn.ɪ.tᵊr.ɪ.zᵊm/ [US] /-t̬ɚ.ɪ-/ *noun* **[U]** a system of controlling a country's economy by limiting how much money is in use at a particular time **monetarist** /ˈmʌn.ɪ.tᵊr.ɪst/ [US] /-t̬ɚ-/ *noun* **[C]**, *adj*: *She's a convinced monetarist.* ○ *monetarist policies*

monetary /ˈmʌn.ɪ.tri/ *adj* relating to the money in a country: *monetary policy* ○ *monetary control* ○ *The monetary unit of the UK is the pound.*

ˈmonetary ˌsystem *noun* **[C]** the system used by a country to provide money and to control the exchange of money

money /ˈmʌn.i/ *noun* **[U]** **1** the coins or notes which are used to buy things, or the amount of these that one person has: *"How much money have you got on you?" "£10 in notes and a few coins."* ○ *We invested the money in a high-interest bank account.* ○ *I wanted to buy it but it* ***cost*** *too much money* (= was too expensive). ○ *We* ***spent*** *so much money redecorating the house that we didn't have any left over for a holiday.* ○ *You can't pay in English money. You'll have to* ***change*** *some money* (= buy some foreign money) *at the bank.* ○ *How much money do you* ***earn*** (= What are you paid to do your job)*?* ○ *He enjoyed acting but he wasn't* ***making*** (= earning) *much money.* ○ *Her investments haven't* ***made*** (= produced as profit) *much money this year.* ○ *They* ***made*** *their money* (= became rich) *in the fashion business.* ○ *He tried to persuade me to* ***put*** *money* ***into*** *the company* (= invest in the company). ○ *We need to* ***raise*** (= collect) *money for a new school pool from the parents.* ○ *Try to* ***save*** (= keep) *some money for your holiday.* ○ *We're* ***saving*** (= not spending as much) *money by using volunteers.* ○ *I didn't like the job, but* ***the*** *money* (= amount of pay) *was good.* ○ *Money is* ***tight/short*** (= We haven't got much money) *at the moment.* ○ *I had some very expensive dental treatment recently – but it was money* ***well spent*** *– it'll save me problems in the future.* **2 money in *sth*** If you say that there is money in something, you mean that the activity will produce a profit: *There's money in sport these days.* ○ *There's money in it for you.*

• **for my money** in my opinion: *For my money, Sunday is the best day to travel because the roads are quiet.*

• **have money** to be rich: *I believe her family has money.*

• **get/have *your* money's worth** to receive good value from something you have paid for: *He's had his money's worth out of that suit – he's been wearing it for years.*

• **be in the money** to suddenly have a lot of money: *If we win this competition we'll be in the money.*

• **be made of money** to be very rich: *No you can't have a new computer game. I'm not made of money, you know.*

• **marry money** to marry a rich person: *One way to get rich is to marry money.*

• **money for old rope** (ALSO **money for jam**) UK money you get for doing something very easy: *Babysitting is money* *for old rope if the children don't wake up.*

• **have money to burn** to spend a lot of money on things that are not necessary: *I don't know what her job is but she certainly seems to have money to burn.*

• **put *your* money where *your* mouth is** INFORMAL to show by your actions and not just your words that you support or believe in something

• **put (your) money on sb/sth 1** to bet on someone or something winning a race or competition: *He put £10 on the horse in the 5 o'clock race.* **2** to strongly believe that someone will do something or that something will happen: *Chris will be promoted – I'd put money on it.*

• **Money talks.** SAYING said about people or organizations that are rich, and can therefore get or do what they want

• **Money doesn't grow on trees.** SAYING said to warn someone that they have to be careful how much money they spend, because there is only a limited amount: *"Mum, I'd like a new bike." "I'll have to think about it – money doesn't grow on trees, you know!"*

• **You pays your money and you takes your chance/choice.** INFORMAL HUMOROUS SAYING said to someone who must decide between different things and accept the results of their decision

moneyed /ˈmʌn.id/ *adj* FORMAL rich: *a moneyed family*

moneybags /ˈmʌn.i.bægz/ *noun* [C] *plural* **moneybags** INFORMAL DISAPPROVING a rich person

moneybox /ˈmʌn.i.bɒks/ ⓤ /-bɑːks/ *noun* [C] MAINLY UK a closed container in which money is kept, especially one with a hole in the top through which coins can be pushed

money-grubbing /ˈmʌn.i.grʌb.ɪŋ/ *adj* DISAPPROVING Someone or something that is money-grubbing has money as their main interest and does anything they can to get lots of it.

moneylender /ˈmʌn.iˌlen.dəʳ/ ⓤ /-dɚ/ *noun* [C] MAINLY DISAPPROVING a person or organization whose job is to lend money to people in return for payment: *Families with money problems often fall into the hands of the moneylenders and get further into debt.*

money-maker /ˈmʌn.i.meɪ.kəʳ/ ⓤ /-kɚ/ *noun* [C] (ALSO **money-spinner**) a product or activity which produces a lot of money:

money ˌmarket *noun* [C or U] the system in which banks and other similar organizations buy and sell money from each other

money-minded /ˈmʌn.iˌmaɪn.dɪd/ *adj* interested in money and good at getting or saving it: *I've never been very money-minded – I leave all my business affairs to my financial adviser.*

money ˌorder US *noun* [C] (UK **postal order**) an official piece of paper with an amount of money written on it, which you send through the post to someone, who can then exchange it for the same amount of money at a post office

money ˌsupply *noun* [C usually sing] all the money which is in use in a country

-monger /-mʌŋ.gəʳ/ ⓤ /-gɚ/ *suffix* MAINLY DISAPPROVING a person who encourages a particular activity, especially one which causes trouble: *They're nothing but a bunch of war-mongers.* ➔See also **ironmonger**; **fishmonger**. **-mongering** /-mʌŋ.gə.rɪŋ/ ⓤ /-gɚ.ɪŋ/ *suffix*: *They accused him of rumour-mongering/scandal-mongering.*

mongol /ˈmɒŋ.gəl/ ⓤ /ˈmɑːŋ-/ *noun* [C] (US ALSO **mongoloid**) OFFENSIVE OLD-FASHIONED a person who has DOWN'S SYNDROME

mongolism /ˈmɒŋ.g-ºl.ɪ.zºm/ ⓤ /ˈmɑːŋ-/ *noun* [U] OFFENSIVE OLD-FASHIONED **Down's syndrome**

mongoose /ˈmɒŋ.guːs/ ⓤ /ˈmɑːŋ-/ *noun* [C] *plural* **mongooses** a small tropical animal with a long tail which eats snakes, rats and birds' eggs

mongrel /ˈmʌŋ.grəl/ *noun* [C] (US INFORMAL ALSO **mutt**) MAINLY DISAPPROVING a dog whose parents are of different breeds

monies /ˈmʌn.iz/ *plural noun* FORMAL amounts of money: *Any monies received from this interest will be treated as capital.*

moniker /ˈmɒn.ɪ.kəʳ/ ⓤ /ˈmɑː.nɪ.kɚ/ *noun* [C] (ALSO **monicker**) HUMOROUS a name or NICKNAME

monitor SCREEN /ˈmɒn.ɪ.təʳ/ ⓤ /ˈmɑː.nɪ.tɚ/ *noun* [C] a device with a screen on which words or pictures can be shown: *a computer monitor* ○ *a TV monitor* ○ *Doctors watched the old man's heartbeat on a monitor.*

monitor WATCH /ˈmɒn.ɪ.təʳ/ ⓤ /ˈmɑː.nɪ.tɚ/ *verb* [T] to watch and check a situation carefully for a period of time in order to discover something about it: *The new findings suggest that women ought to monitor their cholesterol levels.* ○ *The CIA were monitoring* (= secretly listening to) *his phone calls.*

monitor /ˈmɒn.ɪ.təʳ/ ⓤ /ˈmɑː.nɪ.tɚ/ *noun* [C] **1** a person who has the job of watching or noticing particular things: *United Nations monitors were not allowed to enter the area.* **2** a machine which regularly tests something: *a radiation monitor* **3** a child in school who has special jobs to do: *the library monitor*

monk /mʌŋk/ *noun* [C] a member of a group of religious men who do not marry and usually live together in a monastery

monkey ANIMAL /ˈmʌŋ.ki/ *noun* [C] an animal that lives in hot countries, has a long tail and climbs trees. Monkeys are PRIMATES (= the group of animals which are most like humans). ➔See picture **Animals and Birds** on page Centre 4

• **not give a monkey's** UK SLANG If you don't/couldn't give a monkey's about something, you are not at all worried by it: *"Chrissie won't like it." "I don't give a monkey's."*

• **I'll be a monkey's uncle!** OLD-FASHIONED used to show you are very surprised

• **make a monkey out of sb** to make someone appear stupid

monkey CHILD /ˈmʌŋ.ki/ *noun* [C] INFORMAL a child who behaves badly: *They ate all the cakes, the monkeys.* ○ [as form of address] *Hey, put that down, you little monkey!*

monkey COPY /ˈmʌŋ.ki/ *verb* [T] US INFORMAL to copy or MIMIC someone

▲ **monkey about/around (with sth)** *phrasal verb* INFORMAL DISAPPROVING to behave, or to use or move things, in a silly and careless way: *The children were bored and started monkeying around.*

monkey ˌbusiness *noun* [U] behaviour which is not acceptable or is dishonest: *The teacher suspected that there had been some monkey business going on in the class.*

monkey-puzzle (tree) /ˈmʌŋ.ki.pʌz.lˌtriː/ *noun* [C] a type of large evergreen tree with stiff branches which spread out at the side and very dark green sharp leaves

monkey ˌwrench *noun* [C] MAINLY US FOR a tool which can be adjusted to tighten or unfasten any size of nut and bolt

mono SOUND /ˈmɒn.əʊ/ ⓤ /ˈmɑː.noʊ/ *noun* [U] recorded or broadcast sound that comes from a single direction: *The recording was available in mono or stereo.* **mono** /ˈmɒn.əʊ/ ⓤ /ˈmɑː.noʊ/ *adj*: *an old mono record player* ➔Compare **stereo**; **quadraphonic**.

mono DISEASE /ˈmɒn.əʊ/ ⓤ /ˈmɑː.noʊ/ *noun* [U] US INFORMAL FOR **mononucleosis**

mono- SINGLE /mɒn.əʊ-/ ⓤ /mɑː.noʊ-/ *prefix* one; single: *monolingual* ○ *a monorail*

monochrome /ˈmɒn.ə.krəʊm/ ⓤ /ˈmɑː.nə.kroʊm/ *adj* **1** using only black, white and grey, or using only one colour: *Kodak still produces monochrome film.* ○ *The park in winter is a depressing monochrome brown.* **2** MAINLY UK not interesting or exciting: *a monochrome, dreary existence* **monochromatic** /ˌmɒn.əʊ.krəˈmæt.ɪk/ ⓤ /ˌmɑː.noʊ.krəˈmæt̬-/ *adj*

monocle /ˈmɒn.ə.kl̩/ ⓤ /ˈmɑː.nə-/ *noun* [C] a round piece of glass worn, especially in the past, in front of one eye in order to help you to see more clearly

monogamy /məˈnɒg.ə.mi/ ⓤ /məˈnɑː.gə-/ *noun* [U] when someone has a sexual relationship or marriage with only one other person at a time ➔Compare **bigamy**; **polygamy**. **monogamous** /məˈnɒg.ə.məs/ ⓤ /məˈnɑː.gə-/ *adj*: *a monogamous relationship*

monogram /ˈmɒn.ə.græm/ ⓤ /ˈmɑː.nə-/ *noun* [C] a symbol, usually formed from the first letters of a person's names joined together, which is sewn or marked on clothes or other possessions: *handkerchiefs/ towels with his monogram in the corner* **mono-**

grammed /ˈmɒn.ə.græmd/ [US] /ˈmɑː.nə-/ *adj*: *monogrammed envelopes*

monograph /ˈmɒn.ə.grɑːf/ /-græf/ [US] /ˈmɑː.nə.græf/ *noun* [C] a long article or a short book on a particular subject: *He has just published a monograph **on** Beethoven's symphonies.*

monolingual /ˌmɒn.əʊˈlɪŋ.gwəl/ [US] /ˌmɑː.noʊ-/ *adj* speaking or using only one language: *This is a monolingual dictionary.* ➲Compare **bilingual**; **multilingual**.

monolith /ˈmɒn.ə.lɪθ/ [US] /ˈmɑː.nə-/ *noun* [C] a large block of stone standing by itself which was put up by people in the distant past

monolithic /ˌmɒn.əˈlɪθ.ɪk/ [US] /ˌmɑː.nə-/ *adj* DISAPPROVING too large, too regular or without interesting differences, and unwilling or unable to be changed: *monolithic state-run organizations*

monologue /ˈmɒn.əl.ɒg/ [US] /ˈmɑː.nə.lɑːg/ *noun* [C] **1** a long speech by one person: DISAPPROVING *He subjected me to a monologue **on** his last stay in hospital.* **2** a short play for one actor: *Alan Bennett wrote a series of monologues called Talking Heads.*

monomania /ˌmɒn.əʊˈmeɪ.ni.ə/ [US] /ˌmɑː.noʊ-/ *noun* [C or U] when someone is too interested in one thing **monomaniac** /ˌmɒn.əʊˈmeɪ.ni.æk/ [US] /ˌmɑː.noʊ-/ *adj, noun* **monomaniacal** /ˌmɒn.əʊ.məˈnaɪə.kəl/ [US] /ˌmɑː.noʊ-/ *adj*: *His interest in personal fitness borders on the monomaniacal.*

mononucleosis /ˌmɒn.əʊˌnjuː.kliˈəʊ.sɪs/ [US] /ˌmɑː.noʊˌnuː.kliˈoʊ-/ *noun* [U] (INFORMAL **mono**) MAINLY US FOR **glandular fever** (= an infectious disease which makes you feel weak and ill for a long time)

monoplane /ˈmɒn.ə.pleɪn/ [US] /ˈmɑː.nə-/ *noun* [C] an aircraft with a single pair of wings ➲Compare **biplane**.

monopoly /məˈnɒp.əl.i/ [US] /-ˈnɑː.pəl-/ *noun* [C or S] (an organization or group which has) complete control of something, especially an area of business, so that others have no share: *The government is determined to protect its tobacco monopoly.* ○ *Is Microsoft a monopoly?* ○ *The drafting of a new constitution cannot be **a** monopoly **of** the white minority regime* (= other people should do it too). ○ *He does not **have a/the** monopoly **on*** (= He is not the only one who has) *good looks.* **monopolistic** /məˌnɒp.əlˈɪs.tɪk/ [US] /-ˌnɑː.pəˈlɪs-/ *adj* USUALLY DISAPPROVING **monopolize**, UK USUALLY **-ise** /məˈnɒp.əl.aɪz/ [US] /-ˈnɑː.pə.laɪz/ *verb* [T] **1** in business, to control something completely and to prevent other people having any effect on what happens: *The company had monopolized the photography market for so many decades that they didn't worry about competition from other companies.* **2** If someone monopolizes a person or a conversation they talk a lot or stop other people being involved: *She completely monopolized the conversation at lunch.* **monopolization**, UK USUALLY **-isation** /məˌnɒp.əl.aɪˈzeɪ.ʃən/ [US] /-ˌnɑː.pəl-/ *noun* [U]

monorail /ˈmɒn.ə.reɪl/ [US] /ˈmɑː.nə-/ *noun* [C] a railway system which has a single RAIL (= long metal bar on which the train travels), often above ground level, or the train which travels along it

monosodium glutamate /ˌmɒn.əˌsəʊ.di.əmˈgluː.tə.meɪt/ [US] /ˌmɑː.nəˌsoʊ.di.əmˈgluː.t̬ə-/ *noun* [U] (ABBREVIATION **MSG**) a chemical which is sometimes added to food, especially food sold in containers, to improve the taste

monosyllabic /ˌmɒn.əʊ.sɪˈlæb.ɪk/ [US] /ˌmɑː.noʊ-/ *adj* **1** SPECIALIZED containing only one syllable **2** DISAPPROVING saying very little in a way that is rude or unfriendly: *He grunted a monosyllabic reply.* **monosyllabically** /ˌmɒn.əʊ.sɪˈlæb.ɪ.kli/ [US] /ˌmɑː.noʊ-/ *adv* DISAPPROVING **monosyllable** /ˈmɒn.əʊˌsɪl.ə.bl̩/ [US] /ˈmɑː.noʊ-/ *noun* [C] SPECIALIZED a word which contains only one syllable: *'Jump', 'buy' and 'heat' are monosyllables.*

monotheism /ˌmɒn.əʊˈθiː.ɪ.zəm/ [US] /ˌmɑː.noʊ-/ *noun* [U] the belief that there is only one god **monotheistic** /ˌmɒn.əʊ.θiːˈɪs.tɪk/ [US] /ˌmɑː.noʊ-/ *adj*: *The three monotheistic religions with the most followers are Christianity, Judaism and Islam.*

monotonous /məˈnɒt.ən.əs/ [US] /-ˈnɑː.t̬ən-/ *adj* staying the same and not changing and therefore boring: *a monotonous job* ○ *a monotonous voice* ○ *The music became monotonous after a while.* **monotonously** /məˈnɒt.ən.əs.li/ [US] /-ˈnɑː.t̬ən-/ *adv* **monotony** /məˈnɒt.ən.i/ [US] /-ˈnɑː.t̬ən-/ *noun* [U] (ALSO **monotonousness**) *The monotony of motorway driving causes many accidents.* ○ *The routine was the same every day, with nothing to **break/relieve** the monotony.*

monotone /ˈmɒn.ə.təʊn/ [US] /ˈmɑː.nə.toʊn/ *noun* [U] a sound which stays on the same note without going higher or lower: DISAPPROVING *He spoke in a boring monotone.*

Monsignor /ˌmɒnˈsiː.njər/ [US] /ˌmɑːnˈsiː.njɚ/ *noun* [U] (WRITTEN ABBREVIATION **Msgr**) a title used with the name of a Roman Catholic priest of high rank: *Monsignor Healey* ○ [as form of address] *This way please, Monsignor.*

monsoon /mɒnˈsuːn/ [US] /mɑːn-/ *noun* [C] the season of heavy rain during the summer in hot Asian countries: *The failure of **the** monsoon would destroy harvests on which 1000 million people rely.*

monster [CREATURE] /ˈmɒnt.stər/ [US] /ˈmɑːnt.stɚ/ *noun* [C] any imaginary frightening creature, especially one which is large and strange: *a sea monster* ○ *prehistoric monsters* ○ *the Loch Ness monster* **monstrous** /ˈmɒnt.strəs/ [US] /ˈmɑːnt-/ *adj* like a monster: *The illustrations show monstrous beasts with bodies like bears and heads like tigers.*

monster [PERSON] /ˈmɒnt.stər/ [US] /ˈmɑːnt.stɚ/ *noun* [C] a cruel and frightening person: *You'd have to be a monster to hit a child like that.*

monster [LARGE] /ˈmɒnt.stər/ [US] /ˈmɑːnt.stɚ/ *noun* [C] INFORMAL something which is very big, or too big: *You should have seen the onions he grew for the competition – they were monsters!* **monster** /ˈmɒnt.stər/ [US] /ˈmɑːnt.stɚ/ *adj* [before n] *a monster housing development*

monstrosity /mɒnˈstrɒs.ə.ti/ [US] /mɑːnˈstrɑː.sə.t̬i/ *noun* [C] something which is very ugly and usually large: *The new office building is a real monstrosity.*

monstrous /ˈmɒnt.strəs/ [US] /ˈmɑːnt-/ *adj* very bad or cruel: *a monstrous crime* ○ *monstrous cruelty* ○ *But that's monstrous – he can't be allowed to get away with it!* **monstrously** /ˈmɒnt.strə.sli/ [US] /ˈmɑːnt-/ *adv*: *monstrously unfair*

montage /ˈmɒn.tɑːʒ/ [US] /ˈmɑːn-/ *noun* [C or U] a piece of work produced by combining smaller parts, or the process of making such a work: *The ads feature a montage **of** images – people surfing, playing football and basketball.*

month /mʌntθ/ *noun* [C] a period of about four weeks, especially one of the twelve periods into which a year is divided: *I'll be away for a month from mid-June to mid-July.* ○ *February is the shortest month.* ○ *a two-month-old puppy* ○ *The project will be finished **in** the next few months* (= quite soon). ○ *They haven't been in contact with me **for** months* (= a long time). ○ *She has two months' holiday every year.*

• **not in a month of Sundays** If you say that something will not happen in a month of Sundays you mean that it is very unlikely to happen: *He's never going to get that finished in a month of Sundays!*

monthly /ˈmʌnt.θli/ *adj, adv* happening or produced once a month: *monthly payments* ○ *Most of these people are paid monthly.*

monthly /ˈmʌnt.θli/ *noun* [C] a magazine which is published once a month

monument /ˈmɒn.jʊ.mənt/ [US] /ˈmɑːn-/ *noun* [C] **1** a statue or building that is built to honour a special person or event: *In the square in front of the hotel stands a monument **to** all the people killed in the war.* **2** **ancient/historic monument** an old building or place which is an important part of a country's history: *Parts of the Berlin wall are being allowed to stand as historic monuments.*

• **be a monument to *sth*** to be an important and permanent result of an action or characteristic: *The annual arts festival is a monument to her vision and hard work.* ○ *Protesters have called the building a monument to corporate greed.*

monumental /ˌmɒn.jʊˈmen.təl/ [US] /ˌmɑːn.jʊˈmen.t̬əl/ *adj* very big: *a monumental task* ○ *a monumental waste of time* **monumentally** /ˌmɒn.jʊˈmen.təl.i/ [US] /ˌmɑːn.jʊˈmen.t̬əl-/ *adv*: *monumentally dull*

pips (UK)
seeds (US)

core

peel

apple

plum

stone (UK)
pit (US)

peach

apricot

pear

cherries

strawberry

raspberries

lime

orange

grapefruit

segment

satsuma

lemon

pineapple

watermelon

melon

dates

kiwifruit

fig

mango

avocado

grapes

coconut

lychee

banana

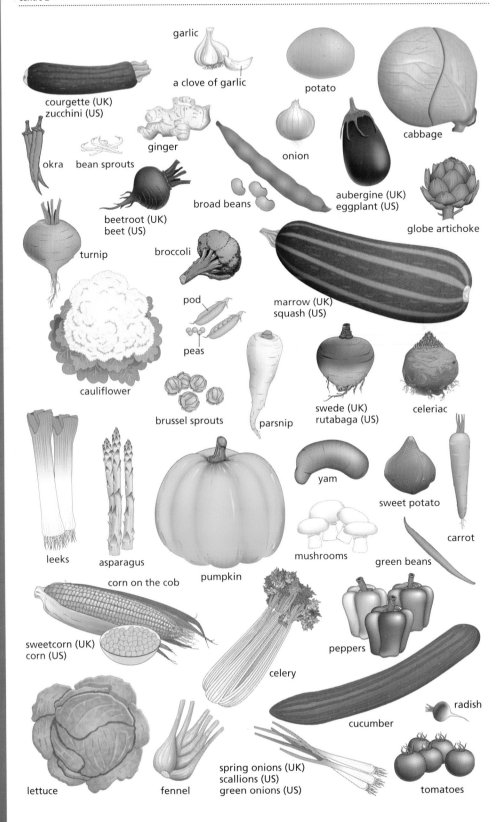

garlic

a clove of garlic

potato

cabbage

courgette (UK)
zucchini (US)

ginger

onion

okra

bean sprouts

aubergine (UK)
eggplant (US)

broad beans

beetroot (UK)
beet (US)

globe artichoke

turnip

broccoli

marrow (UK)
squash (US)

pod

peas

cauliflower

swede (UK)
rutabaga (US)

celeriac

brussel sprouts

parsnip

yam

sweet potato

leeks

asparagus

mushrooms

green beans

carrot

corn on the cob

pumpkin

sweetcorn (UK)
corn (US)

peppers

celery

cucumber

radish

lettuce

fennel

spring onions (UK)
scallions (US)
green onions (US)

tomatoes

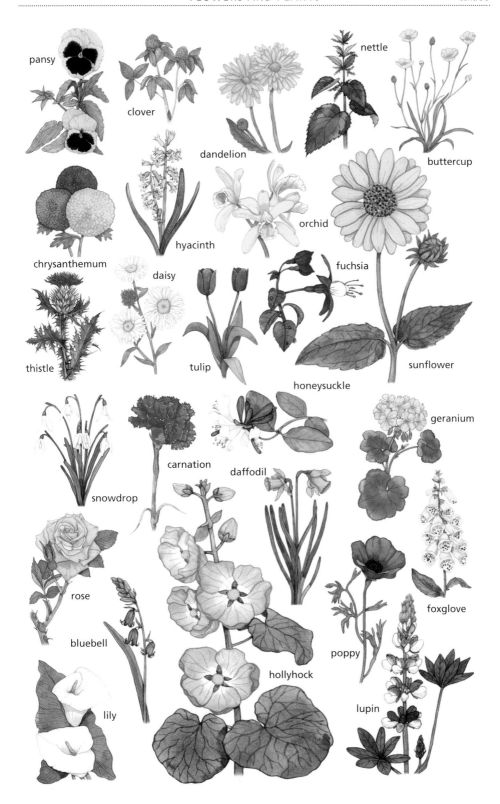

pansy

clover

dandelion

nettle

buttercup

chrysanthemum

hyacinth

orchid

fuchsia

daisy

thistle

tulip

honeysuckle

sunflower

snowdrop

carnation

daffodil

geranium

rose

bluebell

hollyhock

poppy

foxglove

lupin

lily

hump

camel

mane

lion

jaws

crocodile

buffalo

gorilla

hippopotamus

giraffe

tiger

claws

blackbird

elephant

tusks

trunk

monkey

horn

rhinoceros

beak

robin

sparrow

swallow

eagle

gull/seagull

pigeon

owl

hen

peacock

duck

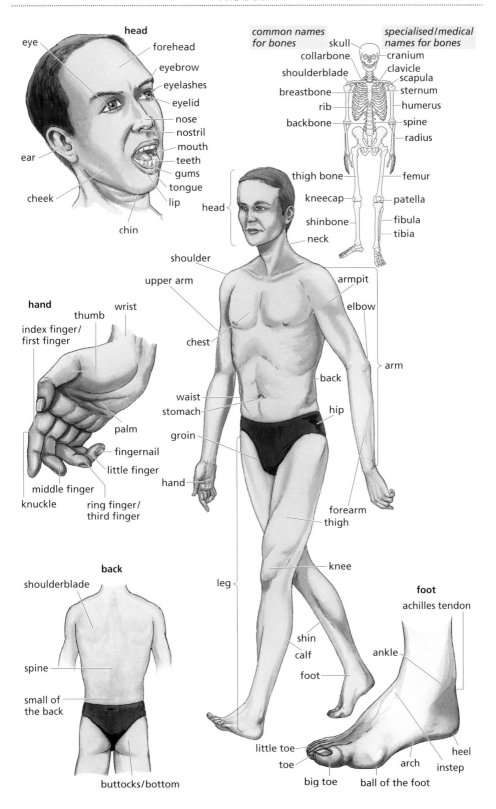

head

eye
forehead
eyebrow
eyelashes
eyelid
nose
nostril
mouth
teeth
gums
tongue
lip
ear
cheek
chin

common names
for bones

specialised/medical
names for bones

skull
collarbone
shoulderblade
breastbone
rib
backbone

cranium
clavicle
scapula
sternum
humerus
spine
radius

thigh bone
kneecap
shinbone

femur
patella
fibula
tibia

head
neck

shoulder
upper arm

armpit
elbow

hand
wrist
thumb
index finger/
first finger

chest

arm

back

waist
stomach
groin

hip

palm
fingernail
little finger
hand
middle finger
knuckle
ring finger/
third finger

forearm
thigh

knee

back
shoulderblade

leg

foot
achilles tendon

shin
calf
foot

ankle

spine

small of
the back

little toe
toe

buttocks/bottom

big toe

ball of the foot

arch

heel
instep

T shirt

jumper (UK)
sweater
pullover

jeans

tie

chinos

waistcoat (UK)
vest (US)

cardigan

jacket

sweatshirt

shirt

trousers

suit

shorts

leggings

bow tie

dungarees (UK)
overalls (US)

tracksuit (UK)
sweats (US)

polo shirt

fleece

jacket

skirt

bra

pants (UK)
panties (US)

overcoat

dress

socks

underpants

vest (UK)
undershirt (US)

boxer shorts

trunks

coat

mini skirt
mini

tights (UK)
pantyhose (US)

bikini

stockings

shoes

sandals

trainers (UK)
sneakers (US)

boots

wellingtons (UK)
rubber boots (US)

belt

anorak

sari

hat

cap

scarf

fringe (UK) bangs (US)

straight

crew cut

spiky

hair band

ponytail

curly

flat top

plait (UK) braid (US)

mohican (UK) mohawk (US)

hair slide (UK) barrette (US)

wavy

skinhead

dreadlocks

cornrows

cap

headscarf

top hat

bowler hat

flat cap

baseball cap

beret

crown

turban

balaclava

straw boater

crash helmet

fedora

bonnet

ear muffs

peak

peaked cap

policeman's helmet

trilby

Stetson™ cowboy hat (US)

sombrero

bobble hat

fez

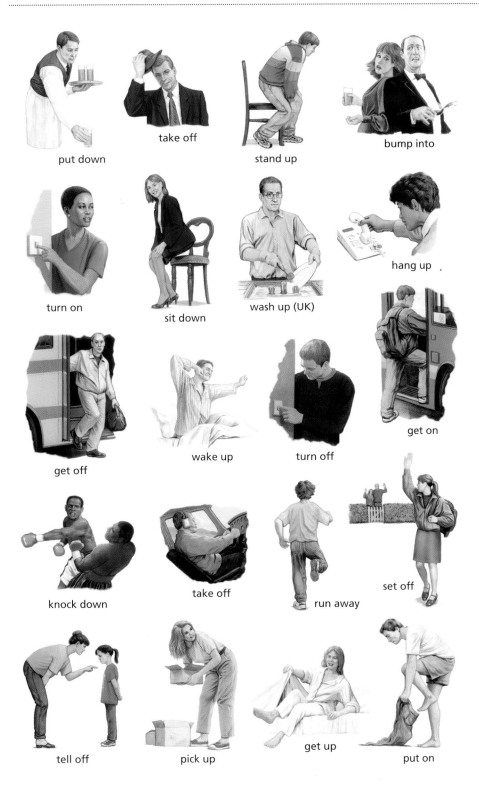

put down

take off

stand up

bump into

turn on

sit down

wash up (UK)

hang up

get off

wake up

turn off

get on

knock down

take off

run away

set off

tell off

pick up

get up

put on

football (UK) soccer (US)

American football (UK)
football (US)

tennis

flag

caddie

club

golf

hole

basketball

cricket

hockey (UK)
field hockey (US)

batter

pitcher

diamond

glove/mit

baseball

table tennis

puck

ice hockey (UK)
hockey (US)

skiing

swimming

hurdles

tape

running

discus

posts

scrum

athletics (UK)
track and field (US)

rugby

long jump

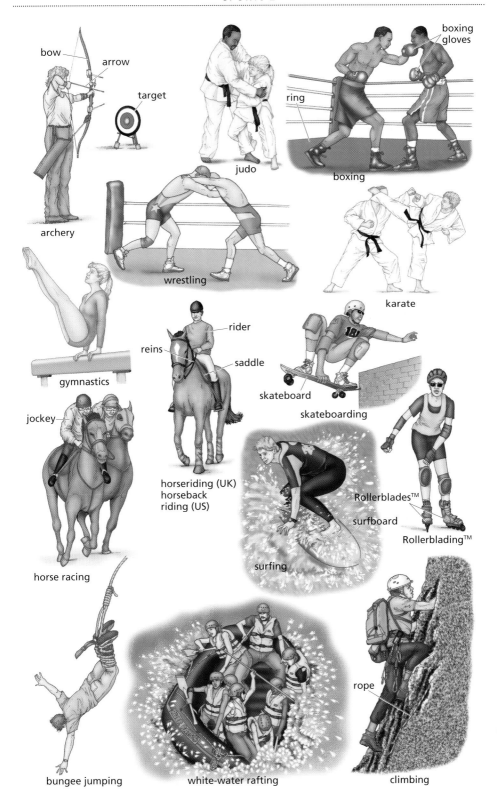

bow

arrow

target

judo

boxing
gloves

ring

boxing

archery

wrestling

karate

rider

reins

saddle

gymnastics

skateboard

skateboarding

jockey

horseriding (UK)
horseback
riding (US)

Rollerblades™

surfboard

Rollerblading™

horse racing

surfing

rope

bungee jumping

white-water rafting

climbing

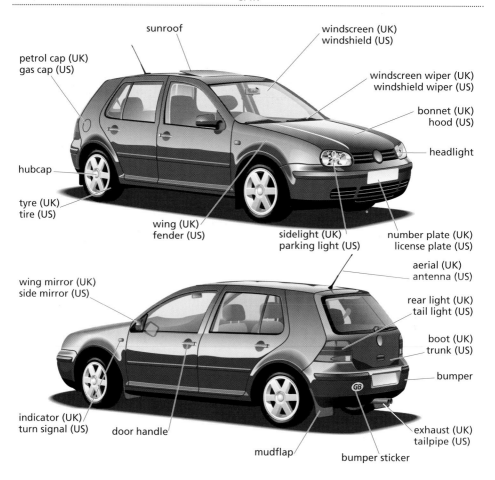

sunroof

windscreen (UK)
windshield (US)

petrol cap (UK)
gas cap (US)

windscreen wiper (UK)
windshield wiper (US)

bonnet (UK)
hood (US)

headlight

hubcap

tyre (UK)
tire (US)

wing (UK)
fender (US)

sidelight (UK)
parking light (US)

number plate (UK)
license plate (US)

aerial (UK)
antenna (US)

wing mirror (UK)
side mirror (US)

rear light (UK)
tail light (US)

boot (UK)
trunk (US)

bumper

indicator (UK)
turn signal (US)

door handle

mudflap

bumper sticker

exhaust (UK)
tailpipe (US)

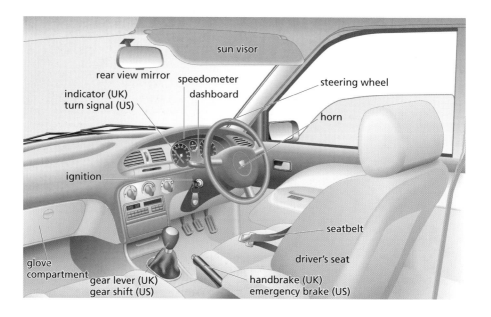

sun visor

rear view mirror

speedometer

steering wheel

indicator (UK)
turn signal (US)

dashboard

horn

ignition

seatbelt

driver's seat

glove
compartment

gear lever (UK)
gear shift (US)

handbrake (UK)
emergency brake (US)

estate (car) (UK)
station wagon (US)

hotrod

Jeep™

saloon (UK) sedan (US)

SUV (US)

fire engine

tow truck
breakdown truck (UK)

coach (UK)
bus (US)

tractor

buggy

limousine/limo

motorbike (UK)
motorcycle

van

convertible

tanker

truck
lorry (UK)

dumper truck (UK)
dump truck (US)

motor home/Winnebago™/RV

school bus

police car

people carrier

caravan (UK)
trailer (US)

racing car

pick up (truck)

hearse

sports car

dustcart (UK)
garbage truck (US)

articulated lorry (UK)
semi (US)

fork-lift
truck

bus

rotor

helicopter

stealth fighter

transport plane

jumbo jet

cockpit

fuselage

plane
airplane(US)
aeroplane (UK)

glider

engine

fighter

wing

landing gear

propellor

biplane

seaplane

microlight

trawler

tanker

warship

hovercraft

1071

canoe

funnel

cruise ship/liner

mast

lifeboat

deck

paddle

anchor

submarine

periscope

ferry

rowing boat (UK)
rowboat (US)

sails

yacht (UK)

oars

motorboat

screen
CPU
printer
CD drive
DVD drive
scanner
web cam
keyboard
mouse
CD-ROM
laptop
speakers
mouse mat (UK)
mouse pad (US)
mobile/mobile phone (UK)
cellphone (US)
earpiece
hands-free kit
Dictaphone™
PDA
Filofax™/personal organizer
business cards
projector
blind
noticeboard (UK)
bulletin board (US)
chart
coathooks
coffee machine
water cooler
filing cabinet
partition
office chair
desk
bin (UK)
trash can (US)
filing tray
pencil
file
calculator
pen
rubber (UK)
eraser (US)
fax (machine)
Post-it™ (note)
photocopier
desk tidy
ruler
stapler
staples

PROGRESS CHART

cafetière

coffee machine

colander

sieve

bread bin (UK)
bread box (US)

kettle

scales (UK)
scale (US)

tin opener (UK)
can opener(US)

grater

teapot

toaster

oven glove (UK)
oven mitt (US)

extractor fan

cupboard

fridge/refrigerator

hob (UK)
stove (US)

sink

tap (UK)
faucet (US)

grill

draining board

freezer

dishwasher

oven

washing machine

grate

peel

slice

spread

chop

mash

grill

fry

boil

Study Sections

These sections give you extra help with particular areas of English. Some deal with useful vocabulary and others give you more support with particular areas of grammar. You should also look at the section 'How to use the dictionary' at the beginning of the book.

Work and jobs

(For more information, look in the dictionary for the words in **bold**.)

A **job** is the thing that you are paid to do. It is a countable noun.
> *I got a job in a bank when I finished college.*

Work is the activity of having a job, being paid, etc. It is an uncountable noun.
> *A lot of people come to London to find work.*

If you work for a person or company, you are an **employee**. Your company is your **employer**. The company **employs** you. If you work for yourself and do not have an employer, you are **self-employed**. If you work for different companies when they need you, you are a **freelance** worker.

Asking about someone's job

What do you do?	*I'm a nurse.*
*What (sort of) **work** do you do?*	*I work **for** a car company **as** a manager.*
*What do you do **for a living**?*	*I work **at/in** the supermarket.*
(formal) *What's your **occupation**?*	*I'm a teacher.*

Types of job

*I've got a **part-time** job two days a week.* (The opposite of part-time is **full-time**. A part-time job can be for a few hours every day or for less than five days in every week.)
*I've got a **temporary** job at the garage until April.* (The opposite of temporary is **permanent**.)

Casual work is a job that you only do sometimes and it is usually not on the same days each week:
> *I do a bit of casual work as a receptionist.*

Leaving a job

The words we use depend on the reason for someone leaving a job:

- A person might choose to leave:
  > *'Are you still working for Kett & Smith?' 'No, I **left** there months ago.'*
  > *I was so angry at the way my boss treated me I **resigned/quit**.*
- An employer might not be able to continue to employ them:
  > *120 people **lost their jobs**/were **laid off**/were **made redundant** when the factory closed.*
- If a person is **dismissed**, **fired** or **sacked**, they leave their job because their employer is not happy with their work or their behaviour.

Not having a job and looking for a job

I haven't got a job at present.
*I'm **unemployed/out of work** at the moment.*
*I'm **looking for** work.*
*I **applied for** a job with Saunders and they've invited me to an interview.*

When a company needs someone to do a job

*The new factory will bring over 500 **jobs** to the area.*
*For information about current **vacancies**, contact our Personnel department.*

Money

(For more information, look in the dictionary for the words in **bold**.)

Ways of paying

You can pay for something

by/in cash   *by cheque* (*UK*) *by check* (*US*)   *by credit card* or *debit card*

Cash is money in the form of notes and coins, rather than cheques.

When you use a **credit card**, you arrange to pay at a later time.

With a **debit card** the money is taken from your bank account automatically.

Using a bank account

A **current account** (*UK*) / **checking account** (*US*) is a bank account which usually earns little or no interest and which you can take money out of at any time. With a **savings/deposit account**, you can earn interest on your money.

Interest is money charged by a bank to people who have borrowed from them, or the money which you receive from a bank after you have left money with them for a period of time.

You can take money out of your bank account by using a **cash machine** (*UK*)/**ATM** (*US*). This is a machine in the wall of the bank or other building. You use a **cash card** (*UK*)/**ATM card** (*US*) to take out the money.

Useful phrases

*I'd like to **pay** this cheque **into** my account and **take out** £50 in cash.*
*You can **withdraw** (= take out) or **deposit** (= put in) money at any time using the machines outside the bank.*
*Could you tell me the **balance on** (= how much money is in) my account?*
*(UK) I have an **overdraft facility** of £500 (= I can borrow up to £500)*
*I hate being **overdrawn/in the red** (= owing money to the bank).*

Saying whether things are cheap or expensive

expensive
↑

*Train travel in the UK is **extortionate** (= too high).*
*House prices in London can be **prohibitive** (= too expensive for people to afford).*
*This car is proving to be very **expensive** to run.*
*The hotel was great but a little **pricey**.*
*That supermarket's a bit **dear**.*
*The house is great and the rent is **reasonable** (= not too expensive).*
*The heating system is very **economical** (= cheap to run).*
*She offered me a **fair** price for my record collection.*
*I booked my holiday at the last moment, so it was **dirt cheap** (= it cost very little money).*
*This coat was half-price, a real **bargain**.*
*The sunglasses are now available in major stores, **a snip** at £25 a pair.*

↓
cheap

*Less than $30 for both of them? What **a steal**!*

Periods of time

Exact periods of time

60 seconds in a **minute**	12 months in a **year**
60 minutes in an **hour**	10 years in a **decade**
24 hours in a **day**	100 years in a **century**
7 days in a **week**	1000 years in a **millennium**

Also, in the UK a **fortnight** is 2 weeks.
> *We're going to Spain for a fortnight.*

Approximate periods of time

Sometimes the words for exact periods of time are also used to talk about approximate periods of time. Usually, this kind of phrase emphasizes how long something is taking.
> *At this rate it'll take **weeks** to finish the project* (= it will take too long).
> *He's been doing the same job for **years and years*** (= a very long time).

Other phrases used for talking about how long something takes
*You're late – I've been waiting (for) **ages**!*
*I've had these boots for **quite a while**.*
*Will the builders be here **long**? Yes, they only started **a short time ago**.*
*She'll be here in **a second/moment/minute**.*
*Would you mind waiting a minute? I'll be with you **presently/shortly**.*

Periods of time in the past and present

These phrases are used to talk in a general way about time in the past or in the present:
> *Punk music was popular **in the late 1970s** and **early 80s**.*
> *Our house was built **in the mid-sixties**.*
> *The hospital dates from **the turn of the century*** (= the beginning of the century).
> *Electric lights were invented near **the end of the nineteenth century**.*
> *Greek civilization was one of the most important **in ancient times**.*
> *Medical science has developed enormously **in modern times**.*
> *I love to hear Grandpa talk about **the old days*** (= the time when he was young).
> ***In those days** it was very difficult to travel across Africa.*
> *Everyone seems to be on the Internet **nowadays/these days**.*
> *I'm really busy with work **at the moment**.*

A period of time from one point of time to another point

Here are some common ways of saying this:
> *We stayed in Brussels **from** Thursday to Monday.*
> *It's open **from** nine o'clock **until/till** half past five.*
> *(US): The performances are Monday **through/thru** Friday* (= they are on Monday, Tuesday, Wednesday, Thursday and Friday).

Relationships

People who are not married

Your **boyfriend** or **girlfriend** is someone with whom you are having a romantic relationship. People who are having a romantic relationship are often referred to as a **couple**.

Why don't we invite the couple next door round for a drink?

If you are having a relationship but are not married and you **live together**, the word **partner** is often used to describe your boyfriend or girlfriend.

Have you met my partner, Tom?

Lover can be used by people in romantic relationships. It is more common to use **girlfriend**, **boyfriend** or **partner** in everyday conversation.

If a couple are **engaged**, they have formally agreed to marry. The person to whom you are **engaged** is your **fiancé** (male) or your **fiancée** (female).

A **single parent**, or **single mother/father** or a **lone parent** is someone who has a child but does not live with a husband, wife or partner.

There are plans to help single mothers back into work.

People who are married

Two people who are married are also referred to as a **couple**. In formal or legal contexts, a person's husband or wife is their **spouse**.

This travel insurance covers both spouse and dependent children.

If a relationship ends

If someone's husband or wife has died, they are a **widow** (female) or a **widower** (male), and the dead person is referred to as their **late husband/wife**.

If a relationship ends you can say the two people have **broken up** or they have **split up**. A previous partner can be an **ex-boyfriend** or **ex-girlfriend**. If you were married to them, they are your **ex-husband** or **ex-wife**. These 'ex' words can all be shortened informally to just '**ex**'.

I hear my ex has moved in with his new girlfriend.

If a married couple **separate** they stop living together, sometimes as part of a legal arrangement. This might be a **trial separation** (a period of separation to find out if the couple want to separate permanently). If the couple **divorce**, they end their marriage through a legal process. They are then both **divorced**.

A new marriage

If one of your parents marries again you have a **stepmother** or **stepfather** and you become a **stepson** or **stepdaughter**.

If your **stepmother** or **stepfather** already has children these become your **stepbrothers** or **stepsisters**.

If one of your parents has another child with a new husband or wife, this is your **half-brother** or **half-sister**.

Telephoning

These are some of the words that you will need if you **phone** (or **telephone**) someone:

Parts of a phone number

If you phone a number such as **00 44 (0)181 8379292** there are three parts to the number.

00 44 is the **country code**	**(0)181** is the **area code**	**8379292** is the **phone number**

The numbers in a phone number are usually pronounced separately: **90233** is pronounced "nine oh two double three".

If you don't know the number you can look it up in the **phone book/telephone directory**, or dial **directory enquiries** (*UK*) /**directory assistance** (*US*) and ask the **operator**. The operator works for the phone company, giving you information and connecting your call if necessary. Usually all phone calls can be made without talking to the operator.

If you phone a large company or organization you may speak to someone in a **call centre**. This is a large office where hundreds of people work answering phone calls.

A **reverse charge call** (*UK*) /**collect call** (*US*) is paid for by the person who receives it, not by the person who makes the call.

Some people have an **answerphone** (MAINLY *UK*)/**answering machine** (MAINLY *US*) which plays a recorded message to you if nobody is able to answer when you phone. In a company or office many people have an electronic system called **voicemail**.

Notice the following uses of **through**:
> *Can I call Japan direct from here, or do I have to* ***go through*** *the operator?*
> *The lines were really busy and I couldn't* ***get through*** *to the airport.*
> *Can you* ***put*** *me* ***through*** *to Miss Shaw on extension 342, please?*

Common phrases meaning to phone someone

She said she'd ***phone/telephone/call/ring*** *(you) tomorrow.*
I'll ***give*** *you a* ***ring/call/phone call***.
I need to ***make*** *a* ***call/phone call*** *(to Brazil).*

Common phrases used when phoning someone

Could/Can I speak to Mr Carter, please?
Is that Karen? Hi, ***this is*** *Barbara/Barbara here.*

Phone problems

I've been trying to get Sonia all morning but her line is always ***engaged*** *(UK)/***busy*** *(US).*
I think you've got a ***wrong number*** *– this is 654731.*
The line's busy – do you want to ***hold the line/hold (on)***?
It's ***a bad/terrible line***, *I can hardly hear you. Can you speak a bit louder?*
Hello, can you connect me to Katie Moore again? We were ***cut off*** *in the middle of our call.*
I tried to use the public phone but it's ***out of order***.

Sounds and smells

Sounds

Be careful to use the right verb with sound.

listen	If you deliberately try to hear something, use the verb **listen**. *I was listening to a CD while I was waiting for Mike.* *Listen! There's that strange noise again!*
hear	If you receive or become aware of sound, use the verb **hear**. *Suddenly, I heard a voice outside.*

The following sentences contain words describing the loudness of a sound. Loud sounds are at the top of the list and quieter sounds are at the bottom. For more information, look in the dictionary for the words in **bold**. The word in brackets tells you the part of speech of the word in bold.

loud

↑

*The winning goal was met with a **deafening** (adjective) roar.*
*They were woken by a **loud** (adjective) bang like a gun going off.*
*Those dogs were making a terrible **racket** (noun) last night.*
*The students held a **noisy** (adjective) demonstration.*
*There was so much traffic **noise** (noun) that he couldn't sleep*
*The **sound** (noun) of voices came from upstairs.*
*Inside the church it was **quiet** (adjective) and peaceful.*
*Her voice sounded **faint** (adjective) and distant.*

↓

quiet *The court was **silent** (adjective) as the men walked in.*

Smells

The verb **smell** can mean different things:

– to become aware of a smell: *I can smell gas!*
– to have a particular smell: *This milk smells bad.*
– to try to breathe in the smell of something: *Smell these flowers.*

There are several words in English meaning a smell. Some refer to pleasant smells while others are used for unpleasant smells. The following list shows pleasant smells at the top and less pleasant smells at the bottom. For more information, look in the dictionary for the words in **bold**. The word in brackets tells you the part of speech of the word in bold.

Good
{ *There was a wonderful **aroma** (noun) of fresh coffee.*
*The roses filled the air with their sweet **fragrance** (noun).*

Neutral
{ *I love the **smell** (noun) of wood smoke.*
*The air was filled with the **scent** (noun) of damp earth.*
*There was a **smell** (noun) of fresh paint.*
*Pure water is completely **odourless** (adjective).*

Bad
{ *Pick up your **smelly** (adjective) socks and put them in the washing machine!*
*Your clothes **stink** (verb) of cigarettes!*
*The **stench** (noun) coming from the toilets made me feel sick.*
*Len **reeks** (verb) of alcohol.*
*The room had a stale **odour** (noun) of cigarettes and beer.*

Computers, text messages, email

Computers

Many words relating to computers have become part of the daily language. Here is a guide to using your computer in English. For more information look in the dictionary for the words in **bold**.

Using a computer

When your computer is ready to use, the first thing you see is the **desktop**. This is an area of the screen that displays **icons** of programs **installed** on your computer. All the programs on the computer are called **software**.

To start using a program, **click** on its icon. This should open in a new area of the screen called a **window**.

When you save information, you can save it to your **hard disk** (also called a **hard drive**) or on a **floppy disk**. Large amounts of information can be **copied** (also **written** or **burned**) onto a **CD**. Most computers also have a **DVD drive** so that you can play **DVDs**.

If your computer **crashes**, you might have to **restart** it.

The Internet

To **surf the Internet** (also called **the Web**), you need to be connected to it with a **modem**. You will also need a **browser**, which is software that enables you to view **web pages**.

To go to a particular **website** you need to type in its **URL** or web address. If you are not sure of the exact web address or want to search for particular information, you can use a **search engine**. Once you have found the **site** you want, you can **browse** the pages using **menus** and **links**. If there is too much text on the screen, you may have to **scroll** down to find what you need.

You can **download** software (programs) from the Internet. This includes **freeware** (which is free) and **shareware** (which you can try for free and pay for later). You need to be careful not to get a computer **virus** from the Internet. You can buy **anti-virus** software to help you do this.

Text messages

Text messages are short written messages between mobile phones. Text messaging is sometimes called **SMS** (short messaging service). Because it takes a long time to type in full words, text messages often contain abbreviations:

B = *be*	**U** = *you*	**@** = *at*
C = *see*	**2** = *to* or *too*	**CU @ 7** = *See you at seven.*
R = *are*	**4** = *for*	**How R U?** = *How are you?*

It is common to miss out vowels in some words:

txt = *text*   **msg** = *message*

other abbreviations include:

b4 = *before*   **l8r** = *later*   **gr8** = *great*   **2day** = *today*   **2morrow** = *tomorrow*

Email

In email and other computer applications (for example **chat rooms**) people also use unusual kinds of English. Internet **abbreviations** are sometimes used, taking the first letter from longer phrases: **Emoticons** or '**smileys**' are also common. These are punctuation marks used to show your feelings. Here are some examples:

INTERNET ABBREVIATIONS			'SMILEYS'		
FYI	=	for your information	;-)	=	joking
BTW	=	by the way	:-)	=	happy
LOL	=	laughing out loud	:-(	=	sad

Writing emails

People communicate using email for many different reasons. It can be used to send single word answers, formal documents or even jokes. The way you write your email depends on how well you know the person you are sending it to. People often write emails in the same way they speak so it is typically less formal than other forms of writing.

the email address of anyone who you want to have a copy of the message

To:	Mairi MacDonald <mmacdonald@cambridge.org>
From:	Harriet Dufton <hdufton@mellor.net>
Subject:	party
Cc:	annbarber@mail.com
Bcc:	
Attached:	C:\My Documents\map.doc;

other computer files which you are sending with the email

Emails often contain symbols known as 'smileys'.

Mairi,

Sat 29th July - We are having a house-warming party and it would be great if you could come - you are more than welcome to stay over -
I think Ann is coming too
:-)

Thanks for your email - I will talk to you properly – email soon - lots to catch up on !!! But I just wanted to check if you could come to our party – if you are able to come then I can pick you up at the station.

Anyway - talk to you soon and hopefully see you soon too !

love

Harriett xxx

Emails can start like ordinary letters "Dear...", but often this is left out. You can start an email without writing anybody's name or with "Hello" or "Hi!"

If you know the other person well, it is not necessary to write in complete sentences.

Notes on writing emails:
- Do not write in capitals because it looks as if you are SHOUTING.
- You can use *asterisks* to emphasise something important: *Please note there is *no* meeting today.*
- Use _underscores_ for titles or something you want to underline.
- /Slashes/ can be used around a word or phrase that you want to put in italics.

Relative clauses

Relative clauses describe or tell us more about a person or thing that has just been mentioned in the sentence.

Relative pronouns are words that act as a subject or object in a relative clause. The following words can be relative pronouns: **that, what, where, when, which, who, whom, why**.

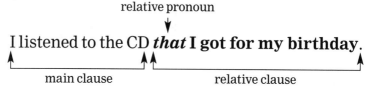

relative pronoun

I listened to the CD *that* I got for my birthday.

main clause   relative clause

Defining relative clauses

These are clauses that tell us exactly who or what is being referred to. Without the defining relative clause the sentence will not make sense. It needs to be there.

PEOPLE	THINGS
*I hate people **who** are insincere*	*I enjoyed the books **that** you lent me.*
For people you can use **who** or **that**, but **who** is more usual. In the above sentence, **who** is the subject of the relative clause.	For things you can use **that** or **which**, but **that** is more usual. In the above sentence, **that** is the object of the relative clause.

You *cannot* miss out the relative pronoun if it is the subject of the relative clause:

~~I hate people are insincere~~

The relative pronoun *can* be missed out if it is the object of the relative clause:

| *I enjoyed the books you lent me.* | OR | *I enjoyed the books you lent me.* |
| *She's the girl that I love.* | OR | *She's the girl I love.* |

Note: There are no commas in defining relative clauses.

Non-defining relative clauses

These are clauses that give us extra information about something or someone already mentioned. The sentence will still make sense without the non-defining relative clause, but the clause gives you extra information.

PEOPLE	THINGS
*The finance minister, **who** has been under pressure to resign, will be holding a press conference today.*	*His latest novel, **which** is set in India, has received good reviews.*
For *people* you must use **who**.	For *things* you must use **which**.

You cannot leave out the relative pronoun in non-defining clauses.

Note: **Who** and **which** are always preceded by a comma in non-defining relative clauses. In spoken English they are preceded by a pause.

Phrasal verbs

A phrasal verb is a verb followed by an adverb or preposition.

    run **away** (verb + adverb)
    look **after** (verb + preposition)

The adverb or preposition in a phrasal verb is also called the **particle**.

A phrasal verb can also be a verb followed by an adverb and a preposition.

    get **on with**
    run **out of**

Some people also call phrasal verbs 'multiword verbs' or 'prepositional verbs'. In the *Cambridge Advanced Learner's Dictionary* they are labelled *phrasal verb*.

Intransitive phrasal verbs

Some phrasal verbs are intransitive and some are transitive. Here is an example of an intransitive phrasal verb, (one not needing an object).

run out   *I went to see if there was any milk left in the fridge but found that we had **run out*** (= there was no milk left in the fridge).

Transitive phrasal verbs

Here is an example of a transitive phrasal verb (one needing an object).

run *sth* up   *Thomas **ran up** huge debts by borrowing money to try to keep the company going.* (= he spent so much that he had very large debts).

In the dictionary we show transitive phrasal verbs by writing the phrasal verb with **'sb'** (short for 'somebody') or **'sth'** (short for 'something'). This shows that the phrasal verb has to have an object. In the example above, we show '**run *sth* up**' because you can only 'run something up', you can't just 'run up'. If a phrasal verb can be transitive and intransitive, we show it like this: **light *(sth)* up**. The bracketed *(sth)* shows that something can 'light up' or it can 'light something up'.

Moving the object with a transitive phrasal verb

If a phrasal verb is transitive, you need to know if you can put an object between the verb and the particle. For example, you can do this with **take off** but not with **look after**.

Take your coat off. ✓   *Look after yourself.* ✓
Take off your coat. ✓   ~~*Look yourself after.*~~ ✗

In the dictionary we use [M] after the phrasal verb to show that the phrasal verb needs an object but that the object can come between the verb and particle, or after the particle. **Take off**, for example, will appear as follows:

take *sth* off [REMOVE] *phrasal verb* [M] to remove something, especially clothes

For more information on phrasal verbs, see the *Cambridge International Dictionary of Phrasal Verbs*. You can also search for phrasal verbs online at http://dictionary.cambridge.org

Determiners

'Determiner' is a general term for words which are used before nouns to show which person or thing is being referred to. Determiners of quantity are used to describe how much or little of something there is. For more information, look in the dictionary for the words in **bold**.

← a complete amount	a large amount			a small amount	zero amount →
all	many		enough	a few	no
every	much			few	neither
each	most			several	
both				a little	
				little	

The following determiners must only be used with *countable nouns* in the plural:

We don't get **many** *tourists* here.
Hold on with **both** *hands*.
We've invited **a few** *friends* to dinner.

We get **several** *letters* a week.
I take **fewer** *trips* abroad these days.
So **few** *people attended*.

Note: **Few** has a negative meaning, and means 'almost no'. **A few** has a positive meaning and means 'some'.

The following determiners must only be used with <u>uncountable nouns</u>:

Will it take **much** <u>time</u>?
Add **a little** <u>salt</u>.

I had **less** <u>money</u> than I thought.
We get so **little** <u>light</u> in this room.

Note: **Little** has a negative meaning, and means 'almost no'. **A little** has a positive meaning and means 'some'.

The following determiners can be used with *countable nouns* in the plural and with <u>uncountable nouns</u>:

Kim's got **more** *bags* than me.
Most *items* of jewellery are made from gold.
All *children* should receive education.
Do you have **enough** *clothes*?
He left **no** *instructions*.

Kim's got **more** <u>luggage</u> than me.
Most <u>gold</u> is used to make jewellery.
All <u>meat</u> is rich in protein.
We don't have **enough** <u>furniture</u>.
There's **no** <u>ice</u> in the fridge.

The following determiners must be used with *singular countable nouns*:

He checked **each** *document* carefully.
Every *child* needs affection.

If you follow one determiner with another determiner (such as *the* or *this*) you usually put **of** between them.

Take **some** bread.
Take **some of** the bread.

Every and *no* cannot be used with *of*. *Every one of* or *none of* is used instead.

Every tree is marked with a cross

Every one of the young trees is marked with a cross.

We have **no** accurate information.

None of this information is accurate.

Modal verbs

A modal verb is a verb that is used before another verb to express meanings such as ability, permission, possibility, necessity or advice.

The modal verbs are **can**, **could**, **may**, **might**, **must**, **ought**, **shall**, **should**, **will** and **would**. **Need** and **used to** can follow some of the grammar patterns of modal verbs, but are also used like ordinary verbs. For more information about any modal verb, look in the dictionary at the entry for the word.

The grammar of modal verbs

- they are usually followed by an infinitive without *to*
  - *You should thank him*
  - ~~*You should to thank him.*~~
- there is no '*s*' for the third person singular
  - *he must, she must, it must*
- they have no infinitive or -ing form
  - ~~*I would like to can go.*~~
- they cannot follow another verb.
  - ~~*I want to can sleep tonight.*~~
- they are not used in future, perfect or continuous tenses
  - ~~*they will might be angry.*~~
  - ~~*they have must leave.*~~
  - ~~*they are canning to speak English*~~.

Example modal verb: can

Look at the extract on the right which is based on what is in the dictionary. From the guidewords, we can see that the modal verb *can* is used to describe the following ideas:

- ability
- permission
- request
- possibility
- polite offers of help

Look at the example sentences. Notice that

- The forms of can for **you** and **she** are the same: *you can, she can*
- When you use modal verbs in questions or negatives you do not use auxiliary verbs such as **do** or **have**: *Can you drive?*

---

can (ABILITY) modal verb
to be able to
Can you drive?
She can speak four languages.
can (PERMISSION) modal verb
INFORMAL to be allowed to, either by general or personal permission
You can park over there.
You can have a piece of cake if you eat your vegetables!
can (REQUEST) modal verb
INFORMAL used informally to request something
If you see Adrian, can you tell him (= please tell him) I'm in London next weekend?
can (POSSIBILITY) modal verb
used to express possibility in the present, although not in the future
You can get stamps from the local newsagents.
can (OFFER) modal verb
used in polite offers of help
Can I help you with those bags?

Homographs: words that are spelled the same

Homographs are words that have the same spelling but have different pronunciation and meaning. In the examples here, the pronunciation is shown at the end of each example.

bow
The actors came back on stage and took a bow. /baʊ/
He learned to hunt with a bow and arrow. UK /bəʊ/ US /boʊ/

close
Close your eyes and count to ten. UK /kləʊz/ US /kloʊz/
Please keep close to the path, it's easy to get lost. UK /kləʊs/ US /kloʊs/

content
Soft drinks have a high sugar content. UK /ˈkɒn.tent/ US /ˈkɑːn.tent/
I was content just to stay at home and read. /kənˈtent/

contract
Your muscles will contract if you get cold. /kənˈtrækt/
The new export contract is worth £16 million. UK /ˈkɒn.trækt/ US /ˈkɑːn.trækt/

desert
He was planning to desert his family and go abroad. UK /dɪˈzɜːt/ US /dɪˈzɜːrt/
It hasn't rained in this part of the desert for years. /ˈdez.ət/

lead
Just follow the signs and they will lead you to the exit. /liːd/
Gold is heavier than lead. /led/

minute
Can I speak to you for a minute, Mr Trent? /ˈmɪnɪt/
We've got a small house with a minute garden. UK /maɪˈnjuːt/ US /maɪˈnuːt/

object
This small stone object is over 5000 years old. UK /ˈɒb.dʒɪkt/ US /ˈɑːb.dʒɪkt/
I strongly object to these cuts in public spending. /əbˈdʒekt/

project
The housing project will create 5000 new homes. UK /ˈprɒdʒ.ekt/ US /ˈprɑː.dʒekt/
He's trying to project a more confident image. /prəˈdʒekt/

refuse
I won't do it – I absolutely refuse! /rɪˈfjuːz/
Put empty bottles here and other refuse in the bin. /ˈref.juːs/

row
I had a blazing row with my girlfriend last night. /raʊ/
I looked quickly along the row of books. UK /rəʊ/ US /roʊ/

tear
She noticed a tear in the corner of his eye. UK /tɪəʳ/ US /tɪr/
To open the packet, tear along the dotted line. UK /teəʳ/ US /ter/

used
There used to be a farm here, years ago. /juːst/
Explosives were used to enter the building /juːzd/

wind
Wind speeds reached 102mph last night. /wɪnd/
You have to wind the handle to the left. /waɪnd/

wound
He wound the rope around his arm. /waʊnd/
In the fight, one young man received a knife wound. /wuːnd/

Homophones – words that sound the same

Homophones are words that sound the same but have a different meaning and spelling. For example:

*My **son** is a doctor*
*The **sun** is really hot today.*

The common homophones on this page are grouped according to the sound that is spelled differently. Words marked *UK* only sound similar in British English. If words are in dark type (e.g. **grate – great**) they are common causes of mistakes for learners.

iː
bean – been
be – bee
feat – feet
flea – flee
heel – he'll – heal
leak – leek
meat – meet
peace – piece
peak – peek
peal – peel
reed – read
sea – see
seam – seem
seen – scene
steal – steel
suite – sweet
weak – week
weave – we've

UK ɔː *US* ɔːr
board – bored
caught – court *UK*
coarse – course
hoarse – horse
sauce – source *UK*
saw – soar *UK*
sort – sought *UK*
warn – worn

eɪ
bale – bail
brake – break
grate – great

male – mail
pain – pane
pair – pear
pray – prey
rain – reign – rein
sale – sail
slay – sleigh
stake – steak
Sunday – sundae
tale – tail
wail – whale
wait – weight
waste – waist
way – weigh

UK aʊ *US* oʊ
groan – grown
hole – whole
know – no
loan – lone
road – rode – rowed
role – roll
row – roe
sew – so
sole – soul

ə
altar – alter
currant – current
gorilla – guerrilla
idol – idle
manner – manor
miner – minor

aɪ
aisle – I'll – isle
aye – eye – I
buy – by – bye
dye – die
hi – high
hire – higher
rye – wry
sight – site
right – write
tyre – tire

UK eaʳ *US* er
air – heir
fair – fare
bare – bear
pair – pear
stair – stare
there – they're – their
ware – wear – where

uː
blew – blue
flew – flu – flue
threw – through
to – too – two

Letter writing

A business letter

Here is an example of a typical business letter, showing how you arrange the different parts on the page. On the opposite page there is an example of a letter that you might write to a friend.

Manesty Clothes Ltd

15 Clifton Court
Manchester MR3 5PY
England
UK
Tel: +44 (0)161 932 2628
Fax: +44 (0)161 932 2884
Email: enquiries@manesty.co.uk

> This is the **letterhead**. It can go on the left, right or in the centre. In the US, it is often on the left.

Production Manager
Suntrek Fabrics
Box 167
Brown Street PO
Singapore

> This is the **salutation**. You do not need to put a comma here. In US letters, you should use a colon.

2nd January 2003

Dear Sir or Madam

> This is the **subject heading**, a summary of the contents of the letter. It helps the reader to quickly understand what the letter is about.

Re: Visit to Singapore

I am now planning my next trip to South East Asia, and would be very pleased if we could meet to discuss our production requirements for next year.

> There is no space here when you start a new paragraph.

I hope to be in Singapore on May 3 or 4. Would it be convenient to visit you on May 3 at 10.30am? I would be grateful if you could tell me exactly where your offices are located.

I look forward to hearing from you.

Yours faithfully

Christine Burrows

C. Burrows
Senior Buyer

> You do not need to put commas after **Dear Sir or Madam** or **Yours faithfully**. Be consistent: if you put a comma after **Dear Sir or Madam**, put one after **Yours faithfully**.

Common phrases used in formal and informal letters

Formal
Thank you for your letter of
22 January concerning...
I am writing to inquire about...
I am writing to inform you that...
I am pleased to inform you that...
I regret to inform you that...
I hope this information has been of use.
Please give my regards to Peter Hogan.
Thank you for all you have done.
I look forward to hearing from you soon.

Informal
Thank you for your letter about...

I'm writing to ask about...
I'm writing to say that...
I'm pleased to say...
I'm sorry to tell you that...
I hope this has been useful.
Regards to Peter.
Thanks for all your help.
Hope to hear from you soon

An example of an informal letter

> 4th Feb 2003
>
> Dear Jo,
>
> Just a quick word to thank you for a brilliant weekend. It was lovely to see you again, and the kids really enjoyed going round London – hope we didn't tire you out too much!
>
> It would be great to see you up in Liverpool some time – it's ages since you've been. We'll be celebrating Jim's fortieth (!) in September, and it would be great if you could come. Anyway, let me know nearer the time if you can make it.
>
> Take care, hope to see you soon.
>
> Love,
>
> Clare xxx

Notes:
- In an informal letter you usually do not write your address but you write the date.
- The style is very much like speech. You can use short forms each as **didn't**. In a formal letter you would not use these.

Regular inflections

Inflections are the way that the ending of a word changes when you use the word in different ways. For example, you say **'I read'** but **'he reads'**.

The inflections of some words are **irregular**, especially the past tense of common verbs (e.g. **buy** changes to **bought** in the past tense). With irregular inflections, you cannot simply work them out . You just have to learn them. All of these **irregular inflections** are shown in the dictionary next to the word that you are looking up.

The two pages here show you what happens with inflections that are not irregular. There are easy rules for **regular inflections** and you can use these rules to work out how a particular word changes.

The following tables show you how nouns, adjectives and verbs change their endings.

Nouns

Most nouns form their plural by adding **-s**.
chair – chairs, plate – plates

Nouns which end in **-s**, **-ss**, **-ch**, **-x** and **-z** make their plurals by adding **–es**
mass – masses, match – matches

Nouns which end in a consonant (e.g. **m, t, p**) + **y** form their plurals by taking away the **-y** and adding **-ies**
baby – babies, university – universities

Nouns which end in a vowel (e.g. **a, e, o**) + **y** form their plurals by adding **-s**
tray – trays, toy – toys

Adjectives

Comparative form of adjectives	this is used to show that someone or something has more of a particular quality than someone or something else	you can either add **-er** to the end of the adjective, or use the word **more** before it (see below)
Superlative form of adjectives	this is used to show that someone or something has more of a particular quality than anyone or anything else	you can either add **-est** to the end of the adjective, or use the word **most** before it (see below)
One-syllable adjectives	these adjectives usually form their comparative and superlative with **-er** and **-est**	*small, **smaller**, **smallest***
Two-syllable adjectives	these adjectives can all form their comparative and superlative with **more** and **most**	*complex, **more** complex, **most** complex*
Three-syllable adjectives	these adjectives usually form their comparative and superlative with **more** and **most**	*beautiful, **more** beautiful, **most** beautiful*

Regular inflections (continued)

Note: Some two-syllable adjectives can form the comparative and superlative with -**er** and -**est** too. The most common of these are:

adjectives ending in -**y** and -**ow**
happy – happier, happiest
noisy – noisier, noisiest
shallow – shallower, shallowest

adjectives ending in -**le**
able – abler, ablest
noble – nobler, noblest
simple – simpler, simplest

some other common two-syllable adjectives which can take -**er** and -**est**
common, cruel, handsome, pleasant, polite, quiet, wicked

When you are using the -**er**, -**est** forms, if the adjective ends in -**e**, take away the -**e** before adding the ending: *pale, paler, palest*

If the adjective ends in -**y**, change this to -**i** before adding the ending: *happy, happier, happiest*

Verbs

For regular verbs add the following endings:

3rd person singular	add -**s**	*pack – pack**s***
Present participle	add -**ing**	*pack – pack**ing***
Past tense and the past participle	add -**ed**	*pack – pack**ed***

Note: For verbs ending in -**s**, -**ss**, -**ch**, -**x**, or -**z** you need to add -**es** for the third person singular ending (e.g. *reach, reaches*), but the present participle, past tense and past participle are the same as other regular verbs: *reach, reaches, reaching, reached*

For verbs ending in -**e**, take away the -**e** before adding the present participle, past tense, and past participle endings: *hate, hates, hating, hated*

For verbs ending in a consonant followed by -**y**, for the present participle take away the -**y** and add -**ies**, and for the past tense and past participle take away the -**y** and add -**ied**: *cry, cries, crying, cried*

Verbs ending in a vowel followed by -**y** are regular: *play, plays, playing, played*

SUMMARY
- If a word has **irregular inflections** these are shown in the dictionary next to the word.
- You can work out all **regular inflections** by using these pages.
- You need to look at the last letters of nouns and verbs to be sure that you have got the right rules for producing their regular inflections.

Punctuation

	Uses	Examples
Capital letter	• for the first letter of a sentence	*Fishing is popular in Britain.*
	• for countries, nationalities, languages, religions, names of people, places, events, organizations, trademarks, days, months, titles	*Portugal, Africa, Russian, Moslem* *Joanne, John, Dubai, Geneva, the World Trade Fair, Jaguar, the Internet, Sunday, February, Mr. / Mrs. / Ms. / Dr. / Professor*
	• for titles of books, films, etc.	*Silence of the Lambs*
	• for abbreviations	*OPEC, AIDS, WWF*
Full stop UK/ period US •	• at the end of a sentence	I'm going for a walk.
	• sometimes after an abbreviation	*Marton Rd. / Mrs. White / Dr. Evans*
	• as the decimal point in figures and amounts of money. This is usually read out as '**point**'	*£3.5 million*
	• to separate parts of email and web addresses. This is read out as '**dot**'	*http://dictionary.cambridge.org*
Question mark ?	• after a direct question • to show doubt	*What's your name?* *Sidney Morgan (1898? – 1972) was little known until after his death.*
Exclamation mark !	• at the end of a sentence in order to show surprise/ shock, etc.	*I can't believe it!* *Ouch! Yes!*
	• to indicate a loud sound	*Bang!*
Comma ,	• between items in a list	*I need peas, butter, sugar and eggs.*
	• to show a pause in a long sentence	*They didn't want to eat before I'd arrived, but I was an hour late.*
	• when you want to add extra information	*Lucy, who I told you about before, will be coming.*
	• before tag questions	*You do love me, don't you?*

	Uses	Examples
Apostrophe '	• for missing letters • for possessives **Note:** 1. words ending in 's' don't need another 's' added 2. **it's** can only be an abbreviation for **it is** or **it has**. There is no apostrophe in the possessive form.	*I'll (I will), it's (it is), don't (do not)* *Noah's bike* *James' house* *It's raining.* *Paris never loses its charm.*
colon :	• to introduce a list or a quotation in a sentence • in the US following the greeting in a business letter	*You need the following: paint, brushes, water, cloths.* *Dear Customer:* *Dear Mr Stein:*
semi-colon ;	• to separate two parts of a sentence	*I spoke to Linda on Monday; she can't come to the meeting tomorrow.*
hyphen –	• to join two words together • to show that a word has been divided and continues on the next line	*blue-black* *Everyone in the room was struck by his air of sadness.*
dash —	• to separate parts of sentences • to mean **to**	*The car – the one with the broken window – was parked outside our house.* *The **London – Edinburgh** train leaves every morning at eight.*
quotation marks/ *UK also* inverted commas ' ' " "	• to show that words are spoken • to show that someone else originally wrote the words **Note:** Single quotation marks are more usual in UK English, and double quotation marks are more usual in US English.	*'I'm tired,' she said.* *"Let's go," he suggested.* *She had described the school as 'not attracting the best pupils'.*

Varieties of English

Labels in the dictionary give information about different varieties of English:

US   American English
AUS   Australian and New Zealand English
UK   British English

As well as British English there are these additional varieties:
Northern English   *Scottish English*   *Irish English*

Differences in words

Differences between varieties of English are clearly marked in the dictionary. For example, this entry shows that **duvet** is British English and that American English has a different word.

---

duvet *UK* /'duː.veɪ/ *US* /–'–/ *noun* [C] (*UK ALSO* **continental quilt**, *US* **comforter**) a large soft flat bag filled with feathers or artificial material used on a bed

---

Grammar differences

The grammars of American and British English are basically quite similar, but here are some important ways in which American English differs from British English:

The past forms of some verbs

In American English some irregular verbs can have a form of the past simple or past participle that is not used in British English.
*He **dived** / (US also) **dove** into the pool.*
*Jake has **got** / (US usually) **gotten** really fat.*

The past simple

In many situations where British English uses the present perfect form of the verb, American English uses the past simple:

UK	US
I think I've lost my camera.	*I think I lost my camera.*
Thanks, but I've already eaten.	*Thanks, but I already ate.*

Different prepositions

UK	US
*The shop is open **from** Monday to Saturday.*	*The shop is open Monday **through** Saturday.*
*It's a quarter **past** seven.*	*It's a quarter **after** seven.*

Differences in spelling

In American English, words tend to be spelt more simply or more like the way they are pronounced. Compare the following British and American spellings:

UK	US	UK	US
equalled	*equaled*	*litre*	*liter*
plough	*plow*	*honour*	*honor*

Australian English usually follows British spellings, although there are some American spellings that are also acceptable.

moo /muː/ *noun* [C] *plural* **moos** (especially in children's books) the noise that a cow makes **moo** /muː/ *verb* [I] **mooing, mooed, mooed**

mooch [MOVE] /muːtʃ/ *verb* [I usually + adv or prep] *INFORMAL* to walk or act slowly and without much purpose: *DISAPPROVING Stop mooching* ***(about/around)*** *in your room and do something useful!*

mooch /muːtʃ/ *noun* [S] *INFORMAL I'm going for a mooch round the shops* (= to look at what is there, not to buy a particular thing).

mooch [OBTAIN] /muːtʃ/ *verb* [I or T] *US SLANG* to obtain something without paying or working for it, or to borrow something without intending to return it: *You're old enough to get a job and stop mooching* ***off*** *your family.* ○ *He mooched a ten* ***off*** *me, and I knew right then I'd never see it again.*

mood /muːd/ *noun* [C] the way you feel at a particular time: *She's* ***in a*** *good/bad mood.* ○ *Her mood seemed to change during the course of the conversation.* ○ *The drink had put him in an amiable mood.* ○ *The public mood changed dramatically after the bombing.* ○ *The mood of the crowd suddenly turned* (= The crowd suddenly became) *aggressive.*

• **be in one of *your* moods** *INFORMAL* If a person is in one of their moods, they are being unfriendly and angry in a way that is typical of them: *Tim's in one of his moods so I'm keeping out of his way.*

• **be in the mood** to feel like doing or having something: *"I'm not really in the mood* ***for*** *shopping."*

• **be in no mood for *sth*/to do *sth*** to not want to do something with someone else, often because you are angry with them: *I was in no mood for chatting.*

moody /ˈmuː.di/ *adj* If someone is moody, they are often unfriendly because they feel angry or unhappy: *a moody teenager* ○ *He can be quite moody.* **moodily** /ˈmuː.dɪ.li/ *adv* **moodiness** /ˈmuː.dɪ.nəs/ *noun* [U]

the moon [PLANET] *noun* **1** [S] the round object which moves in the sky around the Earth and can be seen at night: *What time does the moon* ***rise/set*** (= appear/disappear in the sky)? **2** [U] the shape made by the amount of the moon that you can see at a particular time: *There's no moon* (= You cannot see the moon) *tonight.* ○ *a crescent/full/new moon* **3** [C] a similar round object that moves around another planet: *Jupiter has at least sixteen moons.*

• **many moons ago** *OLD-FASHIONED* a long time ago

• **be over the moon** to be very pleased: *She was over the moon* ***about/with*** *her new bike.*

moonless /ˈmuːn.ləs/ *adj* without light from the moon: *a dark moonless night*

moon [LACK PURPOSE] /muːn/ *verb* [I usually + adv or prep] to move or spend time in a way which shows a lack of interest and no clear purpose: *She was mooning* ***about/around*** *the house all weekend.* ○ *He's been mooning* ***over*** (= looking foolishly at) *those holiday photos all afternoon.*

moonbeam /ˈmuːn.biːm/ *noun* [C] a beam or line of light which comes from the moon

Moonie /ˈmuː.ni/ *noun* [C] a member of the Unification Church, a religious group whose members must obey its rules and teachings completely: *He has joined the Moonies.*

mooning /ˈmuː.nɪŋ/ *noun* [U] *SLANG* showing your naked bottom as a joke or as a protest

moonlight [LIGHT] /ˈmuːn.laɪt/ *noun* [U] the pale light of the moon: *The young lovers sat in the moonlight.*

• **do a moonlight flit** *UK INFORMAL* to leave secretly, especially to avoid paying money that you owe: *When he discovered the police were after him, he did a moonlight flit.*

moonlit /ˈmuːn.lɪt/ *adj* [before n] able to be seen because of the light of the moon: *a bright moonlit night*

moonlight [WORK] /ˈmuːn.laɪt/ *verb* [I] **moonlighted, moonlighted** to work at an additional job, especially without telling your main employer: *A qualified teacher, he moonlighted* ***as*** *a cabbie in the evenings to pay the rent.*

moonlighting /ˈmuːn.laɪ.tɪŋ/ [US] /-t̬ɪŋ/ *noun* [U] *You'll get sacked if the boss finds out you've been moonlighting.*

moonshine [ALCOHOL] /ˈmuːn.ʃaɪn/ *noun* [U] *MAINLY US* alcoholic drink made illegally

moonshine [SPEECH] /ˈmuːn.ʃaɪn/ *noun* [U] *INFORMAL* nonsense; foolish talk

moor [COUNTRYSIDE] /mɔːʳ/ /mʊəʳ/ [US] /mʊr/ *noun* [C] an open area of hills covered with rough grass: *the Yorkshire moors*

moor [TIE] /mɔːʳ/ /mʊəʳ/ [US] /mʊr/ *verb* [I or T] to tie a boat so that it stays in the same place: *We moored further up the river.* ○ *We moored the boat* ***to*** *a large tree root.*

mooring /ˈmɔː.rɪŋ/ /ˈmʊə-/ [US] /ˈmʊr.ɪŋ/ *noun* [C] *We rented a mooring* (= a place to tie a boat).

moorings /ˈmɔː.rɪŋz/ /ˈmʊə-/ [US] /ˈmʊr.ɪŋz/ *plural noun* the ropes or chains which keep a boat from moving away from a particular place

moorhen /ˈmɔː.hen/ /ˈmʊə-/ [US] /ˈmʊr-/ *noun* [C] a small black bird which lives near water

Moorish /ˈmʊə.rɪʃ/ [US] /ˈmʊr.ɪʃ/ *adj* of the Muslim people who were the rulers of Spain from 711 to 1492: *Moorish architecture*

moorland /ˈmɔː.lənd/ /ˈmʊə-/ [US] /ˈmʊr-/ *noun* [C or U] an area of MOOR (= high open countryside with grass and small bushes)

moose (*plural* **moose**) /muːs/ *noun* [C] (*UK OLD-FASHIONED* **elk**) a type of large deer with large flat horns and a long nose which lives in the forests of North America, northern Europe and Asia

moot [DISCUSSION] /muːt/ *verb* [T] *FORMAL* to suggest something for discussion: *The idea was first mooted as long ago as the 1840s.* ○ *His name was mooted as a possible successor.*

moot /muːt/ *adj* tending to be discussed or argued about and having no definite answer: *It's* ***a*** *moot* ***point*** *whether building more roads reduces traffic congestion.*

moot [LEGAL CASE] /muːt/ *noun* [C] *SPECIALIZED* a trial or discussion dealing with an imaginary legal case, performed by students as part of their legal training but in exactly the same way as a real one: *a moot court*

moot /muːt/ *adj MAINLY US LEGAL* having no practical use or meaning: *The district attorney said if McVeigh is given the death penalty and his conviction is upheld on appeal, the state prosecution would become moot.*

mop /mɒp/ [US] /mɑːp/ *noun* [C] a stick with soft material fixed at one end, especially used for washing floors or dishes: *a floor mop* ○ *a dish mop*

mop /mɒp/ [US] /mɑːp/ *verb* [T] **-pp- 1** to use a mop to wash something: *He mopped the bathroom floor.* **2** to use a cloth to remove sweat from the face: *He kept pausing to mop his brow.*

PHRASAL VERBS WITH **mop**

▲ **mop *sth* up** [CLEAN] *phrasal verb* [M] to use a cloth or a mop to remove liquid from the surface of something: *There's milk on the floor over there – could you get a cloth and mop it up?*

▲ **mop *sth* up** [FINISH] *phrasal verb* [M] *INFORMAL* to finish dealing with something: *It took a week to mop up the last of the enemy soldiers* (= defeat them).

mope /məʊp/ [US] /moʊp/ *verb* [I] *DISAPPROVING* to be unhappy and unwilling to think or act in a positive way, especially because of a disappointment: *There's no point in sitting at home and moping – get out there and find yourself another job!*

▲ **mope about/around *(somewhere)*** *phrasal verb* to move about without any particular purpose or energy because you are unhappy or disappointed: *He was driving me mad, moping about the house all day.*

moped /ˈməʊ.ped/ [US] /ˈmoʊ-/ *noun* [C] a small motorcycle which also has PEDALS (= parts which you press with your feet to move forward) which can be used when starting it or travelling up a hill

mopoke /ˈməʊ.pəʊk/ [US] /ˈmoʊ.poʊk/ *noun* [C] **1** a type of Australian and New Zealand OWL whose call sounds like its name **2** *AUS INFORMAL* someone who is stupid or looks very unhappy

moppet /ˈmɒp.ɪt/ [US] /ˈmɑː.pɪt/ *noun* [C] *INFORMAL* an affectionate word for a young child, especially a girl: *a curly-haired moppet*

moral /ˈmɒr.əl/ [US] /ˈmɔːr-/ *adj* **1** relating to the standards of good or bad behaviour, fairness, honesty, etc. which

M

each person believes in, rather than to laws: *It's her moral* ***obligation*** *to tell the police what she knows.* ○ *It is not part of a novelist's job to make a moral* ***judgment.*** ○ *She was the only politician to condemn the proposed law on moral grounds* (= for moral reasons). ○ *The Democrats are attempting to* ***capture the*** *moral* ***high ground*** (= are trying to appear more honest and good than the other political parties). ➲Compare **amoral**; **immoral**. **2** behaving in ways considered by most people to be correct and honest: *She's a very moral woman.* ○ *Oh, stop being so moral!* ○ *Is TV responsible for weakening people's moral* ***fibre*** (= ability to behave well and honestly and work hard)?

moral /ˈmɒr.əl/ [US] /ˈmɔːr-/ *noun* [C] The moral of a story, event or experience is the message which you understand from it about how you should or should not behave: *And the moral* ***of/to*** *the story is that honesty is always the best policy.*

moralist /ˈmɒr.əl.ɪst/ [US] /ˈmɔːr-/ *noun* [C] *DISAPPROVING* a person who tries to force or teach other people to behave in ways he or she considers to be most correct and honest

moralistic /ˌmɒr.əlˈɪs.tɪk/ [US] /ˌmɔːr-/ *adj DISAPPROVING* Someone or something that is moralistic judges people by fixed and possibly unfair standards of right and wrong and tries to force or teach them to behave according to these standards: *Drug addicts need sympathetic, not moralistic, treatment.*

morality /məˈræl.ə.ti/ [US] /mɔːˈræl.ə.t̬i/ *noun* [C or U] a personal or social set of standards for good or bad behaviour and character, or the quality of being right, honest or acceptable: *They argued for a new morality based on self-sacrifice and honesty.* ○ *I have to question the morality* ***of*** *forcing poor people to pay for their medical treatment.*

moralize, *UK USUALLY* **-ise** /ˈmɒr.əl.aɪz/ [US] /ˈmɔːr-/ *verb* [I] *DISAPPROVING* to express judgments about what is morally right and what is wrong: *his parents' self-righteous moralizing*

morally /ˈmɒr.əl.i/ [US] /ˈmɔːr-/ *adv* based on principles that you or people in general consider to be right, honest or acceptable: *Morally you're right, but in practice I don't think it would work.* ○ *For a teacher to hit a child is not just morally wrong but also illegal.* ○ *She thinks she's morally superior to the rest of us.*

morals /ˈmɒr.əlz/ [US] /ˈmɔːr-/ *plural noun* standards for good or bad character and behaviour: *public/private morals* ○ *OLD-FASHIONED DISAPPROVING a person of* ***loose*** *morals* (= whose character or sexual behaviour are considered unacceptable)

morale /məˈrɑːl/ *noun* [U] the amount of confidence felt by a person or group of people, especially when in a dangerous or difficult situation: *A couple of victories would improve the team's morale enormously.* ○ *There have been a lot of recent redundancies so morale is fairly low.*

ˌmoral maˈjority *noun* [U] those people in a society, especially the US in the 20th century, who support severe and old-fashioned Christian standards of behaviour

ˌmoral supˈport *noun* [U] If you give someone moral support, you encourage them and show that you approve of what they are doing, rather than giving them practical help.

ˌmoral ˈvictory *noun* [C] when you prove that your beliefs are right, although you lose an argument

morass /məˈræs/ *noun* [C usually sing] **1** something that is extremely complicated and difficult to deal with and makes any progress almost impossible: *The morass* ***of*** *rules and regulations is delaying the start of the project.* **2** *LITERARY* an area of soft wet ground in which it is easy to get stuck

moratorium /ˌmɒr.əˈtɔː.ri.əm/ [US] /ˌmɔːr.əˈtɔːr.i-/ *noun* [C] *plural* **moratoriums** or **moratoria** *FORMAL* a stopping of an activity for an agreed amount of time: *a five-year worldwide moratorium* ***on*** *nuclear weapons testing*

morbid /ˈmɔː.bɪd/ [US] /ˈmɔːr-/ *adj DISAPPROVING* too interested in unpleasant subjects, especially death: *a morbid fascination with death* **morbidly** /ˈmɔː.bɪd.li/ [US] /ˈmɔːr-/ *adv* **morbidity** /ˌmɔːˈbɪd.ɪ.ti/ [US] /ˌmɔːrˈbɪd.ə.t̬i/ *noun* [U]

mordant /ˈmɔː.dənt/ [US] /ˈmɔːr-/ *adj FORMAL* (especially of humour) cruel; criticizing in an amusing way: *mordant* ***wit/humour*** ○ *a mordant remark* **mordantly** /ˈmɔː.dənt.li/ [US] /ˈmɔːr-/ *adv*

more /mɔːʳ/ [US] /mɔːr/ *determiner, pronoun, adv* **1** a larger or extra number or amount: *Would you like some more food?* ○ *The doctors can't cope with* ***any*** *more patients.* ○ *Add some more cream to the sauce.* ○ *You need to listen more, and talk less!* ○ *More people live in the capital* ***than*** *in the whole of the rest of the country.* ○ *We spent more time on the last job* ***than*** *usual.* ○ *The noise was more* ***than*** *I could bear.* ○ *It was a hundred times more fun* ***than*** *I'd expected.* ○ *She's more* ***of a*** *poet* ***than*** *a novelist.* ○ *Bring as much food as you can –* ***the*** *more,* ***the better.*** **2** used to form the comparative of many adjectives and adverbs: *She couldn't be more beautiful.* ○ *Let's find a more sensible way of doing it.* ○ *You couldn't be more wrong.* ○ *He finds physics* ***far/much*** *more difficult* ***than*** *other science subjects.* ○ *Play that last section more passionately.* **3** used to emphasize the large size of something: *More* ***than*** *20 000 demonstrators crowded into the square.*

• **couldn't agree/disagree more** *FORMAL* If you say that you couldn't agree/disagree more, you mean that you agree/disagree completely.

• **not/no more than** used to emphasize how small an amount is: *There are beautiful mountains not more than ten minutes' drive away.*

• **all the more** even more than before: *Several publishers rejected her book, but that just made her all the more determined.*

• **any more** If you do not do something or something does not happen any more, you have stopped doing it or it does not now happen: *I don't do yoga any more.*

• **more and more** increasingly: *It gets more and more difficult to understand what is going on.*

• **That's more like it!** *INFORMAL* used to show that you think something or someone has improved

• **more often than not** most of the time: *More often than not, a student will come up with the right answer.*

• **more or less 1** mostly: *The project was more or less a success.* **2** approximately: *It's 500 kilos, more or less.* **3** very nearly: *He more or less admitted he'd done it.*

• **more than** very: *It's more than* ***likely*** *that there's oil here under the ground.* ○ *I was more than a little* (= I was very) *curious about the whole business.* ○ *FORMAL We will be more than glad/happy/willing to help you in any way we can.*

• **the more...the more/less** used to say that when an action or event continues, there will be a particular result: *The more he drank, the more violent he became.* ○ *The more he insisted he was innocent, the less they seemed to believe him.*

• **the more the merrier** used to say an occasion will be more enjoyable if lots of people are there: *"Do you mind if I bring a couple of friends to your party?" "Not at all – the more the merrier!"*

USAGE

more

The opposite of **more** is **fewer** for countable nouns and **less** for uncountable nouns.

He takes more exercise now.
He takes less exercise now.
He smokes fewer cigarettes.

moreish /ˈmɔː.rɪʃ/ [US] /ˈmɔːr.ɪʃ/ *adj UK INFORMAL APPROVING* (of food) having a very pleasant taste and making you want to eat more: *These peanuts are very moreish, aren't they?*

moreover /ˌmɔːˈrəʊ.vəʳ/ [US] /ˌmɔːrˈoʊ.vɚ/ *adv FORMAL* (used to add information) also and more importantly: *The whole report is badly written. Moreover, it's inaccurate.*

mores /ˈmɔː.reɪz/ [US] /ˈmɔːr.eɪz/ *plural noun FORMAL* the traditional customs and ways of behaving that are typical of a particular (part of) society: *middle-class mores* ○ *the mores and culture of the Japanese*

morgue /mɔːɡ/ ⓤ /mɔːrɡ/ *noun* [C] MAINLY US FOR **mortuary** (= place where dead bodies are kept)

moribund /ˈmɒr.ɪ.bʌnd/ ⓤ /ˈmɔːr-/ *adj* FORMAL DISAPPROVING (especially of an organization or business) not active or successful: *How can the Trade Department be revived from its present moribund state?*

Mormon /ˈmɔː.mən/ ⓤ /ˈmɔːr-/ *noun* [C] a member of a religious group called the Church of Jesus Christ of Latter-Day Saints, which originated in the US in 1830

morn /mɔːn/ ⓤ /mɔːrn/ *noun* [C] LITERARY a morning: *Yonder breaks a new and glorious morn.*

morning /ˈmɔː.nɪŋ/ ⓤ /ˈmɔːr-/ *noun* [C or U] the part of the day from the time when the sun rises or you wake up until the middle of the day or lunch time: *a beautiful/sunny/wet morning* ○ *I work three mornings a week at the bookshop.* ○ *She only works **in the** mornings.* ○ *What's our schedule for **this** morning?* ○ *I'd like an appointment for **tomorrow** morning, please.* ○ *I'll see you **on** Saturday morning.* ○ *I had too much to drink at Sarah's party, and I felt terrible **the morning after**.*
● **in the morning 1** during the early part of the day: *I listen to the radio in the morning.* **2** at some time between twelve o'clock at night and twelve o'clock in the middle of the day: *The murder took place at four in the morning.* **3** the next morning: *She said she would see you in the morning.*
● **morning, noon and night** all the time: *Our neighbour's baby cries morning, noon and night.*

mornings /ˈmɔː.nɪŋz/ ⓤ /ˈmɔːr-/ *adv* MAINLY US every morning: *Mornings we go running in the park.*

morning-after pill /ˌmɔː.nɪŋˈɑːf.tə.pɪl/ ⓤ /ˌmɔːr.nɪŋˈæf.tɚ-/ *noun* [C usually sing] a pill containing a drug which prevents a woman from getting pregnant if it is taken after she has had sex

'morning ˌdress *noun* [U] (ALSO **morning suit**) a very formal set of clothes worn by some men on occasions such as marriage ceremonies, including a long black or grey coat, STRIPED trousers, and a TOP HAT

'morning ˌsickness *noun* [U] the feeling of wanting to vomit experienced by some women during the first months of pregnancy

the ˌmorning 'star *noun* [S] a planet, especially Venus, which can be seen shining brightly in the east just before or as the sun rises

moron /ˈmɔː.rɒn/ ⓤ /ˈmɔːr.ɑːn/ *noun* [C] INFORMAL a very stupid person: *Some moron smashed into the back of my car yesterday.* ○ [as form of address] *You moron!* **moronic** /məˈrɒn.ɪk/ ⓤ /mɔːˈrɑː.nɪk/ *adj* INFORMAL DISAPPROVING *a moronic grin* ○ *some really moronic suggestions*

morose /məˈrəʊs/ ⓤ /-ˈroʊs/ *adj* unhappy, annoyed and unwilling to speak or smile; SULLEN: *a morose expression* ○ *Why are you so morose these days?* **morosely** /məˈrəʊ.sli/ ⓤ /-ˈroʊ-/ *adv* **moroseness** /məˈrəʊ.snəs/ ⓤ /-ˈroʊ-/ *noun* [U]

morph /mɔːf/ ⓤ /mɔːrf/ *verb* [I or T] to change one image into another, or combine them, using a computer program: *The video showed a man morphing **into** a tiger.*

morpheme /ˈmɔː.fiːm/ ⓤ /ˈmɔːr-/ *noun* [C] SPECIALIZED the smallest bit of language that has its own meaning, either a word or a part of a word: *'Worker' contains two morphemes – 'work' and '-er'.*

morphine /ˈmɔː.fiːn/ ⓤ /ˈmɔːr-/ *noun* [U] a drug made from OPIUM, used to stop people from feeling pain or to make people feel calmer

morphology /mɔːˈfɒl.ə.dʒi/ ⓤ /mɔːrˈfɑː.lə-/ *noun* [U] SPECIALIZED the scientific study of the structure and form of either animals and plants or words and phrases **morphological** /ˌmɔː.fəˈlɒdʒ.ɪ.kəl/ ⓤ /ˌmɔːr.fəˈlɑː.dʒɪ-/ *adj*

morris dancing /ˈmɒr.ɪsˌdɑːnt.sɪŋ/ ⓤ /ˈmɔːr.ɪsˌdænt-/ *noun* [U] a type of traditional English dancing in which a group of people, especially men, dance together, wearing special clothes decorated with little bells **morris dance** /ˈmɒr.ɪsˌdɑːnts/ ⓤ /ˈmɔːr.ɪsˌdænts/ *noun* [C] **morris dancer** /ˈmɒr.ɪsˌdɑːnt.sə/ ⓤ /ˈmɔːr.ɪsˌdænt.sɚ/ *noun* [C]

morrow /ˈmɒr.əʊ/ ⓤ /ˈmɑːr.oʊ/ *noun* [S] LITERARY the next day, or tomorrow: *They arranged to meet **on the** morrow.*

Morse (code) /mɔːsˈkəʊd/ ⓤ /mɔːrsˈkoʊd/ *noun* [U] a system used for sending messages, in which letters and numbers are represented by short and long marks, sounds or flashes of light

morsel /ˈmɔː.səl/ ⓤ /ˈmɔːr-/ *noun* [C] **1** a very small piece of food: *a morsel **of** cheese* ○ *The prisoners ate every last morsel.* **2** a very small piece or amount: *a morsel **of** good news*

mortal /ˈmɔː.təl/ ⓤ /ˈmɔːr.təl/ *adj* LITERARY **1** (of living things, especially people) unable to continue living forever; having to die: *For all men are mortal.* ⊃Compare **immortal**. **2** causing death: *a mortal injury/illness* ○ *men engaged in mortal **combat** (= fighting until one of them dies)* ○ FIGURATIVE *New computing technology dealt a mortal **blow** to the power of the old printing unions.* ⊃Compare **lethal**. **3** **mortal dread/fear/terror** extreme anxiety about or fear of someone or something: *We live in mortal dread of further attacks.* **4** **mortal enemy/danger/threat, etc.** a very serious and dangerous enemy/danger/threat, etc.

mortal /ˈmɔː.təl/ ⓤ /ˈmɔːr.təl/ *noun* [C] LITERARY MAINLY HUMOROUS an ordinary person, rather than a god or a special, important or powerful person: *The police officers guarding the door let in the celebrities, but they prevented us **lesser/mere** mortals from going inside.*

mortality /mɔːˈtæl.ə.ti/ ⓤ /mɔːrˈtæl.ə.ti/ *noun* [U] FORMAL **1** the way that people do not live forever: *Her death made him more aware of his own mortality.* ⊃Compare **immortality** at **immortal**. **2** the number of deaths within a particular society and within a particular period of time: *the mortality **rate*** ○ ***Infant** mortality is much higher in the poorest areas of the city.*

mortally /ˈmɔː.təl.i/ ⓤ /ˈmɔːr.təl-/ *adv* **1** so severe that death is likely: *mortally wounded* **2** extremely: *I hadn't realized I'd upset him but apparently he was mortally offended.*

ˌmortal 'sin *noun* [C usually sing] in the Roman Catholic religion, an action that is so bad that you will be punished forever after your death, if you do not ask for forgiveness from God

COMMON LEARNER ERROR

mortal

Do not use **mortal** to describe an illness that can kill someone. **Mortal** can be used with this meaning but it is a formal, literary word and you should use the word **fatal** instead.

~~We can now cure diseases which were mortal only a few years ago.~~
We can now cure diseases which were fatal only a few years ago.

mortar MIXTURE /ˈmɔː.tə/ ⓤ /ˈmɔːr.tɚ/ *noun* [U] a mixture of sand, water and cement or lime that is used to fix bricks or stones to each other when building walls

mortar GUN /ˈmɔː.tə/ ⓤ /ˈmɔːr.tɚ/ *noun* [C] a large gun with a short wide barrel which fires bombs or other explosives very high into the air, or an explosive device fired from such a gun

mortar BOWL /ˈmɔː.tə/ ⓤ /ˈmɔːr.tɚ/ *noun* [C] a hard strong bowl in which substances are crushed into a powder by hitting or rubbing them with a PESTLE (= heavy tool): *Use a **pestle and** mortar to crush the spices.*

mortarboard /ˈmɔː.tə.bɔːd/ ⓤ /ˈmɔːr.tɚ.bɔːrd/ *noun* [C] (AUS **trencher**) a black hat with a square flat top, worn on formal occasions by some teachers and students at college or university, and in the past by some school teachers

mortgage /ˈmɔː.ɡɪdʒ/ ⓤ /ˈmɔːr-/ *noun* [C] an agreement which allows you to borrow money from a bank or similar organization, especially in order to buy a house or apartment, or the amount of money itself: *They **took out** a £40 000 mortgage (= They borrowed £40 000) to buy the house.* ○ *a monthly mortgage payment*

mortgage /ˈmɔː.ɡɪdʒ/ ⓤ /ˈmɔːr-/ *verb* [T] *The house was mortgaged **up to the hilt** (= The full value of the house had been borrowed).*

mortgagee /ˌmɔː.ɡɪˈdʒiː/ ⓤ /ˌmɔːr-/ *noun* [C] SPECIALIZED a bank or similar organization which gives mortgages to people, especially so that they can buy a house or apartment

mortician /mɔːˈtɪʃ.ᵊn/ [US] /mɔːr-/ *noun* [C] *US FOR* **undertaker**

mortify /ˈmɔː.tɪ.faɪ/ [US] /ˈmɔːr.t̬ə-/ *verb* [T usually passive] to cause someone to feel extremely ashamed: *If I told her that she'd upset him she'd be mortified.* **mortification** /ˌmɔː.tɪ.fɪˈkeɪ.ʃᵊn/ [US] /ˌmɔːr.t̬ə-/ *noun* [U] ***To the** mortification **of** the show's organizers, the top performers withdrew at the last minute.*

mortise, mortice /ˈmɔː.tɪs/ [US] /ˈmɔːr.t̬ɪs/ *noun* [C] *SPECIALIZED* a rectangular hole in a piece of wood, stone, etc. into which another piece is fixed, so that they form a joint

ˈmortise ˌlock *UK,* **mortice lock** *noun* [C] (*US* **deadbolt,** *AUS* **deadlock**) a lock that is enclosed within the edge of a door, so that it cannot be seen or removed when the door is closed

mortuary /ˈmɔː.tjʊ.ri/ [US] /ˈmɔːr.tʃu.er.i/ *noun* [C] **1** *UK* (*US* **morgue**) a building, or a room in a hospital, where dead bodies are kept so that they can be examined before the funeral **2** *US FOR* **funeral parlour**

mosaic /məʊˈzeɪ.ɪk/ [US] /moʊ-/ *noun* [C] a pattern or picture made using many small pieces of coloured stone or glass: *a beautiful 10th century mosaic* ○ *FIGURATIVE The country is now a cultural and social mosaic* (= mixture) *due to the influx of several different ethnic groups.*

mosey /ˈməʊ.zi/ [US] /ˈmoʊ-/ *verb* [I usually + adv or prep] *INFORMAL* to walk or go slowly, usually without a special purpose: *I'll just mosey **on down** to the beach for a while.*

mosh /mɒʃ/ [US] /mɑːʃ/ *verb* [I] *INFORMAL* to dance energetically and violently at a rock concert **mosher** /ˈmɒʃ.əʳ/ [US] /ˈmɑː.ʃɚ/ *noun* [C]

ˈmosh ˌpit *noun* [C or S] *INFORMAL* the area in front of the stage at a rock concert where members of the audience dance energetically and violently

Moslem /ˈmɒz.lɪm/ [US] /ˈmɑː.zlem/ *noun, adj* **Muslim**

mosque /mɒsk/ [US] /mɑːsk/ *noun* [C] a building for Islamic religious activities and worship

mosquito (*plural* **mosquitoes**) /məˈskiː.təʊ/ [US] /-t̬oʊ/ *noun* [C] (*UK INFORMAL* **mozzie/mossie**) a small flying insect that bites people and animals, and sucks their blood: *Some types of the anopheles mosquito transmit malaria to humans.*

mosˈquito ˌnet *noun* [C] a net that hangs over and around a bed to keep insects away from someone who is sleeping

moss /mɒs/ [US] /mɑːs/ *noun* [C or U] a very small green or yellow plant that grows especially in wet earth or on rocks, walls and tree trunks: *The rocks near the river were covered with moss.* **mossy** /ˈmɒs.i/ [US] /ˈmɑː.si/ *adj*: *a mossy tree/rock/lawn*

most /məʊst/ [US] /moʊst/ *determiner, pronoun, adv* **1** the biggest number or amount of; more than anything or anyone else: *What's **the** most you've ever won at cards?* ○ *Which of you earns **the** most money?* ○ *He wanted to do **the** most good he could with the £200, so he gave it to charity.* ○ *The kids loved the fair, but they enjoyed the bumper cars most **of all**.* **2** used to form the superlative of many adjectives and adverbs: *Joanne is **the** most intelligent person I know.* ○ *The department needs three more computers in order to work most effectively* (= to work as effectively as possible). **3** almost all: *I don't eat meat, but I like most types of fish.* ○ *In this school, most **of** the children are from the Chinese community.* **4** *FORMAL* very: *It was a most beautiful morning.* **5** *MAINLY US INFORMAL* almost: *You'll find her in the bar most **every** evening about six o'clock.*

• **make the most of** ***sth*** to take full advantage of something because it may not last long: *It's a lovely day – we must make the most of **it**.*

-most /-məʊst/ [US] /-moʊst/ *suffix* used to mean 'furthest': *John O'Groats is the northernmost part of the British mainland* (= the part that is farther to the north than any other part).

mostly /ˈməʊst.li/ [US] /ˈmoʊst-/ *adv*: *In the smaller villages, it's mostly* (= usually) *very quiet at nights.* ○ *The band are mostly* (= Most of them are) *teenagers, I think.*

MOT /ˌem.əʊˈtiː/ [US] /-oʊ-/ *noun* [C] a test which all British road vehicles more than three years old have to pass each year in order to prove that they are safe to drive: *The car will fail its MOT if we don't get the brakes fixed.* ○ *an MOT certificate* **MOT** /ˌem.əʊˈtiː/ [US] /-oʊ-/ *verb* [T] **MOTing, MOT'd, MOT'd** *I want to **get/have** the car MOT'd before we drive to France.*

mote /məʊt/ [US] /moʊt/ *noun* [C] *LITERARY* something, especially a bit of dust, that is so small it is almost impossible to see

motel /məʊˈtel/ [US] /moʊ-/ *noun* [C] (*US ALSO* **motor inn/lodge**) a hotel by the side of a road, usually with spaces for cars next to each room

moth /mɒθ/ [US] /mɑːθ/ *noun* [C] an insect with wings which is similar to a BUTTERFLY, usually flies at night, and is attracted to light: *Some types of moth eat holes in clothes.*

mothball /ˈmɒθ.bɔːl/ [US] /ˈmɑːθ.bɑːl/ *verb* [T] to stop work on an idea, plan or job, but leaving it in such a way that you can start on it again at some point in the future: *Six coal pits were mothballed in the hope that they could be reopened in a time of better economic conditions.*

moth-eaten /ˈmɒθˌiː.tᵊn/ [US] /ˈmɑːθˌiː.t̬ᵊn/ *adj* If clothing or furniture is moth-eaten, it looks old and has holes in it.

mother [PARENT] /ˈmʌð.əʳ/ [US] /-ɚ/ *noun* [C] a female parent: *My mother was 21 when she got married.* ○ *All the mothers **and fathers** had been invited to the end-of-term concert.* ○ *The little kittens and their mother were all curled up asleep in the same basket.* ○ [as form of address] *FORMAL OR OLD-FASHIONED May I borrow your car, Mother?*

• **the mother of all** ***sth*** *INFORMAL* an extreme example of something: *We got caught in the mother of all storms.*

• **at** ***your*** **mother's knee** *LITERARY* If you learned something at your mother's knee, you learned it when you were a child: *I learned to sew at my mother's knee.*

mother /ˈmʌð.əʳ/ [US] /-ɚ/ *verb* [T] *OFTEN DISAPPROVING* to treat a person with great kindness and affection and to try to protect them from anything dangerous or difficult: *Stop mothering her – she's 40 years old and can take care of herself.*

motherhood /ˈmʌð.ə.hʊd/ [US] /-ɚ-/ *noun* [U] the state or time of being a mother: *I don't feel ready for motherhood yet.*

motherly /ˈmʌð.ᵊl.i/ [US] /-ɚ.li/ *adj* *USUALLY APPROVING* describes a woman who treats other people with a lot of kindness and affection and tries to make certain they are happy

Mother [RELIGIOUS WOMAN] /ˈmʌð.əʳ/ [US] /-ɚ/ *noun* the title of a woman who is in charge of, or who has a high rank within, a convent: *Mother Theresa* ○ *a mother **superior*** ○ [as form of address] *Good morning, Mother.*

mother [SLANG] /ˈmʌð.əʳ/ ʊʃ -‿-/ *noun* [C] *US OFFENSIVE* **motherfucker**

motherboard /ˈmʌð.ə.bɔːd/ [US] /-ɚ.bɔːrd/ *noun* [C] *SPECIALIZED* a PRINTED CIRCUIT BOARD that contains the CPU of a computer and makes it possible for the other parts of a computer to communicate with each other

ˈmother ˌcountry *noun* [S] the country where you were born or which you feel is your original home: *Even though she hasn't lived in Spain for 50 years, she still calls it her mother country.*

ˈmother ˌfigure *noun* [C] a woman who you feel you can ask for help, support or advice

motherfucker /ˈmʌð.əˌfʌk.əʳ/ [US] /-ɚˌfʌk.ɚ/ *noun* [C] (*ALSO* **mother**) **1** *MAINLY US OFFENSIVE* an extremely insulting name for someone you hate or for someone who has made you angry: *If that motherfucker touches my car again, I'll break his fingers!* **2** *US OFFENSIVE* an extremely unpleasant thing: *That was a motherfucker of an exam.* **motherfucking** *adj OFFENSIVE He's a motherfucking son of a bitch.*

mother-in-law /ˈmʌð.ə.rɪnˌlɔː/ [US] /-ɚ.ɪnˌlɑː/ *noun* [C] *plural* **mothers-in-law** the mother of your husband or wife

motherland /ˈmʌð.ə.lænd/ [US] /-ɚ-/ *noun* [U] **fatherland**

motherless /ˈmʌð.ᵊl.i/ [US] /-ɚ.li/ *adj* without a mother: *a poor motherless child*

ˌMother ˈNature *noun* [U] *OFTEN HUMOROUS* nature, especially when considered as a force that controls the weather and all living things: *It is better to try to work with, rather than against, Mother Nature.*

mother-of-pearl /ˌmʌð.ə.rəv'pɜːl/ ⓤ /-ɚ.əv'pɝːl/ *noun* [U] a smooth hard substance forming a layer inside the shells of some sea animals. It is white but also seems to shine with many different colours. It is used to make buttons and for decoration.

Mother's Day /'mʌð.əz,deɪ/ ⓤ /-ɚz-/ *noun* [C usually sing] (*UK ALSO* **Mothering Sunday**) a day each year when people give a card or present to their mother or do something special for her

mother-to-be /ˌmʌð.ə.tə'biː/ ⓤ /-ɚ-/ *noun* [C] a woman who is pregnant

ˌmother ˈtongue *noun* [C usually sing] the first language that you learn when you are a baby, rather than a language learned at school or as an adult

motif /məʊ'tiːf/ ⓤ /moʊ-/ *noun* [C] **1** a pattern or design: *We chose some curtains with a flower motif.* **2** an idea that is used many times in a piece of writing or music: *The motif of betrayal and loss is crucial in all these stories.*

motile /'məʊ.taɪl/ ⓤ /'moʊ.t̬ə l/ *adj SPECIALIZED* (especially of plants, organisms and very small forms of life) able to move by itself **motility** /məʊ'tɪl.ə.ti/ ⓤ /moʊ'tɪl.ə.t̬i/ *noun* [U]

motion [MOVEMENT] /'məʊ.ʃ ə n/ ⓤ /'moʊ-/ *noun* **1** [C or U] the act or process of moving, or a particular action or movement: *The violent motion of the ship upset his stomach.* ○ *He rocked the cradle with a gentle backwards and forwards motion.* ○ *They showed the goal again in slow motion* (= at a slower speed so that the action could be more clearly seen). **2** [C] *UK* a polite way of referring to the process of excretion of solid waste, or the waste itself: *The nurse asked if her motions were regular.*

● **go through the motions** *INFORMAL DISAPPROVING* to do something without caring very much about it or having much interest in it: *He says he's been investigating my complaint, but I feel he's just going through the motions.*

● **put/set** *sth* **in motion** to start a machine or process: *Once the printing processes have been put in motion, they're not so easy to stop.* ○ *We wrote to the passport office to set the whole process in motion.*

motionless /'məʊ.ʃ ə n.ləs/ ⓤ /'moʊ-/ *adj* without moving: *The horse lay motionless on the ground, as if dead.*

motion [SIGNAL] /'məʊ.ʃ ə n/ ⓤ /'moʊ-/ *verb* [I or T; usually + adv or prep] to make a signal to someone, usually with your hand or head: *I saw him motion to the man at the door, who quietly left.* ○ *Her attendants all gathered round her, but she motioned them away.* ○ [+ obj + to infinitive] *He motioned me to sit down.*

motion [SUGGESTION] /'məʊ.ʃ ə n/ ⓤ /'moʊ-/ *noun* [C] a formal suggestion made, discussed and voted on at a meeting: [+ to infinitive] *Someone proposed a motion to increase the membership fee to £500 a year.* ○ *The motion was accepted/passed/defeated/rejected.*

ˌmotion ˈpicture *noun* [C] *US FORMAL FOR* **movie**

ˈmotion ˌsickness *noun* [U] **travel sickness**

motive [REASON] /'məʊ.tɪv/ ⓤ /'moʊ.tɪv/ *noun* [C] a reason for doing something: *Why would she have killed him? She has no motive.* ○ *Does he have a motive for lying about where he was?* ○ *What is the motive behind* (= the reason for) *the bombing?* ○ *I think you should examine/question their motives in offering to lend you the money.* ○ *She denies that she has has an ulterior* (= secret) *motive for making the donation.*

motivate /'məʊ.tɪ.veɪt/ ⓤ /'moʊ.t̬ɪ-/ *verb* **1** [T often passive] to cause someone to behave in a particular way: *Like so many people, he's motivated by greed.* ○ *He is genuinely motivated by a desire to help people.* **2** [T] to make someone want to do something well: [+ to infinitive] *Teaching is all about motivating people to learn.*

motivated /'məʊ.tɪ.veɪ.tɪd/ ⓤ /'moʊ.t̬ɪ.veɪ.t̬ɪd/ *adj: a racially-motivated murder* ○ *Our staff are hard-working and highly motivated* (= enthusiastic).

motivation /ˌməʊ.tɪ'veɪ.ʃ ə n/ ⓤ /ˌmoʊ.t̬ɪ-/ *noun* **1** [U] enthusiasm for doing something: *He's a bright enough student – he just lacks motivation.* ○ *There seems to be a lack of motivation among the staff.* **2** [C] the need or reason for doing something: *What was the motivation*

for the attack? ○ *The motivation behind the decision is the desire to improve our service to our customers.*

motivational /ˌməʊ.tɪ'veɪ.ʃ ə n.ə l/ ⓤ /ˌmoʊ.t̬ɪ-/ *adj* [before n] giving you motivation: *a motivational speaker*

motiveless /'məʊ.tɪv.ləs/ ⓤ /'moʊ.t̬ɪv-/ *adj* without a motive: *an apparently motiveless murder*

motive [MOVEMENT] /'məʊ.tɪv/ ⓤ /'moʊ.tɪv/ *adj* [before n] *SPECIALIZED* (of power or force) causing movement or action

mot juste /ˌməʊ'ʒuːst/ ⓤ /ˌmoʊ-/ *noun* [C usually sing] *plural* **mots justes** *FORMAL* the word or phrase that is exactly right in a particular situation

motley /'mɒt.li/ ⓤ /'mɑːt-/ *adj* [before n] consisting of many different types and therefore appearing strange or of low quality: *There's a motley assortment/collection of old furniture in the house we're renting at the moment.* ○ *The people who turned up to the meeting were a motley crew* (= a group consisting of many different types of people).

motocross /'məʊ.tə.krɒs/ ⓤ /'moʊ.t̬ə.krɑːs/ *noun* [U] (*ALSO* **scrambling**) the sport of racing over rough ground on specially strengthened motorcycles

motor [DEVICE] /'məʊ.tə r/ ⓤ /'moʊ.t̬ɚ/ *noun* [C] a device that changes electricity or fuel into movement and makes a machine work: *The pump is powered by a small electric motor.* ○ *Our washing machine needs a new motor.* ○ *MAINLY UK I've had a new motor* (= engine) *put in my car.* * NOTE: In British and Australian English, **motor** is used mainly for devices powered by electricity. In American English, it is also commonly used for devices powered by petrol, steam, etc.

motor [CAR] /'məʊ.tə r/ ⓤ /'moʊ.t̬ɚ/ *adj* [before n] *MAINLY UK* connected with cars or other vehicles which have engines and use roads: *This has been a difficult year for the motor industry/trade.* ○ *motor insurance*

motor /'məʊ.tə r/ ⓤ /'moʊ.t̬ɚ/ *noun* [C] *MAINLY UK INFORMAL* a car: *Do you know anyone who's looking for a second-hand motor?*

motor /'məʊ.tə r/ ⓤ /'moʊ.t̬ɚ/ *verb* [I] **1** *UK OLD-FASHIONED* to drive: *I was just motoring along, minding my own business, when suddenly I was stopped by the police.* **2** *INFORMAL* to move or increase very quickly: *Shares have motored ahead as profits have risen.*

motoring /'məʊ.tə.rɪŋ/ ⓤ /'moʊ.t̬ɚ-/ *adj* [before n] *MAINLY UK* relating to driving: *motoring costs* ○ *It was the first time he'd been convicted of a motoring offence.*

motorist /'məʊ.tə r.ɪst/ ⓤ /'moʊ.t̬ɚ-/ *noun* [C] a person who drives a car

motorized, *UK USUALLY* **-ised** /'məʊ.tə r.aɪzd/ ⓤ /'moʊ.t̬ə.raɪzd/ *adj* **1** specially fitted with an engine or motor: *a motorized wheelchair* **2** Soldiers who are motorized are provided with wheeled vehicles which have engines: *motorized infantry*

motor [MUSCULAR] /'məʊ.tə r/ ⓤ /'moʊ.t̬ɚ/ *adj* [before n] *SPECIALIZED* relating to muscles that produce movement, or the nerves and parts of the brain that control these muscles: *He has poor motor control/functions.*

motorbike /'məʊ.tə.baɪk/ ⓤ /'moʊ.t̬ɚ-/ *noun* [C] *UK* **1** a motorcycle: *She jumped on her motorbike and raced off down the road.* ⊃See picture **Cars and Trucks** on page Centre 13 **2** *US* a small light motorcycle

motorboat /'məʊ.tə.bəʊt/ ⓤ /'moʊ.t̬ɚ.boʊt/ *noun* [C] a usually small and often fast boat which is powered by an engine ⊃See picture **Planes, Ships and Boats** on page Centre 14

motorcade /'məʊ.tə.keɪd/ ⓤ /'moʊ.t̬ɚ-/ *noun* [C] (*US ALSO* **autocade**) a series of cars and other motor vehicles which moves slowly along a road carrying someone important, especially during an official ceremony

ˈmotor ˌcar *noun* [C] *UK FORMAL* a car

motorcycle /'məʊ.tə.saɪ.kl/ ⓤ /'moʊ.t̬ɚ-/ *noun* [C] (*ALSO* **motorbike**) a vehicle with two wheels and an engine

motorcyclist /'məʊ.tə.saɪ.klɪst/ ⓤ /'moʊ.t̬ɚ-/ *noun* [C] a person who rides a motorcycle

motorhome /'məʊ.tə.həʊm/ ⓤ /'moʊ.t̬ɚ.hoʊm/ *noun* [C] a large motor vehicle that is designed to be lived in while travelling. It contains cooking equipment, one or more beds, and sometimes a toilet. ⊃See picture **Cars and Trucks** on page Centre 13

ˈmotor ˌinn *noun* [C] *US FOR* **motel**

'motor ,lodge noun [C] US FOR **motel**

motorman /'məʊ.tə.mən/ ⓤ /'moʊ.t̬ɚ.mæn/ noun [C] US a driver of an underground train

motormouth /'məʊ.tə.maʊθ/ ⓤ /'moʊ.t̬ə-/ noun [C] MAIN-LY US INFORMAL DISAPPROVING a person who talks quickly and continuously, often without considering what they are saying

'motor ,mower noun [C] a powered machine for cutting grass

,motor 'neurone di,sease noun [U] a disease which causes the muscles to become weak and results in death

'motor ,racing noun [U] the sport of racing extremely fast and powerful cars around a track

'motor ,scooter noun [C] a very light motorcycle with small wheels

'motor ,vehicle noun [C] FORMAL OR LEGAL a vehicle that has an engine: The council has forbidden motor vehicles from entering the city centre.

motorway UK /'məʊ.tə.weɪ/ ⓤ /'moʊ.t̬ə-/ noun [C] (US freeway) a wide road built for fast moving traffic travelling long distances: Because of the bad weather, motorway (driving) conditions are expected to be hazardous tonight.

mottled /'mɒt.l̩d/ ⓤ /'mɑː.t̬l̩d/ adj marked with areas of different colours which do not form a regular pattern: mottled skin

motto /'mɒt.əʊ/ ⓤ /'mɑː.t̬oʊ/ noun [C] plural **mottos** or **mottoes** a short sentence or phrase that expresses a belief or purpose: Her motto is "Work hard, play hard".

mould GROWTH UK, US **mold** /məʊld/ ⓤ /moʊld/ noun [U] a soft green or grey growth which develops on old food or on objects that have been left for too long in warm wet air: There was mould on the cheese.

mouldy UK, US **moldy** /'məʊl.di/ ⓤ /'moʊl-/ adj **1** covered with mould: mouldy bread/cheese **2** not modern or interesting: The city's museums are filled with mouldy **old** collections.

mould SHAPE UK, US **mold** /məʊld/ ⓤ /moʊld/ noun **1** [C] a hollow container with a particular shape into which soft or liquid substances are poured, so that when the substance hardens it takes the shape of the container: a cake/jelly mould **2** [S] If someone is from or in a mould, they have the characteristics typical of a certain type of person: He's **cast in** a very different mould from his brother. ○ He's a player in the Becker mould.

mould UK, US **mold** /məʊld/ ⓤ /moʊld/ verb **1** [T] to make a soft substance a particular shape: This plastic is going to be moulded **into** plates. ○ The children moulded little pots out of/from (= made them by shaping) clay. **2** [T] to try to change or influence someone: He kept trying to mould me **into** something he wanted me to be. **3** [I usually + adv or prep] to fit the body very closely: She was wearing an extremely tight costume which moulded to/round the contours of her body.

moulding UK, US **molding** /'məʊl.dɪŋ/ ⓤ /'moʊl-/ noun [C or U] a piece of wood, plastic, stone, etc. which has been made into a particular shape to decorate the top or bottom of a wall, or a door, window or piece of furniture

moulder /'məʊl.də'/ ⓤ /'moʊl.dɚ/ verb [I] **1** UK (US **molder**) to decay slowly; to ROT: I found these apples mouldering in the cupboard. **2** to be left somewhere and not used or cared for: There's an old bike that's been mouldering **away** in the shed for years.

mouldy /'məʊl.di/ ⓤ /'moʊl-/ adj [before n] UK OLD-FASHIONED SLANG of little value; unpleasant: All he gave me was a mouldy **old** 50p. ⊃See also **mouldy** at **mould** GROWTH.

moult UK, US USUALLY **molt** /məʊlt/ ⓤ /moʊlt/ verb [I] (of a bird or animal) to lose feathers, skin or hair as a natural process at a particular time of year so that new feathers, skin or hair can grow

mound /maʊnd/ noun [C] **1** a large pile of earth, stones etc. like a small hill: a **burial** mound (= a place where people were buried in ancient times) **2** a large pile of something: a mound **of** potatoes/papers **3** US the raised area in baseball from which the PITCHER throws the ball

mount GET ON /maʊnt/ verb [I or T] to get on a horse, bicycle, etc. in order to ride: She mounted her horse and rode off.

mount /maʊnt/ noun [C] FORMAL a horse: an excellent mount for a child

mounted /'maʊn.tɪd/ ⓤ /-t̬ɪd/ adj [before n] describes soldiers or police officers who ride horses while on duty: mounted police officers

mount GO UP /maʊnt/ verb [T] to go up or onto: He mounted the platform and began to speak to the assembled crowd. ○ FORMAL Queen Elizabeth II mounted **the throne** (= became queen) in 1952.

mount INCREASE /maʊnt/ verb [I] to gradually increase, rise, or get bigger: The children's excitement is mounting as Christmas gets nearer.

mounting /'maʊn.tɪŋ/ ⓤ /-t̬ɪŋ/ adj gradually increasing: mounting anxiety/excitement ○ mounting debts

▲ **mount up** phrasal verb to gradually become a large amount: It isn't a good idea to let bills mount up.

mount ORGANIZE /maʊnt/ verb [T] to organize and begin an activity or event: to mount an attack/campaign/challenge/protest ○ to mount an exhibition/display

mount FIX /maʊnt/ verb [T] to fix something on a wall, in a frame etc., so that it can be viewed or used: The children's work has been mounted **on** cards and put up on the walls of the classroom. ○ The CCTV camera is mounted above the main door. **mount** /maʊnt/ noun [C] I'm looking for a piece of card I can use as a mount **for** this picture.

mount GUARD /maʊnt/ verb [T] to place someone on guard: Sentries are mounted outside the palace at all times.

• **mount guard (on/over** sb**)** to guard someone: Armed security officers are employed to mount guard over the president.

Mount MOUNTAIN /maʊnt/ noun (WRITTEN ABBREVIATION **Mt**) used as part of the name of a mountain: Mount Everest ○ Mount Hood

mountain /'maʊn.tɪn/ ⓤ /-t̬ᵊn/ noun [C] **1** a raised part of the Earth's surface, much larger than a hill, the top of which might be covered in snow: The Matterhorn is one of the biggest mountains in Europe. ○ The Rockies are a mountain **chain/range** in the western USA. ○ I'd love to go mountain-**climbing**. ○ We're going to the mountains (= an area where there are mountains) for our holiday. **2** UK a large amount of food which is kept in storage instead of being sold, so that prices for it do not fall: a grain mountain

• **a mountain of** sth a large amount of something: I've got a mountain of work to do.

• **make a mountain out of a molehill** to make a slight difficulty seem like a serious problem: You're making a mountain out of a molehill. You wrote one bad essay – it doesn't mean you're going to fail your exam.

mountaineer /,maʊn.tɪ'nɪə'/ ⓤ /-t̬ᵊn'ɪr/ noun [C] a person who climbs mountains as a sport or job

mountaineering /,maʊn.tɪ'nɪə.rɪŋ/ ⓤ /-t̬ᵊn'ɪr.ɪŋ/ noun [U] the sport or activity of climbing mountains

mountainous /'maʊn.tɪ.nəs/ ⓤ /-t̬ᵊn.əs/ adj **1** having a lot of mountains: a mountainous region **2** very big: mountainous waves

Mountains /'maʊn.tɪnz/ ⓤ /-t̬ᵊnz/ plural noun used as part of a name for a group of mountains: the Blue Ridge Mountains of Virginia

'mountain ,bike noun [C] a bicycle with thick tyres and a lot of gears, originally made for riding on hills and rough ground, but now often used on roads

'mountain ,lion noun [C] US FOR **puma**

mountainside /'maʊn.tɪn.saɪd/ ⓤ /-t̬ᵊn-/ noun [C usually sing] the side or slope of a mountain: Can you see those goats high up **on** the mountainside?

mountaintop /,maʊn.tɪn'tɒp/ ⓤ /-t̬ᵊn'tɑːp/ noun [C] the top of a mountain ⊃See also **peak** MOUNTAIN TOP; **summit** HIGHEST POINT.

Mountie /'maʊn.ti/ ⓤ /-t̬i/ noun [C] INFORMAL a member of the ROYAL CANADIAN MOUNTED POLICE

mourn /mɔːn/ ⓤ /mɔːrn/ verb [I or T] to feel or express great sadness, especially because of someone's death: Queen Victoria mourned Prince Albert/Prince Albert's death for 40 years. ○ She was still mourning **for** her brother. ○ They mourned the **passing of** traditional folk dancing (= felt sad because it had stopped existing).

mourner /ˈmɔː.nəʳ/ [US] /ˈmɔːr.nɚ/ *noun* [C] a person at a funeral: *The dead man's wife and children were the chief mourners.*

mournful /ˈmɔːn.fəl/ [US] /ˈmɔːrn-/ *adj* very sad: *a mournful expression* ○ *mournful music* **mournfully** /ˈmɔːn.fəl.i/ [US] /ˈmɔːrn-/ *adv* **mournfulness** /ˈmɔːn.fəl.nəs/ [US] /ˈmɔːrn-/ *noun* [U]

mourning /ˈmɔː.nɪŋ/ [US] /ˈmɔːr-/ *noun* [U] **1** great sadness felt because someone has died: *Shops will be closed today as a sign of mourning* ***for*** *the king.* ○ *He was* ***in*** *mourning* ***for*** *his wife.* **2** the usually black clothes that are worn in some countries as an expression of sadness about someone's death

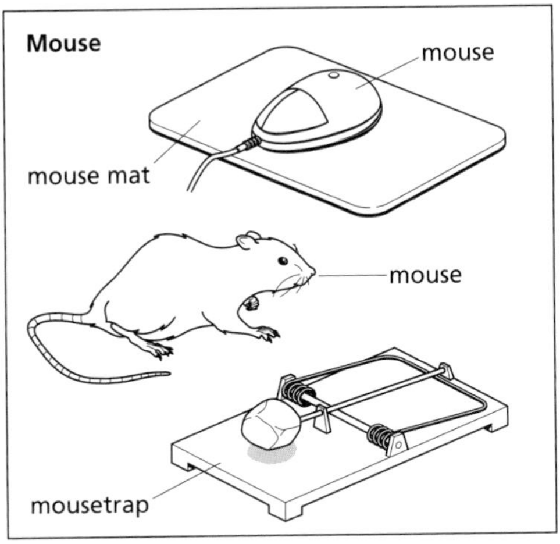
Mouse
mouse
mouse mat
mouse
mousetrap

mouse [ANIMAL] /maʊs/ *noun plural* **mice 1** [C] a small mammal with short fur, a pointed face, and a long tail **2** [C usually sing] a shy, quiet, nervous person

mouser /ˈmaʊ.səʳ/ [US] /-sɚ/ *noun* [C] a cat that catches mice: *She's a good mouser.*

mouse [DEVICE] /maʊs/ *noun* [C] *plural* **mice** a small device which you move across a surface in order to move a POINTER on your computer screen ➲See picture **In the Office** on page Centre 15

ˈ**mouse** ˌ**mat** *UK noun* [C] (*US* **mouse pad**) the special flat piece of material on which you move the MOUSE for your computer

mousetrap /ˈmaʊs.træp/ *noun* [C] a small device that is used in houses and other buildings for catching and killing mice

moussaka /muːˈsɑː.kə/ *noun* [U] a dish, originally from Greece, consisting of meat, tomato and AUBERGINE (= a large purple vegetable) with cheese on top

mousse /muːs/ *noun* [C or U] **1** a light cold food made from eggs mixed with cream: *chocolate mousse* ○ *salmon mousse* **2** a light creamy substance which is put on the hair or skin to improve its appearance or condition: *styling mousse*

moustache, *US USUALLY* **mustache** /mʊˈstɑːʃ/ [US] /ˈmʌs.tæʃ/ *noun* [C] hair which a man grows above his upper lip: *Groucho Marx had a thick black moustache.*

mousy (**mousier**, **mousiest**) /ˈmaʊ.si/ *adj* (*ALSO* **mousey**) **1** describes hair which is brown and not special or attractive **2** shy and nervous and lacking interesting qualities: *A mousy-looking woman accompanied him, his wife I assumed.*

mouth [BODY PART] /maʊθ/ *noun* [C] the opening in the face of a person or animal, consisting of the lips and the space between them, or the space behind containing the teeth and the tongue: *Open your mouth wide and say "Ah".* ○ *You shouldn't put so much food in your mouth at once.* ➲See picture **The Body** on page Centre 5

• **be all mouth** (*UK ALSO* **be all mouth and no trousers**) *INFORMAL* to talk a lot about doing something but never do it: *He says he's going to complain to the manager, but I reckon he's all mouth.*

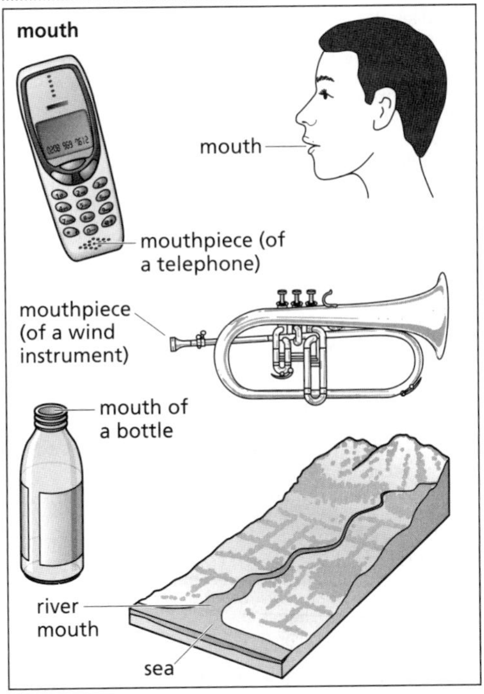
mouth
mouth
mouthpiece (of
a telephone)
mouthpiece
(of a wind
instrument)
mouth of
a bottle
river
mouth
sea

• **be down in the mouth** *INFORMAL* to be sad

• **mouth to feed** someone, especially a new-born baby, for whom you must provide food: *They've got three kids and the husband's just lost his job – the last thing they need is* ***another*** *mouth to feed.*

• **keep *your* mouth shut** *INFORMAL* to not talk about something: *I don't know whether to tell him what I know or keep my mouth shut.*

• **make *sb's* mouth water** If the smell or sight of food makes your mouth water, it makes you want to eat it: *The smell of that bacon cooking is making my mouth water.*

• **Out of the mouths of babes and sucklings.** *LITERARY SAYING* said when a child says something that surprises you because it shows an adult's understanding

mouth /maʊð/ *verb* [T] *It looks to me as if the singers are only mouthing the words* (= forming them with their lips without making any sound). ○ [+ speech] *"Can we go?" mouthed Mary.* ○ *I don't want to stand here listening to you mouthing* (= saying in a way that is not sincere) *excuses.* ➲See also **badmouth**.

-mouthed /-maʊðd/ *suffix*: *a loud-mouthed teenager* (= talking very loudly, especially to attract attention) ○ *a foul-mouthed drunk* (= often swearing) ○ *We stared* ***open****-mouthed* (= in surprise) *as the elephant walked slowly down Fairview Close.*

▲ **mouth off (about *sth*)** *phrasal verb INFORMAL DISAPPROVING* to express your opinions too loudly and publicly: *I had to listen to Michael mouthing off about the government all through lunch.*

▲ **mouth off (to/at *sb*)** *phrasal verb INFORMAL DISAPPROVING* to speak in a rude or offensive way to someone: *She's a typical teenager, coming home late at night and mouthing off to her parents.*

mouth [OPENING] /maʊθ/ *noun* [C usually sing] the opening of a narrow container, the opening of a hole or cave, or the place where a river flows into the sea: *Quebec is at the mouth* ***of*** *the St Lawrence River.*

mouthful [AMOUNT] /ˈmaʊθ.fʊl/ *noun* [C] an amount of food or drink which fills your mouth, or which you put into your mouth at one time: *He only ate a few mouthfuls of meat.*

mouthful [WORD] /ˈmaʊθ.fʊl/ *noun* [U] *INFORMAL* a word or phrase that is difficult to pronounce or that has a lot of

[M]

syllables: *I've always called myself 'Henny' because it's less of a mouthful than 'Henrietta'.*

• **give someone a mouthful** *MAINLY UK INFORMAL* to shout something angry at someone, usually swearing at them: *A taxi driver wound down his window and gave the cyclist a mouthful.*

ˈmouth ˌorgan *noun* [C] a **harmonica**

mouthpiece /ˈmaʊθ.piːs/ *noun* [C] **1** the part of a telephone, musical instrument or other device that goes near or between the lips: *To play the recorder, blow gently* ***into*** *the mouthpiece.* **2** *DISAPPROVING* a person or a newspaper that only expresses the opinions of one particular organization: *This newspaper is just a Republican mouthpiece.*

mouth-to-mouth (resuscitation) /ˌmaʊθ.tə.maʊθ.rɪˌsʌs.ɪˈteɪ.ʃᵊn/ *noun* [U] **artificial respiration**

mouthwash /ˈmaʊθ.wɒʃ/ [US] /-wɑːʃ/ *noun* [C or U] a liquid used for keeping the mouth clean and smelling fresh

mouth-watering /ˈmaʊθˌwɔː.tə.rɪŋ/ [US] /-ˌwɑː.t̬ɚ-/ *adj* describes food that looks as if it will taste good: *Look at those mouth-watering cakes.*

movable /ˈmuː.və.bl̩/ *adj* (*ALSO* **moveable**) able to be moved: *a chair with movable armrests*

ˌmovable ˈfeast *noun* [C] a religious holiday that is not on the same day every year: *Easter is a movable feast.*

move [CHANGE POSITION] /muːv/ *verb* [I or T] **1** to (cause to) change position: *I'm so cold I can't move my fingers.* ○ *Will you help me move this table to the back room?* ○ *Can we move* (= change the time of) *the meeting* ***from*** *2pm* ***to*** *3.30pm?* ○ *Don't move! Stay right where you are.* ○ *I thought I could hear someone moving* ***about/around*** *upstairs.* ○ *If you move* ***along/over/up*** (= go further to the side, back or front) *a bit, Tess can sit next to me.* ○ *Police officers at the scene of the accident were asking passers-by to move* ***along/on*** (= to go to a different place). ○ *Come on, it's time we were moving* (= going to a different place). ○ *Let's stay here tonight, then move* ***on*** (= continue our journey) *tomorrow morning.* **2** to change the position of one of the pieces used in a BOARD GAME: *In chess, the pieces can only move in certain directions.*

• **move heaven and earth** to do everything you can to achieve something: *He'll move heaven and earth to get it done on time.*

• **Move it!** *INFORMAL* used to tell someone to hurry: *Come on, Phil, move it!*

• **not move a muscle** to stay completely still: *She sat without moving a muscle as the nurse put the needle in.*

move /muːv/ *noun* **1** [S] an act of moving: *She held the gun to his head and said, "One move and you're dead!"* ○ *I hate the way my boss* ***watches my every*** *move* (= watches everything I do). **2** [C] in some BOARD GAMES, a change of the position of one of the pieces used to play the game, or a change of position that is permitted by the rules, or a player's turn to move their piece: *It takes a long time to learn all the moves in chess.* ○ *It's your move.*

• **get a move on** *INFORMAL* to hurry: *Come on, you two, get a move on!* ○ *We need to get a move on if we're going to catch that train.*

• **make a move** *UK* (*US* **be on the move**) *INFORMAL* to leave a place: *It's late – I think it's time we made a move.*

• **be on the move** *INFORMAL* **1** to be physically active: *I've been on the move all day and I'm really tired.* **2** to be travelling: *We're going to be on the move all next week, but we'll call you when we get to Edinburgh.*

movement /ˈmuːv.mənt/ *noun* **1** [C or U] a change of position: *He* ***made*** *a sudden movement and frightened the bird away.* ○ *For a long time after the accident, he had no movement* ***in*** (= was unable to move) *his legs.* ○ *Her movements were rather clumsy.* **2** [C] the part of a clock or watch which turns the narrow pointers that show the time

movements /ˈmuːv.mənts/ *plural noun* ***sb's*** **movements** what someone is doing during a particular period: *I don't know his movements this week.*

mover /ˈmuː.vəʳ/ [US] /-vɚ/ *noun* [C] *OLD-FASHIONED* used in descriptions of how someone dances: *He's a great mover.*

moving /ˈmuː.vɪŋ/ *adj* [before n] A moving object is one that moves: *a moving target* ○ *moving* ***parts*** *in a machine*

move [CHANGE PLACE] /muːv/ *verb* [I] to go to a different place to live or work: *We're moving* ***to*** *Paris.* ○ *They've bought a new house, but it will need a lot of work before they can move* ***into*** *it/move* ***in****.* ○ *I hear Paula has moved in* ***with*** *her boyfriend* (= gone to live in his house). ○ *The couple next door moved* ***away*** (= went to live somewhere else) *last year.* ○ *A lot of businesses are moving* ***out of*** *London because it's too expensive.*

• **move house** *UK* to leave your home in order to live in a new one: *We're moving house next week.*

move /muːv/ *noun* [C] when you go to live or work in a different place: *We've had four moves in three years.*

mover *US* /ˈmuː.vəʳ/ [US] /-vɚ/ *noun* [C] (*UK* **remover,** *AUS* **removalist**) someone who helps people move their possessions to a different place to live or work

moving /ˈmuː.vɪŋ/ *noun* [U] *I hate moving* (= going to a different place to live or work).

move [PROGRESS] /muːv/ *verb* [I or T] to (cause to) progress, change or happen in a particular way or direction: *The judge's decision will allow the case to move* ***ahead****.* ○ *If you want to move* ***ahead*** *in your career, you'll have to work harder.* ○ *Share prices moved* ***up/down*** *slowly yesterday.* ○ *Sophie has been moved* ***up/down*** *a grade at school.* ○ *It's time this company moved* ***into*** (= started to take advantage of the benefits of) *the computer age.*

• **move on to higher/better things** *HUMOROUS* to get a better job or improve your life in some way: *I hear you've moved on to higher things.*

movement /ˈmuːv.mənt/ *noun* [U] *There has been little movement in the dollar* (= It has not changed in value very much) *today.*

move [CHANGE OPINION] /muːv/ *verb* [I or T] to (cause to) change an opinion or the way in which you live or work: *He's made up his mind, and nothing you can say will move him* ***on*** *the issue.* ○ *More and more people are moving* ***away from/towards*** *vegetarianism.*

movement /ˈmuːv.mənt/ *noun* [C or U] *There has been a movement* (= change in the way people think and feel) ***towards*** *more women going back to work while their children are still small.* ○ *Recently there has been some movement* ***away from*** *traditional methods of teaching.*

move [FEELINGS] /muːv/ *verb* [T] to cause someone to have strong feelings, such as sadness, sympathy, happiness or admiration: *She said that she was* ***deeply*** *moved by all the letters of sympathy she had received.* ○ *It was such a sad film that it moved him* ***to tears*** (= made him cry).

moved /muːvd/ *adj*: *When she told me about her daughter's death, I was too moved even to speak.*

moving /ˈmuː.vɪŋ/ *adj* causing strong feelings of sadness or sympathy: *a very moving story* ○ *I find some of Brahms's music* ***deeply*** *moving.* **movingly** /ˈmuː.vɪŋ.li/ *adv*: *He spoke movingly about his wife's death.*

move [ACT] /muːv/ *verb* [T] to cause someone to take action: [+ obj + **to** infinitive] *FORMAL I can't imagine what could have moved him* ***to*** *say such a thing.*

move /muːv/ *noun* [C] an action taken to achieve something: *Buying those shares was a* ***good*** *move.* ○ *This move* (= stage in a plan of action) ***towards*** *improving childcare facilities has been widely welcomed.* ○ [+ **to** infinitive] *The council is* ***making*** *a move* (= taking action) ***to*** *ban traffic in some parts of the city.*

• **make the first move** **1** to be the first to take action: *Neither side seems prepared to make the first move towards reaching a peace agreement.* **2** *INFORMAL* to start a romantic or sexual relationship with someone: *She's fancied him for ages, but doesn't want to make the first move.*

moving /ˈmuː.vɪŋ/ *adj* [before n] *Local parents were the moving* ***force/spirit*** *behind the safety improvements at the playground* (= They were the people who made them happen).

move [SELL] /muːv/ *verb* [I or T] to sell: *No one wants to buy these toys – we just can't move them.* ○ *This new shampoo is moving really fast.*

mover /ˈmuː.vəʳ/ [US] /-vɚ/ *noun* [C] a product which sells very well: *These skirts have been one of our best movers this spring.*

move BE WITH PEOPLE /muːv/ *verb* [I + adv or prep] spend time with people: *She moves in/among a very small circle of people.*

move SUGGEST /muːv/ *verb* [I or T] SPECIALIZED to suggest something, especially formally at a meeting or in a court of law: *A vote was just about to be taken when someone stood up and said that they wished to move an amendment.* ○ [+ that] *I should like to move that the proposal be accepted.* ○ *Your Honour, we wish to move for dismissal of the charges.*

mover /ˈmuːvəʳ/ US /-vɚ/ *noun* [C] SPECIALIZED a person who formally makes a suggestion during a formal meeting or discussion

move EXCRETE /muːv/ *verb* [I or T] POLITE WORD (used especially by doctors and nurses) to excrete the contents of the bowels: *The doctor asked him if he'd moved his bowels that day.*

movement /ˈmuːv.mənt/ *noun* [C] POLITE WORD (used especially by doctors and nurses) an act of emptying the bowels: *When did you last have a (bowel) movement?*

PHRASAL VERBS WITH move ▼

▲ **move sb/sth in** *phrasal verb* [M] If the police, army or any group of people in authority move in, or if someone moves them in, they take control or attack, in order to deal with a difficult or dangerous situation: *When a company goes out of business, officials usually move in to take control.* ○ *The decision has been made to move UN troops in to try and stop the fighting.*

▲ **move in on sth/sb** *phrasal verb* If you move in on a person or place, you come close or closer to them in order to attack or take control of them: *Government troops are moving in on the rebel stronghold.*

▲ **move sth off/on (to sth)** *phrasal verb* to change from one subject to another when talking or writing: *Let's move off this subject now, shall we?* ○ *"Can we move on to the next item for discussion, please?"*

▲ **move on** NEW PLACE *phrasal verb* to leave the place where you are staying and go somewhere else: *I've been in Paris long enough – it's time to move on.*

▲ **move on** NEW ACTIVITY *phrasal verb* to start a new activity: *I'd done the same job for years and felt it was time to move on.*

▲ **move out** *phrasal verb* to stop living in a particular home: *Her landlord has given her a week to move out.*

movement GROUP OF PEOPLE /ˈmuːv.mənt/ *group noun* [C] a group of people with a particular set of aims: *the women's movement* ○ *The suffragette movement campaigned for votes for women in Britain and the US.* ○ [+ to infinitive] *a movement to stop animals being killed for their fur*

movement MUSIC /ˈmuːv.mənt/ *noun* [C] one of the main parts of a piece of classical music that is separated from the other parts with pauses: *Beethoven's fifth symphony has four movements.*

the ˌmovers and ˈshakers *plural noun plural* **movers and shakers** people with a lot of power and influence: *It's a play that's attracted the attention of the Broadway movers and shakers.*

movers /ˈmuː.vəz/ US /-vɚz/ *plural noun* (UK FORMAL **(furniture) removers**) MAINLY US, UK INFORMAL people whose job is to help people move their furniture and other possessions when they move to a new home

movie /ˈmuː.vi/ *noun* [C] MAINLY US FOR a cinema film: *My favourite movie is 'Casablanca'.*

the movies *plural noun* MAINLY US a cinema or group of cinemas: *What's on/showing at the movies this week?*

moviegoer US /ˈmuː.vi.ɡəʊ.əʳ/ US /-ˌɡoʊ.ɚ/ *noun* [C] (UK **filmgoer/cinemagoer**) a person who regularly goes to watch films at the cinema **moviegoing** MAINLY US /ˈmuː.vi.ɡəʊ.ɪŋ/ US /-ˌɡoʊ-/ *noun* [U], *adj* [before n] (MAINLY UK **filmgoing/cinemagoing**) *the moviegoing public*

ˈmovie ˌstar MAINLY US *noun* [C] (MAINLY UK **film star**) a very popular and successful movie actor or actress: *Greta Garbo was one of the great movie stars of the 1930s.*

ˈmovie ˌtheater *noun* [C] US FOR cinema: *There's a season of Bergman films on at our local movie theater.*

ˈmoving ˌvan *noun* [C] US FOR **removal van**

mow /məʊ/ US /moʊ/ *verb* [I or T] **mowed**, **mown** or **mowed** to cut plants, such as grass or wheat, which have long thin stems and grow close together: *You can't mow the grass/lawn if it's wet.* ○ *I love the smell of new-mown hay.*

mower /ˈməʊ.əʳ/ US /ˈmoʊ.ɚ/ *noun* [C] a machine for cutting especially grass ⊃See also **lawnmower**.

▲ **mow sb down** *phrasal verb* [M] to kill people, usually in large numbers, by shooting them or driving a vehicle into them: *Three shoppers were mown down this afternoon when a drunken driver lost control of his car.*

mozzarella /ˌmɒt.səˈrel.ə/ US /ˌmɑːt-/ *noun* [U] a soft white Italian cheese

MP /ˌemˈpiː/ *noun* [C] ABBREVIATION FOR **Member of Parliament**: *Tony Blair MP* ○ *Who is the MP for Hertfordshire South?*

MP3 /ˌem.piːˈθriː/ *noun* [C or U] TRADEMARK a computer FILE which stores high-quality sound in a small amount of space, or the technology that makes this possible: *I downloaded their latest album on MP3.*

MPˈ3 ˌplayer *noun* [C] an electronic device or a computer program for playing music which has been stored as MP3 files

mpg /ˌem.piːˈdʒiː/ ABBREVIATION FOR miles per gallon; the number of miles a vehicle travels using one GALLON of fuel: *My car does about 40 mpg.* ○ *How many mpg do you get from your car?*

mph /ˌem.piːˈeɪtʃ/ ABBREVIATION FOR miles per hour: *My car won't do/go more than 70 mph.* ○ *She was caught driving at 120 mph.*

MPhil /ˌemˈfɪl/ *noun* [C] UK ABBREVIATION FOR **Master of Philosophy**: *Alison Wells, MPhil* ○ *He has/is doing an MPhil in psychology.*

MPV /ˌem.piːˈviː/ *noun* [C] ABBREVIATION FOR multi-purpose vehicle: a PEOPLE CARRIER

Mr /ˈmɪs.təʳ/ US /-tɚ/ *noun* [U] **1** a title used before the family name or full name of a man who has no other title, or when addressing a man who holds a particular official position: *Mr Jones/Mr David Jones* ○ [as form of address] *Good afternoon, Mr Dawson.* ○ *We're looking for a Mr* (= a man called) *George Smith.* ○ *It's an honour to have you here today, Mr President.* ⊃Compare **Miss** TITLE; **Mrs**; **Ms**. See also **Messrs**. Compare **madam** WOMAN. **2** used when expressing the idea that a man is typical of or represents a quality, activity or place: *She's still hoping to meet Mr Right* (= the perfect man). ○ *He thinks he's Mr Big* (= that he is very important).

● **no more Mr Nice Guy** INFORMAL something that is said when someone has decided to stop caring about the wishes and feelings of other people: *I've had enough of people taking advantage of me. From now on it's no more Mr Nice Guy.*

MRI /ˌem.ɑːrˈaɪ/ *noun* [U] ABBREVIATION FOR magnetic resonance imaging: a system for producing electronic pictures of the organs inside a person's body, using radio waves and a strong magnetic field

Mrs /ˈmɪs.ɪz/ *noun* [U] **1** a title used before the family name or full name of a married woman who has no other title: *Mrs Wood/Mrs Jean Wood* ○ [as form of address] *Hello, Mrs Grant, how are you today?* ⊃Compare **madam** WOMAN; **Miss** TITLE; **Mr**; **Ms**. **2** used when expressing the idea that a married woman is typical of or represents a quality, activity or place: *Mrs Average* (= a woman who is typical of an ordinary woman)

ms DOCUMENT /ˌemˈes/ *noun* [C] *plural* **mss** WRITTEN ABBREVIATION FOR **manuscript**

Ms TITLE /məz/ US /mɪz/ *noun* [U] a title used before the family name or the full name of a woman, whether she is married or not: *Ms Hill/Ms Paula Hill* ○ [as form of address] *What can I do for you, Ms Wood?* ⊃Compare **Miss** TITLE; **Mr**; **Mrs**.

MS ILLNESS /ˌemˈes/ *noun* [U] ABBREVIATION FOR multiple sclerosis

MSc UK /ˌem.esˈsiː/ *noun* [C] (US **MS**) ABBREVIATION FOR **Master of Science**: *Lynn Kramer MSc* ○ *Phil has/is doing/is studying for an MSc in biochemistry.*

MS-DOS /ˌem.esˈdɒs/ US /-ˈdɑːs/ *noun* [U] TRADEMARK a set of programs for controlling the storage and organization of information on the magnetic discs of personal computers and for controlling access to that information

msec *WRITTEN ABBREVIATION FOR* **millisecond**

MSG /,em.es'dʒi:/ *noun* [U] *ABBREVIATION FOR* **monosodium glutamate**

Msgr *noun* [before n] *WRITTEN ABBREVIATION FOR* **Monsignor**

MSP /,em.es'pi:/ *noun* [C] *ABBREVIATION FOR* Member of the Scottish Parliament

Mt *noun* *WRITTEN ABBREVIATION FOR* **Mount** or **mountain**: *Mt Everest*

MTV /,em.ti:'vi:/ *group noun* [U] *TRADEMARK ABBREVIATION FOR* Music Television: an organization that broadcasts popular music internationally

much [AMOUNT] /mʌtʃ/ *determiner, pronoun, adv* **more, most 1** a large amount or to a large degree: *I don't earn much money.* ○ *You haven't said much, Joan – what do you think?* ○ *I don't think there's much to be gained by catching an earlier train.* ○ *The children never eat (very) much, but they seem quite healthy.* ○ *"Is there any wine left?" "Not much."* ○ *There's not/nothing much to do around here.* ○ *How much (= What amount of) sugar do you take in your coffee?* ○ *How much do these shoes cost?* ○ *I spend too much on clothes.* ○ *I don't have as much time as (= I have less time than) I would like for visiting my friends.* ○ *Because of the rain, we weren't able to spend much of the day on the beach.* ○ *Have you seen/heard much of Polly (= often seen or heard about her) recently?* ○ *I'd very much like to visit them sometime.* ○ *One day I hope I'll be able to do as much (= the same amount) for you as you've done for me.* ○ *Things around here are much as always/usual/ever (= have not changed a lot).* ○ *The two schools are much the same (= very similar).* ○ *Much to our surprise, (= We were very surprised that) they accepted our offer.* ○ *I'm not much good at knitting (= do not do it very well).* ○ *This is a much (= often) discussed issue.* ○ *Brian's become a much (= greatly) changed person since his car accident.* ○ *I've been feeling much healthier (= a lot more healthy) since I became a vegetarian.* ○ *The repairs to our car cost much more than we were expecting.* ○ *I'm very much aware of the problem.* ○ *She's much the best person for the job (= She is certainly better than everyone else).* ○ *I would much rather have my baby at home than in hospital.* ○ *She is as much a friend to me as a mother (= although she is my mother, she is also a friend).* * NOTE: **much** is used with uncountable nouns. ⊃Compare **many** and see Note **many, much or a lot of?** at **many. 2** *INFORMAL* used at the end of a negative sentence to suggest the opposite of what you have just said: *I can see you don't like chocolate – much!*

● **as much 1** If you say that you thought/expected/said as much, it means that something bad that you thought/expected/said would happen has happened: *I knew he'd fail – I said as much at the time.* **2** the same: *Go on, lend me the money – you know I'd do as much for you.*

● **as much as** almost: *He as much as admitted that it was his fault.*

● **as much again** *UK* the same amount again: *My fare was nearly £10, and it was almost as much again for the children.*

● **as much as you can do** *UK* If you say something is as much as you can do, you manage to do it, but with great difficulty: *I felt so ill this morning, it was as much as I could do to get out of bed.*

● **much as** although: *Much as I would like to help you, I'm afraid I'm simply too busy at the moment.*

● **much less** and certainly not: *Tony can barely boil an egg, much less cook dinner.*

● **much too much** a far larger amount of something than you want or need: *You've drunk much too much to drive.*

● **not go much on sth** *UK INFORMAL* to dislike something: *I don't go much on white wine.*

● **not so much sth as sth** If you say that something is not so much one thing as something else, you mean it is more the second thing: *They're not so much lovers as friends.* ○ *I don't feel angry so much as sad.*

● **so much** a particular amount: *By the time you've paid so much for the ferry and so much for the train fare, it would be cheaper to go by plane.*

● **so much for sth** used to express disappointment and annoyance at the fact that a situation is not as you thought it was: *The car's broken down again. So much for our trip to the seaside.*

● **too much** (*ALSO* **a bit (too) much**) **1** more than someone can deal with: *I can't look after six children at my age – it's too much.* **2** unreasonable and unfair: *I think it's a bit much for you to expect me to do all the cleaning.* ○ *And you had to work till eight? That's a bit much!*

muchness /'mʌtʃ.nəs/ *noun* *UK INFORMAL* **be much of a muchness** to be very similar and usually of low quality: *The songs you hear on the radio these days all sound much of a muchness.*

much [GOOD] /mʌtʃ/ *pronoun, adv* (something) of good quality: *He's not much to look at, but he has a wonderful personality.* ○ *I've never been much of a dancer (= good at dancing, or interested in doing it).* ○ *There's not/nothing much on TV tonight.*

muck /mʌk/ *noun* **1** dirt or animal excrement: *You're treading muck into the carpet with your dirty shoes!* ○ *a pile of dog muck* **2** something you consider disgusting or very low quality: *I'm not eating that muck!* ○ *The immigrants were treated like muck (= treated badly, as if they were not important).*

● **Where there's muck there's brass.** *UK SAYING* said to mean that a lot of money can be made from business activities which are dirty or unpleasant

● **make a muck of sth** *INFORMAL* to spoil something or do something very badly: *I've made a muck of it – I'll have to do it again.*

mucky /'mʌk.i/ *adj* **1** *INFORMAL* dirty: *Get your mucky feet off that chair!* ○ *Don't walk all over my clean floor in your mucky boots!* **2** *UK INFORMAL* pornographic: *a mucky book/film/magazine*

muck /mʌk/ *verb*

PHRASAL VERBS WITH **muck** ▼

▲ **muck sb/sth about/around** *phrasal verb* *MAINLY UK INFORMAL* to behave in a silly way, or to treat someone or something in a careless way: *Stop mucking about with those ornaments, you'll break something!* ○ *I'm fed up with them mucking me about and cancelling our arrangements.*

▲ **muck in** *phrasal verb* *UK INFORMAL* to share the work that needs to be done: *She doesn't mind mucking in with the rest of us when there's work to be done.*

▲ **muck (sth) out** *phrasal verb* to clean a place where a large animal lives, especially a STABLE, by removing the excrement and old straw: *She'd spent all morning mucking out the horses.*

▲ **muck sth up** *phrasal verb* [M] *INFORMAL* to spoil something completely, or do something very badly: *I really prepared for the interview because I didn't want to muck it up.* ○ *I mucked up the whole exam!*

muck-up /'mʌk.ʌp/ *noun* [C] *They made a muck-up of our order – it won't be ready till next week now.*

muckraking /'mʌk,reɪ.kɪŋ/ *noun* [U] *DISAPPROVING* the activity, especially of newspapers and reporters, of trying to find out unpleasant information about people or organizations in order to make it public: *There was so much muckraking about his family life that he decided not to stand for election.* **muckraker** /'mʌk,reɪ.kəʳ/ ⓊⓈ /-kɚ/ *noun* [C]

mucous membrane /,mju:.kəs'mem.breɪn/ *noun* [C] *SPECIALIZED* the thin skin that covers the inner surface of parts of the body such as the nose and mouth and produces mucus to protect them

mucus /'mju:.kəs/ *noun* [U] a thick liquid produced inside the nose and other parts of the body: *This drug reduces mucus production in the gut.*

mud /mʌd/ *noun* [U] earth that has become wet and sticky: *The vehicles got bogged down in the heavy mud.* ○ *Modern houses have replaced the one-room mud huts with grass roofs that had been home to generations of peasants.* ○ *These mud flats (= level ground near the sea) are a site of special scientific interest.*

● **Here's mud in your eye!** sometimes said by people in a friendly way just before drinking an alcoholic drink together

• **hurl/throw/sling mud at** ***sb*** to say insulting or unfair things about someone, especially to try to damage their reputation ➲See also **mud-slinging**.
• **Mud sticks.** *UK SAYING* said to mean that people are likely to believe something bad that is said about someone, even if it is not true

muddy /ˈmʌd.i/ *adj* **1** covered by or containing mud: *Don't bring those muddy boots inside!* ○ *muddy water* **2** describes colours that are dark and not bright: *The sitting-room has been painted in muddy browns and greens.*

muddy /ˈmʌd.i/ *verb* [T] to put mud into something or cover something with mud: *Industrial activity has muddied the river.*
• **muddy the waters** to make a situation more confused and less easy to understand or deal with

muddle /ˈmʌd.l̩/ *noun* [U] an untidy or confused state: *The documents were* ***in a*** *muddle.* ○ *Whenever I go abroad I get* ***in a*** *muddle* ***about/over*** (= become confused about) *the money.*

muddled /ˈmʌd.l̩d/ *adj* **1** Things that are muddled are badly organized: *He left his clothes in a muddled pile in the corner.* **2** A person who is muddled is confused: *He became increasingly muddled as he grew older.*

muddle /ˈmʌd.l̩/ *verb*

PHRASAL VERBS WITH **muddle** ▼

▲ **muddle along** *phrasal verb* to continue doing something with no clear purpose or plan: *Decide what you want in life – don't just muddle along.*
▲ **muddle through** *phrasal verb* to manage to do something although you are not organized and do not know how to do it: *I'm afraid I can't help you – you'll just have to muddle through on your own.*
▲ **muddle** ***sth*** **up** [ARRANGE] *phrasal verb* [M] to arrange things in the wrong order: *I've arranged the books alphabetically so don't muddle them up.*
▲ **muddle** ***sb/sth*** **up** [SIMILAR] *phrasal verb* [M] to think that a person or thing is someone or something else because they are very similar: *I often muddle up Richard* ***with*** *his brother.* ○ *It's easy to muddle up some Spanish and Italian words.*

muddle-headed /ˌmʌd.l̩ˈhed.ɪd/ *adj* not thinking clearly or in an organized way

mudflap *UK* /ˈmʌd.flæp/ *noun* [C] (*US* **splash guard**) one of the pieces of rubber which are fixed to a vehicle behind the wheels to prevent dirt and small objects from being thrown up ➲See picture **Car** on page Centre 12

mudflat /ˈmʌd.flæt/ *noun* [C] a flat area of very wet soil near the sea which is covered at HIGH TIDE (= the time when the sea reaches its highest level and comes furthest up the beach)

mudguard /ˈmʌd.gɑːd/ [US] /-gɑːrd/ *noun* [C] (*US USUALLY* **fender**) a curved piece of metal or plastic above the wheels of a bicycle or motorcycle that prevents dirt from getting on the rider

mudpack /ˈmʌd.pæk/ *noun* [C] a special substance that you put on your face and leave for a short time to improve your skin

ˌmud ˈpie *noun* [C] a small round shape made of mud by children playing

mud-slinging, **mudslinging** /ˈmʌdˌslɪŋ.ɪŋ/ *noun* [U] when you say insulting or unfair things about someone, especially to try to damage their reputation: *political mud-slinging*

muesli /ˈmjuːzli/ *noun* [U] a mixture of raw grains, dried fruit and nuts that is eaten with milk as part of the first meal of the day ➲Compare **granola**.

muezzin /muːˈez.ɪn/ *noun* [C] a man who calls Muslims to prayer from the tower of a MOSQUE (= Muslim holy building)

muff [CLOTHING] /mʌf/ *noun* [C] a short tube of fur or warm cloth, into which women in the past put their hands in cold weather in order to keep them warm

muff [SPOIL] /mʌf/ *verb* [T] *INFORMAL* to spoil an opportunity or do something badly: *I only had two lines in the whole play and I muffed them.*

muffin [BREAD] *UK* /ˈmʌf.ɪn/ *noun* [C] (*US* **English muffin**) a small round flat type of bread, usually sliced in two and eaten hot with butter

muffin [CAKE] /ˈmʌf.ɪn/ *noun* [C] a small sweet cake that often has fruit inside it: *blueberry muffins*

muffle [MAKE QUIET] /ˈmʌf.l̩/ *verb* [T] to make a sound quieter and less clear: *The house's windows are double-glazed to muffle the noise of aircraft.* **muffled** /ˈmʌf.l̩d/ *adj*: *I could hear muffled voices next door but couldn't make out any words.* ○ *The muffled roar of traffic could be heard in the distance.*

muffler /ˈmʌf.ləʳ/ [US] /-lɚ/ *noun* [C] *US* a **silencer**

muffle [KEEP WARM] /ˈmʌf.l̩/ *verb* [T] to wear thick warm clothes in order to keep warm: *I was muffled* ***up*** *against the cold in a scarf and hat.*

muffler /ˈmʌf.ləʳ/ [US] /-lɚ/ *noun* [C] *OLD-FASHIONED* a thick SCARF (= long piece of cloth worn around the neck)

mufti /ˈmʌf.ti/ *noun* [U] *OLD-FASHIONED* ordinary clothes worn by people who usually wear uniforms, especially soldiers: *The admiral arrived* ***in*** *mufti.*

mug [CONTAINER] /mʌg/ *noun* [C] **1** a large cup with straight sides used for hot drinks: *I made myself a large mug* ***of*** *cocoa* (= enough to fill a mug) *and went to bed.* **2** *MAINLY US* **beer mug** a heavy glass with a handle and usually with patterns cut into its side, out of which you drink beer

mug [STUPID PERSON] /mʌg/ *noun* [C] *MAINLY UK INFORMAL* a person who is stupid and easily deceived: *He's such a mug, he believes everything she tells him.*
• **a mug's game** *UK INFORMAL* an activity that will not make you happy or successful: *Teaching's a mug's game.*

mug [FACE] /mʌg/ *noun* [C] *INFORMAL MAINLY DISAPPROVING* someone's face: *his* ***ugly*** *mug*

mug [ATTACK] /mʌg/ *verb* [T] **-gg-** to attack a person in a public place and steal their money: *He was mugged in broad daylight.*

mugging /ˈmʌg.ɪŋ/ *noun* [C or U] an act of attacking someone and stealing their money: *Police are concerned that mugging is on the increase.*

mugger /ˈmʌg.əʳ/ [US] /-ɚ/ *noun* [C] a person who attacks people in order to steal their money

▲ **mug** ***(sth)*** **up** *phrasal verb* [M] *UK INFORMAL* to study a subject quickly before taking an exam: *I've got to mug up* ***(on)*** *my History before tomorrow's exam.*

muggins /ˈmʌg.ɪnz/ *noun* [S] *UK HUMOROUS* a stupid person: often used to describe yourself when you have done something silly or when you feel you are being treated unfairly: *I suppose muggins* ***here*** *will have to look after the cat when they go on holiday* (= I will have to do it but I don't want to).

muggy /ˈmʌg.i/ *adj* When the weather is muggy, it is unpleasantly warm and the air contains a lot of water.

ˈmug ˌshot *noun* [C] *SLANG* a photograph taken by the police of a person who has been charged with a crime: *A poster with mug shots of wanted men was on the wall.*

mujaheddin /ˌmʌ.dʒə.həˈdiːn/ *plural noun* Muslim soldiers fighting in support of their political and religious beliefs

mulatto /məˈlæt.əʊ/ /mjuː-/ [US] /-ˈlæ.t̬oʊ/ *noun* [C] an offensive word for someone with one black parent and one white parent

mulberry /ˈmʌl.bᵊr.i/ [US] /-ber-/ *noun* [C] a small soft purple fruit, or the tree that has these fruit

mulch /mʌltʃ/ *noun* [C or U] a covering of decaying leaves that is spread over the soil in order to keep water in it or to improve it

mulch /mʌltʃ/ *verb* [I or T] [+ adv or prep] *Mulch* (= Put mulch) ***around*** *the base of the roses.* ○ *Mulch the roses.*

mule [ANIMAL] /mjuːl/ *noun* [C] an animal whose mother is a horse and whose father is a donkey, which is used especially for transporting loads

mulish /ˈmjuː.lɪʃ/ *adj* describes someone who is very determined and refuses to change their plans for anyone else

mule [PERSON] /mjuːl/ *noun* [C] a person who agrees to carry illegal drugs into another country in return for payment by the person selling the drugs: *These very poor women who are used as mules by drug barons often get long prison sentences.*

mule [SHOE] /mjuːl/ *noun* [C] a woman's shoe or SLIPPER that has no back

mulga /ˈmʌl.gə/ *noun AUS* **1** [C or U] a type of tree found in dry regions, or its wood **2** [S] **the bush** AREA OF LAND: *They live up in the mulga.*

mull /mʌl/ *verb* [T] to heat wine or beer with added sugar and spices: *mulled* ***wine***

▲ **mull *sth* over** *phrasal verb* [M] to think carefully about something for a long time: *I need a few days to mull things over before I decide if I'm taking the job.*

mullah /ˈmʊl.ə/ *noun* [C] an Islamic religious teacher or leader

mullet [FISH] /ˈmʌl.ɪt/ *noun* [C] a small sea fish that can be cooked and eaten: *red mullet*

mullet [HAIR] /ˈmʌl.ɪt/ *noun* [C] *INFORMAL* a men's hairstyle from the 1980's in which the hair on top and at the sides of the head is short and the hair at the back is long

mulligatawny /ˌmʌl.ɪ.gəˈtɔː.ni/ [US] /-ˈtɑː-/ *noun* [U] a very spicy soup that has CURRY POWDER in it

mullioned /ˈmʌl.i.ənd/ *adj* (of windows) having vertical sections, usually made of stone, between the glass parts

multi- /mʌl.ti-/ [US] /-t̬i-/ *prefix* having many: *a multi-coloured skirt* (= a skirt with many colours) ○ *a multi-vitamin tablet* (= a pill which contains several vitamins)

multicultural /ˌmʌl.tiˈkʌl.tʃᵊr.ᵊl/ [US] /-t̬iˈkʌl.tʃɚ-/ *adj* including people who have many different customs and beliefs: *Britain is increasingly a multicultural society.* **multiculturalism** /ˌmʌl.tiˈkʌl.tʃᵊr.ᵊl.ɪ.zᵊm/ [US] /-t̬iˈkʌl.tʃɚ-/ *noun* [U] the existence of several cultures within a society

multi-disciplinary /ˌmʌl.ti.dɪs.əˈplɪn.ᵊr.i/ [US] /-t̬i.dɪs.əˈplɪ.ner-/ *adj* involving different subjects of study in one activity: *a multi-disciplinary course*

multi-ethnic /ˌmʌl.tiˈeθ.nɪk/ [US] /-t̬i-/ *adj* consisting of, or relating to various different races: *Britain is a multi-ethnic society, with many black and Asian people.*

multi-faceted /ˌmʌl.tiˈfæs.ɪ.tɪd/ [US] /-t̬iˈfæs.ɪ.t̬ɪd/ *adj* having many different parts: *It's a multi-faceted business, offering a range of services.*

multifarious /ˌmʌl.tɪˈfeə.ri.əs/ [US] /-t̬ɪˈfer.i-/ *adj FORMAL* of many different types: *The newspaper report detailed the fraudster's multifarious business activities.*

multigym /ˈmʌl.ti.dʒɪm/ [US] /-t̬i-/ *noun* [C] *UK* a machine on which you can do several different exercises to keep your body fit, or a room in which several different exercise machines can be used

multilateral /ˌmʌl.tiˈlæt.ᵊr.ᵊl/ [US] /-t̬iˈlæt̬.ɚ-/ *adj* involving more than two groups or countries: *Seven countries are taking part in the multilateral talks.* ➲Compare **bilateral**; **unilateral**. **multilaterally** /ˌmʌl.tiˈlæt.ᵊr.ᵊl.i/ [US] /-t̬iˈlæt̬.ɚ-/ *adv*

multilingual /ˌmʌl.tiˈlɪŋ.gwəl/ [US] /-t̬ɪ-/ *adj* (of people or groups) able to use more than two languages for communication, or (of a thing) written or spoken in more than two different languages: *a multilingual on-line dictionary* ➲Compare **bilingual**; **monolingual**.

multimedia /ˌmʌl.tiˈmiː.di.ə/ [US] /-t̬i-/ *adj* [before n] using a combination of moving and still pictures, sound, music and words, especially in computers or entertainment: *multimedia software* **multimedia** /ˌmʌl.tiˈmiː.di.ə/ [US] /-t̬i-/ *noun* [U]

multimillionaire /ˌmʌl.tiˌmɪl.jəˈneəʳ/ [US] /-t̬iˌmɪl.jəˈner/ *noun* [C] a person who has money and property worth several million pounds or dollars

multinational /ˌmʌl.tiˈnæʃ.ᵊn.ᵊl/ [US] /-t̬i-/ *adj* involving several different countries, or (of a business) producing and selling goods in several different countries: *The UN has sent a multinational peace-keeping force.* ○ *a major multinational food company* **multinational** /ˌmʌl.tiˈnæʃ.ᵊn.ᵊl/ [US] /-t̬i-/ *noun* [C] a large and powerful company that produces and sells goods in many different countries: *Are multinationals now more powerful than governments?*

multiple [MANY] /ˈmʌl.tɪ.pl̩/ [US] /-t̬ɪ-/ *adj* very many of the same type, or of different types: *The youth died of multiple burns.* ○ *We made multiple copies of the report.* ○ *These children have multiple* (= many different) *handicaps.*

multiple /ˈmʌl.tɪ.pl̩/ [US] /-t̬ɪ-/ *noun* [C] a large company which has shops in many towns

multiple [NUMBER] /ˈmʌl.tɪ.pl̩/ [US] /-t̬ɪ-/ *noun* [C] a number that can be divided by a smaller number an exact number of times: *18 is a multiple* ***of*** *3, because 18 = 3 x 6.*

ˌmultiple ˈbirth *noun* [C] when more than two babies are born to the same woman on one occasion

multiple-choice /ˌmʌl.tɪ.pl̩ˈtʃɔɪs/ [US] /-t̬ɪ-/ *adj* [before n] describes an exam or question in which you are given a list of answers and you have to choose the correct one: *a multiple-choice test*

ˌmultiple scleˈrosis *noun* [U] (*ABBREVIATION* **MS**) a disease in which the covering of the nerves gradually becomes destroyed, damaging a person's speech and sight and ability to move

multiplex /ˈmʌl.tɪ.pleks/ [US] /-t̬ɪ-/ *noun* [C] a very large cinema that has a lot of separate cinemas inside it

multipliˈcation ˌtable *noun* [C] a list that shows the results of multiplying one number by a set of other numbers, usually from one to twelve, used especially by children at school

multiplicity /ˌmʌl.tɪˈplɪs.ɪ.ti/ [US] /-t̬əˈplɪs.ə.t̬i/ *noun* [U] *FORMAL* a large number or wide range (of something): *There is a multiplicity* ***of*** *fashion magazines to choose from.*

multiply /ˈmʌl.tɪ.plaɪ/ [US] /-t̬ɪ-/ *verb* [I or T] to increase greatly in number, or (in mathematics) to add a number to itself a particular number of times: *In warm weather these germs multiply rapidly.* ○ *If you multiply seven* ***by*** *15 you get 105.* ➲Compare **add**; **divide** CALCULATE; **subtract**. **multiplication** /ˌmʌl.tɪ.plɪˈkeɪ.ʃᵊn/ [US] /-t̬ɪ-/ *noun* [U]

multipurpose /ˌmʌl.tɪˈpɜː.pəs/ [US] /-t̬ɪˈpɝː-/ *adj* describes a tool, etc. that can be used in several different ways: *a multipurpose hall*

multiracial /ˌmʌl.tɪˈreɪ.ʃᵊl/ [US] /-t̬ɪ-/ *adj* involving people of several different races: *a multiracial school* ○ *South Africa's first multiracial elections took place in 1994.*

multi-storey *UK* /ˌmʌl.tɪˈstɔː.ri/ [US] /-t̬ɪˈstɔːr.i/ *adj* (*US* **multistory**) describes a building with several floors: *UK a multi-storey car park* ○ *US a multistory apartment block* **multi-storey** /ˌmʌl.tɪˈstɔː.ri/ [US] /-t̬ɪˈstɔːr.i/ *noun* [C] *UK* a multi-storey car park: *I left the car in the multi-storey.*

multitasking /ˌmʌl.tɪˈtɑːs.kɪŋ/ [US] /-t̬ɪˌtæs-/ *noun* [U] **1** the ability of a computer to operate several programs at one time: *The machine allows multitasking without the need to buy extra hardware.* **2** a person's ability to do more than one thing at a time: *Women are often very good at multitasking.*

multitude /ˈmʌl.tɪ.tjuːd/ [US] /-t̬ə.tuːd/ *noun FORMAL* **a multitude of** a large number of people or things: *The city has a multitude of problems, from homelessness to drugs and murder.* ○ *This case has raised a multitude of questions.* **the multitude** *noun* [S] *FORMAL* **1** a large crowd of people: *He stepped out onto the balcony to address the multitude below.* **2** the ordinary people who form the largest group in a society **the multitudes** *plural noun FORMAL* large numbers of people: *the multitudes using the Internet*

• **cover/hide a multitude of sins** *HUMOROUS* to prevent people from seeing or discovering something bad: *Large sweaters are warm and practical and hide a multitude of sins.*

mum [MOTHER] *UK* /mʌm/ *noun* [C] (*US* **mom**) *INFORMAL* mother: [as form of address] *"Happy birthday, Mum."* ○ *All the mums* ***and dads*** *are invited to the school play at the end of the year.*

mum [SECRET] /mʌm/ *adj INFORMAL* **keep mum** to say nothing about a subject: *It's not official yet so keep mum.*

• **Mum's the word.** *SAYING* said when you tell someone, or agree with someone, to keep something a secret: *"I'm not telling people generally yet." "OK, mum's the word!"*

mumble /ˈmʌm.bl̩/ *verb* [I or T] to speak unclearly and quietly so that the words are difficult to understand: *She mumbled* ***something*** *about being too busy.* ○ [+ speech] *"I'm sorry," he mumbled.*

mumbo jumbo /ˌmʌm.bəʊˈdʒʌm.bəʊ/ [US] /-boʊˈdʒʌm.boʊ/ *noun* [U] *INFORMAL* words or activities that are

M

unnecessarily complicated or mysterious and seem meaningless: *You don't believe in horoscopes and all that mumbo jumbo, do you?*

mummy [MOTHER] *UK* /ˈmʌm.i/ *noun* [C] (*US* **mommy**) *CHILD'S WORD FOR* mother: [as form of address] *I want to go home, Mummy.* ○ *Could I speak to your mummy please, Phoebe?*

mummy [BODY] /ˈmʌm.i/ *noun* [C] (especially in ancient Egypt) a dead body that has been preserved from decay by being treated with special substances before being wrapped in cloth

mummify /ˈmʌm.ɪ.faɪ/ *verb* [T] to preserve a dead body as a mummy

mummy's boy *UK* /ˈmʌm.iz,bɔɪ/ *noun* [C usually sing] (*US* **mama's boy**) *DISAPPROVING* a boy or man who appears to do whatever his mother tells him to

mumps /mʌmps/ *noun* [U] an infectious disease that causes painful swelling in the neck and slight fever

mumsy /ˈmʌm.zi/ *adj UK INFORMAL MAINLY DISAPPROVING* describes a woman with an old-fashioned appearance, like that of a traditional mother: *As she became more successful, she changed her mumsy hairstyle for something more glamorous.*

munch /mʌntʃ/ *verb* [I or T] to eat something, especially noisily: *He was munching **on** an apple.* ○ *We watched her munch her way through two packets of peanuts.*

munch /mʌntʃ/ *noun* [U] *UK INFORMAL* food: *Shall we get some munch, then?*

munchies /ˈmʌn.tʃiz/ *plural noun MAINLY US INFORMAL* small light things to eat: *We need a few munchies – some peanuts and crackers.*

the munchies *plural noun INFORMAL* feelings of hunger: ***I've got** the munchies.*

mundane /mʌnˈdeɪn/ *adj* very ordinary and therefore not interesting: *Mundane matters such as paying bills and shopping for food do not interest her.*

mung bean /ˈmʌŋ,biːn/ *noun* [C] a small bean which is often used in Chinese cooking and is eaten when it has grown long SHOOTS

municipal /mjuːˈnɪs.ɪ.pᵊl/ *adj* of or belonging to a town or city: *municipal authorities* ○ *municipal tennis courts* ○ *municipal elections*

municipality /mjuː,nɪs.ɪˈpæl.ə.ti/ [US] /-t̬i/ *noun* [C] a city or town with its own local government, or this local government itself: *The municipality provides services such as electricity, water and rubbish collection.*

munificent /mjuːˈnɪf.ɪ.sᵊnt/ *adj FORMAL* very generous with money: *A former student has donated a munificent sum of money to the college.* **munificence** /mjuːˈnɪf.ɪ.sᵊnts/ *noun* [U] *I thanked them for their munificence.*

munitions /mjuːˈnɪʃ.ᵊnz/ *plural noun* military weapons such as guns and bombs: *The army used precision-guided munitions to blow up enemy targets.* ○ *a munitions depot* ○ *a munitions factory*

mural /ˈmjʊə.rəl/ [US] /ˈmjʊr.ᵊl/ *noun* [C] a large picture that has been painted on the wall of a room or building

murder /ˈmɜː.dəʳ/ [US] /ˈmɝː.dɚ/ *noun* [C or U] the crime of intentionally killing a person: *Two sisters have been **charged with*** (= officially accused of) *murder.* ○ *There were three murders in the town last year.* ○ *The three were **convicted of*** (= proved guilty of) *murder.* ○ *murder **weapon*** (= a weapon used to commit a murder) ➲Compare **manslaughter**; **suicide** DEATH.

• **be murder** *INFORMAL* to be very difficult to do: *It's murder finding a parking space in town.*

murder /ˈmɜː.dəʳ/ [US] /ˈmɝː.dɚ/ *verb* [T] **1** to commit the crime of intentionally killing a person: *Her husband was murdered by gunmen as she watched.* ○ *In the last year, terrorists have murdered several local journalists.* **2** *UK INFORMAL* If you say you will or could murder someone, it means you are very angry with them: *If he's late again, I'll murder him!*

• **could murder sth** *UK INFORMAL* If you say you could murder a type of food or drink, it means you would like to have it now: *I could murder a cup of tea!*

murderer /ˈmɜː.dᵊr.əʳ/ [US] /ˈmɝː.dɚ.ɚ/ *noun* [C] (*OLD-FASHIONED FEMALE* **murderess**) someone who illegally and intentionally kills another person: *A **convicted** murderer was executed in North Carolina yesterday.* ○ *a **mass** murderer* (= someone who has killed a large number of people illegally)

murderous /ˈmɜː.dᵊr.əs/ [US] /ˈmɝː.dɚ-/ *adj* **1** extremely dangerous and likely to commit murder: *He was a murderous gangster.* ○ *She gave me a look of murderous hatred.* **2** *INFORMAL* extremely unpleasant: *The traffic was murderous today.*

murk /mɜːk/ [US] /mɝːk/ *noun* [U] darkness or thick cloud, preventing you from seeing clearly: *It was foggy and the sun shone feebly through the murk.*

murky /ˈmɜː.ki/ [US] /ˈmɝː-/ *adj* **1** dark and dirty or difficult to see through: *The river was brown and murky after the storm.* **2** describes a situation that is complicated and unpleasant, and about which many facts are unclear: *He became involved in the murky world of international drug-dealing.* ○ *I don't want to get into the murky **waters** of family arguments.*

murmur [SPEAK QUIETLY] /ˈmɜː.məʳ/ [US] /ˈmɝː.mɚ/ *verb* [I or T] to speak or say very quietly: [+ speech] *"I love you", she murmured.* ○ *He was murmuring **to himself**.* ○ *HUMOROUS He murmured **sweet nothings*** (= romantic talk) *in her ear.*

murmur /ˈmɜː.məʳ/ [US] /ˈmɝː.mɚ/ *noun* **1** [C] the sound of something being said very quietly: *A murmur **of** agreement came from the crowd.* **2** [S] a soft continuous sound: *The murmur of the waves on the beach lulled me to sleep.*

murmur [COMPLAIN] /ˈmɜː.məʳ/ [US] /ˈmɝː.mɚ/ *verb* [I] to complain about something that you disagree with or dislike, but not in a public way: *They were murmuring **about** the boss's nephew getting the job.*

murmur /ˈmɜː.məʳ/ [US] /ˈmɝː.mɚ/ *noun* [C] a complaint which is expressed privately: *After the report was published, there were murmurs **of discontent** round the office.*

• **without a murmur** without even a small complaint: *For once the children went to bed without a murmur.*

Murphy's law /,mɜː.fizˈlɔː/ [US] /,mɝː.fizˈlɑː/ *noun* [U] (*UK OFFENSIVE ALSO* **Sod's law**) *HUMOROUS* the tendency of things to go wrong: *The bus is always late but today when I was late it came on time – that's Murphy's law I suppose!*

muscle /ˈmʌs.l̩/ *noun* **1** [C or U] one of many tissues in the body that can tighten and relax to produce movement: *neck/back/leg/stomach muscles* ○ *facial muscles* ○ ***bulging/rippling*** (= large and clear to see) *muscles* ○ *He **flexed** his muscles* (= tightened, especially his arm muscles, to make them look large and strong) *so that everyone could admire them.* ○ *These exercises build muscle and increase stamina.* ○ *a muscle **spasm*** (= a sudden uncontrollable tightening movement) **2** [U] the power to do difficult things or to make people behave in a certain way: *This magazine has considerable financial muscle and can afford to pay top journalists.* ○ *The company lacks the marketing muscle to compete with drug giants.*

• **pull a muscle** to injure a muscle by stretching it too far so that it is very painful: *Russell pulled a back muscle early in the game.*

muscular /ˈmʌs.kjʊ.ləʳ/ [US] /-lɚ/ *adj* **1** related to muscles: *muscular **contractions*** ○ *muscular pain* **2** having well-developed muscles: *muscular arms/legs* ○ *He wished he was more muscular.*

musculature /ˈmʌs.kjʊ.lə.tʃəʳ/ [US] /-tʃɚ/ *noun* [U] the position and structure of the muscles: *By looking at the bones of this animal, we can discover quite a lot about its musculature.*

muscly /ˈmʌs.li/ *adj INFORMAL* having a lot of well-developed muscles: *She's got big, muscly legs.*

muscle /ˈmʌs.l̩/ *verb*

▲ **muscle in** *phrasal verb INFORMAL* to force your way into a situation and make certain you are included, although you are not wanted: *I hear Mark's muscled in **on** our meeting.*

muscle-bound /ˈmʌs.l̩.baʊnd/ *adj DISAPPROVING* describes someone who has a lot of very large firm muscles which makes it difficult for them to move normally

muscle-flexing /ˈmʌs.l̩,flek.sɪŋ/ *noun* [U] a public display of military or political power that is intended to

M

worry an opponent: *Opposition groups fear violence, after weeks of military muscle-flexing from the government.*

muscleman /ˈmʌs.l̩.mæn/ *noun* [C] a man who has very large muscles as a result of doing special exercises to improve them

Muscovite /ˈmʌs.kə.vaɪt/ *noun* [C] a person from Moscow

muscular dystrophy /ˌmʌs.kjʊ.ləˈdɪs.trə.fi/ [US] /-lɚ-/ *noun* [U] a serious disease in which a person's muscles gradually weaken until walking is no longer possible

muse [THINK] /mjuːz/ *verb* [I] FORMAL to think about something carefully and for a long time: *I began to muse* ***about/on*** *the possibility of starting my own business.*

muse [IMAGINARY FORCE] /mjuːz/ *noun* [C] LITERARY an imaginary being or force that gives someone ideas and helps them to write, paint or make music: *The muse has left me – I haven't written any poetry for months!* ○ *Juliet was not only the painter's best model but also his muse* (= the person who causes him to have the most ideas for his work).

Muse /mjuːz/ *noun* [C] LITERARY in ancient Greek and Roman stories, one of the nine goddesses who were believed to give encouragement in different areas of literature, art and music

museum /mjuːˈziː.əm/ *noun* [C] a building where objects of historical, scientific or artistic interest are kept: *a museum of modern art* ○ *the Natural History Museum*

muˈseum ˌpiece *noun* [C] HUMOROUS something that is very old-fashioned and should no longer be used: *That old car is a museum piece – you should get a new one.*

mush /mʌʃ/ *noun* [U] **1** INFORMAL any unpleasant thick soft substance, such as food that has been cooked for too long: *If you overcook the cabbage it'll* ***turn to mush.*** **2** If you say your brain has turned to mush it means you cannot think clearly. **3** INFORMAL If you describe something such as a book or film as mush, you mean that it is unpleasantly emotional: *The film was just romantic mush.*

mushy /ˈmʌʃ.i/ *adj* **1** soft and having no firm shape: *Cook the lentils until they are mushy.* ○ DISAPPROVING *The meat was mushy and tasteless.* **2** INFORMAL DISAPPROVING too emotional: *I hate those mushy love stories.*

mushroom /ˈmʌʃ.ruːm/ /-rʊm/ *noun* [C] a fungus with a round top and short stem. Some types of mushroom can be eaten: *wild/cultivated mushrooms* ○ *button* (= very small) *mushrooms* ○ *dried/grilled/stuffed/sliced mushrooms* ○ *cream of mushroom soup* ○ *For this recipe choose mushrooms with large* ***caps*** (= top parts). ○ *Unfortunately some poisonous mushrooms look like* ***edible*** *mushrooms.* ➲Compare **toadstool**. ➲See picture **Vegetables** on page Centre 2

mushroom /ˈmʌʃ.ruːm/ /-rʊm/ *verb* [I] to increase very quickly: *The number of computers in schools has mushroomed in recent years.*

ˈmushroom ˌcloud *noun* [C usually sing] a very large cloud of dust that rises into the air in the shape of a large mushroom especially after a nuclear explosion: *The mushroom cloud over Hiroshima is a horrific image of war.*

ˌmushy ˈpeas *plural noun* UK soft, cooked MARROWFAT PEAS (= a type of large pea)

music /ˈmjuː.zɪk/ *noun* [U] **1** a pattern of sounds made by musical instruments, singing or computers, or a combination of these, intended to give pleasure to people listening to it: *classical/pop/dance/rock music* ○ *a beautiful* ***piece of*** *music* ○ *What sort of music do you listen to?* ○ *They* ***play*** *good music* (= recordings of music) *on this (radio) station.* ○ *I just like* ***making*** *music* (= playing music or singing). ○ *Shall I* ***put on*** *some music* (= play a recording)*?* **2** the art or study of music: *I studied music at college.* ○ *the music business/industry* ○ *music lessons* **3** the written system of symbols representing musical notes: *Can you* ***read*** *music?*

• **be music to *sb's* ears** to be something that you are very pleased to hear: *The rattle of the letterbox was music to my ears – the letter had arrived at last.*

musical /ˈmjuː.zɪ.kəl/ *adj* **1** related to or connected with music: *musical instruments* ○ *Mozart's musical compositions include symphonies and operas.* **2** If you are musical, you have a skill in or great liking for music: *The family all play instruments – they're all very musical.*

musical /ˈmjuː.zɪ.kəl/ *noun* [C] a play or film in which part of the story is sung to music

musicality /mjuː.zɪˈkæl.ə.ti/ [US] /-t̬i/ *noun* [U] skill and good judgment in playing music: *Her natural musicality made this one of the most enjoyable concerts of the year.*

musically /ˈmjuː.zɪ.kli/ *adv*: *It's a school for musically* ***gifted*** *children* (= those who are very good at playing a musical instrument or singing). ○ *Musically speaking* (= referring to the music they produce)*, this band has a lot of talent.*

musicology /ˌmjuː.zɪˈkɒl.ə.dʒi/ [US] /-ˈkɑː.lə-/ *noun* [U] the study of the history, theory and science of music

musicologist /ˌmjuː.zɪˈkɒl.ə.dʒɪst/ [US] /-ˈkɑː.lə-/ *noun* [C] *Arvinda is a respected musicologist.*

ˈmusical ˌbox UK *noun* [C] (US **music box**) a decorative box with a device inside it that plays a tune when you open the lid

ˌmusical ˈchairs *plural noun* a game in which children walk around a group of chairs while music plays. When the music stops they have to sit quickly on a chair, but because there is always one fewer chairs than children, the child that is left standing must leave the game: FIGURATIVE *It's a game of musical chairs* (= a situation in which people change jobs often) *as editors move from one newspaper to another.*

ˈmusic ˌbox *noun* [C] US FOR **musical box**

ˈmusic ˌhall UK *noun* [C or U] (US ALSO **vaudeville**) a type of theatre entertainment in the 1800s and 1900s which included music, dancing and jokes, or the building used for this entertainment

musician /mjuːˈzɪʃ.ən/ *noun* [C] someone who is skilled in playing music, usually as their job: *The concert features dancers, singers and musicians of all nationalities.*

musicianship /mjuːˈzɪʃ.ən.ʃɪp/ *noun* [U] a person's skill in playing a musical instrument or singing: *The sheer musicianship of this young woman is breathtaking.*

music-making /ˈmjuː.zɪkˌmeɪ.kɪŋ/ *noun* [U] the playing or writing of music: *His compositions were influenced by the great tradition of music-making in that country.*

ˈmusic ˌtheatre *noun* [C or U] a type of theatre involving acting and music, performed by a small number of people

musk /mʌsk/ *noun* [U] a substance with a strong sweet smell, used in making perfumes **musky** /ˈmʌs.ki/ *adj*: *Her skin had a warm musky odour.*

musket /ˈmʌs.kɪt/ *noun* [C] a gun with a long barrel, used in the past

Muslim /ˈmʊz.lɪm/ [US] /ˈmɑː.zlem/ *noun* [C] (ALSO **Moslem**) a person who follows the religion of Islam **Muslim** /ˈmʊz.lɪm/ [US] /ˈmɑː.zlem/ *adj*: *a Muslim country/state* ○ *a Muslim family*

muslin /ˈmʌz.lɪn/ *noun* [U] a very thin cotton material: *A 19th-century painting of a girl in a muslin dress hung on the wall.* ○ *The soured milk is strained through muslin to leave a soft ball of cheese ready to be shaped.*

muso /ˈmjuː.zəʊ/ [US] /-zoʊ/ *noun* [C] UK INFORMAL someone who likes popular music very much and knows a lot about it, often having a lot of musical equipment

muss /mʌs/ *verb* [T] MAINLY US to make untidy: *The wind is mussing (up) my hair.*

muss /mʌs/ *noun* US **no muss, no fuss** used to say that something can be done without a lot of difficulty: *If we pack tonight, we can leave first thing in the morning – no muss, no fuss.*

mussel /ˈmʌs.əl/ *noun* [C] a small edible sea animal that lives inside a dark-coloured shell with two parts that close tightly together

must [NECESSARY] STRONG /mʌst/, WEAK /məst/ /məs/ *modal verb* **1** used to show that it is necessary or very important that something happens in the present or future: *Meat must be cooked thoroughly.* ○ *I must get some sleep.* ○ *You mustn't show this letter to anyone else.* ○ *Luggage must not be left unattended* (= it is against the

M

rules). ○ *FORMAL Must you leave so soon?* ○ *FORMAL "Must I sign this?" "No, there's no need."* **2** If you say that you must do something, you mean that you have a definite intention to do something in the future: *I must phone my sister.* ○ *We must get someone to fix that wheel.* ○ *I mustn't bite my nails.* **3** used for emphasis: ***I must say****, you're looking extremely well.* ○ ***I must admit****, I wasn't looking forward to it.* **4** If you tell someone else that they must do something pleasant, you are emphasizing that you think it is a good idea for them to do that: *You must come and stay with us for the weekend.* ○ *We must meet for lunch soon.*

must /mʌst/ *noun* [C] *INFORMAL* something which is necessary: *If you live in the country a car is* ***a*** *must.*

must- /mʌst-/ *prefix INFORMAL* **a must-do/-have/-see, etc.** something that is so good, you must do it, have it or see it: *The cashmere scarf is this season's must-have.* ○ *It's a moderately entertaining film but it's certainly not a must-see.*

COMMON LEARNER ERROR

the past tense of must

In the past tense, **had to** is used instead of **must**.

I'm going to France this evening and I must remember to take my passport with me.
Claudio could not come because he had to go to London.
~~*Claudio could not come because he must go to London.*~~

must [PROBABLY] *STRONG* /mʌst/, *WEAK* /məst/ /məs/ *modal verb* used to show that something is very likely, probable or certain to be true: *Harry's been driving all day – he must be tired.* ○ *There's no food left – we must have eaten it all.* ○ *When you got lost in the forest you must have been very frightened.* ○ *"You must know Frank." "No, I don't."*

mustache /mʊˈstɑːʃ/ [US] /ˈmʌs.tæʃ/ *noun* [C] *US FOR* **moustache**

mustachioed /məˈstæʃ.i.əʊd/ [US] /-oʊd/ *adj MAINLY HUMOROUS* having a large MOUSTACHE (= line of hair above the upper lip): *a mustachioed gentleman*

mustang /ˈmʌs.tæŋ/ *noun* [C] an American wild horse

mustard /ˈmʌs.təd/ [US] /-tɚd/ *noun* [U] a thick yellow or brown sauce that tastes spicy and is eaten cold in small amounts, especially with meat

ˈmustard ˌgas *noun* [U] a very poisonous gas, used as a weapon, that burns the skin, damages organs inside the body and can kill

muster [PRODUCE] /ˈmʌs.təʳ/ [US] /-tɚ/ *verb* [I or T] to produce or encourage especially an emotion or support: *She managed to muster the* ***courage*** *to ask him to the cinema.* ○ *The team will need all the* ***strength*** *they can muster to win this game.* ○ *Opponents are unlikely to be able to muster enough* ***votes*** *to override the veto.*

muster [GATHER] /ˈmʌs.təʳ/ [US] /-tɚ/ *verb* [I or T] (especially of soldiers) to gather together, especially in preparation for fighting, or to cause to do this: *The twelfth division mustered on the hill.* ○ *The general mustered his* ***troops****.*

muster /ˈmʌs.təʳ/ [US] /-tɚ/ *noun* [C] a group of people, especially soldiers, who have been brought together

▲ **muster *sth* up** *phrasal verb* If you muster up a feeling of bravery or energy, you try hard to find that quality in yourself because you need it in order to do something: [+ to infinitive] *She finally mustered up the courage to ask him for more money.*

ˈmuster ˌpoint *noun* [C] (*ALSO* **muster station**) *UK* a place where everyone in an area or on a boat is ordered to go when there is an emergency

mustn't /ˈmʌs.ᵊnt/ *short form of* must not: *You mustn't worry too much about this.*

musty /ˈmʌs.ti/ *adj* smelling unpleasantly old and slightly wet: *musty old books* ○ *a musty smell* ○ *a musty room*

mutate /mjuːˈteɪt/ *verb* [I] to develop new physical characteristics because of a permanent change in the genes. These changes can happen naturally or can be produced by the use of chemicals or radiation: *These bacteria have mutated* ***into*** *forms that are resistant to certain drugs.*

mutation /mjuːˈteɪ.ʃᵊn/ *noun* **1** [U] the way in which genes change and produce permanent differences: *It is well known that radiation can cause mutation.* **2** [C] a permanent change in an organism, or the changed organism itself: *Environmental pressures encourage genes with certain mutations to persist and others to die out.* ○ *These plants* ***carry*** *the mutation* ***for*** *red flowers.*

mutant /ˈmjuː.tᵊnt/ [US] /-t̬ᵊnt/ *noun* [C] **1** an organism that is different from others of its type because of a permanent change in its genes: *These mutants lacked a vital protein which gives them immunity to the disease.* ○ *This mutant* ***gene*** *is thought to cause cancer.* ○ *FIGURATIVE HUMOROUS I'm convinced he's a mutant – he's not a bit like the rest of our family!* **2** *DISAPPROVING* an unpleasant and frightening thing: *The result of these experiments will be a nightmarish world filled with two-headed monsters and other mutants.*

mute /mjuːt/ *adj* (of a person) unable or unwilling to speak, or (of an activity) silent: *a mute child* ○ *The president has* ***remained*** *mute about plans to curtail the number of immigrants.* ○ *I gazed at her in mute* (= silent) *admiration.*

mute /mjuːt/ *noun* [C] **1** a button or other device on a musical instrument that can be fixed in order to make it quieter **2** *OLD-FASHIONED* a person who is not able to speak

mute /mjuːt/ *verb* [T] If you mute a noise, you do something to make it less loud: *Double glazing muted the noise of the traffic.*

muted /ˈmjuː.tɪd/ [US] /-t̬ɪd/ *adj* **1** not loud: *There was polite, muted applause when I finished speaking.* **2** lacking enthusiasm: *The idea received a muted response.* **3** describes a colour which is not bright: *She was dressed in muted shades of blue.*

ˈmute ˌswan *noun* [C] the largest type of swan, which makes no cries when flying

mutilate /ˈmjuː.tɪ.leɪt/ [US] /-t̬ᵊl.eɪt/ *verb* [T] **1** to damage severely, especially by violently removing a part: *Her body had been mutilated beyond recognition.* ○ *Self-hatred apparently drove her to mutilate her own face.* **2** to destroy an idea or a piece of art or entertainment: *They have mutilated a beautiful film by making these changes.* **mutilation** /ˌmjuː.tɪˈleɪ.ʃᵊn/ [US] /-t̬ᵊlˈeɪ-/ *noun* [C or U] *He admitted to the murder and mutilation of between 12 and 16 young men.*

mutiny /ˈmjuː.tɪ.ni/ [US] /-t̬ɪ-/ *noun* [C or U] when a group of people, especially soldiers or sailors, refuse to obey orders and/or attempt to take control from people in authority: *Conditions on the ship were often very bad, and crews were on the point of mutiny.* ○ *There were rumours of mutiny* ***among*** *the troops.* ○ *Soldiers and police killed 250-300 prisoners while crushing mutinies in three jails.* **mutiny** /ˈmjuː.tɪ.ni/ [US] /-t̬ɪ-/ *verb* [I] *The crew mutinied and murdered the ship's captain.* ○ *The troops mutinied* ***against*** *their officers.*

mutineer /ˌmjuː.tɪˈnɪəʳ/ [US] /-t̬ɪˈnɪr/ *noun* [C] someone who takes part in a mutiny **mutinous** /ˈmjuː.tɪ.nəs/ [US] /-t̬ɪ-/ *adj*: *The mutinous sailors took control of the ship.*

mutt [PERSON] /mʌt/ *noun* [C] *MAINLY US INFORMAL* a person who behaves in a silly or careless way: *Come on you mutts, play harder!*

mutt [DOG] /mʌt/ *noun* [C] *MAINLY US* a **mongrel**

mutter /ˈmʌt.əʳ/ [US] /ˈmʌt̬.ɚ/ *verb* [I or T] to speak quietly and in a low voice that is not easy to hear, often when you are anxious or complaining about something: *Stop muttering and speak up!* ○ *He was muttering* ***(away) to*** *himself.* ○ *Laurence muttered something* ***about*** *his wife and left.* ○ *He muttered something* ***under*** *his* ***breath*** *to the person next to him.*

mutter /ˈmʌt.əʳ/ [US] /ˈmʌt̬.ɚ/ *noun* **1** [C or S] (the sound of) words being said very quietly: *I heard the soft mutter of voices in the next room.* **2** [C] a complaint which is made privately: *There were mutters* ***that*** *other departments received more money than ours.*

mutterings /ˈmʌt.ə.rɪŋz/ [US] /ˈmʌt̬.ɚ-/ *plural noun* complaints which are made privately: *There are mutterings* ***of discontent*** *among the staff.*

mutton /ˈmʌt.ᵊn/ [US] /ˈmʌt̬-/ *noun* [U] the meat from an adult sheep eaten as food

M

● **mutton dressed as lamb** *UK INFORMAL DISAPPROVING* a way of describing a woman who is dressed in a style that is more suitable for a younger woman: *Do you think this dress is too young-looking for me? – I don't want to look like mutton dressed as lamb.*

muttonchops /ˈmʌt.ˀn.tʃɒps/ ⓤ /ˈmʌt.ˀn.tʃɑːps/ *plural noun* (*ALSO* **muttonchop whiskers**) long hair growing down each side of a man's face, worn especially in Europe and America in the 19th century

mutual /ˈmjuː.tʃu.əl/ *adj* (of two or more people or groups) feeling the same emotion, or doing the same thing to or for each other: *Theirs was a partnership based on mutual respect, trust and understanding.* ○ *Both countries are acting to their mutual advantage.* ○ *The agreement was terminated by mutual consent.*
mutually /ˈmjuː.tʃu.ə.li/ *adv*: *It will be a mutually bene-ficial project.* ○ *Being rich and being a Socialist are not mutually exclusive* (= they can exist together at the same time).

mutual friend *noun* [C] a person who is the friend of two people who may or may not know each other: *Lynn and Phil met through a mutual friend.*

mutual fund *noun* [C usually sing] *US FOR* **unit trust**

Muzak /ˈmjuː.zæk/ *noun* [U] *TRADEMARK* recorded music that is played quietly and continuously in public places, such as airports, hotels and shops, to make people feel relaxed

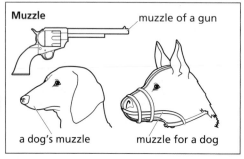

Muzzle

muzzle of a gun

a dog's muzzle

muzzle for a dog

muzzle ANIMAL /ˈmʌz.l̩/ *noun* [C] the mouth and nose of an animal, especially a dog, or a covering put over this in order to prevent the animal from biting
muzzle /ˈmʌz.l̩/ *verb* [T] **1** to put a muzzle on an animal: *Dangerous dogs should be muzzled.* **2** to stop a person or organization from expressing independent opinions: *The new Secrecy Act will muzzle the media and the opposition.*

muzzle GUN /ˈmʌz.l̩/ *noun* [C] the end of a gun barrel, where the bullets come out

muzzy /ˈmʌz.i/ *adj UK* (of a person) confused and unable to think clearly because of tiredness, illness, alcohol or drugs, or (of a situation, plans, language, etc.) not clear or well explained: *Feeling muzzy from the blow on his head, he got up very slowly.* ○ *Until a week ago, the group's objectives were slightly muzzy.* **muzzily** /ˈmʌz.ɪ.li/ *adv* **muzziness** /ˈmʌz.ɪ.nəs/ *noun* [U]

MW *noun* [U] *WRITTEN ABBREVIATION FOR* **medium wave**

MWA /ˌem.dʌbl.juːˈeɪ/ *noun* [C] *ABBREVIATION FOR* Member of the Welsh Assembly

my OF ME /maɪ/ *determiner* **1** of or belonging to me (= the speaker or writer): *my parents* ○ *my feet* ○ *my name* ○ *my jacket* ○ *It wasn't my fault.* ○ *FORMAL She was rather surprised at my asking* (= that I asked) *for the book to be returned.* ⟳See also I LETTER; **me** PERSON; **mine** BELONGING TO ME. **2** my own used to emphasize that something belongs to or is connected with me and no one else: *I want my own car.* ○ *It was my own decision.* ○ *This cake is all my own work* (= I made it without help). **3** used in front of a noun as a way of expressing love or as a polite or humorous form of address: *My darling!* ○ *Do you want any help, my dear?*

myself /maɪˈself/ *pronoun* **1** the reflexive pronoun of I: *I've bought myself a new coat.* ○ *I caught sight of myself in the mirror.* ○ *Yes, I thought to myself, it's time to take a holiday.* **2** used to emphasize 'I' as the subject of a sentence: *I myself don't like a heavy meal at lunchtime.* ○ *I don't like a heavy meal at lunchtime myself.* ○ *I had to do the whole job by myself* (= with no help from other people). ○ *I live by myself* (= alone). ○ *I never get an hour to myself* (= for my own use). **3** used instead of 'I' or 'me': *My husband and myself were delighted with the gift.* ○ *They very kindly invited my sister and myself to the in-auguration.*

● **in myself** *UK INFORMAL* used when describing your state of mind when you are physically ill: *I'm well enough in myself* (= happy) – *I've just got this nagging headache.*

my EXPRESSION /maɪ/ *exclamation OLD-FASHIONED* used to express surprise or pleasure: *My, what delicious food!* ○ *My, oh, my, what a busy day!*

myalgic encephalomyelitis /maɪˌæl.dʒɪk.enˌsef.ə.ləʊ.maɪ.əˈlaɪ.tɪs/ ⓤ /-ˌləʊ.maɪ.əˈlaɪ.t̬əs/ *noun* [U] *UK FOR* **chronic fatigue syndrome**

mycology /maɪˈkɒl.ə.dʒi/ ⓤ /-ˈkɑː.lə-/ *noun* [U] the scientific study of fungi **mycologist** /maɪˈkɒl.ə.dʒɪst/ ⓤ /-ˈkɑː.lə-/ *noun* [C]

mynah (bird) /ˈmaɪ.nəˌbɜːd/ ⓤ /-ˌbɝːd/ *noun* [C] (*AUS* **Indian mynah**) a black or dark brown bird from Asia, some types of which can copy human speech

myopia /maɪˈəʊ.pi.ə/ ⓤ /-ˈoʊ-/ *noun* [U] *SPECIALIZED* inability to see distant things clearly
myopic /maɪˈɒp.ɪk/ ⓤ /-ˈɑː.pɪk/ *adj* **1** *SPECIALIZED* not able to see clearly things that are far away **2** *DISAPPROVING* unable to understand a situation or the way actions will affect it in the future: *Their myopic refusal to act now will undoubtedly cause problems in the future.*

myriad /ˈmɪr.i.əd/ *noun* [C] *LITERARY* a very large number of something: *a myriad of choices* ○ *And now myriads of bars and hotels are opening up along the coast.* **myriad** /ˈmɪr.i.əd/ *adj*: *They offered no solution for all our myriad problems.*

myrrh /mɜːʳ/ ⓤ /mɝː/ *noun* [U] a sticky brown substance with a strong smell which is used in making perfume and INCENSE

myrtle /ˈmɜː.tl̩/ ⓤ /ˈmɝː.t̬l̩/ *noun* [C] a small tree with shiny green leaves, pleasant-smelling white flowers and blue-black fruit

myself /maɪˈself/ *pronoun* ⟳See at **my** OF ME.

mystery /ˈmɪs.tˀr.i/ ⓤ /-t̬ɚ-/ *noun* **1** [C or U] something strange or unknown which has not yet been explained or understood: *How the massive stones were brought here from hundreds of miles away is/remains a mystery.* ○ *The mystery was solved when the police discovered the murder weapon.* ○ *The book tries to explain some of the mysteries of life.* ○ *The details of the scandal remain cloaked/shrouded/wrapped in mystery.* ○ *It's a complete mystery (to me) that/why* (= I do not understand why) *she married him at all!* **2** [C] a book, film or play, especially about a crime or a murder, with a surprise ending which explains all the strange events that have happened: *I really enjoy murder mysteries.* ○ *a mystery writer* **mysterious** /mɪˈstɪə.ri.əs/ ⓤ /-ˈstɪr.i-/ *adj*: *She's an actress whose inner life has remained mysterious, despite the many interviews she has given.* ○ *He died in mysterious circumstances, and there is still a possibility that it was murder.* **mysteriously** /mɪˈstɪə.ri.ə.sli/ ⓤ /-ˈstɪr.i-/ *adv*: *"Perhaps, and perhaps not," she said mysteriously.* ○ *Mysteriously, the light came on, although no one was near the switch.*

mystery play *noun* [C] a religious play based on stories from the Bible and performed especially in Europe between the 11th and 14th centuries

mystery shopper *noun* [C] (*US ALSO* **secret shopper**) someone employed to test the service in shops and businesses by pretending to be a normal customer

mystery tour *noun* [C] *UK* a short journey, especially with a group of other people in a bus, to visit places which are kept secret from you until you get there

mysticism /ˈmɪs.tɪ.sɪ.zˀm/ *noun* [U] the belief that there is hidden meaning in life or that each human being can unite with God
mystic /ˈmɪs.tɪk/ *noun* [C] someone who attempts to be united with God through prayer **mystical** /ˈmɪs.tɪ.kˀl/ *adj* (*ALSO* **mystic**) *a mystical religion*

mystify /ˈmɪs.tɪ.faɪ/ *verb* **[T often passive]** to confuse someone by being or doing something very strange or impossible to explain: *I was mystified by her decision.* ○ *Most Americans seem totally mystified by cricket.*
mystification /ˌmɪs.tɪ.fɪˈkeɪ.ʃᵊn/ *noun* **[U]** when someone or something confuses you by being impossible to understand: *And then, to the audience's mystification, the band suddenly stopped playing.* **mystifying** /ˈmɪs.tɪ.faɪ.ɪŋ/ *adj*: *After ten years her mystifying disappear- ance was still unexplained.* **mystifyingly** /ˈmɪs.tɪ.faɪ.ɪŋ.li/ *adv*

mystique /mɪˈstiːk/ *noun* **[U]** *FORMAL* a quality of being special in a mysterious and attractive way: *There's great mystique* ***attached to/surrounding*** *the life of a movie star.* ○ *Too much publicity has destroyed the mystique of the monarchy.*

myth /mɪθ/ *noun* **1** **[C or U]** an ancient story or set of stories, especially explaining in a literary way the early history of a group of people or about natural events and facts: *ancient myths* ○ *The children enjoyed the stories about the gods and goddesses of Greek and Roman myth.* ○ *Most societies have their own creation myths.* **2** **[C + *that*]** *DISAPPROVING* a commonly believed but false idea: *Statistics* ***disprove*** *the myth* ***that*** *women are worse drivers than men.*
mythical /ˈmɪθ.ɪ.kᵊl/ *adj* **1** existing only in stories: *the mythical island of Atlantis* ○ *a mythical hero* ○ *dragons and other mythical creatures* **2** imaginary or not real: *Start living life here and now instead of waiting for that mythical day when you'll be slim.*
mythological /ˌmɪθ.ᵊlˈɒdʒ.ɪ.kᵊl/ [US] /-əˈlɑː.dʒɪ-/ *adj* connected with myths: *a mythological hero/creature*
mythology /mɪˈθɒl.ə.dʒi/ [US] /-ˈθɑː.lə-/ *noun* **[U]** **1** myths in general: *She's fascinated by the stories of* ***classical*** *mythology* (= ancient Greek and Roman myths). **2** a popular belief that is probably not true: *It's just a piece of* ***popular*** *mythology that people always get sacked when they are away.*
mythologize, *UK USUALLY* **-ise** /mɪˈθɒl.ə.dʒaɪz/ [US] /mɪˈθɑː.lə-/ *verb* **[I or T]** *MAINLY US* to create a false picture of a situation: *People tend to mythologize* ***(about)*** *their youth/the past.*

myxomatosis /ˌmɪk.sə.məˈtəʊ.sɪs/ [US] /-ˈtoʊ-/ *noun* **[U]** an infectious disease of rabbits that usually kills them

M

N

N [LETTER] (*plural* **N's** or **Ns**), **n** (*plural* **n's** or **ns**) /en/ *noun* [C] the 14th letter of the English alphabet: *I think his name begins with an N.* ⊃Compare **nth**.

N [NORTH] *noun* [U], *adj* (UK ALSO **Nth**, US ALSO **No**) WRITTEN ABBREVIATION FOR **north** or **northern**

n [MATHEMATICS] /en/ *noun* [U] **1** used in mathematics to mean a number whose value is not known or not stated: *If 3n = 12, what is the value of n?* **2** used more generally to represent a number that is not known or exact

n [GRAMMAR] WRITTEN ABBREVIATION FOR **noun**

'n' [AND] /-ᵊn-/ *conjunction* NOT STANDARD used in writing to mean 'and': *fish 'n' chips* ○ *rock 'n' roll*

n/a, N/A /ˌenˈeɪ/ WRITTEN ABBREVIATION FOR not applicable: used on a form when you cannot give an appropriate answer to a question

naan (bread) /ˈnɑːnˌbred/ *noun* [C or U] **nan (bread)**

nab /næb/ *verb* [T] **-bb-** INFORMAL to take something suddenly, or to catch or arrest a criminal: *Undercover police officers nabbed* (= caught) *the men at the airport.* ○ *Someone nabbed my apple when I wasn't looking!*

nabob /ˈneɪ.bɒb/ [US] /-bɑːb/ *noun* [C] OLD-FASHIONED a rich or powerful person

nachos /ˈnætʃ.əʊz/ [US] /-tʃoʊz/ *plural noun* small pieces of fried TORTILLA (= flat bread made from maize flour) covered with melted cheese, beans and a spicy sauce
nacho /ˈnætʃ.əʊ/ [US] /-tʃoʊ/ *adj*: *nacho-flavoured chips*

nadir /ˈneɪ.dɪəʳ/ [US] /-dɚ/ *noun* [S] FORMAL the worst moment, or the moment of least hope and least achievement: *The defeat was* ***the*** *nadir* ***of*** *her career.* ⊃Compare **zenith**.

nae /neɪ/ *adv* SCOTTISH ENGLISH OR NORTHERN ENGLISH FOR **no** NOT

naff /næf/ *adj* UK SLANG not stylish or fashionable: *His haircut was a bit naff.*

naff /næf/ *verb*
▲ **naff off** *phrasal verb* UK SLANG used to rudely tell someone to go away because they are annoying you

nag [CRITICIZE] /næg/ *verb* [I or T] **-gg-** to criticize or complain repeatedly in an annoying way: [+ obj + *to* infinitive] *My mum's always nagging me* ***to*** *get my hair cut.* ○ *If she'd only stop nagging* ***at*** *me, I might actually help.* ○ *I'm always nagging him* ***about*** *his diet.*
nagging /ˈnæg.ɪŋ/ *adj* **1** complaining or criticizing: *a nagging voice* **2** describes an unpleasant feeling that continues for a long period of time: *nagging doubts/pain*
nagging /ˈnæg.ɪŋ/ *noun* [U] complaining and criticizing: *I got sick of her constant nagging.*
▲ **nag (away) at** ***sb*** *phrasal verb* If doubts or worries nag (away) at you, you think about them all the time: *The same thought has been nagging away at me since last week.*

nag [HORSE] /næg/ *noun* [C] a horse, especially one that is too old to be useful

nah /næː/ *adv* SLANG FOR **no** NEGATIVE ANSWER

nail [METAL] /neɪl/ *noun* [C] a small thin piece of metal with one pointed end and one flat end which you hit into something with a hammer, especially in order to fasten or join it to something else: *a three-inch nail* ○ *I stepped on a nail sticking out of the floorboards.* ○ ***Hammer*** *a nail into the wall and we'll hang the mirror from it.*
• **another/the final nail in the coffin** an event which causes the failure of something that had already started to fail: *Each successive revelation of incompetence is another nail in the chairman's coffin.* ○ *That report drove the final nail in the company's coffin.*
• **hard/tough as nails** not feeling or showing any emotions such as sympathy, fear or worry ⊃See also **hit the nail on the head** at **hit** TOUCH.
nail /neɪl/ *verb* **1** [T + adv or prep] to fasten something with nails: *She had nailed a small shelf* ***to*** *the door.* ○ *A notice had been nailed* ***up*** *on the wall.* ○ *The lid of the coffin had been nailed* ***down***. **2** [T] SLANG to catch someone, especially when they are doing something wrong, or to make it clear that they are guilty: *The police had been trying to nail those guys for months.*
• **nail** ***your*** **colours to the mast** UK to make it obvious what your opinions or plans are

Nail

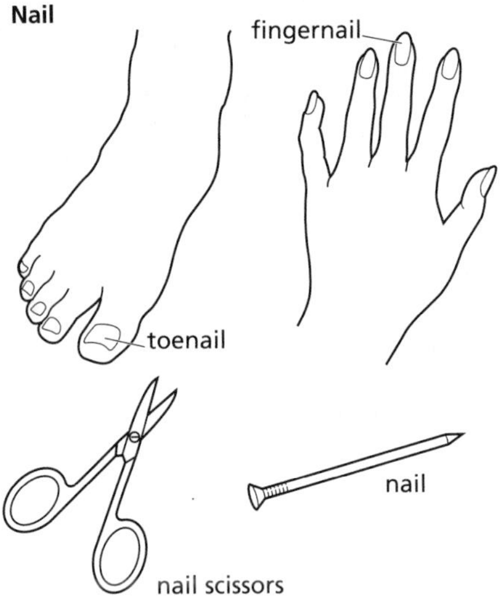

nail [BODY PART] /neɪl/ *noun* [C] a thin hard area that covers the upper side of the end of each finger and each toe: *Stop* ***biting*** *your nails!* ○ *nail clippers* ○ *a nail file*

PHRASAL VERBS WITH **nail**

▲ **nail** ***sth*** **down** [DECISION] *phrasal verb* INFORMAL If you nail down an arrangement or decision, you fix and agree to the details of it: *After a five-hour meeting, we finally nailed down a deal.*
▲ **nail** ***sb*** **down** *phrasal verb* INFORMAL to make someone give you exact details or a firm decision about something: *They nailed him down* ***to*** *a specific time and place.*
▲ **nail** ***sth*** **down** [UNDERSTAND] *phrasal verb* [M] US INFORMAL to understand something completely, or to describe something correctly: *We haven't been able to nail down the cause of the fire yet.*

nail-biting /ˈneɪlˌbaɪ.tɪŋ/ [US] /-t̬ɪŋ/ *adj* [before n] describes a situation that is very exciting or worrying because you do not know how it will end: *Germany won the championship after a nail-biting final.*
nail-biter /ˈneɪlˌbaɪ.təʳ/ [US] /-t̬ɚ/ *noun* [C] a sports event or a film which is exciting because you do not know how it will end: *Saturday's semi-final was a real nail-biter.*

ˈnail ˌbrush *noun* [C] a small stiff brush used for cleaning your nails and your hands

ˈnail ˌfile *noun* [C] a small strip of metal or paper with a rough surface used for making the edges of your nails smooth and curved

ˈnail ˌpolish *noun* [C or U] (UK ALSO **nail varnish**) a coloured liquid which is painted on FINGERNAILS or TOENAILS

ˈnail ˌscissors *plural noun* a small pair of curved scissors used to cut your nails

naive, naïve /naɪˈiːv/ *adj* MAINLY DISAPPROVING too willing to believe that someone is telling the truth, that people's intentions in general are good or that life is simple and fair. People are often naive because they are young and/or have not had much experience of life: *She was very naive to believe that he'd stay with her.* ○ *They make the naive assumption that because it's popular it must be good.* ○ ***It*** *was a little naive* ***of*** *you* ***to*** *think that they would listen to your suggestions.* **naively, naïvely** /naɪˈiː.v.li/ *adv*: *I, perhaps naively, believed he was telling the truth.*

naivety, naïveté /naɪˈiː.vɪ.ti/ [US] /-və.t̬i/ *noun* [U] trust based on lack of experience: DISAPPROVING *He demonstrated a worrying naivety about political issues.* ○ APPROVING *I think her naivety is charming – she's so unspoilt and fresh.*

naked /ˈneɪ.kɪd/ *adj* **1** not covered by clothes: *a naked man* ○ *naked bodies* ○ ***stark** naked* (= completely naked) ○ US INFORMAL *buck/butt naked* (= completely naked) ○ *He was naked **to** the waist* (= not wearing clothes above his waist). ○ *The children were **half** naked* (= partly naked). ○ *They **stripped** naked* (= took off their clothes) *and ran into the sea.* **2** Something that is naked is lacking its usual covering: *a naked flame/light bulb* (= one with nothing surrounding or covering it) ○ *a naked hillside* (= one without trees or plants) **3** [before n] A naked feeling or quality is not hidden, although it is bad: *naked aggression/greed*
• **the naked eye** If something can be seen with the naked eye, it can be seen without the help of an instrument: *This organism is too small to be seen **with** the naked eye.* ○ *The police found traces of blood on his jacket that were **invisible to** the naked eye.*
nakedness /ˈneɪ.kɪd.nəs/ *noun* [U] the state of being naked: *Adam and Eve tried to hide their nakedness with fig leaves.* **nakedly** /ˈneɪ.kɪd.li/ *adv*

namby-pamby /ˌnæm.biˈpæm.bi/ *adj* INFORMAL DISAPPROVING weak, foolish or silly: *She probably regarded us as a bunch of namby-pamby liberals.*

name /neɪm/ *noun* **1** [C] the word or words that a person, thing or place is known by: *"Hi, what's your name?" "My name's Diane."* ○ *Please write your **full*** (= complete) *name **and address** on the form.* ○ *What's the name of that mountain in the distance?* ○ *We finally agreed on the name Luca for our son.* ○ *The students were listed **by** name and by country of origin.* **2** [C usually sing] the opinion or reputation that someone or something has: *She went to court to **clear** her name* (= prove that the bad things said about her were not true). ○ *Their actions **gave** British football a **bad** name in Europe at that time.* ○ *They're trying to restore the **good** name of the manufacturer.* **3** [C] someone who is famous or has a good reputation: *It seemed like all the **big** names in football were there.*
• **by the name of *sth*** FORMAL called: *I've got to talk to a professor by the name of Bin Said.*
• **go by the name of *sth*** to give yourself a name which is not your real name: *In the business world he goes by the name of J. Walter Fortune.*
• **in all but name** existing as a fact but not officially described that way: *She is vice-president in all but name.*
• **in name only** If a situation exists in name only, it is officially described that way, although that description is not true: *A large percentage of the population is Catholic, though many are so in name only.*
• **in the name of *sb*** (ALSO **in *sb's* name**) for someone or belonging to someone: *I've come to collect my tickets – I reserved them by phone yesterday in the name of Tremin.* ○ *The house is in my wife's name.*
• **in the name of *sth*** (ALSO **in *sth's* name**) (said or done) in order to help a particular thing succeed: *Much blood has been spilled in the name of religion.*
• **in the name of *sb/sth*** (ALSO **in *sb's/sth's* name**) doing something as a representative of someone or something: *In old movies the police shouted "Open up in the name of* (= by the right of) *the law" before they broke the door down.* ○ *They were arrested in the name of the king.* ○ *As members of the union, we have the right to know what action the union is taking in our name.*
• **in God/heaven's name** (ALSO **in the name of God/heaven**) used to add force to something which is said, although some people might find the use of 'God' offensive: *What in God's name caused that outburst?* ○ *Why in the name of God didn't you tell me sooner?*
• **make a name for *yourself*** to become famous or respected by a lot of people: *He's made a name for himself **as** a talented journalist.*
• **be a name to conjure with** UK to be a very important name, or an interesting name which gives you a mental picture of something pleasant or exciting: *In those days Churchill was still a name to conjure with.* ○ *The House of the Blue Lagoon – now there's a name to conjure with!*
• ***your* name is mud** INFORMAL If your name is mud, other people are angry with you because of something you have said or done: *If he doesn't turn up tonight, his name will be mud.*
• **the name of the game** INFORMAL the most important part of an activity, or the quality that you most need for that activity: *People say that in politics the name of the game is making the right friends.*
• **take *sb's* name in vain** UK HUMOROUS to criticize someone or talk about someone without respect, especially when they are not there
• **to *your* name** If you have nothing or very little to your name, you own very little or have no money: *He had arrived in America without a cent to his name.*
• **under the name of** using the false name of: *Her detective stories were written under the name of Kramer.*
name /neɪm/ *verb* [T] **1** to give someone or something a name: [+ two objects] *We named our dogs 'Shandy' and 'Belle'.* ○ *A man named Dennis answered the door.* **2** to say what something or someone's name is: *In the first question you had to name three types of monkey.* ○ *He couldn't name his attacker.* **3** to choose someone or something: *Just name the time and I'll be there on the dot.* ○ *Name your conditions/terms/price.* ○ *Ms Martinez has been named **(as)*** (= she will be) *the new Democratic candidate.*
• **name names** to tell someone in authority the names of people involved in a secret or illegal activity
• **name and shame** UK to publicly say that a person, group or business has done something wrong: *The report names and shames companies that are not doing enough to fight industrial pollution.*
• **you name it** used to say there are many things to choose from: *Gin, vodka, whisky, beer – you name it, I've got it.* ○ *I've tried every diet going – you name it, I've tried it.*
• **name the day** to decide the date on which you are going to get married: *When are you going to name the day?*
nameless /ˈneɪm.ləs/ *adj* having no name, or having a name that is not known: *a nameless soldier* ○ *the nameless author of a medieval text*
• **who shall remain nameless** HUMOROUS used when you are telling people about a bad thing that someone else has done: *One boy, who shall remain nameless, has been late every day this week.*
▲ **name *sb/sth* after *sb/sth*** *phrasal verb* (US ALSO **name *sb/sth* for *sb/sth***) to give someone or something the same name as another person or thing: *Paul was named after his grandad.* ○ *She told us about his brother, Apollo, born in 1969 and named for the U.S. astronauts' mission to the moon.*

name-calling /ˈneɪmˌkɔː.lɪŋ/ [US] /-kɑː-/ *noun* [U] when someone insults someone else by calling them rude names

name-dropping /ˈneɪm.drɒp.ɪŋ/ [US] /-drɑːp-/ *noun* [U] DISAPPROVING when someone talks about famous people that they have met, often pretending that they know them better than they really do, in order to appear more important and special **ˈname ˌdrop** *verb* [I] **name-dropper** /ˈneɪmˌdrɒp.əʳ/ [US] /-drɑː.pɚ/ *noun* [C]

namely /ˈneɪm.li/ *adv* used when you want to give more detail or be more exact about something you have just said: *We need to get more teachers into the classrooms where they're most needed, namely in high poverty areas.*

nameplate /ˈneɪm.pleɪt/ *noun* [C] a piece of metal or plastic fastened onto something to show who owns it, who has made it, or who lives or works there: *There was a brass nameplate outside the door saying Dr A. Aslan.*

namesake /ˈneɪm.seɪk/ *noun* [C] a person or thing having the same name as another person or thing

nan /næn/ *noun* [C usually sing] UK INFORMAL FOR **grandmother**: *The kids love staying with their nan at the weekend.*

nana /ˈnæn.ə/ *noun* [C] CHILD'S WORD FOR **grandmother**: [as form of address] *Will you read me a story, Nana?*

ˈnan (ˌbread), **naan (bread)** *noun* [C or U] a flat bread typically eaten with Indian food

N

nandrolone /ˈnæn.drə.ləʊn/ [US] /-loʊn/ *noun* [U] a substance that can improve someone's physical strength and STAMINA (= the ability to do something for a long period) and which is forbidden in most sports competitions

nanny [GRANDMOTHER] /ˈnæn.i/ *noun* [C] *UK INFORMAL FOR* **grandmother**

nanny [JOB] /ˈnæn.i/ *noun* [C] a woman whose job is to take care of a particular family's children
• **the nanny state** *UK DISAPPROVING* a government which tries to give too much advice or make too many laws about how people should live their lives, especially about eating, smoking or drinking alcohol

ˈnanny ˌgoat *noun* [C] a female goat

nanometre *UK* /nænˈɒm.ə.təʳ/ [US] /-ˈɑː.mə.tɚ/ *noun* [C] (*US* **nanometer**) 0.000 000 001 of a metre

nanosecond /ˈnæn.əʊˌsek.ənd/ [US] /-oʊ-/ *noun* [C] 0.000 000 001 seconds

nanotechnology /ˌnæn.əʊ.tekˈnɒl.ə.dʒi/ [US] /-oʊ.tek-ˈnɑː.lə-/ *noun* [U] an area of science which deals with developing and producing extremely small tools and machines by controlling the arrangement of individual atoms

nap [SLEEP] /næp/ *noun* [C] a short sleep, especially during the day: *Grandpa usually **has/takes a** nap after lunch.*
nap /næp/ *verb* [I] **-pp-** *He likes to nap for an hour when he gets home from work.*

nap [CLOTH] /næp/ *noun* [S] the surface of a piece of cloth such as VELVET, consisting of short threads which have been brushed in one direction

napalm /ˈneɪ.pɑːm/ *noun* [U] a substance containing petrol which burns fiercely and is used in bombs, especially to destroy areas of plants so that enemy soldiers cannot hide

nape /neɪp/ *noun* [C usually sing] the back of the neck: *She kissed **the** nape **of** his **neck**.*

napkin /ˈnæp.kɪn/ *noun* [C] (*UK ALSO* **serviette**) a small square piece of cloth or paper used while you are eating for protecting your clothes or to clean your mouth or fingers

ˈnapkin ˌring *noun* [C] a small ring which holds a particular person's cloth napkin between meals when they are not using it

nappy *UK* /ˈnæp.i/ *noun* [C] (*US* **diaper**) a square of thick soft paper or cloth which is fastened around a baby's bottom and between its legs to absorb its urine and excrement: *disposable/reusable nappies* ○ *nappy cream* ○ *She was **changing** the baby's nappy.* ○ *I knew William when he was still **in** nappies* (= when he was a baby).

ˈnappy ˌrash *UK noun* [U] (*US* **diaper rash**) a red painful area of skin on a baby's bottom caused by a wet nappy

narcissism /ˈnɑː.sɪ.sɪ.zəm/ [US] /ˈnɑːr.sə-/ *noun* [U] *DISAPPROVING* too much interest in and admiration for your own physical appearance and/or your own abilities
narcissist /ˈnɑː.sɪ.sɪst/ [US] /ˈnɑːr.sə-/ *noun* [C] someone who has too much admiration for themselves **narcissistic** /ˌnɑː.sɪˈsɪs.tɪk/ [US] /ˌnɑːr.sə-/ *adj*: *a narcissistic personality*

narcissus /nɑːˈsɪs.əs/ [US] /nɑːr-/ *noun* [C] *plural* **narcissuses** or **narcissi** or **narcissus** a yellow, white or orange flower, similar to a DAFFODIL

narcolepsy /ˈnɑː.kəʊ.lep.si/ [US] /ˈnɑːr.kə-/ *noun* [U] a medical condition which makes you go to sleep suddenly and unexpectedly **narcoleptic** /ˌnɑː.kəʊˈlep.tɪk/ [US] /ˌnɑːr.kə-/ *noun* [C], *adj*

narcotic /nɑːˈkɒt.ɪk/ [US] /nɑːrˈkɑː.t̬-/ *noun* [C] **1** *MAINLY US* an illegal drug such as HEROIN or COCAINE: *He faces three years in jail for selling narcotics.* **2** *SPECIALIZED* a drug which makes you want to sleep and prevents you feeling pain: *Morphine is a narcotic.* **narcotic** /nɑːˈkɒt.ɪk/ [US] /nɑːrˈkɑː.t̬-/ *adj*: *narcotic drugs* ○ *a narcotic effect*

nark [ANNOY] /nɑːk/ [US] /nɑːrk/ *verb* [T usually passive] *UK SLANG OLD-FASHIONED* to annoy someone: *I was a bit narked by David's comment.*
nark /nɑːk/ [US] /nɑːrk/ *noun* [C] *AUS* a person who complains and spoils other people's enjoyment
narky /ˈnɑː.ki/ [US] /ˈnɑːr-/ *adj UK SLANG OLD-FASHIONED* easily annoyed: *You were a bit narky with me this morning.*

nark [CRIMINAL] /nɑːk/ [US] /nɑːrk/ *noun* [C] *UK OLD-FASHIONED SLANG* a person, especially a criminal, who gives the police information about other criminals: *a **coppers'** nark*
nark, narc /nɑːk/ [US] /nɑːrk/ *verb* [I] *US SLANG* to secretly tell the police or someone in authority about something bad or illegal that someone has done

nark [POLICE OFFICER] /nɑːk/ [US] /nɑːrk/ *noun* [C] (*ALSO* **narc**) *US SLANG* a police officer whose job is to catch people who produce, sell or use illegal drugs

narrate /nəˈreɪt/[US] /ˈnær.eɪt/ *verb* [T] to tell a story, often by reading aloud from a text, or to describe events as they happen: *Documentaries are often narrated by well-known actors.* ○ *One by one the witnesses narrated the sequence of events which led up to the disaster.*
narration /nəˈreɪ.ʃən/ [US] /nærˈeɪ-/ *noun* **1** [U] the act of telling a story **2** [C or U] a spoken description of events given during a film or television programme: *Dame Judi Dench did the narration for the documentary.*
narrative /ˈnær.ə.tɪv/ [US] /-t̬ɪv/ *noun* [C or U] *FORMAL* a story or a description of a series of events: *It's a moving narrative of wartime adventure.*
narrator /nəˈreɪ.təʳ/ [US] /ˈnær.eɪ.t̬ɚ/ *noun* [C] the character who tells you what is happening in a book or film

narrow /ˈnær.əʊ/ [US] /-oʊ/ *adj* **1** having a small distance from one side to the other, especially in comparison with the length: *a narrow bridge/passage/gap* ○ *a narrow face* ○ *narrow feet* ○ *The little village has very narrow **streets**.* **2** *MAINLY DISAPPROVING* limited to a small area of interest, activity or thought: *They are unable to see beyond the narrow world of the theatre.* ○ *It was regarded as a very narrow interpretation of the law.* ➲See also **narrow-minded**. **3** If you achieve a narrow result, the result could easily have been different because the amount by which you failed or succeeded was very small: *The election was won by the very narrow **margin** of only 185 votes.* ○ *The opposition had a narrow **defeat**.* ○ *We won a narrow **victory**.*
• **a narrow escape** a situation in which you only just avoid danger: *We got out in time but it was a narrow escape.*
• **a narrow squeak** *UK* a success that was almost a failure: *We caught the ferry but it was a narrow squeak.*
narrow /ˈnær.əʊ/ [US] /-oʊ/ *verb* [I or T] to become less wide or to make something less wide: *The road narrows after the bridge.* ○ *He narrowed his **eyes** in suspicion.* ○ *They have narrowed the focus of the investigation, to concentrate on younger adults.* ○ *FIGURATIVE We must strive to narrow the gap between rich and poor.*
narrowly /ˈnær.əʊ.li/ [US] /-oʊ-/ *adv* **1** only by a small amount: *She narrowly missed winning an Oscar.* **2** in a limited way: *a narrowly interpreted law* **3** *FORMAL* carefully or in a way that shows doubt: *The officer looked at him narrowly through half-closed eyes.* **narrowness** /ˈnær.əʊ.nəs/ [US] /-oʊ-/ *noun* [U]
narrows /ˈnær.əʊz/ [US] /-oʊz/ *plural noun* **1** a narrow channel that connects two large areas of water **2** *US* a narrow part of a lake or river
▲ **narrow *sth* down** *phrasal verb* [M] to make a number or list of things smaller and clearer, by removing the things that are least important, necessary or desirable: *We narrowed the list of candidates down **from** ten **to** three.*

ˈnarrow ˌboat *noun* [C] *UK* a **canal boat** ➲Compare **barge** BOAT.

narrow-gauge /ˈnær.əʊ.geɪdʒ/ [US] /-oʊ-/ *adj* [before n] describes a railway with metal tracks that are closer together than the standard British and American distance of 56.5 inches

narrow-minded /ˌnær.əʊˈmaɪn.dɪd/ [US] /-oʊ-/ *adj DISAPPROVING* not willing to accept ideas or ways of behaving that are different from your own: *narrow-minded opinions/views* ○ *a narrow-minded person* ➲Compare **broadminded**. **narrow-mindedness** /ˌnær.əʊˈmaɪn.dɪd.nəs/ [US] /-oʊ-/ *noun* [U] *The villagers displayed the typical narrow-mindedness of a small community.*

NASA /ˈnæs.ə/ *group noun* **[U]** *ABBREVIATION FOR* National Aeronautics and Space Administration: the US government organization that is responsible for space travel and the scientific study of space

nasal /ˈneɪ.zᵊl/ *adj* **1** related to the nose: *nasal passages* ○ *nasal congestion* ○ *the nasal cavity* ○ *a nasal spray* **2** *USUALLY DISAPPROVING* If a person's voice is nasal, it has a particular sound because air is going through their nose when they speak: *a nasal accent* ○ *She spoke in nasal tones.* **nasally** /ˈneɪ.zᵊl.i/ *adv*

nascent /ˈnæs.ᵊnt/ /ˈneɪ.sᵊnt/ *adj FORMAL* only recently formed or started, but likely to grow larger quickly: *a nascent political party* ○ *a nascent problem*

nasturtium /nəˈstɜː.ʃᵊm/ [US] /-ˈstɝː-/ *noun* **[C]** a plant with yellow, red or orange flowers and round leaves

nasty /ˈnɑː.sti/ [US] /ˈnæs.ti/ *adj* **1** bad or very unpleasant: *a nasty shock/surprise* ○ *There's a nasty smell in here.* ○ *He had a nasty cut above the eye.* ○ *She has a nasty **habit** of picking on people in meetings.* **2** unkind: *Don't be so nasty **to** your brother – he's four years younger than you!* **3** dangerous or violent: *In an emergency you could get out through a window, but it would be a nasty drop.* ○ *The situation could **turn*** (= become) *nasty at any moment.* **4** rude or offensive: *She said some quite nasty things about him.*

• **have a nasty feeling** to think that something bad is likely to happen or to be true: *I've got a nasty feeling **that** I forgot to tell Joe I couldn't come.*

• **a nasty piece of work** *INFORMAL* a very unpleasant person

nastily /ˈnɑː.stɪ.li/ [US] /ˈnæs.tɪ-/ *adv*: *He laughed nastily* (= unkindly) *and walked away.* **nastiness** /ˈnɑː.stɪ.nəs/ [US] /ˈnæs.tɪ-/ *noun* **[U]**

natch /nætʃ/ *adv HUMOROUS INFORMAL* naturally; as you would expect: *We're flying – by private plane, natch.*

nation /ˈneɪ.ʃᵊn/ *noun* **1** **[C]** a country, especially when thought of as a large group of people living in one area with their own government, language, traditions, etc: *All the nations of the world will be represented at the conference.* ○ *The Germans, as a nation, are often thought to be well organized.* ○ *Practically the whole nation watched the ceremony on television.* ➲See Note **country, land, nation, or state?** at **country** POLITICAL UNIT. **2** **[S]** a large group of people of the same race who share the same language, traditions and history, but who might not all live in one area: *the Navajo nation*

national /ˈnæʃ.ᵊn.ᵊl/ /ˈnæʃ.nəl/ *adj* relating to or typical of a whole country and its people, rather than to part of that country or to other countries: *a national holiday* ○ *Britain has more than ten national newspapers.* ○ *The company's national headquarters is in Rome.* ○ *The children were wearing traditional national **costume/dress**.* ○ *The government's view is that raising taxes now would not be in the national **interest*** (= would not be good for the country).

national /ˈnæʃ.ᵊn.ᵊl/ /ˈnæʃ.nəl/ *noun* **[C usually pl]** someone who officially belongs to a particular country: *Thirty people, including six UK nationals, were killed in yesterday's plane crash.* ○ *All **foreign** nationals were advised to leave the country following the outbreak of civil war.*

nationality /ˌnæʃ.ᵊnˈæl.ə.ti/ /ˌnæʃˈnæl-/ [US] /-t̬i/ *noun* **1** **[C or U]** the official right to belong to a particular country: *She **has** British nationality.* ○ *What nationality are you?* **2** **[C]** a group of people of the same race, religion, traditions, etc: *At the International School they have pupils of 46 different nationalities.*

nationally /ˈnæʃ.ᵊn.ᵊl.i/ /ˈnæʃ.nə.li/ *adv* by or to everyone in a nation: *She's a nationally known columnist.*

nationalism /ˈnæʃ.ᵊn.ᵊl.ɪ.zᵊm/ /ˈnæʃ.nə.lɪ-/ *noun* **[U]** **1** the desire for and the attempt to achieve political independence for your country or nation **2** a great or too great love of your own country: *The book documents the rise of the political right with its accompanying strands of nationalism and racism.*

nationalist /ˈnæʃ.ᵊn.ᵊl.ɪst/ /ˈnæʃ.nə.lɪst/ *noun* **[C]** a person who wants political independence for their country

nationalist /ˈnæʃ.ᵊn.ᵊl.ɪst/ /ˈnæʃ.nə.lɪst/ *adj* wanting political independence for your country: *a nationalist movement*

nationalistic /ˌnæʃ.ᵊn.ᵊlˈɪs.tɪk/ /ˌnæʃ.nəˈlɪs-/ *adj MAINLY DISAPPROVING* having too much pride in your own country: *a nationalistic viewpoint*

ˌnational ˈanthem *noun* **[C]** a country's official song which is played and/or sung on public occasions

the ˌnational curˈriculum *noun* **[S]** *UK* the set of subjects that children in England and Wales must study from the age of 5 to 16

ˌnational ˈdebt *noun* **[C usually sing]** (*US ALSO* **public debt**) the total amount of money that is owed by a country's government

the ˌNational ˈFront *noun* **[U]** (*ABBREVIATION* **NF**) a small British political party that has extreme views on race

ˌnational ˈgrid *noun* **[S]** *UK* a system of special wires that take electricity from POWER STATIONS (= places where electricity is made) to all parts of a country

the ˌNational ˈHealth ˌService *noun* **[S]** (*ABBREVIATION* **the NHS**) the British service which provides free or cheap medical treatment for everyone and is paid for by taxation: *Can you get acupuncture **on*** (= paid for by) *the National Health Service?* **ˌNational ˈHealth** *adj* (*ALSO* **NHS**) *a National Health hospital* ○ *Is your dentist private or NHS?*

ˌnational ˈholiday *noun* **[C]** (*US ALSO* **federal holiday**) a day when most people in a country do not have to work

ˌNational Inˈsurance *noun* **[U]** a system of taxation in the UK in which the government collects money from companies and workers and makes payments to people who are too old or ill to work or who have no job

nationalize, *UK USUALLY* **-ise** /ˈnæʃ.ᵊn.ᵊl.aɪz/ /ˈnæʃ.nə.laɪz/ *verb* **[T]** (of a government) to take control of a business or industry: *The government recently nationalized the railways.* ✻ NOTE: The opposite is **privatize** or **denationalize**. **nationalization**, *UK USUALLY* **-isation** /ˌnæʃ.ᵊn.ᵊl.aɪˈzeɪ.ʃᵊn/ /ˌnæʃ.nə.laɪ-/ *noun* **[U]** *Nationalization of agriculture is on the government's agenda.*

ˌnational ˈpark *noun* **[C]** an area of a country that is protected by the government because of its natural beauty or because it has a special history

ˌnational ˈservice *noun* **[U]** *UK* the system by which young people, especially men, are ordered by law to spend a period of time in the armed forces: *In some countries, everyone **does** two years' national service after leaving school.* ○ *In Britain, national service was abolished in 1962.* ➲Compare **selective service**.

ˌnational ˈsocialism *noun* **[U]** **Nazism** ➲See at **nazi**.

the ˌNational ˈTrust *noun* **[U]** an organization in the UK which owns and takes care of many beautiful and old buildings and beautiful and important areas of countryside

ˌnation ˈstate *noun* **[C]** an independent country, especially when thought of as consisting of a single large group of people all sharing the same language, traditions and history

nationwide /ˌneɪ.ʃᵊnˈwaɪd/ *adj* existing or happening in all parts of a particular country: *a nationwide network/chain of shops* ○ *a nationwide survey/referendum* **nationwide** /ˌneɪ.ʃᵊnˈwaɪd/ *adv*: *Schools nationwide are experiencing a shortage of teachers.*

native /ˈneɪ.tɪv/ [US] /-t̬ɪv/ *adj* **1** **[before n]** relating to or describing someone's country or place of birth or someone who was born in a particular country or place: *She returned to live and work in her native Japan.* ○ *She's a native Californian.* **2** describes plants and animals which grow naturally in a place, and have not been brought there from somewhere else: *Henderson Island in the Pacific has more than 55 species of native flowering plants.* ○ *The horse is not native **to** America – it was introduced by the Spanish.* **3** **[before n]** relating to the first people to live in an area: *The Aborigines are the native inhabitants of Australia.* ○ *the native population* ○ *native customs and traditions* ➲See also **indigenous**. **4** ***your* native language/tongue** the first language that you learn: *French is his native tongue.* **5** **[before n]** A native ability or characteristic is one that a person or thing has naturally and is part of their basic character: *his native wit* ➲See also **innate**.

native /ˈneɪ.tɪv/ ⓤ /-t̬ɪv/ noun [C] **1** a person who was born in a particular place, or a plant or animal that lives or grows naturally in a place and has not been brought from somewhere else: *a native of Monaco* ○ *The red squirrel is a native of Britain.* **2** OFFENSIVE OLD-FASHIONED someone who lived in a country, especially in Africa, before Europeans went there

• **go native** DISAPPROVING OR HUMOROUS If a person who is in a foreign country goes native, they begin to live and/or dress like the people who live there.

COMMON LEARNER ERROR

natives

Since this word is rather offensive, use alternatives such as 'local people'.

When I'm travelling I'm always interested to find out about the customs of the local people.

~~When I'm travelling I'm always interested to find out about the customs of the natives.~~

Native Aˈmerican noun [C] a member of one of the races who were living in North and South America before Europeans arrived ˌNative Aˈmerican adj

native ˈspeaker noun [C] someone who has spoken a particular language since they were a baby, rather than having learnt it as a child or adult: *All our teachers are native speakers of English.* ○ *a native-speaker dictionary*

the Nativity /ðə.nəˈtɪv.ɪ.ti/ ⓤ /-ə.t̬i/ noun [S] the birth of Jesus Christ, which is celebrated by Christians at Christmas

nativity play /nəˈtɪv.ɪ.ti.pleɪ/ ⓤ /-ə.t̬i-/ noun [C] a play which tells the story of Jesus Christ's birth, usually performed by children at Christmas time

NATO, Nato /ˈneɪ.təʊ/ ⓤ /-t̬oʊ/ group noun [U] ABBREVIATION FOR North Atlantic Treaty Organization: an international military organization consisting of the US, Canada and many European countries

natter /ˈnæt.əʳ/ ⓤ /ˈnæt̬.ɚ/ verb [I] INFORMAL to talk continuously for a long time without any particular purpose: *Once he starts nattering you just can't stop him.* ○ *My mother and her friends natter away on the phone all evening.* **natter** /ˈnæt.əʳ/ ⓤ /ˈnæt̬.ɚ/ noun [C] *We had a long natter over coffee.*

natty /ˈnæt.i/ ⓤ /ˈnæt̬-/ adj OLD-FASHIONED INFORMAL stylish and tidy in every detail: *He's always been a natty dresser.* **nattily** /ˈnæt.ɪ.li/ ⓤ /ˈnæt̬-/ adv

natural EXPECTED /ˈnætʃ.ᵊr.ᵊl/ ⓤ /-ɚ-/ adj normal or expected: *Of course you're upset – it's only natural.* ○ *It's natural that you should feel anxious when you first leave home.* ○ *It's quite natural to experience a few doubts just before you get married.* ➔See also **natural** at **nature** LIFE.

naturally /ˈnætʃ.ᵊr.ᵊl.i/ ⓤ /-ɚ-/ adv as you would expect: *Naturally we want to see as few job losses in the industry as possible.* ○ *"You will try to be tactful when you explain to her why she hasn't been invited, won't you?" "Naturally* (= Yes, obviously).*"*

natural MUSIC /ˈnætʃ.ᵊr.ᵊl/ ⓤ /-ɚ-/ adj [after n] (of a musical note) not SHARP or FLAT: *E natural* ➔See also **natural** at **nature** LIFE.

natural ˈchildbirth noun [U] a method of giving birth in which special preparation and breathing exercises are used to make the birth easier, instead of drugs

natural ˈgas noun [U] gas, found underground, which is used as a fuel

natural ˈhistory noun [U] the study of plants, animals, rocks, etc: *We went to see the dinosaur skeletons in the Natural History Museum.*

naturalize, UK USUALLY **-ise** /ˈnætʃ.ᵊr.ᵊl.aɪz/ ⓤ /-ə.rə.laɪz/ verb [T] to make someone a legal CITIZEN of a country that they were not born in: *a naturalized US citizen* ○ *She has lived in Australia for a long time, and recently she was naturalized.* **naturalization**, UK USUALLY **-isation** /ˌnætʃ.ᵊr.ᵊl.aɪˈzeɪ.ʃᵊn/ ⓤ /-ə.rə.lɪ-/ noun [U]

natural ˈlanguage noun [U] SPECIALIZED language which has developed in the usual way as a method of communicating between people: *Computers are increasingly being used for natural language processing.*

natural reˈsources plural noun things such as minerals, forests, coal, etc. which exist in a place and can be used by people: *Some natural resources, such as natural gas and fossil fuel, cannot be replaced.*

the ˌnatural ˈsciences plural noun subjects such as biology, physics and chemistry in which things that can be seen in nature are studied

natural seˈlection noun [U] the process which results in the continued existence of only the types of animals and plants which are best able to produce young or new plants in the conditions in which they live

natural ˈwastage UK noun [U] (US **attrition**) a reduction in the number of people who work for an organization which is achieved by not replacing those people who leave

nature LIFE /ˈneɪ.tʃəʳ/ ⓤ /-tʃɚ/ noun [U] **1** all the animals, plants, rocks, etc. in the world and all the features, forces and processes that happen or exist independently of people, such as the weather, the sea, mountains, reproduction and growth: *her love of nature* ○ *This new technique of artificially growing cells copies what actually happens in nature.* ○ *a nature article/book/programme* **2 Nature** the force that is responsible for physical life and that is sometimes spoken of as a person: *Feeling tired-out is Nature's way of telling you to rest.* ○ *Nature gave these tiny creatures the ability to reproduce quickly when food is abundant.*

• **go/get back to nature** to start living a more simple life in which you use fewer artificial or processed products

• **let nature take its course** to allow someone or something to live or die naturally: *He could be kept alive artificially, but I think it would be kinder to let nature take its course.*

natural /ˈnætʃ.ᵊr.ᵊl/ ⓤ /-ɚ-/ adj **1** as found in nature and not involving anything made or done by people: *a natural substance* ○ *People say that breast-feeding is better than bottle-feeding because it's more natural.* ○ *He died from natural causes* (= because he was old or ill). ○ *Floods and earthquakes are natural disasters.* **2** describes an ability or characteristic that you were born with: *natural beauty* ○ *a natural talent for sports* ○ *She's a natural blonde* (= Her hair is not artificially made a lighter colour). **3** describes food or drink which is pure and has no chemical substances added to it and is therefore thought to be healthy: *natural mineral water* ○ *natural ingredients* ➔See also **natural** EXPECTED, **natural** MUSIC. **4** *someone's* **natural mother/father/parent** a parent who caused someone to be born, although they might not be their legal parent or the parent who raised them

natural /ˈnætʃ.ᵊr.ᵊl/ ⓤ /-ɚ-/ noun [C] INFORMAL someone who was born with the right characteristics or abilities for doing a particular thing: *She won't have any troubles learning to ride a horse – you can see she's a natural.*

Naturalism /ˈnætʃ.ᵊr.ᵊl.ɪ.zᵊm/ ⓤ /-ɚ.rə.lɪ-/ noun [U] (in art and literature) showing people and experiences as they really are, instead of suggesting that they are better than they really are or representing them in a fixed style: *Strindberg, Ibsen and Chekhov are a few of the dramatists who were influenced by Naturalism.*

naturalist /ˈnætʃ.ᵊr.ᵊl.ɪst/ ⓤ /-ɚ-/ noun [C] **1** a person who studies and knows a lot about plants and animals **2 Naturalist** a person who writes, paints, etc. in the style of Naturalism

naturalistic /ˌnætʃ.ᵊr.ᵊlˈɪs.tɪk/ ⓤ /-ɚ.rəˈlɪs-/ adj **1** similar to what exists in nature: *Most zoos try to exhibit animals in naturalistic settings.* **2** Naturalistic art, literature, acting, etc. shows things as they really are.

naturally /ˈnætʃ.ᵊr.ᵊl.i/ ⓤ /-ɚ-/ adv **1** happening or existing as part of nature and not made or done by people: *A healthy body will be able to fight off the illness naturally without the use of medicine.* **2** having an ability or characteristic from birth: *He's naturally funny – he doesn't even have to try.* **3 come naturally (to sb)** If a particular skill comes naturally (to you), you are able to do it easily, with little effort or learning: *Dancing seemed to come naturally to her.*

naturalness /ˈnætʃ.ᵊr.ᵊl.nəs/ ⓤ /-ɚ-/ noun [U] the quality of being real and not influenced by other people: *the* *naturalness of children* ○ *Her performance was noted for its naturalness.*

> **USAGE**
>
> **nature, the environment and the countryside**
>
> Nature means all the things in the world which exist naturally and were not created by people.
>
> *He's fascinated by wildlife and anything to do with nature.*
>
> The environment means the land, water, and air that animals and plants live in. It is usually used when talking about the way people use or damage the natural world.
>
> *The government has introduced new policies to protect the environment.*
>
> Countryside means land where there are no towns or cities.
>
> *I love walking in the countryside.*

nature [TYPE] /'neɪ.tʃər/ ⓤ /-tʃɚ/ *noun* [S or U] the type or main characteristic of something: *What was the nature of his inquiry?* ○ *Motor-racing is by nature a dangerous sport.*

• **be in the nature of things** to be usual and expected: *There are problems in every relationship – it's in the nature of things.*

• **be the nature of the beast** to be what something is like or what it involves: *Owning a car involves a lot of expense – that's the nature of the beast.*

nature [CHARACTER] /'neɪ.tʃər/ ⓤ /-tʃɚ/ *noun* [C or U] Someone's nature is their character: *As a child Juliana had a lovely nature – everyone liked her.* ○ *It's not really in her nature to be aggressive.* ○ *He is by nature inclined to be rather lazy.* **-natured** /-neɪ.tʃəd/ ⓤ /-tʃɚd/ *suffix*: *He's such a good-natured/sweet-natured little boy.*

'nature re,serve *noun* [C] an area of land which is protected in order to keep safe the animals and plants that live there, often because they are rare

'nature ,strip *noun* [C] AUS a strip of grass, and often trees and other plants, which separates a path used by walkers from the part of a road used by vehicles

'nature ,trail *noun* [C] a path through an area of the countryside which is intended to attract the walker's attention to interesting plants, animals and other features

naturist /'neɪ.tʃʊr.ɪst/ ⓤ /-tʃɚ-/ *noun* [C] FORMAL a NUDIST (= a person who sometimes wears no clothes because they think that this is healthy) **naturism** /'neɪ.tʃʊr.ɪ-zᵊm/ ⓤ /-tʃɚ-/ *noun* [U]

naught [NOTHING] /nɔːt/ ⓤ /nɑːt/ *noun* [U] (ALSO **nought**) OLD USE OR LITERARY nothing: *All our efforts were for naught.* ○ *All their plans came to naught* (= did not achieve anything).

naught [ZERO] /nɔːt/ ⓤ /nɑːt/ *noun* [U] US FOR **nought** ZERO

naughty [BADLY BEHAVED] /'nɔː.ti/ ⓤ /'nɑː.t̬i/ *adj* **1** When children are naughty, or their behaviour is naughty, they behave badly or are not obedient: *Now that's naughty – you mustn't throw food on the floor!* ○ *Our boss treats us all like naughty schoolchildren.* **2** used slightly humorously to describe an adult who has behaved badly or an adult's bad action: *"I'm afraid I borrowed your car without asking." "Yes, that was very naughty of you – I needed it at the weekend!"* **naughtily** /'nɔː.tɪ.li/ ⓤ /'nɑː.t̬ɪ-/ *adv* **naughtiness** /'nɔː.tɪ.nəs/ ⓤ /'nɑː.t̬ɪ-/ *noun* [U]

naughty [SEXUAL] /'nɔː.ti/ ⓤ /'nɑː.t̬i/ *adj* INFORMAL HUMOROUS involving or suggesting sex: *The film was shown on television but they'd cut out all the naughty scenes/(UK) bits.* ○ *He always buys her naughty underwear for her birthday.* **naughtily** /'nɔː.tɪ.li/ ⓤ /'nɑː.t̬ɪ-/ *adv* **naughtiness** /'nɔː.tɪ.nəs/ ⓤ /'nɑː.t̬ɪ-/ *noun* [U]

nausea /'nɔː.zi.ə/ ⓤ /-ʒə/ /'nɑː-/ *noun* [U] when you feel as if you are going to vomit: *Signs of the illness include fever, nausea and vomiting.*

nauseate /'nɔː.zi.eɪt/ ⓤ /'nɑː-/ *verb* [T often passive] FORMAL to cause someone to feel as if they are going to vomit: *He's nauseated by the smell of meat cooking.*

nauseating /'nɔː.zi.eɪ.tɪŋ/ ⓤ /'nɑː.zi.eɪ.t̬ɪŋ/ *adj* **1** making you feel as if you are going to vomit: *the nauseating smell of rotting food* **2** If someone's attitude or behaviour is nauseating, it disgusts you: *Her strongest*

criticism was reserved for the prime minister whom she accused of 'nauseating hypocrisy'. ○ HUMOROUS *She's good at everything she does – it's quite nauseating!*

nauseatingly /'nɔː.zi.eɪ.tɪŋ.li/ ⓤ /'nɑː.zi.eɪ.t̬ɪŋ-/ *adv* **1** in a way that makes you feel as if you want to vomit **2** in a way that disgusts you: *I detest the sort of ads that use nauseatingly cute children and animals.*

nauseous /'nɔː.zi.əs/ /-ʒəs/ ⓤ /'nɑː.ʃəs/ *adj* **1** feeling as if you might vomit: *Roller coasters make me feel nauseous.* **2** FORMAL making you feel as if you might vomit: *the nauseous smell of rotting flesh* ○ HUMOROUS *The bride's mother was wearing a nauseous* (= extremely unattractive) *combination of green and yellow.*

nautical /'nɔː.tɪ.kᵊl/ ⓤ /'nɑː.t̬ɪ-/ *adj* relating to ships, sailing or sailors: *nautical equipment* ○ *You're looking very nautical in your navy blue sweater.* **nautically** /'nɔː.tɪ.kli/ ⓤ /'nɑː.t̬i-/ *adv*

,nautical 'mile *noun* [C] (ALSO **sea mile**) a unit of distance used at sea which is equal to 1852 metres ⊃Compare **mile**.

naval /'neɪ.vᵊl/ *adj* ⊃See at **navy**.

nave /neɪv/ *noun* [C] the long central part of a church, often with AISLES (= long passages) on both sides

navel /'neɪ.vᵊl/ *noun* [C] (INFORMAL **belly button**) the small round part in the middle of the stomach which is left after the UMBILICAL CORD (= long tube of flesh joining the baby to its mother) has been cut at birth

• **gaze at/contemplate your navel** HUMOROUS to spend too much time thinking about yourself and your own problems

navel-gazing /'neɪ.vᵊlˌgeɪ.zɪŋ/ *noun* [U] HUMOROUS DISAPPROVING spending too much time considering your own thoughts, feelings or problems

,navel 'orange *noun* [C] a type of orange that is sweet and usually without seeds

navigable /'næv.ɪ.gə.bl̩/ *adj* (of an area of water) deep, wide or safe enough for a boat to go through: *That stretch of river is too shallow to be navigable.* **navigability** /ˌnæv.ɪ.gəˈbɪl.ɪ.ti/ ⓤ /-ə.t̬i/ *noun* [U]

navigate /'næv.ɪ.geɪt/ *verb* [I or T] **1** to direct the way that a ship, aircraft, etc. will travel, or to find a direction across, along or over an area of water or land, often by using a map: *Sailors have special equipment to help them navigate.* ○ *Even ancient ships were able to navigate large stretches of open water.* ○ *Some migrating birds can navigate by the moon* (= using the moon as a guide). ○ *There weren't any road signs to help us navigate through the maze of one-way streets.* ○ *We had to navigate several flights of stairs to find his office.* **2** to move around a WEBSITE (= an address on the Internet) or between websites: *Their website is fairly plain, but very easy to navigate.*

navigation /ˌnæv.ɪˈgeɪ.ʃᵊn/ *noun* [U] the act of directing a ship, aircraft, etc. from one place to another, or the science of finding a way from one place to another: *In the past, navigation depended on a knowledge of the positions of the stars.* ○ *Mechanics discovered problems with the plane's navigation system.* **navigational** /ˌnæv.ɪ-ˈgeɪ.ʃᵊn.ᵊl/ *adj*: *navigational errors* ○ *navigational equipment*

navigator /'næv.ɪ.geɪ.tər/ ⓤ /-t̬ɚ/ *noun* [C] a person in a vehicle who decides on the direction in which the vehicle travels

navvy /'næv.i/ *noun* [C] UK OLD-FASHIONED INFORMAL a man who is employed to do unskilled physical work, usually building or making roads

navy /'neɪ.vi/ *group noun* [S] the part of a country's armed forces which is trained to operate at sea: *My brother is an officer in the Navy.* ○ *Gabriel joined the navy in 1997.* ○ *a navy ship/vessel*

naval /'neɪ.vᵊl/ *adj* belonging to a country's navy, or relating to military ships: *a naval officer* ○ *naval forces* ○ *a naval museum/battle*

,navy ('blue) *adj, noun* [U] dark blue: *He was wearing a navy sweater.*

nay [EVEN MORE] /neɪ/ *adv* FORMAL used to introduce a second and more extreme phrase in a sentence when the first phrase was not strong enough: *It is my pleasure, nay (my) privilege, to introduce tonight's guest speaker.*

nay [NO] /neɪ/ *adv* NORTHERN ENGLISH FOR no: *Nay lass, don't cry.*

Nazi /ˈnɑːt.si/ *noun* **1** a member of the National Socialist (Workers') Party, led by Adolf Hitler, which controlled Germany from 1933 to 1945 **2** DISAPPROVING someone who is cruel or who demands an unreasonable degree of obedience, or someone who has extreme and unreasonable beliefs about race **Nazi** /ˈnɑːt.si/ *adj*: *a Nazi officer* ○ *Nazi Germany the Nazi occupation of Poland* **Nazism** /ˈnɑːt.sɪ.zᵊm/ *noun* [U]

NB, **nb** /ˌenˈbiː/ FORMAL written before a piece of important information to make readers notice it: *NB Applications received after the closing date will not be accepted.*

NBC /ˌen.biːˈsiː/ *group noun* [U] ABBREVIATION FOR National Broadcasting Company: a company that broadcasts television programmes in the US

NC-17 /ˌen.si.sev.ənˈtiːn/ *adj* used officially in the US to refer to a film which is not considered suitable for children under the age of 17 to watch because it contains sex or violence: *This movie is **rated** NC-17.* ➲Compare **G** FILM, **PG**, **U** FILM, **X** FILM.

NCO /ˌen.siːˈəʊ/ [US] /-ˈoʊ/ *noun* [C] *plural* **NCOs** ABBREVIATION FOR non-commissioned officer: a member of the armed forces who has achieved the rank of officer by rising from the lower ranks rather than by receiving a COMMISSION ➲See also **commissioned officer**.

NE *noun* [U], *adj* ABBREVIATION FOR **northeast** or **northeastern**

Neanderthal /niːˈæn.dəˌtɑːl/ [US] /-dɚ-/ *adj* **1** relating to a type of PRIMITIVE people who lived in Europe and Asia from about 150 000 to 30 000 years ago: *Neanderthal man* **2 neanderthal** (of people or beliefs) very old-fashioned and not willing to change: *He criticized what he described as the 'neanderthal tendencies' of the right wing of the party.* **3** DISAPPROVING (of people) rude or offensive **Neanderthal** /niːˈæn.dəˌtɑːl/ [US] /-dɚ-/ *noun* [C]

near /nɪəʳ/ [US] /nɪr/ *adv, prep* **1** not far away in distance: *Is there a train station near here?* ○ *I'd like to sit near a window, please.* ○ *Don't come too near me – you might catch my cold.* ○ *The hotel is near the airport.* ○ *Which bus stop is nearest (to) your house?* ○ *I was standing just near enough to hear what they were saying.* **2** not far away in time: *As the date of his operation **drew** near, he became more and more anxious.* ○ *Her birthday was getting nearer and I still hadn't bought her a present.* ○ UK *We can decide which route to take nearer the time.* **3** almost in a particular state or condition: *The runners looked near exhaustion.* ○ *I was near **(to)** tears* (= almost cried) *at one point during the film.*

• **nowhere near** not close in distance, time, amount or quality: *The house was nowhere near the sea.* ○ *It's nowhere near time for us to leave yet.* ○ *I'm nowhere near finishing the book – I'm only half-way through it.* ○ *He's nowhere near as tall as his sister.*

• **near enough** INFORMAL almost: *They're the same age or near enough.*

near /nɪəʳ/ [US] /nɪr/ *adj* [before n] **1** not far away in distance, time, characteristics or quality: *Where's the nearest post office?* ○ *My pocket knife is **the** nearest **thing*** (= the most similar thing) ***to** a weapon that I have.* ○ *I couldn't get any cream cheese so I bought the nearest equivalent* (= the most similar thing) *that I could find.* **2** UK Your near relatives are those who are closely related to you, such as your parents, brothers or sisters.

• **in the near future** at a time which is not far away: *All our computer equipment will be replaced in the near future.*

• ***your* nearest and dearest** HUMOROUS your family, especially those that you live with or are very involved with

near- /nɪəʳ-/ [US] /nɪr-/ *prefix* combines with adjectives and nouns to mean 'almost': *We had a near-disaster this morning in the car!* ○ *She was near-hysterical by the time I arrived there.*

near /nɪəʳ/ [US] /nɪr/ *verb* [I or T] to get close to something in distance, time or state: *I'm pleased to say the project is nearing completion.* ○ *As the wedding day neared, I started to have second thoughts about getting married.* ○ *The captain switched on the seat belt sign as we neared the airport.* **nearness** /ˈnɪə.nəs/ [US] /ˈnɪr-/ *noun* [U] *I bought my house because of its nearness **to** the office where I work.*

nearby /ˌnɪəˈbaɪ/ [US] /ˌnɪr-/ *adv, adj* not far away: *If there's a cafe nearby, we could stop for a snack.* ○ *I noticed a policeman standing nearby.* ○ *We stopped at some nearby shops to buy some food.*

near-death experience /ˌnɪəˈdeθ.ɪkˌspɪə.ri.ᵊnts/ [US] /ˌnɪrˈdeθ.ɪkˌspɪr.i-/ *noun* [C] an experience described by some people who have been extremely ill and close to death, in which the person feels as if they have left their body and are watching themselves from above

nearly /ˈnɪə.li/ [US] /ˈnɪr-/ *adv* almost, or not completely: *It's been nearly three months since my last haircut.* ○ *I've nearly finished that book you lent me.* ○ *She's nearly as tall as her father now.* ○ *They'd eaten nearly everything before we arrived.* ○ FIGURATIVE *It was so funny – we nearly died laughing.*

• **not nearly as/so** a lot less: *She's not nearly as beautiful as you said she was.* ○ *My cold isn't nearly so bad as it was.*

• **not nearly enough** much less than you want or need: *There's not nearly enough food for all these people!*

ˌnear ˈmiss [HIT] *noun* [C usually sing] (ALSO **near thing**) a situation in which something almost hits something else: *A Boeing 747 was involved in a near miss with a private aircraft just south of San Francisco.* ○ *That was a near miss – we must have come within an inch of that lorry!*

ˌnear ˈmiss [HAPPEN] *noun* [C usually sing] an attempt to do or achieve something which fails although it almost succeeds

nearside /ˈnɪə.saɪd/ [US] /ˈnɪr-/ *adj* [before n] (ALSO **near**) UK on the left side of something, especially a vehicle or road: *A car pulled out from the nearside lane without signalling.*

nearsighted US /ˌnɪəˈsaɪ.tɪd/ [US] /ˌnɪrˈsaɪ.t̬ɪd/ *adj* (UK **short-sighted**) Someone who is nearsighted cannot see objects clearly when they are far away. **nearsightedness** /ˌnɪəˈsaɪ.tɪd.nəs/ [US] /ˌnɪrˈsaɪ.t̬ɪd.nəs/ *noun* [U]

ˌnear ˈthing *noun* [S] UK a situation in which you almost failed to achieve something and only just succeeded: *We beat them but it was a near thing.* ➲See also **near miss** HIT.

neat [TIDY] /niːt/ *adj* tidy, with everything in its place: *Your house is always so neat – how do you manage it with three children?* ○ *She likes everything neat **and tidy**.* ○ *You've got such neat handwriting.* ○ *They did a very neat job stitching up your knee – there's hardly a scar there.*

neaten /ˈniː.tᵊn/ [US] /-t̬ᵊn/ *verb* [T] to make something tidy: *She's careful to neaten her desk before she leaves in the evening.* ○ *Could you neaten **up** those bookshelves, please?* **neatly** /ˈniːt.li/ *adv*: *His clothes are all neatly folded in their drawers.* **neatness** /ˈniːt.nəs/ *noun* [U] *When writing your homework, remember that neatness is important.*

neat [PERSON] /niːt/ *adj* A neat person likes to keep themselves, their house and their possessions tidy and in good order: *Hassan is the neatest child I've ever met – even his shoes are clean!* ○ *I try to be neat, but my husband is a slob.*

neat [NOTHING ADDED] /niːt/ *adj* (of a strong alcoholic drink) without anything, such as water or ice or another drink, added to it: *I'll have a neat gin, please.* ○ *She likes her whisky neat.*

neat [GOOD] /niːt/ *adj* MAINLY US INFORMAL good: *That video game is really neat!* ○ *Kyle has the neatest mom – she lets him stay up late on the weekends.*

'neath /niːθ/ *prep* LITERARY **beneath**: *'Neath stars and sun we wandered*

nebula /ˈneb.jʊ.lə/ *noun* [C] *plural* **nebulae** or **nebulas** SPECIALIZED a cloud of gas or dust in space, appearing either bright or dark **nebular** /ˈneb.jʊ.ləʳ/ [US] /-lɚ/ *adj*

nebulous /ˈneb.jʊ.ləs/ *adj* (especially of ideas) unclear and lacking form: *She has a few nebulous ideas about what she might like to do in the future, but nothing definite.* **nebulousness** /ˈneb.jʊ.lə.snəs/ *noun* [U]

necessary /ˈnes.ə.ser.i/ *adj* **1** needed in order to achieve a particular result: *He lacks the necessary skills for the job.* ○ *I don't have much time so I won't be staying any* *longer than necessary.* ○ *Just do what's necessary and then leave.* ○ ***If** necessary, we can always change the dates of our trip.* ○ *Is **it** necessary **for** all of us **to** be present at the meeting this afternoon?* ○ *We don't want to take any more luggage with us than is **strictly** necessary.* **2** used in negatives and questions to show that you disapprove of something and do not think it should be used or done: *I really don't think that sort of language is necessary on television.* ○ *Was **it** really necessary **for** you **to** say that?*

necessaries /ˈnes.ə.ser.iz/ *plural noun* the items that are needed, especially for a particular purpose: *He packed drinks, a map and a compass – all the necessaries for a day's walking in the countryside.*

necessarily /ˈnes.ə.ser.ɪl.i/ *adv* used in negatives to mean 'in every case' or 'therefore': *The fact that something is cheap doesn't necessarily mean it's of low quality.* ○ *You may love someone without necessarily wanting to marry them.* ○ *That's **not** necessarily true.*

ˌnecessary ˈevil *noun* [C] something you do not like doing but which you know must be done, or something you do not like but which you must accept: *I think he regards work as a necessary evil.*

necessitate /nəˈses.ɪ.teɪt/ *verb* [T] FORMAL to cause something to be needed, or to make something necessary: *Reduction in government spending will necessitate further cuts in public services.* ○ [+ v-ing] *An important meeting necessitates my being in London on Friday.*

necessity /nəˈses.ɪ.ti/ [US] /-ə.ţi/ *noun* **1** [U] the need for something: *You can come early if you want to, but there's no necessity **for** it.* ○ [+ to infinitive] *Is there any necessity **to** reply to her letter?* ○ *The report stresses the necessity **of** eating plenty of fresh fruit and vegetables.* ○ *With a personal fortune of six million pounds, she certainly doesn't work **out of** necessity* (= because she needs to). ○ *We'll employ extra staff to help out as and when the necessity **arises*** (= when we need to). **2** [C] something that you need, especially in order to live: *We brought only the **bare** necessities with us.* ○ *He regarded music as one of life's necessities.*

• **Necessity is the mother of invention.** SAYING an expression which means that if you really need to do something, you will think of a way of doing it

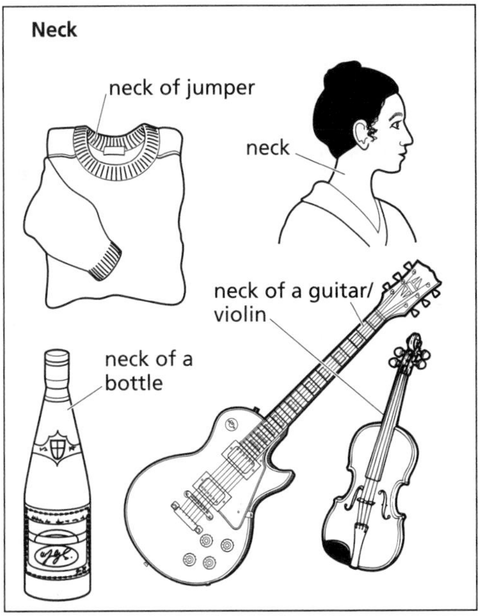

neck [BODY PART] /nek/ *noun* [C] **1** the part of the body which joins the head to the shoulders: *He had the thickest neck I'd ever seen.* ○ *She wore a gold chain around her neck.* ➲See picture **The Body** on page Centre 5 **2** the part of a piece of clothing which goes around a person's neck: *This sweater's too tight at the neck.* ○ *He wasn't wearing a tie and his shirt was open at the neck.* ○ *a low-neck dress* **3** part of a hollow object which is at the top and is narrower than the part below it: *the neck of a bottle/guitar* ➲See also **bottleneck**; **halterneck**; **redneck**; **roughneck**; **turtleneck**.

• **get it in the neck** UK INFORMAL to be punished or severely criticized for something that you have done: *Poor old Bob got it in the neck **for** being late this morning.*

• **neck and neck** If two competitors are neck and neck, they are level with each other and have an equal chance of winning.

• **be up to *your* neck (in *sth*)** INFORMAL to be very busy: *I'd like to help, but I'm up to my neck at the moment.*

• **be up to *your* neck in *sth*** to be very involved in a situation, or to have too much of the thing stated: *She's up to her neck in debt/problems/work.*

• ***this/our, etc.* neck of the woods** INFORMAL this/our, etc. part of a particular area: *We don't often see you in this neck of the woods.*

-necked /-nekt/ *suffix* refers to the type of neck someone or something has, or to the style of a piece of clothing around the neck or the way that it is worn: *a stocky, stiff-necked little man* ○ *a round-necked jumper* ○ *an open-necked shirt*

neck [KISS] /nek/ *verb* [I] OLD-FASHIONED INFORMAL to kiss and hold a person in a sexual way

neckband /ˈnek.bænd/ *noun* [C] a narrow strip which goes round the neck of an item of clothing: *I can't get this sweater over my head – the neckband's too tight.*

neckerchief /ˈnek.ə.tʃiːf/ [US] /-ɚ-/ *noun* [C] *plural* **neckerchiefs** or **neckerchieves** OLD USE a piece of square cloth which is folded and worn around the neck

necklace [JEWELLERY] /ˈnek.ləs/ *noun* [C] a piece of jewellery worn around the neck, such as a chain or a string of decorative stones, BEADS, etc: *a gold/silver/pearl necklace*

necklace [MURDER] /ˈnek.ləs/ *verb* [T] to kill someone by putting a burning rubber tyre around their neck **necklacing** /ˈnek.lə.sɪŋ/ *noun* [C]

neckline /ˈnek.laɪn/ *noun* [C] the shape made by the edge of a dress or shirt at the front of the neck or on the chest: *She wore a dress with a **plunging** neckline* (= one showing part of her breasts).

necktie /ˈnek.taɪ/ *noun* [C] MAINLY US FOR a **tie** (= long piece of material worn under a shirt collar)

necromancy /ˈnek.rəʊ.mænt.si/ [US] /-rə-/ *noun* [U] the practice of claiming to communicate with the dead in order to discover what is going to happen in the future, or BLACK MAGIC (= magic used for bad purposes) **necromancer** /ˈnek.rəʊ.mænt.səʳ/ [US] /-rə.mænt.sɚ/ *noun* [C]

necrophilia /ˌnek.rəʊˈfɪl.i.ə/ [US] /-rə-/ *noun* [U] sexual attraction to or sexual activity with dead bodies **necrophiliac** /ˌnek.rəʊˈfɪl.i.æk/ [US] /-rə-/ *noun* [C] a person who is sexually attracted to or has sex with dead bodies **necrophiliac** /ˌnek.rəʊˈfɪl.i.æk/ [US] /-rə-/ *adj*

necropolis /nekˈrɒp.əl.ɪs/ [US] /nekˈrɑː-/ *noun* [C] an ancient CEMETERY (= piece of ground where people are buried)

nectar /ˈnek.təʳ/ [US] /-tɚ/ *noun* [U] **1** a sweet liquid produced by flowers and collected by bees and other insects: *The bee turns nectar into honey.* **2** in ancient Greek and Roman stories, the drink of the gods: *This wine tastes like nectar* (= tastes excellent).

nectarine /ˈnek.tᵊr.iːn/ [US] /ˌnek.təˈriːn/ *noun* [C] a type of sweet juicy fruit like a PEACH but with a smooth skin

née /neɪ/ *adj* [after n] used after a woman's married name to introduce the family name by which she was known before she married: *Elaine Gibson (née Gillett)*

need [MUST HAVE] /niːd/ *verb* [T] **1** to have to have something, or to want something very much: *Babies need constant care.* ○ *The doctor said I needed an operation.* ○ [+ to infinitive] *I need **to** go to the toilet.* ○ *Most people need **to** feel loved.* ○ [+ obj + to infinitive] *I need you **to** help me choose an outfit.* ○ *I **badly** need* (= strongly want) *a rest from all this.* ○ INFORMAL *I don't need all this hassle.* **2** If you say that someone or something needs something else, you mean that they should have it, or would benefit from

N

having it: *What you need, my son, is a nice hot bowl of soup.* ○ [+ v-ing] *This room needs brightening up a bit.* ○ [+ past participle or + v-ing] *She needs her hair washed/*(UK) *washing.*

• **need *sth* like (*you* need) a hole in the head** *HUMOROUS* to not want or need something at all: *I need all this extra work like I need a hole in the head!*

• **Who needs...?** *MAINLY HUMOROUS* used to mean that the thing referred to is not necessary or useful, or causes trouble: *Men! Who needs them?*

need /niːd/ *noun* **1** [S or U] the state of having to have something that you do not have, especially something that you must have so that you can have a satisfactory life: *Are you **in** need **of** help?* ○ *There's **a** growing need **for** cheap housing in the larger cities.* **2** [C or U] a feeling or state of strongly wanting something: [+ to infinitive] *He seems to have **a** desperate need **to** be loved by everyone.* ○ *I don't know about you but I'm **in** need **of** a drink.* ○ *FORMAL We **have** no need **of** your sympathy.* **3 in need** not having enough money or food: *You just hope that the money goes to those who are most in need.* **4** [U] the state of being necessary: *Help yourself to stationery as the need **arises**.* ○ ***If** need/needs **be*** (= If necessary), *we can take a second car to fit everyone in.* ○ *I don't think there's any need **for** all of us **to** attend the meeting.*

• **be no need to do *sth*** If there is no need to do something, it is not necessary or it is wrong: *There's no need to go to the shops – there's plenty of food in the fridge.* ○ *I understand why she was angry but there was no need to be so rude to him.* ○ *There's no need to shout, for goodness' sake! Just calm down.*

needed /ˈniː.dɪd/ *adj* necessary or wanted: *After six hours work in the garden, we sat down for a **much**-needed rest.* ○ *Most people like to feel needed.*

needs /niːdz/ *plural noun* the things that a person must have in order to have a satisfactory life: *Housing, enough money to live on and education are **basic** needs.* ○ *They don't have enough food to **meet** their needs.*

needy /ˈniː.di/ *adj* **1** poor and not having enough food, clothes, etc: *The proceeds from the sale go to help needy people in the area.* **2** wanting too much attention and love: *Sybil was very insecure and needy.*

the needy *plural noun* poor people: *Let us pray for those who are not so fortunate as ourselves – the sick, the old and the needy.*

N

need [MUST DO] /niːd/ *verb* [+ to infinitive or + infinitive without to] **1** to have (to): [+ to infinitive] *He needs **to** lose a bit of weight.* ○ *I need **to** do some shopping on my way home from work.* ○ [+ infinitive without to] *I don't think we need ask him.* ○ *Nothing need be done about this till next week.* ○ *SLIGHTLY FORMAL "Need we take your mother?" "No, we needn't/I don't think we need."* **2** *UK* ***sb/sth* needn't *do sth*** there is no reason for someone or something to do a particular thing: *You needn't worry – I'm not going to mention it to anyone.* ○ *It's a wonderful way of getting to see Italy, and it needn't cost very much.* **3** *MAINLY UK* ***sb* needn't *do sth*** used, often when you are angry with someone, to say that they should not do a particular thing or that they have no right to do it: *He needn't think I'm driving him all the way there!* ○ *You needn't laugh! It'll be your turn next!* **4 *sb* didn't need to** used to say either that someone did a particular thing although they did not have to, or that they did not do it because they did not have to: *I gave her some extra money – I know I didn't need to but I thought it would be kind.* ○ *"Did you ask Sophia to help?" "I didn't need to – I managed perfectly well on my own."* **5** *MAINLY UK* ***sb* needn't have *done sth*** it was not necessary for someone to have done a particular thing, although they did do it: *You needn't have washed all those dishes, you know – I'd have done them myself when I got home.* ○ *You needn't have worried about the dinner – it was delicious!*

• **Need *you* ask!** used to say that the person asking you something already knows the answer, because it is expected: *"Did he upset a lot of people at the meeting?" "Need you ask!"*

• **I need hardly *do sth*** *SLIGHTLY FORMAL* used to say that what you are going to say is obvious: *I need hardly **say** what a pleasure it is to introduce our speaker.* ○ *I need hardly **remind** you of the seriousness of the situation.*

• **need I say** obviously: *Need I say, I'm extremely sorry to hear the news about your father.*

• **Need I say more?** *HUMOROUS* said after a statement when you expect that someone can guess the result of what you have just said: *Tom was doing the cooking – need I say more?*

needless /ˈniːd.ləs/ *adj* completely unnecessary: *All that needless worrying over what I'd say to him at the party, and he wasn't even there!*

• **needless to say** as you would expect; added to, or used to introduce, a remark giving information which is expected and not surprising: *Needless to say, he'll be off work for a while.*

needlessly /ˈniːd.lə.sli/ *adv* in a way that is not necessary: *She'd worried quite needlessly about whether there would be enough food.*

needle [SEWING TOOL] /ˈniː.dl̩/ *noun* [C] **1** a thin metal pin, used in sewing, which is pointed at one end and has a hole called an EYE at the other end for thread: *a needle and thread* ○ *Here, your eyes are better than mine – could you **thread*** (= put thread through) *this needle for me?* ➲See also **needlework**. **2** a long thin metal stick used with another of the same type to knit: *a **knitting** needle*

• **a needle in a haystack** something which is impossible or extremely difficult to find, especially because the area you have to search is too large: ***looking for/trying to find** a needle in a haystack*

needle [MEDICAL TOOL] /ˈniː.dl̩/ *noun* [C] (*ALSO* **hypodermic needle**) a very thin hollow pointed piece of metal which is attached to a SYRINGE and used to take blood from the body or to put drugs or medicine in

needle [POINTER] /ˈniː.dl̩/ *noun* [C] on a COMPASS or measuring device, the thin moving part which points in a particular direction or points to a particular measurement: *The needle on a compass always points to magnetic north.*

needle [LEAF] /ˈniː.dl̩/ *noun* [C] a thin hard pointed leaf of a PINE tree: *pine needles*

needle [MUSIC] /ˈniː.dl̩/ *noun* [C] *INFORMAL* the part of a RECORD PLAYER which touches the record as it turns round and which is made of a hard material, such as a diamond: *It sounds like the needle on your record player needs to be replaced.*

needle [ANNOY] /ˈniː.dl̩/ *verb* [T] *INFORMAL* to annoy someone, especially by repeated criticism: *His mother was always needling him **about** getting a job.*

needlepoint /ˈniː.dl̩.pɔɪnt/ *noun* [U] the activity of making a picture by sewing onto a piece of cloth

needless /ˈniːd.ləs/ *adj* ➲See at **need** MUST DO.

needlework /ˈniː.dl̩.wɜːk/ [US] /-wɝːk/ *noun* [U] sewing, especially decorative sewing, done by hand with needle and thread

needn't /ˈniː.dᵊnt/ *short form of* need not: *You needn't come until later.*

needy /ˈniː.di/ *plural noun, adj* ➲See at **need** MUST HAVE.

ne'er /neəʳ/ [US] /ner/ *adv LITERARY* never: *Ne'er the night passes without my dreaming of you.*

ne'er-do-well /ˈneə.duː.wel/ [US] /ˈner-/ *noun* [C] *OLD-FASHIONED* someone who is lazy or not willing act in a responsible way

nefarious /nəˈfeə.ri.əs/ [US] /-ˈfer.i-/ *adj FORMAL* (especially of activities) evil or immoral: *The director of the company seems to have been involved in some nefarious practices/**activities**.* **nefariously** /nəˈfeə.ri.ə.sli/ [US] /-ˈfer.i-/ *adv* **nefariousness** /nəˈfeə.ri.ə.snəs/ [US] /-ˈfer.i-/ *noun* [U]

negate /nɪˈɡeɪt/ *verb* [T] *SLIGHTLY FORMAL* to cause something to have no effect and therefore to be useless: *The increase in our profits has been negated by the rising costs of running the business.* **negation** /nɪˈɡeɪ.ʃᵊn/ *noun* [U]

negative [NO] /ˈneɡ.ə.tɪv/ [US] /-t̬ɪv/ *adj* **1** expressing 'no': *We received a negative answer to our request.* * NOTE: The opposite is **affirmative**. **2** A negative sentence or phrase is one which contains a word such as 'not', 'no', 'never' or 'nothing': *'I've never seen him in my life' is a negative sentence.* ○ *'Don't' and 'do not' are negative forms of 'do'.*

negative /ˈneɡ.ə.tɪv/ [US] /-t̬ɪv/ *noun* [C or U] *I didn't hear your answer, Edward — was that a negative?* ○ *I'm* *afraid the reply was definitely in the negative* (= was 'no'). ⊃Compare **affirmative**. **negatively** /'neg.ə.tɪv.li/ ⓤ /-t̬ɪv-/ *adv*

negative ⟨WITHOUT HOPE⟩ /'neg.ə.tɪv/ ⓤ /-t̬ɪv/ *adj* not hopeful, or tending to consider only the bad side of a situation: *a negative attitude* ○ *You're so negative about everything!* ⊃Compare **positive** ⟨HOPEFUL⟩. **negatively** /'neg.ə.tɪv.li/ ⓤ /-t̬ɪv-/ *adv* **negativism** /'neg.ə.tɪ.vɪ.zəm/ ⓤ /-t̬ɪ-/ *noun* [U] (ALSO **negativity**) *There's a real attitude of negativism among the team at the moment.*

negative ⟨ELECTRICITY⟩ /'neg.ə.tɪv/ ⓤ /-t̬ɪv/ *adj* of the type of electrical charge which is carried by electrons ✳ NOTE: The opposite is **positive**.

negative ⟨PHOTOGRAPH⟩ /'neg.ə.tɪv/ ⓤ /-t̬ɪv/ *noun* [C] (INFORMAL **neg**) a piece of film from which a photograph can be produced, and in which light and dark areas appear the opposite way round to the way in which they appear in the photograph: *black-and-white/colour negatives* ○ *I've borrowed the negatives of her wedding photos so I can get some pictures printed.*

negative ⟨TEST RESULTS⟩ /'neg.ə.tɪv/ ⓤ /-t̬ɪv/ *adj* (of a medical test) showing that the patient does not have the disease or condition for which he or she has been tested: *a negative pregnancy test* ○ *The results of his HIV test were negative.* ✳ NOTE: The opposite is **positive**.

negative ⟨BELOW ZERO⟩ /'neg.ə.tɪv/ ⓤ /-t̬ɪv/ *adj* (of a number or amount) less than zero: *negative numbers* ✳ NOTE: The opposite is **positive**.

negative ⟨BLOOD TYPE⟩ /'neg.ə.tɪv/ ⓤ /-t̬ɪv/ *adj* not having the RHESUS FACTOR in the blood

,negative 'equity *noun* [U] UK when someone's house has become less valuable than the amount of money they borrowed in order to buy it

,negative 'pole *noun* [C] SPECIALIZED the part of a battery that releases electrons

neglect /nɪ'glekt/ *verb* [T] **1** to give not enough care or attention to people or things that are your responsibility: *to neglect your appearance/the garden* ○ *He neglects that poor dog – he never takes him for walks or gives him any attention.* ○ *I'm afraid I've rather neglected my studies this week.* **2 neglect to do sth** to not do something, often because you forget: *I'd neglected to give him the name of the hotel where I'd be staying.* ○ *He neglected to mention the fact that we could lose money on the deal.*

neglect /nɪ'glekt/ *noun* [U] when you do not give enough care or attention to someone or something, or the state of not receiving enough care or attention: *Both parents were found guilty of neglect and their child was taken away from them.* ○ *Over the years the church has fallen into a state of neglect.*

neglected /nɪ'glek.tɪd/ *adj* not receiving enough care or attention: *She was distressed at how neglected the children looked.*

neglectful /nɪ'glekt.fˀl/ *adj* not giving enough care and attention to something or someone: *I'm sure my boss thinks I've been neglectful of my duties recently.*

negligée /'neg.lɪ.ʒeɪ/ ⓤ /,--'-/ *noun* [C] (ALSO **negligee**) a woman's decorative DRESSING GOWN (= a loose-fitting coat worn inside the house) made of light material

negligent /'neg.lɪ.dʒˀnt/ *adj* not being careful or giving enough attention to people or things that are your responsibility: *The judge said that the teacher had been negligent in allowing the children to swim in dangerous water.* **negligently** /'neg.lɪ.dʒˀnt.li/ *adv*

negligence /'neg.lɪ.dʒˀnts/ *noun* [U] when you do not give enough care or attention to someone or something: *My mother accuses me of negligence unless I phone her every day.* ○ *medical negligence*

negligible /'neg.lɪ.dʒə.bl̩/ *adj* too slight or small in amount to be of importance: *The difference between the two products is negligible.* ○ *My knowledge of German is negligible.* **negligibly** /'neg.lɪ.dʒə.bli/ *adv*

negotiate ⟨DISCUSS⟩ /nə'gəʊ.ʃi.eɪt/ ⓤ /-'goʊ-/ *verb* [I or T] to have formal discussions with someone in order to reach an agreement with them: *The government has refused to negotiate with the strikers.* ○ *I'm negotiating for a new contract.* ○ *I've managed to negotiate* (= obtain by discussion) *a five per cent pay increase with my boss.*

negotiable /nə'gəʊ.ʃə.bl̩/ ⓤ /-'goʊ.ʃi.ə-/ *adj* able to be discussed or changed in order to reach an agreement: *Everything is negotiable at this stage – I'm ruling nothing out.*

negotiator /nɪ'gəʊ.ʃi.eɪ.tər/ ⓤ /-'goʊ.ʃi.ə.t̬ər/ *noun* [C] someone who tries to help two groups who disagree to reach an agreement with each other, usually as a job: *Some very skilful negotiators will be needed to settle this dispute.*

negotiation /nə,gəʊ.ʃi'eɪ.ʃˀn/ ⓤ /-,goʊ-/ *noun* [C or U] the process of discussing something with someone in order to reach an agreement with them, or the discussions themselves: *The agreement was reached after a series of difficult negotiations.* ○ *The exact details of the agreement are still under negotiation.* ○ *Negotiation for the pay increase is likely to take several weeks.*

negotiate ⟨TRAVEL⟩ /nə'gəʊ.ʃi.eɪt/ ⓤ /-'goʊ-/ *verb* [T] **1** to manage to travel along a difficult route: *The only way to negotiate the muddy hillside is on foot.* **2** to deal with something difficult: *The company's had some tricky problems to negotiate in its first year in business.*

negotiate ⟨EXCHANGE⟩ /nə'gəʊ.ʃi.eɪt/ ⓤ /-'goʊ-/ *verb* [T] SPECIALIZED to obtain or give a sum of money in exchange for a financial document of the same value **negotiable** /nə'gəʊ.ʃə.bl̩/ ⓤ /-'goʊ.ʃi.ə-/ *adj*: *A cheque that is not negotiable* (US ALSO **non negotiable**) *cannot be exchanged for cash and must be paid into a bank account.*

Negro (*plural* **Negroes**), **negro** /'niː.grəʊ/ ⓤ /-groʊ/ *noun* [C] OFFENSIVE OLD-FASHIONED a black person

negroid /'niː.grɔɪd/ *adj* OFFENSIVE OLD-FASHIONED SPECIALIZED having the physical features of a black person from Africa

neigh /neɪ/ *noun* [C] a long loud high call that is produced by a horse when it is excited or frightened **neigh** /neɪ/ *verb* [I] *When he laughs he sounds like a horse neighing.*

neighbour /'neɪ.bər/ ⓤ /-bər/ *noun* [C] **1** UK (US **neighbor**) someone who lives very near to you: *Some of the neighbours have complained about the noise from our party.* ○ *Have you met Pat, my next-door neighbour?* **2** A country's neighbour is one that is next to it: *The relationship between Scotland and its southern neighbour has not always been peaceful.*

neighbourhood UK, US **neighborhood** /'neɪ.bə.hʊd/ ⓤ /-bɚ-/ *noun* [C] the area of a town that surrounds someone's home, or the people who live in this area: *There were lots of kids in my neighbourhood when I was growing up.* ○ *They live in a wealthy/poor/friendly neighbourhood.* ○ *I wouldn't like to live in the neighbourhood of* (= in the area around) *an airport.*
● **in the neighbourhood of** *sth* approximately: *We're hoping to get somewhere in the neighbourhood of £70 000 for our house.*

neighbouring UK, US **neighboring** /'neɪ.bˀr.ɪŋ/ ⓤ /-bɚ-/ *adj* [before n] Neighbouring places are next to or near each other: *neighbouring countries/states* ○ *She married a man from the neighbouring village.*

neighbourly UK, US **neighborly** /'neɪ.bˀl.i/ ⓤ /-bɚ.li/ *adj* friendly or helpful: *It was very neighbourly of you to do her shopping for her.* **neighbourliness** UK, US **neighborliness** /'neɪ.bˀl.ɪ.nəs/ ⓤ /-bɚ.lɪ-/ *noun* [U]

,neighbourhood 'watch UK, US **neighborhood watch** *noun* [C or U] a way of reducing crime by organizing the people who live in an area to watch each other's property and tell the police about possible criminals

neither /'naɪ.ðər/ ⓤ /'niː-/ ⓤ /-ðɚ/ *determiner, pronoun, conjunction, adv* not either of two things or people: *We've got two TVs, but neither works properly.* ○ *Neither of my parents likes my boyfriend.* ○ *Neither one of us is particularly interested in gardening.* ○ *"Which one would you choose?" "Neither. They're both terrible."* ○ *If she doesn't agree to the plan, neither will Tom* (= Tom also will not). ○ *Chris wasn't at the meeting and neither was her assistant.* ○ INFORMAL *"I don't feel like going out this evening." "Me neither."* ○ *On two occasions she was accused of stealing money from the company, but in neither case was there any evidence to support the claims.*
● **neither ... nor** used when you want to say that two or more things are not true: *Neither my mother nor my*

father went to university. ○ *They speak neither French nor German, but a curious mixture of the two.* ○ *I neither know nor care what's happened to him.*

● **be neither one thing nor the other** to be a mixture of two different things, often things that do not combine well: *I prefer a book to be either fact or fiction – this one is neither one thing nor the other!*

● **be neither here nor there** to be unimportant: *It's essential that she has this medicine, and the cost is neither here nor there.*

USAGE

neither... nor

This can be used with a singular or a plural verb.

Neither Jack nor Philip like/likes football.

nelly /'nel.i/ *noun UK OLD-FASHIONED HUMOROUS* **not on your nelly** there is no possibility of that: *"Perhaps you could take Simon to the party." "Not on your nelly!"*

nemesis /'nem.ə.sɪs/ *noun* [C] *plural* **nemeses** *LITERARY* **1** Someone's nemesis is a person or thing that is very difficult for them to defeat. **2** (a cause of) punishment or defeat that is deserved and cannot be avoided: *The tax increases proved to be the President's political nemesis at the following election.*

neo- /ni:.əʊ-/ ⑥ /-oʊ-/ *prefix* new or recent, or in a modern form: *neo-fascist* ○ *neo-Nazi* ○ *neo-realist cinema*

neoclassical /ˌni:.əʊˈklæs.ɪ.kᵊl/ ⑥ /-oʊ-/ *adj SPECIALIZED* made in a style which is based on the art and building designs of ancient Rome and Greece **neoclassicism** /ˌni:.əʊˈklæs.ɪ.sɪ.zᵊm/ ⑥ /-oʊ-/ *noun* [U]

neocolonialism /ˌni:.əʊ.kəˈləʊ.ni.ᵊl.ɪ.zᵊm/ ⑥ /-oʊ.kə-ˈloʊ-/ *noun* [U] political control by a wealthy country of a poorer country that should be independent and free to govern itself **neocolonialist** /ˌni:.əʊ.kəˈləʊ.ni.ᵊl.ɪst/ ⑥ /-oʊ.kəˈloʊ-/ *adj*

neolithic /ˌni:.əʊˈlɪθ.ɪk/ ⑥ /-oʊ-/ *adj* belonging to the period when humans used tools and weapons made of stone and had just developed farming: *neolithic tools/artifacts/settlements* ○ *The neolithic **period** is sometimes called the new stone age.* ➔Compare **palaeolithic**.

neologism /niˈɒl.ə.dʒɪ.zᵊm/ ⑥ /-ˈɑː.lə-/ *noun* [C] *FORMAL* a new word or expression, or a new meaning for an existing word

neon /'ni:.ɒn/ ⑥ /-ɑːn/ *noun* [U] a colourless gas which has no smell, does not react with other chemicals, and shines red when an electric current goes through it: *a neon **light/sign***

neonatal /ˌni:.əʊˈneɪ.tᵊl/ ⑥ /-oʊˈneɪ.t̬ᵊl/ *adj* [before n] of or for babies that were born recently: *Their baby is still in the hospital's neonatal **unit**.*

neophyte /'ni:.əʊ.faɪt/ ⑥ /-oʊ-/ *noun* [C] *FORMAL* someone who has recently become involved in an activity and is still learning about it

nephew /'nef.ju:/ /'nev-/ *noun* [C] a son of your sister or brother or a son of the sister or brother of your husband or wife ➔Compare **niece**.

nepotism /'nep.ə.tɪ.zᵊm/ *noun* [U] *DISAPPROVING* using your power or influence to obtain good jobs or unfair advantages for members of your own family: *He was guilty of nepotism and corruption.* **nepotistic** /ˌnep.ə-ˈtɪs.tɪk/ *adj*

Neptune /'nep.tju:n/ ⑥ /-tu:n/ *noun* [S] the planet eighth in order of distance from the Sun, after Uranus and before Pluto: *Neptune was discovered in 1846.*

nerd /nɜ:d/ ⑥ /nɜ˞:d/ *noun* [C] *INFORMAL DISAPPROVING* a person, especially a man, who is unattractive and awkward or socially embarrassing: *He was a real nerd in high school – I can't believe he's so handsome now.* **nerdy** /'nɜ:.di/ ⑥ /'nɜ˞:-/ *adj*: *He's nice, but kind of nerdy.* ○ *These glasses make me **look/feel** nerdy.*

nerve [FIBRES] /nɜ:v/ ⑥ /nɜ˞:v/ *noun* [C] a group of long thin fibres that carry information or instructions between the brain and other parts of the body: *the optic nerve* ○ *a spinal nerve* ○ *nerve **damage*** ○ *nerve fibres* **nervous** /'nɜ:.vəs/ ⑥ /'nɜ˞:-/ *adj*: *He suffers from a nervous **disorder** (= disease of the nerves).*

nerve [BRAVERY] /nɜ:v/ ⑥ /nɜ˞:v/ *noun* [U] bravery or confidence necessary to do something difficult, unpleasant or rude: *It takes a lot of nerve to be a bomb disposal expert.* ○ *I wanted to ask her out, but I **lost** my nerve and couldn't go through with it.* ○ [+ *to* infinitive] *I didn't have **the** nerve **to** tell him what I really thought of his suggestion.*

nerve yourself *verb* [R] *UK* to make yourself brave enough to do something: [+ *to* infinitive] *It took her several months before she eventually nerved herself **(up) to** invite him to her house.*

● **have nerves of steel** to be very brave: *You need to have nerves of steel to be a fighter pilot.*

nerve [RUDENESS] /nɜ:v/ ⑥ /nɜ˞:v/ *noun* [S or U] the rudeness to do something that you know will upset other people: [+ *to* infinitive] *She's late for work every day, but she still has **the** nerve **to** lecture me about punctuality.* ○ *That man has such a nerve! He's always blaming me for things that are his fault.* ○ *She drove the car into a tree and then told me it was my fault for not concentrating, **of all the** nerve!*

● **hit/touch a (raw) nerve** to upset someone: *She touched a raw nerve when she mentioned that job he didn't get.*

nerve cell *noun* [C] a **neuron**

nerve centre *UK noun* [C] (*US* **nerve center**) a place from which an organization or activity is controlled or managed: *The Pentagon is the nerve centre of the US Armed Forces.*

nerve gas *noun* [U] a poisonous gas, often used as a weapon, that damages the nerves

nerve-racking, **nerve-wracking** /'nɜ:v.ræk.ɪŋ/ ⑥ /'nɜ˞:v-/ *adj* describes something that is difficult to do and causes a lot of worry for the person involved in it: *My wedding was the most nerve-racking thing I've ever experienced.*

nerves /nɜ:vz/ ⑥ /nɜ˞:vz/ *plural noun* [C] worry or anxiety about something that is going to happen: *I never suffer from nerves when I'm speaking in public.* ○ *She was a **bundle of** nerves (= very nervous) before the audition.* ○ *I always have a cigarette to **calm/steady** my nerves (= make me less nervous) before I go on stage.*

● **get on sb's nerves** to annoy someone a lot: *We really got on each other's nerves when we were living together.* ○ *Please stop making that noise! It really gets on my nerves.*

nerveless /'nɜ:v.ləs/ ⑥ /'nɜ˞:v-/ *adj* calm and confident about something difficult that you are doing **nervelessly** /'nɜ:v.lə.sli/ ⑥ /'nɜ˞:v-/ *adv*

nervous /'nɜ:.vəs/ ⑥ /'nɜ˞:-/ *adj* worried and anxious: *Do you **feel/get** nervous during exams?* ○ *I was too nervous to speak.* ○ *She's always been nervous **around** dogs.* ○ *I was very nervous **about** driving again after the accident.* ○ *He had/was of a nervous **disposition**.* **nervously** /'nɜ:.və.sli/ ⑥ /'nɜ˞:-/ *adv*: *He looked nervously over his shoulder, making sure no one else was listening.* **nervousness** /'nɜ:.və.snəs/ ⑥ /'nɜ˞:-/ *noun* [U] *There is growing nervousness **about** the possibility of a war in the region.*

nervous breakdown *noun* [C usually sing] a period of mental illness, usually without a physical cause, which results in anxiety, difficulty in sleeping and thinking clearly, a lack of confidence and hope, and a feeling of great sadness: *He **suffered** a nervous breakdown in his twenties.*

nervous system *noun* [C usually sing] An animal's nervous system consists of its brain and all the nerves in its body which together make movement and feeling possible by sending messages around the body.

nervy /'nɜ:.vi/ ⑥ /'nɜ˞:-/ *adj UK* worried: *I'm always nervy before an exam.*

-ness /-nəs/ *suffix* added to adjectives to form nouns which refer to a quality or a condition: *happiness* ○ *sadness* ○ *nervousness* ○ *selfishness* ○ *kindness*

nest [HOME] /nest/ *noun* [C] **1** a structure built by birds or insects to leave their eggs in to develop, and by some other animals to give birth or live in: *a bird's nest* ○ *a wasps'/hornets' nest* ○ *a rat's nest* ○ *Cuckoos are famous for laying their eggs in the nests of other birds.* ○ *The alligators build their nests out of grass near the water's* *edge.* **2** a comfortable home: *when the children grow up and* ***leave the*** *nest* **3** a place where something unpleasant or unwanted has developed: *The diplomats have been sent home because their embassy has become a nest* ***of*** *spies and espionage.*

nest /nest/ *verb* [I] to build a nest, or live in a nest: *We've got some swallows nesting in our roof at the moment.* ○ *Stone farm buildings are ideal nesting* ***sites*** *for barn owls.*

nest [SET] /nest/ *noun* [C] a set of things that are similar but different in size and have been designed to fit inside each other: *I'd like a nest* ***of*** *tables for the living room.*

nesting /ˈnes.tɪŋ/ *adj: I bought a set of nesting* ***dolls*** *in Moscow.*

ˈnest ˌegg *noun* [C] a sum of money that has been saved or kept for a special purpose: *Regular investment of small amounts of money is an excellent way of building a nest egg.*

ˈnesting ˌbox *UK noun* [C] (*US* **birdhouse**) a box for birds to nest in

nestle /ˈnes.l̩/ *verb* [I or T; + adv or prep] **1** to rest yourself or part of your body in a warm, comfortable and protected position: *She nestled (her head)* ***against*** *his shoulder.* **2** to be in, or put something in, a protected or sheltered position, with bigger things around it: *Bregenz is a pretty Austrian town that nestles* ***between*** *the Alps and Lake Constance.*

nestling /ˈnes.lɪŋ/ /ˈnest.lɪŋ/ *noun* [C] a young bird which has not yet learned to fly and still lives in the nest built by its parents

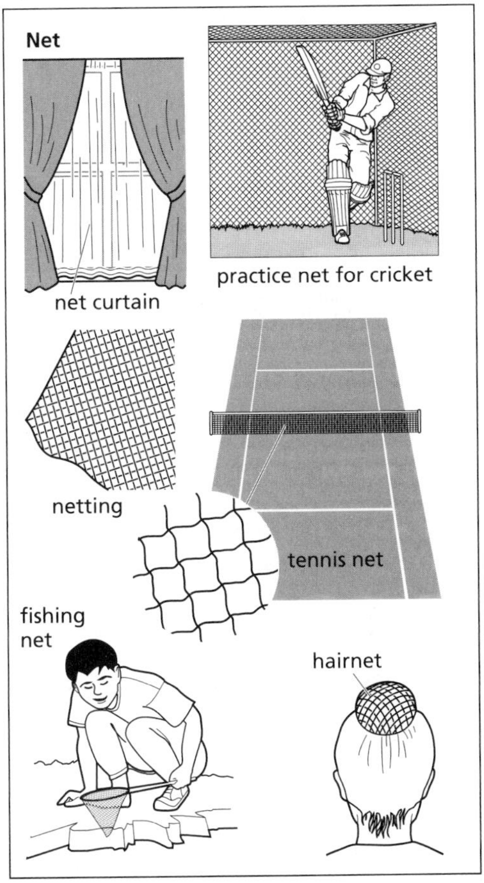
Net
practice net for cricket
net curtain
netting
tennis net
fishing net
hairnet

net [MATERIAL] /net/ *noun* **1** [C or U] material made of threads of rope, string, wire or plastic that are woven loosely so that there are spaces between them, allowing gas, liquid or small objects to go through, or an object made with this material which is used to limit the movement of something: *a fishing net* ○ *a butterfly net* ○ *Dolphins often get tangled in the nets that are used to catch tuna fish.* ○ *The living-room windows have net* ***curtains*** *which let in sunlight but stop passers-by looking in from the street.* **2** [C] a rectangular piece of material made from string which is used to separate the two sides in various sports: *If the ball touches the net during a service in a game of tennis, you have to serve again.* **3** [C] the area surrounded by a piece of material made from string into which a ball or PUCK is put in order to score points in various sports: *His penalty kick placed the ball decisively in the back of the net.* ○ *a basketball net*

net /net/ *verb* [T] **-tt- 1** to catch something using a net: *How many fish did you net this afternoon?* **2** If you net the ball during a game like football, you score a goal: *He secured a dramatic victory for England by netting the ball half a minute before the end of the game.* **3** to obtain something good or to earn a lot of money from something: [+ two objects] *She netted herself a fortune when she sold her company.* ○ *She netted £10 million* ***(for*** *herself) from the sale of her company.* ○ *Mark's netted himself a top job with an advertising company.*

netting /ˈnet.ɪŋ/ [US] /ˈnet̬-/ *noun* [U] material in the form of a net: *Two skiers were injured by safety netting that was too close to the course.*

net [LEFT OVER], *UK ALSO* **nett** /net/ *adj* [before or after n] left when there is nothing else to be subtracted: *I earn £15 000 gross, but my net* ***income*** (= income that is left after tax has been paid) *is about £12 000.* ○ *The net* ***weight*** *of something excludes the weight of the material that it is packed in.* ➲Compare **gross** TOTAL.

the Net *noun* [S] *ABBREVIATION FOR* **the Internet**: *I've found a really useful website about allergies on the Net.*

.net /ˌdɒtˈnet/ [US] /ˌdɑːt-/ network: the part of an Internet address that shows it belongs to a NETWORK or a business

netball /ˈnet.bɔːl/ [US] /-bɑːl/ *noun* [U] *UK* a sport played by two teams of seven players, usually women or girls, in which goals are obtained by throwing a ball through a net hanging from a ring at the top of a pole

nether /ˈneð.əʳ/ [US] /-ɚ/ *adj* [before n] *LITERARY OR HUMOROUS* in a lower position: *The boiler room is somewhere down in the building's nether* ***regions.***

netherworld /ˈneð.ə.wɜːld/ [US] /-ɚ.wɝːld/ *noun* [S] a place, situation or part of society which is hidden, and often unpleasant: *The film shows us a netherworld of drugs and crime.*

netiquette /ˈne.tɪ.ket/ *noun* [U] *SPECIALIZED* the set of rules about behaviour that is acceptable when writing an email or talking to people in a CHAT ROOM (= an address on the Internet where people can talk to each other using email): *It's considered bad netiquette to use capital letters in an email because it looks like YOU ARE SHOUTING.*

netizen /ˈne.tɪ.zən/ *noun* [C] *INFORMAL* a person who uses the Internet

ˌnet reˈsult *noun* [S] the situation that exists at the end of a series of events: *The net result of the changes will be increased fares and reduced services for most rail travellers.*

nettle [PLANT] /ˈnet.l̩/ [US] /ˈnet̬-/ *noun* [C] a wild plant with heart-shaped leaves that are covered in hairs which sting: ***stinging*** *nettles* ○ *nettle soup/tea* ➲See picture **Flowers and Plants** on page Centre 3

nettle [ANNOY] /ˈnet.l̩/ [US] /ˈnet̬-/ *verb* [T often passive] *MAINLY UK* to make someone annoyed or slightly angry: *She looked up at me sharply, clearly nettled by the interruption.*

ˈnettle ˌrash *noun* [U] *UK* a condition that causes slightly raised red or white spots to appear on the skin

network /ˈnet.wɜːk/ [US] /-wɝːk/ *noun* [C] a large system consisting of many similar parts that are connected together to allow movement or communication between or along the parts or between the parts and a control centre: *a television network* ○ *a road/rail network* ○ *a computer network* ○ *Massive investment is needed to modernise the country's* ***telephone*** *network.* ○ *We could reduce our costs by developing a more efficient* ***distribu-***

N

tion network. ○ *a network of spies/a spy network*
network /ˈnet.wɜːk/ [US] /-wɝːk/ *verb* **1** [T] to connect computers together so that they can share information: *Our computer system consists of about twenty personal computers networked* **to** *a powerful file-server.* **2** [I] to meet people who might be useful to know, especially in your job: *I don't really enjoy these conferences, but they're a good opportunity to do some networking.*

neural /ˈnjʊə.rəl/ [US] /ˈnʊr.əl/ *adj* [before n] involving a nerve or the system of nerves that includes the brain: *Some people suffered severe neural damage as a result of the vaccination.*

neuralgia /njʊəˈræl.dʒə/ [US] /nʊrˈæl-/ *noun* [U] severe brief pains felt suddenly along a nerve, especially in the neck or head **neuralgic** /njʊəˈræl.dʒɪk/ [US] /nʊrˈæl-/ *adj*

neur(o)- /njʊə.rəʊ-/ [US] /njʊr.oʊ-/ *prefix* relating to nerves: *neuroscience* ○ *A neurotransmitter is a chemical that nerve cells use to communicate with each other and with muscles.*

neurology /njʊəˈrɒl.ə.dʒi/ [US] /nʊrˈɑː.lə-/ *noun* [U] the study of the structure and diseases of the brain and all the nerves in the body
neurological /ˌnjʊə.rəˈlɒdʒ.ɪ.kəl/ [US] /ˌnʊr.əˈlɑː.dʒɪ-/ *adj* relating to nerves: *neurological disease/damage* ○ *Alzheimer's disease is a neurological* **disorder**.
neurologist /njʊəˈrɒl.ə.dʒɪst/ [US] /nʊrˈɑː.lə-/ *noun* [C] a doctor who studies and treats diseases of the nerves

neuron /ˈnjʊə.rɒn/ [US] /ˈnʊr.ɑːn/ *noun* [C] (*UK ALSO* **neurone**) a nerve cell that carries information between the brain and other parts of the body

neurosis /njʊəˈrəʊ.sɪs/ [US] /nʊrˈoʊ-/ *noun* [C or U] *plural* **neuroses** a mental illness resulting in high levels of anxiety, unreasonable fears and behaviour and, often, a need to repeat actions unnecessarily: *If you want my opinion, I think she's suffering from some form of neurosis.* ○ *She's obsessively clean – it's almost become a neurosis with her.*
neurotic /njʊəˈrɒt.ɪk/ [US] /nʊrˈɑː.t̬ɪk/ *adj* behaving strangely or in an anxious way, often because you have a mental illness: *neurotic behaviour/tendencies* ○ *She's neurotic* **about** *her weight – she weighs herself three times a day.*
neurotic /njʊəˈrɒt.ɪk/ [US] /nʊrˈɑː.t̬ɪk/ *noun* [C] someone who behaves strangely, often because they have a mental illness **neurotically** /njʊəˈrɒt.ɪ.kli/ [US] /nʊrˈɑː.t̬ɪ-/ *adv*

neurosurgeon /ˈnjʊə.rəʊˌsɜː.dʒən/ [US] /ˈnʊr.oʊˌsɝː-/ *noun* [C] a doctor who performs operations involving the brain or nerves **neurosurgery** /ˈnjʊə.rəʊˌsɜː.dʒər.i/ [US] /ˈnʊr.oʊˌsɝː.dʒɚ-/ *noun* [U]

neuter [GRAMMAR] /ˈnjuː.təʳ/ [US] /ˈnuː.t̬ɚ/ *adj SPECIALIZED* relating to a group of nouns in a particular language which have the same grammatical behaviour and which do not usually include words that refer to females or males: *The German word for 'book', 'das Buch', is neuter.* ➲Compare **masculine** GRAMMAR; **feminine** GRAMMAR.

neuter [REMOVE SEX ORGANS] /ˈnjuː.təʳ/ [US] /ˈnuː.t̬ɚ/ *verb* [T] **1** to remove part of an animal's sexual organs, so that it cannot reproduce: *Has your dog been neutered?* **2** to take the power away from something

neutral [NO OPINION] /ˈnjuː.trəl/ [US] /ˈnuː-/ *adj* not saying or doing anything that would encourage or help any of the groups involved in an argument or war: *If there's an argument between my daughter and her mother, it's important that I* **remain** *neutral.* ○ *The peace conference would have to be held in a neutral* **country**. ○ *I'd rather meet on neutral* **ground/territory** (= somewhere not controlled by or connected to either of us) *rather than in his apartment.*
neutral /ˈnjuː.trəl/ [US] /ˈnuː-/ *noun* [C] a neutral person or thing: *Sweden and Switzerland were neutrals during the war.* **neutrality** /njuːˈtræl.ə.ti/ [US] /nuːˈtræl.ə.t̬i/ *noun* [U] *Sweden isn't likely ever to abandon its traditional neutrality.* ○ *The Queen has maintained* **political** *neutrality throughout her reign.*

neutral [NOT NOTICEABLE] /ˈnjuː.trəl/ [US] /ˈnuː-/ *adj* **1** having features or characteristics that are not easily noticed: *Huw wants dark red walls, but I'd rather a more neutral* **colour** *like cream.* **2** describes a chemical substance that is neither an acid nor an ALKALI: *Pure water is neutral and has a pH of 7.* **3** describes an object in physics that has no electrical charge: *Atoms consist of positively-charged protons, negatively-charged electrons and neutral particles called neutrons.*
neutralize, *UK USUALLY* **-ise** /ˈnjuː.trə.laɪz/ [US] /ˈnuː-/ *verb* [T] to make something neutral: *Acidity in soil can be neutralized* (= have the acid removed) *by spreading lime on it.* **neutralization**, *UK USUALLY* **-isation** /ˌnjuː.trə.laɪˈzeɪ.ʃən/ [US] /ˌnuː-/ *noun* [U]

neutral [VEHICLE] /ˈnjuː.trəl/ [US] /ˈnuː-/ *noun* [U] **1** the position of the gears in a vehicle when they are not connected to the engine: *In Britain, you're supposed to put your car* **into** *neutral whenever you stop at a junction.* **2** a state of no activity or development: *After two years* **in** *neutral, the economy is finally moving forward again.*

neutralize, *UK ALSO* **-ise** /ˈnjuː.trə.laɪz/ [US] /ˈnuː-/ *verb* [T] to stop something from having an effect: *to neutralize an acid/odour* ○ *The aerial bombardments have neutralized the threat of artillery attacks on allied ground forces.*
neutralization, *UK ALSO* **-isation** /ˌnjuː.trə.laɪˈzeɪ.ʃən/ [US] /ˌnuː-/ *noun* [U]

neutron /ˈnjuː.trɒn/ [US] /ˈnuː.trɑːn/ *noun* [C] a part of an atom that has no electrical charge ➲Compare **electron**; **proton**.

ˈneutron ˌbomb *noun* [C] a nuclear weapon for use across short distances which is designed to kill people rather than destroy buildings or vehicles: *Neutron bombs release lethal radiation instead of exploding with a lot of heat and wind.*

never /ˈnev.əʳ/ [US] /-ɚ/ *adv* not at any time or not on any occasion: *We've never been to Australia.* ○ *I've never heard anything so ridiculous.* ○ *Let us never forget those who gave their lives for their country.* ○ *Wars never solve anything.* ○ *He threatened to shoot, but I never thought* (= did not think) *he would.* ○ *I never realised you knew my brother.* ○ *It's never* **too late** *to start eating a healthy diet.* ○ *UK INFORMAL "He's never 61!* (= It's difficult to believe he's 61!) *He looks so young."* ○ *UK NOT STANDARD "You stole my drink!" "No, I never* (= I didn't)*."*
• **as never before** in a way that has never been possible before: *Satellite technology offers the opportunity, as never before, for continuous television coverage of major international events.*
• **Never fear!** *OLD-FASHIONED OR HUMOROUS* do not worry: *Never fear! I'll have that leak fixed in a few moments.*
• **never mind 1** used to tell someone not to worry about something because it is not important: *"I'm afraid I've lost that wallet you gave me." "Well, never mind, I can easily buy you another one."* **2 never mind sth** used as a way of emphasizing that, although a particular thing is true, the one you have just mentioned is more important or interesting: *Midsummer House is one of the best restaurants in the country, never mind Cambridge.*
• **never mind that** *INFORMAL* despite the fact that: *He's going on holiday for the third time this year, never mind that he has hardly any money left.*
• **That will never do.** *OLD-FASHIONED* said when you think that something is unacceptable: *"He promised to pay me back last week, but he didn't." "Dear me, that will never do!"*
• **Well, I never (did)!** *OLD-FASHIONED* said when you are very surprised at something: *"Sophie's brother's been married seven times." "Well, I never (did)!"*

COMMON LEARNER ERROR

never

Never has a negative meaning so you do not need 'not' in the same sentence.

I'll never do that again.
~~*I'll not never do that again.*~~

never-ending /ˌnev.əˈrend.ɪŋ/ [US] /-ɚ-/ *adj* describes something that never ends or seems as if it will never end: *Writing a dictionary is a never-ending task.*

the never-never /ðəˌnev.əˈnev.əʳ/ [US] /-ɚˈnev.ɚ/ *UK INFORMAL* **on the never-never** using a system of payment in which part of the cost of something is paid immediately and then small regular payments are made until the debt is reduced to nothing: *I don't like **buying** things on the never-never because they charge you such a lot in interest.*

never-never land /ˌnev.əˈnev.əˌlænd/ [US] /-ɚˈnev.ɚ-/ *noun* [U] an imaginary place where everything is pleasant or perfect in a way that is impossible to achieve in reality: *If he thinks we can get this done by next week, he's **living** in never-never land.*

nevertheless /ˌnev.ə.ðəˈles/ [US] /-ɚ-/ *adv* (*SLIGHTLY FORMAL* **nonetheless**) despite what has just been said or referred to: *I knew a lot about the subject already, but her talk was interesting nevertheless.*

new [RECENTLY CREATED] /njuː/ [US] /nuː/ *adj* recently created or having started to exist recently: *a new car* ○ *She's very creative and always coming up with new ideas.* ○ *What have they decided to call their new baby?* ○ *What's new in the fashion world?* ○ *We have to invest in new technology if we are to remain competitive.* ➲See also **brand new**.

new /njuː/ [US] /nuː/ *noun* [U] *Out with the old and in with the new* (= new things).

new- /njuː-/ [US] /nuː-/ *prefix*: *The government's new-**found*** (= recently found) *enthusiasm for green issues has been welcomed by environmentalists.*

newish /ˈnjuː.ɪʃ/ [US] /ˈnuː.ɪʃ/ *adj INFORMAL* slightly new: *They have a four-bedroom house on a newish estate.*

newly /ˈnjuː.li/ [US] /ˈnuː.li/ *adv* recently: *the newly formed residents' association* ○ *Newly-discovered documents cast doubt on the guilt of the two men.* ➲See also **newlywed**.

newness /ˈnjuː.nəs/ [US] /ˈnuː-/ *noun* [U]

new [DIFFERENT] /njuː/ [US] /nuː/ *adj* [before n] different to one that existed earlier: *Have you met the new secretary?* ○ *She's looking for a new job.* ○ *Have you seen Ann's new house* (= the house that Ann has just started living in)*?* ○ *They've just launched a new generation of computers that are much more powerful than earlier models.*

• **be the new *sth*** used to say that something is now more popular or fashionable than the thing that it replaces: *This season fashion designers have declared that brown is the new black.*

• **feel like a new woman/man** to feel very much better: *That holiday did me the world of good – I feel like a whole new woman since I came back.*

• **A new broom sweeps clean.** *UK SAYING* said when someone new takes control of an organization and makes many changes

• **a new lease of life** *UK* (*US* **a new lease on life**) **1** when you become more energetic and active than before: *His grandchildren have **given** him a new lease of life.* **2** an increase in the period for which something can be used or continued: *The project suddenly **got** a new lease of life when the developers agreed to provide some more funding.*

new [NOT FAMILIAR] /njuː/ [US] /nuː/ *adj* [after v] not yet familiar or experienced: *to be new **to** the area* ○ *She's new **to** the job so you can't expect her to know everything yet.*

new [NOT USED] /njuː/ [US] /nuː/ *adj* not previously used or owned: *Used car sales have risen because of the increased cost of new cars.* ○ *Did you buy your bike new or second-hand?* ➲See also **brand new**.

new [RECENTLY DISCOVERED] /njuː/ [US] /nuː/ *adj* recently discovered or made known: *This new cancer treatment offers hope to many sufferers.* ○ *A retrial can only take place when new evidence has emerged.*

• **That's a new one on me.** *INFORMAL* said when someone has just told you a surprising fact that you did not know before: *"Sian and Richard are getting married." "Really! That's a new one on me!"*

ˌNew ˈAge *noun* [U] a way of life and thinking which developed in the late 1980s which includes a wide range of beliefs and activities based on ideas that existed before modern scientific and economic theories: *Astrology and alternative medicine are part of the New Age **movement**.* **New Ager** /ˌnjuːˈeɪ.dʒəʳ/ [US] /ˌnuːˈeɪ.dʒɚ/ *noun* [C] *Many New Agers are vegetarians and environmentalists.*

ˌNew Age ˈmusic *noun* [U] a type of music which is intended to produce a calm and peaceful state of mind: *My massage therapist always plays New Age music to help me relax.*

ˌNew Age ˈtraveller *noun* [C] *UK* someone who lives in a vehicle and has no permanent home or job, refusing to accept their society's normal ideas and ways of living: *New Age travellers were on the road again today, looking for a place to hold their midsummer festival.*

newbie /ˈnjuː.bi/ [US] /ˈnuː.bi/ *noun* [C] *INFORMAL* a person who has recently started to use a computer or the Internet and does not know how to use it properly

ˌnew ˈblood *noun* [U] people with a lot of energy or fresh ideas who are brought into an organization in order to improve it: *The new blood in the team should improve our chances of victory in next week's match.*

newborn /ˈnjuː.bɔːn/ [US] /ˈnuː.bɔːrn/ *adj* [before n] recently born: *Breast-feeding is extremely beneficial to the health of newborn **babies**.* ○ *FIGURATIVE the newborn democracies of the world*

newcomer /ˈnjuːˌkʌm.əʳ/ [US] /ˈnuːˌkʌm.ɚ/ *noun* [C] someone who has recently arrived in a place or recently become involved in an activity: *We've lived here for 15 years, but we're **relative** newcomers **to** the village.* ○ *The newcomer **on the** radio **scene** is a commercial station devoted to classical music.*

newfangled /ˌnjuːˈfæŋ.gḷd/ [US] /ˌnuː-/ *adj* recently made for the first time, but not necessarily an improvement on what existed before: *I really don't understand these newfangled computer games that my children are always playing.*

ˈnew ˌgirl/ˌboy *noun* [C] *MAINLY UK* **1** a child who has recently started going to a school **2** someone who has recently become involved with an activity or organization: *Mark Kennedy is the new boy in the government.*

newlywed /ˈnjuː.li.wed/ [US] /ˈnuː-/ *noun* [C usually pl] someone who has recently got married: *The hotel has a special discount rate for newlyweds.*

ˌNew ˈMan *noun* [C] *MAINLY UK* a man who believes that women and men are equal and should be free to do the same things, and who does tasks and shows emotions that were traditionally considered only suitable for women: *I'm not particularly what you would call a New Man, but I do cook, and I iron my own shirts.*

ˌnew ˈmedia *plural noun* products and services that provide information or entertainment using computers or the Internet, and not by traditional methods such as television and newspapers: *We must embrace the opportunities presented by the new media.*

ˌnew ˈmoon *noun* [C usually sing; U] the moon when it is shaped like a CRESCENT, or a time when it is shaped like this: *It was dark now and the sliver of a new moon could be seen overhead.* ○ *The team discovered that the planet is 0.02 °C warmer at full moon than at new moon.*

ˌnew poˈtatoes *plural noun* small potatoes that are taken out of the ground earlier than the others in the crop

news /njuːz/ [US] /nuːz/ *noun* [U] **1** information or reports about recent events: *That's the best **(piece of)** news I've heard for a long time!* ○ *We've had no news **of** them since they left for Australia.* ○ *Have you heard the news **about** Tina and Tom? They're getting divorced.* ○ *Do write and tell us all your news.* ○ [+ that] *The news **that** Madge had resigned took everyone by surprise.* ○ *We've got some **good** news for you. We're getting married.* **2 the news** a television or radio programme consisting of reports about recent events: *I usually watch the **early evening/late night** news.* ○ *Was there anything interesting **on** the news this evening?*

• **be good/bad news** to be someone or something that will affect a person or situation well/badly: *He's bad news **for** the company. He should never have been given the job.*

• **be in the news** to be reported about: *They've been in the news a lot recently because of their marital problems.*

• **be news to *sb*** *INFORMAL* to be information that someone did not know before: *"I hear you and Phil are going to Paris for the weekend." "Really? That's news to me."*

• **break (the) news** to tell someone about something bad which has just happened and which has an effect on them: *I was devastated when the doctor broke the news **to***

N

me. ○ *Where were you when the news of Kennedy's assassination **broke** (= became known)?*

• **have news for *sb*** used to say that someone is going to be unpleasantly surprised because something will not be as they want it to be: *I've got news for him, if he thinks he can carry on living here free of charge.*

• **No news is good news.** SAYING said to make someone feel less worried when they have not received information about someone or something, because if something bad had happened, they would have been told about it: *We haven't heard anything from the hospital today, but I suppose no news is good news.*

newsy /ˈnjuː.zi/ [US] /ˈnuː-/ *adj* INFORMAL containing a lot of news that is personal or not very serious: *I got a lovely long newsy letter from Bec.*

ˈnews ˌagency *noun* [C] an organization which supplies reports to newspapers, magazines and broadcasters

newsagent /ˈnjuːzˌeɪ.dʒənt/ [US] /ˈnuːz-/ *noun* [C] UK **1** (ALSO **newsagent's**) a shop whose main business is selling newspapers and magazines: *Do you want anything from the newsagent's apart from a paper?* **2** a person who owns or manages a newsagent's

newscaster /ˈnjuːzˌkɑː.stər/ [US] /ˈnuːzˌkæs.tɚ/ *noun* [C] (UK ALSO **newsreader**) someone who reads out the reports on a television or radio news programme

newscast /ˈnjuːz.kɑːst/ [US] /ˈnuːz.kæst/ *noun* [C] MAINLY US a radio or television programme that consists of news reports

ˈnews ˌconference *noun* [C] MAINLY US a meeting in which someone makes a statement to reporters or answers questions from them: *She **called** a news conference to give her side of the story.* ➲See also **press conference**.

newsflash /ˈnjuːz.flæʃ/ [US] /ˈnuːz-/ *noun* [C] a brief news report on radio or television, giving the most recent information about an important or unexpected event

newsgroup /ˈnjuːz.gruːp/ [US] /ˈnuːz.gruːp/ *noun* [C] a collection of messages that are displayed on the Internet and have been written by people interested in a particular subject: *If you want to read discussions on the latest films, subscribe to a newsgroup.*

newsletter /ˈnjuːzˌlet.ər/ [US] /ˈnuːzˌlet̬.ɚ/ *noun* [C] a printed document containing information about the recent activities of an organization, which is sent regularly to the organization's members: *a **monthly** newsletter*

newspaper /ˈnjuːzˌpeɪ.pər/ [US] /ˈnuːzˌpeɪ.pɚ/ *noun* **1** [C] a regularly printed document consisting of news reports, articles, photographs and advertisements that are printed on large sheets of paper which are folded together but not permanently joined: *Which newspaper do you read regularly?* ○ *a **daily/Sunday** newspaper* **2** [C] an organization which makes and publishes a newspaper: *He wants to work for a newspaper when he leaves school.* **3** [U] old newspapers: *You'd better wrap that mirror up in newspaper before you put it in the car.*

COMMON LEARNER ERROR

in the newspaper

Remember to use the preposition 'in' when you are talking about the things that are written in the newspaper.

I read an article in the newspaper.
~~*I read an article on the newspaper.*~~

newsprint /ˈnjuːz.prɪnt/ [US] /ˈnuːz-/ *noun* [U] cheap, low quality paper that newspapers are printed on

newsreader /ˈnjuːzˌriː.dər/ [US] /ˈnuːzˌriː.dɚ/ *noun* [C] UK FOR **newscaster**

newsreel /ˈnjuːz.riːl/ [US] /ˈnuːz-/ *noun* [C] a short film that consists of news reports, usually one that was made in the past for showing in a cinema: *The movie contains some recently discovered newsreel **footage** of the war.*

newsroom /ˈnjuːz.rʊm/ /-ruːm/ [US] /ˈnuːz-/ *noun* [C] an office at a television or radio station or a newspaper where news is gathered and reports are prepared for broadcasting or publishing

newsstand /ˈnjuːz.stænd/ [US] /ˈnuːz-/ *noun* [C] a table or temporary structure used as a small shop for selling newspapers and magazines outside in public places

newsvendor /ˈnjuːzˌven.dər/ [US] /ˈnuːzˌven.dɚ/ *noun* [C] someone who sells newspapers

newsworthy /ˈnjuːzˌwɜː.ði/ [US] /ˈnuːzˌwɝː-/ *adj* interesting enough to be described in a news report: *Nothing newsworthy ever happens around here. It's so boring.*

newsy /ˈnjuː.zi/ [US] /ˈnuː-/ *adj* ➲See at **news**.

newt /njuːt/ [US] /nuːt/ *noun* [C] a small animal which has a long thin body and tail and short legs, and lives both on land and in water

the ˌNew ˈTestament *noun* [U] the second of the two main parts of the Bible, containing the books written after the birth of Jesus Christ: *the New Testament reading* ➲Compare **the Old Testament**.

ˈnew ˌtown *noun* [C] a British town which did not develop gradually but was established and planned by the government: *Milton Keynes is a new town which was founded in 1967.*

ˌnew ˈwave *noun* [S or U] a fashion in something, such as art, music, cinema or politics, which is intentionally different from traditional ideas in that subject or activity: *Truffaut was an important film director of the French New Wave.* ○ *new-wave music*

ˌnew ˈwave group *noun* [S] people who are doing activities in a new and different way: *the new wave **of** wine producers*

the ˌNew ˈWorld *noun* [S] North, Central and South America ➲Compare **the Old World**.

ˌNew ˈYear, **new year** *noun* [C usually sing] the beginning of the year which is about to begin or has just begun: *I'm spending New Year* (= the first days of the new year) *in Scotland with my parents.* ○ *We'll have to wait until **the** new year before we can make any definite plans.* ○ *Best wishes for Christmas and a **Happy** New Year.*

New Year's Day /ˌnjuːˌjɪəzˈdeɪ/ [US] /ˌnuːˌjɪrz-/ *noun* [U] (US **New Year's**) the first day of the year, which is a public holiday in many countries

New Year's Eve /ˌnjuːˌjɪəzˈiːv/ [US] /ˌnuːˌjɪrz-/ *noun* [U] the last day of the year: *Are you having a New Year's Eve party?* ➲See also **Hogmanay**.

New Year('s) resolution /ˌnjuːˌjɪəzˌrez.əˈluː.ʃən/ [US] /ˌnuːˌjɪrz-/ *noun* [C] a promise that you make to yourself to start doing something good or stop doing something bad on the first day of the year: *"Have you **made** any New Year's resolutions?" "Yes, I'm going to eat more healthily and give up smoking."*

next /nekst/ *adj, pronoun* being the first one after the present one or after the one just mentioned, or being the first after the present moment: *Who works in the office next **to** yours?* ○ *Take the next turning on the right.* ○ *Who do you think will be the next president?* ○ *Nothing really changes around here. One day is pretty much like **the** next.* ○ *(The) next time you want to borrow something, please ask me first.* ○ *I'm so busy it's hard to remember what I'm supposed to be doing **from one moment to the** next.* ○ *She's on holiday for the next few days.* ○ *You'll have to wait until your next birthday for a new bike.* ○ *Can we arrange a meeting for the week after next?* ○ *What do you think you'll be doing this time next year?* ○ *We had a dreadful argument in the restaurant, but he phoned me **the** next **day*** (= the day after) *to apologise.* ○ *Excuse me, it's my turn to be served – I was next.*

• **as much as the next *person*** as much as anyone would: *I enjoy winning awards as much as the next guy, but other things are more important to me.*

• **the next best thing** the thing that is best, if you cannot have or do the thing you really want: *I really wanted to work in television but I ended up in radio, which is the next best thing.*

• **the next thing I knew** INFORMAL used to talk about part of a story that happens in a sudden and surprising way: *A car came speeding round the corner, and the next thing I knew I was lying on the ground.*

next /nekst/ *adv* **1** immediately after: *So what happened next?* ○ *What would you like next?* ○ *First, fry the garlic.*

N

Next, add the ginger. **2** The time when you next do something is the first time you do it again: [+ v-ing] *When are you next going to London?*

• **next to 1** used when describing two people or things that are very close to each other with nothing between them: *Can I **sit** next to the window?* ○ *There was a really strange man standing next to me at the station.* **2** used to mean 'after' when making a choice or a comparison: *I'd say cheese is my favourite food and, next to that, chocolate* (= Cheese is the only food that I like more than chocolate). **3** almost: *They pay me next to **nothing*** (= very little) *but I really enjoy the work.* ○ *It's next to **impossible*** (= extremely difficult) *to find somewhere cheap to live in the city centre.* ○ *We got home in next to **no time*** (= very little time).

• **next up** next in order to appear or happen, often in some form of entertainment: *Next up on Channel 4 is the first episode of a new medical drama set in Chicago.*

ˌnext ˈdoor *adv, adj* in the next room, house or building: *A Russian couple have just moved in next door.* ○ *Who lives next door **to** you?* ○ *Margot is our next-door **neighbour**.*

ˌnext ˈdoor *noun* [U] *UK INFORMAL* the person or people living in the next room, house or building: *Next door's having a party next week, did you know?*

ˌnext ˈdoor *adv* very close: *Would you want to live next door to a nuclear power station?*

ˌnext of ˈkin *noun* [C] *plural* **next of kin** the person or group of people you are most closely related to: *We cannot release the names of the soldiers who were killed until we having informed their next of kin.*

ˌnext to ˈlast *adj* describes the person or thing before the last one: *I was next to last in the steeplechase.* ○ *He injured himself on the next-to-last day of his vacation.*

nexus /ˈnek.səs/ *noun* [C usually sing] *FORMAL* an important connection between the parts of a system or a group of things: *Times Square is the nexus of the New York subway.*

the NHS /ðiˌen.eɪtʃˈes/ *noun* [S] *ABBREVIATION FOR* **the National Health Service**: *Many forms of cosmetic surgery are not **available on*** (= paid for by) *the NHS.* **NHS** /ˌen.eɪtʃˈes/ *adj*: *an NHS hospital*

nib /nɪb/ *noun* [C] a pointed metal part at one end of a pen, which the ink flows through when you write or draw ➲Compare **ballpoint**; **felt-tip (pen)**.

nibble /ˈnɪb.l̩/ *verb* **1** [I or T] to eat something by taking a lot of small bites: *Have you got some peanuts for us to nibble while the party warms up?* ○ *A mouse has nibbled through the computer cables.* ○ *Jenny's hamster's nibbled a hole **in** the sofa.* **2** [T] to bite something gently and repeatedly: *She nibbled his ear.*

nibble /ˈnɪb.l̩/ *noun* **1** [C] when you nibble something: *Just **take/have** a nibble to see if you like the taste.* **2** [S] an expression of interest in something: *Our house was on the market for six months and there wasn't a single nibble.*

nibbles /ˈnɪb.l̩z/ *plural noun UK INFORMAL* small pieces of food that are eaten between or before meals, often with alcoholic drinks: *I bought some crisps and nuts and other nibbles.*

▲ **nibble (away) at *sth*** *phrasal verb* to slowly reduce something: *Even when inflation is low, it nibbles away at people's savings, reducing their value considerably over several years.*

nibs /nɪbz/ *noun OLD-FASHIONED INFORMAL* **his nibs** a man who is in a position of authority or who thinks he is more important than he really is: *Did his nibs say when he would be back in the office?*

NiCad /ˈnaɪ.kæd/ *TRADEMARK* a type of battery that can be RECHARGED (= filled with electricity again and again), and which is used in electronic equipment

nice [PLEASANT] /naɪs/ *adj* pleasant, enjoyable or satisfactory: *Did you have a nice holiday?* ○ *Have a nice day/time!* ○ *This milk doesn't smell very nice.* ○ *Thanks for ringing – **it's** been nice talk**ing** to you.* ○ *Wasn't **it** nice **of** them **to** invite us?*

• **nice and ...** *INFORMAL* pleasantly: *This orange is nice and juicy.*

• **nice work if you can get it** something you say about an easy way of earning money which you would like to do if you could: *She got one million dollars for appearing on television for five minutes – (that's) nice work if you can get it!*

nicely /ˈnaɪ.sli/ *adv* well, pleasantly or satisfactorily: *Those trousers fit you nicely.* ○ *You've painted the woodwork very nicely.* ○ *Bake the mixture for 35 to 40 minutes until the cake is nicely browned.* ○ *They said the baby was **doing** nicely* (= was healthy) *and would soon be back at home.*

• **do nicely** *INFORMAL* to make a large profit: *They did very nicely **from** the sale of their company.*

• **that'll do nicely** used to say that something is satisfactory: *That'll do nicely, thank you.*

nice [KIND] /naɪs/ *adj* kind, friendly or polite: *Jane's new boyfriend is a really nice guy.* ○ *I wish you'd be nice **to** your brother.* ○ ***It** was very nice **of** her **to** drive you home.* ○ *It's not nice to talk with your mouth full.* **nicely** /ˈnaɪ.sli/ *adv*: *Well, I like her – she's always treated me very nicely.* ○ *You can have another biscuit if you ask nicely.*

nice [SLIGHTLY DIFFERENT] /naɪs/ *adj* [before n] *FORMAL* based on very slight differences and needing a lot of careful and detailed thought: *I wasn't convinced by the minister's nice **distinction** between a lie and an untruth.*

nicety /ˈnaɪ.sə.ti/ Ⓤⓢ /-t̬i/ *noun* **1** [C usually pl] a detail or small difference which is only obvious after careful consideration: *They spent a lot of time arguing about **legal** niceties.* ○ *We don't bother with all the **social** niceties here.* **2** [U] *FORMAL* when something is based on very slight differences

nice-looking /ˌnaɪsˈlʊk.ɪŋ/ *adj* attractive: *Isn't Gill's husband nice-looking?*

niche [POSITION] /niːʃ/ Ⓤⓢ /nɪtʃ/ *noun* [C] **1** a job or position which is very suitable for someone, especially one that they like: *Lloyd has **carved/made** a niche for himself as a professional tennis player.* **2** an area or position which is exactly suitable for a small group of the same type: *an ecological niche.*

niche [HOLLOW] /niːʃ/ Ⓤⓢ /nɪtʃ/ *noun* [C] a hollow in a wall, especially one made to put a statue in so that it can be seen

ˈniche ˌmarket *noun* [C] a small area of trade within the economy, often involving specialized products: *Lotus make luxury cars for a small but significant niche market.*

nick [CUT] /nɪk/ *noun* [C] a small cut in a surface or an edge: *Apart from a few nicks in the varnish, the guitar is in very good condition.*

• **in the nick of time** at the last possible moment: *We got there just in the nick of time.*

nick /nɪk/ *verb* [T] to make a small cut in a surface or an edge: *Paintwork on the corner of a stairway tends to get nicked and scratched.*

nick [STEAL] /nɪk/ *verb* [T] *UK INFORMAL* to steal something: *I've had my bike nicked again.* ○ *All right, who's nicked my ruler?*

nick [CATCH] /nɪk/ *verb* [T] *UK SLANG* If the police nick someone, they catch them for committing a crime: *They nicked him **for** driving at seventy in a fifty speed limit area.*

the nick [PRISON] /ðəˈnɪk/ *noun* [S] *UK SLANG* prison: *He's been **in** the nick half his life.*

nick [CONDITION] /nɪk/ *noun* [U] *UK SLANG* a stated condition, especially of health: *He's **in** pretty good nick for a man of his age.* ○ *The car really is **in** excellent nick.*

nickel [METAL] /ˈnɪk.l̩/ *noun* [U] a silvery white metallic element: *a nickel alloy*

nickel [COIN] /ˈnɪk.l̩/ *noun* [C] a US or Canadian coin worth five cents

nickel-and-dime /ˌnɪk.l̩.ənˈdaɪm/ *adj US INFORMAL* describes something that is unimportant, usually because it does not involve much money: *a nickel-and-dime dispute*

nick-nack /ˈnɪk.næk/ *noun* [C] a **knick-knack**

nickname /ˈnɪk.neɪm/ *noun* [C] an informal name for someone or something, especially a name which you are called by your friends or family, usually based on your proper name or your character: *We always use the nickname Beth for our daughter Elizabeth.* ○ *"Darwin" was the nickname he was given at high school, because of his interest in science.* **nickname** /ˈnɪk.neɪm/ *verb* [T + obj + n] *The campsite has been nicknamed 'tent city' by visiting reporters.*

nicotine /ˈnɪk.ə.tiːn/ [US] /-t̬iːn/ *noun* [U] a poisonous chemical found in tobacco which makes people who breathe it in habitually want more of it

ˈnicotine ˌpatch *noun* [C] a small piece of material with nicotine on it which a person can stick onto their skin to help them stop smoking

niece /niːs/ *noun* [C] the daughter of your brother or sister, or the daughter of your husband's or wife's brother or sister ➲Compare **nephew**.

niff /nɪf/ *noun* [C usually sing] *UK INFORMAL* an unpleasant smell: *a nasty niff* **niffy** /ˈnɪf.i/ *adj*

nifty /ˈnɪf.ti/ *adj INFORMAL* good, pleasing or effective: *a nifty piece of work/footwork* ○ *a nifty little gadget*

niggardly /ˈnɪg.əd.li/ [US] /-ɚd-/ *adj DISAPPROVING* slight in amount, quality or effort: *a niggardly donation/amount*

nigger /ˈnɪg.əʳ/ [US] /-ɚ/ *noun* [C] *OFFENSIVE* a black person

niggle [WORRY] /ˈnɪg.l̩/ *verb* [I or T] to worry someone slightly, usually for a long time: *I just can't remember his name – it's been niggling (me) for a couple of weeks.*
niggle /ˈnɪg.l̩/ *noun* [C] a small doubt or worry: *Don't you feel even a slight niggle about the morality of your experiments?* **niggling** /ˈnɪg.l̩.ɪŋ/ /-lɪŋ/ *adj* [before n] *a niggling doubt/fear*

niggle [CRITICIZE] /ˈnɪg.l̩/ *verb* [I or T] to criticize someone about small details or give too much attention to details: *She niggles endlessly* ***over*** *the exact pronunciation.* ○ *The accounts department is niggling me for ten cents they say I owe them.*
niggle /ˈnɪg.l̩/ *noun* [C] *I do have a few minor niggles* (= criticisms) *about the book, but generally it's very good.* **niggling** /ˈnɪg.l̩.ɪŋ/ /-lɪŋ/ *adj* [before n] *a niggling comment/criticism*

nigh /naɪ/ *adv, prep OLD-FASHIONED OR LITERARY* near: *She must have written nigh* ***on*** (= nearly but not quite) *50 books.* ○ ***The time is*** *nigh* (= It is nearly time) *for us to make a decision.*

night [DARK PERIOD] /naɪt/ *noun* [C or U] the part of every 24 hour period when it is dark because there is very little light from the sun: *It gets cold* ***at*** *night.* ○ *I slept really badly* ***last*** *night.* ○ *I* ***spent*** *the night at Ted's.* ○ *He took the night ferry/train.*
• **night after night** every night: *The howling of wild animals kept him awake night after night.*
• **night and day** (*ALSO* **day and night**) all the time: *They've worked night and day to publicise their campaign.*
nightly /ˈnaɪt.li/ *adj, adv* (happening) every night: *Nightly bombardment of the city looks set to continue.*

night [EVENING] /naɪt/ *noun* **1** [C or U] the period of time between the late afternoon and going to bed; the evening: *Shall we go dancing on Saturday night?* ○ *We've been out every night this week.* ○ *She's a singer in a bar* ***by*** *night and a secretary by day.* **2** [S] the evening on which a special event happens: *When's the* ***last*** *night of your show?* ○ *The* ***first/opening*** *night of her new film was a great success.*
• **night after night** every evening: *She stayed in night after night, waiting for him to call.*
• **night-night** *CHILD'S EXPRESSION* used as another way of saying GOOD NIGHT, usually by or to children
• **the other night** on one evening recently: *I saw Naomi at the club the other night.*
• **a night on the town** an evening when you go to various places and enjoy entertainments such as dancing, eating in a restaurant and drinking in a bar: *Let's* ***have/go for*** *a night on the town to celebrate.*
• **a night out** an evening spent at a restaurant, theatre, etc. rather than staying at home: *Let's* ***have*** *a night out together on Saturday – we could go dancing.*
nightly /ˈnaɪt.li/ *adj, adv* (happening) every evening: *They're appearing/performing twice nightly at the Playhouse Theatre.* ○ *a nightly visit/news broadcast*

nightcap [DRINK] /ˈnaɪt.kæp/ *noun* [C] a drink, often an alcoholic drink, which someone has just before they go to bed

nightcap [HAT] /ˈnaɪt.kæp/ *noun* [C] a type of hat made from soft cloth and worn in bed, especially in the past

nightclothes /ˈnaɪt.kləʊðz/ [US] /-kloʊðz/ *plural noun* clothes which are worn in bed

nightclub /ˈnaɪt.klʌb/ *noun* [C] (*INFORMAL* **nightspot**) a place which is open late into the night, where people can go to drink and dance and often see some type of entertainment
nightclubbing /ˈnaɪtˌklʌb.ɪŋ/ *noun* [U] *OLD-FASHIONED FOR* **clubbing**, see at **club** DANCE: *to go nightclubbing*

nightdress *UK* /ˈnaɪt.dres/ *noun* [C] (*US* **nightgown**) a comfortable piece of clothing like a loose dress worn by a woman or a girl in bed

nightfall /ˈnaɪt.fɔːl/ [US] /-fɑːl/ *noun* [U] the time in the evening when it becomes dark

nightgown /ˈnaɪt.gaʊn/ *noun* [C] *US FOR* **nightdress**

nightie /ˈnaɪ.ti/ [US] /-t̬i/ *noun* [C] *INFORMAL FOR* **nightdress**

nightingale /ˈnaɪ.tɪŋ.geɪl/ [US] /-t̬ɪŋ-/ *noun* [C] a small brown European bird known especially for the beautiful song of the male bird which is usually heard during the night

nightlife /ˈnaɪt.laɪf/ *noun* [U] entertainment and social activities which happen in the evening in bars and nightclubs: *There isn't much nightlife at the resort – you'll have to go into the main town for that.*

nightlight /ˈnaɪt.laɪt/ *noun* [C] a light that is not bright which can be left on through the night, especially for a child

nightlong /ˌnaɪtˈlɒŋ/ [US] /-ˈlɑːŋ/ *adj, adv LITERARY* through the night

nightmare /ˈnaɪt.meəʳ/ [US] /-mer/ *noun* [C] **1** a very upsetting or frightening dream: *a terrifying nightmare* ○ *I shouldn't have watched that movie – it'll give me nightmares.* **2** an extremely unpleasant event or experience or possible event or experience: *Being trapped underwater is my* ***worst*** *nightmare.* ○ *The whole journey was a nightmare – we lost our luggage and we arrived two days late.* **nightmarish** /ˈnaɪt.meə.rɪʃ/ [US] /-mer.ɪʃ/ *adj* **nightmarishly** /ˈnaɪt.meə.rɪʃ.li/ [US] /-mer.ɪʃ-/ *adv*

ˈnight ˌowl *noun* [C] *INFORMAL* a person who prefers to be awake and active at night

nights /naɪts/ *adv* at night, especially every night: *Because she's a nurse she often has to* ***work*** *nights.* ○ *US I like to go out nights and sleep during the day.*

ˈnight ˌschool *noun* [C] a series of classes held in the evening, often in a school, especially for adults who work during the day

ˈnight ˌshift *group noun* [S] the group of workers who work for a period during the night
ˈnight ˌshift *noun* [C] a period in the night during which a particular group of people work: *People who work* ***on*** *the night shift are paid more.*

nightshirt /ˈnaɪt.ʃɜːt/ [US] /-ʃɝːt/ *noun* [C] a comfortable piece of clothing like a long loose shirt worn in bed, especially in the past by a man or boy

nightspot /ˈnaɪt.spɒt/ [US] /-spɑːt/ *noun* [C] a **nightclub**

nightstand /ˈnaɪt.stænd/ *noun* [C] (*ALSO* **night table**) *US FOR* **bedside table**

nightstick *US* /ˈnaɪt.stɪk/ *noun* [C] (*UK* **truncheon**) a thick heavy stick used as a weapon by police officers

night-time /ˈnaɪt.taɪm/ *noun* [U] the time in every 24 hour period when it is dark: *It's pretty noisy at night-time.* ○ *a night-time curfew*

ˌnight ˈwatchman *noun* [C] a person who guards a building at night

nightwear /ˈnaɪt.weəʳ/ [US] /-wer/ *noun* [U] clothes worn in bed or while preparing to go to bed

nihilism /ˈnaɪ.ə.lɪ.zᵊm/ *noun* [U] *SPECIALIZED* a belief that all political and religious organizations are bad, or a system of thought which says that there are no principles or beliefs which have any meaning or can be true **nihilist** /ˈnaɪ.ə.lɪst/ *noun* [C] **nihilistic** /ˌnaɪ.əˈlɪs.tɪk/ *adj*

the Nikkei (index) /ðəˌnɪk.eɪˈɪn.deks/ [US] /-ˌniː.keɪ-/ *noun* [S] a list which gives the price of shares in the most important Japanese companies ➲Compare **the Dow Jones (industrial) average**; **the FTSE 100 (Index)**.

nil /nɪl/ *noun* [U] nothing: *She claims that the operating risks are virtually nil.* ○ *UK The challengers lost the game seven-nil* (= zero).

nimble /ˈnɪm.bl̩/ *adj USUALLY APPROVING* quick and exact either in movement or thoughts: *nimble fingers/feet* ○ *His nimble mind calculated the answer before I could key the numbers into my computer.* **nimbly** /ˈnɪm.bli/ *adv* **nimbleness** /ˈnɪm.bl̩.nəs/ *noun* [U]

nimbus /ˈnɪm.bəs/ *noun* [U] *SPECIALIZED* dark-grey cloud which often produces rain or snow ➲Compare **cirrus**; **cumulus**.

Nimby /ˈnɪm.bi/ *noun* [C] *ABBREVIATION FOR* not in my back yard: a person who does not want something unpleasant to be built or done near where they live: *The spokeswoman said that Nimby attitudes were delaying development of the site.* **nimbyism** /ˈnɪm.biː.ɪsm/ *noun* [U] *Residents were accused of nimbyism when they tried to stop the new superstore development.*

nincompoop /ˈnɪŋ.kəm.puːp/ *noun* [C] *INFORMAL* a foolish or stupid person

nine /naɪn/ *determiner, pronoun, noun* the number 9: *eight, nine, ten* ○ *a nine-month prison sentence* ○ *Tiago has nine cousins.* ○ *The birthday girl was wearing a badge with a nine on it.*

• **done/dressed (up) to the nines** *INFORMAL* wearing very stylish and fashionable clothes, often for a particular purpose or occasion: *The doorbell rang and there was Chris, all dressed up to the nines.*

• **be a nine days' wonder** *UK OLD-FASHIONED* to be a cause of great excitement or interest for a short time but then quickly forgotten

• **nine times out of ten** almost always: *Nine times out of ten, you can fix it.* ➲See also **ninety-nine times out of a hundred** at **ninety**.

• **nine to five** describing or relating to work that begins at nine o'clock in the morning and finishes at five, which are the hours worked in many offices from Monday to Friday: *a nine-to-five routine* ○ *She's tired of **working** nine to five.*

ninth /naɪntθ/ *determiner, pronoun, adj, adv, noun* 9th written as a word: *The ninth letter of the alphabet is I.* ○ *The school term ends on **the** ninth (of July).* ○ *She currently is/ranks ninth in the world.*

ninth /naɪntθ/ *noun* [C] one of nine equal parts of something: *A ninth of 27 is 3.*

ninepins /ˈnaɪn.pɪnz/ *plural noun UK* **go down/fall like ninepins** to fall, break or be damaged in large numbers: *Trees were going down like ninepins in the strong wind.*

nineteen /ˌnaɪnˈtiːn/ *determiner, pronoun, noun* the number 19: *eighteen, nineteen, twenty* ○ *They were trapped in the cave for nineteen hours.* ○ *Simson, aged nineteen, was convicted on two charges of burglary.*

nineteenth /ˌnaɪnˈtiːntθ/ *determiner, pronoun, adj, adv, noun* 19th written as a word

• **the nineteenth hole** *INFORMAL* the bar at a GOLF COURSE where people go to socialize after they have finished playing golf

ninety /ˈnaɪn.ti/ [US] /-t̬i/ *determiner, pronoun, noun* the number 90: *eighty, ninety, a hundred* ○ *Ninety percent of the people surveyed were in favour.* ○ *There were about ninety (people) at the party.*

• **ninety-nine times out of a hundred** almost always: *Ninety-nine times out of a hundred everything's fine, but now and then there's a problem.* ➲See also **nine times out of ten** at **nine**.

nineties /ˈnaɪn.tiz/ [US] /-t̬iz/ *plural noun* A person's nineties are the period in which they are aged between 90 and 99: *She was well **into** her nineties when she died.*

the nineties *plural noun* **1** the range of temperature between 90° and 99° Fahrenheit **2** the period of years between 90 and 99 in any century

ninetieth /ˈnaɪn.ti.əθ/ [US] /-t̬i-/ *determiner, pronoun, adj, adv, noun* 90th written as a word: *We're (lying) ninetieth in the competition so far.* ○ *Tomorrow is Aunt Elma's ninetieth (birthday).*

ninja /ˈnɪn.dʒə/ *noun* [C] a Japanese fighter, especially in the past, who moves and acts without being seen and usually carries a short sword

ninny /ˈnɪn.i/ *noun* [C] *OLD-FASHIONED INFORMAL* a foolish person

ninth /naɪntθ/ *pronoun, noun, adj, adv* ➲See at **nine**.

nip [GO QUICKLY] /nɪp/ *verb* [I usually + adv or prep] **-pp-** *UK INFORMAL* to go somewhere quickly or be somewhere for only a short time: *Can you nip **out/round/down** to the shop for me?* ○ *Shall we nip **in** to the cafe for a bite to eat?*

nippy /ˈnɪp.i/ *adj UK INFORMAL* able to change speed and direction easily: *a nippy little car*

nip [PRESS QUICKLY] /nɪp/ *verb* [I or T] **-pp-** to press something quickly and quite hard between two objects, especially sharp objects such as your teeth or nails: *Josie's hamster nipped me.* ○ *When he dropped the crate he nipped his hand.*

• **nip *sth* in the bud** to stop something before it has an opportunity to become established: *Many serious illnesses can be nipped in the bud if they are detected early enough.* ○ *It's important to nip this kind of bullying in the bud.*

nip /nɪp/ *noun* [C] when something nips a person or thing: *I gave my thumb quite a nip with the pliers.*

• **nip and tuck** *MAINLY US* If a competition is nip and tuck, first one side seems to be winning and then the other, so that the result in uncertain: *It was nip and tuck as to who would win the playoffs, but Denver's determination helped them to beat a tough Washington team.*

• **a nip (here) and a tuck (there)** **1** *US INFORMAL* a series of small reductions: *The department made a nip here and a tuck there, but they were still way over budget.* **2** *INFORMAL* **plastic surgery**: *I suspect she's had a nip and tuck to look like that at her age.*

nip [COLD] /nɪp/ *noun INFORMAL* **a nip (in the air)** If there is a nip in the air, the air outside is quite cold: *You can tell winter's on its way – there's a real nip in the air in the mornings.*

nippy /ˈnɪp.i/ *adj INFORMAL* describes weather or air that is quite cold: ***It's** a bit nippy today – you might need a coat.*

nip [DRINK] /nɪp/ *noun* [C] *UK INFORMAL* a small amount of strong alcoholic drink: *a nip of gin/brandy*

Nip [PERSON] /nɪp/ *noun* [C] *OFFENSIVE* a Japanese person

nipper /ˈnɪp.əʳ/ [US] /-ɚ/ *noun* [C] *INFORMAL* a young child

nipple /ˈnɪp.l̩/ *noun* [C] **1** the dark part of the skin which sticks out from the breast of a mammal and through which milk is supplied to the young **2** *US FOR* **teat** BOTTLE

nirvana /nɪəˈvɑː.nə/ [US] /nɚ-/ *noun* [U] **1** a high spiritual state of freedom from all suffering which Buddhists believe can be achieved by removing all personal desires **2** a state of perfection

Nissen hut /ˈnɪs.ənˌhʌt/ *noun* [C] a building shaped like a tube cut in half along the middle made from CORRUGATED iron sheets

nit [PERSON] /nɪt/ *noun* [C] *UK INFORMAL DISAPPROVING* a **nitwit**

nit [EGG] /nɪt/ *noun* [C usually pl] the egg of a LOUSE, which sticks to the fur of an animal or the hair of a person: *A few of the children have **got** nits.*

nite /naɪt/ *noun* [C] *NOT STANDARD FOR* **night**. This word is often used in advertisements.

nitpicking /ˈnɪtˌpɪk.ɪŋ/ *noun* [U] *INFORMAL DISAPPROVING* giving too much attention to unimportant details, especially as a way of criticizing: *If you spent less time nitpicking, you'd get more work done.* **nitpicking** /ˈnɪtˌpɪk.ɪŋ/ *adj*: *a nitpicking attitude*

nitpick /ˈnɪt.pɪk/ *verb* [I] *INFORMAL DISAPPROVING* *Must you nitpick* (= find fault with details) *all the time?* **nitpicker** /ˈnɪtˌpɪk.əʳ/ [US] /-ɚ/ *noun* [C]

nitrate /ˈnaɪ.treɪt/ *noun* [C or U] a chemical which includes NITROGEN and oxygen, often used as a FERTILIZER (= a substance that help plants grow): *potassium/sodium nitrate* ○ *Nitrogen is converted into nitrates in the soil which plants can then use.*

nitric acid /ˌnaɪ.trɪkˈæs.ɪd/ *noun* [U] a transparent colourless liquid which is used in making many chemicals, especially explosives and FERTILIZERS (= substances that help plants grow)

N

nitrogen /ˈnaɪ.trə.dʒən/ *noun* [U] a gas with no colour or taste which forms about 78% of the Earth's atmosphere and is a part of all things which live

nitroglycerine /ˌnaɪ.trəʊˈɡlɪs.ᵊr.iːn/ ⓤ /-troʊˈɡlɪs.ɚ-/ *noun* [U] (*US ALSO* **nitroglycerin**) a very powerful liquid explosive

the nitty-gritty /ðəˌnɪt.iˈɡrɪt.i/ ⓤ /-ˌnɪt.iˈɡrɪt̬-/ *noun* [S] *INFORMAL* the basic facts of a situation: *Let's get down to the nitty-gritty – when can you finish the building and how much will it cost?*

nitwit /ˈnɪt.wɪt/ *noun* [C] (*ALSO* **nit**) *INFORMAL DISAPPROVING* a foolish or stupid person

nix /nɪks/ *verb* [T] *US INFORMAL* to stop, forbid or refuse to accept something: *The film studio nixed her plans to make a sequel.*

nix /nɪks/ *noun* [U], *adv US INFORMAL* All that effort for nix (= nothing). ○ *I suppose mom will say nix to us going* (= say we cannot go) *to the movies.*

no NOT ANY /nəʊ/ ⓤ /noʊ/ *determiner* **1** not any; not one; not a: *There's no butter left.* ○ *There are no pockets in these trousers.* ○ *That's my kind of holiday – no telephone, no TV and no worries.* ○ *There's no chance* (= no possibility) *of us getting there by eight.* **2** used in signs and on notices to show that something is not allowed: *No smoking/fishing.*

• **there's no knowing/telling/saying** *INFORMAL* it is not possible to know what will happen: *She's very unpredictable so there's no knowing how she'll react to the news.*

no NEGATIVE ANSWER /nəʊ/ ⓤ /noʊ/ *adv* used to give negative answers: *"Did you go to the shops?" "No, I forgot."* ○ *"Would you like any more cake?" "No thank you."* ○ *"Have you got any homework tonight?" "No."*

no /nəʊ/ ⓤ /noʊ/ *noun* [C] *plural* **noes 1** a negative answer or reaction: *"Have you had any replies about the camping weekend?" "So far I've had two yeses, a no, and a maybe."* **2** a voter or a vote against a question which is being discussed: *14 ayes to 169 noes – the noes have it.* ➔Compare **aye**.

no NOT /nəʊ/ ⓤ /noʊ/ *adv* not; not any: *The exam is no more difficult than the tests you've been doing in class.* ○ *The issues are of no great interest* (= only a little interest) *to me.*

no. NUMBER, no *noun* [before n] *WRITTEN ABBREVIATION FOR* number: *Do you know the people who live at No. 17?* ○ *The answers to nos 13-20 are on page 21.*

• **No. 10** *WRITTEN ABBREVIATION FOR* **Number Ten**

no-account /ˈnəʊ.əˌkaʊnt/ ⓤ /noʊ-/ *adj* [before n] *US INFORMAL* describes a person of little use or importance: *She left her no-account second husband and moved to Oregon.*

Noah's ark /ˌnəʊ.əzˈɑːk/ ⓤ /ˌnoʊ.əzˈɑːrk/ *noun* ➔See **the ark**.

nob /nɒb/ ⓤ /nɑːb/ *noun* [C] *UK OLD-FASHIONED INFORMAL DISAPPROVING* a rich person whose family has been important for a long time

no-ball /ˌnəʊˈbɔːl/ ⓤ /ˌnoʊˈbɑːl/ *noun* [C] when the ball is BOWLED (= thrown) in cricket and some other games in a way which is not allowed by the rules

nobble CAUSE TO FAIL /ˈnɒb.l̩/ ⓤ /ˈnɑː-/ *verb* [T] *UK SLANG* to make something fail, especially to make a horse in a race fail by giving it drugs

nobble PERSUADE /ˈnɒb.l̩/ ⓤ /ˈnɑː-/ *verb* [T] *UK SLANG* to make someone do what you want them to do, especially using money, threats or other persuasion: *The jury who convicted him were suspected of being nobbled.*

nobble CATCH ATTENTION /ˈnɒb.l̩/ ⓤ /ˈnɑː-/ *verb* [T] *UK SLANG* to intentionally catch the attention of someone so that you can talk to them: *He nobbled her in the corridor to sign the invoice.*

Nobel prize /ˌnəʊ.belˈpraɪz/ ⓤ /ˌnoʊ-/ *noun* [C] any of the six international prizes which are given each year to people who make important discoveries or advances in chemistry, physics, medicine, literature, peace and ECONOMICS: *the Nobel prize for literature*

noble MORAL /ˈnəʊ.bl̩/ ⓤ /ˈnoʊ-/ *adj* moral in an honest, brave and not selfish way: *a noble gesture* ○ *His followers believe they are fighting for a noble cause.* **nobility** /nəʊˈbɪl.ɪ.ti/ ⓤ /noʊˈbɪl.ə.t̬i/ *noun* [U] *nobility of spirit/purpose* ➔See also **the nobility** at **noble** HIGH RANK;

nobility at **noble** ADMIRABLE. **nobly** /ˈnəʊ.bli/ ⓤ /ˈnoʊ-/ *adv*

noble HIGH RANK /ˈnəʊ.bl̩/ ⓤ /ˈnoʊ-/ *adj* belonging to a high social rank in a society, especially by birth: *a noble family*

noble /ˈnəʊ.bl̩/ ⓤ /ˈnoʊ-/ *noun* [C] a person of the highest social group in some countries

the noˈbility *group noun* [S] the people of the highest social rank in a society, considered as a group: *members of the nobility*

noble ADMIRABLE /ˈnəʊ.bl̩/ ⓤ /ˈnoʊ-/ *adj* admirable in appearance or quality: *a noble bearing/gesture* ○ *a building with a noble facade* **nobility** /nəʊˈbɪl.ɪ.ti/ ⓤ /noʊˈbɪl.ə.t̬i/ *noun* [U]

nobleman /ˈnəʊ.bl̩.mən/ ⓤ /ˈnoʊ-/ *noun* [C] a member of the NOBILITY (= the highest social rank in a society)

noblesse oblige /nəʊˌbles.əʊˈbliːʒ/ ⓤ /noʊˌbles.oʊ-/ *noun* [U] *FORMAL* the idea that someone with power and influence should use their social position to help other people

noblewoman /ˈnəʊ.bl̩ˌwʊm.ən/ ⓤ /ˈnoʊ-/ *noun* [C] a female member of the NOBILITY (= the highest social rank in a society)

nobody NO PERSON /ˈnəʊ.bə.di/ /-bɒd.i/ ⓤ /ˈnoʊ.bɑː.di/ *pronoun* (*ALSO* **no one**) not anyone: *Is there nobody here who can answer my question?* ○ *I saw nobody all morning.* ○ *Nobody agreed with me.*

nobody UNIMPORTANT PERSON /ˈnəʊ.bɒd.i/ ⓤ /ˈnoʊ.bɑː.di/ *noun* [C] someone who is completely unimportant: *He's just some nobody trying to get noticed by the press.*

no-brainer /ˌnəʊˈbreɪ.nər/ ⓤ /ˌnoʊˈbreɪ.nɚ/ *noun* [S] *SLANG* something that is very simple to do or to understand: *That last test question was a complete no-brainer.*

no-claims bonus /ˌnəʊˌkleɪmzˈbəʊ.nəs/ ⓤ /ˌnoʊ-ˈboʊ-/ *noun* [C] (*ALSO* **no-claims discount**) *UK* an amount subtracted from the money paid to an INSURANCE company, especially for motor vehicles, because no claims have been made for a particular period

nocturnal /nɒkˈtɜː.nəl/ ⓤ /nɑːkˈtɜː-/ *adj FORMAL* happening in or active during the night, or relating to the night: *nocturnal wanderings* ○ *nocturnal light* ○ *Most bats are nocturnal.* ➔Compare **diurnal**. **nocturnally** /nɒkˈtɜː.nə.li/ ⓤ /nɑːkˈtɜː-/ *adv*

nocturne /ˈnɒk.tɜːn/ ⓤ /ˈnɑːk.tɜːn/ *noun* [C] a gentle piece of classical music

nod /nɒd/ ⓤ /nɑːd/ *verb* [I or T] *-dd-* to move your head down and then up, sometimes repeatedly, especially to show agreement, approval or greeting or to show something by doing this: *Many people in the audience nodded in agreement.* ○ *When I suggested a walk, Elena nodded enthusiastically.* ○ *She looked up and nodded for me to come in.* ➔Compare **shake** MOVE. **nod** /nɒd/ ⓤ /nɑːd/ *noun* [C usually sing] *Chen gave her a nod of recognition across the crowded room.*

• **on the nod** *UK INFORMAL* If a suggestion is approved on the nod, it is accepted without discussion: *The new proposal went through on the nod.*

• **have a nodding acquaintance with sb/sth** to know someone slightly or have a slight knowledge of a subject: *She has only a nodding acquaintance with the issues involved.*

▲ **nod off** *phrasal verb INFORMAL* to begin sleeping, especially not intentionally: *After our busy day we both sat and nodded off in front of the TV.*

node LUMP /nəʊd/ ⓤ /noʊd/ *noun* [C] *SPECIALIZED* a lump or swelling on or in a living object: *a lymph node*

node JOIN /nəʊd/ ⓤ /noʊd/ *noun* [C] *SPECIALIZED* a place where things join, for example lines, or where a leaf and stem join on a plant: *a leaf node* **nodal** /ˈnəʊ.dᵊl/ ⓤ /ˈnoʊ-/ *adj: a nodal point*

nodule /ˈnɒd.juːl/ ⓤ /ˈnɑː.djuːl/ *noun* [C] *SPECIALIZED* a small lump or swelling: *There was a soft nodule on my vocal cord.* **nodular** /ˈnɒd.jʊ.lər/ ⓤ /ˈnɑː.dʒə.lɚ/ *adj*

Noel, Noël /nəʊˈel/ ⓤ /noʊ-/ *noun* [U] Christmas ∗ NOTE: This is mainly used in songs and written greetings.

noes /nəʊz/ ⓤ /noʊz/ *plural of* **no** NEGATIVE ANSWER

no-fault /ˌnəʊˈfɒlt/ ⓤ /ˌnoʊˈfɑːlt/ *adj* [before n] LEGAL describes an agreement or system in which blame can not have to be proved before action can be taken, especially before money can be paid: *a no-fault divorce* ○ *a no-fault compensation/insurance scheme*

no-fly zone /ˌnəʊˈflaɪˌzəʊn/ ⓤ /ˌnoʊˈflaɪˌzoʊn/ *noun* [C] an area above a country which aircraft from other countries may not enter without risking attack: *Aircraft will enforce the no-fly zone to protect UN forces on the ground.*

no-frills /ˌnəʊˈfrɪlz/ ⓤ /ˌnoʊ-/ *adj* [before n] describes a product or a service that is basic and has no luxuries or unnecessary details: *It's a no-frills shop supplying only basic goods at affordable prices.* ○ *a no-frills airline*

no-go area /ˌnəʊˈgəʊˌeə.ri.ə/ ⓤ /ˌnoʊˈgoʊˌer.i-/ *noun* [C] INFORMAL an area, especially in a town, where it is very dangerous to go, usually because a group of people who have weapons prevent the police, army and other people from entering

no-good /ˌnəʊˈgʊd/ ⓤ /ˌnoʊ-/ *adj* [before n] US SLANG DISAPPROVING describes someone who does nothing useful or helpful and is therefore considered to be of little value: *a no-good son of a bitch*

no-holds-barred /ˌnəʊ.həʊldzˈbɑːd/ ⓤ /ˌnoʊ.hoʊldzˈbɑːrd/ *adj* without any limits or controls: *a no-holds-barred interview/account* ○ *Mr. Nixon may well have had a no-holds-barred approach to dealing with political adversaries.*

no-hoper /ˌnəʊˈhəʊp.əʳ/ ⓤ /ˌnoʊˈhoʊ.pɚ/ *noun* [C] UK someone or something which will fail: *He's a real/total no-hoper – he'll never achieve anything.*

noise SOUND /nɔɪz/ *noun* [C or U] (a) sound, especially when it is unwanted, unpleasant or loud: *The noise out in the street was deafening.* ○ *I heard a loud noise and ran to the window.* ○ *traffic/background noise* ○ *dangerously high noise levels*
● **make a noise about sth** INFORMAL to talk about or complain about something a lot: *She's been making a lot of noise about moving to a new house.*
● **make noises** UK INFORMAL **1** to show what you think or feel by what you say, without stating it directly: *She made very positive noises at the interview about me getting the job.* **2** (ALSO **make a noise**) to complain or make trouble: *If things start going badly again, our members are sure to make noises.*
● **make (all) the right/correct, etc. noises** UK to show enthusiasm for something but sometimes not sincerely: *He made all the right noises about my audition but I couldn't tell if he was genuinely impressed.*
noisy /ˈnɔɪ.zi/ *adj* making a lot of noise: *a noisy crowd of fans* ○ *noisy neighbours* **noisily** /ˈnɔɪ.zɪ.li/ *adv*: *A motorbike started up noisily outside.* **noisiness** /ˈnɔɪ.zɪ.nəs/ *noun* [U]
noiseless /ˈnɔɪz.ləs/ *adj* silent: *Above them an eagle circled in noiseless flight.* **noiselessly** /ˈnɔɪz.lə.sli/ *adv*

noise SIGNAL /nɔɪz/ *noun* [U] SPECIALIZED any unwanted change in a signal, especially in a signal produced by an electronic device: *Using a single chip reduces (the) noise on the output signal by 90%.* **noisy** /ˈnɔɪ.zi/ *adj*: *a noisy signal*

noise pol‚lution *noun* [U] noise, such as that from traffic, which upsets people where they live or work and is considered to be unhealthy for them: *to tackle/ease/reduce noise pollution*

noisome /ˈnɔɪ.səm/ *adj* LITERARY very unpleasant and offensive: *a noisome stench*

nomad /ˈnəʊ.mæd/ ⓤ /ˈnoʊ-/ *noun* [C] a member of a group of people who move from one place to another rather than living in one place all of the time: *a tribe of Somalian desert nomads* **nomadic** /nəʊˈmæd.ɪk/ ⓤ /noʊ-/ *adj*: *nomadic people/herdsmen* ○ *a nomadic life/existence*

no-man's-land /ˈnəʊ.mænz.lænd/ ⓤ /ˈnoʊ-/ *noun* **1** [S or U] an area or strip of land which no one owns or controls such as a strip of land between two countries' borders, especially in a war: *to be lost/stranded/stuck in no-man's-land* ○ *They found themselves trapped in the no-man's-land between the two warring factions.* **2** [S] a situation or area of activity where there are no rules or which no one understands or controls because it belongs neither to one type nor another: *The families of people who die in custody are in a legal no-man's-land when they try to discover what went wrong.*

nom de plume /ˌnɒm.dəˈpluːm/ ⓤ /ˌnɑːm-/ *noun* [C] plural **noms de plume** a **pen name**

nomenclature /nəʊˈmeŋ.klə.tʃəʳ/ ⓤ /ˈnoʊ.men.kleɪ.tʃɚ/ *noun* [C or U] SPECIALIZED a system for naming things, especially in a particular area of science: *(the) nomenclature of organic chemicals*

nominal NOT IN REALITY /ˈnɒm.ɪ.nəl/ ⓤ /ˈnɑː.mə-/ *adj* in name or thought but not reality: *She's the nominal head of our college – the real work is done by her deputy.* **nominally** /ˈnɒm.ɪ.nə.li/ ⓤ /ˈnɑː.mə-/ *adv*: *The province is nominally independent.*

nominal SMALL /ˈnɒm.ɪ.nəl/ ⓤ /ˈnɑː.mə-/ *adj* describes a sum of money which is very small compared to an expected price or value: *a nominal sum/charge* ○ *For a nominal fee, they will deliver orders to customers' homes.*

nominate SUGGEST /ˈnɒm.ɪ.neɪt/ ⓤ /ˈnɑː.mə-/ *verb* [T] **1** to officially suggest someone for an election, job, position or honour: *He's been nominated by the Green Party as their candidate in the next election.* ○ *Would you like to nominate anyone for/as director?* **2** to state officially that a film, song, programme, etc. will be included in a competition for a prize: *The film was nominated for an Academy Award.*
nomination /ˌnɒm.ɪˈneɪ.ʃən/ ⓤ /ˌnɑː.mə-/ *noun* [C or U] *There have been two nominations* (= official suggestions) *of suitable people) for the new job.*
nominee /ˌnɒm.ɪˈniː/ ⓤ /ˌnɑː.mə-/ *noun* [C] someone who has been nominated for something: *All nominees for Treasurer will be considered.*

nominate CHOOSE /ˈnɒm.ɪ.neɪt/ ⓤ /ˈnɑː.mə-/ *verb* [T] to officially choose someone for a job or to do something: *She was nominated as the delegation's official interpreter.* ○ [+ to infinitive] *President Yeltsin nominated acting prime minister Sergei Kiriyenko to head the government.*
nomination /ˌnɒm.ɪˈneɪ.ʃən/ ⓤ /ˌnɑː.mə-/ *noun* [C or U] when someone is officially chosen for a job or position: *The nomination of Judge Watkins as head of the inquiry was a surprise.*
nominee /ˌnɒm.ɪˈniː/ ⓤ /ˌnɑː.mə-/ *noun* [C] a person who is officially chosen for a position or job

nominative /ˌnɒm.ɪ.nə.tɪv/ ⓤ /ˌnɑː.mə.nə.tɪv/ *noun, adj* SPECIALIZED (being) a particular form of a noun in particular languages showing the noun to be the subject of a verb

non- /nɒn-/ ⓤ /nɑːn-/ *prefix* used to add the meaning 'not' or 'the opposite of' to adjectives and nouns: *non-sexist* ○ *non-racist* ⊃ Compare **dis-; in-** LACKING; **un-**.

non-addictive /ˌnɒn.əˈdɪk.tɪv/ ⓤ /ˌnɑːn-/ *adj* describes a drug that does not make people who take it want habitually to take more of it

nonagenarian /ˌnɒn.ə.dʒəˈneə.ri.ən/ ⓤ /ˌnɑː.nə.dʒəˈner.i-/ *noun* [C] a person who is between 90 and 99 years old **nonagenarian** /ˌnɒn.ə.dʒəˈneə.ri.ən/ ⓤ /ˌnɑː.nə.dʒəˈner.i-/ *adj*

non-aggression /ˌnɒn.əˈgreʃ.ən/ ⓤ /ˌnɑːn-/ *noun* [U] FORMAL when countries or groups avoid fighting each other: *a non-aggression pact*

non-alcoholic /ˌnɒn.æl.kəˈhɒl.ɪk/ ⓤ /ˌnɑːn.ælkəˈhɑː.lɪk/ *adj* describes a drink that does not contain alcohol: *non-alcoholic beer*

non-aligned /ˌnɒn.əˈlaɪnd/ ⓤ /ˌnɑːn-/ *adj* If a country is non-aligned, it does not support or depend on any powerful country or group of countries.
non-alignment /ˌnɒn.əˈlaɪn.mənt/ ⓤ /ˌnɑːn-/ *noun* [U] the condition or principle of being non-aligned

non-believer /ˌnɒn.bɪˈliː.vəʳ/ ⓤ /ˌnɑːn.bɪˈliː.vɚ/ *noun* [C] a person who has no religious beliefs

non-bio /ˌnɒnˈbaɪ.əʊ/ ⓤ /ˌnɑːnˈbaɪ.oʊ/ *adj* (ALSO **non-biological**) UK describes a washing powder or liquid that does not contain ENZYMES (= special chemical substances) to help clean clothes

nonce word /ˈnɒnts.wɜːd/ ⓤ /ˈnɑːnts.wɜːrd/ *noun* [C] a word invented for a particular occasion or situation

nonchalant /ˈnɒn.tʃəl.ənt/ ⓤ /ˌnɑːn.ʃəˈlɑːnt/ *adj* behaving in a calm manner, often in a way which suggests lack of interest or care: *a nonchalant manner/shrug*

nonchalance /ˈnɒn.tʃəl.ə̩nts/ ⓤ /ˌnɑːn.ʃəˈlɑːnts/ *noun* [U]
nonchalantly /ˈnɒn.tʃ³l.³nt.li/ ⓤ /ˌnɑːn.ʃəˈlɑːnt-/ *adv*

non-combatant /ˌnɒnˈkɒm.bə.t³nt/ ⓤ /ˌnɑːn-
ˈkɑːm.bə.t³nt/ *noun* [C] a person, especially in the armed
forces, who does not fight in a war, for example a priest
or a doctor **non-combatant** /ˌnɒnˈkɒm.bə.t³nt/ ⓤ /ˌnɑːn-
ˈkɑːm.bə.t³nt/ *adj* [before n] *non-combatant troops/ships*

noncommittal /ˌnɒn.kəˈmɪt.³l/ ⓤ /ˌnɑːŋ.kəˈmɪt-/ *adj* not
expressing an opinion or decision: *The ambassador was
typically noncommittal when asked whether further sanctions would be introduced.* **noncommittally** /ˌnɒn.kə-
ˈmɪt.³l.i/ ⓤ /ˌnɑːn.kəˈmɪt-/ *adv*

non compos mentis /ˌnɒn.kɒm.pɒsˈmen.tɪs/ ⓤ /ˌnɑːn-
ˌkɑːm.poʊsˈmen-/ *adj* [after v] describes someone who is
unable to think clearly, especially because of mental illness, and therefore not responsible for their actions

nonconformist /ˌnɒn.kənˈfɔː.mɪst/ ⓤ /ˌnɑːn.kənˈfɔːr-/
noun [C] **1** someone who lives and thinks in a way which
is different from other people **2** a member of a Christian
group which is Protestant but does not belong to the
Church of England **nonconformist** /ˌnɒŋ.kənˈfɔː.mɪst/
ⓤ /ˌnɑːŋ.kənˈfɔːr-/ *adj*: *nonconformist behaviour* ○ *a Nonconformist minister* **nonconformity** /ˌnɒŋ.kənˈfɔː.mə.ti/
ⓤ /ˌnɑːŋ.kənˈfɔːr.mə.t̬i/ *noun* [U] (*ALSO* **nonconformism**) *Her
clothes were an immediate signal of her nonconformity.*

non-contributory /ˌnɒn.kənˈtrɪb.ju.tri/ ⓤ /ˌnɑːn.kən-
ˈtrɪb.jə.tɔːri/ *adj* describes a financial plan or agreement
for an employee which is completely paid for by their
employer: *a non-contributory insurance policy* ○ *a non-
contributory pension plan*

nondescript /ˈnɒn.dɪ.skrɪpt/ ⓤ /ˈnɑːn-/ *adj* very
ordinary, or having no interesting or exciting features
or qualities: *The meteorological bureau is in a nondescript building on the outskirts of town.*

none /nʌn/ *pronoun* not one (of a group of people or
things), or not any: *None of my children has/have blonde
hair.* ○ *"I'd like some more cheese." "I'm sorry there's none
left."* ○ *"Have you any idea how much this cost?" "None at
all/None whatsoever."* ○ *She went to the shop to get
some oranges but they had none.*
• **have none of** *sth FORMAL* to refuse to accept, agree with
or support something: *She tried to persuade him to retire,
but he would have none of it.*
• **none other than** *sb/sth FORMAL* said when you want to
show that someone or something is a surprising or
exciting choice or example: *The first speech was given by
none other than Clint Eastwood.*
• **none the worse/better/richer, etc.** not any worse/
better/richer, etc. than before: *Luckily, the horse seemed
none the worse for his fall.* ○ *Small investors like myself
are probably none the richer after handing over their
financial affairs to professional advisers.*
• **none too** *FORMAL* not very: *He seemed none too **happy,
pleased** at the prospect of meeting the family.*

nonentity /nɒnˈen.tɪ.ti/ ⓤ /ˌnɑːˈnen.t̬ə.t̬i/ *noun* **1** [C] *DIS-
APPROVING* a person without strong character, ideas or
influence: *She was once a political nonentity, but has
since won a formidable reputation as a determined
campaigner.* **2** [U] when something or someone is unknown because they lack any strong character, ideas or
influence: *This collection of essays is saved from nonentity by the stature of the contributors.*

nonetheless /ˌnʌn.ðəˈles/ *adv* (*ALSO* **nevertheless**)
despite what has just been said or done: *There are
serious problems in our country. Nonetheless, we feel this
is a good time to return.*

non-event /ˌnɒn.ɪˈvent/ ⓤ /ˌnɑːn-/ *noun* [C usually sing]
INFORMAL a disappointing occasion which was not interesting, especially one which was expected to be exciting
and important: *The party turned out to be a bit of a non-
event – hardly anybody turned up.*

non-existent /ˌnɒn.ɪɡˈzɪs.t³nt/ ⓤ /ˌnɑːn-/ *adj* describes
something that does not exist or is not present in a
particular place: *Government funding of alternative
health care is virtually non-existent.*

non-fat /ˌnɒnˈfæt/ ⓤ /ˌnɑːn-/ *adj* Non-fat food contains
no fat: *non-fat milk/yoghurt*

non-fiction /ˌnɒnˈfɪk.ʃ³n/ ⓤ /ˌnɑːn-/ *noun* [U] writing
that is about real events and facts, rather than stories

which have been invented ➔Compare **fiction**.

non-flammable /ˌnɒnˈflæm.ə.bl/ ⓤ /ˌnɑːn-/ *adj*
describes something that cannot burn or is very difficult
to burn ✶ NOTE: Do not confuse with *inflammable*. See note at **inflammable**.

nonintervention /ˌnɒn.ɪn.təˈven.tʃ³n/ ⓤ /ˌnɑːˌnɪn.t̬ər-/
noun [U] refusal to take part, especially in a disagreement between countries or within a country: *a policy of
nonintervention*

non-negotiable /ˌnɒn.nəˈɡəʊ.ʃə.bl/ ⓤ /ˌnɑːn.nə-
ˈɡoʊ.ʃi.ə-/ *adj* Something which is non-negotiable cannot
be changed by discussion: *The terms of this agreement
are non-negotiable.*

no-no /ˈnəʊ.nəʊ/ ⓤ /ˈnoʊ.noʊ/ *noun* [C usually sing] *INFORMAL*
something which is thought to be unsuitable or unacceptable: *Total nudity is still a definite no-no on most of
Europe's beaches.*

no-nonsense /ˌnəʊˈnɒn.s³nts/ ⓤ /ˌnoʊˈnɑːn.sents/ *adj*
[before n] practical and serious, and only interested in
doing what is necessary or achieving what is intended,
without silly ideas or methods: *a no-nonsense manner/
leader* ○ *a no-nonsense approach to child-rearing*

non-payment /ˌnɒnˈpeɪ.mənt/ ⓤ /ˌnɑːn-/ *noun* [U] a failure to pay money which is owed: *non-payment of taxes*

nonplussed /ˌnɒnˈplʌst/ ⓤ /ˌnɑːn-/ *adj* surprised, confused and not certain how to react: *I was completely nonplussed by his reply.*

non-profit(-making) /ˌnɒnˈprɒf.ɪt.meɪ.kɪŋ/ ⓤ /ˌnɑːn-
ˈprɑː-/ *adj* (*MAINLY US* **nonprofit**) describes an organization
which does not make a profit, usually intentionally:
*Charities are non-profit-making organizations and get
tax relief.*

non-proliferation /ˌnɒn.prə.lɪf.³rˈeɪ.ʃ³n/ ⓤ
/ˌnɑːn.prə.lɪf.əˈreɪ-/ *noun* [U] the limitation of the spread
and/or amount of something, especially nuclear or
chemical weapons: *a non-proliferation treaty*

non-resident /ˌnɒnˈrez.ɪ.d³nt/ ⓤ /ˌnɑːn-/ *noun* [C] a
person who is not staying or living in or at a place: *The
hotel bar is open to non-residents.* **non-resident** /ˌnɒn-
ˈrez.ɪ.d³nt/ ⓤ /ˌnɑːn-/ *adj*: *During the summer the town
has a large non-resident population of holidaymakers.*

non-returnable /ˌnɒn.rɪˈtɜː.nə.bl/ ⓤ /ˌnɑːn.rɪˈtɜː-/ *adj*
describes something which cannot be returned: *a non-
returnable deposit* ○ *These bottles are non-returnable* (=
cannot be taken back to a shop to be used again).

nonsense /ˈnɒn.s³nts/ ⓤ /ˈnɑːn.sents/ *noun* **1** [C or U] an
idea, something said or written, or behaviour that is
foolish or ridiculous: *This report is nonsense and nothing but a waste of paper.* ○ *The accusations are
(absolute/complete/utter) nonsense.* ○ *Nonsense/Don't
talk nonsense! She's far too ill to return to work!* ○ *You
mustn't upset your sister with any more nonsense about
ghosts.* ○ [+ to infinitive] *It's (a) nonsense to say that he's too
old for the job.* **2** [U] language which cannot be understood because it does not mean anything: *The translation of the instructions was so poor they were just nonsense.*
• **make (a) nonsense of** *sth UK* to make something appear
ridiculous or wrong, or to spoil something: *His repeated
lack of promotion makes nonsense of the theory that if you
work hard you'll be successful.*
• **not stand any nonsense** (*UK ALSO* **stand no nonsense**) to
refuse to accept bad or foolish behaviour: *The new
teacher won't stand any nonsense.*

nonsensical /ˌnɒnˈsent.sɪ.kl/ ⓤ /ˌnɑːn-/ *adj* foolish or
ridiculous: *It's nonsensical to blame all the world's
troubles on one man.* ○ *Their methods of assessment
produce nonsensical results.*

non sequitur /ˌnɒnˈsek.wɪ.təʳ/ ⓤ /ˌnɑːnˈsek.wɪ.t̬ɚ/ *noun*
[C] a statement which does not correctly follow from the
meaning of the previous statement

non-slip /ˌnɒnˈslɪp/ ⓤ /ˌnɑːn-/ *adj* designed to prevent
sliding, especially by being made of sticky material or
having a surface with a special TEXTURE: *a non-slip
surface/grip*

non-smoker /ˌnɒnˈsməʊ.kəʳ/ ⓤ /ˌnɑːnˈsmoʊ.kɚ/ *noun* [C]
a person who does not smoke

non-smoking /ˌnɒnˈsməʊ.kɪŋ/ ⓤ /ˌnɑːnˈsmoʊ-/ *adj* **1**
[before n] describes a person who does not smoke: *non-*

smoking passengers **2** (*ALSO* **no-smoking**) describes a place where people are not allowed to smoke: *Let's get a table in the no-smoking area.* ○ *a non-smoking flight/restaurant*

non-standard [NOT USUAL] /ˌnɒnˈstæn.dəd/ [US] /ˌnɑːnˈstæn.dɚd/ *adj* not normal or usual: *The keyboard was fitted with a non-standard plug.*

non-standard [LANGUAGE] /ˌnɒnˈstæn.dəd/ [US] /ˌnɑːnˈstæn.dɚd/ *adj* describes a word or phrase which is not considered correct by educated speakers of the language

non-starter /ˌnɒnˈstɑː.təʳ/ [US] /ˌnɑːnˈstɑːr.t̬ɚ/ *noun* [C] *INFORMAL* an idea, plan or person with no chance of success: *The proposal was a non-starter from the beginning because there was no possibility of funding.*

non-stick /ˌnɒnˈstɪk/ [US] /ˌnɑːn-/ *adj* describes a cooking pan or tool that has a special surface which prevents food from sticking to it: *a non-stick frying pan*

non-stop /ˌnɒnˈstɒp/ [US] /ˌnɑːnˈstɑːp/ *adj, adv* without stopping or without interruptions: *a non-stop flight* ○ *It felt like we travelled non-stop for the entire week.*

nonunion /ˌnɒnˈjuː.ni.ən/ [US] /ˌnɑːn-/ *adj* describes a company or organization that does not employ workers who belong to a union, or a person who does not belong to a union: *nonunion employers/employees*

non-verbal /ˌnɒnˈvɜː.bəl/ [US] /ˌnɑːnˈvɝː-/ *adj* not using spoken language: *Body language is a potent form of non-verbal* ***communication****.*

non-violence /ˌnɒnˈvaɪə.ləns/ [US] /ˌnɑːn-/ *noun* [U] when someone avoids fighting and physical force, especially when trying to make political change: *The Dalai Lama has always counselled non-violence.* **non-violent** /ˌnɒnˈvaɪə.lənt/ [US] /ˌnɑːn-/ *adj*: *Gandhi was an exponent of non-violent protest.*

non-white /ˌnɒnˈwaɪt/ [US] /ˌnɑːn-/ *noun* [C] *USUALLY OFFENSIVE* a person who is not white **non-white** /ˌnɒnˈwaɪt/ [US] /ˌnɑːn-/ *adj*

noodle /ˈnuː.dl̩z/ *noun* [C usually pl] a food in the form of long thin strips made from flour or rice, water and often egg, which you cook in boiling liquid: *egg/rice noodles* ○ *instant/crispy noodles* ○ *chicken noodle soup*

nook /nʊk/ *noun* [C] *LITERARY* a small space which is hidden or partly sheltered: *a cosy/sheltered/quiet nook*
- **every nook and cranny** every part of a place: *Every nook and cranny of the house was stuffed with souvenirs of their trips abroad.*

nooky, **nookie** /ˈnʊk.i/ *noun* [U] *SLANG* sex

noon /nuːn/ *noun* [U] twelve o'clock in the middle of the day, or about that time: *We used to ski before noon then take a long lunch.* ○ *By noon, we had had ten phone calls.*

ˈno ˌone *pronoun* (*ALSO* **nobody**) no person: *At first I thought there was no one in the room.* ○ *"Who was that on the phone?" "No one you would know."* ○ *I'd like to go to the concert but no one* ***else*** (= no other person) *wants to.* ○ *No-one told me she was ill.*

noose /nuːs/ *noun* **1** [C] one end of a rope tied to form a circle which can be tightened round something such as a person's neck to HANG (= kill) them: *They put him on the back of a horse and looped a noose around his neck.* **2** [S] a serious problem or limitation: *The noose of poverty was* ***tightening*** (= becoming more serious) *daily.*

nope /nəʊp/ [US] /noʊp/ *adv SLANG* no: *"Are you going out tonight?" "Nope."*

noplace /ˈnəʊ.pleɪs/ [US] /ˈnoʊ-/ *adv US INFORMAL FOR* **nowhere**: *Soon there would be noplace for them to go for help.*

nor /nɔːʳ/ [US] /nɔːr/ *conjunction* **1** used before the second or last of a set of negative possibilities, usually after 'neither': *We can neither change nor improve it.* ○ *Strangely, neither Carlo nor Juan saw what had happened.* **2** *MAINLY UK* neither: *"I've never been to Iceland." "Nor have I."* ○ *I can't be at the meeting and nor can Andrew.*

Nordic /ˈnɔː.dɪk/ [US] /ˈnɔːr-/ *adj* from or relating to the people of Scandinavia, Finland or Iceland: *He's a classic Nordic type – tall with blond hair and blue eyes.*

norm /nɔːm/ [US] /nɔːrm/ *noun* [C usually pl] **1** an accepted standard or a way of behaving or doing things that most people agree with: *Europe's varied cultural, political and ethical norms* ○ *accepted social norms* **2 the norm** a situation or type of behaviour that is expected and considered to be typical: *One child per family is fast becoming the norm in some countries.*

normal /ˈnɔː.məl/ [US] /ˈnɔːr-/ *adj* ordinary or usual; the same as would be expected: *a normal working day* ○ *Lively behaviour is normal for a four-year-old child.* ○ ***It's*** *normal for couples* ***to*** *argue now and then.* ○ *They were selling the goods at half the normal cost.* ○ *The temperature was* ***above/below*** *normal for the time of year.* ○ *Things are* ***back to*** *normal now that we've paid off all our debts.*

normality /nɔːˈmæl.ə.ti/ [US] /nɔːrˈmæl.ə.t̬i/ *noun* [U] (*US ALSO* **normalcy**) the state of being normal: *Now that the civil war is over, relative normality has returned to the south of the country.*

normalize, *UK USUALLY* **-ise** /ˈnɔː.mə.laɪz/ [US] /ˈnɔːr-/ *verb* [I or T] to return to the normal or usual situation: *They claim that the new drug normalizes blood pressure.* ○ *Relations between the two countries are gradually normalizing.*

normally /ˈnɔː.mə.li/ [US] /ˈnɔːr-/ *adv* **1** If you normally do something, you usually or regularly do it: *She doesn't normally arrive until ten.* ○ *Normally, I plan one or two days ahead.* **2** If something happens normally, it happens in the usual or expected way: *Is the phone working normally again?*

Norman /ˈnɔː.mən/ [US] /ˈnɔːr-/ *adj* belonging or relating to the people from northern France, especially those who INVADED (= used force to enter) England in 1066 and became its rulers, or to the buildings which were made during their rule: *the Norman invasion/conquest* ○ *a Norman castle/church/cathedral* **Norman** /ˈnɔː.mən/ [US] /ˈnɔːr-/ *noun* [C] *The Anglo-Saxons were defeated by the Normans.*

Norse /nɔːs/ [US] /nɔːrs/ *adj* belonging or relating to the people who lived in Scandinavia in the past, especially the VIKINGS: *Norse mythology* ○ *a Norse god/warrior*

north /nɔːθ/ [US] /nɔːrθ/ *noun* [U] **1** (*ALSO* **North**) (*WRITTEN ABBREVIATION* **N**, *UK ALSO* **Nth**, *US ALSO* **No**) the direction which goes towards the part of the Earth above the equator, opposite to the south, or the part of an area or country which is in this direction: *The points of the compass are North, South, East and West.* ○ *The countryside is more mountainous* ***in the*** *north* ***(of*** *the country).* ○ *Cambridge* ***is/lies to the*** *north* ***of*** *London.* ○ *a north-****facing*** *window* **2 the North** the rich industrial countries of the world, most of which are above the equator **3 the North** the northern states of the middle and eastern part of the US: *The North defeated the South in the American Civil War.*

north /nɔːθ/ [US] /nɔːrθ/ *adj* (*WRITTEN ABBREVIATION* **N**, *UK ALSO* **Nth**, *US ALSO* **No**) **1** (*ALSO* **North**) in or forming the north part of something: *North America/Africa* ○ *the north coast of Iceland* ○ *Our farm is a few miles north of the village.* **2 north wind** a wind coming from the north

north /nɔːθ/ [US] /nɔːrθ/ *adv* towards the north: *Go* ***due*** (= directly) *north for two miles.* ○ *The garden* ***faces*** *north and doesn't get much sun in winter.*
- **up north** *INFORMAL* to or in the north of the country or region: *I live in Cambridge, but my relatives live up north in Manchester.*
- **north of *sth*** used to say that an amount is more than the stated amount: *The share price is expected to rise north of $20.*

northbound /ˈnɔːθ.baʊnd/ [US] /ˈnɔːrθ-/ *adj, adv* going or leading towards the north: *northbound traffic* ○ *A 20-mile jam built up on the northbound lanes near Birmingham.*

northerly /ˈnɔː.ðəl.i/ [US] /ˈnɔːr.ðɚ.li/ *adj* **1** towards or in the north: *They walked in a northerly direction* (= towards the north) *across the desert.* ○ *There are plans to build a hotel on the most northerly* (= nearest the north) *point of the island.* **2 northerly wind** a wind that comes from the north

northern, **Northern** /ˈnɔː.ðən/ [US] /ˈnɔːr.ðɚn/ *adj* (*WRITTEN ABBREVIATION* **N**, *US ALSO* **No**) in or from the north part of an area: *northern Europe* ○ *the Northern Hemisphere*

northerner, **Northerner** /ˈnɔː.ðᵊn.ər/ ⓤⓈ /ˈnɔːr.ðɚ.nɚ/ *noun* [C] a person who comes from the north of a country

northernmost /ˈnɔː.ðᵊn.məʊst/ ⓤⓈ /ˈnɔːr.ðɚn.moʊst/ *adj* furthest towards the north of an area: *Cape Columbia is the northernmost **point** of Canada.*

northward /ˈnɔːθ.wəd/ ⓤⓈ /ˈnɔːrθ.wɚd/ *adv* (ALSO **northwards**) towards the north: *The dust from the volcano spread northward.* ○ *The plane turned northwards.* **northward** /ˈnɔːθ.wəd/ ⓤⓈ /ˈnɔːrθ.wɚd/ *adj*: *She cycled off in a northward **direction**.*

ˌ**North A'merica** *noun* [U] the continent that is to the north of South America, to the west of the Atlantic Ocean and to the east of the Pacific Ocean ˌ**North A'merican** *adj*

northeast /ˌnɔːθˈiːst/ ⓤⓈ /ˌnɔːrθ-/ *noun* [U] **1** (WRITTEN ABBREVIATION **NE**) the direction which is between north and east: *The wind is **in**/coming from **the** northeast.* **2 the Northeast** the area in the northeast of Britain or of another country: *She works in the Northeast.*

northeast /ˌnɔːθˈiːst/ ⓤⓈ /ˌnɔːrθ-/ *adj, adv* in or towards the northeast: *Go northeast for about five miles.* ○ *The town **is/lies** roughly northeast **of** here.*

northeast /ˌnɔːθˈiːst/ ⓤⓈ /ˌnɔːrθ-/ *adj* **northeast wind** a wind that comes from the northeast

northeasterly /ˌnɔːθˈiː.stə.li/ ⓤⓈ /ˌnɔːrˈθiː.stɚ-/ *adj* towards the northeast: *a northeasterly direction*

northeasterly (wind) /ˌnɔːθˈiː.stə.li/ ⓤⓈ /ˌnɔːrˈθiː.stɚ-/ *noun* [C] a wind that comes from the northeast

northeastern /ˌnɔːθˈiː.stᵊn/ ⓤⓈ /ˌnɔːrˈθiː.stɚn/ *adj* (WRITTEN ABBREVIATION **NE**) in or from the northeast: *the Northeastern states* ○ *Northeastern China*

northeastward /ˌnɔːθˈiːs.twəd/ ⓤⓈ /ˌnɔːrˈθiːs.twɚd/ *adv* (ALSO **northeastwards**) towards the northeast: *We travelled northeastwards for about 250 kilometres.* **northeastward** /ˌnɔːθˈiːs.twəd/ ⓤⓈ /ˌnɔːrˈθiːs.twɚd/ *adj*: *They went in a northeastward **direction**.*

the ˌ**Northern 'lights** *plural noun* the aurora borealis

the ˌ**North 'Pole** *noun* [S] the point on the Earth's surface which is furthest north

the ˌ**North-South divide** /ˌnɔːθˌsaʊθ.dɪˈvaɪd/ ⓤⓈ /ˌnɔːrθ-/ *noun* [U] **1** the difference in wealth between the rich countries of the world in the North and the poor countries in the South **2** in Britain, the difference in conditions, especially economic, between the poorer areas in the north and the richer areas in the south of the country

northwest /ˌnɔːθˈwest/ ⓤⓈ /ˌnɔːrθ-/ *noun* [U] **1** (WRITTEN ABBREVIATION **NW**) the direction which is between north and west: *The wind is coming from the northwest.* **2 the Northwest** the area in the northwest of Britain or of another country: *the Northwest of Australia* ○ *Most of the country's industry is in the Northwest.*

northwest /ˌnɔːθˈwest/ ⓤⓈ /ˌnɔːrθ-/ *adj, adv* in or towards the northwest: *the sale of the company's northwest division* ○ *Turn northwest.* ○ *The town **is/lies** about 100 miles northwest **of** Las Vegas.*

northwest /ˈnɔːθ.west/ ⓤⓈ /ˈnɔːrθ-/ *adj* **northwest wind** a wind that comes from the northwest

northwesterly /ˌnɔːθˈwes.tᵊl.i/ ⓤⓈ /ˌnɔːrθˈwes.tɚ.li/ *adj* towards the northwest: *a northwesterly direction* (= towards the northwest)

northwesterly (wind) /ˌnɔːθˈwes.tᵊl.i/ ⓤⓈ /ˌnɔːrθˈwes.tɚ.li/ *noun* [C] a wind that comes from the northwest

northwestern /ˌnɔːθˈwes.tᵊn/ ⓤⓈ /ˌnɔːrθˈwes.tɚn/ *adj* (WRITTEN ABBREVIATION **NW**) in or from the northwest: *northwestern Mexico*

northwestward /ˌnɔːθˈwes.twəd/ ⓤⓈ /ˌnɔːrθˈwes.twɚd/ *adv* (ALSO **northwestwards**) towards the northwest: *The road went northwestwards over the hills.* **northwestward** /ˌnɔːθˈwes.twəd/ ⓤⓈ /ˌnɔːrθˈwes.twɚd/ *adj*: *travelling in a northwestward direction*

Norwegian /nɔːˈwiː.dʒᵊn/ ⓤⓈ /nɔːr-/ *adj* from, belonging to or relating to Norway

Norwegian /nɔːˈwiː.dʒᵊn/ ⓤⓈ /nɔːr-/ *noun* **1** [C] a person from Norway **2** [U] the language of Norway

nos. *plural of* **no.**

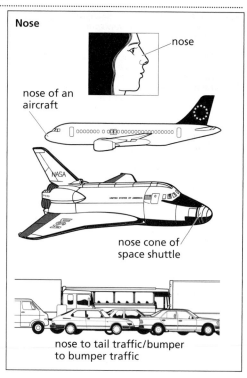

Nose

nose

nose of an aircraft

NASA

nose cone of space shuttle

nose to tail traffic/bumper to bumper traffic

nose BODY PART /nəʊz/ ⓤⓈ /noʊz/ *noun* [C] **1** the part of the face that sticks out above the mouth, through which you breathe and smell: *a large/long/pointed nose* ○ *I've got a sore throat and a **runny** nose* (= liquid coming out of the nose). ○ *Come on now, stop crying – **blow** your nose on my hankie.* ⊃See also **nosy**; **nasal**. ⊃See picture **The Body** on page Centre 5 **2** SPECIALIZED the particular smell of a wine: *a wine praised for its smoky nose*

• **get up** *sb's* **nose** MAINLY UK INFORMAL to annoy someone: *People who drive like that really get up my nose.*

• **have a (good) nose for** *sth* INFORMAL to be good at finding things of the stated type: *She's got a good nose for a bargain.* ○ *As a reporter, he had a nose for a good story.*

• **keep** *your* **nose clean** INFORMAL to avoid getting into trouble: *I'd only been out of prison three months so I was trying to keep my nose clean.*

• **keep** *your* **nose out of** *sth* INFORMAL to not become involved in other people's activities or relationships: *She can't keep her nose out of other people's business.*

• **keep/put** *your* **nose to the grindstone** INFORMAL to work very hard for a long time: *She kept her nose to the grindstone all year and got the exam results she wanted.*

• **nose in the air** describes the way someone behaves when they think they are better than other people and do not want to speak to them: *She walked past me **with** her nose in the air.*

• **have** *your* **nose in a book** to be continually reading: *She's always got her nose in a book.*

• **poke/stick** *your* **nose into** *sth* INFORMAL to try to discover things which are not really related to you: *I wish he'd stop poking his nose into my personal life!*

• **put** *sb's* **nose out of joint** INFORMAL to offend or upset someone, especially by getting something that they were wanting for themselves: *John's nose was really put out of joint when Jane was promoted and he wasn't.*

• **(from) under** *your* **nose** (US ALSO **(out from) under** *your* **nose**) used about something bad which happens in an obvious way but in a way that you do not notice or cannot prevent: *She stole the shoes from right under the assistant's nose.*

• **be (right) under** *your* **nose** to be in a place that you can clearly see: *I spent ages looking for the book and it was right under my nose all the time.* ○ *She shoved the letter* *under her boss's nose* (= made certain he saw it).

-nosed /-nəʊzd/ [US] /-noʊzd/ *suffix* having a nose of the type mentioned: *sharp/snub/hook-nosed* ➲See also **-nosed** at **nose** VEHICLE.

nose [VEHICLE] /nəʊz/ [US] /noʊz/ *noun* [C] the front of a vehicle, especially an aircraft: *The symbol was painted on each side of the plane's nose.*

• **nose to tail** one closely behind the other: *The cars were parked nose to tail down the street.*

nose /nəʊz/ [US] /noʊz/ *verb* [I or T; + adv or prep] to (make a vehicle) move forwards slowly and carefully: *The car nosed **out** of the side street, its driver peering anxiously around.* ○ *He carefully nosed his lorry **into** the small gap.* ➲See also **nose *sth* out**. **-nosed** /-nəʊzd/ [US] /-noʊzd/ *suffix*: *a blunt-nosed missile* ➲See also **-nosed** at **nose** BODY PART.

nose [SEARCH] /nəʊz/ [US] /noʊz/ *verb* [I usually + adv or prep] *INFORMAL* to look around or search in order to discover something, especially something that other people do not want you to find: *There were some journalists nosing **about/around**.* ○ *The police came in and started nosing **into** drawers and looking through papers.*

▲ **nose *sth* out** *phrasal verb* [M] *INFORMAL* to discover something by searching carefully: *He soon nosed out the details of the accident by chatting innocently to people and making some phone calls.*

nosebag /ˈnəʊz.bæg/ [US] /ˈnoʊz-/ *noun* [C] (*US* **feedbag**) a bag for holding food which is hung around a horse's head

nosebleed /ˈnəʊz.bliːd/ [US] /ˈnoʊz-/ *noun* [C] when blood comes out of a person's nose: *She **gets/has** a lot of nosebleeds.*

ˈnose ˌcone *noun* [C] the front part of a spacecraft, aircraft or missile

nosedive /ˈnəʊz.daɪv/ [US] /ˈnoʊz-/ *noun* [C usually sing] **1** a fast and sudden fall to the ground with the front pointing down: *The plane roared overhead and **went into** a nosedive.* **2** a sudden fast fall in prices, value, etc: *There was alarm in the markets when the dollar **took** a nosedive.* **nosedive** /ˈnəʊz.daɪv/ [US] /ˈnoʊz-/ *verb* [I] *Spectators in the crowd watched in horror as the plane nosedived.* ○ *House prices nosedived without warning.*

ˈnose ˌjob *noun INFORMAL* **have a nose job** to have an operation to change the shape of your nose

nosh /nɒʃ/ [US] /nɑːʃ/ *noun* **1** [C or U] *UK OLD-FASHIONED SLANG* food or a meal: *They serve good nosh in the cafeteria.* **2** [U] *US INFORMAL* a small amount of food eaten between meals or as a meal: *I'll just have a little nosh at lunchtime, perhaps a hot dog.*

nosh /nɒʃ/ [US] /nɑːʃ/ *verb* [I] *INFORMAL* to eat: *US We noshed **on** a burger before the match.*

no-show /ˌnəʊˈʃəʊ/ [US] /ˌnoʊˈʃoʊ/ *noun* [C] a person who is expected but does not arrive: *Two important witnesses were no-shows.* ○ *a no-show passenger*

nosh-up /ˈnɒʃ.ʌp/ [US] /ˈnɑːʃ-/ *noun* [C] *UK INFORMAL* a big enjoyable meal: *We had some good nosh-ups on holiday.*

nostalgia /nɒsˈtæl.dʒə/ [US] /nɑːˈstæl-/ *noun* [U] a feeling of pleasure and sometimes slight sadness at the same time as you think about things that happened in the past: *Some people feel nostalgia **for** their schooldays.* ○ *Hearing that tune again **filled** him **with** nostalgia.* ○ *a **wave*** (= sudden strong feeling) ***of** nostalgia* **nostalgic** /nɒsˈtæl.dʒɪk/ [US] /nɑːˈstæl-/ *adj*: *Talking about our old family holidays has made me feel quite nostalgic.* ○ *We'll take a nostalgic look at the musical hits of the '60s.* **nostalgically** /nɒsˈtæl.dʒɪ.kli/ [US] /nɑːˈstæl-/ *adv*: *to look back/talk/think nostalgically*

nostril /ˈnɒs.trəl/ [US] /ˈnɑː.strəl/ *noun* [C] either of the two openings in the nose through which air moves when you breathe: *The horses came to a halt, steam streaming from their nostrils.* ➲See picture **The Body** on page Centre 5

nosy (nosier, nosiest), **nosey** /ˈnəʊ.zi/ [US] /ˈnoʊ-/ *adj DISAPPROVING* too interested in what other people are doing and wanting to discover too much about them: *She was complaining about her nosy parents.* **nosily** /ˈnəʊ.zɪ.li/ [US] /ˈnoʊ-/ *adv*: *"Who was that on the phone?" she asked nosily.* **nosiness** /ˈnəʊ.zɪ.nəs/ [US] /ˈnoʊ-/ *noun* [U]

nosy parker /ˌnəʊ.ziˈpɑː.kəʳ/ [US] /ˌnoʊ.ziˈpɑːr.kɚ/ *noun* [C] *INFORMAL* a person who is nosy

not /nɒt/ [US] /nɑːt/ *adv* **1** used to form a negative phrase after verbs like 'be', 'can', 'have', 'will', 'must', etc. usually used in the short form 'n't' in speech: *He's not fat!* ○ *I won't tell her.* ○ *I can't go.* ○ *Don't you like her?* ○ *It isn't difficult* (= It is easy). ○ *I'm just not interested.* ○ *He's not bad-looking* (= He is quite attractive)*!* ○ *He's not **as** tall as his father.* **2** used to give the next word or group of words a negative meaning: *I told you not to do that.* ○ *I like most vegetables but not cabbage.* ○ *"Come and play football, Dad" "Not now, Jamie."* ○ *It was Yuko who said that, not Richard.* **3** used after verbs like 'be afraid', 'hope', 'suspect', etc. in short, negative replies: *"Is he coming with us?" "I hope not."* ○ *"Have you finished?" "I'm afraid not."* **4** *HUMOROUS* sometimes used at the end of a statement to show that you did not mean what you have said: *That was the best meal I've ever had – not!* **5 if not** used to say what the situation will be if something does not happen: *I hope to see you there but, if not, I'll call you.* **6 or not** used to express the possibility that something might not happen: *Are you going to reply or not?* ○ *I still don't know whether she's coming or not.*

• **not at all 1** used as a polite reply after someone has thanked you: *"Thanks for helping." "Not at all."* **2** used to say 'no' or 'not' strongly: *"Was he a nuisance?" "No, not at all."* ○ *I'm not at all happy about it.*

• **not that 1** used to say you are not suggesting something: *She wouldn't tell me how much it cost – not that I was really interested.* **2** used to say you do not think something is important: *Not that I mind, but why didn't you phone yesterday?*

• **not all that** *INFORMAL* not very: *I'm not all that keen on swimming.*

• **not be up to much** *INFORMAL* to not be of good quality: *The food wasn't up to much.*

COMMON LEARNER ERROR

not...either

The words **not** ... **either** are used to add another piece of negative information.

I'd forgotten my credit card and I didn't have any cash either.
~~*I'd forgotten my credit card and I didn't have any cash neither.*~~
Helen didn't enjoy it either.
~~*Helen didn't enjoy it too.*~~

notable /ˈnəʊ.tə.bl̩/ [US] /ˈnoʊ.t̬ə-/ *adj* important and deserving attention, because very good or interesting: *a notable collection of rare plants* ○ *Getting both sides to agree was a notable achievement.* ○ *This attractive building is particularly notable **for** its garden setting.*

notable /ˈnəʊ.tə.bl̩/ [US] /ˈnoʊ.t̬ə-/ *noun* [C] *LITERARY* an important or famous person: *Other notables among his pupils were the kings of Saudi Arabia and Thailand.*

notably /ˈnəʊ.tə.bli/ [US] /ˈnoʊ.t̬ə-/ *adv* **1** particularly or most importantly: *They have begun attracting investors, most notably big Japanese financial houses.* **2** to an important degree, or in a way which can or should be noticed: *The newspapers are notably biased.*

notarize /ˈnəʊ.tər.aɪz/ [US] /ˈnoʊ.t̬ə.raɪz/ *verb* [T] *US* If a letter or other document is notarized, it is marked by a NOTARY PUBLIC (= a person whose job is to mark documents to make them official): *a notarized affidavit* ○ *The airline requires children travelling alone to have a notarized letter of consent from one or both parents.*

notary (public) /ˌnəʊ.tər.iˈpʌb.lɪk/ [US] /ˌnoʊ.t̬ɚ-/ *noun* [C] *LEGAL* an official who has the legal authority to say that documents are correctly signed or truthful or to make an OATH (= promise) official: *This agreement was drawn up and verified by a notary.*

notation /nəʊˈteɪ.ʃən/ [US] /noʊ-/ *noun* [C or U] a system of written symbols used especially in mathematics or to represent musical notes: *musical/scientific notation* ○ *Did you write things out in **standard** notation?*

notch [CUT] /nɒtʃ/ [US] /nɑːtʃ/ *noun* [C] a V-shaped cut in a hard surface: *The stick has two notches, one at each end.*

notch /nɒtʃ/ [US] /nɑːtʃ/ *verb* [T] to cut a notch in something

N

notch POSITION /nɒtʃ/ ⓤ /nɑːtʃ/ *noun* [C] an imaginary point or position in a system of comparing values, where a higher position is better and a lower position is worse: *Among current players, she is rated a notch **above*** (= is better than) *the rest.*

▲ **notch sth up** *phrasal verb* [M] *INFORMAL* to achieve something: *She has recently notched up her third win at a major tennis tournament.*

note WRITING /nəʊt/ ⓤ /noʊt/ *noun* [C] **1** a short piece of writing: *He left a note to say he would be home late.* ○ *There's a note pinned to the door saying when the shop will open again.* **2** a short explanation or an extra piece of information that is given at the bottom of a page, at the back of a book or on the cover for a piece of recorded music, etc: *For a further explanation see Note 3.* ⊃See also **footnote.**

● **make/take a note** to write something down or remember it carefully: *I'll just take a note **of** your name and address.* ○ *She made a **mental** note **of** the title.* ○ *Make a note to phone again next week.*

notes /nəʊts/ ⓤ /noʊts/ *plural noun* information written on paper: *The wind blew my notes all over the room.* ○ *The journalist **took** notes throughout the interview.*

note SOUND /nəʊt/ ⓤ /noʊt/ *noun* **1** [C] a single sound at a particular level, usually in music, or a written symbol which represents this sound: *high/low notes* ○ *She played three long notes on the piano.* ○ *The engine noise suddenly **changed** its note and rose to a whine.* **2** [S] an emotion or a way of expressing something: *There was **a** note of caution in her letter.* ○ *His speech **struck** just the right note.* ○ *The meeting ended on an optimistic note.*

note MONEY *MAINLY UK* /nəʊt/ ⓤ /noʊt/ *noun* [C] (*US USUALLY* **bill**) a piece of paper money: *a £20 note* ○ *He took a wad of notes from his pocket.*

note NOTICE /nəʊt/ ⓤ /noʊt/ *verb* [T] *SLIGHTLY FORMAL* **1** to notice something: *They noted the consumers' growing demand for quicker service.* ○ [+ (**that**)] *Please note **(that)** we will be closed on Saturday.* ○ [+ question word] *Note how easy it is to release the catch quickly.* **2** to give your attention to something by discussing it or making a written record of it: [+ **that**] *He said the weather was beyond our control, noting **that** last summer was one of the hottest on record.* ○ *In the article, she notes several cases of medical incompetence.*

note /nəʊt/ ⓤ /noʊt/ *noun* [U] *FORMAL* importance, or when something deserves attention: *There was nothing of note in the latest report.*

● **take note of sth** to give attention to something, especially because it is important: *You should take careful note of what she tells you because she knows their strategy well.*

noted /ˈnəʊ.tɪd/ ⓤ /ˈnoʊ.t̬ɪd/ *adj* known by many people, especially because of particular qualities: *Summerhill school is noted **for** its progressive policies.* ○ *She's not noted **for** her patience* (= She is not a patient person).

▲ **note sth down** *phrasal verb* to write something so that you do not forget it: *I noted down his phone number.*

notebook /ˈnəʊt.bʊk/ ⓤ /ˈnoʊt-/ *noun* [C] a book of plain paper or paper with lines, for writing on: *She was jotting things down in a little notebook.*

notebook (com'puter) *noun* [C] a very small computer which you can carry easily ⊃See also **laptop (computer); palmtop (computer).**

notelet /ˈnəʊt.lət/ ⓤ /ˈnoʊt-/ *noun* [C] *UK* a small folded sheet of paper or card, usually with a picture on the front, inside which you write a short letter: *a box of notelets*

notepad /ˈnəʊt.pæd/ ⓤ /ˈnoʊt-/ *noun* [C] a set of sheets of plain or lined paper, joined at the top edge, for writing on: *a plain/ruled notepad* ○ *a reporter's notepad*

notepad (com'puter) *noun* [C] a very small computer which you can carry easily

notepaper /ˈnəʊtˌpeɪ.pər/ ⓤ /ˈnoʊtˌpeɪ.pɚ/ *noun* [U] plain paper for writing letters on: *three sheets/pieces of notepaper* ○ *headed notepaper*

noteworthy /ˈnəʊtˌwɜː.ði/ ⓤ /ˈnoʊtˌwɝː-/ *adj* *SLIGHTLY FORMAL* deserving attention because important or interesting: *a noteworthy example/event* ○ *It is noteworthy **that** one-third of students do not pay any tuition fees.*

○ *King Darius I is noteworthy **for** his administrative reforms, military conquests, and religious toleration.*

nothing /ˈnʌθ.ɪŋ/ *pronoun* not anything: *There's nothing in the drawer – I took everything out.* ○ *Nothing I could say would cheer her up.* ○ *I have nothing new to tell you.* ○ *There's nothing **else*** (= no other thing) *we can do to help.* ○ *There's nothing **much*** (= not very much) *to do in our village.* ○ *The story was nothing **but*** (= only) *lies.* ○ *US The score is Yankees three, Red Sox nothing* (= no points).

● **all or nothing** relates to doing something either completely or not at all: *She either loves you or hates you – it's all or nothing with her.* ○ *The Government has rejected the all-or-nothing **approach** in favour of a compromise solution.*

● **be/mean nothing** to have no importance or value: *Money is nothing **to** him.*

● **it is/was nothing** *INFORMAL* used to tell someone not to worry about, or place special value on, what you are doing or have done: *"You seem very upset." "No, no, it's nothing, I'm OK."* ○ *"It was very kind of you to look after the baby all day." "Oh, it was nothing, I enjoyed it."*

● **be nothing for it** to be nothing else you can do to solve the problem: *There's nothing for it **but to** get some extra help.*

● **be nothing if not generous/honest/thorough, etc.** used to emphasize that someone or something is extremely generous/honest/thorough, etc: *He's nothing if not charming.*

● **there's nothing in sth** used for saying that something you have been told is not true: *I heard a rumour that she's leaving, but apparently there's nothing in it.*

● **be nothing less than sth** used to emphasize how important, special or desirable something is: *Their dream to bring computers and ordinary people together was nothing less than revolutionary.*

● **be/have nothing to do with sb/sth** to have no connection or influence with someone or something: *We are nothing to do with the firm which has the offices next door.* ○ *In the evening he likes to read books and articles which have/are nothing to do with his work.*

● **be/have nothing to do with sb** to be a matter or subject which someone has no good reason to know about or be involved with: *I wish he wouldn't offer advice on my marriage – it's nothing to do with him.*

● **be nothing to it** used to say that something is very easy: *Windsurfing is easy – there's nothing to it.*

● **for nothing 1** free or without paying: *I got this picture for nothing from a friend.* **2** with no good result or for no purpose: *He queued for two hours and **(all)** for nothing – there were no seats left.* ○ *Let us make sure that these brave men did not die for nothing.*

● **like nothing on earth** *INFORMAL* very strange, unusual or unpleasant in appearance, sound or taste: *It looked nice, but it tasted like nothing on earth.*

● **nothing doing** *INFORMAL* used to mean 'no', especially when said in answer to a request: *We asked if she'd come over and help us, but she said, "Nothing doing".*

● **nothing more than** *DISAPPROVING* only: *He dismissed Bryan as nothing more than an amateur.*

● **nothing of the sort/kind** used to emphasize a negative statement: *I told him nothing of the sort* (= I did not tell him anything like that).

● **nothing on 1** no clothes on your body: *She sleeps **with** nothing on.* ○ *I couldn't come to the door – I **had** nothing on!* **2** no arrangements for a stated period: *I've looked in her diary and she **has** nothing on on Tuesday afternoon.* ○ *There's nothing on next Friday – we could hold the meeting then.*

nothing /ˈnʌθ.ɪŋ/ *noun* [C] *INFORMAL* someone of no value or importance: *He's a nothing, a low-down, useless nobody.*

nothing /ˈnʌθ.ɪŋ/ *adv* in no way: *MAINLY UK He had two letters of refusal but, nothing **daunted*** (= not discouraged), *he tried again.*

● **be nothing short of...** used to emphasize a bad situation, quality or type of behaviour: *The party was nothing short of a disaster.* ○ *His behaviour was nothing short of rude.*

• **be nothing special** to not be excellent or not be beautiful: *She's nothing special.*

nothingness /ˈnʌθ.ɪŋ.nəs/ *noun* [U] a state where nothing is present, or where nothing exists that is important or gives meaning to life

notice [SEE] /ˈnəʊ.tɪs/ [US] /ˈnoʊ.t̬ɪs/ *verb* [I or T] to see or become aware of something or someone: *I noticed a crack in the ceiling.* ○ *Mary waved at the man but he didn't seem to notice.* ○ [+ (that)] *He noticed* ***(that)*** *the woman was staring at him.* ○ [+ question word] *Did you notice* ***how*** *she did that?*

notice /ˈnəʊ.tɪs/ [US] /ˈnoʊ.t̬ɪs/ *noun* [U] attention: *It has* ***come to/been brought to*** *my notice* (= I have been told) *that you have been late for work every day this week.*

• **take notice** to give attention to something: *I asked him to drive more slowly, but he didn't take any notice.* ○ *Don't take any notice of/Take no notice of what your mother says – she's just in a bad mood.*

noticeable /ˈnəʊ.tɪ.sə.bl̩/ [US] /ˈnoʊ.t̬ɪ-/ *adj* easy to see or recognize: *There has been a noticeable improvement in Tim's cooking.*

noticeably /ˈnəʊ.tɪ.sə.bli/ [US] /ˈnoʊ.t̬ɪ-/ *adv*: *Fiona had become noticeably thinner* (= so much thinner that it was easy to see).

notice [INFORMATION] /ˈnəʊ.tɪs/ [US] /ˈnoʊ.t̬ɪs/ *noun* **1** [C] (a board, piece of paper, etc. containing) information or instructions: *There was a large notice on the wall saying 'No Parking'.* ○ *I saw a notice in the paper announcing their marriage.* **2** [U] information or a warning given in advance about something that is going to happen in the future: *The next time you visit, can you* ***give*** *me more notice?* ○ *The emergency services are ready to spring into action* ***at a moment's*** *notice.* ○ *The building is closed* ***until further*** *notice* (= until another official announcement is made).

• **at short notice** *UK* (*US* **on short notice**) only a short time before something happens: *I can't cancel my arrangements at such short notice.*

• **give *sb* notice** to ask someone who works for you to leave their job, usually after a particular period of time: *My boss gave me a month's notice.*

• **hand/give in *your* notice** to tell your employer that you intend to leave your job after a particular period of time: *I handed in my notice yesterday.*

notices /ˈnəʊ.tɪ.sɪz/ [US] /ˈnoʊ.t̬ɪ-/ *plural noun* printed statements of opinion in the newspapers about plays, films, books, etc: *The musical has received wonderful notices.*

noticeboard *UK* /ˈnəʊ.tɪs.bɔːd/ [US] /ˈnoʊ.t̬ɪs.bɔːrd/ *noun* [C] (*US* **bulletin board**) a board on a wall on which notices can be fixed: *I've put the list of players up on the noticeboard.* ➲See picture **In the Office** on page Centre 15

notify /ˈnəʊ.tɪ.faɪ/ [US] /ˈnoʊ.t̬ə-/ *verb* [T] to tell someone officially about something: *The school is required to notify parents if their children fail to come to school.* ○ *Has everyone been notified* ***of*** *the decision?* ○ [+ that] *We notified the police* ***that*** *the bicycle had been stolen.*

notifiable /ˈnəʊ.tɪ.faɪ.ə.bl̩/ [US] /ˈnoʊ.t̬ə-/ *adj* describes a disease or offence that must be reported to the authorities: *If the animals have died from a notifiable* ***disease****, their bodies must be burnt.*

notification /ˌnəʊ.tɪ.fɪˈkeɪ.ʃən/ [US] /ˌnoʊ.t̬ə-/ *noun* [C or U] when you tell someone officially about something, or a document which does this: *You must give the bank (a) written notification if you wish to close your account.*

notion /ˈnəʊ.ʃən/ [US] /ˈnoʊ-/ *noun* [C or U] (a) belief or idea: [+ that] *The programme makers reject the notion* ***that*** *seeing violence on television has a harmful effect on children.* ○ *I have only a* ***vague*** *notion* ***of*** *what she does for a living.*

• **have/take a notion to *do sth*** *OLD-FASHIONED* to suddenly want to do something: *I had a notion to write them a letter.*

notional /ˈnəʊ.ʃən.əl/ [US] /ˈnoʊ-/ *adj FORMAL* existing only as an idea, not in reality: *Almost everyone will have to pay a higher tax bill than the notional amount suggested by the Government.*

notorious /nəʊˈtɔː.ri.əs/ [US] /noʊˈtɔːr.i-/ *adj* famous for something bad: *one of Britain's most notorious criminals* ○ *The company is notorious* ***for*** *paying its bills late.*

notoriously /nəʊˈtɔː.ri.ə.sli/ [US] /noʊˈtɔːr.i-/ *adv*: *The crime of rape is notoriously* (= famous as being) ***difficult*** *to prove.*

notoriety /ˌnəʊ.təˈraɪ.ə.ti/ [US] /ˌnoʊ.t̬əˈraɪ.ə.t̬i/ *noun* [U] the state of being famous for something bad: *He* ***achieved/gained*** *notoriety* ***for*** *murdering eleven women in the north of England.*

notwithstanding /ˌnɒt.wɪðˈstæn.dɪŋ/ [US] /ˌnɑːt-/ *prep, adv FORMAL* despite the fact or thing mentioned: *Notwithstanding some members' objections, I think we must go ahead with the plan.* ○ *Injuries notwithstanding, he won the semi-final match.*

nougat /ˈnuː.gɑː/ [US] /ˈnuː.gət/ *noun* [U] a hard chewy white or pink sweet food, usually containing nuts

nought [ZERO] *MAINLY UK* /nɔːt/ [US] /nɑːt/ *noun* [C] (*US USUALLY* **naught**) the number 0 or zero: *He said it was only worth £10, but really you could add a couple of noughts to that* (= it is really worth £1000).

nought [NOTHING] /nɔːt/ [US] /nɑːt/ *noun* [U] **naught** NOTHING

ˌnoughts and ˈcrosses *noun* [U] (*US* **tick-tack-toe**) *UK* a game played on a piece of paper in which two players write either O or X in a pattern of nine squares, which is won by the first player who places three noughts or three crosses in a straight line

noun /naʊn/ *noun* [C] a word that refers to a person, place, thing, event, substance or quality: *'Doctor', 'tree', 'party', 'coal' and 'beauty' are all nouns.*

ˈnoun ˌphrase *noun* [C] a group of words in a sentence which together behave as a noun: *In the sentences 'We took the night train' and 'Do you know the man sitting in the corner', 'the night train' and 'the man sitting in the corner' are noun phrases.*

nourish /ˈnʌr.ɪʃ/ [US] /ˈnɝː-/ *verb* [T] **1** to provide people or living things with food in order to make them grow and keep them healthy: *Children need plenty of good fresh food to nourish them.* ○ *She looks happy and well nourished.* ○ *This cream is supposed to help nourish your skin.* **2** *FORMAL* If you nourish a feeling, belief or plan, you think about it a lot and encourage it: *Lisa has long nourished the hope of becoming a famous writer.*

nourishing /ˈnʌr.ɪ.ʃɪŋ/ [US] /ˈnɝː-/ *adj* A nourishing drink or food makes you healthy and strong: *Sweets aren't very nourishing.*

nourishment /ˈnʌr.ɪʃ.mənt/ [US] /ˈnɝː-/ *noun* [U] *Young babies obtain all the nourishment* (= food to make them healthy) *they need from their mother's milk.*

nous /naʊs/ *noun* [U] *UK INFORMAL* good judgment and practical ability: *Anyone with a bit of nous would have known what to do.*

nouveau riche /ˌnuː.vəʊˈriːʃ/ [US] /-voʊ-/ *adj DISAPPROVING* describes people from a low social class who have recently become very rich and like to show their wealth publicly by spending a lot of money **the nouveau riche** /ðəˌnuː.vəʊˈriːʃ/ [US] /-voʊ-/ *plural noun*: *The restaurant is popular with the city's nouveau riche.*

nouvelle cuisine /ˌnuː.vel.kwɪˈziːn/ *noun* [U] a style of cooking in which food is lightly cooked and served in attractive patterns on the plate in small amounts: *Raymond Blanc, star of nouvelle cuisine, tells Paul Bailey about the philosophy behind his cooking.*

novel [BOOK] /ˈnɒv.əl/ [US] /ˈnɑː.vəl/ *noun* [C] a long printed story about imaginary characters and events: *a paperback novel* ○ ***historical/romantic*** *novels* ○ *Have you read any of Jane Austen's novels?* ○ *His latest novel is selling really well.*

novelist /ˈnɒv.əl.ɪst/ [US] /ˈnɑː.və-/ *noun* [C] a person who writes novels

novel [NEW] /ˈnɒv.əl/ [US] /ˈnɑː.vəl/ *adj* new and original, not like anything seen before: *a novel idea/suggestion* ○ *Keeping a sheep in the garden is a novel way of keeping the grass short!*

novelty /ˈnɒv.əl.ti/ [US] /ˈnɑː.vəl.t̬i/ *noun* **1** [U] the quality of being new and unusual: *The novelty of these toys soon* ***wore off*** *and the children became bored with them.* ○ *In Britain in the 1950s, television had a novelty* ***value****.* **2** [C] something which has not been experienced before and so is interesting: *Tourists are still a novelty on this remote island.* **3** [C] a cheap unusual object such as a small toy, often given as a present: *A Christmas cracker* usually contains a paper hat, a joke and a novelty. ○ *a novelty item*

novella /nəʊˈvel.ə/ [US] /noʊ-/ *noun* [C] *plural* **novellas** or **novelle** a short novel

November /nəʊˈvem.bəʳ/ [US] /noʊˈvem.bɚ/ *noun* [C or U] (WRITTEN ABBREVIATION **Nov**) the eleventh month of the year, after October and before December: *5(th) November/November 5(th)* ○ *Guy Fawkes' Night is* **on** *the fifth of November/November the fifth/*(MAINLY US) *November fifth.* ○ *The factory opened* **last** *November.* ○ *He's starting his new job* **in** *November.*

novice /ˈnɒv.ɪs/ [US] /ˈnɑː.vɪs/ *noun* [C] **1** a person who is not experienced in a job or situation: *I've never driven a car before – I'm a complete novice.* ○ *This is quite a difficult plant for novice gardeners to grow.* **2** a person who is still training to be a monk or a nun

novocaine /ˈnəʊ.və.keɪn/ [US] /ˈnoʊ-/ *noun* [U] (TRADEMARK **Novocain**) a drug given to people to stop them feeling pain, especially during an operation on their teeth

now [AT PRESENT] /naʊ/ *adv* **1** at the present time, not in the past or future: *She used to be a teacher, but now she works in publishing.* ○ *I may eat something later, but I'm not hungry now.* ○ *Many people now own a video recorder.* **2** immediately: *I don't want to wait until tomorrow, I want it now!* **3** used to express how long something has been happening, from when it began to the present time: *She's been a vegetarian* **for** *ten years now.* **4** used in stories or reports of past events to describe a new situation or event: *It was getting dark now and we were tired.* **5** used when describing a situation that is the result of what someone just said or did: *Oh yes, now I know who you mean.*

• **any minute/moment/second/time now** very soon: *Our guests will be arriving any moment now and the house is still a mess.*

• **(every) now and then/again** sometimes, but not very often: *We meet up for lunch now and then, but not as often as we used to.*

• **now for ...** INFORMAL used to introduce a new subject: *And now for what we're going to do tomorrow.*

• **It's now or never.** SAYING said when you must do something immediately, especially because you will not get another chance

• **Now you're talking.** SAYING said when someone makes a suggestion or offer that is better than one that they have already made

now /naʊ/ *noun* [U] the present moment or time: *Now isn't a good time to speak to him.* ○ *I thought you'd have finished* **by** *now.* ○ *You should have mentioned it before* **now**. ○ *That's all* **for** *now* (= until a future point in time).

• **from now on/as from now** from this moment and always in the future: *From now on the gates will be locked at midnight.*

now (that) ... /ˈnaʊˌðət/ /-ðæt/ *conjunction* used to give an explanation of a new situation: *Now I've got a car, I don't get as much exercise as I used to.* ○ *She's enjoying the job now that she's got more responsibility.*

now [IN SPEECH] /naʊ/ *adv* used in statements and questions to introduce or give emphasis to what you are saying: *Now, where did I put my hat?* ○ *There was a knock at the door. Now Jan knew her mother had promised to visit, so she assumed it was her.* ○ *Hurry, now, or you'll miss the bus!* ○ *Sorry, I can't today. Now if you'd asked me yesterday, I would have said yes.*

• **now, now** said when you want to make someone feel better or give them a gentle warning: *Now, now, don't cry.* ○ *Now, now, children, stop fighting!*

• **now then** said to attract attention to what you are going to ask or suggest: *Now then, what's all this fuss about?*

nowadays /ˈnaʊ.ə.deɪz/ *adv* at the present time, in comparison to the past: *Who remembers those films nowadays?* ○ *Nowadays, I bake my own bread rather than buy it.*

nowhere /ˈnəʊ.weəʳ/ [US] /ˈnoʊ.wer/ *adv* **1** in, at or to no place; not anywhere: *These young people have nowhere* **(else)** *to go.* ○ *Nowhere does the article mention the names of the people involved.* **2** not in a successful or a winning position: *The horse I bet on finished nowhere.*

• **from/out of nowhere** very suddenly and unexpectedly: *She said her attacker seemed to* **come** *out of nowhere.* ○ FIGURATIVE *The team has* **come** *from nowhere* (= from a very bad position) *to win football's biggest prize.*

• **go/get/head nowhere** to not have any success or achieve anything: *I'm trying to persuade her to come, but I'm* **getting** *nowhere.* ○ *Bad manners will get you nowhere* (= will not help you to succeed).

• **nowhere to be found** impossible to see or find: *We looked for her everywhere, but she was nowhere to be found.*

no-win /ˌnəʊˈwɪn/ [US] /ˌnoʊ-/ *adj* [before n] INFORMAL describes a set of conditions in which whatever happens there will be an unhappy and unsuccessful result: *to be in a no-win* **situation**

nowt /naʊt/ *pronoun* [U] NORTHERN ENGLISH nothing: *That's got nowt to do with it!* ➲Compare **owt**.

• **There's nowt so queer as folk.** UK INFORMAL SAYING said to emphasize that people sometimes behave in a very strange way

noxious /ˈnɒk.ʃəs/ [US] /ˈnɑːk-/ *adj* FORMAL **1** describes something, especially a gas or other substance, that is poisonous or very harmful: *They died from inhaling noxious fumes.* **2** harmful and unpleasant: *a noxious smell/influence*

nozzle /ˈnɒz.l̩/ [US] /ˈnɑː.zl̩/ *noun* [C] a narrow piece fixed to the end of a tube so that the liquid or air that comes out can be directed in a particular way: *Attach the nozzle to the garden hose before turning on the water.*

nr WRITTEN ABBREVIATION FOR **near**, when used as part of an address: *Bray, nr Dublin*

n't /-ᵊnt/ *short form of* not: *didn't* ○ *mustn't*

nth /enθ/ *adj* [before n] INFORMAL used to describe the most recent in a long series of things, when you do not know how many there are: *I glanced at my watch* **for** *the nth* **time** *that morning.*

• **to the nth degree** as much or as far as possible: *We were questioned to the nth degree.*

nuance /ˈnjuː.ɑːnts/ [US] /ˈnuː-/ *noun* [C] a very slight difference in appearance, meaning, sound, etc: *The painter has managed to capture every nuance* **of** *the woman's expression.* ○ *Linguists explore the nuances* **of** *language.*

nub /nʌb/ *noun* [U] the most important or basic part of something: *What do you think is the nub* **of** *the problem?*

nubile /ˈnjuː.baɪl/ [US] /ˈnuː-/ *adj* describes a woman who is young and sexually attractive: *Rich old men often like to be surrounded by nubile young women.*

nuclear /ˈnjuː.klɪəʳ/ [US] /ˈnuː.klɪr/ *adj* **1** being or using the power produced when the nucleus of an atom is divided or joined to another nucleus: *nuclear energy/power* ○ *a nuclear power plant* ○ *the nuclear industry* ➲See also **nuclear** at **nucleus**. **2** relating to weapons, or the use of weapons, which use the power produced when the nucleus of an atom is divided or joined to another nucleus: *a nuclear war/attack* ○ *nuclear disarmament* ○ *How many nations have a nuclear* **capability** (= have nuclear weapons)*?*

ˌnuclear ˈfamily *noun* [C] SPECIALIZED a family consisting of two parents and their children, but not including aunts, uncles, grandparents, etc. ➲Compare **extended family**.

ˌnuclear ˈfission *noun* [U] SPECIALIZED **fission**

nuclear-free /ˌnjuː.klɪəˈfriː/ [US] /ˌnuː.klɪr-/ *adj* describes an area in which nuclear weapons and nuclear energy are not allowed: *The city has declared itself a nuclear-free* **zone**.

ˌnuclear ˈfusion *noun* [U] SPECIALIZED the process of joining of two nuclei to produce energy

ˌnuclear reˈactor *noun* [C] a large machine which uses nuclear fuel to produce power

ˌnuclear ˈwaste *noun* [U] unwanted, dangerously radioactive material that is made when producing nuclear power: *to dump/dispose of nuclear waste*

nucleic acid /njuːˌkleɪ.ɪkˈæs.ɪd/ [US] /nuː-/ *noun* [C or U] SPECIALIZED a type of acid that exists in all living cells: *DNA and RNA are both nucleic acids.*

nucleus /'njuː.kli.əs/ US /'nuː-/ noun [C] plural **nuclei** or **nucleuses 1** SPECIALIZED the central part of an atom, usually made up of PROTONS and NEUTRONS **2** SPECIALIZED the part of a cell that controls its growth: *DNA is stored in the nucleus of a cell.* **3 the nucleus of sth** the group of people or things which are the most important part of something: *These three players will form the nucleus of a revised and stronger team.*

nuclear /'njuː.klɪəʳ/ US /'nuː.klɪr/ adj SPECIALIZED relating to the nucleus of an atom: *nuclear fission/fusion/physics* ⊃See also **nuclear**.

nude /njuːd/ US /nuːd/ adj not wearing any clothes; naked: *She once posed nude for a magazine.* ○ *Nude sunbathing is only allowed on certain beaches.*

nude /njuːd/ US /nuːd/ noun [C] a picture or other piece of art showing a person who is not wearing any clothes: *The exhibition includes several superb nudes.*
• **in the nude** not wearing any clothes: *The children were running around the garden in the nude.*

nudism /'njuː.dɪ.z³m/ US /'nuː-/ noun [U] the activity of wearing no clothes because you believe that wearing no clothes is healthy

nudist /'njuː.dɪst/ US /'nuː-/ noun [C] someone who practises nudism: *The whole family are committed nudists.* ○ *a nudist beach* (= beach for nudists)

nudity /'njuː.dɪ.ti/ US /'nuː.də.t̬i/ noun [U] when people are not wearing clothes: *The film was criticized for its excessive violence and nudity.*

nudge /nʌdʒ/ verb **1** [T] to push something or someone gently, especially to push someone with your ELBOW (= the middle part of your arm where it bends) to attract their attention: *The children were giggling and nudging each other.* ○ *He nudged the cat off the sofa so that he could sit down.* **2** [I + adv or prep; T] to move slowly and almost reach a higher point or level: *Oil prices continue to nudge higher.* ○ *Peter must be nudging 40 now.*
• **nudge nudge (wink wink)** UK INFORMAL something you say when you want to suggest that there is a sexual meaning in something that has just been said

nudge /nʌdʒ/ noun [C] when you nudge someone or something: *I gave him a nudge to wake him up.*

nugget /'nʌg.ɪt/ noun [C] **1** a small roughly shaped lump, especially of gold **2** a small piece of chicken or fish that has been covered in BREADCRUMBS and fried: *She won't eat anything except chicken nuggets and chips.* **3** something that a person has said or written that is very true or very wise: *a nugget of information/truth* ○ HUMOROUS *What other astonishing nuggets of wisdom do you have for us?*

nuisance /'njuː.s³nts/ US /'nuː-/ noun [C or U] something or someone that annoys you or causes trouble for you: *I've forgotten my umbrella – what a nuisance!* ○ [+ v -ing] *It's such a nuisance having to rewrite those letters.* ○ *I hate to be a nuisance, but could you help me?* ○ *Local residents claimed that the noise was causing a public nuisance.*
• **make a nuisance of yourself** to cause trouble or annoyance to other people

nuke /njuːk/ US /nuːk/ verb [T] **1** SLANG to bomb somewhere with nuclear weapons: *The two countries were threatening to nuke each other.* **2** MAINLY US to heat or cook something in a MICROWAVE OVEN

nuke /njuːk/ US /nuːk/ noun [C] SLANG a nuclear weapon: *'No nukes here!' the banner read.*

null and void /ˌnʌl.ənd'vɔɪd/ adj [after n or v] LEGAL having no legal force: *The change in the law makes the previous agreement null and void.* ○ *The election was declared null and void.*

nullify /'nʌl.ɪ.faɪ/ verb [T] **1** FORMAL to make a legal agreement or decision have no legal force: *The state death penalty law was nullified in 1977.* **2** to cause something to have no value or effect: *All my hard work was nullified when I lost my notes.*

numb /nʌm/ adj **1** If a part of your body is numb, you are unable to feel it, usually for a short time: *I had been lying awkwardly and my leg had gone numb.* ○ *My fingers were numb with cold.* **2** not able to feel any emotions properly or to think clearly, because you are so shocked or frightened, etc: *When she first heard the news, she was numb with disbelief.* ○ *Ever since his girl-*friend left him he has felt numb.

numb /nʌm/ verb [T] to make something or someone feel numb: *The extreme cold numbed her face and hands.* ○ *The children are still numbed by their father's death.*

numbly /'nʌm.li/ adv

numbness /'nʌm.nəs/ noun [U] lack of physical or emotional feeling

number SYMBOL /'nʌm.bəʳ/ US /-bɚ/ noun [C] **1** (a sign or symbol representing) a unit which forms part of the system of counting and calculating: *25, 300 and a billion are all numbers.* ○ *She's very good with numbers* (= good at adding, subtracting, etc.). **2** (WRITTEN ABBREVIATION **no.**) one of a series of the symbols used in counting, which is used to mark a particular example of something: *They live at number 34 Orchard Street.* ○ *Please write your credit card number on this form.* ○ *What's our flight number?* **3** (WRITTEN ABBREVIATION **no.**) a telephone number: *I gave him my number and he promised to call me.*
• **by numbers** UK (US **by the numbers**) done according to a plan that has been decided previously, without using your own imagination and ideas: *This is painting by numbers – there's nothing original here.*
• **have sb's number** SLANG to know a lot about someone and so have an advantage over them: *Don't worry, I've got his number, he doesn't fool me.*
• **your number is up** SLANG When your number is up, you are going to die: *When the plane started to shake, I just thought my number was up.*

number /'nʌm.bəʳ/ US /-bɚ/ verb [T] to give something a number in a series and usually to write this number on it: *All the folders have been carefully numbered and filed away.* ○ *Number the pages from one to ten.*

number AMOUNT /'nʌm.bəʳ/ US /-bɚ/ group noun [S] **1** an amount or total: *The number of people killed in road accidents fell last month.* ○ *There has been an increasing number of cases of the disease.* ○ *A small number of children are educated at home.* ○ SLIGHTLY FORMAL *A large number of invitations has been sent.* ○ *Letters of complaint were surprisingly few in number* (= there were not many of them). ⊃See Note **amount of or number of?** at **amount**. **2** a number of **things** several of a particular type of thing: *I decided not to go, for a number of reasons.* **3** a group of people: *On the trip, one of our number fell ill.*
• **any number of things** a lot of a particular thing: *His shop stocks any number of different kinds of pasta.*
• **beyond/without number** LITERARY too many to count: *An earthquake in the city could result in deaths beyond number.*

number /'nʌm.bəʳ/ US /-bɚ/ verb [L only + n] If people or things number a particular amount, there are this many of them: *After the hurricane the homeless numbered over 200 000.*

numberless /'nʌm.b³l.əs/ US /-bɚ.ləs/ adj LITERARY too many to count: *numberless stars*

numbers /'nʌm.bəz/ US /-bɚz/ plural noun a number of a particular description: *Small numbers of children are educated at home.* ○ *Large numbers of invitations were sent.* ○ *Newspapers are produced in vast numbers.*
• **by (sheer) force/weight of numbers** because the number of people or things was so great: *The crowd managed to force its way in by sheer weight of numbers.*

number PARTICULAR THING /'nʌm.bəʳ/ US /-bɚ/ noun **1** [C] a particular example of something **2** [C] a particular copy of a magazine: *Have you got last week's number of the New Yorker?* ○ *He's got all the back numbers of the magazine.* **3** [C] INFORMAL a piece of clothing, especially a dress, that you admire: *She was wearing a stylish Dior number.* **4** [C] US SLANG a person with a particular characteristic: *He's a real sexy number, don't you think?* **5** [C] a short tune or song: *Sing one of those romantic numbers.* **6** [C usually sing] MAINLY US SLANG something that is often said: *He tried the usual/that old number about how his wife didn't understand him.*
• **do a number on sb** US SLANG to hurt, defeat or embarrass someone: *She really did a number on her old boyfriend, making him beg her to come back and then turning him down.*

N

▲ **number** *sb/sth* **among** *sb/sth phrasal verb* FORMAL If you are numbered among a particular group, you belong to that group: *At one time, the club numbered an archbishop among its members.*

number-crunching /ˈnʌm.bə.krʌn.tʃɪŋ/ ⑪ /-bɚ-/ *noun* [U] mathematical work performed by people or computers which is often quite simple but takes a long time **number-cruncher** /ˈnʌm.bə.krʌn.tʃəʳ/ ⑪ /-bɚ.krʌn.tʃɚ/ *noun* [C] *I'm only a number-cruncher in the accounts department.*

,**number** ˈ**one** YOURSELF *noun* [U] (*US ALSO* **numero uno**) INFORMAL yourself and no one else: *Frank is completely selfish – he only cares about number one.* ◦ *I'm going to* **look out for** *number one* (= take care of myself only).

,**number** ˈ**one** THE BEST *noun* [U] the most important, best, most noticeable or most famous person or organization in a particular area of activity: *She's still the world number one in tennis.* ◦ *I'm your number one fan.*

ˈ**number** ,**plate** *UK noun* [C] (*US* **license plate**) the sign on the front and back of a road vehicle that shows its REGISTRATION NUMBER ⊃See picture **Car** on page Centre 12

,**Number** ˈ**Ten** *group noun* [U] (*WRITTEN ABBREVIATION* **No 10**) the official home of the British Prime Minister in Downing Street, London, or the people who work for or represent the Prime Minister: *Number Ten announced tonight that the election will be on April 6.*

numbskull /ˈnʌm.skʌl/ *noun* [C] a **numskull**

numeral /ˈnjuː.mə.rəl/ ⑪ /ˈnuː-/ *noun* [C] a symbol that represents a number

numerate /ˈnjuː.mə.rət/ ⑪ /ˈnuː-/ *adj* SPECIALIZED able to add, subtract, etc: *Geography graduates are literate and numerate and have very good IT skills.*

numeracy /ˈnjuː.mə.rə.si/ ⑪ /ˈnuː-/ *noun* [U] ability to do basic mathematics: *the latest statistics on the literacy and numeracy of eleven to sixteen-year-olds.*

numerator /ˈnjuː.mə.reɪ.təʳ/ ⑪ /ˈnuː.mə.reɪ.t̬ɚ/ *noun* [C] the number above the line in a fraction: *In the fraction ¾, 3 is the numerator.* ⊃Compare **denominator**.

numerical /njuːˈmer.ɪ.kl̩/ ⑪ /nuː-/ *adj* involving or expressed in numbers: *a numerical calculation* ◦ *numerical skill/ability* ◦ *Keep your files in numerical* **order.** ◦ *The UN forces have a numerical superiority over the rebels* (= There are more of the UN forces). **numerically** /njuːˈmer.ɪ.kli/ ⑪ /nuː-/ *adv*: *to be numerically superior*

numerous /ˈnjuː.mə.rəs/ ⑪ /ˈnuː-/ *adj* many: *We have discussed these plans on numerous occasions.* ◦ *Shops of this type, once rare, are now numerous* (= there are many of them).

numismatics /ˌnjuː.mɪzˈmæt.ɪks/ ⑪ /ˌnuː.mɪzˈmæt̬.ɪks/ *noun* [U] SPECIALIZED the study or collecting of coins, bank notes and medals

numskull, numbskull /ˈnʌm.skʌl/ *noun* [C] INFORMAL a very stupid or silly person: *You've spilt my coffee, you numskull!*

nun /nʌn/ *noun* [C] a member of a female religious group which lives in a convent: *a convent school run by Catholic nuns*

nunnery /ˈnʌn.ə.ri/ ⑪ /-ɚ-/ *noun* [C] LITERARY a convent ⊃Compare **monastery**.

nuptial /ˈnʌp.tʃ⁰l/ *adj* FORMAL belonging or relating to a marriage or the state of being married: *nuptial vows/ promises* ◦ *the nuptial bed*

nuptials /ˈnʌp.tʃ⁰lz/ *plural noun* FORMAL a person's marriage and marriage celebrations: *Sadly we weren't able to attend the nuptials.*

nurse PERSON /nɜːs/ ⑪ /nɝːs/ *noun* [C] **1** (the title given to) a person whose job is to care for people who are ill or injured, especially in a hospital: *He worked as a nurse in a psychiatric hospital.* ◦ *Nurse Millard will be with you shortly.* ◦ [as form of address] *Thank you, Nurse.* **2** OLD-FASHIONED a woman employed to take care of a young child or children

nurse /nɜːs/ ⑪ /nɝːs/ *verb* [T] **1** to care for a person or an animal while they are ill: *He gave up his job so that he could nurse his mother at home.* ◦ *They found an injured cat and carefully nursed it* **back to health** (= until it was well again). **2** to spend a lot of time taking care of some-

thing as it grows or develops: *These young trees are carefully nursed by the head gardener.* ◦ *The project will have to be nursed* **through** *its first few months.* **3** If you nurse an illness or injury, you rest until it gets better: *Robert's in bed nursing a back injury.* **4** to hold a small child in your arms as a way of comforting them: *She nursed the crying child on her lap.* **5** to feel a desire or an emotion for a long time: *She had long nursed a passion for Japanese art.* **6** to hold a drink for a long time without drinking it: *Mark was sitting in the corner nursing an almost empty pint glass.*

nursing /ˈnɜː.sɪŋ/ ⑪ /ˈnɝː-/ *noun* [U] the job of being a nurse: *She studied nursing at Garfield Hospital.*

nurse FEED /nɜːs/ ⑪ /nɝːs/ *verb* [T] When a woman nurses a baby, she feeds it with milk from her breasts.

nursing /ˈnɜː.sɪŋ/ ⑪ /ˈnɝː-/ *adj* [before n] describes a woman who is feeding her baby with her own breast milk: *Nursing* **mothers** *are advised to eat plenty of leafy green vegetables.*

nursemaid /ˈnɜːs.meɪd/ ⑪ /ˈnɝːs-/ *noun* [C] OLD-FASHIONED a woman who takes care of someone else's young children: *I'm not going to be a nursemaid to you – make your own bed!*

nursery FOR CHILDREN /ˈnɜː.s⁰r.i/ ⑪ /ˈnɝː.sɚ-/ *noun* [C] **1** a place where young children and babies are taken care of while their parents are at work: *Does Jake go to a nursery or a childminder?* **2** a room in a house where small children sleep and play

nursery /ˈnɜː.s⁰r.i/ ⑪ /ˈnɝː-/ *adj* [before n] relating to the teaching of children who are between the ages of two or three to five years old: *Do you think the state should provide free nursery* **education***?*

nursery FOR PLANTS /ˈnɜː.s⁰r.i/ ⑪ /ˈnɝː.sɚ-/ *noun* [C] a place where plants and trees are grown, especially for sale

ˈ**nursery** ,**nurse** *noun* [C] *UK* a person who has been trained to take care of young children

ˈ**nursery** ,**rhyme** *noun* [C] a short and usually very old poem or song for young children: *a book of nursery rhymes*

ˈ**nursery** ,**school** *noun* [C] (*US ALSO* **preschool**) a school for children between the ages of two and five

ˈ**nursery** ,**slope** *UK noun* [C] (*US* **bunny slope**) a gentle slope on a mountain used by people learning to ski (= move over snow on two sticks)

nurse's aide /ˌnɜːs.ˈsɪz.eɪd/ ⑪ /ˌnɝː-/ *noun* [C] US FOR **auxiliary nurse**

ˈ**nursing** ,**aid** *noun* [C] AUS FOR **auxiliary nurse**

ˈ**nursing au**,**xiliary** *noun* [C] UK an **auxiliary nurse**

ˈ**nursing** ,**home** *noun* [C] a place where very old people who are ill live and receive medical treatment and care

nurture /ˈnɜː.tʃəʳ/ ⑪ /ˈnɝː.tʃɚ/ *verb* [T] FORMAL **1** to take care of, feed and protect someone or something, especially young children or plants, and help them to develop: *She wants to stay at home and nurture her children.* ◦ *a carefully nurtured garden* **2** to help a plan or a person to develop and be successful: *As a record company director, his job is to nurture young* **talent.** **3** to have a particular emotion, plan or idea for a long time: *Winifred nurtured ambitions for her daughter to be a surgeon.*

nurture /ˈnɜː.tʃəʳ/ ⑪ /ˈnɝː.tʃɚ/ *noun* [U] the way in which children are treated as they are growing, especially as compared with the characteristics they are born with: *Which do you believe has the strongest influence on how children develop – nature or nurture?*

nut FOOD /nʌt/ *noun* [C] the dry fruit of particular trees which grows in a hard shell and can often be eaten: *a Brazil/cashew nut* ◦ *Sprinkle some roasted chopped nuts on top.*

● **a tough/hard nut** someone who is very unpleasant and difficult to deal with: *As a teenager, Jack was a real hard nut, always getting into fights.*

● **a hard/tough nut to crack** a problem that is very difficult to solve or a person who is very difficult to understand

nutty /ˈnʌt.i/ ⑪ /ˈnʌt̬-/ *adj* containing or tasting of nuts **nuttiness** /ˈnʌt.ɪ.nəs/ ⑪ /ˈnʌt̬-/ *noun* [U]

nut METAL OBJECT /nʌt/ *noun* [C] a small piece of metal with a hole in it which a bolt can be screwed into: *Nuts and bolts are used to hold pieces of machinery together.*
• **the nuts and bolts** the practical facts about a particular thing, rather than theoretical ideas about it: *When it came to the nuts and bolts of running a business, he was clearly unable to cope.*

nut PERSON /nʌt/ *noun* [C] INFORMAL **1** a person who is mentally ill or who behaves in a very foolish or stupid or strange way: *What kind of nut would leave a car on a railway track?* **2** someone who is extremely enthusiastic about a particular activity or thing: *Ian's a tennis nut – he plays every day.* ⊃See also **nuts** FOOLISH.
nutty /'nʌt.i/ ⑩ /'nʌt̬-/ *adj* INFORMAL crazy, foolish or strange: *She's got some nutty idea about setting up a school for cats.*
• **be (as) nutty as a fruitcake** INFORMAL to be a very strange or crazy person
nutter /'nʌt.əʳ/ ⑩ /'nʌt̬.ɚ/ *noun* [C] UK INFORMAL someone who is crazy, foolish or strange: *He's a bit of a nutter.*

nut HEAD /nʌt/ *noun* [C] SLANG a person's head: *Come on, use your nut* (= think clearly)*!*
• **do your nut** UK SLANG to become extremely angry: *She'll do her nut when she sees the mess.*
• **be off your nut** SLANG to be very foolish or stupid: *You can't do that! Are you off your nut?*

nutcase /'nʌt.keɪs/ *noun* [C] INFORMAL DISAPPROVING someone who is mentally ill or who behaves in an extremely silly way

nutcracker /'nʌt̩ˌkræk.əʳ/ ⑩ /-ɚ/ *noun* [C] (*UK ALSO* **nutcrackers**) a tool for breaking the shell of a nut, so that you can remove and eat the softer part inside

nuthouse /'nʌt.haʊs/ *noun* [C] OFFENSIVE a **psychiatric hospital**

nutmeg SPICE /'nʌt.meg/ *noun* [C or U] the hard fruit of a tropical tree, or a brown powder made from this and used as a spice for flavouring food: *Grate some nutmeg on top of the pudding.*

nutmeg FOOTBALL /'nʌt.meg/ *verb* [T] **-gg-** MAINLY UK INFORMAL in football, to kick the ball through the legs of an opponent: *Roberts added the second goal five minutes into the second half when he nutmegged Evans.* **nutmeg** /'nʌt.meg/ *noun* [C] INFORMAL

nutrient /'nju:.tri.ənt/ ⑩ /'nu:-/ *noun* [C] SPECIALIZED any substance which plants or animals need in order to live and grow: *It's good soil – full of nutrients.* ○ *A healthy diet should provide all your essential nutrients.*

nutrition /nju:'trɪʃ.ᵊn/ ⑩ /nu:-/ *noun* [U] **1** the substances that you take into your body as food and the way that they influence your health: *Good nutrition is essential if patients are to make a quick recovery.* ○ *improvements in nutrition* **2** the process of taking in and using food, or the scientific study of this: *She's a professor of nutrition at Columbia University.*
nutritional /nju:'trɪʃ.ᵊn.ᵊl/ ⑩ /nu:-/ *adj* (*ALSO* **nutritive**) relating to nutrition: *Chemical sweeteners have no nutri-*

tional value.
nutritious /nju:'trɪʃ.əs/ ⑩ /nu:-/ *adj* containing many of the substances needed for life and growth: *a nutritious diet* ○ *Raw spinach is especially nutritious.*
nutritionist /nju:'trɪʃ.ᵊn.ɪst/ ⑩ /nu:-/ *noun* [C] an expert on the subject of nutrition: *The doctor advised him to see a nutritionist about his diet.*

nuts BODY PART /nʌts/ *plural noun* MAINLY US OFFENSIVE FOR **testicles**

nuts FOOLISH /nʌts/ *adj* [after v] INFORMAL foolish, stupid or strange: [+ *to* infinitive] *You must be nuts to go climbing mountains in winter.*
• **be nuts about/over sth/sb** INFORMAL to be very enthusiastic about an object, activity or person: *Sophie's nuts about dinosaurs.* ○ *I'm nuts over Kevin Costner.*
• **go nuts** INFORMAL to become extremely angry: *My sister will go nuts when she finds out I've wrecked her car.*

nutshell /'nʌt.ʃel/ *noun* **in a nutshell** using as few words as possible: *Well, to put it in a nutshell, we're lost.*

nuttiness /'nʌt.ɪ.nəs/ ⑩ /'nʌt̬-/ *noun* [U] ⊃See at **nut** FOOD.

nutty /'nʌt.i/ ⑩ /'nʌt̬.i/ *adj* ⊃See at **nut** FOOD and **nut** PERSON.

nuzzle /'nʌz.l̩/ *verb* [I + adv or prep; T] to touch, rub or press something or someone gently and/or affectionately, especially with the head or nose, usually with small repeated movements: *My dog came and nuzzled my foot to try and cheer me up.* ○ *The kittens like to nuzzle up against/up to their mother.*

NVQ /ˌen.viːˈkjuː/ *noun* [C] ABBREVIATION FOR National Vocational Qualification: a British qualification in a technical or practical subject which shows that a person has a range of skills useful for employment

NW *noun* [U], *adj* ABBREVIATION FOR **northwest** or **northwestern**

NY /ˌenˈwaɪ/ *noun* [U] (*ALSO* **NYC**) ABBREVIATION FOR New York (City)

nylon /'naɪ.lɒn/ ⑩ /-lɑːn/ *noun* [U] an artificial substance used especially to make clothes, ropes and brushes: *These covers are 100% nylon.* ○ *a nylon shirt/bag*
nylons /'naɪ.lɒnz/ ⑩ /-lɑːnz/ *plural noun* OLD-FASHIONED women's nylon tights or stockings

nymph /nɪmpf/ *noun* [C] (in ancient Greek and Roman traditional stories) a goddess or spirit in the form of a young woman, living in a tree, river, mountain, etc.

nymphet /nɪmpˈfet/ ⑩ /'nɪmp.fət/ *noun* [C] USUALLY HUMOROUS a girl about 10 to 14 years old considered to be sexually attractive

nymphomaniac /ˌnɪmp.fəʊˈmeɪ.ni.æk/ ⑩ /-foʊ-/ *noun* [C] (*INFORMAL* **nympho**) DISAPPROVING a woman who likes to have sex very often, especially with lots of different men **nymphomania** /ˌnɪmp.fəʊˈmeɪ.ni.ə/ ⑩ /-foʊ-/ *noun* [U]

NZ /ˌenˈzed/ ⑩ /-ˈziː/ *noun* [U] ABBREVIATION FOR New Zealand

O

O [LETTER] (*plural* **O's** or **Os**) /əʊ/ [US] /oʊ/ *noun* [C] **1** (*ALSO* **o** (*plural* **o's** or **os**)) the 15th letter of the English alphabet **2** (*ALSO* **o, oh**) used in speech to mean zero: *My phone number is three, one, o, five, one, double o* (= 3105100). ○ *The year 1705 is usually pronounced seventeen o five.*

O [EMOTION] /əʊ/ [US] /oʊ/ *exclamation OLD USE OR LITERARY* used when addressing someone or something, or expressing something in an emotional or formal way: *O Zeus! Hear my prayer.* ➲Compare **oh** EMOTION.

o' /ə/ *prep* **1** used in writing to represent 'of' when its *f* is not pronounced: *a bottle o' beer* **2** used as part of many last names: *Jeanne O'Connor*

:-o *INTERNET SYMBOL FOR* surprised or shouting

:-O *INTERNET SYMBOL FOR* very surprised or shouting loudly

=:-o *INTERNET SYMBOL FOR* frightened or surprised

oaf /əʊf/ [US] /oʊf/ *noun* [C] *OLD-FASHIONED* a stupid, rude or awkward person, especially a man: *a drunken/insensitive/stupid oaf* ○ *You clumsy oaf! You've broken it!* **oafish** /ˈəʊ.fɪʃ/ [US] /ˈoʊ-/ *adj INFORMAL DISAPPROVING oafish behaviour* ○ *an oafish young man* **oafishness** /ˈəʊ.fɪʃ.-nəs/ [US] /ˈoʊ-/ *noun* [U]

oak /əʊk/ [US] /oʊk/ *noun* [C or U] a large tree that is common especially in northern countries, or the hard wood of this tree: *a mighty oak* ○ *The timbers of those old sailing ships were mainly oak.* ○ *an oak table/cupboard*
• **Tall/Great oaks from little acorns grow.** *SAYING* said about organizations or plans which start off very small or simple and become extremely large or successful
oaky /ˈəʊ.ki/ [US] /ˈoʊ-/ *adj* describes wine which has a slightly woody flavour, especially because it has been left to develop in a container made of oak: *a deliciously oaky red wine*

OAP /ˌəʊ.eɪˈpiː/ [US] /ˌoʊ-/ *noun* [C] *UK ABBREVIATION FOR* **old age pensioner**: *OAPs get cheaper bus and train tickets.*

oar /ɔːʳ/ [US] /ɔːr/ *noun* [C] a long pole with a wide flat part at one end which is used for rowing a boat: *a pair of oars* ○ *She dipped her oars into the water and pulled.* ➲Compare **paddle** POLE. ➲See picture **Planes, Ships and Boats** on page Centre 14
• **put/stick *your* oar in** *INFORMAL DISAPPROVING* to say or do something which annoys other people because they have not asked you to join their conversation or activity: *No-one asked him to help – he's always sticking his oar in.*
oarsman /ˈɔːz.mən/ [US] /ˈɔːrz-/ *noun* [C] a person who rows a boat, especially in competitions
oarswoman /ˈɔːzˌwʊm.ən/ [US] /ˈɔːrz-/ *noun* [C] a female oarsman

oarlock /ˈɔː.lɒk/ [US] /ˈɔːr.lɑːk/ *noun* [C] *US FOR* **rowlock**

oasis /əʊˈeɪ.sɪs/ [US] /oʊ-/ *noun plural* **oases** **1** [C] a place in a desert where there is water and therefore plants and trees and sometimes a village or town **2** [S] a calm, pleasant place in the middle of somewhere busy and unpleasant: *Her office was an oasis **of** peace and sanity amid the surrounding chaos.*

oatcake /ˈəʊt.keɪk/ [US] /ˈoʊt-/ *noun* [C] a thin savoury biscuit made from oats, especially common in Scotland

oath [PROMISE] /əʊθ/ [US] /oʊθ/ *noun* [C] a promise, especially that you will tell the truth in a law court: *Medieval knights **took** an oath **of** allegiance/loyalty to their lord.* ○ *The witness placed her hand on the Bible and **took the** oath* (= promised to tell the truth).
• **be under/on oath** to have formally promised to tell the truth: *The judge reminded the witness that she was under oath.*

oath [SWEAR WORD] /əʊθ/ [US] /oʊθ/ *noun* [C] *OLD-FASHIONED* a swear word, especially one which uses a name for God: *muttering/mouthing oaths*

oatmeal /ˈəʊt.miːl/ [US] /ˈoʊt-/ *noun* [U] **1** a type of flour made from oats: *oatmeal porridge* **2** *US FOR* **porridge** FOOD

oats /əʊts/ [US] /oʊts/ *plural noun* a grass-like CEREAL plant, or its seeds which are used in baking and cooking and also to feed animals: *a field of oats* ○ **rolled** *oats* (= oats that have been pressed flat) ○ *porridge oats* ○ *These biscuits contain oats.*
oat /əʊt/ [US] /oʊt/ *adj* [before n] made of or from oats: *oat biscuits* ○ *oat bran/cereal*

OB /ˌəʊˈbiː/ [US] /ˌoʊ-/ *noun* [C] *US INFORMAL FOR* **obstetrician** ➲See at **obstetrics**.

obdurate /ˈɒb.djʊ.rət/ [US] /ˈɑːb.dʊr.ɪt/ *adj FORMAL DISAPPROVING* extremely determined to act in a particular way and not to change despite argument or persuasion: *The President remains obdurate **on** the question of tax cuts.*

obedient /əʊˈbiː.di.ənt/ [US] /oʊ-/ *adj* doing, or willing to do, what you have been told to do by someone in authority: *Students are expected to be quiet and obedient in the classroom.* ○ *an obedient dog* ➲See also **obey**.
* NOTE: The opposite is **disobedient**. **obediently** /əʊˈbiː.di.ənt.li/ [US] /oʊ-/ *adv*: *The dog trotted obediently to his master.*
obedience /əʊˈbiː.di.ənts/ [US] /oʊ-/ *noun* [U] when people or animals are obedient: *He demands unquestioning obedience from his soldiers.*

obeisance /əʊˈbeɪ.sᵊnts/ [US] /oʊ-/ *noun* [C or U] *FORMAL* obedience and respect, or something you do which expresses this: *One by one the noblemen **made** their obeisances* (= bent at the waist) ***to** the Queen.*

obelisk /ˈɒb.ᵊl.ɪsk/ [US] /ˈɑː.bᵊl-/ *noun* [C] a tall stone column with four sloping sides and a pointed top, made in honour of an important person or event

obese /əʊˈbiːs/ [US] /oʊ-/ *adj* extremely fat **obesity** /əʊˈbiː.sɪ.ti/ [US] /oʊˈbiː.sə.t̬i/ *noun* [U] *A diet that is high in fat can lead to obesity.*

obey /əʊˈbeɪ/ [US] /oʊ-/ *verb* [I or T] to act according to what you have been asked or ordered to do by someone in authority or to behave according to a rule, law or instruction: *The soldiers refused to obey **(orders)**.* ○ *to obey the **rules** of international law* ○ *Falling objects obey the **law** of gravity.* ➲See also **obedient**.

obfuscate /ˈɒb.fʌs.keɪt/ [US] /ˈɑːb.fə.skeɪt/ *verb* [T] *FORMAL* to make something less clear and harder to understand, especially intentionally: *She was criticized for using arguments that obfuscated the main issue.* **obfuscation** /ˌɒb.fʌsˈkeɪ.ʃᵊn/ [US] /ˌɑːb.fəˈskeɪ-/ *noun* [U] *They accused the White House of obstruction and obfuscation.*

ob-gyn /ˌɒbˈgaɪn/ [US] /ˌɑːb-/ *noun* [C] *US INFORMAL ABBREVIATION FOR* obstetrician-gynecologist: a medical specialist who deals with pregnancy, birth, and women's reproductive diseases

obituary /əʊˈbɪtʃ.ʊə.ri/ [US] /oʊˈbɪtʃ.u.er.i/ *noun* [C] (*INFORMAL* **obit**) a report, especially in a newspaper, which gives the news of someone's death and details about their life

object [THING] /ˈɒb.dʒɪkt/ [US] /ˈɑːb-/ *noun* [C] a thing that you can see or touch but that is not usually a living animal, plant or person: *a solid/material/physical object* ○ *a collection of precious objects* ○ *Look, there's a strange object in the sky!*
objectification /ɒbˌdʒek.tɪ.fɪˈkeɪ.ʃᵊn/ [US] /ɑːbˌdʒek.t̬ɪ-/ *noun* [U] *SPECIALIZED* treating people like tools or toys, as if they had no feelings, opinions or rights of their own: *Pornography is an example of the objectification of women by men.*

object [PURPOSE] /ˈɒb.dʒɪkt/ [US] /ˈɑːb-/ *noun* [C usually sing] a reason for doing something, or the result you wish to achieve by doing it: ***The** object **of** their expedition was to discover the source of the River Nile.* ➲See also **objective** AIM.
• **the object of the exercise** the desired result of an activity: *In today's session, the object of the exercise is to improve your interpersonal skills.*

object [CAUSE] /ˈɒb.dʒɪkt/ [US] /ˈɑːb-/ *noun* [C usually sing] *SLIGHTLY FORMAL* someone or something that causes particular feelings in or actions by others: *He became an object **of** ridicule among the other workers.*
• **be no object** If something valuable, such as money, is no object, it does not need to be considered as a

problem, because you have a lot of it: *For a millionaire like him, money is no object.*

object GRAMMAR /'ɒb.dʒɪkt/ ⓤ /'ɑːb-/ *noun* [C] (*WRITTEN ABBREVIATION* **obj**) *SPECIALIZED* **1** a person or thing that is affected by the action of a verb or involved in the result of an action, or a noun, pronoun or noun phrase that represents that person or thing: *In the sentence 'I like ice cream', 'ice cream' is the object **of** the verb 'like'.* **2** a word that follows a preposition

object OPPOSE /əb'dʒekt/ *verb* [I] to feel or express opposition to or dislike of something or someone: *Would anyone object if we started the meeting now?* ○ *He objects **to** the label 'magician' which he is often given.* ○ *No-one objected when the boss said it was time to go home.*
objection /əb'dʒek.ʃən/ *noun* [C] *Her objection **to/against** the plan is based on incorrect facts.* ○ *A couple of people **raised/voiced** objections.* ○ [+ that] *The only objection I **have** is **that** it may cost more than expected.*
objectionable /əb'dʒek.ʃən.ə.bl̩/ *adj FORMAL* describes people or things that you dislike or oppose because they are so unpleasant or wrong: *an objectionable smell* ○ *I found the violence in that film really objectionable.*
objector /əb'dʒek.tər/ ⓤ /-tɚ/ *noun* [C] *200 objectors were present at the inquiry.* ○ *a conscientious objector*

objective AIM /əb'dʒek.tɪv/ ⓤ /-tɪv/ *noun* [C] something which you plan to do or achieve: *Her **main/prime** objective now is simply to stay in power.* ○ *Can the sales force **achieve/meet** its financial objectives?* ➔See also **object** PURPOSE.

objective FAIR OR REAL /əb'dʒek.tɪv/ *adj* based on real facts and not influenced by personal beliefs or feelings: *an objective and impartial report* ○ *I can't really be objective when I'm judging my daughter's work.* ✱ NOTE: The opposite is **subjective**. **objectively** /əb'dʒek.tɪv.li/ *adv*: *Judges must weigh the evidence logically and objectively.* **objectivity** /ˌɒb.dʒek'tɪv.ɪ.ti/ ⓤ /ˌɑːb.dʒek'tɪv.ə.ti/ *noun* [U] *Surely true objectivity in a critic is impossible?*

'**object ˌlesson** *noun* [C] *APPROVING* an action or story which teaches you how or how not to act, or which clearly shows the facts of a situation, usually a bad one: *The disaster was an object lesson **in** how not to run a ship.*

object-oriented /'ɒb.dʒɪkt.ˌɔː.ri.en.tɪd/ ⓤ /'ɑːb.dʒɪkt-ˌɔːr.i.en.tɪd/ *adj SPECIALIZED* describes, in computing, something based on groups of information and their effects on each other, rather than on a series of instructions: *C++ is a common object-oriented **programming** language.*

objet d'art /ˌɒb.ʒeɪ'dɑːr/ ⓤ /ˌɑːb.ʒeɪ'dɑːr/ *noun* [C] *plural* **objets d'art** an object, usually a small object, considered to have some worth or value as art

oblige FORCE /ə'blaɪdʒ/ *verb* [T + obj + *to* infinitive] (*MAINLY US OR FORMAL* **obligate**) to force someone to do something, or to make it necessary for someone to do something: *The law obliges companies **to** pay decent wages to their employees.* ○ *Sellers are not legally obliged to accept the highest offer.*
obligation /ˌɒb.lɪ'geɪ.ʃən/ ⓤ /ˌɑː.blə-/ *noun* **1** [C or U] when you are obliged to do something: [+ *to* infinitive] *If you have not signed a contract, you are **under** no obligation to* (= it is not necessary to) *pay them any money.* ○ *You have a **legal** obligation **to*** (= The law says you must) *ensure your child receives a proper education.* **2** [C] something that you must do: *I haven't got time to do his work for him – I've got too many obligations as it is.*
obligatory /ə'blɪg.ə.tər.i/ ⓤ /-tɔːr-/ *adj* **1** describes something you must do because of a rule or law, etc: *The medical examination before you start work is obligatory.* ○ [+ *to* infinitive] *The statute made it obligatory **for** all fit males between 12 and 60 **to** work.* **2** expected because it usually happens: *Some secret service agents turned up, all wearing the obligatory raincoat and hat.* **obliged** /ə-'blaɪdʒd/ *adj* [after v; + *to* infinitive] (*MAINLY US OR FORMAL* **obligated**) *Doctors are legally obliged **to** take certain precautions.* ○ *She feels obliged **to** be nice to Jack because he's her boss.*

oblige HELP /ə'blaɪdʒ/ *verb* [I or T] to please or help someone, especially by doing something they have asked you to do: *We only went to the party to oblige some old friends*

who especially asked us to be there. ○ *We needed a guide and he was only too **happy to** oblige.*
● **be obliged if** *FORMAL* used to ask someone politely to do something: *I'd be obliged if you would complete and return the form as soon as possible.*
● **(be) much obliged** *FORMAL* used to thank someone and say that you are grateful: *"Here's the information you requested." "Oh, (I'm) much obliged (to you)."*
obliging /ə'blaɪ.dʒɪŋ/ *adj APPROVING* willing or eager to help: *He found an obliging doctor who gave him the drugs he needed.* **obligingly** /ə'blaɪ.dʒɪŋ.li/ *adv*
▲ **oblige *sb* with *sth** FORMAL* to help someone by giving them something: *Could you oblige me with a pen and a piece of paper, please?*

oblique DIAGONAL /əʊ'bliːk/ ⓤ /oʊ-/ *adj* **1** having a sloping direction, angle or position: *Through the window came the last few oblique rays of evening sunshine.* ○ *He gave her an oblique **glance**.* **2** *SPECIALIZED* (of an angle) either more or less than 90° **obliquely** /əʊ'bliː.kli/ ⓤ /oʊ-/ *adv*
o,blique ('**stroke**) *noun* [C] *UK FOR* **slash** PUNCTUATION: *Fractions can be written with oblique strokes, for example 2/3.*

oblique INDIRECT /əʊ'bliːk/ ⓤ /oʊ-/ *adj* describes remarks which are indirect, so that the real meaning is not immediately clear: *She made several oblique **references** to the current financial situation.* **obliquely** /əʊ'bliː.kli/ ⓤ /oʊ-/ *adv*

obliterate /ə'blɪt.ər.eɪt/ ⓤ /-'blɪt̬.ə.reɪt/ *verb* **1** [T often passive] to remove all sign of something, either by destroying it or by covering it so that it cannot be seen: *The missile strike was devastating – the target was totally obliterated.* ○ *All of a sudden the view was obliterated by the fog.* **2** [T] to make an idea or feeling disappear completely: *Perhaps she gets drunk to obliterate painful memories.* **obliteration** /əˌblɪt.ər'eɪ.ʃən/ ⓤ /-ˌblɪt̬.ə'reɪ-/ *noun* [U]

oblivion UNCONSCIOUSNESS /ə'blɪv.i.ən/ *noun* [U] the state of being unconscious: *He sought oblivion in a bottle of whisky.*

oblivion NO MEMORY /ə'blɪv.i.ən/ *noun* [U] **1** the state of being completely forgotten: *He was another minor poet, perhaps unfairly consigned **to** oblivion.* ○ *These toys will be around for a year or two, then fade/slide/sink **into** oblivion.* **2** the state of being completely destroyed: *The planes bombed the city **into** oblivion.*

oblivious /ə'blɪv.i.əs/ *adj* not aware of something, especially what is happening around you: *Absorbed in her work, she was totally oblivious **of** her surroundings.* ○ *The government seems oblivious **to** the likely effects of the new legislation.* **obliviously** /ə'blɪv.i.ə.sli/ *adv* **obliviousness** /ə'blɪv.i.ə.snəs/ *noun* [U]

oblong /'ɒb.lɒŋ/ ⓤ /'ɑː.blɑːŋ/ *noun* [C] an object or shape that is longer than it is wide, especially a four-sided flat shape with four angles of 90° and opposite sides of equal length ➔Compare **square** SHAPE. **oblong** /'ɒb.lɒŋ/ ⓤ /'ɑː.blɑːŋ/ *adj*: *an oblong box*

obnoxious /əb'nɒk.ʃəs/ ⓤ /-'nɑːk-/ *adj DISAPPROVING* very unpleasant or rude: *Some of his colleagues say that he's loud and obnoxious.* ○ *When she's in a bad mood she's obnoxious to everyone.* **obnoxiously** /əb'nɒk.ʃə.sli/ ⓤ /-'nɑːk-/ *adv*: *obnoxiously arrogant/drunk* **obnoxiousness** /əb'nɒk.ʃə.snəs/ ⓤ /-'nɑːk-/ *noun* [U]

obo *noun US WRITTEN ABBREVIATION FOR* or best offer; used in advertisements for possessions that people are trying to sell, to show that they will accept slightly less money than the price they are asking for: *Exercise bike for sale – $40 obo.*

oboe /'əʊ.bəʊ/ ⓤ /'oʊ.boʊ/ *noun* [C] a tube-shaped musical instrument which is played by blowing through two reeds at the top while pressing keys and covering holes with your fingers
oboist /'əʊ.bəʊ.ɪst/ ⓤ /'oʊ.boʊ-/ *noun* [C] someone who plays the oboe

obscene /əb'siːn/ *adj* **1** offensive, rude or shocking, usually because too obviously related to sex or showing sex: *In the raid, police found several boxes of obscene videotapes.* ○ *He was jailed for making obscene **phone calls*** (= ones in which unwanted sexual suggestions were made to the listener). ○ *obscene language/graffiti* **2** morally wrong, often describing something that is morally wrong because it is too large: *to make obscene profits* ○ *The salaries some company directors earn are obscene.* **obscenely** /əbˈsiːn.li/ *adv*: *He's obscenely rich/fat/cruel.*

obscenity /əbˈsen.ɪ.ti/ [US] /-ə.t̬i/ *noun* **1** [C or U] when someone or something is obscene: *The people who made that film could be prosecuted for obscenity.* ○ *Such deliberate destruction of the environment is an obscenity* (= an offensive and shocking situation or event). ○ *obscenity laws* **2** [C usually pl] a very offensive or sexually shocking word or sentence: *He was shouting and screaming obscenities.*

obscure [UNKNOWN] /əbˈskjʊəʳ/ [US] /-ˈskjʊr/ *adj* not known to many people: *an obscure island in the Pacific* ○ *an obscure 12th-century mystic* **obscurity** /əbˈskjʊə.rɪ.ti/ [US] /-ˈskjʊr.ə.t̬i/ *noun* [U] *He was briefly famous in his twenties but then* ***sank into*** *obscurity.* ○ *He rose from relative obscurity to worldwide recognition.*

obscure [UNCLEAR] /əbˈskjʊəʳ/ [US] /-ˈskjʊr/ *adj* unclear and difficult to understand or see: *Official policy has changed, for reasons that remain obscure.* ○ *His answers were obscure and confusing.*

obscure /əbˈskjʊəʳ/ [US] /-ˈskjʊr/ *verb* [T] **1** to prevent something from being seen or heard: *Two new skyscrapers had sprung up, obscuring the view from her window.* ○ *The sun was obscured by clouds.* **2** to make something difficult to discover and understand: *Managers deliberately obscured the real situation* ***from*** *federal investigators.* **obscurely** /əbˈskjʊə.li/ [US] /-ˈskjʊr-/ *adv*: *The minister's statement was obscurely worded.* **obscurity** /əbˈskjʊə.rɪ.ti/ [US] /-ˈskjʊr.ə.t̬i/ *noun* [U] *The story is convoluted and opaque, often to the point of total obscurity.*

obsequious /əbˈsiː.kwi.əs/ *adj* FORMAL DISAPPROVING too eager to praise or obey someone: *She is almost embarrassingly obsequious to anyone in authority.*

obserˈvation ˌpost *noun* [C] a place or building from which you can watch someone, especially an enemy

observe [WATCH] /əbˈzɜːv/ [US] /-ˈzɝːv/ *verb* [T] SLIGHTLY FORMAL to watch carefully the way something happens or the way someone does something, especially in order to learn more about it: *The role of scientists is to observe and describe the world, not to try to control it.* ○ [+ question word] *He spent a year in the jungle, observing* ***how*** *deforestation is affecting local tribes.* ○ *Children learn by observing adults.*

observation /ˌɒb.zəˈveɪ.ʃᵊn/ [US] /ˌɑːb.zɚ-/ *noun* [U] when you observe something or someone: ***close*** *observation of nature/human nature/animal behaviour* ○ *The police are keeping the suspect* ***under*** *observation.* ○ *She was admitted to hospital* ***for*** *observation* (= so that doctors could watch her and see if anything was wrong with her).

observatory /əbˈzɜː.və.tri/ [US] /-ˈzɝː.və.tɔːr.i/ *noun* [C] a building from which scientists can watch the planets, the stars, the weather, etc.

observer /əbˈzɜː.vəʳ/ [US] /-ˈzɝː.vɚ/ *noun* [C] a person who watches what happens but has no active part in it: *observers of the political situation/political observers* ○ *UN observers are monitoring the ceasefire.*

observe [NOTICE] /əbˈzɜːv/ [US] /-ˈzɝːv/ *verb* [T] FORMAL to notice or see: *Jack observed a look of anxiety on his brother's face.* ○ [+ question word] *The guards failed to observe* ***who*** *delivered the package.* ○ [+ that] *In all these films one observes* ***that*** *directors are taking a new interest in Native American culture.* ○ [+ infinitive without to] *A teacher observed her climb over the gate.* **observable** /əbˈzɜː.və.bl̩/ [US] /-ˈzɝː-/ *adj*: *There's no observable connection between the two events.* **observably** /əbˈzɜː.və.bli/ [US] /-ˈzɝː-/ *adv*

observant /əbˈzɜː.vᵊnt/ [US] /-ˈzɝː-/ *adj* APPROVING good or quick at noticing things: *"That's a new dress, isn't it?" "Yes, you are observant!"*

observation /ˌɒb.zəˈveɪ.ʃᵊn/ [US] /ˌɑːb.zɚ-/ *noun* [U] when you notice or see something: *She has remarkable* ***powers of*** *observation* (= is very good at noticing things).

observe [SAY] /əbˈzɜːv/ [US] /-ˈzɝːv/ *verb* [T] FORMAL to make a remark about something: [+ speech] *"I've always found German cars very reliable," he observed.* ○ [+ that] *She observed* ***that*** *it would soon be time to stop for lunch.*

observation /ˌɒb.zəˈveɪ.ʃᵊn/ [US] /ˌɑːb.zɚ-/ *noun* [C] FORMAL a remark about something that you have noticed: *The book is full of interesting observations* ***on/about*** *the nature of musical composition.* ○ *May I* ***make*** *an observation?*

observe [OBEY] /əbˈzɜːv/ [US] /-ˈzɝːv/ *verb* [T] FORMAL to obey a law, rule or custom: *People must observe the law. Nobody should be an exception.* ○ *The old people in the village still observe the local traditions.* ○ *Do you observe Passover?*

observance /əbˈzɜː.vᵊnts/ [US] /-ˈzɝː-/ *noun* [C or U] FORMAL when someone obeys a law or follows a religious custom: *Religious observances such as fasting can be hard to follow.*

obsessed /əbˈsest/ *adj* unable to stop thinking about something; too interested in or worried about something: *Why are people so obsessed* ***with*** *money?* ○ *As a society we're obsessed* ***by*** *sex.*

obsess /əbˈses/ *verb* [I or T] If something or someone obsesses you, or if you obsess about something or someone, you think about them all the time: *The whole relationship obsessed me for years.* ○ *She used to obsess* ***about*** *her weight.*

obsession /əbˈseʃ.ᵊn/ *noun* [C or U] something or someone that you think about all the time: *an unhealthy obsession* ***with*** *death* ○ *her chocolate obsession* ○ *He's always wanted to find his natural mother but recently it's become an obsession.* **obsessive** /əbˈses.ɪv/ *adj* (ALSO **obsessional**) *obsessive secrecy* ○ *He's obsessive* ***about*** *punctuality.* ○ *obsessional behaviour* **obsessively** /əbˈses.ɪv.li/ *adv* (ALSO **obsessionally**)

obsessive /əbˈses.ɪv/ *noun* [C] SPECIALIZED an obsessive person

obˌsessive-comˈpulsive disˌorder *noun* [C or U] (ABBREVIATION **OCD**) SPECIALIZED a mental illness which causes the sufferer to do something repeatedly for no reason **obsessive-compulsive** /əbˌses.ɪv.kəmˈpʌl.sɪv/ *adj*

obsidian /ɒbˈsɪd.i.ən/ [US] /ɑːb-/ *noun* [U] a type of almost black glass-like rock

obsolete /ˌɒb.sᵊlˈiːt/ [US] /ˌɑːb-/ *adj* not in use any more, having been replaced by something newer and better or more fashionable: *Gas lamps became obsolete when electric lighting was invented.*

obsolescent /ˌɒb.səˈles.ᵊnt/ [US] /ˌɑːb-/ *adj* FORMAL becoming obsolete: *Much of our existing military hardware is obsolescent.* **obsolescence** /ˌɒb.səˈles.ᵊnts/ [US] /ˌɑːb-/ *noun* [U] *Mobile phone technology is developing so quickly that many customers are concerned about obsolescence.*

• **built-in/planned obsolescence** when a product is intentionally designed and made so that it will not last for a long time

obstacle /ˈɒb.stɪ.kl̩/ [US] /ˈɑːb-/ *noun* [C] something that blocks you so that movement, going forward or action are prevented or made more difficult: *The biggest obstacle in our way was a tree trunk in the road.* ○ *This decision has removed the last obstacle* ***to*** *the hostages' release.*

ˈobstacle ˌcourse *noun* [C] **1** a race in which runners have to climb over, under or through a series of obstacles **2** a series of problems that you have to solve in order to achieve something

obstetrics /ɒbˈstet.rɪks/ [US] /ɑːb-/ *noun* [U] SPECIALIZED the area of medicine which deals with pregnancy and the birth of babies: *obstetrics and gynaecology* **obstetric** /ɒbˈstet.rɪk/ [US] /ɑːb-/ *adj*: *an obstetric nurse*

obstetrician /ˌɒb.stəˈtrɪʃ.ᵊn/ [US] /ˌɑːb-/ *noun* [C] (US INFORMAL **OB**) SPECIALIZED a doctor with special training in how to care for pregnant women and help in the birth of babies

obstinate /ˈɒb.stɪ.nət/ [US] /ˈɑːb.stə-/ *adj* **1** unreasonably determined, especially to act in a particular way and not to change at all, despite argument or persuasion: *He can be very obstinate at times.* ○ *her obstinate refusal to compromise* **2** [before n] describes a problem, situation or thing that is difficult to deal with, remove or defeat: *obstinate weeds* ○ *Invading troops met with obstinate resistance by guerilla forces.* **obstinately** /ˈɒb.stɪ.nət.li/ [US] /ˈɑːb.stə-/ *adv* **obstinacy** /ˈɒb.stɪ.nə.si/ [US] /ˈɑːb.stə-/ *noun* [U]

obstreperous /əbˈstrep.ᵊr.əs/ [US] /ɑːbˈstrep.ɚ.əs/ *adj FORMAL* too eager to have an argument; difficult to deal with and noisy: *obstreperous customers* **obstreperousness** /əbˈstrep.ᵊr.ə.snəs/ [US] /ɑːbˈstrep.ɚ.ə-/ *noun* [U]

obstruct /əbˈstrʌkt/ *verb* [T] **1** to block a road, passage, entrance, etc. so that nothing can go along it, or to prevent something from happening correctly by putting difficulties in its way: *After the earthquake many roads were obstructed by collapsed buildings.* ○ *Her view of the stage was obstructed by a pillar.* ○ *An accident is obstructing traffic on the M11.* **2** to try to stop something from happening or developing: *to obstruct a police investigation* ○ *He got five years in prison for withholding evidence and obstructing the course of justice.*
obstruction /əbˈstrʌk.ʃᵊn/ *noun* [C or U] *There's some sort of obstruction* (= blockage) *on the railway tracks.* ○ *They were charged with obstruction of the police/of justice* (= preventing the police/law courts from doing their jobs). ○ *The referee said it was obstruction* (= that one player had got in the way of another and so prevented them from moving freely).
obstructionism /əbˈstrʌk.ʃᵊn.ɪ.zᵊm/ *noun* [U] *DISAPPROVING* when someone intentionally stops or delays an official process **obstructionist** /əbˈstrʌk.ʃᵊn.ɪst/ *adj*: *obstructionist policies/tactics*
obstructive /əbˈstrʌk.tɪv/ *adj DISAPPROVING* trying to stop someone from doing something by causing problems for them: *We'd have made a decision by now if Jean hadn't been so obstructive.* **obstructively** /əbˈstrʌk.tɪv.li/ *adv* **obstructiveness** /əbˈstrʌk.tɪv.nəs/ *noun* [U]

obtain [GET] /əbˈteɪn/ *verb* [T] *FORMAL* to get something, especially by asking for it, buying it, working for it or producing it from something else: *to obtain permission* ○ *First editions of these books are now almost impossible to obtain.* ○ *In the second experiment they obtained a very clear result.* ○ *Sugar is obtained* ***by*** *crushing and processing sugar cane.*
obtainable /əbˈteɪ.nə.bl̩/ *adj* able to be obtained: *Information on the subject is easily obtainable on the Internet.* * NOTE: The opposite is **unobtainable**.

obtain [EXIST] /əbˈteɪn/ *verb* [I not continuous] *FORMAL* (especially of a situation) to exist: *Conditions of extreme poverty now obtain in many parts of the country.*

obtrude /əbˈtruːd/ *verb* [I or T] *FORMAL* (especially of something unwanted) to make or become too noticeable, especially by interrupting: *I don't want to obtrude* ***upon/on*** *her privacy.*

obtrusive /əbˈtruː.sɪv/ *adj* too noticeable: *The logo was still visible but less obtrusive this time in beige.* ○ *The soldiers were in civilian clothes, to make their presence less obtrusive.* * NOTE: The opposite is **unobtrusive**. **obtrusively** /əbˈtruː.sɪv.li/ *adv* **obtrusiveness** /əbˈtruː.sɪv.nəs/ *noun* [U]

obtuse [ANGLE] /əbˈtjuːs/ [US] /ɑːbˈtuːs/ *adj* (of an angle) more than 90° and less than 180° ➲Compare **acute** ANGLE.

obtuse [STUPID] /əbˈtjuːs/ [US] /-ˈtuːs/ *adj FORMAL* stupid and slow to understand, or unwilling to try to understand: *Surely the answer's obvious – or are you being deliberately obtuse?* **obtusely** /əbˈtjuː.sli/ [US] /ɑːbˈtuː-/ *adv* **obtuseness** /əbˈtjuː.snəs/ [US] /ɑːbˈtuː-/ *noun* [U]

obverse /ˈɒb.vɜːs/ [US] /ɑːbˈvɝːs/ *noun* [U] *FORMAL* the other side of something; opposite: *False humility and its obverse, arrogance, are equally unpleasant.* ○ *Of course,* ***the*** *obverse* ***of*** *the theory may also be true.*
the obverse *noun* [S] *SPECIALIZED* the front side of a coin which has the main picture on it

obviate /ˈɒb.vi.eɪt/ [US] /ˈɑːb-/ *verb* [T] *FORMAL* to remove a difficulty, especially so that action to deal with it becomes unnecessary: *A peaceful solution would obviate* ***the need*** *to send a UN military force.*

obvious /ˈɒb.vi.əs/ [US] /ˈɑːb-/ *adj* clear; easy to see, recognize or understand: [+ (that)] ***It's obvious (that)*** *she doesn't like him.* ○ *They have a small child so* ***for*** *obvious* ***reasons*** *they need money.* ○ *I know you don't like her, but do you have to* ***make*** *it so obvious?* ○ *Am I* ***stating*** *the obvious* (= saying what everyone already knows)*?* ○ *There is no obvious* ***solution***.
obviously /ˈɒb.vi.ə.sli/ [US] /ˈɑːb-/ *adv* in a way that is easy to understand or see: *He was in tears and obviously very upset.* ○ *Obviously the school cannot function without teachers.*

occasion [PARTICULAR TIME] /əˈkeɪ.ʒᵊn/ *noun* [C] **1** a particular time, especially when something happens or has happened: *We met on several occasions to discuss the issue.* ○ *I've heard him be rude to her on a number of occasions.* ○ *I seem to remember that* ***on*** *that occasion he was with his wife.* ➲See Note **possibility, occasion or opportunity?** at **possibility**. **2** a special or formal event: *Sara's party was* ***quite an*** *occasion – there were over a hundred people there.* ○ *At the wedding he sang a song specially written* ***for*** *the occasion.* ○ *I have a suit but I only wear it* ***on special*** *occasions.* ○ *The coronation of a new king is, of course, a* ***historic*** *occasion.* ○ *Congratulations* ***on the*** *occasion* ***of*** *your wedding anniversary.* **3** *FORMAL* an opportunity or reason for doing something or for something to happen: *The 200th anniversary of Mozart's death was the occasion* ***for*** *hundreds of special films, books and concerts.* ○ *An occasion may* ***arise*** *when you can use your knowledge of French.* ○ *The bride* ***took/used*** *the occasion to make a short speech.*
• **have occasion to do *sth*** *FORMAL* to need to do something: *Of course, as a teacher I had authority, but rarely did I have occasion to use it.*
• **on occasion** sometimes but not often: *He has, on occasion, made a small mistake.*

occasion [CAUSE] /əˈkeɪ.ʒᵊn/ *verb* [T] *FORMAL* to cause something: *Her refusal occasioned a lot of trouble.* ○ [+ two objects] *The case occasioned the authorities a lot of worry/ The authorities were occasioned a lot of worry* ***by*** *the case.*

occasional /əˈkeɪ.ʒᵊn.ᵊl/ /-ˈkeɪʒ.nəl/ *adj* not happening or done often or regularly: *I play the occasional game of football.* ○ *He has the occasional cigar after dinner.*
occasionally /əˈkeɪ.ʒᵊn.ᵊl.i/ /-ˈkeɪʒ.nəl-/ *adv* sometimes but not often: *I see him occasionally in town.* ○ *Occasionally I'll have a piece of chocolate, but it's quite rare.*

the Occident /ðiˈɒk.sɪ.dᵊnt/ [US] /-ˈɑːk.sə-/ *noun* [S] *FORMAL* the western part of the world, especially the countries of Europe and America ➲Compare **the Orient**.
occidental /ˌɒk.sɪˈden.tᵊl/ [US] /ˌɑːk.səˈden.t̬ᵊl/ *adj*: *occidental cultures* ➲Compare **oriental** at **the Orient**.

occult /ˈɒk.ʌlt/ /-ˈ-/ [US] /ˈɑː.kʌlt/ *adj* relating to magical powers and activities, such as those of WITCHCRAFT and astrology: *She claims to have occult* ***powers****, given to her by some mysterious spirit.*
the occult *noun* [S] the study of magic or mysterious powers

occupation /ˌɒk.jʊˈpeɪ.ʃᵊn/ [US] /ˌɑː.kjə-/ *noun* [C] *SLIGHTLY FORMAL* **1** a person's job: *In the space marked 'occupation' she wrote 'police officer'.* **2** a regular activity: *It seems to me his favourite occupation is eating.*
occupational /ˌɒk.jʊˈpeɪ.ʃᵊn.ᵊl/ [US] /ˌɑː.kjə-/ *adj* [before n] relating to or caused by your job: *Back problems are an occupational* ***hazard*** (= a risk that you take in a job) *for any desk-bound office worker.* ○ *an occupational* ***disease***

occuˌpational ˈtherapy *noun* [U] a way of treating mentally or physically ill people by getting them to do special activities **occuˌpational ˈtherapist** *noun* [C]

occupy [FILL] /ˈɒk.jʊ.paɪ/ [US] /ˈɑː.kjʊ-/ *verb* [T] **1** to fill, exist in, or use a place or period of time: *The bathroom's occupied – I think John's in there.* ○ *The rest of the time was occupied* ***with*** *writing a report.* ○ *The house hasn't been occupied* (= lived in) ***by*** *anyone for a few months.* ○ *FORMAL A large picture of the battle of Waterloo occupied the space above the fireplace.* **2** to keep someone busy or interested: [R] *On long car journeys I occupy myself with solving maths puzzles.* ○ *All the new toys* ***kept*** *the kids occupied for hours.*
occupancy /ˈɒk.jʊ.pᵊnt.si/ [US] /ˈɑː.kjə-/ *noun* [U] *FORMAL* someone's use of a room or building for the purposes of

O

living or working: *The family's occupancy of the apartment lasted only six months.*

occupant /ˈɒk.jʊ.pᵊnt/ [US] /ˈɑː.kjə-/ *noun* [C] FORMAL **1** a person who lives or works in a room or building: *The previous occupants were an Italian family.* **2** a person who is in a car, room, seat, place or position: *One of the occupants of the car was slightly injured.*

occupier /ˈɒk.jʊ.paɪ.əʳ/ [US] /ˈɑː.kjə.paɪ.ɚ/ *noun* [C] UK someone who lives or works in a room or building: *The envelope was simply addressed to 'The Occupier'.*

occupy [TAKE CONTROL] /ˈɒk.jʊ.paɪ/ [US] /ˈɑː.kjuː-/ *verb* [T] (of an army or group of people) to move into and take control and/or possession of a place: *Troops quickly occupied the city.* ○ *Protesting students occupied the university office for two weeks.* ○ *the occupying forces*

occupation /ˌɒk.jʊˈpeɪ.ʃᵊn/ [US] /ˌɑː.kjə-/ *noun* [U] *the Italian occupation **of** Ethiopia*

occupied /ˈɒk.jʊ.paɪd/ [US] /ˈɑː.kjʊ-/ *adj*: *She spent two years in occupied Paris* (= Paris when it was under foreign control) *during the war.* **occupier** /ˈɒk.jʊ.paɪ.əʳ/ [US] /ˈɑː.kjə.paɪ.ɚ/ *noun* [C usually pl] *The occupiers were driven out after fierce street fighting.*

occur [HAPPEN] /əˈkɜːʳ/ [US] /-ˈkɝː/ *verb* [I] **-rr-** (especially of accidents and other unexpected events) to happen: *An accident involving over ten vehicles has occurred in the east-bound lane.* ○ *If any of these symptoms occur while you are taking the medicine, consult your doctor immediately.*

occurrence /əˈkʌr.ᵊnts/ [US] /-ˈkɝː-/ *noun* [C] something that happens: *Street-fights are an everyday occurrence in this area of the city.*

occur [EXIST] /əˈkɜːʳ/ [US] /-ˈkɝː/ *verb* [I + adv or prep] **-rr-** to exist or be present in, among, etc: *Violence of some sort seems to occur in every society.* ○ *Minerals occur naturally in the earth's crust.*

occurrence /əˈkʌr.ᵊnts/ [US] /-ˈkɝː-/ *noun* [U] the fact of something existing, or how much of it exists: *The study compares the occurrence of heart disease in various countries.*

▲ **occur to *sb*** *phrasal verb* If a thought or idea occurs to you, it comes into your mind: *The thought did occur to me.* ○ [+ that] ***It** never even occurred to us **that** he hadn't been invited.* ○ *Does **it** never occur to you **that** I might like to be on my own occasionally?*

O

ocean /ˈəʊ.ʃᵊn/ [US] /ˈoʊ-/ *noun* **1** [S] a very large area of sea: *These mysterious creatures live at the bottom of **the** ocean.* **2** [C] used in the name of each of the world's five main areas of sea: *the Atlantic/Pacific/Indian/Arctic/Antarctic Ocean*

● **oceans of *sth*** OLD-FASHIONED a lot of something: *We've got oceans of time.*

oceanic /ˌəʊ.ʃiˈæn.ɪk/ [US] /ˌoʊ-/ *adj* SPECIALIZED relating to oceans: *oceanic crust/plates*

oceangoing /ˈəʊ.ʃᵊnˌgəʊ.ɪŋ/ [US] /ˈoʊ.ʃᵊnˌgoʊ-/ *adj* (ALSO **seagoing**) (of a ship, boat, etc.) designed for travelling across large areas of sea: *an oceangoing vessel*

oceanography /ˌəʊ.ʃəˈnɒg.rə.fi/ [US] /ˌoʊ.ʃəˈnɑː.grə-/ *noun* [U] the scientific study of the sea

ochre, US ALSO **ocher** /ˈəʊ.kəʳ/ [US] /ˈoʊ.kɚ/ *noun* [U] a yellowish orange colour, or a substance obtained from the earth which is used for giving this colour to paints

ocker, **okker** /ˈɒk.əʳ/ [US] /ˈɑː.kɚ/ *noun* [C] AUS INFORMAL an Australian who is not well educated and does not behave in a polite way

o'clock /əˈklɒk/ [US] /-ˈklɑːk/ *adv* used after a number from one to twelve to say the time when it is exactly that hour: *It's two o'clock.* ○ *He rang me at four o'clock in the morning.*

OCR /ˌəʊ.siːˈɑːʳ/ [US] /ˌoʊ.siːˈɑːr/ *noun* [U] ABBREVIATION FOR **optical character recognition**: the process by which an electronic device recognizes printed or written letters or numbers

octagon /ˈɒk.tə.gən/ [US] /ˈɑːk.tə.gɑːn/ *noun* [C] a flat eight-sided shape

octagonal /ɒkˈtæg.ᵊn.ᵊl/ [US] /ɑːk-/ *adj*: *an octagonal* (= eight-sided) *tower*

octane /ˈɒk.teɪn/ [US] /ˈɑːk-/ *noun* [U] a chemical in petrol

ˈoctane ˌnumber *noun* [C] (ALSO **octane rating**) a number showing the quality of petrol in representing how well and with how much power it can make an engine work

-octane /-ɒk.teɪn/ [US] /-ɑːk-/ *suffix*: *Racing cars use a **high**-octane* (= powerful) *fuel.*

octave /ˈɒk.tɪv/ [US] /ˈɑːk-/ *noun* [C] SPECIALIZED the space between two musical notes which are eight musical notes apart: *Her remarkable vocal range spanned three and a half octaves.*

octet /ɒkˈtet/ [US] /ɑːk-/ *group noun* [C] a group of eight singers or musicians performing together

octet /ɒkˈtet/ [US] /ɑːk-/ *noun* [C] a piece of music written for eight people

October /ɒkˈtəʊ.bəʳ/ [US] /ɑːkˈtoʊ.bɚ/ *noun* [C or U] (WRITTEN ABBREVIATION **Oct**) the tenth month of the year, after September and before November: *22(nd) October/October 22(nd)* ○ *We're leaving for Italy **on** October the ninth/the ninth of October/*(MAINLY US) *October ninth.* ○ *Sara's birthday is some time **in/during** October.* ○ *It's been the rainiest October for years.*

octogenarian /ˌɒk.təʊ.dʒəˈneə.ri.ən/ [US] /ˌɑːk.toʊ.dʒɪˈner.i-/ *noun* [C] a person who is between 80 and 89 years old

octopus /ˈɒk.tə.pəs/ [US] /ˈɑːk.tə.pəs/ *noun* [C] *plural* **octopuses** or **octopi** a sea creature with a soft oval body and eight TENTACLES (= long arm-like parts)

ocular /ˈɒk.jʊ.ləʳ/ [US] /ˈɑː.kjə.lɚ/ *adj* SPECIALIZED of or related to the eyes or sight

oculist /ˈɒk.jʊ.lɪst/ [US] /ˈɑː.kjə-/ *noun* [C] OLD-FASHIONED FOR **ophthalmologist**, see at **ophthalmology**

OD /ˌəʊˈdiː/ [US] /ˌoʊ-/ *verb* [I] **OD'd, OD'd** **1** SLANG to take an OVERDOSE (= too much) of a drug: *She OD'd **on** heroin and died.* **2** INFORMAL HUMOROUS to have too much of something, often food: *Nothing more for me, thanks. I think I OD'd **on** chocolate cake.* **OD** /ˌəʊˈdiː/ [US] /ˌoʊ-/ *noun* [C] MAINLY US SLANG

odd [STRANGE] /ɒd/ [US] /ɑːd/ *adj* strange or unexpected: *Her father was an odd man.* ○ *What an odd thing to say.* ○ *The skirt and jacket looked a bit odd together.* ○ *That's odd* (= surprising) – *I'm sure I put my keys in this drawer and yet they're not here.* ○ ***It's** odd **that** no-one's seen him.* ○ ***It** must be odd **to** live on the 43rd floor.*

● **the odd one out** (ALSO **the odd man out**) a person or thing that is different from or kept apart from others that form a group or set: *Guess which number of the following sequence is the odd one out.* ○ *She was always the odd one out at school – she didn't have many friends.*

oddity /ˈɒd.ɪ.ti/ [US] /ˈɑː.də.t̬i/ *noun* [C] someone or something that is strange and unusual: *Even today a man who stays at home to look after the children is regarded as something of an oddity.*

oddly /ˈɒd.li/ [US] /ˈɑːd-/ *adv*: *Didn't you think she was behaving rather oddly at the party yesterday?* ○ *Oddly **enough*** (= This is strange/surprising), *she didn't mention anything about the fact that she was getting married.*

oddness /ˈɒd.nəs/ [US] /ˈɑːd-/ *noun* [U]

odd [SEPARATED] /ɒd/ [US] /ɑːd/ *adj* [before n] (of something that should be in a pair or set) separated from its pair or set: *He's got a whole drawer full of odd socks.* ○ *I'd got a few odd* (= I had various) *balls of wool left over.*

odd [NUMBERS] /ɒd/ [US] /ɑːd/ *adj* (of numbers) not able to be divided exactly by two: *3, 5, 7 are all odd numbers.* ○ *The houses on this side of the street have all got odd numbers.*

* NOTE: The opposite is **even**.

odd [NOT OFTEN] /ɒd/ [US] /ɑːd/ *adj* [before n] not happening often: *She does **the** odd teaching **job** but nothing permanent.* ○ *You get **the** odd person who's rude to you but they're generally quite helpful.*

-odd [APPROXIMATELY] /-ɒd/ [US] /-ɑːd/ *suffix* INFORMAL used after a number, especially a number that can be divided by ten, to show that the exact number is not known: *I'd say Robert's about forty-odd – maybe forty-five.*

oddball /ˈɒd.bɔːl/ [US] /ˈɑːd.bɑːl/ *noun* [C] INFORMAL a person whose behaviour is unusual and strange **oddball** /ˈɒd.bɔːl/ [US] /ˈɑːd.bɑːl/ *adj* [before n] *The oddball superstar's habits include watching TV with his chimpanzee.*

odd-job man /ˌɒdˈdʒɒb.mæn/ [US] /ˌɑːd.dʒɑːb-/ *noun* [C] (ALSO **odd-jobber**) a man who is paid to do a variety of jobs, especially in the house or garden

oddments /ˈɒd.mənts/ ⓤ /ˈɑːd-/ *plural noun* MAINLY UK small pieces, usually of cloth, that have been cut from larger pieces: *a few oddments of fabric*

odds /ɒdz/ ⓤ /ɑːdz/ *plural noun* **1** the probability that a particular thing will or will not happen: *If you drive a car all your life, the odds are that you'll have an accident at some point.* ○ *There are heavy odds against people succeeding in such a bad economic climate.* ○ *What are the odds on him being* (= Do you think he will be) *re-elected?* ○ *The odds are stacked against a woman succeeding* (= it is not likely that a woman will succeed) *in the business.* **2** the probability expressed as a number when making a bet: *The odds against my horse winning* (= that it will not win)/*on my horse winning* (= that it will win) *are a hundred to one.* ○ *The odds that the US entrant will win the race are ten to one.*

• **against (all) the odds/against all odds** If you do or achieve something against (all) the odds/against all odds, you do or achieve it although there were a lot of problems and you were not likely to succeed: *Against all the odds, he recovered.*

• **be at odds** to disagree: *They're at odds over the funding of the project.* ○ *Her version of events was at odds with* (= very different from) *the police report.*

• **make no odds** MAINLY UK INFORMAL to not be important, or to not change to situation or result: *I don't mind whether you come or not – it makes no odds to me.*

• **over the odds** UK INFORMAL more than something is really worth: *It's a nice enough car but I'm sure she paid over the odds for it.*

,odds and 'ends INFORMAL *plural noun* (UK SLANG **odds and sods**) various items of different types, usually small and unimportant or of little value: *I've taken most of the big things to the new house, but there are a few odds and ends left to collect.*

odds-on /ˌɒdzˈɒn/ ⓤ /ˌɑːdzˈɑːn/ *adj* very probable: *It's odds-on she'll be late and I've rushed for no reason!* ○ *The odds-on favourite to win in the 3.30 race is Killjoy.*

ode /əʊd/ ⓤ /oʊd/ *noun* [C] a poem expressing the writer's thoughts and feelings about a particular person or subject, usually addressed to that person or subject: *'Ode to a Nightingale' and 'Ode on a Grecian Urn' are poems by Keats.*

odious /ˈəʊ.di.əs/ ⓤ /ˈoʊ-/ *adj* FORMAL extremely un-pleasant; causing and deserving hate: *an odious crime* ○ *an odious little man*

odium /ˈəʊ.di.əm/ ⓤ /ˈoʊ-/ *noun* [U] FORMAL hate and strong disapproval

odometer /əʊˈdɒm.ɪ.təʳ/ ⓤ /oʊˈdɑː.mə.t̬ɚ/ *noun* [C] MAIN-LY US FOR **mileometer**

odour UK, US **odor** /ˈəʊ.dəʳ/ ⓤ /ˈoʊ.dɚ/ *noun* [C or U] SLIGHTLY FORMAL a smell, often one that is unpleasant: *In-side the room there was the unmistakable odour of sweaty feet.* ○ FIGURATIVE *The odour of hypocrisy hung about everything she said.*

odourless UK, US **odorless** /ˈəʊ.də.ləs/ ⓤ /ˈoʊ.dɚ-/ *adj* FORMAL without a smell: *an odourless gas*

odyssey /ˈɒd.ɪ.si/ ⓤ /ˈɑː.dɪ-/ *noun* [C usually sing] LITERARY a long exciting journey: *The film follows one man's odyssey to find the mother from whom he was separated at birth.* ○ FIGURATIVE *a spiritual odyssey*

Oedipus complex /ˌiː.dɪ.pəsˈkɒm.pleks/ ⓤ /-ˈkɑːm-/ *noun* [C usually sing] in psychology, a child's sexual desire for their parent of the opposite sex, especially that of a boy for his mother **oedipal** /ˈiː.dɪ.p³l/ ⓤ /ˈe-/ *adj: Freud argued that all people go through an oedipal phase of sexual development.* ○ *oedipal fantasies*

oenophile /ˈiː.nə.faɪl/ *noun* [C] SPECIALIZED a person who loves wine and knows a lot about it

o'er /ɔːʳ/ ⓤ /ɔːr/ *prep* LITERARY SHORT FORM OF **over**: *O'er land and sea they sped.*

oesophagus UK (*plural* **oesophaguses**), US **esophagus** /ɪˈsɒf.ə.ɡəs/ ⓤ /ɪˈsɑː.fə-/ *noun* [C] SPECIALIZED the tube in the body which takes food from the mouth to the stomach

oestrogen, MAINLY US **estrogen** /ˈiː.strəʊ.dʒ³n/ ⓤ /ˈes.trə-/ *noun* [U] a female hormone that causes develop-ment and change in the reproductive organs

oeuvre /ˈɜː.vrə/ *noun* [C usually sing] LITERARY the complete works of a writer, painter or other artist: *Sadly, I'm not familiar with his oeuvre.*

of POSSESSION WEAK /əv/, STRONG /ɒv/ ⓤ /ɑːv/ *prep* used to show possession, belonging or origin: *a friend of mine* ○ *the president of the United States* ○ *employees of the company* ○ *the colour of his hair* ○ *a habit of mine* ○ *that revolting dog of hers* ○ *the love of a good woman* ○ *the complete plays of* (= written by) *Federico Garcia Lorca*

of AMOUNT WEAK /əv/, STRONG /ɒv/ ⓤ /ɑːv/ *prep* used after words or phrases expressing amount, number or particular unit: *a kilo of apples* ○ *loads of food* ○ *hundreds of people* ○ *most of them* ○ *none of them* ○ *both of us* ○ *a third of all people* ○ *a speck of dust* ○ *a drop of rain*

of CONTAINING WEAK /əv/, STRONG /ɒv/ ⓤ /ɑːv/ *prep* contain-ing: *a bag of sweets* ○ *a bottle of beer* ○ *a book of short stories* ○ *sacks of rubbish* ○ *a class of idiots*

of POSITION WEAK /əv/, STRONG /ɒv/ ⓤ /ɑːv/ *prep* used in expressions showing position: *the top of his head* ○ *the back of your dress* ○ *on the corner of the street* ○ *the front of the queue* ○ *I've never been north of Edinburgh.*

of TYPICAL WEAK /əv/, STRONG /ɒv/ ⓤ /ɑːv/ *prep* typical or characteristic of: *She has the face of an angel.* ○ *That man's got the brain of a donkey!*

of DAYS WEAK /əv/, STRONG /ɒv/ ⓤ /ɑːv/ *prep* used to refer to a particular date in a month: *the eleventh of March* ○ *the first of the month*

of TIME WEAK /əv/, STRONG /ɒv/ ⓤ /ɑːv/ *prep* US used in say-ing what the time is: *It's ten (minutes) of five* (= ten minutes before five o'clock).

of DURING WEAK /əv/, STRONG /ɒv/ ⓤ /ɑːv/ *prep* OLD-FASHIONED during: *I like to relax with a pipe of an even-ing.*

of USED AFTER ADJECTIVES WEAK /əv/, STRONG /ɒv/ ⓤ /ɑːv/ *prep* used to connect particular adjectives with nouns: *fond of swimming* ○ *sick of his excuses* ○ *frightened of spiders*

of JUDGMENT WEAK /əv/, STRONG /ɒv/ ⓤ /ɑːv/ *prep* used after an adjective when judging someone's behaviour: *It was a bit unkind of you to mention her weight.* ○ *Thank you so much for my present. How thoughtful of you.*

of RELATING TO WEAK /əv/, STRONG /ɒv/ ⓤ /ɑːv/ *prep* about; relating to: *Speaking of Elizabeth, here she is.* ○ *One of the advantages of travelling by train is being able to read.* ○ *Let us consider the events of the last five months.* ○ *Of her childhood we know very little.* ○ *And what of* (= Tell me about) *young Adrian? How is he?*

of MADE OF WEAK /əv/, STRONG /ɒv/ ⓤ /ɑːv/ *prep* made or consisting of; having: *dresses of lace and silk* ○ *plates of gold and silver* ○ *a land of ice and snow* ○ *a woman of great charm* ○ *a subject of very little interest*

of SEPARATE FROM WEAK /əv/, STRONG /ɒv/ ⓤ /ɑːv/ *prep* used in expressions showing distance from something in place or time: *We live within a mile of the city centre.* ○ *She came within two seconds of beating the world record.*

of LOSS WEAK /əv/, STRONG /ɒv/ ⓤ /ɑːv/ *prep* used in expres-sions showing loss: *They were robbed of all their savings.* ○ *I feel I've been deprived of your company.*

of THAT IS/ARE WEAK /əv/, STRONG /ɒv/ ⓤ /ɑːv/ *prep* that is/ are: *the problem of homelessness* ○ *a rise of 2% in infla-tion* ○ *the skill of negotiating* ○ *the difficulty of bringing up twins* ○ *the pain of separation* ○ *At the age of six she could read a newspaper.*

of COMPARING WEAK /əv/, STRONG /ɒv/ ⓤ /ɑːv/ *prep* used when comparing related things: *Best of all I liked the green one.* ○ *Worst of all was the food!* ○ *He's the best looking of the three brothers.* ○ *I think that of all his films it's my favourite.*

• **of all people/things/places** used to express the idea that a particular person/thing/place is unlikely or surpris-ing: *Stella, of all people, is the last one I'd expect to see at the club.* ○ *And why did you choose Iceland for a holiday, of all places?*

of DONE TO WEAK /əv/, STRONG /ɒv/ ⓤ /ɑːv/ *prep* done to: *the massacre of hundreds of innocent people* ○ *the oppression of a nation* ○ *the destruction of the rain forest*

of FELT BY _WEAK_ /əv/, _STRONG_ /ɒv/ ⓤ /ɑːv/ _prep_ felt or experienced by: _the suffering of millions_ ○ _the anguish of the murdered child's parents_

of THROUGH _WEAK_ /əv/, _STRONG_ /ɒv/ ⓤ /ɑːv/ _prep_ through; having as the cause: _He died of cancer._ ○ _I didn't have to go there – I did it of my own free will._ ○ _I want to know how it happened because it certainly didn't happen of itself._

OFEX /ˈɒf.eks/ ⓤ /ˈɑːf-/ _noun_ [U] _TRADEMARK_ a British share trading and information service that enables investors to buy and sell shares in companies whose shares are not traded on the London Stock Exchange: _The company plans to join OFEX next year._

off NOT OPERATING /ɒf/ ⓤ /ɑːf/ _adv_ (especially of machines, electrical devices, lights, etc.) not operating because not switched on: _Make sure the computers are all off before you go home._ ○ _**Turn/Switch** the light/engine/television off._

off NOT LIKING /ɒf/ ⓤ /ɑːf/ _prep_ not liking or taking something or someone: _He's been off his food ever since he had the stomach upset._ ○ _I used to love wine but I've **gone** off it_ (= stopped liking it) _recently._ ○ _She's well enough to be off the medicine now._ ○ _The doctor says he can **come** off the tablets._

off AWAY FROM /ɒf/ ⓤ /ɑːf/ _adv, prep_ away from a place or position, especially the present place or position: _He drove off at the most incredible speed._ ○ _Keep the dog on the lead or he'll just run off._ ○ _Someone's run off with_ (= taken) _my pen._ ○ _I'm just going off to the shops._ ○ _If we can get off_ (= leave) _early tomorrow morning we'll avoid most of the traffic._ ○ _I'm off now – see you tomorrow._ ○ _She's off **to** Canada next week._ ○ _I saw her off_ (= said goodbye) _at the station._ ○ _There was a 'keep off the grass' sign._

the off _noun_ [S] _UK INFORMAL_ the act of leaving somewhere: _Are we **ready for** the off, then?_

off REMOVED /ɒf/ ⓤ /ɑːf/ _adv, prep_ used with actions in which something is removed or removes itself from another thing: _Take your jacket off._ ○ _One of my buttons has come off._ ○ _She's had all her hair cut off._ ○ _I can't get the lid off this jar._ ○ _Has anyone taken a book off my desk?_ ○ _He fell off his bike._ ○ _Could you cut me a small piece off that big white cheese?_ ○ _Take your feet off that seat, young man!_ ○ _I don't like taking money off you_ (= asking for money)! ○ _I hope she knows where to get off_ (= leave) _the bus/train._ ○ _Get off me_ (= Stop touching me)! ○ _NOT STANDARD I got the knife off of him before he ran away._

• **off with** _sth_ used as a way of ordering someone to remove something: _Off with his head!_ ○ _Off with your jacket!_

off NEAR TO /ɒf/ ⓤ /ɑːf/ _prep_ near to: _He lives just off the main road._ ○ _It's an island off the east coast of Spain._

off BAD /ɒf/ ⓤ /ɑːf/ _adj_ [after v] (of food and drink) no longer fresh or good to eat because of being too old: _This milk smells off._ ○ _I'd better eat this cheese before it **goes** off._

off NOT AT WORK /ɒf/ ⓤ /ɑːf/ _adv, adj_ not at work; at home or on holiday: _I'm going to **take/have** some time off to work on my house._ ○ _She was off **sick** last week._ ○ _He's off at the moment – can I get him to ring you back?_

off COMPLETELY /ɒf/ ⓤ /ɑːf/ _adv_ in such a way as to be completely absent, especially because of having been used or killed: _It says on the bottle that it kills off all known germs._ ○ _It'll take some time before she manages to **pay** off all her debts._ ○ _The good thing about exercise is that it burns off calories._ ○ _INFORMAL Between us we managed to **finish** off eight bottles of wine._

off BELOW USUAL LEVEL /ɒf/ ⓤ /ɑːf/ _adv, adj_ below the usual standard or rate: _She used to have a lovely voice but I think it's **gone** off recently_ (= is not as good as it was). ○ _I'm having an **off day** today – I just can't seem to do anything right!_

off DISTANT /ɒf/ ⓤ /ɑːf/ _adv, prep_ distant (from) in time or space: _The exams are so **far** off that I'm not even thinking about them yet._ ○ _How far off finishing the project are we_ (= How much more is there to do)? ○ _We've been working on the flat for six months now but we're still **a**_

**long way** off finishing. ○ _We're not far off_ (= We are quite near) _London now._

off STOPPED /ɒf/ ⓤ /ɑːf/ _adj_ [after v] (of an arranged event) stopped or given up in advance: _The wedding's off – she's decided she's too young to settle down._ ○ _INFORMAL It's all off_ (= The relationship is finished) _between Philippa and Mike._

off LESS MONEY /ɒf/ ⓤ /ɑːf/ _adv, prep_ (of money) subtracted from the original price: _You can get some money off if you pay cash._ ○ _There's 40% off this week on all winter coats._ ○ _There was $40 or $50 off most jackets in the shop._

off SEPARATED /ɒf/ ⓤ /ɑːf/ _adv_ in such a way as to be separated: _The police have **shut/closed** off all streets leading to the city._ ○ _The area in the park where the kids play is fenced off for safety reasons._

off GET RID OF /ɒf/ ⓤ /ɑːf/ _adv_ in such a way as to get rid of something: _We went out for a while to **walk** off some of our dinner._ ○ _He's gone to **sleep** off a headache after rather too much wine._ ○ _There's no point in getting upset about such remarks – you've just got to laugh them off._

off PROVIDED FOR /ɒf/ ⓤ /ɑːf/ _adj_ having a particular amount or number, especially of money: _UK How are you off **for** money_ (= Have you got enough/How much have you got)? ○ _Andrew must be so **well**-off_ (= rich) _by now._ ○ _I think they're fairly **badly**-off_ (= poor) _now that David has lost his job._ ○ _I'm quite **well** off **for**_ (= have a lot of) _sweaters._

off NO LONGER SERVED /ɒf/ ⓤ /ɑːf/ _adj_ [after v] (of food in a restaurant) not being served because there is none left: _I'm sorry, sir, the salmon is off._

off RUDE /ɒf/ ⓤ /ɑːf/ _adj_ [after v] _MAINLY UK INFORMAL_ not caring about other people's feelings; rude: _He didn't even ring her up on her birthday – I thought that was **a bit** off._

off KILL /ɒf/ ⓤ /ɑːf/ _verb_ [T] _US SLANG_ to kill someone: _They offed him and dumped his body in the swamp._

offal /ˈɒf.ᵊl/ ⓤ /ˈɑː.fᵊl/ _noun_ [U] (_MAINLY US_ **variety meat**) the organs inside an animal, such as the brain, the heart and the liver, which are eaten as food

off **balance** _adj_ [after v], _adv_ **1** If someone or something is off balance, they are in a position where they are likely to fall or be knocked down: _A gust of wind **knocked/threw** her off balance and she fell._ **2** confused or uncertain about what to do next: _Many Republicans were **thrown** off balance by the Democrats' landslide at the polls._

off **beam** _adj_ [after v] _UK INFORMAL_ wrong: _You're **(way)** off beam there._

offbeat /ˌɒfˈbiːt/ ⓤ /ˌɑːfˈbiːt/ _adj_ unusual and strange and therefore surprising or noticeable: _an offbeat sense of humour_

off-centre _UK_ /ˌɒfˈsen.təʳ/ ⓤ /ˌɑːfˈsen.t̬ɚ/ _adj_ [after v] (_US_ **off-center**) nearly, but not quite, in a central position

off **chance** _noun UK INFORMAL_ **on the off chance** hoping that something may be possible, although it is not likely: _I applied for the job on the off chance, but I didn't seriously expect to get it._

off-colour ILL /ˌɒfˈkʌl.əʳ/ ⓤ /ˌɑːfˈkʌl.ɚ/ _adj_ [after v] _INFORMAL_ slightly ill: _I'm feeling a bit off-colour today._

off-colour SEXUAL /ˌɒfˈkʌl.əʳ/ ⓤ /ˌɑːfˈkʌl.ɚ/ _adj_ describes remarks or jokes about sex that are slightly shocking

off-duty /ˌɒfˈdjuː.ti/ ⓤ /ˌɑːfˈduː.t̬i/ _adj_ When police officers, doctors, guards, etc. are off-duty, they are not working: _He looks completely different when he's off-duty and in his normal clothes._

offence CRIME, _US USUALLY_ **offense** /əˈfents/ _noun_ [C] _LEGAL_ an illegal act; a crime: _a serious/minor offence_ ○ _a criminal/drink-driving offence_ ○ _Driving without a licence is an offence._ ○ _He **committed** several serious offences._ ○ _It's the third time that he's been **convicted** of a drug offence._

offend /əˈfend/ _verb_ [I] _LEGAL_ to commit a crime: _Obviously if a police officer offends it's a fairly serious matter._

offender /əˈfen.dəʳ/ ⓤ /-dɚ/ _noun_ [C] _LEGAL_ a person who is guilty of a crime: _first-time offenders_ ○ _sex offenders_ ○ _young offenders_

offence [UPSET FEELINGS], *US USUALLY* **offense** /əˈfents/ *noun* [U] upset and hurt feelings or feelings of annoyance, often because someone has been rude or shown a lack of respect: *I really didn't mean (to **cause/give**) any offence* (= did not intend to upset anyone) – *I was just stating my opinion.* ○ *Do you think he **took** offence* (= was upset) *at what I said about his hair?* ○ *INFORMAL If you don't mind, I'd rather go on my own – **no** offence (intended), but I think it would be better.*

offend /əˈfend/ *verb* [T] to make someone upset or angry: [+ that] *I think she was a bit offended **that** she hadn't been invited to the party.* ○ *He looked a bit offended when you called him middle-aged.* ○ *If the sight of a few dirty dishes offends you, then I think you've got problems!*

offensive /əˈfent.sɪv/ *adj* **1** causing offence: *This programme contains language that some viewers might find offensive.* ○ *He told some really offensive sexist jokes.* ✻ NOTE: The opposite is **inoffensive**. **2** unpleasant: *offensive smells* **offensively** /əˈfent.sɪv.li/ *adv* **offensiveness** /əˈfent.sɪv.nəs/ *noun* [U]

▲ **offend against *sth*** *phrasal verb FORMAL* to break, or to be in opposition to, a rule or principle or something that people consider to be correct: *Do you suppose it would be offending against good taste to wear a patterned tie with my striped shirt?*

ofˌfender ˈprofile *noun* [C] *SPECIALIZED* a **psychological profile**

offending /əˈfen.dɪŋ/ *adj* [before n] *OFTEN HUMOROUS* unwanted, often because unpleasant and causing problems or inconvenience: *"There's a hair in my soup!" "Well, pass it over here and I'll remove the offending **article**."*

offense /əˈfents/ *noun US SPELLING OF* **offence**

offensive /əˈfent.sɪv/ *noun* [C] a planned military attack: *They **launched** the land offensive in the middle of the night.* ○ *UN troops have gone **on the** offensive* (= started to attack).

• **take the offensive** to attack first

offensive /əˈfent.sɪv/ *adj* used for attacking: *Since the other side had taken offensive action* (= attacked), *we had no choice but to defend ourselves.* ○ *Knives of any sort are classed as offensive **weapons**.*

offer [AGREE TO GIVE] /ˈɒf.əʳ/ [US] /ˈɑː.fɚ/ *verb* **1** [I or T] to ask someone if they would like to have something or if they would like you to do something: [+ two objects] *I feel bad that I didn't offer them any food/offer any food **to** them.* ○ *She was offered a job in Paris.* ○ *Can I offer you* (= Would you like) *a drink?* ○ *"Would you sell me that painting?" "What are you offering* (= What will you pay) ***for** it?"* ○ [+ to infinitive] *My father's offered **to** take us to the airport.* ○ [+ speech] *"I'll do the cooking," he offered.* ○ *"I could help." "No, it's all right, thanks." "Well, don't say I didn't offer."* **2** [T] (*ALSO* **offer up**) to say a prayer or make a SACRIFICE (= an act of killing or giving up something) to a god: *Dear Lord, we offer up our prayers...*

offer /ˈɒf.əʳ/ [US] /ˈɑː.fɚ/ *noun* [C] when someone asks you if you would like to have something or if you would like them to do something: *"If you like I can do some shopping for you." "That's a very kind offer."* ○ *I must say the offer **of** a weekend in Barcelona quite tempts me.* ○ *INFORMAL One day I'll **take** you **up on*** (= accept) *that offer.*

• **make an offer** (*ALSO* **put in an offer**) to state that you would like to buy something, especially a house, at a particular price: *They were asking one hundred and eighty thousand for the place, so I put in an offer of one hundred and seventy.* ○ *I've made an offer **on** a house in the town centre.*

• **on (special) offer** *UK* If goods in a shop are on (special) offer, they are being sold at a lower price than usual.

• **under offer** *UK* If a house is under offer, someone has already suggested a particular price at which they would be willing to buy it.

offering /ˈɒf.ər.ɪŋ/ [US] /ˈɑː.fɚ-/ *noun* [C] something that you give or offer to someone: *a peace offering* ○ *a sacrificial offering*

offer [PROVIDE] /ˈɒf.əʳ/ [US] /ˈɑː.fɚ/ *verb* [T] to provide or supply something: *It's an organization that offers free legal advice to people on low incomes.* ○ *It says in the guide that this area of the countryside offers some of the best walks in England.* ○ [+ two objects] *We are now offering you the chance to buy the complete set of pans at half price.* ○ *Did he offer any explanation for his strange behaviour?* ○ *It doesn't **have much to** offer as a town – its shops are fairly poor and there's only one cinema.*

offhand [NOT INTERESTED] /ˌɒfˈhænd/ [US] /ˌɑːf-/ *adj* (*UK INFORMAL* **offish**) not friendly, and showing lack of interest in other people in a way that seems slightly rude: *I hope I didn't appear offhand **with** her – it's just that I was in such a hurry.* **offhandedly** /ˌɒfˈhæn.dɪd.li/ [US] /ˌɑːf-/ *adv* **offhandedness** /ˌɒfˈhæn.dɪd.nəs/ [US] /ˌɑːf-/ *noun* [U]

offhand [IMMEDIATELY] /ˌɒfˈhænd/ [US] /ˌɑːf-/ *adv* without looking for information and without thinking carefully; immediately: *I can't quote the exact statistics for you offhand, but they're there for you to see in the report.*

office [WORK ROOM] /ˈɒf.ɪs/ [US] /ˈɑː.fɪs/ *noun* [C] **1** a room or part of a building in which people work, especially sitting at tables with computers, telephones, etc., usually as a part of a business or other organization: *the director's office* ○ *office equipment* ○ *I didn't leave the office until eight o'clock last night.* ○ *office workers* ➲See Note **cabinet or office?** at **cabinet** FURNITURE. ➲See picture **In the Office** on page Centre 15 **2** a part of a company: *They've got offices in Paris, London and Madrid.*

Office [GOVERNMENT DEPARTMENT] /ˈɒf.ɪs/ [US] /ˈɑː.fɪs/ *noun* [C] a department of the national government in Britain, or an official government organization: *the Home Office* ○ *the Foreign Office* ○ *the Office of Fair Trading*

office [RESPONSIBILITY] /ˈɒf.ɪs/ [US] /ˈɑː.fɪs/ *noun* [C or U] a position of authority and responsibility in a government or other organization: *the office of vice-president* ○ *As chairman of the association, he **held** office for over twenty years.* ○ *The socialist party have been **in** office* (= governing)/***out of** office* (= not governing) *for almost ten years.* ○ *She's held various offices during her time as a minister.*

officer /ˈɒf.ɪ.səʳ/ [US] /ˈɑː.fɪ.sɚ/ *noun* [C] **1** a person in the armed forces who has a position of authority: *a naval officer* ○ *a top-ranking officer* **2** a person who has a position of authority in an organization: *a careers/customs/personnel officer* **3** a form of address for a member of the police force: *"Were you aware of the speed you were driving at, madam?" "No, officer."* ○ *Officer Clarke will show you where to go, sir.*

official /əˈfɪʃ.əl/ *noun* [C] a person who has a position of responsibility in an organization: *a government/trade-union/council official*

official /əˈfɪʃ.əl/ *adj* **1** relating to a position of responsibility: *He visited China in his official capacity as America's trade representative.* ○ *Number Ten Downing Street is the British prime minister's official residence.* ✻ NOTE: The opposite is **unofficial**. **2** agreed to or arranged by people in positions of authority: *The official photos of the prime minister's tour of India are in the magazine.* ○ *The queen will attend the official opening of the theatre in June.* ○ *There is to be an official inquiry into the incident.* **3** If a piece of information is official, it has been announced publicly with authority: *Their engagement is now official.* ○ *Inflation has fallen below 2%, and that's official.*

officialdom /əˈfɪʃ.əl.dəm/ *noun* [U] *DISAPPROVING* used to refer to those people who have a position of authority, especially in government, usually when they are preventing you from doing what you want to do or are slow or not effective

officialese /əˌfɪʃ.əlˈiːz/ *noun* [U] *US* the language often used in government documents which is formal and often difficult to understand

officially /əˈfɪʃ.əl.i/ *adv*: *The royal engagement was announced officially* (= with authority) *this morning.*

officiate /əˈfɪʃ.i.eɪt/ *verb* [I] *FORMAL* to be in charge of or to lead a ceremony or other public event: *A priest officiated **at** the wedding.*

ˈoffice ˌbuilding *noun* [C] (*UK ALSO* **office block**) a large building which contains offices

ˌoffice ˈhours *plural noun UK* the hours during the day when people who work in offices are usually at work: *I'll have to do it **outside/out of*** (= before or after) *office hours.*

ofˌficial reˈceiver *noun* [C] *UK* a person who is instructed by the government to deal with the income and

O

property of a company or a person after they have gone BANKRUPT (= are unable to pay their debts)

of‚ficial 'secret noun [C] UK a piece of information which is known only by the government and its employees: *She was accused of leaking (= telling) official secrets to the newspapers.*

the Of‚ficial 'Secrets ‚Act noun [S] a law in Britain that forbids government workers to make known particular information which could be used against the government: *She had to **sign** the Official Secrets Act when she started her new job.*

officious /ə'fɪʃ.əs/ adj DISAPPROVING too eager to tell people what to do and having too high an opinion of your own importance: *He's an officious little man and widely disliked in the company.* **officiously** /ə'fɪʃ.ə.sli/ adv **officiousness** /ə'fɪʃ.ə.snəs/ noun [U]

offie /'ɒf.i/ US /'ɑː.fi/ noun [C] UK INFORMAL an **off-licence**

offing /'ɒf.ɪŋ/ US /'ɑː.fɪŋ/ noun **in the offing** likely to happen soon: *With an election in the offing, the prime minister is keen to maintain her popularity.*

offish /'ɒf.ɪʃ/ US /'ɑː.fɪʃ/ adj **1** UK **offhand** NOT INTERESTED **2** US **standoffish**

off-key /‚ɒf'kiː/ US /‚ɑːf-/ adv If you sing or play music off-key, you produce notes which are slightly higher or lower than they should be.

off-licence UK /'ɒf.laɪ.sᵊnts/ US /'ɑːf-/ noun [C] (US **liquor store**) a shop that sells mainly alcoholic drinks to be taken away and drunk at home

off-limits /‚ɒf'lɪm.ɪts/ US /‚ɑːf-/ adj [after v] If an area of land is off-limits, it is forbidden that you enter it.

offline /‚ɒf'laɪn/ US /‚ɑːf-/ adj, adv (of a computer) not connected to or directly controlled by a central system, or not connected to the Internet

offload /‚ɒf'ləʊd/ US /'ɑːf.loʊd/ verb [T] to get rid of something that you do not want by giving it to someone else: *I've managed to offload some of our old furniture **onto** a friend who's just bought a house.*

off-message /‚ɒf'mes.ɪdʒ/ US /‚ɑːf-/ adj [after v], adv UK describes a politician who says things in public which are different from the official ideas of their political party: *He was criticised severely by party leaders for **going** off-message during the debate.*

off-peak /‚ɒf'piːk/ US /‚ɑːf-/ adj not at the most popular and expensive time: *off-peak telephone calls*

off-piste /‚ɒf'piːst/ US /‚ɑːf-/ adj, adv MAINLY UK describes skiing that is done on areas of snow which have not been specially prepared for skiing on

off-putting /‚ɒf'pʊt.ɪŋ/ US /'ɑːf.pʊt.ɪŋ/ adj [after v] slightly unpleasant or worrying so that you are discouraged from getting involved in any way: *He's slightly aggressive, which a lot of people find a bit off-putting when they first meet him.* ○ *What I found off-putting was the amount of work that you were expected to do.*

off-ramp US /'ɒf.ræmp/ US /'ɑːf-/ noun [C] (UK **slip road**) a road for driving off a major road

off-season /'ɒf.siː.zᵊn/ US /'ɑːf-/ noun [S] a period of the year when there is less activity in business: *We tend to go skiing during the off-season because it's cheaper.* **off-season** /'ɒf.siː.zᵊn/ US /'ɑːf-/ adj: *Off-season rates for a double room are about $30 a night.*

offset /‚ɒf'set/ US /‚ɑːf-/ verb [T] **offsetting**, **offset**, **offset** to balance one influence against an opposing influence, so that there is no great difference as a result: *The extra cost of travelling to work is offset **by** the lower price of houses here.* ○ UK *He keeps his petrol receipts because petrol is one of the expenses that he can offset **against tax** (= can show to the government as being a business cost, and so not pay tax).*

offshoot /'ɒf.ʃuːt/ US /'ɑːf-/ noun [C] something which has developed from something larger which already existed: *It's an offshoot **of** a much larger company based in Sydney.*

offshore AT SEA /‚ɒf'ʃɔːʳ/ US /‚ɑːf'ʃɔːr/ adj, adv away from or at a distance from the coast: *offshore engineering* ○ *an offshore breeze* ○ *The wind was blowing offshore.*

offshore IN A DIFFERENT COUNTRY /‚ɒf'ʃɔːʳ/ US /‚ɑːf'ʃɔːr/ adj (of companies and banks) based in a different country

with advantageous tax rules: *offshore banking/funds*

offside NOT ALLOWED /‚ɒf'saɪd/ US /‚ɑːf-/ adj (in particular sports, especially football and hockey) in a position which is not allowed by the rules of the game, often in front of the ball: *the offside rule* **offside** /‚ɒf'saɪd/ US /‚ɑːf-/ noun [U] *Coventry had a goal disallowed for offside.*

offside RIGHT SIDE /'ɒf.saɪd/ US /'ɑːf-/ adj [before n] MAINLY UK (especially of a part of a vehicle or road) on the right side: *The offside rear wheel needs replacing.* **the 'offside** noun [S]

offspring /'ɒf.sprɪŋ/ US /'ɑːf-/ noun [C] plural **offspring 1** the young of an animal: *In the case of the guinea pig, the number of offspring varies between two and five.* **2** HUMOROUS OR FORMAL a person's children: *Tom's sister came round on Saturday with her numerous offspring.*

offstage /‚ɒf'steɪdʒ/ US /‚ɑːf-/ adj **1** off the stage, or happening behind or at the side of the stage, so that people who are watching cannot see: *The main characters are offstage for most of the second act.* **2** describes a performer when they are not performing in a play or film, etc: *Though best known for the funny and outspoken roles that she plays on screen, offstage she is shy and rather serious.* **offstage** /‚ɒf'steɪdʒ/ US /‚ɑːf-/ adv: *He never actually appears in the second half of the play – you just hear his voice offstage.*

off-the-peg UK /‚ɒf.ðə'peg/ US /‚ɑːf-/ adv, adj (US **off-the-rack**, AUS **off-the-hook**) describes clothes that are made and bought in standard sizes and not made especially to fit a particular person: *an off-the-peg suit* ⊃Compare **made-to-measure**.

off-white /‚ɒf'waɪt/ US /‚ɑːf-/ adj, noun [U] white with a little grey or yellow in it: *The walls were painted off-white.*

oft /ɒft/ US /ɑːft/ adv OLD USE OR FORMAL often: *that oft-repeated cliché, 'Time heals'*

often /'ɒf.tᵊn/ US /'ɑːf.tᵊn/ adv frequently; many times: *I often see him in the garden.* ○ **How** often do you wash your hair? ○ *I don't often drink spirits.* ○ *It's not often that you meet someone who you're instantly attracted to.* ○ *I don't see my parents as often as I'd like to.* ○ *Christmas is often mild in this country.*

• **as often as not** (ALSO **more often than not**) usually: *As often as not when I make the effort to visit her, I wonder why I've even bothered.*

ogle /'əʊ.gl̩/ US /'oʊ-/ verb [I or T] to look at someone with obvious sexual interest: *I saw you ogling the woman in the red dress!*

ogre /'əʊ.gəʳ/ US /'oʊ.gɚ/ noun [C] **1** a large frightening character in children's stories who eats children **2** INFORMAL a fierce and frightening person: *The headmaster at my junior school was a real ogre.*

oh EMOTION /əʊ/ US /oʊ/ exclamation **1** used to express a variety of emotions, such as surprise, disappointment and pleasure, often as a reaction to something someone has said: *"He's been married three times." "Oh, really? I didn't know that!"* ○ *"I'm afraid I can't come to the party." "Oh, that's a shame."* ○ *Is that for me? Oh, you're so kind!* ○ *"I'm sorry I forgot to ring you." "Oh, don't worry."* **2** introduces an idea that you have just thought of, or something that you have just remembered: *Oh, I've just thought of a problem.* ○ *Oh, and don't forget to lock the back door.* **3** used with other expressions of disappointment, sadness, anger, annoyance, etc: *Oh dear, what a mess!* ○ *Oh hell, I've left my umbrella behind!* ○ *Oh damn, it's broken!*

oh NUMBER /əʊ/ US /oʊ/ noun [C] (ALSO **o**) sometimes used in writing for the number zero: *My phone number is five, double oh, seven, six, six.*

ohm /əʊm/ US /oʊm/ noun [C] SPECIALIZED the standard unit of electrical RESISTANCE

-oholic /-əʊ.hɒl.ɪk/ US /-ə.hɑː.lɪk/ suffix **-aholic**

OHP /‚əʊ.eɪtʃ'piː/ US /‚oʊ-/ noun [C] ABBREVIATION FOR **overhead projector**

OIC, oic INTERNET ABBREVIATION FOR Oh, I see: used to show that you understand what someone has said

oik /ɔɪk/ noun [C] UK SLANG a rude and unpleasant man from a low social class: *In his latest film he plays a racist oik from the East End of London.*

oil /ɔɪl/ *noun* **1** [U] a thick liquid that comes from under the Earth's surface which is used as a fuel and for making parts of machines move easily: *diesel/lubricating oil* **2** [U] PETROLEUM (= the black oil obtained from under the Earth's surface from which petrol comes): *drilling for oil* ○ *the oil industry* **3** [C or U] a smooth thick liquid produced from plants or animals that is used in cooking: *olive/corn/vegetable/sunflower oil* ➲See also **well-oiled** EFFECTIVE; **well-oiled** DRUNK. **4** [C or U] a smooth thick liquid that is used to improve the appearance or quality of the skin or hair: *a bath/hair oil*

oil /ɔɪl/ *verb* [T] to put oil on something, especially a machine, usually to make it work more easily without sticking

• **oil the wheels** *INFORMAL* to make it easier for something to happen: *An aid programme was established to oil the wheels **of** economic reform in the region.*

oily /ˈɔɪ.li/ *adj* **1** consisting of or similar to oil: *an oily liquid* **2** covered in oil or containing a lot of oil: *an oily rag* ○ *oily fish* ○ *I've got oily skin* (= it produces a lot of oil). **3** too friendly and polite in a way that is not sincere

oils /ɔɪlz/ *plural noun* thick paints with an oil base, used for painting pictures: *Do you paint in oils or watercolours?*

oilcan /ˈɔɪl.kæn/ *noun* [C] a container for oil, especially one with a long thin tube for putting oil on machinery

oilfield /ˈɔɪl.fiːəld/ *noun* [C] an area underground where there is a large amount of oil: *the Saudi Arabian oilfields*

oil-fired /ˈɔɪl.faɪəd/ [US] /-faɪrd/ *adj* describes a heating system that uses REFINED oil (= oil from which unwanted substances have been removed) as a fuel

oilman /ˈɔɪl.mən/ *noun* [C] a man who owns or operates OIL WELLS or who buys and sells oil: *He started off his career as a Texas oilman.*

ˈoil ˌpaint *noun* [U] a thick type of paint with an oil base, used for painting pictures ➲See also **oils** at **oil**.

ˈoil ˌpainting *noun* **1** [C] a picture painted with oil paints **2** [U] the art or process of painting with oil paints

• **be no oil painting** *UK HUMOROUS* to be unattractive: *She's no oil painting but she's got a lovely personality.*

oilrig /ˈɔɪl.rɪg/ *noun* [C] a large structure with equipment for removing oil from under the ground, especially under the sea

oilseed /ˈɔɪl.siːd/ *noun* [U] any of a variety of seeds from cultivated crops which provide oil: *oilseed rape*

oilskin /ˈɔɪl.skɪn/ *noun* [C or U] cotton cloth which has a thin layer of oil on it to make it waterproof, or a piece of protective clothing made out of this cloth: *a hat made of oilskin* ○ *The fishermen were all wearing oilskins* (= clothing made of this cloth).

ˈoil ˌslick *noun* [C] a layer of oil that is floating over a large area of the surface of the sea, usually because an accident has caused it to escape from a ship or container

ˈoil ˌtanker *noun* [C] a ship which carries a large amount of oil

ˈoil ˌwell *noun* [C] a hole made in the ground for the removal of oil

oink /ɔɪŋk/ *noun* [C] *INFORMAL* (especially in children's books) a written representation of the noise that a pig makes

ointment /ˈɔɪnt.mənt/ *noun* [U] a thick oily substance, usually containing medicine, which is put on the skin where it is sore or where there is an injury, in order to cure it: *eye ointment*

okay [AGREED], **OK** /ˌəʊˈkeɪ/ [US] /ˌoʊ-/ /ˈ--/ *adj* [after v], *exclamation INFORMAL* agreed or acceptable: *Is it okay if I bring a friend to the party?* ○ *If it's okay **by/with** you, I'll leave the shopping till tomorrow.* ○ *I'll see you at six-thirty, okay?* ○ *"I'll pay you back tomorrow." "OK, no problem."* ○ *I mean, OK* (= I accept that), *I wasn't exactly polite to him, but I don't think I was that rude!*

okay (**okaying, okayed, okayed**), **OK** (**OKing, OKed, OKed**) /ˌəʊˈkeɪ/ [US] /ˌoʊ-/ /ˈ--/ *verb* [T] *INFORMAL* to agree to something: *Have the committee okayed your proposal?*

the okay, the OK *noun* [S] *INFORMAL* permission: *He's **got** the okay to go ahead with his project.*

okay [SATISFACTORY], **OK** /ˌəʊˈkeɪ/ [US] /ˌoʊ-/ /ˈ--/ *adj INFORMAL* **1** in a satisfactory state or of a satisfactory quality; ALL RIGHT: *How's Paula? Is she okay after her fall yesterday?* ○ *Are you OK? You look a bit pale.* ○ *"Is everything OK with you?" "Yes, fine."* ○ *I'll just check that the car's okay – that was a bit of a bang!* **2** not bad but certainly not good: *"Did you have a good meal last night?" "It was okay, though I've certainly had better."* ○ *Her voice is OK, but it's nothing special.*

okay, OK /ˌəʊˈkeɪ/ [US] /ˌoʊ-/ *adv INFORMAL* in a satisfactory way: *Everything was going OK until the printer stopped working.* ○ *Did you sleep okay?* ○ *I just phoned to make sure that you got there okay.*

okay [EXPRESSION], **OK** /əʊˈkeɪ/ [US] /oʊ-/ /ˈ--/ *exclamation* **1** *INFORMAL* used as a way of showing that you are going to take action or start something new: *Okay, let's go.* ○ *Okay then, if you're ready we'll start.* **2** *NOT STANDARD* used in the middle of a sentence as a way of pausing: *We saw these guys, okay, so we went up to them and started talking.*

okey-doke /ˈəʊ.ki.dəʊk/ [US] /ˈoʊ.ki.doʊk/ *exclamation* (*ALSO* **okey-dokey**) *INFORMAL FOR* **okay** AGREED

okker /ˈɒk.əʳ/ [US] /ˈɑː.kɚ/ *noun* [C] an **ocker**

okra /ˈəʊ.krə/ [US] /ˈoʊ-/ *noun* [U] (*US ALSO* **gumbo**) the small green pods from a tropical plant eaten as a vegetable or used to thicken soups and other dishes, or the plant itself ➲See picture **Vegetables** on page Centre 2

old [EXISTED MANY YEARS] /əʊld/ [US] /oʊld/ *adj* **1** having lived or existed for many years: *an old man* ○ *We're all **getting** older.* ○ *I was shocked by how old he looked.* ○ *Now come on, you're old enough to tie your own shoelaces, Carlo.* ○ *I'm too old **to** be out clubbing every night.* ○ *a beautiful old farm house in the country* ○ *a battered old car* ○ *That's an old joke – I've heard it about a thousand times.* ○ *I think this cheese is a bit old judging by the smell of it.* ➲See Note **elder/eldest** or **old/oldest?** at **elder**. **2** *DISAPPROVING* **too old/a bit old** unsuitable because intended for older people: *Don't you think that book is a bit old for you?*

• **be (as) old as the hills** to be very old

• **the oldest profession in the world** *HUMOROUS* PROSTITUTION (= the job of having sex for money)

the old *plural noun* old people considered together as a group: *A lot of services have been cut that particularly affect the old.*

oldish /ˈəʊl.dɪʃ/ [US] /ˈoʊl-/ *adj* quite old: *"Is she old?" "Oldish – late sixties maybe."*

USAGE

old or elderly?

Elderly is sometimes used instead of **old** when describing a person as it is considered more polite.

an elderly gentleman

old [OF AGE] /əʊld/ [US] /oʊld/ *adj* used to describe or ask about someone's age: *How old is your father?* ○ *Rosie's six years old now.* ○ *It's not very dignified behaviour for a 54-year-old man.* ○ *He's a couple of years older than me.*

COMMON LEARNER ERROR

old

You can give someone's age using **old** in two different ways. You can write the age as three separate words when you name the person first.

My daughter is three years old.

However, when you use **old** before naming the person then you should write the age as one word (eg **three-year-old**) with hyphens. Note that the word **year** does not become **years** when you use **old** like this.

I've got a three-year-old daughter.

old [FROM THE PAST] /əʊld/ [US] /oʊld/ *adj* [before n] **1** from a period in the past; FORMER: *I saw my old English teacher last time I went home.* ○ *He's bought me a smart new camera to replace my old one.* ○ *She showed me her old school.* ○ *I saw an old boyfriend of mine.* ○ *In my old job I wasn't given sick-pay.* **2** **Old English/French, etc.** describes a language when it was in an early stage in its development

• **for old times' sake** If you do something for old times' sake, you do it in order to remember a happy time that you had in the past: *We should all meet up again – just for old times' sake.*
• **of old 1** *LITERARY* in or from the past: *in* ***days*** *of old* **2** *MAINLY UK* for a very long time: *I know him of old.*
• **of the old school** traditional and old-fashioned

old [VERY FAMILIAR] /əʊld/ [US] /oʊld/ *adj* **[before n] 1** (especially of a friend) known for a long time: *She's one of my oldest friends – we met at school.* **2** *INFORMAL* used before someone's name when you are referring to or addressing them, to show that you know them well and like them: *There's old Sara working away in the corner.* ○ *I hear* ***poor*** *old Frank's lost his job.*

ˌold ˈage *noun* **[U]** the period in a person's life when he or she is old: *She became very depressed* ***in*** *her old age.*

ˌold age ˈpension *noun* **[C]** *UK* a PENSION that is paid by the state to people who have stopped working because they have reached a particular age
ˌold age ˈpensioner *noun* **[C]** (*ABBREVIATION* **OAP**) *UK* a person who receives an old age pension from the state

ˌold ˈboy [OLD MAN] *noun* **1 [C]** *MAINLY UK INFORMAL* an old man: *the old boy next door* **2 [as form of address]** *OLD-FASHIONED* a way that some men address male friends that they have known for many years: *Come on, old boy, drink up.*

ˌold ˈboy [STUDENT] *noun* **[C]** *UK* An old boy of a particular school is a man who went to school there as a child: *an old-boy reunion*
• **the old-boy network** *UK* the way in which men who have been to the same expensive school or university help each other to find good jobs: *The old-boy network still operates in some City banks.*

the ˈold ˌcountry *noun* **[S]** the country that a person or a person's family originally came from: *I've no plans to go back to the old country.*

olden /ˈəʊl.dᵊn/ [US] /ˈoʊl-/ *adj* **[before n]** *OLD USE OR LITERARY* from a long time ago: *We didn't have things like televisions and computers* ***in the*** *olden* ***days.*** ○ ***In*** *olden* ***times,*** *people rarely travelled.*

olde-worlde /ˌəʊl.diˈwɜːl.di/ [US] /ˌoʊl.diˈwɝːl-/ *adj UK INFORMAL* old in a very noticeable or artificial way, or made to look old in a way that seems false: *The village is a bit too olde-worlde and more of a museum than a thriving community.*

old-fashioned [THINGS] /ˌəʊldˈfæʃ.ᵊnd/ [US] /ˌoʊld-/ *adj MAINLY DISAPPROVING* not modern, belonging to or typical of a time in the past: *old-fashioned clothes/ideas/furniture*

old-fashioned [PEOPLE] /ˌəʊldˈfæʃ.ᵊnd/ [US] /ˌoʊld-/ *adj MAINLY DISAPPROVING* behaving or thinking in a way that is not modern and is more typical of a time in the past: *She's a bit old-fashioned in her outlook.*

ˌold ˈflame *noun* **[C]** a person that you loved or had a sexual relationship with in the past

ˌold ˈgirl [OLD WOMAN] *noun* **1 [C]** *MAINLY UK INFORMAL* an old woman: *The poor old girl doesn't get out much these days.* **2 [as form of address]** *OLD-FASHIONED* a way that some men address female friends that they have known for many years: *Come on, old girl, we haven't got all day.*

ˌold ˈgirl [STUDENT] *noun* **[C]** *UK* An old girl of a particular school is a woman who went to school there as a child: *an old-girl reunion*

ˌold ˈgrowth *noun* **[U]** *US* trees that have been growing for a very long time

the ˌold ˈguard *group noun* **[S]** those people in an organization or society who oppose change and whose beliefs and ideas belong to a period in the past: *Radical reform was, of course, opposed by the old guard.*

ˌold ˈhand *noun* **[C]** someone who is very experienced and skilled in a particular area of activity: *We should be able to trust Silva to negotiate a good deal for us – he's an old hand* ***at*** *the game.*

ˌold ˈhat *adj* **[after v]** *DISAPPROVING* not modern or exciting: *He may be old hat among the trendy younger generation, but his shows draw more viewers than any other comedian.*

oldie [SONG] /ˈəʊl.di/ [US] /ˈoʊl-/ *noun* **[C]** *INFORMAL* an old popular song: ***golden*** *oldies from the sixties*

oldie [PERSON] /ˈəʊl.di/ [US] /ˈoʊl-/ *noun* **[C]** *INFORMAL* an old person

ˌold ˈlady *noun* **[S]** *SLANG* a man's wife: *I haven't seen your old lady for months, Bill.* ○ *How's* ***the*** *old lady, then?*

ˌold ˈmaid *noun* **[C]** *OLD-FASHIONED* a woman who is not married or has not had a sexual relationship and is not now young

ˌold ˈman *noun* **[S]** *SLANG* someone's father or someone's husband: *Thought I'd take* ***the*** *old man out for a drink tonight.* ○ *My old man's taking me on holiday.*

ˌold ˈmaster *noun* **[C]** a painting by a famous European artist of the past, especially from the 13th to the 17th century

ˈold ˌmoney [PEOPLE] *noun* **[U]** used to refer to rich people whose families have been rich for a long time: *Much of big business is still controlled by old money.*

ˈold ˌmoney [MONEY] *noun* **[U]** a type of money that is no longer used

ˌOld ˈNick *noun* **[S]** *OLD-FASHIONED HUMOROUS* the Devil

old people's home /ˌəʊldˈpiː.pl̩zˌhəʊm/ [US] /ˌoʊldˈpiː.pl̩zˌhoʊm/ *noun* **[C]** a place where old people can live together and be cared for when they are too weak or ill to take care of themselves

old-school /ˈəʊld.skuːl/ [US] /ˈoʊld-/ *adj* old-fashioned: *old-school ideas/traditions* ○ *He was very old-school in his approach to management.*

the ˌold school ˈtie *noun* **[S]** the way in which people who have been to the same expensive private school help each other to find good jobs: *The old school tie still has enormous power in such companies.*

old-style /ˈəʊld.staɪl/ [US] /ˈoʊld-/ *adj* **[before n]** old-fashioned, or based on ideas from the past: *old-style teaching methods* ○ *old-style politics*

the ˌOld ˈTestament *noun* **[S]** one of the two main parts of the Christian Bible, which records the history of the Jewish people before the birth of Christ ➲Compare **the New Testament**.

old-time /ˈəʊld.taɪm/ [US] /ˈoʊld-/ *adj MAINLY US* describes things from a long time ago: *old-time dancing* ○ *old-time movie theaters*

old-timer /ˌəʊldˈtaɪ.məʳ/ [US] /ˈoʊldˌtaɪ.mɚ/ *noun* **[C]** *INFORMAL* an old man, or someone who has been or worked in a place for a long time

old wives' tale /ˌəʊldˈwaɪvzˌteɪl/ [US] /ˌoʊld-/ *noun* **[C]** a piece of advice or a theory, often related to matters of health, that was believed in the past but which we now know to be wrong

ˌold ˈwoman *noun* **[C]** *DISAPPROVING* a man who gets anxious over unimportant matters and details: *You know what an old woman Dave is – he nearly had a fit because he got a few specks of mud on his shoes!*

old-world /ˌəʊldˈwɜːld/ [US] /ˌoʊldˈwɝːld/ [PAST] *adj APPROVING* belonging to or typical of a period in the past: *The town centre retains its old-world* ***charm,*** *with buildings dating from Shakespeare's day.* ➲Compare **olde-worlde**.

the ˌOld ˈWorld [REGION] *noun* **[S]** Asia, Africa and Europe

oleaginous /ˌəʊ.liˈædʒ.ɪ.nəs/ [US] /ˌoʊ-/ *adj FORMAL* extremely polite, kind or helpful in a false way that is intended to benefit yourself

oleander /ˌəʊ.liˈæn.dəʳ/ [US] /ˌoʊ.liˈæn.dɚ/ *noun* **[C or U]** an evergreen Mediterranean tree or bush with strong leaves and white, red or pink flowers

ˈO ˌlevel *noun* **[C]** a public examination in a particular subject that was taken in the past in British schools by children aged 15 or 16, or the qualification obtained: *She's got 10 O levels.* ○ *O levels were replaced by GCSEs in 1988.* ➲Compare **A level**.

olfactory /ɒlˈfæk.tᵊr.i/ [US] /ɑːlˈfæk.ter.i/ *adj* **[before n]** *SPECIALIZED* connected with the ability to smell: *the olfactory nerve*

oligarchy /ˈɒl.ɪ.gɑː.ki/ [US] /ˈɑː.lɪ.gɑːr-/ *group noun* **[C or U]** (government by) a small group of powerful people

oligarch /ˈɒl.ɪ.gɑː.k/ [US] /ˈɑː.lɪ.gɑːrk/ *noun* **[C]** one of the people in an oligarchy

olive /ˈɒl.ɪv/ ⓤ /ˈɑː.lɪv/ *noun* [C] a small bitter green or black fruit that is eaten or used to produce oil, or an evergreen Mediterranean tree on which this fruit grows: *olive groves*
● **hold out/offer an olive branch** to do or say something in order to show that you want to end a disagreement with someone: *He held out an olive branch to the opposition by releasing 42 political prisoners.*

olive 'drab *noun* [U] *US* a greyish green colour that is often used for military uniforms

olive 'oil *noun* [U] a yellow or green oil obtained by pressing ripe olives

-ology /-ɒl.ə.dʒi/ ⓤ /-ɑː.lə.dʒi/ *suffix* the scientific study of a particular subject: *geology* ○ *climatology* **-ological** /-ə.lɑdʒ.ɪ.kᵊl/ ⓤ /-ɑː.dʒɪ-/ *suffix: biological* ○ *technological* **-ologist** /-ɒl.ə.dʒɪst/ ⓤ /-ɑː.lə-/ *suffix: archaeologist*

Olympiad /əʊˈlɪm.pi.æd/ ⓤ /oʊ-/ *noun* [C] an occasion on which the Olympic Games are held

Olympian /əʊˈlɪm.pi.ən/ ⓤ /oʊ-/ *adj* LITERARY having the qualities of a god: *She has maintained an Olympian* ***detachment*** *from* (= avoided being involved with and worried by) *the everyday business of the office.* ➔See also **Olympian** at **Olympics**.

the Olympics /ðiəʊˈlɪm.pɪks/ ⓤ /-oʊ-/ *plural noun* (*ALSO* **the Olympic Games**) a set of international sports competitions that happen once every four years: *The Olympic Games are held in a different country on each occasion.* ○ *the Summer/Winter Olympics* **Olympic** /əʊˈlɪm.pɪk/ ⓤ /-oʊ-/ *adj* [before n] *the International Olympic Committee* ○ *an Olympic gold medallist*

Olympian /əʊˈlɪm.pi.ən/ ⓤ /oʊ-/ *noun* [C] MAINLY US a competitor in the Olympic Games ➔See also **Olympian**.

ombudsman /ˈɒm.bʊdz.mən/ ⓤ /ˈɑːm.bədz-/ *noun* [C] someone who works for a government or large organization and deals with the complaints made against it: *Complaints to the Banking Ombudsman grew by 50 per cent last year.*

omelette, *US ALSO* **omelet** /ˈɒm.lət/ ⓤ /ˈɑː.mə.lət/ *noun* [C] a savoury dish made by mixing together the yellow and transparent parts of an egg and frying it, often with small pieces of other food: *a cheese/mushroom omelette*
● **You can't make an omelette without breaking eggs.** SAYING said about a situation in which it is hard to achieve something important without causing unpleasant effects

omen /ˈəʊ.mən/ ⓤ /ˈoʊ-/ *noun* [C] something that is considered to be a sign of how a future event will take place: *England's victory over France is a* ***good*** *omen* ***for*** *next week's match against Germany.* ○ *a* ***bad*** *omen* ○ *Many people believe that a broken mirror is an omen* ***of*** *bad luck.*

ominous /ˈɒm.ɪ.nəs/ ⓤ /ˈɑː.mə-/ *adj* suggesting that something unpleasant is likely to happen: *There was an ominous* ***silence*** *when I asked whether my contract was going to be renewed.* ○ *The engine had been making an ominous* ***sound*** *all the way from London.* ○ *ominous dark clouds* **ominously** /ˈɒm.ɪ.nə.sli/ ⓤ /ˈɑː.mə-/ *adv: I went into the kitchen and found him lying ominously still on the floor.*

omit /əʊˈmɪt/ ⓤ /oʊ-/ *verb* [T] **-tt-** to fail to include or do something: *She omitted* ***from*** *the list of contributors to the report.* ○ *The Prince's tour conveniently omitted the most deprived areas of the city.* ○ [+ to infinitive] FORMAL *She omitted* ***to*** *mention that she was going to Yorkshire next week.*

omission /əʊˈmɪʃ.ᵊn/ ⓤ /oʊ-/ *noun* [C or U] when something has not been included that should have been: *Measures to control child employment are a* ***glaring*** (= very obvious) *omission* ***from*** *new legislation to protect children.* ○ *There are some serious errors and omissions in the book.* ○ *Many of the fans believe that the omission* ***of*** *Heacock* ***from*** *the team cost England the match.*

omni- /ɒm.ni-/ ⓤ /ɑː.mni-/ *prefix* everywhere or everything: *omnipresent* ○ *omniscient*

omnibus SEVERAL PARTS /ˈɒm.nɪ.bəs/ ⓤ /ˈɑːm-/ *noun* [C] **1** a book consisting of two or more parts that have already been published separately ➔Compare **anthology**. **2** *UK* a programme consisting of two or more parts that have already been broadcast separately: *the omnibus* ***edition*** *of a soap opera*

omnibus TRANSPORT /ˈɒm.nɪ.bəs/ ⓤ /ˈɑːm-/ *noun* [C] OLD USE a bus
● **the man/woman on the Clapham omnibus** *UK* OLD-FASHIONED an imaginary person whose opinions or ideas are considered to be typical of those of ordinary British people: *The man on the Clapham omnibus probably knows nothing about Rwanda.*

omnipotent /ɒmˈnɪp.ə.tᵊnt/ ⓤ /ɑːmˈnɪp.ə.tᵊnt/ *adj* FORMAL having unlimited power; able to do anything: *How can a loving, omnipotent God permit disease, war and suffering?* **omnipotence** /ɒmˈnɪp.ə.tᵊnts/ ⓤ /ɑːmˈnɪp.ə.tᵊnts/ *noun* [U] *God's omnipotence*

omnipresent /ˌɒm.nɪˈprez.ᵊnt/ ⓤ /ˌɑːm-/ *adj* FORMAL present or having an effect everywhere at the same time: *So how did a diminutive Australian soap star get to be an omnipresent icon of style and beauty?* **omnipresence** /ˌɒm.nɪˈprez.ᵊnts/ ⓤ /ˌɑːm-/ *noun* [U] *the omnipresence of the secret police*

omniscient /ɒmˈnɪs.i.ənt/ ⓤ /ɑːmˈnɪʃ.ᵊnt/ *adj* FORMAL having or seeming to have unlimited knowledge: *the omniscient narrator* **omniscience** /ɒmˈnɪs.i.ənts/ ⓤ /ɑːmˈnɪʃ.ᵊnts/ *noun* [U]

omnivorous /ɒmˈnɪv.ᵊr.əs/ ⓤ /ɑːmˈnɪv.ɚ-/ *adj* **1** naturally able to eat both plants and meat: *Pigs are omnivorous animals.* **2** enthusiastic and interested in many different areas of a subject: *an omnivorous* ***reader*** **omnivore** /ˈɒm.nɪ.vɔːʳ/ ⓤ /ˈɑːm.nɪ.vɔːr/ *noun* [C] an animal that is naturally able to eat both plants and meat ➔Compare **carnivore**, **herbivore**.

on ABOVE /ɒn/ ⓤ /ɑːn/ *prep* used to show that something is in a position above something else and touching it, or that something is moving into such a position: *Look at all the books on your desk!* ○ *Ow, you're standing on my foot!* ○ *Your suitcase is on top of the wardrobe.* ○ *They live in that old farmhouse on the hill.* ○ *I got on my bike and left.*

on CONNECTED /ɒn/ ⓤ /ɑːn/ *prep* covering the surface of, being held by, or connected to: *You've got blood on your shirt.* ○ *Which finger do you wear your ring on?* ○ *Can you stand on your head?* ○ *We could hang this picture on the wall next to the door.* ○ *Dogs should be kept on their leads at all times.* ○ *UK We've just moved house and we're not on the phone* (= not connected to the telephone service) *yet.*

on /ɒn/ ⓤ /ɑːn/ *adv, adj* [after v] **1** on your body or someone's body: *It's very cold so* ***put*** *a jumper on.* ○ *She wanders round the house with* ***nothing*** *on.* ○ *Can you remember what he* ***had*** *on* (= was wearing)? ○ *I tried on a few jackets, but none of them looked nice.* **2** covering the surface of something or connected to something: *Screw the lid on tightly.* ○ *Make sure the top's on properly.* ○ *Surgeons have managed to sew a man's ear back on after it was bitten off in a fight.*

on WRITING /ɒn/ ⓤ /ɑːn/ *prep* used to show where something has been written, printed or drawn: *Which page is that curry recipe on?* ○ *His initials were engraved on the back of his watch.* ○ *What's on the menu* (= What food is available) *tonight?*

on RECORDING/PERFORMANCE /ɒn/ ⓤ /ɑːn/ *prep* used to show the form in which something is recorded or performed: *How much data can you store on a floppy disk?* ○ *When's the movie coming out on video?* ○ *I was really embarrassed the first time I saw myself on film.* ○ *What's on television tonight?* ○ *I wish there was more jazz on the radio.*

on PERFORMING /ɒn/ ⓤ /ɑːn/ *adv, adj* [after v] performing: *Hurry up with the make-up – I'm on in ten minutes.* ○ *The audience cheered as the band came on* (= came onto the stage).

on PAIN /ɒn/ ⓤ /ɑːn/ *prep* used to show what causes pain or injury as a result of being touched: *I hit my head on the shelf as I was standing up.* ○ *You'll cut yourself on that knife if you're not careful.*

on TO /ɒn/ ⓤ /ɑːn/ *prep* to or towards: *Our house is the first on the left after the post office.* ○ *The attack on the village lasted all night.* ○ *I wish you wouldn't creep up on me like that!*

on RELATING /ɒn/ ⓤ /ɑːn/ *prep* relating to: *a book on pregnancy* ○ *Her thesis is on Italian women's literature.*

O

○ *The minister has refused to comment on the allegations.* ○ *Criticism has no effect on him.* ○ *Have the police got anything on you* (= have they got any information about you which can be used against you)?

on [MONEY] /ɒn/ ⓤ /ɑːn/ *prep* used to show something for which a payment is made: *He spent eighty pounds on a hat.* ○ *I've wasted a lot of money on this car.* ○ *We made a big profit on that deal.* ○ *How much interest are you paying on the loan?*

on [NECESSARY] /ɒn/ ⓤ /ɑːn/ *prep* used to show a person or thing that is necessary for something to happen or that is the origin of something: *We're relying on you.* ○ *I might come – it depends on Andrew.* ○ *Most children remain dependent on their parents while at university.* ○ *His latest movie is based on a fairy story.*

on [NEXT TO] /ɒn/ ⓤ /ɑːn/ *prep* next to or along the side of: *Cambridge is on the River Cam.* ○ *Our house was on Sturton Street.* ○ *Strasbourg is on the border of France and Germany.*

on [TIME] /ɒn/ ⓤ /ɑːn/ *prep* used to show when something happens: *Many shops don't open on Sundays.* ○ *What are you doing on Friday?* ○ *My birthday's on the 30th of May.* ○ *Would you mind telling me what you were doing on the afternoon of Friday the 13th of March?* ○ *Trains to London leave on* **the** *hour* (= at exactly one o'clock, two o'clock etc.) *every hour.* ○ *On a clear day you can see the mountains from here.* ○ *She was dead on arrival* (= dead when she arrived) *at the hospital.* ○ *Please hand in your keys at reception on your departure from* (= when you leave) *the hotel.*

on [AFTER] /ɒn/ ⓤ /ɑːn/ *prep* happening after and usually because of: *Acting on information given to them anonymously, the police arrested him.* ○ *He inherited a quarter of a million pounds on his mother's death.* ○ *On their return they discovered that their house had been burgled.*

on [TRAVEL] /ɒn/ ⓤ /ɑːn/ *prep* used for showing some methods of travelling: *I love travelling on trains.* ○ *She'll be arriving on the five-thirty train.* ○ *We went to France on the ferry.* ○ *It'd be quicker to get there on foot.* ○ *two figures on horseback* **on** /ɒn/ ⓤ /ɑːn/ *adv*: *The train suddenly started moving as I was getting on.* ○ *Her horse galloped off as soon as she was on.*

on [FOOD/FUEL/DRUG] /ɒn/ ⓤ /ɑːn/ *prep* used to show something which is used as food, fuel or a drug: *What do mice* **live** *on?* ○ *Does this radio* **run** *on batteries?* ○ *Is he on drugs?*

on [FINANCIAL SUPPORT] /ɒn/ ⓤ /ɑːn/ *prep* used to show what is providing financial support or an income: *I've only got £50 a week to* **live** *on at the moment.* ○ *He retired on a generous pension from the company.* ○ *UK She's on* (= earning) *£15 000 a year.*

on [PROCESS] /ɒn/ ⓤ /ɑːn/ *prep* used to show that a condition or process is being experienced: *He accidentally set his bed on* **fire**. ○ *Their flights to Paris are on special* **offer** *at the moment.* ○ *Martin's on* **holiday** *this week.* ○ *I'll be away on a training course next week.* ○ *I often feel carsick when I'm on a long journey.* ○ *Crime is on the increase* (= is increasing) *again.*

● **on the go 1** very busy: *I've been on the go all day and I'm really tired.* **2** *UK* in the process of being produced: *Did you know that she's got a new book on the go* (= being written)*.*

on [INVOLVEMENT] /ɒn/ ⓤ /ɑːn/ *prep* used to show when someone is involved or taking part in something: *I'm working on a new book.* ○ *In the last lesson we were on the causes of the First World War, weren't we?* ○ *"Where had we got up to?" "We were on page 42."*

on [MEMBER] /ɒn/ ⓤ /ɑːn/ *prep* used to show when someone is a member of a group or organization: *Have you ever served on a jury?* ○ *There are no women on the committee.* ○ *How many people are on your staff?* ○ *She's a researcher on a women's magazine.*

on [AGAIN] /ɒn/ ⓤ /ɑːn/ *prep* used to show when something is repeated one or more times: *The government suffered defeat on defeat in the local elections.* ○ *Wave on wave of refugees has crossed the border to escape the fighting.*

on [COMPARISON] /ɒn/ ⓤ /ɑːn/ *prep* used when making a comparison: *£950 is my final offer, and I can't improve on*

it. ○ *The productivity figures are* **down/up** *on last week's.*

on [POSSESSION] /ɒn/ ⓤ /ɑːn/ *prep* [before pronoun] used to show when someone has something with them in their pocket or in a bag that they are carrying: *Have you got a spare cigarette on you?* ○ *I haven't got my driving licence on me.*

on [PAYMENT] /ɒn/ ⓤ /ɑːn/ *prep INFORMAL* used to show who is paying for something: *This meal is on me.* ○ *She had her operation done on the National Health Service.*

on [FAULTY] /ɒn/ ⓤ /ɑːn/ *prep* used to show who suffers when something does not operate as it should: *The phone suddenly went dead on me.* ○ *Their car broke down on them in the middle of the motorway.*

on [TOOL] /ɒn/ ⓤ /ɑːn/ *prep* used when referring to a tool, instrument or system that is used to do something: *I do all my household accounts on computer.* ○ *Chris is on drums and Mike's on bass guitar.* ○ *I'm on the phone.*

on [NOT STOPPING] /ɒn/ ⓤ /ɑːn/ *adv* continuing or not stopping: *If her phone's engaged,* **keep** *on trying.* ○ *Stop talking and* **get** *on with your work.* ○ *If Elise would just* **hang** *on* (= wait) *a little longer she'd certainly get the promotion.* ○ *The noise just* **went** *on and on* (= continued for a long time) *and I thought it would never stop.*

● **be on about** *UK INFORMAL* If you ask someone what they are on about, you are asking them, usually angrily, what they mean: *I dunno what you're on about.*

● **be/go on at** *sb UK* to speak to someone again and again to complain about their behaviour or to ask them to do something: *My parents are always on at us* **about** *having a baby.* ○ *She's been on at me* **to** *get my hair cut.*

on [MOVING FORWARD] /ɒn/ ⓤ /ɑːn/ *adv* in a way which results in forward movement: *You cycle on and I'll meet you there.* ○ *Move on, please, and let the ambulance through.* ○ *When you've finished reading it would you pass it on to Paul?* ○ *They never spoke to each other* **from** **that** *day* (= after that day)*.* ○ *What are you doing* **later** *on?*

on [POSITION] /ɒn/ ⓤ /ɑːn/ *adv* used when talking about the position of one thing compared with the position of another: *It's amazing nobody was injured because the two buses collided* **head** *on* (= the front parts of the buses hit each other)*.* ○ *UK The bike hit our car* **side** *on* (= hit the side of the car rather than the front or back)*.* ○ *UK It would be easier to get the bookcase through the doorway if we turned it* **sideways** *on* (= turned it so that one of its sides is at the front)*.*

on [OPERATING] /ɒn/ ⓤ /ɑːn/ *adv* used to show when something is operating or starting to operate: *Could you* **switch** *on the radio?* ○ *Would you* **turn** *the TV on?* ○ *You* **left** *the bedroom light on.*

on [HAPPENING] /ɒn/ ⓤ /ɑːn/ *adv* happening or planned: *I'm busy tomorrow, but I've got nothing on the day after.* ○ *I've got a lot on at the moment.* ○ *Is the party still on for tomorrow?* ○ *Food had to be rationed when the war was on.* ○ *Are there any good films on* (= being shown) *at the cinema this week?*

● **You're on!** *INFORMAL* used as a way of expressing agreement to something happening: *"I'll give you fifty quid for your bike." "You're on!"*

● **be not on** *MAINLY UK* Something that is not on is unacceptable and should not happen: *You can't be expected to work for nothing – it's not on.*

● **on and off** (ALSO **off and on**) If something happens on and off during a period of time, it happens sometimes: *I've had toothache on and off for a couple of months.*

on [POINTS] /ɒn/ ⓤ /ɑːn/ *prep UK* used to show the number of points a person or team has in a competition: *Clive's team is on five points while Joan's is on seven.*

on-board /ˈɒn.bɔːd/ ⓤ /ˈɑːn.bɔːrd/ *adj* describes items that are carried by a vehicle and form part of it: *In the future, cars equipped with on-board* **computers** *will be able to detect and avoid traffic jams automatically.*

once [ONE TIME] /wʌnts/ *adv* one single time: *I went sailing once, but I didn't like it.* ○ *We have lunch together once a month.*

● **at once** at the same time: *They all started talking at once.*

• **for once** used when something happens that does not usually happen: *For once, the bus came on time.*

• **just this once** used to say that you will only do or request something on this particular occasion: *All right, I'll give you a lift – just this once.*

• **once in a lifetime** only likely to happen once in a person's life: *An opportunity as good as this arises once in a lifetime.*

• **once again** again, as has happened before: *Once again, racist attacks are increasing across Europe.*

• **once and for all** completely and in a way that will finally solve a problem: *Our intention is to destroy their offensive capability once and for all.*

• **(every) once in a while** sometimes but not often: *We meet for lunch once in a while.*

• **once more 1** one more time: *I'd like to visit the colleges once more before we leave.* **2** SLIGHTLY FORMAL again, as has happened before: *I'm pleased that Daniel's working with us once more.*

• **once or twice** a few times: *I've seen him once or twice in town.*

• **once upon a time 1** used at the beginning of children's stories to mean 'a long time ago': *Once upon a time there was a beautiful young princess with long golden hair.* **2** used in a slightly literary way when referring to something that happened in the past, particularly when expressing regret that it no longer happens: *Once upon a time people knew the difference between right and wrong, but nowadays nobody seems to care.*

the once /ðəˈwʌnts/ on a single occasion: *I've only played rugby the once, and I never want to play it again.*

once PAST /wʌnts/ *adv* in the past, but not now: *This house once belonged to my grandfather.* ○ *Computers are much cheaper nowadays than they once were.* ○ *A few kilometres from the crowded beaches of Spain's Mediterranean coast, many once-thriving villages stand deserted and in ruins.*

once AS SOON AS /wʌnts/ *conjunction* as soon as, or from the moment when: *Once I've found somewhere to live I'll send you my address.* ○ *Remember that you won't be able to cancel the contract once you've signed.*

• **at once** immediately: *I knew at once that I'd like it here.*

• **all at once** suddenly and unexpectedly: *All at once there was a loud crashing sound.*

• **Once bitten, twice shy.** SAYING said when you are frightened to do something again because you had an unpleasant experience doing it the first time

once-in-a-lifetime /ˌwʌntˈsɪnəˈlaɪf.taɪm/ *adj* [before n] describes an experience or opportunity that is very special because it is the only time you will be able to benefit from it: *A tour of Australia is a once-in-a-lifetime experience.*

once-over LOOKING /ˈwʌnt.səʊ.vəʳ/ US /-soʊ-/ *noun* INFORMAL **give sth/sb the once-over** to look at and examine something or someone briefly: *The security guards gave me the once-over, but they didn't ask me for any identification.*

once-over CLEANING /ˈwʌnt.səʊ.vəʳ/ US /-soʊ-/ *noun* [S] INFORMAL when you quickly clean a place: *Would you mind giving the carpet a once-over with the vacuum cleaner?*

oncogene /ˈɒŋ.kəʊ.dʒiːn/ US /ˈɑːn.kə-/ *noun* [C] SPECIALIZED a gene that is present in every cell and causes a healthy cell to become cancerous under particular conditions

oncology /ɒŋˈkɒl.ə.dʒi/ US /ɑːnˈkɑː.lə-/ *noun* [U] the study and treatment of TUMOURS (= masses of diseased cells) in the body **oncologist** /ɒŋˈkɒl.ə.dʒɪst/ US /ɑːnˈkɑː.lə-/ *noun* [C]

oncoming /ˈɒn.kʌm.ɪŋ/ US /ˈɑːn-/ *adj* [before n] moving towards you or approaching: *The car veered onto the wrong side of the road and collided with an oncoming truck.* ○ *There seemed to be no way of averting the oncoming crisis.*

one NUMBER /wʌn/ *noun, determiner, pronoun* **1** (the number) 1: *You've got three bags and I've only got one.* ○ *She'll be one year old tomorrow.* ○ *one hundred and ninety-one people* ○ *Americans drive one third of the 400 million cars on the planet.* ○ *Four parcels came this*

morning, but only one was for Mark. **2 one of** a member of a group of people or things: *One of their daughters has just got married.* ○ *PolyGram is one of the world's largest record companies.* ○ *Finding a cure for cancer is one of the biggest challenges facing medical researchers.* ○ *Our organization is just one of **many** charities that are providing famine relief in the region.*

• **a hundred/thousand/million and one** very many: *I can't stand around chatting – I've got a hundred and one things to do this morning.*

• **(all) in one** combined in a single person or object: *With this model you get a radio, CD player and cassette deck all in one.*

• **be a one** UK OLD-FASHIONED INFORMAL to be someone who is amusing in a slightly rude way or in a way that shows a lack of respect: *"He told me I couldn't have the job and I told him I never really wanted it in the first place." "Ooh, you are a one."*

• **be at one** (ALSO **be as one**) SLIGHTLY FORMAL to agree: *We disagree on most things, but on this question we are at one **with** each other.*

• **down in one** INFORMAL If you drink a glass of alcohol down in one, you drink the whole glass without stopping.

• **for one** used to say that you think your opinion or action is right, even if others do not: *The rest of you may disagree, but I, for one, think we should proceed with the plan.*

• **in ones and twos** in small numbers: *The replies came back in ones and twos.*

• **one after another** (ALSO **one after the other**) many, in a series: *I'll eat chocolates one after the other until the box is finished.*

• **one and all** LITERARY everyone: *The news of his resignation came as a surprise to one and all.*

• **one or two** a few: *I'd like to make one or two suggestions.*

one FUTURE TIME /wʌn/ *determiner* used to refer to a time in the future which is not yet decided: *Why don't we meet for lunch one day next week?* ○ *I'd like to go skiing one Christmas.*

• **one day** at some time in the future: *I'd like to go to Berlin again one day.*

one PARTICULAR OCCASION /wʌn/ *determiner* used to refer to a particular occasion while avoiding stating the exact moment: *One night we stayed up talking till dawn.* ○ *He was attacked as I was walking home from work late one afternoon.* ○ *One moment he says he loves me, the next moment he's asking for a divorce.* ○ *She never seems to know what she's doing from one minute to the next.*

one UNKNOWN PERSON /wʌn/ *determiner* FORMAL used before the name of someone who is not known: *Her solicitor is one John Wintersgill.*

one SINGLE /wʌn/ *determiner, pronoun* a single thing; not two or more: *Do you think five of us will manage to squeeze into **the** one car?* ○ *There's too much data to fit onto just **the** one disk.* ○ *Eat them one **at a time** (= separately).* ○ *I think we should paint the bedroom **all** one (= in a single) colour.*

• **one by one** separately, one after the other: *One by one the old buildings in the city have been demolished and replaced with modern tower blocks.* ○ *They entered the room one by one.*

one ONLY /wʌn/ *determiner* used when saying there is no other person or thing: *He's **the** one person you can rely on in an emergency.* ○ *This may be your one **and only** (= only ever) opportunity to meet her.* ○ *My final guest on tonight's show needs no introduction. Please welcome **the** one **and only** Michael Jordan!*

one COMPARISON /wʌn/ *determiner, pronoun* used to talk about one person or thing compared with other similar or related people or things: *Paint one side, leave it to dry, and then paint the other.* ○ *He can't tell one wine from another, so don't give him any of the expensive stuff.* ○ *They look so similar it's often difficult to distinguish one from the other.* ○ *You may have one or the other, but not both.* ○ *Crime and freedom are inseparable. You can't have one without the other.*

• **one way or another 1** in some way that is not stated: *Everyone at the party was related **(in)** one way or* another. **2** in any way that is possible: *These bills have to be paid one way or another.* ○ *We have to make a decision one way or another about what needs to be done.*

one PARTICULAR THING/PERSON /wʌn/ *pronoun* **1** used to refer to a particular thing or person within a group or range of things or people that are possible or available: *I've got a few books on Chinese food. You can borrow one if you like.* ○ *Which one would you like?* ○ *Would you make a copy for everybody in the office and a few extra ones for the visitors.* ○ *"Which cake would you like?" "The one at the front."* ○ *French croissants are so much better than the English ones.* ○ *There were lots of people standing watching, and not one of them offered to help.* ○ *I've received no replies to my job applications – not a single one* (= none). ○ *Chris is the one* (= the person) *with curly brown hair.* **2** INFORMAL **not be one to do sth** to never do something: *I'm not one to criticize other people, as you know.* **3** INFORMAL **be one for sth** to like something very much: *I've never been one for staying out late.* ○ *He's a great one for the ladies.*

● **the one about** INFORMAL the joke about: *Have you heard the one about the Italian, the American and the Australian?*

● **be one of a kind** to be very unusual and special: *He's one of a kind, he really is.* ⊃Compare **be two of a kind** at **two**.

one EMPHASIS /wʌn/ *determiner* MAINLY US used to emphasize an adjective: *His mother is one* (= a very) *generous woman.* ○ *That's one* (= a very) *big ice-cream you've got there.* ○ *It was one hell of a* (= a very great) *shock to find out I'd lost my job.*

one ANY PERSON /wʌn/ *pronoun* FORMAL any person, but not a particular person: *One has an obligation to one's friends.* ○ *One ought to make the effort to vote.* * NOTE: When *one* is used in this way, it makes the speaker sound formal or old-fashioned. Most people use *you* instead in situations that are not formal.

one I OR ME /wʌn/ *pronoun* FORMAL the person speaking or writing: *Of course, one* (= I) *would be delighted to dine with the Queen.* * NOTE: When *one* is used in this way, it makes the speaker sound very formal or old-fashioned. *I* is almost always used instead.

ˌone aˈnother *pronoun* **each other**

one-armed bandit /ˌwʌn.ɑːmd'bæn.dɪt/ ⓤ /-ɑːrmd-/ *noun* [C] UK INFORMAL a type of SLOT MACHINE with a large metal pole on the side that you pull to make it work

one-dimensional MEASURE /ˌwʌn.daɪˈmen.tʃ°n.°l/ *adj* having height or width or length, but not two or all of these

one-dimensional BORING /ˌwʌn.daɪˈmen.tʃ°n.°l/ *adj* boring or lacking variety: *The characters in his novels tend to be rather one-dimensional.*

one-handed /ˌwʌnˈhæn.dɪd/ *adv, adj* using just one hand: *He had injured his left hand and was typing one-handed.*

one-hit wonder /ˌwʌn.hɪtˈwʌn.dəʳ/ ⓤ /-dɚ/ *noun* [C] INFORMAL a performer of popular music who makes one successful recording but then no others

one-horse race /ˌwʌn.hɔːsˈreɪs/ ⓤ /-hɔːrs-/ *noun* [C usually sing] a race or competition which only one of the competitors has a real chance of winning: *This election has been a one-horse race right from the start.*

one-horse town /ˌwʌn.hɔːsˈtaʊn/ ⓤ /-hɔːrs-/ *noun* [C] MAINLY US a town that is small and unimportant

one-liner /ˌwʌnˈlaɪ.nəʳ/ ⓤ /-nɚ/ *noun* [C] INFORMAL a joke or a clever and amusing remark or answer which is usually one sentence long: *There are some very witty one-liners in the film.*

ˌone-man ˈband *noun* [C usually sing] a musician who performs alone, usually outside, carrying and playing several instruments at the same time: FIGURATIVE *The organization seems to have become a one-man band with just one person making all the decisions.*

one-night stand SEX /ˌwʌn.naɪtˈstænd/ *noun* [C] a sexual relationship which lasts for only one night, or a person who you have had this type of relationship with

one-night stand PERFORMANCE /ˌwʌn.naɪtˈstænd/ *noun* [C] a performance which happens only once in a particular place

one-off /ˌwʌnˈɒf/ ⓤ /-ˈɑːf/ *noun* [S] UK something that happens or is made or done only once: *Will you be doing more talks in the future or was that just a one-off?*

one-off UK /ˌwʌnˈɒf/ ⓤ /-ˈɑːf/ *adj* (US **one-shot**) happening only once: *They gave him a one-off payment to compensate for the extra hours that he had to work.*

one-on-one /ˌwʌn.ɒnˈwʌn/ ⓤ /-ɑːn-/ *adv* US In sports, if something is done one-on-one, it means that each player from one team is matched to a single player from the other team. ⊃See also **one-to-one** CONNECTION; **one-to-one** TWO PEOPLE.

one-parent family /ˌwʌn.peə.rənt'fæm.°l.i/ ⓤ /-per.°nt-/ *noun* [C] (ALSO **single-parent family**) a family which includes either a mother or a father but not both

one-person /ˌwʌnˈpɜː.s°n/ ⓤ /-ˈpɜː-/ *adj* [before n] (ALSO **one-man/woman**) describes a play or show which is a performance or show of artistic works by just one person: *This is the first time her one-woman show has been on television.*

one-piece /ˈwʌn.piːs/ *noun* [C] (US USUALLY **one-piece swimsuit**) an item of women's clothing that is worn when swimming or on a beach and consists of a single piece of material rather than a separate top and bottom: *I'd prefer a one-piece to a bikini.*

onerous /ˈəʊ.n°r.əs/ ⓤ /ˈɑː.nɚ-/ *adj* FORMAL difficult to do or needing a lot of effort: *the onerous task of finding a peaceful solution* ○ *the onerous duties of motherhood* **onerousness** /ˈəʊ.n°r.ə.snəs/ ⓤ /ˈɑː.nɚ-/ *noun* [U]

oneself /ˌwʌnˈself/ *pronoun* FORMAL the reflexive form of the pronoun 'one' when it refers to people in general or to the person speaking: *One has to learn to control oneself.* * NOTE: **oneself** is generally considered too formal or old-fashioned. **I** or **you**, and **myself** or **yourself**, are usually used instead.

one-sided /ˌwʌnˈsaɪ.dɪd/ *adj* **1** If a competition is one-sided, one team or player is much better than the other: *a one-sided contest/game* **2** only considering one opinion in an argument in a way that is unfair: *They blamed their defeat on the media's one-sided reporting of the election campaign.* **one-sidedness** /ˌwʌnˈsaɪ.dɪd.nəs/ *noun* [U]

one-size-fits-all /ˌwʌn.saɪz.fɪtsˈɔːl/ ⓤ /-ˈɑːl/ *adj* **1** MAINLY US describes a piece of clothing that is designed to fit a person of any size **2** DISAPPROVING (intended to be) suitable for everyone or every purpose: *a one-size-fits-all approach to education*

one-star /ˌwʌnˈstɑːʳ/ ⓤ /-ˈstɑːr/ *adj* describes a hotel or restaurant which is not especially good but has achieved the lowest acceptable standard in an official quality test

one-stop /ˈwʌn.stɒp/ ⓤ /-stɑːp/ *adj* describes activities that involve stopping at a single place: *We offer our customers one-stop banking services and investment advice.*

one-time /ˈwʌn.taɪm/ *adj* **a one-time teacher/doctor/cleaner, etc.** someone who was a teacher/doctor/cleaner, etc. in the past: *Duggan, a TV presenter and one-time journalist, made the announcement last week.*

one-to-one CONNECTION /ˌwʌn.təˈwʌn/ *adj* Something that is in a one-to-one relationship with another thing strongly influences the way that the other thing changes: *Is there a one-to-one relationship between pay levels and productivity?*

one-to-one TWO PEOPLE /ˌwʌn.təˈwʌn/ *adj* [before n] (US ALSO **one-on-one**) describes an activity in which one person is teaching or giving information to another person: *These children have special educational needs and require one-to-one attention.*

one-track mind /ˌwʌn.trækˈmaɪnd/ *noun* **have a one-track mind** to think about one particular thing and nothing else: *And no, Bill, I wasn't talking about sex – you've got a one-track mind!*

one-two punch /ˌwʌn.tuːˈpʌntʃ/ *noun* [S] US two unpleasant things which happen together: *The weather delivered a one-two punch to gardeners with unseasonal freezing temperatures and strong winds.*

one-upmanship /wʌnˈʌp.mən.ʃɪp/ *noun* [U] DISAPPROVING when someone does or says something in order to prove that they are better than someone else

one-way /ˌwʌnˈweɪ/ *adj* **1** [before n] travelling or allowing travel in only one direction: *I drove the wrong way down a one-way street.* ◦ *US How much is a one-way ticket (UK USUALLY single) to New York?* **2** describes a relationship which is not fair because only one person or group of the two makes any effort

ongoing /ˈɒnˌgəʊ.ɪŋ/ /ˌ-ˈ--/ Ⓤ /ˈɑːnˌgoʊ-/ *adj* continuing to exist or develop, or happening at the present moment: *an ongoing investigation/process/project* ◦ *No agreement has yet been reached and the negotiations are still ongoing.*

onion /ˈʌn.jən/ *noun* [C or U] a vegetable with a strong smell and flavour, made up of several layers surrounding each other tightly in a round shape, usually brown or red on the outside and white inside: *I always cry when I'm chopping onions.* ◦ *Fry the onion and garlic for about two minutes.* ⊃See picture **Vegetables** on page Centre 2

online [INTERNET] /ˈɒn.laɪn/ Ⓤ /ˈɑːn.laɪn/ *adj* [before n] describes products, services or information that can be bought or accessed using the Internet: *an online newspaper/magazine/dictionary* ◦ *online banking/shopping*
• **be online** to be able to use email or the Internet: *I'll send you my email address once I'm online.*
online /ˌɒnˈlaɪn/ Ⓤ /ˌɑːnˈlaɪn/ *adv* bought, accessed, etc. using the Internet: *Have you ever bought anything online?* ◦ *This dictionary went online in 1999.*

online [SYSTEM] /ˌɒnˈlaɪn/ Ⓤ /ˌɑːnˈlaɪn/ *adj* [after v], *adv* connected to a system: *The new power station is expected to be online by July.* ◦ *When will the new factory come online (= start production)?*

onlooker /ˈɒnˌlʊk.əʳ/ Ⓤ /ˈɑːnˌlʊk.ɚ/ *noun* [C] someone who watches something that is happening in a public place but is not involved in it: *A crowd of curious onlookers soon gathered to see what was happening.*

only [SINGLE OR FEW] /ˈəʊn.li/ Ⓤ /ˈoʊn-/ *adj* [before n] used to show that there is a single one or very few of something, or that there are no others: *I was the only person on the train.* ◦ *Is this really the only way to do it?* ◦ *The only thing that matters is that the baby is healthy.* ◦ *It was the only thing I could do under the circumstances.* ◦ *Rita was the only person to complain.*

only [LIMIT] /ˈəʊn.li/ Ⓤ /ˈoʊn-/ *adv* **1** used to show that something is limited to the people, things, amount or activity stated: *At present these televisions are only available in Japan.* ◦ *Only Sue and Mark bothered to turn up for the meeting.* ◦ *This club is for members only.* ◦ *Only an idiot would do that.* ◦ *These shoes only cost £20.* ◦ *Don't worry – it's only a scratch.* ◦ *I was only joking.* ◦ *I was only trying to help.* ◦ *I only arrived half an hour ago.* ◦ *She spoke to me only (= no more than) a few minutes ago on the phone.* ◦ *It's only four o'clock and (=* It is surprising that it is no later than four o'clock because) *it's already getting dark.* ◦ *"Who's there?" "It's only me (= it is not someone you should worry about). I've locked myself out."* ◦ *It's only natural that you should worry about your children.* **2** used to express regret about something that cannot happen when explaining why it cannot happen: *I'd love to go to Australia. I only wish I could afford to.* **3** used when saying that something unpleasant will happen as a result of an action or a failure to act: *If you don't do something about it now it will only get worse.* **4** INFORMAL used to show that you think someone has done something foolish: *She's only locked herself out of her flat again!*
• **have only (got) to** If you say you have only (got) to do something, you mean that it is all you need to do in order to achieve something else: *If you want any help, you have only to ask.* ◦ *You've only got to look at her face to see that she's not well.*
• **if only** used when you want to say how doing something simple would make it possible to avoid something unpleasant: *If only she'd listen to what he's saying, I'm sure they could work it out.*
• **not only ... (but) also** used to say that two related things are true or happened, especially when this is surprising or shocking: *Not only did he turn up late, he also forgot his books.* ◦ *If this project fails it will affect not only our* department, but also the whole organization.
• **only just 1** used to refer to something that happens almost immediately after something else: *People were leaving and I'd only just arrived.* ◦ *We'd only just set off when the car broke down.* **2** almost not: *There was only just enough food to go round.* ◦ *We arrived in time for our flight, but only just (= but we almost did not).*
• **only to do sth** used to show that something is surprising or unexpected when something done earlier is considered: *He spent ages negotiating for a pay increase, only to resign from his job soon after he'd received it.*

only [BUT] /ˈəʊn.li/ Ⓤ /ˈoʊn-/ *conjunction* used to show what is the single or main reason why something mentioned in the first part of the sentence cannot be performed or is not completely true: *I'd invite Frances to the party, only (=* but I will not because) *I don't want her husband to come.* ◦ *I'd phone him myself, only (= but I cannot because) I've got to go out.* ◦ *I'd be happy to do it for you, only (= but) don't expect it to be done before next week.* ◦ *This fabric is similar to wool, only (= except that it is) cheaper.*

only child *noun* [C] *plural* **only children** a child who has no sisters or brothers

on-message /ˌɒnˈmes.ɪdʒ/ Ⓤ /ˌɑːn-/ *adj* [after v], *adv* UK A politician who is on-message says things in public which support the official ideas of their political party: *The candidate is clearly on-message with the Tory party leader.*

ono *noun* UK WRITTEN ABBREVIATION FOR or near(est) offer; used in advertisements for things that people are trying to sell to show that they will accept slightly less money than the price they are asking for: *ladies' bike – excellent condition. £80 ono*

onomatopoeia /ˌɒn.əʊˌmæt.əˈpiː.ə/ Ⓤ /ˌɑː.noʊˌmæt̬.oʊ-/ *noun* [U] SPECIALIZED the creation and use of words which include sounds that are similar to the noises that the words refer to **onomatopoeic** /ˌɒn.əʊˌmæt.əˈpiː.ɪk/ Ⓤ /ˌɑː.noʊˌmæt̬.oʊ-/ *adj*: *"Pop", "boom" and "squelch" are onomatopoeic words.*

on-screen /ˈɒn.skriːn/ Ⓤ /ˈɑːn-/ *adj* [before n], *adv* describes something or someone seen or appearing on a television or computer screen: *Her on-screen husband is also her partner in real life.* ◦ *You can use the device to scan the image and reproduce it on-screen in an electronic format.*

onset /ˈɒn.set/ Ⓤ /ˈɑːn-/ *noun* **the onset of sth** the moment at which something unpleasant begins: *the onset of cancer* ◦ *The new treatment can delay the onset of the disease by several years.*

onshore /ˌɒnˈʃɔːʳ/ Ⓤ /ˈɑːn.ʃɔːr/ *adj*, *adv* moving towards land from the sea, or on land rather than at sea: *onshore winds* ◦ *onshore oil reserves* ⊃Compare **offshore** AT SEA.

onside /ˌɒnˈsaɪd/ Ⓤ /ˌɑːn-/ *adj*, *adv* (in football and some other sports) in a position where you are allowed to kick, throw or receive the ball or PUCK ⊃Compare **offside** NOT ALLOWED.

on-site /ˌɒnˈsaɪt/ Ⓤ /ˌɑːn-/ *adj*, *adv* existing or happening in the place where people are working or involved in a particular activity: *on-site facilities* ◦ *We're meeting the builders on-site tomorrow.*

onslaught /ˈɒn.slɔːt/ Ⓤ /ˈɑːn.slɑːt/ *noun* [C] a very powerful attack: *It is unlikely that his forces could withstand an allied onslaught for very long.* ◦ *Scotland's onslaught on Wales in the second half of the match earned them a 4-1 victory.*

onstage /ˌɒnˈsteɪdʒ/ Ⓤ /ˈɑːn-/ *adv*, *adj* onto or on a stage for a performance: *The audience cheered as the band walked onstage for another encore.* ◦ *onstage violence*

onto, **on to** /ˈɒn.tu/ Ⓤ /ˈɑːn.tu/ *prep* **1** used to show movement into or on a particular place: *I slipped as I stepped onto the platform.* ◦ *The sheep were loaded onto trucks.* ◦ *I've been having problems loading this software onto my computer.* ◦ *Imir's been voted onto the union committee.* ◦ *Hold onto (=* Keep holding) *my hand and you'll be perfectly safe.* **2** used to show that you are starting to talk about a different subject: *How did we get onto this subject?* ◦ *Can we move onto the next item on the agenda?* ◦ *I'd now like to come onto my next point.* **3** UK If you are onto someone, you talk to them, especially to ask them to do something or to complain: *I must* ***get*** *onto the plumber about the shower.* ○ *Dad was onto her again about doing her homework.* **4** knowing about someone or something that can benefit you: *So how did you* ***get*** *onto this deal?* ○ *David* ***put*** *me onto* (= told me about) *a really good restaurant.* ○ *You're onto* ***a good thing*** *with this buy-one-get-one-free offer at the shop.* **5** knowing about something bad someone has done: *He knows we're onto him.* ○ *Who* ***put*** *the police onto* (= told the police about) *her?*

the onus /ðiˈəʊ.nəs/ [US] /-ˈoʊ-/ *noun* **[S]** *FORMAL* the responsibility or duty to do something: **[+ to infinitive]** *The onus is* ***on*** *the landlord* ***to*** *ensure that the property is habitable.* ○ *We are trying to shift the onus* ***for*** *passenger safety onto the government.*

onward /ˈɒn.wəd/ [US] /ˈɑːn.wɚd/ *adj* **[before n]** *FORMAL* moving forward to a later time or a more distant place: *the onward march of time.* ○ *UK If you are continuing on an onward* ***flight****, your bags will be transferred automatically.*

• **onward and upward** becoming more and more successful: *Her publishing career started as an editorial assistant on a women's magazine and it was onward and upward from there.*

onwards *MAINLY UK* /ˈɒn.wədz/ [US] /ˈɑːn.wɚdz/ *adv* (*MAINLY US* **onward**) **1 from 6.30/March/the 1870s, etc. onwards** beginning at a particular time and continuing after it: *I'm usually at home from 5 o'clock onwards.* **2** If you move onwards, you continue to go forwards: *We sailed onwards in a westerly direction.*

onyx /ˈɒn.ɪks/ [US] /ˈɑː.nɪks/ *noun* **[U]** a valuable stone with white and grey strips that is used in jewellery and decorations

oodles /ˈuː.dl̩z/ *plural noun OLD-FASHIONED INFORMAL* a very large amount of something pleasant: *She inherited oodles* ***of*** *money from her uncle.*

ooh /uː/ *exclamation* an expression of surprise, pleasure, approval, disapproval or pain: *Ooh, what a lovely dress!* ○ *Ooh, yes, that would be nice!* ○ *Ooh, that's a bit unkind!*

ooh /uː/ *verb* **[I]**

• **ooh and aah** *INFORMAL* to express admiration: *We watched the fireworks, oohing and aahing with everyone else.*

oomph /ʊmpf/ /uːmpf/ *noun* **[U]** *INFORMAL* power, strength or energetic activity: *You want a car with a bit of oomph.* ○ *It's important to have someone with a bit of oomph in charge of the department.*

oops /uːps/ /ʊps/ *exclamation* (*ALSO* **whoops**) *INFORMAL* an expression of surprise or regret about a mistake or slight accident: *Oops! I've typed two L's by mistake.*

oops-a-daisy /ˈʊp.səˌdeɪ.zi/ *exclamation* (*ALSO* **ups-a-daisy**) *INFORMAL* something said to young children when they fall over

ooze /uːz/ *verb* **[I + adv or prep; T]** to flow slowly out of something through a small opening, or to slowly produce a thick sticky liquid: *Blood was still oozing out of the wound.* ○ *She removed the bandage to reveal a red swollen wound oozing pus.* ○ *The waiter brought her a massive pizza oozing* ***(with)*** *cheese.* ○ *FIGURATIVE* He oozes (= has a lot of) *charm/confidence.*

ooze /uːz/ *noun* **[U]** a thick brown liquid made of earth and water, found at the bottom of a river or lake: *Many millions of years ago, our ancestors climbed out of the primeval ooze onto dry land.*

op [OPERATION] /ɒp/ [US] /ɑːp/ *noun* **[C]** *UK INFORMAL* a medical operation: *How long did you take to recover from your op?*

Op. [MUSIC] *noun ABBREVIATION FOR* **opus**: *Dvorak's Piano Concerto in G Minor, Op. 33*

op [OPPORTUNITY] /ɒp/ [US] /ɑːp/ *noun* **[C]** *US INFORMAL* an opportunity: *a* ***photo*** *op* (= a chance for a politician, etc. to be photographed looking good or doing good things)

opal /ˈəʊ.pəl/ [US] /ˈoʊ-/ *noun* **[C or U]** a precious stone whose colour changes when the position of the person looking at it changes

opalescent /ˌəʊ.pəlˈes.ənt/ [US] /ˌoʊ-/ *adj LITERARY* describes something that reflects light and changes colour like an opal: *the opalescent scales of a fish*

opalescence /ˌəʊ.pəlˈes.ənts/ [US] /ˌoʊ-/ *noun* **[U]**

opaque /əʊˈpeɪk/ [US] /oʊ-/ *adj* **1** preventing light from travelling through, and therefore not transparent or TRANSLUCENT: *opaque glass/tights* **2** *FORMAL* describes writing or speech that is difficult to understand: *I find her poetry rather opaque.* **opaquely** /əʊˈpeɪ.kli/ [US] /oʊ-/ *adv*

opacity /əʊˈpæs.ə.ti/ [US] /oʊˈpæs.ə.t̬i/ *noun* **[U]** *FORMAL* the state of being opaque, or the degree to which something is opaque

ˈop ˌart *noun* **[U]** a type of modern art which uses patterns that do not exist naturally in order to create images which appear to move or to be something that they are not

op. cit. /ˌɒpˈsɪt/ [US] /ˌɑːp-/ *adv FORMAL ABBREVIATION* used by writers to avoid repeating the details of a book or article that has already been referred to: *Johnson (op. cit., page 53) calls this phenomenon 'the principle of minimal effort'.*

OPEC /ˈəʊ.pek/ [US] /ˈoʊ-/ *noun ABBREVIATION FOR* Organization of Petroleum Exporting Countries: a group of countries which produce oil and decide together how much to produce

op-ed /ˌɒpˈed/ [US] /ˌɑːp-/ *adj* **[before n]** *US* describes a piece of writing which expresses a personal opinion and is usually printed in a newspaper opposite the page on which the EDITORIAL is printed: *an op-ed article/column/page* **op-ed** /ˌɒpˈed/ [US] /ˌɑːp-/ *noun* **[U]** *His rebuttal appeared in yesterday's op-ed.*

open [NOT CLOSED] /ˈəʊ.pən/ [US] /ˈoʊ-/ *adj* not closed or fastened: *an open door/window* ○ *An open suitcase lay on her bed.* ○ *You left the packet open.* ○ *Someone had left the window* ***wide*** (= completely) *open.* ○ *He had several nasty open* ***wounds*** (= those which had not begun to heal).

• **greet/welcome** ***sb*** **with open arms** to show someone that you are very pleased to see someone

open /ˈəʊ.pən/ [US] /ˈoʊ-/ *verb* **1** **[I or T]** to move something to a position that is not closed, or to make something change to a position that is not closed: *Could you open the window, please?* ○ *You can open your eyes now – here's your present.* ○ *The flowers open* ***(out)*** *in the morning but close again in the afternoon.* ○ *From the kitchen there is a door which opens* ***(out) into/onto*** *the garden.* ○ *INFORMAL "Open* ***up*** (= Open the door) *– it's the police!" shouted the police officer, banging on the door.* **2** **[T]** to remove or separate part of a container or parcel so that you can see or use what it contains: *Don't open a new bottle just for me.* ○ *I couldn't wait to open the letter.*

• **the earth/ground/floor opens** People say that they wish the earth/floor/ground would open (up) if they are so embarrassed that they want suddenly to disappear: *At that moment the boss walked in and I just wanted the ground to open up and swallow me.*

• **open the door to** ***sth*** to allow something new to start: *The ceasefire has opened the door to talks between the two sides.*

• **open** ***sb's*** **eyes** to make someone aware of something surprising or shocking, which they had not known about or understood before: *She really opened my eyes* ***to*** *how stupid I'd been.*

• **open** ***your*** **heart to someone** to tell someone about your problems and secrets: *She's very understanding – you feel you can really open your heart to her.*

• **open** ***your*** **mouth** to speak or start to speak: *Don't look at me – I never opened my mouth.*

opener /ˈəʊ.pən.əʳ/ [US] /ˈoʊ.pən.ɚ/ *noun* **bottle/can/tin, etc. opener** a device for opening closed containers

opening /ˈəʊ.pən.ɪŋ/ [US] /ˈoʊp.nɪŋ/ *noun* **[C]** a hole or space that something or someone can pass through: *The children crawled through an opening space* ***in*** *the fence.*

COMMON LEARNER ERROR

open or **switch/turn on?**

In some languages the verbs **open** and **close** are used with electrical devices such as TVs and lights. In English, however, you must use the phrasal verbs **switch on/off** or **turn on/off**.

She switched on the light and looked around the room.
~~*She opened the light and looked around the room.*~~
I asked him to turn off the light.

~~I asked him to close the light.~~

COMMON LEARNER ERROR

open and **close**

Be careful not to confuse the adjective and verb forms of these words.

The adjectives are **open** and **closed**.

Is the supermarket open on Sunday?
The museum is closed today.

The verbs are **open** and **close**.

The supermarket opens at 8 a.m.
The museum closes at 5 p.m. tomorrow.

open [READY] /ˈəʊ.pᵊn/ [US] /ˈoʊ-/ *adj* [after v] ready to be used or ready to provide a service: *The supermarket is open till 8.00 p.m.* ○ *The road is open now, but it is often blocked by snow in the winter.* ○ *The new hospital was declared open by the mayor.*

open /ˈəʊ.pᵊn/ [US] /ˈoʊ-/ *verb* **1** [I or T] If a shop or office opens at a particular time of day, it starts to do business at that time: *The café opens at ten o'clock.* ○ *He opens **(up)** his café* (= makes it ready to provide a service) *at ten o'clock.* **2** [T] If someone, usually someone important, opens a building or place or event, they officially state that it is ready to be used or to start operating: *The new hospital will be **officially** opened by the mayor on Tuesday.* **opening** /ˈəʊ.pᵊn.ɪŋ/ [US] /ˈoʊp.nɪŋ/ *noun* [C usually sing] *The **official** opening **of** the new school will take place next month.*

open [NOT DECIDED] /ˈəʊ.pᵊn/ [US] /ˈoʊ-/ *adj* not decided or certain: *We don't have to make a firm decision yet. Let's **leave it** open.* ○ *We can leave our offer open for another week, but we must have your decision by then.* ○ *I want to keep my **options** open, so I'm not committing myself yet.*

open [NOT SECRET] /ˈəʊ.pᵊn/ [US] /ˈoʊ-/ *adj* **1** not secret: *There has been open hostility between them ever since they had that argument last summer.* **2** honest and not secretive: *He's quite open about his weaknesses.* ○ *I wish you'd be more open **with** me, and tell me what you're feeling.* ○ *She has an honest, open face.*

the open *noun* **bring *sth* out into the open** to tell people information that was secret: *It's time this issue was brought out into the open.*

openly /ˈəʊ.pᵊn.li/ [US] /ˈoʊ-/ *adv* without hiding any of your thoughts or feelings: *They were openly contemptuous of my suggestions.* ○ *We discussed our reservations about the contract quite openly.*

openness /ˈəʊ.pᵊn.nəs/ [US] /ˈoʊ-/ *noun* [U] honesty: *If these discussions are to succeed, we'll need openness from/on both sides.*

open [BEGIN] /ˈəʊ.pᵊn/ [US] /ˈoʊ-/ *verb* [I or T] to (cause to) begin: *I would like to open my talk by giving a brief background to the subject.* ○ *I'm going to open an account with another bank.* ○ *The Olympic Games open tomorrow.* ○ *A new radio station is due to open **(up)** next month.* ○ *The film opens* (= will be shown for the first time) *in New York and Los Angeles next week.*

opening /ˈəʊ.pᵊn.ɪŋ/ [US] /ˈoʊp.nɪŋ/ *adj* [before n] happening at the beginning of an event or activity: *her opening remarks* ○ *the opening night*

opening /ˈəʊ.pᵊn.ɪŋ/ [US] /ˈoʊp.nɪŋ/ *noun* [C usually sing] the beginning of something: *The opening of the novel is amazing.*

openers /ˈəʊ.pᵊn.əz/ [US] /ˈoʊ.pᵊn.ɚz/ *plural noun* INFORMAL **for openers** first: *Just for openers, I'd like to ask a question.*

open [NOT ENCLOSED] /ˈəʊ.pᵊn/ [US] /ˈoʊ-/ *adj* not enclosed or covered: *From the garden there was a marvellous view over open **countryside**.* ○ *It's not a good idea to camp in the middle of an open **field*** (= one which is not covered with trees, bushes, etc.). ○ *The survivors were adrift on the open **sea*** (= far from land).

the open *noun* [S] somewhere outside, rather than in a building: *It's good to be **(out) in** the open after being cooped up in an office all day.*

open [AVAILABLE] /ˈəʊ.pᵊn/ [US] /ˈoʊ-/ *adj* [after v] available; not limited: *There are still several possibilities open **to** you.* ○ *The competition is open **to** anyone over the age of sixteen.* ○ *Is the library open **to** the general public?* ○ *Their whole attitude to these negotiations is open **to** criticism* (= can be criticized). ○ *I'd like to think I'm open **to*** (= willing to consider) *any reasonable suggestion.* ○ *An accident would **lay** the whole issue of safety open* (= cause it to be considered).

open /ˈəʊ.pᵊn/ [US] /ˈoʊ-/ *verb* [T] to make something available: *This research opens (up) the possibility of being able to find a cure for the disease.* ○ *The country is planning to open (up) its economy **to** foreign investment.*

opening /ˈəʊ.pᵊn.ɪŋ/ [US] /ˈoʊp.nɪŋ/ *noun* [C] a job or an opportunity to do something: *There's **an** opening **for** an editorial assistant in our department.*

open [COMPUTER] /ˈəʊ.pᵊn/ [US] /ˈoʊ-/ *adj* If a computer document or program is open, it is ready to be read or used: *Make sure the file you're copying to is open before you click 'Paste'.*

open /ˈəʊ.pᵊn/ [US] /ˈoʊ-/ *verb* [T] If you open a computer document or program, you make it ready to read or use: *To open a new document, click 'File', then click 'New'.* ○ *Click the desktop icon to open the Cambridge Advanced Learner's Dictionary.*

PHRASAL VERBS WITH **open** ▼

▲ **open *sth* out/up** *phrasal verb* to make a space larger or less enclosed: *We're going to open up our kitchen by knocking down a couple of walls.*

▲ **open *(sth)* up** [LOCK] *phrasal verb* [M] to open the lock on the door of a building: *The caretaker opens up the school every morning at seven.*

▲ **open *sth* up** [SITUATION] *phrasal verb* [M] to improve a situation by making it less limited: *The government has announced plans to open up access to higher education.*

▲ **open *sth* up** [SHOW] *phrasal verb* [M] to show something that was hidden or not previously known: *The security council debate could open up sharp differences between the countries.*

▲ **open *sb* up** *phrasal verb* INFORMAL to do a medical operation on someone to see inside their body: *When they opened her up, they couldn't find anything wrong with her.*

▲ **open up** [PERSON] *phrasal verb* to start to talk more about yourself and your feelings: *I've never opened up **to** anyone like I do to you.*

ˌopen adˈmissions *noun* [U] (ALSO **open enrollment**) US a system which allows students to go to a college without having any special qualifications for it

ˌopen aˈdoption *noun* [C] MAINLY US an arrangement by which children legally go to live with people who are not their natural parents, but still continue to communicate with their natural parents

open-air /ˌəʊ.pᵊnˈeəʳ/ [US] /ˌoʊ.pᵊnˈer/ *adj* [before n] describes a place that does not have a roof, or an event which takes place outside: *an open-air concert/market*

open-and-shut /ˌəʊ.pᵊn.ənˈʃʌt/ [US] /ˌoʊ-/ *adj* describes a problem or legal matter which is easy to prove or answer: *Our lawyer thinks that we have an open-and-shut **case**.*

ˌopen ˈbook *noun* **be an open book** If someone is an open book, it is easy to know what they are thinking and feeling.

opencast UK /ˈəʊ.pᵊn.kɑːst/ [US] /ˈoʊ.pᵊn.kæst/ *adj* (US **open-cut**) describes a place where minerals, especially coal, are taken from the surface of the ground rather than from passages dug under it, or relating to this way of getting minerals: *opencast mine/mining*

ˌopen ˈclassroom *noun* [U] in the US, a system for educating young children in which classes and activities are informal and changed to suit each child

open-cut /ˈəʊ.pᵊn.kʌt/ [US] /ˈoʊ-/ *adj* US FOR **opencast**

ˈopen ˌday UK *noun* [C] (US **open house**) a day when an organization such as a school, college or factory allows members of the public to go in and see what happens there

open-door /ˌəʊ.pᵊnˈdɔːʳ/ [US] /ˌoʊ.pᵊnˈdɔːr/ *adj* allowing people and goods to come freely into a place or country: *an open-door system* ○ *open-door regulations*

open-ended /ˌəʊ.pᵊnˈen.dɪd/ [US] /ˌoʊ-/ *adj* An open-ended activity or situation does not have a planned ending, so

O

it may develop in several ways: *We are not willing to enter into open-ended discussions.*

ˌopen ˈfire *noun* [C] (*US* **open fireplace**) a space in a wall of a building in which wood or coal is burnt, and which has a chimney inside the wall to take the smoke away, or a fire which burns in such a space: *We roasted chestnuts on the open fire.*

open-handed /ˌəʊ.pᵊnˈhæn.dɪd/ [US] /ˌoʊ-/ *adj* generous: *open-handed assistance*

open-hearted /ˌəʊ.pᵊnˈhɑː.tɪd/ [US] /ˌoʊ.pᵊnˈhɑːr.t̬ɪd/ *adj* Someone who is open-hearted is kind, caring and honest.

open-heart surgery /ˌəʊ.pᵊn.hɑːtˈsɜː.dʒᵊr.i/ [US] /ˌoʊ.pᵊn.hɑːrtˈsɝː.dʒɚ-/ *noun* [U] a medical operation in which the body is cut open and the heart is repaired, while the body's blood is kept flowing by a machine

ˌopen ˈhouse *noun* [U] **1** a situation in which people welcome visitors at any time: *We* ***keep*** *open house, so come and see us any time.* **2** *US* a time when a house or apartment that is being sold can be looked at by the public

ˈopening ˌhours *plural noun UK* the times when a business, such as a bar, restaurant, shop or bank, is open for people to use it

ˌopening ˈnight *noun* [C usually sing] the first night that a play, film, etc. is performed or shown: *The ballet's opening night was a huge success.*

ˈopening ˌtime *noun* [C usually sing] *UK* the time at which a bar or pub opens

ˌopen ˈletter *noun* [C] a letter intended to be read by a lot of people, not just the person it is addressed to: *An open letter to the prime minister, signed by several MPs, appeared in today's papers.*

ˌopen ˈmarket *noun* [S] a situation in which companies can trade freely without limits, and prices are changed by the number of goods and how many people are buying them: *In the meantime, the shares will continue to trade* ***on*** *the open market.*

ˌopen ˈmarriage *noun* [C] a marriage in which both partners are free to have sexual relationships with other people

ˌopen ˈmind *noun* **have/keep an open mind** to wait until you know all the facts before forming an opinion or making a judgement: *We should keep an open mind until all of the evidence is available.*

O

open-minded /ˌəʊ.pᵊnˈmaɪn.dɪd/ [US] /ˌoʊ-/ *adj* willing to consider ideas and opinions that are new or different to your own: *Doctors these days tend to be more open-minded* ***about*** *alternative medicine.* **open-mindedness** /ˌəʊ.pᵊnˈmaɪn.dɪd.nəs/ [US] /ˌoʊ-/ *noun* [U] *She has a reputation for open-mindedness and original thinking.*

open-mouthed /ˌəʊ.pᵊnˈmaʊðd/ [US] /ˌoʊ-/ *adj* with your mouth wide open, especially because you are surprised or shocked: *They stared open-mouthed at the extent of the damage.*

open-necked /ˌəʊ.pᵊnˈnekt/ [US] /ˌoʊ-/ *adj* [before n] describes a shirt which is not fastened at the neck

open-plan /ˌəʊ.pᵊnˈplæn/ [US] /ˌoʊ-/ *adj* describes a room or building which has few or no walls inside, so it is not divided into smaller rooms: *an open-plan office*

ˌopen ˈprison *UK noun* [C] (*US* **minimum-security prison**) a prison where prisoners are not kept inside because they are trusted not to escape

ˌopen ˈsandwich *noun* [C] a single slice of bread with various types of food, such as cold fish or meat, on the top

ˈopen ˌseason *noun* **1** [S or U] the period in the year when it is legal to hunt particular animals ➲Compare **close season**. **2** a situation which allows or causes a particular group of people to be treated unfairly: *To pass this legislation would be to* ***declare*** *open season* ***on*** *homosexuals.*

ˌopen ˈsesame *noun* [C usually sing] a very successful way of achieving something: *A science degree can be an open sesame* ***to*** *a job in almost any field.*

ˌOpen Uniˈversity *noun* [S] *UK* in Britain, a college especially established to educate older people who did not get a degree when they were young. Students study by special television and radio programmes and they usually send their work to their teachers by post.

ˌopen ˈverdict *noun* [C usually sing] *UK LEGAL* a legal decision which records a death but does not state its cause

opera /ˈɒp.ᵊr.ə/ /ˈɒp.rə/ [US] /ˈɑː.pɚ.ə/ *noun* [C or U] musical plays in which most of the words are sung, or a play of this type: *'Carmen' is my favourite opera.* ○ *I've never been a huge fan of opera.* ○ *He goes to* ***the*** *opera* (= to see an opera) *whenever he can.* ○ *an opera singer* ➲Compare **operetta**. **operatic** /ˌɒp.ᵊrˈæt.ɪk/ [US] /ˌɑː.pəˈræt̬-/ *adj*: *an operatic society* ○ *operatic arias* **operatically** /ˌɒp.ᵊrˈæt.ɪ.kli/ [US] /ˌɑː.pəˈræt̬-/ *adv*

ˈopera ˌglasses *plural noun* [C] small BINOCULARS which can be used in large theatres by people sitting far from the stage, so that they can see the performers more clearly

ˈopera ˌhouse *noun* [C] a theatre which is specially designed for operas to be performed in: *the Royal Opera House, Covent Garden*

operate [WORK] /ˈɒp.ᵊr.eɪt/ [US] /ˈɑː.pə.reɪt/ *verb* [I or T] to (cause to) work, be in action or have an effect: *How do you operate the remote control unit?* ○ *Does the company operate a pension scheme?* ○ *For several years she operated a dating agency from her basement flat.* ○ *Changes are being introduced to make the department operate more efficiently.* ○ *Specially equipped troops are operating in the hills.* ○ *We have representatives operating in most countries.* ○ *Exchange rates are currently operating to the advantage of exporters.*

operation /ˌɒp.ᵊrˈeɪ.ʃᵊn/ [US] /ˌɑː.pəˈreɪ-/ *noun* **1** [U] the fact of operating or being active: *There are several reactors of the type* ***in*** *operation* (= working) *at the moment.* ○ *We expect the new scheme for assessing claims to* ***come into*** *operation* (= start working) *early next year.* **2** [U] the way that parts of a machine or system work together, or the process of making parts of a machine or system work together **3** [C] a business organization: *Less profitable business operations will have difficulty in finding financial support.* **4** [C] an activity which is planned to achieve something: *a military/peacekeeping operation.* ○ *Following the earthquake, a large-scale* ***rescue*** *operation was* ***launched.*** ○ [+ to infinitive] *The operation* ***to*** *fly in supplies will begin as soon as possible.* **5** [C] *SPECIALIZED* a mathematical process, such as addition, in which one set of numbers is produced from another

operational /ˌɒp.ᵊrˈeɪ.ʃᵊn.ᵊl/ [US] /ˌɑː.pəˈreɪ-/ *adj* **1** relating to a particular activity: *There are operational advantages in putting sales and admin in the same building.* **2** If a system is operational, it is working: *Repairs have already begun and we expect the factory to be* ***fully*** *operational again with six months.* **operationally** /ˌɒp.ᵊrˈeɪ.ʃᵊn.ᵊl.i/ [US] /ˌɑː.pəˈreɪ-/ *adv*

operative /ˈɒp.ᵊr.ə.tɪv/ [US] /ˈɑː.pɚ.ə.t̬ɪv/ *adj FORMAL* working or being used: *The agreement will not become operative until all members have signed.* * NOTE: The opposite is **inoperative**.

• **the operative word** the most important word in a phrase, which explains the truth of a situation: *He was a painter – 'was' being the operative word since he died last week.*

operative /ˈɒp.ᵊr.ə.tɪv/ [US] /ˈɑː.pɚ.ə.t̬ɪv/ *noun* [C] **1** *FORMAL* a worker, especially one who is skilled in working with their hands: *a factory operative* **2** *MAINLY US* a person who works secretly for an organization: *a CIA operative*

operable /ˈɒp.ᵊr.ə.bl̩/ [US] /ˈɑː.pɚ.ə-/ *adj* able to be used: *There will be a delay before the modified machines are operable.*

operator /ˈɒp.ᵊr.eɪ.təʳ/ [US] /ˈɑː.pə.reɪ.t̬ɚ/ *noun* [C] **1** someone whose job is to use and control a machine or vehicle: *a computer operator* **2** a company that does a particular type of business: *a tour operator* **3** a person who helps to connect people on a telephone system **4** **smooth/clever, etc. operator** a person who deals with people or problems cleverly, especially for their own advantage: *He has shown himself to be a canny operator in wage negotiations.*

operate [MEDICAL PROCESS] /ˈɒp.ᵊr.eɪt/ [US] /ˈɑː.pə.reɪt/ *verb* [I] to cut a body open for medical reasons in order to repair, remove or replace a diseased or damaged part: *If the growth gets any bigger they'll have to operate.* ○ *Are they going to operate* ***on*** *him?*

operation /ˌɒp.ᵊrˈeɪ.ʃᵊn/ [US] /ˌɑː.pəˈreɪ-/ *noun* [C] (*UK INFORMAL* **op**) when a doctor cuts a body for medical reasons in order to repair, remove or replace a diseased or damaged part: *a major/minor/routine operation* ○ *an abdominal/cataract/transplant operation* ○ *He's got to* ***have*** *an operation* ***on*** *his shoulder.* ○ [+ to infinitive] *We will know in a couple of days if the operation* ***to*** *restore her sight was* ***successful***.

operable /ˈɒp.ᵊr.ə.bl/ [US] /ˈɑː.pɚ.ə-/ *adj* able to be treated by operation: *In about half of diagnosed cases, the condition is operable.* * NOTE: The opposite is **inoperable**.

ˈoperating ˌroom *noun* [C] *US FOR* **operating theatre**

ˈoperating ˌsystem *noun* [C] a special program that controls the way a computer system works, especially how its memory is used and the timing of other programs

ˈoperating ˌtable *noun* [C] a special table that a patient lies on during an operation

ˈoperating ˌtheatre *UK noun* [C] (*US* **operating room**) a special room in which people are operated on in a hospital

opeˌrational reˈsearch *UK noun* [U] (*US* **operations research**) *SPECIALIZED* the systematic study of how best to solve problems in business and industry

operetta /ˌɒp.ᵊrˈet.ə/ [US] /ˌɑː.pəˈreṭ-/ *noun* [C or U] amusing plays in which many or all of the words are sung to music and which might include some dancing, or a play of this type

ophˌthalmic opˈtician *noun* [C] *UK FOR* **optician**

ophthalmology /ˌɒf.θælˈmɒl.ə.dʒi/ [US] /ˌɑːf.θælˈmɑː.lə-/ *noun* [U] the scientific study of eyes and their diseases ⮌Compare **optometry**.

ophthalmologist /ˌɒf.θælˈmɒl.ə.dʒɪst/ [US] /ˌɑːf.θælˈmɑː.lə-/ *noun* [C] a doctor who treats eye diseases ⮌Compare **optician**; **optometrist**.

opiate /ˈəʊ.pi.ət/ [US] /ˈoʊ-/ *noun* [C] a drug which contains OPIUM, especially one which causes sleep

opine /əʊˈpaɪn/ [US] /oʊ-/ *verb* [T] *FORMAL* to state something as an opinion: [+ speech] *Power grows from the barrel of a gun, opined Mao Tse-tung.* ○ [+ that] *Ernest Rutherford opined* ***that*** *his work on radioactive substances would be of little or no practical use.*

opinion /əˈpɪn.jən/ *noun* **1** [C] a thought or belief about something or someone: *What's your opinion* ***about/on*** *the matter?* ○ *People tend to* ***have*** *strong opinions on capital punishment.* ○ *He didn't* ***express/give*** *an opinion on the matter.* ○ *Who,* ***in*** *your opinion,* (= Who do you think) *is the best football player in the world today?* ○ *He's very much* ***of the*** *opinion* ***that*** *alternative medicine is a waste of time.* **2** [U] the thoughts or beliefs that a group of people have: *Eventually, the government will have to take notice of* ***public*** *opinion.* ○ *There is a diverse range of opinion on the issue.* ○ *There was a* ***difference of*** *opinion as to the desirability of the project.* ○ *Opinion* ***is divided*** *as to whether the treatment actually works.* ○ *Both performances were excellent, it's simply* ***a matter of*** *opinion as to whose was better.* **3** [C] a judgment about someone or something: *Her opinion* ***of*** *Adam changed after he'd been so helpful at the wedding.* ○ *She* ***has*** *a* ***good/high*** *opinion* ***of*** *his abilities* (= thinks he is good). ○ *I* ***have*** *a rather* ***bad/low/poor*** *opinion* ***of*** *my sister's boyfriend* (= I do not like or approve of him). ○ *He has a very* ***high*** *opinion* ***of himself*** (= thinks he is very skilled/clever in a way that is annoying). **4** [C] a judgment made by an expert: *My doctor has referred me to a specialist for a* ***second*** *opinion on the results of my blood test.*

opinionated /əˈpɪn.jə.neɪ.tɪd/ [US] /-ṭɪd/ *adj DISAPPROVING* describes someone who is certain about what they think and believe, and who expresses their ideas strongly and often: *He was opinionated and selfish, but undeniably clever.*

oˈpinion ˌpoll *noun* [C] when people are asked questions to discover what they think about a subject: *The latest opinion poll shows that the president's popularity has declined.*

opium /ˈəʊ.pi.əm/ [US] /ˈoʊ-/ *noun* [U] a drug made from the seeds of a POPPY (= red flower) and used to control pain or to help people sleep. It can make a person who takes it want more of it and is sometimes used by people to give them temporarily pleasant effects: *an opium addict*

opossum /əˈpɒs.əm/ [US] /-ˈpɑː.səm/ *noun* [C] *MAINLY US* a **possum**

opponent /əˈpəʊ.nənt/ [US] /-ˈpoʊ-/ *noun* [C] **1** a person who disagrees with something and speaks against it or tries to change it: *a political opponent* ○ *Leading opponents* ***of*** *the proposed cuts in defence spending will meet later today.* ⮌See also **oppose**. Compare **proponent**. **2** a person being competed against in a sports event: *In the second game, her opponent hurt her leg and had to retire.*

opportune /ˈɒp.ə.tjuːn/ [US] /ˌɑː.pɚˈtuːn/ *adj FORMAL* happening at a time which is likely to give success or which is convenient: *This would seem to be an opportune* ***moment*** *for reviving our development plan.* ○ *Would* ***it*** *be opportune* ***to*** *discuss the contract now?* * NOTE: The opposite is **inopportune**.

opportunist /ˌɒp.əˈtjuː.nɪst/ [US] /ˌɑː.pɚˈtuː-/ *noun* [C] *USUALLY DISAPPROVING* someone who tries to get power or an advantage in every situation: *He was portrayed as a ruthless opportunist who exploited the publicity at every opportunity.* **opportunism** /ˌɒp.əˈtjuː.nɪ.zᵊm/ [US] /ˌɑː.pɚˈtuː-/ *noun* [U] *political opportunism*

opportunist /ˌɒp.əˈtjuː.nɪst/ [US] /ˌɑː.pɚˈtuː-/ *adj* (*ALSO* **opportunistic**) *USUALLY DISAPPROVING* using a situation to get power or an advantage: *It's said that a barking dog puts off the opportunist thief.* ○ *At half-time, United were leading with two opportunistic goals by Black.* **opportunistically** /ˌɒp.ə.tjuːˈnɪs.tɪ.kli/ [US] /ˌɑː.pɚ.tuːˈnɪs.ṭɪ-/ *adv*

opportunity /ˌɒp.əˈtjuː.nə.ti/ [US] /ˌɑː.pɚˈtuː.nə.ṭi/ *noun* **1** [C or U] an occasion or situation which makes it possible to do something that you want to do or have to do, or the possibility of doing something: *Everyone will* ***have*** *an opportunity to comment.* ○ *I was never given the opportunity* ***of*** *go****ing*** *to college.* ○ [+ to infinitive] *The exhibition is a* ***unique*** *opportunity* ***to*** *see her later work.* ○ *An ankle injury meant she* ***missed*** *the opportunity* ***to*** *run in the qualifying heat.* ○ *FORMAL Please contact us* ***at the earliest*** *opportunity* (= as soon as possible). ○ *He goes fishing* ***at every*** *opportunity* (= as often as possible). ○ *I used to enjoy going to the theatre, but I don't get much opportunity now.* ○ *He had a* ***golden*** (= an extremely good) *opportunity to score in the first half but squandered it.* ⮌See Note **possibility, occasion or opportunity?** at **possibility**. **2** [C] the chance to get a job: *employment/job opportunities* ○ *opportunities for* ***young*** *graduates* ○ *There are far more opportunities now* ***for*** *school leavers than there were fifty years ago.*

opporˈtunity ˌshop *noun* [C] (*INFORMAL* **op-shop**) *AUS FOR* **charity shop**

oppose /əˈpəʊz/ [US] /-ˈpoʊz/ *verb* [T] to disagree with something or someone, often by speaking or fighting against them: *The proposed new examination system has been vigorously opposed by teachers.* ○ *Most of the local residents opposed the closing of their hospital.* ○ [+ v-ing] *I would certainly oppose chang****ing*** *the system.* ⮌See also **opponent**.

opposed /əˈpəʊzd/ [US] /-ˈpoʊzd/ *adj* **be opposed to** ***sth*** to disagree with a principle or plan: *She's opposed to religious education in schools.*

opposing /əˈpəʊ.zɪŋ/ [US] /-ˈpoʊ-/ *adj* [before n] competing or fighting against each other: *Opposing* ***factions*** *on the committee are refusing to compromise.*

opposition /ˌɒp.əˈzɪʃ.ᵊn/ [US] /ˌɑː.pə-/ *noun* [U] strong disagreement: *There is a lot of opposition* ***to*** *the proposed changes.* ○ *The unions are* ***in*** *opposition* ***to*** *the government over the issue of privatization.*

the Opposition *group noun* [S] in some political systems, the elected politicians who belong to the largest party which does not form the government: *the Leader of the Opposition* ○ *The Opposition has/have condemned the Government's proposed tax increases.*

the opposition *group noun* [S] the team or person being played against in a sports competition: *The*

O

opposition has/have some good players so it should be a tough match.

opposite DIFFERENT /'ɒp.ə.zɪt/ ⓤ /'ɑː.pə-/ *adj* completely different: *You'd never know they're sisters – they're completely opposite* **to** *each other in every way.* ○ *Police attempts to calm the violence had the opposite* **effect***.*

opposite /'ɒp.ə.zɪt/ ⓤ /'ɑː.pə-/ *noun* [C **often sing**] something or someone that is completely different from another person or thing: *My father is a very calm person, but my mother is just* **the** *opposite.* ○ *She's turned out to be* **the exact** *opposite of what everyone expected.* ○ **The opposite** *of 'fast' is 'slow'.* ○ *They always say opposites* **attract***.*

opposed /ə'pəʊzd/ ⓤ /-'poʊzd/ *adj* completely different: *Two opposed interpretations of the facts have been presented.* ○ *His view of the situation is* **diametrically** (= very strongly) *opposed* **to** *mine.*

● **as opposed to** rather than: *I'd prefer to go on holiday in May, as opposed to September.*

opposite FACING /'ɒp.ə.zɪt/ ⓤ /'ɑː.pə-/ *adj* **1** being in a position on the other side; facing: *My brother and I live on opposite sides of London.* ○ *The map on the opposite page shows where these birds commonly breed.* ○ *They sat at opposite ends of the table* (**to/from** *each other*), *refusing to talk.* **2** facing the speaker or stated person or thing: *If you want to buy tickets, you need to go to the counter opposite.* ○ *Who owns that shop opposite* (= on the other side of the road)?

opposite /'ɒp.ə.zɪt/ ⓤ /'ɑː.pə-/ *prep* **1** in a position facing someone or something but on the other side: *We're in the building opposite the government offices.* ○ *They sat opposite each other.* ○ *Put a tick opposite* (= next to) *the answer that you think is correct.* **2** **act/play/star opposite** *sb* to act a part in a film or play with someone as a partner: *Katharine Hepburn played opposite Henry Fonda in many films.*

opposite /'ɒp.ə.zɪt/ ⓤ /'ɑː.pə-/ *adv* in a position facing someone or something but on the other side: *She asked the man sitting opposite whether he'd mind if she opened the window.* ○ *The people who live opposite* (= on the other side of the road) *are always making a lot of noise.*

opposite '**number** *noun* [C **usually sing**] a person who has a very similar job or rank to you but in a different organization

the '**opposite** '**sex** *noun* someone who is male if you are female, and female if you are male: *It's not always easy to meet* **members** *of the opposite sex.*

oppress RULE /ə'pres/ *verb* [T **often passive**] to govern people in an unfair and cruel way and prevent them from having opportunities and freedom: *For years now, the people have been oppressed by a ruthless dictator.* **oppressed** /ə'prest/ *adj: oppressed minorities* ○ *the poor and the oppressed*

oppression /ə'preʃ.ən/ *noun* [U] when people are governed in an unfair and cruel way and prevented from having opportunities and freedom: *Every human being has the right to freedom from oppression.* ○ *War, famine and oppression have forced people in the region to flee from their homes.* ○ *the oppression* **of** *women*

oppressive /ə'pres.ɪv/ *adj* cruel and unfair: *an oppressive government/military regime* **oppressively** /ə'pres.ɪv.li/ *adv* **oppressiveness** /ə'pres.ɪv.nəs/ *noun* [U]

oppressor /ə'pres.ər/ ⓤ /-ɚ/ *noun* [C] someone who treats people in an unfair and cruel way and prevents them from having opportunities and freedom: *Sisters, we must rise up and defeat our oppressors.*

oppress MAKE UNCOMFORTABLE /ə'pres/ *verb* [T] to make a person feel uncomfortable or anxious, and sometimes ill: *Strange dreams and nightmares oppressed him.*

oppression /ə'preʃ.ən/ *noun* [U] when someone feels anxious and uncomfortable: *Several people had experienced the same feeling of oppression when they slept in that room.*

oppressive /ə'pres.ɪv/ *adj* **1** causing anxiety: *an oppressive silence* **2** If the weather or heat is oppressive, it is too hot and there is no wind: *We were unable to sleep because of the oppressive heat.* **oppressively** /ə-'pres.ɪv.li/ *adv* **oppressiveness** /ə'pres.ɪv.nəs/ *noun* [U]

opprobrium /ə'prəʊ.bri.əm/ ⓤ /-'proʊ-/ *noun* [U] FORMAL severe criticism and blame: *International opprobrium*

has been heaped on the country following its attack on its neighbours. **opprobrious** /ə'prəʊ.bri.əs/ ⓤ /-'proʊ-/ *adj*

op-shop /'ɒp.ʃɒp/ ⓤ /'ɑːp.ʃɑːp/ *noun* [C] AUS INFORMAL FOR **opportunity shop**

opt /ɒpt/ ⓤ /ɑːpt/ *verb* [I] to make a choice, especially for one thing or possibility in preference to any others: *Mike opted* **for** *early retirement.* ○ [+ **to** infinitive] *Most people opt* **to** *have the operation.*

▲ **opt out** *phrasal verb* to choose not to be part of an activity or to stop being involved in it: *Within any society, there will usually be people who decide to opt out* (= choose to not live the way most people do). ○ *The government has been encouraging individuals to opt out of the state pension scheme.*

opt-out /'ɒpt.aʊt/ ⓤ /'ɑːpt-/ *noun* [C] *Since the opt-out, the hospital has been responsible for its own budgeting.*

optical /'ɒp.tɪ.kəl/ ⓤ /'ɑːp-/ *adj* relating to light or the ability to see: *an optical effect* ○ *an optical microscope/telescope*

optic /'ɒp.tɪk/ ⓤ /'ɑːp-/ *adj* [before n] SPECIALIZED relating to light or the eyes: *the optic nerve* **optically** /'ɒp.tɪ.kli/ ⓤ /'ɑːp-/ *adv*

optics /'ɒp.tɪks/ ⓤ /'ɑːp-/ *noun* [U] the study of light and of instruments using light

optical ,**character** ,**recog'nition** *noun* [U] (ABBREVIATION **OCR**) SPECIALIZED the process by which an electronic device recognizes printed or written letters or numbers

optical '**fibre** *noun* [C] a long thin glass rod through which very large amounts of information can be sent in the form of light ⊃See also **fibre optics**.

optical il'lusion *noun* [C] something that you think you see, but which is not really there

optician /ɒp'tɪʃ.ən/ ⓤ /ɑːp-/ *noun* [C] **1** UK (UK ALSO **ophthalmic optician**, US **optometrist**) someone whose job is examining people's eyes and selling glasses or CONTACT LENSES to correct sight problems ⊃Compare **ophthalmologist** at **ophthalmology**. **2** US FOR **dispensing optician**

optimism /'ɒp.tɪ.mɪ.zəm/ ⓤ /'ɑːp.tə-/ *noun* [U] the tendency to be hopeful and to emphasize the good part of a situation rather than the bad part; the belief that good things will happen in the future: *There was a note of optimism in his voice as he spoke about the company's future.* ○ *Judging from your examination results, I think you have cause/grounds/reason for* **cautious** *optimism about getting a university place.* ✳ NOTE: The opposite is **pessimism**.

optimist /'ɒp.tɪ.mɪst/ ⓤ /'ɑːp.tə-/ *noun* [C] someone who always believes that good things will happen: *She's a* **born** *optimist* (= someone who has always been optimistic). **optimistic** /ˌɒp.tɪ'mɪs.tɪk/ ⓤ /ˌɑːp.tə-/ *adj: She is optimistic* **about** *her chances of winning a gold medal.* **optimistically** /ˌɒp.tɪ'mɪs.tɪ.kli/ ⓤ /ˌɑːp.tə-/ *adv*

optimum /'ɒp.tɪ.məm/ ⓤ /'ɑːp-/ *adj* [before n] (ALSO **optimal**) best; most likely to bring success or advantage: *A mixture of selected funds is an optimum* **choice** *for future security and return on investment.*

optimize, UK USUALLY -**ise** /'ɒp.tɪ.maɪz/ ⓤ /'ɑːp.tə-/ *verb* [T] to make something as good as possible: *We need to optimize our use of the existing technology.*

option /'ɒp.ʃən/ ⓤ /'ɑːp-/ *noun* **1** [C or U] one thing which can be chosen from a set of possibilities, or the freedom to make a choice: *The best option would be to cancel the trip altogether.* ○ *There are various options* **open** *to someone who is willing to work hard.* ○ *They didn't leave him much option – either he paid or they'd beat him up.* **2** [C] SPECIALIZED the right to buy something in the future: *a share option* ○ *The publishers decided not to take up their option* **on** *the paperback version.*

● **have no option (but to do something)** to not have the possibility of doing something else: *After her appalling behaviour, we had no option but to dismiss her.*

● **have/keep** *your* **options open** to wait before making a choice: *I'm going to keep my options open while I find out about college courses abroad.*

optional /'ɒp.ʃən.əl/ ⓤ /'ɑːp-/ *adj* If something is optional, you can choose whether to do it, pay it, buy it, etc: *English is compulsory for all students, but art and music are optional.*

optometrist US /ɒpˈtɒm.ə.trɪst/ US /ɑːpˈtɑːˌmə-/ *noun* [C] (*UK* **optician**) someone whose job is examining people's eyes and selling glasses or CONTACT LENSES to correct sight problems ⊃Compare **ophthalmologist** at **ophthalmology**. **optometry** /ɒpˈtɒm.ə.tri/ US /ɑːpˈtɑːˌmə-/ *noun* [U] MAINLY US ⊃Compare **ophthalmology**.

opulent /ˈɒp.jʊ.lənt/ US /ˈɑːˌpjʊ-/ *adj* expensive and luxurious: *an opulent lifestyle* ○ *an opulent hotel* **opulence** /ˈɒp.jʊ.lənts/ US /ˈɑːˌpjʊ-/ *noun* [U] **opulently** /ˈɒp.jʊ.lənt.li/ US /ˈɑːˌpjʊ-/ *adv*

opus (*plural* **opuses** or *SPECIALIZED* **opera**) /ˈəʊ.pəs/ US /ˈoʊ-/ *noun* [C] **1** (*WRITTEN ABBREVIATION* **Op.**) a piece of music written by a particular musician and given a number relating to the order in which it was published: *Carl Nielsen's Opus 43 quintet* **2** *FORMAL* any work of art: *He showed us his latest opus, a rather awful painting of a vase of flowers.*

or POSSIBILITIES *STRONG* /ɔːʳ/ US /ɔːr/, *WEAK* /əʳ/ US /ɚ/ *conjunction* **1** used to connect different possibilities: *Is it Tuesday or Wednesday today?* ○ *You can pay now or when you come back to pick up the paint.* ○ *Are you listening to me or* **not**? ○ *The patent was granted in* (**either**) *1962 or 1963 – I can't quite remember which.* ○ *It doesn't matter* **whether** *you win or lose – it's taking part that's important.* ○ *There were ten or twelve* (= approximately that number of) *people in the room.* ○ *He was only joking – or was he* (= but it is possible that he was not)? **2** used after a negative verb to mean not one thing and also not another: *The child never smiles or laughs.* ⊃Compare **nor**.

• **or no** *INFORMAL* used to emphasize that the stated thing will not make any difference: *Extra pay or no extra pay, I'm not going to work late again tonight.*

• **or so** *INFORMAL* approximately: *They raised two hundred pounds or so for charity.*

• **or two** *INFORMAL* approximately or a little more than: *I'll be with you in* **a** *minute or two.* ○ *It's* **a** *good year or two since we last met.*

or IF NOT *STRONG* /ɔːʳ/ US /ɔːr/, *WEAK* /əʳ/ US /ɚ/ *conjunction* if not: *You should eat more, or you'll make yourself ill.*

or EXPLAIN *STRONG* /ɔːʳ/ US /ɔːr/, *WEAK* /əʳ/ US /ɚ/ *conjunction* used to show that a word or phrase means the same as, or explains or limits or corrects, another word or phrase: *Rosalind, or Roz to her friends, took the initiative.* ○ *Things have been going quite well recently. Or they were, up until two days ago.*

OR HOSPITAL /ˌəʊˈɑːʳ/ US /ˌoʊˈɑːr/ *noun* [U] *US ABBREVIATION FOR* **operating room**

-or PERFORMER /-əʳ/ US /-ɚ/ *suffix* ⊃See at **-er** PERFORMER.

oracle /ˈɒr.ə.kl̩/ US /ˈɔːr-/ *noun* [C] **1** (especially in ancient Greece) a female priest who gave people wise but often mysterious advice from a god, or the advice given **2** someone who knows a lot about a subject and can give good advice: *Professor Ross is regarded as the oracle on eating disorders.*

oracular /ɒrˈæk.jʊ.ləʳ/ US /ɔːrˈæk.juːˌlɚ/ *adj FORMAL* mysterious and difficult to understand, but probably wise: *an oracular statement*

oral SPOKEN /ˈɔː.rəl/ US /ˈɔːr.əl/ *adj* spoken; not written: *an oral agreement/exam* **oral** /ˈɔː.rəl/ US /ˈɔːr.əl/ *noun* [C] *When do you have your Spanish oral* (= exam in spoken Spanish)? **orally** /ˈɔː.rə.li/ US /ˈɔːr.ə-/ *adv*

oral MOUTH /ˈɔː.rəl/ US /ˈɔːr.əl/ *adj MAINLY SPECIALIZED* of, taken by, or done to the mouth: *oral hygiene* ○ *oral contraceptives* ○ *oral surgery* **orally** /ˈɔː.rə.li/ US /ˈɔːr.ə-/ *adv*: *This medicine is to be taken orally.*

oral ˈhistory *noun* [U] information about an historical event or period which is told to you by people who experienced it

oral ˈsex *noun* [U] the activity of using the tongue and lips to touch someone's sexual organs in order to give pleasure

orange COLOUR /ˈɒr.ɪndʒ/ US /ˈɔːr-/ *adj, noun* [C or U] (of) a colour between red and yellow: *The setting sun filled the sky with a deep orange glow.* **orangeness** /ˈɒr.ɪn.ʒnəs/ US /ˈɔːr-/ *noun* [U]

orange FRUIT /ˈɒr.ɪndʒ/ US /ˈɔːr-/ *noun* [C or U] a round sweet fruit which has a thick orange-coloured skin and an orange-coloured centre divided into many parts: *a glass of orange juice* ⊃See picture **Fruit** on page Centre 1

orangeade /ˌɒr.ɪndʒˈeɪd/ US /ˌɔːr-/ *noun* [U] **1** *UK* (*US* **orange soda**) a fizzy sweet drink, which tastes of oranges: *a can of orangeade* **2** *US FOR* **orange squash**

orange ˈsquash *UK noun* [U] (*US* **orangeade**) a drink that tastes of oranges, made by adding water to very strong orange juice

orang-utan /ɔːˈræŋ.uˌtæn/ /-,--ˈ-/ US /ɔːrˈæŋ-/ *noun* [C] (*ALSO* **orang**) a large ape with reddish brown hair and long arms which lives in the forests of Sumatra and Borneo

oration /ɔːˈreɪ.ʃᵊn/ /ɒrˈeɪ-/ US /ɔːrˈeɪ-/ *noun* [C] *FORMAL* a formal public speech about a serious subject

oratorio /ˌɒr.əˈtɔː.ri.əʊ/ US /ˌɔːr.əˈtɔːr.i.oʊ/ *noun* [C] *plural* **oratorios** a piece of music for orchestra and singers which tells a story, usually on a religious subject, without acting ⊃Compare **cantata**.

oratory /ˈɒr.ə.tᵊr.i/ US /ˈɔːr.ə.tɔːr-/ *noun* [U] *FORMAL* skilful and effective public speaking: *The prime minister has a reputation for powerful oratory.* **orator** /ˈɒr.ə.təʳ/ US /ˈɔːr.ə.tɚ/ *noun* [C] *a skilled orator* **oratorical** /ˌɒr.əˈtɒr.ɪ.kᵊl/ US /ˌɔːr.əˈtɔːr-/ *adj: oratorical skill*

orb /ɔːb/ US /ɔːrb/ *noun* [C] *LITERARY* something in the shape of a sphere: *the glowing orb of the sun*

orbit /ˈɔː.bɪt/ US /ˈɔːr-/ *noun* [C or U] the curved path through which objects in space move around a planet or star: *The satellite is now in a stable orbit.* ○ *Once in space, the spacecraft will go into orbit around the Earth.*

• **go into orbit** *INFORMAL* to increase or succeed very quickly or to be in a state of extreme activity: *Prices have gone into orbit this year.*

orbit /ˈɔː.bɪt/ US /ˈɔːr-/ *verb* [I or T] to follow a curved path around a planet or star: *On this mission the Shuttle will orbit (the Earth) at a height of several hundred miles.* **orbital** /ˈɔː.bɪ.tᵊl/ US /ˈɔːr.bɪ.tᵊl/ *adj: an orbital space station*

ˈorbital ˌroad *noun* [C] *UK* a road which takes traffic around a city rather than through it

orchard /ˈɔː.tʃəd/ US /ˈɔːr.tʃɚd/ *noun* [C] an area of land where fruit trees (but not orange trees or other CITRUS trees) are grown: *an apple/cherry orchard*

orchestra MUSIC /ˈɔː.kɪ.strə/ US /ˈɔːr-/ *group noun* [C] a large group of musicians who play many different instruments together and are led by a CONDUCTOR: *She's a cellist in the City of Birmingham Symphony Orchestra.* **orchestral** /ɔːˈkes.trᵊl/ US /ɔːr-/ *adj: an orchestral arrangement* **orchestrate** /ˈɔː.kɪ.streɪt/ US /ˈɔːr-/ *verb* [T often passive] to arrange or write a piece of music so that it can be played by an orchestra ⊃See also **orchestrate**. **orchestration** /ˌɔː.kɪˈstreɪ.ʃᵊn/ US /ˌɔːr-/ *noun* [C or U]

the orchestra THEATRE *noun* [S] *US FOR* **the stalls** THEATRE

ˈorchestra ˌpit *noun* [S] the area of a theatre in which musicians play their instruments, and which is in front of, or under the front of, the stage

orchestrate /ˈɔː.kɪ.streɪt/ US /ˈɔːr-/ *verb* [T often passive] to arrange something carefully, and sometimes unfairly, so as to achieve a desired result: *Their victory was largely a result of their brilliantly orchestrated election campaign.* ⊃See also **orchestrate** at **orchestra**. **orchestration** /ˌɔː.kɪˈstreɪ.ʃᵊn/ US /ˌɔːr-/ *noun* [U]

orchid /ˈɔː.kɪd/ US /ˈɔːr-/ *noun* [C] a plant with unusually shaped and beautifully coloured flowers ⊃See picture **Flowers and Plants** on page Centre 3

ordain CHURCH /ɔːˈdeɪn/ US /ɔːr-/ *verb* [T often passive] to officially make someone a priest or other religious leader, in a religious ceremony: *He was ordained (as) a priest in Oxford cathedral in 1987.* **ordination** /ˌɔː.dɪˈneɪ.ʃᵊn/ US /ˌɔːr-/ *noun* [C or U] the act or ceremony of making someone a priest or other religious leader

ordain ORDER /ɔːˈdeɪn/ US /ɔːr-/ *verb* [T] *FORMAL* (of God or someone in authority) to order something to happen: *There is strong support here for the tough economic* reforms ordained in the federal capital, Prague. ○ [+ that] HUMOROUS The council, in its wisdom, has ordained **that** all the local libraries will close on Mondays.

ordeal /ɔːˈdiːəl/ US /ɔːr-/ noun [C] a very unpleasant and painful or difficult experience: The hostages' ordeal came to an end when soldiers stormed the building.

order PURPOSE /ˈɔː.dəʳ/ US /ˈɔːr.dɚ/ noun **in order to/in order for/in order that** with the aim of achieving something: He came home early in order to see the children before they went to bed. ○ I agreed to her suggestion in order **not** to upset her.

order ARRANGEMENT /ˈɔː.dəʳ/ US /ˈɔːr.dɚ/ noun [U] the way in which people or things are arranged, either in relation to one another or according to a particular characteristic: The children lined up **in order** of age/height. ○ I can't find the file I need because they're all **out of order** (= they are no longer arranged in the correct way). ○ Put the files in **alphabetical/chronological order**. ○ MAINLY UK Here's the **running** order for the concert (= the order in which each item will happen). ⊃See also order CORRECT BEHAVIOUR; order TIDY.
• **the order of the day 1** FORMAL in parliament or in formal meetings, the list of matters to be discussed on a particular day **2** INFORMAL something that is very common or important: On these TV channels, quiz shows and repeats are becoming the order of the day.

order /ˈɔː.dəʳ/ US /ˈɔːr.dɚ/ verb [T] to arrange a group of people or things in a list from first to last: I've ordered the application forms **into** three groups.
• **order your thoughts** to plan what you want to say or do: Just give me a moment to order my thoughts, and then I'll explain the system to you.

order REQUEST /ˈɔː.dəʳ/ US /ˈɔːr.dɚ/ verb [I or T] to ask for something to be made, supplied or delivered, especially in a restaurant or shop: I ordered some pasta and a mixed salad. ○ [+ two objects] There are no shirts left in this size but we could order one **for** you/order you one.

order /ˈɔː.dəʳ/ US /ˈɔːr.dɚ/ noun [C] **1** a request to make, supply or deliver food or goods: "Can I **take** your order now?" said the waiter. ○ I would like to **place** (= make) an order for a large pine table. **2** a product or a meal which has been requested by a customer: The shop phoned to say your order has come in. **3 be on order** If something is on order, you have requested it but have not yet received it: The new drilling equipment has been on order for several weeks. **4 do/make sth to order** to do or make something especially for a person who has requested it: We make wedding cakes to order.

order CORRECT BEHAVIOUR /ˈɔː.dəʳ/ US /ˈɔːr.dɚ/ noun [U] a situation in which rules are obeyed and people do what they are expected to do: The teacher found it hard to **keep** her class **in order**. ○ As the demonstration began to turn violent, the police were called in to **restore** order. ○ After some heated discussion, the chair **called** the meeting **to order** (= told everyone to stop talking so that the meeting could continue). ○ His behaviour in the meeting was **out of order** (= not suitable for the situation). ○ UK Is it **in order** (= allowed) for me to park my car outside the building?
• **Order! Order!** FORMAL an expression used in parliament or a formal meeting to get people's attention and make them stop talking, so that the meeting or discussion can start or continue

order INSTRUCTION /ˈɔː.dəʳ/ US /ˈɔːr.dɚ/ noun [C] **1** something you are told to do by someone else and which you must do: Clean up this room immediately – and that's an order! ○ The soldiers fired as soon as their commander **gave** the order. ○ Soldiers must **obey** orders. ○ The road was closed all day **by order** of the police. ⊃Compare request. **2** an official instruction telling someone what they can or cannot do, or a written instruction to a bank to pay money to a particular person
orders /ˈɔː.dəz/ US /ˈɔːr.dɚz/ plural noun: What are your orders (= What have you been told you must do)? ○ My orders are **to search everyone's bag as they come in.** ○ We are **under** orders (= We have been told) not to allow anyone into the building.
• **orders are orders** said when you have to do something because someone in authority has told you to, and usually when you do not really approve of it: Nobody wants

to do it, but orders are orders, so let's start.

order /ˈɔː.dəʳ/ US /ˈɔːr.dɚ/ verb [T] If a person in authority orders someone to do something, or orders something to be done, they tell someone to do it: The management has ordered a cutback in spending. ○ [+ speech] "Wait over there," she ordered. ○ [+ to infinitive] They ordered him **to** leave the room.

order TIDY /ˈɔː.dəʳ/ US /ˈɔːr.dɚ/ noun [U] **1** when everything is arranged in its correct place: The house was so untidy that she spent the whole day trying to establish some sort of order. **2 leave/put sth in order** to organize something well: I try to leave my desk in order when I go home. ○ He put his **affairs** in order (= made special arrangements for his personal and business matters) before he went into hospital.
ordered /ˈɔː.dəd/ US /ˈɔːr.dɚd/ adj (ALSO **well-ordered**) carefully arranged or controlled: a well-ordered (= tidy) room
orderly /ˈɔː.dəl.i/ US /ˈɔːr.dɚ.li/ adj well arranged or organized: She put the letters in three orderly piles. ○ Form an orderly queue. ○ During the bomb scare, the customers were asked to proceed **in an** orderly fashion out of the shop. ⊃See also orderly HOSPITAL WORKER; orderly SOLDIER.

order STATE /ˈɔː.dəʳ/ US /ˈɔːr.dɚ/ noun [U] the state of working correctly or of being suitable for use: TV for sale **in (good) working** order. ○ Are your immigration papers in order (= legally correct)? ○ The coffee machine is **out of** order (= not working). ⊃See also order ARRANGEMENT, order CORRECT BEHAVIOUR.

order SYSTEM /ˈɔː.dəʳ/ US /ˈɔːr.dɚ/ noun [C] a social or political system: The collapse of Communism at the end of the 1980s encouraged hopes of a new world order.

order GROUP OF PEOPLE /ˈɔː.dəʳ/ US /ˈɔːr.dɚ/ group noun **1** [C] a group of people who join together for religious or similar reasons and live according to particular rules: religious/holy orders ○ monks of the Cistercian/Franciscan Order **2** [S] a group which people are made members of as a reward for services they have done for their country: He was made a knight of the Order of the Garter. **3** UK OLD-FASHIONED DISAPPROVING **the lower orders** the poorest social groups in society

order TYPE /ˈɔː.dəʳ/ US /ˈɔːr.dɚ/ noun [U] the type or size of something: These were problems of a completely different order from anything we had faced before. ○ FORMAL No successful business can be run without skills **of the highest** order (= great skills).
• **of the order of** (UK ALSO **in the order of**) approximately: "How much is the project going to cost?" "Something in the order of £500."

order BIOLOGY /ˈɔː.dəʳ/ US /ˈɔːr.dɚ/ noun [C] SPECIALIZED (used in the CLASSIFICATION of plants and animals) a group of related plants or animals: An order is below a class and above a family.

PHRASAL VERBS WITH **order** ▼

▲ **order sb about/around** phrasal verb DISAPPROVING to tell someone what they should do in an unpleasant or forceful way, especially continually: You can't just come in here and start ordering people around.

▲ **order sth in** phrasal verb [M] US to order food that is ready to eat to be brought to your home or to the place where you work: I think I'll stay home tonight, order in a pizza and watch a video.

'order ,book noun [C] a book in which a company or shop keeps a record of customers' orders

'order ,form noun [C] a printed form which a customer uses to request goods or a service

orderly HOSPITAL WORKER /ˈɔː.dəl.i/ US /ˈɔːr.dɚ.li/ noun [C] a hospital worker who does jobs for which no training is necessary, such as helping the nurses or carrying heavy things: He has a part-time job as a **hospital** orderly. ⊃See also orderly at order TIDY.

orderly SOLDIER /ˈɔː.dəl.i/ US /ˈɔːr.dɚ.li/ noun [C] a soldier who acts as an officer's servant

,order of 'magnitude noun [C usually sing] the approximate size of something, especially a number: The country's debt this year will be **of** the same order of magnitude as it was last year.

'order ,paper *noun* [C] in parliament, a list which shows the order in which matters will be discussed on a particular day

ordinal (number) /ˌɔː.dɪ.nəlˈnʌm.bəʳ/ US /ˌɔːr.dən.əlˈnʌm.bəʳ/ *noun* [C] a number like 1st, 2nd, 3rd, 4th, which shows the position of something in a list of items: *Ordinal numbers are used in these sentences: 'She was fifth in the race' and 'They celebrated the 200th anniversary of the university's foundation'.* ➜Compare **cardinal (number).**

ordinance /ˈɔː.dɪ.nənts/ US /ˈɔːr.dən.ənts/ *noun* [C] FORMAL a law or rule made by a government or authority: *City Ordinance 126 forbids car parking in this area of New York.*

ordinary /ˈɔː.dɪ.nə.ri/ US /ˈɔːr.dən.er-/ *adj* not different or special or unexpected in any way; usual: *an ordinary neighbourhood* ○ *Readers of the magazine said they wanted more stories about ordinary people and less stories about the rich and famous.* ○ *Her last concert appearance in Britain was **no** ordinary* (= a very special) *performance.* ○ *For the police, the incident seemed **nothing out of the** ordinary/did not seem **out of the** ordinary* (= it was not unusual).
• **in the ordinary way** UK normally, or in the way that usually happens: *If we hadn't seen the TV programme, we would have carried on giving money to the charity in the ordinary way.*

ordinarily /ˈɔː.dɪ.nə.rə.li/ /ˌɔː.dən'er.ɪ-/ US /ˈɔːr.dən'er-/ *adv* usually: *Ordinarily, we send a reminder about a month before payment is required.*

ordinariness /ˈɔː.dɪ.nə.rɪ.nəs/ US /ˌɔːr.dən'er-/ *noun* [U] *She expected him to act like a star, but she was surprised at his very ordinariness* (= how ordinary he was).

ordination /ˌɔː.dɪ'neɪ.ʃən/ US /ˌɔːr.dən'eɪ-/ *noun* [U] ➜See at **ordain** CHURCH.

the Ordnance Survey /ðiˌɔːd.nənts'sɜː.veɪ/ US /-ˌɔːrd.-nənts'sɜːr-/ *noun* [S] the government organization which makes detailed official maps of Britain and Northern Ireland

ore /ɔːʳ/ US /ɔːr/ *noun* [C or U] rock or soil from which metal can be obtained: *iron/copper ore*

oregano /ˌɒr.ɪ'gɑː.nəʊ/ US /ɔː'reg.ə.noʊ/ *noun* [U] a herb whose dried leaves are used in cooking to add flavour, especially in Italian cooking

.org /ˌdɒt'ɔːg/ /ˌdɑːt'ɔːrg/ INTERNET ABBREVIATION FOR organization: used to show that an Internet address belongs to an organization which does not intentionally make a profit: *You can search Cambridge dictionaries on-line at www.dictionary.cambridge.org.*

organ BODY PART /ˈɔː.gən/ US /ˈɔːr-/ *noun* [C] a part of the body of an animal or plant which performs a particular job: *an external/internal/reproductive organ* ○ *an organ donor/transplant*

organ INSTRUMENT /ˈɔː.gən/ US /ˈɔːr-/ *noun* [C] a musical instrument with a keyboard in which sound is produced by air being forced through pipes of different sizes and lengths when you press the keys with your hands or feet, or in which sound is produced electronically: *Electronic organs are much smaller and cheaper than pipe organs.*

organist /ˈɔː.gən.ɪst/ US /ˈɔːr-/ *noun* [C] a person who plays an organ, especially in a church or as a job

organ NEWSPAPER /ˈɔː.gən/ US /ˈɔːr-/ *noun* FORMAL **the organ of sth** a newspaper or broadcasting station produced by a particular organization and giving only the opinions of that organization: *The newspaper Pravda was the official organ of the Communist Party in the Soviet Union.*

'organ ,grinder *noun* [C] OLD-FASHIONED a person who earns money in the street by playing a type of organ that is operated by turning a handle

organic LIVING /ɔː'gæn.ɪk/ US /ɔːr-/ *adj* **1** being or coming from living plants and animals: *A quarter of the contents of an average family's dustbin is organic **matter**.* ✳ NOTE: The opposite is **inorganic**. **2** FORMAL (of a disease or illness) producing a physical change in the structure of an organ or part of the body **3** SPECIALIZED (of a chemical substance) containing carbon: *Organic chemicals are*

used in the manufacture of plastics, fibres, solvents and paints.

organic NO CHEMICALS /ɔː'gæn.ɪk/ US /ɔːr-/ *adj* not using artificial chemicals in the growing of plants and animals for food: *organic food/fruit/farms/farmers* **organically** /ɔː'gæn.ɪ.kli/ US /ɔːr-/ *adv*: *The wine is made from organically grown grapes.*

or,ganic 'chemistry *noun* [U] the scientific study of chemical substances which contain carbon, including artificial substances such as plastics

organism /ˈɔː.gən.ɪ.zəm/ US /ˈɔːr-/ *noun* [C] a single living plant, animal, virus, etc: *Amoebae and bacteria are single-celled organisms.* ➜See also **microorganism.**

organization, UK USUALLY **-isation** /ˌɔː.gən.aɪ'zeɪ.ʃən/ US /ˌɔːr-/ *noun* [C] a group of people who work together in a structured way for a shared purpose: *the World Health Organization* ○ *The article was about the international aid organizations.* ➜See also **organization** at **organize** ARRANGE; **organize** MAKE A SYSTEM.

organize ARRANGE, UK USUALLY **-ise** /ˈɔː.gən.aɪz/ US /ˈɔːr-/ *verb* [T] to make arrangements for something to happen: *They organized a meeting between the teachers and students.* ○ [+ to infinitive] UK *She had organized a car **to** meet me at the airport.*
• **couldn't organize a piss-up in a brewery** UK OFFENSIVE said about someone who is completely unable to organize things

organization, UK USUALLY **-isation** /ˌɔː.gən.aɪ'zeɪ.ʃən/ US /ˌɔːr-/ *noun* [U] the planning of an activity or event: *He didn't want to be involved in the organization **of/for** the conference, although he was willing to attend and speak.* ➜See also **organization**. **organized**, UK USUALLY **-ised** /ˈɔː.gən.aɪzd/ US /ˈɔːr-/ *adj*: *I don't like going on organized tours.* **organizer**, UK USUALLY **-iser** /ˈɔː.gən.aɪ.zəʳ/ US /ˈɔːr.gən.aɪ.zəʳ/ *noun* [C] *There aren't enough seats for all the guests – I must tell the organizers.*

organize MAKE A SYSTEM, UK USUALLY **-ise** /ˈɔː.gən.aɪz/ US /ˈɔːr-/ *verb* [T] to do or arrange something according to a particular system: *The books were organized on the shelves according to their size.* ○ INFORMAL *My mother is always trying to organize me* (= make me do things in the way she likes).

organization, UK USUALLY **-isation** /ˌɔː.gən.aɪ'zeɪ.ʃən/ US /ˌɔːr-/ *noun* [U] the way in which something is done or arranged ➜See also **organization**. **organizational**, UK USUALLY **-isational** /ˌɔː.gən.aɪ'zeɪ.ʃən.ᵊl/ US /ˌɔːr-/ *adj* [before n] *She is looking for a personal assistant with good organizational skills.*

organized, UK USUALLY **-ised** /ˈɔː.gən.aɪzd/ US /ˈɔːr-/ *adj* **1** arranged according to a particular system: *The letters had been placed in organized piles, one for each letter of the alphabet.* ✳ NOTE: The opposite is **disorganized**. **2** describes someone who is able to plan things carefully and keep things tidy: *She's not a very organized person and she always arrives late at meetings.* **organizer**, UK USUALLY **-iser** /ˈɔː.gən.aɪ.zəʳ/ US /ˈɔːr.gən.aɪ.zəʳ/ *noun* [C] *We need someone who is a good organizer.*

,organized 'crime *noun* [U] criminal organizations which plan and commit crime, or the crimes which are committed by such organizations: *The murders may have been linked to organized crime.*

organophosphate /ˌɔː.gæn.əʊ'fɒs.feɪt/ US /ɔːr,gæn.oʊ-'fɑːs.feɪt/ *noun* [C] a chemical used for killing insects and small animals that damage crops: *organophosphate pesticides/poisoning*

orgasm /ˈɔː.gæz.ᵊm/ US /ˈɔːr-/ *noun* [C or U] the moment of greatest pleasure and excitement in sexual activity: *to have an orgasm* ○ *to achieve/reach orgasm* **orgasm** /ˈɔː.gæz.ᵊm/ US /ˈɔːr-/ *verb* [I]

orgasmic /ɔː'gæz.mɪk/ US /ɔːr-/ *adj* **1** relating to orgasm **2** INFORMAL producing feelings of great pleasure or excitement: *Their chocolate mousse is simply orgasmic.*

orgy /ˈɔː.dʒi/ US /ˈɔːr-/ *noun* [C] **1** an occasion when a group of people behave in a wild uncontrolled way, especially involving sex, alcohol or illegal drugs: *drunken orgies* **2** DISAPPROVING **an orgy of sth** a period when there is too much of something, usually a bad or harmful activity: *The protest degenerated into an orgy of looting and shooting.* ○ *When she got her first salary* *cheque, she indulged in an orgy of spending.*

orgiastic /ˌɔː.dʒiˈæs.tɪk/ Ⓤ /ˌɔːr-/ *adj FORMAL* describes an activity which involves wild uncontrolled behaviour and feelings of great pleasure and excitement

the Orient /ðiˈɔː.ri.ənt/ Ⓤ /-ˈɔːri-/ *noun* [S] *OLD-FASHIONED* the countries in the east and south-east of Asia ⊃Compare **the Occident. oriental** /ˌɔː.riˈen.tᵊl/ Ⓤ /ˌɔːr.i-ˈen.tᵊl/ *adj: oriental cuisine/fruits/plants* ⊃Compare **occidental** at the occident.

orientalist /ˌɔː.riˈen.tᵊl.ɪst/ Ⓤ /ˌɔːr.iˈen.tᵊl-/ *noun* [C] *SPECIALIZED* a person who studies the languages and culture of countries in the east and south-east of Asia

orientate *yourself* FIND DIRECTION *UK adj verb* [R] (*US* **orient**) to discover your position in relation to your surroundings: *If you get lost while you are out walking, try to use the sun to orientate yourself.*

orientation /ˌɔː.ri.enˈteɪ.ʃᵊn/ Ⓤ /ˌɔːr.i-/ *noun* [U] *FORMAL* arrangement: *The building has an east-west orientation* (= It is built on a line between east and west).

orienteering /ˌɔː.ri.ənˈtɪə.rɪŋ/ Ⓤ /ˌɔːr.i.enˈtɪr.ɪŋ/ *noun* [U] a sport in which you have to find your way to somewhere on foot as quickly as possible by using a map and a COMPASS

orientate AIM *UK* /ˈɔː.ri.ən.teɪt/ Ⓤ /ˈɔːr.i-/ *verb* [T usually + adv or prep] (*US* **orient**) to aim something at someone or something, or make something suitable for a particular group of people: *It is essential that the public sector orientates itself more towards the consumer.*

orientated *UK* /ˌɔː.ri.ənˈteɪ.tɪd/ Ⓤ /ˌɔːr.i.enˈteɪ.t̬ɪd/ *adj* (*US* **oriented**) directed towards or interested in something: *The industry is heavily orientated towards export markets.*

-orientated *UK* /-ɔː.ri.en.teɪ.tɪd/ Ⓤ /-ɔːr.i.en.teɪ.t̬ɪd/ *suffix* (*US* **-oriented**) showing the direction in which something is aimed: *She wants to turn the company into a profit-orientated organization.*

orientation /ˌɔː.ri.enˈteɪ.ʃᵊn/ Ⓤ /ˌɔːr.i-/ *noun* [U] the particular interests, activities or aims that someone or something has: *We employ people without regard to their political or sexual orientation.*

orifice /ˈɒr.ɪ.fɪs/ Ⓤ /ˈɔːr.ə-/ *noun* [C] an opening or hole, especially one in the body, such as the mouth: *HUMOROUS I was stuffing cake into every available orifice.* ∘ *FORMAL The driver was bleeding from every orifice.*

origami /ˌɒr.ɪˈɡɑː.mi/ Ⓤ /ˌɔːr-/ *noun* [U] the art of making objects for decoration by folding sheets of paper into shapes: *Origami comes from Japan, where it is still widely practised.*

origin /ˈɒr.ɪ.dʒɪn/ Ⓤ /ˈɔːr.ə-/ *noun* **1** [C] (*ALSO* **origins**) the beginning or cause of something: *It's a book about the origin of the universe.* ∘ *Her unhappy childhood was the origin of her problems later in life.* ∘ *What's the origin of this saying?* (= Where did it come from?) **2** [U] where a person was born: *He is of North African origin.* ∘ *What is your country of origin?* **3** [U] where an object was made: *The furniture was French in origin.*

origins /ˈɒr.ɪ.dʒɪnz/ Ⓤ /ˈɔːr.ə-/ *plural noun*: *The story has obscure origins* (= No one knows how it started). ∘ *The president's family was of humble origins* (= They were poor people without a good position in society).

original /əˈrɪdʒ.ɪ.nəl/ *noun* [C] **1** the first one made and not a copy: *Can you let me have the original of your report? I can't read this photocopy.* **2** a piece of work by a famous artist or *DESIGNER* and not a copy by someone else: *If the painting is an original, it will be very valuable.*

• **in the original** If you read something in the original, you read it in the language in which it was first written.

original /əˈrɪdʒ.ɪ.nəl/ *adj* [before n] **1** existing since the beginning, or being the earliest form of something: *Is this the original fireplace?* ∘ *The gardens have recently been restored to their original glory.* ⊃See also **original. 2** describes a piece of work, such as a painting, etc. produced by the artist and not a copy: *an original drawing/manuscript* ∘ *Is this an original Rembrandt* (= Was it painted by him)?

originally /əˈrɪdʒ.ɪ.nə.li/ *adv* first of all: *Originally it was a bedroom, but we turned it into a study.*

originate /əˈrɪdʒ.ɪ.neɪt/ *verb* **1** [I] coming from a particular place, time, situation, etc: *Although the*

technology originated in the UK, it has been developed in the US. ∘ *The game is thought to have originated among the native peoples of Alaska.* **2** [T] to start something or cause it to happen: *Who originated the saying 'Small is beautiful'?*

originator /əˈrɪdʒ.ɪ.neɪ.tər/ Ⓤ /-t̬ə-/ *noun* [C] the person who first thinks of something and causes it to happen: *He is best known as the originator of a long-running TV series.*

original /əˈrɪdʒ.ɪ.nəl/ *adj MAINLY APPROVING* not the same as anything or anyone else and therefore special and interesting: *original ideas/suggestions/work* ∘ *She's a highly original young designer.* ⊃See also **original** at **origin.** * NOTE: The opposite is **unoriginal. originality** /əˌrɪdʒ.ɪˈnæl.ə.ti/ Ⓤ /-t̬i/ *noun* [U] *We were impressed by the originality of the children's work especially their ice sculptures.*

oˌriginal ˈsin *noun* [U] in the Christian religion, the idea that all human beings are born with a tendency to be evil

oriole /ˈɔː.ri.əʊl/ Ⓤ /ˈɔːr.i.oʊl/ *noun* [C] a type of colourful European or North American bird

ornament /ˈɔː.nə.mənt/ Ⓤ /ˈɔːr-/ *noun* **1** [C] an object which is beautiful rather than useful: *a glass ornament* ∘ *garden ornaments such as statues and fountains* **2** [U] *FORMAL* decoration which is added to increase the beauty of something: *The building relies on clever design rather than on ornament for its impressive effect.*

ornament /ˈɔː.nə.ment/ Ⓤ /ˈɔːr-/ *verb* [T] *SLIGHTLY FORMAL* to add decoration to something: *She ornamented her letters with little drawings in the margin.*

ornamental /ˌɔː.nəˈmen.tᵊl/ Ⓤ /ˌɔːr.nəˈmen.tᵊl/ *adj* beautiful rather than useful: *a bowl of ornamental china fruit* ∘ *The handles on each side of the box are purely ornamental* (= They are for decoration only).

ornamentation /ˌɔː.nə.menˈteɪ.ʃᵊn/ Ⓤ /ˌɔːr-/ *noun* [U] *SLIGHTLY FORMAL* decoration: *a plain gold ring with no ornamentation*

ornate /ɔːˈneɪt/ Ⓤ /ɔːr-/ *adj* having a lot of complicated decoration: *a room with an ornate ceiling and gold mirrors* **ornately** /ɔːˈneɪt.li/ Ⓤ /ɔːr-/ *adv: a pair of ornately carved doors*

ornery /ˈɔː.nə.ri/ Ⓤ /ˈɔːr-/ *adj US* tending to get angry and argue with people: *He had been in an ornery mood all day, rowing with his wife and his boss.*

ornithology /ˌɔː.nɪˈθɒl.ə.dʒi/ Ⓤ /ˌɔːr.nəˈθɑː.lə-/ *noun* [U] *SPECIALIZED* the study of birds **ornithological** /ˌɔː.nɪ.θə-ˈlɒdʒ.ɪ.kᵊl/ Ⓤ /ˌɔːr.nə.θəˈlɑː.dʒɪ-/ *adj* [before n]

ornithologist /ˌɔː.nɪˈθɒl.ə.dʒɪst/ Ⓤ /ˌɔːr.nəˈθɑː.lə-/ *noun* [C] *SPECIALIZED* a person whose job is to study birds

orphan /ˈɔː.fᵊn/ Ⓤ /ˈɔːr-/ *noun* [C] a child whose parents are dead: *The civil war is making orphans of many children.*

orphan /ˈɔː.fᵊn/ Ⓤ /ˈɔːr-/ *verb* [T] *He was orphaned as a baby* (= His parents died when he was a baby). ∘ *The children were orphaned by the war* (= their parents were killed in the war).

orphanage /ˈɔː.fᵊn.ɪdʒ/ Ⓤ /ˈɔːr-/ *noun* [C] a home for children whose parents are dead or unable to care for them

orthodontics /ˌɔː.θəʊˈdɒn.tɪks/ Ⓤ /ˌɔːr.θoʊˈdɑːn.t̬ɪks/ *noun* [U] *SPECIALIZED* the job or activity of correcting the position of teeth and dealing with and preventing problems of the teeth **orthodontic** /ˌɔː.θəʊˈdɒn.tɪk/ Ⓤ /ˌɔːr.θoʊˈdɑːn.t̬ɪk/ *adj* [before n] *Does she need orthodontic treatment to have her teeth straightened?*

orthodontist /ˌɔː.θəʊˈdɒn.tɪst/ Ⓤ /ˌɔːr.θoʊˈdɑːn.t̬ɪst/ *noun* [C] *SPECIALIZED* a person whose job is to correct the position of the teeth, etc.

orthodox /ˈɔː.θə.dɒks/ Ⓤ /ˈɔːr.θə.dɑːks/ *adj* **1** (of beliefs, ideas or activities) considered traditional, normal and acceptable by most people: *orthodox treatment/methods* ∘ *orthodox views/opinions* ∘ *We would prefer a more orthodox approach/solution to the problem.* ⊃Compare **heterodox. 2** (of religious people) having more traditional beliefs than other people in the same religious group: *orthodox Christians/Jews/Muslims* **3** **the (Greek/Russian/Eastern) Orthodox Church** a part of the Christian Church, with many members in Greece, Russia and eastern Europe

orthodoxy /ˈɔː.θə.dɒk.si/ ⓤ /ˈɔːr.θə.dɑːk-/ *noun* **1** [C] the generally accepted beliefs of society at a particular time: *The current economic orthodoxy is of a free market and unregulated trade.* **2** [C or U] the traditional beliefs of a religious group or political party: *She is a strict defender of Catholic orthodoxy.* **3** [U] the degree to which someone believes in traditional religious or political ideas: *His orthodoxy began to be seriously questioned by his parish priest.*

ˌorthodox ˈmedicine *noun* [U] using drugs and operations to cure illness: *She is a cancer sufferer who has rejected orthodox medicine and turned instead to acupuncture, aromatherapy and other forms of alternative medicine.*

orthography /ɔːˈθɒg.rə.fi/ ⓤ /ɔːrˈθɑː.grə-/ *noun* [U] SPECIALIZED the accepted way of spelling and writing words **orthographic** /ˌɔː.θəʊˈgræf.ɪk/ ⓤ /ˌɔːr.θə-/ *adj* [before n] **orthographically** /ˌɔː.θəʊˈgræf.ɪ.kli/ ⓤ /ˌɔːr.θə-/ *adv*

orthopaedics UK /ˌɔː.θəˈpiː.dɪks/ ⓤ /ˌɔːr.θə-/ *plural noun* (MAINLY US **orthopedics**) SPECIALIZED the treatment or study of bones which have not grown correctly or which have been damaged

orthopaedic UK, MAINLY US **orthopedic** /ˌɔː.θəʊˈpiː.dɪk/ ⓤ /ˌɔːr.θə-/ *adj* [before n] SPECIALIZED **1** relating to orthopaedics: *an orthopaedic surgeon/specialist/hospital* **2** designed to prevent or treat bone injuries: *an orthopaedic mattress* ○ *orthopaedic shoes*

OS /ˌəʊˈes/ ⓤ /ˌoʊ-/ *noun* [U] ABBREVIATION FOR the **Ordnance Survey**

Oscar /ˈɒs.kəʳ/ ⓤ /ˈɑː.skɚ/ *noun* [C] TRADEMARK one of a set of American prizes given each year to the best film, the best actor or actress in any film and to other people involved in the production of films: *The movie won Oscars for best costumes and best screenplay in this year's awards.* ○ *The Oscar* **ceremony** *takes place in March every year.*

oscillate /ˈɒs.ɪ.leɪt/ ⓤ /ˈɑː.sᵊl.eɪt/ *verb* [I] **1** to move repeatedly from one position to another: *The needle on the dial oscillated* **between** *'full' and 'empty'.* **2** FORMAL If you oscillate between feelings or opinions, you change repeatedly from one to the other: *My emotions oscillate* **between** *desperation and hope.* **3** SPECIALIZED (of a wave or electric current) to change regularly in strength or direction **oscillation** /ˌɒs.ɪˈleɪ.ʃᵊn/ ⓤ /ˌɑː.sᵊlˈeɪ-/ *noun* [C or U] FORMAL OR SPECIALIZED

oscilloscope /əˈsɪl.ə.skəʊp/ ⓤ /-skoʊp/ *noun* [C] a device which represents a changing amount on a screen in the form of a wavy line

osmosis /ɒzˈməʊ.sɪs/ ⓤ /ɑːzˈmoʊ-/ *noun* [U] SPECIALIZED **1** the process in plants and animals by which a liquid moves gradually from one part of the body or the plant to another through a MEMBRANE (= cell covering): *Fluid flows back into the tiny blood vessels* **by** *osmosis.* **2** the way in which ideas and information gradually spread between people: *The children were never taught the songs, they just listened to other children singing them and learned them* **by** *osmosis.* ○ *Reading is not picked up* **by a process of** *osmosis, but needs to be taught.* **osmotic** /ɒzˈmɒt.ɪk/ ⓤ /ɑːzˈmɑː.t̬ɪk/ *adj* [before n] *an osmotic process*

osprey /ˈɒs.preɪ/ ⓤ /ˈɑː.spri/ *noun* [C] a large fish-eating bird with black and white feathers

ossify /ˈɒs.ɪ.faɪ/ ⓤ /ˈɑː.sə-/ *verb* **1** [I or T] FORMAL DISAPPROVING If habits or ideas ossify, or if something ossifies them, they become fixed and unable to change: *Years of easy success had ossified the company's thinking and it never faced up to the challenge of the new technology.* **2** [I] SPECIALIZED If body tissue ossifies, it hardens and changes into bone. **ossification** /ˌɒs.ɪ.fɪˈkeɪ.ʃᵊn/ ⓤ /ˌɑː.sə-/ *noun* [U] **ossified** /ˈɒs.ɪ.faɪd/ ⓤ /ˈɑː.sə-/ *adj*

ostensible /ɒsˈten.sɪ.bl̩/ ⓤ /ɑːˈstent-/ *adj* [before n] FORMAL appearing or claiming to be one thing when it is really something else: *Their ostensible goal was to clean up government corruption, but their real aim was to unseat the government.* **ostensibly** /ɒsˈten.sɪ.bli/ ⓤ /ɑːˈstent-/ *adv*: *He has spent the past three months in*

Florida, ostensibly for medical treatment, but in actual fact to avoid prosecution for a series of notorious armed robberies.

ostentatious /ˌɒs.tenˈteɪ.ʃəs/ ⓤ /ˌɑː.stən-/ *adj* DISAPPROVING too obviously showing your money, possessions or power, in an attempt to make other people notice and admire you: *They criticized the ostentatious lifestyle of their leaders.* ○ *an ostentatious gesture/manner* **ostentation** /ˌɒs.tenˈteɪ.ʃᵊn/ ⓤ /ˌɑː.stən-/ *noun* [U] *Her luxurious lifestyle and personal ostentation were both hated and envied.* **ostentatiously** /ˌɒs.tenˈteɪ.ʃə.sli/ ⓤ /ˌɑː.stən-/ *adv* DISAPPROVING *The room was ostentatiously decorated in white and silver.* ○ *He took out his gold watch and laid it ostentatiously* (= very obviously so everyone would notice) *on the table in front of him.*

osteoarthritis /ˌɒs.ti.əʊ.ɑːˈθraɪ.tɪs/ ⓤ /ˌɑː.sti.oʊ.ɑːrˈθraɪ.t̬əs/ *noun* [U] a disease which causes pain and stiffness in the joints

osteopath /ˈɒs.ti.əʊ.pæθ/ ⓤ /ˈɑː.sti.oʊ-/ *noun* [C] a person who is trained to treat injuries to bones and muscles using pressure and movement **osteopathy** /ˌɒs.tiˈɒp.ə.θi/ ⓤ /ˌɑː.stiˈɑː.pə-/ *noun* [U] the treatment of injuries to bones and muscles using pressure and movement

osteoporosis /ˌɒs.ti.əʊ.pəˈrəʊ.sɪs/ ⓤ /ˌɑː.sti.oʊ.pəˈroʊ-/ *noun* [U] a disease which causes the bones to weaken and become easily broken: *Osteoporosis afflicts many older women.*

ostracize, UK USUALLY **-ise** /ˈɒs.trə.saɪz/ ⓤ /ˈɑː.strə-/ *verb* [T] to avoid someone intentionally or to prevent them from taking part in the activities of a group: *His colleagues ostracized him after he criticized the company in public.* **ostracism** /ˈɒs.trə.sɪ.zᵊm/ ⓤ /ˈɑː.strə-/ *noun* [U] *AIDS victims often experience social ostracism and discrimination.*

ostrich BIRD /ˈɒs.trɪtʃ/ ⓤ /ˈɑː.strɪtʃ/ *noun* [C] a very large bird from Africa which cannot fly: *The ostrich is the fastest animal on two legs.*

ostrich PERSON /ˈɒs.trɪtʃ/ ⓤ /ˈɑː.strɪtʃ/ *noun* [C] INFORMAL someone who says that a problem does not exist, because they do not want to deal with it: *If you're an ostrich about your debts, you're only going to make matters worse: it would be much better to take your head out of the sand and face facts, however unpleasant.*

OTE /ˌəʊ.tiːˈiː/ ⓤ /ˌoʊ.t̬iː-/ *noun* UK ABBREVIATION FOR on target earnings: used in job advertisements to show how much money it is possible to earn if the person doing the job sells an amount of goods or services, or does an amount of work, stated by the employer

other PART OF A SET /ˈʌð.əʳ/ ⓤ /-ɚ/ *determiner, pronoun* the second of two things or people, or the item or person that is left in a group or set of things: *I've found one earring – do you know where* **the** *other* **one** *is?* ○ *Hold the racquet in one hand and the ball in* **the** *other.* ○ *Some people prefer a vegetarian diet, while others prefer a meat-based diet.* ○ *She gave me one book last week and promised to bring* **the** *others on Wednesday.* ⊃See also **each other**.

other /ˈʌð.əʳ/ ⓤ /-ɚ/ *determiner* the opposite: *Put the chair at the other* **end** *of the desk.* ○ *The man was waiting on the other* **side** *of the street.*

other ADDITIONAL /ˈʌð.əʳ/ ⓤ /-ɚ/ *determiner* **1** additional to the item or person already mentioned: *The product has many other time-saving features.* ○ *There is no other work available at the moment.* ○ *There is only one other person who could help us.* ○ *Are there any other people we should speak to?* ⊃See also **another** ADDITIONAL. **2** used at the end of a list to show that there are more things, without being exact about what they are: *The plan has been opposed by schools, businesses and other local organizations.* ○ *These two books will be especially useful for editors, journalists and other professional users of the language.*

others /ˈʌð.əz/ ⓤ /-ɚz/ *pronoun* **1** additional ones: *I only know about this book, but there might be others* (= other books). **2** people in general, not including yourself: *You shouldn't expect others to do your work for you.*

other DIFFERENT /'ʌð.əʳ/ US /-ɚ/ *determiner* **1** different from the item or person already mentioned: *I've no cash – is there no other way of paying?* ○ *He likes travelling abroad and learning about other people's customs and traditions.* ⊃See also **another** DIFFERENT. **2** referring to a time in the recent past without saying exactly when it was: *I saw him just the other day/night/week.*

• **in other words** used to introduce an explanation that is simpler than the one given earlier: *He was economical with the truth – in other words, he was lying.*

• **other than 1** FORMAL different from or except: *Holidays other than those in this brochure do not have free places for children.* ○ *The form cannot be signed by anyone other than yourself.* **2** in a negative sentence, used to mean 'except': *There's nothing on TV tonight, other than rubbish.*

• **or other** INFORMAL used when you cannot or do not want to be exact about the information you are giving: *The event was held in some park or other.* ○ *We'll find someone or other to help us.*

otherness /'ʌð.ə.nəs/ US /-ɚ-/ *noun* [U] FORMAL being or feeling different in appearance or character from what is familiar, expected or generally accepted: *In the film, he is able to depict the sense of otherness and alienation that many teenagers feel.*

,**other 'half** *noun* [C usually sing] INFORMAL a person's husband, wife or usual partner: *Bring your other half next time you come.*

otherwise /'ʌð.ə.waɪz/ US /-ɚ-/ *adv* **1** differently, or in another way: *The police believe he is the thief, but all the evidence suggests otherwise* (= that he is not). ○ *Under the Bill of Rights, a person is presumed innocent until proved otherwise* (= guilty). ○ *Protestors were executed, jailed or otherwise persecuted.* ○ *Marion Morrison, otherwise known as the film star John Wayne, was born in 1907.* ○ FORMAL *I can't meet you on Tuesday – I'm otherwise engaged/occupied* (= doing something else). **2** except for what has just been referred to: *The bike needs a new saddle, but otherwise it's in good condition.* ○ *The poor sound quality ruined an otherwise splendid film.*

• **or otherwise** used to refer to the opposite of the word which comes before it: *Hand in your exam papers, finished or otherwise* (= or not finished).

otherwise /'ʌð.ə.waɪz/ US /-ɚ-/ *conjunction* used after an order or suggestion to show what the result will be if you do not follow that order or suggestion: *I'd better write it down, otherwise I'll forget it.* ○ *Phone home, otherwise your parents will start to worry.*

otherwise /'ʌð.ə.waɪz/ US /-ɚ-/ *adj* [after v] FORMAL used to show that something is completely different from what you think it is or from what was previously stated: *He might have told you he was a qualified electrician, but the truth is quite otherwise.*

otherworldly /,ʌð.ə'wɜːld.li/ US /-ɚ'wɝːld-/ *adj* more closely connected to spiritual things than to the ordinary things of life: *The children in the picture look delicate and otherworldly, as though they had never run or shouted.*

otiose /'əʊ.ti.əʊs/ /-ʃi-/ US /'oʊ.ti.oʊs/ *adj* FORMAL describes a word or phrase, or sometimes an idea, that is unnecessary or has been used several times: *The use of the word 'recumbent' is surely otiose after the word 'recline'.*

OTOH, otoh INTERNET ABBREVIATION FOR on the other hand ⊃See **on the one hand ... on the other hand** at **hand** BODY PART.

OTT /,əʊ.tiː'tiː/ US /,oʊ-/ *adj* UK ABBREVIATION FOR **over the top** ⊃See at **top** HIGHEST PART.

otter /'ɒt.əʳ/ US /'ɑː.t̬ɚ/ *noun* [C] a four-legged mammal with short brown fur which swims well and eats fish

ouch /aʊtʃ/ *exclamation* **1** used to express sudden physical pain: *Ouch, you're hurting me!* **2** HUMOROUS used in answer to something unkind that someone says: *"I really think you're much too fat, Dorothy." "Ouch, that was a bit unkind."*

ought DUTY /ɔːt/ US /ɑːt/ *modal verb* used to show when it is necessary, desirable or advantageous to perform the activity referred to by the following verb: *You ought to be kinder to him.* ○ *We ought not/oughtn't to have*

agreed without knowing what it would cost. ○ *"We ought to be getting ready now." "Yes, I suppose we ought (to)."*

ought PROBABLE /ɔːt/ US /ɑːt/ *modal verb* used to express something that you expect will happen: *He ought to be home by seven o'clock.* ○ *They ought to have arrived at lunchtime but the flight was delayed.* ○ *If you show the receipt, there ought not/oughtn't to be any difficulty getting your money back.*

oughtn't /'ɔː.t̬ənt/ US /'ɑː-/ short form of ought not: *He oughtn't to do that.*

ouija board /'wiː.dʒi,bɔːd/ US /-,bɔːrd/ *noun* [C] TRADE-MARK a board marked with letters of the alphabet and numbers, which people use in the belief that it will help them receive messages from people who are dead

ounce /aʊnts/ *noun* [C] **1** (WRITTEN ABBREVIATION OZ) a unit of weight equal to approximately 28 grams: *There are 16 ounces in one pound.* ○ *a 12-oz pack of bacon* **2** INFORMAL a very small amount: *She can eat as much as she wants and she never puts on an ounce* (= her weight does not increase). ○ *If he's got an ounce of common sense, he'll realise that this project is bound to fail.*

our /aʊəʳ/ /ɑːʳ/ US /aʊɚ/ *determiner* of or belonging to us: *We bought our house several years ago.* ○ *He walked off and left us on our own.* ○ *Drugs are one of the greatest threats in our society.* ○ *There's no point in our buying a new car this year.* **ours** /aʊəz/ /ɑːz/ US /aʊɚz/ *pronoun*: *Which table is ours?* ○ *He's a cousin of ours.* ○ *Ours is the red car parked over there.* ○ *Ours is a huge country.*

ourselves /,aʊə'selvz/ /,ɑː-/ US /,aʊɚ-/ *pronoun* **1** the reflexive form of the pronoun 'we': *We promised ourselves a good holiday this year.* ○ *Will we be able to do it ourselves or will we need help?* ○ *It's a big garden, but we do all the gardening (by) ourselves* (= without other people's help). ○ *The hotel was very quiet so we had the swimming pool all to ourselves* (= we did not have to share it with other people). **2** FORMAL used to emphasize the subject: *We ourselves realize that there are flaws in the scheme.*

,**Our 'Father** *noun* [U] INFORMAL the Lord's Prayer

,**Our 'Lady** *noun* (in some parts of the Christian religion) a name for Mary, the mother of Jesus

oust /aʊst/ *verb* [T] to force someone to leave a position of power, job, place or competition: *The president was ousted (from power) in a military coup in January 1987.* ○ *Police are trying to oust drug dealers from the city centre.* ○ *The champions were defeated by Arsenal and ousted from the League Cup.*

ouster /'aʊ.stəʳ/ US /-stɚ/ *noun* [C or U] US the removal of someone from an important position or job: *The committee's chairperson is facing a possible ouster.*

out MOVE OUTSIDE /aʊt/ *adv, prep* used to show movement away from the inside of a place or container: *She opened the window and stuck her head out.* ○ *The bag burst and the apples fell out.* ○ *I jumped out of bed and ran downstairs.* ○ *He leaned out the window.* ○ *He opened the drawer and took out a pair of socks.* ○ *Get out!* ○ *Out you go* (= Go out)*!* ○ *My secretary will see you out* (= go with you to the door). ○ *Turn the trousers inside out* (= put the inside on the outside).

• **Out with it!** INFORMAL said to someone when you want them to tell you something which they do not want you to know: *What did he say, then? Come on, out with it!*

out OUTSIDE /aʊt/ *adv* outside a building or room: *It's bitterly cold out, today.* ○ *Would you like to wait out here, and the doctor will come and fetch you in a minute?* ○ *Danger! Keep out* (= Do not enter)*!*

• **out and about** active; doing the things you usually do: *The doctor says she's making a good recovery from the infection and she should be out and about in a few days' time.*

out ABSENT /aʊt/ *adj* [after v] **1** absent for a short time from the place where you live or work: *I came round to see you this morning, but you were out.* ○ *Someone phoned for you while you were out.* **2** when someone is away from the main office in order to do a particular job: *The thieves were spotted by a postman out on his rounds* (= as he was delivering the post). ○ *The police were out in force* (= There were a lot of police) *at the football match.* **3** In a library, if a book is out, it has been borrowed by someone: *Both copies of 'Wuthering Heights' were out.*

out /aʊt/ *adv* used to refer to when someone goes away from home for a social activity: *I can't go out tonight – I've got work to do.* ○ *Do you want to eat out* (= eat in a restaurant) *tonight?* ○ *He's asked me out* (= asked me to go with him) *to the cinema next week.*

out [DISAPPEAR] /aʊt/ *adv* to the point where something is removed or disappears: *The stain won't come out.* ○ *Cross out any words that are not on the list.* ○ *Never use water to put out fires in electrical equipment.* ○ *Our time/money/patience ran out.*

• **out of** when no more of something is available: *We're nearly out of petrol.* ○ *I'm **running** out of patience/time/money.*

out /aʊt/ *adj* [after v] If a light or fire is out, it is no longer shining or burning: *When we got home, all the lights were out.* ○ *Is that fire completely out?*

out [GIVE] /aʊt/ *adv* to many people: *The teacher **gave** out photocopies to all the children.* ○ *Greenpeace **sent** a letter out to all its supporters.*

out [MOVE AWAY] /aʊt/ *adv* spreading out from a central point over a wider area: *The police search party **spread** out across the fields.*

out [VERY] /aʊt/ *adv* used to make the meaning of a word stronger: *Your room needs a good clean out.* ○ *We walked all day and were tired out/*(MAINLY US) *all played out* (= very tired) *by the time we got home.* ○ *It's up to you to **sort** this out* (= solve it completely).

out [LOUD] /aʊt/ *adv* used with verbs describing sounds to emphasize the loudness of the sound: *He **cried** out in pain as he hit his head.* ○ *Charlie Chaplin films always make me laugh out loud.*

out [FAR AWAY] /aʊt/ *adv* a long distance away from land, a town or your own country: *The fishing boats were out at sea for three days.* ○ *They live out in the countryside, miles from anywhere.* ○ *He lived out in Zambia for seven years.* ○ MAINLY US *The weather's better out **west*** (= a long distance away in the west of the country).

out [AVAILABLE] /aʊt/ *adj* [after v], *adv* When a book, magazine, film or musical recording is out, it is available to the public: *Is the new Harry Potter book out yet?* ○ *The new Spielberg movie **comes** out in August.*

out [MADE PUBLIC] /aʊt/ *adj* [after v], *adv* INFORMAL **1** (of information) no longer kept secret: *You can't hide your gambling any longer – the secret's out.* **2** (of a homosexual) not keeping their sexual preferences a secret: *She's been out for three years.* ○ *Don't let his sister know he's gay, because he hasn't **come** out **to** his family yet.*

out /aʊt/ *verb* [T often passive] If a famous person is outed, their HOMOSEXUALITY (= sexual attraction to people of their own sex) is made public when they want to keep it secret: *Hardly a week went by without someone famous being outed.* **outing** /ˈaʊ.tɪŋ/ [US] /-t̬ɪŋ/ *noun* [C or U] *There have been several outings of well-known film stars recently.* ➲See also **outing**.

out [APPEAR] /aʊt/ *adj* [after v], *adv* able to be seen: *The stars are out tonight.* ○ *The rain stopped and the sun **came** out* (= appeared). ○ *In spring all the flowers came out* (= their petals opened).

out [UNCONSCIOUS] /aʊt/ *adv, adj* [after v] unconscious or sleeping: *He **passes** out* (= loses consciousness) *at the sight of blood.* ○ *I was hit on the head, and I must have been out **cold*** (= completely unconscious) *for about ten minutes.*

out [FINISHED] /aʊt/ *adj* [after v] used to show that a period of time is finished: *I think I can finish this project before the month's out.*

out [DEFEATED] /aʊt/ *adj* [after v], *adv* **1** (in sport) no longer able to play because your turn has finished: *Two of the best players on the team were out after ten minutes.* ○ *New Zealand were all out **for** 246* (= The team finished with a score of 246). **2** (in politics) no longer able to govern because you have lost an election: *The Social Democrats were voted out after 15 years in power.*

out [BALL] /aʊt/ *adj* [after v] (of a ball in a sport such as tennis) landing beyond one of the lines which mark the area where the game is played: *He thought the ball had bounced on the line, but the umpire said it was out.*

out [COAST] /aʊt/ *adv, adj* [after v] away from the coast or beach: *Is the tide coming in or going out?* ○ *You can only see the beach when the **tide** is out.*

out [NOT ACCEPTABLE] /aʊt/ *adj* [after v] INFORMAL not acceptable or not possible: *Smoking is definitely out among my friends.* ○ *The option of taking on more staff is out at present.*

out [NOT FASHIONABLE] /aʊt/ *adj* [after v], *adv* INFORMAL no longer fashionable or popular: *Every month the magazine lists what's out and what's in* (= fashionable). ○ *Trousers like that **went** out* (= stopped being fashionable) *in the 70s.*

out [NOT ACCURATE] /aʊt/ *adj* [after v] INFORMAL not accurate: *Our estimates were only out by a few dollars.* ○ *You were 25cm out in your measurements.* ○ *Those sales figures were **way** out* (= completely wrong). ○ US *I'm out $25 on this trip* (= It cost me $25 more than expected).

out [EXISTING] /aʊt/ *adv* INFORMAL (used with superlatives) available or in existence: *This is the best automatic camera out.* ○ *I think he's the greatest footballer out.*

out [INTEND] /aʊt/ *adj* INFORMAL **out for/to** doing something, or intending to do or get something, for an often selfish or unpleasant reason: *She doesn't usually help the charity – she's only out for the publicity.* ○ [+ **to** infinitive] *He's always been out **to** cause trouble between us.*

out [EXCUSE] /aʊt/ *noun* [C usually sing] INFORMAL an excuse or reason for avoiding an unpleasant situation: *We must arrange the negotiations so we have an out if we need it.*

out- [NOT CENTRAL] /aʊt-/ *prefix* used to add the meaning 'not central' to nouns and adjectives: *the outskirts of town* (= the areas that form the edge of the town)

out- [FURTHER] /aʊt-/ *prefix* used to add the meaning 'going beyond' or 'being better than' to verbs: *She doesn't drink or smoke and I'm sure she'll outlive* (= live longer than) *us all.*

out- [AWAY FROM] /aʊt-/ *prefix* used to add the meaning 'out of' or 'away from' to nouns and adjectives: *She turned away from their outstretched hands* (= hands held out).

outage /ˈaʊ.tɪdʒ/ [US] /-t̬ɪdʒ/ *noun* [C] US a period when a service, such as electricity, is not available: *The radio news reported **power** outages affecting 50 homes.*

out-and-out /ˌaʊ.təˈnaʊt/ [US] /ˌaʊ.t̬ə-/ *adj* [before n] complete or in every way, used to emphasize an unpleasant quality of a person or thing: *That's an out-and-out lie!* ○ *The whole project was an out-and-out disaster.*

the outback /ðiˈaʊt.bæk/ *noun* [S] the areas of Australia that are far away from towns and cities, especially the desert areas in central Australia

outbid /ˌaʊtˈbɪd/ *verb* [T] **outbidding, outbid, outbid** to offer to pay a higher price for something than someone else, especially at an auction: *The retail group outbid all three competitors **for** space in the shopping centre.*

outboard (motor) /ˌaʊt.bɔːdˈməʊ.tə[r]/ [US] /-bɔːrd-ˈmoʊ.t̬ɚ/ *noun* [C] **1** a motor with a PROPELLER, designed to be fixed to the back of a small boat **2** a boat with an outboard motor

outbound /ˈaʊt.baʊnd/ *adj* travelling away from a particular point: *There has been an increase in outbound **traffic** leaving London airport for the Mediterranean resorts.*

out-box /ˈaʊt.bɒks/ [US] /-bɑːks/ *noun* [C] **1** US FOR **out-tray** **2** a place on a computer where copies of email messages which you send are kept

outbreak /ˈaʊt.breɪk/ *noun* [C] a sudden beginning of something, especially of a disease or something else dangerous or unpleasant: *an outbreak **of** cholera/food poisoning/rioting/war* ○ *Last weekend saw further thundery outbreaks.*

outbuilding /ˈaʊtˌbɪl.dɪŋ/ *noun* [C] a usually small building near to and on the same piece of land as a larger building: *The stables and other outbuildings were sold together with the main house.*

outburst /ˈaʊt.bɜːst/ [US] /-bɝːst/ *noun* [C] a sudden forceful expression of emotion, especially anger: *a violent outburst* ○ *an outburst **of** creative activity* ○ *Her comments provoked an outburst **of** anger from the boss.*

outcast /ˈaʊt.kɑːst/ ⓤ /-kæst/ *noun* [C] a person who has no place in their society or in a particular group, because the society or group refuses to accept them: *She has spent her life trying to help gypsies, beggars and other **social** outcasts.* ○ *She was a political outcast after the Party expelled her in 1982.*

outclass /ˌaʊtˈklɑːs/ ⓤ /-ˈklæs/ *verb* [T] to be much better than someone or something: *The latest 500 cc road bike easily outclasses all the competition.*

outcome /ˈaʊt.kʌm/ *noun* [C usually sing] a result or effect of an action, situation, etc: *It's too early to predict the outcome **of** the meeting.*

outcrop /ˈaʊt.krɒp/ ⓤ /-krɑːp/ *noun* [C] a large rock or group of rocks that sticks out of the ground

outcry /ˈaʊt.kraɪ/ *noun* [C] a strong expression of anger and disapproval about something, made by a group of people or by the public: *The release from prison of two of the terrorists has provoked a **public** outcry.*

outdated /ˌaʊtˈdeɪ.tɪd/ ⓤ /-t̬ɪd/ *adj* old-fashioned and therefore not as good or as fashionable as something modern: *outdated weapons/ideas* ○ *Nowadays this technique is rather outdated.* ⊃See also **out of date** at **date** DAY.

outdistance /ˌaʊtˈdɪs.tᵊnts/ *verb* [T] to be faster in a race than other competitors, or (more generally) to be much better than someone: *The company outdistance their nearest business competitors **by** a long way.*

outdo /ˌaʊtˈduː/ *verb* [T] **outdid, outdone** to be, or do something, better than someone else: *He always tries to outdo everybody else in the class.*
• **not to be outdone** not wanting someone else to do something better than you: *Pat was wearing an outrageous backless purple dress, so, not to be outdone, I put on my new gold and black trouser suit.*

outdoor /ˈaʊt.dɔːʳ/ ⓤ /-dɔːr/ *adj* [before n] **1** existing, happening or done outside, rather than inside a building: *an outdoor swimming pool/festival* ○ *outdoor clothes* **2** liking or relating to outdoor activities, such as walking and climbing: *Sara's not really the outdoor **type**.*

outdoors /ˌaʊtˈdɔːz/ ⓤ /-ˈdɔːrz/ *adv, noun* outside: *If the weather's good, we'll eat outdoors* (= not in a building). ○ *Every year he takes a month off work to go trekking in **the great** outdoors* (= in the countryside, far away from towns). ⊃See also **out of doors** at **door**.

outer /ˈaʊ.təʳ/ ⓤ /-t̬ɚ/ *adj* [before n] at a greater distance from the centre: *outer London* ○ *the outer lane of the motorway*

outermost /ˈaʊ.tə.məʊst/ ⓤ /-t̬ɚ.moʊst/ *adj* [before n] at the greatest distance from the centre: *These spacecraft may send back data about the outermost **reaches** of the solar system.*

ˌouter ˈspace *noun* [U] the part of space that is very far away from Earth

the outfield /ðiˈaʊt.fiːld/ *noun* [S] the part of a cricket or baseball field that is the longest distance away from the BATTER (= person trying to hit the ball), or the group of players there: *He can play **in** the outfield.* ⊃Compare **the infield**. **outfielder** /ˈaʊt.fiːl.dəʳ/ ⓤ /-dɚ/ *noun* [C] *He was a star outfielder for the Brooklyn Dodgers.*

outfight /ˌaʊtˈfaɪt/ *verb* [T] **outfought, outfought** to fight better than someone: *The former heavyweight champion was outwitted and outfought.*

outfit CLOTHES /ˈaʊt.fɪt/ *noun* [C] a set of clothes worn for a particular occasion or activity: *I've got a cowboy outfit for the fancy dress party.*

outfit /ˈaʊt.fɪt/ *verb* [T often passive] **outfitting, outfitted, outfitted** to provide someone or something with equipment or clothes: *The ambulances have all been outfitted with new radios.*
outfitters /ˈaʊt.fɪt.əz/ ⓤ /-ˌfɪt̬.ɚz/ *plural noun* OLD-FASHIONED a shop that sells a particular type of clothes, especially men's clothes or uniforms: *a gentlemen's outfitters*

outfit GROUP /ˈaʊt.fɪt/ *group noun* [C] INFORMAL an organization, company, team, military unit, etc: *He has recently set up his own research outfit, which has as yet no name.*

outflank /ˌaʊtˈflæŋk/ *verb* [T] **1** to move forward past an enemy position in order to attack it from the side or from the back **2** to do better than an opponent by gaining an advantage over them: *The government has outflanked the opposition by cutting taxes.*

outflow /ˈaʊt.fləʊ/ ⓤ /-floʊ/ *noun* [C] a movement away from a place: *I'm trying to measure the outflow **of** water/sewage from that pipe.* ○ *The central bank has announced controls on **capital** outflows.*

outgoing FRIENDLY /ˌaʊtˈgəʊ.ɪŋ/ ⓤ /ˈaʊt.goʊ-/ *adj* APPROVING (of a person) friendly and energetic and finding it easy and enjoyable to be with others: *Sales reps need to be outgoing, because they are constantly meeting customers.* ○ *She has an outgoing personality.*

outgoing LEAVING /ˌaʊtˈgəʊ.ɪŋ/ ⓤ /-ˌgoʊ-/ *adj* [before n] leaving a place, or leaving a job, having finished a period of time in it: *Outgoing flights are booked until January 15th.* ○ *the outgoing vice-president/chairman/governor*

outgoings /ˈaʊt.gəʊ.ɪŋz/ ⓤ /-ˌgoʊ-/ *plural noun* UK amounts of money that regularly have to be spent, for example to pay for heating or rent

outgrow /ˌaʊtˈgrəʊ/ ⓤ /-ˈgroʊ/ *verb* [T] **outgrew, outgrown 1** to grow bigger than or too big for something: *My seven-year-old had new shoes in April and he's already outgrown them* (= his feet have grown too large for them). ○ *The company outgrew* (= became too large for) *its office space.* **2** to lose interest in an idea or activity as you get older and change: *He eventually outgrew his adolescent interest in war and guns.*

outgrowth /ˈaʊt.grəʊθ/ ⓤ /-groʊθ/ *noun* [C] **1** SPECIALIZED a growth on the outside of an animal or plant: *Antlers are the bony outgrowths on the heads of deer.* **2** a result or development: *This policy is just an outgrowth of earlier decisions.*

outgun /ˌaʊtˈgʌn/ *verb* [T] **-nn- 1** to win a war or fight by having more weapons than the other side: *Despite being heavily outgunned, the rebel forces seem to have held on to the south side of the city.* **2** to beat a person or team by using greater skill: *Arsenal were outgunned by Norwich in Saturday's game.*

outhouse /ˈaʊt.haʊs/ *noun* [C] **1** a small building joined to or near to a larger one **2** US a toilet in an OUTBUILDING

outing /ˈaʊ.tɪŋ/ ⓤ /-t̬ɪŋ/ *noun* [C] when a group of people go on a short journey, usually for pleasure or education: *Rosie's **going on** a class/school outing **to** the Museum of Modern Art.* ⊃See also **outing** at **out** MADE PUBLIC.

outlandish /ˌaʊtˈlæn.dɪʃ/ *adj* DISAPPROVING strange and unusual and difficult to accept or like: *an outlandish hairstyle/outfit* **outlandishly** /ˌaʊtˈlæn.dɪʃ.li/ *adv* **outlandishness** /ˌaʊtˈlæn.dɪʃ.nəs/ *noun* [U]

outlast /ˌaʊtˈlɑːst/ ⓤ /-ˈlæst/ *verb* [T] to live or exist, or to stay energetic and determined, longer than another person or thing: *The queen outlasted all her children.* ○ *The Orioles outlasted the Yankees, finally winning 10 to 9.*

outlaw /ˈaʊt.lɔː/ ⓤ /-lɑː/ *noun* [C] (especially in the past) a person who has broken the law and who lives separately from the other parts of society because they want to escape legal punishment: *Robin Hood was an outlaw who lived in the forest and stole from the rich to give to the poor.*

outlaw /ˈaʊt.lɔː/ ⓤ /-lɑː/ *verb* [T] to make something illegal or unacceptable: *The new law will outlaw smoking in public places.*

outlay /ˈaʊt.leɪ/ *noun* [C] an amount of money spent for a particular purpose, especially as a first investment in something: *For an **initial** outlay **of** £2000 to buy the equipment, you should be earning up to £500 a month if the product sells well.*

outlet WAY OUT /ˈaʊt.let/ *noun* [C] **1** a way, especially a pipe or hole, for liquid or gas to go out: *a waste water outlet* ○ *an outlet pipe* **2** a way in which emotion or energy can be expressed or made use of: *Her work **provided** no outlet for her energies and talents.* ○ *Writing poetry was his only form of emotional outlet.*

outlet SHOP /ˈaʊt.let/ *noun* [C] a shop that is one of many owned by a particular company and that sells the goods which the company has produced: *a fast-food outlet* ○ *a retail outlet*

outlet ELECTRICITY /ˈaʊt.let/ *noun* [C] US FOR **power point**

ˈoutlet ˌmall *noun* [C] a large group of shops, usually situated outside of towns or cities, which sell clothes, goods, etc. for a reduced price: *In the last ten years, outlet malls have sprung up all over the country.*

outline /ˈaʊt.laɪn/ *noun* [C] **1** the main shape or edge of something, without any details: *She drew the outline **of** the boat and then coloured it in.* **2** a description of the main facts about something: *If you read the minutes of the meeting, they'll give you a broad outline **of** what was discussed.* ○ *Some novelists start by writing an outline* (= plan of the main points of the story).

• **in outline** as a shape with an edge but without any details: *The mountain was visible only in outline as the light faded.*

outline /ˈaʊt.laɪn/ *verb* [T] **1** to draw the main shape or edge of something: *The area we're interested in is outlined **in** red on the map.* **2** to give the main facts about something: *At the interview she outlined what I would be doing.*

outlive /ˌaʊtˈlɪv/ *verb* [T] to live or exist longer than someone or something: *He outlived all of his brothers.*

• **outlive *your* usefulness** to no longer be useful: *This old system has outlived its usefulness.*

outlook [FUTURE SITUATION] /ˈaʊt.lʊk/ *noun* [C usually sing] the likely future situation: *The outlook **for** the economy is bleak.* ○ *The outlook **for** today is cloudy and dry at first with showers later.*

outlook [OPINION] /ˈaʊt.lʊk/ *noun* [C usually sing] a person's way of understanding and thinking about something: *He has a fairly positive outlook **on** life.*

outlook [VIEW] /ˈaʊt.lʊk/ *noun* [C] *FORMAL* a view: *From the top of the tower, the outlook over the city was breathtaking.*

outlying /ˈaʊtˌlaɪ.ɪŋ/ *adj* [before n] far away from main towns and cities, or far from the centre of a place: *Many of the pupils travel in by bus from outlying areas.*

outmanoeuvre *UK*, *US* **outmaneuver** /ˌaʊt.məˈnuː.vəʳ/ [US] /-vɚ/ *verb* [T] to cleverly obtain an advantage over someone, especially a competitor: *In the negotiations, he outmanoeuvred his rivals by offering a higher price.*

outmoded /ˌaʊtˈməʊ.dɪd/ [US] /-ˈmoʊ-/ *adj DISAPPROVING* old-fashioned; no longer modern, useful or necessary: *Outmoded working practices are being phased out.*

outnumber /ˌaʊtˈnʌm.bəʳ/ [US] /-bɚ/ *verb* [T] to be greater in number than someone or something: *In our office, the women outnumber the men 3 to 1.*

ˈout ˌof [NO LONGER IN] *prep* **out of *somewhere/sth*** no longer in a stated place or condition: *An apple rolled out of the bag.* ○ *Professor Aitchison is out of **town** this week.* ○ *The patient is now out of **danger**.* ○ *The coffee machine is out of **order*** (= does not work). ○ *Both she and her husband are out of **work*** (= no longer have jobs).

ˈout ˌof [MADE FROM] *prep* (*ALSO* **of**) used to show what something is made from: *The dress was made out of velvet.*

ˈout ˌof *prep* describes the origin of something: *She dresses like a character out of a 19th century novel.* ○ *I paid for the computer out of* (= using some of) *my savings.*

ˈout ˌof [BECAUSE OF] *prep* used to show the reason why someone does something: *I took the job out of necessity because we had no money left.* ○ *You might like to come and see what we're doing out of interest* (= because I think you might be interested).

ˈout ˌof [FROM AMONG] *prep* from among an amount or number: *Nine out of ten people said they liked the product.* ○ *No one got 20 out of 20* (= all the answers correct) *in the test.*

ˈout ˌof [NOT INVOLVED] *prep* [after v] no longer involved in: *He missed two practice sessions so he's out of the team.* ○ *I'm out of the habit of cycling to work.*

• **out of it** *INFORMAL* **1** not aware of your surroundings or condition as a result of taking alcohol or drugs: *She was lying on the sofa, totally out of it.* **2** unhappy because you are not included in what is happening: *I didn't know anyone at the party and I felt really out of it.*

• **out of *your* mind/head** *INFORMAL* extremely foolish: *He must be out of his mind to have spent that much money on an old car!*

out-of-court /ˌaʊt.əvˈkɔːt/ [US] /ˌaʊt̬.əvˈkɔːrt/ *adj* [before n], *adv* agreed without involving a trial in a law court: *an out-of-court **settlement*** ○ *My lawyer wants to **settle** out of court.*

ˌout-of-ˈdate *adj* **1** If clothes, colours, styles, etc. are out-of-date, they are old and not fashionable: *That radio looks so out of date.* **2** If information is out-of-date, it is old and not useful or correct: *an out-of-date phone directory* ○ *I have a map but I'm afraid it's out-of-date.* **3** If food is out-of-date, it is old and not now safe to eat.

out-of-pocket expenses /ˌaʊt.əvˌpɒk.ɪt.ɪkˈspent.sɪz/ [US] /ˌaʊt̬.əvˌpɑː.kɪt-/ *plural noun* money that you spend on things such as food and travel while you are working for someone else: *All out-of-pocket expenses will be reimbursed by the company.*

out-of-town /ˌaʊt.əvˈtaʊn/ [US] /ˌaʊt̬.əv-/ *adj* [before n] describes shops, and other services, situated outside the town: *an out-of-town shopping centre*

outpace /ˌaʊtˈpeɪs/ *verb* [T] to move or develop faster than someone or something else: *Ovett managed to outpace every other runner.* ○ *The company has completely outpaced its rivals in the market.*

outpatient /ˈaʊt.peɪ.ʃᵊnt/ *noun* [C] a person who goes to a hospital for treatment, but who does not stay any nights there: *an outpatient clinic* ➲Compare **inpatient**.

outperform /ˌaʊt.pəˈfɔːm/ [US] /-pɚˈfɔːrm/ *verb* [T] to do well in a particular job or activity compared to others of a similar type: *The Peugeot engine has consistently outperformed its rivals this season.*

outplay /ˌaʊtˈpleɪ/ *verb* [T] to play a game more cleverly and successfully than another person or team: *The French chess players were completely outplayed by the Russian team.*

outpost /ˈaʊt.pəʊst/ [US] /-poʊst/ *noun* [C] a place, especially a small group of buildings or a town, which maintains the authority or business interests of a distant government or company: *a police/military/colonial outpost*

outpouring /ˈaʊtˌpɔː.rɪŋ/ [US] /-ˌpɔːr.ɪŋ/ *noun* [C] **1** an uncontrollable expression of strong feeling: *His death at the age of 35 has occasioned an outpouring **of** grief.* **2** *MAINLY HUMOROUS* a very large number of things produced at the same time: *Last year saw an outpouring **of** cookery books.*

output /ˈaʊt.pʊt/ *noun* [U] an amount of something produced by a person, machine, factory, country, etc: *Last year British manufacturing output fell by 14%.*

outrage /ˈaʊt.reɪdʒ/ *verb* [T] (especially of an unfair action or statement) to cause someone to feel very angry, shocked or upset: *Local people were outraged **at** the bombing.* ○ *A proposed 5% pay cut has outraged staff at the warehouse.*

outraged /ˈaʊt.reɪdʒd/ *adj* feeling outrage: *Many outraged viewers wrote to the BBC to complain.*

outrage /ˈaʊt.reɪdʒ/ *noun* **1** [U] a feeling of anger and shock: *These murders have provoked outrage across the country.* ○ *Many politicians and members of the public expressed outrage at the verdict.* **2** [C] a shocking, morally unacceptable and usually violent action: *The bomb, which killed 15 people, was the worst of a series of terrorist outrages.* ○ [+ that] ***It's** an outrage* (= it is shocking and morally unacceptable) ***that** so much public money should have been wasted in this way.*

outrageous /ˌaʊtˈreɪ.dʒəs/ *adj* **1** shocking and morally unacceptable: *The judge criticized the "outrageous greed" of some of the lawyers.* ○ [+ that] ***It** is outrageous **that** these buildings remain empty while thousands of people have no homes.* ○ *These prices are just outrageous* (= much too high). **2** describes something or someone that is shocking because they are unusual or strange: *outrageous clothes/behaviour* ○ *an outrageous character* **outrageously** /ˌaʊtˈreɪ.dʒə.sli/ *adv*: *outrageously high prices*

outran /ˌaʊtˈræn/ *past simple of* **outrun**

outrank /ˌaʊtˈræŋk/ *verb* [T] to have a higher rank than someone: *As a Chief Superintendent, she outranked all the other police officers in the room.*

outré /ˈuː.treɪ/ *adj FORMAL* unusual, strange and shocking, especially in an amusing way: *He wrote an outré comedy about Hitler's childhood.*

O

outreach /ˈaʊt.riːtʃ/ *adj* **[before n]** when an organization brings medical or similar services to people at home or to where they spend time: *an outreach worker/centre* ○ *An AIDS outreach program for prostitutes on the streets.*

outrider /ˈaʊtˌraɪ.dəʳ/ [US] /-dɚ/ *noun* **[C]** a person, especially a police officer, who rides on a motorcycle next to or in front of an official vehicle

outright /ˌaʊtˈraɪt/ *adv* completely or immediately: *I think cigarette advertising should be banned outright.* ○ *The driver and all three passengers were **killed** outright.*

outright /ˈaʊt.raɪt/ *adj* **[before n]** complete: *Outsiders are regarded with outright hostility.* ○ *There was no outright winner in the election.*

outrun /ˌaʊtˈrʌn/ *verb* **[T] outrunning, outran, outrun 1** to move faster or further than someone or something: *The thieves easily outran the policewoman who was chasing them.* **2** to develop faster or further than something: *In the future, demand for metals like tungsten will outrun supply.*

outs /aʊts/ *plural noun* US INFORMAL **on the outs** People who are on the outs have argued and are not now friendly with each other: *Lizzie and Tyler are on the outs again.*

outscore /ˌaʊtˈskɔːʳ/ [US] /-ˈskɔːr/ *verb* **[T]** MAINLY US to score more points than another player or team in a competition: *Johnson outscored his nearest rival by 30 points.*

outsell /ˌaʊtˈsel/ *verb* **[T] outsold, outsold** (of a product) to be sold in greater numbers than another product: *CDs soon began to outsell records.*

the outset /ðiˈaʊt.set/ *noun* **[S]** the beginning: *I told him **at/from** the outset I wasn't interested.*

outshine /ˌaʊtˈʃaɪn/ *verb* **[T] outshone, outshone** to be much more skilful and successful than someone: *Ben Palmer easily outshone his rivals in the 200 metre freestyle.*

outside [OUTER PART] /ˌaʊtˈsaɪd/ /ˈ--/ *noun* **[C usually sing]** the outer part or side of something: *The outside of the house needs painting.* ○ *The house looks larger when looked at from **the** outside.* ○ *The company needs to get help from outside* (= from people who work for other organizations). ➲Compare **inside** INNER PART.

• **at the outside** used to say that an amount is the most possible in a situation: *The job will take about ten days at the outside.*

outside /ˌaʊtˈsaɪd/ *adj, adv, prep* **1** **[before n]** not inside a building: *It was a lovely day outside.* ○ *Since it's such a nice day shall we eat/sit/go outside?* ○ *an outside light/toilet* **2** **[before n]** coming from another place or organization: *The company has called in outside experts.* **3 outside call/line** a telephone call or connection going outside the place where you are **4** **[before n]** the most that would be allowed: *The outside limit/figure would be £350.*

outside /ˌaʊtˈsaɪd/ *adv, prep* **1** not in a particular building or room, but near it: *She sat for two hours on the floor outside his room.* **2** not in a particular place: *Nobody outside this room must ever know what we have discussed.* **3** beyond or not within or part of something: *I'm afraid that would be outside my job description.*

• **outside of** MAINLY US except for: *Outside of us three, no one knows anything about the problem, yet.*

• **the outside world** (ALSO **the world outside**) things that are common in normal society, but which you have no experience of: *An over-protected childhood meant that at the age of 22 she had no idea about the outside world.*

outsider /ˌaʊtˈsaɪ.dəʳ/ [US] /-dɚ/ *noun* **[C]** **1** a person who is not involved with a particular group of people or organization or who does not live in a particular place: *Outsiders have a glamorized idea of what it is like to work for the BBC.* **2** a person who is not liked or accepted as a member of a particular group, organization or society and who feels different from those people who are accepted as members: *As a child he was very much an outsider, never participating in the games other children played.*

outside [SLIGHT] /ˈaʊt.saɪd/ *adj* **[before n]** slight: *There's still an outside **chance/possibility** that Scotland will get through into the World Cup.*

outsider /ˌaʊtˈsaɪ.dəʳ/ [US] /-dɚ/ *noun* **[C]** *The race was won by a **rank** outsider* (= a person or animal with only a slight chance of winning).

ˌoutside ˈbroadcast *noun* **[C]** (US **remote broadcast**) a broadcast made away from the television or radio station

ˌoutside ˈlane [ROAD] *noun* **1** **[S]** (INFORMAL **outside**) UK the part of the road nearest the vehicles going in the opposite direction, used especially by faster vehicles: *She cruised by at 160 kilometres per hour **on** the outside/**in** the outside lane.* **2** **[C]** US the part of the road nearest the edge, especially used by slower vehicles

ˌoutside ˈlane [RACE TRACK] *noun* **[S]** the part of a race track that is furthest from the centre

outsize /ˈaʊt.saɪz/ *adj* **[before n]** (especially of clothing) much larger than usual: *They specialize in outsize clothes.*

the outskirts /ðiˈaʊt.skɜːts/ [US] /-skɜːrts/ *plural noun* the areas that form the edge of a town or city: *The factory is **in/on** the outskirts **of** New Delhi.*

outsmart /ˌaʊtˈsmɑːt/ [US] /-ˈsmɑːrt/ *verb* **[T]** to **outwit**

outsold /ˌaʊtˈsəʊld/ [US] /-ˈsoʊld/ *past simple and past participle of* **outsell**

outsource /ˈaʊt.sɔːs/ [US] /-sɔːrs/ *verb* **[I or T]** If a company outsources, it pays to have part of its work done by another company: *Unions are fighting a plan by universities to outsource all non-academic services.* ○ *Some companies outsource to cheaper locations to cut costs.* **outsourcing** /ˈaʊtˌsɔː.sɪŋ/ [US] /-ˌsɑː-/ *noun* **[U]** *The management guaranteed that outsourcing wouldn't mean job losses.*

outspoken /ˌaʊtˈspəʊ.kᵊn/ [US] /-ˈspoʊ-/ *adj* expressing strong opinions very directly without worrying if other people are offended: *outspoken comments* ○ *Mr Masack is an outspoken critic of the present government.*

outspread /ˌaʊtˈspred/ *adj* spread as far as possible: *a bronze angel with outspread wings*

outstanding [EXCELLENT] /ˌaʊtˈstæn.dɪŋ/ *adj* excellent; clearly very much better than what is usual: *an outstanding performance/writer/novel/year* ○ *It's an area of outstanding natural beauty.* **outstandingly** /ˌaʊtˈstæn.dɪŋ.li/ *adv*: *He was an outstandingly successful mayor from 1981 to 1984.*

outstanding [NOT FINISHED] /ˌaʊtˈstæn.dɪŋ/ *adj* not yet paid, solved or done: *$450 million in outstanding debts* ○ *There are still a couple of problems outstanding.*

outstay /ˌaʊtˈsteɪ/ *verb* **outstay *your* welcome** to continue to stay in a place although other people want you to leave: *They were busy so I left – I didn't want to outstay my welcome.*

outstretched /ˌaʊtˈstretʃt/ *adj* reaching out as far as possible: *He ran up to her, his arms outstretched.* ○ *She put some pesos into the little girl's outstretched hand.*

outstrip /ˌaʊtˈstrɪp/ *verb* **[T]** **-pp-** to be or become greater in amount, degree or success than something or someone: *The demand for firewood now far outstrips supply.*

outta, **outa** /ˈaʊ.tə/ [US] /-t̬ə/ *prep* MAINLY US INFORMAL out of: *We'd better get outta here, man!* ○ *I'm outta here* (= I'm leaving).

out-take /ˈaʊt.teɪk/ *noun* **[C]** a short part of a film or television programme or music recording that was removed and not included, usually because it contains mistakes: *They showed a video of amusing out-takes from various films.*

out-tray UK /ˈaʊt.treɪ/ *noun* **[C]** (US **out-box**) a flat open container on a desk for letters and other documents that have already been dealt with and are waiting to be sent to someone else or put away: *The letter is **in** your out-tray.*

outvote /ˌaʊtˈvəʊt/ [US] /-ˈvoʊt/ *verb* **[T]** to defeat someone by winning a greater number of votes: *The Democrats were outvoted, as usual.* ○ INFORMAL *I suggested we should go for a pizza, but I was outvoted* (= most people did not want to) *so we went for a curry.*

outward /ˈaʊt.wəd/ [US] /-wɚd/ *adj* **1** **[before n]** relating to how people, situations or things seem to be, rather than how they are inside: *The outward **appearance** of the building has not changed at all in 200 years.* ○ *If he is* *suffering, he certainly shows no outward **sign** of it.* ○ **To all** *outward **appearances** everything was fine, but under the surface the marriage was very shaky.* ⊃Compare **inward**. **2** *away from the centre: outward investment (=* investment in other companies/countries) ○ *We have the chance to build an outward-**looking** Europe that lives up to its global responsibilities.* **outwardly** /ˈaʊt.wəd.li/ ⓤ /-wɚd-/ *adv: Outwardly, he seemed happy enough.*

outward-bound /ˌaʊt.wədˈbaʊnd/ ⓤ /-wɚd-/ *adj* [before n] describes a ship or passenger going away from home: *At the port she managed to get a passage on an outward-bound ship.*

outwards /ˈaʊt.wədz/ ⓤ /-wɚdz/ *adv* (*MAINLY US* **outward**) *going or pointing away from a particular place or towards the outside: The door opens outwards.* ○ *It's much healthier to direct your emotions outwards than to bottle them up inside you.* ✳ NOTE: The opposite is **inwards**. **outward** /ˈaʊt.wəd/ ⓤ /-wɚd/ *adj* [before n] *The outward flight/journey took eight hours.*

outweigh /ˌaʊtˈweɪ/ *verb* [T] *to be greater or more important than something else: The benefits of this treatment far outweigh any risks.*

outwit (**-tt-**) /ˌaʊtˈwɪt/ *verb* [T] (*ALSO* **outsmart**) *to obtain an advantage over someone by acting more cleverly and often by using a trick: In the story, the cunning fox outwits the hunters.*

outworn /ˌaʊtˈwɔːn/ ⓤ /-ˈwɔːrn/ *adj* (especially of an idea or phrase) *old-fashioned and used too often in the past, so no longer useful or important*

ouzo /ˈuː.zəʊ/ ⓤ /-zoʊ/ *noun* [C or U] *plural* **ouzos** *a Greek alcoholic drink flavoured with* ANISEED, *which turns white if mixed with water: She ordered a couple of ouzos (=* glasses of ouzo).

ova /ˈəʊ.və/ ⓤ /ˈoʊ-/ *plural of* **ovum**

oval /ˈəʊ.vəl/ ⓤ /ˈoʊ-/ *adj* shaped like a circle that is flattened either at one place or at two opposite places, so that it is like either an egg or an ELLIPSE: *an oval mirror* ○ *an oval face* **oval** /ˈəʊ.vəl/ ⓤ /ˈoʊ-/ *noun* [C] *Her eyes were large ovals.*

the ˌOval ˈOffice *noun* [S] *the office of the US President, in Washington: The President delivered his speech from the Oval Office.* ○ *FIGURATIVE It now seems unlikely that the Democratic nominee will reach the Oval Office (=* become President).

ovary /ˈəʊ.vər.i/ ⓤ /ˈoʊ-/ *noun* [C] *either of the pair of organs in a woman's body which produce eggs, or the part of any female animal or plant that produces eggs or seeds* **ovarian** /əʊˈveə.ri.ən/ ⓤ /oʊˈver.i-/ *adj: ovarian cancer* ○ *an ovarian cyst*

ovation /əʊˈveɪ.ʃən/ ⓤ /oʊ-/ *noun* [C] *when a crowd of people express great enjoyment and/or approval of something with loud and long clapping: She was given a **standing** ovation (=* the crowd stood up while they clapped, to show respect) *at the end of her speech.*

oven /ˈʌv.ən/ *noun* [C] *the part of a cooker with a door, which is used to cook food: a conventional/gas/fan-assisted oven* ○ *a microwave oven* ○ *a cool/medium/hot oven* ○ *Place the cake **in** the oven at 200°C.* ○ *Calcutta in summer is **like an** oven (=* extremely and uncomfortably hot). ⊃See picture **In the Kitchen** on page Centre 16
ovenable /ˈʌv.ən.ə.bl̩/ *adj* able to be cooked in an oven: *a packet of ovenable chips*
ovenproof /ˈʌv.ən.pruːf/ *adj* able to be used in an oven: *Is this dish definitely ovenproof?*

ˈoven ˌgloves *noun* [C] (*US* **oven mitts**) *UK* thick cloth coverings for the hands used for taking hot things out of an oven ⊃See picture **In the Kitchen** on page Centre 16

oven-ready /ˌʌv.ənˈred.i/ *adj* sold already prepared for cooking: *an oven-ready chicken*

ovenware /ˈʌv.ən.weər/ ⓤ /-wer/ *noun* [U] food containers in which food can be cooked

over [HIGHER POSITION] /ˈəʊ.vər/ ⓤ /ˈoʊ.vɚ/ *prep* **1** above or higher than something else, sometimes so that one thing covers the other; above: *The sign over the door said "Exit".* ○ *She held the umbrella over both of us.* ○ *Helicopters dropped leaflets over the city.* ○ *I put my hands over my eyes/ears because I couldn't bear to watch/listen.* ○ *I couldn't hear what she was saying over the noise of the planes taking off (=* the aircraft were

louder than her voice). ⊃Compare **under** LOWER POSITION. **2** sometimes used when talking about a calculation in which one number is divided by another number: *40 over 7 is roughly 6.*

over /ˈəʊ.vər/ ⓤ /ˈoʊ.vɚ/ *adv: A man came to paint over (=* cover with paint) *the cracks in the wall.*
over- /ˈəʊ.vər-/ ⓤ /ˈoʊ.vɚ-/ *prefix above: She was knocked off her bicycle by an overhanging branch.*

over [ACROSS] /ˈəʊ.vər/ ⓤ /ˈoʊ.vɚ/ *prep* **1** across from one side to the other, especially by going up and then down: *She jumped over the gate.* ○ *The road goes over the mountains, not through a tunnel.* ○ *She is always chatting with her neighbour over the garden wall.* ○ *From the top of the tower you could see for miles over the city.* ○ *Tanks travel over the most difficult ground.* **2** on the other side of: *The story continues over the page.*
● **be all over** *sb INFORMAL* to be touching someone in a sexual way everywhere on their body: *She was all over him, kissing him and stroking him.*
● **all over** *somewhere* everywhere in a particular place: *Soon the news was all over town.*
over /ˈəʊ.vər/ ⓤ /ˈoʊ.vɚ/ *adv* **1** across; from one side or place to another: *She leaned over and kissed me.* ○ *A fighter plane flew over.* ○ *Why don't you come over (=* come to my house) *for dinner on Thursday?* ○ *I've got a friend over from Canada this week (=* A friend came from Canada and is staying with me). ○ *Now we're going over to (=* there will be a broadcast from) *Wembley for commentary on the Cup Final.* ○ *Come over **here** (=* to this place from where you are) *– it's warmer.* ○ *Who's that man over **there** (=* in that place)? **2** describes the way an object moves or is moved so that a different part of it is facing up: *She turned another page over.* ○ *The dog rolled over onto its back.* ○ *The children rolled over **and over** (=* turned over many times) *down the gentle slope.* **3** changing or exchanging position: *Would you mind **changing/swapping** those plates over?* ○ *She **changed** over to editing **from** marketing.* ○ *Why should we **hand** over the money **to** the Russians?* ○ *I've done all I can – now it's over to you (=* it's your turn to take action). **4** said when you are talking to someone by radio, to mean that you have finished speaking and will wait for their answer: *"This is flight 595X. Do you read me? Over."*
● **Over and out.** said when you are talking to someone by radio in order to end the conversation: *"Thank you, control tower. Over and out."*
over- /ˈəʊ.vər-/ ⓤ /ˈoʊ.vɚ-/ *prefix across: Of course, the overland route is much slower than going by air.*

over [MORE THAN] /ˈəʊ.vər/ ⓤ /ˈoʊ.vɚ/ *prep* **1** more than: *Most of the carpets cost/are over £100.* ○ *Children over the age of 12 (=* older than 12) *must have full-price tickets.* ○ *I value quality of life over money.* **2** increasing beyond a particular limit or point: *They are already $25 million over budget.*
● **over and above** in addition to: *They receive extra money over and above the usual welfare payments.*
over /ˈəʊ.vər/ ⓤ /ˈoʊ.vɚ/ *adv* more than a particular amount or level: *People who are 65 years old **and** over can get half-price tickets.*
over- /ˈəʊ.vər-/ ⓤ /ˈoʊ.vɚ-/ *prefix more than: a club for the over-50s*

over- [TOO MUCH] /ˈəʊ.vər-/ ⓤ /ˈoʊ.vɚ-/ *prefix too much or more than usual: The children got rather over-excited (=* too excited).

over [DOWN] /ˈəʊ.vər/ ⓤ /ˈoʊ.vɚ/ *adv, prep* from a higher to a lower position; down: *The little boy **fell** over and started to cry.* ○ *He was run/knocked over by a taxi.* ○ *She tripped over the rug.*
over /ˈəʊ.vər/ ⓤ /ˈoʊ.vɚ/ *prep* falling off a steep place: *Harold jumped out of the car just before it went over the cliff.*

over [USING] /ˈəʊ.vər/ ⓤ /ˈoʊ.vɚ/ *prep* using: *They spoke over the phone.* ○ *We heard the news over the radio.*

over [OTHER SIDE] /ˈəʊ.vər/ ⓤ /ˈoʊ.vɚ/ *prep* on the other side of: *There's a pub over the road we could go to.*

over [DURING] /ˈəʊ.vər/ ⓤ /ˈoʊ.vɚ/ *prep* during something, or while doing something: *I was in Seattle over the summer.* ○ *Shall we discuss it over lunch/over a drink?* ○ *They took/spent an hour over lunch (=* Their meal lasted an hour). ○ *It's fascinating to watch how a baby changes and develops over **time*** (= as time passes).

over CONTROL /ˈəʊ.vəʳ/ ⓤ /ˈoʊ.vɚ/ *prep* in control of or in-structing someone or something: *A good teacher has an easy authority over a class.* ○ *She's a sales manager but she has a regional sales director over* (= with a higher rank than) *her.* ○ *The victory over the French at Waterloo was Wellington's greatest triumph.*

over CONNECTED WITH /ˈəʊ.vəʳ/ ⓤ /ˈoʊ.vɚ/ *prep* (referring to a cause of interest, worry, discussion, etc.) connected with or about: *There's no point in arguing over something so unimportant.* ○ *I need time to talk/think over your proposal* (= to discuss/consider it carefully). ○ *The legal battle was over who should have custody of the child.*

over EXTRA /ˈəʊ.vəʳ/ ⓤ /ˈoʊ.vɚ/ *adv* extra; not used: *I have some American dollars left over from the last time I was there.* ○ *UK When all the guests had gone, we realized there was lots of food over.*

over FINISHED /ˈəʊ.vəʳ/ ⓤ /ˈoʊ.vɚ/ *adj* [after v] (especially of an event) completed: *I'll be glad when the competition is over.* ○ *I used to have a thriving business and a happy marriage, but that's **all** over now* (= finished).
● **over and done with** completely finished: *She gets unpleasant tasks over and done with as quickly as possible.*

over AGAIN /ˈəʊ.vəʳ/ ⓤ /ˈoʊ.vɚ/ *adv* US again or repeatedly: *You've ruined it – now I'll have to **do** it over!*
● **over and over (again)** happening or done many times: *I read the article over and over till it made sense.*

over FEELING BETTER /ˈəʊ.vəʳ/ ⓤ /ˈoʊ.vɚ/ *prep* **be/get over sth** to feel physically or mentally better after an illness or an upsetting experience: *It takes you a while to get over an illness like that.* ○ *His girlfriend finished with him last year and he's not over her yet.* ○ *He's not fully recovered, but he's over **the worst*** (= has experienced the worst stage of the illness and is now improving).

over CRICKET /ˈəʊ.vəʳ/ ⓤ /ˈoʊ.vɚ/ *noun* [C] (in cricket) a set of six BOWLS (= throws) from the same end of the field

overact /ˌəʊ.vəˈrækt/ ⓤ /ˌoʊ.vɚˈækt/ *verb* [I or T] DIS-APPROVING to make your voice and movements express emotions too strongly when acting in a play ∗ NOTE: Do not confuse with **overreact**.

overage /ˌəʊ.vəˈreɪdʒ/ ⓤ /ˌoʊ.vɚˈeɪdʒ/ *adj* older than a particular age and therefore no longer allowed to do or have particular things: *She lost her place on the youth team when the manager discovered she was overage.*

overall /ˌəʊ.vəˈrɔːl/ ⓤ /ˌoʊ.vɚˈɑːl/ *adj* [before n], *adv* in general rather than in particular, or including all the people or things in a particular group or situation: *The overall situation is good, despite a few minor problems.* ○ *Overall, it has been a good year.* ○ *The overall winner, after ten games, will receive $250 000.*

overalls /ˈəʊ.vəˈrɔːlz/ ⓤ /ˈoʊ.vɚ.ɑːlz/ *plural noun* **1** UK (US **coveralls**) a piece of clothing that covers both the upper and lower parts of the body and is worn especially over other clothes to protect them: *She put on some overalls and got out a tin of paint.* **2** US FOR **dungarees**

overarching /ˌəʊ.vəˈrɑː.tʃɪŋ/ ⓤ /ˌoʊ.vɚˈɑːr-/ *adj* [before n] FORMAL most important, because including or affecting all other areas: *a grand overarching strategy* ○ *The overarching theme of the election campaign was tax cuts.*

overarm /ˈəʊ.vəˈrɑːm/ ⓤ /ˈoʊ.vɚˈɑːrm/ *adj*, *adv* (especially of a throw) made with the arm moving above the shoulder: *an overarm throw/serve* ○ *Bowl it overarm.*

overate /ˌəʊ.vəˈret/ /-reɪt/ ⓤ /ˌoʊ.vɚˈeɪt/ *past simple of* **overeat**

overawe /ˌəʊ.vəˈrɔː/ ⓤ /ˌoʊ.vɚˈɑː/ *verb* [T usually passive] to cause someone to feel a mixture of extreme respect and fear: *Some of the players were totally overawed by playing their first game at the national stadium.*

overbalance /ˌəʊ.vəˈbæl.ᵊnts/ ⓤ /ˌoʊ-/ *verb* [I] to lose balance and therefore fall or nearly fall: *Halfway along the wall he overbalanced and fell.*

overbearing /ˌəʊ.vəˈbeə.rɪŋ/ ⓤ /ˌoʊ.vɚˈber.ɪŋ/ *adj* DIS-APPROVING too confident and too determined to tell other people what to do, in a way that is unpleasant: *Milligan had a pompous, overbearing father.*

overbid /ˌəʊ.vəˈbɪd/ ⓤ /ˌoʊ.vɚ-/ *verb* [I or T] **overbidding, overbid, overbid** to offer more money than someone in an attempt to buy something, or to offer too much money in an attempt to buy something: *They were overbid by a Japanese firm.* ○ *The Commission felt the company were overbidding and gave the franchise to their competitors instead.*

overblown /ˌəʊ.vəˈbləʊn/ ⓤ /ˌoʊ.vɚˈbloʊn/ *adj* DIS-APPROVING bigger or more impressive than it should be: *an overblown news story* ○ *Sir Neville's conducting is precise and delicate, never overblown.*

overboard /ˈəʊ.vəˈbɔːd/ /ˌ--ˈ-/ ⓤ /ˈoʊ.vɚˈbɔːrd/ *adv* over the side of a boat or ship and into the water: *Someone had **fallen** overboard.*
● **go overboard** INFORMAL to do something too much, or to be too excited or eager about something: *I don't suppose there'll be more than six people eating so I wouldn't go overboard with the food.*
● **chuck/throw/toss sth/sb overboard** INFORMAL to get rid of something or someone: *She threw $2 million of energy shares overboard and bought computer technology shares instead.*

overbook /ˌəʊ.vəˈbʊk/ ⓤ /ˌoʊ.vɚ-/ *verb* [I or T] to sell more tickets or places for an aircraft, holiday, etc. than are available: *The hotel was overbooked.* ○ *There was no seat for me on the plane, because the airline had overbooked.*

overburden /ˌəʊ.vəˈbɜː.dᵊn/ ⓤ /ˌoʊ.vɚˈbɜː-/ *verb* [T often passive] to make someone or something work too hard or carry, contain or deal with too much: *Insurance companies are already overburdened **with** similar claims.* ○ *Now 5000 new children will be attending the district's already overburdened school system.*

overcast /ˈəʊ.vəˈkɑːst/ /ˌ--ˈ-/ ⓤ /ˈoʊ.vɚˈkæst/ *adj* cloudy and therefore not bright and sunny: *The sky/weather was overcast.* ○ *a depressing, overcast winter morning*

overcharge /ˌəʊ.vəˈtʃɑːdʒ/ ⓤ /ˌoʊ.vɚˈtʃɑːrdʒ/ *verb* [I or T] to charge someone either more than the real price or more than the value of the product or service: *The shop overcharged me (**by** £10).* ○ [+ two objects] *They overcharged her £45.*

overcoat /ˈəʊ.vəˈkəʊt/ ⓤ /ˈoʊ.vɚˈkoʊt/ *noun* [C] a long thick coat worn in cold weather ⊃See picture **Clothes** on page Centre 6

overcome DEAL WITH /ˌəʊ.vəˈkʌm/ ⓤ /ˌoʊ.vɚ-/ *verb* [I or T] **overcame, overcome** to defeat or succeed in controlling or dealing with something: *Juventus overcame Ajax in a thrilling match.* ○ *to overcome **difficulties/obstacles/ problems/resistance*** ○ *Eventually she managed to overcome her shyness in class.* ○ *Twenty thousand demonstrators sang "We shall overcome" as they marched through Washington today.*

overcome UNABLE TO ACT /ˌəʊ.vəˈkʌm/ ⓤ /ˌoʊ.vɚ-/ *verb* [T usually passive] **overcame, overcome** to prevent someone from being able to act or think in the usual way: *They were overcome **by** fumes from the fire and had to be carried out of their houses.* ○ *Overcome **with/by** emotion, she found herself unable to speak for a few minutes.*

overcompensate /ˌəʊ.vəˈkɒm.pən.seɪt/ ⓤ /ˌoʊ.vɚˈkɑːm-/ *verb* [I] to try too hard to correct a problem, therefore creating a new problem: *Chris is one of those small men who overcompensate **for** their lack of height **with** a larger than life personality.*

overcook /ˌəʊ.vəˈkʊk/ ⓤ /ˌoʊ.vɚ-/ *verb* [T often passive] to cook food for longer than necessary, reducing its quality as a result: *The chicken was overcooked and dry.*

overcrowded /ˌəʊ.vəˈkraʊ.dɪd/ ⓤ /ˌoʊ.vɚ-/ *adj* containing too many people or things: *overcrowded cities/ prisons/schools* ○ *The world market for telecommunications is already overcrowded **with** businesses.* **overcrowding** /ˌəʊ.vəˈkraʊ.dɪŋ/ ⓤ /ˌoʊ.vɚ-/ *noun* [U] *Investment in the railway network would reduce overcrowding on the roads.* **overcrowd** /ˌəʊ.vəˈkraʊd/ ⓤ /ˌoʊ.vɚ-/ *verb* [T]

overdeveloped /ˌəʊ.və.dɪˈvel.əpt/ ⓤ /ˌoʊ.vɚ-/ *adj* having developed too much: *I don't like body builders who are so overdeveloped you can see the veins in their bulging muscles.*

overdo /ˌəʊ.vəˈduː/ ⓤ /ˌoʊ.vɚ-/ *verb* [T] **overdid, overdone** to do something in a way that is too extreme: *After a heart attack you have to be careful not to overdo it/*

things (= you have to work and live calmly).

overdone /ˌəʊ.vəˈdʌn/ [US] /ˌoʊ.vɚ-/ *adj* (especially of meat) cooked too long: *The roast lamb was dry and overdone.*

overdose /ˈəʊ.və.dəʊs/ [US] /ˈoʊ.vɚ.doʊs/ *noun* [C] **1** (*INFORMAL* **OD**) too much of a drug taken or given at one time, either intentionally or by accident: *When he was 17 he **took** an overdose **of** sleeping pills and nearly died.* ○ *Jimi Hendrix died of a **drug(s)** overdose.* **2** *HUMOROUS* too much of something: *I was suffering from an overdose of culture.*
overdose /ˈəʊ.və.dəʊs/ [US] /ˈoʊ.vɚ.doʊs/ /ˌ--ˈ-/ *verb* [I] **1** (*INFORMAL* **OD**) to take too much of a drug: *She overdosed **on** aspirin and died.* **2** to have too much of something: *HUMOROUS I think I've just overdosed **on** cheesecake!*

overdraft /ˈəʊ.və.drɑːft/ [US] /ˈoʊ.vɚ.dræft/ *noun* [C] an amount of money that a customer with a bank account is temporarily allowed to owe to the bank, or the agreement which allows this: *to **run up/pay off** an overdraft* ○ *The bank offers overdraft **facilities**.*

overdrawn /ˌəʊ.vəˈdrɔːn/ [US] /ˌoʊ.vɚˈdrɑːn/ *adj* having taken more money out of your bank account than the account contained, or (of a bank account) having had more money taken from it than was originally in it: *They were overdrawn **by** £150, so they couldn't write any cheques.* ○ *The account was overdrawn.* **overdraw** /ˌəʊ.vəˈdrɔː/ [US] /ˌoʊ.vɚˈdrɑː/ *verb* [I or T] **overdrew**, **overdrawn** *I overdrew my account **by** £20.*

overdressed /ˌəʊ.vəˈdrest/ [US] /ˌoʊ.vɚ-/ *adj* wearing clothes that are too formal or splendid for a particular occasion: *Everyone else was wearing jeans so I felt a bit overdressed in my best suit.*

overdrive /ˈəʊ.və.draɪv/ [US] /ˈoʊ.vɚ-/ *noun* [U] a state of great activity, effort or hard work: *The official propaganda machine **went into** overdrive when war broke out.* ○ *The cast were **in** overdrive, rehearsing for the first performance.*

overdue /ˌəʊ.vəˈdjuː/ [US] /ˌoʊ.vɚˈduː/ *adj* not done or happening when expected or when needed; late: *My library books are a week overdue.* ○ *The baby is two weeks overdue* (= The baby was expected to be born two weeks ago). ○ *Changes to the tax system are **long** overdue.* ○ *She feels she's overdue **for** promotion.*

overeat /ˌəʊ.vəˈriːt/ [US] /ˌoʊ.vɚˈiːt/ *verb* [I] **overate**, **overeaten** to eat more food than your body needs, especially so that you feel uncomfortably full **overeating** /ˌəʊ.vəˈriː.tɪŋ/ [US] /ˌoʊ.vɚˈiː.t̬ɪŋ/ *noun* [U] *Overeating is surely the main cause of obesity.*

overestimate /ˌəʊ.vəˈres.tɪ.meɪt/ [US] /ˌoʊ.vɚˈes-/ *verb* [I or T] to think that something is or will be greater, more extreme or more important than it really is: *The benefits of nuclear technology, she said, had been grossly overestimated.* ○ *They were forced to the conclusion that they had overestimated him/his abilities.* ○ *I overestimated and there was a lot of food left over after the party.* **overestimate** /ˌəʊ.vəˈres.tɪ.mət/ [US] /ˌoʊ.vɚˈes-/ *noun* [C]

overexpose /ˌəʊ.və.rɪkˈspəʊz/ [US] /ˌoʊ.vɚ.ɪkˈspoʊz/ *verb* [T usually passive] to give too much light to a piece of photographic film when taking a photograph: *Unfortunately the light was too bright and my photos were all overexposed.*

overflow /ˌəʊ.vəˈfləʊ/ [US] /ˌoʊ.vɚˈfloʊ/ *verb* **1** [I or T] When a liquid overflows, it flows over the edges of a container, etc. because there is too much of it: *The milk overflowed when I poured it into the jug.* ○ *Because of heavy rain, the river may overflow its banks.* **2** [I or T] If a container or a place overflows, whatever is inside it starts coming out because it is too full: *Oh no, the bath is overflowing all over the floor.* ○ *The bin was overflowing **with** rubbish.* **3** [I] When a place overflows, or people or things overflow from somewhere, some people or things have to come out because it cannot contain them all: *The pub was so full that people were overflowing **into/onto** the street.* ○ *The train was **(full to)** overflowing* (= so full that there was not space for any more passengers). ○ *His room is overflowing **with*** (= contains a lot of) *books.* **4** [I] If you overflow with thoughts or feelings, you express them strongly: *They were **(full to)** overflowing **with** emotion at the birth of their baby.* ○ *Suddenly, her anger overflowed.*
• **to overflowing** so that water or another substance is almost coming over the top: *Someone has filled the bath **(full) to** overflowing.*
overflow /ˈəʊ.və.fləʊ/ [US] /ˈoʊ.vɚ.floʊ/ *noun* [S or U] an amount of liquid or number of people that cannot fit in a space: *I put a bucket underneath to catch the overflow **from** the water tank.* ○ *We can't cope with this overflow **of** patients **from** the other hospitals.*

ˈoverflow ˌpipe *noun* [C] (*ALSO* **overflow**) a pipe that carries away water that is not needed

overgrown [COVERED] /ˌəʊ.vəˈgrəʊn/ [US] /ˌoʊ.vɚˈgroʊn/ *adj* covered with plants that are growing thickly and in an uncontrolled way: *The field is overgrown **with** weeds.*

overgrown [TOO LARGE] /ˌəʊ.vəˈgrəʊn/ [US] /ˌoʊ.vɚˈgroʊn/ *adj DISAPPROVING* describes something that has grown too large
• **overgrown schoolboy/schoolgirl** *DISAPPROVING* an adult who behaves like a child: *Jim is just an overgrown schoolboy.*

overhand /ˈəʊ.və.hænd/ [US] /ˈoʊ.vɚ-/ *adj, adv US FOR* **overarm**

overhang /ˌəʊ.vəˈhæŋ/ [US] /ˌoʊ.vɚ-/ *verb* [T] **overhung**, **overhung** **1** (of something at a higher level) to stick out over something at a lower level: *Several large trees overhang the path.* **2** to have a negative effect on a situation: *Overhanging the controversy is the question of how much the government knew about the arms deal.*
overhang /ˈəʊ.və.hæŋ/ [US] /ˈoʊ.vɚ-/ *noun* [C] the part of a rock or roof that sticks out over something below: *The church is unsafe because it was built on an overhang.*
overhanging /ˈəʊ.vəˌhæŋ.ɪŋ/ [US] /ˈoʊ.vɚ-/ /ˌ--ˈ--/ *adj*: *the overhanging branches of a tree*

overhaul /ˈəʊ.və.hɔːl/ [US] /ˈoʊ.vɚ.hɑːl/ *verb* [T] to repair or improve something so that every part of it works properly: *I got the engine overhauled.* ○ *The government plans to overhaul the health service.* **overhaul** /ˈəʊ.və.hɔːl/ [US] /ˈoʊ.vɚ.hɑːl/ *noun* [C] *I took my motorbike in for an overhaul.*

overhead /ˈəʊ.və.hed/ [US] /ˈoʊ.vɚ-/ *adj, adv* above your head, usually in the sky: *overhead cables* ○ *A flock of geese flew overhead.* ○ *This room needs overhead lighting* (= lights in the ceiling).

overhead (transparency) /ˌoʊ.və.hed.trænˈspær.ᵊnt.si/ [US] /ˌoʊ.vɚ.hed.trænˈsper-/ *noun* [C] a transparent sheet used for showing text or pictures with an OVERHEAD PROJECTOR

ˌoverhead ˈprojector *noun* [C] (*ABBREVIATION* **OHP**) a device which makes large images from a flat transparent sheet and shows them on a white screen or wall ⊃See picture **In the Office** on page Centre 15

overheads *UK* /ˈəʊ.və.hedz/ [US] /ˈoʊ.vɚ-/ *plural noun* (*US* **overhead**) the regular and necessary costs, such as rent and heating that are involved in operating a business: *We need to reduce our overheads.* ○ *Many businesses are moving out of New York because the overhead there is so high.* **overhead** /ˈəʊ.və.hed/ [US] /ˈoʊ.vɚ-/ *adj* [before n] *One way of increasing profit margins is to cut overhead costs.*

overhear /ˌəʊ.vəˈhɪəʳ/ [US] /ˌoʊ.vɚˈhɪr/ *verb* [I or T] **overheard**, **overheard** to hear what other people are saying unintentionally and without their knowledge: *I overheard a very funny conversation on the bus this morning.* ○ [+ obj + v-ing] *He overheard his daughter telling her teddy not to be so naughty.* ○ [+ obj + infinitive without *to*] *We overheard them say that they didn't really like the meal.* ○ *I'm sorry, I couldn't help overhearing.*

overheat /ˌəʊ.vəˈhiːt/ [US] /ˌoʊ.vɚ-/ *verb* **1** [I or T] to (cause to) become hotter than necessary or desirable: *I think the engine is overheating.* ○ *It isn't healthy to overheat your house.* **2** [I] If an economy overheats, it grows very quickly, so that prices, etc. increase quickly.
overheated /ˌəʊ.vəˈhiː.tɪd/ [US] /ˌoʊ.vɚˈhiː.t̬ɪd/ *adj* If a situation is/gets overheated, strong feelings, especially anger, are expressed: *Things got a bit overheated at the meeting.*

overhung /ˌəʊ.vəˈhʌŋ/ [US] /ˌoʊ.vɚ-/ *past simple and past participle of* **overhang**

overindulge /ˌəʊ.və.rɪnˈdʌldʒ/ [US] /ˌoʊ.vɚ.ɪn-/ *verb* [I or T] to allow yourself or someone else to have too much of

O

something enjoyable, especially food or drink: *I wish I hadn't overindulged so much* (= had so much to eat and drink) *last night.* ○ *It's not good for children to be over-indulged* (= always given what they want).

overindulgence /ˌəʊ.və.rɪnˈdʌldʒ.ᵊnts/ Ⓤ /ˌoʊ.vɚ.ɪn-/ noun [U] *For many Americans, Thanksgiving is a time of overindulgence* (= eating and drinking too much).

overjoyed /ˌəʊ.vəˈdʒɔɪd/ Ⓤ /ˌoʊ.vɚ-/ adj **[after v]** extremely pleased and happy: *We're overjoyed at your news.* ○ **[+ to infinitive]** *Helen was overjoyed to hear that she had got the job.* ○ **[+ that]** *I'm overjoyed that you're com-ing to visit me.*

overkill /ˈəʊ.və.kɪl/ Ⓤ /ˈoʊ.vɚ-/ noun [U] DISAPPROVING much more of something than is needed, resulting in less effectiveness: *Should I add an explanation, or would that be overkill?*

overland /ˈəʊ.və.lænd/ Ⓤ /ˈoʊ.vɚ-/ adj, adv (of travel) across the land in a vehicle, on foot or on a horse; not by sea or air: *an overland trip across Australia* ○ *We drove overland.*

overlap /ˌəʊ.vəˈlæp/ Ⓤ /ˌoʊ.vɚ-/ verb -pp- **1** [I or T] to cover something partly by going over its edge; to cover part of the same space: *The fence is made of panels which overlap (each other).* **2** If two or more activities, subjects or periods of time overlap, they have some parts which are the same: *My musical tastes don't overlap with my brother's at all.*

overlap /ˈəʊ.və.læp/ Ⓤ /ˈoʊ.vɚ-/ noun [C or U] the amount by which two things or activities cover the same area: *The roof tiles will need an overlap of several centimetres.* ○ *There are some overlaps between the products of the two companies.*

overlapping /ˈəʊ.vəˌlæp.ɪŋ/ Ⓤ /ˈoʊ.vɚ-/ /ˌ--ˈ--/ adj: *The overlapping slates of the roofs in the mountain village resembled fish scales.* ○ *The word has two separate but overlapping meanings* (= parts of the meanings are the same).

overlay /ˌəʊ.vəˈleɪ/ Ⓤ /ˌoʊ.vɚ-/ verb [T often passive] over-laid, overlaid **1** to cover something with a layer of some-thing: *The foundation of the house is built from rubble overlaid with concrete.* **2** LITERARY be overlaid with sth to have a particular quality added to it which influences its character: *Her new novel is overlaid with political concerns.*

overlay /ˈəʊ.və.leɪ/ Ⓤ /ˈoʊ.vɚ-/ noun [C] *The wood frame has a gold overlay* (= thin covering of gold).

overleaf /ˌəʊ.vəˈliːf/ Ⓤ /ˌoʊ.vɚ-/ adv on the other side of the page: *See overleaf for a list of abbreviations.*

overload /ˌəʊ.vəˈləʊd/ Ⓤ /ˌoʊ.vɚˈloʊd/ verb [T] overloaded or UK ALSO overladen **1** to put too large a load in or on something: *Don't overload the washing machine, or it won't work properly.* **2** to put too much electricity through an electrical system

overload /ˈəʊ.və.ləʊd/ Ⓤ /ˈoʊ.vɚ.loʊd/ noun [C or U] *People today suffer from information overload* (= being given too much information). ○ *There was an overload on the electrical circuit and the fuse blew.*

overloaded /ˌəʊ.vəˈləʊ.dɪd/ Ⓤ /ˌoʊ.vɚˈloʊ-/ adj having or supplied with too much of something: *The market is already overloaded with car magazines – why would any-one want to produce another one?*

overlong /ˌəʊ.vəˈlɒŋ/ Ⓤ /ˌoʊ.vɚˈlɑːŋ/ adj too long: *I en-joyed the film, but I thought it was overlong.*

overlook VIEW /ˌəʊ.vəˈlʊk/ Ⓤ /ˌoʊ.vɚ-/ verb [T] to provide a view of, especially from above: *Our hotel room over-looked the harbour.* ○ *The house is surrounded by trees, so it's not overlooked at all* (= it cannot be seen from any other buildings).

overlook /ˈəʊ.və.lʊk/ Ⓤ /ˈoʊ.vɚ-/ noun [C] US a **view-point** VIEW: *There are lots of scenic overlooks along the road from New York to Montreal.*

overlook NOT NOTICE /ˌəʊ.vəˈlʊk/ Ⓤ /ˌoʊ.vɚ-/ verb [T] to fail to notice or consider something: *I think there is one key fact that you have overlooked.* ○ *No one will be over-looked in the selection of the team.* See Note **oversee** or **overlook?** at **oversee**.

overlook FORGIVE /ˌəʊ.vəˈlʊk/ Ⓤ /ˌoʊ.vɚ-/ verb [T] to for-give or pretend not to notice something: *I'm prepared to*

overlook his behaviour this time. See Note **oversee or overlook** at **oversee**.

overlord /ˈəʊ.və.lɔːd/ Ⓤ /ˈoʊ.vɚ.lɔːrd/ noun [C] a person in a position of power, especially in the past

overly /ˈəʊ.vᵊl.i/ Ⓤ /ˈoʊ.vɚ.li/ adv (ALSO over) too; very: *Earlier sales forecasts were overly optimistic.* ○ *His films have been criticized for being overly violent.*

overmanned /ˌəʊ.vəˈmænd/ Ⓤ /ˌoʊ.vɚ-/ adj having more employees than are needed; OVERSTAFFED

overmuch /ˌəʊ.vəˈmʌtʃ/ Ⓤ /ˌoʊ.vɚ-/ adv, adj (especially in negatives) too much or very much: *At least he didn't suffer overmuch before he died.* ○ *I don't have overmuch confidence in Hal.*

overnight /ˌəʊ.vəˈnaɪt/ Ⓤ /ˌoʊ.vɚ-/ adj, adv **1** for or during the night: *an overnight stop in Paris* ○ *You can stay overnight if you want to.* ○ *Don't forget to pack an overnight bag* (= a bag for things that you need when you stay away from home for a night). **2** suddenly and unexpectedly: *She became a star overnight.* ○ *The book was an overnight success.*

overpass /ˈəʊ.və.pɑːs/ Ⓤ /ˈoʊ.vɚ.pæs/ noun [C] US FOR **fly-over** BRIDGE

overpay /ˌəʊ.vəˈpeɪ/ Ⓤ /ˌoʊ.vɚ-/ verb [T often passive] over-paid, overpaid to pay someone too much: *I felt I should tell my boss she'd overpaid me by £50.* ○ DISAPPROVING City lawyers are grossly overpaid for what they do.

overplay /ˌəʊ.vəˈpleɪ/ Ⓤ /ˌoʊ.vɚ-/ verb [T] to make some-thing seem more important than it really is: *I think she's overplaying the significance of his remarks.*

● **overplay your hand** to spoil your chance of success by saying or doing too much

overpopulated /ˌəʊ.vəˈpɒp.jʊ.leɪ.tɪd/ Ⓤ /ˌoʊ.vɚˈpɑː.pjə.leɪ.tɪd/ adj If a country or city, etc. is overpopulated, it has too many people for the amount of food, materials and space available there. **overpopula-tion** /ˌəʊ.vəˌpɒp.jʊˈleɪ.ʃᵊn/ Ⓤ /ˌoʊ.vɚˌpɑː.pjə-/ noun [U] *Overpopulation is one of the country's most pressing social problems.*

overpower /ˌəʊ.vəˈpaʊəʳ/ Ⓤ /ˌoʊ.vɚˈpaʊɚ/ verb [T] **1** to defeat someone by having greater strength or power: *The gunman was finally overpowered by three security guards.* **2** If a smell or feeling overpowers you, it is so strong that it makes you feel weak or ill: *The smell of gas/heat overpowered me as I went into the house.*

overpowering /ˌəʊ.vəˈpaʊə.rɪŋ/ Ⓤ /ˌoʊ.vɚˈpaʊɚ.ɪŋ/ adj too strong: *Firefighters were driven back by the over-powering heat of the flames.* ○ *There's an overpowering smell of garlic in the kitchen.* ○ *He's suffering from over-powering feelings of guilt.*

overpriced /ˌəʊ.vəˈpraɪst/ Ⓤ /ˌoʊ.vɚ-/ adj too expensive: *These shoes are very nice, but they're terribly overpriced.*

overproduce /ˌəʊ.və.prəˈdjuːs/ Ⓤ /ˌoʊ.vɚ.prəˈduːs/ verb [I or T] to produce more of something than is needed, or to produce too much **overproduction** /ˌəʊ.və.prəˈdʌk.ʃᵊn/ Ⓤ /ˌoʊ.vɚ-/ noun [C or U] *The company is in a bad financial position because of overproduction and distribu-tion problems.*

overprotective /ˌəʊ.və.prəˈtek.tɪv/ Ⓤ /ˌoʊ.vɚ-/ adj wishing to protect someone too much, especially a child: *The children of overprotective parents are sometimes rather neurotic.*

overqualified /ˌəʊ.vəˈkwɒl.ɪ.faɪd/ Ⓤ /ˌoʊ.vɚˈkwɑː.lɪ-/ adj having more knowledge, skill and/or experience than is needed (for a particular job): *The problem with employing people who are overqualified for the job is that they often don't stay in it for long.*

overran /ˌəʊ.vəˈræn/ Ⓤ /ˌoʊ.vɚ-/ past simple and past participle of **overrun**

overrate /ˌəʊ.vəˈreɪt/ Ⓤ /ˌoʊ.vɚ-/ verb [T often passive] to have too good an opinion of something: *Be careful not to overrate the opposition.* **overrated** /ˌəʊ.vəˈreɪ.tɪd/ Ⓤ /ˌoʊ.vɚˈreɪ.tɪd/ /ˈ--ˌ--/ adj: *In my opinion, she's a hugely overrated singer.*

overreach yourself /ˌəʊ.vəˈriːtʃ/ Ⓤ /ˌoʊ.vɚ-/ verb [R] to fail by trying to achieve, spend or do more than you can manage: *Companies that overreach themselves soon find themselves in debt.*

overreact /ˌəʊ.və.riˈækt/ Ⓤ /ˌoʊ.vɚ-/ verb [I] to react in an extreme, especially an angry or frightened, way: *You* *must learn not to overreact **to** criticism.* **overreaction** /ˌəʊ.və.riˈæk.ʃən/ [US] /ˌoʊ.vɚ-/ *noun* [C or U]

override [NOT ACCEPT] /ˌəʊ.vəˈraɪd/ [US] /ˌoʊ.vɚ-/ *verb* [T] **overrode, overridden 1** (of a person who has the necessary authority) to refuse to accept or to decide against a previous decision, an order, a person, etc: *Every time I make a suggestion at work, my boss overrides me/it.* ○ *The President used his veto to override the committee's decision.* **2** to operate an automatic machine by hand: *He overrode the autopilot when he realised it was malfunctioning.* **3** to take control over something, especially in order to change the way it operates: *The pills are designed to override your body's own hormones.*
override /ˌəʊ.vəˈraɪd/ [US] /ˌoʊ.vɚ-/ *noun* [C] **1** a device that changes the control of a machine or system in special situations, especially from automatic to MANUAL: *The heating system has a manual override.* **2** in American politics, the refusal of an elected group of people to accept a decision made by an elected leader: *The vote fell short of the majority needed for an override **of** the Governor's veto.*

override [MORE IMPORTANT] /ˌəʊ.vəˈraɪd/ [US] /ˌoʊ.vɚ-/ *verb* [T] **overrode, overridden** to be more important than something: *Parents' concern for their children's future often overrides all their other concerns.*
overriding /ˌəʊ.vəˈraɪ.dɪŋ/ [US] /ˌoʊ.vɚ-/ *adj* [before n] more important than anything else: *The government's overriding **concern** is to reduce inflation.*

overripe /ˌəʊ.vəˈraɪp/ [US] /ˌoʊ.vɚ-/ *adj* too ripe; starting to decay

overrule /ˌəʊ.vəˈruːl/ [US] /ˌoʊ.vɚ-/ *verb* [T] *FORMAL* (of a person who has official authority) to decide against a decision that has already been made: *In tennis, the umpire can overrule the line judge.*

overrun [FILL] /ˌəʊ.vəˈrʌn/ [US] /ˌoʊ.vɚ-/ *verb* [T] **overrunning, overran, overrun** If unwanted people or things overrun, they fill a place quickly and in large numbers: *Rebel soldiers overran the embassy last night.* ○ *Our kitchen is overrun **with** cockroaches.*

overrun [GO BEYOND] /ˌəʊ.vəˈrʌn/ [US] /ˌoʊ.vɚ-/ *verb* [I or T] **overrunning, overran, overrun** to continue beyond an intended limit, especially a finishing time or a cost: *My evening class overran by ten minutes.* ○ *It looks as if we're going to overrun our budget.* **overrun** /ˌəʊ.vəˈrʌn/ [US] /ˌoʊ.vɚˈrʌn/ *noun* [C]

overseas /ˌəʊ.vəˈsiːz/ [US] /ˌoʊ.vɚ-/ /ˈ---/ *adj, adv* in, from or to other countries: *We need to open up overseas markets.* ○ *There are a lot of overseas students in Cambridge.* ○ *My brother is a student overseas.* ○ *Many more people go/travel/live/work overseas these days.*

oversee /ˌəʊ.vəˈsiː/ [US] /ˌoʊ.vɚ-/ *verb* [T] **overseeing, oversaw, overseen** to watch or organize a job or an activity to make certain that it is being done correctly: *As marketing manager, her job is to oversee all the company's advertising.*
overseer /ˈəʊ.vəˌsiː.əʳ/ [US] /ˈoʊ.vɚˌsiː.ɚ/ *noun* [C] *MAINLY OLD USE* a person whose job it is to make certain that employees are working or that an activity is being done correctly

COMMON LEARNER ERROR

oversee or overlook?

Oversee cannot be used to mean 'to fail to notice or consider something'. The correct word for this meaning is **overlook**.

Two important facts have been overlooked in this case.
~~*Two important facts have been overseen in this case.*~~

oversell /ˌəʊ.vəˈsel/ [US] /ˌoʊ.vɚ-/ *verb* [T] **oversold, oversold** *MAINLY US* to sell more than is available: *The flight had been oversold.*

oversexed /ˌəʊ.vəˈsekst/ [US] /ˌoʊ.vɚ-/ *adj* having too much desire for sex

overshadow /ˌəʊ.vəˈʃæd.əʊ/ [US] /ˌoʊ.vɚˈʃæd.oʊ/ *verb* [T often passive] **1** to cause someone or something to seem less important or less happy: *Karen has always felt overshadowed by her famous elder sister.* ○ *My happiness was overshadowed by the bad news.* **2** (of a building) to be much taller than another building and therefore block the sun from it: *Grand Central Station in New York is overshadowed by the PanAm building.*

overshoes /ˈəʊ.və.ʃuːz/ [US] /ˈoʊ.vɚ-/ *plural noun* (*US ALSO* **galoshes**) waterproof shoes, usually made of rubber, for wearing over an ordinary shoe in the rain or snow

overshoot /ˌəʊ.vəˈʃuːt/ [US] /ˌoʊ.vɚ-/ *verb* [T] **overshot, overshot** to go beyond the end of or past something, without intending to: *The plane overshot the **runway** and finished up in the water.*

oversight /ˈəʊ.və.saɪt/ [US] /ˈoʊ.vɚ-/ *noun* [C or U] a mistake made because of a failure to notice something: *They claimed it was simply (an) oversight.*

oversimplify /ˌəʊ.vəˈsɪm.plɪ.faɪ/ [US] /ˌoʊ.vɚˈsɪm.plə-/ *verb* [I or T] to describe or explain something in such a simple way that it is no longer right or true: *The TV documentary grossly oversimplified the problem.* **oversimplification** /ˌəʊ.vəˌsɪm.plɪ.fɪˈkeɪ.ʃən/ [US] /ˌoʊ.vɚˌsɪm.plə-/ *noun* [C or U]

oversize /ˈəʊ.və.saɪz/ [US] /ˈoʊ.vɚ-/ *adj* (*ALSO* **oversized**) *MAINLY US* bigger than usual; too big: *My daughter loves to wear oversize clothes.*

oversleep /ˌəʊ.vəˈsliːp/ [US] /ˌoʊ.vɚ-/ *verb* [I] **overslept, overslept** to sleep for longer than you intended to and so wake up late: *I missed the train this morning because I overslept again.*

oversold /ˌəʊ.vəˈsəʊld/ [US] /ˌoʊ.vɚˈsoʊld/ *past simple and past participle of* **oversell**

overspend /ˌəʊ.vəˈspend/ [US] /ˌoʊ.vɚ-/ *verb* [I or T] **overspent, overspent** to (cause to) spend more money than you should: *The council seems likely to overspend this year.* ○ *The hospital has already overspent **(on)** its drugs **budget**.* **overspend** /ˈəʊ.və.spend/ [US] /ˈoʊ.vɚ-/ *noun* [S] *UK We're expecting to have a £5 million **(budget)** overspend this year.* **overspending** /ˌəʊ.vəˈspen.dɪŋ/ [US] /ˌoʊ.vɚ-/ *noun* [U]

overspill /ˈəʊ.və.spɪl/ [US] /ˈoʊ.vɚ-/ *noun* [U] *UK* people who move out of a crowded city and into other towns or villages near the city: *the overspill **from** London/the London overspill* ○ *an overspill housing estate.*

overstaffed /ˌəʊ.vəˈstɑːft/ [US] /ˌoʊ.vɚˈstæft/ *adj* (*ALSO* **overmanned**) having more employees than are needed: *The department has been accused of being inefficient and hugely overstaffed.*

overstate /ˌəʊ.vəˈsteɪt/ [US] /ˌoʊ.vɚ-/ *verb* [T] to describe or explain something in a way that makes it seem more important or serious than it really is: *The impact of the new legislation has been greatly overstated.* ○ *The shareholders seem to think that the executive board is overstating the **case** for a merger.* * NOTE: The opposite is **understate**.
overstatement /ˌəʊ.vəˈsteɪt.mənt/ /ˈ--ˌ--/ [US] /ˌoʊ.vɚ-/ *noun* [C or U] when someone describes or explains something in a way that makes it seem more important or serious than it really is: *It would be an overstatement to say that Lewis deserved to win the race.*

overstay /ˌəʊ.vəˈsteɪ/ [US] /ˌoʊ.vɚ-/ *verb* [T] to stay longer in a place than you are allowed or wanted: *Be careful not to overstay your visa.* ○ *They left the party at 11pm, careful not to overstay their welcome.*

overstep /ˌəʊ.vəˈstep/ [US] /ˌoʊ.vɚ-/ *verb* [T] **-pp-** to go beyond what is considered acceptable or correct: *The bad language in that play overstepped the **limits/boundaries** of what ought to be allowed on television.* ○ *I think you're overstepping your authority.*
• **overstep the mark** to behave in a completely unacceptable way: *You've overstepped the mark this time, Simpson – you're fired!*

overstock /ˌəʊ.vəˈstɒk/ [US] /ˌoʊ.vɚˈstɑːk/ *verb* [I or T] to (cause to) have more goods or supplies than are needed: *The shop is overstocked **(with** shoes).*

oversubscribed /ˌəʊ.və.səbˈskraɪbd/ [US] /ˌoʊ.vɚ-/ *adj* when people still want to buy things, especially shares or tickets, although all of them are already sold: *The $400 million oil company share issue was three times oversubscribed.*

overt /əʊˈvɜːt/ /ˈ--/ [US] /oʊˈvɝːt/ *adj* done or shown publicly or in an obvious way; not secret: *overt criticism* ○ *overt racism* ○ *He shows no overt signs of his unhappiness.* ⊃Compare **covert**. **overtly** /əʊˈvɜːt.li/ /ˈ---/ [US]

O

/oʊˈvɝːt-/ *adv*: *It was an overtly sexual advertising campaign.*

overtake [GO PAST] /ˌəʊ.vəˈteɪk/ [US] /ˌoʊ.vɚ-/ *verb* **overtook, overtaken** **1** [T] to go beyond something by being a greater amount or degree: *Our US sales have now overtaken our sales in Europe.* ○ *We'd planned to hold a meeting tomorrow, but **events** have overtaken us* (= things have changed). **2** [I or T] UK (US **pass**) to come from behind another vehicle or a person and move in front of it: *Always check your rear view mirror before you overtake (another car).*

overtake [HAPPEN] /ˌəʊ.vəˈteɪk/ [US] /ˌoʊ.vɚ-/ *verb* [T] **overtook, overtaken** to happen to a person or a place suddenly and unexpectedly: *The family was overtaken by tragedy several years ago, and they still haven't recovered.*

overˈtaking ˌlane UK *noun* [C usually sing] (US **passing lane**) the part of a motorway that is used for passing other vehicles and is nearest the centre of the road

overtax [MONEY] /ˌəʊ.vəˈtæks/ [US] /ˌoʊ.vɚ-/ *verb* [T] to demand too much tax from someone or to put too much tax on goods: *I've been overtaxed this month.* ○ *Food should not be overtaxed.*

overtax [DIFFICULTY] /ˌəʊ.vəˈtæks/ [US] /ˌoʊ.vɚ-/ *verb* [T] to cause to feel tired or confused as a result of doing too much or doing something too difficult: [R] *Remember you've been ill, and don't overtax yourself.* ○ *This problem is overtaxing my brain.*

overthrow [DEFEAT] /ˌəʊ.vəˈθrəʊ/ [US] /ˌoʊ.vɚˈθroʊ/ *verb* [T] **overthrew, overthrown** to remove someone from power, using force; to defeat: *He said that Allende's government in Chile was overthrown by the army and the CIA in 1973.* **overthrow** /ˈəʊ.və.θrəʊ/ [US] /ˈoʊ.vɚ.θroʊ/ *noun* [C usually sing] *the overthrow **of** the monarchy*

overthrow [THROW] /ˈəʊ.və.θrəʊ/ [US] /ˈoʊ.vɚ.θroʊ/ /ˌ--ˈ-/ *verb* [I or T] **overthrew, overthrown** US to throw a ball beyond the person or object you intended to throw to: *Joe Montana overthrew (the pass).* **overthrow** /ˈəʊ.və.θrəʊ/ [US] /ˈoʊ.vɚ.θroʊ/ *noun* [C usually sing] when a ball is thrown too far

overtime /ˈəʊ.və.taɪm/ [US] /ˈoʊ.vɚ-/ *noun* [U], *adv* **1** (time spent working) beyond the usual time needed or expected in a job: *They're **doing/working** overtime to get the job finished on time.* ○ *Everyone is **on** overtime* (= being paid extra for working beyond the usual time) *this weekend.* **2** US FOR **extra time** **overtime** /ˈəʊ.və.taɪm/ [US] /ˈoʊ.vɚ-/ *noun* [U] extra payment for working beyond the usual time: *I earn overtime for working after 6.00 p.m.*

overtired /ˌəʊ.vəˈtaɪəd/ [US] /ˌoʊ.vɚˈtaɪrd/ *adj* extremely tired, often so that you can not sleep

overtly /əʊˈvɜːt.li/ /ˈ---/ [US] /oʊˈvɝːt-/ *adv* ➲See at **overt**.

overtone /ˈəʊ.və.təʊn/ [US] /ˈoʊ.vɚ.toʊn/ *noun* [C usually pl] something that is suggested, but is not clearly stated: *The concert was supposed to be a charity event but it **had** strong political overtones.* ○ *There was an overtone **of** regret in his farewell speech.*

overtook /ˌəʊ.vəˈtʊk/ [US] /ˌoʊ.vɚ-/ *past simple of* **overtake**

overture [MUSIC] /ˈəʊ.və.tjʊəʳ/ [US] /ˈoʊ.vɚ.tʃɚ/ *noun* [C] a piece of music which is an introduction to a longer piece, especially an opera: *the overture **to** "The Magic Flute"*

overture [APPROACH] /ˈəʊ.və.tjʊəʳ/ [US] /ˈoʊ.vɚ.tʃɚ/ *noun* [C usually pl] an approach made to someone in order to offer something: *overtures **of** friendship.* ○ *Neither side in the conflict seems willing to **make** peace overtures.* ○ INFORMAL *So he's been **making** overtures* (= showing a sexual interest), *has he?*

overturn /ˌəʊ.vəˈtɜːn/ [US] /ˌoʊ.vɚˈtɝːn/ *verb* **1** [I or T] to (cause to) turn over: *The car skidded off the road, hit a tree and overturned.* ○ *The burglars had overturned all the furniture in the house.* **2** [T] FORMAL to change a legal decision: *The Court of Appeal overturned the earlier decision.*

overuse /ˌəʊ.vəˈjuːz/ [US] /ˌoʊ.vɚ-/ *verb* [T] to use something too often or too much: *I tend to overuse certain favourite expressions.* **overuse** /ˌəʊ.vəˈjuːs/ [US] /ˌoʊ.vɚ-/ *noun* [U] *The overuse of X-rays may be causing 250 deaths each year.*

overvalue /ˌəʊ.vəˈvæl.juː/ [US] /ˌoʊ.vɚ-/ *verb* [T] to put too high a value on something: *The company is overvalued on the stock market.*

overview /ˈəʊ.və.vjuː/ [US] /ˈoʊ.vɚ-/ *noun* [C] a short description of something which provides general information about it, but no details: *I'll **give** you a brief overview **of** what the job involves.*

overweening /ˌəʊ.vəˈwiː.nɪŋ/ [US] /ˌoʊ.vɚ-/ *adj* [before n] FORMAL DISAPPROVING showing too much pride or confidence in yourself: *overweening pride/arrogance/vanity* ○ *She is driven by overweening ambition.* **overweeningly** /ˌəʊ.vəˈwiː.nɪŋ.li/ [US] /ˌoʊ.vɚ-/ *adv*

overweight /ˌəʊ.vəˈweɪt/ /ˈ---/ [US] /ˌoʊ.vɚ-/ *adj* **1** fat: *He used to be very overweight.* ○ *I'm only a few kilos overweight, but I just can't seem to lose them.* ○ *an overweight man/woman/child* * NOTE: The opposite is **underweight**. **2** heavier than is allowed: *If your luggage is overweight, you have to pay extra.*

overwhelm /ˌəʊ.vəˈwelm/ [US] /ˌoʊ.vɚ-/ *verb* **1** [T] to defeat someone or something by using a lot of force: *Government troops have overwhelmed the rebels and seized control of the capital.* **2** [T usually passive] to cause someone to feel sudden strong emotion: *They were overwhelmed **with/by** grief when their baby died.* ○ *I was quite overwhelmed by all the flowers and letters of support I received.* **3** [T] LITERARY If water overwhelms a place, it covers it suddenly and completely.
overwhelming /ˌəʊ.vəˈwel.mɪŋ/ [US] /ˌoʊ.vɚ-/ *adj* **1** difficult to fight against: *She felt an overwhelming **urge/desire/need** to tell someone about what had happened.* **2** very great or very large: *She said how much she appreciated the overwhelming generosity of the public in responding to the appeal.* ○ *An overwhelming **majority** have voted in favour of the proposal.*
overwhelmingly /ˌəʊ.vəˈwel.mɪŋ.li/ [US] /ˌoʊ.vɚ-/ *adv*: *The team were overwhelmingly* (= strongly or completely) *defeated in yesterday's game.*

overwork /ˌəʊ.vəˈwɜːk/ [US] /ˌoʊ.vɚˈwɝːk/ *verb* [I or T] to (cause someone to) work too much: *You look exhausted – I hope they're not overworking you.*
overworked /ˌəʊ.vəˈwɜːkt/ [US] /ˌoʊ.vɚˈwɝːkt/ *adj* **1** having to work too much: *an overworked civil servant* ○ *I'm overworked **and underpaid**.* **2** used to describe language that has been used too much and has lost its meaning: *The article was full of overworked expressions.*
overwork /ˈəʊ.və.wɜːk/ [US] /ˈoʊ.vɚ.wɝːk/ *noun* [U] *He was made ill by overwork* (= working too much).

overwrite /ˌəʊ.vəʳˈraɪt/ [US] /ˌoʊ.vɚ-/ *verb* **overwrote, overwritten** **1** [I or T] to write something in a way which is not clear and simple or is more detailed than it needs to be: *His new book is massively overwritten.* ○ *She's one of those authors who has a tendency to overwrite.* **2** [T] If you overwrite a computer file, you replace it with a different one.

overwrought /ˌəʊ.vəʳˈrɔːt/ [US] /ˌoʊ.vɚˈrɑːt/ *adj* in a state of being upset, nervous and anxious: *She was so tired and overwrought that she burst into tears.* ○ *He was in an overwrought **state/condition** for weeks after the accident.*

ovulate /ˈɒv.jʊ.leɪt/ [US] /ˈɑː.vjuː-/ *verb* [I] (of a woman or female animal) to produce an egg from which a baby can be formed: *Some women take drugs to help them ovulate.* **ovulation** /ˌɒv.jʊˈleɪ.ʃən/ [US] /ˌɑː.vjuː-/ *noun* [U] when a woman or female animal produces an egg

ovum /ˈəʊ.vəm/ [US] /ˈoʊ-/ *noun* [C] *plural* **ova** SPECIALIZED a reproductive cell produced by a woman or female animal: *If two ova are fertilized at the same time, the mother will have twins.*

ow /aʊ/ *exclamation* used to express sudden pain: *Ow, stop it, you're hurting me!* ➲See also **ouch**.

owe [HAVE DEBTS] /əʊ/ [US] /oʊ/ *verb* [T] to need to pay or give something to someone because they have lent money to you, or in exchange for something they have done for you: [+ two objects] *I owe Janet ten pounds.* ○ *We still owe $1000 **on** our car* (= We still need to pay $1000 before we own our car). ○ *I owe you a drink **for** helping me move.* ○ *I think you owe* (= should give) *me an explanation/apology.* ➲See also **IOU**.

O

• **I owe *you* (one)** *INFORMAL* used as a way to thank someone for helping you and showing that you will do something for them in the future: *Thanks for the help, Bill – I owe you one.*
• **owe *sb* a living** *INFORMAL* to have to provide money for someone to live on, whether they deserve it or not: *He seems to think **the world** owes him a living.* ○ *No one owes you a living.*
• **owe it to *yourself*** to deserve and need to do something which will be good for you: *Take a few days off work – you owe it to yourself.*
owing /ˈəʊ.ɪŋ/ [US] /ˈoʊ-/ *adj* **[after v]** *UK* still to be paid: *We have several hundred pounds owing **on** our car.*

owe [AS A RESULT] /əʊ/ [US] /oʊ/ *verb* **[T]** to have success, happiness, a job, etc. only because of what someone has given you or done for you or because of your own efforts: *I owe my success **to** my education.* ○ *He owes his life **to** the staff at the hospital.* ○ *I owe everything* (= I am very grateful) *to my parents.*
ˈowing ˌto *prep* because of: *The concert has been cancelled owing to lack of support.*

owl /aʊl/ *noun* **[C]** a bird with a flat face, large eyes, and strong curved nails, which hunts small mammals at night ➲See picture **Animals and Birds** on page Centre 4
owlish /ˈaʊ.lɪʃ/ *adj* A person who is owlish has a round face, usually wears glasses, and looks serious and intelligent: *He was an owlish figure, sitting in the corner of the library.* **owlishly** /ˈaʊ.lɪʃ.li/ *adv*: *He peered owlishly over his glasses.*

own [BELONGING] /əʊn/ [US] /oʊn/ *determiner, pronoun* belonging to or done by a particular person or thing: *Each neighbourhood in New York has its own characteristics.* ○ *I'd like to have my **very** own apartment.* ○ *He wanted an apartment **of** his own.* ○ *She makes **all** her own clothes.* ○ *I'm going to be out tonight, so you'll have to get your own dinner* (= prepare it yourself). ○ *Was that your own idea or did someone suggest it to you?* ○ *You'll have to make up your own mind* (= decide by yourself) *what you want to do.* ○ *I'd never have believed it if I hadn't **seen it with** my own **eyes/heard it with** my own **ears**.* ○ *"Is that your mum's car?" "No, it's my own* (= it belongs to me)." ○ *James Joyce wrote in a style that was **all** his own* (= that was not like that of anyone else). ○ *We like to take care of our own* (= take care of people who are members of our family, or who work for us).
• **come into *your* own** to be very useful or successful in a particular situation: *Eileen really comes into her own in a crisis.*
• **in *your* own time 1** *MAINLY UK* If you do something in your own time, you do it at the speed at which you want to work. **2** *UK* (*US* **on *your* own time**) during the time when you are not officially working: *You may only use company computers to access the Web in your own time.*
• **for its own sake** If you do something for its own sake, you do it because it is interesting and enjoyable, and not because you have or need to do it: *I study for its own sake.*
• **get *your* own back (on *sb*)** *UK INFORMAL* to do something unpleasant to someone because they have done something unpleasant to you: *I'll get my own back on her one day.*
• **get *your* own way** to persuade other people to allow you to do what you want: *My little brother always gets his own way.*
• **be *your* own person/woman/man** to be in control of your life and not allowing other people to tell you what to do: *Nobody tells me how to live my life – I'm my own man.*
• **make *sth* (all) *your* own** If you make a piece of music, etc. (all) your own, you make it famous by the way you perform it.
• **(all) on *your* own 1** alone: *I like living on my own.* **2** without any help: *I did my buttons up all on my own, Mummy.*
• **on *your* own head be it** used to tell someone that they will have to take full responsibility for what they plan to do
• ***your* own flesh and blood** your family or relatives: *It's hard to believe that he could treat his own flesh and blood so badly.*
own /əʊn/ [US] /oʊn/ *verb* **[T not continuous]** to have something that legally belongs to you: *We own our house.* ○ *I've never owned a suit in my life.*
• **as if *you* owned the place** *UK* (*US* **like *you* owned the place**) *DISAPPROVING* in a way that is too confident: *He walked into the office as if he owned the place.*
-owned /-əʊnd/ [US] /-oʊnd/ *suffix* belonging to or controlled by: *a family-owned business* ○ *state-owned industry*
owner /ˈəʊ.nəʳ/ [US] /ˈoʊ.nɚ/ *noun* **[C]** someone who owns something: *Are you the owner **of** this car?* ○ *We still haven't found the dog's owner.*
ownership /ˈəʊ.nə.ʃɪp/ [US] /ˈoʊ.nɚ-/ *noun* **[U]** when you own something: *Do you have any proof of ownership **of/for** this car?* ○ *Rates of home ownership have remained relatively constant.*

own [ADMIT] /əʊn/ [US] /oʊn/ *verb* **[I]** *OLD-FASHIONED* to admit: **[+ (that)]** *I own **(that)** I was not very happy with the group's decision.*
▲ **own up** *phrasal verb* to admit that you have done something wrong: *No one has owned up **to** stealing the money.*

ˌown ˈbrand *UK noun* **[C]** (*US* **store brand,** *AUS* **generic brand**) a product that is advertised with the name of the shop where you buy it, rather than the name of the company that made it

owner-occupied /ˌəʊ.nəˈɒk.jʊ.paɪd/ [US] /ˌoʊ.nɚˈɑː.kjʊ-/ *adj UK* describes houses or flats that have been bought by the people who live in them **owner-occupier** /ˌəʊ.nəˈɒk.jʊ.paɪ.əʳ/ [US] /ˌoʊ.nɚˈɑː.kjʊ.paɪ.ɚ/ *noun* **[C]**

ˌown ˈgoal *noun* **[C] 1** *UK* in sport, a point scored unintentionally by a player for the opposing team: *Our team lost when we **scored** an own goal late in the second half.* **2** *UK* an act which unintentionally helps someone else and is harmful to yourself

owt /aʊt/ *pronoun NON STANDARD NORTHERN ENGLISH* **anything**: *I haven't heard owt about it.* ○ *Is there owt to drink?* ➲Compare **nowt**.

ox /ɒks/ [US] /ɑːks/ *noun* **[C]** *plural* **oxen** a bull which has had its reproductive organs removed, used in the past for pulling loads on farms, or, more generally, any adult of the cattle family

Oxbridge /ˈɒks.brɪdʒ/ [US] /ˈɑːks-/ *noun* **[U]** *UK* the universities of Oxford and Cambridge, considered as a unit separate from other universities in Britain: *Many members of the British government went to Oxbridge* (= a college at either Oxford or Cambridge).
Oxbridge /ˈɒks.brɪdʒ/ [US] /ˈɑːks-/ *adj*: *She's an Oxbridge student* (= a student from Oxford or Cambridge). ○ *He's very Oxbridge in his manner* (= behaves as if he went to a college in Oxford or Cambridge). ➲Compare **redbrick**.

Oxfam /ˈɒks.fæm/ [US] /ˈɑːks-/ *group noun* **[U]** *ABBREVIATION FOR* Oxford Committee for Famine Relief: a UK-based organization which works to help people who are extremely poor and suffering

oxide /ˈɒk.saɪd/ [US] /ˈɑːk-/ *noun* **[C or U]** a chemical combination of oxygen and one other element: *iron oxide* ○ *an oxide **of** copper*
oxidize, *UK USUALLY* **-ise** /ˈɒk.sɪ.daɪz/ [US] /ˈɑːk-/ *verb* **1 [I]** If a substance oxidizes, it combines with oxygen to form another substance: *Iron oxidizes to form rust.* **2 [T]** to combine a substance with oxygen **oxidization,** *UK USUALLY* **-isation** /ˌɒk.sɪ.daɪˈzeɪ.ʃᵊn/ [US] /ˌɑːk-/ *noun* **[U]** (*US USUALLY* **oxidation**)

oxtail /ˈɒks.teɪl/ [US] /ˈɑːks-/ *noun* **[C or U]** meat from the tail of an ox, or the tail itself: *oxtail **soup*** ○ *I bought an oxtail to make some soup.*

oxyacetylene /ˌɒk.si.əˈset.ᵊl.iːn/ [US] /ˌɑːk.si.əˈset̬-/ *noun* **[U]** *SPECIALIZED* a mixture of oxygen and ACETYLENE (= a gas) that produces a hot bright flame, and that can be used for cutting metal: *an oxyacetylene lamp/torch*

oxygen /ˈɒk.sɪ.dʒən/ [US] /ˈɑːk-/ *noun* **[U]** a colourless gas that forms a large part of the air on Earth and which is needed by people, animals and plants to live

oxygenate /ˈɒk.sɪ.dʒə.neɪt/ [US] /ˈɑːk-/ *verb* [T] to add oxygen to something: *Fish tanks often have a pump which oxygenates the water.*

ˈoxygen ˌmask *noun* [C] a piece of equipment which can be put over a person's nose and mouth to supply them with oxygen

ˈoxygen ˌtent *noun* [C] a clear covering put over the head and upper body of an ill person to provide oxygen to help them breathe

oxymoron /ˌɒk.sɪˈmɔː.rɒn/ [US] /ˌɑːk.sɪˈmɔːr.ɑːn/ *noun* [C] two words used together which have, or seem to have, opposite meanings

oyster /ˈɔɪ.stəʳ/ [US] /-stɚ/ *noun* [C] a large flat sea creature that lives in a shell, some types of which can be eaten either raw or cooked, and other types of which produce PEARLS (= small round white precious stones)

ˈoyster ˌbed *noun* [C] an area at the bottom of the sea where oysters live

oz [WEIGHT] *noun* [C] *plural* **oz** *WRITTEN ABBREVIATION FOR* **ounce**: *Add 8 oz **of** flour.*

Oz [COUNTRY] /ɒz/ [US] /ɑːz/ *noun UK INFORMAL* Australia

ozone /ˈəʊ.zəʊn/ [US] /ˈoʊ.zoʊn/ *noun* [U] **1** a poisonous form of oxygen **2** *UK INFORMAL* air that is clean and pleasant to breathe, especially near the sea

ozone-friendly /ˌəʊ.zəʊnˈfrend.li/ [US] /ˌoʊ.zoʊn-/ *adj* describes a product which does not produce gases that are harmful to THE OZONE LAYER: *ozone-friendly packaging* ○ *an ozone-friendly refrigerator*

the ˈozone ˌlayer *noun* [U] a layer of air high above the Earth, which contains a lot of ozone, and which prevents harmful ULTRAVIOLET light from the sun from reaching the Earth

P

P [LETTER] (*plural* **P's** or **Ps**), **p** (*plural* **p's** or **ps**) /piː/ *noun* [C] the 16th letter of the English alphabet

P [SIGN] /piː/ *noun* [U] UK WRITTEN ABBREVIATION FOR **parking**, see at **park** STOP, used especially on road signs

p [MONEY] /piː/ *noun* [C] *plural* **p** UK ABBREVIATION FOR **penny** or **pence**: *Could you lend me 50p?* ○ *This packet of crisps costs 25p.* ○ *I need a 1p/5p/20p* ***coin/piece***.

p [PAGE] *noun* [C] *plural* **pp** WRITTEN ABBREVIATION FOR **page** PAPER: *See p. 27.* ○ *The references are on pp. 256-264.*

:-P INTERNET SYMBOL FOR tongue sticking out: used when you want to be rude to someone

pa [FATHER] /pɑː/ *noun* [C] OLD-FASHIONED INFORMAL FOR father ➲Compare **ma** MOTHER.

pa [EVERY YEAR], **p.a.** /ˌpiː'eɪ/ *adv* ABBREVIATION FOR **per annum** (= each year): *a salary of £20 000 p.a.*

PA [WORK] /ˌpiː'eɪ/ *noun* [C] UK ABBREVIATION FOR personal assistant: someone whose job is helping someone in a higher position, especially writing letters, arranging meetings, and making telephone calls: *Chris works as a PA* ***to*** *the managing director.*

pace [SPEED] /peɪs/ *noun* [U] **1** the speed at which someone or something moves, or with which something happens or changes: *a slow/fast pace* ○ *When she thought she heard someone following her, she* ***quickened*** *her pace.* ○ *Could you slow down a bit – I can't* ***keep*** *pace* ***with*** (= walk or run as fast as) *you.* ○ *For many years this company has* ***set*** *the pace* (= has been the most successful company) *in the communications industry.* ○ *These changes seem to me to be happening* ***at*** *too fast a pace.* ○ *I don't like the pace* ***of*** *modern life.* ➲See also **pacemaker** RUNNER; **pacemaker** DEVICE. **2 force the pace** to make other people in a race go faster by going faster yourself

pace /peɪs/ *verb* [T] to establish a speed for someone who is training for a race or running in a race, for example by running with them

pace *yourself* *verb* [R] to be careful not to do something too quickly so that you do not get too tired to finish it

pacy, pacey (**pacier, paciest**) /'peɪ.si/ *adj* UK A pacy novel/story/film etc. contains a lot of action or events which happen quickly.

pace [STEP] /peɪs/ *noun* [C] a single step, or the distance you move when you take a single step: *Take two paces forwards/backwards.* ○ *The runner collapsed just a few paces from the finish.*

• **put *sb/sth* through *their* paces** to make someone show their skills or knowledge, or to make something show its good qualities: *All the candidates were put through their paces during the television debate.*

pace /peɪs/ *verb* [I + adv or prep; T] to walk with regular steps in one direction and then back again, usually because you are anxious or worried: *He paced the room nervously.* ○ *He paced* ***up and down***, *waiting for the doctor to call.*

▲ **pace *sth* off/out** *phrasal verb* to measure a distance by taking steps of equal size across it and counting them: *You can get a rough idea of the size of the room by pacing it out.*

pacemaker [RUNNER] /'peɪsˌmeɪ.kəʳ/ [US] /-kɚ/ *noun* [C] (ALSO **pace-setter**) the person or animal that establishes the speed in a race, or a person or organization that is an example for others by being successful

pacemaker [DEVICE] /'peɪsˌmeɪ.kəʳ/ [US] /-kɚ/ *noun* [C] a small device which is put inside someone's chest in order to help their heart beat at the correct speed

the ˌPacific 'Rim *noun* [S] the countries on the edge of the PACIFIC OCEAN such as Japan, Australia and the West coast of the US: *We supply systems for clients* ***on*** *the Pacific rim.*

pacifism /'pæs.ɪ.fɪ.zᵊm/ *noun* [U] the belief that war is wrong, and therefore that to fight in a war is wrong

pacifist /'pæs.ɪ.fɪst/ *noun* [C] someone who believes in pacifism: *The pacifist movement is gaining increasing support among young people.*

pacify [CALM] /'pæs.ɪ.faɪ/ *verb* [T] to cause someone who is angry or upset to be calm and satisfied: *He pacified his crying child* ***with*** *a bottle.* ○ *It was difficult for the police to pacify the angry crowd.* **pacification** /ˌpæs.ɪ.fɪ'keɪ.ʃᵊn/ *noun* [U]

pacifier /'pæs.ɪ.faɪ.əʳ/ [US] /-ɚ/ *noun* [C] **1** something that makes people calm when they are angry or upset **2** US FOR **dummy** FOR BABY

pacify [PEACE] /'pæs.ɪ.faɪ/ *verb* [T] to bring peace to a place or end war in a place: *A UN force has been sent in to try and pacify the area worst affected by the civil war.*

pacific /pə'sɪf.ɪk/ *adj* peaceful or helping to cause peace **pacifically** /pə'sɪf.ɪ.kli/ *adv* **pacification** /ˌpæs.ɪ.fɪ'keɪ.ʃᵊn/ *noun* [U]

pack [PUT INTO] /pæk/ *verb* **1** [I or T] to put something into a bag, box, etc: *We're leaving early tomorrow morning, so you'd better pack* (= put clothes and other possessions into a bag or bags) *tonight.* ○ *She packed a small* ***suitcase*** *for the weekend.* ○ *He just packed his* ***bags*** *and walked out on his wife and children.* ○ *I haven't packed my clothes* (= put them into a bag etc.) *yet.* ○ [+ two objects] *Could you pack me a spare pair of shoes, please/pack a spare pair of shoes* ***for*** *me, please?* ○ *These books need to be packed* ***in/into*** *a box.* **2** [T] to put a protective material around something before it is put into a bag, box, etc. so that it will not break or be damaged: *She packed the vase in tissue paper to protect it.*

pack /pæk/ *noun* [C] (US ALSO **backpack**) a type of bag which you usually carry on your back when you are travelling ➲See also **backpack**.

packed /pækt/ *adj* **be packed** to have put your things into a bag or box, etc: *Are you packed yet?* ○ *I'm all packed and ready to go.*

packer /'pæk.əʳ/ [US] /-ɚ/ *noun* [C] a person, company or machine which puts goods into boxes or food into containers

packing /'pæk.ɪŋ/ *noun* [U] **1** when you put things into boxes, bags, etc: *He always* ***does*** *his own packing.* ➲See also **postage and packing**. **2** protective material that you put around something to keep it from being damaged

pack [FILL] /pæk/ *verb* [I usually + adv or prep; T] to come or bring together in large numbers or to fill a space: *Thousands of fans are packing* ***into*** *the stadium.* ○ *Fans packed the stadium to watch the final match.* ○ *The people on the bus were packed* ***(together) like sardines*** (= there were many of them very close together).

packed /pækt/ *adj* completely full: *The train was so packed that I couldn't find a seat.* ○ *This book is packed* ***with*** *useful information.*

-packed /-pækt/ *suffix* full of the thing described: *a fun-packed day* ○ *an action-packed film*

pack [MASS] /pæk/ *verb* [I or T; usually + adv or prep] to (cause to) form into a solid mass: *The wind has packed the snow against the garage door.* ○ *The snow has packed* ***down*** *tightly, making the streets dangerous to walk on.*

pack /pæk/ *noun* [C] **1** a thick mass of a substance, often like clay, which is used as a beauty treatment for the face **2** a thick mass of cloth, etc. which can be put on an injury to stop any bleeding or swelling: *Hold this ice pack to your head to stop the bruising.* ➲See also **compress** CLOTH.

pack [GROUP] /pæk/ *noun* [C] **1** a group, set or collection of something: *The* ***information*** *pack consists of a brochure and a map.* **2** a group of animals such as dogs, which live and/or hunt together: *a wolf pack* ○ *a pack of wild dogs* **3** an organized group of children who are BROWNIES or CUBS: *My uncle was the leader of my Cub pack.* **4** (US ALSO **deck**) a set of playing cards: *a pack of cards* **5** MAINLY DISAPPROVING a group of similar people, especially one which contains people whose activities you do not approve of: *a pack* ***of*** *thieves* ○ *A pack* ***of*** *journalists was waiting outside the White House.* ➲See also **gang**.

pack [CONTAINER] /pæk/ *noun* [C] US FOR **packet** (= a paper or cardboard container): *a pack* ***of*** *cigarettes/gum*

-pack /-pæk/ *suffix* used in combination with an amount to show that that many of a particular type of goods have been wrapped and are being sold together: *a six-pack of beer* ○ *a twin-pack of soap* ○ *a multi-pack of toilet paper*

pack CARRY /pæk/ *verb* [T] *US SLANG* to carry something, especially a gun: *to pack a **gun*** ○ *Each missile packs several warheads.* ○ *FIGURATIVE This gun packs (= has) a lot of firepower.*

• **pack a punch** *INFORMAL* to have a lot of force or a great effect: *His speech packed quite a punch.* ○ *These cocktails taste quite innocent, but they really pack a punch!*

PHRASAL VERBS WITH **pack** ▼

▲ **pack sth away** *phrasal verb* **1** to put something into a bag or container, or to put something in the place where it is usually kept: *Come on, children, it's time to pack away your toys.* **2** *INFORMAL* to eat a lot of food: *She's tiny but she can really pack away the biscuits.*

▲ **pack sth in** STOP *phrasal verb* [M] *INFORMAL* to stop doing something: *This course is really tough, – sometimes I feeling like packing **it all** in.*

▲ **pack sb in** *phrasal verb* [M] *UK INFORMAL* to end your relationship with someone, or to stop meeting or spending time with them: "*Is Emma still seeing Joe?*" "*No, she's packed him in.*"

,**Pack it 'in!** *exclamation UK INFORMAL* said to rudely tell someone to stop doing something that is annoying you

▲ **pack sb in** LARGE NUMBER *phrasal verb* [M] If an entertainment or exhibition packs people in, a large number of people come to see it: *Spielberg's new film is packing in the crowds.* ○ *The latest computer exhibition is really packing them in.*

▲ **pack sth/sb in** *phrasal verb* [M] *INFORMAL* to manage to include a large number of things, activities or people: *We were only there four days but we packed a lot in.*

▲ **pack sth into sth** *phrasal verb* to manage to do a lot of activities in a limited period of time: *We packed a lot of sightseeing into our weekend in New York.*

▲ **pack sb off** *phrasal verb* [M] *INFORMAL* to send someone to another place: *We've packed the kids off for the weekend.* ○ *I packed her off **to** my sister's.*

▲ **pack sth/somewhere out** *phrasal verb UK INFORMAL* to make a place very full: *100 000 football supporters packed out Wembley Stadium to see the game.*

be ,packed 'out *INFORMAL* to be full of people: *The bar was packed out last night.*

▲ **pack up** STOP WORKING *phrasal verb UK INFORMAL* If a machine packs up, it stops operating: *My camera has packed up.*

▲ **pack up (sth)** *phrasal verb* [M] *UK INFORMAL* to stop working or doing another regular activity: *She packed up her job, and went off to Australia.* ○ [+ v-ing] *It's time you packed up smoking.*

▲ **pack (sth) up** COLLECT *phrasal verb* [M] to collect all your things together when you have finished doing something: *I'm about to pack up my things and go home.*

package /'pæk.ɪdʒ/ *noun* [C] **1** a parcel: *The postman has just delivered a package for you.* ○ *The package was wrapped in plain brown paper.* **2** *US FOR* **packet**: *a package of cookies* **3** a related group of things when they are offered together as a single unit: *The computer comes with a **software** package.* ○ *The **aid** package for the earthquake-hit area will include emergency food and medical supplies.*

• **Good things come in small packages.** *SAYING* said to emphasize that something does not need to be big in order to be good

package /'pæk.ɪdʒ/ *verb* [T] **1** to put goods into boxes or containers to be sold: *These organic olives are packaged **in** recycled glass containers.* **2** to show someone or something in an attractive way so that people will like or buy them: *As a young film star, she was packaged **as** a sex symbol.*

packaging /'pæk.ɪ.dʒɪŋ/ *noun* [U] the materials in which objects are wrapped before being sold: *All our packaging is biodegradable.*

'**package ,deal** *noun* [C] a set of arrangements that must be accepted together and not separately

'**package ,store** *noun* [C] *US FOR* **off-licence**

,**package ,tour** *noun* [C] (*UK ALSO* **package holiday,** *AUS ALSO* **holiday package**) a holiday at a fixed price in which the travel company arranges your travel, hotels and sometimes meals for you: *We bought a cheap package tour to Spain and stayed in a big hotel by the sea.*

'**pack ,animal** *noun* [C] animals such as horses, which are used to transport things on their backs

packed /pækt/ *adj* ➔See at **pack** PUT INTO, **pack** FILL.

,**packed 'lunch** *UK noun* [C] (*US* **box lunch,** *AUS* **cut lunch**) a light meal put in a container, usually to take with you somewhere to be eaten later

packer /'pæk.əʳ/ ⑩ /-ɚ/ *noun* [C] ➔See at **pack** PUT INTO.

packet /'pæk.ɪt/ *noun* [C] **1** *MAINLY UK* a small paper or cardboard container in which a number of small objects are sold: *a packet **of** cereal/biscuits/crisps* ○ *a packet of chewing gum/cigarettes* ○ *How many seeds are there in a packet?* ➔Compare **parcel**. **2** (*US* **package**) *UK OFFENSIVE FOR* a man's sex organs **3** *UK INFORMAL* **a packet** a large amount of money: *That house must have **cost** a packet!* ○ *Someone's **making** a packet out of this business.*

'**pack ,ice** *noun* [U] a large mass of ice floating in the sea that has been formed by smaller pieces of ice being forced together

packing /'pæk.ɪŋ/ *noun* [U] ➔See at **pack** PUT INTO.

'**packing ,case** *UK noun* [C] (*US* **packing crate**) a large strong box for transporting things: *I don't think we've got enough packing cases for all the kitchen equipment.*

pact /pækt/ *noun* [C] a formal agreement between two people or groups of people: *The United States and Canada have **signed** a free-trade pact.* ○ [+ **to** infinitive] *The Liberal Democrats may **form** a pact **with** Labour **to** try to beat the Conservatives in the next election.*

pacy /'peɪ.si/ *adj* ➔See at **pace** SPEED.

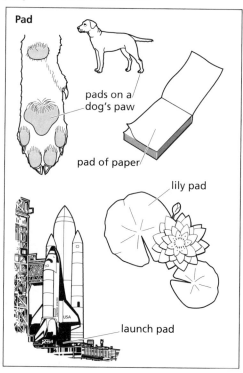

Pad

pads on a dog's paw

pad of paper

lily pad

launch pad

pad MATERIAL /pæd/ *noun* [C] a piece of soft thick cloth or rubber which is used to protect a part of the body, give shape to something or clean something: *a knee/shoulder pad* ○ *Footballers often wear **shin** pads to protect their legs.* ○ *In the 1980s, **shoulder** pads were very fashionable in women's clothes.* ○ *She wiped her eye make-up off with a cotton wool pad.*

pad /pæd/ *verb* [T] **-dd-** to put pieces of soft material in something to make it soft, give it a different shape, or protect what is inside: *These walking boots are padded with shock-resistant foam.*

padded /ˈpæd.ɪd/ *adj* containing a layer of soft material used for protection or to give shape: *It's a short jacket with padded* ***shoulders.*** ○ *a padded* ***bra*** (= one with extra layers of material in it to make the breasts seem bigger)

padding /ˈpæd.ɪŋ/ *noun* [U] **1** the pieces of material used to protect something or give it shape **2** unnecessary words or information added to a speech or piece of writing: *It could have been an interesting essay, but there was too much padding.*

pad [PAPER] /pæd/ *noun* [C] a number of pieces of paper that have been fastened together along one side, which is used for writing or drawing on: *I have a pad and pencil for taking notes.* ○ *I always keep a pad* ***of paper*** *by the phone.* ➲See also **notepad**.

pad [FLAT SURFACE] /pæd/ *noun* [C] **1** a hard flat area of ground where helicopters can take off and land, or from which rockets are sent: *The hotel has its own helicopter pad.* ○ *Missiles have been launched from their pads deep in enemy territory.* **2** one of the large flat leaves of a WATER LILY: *a lily pad*

pad [FOOT] /pæd/ *noun* [C] the soft part at the bottom of a cat or dog's PAW (= foot)

pad [HOUSE] /pæd/ *noun* [C] *OLD-FASHIONED SLANG* a person's house or apartment: *a bachelor pad*

▲ **pad *sth* out** *phrasal verb* [M] If you pad out a speech or piece of writing, you add unnecessary words or information to make it longer or to hide the fact that you are not saying anything very important.

ˌpadded ˈcell *noun* [C usually sing] a room in a mental hospital that has very soft walls to stop a seriously mentally ill person from hurting themselves

paddle [POLE] /ˈpæd.l̩/ *noun* [C] **1** a short pole with a wide flat part at one end or both ends, used for moving a small boat or CANOE through the water ➲See picture **Planes, Ships and Boats** on page Centre 14 **2** a blade on a paddle wheel

paddle /ˈpæd.l̩/ *verb* **1** [I or T] to push a pole with a wide end through the water in order to make a boat move **2** [I] to swim by moving your feet and hands up and down **3** [T] *US* to hit a child on the bottom with a short, wide piece of wood

paddle [WALK] *UK* /ˈpæd.l̩/ *verb* [I] (*US* **wade**) to walk with bare feet through shallow water, often at the edge of the sea: *We rolled up our trousers and paddled along the seashore.*

paddle *UK* /ˈpæd.l̩/ *noun* [C usually sing] (*US* **wade**) a walk through shallow water, especially at the edge of the sea: *Shall we go for a paddle?*

ˈpaddle ˌsteamer *UK noun* [C] (*US* **paddle wheeler**) a large boat that uses a paddle powered by steam to move through the water

ˈpaddle ˌwheel *noun* [C] a type of wheel with small flat blades fixed around the edge which makes a boat move through the water or which operates a piece of machinery

ˈpaddling ˌpool *UK noun* [C] (*US* **wading pool**) a shallow pool that small children can play in

paddock /ˈpæd.ək/ *noun* [C] **1** a small field where animals, especially horses, are kept **2** *AUS* a field of any size which is used for farming **3** *SPECIALIZED* an enclosed area where horses are shown to the public before a race

Paddy [PERSON] /ˈpæd.i/ *noun* [C] *OFFENSIVE* an Irish person

paddy [ANGRY] /ˈpæd.i/ *noun* [C usually sing] *UK OLD-FASHIONED INFORMAL* a very angry state: *There's no need to get* ***in/ into*** *a paddy.*

ˈpaddy ˌfield *UK noun* [C] (*US* **rice paddy**) a field planted with rice growing in water

ˈpaddy ˌwagon *noun* [C] *US* an enclosed police vehicle used for transporting prisoners

padlock /ˈpæd.lɒk/ [US] /-lɑːk/ *noun* [C] a small metal lock with a U-shaped bar

padlock /ˈpæd.lɒk/ [US] /-lɑːk/ *verb* [T] to fasten something using a padlock: *The box was securely padlocked and no one had the key.*

padre /ˈpɑː.dreɪ/ [US] /-dri/ *noun* [C] a Christian priest, especially in the armed forces

paean /ˈpiː.ən/ *noun* [C] *LITERARY* a song, film or piece of writing that praises someone or something very enthusiastically: *The song is a paean* ***to*** *solitude and independence.*

paederast /ˈped.ər.æst/ [US] /-dɚ-/ *noun* [C] *UK OLD-FASHIONED FOR* **pederast**

paediatrician *UK, US* **pediatrician** /ˌpiː.di.əˈtrɪʃ.ən/ *noun* [C] a doctor who has special training in medical care for children

paediatric *UK, US* **pediatric** /ˌpiː.diˈæt.rɪk/ *adj* relating to the medical care of children: *paediatric medicine* ○ *a paediatric hospital*

paediatrics *UK* /ˌpiː.diːˈæt.rɪks/ *noun* [U] (*US* **pediatrics**) the science or study of medical care for children: *She specializes in paediatrics.*

paedophile *UK, US* **pedophile** /ˈpiː.dəʊ.faɪl/ [US] /ˈped.oʊ-/ *noun* [C] a person, especially a man, who is sexually interested in children **paedophilia** *UK, US* **pedophilia** /ˌpiː.dəʊˈfɪl.i.ə/ [US] /ˌped.oʊˈfiː.li-/ *noun* [U]

ˈpaedophile ˌring *noun* [C] a group of people who take part in illegal sexual activity involving children

paella /paɪˈel.ə/ [US] /pɑːˈjel-/ *noun* [C or U] a Spanish dish consisting of rice mixed with vegetables, fish and chicken

pagan /ˈpeɪ.gən/ *adj* **1** belonging to a religion which worships many gods, especially one which existed before the main world religions: *a pagan religion* ○ *The Easter egg has both pagan and Christian origins.* **2** relating to religious beliefs that do not belong to any of the main religions of the world: *a pagan festival*

pagan /ˈpeɪ.gən/ *noun* [C] **1** a person who has pagan beliefs **2** *HUMOROUS* a person who has no religious beliefs

paganism /ˈpeɪ.gən.ɪ.zəm/ *noun* [U]

page [PAPER] /peɪdʒ/ *noun* [C] (*WRITTEN ABBREVIATION* **p**) **1** a side of one of the pieces of paper in a book, newspaper or magazine, usually with a number printed on it: *For details on how to enter the competition, see page 134.* ○ *The article appeared on the* ***front*** *page of the Guardian.* **2** one of the sheets of paper in a book, newspaper or magazine: *Several pages have been torn out of this book.*

• **page in/of history** *LITERARY* an important part of the history of a place, time or group of people: *The signing of the peace treaty will be seen as a glorious page in our country's history.*

pagination /ˌpædʒ.ɪˈneɪ.ʃən/ [US] /-ənˈeɪ-/ *noun* [U] *SPECIALIZED* the way in which the pages of a book or document, etc. are numbered

page [COMPUTER] /peɪdʒ/ *noun* [C] (*ALSO* **web page**) one part of a WEBSITE (= area of information on the Internet) ➲See also **home page**.

page [CALL] /peɪdʒ/ *verb* [T] **1** to call a person using a LOUDSPEAKER (= an electric device for making sounds louder) in a public place: *He was paged at the airport and told to return home immediately.* **2** to send a message to someone's PAGER (= small piece of electronic equipment that receives signals): *Have you tried to page him?*

pager /ˈpeɪ.dʒər/ [US] /-dʒɚ/ *noun* [C] (*UK ALSO* **bleeper,** *US ALSO* **beeper**) a small device that you carry or wear, which moves or makes a noise to tell you that someone wants you to telephone them

page [BOY] /peɪdʒ/ *noun* [C] (in the past) a boy who worked as a servant for a knight and who was learning to become a knight ➲Compare **pageboy** BOY.

pageant /ˈpædʒ.ənt/ *noun* [C] **1** *UK* a show, usually performed outside, that consists of people wearing traditional clothing and acting out historical events: *Our youngest son is taking part in the school pageant.* **2** *US* a competition for young women in which they are judged on their beauty and other qualities: *a* ***beauty*** *pageant* **3** any colourful and splendid show or ceremony

pageantry /ˈpædʒ.ən.tri/ *noun* [U] splendid, colourful and very expensive ceremonies: *She loved the pageantry and tradition of the Royal Family.*

pageboy [BOY] /ˈpeɪdʒ.bɔɪ/ *noun* [C] a young boy who is one of the people to go with the BRIDE (= the woman who

P

is getting married) into the church: *The little pageboys were dressed in kilts and the bridesmaids in pink dresses.* ➲Compare **page** BOY.

pageboy [HAIR] /ˈpeɪdʒ.bɔɪ/ *noun* [C] a hairstyle, mainly for women, in which the hair is straight and quite short and turns under at the ends

ˌpage ˈthree ˌgirl *noun* [C] *UK* a young woman who appears with naked breasts in photographs for some popular newspapers in the UK

page-turner /ˈpeɪ.dʒˌtɜː.nəʳ/ [US] /-ˌtɝː.nɚ/ *noun INFORMAL* a book that is so exciting that you have to read it quickly: *Her latest novel is a real page-turner.*

pagoda /pəˈɡəʊ.də/ [US] /-ˈɡoʊ-/ *noun* [C] a tall religious building in Asia with many levels, each of which has a curved roof

paid [PAY] /peɪd/ *past simple and past participle of* **pay**

paid [GIVEN MONEY] /peɪd/ *adj* **1** being given money for something: *Are you looking for paid work* (= work for which you are given money) *or voluntary work?* ○ *paid employment* ○ *paid (UK) holiday/ (US) vacation* ○ *paid leave* **2** used in combination to refer to the amount of money which someone is given for their work: ***low**-paid workers* ○ *a **well**-paid job*

paid-up /ˌpeɪdˈʌp/ *adj* **1 paid-up member** someone who has paid the money necessary to be a member of a particular organization **2** *UK INFORMAL* describes someone who is a loyal and enthusiastic member of a group

pail /peɪl/ *noun* [C] *MAINLY US* a **bucket**: *Fill the pail with sand.* ○ *It took several pails of water* (= the amount a pail contains) *to put out the fire.*

pain /peɪn/ *noun* [C or U] **1** a feeling of physical suffering caused by injury or illness: *Her symptoms included abdominal pain and vomiting.* ○ *Are you **in*** (= suffering from) *pain?* ○ *She was in **constant** pain.* ○ *These tablets should help to **ease** the pain.* ○ *I felt a **sharp** pain **in** my foot.* ○ *He's been suffering various **aches and** pains for years.* **2** emotional or mental suffering: *It's a film about the pains and pleasures of parenthood.* ○ *The parents are still in great pain **over** the death of their child.*

• **a pain (in the neck)** *INFORMAL* someone or something that is very annoying: *That child is a **real** pain in the neck.*

• **a pain in the arse/backside** *UK* (*US* **pain in the ass/butt**) *OFFENSIVE* someone or something that is very annoying: *The kids were a real pain in the arse.*

• **on/under pain of death** *FORMAL* If you are told to do something on/under pain of death, you will be killed if you do not do it.

pain /peɪn/ *verb* [T] *FORMAL* If something pains you, it causes you to feel sad and upset: [+ *to* infinitive] ***It** pains me **to** see animals being mistreated.*

pains /peɪnz/ *plural noun* **1 be at pains to do *sth*** to make a lot of effort to do something: *She is at pains to point out how much work she has done.* **2 go to/take great pains to do *sth*** to make a lot of effort to do something: *I went to great pains to select the best staff available.*

pained /peɪnd/ *adj* If you look or sound pained, you show that you are upset or offended: *a pained expression*

painful /ˈpeɪn.fəl/ *adj* **1** causing emotional or physical pain: *The old photograph brought back painful memories.* ○ *A painful injury forced her to withdraw from the game.* **2** If something is painful to watch or listen to, it is so bad that it makes you feel embarrassed: *It was painful to listen to his pathetic excuses.*

painfully /ˈpeɪn.fəl.i/ *adv* **1** in a way that causes pain: *Without surgery, this animal will die slowly and painfully.* **2** used to emphasize a quality, action or situation that is unpleasant or not desirable: *I am painfully aware that I have made mistakes.* ○ *It was a painfully slow journey.*

painless /ˈpeɪn.ləs/ *adj* **1** causing no physical pain: *a painless medical procedure* **2** describes something that causes no problems: *a painless solution to a problem*

painlessly /ˈpeɪn.lə.sli/ *adv*: *The laser beam heals the eye painlessly.*

painkiller /ˈpeɪnˌkɪl.əʳ/ [US] /-ɚ/ *noun* [C] medicine used to reduce or remove physical pain: *The body produces chemicals which are natural painkillers.* **painkilling** /ˈpeɪŋˌkɪl.ɪŋ/ *adj* [before n] *This tiny capsule contains two types of effective painkilling **ingredients**.*

painstaking /ˈpeɪnzˌteɪ.kɪŋ/ *adj* extremely careful and correct, and using a lot of effort: *It took months of painstaking research to write the book.* ○ *He was described by his colleagues as a painstaking journalist.*

painstakingly /ˈpeɪnzˌteɪ.kɪŋ.li/ *adv* in a way that shows you have taken a lot of care or made a lot of effort: *She painstakingly explained how the machine worked.*

paint /peɪnt/ *noun* [C or U] a coloured liquid that is put on a surface such as a wall to decorate it: *a (UK) tin/(US) can of paint* ○ *This wall needs another **coat** of paint.* ○ *Caution! Wet paint.* ○ *gloss/(UK) matt/(US) matte paint* ○ *There were so many paints* (= types of paint) *to choose from that I couldn't decide which to buy.*

paint /peɪnt/ *verb* **1** [I or T] to cover a surface with paint: [+ obj + adj] *We've painted the bedroom blue.* ○ *I've been painting all morning.* ○ *I'll need to paint **over*** (= cover with another layer of paint) *these dirty marks on the wall.* **2** [I or T] to make a picture using paints: *All these pictures were painted by local artists.* **3** [T + obj + n] If someone paints their nails or face, they put make-up on that part of their body: *She painted her nails a bright red.*

• **paint a bleak/gloomy/rosy, etc. picture of *sth*** to describe something in a particular way: *He painted a rosy picture of family life.* ○ *She paints a gloomy picture of the future.*

• **paint the town (red)** to go out and enjoy yourself, often drinking a lot of alcohol, usually in order to celebrate something

paints /peɪnts/ *plural noun* tubes of paint or blocks of dried paint used for making pictures: *oil paints*

painter /ˈpeɪn.təʳ/ [US] /-t̬ɚ/ *noun* [C] **1** someone who paints pictures **2** someone whose job is to paint surfaces, such as walls and doors

painting /ˈpeɪn.tɪŋ/ [US] /-t̬ɪŋ/ *noun* **1** [C or U] a picture made using paint: *The walls are covered in oil paintings.* ○ *an exhibition of 19th-century French painting* **2** [U] the skill or activity of making a picture or putting paint on a wall: *We were taught painting and drawing at art college.* ○ *When we bought the house, we had to do a lot of painting and redecorating.*

paintball /ˈpeɪnt.bɔːl/ [US] /-bɑːl/ *noun* [U] a game in which people dress up in military clothing, go out into the countryside and attempt to shoot each other with guns that fire paint rather than bullets

paintbox /ˈpeɪnt.bɒks/ [US] /-bɑːks/ *noun* [C] a box containing paints for making pictures

paintbrush /ˈpeɪnt.brʌʃ/ *noun* [C] a brush used for putting paint on a surface or on a picture

ˈpaint ˌstripper *noun* [U] *UK* a liquid used to remove old paint from wooden surfaces

ˈpaint ˌthinner *noun* [U] a liquid that you add to paint to make it less thick or to remove paint from brushes

paintwork /ˈpeɪnt.wɜːk/ [US] /-wɝːk/ *noun* [U] the covering of paint on a surface: *The car's paintwork has been scratched.*

pair /peəʳ/ [US] /per/ *noun* [C] **1** two things of the same appearance and size that are intended to be used together, or something that consists of two parts joined together: *a pair **of** shoes/gloves* ○ *a pair **of** scissors/glasses* ○ *I can't find a matching pair of socks.* ○ *He packed two pairs of trousers and four shirts.* ○ *I'd like you to do this exercise **in** pairs* (= in groups of two). **2** two people who have a romantic relationship or are doing something together: *They seem a very happy pair.* ○ *What have you pair been up to?* **3** two animals that come together to have sex and produce young: *a breeding pair* ○ *a mated pair of swans*

pair /peəʳ/ [US] /per/ *verb*

PHRASAL VERBS WITH **pair**

▲ **pair off** *phrasal verb* to begin a romantic or sexual relationship with someone: *All my friends seem to be pairing off and getting married.* ○ *Ravens nest very early in the spring and they pair off in the late autumn.*

▲ **pair *sb* off** *phrasal verb* [M] to introduce two people to each other so that they will start a romantic relation-

ship: *I managed to pair my best friend Sue off* ***with*** *Mike.*
▲ **pair (sb) off** *phrasal verb* [M] If a group of people pair off, they divide into pairs in order to do something, and if you pair them off, you divide them into pairs: *The students paired off to practise their conversational skills.*
▲ **pair up** *phrasal verb* to join together temporarily with another person in order to do something: *Everyone should pair up for the next dance.*

paisley /ˈpeɪz.li/ *noun* [C or U] a colourful pattern of curved shapes, usually on cloth: *My sister loves paisley.* ○ *a paisley tie*

pajamas /pɪˈdʒɑː.məz/ [US] /-ˈdʒæm.əz/ *plural noun* US FOR **pyjamas**

Paki /ˈpæk.i/ *noun* [C] *OFFENSIVE* a person from Pakistan

pal /pæl/ *noun* [C] *INFORMAL* **1** a friend: *You're my* ***best*** *pal.* ○ *It's my* ***old*** *pal Pete!* **2** sometimes used when talking to a man who is annoying you: *Look, pal, you're asking for trouble.*
pally /ˈpæl.i/ *adj INFORMAL* friendly: *They've become very pally (****with*** *each other).* ○ *Suddenly she started acting very pally* ***towards*** *me.*

pal /pæl/ *verb* **-ll-**

PHRASAL VERBS WITH **pal**

▲ **pal around** *phrasal verb US INFORMAL* to spend time with someone that you are very friendly with: *He used to pal around* ***with*** *one of the president's sons.*
▲ **pal up** *phrasal verb UK OLD-FASHIONED* to become friends with someone: *I've palled up* ***with*** *some people from work and we're going on holiday together.*

palace /ˈpæl.ɪs/ *noun* [C] **1** a large house that is the official home of a king, queen or other person of high social rank: *a royal/presidential palace* ○ *The Queen has agreed to open Buckingham Palace to the public.* **2** *OLD-FASHIONED* used in the names of large buildings, such as cinemas or places where people go dancing: *An old movie palace is being restored.*
the Palace *group noun* [S] used when referring to the people who live in a palace: *The Palace has issued a statement criticizing the newspaper report.* ○ *A spokesman for the Palace has denied the accusation.*
palatial /pəˈleɪ.ʃəl/ *adj* describes a house that is very large and splendid

ˌpalace ˈcoup *noun* [C] (*ALSO* **palace revolution**) a situation in which a leader is removed from power by the people who have worked with him or her: *A palace coup led by General Rodriguez has toppled the dictator.*

palaeo-, *US ALSO* **paleo-** /pæl.i.əʊ-/ /peɪ.li.əʊ-/ [US] /peɪ.li.oʊ-/ *prefix* ancient; from a time before history was being recorded: *palaeobotany*

palaeolithic, *US ALSO* **paleolithic** /ˌpæl.i.əʊˈlɪθ.ɪk/ [US] /ˌpeɪ.li.oʊ-/ *adj* belonging to the period when humans used tools and weapons made of stone: *The Palaeolithic* ***Period*** *is sometimes called the Old Stone Age.* ⊃Compare **neolithic**.

palaeontology, *US ALSO* **paleontology** /ˌpæl.i.ɒnˈtɒl.ə.dʒi/ [US] /ˌpeɪ.li.ɑːnˈtɑː.lə-/ *noun* [U] the study of FOSSILS (= preserved bones or shells) as a way of getting information about the history of life on Earth and the structure of rocks **palaeontologist**, *US ALSO* **paleontologist** /ˌpæl.i.ɒnˈtɒl.ə.dʒɪst/ [US] /ˌpeɪ.li.ɑːnˈtɑː.lə-/ *noun* [C]

palate /ˈpæl.ət/ *noun* **1** [C] the top part of the inside of your mouth **2** [C usually sing] a person's ability to taste and judge good food and wine: *a* ***discriminating*** *palate*
palatable /ˈpæl.ə.tə.bl̩/ [US] /-t̬ə-/ *adj* **1** *FORMAL* describes food or drink that has a pleasant taste: *a very palatable wine* ○ *The meal was barely palatable.* * NOTE: The opposite is **unpalatable**. **2** acceptable: *I'm afraid the members won't find all these changes very palatable.*

palatial /pəˈleɪ.ʃəl/ *adj* ⊃See at **palace**.

palaver /pəˈlɑː.vəʳ/ [US] /-ˈlæv.ɚ/ *noun* [S or U] *INFORMAL* unnecessary inconvenience and trouble: *Organizing the annual office lunch was such a palaver, I swore I'd never do it again.*

pale /peɪl/ *adj* **1** describes someone's face or skin if it has less colour than usual, for example when they are ill or frightened, or if it has less colour than people generally have: *You're looking pale – do you feel ill?* ○ *She has a naturally pale complexion and dark hair.* ⊃See **beyond the pale** at **beyond** OUTSIDE A LIMIT. **2** describes light or a colour that is not bright or strong: *She wore a pale blue hat.* ○ *pale winter sunlight*
pale /peɪl/ *verb* [I] If a person's face pales, it loses its usual colour: *His face paled and he looked as if he might faint.*
• **pale in comparison** (*ALSO* **pale beside** ***sth/sb***) to seem much less serious or important when compared with someone or something else: *I thought I was badly treated but my experiences pale in comparison with yours.*
• **pale into insignificance** to seem completely unimportant when compared with something else: *Everything else that happened in my life pales into insignificance beside that one event.*
paleness /ˈpeɪl.nəs/ *noun* [U] the state of being pale
palish /ˈpeɪ.lɪʃ/ *adj*: *The sky was a palish* (= quite pale) *blue.*

ˌpale ˈale *noun* [C or U] a type of beer that does not contain much alcohol and is often sold in bottles

ˌpale imiˈtation *noun* [C] something that is similar to but not as good as something else: *Modern luxury ships are a pale imitation* ***of*** *the glamour and style of the early ocean liners.*

paleo- /pæl.i.əʊ-/ /peɪ.li.əʊ-/ [US] /peɪ.li.oʊ-/ *prefix ANOTHER SPELLING OF* **palaeo-**

paleolithic /ˌpæl.i.əʊˈlɪθ.ɪk/ [US] /ˌpeɪ.li.oʊ-/ *adj ANOTHER SPELLING OF* **palaeolithic**

paleontology /ˌpæl.i.ɒnˈtɒl.ə.dʒi/ [US] /-ˈtɑː.lə-/ *noun* [U] *ANOTHER SPELLING OF* **palaeontology**

Palestinian /ˌpæ.ləˈstɪn.i.ən/ *adj* from, belonging to or relating to Palestine: *Representatives of the Palestinian Authority attended the meeting.* ○ *the Palestinian people*
Palestinian /ˌpæ.ləˈstɪn.i.ən/ *noun* [C] a person from Palestine, especially a member of the Arab people of Palestine

palette /ˈpæl.ət/ *noun* **1** [C] a thin board with curved edges and a hole for your thumb, used by an artist to mix their paints on while they are painting **2** [C usually sing] *SPECIALIZED* the range of colours that an artist usually paints with: *Matisse's palette typically consists of bright blues, greens and oranges.*

ˈpalette ˌknife *noun* [C] a knife with a wide thin blade, a rounded end and no sharp edge, used to mix paints together and also to spread soft substances when cooking

palindrome /ˈpæl.ɪn.drəʊm/ [US] /-droʊm/ *noun* [C] a word or group of words that is the same whether you read it forwards from the beginning or backwards from the end: *"Refer" and "level" are palindromes.*

paling /ˈpeɪ.lɪŋ/ *noun* [C] a fence made from long thin pieces of wood: *He has just put up a paling around the house.*

palisade /ˌpæl.ɪˈseɪd/ [US] /ˈ---/ *noun* [C] a strong fence made out of wooden or iron poles that is used to protect people or a place from being attacked

palisades /ˌpæl.ɪˈseɪdz/ [US] /ˈ---/ *plural noun US* a line of cliffs by the sea or a river

pall [BECOME BORING] /pɔːl/ [US] /pɑːl/ *verb* [I] to become less interesting or enjoyable: *The pleasure of not having to work quickly palled.*

pall [CLOUD] /pɔːl/ [US] /pɑːl/ *noun* **1** [C] a thick dark cloud of smoke: *Palls* ***of*** *smoke obscured our view.* **2** [S] a negative atmosphere: *The bad news* ***cast*** *a pall* ***over*** *the evening.* ○ *A pall of embarrassment descended on the room.*

pall [CLOTH] /pɔːl/ [US] /pɑːl/ *noun* [C] **1** a cloth used to cover a coffin at a funeral **2** *US* the coffin itself at a funeral

pallbearer /ˈpɔːl̩beə.rəʳ/ [US] /ˈpɑːl̩ber.ɚ/ *noun* [C] a person who helps to carry a coffin at a funeral or who walks beside the people carrying it

pallet /ˈpæl.ɪt/ *noun* [C] a flat wooden structure onto which heavy goods are loaded so that they can be moved using a FORK-LIFT TRUCK (= a small vehicle with two strong bars of metal on the front which is used for lifting heavy goods)

palliative /ˈpæl.i.ə.tɪv/ [US] /-t̬ɪv/ *noun* [C] **1** *SPECIALIZED* a drug or medical treatment that reduces pain without

P

curing the cause of the pain **2** *FORMAL* something that makes a problem seem less serious but does not solve the problem or make it disappear: *We want long-term solutions, not short-term palliatives.* **palliative** /ˈpæl.i.ə.tɪv/ [US] /-t̬ɪv/ *adj SPECIALIZED palliative care*

pallid /ˈpæl.ɪd/ *adj* **1** very pale, in a way that looks unattractive and unhealthy: *Next to his tanned face, hers seemed pallid and unhealthy.* **2** lacking enthusiasm or excitement: *This is a pallid production of what should be a great ballet.*

pallor /ˈpæl.əʳ/ [US] /-ɚ/ *noun* [U] the state of being very pale: *The **deathly** pallor of her skin was frightening.*

pally /ˈpæl.i/ *adj*: See at **pal**.

palm /pɑːm/ *noun* [C] **1** the inside part of your hand from your wrist to the base of your fingers: *This tiny device fits into **the palm of your hand**.* ➲See picture **The Body** on page Centre 5 **2 read *sb's* palm** to look at the lines on the inside of someone's hand and tell them what these lines say about their character and their future

• **have *sb* in the palm of *your* hand** (*ALSO* **have *sb* eating out of the palm of *your* hand**) to have complete control over someone and to be able to make them do anything you want them to: *He had the audience in the palm of his hand.*

palm /pɑːm/ *verb* [T] to make something seem to disappear by hiding it in the palm of your hand as part of a trick, or to steal something by picking it up in a way that will not be noticed: *I suspected that he had palmed a playing card.*

PHRASAL VERBS WITH **palm** ▼

▲ **palm *sth* off** *phrasal verb* [M] to give away something, or persuade someone to accept something, because you do not want it and you know it has no value: *She tried to palm her old car off **on** me.*

▲ **palm *sb* off with *sth*** *phrasal verb* to give someone an untrue or unsatisfactory answer, or to give them something that has no value in order to try to satisfy them and make them go away: *You're not going to palm me off with that feeble excuse.*

palmist /ˈpɑː.mɪst/ *noun* [C] (*ALSO* **palm reader**) a person who looks at the lines on the inside of your hand and tells you what these lines say about your character and your future

palmistry /ˈpɑː.mɪ.stri/ *noun* [U] (*ALSO* **palm reading**) the skill and activity of looking at the lines on the inside of people's hands and claiming to be able to see signs about their character and future

ˈpalm ˌoil *noun* [C or U] an oil obtained from the nuts of some types of palm, used in some foods and to make soap

ˌPalm ˈSunday *noun* [C or U] the Sunday before EASTER (= a Christian religious holiday) in Christian religions

palmtop (computer) /ˌpɑːm.tɒp.kəmˈpjuː.təʳ/ [US] /-tɑːp.kəmˈpjuː.t̬ɚ/ *noun* [C] a type of computer which is small enough to fit in your hand

ˈpalm (ˌtree) *noun* [C] a tree that grows in hot countries and has a tall trunk with a mass of long pointed leaves at the top: *date palms* ○ *palm **fronds*** ○ *The island has long golden beaches fringed by palm trees.*

palomino (*plural* **palominos**) /ˌpæl.əˈmiː.nəʊ/ [US] /-noʊ/ *noun* [C] (*ALSO* **palamino**) a horse that is golden in colour with a white MANE (= neck hair) and tail

palpable /ˈpæl.pə.bl̩/ *adj* so obvious that it can easily be seen or known, or (of a feeling) so strong that it seems as if it can be touched or physically felt: *a palpable **effect*** ○ *Her joy was palpable.*

palpably /ˈpæl.pə.bli/ *adv*: *The system was palpably* (= very obviously) *unfair.*

palpitate /ˈpæl.pɪ.teɪt/ [US] /-pə-/ *verb* [I] (of the heart) to beat very fast and irregularly: *My heart was palpitating **with** fear.*

palpitations /ˌpæl.pɪˈteɪ.ʃənz/ [US] /-pə-/ *plural noun* **1** when your heart beats too quickly or irregularly: *He ended up in hospital with heart palpitations.* **2** *HUMOROUS* **have palpitations** to be very shocked: *My mother will have palpitations when she sees my new boyfriend.*

paltry /ˈpɔːl.tri/ [US] /ˈpɑːl-/ *adj* **1** (of a sum of money) very small and of little or no value: *Student grants these days are paltry, and many students have to take out loans.* ○ *The company offered Jeremy a paltry **sum** which he refused.* **2** low in quality: *She made some paltry **excuse** and left.*

pampas /ˈpæm.pəs/ *group noun* [S or U] the large flat areas of land covered in grass in parts of South America

ˈpampas ˌgrass *noun* [U] tall grass with silver-coloured flowers

pamper /ˈpæm.pəʳ/ [US] /-pɚ/ *verb* [T] to treat a person or an animal in a special way by making them as comfortable as possible and giving them whatever they want: *She pampers her dog **with** the finest steak and salmon.* ○ *Why not pamper yourself after a hard day **with** a hot bath scented with oils?* **pampered** /ˈpæm.pəd/ [US] /-pɚd/ *adj*: *He was a pampered rich kid who was driven to school in a limousine.*

pamphlet /ˈpæm.flət/ *noun* [C] a thin book with only a few pages which gives information or an opinion about something

pan [CONTAINER] /pæn/ *noun* [C] **1** a metal container that is round and often has a long handle and a lid, used for cooking things on top of a cooker: *Heat the milk in a small pan.* ○ *This dishwasher even washes **pots and pans*** (= different types of pan). **2** *MAINLY US* a metal container used for cooking things inside the cooker

pan [TOILET] /pæn/ *noun* [C] *UK* the bowl-shaped part of a toilet

• **go down the pan** *SLANG* to fail or to be lost or destroyed: *We don't want to see our business go down the pan.*

pan [MOVE SLOWLY] /pæn/ *verb* [I] **-nn-** (of a film camera) to move slowly from one side to another or up and down: *In the first scene, the camera pans slowly **across** the room.*

pan [CRITICIZE] /pæn/ *verb* [T] **-nn-** *INFORMAL* to criticize something severely: *The critics panned the film version of the novel.*

pan- [INCLUDING] /pæn-/ *prefix* including or relating to all the places or people in a particular group: *a pan-American conference* ○ *a pan-European summit* ○ *the Pan-African Congress*

▲ **pan out** *phrasal verb INFORMAL* to develop in a particular way or in a successful way: *We'll have to see how things pan out.* ○ *Their attempt to start a new business didn't pan out.*

panacea /ˌpæn.əˈsiː.ə/ *noun* [C usually sing] **1** *DISAPPROVING* something that will solve all problems: *Technology is not a panacea **for** all our problems.* **2** something that will cure all illnesses

panache /pəˈnæʃ/ *noun* [U] a stylish, original and very confident way of doing things that makes people admire you: *The orchestra played with great panache.* ○ *He dressed with panache.*

panama (hat) /ˌpæn.ə.mɑːˈhæt/ *noun* [C] a man's pale-coloured hat that is made from straw

panatella /ˌpæn.əˈtel.ə/ *noun* [C] a long thin cigar

pancake /ˈpæn.keɪk/ *noun* [C] **1** *UK* (*MAINLY US* **crepe**) a very thin flat round cake made from a mixture of flour, milk and egg, which is fried on both sides: *Do you want a sweet pancake or a savoury one?* **2** *US* a sweet thick round cake made from flour, sugar, milk and eggs, which is cooked in a pan and eaten with MAPLE SYRUP, usually for breakfast: *a **stack** of pancakes*

ˈPancake ˌDay *UK INFORMAL noun* [C usually sing] (*ALSO* **Shrove Tuesday,** *US INFORMAL* **Pancake Tuesday**) the day before LENT (= a religious period in the Christian religion) starts, when pancakes are traditionally eaten

ˌpancake ˈlanding *noun* [C] when an aircraft lands without using its wheels by dropping onto the ground from a low height, because it has a problem and cannot continue to fly

pancreas /ˈpæŋ.kri.əs/ *noun* [C] an organ in the body that produces INSULIN (= a chemical substance that controls the amount of sugar in the blood) and substances which help to digest food so that it can be used by the body

pancreatic /ˌpæŋ.kriˈæt.ɪk/ [US] /-ˈæt̬-/ *adj*: *pancreatic cancer*

panda (*plural* **pandas** or **panda**) /ˈpæn.də/ *noun* [C] (*ALSO* **giant panda**) a large black and white mammal similar to a bear, that lives in forests in China

pandemic /pænˈdem.ɪk/ *adj SPECIALIZED* (of a disease) existing in almost all of an area or in almost all of a group of people, animals or plants: *In some parts of the world malaria is still pandemic.* **pandemic** /pænˈdem.ɪk/ *noun* [C] *a pandemic* ***of*** *influenza* ○ *an influenza pandemic*

pandemonium /ˌpæn.dəˈməʊ.ni.əm/ [US] /-ˈmoʊ-/ *noun* [U] a situation in which there is a lot of noise and confusion because people are excited, angry or frightened: *Pandemonium reigned in the hall as the unbelievable election results were read out.* ○ *the pandemonium of the school playground*

pander /ˈpæn.dəʳ/ [US] /-dɚ/ *verb*

▲ **pander to** ***sb/sth*** *phrasal verb DISAPPROVING* to do or provide exactly what a person or group wants, especially when it is not acceptable, reasonable or approved of, usually in order to get some personal advantage: *It's not good the way she panders to his every whim.* ○ *Political leaders almost inevitably pander to big business.*

Pandora's box /pænˌdɔː.rəzˈbɒks/ [US] /-ˌdɔːr.əzˈbɑːks/ *noun* [S] something which creates a lot of new problems that you did not expect: *Sadly, his reforms* ***opened up*** *a Pandora's box of domestic problems.*

P&P /ˌpiː.ənˈpiː/ *noun* [U] *UK ABBREVIATION FOR* **postage and packing**: *The books cost £12.50 plus P&P.*

pane /peɪn/ *noun* [C] a flat piece of glass, used in a window or door: *a window pane*

panegyric /ˌpæn.əˈdʒɪr.ɪk/ *noun* [C] *FORMAL* a speech or piece of writing that praises someone greatly and does not mention anything bad about them: *She delivered a panegyric* ***on*** *the President-elect.*

panel [TEAM] /ˈpæn.əl/ *group noun* [C] a small group of people chosen to give advice, make a decision, or publicly discuss their opinions as entertainment: *The competition will be judged by a panel* ***of*** *experts.* **panellist** *UK, US* **panelist** /ˈpæn.əl.ɪst/ *noun* [C] *Panellists on the Arts Review Board serve for a maximum of three years.*

panel [PART] /ˈpæn.əl/ *noun* [C] a flat, usually rectangular part, or piece of wood, metal, cloth, etc., that fits into or onto something larger: *a beautiful old door with oak panels* ○ *White silk panels were inset into the sides of the dress.* ○ *At the bottom of each page is a panel with grammatical information.* **panel** /ˈpæn.əl/ *verb* [T] **-ll-** or *US USUALLY* **-l-** *The walls of the dining hall were panelled* ***in*** *oak.* ○ *a panelled room/wall/door* **panelling** *UK, US USUALLY* **paneling** /ˈpæn.əl.ɪŋ/ *noun* [U] *wood panelling*

panel [CONTROL BOARD] /ˈpæn.əl/ *noun* [C] a board or surface which has controls and other devices on it for operating an aircraft or other large machine: *a* ***control/instrument*** *panel*

panettone /ˌpæn.əˈtəʊ.ni/ [US] /-ɪˈtoʊ-/ *noun* [C or U] an Italian Christmas cake containing dried fruit and nuts

pan-fry /ˈpæn.fraɪ/ *verb* [T] to cook food in a pan in a small amount of oil or fat: *pan-fried lobster*

pang /pæŋ/ *noun* [C] a sudden sharp feeling, especially of painful emotion: *a pang* ***of*** *jealousy* ○ *We hadn't eaten since yesterday and the* ***hunger*** *pangs were getting harder to ignore.*

panhandle [AREA] /ˈpænˌhæn.dl̩/ *noun* [C] *US* a long thin piece of land joined to a larger area: *the Texas panhandle*

panhandle [ASK] /ˈpænˌhæn.dl̩/ *verb* [I or T] *US INFORMAL* to ask people that you do not know for money, especially in a public place: *He was arrested for panhandling.* **panhandler** /ˈpænˌhænd.ləʳ/ [US] /-lɚ/ *noun* [C] *US*

panic /ˈpæn.ɪk/ *noun* [C usually sing; U] a sudden strong feeling of anxiety or fear that prevents reasonable thought and action: *a state of panic* ○ *Panic* ***spread*** *through the crowd as the bullets started to fly.* ○ *Carmel was* ***in*** *a panic about her exam.* ○ *He* ***got in(to)*** *a panic that he would forget his lines on stage.*

panic /ˈpæn.ɪk/ *verb* [I or T] **panicking, panicked, panicked** to suddenly feel so worried or frightened that you cannot think or behave calmly or reasonably: *Don't panic! Everything will be okay.* ○ *The sound of gunfire panicked the crowd.* ○ *The boss always panics* ***over/about*** *the budget every month.* **panicky** /ˈpæn.ɪ.ki/ *adj INFORMAL a panicky feeling/expression/action* ○ *Is he the panicky type?*

ˈpanic atˌtack *noun* [C] a sudden period of severe anxiety in which your heart beats fast, you have trouble breathing and you feel as if something very bad is going to happen

ˈpanic ˌbutton *noun* [C usually sing] a device, usually a button, that is used to call for help by someone in a dangerous situation

• **hit/press/push the panic button** to do something quickly without thinking about it in order to deal with a difficult or worrying situation

ˈpanic ˌbuying *noun* [U] when many people suddenly buy as much food, fuel, etc. as they can because they are frightened about something bad such as a war that is going to happen soon: *The government admitted that there was a petrol shortage, but warned people against panic buying.*

ˈpanic ˌselling *noun* [U] when many people suddenly start to sell company shares that they own, because their value is being reduced

ˈpanic ˌstations *plural noun UK INFORMAL* a situation in which people feel anxious because things need to be done quickly: *Two weeks before an exam it's always panic stations as I realise how much I still have to do.*

panic-stricken /ˈpæn.ɪkˌstrɪk.ən/ *adj* very frightened and anxious about a situation, and therefore unable to think clearly or act reasonably: *The streets were full of panic-stricken people trying to escape the tear gas.*

pannier /ˈpæn.i.əʳ/ [US] /-jɚ/ *noun* [C] a bag or similar container, especially one of a pair that hang on either side of a bicycle, motorcycle, or animal such as a horse or donkey

panoply /ˈpæn.ə.pli/ *noun* [U] *FORMAL* a wide range or collection of different things: *There is a whole panoply* ***of*** *remedies and drugs available to the modern doctor.*

panorama /ˌpæn.ərˈɑː.mə/ [US] /-əˈræm.ə/ *noun* [C] **1** a view of a wide area: *From the hotel roof you can enjoy a panorama of the whole city.* **2** a view, description or study of events or activities: *The investigation revealed a panorama of corruption and illegal dealings.* **panoramic** /ˌpæn.ərˈæm.ɪk/ [US] /-əˈræm-/ *adj*: *a wonderful panoramic* ***view*** *of the countryside*

panpipes /ˈpæn.paɪps/ *plural noun* a musical instrument made of short tubes of different lengths joined together, which you play by blowing across the open ends

ˈpan ˌscourer *noun* [C] a **scourer** ➲See at **scour** CLEAN.

pansy [PLANT] /ˈpæn.zi/ *noun* [C] a small garden plant with flowers of many different colours which have rounded petals ➲See picture **Flowers and Plants** on page Centre 3

pansy [PERSON] /ˈpæn.zi/ *noun* [C] *OFFENSIVE OLD-FASHIONED* a man who behaves in a way that is considered to be more typical of a woman

pant /pænt/ *verb* [I] to breathe quickly and loudly through your mouth, usually because you have been doing something very energetic: *Matteo arrived at the top of the hill, panting and covered in sweat.* ○ [+ speech] *"Hurry! They're almost here," she panted* (= said while panting).

▲ **pant for/after** ***sb/sth*** *phrasal verb UK* to want someone or something very much: *The newspapers are panting for details of the scandal.*

pantheism /ˈpænt.θi.ɪ.zəm/ *noun* [U] belief in many or all gods, or the belief that God exists in and is the same as all things, animals and people within the universe **pantheist** /ˈpænt.θi.ɪst/ *noun* [C], *adj* **pantheistic** /ˌpænt.θiˈɪs.tɪk/ *adj* (*ALSO* **pantheist**)

pantheon /ˈpænt.θi.ən/ [US] /-ɑːn/ *noun* [C usually sing] *FORMAL* a small group of people who are the most famous, important and admired in their particular area of activity: *Don't you agree that Malcolm X definitely has a place in* ***the*** *pantheon* ***of*** *black civil rights heroes?*

panther /ˈpænt.θəʳ/ [US] /-θɚ/ *noun* [C] *plural* **panthers** or **panther** a black LEOPARD (= large wild cat)

P

panties /ˈpæn.tiz/ ⓤ /-ţiz/ *plural noun* (*UK ALSO* **pants**) women's and girls' UNDERPANTS ⊃See picture **Clothes** on page Centre 6

pantomime /ˈpæn.tə.maɪm/ ⓤ /-ţə-/ *noun* **1** [C] (*UK INFORMAL* **panto**) (in Britain) an amusing musical play based on traditional children's stories, performed especially at Christmas **2** [C or U] **mime**: *It's an evening of music, drama and pantomime.*

,**pantomime 'horse** *noun* [C] *UK* two people pretending humorously to be a horse by dressing in special clothes and standing one behind the other so that the front person appears as the horse's front half and the person behind forms the back part

pantry /ˈpæn.tri/ *noun* [C] a small room or large cupboard in a house where food is kept

pants [CLOTHES] /pænts/ *plural noun* **1** *UK* **underpants** ⊃See picture **Clothes** on page Centre 6 **2** *US FOR* trousers: *a pair of pants*
• **wet** *your* **pants** to urinate in your clothes: *Tilly had wet her pants so I was looking for somewhere to change her.*
• **piss/shit** *your* **pants** OFFENSIVE to suddenly feel very frightened: *I shit my pants when all the lights went out.*
• **beat/bore/scare, etc. the pants off** *sb* INFORMAL to defeat/bore/frighten, etc. someone completely: *Sunbathing bores the pants off me.*

pants [BAD] /pænts/ *adj* [after v] *UK SLANG* worthless, useless or of bad quality: *This music is pants.*

pantsuit /ˈpænt.sjuːt/ ⓤ /-suːt/ *noun* [C] *US FOR* **trouser suit**

pantyhose /ˈpæn.ti.həʊz/ ⓤ /-ţi.hoʊz/ *plural noun* *US FOR* tights ⊃See picture **Clothes** on page Centre 6

panty liner /ˈpæn.ti,laɪ.nəʳ/ ⓤ /-ţi,laɪ.nɚ/ *noun* [C] a small length of absorbent material which can be stuck to the inside of a woman's underpants

pap [FOOD] /pæp/ *noun* [U] *INFORMAL DISAPPROVING* food which is soft and has little taste
pappy /ˈpæp.i/ *adj* describes food that is unpleasantly soft or watery: *pappy pasta*

pap [ENTERTAINMENT] /pæp/ *noun* [U] *INFORMAL DISAPPROVING* television, cinema or literature which is entertaining, but has no artistic or educational value **pappy** /ˈpæp.i/ *adj*: *It's just another pappy novel.*

papa /pəˈpɑː/ ⓤ /ˈpɑː.pə/ *noun* [C] *UK OLD-FASHIONED FORMAL OR US INFORMAL* father: [as form of address] *"Why is the sky blue, Papa?" she asked.*

the papacy /ðəˈpeɪ.pə.si/ *noun* [S] the position or authority of the pope, or the length of time that a particular person is pope

papal /ˈpeɪ.pᵊl/ *adj* connected with the position or authority of the pope: *a papal messenger/ announcement/election*

paparazzi /ˌpæp.ᵊrˈæt.si/ ⓤ /ˌpɑː.pɑːˈrɑːt.si/ *plural noun* the photographers who follow famous people everywhere they go in order to take photographs of them for newspapers and magazines

papaya /pəˈpaɪ.ə/ *noun* [C or U] (*ALSO* **pawpaw**) a large oval fruit with a yellowish skin and sweet orange flesh, or the tropical tree on which this grows

paper /ˈpeɪ.pəʳ/ ⓤ /-pɚ/ *noun* **1** [U] thin flat material which is made from crushed wood or cloth and is used for writing, printing or drawing on: *a piece/sheet of paper* ○ *a pack of* **writing** *paper* ○ *Dictionaries are usually printed on thin paper.* ○ *a paper bag* ○ *This card is printed on* **recycled** *paper* (= paper made from used paper). ○ *Get the idea* **down** *on paper* (= write it) *before you forget it.* ○ *She works* **on** *paper* (= writes things on paper) *because she hates computers.* **2** [C] a newspaper: *a daily/weekly/local/national paper* ○ *The photo was on the front page of all the papers.* **3** [C] *UK* a set of printed questions in an exam: *Candidates must answer two questions from each paper.* ○ *The geography paper is not till next week.* **4** [C] a piece of writing on a particular subject written by an expert and usually published in a book or JOURNAL, or read aloud to other people: *He's giving a paper* **on** *thermodynamics at a conference at Manchester University.* **5** [C] *US FOR* **essay** WRITING: *Mr Jones thought my history paper was terrific.*

• *sb* **couldn't act/argue/fight, etc.** *their* **way out of a paper bag** HUMOROUS said about someone you think has no energy or ability
• **on paper** refers to a quality that an idea, plan or person, etc. seems to have when you read about them, but which might not show the real or complete situation: *The design certainly* **looks good** *on paper.* ○ *Several candidates seemed suitable on paper but failed the interview.*

paper /ˈpeɪ.pəʳ/ ⓤ /-pɚ/ *verb* [T] to cover a wall, room, etc. with wallpaper

papers /ˈpeɪ.pəz/ ⓤ /-pɚz/ *plural noun* official documents, especially ones that show who you are: *The border guards stopped me and asked to see my papers.*

papery /ˈpeɪ.pᵊr.i/ ⓤ /-pɚ.i/ *adj* thin and dry like paper: *The skin on his hands was wrinkled and papery.*

▲ **paper over** *sth phrasal verb* to hide an unpleasant situation, especially a problem or disagreement, in order to make people believe that it does not exist or is not serious: *He tried to paper over the country's deepseated problems.*
• **paper over the cracks** to hide problems, especially arguments between people, in order to make a situation seem better than it really is: *She tried to paper over the cracks, but I could see that the relationship was failing.*

paperback /ˈpeɪ.pə.bæk/ ⓤ /-pɚ-/ *noun* [C] a book with a cover made of thin card: *a best-selling paperback* ○ *I'll buy some paperbacks at the airport.* ○ *It will be published* **in** *paperback* (= as a paperback) *in March.* ⊃Compare **hardback**; **softback**.

paperbark /ˈpeɪ.pə.bɑːk/ ⓤ /-pɚ.bɑːrk/ *noun* [C] an Australian tree with thin BARK that can be removed in large pieces

'**paper ,clip** *noun* [C] a small piece of bent wire used for holding pieces of paper together

'**paper ,knife** *UK noun* [C] (*US* **letter opener**) a knife for opening envelopes that is not sharp and is often decorative

,**paper 'money** *noun* [U] money in paper form, rather than coins

,**paper 'profit** *noun* [C or U] a profit that is shown in financial records but which has not yet been made by a company, especially because it is waiting for payments it is owed: *The company made a paper profit last year, but they still got rid of six employees.*

'**paper ,round** *UK noun* [C] (*US* **paper route**) the job, usually done by children, of delivering newspapers to people's homes

'**paper ,shop** *noun* [C] *UK* a shop which sells newspapers

,**paper 'thin** *adj* very thin: *paper thin layers of pastry* ○ FIGURATIVE *The walls were paper thin and I could hear everything!*

,**paper 'tiger** *noun* [C] DISAPPROVING something, such as an enemy or foreign country, which seems very strong and very dangerous, but which is really weak and harmless: *The Soviet Union was suddenly revealed as a paper tiger.*

,**paper 'towel** *noun* [C] a sheet of soft thick paper used for drying your hands, cleaning objects, removing liquids, etc.

'**paper ,trail** *noun* [C usually sing] MAINLY US a series of documents that show a record of your activities

paperweight /ˈpeɪ.pə.weɪt/ ⓤ /-pɚ-/ *noun* [C] a small heavy object which is put on top of pieces of paper to keep them in position

paperwork /ˈpeɪ.pə.wɜːk/ ⓤ /-pɚ.wɜːrk/ *noun* [U] **1** the part of a job which involves writing letters and reports and keeping records **2** the written records connected with a particular job, deal, journey, etc: *I've kept all the paperwork for the car.*

papier-mâché /ˌpæp.i.eɪˈmæʃ.eɪ/ ⓤ /ˌ----'-/ *noun* [U] pieces of paper mixed with glue or with flour and water and used to make decorative objects or models **papier-mâché** /ˌpæp.i.eɪˈmæʃ.eɪ/ ⓤ /ˌ----'-/ *adj*: *a papier-mâché mask*

papist /ˈpeɪ.pɪst/ *noun* [C] OFFENSIVE a Roman Catholic **papist** /ˈpeɪ.pɪst/ *adj*

papoose /pə'puːs/ ⓤ /pæp'uːs/ *noun* [C] OLD-FASHIONED a NATIVE AMERICAN baby or small child

pappy /'pæp.i/ *adj* ➲See at **pap** ENTERTAINMENT.

paprika /'pæp.rɪ.kə/ /pə'priː-/ *noun* [U] a red powder used as a spice to give a slightly hot flavour to food, especially in meat dishes

'**Pap ,smear** *noun* [C] US FOR **smear (test)**

papyrus /pə'paɪə.rəs/ ⓤ /-'paɪ-/ *noun* [C or U] *plural* **papyruses** or **papyri** a tall grass-like plant that grows in or near water, especially in North Africa, or paper made from this plant, especially by ancient Egyptians

par EQUAL /pɑːʳ/ ⓤ /pɑːr/ *noun* **on a par (with** *sb/sth*) the same as or equal to someone or something: *The regeneration of the city's downtown dock front will put it on a par with Nice or Cannes.*

par STANDARD /pɑːʳ/ ⓤ /pɑːr/ *noun* [U] **1** the usual standard or condition **2** the expected number of times in golf that a good player should have to hit the ball in order to get it into a hole or into all the holes: *Tiger Woods finished the round 10 **below/under** par.* **3** SPECIALIZED **par (value)** the original value of a share in a business
• **below/under par 1** ill: *Are you **feeling** a bit under par?* **2** worse than the usual or expected standard
• **be up to par** to be of the usual or expected standard: *Her work hasn't been up to par lately.*
• **be par for the course** DISAPPROVING If a type of behaviour, event or situation is par for the course, it is not good but it is normal or as you would expect: *The school budget is going to be cut again this year, but then that's par for the course.*

para- BEYOND /pær.ə-/ ⓤ /per.ə-/ *prefix* beyond: *Parapsychology is the study of abilities that go beyond what is natural and normal.* ○ *paranormal phenomena*

para- SIMILAR /pær.ə-/ ⓤ /per.ə-/ *prefix* similar to, or helping to do a similar job: *a paramedic* ○ *paramilitary*

para SOLDIER /'pær.ə/ ⓤ /'per.ə/ *noun* [C] MAINLY UK INFORMAL FOR **paratrooper**

para TEXT /'pær.ə/ ⓤ /'per.ə/ *noun* [C] ABBREVIATION FOR **paragraph**: *Paras 5 and 6 will have to be rewritten.*

parable /'pær.ə.bl̩/ ⓤ /'per-/ *noun* [C] a short simple story which teaches or explains an idea, especially a moral or religious idea

parabola /pə'ræb.ᵊl.ə/ *noun* [C] SPECIALIZED a type of curve such as that made by an object that is thrown up in the air and falls to the ground in a different place **parabolic** /,pær.ə'bɒl.ɪk/ ⓤ /,per.ə'baː.lɪk/ *adj*: *a parabolic curve/trajectory*

paracetamol UK /,pær.ə'siː.tə.mɒl/ ⓤ /,per.ə'siː.tə.maːl/ *noun* [C or U] (US **acetaminophen**) a drug used to reduce pain

parachute /'pær.ə.ʃuːt/ ⓤ /'per-/ *noun* [C] a piece of equipment made of a large piece of special cloth which is fastened to someone or something that is dropped from an aircraft, in order to make them fall slowly and safely to the ground
parachute /'pær.ə.ʃuːt/ ⓤ /'per-/ *verb* **1** [I usually + adv or prep] to jump from an aircraft using a parachute: *The plan is to parachute into the town.* **2** [T usually + adv or prep] to drop someone or something from an aircraft by parachute: [often passive] *Thousands of leaflets were parachuted behind enemy lines.*

parachutist /'pær.ə.ʃuː.tɪst/ ⓤ /'per.ə.ʃuː.t̬ɪst/ *noun* [C] someone who jumps out of an aircraft wearing a parachute on their back, especially as a sport or a military job

parade /pə'reɪd/ *noun* [C] **1** a large number of people walking or in vehicles, all going in the same direction, usually as part of a public celebration of something: *a victory parade* **2** a series of people or things that appear one after the other: *For three hours a committee of state senators listened to a parade of local residents giving their opinions.* **3** UK a row of shops **4** UK **Parade** used in the names of some roads: *It's a small road off Park Parade.*
• **on parade** When soldiers are on parade they march and practise military movements in front of important officials or as part of a public celebration or ceremony: *The entire regiment was on parade.*

parade /pə'reɪd/ *verb* **1** [I or T usually + adv or prep] (of a group) to walk or march somewhere, usually as part of a public celebration: *The Saint Patrick's Day marchers paraded up Fifth Avenue, past the cathedral.* ○ *In ancient Rome, captured generals were paraded through the streets in chairs.* **2** [I or T] to show something in an obvious way in order to be admired: *It's sickening the way he parades his wealth, his car and his expensive clothes.* ○ *The children paraded **about/around** in their new clothes.*

pa'rade ,ground *noun* [C usually sing] a large flat area where soldiers march and practise military movements

paradigm /'pær.ə.daɪm/ ⓤ /'per-/ *noun* [C] FORMAL a model of something, or a very clear and typical example of something: *Some of these educators are hoping to produce a change in the current cultural paradigm.* **paradigmatic** /,pær.ə.dɪg'mæt.ɪk/ ⓤ /,per.ə.dɪg'mæt̬-/ *adj*

'**paradigm ,shift** *noun* [C] FORMAL when the usual and accepted way of doing or thinking about something is changed

paradise /'pær.ə.daɪs/ ⓤ /'per-/ *noun* [C usually sing; U] **1** a place or condition of great happiness where everything is exactly as you would like it to be: *a tropical paradise* ○ *His idea of paradise is to spend the day lying on the beach.* ○ *This mall is a shopper's paradise.* **2 Paradise** Heaven: *They believe they'll go to Paradise after they die.* **3 Paradise** the GARDEN OF EDEN (= the place where Adam and Eve lived, in the Bible story)

paradox /'pær.ə.dɒks/ ⓤ /'per.ə.daːks/ *noun* [C or U] a situation or statement which seems impossible or is difficult to understand because it contains two opposite facts or characteristics: [+ that] *It's a curious paradox that drinking a lot of water can often make you feel thirsty.* **paradoxical** /,pær.ə'dɒk.sɪ.kᵊl/ ⓤ /,per.ə'daːk-/ *adj*: *It seems paradoxical to me, but if you drink a cup of hot tea it seems to cool you down.* **paradoxically** /,pær.ə'dɒk.sɪ.kli/ ⓤ /,per.ə'daːk-/ *adv*

paraffin UK /'pær.ə.fɪn/ ⓤ /'per-/ *noun* [U] (US **kerosene**) a clear liquid with a strong smell made from coal or PETROLEUM and used as a fuel, especially in heaters and lights

,**paraffin ('wax)** *noun* [U] a white wax made from PETROLEUM or coal, used especially to make candles

paragliding /'pær.ə,glaɪ.dɪŋ/ ⓤ /'per-/ *noun* [U] the sport of jumping out of an aircraft with a special parachute that allows you to travel a long horizontal distance before you land

paragon /'pær.ə.gən/ ⓤ /'per.ə.gaːn/ *noun* [C] a person or thing that is perfect or has an unusually large amount of a particular good characteristic: *In the novel, Constanza is a paragon **of** virtue who would never compromise her reputation.*

paragraph /'pær.ə.grɑːf/ ⓤ /'per.ə.græf/ *noun* [C] (WRITTEN ABBREVIATION **para**) a short part of a text, consisting of at least one sentence and beginning on a new line. It usually deals with a single event, description, idea, etc.

parakeet /,pær.ə'kiːt/ /'---/ ⓤ /'per.ə.kiːt/ *noun* [C] a small parrot with a long tail

parallel POSITION /'pær.ə.lel/ ⓤ /'per-/ *adj* If two or more lines, streets, etc. are parallel, the distance between them is the same all along their length: *Draw a pair of parallel lines.* ○ *Hills Road is parallel **to** Mill Road.*
parallel /'pær.ə.lel/ ⓤ /'per-/ *noun* **1 parallel (line)** a line that is always at the same distance from another line **2** one of a number of imaginary lines around the Earth always at the same distance from the equator: *Cambridge lies near the 52nd parallel.*
• **in parallel** SPECIALIZED If two or more parts of an electrical system are in parallel, they are arranged in a way that means they both receive the same amount of electricity.
parallel /'pær.ə.lel/ ⓤ /'per-/ *adv*: *It's a quiet street running* (= positioned) *parallel **to** the main road.*

parallel SIMILARITY /'pær.ə.lel/ ⓤ /'per-/ *noun* [C] something very similar to something else, or a similarity between two things: *I'm trying to see if there are any obvious parallels **between** the two cases.* ○ *It would be*

easy to ***draw*** (= make) *a parallel* ***between*** *the town's history and that of its football club.*
• **have no parallel** (*ALSO* **be without parallel**) If something has no parallel or is without parallel, there is nothing similar to it or of the same high quality as it: *These beautiful African churches have no parallel in Europe.*
parallel /ˈpær.ə.lel/ [US] /ˈper-/ *adj* describes an event or situation that happens at the same time as and/or is similar to another one: *a parallel example* ○ *Parallel experiments are being conducted in Rome, Paris and London.*
parallel /ˈpær.ə.lel/ [US] /ˈper-/ *verb* [T] to happen at the same time as something else, or be similar or equal to something else: *The events of the last ten days in some ways parallel those before the 1978 election.* ➲Compare **unparalleled**.

the ˌparallel ˈbars *plural noun* a piece of equipment used in GYMNASTICS, consisting of two horizontal bars fastened to four poles and used for exercising and competing

parallelogram /ˌpær.əˈlel.ə.græm/ [US] /ˌper-/ *noun* [C] *SPECIALIZED* a flat shape which has four sides. The two sets of opposite sides are parallel and of equal length to each other.

ˌparallel ˈparking *noun* [U] when you park vehicles along or parallel to the side of the road, rather than facing into the side of the road

ˌparallel ˈprocessing *noun* [U] *SPECIALIZED* when a computer does two or more pieces of work at the same time

paralyse *UK, US* **paralyze** /ˈpær.ᵊl.aɪz/ [US] /ˈper-/ *verb* [T] **1** to cause a person, animal or part of the body to lose the ability to move or feel: *The drug paralyses the nerves so that there is no feeling or movement in the legs.* **2** to cause a person, group or organization to stop working or acting normally: *A sudden snowstorm paralysed the city.*
paralysed *UK, US* **paralyzed** /ˈpær.ᵊl.aɪzd/ [US] /ˈper-/ *adj* unable to move or act: *The accident left her paralysed* ***from*** *the waist down.* ○ *The government seems paralysed* ***by/with*** *indecision.* ○ *She was paralysed* ***with*** *fear.*
paralysis /pəˈræl.ə.sɪs/ *noun* [C or U] *plural* **paralyses** **1** when you are unable to move all or part of your body because of illness or injury: *Some nervous disorders can produce paralysis.* **2** when you are unable to take action: *political paralysis*
paralytic /ˌpær.əˈlɪt.ɪk/ [US] /ˌper.əˈlɪţ-/ *adj* **1** *UK INFORMAL* extremely drunk **2** related to or connected with paralysis: *a paralytic illness*

paramedic /ˌpær.əˈmed.ɪk/ [US] /ˌper.əˈmed-/ *noun* [C] a person who is trained to do medical work, especially in an emergency, but who is not a doctor or nurse

parameter /pəˈræm.ɪ.təʳ/ [US] /-ə.ţɚ/ *noun* [C usually pl] a set of facts or a fixed limit which establishes or limits how something can or must happen or be done: *The researchers must keep within the parameters of the experiment.* ○ *The central office sets/establishes the parameters which guide policy at the local level.*

paramilitary /ˌpær.əˈmɪl.ɪ.tri/ [US] /ˌper.əˈmɪl.ə.ter.i/ *adj* **1** describes a group which is organized like an army but is not official and often not legal **2** connected with and helping the official armed forces: *In some countries, police and fire officers have paramilitary training.*
paramilitary /ˌpær.əˈmɪl.ɪ.tri/ [US] /ˌper.əˈmɪl.ə.ter.i/ *noun* [C] a person who belongs to a paramilitary organization

paramount /ˈpær.ə.maʊnt/ [US] /ˈper-/ *adj FORMAL* more important than anything else: *There are many priorities, but reducing the budget deficit is paramount/is* ***of*** *paramount* ***importance***.

paramour /ˈpær.ə.mɔːʳ/ [US] /ˈper.ə.mʊr/ *noun* [C] *OLD USE OR LITERARY* a lover

paranoia /ˌpær.əˈnɔɪ.ə/ [US] /ˌper-/ *noun* **1** [C or U] an extreme and unreasonable feeling that other people do not like you or are going to harm or criticize you: *There's a lot of paranoia* ***about*** *crime at the moment.* **2** [U] *SPECIALIZED* Someone who has paranoia has unreasonable false beliefs as a part of another mental illness, for example SCHIZOPHRENIA.
paranoid /ˈpær.ᵊn.ɔɪd/ [US] /ˈper.ə.nɔɪd/ *adj* **1** feeling extremely anxious and worried because you believe that other people do not like you or are trying to harm you: *He started feeling paranoid and was convinced his boss was going to fire him.* **2** *SPECIALIZED* suffering from a mental illness in which you believe that other people are trying to harm you: *He was diagnosed as a paranoid* ***schizophrenic***. ○ *paranoid delusions*
paranoiac /ˌpær.əˈnɔɪ.æk/ [US] /ˌper-/ *noun* [C] someone who is paranoid

paranormal /ˌpær.əˈnɔː.məl/ [US] /ˌper.əˈnɔːr-/ *adj* impossible to explain by known natural forces or by science: *paranormal powers/events/forces* ○ *This book is about people who claim to have paranormal abilities such as ESP and mind-reading.*
the paranormal *noun* [S] all the things that are impossible to explain by known natural forces or by science: *investigations into the paranormal*

parapet /ˈpær.ə.pet/ [US] /ˈper-/ *noun* [C] a low wall along the edge of a roof, bridge, etc.
• **put *your* head over/above the parapet** *UK* to be brave enough to state an opinion that might upset someone

paraphernalia /ˌpær.ə.fəˈneɪ.li.ə/ [US] /ˌper.ə.fɚˈneɪl.jə/ *noun* [U] all the objects needed for or connected with a particular activity: *We sell pots, gloves, seeds and other gardening paraphernalia.* ○ *Bags of cocaine and all sorts of drug paraphernalia were seized at the airport.*

paraphrase /ˈpær.ə.freɪz/ [US] /ˈper-/ *verb* [I or T] to repeat something written or spoken using different words, often in a humorous form or in a simpler and shorter form that makes the original meaning clearer **paraphrase** /ˈpær.ə.freɪz/ [US] /ˈper-/ *noun* [C] *She gave us a quick paraphrase* ***of*** *what had been said.*

paraplegia /ˌpær.əˈpliː.dʒə/ [US] /ˌper-/ *noun* [U] *SPECIALIZED* loss of the ability to move or feel in the legs and lower part of the body, usually because of a severe injury to the spine (= bones in the centre of the back) **paraplegic** /ˌpær.əˈpliː.dʒɪk/ [US] /ˌper-/ *adj, noun* [C] *Is he paraplegic?* ○ *She does a lot of work with paraplegics.*

parapsychology /ˌpær.ə.saɪˈkɒl.ə.dʒi/ [US] /ˌper.ə.saɪˈkɑː.lə-/ *noun* [U] the study of mental abilities, such as knowing the future or TELEPATHY, which seem to go against or be beyond the known laws of nature and science

Paraquat /ˈpær.ə.kwɒt/ [US] /ˈper.ə.kwɑːt/ *noun* [U] *TRADEMARK* a very strong liquid poison used to kill unwanted plants

parasailing /ˈpær.əˌseɪ.lɪŋ/ [US] /ˈper-/ *noun* [U] a sport in which you wear a PARACHUTE and are pulled behind a motor boat in order to sail through the air

parascending /ˈpær.əˌsen.dɪŋ/ [US] /ˈper-/ *noun* [U] a sport in which you wear a parachute and you are connected by a long rope to a car or boat which pulls you up into the air as it moves forward on the ground or on water

parasite /ˈpær.ə.saɪt/ [US] /ˈper-/ *noun* [C] **1** an animal or plant that lives on or in another animal or plant of a different type and feeds from it: *The older drugs didn't deal effectively with the malaria parasite.* **2** *DISAPPROVING* a person who is useless and lives by other people's work: *Financial speculators are parasites* ***upon*** *the national economy.*
parasitic /ˌpær.əˈsɪt.ɪk/ [US] /ˌper.əˈsɪţ-/ *adj* (*ALSO* **parasitical**) caused by or connected with a parasite: *a parasitic disease* ○ *parasitic insects* **parasitism** /ˈpær.ə.saɪ.tɪ.zᵊm/ *noun* [U]

parasol /ˈpær.ə.sɒl/ [US] /ˈper.ə.sɑːl/ *noun* [C] a type of SUNSHADE (= round cloth-covered frame on a stick) carried especially by women in the past, to give protection from the sun

parathyroid (gland) /ˌpær.əˈθaɪə.rɔɪdˌglænd/ [US] /ˌper.əˈθaɪ-/ *noun* [C] *SPECIALIZED* any of four GLANDS (= small organs in the body) that control the amount of the chemicals CALCIUM and PHOSPHORUS in the body

paratroops /ˈpær.ə.truːps/ [US] /ˈper-/ *plural noun* (*UK INFORMAL* **paras**) (a military unit of) soldiers trained to be dropped from an aircraft with a parachute **paratrooper** /ˈpær.əˌtruː.pəʳ/ [US] /ˈper.əˌtruː.pɚ/ *noun* [C] (*UK INFORMAL* **para**) *Paratroopers were dropped behind enemy lines to capture key points on the roads into the city.*

P

parboil /ˈpɑː.bɔɪl/ [US] /ˈpɑːr-/ *verb* [T] to boil food for a short time until it is partly cooked

parcel /ˈpɑː.səl/ [US] /ˈpɑːr-/ *noun* [C] **1** *MAINLY UK* (*MAINLY US* **package**) an object or collection of objects wrapped in paper, especially so that it can be sent by post: *a food parcel* ○ *The parcel was wrapped in plain brown paper.* **2** *MAINLY US SPECIALIZED* an area of land: *a 60-acre parcel*

parcel /ˈpɑː.səl/ [US] /ˈpɑːr-/ *verb* -ll- or *US USUALLY* -l-

PHRASAL VERBS WITH **parcel**

▲ **parcel *sth* out** *phrasal verb* [M often passive] to divide something and give the separate parts to different people: *The bigger farms were parcelled out after the revolution in 1973.* ○ *She parcelled out the gifts* ***to*** *the other children.*

▲ **parcel *sth* up** *phrasal verb* [M] *MAINLY UK* to wrap something and make it into a parcel: *Parcel up the tins and we'll send them off tomorrow.*

ˈparcel ˌbomb *noun* [C] *UK* a bomb wrapped up as a parcel and sent by post

ˈparcel ˌpost *noun* [U] the system in which parcels are sent by post: *The cheapest way to send it would be by parcel post.*

parched /pɑːtʃt/ [US] /pɑːrtʃt/ *adj* **1** (especially of earth or crops) dried out because of too much heat and not enough rain: *parched earth/fields/corn* ○ *It was the height of summer and the land was parched and brown.* **2** *INFORMAL* extremely thirsty: *I must get a drink – I'm absolutely parched!*

parchment /ˈpɑːtʃ.mənt/ [US] /ˈpɑːrtʃ-/ *noun* **1** [U] the thin dried skin of some animals which was used in the past for writing on, or a high quality paper made to look like this, or a document written on either of these materials: *ancient parchment* ○ *He'd been ill for a long time, and his skin was like parchment.* **2** [C] a document written on parchment: *A framed parchment hung on the wall.*

pardner /ˈpɑːd.nər/ [US] /ˈpɑːrd.nɚ/ *noun* [C] *US HUMOROUS* used as an informal form of address, usually between men: ***Howdy*** *pardner!*

pardon /ˈpɑː.dən/ [US] /ˈpɑːr-/ *verb* [T] **1** to forgive someone for something they have said or done. This word is often used in polite expressions: *Pardon my ignorance, but what exactly is ergonomics?* ○ [+ v-ing] *Pardon me interrupting, but there's a client to see you.* **2** If someone who has committed a crime is pardoned, they are officially forgiven and their punishment is stopped: *Large numbers of political prisoners have been pardoned and released by the new president.*

• **if you'll pardon the expression** said before or after using language which other people might consider shocking: *The man doesn't know his arse from his elbow, if you'll pardon the expression.*

pardon /ˈpɑː.dən/ [US] /ˈpɑːr-/ *noun* [C] when someone who has committed a crime is officially forgiven: *He had actively sought a pardon from the president.*

pardon /ˈpɑː.dən/ [US] /ˈpɑːr-/ *exclamation* **1** (*US ALSO* **pardon me**) used to politely ask someone to repeat something they have said because you have not heard it ➲See also **I beg your pardon** at **beg**. **2** (*US ALSO* **pardon me**, *FORMAL OR HUMOROUS* **I beg your pardon**) used to show that someone has said something that offends you: *"Women tend to make fairly useless drivers, anyway." "I beg your pardon!"*

• **pardon (me)** (*FORMAL* **I beg your pardon**) used to say that you are sorry for doing something wrong or for being rude

• **Pardon me for breathing/existing/living!** *INFORMAL* used to tell someone that you think they have just answered or spoken to you in an unreasonably critical or rude way: *"If you're going to get in my way, James, could you just leave the kitchen?" "Oh, pardon me for breathing!"*

pardonable /ˈpɑː.dən.ə.bl/ [US] /ˈpɑːr-/ *adj* able to be forgiven: *a pardonable mistake* **pardonably** /ˈpɑː.dən.ə.bli/ [US] /ˈpɑːr-/ *adv*

pare /peər/ [US] /per/ *verb* [T often + adv or prep] **1** to cut away the outer layer from something, especially a fruit or a vegetable: *He was busy paring apples in the kitchen.* ○ *Pare* ***off*** *any bits of the carrots that don't look very nice.* **2** to reduce something, especially by a large amount: *The three-hour play has been pared* ***(down)*** *to two hours.*

• **pare *sth* (down) to the bone** to reduce something to a level at which only what is necessary is left

paring /ˈpeə.rɪŋ/ [US] /ˈper.ɪŋ/ *noun* [C usually pl] a thin piece that has been cut away from something: *We feed most of our vegetable parings to the guinea pigs.*

parent /ˈpeə.rənt/ [US] /ˈper.ənt/ *noun* [C] a mother or father of a person or an animal: *I'm going to meet Richard's parents for the first time this weekend.*

parentage /ˈpeə.rən.tɪdʒ/ [US] /ˈper.ən.t̬ɪdʒ/ *noun* [U] When you refer to a person's parentage, you mean their parents and/or their parent's country and social class: *The novel starts when a child of unknown parentage is left at the house of the local priest.* ○ *She is of mixed Australian and Japanese parentage.*

parental /pəˈren.təl/ [US] /-t̬əl/ *adj* connected with parents or with being a parent: *parental advice/influence* ○ *The government repeatedly stressed its support for parental* ***choice*** *in the selection of a child's school.*

parenthood /ˈpeə.rənt.hʊd/ [US] /ˈper.ənt-/ *noun* [U] the state of being a parent: *The prospect of parenthood filled her with horror.*

parenting /ˈpeə.rən.tɪŋ/ [US] /ˈper.ən.t̬ɪŋ/ *noun* [U] the raising of children and all the responsibilities and activities that are involved in it

paˌrental ˈleave *noun* [U] time that a parent is allowed to spend away from work to look after their baby

ˌparent ˈcompany *noun* [C] a company which controls other smaller companies

parentheses *MAINLY US* /pəˈrent.θə.siːz/ *plural noun* (*UK USUALLY* **(round) brackets**) the ( ) punctuation marks that are put around a word, phrase or sentence in a piece of writing to show that what is inside them should be considered as separate from the main part: *The students' first names are shown* ***in*** *parentheses.*

parenthesis /pəˈrent.θə.sɪs/ *noun* [C] *plural* **parentheses** **1** a remark which is added to a sentence, often to provide an explanation or additional information, and which is separated from the main part of the sentence by commas, **brackets** SYMBOL or **dashes**: *The sentence 'Her youngest sister – the one who lives in Australia – is coming over next summer' contains a parenthesis.* **2 in parenthesis** If, while you are talking, you say something in parenthesis, you say it as an addition and then continue with the main part of the sentence: *Of his origins he said very little, merely mentioning in parenthesis that his background was poor.*

parenthetical /ˌpær.ənˈθet.ɪ.kəl/ [US] /ˌper.ənˈθet̬-/ *adj* (*ALSO* **parenthetic**) *FORMAL* describes a remark which is said in addition to the main part of what you are saying **parenthetically** /ˌpær.ənˈθet.ɪ.kli/ [US] /ˌper.ənˈθet̬-/ *adv*

parent-teacher association /ˌpeə.rənt-ˈtiː.tʃə.rə.səʊ.si.eɪ.ʃən/ [US] /ˌper.əntˈtiː.tʃɚ.ə.soʊ-/ *noun* [C] (*ABBREVIATION* **PTA**, *US* **parent-teacher organization**) an organization run by teachers and the parents of children at a school which tries to help the school, especially by arranging activities that raise money for it

par excellence /ˌpɑːrˈeks.əl.ɑ̃ns/ [US] /ˌpɑːrˌek.səˈlɑːnts/ *adj* [after n] You describe something as par excellence when it is the best example of its type: *This is undoubtedly the cooking chocolate par excellence.*

pariah /pəˈraɪə/ *noun* [C] a person who is not accepted by a social group, especially because he or she is not liked, respected or trusted

paring /ˈpeə.rɪŋ/ [US] /ˈper.ɪŋ/ *noun* [C usually pl] ➲See at **pare**.

ˈparing ˌknife *noun* [C] a small knife which is used to cut away a thin outer layer of something, especially fruit

parish /ˈpær.ɪʃ/ [US] /ˈper-/ *noun* [C] (in some Christian groups) an area cared for by one priest and which has its own church, or (in England) the smallest unit of local government: *the parish church/magazine/priest/register* ➲See also **parochial** OF A CHURCH.

parishioner /pəˈrɪʃ.ən.ər/ [US] /-ɚ/ *noun* [C] a member of a particular parish under the care of a priest, especially one who frequently goes to its church

ˌparish ˈclerk *noun* [C] an official whose duties are connected with a church

P

,parish 'council noun [C] a group of people who are elected to make decisions for their parish

parity /'pær.ə.ti/ Ⓤ /'per.ə.ţi/ noun [U] equality, especially of pay or position: *British nurses would like to see pay parity with nurses in other major European countries.*

park AREA OF LAND /pɑːk/ Ⓤ /pɑːrk/ noun [C] **1** a large enclosed area of land with grass and trees, which is specially arranged so that people can walk in it for pleasure or children can play in it: *Central Park* ○ *Hyde Park* ○ *We watched the joggers in the park.* **2** UK an area of land around a large house in the countryside **3** US an area of land for playing sports

park STOP /pɑːk/ Ⓤ /pɑːrk/ verb **1** [I or T] to put a vehicle in a place where it can stay for a period of time, usually while you leave it: *Where have you parked?* ○ *Just park your car in the driveway.* **2** [T + adv or prep] INFORMAL to put yourself or something in a particular place for a long time, often causing annoyance to others: [R] *He parked himself in front of the TV and stayed there all afternoon.* ○ *She's parked an enormous pile of papers on my desk and I haven't a clue what to do with them.*

parking /'pɑː.kɪŋ/ Ⓤ /'pɑːr-/ noun [U] leaving a vehicle in a particular place for a period of time: *a parking place/space* ○ *He was fined for illegal parking.* ○ *Parking fines are given for parking offences/violations.* ○ US *a parking lot*

parka /'pɑː.kə/ Ⓤ /'pɑːr-/ noun [C] **1** a knee-length, often waterproof, coat with a HOOD (= head cover) **2** US FOR **anorak** COAT

'parking ,brake noun [C usually sing] US FOR **handbrake**

'parking ,garage noun [C] US a building for parking cars: *an underground parking garage*

'parking ,light noun [C] US FOR **sidelight** ⊃See picture **Car** on page Centre 12

'parking ,lot noun [C] US an outside CAR PARK (= area of ground for parking cars)

'parking ,meter noun [C] a device at the side of the road that you put money into so that you can leave your vehicle there for a particular amount of time

'parking ,ticket noun [C] an official notice which is attached to your vehicle when you have parked illegally, and which tells you that you must pay a particular amount of money as punishment

Parkinson's (disease) /'pɑː.kɪn.sᵊnz.dɪˌziːz/ Ⓤ /'pɑːr-/ noun [U] a disease of the nervous system which causes the muscles to become stiff and the body to shake, and which gradually gets worse as a person gets older

Parkinson's law /'pɑː.kɪn.sᵊnz.lɔː/ Ⓤ /'pɑːr.kɪn.sᵊnz.lɑː/ noun [U] HUMOROUS the idea that any piece of work will increase to fill as much time as you have to do it in

'park ,keeper noun [C] UK a person who is in charge of and takes care of a public park

parkland /'pɑːk.lænd/ Ⓤ /'pɑːrk-/ noun [U] an area of open land with grass and trees: *The college is surrounded by 70 acres of parkland.*

parkway /'pɑːk.weɪ/ Ⓤ /'pɑːrk-/ noun [C] US a wide road, usually divided, with an area of grass and trees on both sides and in the middle

parky /'pɑː.ki/ Ⓤ /'pɑːr-/ adj [usually after v] UK INFORMAL (of weather or the conditions in a room) quite cold: *It's a bit parky today, love – you'll want your coat!*

parlance /'pɑː.lənts/ Ⓤ /'pɑːr-/ noun [U] FORMAL a group of words or style of speaking used by a particular group of people: *Oral contraceptives are collectively referred to in common parlance as 'the pill'.* ○ *business/legal parlance*

parlay /'pɑː.li/ Ⓤ /'pɑːr.leɪ/ verb [T] MAINLY US to use or develop money, skills, etc. in a way that makes more money or leads to success: *They parlayed a small inheritance into a vast fortune.*

parley /'pɑː.li/ Ⓤ /'pɑːr-/ noun [C] OLD-FASHIONED OR HUMOROUS a discussion between two groups of people, especially one that is intended to end an argument **parley** /'pɑː.li/ Ⓤ /'pɑːr-/ verb [I] OLD-FASHIONED *After some serious parleying, both sides agreed to settle their differences.*

parliament /'pɑː.lɪ.mənt/ Ⓤ /'pɑːr.lə-/ noun **1** [C or U] in some countries, the group of (usually) elected politicians or other people who make the laws for their country: *On Tuesday the country's parliament voted to establish its own army.* ○ *She was elected to Parliament in 1997.* **2** [C] a particular period of time during which a parliament is operating, between either holidays or elections

parliamentarian /ˌpɑː.lɪ.menˈteə.ri.ən/ Ⓤ /ˌpɑːr.lə.menˈter.i-/ noun [C] **1** a member of a parliament, especially one who is respected for his or her experience and skill **2** US someone who is an expert on the rules and methods used by a group that makes laws or decisions

parliamentary /ˌpɑː.lɪˈmen.tᵊr.i/ Ⓤ /ˌpɑːr.ləˈmen.ţɚ-/ adj: *a parliamentary candidate/debate/election/session* ○ *parliamentary procedures/rules*

parlour SHOP UK, US **parlor** /'pɑː.ləʳ/ Ⓤ /'pɑːr.lɚ/ noun [C] a shop which provides a stated type of personal service or sells a stated product: *a beauty parlour* ○ *an ice-cream/pizza parlour*

parlour ROOM UK, US **parlor** /'pɑː.ləʳ/ Ⓤ /'pɑːr.lɚ/ noun [C] (especially in the past) a room in a private house used for relaxing, especially one which was kept tidy for the entertaining of guests: *the front parlour* ○ *an Edwardian parlour*

'parlour ,game UK, US **parlor game** noun [C] OLD-FASHIONED a game played inside a house, usually involving words or acting

parlous /'pɑː.ləs/ Ⓤ /'pɑːr-/ adj FORMAL very bad, dangerous or uncertain: *Relations between the two countries have been in a parlous condition for some time.* ○ *I'd like to buy a new car, but my finances are in such a parlous state that I can't afford to.*

parmesan (cheese) /ˌpɑː.mɪˈzæn'tʃiːz/ Ⓤ /ˌpɑːr.məˈzɑːn-/ noun [U] a hard dry Italian cheese used especially in cooking and for scattering on particular types of Italian food, such as pasta

parochial OF A CHURCH /pəˈrəʊ.ki.əl/ Ⓤ /-ˈroʊ-/ adj connected with a PARISH (= an area which has its own church or priest): *parochial boundaries*

parochial LIMITED /pəˈrəʊ.ki.əl/ Ⓤ /-ˈroʊ-/ adj DISAPPROVING showing interest only in a narrow range of matters, especially those which directly influence yourself, your town or your country: *a parochial view/opinion* ○ *Although it's just the local paper, it somehow manages not to be too parochial in its outlook.* **parochially** /pəˈrəʊ.ki.ə.li/ Ⓤ /-ˈroʊ-/ adv **parochialism** /pəˈrəʊ.ki.ə.lɪ.zᵊm/ Ⓤ /-ˈroʊ-/ noun [U] *political parochialism*

paˈrochial ,school noun [C] US a school which is controlled by a religious organization, and which usually receives no money from the government

parody /'pær.ə.di/ Ⓤ /'per-/ noun **1** [C or U] writing, music, art, speech, etc. which intentionally copies the style of someone famous or copies a particular situation, making the features or qualities of the original more noticeable in a way that is humorous: *He was an eighteenth-century author who wrote parodies of other people's works.* ○ *There is a hint of self-parody in his later paintings.* ⊃Compare **travesty**. **2** [C] DISAPPROVING something which so obviously fails to achieve the effect that was intended that it is ridiculous: *"It was a parody of a trial," said one observer.*

parodist /'pær.ə.dɪst/ Ⓤ /'per-/ noun [C] a person who writes parodies

parody /'pær.ə.di/ Ⓤ /'per-/ verb [T] to copy the style of someone or something in a humorous way: *One of the papers is running a competition in which you've got to parody a well-known author.*

parole /pəˈrəʊl/ Ⓤ /-ˈroʊl/ noun [U] when a prisoner is released before their period in prison is finished, with the agreement that they will behave well: *He's been released on parole.* ○ *She hopes to be eligible for parole in 3 years.* ○ *Reynolds was sentenced to life without parole.* **parole** /pəˈrəʊl/ Ⓤ /-ˈroʊl/ verb [T]

paroxysm /'pær.ɒk.sɪ.zᵊm/ Ⓤ /'per.ək-/ noun [C] a sudden and powerful expression of strong feeling, especially one that you cannot control: *In a sudden paroxysm of jealousy he threw her clothes out of the window.* ○ *paroxysms of laughter*

parquet /'pɑː.keɪ/ Ⓤ /'pɑːr.keɪ/ noun [U] floor covering that consists of small rectangular blocks of wood arranged in a pattern ⊃See also **woodblock**.

parricide /ˈpær.ɪ.saɪd/ ⓤ /ˈper.ə-/ noun LEGAL **1** [C or U] the crime of murdering a close relative, especially a parent ⊃Compare **matricide**; **patricide**. **2** [C] a person who has killed their father, mother or a close relative

parrot /ˈpær.ət/ ⓤ /ˈper-/ noun [C] a tropical bird with a curved beak, which is often kept as a pet and can be trained to copy the human voice
parrot /ˈpær.ət/ ⓤ /ˈper-/ verb [T] DISAPPROVING to repeat exactly what someone else says, without understanding it or thinking about its meaning: She doesn't have an original thought in her head – she just parrots anything that Sara says.

parrot-fashion /ˈpær.ət,fæʃ.ᵊn/ ⓤ /ˈper-/ adv UK If you learn or repeat a piece of text parrot-fashion, you learn or repeat the exact words, usually without understanding them.

parry /ˈpær.i/ ⓤ /ˈper-/ verb [T] **1** to defend yourself from a weapon or an attack by pushing the weapon away or by putting something between your body and the weapon **2** to manage cleverly to avoid dealing with a difficult question or some criticism: Predictably the president parried enquiries about the arms scandal. **parry** /ˈpær.i/ ⓤ /ˈper-/ noun [C]

parse /pɑːs/ ⓤ /pɑːrs/ verb [T] SPECIALIZED to separate a sentence into grammatical parts, such as subject, verb, etc.

Parsee, Parsi /ˌpɑːˈsiː/ ⓤ /ˈpɑːr.siː/ noun [C] a member of a religious group found mainly in western India, whose religion, ZOROASTRIANISM, started in Persia (ancient Iran) **Parsee, Parsi** /ˌpɑːˈsiː/ ⓤ /ˈpɑːr.siː/ adj

parsimonious /ˌpɑː.sɪˈməʊ.ni.əs/ ⓤ /ˌpɑːr.səˈmoʊ-/ adj FORMAL DISAPPROVING not willing to spend money or give something: She's too parsimonious to heat the house properly. ○ FIGURATIVE I think that politicians are often rather parsimonious with the (= do not tell the complete) truth. **parsimoniously** /ˌpɑː.sɪˈməʊ.ni.ə.sli/ ⓤ /ˌpɑːr.-səˈmoʊ-/ adv **parsimony** /ˈpɑː.sɪ.mə.ni/ ⓤ /ˈpɑːr.sə.moʊ-/ noun [U]

parsley /ˈpɑː.sli/ ⓤ /ˈpɑːr-/ noun [U] a herb with curly or flat leaves, used to add flavour to food and also to make it look attractive

parsnip /ˈpɑː.snɪp/ ⓤ /ˈpɑːr-/ noun [C or U] a long cream-coloured root of a plant, eaten as a vegetable: boiled/roasted parsnips ⊃See picture **Vegetables** on page Centre 2

parson /ˈpɑː.sᵊn/ ⓤ /ˈpɑːr-/ noun [C] OLD-FASHIONED OR HUMOROUS any Christian priest
parsonage /ˈpɑː.sᵊn.ɪdʒ/ ⓤ /ˈpɑːr-/ noun [C] OLD-FASHIONED a house that was built for a parson

part [SOME] /pɑːt/ ⓤ /pɑːrt/ noun [U] some but not all of a thing: Part of my steak isn't cooked properly. ○ Part of this form seems to be missing. ○ I think part of her problem is that she doesn't listen carefully enough to what other people say.
• **in part** partly, or to some degree: The deadline for applications is being extended, in part because of the postal strike.
• **in (a) large part** to an important degree: How quickly we can finish the project depends in (a) large part on when we get the payments through.
• **for the most part** mostly or usually: He was, for the most part, quite helpful.
• **be part and parcel of sth** to be a necessary feature of a particular experience, which cannot be avoided: Being recognized in the street is part and parcel of being a celebrity.
• **part of the furniture** something or someone so familiar that you no longer notice them
part /pɑːt/ ⓤ /pɑːrt/ adj [before n] He's (a) part **owner** of a racehorse (= he shares the ownership of it with other people). **part** /pɑːt/ ⓤ /pɑːrt/ adv: He's part African – his father was born in Somalia. ○ The exam is part spoken and part written. **partly** /ˈpɑːt.li/ ⓤ /ˈpɑːrt-/ adv: His attractiveness is partly due to his self-confidence. ○ The house is partly owned by her father.

part [SEPARATE PIECE] /pɑːt/ ⓤ /pɑːrt/ noun [C] **1** a separate piece of something, or a piece which combines with other pieces to form the whole of something: We learned about all the different parts of the digestive system. ○ The lower part of her spine was crushed in the accident. ○ I think there's always a part of you that doubts what you're doing. ○ Fresh fruit and vegetables form an essential/important part of a healthy diet. ○ There'll be snow in parts (= particular areas) of the Midlands tonight. **2** one of the pieces that together form a machine or some type of equipment: He works for a company that makes aircraft parts. **3** a single broadcast of a series of television or radio programmes or a division of a story: Next week we publish part three of 'The Diana Diaries'. ○ The programme will be shown in two parts. **4** one of two or more equal, or almost equal, measures of something: Mix one part of the medicine with three parts water. **5** one of the characters in a film, play or dance, or the words, actions or movements that are said or done by that character: He's got a small part in the school play. ○ She plays the part of the sexy blonde waitress. **6** the music that a particular musician plays in a group
• **dress/look/act the part** to look suitable or behave in a suitable way for a particular situation: If you're going to be a high-powered businesswoman, you've got to look the part.
• **the best/better part of** most of: I spent the better part of a day cleaning that kitchen!
parts /pɑːts/ ⓤ /pɑːrts/ plural noun INFORMAL these **parts** used to refer to an area of the country: We don't see many foreigners in these parts.

part [SEPARATE] /pɑːt/ ⓤ /pɑːrt/ verb **1** [I or T] to separate or cause to separate: The curtains parted, revealing a darkened stage. ○ To be parted **from** him even for two days made her sad. **2** [T] If you part your hair, you arrange it so that it falls on either side of your head by separating it with a line down the middle or on one side. **3** [I] FORMAL If two people part, they leave each other, often at the end of a relationship: I'm afraid we parted on rather bad terms.
• **part company** If two people part company, they end their relationship: The world's number one tennis player and his coach parted company earlier this month.
parted /ˈpɑː.tɪd/ ⓤ /ˈpɑːr.t̬ɪd/ adj: On his wall he has a poster of Marilyn Monroe, her lips forever parted (= separated) in anticipation.
parting /ˈpɑː.tɪŋ/ ⓤ /ˈpɑːr.t̬ɪŋ/ noun **1** [C or U] when you are separated from another person, often for a long time: They'd had an amicable parting. ○ The pain of parting had lessened over the years. **2** [C] UK (US **part**) a line on someone's head made by brushing the hair in two different directions: a centre/side parting
• **parting of the ways** the point at which two people or organizations separate: The parting of the ways came after a series of disagreements between the singer and his song-writer.
parting /ˈpɑː.tɪŋ/ ⓤ /ˈpɑːr.t̬ɪŋ/ adj [before n] done while leaving or separating: a parting glance/remark ⊃See also **parting shot**.
▲ **part with sth** phrasal verb to give something to someone else, especially when you do not want to: I was going to give away her old baby clothes, but I couldn't bring myself to part with them.

part [INVOLVEMENT] /pɑːt/ ⓤ /pɑːrt/ noun [U] involvement in or responsibility for an activity or action: He admitted his part in the robbery. ○ I want no part in/of your crazy schemes!
• **take part** to be involved in an activity with other people: She doesn't usually take part in any of the class activities.
• **take sb's part** to support someone: For once, my brother took my part in the argument.

part [HAIR] US /pɑːt/ ⓤ /pɑːrt/ noun [C] (UK **parting**) a line on someone's head made by brushing the hair in two different directions

partake [EAT/DRINK] /pɑːˈteɪk/ ⓤ /pɑːr-/ verb [I] **partook**, **partaken** OLD-FASHIONED OR HUMOROUS to eat or drink: Would you care to partake **of** a little wine with us?

partake [TAKE PART] /pɑːˈteɪk/ ⓤ /pɑːr-/ verb [I] **partook**, **partaken** OLD-FASHIONED OR FORMAL to become involved with or take part in something: She was happy to partake **in** the festivities.

P

ˌpart exˈchange *noun* [C] *UK* a way of paying for a new object that involves giving your old one as part of the payment: *I might offer them my old camera* ***in/as*** *part exchange for a new one.*

parthenogenesis /ˌpɑː.θə.nəʊˈdʒen.ə.sɪs/ [US] /ˌpɑːr.θə.noʊˈdʒen-/ *noun* [U] *SPECIALIZED* a type of reproduction in which the young develop from eggs which have not been FERTILIZED (= united with the male sexual cells)

partial [NOT COMPLETE] /ˈpɑː.ʃəl/ [US] /ˈpɑːr-/ *adj* not complete: *The general has ordered a partial* ***withdrawal*** *of troops from the area.* **partially** /ˈpɑː.ʃəl.i/ [US] /ˈpɑːr-/ *adv: The meat was only partially cooked.*

partial [UNFAIR] /ˈpɑː.ʃəl/ [US] /ˈpɑːr-/ *adj* influenced by your personal preference for or approval of something, so that you do not judge fairly: *The reporting in the papers is entirely partial and makes no attempt to be objective.* * NOTE: The opposite is **impartial**. **partiality** /ˌpɑː.ʃiˈæl.ə.ti/ [US] /ˌpɑːr.ʃiˈæl.ə.t̬i/ *noun* [U] *The judges have been heavily criticized for their partiality in the whole affair.* * NOTE: The opposite is **impartiality**.

partial [LIKING] /ˈpɑː.ʃəl/ [US] /ˈpɑːr-/ *adj* [after v] *OLD-FASHIONED OR FORMAL* having a liking for something: *I'm rather partial* ***to*** *red wine.* **partiality** /ˌpɑː.ʃiˈæl.ə.ti/ [US] /ˌpɑːr.ʃiˈæl.ə.t̬i/ *noun* [U] *He has a partiality* ***for*** *expensive suits.*

ˌpartially ˈsighted *adj* People who are partially sighted are not completely blind but are able to see very little.

participate /pɑːˈtɪs.ɪ.peɪt/ [US] /pɑːrˈtɪs.ə-/ *verb* [I] to take part in or become involved in an activity: *She never participates* ***in*** *any of our discussions, does she?* **participation** /pɑːˌtɪs.ɪˈpeɪ.ʃən/ [US] /pɑːrˌtɪs.ə-/ *noun* [U] when you take part or become involved in something **participant** /pɑːˈtɪs.ɪ.pənt/ [US] /pɑːrˈtɪs.ə-/ *noun* [C] a person who takes part in or becomes involved in a particular activity **participatory** /pɑːˌtɪ.sɪˈpeɪ.tər.i/ [US] /pɑːrˈtɪs.ə.pə.tɔːr-/ *adj: Participatory sports are becoming more popular.*

participle /pɑːˈtɪs.ɪ.pl̩/ [US] /ˈpɑːr.tɪ.sɪ-/ *noun* [C] the form of a verb that usually ends in 'ed' or 'ing' and is used to form some tenses and as an adjective: *In the sentences 'He's sleeping' and 'I've already eaten', the words 'sleeping' and 'eaten' are both participles.*

particle [SMALL PIECE] /ˈpɑː.tɪ.kl̩/ [US] /ˈpɑːr.t̬ə-/ *noun* [C] an extremely small piece of matter: *Dust particles must have got into the motor, which is why it isn't working properly.* ○ *Electrons and protons are atomic particles.*

particle [GRAMMAR] /ˈpɑː.tɪ.kl̩/ [US] /ˈpɑːr.t̬ə-/ *noun* [C] a word or a part of a word which has a grammatical purpose but often has little or no meaning: *In the sentence 'I tidied up the room', the adverb 'up' is a particle.*

ˈparticle acˌcelerator *noun* [C] in physics, a machine which makes extremely small pieces of matter travel at very high speeds, so that scientists can study the way they behave

particular [SPECIAL] /pəˈtɪk.jʊ.ləʳ/ [US] /pɚˈtɪk.jə.lɚ/ *adj* [before n] **1** special, or this and not any other: *She wanted a particular type of cactus.* ○ *He wouldn't take just any book – he had to have this particular one!* ○ *"Why did you ask?" "Oh, no particular reason, just making conversation."* **2** *FORMAL* **the particular** If you are considering the particular, you are considering single examples rather than general matters or ideas: *The report focuses on the particular rather than the general and so doesn't draw any overall conclusions.*

• **in particular** especially: *What in particular did you like about the last apartment that we saw?* ○ *Are you looking for anything in particular?*

particularly /pəˈtɪk.jʊ.lə.li/ [US] /pɚˈtɪk.jə.lɚ.li/ *adv* especially, or more than usual: *We're particularly interested to hear from people who speak two or more European languages.* ○ *I didn't particularly want to go, but I had to.*

particularity /pəˌtɪk.jʊˈlær.ə.ti/ [US] /pɚˌtɪk.jəˈler.ə.t̬i/ *noun* [U] *FORMAL* the quality of being exact or very detailed

particularities /pəˌtɪk.jʊˈlær.ə.tiz/ [US] /pɚˌtɪk.jəˈler.ə.t̬iz/ *plural noun FORMAL* details: *The particularities* ***of*** *the case have not been revealed.*

particulars /pəˈtɪk.jʊ.ləz/ [US] /pɚˈtɪk.jə.lɚz/ *plural noun* details or information about a person or an event, especially when officially recorded: *There's a form for you to note down all your particulars.*

particular [NOT EASILY SATISFIED] /pəˈtɪk.jʊ.ləʳ/ [US] /pɚˈtɪk.jə.lɚ/ *adj* [after v] not easily satisfied and demanding that close attention should be given to every detail: *He's very particular* ***about*** *the kitchen – everything has to be perfectly clean and in its place.* ○ *She's very particular* ***about*** *what she eats.*

particulate /pəˈtɪ.kjuː.lət/ *noun* [C usually pl] *SPECIALIZED* an extremely small piece of dirt, especially one produced by road vehicles, which causes serious pollution

ˌparting ˈshot *noun* [C] a remark which you do not make until you are leaving, so that it has a stronger effect: *"And the dress that you bought me doesn't fit either!" was her parting shot.*

partisan [UNFAIR], **partizan** /ˌpɑː.tɪˈzæn/ /ˈ---/ [US] /ˈpɑːr.t̬ɪ.zən/ *adj* strongly supporting a person, principle or political party, often without considering or judging the matter very carefully: *The audience was very partisan, and refused to listen to her speech.* ○ *partisan politics* ➲See also **bipartisan**. **partisanship**, **partizanship** /ˌpɑː.tɪˈzæn.ʃɪp/ /ˈ----/ [US] /ˈpɑːr.t̬ɪ.zən-/ *noun* [U] *There was a certain partisanship about the way that votes were cast.*

partisan [PERSON], **partizan** /ˌpɑː.tɪˈzæn/ /ˈ---/ [US] /ˈpɑːr.t̬ɪ.zən/ *noun* [C] **1** (in a country which has been defeated) a member of a secret armed force whose aim is to fight against the enemy which is controlling the country **2** someone who supports a person, principle or political party

partition [DIVIDING STRUCTURE] /pɑːˈtɪʃ.ən/ [US] /pɑːr-/ *noun* [C] a vertical structure like a thin wall which separates one part of a room or building from another: *The partitions* ***between*** *the toilets were very thin.* ➲See picture **In the Office** on page Centre 15 **partition** /pɑːˈtɪʃ.ən/ [US] /pɑːr-/ *verb* [T] *Why don't you partition that large room* ***into*** *a lounge and a dining-room?*

partition [NATIONAL DIVISION] /pɑːˈtɪʃ.ən/ [US] /pɑːr-/ *noun* [U] the dividing of a country into separate countries or areas of government: *The partition* ***of*** *India occurred in 1948.* **partition** /pɑːˈtɪʃ.ən/ [US] /pɑːr-/ *verb* [T] *Ireland was partitioned in 1921.*

partly /ˈpɑːt.li/ [US] /ˈpɑːrt-/ *adv:* ➲See at **part** SOME.

partner /ˈpɑːt.nəʳ/ [US] /ˈpɑːrt.nɚ/ *noun* [C] **1** a person you are closely involved with in some way: *He gave up his job as a police officer after his partner was killed.* ○ *The two companies are partners in a contract to build a new power station.* **2** one of the owners of a company: *He's a partner* ***in*** *an insurance company/a law firm.* **3** the person you are married to or living with as if you were married to them, or the person you are having a sexual relationship with **4** one of a pair of dancers or one of a pair who are playing a sport or a game together, especially when the pair are playing as a team **partner** /ˈpɑːt.nəʳ/ [US] /ˈpɑːrt.nɚ/ *verb* [T] If you partner someone in a sport, a game or a dance, you act as their partner. **partnership** /ˈpɑːt.nə.ʃɪp/ [US] /ˈpɑːrt.nɚ-/ *noun* **1** [C or U] the state of being a partner **2** [C] a company which is owned by two or more people: *the John Lewis Partnership*

ˌpart of ˈspeech *noun* [C] (*SPECIALIZED* **word class**) one of the grammatical groups, such as noun, verb and adjective, into which words are divided depending on their use

partook /pɑːˈtʊk/ [US] /pɑːr-/ *past simple of* **partake**

partridge /ˈpɑː.trɪdʒ/ [US] /ˈpɑːr-/ *noun* [C] *plural* **partridge** or **partridges** a bird with a round body and a short tail which is sometimes hunted for food or for sport

part-time /ˌpɑːtˈtaɪm/ [US] /ˌpɑːrt-/ *adv, adj* If you work part-time or do part-time work, you work for only some of the day or the week: *a part-time job* ➲Compare **full-time** WORK/EDUCATION.

part-timer /ˌpɑːtˈtaɪ.məʳ/ ⑩ /ˌpɑːrtˈtaɪ.mɚ/ *noun* [C] someone who works part-time

parturition /ˌpɑːtjʊəˈrɪʃ.ən/ ⑩ /ˌpɑːr.tuːˈrɪʃ-/ *noun* [U] SPECIALIZED the act of giving birth

party CELEBRATION /ˈpɑː.ti/ ⑩ /ˈpɑːr.t̬i/ *noun* [C] a social event where a group of people meet to talk, eat, drink, dance, etc., often in order to celebrate a special occasion: *a birthday party* ○ *a farewell party* ○ *a dinner party* (= a small sometimes formal party where a meal is eaten) ○ *a (UK)* **fancy-dress**/(US) **costume** *party* (= a party where people wear clothes that make them look like someone or something else) ○ *Peter* **has/gives/throws** *really wild parties.*
• **bring** *sth* **to the party** to provide something as part of an arrangement: *So what's Carter's involvement in all of this? What's he bringing to the party?*

party /ˈpɑː.ti/ ⑩ /ˈpɑːr.t̬i/ *verb* [I] to enjoy yourself by drinking and dancing, especially at a party: *Let's party!* ○ *They partied till dawn.*

party POLITICAL GROUP /ˈpɑː.ti/ ⑩ /ˈpɑːr.t̬i/ *group noun* [C] an organization of people with particular political beliefs which competes in elections to try to win positions in local or national government: *the Democratic Party* ○ *the Green party* ○ *the Conservative party* ○ *The Labour party has/have just elected a new leader.* ○ *He was elected as party* **leader** *in 2001.* ○ *They contacted party* **members** *from across the nation to ask for their support.*

party VISITING GROUP /ˈpɑː.ti/ ⑩ /ˈpɑːr.t̬i/ *group noun* [C] a group of people who are involved in an activity together, especially a visit: *a party of tourists* ○ *Most museums give a discount to* **school** *parties.*

party INVOLVEMENT /ˈpɑː.ti/ ⑩ /ˈpɑːr.t̬i/ *noun* [C] one of the people or groups of people involved in an official argument, arrangement or similar situation: *The UN called on all parties* **in** *the conflict to take a positive stance towards the new peace initiative.* ○ *It's often difficult to establish who the* **guilty** *party is following a road accident.*
• **be (a) party to** *sth* to be involved in something, especially something bad

party ˌanimal *noun* [C] INFORMAL someone who enjoys parties and party activities very much and goes to as many as possible: *Sarah's a real party animal – she likes to dance all night.*

ˌparty ˈfaithful *plural noun* people who have been loyal members or supporters of a party for a long time: *This policy may appeal to the party faithful, but will it gain the support of uncommitted voters?*

ˈparty ˌfavor *noun* [C usually pl] US small presents given to guests, usually children, at a party: *He handed out the party favors as we were leaving.*

the ˌparty ˈline POLITICS *noun* [S] the official ideas and aims of a political party: *Her speech deviated little from the official party line.*

ˈparty ˌline TELEPHONE *noun* [C] a telephone connection which is shared by two or more customers with separate telephones

ˈparty ˌpiece *noun* [C] UK HUMOROUS a short performance or an action done in public, especially one showing an unusual or amusing skill

ˌparty political ˈbroadcast UK *noun* [C] (US **paid political broadcast**) a short television or radio programme in which a politician talks about their party's ideas and plans in order to try to win more support

ˌparty ˈpolitics *plural noun* political activity and discussion within or relating to political parties rather than the whole country

party pooper /ˈpɑː.tiˌpuː.pəʳ/ ⑩ /ˈpɑːr.t̬iˌpuː.pɚ/ *noun* [C] HUMOROUS someone who spoils other people's enjoyment by disapproving of or not taking part in a particular activity

ˈparty ˌpopper *noun* [C] a small device, held in the hand, which makes a loud noise and scatters strips of coloured paper when you pull the string at the top of it

ˌparty ˈwall UK *noun* [C] (US **common wall**) a wall which divides two buildings that are joined together and belongs to both of them

parvenu /ˈpɑː.və.njuː/ ⑩ /ˈpɑːr-/ *noun* [C] FORMAL DISAPPROVING someone from a low social position who has suddenly become rich or successful

pas de deux /ˌpɑː.dəˈdɜː/ *noun* [C] *plural* **pas-de-deux** (in ballet) a dance for two people, usually a man and a woman

pass GO PAST /pɑːs/ ⑩ /pæs/ *verb* **1** [I or T] to go past something or someone or move in relation to it: *I passed him on the stairs this morning.* ○ *You should only pass a slower vehicle if it is safe to do so.* ○ *If you pass a supermarket, could you get me some milk?* ○ *I was just passing* **by** (= going past the place where you are), *so I thought I'd drop in for a chat.* ○ *A momentary look of anxiety passed* **across** *his face.* ○ *A cloud passed* **over** *the sun.* **2** [T] to go past a particular point in time: *Don't buy goods which have passed their sell-by date.* **3** [I] If you say a state or feeling will pass, you mean it will disappear: *Don't worry, his depression is only temporary – it'll soon pass.*
• **pass (all) belief** UK to be (extremely) difficult to believe: *It passes all belief* **that** *he could have been so selfish.*

passable /ˈpɑː.sə.bl̩/ ⑩ /ˈpæs.ə-/ *adj* possible to travel on: *Because of the heavy snow, roads were passable only with care in parts of Northern England.*

passer-by /ˌpɑː.səˈbaɪ/ ⑩ /ˌpæs.ɚ-/ *noun* [C] *plural* **passers-by** someone who is going past a particular place, especially when something unusual happens: *The gunmen opened fire, killing a policeman and a passer-by.*

passing /ˈpɑː.sɪŋ/ ⑩ /ˈpæs.ɪŋ/ *adj* [before n] **1** moving past: *A passing motorist stopped and gave her a lift to the nearby town.* **2** lasting only for a short time and not important or complete: *The elephants and giraffes got only a passing* **glance** *from the teenagers heading from the car park to the games arcade.* ○ *The matter is only of passing scientific interest.*
• **a passing resemblance** a slightly similar appearance: *He bears more than a passing resemblance* **to** (= he is noticeably similar to) *the young Marlon Brando.*

passing /ˈpɑː.sɪŋ/ ⑩ /ˈpæs.ɪŋ/ *noun* **in passing** If something is said in passing, it is said while talking about something else and is not the main subject of a conversation: *When asked if he had told the police about the incident, Mr Banks said he had* **mentioned** *it in passing to a detective.*

pass GIVE /pɑːs/ ⑩ /pæs/ *verb* **1** [T] to give something to someone: *Could you pass the salt please?* ○ *I asked if I could see the letter, so she passed it* **to** *me reluctantly.* ○ [+ two objects] *Gerald passed me the note./Gerald passed the note to me.* ○ *Genes are the instructions by which parents' characteristics are passed* **on to** *their children.* **2** [I or T] In several sports, if you pass the ball, you kick, throw or hit it to someone in your team. **3** [T] If you pass money, you give someone false or stolen money without telling them: [+ two objects] *I haven't trusted him since he passed me a forged £5 note.* ○ *She was arrested for passing stolen cheques.*
• **pass the hat around/round** to try to collect money by asking people or organizations

pass /pɑːs/ ⑩ /pæs/ *noun* [C] a movement of the ball from one player to another member of the same team in a team sport

pass SUCCEED /pɑːs/ ⑩ /pæs/ *verb* [I or T] to be successful in an exam, course, etc: *Guess what? I've passed my driving test!* ○ *The exam is so hard that only 5% of all applicants pass.*
• **pass muster** to reach an acceptable standard: *New teams won't be admitted to the league if their stadiums don't pass muster.*

pass /pɑːs/ ⑩ /pæs/ *noun* [C] **1** UK a successful result in an exam: *Jonathon Hill achieved grade A passes at A-level.* **2** US a mark given to a student to show that they have successfully completed a course or an exam that they will not be given a GRADE (= numbered mark) for: *I got a pass in my World Lit course.*

passable /ˈpɑː.sə.bl̩/ ⑩ /ˈpæs.ə-/ *adj* satisfactory but not excellent: *Mary can speak passable Russian.* **passably** /ˈpɑː.sə.bli/ ⑩ /ˈpæs.ə-/ *adv*

pass TIME /pɑːs/ ⑩ /pæs/ *verb* **1** [I] When time passes, it goes past: *Time seems to pass* **(by)** *so slowly when you're bored.* ○ *I was a bit worried about the party, but the even-*

ing passed without any great disasters. **2** [T] If you pass time, you do something to stop yourself being bored during that period: *The visitors pass their days swimming, windsurfing and playing volleyball.*

• **pass the time of day** to have a short informal conversation: *I was just passing the time of day with her.*

passing /ˈpɑː.sɪŋ/ ⓤ /ˈpæs.ɪŋ/ *adj* [before n] describes a period of time that is going past: *The situation seems to become more hopeless with each/every passing day.*

passing /ˈpɑː.sɪŋ/ ⓤ /ˈpæs.ɪŋ/ *noun* **1 the passing of time/the years** the way that time passes: *My parents seem to have mellowed with the passing of the years.* **2** the death of someone or something: *Ten years after her death, the public still mourns her passing.* ○ *the passing of the old year*

pass APPROVE /pɑːs/ ⓤ /pæs/ *verb* [T] (of an official group of people) to give approval to something, especially by voting to make it law: *The government passed a law to restrict the sale of guns.* ○ UK *The restaurant was serving meat that had not been passed as fit for human consumption.*

pass JUDGE /pɑːs/ ⓤ /pæs/ *verb* **1 pass judgment/comment, etc.** to express a judgment or opinion about something, especially someone else's behaviour: *As a convicted criminal, he's in no position to pass judgment (on the rest of us).* **2 pass sentence** to state, as a judge, what a criminal's official punishment will be

pass EXCRETE /pɑːs/ ⓤ /pæs/ *verb* [T] FORMAL **1** to excrete something: *to pass urine* **2 pass blood** to excrete blood in your urine or FAECES (= solid waste): *If you pass blood, you should see your doctor.*

• **pass water** POLITE EXPRESSION FOR **urinate**

pass NOT PLAY /pɑːs/ ⓤ /pæs/ *verb* [I] to choose not to play in a part of a card game or not to answer a question in a QUIZ

pass CHANGE /pɑːs/ ⓤ /pæs/ *verb* [I usually + adv or prep] to change from one state to another: *Wax passes from solid to liquid when you heat it.*

pass PATH /pɑːs/ ⓤ /pæs/ *noun* [C] a path or road between or over mountains: *a mountain pass*

pass DOCUMENT /pɑːs/ ⓤ /pæs/ *noun* [C] an official document or ticket which shows that you have the right to go somewhere or use a particular form of transport: *a bus pass* ○ *a boarding pass* ○ *My guest pass allows me to use the club's facilities free of charge.*

pass SEXUAL ACTION /pɑːs/ ⓤ /pæs/ *INFORMAL* **make a pass at sb** to speak to or touch someone in a way that shows you would like to start a sexual relationship with them

pass BAD SITUATION /pɑːs/ ⓤ /pæs/ *noun* [S] a difficult or unpleasant condition: *If I'd been aware things had reached such a pass, I'd have told the police.* ○ UK *It's come to a pretty pass* (= It's a bad situation) *when you can't even have a few quiet drinks with some friends.*

PHRASAL VERBS WITH **pass** ▼

▲ **pass sth around** *phrasal verb* [M] US FOR **pass [sth] round**

▲ **pass as/for sth/sb** *phrasal verb* to appear to be someone or something else, or to cause people to believe that they are: *I really want to go and see the film, but I don't think I'd pass for 18.* ○ *Do you think this jacket and trousers will pass as a suit? They're almost the same colour.*

▲ **pass away/on** *phrasal verb* POLITE EXPRESSION FOR **die** STOP LIVING: *She's terribly upset because her father passed away last week.*

▲ **pass sb by** *phrasal verb* If an event or opportunity passes you by, you do not properly notice it, or get pleasure or benefit from it: *Do you ever feel that life is passing you by?*

▲ **pass sth down** *phrasal verb* [M often passive] to teach or give something to someone who will be alive after you have died: *His is a family trade, passed down from generation to generation.*

▲ **pass off** UK *phrasal verb* [+ adv] (US **come off**) to happen: *The pop festival passed off peacefully, despite the fears of local residents.*

▲ **pass sth/sb off as sth/sb** *phrasal verb* [M] to pretend that something or someone is a particular thing or person when they are not: *The dealer was trying to pass off*

fakes as valuable antiques. ○ *It's hard to believe anyone would try to pass this nonsense off as literature.*

▲ **pass sth on** TELL *phrasal verb* [M] to tell someone something that another person has told you: *If he provided us with any information, no one passed it on to me.*

▲ **pass sth on** GIVE *phrasal verb* [M] to give someone something that another person has given you: *Could you pass it on to Laura when you've finished reading it?*

▲ **pass sth on** DISEASE *phrasal verb* [M] to give a disease to another person: *It's possible to pass on the virus to others through physical contact.*

▲ **pass out** BECOME UNCONSCIOUS *phrasal verb* to become unconscious for a short time, for example when ill, badly hurt or drunk: *I was hit on the head and passed out.*

▲ **pass out** LEAVE COLLEGE *phrasal verb* UK to leave a military college after successfully completing the course: *The new officers passed out from Britannia Royal Naval College on Thursday 1 August.*

passing 'out *noun* [S] *His parents attended the passing-out ceremony.*

▲ **pass sth out** GIVE *phrasal verb* [M] US to give something to each person in a group of people: *The teacher passed out the test booklets.*

▲ **pass sb/sth over** *phrasal verb* [M] to ignore or to not give attention to someone or something: *The woman alleges that her employers passed her over for promotion because she was pregnant.*

▲ **pass sth round** UK *phrasal verb* [M] (US **pass sth around**) to offer something to each person in a group of people: *Could you do me a favour and pass these sandwiches round?*

▲ **pass sth up** *phrasal verb* [M] to fail to take advantage of an opportunity: *I can't believe she passed up the chance to go to South America.* ○ *He's never one to pass up a free meal.*

passage CONNECTING WAY /ˈpæs.ɪdʒ/ *noun* [C] **1** (ALSO **passageway**) a usually long and narrow part of a building with rooms on one or both sides, or an enclosed path which connects places: *A narrow passage led directly through the house into the garden.* ○ *The bathroom's on the right at the end of the passage.* **2** a hollow part of the body through which something goes: *the nasal passages* ○ *the anal passage*

passage PART /ˈpæs.ɪdʒ/ *noun* [C] a short piece of writing or music which is part of a larger piece of work: *Several passages from the book were printed in a national newspaper before it was published.*

passage TRAVEL /ˈpæs.ɪdʒ/ *noun* **1** [U] FORMAL travel, especially as a way of escape: *The gunman then took a hostage and demanded a plane and safe passage to an unspecified destination.* **2** OLD-FASHIONED a journey, especially over the sea: *He had booked his passage to Rio de Janeiro.* **3** OLD-FASHIONED **work your passage** to do work on a ship during your journey instead of paying for a ticket

passage MOVEMENT /ˈpæs.ɪdʒ/ *noun* [U] an act of moving through somewhere: *Many meteors disintegrate during their passage through the atmosphere.* ○ *The government prohibits the passage of foreign troops and planes across its territory.*

passage TIME /ˈpæs.ɪdʒ/ *noun* LITERARY **the passage of time** the action of time going past: *Memories fade with the passage of time.*

passage LAW /ˈpæs.ɪdʒ/ *noun* [U] FORMAL the official approval of something, especially a new law: *He again urged passage of a constitutional amendment outlawing abortion.*

passbook /ˈpɑːs.bʊk/ ⓤ /ˈpæs-/ *noun* [C] a small book that is used to officially record how much money is in a customer's bank account

pass de,gree DEGREE *noun* [C] UK a degree given to university or college students who have passed their exams, but not well enough to get an HONOURS degree

pass de,gree DEGREE COURSE *noun* [C] AUS a degree course which is designed to be completed in three years instead of the usual four

passé /pɑːˈseɪ/ ⓤ /pæsˈeɪ/ *adj* DISAPPROVING no longer fashionable: *Wines from that region were quite popular* *for a while, but now they're rather passé.*

passenger /ˈpæs.ᵊn.dʒəʳ/ ⓤ /-dʒɚ/ *noun* [C] **1** a person who is travelling in a vehicle but is not driving it, flying it or working on it: *airline/rail/train/car passengers* **2 passenger train** a train carrying people rather than goods: *The two passenger trains involved in the accident had both come from south-west London.*

pass-fail /ˌpɑːsˈfeɪl/ ⓤ /ˌpæs-/ *adj* MAINLY US If an exam or course is pass-fail, no mark is given for it, and the only thing the students are told about their performance is whether or not they have passed.

passing ˌlane *noun* [C usually sing] US FOR **overtaking lane**

passing ˌshot *noun* [C] when you successfully hit the ball past the other player in tennis

passion FEELING /ˈpæʃ.ᵊn/ *noun* [C or U] a very powerful feeling, for example of sexual attraction, love, hate, anger or other emotion: *Football arouses a good deal of passion among its supporters.* ○ *At school, his early interest in music developed into an abiding passion.* ○ *Politics and philosophy were his lifelong passions.*
• **a passion for sth** an extreme interest in or desire for doing something, such as a hobby, activity, etc: *Anton has a consuming passion for science fiction.*
passions /ˈpæʃ.ᵊnz/ *plural noun* very powerful feelings: *Touch a man's property and his passions are immediately aroused.*
• **passions run high** a way of describing a time when people feel strong emotions about a particular subject: *Passions run very high at election time.*
passionate /ˈpæʃ.ᵊn.ət/ ⓤ /-ə.nɪt/ *adj* having very strong feelings or emotions: *a passionate speech* ○ *a passionate kiss/embrace* ○ *The Italians are said to be the most passionate people in Europe.* ○ *The child's mother made a passionate plea for help.* ○ *Joe is passionate about baseball* (= he likes it very much). **passionately** /ˈpæʃ.ᵊn.ət.li/ ⓤ /-ə.nɪt-/ *adv*: *I walked into the room and found them kissing passionately.* ○ *Ann has always believed passionately in women's rights.*
passionless /ˈpæʃ.ᵊn.ləs/ *adj* DISAPPROVING without any passion: *They had a passionless marriage.* ○ *This music is passionless.*

the ˈPassion RELIGION *noun* [S] in CHRISTIANITY, the suffering and death of Jesus Christ

passion ˌflower *noun* [C] a tropical climbing plant with large colourful flowers and edible fruits called passion fruits

passion ˌfruit *noun* [C or U] a small fruit with thick purple or yellow skin and many seeds

passion ˌplay *noun* [C] a play that tells the story of the suffering and death of Jesus Christ

passive BEHAVIOUR /ˈpæs.ɪv/ *adj* OFTEN DISAPPROVING not acting to influence or change a situation; allowing other people to be in control: *He's very passive in the relationship.* ○ *Men have always played an active part in leading worship while women have been confined to more passive roles.* ⊃See also **impassive**. Compare **active** BUSY/INVOLVED. **passively** /ˈpæs.ɪv.li/ *adv*: *He tends to wait passively for his boss to tell him what to do.*
passivity /pæsˈɪv.ɪ.ti/ ⓤ /-ə.t̬i/ *noun* [U] the quality or state of being passive

the passive GRAMMAR *noun* [S] SPECIALIZED a way of structuring a sentence so that the grammatical subject is the person or thing which experiences the effect of an action, rather than the person or thing which causes the effect: *When changed into the passive, 'The dog chased the cat' becomes 'The cat was chased by the dog'.* ⊃Compare **active** GRAMMAR. **passive** /ˈpæs.ɪv/ *adj*: *'He was released from prison,' is a passive sentence.*
passivize, UK USUALLY **-ise** /ˈpæs.ɪ.vaɪz/ *verb* [T] SPECIALIZED to change a verb or sentence into the passive
passivization, UK USUALLY **-isation** /ˌpæs.ɪ.vaɪˈzeɪ.ʃᵊn/ ⓤ /-ɪ.vɪ-/ *noun* [U] SPECIALIZED the process of changing a verb or sentence into the passive

passive reˈsistance *noun* [U] when you show your opposition to something in a peaceful way rather than acting violently: *The Mahatma instigated several campaigns of passive resistance against the British government in India.*

passive ˈsmoking *noun* [U] the unwanted breathing in of other people's cigarette smoke, especially by people who do not smoke: *Doctors say passive smoking has caused his lung cancer.*

passkey /ˈpɑːs.kiː/ ⓤ /ˈpæs-/ *noun* [C] a key for a door that is only given to people who are allowed to enter

ˈpass ˌmark UK *noun* [C] (US **passing mark**) the number of points that must be achieved in order to be successful in an exam

Passover /ˈpɑːsˌəʊ.vəʳ/ ⓤ /ˈpæsˌoʊ.vɚ/ *noun* [C or U] (ALSO **Pesach**) a Jewish celebration in March or April every year to remember the escape of the Jews from Egypt

passport /ˈpɑːs.pɔːt/ ⓤ /ˈpæs.pɔːrt/ *noun* [C] **1** an official document containing personal information and usually a photograph which allows a person to travel to foreign countries and to prove who they are: *Many refugees have arrived at the border without passports.* ○ *He was a German, travelling on a Swiss passport.* ○ *passport control* (= the examining of travellers' passports) ○ *a passport photo* **2 a passport to sth** a certain way of obtaining something you want: *Many students opt for business studies simply because it sounds like a passport to a good job.* ○ *Beauty alone can be a passport to success.*

ˈpass ˌrate *noun* [C] the number of people, shown as a percent, who were successful in a particular exam

password /ˈpɑːs.wɜːd/ ⓤ /ˈpæs.wɜːd/ *noun* [C] a secret word or combination of letters or numbers which is used for communicating with another person or with a computer to prove who you are: *I can't let you in unless you give the password.* ○ *You can't gain access to the computer system without entering your password.*

the past TIME BEFORE *noun* [S] **1** the period before and until, but not including, the present time: *Evolution can explain the past, but it can never predict the future.* ○ *In the past, this sort of work was all done by hand.* ○ *By winning the 1500 metres, he joins some of the great names of the past.* **2 a past** a part of someone's life in which they did immoral things: *He's a man with a past.*
past /pɑːst/ ⓤ /pæst/ *adj* **1** used to refer to a period of time before and until the present: *The average temperature worldwide has risen by about one degree Fahrenheit in the past 100 years.* ○ *I've been walking 3 miles a day for the past 30 years.* ○ *He was the fifth climber to die on these mountains over the past two days.* ○ *In centuries/years past* (= Many centuries/years ago) *even visiting the next village was considered a long journey.* **2** [before n] having happened or existed before now: *I know from past experience that you can't judge someone by their appearance.* ○ *The Prime Minister's family have been instructed not to discuss his past life with the press.* **3** [after v] finished: *I'm feeling much better now that the cold weather is past.*

the past GRAMMAR *noun* [S] the form of a verb used to describe actions, events or states that happened or existed before the present time: *The past of 'change' is 'changed'.* **past** /pɑːst/ ⓤ /pæst/ *adj* [before n] *'Must' doesn't have a past form.*

past BEYOND /pɑːst/ ⓤ /pæst/ *prep, adv* **1** in or to a position that is beyond a particular point: *I live on Station Road, just past the post office.* ○ *Three boys went past us on mountain bikes.* ○ *Was that Peter who just jogged past in those bright pink shorts?* **2** used to say what the time is when it is a particular number of minutes after an hour: *It's 5/10/a quarter/20/25/half past three.* ○ *I've got to leave at twenty past or I'll miss that train.*
past /pɑːst/ ⓤ /pæst/ *prep* beyond a particular age or a particular point: *She's past the age where she needs a babysitter.* ○ *Do what you want, I'm past caring* (= I don't care any longer).
• **be past it** INFORMAL, MAINLY HUMOROUS to be too old to do something: *Don't ask Andy to enter the race – he's past it!*
• **not put it past sb (to do sth)** INFORMAL to not be surprised if someone does something bad, because it is a typical thing for them to do: *Perhaps Helena told him – I wouldn't put it past her.*

pasta /ˈpæs.tə/ ⓤ /ˈpɑː.stə/ *noun* [U] a food made from flour, water and sometimes egg which is cooked and usually served with a sauce. It is made in various shapes which have different names: *Spaghetti, lasagne,* *vermicelli, ravioli and canneloni are all types of pasta.*

the ˌpast conˈtinuous *noun* **[S]** (*ALSO* **the past progressive**) the grammatical tense used to describe an action which someone was doing or an event which was happening at a particular time. It is made with 'was' or 'were' and the *-ing* form of a verb: *'I was cooking' is an example of the past continuous.*

paste [STICKY SUBSTANCE] /peɪst/ *noun* **[U]** **1** a thick soft sticky substance made by mixing a liquid with a powder especially to make a type of glue: *flour-and-water paste* ○ *wallpaper paste* **2** a thick soft substance made by crushing and mixing things such as fish, fruit or vegetables for food: *tomato/anchovy/curry paste*

paste /peɪst/ *verb* **1** **[T usually + adv or prep]** to stick something to something, especially with paste: *You can make your own distorting mirror by pasting a sheet of kitchen foil* ***to*** *a piece of thin cardboard.* **2** **[I or T]** to move a piece of text to a particular place in a computer document: *Cut that paragraph and then paste it at the end of the page.*

paste [HARD MATERIAL] /peɪst/ *noun* **[U]** *SPECIALIZED* a hard type of glass used to make artificial jewels: *Are these real diamonds or paste?*

pasteboard /ˈpeɪst.bɔːd/ Ⓤⓢ /-bɔːrd/ *noun* **[U]** a type of thick cardboard made from sheets of paper that have been glued together

pastel [MATERIAL] /ˈpæs.tᵊl/ Ⓤⓢ /pæsˈtel/ *noun* **[C or U]** a colouring material which can be powdery or slightly shiny and is usually in the shape of a small stick, or a picture made by using this: *Do you like working with pastels/in pastel?* ○ *The show includes eighty-five paintings, pastels and sculptures.*

pastel [COLOUR] /ˈpæs.tᵊl/ Ⓤⓢ /pæsˈtel/ *noun* **[C]** a colour that is pale and soft

pastel /ˈpæs.tᵊl/ Ⓤⓢ /pæsˈtel/ *adj* **[before n]** *Their house is decorated in pastel* ***shades*** (= soft pale colours).

paste-up /ˈpeɪst.ʌp/ *noun* **[C]** *SPECIALIZED* a piece of paper to which text and pictures have been fixed while designing a magazine or book

pasteurize, *UK USUALLY* **-ise** /ˈpæs.tʃᵊr.aɪz/ /ˈpɑːs-/ Ⓤⓢ /ˈpæs.tʃə.raɪz/ *verb* **[T]** to heat something, especially milk, at a controlled temperature for a fixed period of time in order to kill bacteria: *pasteurized milk/cheese* ○ *pasteurised beer* **pasteurization**, *UK USUALLY* **-isation** /ˌpæs.tʃᵊr.aɪˈzeɪ.ʃᵊn/ /ˌpɑːs-/ Ⓤⓢ /ˌpæs.tʃɚ.ɪ-/ *noun* **[U]**

pastiche /pæsˈtiːʃ/ Ⓤⓢ /pɑːˈstiːʃ/ *noun* **[C or U]** a piece of art, music, literature, etc. which intentionally copies the style of someone else's work or is intentionally in various styles, or the practice of making art in either of these ways: *The film is a skilful, witty pastiche* ***of*** *'Jaws'.*

pastille /ˈpæs.tᵊl/ *noun* **[C]** a type of small round sweet that can be sucked or chewed: *a throat pastille* (= a sweet for people with a cough or a sore throat)

pastime /ˈpɑːs.taɪm/ Ⓤⓢ /ˈpæs-/ *noun* **[C]** an activity which is done for enjoyment; a hobby: *Do-it-yourself is the nation's most popular pastime.* ○ *FIGURATIVE* *Suing people, especially doctors, is a national pastime* (= common activity) *in America.*

pasting /ˈpeɪ.stɪŋ/ *noun* **[S]** *MAINLY UK INFORMAL* a severe beating, severe criticism, or a severe defeat in a game or competition: *The England team* ***got/took*** *a pasting in the semi-final.*

pastis /pæsˈtiːs/ *noun* **[C or U]** an alcoholic drink which is flavoured with ANISEED, or a glass of this

ˌpast ˈmaster *noun* **[C]** a person who is very skilled in a particular activity: *Joe is a past master* ***at*** *getting invitations to parties.*

pastor /ˈpɑː.stəʳ/ Ⓤⓢ /ˈpæs.tɚ/ *noun* **[C]** a leader of a Christian group or church, especially one which is Protestant

pastoral [CARE] /ˈpɑː.stᵊr.ᵊl/ Ⓤⓢ /ˈpæs.tɚ-/ *adj* describes the part of the work of teachers and priests that involves giving help and advice about personal matters: *A priest's pastoral* ***duties*** *include helping the poor and sick.*

pastoral [ART] /ˈpɑː.stᵊr.ᵊl/ Ⓤⓢ /ˈpæs.tɚ-/ *adj* describes a piece of art, writing or music that represents the pleasant and traditional features of the countryside: *The painting depicts an idyllic pastoral scene of shepherds watching over their grazing sheep.*

ˈpastoral ˌfarming *noun* **[U]** farming which involves keeping sheep, cattle, etc.

ˌpast parˈticiple *noun* **[C]** the form of a verb, usually made by adding *-ed*, which is used in some grammatical structures such as the passive or PERFECT tenses: *The past participle of 'cook' is 'cooked'.*

the ˌpast ˈperfect *noun* **[S]** (*ALSO* **the pluperfect**) the grammatical tense used to describe an action that had already finished when another action happened. It is made with 'had' and a past participle: *'I had just cooked' is an example of the past perfect, and 'I had just been cooking' is an example of the past perfect* ***continuous.***

pastrami /pæsˈtrɑː.mi/ Ⓤⓢ /pə-/ *noun* **[U]** spicy smoked beef usually cut in thin slices and eaten cold on bread

pastry /ˈpeɪ.stri/ *noun* **1** **[U]** a food made from a mixture of flour, fat and water, which is rolled flat and wrapped round or put over or under other foods and baked: *shortcrust/puff/filo/choux/flaky pastry* ○ *Ann makes delicious pastry – you should try her apple pie.* ➲See also **Danish pastry**. **2** **[C]** a type of sweet cake made of special pastry and usually containing something such as fruit or nuts: *We were offered a selection of cakes and pastries with our tea.*

the ˌpast ˈsimple *noun* **[S]** (*ALSO* **the simple past**) the form of a verb used to describe an action which happened before the present time and is no longer happening. It is usually made by adding *-ed*: *The past simple of 'cook' is 'cooked'.*

the ˌpast ˈtense *noun* **[S]** used generally to describe grammatical structures that describe actions which have now finished. It is used by some people to refer to the PAST SIMPLE: *Add -ed to all these verbs to put them* ***in*** *the past tense.* ○ *I think her husband must be dead – she always talks about him* ***in*** *the past tense.*

pasture /ˈpɑːs.tʃəʳ/ Ⓤⓢ /ˈpæs.tʃɚ/ *noun* **[C or U]** grass or similar plants suitable for animals such as cows and sheep to eat, or an area of land covered in this: *The sheep were grazing on the lush green pastures.* ○ *Some fields are planted with crops for several years, and then returned to pasture for the cattle.*

• **put *sb* out to pasture** *INFORMAL* to stop someone working in their job because they are too old to be useful

• **greener pastures** (*UK ALSO* **pastures new**, *US ALSO* **new pastures**) a new place or activity that offers new opportunities: *Many scientists working for the government have left for greener pastures in the private sector.* ○ *She's giving up her job and moving on to pastures new.*

pasty [FOOD] /ˈpæs.ti/ *noun* **[C]** a small container made of pastry with a savoury filling such as meat, vegetables or cheese: *a cheese-and-onion pasty*

pasty [APPEARANCE] /ˈpeɪ.sti/ *adj* *DISAPPROVING* (of someone's face or skin) very pale and unhealthy looking: *He's a rather unattractive man with long greasy hair and pasty skin.*

pasty-faced /ˈpeɪ.sti.feɪst/ *adj* looking pale and ill

PA (system) /ˌpiːˈeɪˌsɪs.təm/ *noun* **[C usually sing]** *ABBREVIATION FOR* **public address system** (= equipment for making sound, especially someone's voice, louder in a public place): *They've just announced* ***on*** *the PA that our flight's been delayed.*

pat [TOUCH] /pæt/ *verb* **[T]** **-tt-** to touch someone or something gently and usually repeatedly with the hand flat: *He patted my head/patted me* ***on*** *the head affectionately.* ○ *I bent down to pat the little puppy.*

• **pat *sb* on the back** to praise someone for doing something good

pat /pæt/ *noun* **[C]** when you pat a person or animal: *I* ***gave*** *the little boy a pat* ***on*** *the head.*

• **a pat on the back** praise: *I* ***got*** *a pat on the back* ***from*** (= was praised by) *my boss.*

pat [PIECE] /pæt/ *noun* **[C]** a small flat piece, especially of butter

pat [WITHOUT THOUGHT] /pæt/ *adj* *USUALLY DISAPPROVING* describes an answer or remark that someone has previously prepared, so that they say it quickly and without any real thought: *The minister came out with a pat answer/response.*

• **have/know *sth* off pat** *UK* (*US* **have/know *sth* down pat**) to know something so well that you can say or do it without having to try or think: *I'd given the talk so many times I had it off pat.*

patch AREA /pætʃ/ *noun* [C] **1** a small area which is different in some way from the area that surrounds it: *Our dog has a black patch on his back.* ○ *The hotel walls were covered in damp patches.* ○ *There were lots of icy patches on the road this morning.* ○ *This story is good in patches* (= some parts are good), *but I wouldn't really recommend it.* **2** INFORMAL a local area within which someone works: *He's been working as a policeman on the same patch for twenty years.*

● **go through a bad/difficult/rough/sticky patch** INFORMAL to experience a lot of problems in a period in your life: *Andy's going through a bit of a rough patch at the moment – his wife wants a divorce.*

● **not be a patch on** *sth* UK INFORMAL to be much less good than something: *This new washing machine isn't a patch on our old one.*

patchy /'pætʃ.i/ *adj* **1** only existing or happening in some parts: *The varnish is a bit patchy on this table.* ○ *Southeast England will start with some patchy rain/ patchy cloud at first.* **2** sometimes good and sometimes bad: *Matthew found the service offered by estate agents extremely patchy.* **patchily** /'pætʃ.ɪ.li/ *adv* **patchiness** /'pætʃ.ɪ.nəs/ *noun* [U]

patch PIECE OF MATERIAL /pætʃ/ *noun* [C] **1** a small piece of material fixed over something to cover it: *I'll have to sew a patch onto these jeans – they're ripped at the knee.* **2** a small piece of material which can be stuck to the skin, from which particular substances can be absorbed into the body: *Some people wear nicotine patches to help them give up smoking.* **3** an **eye-patch**

patch /pætʃ/ *verb* [T] to put a patch on something

patch CONNECT /pætʃ/ *verb* [T usually + adv or prep] SPECIALIZED to connect electronic or telephone equipment to a system

patch COMPUTER /pætʃ/ *noun* [C] a small computer program that can be added to an existing program in order to make the existing program work properly: *I downloaded a patch from their website.* ⊃Compare **plugin**.

PHRASAL VERBS WITH **patch** ▼

▲ **patch** *sth* **together** *phrasal verb* [M] to arrange something very quickly but not very carefully: *There is much disagreement, but the group of countries is trying to patch together a treaty on defence.*

▲ **patch** *sth* **up** *phrasal verb* **1** [M] to try to improve a relationship after there have been problems: *Jackie and Bill are still trying to patch up their marriage.* ○ *Did you manage to patch things up with Jackie after your row?* **2** to repair something, especially in a basic and temporary way

▲ **patch** *sb/sth* **up** *phrasal verb* to give basic medical care to someone that helps them temporarily: *If you've cut your hand, the first aider will patch you up.*

patch pocket *noun* [C] a square of material sewn onto the outside of a piece of clothing for carrying things in: *a skirt with two patch pockets*

patchwork /'pætʃ.wɜːk/ US /-wɜːk/ *noun* **1** [U] cloth which is made by sewing together a lot of smaller usually square pieces of cloth with different patterns and colours, or the activity of doing this: *a patchwork quilt/ jacket* ○ *The old lady sat in the corner doing patchwork.* **2** [S] a mixture of different things: *We looked out of the aircraft window down onto the patchwork of fields below.*

pate /peɪt/ *noun* [C] OLD-FASHIONED OR HUMOROUS the top of a person's head

pâté /'pæ.teɪ/ US /-'-/ *noun* [C or U] a thick smooth soft savoury mixture made from meat, fish or vegetables: *liver/salmon/vegetarian pâté*

patella /pə'tel.ə/ *noun* [C] *plural* **patellae** SPECIALIZED a **kneecap** (= bone) ⊃See picture **The Body** on page Centre 5

patent LEGAL RIGHT /'peɪ.tᵊnt/ US /'pæt.ᵊnt/ *noun* [C] the official legal right to make or sell an invention for a particular number of years: *In 1880 Alexander Graham Bell was granted a patent on an apparatus for signalling and communicating called a Photophone.* ○ *The company took out/filed a patent on a genetically engineered*

tomato that remains firm longer than untreated tomatoes. **patent** /'peɪ.tᵊnt/ US /'pæt.ᵊnt/ *adj* [before n] *a patent screwdriver* **patent** /'peɪ.tᵊnt/ US /'pæt.ᵊnt/ *verb* [T] *If you don't patent your invention, other people may make all the profit out of it.*

patentee /ˌpeɪ.tᵊn'tiː/ US /ˌpæt.ᵊn'tiː/ *noun* [C] SPECIALIZED the person or organization that owns the legal right to make or sell something

patent SHINY /'peɪ.tᵊnt/ US /'pæt.ᵊnt/ *adj* **patent leather** leather that has a very shiny surface: *black patent leather shoes*

patent OBVIOUS /'peɪ.tᵊnt/ US /-tᵊnt/ *adj* [before n] FORMAL very obvious: *a patent lie* ○ *a patent disregard of the law* ○ *"No," he replied, with patent distaste.* **patently** /'peɪ.tᵊnt.li/ US /-tᵊnt-/ *adv*: *She was patently lying.* ○ *It's patently obvious that he doesn't care.*

patent 'medicine *noun* [C] a medicine, usually not very powerful, which you can buy from a shop without the written permission of a doctor

pater /'peɪ.tər/ US /'pɑː-/ US /'pɑː.t̬ər/ *noun* [C] UK OLD-FASHIONED FORMAL father

paternal /pə'tɜː.nᵊl/ US /-'tɜː-/ *adj* of or like a father: *He's very paternal* (= showing the affectionate feelings of a father) *– it's lovely to see him with the baby.* ○ *My paternal grandparents* (= My father's parents) *were Irish.* ⊃Compare **maternal**. **paternally** /pə'tɜː.nə.li/ US /-'tɜː-/ *adv*

paternity /pə'tɜː.nɪ.ti/ US /-'tɜː.nə.t̬i/ *noun* [U] **1** the fact of being a father or connected with being a father: *Increasingly, the unmarried father of a child in Europe registers his paternity at the baby's birth.* ○ *Does your firm give paternity leave* (= time a man is allowed away from work when his wife or partner is having a child)? **2** FORMAL the origin of an idea or invention

paternalism /pə'tɜː.nə.lɪ.zᵊm/ US /-'tɜː-/ *noun* [U] USUALLY DISAPPROVING an attitude of people in authority which results in them making decisions for other people which are often beneficial but which prevent those people from taking responsibility for their own lives **paternalist** /pə'tɜː.nə.lɪst/ US /-'tɜː-/ *noun* [C] **paternalistic** /pəˌtɜː.nə-'lɪs.tɪk/ US /-ˌtɜː.nə'lɪs-/ *adj* MAINLY DISAPPROVING

path TRACK /pɑːθ/ US /pæθ/ *noun* [C] a route or track between one place and another, or the direction in which something is moving: *a garden path* ○ *a concrete path* ○ *a well-trodden path* ○ *This is the path to the cliffs.* ○ *It will be several days before snowploughs clear a path (through) to the village.* ○ *They followed the path until they came to a gate.* ○ *A fierce fire is still raging through the forest, burning everything in its path* (= as it moves forward). ○ *The Weather Service issues warnings to people in the path of a hurricane* (= in the area in which it is moving). ○ *The charged particles move in spiral paths.* ○ FIGURATIVE *His path through life was never easy.*

● **paths cross** If two people's paths cross, they meet: *It was a pleasure meeting you – I hope our paths cross again.*

path ACTIONS /pɑːθ/ US /pæθ/ *noun* [C] a set of actions, especially ones which lead to a goal or result: *The path to success is fraught with difficulties.*

pathetic SAD /pə'θet.ɪk/ US /-'θet̬-/ *adj* causing feelings of sadness, sympathy or sometimes lack of respect, especially because a person or an animal is suffering: *The refugees were a pathetic sight – starving, frightened and cold.* ○ *After the accident he became a pathetic figure, a shadow of his former self.* ⊃See also **pathos**. **pathetically** /pə'θet.ɪ.kli/ US /-'θet̬-/ *adv*: *Other former captives spoke of pathetically inadequate food rations.*

pathetic UNSUCCESSFUL /pə'θet.ɪk/ US /-'θet̬-/ *adj* DISAPPROVING causing a lack of respect, often because unsuccessful or lacking ability, effort or bravery: *a pathetic attempt/ joke/excuse* ○ *Are you telling me you're frightened to speak to her? Don't be so pathetic!* **pathetically** /pə-'θet.ɪ.kli/ US /-'θet̬-/ *adv*: *My parents' advice on sex was pathetically inadequate.*

pathogen /'pæθ.ə.dʒᵊn/ *noun* [C] any small organism, such as a virus or a BACTERIUM which can cause disease: *a dangerous pathogen* **pathogenic** /ˌpæθ.ə'dʒen.ɪk/ *adj*

P

pathological /ˌpæθ.əˈlɒdʒ.ɪ.kᵊl/ ⑩ /-ˈlɑː.dʒɪ-/ *adj INFORMAL* (of a person) unable to control part of their behaviour; unreasonable: *I've got a pathological fear of heights.* ○ *Anthony's a pathological **liar**.* **pathologically** /ˌpæθ.əˈlɒdʒ.ɪ.kli/ ⑩ /-ˈlɑː.dʒɪ-/ *adv*

pathology /pəˈθɒl.ə.dʒi/ ⑩ /-ˈθɑː.lə-/ *noun* [U] the scientific study of disease
pathologist /pəˈθɒl.ə.dʒɪst/ ⑩ /-ˈθɑː.lə-/ *noun* [C] an expert in the study of diseases, especially someone who examines a dead person's body and cuts it open to discover how they died **pathological** /ˌpæθ.əˈlɒdʒ.ɪ.kᵊl/ ⑩ /-ˈlɑː.dʒɪ-/ *adj: a pathological condition/complaint* **pathologically** /ˌpæθ.əˈlɒdʒ.ɪ.kli/ ⑩ /-ˈlɑː.dʒɪ-/ *adv*

pathos /ˈpeɪ.θɒs/ ⑩ /-θɑːs/ *noun* [U] *LITERARY* the power of a situation, piece of writing, work of art or person to cause feelings of sadness, especially because of sympathy: *There's a pathos in his performance which he never lets slide into sentimentality.*

pathway /ˈpɑːθ.weɪ/ ⑩ /ˈpæθ-/ *noun* [C] **1** *SLIGHTLY FORMAL* a track which a person can walk along: *New pedestrian pathways are being built alongside the road.* **2** a **path** (= set of actions that you take in life): *Working your way up through a company is a difficult pathway.* **3** *SLIGHTLY FORMAL* a set of connected chemical reactions in biology

patience /ˈpeɪ.ʃᵊnts/ *noun* [U] **1** the ability to wait, or to continue doing something despite difficulties, or to suffer without complaining or becoming annoyed: *You have to have such a lot of patience when you're dealing with kids.* ○ *In the end I **lost** my patience and shouted at her.* ○ *He's a good teacher, but he doesn't have much patience **with** the slower pupils.* ○ *Making small-scale models **takes/requires** a great deal of patience.* ○ *Their youngest son was beginning to **try** my patience* (= annoy me). ○ *Patience – they'll be here soon!* ✳ NOTE: The opposite is **impatience**. **2** *UK* (*US* **solitaire**) a game played with cards by one person
• **have the patience of a saint** to always be calm and never let anything upset you

patient /ˈpeɪ.ʃᵊnt/ *adj* having patience: *Dinner will be ready in half an hour – just be patient!* ○ *Be patient **with** her – she's very young.* ✳ NOTE: The opposite is **impatient**. **patiently** /ˈpeɪ.ʃᵊnt.li/ *adv: There was a queue of people **waiting** patiently for the bus to arrive.*

patient /ˈpeɪ.ʃᵊnt/ *noun* [C] a person who is receiving medical care, or who is cared for by a particular doctor or dentist when necessary: *I'm a patient of Dr Stephens, please could I make an appointment to see her?*

patina /ˈpæt.ɪ.nə/ ⑩ /ˈpæt̬.ᵊn.ə/ *noun* **1** [S] a thin surface layer which develops on something because of use, age or chemical action: *His tomb was covered with **a** yellow patina **of** lichen.* **2** [S] *FORMAL* something which makes someone or something seem to be something which they are not: *Beware their patina of civility, it's only an act.* **3** [U] *SPECIALIZED* a blue-green layer that forms on copper, brass or BRONZE

patio /ˈpæt.i.əʊ/ ⑩ /ˈpæt̬.i.oʊ/ *noun* [C] *plural* **patios** an area outside a house with a solid floor but no roof which is used, especially for eating, in good weather: *In the summer we have breakfast out **on** the patio.*

patisserie /pəˈtiː.sᵊr.i/ ⑩ /ˈpæt̬.ɪs.ᵊr-/ *noun* **1** [U] cakes made in the French style **2** [C] a shop that sells these cakes

patois /ˈpæt.wɑː/ *noun* [C or U] *plural* **patois** the form of a language spoken by people in a particular area which is different from the standard language of the country: *the local patois*

patriarch /ˈpeɪ.tri.ɑːk/ ⑩ /-ɑːrk/ *noun* [C] a bishop in particular Eastern Christian churches

patriarchy /ˈpeɪ.tri.ɑː.ki/ ⑩ /-ɑːr-/ *noun* [C or U] a society in which the oldest male is the leader of the family, or a society controlled by men in which men use their power to their own advantage: *Patriarchy has not disappeared – it has merely changed form.* ○ *She rails against patriarchy and hierarchy.* ⊃Compare **matriarchy** at **matriarch**.
patriarch /ˈpeɪ.tri.ɑːk/ ⑩ /-ɑːrk/ *noun* [C] the male leader of a family ⊃Compare **matriarch**. **patriarchal** /ˌpeɪ.tri-

ˈɑː.kᵊl/ ⑩ /-ˈɑːr-/ *adj: patriarchal structure* ○ *a patriarchal society*

patrician /pəˈtrɪʃ.ᵊn/ *adj FORMAL* of or like a person of high social rank **patrician** /pəˈtrɪʃ.ᵊn/ *noun* [C]

patricide /ˈpæt.rɪ.saɪd/ ⑩ /-rə-/ *noun* [U] the crime of killing your own father ⊃Compare **matricide; parricide**.

patriot /ˈpæt.ri.ət/ /ˈpeɪ.tri-/ ⑩ /ˈpeɪ.tri.ɑːt/ *noun* [C] a person who loves their country and, if necessary, will fight for it
patriotic /ˌpæt.riˈɒt.ɪk/ ⑩ /ˌpeɪ.triˈɑː.t̬ɪk/ *adj* showing love for your country and pride in it: *patriotic fervour/ pride* ○ *Many Americans felt it was their patriotic **duty** to buy bonds to support the war effort.* **patriotically** /ˌpæt.riˈɒt.ɪ.kli/ ⑩ /ˌpeɪ.triˈɑː.t̬ɪ.kli/ *adv*
patriotism /ˈpæt.ri.ə.tɪ.zᵊm/ /ˈpeɪ.tri-/ ⑩ /ˈpeɪ.tri-/ /-t̬ɪ-/ *noun* [U] when you love your country and are proud of it

patrol /pəˈtrəʊl/ ⑩ /-ˈtroʊl/ *verb* [I or T] **-ll-** (especially of soldiers or the police) to go around an area or a building to see if there is any trouble or danger: *The whole town is patrolled by police because of the possibility of riots.* ○ *A security guard with a dog patrols the building site at night.* ○ *Coastguards found a deserted boat while patrolling (along) the coast.*
patrol /pəˈtrəʊl/ ⑩ /-ˈtroʊl/ *noun* [C or U] the act of looking for trouble or danger in a building or area: *a highway patrol* ○ *Three reconnaissance aircraft are permanently **on** patrol.*
patrol /pəˈtrəʊl/ ⑩ /-ˈtroʊl/ *group noun* [C] a small group of soldiers or military ships, aircraft or vehicles, especially one which patrols an area: *Our forward patrol has/ have spotted the enemy.*

paˈtrol ˌcar *noun* [C] an official car used by the police

paˈtrol ˌofficer *noun* [C] (*MALE ALSO* **patrolman**) *US* a police officer who wears a uniform and patrols a particular area

paˈtrol ˌwagon *noun* [C] (*ALSO* **paddy wagon**) *US* an enclosed police vehicle used for transporting prisoners

patron SUPPORTER /ˈpeɪ.trᵊn/ *noun* [C] a person or group that supports an activity or organization, especially by giving money: *The Princess Royal is a well-known patron of several charities.*
patronage /ˈpæt.rə.nɪdʒ/ /ˈpeɪ.trᵊn-/ ⑩ /ˈpeɪ.trᵊn-/ /ˈpæt.-rᵊn-/ *noun* [U] the support given to an organization by someone: *The Conservative Party **enjoys** the patronage of much of the business community.*

patron CUSTOMER /ˈpeɪ.trᵊn/ *noun* [C] *FORMAL* a person who uses a particular shop, restaurant, hotel, etc., especially regularly; a customer: *Will patrons kindly note that this shop will be closed on 17th July.*
patronage /ˈpæt.rə.nɪdʒ/ /ˈpeɪ.trᵊn-/ ⑩ /ˈpeɪ.trᵊn-/ /ˈpæt.-rᵊn-/ *noun* [U] *FORMAL* the business given to a shop or restaurant, etc. by its customers: *We would like to thank all of our customers for their patronage in the past.*
patronize, *UK USUALLY* **-ise** /ˈpæt.rə.naɪz/ ⑩ /ˈpeɪ.trᵊn-/ /ˈpæt.rᵊn-/ *verb* [T] *FORMAL* to be a regular customer of a shop or restaurant, etc: *We always patronize Beaumont's – the food is so good there.*

patronage /ˈpæt.rə.nɪdʒ/ /ˈpeɪ.trᵊn-/ ⑩ /ˈpeɪ.trᵊn-/ /ˈpæt.rᵊn-/ *noun* [U] *MAINLY DISAPPROVING* the power of a person to give someone an important job or position: *Patronage is a potent force if used politically.*

patronize, *UK USUALLY* **-ise** /ˈpæt.rə.naɪz/ ⑩ /ˈpeɪ.trᵊn-/ /ˈpæt.rᵊn-/ ⑩ /ˈpeɪ.trə-/ *verb* [T] *DISAPPROVING* to speak to or behave towards someone as if they are stupid or unimportant: *Stop patronising me – I understand the play as well as you do.* **patronizing**, *UK USUALLY* **-ising** /ˈpæt.rə.naɪ.zɪŋ/ ⑩ /ˈpeɪ.trᵊn.aɪ-/ /ˈpæt.rᵊn.aɪ-/ *adj: It's that patronizing tone of hers that I can't bear.*

ˌpatron ˈsaint *noun* [C] a Christian saint who is believed to give special help to a particular place, activity, person or type of object: *St. John Bosco is the patron saint of Turin.*

patsy /ˈpæt.si/ *noun* [C] *US SLANG* a person whom it is easy to cheat or make suffer

patter SPEECH /ˈpæt.əʳ/ ⑩ /ˈpæt̬.ɚ/ *noun* [U] continuous and sometimes amusing speech or talk, often learned in advance, especially used by someone trying to sell things or by an entertainer: *He should succeed – he* *dresses well and his **sales** patter is slick and convincing.*

patter [SOUND] /ˈpæt.əʳ/ [US] /ˈpæt̬.ɚ/ *noun* **[S]** the sound of a lot of things gently and repeatedly hitting a surface: *I find **the** patter **of** rain on the roof soothing.*

• **the patter(ing) of tiny feet** *HUMOROUS* something that you say which means that someone is going to have a baby: *Are you telling me we're going to be hearing the patter of tiny feet?*

patter /ˈpæt.əʳ/ [US] /ˈpæt̬.ɚ/ *verb* **[I usually + adv or prep]** to make the sound of a lot of things gently and repeatedly hitting a surface: *I heard the rain patter **against/on** the window.* ○ *We could hear mice pattering **about/around** looking for food.*

pattern [WAY] /ˈpæt.ᵊn/ [US] /ˈpæt̬.ɚn/ *noun* **[C]** a particular way in which something is done, organized or happens: *The pattern of family life has been changing over recent years.* ○ *A pattern is beginning to emerge from our analysis of the accident data.* ○ *In this type of mental illness, the usual pattern is bouts of depression alternating with elation.* ○ *Many **behaviour(al)** patterns have been identified in the chimp colony.*

pattern [ARRANGEMENT] /ˈpæt.ᵊn/ [US] /ˈpæt̬.ɚn/ *noun* **[C]** any regularly repeated arrangement, especially a design made from repeated lines, shapes or colours on a surface: *Look, the frost has made a beautiful pattern on the window.* ○ *I've never really cared for **floral** patterns.* **patterned** /ˈpæt.ᵊnd/ [US] /ˈpæt̬.ɚnd/ *adj*: *patterned textiles/wallpaper*

pattern [EXAMPLE] /ˈpæt.ᵊn/ [US] /ˈpæt̬.ɚn/ *noun* **[C usually sing]** something which is used as an example, especially to copy: *The design is so good it's sure to **set the** pattern for many others.*

pattern [DRAWING] /ˈpæt.ᵊn/ [US] /ˈpæt̬.ɚn/ *noun* **[C]** a drawing or shape used to show how to make something: *a knitting pattern* ○ *a dress pattern* ○ *Cut out all of the pieces from the paper pattern and pin them on the cloth.*

pattern [PIECE] /ˈpæt.ᵊn/ [US] /ˈpæt̬.ɚn/ *noun* **[C]** a small piece of cloth or paper taken from a usual-sized piece and used to show what it looks like; a SAMPLE: *a pattern book*

pattern /ˈpæt.ᵊn/ [US] /ˈpæt̬.ɚn/ *verb*

▲ **pattern *yourself* on *sb/sth*** *phrasal verb* **[R]** to copy something or someone: *She patterns herself **on** her big sister.*

patty /ˈpæt.i/ [US] /ˈpæt̬-/ *noun* **[C]** a piece of food made into a disc shape which is then cooked: *minced meat patties/sweet corn patties*

paucity /ˈpɔː.sɪ.ti/ [US] /ˈpɑː.sə.t̬i/ *noun* **[S]** *FORMAL* a lack of something: *There is a paucity **of** information on the ingredients of many cosmetics.*

paunch /pɔːntʃ/ [US] /pɑːntʃ/ *noun* **[C]** a fat stomach, especially on a man **paunchy** /pɔːn.tʃi/ [US] /pɑːn-/ *adj* **paunchiness** /ˈpɔːn.tʃɪ.nəs/ [US] /ˈpɑːn-/ *noun* **[U]**

pauper /ˈpɔː.pəʳ/ [US] /ˈpɑː.pɚ/ *noun* **[C]** a very poor person

pause /pɔːz/ [US] /pɑːz/ *noun* **[C]** a short period in which something such as a sound or an activity is stopped before starting again: *There will be a brief pause **in** the proceedings while the piano is moved into place.* ○ *After a long, awkward pause someone asked a question.* ○ *She spoke for three quarters of an hour without so much as a pause.* ○ *There followed a **pregnant*** (= filled with meaning) *pause in which neither of them knew what to say.*

• **give *sb* pause** *FORMAL* to cause someone to stop and think about what they were doing or intending to do

pause /pɔːz/ [US] /pɑːz/ *verb* **[I]** to stop doing something for a short time: *He paused and thought for a moment.* ○ *She paused to get her breath back and then carried on jogging.*

pave /peɪv/ *verb* **[T]** to cover an area of ground with a hard flat surface of pieces of stone, concrete or bricks: *The area from the shops to the beach is paved **with** bricks set in patterns.*

• **paved with gold** used about a city to mean that it is easy to make money there: *Unemployed youngsters still come to London in their hundreds thinking that **the streets are** paved with gold.*

• **pave the way** If something paves the way for/to something else, it makes the other thing possible: *Scientists hope that data from the probe will pave the way for a more detailed exploration of Mars.*

paving /ˈpeɪ.vɪŋ/ *noun* **[U]** a paved area, or material used to pave an area

pavement /ˈpeɪv.mənt/ *noun* **[C]** **1** *UK* (*US* **sidewalk**) a path with a hard surface beside one or both sides of a road, that people walk on: *Keep to the pavement, Rosie, there's a good girl.* **2** *US* the surface of a road when it has been covered with concrete or TARMAC

ˈpavement ˌartist *UK noun* **[C]** (*US* **sidewalk artist**) a person who draws pictures on a pavement using coloured CHALKS, especially so that people who walk past will give small amounts of money

pavilion [BUILDING] /pəˈvɪl.jən/ *noun* **[C]** **1** *UK* a building beside a sports field, especially one where cricket is played, used by the players and sometimes by people watching the game **2** *US* one of a group of related buildings: *the West Pavilion of Central General Hospital* **3** *US* a large building in which sports or entertainment take place

pavilion [TEMPORARY STRUCTURE] /pəˈvɪl.jən/ *noun* **[C]** a temporary structure, such as a large tent, especially used at public events or for shows

ˈpaving ˌstone *noun* **[C]** *MAINLY UK* a flat piece of stone, usually used in groups to cover a path or an area

pavlova /pævˈləʊ.və/ [US] /pɑːvˈloʊ-/ *noun* **[C or U]** a sweet cold dish consisting of a MERINGUE (= the transparent part of an egg cooked slowly with sugar) with a layer of fruit and cream on top

paw /pɔː/ [US] /pɑː/ *noun* **1** **[C]** the foot of an animal which has claws or nails, such as a cat, dog or bear: *I found paw **prints** in the kitchen.* ⊃Compare **hoof**. **2** **[C usually plural]** *INFORMAL HUMOROUS* a human hand: *Take your filthy paws off my nice clean washing!*

paw /pɔː/ [US] /pɑː/ *verb* **1** **[I or T]** to touch something with a paw: *When their dog heard them it began pawing **(at)** the ground in excitement.* **2** **[T]** *INFORMAL* to feel or touch someone roughly with the hands, especially in an unpleasant sexual way

pawn [GAME PIECE] /pɔːn/ [US] /pɑːn/ *noun* **[C]** **1** any one of the eight least valuable pieces in the game of chess which are all the same **2** a person who does not have any real power but is used by others to achieve something: *The refugees are pawns **in** an international political dispute.*

pawn [MONEY] /pɔːn/ [US] /pɑːn/ *verb* **[T]** to leave a possession with a PAWNBROKER, for which they give money but which they can also sell if the money is not paid back within a particular time: *Of all items pawned, jewellery is the most common.* **pawn** /pɔːn/ [US] /pɑːn/ *noun* **[U]**

pawnbroker /ˈpɔːnˌbrəʊ.kəʳ/ [US] /ˈpɑːnˌbroʊ.kɚ/ *noun* **[C]** a person who lends money in exchange for items which they can sell if the person leaving them does not pay an agreed amount of money in an agreed time

ˈpawn ˌshop *noun* **[C]** (*ALSO* **pawnbroker's**) a shop where a pawnbroker operates their business

pawpaw /ˈpɔː.pɔː/ [US] /ˈpɑː.pɑː/ *noun* **[C or U]** **1** *OLD-FASHIONED FOR* **papaya** **2** (*ALSO* **papaw**) *US* (the fruit of) a type of tree that grows in central and southern parts of the US

pay [BUY] /peɪ/ *verb* **[I or T]** **paid, paid** to give money to someone for something you want to buy or for services provided: *How much did you pay **for** the tickets?* ○ *I pay my taxes.* ○ *Will you pay these cheques **into** (US USUALLY **deposit** these checks **in**) my account for me?* ○ **[+ two objects]** *I'll pay you the fiver **back** tomorrow.* ○ *I paid the driver **(in/with)** cash.* ○ *Would you prefer to pay **with/by** cash, cheque or credit card?* ○ **[+ obj + to infinitive]** *I think we'll need to pay a builder **to** take this wall down.* ○ *Did Linda pay you **for** looking after her cats while she was away?* ○ *I paid **(out)** a lot of money to get the washing machine fixed and it still doesn't work!*

• **pay dividends** If something you do pays dividends, it causes good results at a time in the future: *All that extra training is paying dividends.*

• **You pays your money and you takes your choice/chance.** *INFORMAL SAYING* You are responsible for your decisions and cannot blame anyone else when what you have chosen is not successful.

P

• **pay *your* dues** to do something that you do not enjoy in order to have something that you want, or because you feel it is your duty

• **pay for itself** If something pays for itself, it works so well that it saves the same amount of money that it cost: *The advertising should pay for itself.*

• **pay the price** to experience the bad result of something you have done: *If you abuse your body now, you'll pay the price when you're older.*

• **pay the ultimate price** to die because of something you have done, especially something you do for moral reasons: *If our soldiers have to pay the ultimate price for defending their country, then so be it.*

• **pay through the nose** *INFORMAL* to pay too much money for something: *We paid through the nose to get the car fixed and it still doesn't go properly.*

• **pay top dollar** *US* to pay a lot of money for something

• **pay *your* way** to pay for yourself rather than allowing someone else to pay

• **He who pays the piper calls the tune.** *SAYING* said to emphasize that the person who is paying someone to do something can decide how it should be done

payable /ˈpeɪ.ə.bl̩/ *adj* **[after v]** **1** that should be paid: *Interest payments are payable monthly.* **2** If a cheque is payable to a person or an organization, the money will be paid to them because their name is written on it: *Please make your cheque payable to WWF.*

payee /peɪˈiː/ *noun* **[C]** *SPECIALIZED* a person who money is paid to or should be paid to

payer /ˈpeɪ.əʳ/ [US] /ˈpeɪ.ɚ/ *noun* **1 good/bad payer** a person who usually pays on time/late **2** used as a combining form: *a tax payer*

payment /ˈpeɪ.mənt/ *noun* **1 [C or U]** an amount of money paid: *Usually we ask for payment on receipt of the goods.* ○ *We need a deposit of £165 followed by twelve monthly payments of £60.* ○ *When is the first payment* ***due?*** **2 [S or U]** reward: *Verbal abuse was hardly the payment I expected* ***for*** *my troubles.* **3 back payment** a sum of money received by an employee because of a pay rise at an earlier time

COMMON LEARNER ERROR

pay for

Remember that **pay** is always followed by the preposition 'for' if there is a direct object, except in certain phrases such as 'pay a bill/fine/etc.'

You have to pay for the tickets in advance, I'm afraid.

~~*You have to pay the tickets in advance, I'm afraid.*~~

USAGE

pay, wage, salary, or **income?**

Pay is a general word which means the money that you receive for working.

Doctors usually get more pay than teachers.

A **wage** is an amount of money you receive each day or week. It is often paid in CASH (= notes and coins).

His weekly wage is $400.

A **salary** is the money you receive each month. A person's **salary** is often expressed as the total amount in a year.

His salary is £20, 000.

Your **income** is the total amount of money that you earn by working or investing money.

She has a monthly income of £1, 400.

pay [WORK] /peɪ/ *verb* **[I or T] paid, paid** to give money to someone for work which they have done: *The company pays £220 a week* ***for*** *people to act as couriers.* ○ *Accountancy may be boring but at least it pays* ***well.*** ○ *Most of these women are very* ***poorly*** *paid and work in terrible conditions.*

pay /peɪ/ *noun* **[U]** the money you receive for doing a job: *UK Any pay* ***rise*** *(US USUALLY* ***raise****) must be in line with inflation.* ○ *It's a nice job but the pay is appalling.*

• **be in the pay of *sb*** to work for someone, especially secretly

pay [PROFIT] /peɪ/ *verb* **[I] paid, paid** to give a profit, advantage or benefit to someone or something: *It never pays* ***to*** *take risks where human safety is concerned.*

pay [GIVE] /peɪ/ *verb* **[T] paid, paid** to give or do something: *Please pay* ***attention,*** *I've got something important to say.* ○ *The commander paid* ***tribute to*** *the courage of his troops.* ○ *It's always nice to be paid* ***a compliment.*** ○ *A crowd of mourners gathered to pay* ***their respects to*** *the dead man.*

• **pay *(sb)* a call** to visit someone: *I'll pay you a call when I'm in the area.* ○ *If you leave your address, I'll pay a call* ***on*** *you when I'm in the area.*

• **put paid to *sth*** *UK* to finish or destroy something: *A knee injury has put paid to her chances of getting into the final.*

PHRASAL VERBS WITH **pay** ▼

▲ **pay *sb/sth* back** [MONEY] *phrasal verb* **[M]** to pay someone the money that you owe them: *Can you lend me a fiver? I'll pay you/it back tomorrow.*

▲ **pay *sb* back** [UNKIND ACT] *phrasal verb* to do something unpleasant to someone because they have done something unpleasant to you: *He swore he'd pay her back* ***for*** *all she'd done to him.*

▲ **pay for *sth*** *phrasal verb* to be punished for doing something bad to someone else, or to suffer because of a mistake that you made: *We all pay for our mistakes in some way at some time.* ○ *He tricked me and I'm going to make him pay for it!*

▲ **pay *sth* in** *phrasal verb* **[M]** (*US USUALLY* **deposit**) to put money into a bank account: *If you go to the bank, will you pay these cheques in for me?*

▲ **pay off** [SUCCESS] *phrasal verb* If something you have done pays off, it is successful: *All her hard work paid off in the end, and she finally passed the exam.*

payoff /ˈpeɪ.ɒf/ [US] /-ɑːf/ *noun* **[C]** *INFORMAL* the result of a set of actions, or an explanation at the end of something: *The payoff for years of research is a microscope which performs better than all of its competitors.*

▲ **pay *sth* off** [MONEY] *phrasal verb* **[M]** to pay back money that you owe: *We should be able to pay off the debt within two years.*

▲ **pay *sb* off** *phrasal verb* **[M]** **1** If your employer pays you off, they pay you for the last time and then end your job, because now they do not need you or could not pay you in the future. **2** *INFORMAL* to give someone money so that they will not do or say something, or so that they will go away: *There were rumours that key witnesses had been paid off to keep quiet.*

payoff /ˈpeɪ.ɒf/ [US] /-ɑːf/ *noun* **[C]** money paid to someone, especially so that they do not cause trouble or so that they will do what you want them to: *It has been alleged that the minister received a secret payoff from an arms dealer.*

▲ **pay *(sth)* out** [MONEY] *phrasal verb* **[M]** to spend a lot of money on something, or to pay a lot of money to someone: *I've just paid out £500 on getting the car fixed.*

payout /ˈpeɪ.aʊt/ *noun* **[C]** a large sum of money which is paid to someone: *With this insurance policy there is a maximum payout of £2500.*

▲ **pay *sth* out** [ROPE] *phrasal verb* **[M]** to release a piece of rope or CABLE in a controlled way

▲ **pay up** *phrasal verb INFORMAL* to give someone the money that you owe them, especially when you do not want to: *Eventually they paid up, but only after receiving several reminders.*

pay-as-you-go /ˌpeɪ.əz.jəˈgəʊ/ [US] /-ˈgoʊ/ *adj* **[before n]** describes a system in which you pay for a service before you use it and you cannot use more than you have paid for: *a pay-as-you-go mobile phone*

payback /ˈpeɪ.bæk/ *noun* **[C or U]** *MAINLY US* an advantage received from something, especially the profit from a financial investment: *The payback for reorganization should be increased productivity.*

ˈpayback ˌperiod *noun* **[C or U]** the amount of time it takes to get back the sum of money originally invested in something

paycheck /ˈpeɪ.tʃek/ *noun* **[C]** *US FOR* **pay packet**

ˈpay ˌclaim *noun* **[C]** *UK* a demand for an increase in pay: *As expected, management said the workers' pay claim was too high.*

payday /ˈpeɪ.deɪ/ *noun* [U] the day on which a worker receives their pay

PAYE /ˌpiː.eɪ.waɪˈiː/ *noun* [U] *UK ABBREVIATION FOR* Pay As You Earn: a system for collecting income tax in which a person's tax is subtracted and sent to the government by their employer before they are paid

payload /ˈpeɪ.ləʊd/ [US] /-loʊd/ *noun* [C] the amount of goods or people which a vehicle, such as an aircraft, can carry, or the explosive which a missile carries, or the equipment carried in a spacecraft

paymaster /ˈpeɪˌmɑː.stəʳ/ [US] /-ˌmæs.tɚ/ *noun* [C] a person or an organization that pays for something to happen and therefore has or expects to have some control over it: *The government accused the opposition parties of being controlled by trade union paymasters.*

payment /ˈpeɪ.mənt/ *noun* ➲See at **pay** BUY.

payola /peɪˈəʊ.lə/ [US] /-ˈoʊ-/ *noun* [C or U] *MAINLY US OLD-FASHIONED INFORMAL* a secret payment to someone for doing an illegal business action

ˈpay ˌpacket *UK noun* [C] (*US* **paycheck**) the amount of money a person earns: *It's easy to go on expensive holidays when you have a pay packet the size of hers.*

pay-per-view /ˌpeɪ.pəˈvjuː/ [US] /-pɚ-/ *noun* [U] a system for television in which viewers pay for particular programmes which they watch: *pay-per-view television/channels* ○ *We watched the Lewis-Holyfield fight* **on** *pay-per-view.*

ˈpay ˌphone *noun* [C] a public telephone which is made to operate by putting coins into it

ˈpay ˌrise *UK noun* [C] (*US* **pay raise**) an increase in the fixed amount of money you earn for doing your job

payroll /ˈpeɪ.rəʊl/ [US] /-roʊl/ *noun* **1** [C] a list of the people employed by a company showing how much each one earns: *a payroll tax* ○ *McDermot Software is growing fast, adding another 100 employees to its payroll over the last year.* **2** [C usually sing] the total amount of money paid to the people employed by a particular company: *With debts of $4 million and a monthly payroll of $1.2 million, the venture is clearly heading for trouble.*

payslip /ˈpeɪ.slɪp/ *noun* [C] a piece of paper given to someone who is employed to show how much money they have earned and how much tax has been subtracted

ˌpay tˈv *noun* [U] (*ALSO* **pay television**) television stations that you must pay to watch: *Do you have pay tv?*

PBS /ˌpiː.biːˈes/ *noun* [U] *ABBREVIATION FOR* Public Broadcasting Service: a US organization broadcasting generally educational television programmes which is paid for by the people who watch it rather than from advertising

PC [COMPUTER], **pc** /ˌpiːˈsiː/ *noun* [C] *ABBREVIATION FOR* **personal computer**: *The price of PCs has been tumbling recently.*

PC [POLICE] /ˌpiːˈsiː/ *noun* [C] *UK ABBREVIATION FOR* **police constable**: *PC Owens* ➲See also **WPC**.

PC [CORRECT] /ˌpiːˈsiː/ *adj ABBREVIATION FOR* **politically correct**

pc *WRITTEN ABBREVIATION FOR* **percent**: *an increase of 22 pc*

PCB /ˌpiː.siːˈbiː/ *noun* [C or U] *ABBREVIATION FOR* polychlorinated biphenyl: one of several harmful chemicals which is used in industry

pcm, **p.c.m.** /ˌpiː.siːˈem/ *adv UK ABBREVIATION FOR* **per calendar month**: *Fully furnished house to let, £650 pcm, quiet location.*

PDA /ˌpiː.diːˈeɪ/ *noun* [C] *ABBREVIATION FOR* **personal digital assistant** (= a small computer that you can carry with you) ➲See picture **In the Office** on page Centre 15

PDF /ˌpiː.diːˈef/ *noun* [C or U] *ABBREVIATION FOR* portable document format: a system for storing and moving documents between computers that only allows the contents to be viewed or printed, or a document created using this system: *a PDF file*

PDQ /ˌpiː.diːˈkjuː/ *adv INFORMAL* pretty damn quick: very quickly or soon: *The phone bill's overdue – we need to pay it PDQ.*

PE /ˌpiːˈiː/ *noun* [U] *ABBREVIATION FOR* **physical education**

pea /piː/ *noun* [C] a round green seed, several of which grow in a pod, eaten as a vegetable: *frozen/dried peas* ○ *pea soup* ➲See picture **Vegetables** on page Centre 2

pea-brained /ˈpiː.breɪnd/ *adj INFORMAL* extremely stupid

pea-brain /ˈpiː.breɪn/ *noun* [C] *INFORMAL* a pea-brained person

peace [NO VIOLENCE] /piːs/ *noun* [U] freedom from war and violence, especially when people live and work together happily without disagreements: *peace talks/proposals* ○ *a peace conference/initiative* ○ *Now that the war is over may there be* ***a lasting*** *peace between our nations.* ○ *Peace lasted in Europe for just over 20 years after 1918 before war broke out again.* ○ *She's very good at* ***keeping*** *(the) peace within the family.* ○ *The police act on the public's behalf to* ***keep the*** *peace.* ○ *Stop fighting you two – shake hands and* ***make*** *(your) peace (with each other)!*

peaceful /ˈpiːs.fᵊl/ *adj* without violence: *peaceful demonstrators* ○ *She hoped the different ethnic groups in the area could live together in peaceful co-existence.* **peacefully** /ˈpiːs.fᵊl.i/ *adv* **peacefulness** /ˈpiːs.fᵊl.nəs/ *noun* [U]

peaceable /ˈpiː.sə.bl̩/ *adj* **1** without violence; peaceful: *They believe only in peaceable, non-violent protest.* **2** avoiding arguments: *a peaceable person* **peaceably** /ˈpiː.sə.bli/ *adv*

peace [CALM] /piːs/ *noun* [U] calm and quiet; lack of interruption or annoyance from worry, problems, noise or unwanted actions: *You'll need peace* ***and quiet*** *to study.* ○ *He says he's* ***at*** *peace when he's walking in the mountains.* ○ *Go away and* ***leave*** *us to finish our dinner* ***in*** *peace.* ○ *For everyone's peace* ***of mind*** *go back and check you locked the door.* ○ *There'll be* ***no*** *peace until she gets what she wants.* ○ *I didn't agree with what she said but I* ***held*** *my peace* (= did not say anything).

• **at peace** a gentle way of saying that someone is dead: *Now she is at peace and her suffering is over.*

• **be at peace with the world** to be feeling calm and happy because you are satisfied with your life

peaceful /ˈpiːs.fᵊl/ *adj* quiet and calm: *a peaceful afternoon/place* **peacefully** /ˈpiːs.fᵊl.i/ *adv*: *He was back in her arms and she could once again sleep peacefully.* **peacefulness** /ˈpiːs.fᵊl.nəs/ *noun* [U] *A kind of peacefulness overcame him as he stared up at the stars.*

the ˈPeace ˌCorps *group noun* [S] an organization in the US which sends people to work as VOLUNTEERS (= people who work without being paid) in poor countries

ˈpeace ˌdividend *noun* [C usually sing] the money saved by a country when it no longer needs to make or buy weapons because the threat of war has grown less

peacekeeping /ˈpiːsˌkiː.pɪŋ/ *noun* [U] the activity of preventing war and violence, especially the use of armed forces not involved in a disagreement to prevent fighting in an area: *a peacekeeping force/mission* **peacekeeper** /ˈpiːsˌkiː.pəʳ/ [US] /-pɚ/ *noun* [C]

peace-loving /ˈpiːsˌlʌv.ɪŋ/ *adj* liking peace and trying to live and act in a way which will bring it: *a peace-loving people/nation*

peacemaker /ˈpiːsˌmeɪ.kəʳ/ [US] /-kɚ/ *noun* [C] a person who tries to establish peace between people

ˈpeace ˌoffering *noun* [C] something said or given by a person to show that they want to be friendly, especially to someone they have argued with

ˈpeace ˌpipe *noun* [C] a decorated tobacco PIPE used by Native Americans at ceremonial events, especially as a sign of peace

ˈpeace ˌsign *noun* [C] a sign made with the hand by holding it with the palm forward and the first two fingers in the shape of a V, used to express peace ➲See also **V-sign**.

peacetime /ˈpiːs.taɪm/ *noun* [U] a period of time when a country is not at war ➲Compare **wartime**.

peach [FRUIT] /piːtʃ/ *noun* [C or U] a round fruit with juicy sweet yellow flesh, slightly furry red and yellow skin and a large seed in its centre: *Would you like peaches* ***and cream*** *for dessert?* ➲See picture **Fruit** on page Centre 1

peach [COLOUR] /piːtʃ/ *adj, noun* [U] (having) a pale pinkish orange colour

peach EXCELLENT /piːtʃ/ *noun* [S] INFORMAL someone or something which is excellent or very pleasing
peachy /'piː.tʃi/ *adj* INFORMAL very good
peach Melba /ˌpiːtʃ'mel.bə/ *noun* [C or U] a sweet food made from half a peach, ice cream and pressed RASPBERRIES
peacock /'piː.kɒk/ ⓤ /-kɑːk/ *noun* [C] **1** a large bird, the male of which has very long tail feathers which it can spread out to show bright colours and eye-like patterns ⊃See picture **Animals and Birds** on page Centre 4 **2** OLD-FASHIONED DISAPPROVING a man is who is very proud of his appearance and gives a lot of attention to his clothes and the way he dresses
peacock 'blue *noun* [U], *adj* a bright, slightly greenish-blue colour
pea 'green *noun* [U], *adj* a bright yellowish green colour
peahen /'piː.hen/ *noun* [C] a female PEACOCK
peak HIGHEST POINT /piːk/ *noun* [C] the highest, strongest or best point, value or level of skill: *Holiday flights **reach** a peak during August.* ○ *Beat the egg whites until they are stiff enough to form firm peaks.* ○ *We saw a victory by an athlete **at** the very peak of her fitness and career.*
peak /piːk/ *verb* [I] to reach the highest, strongest or best point, value or level of skill: *Official figures show that unemployment peaked in November.*
peak /piːk/ *adj* [before n] *Traffic congestion is really bad at peak* (= the most busy) ***periods.*** ○ *It is most expensive to advertise at peak viewing times* (= those with the most people watching). ○ *Don't go there in the peak* (= busiest) ***season*** *– it'll be hot and crowded.*
peak MOUNTAIN TOP /piːk/ *noun* [C] the pointed top of a mountain, or the mountain itself: *It is one of the most difficult peaks to climb.*
peak HAT PART MAINLY UK /piːk/ *noun* [C] (US USUALLY **visor**) the flat curved part of a CAP which goes above the eyes of the person who is wearing it ⊃See picture **Hairstyles and Hats** on page Centre 8 **peaked** /piːkt/ *adj: a peaked cap* ⊃See picture **Hairstyles and Hats** on page Centre 8
peaky MAINLY UK /'piː.ki/ *adj* (US USUALLY **peaked**) INFORMAL slightly ill, often looking pale: *You look **a bit peaky**, love, are you all right?*
peal RING /piːl/ *verb* [I] When bells peal, they ring with a loud sound: *After their wedding the bells pealed **out** from the tower.* **peal** /piːl/ *noun* [C] *When we heard the peal of (the) bells, we knew a truce had been declared.*
peal LOUD SOUND /piːl/ *noun* [C] a long loud sound or series of sounds, especially of laughter or thunder: *Her suggestion was met with peals **of laughter***. ○ *A loud peal **of thunder** woke him from restless sleep.*
peanut /'piː.nʌt/ *noun* [C UK SPECIALIZED ALSO **groundnut**) an oval-shaped nut that grows underground in pairs inside a thin brown shell: *peanut/groundnut oil* ○ *salted/dry-roast(ed) peanuts*
peanut 'butter *noun* [U] a soft pale brown substance made from crushed peanuts which is often eaten spread on bread
peanuts /'piː.nʌts/ *plural noun* INFORMAL something so small it is not worth considering, especially a sum of money: *They **pay** people peanuts in that organization.*
pear /peəʳ/ ⓤ /per/ *noun* [C or U] a sweet juicy fruit with a green skin which has a round base and is slightly pointed towards the stem ⊃See picture **Fruit** on page Centre 1
pearl /pɜːl/ ⓤ /pɝːl/ *noun* **1** [C or U] a small round object, usually white, that forms around a grain of sand inside the shell of especially an OYSTER (= a sea animal with a large flat shell), which is very valuable and is used to make jewellery: *a string of pearls* ○ *a pearl necklace* **2** an artificially made pearl: *cultured pearls* **3** [C] LITERARY a small drop of liquid: *There were pearls **of** dew on the grass.* **4** [U] the creamy white shiny colour of pearl or a pale colour **5** [U] **mother-of-pearl**: *pearl buttons*
• **a pearl of great price** UK FORMAL something that is very rare and is considered very important: *Inexhaustible patience is a pearl of great price.*
pearls /pɜːlz/ ⓤ /pɝːlz/ *plural noun* jewellery made from pearls: *He gave her pearls for her birthday.*

pearly /'pɜː.li/ ⓤ /'pɝː-/ *adj* white and shiny, like a pearl: *pearly white teeth*
'pearl ˌdiver *noun* [C] a person who swims deep down into the sea to find shells containing pearls
the ˌpearly 'gates *plural noun* [U] HUMOROUS the imaginary entrance to heaven
pear-shaped /'peə.ʃeɪpt/ ⓤ /'per-/ *adj* shaped like a pear: *a pear-shaped physique*
• **go pear-shaped** UK INFORMAL If a plan goes pear-shaped, it fails: *We'd planned to go away for the weekend, but it **all** went pear-shaped.*
peasant /'pez.ᵊnt/ *noun* [C] **1** a person who owns or rents a small piece of land and grows crops, keeps animals, etc. on it, especially one who has a low income, very little education and a low social position. This is usually used of someone who lived in the past or of someone in a poor country: *Tons of internationally donated food was distributed to the starving peasants.* ○ *Most of the produce sold in the market is grown by peasant farmers.* ○ *Peasant women with scarves around their heads were working in the fields.* **2** INFORMAL DISAPPROVING a person who is not well educated or is rude and does not behave well: *Joe's a real peasant.*
peasantry /'pez.ᵊn.tri/ *noun* [U] especially in the past, all the people who were peasants
peashooter /'piːˌʃuː.təʳ/ ⓤ /-t̬ɚ/ *noun* [C] **1** a long thin tube through which small objects, especially dried peas, can be blown in order to hit something **2** US a small weapon, especially a gun, which is not very effective
pea-souper /ˌpiː'suː.pəʳ/ ⓤ /-pɚ/ *noun* [C] (US **pea soup**) UK OLD-FASHIONED INFORMAL a very dense fog
peat /piːt/ *noun* [U] a dark brown earth-like substance which was formed by plants dying and becoming buried. It is sometimes added to ordinary garden earth to improve it and is sometimes used as fuel **peaty** /'piː.ti/ ⓤ /-t̬i/ *adj: a dark peaty brown* ○ *a strong peaty smell* ○ *peaty soil*
'peat ˌbog *noun* [C] an area of land from which peat is taken
pebble /'peb.l̩/ *noun* [C] a small smooth round stone, especially one found on a beach or in a river: *This part of the coast has pebble beaches.* **pebbled** /'peb.l̩d/ *adj* (ALSO **pebbly**)
pecan /pɪ'kæn/ ⓤ /-'kɑːn/ *noun* [C] a type of nut which is long with an uneven surface and which has a smooth reddish shell: *chopped pecans* ○ *pecan pie*
peccadillo /ˌpek.ə'dɪl.əʊ/ ⓤ /-oʊ/ *noun* [C] *plural* **peccadillos** or **peccadilloes** a small fault or a not very bad action: *a youthful peccadillo* ○ *He dismissed what had happened as a mere peccadillo.*
peck /pek/ *verb* **1** [I or T] When a bird pecks, it bites, hits or picks up something small with its beak: *The birds learn to peck holes in the foil milk bottle tops.* ○ *Geese were pecking around for food.* ○ *Chickens pecked **at** the seeds which covered the ground.* **2** [T] to give someone a quick kiss, especially on the side of the face: *He pecked his aunt **on the cheek**.*
peck /pek/ *noun* [C] *She gave me the usual peck **on the cheek*** (= quick kiss).
▲ **peck at** *sth phrasal verb* to eat small quantities of something without any enthusiasm
pecker PENIS /'pek.əʳ/ ⓤ /-ɚ/ *noun* [C] OFFENSIVE FOR **penis**
pecker STAY HAPPY /'pek.əʳ/ ⓤ /-ɚ/ *noun* UK OLD-FASHIONED INFORMAL **keep** your **pecker up** to try to stay happy when things are difficult
'pecking ˌorder *noun* [C usually sing] an informal social system in which some people or groups know they are more or less important than others: *There's a clearly established pecking order in this office.* ○ *He started as a clerk but gradually rose in the pecking order.*
peckish /'pek.ɪʃ/ *adj* UK slightly hungry: *By ten o'clock I was feeling rather peckish, even though I'd had a large breakfast.*
pectin /'pek.tɪn/ *noun* [U] a chemical found in some fruits which helps to make liquid firm when making jam
pectoral /'pek.tᵊr.ᵊl/ ⓤ /-tɔːr-/ *adj* SPECIALIZED of the chest: *He flexed his pectoral **muscles**.*

pectorals /'pek.t³r.ºlz/ ⓤ /-tɔːr-/ *plural noun* (INFORMAL **pecs**) SPECIALIZED chest muscles

peculiar STRANGE /pɪˈkjuː.li.əʳ/ ⓤ /-ˈkjuːl.jɚ/ *adj* unusual and strange, sometimes in an unpleasant way: *She has the most peculiar ideas.* ○ *What a peculiar smell!* ○ *It's peculiar that they didn't tell us they were going away.* ○ *UK The video on road accidents made me* **feel** *rather peculiar* (= ill). **peculiarly** /pɪˈkjuː.li.ə.li/ ⓤ /-ˈkjuːl.jɚ-/ *adv*: *He looked at me most peculiarly.* ○ *The streets were peculiarly quiet for the time of day.*

peculiarity /pɪˌkjuː.liˈær.ə.ti/ ⓤ /-ˈer.ə.t̬i/ *noun* [C or U] the quality of being strange or unfamiliar, or an unusual characteristic or habit: *You couldn't help but be aware of the peculiarity* **of** *the situation.* ○ *Well, we all have our little peculiarities, don't we?*

peculiar BELONGING TO /pɪˈkjuː.li.əʳ/ ⓤ /-ˈkjuːl.jɚ/ *adj* belonging to, relating to or found in only particular people or things: *He gets on with things in his own peculiar way/manner/fashion.* ○ *They noted that special manner of walking which was peculiar* **to** *her alone.* ○ *This type of building is peculiar* **to** *the south of the country.* **peculiarly** /pɪˈkjuː.li.ə.li/ ⓤ /-ˈkjuːl.jɚ-/ *adv*

peculiarity /pɪˌkjuː.liˈær.ə.ti/ ⓤ /-ˈer.ə.t̬i/ *noun* [C] something which is typical of one person, group or thing: *This technique is applicable to a wide variety of crops, but some modifications may be necessary to accommodate the peculiarities of each type.*

peculiarly /pɪˈkjuː.li.ə.li/ ⓤ /-ˈkjuːl.jɚ-/ *adv* SLIGHTLY OLD-FASHIONED OR LITERARY very or especially: *It's peculiarly painful where I burnt my hand.* ○ *She's a peculiarly attractive woman.* ⊃See also **peculiarly** at **peculiar** STRANGE; **peculiar** BELONGING TO.

pecuniary /pɪˈkjuː.nj³r.i/ ⓤ /-ni.er-/ *adj* FORMAL relating to money: *pecuniary interest/loss/benefit* ○ *a pecuniary matter*

pedagogue /'ped.ə.gɒg/ ⓤ /-gɑːg/ *noun* [C] **1** DISAPPROVING a teacher who gives too much attention to formal rules and is not interesting **2** OLD USE any teacher

pedagogy /'ped.ə.gɒdʒ.i/ ⓤ /-gɑː.dʒi/ *noun* [U] SPECIALIZED the study of the methods and activities of teaching **pedagogic** /ˌped.əˈgɒdʒ.ɪk/ ⓤ /-ˈgɑː.dʒɪk/ *adj* (ALSO **pedagogical**)

pedagogically /ˌped.əˈgɒdʒ.ɪ.kli/ ⓤ /-ˈgɑː.dʒɪ-/ *adv* SPECIALIZED *The minister's reforms are pedagogically questionable* (= not based on good teaching theory).

pedal /'ped.ºl/ *noun* [C] a small part of a machine or object which is pushed down with the foot to operate or move the machine or object: *the brake/accelerator pedal* ○ *This sewing machine is operated by a* **foot** *pedal.* ○ *He stood up on the pedals of his bike to get extra power as he cycled up the hill.*

pedal /'ped.ºl/ *adj* [before n] operated by a pedal or pedals: *a pedal bike/boat/car* ○ *She emptied the ashtray into the pedal bin.*

pedal /'ped.ºl/ *verb* [I or T] **-ll-** or *US USUALLY* **-l-** to push the pedals of a bicycle round with your feet: *He struggled to pedal his bicycle up the hill.* ○ *We were pedalling like mad* (= very fast) *against the wind, but didn't seem to be getting anywhere.* ⊃See also **backpedal**.

pedalo *UK* (*plural* **pedalos**) /'ped.ºl.əʊ/ ⓤ /-oʊ/ *noun* [C] (US **pedal boat**) a small boat which is moved by pushing PEDALS with the feet

pedant /'ped.ºnt/ *noun* [C] DISAPPROVING a person who is too interested in formal rules and small unimportant details

pedantic /pəˈdæn.tɪk/ ⓤ /ped'æn-/ *adj* DISAPPROVING giving too much attention to formal rules or small details: *They were being unnecessarily pedantic by insisting that Berry himself, and not his wife, should have made the announcement.* **pedantically** /pəˈdæn.tɪ.kli/ ⓤ /ped'æn-/ *adv* **pedantry** /'ped.ºn.tri/ *noun* [U] *There was a hint of pedantry in his elegant style of speaking.*

peddle /'ped.l/ *verb* [T] MAINLY DISAPPROVING **1** to sell things, especially by taking them to different places: *These products are generally peddled (from) door to door.* ○ *He travels around, peddling his* **wares.** **2** If you peddle stories or information, you spread them by telling different people: *The organization has peddled the myth that they are supporting the local population.*

peddler /'ped.ləʳ/ ⓤ /-lɚ/ *noun* [C] **1** (MAINLY UK **pedlar**) especially in the past, a person who travelled to different places to sell small goods, usually by going from house to house **2** (MAINLY UK **pedlar**) DISAPPROVING someone who gives ideas to other people: *a peddler of New Age philosophies* **3** OLD-FASHIONED **(drug) peddler** someone who sells illegal drugs to people

pederast, UK OLD-FASHIONED **paederast** /'ped.³r.æst/ ⓤ /-dɚ-/ *noun* [C] a man who has illegal sex with a young boy

pedestal /'ped.ə.st³l/ *noun* [C] a long thin column which supports a statue, or a tall column-like structure on which something rests: *In the riot, the statues were toppled from their pedestals.* ○ *A flower arrangement in a large basket stood on a (flower) pedestal in the corner of the room.*

● **put** *sb* **on a pedestal** to believe that someone is perfect ⊃Compare **knock** someone **off** their **pedestal** at **knock** HIT.

pedestrian WALKER /pəˈdes.tri.ən/ *noun* [C] a person who is walking, especially in an area where vehicles go: *A few pedestrians carrying their evening shopping sheltered from the rain in doorways.* ○ *The death rate for pedestrians hit by cars is unacceptably high.*

pedestrianize, UK USUALLY **-ise** /pəˈdes.tri.ə.naɪz/ *verb* [T] to make an area into one where vehicles are not allowed to go: *They are pedestrianizing the town square.*

pedestrian NOT INTERESTING /pəˈdes.tri.ən/ *adj* FORMAL DISAPPROVING not interesting; showing very little imagination: *Her books, with few exceptions, are workmanlike but pedestrian.* ○ *His speech was long and pedestrian.*

pe,destrian 'crossing *noun* [C] (*US ALSO* **crosswalk**) a marked place in a road where traffic must stop to allow people to walk across ⊃Compare **pelican crossing**; **zebra crossing**.

pe,destrian 'precinct *noun* [C] (*US USUALLY* **pedestrian mall**) a covered area with shops where vehicles are not allowed

pediatrician /ˌpiː.di.əˈtrɪʃ.ºn/ *noun* [C] MAINLY US FOR **paediatrician** **pediatric** /ˌpiː.diˈæt.rɪk/ *adj* MAINLY US

pedicure /'ped.ɪ.kjʊəʳ/ ⓤ /-kjʊr/ *noun* [C or U] (a) beauty treatment for the feet which involves cutting and sometimes painting the nails, and softening or MASSAGING (= rubbing) the skin ⊃Compare **manicure**.

pedigree /'ped.ɪ.griː/ *noun* **1** [C] a list of the parents and other relatives of an animal: *The breeder showed us the dog's pedigree.* ○ *He breeds pedigree poodles/cattle* (= ones whose parents and other relatives are all of the same breed). **2** [C or U] a person's family history, education and experience, or the history of an idea or activity: *His voice and manner suggested an aristocratic pedigree.* ○ *Isolationism has a long and respectable pedigree in American history.*

pediment /'ped.ɪ.mənt/ *noun* [C] SPECIALIZED a triangular part at the top of the front of a building which supports the roof and which is often decorated

pedlar /'ped.ləʳ/ ⓤ /-lɚ/ *noun* [C] ⊃See at **peddle**.

pedometer /peˈdɒm.ɪ.təʳ/ ⓤ /pɪˈdɑː.mə.t̬ɚ/ *noun* [C] a device which measures how far someone has walked by counting the number of times the feet are raised and put down again

pedophile /'piː.dəʊ.faɪl/ ⓤ /'ped.oʊ-/ *noun* [C] MAINLY US FOR **paedophile** **pedophilia** /ˌpiː.dəˈfɪl.i.ə/ *noun* [U] MAINLY US

pee /piː/ *verb* [I or T] INFORMAL FOR **urinate**

pee /piː/ *noun* INFORMAL **1** [U] urine **2** [S] when you URINATE: *I must go for/must have a pee.*

peek /piːk/ *verb* [I] **1** to look, especially for a short time or while trying to avoid being seen: *Close your eyes. Don't peek. I've got a surprise for you.* ○ *I peeked out the window to see who was there.* ○ *The children peeked over the wall to see where the ball had gone.* ○ *The film peeks behind the scenes of a multinational corporation.* **2 peek out/through,** etc. to stick out slightly and be partly seen: *I could just see her petticoat peeking out from under her skirt.*

peek /piːk/ *noun* INFORMAL **have/take a peek** to look at something for a short time: *If I'm passing by I might take a peek at the new premises.*

peek-a-boo /ˌpiːk.əˈbuː/ *noun* [U] (*UK ALSO* **peep-bo**) a game played with very young children in which you hide your face, especially with your hands, and then suddenly take your hands away saying "peek-a-boo"

peel [FOOD] /piːl/ *verb* [T] to remove the skin of fruit and vegetables: *Peel, core and chop the apples.* ➲See picture **In the Kitchen** on page Centre 16
peel /piːl/ *noun* [U] the skin of fruit and vegetables, especially after it has been removed: *apple peel* ○ *potato peel* ○ *The dessert was decorated with strips of lemon peel.* ○ *What shall I do with the peel?* ➲See picture **Fruit** on page Centre 1
peeler /ˈpiː.ləʳ/ [US] /-lɚ/ *noun* [C] a utensil for removing the skin of fruit and vegetables: *a vegetable/potato peeler*
peelings /ˈpiː.lɪŋz/ *plural noun* the unwanted pieces of fruit or vegetable skin which have been taken off: *potato/apple peelings* ○ *Put the vegetable peelings on the compost heap.*

peel [COVERINGS] /piːl/ *verb* [I or T; usually + adv or prep] If a layer or covering peels, it slowly comes off, and if you peel a layer or covering, you remove it slowly and carefully: *We peeled the wallpaper **off** the walls.* ○ *Peel **off** the backing strip and press the label down firmly.* ○ *The posters were peeling **away from** the damp walls.* ○ *The new paint is already starting to crack and peel.*

peel [BODY] /piːl/ *verb* [I] If you peel, or part of your body or your skin peels, parts of the top layer of your skin comes off because you are burnt from being in the sun: *My back is peeling.*
▲ **peel away/off** *phrasal verb* [M] When separate vehicles, people or animals peel away/off, they leave the group or structure they were part of and move away in a different direction: *One motorbike peeled away **from** the formation and circled round behind the rest.*

peep [LOOK] /piːp/ *verb* [I usually + adv or prep] to secretly look at something for a short time, usually through a hole: *I saw her peeping **through** the curtains/**into** the room.*
peep /piːp/ *noun* [S] a quick look: ***Take/Have a** peep **at** what it says in this letter.*

peep [APPEAR] /piːp/ *verb* [I usually + adv or prep] to appear slowly and not be completely seen: *A few early flowers had peeped up through the snow.* ○ *The cat's tail was peeping **out** from under the bed.*

peep [SOMETHING SAID] /piːp/ *noun* [S] *INFORMAL* a statement, answer or complaint: *No one has **raised a** peep about this dreadful behaviour.* ○ *One more peep **out of** you and there'll be no television tomorrow.* ○ *There hasn't been **a** peep **out of*** (= any form of communication from) *my sister for a couple of weeks.*

P

peep [NOISE] /piːp/ *noun* [C] the weak high noise made by young birds **peep** /piːp/ *verb* [I]

peephole /ˈpiːp.həʊl/ [US] /-hoʊl/ *noun* [C] (*UK ALSO* **spyhole**) a small hole in a door or a wall through which you can look, especially without being seen: *I have a security peephole in my front door.*

ˌpeeping ˈTom *noun* [C] *DISAPPROVING* a man who tries to secretly watch women when they are wearing no clothes

peepshow /ˈpiːp.ʃəʊ/ [US] /-ʃoʊ/ *noun* [C] **1** a short, sexually exciting performance or film that someone pays to watch through a window in a small room **2** especially in the past, a sexually exciting picture or film, watched on a machine through a small hole

peer [LOOK] /pɪəʳ/ [US] /pɪr/ *verb* [I usually + adv or prep] to look carefully or with difficulty: *When no one answered the door, she peered **through** the window to see if anyone was there.* ○ *The driver was peering into the distance trying to read the road sign.*

peer [HIGH RANK] /pɪəʳ/ [US] /pɪr/ *noun* [C] in Britain, a person who has a high social position and any of a range of titles, including BARON, EARL and duke, or a LIFE PEER: *a hereditary peer* ○ *a Conservative peer*
peerage /ˈpɪə.rɪdʒ/ [US] /ˈpɪr.ɪdʒ/ *noun* **1** [C usually sing] the position of being a peer: *She was given a peerage.* ○ *He was **elevated to** the peerage after distinguished service in industry.* **2** [C] a book containing information about peers who are not LIFE PEERS and their family history
the peerage *group noun* [S] the group of people who are peers, either because of their families or because they are LIFE PEERS

peer [EQUAL] /pɪəʳ/ [US] /pɪr/ *noun* [C] a person who is the same age or has the same social position or the same abilities as other people in a group: *Do you think it's true that teenage girls are less self-confident than their male peers?* ○ *He wasn't a great scholar, but as a teacher he had few peers* (= not many people had the same ability as him).
peerless /ˈpɪə.ləs/ [US] /ˈpɪr-/ *adj FORMAL* describes something that is better than any other of its type: *peerless beauty/ability*

peeress /ˈpɪə.rəs/ /-ˈ-/ [US] /ˈpɪr.ɪs/ *noun* [C] a female **peer** HIGH RANK

ˈpeer ˌgroup *group noun* [C usually sing] the people who are approximately the same age as you and come from a similar social group: *These children scored significantly lower on intelligence tests than others in their peer group.*

ˌpeer of the ˈrealm *noun* [C] a member of the HOUSE OF LORDS (= the part of the British parliament which is not elected) who is not a LIFE PEER

ˈpeer ˌpressure *noun* [U] (*UK* **peer group pressure**) the strong influence of a group, especially of children, on members of that group to behave as everyone else does: *There is tremendous peer pressure to wear fashionable clothes.*

peeved /piːvd/ *adj INFORMAL* annoyed: *He was peeved because we didn't ask him what he thought about the idea.* **peeve** /piːv/ *verb* [T] *What peeved her most was his thoughtlessness.* ○ [+ that] ***It** peeves me **that** she didn't bother to phone.*
peevish /ˈpiː.vɪʃ/ *adj* easily annoyed: *a peevish, bad-tempered person* **peevishly** /ˈpiː.vɪʃ.li/ *adv*: *"I thought you might have helped," she replied peevishly.*

peewit /ˈpiː.wɪt/ *noun* [C] a **lapwing**

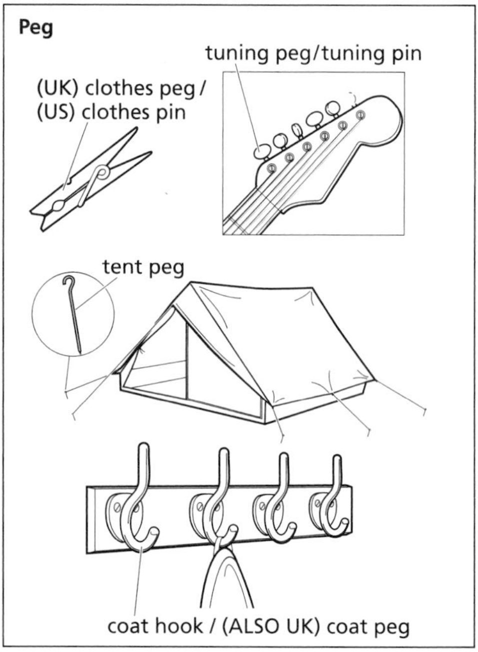
Peg
tuning peg/tuning pin
(UK) clothes peg /
(US) clothes pin
tent peg
coat hook / (ALSO UK) coat peg

peg [HOOK] /peg/ *noun* **1** [C] a small stick or hook which sticks out from a surface and from which objects, especially clothes, can hang: *He took off his coat/hat and hung it **on** the peg.* **2** [S] a reason for discussing something further: *They decided to use the anniversary as the peg **for**/a peg **on which to hang** a TV documentary.*
• **bring/take** *sb* **down a peg (or two)** *INFORMAL* to show someone that they are not as important as they thought they were

peg [FIXING DEVICE] /peg/ *noun* [C] a device which is used to fix something into a particular place: *UK There aren't enough pegs (ALSO* **clothes pegs**, *US* **clothes pins**) *to hang all this washing on the line.* ○ *Hammer the pegs (ALSO* **tent pegs**) *firmly into the ground.*
peg /peg/ *verb* **-gg- 1** [T usually + adv or prep] to fix something in place with pegs: *Make sure the tarpaulin is securely pegged* **down**. ○ *I'll peg* **out** *the clothes before I go to work.* **2** [T] to arrange something so that it stays at a particular level: *The agreement works because member nations haven't tried to peg prices.*

peg [BASEBALL] /peg/ *noun* [C] *US INFORMAL* a low fast throw in baseball
peg /peg/ *verb* [T] **-gg-** *US INFORMAL Mattingly pegged* (= threw) *the ball to Stanley.*

PHRASAL VERBS WITH **peg**

▲ **peg out** [DIE] *phrasal verb UK SLANG* **1** to die **2** to stop working: *The car finally pegged out about 20 miles from home.*
▲ **peg *sth* out** [MARK] *phrasal verb* [M] If you peg out an area, you mark the edges of it by hitting short sticks into the ground.

pejorative /pɪˈdʒɒr.ə.tɪv/ [US] /-ˈdʒɔːr.ə.t̬ɪv/ *adj FORMAL* disapproving or suggesting that something is not good or is of no importance: *Make sure students realise that 'fat' is an unflattering or pejorative word.* ○ *It comes as quite a shock to still hear a judge describing a child as 'illegitimate', with all the pejorative overtones of that word.*

pekinese (*plural* **pekinese** or *UK* **pekineses**), **pekingese** /ˌpiː.kɪˈniːz/ *noun* [C] (*ALSO* **peke**) a small dog with long soft hair and a wide flat nose

pelican /ˈpel.ɪ.kən/ *noun* [C] a large bird which catches fish and carries them in the lower part of its beak, which is like a bag

ˌpelican ˈcrossing *noun* [C] *UK* a marked place in the road in Britain, with a set of lights beside the road and a device which people can press to make the red light show and the traffic stop, allowing them to cross ➲Compare **pedestrian crossing**; **zebra crossing**.

pellet /ˈpel.ət/ *noun* [C] **1** a small hard ball or tube-shaped piece of any substance: *iron/lead/wax/plastic/paper pellets* ○ *food pellets* **2** the excrement of particular animals: *rabbit/sheep pellets* **3** small metal objects that are shot from some types of gun: *airgun pellets* ○ *shotgun pellets* ○ *a pellet* **gun**

pell-mell /ˌpelˈmel/ *adv OLD-FASHIONED* very fast and not organized: *At the sound of the alarm bell, the customers* **ran** *pell-mell for the doors.*

pelmet /ˈpel.mət/ *noun* [C] (*US USUALLY* **valance**) a narrow strip of wood or cloth which is fixed above a window or door and which hides the top of the curtains

pelt [THROW] /pelt/ *verb* [T] to throw a number of things quickly at someone or something: *We saw rioters pelting police* **with** *bricks and bottles.*
● **pelt (down)** to rain heavily: ***It's pelting down (with rain)***.

pelt [RUN] /pelt/ *verb* [I + adv or prep] *INFORMAL* to run fast: *The children pelted down the bank, over the bridge and along the path.*
pelt /pelt/ *noun UK* **at full pelt** running as fast as possible

pelt [SKIN] /pelt/ *noun* [C] the skin and fur of a dead animal, or the skin with the fur removed

pelvis /ˈpel.vɪs/ *noun* [C] the bones which form a bowl-shaped structure in the area below the waist at the top of the legs, and to which the leg bones and spine are joined **pelvic** /ˈpel.vɪk/ *adj*: *the pelvic region/area*

pen [WRITING DEVICE] /pen/ *noun* [C] a long thin object used for writing or drawing with ink: *a fountain/ballpoint/felt-tip pen* ○ *Don't write* **in** (= using a) *pen, or you won't be able to rub out any mistakes you make.* ➲See picture **In the Office** on page Centre 15
● **put/set pen to paper** to start to write: *It's time you put pen to paper and replied to that letter from your mother.*
● **The pen is mightier than the sword.** *SAYING* said to emphasize that thinking and writing have more influence on people and events than the use of force or violence
pen /pen/ *verb* [T] **-nn-** *FORMAL* to write something: *She penned a note of thanks to her hostess.*

pen [ENCLOSED SPACE] /pen/ *noun* [C] **1** a small area surrounded by a fence, especially one in which animals are kept: *a sheep/pig pen* ➲See also **playpen**. **2** *US SLANG FOR* **penitentiary**: *He served nine years in the* **state** *pen.*
▲ **pen *sb* in/up** *phrasal verb* [often passive] to keep people or animals in a small area: *The sheep were penned in behind the barn.* ○ *The soldiers were penned up in their barracks.*

penal [PUNISHING] /ˈpiː.nəl/ *adj* [before n] of or connected with punishment given by law: *Many people believe that execution has no place in the penal* **system** *of a civilized society.* ○ *He had been in and out of penal institutions* (= prison) *from the age of 16.*
penalize, *UK USUALLY* **-ise** /ˈpiː.nə.laɪz/ *verb* [T] **1** to cause someone a disadvantage: *The present tax system penalizes poor people.* ○ *The scheme should ensure that borrowers are not penalized by sudden rises in mortgage rates.* **2** to punish someone for breaking a rule: *He was penalized early in the match* **for** *dangerous play.*
penalty /ˈpen.əl.ti/ [US] /-t̬i/ *noun* [C] **1** a punishment, or the usual punishment, for doing something that is against a law: *The law carries a penalty* **of** *up to three years in prison.* ○ *They asked for the* **maximum** *penalty* **for** *hoax calls to be increased to one year.* ○ *The protesters were told to clear the area around the building,* **on** *penalty* **of** (= the punishment would be) *arrest if they did not.* **2** a type of punishment, often involving paying money, that is given to you if you break an agreement or do not follow rules: *Currently, ticket holders* **pay** *a penalty equal to 25% of the ticket price when they change their flight plans.* ○ *There was a penalty* **clause** *which said you had to pay half the cost if you cancelled your booking.* **3** an advantage given in some sports to a team or player when the opposing team or player breaks a rule: *The referee* **awarded** (= gave) *a penalty* **kick**. ○ *Hysen handled the ball and* **conceded** *the penalty that gave Manchester United the lead.*

penal [CAUSING DISADVANTAGE] /ˈpiː.nəl/ *adj UK* having a harmful effect; causing disadvantage: *They complained about the penal and counter-productive tax rates.* ○ *Employees regarded the childcare charges as penal.*
penalty /ˈpen.əl.ti/ [US] /-t̬i/ *noun* [C] *Loss of privacy is one of the penalties* (= disadvantages) **of** *success.* ○ *She has* **paid** *a heavy penalty* (= suffered serious disadvantages) **for** *speaking the truth.*

ˈpenal ˌcode *noun* [C] the system of legal punishment of a country

ˈpenal ˌcolony *noun* [C] (*ALSO* **penal settlement**) a type of prison, which is often in a place far away from other people

ˌpenal reˈform *noun* [C or U] the attempt to improve the system of legal punishment: *She is a spokesperson for the Howard League for Penal Reform.*

ˈpenalty ˌarea *noun* [C usually sing] (*ALSO* **penalty box**) in football, the area marked with white lines in front of the goal

ˈpenalty ˌbox *noun* [C usually sing] in ICE HOCKEY, an area where players must sit when they are given a penalty

ˌpenalty ˈshoot-out *noun* [C] a way of deciding who will win a football game in which both teams finished with the same number of goals, by each team taking turns to have a set number of kicks at the goal

ˈpenalty ˌspot *noun* [S] in football, the place marked with a white spot from which a penalty kick is taken

penance /ˈpen.ənts/ *noun* [C or U] an act which shows that you regret something that you have done, sometimes for religious reasons: *As a penance, she said she would buy them all a box of chocolates.* ○ *They are* **doing** *penance* **for** *their sins.*

pence /pents/ *plural of* PENNY (= a unit of money) ➲See also **sixpence**; **tuppence**.

penchant /ˈpɒ̃n.ʃɒ̃n/ [US] /ˈpen.tʃənt/ *noun* [C usually sing] a liking for, an enjoyment of, or a habit of doing something, especially something that other people might not like: *a penchant* **for** *melodrama/skiing/exotic clothes*

P

○ *Her penchant* ***for*** *disappear****ing*** *for days at a time worries her family.*

pencil /ˈpent.sᵊl/ *noun* [C] **1** a long thin usually wooden object for writing or drawing, with a sharp black or other coloured point, made from a type of carbon, at one end: *a box of coloured pencils* ○ *pens and pencils* ○ *He sat with his pencil* ***poised****, ready to take notes.* ○ *The pencil's* ***blunt*** *– you'd better* ***sharpen*** *it* (= make its point sharp). ○ *Write your comments in the margin of the report* ***in*** (= using) *pencil.* ○ *a pencil sharpener* ➲See picture **In the Office** on page Centre 15 **2** the form of some types of make-up: *an eyebrow pencil* ○ *a lip pencil* **3** *LITERARY* a thin beam of light: *A pencil of light showed as the door opened slightly.*

pencil /ˈpent.sᵊl/ *adj* [before n] describes something that has been drawn with a pencil: *pencil sketches/drawings* ○ *Cut on or just inside the pencil* ***line****.*

● **put/set pencil to paper** to write: *Everyone should put pencil to paper and complain about the proposal.*

pencil /ˈpent.sᵊl/ *verb* [T] -ll- or *US USUALLY* -l- to write something with a pencil **pencilled**, *US ALSO* **penciled** /ˈpent.sᵊld/ *adj*: *pencilled comments/notes*

▲ **pencil** ***sth/sb*** **in** *phrasal verb* [M] to arrange for something to happen or for someone to do something on a particular date or occasion, knowing that the arrangement might be changed later: *We'll pencil in the dates for the next two meetings and confirm them later.*

ˈpencil ˌpusher *noun* [C] *US FOR* **pen pusher**

ˈpencil ˌskirt *noun* [C] a long narrow skirt

pencil-thin /ˌpent.sᵊlˈθɪn/ *adj* very thin: *a pencil-thin fashion model*

pendant /ˈpen.dᵊnt/ *noun* [C] a piece of jewellery which is worn round the neck, consisting of a long chain with an object hanging from it, or the object itself: *She was wearing a crystal pendant.* ○ *It was a beautiful necklace with a diamond pendant.* ➲See also **pendent**.

pendent /ˈpen.dᵊnt/ *adj* (*ALSO* **pendant**) *FORMAL* hanging from or over something: *pendent branches* ○ *a pendent lampshade* ➲See also **pendant**.

pending /ˈpen.dɪŋ/ *adj* about to happen or waiting to happen: *There were whispers that a deal was pending.* ○ *The pending releases of the prisoners are meant to create a climate for negotiation.*

pending /ˈpen.dɪŋ/ *prep FORMAL* used to say that one thing must wait until another thing happens: *The identity of the four people was not made public, pending (the) notification of relatives.* ○ *Flights were suspended pending (an) investigation of the crash.*

pendulous /ˈpen.djʊ.ləs/ [US] /-dʒə.ləs/ *adj FORMAL* hanging down loosely: *pendulous blossoms*

pendulum /ˈpen.djʊ.ləm/ [US] /-dʒə.ləm/ *noun* **1** [C] a device consisting of a weight on a stick or thread which moves from one side to the other, especially one which forms a part of some types of clocks: *The pendulum in the grandfather clock* ***swung*** *back and forth.* ○ *The spaceship's jets were fired periodically to dampen a side-to-side pendulum* ***motion*** *that had developed.* **2** [S] a change, especially from one opinion to an opposite one: *As so often in education,* ***the*** *pendulum has* ***swung back*** *to the other extreme and testing is popular again.*

penetrate [MOVE] /ˈpen.ɪ.treɪt/ *verb* **1** [I or T] to move into or through something: *Amazingly, the bullet did not penetrate his brain.* ○ *In a normal winter, the frost penetrates deeply enough to kill off insect eggs in the soil.* ○ *The organization had been penetrated by a spy.* ○ *The company has been successful in penetrating overseas markets this year.* **2** [T] If your eyes penetrate dark surroundings, you manage to see through them: *Our eyes couldn't penetrate the dark/****the gloom*** *of the inner cave.*

penetration /ˌpen.ɪˈtreɪ.ʃᵊn/ *noun* [U] **1** a movement into or through something or someone: *Sunscreens can help reduce the penetration of ultraviolet rays into the skin.* ○ *The company is trying to increase its penetration of the market.* **2** the act of a man putting his penis into his sexual partner's vagina or anus during sexual activity

penetrative /ˈpen.ɪ.trə.tɪv/ [US] /-treɪ.t̬ɪv/ *adj*: *a penetrative attack* ○ *penetrative sex*

penetrate [UNDERSTAND] /ˈpen.ɪ.treɪt/ *verb* [I or T] to study or INVESTIGATE something in order to understand: *It's hard to penetrate her mind.* ○ *He penetrates deeper into the artist's life in the second volume of his autobiography.*

penetration /ˌpen.ɪˈtreɪ.ʃᵊn/ *noun* [U] *FORMAL* someone's ability to understand quickly and well

penetrating /ˈpen.ɪ.treɪ.tɪŋ/ [US] /-t̬ɪŋ/ *adj* **1** describes a way of looking at someone in which you seem to know what they are thinking ➲See also **penetrating**. **2 penetrating mind** a mind which understands things quickly and well

penetrative /ˈpen.ɪ.trə.tɪv/ [US] /-treɪ.t̬ɪv/ *adj* showing understanding: *a penetrative remark*

penetrating /ˈpen.ɪ.treɪ.tɪŋ/ [US] /-t̬ɪŋ/ *adj* very loud: *I heard a penetrating scream.* ○ *He has a very penetrating voice.* ➲See also **penetrating** at **penetrate** UNDERSTAND.

penguin /ˈpeŋ.gwɪn/ *noun* [C] a black and white sea bird which cannot fly but uses its small wings to help it swim

penicillin /ˌpen.əˈsɪl.ɪn/ *noun* [U] *SPECIALIZED* a type of medicine which kills bacteria; a type of ANTIBIOTIC

penile /ˈpiː.naɪl/ *adj SPECIALIZED* of the penis

peninsula /pəˈnɪnt.sjʊ.lə/ [US] /-sə-/ *noun* [C] a long piece of land which sticks out from a larger area of land into the sea or into a lake: *the Korean/Arabian/Florida Peninsula*

penis /ˈpiː.nɪs/ *noun* [C] the part of a male's body which is used for urinating and in sexual activity

penitent /ˈpen.ɪ.tᵊnt/ *adj FORMAL* feeling or showing regret for something you have done because you feel it was wrong: *"I'm sorry," she said with a penitent smile.* ○ *It was hard to be angry with him when he looked so penitent.* **penitence** /ˈpen.ɪ.tᵊnts/ *noun* [U]

penitent /ˈpen.ɪ.tᵊnt/ *noun* [C] *FORMAL* a person who is performing a formal religious act to show regret for something they have done wrong **penitently** /ˈpen.ɪ.tᵊnt.li/ *adv*

penitentiary /ˌpen.ɪˈten.tʃᵊr.i/ [US] /-tʃə.riː/ *noun* [C] *US FOR* a **prison** (= building in which criminals are kept)

penknife /ˈpen.naɪf/ *noun* [C] (*ALSO* **pocketknife**) a small knife which folds into a case and is usually carried in a pocket

ˈpen ˌlid *UK noun* [C] (*US* **pen cap**) a cover which goes over the top of a pen to stop the ink from escaping

penlight /ˈpen.laɪt/ *noun* [C] *US* a small TORCH about the size and shape of a pen

ˈpen ˌname *noun* [C] a name chosen by a writer to use instead of using their real name when publishing books

pennant /ˈpen.ᵊnt/ *noun* [C] **1** a triangular-shaped flag **2** a flag which is the symbol to show that a particular baseball team is the winner among the group of teams which it plays in: *Divisional winners meet in the final to decide the pennant.*

penny (*plural* **pence** or **p** or **pennies**) /ˈpen.i/ *noun* [C] **1** (*ABBREVIATION* **p**) the smallest unit of money in Britain of which there are 100 in a pound, or a small coin worth this much. You use 'pence' or, more informally, 'p' when you are speaking of the units of money and pennies when you are speaking of the coins themselves: *Could you lend me 50 pence/50p please?* ○ *I found a ten/twenty/fifty pence* ***piece*** (= a coin of this value) *in the phone booth.* ○ *I keep pennies and other small coins in a jar.* **2** in the US and Canada, a cent or a coin of this value **3** (*ALSO* **old penny,** *ABBREVIATION* **d**) in Britain before 1971, a large coin. There were twelve pennies in a SHILLING. **4** used when speaking of the smallest amount of money possible: *Buy a TV now and it won't cost you a penny* (= will cost nothing) *for 3 months.* ○ *It was an expensive meal but worth every penny.*

● **In for a penny, (in for a pound)** *UK* something you say which means that since you have started something or are involved in it, you should complete the work although it has become more difficult or complicated than you had expected

● **the penny drops** *UK INFORMAL* If the penny drops, you suddenly understand something: *She looked confused for a moment, then suddenly the penny dropped.*

● **(a) penny for your thoughts** said when you want to know what another person is thinking, usually because they have been quiet for a while

• **not have a penny to *your* name** (*ALSO* **not have two pennies to rub together**) to be very poor

• **be penny-wise and pound-foolish** *OLD-FASHIONED* to be extremely careful about small amounts of money and not careful enough about larger amounts of money

• **be two/ten a penny** *UK* (*US* **be a dime a dozen**) to be very common: *Antique toy cars are ten a penny nowadays.*

-penny /-pə.ni/ *suffix UK* used in the past with numbers to show how many pence something cost: *a fourpenny ice-cream*

penniless /ˈpen.i.ləs/ *adj* having no money: *She fell in love with a penniless artist.*

pennyworth /ˈpen.i.wəθ/ /ˈpen.əθ/ *US* /ˈpen.i.wɚθ/ *noun* [S] **1** (*UK* **penn'orth**) *OLD-FASHIONED* as much of something as could be bought for a penny **2** a small amount of something: *It won't make **a pennyworth of** difference to me.*

penny-ante /ˈpen.iˌæn.ti/ *US* /-ˌti/ *adj US* of little value or importance: *He was proposing some penny-ante increase in child-care that amounted to an extra ten dollars a week.*

penny-farthing /ˌpen.iˈfɑː.ðɪŋ/ *US* /-ˈfɑːr-/ *noun* [C] a type of bicycle used in the past which had a very large front wheel and a small back wheel

penny-pinching /ˈpen.iˌpɪn.tʃɪŋ/ *adj* [before n] unwilling to spend money: *I became tired of his penny-pinching friends.* **penny-pinching** /ˈpen.iˌpɪn.tʃɪŋ/ *noun* [U] *Local residents have accused the council of penny-pinching.*

ˌpenny ˈwhistle *noun* [C] a small cheap musical instrument shaped like a tube with holes along one side and a part for your mouth at one end that you blow into

ˈpen ˌpal *noun* [C] (*UK* **pen friend**) someone you exchange letters with as a hobby but whom you usually have not met: *I've got a pen pal in Australia.*

ˈpen ˌpusher *UK noun* [C] (*US* **pencil pusher**) *DISAPPROVING* a person who has an office job that is not interesting

pension /ˈpent.ʃ⁵n/ *noun* [C] a sum of money paid regularly by the government or a private company to a person who does not work any more because they are too old or they have become ill: *They find it hard to live on their state pension.* ○ *He won't be able to **draw** (= receive) his pension until he's 65.*

pensionable /ˈpent.ʃ⁵n.ə.bl̩/ *adj UK* allowing someone to receive a pension: *She is of pensionable **age** (= is old enough to claim a pension).* ○ *a pensionable job*

pensioner *MAINLY UK* /ˈpent.ʃ⁵n.ə⁵/ *US* /-ɚ/ *noun* [C] (*UK ALSO* **old age pensioner**) a person who receives a pension, especially the government pension given to old people: *Students and pensioners are entitled to a discount.*

pension /ˈpent.ʃ⁵n/ *verb*

PHRASAL VERBS WITH **pension** ▼

▲ **pension** *sb* **off** GIVE MONEY *phrasal verb* [often passive] *MAINLY UK* to make someone leave their job and give them a PENSION, usually because of their age: *Workers in the company are being pensioned off at 50.*

▲ **pension** *sth* **off** STOP USING *phrasal verb* [M] to stop using something, usually a machine, because it is old and has become too much: *After flying for 38 years, their Wessex helicopter is about to be pensioned off.*

ˈpension ˌfund *noun* [C] a supply of money which many people pay into, especially employees of a company, and which is invested in order to provide them with a pension when they are older

ˈpension ˌplan *noun* [C] (*UK* **pension scheme**) a financial plan that allows you to receive money after you or your employer have paid money into it for a number of years

pensive /ˈpent.sɪv/ *adj* thinking in a quiet way, often with a serious expression on your face: *She became withdrawn and pensive, hardly speaking to anyone.* **pensively** /ˈpent.sɪv.li/ *adv*: *He gazed pensively at the glass in front of him, lost in thought.*

pentagon SHAPE /ˈpen.tə.g⁵n/ *US* /-tə.gɑːn/ *noun* [C] a five-sided shape with five angles

the Pentagon BUILDING *noun* [S] the building in Washington where the US Defense Department is based, or the US Defense Department itself: *The Pentagon is aim-*

ing to cut US forces by over 25 per cent in the next five years.

pentathlon /penˈtæθ.lɒn/ *US* /-lɑːn/ *noun* [C] a sports event in which athletes compete in five different sports: *The pentathlon consists of running, swimming, riding, shooting, and fencing.* ⊃Compare **biathlon**; **decathlon**; **heptathlon**.

pentathlete /penˈtæθ.liːt/ *noun* [C] a person who competes in pentathlons

Pentecost /ˈpen.tɪ.kɒst/ *US* /-tɪ.kɑːst/ *noun* **1** [C or U] in the Jewish religion, a holy day that comes 50 days after PASSOVER **2** [U] in the Christian religion, a holy day that is the seventh Sunday after EASTER

Pentecostalism /ˌpen.tɪˈkɒs.t⁵l.ɪ.z⁵m/ *US* /-ˈkɑː.st⁵l-/ *noun* [U] a modern section of the Christian religion which began in the US in 1901, whose members believe that everything written in the Bible is true **Pentecostal** /ˌpen.tɪˈkɒs.t⁵l/ *US* /-tɪˈkɑː.st⁵l/ *adj, noun* [C]

penthouse /ˈpent.haʊs/ *noun* [C] a luxurious apartment or set of rooms at the top of a hotel or tall building: *The singer is staying in a penthouse **suite** (= set of rooms) in the Hilton.*

Pentium /ˈpen.tiəm/ *noun* [C] *TRADEMARK* a very fast PROCESSOR (= part of a computer that deals with information and instructions), or a computer with this: *a Pentium processor/chip* ○ *a Pentium computer*

pent-up /ˌpentˈʌp/ *adj* Pent-up feelings are not allowed to be expressed or released: *Screaming at the top of your voice is a good way of venting pent-up frustration.*

penultimate /pəˈnʌl.tɪ.mət/ *US* /pɪˈnʌl.tə.mət/ *adj* [before n] *FORMAL* second from the last: *It's the penultimate episode of the series tonight.*

penury /ˈpen.jʊ.ri/ *US* /-jʊr.i/ *noun* [U] *FORMAL* the state of being extremely poor

peony /ˈpiː.ə.ni/ *noun* [C] a garden plant with large red, pink or white flowers

people /ˈpiː.pl̩/ *plural noun* **1** men, women and children: *Many people never take any exercise.* ○ *We've invited thirty people to our party.* **2** used to refer to persons in general or everyone, or informally to the group of people that you are speaking to: *People will think you've gone mad.* ○ *People like to be made to feel important.* ○ *Now that we've discussed our problems, are people happy with the decisions taken?* **3** men and women who are involved in a particular type of work: *We'll have to get the people from the tax office to look at these accounts.* ○ *Most of her friends are media people.* **4** **the people** the large number of ordinary men and women who do not have positions of power in society: *She claims to be the voice of the people.* ○ *The President has lost the support of the people.* ○ *the people's Princess* **5** *INFORMAL* **sb's people** the people to whom someone is related: *Her people come from Scotland originally.*

• **of all people** used to show that you are especially surprised at a particular person's behaviour because it does not seem typical of them: *I thought that you, of all people, would believe me!*

• **man/woman of the people** a person, usually involved in politics, who is liked by a lot of ordinary people and seems to understand and like them

people /ˈpiː.pl̩/ *group noun* [C] **1** all the men, women and children who live in a particular country: *The French are known as a food-loving people.* **2** a society: *Customs similar to this one are found among many peoples of the world.*

people /ˈpiː.pl̩/ *verb*

▲ **people** *sth/somewhere* **by/with** *sb phrasal verb* If something or somewhere is peopled by/with a particular type of person, it is filled with them: *Her novels are peopled with the rich and beautiful.*

ˈpeople ˌcarrier *noun* [C] a large, high car which can carry more people than a normal car ⊃See picture **Cars and Trucks** on page Centre 13

pep /pep/ *noun* [U] *INFORMAL* energy, or a willingness to be active

pep /pep/ *verb*

▲ **pep** *sb/sth* **up** *phrasal verb* [M] to make someone or something more energetic or interesting: *A good night's* *sleep will pep you up.* ○ *The show needs to be pepped up with some decent songs.*

pepper [POWDER] /'pep.ə^r/ ⓤ /-ɚ/ *noun* [U] a greyish black or creamy coloured powder produced by crushing dry PEPPERCORNS, which is used to give a spicy hot taste to food: *freshly ground black pepper* ○ ***salt and** pepper*

peppery /'pep.ᵊr.i/ ⓤ /-ɚ.i/ *adj* having a spicy flavour like pepper: *This salad has a sharp peppery flavour.*

pepper [VEGETABLE] /'pep.ə^r/ ⓤ /-ɚ/ *noun* [C] a vegetable that is usually green, red or yellow, has a rounded shape and is hollow with seeds in the middle: *a red/green pepper* ○ *Peppers are usually cooked with other vegetables or eaten raw in salads.* ○ ***Red** peppers are ideal for roasting in the oven.* ⊃See picture **Vegetables** on page Centre 2

pepper /'pep.ə^r/ ⓤ /-ɚ/ *verb*

PHRASAL VERBS WITH **pepper** ▼

▲ **pepper *sth* with *sth*** [HIT] *phrasal verb* to hit something repeatedly with small objects: *The city's walls were peppered with bullets.*

▲ **pepper *sth* with *sth*** [INCLUDE] *phrasal verb* [often passive] If you pepper a speech or piece of writing with something, you include a lot of that particular thing: *The letter was peppered with exclamation marks.*

pepper-and-salt *UK* /ˌpep.ə.rᵊn'sɒlt/ ⓤ /-ɚ.ᵊn'sɑːlt/ *adj* [before n] (*US* **salt-and-pepper**) describes hair that is a mixture of dark hairs and grey or white hairs

peppercorn /'pep.ə.kɔːn/ ⓤ /-ɚ.kɔːrn/ *noun* [C] a small dried fruit that looks like a seed and is crushed to produce pepper

ˌpeppercorn 'rent *noun* [C] *UK* a very small amount of money that you pay as rent

'pepper ˌmill *noun* [C] a small device, the top part of which you turn by hand to crush the PEPPERCORNS inside it to produce pepper

peppermint /'pep.ə.mɪnt/ ⓤ /-ɚ-/ *noun* **1** [U] a strong fresh flavouring obtained from a type of mint plant, used especially to flavour sweets: *She drinks peppermint-flavoured tea.* **2** [C] a hard white sweet that has the flavour of peppermint: *You can eat a peppermint as a breath freshener.*

pepperoni /ˌpep.ə'rəʊni/ ⓤ /-'roʊni/ *noun* [U] a spicy PORK or beef sausage, used especially on PIZZA: *a pepperoni pizza*

'pepper ˌpot *UK noun* [C] (*US* **pepper shaker**) a small container with several holes in the top that contains pepper

'pep ˌpill *noun* [C] a pill containing a drug that gives you more energy and makes you feel happier

'pep ˌtalk *noun* [C] a short speech intended to encourage people to work harder or try to win a game or competition: *The boss gave the staff a pep talk this morning in an attempt to boost sales.*

per STRONG /pɜː^r/ ⓤ /pɜː/, WEAK /pə^r/ ⓤ /pɚ/ *prep* used when expressing rates, prices or measurements to mean for each: *The meal will cost $20 per person.* ○ *The car was travelling at 70 miles per hour (70 mph).* ○ *There are more cafés per square mile here than anywhere else in the country.* ⊃See also **percent**.

● **as per instructions** FORMAL according to the instructions: *I had two spoonfuls after lunch, as per instructions.*

● **as per usual/normal** as usual: *Carlo turned up without any money, as per usual.*

perambulate /pə'ræm.bjʊ.leɪt/ *verb* [I] OLD USE to walk about for pleasure

perambulator /pə'ræm.bjʊ.leɪ.tə^r/ ⓤ /-t̬ɚ/ *noun* [C] UK OLD-FASHIONED FORMAL FOR **pram**

per 'annum *adv* (WRITTEN ABBREVIATION **pa**) FORMAL used in finance and business when referring to an amount that is produced, sold or spent each year: *The country exports goods worth $600 million per annum.*

per 'calendar ˌmonth *adv* (WRITTEN ABBREVIATION **pcm**) *UK FORMAL* used in finance and business when referring to an amount that is produced, sold or spent each month: *The rent for this apartment is $600 per calendar month.*

per capita /pə'kæp.ɪ.tə/ ⓤ /pɚ'kæp.ɪ.t̬ə/ *adv, adj FORMAL* If you state an amount per capita, you mean that

amount for each person: *France and Germany invest far more per capita in public transport than Britain.* ○ *The per capita income in the country is very low.*

perceive [SEE] /pə'siːv/ ⓤ /pɚ-/ *verb* [T] to see something or someone, or to become aware of something that is obvious: *Bill perceived a tiny figure in the distance.* ○ *I perceived a note of unhappiness in her voice.* ○ *Perceiving **that** he wasn't happy with the arrangements, I tried to book a different hotel.*

perceive [BELIEVE] /pə'siːv/ ⓤ /pɚ-/ *verb* [T] to come to an opinion about something, or have a belief about something: *How do the French perceive the British?* ○ *Women's magazines are often perceived **to be** superficial.*

percent, per cent /pə'sent/ ⓤ /pɚ-/ *adv* for or out of every 100, shown by the symbol %: *You got 20 percent **of** the answers right – that means one in every five.* ○ *Only 40% of people bothered to vote in the election.*

percentage /pə'sen.tɪdʒ/ ⓤ /pɚ'sen.t̬ɪdʒ/ *noun* **1** [C] an amount of something, often expressed as a number out of 100: *What percentage of women return to work after having a baby?* ○ *Interest rates have risen by two percentage **points**.* **2** [U] *US INFORMAL* an advantage: *There's no percentage in working such long hours.*

percentile /pə'sen.taɪl/ ⓤ /pɚ-/ *noun* [C] SPECIALIZED one of the points into which a large range of numbers, results, etc. is divided to make 100 equal-sized groups: *That score puts you on the 97th percentile.*

perceptible /pə'sep.tə.bl̩/ ⓤ /pɚ-/ *adj* that can be seen, heard or noticed: *There was a **barely** perceptible movement in his right arm.* ○ *The past year has seen a perceptible improvement in working standards.* **perceptibly** /pə'sep.tə.bli/ ⓤ /pɚ-/ *adv*: *The mood had changed perceptibly.*

perception [BELIEF] /pə'sep.ʃᵊn/ ⓤ /pɚ-/ *noun* [C] a belief or opinion, often held by many people and based on appearances: *We have to change the public's perception that money is being wasted.* ○ *These photographs will affect people's perceptions of war.*

perception [SIGHT] /pə'sep.ʃᵊn/ ⓤ /pɚ-/ *noun* [U] **1** an awareness of things through the physical senses, especially sight: *Drugs can alter your perception of reality.* **2** someone's ability to notice and understand things that are not obvious to other people: *She has extraordinary powers of perception for one so young.* ○ *He's not known for his perception.*

perceptive /pə'sep.tɪv/ ⓤ /pɚ-/ *adj* very good at noticing and understanding things that many people do not notice: *Her books are full of perceptive insights into the human condition.* **perceptively** /pə'sep.tɪv.li/ ⓤ /pɚ-/ *adv*: *He has spoken perceptively on many subjects.* **perceptiveness** /pə'sep.tɪv.nəs/ ⓤ /pɚ-/ *noun* [U]

perch [SIT] /pɜːtʃ/ ⓤ /pɜːtʃ/ *verb* **1 perch in/on, etc. *sth*** to sit on or near the edge of something: *We perched on bar stools and had a beer.* ○ *A blackbird was perching on the gate.* **2** to be in a high position or in a position near the edge of something, or to put something in this position: *The village is perched on top of a high hill.*

perch /pɜːtʃ/ ⓤ /pɜːtʃ/ *noun* [C] *plural* **perch** *or US ALSO* **perches 1** a place where a bird sits, especially a thin rod in a cage **2** a seat or other place high up, often giving a good view of something below: *We watched the parade from our perch on the scaffolding.*

perch [FISH] /pɜːtʃ/ ⓤ /pɜːtʃ/ *noun* [C or U] *plural* **perch** *or US ALSO* **perches** a fish that lives in lakes and rivers and is eaten as food

perchance /pə'tʃɑːnts/ ⓤ /pɚ'tʃænts/ *adv* OLD USE by chance; possibly: *Do you know her, perchance?*

percipient /pə'sɪp.i.ənt/ ⓤ /pɚ-/ *adj FORMAL* good at noticing and understanding things

percolate /'pɜː.kᵊl.eɪt/ ⓤ /'pɜː-/ *verb* [I] **1** If a liquid percolates, it moves slowly through a substance with very small holes in it: *Sea water percolates down through the rocks.* **2** to spread slowly: *The news has begun to percolate **through** the staff.*

percolator /'pɜː.kᵊl.eɪ.tə^r/ ⓤ /'pɜː.kᵊl.eɪ.t̬ɚ/ *noun* [C] a device for making coffee in which hot water passes through crushed coffee beans into a container below

percussion /pə'kʌʃ.ᵊn/ ⓤ /pɚ-/ *noun* [U] musical instruments that you play by hitting them with your hand or object such as a stick: *Drums, tambourines and cymbals are all percussion instruments.* ○ *Jean plays the guitar and her brother is* **on** *percussion* (= plays percussion instruments). ➲Compare **brass** MUSICAL INSTRUMENTS; **woodwind**.

percussionist /pəˈkʌʃ.ən.ɪst/ [US] /pɚ-/ *noun* [C] a person who plays percussion instruments

percussive /pəˈkʌs.ɪv/ [US] /pɚ-/ *adj* relating to percussion instruments

perdition /pəˈdɪʃ.ən/ [US] /pɚ-/ *noun* [U] *LITERARY* a state of punishment which goes on for ever, suffered by evil people after death

peregrination /ˌper.ə.grɪˈneɪ.ʃən/ *noun* [C] *FORMAL* a long journey in which you travel to various different places, especially on foot

peregrine falcon /ˌper.ə.grɪnˈfɒl.kən/ [US] /-ˈfɑːl-/ *noun* [C] a large bird with a dark back and wings and a lightly coloured front, which catches mice and other small animals

peremptory /pəˈremp.tər.i/ [US] /-tɚ-/ *adj* expecting to be obeyed immediately and without questioning: *He started issuing peremptory instructions.* ○ *She was highly critical of the insensitive and peremptory way in which the cases had been handled.* **peremptorily** /pəˈremp.trə.li/ *adv*: *"Now," he said peremptorily, "Step forward and state your name."*

perennial [TIME] /pəˈren.i.əl/ *adj* lasting a very long time, or happening repeatedly or all the time: *The film 'White Christmas' is a perennial favourite.* ○ *We face the perennial problem of not having enough money.* ➲Compare **annual** EVERY YEAR; **biennial**. **perennially** /pəˈren.i.ə.li/ *adv*: *She seems to be perennially short of money.*

perennial [PLANT] /pəˈren.i.əl/ *noun* [C] a plant that lives for several years: *Roses and geraniums are perennials, flowering year after year.* ➲Compare **annual** PLANT.

perestroika /ˌper.əˈstrɔɪ.kə/ *noun* [U] the political, social and economic changes which happened in the USSR during the late 1980s

perfect [WITHOUT FAULT] /ˈpɜː.fekt/ [US] /ˈpɝː-/ *adj* **1** complete and correct in every way, of the best possible type or without fault: *a perfect day* ○ *What is your idea of perfect happiness?* ○ *This church is a perfect example of medieval architecture.* ○ *You have a perfect English accent.* ○ *The car is five years old but is in almost perfect condition.* ○ *She thought at last she'd found the perfect man.* **2** used to emphasize a noun: *It makes perfect sense.* ○ *a perfect stranger*

perfect /pəˈfekt/ [US] /pɝː-/ *verb* [T] to make something free from faults: *He is keen to perfect his golfing technique.*

perfectly /ˈpɜː.fekt.li/ [US] /ˈpɝː-/ *adv* **1** in a perfect way: *The jacket fits perfectly, the skirt not so well.* ○ *They're perfectly suited.* **2** used to emphasize the word that follows: *To be perfectly honest, I don't care any more.* ○ *You know perfectly well what the matter is.* ○ *I made it perfectly clear to him what I meant.* ○ *I was perfectly happy on my own.*

perfection /pəˈfek.ʃən/ [US] /pɚ-/ *noun* [U] **1** the state of being complete and correct in every way: *In his quest for physical perfection, he spends hours in the gym.* **2 to perfection** extremely well: *The fish was cooked to perfection.*

the perfect [PAST TENSE] *noun* [S] *SPECIALIZED* the tense of a verb that shows action that has happened in the past or before another time or event: *In English, the perfect is formed with 'have' and the past participle of the verb.* **perfect** /pəˈfekt/ [US] /pɝː-/ *adj*: *the present perfect tense*

perfectionist /pəˈfek.ʃən.ɪst/ [US] /pɚ-/ *noun* [C] a person who wants everything to be perfect and demands the highest standards possible: *She's such a perfectionist that she notices even the tiniest mistakes.*

perfectionism /pəˈfek.ʃən.ɪ.zəm/ [US] /pɚ-/ *noun* [U] the wish for everything to be correct: *Obsessive perfectionism can be very irritating.*

ˌperfect parˈticiple *noun* [C] another word for **past participle**

perfidious /pəˈfɪd.i.əs/ [US] /pɚ-/ *adj LITERARY* unable to be trusted, or showing a lack of loyalty: *She described the new criminal bill as a perfidious attack on democracy.*

perfidy /ˈpɜː.fɪ.di/ [US] /ˈpɝː.fə-/ *noun* [U] *LITERARY* behaviour which is not loyal

perforate /ˈpɜː.fər.eɪt/ [US] /ˈpɝː.fə.reɪt/ *verb* [T] to make a hole or holes in something: *He suffered from bruises and a perforated eardrum in the accident.*

perforated /ˈpɜː.fər.eɪ.tɪd/ [US] /ˈpɝː.fə.reɪ.t̬ɪd/ *adj* If paper or another material is perforated, it has a series of small holes made in it, often so that it will tear easily or allow light or air to enter: *The windows have been covered with perforated metal screens.* **perforation** /ˌpɜː.fərˈeɪ.ʃən/ [US] /ˌpɜː.fəˈreɪ-/ *noun* [C or U] *A tea bag is full of tiny perforations.*

perforce /pəˈfɔːs/ [US] /pɚˈfɔːrs/ *adv OLD-FASHIONED FORMAL* because it is necessary

perform [DO] /pəˈfɔːm/ [US] /pɚˈfɔːrm/ *verb* [T] **1** to do an action or piece of work: *Computers can perform a variety of tasks.* ○ *The operation will be performed next week.* ○ *Most of the students performed well in the exam.* **2 perform well/badly** to operate/not operate satisfactorily: *The equipment performed well during the tests.* ○ *These tyres perform badly/poorly in hot weather.*

performance /pəˈfɔː.mənts/ [US] /pɚˈfɔːr-/ *noun* [C or U] how well a person, machine, etc. does a piece of work or an activity: *Some athletes take drugs to improve their performance.* ○ ***High****-performance* (= Fast, powerful and easy to control) *cars are the most expensive.* ○ *This was a very* ***impressive*** *performance by the young player, who scored 12 points within the first 10 minutes.*

performer /pəˈfɔː.məʳ/ [US] /pɚˈfɔːr.mɚ/ *noun* [C] If you are a particular type of performer, you are able to do the stated thing well or badly: *The British boat was the star performer in the race.*

perform [ENTERTAIN] /pəˈfɔːm/ [US] /pɚˈfɔːrm/ *verb* [I or T] to entertain people by dancing, singing, acting or playing music: *She composes and performs her own music.* ○ *A major Hollywood star will be performing on stage tonight.* ○ *The council plans to ban circuses with performing animals.*

performance /pəˈfɔː.mənts/ [US] /pɚˈfɔːr-/ *noun* [C] **1** the action of entertaining other people by dancing, singing, acting or playing music: *a performance of Arthur Miller's play, 'The Crucible'* ○ *She* ***gave*** *a superb performance as Lady Macbeth.* **2** *MAINLY UK INFORMAL* **a performance** an action or behaviour that involves a lot of attention to detail or to small matters that are not important: *Cleaning the oven is such a performance.* ○ *What a performance! Please stop shouting!* **3 repeat performance** when an event or a situation happens again: *The police hope to avoid a repeat performance of last year, when the festivities turned into rioting.*

performer /pəˈfɔː.məʳ/ [US] /pɚˈfɔːr.mɚ/ *noun* [C] a person who entertains people by acting, singing, dancing or playing music: *He's a brilliant performer.*

perˈformance ˌart *noun* [C or U] a type of theatrical entertainment in which the artist's personality and the way in which they create and develop their ideas form part of the show

the perˌforming ˈarts *plural noun* forms of entertainment such as acting, dancing and playing music

perfume /ˈpɜː.fjuːm/ [US] /pɝːˈfjuːm/ *noun* **1** [C or U] a liquid with a pleasant smell, usually made from oils taken from flowers or spices, which is often used on the skin: *What perfume are you wearing?* ○ *She adores French perfume.* **2** [U] a pleasant natural smell: *The perfume of the roses filled the room.* **perfume** /ˈpɜː.fjuːm/ [US] /ˈpɝː-/ *verb* [T] *In the evening, the flowers perfume the air.* **perfumed** /ˈpɜː.fjuːmd/ [US] /ˈpɝː-/ *adj*: *perfumed bath oil* ○ *expensively-perfumed women*

perfunctory /pəˈfʌŋk.tər.i/ [US] /pɚˈfʌŋk.tɚ.i/ *adj* done quickly, without taking care or interest: *His smile was perfunctory.* **perfunctorily** /pəˈfʌŋk.tər.əl.i/ [US] /pɚˈfʌŋk.tɚ.ə.li/ *adv*: *The two heads of state shook hands perfunctorily for the photographers.*

pergola /ˈpɜː.gəl.ə/ [US] /ˈpɝː-/ *noun* [C] a frame in a garden that climbing plants can grow over and which you can walk through

perhaps /pəˈhæps/ /præps/ [US] /pɚˈhæps/ *adv* **1** used to show that something is possible or that you are not

P

certain about something: *He hasn't written to me recently – perhaps he's lost my address.* ○ *Perhaps the most important question has not been asked.* ○ *We plan to travel to Europe – to Spain or Italy perhaps.* ➲See also **maybe**. **2** used to show that a number or amount is approximate: *There were perhaps 500 people at the meeting.* **3** used when making polite requests or statements of opinion: *"I never remember people's birthdays." "Well, perhaps you should."*

peril /ˈper.əl/ *noun* [C or U] *FORMAL* **1** great danger, or something that is very dangerous: *I never felt that my life was **in** peril.* ○ *The journey through the mountains was fraught with peril* (= full of dangers). ○ *Teenagers must be warned about **the** perils **of** unsafe sex.* **2 do sth at *your* peril** to do something that might be very dangerous for you: *We underestimate the destructiveness of war at our peril.*

perilous /ˈper.əl.əs/ *adj FORMAL* extremely dangerous: *The country roads are quite perilous.* **perilously** /ˈper.əl.ə.sli/ *adv*: *She **came** perilously **close** to getting herself killed in her attempt to break the world record.*

perimeter /pəˈrɪm.ɪ.təʳ/ [US] /-ˈrɪm.ə.t̬ɚ/ *noun* [C] **1** the outer edge of an area of land or the border around it: *Protesters cut a hole in the perimeter fence.* ○ *A river runs along one side of the field's perimeter.* **2** *SPECIALIZED* the length of the outer edge of a shape

period [TIME] /ˈpɪə.ri.əd/ [US] /ˈpɪr.i-/ *noun* [C] **1** a length of time: *Her work means that she spends long periods away from home.* ○ *Unemployment in the first half of 1993 was 2% lower than **in** the same period the year before.* ○ *Fifteen people were killed **in/over** a period **of** four days.* ○ *The study will be carried out **over** a six-month period.* **2** in school, a division of time in the day when a subject is taught: *We have six periods of science a week.* **3** a fixed time during the life of a person or in history: *Most teenagers go through a rebellious period.* ○ *The house was built during the Elizabethan period.*

period /ˈpɪə.ri.əd/ [US] /ˈpɪr.i-/ *adj* **period costume/dress/furniture** the clothes or furniture of a particular time in history: *They performed 'Julius Caesar' in period dress.*

period [BLEEDING] /ˈpɪə.ri.əd/ [US] /ˈpɪr.i-/ *noun* [C] the bleeding from a woman's womb that happens once a month when she is not pregnant: *period pains* ○ *She'd missed a period and was worried.*

period [MARK] /ˈpɪə.ri.əd/ [US] /ˈpɪr.i-/ *noun* [C] **1** *MAINLY US FOR* **full stop** **2** *MAINLY US* said at the end of a statement to show that you believe you have said all there is to say on a subject and you are not going to discuss it any more: *There will be no more shouting, period!*

periodic /ˌpɪə.riˈɒd.ɪk/ [US] /ˌpɪr.iˈɑː.dɪk/ *adj* happening repeatedly over a period of time: *He suffers periodic mental breakdowns.*

periodically /ˌpɪə.riˈɒd.ɪ.kli/ [US] /ˌpɪr.iˈɑː.dɪ-/ *adv*: *The equipment should be tested periodically* (= at regular times).

periodical /ˌpɪə.riˈɒd.ɪ.kəl/ [US] /ˌpɪr.iˈɑː.dɪ-/ *noun* [C] a magazine or newspaper, especially on a serious subject, that is published regularly: *She has written for several legal periodicals.*

the ˌperiodic ˈtable *noun* [S] *SPECIALIZED* an arrangement of the symbols of chemical elements, usually in rows and columns, showing similarities in chemical behaviour, especially between elements in the same columns

ˈperiod ˌpiece *noun* [C usually sing] *INFORMAL* something such as a book or a film that is very old-fashioned, often in a way that is amusing to people now

peripatetic /ˌper.ɪ.pəˈtet.ɪk/ [US] /-ˈtet̬-/ *adj FORMAL* travelling around to different places, usually because you work in more than one place: *a peripatetic music teacher*

periphery /pəˈrɪf.ər.i/ [US] /-ˈrɪf.ɚ-/ *noun* [C usually sing] **1** the outer edge of an area: *Houses have been built on the periphery of the factory site.* ○ *The ring road runs around the periphery of the city centre.* **2** the less important part of a group or activity: *Many women feel they are being kept on the periphery of the armed forces.*

peripheral /pəˈrɪf.ər.əl/ [US] /-ˈrɪf.ɚ-/ *adj* **1** describes something that is not as important as something else: *The book contains a great deal of peripheral detail.* **2** happening at the edge of something: *A figure came into my peripheral vision.*

peripheral /pəˈrɪf.ər.əl/ [US] /-ˈrɪf.ɚ-/ *noun* [C] *SPECIALIZED* a piece of equipment, such as a printer, that can be connected to a computer

periscope /ˈper.ɪ.skəʊp/ [US] /-skoʊp/ *noun* [C] a long vertical tube containing a set of mirrors which gives you a view of what is above you when you look through the bottom of the tube: *Periscopes are used in submarines to allow you to look above the surface of the water.* ➲See picture **Planes, Ships and Boats** on page Centre 14

perish /ˈper.ɪʃ/ *verb* [I] **1** to die, especially in an accident or by being killed, or to be destroyed: *Three hundred people perished in the earthquake.* ○ *He believes that Europe must create closer ties or it will perish.* **2** *UK* If material such as rubber or leather perishes, it decays and starts to break into pieces: *Sunlight has caused the rubber to perish.*

• **perish the thought** *HUMOROUS OR INFORMAL* said to show that you hope that something that has been suggested will never happen: *Me, get married? Perish the thought!*

perishable /ˈper.ɪ.ʃə.bl̩/ *adj* describes food that decays quickly: *It's important to store perishable food in a cool place.*

perishables /ˈper.ɪ.ʃə.bl̩z/ *plural noun* items of food that decay quickly

perished /ˈper.ɪʃt/ *adj* [after v] *UK INFORMAL* extremely cold: *Her hands were perished.* ○ *I'm perished **with cold**.*

perisher /ˈper.ɪ.ʃəʳ/ [US] /-ʃɚ/ *noun* [C] *UK OLD-FASHIONED INFORMAL* a child who is being annoying

perishing [COLD] /ˈper.ɪ.ʃɪŋ/ *adj UK INFORMAL* extremely cold: *Wear your coat, **it's** perishing out there!* ○ *He's out there in the perishing **cold**.*

perishing [ANNOYED] /ˈper.ɪ.ʃɪŋ/ *adj OLD-FASHIONED* used to show your annoyance about something: *Now I've gone and lost my perishing keys!*

peritonitis /ˌper.ɪ.təʊˈnaɪ.tɪs/ [US] /-t̬əˈnaɪ.t̬ɪs/ *noun* [U] *SPECIALIZED* a serious medical condition in which the inside wall of the ABDOMEN (= lower part of the body containing the stomach and intestines) becomes very sore and larger than its usual size, especially because of infection

periwinkle [PLANT] /ˈper.ɪˌwɪŋ.kl̩/ *noun* [C] an evergreen plant with small blue flowers

periwinkle [SEA CREATURE] /ˈper.ɪˌwɪŋ.kl̩/ *noun* [C] *US FOR* **winkle**

perjure *yourself* /ˈpɜː.dʒəʳ/ [US] /ˈpɝː.dʒɚ/ *verb* [R] *LEGAL* to tell a lie in a law court, after promising formally to tell the truth: *The judge warned the witness not to perjure herself.* **perjured** /ˈpɜː.dʒəd/ [US] /ˈpɝː.dʒɚd/ *adj*: *a perjured testimony* **perjurer** /ˈpɜː.dʒər.əʳ/ [US] /ˈpɝː.dʒɚ.ɚ/ *noun* [C]

perjury /ˈpɜː.dʒər.i/ [US] /ˈpɝː.dʒɚ-/ *noun* [U] *LEGAL* the crime of telling lies in court when you have promised to tell the truth: *She was sentenced to two years in jail for **committing** perjury* (= telling lies in a law court).

perk [ADVANTAGE] /pɜːk/ [US] /pɝːk/ *noun* [C] **1** *INFORMAL* an advantage or benefit, such as money or goods, which you are given because of your job: *A company car and a mobile phone are some of the perks that come with the job.* **2** an advantage: *Having such easy access to some of the best cinema and theatre is one of the perks of living in Sydney.*

PHRASAL VERBS WITH **perk** ▼

▲ **perk *(sb)* up** [BECOME HAPPY] *phrasal verb* [M] to become or cause someone to become happier, more energetic or active: *She perked up as soon as I mentioned that Charles was coming to dinner.* ○ *He perked up **at** the news.* ○ *Would you like a cup of coffee? It might perk you up a bit.*

▲ **perk up** [IMPROVE] *phrasal verb INFORMAL* to improve or become more exciting: *Share prices perked up slightly before the close of trading.*

perky /ˈpɜː.ki/ [US] /ˈpɝː-/ *adj* happy and full of energy: *You look very perky this morning.*

perkily /ˈpɜː.kɪ.li/ [US] /ˈpɝː-/ *adv*: *"Does anyone want to come out jogging with me?" he said perkily.*
perkiness /ˈpɜː.kɪ.nəs/ [US] /ˈpɝː-/ *noun* [U]

perm /pɜːm/ [US] /pɝːm/ *noun* [C] (*US OR FORMAL* **permanent (wave)**) a chemical process which makes your hair wavy or curly, or a hair style which is created in this way: *Is your hair naturally curly or have you had a perm?* **perm** /pɜːm/ [US] /pɝːm/ *verb* [T] *I'm going to get my hair permed on Saturday.*

permafrost /ˈpɜː.mə.frɒst/ [US] /ˈpɝː.mə.frɑːst/ *noun* [U] *SPECIALIZED* an area of land which is permanently frozen, whose surface melts in the summer and freezes again in the autumn

permanent /ˈpɜː.mə.nənt/ [US] /ˈpɝː-/ *adj* **1** lasting for a long time or forever: *She is looking for a permanent place to stay.* ○ *Are you looking for a temporary or a permanent job?* ○ *The disease can cause permanent damage to the brain.* ○ *A semi-permanent hair dye will wash out after about three months.* ○ *He entered the United States in 1988 as a permanent resident because of his marriage to a U.S. citizen.* **2** describes something that exists or happens all the time: *Mont Blanc has a permanent snow cap.* ○ *Our office is in a permanent state of chaos.*
permanent /ˈpɜː.mə.nənt/ [US] /ˈpɝː-/ *noun* [C] *US FOR* **perm**
permanently /ˈpɜː.mə.nənt.li/ [US] /ˈpɝː-/ *adv* always or forever: *Smoking is likely to damage your health permanently.* ○ *Michael and his family have settled permanently in the States.* ○ *I seem to be permanently broke.*
permanence /ˈpɜː.mə.nənts/ [US] /ˈpɝː-/ *noun* [U] (*FORMAL* **permanency**) staying the same or continuing for a long time: *A loving family environment gives children that sense of stability and permanence which they need.* * NOTE: The opposite is **impermanence**.

ˌpermanent ˈsecretary *noun* [C] *UK* a government official who belongs to the CIVIL SERVICE (= the official departments responsible for putting government plans into action) rather than an elected government

ˌpermanent ˈwave *noun* [C] *FORMAL FOR* **perm**

permeate /ˈpɜː.mi.eɪt/ [US] /ˈpɝː-/ *verb* [I usually + adv or prep; T] *FORMAL* to spread through something and be present in every part of it: *Dissatisfaction with the government seems to have permeated every section of society.* ○ *A foul smell of stale beer permeated the whole building.* ○ *The table has a plastic coating which prevents liquids from permeating **into** the wood beneath.*
permeable /ˈpɜː.mi.ə.bl̩/ [US] /ˈpɝː-/ *adj FORMAL* If a substance is permeable, it allows liquids or gases to go through it: *Certain types of sandstone are permeable **to** water.* ○ *The solvent passes through the permeable **membrane** to the solution.* ○ *Soft and **gas**-permeable contact lenses are kinder to the eyes than hard lenses.* * NOTE: The opposite is **impermeable**.
permeability /ˌpɜː.mi.əˈbɪl.ɪ.ti/ [US] /ˌpɝː.mi.əˈbɪl.ə.t̬i/ *noun* [U] *FORMAL* the ability of a substance to allow gases or liquids to go through it: *Chalk has a **high** permeability* (= liquids easily pass through it).

perˌmissive soˈciety *noun* [C usually sing] *UK MAINLY DISAPPROVING* the type of society that has existed in most of Europe, Australia and North America since the 1960s, in which there is a great amount of freedom of behaviour, especially sexual freedom

permit /pəˈmɪt/ [US] /pɚ-/ *verb* **-tt- 1** [T] *SLIGHTLY FORMAL* to allow something: *The regulations do not permit much flexibility.* ○ [+ v-ing] *The prison authorities permit visiting only once a month.* ○ [+ obj + to infinitive] *The security system will not permit you **to** enter without the correct password.* ○ *As it was such a special occasion, she permitted herself a small glass of champagne.* ○ *FORMAL The law permits **of** no other interpretation.* * NOTE: *Permit* is more formal than *allow*. **2** [I] *FORMAL* to make something possible: *The Chancellor is looking to lower interest rates, when economic conditions permit.* ○ *We have arranged to play tennis on Saturday, **weather** permitting* (= if the weather is good enough).
permit /ˈpɜː.mɪt/ [US] /ˈpɝː-/ *noun* [C] an official document that allows you to do something or go somewhere: *a work/travel/parking permit* ○ *She has managed to obtain a temporary residence permit.* ○ [+ to infinitive] *Do you need a permit **to** work here?*
permissible /pəˈmɪs.ə.bl̩/ [US] /pɚ-/ *adj FORMAL* allowed: [+ to infinitive] *Is **it** permissible **to** park my car here?* ○ *a permissible level for vehicle exhaust emissions*
permission /pəˈmɪʃ.ən/ [US] /pɚ-/ *noun* [U] If someone is given permission to do something, they are allowed to do it: [+ to infinitive] *You will need permission from the council **to** extend your garage.* ○ *Official permission has been **granted** for more building near the river.* ○ *The authorities have **refused** permission for the demonstration to take place.* ○ ***Planning** permission was refused for the hypermarket after a three-week inquiry.*
permissive /pəˈmɪs.ɪv/ [US] /pɚ-/ *adj* A person or society that is permissive allows behaviour which other people might disapprove of: *It's a very permissive school where the children are allowed to do whatever they like.* ○ *He claims that society has been far too permissive **towards** drug taking.* **permissiveness** /pəˈmɪs.ɪv.nəs/ [US] /pɚ-/ *noun* [U] *She attributed the social and economic problems of the 1980s to the permissiveness of the 1960s.* ○ *He remembers the 1960s as being an era of **sexual** permissiveness.*

permutation /ˌpɜː.mjʊˈteɪ.ʃən/ [US] /ˌpɝː.mjuː-/ *noun* **1** [C usually pl] *FORMAL* any of the various ways in which a set of things can be ordered: *There are 120 permutations **of** the numbers 1, 2, 3, 4 and 5: for example, 1, 3, 2, 4, 5 or 5, 1, 4, 2, 3.* ○ *He made six separate applications for a total of 39 000 shares, using permutations of his surname and Christian names.* **2** [C] one of several different forms: *The company has had five different names in its various permutations over the last few years.*

pernicious /pəˈnɪʃ.əs/ [US] /pɚ-/ *adj FORMAL* having a very harmful effect or influence: *The cuts in government funding have had a pernicious effect on local health services.*

pernickety /pəˈnɪk.ɪ.ti/ [US] /pɚˈnɪk.ə.t̬i/ *adj* (*US USUALLY* **persnickety**) *DISAPPROVING* giving too much attention to small unimportant details in a way that annoys other people: *As a writer, he is extremely pernickety about using words correctly.*

peroxide /pəˈrɒk.saɪd/ [US] /pəˈrɑːk-/ *noun* [C or U] (*SPECIALIZED* **hydrogen peroxide**) a liquid chemical used to make hair very pale in colour or to kill bacteria: *Peroxide is a bleach and an antiseptic.* ○ *Peroxides are found in household detergents.* ○ *She has dyed her brown hair peroxide **blonde**.*

perpendicular /ˌpɜː.pənˈdɪk.jʊ.ləʳ/ [US] /ˌpɝː.pənˈdɪk.juː.lɚ/ *adj* **1** *FORMAL* at an angle of 90° to a horizontal line or surface: *We scrambled up the nearly perpendicular side of the mountain.* **2** *SPECIALIZED* at an angle of 90° to another line or surface: *The wheel rotates about an axis which is perpendicular **to** the plane.*
perpendicular /ˌpɜː.pənˈdɪk.jʊ.ləʳ/ [US] /ˌpɝː.pənˈdɪk.juː.lɚ/ *noun* [C] *SPECIALIZED* **1** a perpendicular line: *Draw a perpendicular from the vertex of the triangle to its base.* **2 the perpendicular** a perpendicular position or direction: *The wall was leaning at an angle of ten degrees to the perpendicular.* **perpendicularly** /ˌpɜː.pənˈdɪk.jʊ.lə.li/ [US] /ˌpɝː.pənˈdɪk.juː.lɚ-/ *adv FORMAL OR SPECIALIZED*

perpetrate /ˈpɜː.pə.treɪt/ [US] /ˈpɝː-/ *verb* [T] *FORMAL* to commit a crime, or a violent or harmful act: *In Britain, half of all violent crime is perpetrated by people who have been drinking alcohol.* ○ *Federal soldiers have been accused of perpetrating atrocities **against** innocent people.* **perpetration** /ˌpɜː.pəˈtreɪ.ʃən/ [US] /ˌpɝː-/ *noun* [U] *Human rights activists have accused the country's government of a systematic perpetration of violence **against** minority groups.*
perpetrator /ˈpɜː.pə.treɪ.təʳ/ [US] /ˈpɝː.pə.treɪ.t̬ɚ/ *noun* [C] (*US OLD-FASHIONED SLANG* **perp**) *FORMAL* someone who has committed a crime, or a violent or harmful act: *The perpetrators of the massacre must be brought to justice as war criminals.*

perpetual /pəˈpetʃ.u.əl/ [US] /pɚˈpetʃ-/ *adj* **1** continuing forever in the same way: *They lived in perpetual fear of being discovered and arrested.* ○ *He has hard, cold eyes and his mouth is set in a perpetual sneer.* ○ *a perpetual student* **2** frequently repeated: *perpetual vandalism*
perpetually /pəˈpetʃ.u.ə.li/ [US] /pɚˈpetʃ-/ *adv*: *She's*

perpetually asking me for money.

perpetuate /pə'petʃ.u.eɪt/ ⓤ /pɚ'petʃ-/ *verb* [T] FORMAL to cause something to continue: *Increasing the supply of weapons will only perpetuate the violence and anarchy.* ○ *The aim of the association is to perpetuate the skills of traditional furniture design.* **perpetuation** /pə,petʃ.u-'eɪ.ʃ°n/ ⓤ /,pɚ.petʃ-/ *noun* [U] *The lack of military action from other countries has contributed to the perpetuation of the civil war.*

perpetuity /,pɜː.pə'tʃuː.ə.ti/ ⓤ /,pɜː.pə'tuː.ə.t̬i/ *noun* FORMAL **in perpetuity** for ever

perplex /pə'pleks/ ⓤ /pɚ-/ *verb* [T] to confuse and worry someone slightly by being difficult to understand or solve: *The disease has continued to perplex doctors.* **perplexed** /pə'plekst/ ⓤ /pɚ-/ *adj*: *The students looked perplexed, so the teacher tried to explain once again.* **perplexing** /pə'plek.sɪŋ/ ⓤ /pɚ-/ *adj*: *They find the company's attitude perplexing and unreasonable.* **perplexity** /pə'plek.sɪ.ti/ ⓤ /pɚ'plek.sə.t̬i/ *noun* [C or U] *She stared at the instruction booklet in complete perplexity.* ○ *the perplexities of life*

per 'se *adv* FORMAL by or of itself: *Research shows that it is not divorce per se that harms children, but the continuing conflict between parents.*

persecute /'pɜː.sɪ.kjuːt/ ⓤ /'pɜː-/ *verb* [T] to treat someone unfairly or cruelly over a long period of time because of their race, religion, or political beliefs or to annoy someone by refusing to leave them alone: *Religious minorities were persecuted and massacred during the ten-year regime.* ○ *His latest film is about the experience of being persecuted for being gay.* ○ *Ever since the news broke about her divorce, she has been persecuted by the tabloid press.* **persecution** /,pɜː.sɪ'kjuː.ʃ°n/ ⓤ /,pɜː-/ *noun* [C or U] *They left the country out of fear of persecution.* ○ *refugees escaping from political persecution*

persecutor /'pɜː.sɪ.kjuː.tər/ ⓤ /'pɜː.sɪ.kjuː.t̬ɚ/ *noun* [C] *The country's native people rose up against their persecutors* (= the people who had treated them cruelly). ○ *The clergy were the main persecutors of witches in the Middle Ages.*

perse'cution ,complex *noun* [C] If someone has a persecution complex, they suffer from the feeling that other people are trying to harm them.

persevere /,pɜː.sɪ'vɪər/ ⓤ /,pɜː.sə'vɪr/ *verb* [I] MAINLY APPROVING to try to do or continue doing something in a determined way, despite having problems: *It looks as if the policy will be a success, providing that the government perseveres and does not give in to its critics.* ○ *The education director is persevering in his attempt to obtain additional funding for the school.* ○ *Despite receiving little support, the women are persevering with their crusade to fight crime.*

perseverance /,pɜː.sɪ'vɪə.rənts/ ⓤ /,pɜː.sə'vɪr.°nts/ *noun* [U] MAINLY APPROVING continued effort and determination: *Through hard work and perseverance, he worked his way up from being a teacher in a village school to the headmaster of a large comprehensive.* **persevering** /,pɜː.sɪ-'vɪə.rɪŋ/ ⓤ /,pɜː.sə'vɪr.ɪŋ/ *adj*: *She was persevering enough to reach the height of her ambition and become the managing director of the company.*

Persian cat /,pɜː.ʒən'kæt/ ⓤ /,pɜː-/ *noun* [C] a type of cat with long hair, short thick legs and a round face

persimmon /pə'sɪm.ən/ ⓤ /pɚ-/ *noun* [C] a very sweet orange-coloured tropical fruit

persist /pə'sɪst/ ⓤ /pɚ-/ *verb* [I] **1** If an unpleasant feeling or situation persists, it continues to exist: *If the pain persists, consult a doctor.* ○ *The cold weather is set to persist throughout the week.* **2** to try to do or continue doing something in a determined but often unreasonable way: *If he persists in asking awkward questions, then send him to the boss.* ○ *The government is persisting with its ambitious public works programme.*

persistence /pə'sɪs.t°nts/ ⓤ /pɚ-/ *noun* [U] when someone or something persists: *Most financial analysts have been surprised by the persistence of the recession.* ○ *Her persistence and enthusiasm have helped the group to achieve its international success.*

persistent /pə'sɪs.t°nt/ ⓤ /pɚ-/ *adj* **1** lasting for a long time or difficult to get rid of: *a persistent smell/skin rash*

○ *Symptoms of the illness include a high temperature and a persistent dry cough.* ○ *There have been persistent **rumours** that the managing director might take early retirement.* **2** Someone who is persistent continues doing something or tries to do something in a determined but often unreasonable way: *Be persistent – don't give up.* ○ *He has been a persistent critic of the president.* ○ *She is a persistent **offender** and has been arrested five times this year for shoplifting.* **persistently** /pə'sɪs.t°nt.li/ ⓤ /pɚ-/ *adv*: *They have persistently ignored our advice.*

per,sistent ,vegetative 'state *noun* [U] SPECIALIZED a medical condition in which a person's brain shows no sign of activity and they have to be kept alive by drugs and machines

persnickety /pə'snɪk.ɪ.ti/ ⓤ /pɚ'snɪk.ə.t̬i/ *adj* US FOR **pernickety**

person /'pɜː.s°n/ ⓤ /'pɜː-/ *noun* [C] *plural* **people** *or* FORMAL OR LEGAL **persons 1** a man, woman or child: *Who was the first person to swim the English Channel?* ○ *A meal at the restaurant costs about $70 for two people.* ○ LEGAL *Four persons have been charged with the murder.* **2** used when describing someone and their particular type of character: *She's an extremely kind person.* ○ *He's nice enough **as a** person, but he's not the right man for this job.* ○ INFORMAL *I don't think of him as a book person* (= a person who likes books). **3** SPECIALIZED used in grammar to describe the verbs and pronouns that refer to the different people in a conversation. The first person ('I' or 'we') refers to the person speaking, the second person ('you') refers to the person being spoken to and the third person ('he', 'she', 'it' or 'they') refers to another person or thing being spoken about or described: *The novel is written in the first person, so that the author and narrator seem to be the same.* ○ *'Are' is the second person plural of the verb 'to be'.*

● **in person** If you do something or go somewhere in person, you do it or go there yourself: *If you can't be there in person, the next best thing is watching it on TV.*

● **in the person of sb** FORMAL in the form of someone: *The editorial board has an expert with a world-wide reputation in the person of Professor Jameson.*

● **on/about your person** FORMAL in a pocket, bag, or something else that you are holding: *Do you have about your person such a thing as a lighter?*

-person /-pɜː.s°n/ ⓤ /-pɜː-/ *suffix* used to combine with nouns to form new nouns referring to the particular job or duty that someone has. It is often used instead of *-man* or *-woman* to avoid making an unnecessary statement about the sex of the particular person: *spokesperson* ○ *chairperson* ○ *business people*

personal /'pɜː.s°n.°l/ ⓤ /'pɜː.s°n.°l/ *adj* **1** relating or belonging to a single or particular person rather than to a group or an organization: *My personal **opinion/view** is that the students should be doing more work outside the classroom.* ○ *Her uncle takes a personal interest in her progress.* ○ *She has her own personal secretary/bodyguard/fitness instructor.* ○ *Passengers are reminded to take all their personal **belongings** with them when they leave the plane.* **2** A personal action is one which is done by someone directly rather than getting another person to do it: *The health minister made a personal **appearance** at the hospital.* ○ *I will give the matter my personal **attention**.* **3** private or relating to someone's private life: *The letter was marked 'Personal. Strictly confidential.'* ○ *Do you mind if I ask you a personal question?* ○ *His resignation was apparently for personal rather than professional reasons.* ○ *For such a famous, wealthy man, his personal **life** was surprisingly simple and ordinary.* **4** relating to your body or appearance: *She is obsessed with personal **hygiene**.* **5 personal remark/comment** an intentionally offensive remark about someone's character or appearance: *Did you have to make such a personal remark about her new haircut?* **6** INFORMAL **get personal** to start being rude to someone about their character or appearance: *As long as the criticism is honestly given and doesn't get personal, I can handle it.*

personally /'pɜː.s°n.°l.i/ ⓤ /'pɜː.r.s°n.°l.i/ *adv* **1** used when you give your opinion: *Personally (speaking), I* *think the show is going to be a great success.* **2** affecting you and not anyone else: *He believes that parents should be made personally responsible for their children's behaviour.* **3** done by you and not by someone else: *These figures should be correct because I've checked them personally.* **4 take *sth* personally** to think that someone is offending you when they are not: *These are general criticisms which should not be taken personally* (= They are not meant to criticize any one person in particular).

personality /ˌpɜː.sᵊnˈæl.ə.ti/ [US] /ˌpɝː.sᵊnˈæl.ə.t̬i/ *noun* **1** [C or U] the type of person you are, which is shown by the way you behave, feel and think: *She has a very warm personality.* ○ *He is well qualified for the job, but he does lack personality* (= he is a boring person). **2** [C] a famous person: *The show is hosted by a popular TV personality.*

personalize, *UK USUALLY* **-ise** /ˈpɜː.sᵊn.ᵊl.aɪz/ [US] /ˈpɝː-/ *verb* [T] **1** If you personalize an object, you change it or add to it so that it is obvious that it belongs to or comes from you: *The computer allows you to personalize standard letters by adding a greeting to each one.* ○ *She had done little to personalize her room, except hang a few posters on the walls.* **2** to make something suitable for the needs of a particular person: *She hired a trainer to create a personalized exercise schedule to get her into shape.* **3** If you personalize a subject, you make people feel more emotionally involved in it by giving examples about real people: *By telling people about her accident, she personalizes the numbing figure of road accidents that happen every year.* **4** *DISAPPROVING* If you personalize an argument or discussion, you start to criticize someone's bad qualities instead of discussing the facts.

personalized, *UK USUALLY* **-ised** /ˈpɜː.sᵊn.ᵊl.aɪz/ [US] /ˈpɝː-/ *adj* describes an object that has someone's name on it, or that has been made for a particular person: *His car has a personalized number plate – TJ 1.*

persona /pəˈsəʊ.nə/ [US] /pɚˈsoʊ-/ *noun* [C] *plural* **personae** or **personas** the particular type of character that a person seems to have, which is often different from their real or private character: *He had a shy, retiring side to his personality that was completely at odds with his **public** persona.*

personable /ˈpɜː.sᵊn.ə.bl̩/ [US] /ˈpɝː-/ *adj FORMAL* having a pleasant appearance and character: *She is intelligent, hard-working and personable.*

personage /ˈpɜː.sᵊn.ɪdʒ/ [US] /ˈpɝː-/ *noun* [C] *FORMAL* an important or famous person

ˌpersonal ˈad *noun* [C] an advertisement that you put in a newspaper or magazine, often in order to find a sexual partner: *He placed/put a personal ad in The Times.*

ˌpersonal alˈlowance *noun* [C] *UK SPECIALIZED* an amount of money that you can earn before you start to be taxed

ˈpersonal ˌcolumn *UK noun* [C] (*US* **the personals**) the part of a newspaper or magazine which contains short advertisements and private messages

ˌpersonal comˈputer *noun* [C] (*ABBREVIATION* **PC**) a medium-sized computer which is used mainly by people at home rather than by large organizations

ˌpersonal ˌdigital asˈsistant *noun* [C] (*ABBREVIATION* **PDA**) a small computer that you can carry with you

ˌpersonal efˈfects *plural noun FORMAL* things that you own which you often carry with you, such as keys or clothing: *After she had identified the body of her husband, the police asked her to collect his personal effects.*

ˌpersonal identifiˈcation ˌnumber *noun* [C] *FORMAL FOR* **PIN (number)**

personˈality ˌclash *noun* [C] when two or more people have very different characters and are unable to have a good relationship with each other: *There's a real personality clash between two of the directors.*

personˈality ˌcult *noun* [C] *DISAPPROVING* officially organized admiration and love for a particular person, especially a political leader

ˌpersonal ˈorganizer *noun* [C] a small book or electronic device in which information is stored, such as names, addresses, telephone numbers and dates of meeting, and which people use to help organize their time ⊃See picture **In the Office** on page Centre 15

ˌpersonal ˈpronoun *noun* [C] *SPECIALIZED* in grammar, a word such as 'I', 'you' and 'they' which refers to a person in speech or in writing

ˌpersonal ˈproperty *noun* [U] *LEGAL* the things you own which you can take with you, such as money, vehicles or furniture

ˌpersonal ˈstereo *noun* [C] (*TRADEMARK* **Walkman**) a small electronic machine that plays music and which has HEADPHONES so that you can listen to music while you are doing other things

ˈpersonal ˌtouch *noun* [C] an original or special quality, or something that is done for every single person in a group in order to make them feel special: *The chairman of the bank believes in the personal touch and always sends a signed letter to each customer.* ○ *Cullinan's tasty offering **adds a** personal touch to classic recipe.*

ˌpersonal ˈtrainer *noun* [C] someone whose job is to help you become stronger and healthier by deciding which exercises you should do and showing you how to do them: *Sandy works out with her personal trainer every week.*

persona non grata /pəˌsəʊ.nəˌnɒŋˈgrɑː.tə/ [US] /pɚˌsoʊ.nəˌnɑːnˈgrɑː.t̬ə/ *noun* [C not after *the*] *plural* **personae non gratae** **1** *SPECIALIZED* a person who is not wanted or welcome in a particular country, because they are unacceptable to its government: *Several embassy staff were **declared** persona non grata and asked to leave the country within 48 hours.* **2** someone who is not popular or accepted by others: *From the look on their faces, I was obviously persona non grata.*

personify /pəˈsɒn.ɪ.faɪ/ [US] /pɚˈsɑː.nɪ-/ *verb* [T] **1** to be a perfect example of something: *These louts personify all that is wrong with our society today.* **2** *SPECIALIZED* to treat something as if it were in the form of a human being: *In Greek myth, love is personified by the goddess Aphrodite.* **personification** /pəˌsɒn.ɪ.fɪˈkeɪ.ʃᵊn/ [US] /pɚˌsɑː.nɪ-/ *noun* [C usually sing; U] *She played a character who was the personification **of** evil.* **personified** /pəˈsɒn.ɪ.faɪd/ [US] /pɚˈsɑː.nɪ-/ *adj* [after n] *She is charm personified.*

personnel /ˌpɜː.sᵊnˈel/ [US] /ˌpɝː-/ *group noun* [U] **1** the people who are employed in a company, organization or one of the armed forces: *The new director is likely to make major changes in personnel.* ○ *military personnel* **2** the department of a company or organization that deals with its employees when they first join, when they need training or when they have any problems: *Personnel will help you find a flat to rent.* ○ *For more information about the job, please contact the personnel **manager**.*

personˈnel ˌcarrier *noun* [C] an armed transport vehicle used by the army

person-to-person /ˌpɜː.sᵊn.təˈpɜː.sᵊn/ [US] /ˌpɝː.sᵊn.təˈpɝː.sᵊn/ *adj US* describes a telephone call where you ask the OPERATOR (= a person who helps connect people on a telephone system) to allow you to speak directly to a particular person

person-to-person /ˌpɜː.sᵊn.təˈpɜː.sᵊn/ [US] /ˌpɝː.sᵊn.təˈpɝː.sᵊn/ *adv MAINLY US* If you talk to or meet someone person-to-person, you talk to or meet them directly.

perspective [THOUGHT] /pəˈspek.tɪv/ [US] /pɚ-/ *noun* [C] a particular way of considering something: *Her attitude lends a fresh perspective to the subject.* ○ *He writes **from** a Marxist perspective.* ○ *Because of its geographical position, Germany's perspective **on** the situation in Eastern Europe is rather different from Britain's.*

• **get/keep *sth* in perspective** to think about a situation or problem in a wise and reasonable way: *You must keep things in perspective – the overall situation isn't really that bad.*

• **put *sth* in(to) perspective** to compare something to other things so that it can be accurately and fairly judged: *Total investments for this year reached £53 million and, to put this into perspective, investments this year were double those made in 2001.*

perspective [ART] /pəˈspek.tɪv/ [US] /pɚ-/ *noun* [U] the way that objects appear smaller when they are further away

P

and the way parallel lines appear to meet each other at a point in the distance: *In 15th-century Italy, artists rediscovered the rules of perspective.*

• **in perspective** An object or person that is in perspective has the correct size and position in comparison with other things in the picture.

• **out of perspective** An object or person that is out of perspective does not have the correct size or position in comparison with other things in the picture, and therefore does not look real or natural.

Perspex *UK TRADEMARK* /'pɜː.speks/ ⓤ /'pɝː-/ *noun* [U] (*US TRADEMARK* **Plexiglas**) a strong transparent plastic which is sometimes used instead of glass

perspicacious /ˌpɜː.spɪˈkeɪ.ʃəs/ ⓤ /ˌpɝː-/ *adj FORMAL APPROVING* quick in noticing, understanding or judging things accurately: *His perspicacious grandfather had bought the land as an investment, guessing that there might be gold underground.*

perspicacity /ˌpɜː.spɪˈkæs.ə.ti/ ⓤ /ˌpɝː.spɪˈkæs.ə.t̬i/ *noun* [U] *FORMAL APPROVING* the ability to understand things quickly and make accurate judgments: *a woman of exceptional perspicacity*

perspire /pəˈspaɪəʳ/ ⓤ /pɚˈspaɪɚ/ *verb* [I] *FORMAL OR POLITE WORD FOR* **sweat** (= to excrete liquid through the skin): *He was perspiring in his thick woollen suit.* ○ *The journalists and camera crews began to perspire in the heat as they stood waiting for the president to appear.*

perspiration /ˌpɜː.spəˈreɪ.ʃən/ ⓤ /ˌpɝː.spəˈreɪ-/ *noun* [U] *POLITE WORD FOR* **sweat** (= colourless liquid excreted through the skin): *During the break between games, she had a drink of water and wiped the perspiration off her face and arms with a towel.* ○ *Beads* (= Drops) *of perspiration glistened on his brow.*

persuade /pəˈsweɪd/ ⓤ /pɚ-/ *verb* [T] to make someone do or believe something by giving them a good reason to do it or by talking to them and making them believe it: *If she doesn't want to go, nothing you can say will persuade her.* ○ [+ (that)] *It's no use trying to persuade him* (that) *you're innocent.* ○ [+ to infinitive] *He is trying to persuade local and foreign businesses to invest in the project.* ○ *Using a bunch of bananas, the zoo-keeper persuaded the monkey back into its cage.* ○ *FORMAL The first priority is to persuade the management of the urgency of this matter.* ○ *Her legal advisers persuaded her into/out of mentioning* (= to mention/not to mention) *the names of the people involved in the robbery.*

persuasion /pəˈsweɪ.ʒən/ ⓤ /pɚ-/ *noun* [U] *It took a lot of persuasion to convince the committee of the advantages of the new scheme.* ○ *She will help you – she just needs a bit of gentle persuasion.* ○ *The occasion will be a test of the senator's powers of persuasion* (= his ability to persuade people). ⊃See also **persuasion**.

persuasive /pəˈsweɪ.sɪv/ ⓤ /pɚ-/ *adj* making you want to do or believe a particular thing: *a persuasive speaker/speech* ○ *Your arguments are very persuasive.* **persuasively** /pəˈsweɪ.sɪv.li/ ⓤ /pɚ-/ *adv* **persuasiveness** /pəˈsweɪ.sɪv.nəs/ ⓤ /pɚ-/ *noun* [U]

persuasion /pəˈsweɪ.ʒən/ ⓤ /pɚ-/ *noun* [C] a particular set of beliefs, especially religious: *We need a society which welcomes people of all religious persuasions.* ⊃See also **persuade**.

pert /pɜːt/ ⓤ /pɝːt/ *adj* **1** attractively small and firm, as a description of a part of the body: *a pert bottom/nose* **2** describes behaviour or qualities, especially in a young woman, that are amusing because they show a slight lack of respect: *a pert answer/glance/smile*

pertain /pəˈteɪn/ ⓤ /pɝː-/ *verb*

▲ **pertain to** *sth phrasal verb FORMAL* to be connected with a particular subject, event or situation: *We are only interested in the parts of the proposals that pertain to local issues.*

pertinacious /ˌpɜː.tɪˈneɪ.ʃəs/ ⓤ /ˌpɝː.t̬ənˈeɪ-/ *adj FORMAL* very determined and refusing to be defeated by problems: *Like most successful politicians, she is pertinacious and single-minded in the pursuit of her goals.*

pertinent /'pɜː.tɪ.nənt/ ⓤ /'pɝː.t̬ən.ənt/ *adj FORMAL* relating directly to the subject being considered: *a pertinent question/remark* ○ *Chapter One is pertinent to the post-*

war period. ✻ NOTE: The opposite is **irrelevant**. Do not confuse with **impertinent** (= rude).

perturb /pəˈtɜːb/ ⓤ /pɚˈtɝːb/ *verb* [T] *FORMAL* to worry someone: *News of the arrest perturbed her greatly.*

perturbation /ˌpɜː.təˈbeɪ.ʃən/ ⓤ /ˌpɝː.t̬ɚ-/ *noun* **1** [U] *FORMAL* worry **2** [C or U] *SPECIALIZED* a small change in the regular movement of an object: *Perturbations in the orbit of the planet Uranus led to the discovery of Neptune in 1846.*

perturbed /pəˈtɜːbd/ ⓤ /pɚˈtɝːbd/ *adj FORMAL* worried: *He didn't seem unduly/overly perturbed by the news.*

peruse /pəˈruːz/ *verb* [T] *FORMAL* to read through something, especially in order to find the part you are interested in: *He opened a newspaper and began to peruse the personal ads.*
perusal /pəˈruː.zəl/ *noun* [S or U] *FORMAL* a brief perusal (= a quick read) ○ *He sent a copy of the report to the governors for their perusal* (= for them to read).

perv /pɜːv/ ⓤ /pɝːv/ *noun* [C] *UK INFORMAL FOR* **pervert**

pervade /pəˈveɪd/ ⓤ /pɚ-/ *verb* [T] *FORMAL* When qualities, characteristics or smells pervade a place or thing, they spread through it and are present in every part of it: *The film is a reflection of the violence that pervades American culture.*

pervasive /pəˈveɪ.sɪv/ ⓤ /pɚ-/ *adj FORMAL* present or noticeable in every part of a thing or place: *The influence of Freud is pervasive in her books.* ○ *a pervasive smell of diesel* ○ *Reforms are being undermined by the all-pervasive corruption in the country.* **pervasively** /pəˈveɪ.sɪv.li/ ⓤ /pɚ-/ *adv* **pervasiveness** /pəˈveɪ.sɪv.nəs/ ⓤ /pɚ-/ *noun* [U]

perverse /pəˈvɜːs/ ⓤ /pɚˈvɝːs/ *adj DISAPPROVING* strange and not what most people would expect or enjoy: *Jack was being perverse and refusing to agree with anything we said.* ○ *She took a perverse pleasure in hearing that her sister was getting divorced.* **perversely** /pəˈvɜː.sli/ ⓤ /pɚˈvɝː-/ *adv*: *The best way to understand this book is to start, perversely, at the end.* **perversity** /pəˈvɜː.sə.ti/ ⓤ /pɚˈvɝː.sə.t̬i/ *noun* [U] ⊃See also **perversity** at **pervert**.

pervert /pəˈvɜːt/ ⓤ /pɚˈvɝːt/ *verb* [T] *DISAPPROVING* to change something so that it is not what it was or should be, or to influence someone in a harmful way: *Her ideas have been shamelessly perverted to serve the president's propaganda campaign.* ○ *The history teacher tried to pervert* (= persuade into unacceptable sexual activity) *the boys by showing them pornographic magazines.*

• **pervert the course of justice** *LEGAL* to act illegally to avoid punishment or to get the wrong person punished: *The two police officers were charged with perverting the course of justice by fabricating evidence in the trial.*

pervert /'pɜː.vɜːt/ ⓤ /'pɝː.vɝːt/ *noun* [C] (*UK INFORMAL* **perv**) *DISAPPROVING* a person whose sexual behaviour is considered strange and unpleasant by most people

perverted /pəˈvɜː.tɪd/ ⓤ /pɚˈvɝː.t̬ɪd/ *adj DISAPPROVING* considered strange and unpleasant by most people: *She told him he had a sick and perverted mind.* ○ *He used a perverted form of socialism to incite racial hatred.*

perversion /pəˈvɜː.ʒən/ ⓤ /pɚˈvɝː-/ *noun* [C or U] *DISAPPROVING* **1** sexual behaviour which is considered strange and unpleasant by most people: *The novels of the Marquis de Sade deal with sexual perversion.* **2** the changing of something so that it is not what it was or should be: *His testimony was clearly a perversion of the truth.* **perversity** /pəˈvɜː.sə.ti/ ⓤ /pɚˈvɝː.sə.t̬i/ *noun* [C or U] *The author of the book seems to be obsessed with sexual perversity and death.* ⊃See also **perversity** at **perverse**.

peseta /pəˈseɪ.tə/ ⓤ /-t̬ə/ *noun* [C] the standard unit of money used in Spain before they started using the euro

pesky /'pes.ki/ *adj* [before n] *INFORMAL* annoying or causing trouble: *Those pesky kids from next door have let down my car tyres again!*

peso /'peɪ.səʊ/ ⓤ /-soʊ/ *noun* [C] the standard unit of money used in Argentina, Chile, Colombia, Cuba, the Dominican Republic, Mexico, the Philippines and Uruguay

pessimism /'pes.ɪ.mɪ.zəm/ *noun* [U] the tendency to emphasize or think of the bad part of a situation rather than the good part, or the feeling that bad things are more likely to happen than good things: *There is now a mood of deepening pessimism **about/over** the economy.* ○ *An underlying pessimism infuses all her novels.* ✻ NOTE: The opposite is **optimism**. **pessimist** /ˈpes.ɪ.mɪst/ *noun* [C] *Don't be such a pessimist!*

pessimistic /ˌpes.ɪˈmɪs.tɪk/ *adj*: *The tone of the meeting was very pessimistic.* ○ *The doctors are pessimistic* (= not hopeful) ***about** his chances of recovery.* **pessimistically** /ˌpes.ɪˈmɪs.tɪ.kli/ *adv*

pest /pest/ *noun* [C] **1** an insect or small animal which is harmful or which damages crops: *common pests such as rats, mice or cockroaches* **2** INFORMAL an annoying person, especially a child: *Put that back, you little pest!*

pester /ˈpes.təʳ/ [US] /-t̬ɚ/ *verb* [T] to behave in an annoying manner towards someone by doing or asking for something repeatedly: *At the frontier, there were people pestering tourists **for** cigarettes, food or alcohol.* ○ [+ to infinitive] *John has been pestering her **to** go out with him all month.*

pesticide /ˈpes.tɪ.saɪd/ [US] /-t̬ə-/ *noun* [C or U] a chemical substance used to kill harmful insects, small animals, wild plants and other unwanted organisms: *The pesticides that farmers spray on their crops kill pests but they can also damage people's health.* ➲Compare **herbicide**; **insecticide**.

pestilence /ˈpes.tɪ.lənts/ [US] /-t̬əl.ənts/ *noun* [C or U] FORMAL any very serious infectious disease that spreads quickly and kills large numbers of people

pestle /ˈpes.l̩/ *noun* [C] a heavy stick made of clay, stone or metal, with a thick rounded end, which is used for crushing substances in a MORTAR (= a small strong bowl) by hitting or rubbing them: *Crush the garlic into a paste using a pestle and mortar.*

pesto /ˈpes.təʊ/ [US] /-toʊ/ *noun* [U] a green sauce which is used in Italian cooking, especially on pasta: *Pesto is made of basil leaves, parmesan cheese, pine nuts, garlic and olive oil which have all been crushed together.*

pet [ANIMAL] /pet/ *noun* [C] **1** an animal which is kept in the home as a companion and treated affectionately: *They have several pets – a dog, two rabbits and a guinea pig.* ○ *a pet snake* **2** DISAPPROVING **be *sb's* pet** to be the person that someone in authority likes best and treats better than anyone else: *The other children hated her because she was the **teacher's** pet.* **3** INFORMAL APPROVING a kind person who is easy to like: *He's always sending me flowers – he's a real pet!* **4** UK INFORMAL an affectionate way of addressing someone, especially a woman or a child: *Thank you, pet.*

pet /pet/ *adj* **pet theory/subject/hate, etc.** a theory/subject/hate, etc. that is special and important to you: *Football is one of her pet hates.*

pet [TOUCH] /pet/ *verb* **-tt- 1** [T] If you pet an animal, child, etc., you touch them gently and affectionately with your hands: *Our dog loves to be petted and tickled behind the ears.* **2** [I] INFORMAL If two people are petting, they are kissing and touching each other in a sexual way. ➲See also **heavy petting**.

petal /ˈpet.əl/ [US] /ˈpet̬-/ *noun* [C] **1** any of the usually brightly coloured parts that together form most of a flower: *rose petals* **2** UK INFORMAL used as an affectionate form of address: *What did you say, petal?* **-petalled**, US USUALLY **-petaled** /-pet.əld/ [US] /-pet̬-/ *suffix*: *a 5-petalled flower* ○ *a white-petalled rose*

petard /petˈɑːd/ [US] /pɪˈtɑːrd/ *noun* **be hoist(ed) with/by *your* own petard** ➲See at **hoist**.

peter /ˈpiː.təʳ/ [US] /-t̬ɚ/ *noun* [C] MAINLY US OFFENSIVE a penis
▲ **peter out** *phrasal verb* to gradually stop or disappear: *The fighting which started in the night had petered out by morning.* ○ *The track petered out after a mile or so.*

petit bourgeois, UK ALSO **petty bourgeois** /ˌpet.iˈbɔː.ʒwɑː/ [US] /pəˌtiː.bʊrˈʒwɑː/ *adj* MAINLY DISAPPROVING belonging to the lower middle social class, or having the characteristics that are connected with this class, such as valuing money and possessions too much and not trusting new or different ideas: *petit bourgeois prejudices*

the petite bourgeoisie, the petty bourgeoisie /ðəˌpet.ɪˌbɔː.ʒwɑːˈziː/ [US] /-pəˌtiː.bʊr-/ *group noun* [S] MAINLY DISAPPROVING people who are petit bourgeois, considered as a group

petite /pəˈtiːt/ *adj* **1** APPROVING If a woman or girl is petite, she is small and thin in an attractive way: *She was dark and petite, as all his wives had been.* **2** of a clothing size that is for small women

petit four (*plural* **petits fours**) /ˌpet.iˈfɔːʳ/ [US] /ˌpet̬.iˈfɔːr/ *noun* [C] (US ALSO **petit fours**) a small cake or biscuit, usually served at the end of a meal with coffee

petition /pəˈtɪʃ.ən/ *noun* [C] **1** a document signed by a large number of people demanding or requesting some action from the government or another authority: *I signed a petition **against** the proposed closure of the local hospital today.* **2** LEGAL a formal letter to a court of law requesting a particular legal action: *She's **filing** a petition **for** divorce.* **petition** /pəˈtɪʃ.ən/ *verb* [I or T] *They're petitioning **for/about** better facilities for disabled people on public transport.* ○ [+ obj + to infinitive] *I think we should petition the government **to** increase the grant for the project.* ○ LEGAL *She is petitioning **for** a re-trial.*

petitioner /pəˈtɪʃ.ən.əʳ/ [US] /-ɚ/ *noun* [C] **1** a person who organizes or signs a petition **2** LEGAL a person who is requesting action from a court of law

petit pois /ˌpet.iˈpwɑː/ [US] /pəˌtiː-/ *plural noun* MAINLY UK small peas

ˌ**pet** ˈ**name** *noun* [C] an informal affectionate name given to someone by their family or friends

petrel /ˈpet.rəl/ *noun* [C] a sea bird with a curved beak, which spends most of its life flying over the sea

petri dish /ˈpet.riˌdɪʃ/ [US] /ˈpiː.tri-/ *noun* [C] a small clear round dish with a cover, which is used in scientific tests, especially for the growing of bacteria

petrify [FRIGHTEN] /ˈpet.rə.faɪ/ *verb* [T] to frighten someone greatly, especially so that they are unable to move or speak: *I think you petrified poor Jeremy – he never said a word the whole time you were here.*

petrified /ˈpet.rə.faɪd/ *adj* extremely frightened: *I stood petrified as the most enormous dog I've ever seen came bounding up to me.* ○ *She's petrified **of** being on her own in the house at night.*

petrify [CHANGE TO STONE] /ˈpet.rə.faɪ/ *verb* [I] If dead things petrify, they change to a substance like stone over a long period of time.

petrified /ˈpet.rə.faɪd/ *adj* **1** having changed to a substance like stone: *a petrified tree/shell* **2** LITERARY describes something that has stopped changing and developing, and often belongs to the past **petrifaction** /ˌpet.rɪˈfæk.ʃən/ *noun* [U] (ALSO **petrification**) SPECIALIZED

petrochemical /ˌpet.rəʊˈkem.ɪ.kəl/ [US] /-roʊ-/ *noun* [C] any chemical substance obtained from PETROLEUM or natural gas: *the petrochemical industry*

petrodollar /ˈpet.rəʊˌdɒl.əʳ/ [US] /-roʊˌdɑː.lɚ/ *noun* [C] a unit of money earned by countries that produce PETROLEUM for sale to other countries: *Petrodollars have maintained Kuwait's wealth.*

petrol UK /ˈpet.rəl/ *noun* [U] (US **gas**) a liquid obtained from PETROLEUM, used especially as a fuel for cars, aircraft and other vehicles: *a petrol tank/pump/station* ○ *lead-free/unleaded/high-octane petrol* ○ *I'm a bit **low on*** (= I haven't got much) *petrol.*

ˈ**petrol** ˌ**bomb** *noun* [C] a bottle filled with petrol or other liquid fuel with a piece of cloth in its top, which is set on fire and thrown: *The rioters were throwing petrol bombs.* **petrol-bomb** /ˈpet.rəl.bɒm/ [US] /-bɑːm/ *verb* [T]

petroleum /pəˈtrəʊ.li.əm/ [US] /-ˈtroʊ-/ *noun* [U] a dark thick oil obtained from under the ground, from which various substances including petrol, PARAFFIN and DIESEL oil are produced

peˌ**troleum** ˈ**jelly** *noun* [U] a clear jelly-like substance made from petroleum, used as a base for medicines which are rubbed into the skin, and also for making parts in a machine move easily against each other

ˈ**petrol** ˌ**station** UK *noun* [C] (US **gas station**) a place where fuel is sold for road vehicles, often with a small shop and public toilets

ˈ**pet** ˌ**sit** *verb* [I or T] to look after someone's pet while they are away from their home **pet-sitter** /ˈpetˌsɪt.əʳ/ [US] /-ˌsɪt̬-/ *noun* [C] **pet-sitting** /ˈpetˌsɪt.ɪŋ/ [US] /-ˌsɪt̬-/ *noun* [U]

P

petticoat /'pet.ɪ.kəʊt/ ⓤ /'pet̬.ɪ.koʊt/ *noun* [C] OLD-FASHIONED a **slip** UNDERWEAR

pettifogging /'pet.ɪ.fɒg.ɪŋ/ ⓤ /'pet̬.ɪ.fɑː.gɪŋ/ *adj* OLD-FASHIONED DISAPPROVING **1** Pettifogging people give too much attention to small unimportant details in a way that shows a limited mind: *pettifogging lawyers* **2** Pettifogging rules or details are too small and unimportant to give attention to.

petting ,zoo *noun* [C] US an open area where small or young animals are kept which children can hold, touch and sometimes feed

petty /'pet.i/ ⓤ /'pet̬-/ *adj* **1** [before n] DISAPPROVING unimportant and not worth giving attention to: *Prisoners complain that they are subjected to too many petty rules and restrictions.* **2** [after n] complaining too much about unimportant things: *Don't be so petty!* **pettiness** /'pet.i.nəs/ ⓤ /'pet̬-/ *noun* [U] DISAPPROVING *It was the pettiness of their arguments that irritated her.*

,petty 'bourgeois *adj* UK FOR **petit bourgeois**

,petty 'cash *noun* [U] a small amount of money kept in an office for buying cheap items: *Take the money for stamps out of petty cash.*

,petty 'crime *noun* [C or U] a type of crime which is not considered serious when compared with some other crimes: *petty crime such as shoplifting*

,petty 'officer *noun* [C] (WRITTEN ABBREVIATION **PO**) a rank in a navy, below the officers but above the ordinary sailors: *Chief Petty Officer*

petulant /'pet.jə.lənt/ *adj* DISAPPROVING easily annoyed and complaining in a childish and rude way **petulantly** /'pet.jə.lənt.li/ *adv:* *"Well, he didn't invite me to his party so I'm certainly not inviting him to mine!" she said petulantly.* **petulance** /'pet.jə.lənts/ *noun* [U]

petunia /pə'tjuː.ni.ə/ ⓤ /-'tuː.njə/ *noun* [C] a garden plant grown for its white, pink, purple or red bell-shaped flowers

pew /pjuː/ *noun* [C] a long wooden seat with a high back, which a row of people sit on in a church
• **Take a pew!** UK HUMOROUS Sit down!

pewter /'pjuː.tər/ ⓤ /-t̬ɚ/ *noun* [U] a bluish grey metal which is a mixture of TIN and lead: *a pewter plate/tankard*

peyote /peɪ'əʊ.ti/ ⓤ /-'oʊ.t̬i/ *noun* [C] US a type of CACTUS (= a desert plant), part of which can be taken as a drug that makes you HALLUCINATE (= see things which do not exist), or the drug itself ⓉSee also **mescalin**.

pfft /fʌt/ ⓤ /fət/ *exclamation* US FOR **phut**

PG FILM /ˌpiː'dʒiː/ *adj, noun* parental guidance; refers to a film that contains slightly sexual or violent parts which parents might not consider suitable for young children: *Her latest film is classified/rated (as) PG.* ○ *The film's a PG.* ⓉCompare **G** FILM; **NC-17**; **U** FILM; **X** FILM.

pg PAGE *noun* [C] MAINLY US WRITTEN ABBREVIATION FOR **page** PAPER: *See pgs. 67-69.*

PG-13 /ˌpiːˌdʒiːˈθɜːˈtiːn/ ⓤ /-ˈθɝː-/ *noun* [C] in the US, a symbol that marks a film that parents are strongly warned might not be suitable for children under the age of 13

PGCE /ˌpiːˌdʒiːˌsiːˈiː/ *noun* [C usually sing] ABBREVIATION FOR **Postgraduate Certificate in Education**

pH /ˌpiːˈeɪtʃ/ *noun* [C usually sing] a number which shows how strongly acid or ALKALINE a substance is, in a range from 0 to 14: *Below pH 6.5 is acid, above pH 7.5 is alkaline.* ○ *The soil in our garden has a low/high pH.*

phagocyte /'fæg.əʊ.saɪt/ ⓤ /-oʊ-/ *noun* [C] SPECIALIZED a type of cell in the body which can surround things and swallow them, especially a white blood cell which protects the body against infection by destroying bacteria

phalanx /'fæl.æŋks/ ⓤ /'feɪ.læŋks/ *group noun* [C] *plural* **phalanxes** or **phalanges** FORMAL a large group of people standing very close to each other, usually for the purposes of defence or attack: *Bodyguards formed a solid phalanx around the singer so that photographers couldn't get close.*

phallocentric /ˌfæl.əʊ'sen.trɪk/ ⓤ /-oʊ-/ *adj* FORMAL having the male, or male sexual feelings or activity, as the main subject of interest: *phallocentric eroticism/literature*

phallus /'fæl.əs/ *noun* [C] FORMAL an image or a model of the penis, especially one representing the power of men to reproduce, or a penis: *These primitive peoples are believed to have worshipped the phallus as a symbol of regeneration.* **phallic** /'fæl.ɪk/ *adj* symbolic of, shaped like, or related to the penis: *phallic symbolism/imagery*

phantasm /'fæn.tæz.ᵊm/ *noun* [C] LITERARY something which is seen or imagined but is not real

phantasmagoria /ˌfæn.tæz.mə'gɔː.ri.ə/ ⓤ /-'gɔːr.i.ə/ *noun* [S] LITERARY a fast-changing and confused group of real or imagined images, one following the other as in a dream

phantom /'fæn.t̬ᵊm/ ⓤ /-t̬ᵊm/ *noun* [C] a spirit of a dead person believed by some to visit the living as a pale, almost transparent form of a person, animal or other object; a ghost: *A phantom coach is said to pass through the grounds of this house when there's a full moon.* ○ HUMOROUS *The phantom wine-drinker has been around – this was almost a full bottle when I put it in the fridge* (= an unknown person has been drinking the wine)*!*

phantom /'fæn.t̬ᵊm/ ⓤ /-t̬ᵊm/ *adj* [before n] describes something that you imagine exists or that appears to exist, although in fact it does not: *Although she had to have her leg amputated, she still feels as though she's got a phantom limb.* ○ *They discovered it was a phantom organization set up for the processing of drug profits.* ○ UK *Although she grew bigger and felt ill, she later discovered it was a phantom* (US **false**) **pregnancy**.

pharaoh /'feə.rəʊ/ ⓤ /'fer.oʊ/ *noun* [C] (the title of) a king of ancient Egypt

pharisee /'fær.ɪ.siː/ ⓤ /'fer-/ *noun* **1 Pharisee** a member of an ancient group of Jews, written about in the Bible, who believed in obeying religious laws very carefully and separated themselves from the ordinary people **2** DISAPPROVING a person who thinks they are very religious, but who does not care about others

pharmaceutical /ˌfɑː.mə'suː.tɪ.kᵊl/ ⓤ /ˌfɑːr.mə'suː.t̬ɪ-/ *adj* connected with the production of medicines: *the pharmaceutical industry* ○ *a pharmaceutical company/product/journal* **pharmaceutical** /ˌfɑː.mə'suː.tɪ.kᵊl/ ⓤ /ˌfɑːr.mə'suː.t̬ɪ-/ *noun* [C usually pl] SPECIALIZED a medicine

pharmacist /'fɑː.mə.sɪst/ ⓤ /'fɑːr-/ *noun* [C] a person who is trained to prepare medicines and who works in a hospital or shop

pharmacology /ˌfɑː.mə'kɒl.ə.dʒi/ ⓤ /ˌfɑːr.mə'kɑː.lə-/ *noun* [U] the study of medicines and drugs, including their action, their use and their effects on the body **pharmacologist** /ˌfɑː.mə'kɒl.ə.dʒɪst/ ⓤ /ˌfɑːr.mə'kɑː.lə-/ *noun* [C] a person who has studied pharmacology

pharmacy /'fɑː.mə.si/ ⓤ /'fɑːr-/ *noun* **1** [C] a shop or part of a shop in which medicines are prepared and sold ✳ NOTE: A shop which sells medicines is also called a *drugstore* in American English, and a *chemist* or *chemist's* in British English. **2** [C] part of a hospital where medicines are prepared **3** [U] the activity or study of medicine preparation

pharynx /'fær.ɪŋks/ *noun* [C] SPECIALIZED the soft part at the top of the throat which connects the mouth and nose to the OESOPHAGUS (= the tube which takes food to the stomach) and the LARYNX (= the hollow organ between the nose and lungs)

phase /feɪz/ *noun* [C] **1** any stage in a series of events or in a process of development: *The project is only in the initial phase as yet, but it's looking quite promising.* ○ *We're entering a new phase in international relations.* **2** a period of strange or difficult behaviour, especially that a young child or person goes through, that will stop after a while: *When I was in my early teens I went through a phase of only ever wearing black.* **3** The phases of the moon are the regular changes in its shape as it appears to us on Earth.
• **in phase/out of phase** If two things are happening in/out of phase they are reaching the same or related stages at the same time/at different times.

phase /feɪz/ *verb* [T often passive] to introduce something in stages over a particular period of time: *The reduction* *in armed forces will be phased over the next ten years.*

PHRASAL VERBS WITH **phase** ▼

▲ **phase** *sth* **in** *phrasal verb* [M] to introduce something gradually or in stages: *They will phase the new health care system in over a period of five years.*

▲ **phase** *sth* **out** *phrasal verb* [M] to remove or stop using something gradually or in stages

PhD /ˌpiːˌeɪtʃˈdiː/ *noun* [C] (*ALSO* **D Phil**) *ABBREVIATION FOR* doctor of philosophy: the highest college or university degree, or someone who has this: *a PhD student/thesis* ○ *Susannah has a PhD in Italian literature.* ○ *She's a PhD.*

pheasant /ˈfez.ᵊnt/ *noun* [C or U] *plural* **pheasants** or **pheasant** a large bird with a rounded body and long tail, which spends a lot of time on the ground and is often shot for sport and food

phenom /fəˈnɒm/ ⑩ /-ˈnɑːm/ *noun* [C] *US SLANG* someone or something extremely successful, especially someone young in sports who achieves a lot very quickly: *In less than a year, the 21-year-old phenom has gone from being a college athlete with great potential to perhaps the best player in baseball.*

phenomenon EXISTING THING /fəˈnɒm.ɪ.nən/ ⑩ /-ˈnɑː.mə.nɑːn/ *noun* [C] *plural* **phenomena** something that exists and can be seen, felt, tasted, etc., especially something which is unusual or interesting: *Gravity is a natural phenomenon.* ○ *Do you believe in the paranormal and other psychic phenomena?* ○ *There's evidence to suggest that child abuse is not just a recent phenomenon.*

phenomenon SUCCESS /fəˈnɒm.ɪ.nən/ ⑩ /-ˈnɑː.mə.nɑːn/ *noun* [C] *plural* **phenomena** someone or something extremely successful, often because of special qualities or abilities: *The Beatles were a phenomenon – nobody had heard anything like them before.* **phenomenal** /fəˈnɒm.ɪ.nᵊl/ ⑩ /-ˈnɑː.mə-/ *adj*: *Her rise to fame was quite phenomenal – in less than two years she was a household name.* **phenomenally** /fəˈnɒm.ɪ.nᵊl.i/ ⑩ /-ˈnɑː.mə-/ *adv*: *His first novel was phenomenally successful.*

phenotype /ˈfiː.nəʊ.taɪp/ ⑩ /-noʊ-/ *noun* [C] *SPECIALIZED* the physical characteristics of something living, especially those characteristics which can be seen ⊃Compare **genotype**.

pheromone /ˈfer.ə.məʊn/ ⑩ /-moʊn/ *noun* [C] *SPECIALIZED* a chemical substance which an animal releases that influences the behaviour of another creature of the same type, for example by attracting it sexually

Phew! /fjuː/ *exclamation* (*ALSO* **Whew!**) *INFORMAL MAINLY HUMOROUS* used when you are happy that something difficult or dangerous has finished or is not going to happen, or when you are tired or hot: *Phew! I'm so glad I don't have to give that speech.* ○ *Phew, it's boiling in here!*

phial *MAINLY UK OLD-FASHIONED* /faɪəl/ *noun* [C] (*US USUALLY* **vial**) a small glass bottle, especially one containing liquid medicine: *a phial of opium/poison*

Phi Beta Kappa /ˌfaɪˌbiːtə ˈkæp.ə/ ⑩ /-ˌbeɪ.t̬ə-/ *noun* [C or U] a national organization in the US whose members are elected because they have achieved a very high level in their studies at colleges or universities, or a member of this organization

philanderer /fɪˈlæn.dᵊr.əʳ/ ⑩ /-dɚ.ɚ/ *noun* [C] *OLD-FASHIONED DISAPPROVING* a man who enjoys having sex with a lot of different women without becoming emotionally involved with any of them **philandering** /fɪˈlæn.dᵊr.ɪŋ/ ⑩ /-dɚ.ɪŋ/ *adj, noun* [U]

philanthropic /ˌfɪl.ənˈθrɒp.ɪk/ ⑩ /-ænˈθrɑː.pɪk/ *adj FORMAL* helping poor people, especially by giving them money **philanthropist** /fɪˈlæn.θrə.pɪst/ *noun* [C] a philanthropic person: *a donation from a wealthy 19th-century philanthropist* **philanthropy** /fɪˈlæn.θrə.pi/ *noun* [U]

philately /fɪˈlæt.ᵊl.i/ ⑩ /-ˈlæt̬-/ *noun* [U] *SPECIALIZED* the collecting and study of stamps and postal history as a hobby

philatelist /fɪˈlæt.ᵊl.ɪst/ ⑩ /-ˈlæt̬-/ *noun* [C] *SPECIALIZED* a person who collects or studies stamps and postal history

-phile /-faɪl/ ⑩ /-fɪl/ *suffix* someone who enjoys a particular thing or has it as a hobby, or who likes a particular place: *A bibliophile likes books and an oenophile enjoys wine.* ○ *An Anglophile likes England or Britain.*

Philharmonic /ˌfɪl.hɑːˈmɒn.ɪk/ ⑩ /-hɑːrˈmɑː.nɪk/ *adj* [before n] used in the names of musical groups, especially orchestras: *the Vienna Philharmonic Orchestra.*

philistine /ˈfɪl.ɪ.staɪn/ ⑩ /-stiːn/ *noun* [C] **1** *DISAPPROVING* a person who refuses to see the beauty or the value of art, literature, music or culture in any form: *I wouldn't have expected them to enjoy a film of that quality anyway – they're just a bunch of philistines!* **2 Philistine** one of a race of people who lived in the coastal area of the SE Mediterranean in ancient times and were often at war with the Israelites

philology /fɪˈlɒl.ə.dʒi/ ⑩ /-ˈlɑː.lə-/ *noun* [U] *OLD-FASHIONED* the study of language, especially its history and development ⊃See also **linguistics**. **philological** /ˌfɪl.əˈlɒdʒ.ɪ.kᵊl/ ⑩ /-ˈlɑː.dʒɪ-/ *adj*

philosophy /fɪˈlɒs.ə.fi/ ⑩ /-ˈlɑː.sə-/ *noun* **1** [U] the use of reason in understanding such things as the nature of reality and existence, the use and limits of knowledge and the principles that govern and influence moral judgment: *René Descartes is regarded as the founder of modern philosophy.* ⊃See also **PhD**. **2** [C] a particular system of beliefs, values and principles: *the Ancient Greek philosophy of Stoicism* **3** [C usually sing] *INFORMAL* someone's approach to life and their way of dealing with it: *Live now, pay later – that's my philosophy of life!* **philosopher** /fɪˈlɒs.ə.fəʳ/ ⑩ /-ˈlɑː.sə.fɚ/ *noun* [C] someone who studies or writes about the meaning of life: *Plato was a Greek philosopher.* **philosophical** /ˌfɪl.əˈsɒf.ɪ.kᵊl/ ⑩ /-ˈsɑː.fɪ-/ *adj* **1** relating to the study or writing of philosophy: *philosophical writings/essays* **2** If you are philosophical in your reaction to something which is not satisfactory, you accept it calmly and without anger, understanding that failure and disappointment are a part of life. **philosophically** /ˌfɪl.əˈsɒf.ɪ.kli/ ⑩ /-ˈsɑː.fɪ-/ *adv* calmly accepting a difficult situation **philosophize**, *UK USUALLY* **-ise** /fɪˈlɒs.ə.faɪz/ ⑩ /-ˈlɑː.sə-/ *verb* [I] *MAINLY DISAPPROVING* to talk for a long time about subjects such as the nature and meaning of life: *Students, she complained, had nothing better to do than spend whole days philosophizing about the nature of truth.*

phlegm SUBSTANCE /flem/ *noun* [U] a thick mucus that is produced especially when you have a cold

phlegm CALMNESS /flem/ *noun* [U] *FORMAL* the ability to stay calm and not get emotional or excited about things even in a difficult or dangerous situation **phlegmatic** /flegˈmæt.ɪk/ ⑩ /-ˈmæt̬-/ *adj FORMAL* describes someone who tends not to get emotional or excited about things: *As a footballer his great asset was his calm, phlegmatic manner.*

-phobe /-fəʊb/ ⑩ /-foʊb/ *suffix* someone who hates something: *An Anglophobe is a person who hates England or Britain.*

phobia /ˈfəʊ.bi.ə/ ⑩ /ˈfoʊ.bjə/ *noun* [C] an extreme fear of a particular thing or situation, especially one that cannot be reasonably explained: *I've got a phobia about/of worms.* **-phobia** /-fəʊ.bi.ə/ ⑩ /-foʊ.bjə/ *suffix*: *Xenophobia means hatred of foreigners.* **phobic** /ˈfəʊ.bɪk/ ⑩ /ˈfoʊ-/ *adj, noun* [C] *I wouldn't describe myself as (a) phobic but I don't like heights.*

phobic /ˈfəʊ.bɪk/ ⑩ /ˈfoʊ-/ *adj INFORMAL* having a strong dislike of something: *Why are so many companies phobic about employing fat people?*

phoenix /ˈfiː.nɪks/ *noun* [C usually sing] in ancient stories, an imaginary bird which set fire to itself every 500 years and was born again, rising from its ASHES (= the powder left after its body has been burnt): *The town was bombed but was then rebuilt and rose from the ashes like a/the phoenix* (= was just as good as before).

phone /fəʊn/ ⑩ /foʊn/ *noun* **1** [C or U] (*FORMAL* **telephone**) a device which uses either a system of wires, along which electrical signals are sent, or a system of radio signals to enable you to speak to someone in another place who has a similar device: *Just then, his mobile phone **rang**.* ○ *Could you **answer** the phone?* ○ *We speak **on the/by** phone about twice a week.* ○ *You had three phone **calls** this morning.* ○ *If the phone **lines** are busy, please try again later.* **2** [C] the part of a telephone that you hold to your mouth and ear and that you speak into: *Could you **pick** the phone **up** for me – my hands are wet.* ○ *I **left** the phone **off the hook**, so it wouldn't ring.* ○ *I was so angry I just **put/slammed** the phone **down (on** her)* (= replaced it before our conversation was finished).

• **be on the phone 1** to be using the telephone: *That son of mine is on the phone all day!* **2** *UK* to have a telephone in the home: *Are the Middletons on the phone, do you know?*

phone /fəʊn/ [US] /foʊn/ *verb* [I or T] to communicate with someone by telephone: *She phoned just after lunch.* ○ *He's phoned me **(up)** every day this week.*

PHRASAL VERBS WITH **phone**

▲ **phone in** [WORK] *phrasal verb* to telephone the place where you work in order to tell your employer something: *She phoned in **sick*** (= saying that she was ill) *this morning.*

▲ **phone in** [PROGRAMME] *phrasal verb* to telephone a television or radio programme in order to express your opinion on a matter: *Over three hundred people phoned in to complain.*

'phone ˌbanking *noun* [U] when customers use the telephone to access an automatic system which allows them to organize, examine and make changes to their bank accounts, investments, etc., or when banks operate a system of this type: *They recently launched a new phone banking **service**.*

'phone ˌbook *noun* [C] *INFORMAL* a **telephone directory**: *Is he in the (phone) book?*

'phone ˌbooth *noun* [C] **1** *UK* a place in a public building, often partly enclosed, where there is a public telephone **2** *US FOR* **phone box**

'phone ˌbox *UK noun* [C] (*US* **phone booth**) a small structure with a door, found outside in public places, containing a public telephone

'phone ˌcall *noun* [C] when you use the telephone: *Will you excuse me? I've got to **make a** phone call.*

P

'phone ˌcard, phonecard *noun* [C] *UK* a small card which is used to operate a public telephone

phone-in *UK* /'fəʊn.ɪn/ [US] /'foʊn-/ *noun* [C] (*US* **call-in**) a television or radio programme in which members of the public telephone to express their opinions or ask questions

'phone ˌsex *noun* [U] the activity of talking on the telephone with someone about sex in order to become sexually excited: *She accused him of **having** phone sex with prostitutes while she was away on business trips.*

phone-tapping /'fəʊnˌtæp.ɪŋ/ [US] /'foʊn-/ *noun* [U] the activity of secretly fitting a special device to someone's telephone in order to listen to their telephone conversations without them knowing

phonetic /fəʊ'net.ɪk/ [US] /foʊ'neṭ-/ *adj SPECIALIZED* **1** using special signs to represent the different sounds made by the voice in speech: *Pronunciations are shown in this dictionary using the International Phonetic Alphabet.* **2** A spelling system can be described as phonetic if you can understand how words are pronounced simply by looking at their spelling. **phonetically** /fəʊ'net.ɪ.kli/ [US] /foʊ'neṭ-/ *adv*: *She pronounced Leicester phonetically as "Ley-ces-ter", but really we say "Lester".*

phonetics /fəʊ'net.ɪks/ [US] /foʊ'neṭ-/ *noun* [U] *SPECIALIZED* the study of the sounds made by the human voice in speech

phoney (**phonier, phoniest**), *US ALSO* **phony** /'fəʊ.ni/ [US] /'foʊ-/ *adj INFORMAL DISAPPROVING* not sincere or not real: *All salespeople seem to have the same phoney smile.* ○ *He gave the police a phoney address.* **phoney**, *US ALSO* **phony** /'fəʊ.ni/ [US] /'foʊ-/ *noun* [C] *I don't trust him – I think he's a phoney.*

ˌphoney 'war *noun* [C usually sing] (*ALSO* **phony war**) *UK* a period during a war when there is no fighting and the situation appears calm

phonograph /'fəʊ.nə.grɑːf/ [US] /'foʊ.noʊ.græf/ *noun* [C] *US OLD USE FOR* **record player**

phonology /fəʊ'nɒl.ə.dʒi/ [US] /fə'nɑː.lə-/ *noun* [U] *SPECIALIZED* the study of sounds in a particular language or in languages generally **phonological** /ˌfɒn.ə'lɒdʒ.ɪ.kəl/ [US] /ˌfoʊ.nə'lɑː.dʒɪ-/ *adj*

phooey /'fuː.i/ *exclamation INFORMAL HUMOROUS* used to express disappointment or a lack of respect for something

phosphate /'fɒs.feɪt/ [US] /'fɑːs-/ *noun* [C] a chemical compound which contains PHOSPHORUS: *Most fertilizers contain nitrogen and phosphates.*

phosphorescent /ˌfɒs.fər'es.ənt/ [US] /ˌfɑːs.fə'res-/ *adj SPECIALIZED* giving off light after radiation has hit it **phosphorescence** /ˌfɒs.fər'es.ənts/ [US] /ˌfɑːs.fə'res-/ *noun* [U]

phosphorus /'fɒs.fər.əs/ [US] /'fɑːs.fɚ.əs/ *noun* [U] a poisonous yellowish white or (more rarely) red or black element that shines in the dark and burns when in the air

phosphoric /fɒs'fɒr.ɪk/ [US] /fɑːs'fɔːr-/ *adj* (*ALSO* **phosphorous**) of or containing phosphorus: *phosphoric acid*

photo [PHOTOGRAPH] /'fəʊ.təʊ/ [US] /'foʊ.ṭoʊ/ *noun* [C] *plural* **photos** *INFORMAL* a photograph: *She **took** a lot of photos **of** the kids.* ○ *Would you like to see my holiday/wedding photos?*

photo- /fəʊ.təʊ-/ [US] /foʊ.ṭoʊ-/ *prefix* connected with photography: *photojournalism*

photo- [LIGHT] /fəʊ.təʊ-/ [US] /foʊ.ṭoʊ-/ *prefix* connected with or produced by light: *photosynthesis*

'photo ˌalbum *noun* [C] a type of book in which you keep photos

'photo ˌcall *noun* [C] an occasion when people at a formal event are asked to have their photograph taken together, or when photographers are officially invited to take photographs of a famous person: *After the conference, there was the usual photo call for everybody involved.*

photocell /'fəʊ.təʊ.sel/ [US] /'foʊ.ṭoʊ-/ *noun* [C] (*ALSO* **photoelectric cell**) an electrical device which produces a current or a VOLTAGE when light shines on it: *Photocells are used in burglar alarms.*

photochemical /ˌfəʊ.təʊ'kem.ɪ.kəl/ [US] /ˌfoʊ.ṭoʊ-/ *adj SPECIALIZED* relating to the effect of light on some chemicals

ˌphotochemical 'smog *noun* [C or U] a fog caused by light from the sun shining on chemicals in the air produced by traffic and industry

photocopiable /ˌfəʊ.təʊ'kɒ.pɪ.ə.bəl/ [US] /ˌfoʊ.ṭoʊ'kɑː.pɪ.ə.bəl/ *adj* If a page in a book is photocopiable, you can make copies of it legally.

photocopier /'fəʊ.təʊˌkɒp.i.ər/ [US] /'foʊ.ṭoʊˌkɑː.pi.ɚ/ *noun* [C] a machine which makes copies of documents using a photographic process ➲See picture **In the Office** on page Centre 15

photocopy /'fəʊ.təʊˌkɒp.i/ [US] /'foʊ.ṭoʊˌkɑː.pi/ *noun* [C] a photographic copy of a document made on a photocopier: *I'll just **make** a photocopy **of** the agreement.* **photocopy** /'fəʊ.təʊˌkɒp.i/ [US] /'foʊ.ṭoʊˌkɑː.pi/ *verb* [T] *Could you photocopy those three pages for me, please?*

photoelectric /ˌfəʊ.təʊ.ɪ'lek.trɪk/ [US] /ˌfoʊ.ṭoʊ-/ *adj* of or using an electrical current or VOLTAGE which is produced because of light

ˌphotoelectric 'cell *noun* [C] a **photocell**

ˌphoto 'finish *noun* [C] the end of a race when the competitors are so close that a photograph has to be examined in order to discover who has won

Photofit (picture) /ˌfəʊ.təʊ.fɪt'pɪk.tʃər/ [US] /ˌfoʊ.ṭoʊ'pɪk.tʃɚ/ *noun* [C] *UK TRADEMARK* a picture which represents as closely as possible a person's memory of a criminal's face, made by putting together photographs of eyes, nose, hair, etc. from a set showing different types of facial features ➲See also **Identikit**.

photo frame noun [C] a flat object with a clear front surface used to display a photograph in

photogenic /ˌfəʊ.təʊˈdʒen.ɪk/ ⓤⓢ /ˌfoʊ.toʊ-/ adj having a face that looks attractive in photographs

photograph /ˈfəʊ.tə.grɑːf/ ⓤⓢ /ˈfoʊ.toʊ.græf/ noun [C] (INFORMAL **photo**) a picture produced using a camera: *a colour/black-and-white photograph* ∘ *aerial photographs* ∘ *nude photographs* ∘ *My parents took a lot of photographs of us when we were small.* **photograph** /ˈfəʊ.tə.grɑːf/ ⓤⓢ /ˈfoʊ.toʊ.græf/ verb [T] *I prefer photographing people rather than places.* ∘ [+ obj + v-ing] *MacKay was photographed leaving the building.*
• **photograph well/badly** to appear attractive/unattractive in photographs

photographer /fəˈtɒg.rə.fəʳ/ ⓤⓢ /-ˈtɑː.grə.fɚ/ noun [C] a person who takes photographs, either as a job or hobby: *a fashion/press/amateur photographer* **photographic** /ˌfəʊ.təˈgræf.ɪk/ ⓤⓢ /ˌfoʊ.tə-/ adj: *photographic equipment/film/materials* ∘ *photographic skills* ∘ *Her paintings are almost photographic in their detail and accuracy.* **photographically** /ˌfəʊ.təˈgræf.ɪ.kli/ ⓤⓢ /ˌfoʊ.tə-/ adv **photography** /fəˈtɒg.rə.fi/ ⓤⓢ /-ˈtɑː.grə-/ noun [U] (the activity or job of taking) photographs or films: *She's doing an evening class in photography.* ∘ *The film won an award for its photography.*

photographic memory noun [C usually sing] If you have a photographic memory, you are able to remember things in exact detail.

photojournalism /ˌfəʊ.təʊˈdʒɜː.nəl.ɪ.zəm/ ⓤⓢ /ˌfoʊ.toʊ-ˈdʒɜː-/ noun [U] (the activity of creating) a news article using mainly photographs **photojournalist** /ˌfəʊ.təʊ-ˈdʒɜː.nəl.ɪst/ ⓤⓢ /ˌfoʊ.toʊˈdʒɜː-/ noun [C]

photon /ˈfəʊ.tɒn/ ⓤⓢ /ˈfoʊ.tɑːn/ noun [C] SPECIALIZED a single unit of light

photo opportunity noun [C] an occasion when a politician or famous person is photographed doing something that will gain them popularity with the public

photosensitive /ˌfəʊ.təʊˈsent.sɪ.tɪv/ ⓤⓢ /ˌfoʊ.toʊ-ˈsent.sə-/ adj reacting to light: *a photosensitive lens/chemical/surface*

photo session noun [C] an occasion arranged for newspaper photographers to take photographs of politicians or other famous people

Photostat /ˈfəʊ.təʊ.stæt/ ⓤⓢ /ˈfoʊ.toʊ-/ noun [C] TRADEMARK a machine used especially in the past to make photographic copies of documents, or a copy made by such a machine **photostat** /ˈfəʊ.təʊ.stæt/ ⓤⓢ /ˈfoʊ.toʊ-/ verb [T] -tt-

photosynthesis /ˌfəʊ.təʊˈsɪnt.θə.sɪs/ ⓤⓢ /ˌfoʊ.toʊ-/ noun [U] the process by which a plant uses the energy from the light of the sun to produce its own food **photosynthesize**, UK USUALLY **-ise** /ˌfəʊ.təʊˈsɪnt.θə.saɪz/ ⓤⓢ /ˌfoʊ.toʊ-/ verb [I or T]

phrasal verb /ˌfreɪ.zəlˈvɜː.b/ ⓤⓢ /-ˈvɜː.b/ noun [C] a phrase which consists of a verb in combination with a preposition or adverb or both, the meaning of which is different from the meaning of its separate parts: *'Look after', 'work out' and 'make up for' are all phrasal verbs.*

phrase GRAMMAR /freɪz/ noun [C] a group of words which is part rather than the whole of a sentence ⇒See also **phrasebook**.

phrase EXPRESSION /freɪz/ noun [C] a short group of words which are often used together and have a particular meaning: *We are governed, in Lord Hailsham's famous phrase, by an 'elective dictatorship'.*

phrase /freɪz/ verb [T usually + adv or prep] to express something with a particular choice of words: *The declaration was carefully/cleverly/tactfully, etc. phrased.*

phraseology /ˌfreɪ.ziˈɒl.ə.dʒi/ ⓤⓢ /-ˈɑː.lə-/ noun [U] the way in which language is used, especially in the choice of words and expressions

phrasing /ˈfreɪ.zɪŋ/ noun [U] the choice of words by which something is expressed: *The phrasing of the contract is rather ambiguous.*

phrase MUSIC /freɪz/ noun [C] SPECIALIZED a small group of notes forming a unit of a tune

phrasing /ˈfreɪ.zɪŋ/ noun [U] SPECIALIZED the way in which a singer or musician divides the tune into

separate parts: *Her phrasing, as ever, is faultless.*

phrasebook /ˈfreɪz.bʊk/ noun [C] a small book containing helpful groups of sentences and words in a particular foreign language, intended for use by travellers: *a Spanish phrasebook*

phut /fʌt/ ⓤⓢ /fət/ noun UK INFORMAL **go phut** If a machine goes phut, it suddenly stops working.

phyllo (pastry) /ˌfiː.ləʊˈpeɪ.stri/ ⓤⓢ /-loʊ-/ noun [U] US FOR **filo (pastry)**

phylum /ˈfaɪ.ləm/ noun [C] SPECIALIZED a major division in a TAXONOMIC (= scientific naming and organization system) relating to animals: *Members of the largest and most diverse phylum of animals (Arthropoda), have segmented bodies and an external skeleton.*

physical BODY /ˈfɪz.ɪ.kəl/ adj **1** connected with the body: *physical exercise/fitness/strength/disabilities* ∘ *I'm not a very physical sort of person* (= I don't enjoy physical activities). ⇒See also **physical** at **physics**. Compare **mental**. **2** INFORMAL violent: *The referee stepped in because the game had started to get a bit physical.* **3** sexual: *There was obviously a great physical attraction between them.*
physical /ˈfɪz.ɪ.kəl/ noun [C] (UK ALSO **medical**) an examination of a person's body by a doctor in order to discover if that person is healthy, sometimes done before a person can be accepted for a particular job
physically /ˈfɪz.ɪ.kli/ adv: *Physically I find him very attractive.* ∘ *The protestors had to be physically removed from the room* (= they were taken away). ∘ *The work is physically demanding* (= you have to work hard in a way that makes your body tired). ∘ *Special holidays are available for physically handicapped/disabled people* (= those lacking the full use of part of their body).

physical REAL /ˈfɪz.ɪ.kəl/ adj relating to things you can see or touch, or relating to the laws of nature: *the physical world* ∘ *All physical objects occupy space.* ⇒See also **physical** BODY; **physical** at **physics**. **physically** /ˈfɪz.ɪ.kli/ adv: *No one could have climbed that wall – it's physically impossible.*

physical education noun [U] (ABBREVIATION **PE**) classes at school in which children do exercise and learn to play sport, or the area of study relating to such classes

physical geography noun [U] the study of the natural features of the Earth, such as mountains and rivers

physical jerks plural noun UK OLD-FASHIONED exercises that people do in order to be healthy

physical sciences plural noun the sciences such as physics, chemistry and astronomy that examine matter and energy and the way the universe behaves

physical therapy noun [U] US FOR **physiotherapy** **physical therapist** noun [C]

physician MAINLY US OR FORMAL /fɪˈzɪʃ.ən/ noun [C] (UK USUALLY **doctor**) a medical doctor, especially one who has general skill and is not a SURGEON

physics /ˈfɪz.ɪks/ noun [U] the scientific study of matter and energy and the effect that they have on each other: *nuclear physics* ∘ *a physics lab*
physical /ˈfɪz.ɪ.kəl/ adj connected with physics: *physical laws* ⇒See also **physical** BODY; **physical** REAL.
physicist /ˈfɪz.ɪ.sɪst/ noun [C] a person who studies physics or whose job is connected with physics

physio /ˈfɪz.i.əʊ/ ⓤⓢ /-oʊ/ noun plural **physios** UK INFORMAL FOR **1** [C] **physiotherapist 2** [U] **physiotherapy**

physiognomy /ˌfɪz.iˈɒn.ə.mi/ ⓤⓢ /-ˈɑː.nə-/ noun [U] FORMAL the physical appearance of the face

physiology /ˌfɪz.iˈɒl.ə.dʒi/ ⓤⓢ /-ˈɑː.lə-/ noun [U] (the scientific study of) the way in which the bodies of animals and plants work **physiological** /ˌfɪz.i.əˈlɒdʒ.ɪ.kəl/ ⓤⓢ /-ˈlɑː.dʒɪ-/ adj
physiologist /ˌfɪz.iˈɒl.ə.dʒɪst/ ⓤⓢ /-ˈɑː.lə-/ noun [C] a person who studies physiology

physiotherapy /ˌfɪz.i.əʊˈθer.ə.pi/ ⓤⓢ /-oʊ-/ noun [U] (INFORMAL **physio**, US **physical therapy**) the treatment of muscle stiffness, pain and injury, especially by rubbing and moving the sore parts

physiotherapist /ˌfɪz.i.əʊˈθer.ə.pɪst/ ⓤⓢ /-oʊ-/ noun [C] (INFORMAL **physio**, US **physical therapist**) someone who treats people using physiotherapy

physique /fɪˈziːk/ *noun* [C] the shape and size of a human body: *He has a very powerful, muscular physique.*

pi, π /paɪ/ *noun* [U] a Greek letter, especially used in mathematics as a symbol for the number (approximately 3.14) used to calculate the size of circles

piano /piˈæn.əʊ/ ⓊⓈ /-oʊ/ *noun* [C or U] *plural* **pianos** a large musical instrument with a row of black and white keys which are pressed to play notes: *We're buying a new piano.* ○ *I play the piano.* ○ MAINLY US OR SPECIALIZED *She used to play piano in a jazz band.* ○ *The music was written for piano.* ○ *We all joined in the song, with Pat* **at** *the piano/***on** *piano.*

pianist /ˈpiː.ˀn.ɪst/ *noun* [C] someone who plays the piano: *a concert pianist* ○ *a jazz pianist*

pi'ano ,lid *noun* [C] the lid of a piano

pi'ano ,stool *noun* [C] a type of chair without a back or sides which is used when playing the piano

pi'ano ,tuner *noun* [C] a person whose job is to make certain that a piano is producing the correct notes by testing it and adjusting the tightness of the strings

piazza /piˈæt.sə/ ⓊⓈ /-ˈɑːt-/ *noun* [C] especially in Italy, an open area with a hard surface in a town, especially where there is no traffic ⊃See also **square** SHAPE.

pic /pɪk/ *noun* [C] INFORMAL FOR **photograph**: *Would you like to see my holiday pics?*

picador /ˈpɪk.ə.dɔːr/ ⓊⓈ /-dɔːr/ *noun* [C] someone, usually a man, who pushes sharp sticks into bulls during a BULLFIGHT ⊃Compare **matador**; **toreador**.

picayune /ˌpɪk.əˈjuːn/ /'---/ *adj* having little value or importance: *The misery suffered in this war makes your own problems seem pretty picayune.*

piccalilli /ˌpɪk.əˈlɪl.i/ ⓊⓈ /'----/ *noun* [U] small pieces of different vegetables preserved in a yellow sauce, made with MUSTARD, which has a hot taste. It is usually eaten with cold meat.

piccolo /ˈpɪk.ə.ləʊ/ ⓊⓈ /-loʊ/ *noun* [C] *plural* **piccolos** a musical instrument, like a small FLUTE, which makes a high sound

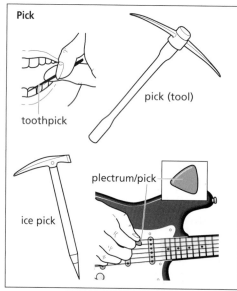

Pick

toothpick

pick (tool)

plectrum/pick

ice pick

pick CHOOSE /pɪk/ *verb* [T] **1** to take some things and leave others; to choose: *Pick a card from the pack.* ○ *One of my sisters has been picked* **for** *the Olympic team.* ○ [+ obj + to infinitive] *She was picked* **to** *play for the team.* ○ *The police asked him if he could pick (***out***) the killer from a series of photos.* ○ *The fairest way to decide the winner is to pick a name* **out of a hat/at random** (= without looking or choosing). ○ *They picked their* **way** (= carefully chose a route) *down the broken steps.* ○ *He's brilliant at picking* **winners** (= choosing what will be successful). **2** OFTEN

DISAPPROVING **pick and choose** to take some things but not others: *The richest universities can pick and choose which students they take.*

• **pick a fight/quarrel/argument** to start a fight/quarrel/argument with someone: *He'd had too much to drink and tried to pick a fight with the bartender.*

• **pick on someone** *your* **own size** said to someone who wants to fight a person who is smaller than them: *Just leave me alone, will you? Why don't you go and pick on someone your own size?*

• **pick 'n' mix** UK a system in a shop where you can choose a few of several different small things, especially sweets

pick /pɪk/ *noun* [U] choice

• **have your pick** to have a large choice available: *The plane was fairly empty so we had our pick* **of** *seats.*

• **take your pick** to choose the one(s) you want from the variety available: *The shirts come in five different colours – just take your pick.*

• **the pick of** *sth* (ALSO **the pick of the bunch**) the best of a group of people or things: *The pick of this year's 3-year-old racehorses is Galileo.* ○ *There were a lot of very amusing entries, but the pick of the bunch came from John Robinson.*

picker /ˈpɪk.ər/ ⓊⓈ /-ər/ *noun* [C] MAINLY US Traditional stock **pickers** (= people who choose companies in which others should invest) *are being replaced by computer programs.*

picky /ˈpɪk.i/ *adj* INFORMAL DISAPPROVING describes someone who is very careful about choosing only what they like: *The children are such picky* **eaters**. ○ *Big companies can afford to be picky about who they hire.*

pick REMOVE /pɪk/ *verb* **1** [I or T] to remove separate items or small pieces from something, especially with the fingers: *Machines pick the fruit (***from/off** *the trees).* ○ *I picked a piece of fluff* **off** *my shiny black suit.* ○ *The child continued picking (***at***) a sore on his leg* (= trying to remove parts of it with his fingers). ○ [+ obj + adj] *The carcass had been picked* **clean** (= all the flesh had been removed) *by other animals and birds.* ○ DISAPPROVING *He kept picking his* **nose** (= removing mucus from it with his finger). **2** [T] When you pick a string on a guitar or similar instrument, you pull it quickly and release it suddenly with your fingers to produce a note.

• **pick** *yourself* **up off the floor** to make improvements to your life after a bad period

• **pick** *sb's* **brains** to ask someone who knows a lot about a subject for information or their opinion: *I was picking Simon's brains about which computer to buy.*

• **pick holes in** *sth* DISAPPROVING to find mistakes in something someone has done or said, to show that it is not good or not correct ⊃See also **pick/pull to pieces** at **piece** PART.

• **pick** *sb's* **pocket** to steal small objects, especially money, from your pockets or bag ⊃See also **pickpocket**

• **pick up the bill/tab** (US ALSO **pick up the check**) INFORMAL to pay for what has been bought, especially a meal in a restaurant

• **pick up the pieces** to try to return to a satisfactory situation: *The fire was a blow, but we were determined to pick up the pieces and get the business back on its feet.*

• **pick up the thread(s)** to start again after an interruption: *Picking up the threads* **of** *our discussion, let's return to the topic of factory farming.*

picker /ˈpɪk.ər/ ⓊⓈ /-ər/ *noun* [C] a person or a machine that picks crops

pick TOOL /pɪk/ *noun* [C] **1** a pickaxe: *picks and shovels* **2** especially in combinations, a sharp pointed tool: *a toothpick*

pick MUSIC /pɪk/ *noun* [C] a **plectrum**

PHRASAL VERBS WITH **pick** ▼

▲ **pick at** *sth phrasal verb* DISAPPROVING to eat only a little bit of your food, showing no interest or enjoyment while you eat it: *Charles picked at his food in a bored fashion.* ⊃See also **picky** at **pick** CHOOSE.

▲ **pick** *sb/sth* **off** SHOOT *phrasal verb* [M] to shoot at one particular person, animal or vehicle which you have chosen from a group: *The snipers picked the soldiers off one by one as they ran for cover.*

▲ **pick on** ***sb*** *phrasal verb* to criticize, punish or be unkind to the same person frequently and unfairly: *He gets picked on by the other boys because he's so small.* ○ *Why don't you pick on* ***someone your own size?***

▲ **pick** ***sb/sth*** **out** [RECOGNIZE] *phrasal verb* [M] to recognize, find or make a choice among different people or items in a group: *Can you pick out the three deliberate mistakes in this paragraph?* ○ *The critics picked him out as the outstanding male dancer of the decade.*

▲ **pick** ***sb/sth*** **out** [EMPHASIZE] *phrasal verb* [M] to choose and emphasize, make clearer or HIGHLIGHT someone or something: *The ship's name was picked out* ***in*** *bright gold letters along her stern.*

▲ **pick** ***sth*** **out** [PLAY] *phrasal verb* [M] If you pick out a tune, you play it slowly or with difficulty, note by note: *I can pick out a simple tune on the piano, but that's about it.*

▲ **pick over** ***sth*** *phrasal verb* [M] to look carefully at a group of things, choosing the ones you want or getting rid of the ones you do not want: *All the clothes at the sale had been thoroughly picked over and there was nothing nice left.*

▲ **pick** ***sb/sth*** **up** [LIFT] *phrasal verb* [M] to lift someone or something using your hands: *If she starts to cry, pick her up and give her a cuddle* ○ *I picked up the kids' clothes that were lying on the floor.* ○ *I went to pick up the phone/receiver, but it had stopped ringing.* ➲See picture **Phrasal Verbs** on page Centre 9

• **pick up the phone** *INFORMAL* to make a telephone call to someone: *If you need me, you just have to pick up the phone.*

▲ **pick** ***sb/sth*** **up** [COLLECT] *phrasal verb* [M] to collect, or to go and get, someone or something: *When you're in town could you pick up the books I ordered?* ○ *Whose turn is it to pick the children up after school?* ○ *The crew of the sinking tanker were picked up* (= saved from the sea) *by helicopter.*

pick-up /ˈpɪk.ʌp/ *noun* [C] *INFORMAL* **1** the act of picking someone or something up, or the place where it happens: *The pick-up* ***point*** *for the long-distance coaches is now in the new bus station.* **2** a person who is picked up: *The taxi driver said I was the first pick-up that he'd had all evening.*

▲ **pick** ***sth*** **up** [BUY] *phrasal verb* [M] to buy something cheaply: *She picked up some real* ***bargains*** *in the sale.*

▲ **pick** ***sth*** **up** [WIN] *phrasal verb* [M] to win or get a prize or something that gives you an advantage, such as votes or support: *The People's Front expect to pick up a lot more votes in this year's elections.*

▲ **pick** ***sth*** **up** [SIGNAL] *phrasal verb* [M] (of a piece of electrical equipment) to receive a signal: *Can you pick up* (= receive broadcasts from) *Moscow* ***on*** *your radio?*

pick-up /ˈpɪk.ʌp/ *noun* [C] a device on an electrical musical instrument or a record player which causes sounds to be produced or made louder

▲ **pick** ***sth*** **up** [LEARN] *phrasal verb* [M] **1** to learn a new skill or language by practising it rather than being taught it: *Don't bother with the computer manual – you'll pick it up as you go along.* ○ *When you live in a country you soon pick up the language.* **2** to learn interesting or useful information from someone or something: *The nurse had picked up the information from a conversation she overheard.*

▲ **pick** ***sth*** **up** [NOTICE] *phrasal verb* [M] to notice and react to something: *Police dogs picked up the scent of the two men from clothes they had left behind.*

▲ **pick** ***sth*** **up** [BECOME ILL] *phrasal verb* [M] to catch an illness from someone or something, caused by bacteria or a virus: *He picked up malaria when he was visiting the country on business.*

▲ **pick** ***(sth)*** **up** [START AGAIN] *phrasal verb* [M] to start again after an interruption; to return to something: *The author picks the same theme up again on page ten.* ○ *After lunch shall we pick up* ***where we left off*** *yesterday?*

▲ **pick** ***sb*** **up** [ARREST] *phrasal verb* [M] *UK INFORMAL* (of the police) to stop someone and take them to a police station in order to question them or arrest them: *He was picked up by the police* ***for*** *drug dealing.* ○ *The police picked her up just outside Canterbury.* ○ *The police picked her up just outside Canterbury.*

▲ **pick** ***sb*** **up** [MEET] *phrasal verb* [M] *INFORMAL* to start a sexual or romantic relationship with someone you do not know, by talking to them and giving them a lot of attention: *He said he'd picked the woman up in a bar.*

▲ **pick up** [INCREASE] *phrasal verb* [I or T] to increase or improve: *The truck picked up* ***speed*** *slowly.* ○ *The wind always picks up in the evening.* ○ *The number of applicants will pick up during the autumn.* ○ *His spirits picked up when he got the good news.* ○ *Her career only began to pick up when she was in her forties.*

pick-up /ˈpɪk.ʌp/ *noun* [S] **1** an increase or improvement: *There's been a pick-up in the share value.* **2** *US* **have good/bad pick-up** (of a car) to be able/unable to increase speed quickly

▲ **pick** ***sb*** **up on** ***sth*** [CRITICIZE] *phrasal verb* to criticize someone about something they have said: *"I want to pick you up on the point you made a few minutes ago about personal morality, Archbishop."* ○ *His teacher picked him up on his pronunciation.*

▲ **pick up on** ***sth*** [RETURN] *phrasal verb* to start talking again about something that someone said previously: *Can I just pick up on your first point again, please?*

▲ **pick up on** ***sth*** [NOTICE] *phrasal verb* to notice something that other people have not noticed: *Only one newspaper picked up on the minister's statement.*

pickaxe, *US* **pickax** /ˈpɪk.æks/ *noun* [C] (*ALSO* **pick**) a tool for breaking hard surfaces, which has a long wooden handle and a curved metal bar with a sharp point

picket /ˈpɪk.ɪt/ *noun* [C] **1** a worker or group of workers who protest outside a building to prevent other workers from going inside, especially because they have a disagreement with their employers: *There were pickets outside the factory gates.* **2** the occasion on which this happens: *The union organised a month-long picket.*
picket /ˈpɪk.ɪt/ *verb* [I or T] *They picketed the burger restaurant and handed out leaflets to potential customers.*
picketer /ˈpɪk.ɪ.təʳ/ [US] /-t̬ɚ/ *noun* [C] a person who stands outside a building as part of a picket **picketing** /ˈpɪk.ɪ.tɪŋ/ [US] /-t̬ɪŋ/ *noun* [U] *The proposed new law would ban picketing.*

ˈpicket ˌfence *noun* [C] a low fence made of a row of flat sticks which are pointed at the top and often painted white

ˈpicket ˌline *noun* [C] a group of workers acting as pickets: *Journalists interviewed the union officials* ***on*** *the picket line.* ○ *The van drivers refused to* ***cross*** *the picket line* (= to go past the pickets).

pickings /ˈpɪk.ɪŋz/ *plural noun* money which can be earned easily or dishonestly: *The street-sellers are lured to the town by the* ***rich/easy*** *pickings that are to be had from foreign tourists.*

pickle /ˈpɪk.l̩/ *noun* **1** [C or U] (a sauce made from) vegetables or fruit which have been preserved in a vinegar sauce or salty water: *cheese and pickle sandwiches* ○ *Have some pickles with your salad.* **2** [C] *US* a CUCUMBER which has been preserved in vinegar or salty water, or slices of this: *a sweet/sour pickle*

• **be in a (pretty/right) pickle** *OLD-FASHIONED* to be in a difficult situation

pickle /ˈpɪk.l̩/ *verb* [T] to preserve vegetables or fruit in a vinegar sauce or salty water: *The onions had been pickled* ***in*** *brine.*
pickled /ˈpɪk.l̩d/ *adj* **1** preserved in vinegar: *pickled onions/gherkins/herring* **2** *OLD-FASHIONED INFORMAL* drunk: *I got really pickled at Pat's party.*

pick-me-up /ˈpɪk.mɪ.ʌp/ *noun* [C] something which makes you feel better, often a drink or a TONIC (= a type of medicine): *It is traditional around here to drink brandy with coffee as a morning pick-me-up.*

pickpocket /ˈpɪkˌpɒk.ɪt/ [US] /-ˌpɑː.kɪt/ *noun* [C] a thief who steals things out of pockets or bags, especially in a crowd

ˈpick-up ˌtruck *noun* [C] a small vehicle with an open part at the back in which goods can be carried ➲See picture **Cars and Trucks** on page Centre 13

picky /ˈpɪk.i/ *adj* ➲See at **pick** CHOOSE.

pick-your-own /ˌpɪk.jəˈrəʊn/ [US] /-jɚˈoʊn/ *adj* [before n] (*WRITTEN ABBREVIATION* **PYO**) relating to the activity of picking fruit or vegetables yourself at a farm and then paying for the amount you have picked: *pick-your-own strawberries* ○ *a pick-your-own farm*

picnic /ˈpɪk.nɪk/ *noun* [C] an occasion when you take a meal with you to eat outside in an informal way, or the food itself: *If the weather's nice we could* ***have*** *a picnic in the park.* ○ *Why don't you* ***take*** *a picnic with you?* ○ *a picnic area/lunch/table* ○ *a picnic basket/hamper*

• **be no picnic** INFORMAL to be a difficult or unpleasant situation: *Being a single parent is no picnic, I can tell you.*

picnic /ˈpɪk.nɪk/ *verb* [I] **picnicking**, **picnicked**, **picnicked** to have a picnic somewhere: *There were several families picnicking on the river bank.* **picnicker** /ˈpɪk.nɪ.kəʳ/ [US] /-kɚ/ *noun* [C]

pictorial /pɪkˈtɔː.ri.əl/ [US] /-ˈtɔːr.i-/ *adj* shown in the form of a picture or photograph: *The exhibition is a pictorial history/record of the town in the 19th century.* **pictorially** /pɪkˈtɔː.ri.ə.li/ [US] /-ˈtɔːr.i-/ *adv*

picture [IMAGE] /ˈpɪk.tʃəʳ/ [US] /-tʃɚ/ *noun* [C] **1** a drawing, painting or photograph, etc: *Atticus* ***drew/painted*** *a picture* ***of*** *my dog.* ○ *We* ***took*** *a picture of* (= photographed) *the children on their new bicycles.* ○ *I hate having my picture taken* (= being photographed). **2** an image seen on a television or cinema screen: *We can't get a clear picture.* **3** something you produce in your mind, by using your imagination or memory: *I have a very* ***vivid*** *picture of the first time I met Erik.*

• **face is a picture** UK If someone's face is a picture, they look very surprised or angry: *Her face was a picture when I told her the price.*

• **be a picture** MAINLY UK to look beautiful: *The garden was a picture with all the roses in bloom.*

• **be the picture of health/innocence, etc.** to look very healthy, innocent, etc: *I can't believe there's anything seriously wrong with him – he's the picture of health.*

• **Every picture tells a story.** SAYING said when what has really happened in a situation is clear because of the way that someone or something looks

the pictures *plural noun* OLD-FASHIONED the cinema: *Let's go to the pictures tonight.*

picture /ˈpɪk.tʃəʳ/ [US] /-tʃɚ/ *verb* [T] to imagine something: *Picture* ***the scene*** *– the crowds of people and animals, the noise, the dirt.* ○ [+ v-ing] *Try to picture yourself lying on a beach in the hot sun.* ○ [+ question word] *Picture* ***to yourself how*** *terrible that day must have been.* ○ FORMAL *He was pictured* (= An artist had painted him) ***as*** *a soldier in full uniform.*

P

picture [IDEA] /ˈpɪk.tʃəʳ/ [US] /-tʃɚ/ *noun* [S] **1** (an idea of) a situation: *After watching the news, I had a clearer picture* ***of*** *what was happening.* ○ *The picture emerging in reports from the battlefield is one of complete confusion.* **2** a situation described in a particular way: FIGURATIVE *The experts are* ***painting*** *a gloomy/brighter/rosy picture of the state of the economy.*

• **get the picture** to understand: *It's all right, don't say any more – I get the picture.*

• **keep *sb* in the picture** to keep someone informed about a situation: *I use the radio to keep me in the picture about what's happening abroad.*

• **put *sb* in the picture** to inform someone about a situation: *His lawyer put him in the picture about what had happened since his arrest.*

• **out of the picture 1** not important to or not involved in a situation: *He used to be in the team, but he's gradually drifted out of the picture.* **2** unnecessary in a particular situation: *The new systems* ***cut*** *humans out of the picture altogether.*

ˈpicture ˌbook *noun* [C] a book, especially for young children, which has a lot of pictures and not many words

ˈpicture ˌframe *noun* [C] a frame into which a picture fits

ˌpicture ˈpostcard [CARD] *noun* [C] (ALSO **postcard**) a POSTCARD with a picture, usually a photograph of a place, on one side

picture-postcard [ATTRACTIVE] /ˌpɪk.tʃəˈpəʊst.kɑːd/ [US] /-tʃɚˈpoʊst.kɑːrd/ *adj* [before n] describes a place that is extremely attractive: *a picture-postcard cottage/village* ○ DISAPPROVING *I hate picture-postcard prettiness.*

picturesque /ˌpɪk.tʃəˈresk/ [US] /-tʃəˈresk/ *adj* (especially of a place) attractive in appearance, especially in an old-fashioned way: *the picturesque narrow streets of the old city* **picturesquely** /ˌpɪk.tʃəˈres.kli/ [US] /-tʃəˈres-/ *adv* **picturesqueness** /ˌpɪk.tʃəˈresk.nəs/ [US] /-tʃəˈresk-/ *noun* [U]

ˈpicture ˌwindow *noun* [C] a large window positioned so that you can see an attractive view

piddle /ˈpɪd.l̩/ *noun* [S or U] INFORMAL urine, or an act of urinating: *There was piddle all over the floor.* ○ *One minute - I just need a piddle.*

piddle /ˈpɪd.l̩/ *exclamation* INFORMAL an expression of slight annoyance: *Oh piddle! I've broken another glass.*

piddle /ˈpɪd.l̩/ *verb* [I]

piddling /ˈpɪd.l̩.ɪŋ/ /ˈpɪd.lɪŋ/ *adj* INFORMAL DISAPPROVING very small or unimportant: *They are making piddling profits of less than £20 000.*

pidgin /ˈpɪdʒ.ɪn/ *noun* [C or U] **1** a language which has developed from a mixture of two languages. It is used as a way of communicating by people who do not speak each other's languages **2** INFORMAL **pidgin English/French, etc.** English/French, etc. when it is spoken in a simple way, often with many mistakes, either by a foreigner or to a foreigner: *"He come here?" he asked* ***in*** *pidgin English.*

pie /paɪ/ *noun* [C or U] a type of food made with meat, vegetables or fruit covered in pastry and baked: *Would you like some more pork pie?* ○ *a pecan/pumpkin/apple pie*

• **pie in the sky** something that you hope will happen but which is very unlikely to happen: *Their plans to set up their own business are just pie in the sky.*

piebald /ˈpaɪ.bɔːld/ [US] /-bɑːld/ *adj* (of an animal, especially a horse) having a pattern of two different colours on its hair, especially black and white: *piebald ponies*

piece [PART] /piːs/ *noun* [C] a part of something: *a piece* ***of*** *cloth torn from her coat* ○ *He cut the cake into six pieces.* ○ *This jigsaw puzzle has two pieces missing.* ○ *The vase lay on the floor* ***in*** *pieces* (= broken into small parts). ○ *She tried to* ***break/tear*** *a small piece* ***off*** *the edge.* ○ *The building was taken apart and reassembled piece* ***by*** *piece* (= one part after another) *in America.*

• **in one piece** as a single item and not divided into smaller pieces: *We want to sell the business in one piece.*

• **(all) in one piece** not damaged: *The radio had been stolen, but otherwise we got the car back (all) in one piece.*

• **piece of cake** INFORMAL something which is very easy to do: *The exam was a piece of cake.*

• **give *sb* a piece of your mind** INFORMAL to speak angrily to someone about something they have done wrong: *I'm going to give that mechanic a piece of my mind if the car's not fixed this time.*

• **come/fall to pieces** to break apart into smaller parts: *The glass must have been cracked – it just fell to pieces in my hand.* ○ *His clothes were dirty and falling to pieces.*

• **come to pieces** UK If something comes to pieces, it has been designed so that it can be divided into smaller parts.

• **go/fall to pieces 1** If someone goes/falls to pieces, they become unable to think clearly and control their emotions because of something unpleasant or difficult that they have experienced: *She just goes* ***(all)*** *to pieces in exams.* **2** If an organization or system goes/falls to pieces, it fails: *Their marriage began to fall to pieces after only a few months.*

• **pick/pull *sb/sth* to pieces** INFORMAL to criticize someone or something severely: *The moment she left, the rest of the family started to pull her to pieces.*

• **take *sth* to pieces** UK to separate something into smaller parts: *If you take the bookcase to pieces, it will fit in the back of your car.*

COMMON LEARNER ERROR

piece

piece cannot be used to mean one of the rooms in a building. You should use the word **room** instead

~~There are en suite bathrooms with every piece.~~
There are en suite bathrooms with every room.

piece [ITEM] /piːs/ *noun* [C] **1** a single item of a particular type: *a piece **of** furniture/clothing/equipment* ○ *a piece* (= whole sheet) *of paper* ○ *a piece **of*** (= an item made of) *china* ○ *a piece **of** information/advice* **2** something which has been created by an artist, musician or writer: *an orchestral/piano/instrumental piece* ○ *a skilful piece **of** work/research* ○ *Did you read that piece* (= article) *in the newspaper?* **3** a single item which forms part of a set: *a chess piece* **4** a coin with a stated value: *Could you swap me a 20p piece for two tens?*
• **piece of ass** *US OFFENSIVE* used to refer to a woman as a sexually attractive object
-piece /-piːs/ *suffix*: *a five-piece band* (= with five players)

piece [GUN] /piːs/ *noun* [C] *OLD-FASHIONED* a gun: *an artillery piece* ○ *US SLANG He was carrying a piece when he was arrested.*

piece /piːs/ *verb*
▲ **piece *sth* together** *phrasal verb* [M] to create something by joining the separate parts of it together or by joining different things together: *The ancient skull of Peking Man has been pieced together **from** fragments.* ○ *Kevin has done a great job to piece together a tremendous team.* ○ *The police are collecting clues in order to piece together the details of the day she died.*

pièce de résistance /piˌes.də.reɪ.zɪˈstɑ̃ːs/ *noun* [S] the best and most impressive thing, often the last in a series of things: *The pièce de résistance of his stage act was a brilliant Elvis Presley impression.*

piecemeal /ˈpiːs.miːl/ *adv, adj OFTEN DISAPPROVING* not done according to a plan but done at different times in different ways: *Unfortunately, everything is being done piecemeal.*

ˌpieces of ˈeight *plural noun* (in the past) coins used in Spain

piecework /ˈpiːs.wɜːk/ [US] /-wɝːk/ *noun* [U] *SPECIALIZED* work for which the amount of pay depends on the number of items completed rather than the time spent making them

ˈpie ˌchart *noun* [C] a circle which is divided from its centre into several parts to show how a total amount is divided up

ˈpie ˌcrust *noun* [C] the pastry on the bottom and sometimes covering a PIE

pied /paɪd/ *adj* [before n] *SPECIALIZED* (used especially in the names of birds) having fur or feathers of two or more colours, usually black and white: *pied kingfishers*

pied à terre /piˌeɪ.dætˈeəʳ/ [US] /-ˈer/ *noun* [C] *plural* **pieds à terre** a small house or apartment in a town or city which someone owns or rents in addition to their main home and which they use when visiting that town or city for a short time

pie-eyed /ˌpaɪˈaɪd/ *adj INFORMAL* very drunk

pier [PLATFORM] /pɪəʳ/ [US] /pɪr/ *noun* [C] **1** a long structure sticking out from the land over the sea, along which people can walk or to which large boats can be tied and which sometimes has restaurants, etc. on it **2** a low structure built at the edge of water, used especially for getting into and out of boats

pier [COLUMN] /pɪəʳ/ [US] /pɪr/ *noun* [C] *SPECIALIZED* a strong thick column used to support a wall, roof or other structure

pierce /pɪəs/ [US] /pɪrs/ *verb* **1** [I + adv or prep; T] to go into or through something, making a hole in it using a sharp point: *The needle pierces the fabric four times a second.* ○ *I couldn't wear these earrings because my ears aren't pierced.* ○ *The gun fires a shell capable of piercing the armour of an enemy tank.* ○ *The hole they drilled pierces 6 km **into** the earth's crust.* **2** [T] (of a light, sound, etc.) to suddenly be seen or heard, despite darkness, noise, etc: *A few rays of sunlight pierced the smoke.*
piercing /ˈpɪə.sɪŋ/ [US] /ˈpɪr-/ *adj* **1** going through or into something: *Troops have been issued with new **armour**-piercing anti-tank grenades.* ○ *FIGURATIVE We shivered in the piercing wind.* **2** describes a sound that is high, loud and unpleasant: *piercing screams* **3 a piercing criticism/question/remark, etc.** a criticism/question/remark, etc. which is unpleasant or uncomfortable because it is strong or it makes you think about or discuss something which you would prefer not to: *She hadn't really meant to lie, but their piercing questions had forced her to.* **4 piercing eyes/look/gaze/glance, etc.** used to describe when a person looks very carefully at someone or something, especially when they are trying to discover something, often making people feel uncomfortable: *Sherlock Holmes gave him a piercing glance.* ○ *FIGURATIVE He looked straight at me with his piercing blue eyes.*
piercing /ˈpɪə.sɪŋ/ [US] /ˈpɪr-/ *noun* [C or U] a hole made in the body for wearing jewellery, or the process of making such a hole: *He has several tattoos and multiple piercings.* **piercingly** /ˈpɪə.sɪŋ.li/ [US] /ˈpɪr-/ *adv*

pierhead /ˈpɪə.hed/ [US] /ˈpɪr-/ *noun* [C usually sing] the part of a PIER that is furthest from the land

piety /ˈpaɪ.ə.ti/ [US] /ˈpaɪə.t̬i/ *noun* [U] *FORMAL* ➲See at **pious** RELIGIOUS.

piezoelectric /ˌpiː.zəʊ.ɪˈlek.trɪk/ [US] /paɪˌiː.zoʊ-/ *adj SPECIALIZED* producing electrical power by putting pressure on particular types of stone: *a piezoelectric device*

piffle /ˈpɪf.l̩/ *noun* [U] *OLD-FASHIONED INFORMAL* nonsense: *Jo really does talk a lot of piffle sometimes.*

piffling /ˈpɪf.l̩.ɪŋ/ /ˈpɪf.lɪŋ/ *adj INFORMAL* extremely unimportant or small: *piffling details* ○ *a piffling amount*

pig [ANIMAL] /pɪg/ *noun* [C] (*US ALSO* **hog**) a large pink, brown or black farm animal with short legs and a curved tail, kept for its meat: *The meat produced from a pig is called pork, bacon or ham.* ○ *They have a large pig farm.*
• **a pig in a poke** something that you buy or accept without first seeing it or finding out whether it is good
• **Pigs might fly.** *HUMOROUS SAYING* said when you think that there is no chance at all of something happening: *"I'll have finished it by tomorrow." "And pigs might fly!"*
• **make a pig's ear of *sth*** *UK INFORMAL* to do something badly, wrongly or awkwardly: *He's made a real pig's ear of that bookcase he was supposed to be making.*
piggy /ˈpɪg.i/ *adj INFORMAL DISAPPROVING* like a pig: *He's got little piggy eyes.*
piggy /ˈpɪg.i/ *noun* [C] *CHILD'S WORD* a pig: *Look at those lovely little piggies, Martha!*
piglet /ˈpɪg.lət/ *noun* [C] a baby pig: *The sow had eight piglets.*

pig [UNPLEASANT PERSON] /pɪg/ *noun* [C] **1** *INFORMAL* a person who is unpleasant and difficult to deal with: *He was an absolute pig to her.* ○ *He's a real pig of a man.* **2** *OFFENSIVE* a police officer **3** *UK INFORMAL* **be a pig to do/play, etc.** to be very difficult or unpleasant to do/play, etc: *It's a beautiful piece of music but it's a pig to play.*

pig [EATS TOO MUCH] /pɪg/ *noun* [C] *INFORMAL* a person who eats too much: *You **greedy** pig! You're not having another chocolate biscuit!*
• **make a pig of *yourself*** *DISAPPROVING* to eat too much: *They made complete pigs of themselves at the dinner.*

pig /pɪg/ *verb* **-gg-**
▲ **pig out** *phrasal verb INFORMAL* to eat a lot or too much: *We pigged out **on** all the lovely cakes and pastries.*

pigeon /ˈpɪdʒ.ən/ *noun* [C or U] a large usually grey bird, which is often seen in towns sitting on buildings in large groups, and is sometimes eaten as food ➲See picture **Animals and Birds** on page Centre 4
• **be not *your* pigeon** *UK OLD-FASHIONED* to not be your responsibility: *Transport? That's not my pigeon – ask Danny.*

pigeon-chested /ˌpɪdʒ.ənˈtʃes.tɪd/ *adj* (of a person) having a narrow chest that sticks out more than usual at the front

ˈpigeon ˌfancier *noun* [C] *UK* someone who keeps PIGEONS as pets

pigeonhole /ˈpɪdʒ.ən.həʊl/ [US] /-hoʊl/ *noun* [C] one of a set of small boxes, open at the front, in which letters and messages are left for different people: *Leave the report **in** my pigeonhole when you've read it.*
• **put *sth/sb* in a pigeonhole** *USUALLY DISAPPROVING* to form a very fixed, often wrong, opinion about what type of person or thing someone or something is
pigeonhole /ˈpɪdʒ.ən.həʊl/ [US] /-hoʊl/ *verb* [T] *USUALLY DISAPPROVING* to have an often unfair idea of what type

someone or something is: *He is a film producer who can't be conveniently pigeonholed.*

pigeon-toed /ˈpɪdʒ.ən.təʊd/ [US] /-toʊd/ *adj* A person who is pigeon-toed bends their feet in towards each other when they walk.

piggy /ˈpɪg.i/ *adj, noun* [C] ⊃See at **pig** ANIMAL.

ˈpiggyback (ˌride) *noun* [C] a ride on someone's back with your arms round their neck and your legs round their waist: *I **gave** her a piggyback ride.*

piggyback /ˈpɪg.i.bæk/ *adv* on someone's back, or on the back of something: *Martha **rode** piggyback **on** her dad.* ○ *Dom **carried** his daughter piggyback when she got too tired to walk.*

piggyback /ˈpɪg.i.bæk/ *verb* [I] to use something that someone else has made or done in order to get an advantage: *Everyone wants to piggyback **on** the phenomenal success of the X Files.*

ˈpiggy ˌbank *noun* [C] a small container, sometimes in the shape of a pig, which is used by children for saving money

ˌpiggy in the ˈmiddle *noun* **1** [U] *UK* a game in which two people throw a ball to each other over the head of a person who stands between them and tries to catch it **2** [C usually sing] someone who is in a difficult situation because they know two people who are arguing and they do not want to become involved

pigheaded /ˌpɪgˈhed.ɪd/ /ˈ-ˌ--/ *adj DISAPPROVING* showing unreasonable support for an opinion or plan of action and refusing to change or listen to different opinions

pigheadedly /ˌpɪgˈhed.ɪd.li/ *adv* **pigheadedness** /ˌpɪgˈhed.ɪd.nəs/ *noun* [U]

ˈpig ˌiron *noun* [U] a type of iron which is not pure

piglet /ˈpɪg.lət/ *noun* [C] ⊃See at **pig** ANIMAL.

pigment /ˈpɪg.mənt/ *noun* [C or U] a substance which gives something a particular colour when it is present in it or is added to it: *Melanin is the dark brown pigment of the hair, skin and eyes which is present in varying amounts in every human being.* ○ *Pigment is mixed into oil, glue, egg, etc. to make different types of paint.*

pigmentation /ˌpɪg.mənˈteɪ.ʃᵊn/ *noun* [U] the natural colour of something, usually a living thing **pigmented** /pɪgˈmen.tɪd/ [US] /ˈpɪg.mən.t̬ɪd/ *adj*: *pigmented tissue/skin/areas*

Pigmy /ˈpɪg.mi/ *noun* [C], *adj* **Pygmy**

pigskin /ˈpɪg.skɪn/ *noun* **1** [U] leather made from the skin of pigs: *pigskin gloves/shoes* **2** [C] *US INFORMAL* the ball used to play American football

pigsty /ˈpɪg.staɪ/ *noun* [C] (*US ALSO* **pigpen**) **1** the building and enclosed area where pigs are kept **2** a dirty or untidy place: *Your bedroom's a pigsty!*

pigswill *UK* /ˈpɪg.swɪl/ *noun* [U] (*US* **swill**) **1** waste human food that is fed to pigs **2** *INFORMAL* bad or unpleasant food: *I can't eat this pigswill! Take it away!*

pigtail /ˈpɪg.teɪl/ *noun* [C] a length of hair which is tied at the back of the head or at each side of the head, sometimes in a PLAIT (= twist): *A little girl **in** pigtails presented the bouquet.*

pike [FISH] /paɪk/ *noun* [C] *plural* **pike** a large fish which lives in lakes and rivers and eats other fish

pike [ROAD] /paɪk/ *noun* [C] *plural* **pikes** *US FOR* **turnpike**: *the Leesburg Pike*

pike [WEAPON] /paɪk/ *noun* [C] *plural* **pikes** a long sharp stick used in the past as a weapon by soldiers on foot: *A soldier with a pike could bring down a knight on a charging horse.*

pike [HILL] /paɪk/ *noun* [C] *plural* **pikes** *NORTHERN ENGLISH* a hill in northern England with a pointed top

piker /ˈpaɪ.kəʳ/ [US] /-kɚ/ *noun* [C] *AUS INFORMAL* a person who avoids getting into difficult or dangerous situations

pikestaff /ˈpaɪk.stɑːf/ [US] /-stæf/ *noun* **be (as) plain as a pikestaff** ⊃See at **plain** CLEAR.

Pilates /ˌpəˈlɑː.tiːz/ *noun* [U] *TRADEMARK* a system of physical exercise involving controlled movements, stretching and breathing

pilau /ˈpiː.laʊ/ [US] /pɪˈlɔː/ *noun* [C or U] (*US USUALLY* **pilaf**) rice cooked in spicy liquid, often with vegetables or meat added: *a delicious mushroom pilau* ○ *barbecued pork with pilau **rice***

pilchard /ˈpɪl.tʃəd/ [US] /-tʃɚd/ *noun* [C] a small edible fish that lives in the sea: *a **tin of** pilchards in tomato sauce*

pile [AMOUNT] /paɪl/ *noun* [C] objects positioned one on top of another: *a large pile **of** sand* ○ *a pile **of** books* ○ *a pile **of** dirty clothes* ○ *INFORMAL I've got piles/a pile* (= a lot) *of things to do today.*

• **make a pile** *INFORMAL* to earn a large amount of money: *He made a pile selling computers and retired by the time he was forty.*

pile /paɪl/ *verb* [I or T +adv or prep] (*ALSO* **pile up**) to arrange objects into a pile: *We piled plenty of logs **up** next to the fire.* ○ *Please pile your homework books neatly **on** the table as you leave.* ○ *Her plate was piled **(high) with** salad.* ○ *Snow had piled up against the walls of the house.*

• **pile it high and sell it cheap** *MAINLY UK SAYING* said when a shop sells large amounts of a product at cheap prices

• **pile it on** *INFORMAL* to say too much, especially giving too much emphasis: *You're really piling it on with the compliments tonight, Gareth, aren't you!*

• **pile on the agony** *UK INFORMAL* to enjoy emphasizing how bad a situation is: *Okay, I'll give you some money – just stop piling on the agony.*

PHRASAL VERBS WITH **pile** ▼

▲ **pile *(sth)* up** [FORM A PILE] *phrasal verb* [M] to form a pile, or to put a lot of things into a pile

▲ **pile *(sth)* up** [INCREASE] *phrasal verb* (of something bad) to increase: *Unpaid bills began to pile up alarmingly.* ○ *They piled up such a huge debt that they soon went bankrupt.*

pile [COLUMN] /paɪl/ *noun* [C] a strong column or post of wood, steel or concrete which is pushed into the ground to help support a building

pile [MOVE] /paɪl/ *verb* [I usually + adv or prep] *INFORMAL* (of a group of people) to move together, especially in an uncontrolled way: *As soon as the train stopped, they all piled **in/out**.*

pile [SURFACE] /paɪl/ *noun* [S] the soft surface made by the ends of many short threads on a carpet or on cloth such as VELVET: *a luxurious **deep**-pile carpet*

pile [BUILDING] /paɪl/ *noun* [C] *MAINLY HUMOROUS* a large building: *They've got a great big Victorian pile somewhere out in the country.*

pile-driver /ˈpaɪlˌdraɪ.vəʳ/ [US] /-vɚ/ *noun* [C] a powerful machine which hammers PILES (= strong posts) into the ground

piles /paɪlz/ *plural noun INFORMAL* **haemorrhoids**

pile-up /ˈpaɪl.ʌp/ *noun* [C] a traffic accident involving several vehicles which hit each other

pilfer /ˈpɪl.fəʳ/ [US] /-fɚ/ *verb* [I or T] to steal things of small value: *He was caught pilfering (sweets) **from** the shop.*

pilgrim /ˈpɪl.grɪm/ *noun* [C] a person who makes a journey, which is often long and difficult, to a special place for religious reasons

pilgrimage /ˈpɪl.grɪ.mɪdʒ/ *noun* [C or U] **1** a special journey made by a pilgrim: *Most Muslims try to **make a** pilgrimage/**go on a** pilgrimage **to** Mecca at least once in their life.* **2** a journey to a place which is considered special, and which you visit to show your respect: *For many football fans, the national ground is **a place of** pilgrimage.*

the ˌPilgrim ˈFathers *plural noun* the group of English people who sailed to North America on the ship 'Mayflower' where they formed Plymouth Colony, Massachusetts in 1620

pill [MEDICINE] /pɪl/ *noun* [C] **1** a small solid piece of medicine which a person swallows without chewing: *a sleeping pill* ○ *a vitamin pill* ○ *My mother **takes** three or four pills a day.* ○ *Jamie's always had trouble **swallowing** pills.* **2 the pill** a type of pill for women which is taken every day in order to prevent them from becoming pregnant: *Are you **on** the pill?*

• **sugar the pill** *UK* (*US* **sweeten the pill**) to make something bad seem less unpleasant: *Plans to improve public services are a way of sugaring the pill of increased taxation.*

pill [PERSON] /pɪl/ *noun* [C] *US* an annoying person: *Jennifer was being such a pill today.*

pill [CLOTHING] *US* /pɪl/ *verb* [I] (*UK* **bobble**) If a piece of clothing or material pills, it develops small balls of threads on its surface. **pill** *US* /pɪl/ *noun* [C] (*UK* **bobble**) *She sat there sulking and picking the pills off her sweater.*

pillage /ˈpɪl.ɪdʒ/ *verb* [I or T] *FORMAL* to steal something from a place or a person by using violence, especially during war: *Works of art were pillaged* ***from*** *many countries in the dark days of the Empire.* **pillage** /ˈpɪl.ɪdʒ/ *noun* [U]

pillar /ˈpɪl.əʳ/ [US] /-ɚ/ *noun* [C] **1** a strong column made of stone, metal or wood which supports part of a building: *A row of reinforced concrete pillars supports the bridge.* ○ *FIGURATIVE a pillar* ***of*** *smoke/flame* **2 pillar of *sth*** a very important member or part of a group, organization, system, etc: *Mrs Maple is a pillar of the local church.* ○ *Equality is one of the pillars of socialism.*

• **from pillar to post** If someone goes from pillar to post, they are forced to keep moving from one place to another: *My parents were always on the move and so my childhood was spent being dragged from pillar to post.*

pillar-box /ˈpɪl.ə.bɒks/ [US] /-ɚ.bɑːks/ *noun* [C] *UK* a tall red box for posting letters

pillbox [CONTAINER] /ˈpɪl.bɒks/ [US] /-bɑːks/ *noun* [C] a small container which pills are carried in

pillbox [BUILDING] /ˈpɪl.bɒks/ [US] /-bɑːks/ *noun* [C] a small very strong building with narrow holes in the walls through which guns can be fired

pillion /ˈpɪl.i.ən/ [US] /-jən/ *noun* [C] *UK* a seat or place behind the person riding a motorcycle where a passenger can sit: *a pillion seat/passenger* **pillion** /ˈpɪl.i.ən/ [US] /ˈ-jən/ *adv*: *You get a bit uncomfortable after* ***riding*** *pillion for a couple of hours.*

pillock /ˈpɪl.ək/ *noun* [C] *UK OFFENSIVE* a stupid or silly person: *You pillock, look what you've done!*

pillory /ˈpɪl.ᵊr.i/ [US] /-ɚ.i/ *verb* [T] to severely criticize someone, especially in a public way: *Although regularly pilloried by the press as an obnoxious loudmouth, he is, nonetheless, an effective politician.*

pillow /ˈpɪl.əʊ/ [US] /-oʊ/ *noun* [C] **1** a rectangular cloth bag filled with soft material, such as feathers or artificial fibres, used for resting your head on in bed: *Do you prefer a feather pillow or a foam pillow?* **2** *US FOR* **cushion** (= bag of soft material for sitting or leaning on)

pillowcase /ˈpɪl.əʊ.keɪs/ [US] /-oʊ-/ *noun* [C] (*ALSO* **pillowslip**) a cloth cover for a pillow which can easily be removed and washed

ˈpillow ˌtalk *noun* [U] conversation between lovers in bed

pill-popping /ˈpɪlˌpɒp.ɪŋ/ [US] /-pɑː.pɪŋ/ *noun* [U] *INFORMAL* taking pills, especially when this is a habit or when the pills are illegal drugs

pilot [AIRCRAFT] /ˈpaɪ.lət/ *noun* [C] a person who flies an aircraft: *a fighter/helicopter/bomber/airline pilot* **pilot** /ˈpaɪ.lət/ *verb* [T] *She piloted the aircraft to safety after one of the engines failed.*

pilot [TEST] /ˈpaɪ.lət/ *adj* [before n] describes a plan, product or system that is used to test how good something is before introducing it: *If the (UK) pilot* ***scheme****/(US) pilot* ***program*** *is successful many more homes will be offered the new television service.*

pilot /ˈpaɪ.lət/ *noun* [C] a programme which is made to introduce and test the popularity of a new radio or television series: *If you'd seen the pilot, you'd know why they decided not to make a complete series of programmes!* **pilot** /ˈpaɪ.lət/ *verb* [T] *We shall pilot several new cosmetic products* ***to*** *selected potential purchasers.*

pilot [INTRODUCE] /ˈpaɪ.lət/ *verb* [T usually + adv or prep] *MAINLY UK* to be responsible for introducing a new law or system and making certain it is established: *Twenty years ago he piloted a bill* ***through*** *Parliament on working conditions.*

pilot [SHIP] /ˈpaɪ.lət/ *noun* [C] a person with detailed knowledge of an area of water, such as that around a port, who goes onto a ship to direct it safely **pilot** /ˈpaɪ.lət/ *verb* [T]

ˈpilot (ˌlight) *noun* [C] a small flame which burns all the time in a gas device, such as a cooker or a water heater, and which starts the main flame burning when the gas is turned on

pimento (*plural* **pimentos**) /pɪˈmen.təʊ/ [US] /-toʊ/ *noun* [C or U] (*US USUALLY* **pimiento**) a sweet red pepper

Pimm's /pɪmz/ *noun* [C or U] *UK TRADEMARK* a pink alcoholic drink usually drunk with ice in the summer

pimp /pɪmp/ *noun* [C] a man who controls prostitutes, especially by finding customers for them, and takes some of the money that they earn **pimp** /pɪmp/ *verb* [I]

pimple /ˈpɪm.pl̩/ *noun* [C] a small raised spot on the skin which is temporary **pimply** /ˈpɪm.pl̩.i/ /ˈ-pli/ *adj* (*ALSO* **pimpled**) *a pimply face* ○ *a pimply adolescent boy*

pin [METAL STICK] /pɪn/ *noun* [C] **1** a small thin piece of metal with a point at one end, especially used for temporarily holding pieces of cloth together: *I'll keep the trouser patch in place with pins while I sew it on.* **2** a thin piece of metal: *If you pull the pin out of a hand-grenade, it'll explode.* ○ *Is it a two-pin plug or a three-pin plug?* ○ *Doctors inserted a metal pin in his leg to hold the bones together.* **3** a decorative object, used as jewellery: *a hat/tie pin* **4** *US FOR* **brooch**

• **be on pins and needles** *US* to be nervously waiting to find out what is going to happen

pin /pɪn/ *verb* **-nn- 1** [T + adv or prep] to fasten something with a pin: *A large picture of the president was pinned* ***to/(up) on*** *the office wall.* ○ *She had pinned* ***up*** *her lovely long hair.* **2** [T] *US OLD-FASHIONED* When a young man pins a young woman, he gives her a piece of jewellery to show that they love each other.

• **pin *your* hopes on *sth/sb*** to hope very much that something or someone will help you to achieve what you want

pin [PREVENT MOVEMENT] /pɪn/ *verb* [T + adv or prep] **-nn-** to force someone or something to stay in a particular place by putting weight on them: *She was pinned* ***(down) under*** *a pile of rubble.* ○ *A huge guy leapt out at Chris and pinned him* ***(up) against*** *the wall.*

• **pin back *your* ears** (*ALSO* **pin *your* ears back**) *UK INFORMAL* to listen carefully

pin [LEG] /pɪn/ *noun* [C usually pl] *OLD-FASHIONED HUMOROUS* a leg: *Grandpa's very old now and he's a bit shaky on his pins.*

PHRASAL VERBS WITH **pin**

▲ **pin *sb* down** [SURROUND] *phrasal verb* [M] to stop someone from escaping by surrounding them and shooting at them if they try to escape: [often passive] *Government forces were pinned down by resistance fighters 30 miles north of the capital.*

▲ **pin *sb* down** [GET DETAILS] *phrasal verb* [M] to make someone provide details about something or make a decision about something: *I've tried asking Stephanie, but she's proving difficult to pin down* ***to*** *a particular date.*

▲ **pin *sth* down** *phrasal verb* [M] to discover exact details about something: *We can't pin down where the leak came from.*

▲ **pin *sth* on *sb*** *phrasal verb* (*ALSO* **hang *sth* on *sb***) to blame someone for something, especially for something they did not do: *You can't pin* ***the blame*** *on her – she wasn't even there when the accident happened.*

pinafore [LOOSE CLOTHING] *UK* /ˈpɪn.ə.fɔːʳ/ [US] /-fɔːr/ *noun* [C] (*INFORMAL* **pinny**) a piece of clothing worn by women over the front of other clothes to keep them clean while doing something dirty, especially cooking

pinafore [DRESS] *UK* /ˈpɪn.ə.fɔːʳ/ [US] /-fɔːr/ *noun* [C] (*US* **jumper**) a loose dress with no sleeves which is usually worn over other clothing such as a shirt

pinball /ˈpɪn.bɔːl/ [US] /-bɑːl/ *noun* [U] a game played on a special machine like a large box on legs in which the player keeps a small ball bouncing between devices to win points

ˈpinball maˌchine *noun* [C] a machine for playing pinball on

pince-nez /ˌpæ̃ːnsˈneɪ/ *noun* [C] *plural* **pince-nez** (especially in the past) glasses held on a person's nose by a spring rather than by pieces which fit around their ears: *He wore* ***(a pair of)*** *pince-nez.*

P

pincer /ˈpɪnt.səʳ/ [US] /-sɚ/ *noun* [C usually pl] one of a pair of curved claws of an animal such as a crab

ˈpincer ˌmovement *noun* [C usually sing] a type of attack in which two parts of an army follow curved paths towards each other in an attempt to surround and then defeat the enemy

pincers /ˈpɪnt.səz/ [US] /-sɚz/ *plural noun* a tool for holding or pulling something, made of two curved metal bars which move against each other so that when the handles are pushed together the other ends close tightly

pinch [PRESS] /pɪntʃ/ *verb* [I or T] to squeeze something, especially someone's skin, strongly between two hard things such as a finger and a thumb, usually causing pain: *Ouch! Stop pinching (me)! ○ These shoes are too tight, they pinch (my feet).*

pinch *yourself* *verb* [R] You say that you have to pinch yourself if you cannot really believe something that has happened because it is so good or so strange: *I can't believe that he's back from Canada and he's mine – I keep having to pinch myself to make sure I'm not dreaming.*

• **pinch pennies** (*UK ALSO* **pinch and scrape**) *OLD-FASHIONED* to spend as little money as possible: *When we were first married we had to pinch pennies just to get by.*

pinch /pɪntʃ/ *noun* [C usually sing] when you pinch something or someone: *She **gave** Emma a painful pinch **on** the arm.*

• **at a pinch** *UK* (*US* **in a pinch**) Something that you can do at a pinch can be done if it is really necessary, but it will be difficult, not perfect, or not what you would really like: *I need £2000 to set up the business, but I suppose £1500 would do at a pinch.*

pinch [STEAL] /pɪntʃ/ *verb* [T] *INFORMAL* to steal something: *Right, who's pinched my chair?*

pinch [AMOUNT] /pɪntʃ/ *noun* [C] a small amount of something, such as a powder, especially the amount which a person can hold between their first finger and thumb: *While the tomatoes are cooking add a pinch **of** salt/sugar/dried thyme ○ FIGURATIVE Opinion polls on subjects like this should be **taken with** a pinch **of** scepticism.*

pinched /pɪntʃt/ *adj* describes someone's face when it is thin and pale: *He had that pinched look which suggests poverty and lack of nourishment.*

pincushion /ˈpɪŋˌkʊʃ.ᵊn/ [US] /ˈpɪn-/ *noun* [C] a small soft object into which pins can be pushed to keep them safely until you need them

ˌpine (aˈway) *verb* [I] to become increasingly thin and weak because of unhappiness, especially after the death of a loved person: *Carter died in 1904 after an accident and Leno pined away and died in London six months later.*

pine /paɪn/ *verb*

▲ **pine for *sth/sb*** *phrasal verb* to want something or someone very much, usually when it would be impossible to have them, or when they have gone away: *He's still pining for his ex-girlfriend.*

pineapple /ˈpaɪnˌæp.l̩/ *noun* [C or U] (the juicy yellow flesh of) a large tropical fruit with a rough orange or brown skin and pointed leaves on top: *tinned pineapples ○ pineapple juice* ➲See picture **Fruit** on page Centre 1

ˈpine ˌcone *noun* [C] the hard egg-shaped part of the pine tree which opens and releases seeds

ˈpine ˌneedle *noun* [C] the thin pointed leaf of a pine tree

ˈpine ˌnut *noun* [C] (*UK* **pine kernel**) the white seed of the pine tree, often used in cooking

ˈpine (ˌtree) *noun* [C or U] an evergreen tree that grows in cooler areas of the world: *a plantation of pines ○ a pine forest*

pine /paɪn/ *noun* [U] the wood of pine trees, which is usually pale in colour: *pine furniture ○ Pine is a softwood.*

piny, piney /ˈpaɪ.ni/ *adj*

ping /pɪŋ/ *verb* [I] to make a short sharp sound: *We heard a small stone ping against our window.* **ping** /pɪŋ/ *noun* [C]

ping /pɪŋ/ *noun, verb* [I] *US FOR* **pink** ENGINE NOISE

Ping-Pong /ˈpɪŋ.pɒŋ/ [US] /-pɑːŋ/ *noun* [U] *INFORMAL AND TRADEMARK FOR* **table tennis** ➲See picture **Sports** on page Centre 10

pinhead [SMALL] /ˈpɪn.hed/ *noun* [C] the very small round end of a pin: *The fault was caused by a hole no larger than a pinhead.*

pinhead [PERSON] /ˈpɪn.hed/ *noun* [C] *INFORMAL* a stupid person

pinhole /ˈpɪn.həʊl/ [US] /-hoʊl/ *noun* [C] a very small hole made by or as if by a pin

pinion [HOLD] /ˈpɪn.jən/ *verb* [T] to hold someone, especially by the arms, to prevent them from moving: *He was pinioned **to** the wall by two men while another one repeatedly punched him.*

pinion [DEVICE] /ˈpɪn.jən/ *noun* [C] a small wheel with teeth-like parts around its edge which fit against similar parts on a larger wheel or a RACK (= bar with teeth-like parts): *a rack-and-pinion assembly*

pink [COLOUR] /pɪŋk/ *adj* of a pale red colour: *pretty pink flowers ○ Have you been in the sun? Your nose is a bit pink.*

pink /pɪŋk/ *noun* [C or U] a pale red colour: *She's very fond of pink.*

• **in the pink** *MAINLY HUMOROUS* in very good health

pinkish /ˈpɪŋ.kɪʃ/ *adj* slightly pink: *a pinkish blue* **pinkness** /ˈpɪŋk.nəs/ *noun* [U]

pink [PLANT] /pɪŋk/ *noun* [C] a small garden plant which has sweet-smelling pink, white or red flowers and narrow grey-green leaves, or one of its flowers

pink [ENGINE NOISE] *UK* /pɪŋk/ *verb* [I] (*US* **ping**) When a car engine pinks, it makes a high knocking sound because the fuel is not burning correctly.

pink [POLITICS] /pɪŋk/ *adj OLD-FASHIONED DISAPPROVING* (slightly) supporting SOCIALIST ideas and principles **pinko** /ˈpɪŋ.kəʊ/ [US] /-koʊ/ *noun* [C] *plural* **pinkos** or **pinkoes**

pink [HOMOSEXUAL] /pɪŋk/ *adj* connected with homosexual people: *the growth in the pink economy*

pink-collar /ˌpɪŋkˈkɒl.əʳ/ [US] /-ˈkɑː.lɚ/ *adj MAINLY US* describes a job that is traditionally done by a woman: *Until recently secretarial work and nursing were very much pink-collar professions.*

pinkie, pinky /ˈpɪŋ.ki/ *noun* [C] *US AND SCOTTISH ENGLISH INFORMAL FOR* **little finger**: *a pinkie ring*

ˈpinking ˌshears *plural noun* special scissors with V-shaped teeth along the blades which make an uneven edge when they cut cloth, so that threads do not easily come out

the ˌpink ˈpound *UK noun* [S] (*US* **the pink dollar**) the money which all homosexuals together have available to spend: *Companies are becoming aware of the power of the pink pound.*

ˌpink ˈslip *noun* [C] *US INFORMAL* a document given to a person telling them that they do not have a job any more

pink-slip /ˌpɪŋkˈslɪp/ *verb* [T often passive] *US INFORMAL* to get rid of someone or something that is no longer needed

ˈpin ˌmoney *noun* [U] a small amount of extra money which a person earns to buy things they want but do not need

pinnacle [SUCCESS] /ˈpɪn.ə.kl̩/ *noun* [C usually sing] the most successful or admirable part of a system or achievement: *By the age of thirty-two she had **reached the** pinnacle **of** her career.*

pinnacle [TOP] /ˈpɪn.ə.kl̩/ *noun* [C] a small pointed tower on top of a building, or the top part of a mountain: *LITERARY The pinnacles of the Himalayas were visible above the clouds.*

ˈPIN (ˌnumber) *noun* [C] *ABBREVIATION FOR* **personal identification number**: a secret number which a person uses together with a special card to obtain money from their bank account from a machine outside the bank

pinny /ˈpɪn.i/ *noun* [C] *UK INFORMAL FOR* **pinafore** LOOSE CLOTHING

pinpoint [POSITION] /ˈpɪn.pɔɪnt/ [US] /ˈpɪn-/ *verb* [T] **1** to find out or say the exact position in space or time of something: *It is not possible to pinpoint precisely the time of death.* **2** to discover or describe the exact facts about something: *Emergency workers at the site are still unable to pinpoint the cause of the explosion.*

pinpoint /ˈpɪn.pɔɪnt/ ⑤ /ˈpɪn-/ adj [before n] very exact: *The computer will calculate your position with pinpoint accuracy.*

pinpoint [SMALL AREA] /ˈpɪn.pɔɪnt/ ⑤ /ˈpɪn-/ noun [C] a very small dot of something: *a pinpoint of light*

pinprick /ˈpɪn.prɪk/ ⑤ /ˈpɪn-/ noun [C usually pl] something which is slightly annoying for a short time: *You have to ignore the pinpricks and just get on with the job.*

pins and ˈneedles plural noun If someone has pins and needles in a part of their body they feel slight sharp pains in it, usually just after they have moved from being still in one position for a long time.

pinstripe /ˈpɪn.straɪp/ noun [U] a usually dark cloth with a pattern of narrow, usually paler, parallel lines: *He was wearing a pinstripe suit.* **pinstriped** /ˈpɪn.straɪpt/ adj

pinstripes /ˈpɪn.straɪps/ plural noun suits made of pinstriped cloth: *She watched the businessmen walk past in their pinstripes.*

pint /paɪnt/ noun [C] **1** a measure for liquid equal to about half a litre: *a pint of milk* ○ *a pint of beer* **2** UK INFORMAL a pint of beer: *He usually goes out for a pint at lunchtime.*

pinta /ˈpaɪn.tə/ ⑤ /-t̬ə/ noun [C usually sing] UK OLD-FASHIONED INFORMAL a pint of milk

pint-size(d) /ˈpaɪnt.saɪzd/ adj INFORMAL (of a person) small and not important: *Don't worry about him, he's just a pint-sized nobody.*

pin-up /ˈpɪn.ʌp/ noun [C] **1** a picture of a sexually attractive and usually famous person, especially someone wearing few clothes: *Every wall in her bedroom was covered with pin-ups of her favourite pop star.* **2** INFORMAL a person who is seen in pin-ups: *With his perfect college-boy looks, he's the latest teenage pin-up.*

pinwheel /ˈpɪn.wiːl/ noun [C] US FOR **windmill** (= a child's toy)

pioneer /ˌpaɪəˈnɪər/ ⑤ /-ˈnɪr/ noun [C] **1** a person who is one of the first people to do something: *one of the pioneers of modern science* ○ *a pioneer heart surgeon* **2** a person who goes to an area and establishes farms, houses, etc: *The pioneers went west across North America, cutting down forests and planting new crops.* **pioneer** /ˌpaɪəˈnɪər/ ⑤ /-ˈnɪr/ verb [T] *It was universities that pioneered these new industries.* **pioneering** /ˌpaɪəˈnɪə.rɪŋ/ ⑤ /-ˈnɪr.ɪŋ/ adj: *pioneering techniques*

pious [RELIGIOUS] /ˈpaɪ.əs/ adj strongly believing in religion, and living in a way which shows this belief: *She is a pious follower of the faith, never missing her prayers.* **piously** /ˈpaɪ.ə.sli/ adv **piety** /ˈpaɪ.ə.ti/ ⑤ /ˈpaɪ.ə.t̬i/ noun [U] (ALSO **piousness**) FORMAL

pious [PRETENDING] /ˈpaɪ.əs/ adj **1** DISAPPROVING pretending to have sincere feelings: *Quit the pious apologies – I know you don't really care.* **2** UK **pious hope** something which is unlikely to happen. **piously** /ˈpaɪ.ə.sli/ adv

pip [SEED] /pɪp/ noun [C] UK one of the small seeds of an edible fruit such as an apple or an orange ⊃Compare **stone** SEED. ⊃See picture **Fruit** on page Centre 1

pip [BEAT] /pɪp/ verb [T] -pp- UK INFORMAL to beat someone either by a very small amount or right at the end of a competition: *I got through to the final interview, but I was pipped at the post (= in the final stage) by a candidate with better qualifications.*

pip [SOUND] /pɪp/ noun [C usually pl] MAINLY UK a short high sound, especially one of a series: *She turned on the radio and heard the five o'clock pips.*

pipe [TUBE] /paɪp/ noun [C] a tube inside which liquid or gas flows from one place to another: *a water/gas/sewer pipe* ○ *a burst/fractured/leaking pipe* **pipe** /paɪp/ verb [T usually passive + adv or prep] *Hot water is piped to all apartments from the central boiler room.* ○ FIGURATIVE *Music is piped throughout the hotel complex.*
piping /ˈpaɪ.pɪŋ/ noun [U] pipes in general or a particular system of pipes

pipe [TOBACCO] /paɪp/ noun [C] a short narrow tube with a small container at one end, used for smoking especially tobacco: *I ordered some tea for myself and lit my pipe.*
● **Put/Stick that in your pipe and smoke it!** OLD-FASHIONED OR HUMOROUS a rude way of telling someone that they must accept what you have just said, even if they do not like it

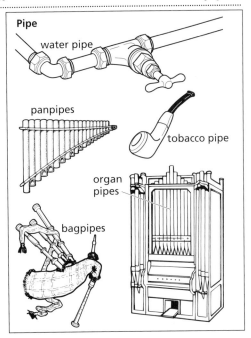

Pipe

water pipe
panpipes
tobacco pipe
organ pipes
bagpipes

pipe [SPEAK] /paɪp/ verb [T] to speak or sing in a high voice

pipe [INSTRUMENT] /paɪp/ noun [C] **1** a simple musical instrument made of a short narrow tube which is played by blowing through it **2** the metal or wood tubes in an organ through which air is pushed to make sound
pipes /paɪps/ plural noun another word for **bagpipes**
piper /ˈpaɪ.pər/ ⑤ /-pɚ/ noun [C] someone who plays a pipe (= a short narrow tube played by blowing through it) or the BAGPIPES: *We could hear a lone piper player playing in the distance.*

PHRASAL VERBS WITH **pipe** ▼

▲ **pipe down** phrasal verb INFORMAL to stop talking or making unnecessary noise: *Will you please pipe down, you two? I'm trying to read!*

▲ **pipe up** phrasal verb INFORMAL to suddenly start to speak or make a noise: *In the silence that followed, a lone voice piped up from the back of the room.*

ˈpipe ˌcleaner noun [C] a piece of wire covered with soft fibres which is used to clean a pipe

ˌpiped ˈmusic noun [U] OFTEN DISAPPROVING **Muzak**

ˈpipe ˌdream noun [C] (of an idea or plan) impossible or very unlikely to happen: *Her plans are not realistic – they'll never be more than a pipe dream.*

pipeline /ˈpaɪp.laɪn/ noun [C] a very long large tube, often underground, through which liquid or gas can flow for long distances
● **in the pipeline** being planned: *The theatre company has several new productions in the pipeline for next season.*

pipette /pɪˈpet/ ⑤ /paɪ-/ noun [C] a thin glass tube used especially in biology and chemistry for measuring or moving a small amount of liquid

piping /ˈpaɪ.pɪŋ/ noun **1** [C or U] a narrow strip of cloth used to decorate the edges of clothes or furniture **2** [U] UK (US **decoration**) a narrow line of ICING (= covering made with sugar) used to decorate a cake

ˌpiping ˈhot adv USUALLY APPROVING describes very hot food or drinks

pipsqueak /ˈpɪp.skwiːk/ noun [C] INFORMAL someone who is unimportant and does not deserve respect: *You little pipsqueak!*

piquant [INTERESTING] /ˈpiː.kənt/ adj SLIGHTLY FORMAL interesting and exciting, especially because mysterious: *More piquant details of their private life were revealed.*

piquancy /ˈpiː.kənt.si/ *noun* [U] **piquantly** /ˈpiː.kənt.li/ *adv*

piquant [SPICY] /ˈpiː.kənt/ *adj* having a pleasant sharp or spicy taste: *a piquant mixture of spices* **piquancy** /ˈpiː.kənt.si/ *noun* [U] **piquantly** /ˈpiː.kənt.li/ *adv*

pique /piːk/ *noun* [U] a feeling of anger and annoyance, especially caused by damage to your feeling of pride in yourself: *He stormed from the room **in a fit of** pique, shouting that he had been misunderstood.* **piqued** /piːkt/ *adj*

piranha /pɪˈrɑː.nə/ [US] /pəˈrɑː.njə/ *noun* [C] *plural* **piranhas** or **piranha** a fierce fish which lives in South American rivers, has sharp teeth and eats meat

pirate [SAILOR] /ˈpaɪ.rət/ [US] /ˈpaɪr.ət/ *noun* [C] a person who sails in a ship and attacks other ships in order to steal from them **piracy** /ˈpaɪ.rə.si/ [US] /ˈpaɪr.ə-/ *noun* [U] *Piracy is alive and flourishing on the world's commercial sea-lanes.* **piratical** /paɪˈræt.ɪ.kəl/ [US] /-ˈræṭ-/ *adj* FORMAL

pirate [COPY] /ˈpaɪ.rət/ [US] /ˈpaɪr.ət/ *verb* [T] to illegally copy a computer program, music, a film, etc. and sell it **pirated** /ˈpaɪ.rə.tɪd/ [US] /ˈpaɪr.ə.ṭɪd/ *adj*: *a pirated video* ○ *pirated software*

pirate /ˈpaɪ.rət/ [US] /ˈpaɪr.ət/ *noun* [C] **1** a person who pirates music, films, computer programs, etc: *software pirates* **2 pirate radio station** a radio station that broadcasts without official permission **piracy** /ˈpaɪ.rə.si/ [US] /ˈpaɪr.ə-/ *noun* [U] *software/video piracy*

pirouette /ˌpɪr.uˈet/ *noun* [C] a fast turn of the body on the toes or the front part of the foot, performed especially by a ballet dancer **pirouette** /ˌpɪr.uˈet/ *verb* [I]

Pisces /ˈpaɪ.siːz/ *noun* [C or U] the twelfth sign of the zodiac, relating to the period 20 February to 20 March, represented by two fish, or a person born during this period **Piscean** /ˈpaɪ.si.ən/ /-ˈ--/ [US] /ˈpaɪ.si-/ *noun* [C]

piss /pɪs/ *noun* [S or U] *OFFENSIVE* urine: *There was piss all over the floor.* ○ *I need **a** piss.* ○ *He's **having a** piss.*

• **take the piss (out of)** ***sb or sth*** *UK OFFENSIVE* to make a joke about someone or make them look silly: *They're always taking the piss out of him because he's a Barry Manilow fan.*

piss /pɪs/ *verb* [I] *OFFENSIVE* to pass urine: *That dog keeps pissing **on** our fence.*

piss *yourself* *verb* [R] *OFFENSIVE* to urinate over yourself and the clothes you are wearing

• **piss *yourself* (laughing)** *OFFENSIVE* to laugh very much: *There I was writhing in agony on the floor and you lot were pissing yourselves laughing!*

• **be pissing in the wind** *OFFENSIVE* to be trying to do something when there is no hope of succeeding: *You can try to change her mind if you like, but you'll be pissing in the wind.*

PHRASAL VERBS WITH **piss** ▼

▲ **piss *(sb)* about/around** *phrasal verb* [I or T] *UK OFFENSIVE* to behave in a stupid way or to treat someone badly: *Look, we haven't got much time so stop pissing about.* ○ *Stop pissing me about and just tell me where they are.*

▲ **piss *sth* away** *phrasal verb* [M] *OFFENSIVE* to waste an opportunity: *This is your last chance to win the league so don't piss it away.*

▲ **piss down** *phrasal verb* [I] *UK OFFENSIVE* to rain heavily: ***It's** really pissing **(it)** down here at the moment.*

▲ **piss off** [GO] *phrasal verb UK OFFENSIVE* to leave or go away, used especially as a rude way of telling someone to go away: *Everyone just pissed off and left me to clean up.* ○ *Why don't you just piss off – you've caused enough problems already!*

▲ **piss *sb* off** [ANNOY] *phrasal verb* (*ALSO* **pee *sb* off**) *OFFENSIVE* to annoy someone: *He never does any washing-up and it's starting to piss me off.*

ˌpissed ˈoff *adj* [after v] (*US ALSO* **pissed**) *UK OFFENSIVE* annoyed: *He'd kept me waiting for an hour so I was pissed off to start with.* ○ *She seemed a bit pissed off that she hadn't been invited.*

ˈpiss ˌartist *noun* [C] **1** *UK OFFENSIVE* someone who does not do things correctly **2** someone who is often drunk

pissed /pɪst/ *adj* [after v] *UK OFFENSIVE* drunk: *I can't remember – I was pissed at the time.*

• **pissed as a newt/fart** (*ALSO* **pissed out of *your* brain/head/mind**) *UK OFFENSIVE* very drunk

pisser /ˈpɪs.ər/ [US] /-ɚ/ *noun* [C] **1** *US OFFENSIVE* something which is of very bad quality: *There was some pisser of a film about a boy and his dog on TV last night.* **2** *US OFFENSIVE* something extremely good or humorous: *It was a pisser of a party!* **3** *OFFENSIVE* something that is very annoying or inconvenient: *"I've got to work late tonight." "What a pisser!"*

pisshead /ˈpɪs.hed/ *noun* [C] *UK OFFENSIVE* a person who drinks a lot of alcohol very often

pissoir /ˈpɪs.wɑːr/ /piːˈswɑːr/ [US] /piːˈswɑːr/ *noun* [C] a small building in which people, especially men, can urinate; a public toilet

piss-poor /ˈpɪs.pɔːr/ [US] /-pʊr/ *adj OFFENSIVE* having very little money, or being of very low quality: *We were piss-poor.* ○ *a piss-poor film*

pisspot /ˈpɪs.pɒt/ [US] /-pɑːt/ *noun* [C] *AUS SLANG* a person who drinks a lot of alcohol very often: *Patrick's a real pisspot.*

piss-take /ˈpɪs.teɪk/ *noun* [C] *UK OFFENSIVE* **1** an act of making someone or something look silly: *He told me I'd won and I thought it was just a piss-take.* **2** when someone copies someone else's behaviour and manner in an amusing way: *He **did** a piss-take **of** Fiona.*

piss-up /ˈpɪs.ʌp/ *noun* [C] *UK OFFENSIVE* an occasion when a lot of alcohol is drunk

pistachio (nut) /pɪˈstæʃ.i.əʊˌnʌt/ [US] /-oʊ-/ *noun* [C] a nut with a hard shell which contains an edible green seed

piste /piːst/ *noun* [C] a snow-covered area or track which is suitable for skiing on

pistol /ˈpɪs.təl/ *noun* [C] a small gun which is held in and fired from one hand: *a loaded pistol* ○ *an automatic pistol*

pistol-whip /ˈpɪs.təl.wɪp/ *verb* [T] *US* to hit someone with a pistol many times

piston /ˈpɪs.tən/ *noun* [C] a short solid piece of metal which moves up and down inside a cylinder in an engine to press the fuel into a small space and to send the power produced by it to the wheels

pit [HOLE] /pɪt/ *noun* [C] **1** a large hole in the ground, or a slightly low area in any surface: *They'd dug a shallow pit and left the bodies in it.* ○ *These pits in my skin are from when I had chickenpox.* ➲See also **armpit**; **sandpit**; **the pits** BAD. **2** a coal mine or an area of land from which a natural substance is taken by digging: *The coal-mining industry wants new pits to be opened.* ○ *a gravel/chalk pit* **3** *SLANG* a very untidy or dirty place: *I'm afraid my room is a complete pit!*

the pit *noun* [C usually sing] in a theatre, the seats at the lowest level, or the ORCHESTRA PIT

• **pit of *your* stomach** the part of the body in which people say they feel fear or nervousness: *I got a sick feeling/a knot in the pit of my stomach when the news of the attack was announced.*

pitted /ˈpɪt.ɪd/ [US] /ˈpɪṭ-/ *adj* marked with holes or low areas: *He'd had bad acne as a youth and his face was pitted* (= marked) ***with** pockmarks.*

pit [SEED] /pɪt/ *noun* [C], *verb* [T] **-tt-** *US FOR* **stone** SEED ➲See picture **Fruit** on page Centre 1

pitted /ˈpɪt.ɪd/ [US] /ˈpɪṭ-/ *adj US FOR* **stoned** (= with the stone removed)

▲ **pit *sb/sth* against *sb/sth*** *phrasal verb* to cause one person, group or thing to fight against or be in competition with another: *It was a bitter civil war, that pitted neighbour against neighbour.* ○ [R] *The climbers pitted themselves against the mountain.*

• **pit *your* wits against *sb/sth*** to see if you can be cleverer than someone or something: *Would you like to pit your wits against our quiz champion?*

ˌpit bull (ˈterrier) *noun* [C] a dog of a fierce, quite small breed, used especially for fighting other dogs so that people can gamble on the result

pitch [SPORTS FIELD] *UK* /pɪtʃ/ *noun* [C] (*US* **field**) an area marked for playing particular sports, especially football: *a football/hockey/cricket pitch* ○ *Supporters **invaded*** (= ran onto) *the pitch.*

pitch [MOVE] /pɪtʃ/ *verb* [I or T; usually + adv or prep] to move or be moved suddenly, especially by throwing: *She pitched the stone* ***into*** *the river.* ○ *He pitched the ball too short and the batsman hit it for six.* ○ *The ball pitched* (= landed) *short.* ○ *The bike hit a rut and I was pitched* ***(forward) onto*** *the road.* ○ *The ship pitched* ***up and down/from side to side*** *in the rough seas.*
• **be pitched into** ***sth*** to suddenly experience a bad feeling: *He was pitched* ***(headlong)*** *into despair by what happened to him in his final year at college.*

pitch [BASEBALL] /pɪtʃ/ *verb* [I or T] in baseball, to throw a ball towards the player with the bat in order for them to try to hit it: *Who will be pitching first for the White Sox this evening?*
pitch /pɪtʃ/ *noun* [C] a throw in a baseball game: *a good/bad pitch*
pitcher /ˈpɪtʃ.əʳ/ [US] /-ɚ/ *noun* [C] a player who pitches the ball in a baseball game ➲See picture **Sports** on page Centre 10

pitch [LEVEL] /pɪtʃ/ *noun* **1** [C or U] the level or degree of something: *The piano and organ were tuned to the same pitch* (= note). ○ *If you teach children and adults in the same class, it's difficult to get the pitch* (= level of difficulty or interest) *right.* **2** [S] the level of a feeling: *By this time their disagreement had reached* ***such a*** *pitch that there was no hope of an amicable conclusion.* ○ *The children were* ***at fever*** *pitch* (= very excited) *the day before the party.*
pitch /pɪtʃ/ *verb* [T] *The tune was pitched* (= the notes in it were) *too high for me to reach the top notes.* ○ *A teacher's got to pitch a lesson* ***at*** *the right level for the students.* **-pitched** /-pɪtʃt/ *suffix*: *a high-pitched voice/scream*

pitch [PERSUASION] /pɪtʃ/ *noun* [C] **1** a speech or act which attempts to persuade someone to buy or do something: *The man in the shop gave me his* ***(sales)*** *pitch about quality and reliability.* ○ *She* ***made*** *a pitch* ***for*** *the job but she didn't get it.* ○ [+ **to** infinitive] *The city* ***made*** *a pitch* ***to*** *stage the Olympics.* **2** *UK* a place in a public area where a person regularly sells goods or performs: *The flower seller was at his usual pitch outside the station.*
pitch /pɪtʃ/ *verb* [I or T] *MAINLY US* to try to persuade someone to do something: *She pitched her idea* ***to*** *me over a business lunch.* ○ *They are pitching* ***for*** *business at the moment.*

pitch [TENT] /pɪtʃ/ *verb* [T] to put up a tent and fix it into position: *We pitched camp/our tent in the shade.*
pitch *UK* /pɪtʃ/ *noun* [C] (*US* **site**) the piece of ground on which you camp: *We chose a large level grassy pitch for our caravan.*

pitch [SLOPE] /pɪtʃ/ *noun* [U] the amount of slope, especially of a roof: *This roof has a very* ***steep/high/gentle/low*** *pitch.* **pitch** /pɪtʃ/ *verb* [I usually + adv or prep] **pitched** /pɪtʃt/ *adj*: *The garage has a pitched roof, not a flat one.*

pitch [BLACK SUBSTANCE] /pɪtʃ/ *noun* [U] a thick black substance which was used in the past to make wooden ships and buildings waterproof

PHRASAL VERBS WITH **pitch**

▲ **pitch in** *phrasal verb INFORMAL* to start to do something as part of a group, especially something helpful: *If we all pitch in together, it shouldn't take too long.* ○ [+ **to** infinitive] *When I bought this house, all my friends pitched in to help fix it up.* ○ *My brother pitched in* ***with*** *an offer of transport.* ○ *After we had seen the video everyone started pitching in* ***with*** *comments on its faults.*
▲ **pitch into** ***sb/sth*** *phrasal verb INFORMAL* to criticize or attack someone or something forcefully: *He pitched into me as soon as I arrived, asking where the work was.*
▲ **pitch up** *phrasal verb INFORMAL* to arrive in a place: *Gerald finally pitched up two hours late.*

ˌpitch ˈdark *adj* (*ALSO* **pitch black**) extremely dark: *a moonless pitch-black night* **ˌpitch ˈdarkness** *noun* [U] (*ALSO* **pitch blackness**) *Suddenly the lights went out, and the house was left* ***in*** *pitch darkness.*

ˌpitched ˈbattle *noun* [C] a large fight, or a battle in which both sides stay in the same place: *A pitched battle* ***between*** *the two sets of fans developed on the terraces after the match was over.*

pitcher /ˈpɪtʃ.əʳ/ [US] /-ɚ/ *noun* [C] **1** *UK* a large container with a wide round base, straight sides and a narrow opening at the top, used in the past for holding water or another liquid: *an earthenware pitcher* **2** *US FOR* **jug** CONTAINER: *a pitcher* ***of*** *beer/water/lemonade* ➲See also **pitcher** at **pitch** BASEBALL.

pitchfork /ˈpɪtʃ.fɔːk/ [US] /-fɔːrk/ *noun* [C] a tool with a long handle and two or three large curved metal points used for moving hay or straw

pitchfork /ˈpɪtʃ.fɔːk/ [US] /-fɔːrk/ *verb*
▲ **pitchfork** ***sb*** **into** ***sth*** *phrasal verb* to cause someone suddenly to be in a particular situation, usually a difficult one, especially when they are not ready: *Her father died when she was 22, and she was pitchforked into the running of the estate.*

piteous /ˈpɪt.i.əs/ [US] /ˈpɪt̬-/ *adj* causing you to feel sadness and sympathy: *The kitten gave a piteous cry.* **piteously** /ˈpɪt.i.ə.sli/ [US] /ˈpɪt̬-/ *adv*: *She wept piteously.* **piteousness** /ˈpɪt.i.ə.snəs/ [US] /ˈpɪt̬-/ *noun* [U]

pitfall /ˈpɪt.fɔːl/ [US] /-fɑːl/ *noun* [C usually pl] a likely mistake or problem in a situation: *The store* ***fell into*** *one of the major pitfalls of small business, borrowing from suppliers by paying bills late.* ○ *There's a video that tells new students about pitfalls to* ***avoid***.

pith /pɪθ/ *noun* [U] the white substance between the skin and the flesh of CITRUS fruits such as oranges, or the soft white inner part of the stem of some plants **pithy** /ˈpɪθ.i/ *adj*: *a pithy orange* ➲See also **pithy**.

pithead /ˈpɪt.hed/ *noun* [C usually sing] *MAINLY UK* the area and buildings at the entrance to a mine ➲See also **pit** HOLE.

ˈpith ˌhelmet *noun* [C] (*ALSO* **topee**) a large hard white hat worn to give protection from the sun. It was worn in the past by Europeans who were in hot countries.

pithy /ˈpɪθ.i/ *adj* (of speech or writing) short and clever; expressing an idea cleverly in a few words: *a pithy remark* ➲See also **pithy** at **pith**. **pithily** /ˈpɪθ.ɪ.li/ *adv*

pitiable /ˈpɪt.i.ə.bl̩/ [US] /ˈpɪt̬-/ *adj* ➲See at **pity**.

pitiful /ˈpɪt.i.fᵊl/ [US] /ˈpɪt̬-/ *adj* ➲See at **pity**.

pitiless /ˈpɪt.i.ləs/ [US] /ˈpɪt̬-/ *adj* ➲See at **pity**.

ˈpit ˌpony *noun* [C] a small horse used in the past to pull loads down mines

the pits [BAD] /ðəˈpɪts/ *plural noun INFORMAL* something that is of extremely low quality: *The hotel we stayed in was the pits!*

the pits [REPAIR AREA] /ðəˈpɪts/ *plural noun* the area next to a motor race track where the cars are given fuel or repaired during a race

pit stop /ˈpɪt.stɒp/ [US] /-stɑːp/ *noun* [C] **1** when a driver in a motor race stops in THE PITS: *to* ***make*** *a pit stop* **2** a short stop that you make during a long car journey in order to rest and eat: *We* ***made*** *a quick pit stop in York before continuing on our journey.*

pitta (bread), *US* **pita (bread)** /ˈpɪt.əˌbred/ *noun* [U] flat hollow bread in an oval shape

pittance /ˈpɪt.ᵊnts/ [US] /ˈpɪt̬-/ *noun* [C usually sing] *DISAPPROVING* a very small amount of money, especially money received as payment, income or a present: *He works hard but he's* ***paid*** *a pittance.*

pitter-patter /ˈpɪt.əˌpæt.əʳ/ [US] /ˈpɪt̬.ɚˌpæt̬.ɚ/ *noun* [S] a quick light knocking sound: *I heard* ***the*** *pitter-patter* ***of tiny feet*** (= the noise of children running). **pitter-patter** /ˈpɪt.əˌpæt.əʳ/ [US] /ˈpɪt̬.ɚˌpæt̬.ɚ/ *verb* [I + adv or prep] *The rain pitter-pattered on the roof.* **pitter-patter** /ˈpɪt.əˌpæt.əʳ/ [US] /ˈpɪt̬.ɚˌpæt̬.ɚ/ *adv*

pituitary (gland) /pɪˈtjuː.ɪ.tᵊr.iˌglænd/ [US] /-ˈtuː.ə.ter-/ *noun* [C usually sing] *SPECIALIZED* a small organ at the base of the brain which controls the growth and activity of the body by producing hormones

pity /ˈpɪt.i/ [US] /ˈpɪt̬-/ *noun* **1** [U] a feeling of sympathy and understanding for someone else's unhappiness or difficult situation: *The girl stood gazing* ***in/with*** *pity at the old lion in the cage.* ○ *We* ***took*** *pity* ***on*** (= felt sorry for and therefore helped) *a couple of people waiting in the rain for a bus and gave them a lift.* ➲See also **self-pity**. **2** [S] If something is described as a pity, it is disappointing or not satisfactory: *"Can't you go to the party? Oh, that's* ***(such) a*** *pity."* ○ [+ (**that**)] *Pity* ***(that)*** *you*

P

didn't remember to give me the message. ○ [+ that] *The pity was that so few people bothered to come.* ○ *We'll have to leave early, more's the pity* (= and I am unhappy about it). ○ *"What a pity you're ill!"*

pity /ˈpɪt.i/ ⓤ /ˈpɪt̬-/ *verb* [T] to feel sympathy for someone: *Pity* (= Feel sorry for) *those on the street with no home to go to.*

pitiful /ˈpɪt.i.f³l/ ⓤ /ˈpɪt̬-/ *adj* (FORMAL **pitiable**) **1** making people feel sympathy: *The refugees arriving at the camp had pitiful stories to tell.* **2** describes something that you consider is bad or not satisfactory or not enough: *a pitiful state of affairs* ○ *The amount of time and money being spent on researching this disease is pitiful.* **pitifully** /ˈpɪt.i.f³l.i/ ⓤ /ˈpɪt̬-/ *adv* (FORMAL **pitiably**) **pitifulness** /ˈpɪt.i.f³l.nəs/ ⓤ /ˈpɪt̬-/ *noun* [U]

pitiless /ˈpɪt.i.ləs/ ⓤ /ˈpɪt̬-/ *adj* **1** cruel and having no pity: *the dictator's pitiless rule* ○ *a pitiless critic* **2** severe and unpleasant: *He told us his story in pitiless detail.* ○ *Few people were out in the pitiless midday sun.* **pitilessly** /ˈpɪt.i.lə.sli/ ⓤ /ˈpɪt̬-/ *adv* **pitilessness** /ˈpɪt.i.lə.snəs/ ⓤ /ˈpɪt̬-/ *noun* [U]

pivot /ˈpɪv.ət/ *noun* [C] **1** a fixed point supporting something which turns or balances **2** the central or most important person or thing in a situation: *The former guerrilla leader has become the pivot on which the country's emerging political stability **turns/revolves** (= it depends on him).* **pivotal** /ˈpɪv.ə.t³l/ ⓤ /-t̬³l/ *adj* central and important: *a pivotal figure/role/idea*

pixel /ˈpɪk.s³l/ *noun* [C] SPECIALIZED the smallest unit of an image on a television or computer screen

pixellated, **pixelated** /ˈpɪk.s³l.eɪ.tɪd/ ⓤ /-t̬ɪd/ *adj* A pixellated image is made up of PIXELS (= extremely small dots on a computer screen that viewed together make an image).

pixie, **pixy** /ˈpɪk.si/ *noun* [C] (especially in children's stories) a small imaginary person

pizza /ˈpiːt.sə/ *noun* [C or U] (US OLD-FASHIONED ALSO **pizza pie**) a large circle of flat bread baked with cheese, tomatoes, and sometimes meat and vegetables spread on top: *a slice of pizza* ○ *I like a lot of different pizza **toppings**.* ○ *deep* (UK) **pan**/(US) **dish** *pizza*

pizza-face /ˈpiːt.sə.feɪs/ *noun* [as form of address] SLANG DISAPPROVING a person whose face has a lot of spots and PIMPLES on it

pizza parlour UK, US **pizza parlor** *noun* [C] a **pizzeria**

pizzazz, **pzazz** /pɪˈzæz/ *noun* [U] INFORMAL APPROVING the quality of noticeable and energetic excitement: *Their performance was full of pizzazz.*

pizzeria /ˌpiːt.səˈriː.ə/ *noun* [C] a restaurant that sells PIZZA

pizzicato /ˌpɪt.sɪˈkɑː.təʊ/ ⓤ /-t̬oʊ/ *adj, adv* SPECIALIZED played by PLUCKING the strings of a musical instrument such as a violin or CELLO with the fingers instead of using a bow

pl ABBREVIATION FOR **plural** GRAMMAR

placard /ˈplæk.ɑːd/ ⓤ /-ɑːrd/ *noun* [C] a large piece of card, paper, etc. with a message written or printed on it, often carried in public places by people who are complaining about something: *Demonstrators marched past **holding/waving** placards that said, 'Send food, not missiles'.*

placate /pləˈkeɪt/ ⓤ /ˈpleɪ.keɪt/ *verb* [T] to stop someone from feeling angry: *Outraged minority groups will not be placated by promises of future improvements.* **placatory** /pləˈkeɪ.t³r.i/ ⓤ /ˈpleɪ.kə.tɔːr-/ *adj* FORMAL trying to avoid making someone angry: *The tone of the letter was placatory.*

place AREA /pleɪs/ *noun* **1** [C] an area, town, building, etc: *Her garden was a cool pleasant place to sit.* ○ *What was the name of that place we drove through on the way to New York?* ○ *They decided to go to a pizza place.* ○ *There are several places **of interest** to visit in the area.* ○ *It's important to feel comfortable in your place of **work**.* ⊃See Note **take part** or **take place?** at **take** ACCEPT. **2** [C] INFORMAL someone's home: *I'm looking for a place to live.* ○ *We'll have the meeting at my place.* **3** [U] a suitable area, building, situation or occasion: *University is a great place **for** making new friends.* ○ [+ to infinitive] *This*

*meeting **isn't** the place **to** discuss your problems, I'm afraid.*

• **all over the place 1** scattered in a lot of different places in an untidy way: *There were dirty dishes and clothes all over the place.* **2** in every place: *You can buy T-shirts like this all over the place.* **3** INFORMAL not correct or suitable: *His drumming was all over the place.*

• **go places** INFORMAL to be likely to be successful in the future: *They said that the group was clearly going places.*

place POSITION /pleɪs/ *noun* [C] **1** a position in relation to other things or people: *His leg was broken in two places.* ○ *When you've finished, put the book back **in** its place on the shelf.* ○ *This plant needs a warm, sunny place.* ○ *Will you **keep** my place **(in the queue)** (= allow me to come back to the same position)?* ○ *She spoke to me and I **lost** my place in the book* (= I forgot where I had been reading). ⊃See also **decimal place**. **2** the seat you will sit in on a particular occasion, or the seat where you usually sit, in the theatre, a class, a train, etc: *My ticket says 6G but there's someone sitting in my place.* ○ *The children collected their prizes and then went back to their places.* ○ ***Save** me a place* (= Keep a seat for me until I arrive) *near the front.* **3** the space at a table where one person will sit and eat, usually with a plate and eating utensils arranged on it: *The waiter showed us to our places and gave us each a menu.* ○ *He **laid** six places at the table.* **4** a position in an organization, a system or competition: *She's got a place **at** university* ○ *She's got a place* (UK) **on**/(US) **in** *a fine-arts course.* ○ *Our team finished **in** second place.* ○ *He **took** third place/*(UK ALSO) **got a** *third place* (= was the third to finish) *in the marathon last year.* **5** US used after words such as 'any' and 'some' as a different way of saying 'anywhere', 'somewhere', etc: *I know I left that book some place – now, where was it?* ○ *That bar was like no place I'd ever been before.*

• **in place 1** If something is in place, it is in its usual or correct position: *The chairs are all in place.* ○ *He screwed the shelf in place.* **2** organized: *The arrangements are all in place for the concert next Thursday.*

• **in place of sb/sth** instead of someone or something: *You can use margarine in place of butter in some recipes.*

• **in the first/second place** used to separate and emphasize reasons or opinions: *I don't want to go yet – in the first place I'm not ready, and in the second place it's raining.* ⊃See also **in the first place** at **first**.

• **out of place** in the wrong place or looking wrong: *The boy looked uncomfortable and out of place among the adults.*

• **place in the sun** an advantageous position: *He certainly earned his place in the sun.*

• **take place** to happen: *The concert takes place next Thursday.*

• **take the place of sb/sth** to be used instead of someone or something

• **A place for everything and everything in its place.** SAYING This means that the best way to stay tidy and well organized is to keep things in their correct positions.

• **take first/second place** to be the most important consideration/a less important consideration: *Work takes second place.*

place /pleɪs/ *verb* **1** [I or T] to put something in a particular position: *She placed the letter in front of me.* ○ *She placed her name on the list of volunteers.* ○ *I'd place him among the ten most brilliant scientists of his age.* ○ [+ obj + adj] *The horse was placed first/second/third in its first race* (= finished the race in first/second/third position). **2 place an advertisement/bet/order, etc.** to arrange to have an advertisement, bet, order, etc.: *They placed the order for the furniture six weeks ago.* ○ *They were placing bets* (= gambling) *on who would win.* **3 place emphasis/importance, etc. on sth** to give something emphasis, importance, etc: *She placed the emphasis on the word 'soon'.* ○ *He placed importance on a comfortable lifestyle* (= It was important to him). **4** [T] to find someone a job: *The students are placed **in/with** companies for a period of work experience.*

• **How are you placed for...?** UK INFORMAL used to ask someone whether they have enough money, time, etc: *How are you placed for money?* ○ *How are you placed for Tuesday night* (= Are you busy on Tuesday night)?

placement /ˈpleɪs.mənt/ *noun* [C or U] the temporary position or job someone has in an organization: *I think we can **find** a placement for you in the accounts department.* ○ *The trainee teachers **do** a school placement in the summer term.*

place [RECOGNIZE] /pleɪs/ *verb* [T] to recognize someone or remember where you have seen them or how you know them: *She looks familiar but I can't place her – did she use to work here?*

place [DUTY] /pleɪs/ *noun* [U] *SLIGHTLY OLD-FASHIONED* what a person should do or is allowed to do, especially according to the rules of society: [+ *to* infinitive] *It's not your place **to** tell me what to do.* ○ *I'm not going to criticize his lordship – I **know** my place* (= I know that I am of lower social rank).

• **put *sb* in *their* place** to tell or show someone that they are less important than they thought they were: *When he tried to take charge, she soon put him in his place.*

placebo /pləˈsiː.bəʊ/ [US] /-boʊ/ *noun* [C] *plural* **placebos** **1** a substance given to someone who is told that it is a particular medicine, either to make them feel as if they are getting better or to compare the effect of the particular medicine when given to others: *She was only given a placebo, but she claimed she got better – that's the placebo **effect**.* **2** something that is given to try to satisfy a person who has not been given the thing they really want: *These small concessions have been made as a placebo to stop the workers making further demands.*

ˈplace ˌcard *noun* [C] a card with someone's name on it, which is put in the space at a table where they will sit, especially at a formal meal

ˈplace ˌmat *noun* [C] a decorative piece of card, cloth, wood, plastic etc. on which someone's plate and eating utensils are put on a table

ˈplace ˌname *noun* [C] the official name of a town or an area: *York and Toledo are place names.*

placenta /pləˈsen.tə/ [US] /-t̬ə/ *noun* [C] *plural* **placentas** or **placentae** *SPECIALIZED* the temporary organ which feeds a FOETUS (= developing baby) inside its mother's womb

ˌplace of ˈworship *noun* [C] a building for religious services, such as a church, TEMPLE, etc.

ˈplace ˌsetting *noun* [C] the glasses, plates, knives and forks, etc. which one person needs for eating a meal, arranged on a table

placid /ˈplæs.ɪd/ *adj* having a calm appearance or characteristics: *a slow-moving and placid river* ○ *the placid pace of village life* ○ *She was a very placid* (= calm and not easily excited) *child who slept all night and hardly ever cried.* **placidly** /ˈplæs.ɪd.li/ *adv* **placidness** /ˈplæs.ɪd.nəs/ *noun* [U] (*ALSO* **placidity**)

plagiarize, *UK USUALLY* **-ise** /ˈpleɪ.dʒər.aɪz/ [US] /-dʒə.raɪz/ *verb* [I or T] to use another person's idea or a part of their work and pretend that it is your own: *The book contains numerous plagiarized passages.* ○ *If you compare the two books side by side, it is clear that the author of the second has plagiarized **(from** the first).* **plagiarism** /ˈpleɪ.dʒər.ɪ.zəm/ [US] /-dʒɚ.ɪ-/ *noun* [U] **plagiarist** /ˈpleɪ.dʒər.ɪst/ [US] /-dʒɚ.ɪst/ *noun* [C]

plague [CAUSE PAIN/TROUBLE] /pleɪɡ/ *verb* [T] **1** to cause worry, pain or difficulty to someone or something over a period of time: *Financial problems have been plaguing their new business partners.* ○ *My shoulder's been plaguing me all week.* **2** to annoy someone, especially by asking continual questions: *The children plagued him **with** questions all through lunch.* ○ *He's been plaguing me **for** a loan of the book.*

plague [DISEASE] /pleɪɡ/ *noun* [C or U] **1** BUBONIC PLAGUE or (an attack of) any serious disease which kills many people **2 a plague of *sth*** a large number of things which are unpleasant or likely to cause damage: *a plague of insects* ○ *HUMOROUS A plague of journalists descended on the town.*

plaice /pleɪs/ *noun* [C or U] *plural* **plaice** a sea fish with a flat circular body, or its flesh eaten as food

plaid /plæd/ *noun* [U] *MAINLY US FOR* **tartan**

plain [WITH NOTHING ADDED] /pleɪn/ *adj* **1** not decorated in any way; with nothing added: *She wore a plain black dress.* ○ *We've chosen a plain carpet* (= one without a pattern) *and patterned curtains.* ○ *He prefers plain food – nothing too fancy.* ○ *We're having plain blue walls in the dining room.* ○ *a catalogue sent in a plain brown envelope* ○ *a plain style of architecture* ○ *plain* (= with no added fruit or sugar) *yoghurt* **2 plain paper** paper which has no lines on it: *a letter written on plain paper* **plainly** /ˈpleɪn.li/ *adv: a plainly furnished room* **plainness** /ˈpleɪn.nəs/ *noun* [U]

plain [CLEAR] /pleɪn/ *adj* obvious and clear to understand: ***It's** quite plain **that** they don't want to speak to us.* ○ *The reason is perfectly plain.* ○ *I **made it** quite plain **(that)*** (= explained clearly that) *I wasn't interested.*

• **be (as) plain as the nose on *your* face** (*ALSO* **be (as) plain as a pikestaff**) to be very obvious: *He's not happy here – that's as plain as the nose on your face.*

• **be plain sailing** *UK* (*US ALSO* **be smooth sailing**) to be easy and without problems: *The roads were busy as we drove out of town, but after that it was plain sailing.*

plainly /ˈpleɪn.li/ *adv* clearly or obviously: *This is plainly wrong.* ○ *Every footstep could be plainly heard.* ○ *The men had plainly lied.* ○ *Plainly, a great deal of extra time will be needed for the security checks.* ○ *The incentive to sell more is large – and it plainly works.* **plainness** /ˈpleɪn.nəs/ *noun* [U]

plain [COMPLETE] /pleɪn/ *adj* [before n] (used for emphasis) complete: *It was plain stupidity on Richard's part.*

plain /pleɪn/ *adv INFORMAL* completely: *I mean, taking the wrong equipment with you – that's just plain **stupid**.*

plain [NOT BEAUTIFUL] /pleɪn/ *adj* (especially of a woman or girl) not beautiful: *She had been a very plain child.* **plainness** /ˈpleɪn.nəs/ *noun* [U]

plain [LAND] /pleɪn/ *noun* [C] (*ALSO* **plains**) a large area of flat land: *the coastal plain* ○ *High mountains rise above the plain.*

plain [STITCH] /pleɪn/ *noun* [U] a type of simple stitch in knitting: *a row of plain and two rows of purl*

ˌplain ˈchocolate *noun* [C or U] **1** *UK FOR* **dark chocolate** ➲Compare **milk chocolate**. **2** *AUS FOR* **milk chocolate**

ˌplain ˈclothes *plural noun* ordinary clothes when worn by police when they are working: *There were police **in** plain clothes in the crowd.* **ˌplain-ˈclothes** *adj* [before n] *plain-clothes police officers/detectives*

ˌplain ˈEnglish *noun* [U] clear simple language: *Why can't they write these instructions in plain English?*

ˌplain ˈflour *UK noun* [C or U] (*US* **all-purpose flour**) flour that contains no chemical to make cakes RISE (= become large when cooked) ➲Compare **self-raising flour**.

plainsong /ˈpleɪn.sɒŋ/ [US] /-sɑːŋ/ *noun* [U] (*ALSO* **plainchant**) a type of simple group singing without instruments, used especially in the past in the Christian church

ˌplain ˈspeaking *noun* [U] when you say clearly and honestly what you think without trying to be polite: *It's time for some plain speaking.* **plain-spoken** /ˌpleɪnˈspəʊ.kən/ [US] /-ˈspoʊ-/ *adj: He's very plain-spoken.*

plaintiff /ˈpleɪn.tɪf/ [US] /-t̬ɪf/ *noun* [C] *LEGAL* someone who makes a legal complaint against someone else in court ➲Compare **defendant** at **defend**.

plaintive /ˈpleɪn.tɪv/ [US] /-t̬ɪv/ *adj* describes something which sounds slightly sad: *the plaintive sound of the bagpipes* ○ *"What about me?" came a plaintive voice.* **plaintively** /ˈpleɪn.tɪv.li/ [US] /-t̬ɪv-/ *adv: "I've broken my glasses," he said plaintively.* **plaintiveness** /ˈpleɪn.tɪv.nəs/ [US] /-t̬ɪv-/ *noun* [U]

plain-vanilla /ˌpleɪn.vəˈnɪl.ə/ *adj* describes a product or service that is basic and has no special features: *I just want a plain-vanilla bank account with low charges.*

plait /plæt/ *verb* [I or T] (*US USUALLY* **braid**) to join three or more lengths of hair or string-like material by putting them over each other in a special pattern: *She plaited the horse's tail.* ○ *a plaited leather bracelet/belt*

plait /plæt/ *noun* [C] (*US USUALLY* **braid**) a length of hair or other material which is divided into three parts which are then crossed over each other in a special pattern: *She usually wears her hair **in a** plait/**in** two plaits.* ➲See picture **Hairstyles and Hats** on page Centre 8

plan [DECISION] /plæn/ *noun* [C] **1** a set of decisions about how to do something in the future: *a company's business plan* ○ *a negotiated peace plan* ○ *a five-year plan*

P

○ *holiday plans* ○ *What are your plans for this weekend?*
○ [+ *to* infinitive] *My plan is to hire a car when I arrive in America and travel about.* **2** a type of arrangement for financial investment: *a pension/savings plan*

• **go according to plan** to happen in the way you intend: *Events of this type rarely go according to plan.*

plan /plæn/ *verb* **-nn-** **1** [I + adv or prep; T] to think about and decide what you are going to do or how you are going to do something: *She helped them to plan their route.* ○ *If we plan carefully, we should be able to stay within our budget.* ○ [+ question word] *She's already planning how to spend her prize money.* **2** [I or T] to intend to do something or that an event or result should happen: *Our meeting wasn't planned – it was completely accidental.* ○ [+ *to* infinitive] *I'm not planning to stay here much longer.* ○ [+ adv or prep] *We only planned for six guests, but then someone brought a friend.*

planner /'plæn.ə'/ ⓤ /-ɚ/ *noun* [C] a person who makes decisions about how something will be done in the future: *a systems planner* **planning** /'plæn.ɪŋ/ *noun* [U] *Events like these take months of careful planning.*

plan [DRAWING] /plæn/ *noun* [C] a drawing of a building, town, area, vehicle, machine, etc. which only shows its shape from above, its size, and the position of important details: *a street plan* (= a type of map of a town showing the roads) ○ *a seating plan* (= a drawing which shows where each person will sit)

plans /plænz/ *plural noun* drawings from which something is made or built: *The architect showed us the house plans that she had drawn up.* ○ *I'll send a set of plans for the new machine.*

plan /plæn/ *verb* [T] **-nn-** to design a building or structure: *The people who planned Britain's new towns had a vision of clean modern housing for everyone.*

planner /'plæn.ə'/ ⓤ /-ɚ/ *noun* [C] a person whose job is to decide how land in a particular area is to be used, what is to be built on it, etc. and who designs plans for it: *a town/urban/environmental/local planner*

planning /'plæn.ɪŋ/ *noun* [U] the process of deciding how land in a particular area will be used and designing plans for it: *town/environmental/urban planning* ○ *the planning department of the local council*

PHRASAL VERBS WITH **plan** ▼

▲ **plan on doing** *sth phrasal verb* to intend to do something: *We were planning on just having a snack and catching the early train.*

▲ **plan on sb/sth doing** *sth phrasal verb* to realize that someone might do something or that something might happen and to make arrangements to deal with the situation: *They hadn't planned on the whole family coming.*

▲ **plan** *sth* **out** *phrasal verb* [M] to think about and decide what you are going to do or how you are going to do something: *I've planned out the day – train to town, some shopping, then a slap-up meal and a show.*

plane [AIRCRAFT] /pleɪn/ *noun* [C] (UK ALSO **aeroplane**, US ALSO **airplane**) a vehicle designed for air travel, which has wings and one or more engines: *a fighter/transport/passenger plane* ○ *We'll be boarding the plane in about 20 minutes.* ○ *He hates travelling by plane.* ○ *a plane ticket* ⊃See picture **Planes, Ships and Boats** on page Centre 14

plane [SURFACE] /pleɪn/ *noun* [C] SPECIALIZED in mathematics, a flat or level surface which continues in all directions: *an inclined plane*
plane /pleɪn/ *adj* [before n] SPECIALIZED flat: *a plane edge/surface*

plane [LEVEL] /pleɪn/ *noun* [C] a particular level or standard: *The poet's treatment of the subject lifts it to a mystical plane.* ○ *His work is on a completely different plane from* (= is much better than) *that of other crime writers.*

plane [TOOL] /pleɪn/ *noun* [C] a tool which is used to make wooden surfaces and edges flat and smooth by removing small strips of the wood **plane** /pleɪn/ *verb* [T] *You'll have to plane some more off the bottom of the door – it's still sticking.*

planet /'plæn.ɪt/ *noun* [C] an extremely large round mass of rock and metal, such as Earth, or of gas, such as Jupiter, which moves in a circular path around the Sun or another star: *the planet Earth/Venus* ○ *Might there be intelligent life on other planets?*

• **be on another planet** INFORMAL to not give attention to what is happening around you and to think differently from other people: *Some days that girl seems as if she's on another planet.*

planetary /'plæn.ɪ.t³r.i/ ⓤ /-ˌter-/ *adj* relating to planets: *planetary science/motion* ⊃See also **interplanetary**.

planetarium /ˌplæn.ɪ.ˈteə.ri.əm/ ⓤ /-ˈter.i-/ *noun* [C] *plural* **planetariums** or **planetaria** a building in which moving images of the sky at night are shown using a special machine

plane (tree) *noun* [C] a large tree with wide leaves and spreading branches that grows especially in towns

plank [FLAT PIECE] /plæŋk/ *noun* [C] a long narrow flat piece of wood or similar material, of the type used for making floors: *oak/concrete planks* ○ *a plank of wood* ○ *We used a plank to cross the ditch.*

planking /'plæŋ.kɪŋ/ *noun* [U] an area of planks used to form a surface: *rotten planking*

plank [PRINCIPLE] /plæŋk/ *noun* [C] LITERARY an important principle on which the activities of a group, especially a political group, are based: *Educational reform was one of the main planks of their election campaign.* ○ *The party's policy is based on five central planks.*

plankton /'plæŋk.tən/ *noun* [U] very small plants and animals which float on the surface of the sea and on which other sea animals feed

planning per'mission UK *noun* [U] (US **building permit**) an official agreement that something new can be built or an existing building can be changed

plant [LIVING THING] /plɑːnt/ ⓤ /plænt/ *noun* [C] a living thing which grows in earth, in water or on other plants, and usually has a stem, leaves, roots and flowers and produces seeds: *native plants and animals* ○ *garden/greenhouse/indoor plants* ○ *a tomato plant* ⊃See also **houseplant**. ✳ NOTE: Trees are plants, but the word is mainly used for those plants which are smaller than trees. ⊃See picture **Flowers and Plants** on page Centre 3

plant /plɑːnt/ ⓤ /plænt/ *verb* [T] **1** to put a plant into the ground or into a container of earth so that it will grow: *We planted trees and bushes in our new garden.* ○ *Hyacinth bulbs planted in pots now will flower early in the spring.* **2** If you plant a particular area, you put plants into the ground there: *The plot was surrounded by a stone wall and planted with flowering trees.* ○ *a densely planted garden* (= one in which the plants are close together)

planter /'plɑːn.tə'/ ⓤ /'plæn.tɚ/ *noun* [C] **1** someone who grows a particular crop in a hot part of the world: *a tea/rubber planter* **2** a large container in which plants are grown for decoration **3** a machine used to plant crops: *a potato planter* **planting** /'plɑːn.tɪŋ/ ⓤ /'plæn.tɪŋ/ *noun* [C or U] *Heavy rain delayed planting in parts of Indiana.*

plant [PUT] /plɑːnt/ ⓤ /plænt/ *verb* **1** [T + adv or prep] to put something firmly and strongly in a particular place: [R] *My brother planted himself on the sofa in front of the television.* ○ *He planted a kiss on her forehead/a blow on his opponent's jaw.* **2** [T usually + adv or prep] to cause an idea or story to exist: *That incident planted doubts about him in my mind.* ○ *Who planted these rumours?*

plant [PUT SECRETLY] /plɑːnt/ ⓤ /plænt/ *verb* [T usually + adv or prep] INFORMAL to put something or someone in a position secretly, especially in order to deceive someone: *She insisted that the drugs had been planted on her without her knowledge.* ○ *The bomb was planted in the station waiting room.*
plant /plɑːnt/ ⓤ /plænt/ *noun* [C usually sing] something illegal or stolen that has been put secretly in a person's clothing or among the things that belong to them to make them seem guilty of a crime: *He insisted the money was a plant.*

plant [BUILDING/MACHINES] /plɑːnt/ ⓤ /plænt/ *noun* **1** [U] machines used in industry: *The industry was accused of having invested little in workers, plant or infrastructure.*

2 [C] a factory in which such machines are used: *Two more car-assembly plants were closed by the strike.* **3** [U] *UK* a large heavy machine or vehicle used in industry, for building roads, etc: *The sign by the roadworks said 'Slow – heavy plant crossing'.* ○ *The firm's main business was plant hire.*

▲ **plant** *sth* **out** *phrasal verb* [M] to put a plant into the ground outside to continue growing: *Plant out the geraniums in early June.*

plantain /ˈplæn.tɪn/ *noun* [C or U] a tropical fruit similar to a BANANA with green skin, or the plant that produces this fruit

plantation /plænˈteɪ.ʃªn/ /plɑː-/ ⑩ /plæn-/ *noun* [C] **1** a large farm, especially in a hot part of the world, on which a particular type of crop is grown: *a tea/cotton/ rubber plantation* **2** an area where trees are grown for wood: *plantations of fast-growing conifers*

plaque FLAT OBJECT /plɑːk/ /plæk/ ⑩ /plæk/ *noun* [C] **1** a flat piece of metal, stone, wood or plastic with writing on it which is fixed to a wall, door or other object: *There was a brass plaque outside the surgery listing the various dentists' names and qualifications.* ○ *Her Majesty later unveiled a commemorative plaque.* ⊃See also **plate** FLAT PIECE. **2** *UK* **blue plaque** a plaque on the wall of a house which shows that someone famous once lived there: *The blue plaque said 'Charles Darwin, biologist, lived here'.*

plaque SUBSTANCE /plɑːk/ /plæk/ ⑩ /plæk/ *noun* [U] a substance containing bacteria that forms on the surface of teeth

plasma BLOOD /ˈplæz.mə/ *noun* [U] (*ALSO* **blood plasma**) the pale yellow liquid that forms 55% of human blood and contains the blood cells

plasma HOT SUBSTANCE /ˈplæz.mə/ *noun* [U] a very hot gas found, for example, inside the sun and other stars: *solar plasma* ○ *plasma physics*

plaster SUBSTANCE /ˈplɑː.stəʳ/ ⑩ /ˈplæs.tə/ *noun* [U] a substance which becomes hard as it dries and is used especially for spreading on walls and ceilings in order to give a smooth surface: *The plaster on the walls was cracked and flaking.* ⊃See also **plasterboard**.

• **in plaster** *UK* (*US* **in a cast**) If a part of your body is in plaster, it has a PLASTER CAST (= protective covering) around it to protect it while the bone heals: *My leg was in plaster for about six weeks.*

plaster /ˈplɑː.stəʳ/ ⑩ /ˈplæs.tə/ *verb* **1** [T] to spread plaster on a surface **2** [T + adv or prep] to make something stick in a flat smooth layer: *The torrential rain had plastered her hair to her head.* **3** [T usually + adv or prep] *INFORMAL* to cover a surface or an object with something completely or thickly: *She had plastered her bedroom walls with photos of pop stars.* ○ *The car was plastered with mud.* ○ *The story was plastered all over* (= printed so that it completely covered) *the front page of the newspaper.* **plastering** /ˈplɑː.stªr.ɪŋ/ ⑩ /ˈplæs.tə.ɪŋ/ *noun* [U] *There's only the plastering left to be done.*

plasterer /ˈplɑː.stªr.əʳ/ ⑩ /ˈplæs.tə.ə/ *noun* [C] a person whose job is to cover walls and ceilings with plaster

plaster STICKY MATERIAL *UK* /ˈplɑː.stəʳ/ ⑩ /ˈplæs.tə/ *noun* [C or U] (*UK ALSO* **sticking plaster,** *US TRADEMARK* **Band-Aid**) a small piece of sticky material used to cover and protect a cut in the skin: *a box of waterproof plasters* ○ *Put a plaster on it so that it doesn't get infected.*

plasterboard /ˈplɑː.stə.bɔːd/ ⑩ /ˈplæs.tə.bɔːrd/ *noun* [U] material consisting of two sheets of heavy paper with a layer of plaster between them, used to make walls and ceilings before putting on a top layer of plaster

plaster cast *noun* [C] **1** (*ALSO* **cast**) a protective covering for a broken bone, made of PLASTER OF PARIS **2** a copy of a statue or similar object, made of PLASTER OF PARIS

plastered /ˈplɑː.stəd/ ⑩ /ˈplæs.təd/ *adj* [after v] *INFORMAL* extremely drunk: *They went out to the pub and got plastered.*

plaster of Paris /ˌplɑː.stə.rəvˈpær.ɪs/ ⑩ /ˌplæs.tə.əvˈper-/ *noun* [U] a mixture of a white powder and water which becomes hard quickly as it dries and is used especially to make PLASTER CASTS

plastic SUBSTANCE /ˈplæs.tɪk/ *noun* [C or U] an artificial substance that can be shaped when soft into many different

forms and has many different uses: *He put a sheet of plastic over the broken window.* ○ *Those flowers aren't real – they're made of plastic.*

plastic /ˈplæs.tɪk/ *adj* **1** made of plastic: *a plastic bag/ box/cup* **2** *DISAPPROVING* artificial or false: *I hate the hostesses' false cheerfulness and plastic smiles.*

plastics /ˈplæs.tɪks/ *noun* [U] the process or business of producing plastic: *The company has moved into plastics.* ○ *the plastics industry*

plastic SOFT /ˈplæs.tɪk/ *adj* soft enough to be changed into a new shape: *Clay is a very plastic material.* ○ *This metal is plastic at high temperatures.* **plasticity** /plæs-ˈtɪs.ɪ.ti/ ⑩ /plæsˈtɪs.ə.t̬i/ *noun* [U]

plastic bullet *noun* [C] a large bullet made of hard plastic that is intended to hurt but not kill people

plastic explosive *noun* [U] a soft explosive substance that is used to make bombs and can be easily formed into different shapes: *They used plastic explosive to blow up the bridge.*

Plasticine /ˈplæs.tə.siːn/ /ˈplɑː.stə-/ ⑩ /ˈplæs.tɪ-/ *noun* [U] *UK TRADEMARK* a soft clay-like substance produced in different colours, used especially by children to make shapes and models

plastic (money) *noun* [U] CREDIT CARDS or DEBIT CARDS, rather than money in the form of notes, coins or cheques: *I'd prefer a restaurant where they take plastic.*

plastic surgery *noun* [U] a medical operation to bring a damaged area of skin, and sometimes bone, back to a usual appearance, or to improve a person's appearance: *Several of the crash victims had to have extensive plastic surgery.* ○ *She had plastic surgery on her nose to straighten it.*

plastic wrap *noun* [U] *US FOR* **clingfilm**

plate DISH /pleɪt/ *noun* [C] **1** a flat, usually round dish with a slightly raised edge that you eat from or serve food from: *paper/plastic/china plates* ○ *a dinner/salad plate* ○ *clean/dirty plates* ○ *There's still lots of food on your plate.* **2** (*ALSO* **plateful**) an amount of food on a plate: *Stephen ate three plates of spaghetti.*

• **give/hand** *sth* **to** *sb* **on a plate** *INFORMAL* to allow someone to get or win something very easily: *They were handed the contract on a plate.* ○ *Arsenal handed the game to them on a plate.*

• **have** *sth* **on your plate** *INFORMAL* to have something, usually a large amount of important work, to deal with: *She's got a lot on her plate – especially with two new projects starting this week.* ○ *The aid agencies have (more than) enough on their plate without having unnecessary visitors to look after.*

plateful /ˈpleɪt.fʊl/ *noun* [C] all that there is on one plate: *I offered him a biscuit and he ate the whole plateful.*

plate FLAT PIECE /pleɪt/ *noun* [C] **1** a flat piece of something that is hard and does not bend: *Thick bony plates protected the dinosaur against attack.* ○ *The ship's deck is composed of steel plates.* ⊃See also **license plates**; **number plates. 2** *SPECIALIZED* a flat piece of metal with words and/or pictures on it that can be printed

plate THIN LAYER /pleɪt/ *verb* [T] to cover a metal object with a thin layer of another metal, especially gold or silver: *We normally plate the car handles with nickel and then chrome.*

plate /pleɪt/ *noun* [U] **1** ordinary metal with a layer of another metal on top: *The knives and forks are silver plate.* **2** objects, especially plates, dishes and cups, completely made of a valuable metal such as gold or silver: *The thieves got away with £15 000 worth of church plate.* **plating** /ˈpleɪ.tɪŋ/ ⑩ /-t̬ɪŋ/ *noun* [U] *gold/silver plating* **-plated** /-pleɪ.tɪd/ ⑩ /-t̬ɪd/ *suffix*: *gold-plated earrings are much cheaper than solid gold ones.*

plate PICTURE /pleɪt/ *noun* [C] *SPECIALIZED* a picture, especially in colour, in a book: *The three birds differ in small features (see Plate 4).*

the plate BASEBALL *noun* [S] *US INFORMAL FOR* **home plate**

plateau /ˈplæt.əʊ/ ⑩ /plætˈoʊ/ *noun* [C] *plural UK* **plateaux** or *US ALSO* **plateaus 1** a large flat area of land that is high above sea level **2** a period during which there are no large changes: *The US death rate reached a plateau in the 1960s, before declining suddenly.*

plateau /ˈplæt.əʊ/ [US] /plætˈoʊ/ *verb* [I] to reach a particular level and then stay the same: *I'd been losing about a pound a week on my diet, but recently I've plateaued and haven't lost an ounce.* ○ *The economic slowdown has caused our sales to plateau.*

ˌplate ˈglass *noun* [U] large sheets of glass used especially as windows and doors in shops and offices: *a plate-glass window*

platelet /ˈpleɪt.lət/ *noun* [C] *SPECIALIZED* a very small cell in the blood that makes the blood thicker and more solid in order to stop bleeding caused by an injury

platform [STRUCTURE] /ˈplæt.fɔːm/ [US] /-fɔːrm/ *noun* [C] **1** a flat raised area or structure **2** a long flat raised structure at a railway station, where people get on and off trains: *The train for Cambridge will depart from platform 9.* **3** the raised part of the floor in a large room, from which you make a speech or give a musical performance: *Speaker after speaker* ***mounted/took the*** *platform to denounce the policy.* ○ *This brilliant young violinist has appeared on* ***concert*** *platforms all round the world.*

• **share a platform** to give speeches or to perform at the same public event: *It was the first time a Green politician and a Labour minister had shared a platform .*

platform [IDEAS] /ˈplæt.fɔːm/ [US] /-fɔːrm/ *noun* **1** [C usually sing] an opportunity to make your ideas or beliefs known publicly: *By refusing to give us a grant to make this programme, they are denying us a platform.* **2** [S] all the things that a political party promises to do if they are elected: *We campaigned on a platform of low taxation.*

platform [COMPUTING] /ˈplæt.fɔːm/ [US] /-fɔːrm/ *noun* [C] describes the type of computer system you are using, in connection with the type of SOFTWARE (= computer programs) you can use on it: *This new personal banking software can be used with any Windows platform.*

ˌplatform ˈshoes *plural noun* (*ALSO* **platforms**) shoes with extremely thick soles which raise the feet from the ground more than usual

platinum /ˈplæt.ɪ.nəm/ [US] /ˈplæt.nəm/ *noun* [U] an extremely valuable metal that is silvery in colour, used in jewellery and in industry: *a platinum wedding ring*

ˌplatinum ˈblonde *adj* describes hair that is so pale it is almost white **ˌplatinum ˈblonde** *noun* [C] *She's a platinum blonde.*

ˌplatinum ˈdisc *noun* [C] a prize given to the performer(s) of a popular song, or a collection of popular songs, when a very large number of copies of the recording of it have been sold ➲Compare **gold disc**.

P

platitude /ˈplæt.ɪ.tjuːd/ [US] /ˈplæt̬.ə.tuːd/ *noun* [C] *DISAPPROVING* a remark or statement that may be true but is boring and meaningless because it has been said so many times before: *Milosevic doesn't* ***mouth*** *platitudes about it not mattering who scores as long as the team wins.* **platitudinous** /ˌplæt.ɪˈtjuː.dɪ.nəs/ [US] /ˌplæt̬.əˈtuː.-dᵊn-/ *adj FORMAL DISAPPROVING*

platonic /pləˈtɒn.ɪk/ [US] /-ˈtɑː.nɪk/ *adj* A platonic relationship or emotion is affectionate but not sexual: *She knew he fancied her, but preferred to keep their relationship platonic.*

platoon /pləˈtuːn/ *group noun* [C] a small group of about 10 or 12 soldiers, with a LIEUTENANT in charge of it

platter /ˈplæt.əʳ/ [US] /ˈplæt̬.ɚ/ *noun* [C] a large plate used for serving food, or a meal with one type of food served on a large plate: *a fish platter*

platypus /ˈplæt.ɪ.pəs/ [US] /ˈplæt̬-/ *noun* [C] (*ALSO* **duck-billed platypus**) an Australian river mammal with a wide beak whose young are born from eggs

plaudit /ˈplɔː.dɪt/ [US] /ˈplɑː-/ *noun* [C usually pl] *FORMAL* praise: *She's received plaudits for her work with homeless people.* ○ *The quality of his photography* ***earned/won*** *him plaudits from the experts.*

plausible /ˈplɔː.zə.bl̩/ [US] /ˈplɑː-/ *adj* **1** seeming likely to be true, or able to be believed: *a plausible explanation/excuse* **2** *DISAPPROVING* describes someone who appears to be honest and truthful, even if they are not: *a plausible salesman* **plausibly** /ˈplɔː.zə.bli/ [US] /ˈplɑː-/ *adv: February's figures cannot plausibly be blamed on flukes or special factors.* **plausibility** /ˌplɔː.zəˈbɪl.ɪ.ti/ [US] /ˌplɑː.-zəˈbɪl.ə.t̬i/ *noun* [U] *In Chapter 2 she goes on to test the plausibility of these assumptions.*

play [ENJOY] /pleɪ/ *verb* [I] When you play, especially as a child, you spend time doing an enjoyable and/or amusing activity: *The children spent the afternoon playing in the garden.* ○ *My daughter used to play* ***with*** *the kids next door.*

play /pleɪ/ *noun* [U] activity that is not serious but done for enjoyment, especially when children enjoy themselves with toys and games: *The kids don't get much time for play in the evenings.* ○ *We watched the children* ***at*** *play in the park.*

• **play on words** an amusing use of a word with more than one meaning or that sounds like another word: *The name of the shop – 'Strata Various' – is a play on words, because it sounds like 'Stradivarius', the famous violin maker.*

playful /ˈpleɪ.fᵊl/ *adj* funny and not serious: *a playful exchange of insults* ○ *He was in a playful mood.* **playfully** /ˈpleɪ.fᵊl.i/ *adv* **playfulness** /ˈpleɪ.fᵊl.nəs/ *noun* [U]

play [GAME] /pleɪ/ *verb* **1** [I or T] to take part in a game or other organized activity: *Do you want to play cards/football (****with*** *us)?* ○ *Irene won't be able to play* ***in*** *the match on Saturday.* ○ *Which team do you play* ***for****?* ○ *Luke plays centre-forward* (= plays in that position within the team). **2** [T] to compete against a person or team in a game: *Who are Aston Villa playing next week?* **3** [T] to hit or kick a ball in a game: *He played the ball back* ***to*** *the goalkeeper.* ○ *A good snooker player takes time deciding which shot to play.* **4** [T] to choose a card, in a card game, from the ones you are holding and put it down on the table: *She played the ace of spades.*

• **play ball** *INFORMAL* to agree to work with or help someone in the way they have suggested: *The family wanted him to be looked after at home, but the insurance company refused to play ball.*

• **play *your* cards right** to behave in the right way so that you get an advantage or succeed in something: *If you play your cards right, you could make quite a lot of money out of this.*

• **play both ends against the middle** to try to get opposing people or groups to fight or disagree so that you will gain something from the situation

• **play fair** to act in a fair and honest way: *It wasn't really playing fair not to tell her the job was already filled.*

• **play the field** to maintain an interest in a number of people or things, especially to become romantically or sexually involved with a number of partners: *Becky's not ready to settle down with one man – she enjoys playing the field too much.*

• **play footsie** to touch someone's feet with your own under the table, usually in order to show sexual interest in them: *She kicked off her shoes and started playing footsie* ***with*** *him.*

• **play the game** to behave fairly: *You should have told them – it wasn't playing the game to keep it secret.*

• **play games** to try to deceive someone: *Don't play games* ***with*** *me!*

• **play hardball** *MAINLY US INFORMAL* to be firm and determined in order to get what you want: *He's a nice guy, but he can play hardball when he needs to.*

• **play for time** to delay until you are ready: *We can't sign the agreement yet – we'll have to play for time.*

play /pleɪ/ *noun* **1** [U] the activity of taking part in a sport or a game: *Rain stopped play during the final of the National Tennis Championship.* **2** [C] *US* a plan or a small set of actions in sport: *The new pitcher made a great play on that throw to first base.*

• **in/out of play** describes a ball that is/is not in a position where it can be hit, kicked, etc: *The ball had gone out of play.* ○ *She managed to keep the ball in play.*

• **make a play for *sth/sb*** to try to obtain something, or start a relationship with someone, sometimes by using a plan: *I wouldn't have made a play for him if I'd known he was married.*

player /ˈpleɪ.əʳ/ [US] /-ɚ/ *noun* [C] **1** someone who takes part in a game or sport: *Each player takes three cards.* ○ *The team has many talented players.* **2** someone who is very involved in an activity or organization: *She was a* ***leading/key*** *player in the reorganization of the health service.*

play [ACT] /pleɪ/ *verb* **1** [I or T] to perform an entertainment or a particular character in a play, film or other entertainment: *In the film version, Kenneth Branagh played the hero.* ○ *North-West Opera played* ***to*** *full houses every night.* ○ *I didn't realize that 'Macbeth' was playing* (= being performed) ***at*** *the Guildhall.* **2** [T] to behave or pretend in a particular way, especially in order to produce a particular effect or result: *to play dead/dumb* ○ *Would you mind playing* ***host*** (= entertaining the guests)*?*

• **play God** to act as if you are in total control of something: *Genetic engineers should not be allowed to play God, interfering with the basic patterns of Nature.*

• **play it cool** to behave in a calm, controlled way, often intentionally appearing not to be interested in the thing that you particularly want to get: *Play it cool – don't let them know how much you need the money.*

• **play *sth* by ear** to decide how to deal with a situation as it develops, rather than acting according to plans made earlier: *I don't know how long I'll continue touring with the band. We've always said we'll just play it by ear.*

• **play to the gallery** to behave in a way intended to make people admire or support you: *Politicians these days are more interested in playing to the gallery than exercising real influence on world events.*

• **play hard to get** to pretend that you are less interested in someone than you really are as a way of making them more interested in you, especially at the start of a romantic relationship: *Why won't you call him back? Are you playing hard to get?*

• **play (merry) hell with *sth*** *INFORMAL* to seriously damage or confuse something: *The power cuts played hell with our computers.*

• **play a joke/trick** to deceive someone for amusement or in order to get an advantage over them: *She loves playing practical jokes* ***on*** *her friends.*

• **play a joke/trick on *sb*** to confuse someone or cause problem for them: *I thought I heard something – my* ***ears*** *must have been playing tricks on me.* ○ *Fate played a cruel trick on him when he was badly injured in his first international game.*

• **play a part** to help to achieve something: *My thanks to everyone who has played a part* ***in*** *saving the hospital.*

• **play (it) safe** to be careful and not take risks: *To play safe, I'd allow an extra ten minutes, just in case.*

• **play silly buggers** *UK SLANG* to behave in a silly, stupid or annoying way: *There'll be a serious accident sooner or later if people don't stop playing silly buggers.*

play /pleɪ/ *noun* [C] a piece of writing that is intended to be acted in a theatre or on radio or television: *a radio play* ○ *"Did you see the play* (= the performance of the play) *on Thursday?" "No, I went on Wednesday night."*

player /ˈpleɪ.əʳ/ [US] /-ɚ/ *noun* [C] **1** *OLD USE* an actor **2** used in the names of some theatre companies: *the Shakespeare Players*

play [PRODUCE SOUNDS/PICTURES] /pleɪ/ *verb* [I or T] **1** to perform music on an instrument or instruments: *He learned to play the clarinet at the age of ten.* ○ [+ two objects] *Play us a song!/Play a song* ***for*** *us!* ○ *On Radio London they play African and South American music as well as rock and pop.* ○ *They could hear a jazz band playing in the distance.* ○ *Play* ***up*** *a bit* (= play louder) *– I can hardly hear you!* **2** to (cause a machine to) produce sound or a picture: *Play the last few minutes of the video again.* ➲See also **playback**.

• **play second fiddle** to be less important or in a weaker position than someone else: *I'm not prepared to play second fiddle* ***to*** *Christina any more – I'm looking for another job!*

playable /ˈpleɪ.ə.bl̩/ *adj* describes a piece of music that is not too difficult for someone to play

player /ˈpleɪ.əʳ/ [US] /-ɚ/ *noun* [C] **1** a person who plays a musical instrument: *a recorder/piano player* **2** a machine for playing music, sound or pictures: *a CD/tape/video player*

play [MOVE] /pleɪ/ *verb* **1** [I or T] to direct or be directed over or onto something: *Firefighters played their* ***hoses onto*** *the base of the fire.* ○ *A fountain was playing* (= sending out water) *in the courtyard outside.* **2** [I + adv or prep] (of something you see, such as light) to move quickly or be seen briefly: *A smile played* ***across/over/on*** *his lips.*

play /pleɪ/ *noun* [U] **1** movement: *the play of moonlight* ***across*** *the water* ○ *the play of emotion* ***across/on*** *his face* **2** when a rope or a structure is free to move, especially a small distance: *Aircraft wings are designed to have a certain amount of play in them.*

• **come into play** (*ALSO* **bring *sth* into play**) If something comes into play, it starts to have a use or an effect in a particular situation, and if it is brought into play, it is given a use or an effect: *In the summer months a different set of climatic factors come into play.* ○ *All the resources and staff available were brought into play to cope with the crisis.*

play [RISK MONEY] /pleɪ/ *verb* [T] to risk money, especially on the results of races or business deals, hoping to win more money: *He plays* ***the horses/the stock market.***

PHRASAL VERBS WITH **play**

▲ **play along** *phrasal verb* to do what someone asks you to do, for a limited period of time: *I know you don't like Jack's idea, but just play along* ***with*** *him for a while.*

▲ **play around** [SILLY] *phrasal verb* (*UK ALSO* **play about**) *INFORMAL* to behave in a silly way: *Stop playing around and get on with your homework!* ○ *I wish you wouldn't play about with that – you'll break it.*

▲ **play around** [SEX] *phrasal verb* (*UK ALSO* **play about**) *INFORMAL DISAPPROVING* If someone who is married or has a serious relationship plays around, they have sex with another person or people: *If she finds out he's been playing around* ***with*** *his secretary, there'll be trouble.*

▲ **play around/about with *sth*** *phrasal verb* to experiment with different methods or different things, before deciding which one to choose: *We've been playing around with* ***ideas*** *for a new TV show.* ○ *Why don't you play about with the different fonts on the computer and see which one you want to use?*

▲ **play at *sth*** *phrasal verb* **1** to pretend to be a particular person or to do a particular thing, usually as a game: *The children were playing at Batman and Robin.* **2** to do something for enjoyment or interest, or without much care and effort, not in a serious way or as a job: *She's only playing at being an actress – she's going off to law school next year.*

• **be playing at *sth*** *UK* If you ask what someone is playing at, you are angry because they are doing something stupid: *What on earth/the hell were you playing at? – You could have got us all killed!*

▲ **play *sth* back** *phrasal verb* [M] If you play back something that has been recorded, you put it through a machine so that you can listen to it or watch it: *The message I recorded for the answering machine sounded terrible when I played it back.*

playback /ˈpleɪ.bæk/ *noun* [C or U] when you play a recording again in order to hear or see something again: *Let's have a playback of those last few frames.* ➲See also **replay** RECORDING.

▲ **play *sth* down** *phrasal verb* [M] to make something seem less important or less bad than it really is: *Military spokespeople tried to play down the seriousness of the disaster.*

▲ **play off** *phrasal verb* to play a game, in a team sport, to decide which side will win: *United and Rangers are playing off for the championship.*

playoff /ˈpleɪ.ɒf/ [US] /-ɑːf/ *noun* [C usually sing] an extra game in a competition played between teams or competitors who have both got the same number of points, in order to decide who wins the competition

▲ **play *sb/sth* off against *sb/sth*** *phrasal verb* [M] to encourage one person or group to compete or argue with another, hoping to get some advantage from this situation: *Management policy seemed to be to play one department off against another.*

▲ **play on/upon *sth*** *phrasal verb* If you play on/upon someone's feelings, you encourage and make unfair use of these feelings in order to get an advantage for yourself: *I hate marketing strategies that play on people's fears and prejudices.*

▲ **play *sth* out** *phrasal verb* [M] to pretend that an imaginary situation or event is really happening: *In the*

P

psychotherapy group, patients were free to play out their fantasies.

▲ **play out** *phrasal verb MAINLY US* When a situation plays out, it happens and develops: *The debate will play out in the meetings and in the media over the next week or two.*

ˌ**play *itself* ˈout** If a situation plays itself out, it develops until nothing more can happen and it is no longer very important: *We were forced to stand back and let the crisis play itself out.*

played-out /ˌpleɪdˈaʊt/ *adj INFORMAL* tired and no longer having power or effectiveness: *I'm about played-out, Jack – it's time I retired.* ○ *FIGURATIVE They won't get people to vote for those played-out old policies.*

▲ **play *sth* up** [EMPHASIZE] *phrasal verb* **[M]** to emphasize a particular quality or part of something, or make it seem more important than it really is, usually for your own advantage: *The official report plays up the likely benefits of the scheme, but glosses over the costs.*

▲ **play *(sb)* up** [CAUSE PAIN] *phrasal verb UK INFORMAL* to cause someone pain: *His knee's been playing him up again.* ○ *My stomach was playing up so I had to go home.*

▲ **play up** [CHILD] *phrasal verb UK* When children play up, they behave badly: *The boys have been playing up at school again.*

▲ **play up** [MACHINE] *phrasal verb* If a machine plays up, it does not work as it should: *The starter motor was playing up again.*

▲ **play up to *sb*** *phrasal verb* to try to make someone like you and treat you well by behaving in a way you think will please them: *Julia knows how to play up to the supervisors – she can always get time off work when she wants it.*

▲ **play with *sth*** [IDEA] *phrasal verb* to consider an idea or plan: *Patricia and I were playing **(around)** with the **idea/possibility** of moving to Glasgow.*

• **have *sth* to play with** *INFORMAL* If you have a particular amount of time or money to play with, that amount is available for you to use: *Having only £200 to play with, they bought a second-hand piano.*

▲ **play with *sth*** [SUBSTANCE] *phrasal verb DISAPPROVING* to keep touching and moving something around with no purpose or interest: *Stop playing with your hair!* ○ *She was just playing with her food – she didn't eat a mouthful.*

▲ **play with *yourself*** [SEX] *phrasal verb* **[R]** *OFFENSIVE FOR* **masturbate**

• **Go play with yourself!**/ *OFFENSIVE* a rude way of telling someone to go away and stop annoying you: *Oh, go play with yourself!*

P

playacting /ˈpleɪ.æk.tɪŋ/ Ⓤⓢ /-t̬ɪŋ/ *noun* **[U]** when you behave in a way that does represent your true feelings in order to hide them from other people or to amuse others: *Don't take any notice of him – he's just playacting.*
play-act /ˈpleɪ.ækt/ *verb* **[I]**

playbill /ˈpleɪ.bɪl/ *noun* **[C]** a piece of paper advertising a play and giving information about where and when it is being performed

playboy /ˈpleɪ.bɔɪ/ *noun* **[C]** a rich man who spends his time and money on luxuries and a life of pleasure: *a playboy lifestyle*

Play-Doh /ˈpleɪ.dəʊ/ Ⓤⓢ /-doʊ/ *noun* **[U]** *TRADEMARK* a soft substance produced in different colours, used especially by children to make shapes and models

playful /ˈpleɪ.fəl/ *adj* ➲See at **play** ENJOY.

playground /ˈpleɪ.graʊnd/ *noun* **1** **[C]** an area designed for children to play in outside, especially at a school **2** **[S]** a place where a particular group of people enjoy themselves: *This area of the coast is the playground **of** the rich and famous.* **3** **[C]** *US FOR* **recreation ground**

playgroup /ˈpleɪ.gruːp/ *noun* **[C]** (*ALSO* **playschool**) *UK* an organized group for children aged between 3 and 5 to play and learn together informally at regular times in a place outside their homes, run by parents or trained leaders

playhouse [THEATRE] /ˈpleɪ.haʊs/ *noun* **[C]** a theatre. This is now only used in the names of theatres: *the La Jolla Playhouse in San Diego* ○ *the Edinburgh Playhouse*

playhouse [TOY HOUSE] /ˈpleɪ.haʊs/ *noun* **[C]** (*UK ALSO* **Wendy house**) a small structure that looks like a house, for children to play in

ˈ**playing ˌcard** *noun* **[C]** one of a set of 52 small rectangular pieces of stiff paper, each with a number and a design showing one of four suits printed on it, used in games

ˈ**playing ˌfield** *noun* **[C]** a large area of ground where sport is played: *The school playing fields were marked out for football and rugby.*

playmate /ˈpleɪ.meɪt/ *noun* **[C]** a friend, especially another child, with whom a child plays often: *We were childhood playmates.*

playpen /ˈpleɪ.pen/ *noun* **[C]** a small structure with bars or a net around the sides but open at the top, which you can put a baby in to play safely

playroom /ˈpleɪ.rʊm/ /-ruːm/ *noun* **[C]** a room intended for children to play in

playschool /ˈpleɪ.skuːl/ *noun* **[C]** *UK* a **playgroup**

PlayStation /ˈpleɪˌsteɪ.ʃən/ *noun* **[C]** *TRADEMARK* a machine that you use to play games on your television

plaything /ˈpleɪ.θɪŋ/ *noun* **[C]** **1** an object used for pleasure or amusement, such as a child's toy: *I keep all the children's playthings in that big cupboard.* ○ *"Limousines and yachts are the playthings of the rich," he said dismissively.* **2** someone who is considered or treated without respect and forced to do things for someone else's pleasure or benefit: *These men's magazines just treat women as playthings.*

playtime /ˈpleɪ.taɪm/ *noun* **[U]** a period of time, especially during school hours, when children can play outside: *You'll have to stay in at playtime today, because it's raining.*

playwright /ˈpleɪ.raɪt/ *noun* **[C]** a person who writes plays

plaza /ˈplɑː.zə/ *noun* **[C]** **1** an open area or square in a town, especially in Spanish-speaking countries **2** a group of buildings including shops designed as a single development within a town

plc, PLC /ˌpiː.elˈsiː/ *noun* **[C]** *ABBREVIATION FOR* public limited company: a British company whose shares can be bought and sold by the public and whose debts are limited if it fails financially: *J Sainsbury plc*

.plc.uk /dɒt.piː.eˌlsiː.dɒt.juːˈkeɪ/ Ⓤⓢ /dɑːt.piː.eˌlsiː.dɑːt-/ the last part of an Internet address of a British company whose shares can be bought by members of the public

plea [REQUEST] /pliː/ *noun* **[C]** *FORMAL* an urgent and emotional request: *He **made** a plea **for** help/mercy.*

plea [STATEMENT] /pliː/ *noun* **[C]** *LEGAL* the answer that a person gives in court to the accusation that they have committed a crime: *Mr Wilson **entered** a plea **of** not guilty.*

ˈ**plea ˌbargaining** *noun* **[U]** when an agreement is made that someone accused of a crime will not be charged with a more serious crime if they admit that they are guilty of a less serious one

plead [REQUEST] /pliːd/ *verb* **[I]** **pleaded** or *US ALSO* **pled**, **pleaded** or *US ALSO* **pled** to make an urgent, emotional statement or request for something: *He was on his knees, pleading **for** mercy/forgiveness.* ○ *She appeared on television to plead **with** the kidnappers.* ○ **[+ speech]** *"Give us more time," they pleaded.* **pleading** /ˈpliː.dɪŋ/ *adj*: *a pleading tone of voice* **pleadingly** /ˈpliː.dɪŋ.li/ *adv*

plead [STATE] /pliːd/ *verb* **[I; L only + adj; T]** **pleaded** or *US ALSO* **pled, pleaded** or *US ALSO* **pled** *FORMAL* to make a statement of what you believe to be true, especially in support of something or someone or in answer to an accusation in a law court: *LEGAL The defendant pleaded **not guilty/innocent** to robbery with violence.* ○ *LEGAL They paid a high-powered attorney to plead their **case*** (= argue for them in court). ○ *LEGAL The judge ruled her unfit to plead* (= to answer a legal charge) *on the grounds of insanity.*

• **plead ignorance** *FORMAL* to say that you do not know about something: *He pleaded ignorance when they found the package in his suitcase.*

pleasant /ˈplez.ənt/ *adj* enjoyable, attractive, friendly, or easy to like: *a pleasant climate/smile/person* ○ *a pleasant day/surprise* ○ *Harold did his best to be* *pleasant* **to** *the old man.* ○ *It was pleasant* **to** *sit down after standing for hours.* **pleasantly** /ˈplez.ᵊnt.li/ *adv: They treated me pleasantly enough.* ○ *Jacqui was pleasantly* **surprised** *to get a B for history.* **pleasantness** /ˈplez.ᵊnt.nəs/ *noun* [U]

pleasantry /ˈplez.ᵊn.tri/ *noun* [C usually pl] *FORMAL* a polite and often slightly amusing remark, usually made to help other people feel relaxed: *After* **exchanging** *pleasantries, the delegation revealed the purpose of their visit.*

please POLITE REQUEST /pliːz/ *exclamation* **1** used to make a request more polite: *Could I have two cups of coffee and a tea, please?* ○ *Please remember to close the windows before you leave.* **2** used to add force to a request or demand: *Please, David, put the knife down.* ○ *Oh, please. Do shut up!* **3** *UK* used especially by children to a teacher or other adult in order to get their attention: *Please, Miss, I know the answer!* **4** used when accepting something politely or enthusiastically: *"More potatoes?" "Please."* ○ *"May I bring my husband?" "Please do."* ○ *MAINLY UK "Oh, yes please," shouted the children, when I suggested a trip to the zoo.*
• **if you please** *OLD-FASHIONED OR FORMAL* used to make a request more polite: *Take your seats, ladies and gentlemen, if you please.*

please MAKE HAPPY /pliːz/ *verb* **1** [I or T] to make someone feel happy or satisfied, or to give someone pleasure: *I only got married to please my parents.* ○ *He was always a good boy, very friendly and eager to please.* ○ [+ obj + to infinitive] *It always pleases me* **to** *see a well-designed book!* **2** [I] *SLIGHTLY FORMAL* to want, like or choose, when used with words such as 'whatever', 'whoever' and 'anywhere': *She thinks she can just do* **whatever/as** *she pleases.* ○ *I shall go out with whoever I please.*
• **please God** used to express a strong hope: *It'll be finished by Christmas, please God.*
• **please yourself** *INFORMAL* to do whatever you choose to do, often used in a slightly rude way by someone who does not agree with or care about what you to do: *"I can't stand this place – I'm going home." "Please yourself."*

pleased /pliːzd/ *adj* happy or satisfied: *a pleased expression/smile* ○ *Are you pleased* **about** *John's promotion?* ○ *We're so pleased* **that** *you're able to come to the wedding.* ○ *I'm really pleased* **with** *your work this term.* ○ *I'm pleased* **to** *hear you're feeling better.*
• **be pleased to** *do sth* to be very willing to do something: *The personnel manager will be pleased to advise you.* ○ *I'm* **only too** (= very) *pleased to help.*
• **(as) pleased as Punch** *OLD-FASHIONED* very pleased: *She was as pleased as Punch about the news.*
• **(I'm) pleased to meet you** a polite way of greeting someone when you meet them for the first time
• **pleased with** *yourself* happy and satisfied about something good that you have done or that has happened to you: *Simon's looking very pleased with himself today.*

pleasing /ˈpliː.zɪŋ/ *adj FORMAL* giving a feeling of satisfaction or enjoyment: *a pleasing performance* ○ *The music was very pleasing* **to** *the ear* (= to listen to). ○ *It was pleasing* **to** *know that the presentation had gone so well.* **pleasingly** /ˈpliː.zɪŋ.li/ *adv: pleasingly smooth/soft*

please ANNOYANCE /pliːz/ *FORMAL* **if you please** used to express surprise and annoyance: *They want £200, if you please, just to replace a couple of broken windows!* ➔See also **if you please** at **please** POLITE REQUEST.

pleasure /ˈpleʒ.əʳ/ ⓤ /-ɚ-/ *noun* [C or U] enjoyment, happiness or satisfaction, or something that gives this: *His visits gave his grandparents such pleasure.* ○ *Why do so many boys* **take** *pleasure* **in** *torturing insects and small animals.* ○ [+ to infinitive] *It was such a pleasure* **to** *meet you.* ○ *He wrote an article on the pleasures and pains* **of** *camping.* ○ *Smoking is one of my few pleasures.*
• **it's a pleasure** (*ALSO* **it's** *my* **pleasure**) a polite way of replying to someone who has thanked you: *"It was so kind of you to give us a lift." "Don't mention it – it was a pleasure."*
• **with pleasure** *FORMAL* willingly: *"Would you mind holding the door open for me, please?" "Oh, with pleasure."*

pleasurable /ˈpleʒ.ᵊr.ə.bl̩/ ⓤ /-ɚ.ɚ-/ *adj SLIGHTLY FORMAL* enjoyable: *a pleasurable evening/meal* ○ *a pleasurable sensation*

pleat /pliːt/ *noun* [C] a narrow fold in a piece of cloth made by pressing or sewing two parts of the cloth together **pleated** /ˈpliː.tɪd/ ⓤ /-t̬ɪd/ *adj: a pleated skirt*

pleb /pleb/ *noun* [C] *INFORMAL DISAPPROVING* a person of a low social class **plebby** /ˈpleb.i/ *adj: I can't bear her plebby friends.*

plebeian /pləˈbiː.ən/ *adj FORMAL DISAPPROVING* belonging to a low social class: *He used to make fun of what he called her 'plebeian origins'.* ○ *He retained a plebeian taste in food and drink.*

plebiscite /ˈpleb.ɪ.sɪt/ ⓤ /-ə.saɪt/ *noun FORMAL* a **referendum**

plectrum (*plural* **plectrums** or **plectra**) /ˈplek.trəm/ *noun* [C] (*INFORMAL* **pick**) a small thin piece of plastic, metal etc. which is held between the fingers and thumb and used for playing instruments such as the guitar

pled /pled/ *US AND SCOTTISH ENGLISH past simple and past participle of* **plead**

pledge /pledʒ/ *noun* [C] a serious or formal promise, especially one to give money or to be a friend, or something that you give as a sign that you will keep a promise: [+ *to* infinitive] *All the candidates have* **given/made** *pledges* **not** *to raise taxes if they are elected.* ○ *Thousands of people* **made** *pledges* (= promised to give money) *to the Children in Need charity campaign.* ○ *I give you this ring as a pledge* **of** *my everlasting love for you.*
• **take/sign the pledge** *UK OLD-FASHIONED OR HUMOROUS* to make a formal promise to stop drinking alcohol: *What's this then, you're only drinking orange juice – have you signed the pledge or something?*

pledge /pledʒ/ *verb* [T] to make a serious or formal promise to give or do something: *We are asking people to pledge their* **support** *for our campaign.* ○ *If you join the armed forces, you have to pledge* **allegiance** *to your country.* ○ *So far, £50 000 has been pledged* (= people have promised to pay this amount) *in response to the appeal.* ○ [+ *to* infinitive] *Both sides have pledged* **to** *end the fighting.* ○ *I've been pledged* **to** *secrecy.*

plenary /ˈpliː.nə.ri/ ⓤ /-nɚ.i/ *adj SPECIALIZED* describes a meeting at which all the members of a group or organization are present, especially at a *CONFERENCE*: *a plenary session of the UN Security Council*

plenary /ˈpliː.nə.ri/ ⓤ /-nɚ.i/ *noun* [C] *SPECIALIZED* a plenary meeting

plenipotentiary /ˌplen.ɪ.pəʊˈten.tʃ·r.i/ ⓤ /-poʊˈten.tʃi.er-/ *noun* [C] *OLD-FASHIONED FORMAL* a person who has the authority to act as the representative of his or her country, especially in another country **plenipotentiary** /ˌplen.ɪ.pəʊˈten.tʃ·r.i/ ⓤ /-poʊˈten.tʃi.er-/ *adj: a plenipotentiary diplomat/role*

plenty /ˈplen.ti/ ⓤ /-t̬i/ *pronoun, noun, adv* (the state of having) enough or more than enough, or a large amount: *"Would you like some more wine?" "No thanks, I've had plenty."* ○ *Don't grab at the balloons, children – there are plenty* **for** *everyone.* ○ *We've got plenty* **of** *time before we need to leave for the airport.* ○ *They've always had plenty* **of** *money.* ○ *There's plenty* **to** *do here.* ○ *US INFORMAL This car cost me plenty* (= a lot of money). ○ *There's plenty* **more** *beer in the fridge.*
• **be plenty more where** *sb/sth* **came from** *INFORMAL* to be a lot more things or people of the same type available: *Have another sandwich – there's plenty more where that came from.*

plentiful /ˈplen.tɪ.fᵊl/ ⓤ /-t̬ɪ-/ *adj* If something is plentiful, there is a lot of it available: *Strawberries are plentiful in the summer.* ○ *I took a plentiful* **supply** *of games to keep the children amused.* **plentifully** /ˈplen.tɪ.fᵊl.i/ ⓤ /-t̬ɪ-/ *adv*

plethora /ˈpleθ.ᵊr.ə/ ⓤ /-ɚ.ə/ *noun* [S] *SLIGHTLY FORMAL* a very large amount of something, especially a larger amount than you need, want or can deal with: *There's* **a** *plethora* **of** *books about the royal family.* ○ *The plethora* **of** *rules and regulations is both contradictory and confusing.*

P

pleurisy /ˈplʊə.rə.si/ [US] /ˈplʊr.ə-/ *noun* [U] a serious illness in which the covering of the lungs becomes red and swollen, and which causes sharp pain when breathing

Plexiglas /ˈplek.si.glɑːs/ [US] /-glæs/ *noun* [U] *US TRADEMARK FOR* **Perspex**

pliable /ˈplaɪ.ə.bl̩/ *adj* **1** A pliable substance bends easily without breaking or cracking: *Some kinds of plastic become pliable if they're heated.* **2** *OFTEN DISAPPROVING* A pliable person is easily influenced and controlled by other people: *He wanted a sweet, pliable, obedient wife.* **pliability** /ˌplaɪ.əˈbɪl.ɪ.ti/ [US] /-ə.t̬i/ *noun* [U]

pliant /ˈplaɪ.ᵊnt/ *adj* **1** Pliant people are easily influenced or controlled by other people: *I don't think it's a good thing for children to be too pliant.* **2** able to bend easily without breaking: *These toys are made of pliant rubber, so they won't break.* **3** being able and willing to accept change or new ideas: *The management has adopted a more pliant position, and has agreed to listen to the staff's requests.* **pliancy** /ˈplaɪ.ᵊnt.si/ *noun* [U] **pliantly** /ˈplaɪ.ᵊnt.li/ *adv*

pliers /ˈplaɪ.əz/ [US] /-ɚz/ *plural noun* a small tool with two handles for holding or pulling small things like nails, or for cutting wire: *Pass me that* ***pair of*** *pliers, please.*

plight [CONDITION] /plaɪt/ *noun* [S] an unpleasant condition, especially a serious, sad or difficult one: ***the plight of*** *the poor/homeless* ○ *Few of us can be unmoved by the plight of the Romanian orphans.*

plight [MARRY] /plaɪt/ *verb OLD USE OR HUMOROUS* **plight** ***your*** **troth** to (promise to) marry

plimsoll /ˈplɪmp.sᵊlz/ *noun* [C] *UK OLD-FASHIONED* a flat light shoe made of heavy cloth with a rubber sole, worn especially for sports

Plimsoll line /ˈplɪm.sɒlˌlaɪn/ [US] /ˈplɪm.sɑːl̩laɪn/ *noun* [C usually sing] (*ALSO* **Plimsoll mark**) a line painted on the outside of a ship which shows how deep it is legally allowed to go down into the water when it is loaded

plinth /plɪntθ/ *noun* [C] a square block, especially of stone, on which a column or a statue stands

plod [WALK] /plɒd/ [US] /plɑːd/ *verb* [I + adv or prep] **-dd-** to walk taking slow steps, as if your feet are heavy: *We plodded through the mud.* ○ *Despite the wind and the rain, they plodded* ***on*** *until they reached the cottage.*

plod [WORK] /plɒd/ [US] /plɑːd/ *verb* [I + adv or prep] **-dd-** to work slowly and continuously, but without imagination, enthusiasm or interest: *For years, he's plodded* ***away at*** *the same dull routine job.* ○ *Alex is just plodding* ***along*** *at school, making very little progress.* **plodder** /ˈplɒd.əʳ/ [US] /ˈplɑː.dɚ/ *noun* [C] *Dennis is a bit of a plodder, but he gets the job done in the end.* **plodding** /ˈplɒd.ɪŋ/ [US] /ˈplɑː.dɪŋ/ *adj*

plonk [SOUND] /plɒŋk/ [US] /plɑːŋk/ *noun* [U] (*US ALSO* **plunk**) *INFORMAL* a hollow sound like that made when an object is dropped heavily onto a surface: *the plonk of a tennis ball*

plonk /plɒŋk/ [US] /plɑːŋk/ *adv* (*US ALSO* **plunk**) *INFORMAL* making a plonk sound: *I heard something go plonk.* ○ *An apple landed plonk* ***on*** *the ground.*

plonk /plɒŋk/ [US] /plɑːŋk/ *verb* [I usually + adv or prep] (*US ALSO* **plunk**) *INFORMAL I really enjoy plonking* ***away on*** *the piano* (= playing, usually not very well, by hitting the keys hard).

plonk [PUT] /plɒŋk/ [US] /plɑːŋk/ *verb* [I or T; usually + adv or prep] (*US USUALLY* **plunk**) *INFORMAL* to put something down heavily and without taking care: *Just plonk the shopping* ***(down) on*** *the table, and come and have a cup of tea.* ○ [R] *Come in and plonk yourselves* ***(down)*** (= sit down) *anywhere you like.*

plonk [WINE] /plɒŋk/ [US] /plɑːŋk/ *noun* [U] *MAINLY UK INFORMAL* cheap wine, especially wine that is not of good quality: *We had pizza and a bottle of plonk.*

plonker /ˈplɒŋ.kəʳ/ [US] /ˈplɑːŋ.kɚ/ *noun* [C] *UK INFORMAL* a foolish or stupid person: *What did you do that for, you plonker?*

plop [SOUND] /plɒp/ [US] /plɑːp/ *noun* [S] *INFORMAL* a soft sound like that of something solid dropping lightly into a liquid: *The stone fell into the water with* ***a*** *plop.* **plop** /plɒp/ [US] /plɑːp/ *adv: Her earring went plop into the soup.*

plop /plɒp/ [US] /plɑːp/ *verb* [I usually + adv or prep] **-pp-** *INFORMAL* to fall with a soft sound: *I noticed drops of water plopping* ***onto*** *the carpet.*

plop [PUT] /plɒp/ [US] /plɑːp/ *verb* [I or T; + adv or prep] **-pp-** to sit down or land heavily or without taking care, or to put something down without taking care: *He came and plopped* ***down*** *next to me.* ○ *Lynn plopped a paper cup* ***down*** *beside her.*

plot [SECRET PLAN] /plɒt/ [US] /plɑːt/ *noun* [C] a secret plan made by several people to do something that is wrong, harmful or not legal, especially to do damage to a person or a government: *The plot was discovered before it was carried out.* ○ [+ to infinitive] *The police have* ***foiled*** *a plot* ***to*** *assassinate the president.*

• **The plot thickens.** *HUMOROUS* said when a situation suddenly becomes more complicated or mysterious: *"Now there are two men phoning her up all the time." "The plot thickens!"*

plot /plɒt/ [US] /plɑːt/ *verb* **-tt- 1** [I or T] to make a secret plan to do something wrong, harmful or illegal: *The army is plotting the overthrow of the government.* ○ *I can't believe that he's plotting* ***against*** *his own father.* ○ [+ to infinitive] *They're plotting* ***(together) to*** *take over the company.* **2** [T] *HUMOROUS* to make a secret plan to do something amusing or fun to or for someone: [+ to infinitive] *They're plotting* ***to*** *play a trick on their brother.* ○ *He's plotting a surprise party for his wife's birthday.*

plotter /ˈplɒt.əʳ/ [US] /ˈplɑː.t̬ɚ/ *noun* [C] someone who plots

plot [STORY] /plɒt/ [US] /plɑːt/ *noun* [C] the story of a book, film, play, etc: *The film has a very simple plot.* ○ *The plots* ***of*** *his books are basically all the same.*

plot /plɒt/ [US] /plɑːt/ *verb* [T] **-tt-** to write the plot for something: *So far I've only plotted* ***(out)*** *the story in a rough form.*

plot [MARK] /plɒt/ [US] /plɑːt/ *verb* [T] **-tt- 1** to mark or draw something on a piece of paper or a map **2** to make marks to show the position, movement or development of something, usually in the form of lines or curves between a series of points on a map or piece of paper: *Radar operators plotted the* ***course*** *of the incoming missile.* ○ *We've plotted our projected costs for the coming year, and they show a big increase.*

plotter /ˈplɒt.əʳ/ [US] /ˈplɑː.t̬ɚ/ *noun* [C] a device which marks things, such as the position of a ship or aircraft, on a map or piece of paper

plot [GROUND] /plɒt/ [US] /plɑːt/ *noun* [C] **1** a small piece of land that has been marked or measured for a particular purpose: *a vegetable plot* ○ *There are several plots* ***of land*** *for sale.* **2** *US FOR* **ground plan** BUILDING

plough *UK, US* **plow** /plaʊ/ *noun* [C] a large farming tool with blades which digs the earth in fields so that seeds can be planted ➲See also **snowplough** VEHICLE.

• **under the plough** *FORMAL* describes land on which crops are grown: *These fields have been under the plough for centuries.*

the Plough *UK noun* [S] (*US* **the Big Dipper**) a group of seven bright stars, which can only be seen in the northern part of the world

plough *UK, US* **plow** /plaʊ/ *verb* [I or T] to dig land with a plough: *Farmers start ploughing in the spring.* ○ *We're going to plough the top field next week.* ○ *Large areas of grazing land have been ploughed* ***up*** *to grow wheat.*

ploughed *UK, US* **plowed** /plaʊd/ *adj* dug ready for planting seeds: *You shouldn't walk over ploughed* ***fields.***

PHRASAL VERBS WITH **plough**

▲ **plough *sth* back/in** [DIG] *phrasal verb* to dig the roots and other remaining parts of a crop into the earth to make the soil more healthy

▲ **plough *sth* back** [SPEND] *phrasal verb* to spend the money that a business has earned on improving that business: *All the profits are being ploughed back* ***into*** *the company.*

▲ **plough into *sth/sb*** [HIT] *phrasal verb* If a vehicle ploughs into something or someone, it hits the object or person with great force: *Many people were injured when the train came off the rails and ploughed into the bank.*

▲ **plough *sth* into *sth*** [INVEST] *phrasal verb INFORMAL* to invest money in a business, especially to help make it

P

successful or to make more money: *They ploughed all their savings into their daughter's business.*

▲ **plough on** *phrasal verb* to continue doing something although it is difficult or boring: *He could see that she didn't like what he was saying, but he ploughed on* (= continued talking) *regardless.* ○ *It would be a mistake to plough on* ***with*** *this scheme – it'll never work.*

▲ **plough through** ***sth*** *phrasal verb* **1** *INFORMAL* to go through a substance or an area of something with difficulty: *We ploughed through the mud.* **2** to finish reading, eating or dealing with something with difficulty: *I've got an enormous pile of papers to plough through.* ○ *You'll never manage to plough through all that food.*

ploughman's (lunch) /ˌplaʊ.mənzˈlʌntʃ/ *noun* [C] *plural* **ploughman's (lunches)** *UK* a small meal of bread, cheese and PICKLE eaten in the middle of the day, especially served in a pub: *I had a ploughman's in The Bull.*

ploughshare *UK, US* **plowshare** /ˈplaʊ.ʃeəʳ/ [US] /-ʃer/ *noun* [C] the sharp blade of a PLOUGH

plover /ˈplʌv.əʳ/ [US] /-ɚ/ *noun* [C] *plural* **plovers** or **plover** a bird with a short tail and long legs, which is found mainly by the sea or in areas covered with grass

ploy /plɔɪ/ *noun* [C] something that is done or said in order to get an advantage, often dishonestly: *There are various ploys we can* ***use*** *if necessary.* ○ [+ **to infinitive**] *He only said he had a meeting as a ploy* ***to*** *get her to leave.*

pluck [REMOVE] /plʌk/ *verb* **1** [T] to pull something, especially with a sudden movement, in order to remove it: *Caged birds sometimes pluck* ***out*** *their breast feathers.* ○ *He plucked the letter* ***from/out of*** *my hand, and ran off with it.* ○ *Do you pluck your eyebrows* (= remove some of the hairs from them to give them a better shape)*?* **2** [T] to remove the feathers from a chicken or other bird so that it can be cooked and eaten **3** [T **usually passive**] to remove someone suddenly from a situation that is ordinary: *He was plucked* ***from obscurity*** *to star in the film.* **4** [T] to remove someone quickly from a dangerous or difficult situation: *The last passengers were plucked* ***from*** *the ship just seconds before it sank.*

● **pluck** ***sth*** **out of the air** to say something quickly, usually because a reply is expected, without having thought about it or made certain it is correct: *"Where did you get those figures from?" "Oh, I just plucked them out of the air."*

pluck [BRAVERY] /plʌk/ *noun* [U] *INFORMAL* bravery and a strong desire to succeed: *She* ***showed*** *a lot of pluck in standing up to her boss.*

● **pluck up** ***your*** **courage** (*ALSO* **pluck up (the) courage to** ***do sth***) *INFORMAL* to force yourself to be brave enough to do something, although you are frightened or anxious about it: *He finally plucked up courage to ask her to marry him.* ○ *I'd love to do a parachute jump, but I can't pluck up the/enough courage.*

plucky /ˈplʌk.i/ *adj INFORMAL* brave: *It was plucky of you to chase after the burglar.*

pluck [MUSIC] /plʌk/ *verb* [I **or** T] (*US ALSO* **pick**) to pull and then release the strings of a musical instrument with your finger to play notes: *He sat on the bed, idly plucking* ***(at)*** *the strings of his guitar.*

▲ **pluck at** ***sth*** *phrasal verb* to pull something with your fingers again and again, using quick, small movements: *I felt a small hand plucking at my jacket.*

plug [ELECTRICAL DEVICE] /plʌg/ *noun* [C] **1** a small plastic or rubber object with two or three metal pins which is fixed to the end of a wire on a piece of electrical equipment, and which is pushed into a special opening in a wall in order to connect the equipment to a supply of electricity: *a three-pin/two-pin plug* ○ *to fit/change a plug* ○ *If a plug is wired incorrectly, it can be dangerous.* **2** *MAINLY UK INFORMAL* an electric SOCKET: *Is there a plug in the bedroom that I can use for my hairdryer?* **3** *US FOR* **jack plug 4** *INFORMAL FOR* **spark plug** ENGINE

plug [FOR HOLE] /plʌg/ *noun* [C] **1** a small piece of rubber, plastic, wood, etc. that fits into a hole in order to close it ➲See also **earplug**. **2** a round piece of rubber or plastic that fits into the hole in a sink or a bath: *a bath plug* ○ *Put the plug in the sink and run some water.* **3** a small piece of plastic or wood that you put into a hole in a

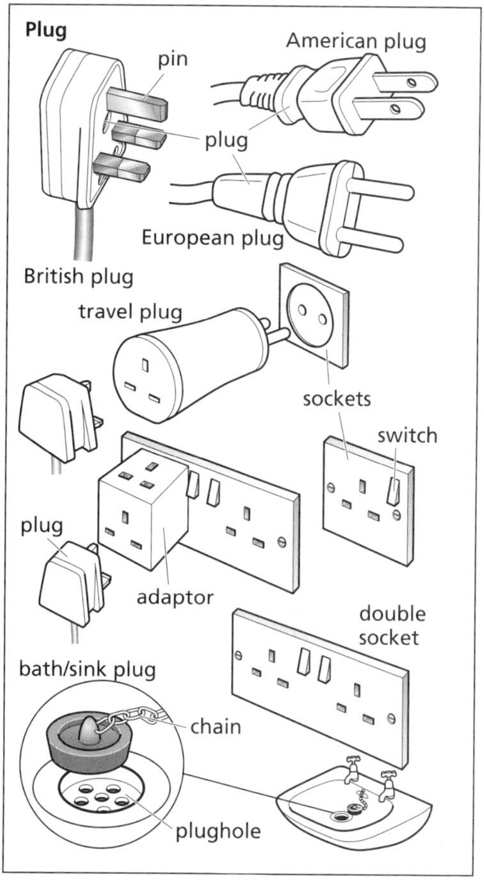
Plug
pin
American plug
plug
European plug
British plug
travel plug
sockets
switch
plug
adaptor
double socket
bath/sink plug
chain
plughole

wall before putting a screw into it **4** a small, tightly twisted or squeezed piece of material such as COTTON WOOL

plug /plʌg/ *verb* [T] **-gg-** to fill a hole with a piece of suitable material: *Have you plugged that leak* (= stopped it by filling the hole) *in the pipe?* ○ *My nose was bleeding and I plugged it* ***with*** *cotton wool.*

plug [ADVERTISE] /plʌg/ *verb* [T] **-gg-** to advertise something by talking about it a lot or praising it, especially on the radio or television: *That interview was just a way for him to plug his new book.* ○ *They're plugging this new chocolate bar everywhere at the moment.*

plug /plʌg/ *noun* [C] the act of telling people publicly about a product, event, etc: *She never misses an opportunity to get in a plug* ***for*** *her new film.*

plug [SHOOT] /plʌg/ *verb* [T] **-gg-** *US SLANG* to shoot someone with a gun: *Sure, boss, we plugged the guy* ***(full of lead)****.*

PHRASAL VERBS WITH **plug** ▼

▲ **plug away** *phrasal verb INFORMAL* to work hard and in a determined way, especially at something that you find difficult: *Katie has been plugging away* ***at*** *her homework for hours.*

▲ **plug** ***(sth)*** **in/plug** ***(sth)*** **into** ***sth*** *phrasal verb* to connect an electrical device to an electrical system or device so that it can be used, by pushing its plug into a SOCKET: *Of course the radio isn't working – you haven't plugged it in!* ○ *I want to plug the kettle into the right-hand socket.* ○ *Can you show me where the microphone plugs into the tape recorder?* ○ *The keyboard plugs in at the back of the computer.*

▲ **plug** ***(sth/sb)*** **into** ***sth*** *phrasal verb INFORMAL* to make something or someone fit well or have good connections with something: *This new product line should be able to plug into our existing distribution* ***network****.*

ˌplug and ˈplay *noun* [U] (*WRITTEN ABBREVIATION* **PnP**) a feature of a computer system which allows an electronic device to be used as soon as it is connected to a computer

plughole /ˈplʌg.həʊl/ ⓤ /-hoʊl/ *noun* [C] a hole in a bath, sink, etc. through which water flows away and into which you can put a PLUG FOR HOLE

plugin, **plug-in** /ˈplʌg.ɪn/ *noun* [C] a small computer program that makes a larger one work faster or have more features ⊃Compare **patch** COMPUTER.

plum FRUIT /plʌm/ *noun* [C or U] a small round fruit with a thin smooth red, purple or yellow skin, sweet soft flesh, and a single large hard seed: *plum jam* ○ *a plum tree* ⊃See picture **Fruit** on page Centre 1
plum /plʌm/ *adj* (*ALSO* **plum-coloured**) having a dark red-dish purple colour: *a plum-coloured dress*
plummy /ˈplʌm.i/ *adj* having the taste or dark reddish purple colour of plums: *This wine has an almost plummy flavour.* ⊃See also **plummy**.

plum GOOD /plʌm/ *adj* [before n] **plummer**, **plummest** very good and worth having: *How did you manage to get such a plum job?*

plumage /ˈpluː.mɪdʒ/ *noun* [U] a bird's covering of feathers: *Male peacocks have beautiful plumage.*
plume /pluːm/ *noun* **1** [C usually pl] a large feather: *fans made of ostrich plumes* ⊃See also **nom de plume**. **2** [C] a decoration which looks like several large feathers tied together and which is worn on the heads of horses or the hats of soldiers during particular ceremonies: *The coffin was drawn by horses with black plumes.* **3** a **plume of dust/smoke, etc.** a tall, thin mass of smoke, dust or similar substance, that rises up into the air: *After the explosion, a plume of smoke could be seen in the sky for miles around.*
plumed /pluːmd/ *adj* [before n] *The dancers wore plumed headdresses* (= with a decoration which looked like several large feathers tied together).

plumb WATER /plʌm/ *verb* [T] to supply a building or a device with water pipes, or to connect a building or a device to a water pipe: *We've discovered that our house isn't plumbed properly.* ○ *I think we can plumb the new bath into the existing pipes.* ○ *Have you plumbed the dishwasher in yet?*
plumber /ˈplʌm.əʳ/ ⓤ /-ɚ/ *noun* [C] a person whose job is to supply and connect, or repair water pipes, baths, toi-lets, etc: *When is the plumber coming to mend the burst pipe?*
plumbing /ˈplʌm.ɪŋ/ *noun* [U] **1** the water pipes and similar systems in a building: *There's something wrong with the plumbing.* **2** the work of connecting water and other pipes in a building: *We did all the plumbing (work) in our house ourselves.*

plumb EXACTLY /plʌm/ *adv* *INFORMAL* exactly: *The hotel is plumb in the middle of the town.* ○ *He hit me plumb on the nose.*

plumb COMPLETELY /plʌm/ *adv* *US INFORMAL* completely: *I plumb forgot your birthday.*

plumb STRAIGHT /plʌm/ *adj* [after v] *SPECIALIZED* exactly straight, usually describing a vertical surface or line: *When you hang a door, you need to make sure that it is both level and plumb.*
● **out of plumb** not straight vertically: *The external wall is out of plumb by half a metre.*

plumb DEEP /plʌm/ *verb* [T] **1** *SPECIALIZED* to measure how deep something is, especially water **2** to understand or discover all about something: *Now that she had begun, she wanted to plumb her own childhood further.*
● **plumb the depths** to reach the lowest point: *Roy plumbed the depths of despair when his wife left him.* ○ *HUMOROUS They must be really plumbing the depths* (= must have been unable to find anyone better) *if they're offering the job to her.*

ˈplumb ˌline *noun* [C] a piece of string with a weight fixed to one end, which is used either to test whether something is vertical, such as a wall, is exactly straight, or to find the depth of water

plume /pluːm/ *noun* [C] ⊃See at **plumage**.

plumed /pluːmd/ *adj* [before n] ⊃See at **plumage**.

plummet /ˈplʌm.ɪt/ *verb* [I] to fall very quickly and suddenly: *House prices have plummeted in recent months.* ○ *Several large rocks were sent plummeting down the mountain.* ○ *She fell from the top of the slide and plummeted to the ground.*

plummy /ˈplʌm.i/ *adj* describes a low voice or way of speaking using lengthened vowels, of a type thought to be typical of the British upper social class: *a plummy voice* ○ *a plummy Home Counties accent* ⊃See also **plummy** at **plum** FRUIT.

plump /plʌmp/ *adj* **1** having a pleasantly soft rounded body or shape: *a nice plump chicken* ○ *plump juicy grapes* ○ *a child with plump rosy cheeks* **2** *POLITE WORD FOR* fat: *He's got rather plump since I last saw him.*
plump /plʌmp/ *verb* [T] to shake and push something to make it round and soft: *My aunt was busy straightening furniture and plumping cushions.* ○ *Let me plump up your pillows for you.* **plumpness** /ˈplʌmp.nəs/ *noun* [U]

PHRASAL VERBS WITH **plump** ▼

▲ **plump (sb/sth) down** *phrasal verb* [M] *INFORMAL* to sit down suddenly and heavily, or to put an object or child down suddenly and without taking care: *She plumped down next to me on the sofa.* ○ [R] *He rushed in and plumped himself down in a chair.* ○ *Joan sat down at the front of the bus, and plumped her bags down beside her.*

▲ **plump for sth/sb** *phrasal verb* *UK INFORMAL* to choose something or someone, especially after taking time for careful thought: *I'm going to plump for the vegetable curry.* ○ *Which film did you plump for in the end?*

ˌplum ˈpudding *noun* [C or U] *US OR UK OLD-FASHIONED* Christmas pudding

plunder /ˈplʌn.dəʳ/ ⓤ /-dɚ/ *verb* **1** [I or T] to steal goods violently from a place, especially during a war: *After the president fled the country, the palace was plundered by soldiers.* ○ *Tragically, the graves were plundered and the grave-goods scattered.* **2** [T] to steal or remove something precious from something, in an immoral or un-necessarily severe way: *Someone has been plundering funds from the company.* ○ *The future of our planet is in danger if we continue to plunder it as we do.*
plunder /ˈplʌn.dəʳ/ ⓤ /-dɚ/ *noun* [U] **1** when goods are stolen from a place especially violently or during a war, or these stolen goods: *Residents in the villages under attack have been unable to protect their homes from plunder.* ○ *The thieves hid their plunder in the woodshed.* **2** when something is removed in an immoral or un-necessarily severe way: *We need to put a stop to the plunder of the rain forest.* **plunderer** /ˈplʌn.dʳr.əʳ/ ⓤ /-dɚ.ɚ/ *noun* [C]

plunge /plʌndʒ/ *verb* [I or T; usually + adv or prep] to (cause someone or something to) move or fall suddenly and often a long way forward, down or into something: *We ran down to the beach and plunged into the sea.* ○ *The car went out of control and plunged over the cliff.* ○ *Cook the peas by plunging them into boiling water.* ○ *Niagara Falls plunges 55.5 metres.* ○ *The fall in demand caused share prices to plunge.* ○ *Our income has plunged dramatically.*
plunge /plʌndʒ/ *noun* [C] **1** a sudden movement or fall forward, down or into something: *I really enjoyed my plunge* (= jumping in and swimming) *in the pool.* **2** a sudden and large fall in value or level: *We are expecting a plunge in profits this year.*
● **take the plunge** to make a decision to do something, especially after thinking about it for a long time: *They're finally taking the plunge and getting married.*
plunging /ˈplʌn.dʒɪŋ/ *adj* describes something that plunges or that has a shape which plunges: *plunging sales figures* ○ *a dress with a plunging neckline* (= hav-ing a deep curve at the neck to show part of the breasts)

PHRASAL VERBS WITH **plunge** ▼

▲ **plunge in/plunge into sth** *phrasal verb* to suddenly start doing something actively or enthusiastically: *Two months before his exams, he suddenly plunged into his studies.* ○ *He took a deep breath and plunged into his speech.*

▲ **plunge** ***(sb/sth)*** **into** ***sth*** *phrasal verb* **[often passive]** to suddenly experience a bad situation or unhappiness, or to make someone or something suddenly experience a bad situation or unhappiness: *The country was plunged into recession.* ○ *He was plunged into despair when his wife left him.*

plunger /ˈplʌn.dʒəʳ/ [US] /-dʒɚ/ *noun* **[C]** **1** a SUCTION device consisting of a cup-shaped piece of rubber on the end of a stick, used to get rid of blockages in pipes **2** a part of a device which you push down into it: *He pressed down the plunger of his cafetiere.*

plunk /plʌŋk/ *noun, verb* *US FOR* **plonk** SOUND, **plonk** PUT

pluperfect /ˌpluːˈpɜː.fekt/ [US] /ˈpluːˌpɝː-/ *noun, adj* *SPECIALIZED* **the past perfect**

plural [GRAMMAR] /ˈplʊə.rəl/ [US] /ˈplʊr.əl/ *noun* **[C or U]** (*WRITTEN ABBREVIATION* **pl**) a word or form which expresses more than one: *'Geese' is the plural of 'goose'.* ○ *'Woman' in the plural is 'women'.* ➲Compare **singular** GRAMMAR. **plural** /ˈplʊə.rəl/ [US] /ˈplʊr.əl/ *adj*: *'Cattle' and 'trousers' are both plural nouns.*

plurality /plʊəˈræl.ə.ti/ [US] /plʊˈræl.ə.t̬i/ *noun* **[U]** the state of being plural ➲See also **plurality** at **plural** DIFFERENT.

pluralize, *UK USUALLY* **-ise** /ˈplʊə.rə.laɪz/ [US] /ˈplʊr.əl.aɪz/ *verb* **[T]** *Certain nouns, such as 'guilt', cannot be pluralized* (= made into a form in which they express more than one).

plural [DIFFERENT] /ˈplʊə.rəl/ [US] /ˈplʊr.əl/ *adj FORMAL* **1** consisting of a lot of different races or types of people or of different things: *We need to recognize that we are now living in a plural* ***society***. **2** for or relating to more than one person or thing: *Very few countries allow people to have plural citizenship* (= citizenship of more than one country).

pluralism /ˈplʊə.rə.lɪ.zəm/ [US] /ˈplʊr.əl.ɪ-/ *noun* **[U]** **1** the existence of different types of people, who have different beliefs and opinions, within the same society: *After years of state control, the country is now moving towards* ***political/religious/cultural*** *pluralism.* **2** the belief that the existence of different types of people within the same society is a good thing: *They are committed to democracy, human rights and pluralism.*

pluralist /ˈplʊə.rə.lɪst/ [US] /ˈplʊr.əl.ɪst/ *adj* (*ALSO* **pluralistic**) including or considering many different types of people, with different beliefs, opinions and needs: *A pluralist society allows its members to express their beliefs freely.* ○ *We need to take a pluralistic approach to education.*

pluralist /ˈplʊə.rə.lɪst/ [US] /ˈplʊr.əl.ɪst-/ *noun* **[C]** a person who believes that the existence of different types of people, beliefs and opinions within a society is a good thing

plurality /plʊəˈræl.ə.ti/ [US] /plʊˈræl.ə.t̬i/ *noun* **[C usually sing]** **1** *FORMAL* a large number of different types of something: *There was* ***a*** *marked plurality* ***of*** *opinions/views among the people attending the meeting.* ➲See also **plurality** at **plural** GRAMMAR. **2** *SPECIALIZED* **have/win a plurality** to receive more votes in an election than any other person or party, but not more than the total number of votes which the other people or parties have received: *He won a 48 percent plurality* ***of*** *the vote rather than an outright majority.*

plus [ADDITION] /plʌs/ *prep* added to: *What is six plus four?* ○ *The rent will be £75 a week, plus* (= added to the cost of) *gas and electricity.*

plus /plʌs/ *prep, conjunction* and also: *There will be two adults travelling, plus three children.* ○ *INFORMAL Let's not go on holiday in August – it'll be too hot – plus it'll be more expensive.*

plus /plʌs/ *adj* **1** **[before n]** describes a stated number or amount more than zero: *Plus 8 is eight more than zero.* ○ *The temperature is expected to be no more than plus two (degrees).* **2** **[after n]** more than the number or amount mentioned: *temperatures of 40 plus* ○ *Those cars cost £15 000 plus.* **3** **[after n]** used by teachers after a letter, such as B or C, to show that the standard of a piece of work is slightly higher than the stated mark: *I got C plus/C+ for my essay.*

plus [ADVANTAGE] /plʌs/ *noun* **[C]** *plural* **pluses** or **plusses** *INFORMAL* an advantage or a good feature: *Your teaching experience will be a plus in this job.* **plus** /plʌs/ *adj* **[before n]** *The house is near the sea, which is a plus* ***factor*** *for us.* ○ *UK The fact that the flight goes from our nearest airport is a real plus* ***point***.

ˌplus ˈfours *plural noun* trousers with legs that are wide above the knee but which end in a tightly-fitted strip just below the knee, sometimes worn by men playing golf

plush [LUXURIOUS] /plʌʃ/ *adj INFORMAL* luxurious; expensive, comfortable and of high quality: *He took me out to a really plush restaurant.*

plush [CLOTH] /plʌʃ/ *noun* **[U]** thick soft cloth, with a surface like short fur, which is used especially for covering furniture: *a plush(-covered) sofa* ○ *2 metres of dark red plush* ○ *plush cushions/curtains*

ˈplus (ˌsign) *noun* **[C]** the + sign, written between two numbers to show that they should be added together

Pluto /ˈpluː.təʊ/ [US] /-t̬oʊ/ *noun* **[S]** the planet ninth and most distant from the Sun, more distant than Neptune

plutocracy /pluːˈtɒk.rə.si/ [US] /-ˈtɑː.krə-/ *noun* **1** **[U]** a system of government in which the richest people in a country rule or have power: *It's time we put an end to plutocracy.* **2** **[C]** a country where the richest people have power

plutocracy /pluːˈtɒk.rə.si/ [US] /-ˈtɑː.krə-/ *group noun* **[S]** the richest people in a country who have power in it

plutocrat /ˈpluː.təʊ.kræt/ [US] /-t̬ə-/ *noun* **[C]** someone who obtains power because they are rich: *The country has long been run by plutocrats.* **plutocratic** /ˌpluː.təʊˈkræt.ɪk/ [US] /-toʊˈkræt̬-/ *adj*

plutonium /pluːˈtəʊ.ni.əm/ [US] /-ˈtoʊ-/ *noun* **[U]** a metallic element that is used in the production of nuclear power, and in nuclear weapons

ply [THICKNESS] /plaɪ/ *noun* **[U]** **1** the particular number of threads from which wool or rope, etc. is made, used as a measure of its thickness: *six balls of four-ply (wool)* ○ *What ply do you need for that knitting pattern?* **2** the particular number of layers from which PLYWOOD or TISSUE is formed, used as a measure of its thickness: *Will* ***three-ply*** (= wood made from three layers stuck together) *be strong enough for making a shelf?*

ply [WORK] /plaɪ/ *verb* **[T]** **1** to sell or to work regularly at something, especially a job involving selling things: *Fishermen in small boats ply their* ***trade*** *up and down the coast.* ○ *Dealers are openly plying drugs in school playgrounds.* ○ *The market traders were loudly plying their* ***wares***. **2** **ply for business/trade, etc.** to try to get customers for your business in a public place, for example, as a taxi driver, by driving around or waiting in a regular place: *UK There are never any taxis plying for trade/hire in our area.* ○ *I noticed a couple of prostitutes plying for business on the corner.*

ply [TRAVEL] /plaɪ/ *verb* **[I + adv or prep; T]** *OLD-FASHIONED* When a form of transport plies a particular route, it makes that journey regularly: *High-speed trains regularly ply* ***between*** *Paris and Lyons.* ○ *This airline has been plying the transatlantic* ***route*** *for many years.*

▲ **ply** ***sb*** **with** ***sth*** *phrasal verb* **1** to keep giving a person something, usually food or drink: *John's been plying me with drinks all evening.* **2** to keep giving someone work or forms to complete, or asking them questions: *We plied Charlie with questions about his trip round the world.*

plywood /ˈplaɪ.wʊd/ *noun* **[U]** wood that consists of several thin layers of wood stuck together: *a box made of plywood* ○ *a cheap plywood door*

p.m. [TIME], **pm** /ˌpiːˈem/ *ABBREVIATION* used when referring to a time in the afternoon or evening or at night: *We'll be arriving at about 4.30 p.m.* ○ *The 6pm train is usually very crowded.* ➲Compare **a.m.** MORNING.

PM [POLITICS] /ˌpiːˈem/ *noun* **[C]** *UK INFORMAL ABBREVIATION FOR* **prime minister**: *The PM wants to see you.*

PMS /ˌpiː.emˈes/ *noun* **[U]** *ABBREVIATION FOR* **premenstrual syndrome** (= a condition in which some women experience unpleasant physical and emotional feelings for a few days before their period)

PMT /ˌpiː.emˈtiː/ *noun* **[U]** *UK ABBREVIATION FOR* **premenstrual tension**: another name for **PMS**: *She gets terrible PMT.* ➲See **premenstrual syndrome**.

pneumatic /njuːˈmæt.ɪk/ [US] /nuːˈmæt̬-/ *adj* **1** operated by air pressure: *Our car has pneumatic* ***brakes***. **2** con-

P

taining air: *Pneumatic **tyres** were invented in 1888 by John Dunlop.* **pneumatically** /njuː'mæt.ɪ.kli/ ⓤ /nuː'mæt̬-/ *adv*

pneu,matic 'drill *noun* [C] (*US ALSO* **jackhammer**) a powerful tool which is held in the hand and operates by air pressure, used for breaking hard surfaces such as roads

pneumonia /njuː'məʊ.ni.ə/ ⓤ /nuː'moʊ.njə/ *noun* [U] a serious illness in which one or both lungs become red and swollen and filled with liquid: *People who are bedridden can easily **get** pneumonia.*
• **catch/get pneumonia** *INFORMAL* to make yourself ill by getting too cold: *She'll catch pneumonia going out without a coat in this weather!*

PO SERVICE /ˌpiː'əʊ/ ⓤ /-'oʊ/ *noun* [S] *ABBREVIATION FOR* the **Post Office**

PO RANK /ˌpiː'əʊ/ ⓤ /-'oʊ/ *noun* *WRITTEN ABBREVIATION FOR* **petty officer**: *PO McLintock*

poach COOK /pəʊtʃ/ ⓤ /poʊtʃ/ *verb* [T] to cook something such as a fish, or an egg with its shell removed, by putting it in gently boiling water or other liquid: *We had poached eggs for breakfast.* ○ *Do you like pears poached in red wine?*

poach TAKE /pəʊtʃ/ ⓤ /poʊtʃ/ *verb* [I or T] **1** to catch and kill animals without permission on someone else's land: *The farmer claimed that he shot the men because they were poaching on his land.* **2** to take and use for yourself unfairly or dishonestly something, usually an idea, that belongs to someone else: *Jeff always poaches my **ideas**, and then pretends that they're his own.* **3** *DISAPPROVING* to persuade someone who works for someone else to come and work for you: *They were furious when one of their best managers was poached by another company.*
poacher /'pəʊ.tʃəʳ/ ⓤ /'poʊ.tʃɚ/ *noun* [C] someone who catches and kills animals illegally
• **poacher turned gamekeeper** someone who opposed people in authority in the past but who now has a position of authority themselves

ˌPˈO ˌBox *noun* [C] a numbered box in a POST OFFICE to which your letters and parcels can be sent and from which you can collect them: *Write to PO Box 123.* ○ *a PO Box number*

pocket BAG /'pɒk.ɪt/ ⓤ /'pɑː.kɪt/ *noun* [C] **1** a small bag for carrying things in, which is made of cloth and sewn into the inside or onto the outside of a piece of clothing: *a jacket/trouser/coat pocket* ○ *a hip/breast pocket* ○ *She thrust her hands deep **in/into** her pockets.* ○ *He took some coins **from/out** of his pocket.* **2** a container, usually made of cloth, which is sewn into or onto a bag or fixed to a seat or door in a vehicle: *Sarah put her maps in the outside pocket of her rucksack.* ○ *The safety instructions are in the pocket **of** the seat in front of you.* **3** one of several holes around the edge of a BILLIARD or SNOOKER table, into which balls are hit **4** *INFORMAL* the amount of money that someone has for spending: *You need **deep** pockets* (= a lot of money) *if you're involved in a long law suit.* ○ *I paid for my ticket **out of** my **own** pocket* (= with my own money)*, but I can claim the cost of it back from my employer.*
• **be/live in each other's pockets** *DISAPPROVING* to be with each other all the time and very dependent on each other: *I don't think it's healthy the way you two are always in each other's pockets.*
• **in *sb's* pocket** *DISAPPROVING* in a situation where someone has power or control over you: *The head teacher **has** the school governors completely in her pocket/The school governors **are** completely in the head teacher's pocket.*
• **have *sth* in your pocket** *INFORMAL* to be certain to win or succeed at something: *Last year's winners again have the championship firmly in their pocket.*
• **in/out of pocket** *UK* having more/less money than you started with after an activity involving money: *Even when we've paid all our expenses, we should still be several hundred pounds in pocket.* ○ *The last time I went to the pub with you, I ended up seriously out of pocket!*

pocket /'pɒk.ɪt/ ⓤ /'pɑː.kɪt/ *verb* [T] **1** to put something into your pocket: *He carefully pocketed his change.* **2** to hit a BILLIARD or SNOOKER ball into a pocket: *Davis pocketed the black to win the game.* **3** to take something for yourself, especially dishonestly: *I'll tell them I sold it for*

£20, not £25, then I can pocket the rest.

pocket /'pɒk.ɪt/ ⓤ /'pɑː.kɪt/ *adj* [before n] describes something that is small enough to put in your pocket, or that you regularly carry in your pocket: *a pocket dictionary* ○ *a pocket diary* ○ *a pocket calculator*

pocketful /'pɒk.ɪt.fʊl/ ⓤ /'pɑː.kɪt-/ *noun* [C] as many or as much of something as a pocket will hold: *She always takes a pocketful **of** tissues with her when she takes the children out.* ○ *INFORMAL They won pocketfuls* (= a large amount) *of money playing cards.*

pocket GROUP/AREA /'pɒk.ɪt/ ⓤ /'pɑː.kɪt/ *noun* [C] a group, area or mass of something which is separate and different from what surrounds it: *Among the staff there are some pockets **of** resistance* (= some small groups of them are opposed) *to the planned changes.* ○ *The pilot said that we were going to encounter a pocket **of** turbulence* (= an area of violently moving air).

pocketbook /'pɒk.ɪt.bʊk/ ⓤ /'pɑː.kɪt-/ *noun* [C] *US* **1** a woman's HANDBAG: *I need a new pocketbook to go with these shoes.* **2** *sb's* **pocketbook** the money that someone has or their ability to pay for things: *These new tax arrangements will hit everyone's pocketbook.* ○ *Voters don't all realize how much the results could affect their pocketbooks.*

pocket-handkerchief CLOTH /ˌpɒk.ɪt'hæŋ.kə.tʃiːf/ ⓤ /ˌpɑː.kɪt'hæŋ.kɚ-/ *noun* [C] *OLD-FASHIONED FOR* **handkerchief**

pocketknife /'pɒk.ɪt.naɪf/ ⓤ /'pɑː.kɪt-/ *noun* [C] *plural* **pocketknives** a **penknife**

'pocket ˌmoney CHILD'S MONEY *MAINLY UK noun* [U] (*US* **allowance**) an amount of money which parents regularly give to their child to spend as they choose: *My mum gives me £5 a week pocket money.*

'pocket ˌmoney ADULT'S MONEY *noun* [U] **1** money for spending on your own personal things: *I make a little pocket money delivering catalogues.* **2** *UK INFORMAL* not enough money: *I work really hard at this job, and all I get paid is pocket money.*

pocket-sized /'pɒk.ɪt.saɪzd/ ⓤ /'pɑː.kɪt-/ *adj* small enough to fit in your pocket: *pocket-sized dictionaries*

ˌpocket 'veto *noun* [C usually sing] *US* when the government intentionally stops suggested laws being introduced by failing to sign for them before the government finishes its business for the year

pockmark /'pɒk.mɑːk/ ⓤ /'pɑːk.mɑːrk/ *noun* [C] a small hollow on your skin that is left after a spot caused by a disease, such as CHICKENPOX or SMALLPOX, has healed: *a face covered with pockmarks*
pockmarked /'pɒk.mɑːkt/ ⓤ /'pɑːk.mɑːrkt/ *adj* (*ALSO* **pocked**) **1** marked with pockmarks: *a pockmarked face* **2** describes a surface with a lot of holes or low areas in it: *The houses in the village were pockmarked **with** bullet holes.*

pod PLANT PART /pɒd/ ⓤ /pɑːd/ *noun* [C] a long, narrow, flat part of some plants, such as beans and peas, which contains the seeds and usually has a thick skin: *seed pods* ○ *a pea/vanilla pod* ⊃See picture **Vegetables** on page Centre 2

pod AIRCRAFT PART /pɒd/ ⓤ /pɑːd/ *noun* [C] a long narrow container which is fixed to an aircraft for carrying engines, weapons, extra fuel, etc: *an escape/storage/ accommodation pod* ○ *a space pod*

podgy *UK* /'pɒdʒ.i/ ⓤ /'pɑː.dʒi/ *adj* (*MAINLY US* **pudgy**) *INFORMAL DISAPPROVING* slightly fat: *a podgy face* ○ *pudgy fingers* **podginess** *UK* /'pɒdʒ.ɪ.nəs/ ⓤ /'pɑː.dʒɪ-/ *noun* [U] (*MAINLY US* **pudginess**) *INFORMAL*

podiatrist /pə'daɪ.ə.trɪst/ *noun* [C] *MAINLY US FOR* **chiropodist podiatry** /pə'daɪ.ə.tri/ *noun* [U] *MAINLY US*

podium /'pəʊ.di.əm/ ⓤ /'poʊ-/ *noun* [C] *plural* **podiums** or **podia** a raised area on which a person stands to speak to a large number of people, to CONDUCT music, or to receive a prize in a sports competition: *Tears ran down her face as she stood on the winner's podium.*

poem /'pəʊ.ɪm/ ⓤ /'poʊ.əm/ *noun* [C] a piece of writing in which the words are arranged in separate lines, often ending in rhyme, and are chosen for their sound and for the images and ideas they suggest: *a book of love poems* ○ *The poet recited some of her recent poems.*

poet /ˈpəʊ.ɪt/ [US] /ˈpoʊ.ət/ *noun* [C] a person who writes poems

poetic /pəʊˈet.ɪk/ [US] /poʊˈeţ-/ *adj* (*ALSO* **poetical**) **1** like or relating to poetry or poets: *a collection of Dryden's poetical works* (= poems) ○ *The story is written in richly poetic* ***language***. **2** *APPROVING* very beautiful or expressing emotion: *Deanne Sokolin creates abstract, mournfully poetic black-and-white images of wrapped objects.* **poetically** /pəʊˈet.ɪ.kli/ [US] /poʊˈeţ-/ *adv*

poetry /ˈpəʊ.ɪ.tri/ [US] /ˈpoʊ.ə-/ *noun* [U] **1** poems in general as a form of literature: *contemporary poetry and prose* ○ *She started writing poetry at a young age.* **2** a very beautiful or emotional quality: *This film* ***has*** *a savage poetry and brilliance.*

poˌetic ˈjustice *noun* [U] when something happens to a person that seems particularly fair and deserved, usually because of the bad things that person has done: *What poetic justice that Brady has to go to court to plead to be allowed to die, just like his innocent victims pleaded to be allowed to live.*

poˌetic ˈlicence *noun* [C] when a poet or writer changes particular facts and rules to make the story they are telling more interesting or effective: *She used a fair amount of poetic licence when describing her life in rural France.*

ˌPoet ˈLaureate *noun* [C usually sing] in Britain, a poet specially honoured by the king or queen, who is asked to write poems about important public occasions: *that most illustrious Poet Laureate, Alfred Lord Tennyson*

po-faced /ˌpəʊˈfeɪst/ [US] /ˌpoʊ-/ *adj* **1** *UK INFORMAL DISAPPROVING* too serious and disapproving: *Two po-faced men came to inspect the house.* ○ *The film is serious but not po-faced.* **2** *INFORMAL* describes someone whose face shows a serious, disapproving or empty expression: *She* ***remained*** *po-faced all evening, even when the rest of us were in stitches at Bob's jokes.*

pogo stick /ˈpəʊ.gəʊˌstɪk/ [US] /ˈpoʊ.goʊ-/ *noun* [C] a children's toy made of a long metal stick with a bar to hold across the top, and a large spring and a bar for your feet at the bottom, used to bounce around on

pogrom /ˈpɒg.rəm/ [US] /ˈpoʊ.grəm/ *noun* [C] an act of organized cruelty or killing which is done to a large group of people because of their race or religion: *The famines and pogroms in 19th-century Eastern Europe forced many Jewish refugees to emigrate.*

poignant /ˈpɔɪ.njənt/ *adj* causing or having a particularly sharp feeling of sadness: *The photograph awakens poignant memories of happier days.* ○ ***It*** *is especially poignant* ***that*** *he died on the day before the wedding.* **poignantly** /ˈpɔɪ.njənt.li/ *adv* **poignancy** /ˈpɔɪ.njənt.si/ *noun* [U] *The poem has* ***a*** *haunting poignancy.*

poinsettia /ˌpɔɪntˈset.i.ə/ [US] /-ˈseţ-/ *noun* [C] a tropical plant with groups of bright red leaves which look like flowers

point [SHARP END] /pɔɪnt/ *noun* [C] the sharp end of something, such as a knife: *The knife landed with its point sticking into the floor.* ○ *Be careful with that needle – it has a very sharp point.* ➲See also **gunpoint**.

pointed /ˈpɔɪn.tɪd/ [US] /-ţɪd/ *adj* A pointed object has a thin sharp end or becomes much narrower at one end: *He's got funny little pointed ears.* ➲See also **pointed**.

pointy /ˈpɔɪn.ti/ [US] /-ţi/ *adj INFORMAL She was wearing a pointy hat* (= a hat shaped into a point).

point [PIECE OF LAND] /pɔɪnt/ *noun* [C] a long thin area of land that stretches out into the sea: *Spurn Point*

point [SHOW] /pɔɪnt/ *verb* **1** [I] to direct other people's attention to something by holding out your finger towards it: *"Look at that!" she said, pointing* ***at*** *the hole in the door.* ○ *Small children are often told that it's rude to point.* **2** [T] to hold something out in the direction of someone or something: *He said that the man had pointed a knife* ***at*** *him.* **3** [I] If something points in a particular direction, it is turned towards that direction: *The road sign points left.* ○ *All the cars were pointing in the same direction.* ○ *There was an arrow pointing* ***to*** *the door.*

pointer /ˈpɔɪn.təʳ/ [US] /-ţɚ/ *noun* [C] **1** something that is used for pointing at things, such as a long thin stick that you hold to direct attention to a place on a map or words on a board, or a **cursor** **2** a helpful piece of advice or information: *This booklet gives some useful pointers* ***on*** *what to expect when you arrive.* **3** something which shows you an existing or developing situation: *The performance of the car industry is a (good) pointer to the general economic health of the country.* **4** a hunting dog that has been trained to stand very still with its nose pointing towards the animals and birds that are being hunted

point [IDEA EXPRESSED] /pɔɪnt/ *noun* **1** [C] an idea, opinion or piece of information that is said or written: *I'd like to discuss the first point in your essay.* ○ *You* ***made*** *some interesting points in your speech.* **2** **the/sb's point** the meaning or most important part of what someone says or writes: *The point is, if you don't claim the money now you might never get it.* ○ *I think you* ***missed*** (= did not understand) *the point of what she was saying.* ○ ***I take*** *your point/Point* ***taken*** (= I understand that what you are saying is important). ○ *Please* ***get to*** *the point* (= say the thing that is most important to you). ○ *He hasn't got much money, but that's not the point* (= that is not the important thing). **3** [S] an opinion or fact that deserves to be considered seriously, or which other people agree is true: *Yes, I can* ***see*** *your point/you've* ***got*** *a point* ***there***. ○ *OK, you've* ***made*** *your point* (= told us your opinion) *– there's no need to go on about it.*

• **beside the point** not important or not related to the subject being discussed: *The fact that he doesn't want to come is beside the point – he should have been invited.*

• **to the point** expressing something very important or suitable for the subject being discussed: *Her comments on my work were very apt and to the point.*

• **make a point of *doing sth*** to always do something or to take particular care to do something: *She makes a point of keeping all her shopping receipts.*

• **my point exactly** said in answer to something that someone has just said when you believe it yourself, or when you have said it yourself earlier: *"So even if we got the funding, we still couldn't get the project started." "My point exactly."*

• **that's a (good) point** said to show that what someone has just said is true or important: *"We'll take the bus." "But we haven't got any money for the fare." "That's a point."*

point [CHARACTERISTIC] /pɔɪnt/ *noun* [C] a particular quality or characteristic of a person or thing: *There are various points to look out for when you're judging dogs in a competition.* ○ *He's boring, but I suppose he has his* ***good*** *points.* ○ *I think her kindness is one of her* ***strong*** *points* (= one of her good qualities).

point [TIME OR PLACE] /pɔɪnt/ *noun* [C] **1** a particular time or stage reached in a process: ***At*** *that point, a soldier opened fire on the car.* ○ *I was completely lost at one point.* ○ [+ question word] *It was so confusing that eventually it* ***got to*** *the point* ***where*** *no one knew what was going on.* ○ *I said I'd tell her the bad news, but when* ***it came to the point*** (= when I had to do it), *I couldn't.* **2** a particular place: *the point where the road bends* ○ *This is a good point from which to watch the race.* **3** **boiling/melting/freezing, etc. point** the temperature at which a substance boils/melts/freezes, etc.

• **be on the point of *(doing) sth*** to be going to do something very soon: *As we were on the point of giving up hope, a letter arrived.* ○ *She was so tired that she was on the point of collapse.*

• **up to a point** partly, or to a limited degree: *Of course there is some truth in all this, but* ***only*** *up to a point.* ○ *The new traffic scheme worked up to a point, but it had its problems.*

point [PURPOSE] /pɔɪnt/ *noun* [U] purpose or usefulness: *I see little point* ***in*** *discussing this further.* ○ *I'd like to write to him, but* ***what's the*** *point? He never writes back.* ○ [+ v-ing] *INFORMAL There's no point arguing about it – we're going and that's that.*

pointless /ˈpɔɪnt.ləs/ *adj* Something that is pointless has no purpose and it is a waste of time doing it: *This is a pointless exercise.* ○ ***It*** *seemed pointless* ***to*** *continue.* ○ *INFORMAL* ***It's*** *pointless arguing with him.* **pointlessly** /ˈpɔɪnt.lə.sli/ *adv*: *Innocent lives were cruelly and pointlessly wiped out.* **pointlessness** /ˈpɔɪnt.lə.snəs/ *noun* [U] *a poem about the pointlessness of life*

point [UNIT] /pɔɪnt/ *noun* [C] **1** a mark or unit for counting, especially how much a person or team has scored in a sport: *The youngest skier won the most points.* ○ *He won the world heavyweight boxing championship* ***on*** *points* (= as a result of the points that he had won). ○ *Interest rates have risen by two percentage points* (= 2%). **2** *SPECIALIZED* a unit used for measuring the size of printed letters, equal to about 0.3 mm: *The large letters are* ***in*** *7¾ point type, and the small letters are* ***in*** *6 point.*

point [SIGN] /pɔɪnt/ *noun* [C] a small round spot that is used in numbers to separate whole numbers from parts of numbers: *One kilogram equals two point two* (= 2.2) *pounds.* ○ *The error occurred when someone left out the* ***decimal*** *point.*

point [ELECTRIC] /pɔɪnt/ *noun* [C] **1** *UK* a SOCKET to which a wire from a piece of electrical equipment is connected in order to supply it with electricity or a radio, television or other signal: *a TV antenna point* ○ *There is a telephone point in every room.* **2** *SPECIALIZED* in some car engines, either of two parts that permit or prevent the flow of electricity: *He checked the points and plugs and topped up the oil.*

point [MARK] /pɔɪnt/ *noun* [C] **1** a small round mark on a line, plan or map to show the position of something: *Join the points A and B together on the diagram with a straight line.* **2** a mark on a COMPASS which shows direction, such as North, South, East and West **3** a very small round light that you can see in the distance: *I could just make out the tiny points of a car's headlights far away.*

PHRASAL VERBS WITH **point** ▼

▲ **point** ***(sth/sb)*** **out** *phrasal verb* [M] to make a person notice someone or something, usually by telling them where they are or by holding up one of your fingers towards them: *If you see her, please point her out* ***to*** *me.* ○ *The tour guide pointed out the inscription that runs round the inside of the dome.*

▲ **point** ***sth*** **out** *phrasal verb* [M] to tell someone about some information, often because you believe they are not aware of it or have forgotten it: [+ **that**] *He was planning to book a rock-climbing holiday, till I pointed out* ***that*** *Denis is afraid of heights.* ○ [+ **question word**] *I feel I should point out* ***how*** *dangerous it is.*

COMMON LEARNER ERROR

point out

Don't forget the preposition 'out' in this phrasal verb.

Psychologists point out the importance for children of having contact with both parents.

~~*Psychologists point the importance for children of having contact with both parents.*~~

▲ **point to/towards** ***sth*** *phrasal verb* to make it seem likely that a particular fact is true or that a particular event will happen: *All the evidence points to suicide.*

▲ **point** ***sth*** **up** *phrasal verb FORMAL* to emphasize a problem or fact, so that people are more aware of it: *It was a badly researched documentary which glossed over important questions while pointing up trivial ones.*

point-blank [VERY CLOSE] /ˌpɔɪnt'blæŋk/ /'--/ *adv, adj* [**before n**] describes shooting from a gun that is fired from extremely close to the target or when almost touching it: *Two bullets were* ***fired*** *into the car* ***at*** *point-blank* ***range.*** ○ *a point-blank shot*

point-blank [NOT POLITE] /ˌpɔɪnt'blæŋk/ /'--/ *adv* saying something very clearly in very few words, without trying to be polite or pleasant: *He asked me to work at the weekend, but I* ***refused*** *point-blank.*

pointed /'pɔɪn.tɪd/ [US] /-t̬ɪd/ *adj* describes a remark, question or manner that is intended as a criticism of the person to whom it is directed: *My aunt made a few pointed remarks about my taste in clothes.* ➲See also **pointed** at **point** SHARP END.

pointedly /'pɔɪn.tɪd.li/ [US] /-t̬ɪd-/ *adv* in a very obvious way, usually to express criticism or disapproval: *He pointedly ignored her after the show.*

pointer /'pɔɪn.təʳ/ [US] /-t̬ɚ/ *noun* [C] ➲See at **point** SHOW.

Pointillism /'pɔɪn.tɪ.lɪ.zəm/ /'pwæn-/ [US] /'pwæn.tə.lɪ-/ *noun* [U] *SPECIALIZED* a style of painting developed in France at the end of the 19th century in which a painting is created out of small spots of pure colour which seem to mix when seen from far away **Pointillist** /'pɔɪn.tɪ.lɪst/ /'pwæn-/ [US] /'pwæn.tə-/ *adj, noun* [C] *Seurat's 'Une Baignade' is a well-known Pointillist painting.* ○ *Seurat and Signac were two of the most famous Pointillists.*

pointless /'pɔɪnt.ləs/ *adj* ➲See at **point** PURPOSE.

ˌpoint of no re'turn *noun* [S] the stage at which it is no longer possible to stop what you are doing and when its effects cannot now be avoided or prevented: *Russia, he said, had* ***reached*** *the point of no return on the road to reform and had to go forward.* ○ *Scientists fear that global warming has gone beyond the point of no return.*

ˌpoint of 'order *noun* [**C usually sing**] *FORMAL* an occasion on which a person in a formal meeting states their belief that a rule of the meeting has been broken: *I would like to* ***raise*** *a point of order.*

ˌpoint of 'view *noun* [C] *plural* **points of view** **1** a way of considering something: ***From*** *a purely practical point of view, the house is too small.* ○ *From a medical point of view, there was no need for the operation.* **2** an opinion: *You have to be willing to* ***see*** (= understand) *other people's points of view.* ○ *I appreciate that* ***from*** *your point of view it's an unwelcome development.*

points [FEET] /pɔɪnts/ *plural noun SPECIALIZED* the toes of a ballet dancer's shoes: *She is learning how to dance on her points.* **point** /pɔɪnt/ *adj* [**before n**] *a pair of point shoes* ○ *Today we'll do some point work.*

points [RAILWAY] /pɔɪnts/ *plural noun* (*US USUALLY* **switches**) a place on a railway track where the RAILS (= metal bars on which the trains travel) can be moved to allow a train to change from one track to another: *The train rattled as it went over the points.*

pointy /'pɔɪn.ti/ [US] /-t̬i/ *adj INFORMAL* ➲See at **point** SHARP END.

poise /pɔɪz/ *noun* [U] *APPROVING* calm confidence in a person's way of behaving, or a quality of grace and balance in the way a person holds or moves their body: *He looked embarrassed for a moment, then quickly regained his poise.* ○ *Her confidence and poise show that she is a top model.*

poised /pɔɪzd/ *adj APPROVING* showing very calm and controlled behaviour

poised /pɔɪzd/ *adj* [**after v**] **1** describes an object or a part of your body that is completely still but ready to move at any moment: *My pencil was poised over the page, ready to take down her words.* **2** ready to do a particular thing at any moment: [+ **to infinitive**] *The company is poised* ***to*** *launch its new advertising campaign.* ○ *The military forces are poised* ***for*** *attack.*

poison /'pɔɪ.zən/ *noun* [**C or U**] a substance that can make people or animals ill or kill them if they eat or drink it: *The pest control officer put bowls of rat poison in the attic.* ○ *Her drink had been laced with a* ***deadly*** *poison.*

• **Name your poison.** (*ALSO* **What's your poison?**) *HUMOROUS* used to ask what type of alcoholic drink someone would like

poison /'pɔɪ.zən/ *verb* [T] **1** to kill a person or animal or to make them very ill by giving them poison: *Four members of the family had been poisoned, but not fatally.* **2** to put poison in someone's food or drink: *He said that someone had poisoned his coffee.* **3** to add dangerous chemicals or other harmful substances to something such as water or air: *The chemical leak had poisoned the water supply.* **4** to spoil a friendship or another situation, by making it very unpleasant: *The long dispute has poisoned relations between the two countries.*

• **poison** ***sb's*** **mind** *DISAPPROVING* to make someone believe unpleasant things about another person which are not true: *Don't listen to her lies – she's just trying to poison your mind* ***against*** *me.*

poisoner /'pɔɪ.zən.əʳ/ [US] /-ɚ/ *noun* [C] a person who has killed or harmed someone using poison

poisoning /ˈpɔɪ.zᵊn.ɪŋ/ *noun* [U] an illness caused by eating, drinking or breathing a dangerous substance: *alcohol/lead poisoning*

poisonous /ˈpɔɪ.zᵊn.əs/ *adj* **1** very harmful and able to cause illness or death: *poisonous chemicals* ○ *Can you tell the the difference between poisonous mushrooms and edible varieties?* **2** very unpleasant and hurtful: *He said some poisonous things to me.*

poisoned ˈchalice *noun* [S] something which seems very good when it is first received, but which in fact does great harm to the person who receives it: *The leadership of the party turned out to be a poisoned chalice.*

poison ˈgas *noun* [U] a gas that is used to kill people, especially in a war

poison ˈivy *noun* [C or U] a North American plant which causes your skin to itch and turn red if you touch its leaves

poison-pen letter /ˌpɔɪ.zᵊnˈpen.let.əʳ/ US /-ˌlet.ɚ/ *noun* [C] a letter in which very unkind or unpleasant things are written about the person it is sent to, in order to offend or upset them

poke PUSH /pəʊk/ US /poʊk/ *verb* [T] to push a finger or other pointed object quickly into someone or something: *You'll poke someone **in** the eye with that umbrella if you're not careful!* ○ *Two kids were poking a stick **into** the drain.*
● **poke fun** at *sb* to make someone seem ridiculous by making jokes about them or laughing unkindly at them
poke /pəʊk/ US /poʊk/ *noun* [C] when you poke someone or something: *She **gave** me a poke **in** the stomach.*

poke APPEAR /pəʊk/ US /poʊk/ *verb* [I or T; usually + adv or prep] to (cause something to) appear or stretch out from behind or through something else: *Cathy poked her head round the door to say hello.* ○ *The first green shoots are poking **up**/**through** the soil.*
▲ **poke around** *phrasal verb* (UK ALSO **poke about**) INFORMAL to search for something by moving things about, usually not in a very careful or organized way: *I was poking about **in** the drawer, looking for the key, when I found this!*

poker GAME /ˈpəʊ.kəʳ/ US /ˈpoʊ.kɚ/ *noun* [U] a game played with cards in which people try to win money from each other

poker TOOL /ˈpəʊ.kəʳ/ US /ˈpoʊ.kɚ/ *noun* [C] a long thin metal stick that you use to move around coal or wood in a fire so that it burns better

poker-faced /ˈpəʊ.kə.feɪst/ US /ˈpoʊ.kɚ-/ *adj* describes someone whose face does not show what they are thinking or feeling: *She sat poker-faced all the way through the film.* **ˈpoker ˌface** *noun* [C] *to wear/keep a poker face*

poky SMALL (**pokier, pokiest**), **pokey** /ˈpəʊ.ki/ US /ˈpoʊ-/ *adj* UK INFORMAL describes a room, house or other place which is unpleasantly small and uncomfortable: *They live in a poky little flat.*

poky SLOW (**pokier, pokiest**), **pokey** /ˈpəʊ.ki/ US /ˈpoʊ-/ *adj* US INFORMAL slow: *I wish you wouldn't be so poky when you're getting ready.*

polar /ˈpəʊ.ləʳ/ US /ˈpoʊ.lɚ/ *adj* ➡See at **pole** OPPOSITE; **pole** PLACE.

polar ˈbear *noun* [C] a bear with white fur that lives near the North Pole

polarity /pəʊˈlær.ə.ti/ US /poʊˈler.ə. t̬i/ *noun* [U] ➡See at **pole** OPPOSITE.

polarize, UK USUALLY **-ise** /ˈpəʊ.lə.raɪz/ US /ˈpoʊ-/ *verb* [T] to cause something, especially something that contains different people or opinions, to divide into two completely opposing groups: *The debate is becoming polarized and there seems to be no middle ground.* **polarization**, UK USUALLY **-isation** /ˌpəʊ.lə.raɪˈzeɪ.ʃᵊn/ US /ˌpoʊ.lɚ.ɪ-/ *noun* [U] *The polarization of society **into** rich and poor can clearly be seen in the city centres.*

Polaroid /ˈpəʊ.lᵊr.ɔɪd/ US /ˈpoʊ.lə.rɔɪd/ *noun* [C] TRADEMARK a camera that takes a picture and prints it after a few seconds, or a photograph taken with this type of camera: *Did you take these with a Polaroid?* ○ *Please send us your Polaroids and the best ones will be published.*

pole STICK /pəʊl/ US /poʊl/ *noun* [C] a long thin stick of wood or metal, often used standing straight up in the ground to support things: *a telegraph/electricity pole* ○ *A flag fluttered from a forty-foot pole.*

pole PLACE /pəʊl/ US /poʊl/ *noun* [C] either of the two points at the most northern and most southern ends of the Earth, around which the Earth turns: *the North/South Pole* ○ *Most weather satellites are stationed over the Equator or travel over the poles.*
polar /ˈpəʊ.ləʳ/ US /ˈpoʊ.lɚ/ *adj* relating to the North or South Pole or the areas around them: *the polar ice caps*

pole OPPOSITE /pəʊl/ US /poʊl/ *noun* [C] either of two completely opposite or different opinions, positions or qualities: *These two men might be thought to represent the opposite poles of economic ideology.*
● **poles apart** completely opposite: *My sister and I are poles apart in personality.*
polar /ˈpəʊ.ləʳ/ US /ˈpoʊ.lɚ/ *adj* Polar opposites are complete opposites: *The novel deals with the polar opposites of love and hate.*
polarity /pəʊˈlær.ə.ti/ US /poʊˈler.ə.t̬i/ *noun* [U] the quality of being opposite: *The film is based on the polarity of the two main characters.*

Pole PERSON /pəʊl/ US /poʊl/ *noun* [C] a person from Poland
Polish /ˈpəʊ.lɪʃ/ US /ˈpoʊ-/ *adj* Someone or something Polish is from Poland.
Polish /ˈpəʊ.lɪʃ/ US /ˈpoʊ-/ *noun* [U] the language of Poland

poleaxe /ˈpəʊl.æks/ US /ˈpoʊl-/ *verb* [T] **1** to hit someone so hard that they fall down: *Blake was poleaxed by a missile thrown from the crowd.* **2** INFORMAL to give someone such a great shock that they do not know what to do: *He was completely poleaxed when his wife left him.*

polecat /ˈpəʊl.kæt/ US /ˈpoʊl-/ *noun* [C] a small wild fierce animal that lives in Europe, Asia and North Africa, which has dark brown fur and a strong, unpleasant smell

polemic /pəˈlem.ɪk/ *noun* [C] FORMAL a piece of writing or a speech in which a person strongly attacks or defends a particular opinion, person, idea or set of beliefs: *She has published a fierce anti-war polemic.* **polemical** /pəˈlem.ɪ.kᵊl/ *adj*: *a polemical essay*

ˈpole poˌsition *noun* [C or U] the starting position on the inside of the front row in a motor race or similar racing competition, which is generally considered to be best and is given to the competitor who achieves the fastest qualifying time: *Damon Hill is **in** pole position for today's Belgian Grand Prix.*

the ˈPole ˌStar *noun* [U] a star that can be seen by people in the northern part of the world and always shows where north lies

the ˈpole ˌvault *noun* [S] a sports competition in which you jump over a high bar using a long stick to push you off the ground: *She won silver in the pole vault for Australia.* ○ *world pole vault champion* **pole vaulter** /ˈpəʊlˌvɒl.təʳ/ US /ˈpoʊlvɑːl.t̬ɚ/ *noun* [C]

police /pəˈliːs/ *plural noun* **1** the official organization that is responsible for protecting people and property, making people obey the law, finding out about and solving crime, and catching people who have committed a crime: *I think you should call **the** police.* ○ ***The** police are investigating fraud allegations against him.* **2** members of this organization: *There should be more police patrolling the area on foot.*
police /pəˈliːs/ *verb* [T] **1** to control or guard a public event or area by members of the police or a similar force: *The march will be heavily policed by an anti-riot unit.* **2** to control the way in which a possibly dangerous substance is dealt with or activity is done: *The use of these chemicals must be carefully policed.*

poˈlice ˌcar *noun* [C] an official car used by the police ➡See picture **Cars and Trucks** on page Centre 13

poˌlice ˈconstable *noun* [C] (ABBREVIATION **PC**) in the UK, a police officer of the lowest rank

poˈlice deˌpartment *noun* [C] US in the US, the police force in an area or city

poˈlice ˌforce *group noun* [C] the police in a country or area: *More young people are needed to **join** the police force.* ○ *the Metropolitan Police Force*

policeman /pəˈliːs.mən/ *noun* [C] a male member of a police force

poˈlice ˌofficer *noun* [C] a male or female member of the police force

poˈlice ˌstate *noun* [C usually sing] *DISAPPROVING* a country in which the government uses the police to severely limit people's freedom

poˈlice ˌstation *noun* [C] the local office of the police in a town or part of a city: *He was taken to the police station for questioning.*

policewoman /pəˈliːsˌwʊm.ən/ *noun* [C] a female member of a police force

policy [PLAN] /ˈpɒl.ə.si/ [US] /ˈpɑː.lə-/ *noun* [C] a set of ideas or a plan of what to do in particular situations that has been agreed officially by a group of people, a business organization, a government or a political party: *They believe that the European Community needs a common foreign and security policy.* ○ *What is your party's policy* ***on*** *immigration?*

policy-making /ˈpɒl.ə.siˌmeɪ.kɪŋ/ [US] /ˈpɑː.lə-/ *noun* [U] the activity of deciding on new policies

policy [DOCUMENT] /ˈpɒl.ə.si/ [US] /ˈpɑː.lə-/ *noun* [C] a document showing an agreement you have made with an insurance company: *You should check your policy to see if you're covered for flood damage.*

polio /ˈpəʊ.li.əʊ/ [US] /ˈpoʊ.li.oʊ/ *noun* [U] (*SPECIALIZED* **poliomyelitis**) a serious infectious disease that can cause permanent PARALYSIS (= inability to move the body): *a polio vaccination programme* ○ *Now 95 per cent of UK babies are* ***immunised against*** *diphtheria, tetanus, polio, measles, mumps and rubella before they are a year old.*

polish /ˈpɒl.ɪʃ/ [US] /ˈpɑː.lɪʃ/ *verb* [T] to rub something using a piece of cloth or brush to clean it and make it shine: *to polish the furniture* ○ *Polish your shoes regularly to protect the leather.*

polish /ˈpɒl.ɪʃ/ [US] /ˈpɑː.lɪʃ/ *noun* **1** [S] when you polish something: *I'll just* ***give*** *my shoes* ***a*** *quick polish.* **2** [C or U] a cream or other substance that you use to clean something: *shoe/furniture/silver polish* **3** [U] skill or quality: *It's a lively, good-hearted film but it lacks a little polish.* ○ *This is a musical with polish and wit.*

polished /ˈpɒl.ɪʃt/ [US] /ˈpɑː.lɪʃt/ *adj* **1** having been polished: *a highly polished floor* **2** describes a person who has style and confidence: *He's suave, polished and charming.* **3** showing great skill: *The dancers gave a polished performance.*

PHRASAL VERBS WITH **polish**

▲ **polish** ***sth*** **off** *phrasal verb* [M] *INFORMAL* to finish something quickly and easily, especially a lot of food or work: *He polished off the whole pie.* ○ *I polished off three essays in one week.*

▲ **polish** ***sth/sb*** **off** *phrasal verb* [M] *INFORMAL* to defeat a competitor easily: *Arsenal polished off Chelsea 5-0 in Saturday's match.*

▲ **polish** ***sb*** **off** *phrasal verb* [M] *MAINLY US INFORMAL* to kill someone: *He was accused of polishing off his former partner.*

▲ **polish** ***sth*** **up** [OBJECT] *phrasal verb* [M] to rub or brush an object to make it shine, especially a metal or wooden object: *Robert was polishing up some old silver candlesticks.*

▲ **polish** ***sth*** **up** [SKILL] *phrasal verb* [M] to improve a skill, especially when you have allowed it to become less good over a period of time: *I really must polish up my Japanese before we visit Japan next year.*

the politburo /ðəˈpɒl.ɪtˌbjʊə.rəʊ/ [US] /-ˈpɑː.lɪtˌbjʊr.oʊ/ *group noun* [S] the main government group in a Communist country, which makes all the important decisions

polite /pəˈlaɪt/ *adj* **1** behaving in a way that is socially correct and shows awareness of and caring for other people's feelings: *I'm afraid I wasn't very polite to her.* ○ *She sent me a polite letter thanking me for my invitation.* ○ *He was too polite to point out my mistake.* **2** socially correct rather than friendly: *polite conversation* **3** *OLD-FASHIONED OR HUMOROUS* **polite society/company** people who have been taught how to behave in a socially correct way: *Sex never used to be discussed* ***in*** *polite society.*

politely /pəˈlaɪt.li/ *adv* **1** in a polite way: *He told them politely to leave him in peace.* **2** without enthusiasm: *The audience clapped politely.* **politeness** /pəˈlaɪt.nəs/ *noun* [U]

politic /ˈpɒl.ɪ.tɪk/ [US] /ˈpɑː.lə-/ *adj* [+ *to* infinitive] *FORMAL* wise and showing the ability to make the right decisions: ***It*** *would not be politic* ***for*** *you* ***to*** *be seen there.*

poˌlitical aˈsylum *noun* [U] the protection given by a government to foreign people who have left their own country because they disagree with their own government: *The number of people* ***seeking*** *political asylum in Britain has risen dramatically.*

poˌlitically corˈrect *adj* (*ABBREVIATION* **PC**) **1** describes someone who believes that language and actions which could be offensive to others, especially those relating to sex and race, should be avoided **2** describes a word or expression that is used instead of another one to avoid being offensive: *Some people think that 'fireman' is a sexist term, and prefer the politically correct term 'firefighter'.* **poˌlitical corˈrectness** *noun* [U]

poˌlitical ˈprisoner *noun* [C] someone who is put in prison for expressing disapproval of their own government, or for belonging to an organization, race or social group not approved of by that government

poˌlitical ˈscience *noun* [U] the study of how people obtain or compete for power and how it is used in governing a country

politics /ˈpɒl.ɪ.tɪks/ [US] /ˈpɑː.lə-/ *noun* [U] **1** the activities of the government, members of law-making organizations or people who try to influence the way a country is governed: *Joe is very active in left-wing politics.* **2** the job of holding a position of power in the government: *The group is campaigning to get more women into politics.* ○ *He is planning to retire from politics next year.* **3** the study of the ways in which a country is governed: *She read politics at Leicester University.*

politics /ˈpɒl.ɪ.tɪks/ [US] /ˈpɑː.lə-/ *plural noun* **1** ***sb's*** **politics** someone's opinions about how a country should be governed: *Her politics have become more liberal over the past few years.* **2** the relationships within a group or organization which allow particular people to have power over others: *I don't like to get involved in* ***office*** *politics.*

• **play politics** *UK* to use a situation or the relationships between people for your own advantage: *He accused councillors of playing politics* ***with*** *children's education.*

political /pəˈlɪt.ɪ.kəl/ [US] /-ˈlɪt̬.ə-/ *adj* relating to politics: *political leaders* ○ *There are two political parties in the US – the Democratic Party and the Republican Party.* ○ *Education is back at the top of the political* ***agenda*** (= the matters that the government is considering).

politically /pəˈlɪt.ɪ.kli/ [US] /-ˈlɪt̬.ə-/ *adv*: *to be politically naive*

politician /ˌpɒl.ɪˈtɪʃ.ən/ [US] /ˌpɑː.lə-/ *noun* [C] a member of a government or law-making organization: *a distinguished/disgraced politician*

politicize, *UK USUALLY* **-ise** /pəˈlɪt.ɪ.saɪz/ [US] /-ˈlɪt̬.ə-/ *verb* [T often passive] to make something or someone political, or more involved in or aware of political matters: *The whole issue has become increasingly politicized.* ○ *a highly politicized debate*

politicking /ˈpɒl.ɪ.tɪ.kɪŋ/ [US] /ˈpɑː.lə-/ *noun* [U] *MAINLY DISAPPROVING* the activity of trying to persuade or even force others to vote or a particular political party or CANDIDATE

polka /ˈpɒl.kə/ [US] /ˈpoʊl-/ *noun* [C] a fast active dance that was popular in the 19th century, or a piece of music that can be used for this dance

ˈpolka ˌdot *noun* [C usually pl] one of a large number of small round spots that are printed in a regular pattern on cloth: *a shocking pink dress with white polka dots* ○ *a polka-dot bikini/bow tie*

poll [OPINION] /pəʊl/ [US] /poʊl/ *noun* [C] a study in which people are asked for their opinions about a subject or person: *We're* ***carrying out/conducting*** *a poll to find out what people think about abortion.* ○ *The latest*

opinion *poll puts the Democrats in the lead.*
poll /pəʊl/ [US] /poʊl/ *verb* [T] to ask a person for their opinion as part of a general study of what people think about a subject: *Half the people polled said they would pay more for environmentally-friendly food.*
pollster /ˈpəʊl.stəʳ/ [US] /ˈpoʊl.stɚ/ *noun* [C] a person who performs opinion polls

poll [ELECTION] /pəʊl/ [US] /poʊl/ *verb* [T] When a person or a political party polls a particular number of votes in an election, they receive that number: *With nearly all the votes counted, Mr Soto had polled 67% of the vote.*
the polls *plural noun* the places where people vote in a political election: *The TV stations agreed not to announce the projected winner until after the polls closed.*
• **go to the polls** to vote: *The country will go to the polls on September 13th.*

pollen /ˈpɒl.ən/ [US] /ˈpɑː.lən/ *noun* [U] a powder produced by the male part of a flower, which is carried by insects or the wind and causes the female part of the same type of flower to produce seeds **pollinate** /ˈpɒl.ə.neɪt/ [US] /ˈpɑː.lə-/ *verb* [T] *Bees pollinate the plants by carrying the pollen from one flower to another.* **pollination** /ˌpɒl.əˈneɪ.ʃᵊn/ [US] /ˌpɑː.lə-/ *noun* [U] *Many species of tree depend on the wind for pollination.*

ˈpollen ˌcount *noun* [C] a measurement of the amount of pollen in the air: *The pollen count is high today, which is bad news for hay fever sufferers.*

ˈpolling ˌbooth *noun* [C] *UK* a small, partly enclosed area in a polling station where you can vote in private

ˈpolling ˌday *UK noun* [U] (*US USUALLY* **election day**) the day when people vote in an election

ˈpolling ˌstation *noun* [C] (*US ALSO* **polling place**) a place where people go to vote in an election

pollute /pəˈluːt/ *verb* [T] to make an area or substance, usually air, water or earth, dirty or harmful to people, animals and plants, especially by adding harmful chemicals: *The fertilizers and pesticides used on many farms are polluting the water supply.* ○ *We won't invest in any company that pollutes the environment.* ○ *FIGURATIVE Many Americans complain that broadcasters pollute the airwaves with violence, sensationalism and sleaze.*
pollutant /pəˈluː.tᵊnt/ [US] /-t̬ᵊnt/ *noun* [C] a substance that pollutes: *Sulphur dioxide is one of several pollutants that are released into the atmosphere by coal-fired power stations.*
polluter /pəˈluː.təʳ/ [US] /-t̬ɚ/ *noun* [C] a person or organization that pollutes
pollution /pəˈluː.ʃᵊn/ *noun* [U] damage caused to water, air, etc. by harmful substances or waste: *air/water pollution* ○ *The manifesto includes tough measures to tackle road congestion and* ***environmental*** *pollution.*

pollyanna /ˌpɒl.iˈæn.ə/ [US] /ˌpɑː.li-/ *noun* [C] *OLD-FASHIONED* a person who believes that good things are more likely to happen than bad things, even when this is very unlikely

polo /ˈpəʊ.ləʊ/ [US] /ˈpoʊ.loʊ/ *noun* [U] a game played between two teams who ride horses and carry long wooden hammers with which they hit a small hard ball, trying to score goals: *Prince Charles is a keen polo player.*

ˈpolo ˌneck *UK noun* [C] (*US* **turtleneck**) **1** a high round collar that folds over on itself and covers the neck: *I'd prefer a sweater with a polo neck.* **2** a jumper or shirt with a polo neck: *Why don't you wear your black polo neck?* **polo-necked** /ˈpəʊ.ləʊ.nekt/ [US] /ˈpoʊ.loʊ-/ *adj* [before n] *UK a polo-necked jumper*

ˈpolo ˌshirt *noun* [C] an informal style of cotton shirt, with short sleeves, a collar and some buttons at the neck ➲See picture **Clothes** on page Centre 6

poltergeist /ˈpɒl.tə.ɡaɪst/ [US] /ˈpoʊl.t̬ɚ-/ *noun* [C] a spirit or ghost-like force that moves furniture and throws objects around in a house

poly [COLLEGE] /ˈpɒl.i/ [US] /ˈpɑː.li/ *noun* [C] *INFORMAL FOR* **polytechnic**

poly- [MANY] /pɒl.i-/ [US] /pɑː.li-/ *prefix* many: *a polytheistic* (= believing in many gods) *society* ○ *a polymath* (= person who knows a lot about many different subjects.)

polyester /ˌpɒl.iˈes.təʳ/ [US] /ˌpɑː.liˈes.tɚ/ *noun* [U] a type of artificial cloth: *a polyester shirt*

polyethylene /ˌpɒl.iˈeθ.ɪ.liːn/ [US] /ˌpɑː.liˈeθ.ə-/ *noun* [U] *US FOR* **polythene**

polygamy /pəˈlɪɡ.ə.mi/ *noun* [U] the fact or custom of being married to more than one person at the same time
polygamist /pəˈlɪɡ.ə.mɪst/ *noun* [C] **polygamous** /pəˈlɪɡ.ə.məs/ *adj*: *a polygamous society*

polyglot /ˈpɒl.ɪ.ɡlɒt/ [US] /ˈpɑː.lɪ.ɡlɑːt/ *adj FORMAL* **1** speaking or using several different languages: *She was reading a polyglot bible, with the text in English, Latin and Greek.* **2** containing people from many different and distant places: *New York is an exciting polyglot city.* **polyglot** /ˈpɒl.ɪ.ɡlɒt/ [US] /ˈpɑː.lɪ.ɡlɑːt/ *noun* [C] *My tutor's something of a polyglot – she speaks seven languages.*

polygon /ˈpɒl.ɪ.ɡɒn/ [US] /ˈpɑː.lɪ.ɡɑːn/ *noun* [C] *SPECIALIZED* a flat shape with three or more straight sides: *Triangles and squares are polygons.*

polygraph /ˈpɒl.ɪ.ɡrɑːf/ [US] /ˈpɑː.lɪ.ɡræf/ *noun* [C] *SPECIALIZED* a **lie detector**

polyhedron /ˌpɒl.iˈhiː.drən/ [US] /ˌpɑː.lɪˈhiː.drɑːn/ *noun* [C] *SPECIALIZED* a solid shape with four or more flat surfaces: *A cube is a polyhedron.*

polymath /ˈpɒl.ɪ.mæθ/ [US] /ˈpɑː.lɪ-/ *noun* [C] *FORMAL APPROVING* a person who knows a lot about many different subjects

polymer /ˈpɒl.ɪ.məʳ/ [US] /ˈpɑː.lɪ.mɚ/ *noun* [C] *SPECIALIZED* a chemical substance consisting of large molecules made from many smaller and simpler molecules: *Many polymers, such as nylon, are artificial.* ○ *Proteins and DNA are* ***natural*** *polymers.*

polymorphous /ˌpɒl.ɪˈmɔː.fəs/ [US] /ˌpɑː.lɪˈmɔːr-/ *adj FORMAL* having or experiencing many different forms or stages of development: *Intelligence is a polymorphous concept.*

polyp [ANIMAL] /ˈpɒl.ɪp/ [US] /ˈpɑː.lɪp/ *noun* [C] a small simple tube-shaped water animal

polyp [GROWTH] /ˈpɒl.ɪp/ [US] /ˈpɑː.lɪp/ *noun* [C] *SPECIALIZED* a small mass of diseased cells that grows in the body, and is usually harmless

polyphony /pəˈlɪf.ᵊn.i/ *noun* [U] *SPECIALIZED* music in which several different tunes are played or sung at the same time **polyphonic** /ˌpɒl.ɪˈfɒn.ɪk/ [US] /ˌpɑː.lɪˈfɑː.nɪk/ *adj*: *polyphonic music* ○ *a 32-voice polyphonic synthesizer*

polystyrene /ˌpɒl.ɪˈstaɪə.riːn/ [US] /ˌpɑː.lɪˈstaɪ-/ *noun* [U] (*US USUALLY TRADEMARK* **Styrofoam**) a light usually white plastic used especially for putting around delicate objects inside containers to protect them from damage, or for putting around something to prevent it from losing heat: *polystyrene cups/plates* ○ *The ceiling was covered with polystyrene insulation tiles.*

polysyllabic /ˌpɒl.ɪ.sɪˈlæb.ɪk/ [US] /ˌpɑː.lɪ.sɪ-/ *adj SPECIALIZED* containing three or more syllables: *The word 'internationalism' is polysyllabic.*

polytechnic /ˌpɒl.ɪˈtek.nɪk/ [US] /ˌpɑː.lɪ-/ *noun* [C] (*INFORMAL* **poly**) (especially in Britain before 1992) a college where students study for degrees, especially in technical subjects, or train for particular types of work: *a polytechnic student/course* ○ *I considered applying to university, but I eventually decided to go to the local poly.* ➲Compare **university**.

polytheism /ˈpɒl.ɪ.θiː.ɪ.zᵊm/ /ˌ--ˈ---/ [US] /ˈpɑː.lɪ-/ *noun* [U] *SPECIALIZED* belief in many different gods **polytheistic** /ˌpɒl.ɪ.θiˈɪs.tɪk/ [US] /ˌpɑː.lɪ-/ *adj*: *Ancient Egyptian society was polytheistic.*

polythene /ˈpɒl.ɪ.θiːn/ [US] /ˈpɑː.lɪ-/ *noun* [U] (*US ALSO* **polyethylene**) a light usually thin soft plastic, often used for making bags or for keeping things dry or fresh: *a polythene* ***bag*** ○ *They covered the broken windows with sheets of polythene.*

polyunsaturate /ˌpɒl.i.ʌnˈsæt.jʊ.rət/ [US] /ˌpɑː.li-/ *noun* [C usually pl; U] a type of fat found in some vegetable oils which is thought to be more healthy to eat than SATURATES (= fat from meat, milk and cheese): *This margarine is* ***high in*** *polyunsaturates.* ➲Compare **saturate** FAT.

polyunsaturated /ˌpɒl.i.ʌnˈsætʃ.ᵊr.eɪ.tɪd/ [US] /ˌpɑː.li.ʌnˈsætʃ.ə.reɪ.t̬ɪd/ *adj SPECIALIZED* describes a fat or oil which

P

has a chemical structure that does not easily change into CHOLESTEROL (= a fatty substance that can cause heart disease): *polyunsaturated margarine/vegetable oil*

polyurethane /ˌpɒl.ɪˈjʊə.rə.θeɪn/ [US] /ˌpɑː.lɪˈjʊr.ə-/ *noun* [U] a plastic used especially as a type of varnish or as a protection for delicate objects

pom /pɒm/ [US] /pɑːm/ *noun* [C] (*ALSO* **pommy**) *AUS INFORMAL DISAPPROVING* an English person

pomander /pəˈmæn.dəʳ/ [US] /ˈpoʊ.mæn.dɚ/ *noun* [C] an object containing dried herbs, spices, flowers, etc., used to make a room, drawer or cupboard smell pleasant

pomegranate /ˈpɒm.ɪˌgræn.ɪt/ [US] /ˈpɑːmˌgræn-/ *noun* [C] a round thick-skinned fruit containing a mass of red juicy seeds

pommel [ROUND PART] /ˈpɒm.əl/ [US] /ˈpʌm-/ *noun* [C] **1** the usually rounded part that sticks up at the front of a saddle **2** the rounded part on the end of a sword handle

pomp /pɒmp/ [US] /pɑːmp/ *noun* [U] splendid and colourful ceremony, especially traditional ceremony on public occasions: *The Prime Minister was received with all the traditional pomp* ***and ceremony*** *that is laid on for visiting heads of government.* ○ *Despite all the pomp* ***of*** *his office/position, he has only limited powers.*

● **pomp and circumstance** formal ceremony: *After two hours of pomp and circumstance, the diplomas were awarded and the audience went wild.*

pompadour /ˈpɒm.pə.dɔːʳ/ [US] /ˈpɑː.m.pə.dɔːr/ *noun* [C] *US FOR* **quiff**

pompom /ˈpɒm.pɒm/ [US] /ˈpɑː.m.pɑːm/ *noun* [C] a small ball of wool or other material used as a decoration, especially on the top of a hat

pompous /ˈpɒm.pəs/ [US] /ˈpɑːm-/ *adj DISAPPROVING* too serious and full of importance: *He's a pompous old prig who's totally incapable of taking a joke.* ○ *He can sometimes* ***sound*** *a bit pompous when he talks about acting.* **pompously** /ˈpɒm.pə.sli/ [US] /ˈpɑːm-/ *adv* **pomposity** /pɒmˈpɒs.ə.ti/ [US] /pɑːmˈpɑː.sə.t̬i/ *noun* [U] (*ALSO* **pompousness**)

ponce [CRIMINAL] /pɒnts/ [US] /pɑːnts/ *noun* [C] *UK INFORMAL* a man who controls prostitutes and takes a large part of the money that they earn for himself

ponce [MAN] /pɒnts/ [US] /pɑːnts/ *noun* [C] *UK INFORMAL DISAPPROVING* a man who does not behave, dress or speak in a traditionally male way, especially one who behaves in a very careful way: *Don't be such a ponce! Pick the spider up – it won't hurt you!* **poncy** /ˈpɒnt.si/ [US] /ˈpɑːnt-/ *adj*: *a poncy flowery shirt*

ponce /pɒnts/ [US] /pɑːnts/ *verb*

PHRASAL VERBS WITH **ponce**

▲ **ponce about/around** [LIKE A WOMAN] *phrasal verb UK INFORMAL DISAPPROVING* If a man ponces about/around, he behaves or dresses more like a woman than like a man: *He was poncing around in a pair of fluffy slippers/yellow silk dressing gown.*

▲ **ponce about/around** [UNHELPFUL] *phrasal verb INFORMAL DISAPPROVING* to waste time doing silly things that do not achieve anything or help anyone: *There's no time for poncing around – we've got to get these boxes packed by this evening.*

poncho /ˈpɒn.tʃəʊ/ [US] /ˈpɑːn.tʃoʊ/ *noun* [C] *plural* **ponchos** a piece of clothing made of a single piece of material, with a hole in the middle through which you put your head

pond /pɒnd/ [US] /pɑːnd/ *noun* [C] an area of water smaller than a lake, often artificially made: *a duck pond*

ponder /ˈpɒn.dəʳ/ [US] /ˈpɑːn.dɚ/ *verb* [I or T] *FORMAL* to think carefully about something, especially for a noticeable length of time: *She sat back for a minute to ponder her next move in the game.* ○ [+ question word] *Journalists pondered* ***why*** *the leading goal-scorer of the World Cup had not scored all season.*

ponderous /ˈpɒn.dər.əs/ [US] /ˈpɑːn.dɚ-/ *adj FORMAL MAINLY DISAPPROVING* **1** slow and awkward because of being very heavy or large: *He had a rather slow and ponderous manner.* **2** If a book, speech or style of writing or speaking is ponderous, it is boring because it is too slow, long or serious: *The ponderous reporting style makes the evening news dull viewing.* **ponderously** /ˈpɒn.dər.ə.sli/ [US] /ˈpɑːn.dɚ-/ *adv*

pong /pɒŋ/ [US] /pɑːŋ/ *noun* [C] *UK HUMOROUS* an unpleasant smell: *What a pong!* **pong** /pɒŋ/ [US] /pɑːŋ/ *verb* [I] *After a couple of days of continuous use, the costumes began to pong.*

pontiff /ˈpɒn.tɪf/ [US] /ˈpɑːn.t̬ɪf/ *noun* [C] *FORMAL FOR* **pope** (= leader of the Roman Catholic Church)

pontificate /pɒnˈtɪf.ɪ.kət/ [US] /pɑːn-/ *noun* [C] *FORMAL* a pope's period of office: *The decision was made during the pontificate of Pope John XX.*

pontificate /pɒnˈtɪf.ɪ.keɪt/ [US] /pɑːn-/ *verb* [I] *DISAPPROVING* to speak or write and give your opinion about something as if you knew everything about it and as if only your opinion was correct: *I think it should be illegal for non-parents to pontificate* ***on/about*** *parenting.*

pontoon [BRIDGE] /pɒnˈtuːn/ [US] /pɑːn-/ *noun* [C] a small flat boat or a metal structure of a similar shape used especially to form or support a temporary floating bridge: *Military engineers hurriedly constructed a pontoon* ***bridge*** *across the river.*

pontoon [GAME] /pɒnˈtuːn/ [US] /pɑːn-/ *noun* [U] *UK FOR* **blackjack** CARD GAME

pony /ˈpəʊ.ni/ [US] /ˈpoʊ-/ *noun* [C] a small type of horse: *As a young girl, she spent every weekend riding her pony.*

ponytail /ˈpəʊ.ni.teɪl/ [US] /ˈpoʊ.ni.teɪl/ *noun* [C] a hairstyle in which the hair is tied up high at the back of the head so that it hangs down like a horse's tail ➲Compare **pigtail**; **plait**. ➲See picture **Hairstyles and Hats** on page Centre 8

ˈ**pony** ˌ**trekking** *noun* [U] *UK* riding horses through the countryside, especially as a holiday activity: *How much does it cost to* ***go*** *pony trekking for an afternoon?*

poo *UK* /puː/ *noun* [C or U] (*US* **poop**) *CHILD'S WORD* (a piece of) excrement: *Ugh, it looks like poo!* ○ *Have you* ***done*** *a poo, Ellie?* **poo** *UK* /puː/ *verb* [I] (*US* **poop**) *INFORMAL Ten minutes after we'd left home, Anna announced that she needed to poo.*

pooch /puːtʃ/ *noun* [C] *INFORMAL MAINLY HUMOROUS* a dog: *a* ***pampered*** *pooch* ○ *a big cuddly/cute little pooch*

poodle /ˈpuː.dl̩/ *noun* [C] a dog with curly hair that is usually cut short, except on its head, tail and legs: *a miniature poodle*

● **be** ***sb's*** **poodle** *UK HUMOROUS DISAPPROVING* to be too willing to support or be controlled by someone in authority: *They accused the Labour party of being the unions' poodle.*

poof [PERSON], **pouf** /pʊf/ *noun* [C] (*ALSO* **poofter**) *MAINLY UK OFFENSIVE* a homosexual man

poof [MAGIC] /pʊf/ *exclamation* used to show that something has happened suddenly or by magic: *He waved his hand over the empty box and – poof! – a dove appeared.*

pooh /puː/ *exclamation INFORMAL* said when you smell something unpleasant: *Pooh! Something stinks in here.*

pooh-pooh /ˌpuːˈpuː/ *verb* [T] *INFORMAL* to express an opinion that an idea or suggestion is silly or worthless: *The Government has pooh-poohed the idea that primary schools will begin to select pupils.*

pool [LIQUID] /puːl/ *noun* [C] **1** a small area of usually still water: *We looked for crabs in the* ***rock*** *pools along the seashore.* **2** a small amount of liquid on a surface: *a pool of blood/oil* ○ *FIGURATIVE a pool of light* **3** a **swimming pool**: *I spent most of my holiday lying/sunbathing by the pool.*

pool [COLLECTION] /puːl/ *noun* [C] a number of people or a quantity of a particular thing, such as money, collected together for shared use by several people or organizations: *Patrick crashed a Ford that he'd borrowed from the* ***car*** *pool at work.* ○ *As unemployment rises, the pool of cheap labour increases.* **pool** /puːl/ *verb* [T] *Three schools in Putney have pooled their* ***resources/money*** *in order to buy an area of waste ground and turn it into a sports field.*

pool [GAME] /puːl/ *noun* [U] a game in which two people use CUES (= long thin poles) to hit 16 coloured balls into six holes around the edge of a large cloth-covered table: *a pool table/room/hall* ○ *MAINLY US INFORMAL Do you want to* ***shoot*** (= play) *some pool?* ➲Compare **snooker** GAME.

the pools *plural noun* (*ALSO* **football pools**) *UK* a type of gambling in which people risk a small amount of money and try to guess the results of football matches correctly and win a lot of money: *They* ***do*** *the pools every week.*

poop [EXCREMENT] /puːp/ *noun* [U] *MAINLY US INFORMAL* excrement, especially dogs' excrement on the ground in public places **poop** /puːp/ *verb* [I] *Your puppy's just pooped right outside my front door.*

poop [TIRED] /puːpt/ *verb US INFORMAL* **be pooped** to be very tired: *I'm pooped! I must get some sleep.*

▲ **poop out** *phrasal verb US INFORMAL* to become very tired and unable to continue working or operating: *I just poop out if I stay up too late.*

▲ **poop *sb* out** *phrasal verb US INFORMAL* to make someone very tired: *All that dancing has really pooped me* ***out.***

the poop [INFORMATION] *noun OLD-FASHIONED US SLANG* information: *Did you get the poop on all the candidates?*

pooper scooper /ˈpuː.pəˌskuː.pəʳ/ [US] /ˈpuː.pɚˌskuː.pɚ/ *noun* [C] (*ALSO* **poop scoop**) *INFORMAL* a tool like a small SPADE, used for picking up and taking away dog excrement from public places

poor [NO MONEY] /pɔːʳ/ [US] /pʊr/ *adj* **1** having little money and/or few possessions: *Most of the world's poorest countries are in Africa.* ○ *He came from a poor immigrant family.* * NOTE: The opposite is **rich**. **2 be poor in *sth*** to have very little of a particular substance or quality: *Unfortunately, Iceland is poor in natural resources.*

• **poor relation** something or someone similar to but less important than another thing or person, and that people do not consider equally valuable: *The air force and navy were modernised but the army, very much* ***the*** *poor relation, was not.*

the poor *plural noun* poor people considered together as a group: *housing for the poor*

poor [BAD] /pɔːʳ/ [US] /pʊr/ *adj* not good, being of a very low quality, quantity or standard: *a poor harvest* ○ *Last year's exam results were fairly poor.* ○ *I was always very poor* ***at*** *maths at school.* ○ *Dad had been in poor* ***health*** *for several years.* ○ *At last month's meeting, attendance was poor.*

• **come/be a poor second/third, etc.** to be considered much lower in value, quality or importance than the one/two, etc. other things or people mentioned: *For Jackie, I'm afraid, money is always of first importance and the children come a poor second.*

poorly /ˈpɔː.li/ [US] /ˈpʊr-/ *adv INFORMAL* not well: *A business as poorly managed as that one doesn't deserve to succeed.* ➲See also **poorly**.

• **think poorly of *sb/sth*** *OLD-FASHIONED* to have a low opinion of someone or something

poor [DESERVING SYMPATHY] /pɔːʳ/ [US] /pʊr/ *adj* [before n] deserving sympathy: *That cold sounds terrible, you poor thing!* ○ *Look at that dog – the poor thing only has three legs.*

poorhouse /ˈpɔː.haʊs/ [US] /ˈpʊr-/ *noun* [C] *OLD USE* a building, in the past, in which extremely poor people could live and be fed and which was paid for by the public ➲Compare **workhouse**.

poorly /ˈpɔː.li/ [US] /ˈpʊr-/ *adj* [after v] *UK* ill: *He says he's* ***feeling*** *poorly and he's going back to bed.* ➲See also **poorly** at **poor** BAD.

ˌpoorly ˈoff *adj* [after v] poor, having little money and/or few possessions: *The country was so poorly off it had to close many of its embassies abroad.*

pop [SOUND] /pɒp/ [US] /pɑːp/ *verb* **-pp- 1** [I or T] to (cause something to) make a short explosive sound, often by bursting something: *The kids were popping all the birthday balloons.* ○ *The music played and champagne corks popped.* **2** [I] If your ears pop, you experience a strange noise and feeling in your ears as a result of a sudden change in air pressure: *My ears always pop as the plane comes in to land.* **pop** /pɒp/ [US] /pɑːp/ *noun* [C] *I heard a pop and the lights went out.*

• **go pop** *HUMOROUS* to explode: *If I eat any more I'm going to go pop!*

pop [MOVE] /pɒp/ [US] /pɑːp/ *verb* [I + adv or prep] **-pp-** to move quickly and suddenly, especially from an enclosed space: *When you open the box, a clown pops* ***out.***

• ***your*** **eyes pop out of *your* head** *INFORMAL* a way of describing the way you look when you are extremely surprised to see something or someone: *When she saw the amount written on the cheque, her eyes* ***nearly*** *popped out of her head.*

pop [GO] /pɒp/ [US] /pɑːp/ *verb* [I + adv or prep] **-pp-** *MAINLY UK INFORMAL* to go to a particular place: *I've just got to pop* ***into*** *the bank to get some money.* ○ *Paula popped* ***out*** *for a minute.* ○ *Would you pop* ***upstairs*** *and see if Grandad is okay?* ○ *Why don't you pop* ***in/over*** *and see us this afternoon?*

pop [PUT] /pɒp/ [US] /pɑːp/ *verb* [T + adv or prep] **-pp-** *INFORMAL* **1** to put or take something quickly: *If you pop the pizza* ***in*** *the oven now, it'll be ready in 15 minutes.* ○ *He popped his head* ***into*** *the room/****round*** *the door and said "Lunchtime!"* ○ *Pop your shoes* ***on*** *and let's go.* **2 pop pills** to take pills regularly, especially ones containing an illegal drug: *A decade of heavy drinking and popping pills ruined her health.*

• **pop *your* clogs** *UK HUMOROUS* to die: *I think I'll leave all my money to charity when I pop my clogs.*

• **pop the question** to ask someone to marry you: *So did he pop the question, then?*

pop [MUSIC] /pɒp/ [US] /pɑːp/ *noun* [U] (*FORMAL* **popular music**) modern popular music, usually with a strong beat, created with electrical or electronic equipment, and easy to listen to and remember: *pop music* ○ *a pop concert/song* ○ *What do you want to listen to – jazz, classical or pop?* ○ *The song reached No. 32 in the pop* ***charts.*** ○ *She wants to be a pop* ***singer/star*** *like Madonna.*

pop [FATHER] /pɒp/ [US] /pɑːp/ *noun MAINLY US INFORMAL* a father: [as form of address] *Hey Pop, can I do anything to help?*

pop [DRINK] /pɒp/ [US] /pɑːp/ *noun* [U] (*US USUALLY* **soda**) *OLD-FASHIONED INFORMAL* a sweet fizzy drink, usually flavoured with fruit: *a bottle of pop*

pop [CRITICISM] /pɒp/ [US] /pɑːp/ *noun UK INFORMAL* **take a pop at *sb*** to criticize someone, especially in public: *She never expected anyone from her own family to take a pop at her.*

pop [OCCASION/ITEM] /pɒp/ [US] /pɑːp/ *noun* [C usually sing] *US INFORMAL* each particular occasion or item in a series: *She gives lectures and gets paid $5 000* ***a*** *pop.*

pop. [PEOPLE] /pɒp/ [US] /pɑːp/ *ABBREVIATION FOR* **population**: *During the 18th and 19th centuries, the village (pop. 3915) was a bustling river port.*

PHRASAL VERBS WITH **pop**

▲ **pop off** *phrasal verb HUMOROUS* to die: *You're all just waiting till I pop off so you can get your hands on my money.*

▲ **pop *sb* off** *phrasal verb HUMOROUS* to kill someone

▲ **pop up** *phrasal verb INFORMAL* to appear or happen, especially suddenly or unexpectedly: *She's one of those film stars who pops up everywhere, on TV, in magazines, on Broadway.* ○ *The words 'Hard disk failure – program aborted' popped up on the screen.*

pop-up /ˈpɒp.ʌp/ [US] /ˈpɑːp-/ *noun* [C] (*ALSO* **pop fly**) in baseball, a ball which is hit very high in the air but not very far

pop-up /ˈpɒp.ʌp/ [US] /ˈpɑːp-/ *adj* **pop-up machine/book, etc.** a machine, book, etc. which has parts that push out from a surface or from inside: *a pop-up toaster* ○ *a pop-up children's book* ➲See also **pop-up (menu)**.

ˈpop ˌart *noun* [U] a type of modern art that started in the 1960s and uses images and objects from ordinary life: *Andy Warhol's pictures of soup cans are a famous example of pop art.*

popcorn /ˈpɒp.kɔːn/ [US] /ˈpɑːp.kɔːrn/ *noun* [U] seeds of maize that are heated until they burst open and become soft and light, usually flavoured with salt, butter or sugar: *a tub of popcorn*

ˌpop ˈculture *noun* [U] music, TV, cinema, literature, etc. that is popular and enjoyed by ordinary people, rather than specialists or highly educated people

pope /pəʊp/ [US] /poʊp/ *noun* [C] (the title of) the leader of the Roman Catholic Church: *Pope John Paul II* ➲See also **the papacy**; **pontiff**.

pop-eyed /ˈpɒp.aɪd/ [US] /ˈpɑːp-/ *adj* INFORMAL having your eyes wide open with surprise or excitement: *The children were pop-eyed* ***with*** *excitement.*

ˈpop ˌgroup *group noun* [C] a small group of people who play and/or sing pop music together: *The Beatles will always be the world's most famous pop group.*

poplar /ˈpɒp.ləʳ/ [US] /ˈpɑː.plɚ/ *noun* [C] a tall tree with branches that form a thin pointed shape: *a tall row of poplars*

poplin /ˈpɒp.lɪn/ [US] /ˈpɑː.plɪn/ *noun* [U] a type of slightly shiny cotton cloth: *a summery poplin dress* ○ *100%* ***cotton*** *poplin*

poppadum, poppadom /ˈpɒp.ə.dɒm/ [US] /ˈpɑː.pə-/ *noun* [C] a very thin flat circular Indian bread that breaks easily into pieces

popper [FASTENER] /ˈpɒp.əʳ/ [US] /ˈpɑː.pɚ/ *noun* [C] UK INFORMAL a **press stud**

popper [DRUG] /ˈpɒp.əz/ [US] /ˈpɑː.pɚz/ *noun* [C usually pl] SLANG the drug AMYL NITRITE, usually in a small container

poppet /ˈpɒp.ɪt/ [US] /ˈpɑː.pɪt/ *noun* [C] UK INFORMAL a person, especially a child, that you like or love: [as form of address] *Come on, poppet, it's time for bed.* ○ *Oh, Becky's a real poppet – such a sweet girl.*

ˌpop psyˈchology *noun* [U] theories and advice about people's behaviour that are easily understood and intended to help people improve their lives: *Why is it women that buy the majority of pop psychology, self-help manuals?*

poppy /ˈpɒp.i/ [US] /ˈpɑː.pi/ *noun* [C] a plant with large delicate flowers, which are typically red, and small black seeds ➲See picture **Flowers and Plants** on page Centre 3

poppycock /ˈpɒp.ɪ.kɒk/ [US] /ˈpɑː.pɪ.kɑːk/ *noun* [U] OLD-FASHIONED DISAPPROVING nonsense: *He dismissed the allegations as poppycock.*

Popsicle /ˈpɒp.sɪ.kl̩/ [US] /ˈpɑːp-/ *noun* [C] US TRADEMARK FOR **ice lolly**

the populace /ðəˈpɒp.jʊ.ləs/ [US] /-ˈpɑː.pjə-/ *group noun* [S] FORMAL the ordinary people who live in a particular country or place: *Some studies show that workers in the nuclear industry are more likely than the* ***general*** *populace to get cancer.*

popular [LIKED] /ˈpɒp.jʊ.ləʳ/ [US] /ˈpɑː.pjə.lɚ/ *adj* liked, enjoyed or supported by many people: *She's the most popular teacher in school.* ○ *That song was popular* ***with*** *people from my father's generation.* ○ *Walking is a popular form of exercise in Britain.* ○ *How popular is Madonna* ***among/with*** *teenagers?* ○ INFORMAL *Jan wasn't very popular* (= people were annoyed by her) *when she opened all the windows on that cold day.* ∗ NOTE: The opposite is UNPOPULAR.

popularity /ˌpɒp.jʊˈlær.ə.ti/ [US] /ˌpɑː.pjəˈler.ə.t̬i/ *noun* [U] when something is liked, enjoyed or supported by many people: *the increasing popularity of organic food*

popularize, UK USUALLY **-ise** /ˈpɒp.jʊ.lə.raɪz/ [US] /ˈpɑː.pjə-/ *verb* [T] to make something become popular: *It was Luciano Pavarotti in the 1980s who really popularized opera.* **popularization**, UK USUALLY **-isation** /ˌpɒp.jʊ.lə.raɪˈzeɪ.ʃᵊn/ [US] /ˌpɑː.pjə.lɚ.ɪ-/ *noun* [U]

popular [GENERAL] /ˈpɒp.jʊ.ləʳ/ [US] /ˈpɑː.pjə.lɚ/ *adj* [before n] for or involving ordinary people rather than specialists or highly educated people: *popular music/entertainment/culture* ○ *The issue was virtually ignored by the popular press.* ○ *The popular myth is that air travel is more dangerous than travel by car or bus.*

popularize, UK USUALLY **-ise** /ˈpɒp.jʊ.lə.raɪz/ [US] /ˈpɑː.pjə-/ *verb* [T] to make something known and understood by ordinary people: *Television has an important role to play in popularizing new scientific ideas.* **popularization**, UK USUALLY **-isation** /ˌpɒp.jə.lə.raɪˈzeɪ.ʃᵊn/ [US] /ˌpɑː.pjə.lɚ.ɪ-/ *noun* [U] **popularly** /ˈpɒp.jʊ.lə.li/ [US] /ˈpɑː.pjə.lɚ-/ *adv*: *In Britain, BSE is popularly known as Mad Cow Disease.*

ˌpopular ˈmusic *noun* [U] FORMAL FOR **pop** MUSIC

population /ˌpɒp.jʊˈleɪ.ʃᵊn/ [US] /ˌpɑː.pjə-/ *group noun* [C] **1** all the people living in a particular country, area or place: *Ten per cent of* ***the*** *population lived in poverty.* ○ *In 1992* ***the*** *population of Cairo was approximately 6 500 000.* ○ *We have a growing/shrinking population.* ○ *Throughout the war, there were horrific casualties amongst the civilian populations of both countries.* ○ *The UN is investigating new methods of population* ***control*** (= limiting the growth of the number of people). ○ *The country is facing a population* ***explosion*** (= sudden growth in the number of people). **2** all the people or animals of a particular type or group who live in one country, area or place: *There's been a 9% rise in the prison population* (= the number of people in prison). ○ *The dolphin population has been decimated by tuna fishing.*

populate /ˈpɒp.jʊ.leɪt/ [US] /ˈpɑː.pjə-/ *verb* **1** [T usually passive] If an area is populated by people or animals, they live in that area: *The inner cities are no longer densely populated.* ○ *The river is populated mainly by smaller species of fish.* **2** [T] to live in an area or place: *The settlers began to move inland and populate the river valleys.*

populous /ˈpɒp.jʊ.ləs/ [US] /ˈpɑː.pjə-/ *adj* FORMAL A populous country, area or place has a lot of people living in it: *China is the world's most populous country.*

populism /ˈpɒp.jʊ.lɪ.zᵊm/ [US] /ˈpɑː.pjə-/ *noun* [U] MAINLY DISAPPROVING political ideas and activities that are intended to represent ordinary people's needs and wishes: *Their ideas are simple populism – tax cuts and higher wages.*

populist /ˈpɒp.jʊ.lɪst/ [US] /ˈpɑː.pjə-/ *adj* representing or connected with the ideas and opinions of ordinary people: *a populist manifesto* ○ *a populist leader* **populist** /ˈpɒp.jʊ.lɪst/ [US] /ˈpɑː.pjə-/ *noun* [C] *a political party dominated by populists*

pop-up (menu) /ˌpɒp.ʌpˈmen.juː/ *noun* [C] in computing, a list of choices that is shown on the screen when the user requests it: *Select the option you want from the pop-up (menu).*

p.o.q. /ˌpiː.əʊˈkjuː/ [US] /-oʊˈ-/ *verb* [I] AUS INFORMAL to leave quickly

porcelain /ˈpɔː.sᵊl.ɪn/ [US] /ˈpɔːr-/ *noun* [U] **1** a hard but delicate shiny white substance made by heating a special type of clay to a high temperature, used to make cups, plates, decorations, etc: *a porcelain dish* ○ *The tea cups are (made of) porcelain.* **2** cups, plates and decorations, etc. made of porcelain: *He had a fine collection of Meissen porcelain.*

porch /pɔːtʃ/ [US] /pɔːrtʃ/ *noun* [C] **1** a covered structure in front of the entrance to a building **2** US a **veranda**: *We sat out on the porch to cool off.*

porcupine /ˈpɔː.kjʊ.paɪn/ [US] /ˈpɔːr-/ *noun* [C] an animal with a protective covering of long sharp QUILLS (= stiff needle-like hairs) on its back

pore /pɔːʳ/ [US] /pɔːr/ *noun* [C] a very small hole in the skin of people or other animals, or a similar hole on the surface of plants or rocks: *Sweat passes through the pores and cools the body down.* ○ *Pimples form when pores become blocked with dirt.*

porous /ˈpɔː.rəs/ [US] /ˈpɔːr.əs/ *adj* **1** describes something that has many small holes, so liquid or air can pass through, especially slowly: *porous soil with good drainage* ○ *porous brick walls* ○ *a porous polymer membrane* **2** not protected enough to stop people going through: *The border in this region is porous and many refugees have simply walked across.*

porosity /pɔːˈrɒs.ə.ti/ [US] /pɔːrˈɑː.sə.t̬i/ *noun* [U] SPECIALIZED the state of being porous

pore /pɔːʳ/ [US] /pɔːr/ *verb*

▲ **pore over** ***sth*** *phrasal verb* to look at and study something, usually a book or document, carefully: *She spends her evenings poring over textbooks.* ○ *He pored over the letter searching for clues about the writer.*

pork /pɔːk/ [US] /pɔːrk/ *noun* [U] meat from a pig, eaten as food: *a pork chop* ○ *pork sausages*

porky /ˈpɔː.ki/ [US] /ˈpɔːr-/ *adj* INFORMAL DISAPPROVING fat: *He's been looking a bit porky since he gave up smoking.*

porker /ˈpɔː.kəʳ/ [US] /ˈpɔːr.kɚ/ *noun* [C] a pig, especially one raised to produce meat

pork-barrel /ˈpɔːkˌbær.ᵊl/ [US] /ˈpɔːrkˌber-/ *adj* [before n] US SLANG DISAPPROVING involving the spending of large amounts of money in an area in order to become more popular with local voters: *pork-barrel projects/spending*

porkie /ˈpɔː.ki/ [US] /ˈpɔːr-/ *noun* [C usually pl] (*ALSO* **pork pie**) *UK HUMOROUS SLANG* a lie: *Have you been **telling** porkies again?*

ˌpork ˈpie [FOOD] *noun* [C] *MAINLY UK* a small round pastry case filled with cooked pork, eaten cold

ˌpork ˈpie [LIE] *noun* [C] *UK HUMOROUS SLANG* another word for **porkie**

pork scratchings *UK* /ˌpɔːkˈskrætʃ.ɪŋz/ [US] /ˌpɔːrk-/ *plural noun* (*US* **pork rinds**) small hard pieces of fried pork skin eaten cold and usually sold in bags

porn /pɔːn/ [US] /pɔːrn/ *noun* [U] *INFORMAL FOR* **pornography**: *Some of those photos they show in tabloid newspapers are nothing but porn.*

porn /pɔːn/ [US] /pɔːrn/ *adj* (*ALSO* **porno**) *INFORMAL FOR* **pornographic**: *a porn shop* ○ *porn movies* ○ *porno magazines*

pornography /pɔːˈnɒg.rə.fi/ [US] /pɔːrˈnɑː.grə-/ *noun* [U] (*INFORMAL* **porn**) *DISAPPROVING* books, magazines, films, etc. with no artistic value which describe or show sexual acts or naked people in a way that is intended to be sexually exciting but would be considered unpleasant or offensive by many people: *a campaign against pornography* ○ ***hard(-core)*** (= very detailed) *porn* ○ ***soft(-core)*** (= not very detailed) *porn*

pornographer /pɔːˈnɒg.rə.fəʳ/ [US] /pɔːrˈnɑː.grə.fɚ/ *noun* [C] *DISAPPROVING* a person who makes or sells pornography **pornographic** /ˌpɔː.nəˈgræf.ɪk/ [US] /ˌpɔːr-/ *adj* (*INFORMAL* **porn, porno**) *The part of the film judged to be pornographic was cut from the final version.*

porous /ˈpɔː.rəs/ [US] /ˈpɔːr.əs/ *adj* ➲See at **pore**.

porpoise /ˈpɔː.pəs/ [US] /ˈpɔːr-/ *noun* [C] a mammal that lives in the sea, swims in groups and looks similar to a DOLPHIN but has a shorter rounder nose

porridge [FOOD] *MAINLY UK* /ˈpɒr.ɪdʒ/ [US] /ˈpɔːr-/ *noun* [U] (*US USUALLY* **oatmeal**) a thick soft food made from oats boiled in milk or water, eaten hot for breakfast

porridge [PRISON] /ˈpɒr.ɪdʒ/ [US] /ˈpɔːr-/ *noun* [U] *UK SLANG* a period of time spent in prison: *He **did** ten years porridge for armed robbery.*

port [TOWN] /pɔːt/ [US] /pɔːrt/ *noun* [C or U] a town by the sea or by a river which has a harbour, or the harbour itself: *a naval/fishing/container port* ○ *We had a good view of all the ships **coming into/leaving** port.*

port [CONNECTION] /pɔːt/ [US] /pɔːrt/ *noun* [C] *SPECIALIZED* a part of a computer where wires from other pieces of equipment, such as a printer, can be connected

port [LEFT] /pɔːt/ [US] /pɔːrt/ *noun* [U] *SPECIALIZED* the left side of a ship or aircraft ✻ NOTE: The opposite is **starboard**.

port [WINE] /pɔːt/ [US] /pɔːrt/ *noun* [U] a strong sweet wine made in Portugal

port [BAG] /pɔːt/ [US] /pɔːrt/ *noun* [C] *AUS* a case or bag

portable /ˈpɔː.tə.bl̩/ [US] /ˈpɔːr.t̬ə-/ *adj* (designed to be) light and small enough to be easily carried or moved: *a portable radio/telephone/computer* **portability** /ˌpɔː.təˈbɪl.ɪ.ti/ [US] /ˌpɔːr.t̬əˈbɪl.ə.t̬i/ *noun* [U] *The advantage of the smaller model is its greater portability.*

Portakabin /ˈpɔː.təˌkæb.ɪn/ [US] /ˈpɔːr.t̬ə-/ *noun* [C] *UK TRADEMARK* a small building that is designed to be moved from place to place and is used as a temporary office, school or home, especially when building work is being done

portal /ˈpɔː.təl/ [US] /ˈpɔːr.t̬əl/ *noun* [C] *SPECIALIZED* a page on the Internet that people use to search THE WORLD WIDE WEB and that enables them to access useful information such as news, weather and travel, or a company that provides these pages

portals /ˈpɔː.təlz/ [US] /ˈpɔːr.t̬əlz/ *plural noun FORMAL* a large and important-looking entrance to a building: *Passing through the portals of the BBC for the first time, she felt slightly nervous.*

portcullis /ˌpɔːtˈkʌl.ɪs/ [US] /ˌpɔːrt-/ *noun* [C] a strong gate made of bars with points at the bottom that hangs above the entrance to a castle and in the past was brought down to the ground in order to close the entrance against enemies

portend /pɔːˈtend/ [US] /pɔːr-/ *verb* [T] *FORMAL* to be a sign that something bad is likely to happen in the future: *It was a deeply superstitious country, where earthquakes were commonly believed to portend the end of dynasties.*

portent /ˈpɔː.tent/ [US] /ˈpɔːr-/ *noun* [C] *Is it true that cows lying down in a field are a portent **of** rain?*

portentous /pɔːˈten.təs/ [US] /pɔːrˈten.t̬əs/ *adj* **1** *FORMAL DISAPPROVING* too serious and trying to be very important: *The problem with the book is that it sometimes descends into portentous philosophizing.* **2** *LITERARY* Portentous events, statements or signs are important because they show that something unpleasant is very likely to happen: *The report contains numerous portentous references to a future environmental calamity.*

portentously /pɔːˈten.tə.sli/ [US] /pɔːrˈten.t̬ə-/ *adv FORMAL DISAPPROVING*

porter /ˈpɔː.təʳ/ [US] /ˈpɔːr.t̬ɚ/ *noun* [C] **1** a person whose job is to carry things, especially traveller's bags at railway stations, airports, etc: *There aren't any porters, so we'll have to find a trolley for the luggage.* **2** *UK* (*US* **doorman**) someone whose job is to take care of a building and be present at its entrance in order to help visitors: *The hotel porter opened the door for me and then called a taxi for me.* **3** *US* a person whose job is to help travellers who are spending the night on a train by arranging their bed, looking after their bags, etc.

portfolio [CASE] /ˌpɔːtˈfəʊ.li.əʊ/ [US] /ˌpɔːrtˈfoʊ.li.oʊ/ *noun* [C] *plural* **portfolios** **1** a large thin case used for carrying drawings, documents, etc. **2** a collection of drawings, documents, etc. that represent a person's, especially an artist's, work: *She's trying to build up a portfolio **of work** to show during job interviews.*

portfolio [INVESTMENTS] /ˌpɔːtˈfəʊ.li.əʊ/ [US] /ˌpɔːrtˈfoʊ.li.oʊ/ *noun* [C] *plural* **portfolios** *SPECIALIZED* a collection of company shares and other investments that are owned by a particular person or organization

portfolio [JOB] /ˌpɔːtˈfəʊ.li.əʊ/ [US] /ˌpɔːrtˈfoʊ.li.oʊ/ *noun* [C] *plural* **portfolios** *UK SPECIALIZED* a particular job or area of responsibility of a member of a government: *The Prime Minister offered her the foreign affairs portfolio.*

• **without portfolio** In Britain, a minister without portfolio is an important government official who is not in charge of a particular department, but who still takes part in the decisions of the government.

porthole /ˈpɔːt.həʊl/ [US] /ˈpɔːrt.hoʊl/ *noun* [C] a small usually round window in the side of a ship or aircraft

portico /ˈpɔː.tɪ.kəʊ/ [US] /ˈpɔːr.t̬ɪ.koʊ/ *noun* [C] *plural* **porticoes** or **porticos** a covered entrance to a building, usually a large and splendid building, which is supported by columns

P

portion /ˈpɔː.ʃən/ [US] /ˈpɔːr-/ *noun* [C] **1** a part or share of something larger: *A large/major portion **of** the company's profit goes straight back into new projects.* ○ *I accept my portion **of** the blame.* **2** the amount of a particular food that is served to one person, especially in a restaurant or a shop which sells food ready to be eaten: *The portions are very **generous** in this restaurant.*

portion /ˌpɔː.ʃən/ [US] /ˌpɔːr-/ *verb*

▲ **portion *sth* out** *phrasal verb* [M] to share something out: *We'll have to portion the money out **among/between** the six of us.* ➲See also **apportion**.

portly /ˈpɔːt.li/ [US] /ˈpɔːrt-/ *adj* (especially of middle-aged or old men) fat and round: *He was a portly figure in a tight-fitting jacket and bow tie.*

portmanteau [BAG] /pɔːtˈmæn.təʊ/ [US] /pɔːrtˈmæn.toʊ/ *noun* [C] *plural* **portmanteaus** or **portmanteaux** *OLD-FASHIONED* a large case for carrying clothes while travelling, especially one which opens out into two parts

portmanteau [GENERAL] /pɔːtˈmæn.təʊ/ [US] /pɔːrtˈmæn.toʊ/ *adj* [before n] consisting of a wide range of items that are considered as a single item: *The Official Secrets Act was described as a piece of portmanteau legislation, covering everything from nuclear weapons to army boots.*

ˌport of ˈcall *noun* [C] a place where you stop for a short time, especially on a journey

portrait /ˈpɔː.trət/ /-treɪt/ [US] /ˈpɔːr.trɪt/ *noun* [C] **1** a painting, photograph, drawing, etc. of a person or, less commonly, of a group of people: *She's commissioned an artist to paint her portrait/paint a portrait **of** her.* ○ *a portrait gallery* ○ *a portrait painter* **2** A film or book which is a portrait of something is a detailed description or representation of it: *Her latest novel paints a very* *vivid portrait **of** the aristocracy in the 1920s.*

portraiture /ˈpɔː.trɪ.tʃə/ [US] /ˈpɔːr.trɪ.tʃɚ/ *noun* [U] *SPECIALIZED* the practice or art of making portraits

portray /pɔːˈtreɪ/ [US] /pɔːr-/ *verb* [T] **1** to represent or describe someone or something in a painting, film, book or other artistic work: *The painting portrays a beautiful young woman in a blue dress.* ○ *The writer portrays life in a small village at the turn of the century.* **2 portray *sb* as *sth*** If a person in a film, book, etc. is portrayed as a particular type of character, they are represented in that way: *The father in the film is portrayed as a fairly unpleasant character.* **portrayal** /pɔːˈtreɪ.ᵊl/ [US] /pɔːr-/ *noun* [C] *His latest film is a fairly grim portrayal **of** wartime suffering.*

Portuguese /ˌpɔː.tʃʊˈgiːz/ /ˌpɔːr-/ *adj* from, belonging to or relating to Portugal: *Portuguese food/customs*

Portuguese /ˌpɔː.tʃʊˈgiːz/ /ˌpɔːr-/ *noun* **1** [U] the language of Portugal **2** [C] a person from Portugal: *There are six Spaniards and a Portuguese in the class.*

pose [CAUSE] /pəʊz/ [US] /poʊz/ *verb* [T] to cause something, especially a problem or difficulty: *Nuclear weapons pose **a threat** to everyone.*

pose [ASK] /pəʊz/ [US] /poʊz/ *verb* [T] to ask a question, especially in a formal situation such as a meeting: *Can we go back to the question that Helena posed earlier?*

poser /ˈpəʊ.zəʳ/ [US] /ˈpoʊ.zɚ/ *noun* [C] *INFORMAL* a problem or question that is difficult to solve or answer: *Who was the last woman to win three Olympic gold medals? That's quite a poser.*

pose [POSITION] /pəʊz/ [US] /poʊz/ *verb* [I] to move into and stay in a particular position, in order to be photographed, painted, etc: *We all posed **for** our photographs next to the Statue of Liberty.*

pose /pəʊz/ [US] /poʊz/ *noun* [C] a particular position in which a person stands, sits, etc. in order to be photographed, painted, etc: *He **adopted/assumed/struck*** (= moved into) *an elegant pose.*

pose [PRETEND] /pəʊz/ [US] /poʊz/ *verb* [I] to pretend to be something that you are not or to have qualities that you do not possess, in order to be admired or attract interest: *He doesn't really know a thing about the theatre – he's just posing!*

pose /pəʊz/ [US] /poʊz/ *noun* [C usually sing] when someone pretends to have qualities that they do not possess: *She likes to appear as if she knows all about the latest films and art exhibitions, but it's all a pose* (= she's pretending and it's not true).

poseur /ˈpəʊ.zəʳ/ [US] /ˈpoʊ.zɚ/ *noun* [C] (*ALSO* **poser**) *DISAPPROVING* someone who pretends to be something they are not, or to have qualities that they do not possess: *You look like a real poseur in your fancy sports car with your expensive clothes!*

posey /ˈpəʊ.zi/ [US] /ˈpoʊ-/ *adj* **posier, posiest** *UK INFORMAL DISAPPROVING* expensive and fashionable, in a way that is intended to impress: *I resent paying extra for my drink just because it's in a posey bottle!*

▲ **pose as *sb*** *phrasal verb* If you pose as a particular person, you pretend to be that person in order to deceive people: *He's posing **as** her date, but he's really her bodyguard.*

posh /pɒʃ/ [US] /pɑːʃ/ *adj* **1** *INFORMAL* (of places and things) expensive and of high quality: *He takes her to some really posh restaurants.* **2** *UK INFORMAL* (of people and their voices) from a high social class: *A woman with a very posh accent telephoned for him earlier.* **posh** /pɒʃ/ [US] /pɑːʃ/ *adv UK NOT STANDARD She talks dead posh.*

posit /ˈpɒz.ɪt/ [US] /ˈpɑː.zɪt/ *verb* [T] *FORMAL* to suggest something as a basic fact or principle from which a further idea is formed or developed: [+ **that**] *If we posit **that** wage rises cause inflation, it follows that we should try to minimize them.*

position [PLACE] /pəˈzɪʃ.ᵊn/ *noun* **1** [C] the place where something or someone is, often in relation to other things: *Well, I've found our position on the map if you want to see where we are.* ○ *You've moved the furniture around – the sofa is **in** a different position.* ○ *I didn't know you played hockey – what position* (= place or job in the team) *do you play?* **2** [C or U] the place where people are sent in order to carry out a course of action: *The troops took up their battle positions at the front line.* ○ *As soon as his officers were **in** position/had moved **into** position, the police commander walked up the path towards the house.*

position /pəˈzɪʃ.ᵊn/ *verb* [T usually + adv or prep] to put something or someone in a particular place: *The army had been positioned to the north and east of the city.* ○ [R] *When it came to seating people for dinner, I positioned myself as far away from him as possible.*

positional /pəˈzɪʃ.ᵊn.ᵊl/ *adj* relating to position, especially in sports: *The Brazilian side had made eight changes, six of them positional.*

position [RANK] /pəˈzɪʃ.ᵊn/ *noun* [C] **1** a rank or level in a company, competition or society: *Whether or not you're given a car depends on your position **in** the company.* ○ *UK She finished the race **in** third position.* **2** a job: *She applied for a position in the firm that I work for.*

position [SITUATION] /pəˈzɪʃ.ᵊn/ *noun* [C usually sing] a situation: *My financial position is rather precarious at the moment.* ○ *When two of your best friends argue it **puts** you **in** a very awkward position.*

• **be in a position to do *sth*** to be able to do something, usually because you have the necessary experience, authority or money: *I'm not in a position to reveal any of the details of the project at present.* ○ *I'm sure they'd like to help her out financially but they're not in a position to do so.*

position [OPINION] /pəˈzɪʃ.ᵊn/ *noun* [C usually sing] *FORMAL* an opinion: *What's the company's position **on** recycling?* ○ *He **takes** the position* (= believes) *that individuals have a responsibility to look after themselves.*

position [ARRANGEMENT OF BODY] /pəˈzɪʃ.ᵊn/ *noun* [C] the way in which something is arranged: *I go to sleep on my back but I always wake up in a different position.* ○ *Keep the bottles in an upright position.* ○ *This is not a very comfortable position.*

positive [CERTAIN] /ˈpɒz.ə.tɪv/ [US] /ˈpɑː.zə.t̬ɪv/ *adj* certain and without any doubt: *Are you positive **(that)** you saw me switch the iron off?* ○ *"Are you sure it's okay for me to use your mother's car?" "Positive."* ○ *"It was him – I saw him take it." "Are you positive **about** that?"* **positively** /ˈpɒz.ə.tɪv.li/ [US] /ˈpɑː.zə.t̬ɪv-/ *adv: He said quite positively that he would come, so I've saved a place for him.* **positiveness** /ˈpɒz.ə.tɪv.nəs/ [US] /ˈpɑː.zə.t̬ɪv-/ *noun* [U]

positive [HOPEFUL] /ˈpɒz.ə.tɪv/ [US] /ˈpɑː.zə.t̬ɪv/ *adj* hopeful and confident, or giving cause for hope and confidence: *a positive attitude* ○ *On a more positive note, we're seeing signs that the housing market is picking up.* ○ *The past ten years have seen some very positive developments in East-West relations.* ○ *There was a very positive response to our new design – people seemed very pleased with it.* * NOTE: The opposite is **negative**.

positively /ˈpɒz.ə.tɪv.li/ [US] /ˈpɑː.zə.t̬ɪv-/ *adv: I don't respond very positively* (= in a good way) *to being bossed around – it just makes me angry.* **positiveness** /ˈpɒz.ə.tɪv.nəs/ [US] /ˈpɑː.zə.t̬ɪv-/ *noun* [U]

positive [TEST RESULTS] /ˈpɒz.ə.tɪv/ [US] /ˈpɑː.zə.t̬ɪv/ *adj* (of a medical test) showing the presence of the disease or condition for which the person is being tested: *a positive pregnancy test* ○ *He's HIV positive.* ○ *She **tested** positive **for** hepatitis.* * NOTE: The opposite is **negative**. **positiveness** /ˈpɒz.ə.tɪv.nəs/ [US] /ˈpɑː.zə.t̬ɪv-/ *noun* [U]

positive [COMPLETE] /ˈpɒz.ə.tɪv/ [US] /ˈpɑː.zə.t̬ɪv/ *adj* [before n] (used to add force to an expression) complete: *Far from being a nuisance, she was a positive joy to have around.*

positively /ˈpɒz.ə.tɪv.li/ [US] /ˈpɑː.zə.t̬ɪv-/ *adv INFORMAL That sales assistant was positively rude to me!*

positive [ABOVE ZERO] /ˈpɒz.ə.tɪv/ [US] /ˈpɑː.zə.t̬ɪv/ *adj* (of a number or amount) more than zero: *Two is a positive number.* * NOTE: The opposite is **negative**.

positive [ELECTRICITY] /ˈpɒz.ə.tɪv/ [US] /ˈpɑː.zə.t̬ɪv/ *adj* being the type of electrical charge which is carried by PROTONS * NOTE: The opposite is **negative**.

positive [BLOOD TYPE] /ˈpɒz.ə.tɪv/ [US] /ˈpɑː.zə.t̬ɪv/ *adj* having the RHESUS FACTOR in the blood: *My blood type is O positive.*

ˌpositive discrimiˈnation *noun* [U] *UK* the practice of giving advantage to those groups in society which are often treated unfairly, usually because of their race or their sex

positive 'vetting *noun* [U] *UK* the detailed examination of a person's past, political beliefs, etc. in order to discover if they are suitable for a government job which might involve dealing with secret information

positron /'pɒz.ɪ.trɒn/ ⓤ /'paː.zɪ.traːn/ *noun* [C] *SPECIALIZED* an extremely small piece of matter with a positive electrical charge, having the same mass as an ELECTRON

poss /pɒs/ ⓤ /paːs/ *adj* [after v] *UK INFORMAL FOR* possible: *I want it done as soon as poss really.*

posse /'pɒs.i/ ⓤ /'paː.si/ *group noun* [C] **1** a group of people who have gathered for the same purpose: *The disgraced minister walked swiftly from the car to his house pursued by a whole posse of reporters.* **2** in the past, a group of men in the US who were gathered together to catch a criminal: *The sheriff rounded up a posse and went after the bank robbers.* **3** *SLANG* a group of friends: *I was hanging with my posse.*

possess OWN /pə'zes/ *verb* [T] to have or own something, or to have a particular quality: *I don't possess a single DVD* (= I don't have even one DVD). ○ *In the past the root of this plant was thought to possess magical powers which could cure baldness.*

possessed /pə'zest/ *adj FORMAL* **be possessed of sth** to own something or have something as a quality: *He was possessed of a large fortune, but sadly no brains to speak of.*

possession /pə'zeʃ.ˀn/ *noun* **1** [U] when you have or own something: *The possession of large amounts of money does not ensure happiness.* ○ *FORMAL I have in my possession a letter which may be of interest to you.* ○ *FORMAL He was found in possession of explosives.* **2** [C usually pl] something that you own or that you are carrying with you at any time: *Please remember to take all your personal possessions with you when you leave the aircraft.* **3** [C usually pl] the countries that are ruled by another country: *a former overseas possession* **4** *LEGAL* **get/take possession of sth** to start to use and control a building or piece of land, whether you own it or not: *We've already bought the house but we won't take possession of it until May.*

possessive /pə'zes.ɪv/ *adj* **1** If you are possessive about something that you own, you do not like lending it to other people or sharing it with other people: *He's a bit possessive about his CDs – I wouldn't dare ask to borrow them.* **2** Someone who is possessive in his or her feelings and behaviour towards or about another person wants to have all of that person's love and attention and will not share it with anyone else: *a possessive mother* ○ *Her boyfriend was getting too possessive so she finished with him.* **3** In grammar, a possessive word, form etc. shows who or what something belongs to: *'Mine' and 'yours' are possessive **pronouns**.*

possessor /pə'zes.əʳ/ ⓤ /-ɚ/ *noun* [C usually sing] *FORMAL OR HUMOROUS* someone who owns something: *I'm pleased to say that I'm now the **proud** possessor of a driving licence!*

possess CONTROL /pə'zes/ *verb* [T] (of a desire or an idea) to take control over a person's mind, making that person behave in a very strange way: [+ to infinitive] *Whatever possessed him to wear that appalling jacket!*

possessed /pə'zest/ *adj* [after v] Someone who is possessed is thought to be controlled by an evil spirit.
• **like a man/woman possessed** in a wild and uncontrolled way: *He's been running around the office this morning like a man possessed.*

possibility /ˌpɒs.ə'bɪl.ɪ.ti/ ⓤ /ˌpaː.sə'bɪl.ə.t̬i/ *noun* **1** [C or U] a chance that something may happen or be true: *It's not likely to happen but I wouldn't **rule out** the possibility.* ○ *The forecast said that there's a possibility of snow tonight.* ○ [+ (that)] *There's a distinct possibility (that) I'll be asked to give a speech.* ○ *Is there any possibility (that) you could pick me up from the station?* ✳ NOTE: The opposite is **impossibility**. **2** [C] something that you can choose to do in a particular situation: *We could take on extra staff – that's one possibility.* ○ *"Have you decided what to do?" "No, I'm still considering the various possibilities."*

COMMON LEARNER ERROR

Possibility, occasion or opportunity?

A **possibility** is a chance that something may happen or be true. Possibility cannot be followed by an infinitive.

Is there a possibility of finding a cure for AIDS?
~~Is there a possibility to find a cure for AIDS?~~

An **occasion** is an event, or a time when something happens. Occasion does not mean 'chance' or 'opportunity'.

Birthdays are always special occasions.

An **opportunity** is a possibility of doing something, or a situation which gives you the possibility of doing something.

The trip to Paris gave me an opportunity to speak French.
Students had the opportunity to ask questions during the lecture.
I have more opportunity to travel than my parents did.
~~I have more possibility to travel than my parents did.~~

---

possible ACHIEVABLE /'pɒs.ə.bl̩/ ⓤ /'paː.sə-/ *adj* able to be done or achieved, or able to exist: *I can't get it all done by Friday – it's just not possible.* ○ *Is it possible to buy tickets in advance?* ○ *We need to send that letter off **as soon as** possible.* ○ *They got as far as was **humanly** possible* (= as far as anyone could have) *before turning back.* ✳ NOTE: The opposite is **impossible**.

possibly /'pɒs.ə.bli/ ⓤ /'paː.sə-/ *adv* **1** used with 'can' or 'could' for emphasis: *He **can't** possibly have drunk all that on his own!* ○ *We did all that we possibly **could** to persuade her to come.* **2** used in polite requests: *Could I possibly ask you to move your chair a little?* **3** used in polite refusals of offers: *"Have another chocolate." "No, really, I **couldn't** possibly."*

possible UNCERTAIN /'pɒs.ə.bl̩/ ⓤ /'paː.sə-/ *adj* [+ (that)] that might or might not happen: *It's possible (that) Mira might turn up tonight.* ○ *"Do you think he'll end up in prison?" "It's very possible."* ○ *That's one possible solution to the problem.* ⊃Compare **probable**.
• **anything's possible** anything could happen: *Well, if your brother can find a woman who's willing to marry him then I suppose anything's possible.*

possibly /'pɒs.ə.bli/ ⓤ /'paː.sə-/ *adv* **1** used when something is not certain: *He may possibly decide not to come, in which case there's no problem.* **2** used to agree or disagree when some doubt is involved: *"Do you think this skirt might be too small for her?" "(Very) possibly – she has put on a bit of weight." ○ "Will he come?" "Possibly not."*

possum (*plural* **possums** or **possum**) /'pɒs.əm/ ⓤ /'paː.səm/ *noun* [C] (*US USUALLY* **opossum**) a small animal which lives in trees and has thick fur, a long nose and a tail without hair

post LETTERS /pəʊst/ ⓤ /poʊst/ *noun* [U] **1** *MAINLY UK* (*US USUALLY* **mail**) letters and parcels that are delivered to homes or places of work: *I'd been away for a few days so I had a lot of post waiting for me.* ○ *Unless it's marked 'private', my secretary usually **opens** my post.* ○ *Has the post **come/arrived** yet?* **2** *MAINLY UK* (*US USUALLY* **mail**) the public system that exists for the collecting and delivering of letters: *My letter must have got lost **in the** post.* ○ *If you don't want to take it there, you can just send it **by** post.* **3** *UK* the time during the day when letters, etc. are collected or delivered: *I **missed** the post this morning.* ○ *Did you manage to **catch** the post?*

post /pəʊst/ ⓤ /poʊst/ *verb* [T] *UK* (*US* **mail**) to send a letter or parcel by post: *Did you remember to post my letter?* ○ *I must post that parcel **(off)** or she won't get it in time for her birthday.* ○ [+ two objects] *Could you post me the details/post the details **to** me?* **2** *UK* to put an object through a LETTERBOX (= special opening in a door): *Just post the key through the door after you've locked it.*

postage /'pəʊ.stɪdʒ/ ⓤ /'poʊ-/ *noun* [U] the money that you pay for sending letters and parcels through the post: *Please enclose £15.99, plus £2 for postage.*

postal /'pəʊ.stˀl/ ⓤ /'poʊ-/ *adj* relating to post or to the public service that collects and delivers the post: *postal charges* ○ *the postal service* ○ *a postal strike* ○ *postal workers*

post POLE /pəʊst/ ⓤ /poʊst/ *noun* [C] **1** a vertical stick or pole fixed into the ground, usually to support something or mark a position **2** used as a combining form: *a lamp-*

P

post ○ *a signpost* **3 the post** in the sport of horse racing, the place where the race finishes or, less often, the place from which the race starts **4 the post** in sports such as football, a GOALPOST (= either of two vertical posts marking the area in which the ball is kicked to score points) ➲See picture **Sports** on page Centre 10

post [JOB] /pəʊst/ ⑩ /poʊst/ *noun* [C] a job in a company or organization: *Teaching posts are advertised in Tuesday's edition of the paper.* ○ *She's held the post for thirteen years.* ○ *They have several vacant posts.*

posting UK /ˈpəʊ.stɪŋ/ ⑩ /poʊ-/ *noun* [C] (*US USUALLY* **post**) a job, often within the same organization that you are working for, which involves going to a different country or town: *If you were offered an overseas posting, would you take it?*

post [STICK] /pəʊst/ ⑩ /poʊst/ *verb* [T] **1** to stick or pin a notice on a wall in order to make it publicly known: *Company announcements are usually posted (up) on the noticeboard.* **2** to leave an electronic message on a WEBSITE (= an address on the Internet): *Somebody's been posting obscene messages in this chat room.*

post [PLACE] /pəʊst/ ⑩ /poʊst/ *noun* [C] the particular place where someone works, especially where a soldier is told to be for military duty, usually as a guard: *The soldier was disciplined for deserting his post.* ○ *I was ordered to remain at my post until the last customer had left.*

post /pəʊst/ ⑩ /poʊst/ *verb* [T] to send someone to a particular place to work: *He's been posted to Pakistan for six months.* ○ *Guards were posted at all the doors.*

post [PAY] /pəʊst/ ⑩ /poʊst/ *verb* [T] US to pay money, especially so that a person who has been accused of committing a crime can be free until their trial: *She has agreed to post bail for her brother.*

post- [AFTER] /pəʊst-/ ⑩ /poʊst-/ *prefix* after or later than: *postgraduate* ○ *postoperative* ○ *He took a post-lunch nap.*

‚postage and ˈpacking UK *noun* [U] (*US* **shipping and handling**) a charge for the cost of having something put into a container and then posted to you

ˈpostage ‚stamp *noun* [C] *FORMAL* a **stamp** LETTER

ˈpostal ‚ballot UK *noun* [C] (*US* **absentee ballot**) a system of voting in which people send their votes by post

ˈpostal ‚order UK *noun* [C] (*US* **money order**) an official piece of paper with an amount of money written on it, which you post to someone who can then exchange it for the same amount of money at a POST OFFICE

postbag UK /ˈpəʊst.bæg/ ⑩ /poʊst-/ *noun* (*UK ALSO AND US* **mailbag**) **1** [U] the number of letters received at one time or on one subject: *It was clear from our postbag that viewers were unhappy about the programme.* **2** [C] a large strong bag used by THE POST OFFICE for transporting and carrying letters and parcels

postbox UK /ˈpəʊst.bɒks/ ⑩ /poʊst.bɑːks/ *noun* [C] (*US* **mailbox**) a metal container in the street or other public place in which you can post letters. In Britain these are bright red.

postcard /ˈpəʊst.kɑːd/ ⑩ /poʊst.kɑːrd/ *noun* [C] a card, often with a photograph or picture on one side, which can be addressed and sent without an envelope

postcode /ˈpəʊst.kəʊd/ ⑩ /poʊst.koʊd/ *noun* [C] UK in Britain, a short series of letters and numbers that is part of a postal address ➲See also **zip code**.

post-coital /ˌpəʊstˈkɔɪ.tᵊl/ ⑩ /poʊstˈkɔɪ.t̬ᵊl/ *adj* [before n] *FORMAL* happening or existing after sexual INTERCOURSE: *post-coital contraception*

postdate /ˌpəʊstˈdeɪt/ /ˈ--/ ⑩ /poʊstˈdeɪt/ *verb* [T] **1** to happen or exist after something: *Most manuscripts post-date the stories which had circulated by word of mouth for centuries.* ➲Compare **backdate**; **predate**. **2** to write a date on a document, such as a cheque or letter, that is later than the date on which you are writing it, usually to get some advantage: *Luckily, she let me postdate the cheque until the end of the month when I get paid.*

poster /ˈpəʊ.stəʳ/ ⑩ /poʊ.stɚ/ *noun* [C] a large printed picture, photograph or notice which you stick or pin to a wall or board, usually for decoration or to advertise something: *The children put up posters on the classroom walls.* ○ *We noticed a poster advertising a circus.* ➲See also **poster paint**.

ˈposter ‚colour *noun* [C or U] UK FOR **poster paint**

poste restante UK /ˌpəʊstˈres.tɑːnt/ /-tɑ̃ːnt/ ⑩ /ˌpoʊst.resˈtɑːnt/ *noun* [U] (*US* **general delivery**) a system in which a POST OFFICE keeps someone's post until they can collect it, usually used by people who are travelling **poste restante** UK /ˌpəʊstˈres.tɑːnt/ /-tɑ̃ːnt/ ⑩ /ˌpoʊst.resˈtɑːnt/ *adv* (*US* **general delivery**) *I don't know the name of her hotel, so I'm sending her mail poste restante.*

posterior /pɒsˈtɪə.ri.əʳ/ ⑩ /pɑːˈstɪr.i.ɚ/ *adj* [before n] *FORMAL* positioned at or towards the back, or later in time ➲Compare **anterior**.

posterior /pɒsˈtɪə.ri.əʳ/ ⑩ /pɑːˈstɪr.i.ɚ/ *noun* *HUMOROUS* *your* **posterior** your bottom: *If you would kindly move your posterior just a fraction to the right, I might get by.*

posterity /pɒsˈter.ə.ti/ ⑩ /pɑːˈster.ə.t̬i/ *noun* [U] *FORMAL* the people who will exist in the future: *Every attempt is being made to ensure that these works of art are pre-served for posterity.*

ˈposter ‚paint *noun* [C or U] brightly coloured paint used for painting pictures ➲See also **poster**.

post-free /ˌpəʊstˈfriː/ ⑩ /ˌpoʊst-/ *adv, adj* (*ALSO* **post-paid**) UK used when something is sent by post without any money having to be paid: *Send for an educational video post-free.* ○ *The guidebook costs £10.95 post-free.*

postgraduate /ˌpəʊstˈgræd.ʒ.u.ət/ ⑩ /ˌpoʊstˈgrædʒ.u-/ *noun* [C] (*US USUALLY* **graduate**) a student who has already obtained one degree and is studying at a university for a more advanced qualification **postgraduate** /ˌpəʊst-ˈgrædʒ.u.ət/ ⑩ /ˌpoʊstˈgrædʒ.u-/ *adj* [before n] (*MAINLY US* **graduate**) *postgraduate studies/research* ○ *a postgraduate degree in microbiology*

Post‚graduate Cer‚tificate in Edu'cation *noun* [C *usually sing*] (*ABBREVIATION* **PGCE**) a British teaching qualification for people who already have a university degree: *It takes a year to do a PGCE and then you can teach in a primary or secondary school.*

posthaste /ˌpəʊstˈheɪst/ ⑩ /ˌpoʊst-/ *adv* *OLD-FASHIONED* *FORMAL* as fast as possible: *They travelled posthaste to Rome to collect the award.*

posthumous /ˈpɒs.tjʊ.məs/ ⑩ /ˈpɑːs.tʃə-/ *adj* *FORMAL* happening after a person's death: *a posthumous award* **posthumously** /ˈpɒs.tjʊ.mə.sli/ ⑩ /ˈpɑːs.tʃə-/ *adv*: *His last novel was published posthumously.*

postie /ˈpəʊs.tiː/ ⑩ /poʊs-/ *noun* [C] UK INFORMAL FOR **postman**

post-industrial /ˌpəʊst.ɪnˈdʌs.tri.əl/ ⑩ /ˌpoʊst-/ *adj* belonging or relating to an economy that is no longer based on heavy industry, such as the making of large machines: *Service industries such as tourism have become more important in the post-industrial age.*

Post-it (note) /ˈpəʊst.ɪt.nəʊt/ ⑩ /ˈpoʊst.ɪt.noʊt/ *noun* [C] *TRADEMARK* a small coloured piece of paper for short messages which can be stuck temporarily to something else ➲See picture **In the Office** on page Centre 15

postman UK /ˈpəʊst.mən/ ⑩ /poʊst-/ *noun* [C] (*UK INFOR-MAL* **postie**, *US* **mailman**) someone whose job is to deliver and collect letters and parcels that are sent by post

postmark /ˈpəʊst.mɑːk/ ⑩ /poʊst.mɑːrk/ *noun* [C] an official mark stamped on a letter or parcel, typically showing the place that it was sent from and the time or date that it was sent **postmark** /ˈpəʊst.mɑːk/ ⑩ /poʊst.mɑːrk/ *verb* [T]

postmaster /ˈpəʊst.mɑː.stəʳ/ ⑩ /poʊst.mæs.tɚ/ *noun* [C] a person who is in charge of a POST OFFICE

postmistress /ˈpəʊst.mɪs.trəs/ ⑩ /poʊst-/ *noun* [C] a woman who is in charge of a POST OFFICE

post-modernism /ˌpəʊstˈmɒd.ᵊn.ɪ.zᵊm/ ⑩ /ˌpoʊst-ˈmɑː.dɚ.nɪ-/ *noun* [U] a style of art, writing, music, theatre and especially ARCHITECTURE (= the designing of buildings), popular in the West in the 1980s and 1990s, which includes features from several different periods in the past or from the present and past **post-modern** /ˌpəʊstˈmɒd.ᵊn/ ⑩ /ˌpoʊstˈmɑː.dɚn/ *adj* (*ALSO* **post-modernist**) *a post-modern building* ○ *a post-modernist critique*

post-mortem (examination) /ˌpəʊstˈmɔː.təm.ɪg-ˌzæm.ɪˈneɪ.ʃᵊn/ ⑩ /ˌpoʊstˈmɔːr.t̬əm-/ *noun* [C] **1** a medical examination of a dead person's body in order to find out the cause of death; an **autopsy 2** *INFORMAL* a discussion of an event after it has happened, especially of what was wrong with it or why it failed: *After we've played a match, there's usually a post-mortem over a few beers.*

postnatal /ˌpəʊstˈneɪ.tᵊl/ [US] /ˌpoʊstˈneɪ.t̬ᵊl/ *adj* relating to the period of time immediately after a baby has been born: *postnatal care* ○ *postnatal depression* ⊃Compare **antenatal**; **prenatal**.

postnuptial /ˌpəʊstˈnʌp.tʃᵊl/ [US] /ˌpoʊst-/ *adj* done after marriage or relating to the period after marriage

ˈpost ˌoffice [SHOP] *noun* [C] a place where stamps are sold and from where letters and parcels are sent

the ˈPost ˌOffice [ORGANIZATION] *noun* [S] the organization which is in charge of the postal service in the UK

post-operative /ˌpəʊstˈɒp.ᵊr.ə.tɪv/ [US] /ˌpoʊstˈɑː.pɚ-/ *adj* SPECIALIZED relating to the period of time which immediately follows a medical operation: *post-operative care* ○ *post-operative infection*

postpartum, **post-partum** /ˌpəʊstˈpɑː.tᵊm/ [US] /ˌpoʊstˈpɑːr.t̬ᵊm/ *adj* after giving birth: *postpartum depression/pain*

postpone /pəʊstˈpəʊn/ /pəst-/ [US] /poʊstˈpoʊn/ *verb* [T] to delay an event and plan or decide that it should happen at a later date or time: *They decided to postpone their holiday* ***until*** *next year.* ○ [+ v-ing] *We've had to postpone going to France because the children are ill.* **postponement** /pəʊstˈpəʊn.mənt/ /pəst-/ [US] /poʊstˈpoʊn-/ *noun* [C or U] *We were disappointed by yet another postponement of our trip.*

postprandial /ˌpəʊstˈpræn.di.əl/ [US] /ˌpoʊst-/ *adj* FORMAL happening after lunch or dinner: *He took the usual postprandial stroll around the grounds of his house.*

postscript /ˈpəʊst.skrɪpt/ [US] /ˈpoʊst-/ *noun* [C] **1** (ABBREVIATION **PS**) a short remark or message added to the bottom of a letter after you have signed your name, usually introduced by the abbreviation PS: *There was the usual romantic postscript at the end of his letter – PS I love you.* **2** any written or spoken addition to something already finished: *As a postscript* ***to*** *that story I told you last week, it turned out that the woman was his sister-in-law.*

postseason /ˈpəʊstˌsiː.zᵊn/ [US] /ˈpoʊst-/ *adj* MAINLY US describes games that are played after the end of the sports season: *The Garden State Bowl kicks off the post-season college football games.* **postseason** /ˈpəʊstˌsiː.zᵊn/ [US] /ˈpoʊst-/ *noun* [C] *The Indians have won three straight one-run games in the postseason.*

post-traumatic stress disorder /ˌpəʊst.trɔːˌmæt.ɪkˈstres.dɪˌsɔː.dəʳ/ [US] /ˌpoʊst.trɑːˌmæt̬.ɪkˈstres.dɪˌsɔːr.dɚ/ *noun* [U] (ABBREVIATION **PTSD**) SPECIALIZED a mental condition in which a person suffers severe anxiety and DEPRESSION after a very frightening or shocking experience, such as an accident or a war

postulate /ˈpɒs.tjʊ.leɪt/ [US] /ˈpɑː.stjə-/ *verb* [I or T] FORMAL to suggest a theory, idea, etc. as a basic principle from which a further idea is formed or developed: *It was the Greek astronomer, Ptolemy, who postulated* ***that*** *the Earth was at the centre of the universe.*
postulate /ˈpɒs.tjʊ.lət/ [US] /ˈpɑː.stjə-/ *noun* [C] FORMAL an idea that is suggested or accepted as a basic principle before a further idea is formed or developed from it

posture [POSITION OF BODY] /ˈpɒs.tʃəʳ/ [US] /ˈpɑːs.tʃɚ/ *noun* [C or U] the way in which someone usually holds their shoulders, neck and back, or a particular position in which someone stands, sits, etc: *She's got very good/bad posture.* ○ *He always* ***adopts/assumes*** (= moves into) *the same posture for the cameras.*

posture [OPINION] /ˈpɒs.tʃəʳ/ [US] /ˈpɑːs.tʃɚ/ *noun* [C usually sing] a way in which a government or other organization thinks about and/or deals with a particular matter: *For the third time this week the opposition has attacked the government's posture* ***on*** *defence.* ○ *The tone of the feminist speakers suggested they were adopting a rather defensive posture.*

posturing /ˈpɒs.tʃᵊr.ɪŋ/ [US] /ˈpɑːs.tʃɚ-/ *noun* [U] DISAPPROVING behaviour or speech which is intended to attract attention and interest, or to make people believe something that is not true: *His writing has been dismissed as mere intellectual posturing.* **posture** /ˈpɒs.tʃəʳ/ [US] /ˈpɑːs.tʃɚ/ *verb* [I]

post-war /ˈpəʊst.wɔː/ [US] /ˈpoʊst.wɔːr/ *adj* happening or existing in the period after a war, especially the First or Second World War: *post-war Europe* ○ *the post-war period* ⊃Compare **pre-war**.

posy /ˈpəʊ.zi/ [US] /ˈpoʊ-/ *noun* [C] **1** UK AND US a small BUNCH of cut flowers: *a posy of violets* **2** US a flower: *a delicate yellow posy*

pot [CONTAINER] /pɒt/ [US] /pɑːt/ *noun* [C] **1** any of various types of container, usually round, especially one used for cooking food: *Fill a large pot with salted water and bring it to the boil.* ○ *There's plenty of cupboard space in the kitchen for all your pots* ***and pans***. ⊃See also **flowerpot**; **teapot**. **2** MAINLY UK any of a variety of containers, with or without a lid, especially for storing food or liquids: *a pot of cream/jam/paint/ink* **3** the amount that is contained inside a pot: *I've just drunk a whole pot of tea!* ○ *She'd made a large pot of chicken soup.* **4** used in combination to refer to a container of a stated type: *a coffee pot* ○ *a flowerpot* ○ *a teapot* **5** a dish, bowl, etc. made by hand out of clay
pots /pɒtz/ [US] /pɑːtz/ *plural noun* UK **pots of** ***sth*** a large amount of something: *She's got pots of* ***money*** (= She's very rich).
pot /pɒt/ [US] /pɑːt/ *verb* [T] **-tt-** to put a plant into a container to grow: *I'm just going to pot* ***(up)*** *these seedlings.*
potted /ˈpɒt.ɪd/ [US] /ˈpɑː.t̬ɪd/ *adj* **1 potted plant** a plant which is grown in a pot **2** UK describes cooked food, especially meat or fish, which is preserved in a closed container: *potted meat/shrimps* **3** UK INFORMAL describes a form of a story or book that has been made shorter and simpler and contains only the main facts or features: *They publish a potted* ***version*** *of Shakespeare's plays especially for children.*
potter /ˈpɒt.əʳ/ [US] /ˈpɑː.t̬ɚ/ *noun* [C] a person who makes dishes, plates and other objects from clay, usually by hand on a special wheel
pottery /ˈpɒt.ᵊr.i/ [US] /ˈpɑː.t̬ɚ-/ *noun* [U] **1** the activity or skill of making clay objects by hand **2** objects that are made out of clay by hand: *They sell pottery and other handmade goods.*

pot [TOILET] /pɒt/ [US] /pɑːt/ *noun* [C] a **potty** (= bowl used by children as a toilet)

pot [DRUG] /pɒt/ [US] /pɑːt/ *noun* [U] US SLANG OR UK OLD-FASHIONED SLANG **cannabis**: *a pot smoker*

pot [SHOOT] /pɒt/ [US] /pɑːt/ *verb* [I or T] **-tt-** MAINLY UK to shoot birds or small animals for food, or to shoot (at) them without taking careful aim: *He strolled through the fields, potting* ***(at)*** *the occasional rabbit.*

pot [HIT] /pɒt/ [US] /pɑːt/ *verb* [T] **-tt-** UK in games such as snooker, to hit a ball so that it falls into one of the holes at the edge of the table
pot /pɒt/ [US] /pɑːt/ *noun* [C] UK *Dawson made a difficult pot* (= act of hitting the ball into a hole) *look very easy.*

pot [STOMACH] /pɒt/ [US] /pɑːt/ *noun* [C usually sing] MAINLY HUMOROUS a **potbelly**

pot [BAD STATE] /pɒt/ [US] /pɑːt/ *noun* INFORMAL **go to pot** to be damaged or spoiled through lack of care or effort: *I'm afraid I've let the garden go to pot this summer.*

potage /pəˈtɑːʒ/ /ˈpɒt.ɪdʒ/ [US] /ˈpɑː.t̬ɪdʒ/ *noun* [U] OLD USE thick soup, especially one made from vegetables

potash /ˈpɒt.æʃ/ [US] /ˈpɑː.t/- *noun* [U] a white powder containing POTASSIUM which is put on the earth to make crops grow better

potassium /pəˈtæs.i.əm/ *noun* [U] a silvery-white element which, when combined with other elements, is used in the production of soap, glass and FERTILIZERS (= substances which help plants to grow)

potato /pəˈteɪ.təʊ/ [US] /-t̬oʊ/ *noun* [C or U] *plural* **potatoes** a round vegetable which grows underground and has white flesh with light brown, red or pink skin, or the plant on which these grow: *boiled/roasted/fried potatoes* ○ *mashed potato/mashed potatoes* ⊃See picture **Vegetables** on page Centre 2

poˈtato ˌchip *noun* [C] US FOR **crisp** POTATO

poˌtato ˈsalad *noun* [C] small pieces of cooked potato mixed with MAYONNAISE (= a thick cold white sauce)

potbelly /ˌpɒtˈbel.i/ [US] /ˌpɑːt-/ *noun* [C] (ALSO **pot**) a noticeably fat, round stomach: *After twenty years of heavy beer-drinking he has a massive potbelly.*

P

potbellied /ˌpɒtˈbel.id/ /ˈ-ˌ--/ [US] /ˌpɑːt-/ *adj*: *Who's that potbellied man sitting over there?*

potboiler /ˈpɒtˌbɔɪ.ləʳ/ [US] /ˈpɑːtˌbɔɪ.lɚ/ *noun* [C] *DISAPPROVING* an artistic work, usually of low quality, that has been created quickly just to earn money: *Her most recent potboiler was one of last year's bestselling paperbacks.*

pot-bound *UK* /ˈpɒt.baʊnd/ [US] /ˈpɑːt-/ *adj* (*US* **rootbound**) If a plant is pot-bound, its roots have filled the container it is growing in and it stops growing well.

potency /ˈpəʊ.tᵊnt.si/ [US] /ˈpoʊ.t̬ᵊnt-/ *noun* [U] **1** strength, influence or effectiveness: *This new drug's potency is not yet known.* ○ *He owed his popular support to the potency of his propaganda machine.* **2** a man's ability to have sex: *Consuming large amounts of alcohol can significantly reduce a man's potency.* ➲Compare **impotence** at **impotent** SEXUAL PROBLEM.

potent /ˈpəʊ.tᵊnt/ [US] /ˈpoʊ.t̬ᵊnt/ *adj* very powerful, forceful or effective: *Surprise remains the terrorists' most potent **weapon**.* ○ *The Berlin Wall was a potent **symbol** of the Cold War.* ○ *This is a very potent **drug** and can have unpleasant side-effects.* **potently** /ˈpəʊ.tᵊnt.li/ [US] /ˈpoʊ.t̬ᵊnt-/ *adv*: *His arguments were strong, and potently deployed.*

potentate /ˈpəʊ.tᵊn.teɪt/ [US] /ˈpoʊ.t̬ᵊn-/ *noun* [C] *LITERARY* a ruler who has a lot of power, especially one whose power is not limited, for example by the existence of a parliament

potential /pəʊˈten.tʃᵊl/ [US] /poʊ-/ *adj* [before n] possible when the necessary conditions exist: *A number of potential **buyers** have expressed interest in the company.* ○ *Many potential **customers** are waiting for a fall in prices before buying.* ○ *The accident is a grim reminder of the potential **dangers** involved in North Sea oil production.*

potential /pəʊˈten.tʃᵊl/ [US] /poʊ-/ *noun* [U] someone's or something's ability to develop, achieve or succeed: *The region has **enormous** potential **for** economic development.* ○ *I don't feel I'm **achieving** my **full** potential in my present job.* ○ [+ to infinitive] *You have the potential **to** reach the top of your profession.* ○ *I think this room has got a lot of potential* (= could be very good if some changes were made to it).

potentially /pəʊˈten.tʃᵊl.i/ [US] /poʊ-/ *adv* possibly: *Hepatitis is a potentially **fatal** disease.* ○ *This crisis is potentially the most **serious** in the organization's history.*

potentiality /pəʊˌten.tʃiˈæl.ə.ti/ [US] /poʊˌten.tʃiˈæl.ə.t̬i/ *noun* [C or U] *FORMAL* an ability for development, achievement or success which is natural or has not been used: [+ to infinitive] *The army's potentiality **to** intervene in politics remains strong.*

pothead /ˈpɒt.hed/ [US] /ˈpɑːt-/ *noun* [C] *OLD-FASHIONED INFORMAL* someone who uses CANNABIS regularly

potholder /ˈpɒtˌhəʊl.dəʳ/ [US] /ˈpɑːtˌhoʊl.dɚ/ *noun* [C] *MAINLY US* a thick protective piece of material used when removing hot dishes or pans from a cooker

pothole [ROADS] /ˈpɒt.həʊl/ [US] /ˈpɑːt.hoʊl/ *noun* [C] **1** a hole in a road surface which results from gradual damage caused by traffic and/or weather: *The car's suspension is so good that when you hit a pothole you hardly notice it.* **2** a problem: *The road to economic recovery is full of potholes.*

potholed /ˈpɒt.həʊld/ [US] /ˈpɑːt.hoʊld/ *adj* describes a road that contains a lot of potholes: *The cottage is situated in the middle of a wood at the end of a narrow potholed lane.*

pothole [UNDERGROUND] /ˈpɒt.həʊl/ [US] /ˈpɑːt.hoʊl/ *noun* [C] a deep hole formed underground in LIMESTONE areas by the gradual rubbing and dissolving action of water flowing through the stone

potholing *UK* /ˈpɒtˌhəʊ.lɪŋ/ [US] /ˈpɑːtˌhoʊ-/ *noun* [U] (*US* **spelunking**) a sport which involves climbing into and around underground caves **potholer** *UK* /ˈpɒtˌhəʊ.ləʳ/ [US] /ˈpɑːtˌhoʊ.lɚ/ *noun* [C] (*US* **spelunker**)

potion /ˈpəʊ.ʃᵊn/ [US] /ˈpoʊ-/ *noun* [C] **1** a liquid that is believed to have a magical effect on someone who drinks it: *a love/magic potion* **2** *MAINLY DISAPPROVING* a liquid or substance that is said to cure an illness or a condition, but which is not a medicine: *Americans are said to spend more on pills and potions than any other nation.*

ˌpot ˈluck *noun* **1** [U] anything that is available or is found by chance, rather than something chosen, planned or prepared: *We had no idea which hotel would be best, so we just **took** pot luck **with** the first one on the list.* ○ *Mary's welcome to stay for dinner if she doesn't mind **taking** pot luck* (= having whatever is available). **2** [C] *MAINLY US* an informal meal where guests bring a different dish which is then shared with the other guests: *a pot luck **dinner*** ○ *We're having a pot luck on Saturday.*

ˈpot ˌplant *noun* [C] **1** *UK* a **houseplant** **2** *US INFORMAL* a CANNABIS plant

potpourri /ˌpəʊ.pəˈriː/ [US] /ˌpoʊ-/ *noun* **1** [U] a mixture of dried petals and leaves from various flowers and plants that is used to give a room a pleasant smell: *a bowl of potpourri* **2** [S] an unusual or interesting mixture of things: *Her new TV show will be a potpourri **of** arts and media reports.*

ˈpot ˌroast *noun* [C] a piece of beef that is cooked slowly in a covered dish with a small amount of liquid and sometimes vegetables: *We usually have a pot roast for Sunday lunch.*

potshot /ˈpɒt.ʃɒt/ [US] /ˈpɑːt.ʃɑːt/ *noun* [C] **1** (*UK ALSO* **pot**) a shot which is fired carelessly or with little preparation: *He was **taking** potshots **at** neighbourhood cats.* **2** a criticism: *The recent criticism of his leadership has included potshots from several leading political journalists.*

potter *UK* /ˈpɒt.əʳ/ [US] /ˈpɑː.t̬ɚ/ *verb* [I usually + adv or prep] (*US USUALLY* **putter**) to move about without hurrying and in a relaxed and pleasant way: *I spent the afternoon pottering **around** the garden doing a few odd jobs.* ○ *He doesn't drive very fast – he tends to potter **along**.* **potter** /ˈpɒt.əʳ/ [US] /ˈpɑː.t̬ɚ/ *noun* [S] *UK* *I'm just going into town for **a** potter **round** the shops.*

potter's wheel /ˌpɒt.əzˈwiːl/ [US] /ˌpɑː.t̬ɚz-/ *noun* [C usually sing] a machine with a horizontal spinning disc on which clay is shaped into decorative or useful objects

ˈpotting ˌshed *noun* [C] *MAINLY UK* a small building in a garden in which plant containers, young plants, seeds, tools, etc. are kept

potty [SILLY] /ˈpɒt.i/ [US] /ˈpɑː.t̬i/ *adj UK INFORMAL* **1** silly or foolish: *She must have been potty to sell that car so cheaply.* ○ *I'd go potty if I had to work here all the time.* **2** **be potty about *sth/sb*** to like something very much: *He's potty about old cars.*

• **drive *sb* potty** *UK INFORMAL* to annoy someone a lot: *The noise from our next-door neighbours is driving us potty.*

pottiness /ˈpɒt.ɪ.nəs/ [US] /ˈpɑː.t̬ɪ-/ *noun* [U]

potty [TOILET] /ˈpɒt.i/ [US] /ˈpɑː.t̬i/ *noun* [C] (*ALSO* **pot**) *MAINLY UK* a bowl, sometimes with a handle, which young children sit on and use as a toilet: *Don't forget to sit Jamie on the potty before you take him to the zoo.*

ˈpotty ˌchair *noun* [C] a small chair with a hole in the seat and a bowl fixed under it for teaching young children to use the toilet

potty-trained /ˈpɒt.i.treɪnd/ [US] /ˈpɑː.t̬i-/ *adj* (*ALSO* **toilet-trained**) describes children who know how to use a potty or toilet and no longer need to wear NAPPIES to protect their clothing: *By what age are children usually potty-trained?*

potty-training /ˈpɒt.iˌtreɪ.nɪŋ/ [US] /ˈpɑː.t̬i-/ *noun* [U] (*ALSO* **toilet-training**) teaching a child how to use a potty

pouch /paʊtʃ/ *noun* [C] **1** a bag or soft container for a small object or a small amount of something: *All our electric shavers are supplied with a free travel pouch.* ○ *Food sealed in foil pouches lasts for a long time.* **2** a pocket on the lower part of the body of some female animals in which their young are carried and protected after they are born: *Kangaroos carry their young in pouches.* **3** a bag formed from skin in the mouths of some animals, used for carrying and storing food

pouf [SEAT], **pouffe** /puːf/ *noun* [C] (*US* **ottoman**) a soft round or square seat with no back or sides, used for sitting on or resting your feet on

pouf [PERSON] /pʊf/ *noun* [C] *UK OFFENSIVE* a **poof** (= homosexual man)

P

poultice /ˈpəʊl.tɪs/ [US] /ˈpoʊl.t̬ɪs/ *noun* [C] a piece of cloth covered with a thick, often warm substance, which is wrapped around an injury to reduce pain or swelling

poultry /ˈpəʊl.tri/ [US] /ˈpoʊl-/ *plural noun* birds, such as chickens, that are bred for their eggs and meat: *Some poultry farmers keep turkeys and ducks as well as chickens.*
poultry /ˈpəʊl.tri/ [US] /ˈpoʊl-/ *noun* [U] the meat from birds such as chickens

pounce /paʊnts/ *verb* [I] to jump or move quickly in order to catch or take hold of something: *The cat sat in the tree ready to pounce* ***on*** *the ducks below.* ○ *The police were waiting to pounce when he arrived at the airport.*

PHRASAL VERBS WITH **pounce**

▲ **pounce on** ***sth*** [CRITICIZE] *phrasal verb* to immediately criticize a mistake: *He knows that his critics are waiting to pounce on any slip that he makes.*
▲ **pounce on** ***sth*** [ACCEPT] *phrasal verb* to accept something quickly and with enthusiasm: *I think if she were given the opportunity to work here, she'd pounce on it.*

pound [MONEY] /paʊnd/ *noun* [C] (*SYMBOL* **£**) the standard unit of money in the UK and some other countries: *a one-pound/two-pound coin* ○ *There are one hundred pence in a pound.* ○ *They stole jewellery valued at £50 000* (= 50 000 pounds). ○ *"Have you got any change?" "Sorry, I've only got a five-pound* ***note****.*
the pound *noun* [S] (*SYMBOL* **£**) the type of money used in Britain: *The devaluation of* ***the*** *pound will make British goods more competitive abroad.* ○ *On the foreign exchanges the pound rose two cents against the dollar to $1.52.*

pound [WEIGHT] /paʊnd/ *noun* [C] (*WRITTEN ABBREVIATION* **lb**) a unit for measuring weight: *One pound is approximately equal to 454 grams.* ○ *One kilogram is roughly the same as 2.2 lbs.* ○ *There are 16 ounces in one pound.* ○ *Ann's baby weighed eight and a half pounds at birth.*
• ˌ**pound of** ˈ**flesh** *DISAPPROVING* something which you have the right to receive but which is unreasonable to demand from someone
-pounder /-paʊn.dəʳ/ [US] /-dɚ/ *suffix INFORMAL "What sort of burger do you want?" "I think I'll have a* ***quarter****-pounder* (= one containing a quarter of a pound of meat)*."* ○ *MAINLY US The newest member of the team is a 23-year-old, 212-pounder* (= person weighing 212 pounds) *from Miami.*

pound [HIT] /paʊnd/ *verb* [I or T] to hit or beat repeatedly with a lot of force, or to crush something by hitting it repeatedly: *I could feel my heart pounding as I went on stage to collect the prize.* ○ *Nearly 50 people are still missing after the storm pounded the coast.* ○ *The city was pounded* ***to*** *rubble during the war.* ○ *He pounded* ***on*** *the door demanding to be let in.* ○ *She was pounding* ***away*** *on her typewriter until four in the morning.*
pounding /ˈpaʊn.dɪŋ/ *noun* [C or S] *The city received heavy poundings* (= attacks) *from the air every night last week.*
• **take/get a pounding** to receive a lot of criticism: *The movie took quite a pounding from the critics.*
▲ **pound away at** ***sth/sb*** *phrasal verb* to criticize something or try to get someone to do something: *The campaigners have promised to* ***keep*** *pounding away at the council until the decision to build the road is reversed.*

ˈ**pound** ˌ**sign** *noun* [U] the symbol £

ˌ**pound** ˈ**sterling** *noun* [C] the official name of the pound used as money in the UK

pour [CAUSE TO FLOW] /pɔːʳ/ [US] /pɔːr/ *verb* [I or T] to make a substance flow from a container, especially into another container, by raising just one side of the container that the substance is in: *I spilled the juice while I was pouring it.* ○ *Pour the honey* ***into*** *the bowl and mix it thoroughly with the other ingredients.* ○ [+ two objects] *Would you like me to pour you some more wine?* ○ *Would you like to pour* (= pour a drink into a glass or cup) *while I open some bags of nuts?*
• **pour oil on troubled waters** *UK* to do or say something in order to make people stop arguing and become calmer: *My husband's always arguing with my father, and I'm the one who has to pour oil on troubled waters.*

pour [FLOW QUICKLY] /pɔːʳ/ [US] /pɔːr/ *verb* [I or T; usually + adv or prep] to (cause to) flow quickly and in large amounts: *The bus was pouring* ***out*** *thick black exhaust fumes.* ○ *The government has been pouring money* ***into*** *inefficient state-owned industries and the country can no longer afford it.* ○ *I felt a sharp pain and looked down to see blood pouring* ***from*** *my leg.* ○ *Refugees have been pouring* ***into*** *neighbouring countries to escape the civil war.* ○ *The sweat was pouring* ***down*** *her face by the end of the race.* ○ *It looks as though* ***it's*** *about to pour* ***(with rain)****.* ○ *I was standing in* ***the*** *pouring* ***rain*** *for an hour waiting for my bus.*
• **pour scorn on** ***sb/sth*** to say a person or thing is ridiculous and worthless: *Critics of the President have been pouring scorn on the plan ever since it was first proposed.*
▲ **pour** ***sth*** **out** *phrasal verb* [M] to tell all your worries, problems or feelings to someone, especially privately or secretly: *He spends every lunchtime pouring out his emotional problems to me and expects me to find a solution.* ○ *I poured my* ***heart*** *out to him* (= told him about all my feelings) *and then he told all his friends what I'd said.*

pout /paʊt/ *verb* [I or T] to push the lower lip forward to express annoyance, or to push both lips forward in a sexually attractive way: *Vanessa always pouts if she doesn't get what she wants.* ○ *Caroline pouts her lips when she's putting on lipstick.* **pout** /paʊt/ *noun* [C] *She didn't say anything but I could tell from her pout that she wasn't very pleased.*

poverty /ˈpɒv.ə.ti/ [US] /ˈpɑː.vɚ.t̬i/ *noun* [U] **1** the condition of being extremely poor: *Two million people in the city live in* ***abject*** (= very great) *poverty.* ○ *He emigrated to Australia to escape the* ***grinding*** (= very great) *poverty of his birthplace.* ○ *Helping to alleviate poverty in developing countries also helps to reduce environmental destruction.* **2** *FORMAL* **a poverty of** ***sth*** a lack of something or when the quality of something is extremely low: *There is a disappointing poverty of creativity in their work.*

ˈ**poverty** ˌ**line** *noun* [U] the official level of income which is needed to achieve a basic living standard with enough money for things such as food, clothing and a place to live: *In 1991 almost 36 million Americans were* ***living below*** *the poverty line.*

poverty-stricken /ˈpɒv.ə.tiˌstrɪk.ən/ [US] /ˈpɑː.vɚ.t̬i-/ *adj* describes a person or place suffering from the effects of being extremely poor: *Some beggars are neither poverty-stricken nor homeless.* ○ *There are few jobs for the peasants who have flooded into the cities from the poverty-stricken countryside in search of work.*

ˈ**poverty** ˌ**trap** *noun* [U] *UK* a situation in which someone would be even poorer or not noticeably richer if they had a job because they would no longer receive financial help from the government: *He's* ***caught in*** *the poverty trap and will only be five pounds a week better off if he accepts the job.*

POW [PRISONER], *UK ALSO* **PoW** /ˌpiː.əʊˈdʌb.l̩.juː/ [US] /-oʊ-/ *noun* [C] *ABBREVIATION FOR* **prisoner of war**: *He was a POW during the Vietnam war.* ○ *a POW camp*

pow [NOISE] /paʊ/ *exclamation INFORMAL* (especially in children's cartoons) a word which represents the noise of an explosion or a gun being fired: *When I shout "Pow!" that means I've shot you and you've got to pretend to be dead.*

powder /ˈpaʊ.dəʳ/ [US] /-dɚ/ *noun* **1** [C or U] a solid substance that consists of extremely small pieces, is soft and easy to divide, and tends to have the same shape as the container that it is in: *curry/chilli powder* ○ *talcum powder* ○ *A packet of white powder was found and police scientists are analysing it.* ○ *You'll get more flavour from the spices if you grind them into a powder.* ○ *UK Why are there so many adverts for* ***washing*** *powders on TV?* ○ *You can buy milk in powder form.* ➲See also **gunpowder**. **2** [U] a soft dry substance which is spread over the skin of the face, in order to stop the skin from looking oily: *face powder* ○ *Dust the face lightly with powder.* **3** [U] fallen snow that is loose and dry and has not begun to melt: *I love skiing in deep powder.*

powder /ˈpaʊ.dəʳ/ [US] /-dɚ/ *verb* [T] to put powder on someone's skin: *Powder the baby's bottom to stop it chafing.*

• **powder *your* nose** a polite or humorous way of saying that you are going to go to the toilet: *Would you get me another drink while I go and powder my nose?*

powdered /ˈpaʊ.dəd/ [US] /-dɚd/ *adj* in the form of a powder or covered with a powder: *Shall I put some powdered* ***milk*** *in your coffee?* ○ *Her face was heavily powdered.* **powdery** /ˈpaʊ.dᵊr.i/ [US] /-dɚ-/ *adj*: *The snow was fresh and powdery.*

ˌpowdered ˈsugar *noun* [U] *US FOR* **icing sugar**

ˈpowder ˌkeg *noun* [C] a situation or a place that could easily become extremely dangerous: *The build-up of forces in the region is creating a powder keg.* ○ *The new tax is a* ***political*** *powder keg which could result in widespread violence.*

ˈpowder ˌpuff *noun* [C] a round piece of soft material which is used for putting powder on the face or body

ˈpowder ˌroom *noun* [C usually sing] a polite word for a women's toilet in a public building, such as a restaurant, hotel, theatre, etc.

power [CONTROL] /paʊəʳ/ [US] /paʊɚ/ *noun* [U] **1** ability to control people and events: *I've no power* ***over*** *him – he does what he wants to.* ○ *Once nicotine has you* ***in*** *its power, it's very difficult to stop smoking.* ○ *She has the power to charm any man she meets.* **2** the amount of political control a person or group has in a country: *Does the President have more power than the Prime Minister?* ○ *How long has the Conservative Party been* ***in*** *power?* ○ *The army* ***seized*** *power after five days of anti-government demonstrations.*

powerful /ˈpaʊə.fᵊl/ [US] /ˈpaʊɚ-/ *adj* having a lot of power: *The President is more powerful than the Prime Minister.* ○ *She's the most powerful person in the organization.*

powerless /ˈpaʊə.ləs/ [US] /ˈpaʊɚ-/ *adj* having no power: *The villagers are powerless* ***against*** *the armed invaders.* ○ *The police seem to be powerless* (= unable) ***to*** *prevent these attacks.* **powerlessness** /ˈpaʊə.lə.snəs/ [US] /ˈpaʊɚ-/ *noun* [U] *A significant cause of stress in the workplace is a sense of powerlessness and lack of control.*

power [PERSON WITH CONTROL] /paʊəʳ/ [US] /paʊɚ/ *noun* [C] a person, organization or country that has control over others, often because of wealth, importance or great military strength: *Spain was an important* ***military*** *power in the 16th century.* ○ *Germany is on its way to becoming a* ***world*** *power with a permanent seat on the UN Security Council.* ○ *She is an increasingly important power* ***in the*** *company.*

• **the power behind the throne** someone who does not have an official position in a government or organization but who secretly controls it

• **the powers that be** important people who have authority over others: *It's up to the powers that be to decide what should be done next.*

power [OFFICIAL RIGHT] /paʊəʳ/ [US] /paʊɚ/ *noun* [U] an official or legal right to do something: [+ to infinitive] *I'd like to help but I don't have the power* ***to*** *intervene in this dispute.* ○ *It's not* ***in*** *your power* ***to*** *cancel the order.* ○ *I can't give you a refund – I'm afraid it's not* ***within*** *my power.*

powers /paʊəz/ [US] /paʊɚz/ *plural noun* authority: *You were acting* ***beyond*** *your powers when you agreed to give her a pay rise.* ○ *Visitors to the city are respectfully reminded of the council's powers* ***to*** *remove illegally parked vehicles.*

power [ABILITY] /paʊəʳ/ [US] /paʊɚ/ *noun* [U] a natural skill or an ability to do something: *He was so shocked by what happened to his parents that he lost the power* ***of*** *speech.* ○ [+ to infinitive] *The surgeon did everything* ***in*** *her power* ***to*** *save him.*

powers /paʊəz/ [US] /paʊɚz/ *plural noun* abilities: *My mental powers aren't as good as they used to be.*

power [STRENGTH] /paʊəʳ/ [US] /paʊɚ/ *noun* [U] strength: *Our car doesn't have enough power to tow a trailer.* ○ *Weightlifters have tremendous power in their arms and legs.* ○ *Scientists are working to harness the power of the atom.* ○ *The economic power of many Asian countries has grown dramatically in recent years.*

• **do *sb* a power of good** *UK* to be extremely good for someone: *He's been working too hard and some time off would do him a power of good.*

• **More power to *your* elbow!** *UK* (*US* **More power to you!**) an expression of praise or admiration for someone's success or bravery: *"I've decided to quit my job and set up my own business." "Well, good for you. More power to your elbow!"*

power /paʊəʳ/ [US] /paʊɚ/ *verb* [I usually + adv or prep] to act with great strength or in a forceful way: *Halfway through, she powered into the lead and went on to win the race.*

powerful /ˈpaʊə.fᵊl/ [US] /ˈpaʊɚ-/ *adj* **1** having a lot of strength or force: *She's an extremely powerful runner.* ○ *The picture quality is bad because the TV signal isn't powerful enough.* **2** having a very great effect: *a powerful drug* ○ *Her speech about cruelty to children was very powerful.*

powerfully /ˈpaʊə.fᵊl.i/ [US] /ˈpaʊɚ-/ *adv*: *He argued powerfully and persuasively against capital punishment.* ○ *She kicked the ball so powerfully that it flew over the hedge.* ○ *Klaus is a very powerfully-****built*** *man* (= has a body with large strong muscles).

power [ELECTRICITY] /paʊəʳ/ [US] /paʊɚ/ *noun* [U] electricity, particularly when considering its use or production: *You should disconnect the power before attempting to repair electrical equipment.* ○ *Our building lost power* (= the electricity was stopped) *during the storm.* ○ *power* ***cables/lines***

power [ENERGY] /paʊəʳ/ [US] /paʊɚ/ *noun* [U] the rate at which energy is used, or the ability to produce energy: *The ship was only slightly damaged in the collision and was able to sail into port under its own power.* ○ *SPECIALIZED The power* ***(rating)*** *of my amplifier is forty watts per channel.*

power /paʊəʳ/ [US] /paʊɚ/ *verb* [T] to provide a machine with energy and the ability to operate: *Buses and trucks are usually powered by diesel engines.* ○ *In the future electricity will be used to power road vehicles.*

-powered /-paʊəd/ [US] /-paʊɚd/ *suffix*: *a battery-powered radio* ○ *nuclear-powered submarines* ○ *My calculator doesn't need batteries because it's* ***solar****-powered* (= it obtains its energy from the sun).

▲ **power *(sth)* up** *phrasal verb* [M] *MAINLY US* If something that needs power or energy powers up, or if someone powers it up, it is turned on or prepared so that it is ready for use or action: *The computer takes a few seconds to power up after it's been switched on.* ○ *College baseball teams across the country are powering up for the new season.*

power [IMAGE SIZE] /paʊəʳ/ [US] /paʊɚ/ *noun* [U] the amount by which an image is increased by a device used for seeing things that are very small or a long distance away: *What's the magnification power of your binoculars?* ○ *You'll need a very high-power microscope to see something as small as that.* ○ *A low-power telescope is enough if you only want to look at the moon.* **powerful** /ˈpaʊə.fᵊl/ [US] /ˈpaʊɚ-/ *adj*: *You'd need an extremely powerful microscope to see something so small.*

power [MATHEMATICS] /paʊəʳ/ [US] /paʊɚ/ *noun* [U] *SPECIALIZED* the number of times that a number is to be multiplied by itself: *2* ***to the*** *fourth power is 2 times 2 times 2 times 2, which equals 16.* ○ *3* ***to the*** *power 4 is usually written as* 3^4.

power(-assisted) steering /ˌpaʊə.rəˌsɪs.tɪdˈstɪə.rɪŋ/ [US] /ˌpaʊɚ.əˌsɪs.tɪdˈstɪr.ɪŋ/ *noun* [U] a system for changing the direction in which a road vehicle is moving by using power from the engine to help the driver turn the vehicle: *Power steering, electric windows and central locking are standard features on all models.*

ˈpower ˌbase *noun* [C usually sing] an area of a country or a group of people on which someone's power depends: *The industrial cities are the Labour Party's traditional power base.*

powerboat /ˈpaʊə.bəʊt/ [US] /ˈpaʊɚ.boʊt/ *noun* [C] a small boat with a powerful engine which can travel very fast and is used in races

P

ˈpower ˌbreakfast/ˌlunch *noun* [C] *HUMOROUS* an occasion at which people eat while they are working and talking about business

ˈpower ˌbroker *noun* [C] someone who has a big influence on decisions about who should possess political power

ˈpower ˌcut *UK noun* [C] (*US* **power outage**) an accidental or intentional interruption in the supply of electricity: *Storms caused power cuts in hundreds of homes last night.*

ˈpower ˌdressing *noun* [U] a style of dressing in which business people wear formal clothes to make them seem powerful

powerhouse /ˈpaʊə.haʊs/ [US] /ˈpaʊr-/ *noun* [C usually sing] a country, organization or person with a lot of influence, power or energy: *Germany is an economic powerhouse.* ○ *The university is no longer the academic powerhouse that it once was.* ○ *She's a powerhouse **of** original ideas and solutions.*

ˌpower of atˈtorney *noun* [C or U] *LEGAL* the legal right to act for someone else in their financial or business matters, or the document which gives someone this right

ˈpower ˌplant *noun* [C] *US FOR* **power station**

ˈpower ˌpoint *UK noun* [C] (*US* **electrical outlet**) a device to which an item of electrical equipment can be connected in order to provide it with electricity

ˈpower ˌpolitics *plural noun* the threat or use of military force to end an international disagreement: *Woodrow Wilson hoped the League of Nations would replace power politics with international cooperation.*

power-sharing /ˈpaʊə.ʃeə.rɪŋ/ [US] /ˈpaʊr.ʃer.ɪŋ/ *noun* [U] when two people or groups share responsibility for running a government, organization, etc: *a power-sharing arrangement/scheme*

the ˌpowers of ˈdarkness *plural noun* evil spiritual forces: *Throughout the play, Macbeth struggles with the powers of darkness.*

ˈpower ˌstation *noun* [C] (*US ALSO* **power plant**) a factory where electricity is produced

ˈpower ˌstructure *noun* [C] a way in which power is organized or shared in an organization or society: *The president has promised a new constitution and the creation of democratic power structures.*

ˈpower ˌstruggle *noun* [C] a fierce, unpleasant or violent competition for power

ˈpower ˌtool *noun* [C] a tool that operates with an electric motor

ˈpower ˌvacuum *noun* [C usually sing] a condition that exists when someone has lost control of something and no one has replaced them: *She was quick to **fill** the power vacuum that was left by the sudden death of the managing director.*

powwow /ˈpaʊ.waʊ/ *noun* **1** [C] a meeting or gathering of Native Americans for making decisions or for having spiritual ceremonies or celebrations **2** [C usually sing] *HUMOROUS* a meeting where something important is discussed: *My brother's getting divorced so I'm going home for a family powwow this weekend.*

the pox /ðəˈpɒks/ [US] /-ˈpɑːks/ *noun* [S] *OLD-FASHIONED INFORMAL FOR* **syphilis** ➲See also **chickenpox**; **cowpox**; **smallpox**.

poxy /ˈpɒk.si/ [US] /ˈpɑːk-/ *adj UK INFORMAL* having little value, importance or influence: *She lives in a poxy little village in the middle of nowhere.*

pp [PAGES] *plural noun WRITTEN ABBREVIATION FOR* pages: *This matter is discussed in more detail on pp 101-123.*

pp [DOCUMENTS] *prep UK FORMAL* used to show when someone has signed a document for a person who is not available to sign it: *I hope to hear from you soon. Yours sincerely, Chris Smith, pp Rebecca Collings.*

PPS /ˌpiː.piːˈes/ *adv* used when an additional short message is added to the end of a letter after a message has already been added: *PS I forgot to invite you to our party next Sunday at six. PPS Please tell Ellis that he's welcome to come too.* ➲See also **PS**.

PR [ADVERTISING] /ˌpiːˈɑːʳ/ [US] /-ˈɑːr/ *noun* [U] *ABBREVIATION FOR* **public relations**: *The company's putting out a lot of PR about the new product line.* ○ *They've decided to hire a PR **firm** to improve their public image.* ○ *a PR exercise/campaign*

PR [VOTING] /ˌpiːˈɑːʳ/ [US] /-ˈɑːr/ *noun* [U] *ABBREVIATION FOR* **proportional representation**: *Do you think a system of PR makes elections fairer?*

practicable /ˈpræk.tɪ.kə.bl̩/ *adj FORMAL* able to be done or put into action: *The troops will be brought home as soon as practicable.* ○ *It is not practicable **to** complete the tunnel before the end of the year.* ✻ NOTE: The opposite is **impracticable**. **practicability** /ˌpræk.tɪ.kəˈbɪl.ɪ.ti/ [US] /-ə.t̬i-/ *noun* [U] *Many people have expressed serious doubts about the practicability of the proposed schedule for next year.*

practical [EXPERIENCE] /ˈpræk.tɪ.kəl/ *adj* relating to experience, reality or action rather than ideas or imagination: *Qualifications are important but practical **experience** is always an advantage.* ○ *The service offers young people practical **advice** on finding a job.* ○ *What's the use of theoretical knowledge that has no practical **application**?*

• **for all practical purposes** in reality: *Dr Frampton is in charge, but for all practical purposes, her assistant runs the office.*

practical /ˈpræk.tɪ.kəl/ *noun* [C] a class or examination in a scientific or technical subject in which students do things rather than just write or talk about them: *We had to dissect a worm and a frog in our biology practical today.*

practicalities /ˌpræk.tɪˈkæl.ɪ.tiz/ [US] /-ə.t̬iz/ *plural noun* the conditions which result from an idea becoming reality: *The practicalities of having two young children and working full time meant we had to employ a nanny.* ○ *It sounds like a good idea, but you ought to consider the practicalities before you put it into action.* **practically** /ˈpræk.tɪ.kli/ *adv*: *Many people have offered to help, but there is little they can do practically.* ○ *Theoretically, it's a good idea to live without a car, but practically **speaking**, it would be difficult to manage without one.* ➲See also **practically**.

practical [SUITABLE] /ˈpræk.tɪ.kəl/ *adj* suitable for the situation in which something is used: *I tend to wear clothes that are practical rather than fashionable.* ○ *Heavy boots aren't very practical for running.* ✻ NOTE: The opposite is **impractical**. **practicality** /ˌpræk.tɪˈkæl.ɪ.ti/ [US] /-ə.t̬i/ *noun* [U] *I bought these shoes for their practicality not their appearance.*

practical [EFFECTIVE] /ˈpræk.tɪ.kəl/ *adj APPROVING* able to provide effective solutions to problems: *She has a lot of interesting ideas, but they're not very practical.* ○ *We need someone practical who can cope with a crisis.* ✻ NOTE: The opposite is **impractical**. **practicality** /ˌpræk.tɪˈkæl.ɪ.ti/ [US] /-ə.t̬i/ *noun* [U] *Jonathan has demonstrated enormous practicality in his successful management of the shop.*

practical [POSSIBLE] /ˈpræk.tɪ.kəl/ *adj* able to be done or put into action: *It's simply not practical **to** divide the work between so many people.* ✻ NOTE: The opposite is **impractical**. **practicality** /ˌpræk.tɪˈkæl.ɪ.ti/ [US] /-ə.t̬i/ *noun* [U] *Your suggestion is appealing in theory, but it lacks practicality.*

ˌpractical ˈjoke *noun* [C] a joke which makes someone seem foolish and involves a physical action rather than words: *She glued her boss's cup and saucer together as a practical joke.* **ˌpractical ˈjoker** *noun* [C]

practically /ˈpræk.tɪ.kli/ *adv* almost or very nearly: *She blamed me for practically every mistake in the report.* ○ *These changes would cost us practically **nothing**.* ○ *It's practically **impossible** for me to get home in less than an hour.* ○ *They used to argue all the time and now they've practically **stopped** talking to each other.* ➲See also **practically** at **practical** EXPERIENCE.

practice [ACTION] /ˈpræk.tɪs/ *noun* [U] action rather than thought or ideas: *It seemed like a good idea before we started, but **in** practice it was a disaster.* ○ *Officially, Robert's in charge, but **in** practice Hannah runs the office.* ○ *I can't see how your plan is going to work **in** practice.* ○ *How do you intend to **put** these proposals **into** practice, Mohamed?*

P

practice [REGULAR ACTIVITY] /ˈpræk.tɪs/ *noun* [C or U] something that is usually or regularly done, often as a habit, tradition or custom: *What can European companies learn from Japanese business practices?* ○ *It's **common** practice in the States to tip the hairdresser.* ○ *This is a cruel practice which should be banned immediately.* ○ *What is **standard** practice* (= What is usually done) *in a situation like this?* ○ *Newspaper editors have agreed a new **code of** practice on the invasion of privacy.*

• **make a practice of *sth*** *UK OLD-FASHIONED* to do something regularly: *I'll do your washing for you this time, but I'm not going to make a practice of it.*

practise *UK, US* **practice** /ˈpræk.tɪs/ *verb* [T] to do something regularly, often according to a custom, religion or set of rules, or as a habit: *The new government has promised all citizens the right to practise their religion.* ○ *Practising safe sex is an important way of avoiding HIV infection.* ○ *The company denies that it has practised discrimination against any of its employees.*

• **practise what *you* preach** to do the things that you advise other people to do: *He's such a hypocrite! He never practises what he preaches.*

practising *UK, US* **practicing** /ˈpræk.tɪ.sɪŋ/ *adj* [before n] actively involved in a religion: *a practising Muslim/Jew/Christian*

practise [TRAIN] *UK, US* **practice** /ˈpræk.tɪs/ *verb* [I or T] to do or play something regularly or repeatedly in order to become skilled at it: *I'm quite good at tennis but I need to practise my serve.* ○ *She practises the violin every day.* ○ [+ v-ing] *His written French is very good but he needs to practise speak**ing** it.*

practice /ˈpræk.tɪs/ *noun* [C or U] when you do something regularly or repeatedly to improve your skill at doing it: *I need to get some more practice before I take my driving test.* ○ *Are you coming to cricket practice this evening?* ○ *She's never at home because she spends all her free time at hockey practices.* ○ *You'll gradually get better at it – it's just a question of practice.* ○ *I'm a bit **out of** practice* (= I haven't had any recent experience) *but I'd love to play.* ○ *Do you mind if I have a few practice shots before we start the game?*

• **Practice makes perfect.** *SAYING* said to encourage someone to continue to do something many times, so that they will learn to do it very well

practised *UK, US* **practiced** /ˈpræk.tɪst/ *adj* **1** very good at doing something because you have a lot of experience of doing it: *She is a confident and practised speaker who always impresses her audience.* ○ *He is practised **in** the art of public debate.* ○ *We need someone who is practised **at** negotiating business deals.* **2** *FORMAL* describes a skill that has been obtained from a lot of practice: *She performed the song with practised skill.*

practise [WORK] *UK, US* **practice** /ˈpræk.tɪs/ *verb* [I or T] to work in an important skilled job for which a lot of training is necessary: *How long have you been practising **as** a dentist?* ○ *She practised medicine for twenty years before she became a writer.*

practice /ˈpræk.tɪs/ *noun* [C] a job or business which involves a lot of skill or training: *a dental/medical/veterinary/legal practice* ○ *Our practice is responsible for about five thousand patients in this part of Leeds.* ○ *She's decided to leave the Health Service and join a **private** practice.*

practising *UK, US* **practicing** /ˈpræk.tɪ.sɪŋ/ *adj* [before n] actively involved in a job: *a practising doctor/lawyer* ○ *The number of practising doctors is falling even though more people are qualifying in medicine.*

practitioner /prækˈtɪʃ.ən.əʳ/ [US] /-ɚ/ *noun* [C] *SLIGHTLY FORMAL* someone involved in a skilled job or activity: *Elizabeth Quan is a London-based practitioner of traditional Chinese medicine.* ○ *She was a **medical** practitioner* (= a doctor) *before she entered politics.* ➲See also **GP**.

pragmatic /prægˈmæt.ɪk/ [US] /-ˈmæt̬-/ *adj MAINLY APPROVING* solving problems in a realistic way which suits the present conditions rather than obeying fixed theories, ideas or rules: *In business, the pragmatic **approach** to problems is often more successful than an idealistic one.*

pragmatically /prægˈmæt.ɪ.kli/ [US] /-ˈmæt̬-/ *adv MAINLY APPROVING* in a pragmatic way: *It is intended that these guidelines should be applied flexibly and pragmatically.*

pragmatism /ˈpræg.mə.tɪ.zᵊm/ [US] /-t̬ɪ-/ *noun* [U] *MAINLY APPROVING* when you deal with a problem in a realistic way rather than obeying fixed theories, ideas or rules: *The council has operated much more effectively since pragmatism replaced political dogma.* **pragmatist** /ˈpræg.mə.tɪst/ [US] /-t̬ɪst/ *noun* [C] *She rose to power by being a political pragmatist who took advantage of every opportunity that presented itself.*

prairie /ˈpreə.ri/ [US] /ˈprer.i/ *noun* [C or U] a wide area of flat land without trees in Canada and the northern US

ˈprairie ˌdog [C] a small wild mammal that lives on the prairies of Canada and the US

praise [SHOW APPROVAL] /preɪz/ *verb* [T] to express admiration or approval about the achievements or characteristics of a person or thing: *He should be praised **for** his honesty.* ○ *My parents always praised me when I did well at school.* ○ *He was **highly** praised for his research on heart disease.*

praise /preɪz/ *noun* [U] when you say or show your admiration and approval for someone or something: *They deserve praise **for** all their hard work.* ○ *His economic policies have **won** widespread praise for reducing government debt.* ○ *Praise from Adrian is (high) praise **indeed*** (= Praise from Adrian is particularly special because he rarely praises anyone).

praiseworthy /ˈpreɪzˌwɜː.ði/ [US] /-ˌwɝː-/ *adj* deserving praise: *His actions during the crisis were truly praiseworthy.*

praise [GOD] /preɪz/ *verb* [T] to honour, worship and express admiration for a god: *They sang hymns praising God.*

praise /preɪz/ *noun* [U] *FORMAL* expression of respect and worship to a god: *As we **give** praise to God, let us remember those who are less fortunate than ourselves.*

praline /ˈprɑː.liːn/ [US] /ˈpreɪ-/ *noun* [C or U] a mixture of crushed nuts and burnt sugar that is used in sweet dishes and chocolates: *almond/hazelnut praline*

pram *UK* /præm/ *noun* [C] (*US* **baby carriage**) a vehicle for moving a baby around which consists of a small enclosed bed supported by a frame on four wheels: *I saw her **pushing** a pram down the street.*

prance /prɑːnts/ [US] /prænts/ *verb* **1** [I +adv or prep] to walk in an energetic way and with more movement than necessary: *It's pathetic to see fifty-year-old rock stars prancing **around** on stage as if they were still teenagers.* ○ *She pranced into the office and demanded to speak to the manager.* **2** [I] When a horse prances it takes small, quick steps and raises its legs higher than usual.

prang /præŋ/ *verb* [T] *UK INFORMAL* to damage a vehicle slightly in a road accident: *She pranged her mother's car a week after she passed her driving test.*

prang *UK* /præŋ/ *noun* [C] (*US* **fender bender**) *INFORMAL* a road accident in which the vehicles involved are only slightly damaged

prank /præŋk/ *noun* [C] a trick that is intended to be amusing but not to cause harm or damage: *When I was at school we were always **playing** pranks **on** our teachers.* ○ *I've had enough of your **childish** pranks.*

prankster /ˈpræŋk.stəʳ/ [US] /-stɚ/ *noun* [C] someone who performs pranks on people

prat /præt/ *noun* [C] *UK INFORMAL* someone who behaves stupidly or lacks ability: *He looked a right prat in that pink suit.* ○ *You've made me spill my drink, you prat!* ○ *Occasionally I'll have a few too many drinks at a party and **make a** prat **of myself*** (= behave stupidly).

prat /præt/ *verb*

▲ **prat about/around** *phrasal verb UK INFORMAL* to behave stupidly, particularly when you should be behaving in a responsible way: *Oh for goodness sake, stop pratting around and get on with your work!*

pratfall /ˈpræt.fɔːl/ [US] /-fɑːl/ *noun* [C] **1** *MAINLY US* a fall in which a person lands on their bottom, especially for an amusing effect in a play, film, etc. **2** an embarrassing defeat or failure: *Most of us get over the pratfalls of childhood.*

P

prattle /ˈpræt.l̩/ ⓤ /ˈpræt̬-/ *verb* [I] to talk foolishly or childishly for a long time about something unimportant or without saying anything important: *She'd have prattled **on about** her new job for the whole afternoon if I'd let her.* ○ *Stop your prattling and go to sleep!* **prattle** /ˈpræt.l̩/ ⓤ /ˈpræt̬-/ *noun* [U] *His speech contained nothing new and was full of political prattle and clichés.* **prattler** /ˈpræt.l̩.ə^r/ /-l̩.ə^r/ ⓤ /ˈpræt̬.l̩.ɚ/ *noun* [C] *Fiona's such a prattler – I wish she'd get to the point of what she wants to say.*

prawn MAINLY UK /prɔːn/ ⓤ /prɑːn/ *noun* [C] (*US USUALLY* **shrimp**) a small edible sea animal with a shell and ten legs: *Prawns are grey when they're raw, and turn pink when they're cooked.* ○ *peeled prawns*

pray SPEAK TO GOD /preɪ/ *verb* **1** [I or T] to speak to a god either privately or in a religious ceremony in order to express love, admiration or thanks or in order to ask for something: *She knelt and prayed silently.* ○ *Let us pray **for** the victims of this terrible disaster.* ○ [+ *that*] *We've been praying to God **that** your son will make a complete recovery.* ○ *FORMAL You must pray* (= ask for) *God's forgiveness for what you have done.* **2** [I] to hope for something very much: *We're praying **for** good weather for tomorrow's cricket match.*

prayer /preə^r/ ⓤ /prer/ *noun* **1** [C] the words that someone says or thinks when they are praying: *a prayer **of** thanks* ○ *She always **says** her prayers* (= prays) *before she goes to sleep.* ○ *We thought he'd been killed, but our prayers were **answered** when he arrived home unexpectedly.* ○ *a prayer book* **2** [U] the act or ceremony in which someone prays: *I found her **kneeling in** prayer at the back of the church.* ○ *The prisoners find their only solace in prayer.*

• **not have a prayer** to have no chance of succeeding: *She hasn't a prayer **of** winning the competition.*

pray PLEASE /preɪ/ *adv OLD USE OR FORMAL* a forceful way of saying 'please': *Pray tell your sister that I long to see her.* ○ *And where have you been, pray **tell**?*

'prayer ,mat *noun* [C] a small piece of thick cloth on which a Muslim goes down on his knees and bends his body down to the ground when praying

,praying 'mantis *noun* [C] a **mantis** (= large green insect)

pre- /priː-/ *prefix* before (a time or an event): *a pre-flight check* ○ *a pre-lunch drink* ○ *pre-industrial societies*

preach SPEAK IN CHURCH /priːtʃ/ *verb* [I or T] (especially of a priest in a church) to give a religious speech: *Father Martin preached to the assembled mourners.* ○ *During the sermon, he preached about the need for forgiveness.* **preacher** /ˈpriː.tʃə^r/ ⓤ /-tʃɚ/ *noun* [C] a person, usually a priest, who gives a religious speech

preach PERSUADE /priːtʃ/ *verb* [T] to try to persuade other people to believe in a particular belief or follow a particular way of life: *They preach the abolition of established systems but propose nothing to replace them.*

• **preach to the converted** (*ALSO* **preach to the choir**) to try to persuade people to believe things which they already believe: *You needn't bother telling us how recycling helps the environment, because you're preaching to the converted.*

preach ADVISE /priːtʃ/ *verb* [I] *DISAPPROVING* to give unwanted advice, especially about moral matters, in a boring way: *He's such a pain – he's always preaching **about** the virtues of working hard and getting up early.* ○ *My mother's always preaching **at/to** me **about** keeping my room tidy.*

preamble /ˈpriː.æm.bl̩/ /priˈæm-/ *noun* **1** [C] *SPECIALIZED* an introduction to a speech or piece of writing **2** [U] talk or activity not connected with the most important matter

prearranged /ˌpriː.əˈreɪndʒd/ *adj* arranged in advance: *a prearranged visit* ○ *At a prearranged **signal**, everyone started moving forwards.*

prebuilt /ˌpriːˈbɪlt/ *adj US FOR* **prefabricated**

precancerous /ˌpriːˈkænt.s^ər.əs/ ⓤ /-sɚ.əs/ *adj SPECIALIZED* (especially of cells) showing signs of developing into a cancer: *a precancerous **growth***

precarious /prɪˈkeə.ri.əs/ ⓤ /-ˈker.i-/ *adj* **1** in a dangerous state because not safe or firmly fixed: *The lorry was lodged in a very precarious way, with its front wheels hanging over the cliff.* **2** A precarious situation is likely to get worse: *Many borrowers now find themselves caught in a precarious financial position.*

precariously /prɪˈkeə.ri.ə.sli/ ⓤ /-ˈker.i-/ *adv* in a way that is likely to fall, be damaged, fail, etc: *Her suitcase was precariously **balanced** on the tiny luggage rack above her head.* ○ *He lived rather precariously from one day to the next, never knowing where his next meal was coming from.* **precariousness** /prɪˈkeə.ri.ə.snəs/ ⓤ /-ˈker.i-/ *noun* [U]

precast /ˌpriːˈkɑːst/ ⓤ /ˈpriː.kæst/ *adj* (especially of concrete) formed into a particular shape and allowed to become solid before being used: *precast concrete slabs*

precaution /prɪˈkɔː.ʃ^ən/ ⓤ /-ˈkɑː-/ *noun* [C] an action which is done to prevent something unpleasant or dangerous happening: *Many people have been stockpiling food as a precaution **against** shortages.* ○ *They failed to **take** the necessary precautions to avoid infection.* **precautionary** /prɪˈkɔː.ʃ^ən.^ər.i/ ⓤ /-ˈkɑː.ʃ^ən.er-/ *adj: The company has withdrawn the drug as a precautionary **measure**.*

precautions /prɪˈkɔː.ʃ^ənz/ ⓤ /-ˈkɑː-/ *plural noun* a polite way of referring to CONTRACEPTION (= methods that prevent a woman becoming pregnant): *If you're going to have sex, make sure you **take** precautions.*

precede /prɪˈsiːd/ ⓤ /priː-/ *verb* [T] to be or go before something or someone in time or space: *Boutros Boutros-Ghali preceded Kofi Annan as the Secretary-General of the UN.* ○ *It would be helpful if you were to precede the report **with** an introduction.*

preceding /prɪˈsiː.dɪŋ/ ⓤ /priː-/ *adj* [before n] existing or happening before someone or something: *The paintings are a development of ideas she explored in the preceding decade.* ○ *In conclusion, I hope the preceding arguments have convinced you of the need for action.*

precedence /ˈpres.ɪ.d^ənts/ ⓤ /-ə.dents/ *noun* [U] **1** the condition of being dealt with before other things or of being considered more important than other things: *Precedence must be **given** to the injured in the evacuation plans.* ○ *Business people often think that fluency and communication **take** precedence **over** grammar when speaking.* **2** *FORMAL* the order of importance given to people in particular societies, groups or organizations: *The **order of** precedence for titled nobility in Britain is duke, marquis, earl, viscount, baron.*

precedent /ˈpres.ɪ.d^ənt/ ⓤ /-ə.dent/ *noun* **1** [C] an action, situation or decision which has already happened and which can be used as a reason why a similar action or decision should be performed or taken: *There are several precedents **for** promoting people who don't have formal qualifications.* ○ *Some politicians fear that agreeing to the concession would **set** a dangerous precedent.* **2** [U] the way that something has been done in the past which therefore shows that it is the correct way: *Would it be **breaking with** precedent for the bride to make a speech?* **3** [C] *LEGAL* a decision about a particular law case which makes it likely that other similar cases will be decided in the same way: *The judgment on pension rights has **established/set** a precedent.*

precept /ˈpriː.sept/ *noun* [C] *FORMAL* a rule for action or behaviour, especially obtained from moral consideration: *This policy goes against common precepts **of** decency.*

precinct SHOPPING AREA /ˈpriː.sɪŋkt/ *noun* [C] *UK* part of a city or a town in which vehicles are not allowed and which is used for a special purpose, especially shopping: *a shopping precinct* ○ *a pedestrian/pedestrianized precinct*

precinct CITY AREA /ˈpriː.sɪŋkt/ *noun* [C] *US* a division of a city or a town, especially an area protected by a particular unit of the police or a division used for voting purposes: *The voter turnout in most precincts is expected to be high.*

precincts /ˈpriː.sɪŋkts/ *plural noun* (*ALSO* **precinct**) *MAINLY UK FORMAL* the area which surrounds a building or place, especially when enclosed by a wall: *A tunnel entrance was found within **the** precincts **of** the prison camp.*

precious [VALUABLE] /ˈpreʃ.əs/ *adj* of great value because of being rare, expensive or important: *a precious gift* ○ *a precious moment/memory* ○ *Clean water is a precious commodity in many parts of the world.* ○ *You're so precious **to** me.*

precious [VERY] /ˈpreʃ.əs/ *adv* INFORMAL very: *A lot of people will start, but precious **few** will finish.* ○ *Be careful – you'll be precious **little** help if you come back injured.*

precious [UNNATURAL] /ˈpreʃ.əs/ *adj* MAINLY UK DISAPPROVING behaving in a very formal and unnatural way by giving too much attention to unimportant details and trying too hard to be perfect: *He's so precious **about** his work that he never gets anything done.* ○ *Don't you hate the precious **way** she speaks, pronouncing each single consonant so precisely.*

preciously /ˈpreʃ.ə.sli/ *adv* DISAPPROVING in a way that is too formal and unnatural: *He speaks too preciously for my liking.* **preciousness** /ˈpreʃ.ə.snəs/ *noun* [U]

precious [DISLIKE] /ˈpreʃ.əs/ *adj* **[before n]** INFORMAL used to express dislike and/or annoyance: *You and your precious car – it's all you're interested in!*

ˌprecious ˈmetal *noun* [C] a metal which is valuable and usually rare: *Platinum and gold are precious metals.*

ˌprecious ˈstone *noun* [C] (US ALSO **precious gem**) a valuable stone which is used in jewellery: *The crown, decorated with diamonds and other precious stones, was exhibited in a special case.*

precipice /ˈpres.ɪ.pɪs/ *noun* [C] **1** a very steep side of a cliff or a mountain: *The film opens with a shot of a climber dangling from a precipice.* **2** a dangerous situation which could lead to harm or failure: *This latest tax increase may push many small companies over the financial precipice.*

precipitous /prɪˈsɪp.ɪ.təs/ [US] /priːˈsɪp.ɪ.t̬əs/ *adj* **1** If a slope is precipitous, it is very steep: *a precipitous mountain path* **2** If a reduction or increase is precipitous, it is fast or great: *Over the past 18 months, there has been a precipitous **fall** in car sales.* **precipitously** /prɪˈsɪp.ɪ.tə.sli/ [US] /priːˈsɪp.ɪ.t̬ə-/ *adv*: *The price of shares in the company dropped precipitously with the news of poor sales figures.*

precipitate [MAKE HAPPEN] /prɪˈsɪp.ɪ.teɪt/ *verb* [T] FORMAL to make something happen suddenly or sooner than expected: *An invasion would certainly precipitate a political crisis.* ○ *Fear of losing her job precipitated* (= suddenly forced) *her **into** action.*

precipitate /prɪˈsɪp.ɪ.tət/ [US] /priːˈsɪp.ɪ.tɪt/ *adj* (ALSO **precipitous**) FORMAL If an action is precipitate, it is done sooner or faster that expected and without enough thought or preparation: *Don't be precipitate – think it through before you make a decision.*

precipitately /prɪˈsɪp.ɪ.tət.li/ [US] /priːˈsɪp.ɪ.tɪt-/ *adv* FORMAL in a way that is too sudden and without consideration: *Scientists are annoyed that the research programme has been abandoned so precipitately.*

precipitation /prɪˌsɪp.ɪˈteɪ.ʃən/ [US] /priː-/ *noun* [U] FORMAL *The prime minister has been accused of acting with precipitation* (= too quickly) *over the crisis.*

precipitate [CHEMISTRY] /prɪˈsɪp.ɪ.tət/ [US] /priːˈsɪp.ɪ.tɪt/ *noun* **[C or U]** SPECIALIZED a solid substance which is produced from a liquid during a chemical process: *After filtration, the precipitate was dried at 90°C.*

precipitate /prɪˈsɪp.ɪ.teɪt/ *verb* **[I or T]** SPECIALIZED If a liquid precipitates, substances in it become solid and separate from the liquid: *Cooling the beaker helps precipitate the compound.* ○ *If any organic salt is formed, it will precipitate **(out)** immediately.* **precipitation** /prɪˌsɪp.ɪˈteɪ.ʃən/ [US] /priː-/ *noun* [U] *The compound is finally obtained by precipitation.*

precipitate [THROW] /prɪˈsɪp.ɪ.teɪt/ *verb* **[T usually + adv or prep]** FORMAL to throw someone or something from a height with great force

precipitation /prɪˌsɪp.ɪˈteɪ.ʃən/ [US] /priː-/ *noun* [U] SPECIALIZED water which falls from the clouds towards the ground, especially as rain or snow: *Hail and sleet are types of precipitation.* ○ *The forecast is for dry, cloudy weather with no precipitation expected.*

précis /ˈpreɪ.si/ *noun* [C] a short form of a text which briefly gives only the important parts: *You have all been given a précis **of** the report.* **précis** /ˈpreɪ.si/ *verb* [T] *If I may précis the president's words – "This country will never give in to terrorism."*

precise [EXACT] /prɪˈsaɪs/ [US] /prə-/ *adj* exact and accurate: *The bunker's precise location is a closely guarded secret.* ○ *He caught me at the precise **moment** that I fainted.* ○ *There was a good turnout for the meeting – twelve of us **to be** precise.*

precisely /prɪˈsaɪ.sli/ [US] /prə-/ *adv* **1** exactly: *The fireworks begin at eight o'clock precisely.* ○ *What do you think the problem is, precisely?* **2** used to emphasize what you are saying: *"You look tired – you should go home and rest." "I'm going to do precisely that."* ○ *But it's precisely because of the noise that they're thinking of moving.* **3** used to express complete agreement with someone or suggest that what they have said is obvious: *"It would be stupid to attempt the journey in the dark." "Precisely," he answered.*

precision /prɪˈsɪʒ.ən/ [US] /prə-/ *noun* [U] the quality of being exact: *Great precision is required to align the mirrors accurately.* ○ *Precision **bombing** was used to destroy enemy airbases and armaments factories.*

COMMON LEARNER ERROR

precise

You cannot use **precise** as a verb. It is only an adjective. If you want to use a verb with a similar meaning, you can use words such as **specify, explain, make clear**.

~~*Your advertisement doesn't precise whether flights are included in the price.*~~
Your advertisement doesn't explain whether flights are included in the price.

precise [CAREFUL] /prɪˈsaɪs/ [US] /prə-/ *adj* APPROVING very careful and accurate, especially about small details: *Years of doing meticulous research had made her very precise in her working methods.*

precisely /prɪˈsaɪ.sli/ [US] /prə-/ *adv* APPROVING carefully and accurately: *He works slowly and precisely whereas I tend to rush things and make mistakes.*

precision /prɪˈsɪʒ.ən/ [US] /prə-/ *noun* [U] APPROVING the qualities of being careful and accurate: *His books are a pleasure to read because he writes with such clarity and precision.*

preˈcision ˌinstrument *noun* [C] (ALSO **precision tool**) a tool which can be controlled very accurately and which produces very accurate results

preclude /prɪˈkluːd/ [US] /prə-/ *verb* [T] FORMAL to prevent something or make it impossible, or prevent someone from doing something: *His contract precludes him **from** discussing his work with anyone outside the company.* ○ *The fact that your application was not successful this time does not preclude the possibility of you applying again next time.* **preclusion** /prɪˈkluː.ʒən/ [US] /prə-/ *noun* [U] *Your age should not act as a preclusion **to** you being accepted on the university course.*

precocious /prɪˈkəʊ.ʃəs/ [US] /prə-/ *adj* **1** (especially of children) showing unusually early mental development or achievement: *A precocious child, she went to university at the age of 15.* ○ *She recorded her first CD at the precocious age of 12.* **2** MAINLY DISAPPROVING describes a child who behaves as if they are much older than they are: *a precocious little brat*

precociously /prɪˈkəʊ.ʃə.sli/ [US] /prə-/ *adv* in a way that is unnaturally advanced or developed **precociousness** /prɪˈkəʊ.ʃə.snəs/ [US] /prə-/ *noun* [U] (FORMAL **precocity**)

precognition /ˌpriː.kɒgˈnɪʃ.ən/ [US] /-kɑːg-/ *noun* [U] SPECIALIZED knowledge of a future event, especially when it is obtained by a direct message to the mind, such as in a dream, rather than by reason **precognitive** /ˌpriːˈkɒg.nɪ.tɪv/ [US] /-ˈkɑːg.nɪ.t̬ɪv/ *adj*: *She claims she has precognitive **abilities** and that she can foresee events before they actually happen.*

pre-Columbian /ˌpriː.kəˈlʌm.bi.ən/ *adj* related to or from America in the period before Columbus arrived in 1492

preconceived /ˌpriː.kənˈsiːvd/ *adj* MAINLY DISAPPROVING (of an idea or an opinion) formed too early, especially without enough consideration or knowledge: *You must* judge each film on its own merits, without any pre-conceived **notions** about what it's like.

preconception /ˌpriːkənˈsep.ʃ°n/ noun [C] MAINLY DIS-APPROVING an idea or opinion formed before enough in-formation is available to form it correctly: Try to go into the meeting without too many preconceptions **about** what the other group want.

precondition /ˌpriːkənˈdɪʃ.°n/ noun [C] something which must happen or be true before it is possible for something else to happen: A halt to the fighting is a pre-condition **for** negotiations.

precook /ˌpriːˈkʊk/ verb [T] to cook food in advance so that it can be heated and then eaten at a later time pre-cooked /ˌpriːˈkʊkt/ adj: Sales of precooked **meals** have risen sharply over the past few years.

precursor /ˌpriːˈkɜː.sə°/ ⓤ /-ˈkɜː.sɚ/ noun [C] SLIGHTLY FORMAL something which happened or existed before another thing, especially if it either developed into it or had an influence on it: Sulphur dioxide is the main pre-cursor **of** acid rain. ◦ Biological research has often been a precursor **to** medical breakthroughs which benefit patients.

predate /ˌpriːˈdeɪt/ verb [T] SLIGHTLY FORMAL to have existed or happened before another thing: These cave paintings predate any others which are known. ⊃Compare **backdate**; **postdate**.

predator /ˈpred.ə.tə°/ ⓤ /-t̬ɚ/ noun [C] **1** an animal that hunts, kills and eats other animals: lions, wolves and other predators **2** DISAPPROVING someone who follows people in order to harm them or commit a crime against them: a sexual predator ◦ In court, he was accused of being a merciless predator who had tricked his grand-mother out of her savings.
predatory /ˈpred.ə.t°r.i/ ⓤ /-tɔːr-/ adj **1** A predatory animal kills and eats other animals: The owl is a pre-datory bird which kills its prey with its claws. **2** MAINLY DISAPPROVING A predatory person or organization tries to obtain something that belongs to someone else: The company spent much effort in avoiding takeover bids from predatory competitors. **3** DISAPPROVING describes someone who expresses sexual interest in a very obvious way: I hate going to bars on my own because men look at you in such a predatory way.

predatory 'pricing noun [U] SPECIALIZED when a company offers goods at such a low price that other companies cannot compete with it: The airline has re-duced its prices so sharply that it has been accused of pre-datory pricing.

predecease /ˌpriː.dɪˈsiːs/ ⓤ /-diː-/ verb [T] FORMAL OR LEGAL to die before someone else: Her husband pre-deceased her by five years.

predecessor /ˈpriː.dɪˌses.ə°/ ⓤ /ˈpred.ə.ses.ɚ/ noun [C] someone who had a job or a position before someone else, or something which comes before another thing in time or in a series: My predecessor worked in this job for twelve years. ◦ The latest Ferrari is not only faster than its predecessors but also more comfortable.

predestination /ˌpriːˌdes.tɪˈneɪ.ʃ°n/ noun [U] the belief that people have no control over events because these things are controlled by God or by FATE
predestined /ˌpriːˈdes.tɪnd/ adj If an action or event is predestined, it is controlled by God or by FATE: It seems the expedition is predestined **to** fail because there have been so many problems.

predetermine /ˌpriː.dɪˈtɜː.mɪn/ ⓤ /-diːˈtɜː.mən/ verb [T] SLIGHTLY FORMAL to decide or arrange something at an earlier time: It's impossible to say how much a person's behaviour is predetermined by their genes. pre-determined /ˌpriː.dɪˈtɜː.mɪn/ ⓤ /-diːˈtɜː.mən/ adj: At a predetermined **time**, we'll all shout 'Happy Birthday, Dave'. predetermination /ˌpriːˌdɪˌtɜː.mɪˈneɪ.ʃ°n/ ⓤ /-diːˌtɜː.mə-/ noun [U] FORMAL

predeterminer /ˌpriːˈdɪˈtɜː.mɪ.nə°/ ⓤ /-diːˈtɜː.mə.nɚ/ noun [C] SPECIALIZED in grammar, a word which is some-times used before a determiner to give more informa-tion about a noun in a noun phrase: In the phrases 'all these children' and 'once a day', the words 'all' and 'once' are predeterminers.

predicament /prɪˈdɪk.ə.mənt/ ⓤ /prə-/ noun [C] SLIGHTLY FORMAL an unpleasant situation which is difficult to get out of: She is hoping to get a loan from her bank to help her out of her financial predicament. ◦ I'm in a bit of a predicament because I've accidentally accepted two invita-tions to dinner on the same night.

predicate SENTENCE PART /ˈpred.ɪ.kət/ ⓤ /-kɪt/ noun [C] SPECIALIZED in grammar, the part of a sentence which contains the verb and gives information about the sub-ject: In the sentence 'We went to the airport', 'went to the airport' is the predicate.

predicate STATE /ˈpred.ɪ.keɪt/ verb [T] FORMAL to state that something is true: [+ that] It would be unwise to pre-dicate **that** the disease is caused by a virus before further tests have been carried out.
• **be predicated on** sth FORMAL If an idea or argument is predicated on something, it depends on the existence or truth of this thing: The sales forecast is predicated on the assumption that the economy will grow by four per cent this year.

predicative /prɪˈdɪk.ə.tɪv/ ⓤ /ˈpred.ɪ.keɪ.t̬ɪv/ adj SPECIALIZED (in grammar, especially of adjectives or phrases) following a verb: In the sentence 'She is happy', 'happy' is a predicative adjective. ⊃Compare **attributive**.

predict /prɪˈdɪkt/ verb [T] to say that an event or action will happen in the future, especially as a result of know-ledge or experience: It's still not possible to accurately predict the occurrence of earthquakes. ◦ [+ that] Who could have predicted **that** within ten years he'd be in charge of the whole company? ◦ [+ to infinitive] The hurricane is pre-dicted **to** reach the coast tomorrow morning. ◦ [+ question word] No one can predict **when** the disease will strike again.
predictable /prɪˈdɪk.tə.bl/ adj **1** Something which is predictable happens in a way or at a time which you know about before it happens: Comets appear at predict-able times. ∗ NOTE: The opposite is **unpredictable**. **2** DISAPPROV-ING happening or behaving in a way that you expect and not unusual or interesting: The ending to the film was just so predictable.
predictably /prɪˈdɪk.tə.bli/ adv as expected: Predictably, after the initial media interest, the refugees now seem to have been forgotten.
predictability /prɪˌdɪk.tə.ˈbɪl.ɪ.ti/ ⓤ /-ə.t̬i/ noun [U] the state of knowing what something is like, when some-thing will happen, etc: Although her job is boring and monotonous, she likes the sense of predictability and security that it gives her.
predictive /prɪˈdɪk.tɪv/ adj FORMAL relating to the ability to predict: The predictive value of this new method of analysis has still to be proven.

prediction /prɪˈdɪk.ʃ°n/ noun [C or U] when you say what will happen in the future: Please don't ask me to **make** any predictions **about** tomorrow's meeting. ◦ [+ that] No one believed her prediction **that** the world would end on November 12.

predigested /ˌpriː.daɪˈdʒes.tɪd/ adj SLIGHTLY DISAPPROV-ING (of information) made simpler or easier to under-stand, especially by removing any parts which would make a person have to think hard: The booklet presents information about the project in a predigested form and explains things in an easy, non-technical way.

predilection /ˌpriː.dɪˈlek.ʃ°n/ ⓤ /ˌpred.°lˈek-/ noun [C] SLIGHTLY FORMAL a strong liking: Ever since she was a child, she has had a predilection **for** spicy food.

predispose /ˌpriː.dɪˈspəʊz/ ⓤ /-ˈspoʊz/ verb
▲ **predispose** sb **to/towards** sth phrasal verb FORMAL to make someone more likely to behave in a particular way or to suffer from a particular illness or condition: Smoking predisposes you to lung cancer. ◦ His family background predisposes him to support the Democrats.

predisposed /ˌpriː.dɪˈspəʊzd/ ⓤ /-ˈspoʊzd/ adj be pre-disposed **to/towards** sth to be more likely than other people to have a medical condition or to behave in a particular way: Researchers have discovered that the children of these patients are genetically predisposed to cancer. ◦ The president is predisposed towards negotia-tion and favours a peaceful way of resolving the crisis.

P

predisposition /ˌpriː.dɪ.spəˈzɪʃ.ᵊn/ *noun* [C] FORMAL the state of being likely to behave in a particular way or to suffer from a particular disease: *She has an annoying predisposition* **to** *find fault wherever she goes.* ○ *There is evidence that a predisposition* **to(wards)** *asthma runs in families.*

predominant /prɪˈdɒm.ɪ.nənt/ [US] /-ˈdɑː.mə-/ *adj* more noticeable or important, or larger in number, than others: *Research forms the predominant part of my job.* ○ *Dancers have a predominant role in this performance.* **predominantly** /prɪˈdɒm.ɪ.nənt.li/ [US] /-ˈdɑː.mə-/ *adv* mostly or mainly: *a predominantly Muslim community* ○ *She is predominantly a dancer, but she also sings.* **predominance** /prɪˈdɒm.ɪ.nənts/ [US] /-ˈdɑː.mə-/ *noun* [U] **1** when one person or group of people has more importance or power than others **2 a predominance of *sth*** a situation in which one type of person or thing within a set is the largest in number: *There is a predominance of people with an arts degree on the board of governors.* **predominate** /prɪˈdɒm.ɪ.neɪt/ [US] /-ˈdɑː.mə-/ *verb* [I] to be the largest in number or the most important: *In industrial areas, the dark-coloured variety of the moth now predominates.*

preemie US /ˈpriː.mi/ *noun* [C] (AUS **premmie**) INFORMAL a baby that is born earlier than expected

pre-eminent /ˌpriːˈem.ɪ.nənt/ *adj* FORMAL more important or better than others: *She is the pre-eminent authority in her subject.* **pre-eminence** /ˌpriːˈem.ɪ.nənts/ *noun* [U] *His pre-eminence in his subject is internationally recognized.*

pre-eminently /ˌpriːˈem.ɪ.nənt.li/ *adv* FORMAL mainly, or to a very great degree: *The arts festival is pre-eminently a festival of theatre.*

pre-empt /ˌpriːˈempt/ *verb* [T] **1** to do or say something before someone so that you make their words or actions unnecessary or ineffective: *The minister held a press conference in order to pre-empt criticism in the newspapers.* **2** US to replace one television programme with another, usually more important one: *All the networks pre-empted their regular schedules to broadcast news of the hijacking.*

pre-emptive /ˌpriːˈemp.tɪv/ *adj* SLIGHTLY FORMAL describes something that is done before other people can act, especially to prevent them from doing something else: *The Treasury has decided to raise interest rates as a pre-emptive* **measure** *against inflation.* ○ *The prime minister authorized a pre-emptive air* **strike** *against the rebels.*

preen [MAKE TIDY] /priːn/ *verb* [I or T] **1** (of a bird) to clean and arrange its feathers using its beak **2** DISAPPROVING to spend time making yourself look attractive: *Roald always spends ages preening (himself) before he goes out.*

preen [FEEL PROUD] /priːn/ *verb* [T] DISAPPROVING to feel very proud or satisfied with yourself because of an action or quality: *The government is publicly preening itself* **on** *the latest trade figures.* ○ *The company preened itself* **for** *hav***ing** *taken on so many new employees last year.*

pre-exist /ˌpriː.ɪɡˈzɪst/ *verb* [I or T] FORMAL to exist before something else: *Dinosaurs pre-existed human beings* **by** *many millions of years.* **pre-existing** /ˌpriː.ɪɡˈzɪs.tɪŋ/ *adj*: *a pre-existing medical condition*

prefab /ˈpriː.fæb/ *noun* [C] INFORMAL a small house which can be built quickly from pieces which have been made in a factory: *After World War Two, lots of prefabs were put up to ease the housing crisis.*

prefabricated /ˌpriːˈfæb.rɪ.keɪ.tɪd/ [US] /-t̬ɪd/ *adj* (INFORMAL **prefab**) describes buildings or objects built from parts which have been made in a factory and can be put together quickly: *a prefabricated* **house** **prefabrication** /ˌpriː.fæb.rɪˈkeɪ.ʃᵊn/ *noun* [U]

preface /ˈpref.ɪs/ *noun* [C] **1** an introduction at the beginning of a book explaining its aims: *In his preface, the author says that he took eight years to write the book.* **2 a preface to *sth*** an event which comes before something more important: *We're hoping these talks could be a preface to peace.*

preface /ˈpref.ɪs/ *verb* [T] FORMAL If you preface your words or actions with something else, you say or do this other thing first: *Each work is prefaced* **by** *a descriptive note and concludes with an author's note.* ○ *I should like to preface my response* **with** *the following observation.* **prefatory** /ˈpref.ə.tᵊr.i/ [US] /-tɔːr-/ *adj* FORMAL coming at the beginning of a piece of writing or a speech; INTRODUCTORY: *After a few prefatory* **comments/remarks**, *she began her speech.*

prefect [OFFICIAL] /ˈpriː.fekt/ *noun* [C] (in some countries) a very important official in the government or the police: *He has been appointed Prefect of Bologna.*

prefect [STUDENT] /ˈpriː.fekt/ *noun* [C] UK (in some British and Australian schools) an older student who is given some authority and helps to control the younger students

prefer [CHOOSE] /prɪˈfɜːʳ/ [US] /-ˈfɝː/ *verb* [T] **-rr-** to like, choose or want one thing rather than another: *Do you prefer hot or cold weather?* ○ *I prefer red wine* **to** *white.* ○ [+ v-ing] *He prefers watch***ing** *rugby to play***ing** *it.* ○ [+ to infinitive] *I'd prefer not* **to** *discuss this issue.* ○ FORMAL *I'd prefer you not* **to** *smoke* (= I would like it better if you did not smoke), *please.* **preferred** /prɪˈfɜːd/ [US] /-ˈfɝːd/ *adj* liked or wanted more than anything else: *The earlier train would be my preferred* **option**. **preferable** /ˈpref.ᵊr.ə.bl̩/ [US] /-ɚ.ə-/ *adj* better or more suitable: *Surely a diplomatic solution is preferable* **to** *war.* **preferably** /ˈpref.ᵊr.ə.bli/ [US] /-ɚ.ə-/ *adv* if possible: *Water the plants twice a week, preferably in the morning.*

prefer [ACCUSE] /prɪˈfɜːʳ/ [US] /-ˈfɝː/ *verb* [T] **-rr-** UK LEGAL to make an official accusation: *The police have decided not to prefer* **charges** *against them because of insufficient evidence.*

preference /ˈpref.ᵊr.ᵊnts/ [US] /-ɚ-/ *noun* [C or U] **1** when you like something or someone more than another person or thing: *Her preference is* **for** *comfortable rather than stylish clothes.* ○ *I have a preference* **for** *sweet food over spicy.* ○ *Choosing furniture is largely a matter of* **personal** *preference.* ○ *It would be wrong to discriminate against a candidate because of their* **sexual** *preference* (= the sex of the people they are sexually attracted to). **2** an advantage which is given to a person or a group of people: *We give preference* **to** *those who have worked with us for a long time.* ○ *Special preferences were offered initially to encourage investment.*

• **in preference to *sth*** If you choose one thing in preference to another thing, you choose it because you like or want it more than the other thing: *He studied chemistry in preference to physics at university.*

preferential /ˌpref.ᵊrˈen.tʃᵊl/ [US] /-əˈren-/ *adj* [before n] describes something you are given which is better than what other people receive: *Inmates claimed that some prisoners had received preferential* **treatment**. ○ *Single mothers have been given preferential access to council housing.* **preferentially** /ˌpref.ᵊrˈen.tʃᵊl.i/ [US] /-əˈren-/ *adv*

prefigure /priːˈfɪɡ.əʳ/ [US] /-jɚ/ *verb* [T] FORMAL to show or suggest that something will happen in the future: *His paintings prefigure the development of perspective in Renaissance art.*

prefix [GRAMMAR] /ˈpriː.fɪks/ *noun* [C] a letter or group of letters added to the beginning of a word to make a new word: *In the word 'unimportant', 'un-' is a prefix.* ⊃See also **affix** WORD PART. Compare **suffix**.

prefix [TELEPHONE] /ˈpriː.fɪks/ *noun* [C] UK a **dialling code**

ˈpregnancy ˌtest *noun* [C usually sing] a chemical test performed on a woman's urine which shows if she is pregnant or not

pregnant [FEMALE] /ˈpreg.nənt/ *adj* (of a woman and some female animals) having young developing inside the womb: *She's five and a half months pregnant.* ○ *My mother stopped smoking when she* **became** *pregnant.* ○ *He believes that men who* **get** (= make) *young girls pregnant should be severely punished.* ○ *My sister is pregnant* **with** *twins.* **pregnancy** /ˈpreg.nənt.si/ *noun* [C or U] *Most women feel sick in the mornings during their first months of pregnancy.* ○ *My first pregnancy was very straightforward – there were no complications.*

pregnant [MEANING] /ˈpreg.nənt/ *adj* filled with meaning or importance which has not yet been expressed or understood: *There followed a pregnant* ***pause*** *in which both knew what the other was thinking but neither knew what to say.*

preheat /ˌpriːˈhiːt/ *verb* [T] to heat a cooker to a particular temperature before putting food in it: *Preheat the oven to 180°C.* ○ *a preheated oven*

prehensile /prɪˈhent.saɪl/ [US] /priːˈhent.sɪl/ *adj* SPECIALIZED (of parts of the body) able to hold on to things, especially by curling around them: *a prehensile tail*

prehistory /priːˈhɪs.tᵊr.i/ [US] /-t̬ɚ.i/ *noun* [U] the period of human history before there were written records of events: *Human prehistory is divided into three successive periods: the Stone Age, the Bronze Age and the Iron Age.* **prehistoric** /ˌpriː.hɪˈstɒr.ɪk/ [US] /-hɪˈstɔːr-/ *adj* **1** describing the period before there were written records: *prehistoric man/humans/animals* ○ *Painting originated* ***in*** *prehistoric* ***times***. **2** INFORMAL DISAPPROVING very old-fashioned: *He has prehistoric views about women who have careers.*

prejudge /ˌpriːˈdʒʌdʒ/ *verb* [T] DISAPPROVING to form an opinion about a situation or a person before knowing or considering all of the facts: *Let's not prejudge the situation – we need to hear both sides of the story first.* **prejudgment** /ˌpriːˈdʒʌdʒ.mənt/ *noun* [C or U] (ALSO **prejudgement**) *You shouldn't make any sort of prejudgment about her before you've even met her.*

prejudice /ˈpredʒ.ʊ.dɪs/ *noun* [C or U] an unfair and unreasonable opinion or feeling, especially when formed without enough thought or knowledge: *Laws against* ***racial*** *prejudice must be strictly enforced.* ○ [+ **that**] *The campaign aims to dispel the prejudice* ***that*** *AIDS is confined to the homosexual community.* ○ *He claims that prejudice* ***against*** *homosexuals would cease overnight if all the gay stars in the country were honest about their sexuality.*

• **without prejudice to *sth*** FORMAL OR LEGAL If a decision or action is made without prejudice to a right or claim, it is made without having an effect on that right or claim: *My client accepts the formal apology without prejudice to any further legal action she may decide to take.*

prejudice /ˈpredʒ.ʊ.dɪs/ *verb* [T] **1** Someone or something that prejudices you influences you unfairly so that you form an unreasonable opinion about something: *His comments may have prejudiced the voters* ***against*** *her.* **2** FORMAL Something or someone that prejudices something else has a harmful influence on it: *The fact that you were late all this week may prejudice your chances of getting a promotion.*

prejudiced /ˈpredʒ.ʊ.dɪst/ *adj* DISAPPROVING showing an unreasonable dislike for something or someone: *The campaign is designed to make people less prejudiced about AIDS.* ○ *The media has been accused of presenting a prejudiced view of people with disabilities.* ○ *Some companies are prejudiced* ***against*** *taking on employees who are over the age of 40.*

prejudicial /ˌpredʒ.ʊˈdɪʃ.ᵊl/ *adj* SLIGHTLY FORMAL harmful or influencing people unfairly: *The judge decided that allowing the videotape as evidence would be prejudicial* ***to*** *the outcome of the trial.*

prelate /ˈprel.ɪt/ *noun* [C] an official of high rank in the Christian religion, such as a bishop or an ABBOT

prelim /ˈpriː.lɪm/ /prɪˈlɪm/ *noun* [C usually pl] INFORMAL a sports event or an exam which acts as a preparation for a more important event that will follow

preliminary /prɪˈlɪm.ɪ.nᵊr.i/ [US] /-ə.ner-/ *adj* [before n] coming before a more important action or event, especially introducing or preparing for it: *Preliminary results show that the vaccine is effective, but this has to be confirmed by further medical trials.* ○ *We've decided to change the design based on our preliminary findings.* **preliminary** /prɪˈlɪm.ɪ.nᵊr.i/ [US] /-ə.ner-/ *noun* [C usually pl] *After a few polite preliminaries* (= introductions), *we stated our main ideas and intentions.* ○ *The French team finished first in the competition preliminaries* (= the first part of the competition).

preliterate /ˌpriːˈlɪt.ᵊr.ət/ [US] /-ˈlɪt̬.ɚ.ət/ *adj* SPECIALIZED (of a society) not having a written language: *a preliterate tribe*

prelude [INTRODUCTION] /ˈprel.juːd/ *noun* [C usually sing] something that comes before a more important event or action which introduces or prepares for it: *The changes are seen as a prelude* ***to*** *wide-ranging reforms.*

prelude [MUSIC] /ˈprel.juːd/ *noun* [C] SPECIALIZED **1** a short piece of music which introduces the main work **2** a short independent piece of music written especially for the piano

premarital /ˌpriːˈmær.ɪ.tᵊl/ [US] /-ˈmer.ə.t̬ᵊl/ *adj* before marriage: *premarital* ***sex*** ○ *premarital counselling*

premature /ˈprem.ə.tʃəʳ/ /-tjʊəʳ/ /ˌ--ˈ-/ [US] /ˌpriː.məˈtʊr/ *adj* happening or done too soon, especially before the natural or desired time: *premature birth/death* ○ *a premature* ***baby*** ○ *Their criticisms seem premature considering that the results aren't yet known.* **prematurely** /ˈprem.ə.tʃə.li/ /-tjʊə-/ /ˌ--ˈ--/ [US] /ˌpriː.məˈtʊr-/ *adv*: *Their baby was born prematurely and weighed only 1 kilogram.* ○ *His stressful job made him go prematurely grey* (= made his hair turn grey at a young age).

premeditated /ˌpriːˈmed.ɪ.teɪ.tɪd/ [US] /-t̬ɪd/ *adj* (especially of a crime or something unpleasant) done after being thought about or carefully planned: *premeditated murder* ○ *a premeditated attack* ○ *The assault was premeditated and particularly brutal.* ✻ NOTE: The opposite is **unpremeditated**. **premeditation** /ˌpriː.med.ɪˈteɪ.ʃᵊn/ *noun* [U] SLIGHTLY FORMAL

premenstrual /ˌpriːˈment.stru.əl/ [US] /-strəl/ *adj* [before n] of the time just before a woman's period

premenstrual syndrome /ˌpriː.ment.stru.əlˈsɪn.drəʊm/ [US] /-strəlˈsɪn.droʊm/ [U] (UK ALSO **premenstrual tension**) a condition in which some women experience pain and swelling in particular parts of their bodies, and feelings such as anxiety, anger, or unhappiness for a few days before their period

premier [LEADER] /ˈprem.i.əʳ/ [US] /prɪˈmɪr/ *noun* [C] (especially used in news reports) the leader of the government of a country, or of a large part of a country

premier [BEST] /ˈprem.i.əʳ/ [US] /prɪˈmɪr/ *adj* [before n] best or most important: *He's one of the nation's premier scientists.*

première /ˈprem.i.eəʳ/ [US] /prɪˈmɪr/ *noun* [C] the first public performance of a play or any other type of entertainment: *The* ***world*** *première* ***of*** *the opera will be at the Metropolitan Opera House in New York.* **première** /ˈprem.i.eəʳ/ [US] /prɪˈmɪr/ *verb* [T] *The play was premièred in New York.*

premise /ˈprem.ɪs/ *noun* [C] an idea or theory on which a statement or action is based: [+ **that**] *They had started with the premise* ***that*** *all men are created equal.* ○ *The research project is based on the premise stated earlier.* **premise** /prɪˈmaɪz/ /ˈprem.ɪs/ *verb* [T] FORMAL to base a theory, argument, etc. on an idea, thought, or belief: *He premised his argument* ***on*** *several incorrect assumptions.*

premises /ˈprem.ɪ.sɪz/ *plural noun* the land and buildings owned by someone, especially by a company or organization: *The company is relocating to new premises.* ○ *There is no smoking allowed anywhere on school premises.* ○ *The ice cream is made* ***on the*** *premises* (= in the building where it is sold). ○ *The security guards escorted the protesters* ***off*** (= away from) *the premises.*

premium [EXTRA] /ˈpriː.mi.əm/ *noun* [C] an amount which is more than usual: *We're willing to pay a premium for the best location.* ○ *Because of their location, these offices* ***attract*** *a premium.* ○ *The modified cars are available* ***at*** *a premium* ***of*** *5%* ***over*** *the original price.* ○ *The busy shopper* ***puts*** *a premium* ***on*** (= appreciates and will pay more for) *finding everything in one big store.* **premium** /ˈpriː.mi.əm/ *adj* describes something that is of higher than usual quality: *premium ice cream* ○ *The building is on a premium site.*

• **be at a premium** to be not common and therefore valuable: *Free time is at a premium for working parents.*

premium [PAYMENT] /ˈpriː.mi.əm/ *noun* [C] an amount of money paid to obtain insurance: *Car insurance premiums have increased this year.* ○ *The premiums* ***for*** *healthcare plans are high.*

ˈpremium ˌbond *noun* [C] UK a BOND (= numbered ticket) which you can buy as part of a government system in which you have the chance every month to win a prize of money

premium (**'gas**) *noun* [U] *US FOR* **four-star (petrol)**

'premium ,rate *adj* describes a telephone number or service that costs more to call than a normal telephone number: *a premium rate number/line/service* ○ *You had to call a premium rate line to enter the contest.*

premmie /'prem.i/ *noun* [C] *AUS FOR* **preemie**

premonition /,prem.ə'nɪʃ.ə n/ /,priː.mə-/ *noun* [C] a feeling that something, especially something unpleasant, is going to happen: [+ *that*] *He had a premonition that his plane would crash, so he took the train.* ○ *She had a sudden premonition of what the future might bring.*

prenatal /,priː'neɪ.t ə l/ /-t ə l/ *adj* [before n] *US FOR* **antenatal**

prenuptial /,priː'nʌp.tʃ ə l/ *adj* before getting married

,prenuptial a'greement *noun* [C] (*INFORMAL* **pre-nup**) an official document signed by two people before they get married which says what will happen to their possessions and/or children if they DIVORCE (= officially stop being married): *He asked her to sign a prenuptial agreement when they got engaged.*

preoccupy /,priː'ɒk.jʊ.paɪ/ /-'ɑː.kjuː-/ *verb* [T] to be the main thought in someone's mind, causing other things to be forgotten: *Economic concerns are preoccupying the voters in this election.*

preoccupied /,priː'ɒk.jʊ.paɪd/ /-'ɑː.kjuː-/ *adj* thinking or worrying about something too much: *She's been very preoccupied recently because her mother has been very ill.* ○ *Why is the media so preoccupied with the love lives of politicians?* **preoccupation** /pri:,ɒk.jʊ'peɪ.ʃ ə n/ /-,ɑː.kjuː-/ *noun* [C or U] *My main preoccupation now is trying to keep life normal for the sake of my two boys.* ○ *Lately, his preoccupation with football had caused his marks at school to slip.*

preordain /,priː.ɔː'deɪn/ /-ɔːr-/ *verb* [T] *FORMAL* (especially of a power thought to be greater than ordinary people) to decide or fix what will happen in a way that cannot be changed or controlled: [+ *to infinitive*] *Illness and suffering seemed (to be) preordained to be her lot.* ○ *His life seems to have followed a preordained path/direction.*

prep SCHOOL WORK /prep/ *noun* [U] *UK* school work that students, especially students at PRIVATE SCHOOL and PUBLIC SCHOOL, do at home or not during lesson time: *Have you got much prep tonight?*

prep GRAMMAR /prep/ *ABBREVIATION FOR* **preposition**

prepacked /,priː'pækt/ *adj* (*US USUALLY* **prepackaged**) wrapped or put into a container before being sold: *The nails come prepacked in small boxes.*

prepaid /,priː'peɪd/ *adj* paid in advance: *Admission tickets are $20 prepaid, $25 at the door.*

preparation /,prep.ə r'eɪ.ʃ ə n/ *noun* [U] the things that you do or the time that you spend preparing for something: *The teacher didn't seem to have done much preparation for the class.* ○ *The team blamed injuries and lack of preparation for their failure to win.* ○ *Yasmin assisted in the preparation of this article.*

preparations /,prep.ə r'eɪ.ʃ ə nz/ /-ə'reɪ-/ *plural noun* plans or arrangements that you make to prepare for something: [+ *to infinitive*] *We are making preparations to fly Mr Goodall to the nearest hospital.* ○ *Preparations for the opening ceremony are well under way.*

preparation /,prep.ə r'eɪ.ʃ ə n/ /-ə'reɪ-/ *noun* [C] a mixture of substances, often for use as a medicine: *a preparation for nappy rash*

preparatory /prɪ'pær.ə.t ə r.i/ /-'per.ə.tɔːr-/ *adj* done in order to get ready for something: *preparatory work* ○ *Differences over these issues narrowed during the preparatory meetings/talks.*

pre'paratory ,school *noun* [C] *FORMAL FOR* **prep school**

prepare /prɪ'peə r/ /-'per/ *verb* [I or T] **1** to make or get something or someone ready for something that will happen in the future: *Have you prepared for your interview?* ○ *She'll prepare the food ahead of time and freeze it.* ○ *This course aims to prepare students for middle and senior managerial positions.* ○ [+ *obj* + *to infinitive*] *Are the players mentally and physically prepared to play a tough game?* ○ *The meal took two hours to prepare.* **2** to expect

that something will happen and to be ready for it: [+ *to infinitive*] *It almost seems as if she is preparing to die.* ○ [R] *You need to prepare yourself for a long wait.*

prepared /prɪ'peəd/ /-'perd/ *adj* **1** ready to deal with a situation: *When she called on me, I wasn't prepared.* ○ *They were prepared for the worst.* **2** made earlier: *The spokesperson read a prepared statement.* **3** be prepared to do sth to be willing, or happy to agree to do something: *Would you be prepared to help me get things ready for the party?* ○ *People are not really prepared to talk about these kinds of personal problems.*

preparedness /prɪ'peəd.nəs/ /-'perd-/ *noun* [U] *SLIGHTLY FORMAL* when you are prepared for a particular situation: *The army is in a state of preparedness for war.*

pre-pay /,priː'peɪ/ *adj* [before n] describes a MOBILE PHONE (= a telephone that you can carry with you) which you must pay to use before you are able use it

preponderance /prɪ'pɒn.d ə r.ə nts/ /-'pɑːn.də-/ *noun* [S] *FORMAL* the largest part or greatest amount: *The preponderance of evidence suggests that he's guilty.*

preponderant /prɪ'pɒn.d ə r.ə nt/ /-'pɑːn.də-/ *adj* *FORMAL* important or large: *Music does not play a very preponderant role in the school's teaching.*

preponderantly /prɪ'pɒn.d ə r.ə nt.li/ /-'pɑːn.də-/ *adv* *FORMAL* mostly or mainly: *Industry is still a preponderantly male environment.* **preponderate** /prɪ'pɒn.d ə r.eɪt/ /-'pɑːn.də-/ *verb* [I] *Although it was a mixed class, girls preponderated.*

preposition /,prep.ə'zɪʃ.ə n/ *noun* [C] in grammar, a word which is used before a noun, a NOUN PHRASE or a pronoun, connecting it to another word: *In the sentences 'We jumped in the lake', and 'She drove slowly down the track', 'in' and 'down' are prepositions.* **prepositional** /,prep.ə'zɪʃ.ə n.ə l/ *adj* [before n] *a prepositional phrase*

prepossessing /,priː.pə'zes.ɪŋ/ *adj* interesting, noticeable or attractive: *He wasn't a very prepossessing sort of person.* ○ *The box didn't look very prepossessing, but the necklace inside was beautiful.*

preposterous /prɪ'pɒs.t ə r.əs/ /-'pɑː.stə-/ *adj* *FORMAL* very foolish or ridiculous: *The very idea is preposterous!* ○ *a preposterous suggestion*

preppy, **preppie** /'prep.i/ *noun* [C] *MAINLY US* a young person from a rich family who goes to an expensive school and who wears expensive, tidy clothes **preppy** /'prep.i/ *adj*: *preppy clothes*

'prep ,school *noun* [C] in Britain, a PRIVATE SCHOOL (= a school paid for by parents not the government), for children, especially boys, between the ages of 7 and 13, who will then usually go to PUBLIC SCHOOL, and in the US, a private school for children over the age of 11, which prepares them to go to college

prep-time /'prep.taɪm/ *noun* [U] *US* a period when teachers are at school but do not teach, and are therefore able to prepare for later classes

pre-pubescent /,priː'pjuː'bes.ə nt/ *adj* relating to the period before children start to develop adult sexual characteristics: *pre-pubescent girls/boys/children*

prequel /'priː.kwəl/ *noun* [C usually sing] a film, book or play which develops the story of an earlier film, etc. by telling you what happened before the events in the first film, etc: *Jean Rhys's novel 'Wide Sargasso Sea' is a prequel to Charlotte Bronte's 'Jane Eyre'.* ⊃Compare **sequel**.

Pre-Raphaelite /,priː'ræf.ə l.aɪt/ /-i.ə l-/ *noun* [C] a member of a 19th century group of British painters who were influenced by the style of painting of the 14th and 15th centuries

Pre-Raphaelite /,priː'ræf.ə l.aɪt/ /-i.ə l-/ *adj* belonging or relating to the Pre-Raphaelites, or typical of their style of painting: *a Pre-Raphaelite artist/painter* ○ *She was a woman of Pre-Raphaelite beauty* (= had pale skin and long wavy reddish-brown hair, like the women often painted by the Pre-Raphaelites).

prerecord /,priː.rɪ'kɔːd/ /-'kɔːrd/ *verb* [T] to record especially music or speech in order to use it at a later time: *Is this a live broadcast, or was it prerecorded?*

prerequisite /,priː'rek.wɪ.zɪt/ *noun* [C] *FORMAL* something which must exist or happen before something else can exist or happen: *Passing a written exam is a pre-*

requisite for taking the advanced course. ○ *Public support is a prerequisite **for/to** the success of this project.* ○ *They had to agree to certain conditions as a prerequisite **of** being lent the money.*

prerogative /prɪˈrɒg.ə.tɪv/ [US] /-ˈrɑː.gə.t̬ɪv/ *noun* [C usually sing] FORMAL something which some people are able or allowed to do or have, but which is not possible or allowed for everyone: *Alex makes all the big decisions – that's his prerogative as company director.* ○ *Skiing used to be the prerogative **of** the rich, but now a far wider range of people do it.* ○ ***the Royal** Prerogative* (= the special rights of the ruling king or queen)

Pres. /prez/ *noun* WRITTEN ABBREVIATION FOR **President**: *Pres. Kennedy*

presage /ˈpres.ɪdʒ/ /prɪˈseɪdʒ/ *verb* [T] FORMAL to show or suggest that something, often something unpleasant, will happen: *But still the economy is not showing signs of any of the excesses that normally presage a recession.*

Presbyterian /ˌprez.bɪˈtɪə.ri.ən/ [US] /-bɪˈtɪr.i-/ *adj* relating or belonging to a Christian group which has members especially in Scotland and the US **Presbyterian** /ˌprez.bɪˈtɪə.ri.ən/ [US] /-bɪˈtɪr.i-/ *noun* [C]

preschool /ˈpriː.skuːl/ *adj* [before n] of or relating to children who have not yet gone to school, and their activities: *a preschool playgroup* ○ *preschool children/toys*

preschool /ˈpriː.skuːl/ *noun* [C or U] US a school for children who are younger than five years old

preschooler /ˈpriːˌskuː.ləʳ/ [US] /-lɚ/ *noun* [C] US a child who is under five years old and therefore does not go to formal school

prescient /ˈpres.i.ənt/ *adj* FORMAL knowing or suggesting correctly what will happen in the future: *a prescient warning* **prescience** /ˈpres.i.ənts/ *noun* [U] *the prescience of her remarks*

prescribe [GIVE MEDICAL TREATMENT] /prɪˈskraɪb/ *verb* [T often passive] (of a doctor) to say what medical treatment someone should have: *The drug is often prescribed **for** ulcers.* ○ [+ two objects] *I've been prescribed painkillers.* **prescribed** /prɪˈskraɪbd/ *adj*: *The patient was taking a widely prescribed sedative.*

prescription /prɪˈskrɪp.ʃᵊn/ *noun* [C] a piece of paper on which a doctor writes the details of the medicine or drugs that someone needs: *a doctor's prescription* ○ *a prescription **for** sedatives* ○ UK *The doctor should give you a **repeat** prescription* (= another piece of paper allowing more of the same medicine to be given, often without the person seeing the doctor again). ○ *These drugs are only available **on** prescription* (= with a prescription from a doctor). ○ *Prescription **charges*** (= the standard amount of money you pay for any medicine prescribed by a doctor) *are rising in June.*

prescribe [GIVE RULE] /prɪˈskraɪb/ *verb* [T] FORMAL to tell someone what they must have or do; to give something as a rule: *Penalties for not paying taxes are prescribed by law.* ○ [+ that] *The law prescribes **that** all children must go to school.* ○ [+ question word] *Grammatical rules prescribe **how** words may be used together.*

prescribed /prɪˈskraɪbd/ *adj*: *The product will have to meet internationally prescribed* (= demanded) *standards.*

prescription /prɪˈskrɪp.ʃᵊn/ *noun* [C or U] FORMAL when someone says what someone else must have or do: *So what is his prescription **for** success?*

prescriptive /prɪˈskrɪp.tɪv/ *adj* FORMAL MAINLY DISAPPROVING saying exactly what must happen, especially by giving an instruction or making a rule: *Most teachers think the government's guidelines on homework are too prescriptive.*

preˈscription ˌdrug *noun* [C] a drug which can only be bought if a doctor orders it for you ➲Compare **over the counter** at **counter** SURFACE.

pre-season UK, US **preseason** /ˈpriːˌsiː.zᵊn/ *adj* [before n] in sports, happening before the main period of competition: *a pre-season match/game* ○ *Manchester United and Arsenal were the pre-season favourites.*

pre-season UK, US **preseason** /ˈpriːˌsiː.zᵊn/ *noun* [C usually sing] in sports, a short period of competition before the main period: *Barkley suffered a strained thigh muscle late in the preseason.* ○ *David Beckham had a great pre-season.*

ˌpresence of ˈmind *noun* [U] APPROVING the ability to make good decisions and to act quickly and calmly in a difficult situation or an emergency: *When the gunmen came into the bank, she **had** the presence of mind to press the alarm.*

present [SOMETHING GIVEN] /ˈprez.ᵊnt/ *noun* [C] (UK INFORMAL **prezzie or pressie**) something which you are given, without asking for it, on a special occasion, especially to show friendship, or to say thank you: *a birthday/Christmas/wedding present* ○ *They gave me theatre tickets as a present.*

present [NOW] /ˈprez.ᵊnt/ *noun* **the present** the period of time which is happening now, not the past or the future; now: *That's all for the present.* ○ *The play is set **in** the present.* ➲See also **presently** NOW.

• **at present** FORMAL now: *"Are you busy?" "Not at present."* ○ *At present she's working abroad.*

present /ˈprez.ᵊnt/ *adj* [before n] happening or existing now: *I don't have her present address.* ○ *Please state your present occupation and salary.*

present [PLACE] /ˈprez.ᵊnt/ *adj* [after v] in a particular place: *The whole family was present.* ○ *There were no children present.*

• **present company excepted** used to show that a criticism or a rude remark does not refer to the people you are talking to: *People here just don't know how to dress, present company excepted.*

presence /ˈprez.ᵊnts/ *noun* **1** [S] when someone or something is in a place: *She was overawed by the presence **of** so many people.* ○ *The presence **of** pollen in the atmosphere causes hay fever in some people.* ○ *He's usually quite polite **in** my **presence**.* ○ *The document was signed **in the presence of** two witnesses.* **2** [C usually sing] a feeling that someone is still in a place although they are not there or are dead: *His daughter's presence seemed to fill her empty bedroom.* **3** [S] a group of police or soldiers who are watching or controlling a situation: *The United Nations has maintained a presence in the region for some time.* ○ *There was a strong police presence at the demonstration.* **4** [U] APPROVING a quality that makes people notice or admire you, even when you are not speaking: *stage presence* ○ *He stood there in the corner of the room, a dark, **brooding*** (= worrying) *presence.*

• **make *your* presence felt** to have a strong effect on other people or on a situation: *The new police chief has really made his presence felt.*

present [GIVE] /prɪˈzent/ *verb* [T] to give, provide or make known: *The winners were presented **with** medals.* ○ *The letter presented the family **with** a **problem** that would be difficult to solve.* ○ *The documentary presented us **with** a balanced view of the issue.* ○ *He presented the report **to** his colleagues at the meeting.* ○ *The classroom presented a cheerful busy atmosphere **to** the visitors* (= appeared to them to have this). ○ *The school is presenting* (= performing) *'West Side Story' as its end-of-term production.*

preˈsent itˌself /prɪˈzent/ *verb* [R] If something presents itself, it happens: *An **opportunity** suddenly presented itself.*

presentation /ˌprez.ᵊnˈteɪ.ʃᵊn/ *noun* **1** [C] a talk giving information about something: *The speaker gave an interesting presentation on urban transport.* **2** [C] an occasion when prizes, qualifications, etc. are formally given to those who have won or achieved them: *The presentation of prizes and certificates will take place in the main hall.* **3** [U] the way something looks when it is shown to other people, or the way someone looks: *Presentation is important if you want people to buy your products.*

present [INTRODUCE] /prɪˈzent/ *verb* [T] **1** UK to introduce a television or radio show: *She presents the late-night news.* **2** FORMAL to introduce a person: *May I present Professor Carter?* ○ *Later on I'd like to present you **to** the headteacher.*

preˈsent *yourself* /prɪˈzent/ *verb* [R] to arrive somewhere and introduce yourself: *He presented himself at the doctor's at 9.30 a.m. as arranged.*

presenter /prɪˈzen.təʳ/ [US] /-t̬ɚ/ *noun* [C] UK someone who introduces a television or radio show: *a news/sports presenter* ○ *children's television presenters*

presentable /prɪˈzen.tə.bļ/ ⓤ /-t̬ə-/ *adj* looking suitable or good enough, especially in the way you are dressed: *Jeremy was looking quite presentable in a suit and tie.* ○ *I've got to have a wash and make myself presentable for our guests.*

the present continuous (,**tense**) *noun* [S] the tense which you use to refer to actions or events that are happening now or developing: *The sentences 'The children are watching television' and 'The weather is getting colder' are in the present continuous.*

present-day /ˌprez.ᵊntˈdeɪ/ *adj* [before n] existing now: *present-day attitudes*

presenteeism /prə.zənˈtiː.ɪzm/ *noun* [U] the practice of staying at work longer than usual to show that you work hard and are important to your employer: *Job insecurity is making presenteeism increasingly common.*

presentiment /prɪˈzen.tɪ.mənt/ *noun* [C] FORMAL a feeling that something, especially something unpleasant, is going to happen; a PREMONITION: *She had had a presentiment of what might lie ahead.*

presently SOON /ˈprez.ᵊnt.li/ *adv* OLD-FASHIONED soon; not at the present time but in the future, after a short time: *The room was hot and presently her eyes grew heavy and she began to feel sleepy.*

presently NOW /ˈprez.ᵊnt.li/ *adv* MAINLY UK FORMAL now; at the present time: *Of 200 boats, only 20 are presently operational.* ○ *Three sites are presently under consideration for the new hotel.*

,**present par'ticiple** *noun* [C] a form of a verb which in English ends in '-ing' and comes after another verb to show continuous action. It is used to form THE PRESENT CONTINUOUS (TENSE): *In the sentences 'The children are watching television', 'The weather is getting colder' and 'I heard him singing', 'watching', 'getting' and 'singing' are present participles.*

the present perfect (,**tense**) *noun* [S] the tense which you use to refer to actions or events which have been completed or which have happened in a period of time up to now: *The sentences 'She has broken her leg' and 'I have never been to Australia' are all in the present perfect.*

the present simple (,**tense**) *noun* [C or U] the tense which you use to refer to events, actions and conditions which are happening all the time, or exist now: *The sentences 'I live in Madrid', 'She doesn't like cheese' and 'I think you're wrong' are all in the present simple.*

preser'vation ,order *noun* [C] UK an official decision that a building or area has special value and must be kept in good condition: *This avenue of mature trees has a preservation order on it.*

preserve KEEP /prɪˈzɜːv/ ⓤ /-ˈzɝːv/ *verb* [T] **1** to keep something as it is, especially in order to prevent it from decaying or being damaged or destroyed; to CONSERVE: *to preserve the environment* ○ *We want to preserve the character of the town while improving the facilities.* ○ *The agreement preserved our right to limit trade in endangered species.* ○ *Putting varnish on wood is a way of preserving it.* ○ *I need to get out of the house from time to time just to preserve (= prevent me from losing) my sanity.* ○See also **well-preserved. 2** to treat food in a particular way so that it can be kept for a long time without going bad: *preserved fruit* ○ *oranges preserved in brandy*

preservative /prɪˈzɜː.və.tɪv/ ⓤ /-ˈzɝː.və.t̬ɪv/ *noun* **1** [C or U] a substance used to prevent decay in wood: *a timber/wood preservative* ○ *The fence has been treated with preservative.* **2** [C] a chemical used to stop food from decaying: *This bread is completely free from artificial preservatives.* ○ *No added preservatives.* ○ *natural preservatives*

preservation /ˌprez.əˈveɪ.ʃᵊn/ ⓤ /-ɚ-/ *noun* [U] when you keep something the same or prevent it from being damaged: *building preservation* ○ *wood preservation* ○ *There is great public concern about some of the chemicals used in food preservation.* ○ *The cathedral is in a poor state of preservation (= has not been kept in good condition).* ○ *The prime minister has said that the government is committed to the preservation (= protection) of the country's national interests.* ○ *She belongs to* the Association for the Preservation of Civil War Sites ○See also **self-preservation.**

preservationist /ˌprez.əˈveɪ.ʃᵊn.ɪst/ ⓤ /-ɚ-/ *noun* [C] MAINLY US someone who works to prevent old buildings and areas of the countryside from being destroyed or damaged

preserve FOOD /prɪˈzɜːv/ ⓤ /-ˈzɝːv/ *noun* [C or U] a food made from fruit or vegetables boiled with sugar and water until it becomes like a firm sauce: *apricot preserve* ○ *jars of preserves* ○See also **conserve** FOOD.

preserve SEPARATE ACTIVITY /prɪˈzɜːv/ ⓤ /-ˈzɝːv/ *noun* [S] an activity which only one person or a particular type of person does or is responsible for: *Owning racehorses is the preserve of the rich.* ○ *Sport used to be a male preserve.*

preserve SEPARATE PLACE /prɪˈzɜːv/ ⓤ /-ˈzɝːv/ *noun* [C or U] FOR **reserve** (= an area of land kept in its natural state, especially for wild animals to live in to be protected)

preset /ˌpriːˈset/ *verb* [T] presetting, preset, preset to prepare a machine in advance so it will operate or stop later, or to arrange for or agree to something in advance: [+ to infinitive] *I'll preset the oven to come on at 5 p.m.* ○ *The agenda for the meeting has been preset.* **preset** /ˈpriː.set/ *adj*: *a preset button* ○ *We have a device which switches the lights on at a preset time in the evening.* ○ *The shares will be sold at a preset price.*

preshrunk /ˌpriːˈʃrʌŋk/ *adj* (of clothes) SHRUNK (= made smaller) by washing before being sold: *preshrunk jeans*

preside /prɪˈzaɪd/ *verb* [I] to be in charge of a formal meeting or ceremony: *Who would be the best person to preside at/over the public enquiry?* **presiding** /prɪˈzaɪ.dɪŋ/ *adj: the presiding judge*

▲ **preside over sth** *phrasal verb* to be in charge of a situation, especially a formal meeting or a trial: *Judge Langdale is to preside over the official enquiry into the case.* ○ *This government has presided over some of the most significant changes in education this century.*

president POLITICS /ˈprez.ɪ.dᵊnt/ *noun* [C] (the title given to) the person who has the highest political position in a country which is a REPUBLIC and who, in some of these countries, is the leader of the government: *President Kennedy* ○ *the President of France* ○ [as form of address] *Thank you, Mr/Madam President.* **presidential** /ˌprez.ɪˈden.tʃᵊl/ *adj* [usually before n] *a presidential candidate/campaign/election*

presidency /ˈprez.ɪ.dᵊnt.si/ *noun* [C usually sing] the job of being president, or the period when someone is a president: *He has announced that he is running for the presidency.* ○ *She won the presidency by a wide margin.*

president ORGANIZATION /ˈprez.ɪ.dᵊnt/ *noun* [C] the person who has the highest position in an organization or, especially in the US, in a company: *a former President of the Royal Society* ○ MAINLY US *She's a friend of the president of the bank.* **presidential** /ˌprez.ɪˈden.tʃᵊl/ *adj* [before n] *'Art and the Community' was the theme of her presidential address to the annual meeting.* **presidency** /ˈprez.ɪ.dᵊnt.si/ *noun* [C or U]

press PUSH /pres/ *verb* **1** [I or T; usually + adv or prep] to push something firmly, often without causing it to move permanently further away from you: *Press the button to start the machine.* ○ *He pressed his face against the window.* ○ *Can you press a bit harder on my shoulders, please?* ○ *The crowd pressed against the locked doors trying to get into the building.* ○ *Press down firmly on the lever.* **2** [T] to make clothes smooth by ironing them: *I'll just press these trousers.* **3** [T] to put a weight on fruit in order to remove the juice: *to press grapes* **4** [T] to make a record or CD: *Over 3000 copies of the CD were pressed and sent some out to college radio stations.* **5** [T] to make something flat and firm by putting it under something heavy: *The children pressed some flowers.* ○ *pressed turkey breast*

press /pres/ *noun* **1** [C usually sing] a firm push against something using the fingers: *To start the machine, just give this button a press.* **2** [S] when you make cloth smooth with an iron: *Can you give this shirt a quick press?* **3** [C] a piece of equipment which is used to put weight on something in order to crush it, remove liquid from it or to make it flat: *a garlic/trouser/wine press*

pressure /ˈpreʃ.əʳ/ ⓤⓢ /-ɚ/ noun **1** [U] the force you produce when you press something: *He put too much pressure on the door handle and it snapped.* ○ *You can stop bleeding by **applying** pressure close to the injured area.* **2** [C or U] the force that a liquid or gas produces when it presses against an area: *gas/water pressure* ○ *The new material allows the company to make gas pipes which withstand higher pressures.* ○ *The gas is stored **under** pressure* (= in a container which keeps it at a higher pressure than it would usually have).

pressurized, UK USUALLY **-ised** /ˈpreʃ.ʳr.aɪzd/ ⓤⓢ /-ə.raɪzd/ *adj* If a container is pressurized, the air pressure inside it is higher than the air pressure outside it: *a pressurized tank* ○ *Aircraft cabins are pressurized.*

pressurization, UK USUALLY **-isation** /ˌpreʃ.ʳr.aɪˈzeɪ.ʃʳn/ ⓤⓢ /-ɚ.ɪ-/ *noun* [U] the state of being pressurized

press PERSUADE /pres/ *verb* [T] **1** to try hard to persuade someone to do something: [+ obj + *to* infinitive] *The committee pressed him **to** reveal more information.* ○ *He's pressing me **for** an answer.* ○ *Can I press you further **on** (= persuade you to say more about) this issue?* **2** **press charges** to complain officially about someone in a court of law: *The family have decided not to press charges **against** him.* **3** **press a case/claim** to continue to try to make people accept your demands: *Once again he tried to press his case **for** promotion.*

• **press home** your advantage to use an advantage that you already have in order to succeed

• **press sth/sb into service** to use something or someone that is not completely suitable because nothing or no one more suitable is available: *The car's broken down so I've had to press my old bike back into service.*

pressure /ˈpreʃ.əʳ/ ⓤⓢ /-ɚ/ *noun* **1** [U] when someone tries to make someone else do something by arguing, persuading, etc: *public/political pressure* ○ *Teachers are **under** increasing pressure to work longer hours.* ○ [+ to infinitive] *Pressure **to** abandon the new motorway is increasing.* ○ *The government is facing pressure **from** environmental campaigners.* ○ *He only asked her **under** pressure **from** his wife* (= because his wife forced him to). ○ *She's **putting** pressure **on** him* (= trying to persuade him) *to get married.* ○ FORMAL *The international community is trying to **bring** pressure to **bear** on the government* (= trying to persuade them) *to resolve the situation.* **2** [C or U] a difficult situation that makes you feel worried or unhappy: *She's got a lot of pressure **on** her at work just now.* ○ *Be nice to him – he's been **under** a lot of pressure recently.* ○ *Can you work well **under** pressure?* ○ *the pressures of work*

pressurize, UK USUALLY **-ise** /ˈpreʃ.ʳr.aɪz/ ⓤⓢ /-ɚ-/ *verb* [T] (MAINLY US **pressure**) to strongly persuade someone to do something they do not want to do: *He was pressurized **into** signing the agreement.*

the press NEWSPAPERS *group noun* [S] newspapers and magazines, and those parts of television and radio which broadcast news, or reporters and photographers who work for them: *The incident has been widely reported **in** the press.* ○ *press reports/coverage* ○ *press reporters/photographers* ○ *the local/national press* ○ *The charity invited the press* (= reporters and photographers) *to a presentation of its plans for the future.* ○ *The press was/were out in force at the awards ceremony.* ○ *The **freedom of the** press* (= the right of newspapers to publish news and opinions without being controlled by the government) *must be upheld.*

press /pres/ *noun* [S or U] the judgment that is given of someone or something in the newspapers or on radio or television: *What kind of press did his play get?* ○ UK *The play has **had** a good/bad press.* ○ US *The play has **had** good/bad press.*

press BOOKS /pres/ *noun* [C] a business which prints and produces books and similar items: *Cambridge University Press*

press PRINTING MACHINE /pres/ *noun* [C] a machine that is used for printing: *a printing press*

• **go to press** to start to be printed: *The newspaper will go to press at midnight.*

PHRASAL VERBS WITH **press** ▼

▲ **press on/ahead** CONTINUE *phrasal verb* to start or continue doing something in a determined way, often despite problems: *It was pouring with rain, but we pressed on **regardless**.* ○ *The government is pressing ahead **with** its plans to reorganize the health service.*

▲ **press sth on sb** GIVE *phrasal verb* to give something to someone and not allow them to refuse to accept it: *All the children had sweets and presents pressed on them by the visitors.*

the ˈPress Associˌation *noun* [S] (ABBREVIATION **PA**) an organization which supplies news reports to newspapers, magazines, and broadcasting and Internet companies

ˈpress ˌbaron *noun* [C] a person who owns several newspapers and sometimes controls what they publish

ˈpress ˌbox *noun* [C usually sing] a room or other area kept for reporters to work in, especially at sports events

ˈpress ˌconference *noun* [C] a meeting at which a person or organization makes a public statement and reporters can ask questions

ˈpress ˌcutting *noun* [C] a piece cut out of a newspaper

pressed /prest/ *adj* **be pressed for time/money/space, etc.** to be in a difficult situation because you do not have enough time/money/space, etc: *I'm a bit pressed for time – could we meet later?*

ˈpress ˌgallery *noun* [C usually sing] in a parliament or other place where laws are made, the upper part of a room where reporters sit to watch what is happening below

press-gang /ˈpres.gæŋ/ *verb* [T] INFORMAL to force or strongly persuade someone to do something they do not want to do: *I've been press-ganged **into** taking the kids swimming.*

pressing URGENT /ˈpres.ɪŋ/ *adj* urgent or needing to be dealt with immediately: *a pressing need for housing* ○ *a pressing issue* ○ *The most pressing question is what do we do next?*

pressing CD /ˈpres.ɪŋ/ *noun* [C] a large number of CDs, records, etc. produced at one time

ˈpress ˌrelease *noun* [C] a public statement given to the press to publish if they wish

ˈpress ˌsecretary *noun* [C] someone who works for a political leader or organization and makes statements to the press or answers questions for them

ˈpress ˌstud UK *noun* [C] (US **snap**) a small clothes fastener with two usually round parts, one of which is pushed into the other

press-up UK /ˈpres.ʌp/ *noun* [C] (US **push-up**) a physical exercise in which you lie flat with your face towards the floor, and try to push up your body with your arms, while keeping your legs and your back straight: *I do twenty press-ups every morning.*

ˈpressure ˌcooker *noun* [C] a cooking pan with a tightly fitting lid which allows food to cook quickly in steam under pressure

ˈpressure ˌgroup *noun* [C] a group of people who work together to try to influence what other people or the government think about a particular subject, in order to achieve the things they want

ˈpressure ˌpoint BODY *noun* [C] a place on the body where an ARTERY (= tube carrying blood from the heart) is close to the surface of the skin, which means that it can be pressed to partly stop the flow of blood

ˈpressure ˌpoint SITUATION *noun* [C] a place or situation which is likely to cause trouble: *Hospitals are a pressure point for the entire health system.*

prestige /presˈtiːdʒ/ *noun* [U] respect and admiration given to someone or something, usually because of a reputation for high quality, success or social influence: *The company has gained international prestige.* ○ *Many people are attracted by the prestige **of** working for a top company.*

prestige /presˈtiːdʒ/ *adj* [before n] causing admiration because connected with luxury or power: *a prestige address/car/job/label*

P

prestigious /presˈtɪdʒ.əs/ *adj* greatly respected and admired, usually because of being important: *a prestigious literary award* ○ *a prestigious university*

prestressed /ˌpriːˈstrest/ *adj* describes concrete or a similar material that has been made stronger by having tightly stretched wires put inside it

presume BELIEVE /prɪˈzjuːm/ US /-ˈzuːm/ *verb* [T] to believe something to be true because it is very likely, although you are not certain: [+ (that)] *I presume (that) they're not coming, since they haven't replied to the invitation.* ○ [+ speech] *You are Dr Smith, I presume?* ○ *"Are we walking to the hotel?" "I presume not/so."* ○ [+ obj + adj] *The boat's captain is missing, presumed dead* (= it is believed that he is dead). ○ *In British law, you are presumed innocent until you are proved guilty.* ○ [+ obj + to infinitive] *The universe is presumed to contain many other planets with some form of life.*

presumably /prɪˈzjuː.mə.bli/ US /-ˈzuː-/ *adv* used to say what you think is the likely situation: *They can presumably afford to buy a bigger apartment.* ○ *Presumably he just forgot to send the letter.*

presumption /prɪˈzʌmp.ʃᵊn/ *noun* [C or U] when you believe that something is true without having any proof: *The presumption of innocence is central to British law.* ○ *There is no scientific evidence to support such presumptions.* ○ [+ that] *The decision is based on the presumption that all information must be freely available.*

presume BE RUDE /prɪˈzjuːm/ US /-ˈzuːm/ *verb* [I] to do something although you know that you do not have a right to do it: [+ to infinitive] *I wouldn't presume to tell you how to do your job, but shouldn't this piece go there?* ○ *I don't wish to presume* (= make a suggestion although I have no right to), *but don't you think you should apologize to her?* ○ *He presumes on* (= takes unfair advantage of) *her good nature.*

presumptuous /prɪˈzʌmp.ʃəs/ *adj* A person who is presumptuous shows a lack of respect for others by doing things they have no right to do: *It would be presumptuous of me to comment on the matter.* **presumptuously** /prɪˈzʌmp.ʃə.sli/ *adv* **presumptuousness** /prɪˈzʌmp.ʃə.snəs/ *noun* [U] (*FORMAL* **presumption**)

presuppose /ˌpriː.səˈpəʊz/ US /-ˈpoʊz/ *verb* [T] **1** to think that something is true in advance without having any proof: [+ that] *You're presupposing that he'll have told her – but he may not have.* **2** *FORMAL* If an idea or situation presupposes something, that thing must be true for the idea or situation to work: *Investigative journalism presupposes some level of investigation.* ○ [+ that] *All this presupposes that he'll get the job he wants.*

presupposition /ˌpriː.sʌp.əˈzɪʃ.ᵊn/ *noun* [C or U] *Your actions are based on some false presuppositions* (= things that you think without knowing the truth). ○ *This is all presupposition – we must wait until we have some hard evidence.*

pretax /ˌpriːˈtæks/ *adj* before tax is paid: *She predicts pretax earnings of over $13m for the company this year.* ○ *pretax profits/losses*

pretend /prɪˈtend/ *verb* [I] **1** to behave as if something is true when you know that it is not, especially in order to deceive people or as a game: [+ (that)] *He pretended (that) he didn't mind, but I knew that he did.* ○ *The children pretended (that) they were dinosaurs.* ○ [+ to infinitive] *Were you just pretending to be interested?* ○ *She's not really hurt – she's only pretending.* ○ *Of course I was angry – I can't pretend otherwise.* **2** *FORMAL* **not pretend to do sth** to not claim something that is false: *I don't pretend to be an expert on the subject.*

pretended /prɪˈten.dɪd/ *adj* [before n] false: *his pretended enthusiasm/interest*

pretence, *US USUALLY* **pretense** /prɪˈtens/ *noun* [U] a way of behaving that is intended to deceive people: *She made absolutely no pretence of being interested.* ○ *They kept up* (= continued) *a pretence of normality as long as they could.* ○ *The army has given up any pretence of neutrality in the war.* ⊃See also **pretentious**.

pretender /prɪˈten.dəʳ/ US /-dɚ/ *noun* [C] a person who claims to have a right to the high position that someone else has, although other people disagree with this: *The rebel forces are led by the pretender to the throne* (= person who wants to replace the present king or queen).

pretension /prɪˈten.ʃᵊn/ *noun* [C usually pl] a claim or belief that you can succeed or that you are important or have serious value: *The Chronicle has pretensions to being a serious newspaper.* ○ *United's championship pretensions took a dent when they were beaten 5-1 by Liverpool.*

pretentious /prɪˈten.ʃəs/ *adj* *DISAPPROVING* trying to appear or sound more important or clever than you are, especially in matters of art and literature: *a pretentious art critic* ○ *The novel deals with grand themes, but is never heavy or pretentious.* **pretentiously** /prɪˈten.ʃə.sli/ *adv* **pretentiousness** /prɪˈten.ʃə.snəs/ *noun* [U] (*ALSO* **pretension**) *I couldn't believe the pretentiousness of the book.*

preternatural /ˌpriː.təˈnætʃ.ᵊr.ᵊl/ US /-tɚˈnætʃ.ɚ-/ *adj* *FORMAL* more than is usual or natural: *Anger gave me preternatural strength, and I managed to force the door open.* **preternaturally** /ˌpriː.təˈnætʃ.ᵊr.ᵊl.i/ US /-tɚˈnætʃ.ɚ-/ *adv*: *The house seemed preternaturally silent.*

pretext /ˈpriː.tekst/ *noun* [C] a pretended reason for doing something that is used to hide the real reason: *The border dispute was used as a pretext for military intervention.* ○ *I called her on the pretext of needing more information.* ○ *He came round to see her on some flimsy* (= obviously false) *pretext.*

pretty PLEASANT /ˈprɪt.i/ US /ˈprɪt̬-/ *adj* pleasant to look at, or (especially of girls or women or things connected with them) attractive or charming in a delicate way: *That's a pretty hat you're wearing.* ○ *The sofa was covered in very pretty flowery material.* ○ *She's got such a pretty daughter.*

• **a pretty pass** *OLD-FASHIONED* a bad situation: *Things have come to a pretty pass when a referee can no longer be trusted.*

• **cost sb a pretty penny** to be very expensive: *That coat must have cost you a pretty penny!*

• **not be a pretty sight** *HUMOROUS* to be unattractive or unpleasant to look at: *I can tell you, first thing in the morning he's not a pretty sight.*

prettily /ˈprɪt.ɪ.li/ US /ˈprɪt̬-/ *adv* in a pretty way: *The menus are printed on prettily illustrated cards.* ○ *She danced prettily.* **prettiness** /ˈprɪt.ɪ.nəs/ US /ˈprɪt̬-/ *noun* [U]

pretty QUITE /ˈprɪt.i/ US /ˈprɪt̬-/ *adv* *INFORMAL* **1** quite, but not extremely: *The house has four bedrooms, so it's pretty big.* ○ *I'm pretty sure it was her.* ○ *I've got a pretty good idea of how to get there.* **2 pretty much/well** almost: *I've pretty much finished here.* ○ *She knows pretty well everything there is to know on the subject.*

pretty-pretty *adj* *UK DISAPPROVING* describes something that has had too much decoration added to it by someone trying too hard to make it pretty

pretzel /ˈpret.sᵊl/ *noun* [C] a hard salty biscuit that has been baked especially in stick or knot shapes

prevail /prɪˈveɪl/ *verb* [I] *FORMAL* **1** to get control or influence: *I am sure that common sense will prevail in the end.* ○ *And did reason prevail over* (= become a more powerful influence than) *emotion?* **2** to be common among a group of people or area at a particular time: *This attitude still prevails among the middle classes.*

prevailing /prɪˈveɪ.lɪŋ/ *adj* **1** existing in a particular place or at a particular time: *the prevailing attitude* ○ *The prevailing mood is one of optimism.* **2 prevailing wind** a wind which usually blows in a particular place: *The town is kept cool by the prevailing westerly winds.*

▲ **prevail on/upon sb** *phrasal verb* [+ to infinitive] *FORMAL* to persuade someone to do something that they do not want to do: *He was eventually prevailed upon to accept the appointment.*

prevalent /ˈprev.ᵊl.ᵊnt/ *adj* existing very commonly or happening frequently: *These diseases are more prevalent among young children.* ○ *Trees are dying in areas where acid rain is most prevalent.* **prevalence** /ˈprev.ᵊl.ᵊnts/ *noun* [U] *the prevalence of smoking amongst teenagers*

prevaricate /prɪˈvær.ɪ.keɪt/ US /-ˈver-/ *verb* [I] *FORMAL* to avoid telling the truth or saying exactly what you think: *He accused the minister of prevaricating.* **prevarication** /prɪˌvær.ɪˈkeɪ.ʃᵊn/ US /-ˌver-/ *noun* [U] *All my attempts* to question the authorities on the subject were met by evasion and prevarication.

prevent /prɪˈvent/ *verb* [T] to stop something from happening or someone from doing something: *Label your suitcases to prevent confusion.* ○ [+ **v-ing**] *His disability prevents him (from) driving.*
preventable /prɪˈven.tə.bl̩/ ⓤⓢ /-t̬ə-/ *adj* able to be prevented: *preventable accidents/injuries*
prevention /prɪˈven.ʃ³n/ *noun* [U] when you stop something from happening or stop someone from doing something: *crime prevention* ○ *The organization is committed to AIDS prevention and education.*
• **Prevention is better than cure.** *UK* (*US* **An ounce of prevention is worth a pound of cure.**) *SAYING* It is better to stop something bad from happening than it is to deal with it after it has happened.
preventive /prɪˈven.tɪv/ ⓤⓢ /-t̬ɪv/ *adj* [before n] (*ALSO* **preventative**) intended to stop something before it happens: *In the past 10 years, preventive measures have radically reduced levels of tooth decay in children.* ○ *preventative medicine*

COMMON LEARNER ERROR

prevent or **protect**?

Prevent means to stop something from happening.
Wearing sunscreen can help prevent skin cancer.

Protect means to keep someone or something safe from bad things.
The police wear bulletproof vests to protect themselves.

preview /ˈpriː.vjuː/ *noun* [C] an opportunity to see something such as a film or a collection of works of art before it is shown to the public, or a description of something such as a television programme before it is shown to the public
preview /ˈpriː.vjuː/ *verb* [I or T] *Miller's new play is previewing* (= being performed publicly before it officially opens) *at the Theatre Royal tomorrow.* ○ *On page 11, Sally Gaines previews* (= describes) *next week's films on TV.*

previous /ˈpriː.vi.əs/ *adj* [before n] happening or existing before something or someone else: *The previous owner of the house had built an extension on the back.* ○ *Training is provided, so no previous experience is required for the job.* ○ *He has two daughters from a previous marriage.*
previously /ˈpriː.vi.ə.sli/ *adv* before the present time or the time referred to: *She was previously employed as a tour guide.* ○ *I had posted the card two months previously.*

pre-war /ˌpriːˈwɔːʳ/ ⓤⓢ /-ˈwɔːr/ *adj* happening before a war, especially the Second World War: *the pre-war years* ⊃Compare **post-war**.

prey /preɪ/ *noun* [U] an animal that is hunted and killed for food by another animal: *A hawk hovered in the air before swooping on its prey.*
• **be easy prey** to be easy to deceive or be taken advantage of: *Homeless young people are easy prey for drug-dealers and pimps.*
• **be/fall prey to sth** to be hurt or deceived by someone or something bad: *Small children are prey to all sorts of fears.*
prey /preɪ/ *verb*

PHRASAL VERBS WITH prey ▼

▲ **prey on sth** *phrasal verb* If an animal preys on another animal, it catches and eats it: *The spider preys on small flies and other insects.*
• **prey on sb** *phrasal verb* to hurt or deceive a group of people, especially people who are weak or can easily be hurt or deceived: *He would attack at night, preying on lone women in their twenties or thirties.*
• **prey on your mind** If a problem preys on your mind, you think about it and worry about it a lot: *I lost my temper with her the other day and it's been preying on my mind ever since.*

prezzie /ˈprez.i/ *noun* [C] *UK INFORMAL FOR* **present** SOMETHING GIVEN

priapic /praɪˈæp.ɪk/ *adj* *MAINLY DISAPPROVING* relating to male sexual activity and interests: *His latest film has*

been condemned as the priapic fantasies of an old man.

price /praɪs/ *noun* [C] the amount of money for which something is sold: *The price of oil has risen sharply.* ○ *House prices have been falling.* ○ *We thought they were asking a very high/low price.* ○ *The large supermarkets are offering big price cuts.*
• **at any price** If you want something at any price, you are willing to do anything in order to get it: *He wanted success at any price.*
• **not at any price** used to say that you would never do something: *I wouldn't invite her again at any price.*
• **at/for a price** If you can buy or obtain something at/for a price, you either have to pay a lot of money or be involved in something unpleasant in order to get it: *You can buy the best of gourmet cuisine here, for a price.*
• **What price fame/victory/success, etc.?** said when you think it is possible that the fame/success, etc. that has been achieved was not worth all the suffering it has caused: *What price victory when so many people have died in the struggle?*
price /praɪs/ *verb* **1** [T often passive] to say what the price of something is: *The car is priced at £28 000.* ○ *There is a lack of reasonably priced housing for rent.* **2** [T] to discover how much something costs: *We went around all the travel agents pricing the different tours.*
• **price yourself out of the market** If a company prices itself out of the market, it charges so much for a product or service that no one wants to buy it.
priceless /ˈpraɪ.sləs/ *adj* **1** describes an object which has such a high value, especially because it is rare, that the price of it cannot be calculated: *A priceless collection of vases was destroyed.* ○ *FIGURATIVE Her knowledge and experience would make her a priceless* (= extremely useful) *asset to the team.* **2** *INFORMAL* extremely amusing to see or hear: *You should have seen the look on her face when I told her – it was priceless!*
pricey (**pricier**, **priciest**), **pricy** /ˈpraɪ.si/ *adj* *INFORMAL* expensive: *It's a bit pricey but the food is wonderful.*

COMMON LEARNER ERROR

price or **prize**?

These two words sound similar but have different spellings and very different meanings.

Price means 'the amount of money that you pay to buy something'.
The price of oil has risen by 20%.
~~The prize of oil has risen by 20%.~~

Prize means 'something valuable that is given to someone who wins a competition or who has done good work'.
She won first prize in the competition.
~~She won first price in the competition.~~

price-conscious /ˈpraɪsˌkɒn.tʃəs/ ⓤⓢ /-ˌkɑːn-/ *adj* aware of how much things cost and avoiding buying expensive things: *price-conscious shoppers*
price-sensitive /ˈpraɪsˌsen.sɪ.tɪv/ ⓤⓢ /-sə.t̬ɪv/ *adj* describes a product whose sales are influenced by price rather than quality
price tag *noun* [C] (*ALSO* **price ticket**) a piece of paper with a price on which is fixed to a product, or the amount that something costs: *How much is it? – I can't find the price tag.* ○ *These suits have designer names and a price ticket to match.*
price war *noun* [C] a situation in which different companies compete with each other by lowering prices: *A supermarket price war has led to lower profit margins.*

prick MAKE HOLES /prɪk/ *verb* [T] to make a very small hole or holes in the surface of something, sometimes in a way which causes pain: *Prick the skin of the potatoes with a fork before baking them.* ○ *She pricked the balloon with a pin and it burst with a loud bang.*
• **prick the bubble (of sth)** to make someone suddenly understand the unpleasant truth of a situation
• **prick sb's conscience** to make someone do something because they feel guilty: *Dan's mentioning Julia pricked my conscience and I gave her a call.*

prick [BODY PART] /prɪk/ *noun* **[C]** *OFFENSIVE* a penis

prick [MAN] /prɪk/ *noun* **[C]** *OFFENSIVE* a stupid man: *I'm not wearing that – I'd look a right prick.*

▲ **prick (sth) up** *phrasal verb* **[M] 1** When an animal pricks its ears up, or when its ears prick up, it puts its ears up straight because it is listening attentively to a small or distant sound. **2** If you prick up your ears, or if your ears prick up, you suddenly begin to listen very attentively because you have heard something interesting: *I overheard them mentioning my name and pricked up my ears.*

prickle /ˈprɪk.l̩/ *noun* **[C] 1** one of several thin sharp points that stick out of a plant or animal: *The fruit can be eaten once the prickles have been removed.* **2** a feeling as if a lot of little points are sticking into your body: *I felt a hot prickle of embarrassment spread across my cheeks.*

prickle /ˈprɪk.l̩/ *verb* **1 [T]** If thin sharp objects prickle you, they cause slight pain by touching against your skin: *She lay on the grass and the stiff dry grass prickled the back of her legs.* **2 [I]** If part of your body prickles, it feels as if a lot of sharp points are touching it because you are frightened or excited: *Turner started to be worried and felt the back of his neck prickle.*

prickly /ˈprɪk.l̩.i/ /-li/ *adj* **1** covered with prickles: *Chestnuts had burst out of their prickly green husks.* ○ *I find this sweater a bit prickly* (= it makes the skin sore). **2** *INFORMAL* unfriendly and slightly rude: *She was asked a couple of questions about her private life and got a bit prickly.*

ˌprickly ˈheat *noun* **[U]** **heat rash**

ˌprickly ˈpear *noun* **[C]** a type of CACTUS (= desert plant) that has oval edible fruit with sharp spines on them

prick-tease /ˈprɪk.tiːz/ *noun* **[C]** (*ALSO* **prick-teaser**) *OFFENSIVE* a woman who tries to make a man sexually excited but does not intend to have sex with him

pride [SATISFACTION] /praɪd/ *noun* **[U]** a feeling of pleasure and satisfaction that you get because you or people connected with you have done or possess something good: *She felt a great sense of pride as she watched him accept the award.* ○ *He felt such pride walking his little daughter down the street.* ➲See also **proud** SATISFIED.

• **take pride in *sth/sb*** to feel very pleased about something or someone that you are closely connected with: *If you don't take professional pride in your work, you're probably in the wrong job.*

• **be the pride of *somewhere/sth*** to be something or someone that a particular place or group of people is very proud of: *This village is the pride of East Sussex.*

• **be *your* pride and joy** to be something or someone that is very important to you and that gives you a lot of pleasure: *He spends hours cleaning that motorcycle – it's his pride and joy.*

• **have/take pride of place** to have the most important position in a group of things: *A portrait of the earl takes pride of place in the entrance hall.*

pride [RESPECT FOR YOURSELF] /praɪd/ *noun* **[U]** your feelings of your own worth and respect for yourself: *She has too much pride to accept any help.* ○ *The country's national pride has been dented* (= damaged) *by its sporting failures.*

pride [FEELING OF IMPORTANCE] /praɪd/ *noun* **[U]** *DISAPPROVING* the belief that you are better or more important than other people: *Pride was his downfall.* ➲See also **proud** FEELING IMPORTANT.

• **Pride comes/goes before a fall.** *SAYING* said to emphasize that if you are too confident about your abilities, something bad will happen which shows that you are not as good as you think

pride [LIONS] /praɪd/ *noun* **[C]** a group of lions

pride /praɪd/ *verb*

▲ **pride *yourself* on *sth*** *phrasal verb* **[R]** to value a skill or good quality that you have: *He prides himself on his loyalty to his friends.*

priest /priːst/ *noun* **[C]** a person, usually a man, who has been trained to perform religious duties in the Christian Church, especially the Roman Catholic Church, or a person with particular duties in some other religions: *Father O'Dooley was ordained a priest in 1949.* ○ *Many in the Anglican Church are still opposed to women priests.*

priestess /ˌpriːˈstes/ /ˈ--/ *noun* **[C]** a woman in particular non-Christian religions who performs religious duties

the priesthood /ðəˈpriːst.hʊd/ *noun* **[S]** the position of being a priest: *He left the priesthood to get married.*

priestly /ˈpriːst.li/ *adj* relating to or like a priest

prig /prɪg/ *noun* **[C]** *DISAPPROVING* a person who obeys the rules of correct behaviour and considers himself or herself to be morally better than other people

priggish /ˈprɪg.ɪʃ/ *adj DISAPPROVING* like a prig: *I found him priggish and cold.*

prim /prɪm/ *adj* **primmer, primmest** *DISAPPROVING* very formal and correct in behaviour and easily shocked by anything rude: *She's much too prim **and proper** to drink pints of beer.* **primly** /ˈprɪm.li/ *adv*: *A primly dressed young woman ran up to the car.*

prima ballerina /ˌpriː.mə.bæl.əˈriː.nə/ [US] /-ɚˈiː-/ *noun* **[C usually sing]** the most important female dancer in a ballet company

primacy /ˈpraɪ.mə.si/ *noun* **[U]** *FORMAL* the state of being the most important thing: *The government insists on the primacy **of** citizens' rights.*

prima donna /ˌpriː.məˈdɒn.ə/ [US] /-ˈdɑː.nə/ *noun* **[C usually sing] 1** the most important female singer in an opera company **2** *DISAPPROVING* someone who demands to be treated in a special way and is difficult to please: *I had to entertain visiting authors and some of them were real prima donnas.* **prima donna-ish** /ˌpriː.məˈdɒn.ə.ɪʃ/ [US] /-ˈdɑː.nə-/ *adj DISAPPROVING prima donna-ish behaviour*

primaeval /ˌpraɪˈmiː.vəl/ *adj* ➲See **primeval**.

prima facie /ˌpraɪ.məˈfeɪ.ʃi/ *adj* **[before n]** *FORMAL OR LEGAL* at first sight (= based on what seems to be the truth when first seen or heard): *There is prima facie **evidence** that he was involved in the fraud.* ○ *For millions of Americans witnessing the event, it was a prima facie **case** of police brutality.*

primal /ˈpraɪ.məl/ *adj* **[before n] 1** relating to the time when human life on Earth began: *The universe evolved from a densely packed primal inferno.* **2** *FORMAL* basic and connected with an early stage of development: *a primal urge to connect with nature* ○ *primal fears*

primary [MOST IMPORTANT] /ˈpraɪ.mə.ri/ [US] /-mɚ.i/ *adj* more important than anything else; main: *The Red Cross's primary concern is to preserve and protect human life.* ○ *The primary responsibility lies with those who break the law.*

primarily /praɪˈmer.ɪ.li/ *adv* mainly: *We're primarily concerned with keeping expenditure down.* ○ *Soccer is primarily a winter game.*

primary [EDUCATION] /ˈpraɪ.mə.ri/ [US] /-mɚ.i/ *adj* **[before n]** *UK* of or for the teaching of young children, especially those between five and eleven years old: *primary education* ○ *a primary **school***

primary [EARLIEST] /ˈpraɪ.mə.ri/ [US] /-mɚ.i/ *adj* happening first: *the primary stages of development*

primary [ELECTION] /ˈpraɪ.mə.ri/ [US] /-mɚ.i/ *noun* **[C]** in the United States, an election in which people who belong to a political party choose who will represent that party in an election for political office

ˌprimary ˈcolour *noun* **[C]** one of the three colours, which in paint, etc. are red, yellow or blue, that can be mixed together in different ways to make any other colour

primate [ANIMAL] /ˈpraɪ.meɪt/ /-mət/ *noun* **[C]** *SPECIALIZED* a member of the most developed and intelligent group of mammals, including humans, monkeys and apes

primate [PRIEST] /ˈpraɪ.meɪt/ /-mət/ *noun* **[C]** *SPECIALIZED* a priest with the highest position in his country: *He was made the Roman Catholic Primate of All Ireland last year.*

prime [MAIN] /praɪm/ *adj* **[before n] 1** main or most important: *This is a prime **example** of 1930s architecture.* ○ *the prime suspect in a murder investigation* ○ *a prime source of evidence* ○ *The president is a prime* (= likely) ***target*** *for the assassin's bullet.* **2** of the best quality: *prime beef* ○ *The hotel is in a prime location in the city centre.*

prime [BEST STAGE] /praɪm/ *noun* **[S]** the period in your life when you are most active or successful: *This is a dancer*

P

in her prime. ○ *Middle age can be the prime* **of life** *if you have the right attitude.* ○ *I suspect this cheese is* **past its** *prime.*

prime PREPARE /praɪm/ *verb* [T] **1** to tell someone something that will prepare them for a particular situation: *I'd been primed so I knew not to mention her son.* **2** to cover the surface of wood with a special paint before the main paint is put on **3** to make a bomb or gun ready to explode or fire

primer /'praɪ.mə^r/ ⓤ /-mɚ/ *noun* **1** [C or U] a type of paint that you put on a wooden surface before the main paint is put on: *It's best to use a* **coat of** *primer before the top coat.* **2** [C] OLD-FASHIONED a small book containing basic facts about a subject, used especially when you are beginning to learn about that subject

,**prime** '**minister** *noun* [C usually sing] (UK INFORMAL ABBREVIATION **PM**) the leader of the government in some countries

,**prime** '**mover** *noun* [C usually sing] someone who has a lot of influence in starting something important: *He was a prime mover* **in** *developing a new style of customer-friendly bookshops in the UK.*

,**prime** '**number** *noun* [C] SPECIALIZED a number that cannot be divided by any other number except itself and the number 1: *2, 3 and 7 are prime numbers.*

'**prime** ,**time** *noun* [U] in television and radio broadcasting, the time when the largest number of people are watching or listening: *prime time TV* ○ *The interview will be broadcast during prime time.*

primeval, MAINLY UK **primaeval** /praɪˈmiː.v^əl/ *adj* ancient; existing at or from a very early time: *primeval forests*

primitive /'prɪm.ɪ.tɪv/ ⓤ /-t̬ɪv/ *adj* **1** relating to human society at a very early stage of development, with people living in a simple way without machines or a writing system: *Primitive races colonized these islands 2000 years ago.* ○ *primitive man* ○ *The spiny anteater is a mammal, although a very primitive one.* **2** DISAPPROVING describes living conditions that are basic, unpleasant and uncomfortable: *Early settlers had to cope with very primitive living conditions.*

primly /'prɪm.li/ *adv* ⊃See at **prim.**

primogeniture /ˌpraɪ.məʊˈdʒen.ɪ.tʃə^r/ ⓤ /-moʊ-'dʒen.ɪ.tʃɚ/ *noun* [U] SPECIALIZED the custom by which all of a family's property goes to the oldest son when the father dies

primordial /praɪˈmɔː.di.əl/ ⓤ /-ˈmɔːr-/ *adj* FORMAL **1** existing at or since the beginning of the world or the universe: *The planet Jupiter contains large amounts of the primordial gas and dust out of which the solar system was formed.* **2** basic and connected with an early stage of development

pri,**mordial** '**soup** *noun* [U] a liquid substance that existed on Earth before there were any plants, animals or humans

primrose /'prɪm.rəʊz/ ⓤ /-roʊz/ *noun* [C] a wild plant with pale yellow flowers

primula /'prɪm.jʊ.lə/ *noun* [C] SPECIALIZED any of a group of wild plants with white, yellow, pink or purple flowers

Primus (stove) /'praɪ.məs,stəʊv/ ⓤ /-,stoʊv/ *noun* [C] TRADEMARK a small cooker that burns PARAFFIN

prince /prɪn^ts/ *noun* [C] **1** an important male member of a royal family, especially a son or grandson of the king or queen: *Prince Edward* ○ *Prince Juan Carlos of Spain became king in 1975.* **2** a male ruler of a country, usually a small country: *Prince Rainier is the ruling prince of Monaco.* **3** LITERARY **prince among/of sth** a man who is excellent at something: *that prince of flautists, William Bennett*

principality /ˌprɪn^t.sɪˈpæl.ɪ.ti/ ⓤ /-ə.t̬i/ *noun* [C] a country ruled by a prince, or from which a prince takes his title: *Monaco is a principality.*

,**Prince** '**Charming** *noun* [S] HUMOROUS A woman's Prince Charming is her perfect partner: *How much time have you wasted sitting around waiting for Prince Charming to appear?*

,**Prince** '**Consort** *noun* [C usually sing] the title sometimes given to the husband of a ruling queen

princely /'prɪn^ts.li/ *adj* HUMOROUS **the princely sum of** used to refer to a surprisingly small amount of money: *She acquired the painting at a jumble sale for the princely sum of 25p.*

the ,**Prince of** '**Darkness** *noun* [S] LITERARY the Devil (= the main evil spirit in the Christian religion)

Prince of Wales /ˌprɪn^ts.əvˈweɪlz/ *noun* [C usually sing] in Britain, a title given to the oldest son of the king and queen who will become king when they die

princess /prɪnˈses/ /'--/ *noun* [C] an important female member of a royal family, especially a daughter or granddaughter of a king and queen, or the wife of a PRINCE: *Lady Diana Spencer became Princess Diana when she married Prince Charles.*

principal MAIN /'prɪn^t.sɪ.p^əl/ *adj* [before n] first in order of importance: *Iraq's principal export is oil.* ○ *He was principal dancer at the Dance Theatre of Harlem.* ○ *That was my principal reason for moving.*

principally /'prɪn^t.sɪ.pli/ *adv* mainly: *The advertising campaign is aimed principally at women.*

principal PERSON /'prɪn^t.sɪ.p^əl/ *noun* [C] US the person in charge of a school or college for children aged between approximately 11 and 18

principal MONEY /'prɪn^t.sɪ.p^əl/ *noun* [C usually sing] SPECIALIZED an amount of money which someone has invested in a bank or lent to a person or organization so that they will receive interest on it from the bank, person or organization: *She lives off the interest and tries to keep the principal intact.*

,**principal** '**boy** *noun* [C] UK the most important male character in a PANTOMIME (= musical play for children), played by a woman

principle BASIC IDEA /'prɪn^t.sɪ.pl/ *noun* [C] a basic idea or rule that explains or controls how something happens or works: *the principles of the criminal justice system* ○ *The country is run* **on** *socialist principles.* ○ *The machine works according to the principle* **of** *electromagnetic conduction.* ○ *The organization works* **on** *the principle* **that** *all members have the same rights.* ⊃See also **first principles.**

● **in principle** If you agree with or believe something in principle, you agree with the idea in general, although you might not support it in reality or in every situation: *In principle I agree with the idea, but in practice it's not always possible.* ○ *They have approved the changes in principle.*

principle MORAL RULE /'prɪn^t.sɪ.pl/ *noun* [C or U] APPROVING a moral rule or standard of good behaviour: *She doesn't have any principles.* ○ *He was a man of principle.* ○ *Anyway, I can't deceive him – it's* **against** *all my principles.* ○ *I never gamble,* **as a matter of** *principle* (= because I believe it is wrong). ○ *She'd never ask to borrow money,* **on** *principle.*

principled /'prɪn^t.sɪ.pld/ *adj* FORMAL **1** always behaving in an honest and moral way: *She was a very principled woman.* **2** based on moral rules: *The Church is taking a principled stand against the conflict.*

print TEXT /prɪnt/ *noun* [U] **1** letters, numbers, words or symbols that have been produced on paper by a machine using ink: *The title is in bold print.* ○ *This novel is available in large print for readers with poor eyesight.* ○ *The book was rushed* **into** *print* (= was produced and published) *as quickly as possible.* ○ *The print quality* (= The quality of the text produced) *of the new laser printer is excellent.* **2** newspapers and magazines: *The debate is still raging, both* **in** *print and on the radio and television.*

● **in/out of print** If a book is in print, it is possible to buy a new copy of it, and if it is out of print, it is not now possible: *Is her work still in print?* ○ *Classic literature never* **goes** *out of print.*

print /prɪnt/ *verb* **1** [I or T] to produce writing or images on paper or other material with a machine: *The leaflets will be printed* **on** *recycled paper.* ○ *I'm waiting for a document to print.* **2** [T] to include a piece of writing in a newspaper or magazine: *Some newspapers still refuse to print certain swear words.* ○ *They printed his letter in Tuesday's paper.* **3** [T] to produce a newspaper, magazine or book in large quantities: *20 000 copies of the novel will be printed in hardback.*

printable /ˈprɪn.tə.bl̩/ [US] /-t̬ə-/ *adj* If something that you say is not printable, it is too rude or offensive to be included in a newspaper or magazine: *He let out a torrent of abuse, none of it printable in a respectable daily newspaper.*

printed /ˈprɪn.tɪd/ [US] /-t̬ɪd/ *adj* **the printed word** information in the form of books, newspapers and magazines: *Children who watch TV all the time have no real interest in the printed word.*

printer /ˈprɪn.təʳ/ [US] /-t̬ɚ/ *noun* [C] **1** a machine that is connected to a computer and prints onto paper using ink: *a bubble-jet/dot-matrix/laser printer* ➲See picture **In the Office** on page Centre 15 **2** a person whose job is to print books, newspapers and magazines

printing /ˈprɪn.tɪŋ/ [US] /-t̬ɪŋ/ *noun* **1** [U] the activity or business of producing writing or images on paper or other material with a machine: *She runs her own printing business.* **2** [C] the number of copies of a book which the PUBLISHER (= company that prints books) has produced: *The publishers produced a first printing of 2500.*

print [PICTURE] /prɪnt/ *noun* [C] a photographic copy of a painting, or a picture made by pressing paper onto a special surface covered in ink, or a single photograph from a film: *a print of Van Gogh's 'Sunflowers'* ○ *a signed Hockney print* ○ *I'd like a second set of prints of this film, please.* **print** /prɪnt/ *verb* [T] *Photographs are better if they are printed* ***from*** *the original negative.*

print [PATTERN] /prɪnt/ *noun* [C] any type of pattern produced using ink on a piece of clothing: *a floral/paisley print*

print /prɪnt/ *verb* [T] to produce a pattern on material or paper: *The designs are printed onto the fabric by hand.*

print [WRITE] /prɪnt/ *verb* [I or T] to write without joining the letters together: *Please print your name clearly below your signature.*

print [FINGER] /prɪnt/ *noun* [C] INFORMAL FOR **fingerprint**: *The burglar had left his prints all over the window.*

▲ **print *sth* out** *phrasal verb* [M] to produce a printed copy of a document that has been written on a computer: *Could you print out a copy of that letter for me?*

ˌprinted ˈcircuit (ˌboard) *noun* [C] a set of electrical connections made by thin lines of metal fixed onto a surface

ˈprinted ˌmatter *noun* [U] documents or books that can be sent by post at a special low cost

ˈprinting ˌpress *noun* [C] a machine that prints books, newspapers or magazines

printout /ˈprɪnt.aʊt/ *noun* [C] text produced by a computer printer: *There were pages of* ***computer*** *printout all over the desk.*

ˈprint ˌrun *noun* [C] the number of copies of a book produced at one time

prion /ˈpraɪ.ɒn/ [US] /-ɑːn/ *noun* [C] SPECIALIZED a small piece of protein which is thought to cause certain brain diseases, such as BSE and CJD

prior [EARLIER] /praɪəʳ/ [US] /praɪr/ *adj* [before n] **1** SLIGHTLY FORMAL existing or happening before something else, or before a particular time: *The course required no prior knowledge of Spanish.* ○ *They had to refuse the dinner invitation because of a prior* ***engagement*** (= something already planned for that time). ➲See also **prior** at **priory**. **2 prior to *sth*** before a particular time or event: *the weeks prior to her death*

prior [MORE IMPORTANT] /praɪəʳ/ [US] /praɪr/ *adj* [before n] FORMAL more important: *Mothers with young children have a prior* ***claim*** *on funds.*

priority /praɪˈɒr.ɪ.ti/ [US] /-ˈɔːr.ə.t̬i/ *noun* [C or U] something that is very important and must be dealt with before other things: *The management did not seem to consider office safety to be a priority.* ○ *My* ***first/top*** *priority is to find somewhere to live.* ○ *You have to learn to* ***get*** *your priorities* ***right/straight*** (= decide which are the most important jobs or problems and deal with them first). ○ *Mending the lights is a priority task* (= more important than other jobs). ○ *Banks normally* ***give*** *priority* ***to*** *large businesses when deciding on loans* (= They deal with them first because they consider them most important). ○ *Official business requirements obviously* ***take/have*** *priority* ***over*** *personal requests* (= Official business matters will be dealt with first).

prioritize, UK USUALLY **-ise** /praɪˈɒr.ɪ.taɪz/ [US] /-ˈɔːr.ə-/ *verb* [I or T] to decide which of a group of things are the most important so that you can deal with them first: *You must learn to prioritize your work.*

priory /ˈpraɪə.ri/ [US] /praɪr.i/ *noun* [C] a building where monks or nuns live, work and pray

prior /praɪəʳ/ [US] /praɪr/ *noun* [C] a man who is in charge of a priory or who is second in charge of an ABBEY ➲See also **prior** EARLIER; **prior** MORE IMPORTANT.

prioress /ˈpraɪə.res/ [US] /ˈpraɪ-/ *noun* [C] a female prior

prise /praɪz/ *verb* [T] UK FOR **prize** LIFT

prism /ˈprɪz.ᵊm/ *noun* [C] a transparent glass or plastic object which separates white light that passes through it into different colours

prison /ˈprɪz.ᵊn/ *noun* **1** [C or U] a building where criminals are forced to live as a punishment: *a prison cell/sentence/warder* ○ *Conditions in the prison are said to be appalling.* ○ *He's spent a lot of time* ***in*** *prison.* ○ *She* ***went to/was sent to*** *prison for six months.* ○ *It was a* ***maximum-security*** *prison* (= intended to be especially difficult to escape from). ○ *They should* ***put*** *him* ***in*** *prison and throw away the key!* **2** [U] the system of keeping people in prisons: *the prison service* ○ *Do you think prison works?* ○ *Prison* (= the time he had spent in prison) *hadn't changed him at all.* **3** [C] a situation or relationship from which it is difficult to escape: *She felt that her marriage had become a prison.*

prisoner /ˈprɪz.ᵊn.əʳ/ [US] /-ɚ/ *noun* [C] a person who is kept in prison as a punishment: *Prisoners climbed onto the prison roof to protest at the conditions inside the prison.* ➲See also **political prisoner**.

• **hold/keep/take *sb* prisoner** to catch someone and guard them so that they can not escape: *Of 10 000 troops, 7000 were killed, wounded or taken prisoner.* ○ *The pilot and several passengers were held prisoner by the gunmen for 57 hours.*

ˈprison ˌcamp *noun* [C] a place where people, usually prisoners of war or political prisoners, are forced to stay: *He was captured by enemy forces and sent to a prison camp for the rest of the war.*

ˌprisoner of ˈconscience *noun* [C] someone kept in prison because their political or religious beliefs are different from those of the government

ˌprisoner of ˈwar (*plural* **prisoners of war**) *noun* [C] (ABBREVIATION **POW**) a member of the armed forces who has been caught by enemy forces during a war: *a prisoner of war camp*

prissy /ˈprɪs.i/ *adj* DISAPPROVING always behaving and dressing in a way that is considered correct and that does not shock: *a prissy sort of a woman* **prissily** /ˈprɪs.ɪ.li/ *adv*

pristine /ˈprɪs.tiːn/ [US] /prɪˈstiːn/ *adj* FORMAL APPROVING new or almost new, and in very good condition: *We've just moved into our pristine new offices.* ○ *Washing machine for sale – only 2 months old and* ***in*** *pristine* ***condition.***

private [PERSONAL] /ˈpraɪ.vət/ *adj* **1** only for one person or group and not for everyone: *She has a small office which is used for private discussions.* ○ *I caught him looking through my private papers.* ○ *The sign on the gate said 'Private* ***Property*** *– No Admittance.'* **2** describes activities which involve personal matters or relationships and are not connected with your work: *Apparently in interviews he refuses to talk about his private* ***life.*** **3** describes thoughts and opinions which are secret and which you do not discuss with other people: *Although I support the project in public, my private opinion is that it will fail.* ○ *This is a private matter.* **4** describes a place which is quiet and where there are no other people to see or hear you: *Is there somewhere private where we can talk?* **5** describes someone who does not like to talk about their personal feelings and thoughts: *She's quite a private person.*

• **in private** If you talk to someone or do something in private, you do it without other people being present: *Jamie wants to speak to me in private.*

P

privately /ˈpraɪ.vət.li/ *adv*: *She spoke privately* (= without other people present) *with the manager.* ○ *Despite his public support, privately* (= secretly) *he was worried.*

privacy /ˈprɪv.ə.si/ [US] /ˈpraɪ.və-/ *noun* [U] **1** someone's right to keep their personal matters and relationships secret: *The new law is designed to protect people's privacy.* **2** the state of being alone: *I hate sharing a bedroom – I never get any privacy.*

private [NOT OFFICIAL] /ˈpraɪ.vət/ *adj* controlled or paid for by a person or company and not by the government: *private education/healthcare* ○ *a private doctor/dentist* ○ *Banks should be supporting small private businesses.* ○ *The finance for the project will come from both the government and **the** private **sector*** (= private businesses). **privately** /ˈpraɪ.vət.li/ *adv*: *a privately-owned business*

privatize, *UK USUALLY* **-ise** /ˈpraɪ.və.taɪz/ *verb* [T] If a government privatizes an industry, company or service that it owns and controls, it sells it so that it becomes privately owned and controlled: *I bought shares in British Gas when it was privatized.* **privatization**, *UK USUALLY* **-isation** /ˌpraɪ.vɪ.taɪˈzeɪ.ʃᵊn/ [US] /-t̬ɪ-/ *noun* [U] *The last few years have seen the privatization of many industries previously owned by the state.*

private [SOLDIER] /ˈpraɪ.vət/ *noun* [C] a soldier of the lowest rank in an army

ˌprivate deˈtective/inˈvestigator *noun* [C] (*INFORMAL* **private eye**) a person whose job is discovering information about people. A private detective is not a government employee or a police officer: *She **hired** a private detective to find out if her husband was having an affair.*

ˌprivate ˈenterprise *noun* [U] industry and businesses owned by ordinary people, not by the government

ˌprivate ˈmeans *plural noun* (*UK ALSO* **private income**) income that you receive from your family, investments, or land, and not from a job

ˌprivate ˈparts *plural noun* (*INFORMAL* **privates**) *POLITE WORD FOR* sexual organs: *He grabbed a towel to cover his private parts.*

ˌprivate ˈschool *noun* [C] a school which does not receive financial support from the government ➲See Note **schools** at **public school** EXPENSIVE SCHOOL.

privation /praɪˈveɪ.ʃᵊn/ *noun* [C or U] *FORMAL* a lack of the basic things that are necessary for an acceptable standard of living: *Economic privation is pushing the poor towards crime.* ○ *Several villages **suffered** serious privations during their long isolation during the war.*

privet /ˈprɪv.ɪt/ *noun* [U] an evergreen bush, which is often grown as a HEDGE around the edges of gardens

privilege /ˈprɪv.ᵊl.ɪdʒ/ *noun* **1** [C or U] an advantage that only one person or group of people has, usually because of their position or because they are rich: *Healthcare should be a right, not a privilege.* ○ *Senior management **enjoy** certain privileges, such as company cars and private healthcare.* **2** [S] an opportunity to do something special or enjoyable: *I had the privilege **of** interviewing Picasso in the 1960s.* ○ ***It** was a real privilege **to** meet her.* **3** [U] the way in which rich people or people from a high social class have most of the advantages in society: *a life of privilege* **4** [C or U] *SPECIALIZED* the special right that some people in authority have which allows them to do or say things that other people are not allowed to: *diplomatic/parliamentary privilege*

privileged /ˈprɪv.ᵊl.ɪdʒd/ *adj* **1** having a privilege: *As an ambassador, she enjoys a very privileged status.* ○ [+ to infinitive] *I have been privileged **to** work with the pioneers of silicon technology.* **2** *SPECIALIZED* describes information that is secret and does not have to be given even in a court of law

privy [AWARE] /ˈprɪv.i/ *adj FORMAL* **be privy to *sth*** to be told information that is not told to many people: *I was never privy to conversations between top management.*

privy [TOILET] /ˈprɪv.i/ *noun* [C] *OLD USE* a toilet, especially in a very small building in the garden of a house

the ˌPrivy ˈCouncil *noun* [S] in Britain, a group of people of high rank in politics who sometimes advise the king or queen but who have little power **ˌPrivy ˈCouncillor** *noun* [C]

prize [REWARD] /praɪz/ *noun* [C] **1** something valuable, such as an amount of money, that is given to someone who succeeds in a competition or game or that is given to someone as a reward for doing very good work: *The critics' prize **for** best film was won by Marc Abbott for 'Belly Laugh'.* ○ *I **won** a prize in the raffle.* ○ *The **first*** (= main) *prize is a weekend for two in Bruges.* ○ *The prize **money** for literary competitions can be as high as £40 000.* ➲See Note **price or prize?** at **price**. **2** something important and valuable which is difficult to achieve or obtain: *The prize would be her hand in marriage.*

• **no prizes for guessing *sth*** something you say when it is very easy to guess something: *No prizes for guessing where Daniel is.*

prize /praɪz/ *adj* [before n] **1** A prize animal, flower or vegetable is one that has won or deserves to win a prize in a competition because it is of very good quality: *a prize bull* ○ *a prize marrow* **2** describes something which is a very good or important example of its type: *prize assets* ○ *SLIGHTLY OLD-FASHIONED Some prize **idiot*** (= extremely foolish person) *forgot to lock the door.*

prize /praɪz/ *verb* [T often passive] to think that someone or something is very valuable or important: *In parts of Asia this plant is prized **for** its medicinal qualities.* ○ *I prize that intimacy above everything.*

prized /praɪzd/ *adj* considered valuable and important: *The 1961 vintage is **highly** prized among wine connoisseurs.* ○ *Her photograph is among my most prized **possessions**.*

prize [LIFT], *UK ALSO* **prise** /praɪz/ *verb* [T + adv or prep] to move or lift something by pressing a tool against a fixed point: *I prized the lid **off** with a spoon.* ○ *The window had been prized **open** with a jemmy.*

▲ **prize *sth* out of *sb*** *phrasal verb* to get something from someone with difficulty, especially information or money: *He's so secretive – you'll have a hard time prizing any information out of him.*

prizefighter /ˈpraɪzˌfaɪ.təʳ/ [US] /-t̬ɚ/ *noun* [C] a boxer who fights to win money

prizefight /ˈpraɪz.faɪt/ *noun* [C] a boxing competition in which people fight to win money

prize-winning /ˈpraɪzˌwɪn.ɪŋ/ *adj* [before n] having won a prize: *a prize-winning film/novel* ○ *a Nobel-prize-winning novelist*

pro- /prəʊ-/ [US] /proʊ-/ *prefix* supporting or approving of something: *pro-American* ○ *pro-democracy demonstrations* ➲Compare **anti-**.

pro /prəʊ/ [US] /proʊ/ *adj, prep*: *Are you pro or anti* (= Do you support or are you against) *the new bill?*

pro [SPORTSPERSON] /prəʊ/ [US] /proʊ/ *noun* [C] *plural* **pros** *INFORMAL* a person who plays sport as a job rather than as a hobby: *a tennis pro* ○ *a pro golfer*

pro [ADVANTAGE] /prəʊ/ [US] /proʊ/ *noun* [C] *plural* **pros** an advantage or a reason for doing something: *One of the big pros **of** living in Madrid is the night life.* ○ *We're just weighing up the pros **and cons*** (= advantages and disadvantages) *of moving to a bigger house.*

proactive /ˌprəʊˈæk.tɪv/ [US] /ˌproʊ-/ *adj* taking action by causing change and not only reacting to change when it happens: *Companies are going to have to be more proactive about environmental management.* ○ *a proactive approach/role* **proactively** /ˌprəʊˈæk.tɪv.li/ [US] /ˌproʊ-/ *adv*

pro-am /ˌprəʊˈæm/ [US] /ˌproʊ-/ *adj* describes a competition in which the teams include PROFESSIONALS (= people who compete as a job) and AMATEURS (= people who compete for pleasure): *a pro-am golf competition*

probable /ˈprɒb.ə.bl̩/ [US] /ˈprɑː.bə-/ *adj* likely to be true or likely to happen: *The probable cause of death was heart failure.* ○ *An election in June seems increasingly probable.* ○ [+ that] ***It** is probable **that** share prices will fall still further.* ➲Compare **possible** UNCERTAIN. ✻ NOTE: The opposite is **improbable**.

probability /ˌprɒb.əˈbɪl.ɪ.ti/ [US] /ˌprɑː.bəˈbɪl.ə.t̬i/ *noun* [C or U] the likelihood of something happening or being true: *What is the probability **of** winning?* ○ *The probability **of** getting all the answers correct is about one in ten.*

[P]

○ ***There's a high/strong probability (that)*** (= It is very likely that) *she'll be here.* ○ *Until yesterday, the project was just a possibility, but now it has become a real probability* (= it is likely that it will happen).

• **in all probability** used to mean that something is very likely: *She will, in all probability, have left before we arrive.*

probably /ˈprɒb.ə.bli/ [US] /ˈprɑː.bə-/ *adv* used to mean that something is very likely: *I'll probably be home by midnight.* ○ *I'm probably going – it depends on the weather.* ○ *He probably didn't even notice.* ○ *Probably the best thing to do is to call them before you go.*

probate /ˈprəʊ.beɪt/ [US] /ˈproʊ-/ *noun* [U] **1** LEGAL the legal process of deciding whether or not a person's will has been made correctly and that the information it contains is correct: *Before probate can be* ***granted****, all business assets have to be identified and valued.* **2** AUS LEGAL **death duty**

probate /ˈprəʊ.beɪt/ [US] /ˈproʊ-/ *verb* [T] US LEGAL to prove that a person's will has been made correctly and that the information it contains is correct

probation /prəʊˈbeɪ.ʃən/ [US] /proʊ-/ *noun* [U] **1** a period of time when a criminal must behave well and not commit any more crimes in order to avoid being sent to prison: *He was fined and given two years' probation.* ○ *The judge* ***put*** *him* ***on*** *probation for two years.* ○ *He served a year in prison and was then* ***let out on*** *probation.* **2** a period of time at the start of a new job when you are watched and tested to see if you are suitable for the job: *a period of probation* **3** US a period of time in which a student who has behaved badly must improve their work or behaviour in order to stay in a school: *Gene's* ***on*** *probation this semester.* **probationary** /prəʊˈbeɪ.ʃən.ər.i/ [US] /proʊˈbeɪ.ʃən.er-/ *adj*: *a probationary period*

probationer /prəʊˈbeɪ.ʃən.əʳ/ [US] /proʊˈbeɪ.ʃən.ɚ/ *noun* [C] **1** a criminal on probation **2** a person such as a police officer or teacher who has recently passed their final exams and who is doing their first year of work

proˈbation ˌofficer *noun* [C] a person whose job is to regularly see people who have committed crimes and who are on probation, and to help them live honestly

probe /prəʊb/ [US] /proʊb/ *verb* [I or T] **1** to try to discover information that other people do not want you to know, by asking questions in an indirect careful way: *The interviewer probed deep* ***into*** *her private life.* ○ *Detectives questioned him for hours, probing* ***for*** *any inconsistencies in his story.* ○ *The article probes* (= tries to describe and explain) *the mysteries of nationalism in modern Europe.* **2** to examine something with a tool, especially in order to find something that is hidden: *They probed* ***in/into*** *the mud with a special drill.*

probe /prəʊb/ [US] /proʊb/ *noun* [C] **1** an attempt to discover information by asking a lot of questions: *an FBI probe* ***into*** *corruption* ○ *a Justice Department probe* ***into*** *the Democrats' fund raising* **2** SPECIALIZED a long thin metal tool used by doctors to examine inside someone **3** SPECIALIZED a device that is put inside something to test or record information ➲See also **space probe**.

probing /ˈprəʊ.bɪŋ/ [US] /ˈproʊ-/ *adj* intended to get information: *She asked me a few probing* ***questions****.*

probity /ˈprəʊ.bɪ.ti/ [US] /ˈproʊ.bə.t̬i/ *noun* [U] FORMAL complete honesty: *Her probity and integrity are beyond question.*

problem /ˈprɒb.ləm/ [US] /ˈprɑː.bləm/ *noun* [C] **1** a situation, person or thing that needs attention and needs to be dealt with or solved: *financial/health problems* ○ *Our main problem is lack of cash.* ○ *I'm* ***having*** *problems* ***with*** *my computer.* ○ *No one has* ***solved*** *the problem* ***of*** *what to do with radioactive waste.* ○ *The very high rate of inflation* ***poses/presents*** (= is) *a serious problem for the government.* ○ *When is the government going to* ***tackle*** (= deal with) *the problem of poverty in the inner cities?* ○ [+ v-ing] *Did you have any problems* (= difficulties) *getting here?* ○ *I'd love to come –* ***the only*** *problem* ***is*** *I've got friends staying that night.* ➲See Note **trouble or problem?** at **trouble** DIFFICULTIES. **2** a question in mathematics which needs an answer: *We were given ten problems to solve.* **3 problem child/family, etc.** a child, etc. whose behaviour is bad

• **have a problem with *sth/sb*** INFORMAL to find something or someone annoying or offensive: *I have a real problem with people who use their mobile phones on the train.* ○ *She can smoke – I don't have a problem with that.*

• **No problem.** INFORMAL **1** said to show that you will or can do what someone has asked you to: *"Can you get me to the station by 11.30?" "No problem."* **2** used as a friendly answer when someone thanks you for something you have done: *"Thanks for the lift." "No problem."*

problematic /ˌprɒb.ləˈmæt.ɪ.kəl/ [US] /ˌprɑː.bləˈmæt̬-/ *adj* (ALSO **problematical**) full of problems or difficulties: *Getting everyone there on time might prove problematic.*

problematically /ˌprɒb.ləˈmæt.ɪ.kli/ [US] /ˌprɑː.bləˈmæt̬-/ *adv*

proboscis /prəˈbɒs.ɪs/ [US] /proʊˈbɑː.sɪs/ *noun* [C] *plural* **probosces** SPECIALIZED the long nose of some animals, or the long tube-like mouth of some insects: *An elephant's trunk is a proboscis.*

probs /prɒbz/ [US] /prɑːbz/ *plural noun* UK INFORMAL **no probs** used to tell someone that you can do something or deal with a situation easily and without problems: *Don't worry, I'll fix it or give you a new one. No probs!*

procedure /prəˈsiː.dʒəʳ/ [US] /-dʒɚ/ *noun* **1** [C or U] a set of actions which is the official or accepted way of doing something: *The company has new procedures* ***for*** *dealing with complaints.* ○ *You must* ***follow*** *correct procedure at all times.* **2** [C] a medical operation: *It's a routine/standard surgical procedure.* **3** [C] SPECIALIZED in computing, part of a program which performs a particular job and which is operated by the main part of the program when it is needed **procedural** /prəˈsiː.djʊ.rəl/ [US] /-dʒɚ.əl/ *adj*: *procedural errors/matters*

proceed /prəʊˈsiːd/ [US] /proʊ-/ *verb* [I] **1** SLIGHTLY FORMAL to continue as planned: *His lawyers have decided not to proceed* ***with*** *the case.* ○ *Preparations for the festival are now proceeding smoothly.* **2 proceed to do *sth*** to do something after you have done something else: *She sat down and proceeded to tell me about her skiing holiday.* ○ HUMOROUS *He told me he was on a diet and then proceeded to eat a plateful of chips!* **3** FORMAL to move forward or travel in a particular direction: *Passengers for Madrid should proceed to gate 26 for boarding.*

▲ **proceed against *sb*** *phrasal verb* LEGAL to start to take legal action against someone: *Lack of evidence meant that the Council could not proceed against Mr Naylor.*

proceedings [EVENTS] /prəʊˈsiː.dɪŋz/ [US] /proʊ-/ *plural noun* FORMAL **1** a series of events that happen in a planned and controlled way: *Millions of people watched the proceedings on television.* ○ *The Chairperson opened the proceedings with a short speech.* **2** a complete written record of what is said or done during a meeting ➲Compare **the minutes**.

proceedings [LEGAL ACTION] /prəʊˈsiː.dɪŋz/ [US] /proʊ-/ *plural noun* LEGAL legal action: *Allegations of sexual harassment have led to* ***disciplinary*** *proceedings being taken* ***against*** *three naval officers.* ○ *I* ***started/took legal*** *proceedings to try to have him taken away from his parents permanently.*

proceeds /ˈprəʊ.siːdz/ [US] /ˈproʊ-/ *plural noun* the amount of money received from a particular event or activity or when something is sold: ***The*** *proceeds* ***of*** *today's festival will go to several local charities.* ○ *It says on the back of the card 'all proceeds to charity'.*

process /ˈprəʊ.ses/ [US] /ˈprɑː-/ *noun* [C] **1** a series of actions that you take in order to achieve a result: *the peace process* ○ *Increasing the number of women in top management jobs will be a slow process.* ○ *This decision may delay the process* ***of*** *European unification.* ○ *The party has begun the* ***painful*** (= difficult) *process of rethinking its policies and strategy.* ○ *Going to court to obtain compensation is a long process.* ○ *She arrived at the correct answer by a process* ***of elimination*** (= by deciding against each answer that was unlikely to be correct until only one was left). **2** a series of changes that happen naturally: *the digestive process* ○ *the ageing process* ○ *It's all part of the learning process.* **3** a method of producing goods in a factory by treating raw materials: *They have developed a new process for extracting aluminium from bauxite.*

• **be in the process of** ***doing sth*** to have started doing something: *We're still in the process of decorating the house.*
• **in the process** If you are doing something, and you do something else in the process, the second thing happens as a result of doing the first thing: *I stood up to say hello and spilt my drink in the process.*
process /ˈprəʊ.ses/ [US] /ˈprɑː-/ *verb* [T] **1** to deal with documents in an official way: *Visa applications take 28 days to process.* **2** If a computer processes information, it performs a particular series of operations on the information, such as a set of calculations. **3** to prepare, change or treat food or raw materials as a part of an industrial operation: *a waste processing plant* **4** to make pictures from photographic film: *I need to get those films processed.*
processed /ˈprəʊ.sest/ [US] /ˈprɑː-/ *adj* describes food which has been treated with chemicals that preserve it or give it extra taste or colour: *processed cheese/meat* ○ *highly processed convenience foods* **processing** /ˈprəʊ.ses.ɪŋ/ [US] /ˈprɑː-/ *noun* [U] *data processing*
procession /prəˈseʃ.ən/ *noun* **1** [C] a line of people who are all walking or travelling in the same direction, especially in a formal way as part of a religious ceremony or public celebration: *a wedding/funeral procession* ○ *The festival will open with a procession led by the mayor.* **2** [S] a series of people or things, one after the other: *My day has just been a never-ending procession* ***of*** *visitors.*
processional /prəˈseʃ.ən.əl/ *adj* [before n] used in a procession: *There was tight security along the processional route.*
process /prəˈses/ *verb* [I + adv or prep] FORMAL to walk slowly: *We watched them process down the aisle.*
processor /ˈprəʊ.ses.əʳ/ [US] /ˈprɑː.ses.ɚ/ *noun* [C] the part of a computer that performs operations on the information that is put into it ➲See also **microprocessor**.
pro-choice /ˌprəʊˈtʃɔɪs/ [US] /ˌproʊ-/ *adj* supporting the belief that a pregnant woman should have the freedom to choose an abortion if she does not want to have a baby: *pro-choice activists/demonstrators* ➲Compare **anti-choice** and **pro-life**.
proclaim [ANNOUNCE] /prəʊˈkleɪm/ [US] /proʊ-/ *verb* [T] FORMAL to announce something publicly or officially, especially something positive: *All the countries have proclaimed their loyalty to the alliance.* ○ *Republican party members were confidently proclaiming victory even as the first few votes came in.* ○ [+ that] *It was the famous speech in which he proclaimed* ***that*** *socialism was dead.* ○ [+ two objects] *She was proclaimed Queen at the age of thirteen after the sudden death of her father.*
proclamation /ˌprɒk.ləˈmeɪ.ʃən/ [US] /ˌprɑː.klə-/ *noun* [C or U] an official announcement: *to issue a proclamation* ○ *A bloody civil war followed the proclamation of an independent state.*
proclaim [SHOW] /prəʊˈkleɪm/ [US] /proʊ-/ *verb* [T] LITERARY to show something or make it clear: *Wearing scarves and hats which proclaimed their allegiance, the football fans flooded into the bar.*
proclivity /prəˈklɪv.ɪ.ti/ [US] /-ə.t̬i/ *noun* [C] FORMAL a tendency to do or like something, especially something immoral: *the* ***sexual*** *proclivities of celebrities* ○ *his proclivity* ***for*** *shapely blondes*
procrastinate /prəʊˈkræs.tɪ.neɪt/ [US] /proʊ-/ *verb* [I] to keep delaying something that must be done, often because it is unpleasant or boring: *I know I've got to deal with the problem at some point – I'm just procrastinating.*
procrastination /prəʊˌkræs.tɪˈneɪ.ʃən/ [US] /proʊ-/ *noun* [U]
procreate /ˈprəʊ.kri.eɪt/ [US] /ˈproʊ-/ *verb* [I] FORMAL to produce young: *While priests were denied the right to marry and procreate, he said, their situation would remain impossible.* **procreation** /ˌprəʊ.kriˈeɪ.ʃən/ [US] /ˌproʊ-/ *noun* [U] *Some people believe that sex should only be for the purpose of procreation.*
proctor /ˈprɒk.təʳ/ [US] /ˈprɑːk.t̬ɚ/ *verb* [I or T] US FOR **invigilate**
procure /prəˈkjʊəʳ/ [US] /-ˈkjʊr/ *verb* FORMAL **1** [T] to obtain something, especially after an effort: *She's managed somehow to procure his telephone number.* ○ [+ two objects] *He'd procured us seats in the front row.* **2** [I or T] to obtain a prostitute for someone else to have sex with
procurement /prəˈkjʊə.mənt/ [US] /-ˈkjʊr-/ *noun* [U] FORMAL the obtaining of supplies: *They are reported to have a substantial budget for the procurement* ***of*** *military supplies.*
procurer /prəˈkjʊə.rəʳ/ [US] /-ˈkjʊr.ɚ/ *noun* [C] FORMAL a person who obtains prostitutes for people who want to have sex with them
prod /prɒd/ [US] /prɑːd/ *verb* **-dd- 1** [I or T] to push something or someone with your finger or with a pointed object: *I prodded her in the back to get her attention.* ○ *She prodded the cake with her fork to see if it was cooked.* ○ *He prodded* ***at*** *the fish with his fork a few times, but he didn't eat a mouthful.* **2** [T] to encourage someone to take action, especially when they are being slow or unwilling: *He gets things done, but only after I've prodded him* ***into doing*** *them.*
prod /prɒd/ [US] /prɑːd/ *noun* **1** [C] an act of pushing something or someone with your finger or with a pointed object: *He* ***gave*** *her a prod in the ribs.* **2** [S] encouragement to do something: *She hasn't ordered that book for me yet – I must* ***give*** *her a prod.*
prodigal /ˈprɒd.ɪ.gəl/ [US] /ˈprɑː.dɪ-/ *adj* FORMAL wasteful with money; tending to spend large amounts without thinking of the future: *There have been rumours that he has been prodigal* ***with*** *company funds.* **prodigality** /ˌprɒd.ɪˈgæl.ɪ.ti/ [US] /ˌprɑː.dɪˈgæl.ə.t̬i/ *noun* [U] **prodigally** /ˈprɒd.ɪ.gli/ [US] /ˈprɑː.dɪ-/ *adv*
ˌprodigal ˈson *noun* [C usually sing] a man or boy who has left his family in order to do something that the family disapprove of and has now returned home feeling sorry for what he has done: FIGURATIVE *Manchester City football club sees the return of the prodigal son tonight with Black once again in the side after a season away.*
prodigious /prəˈdɪdʒ.əs/ *adj* FORMAL extremely great in ability, amount or strength: *She wrote a truly prodigious number of novels.* ○ *She was a prodigious musician.* ○ *He had a prodigious appetite for both women and drink.* **prodigiously** /prəˈdɪdʒ.ə.sli/ *adv*: *He was a prodigiously gifted artist.*
prodigy /ˈprɒd.ɪ.dʒi/ [US] /ˈprɑː.də-/ *noun* [C] someone with a very great ability which usually shows itself when that person is a young child: *The 16-year-old tennis prodigy is the youngest player ever to reach the Olympic finals.* ○ *He read in the paper about a mathematical prodigy who was attending university at the age of 12.* ➲See also **child prodigy**.
produce [MAKE] /prəˈdjuːs/ [US] /-ˈduːs/ *verb* [T] **1** to make something or bring something into existence: *France produces a great deal of wine for export.* ○ *Red blood cells are produced in the bone marrow.* ○ *She works for a company that produces* (= makes for sale) *electrical goods.* ○ *I was wondering whether I could produce a meal out of what's left in the fridge.* ○ *She's asked me to produce a report on the state of the project.* **2** When animals produce young, they give birth to them: *Our cat produced four kittens during the course of the night.* ○ HUMOROUS *All our friends seem to be busy producing offspring at the moment.*
produce /ˈprɒd.juːs/ [US] /ˈprɑː.djuːs/ *noun* [U] food or any other substance or material that is grown or obtained through farming, especially that which is produced in large amounts: *agricultural/dairy/fresh produce*
producer /prəˈdjuː.səʳ/ [US] /-ˈduː.sɚ/ *noun* [C] a company, country or person that provides goods, especially those which are produced by an industrial process or grown or obtained through farming, usually in large amounts: *egg producers* ○ *gas/oil producers* ○ *Australia is one of the world's main producers* ***of*** *wool.*
product /ˈprɒd.ʌkt/ [US] /ˈprɑː.dʌkt/ *noun* [C or U] **1** something that is made to be sold, usually something that is produced by an industrial process or, less commonly, something that is grown or obtained through farming: *They do a range of skin-care products.* ○ *The product is so good it sells itself.* ○ *I'm trying to cut down on* ***dairy*** *products.* ➲See also **by-product**. **2 a/the product of** ***sth*** a/the result of something: *A figure like that is usually the product of many hours spent in the gym.* ○ *She had a*

P

very happy childhood, and I guess her confidence is a product of that.

production /prə'dʌk.ʃⁿn/ *noun* [U] **1** the process of making or growing goods to be sold: *Coke is used in the production of steel.* ○ *We saw a quick film showing the various stages in the production of glass.* ○ *The company's new model will be going into production early next year.* **2** the amount of something that is made or grown by a country or a company: *Swedish industrial production has fallen steadily this year.* ○ *Wheat production has risen over the years.*

productive /prə'dʌk.tɪv/ *adj* **1** resulting in or providing a large amount or supply of something: *In order to turn the deserts into fertile and productive land, engineers built an 800-mile canal.* ○ *He had an amazingly productive five years in which he managed to write four novels.* ✳ NOTE: The opposite is **unproductive**. **2** having positive results: *We had a very productive meeting – I felt we sorted out a lot of problems.* ○ *Theirs was a very productive partnership.*

productively /prə'dʌk.tɪv.li/ *adv*: *Their working system is based on the belief that people work more productively* (= produce better results) *in a team.*

productivity /ˌprɒd.ʌk'tɪv.ɪ.ti/ ⓤ /ˌproʊ.dək'tɪv.ə.ti/ *noun* [U] the rate at which a company or country makes goods, usually judged in connection with the number of people and the amount of materials necessary to produce the goods: *Studies show that if a working environment is pleasant, productivity increases.* ○ *a productivity bonus/incentive* ○ *Productivity in the steel industry improved by 5% last year.*

produce FILM/BROADCASTING /prə'dju:s/ ⓤ /-'du:s/ *verb* [T] to organize the practical and financial matters connected with the preparation of a film, play or television or radio programme ⊃Compare **direct** CONTROL.

producer /prə'dju:.sə'/ ⓤ /-'du:.sɚ/ *noun* [C] a person who makes the practical and financial arrangements needed to make a film, play, television or radio programme: *a film/Hollywood/movie producer* ⊃Compare **director** at **direct** CONTROL.

production /prə'dʌk.ʃⁿn/ *noun* **1** [C or U] the activity of organizing the practical and financial matters connected with the preparation of a film, play or television or radio programme: *She's hoping to get into television production.* ○ *Disney's latest production* (= film) *looks likely to be their most successful one ever.* **2** [C] a particular series of performances of a theatrical entertainment such as a play or opera: *They're doing a new production of Macbeth at the National Theatre.*

produce RECORDING /prə'dju:s/ ⓤ /-'du:s/ *verb* [T] to be in charge of making a musical recording and to be responsible for the arrangement of the music, the combination of the different instruments or voices and the general sound of it

producer /prə'dju:.sə'/ ⓤ /-'du:.sɚ/ *noun* [C] a person who makes the practical and financial arrangements needed to make a CD or other recording: *a record producer*

production /prə'dʌk.ʃⁿn/ *noun* [U] the preparation and general quality of a musical recording's sound, showing the way in which the music was recorded rather than the quality of the singing and the music: *George Martin did the production on the Beatles records.*

produce BRING OUT /prə'dju:s/ ⓤ /-'du:s/ *verb* [T] to bring something out from somewhere and show it: *He produced a letter from his desk which he asked me to read.* ○ *One of the men suddenly produced a knife from his pocket.*

production /prə'dʌk.ʃⁿn/ *noun* [U] FORMAL Entry to the club is only permitted **on production** (= the showing) *of a membership card.*

produce CAUSE /prə'dju:s/ ⓤ /-'du:s/ *verb* [T] to cause a reaction or result: *The prime minister's speech produced an angry response from the opposition.* ○ *Her remarks produced an awkward silence.* ○ *If used on delicate skin, this cream may produce a stinging sensation.*

produce RESULT IN /prə'dju:s/ ⓤ /-'du:s/ *verb* [T] to result in or discover something, especially proof: *A lengthy police investigation failed to produce any evidence on which the suspect could be convicted.*

product /'prɒd.ʌkt/ ⓤ /'prɑ:.dʌkt/ *noun* [C] SPECIALIZED the result obtained when two or more numbers are multiplied together: *The product of six and three is eighteen.* ⊃See also **product** at **produce** MAKE.

pro'duction ˌline *noun* [C] a line of machines and workers in a factory which a product moves along while it is being built or produced. Each machine or worker performs a particular job, which must be completed before the product moves to the next position in the line.

'product ˌplacement *noun* [C or U] when a company advertises a product by supplying it for use in films or television programmes

Prof. *noun* [C] WRITTEN ABBREVIATION FOR **Professor**: *Prof. Tina Pritchard*

prof /prɒf/ ⓤ /prɑ:f/ *noun* [C] INFORMAL a **professor**

profane AGAINST RELIGION /prə'feɪn/ *adj* FORMAL showing a lack of respect for a god or a religion, often through language: *profane language* ○ *Funny, profane and fearless, she has become one of America's biggest television celebrities.*

profanity /prə'fæn.ɪ.ti/ ⓤ /-ə.ţi/ *noun* FORMAL **1** [U] (an example of) showing a lack of respect for a god or a religion, especially through language **2** [C] an offensive or OBSCENE word or phrase: *It was the song's opening line, a series of profanities, that caused the record to be banned on the radio station.*

profane NOT SPIRITUAL /prə'feɪn/ *adj* FORMAL not connected with religion or spiritual matters; SECULAR: *sacred and profane art*

profess /prə'fes/ *verb* [T] to claim something, sometimes in a way which is not sincere: [+ to infinitive] *She professes not to be interested in money.* ○ *I don't profess to know all the details about the case.* ○ *She professes ignorance of the whole affair, though I'm not sure I believe her.*

professed /prə'fest/ *adj* [before n] **1** describes a belief which someone has made known: *She is a professed monarchist.* **2** describes a belief or feeling which someone claims to have or feel but which is probably not really held or felt: *His professed love of women seems a little odd when you consider how he treats them.*

profession /prə'feʃ.ⁿn/ *noun* [C] a statement about what someone feels, believes or intends to do, often made publicly: *The government's professions of commitment to the environment seem less believable every day.* ○ *his professions of love*

profession /prə'feʃ.ⁿn/ *group noun* [C] **1** any type of work which needs special training or a particular skill, often one which is respected because it involves a high level of education: *He left the teaching profession in 1965 to set up his own business.* ○ *The report notes that forty per cent of lawyers entering the profession are women.* ○ *Teaching as a profession is very underpaid.* ○ *He's a doctor by profession.* **2** the people who do a type of work, considered as a group: *There's a feeling among the nursing profession that their work is undervalued.* **3** the professions jobs which need special training and skill, such as being a doctor or lawyer, but not work in business or industry

professional /prə'feʃ.ⁿn.ⁿl/ *adj* **1** related to work that needs special training or education: *Chris, you're a nurse, so can I ask your professional opinion on bandaging ankles?* ○ *Both doctors have been charged with professional misconduct* (= bad or unacceptable behaviour in their work). ⊃Compare **amateur**. **2** APPROVING having the qualities that you connect with trained and skilled people, such as effectiveness, skill, organization and seriousness of manner: *It would look more professional if the letter was typed.* ○ *She always looks very professional in her smart suits.* ○ *You've done a very professional job stripping that floor!* **3** describes someone who does as a job what people usually do as a hobby: *She's a professional dancer/photographer.* ○ *He's a runner who's just turned professional.* (= His running used to be a hobby, but now it is his job.) **4** having the type of job that is respected because it involves a high level of education and training: *Room for rent in shared house – would suit professional person.* ○ *a bar full of young professional types in suits*

professional /prəˈfeʃ.ˀn.ˀl/ *noun* [C] **1** a person who has the type of job that needs a high level of education and training: *health professionals* ⊃Compare **amateur**. **2** INFORMAL someone who has worked hard in the same type of job for a long time and has become skilled at dealing with any problem that might happen: *I thought the whole meeting was going to fall apart but you rescued it like a true professional!* ○ *the consummate professional* **3** a person who does as a job what people usually do as a hobby: *He's only been playing football as a professional for two years.* **4** a sportsperson, especially a golf or tennis player, who is employed by a CLUB GROUP to train its members in a particular sport

professionally /prəˈfeʃ.ˀn.ˀl.i/ *adv*: *I think next time we need any decorating we'll get it done professionally* (= by skilled people). ○ *He started to sing professionally* (= for money) *after leaving college.* ○ *Are you asking for my opinion of him personally or professionally?*

professionalism /prəˈfeʃ.ˀn.ˀl.ɪ.zˀm/ *noun* [U] the combination of all the qualities that are connected with trained and skilled people: *He praised her professionalism and dynamism.*

COMMON LEARNER ERROR

profession (spelling)

Many learners make mistakes when spelling this word and related words. The correct spelling has 'f' and 'ss'.

Engineering was her chosen profession.

---

proˌfessional adˈvice *noun* [U] advice from a lawyer or an ACCOUNTANT (= someone who deals with money matters)

proˌfessional ˈfoul *noun* [C] in football, an intentional FOUL (= act which breaks the rules), especially one which is intended to prevent the other team from scoring a goal

proˌfessional ˈhelp *noun* [U] POLITE EXPRESSION FOR help from a PSYCHIATRIST (= a doctor trained in treating mental illnesses): *Personally, I think he should get some professional help.*

professor /prəˈfes.ər/ ⓤ /-ɚ/ *noun* [C] a teacher of the highest rank in a department of a British university, or a teacher of high rank in an American university or college: *Professor Stephen Hawking* ○ *a professor of sociology* ○ *a sociology professor*

professorial /ˌprɒf.əˈsɔː.ri.əl/ ⓤ /ˌprɑː.fəˈsɔːr.i-/ *adj* FORMAL like a professor: *He retains an almost professorial air.*

professorship /prəˈfes.ə.ʃɪp/ ⓤ /-ɚ-/ *noun* [C] the position of professor in a university

proffer /ˈprɒf.ər/ ⓤ /ˈprɑː.fɚ/ *verb* [T] FORMAL to offer something by holding it out, or to offer advice or an opinion: *He shook the warmly proffered hand.* ○ *I didn't think it wise to proffer an opinion.*

proficient /prəˈfɪʃ.ˀnt/ *adj* skilled and experienced: *a proficient swimmer* ○ *She's proficient in two languages.* ○ *It takes a couple of years of regular driving before you become proficient at it.* **proficiency** /prəˈfɪʃ.ˀnt.si/ *noun* [U] *It said in the job ad that they wanted proficiency in at least two languages.*

profile SIDE VIEW /ˈprəʊ.faɪl/ ⓤ /ˈproʊ-/ *noun* [C] a side view of a person's face: *Drawing profiles is somehow easier than drawing the full face.* ○ *a strong profile* ○ *The actor is photographed in profile, smoking a cigarette.*

profile SHORT DESCRIPTION /ˈprəʊ.faɪl/ ⓤ /ˈproʊ-/ *noun* [C] a short description of someone's life, work, character, etc. **profile** /ˈprəʊ.faɪl/ ⓤ /ˈproʊ-/ *verb* [T] *Every week in the books section of the paper they profile a different author.*

profile ATTENTION /ˈprəʊ.faɪl/ ⓤ /ˈproʊ-/ *noun* [C] the amount of public attention and notice that something receives: *We need to increase our company's profile in Asia.* ○ *There is a growing number of women in high-profile positions* (= positions where they are noticed) *in the government.*

• **keep a low profile** to avoid attracting attention to yourself: *He's been in a bit of trouble recently so he's trying to keep a low profile.*

profiling /ˈprəʊ.faɪ.lɪŋ/ ⓤ /ˈproʊ-/ *noun* [U] the activity of collecting information about someone, especially a criminal, in order to give a description of them ⊃See also **psychological profile**.

profit /ˈprɒf.ɪt/ ⓤ /ˈprɑː.fɪt/ *noun* **1** [C or U] money which is earned in trade or business, especially after paying the costs of producing and selling goods and services: *She **makes** a big profit from selling waste material to textile companies.* ○ *A year ago the Tokyo company had a **pretax** profit of 35 million yen.* ○ *Company profits are down on last year's figures.* ○ *You don't expect to make much profit within the first couple of years of setting up a company.* ○ *He sold his house **at a** huge profit.* **2** [U] the benefit or advantage that can be achieved by a particular action or activity: *There's no profit to be **gained** from endlessly discussing whose fault it was.*

profitable /ˈprɒf.ɪ.tə.bl̩/ ⓤ /ˈprɑː.fɪ.tə-/ *adj* resulting in or likely to result in a profit or an advantage: *Over the years it has developed into a highly profitable business.* ○ *I made profitable use of my time* (= used my time to get advantages or benefits), *mixing with a lot of different people and practising my Spanish.* ✳ NOTE: The opposite is **unprofitable**.

profitably /ˈprɒf.ɪ.tə.bli/ ⓤ /ˈprɑː.fɪ.tə-/ *adv*: *It was several months before the company started to trade profitably* (= making money). ○ *Use your time profitably* (= use it to get advantages or benefits). **profitability** /ˌprɒf.ɪ.təˈbɪl.ɪ.ti/ ⓤ /ˌprɑː.fɪ.təˈbɪl.ə.ti/ *noun* [U] *The company needs to return to profitability extremely soon.*

profiteer /ˌprɒf.ɪˈtɪər/ ⓤ /ˌprɑː.fɪˈtɪr/ *noun* [C] DISAPPROVING a person who takes advantage of a situation in which other people are suffering to make a profit, often by selling at a high price goods which are difficult to obtain: *a war profiteer* **profiteering** /ˌprɒf.ɪˈtɪə.rɪŋ/ ⓤ /ˌprɑː.fɪˈtɪr.ɪŋ/ *noun* [U] *The pharmaceutical company has been charged with profiteering from the AIDS crisis.*

profit /ˈprɒf.ɪt/ ⓤ /ˈprɑː.fɪt/ *verb*

▲ **profit from** *sth phrasal verb* **1** to earn money from something: *A lot of companies will profit from the fall in interest rates.* **2** to achieve an advantage from something: *I profited enormously from work**ing** with her.*

profiterole /prəˈfɪt.ˀr.əʊl/ ⓤ /ˈfɪt.ə.roʊl/ *noun* [C usually pl] a small pastry cake with a cream filling and a covering of chocolate sauce, usually served in a pile

ˈprofit ˌmargin *noun* [C] the profit that can be made in a business after the costs have been subtracted: *Many small companies operate on very **narrow** profit margins.*

ˈprofit ˌsharing *noun* [U] the system of sharing the profits that a company makes between all the people who work for it

profligate /ˈprɒf.lɪ.gət/ ⓤ /ˈprɑː.flɪ-/ *adj* FORMAL wasteful with money: *She is well-known for her profligate spending habits.* **profligacy** /ˈprɒf.lɪ.gə.si/ ⓤ /ˈprɑː.flɪ-/ *noun* [U] *The profligacy of the West shocked him.*

pro forma /ˌprəʊˈfɔː.mə/ ⓤ /ˌproʊˈfɔːr-/ *adj* [before n], *adv* FORMAL describes words or actions that are usual or done in the usual way: *a pro forma declaration of loyalty*

pro forma (invoice) /ˌprəʊˌfɔːˈməˈɪn.vɔɪs/ ⓤ /ˌproʊˌfɔːr-/ *noun* [C] SPECIALIZED a list of items that have been ordered which is sent with their prices to a customer so that the items can be paid for before they are delivered

profound EXTREME /prəˈfaʊnd/ *adj* felt or experienced very strongly or in an extreme way: *His mother's death when he was aged six had a very profound effect on him.* ○ *The invention of the contraceptive pill brought about profound changes in the lives of women.* ○ *Those two lines of poetry express perfectly the profound sadness of loss.* ○ *My grandfather has a profound mistrust of anything new or foreign.* ○ *There was a note of profound irritation in his voice.* **profoundly** /prəˈfaʊnd.li/ *adv*: *Society has changed so profoundly over the last fifty years.* ○ *We are all profoundly grateful for your help and encouragement.* **profundity** /prəˈfʌn.dɪ.ti/ ⓤ /-də.t̬i/ *noun* [U] FORMAL

profound SHOWING UNDERSTANDING /prəˈfaʊnd/ *adj* showing a clear and deep understanding of serious matters: *profound truths/wisdom* ○ *The review that I read said that it was 'a thoughtful and profound film'.* ○ *"Dying is easy – it's living that's the problem." "That was very profound of you, Steven."*

profundity /prəˈfʌn.dɪ.ti/ [US] /-də.ţi/ *noun* FORMAL **1** [U] the quality of showing a clear and deep understanding of serious matters: *the profundity of his remarks* **2** [C usually pl] a remark or thought that shows, or is intended to show, great understanding: *We would sit up all night exchanging profundities.*

profuse /prəˈfjuːs/ *adj* produced or given in large amounts: *She was admitted to St Mary's Hospital with profuse bleeding.* ○ *The company accepted blame and sent us profuse* ***apologies***. **profusely** /prəˈfjuː.sli/ *adv*: *She apologized/thanked us profusely.* ○ *He was bleeding/sweating profusely.*

profusion /prəˈfjuː.ʒᵊn/ *noun* [S or U] FORMAL an extremely large amount of something: *I was remarking on the recent profusion of books and articles on the matter.* ○ *She'd never seen flowers so beautiful and* ***in*** *such profusion.*

progenitor /prəʊˈdʒen.ɪ.təʳ/ [US] /proʊˈdʒen.ɪ.ţɚ/ *noun* [C] FORMAL a person who first thinks of something and causes it to happen: *Marx was the progenitor of communism.*

progeny /ˈprɒdʒ.ə.ni/ [US] /ˈprɑː.dʒə-/ *plural noun* FORMAL the young or OFFSPRING of a person, animal or plant: *His numerous progeny are scattered all over the country.*

progesterone /prəʊˈdʒes.tᵊr.əʊn/ [US] /proʊˈdʒes.tə.roʊn/ *noun* [U] a female hormone which causes the womb to prepare for pregnancy

prognosis (*plural* **prognoses**) /prɒgˈnəʊ.sɪs/ [US] /prɑːgˈnoʊ-/ *noun* [C] **1** (ALSO **prognostication**) FORMAL a doctor's judgment of the likely or expected development of a disease or of the chances of getting better: *The prognosis after the operation was for a full recovery.* **2** a statement of what is judged likely to happen in the future, especially in connection with a particular situation: *I was reading a gloomy economic prognosis in the paper this morning.*

program /ˈprəʊ.græm/ [US] /ˈproʊ-/ *noun* [C] **1** a series of instructions which can be put into a computer in order to make it perform an operation: *a* ***computer*** *program* ○ *She's* ***written*** *a program to find words which frequently occur together.* **2** AUS USUALLY AND US a **programme**

program /ˈprəʊ.græm/ [US] /ˈproʊ-/ *verb* [T] **-mm- 1** to write a series of instructions which make a computer perform a particular operation: [+ to infinitive] *She programmed the computer* ***to*** *calculate the rate of exchange in twelve currencies.* **2** US FOR **programme** INSTRUCT

programmer /ˈprəʊ.græm.əʳ/ [US] /ˈproʊ.græm.ɚ/ *noun* [C] (ALSO **computer programmer**) a person whose job is to produce computer programs

programming /ˈprəʊ.græm.ɪŋ/ [US] /ˈproʊ-/ *noun* [U] when someone writes computer programs

COMMON LEARNER ERROR

program or **programme?**

Computer program is spelt **program** in both British English and American English.

a new computer program

In British English, **programme** is the spelling used for all other meanings.

a television programme
a theatre programme
What's the programme for the week's activities?

In American English, **program** is the spelling used for all meanings.

---

programme [BROADCAST] UK, US **program** /ˈprəʊ.græm/ [US] /ˈproʊ-/ *noun* [C] a broadcast on television or radio: *It's one of those arts programmes late at night.* ○ *It's my favourite TV programme – I never miss an episode.* ➲See Note **program or programme?** at **program**.

programme [THIN BOOK] UK, US **program** /ˈprəʊ.græm/ [US] /ˈproʊ-/ *noun* [C] a thin book or piece of paper giving information about a play or musical or sports event, usually bought at the theatre or place where the event happens: *I looked in the programme to find out the actor's name.*

programme [PLAN] UK, US **program** /ˈprəʊ.græm/ [US] /ˈproʊ-/ *noun* [C] a plan of activities to be done or things to be achieved: *The school offers an exciting and varied programme of social events.* ○ *The rail system is to put twenty million pounds into its modernisation programme.* ○ *I'm running three mornings a week – it's all part of my fitness programme.*

programme [INSTRUCT] /ˈprəʊ.græm/ [US] /ˈproʊ-/ *verb* [T + obj + to infinitive] **1** UK (US **program** (**-mm-**)) to instruct a device or system to operate in a particular way or at a particular time: *I've programmed the video to start recording at 10 o'clock.* **2 be programmed to do sth** to always do or think a particular thing, although you do not try to: *I'm programmed to wake up at seven.*

programmable /prəʊˈgræm.ə.bl̩/ /ˈprəʊ.græm-/ [US] /ˈproʊ.græm.ə-/ *adj* able to be programmed

progress /ˈprəʊ.gres/ [US] /ˈprɑː-/ *noun* [U] **1** advancement to an improved or more developed state, or to a forward position: *Technological progress has been so rapid over the last few years.* ○ *I'm not* ***making*** *much progress with my Spanish.* ○ *The doctor said that she was* ***making*** *good progress* (= getting better after a medical operation or illness). ○ *The recent free elections mark the next step in the country's progress* ***towards*** *democracy.* ○ *The yacht's crew said that they were* ***making*** *relatively slow progress north-easterly.* **2** FORMAL **in progress** happening or being done now: *Repair work is in progress on the southbound lane of the motorway and will continue until June.*

progress /prəˈgres/ *verb* [I] **1** to improve or develop in skills, knowledge, etc: *My Spanish never really progressed* ***beyond*** *the stage of being able to order drinks at the bar.* ➲Compare **regress**. **2** to continue gradually: *As the war progressed more and more countries became involved.* ○ *We started off talking about the weather and gradually the conversation progressed* ***to*** *politics.*

progression /prəˈgreʃ.ᵊn/ *noun* [C or U] when something or someone changes to the next stage of development: *Drugs can slow down the progression of the disease.* ○ *The novel follows the progression of a woman from youth to middle age.* ○ *She'd always worked with old people so becoming a nurse was a* ***logical/natural*** *progression.*

progressive /prəˈgres.ɪv/ *adj* **1** developing or happening gradually: *There's been a progressive decline in the standard of living over the past few years.* ○ *a progressive disease* **2** describes ideas or systems which are new and modern, encouraging change in society or in the way that things are done: *progressive ideas/attitudes* ○ *The left of the party is pressing for a more progressive social policy.* ○ *a progressive school* **3** describes a tax system in which the rate of tax is higher on larger amounts of money **4** describes the form of a verb which is used to show that the action is continuing. It is formed with the verb 'be' followed by the present participle (= *-ing* form of the verb): *'He's working hard at the moment' is an example of the* ***present*** *progressive form of the verb 'work'.* ○ *'I was eating when the phone rang' is an example of the* ***past*** *progressive.*

progressive /prəˈgres.ɪv/ *noun* [C] a person who supports new ideas and social change, especially one who belongs to a political party ➲Compare **reactionary**.

progressively /prəˈgres.ɪv.li/ *adv* gradually: *My eyesight has got progressively worse over the years.*

prohibit /prəˈhɪb.ɪt/ *verb* **1** [T often passive] to officially forbid something: *Motor vehicles are prohibited* ***from*** *driving in the town centre.* ○ *The government introduced a law prohibiting tobacco advertisements on TV.* ○ *Parking is* ***strictly*** *prohibited between these gates.* **2** [T] to prevent a particular activity by making it impossible: *The loudness of the music prohibits serious conversation in most nightclubs.*

prohibition /ˌprəʊ.hɪˈbɪʃ.ᵊn/ [US] /ˌproʊ-/ *noun* [C or U] **1** when something is officially forbidden, or an order forbidding something: *London Transport has announced a prohibition* ***on*** *smoking on buses.* ○ *The environmental group is demanding a complete prohibition* ***against*** *the hunting of whales.* ○ *It's my feeling that the money spent on drug prohibition would be better spent on information and education.* **2 Prohibition** the period from 1920 to 1933 when the production and sale of alcohol was forbidden in the US

prohibitive /prə'hɪb.ɪ.tɪv/ ⑩ /-t̬ɪv/ *adj* If the cost of something is prohibitive, it is too expensive for most people: *Hotel prices in the major cities are high but not prohibitive.*
prohibitively /prə'hɪb.ɪ.tɪv.li/ ⑩ /-t̬ɪv-/ *adv*: *Property in the area tends to be prohibitively expensive* (= so expensive that you can not buy it).

project PIECE OF WORK /'prɒdʒ.ekt/ ⑩ /'prɑː.dʒekt/ *noun* [C] **1** a piece of planned work or an activity which is completed over a period of time and intended to achieve a particular aim: *the Kings Cross housing project* ○ *a scientific research project* ○ *Her latest project is a film based on the life of a nineteenth-century music hall star.* ○ *My next project is decorating the kitchen.* **2** a study of a particular subject done over a period of time, especially by students: *He's **doing** a class project **on** pollution.* ○ *In our third year at college everyone had to do a special project.*

project CALCULATE /prə'dʒekt/ *verb* [T usually passive] to calculate an amount or number expected in the future from information already known: [+ to infinitive] *Government spending is projected **to** rise by 3% next year.*
projected /prə'dʒek.tɪd/ *adj*: *The projected* (= planned) *extension to the motorway near London is going to cost over £4 million.*
projection /prə'dʒek.ʃən/ *noun* [C] a calculation or guess about the future based on information that you have: *The company has failed to achieve last year's sales projections by thirty percent.* ⊃See also **projection**; **projection** at **project** MAKE AN IMAGE and **project** STICK OUT.

project THROW /prə'dʒekt/ *verb* [T] to throw or direct something forwards, with force: *Ninety percent of the projected missiles will hit their target.*
• **project *your* voice** to sing or speak loudly and clearly: *It's a big theatre so you really have to project your voice if you're going to be heard at the back.*
projectile /prə'dʒek.taɪl/ ⑩ /-t̬əl/ *noun* [C] SPECIALIZED an object that is thrown or fired forwards, especially from a weapon: *The second projectile exploded after hitting a tank.*

project MAKE AN IMAGE /prə'dʒekt/ *verb* [T] **1** to cause a film, image or light to appear on a screen or other surface: *Laser images were projected **onto** a screen.* **2** SPECIALIZED to wrongly imagine that someone else is feeling a particular emotion or desire when in fact it is you who feels this way: *I suspect he's projecting his fears **onto** you.* **3** If you project a particular quality, that quality is what most people notice about you: *Recently the president has sought to project a much tougher **image**.*
projection /prə'dʒek.ʃən/ *noun* [U] when a film or an image is projected onto a screen or wall ⊃See also **projection**; **projection** at **project** CALCULATE and **project** STICK OUT.
projectionist /prə'dʒek.ʃən.ɪst/ *noun* [C] a person whose job is to operate a projector in a cinema
projector /prə'dʒek.tər/ ⑩ /-t̬ər/ *noun* [C] a device for showing films or images on a screen or other surface

project STICK OUT /prə'dʒekt/ *verb* [I + adv or prep] to stick out over an edge or from a surface: *The hotel dining room projects out over the water.*
projection /prə'dʒek.ʃən/ *noun* [C] something that projects from a surface or beyond the edge of something
projection /prə'dʒek.ʃən/ *noun* [C] SPECIALIZED a drawn representation of a solid shape or a line as seen from a particular direction ⊃See also **projection** at **project** CALCULATE, **project** MAKE AN IMAGE and **project** STICK OUT.

prolapse /'prəʊ.læps/ ⑩ /'proʊ-/ *noun* [C] SPECIALIZED a medical condition in which an organ has moved down out of its usual position: *a rectal prolapse/a prolapse of the rectum* **prolapsed** /'prəʊ.læpst/ ⑩ /'proʊ-/ *adj*: *a prolapsed womb*

the proletariat /ðə,prəʊ.lɪ'teə.ri.ət/ ⑩ /-,prɒl.ɪ-/ ⑩ /-,proʊ.-lə'ter.i-/ *group noun* [S] the class of people who do unskilled jobs in society and own little or no property
proletarian /,prəʊ.lɪ'teə.ri.ən/ ⑩ /,proʊ.lə'ter.i-/ *noun* [C] (INFORMAL **prole**) MAINLY DISAPPROVING a member of the proletariat **proletarian** /,prəʊ.lɪ'teə.ri.ən/ ⑩ /,proʊ.lə-'ter.i-/ *adj*

pro-life /,prəʊ'laɪf/ ⑩ /,proʊ-/ *adj* opposed to the belief that a pregnant woman should have the freedom to choose an abortion if she does not want to have a baby ⊃Compare **pro-choice**.

proliferate /prə'lɪf.ər.eɪt/ ⑩ /-ə.reɪt/ *verb* [I] FORMAL to increase greatly and suddenly in number: *Small businesses have proliferated in the last ten years.*
proliferation /prə,lɪf.ər'eɪ.ʃən/ ⑩ /-ə'reɪ-/ *noun* [U] *The past two years have seen the proliferation of TV channels.*

prolific /prə'lɪf.ɪk/ *adj* producing a great number or amount of something: *He was probably the most prolific songwriter of his generation.* ○ *Rabbits and other rodents are prolific* (= have a lot of babies).

prolix /'prəʊ.lɪks/ ⑩ /'proʊ-/ *adj* FORMAL DISAPPROVING using too many words and therefore boring or difficult to read or listen to; VERBOSE: *The author's prolix style has done nothing to encourage sales of the book.*

prologue /'prəʊ.lɒg/ ⑩ /'proʊ.lɑːg/ *noun* **1** [C] (US ALSO **prolog**) a part that comes at the beginning of a play, story or long poem, often giving information about events that have happened before the time when the play, story or poem begins ⊃Compare **epilogue**. **2** [S] LITERARY a series of events related to the main event and which happen before it: INFORMAL *A series of internal struggles was the prologue **to** full-scale civil war.*

prolong /prə'lɒŋ/ ⑩ /-'lɑːŋ/ *verb* [T] to make something last a longer time: *We were having such a good time that we decided to prolong our stay by another week.* ○ *She chewed each delicious mouthful as slowly as she could, prolonging the pleasure.* **prolongation** /,prəʊ.lɒŋ'geɪ.-ʃən/ ⑩ /,proʊ.lɑːŋ-/ *noun* [U]
prolonged /prə'lɒŋd/ ⑩ /-'lɑːŋd/ *adj* continuing for a long time: *Prolonged use of the drug is known to have harmful side-effects.*

prom PARTY /prɒm/ ⑩ /prɑːm/ *noun* [C] US a formal party held for older students at the end of the school year, at which there is dancing: *Who are you taking to the Senior Prom?*

prom PATH /prɒm/ ⑩ /prɑːm/ *noun* INFORMAL FOR **promenade**

promenade /,prɒm.ə'nɑːd/ ⑩ /,prɑː.mə'neɪd/ *noun* [C] (INFORMAL **prom**) a path for walking on, especially one built next to the sea: *We strolled along on the promenade eating ice-creams.*
promenade /,prɒm.ə'nɑːd/ ⑩ /,prɑː.mə'neɪd/ *verb* [I] OLD-FASHIONED to walk slowly along a road or path for relaxation and pleasure

prominent /'prɒm.ɪ.nənt/ ⑩ /'prɑː.mə-/ *adj* **1** very well known and important: *a prominent Democrat* ○ *a prominent member of the Saudi royal family* ○ *The government should be playing a more prominent role in promoting human rights.* **2** sticking out from a surface: *She has a rather prominent chin/nose.* **3** describes something that is in a position in which it is easily seen: *New books are displayed in a prominent **position** on tables at the front of the shop.*
prominently /'prɒm.ɪ.nənt.li/ ⑩ /'prɑː.mɪ-/ *adv*: *A photograph of her daughter was prominently displayed* (= in a position where it could be seen) *on her desk.*
prominence /'prɒm.ɪ.nənts/ ⑩ /'prɑː.mə-/ *noun* [U] *Most of the papers **give** prominence **to*** (= put in a noticeable position) *the same story this morning.* ○ *It's the first time that a lawyer of such prominence* (= fame and importance) *has been given the freedom to air his views on TV.* ○ *Elton was one of the comedians who **came to/rose to/gained** prominence* (= became famous) *in the 1980s.*

promiscuous /prə'mɪs.kju.əs/ *adj* DISAPPROVING (of a person) having a lot of different sexual partners or sexual relationships, or (of sexual habits) involving a lot of different partners: *I suppose I was quite promiscuous in my youth.* ○ *It's an often repeated fallacy that homosexual men have more promiscuous lifestyles than heterosexuals.*
promiscuously /prə'mɪs.kju.ə.sli/ *adv*
promiscuity /,prɒm.ɪ'skjuː.ɪ.ti/ ⑩ /,prɑː.mɪ'skjuː.ə.t̬i/ *noun* [U] when someone is promiscuous

promise SAY CERTAINLY /'prɒm.ɪs/ ⑩ /'prɑː.mɪs/ *verb* [I or T] to tell someone that you will certainly do something: [+ to infinitive] *He promised faithfully **to** call me every week.*

P

○ [+ that] *The government have promised* ***that*** *they'll reduce taxes.* ○ [+ (that)] *Promise me* ***(that)*** *you won't tell him.* ○ *I'll have a look for some while I'm at the shops but I'm not promising anything.* ○ *Can I have that book back when you've finished because I've promised it* (= I have said I will give it) ***to*** *Sara.* ○ [+ two objects] *Her parents promised her a new car if she passed her exams.* ○ *I've promised myself a long bath when I get through all this work.* ○ [+ speech] *"I'll come round and see you every day," she promised.* ○ *"I won't do anything dangerous." "You promise?" "I promise."* ○ *"I won't have time to take you shopping this afternoon." "But you promised!"*

• **promise *sb* the earth/moon** *INFORMAL* to say that you will do much greater things than you will ever be able to achieve: *Like most governments in their first term of office, they promised the earth.*

promise /ˈprɒm.ɪs/ [US] /ˈprɑː.mɪs/ *noun* [C] when you say that you will certainly do something: *I'll tidy my things away tonight – and that's a promise!* ○ *I'll try to get back in time, but I'm not* ***making*** *any promises.*

• **keep/break a promise** to do/not do what you said that you would do: *If I make a promise, I like to keep it.*

• **Promises, promises!** *INFORMAL* something that you say when someone says they will do something and you do not believe them: *"When I've got some time I'll show you everything." "Promises, promises!"*

COMMON LEARNER ERROR

promise

When you use the expression '**promise** someone something', no preposition is needed after the verb.

He promised his mum he would clean his room.
~~*He promised to his mum he would clean his room.*~~

promise [BE EXPECTED] /ˈprɒm.ɪs/ [US] /ˈprɑː.mɪs/ *verb* **promise to be good/exciting, etc.** to be expected to be good/exciting, etc: *It promises to be a really exciting match.*

promise /ˈprɒm.ɪs/ [US] /ˈprɑː.mɪs/ *noun* [U] when someone or something is likely to develop successfully and people expect this to happen: *His English teacher had written on his report that he* ***showed*** *great promise.* ○ *As a child I was quite a good dancer, but I didn't fulfil my early promise.*

promising /ˈprɒm.ɪ.sɪŋ/ [US] /ˈprɑː.mɪ-/ *adj* Something which is promising shows signs that it is going to be successful or enjoyable: *They won the award for the most promising new band of the year.* ○ *"How's your new venture going?" "It's looking quite promising."* ○ *It's a great restaurant but it doesn't look at all promising from the outside.* * NOTE: The opposite is **unpromising**. **promisingly** /ˈprɒm.ɪ.sɪŋ.li/ [US] /ˈprɑː.mɪ-/ *adv*: *The film starts promisingly enough but it doesn't maintain the interest level.*

ˈPromised ˌLand *noun* [U] in the Bible, the land of Canaan, promised by God to Abraham and his race: *FIGURATIVE America was the Promised Land for many immigrant families.*

promissory note /ˈprɒm.ɪ.sᵊr.iˌnəʊt/ [US] /ˈprɑː.mɪ.sɔːr.i-ˌnoʊt/ *noun* [C] *SPECIALIZED* a document which contains a promise to pay a stated amount of money to a stated person either on a fixed date or when the money is demanded

promo /ˈprəʊ.məʊ/ [US] /ˈproʊ.moʊ/ *noun* [C] *plural* **promos** **1** *INFORMAL* a short film which is made to advertise a product, especially a record of modern popular music **2** *US* an advertisement, broadcast announcement, discussion with a writer, film producer, actor, etc. which is designed to give attention to a book or film in order to increase sales

promontory /ˈprɒm.ən.tri/ [US] /ˈprɑː.mən.tɔːr-/ *noun* [C] (*ALSO* **headland**) a narrow area of high land that sticks out into the sea

promote [ENCOURAGE] /prəˈməʊt/ [US] /-ˈmoʊt/ *verb* [T] to encourage the popularity, sale, development or existence of something: *Advertising companies are always having to think up new ways to promote products.* ○ *The Institute is intended to promote an understanding of the politics and culture of the Arab world.* ○ *Greenpeace works to promote awareness of the dangers that threaten our planet today.* ○ *It has long been known that regular exercise promotes all-round good health.*

promoter /prəˈməʊ.təʳ/ [US] /-ˈmoʊ.t̬ɚ/ *noun* [C] **1** someone who tries to encourage something to happen or develop: *a promoter* ***of*** *peace/sexual equality* **2** a person who organizes and arranges finance for sports and musical events: *a boxing/rock concert promoter*

promotion /prəˈməʊ.ʃᵊn/ [US] /-ˈmoʊ-/ *noun* **1** [C or U] activities to advertise something: *a* ***sales*** *promotion* ○ *There was a promotion in the supermarket and they were giving away free glasses of wine.* ○ *Obviously as sales manager he'll be very involved in the promotion and marketing of the product.* **2** [U] when something is encouraged to happen or develop: *the promotion of a healthy lifestyle*

promotional /prəˈməʊ.ʃᵊn.ᵊl/ [US] /-ˈmoʊ-/ *adj* intended to advertise something: *a promotional campaign/video* ○ *The writer recently went on a promotional tour of his homeland.*

promote [RAISE] /prəˈməʊt/ [US] /-ˈmoʊt/ *verb* [T often passive] **1** to raise someone to a higher or more important position or rank: *If I'm not promoted within the next two years, I'm going to change jobs.* ○ *She's just been promoted* ***to*** *senior sales rep.* ○ *If Coventry City win this match, they'll be promoted* ***to*** *the Premier League.* * NOTE: The opposite is **demote**. **2** *US* If a student is promoted, they go up to the next higher GRADE (= level in school).

promotion /prəˈməʊ.ʃᵊn/ [US] /-ˈmoʊ-/ *noun* [C or U] when someone is raised to a higher or more important position or rank: *Did Steve* ***get****/Was Steve* ***given*** *the promotion he wanted?* ○ *The job offers excellent promotion* ***prospects****.* ○ *Fiorentina's win against Palermo last night has considerably increased their chances of promotion this season.*

prompt [CAUSE] /prɒmpt/ [US] /prɑːmpt/ *verb* [T] **1** to make something happen: *The bishop's speech has prompted an angry response from both political parties.* ○ *Recent worries over the president's health have prompted speculation over his political future.* **2 prompt *sb* to do *sth*** to make someone decide to say or do something: *What prompted you to say that?* ○ *I don't know what prompted him to leave.* **3** to help someone, especially an actor, to remember what they were going to say or do: *I forgot my line and had to be prompted.*

prompt /prɒmpt/ [US] /prɑːmpt/ *noun* [C] **1** a sign on a computer screen which shows that the computer is ready to receive your instructions **2** words which are spoken to an actor who has forgotten what he or she is going to say during the performance of a play **3** (*ALSO* **prompter**) a person whose job is to help actors, during a performance, to remember words that they have forgotten

prompting /ˈprɒmp.tɪŋ/ [US] /ˈprɑːmp-/ *noun* [C or U] when you try to make someone say something: [+ *to* infinitive] *Kids of that age really shouldn't need prompting* ***to*** *say thank you for things.* ○ *Amazingly – without any prompting – my husband actually said how nice I looked in my new dress!*

prompt [QUICK] /prɒmpt/ [US] /prɑːmpt/ *adj* (of an action) done quickly and without delay, or (of a person) acting quickly or arriving at the arranged time: *They've written back already – that was a very prompt reply.* ○ *They're usually fairly prompt in dealing with enquiries.* ○ *Try to be prompt because we'll be very short of time.*

prompt /prɒmpt/ [US] /prɑːmpt/ *adv* at the time stated and no later: *We'll be leaving at six o'clock prompt.*

promptly /ˈprɒmpt.li/ [US] /ˈprɑːmpt-/ *adv*: *We'll have to leave fairly promptly* (= on time) *if we want to catch that train.* ○ *We try to answer readers' letters as promptly* (= quickly) *as we can.* ○ *She promised she'd keep it secret and promptly* (= immediately after) *went and told Ben!*

promulgate [SPREAD] /ˈprɒm.ᵊl.geɪt/ [US] /ˈprɑː.məl-/ *verb* [T] *FORMAL* to spread beliefs or ideas among a lot of people

promulgation /ˌprɒm.ᵊlˈgeɪ.ʃᵊn/ [US] /ˌprɑː.məl-/ *noun* [U]

promulgate [ANNOUNCE] /ˈprɒm.ᵊl.geɪt/ [US] /ˈprɑː.məl-/ *verb* [T] *FORMAL* to announce something publicly, especially a new law: *The new law was finally promulgated in*

P

the autumn of last year. **promulgation** /ˌprɒm.əlˈgeɪ.ʃən/ [US] /ˌprɑː.məl-/ *noun* [U]

pron *noun* ABBREVIATION FOR **pronoun**

prone [TENDING] /prəʊn/ [US] /proʊn/ *adj* **be prone to** ***sth/do sth*** tending to suffer from an illness or show a particular negative characteristic: *I've always been prone to headaches.* ○ *He was prone to depressions even as a teenager.* ○ *She's prone to exaggerate, that's for sure.* **-prone** /-prəʊn/ [US] /-proʊn/ *suffix*: *accident-prone* (= often having accidents) ○ *injury-prone* (= often getting injuries)

prone [LYING DOWN] /prəʊn/ [US] /proʊn/ *adj* FORMAL lying on the front with the face down: *The photograph showed a man lying prone on the pavement, a puddle of blood about his head.*

prong /prɒŋ/ [US] /prɑːŋ/ *noun* [C] one of two or more long sharp points on an object, especially a fork **-pronged** /-prɒŋd/ [US] /-prɑːŋd/ *suffix* **two-pronged/three-pronged, etc.** having the stated number of prongs: FIGURATIVE *To tackle inflation the government have evolved a three-pronged strategy* (= a plan that involves three ways of dealing with the problem).

pronoun /ˈprəʊ.naʊn/ [US] /ˈproʊ-/ *noun* [C] a word which is used instead of a noun or a noun phrase: *Pronouns are often used to refer to a noun that has already been mentioned.* ○ *'She', 'it' and 'who' are all examples of pronouns.* **pronominal** /prəʊˈnɒm.ɪ.nəl/ [US] /proʊˈnɑː.mə-/ *adj* SPECIALIZED

pronounce [MAKE SOUND] /prəˈnaʊnts/ *verb* [T] to say a word or a letter in a particular way: *How do you pronounce your surname?* ○ *She pronounced his name so badly he didn't even recognise it.* ○ *Sade, pronounced shah-day, is a singer.* **pronunciation** /prəˌnʌnt.siˈeɪ.ʃən/ *noun* [C or U] how words are pronounced: *English pronunciation is notoriously difficult.* ○ *There are two different pronunciations of this word.*

pronounce [TO STATE] /prəˈnaʊnts/ *verb* [T] FORMAL to state something officially or with certainty: [+ obj + n or adj] *He was taken to the hospital where he was pronounced dead on arrival.* ○ *The jury pronounced him guilty.* ○ *He gazed vacantly while the verdict and sentence were pronounced.* ○ *She surveyed the building and pronounced herself pleased with their work.* ○ [+ that] *The government pronounced* ***that*** *they are no longer a nuclear state.* ○ *"Have I met him?" "You have indeed – I recall you pronounced the man* (= said that he was) *a fool."* ○ *The dessert was tried and pronounced delicious.* **pronouncement** /prəˈnaʊnt.smənt/ *noun* [C] FORMAL an official announcement: *The treasurer has been taking a more optimistic view of economic recovery in his recent public pronouncements.*

▲ **pronounce on/upon** ***sth*** *verb* [T] FORMAL to give a judgement or opinion about something: *I'd rather not go pronouncing on a subject that I know so little about.*

pronounced /prəˈnaʊntst/ *adj* very noticeable or certain: *I'm told I have a very pronounced English accent when I speak French.* ○ *She's a woman of very pronounced views which she is not afraid to air.*

pronto /ˈprɒn.təʊ/ [US] /ˈprɑːn.t̬oʊ/ *adv* INFORMAL quickly and without delay: *I'll send those off pronto, before I forget.*

proof [SHOWING TRUTH] /pruːf/ *noun* [C or U] a fact or piece of information which shows that something exists or is true: [+ that] *Do they have any proof* ***that*** *it was Hampson who stole the goods?* ○ *I have a suspicion that he's having an affair, though I don't have any* ***concrete*** (= definite) *proof.* ○ *If anyone needs proof* ***of*** *Andrew Davies' genius as a writer, this novel is it.* ○ *"How old are you?" "Twenty-one." "Have you got any proof on you?"* ○ *Keep your receipt as proof* ***of*** *purchase.* ➲See **burden of proof** at **burden**.

• **The proof of the pudding (is in the eating).** SAYING said to mean that you can only judge the quality of something after you have tried, used or experienced it

prove /pruːv/ *verb* [T] **proved, proved,** MAINLY US **proven** to show that something is true: [+ that] *They suspected that she'd killed him but they could never actually prove* ***that*** *it was her.* ○ [+ adj] *They proved him* ***innocent/guilty.*** ○ *Under the present system, you're innocent until proven guilty.* ○ [+ question word] *"I spent thirty pounds in the pub last night." "That just* ***goes to*** *prove* ***what*** *an idiot you are!"* ○ *Computers have been used to prove mathematical theorems.* ○ *That theory was proved false.* ○ *He's so aggressive – it's as if he's always trying to prove something.* ➲See also **prove** SHOW. **proven** /ˈpruː.vən/ /ˈprəʊ-/ *adj*: *You've got a proven work record, which gives you a big advantage.*

-proof [PROTECTED] /-pruːf/ *suffix* protecting against, or not damaged by, a particular thing: *a bullet-proof vest* ○ *a waterproof/wind-proof jacket* ○ *frost-proof pots for the garden*

proof /pruːf/ *adj* FORMAL *No household security devices are proof* ***against*** (= protect completely against) *the determined burglar.* ○ *Her virtue would be proof* ***against*** *his charms.*

proof /pruːf/ *verb* [T] to treat a surface with a substance which will protect it against something, especially water

proof [PRINTED COPY] /pruːf/ *noun* [C] a printed copy of something which is examined and corrected before the final copies are printed: *I was busy correcting proofs.*

proof [ALCOHOL] /pruːf/ *adj* [after n] of the stated alcoholic strength, a higher number meaning a greater amount of alcohol: *It says on the bottle that it's 60 percent proof.*

ˌproof ˈpositive *noun* [U] facts that cannot be doubted: *The strength of reaction to the article is proof positive that this is a very important issue.*

proofread /ˈpruːf.riːd/ *verb* [I or T] to find and correct mistakes in PROOFS (= copies of printed text) before the final copies are printed **proofreader** /ˈpruːfˌriː.dəʳ/ [US] /-dɚ/ *noun* [C] a person whose job is to correct mistakes in books before they are printed **proofreading** /ˈpruːfˌriː.dɪŋ/ *noun* [U] *Most of the errors were corrected at the proofreading stage.*

prop [SUPPORT] /prɒp/ [US] /prɑːp/ *verb* [T + adv or prep] **-pp-** to support something physically, often by leaning it against something else or putting something under it: *I propped my bike* ***(up) against*** *the wall.* ○ *She was sitting at the desk with her chin propped* ***on*** *her hands.* ○ *This window keeps on closing – I'll have to prop it* ***open*** *with something.* **prop** /prɒp/ [US] /prɑːp/ *noun* [C] an object which is used to support something by holding it up: *I need some sort of a prop to keep the washing line up.* ○ FIGURATIVE *A lot of people use cigarettes as a sort of* ***social*** *prop* (= to make them feel more confident).

prop [FILM/THEATRE] /prɒp/ [US] /prɑːp/ *noun* [C usually pl] an object used by the actors performing in a play or film: *The set is minimal and the only props used in the show are a table, a chair and a glass of water.*

prop [AIRCRAFT/SHIP] /prɒp/ [US] /prɑːp/ *noun* [C] INFORMAL FOR **propeller**

▲ **prop** ***sth*** **up** *phrasal verb* [M] **1** to lift and give support to something by putting something under it: *He was sitting upright in his hospital bed, propped up by pillows.* ○ *There were the usual bunch of drinkers propped up at* (= leaning against) *the bar.* **2** to give support to something, especially a country or organization, so that it can continue to exist in a difficult situation: *How long is the government likely to survive without the US military force there to prop it up?*

propaganda /ˌprɒp.əˈgæn.də/ [US] /ˌprɑː.pə-/ *noun* [U] MAINLY DISAPPROVING information, ideas, opinions or images, often only giving one part of an argument, which are broadcast, published or in some other way spread with the intention of influencing people's opinions: *political/wartime propaganda* ○ *At school we were fed communist/right-wing propaganda.* ○ *One official dismissed the ceasefire as a mere propaganda exercise.* **propagandist** /ˌprɒp.əˈgæn.dɪst/ [US] /ˌprɑː.pə-/ *noun* [C], *adj*: *Communist/Nazi/Republican/right-wing propagandists* *The papers were full of the most blatant propagandist nonsense.* **propagandize,** UK USUALLY **-ise** /ˌprɒp.əˈgæn.daɪz/ [US] /ˌprɑː.pə-/ *verb* [I] FORMAL MAINLY DISAPPROVING

propagate /ˈprɒp.ə.geɪt/ [US] /ˈprɑː.pə-/ *verb* **1** [I or T] to produce a new plant from a parent plant: *Most house plants can be propagated from stem cuttings.* ○ *Plants*

[P]

needs certain conditions to propagate. **2** *FORMAL* (of a plant or animal) to reproduce **3** **[T]** *FORMAL* to spread opinions, lies or religions among a lot of people: *The government have tried to propagate the belief that this is a just war.* ○ *Such lies are propagated in the media.* **propagation** /ˌprɒp.əˈgeɪ.ʃᵊn/ [US] /ˌprɑː.pə-/ *noun* **[U]**
propagator /ˈprɒp.ə.geɪ.təʳ/ [US] /ˈprɑː.pə.geɪ.t̬ɚ/ *noun* **[C]** *SPECIALIZED* a box in which seeds or young plants are grown, that has a transparent cover and is sometimes heated

propane /ˈprəʊ.peɪn/ [US] /ˈproʊ-/ *noun* **[U]** a colourless gas used as fuel, especially in cooking and heating

propel /prəˈpel/ *verb* **[T]** **-ll-** **1** to push or move something somewhere, often with a lot of force: *a rocket propelled through space* ○ *The Kon-Tiki sailed across the Pacific Ocean propelled by wind power.* **2** **propel *sb* into/to/towards *sth*** to cause someone to do an activity or be in a situation: *The film propelled him to international stardom.*
propellant /prəˈpel.ənt/ *noun* **[C or U]** **1** an explosive substance or fuel which causes something to move forwards **2** a gas which is used in AEROSOLS to force the liquid out in very small drops
propeller /prəˈpel.əʳ/ [US] /-ɚ/ *noun* **[C]** (*INFORMAL* **prop**) a device which causes a ship or aircraft to move, consisting of two or more blades which turn round at high speed ➲See picture **Planes, Ships and Boats** on page Centre 14
propulsion /prəˈpʌl.ʃᵊn/ *noun* **[U]** a force that pushes something forward: *wind propulsion* ○ *a propulsion system* ➲See also **jet propulsion**.

proˌpelling ˈpencil *UK noun* **[C]** (*US* **mechanical pencil**) a pencil in which the LEAD is pushed out by turning or pressing a part of the pencil

propensity /prəˈpen.sɪ.ti/ [US] /-sə.t̬i/ *noun* **[C]** *FORMAL* a tendency towards a particular way of behaving, especially a bad one: **[+ to infinitive]** *She's inherited from her father a propensity **to** talk too much.* ○ *He's well-known for his natural propensity **for** indiscretion.*

proper [REAL] /ˈprɒp.əʳ/ [US] /ˈprɑː.pɚ/ *adj* **[before n]** real, satisfactory, suitable or correct: *This is Sara's first proper job – she usually does temporary work just for the money.* ○ *If you're going to walk those sort of distances you need proper walking boots.* ○ *I would have done the job myself but I didn't have the proper equipment.* ○ *I've had sandwiches but I haven't eaten a proper meal.* ○ *She likes everything to be in its proper place.*
proper /ˈprɒp.əʳ/ [US] /ˈprɑː.pɚ/ *adv UK NOT STANDARD* sometimes used instead of the adverb 'properly' to describe how someone speaks: *She was an educated lady so she **talked** proper.*
properly /ˈprɒp.ᵊl.i/ [US] /ˈprɑː.pɚ.li/ *adv* correctly, or in a satisfactory way: *It's still not working properly.* ○ *I'm not properly dressed for this sort of weather.* ○ *I think you should take it somewhere to have it mended properly.* ○ *Come on, Evie, speak properly – you're not a baby any more!*
• **properly speaking** *FORMAL* really: *It's not, properly speaking, champagne but it is very similar.*

proper [SOCIALLY ACCEPTABLE] /ˈprɒp.əʳ/ [US] /ˈprɑː.pɚ/ *adj* showing standards of behaviour that are socially and morally acceptable: **[+ to infinitive]** *In those days **it** was considered not quite proper for young ladies **to** be seen talking to men in public.* ○ *She was very proper, my grandmother – she'd never go out without wearing her hat and gloves.*
properly /ˈprɒp.ᵊl.i/ [US] /ˈprɑː.pɚ.li/ *adv FORMAL Most vegetables should be eaten with a fork but asparagus can be properly* (= politely) *eaten with the fingers.*
propriety /prəˈpraɪə.ti/ [US] /-t̬i/ *noun* **[U]** *FORMAL* correct moral behaviour or actions: *The director insisted that there was no question as to the propriety of how the funds were raised.* ○ *She was careful always to behave with propriety.*
proprieties /prəˈpraɪə.tiz/ [US] /-t̬iz/ *plural noun FORMAL* the rules of polite social behaviour: *They'd invited us to dinner so we thought we'd better **observe** the proprieties and invite them back.*

proper [MAIN] /ˈprɒp.əʳ/ [US] /ˈprɑː.pɚ/ *adj* **[after n]** belonging to the main, most important or typical part: *It's a suburb of Manchester really – I wouldn't call it Manchester proper.*

proper [COMPLETE] /ˈprɒp.əʳ/ [US] /ˈprɑː.pɚ/ *adj UK INFORMAL* complete: *I've got myself into a proper mess!*

ˌproper ˈfraction *noun* **[C]** *SPECIALIZED* a fraction in which the number below the line is larger than the number above it: *¾ and ⅝ are proper fractions.*

ˈproper ˌnoun *noun* **[C]** *SPECIALIZED* the name of a particular person, place or object that is spelt with a capital letter: *Examples of proper nouns in English are Joseph, Vienna and the White House.* ➲Compare **common noun**.

property [THINGS OWNED] /ˈprɒp.ə.ti/ [US] /ˈprɑː.pɚ.t̬i/ *noun* **1** **[U]** an object or objects that belong to someone: *The club does not accept responsibility for loss of or damage to club members' **personal** property.* ○ *Both books have 'property of Her Majesty's Government' stamped inside them.* ○ *Children need to be taught to have respect for other people's property.* **2** **[C or U]** a building or area of land, or both together: *He owns a number of properties in the centre of London.* ○ *The notice said 'Private Property, Keep Off.* ○ *Yes, I've bought my own house – I'm now a **man/woman of** property!* **3** **[U]** *SPECIALIZED* the legal right to own and use something

property [QUALITY] /ˈprɒp.ə.ti/ [US] /ˈprɑː.pɚ.t̬i/ *noun* **[C]** a quality in a substance or material, especially one which means that it can be used in a particular way: *One of the properties of copper is that it conducts heat and electricity very well.* ○ *We value herbs for their taste, but we forget that they also have medicinal properties.*

ˈproperty deˌveloper *noun* **[C]** a person whose job involves buying and selling buildings and land, and arranging for new buildings to be built

prophecy /ˈprɒf.ə.si/ [US] /ˈprɑː.fə-/ *noun* **1** **[C]** a statement that says what is going to happen in the future, especially one which is based on what you believe about a particular matter rather than existing facts: *The minister suggested that the dire prophecies of certain leading environmentalists were somewhat exaggerated.* ○ *These doom and gloom prophecies are doing little to help the economy.* **2** **[U]** *FORMAL* the ability to say what is going to happen in the future
prophesy /ˈprɒf.ə.saɪ/ [US] /ˈprɑː.fə-/ *verb* **[I or T]** to say that you believe something will happen in the future: *Few could have prophesied this war.* ○ **[+ that]** *He prophesied **that** the present government would only stay four years in office.* ○ **[+ question word]** *I wouldn't like to prophesy **what** will happen to that marriage!*
prophet /ˈprɒf.ɪt/ [US] /ˈprɑː.fɪt/ *noun* **[C]** **1** a person who is believed to have a special power which allows them to say what a god wishes to tell people, especially about things that will happen in the future: *an Old Testament prophet* ○ *Let us hear the words of the prophet Isaiah on the coming of the Prince of Peace.* **2** a person who supports a new system of beliefs and principles: *Rousseau, that great prophet of the modern age*
• **the Prophet** Mohammed, the man who made Islam known to the world through the Koran
• **prophet of doom** *DISAPPROVING* someone who always expects bad things to happen: *The prophets of doom have been predicting the end of European cinema for the last ten years.*
prophetic /prəˈfet.ɪk/ [US] /-ˈfet̬-/ *adj* saying correctly what will happen in the future: *Much of Orwell's writing now seems grimly prophetic.* **prophetically** /prəˈfet.ɪ.kli/ [US] /-ˈfet̬-/ *adv*

prophetess /ˌprɒf.ɪˈtes/ /ˈ---/ [US] /ˈprɑː.fɪ.t̬əs/ *noun* **[C]** a female prophet

prophylactic /ˌprɒf.ɪˈlæk.tɪk/ [US] /ˌprɑː.fɪˈlæk.t̬ɪk/ *adj SPECIALIZED* preventing disease: *Some dentists are convinced that the addition of fluoride in water is ineffective as a prophylactic treatment.*
prophylactic /ˌprɒf.ɪˈlæk.tɪk/ [US] /ˌprɑː.fɪ-/ *noun* **[C]** **1** *SPECIALIZED* something which is intended to prevent disease **2** *MAINLY US* a condom

propitiate /prəˈpɪʃ.i.eɪt/ *verb* **[T]** *FORMAL* to please and make calm a god or person who is annoyed with you: *In those days people might sacrifice a goat or sheep to propitiate an angry god.* ○ *The radicals in the party were*

P

clearly sacked to propitiate the conservative core.
propitiation /prəˌpɪʃ.iˈeɪ.ʃən/ *noun* [U]
propitiatory /prəˌpɪʃ.iˈeɪ.tər.i/ [US] /prəˈpɪʃ.i.ə.tɔːr-/ *adj* *FORMAL* intended to please someone and make them calm: *a propitiatory gesture*

propitious /prəˈpɪʃ.əs/ *adj FORMAL* likely to result in or showing signs of success: *With the economy in the worst recession for thirty years, it was scarcely the most propitious time to start up a company.* **propitiously** /prəˈpɪʃ.ə.sli/ *adv*

proponent /prəˈpəʊ.nənt/ [US] /-ˈpoʊ-/ *noun* [C] a person who speaks publicly in support of a particular idea or plan of action: *He is one of the leading proponents* ***of*** *capital punishment.* ⊃Compare **opponent**.

proportion /prəˈpɔː.ʃən/ [US] /-ˈpɔːr-/ *noun* **1** [C + sing or pl v] the number or amount of a group or part of something when compared to the whole: *Children make up a large proportion* ***of*** *the world's population.* ○ *A higher proportion* ***of*** *women now smoke than used to be the case.* ○ *The report shows that poor families spend a larger proportion* ***of*** *their income on food.* **2** [U] the number, amount or level of one thing when compared to another: *The proportion* ***of*** *women* ***to*** *men at my college was about five to one.* ○ *The chart shows how weight increases* ***in*** *proportion* ***to*** *height* (= the increase in weight depends on the increase in height). ○ *The level of crime in an area is almost always* ***in direct*** *proportion* ***to*** *the number of unemployed.* **3** [C or U] the correct or most attractive relationship between the size of different parts of the same thing or between one thing and another: *Your legs are very much* ***in*** *proportion* ***to*** (= the right size for) *the rest of your body.* ○ *His feet seem very small* ***in*** *proportion* ***to*** *his body.* ○ *My head was much nearer the camera than the rest of me so I'm all* ***out of*** *proportion.* **4** [U] used in a number of phrases to mean importance and seriousness: *You've got to keep a* ***sense of*** *proportion* (= the ability to understand what is important and what is not). ○ *I think a certain amount of worry about work is very natural, but you've got to* ***keep it in*** *proportion* (= judge correctly its seriousness).
• **blow *sth* out of proportion** to treat a particular event or problem far too seriously: *It's ridiculous – we have a tiny disagreement and you blow the whole thing out of proportion!* ○ *Of course, when the papers get hold of a story, it's blown out of* ***all*** *proportion.*
proportioned /prəˈpɔː.ʃənd/ [US] /-ˈpɔːr-/ *adj* having parts of the size or shape that is described: *We wandered through the beautifully proportioned rooms of the Winter Palace.* ○ *She has the dancer's finely proportioned physique.* ○ *HUMOROUS The* ***generously*** *proportioned* (= fat) *singer has to have all his garments specially made.*
proportional /prəˈpɔː.ʃən.əl/ [US] /-ˈpɔːr-/ *adj* (*ALSO* **proportionate**) If two amounts are proportional, they change at the same rate so that the relationship between them does not change: *Weight is proportional* ***to*** *size.*
proportionally /prəˈpɔː.ʃən.əl.i/ [US] /-ˈpɔːr-/ *adv* (*ALSO* **proportionately**) *Unemployment is proportionally much higher in the north of the country.*
proportions /prəˈpɔː.ʃənz/ [US] /-ˈpɔːr-/ *plural noun* the size, shape or level of something: *a building of elegant proportions* ○ *I'm not very good at drawing people – I can never get the proportions right.* ○ *HUMOROUS She's a woman of generous proportions* (= she is fat). ○ *A small worry in the back of your mind can for no apparent reason* ***assume/take on*** *massive proportions in the middle of the night.*

proˌportional representˈation *noun* [U] (*ABBREVIATION* **PR**) a political system in which parties are represented in parliament according to the number of people who voted for them

propose [SUGGEST] /prəˈpəʊz/ [US] /-ˈpoʊz/ *verb* **1** [T] to offer or state a possible plan or action for other people to consider: [+ *that*] *I propose* ***that*** *we wait until the budget has been announced before committing ourselves to any expenditure.* ○ [+ v-*ing*] *He proposed deal****ing*** *directly with the suppliers.* ○ *She proposed a boycott of the meeting.* ○ *He proposed a* ***motion*** *that the chairman resign.* **2** [T] to suggest someone for a position or for membership of an organization: *To be nominated for union president you need one person to propose you and another to second you.* **3** [I] to ask someone to marry you: *I remember the night your father proposed* ***to*** *me.*
• **propose a toast** to ask people gathered at a formal social occasion to express their good wishes or respect for someone by holding up their glasses, usually of alcohol, at the same time and then drinking from them: *Now, if you'd all please raise your glasses, I'd like to propose a toast* ***to*** *the bride and groom.*
proposal /prəˈpəʊ.zəl/ [US] /-ˈpoʊ-/ *noun* [C] **1** a suggestion, sometimes a written one: *Congress has rejected the latest economic proposal* ***put forward*** *by the president.* ○ [+ *to* infinitive] *There has been an angry reaction to the government's proposal* ***to*** *reduce unemployment benefit.* ○ *Have you read Steve's proposals for the new project?* ○ [+ *that*] *There was anger at the proposal* ***that*** *a UN peacekeeping force should be sent to the area.* **2** an offer of marriage
proposer /prəˈpəʊ.zər/ [US] /-ˈpoʊ.zɚ/ *noun* [C] **1** a person who suggests a subject for discussion: *The proposer of the motion tonight is Jonathan Hesk.* **2** a person who suggests someone's name for a position or for membership of an organization
proposition /ˌprɒp.əˈzɪʃ.ən/ [US] /ˌprɑː.pə-/ *noun* **1** [C] an offer or suggestion, usually in business: *He wrote to me last week regarding a business proposition he thought might interest me.* ○ *I've* ***put*** *my proposition* ***to*** *the company director for his consideration.* **2** an idea or opinion: *They were debating the proposition that 'All people are created equal'.*
proposition /ˌprɒp.əˈzɪʃ.ən/ [US] /ˌprɑː.pə-/ *verb* [T] to ask someone with whom you are not having a sexual relationship if they would like to have sex with you: *I was propositioned by a complete stranger.*

COMMON LEARNER ERROR

propose/proposal

Propose and **proposal** are quite formal words that are usually only used when suggesting a plan or idea in politics or business.

The government has proposed a package of measures to cut inflation.

Suggest or **recommend** are the normal words used when suggesting a plan or idea.

As you don't have much time, I suggest you fly to Edinburgh.
~~*As you don't have much time, I propose you fly to Edinburgh.*~~

Propose and **proposal** are not used when you are giving something to someone or asking them to do something with you. The normal words here are 'offer' and 'invite'.

I decided to accept the job offer.
~~*I decided to accept the job proposal.*~~

Propose is not used to talk about the services which are available somewhere. The normal verb here is 'offer'.

Does your resort offer any sporting facilities?
~~*Does your resort propose any sporting facilities?*~~

propose [INTEND] /prəˈpəʊz/ [US] /-ˈpoʊz/ *verb* [T] *FORMAL* to intend to do something: [+ *to* infinitive] *How do you propose* ***to*** *complete the project in such a short time scale?* ○ [+ v-*ing*] *How do you propose tackl****ing*** *this problem?* ○ *I do not propose* ***to*** *reveal details at this stage.* ○ *What we are proposing is a radical change in approach.* **proposed** /prəˈpəʊzd/ [US] /-ˈpoʊzd/ *adj*: *There have been huge demonstrations against the proposed factory closure.*

propound /prəˈpaʊnd/ *verb* [T] *FORMAL* to suggest a theory, belief or opinion for other people to consider: *It was Ptolemy who propounded the theory that the earth was at the centre of the universe.*

proprietor /prəˈpraɪə.tər/ [US] /-t̬ɚ/ *noun* [C] a person who owns a particular type of business, especially a hotel, a shop or a company that makes newspapers: *a hotel/newspaper proprietor*
proprietorial /prəˌpraɪəˈtɔː.ri.əl/ [US] /-ˈtɔːr.i-/ *adj* relating to or like an owner: *He put a proprietorial arm around her.*
proprietary /prəˈpraɪə.tri/ [US] /-ter.i/ *adj* **1** [before n] relating to ownership, or relating to or like an owner: *I just assumed he owned the place – he had a proprietary air about him.* **2** describes goods which are made and sent out by a particular company whose name is on the product: *proprietary medicines*

P

proprietress /prəˈpraɪə.trəs/ [US] /proʊ-/ *noun* [C] *OLD-FASHIONED* a female proprietor

propriety /prəˈpraɪə.ti/ [US] /-ţi/ *noun* [U] ➲See at **proper** SOCIALLY ACCEPTABLE.

propulsion /prəˈpʌl.ʃᵊn/ *noun* ➲See at **propel**.

pro rata /ˌprəʊˈrɑː.tə/ [US] /ˌproʊˈreɪ.ţə/ *adj, adv FORMAL* calculated according to, or as a share of, the fixed rate for a larger total amount: *a pro rata payment/pay increase* ○ *It's £20 000 pro rata, but I'm doing half the full number of hours, so I'll be getting ten thousand.*

prosaic /prəˈzeɪ.ɪk/ *adj FORMAL* lacking interest, imagination and variety; boring: *If only she'd been called 'Camilla' or 'Flavia' instead of the prosaic 'Jane'.* ○ *He asked if I'd got my black eye in a fight – I told him the prosaic truth that I'd banged my head on a door.*

prosciutto /prəˈʃuː.təʊ/ [US] /-ţoʊ/ *noun* [U] Italian HAM (= meat from the shoulder or leg of a pig), served in very thin slices

proscribe /prəʊˈskraɪb/ [US] /proʊ-/ *verb* [T] *FORMAL* (of a government or other authority) to forbid something: *The Broadcasting Act allows ministers to proscribe any channel that offends against good taste and decency.* ○ *The Athletics Federation have banned the runner from future races for using proscribed drugs.* **proscription** /prəʊˈskrɪp.ʃᵊn/ [US] /proʊ-/ *noun* [U]

prose /prəʊz/ [US] /proʊz/ *noun* [U] written language in its ordinary form rather than poetry: *I've always preferred reading prose to poetry.* ➲Compare **verse**.

prosecute [LEGAL] /ˈprɒs.ɪ.kjuːt/ [US] /ˈprɑː.sɪ-/ *verb* [I or T] to officially accuse someone of committing a crime in a court of law, or (of a lawyer) to try to prove that a person accused of committing a crime is guilty of that crime: *Shoplifters will be prosecuted.* ○ *He was prosecuted **for** fraud.* ○ *Any manufacturer who does not conform to the standards could be prosecuted under the Consumers Protection Act, 1987.* ○ *The victim has said that she will not prosecute.* ➲Compare **defend**.

prosecution /ˌprɒs.ɪˈkjuː.ʃᵊn/ [US] /ˌprɑː.sɪ-/ *noun* [C or U] when someone is prosecuted: *A number of the cases have resulted in successful prosecution.* ○ *Doctors guilty of neglect are **liable to** prosecution.*

the prose'cution *group noun* [S] the lawyers in a trial who try to prove that a person accused of committing a crime is guilty of that crime: *His plea of guilty to manslaughter was not accepted by the prosecution.* ○ *The prosecution alleged that he lured the officer to his death by making an emergency call.*

prosecutor /ˈprɒs.ɪ.kjuː.təʳ/ [US] /ˈprɑː.sɪ.kjuː.ţɚ/ *noun* [C] a legal representative who officially accuses someone of committing a crime, especially in a court of law

prosecute [CONTINUE] /ˈprɒs.ɪ.kjuːt/ [US] /ˈprɑː.sɪ-/ *verb* [T] *FORMAL* to continue to take part in a planned group of activities, especially a war: *He seemed convinced that the US would prosecute the war to its end.* **prosecution** /ˌprɒs.ɪˈkjuː.ʃᵊn/ [US] /ˌprɑː.sɪ-/ *noun* [U]

proselytize, *UK USUALLY* **-ise** /ˈprɒs.ᵊl.ɪ.taɪz/ [US] /ˈprɑː.sə.lɪ-/ *verb* [I] *FORMAL DISAPPROVING* to try to persuade someone to change their religious or political beliefs or their way of living to your own: *He was also remarkable for the proselytizing zeal with which he wrote his political pamphlets.* ○ *The television has provided the evangelists with yet another platform for their proselytizing.* **proselytizer**, *UK USUALLY* **-iser** /ˌprɒs.ᵊl.ɪˈtaɪ.zəʳ/ [US] /ˌprɑː.səl.ɪ.taɪ.zɚ/ *noun* [C] *FORMAL*

prospect [POSSIBILITY] /ˈprɒs.pekt/ [US] /ˈprɑː.spekt/ *noun* **1** [C or U] the possibility that something good might happen in the future: *Is there any prospect **of** the weather improving?* ○ *There seems little prospect **of** an end to the dispute.* ○ [+ that] *There's not much prospect **that** this war will be over soon.* ○ *There's **every** prospect **of** success.* **2** [S] the idea of something that will or might happen in the future: *The prospect **of** spending three whole days with her fills me with horror.* ○ *I'm very excited **at the** prospect **of** seeing her again.* ○ *We face the prospect of having to start all over again.* **3** [C] a person who might be chosen, for example as an employee: *We'll be interviewing four more prospects for the posts this afternoon.*

prospects /ˈprɒs.pekts/ [US] /ˈprɑː.spekts/ *plural noun* the possibility of being successful, especially at work: *She's hoping the course will improve her **career** prospects.* ○ *Prospects **of/for** (= Opportunities for) employment remain bleak for most people in the area.*

prospective /prəˈspek.tɪv/ *adj* **prospective buyers/employers/parents, etc.** people who are expected to buy something/employ someone/become a parent, etc: *We've had three sets of prospective buyers looking round the house.*

prospect [SEARCH] /prəˈspekt/ *verb* [I] to search for gold, oil or other valuable substances on or under the surface of the earth: *to prospect **for** oil/gold* **prospector** /prəˈspek.təʳ/ [US] /-ţɚ/ *noun* [C]

prospect [VIEW] /ˈprɒs.pekt/ [US] /ˈprɑː.spekt/ *noun* [C] *FORMAL* a good view of a large land area or of a city: *From the restaurant there was a marvellous prospect **of/over** Sienna and the countryside beyond.*

prospectus /prəˈspek.təs/ *noun* [C] a document giving details of a college, school or business and its activities: *I picked up a really impressive prospectus for Shirley Heath Junior School.*

prosper /ˈprɒs.pəʳ/ [US] /ˈprɑː.spɚ/ *verb* [I] (of a person or a business) to be or become successful, especially financially: *A lot of microchip manufacturing companies prospered at that time.*

prosperity /prɒsˈper.ɪ.ti/ [US] /prɑːˈsper.ə.ţi/ *noun* [U] the state of being successful and having a lot of money: *A country's future prosperity depends, to an extent, upon the quality of education of its people.* ○ *The war was followed by a long period of peace and prosperity.*

prosperous /ˈprɒs.pᵊr.əs/ [US] /ˈprɑː.spɚ-/ *adj* successful, usually by earning a lot of money: *In a prosperous country like this, no one should go hungry.* **prosperously** /ˈprɒs.pᵊr.ə.sli/ [US] /ˈprɑː.spɚ-/ *adv*

prostate (gland) /ˈprɒs.teɪtˌglænd/ [US] /ˈprɑː.steɪt-/ *noun* [C] an organ in male mammals situated near to the penis, which produces a liquid that mixes with and carries sperm: *He has prostate trouble.* ○ *prostate cancer*

prosthesis /ˈprɒs.θiː.sɪs/ [US] /ˈprɑːs-/ *noun* [C] *plural* **prostheses** *SPECIALIZED* an artificial body part, such as an arm, foot or tooth, which replaces a missing part **prosthetic** /prɒsˈθet.ɪk/ [US] /prɑːsˈθeţ-/ *adj*: *a prosthetic hand*

prostitute [PERSON] /ˈprɒs.tɪ.tjuːt/ [US] /ˈprɑː.stɪ.tuːt/ *noun* [C] a person who has sex with someone for money

prostitute *yourself* *verb* [R] *FORMAL* to have sex for money

prostitution /ˌprɒs.tɪˈtjuː.ʃᵊn/ [US] /ˌprɑː.stɪˈtuː-/ *noun* [U] the work of a prostitute: *Poverty drove her to prostitution.*

prostitute [USE BADLY] /ˈprɒs.tɪ.tjuːt/ [US] /ˈprɑː.stɪ.tuːt/ *verb* [T] *FORMAL DISAPPROVING* to use yourself or your abilities or beliefs in a way which does not deserve respect, especially in order to get money: *Some critics say he prostituted his musical skills by going into pop rather than staying with classical music.* ○ [R] *He went to work in Hollywood and was accused of prostituting himself.*

prostrate [LYING] /ˈprɒs.treɪt/ [US] /ˈprɑː.streɪt/ *adj* lying with the face down and arms stretched out, especially in obedience or worship

prostrate *yourself* /prɒsˈtreɪt/ /prəˈstreɪt/ [US] /ˈprɑː.streɪt/ *verb* [R] to lie with the face down and arms stretched out, especially in obedience or worship

prostration /prɒsˈtreɪ.ʃᵊn/ [US] /prɑːˈstreɪ-/ *noun* [C or U]

prostrate [VERY TIRED] /ˈprɒs.treɪt/ [US] /ˈprɑː.streɪt/ *adj* (*ALSO* **prostrated**) having lost all strength or all determination because of an illness or an extremely bad experience: *A woman, prostrate with grief, lay wailing on the ground.*

protagonist [SUPPORTER] /prəˈtæg.ᵊn.ɪst/ *noun* [C] an important supporter of an idea or political system: *Key protagonists **of** the revolution were hunted down and executed.* ➲Compare **antagonist** at **antagonism**.

protagonist [CHARACTER] /prəˈtæg.ᵊn.ɪst/ *noun* [C] *FORMAL* one of the main characters in a story or a play

protean /prəʊˈtiː.ən/ [US] /ˈproʊ.ţi-/ *adj LITERARY* easily and continually changing; VARIABLE: *the protean talents of this comedian*

protease /ˈprəʊ.tiː.eɪz/ [US] /ˈproʊ.t̬i-/ *noun* [C] *SPECIALIZED* an ENZYME which causes proteins to break into smaller pieces

protease inhibitor /ˈprəʊ.ti.eɪz.ɪnˌhɪb.ɪ.təʳ/ [US] /ˈproʊ.t̬i.eɪz.ɪnˌhɪb.ɪ.t̬ɚ/ *noun* [C] *SPECIALIZED* a drug for treating HIV which works by preventing the virus reproducing

protect /prəˈtekt/ *verb* **1** [I or T] to keep someone or something safe from injury, damage or loss: *clothing that protects you **against** the cold* ○ *It's important to protect your skin **from** the harmful effects of the sun.* ○ *Surely the function of the law is to protect everyone's rights.* ○ *Of course the company will act to protect its financial interests in the country if war begins.* ○ *Patients' names have been changed to protect their privacy.* ○ *Public pressure to protect the environment is strong and growing.* ○ *Vitamin C may help protect **against** cancer.* ➲See Note **prevent or protect?** at **prevent**. **2** [T] If a government protects a part of its country's trade or industry, it helps it by taxing goods from other countries. **3** [T] to provide someone with insurance against injury, damages, etc.

protected /prəˈtek.tɪd/ *adj*: *Dolphins are a protected **species*** (= it is illegal to harm or kill them).

protection /prəˈtek.ʃᵊn/ *noun* [U] **1** the act of protecting or state of being protected: *Their flimsy tent **gave/offered** little protection **against** the severe storm.* ○ *Round-the-clock police protection is given to all senior politicians.* ○ *New legislation still does not offer adequate protection **for** many endangered species.* ○ *Always wear goggles as a protection **for** your eyes when using the machines.* ○ *The insurance policy provides protection* (= will make a financial payment) *in case of accidental loss of life or serious injury.* **2** *INFORMAL FOR* **protection money** **3** a CONDOM (= thin rubber covering for the penis) used as a way of preventing pregnancy or the spread of disease: *Did you use any protection?*

protective /prəˈtek.tɪv/ *adj* **1** giving protection: *protective clothing* ○ *a protective mask and goggles* **2** wanting to protect someone from criticism, hurt, danger, etc. because you like them very much: *It's easy to be too protective **towards/of** your children.* ○ *She's fiercely protective **of** the man she married 29 years ago.* **protectively** /prəˈtek.tɪv.li/ *adv*: *He put an arm around her shoulder protectively.* **protectiveness** /prəˈtek.tɪv.nəs/ *noun* [U]

protectionism /prəˈtek.ʃᵊn.ɪ.zᵊm/ *noun* [U] *DISAPPROVING* the actions of a government to help its country's trade or industry by taxing goods bought from other countries **protectionist** /prəˈtek.ʃᵊn.ɪst/ *adj*

protector /prəˈtek.təʳ/ [US] /-t̬ɚ/ *noun* [C] **1** someone who protects someone or something: *Philip II considered himself the protector of the Catholic Church.* ○ *She has a reputation for being an ardent protector of individuals' liberties.* **2** a device that protects someone: *All flat jockeys are required to wear a back and chest protector.*

protectorate /prəˈtek.tᵊr.ət/ [US] /-tɚ-/ *noun* [C] a country which is generally controlled and defended by a more powerful country ➲See Note **prevent** or **protect?** at **prevent**.

proˈtection ˌmoney *noun* [U] money that criminals take from people in exchange for agreeing not to hurt them or damage their property

proˌtective ˈcustody *noun* [U] a safe place, sometimes prison, where someone is kept by the police for their own safety

protégé /ˈprɒt.ə.ʒeɪ/ [US] /ˈprɑː.t̬ə-/ *noun* [C] a young person who is helped and taught by an older and usually famous person: *Shapur's restaurant is full every night as trendy Londoners enjoy the wonders of his young protégé, chef Glyn Fussell.* ➲Compare **mentor**.

protein /ˈprəʊ.tiːn/ [US] /ˈproʊ-/ *noun* [C or U] one of the many substances found in food such as meat, cheese, fish or eggs, that is necessary for the body to grow and be strong

pro tem /ˌprəʊˈtem/ [US] /ˌproʊ-/ *adv, adj* now and for only a short period after; temporarily: *Phil is taking over from David on a pro tem basis.* ○ [after n] *US mayor/president pro tem*

protest /ˈprəʊ.test/ [US] /ˈproʊ-/ *noun* **1** [C or U] a strong complaint expressing disagreement, disapproval or opposition: *Protests have been **made/registered** by many people who would be affected by the proposed changes.* ○ *A formal protest was made by the German team **about** their disqualification from the relay final.* ○ *Conservation groups have united **in** protest **against** the planned new road.* **2** [C] an occasion when people show that they disagree with something by standing somewhere, shouting, carrying signs, etc: *a public protest **against** the war* ○ *a peaceful/violent protest*

• **under protest** If something is done under protest, it is done unwillingly: *I only went to the meeting under protest.*

protest /prəˈtest/ [US] /ˈproʊ.test/ *verb* [I or T] **1** to show that you disagree with something by standing somewhere, shouting, carrying signs, etc: *A big crowd of demonstrators were protesting **against** cuts in health spending.* ○ *US Outside, a group of students were protesting research cuts.* **2** to say something forcefully or complain about something: *A lot of people protested **about** the new working hours.* ○ *They protested bitterly **to** their employers, but to no avail.* ○ [+ that] *A young girl was crying, protesting **that** she didn't want to leave her mother.* ○ *All through the trial he protested his **innocence*** (= strongly said he was not guilty).

• **protest too much** to express an opinion or state a fact so strongly or so often that people start to doubt that you are telling the truth: *She keeps trying to impress on me how she doesn't fancy him but does she protest too much?*

protester, protestor /prəˈtes.təʳ/ [US] /-tɚ/ *noun* [C] someone who shows that they disagree with something by standing somewhere, shouting, carrying signs, etc.

protestation /ˌprɒt.esˈteɪ.ʃᵊn/ [US] /ˌprɑː.t̬esˈteɪ-/ *noun* [C usually pl] *FORMAL* when someone says something forcefully or complains about something: *Ignoring my protestations* (= strong expressions of disagreement), *they went ahead and chopped the tree down.* ○ *Their protestations* (= strong expressions) ***of** loyalty seem rather hollow in view of the way they behaved.*

Protestant /ˈprɒt.ɪ.stᵊnt/ [US] /ˈprɑː.t̬ɪ-/ *noun* [C] a member of the parts of the Christian Church which separated from the Roman Catholic Church during the 16th century **Protestantism** /ˈprɒt.ɪ.stᵊn.tɪ.zᵊm/ [US] /ˈprɑː.t̬ɪ-/ *noun* [U] **Protestant** /ˈprɒt.ɪ.stᵊnt/ [US] /ˈprɑː.t̬ɪ-/ *adj*: *a Protestant minister*

• **the Protestant work ethic** the belief that work is valuable as an activity, as well as for what it produces

ˈprotest ˌmarch *noun* [C] an occasion when people show that they disagree with something by walking somewhere, often shouting and carrying signs, etc.

ˈprotest ˌsong *noun* [C] a song which expresses disapproval, usually about a political subject

prot(o)- /prəʊ.təʊ-/ [US] /proʊ.t̬oʊ-/ *prefix* first, especially from which other similar things develop; original: *protoplasm* ○ *a prototype*

protocol [RULES] /ˈprəʊ.tə.kɒl/ [US] /ˈproʊ.t̬ə.kɑːl/ *noun* [U] the system of rules and acceptable behaviour used at official ceremonies and occasions: *a breach of Royal protocol* ○ *diplomatic protocol*

protocol [AGREEMENT] /ˈprəʊ.tə.kɒl/ [US] /ˈproʊ.t̬ə.kɑːl/ *noun* [C] a formal international agreement: *The Geneva Protocol of 1925 prohibits the use of poisonous gases in war.*

protocol [COMPUTING] /ˈprəʊ.tə.kɒl/ [US] /ˈproʊ.t̬ə.kɑːl/ *noun* [C] *SPECIALIZED* a computer language enabling computers that are connected to each other to communicate

proton /ˈprəʊ.tɒn/ [US] /ˈproʊ.tɑːn/ *noun* [C] a type of ELEMENTARY PARTICLE (= very small piece of matter) which has a positive electrical charge and is found in the nucleus of all atoms ➲Compare **electron**; **neutron**.

protoplasm /ˈprəʊ.tə.plæz.ᵊm/ [US] /ˈproʊ.t̬ə-/ *noun* [U] the transparent liquid which is inside all living cells

prototype /ˈprəʊ.tə.taɪp/ [US] /ˈproʊ.t̬ə-/ *noun* [C] the first example of something, such as a machine or other industrial product, from which all later forms are developed: *a prototype **for/of** a new car*

protozoan /ˌprəʊ.təʊˈzəʊ.ən/ [US] /ˌproʊ.t̬əˈzoʊ-/ *noun* [C] *plural* **protozoans** or **protozoa** *SPECIALIZED* any of various types of very small, usually single-celled animal which do not have a spine: *Amoebas are protozoans.* **protozoan** /ˌprəʊ.təʊˈzəʊ.ən/ [US] /ˌproʊ.t̬əˈzoʊ-/ *adj*

protracted /prəˈtræk.tɪd/ *adj* lasting for a long time or made to last longer: *protracted negotiations* ○ *a protracted argument/discussion* **protract** /prəˈtrækt/ *verb* [T] FORMAL *I have no desire to protract the process.* **protraction** /prəˈtræk.ʃᵊn/ *noun* [U]

protractor /prəˈtræk.təʳ/ *noun* [C] a device used for measuring and drawing angles. It is usually in the form of half a circle made from transparent plastic with degrees marked on it.

protrude /prəˈtruːd/ *verb* [I] to stick out from or through something: *A rotting branch protruded* ***from*** *the swamp like a ghostly arm.* ○ *protruding ears/teeth*
protrusion /prəˈtruː.ʒᵊn/ *noun* [C or U] something that sticks out from a surface, or the act of doing this: *It has a series of protrusions along its back.* ○ *The condition results in weight loss, rapid heart beat and protrusion of the eyes.*

protuberance /prəˈtjuː.bᵊr.ᵊnts/ [US] /-ˈtuː-/ *noun* [C] FORMAL something that sticks out from a surface: *If the plant has been infected you will see dark protuberances along the stems.*
protuberant /prəˈtjuː.bᵊr.ᵊnt/ [US] /-ˈtuː.bɚ-/ *adj* FORMAL sticking out: *He stared at me with blue, slightly protuberant eyes.*

proud [SATISFIED] /praʊd/ *adj* feeling pleasure and satisfaction because you or people connected with you have done or possess something good: *You must be very proud* ***of*** *your son.* ○ *We're particularly proud* ***of*** *our company's environmental record.* ○ *When she received her prize I think I was the proudest parent on the face of the Earth.* ○ [+ **to** infinitive] *I'm very proud* ***to*** *have been involved in this project.* ○ [+ (**that**)] *I was so proud* ***(that)*** *my son had been chosen for the national team.* ➲See also **house-proud**; **pride** SATISFACTION.
• **do *sb* proud 1** UK OLD-FASHIONED to treat someone who is visiting you very well, especially by giving them a lot of food: *We had a lovely tea – Sheila did us proud.* **2** INFORMAL to make someone proud of you by doing something very well: *Once again, the armed forces have done us proud.*
proudly /ˈpraʊd.li/ *adv* in a proud way: *He proudly held out his trophy for us to admire.* ○ *Elaine and Ian Gibson proudly announce the birth of their son, John Maurice.* ○ *There were photographs of all her children proudly displayed on the mantelpiece.*

proud [RESPECTING YOURSELF] /praʊd/ *adj* APPROVING having or showing self-respect: *We Albanians are a proud people.* ○ *He might be poor but he's also proud, and he won't be pushed around by anyone.* ➲See also **pride** RESPECT FOR YOURSELF. **proudly** /ˈpraʊd.li/ *adv*

proud [FEELING IMPORTANT] /praʊd/ *adj* DISAPPROVING feeling that you are better and more important than other people: *Come on, admit you're wrong and don't be so proud.* ○ *She knows she's lost, but she's* ***too*** *proud* ***to*** *admit it.* ➲See also **pride** FEELING OF IMPORTANCE. **proudly** /ˈpraʊd.li/ *adv*

proud [STICKING OUT] /praʊd/ *adj, adv* MAINLY UK SPECIALIZED sticking out from the surrounding area: *Sand the surface with abrasive paper until no flakes of paint stand proud* ***of*** *the surface.*

prove [SHOW] /pruːv/ *verb* [T; L only + adj or n] **proved, proved,** MAINLY US **proven 1** to show a particular result after a period of time: *The operation proved a complete success.* ○ *The dispute over the song rights proved impossible to resolve.* ○ [L (+ **to be**)] *The new treatment has proved* ***to be*** *a disaster.* **2 prove yourself** to show that you are good at something: *I wish he'd stop trying to prove himself all the time.*

prove [TRUE] /pruːv/ *verb* [T] **proved, proved,** MAINLY US **proven** ➲See at **proof** SHOWING TRUTH.

provenance /ˈprɒv.ᵊn.ənts/ [US] /ˈprɑː.vᵊn-/ *noun* [U] FORMAL the place of origin of something: *jewels of uncertain provenance* ○ *This raised doubts about the provenance of the painting.* ○ *I don't need to see a label to identify the provenance of a garment that someone is wearing.*

proverb /ˈprɒv.ɜːb/ [US] /ˈprɑː.vɝːb/ *noun* [C] a short sentence, etc., usually known by many people, stating something commonly experienced or giving advice: *The appetite, says the proverb, grows with eating.* ○ [+ **that**] *There is an old Arab proverb* ***that*** *everything you write or speak should pass through three gates: Is this kind? Is this necessary? Is this true?*
proverbial /prəˈvɜː.bi.əl/ [US] /-ˈvɝː-/ *adj* **1** as used in a proverb or other phrase: *He's got to pull the proverbial finger out.* **2** well known: *his proverbial good humour* **proverbially** /prəˈvɜː.bi.ə.li/ [US] /-ˈvɝː-/ *adv*

provide [SUPPLY] /prəˈvaɪd/ *verb* [T] to give someone something that they need: *This booklet provides useful information about local services.* ○ *All meals are provided throughout the course.* ○ *The author provides no documentary references to support her assertions.* ○ *We have concerns about whether the government will be able to provide viable social services* ***for*** *poorer families/ provide poorer families* ***with*** *viable social services.* ○ *Putting more police on patrol doesn't provide a real solution to the problem of increasing violence.*
provider /prəˈvaɪ.dəʳ/ [US] /-dɚ/ *noun* [C] someone who provides something: *an Internet service provider* ○ *The bank is now a major provider of financial services to industry.* ○ *Until her illness she was the main provider* (= earned most of the money) *in the family.*
provision /prəˈvɪʒ.ᵊn/ *noun* [C or U] **1** when something is provided: ***The*** *provision* ***of*** *good public transport will be essential for developing the area.* ○ *Of course there's provision in the plan* ***for*** *population increase.* ○ *When designing buildings in this area, you have to* ***make*** *provision* ***against*** *earthquakes.* ➲See also **provisions**. **2 make provision for *sth*** to make arrangements to deal with something, often financial arrangements: *He hasn't made any provision for his retirement yet.*

COMMON LEARNER ERROR

provide with

Remember to use the preposition 'with' in the phrase '**provide** someone **with** something'.

Could you provide us with a list of hotels in the area?
~~*Could you provide us a list of hotels in the area?*~~

provide [LAW] /prəˈvaɪd/ *verb* [+ **that**] FORMAL (of a law or decision) to state that something must happen if particular conditions exist: *Section 17 provides* ***that*** *all decisions must be circulated in writing.*
provision /prəˈvɪʒ.ᵊn/ *noun* [C] a statement within an agreement or a law that a particular thing must happen or be done, especially before another can be: *We have inserted certain provisions into the treaty to safeguard foreign workers.* ○ [+ **that**] *She accepted the job with the provision* ***that*** *she would be paid expenses for relocating.*

PHRASAL VERBS WITH **provide** ▼

▲ **provide against *sth*** *phrasal verb* FORMAL to make plans in order to prevent or deal with a bad situation: *Beach operators do not have a legal obligation to provide against injury or drowning.*
▲ **provide for *sb*** [LOOK AFTER] *phrasal verb* to give someone the things they need such as money, food or clothes: *He has a wife and two young children to provide for.*
▲ **provide for *sth*** [PLAN FOR] *phrasal verb* **1** to make plans in order to deal with a possible event in the future: *We must provide for depreciation when calculating the costs.* **2** FORMAL If a law or agreement provides for something, it allows it to happen or exist: *Current legislation provides for the detention of those suspected of terrorism.*

proˈvided (that) *conjunction* (ALSO **providing (that)**) if, or only if: *He's welcome to come along, provided that he behaves himself.*

providence /ˈprɒv.ɪ.dᵊnts/ [US] /ˈprɑː.və-/ *noun* [U] an influence which is not human in origin and is thought to control whether or not people receive the things which they need: *divine providence*

provident /ˈprɒv.ɪ.dᵊnt/ [US] /ˈprɑː.və-/ *adj* FORMAL APPROVING making arrangements for future needs, especially by saving money **providently** /ˈprɒv.ɪ.dᵊnt.li/ [US] /ˈprɑː.və-/ *adv*

providential /ˌprɒv.ɪˈden.tʃᵊl/ [US] /ˌprɑː.və-/ *adj FORMAL* happening exactly when needed but without being planned: *a providential opportunity* **providentially** /ˌprɒv.ɪˈden.tʃᵊl.i/ [US] /ˌprɑː.və-/ *adv*

province [REGION] /ˈprɒv.ɪnts/ [US] /ˈprɑː.vɪnts/ *noun* [C] an area which is governed as part of a country or an empire: *the Canadian province of Alberta* **provincial** /prəˈvɪn.tʃᵊl/ *adj*: *provincial governments* ➲See also **provincial** at **the provinces**.

province [SUBJECT] /ˈprɒv.ɪnts/ [US] /ˈprɑː.vɪnts/ *noun SLIGHTLY FORMAL* **sb's province** a subject or activity of special interest, knowledge or responsibility: *Renaissance art is not really his province – he specializes in the modern period.* ○ *Marketing is within the province **of** the sales department.*

the provinces *plural noun* the parts of a country that are not the capital city

provincial /prəˈvɪn.tʃᵊl/ *noun* [C] *MAINLY DISAPPROVING* a person who comes from somewhere in a country outside its capital city

provincial /prəˈvɪn.tʃᵊl/ *adj* **1** in or from the parts of the country that are not the capital city: *The majority of young professionals in the capital have moved there from provincial towns.* ➲See also **provincial** at **province** REGION. **2** *DISAPPROVING* having attitudes and ideas which are old fashioned and simple: *provincial attitudes*

provincialism /prəˈvɪn.tʃᵊl.ɪ.zᵊm/ *noun* [U] *DISAPPROVING*

ˈproving ˌground *noun* [C usually sing] a situation or place where something such as a new theory or machine can be tested

provision /prəˈvɪʒ.ᵊn/ *noun* ➲See at **provide** SUPPLY; LAW

provisional /prəˈvɪʒ.ᵊn.ᵊl/ *adj* for the present time but likely to change; temporary: *a provisional government* ○ *These dates are only provisional.* **provisionally** /prəˈvɪʒ.ᵊn.ᵊl.i/ *adv*: *Club members have provisionally agreed to the changes.*

proˌvisional ˈlicence *UK noun* [C] (*US* **learner's permit**) an official document which a person has to have when they are learning to drive

provisions /prəˈvɪʒ.ᵊnz/ *plural noun* supplies of food and other necessary things: *provisions for the journey*

provision /prəˈvɪʒ.ᵊn/ *verb* [T] *FORMAL* to supply with food and other necessary things

proviso /prəˈvaɪ.zəʊ/ [US] /-zoʊ/ *noun* [C] *plural* **provisos** a statement in an agreement, saying that a particular thing must happen before another can: [+ that] *He was released from prison **with/on** the proviso **that** he doesn't leave the country.*

provoke [ANGER] /prəˈvəʊk/ [US] /-ˈvoʊk/ *verb* [T] to make or try to make a person or an animal angry: *It was a vicious-looking dog and I didn't want to provoke it.* ○ *He was clearly trying to get at me but I refused to be provoked.* ○ *I was provoked **into** the argument.*

provocation /ˌprɒv.əˈkeɪ.ʃᵊn/ [US] /ˌprɑː.və-/ *noun* [C or U] an action or statement that is intended to make someone angry: *He'd fly into a rage **at the slightest** provocation.*

provocative /prəˈvɒk.ə.tɪv/ [US] /-ˈvɑː.kə.t̬ɪv/ *adj* **1** causing an angry reaction, usually intentionally: *a provocative question/remark* ○ *In a deliberately provocative speech, she criticised the whole system of government.* **2** If behaviour or clothing is provocative, it is intended to cause sexual desire: *She slowly leaned forward in a provocative way.*

provocatively /prəˈvɒk.ə.tɪv.li/ [US] /-ˈvɑː.kə.t̬ɪv-/ *adv*: *She dresses very provocatively* (= intending to cause sexual desire).

provoke [CAUSE REACTION] /prəˈvəʊk/ [US] /-ˈvoʊk/ *verb* [T] to cause a reaction, especially a negative one: *The prospect of increased prices has already provoked an outcry.* ○ *Test results provoked worries that the reactor could overheat.*

provocative /prəˈvɒk.ə.tɪv/ [US] /-ˈvɑː.kə.t̬ɪv/ *adj* causing thought about interesting subjects: *The programme will take a detailed and provocative look at the problem of homelessness.* **provocatively** /prəˈvɒk.ə.tɪv.li/ [US] /-ˈvɑː.kə.t̬ɪv-/ *adv*

provost /ˈprɒv.əst/ [US] /ˈprɑː.vəst/ *noun* [C] **1** *UK* (in some universities) the person in charge of a particular college: *the Provost of King's College, Cambridge* **2** *US* an important official who helps to run a college or university

prow /praʊ/ *noun* [C] the front part of a boat or ship

prowess /ˈpraʊ.es/ *noun* [U] *SLIGHTLY FORMAL* great ability or skill: *athletic/sporting prowess* ○ *He's always boasting about his **sexual** prowess.*

prowl /praʊl/ *verb* [I or T] to move around quietly in a place trying not to be seen or heard, such as when hunting: *There have been reports of a masked man prowling in the neighbourhood.* ○ *At night, adult scorpions prowl the desert **for*** (= trying to catch) *insects.* ○ *INFORMAL Unable to sleep, he prowled* (= walked without purpose) ***(about/around)*** *the hotel corridors.*

prowl /praʊl/ **be on the prowl** to be moving around quietly in a place trying not to be seen or heard: *There was a fox on the prowl earlier.*

prowler /ˈpraʊ.ləʳ/ [US] /-lɚ/ *noun* [C] someone who moves around quietly in a place, trying not to be seen, often before committing a crime

proximity /prɒkˈsɪm.ɪ.ti/ [US] /prɑːkˈsɪm.ə.t̬i/ *noun* [U] *FORMAL* the state of being near in space or time: *The best thing about the location of the house is its proximity **to** the town centre.*

proxy /ˈprɒk.si/ [US] /ˈprɑːk-/ *noun* [C or U] authority given to a person to act for someone else, such as by voting for them in an election, or the person who this authority is given to: *a proxy vote* ○ *My brother's voting for me **by** proxy in the club elections.* ○ *Can I nominate someone as a proxy to sign for me?*

Prozac /ˈprəʊ.zæk/ [US] /ˈproʊ-/ *noun* [U] *TRADEMARK* a drug which is used to treat DEPRESSION (= a mental illness that makes you feel extremely unhappy) and ANXIETY (= a mental illness that makes you feel very worried)

prude /pruːd/ *noun* [C] *DISAPPROVING* a person who is easily shocked by rude things, especially those of a sexual type: *Don't be such a prude.* **prudish** /ˈpruː.dɪʃ/ *adj*: *I don't consider myself prudish but I do think the sex scenes in the film were a bit excessive.* **prudishly** /ˈpruː.dɪʃ.li/ *adv* **prudishness** /ˈpruː.dɪʃ.nəs/ *noun* [U] (*ALSO* **prudery**)

prudent /ˈpruː.dᵊnt/ *adj SLIGHTLY FORMAL* avoiding risks and uncertainties; careful: [+ to infinitive] ***It's** always prudent **to** read a contract properly before signing it.* * NOTE: The opposite is **imprudent**. **prudently** /ˈpruː.dᵊnt.li/ *adv* **prudence** /ˈpruː.dᵊnts/ *noun* [U] *The firm was commended for its financial prudence.*

prune [CUT] /pruːn/ *verb* [T] **1** to cut off branches from a tree, bush or plant, especially so that it will grow better in future: *She spent the afternoon pruning roses.* **2** to reduce something by removing things which are not necessary: *Arco has reacted to the loss in revenue by pruning **(back)** its expansion plans.* ○ *I felt his essay needed a little pruning.*

prune [FRUIT] /pruːn/ *noun* [C] a dried PLUM

ˈpruning ˌshears *plural noun US* SECATEURS (= a tool for pruning)

prurient /ˈprʊə.ri.ənt/ [US] /ˈprʊr.i-/ *adj FORMAL DISAPPROVING* too interested in the details of another person's sexual behaviour: *He denied that the article had been in any way prurient.* **pruriently** /ˈprʊə.ri.ənt.li/ [US] /ˈprʊr.i-/ *adv*: *Newspapers often delve pruriently into people's private lives.* **prurience** /ˈprʊə.ri.ənts/ [US] /ˈprʊr.i-/ *noun* [U]

prussic acid /ˌprʌs.ɪkˈæs.ɪd/ *noun* [U] *OLD-FASHIONED* a very poisonous acid, a type of CYANIDE

pry [ASK QUESTIONS] /praɪ/ *verb* [I] *DISAPPROVING* to try to obtain private facts about a person: *As a reporter, I was paid to pry **into** other people's lives.* ○ *I hope you don't think I'm prying, but has your boyfriend ever lived with anyone before?* ○ *She wanted a private holiday **away from** prying **eyes*** (= where no one would be trying to see her).

pry [OPEN] /praɪ/ *verb* [T] *MAINLY US* to move or lift something by pressing a tool against a fixed point: [+ adj] *The car trunk had been pried **open** and all her equipment was gone.*

PS /ˌpiːˈes/ *noun* [C] used when you want to add extra information at the end of a letter or email: *Love from Sophie. PS Say hi to Gemma.* ○ *She **added** a PS asking for your address.*

psalm /sɑːm/ *noun* [C] a holy poem or song, especially one of the 150 grouped together in the Bible

pseud /suːd/ *noun* [C] *UK INFORMAL DISAPPROVING* a person who tries to seem to have detailed knowledge or excellent judgment of a subject, especially in art, literature, music, etc: *He's such a pseud, with his talk of 'lambent harmonies' and 'melting arpeggios'.* **pseudy** /ˈsuː.di/ *adj*: *I have to say, I don't have much time for the pseudy vocabulary of wine snobs.*

pseud(o)- /suː.dəʊ/ [US] /-doʊ/ *prefix MAINLY DISAPPROVING* not real; pretended: *pseudo-religious* ○ *a pseudo-intellectual*

pseudonym /ˈsuː.də.nɪm/ *noun* [C] a name which a person, such as a writer, uses instead of their real name, especially on their work: *She writes* ***under*** *a pseudonym.* ○ *George Orwell was a pseudonym – his real name was Eric Blair.* **pseudonymous** /suːˈdɒn.ɪ.məs/ [US] /-ˈdɑː.nɪ-/ *adj SPECIALIZED pseudonymous literature*

pseudo-science /ˈsuː.dəʊ.saɪənts/ [US] /-doʊ-/ *noun* [C usually sing] a system of thought or a theory which is not formed in a scientific way

psoriasis /səˈraɪə.sɪs/ *noun* [U] a disease in which areas of skin turn red and are covered with small dry pieces of skin

psst /pst/ *exclamation* a sound made to get someone's attention, especially without other people noticing: *Psst, what's the time?*

psych /saɪk/ *verb*

PHRASAL VERBS WITH **psych** ▼

▲ **psych** ***sb*** **out** *phrasal verb* [M] *INFORMAL* to behave in a very confident or forceful way in order to make a competitor, especially in a sports event, feel less confident: *Both athletes were trying to psych each other out before the race.*

▲ **psych** ***yourself*** **up** *phrasal verb* [R] *INFORMAL* to try to make yourself feel confident and ready to do something difficult: *I have to spend a little time on my own before I give a speech, psyching myself up.*

psyche /ˈsaɪ.ki/ *noun* [C usually sing] the mind, or the deepest thoughts, feelings or beliefs of a person or group: *the male psyche* ○ *Peru is a very traditional country, and embedded in its psyche is a love of ceremony.*

psychedelic /ˌsaɪ.kəˈdel.ɪk/ *adj* **1** (of a drug) causing effects on the mind, such as feelings of deep understanding or seeing strong images: *psychedelic drugs* **2** Psychedelic art or clothing has bright colours and strange patterns of a type which might be experienced by taking psychedelic drugs.

psychiˈatric ˌhospital *noun* [C] a place where people who are mentally ill stay and receive treatment

psychiatry /saɪˈkaɪə.tri/ *noun* [U] the part of medicine which studies mental illness ➲Compare **psychology**. **psychiatric** /ˌsaɪ.kiˈæt.rɪk/ *adj*: *psychiatric treatment* ○ *a psychiatric patient* ○ *the hospital's psychiatric unit* **psychiatrically** /ˌsaɪ.kiˈæt.rɪk.li/ *adv* **psychiatrist** /saɪˈkaɪə.trɪst/ /sɪ-/ *noun* [C] a doctor who is also trained in psychiatry

psychic [KNOWING] /ˈsaɪ.kɪk/ *adj* having a special mental ability, for example so that you are able to know what will happen in the future or know what people are thinking: *psychic powers* **psychic** /ˈsaɪ.kɪk/ *noun* [C] *a gifted psychic* (= person with these abilities) **psychical** /ˈsaɪ.kɪk.əl/ *adj* [before n] *The Society for Psychical Research is investigating reports of a ghost at the old vicarage.* **psychically** /ˈsaɪ.kɪk.li/ *adv*

psychic [MENTAL] /ˈsaɪ.kɪk/ *adj* (especially of an illness) of the mind rather than the body: *psychic problems* **psychically** /ˈsaɪ.kɪk.li/ *adv*

psycho /ˈsaɪ.kəʊ/ [US] /-koʊ/ *noun* [C] *plural* **psychos** *INFORMAL* someone who is crazy and frightening: *The man's a psycho.* **psycho** /ˈsaɪ.kəʊ/ [US] /-koʊ/ *adj*: *He suddenly* ***went*** *psycho and started shooting in all directions.*

psych(o)- /saɪ.kəʊ/ [US] /-koʊ/ *prefix* of the mind or mental processes: *psychopharmacology* (= the study of drugs which affect the mind)

psychoanalysis /ˌsaɪ.kəʊ.əˈnæl.ə.sɪs/ [US] /-koʊ-/ *noun* [U] any of a number of the theories of the human personality, which attempt to examine a person's unconscious mind to discover the hidden causes of their mental problems: *Sigmund Freud is known as the father of psychoanalysis.* **psychoanalyse** *UK, US* **psychoanalyze** /ˌsaɪ.kəʊˈæn.əl.aɪz/ [US] /-koʊ-/ *verb* [T] to examine someone or treat them using psychoanalysis **psychoanalyst** /ˌsaɪ.kəʊˈæn.əl.ɪst/ [US] /-koʊ-/ *noun* [C] (*ALSO* **analyst**) **psychoanalytic** /ˌsaɪ.kəʊˈæn.əl.ɪ.tɪk/ [US] /-koʊˈæn.əl.ɪ.t̬ɪk/ *adj* relating to psychoanalysis

psychobabble /ˈsaɪ.kəʊˌbæb.l̩/ [US] /-koʊ-/ *noun* [U] *INFORMAL DISAPPROVING* language using lots of words and expressions taken from psychology

psychokinesis /ˌsaɪ.kəʊ.kɪˈniː.sɪs/ [US] /-koʊ-/ *noun* [U] changing the state or position of a physical object, using only the power of the mind **psychokinetic** /ˌsaɪ.kəʊ.kɪˈnet.ɪk/ [US] /-koʊ.kɪˈnet̬-/ *adj*

psychoˌlogical ˈmoment *noun* [S] the time when something is most likely to be accepted: *They chose the right psychological moment to announce the plans.*

psychoˌlogical ˈprofile *noun* [C] (*SPECIALIZED* **offender profile**) a description of the likely character, behaviour and interests of a violent criminal which is based on evidence collected from the place where a crime was committed **psychoˌlogical ˈprofiling** *noun* [U] (*SPECIALIZED* **offender profiling**)

psychoˌlogical ˈwarfare *noun* [U] the use of activities which cause fear and anxiety in the people you want to influence without hurting them physically

psychology /saɪˈkɒl.ə.dʒi/ [US] /-ˈkɑː.lə-/ *noun* [U] the scientific study of the way the human mind works and how it influences behaviour, or the influence of a particular person's character on their behaviour: *She studied psychology at Harvard.* ○ *a lecturer in psychology* ○ *child psychology* ○ *the psychology* ***of*** *the soldier* ➲Compare **psychiatry**. **psychological** /ˌsaɪ.kəlˈɒdʒ.ɪ.kəl/ [US] /-kəˈlɑː.dʒɪ-/ *adj* **1** relating to the human mind and feelings: *psychological problems* ○ *He claims that the constant aircraft noise has a bad psychological effect on the residents.* ○ *We are concerned with the physical and psychological well-being of our employees.* **2** (of an illness or other physical problem) caused by anxiety or sadness: *I suspect his headaches are purely psychological.* **psychologically** /ˌsaɪ.kəlˈɒdʒ.ɪ.kli/ [US] /-kəˈlɑː.dʒɪ-/ *adv*: *psychologically disturbed* **psychologist** /saɪˈkɒl.ə.dʒɪst/ [US] /-ˈkɑː.lə-/ *noun* [C] someone who studies the human mind and human emotions and behaviour, and how different situations have an effect on them: *a child psychologist* ○ *an educational psychologist* ○ *She spent 15 years as a* ***clinical*** *psychologist with the Northumberland Health Authority.*

psychopath /ˈsaɪ.kə.pæθ/ *noun* [C] **1** (*INFORMAL* **psycho**) someone who is very mentally ill and dangerous **2** *SPECIALIZED* in psychology, a person who has no feeling for other people, does not think about the future and does not feel bad about anything they have done in the past **psychopathic** /ˌsaɪ.kəˈpæθ.ɪk/ *adj* (*INFORMAL* **psycho**) *A series of unsolved murders on the island has raised fears that a psychopathic serial killer is on the loose.*

psychopathology /ˌsaɪ.kəʊ.pəˈθɒl.ə.dʒi/ [US] /-koʊ.pəˈθɑː.lə-/ *noun* [U] the study of mental diseases: *She's doing an MPhil in psychopathology.*

psychosis /saɪˈkəʊ.sɪs/ [US] /-ˈkoʊ-/ *noun* [C or U] *plural* **psychoses** any of a number of the more severe mental diseases that make you believe things that are not real: *She fell into a drug-induced psychosis.* **psychotic** /saɪˈkɒt.ɪk/ [US] /-ˈkɑː.t̬ɪk/ *adj* suffering from psychosis: *a psychotic disorder* ○ *His dislike of women bordered on the psychotic.*

psychosomatic /ˌsaɪ.kəʊ.səˈmæt.ɪk/ [US] /-koʊ.soʊˈmæt̬-/ *adj* (of an illness) caused by anxiety and worry and not by an infection or injury: *a psychosomatic illness*

psychotherapy /ˌsaɪ.kəʊˈθer.ə.pi/ [US] /-koʊ-/ *noun* [U] the treatment of mental illness by discussing the problems which caused it with the sufferer, instead of using drugs or operations

P

psychotherapist /ˌsaɪ.kəˈθer.ə.pɪst/ *noun* [C] someone who gives people psychotherapy: *He sees a psychotherapist twice a week.*

pt [PART] *noun* [C] *WRITTEN ABBREVIATION FOR* part, when referring to a section of a document: *See pt 3 for further details.*

pt [MEASUREMENT] *noun* [C] *WRITTEN ABBREVIATION FOR* **pint**: *Add 1 pt of water and bring to the boil.*

pt [PLACE] *WRITTEN ABBREVIATION FOR* **point** PIECE OF LAND: *Spurn Pt*

pt [POINT] *noun* [C] *WRITTEN ABBREVIATION FOR* **point** UNIT: *He needs a good high jump to score more than 9000 pts.*

PTA /ˌpiː.tiːˈeɪ/ *noun* [C] *ABBREVIATION FOR* **parent-teacher association**: *a PTA meeting*

pterodactyl /ˌter.əˈdæk.tɪl/ [US] /-təl/ *noun* [C] a very large flying animal that lived many millions of years ago

PTO [INSTRUCTION] /ˌpiː.tiːˈəʊ/ [US] /-ˈoʊ/ *ABBREVIATION FOR* please turn over: written at the bottom of a page to show that there is more information on the other side

PTO [ORGANIZATION] /ˌpiː.tiːˈəʊ/ [US] /-ˈoʊ/ *noun* [C] *MAINLY US ABBREVIATION FOR* **parent-teacher organization** ➲See **parent-teacher association**.

Pty *adj* [after n] *ABBREVIATION FOR* **Proprietary**, used in the names of private companies in Australia, New Zealand and South Africa whose owners are responsible for only a limited amount of the companies' debts: *Mackenzie Investments Pty*

pub *UK* /pʌb/ *noun* [C] (*FORMAL* **public house**) a building in Britain where alcoholic drinks can be bought and drunk and where food is often available: *Do you want to **go to/** (INFORMAL) **go down** the pub after work?* ○ *our local pub* ○ *a pub lunch.* ➲See also **publican**; **local** PUB.

ˈpub ˌcrawl *noun* [C] *UK INFORMAL* a visit to several pubs, one after the other, having a drink or drinks at each one: *We **went on** a pub crawl on Saturday night.*

pube /pjuːb/ *noun* [C often pl] *INFORMAL* one of the short curly hairs which grow around the sexual organs on the outside of the body of a person who is old enough to reproduce

puberty /ˈpjuː.bə.ti/ [US] /-bɚ.t̬i/ *noun* [U] the stage in a person's life when they develop from a child into an adult because of changes in their body that make them able to have children: ***At** puberty, pubic hair develops and girls begin to menstruate.*

pubescent /pjuːˈbes.ənt/ *adj* describes someone who is at the stage in their life when they are developing from a child into an adult and becoming able to have children: *pubescent girls/boys*

ˈpub ˌgrub *noun* [U] *UK INFORMAL* meals that are served in a pub

pubic /ˈpjuː.bɪk/ *adj* [before n] of or near the sexual organs on the outside of a person's body: *pubic **hair*** ○ *the pubic area*

public [PEOPLE] /ˈpʌb.lɪk/ *adj* relating to or involving people in general, rather than being limited to a particular group of people: *Public opinion* (= the opinions of most people) *has turned against him.* ○ *Is it really **in the** public **interest*** (= useful to people) *to publish this information?* ○ *We need to increase public **awareness** of the disease.* ○ *Peaceful demonstrations that do not cause a public **nuisance*** (= do not harm other people) *are a fundamental right in any truly democratic country.* ○ *The government has had to bow to public **pressure** on the issue.* ○ *The information only became public after his death.* ○ *The results will not be **made** public* (= told to everyone) *until tomorrow.* ○ *We will not **go** public **with*** (= tell people in general) *the results until tomorrow.*

• **be in the public eye** to be famous and written about in newspapers and magazines and seen on television

• **public enemy number one/No. 1** someone or something that many people do not like or approve of

the public *group noun* [S] all ordinary people: *The public has a right to know about this.* ○ *The palace and its grounds are **open to** the public* (= people can visit) *during the summer months.* ○ *When will the product be available to the **general** public* (= all ordinary people)*?* ○ ***Members of** the public were asked about their shopping habits.*

public /ˈpʌb.lɪk/ *group noun* [U] **1** the group of people who are involved with you or your organization, especially in a business relationship: *Newspapers publish these outrageous stories because they know what their public wants.* **2 in public** in a place where people can see you: *I'd never behave like that in public.* ➲Compare **in private** at **private** PERSONAL.

publicly /ˈpʌb.lɪ.kli/ *adv* If something is done publicly, it is done so that everyone can know about it: *The company publicly apologized and agreed to contribute some money to charity.* ○ *He certainly wouldn't stand for being publicly **humiliated** like that.*

public [GOVERNMENT] /ˈpʌb.lɪk/ *adj* provided by the government from taxes to be available to everyone: *public funds/services/spending* ○ *public buildings* ○ *a public library* ○ *She works in **the** public **sector*** (= for a government organization). ○ *He is unlikely to **hold** public **office*** (= have an important job in national or local government). **publicly** /ˈpʌb.lɪ.kli/ *adv*: *The new railway will not be publicly **funded**.*

public [PLACE] /ˈpʌb.lɪk/ *adj* describes a place where a lot of people are: *It's too public here – let's go back to my room to talk.*

ˌpublic adˈdress ˌsystem *noun* [C] (*ABBREVIATION* **PA**) equipment for making sound louder in a public place

publican /ˈpʌb.lɪ.kən/ *noun* [C] *UK* the manager of a pub

publication /ˌpʌb.lɪˈkeɪ.ʃən/ *noun* **1** [U] the act of making information or stories available to people in a printed form: *The brochure will be ready for publication in September.* ○ *Will you arrange the publication **of** the names of the winners?* ○ *When is the publication **date*** (= When will the book be available to buy)*?* ➲See also **publish**. **2** [C] a book, magazine, newspaper or document in which information or stories are published: *Our latest publication is a magazine for health enthusiasts.*

ˌpublic ˈbar *noun* [C] a drinking room in a pub with plainer furniture and sometimes lower prices than in the other drinking rooms

ˌpublic ˈcompany *noun* [C] a business which is owned by many people who have bought shares in it

ˌpublic conˈvenience *noun* [C] *MAINLY UK FORMAL* a building containing toilets that are available for everyone to use

the ˌpublic doˈmain *noun* **be in the public domain** If something such as a book, song, computer program, etc. is in the public domain, no one has the right to control its use and anyone may use it without charge.

ˌpublic doˈmain *adj* [before n] not secret; able to be known about or used by anyone: *public domain software*

ˌpublic ˈfigure *noun* [C] someone who is famous because of what they do, and is written about in newspapers and magazines or is often on television or the radio

ˌpublic ˈholiday *noun* [C] a day when almost everyone in a particular country does not have to go to work or school: *New Year's Day is a public holiday in many countries.*

ˌpublic ˈhouse *noun* [C] *UK FORMAL FOR* **pub**

ˌpublic ˈhousing *noun* [U] *US FOR* **council housing**

publicity /pʌbˈlɪs.ɪ.ti/ [US] /-ə.t̬i/ *noun* [U] the activity of making certain that someone or something attracts a lot of interest or attention from many people, or the attention received as a result of this activity: *He attracted a lot of **adverse/bad** publicity with his speech about unmarried mothers.* ○ *Her first novel was published last year **in a blaze of*** (= with a lot of) *publicity.* ○ *We have planned an exciting publicity **campaign** with our advertisers.* ○ *The publicity **generated** by the court case has given a welcome boost to our sales.* ○ *The normally publicity-**shy** director will be making several public appearances for the launch of the movie.* ○ *The enormous publicity surrounding the case will make it very difficult to hold a fair trial.* ○ *The pop group's arrival by hot-air balloon was just a publicity **stunt*** (= an unusual way of attracting the public's attention).

• **Any publicity is good publicity.** (*ALSO* **There's no such thing as bad publicity.**) *SAYING* said to emphasize that it is better that something receives bad publicity than no publicity at all

P

publicist /ˈpʌb.lɪ.sɪst/ *noun* [C] someone who arranges publicity for a person or organization by giving information to reporters and broadcasters and arranging public meetings and special events

publicize, *UK USUALLY* **-ise** /ˈpʌb.lɪ.saɪz/ *verb* [T] to make information about something generally available: *Attitudes seem to be changing as a result of recent* ***highly*** *publicized* ***cases*** *of sexual harassment.* ○ *The event was* ***well*** *publicized all over town.* ○ *The work of the charity has been* ***widely*** *publicized throughout the media.*

ˌpublic ˈlibrary *noun* [C] a building where people can read or borrow books without having to pay

ˌpublic ˈprosecutor *noun* [C] *LEGAL* a lawyer who acts for the government against a criminal in court

the ˌpublic ˈpurse *noun* [S] *MAINLY UK* money from the government: *People should provide for their own retirement and not expect to be supported by the public purse.*

ˌpublic reˈlations *noun* [U] (*ABBREVIATION* **PR**) the activity of keeping good relationships between an organization and the people outside it: *Environmentalists attacked the company's ad as a public-relations* ***exercise****.*

ˌpublic ˈschool [EXPENSIVE SCHOOL] *noun* [C or U] in England, an expensive type of PRIVATE SCHOOL (= school paid for by parents not by the government)

USAGE

public schools

In England, schools provided by the government, where people do not have to pay, are called **state schools**. The term **public school** describes very expensive schools of a high academic standard which are for the children of very rich people often of a high social class. **Private school** or **independent school** are more general terms for schools where people have to pay.

In the US, Scotland and Australia, **public schools** are free schools provided by the government.

ˌpublic ˈschool [FREE SCHOOL] *noun* [C or U] *US* in Scotland, Australia and the US, a free school provided by the government

ˌpublic ˈservant *noun* [C] a government employee

public-spirited /ˌpʌb.lɪkˈspɪr.ɪ.tɪd/ Ⓤⓢ /-t̬ɪd/ *adj APPROVING* wanting to help people generally: *You pick litter up in the park? That's very public-spirited of you!*

ˌpublic ˈtransport *UK noun* [U] (*US* **public transportation**) a system of vehicles such as buses and trains which operate at regular times on fixed routes and are used by the public: *Greater investment in public transport would keep more cars off the roads.*

ˌpublic uˈtility *noun* [C] an organization that supplies the public with water, gas or electricity

publish /ˈpʌb.lɪʃ/ *verb* [T] to make information available to people, especially in a book, magazine or newspaper, or to produce and sell a book, magazine or newspaper: *She's just had an article published in their weekend supplement.* ○ *The Government publishes figures every six months showing how many people are unemployed.* ○ *The names of the winners of the competition will be published in June.* ○ *She was only 19 when her first novel was published.* ➲See also **publication**.

publisher /ˈpʌb.lɪ.ʃəʳ/ Ⓤⓢ /-ʃɚ/ *noun* [C] **1** an organization which prints text or music **2** an employee of a publishing company who has responsibility for deciding what is published **publishing** /ˈpʌb.lɪ.ʃɪŋ/ *noun* [U] *a career in publishing*

ˈpublishing ˌhouse *noun* [U] a company which publishes books

puce /pjuːs/ *noun* [U], *adj* (being) a dark brownish purple colour: *Her face turned puce with rage.*

puck /pʌk/ *noun* [C] a small hard rubber disc which is used instead of a ball in ICE HOCKEY (= a game played on ice) ➲See picture **Sports** on page Centre 10

pucker /ˈpʌk.əʳ/ Ⓤⓢ /-ɚ/ *verb* [I or T] (*ALSO* **pucker up**) to tighten skin or cloth until small folds appear or (of skin or cloth) to form small folds: *He puckered his lips and kissed her.* ○ *Her mouth puckered and I thought she was going to cry.* ○ *puckered seams* **pucker** /ˈpʌk.əʳ/ Ⓤⓢ /-ɚ/ *noun* [C]

puckish /ˈpʌk.ɪʃ/ *adj LITERARY* liking to make jokes about other people and play harmless tricks on them: *a puckish sense of humour* ○ *a puckish grin*

pud /pʊd/ *noun* [C or U] *UK INFORMAL FOR* **pudding**: *What's for pud?*

pudding [SWEET FOOD] /ˈpʊd.ɪŋ/ *noun* **1** [C or U] *UK* a sweet and usually hot dish made with pastry, flour, bread or rice and often fruit: *a sticky toffee/treacle pudding* ○ *Is there any more rice pudding?* **2** [U] *US* a sweet soft food made from milk, sugar, eggs and flavouring which is eaten cold: *chocolate/vanilla/butterscotch pudding* **3** [U] (*INFORMAL* **pud**) *UK* the final part of a meal when a sweet dish is eaten; DESSERT: ***What's for*** *pudding?* ○ *I thought we'd* ***have*** *trifle* ***for*** *pudding.*

• **be in the pudding club** *UK OLD-FASHIONED* to be pregnant

• **over-egg the pudding** *UK* to spoil something by trying too hard to improve it

pudding [SAVOURY FOOD] /ˈpʊd.ɪŋ/ *noun* [C or U] (*INFORMAL* **pud**) *UK* a hot savoury dish made with pastry or flour, which contains or is eaten with meat: *steak and kidney pudding*

ˈpudding ˌbasin *noun* [C] *UK* a large bowl which is used for making PUDDINGS

pudding-basin haircut /ˌpʊd.ɪŋˌbeɪ.sᵊnˈheə.kʌt/ Ⓤⓢ /-ˈher-/ *noun* [C] *UK* a short hairstyle which is not fashionable and looks as if it has been created by putting a pudding basin over your head and cutting round the edge of it

puddle /ˈpʌd.l̩/ *noun* [C] a small pool of liquid on the ground, especially from rain

pudgy /ˈpʌdʒ.i/ *adj MAINLY US* short and fat: *I was a pudgy child.* **pudginess** /ˈpʌdʒ.ɪ.nəs/ *noun* [U]

puerile /ˈpjʊə.raɪl/ Ⓤⓢ /ˈpjʊr.ɪl/ *adj DISAPPROVING* behaving in a silly way, not like an adult: *I find his sense of humour rather puerile.* **puerility** /pjʊəˈrɪl.ɪ.ti/ Ⓤⓢ /pjʊrˈɪl.ə.t̬i/ *noun* [U]

puff [BREATHE] /pʌf/ *verb* [I] to breathe fast and with difficulty, usually because you have been doing exercise: *He came puffing up the stairs.* ○ [+ speech] *"I ran all the way home," she puffed* (= said while puffing).

• **puff and pant** to breathe fast and with difficulty, usually because you have been doing exercise

puff /pʌf/ *noun INFORMAL* **be out of puff** to be breathing with difficulty because you have been doing physical exercise

ˌpuffed (ˈout) *UK adj* [after v] (*US* **pooped**) *INFORMAL* breathing with difficulty because you have been doing physical exercise: *I can't walk any further – I'm puffed!*

puff [SMOKE] /pʌf/ *verb* [I or T] to smoke tobacco: *She was puffing* ***on*** *a cigarette at the time.* ○ *He sat there, puffing* ***away at*** *a cigarette.*

puff /pʌf/ *noun* [C] an act of smoking: *She* ***took a*** *puff* ***on*** *her cigarette and thought for a moment.*

puff [SMALL AMOUNT] /pʌf/ *noun* [C] a small amount of smoke, air or something that can rise into the air in a small cloud: *Sean blew a puff* ***of smoke*** *at his reflection in the mirror.* ○ *He hit the ground with his stick and a puff* ***of*** *dust rose up into the air.*

• **vanish/go up/disappear in a puff of smoke** *INFORMAL* to disappear suddenly and completely: *One moment he was standing behind me, the next he had vanished in a puff of smoke.* ○ *All his hard work seemed to be going up in a puff of smoke.*

puff /pʌf/ *verb* [I or T] to blow out in clouds, or make steam or smoke do this: *He puffed a cloud of cigarette smoke into my eyes.* ○ *The chimney was puffing* ***out*** *clouds of smoke.*

puff [CAKE] /pʌf/ *noun* [C] a type of sweet cake or savoury food which is made from puff pastry and is filled with different food: *a cream/jam puff* ○ *cheese puffs*

puff [PRAISE] /pʌf/ *noun* [C] (*US ALSO* **puff piece**) *INFORMAL MAINLY DISAPPROVING* a piece of writing or speech which praises something too much

PHRASAL VERBS WITH **puff** ▼

▲ **puff** ***sth*** **out** *phrasal verb* [M] to make your chest or your face become bigger by filling it with air: *He puffed out his cheeks and sat back in his chair.*

P

▲ **puff up** *phrasal verb* If part of your body puffs up, it becomes bigger because it is infected or injured: *My leg puffed up all round the insect bite.*

▲ **puff *sth* up** *phrasal verb* **[M]** to become larger or full of air, or to make something become larger in this way: *When the pastry is golden and puffed up, take the pie out of the oven.*

ˈpuff ˌadder *noun* **[C]** a poisonous African snake which swells to a larger size when it is attacked

puffball /ˈpʌf.bɔːl/ [US] /-bɑːl/ *noun* **[C]** a large white round edible fungus

ˌpuff(ed) ˈsleeve *noun* **[C usually pl]** a short sleeve which swells out into a ball shape

puffer train /ˈpʌf.əˌtreɪn/ [US] /-ɚ-/ *noun* **[C]** *CHILD'S WORD* a steam train (= train powered by steam)

puffin /ˈpʌf.ɪn/ *noun* **[C]** a sea bird which lives in northern parts of the world and has a large brightly coloured beak

ˌpuff ˈpastry *noun* **[U]** pastry with lots of thin layers which swells to a larger size when cooked

puffy /ˈpʌf.i/ *adj* If the skin around your eyes is puffy, it is slightly swollen: *His eyes were still puffy with sleep.*

pug /pʌg/ *noun* **[C]** a small dog with a flat face and a short wide nose

pugnacious /pʌgˈneɪ.ʃəs/ *adj FORMAL* wanting to start an argument or fight, or expressing an argument or opinion very forcefully: *I found him pugnacious and arrogant.* **pugnacity** /pʌgˈnæs.ɪ.ti/ [US] /-ə.t̬i/ *noun* **[U]** (*ALSO* **pugnaciousness**)

puke /pjuːk/ *verb* **[I or T]** *SLANG* to vomit: *The baby puked all down my shirt.* ○ *She puked her dinner **up** again.*

• **It makes me (want to) puke.** *SLANG* used to say that something makes you very upset or angry

puke /pjuːk/ *noun* **[U]** *SLANG* vomit: *The floor was covered with puke.*

pukka /ˈpʌk.ə/ *adj* **1** *OLD-FASHIONED* real: *a nice little Italian restaurant serving pukka pizzas and pasta* **2** *SLANG* of excellent quality: *I've had some pukka food there.* **3** extremely formal and educated: *He's not one of the pukka types she usually favours.*

pulchritude /ˈpʌl.krɪ.tjuːd/ [US] /-tuːd/ *noun* **[U]** *FORMAL* beauty, especially a woman's beauty **pulchritudinous** /ˌpʌl.krɪˈtjuːd.ɪ.nəs/ [US] /-ˈtuːd-/ *adj*

pull [MOVE TOWARDS YOU] /pʊl/ *verb* **[I or T]** to move something towards yourself, sometimes with great physical effort: *Could you help me move this bookcase over there? You pull and I'll push.* ○ *He pulled the chair away from the desk.* ○ *He pulled the heavy box across the floor to the door.* ○ **[+ obj + adj]** *He pulled the door open.* ○ *The car was pulling a caravan.* ○ *The sun was so strong we had to pull **down** the blinds.* ○ *She pulled **out** the drawer.*

• **pull *sth* out of the bag/hat** to do something unexpected which suddenly improves a bad situation

• **pull the rug from under sb's feet** to suddenly take away help or support from someone, or to suddenly do something which causes many problems for them

• **pull a gun/knife, etc. on *sb*** to suddenly take out a weapon and threaten someone with it

• **pull a fast one** *INFORMAL* to successfully deceive someone: *It's never worth that much – I think he pulled a fast one **on** you.*

• **Pull the other leg/one (it's got bells on)!** *INFORMAL HUMOROUS* used when you do not believe what someone has just said: *Helen, mountain climbing? Pull the other one – she can't even climb a ladder without feeling sick!*

• **pull the plug** to do something which prevents an activity from continuing, especially to stop giving money: *If the viewing figures drop much further, the TV company will probably pull the plug **on** the whole series.*

• **not pull any/*your* punches** to speak in an honest way without trying to be kind: *Her image is that of an investigative reporter who doesn't pull any punches.*

• **pull rank** to use the power that your position gives you over someone in order to make them do what you want: *He doesn't have the authority to pull rank **on** me any more.*

• **pull *your* socks up** *INFORMAL* to make an effort to improve your work or behaviour because it is not good enough: *He's going to have to pull his socks up if he wants to stay in the team.*

• **pull out all the stops** to do everything you can to make something successful: *They pulled out all the stops for their daughter's wedding.*

• **pull strings** to secretly use the influence you have over important people in order to get something or to help someone: *I may be able to pull a few strings if you need the document urgently.*

• **pull the strings** to be in control of an organization, often secretly: *I want to know who's pulling the strings around here.*

• **pull *your* weight** to work as hard as other people in a group: *The others had complained that Sarah wasn't pulling her weight.*

pull /pʊl/ *noun* **1** **[C usually sing]** when you pull something towards yourself: ***Give** the rope a hard pull.* **2** **[C]** something that you pull to make something work or to open something: *a curtain pull* ○ *a drawer pull*

pull [REMOVE] /pʊl/ *verb* **[T]** to take something out of or away from a place, especially using physical effort: *He pulled **off** his sweater.* ○ *The dentist pulled both teeth **out**.* ○ *I spent the morning pulling **up** the weeds in the flowerbeds.* ○ *He put his hands on the side of the pool and pulled himself **out** of the water.* ○ *I watched an old woman pull herself **up** the stairs, holding on to a rail.*

pull [ATTRACT] /pʊl/ *verb* **1** **[T]** to attract a person or people: *The show has certainly pulled **(in) the crowds**.* **2** **[I or T]** *UK INFORMAL* to succeed in starting a sexual relationship with someone: *He certainly knows how to pull **the birds*** (= attract female sexual partners). ○ *Did Tracy pull at the nightclub last night?*

pull /pʊl/ *noun* **1** **[C]** something which attracts people: *"How can we persuade people to come to the meeting?" "A glass of wine is quite a good pull."* **2** **[U]** the physical or emotional power to attract: *The greater the mass of an object, the greater its gravitational pull.* ○ *The movie's all-star cast should give it a lot of pull.* **3** **[U]** influence: *He's still got quite a bit of pull in the club – he could probably get you elected.*

• **be on the pull** *UK INFORMAL* to be trying to find someone to have sex with: *Michael was out on the pull again last night.*

pull [MOVE] /pʊl/ *verb* **[I + adv or prep]** to move in the stated direction: *During the last lap of the race one of the runners began to pull **ahead**.* ○ *We waved as the train pulled **out of** the station.* ○ *Our armies are pulling **back** on all fronts.*

pull [INJURE] /pʊl/ *verb* **[T]** to injure a muscle by stretching it too much: *I pulled a muscle in my back lifting some drawers.* ○ *He pulled a hamstring.*

pull [DISHONEST] /pʊl/ *verb* **[T]** *SLANG* to perform a dishonest action: *The gang that pulled the bank robbery were all arrested.* ○ *No one's gonna pull that kind of trick **on** me!*

PHRASAL VERBS WITH **pull** ▼

▲ **pull *sth/sb* apart** [SEPARATE] *phrasal verb* **[M]** to separate two things or people: *They went for each other with their fists and had to be pulled apart.*

▲ **pull *sth* apart** [DESTROY] *phrasal verb* **[M]** to destroy something by tearing it into pieces

▲ **pull *sth* apart** [CRITICIZE] *phrasal verb* **[M]** to say that something, usually a piece of work, is very bad: *The last essay I gave him he completely pulled apart.*

▲ **pull at *sth*** *phrasal verb* to pull something briefly and usually repeatedly: *The child pulled at his sleeve to catch his attention.* ○ *He pulled at his ear as he spoke.*

▲ **pull away** [VEHICLE] *phrasal verb* If a vehicle pulls away, it starts moving: *There was a roar and a cloud of smoke as the car pulled away from the traffic lights.*

▲ **pull away** [PERSON] *phrasal verb* If you pull away from someone who is holding you, you suddenly move your body backwards, away from them: *She pulled away just as he was about to kiss her.*

▲ **pull back *(from sth)*** [NOT CONTINUE] *phrasal verb MAINLY US* to decide not to do or involve yourself with something when you were previously going to: *It is rumoured that the company intends to pull back from petrochemicals.*

P

▲ **pull** ***sth*** **back** [SCORE] *phrasal verb* [M] If a team that is losing pulls a goal back or pulls points back, it scores a goal or wins some points.

▲ **pull** ***sth*** **down** [BUILDING] *phrasal verb* [M] to destroy a building: *They pulled down the warehouse to build a new supermarket.*

▲ **pull down** ***sth*** [MONEY] *phrasal verb* US INFORMAL to earn a stated amount of money: *Between them they must be pulling down over $100 000 a year.*

▲ **pull in/pull into** ***somewhere*** [MOVE] *phrasal verb* If a vehicle pulls in or pulls into somewhere, it moves in that direction and stops there: *He pulled in at the side of the road.* ○ *I pulled into the empty parking space.*

▲ **pull** ***sb*** **in** [ARREST] *phrasal verb* [M] MAINLY US INFORMAL If the police pull you in, they arrest you: *The police pulled in scores of protesters during the demonstration.*

▲ **pull** ***sth*** **off** [SUCCEED] *phrasal verb* [M] INFORMAL to succeed in doing something difficult or unexpected: *The central bank has pulled off one of the biggest financial rescues of recent years.*

▲ **pull off** [MOVE AWAY] *phrasal verb* UK If a vehicle pulls off, it starts moving: *The car pulled off and sped up the road.*

▲ **pull** ***sth*** **on** *phrasal verb* [M] to put on clothes quickly: *I pulled on my jeans and ran downstairs.*

▲ **pull out** [VEHICLE] *phrasal verb* If a vehicle pulls out, it starts moving onto a road or onto a different part of the road: *A car pulled right out in front of me.*

▲ **pull** ***(sb/sth)*** **out** [AREA] *phrasal verb* [M] If soldiers or military forces pull out or are pulled out, they move out of an area because they have been ordered to.

pull-out /ˈpʊl.aʊt/ *noun* [C usually sing] the removal of soldiers from an area where there has been fighting

▲ **pull** ***(sb/sth)*** **out** [ACTIVITY] *phrasal verb* [M] to stop being involved in an activity or agreement: *He pulled out* ***of*** *the deal at the last moment.* ○ *They've pulled all their athletes out of the competition.*

▲ **pull over** *phrasal verb* If a vehicle pulls over, it moves to the side of the road and stops: *Just pull over here, and I'll get out and walk the rest of the way.*

▲ **pull through** ***(sth)*** [LIVE] *phrasal verb* to become well again after a serious illness, especially when you might have died: *They said the operation had been successful and they expected his wife to pull through.*

▲ **pull** ***(sb)*** **through** ***(sth)*** [MANAGE] *phrasal verb* to succeed in dealing with a difficult period, or to help someone do this: *He'd never have managed on his own, but his colleagues have pulled him through.* ○ *It was a crisis year for the company, but we have pulled through.*

▲ **pull** ***yourself*** **together** [CALM] *phrasal verb* [R] to become calm and behave normally again after being angry or upset: *Just pull yourself together. There's no point crying about it.*

▲ **pull together** [COMBINE] *phrasal verb* to work hard as a group in order to achieve something: *We don't have much time but if we all pull together we should get the job done.*

▲ **pull** ***sb*** **up** [CRITICIZE] *phrasal verb* to tell someone that they have done something wrong: *She's always pulling me up* ***for/over*** *my bad spelling.*

▲ **pull up** [STOP] *phrasal verb* When a car or someone driving a car pulls up, the driver stops the car, often for a short time: *A car pulled up outside my house.*

• **pull up short** to stop suddenly in a vehicle: *A dog suddenly ran across the road and I had to pull up short.*

• **pull** ***sb*** **up short** to surprise someone, often so that they stop what they are doing: *Seeing her picture in the paper pulled me up short.*

ˈpull ˌdate *noun* [C] US FOR **sell-by date**

pull-down menu /ˈpʊl.daʊnˌmen.juː/ *noun* [C] a list of instructions on a computer screen, which is kept out of view until you choose to see it: *Click 'Tools', then select 'Options' from the pull-down menu.*

pulley /ˈpʊl.i/ *noun* [C] a piece of equipment for moving heavy objects up or down, consisting of a small wheel over which a rope or chain fixed to the object can be easily pulled or released slowly: *The blocks of stone had to be lifted into position with a system of pulleys.*

pull-in UK INFORMAL /ˈpʊl.ɪn/ *noun* [C] (US **rest stop**) a place at the side of a road where vehicles can stop and where it is sometimes possible to buy food and drinks

ˈpulling ˌpower *noun* [U] the ability to attract people: *Although she hasn't made a movie for four years, her pulling power is as great as ever.* ○ *Circuses don't seem to have much pulling power these days.*

pull-out /ˈpʊl.aʊt/ *adj* **pull-out bed/table, etc.** a piece of furniture that can be pulled into position when you want to use it and folded away when you do not

pull-out (section) /ˈpʊl.aʊt/ *noun* [C] in a magazine or newspaper, a set of pages that are intended to be taken out and used separately: *a 16-page pull-out* ○ *There's a pull-out on hair care in next week's issue.*

pullover /ˈpʊl|əʊ.vəʳ/ [US] /-ˌoʊ.vɚ/ *noun* [C] (US USUALLY **sweater,** AUS USUALLY **jumper**) a piece of clothing which is made of a warm material such as wool, has long sleeves, and is worn over the top part of the body and put on by pulling it over your head ➲See picture **Clothes** on page Centre 6

pull-tab /ˈpʊl.tæb/ *noun* [C] US FOR **ring-pull**

pulmonary /ˈpʊl.mə.nə.ri/ [US] /-ner.i/ *adj* SPECIALIZED relating to the lungs: *the pulmonary artery*

pulp /pʌlp/ *noun* **1** [S or U] a soft wet mass: *Mash the bananas* ***to a*** *pulp and then mix in the yoghurt.* **2** [U] small pieces of paper, cloth or wood mixed with water until they form a soft wet mass, used for making paper: *wood pulp* ○ *a pulp mill* **3** [U] DISAPPROVING books and magazines which are of low quality in the way they are produced and the stories and articles they contain: *pulp fiction*

• **beat** ***sb*** **to a pulp** INFORMAL to hit someone repeatedly until they are badly injured

pulp /pʌlp/ *verb* [T] to make something into a pulp: *Old newspapers are pulped and recycled.*

pulpit /ˈpʊl.pɪt/ *noun* [C] a raised place in a church, with steps leading up to it, from which the priest speaks to the people during a religious ceremony

pulsar /ˈpʌl.sɑːʳ/ [US] /-sɑːr/ *noun* [C] SPECIALIZED a very small dense star that sends out radio waves

pulsate /pʌlˈseɪt/ [US] /ˈ--/ *verb* [I] to beat or move with a strong, regular rhythm: *The whole room was pulsating* ***with*** *music.*

pulsating /pʌlˈseɪ.tɪŋ/ [US] /ˈpʌl.seɪ.t̬ɪŋ/ *adj* very lively and exciting: *Rue St. Denis is the pulsating heart of French street life in Montreal.* **pulsation** /pʌlˈseɪ.ʃᵊn/ *noun* [C or U]

pulse /pʌls/ *noun* [C] **1** the regular beating of the heart, especially when it is felt at the wrist or side of the neck: *The child's pulse was* ***strong/weak.*** ○ *Exercise increases your pulse* ***rate.*** **2 take** ***sb's*** **pulse** to hold someone's wrist and count how many times their heart beats in one minute **3** a short burst of energy which is repeated regularly, such as a brief loud sound or a brief flash of light: *The data, normally transmitted electronically, can be changed into pulses of light.*

• **have/keep** ***your*** **finger on the pulse** to be/stay familiar with the most recent changes or improvements: *The situation changes daily, so you've got to keep your finger on the pulse.*

• **set** ***your*** **pulse racing** (ALSO **quicken** ***your*** **pulse**) to make you excited: *This is a movie that will set your pulse racing.*

pulse /pʌls/ *verb* [I] to move or beat with a strong, regular rhythm: *I could feel the blood pulsing through my veins.*

pulses /ˈpʌl.sɪz/ *plural noun* SPECIALIZED seeds such as beans or peas which are cooked and eaten: *Pulses include peas, lentils and chickpeas.*

pulverize, UK USUALLY **-ise** /ˈpʌl.vᵊr.aɪz/ [US] /-və.raɪz/ *verb* [T] **1** to press or crush something until it becomes powder or a soft mass: *pulverized coal/bones* **2** INFORMAL to defeat someone easily **pulverization**, UK USUALLY **-isation** /ˌpʌl.vᵊr.aɪˈzeɪ.ʃᵊn/ [US] /-vɚ.ɪ-/ *noun* [U]

puma MAINLY UK /ˈpjuː.mə/ *noun* [C] (MAINLY US **cougar**) a large brown wild cat that lives in North and South America

pumice (stone) /ˈpʌm.ɪsˌstəʊn/ [US] /-ˌstoʊn/ *noun* [C or U] a type of grey light stone which is used in pieces or as a powder for rubbing things to make them smooth: *Pumice is produced in volcanic eruptions.* ○ *You can use a* *pumice stone in the bath to remove dry skin from your feet.*

pummel /'pʌm.ªl/ *verb* [T] -ll- *or US USUALLY* -l- **1** to hit someone or something repeatedly, especially with your fists: *The boxer had pummelled his opponent into submission by the end of the fourth round.* **2** *INFORMAL* to defeat someone easily at a sport: *They were pummelled in the second round.* **pummelling**, *US USUALLY* **pummeling** /'pʌm.ªl.ɪŋ/ *noun* [C]

pump DEVICE /pʌmp/ *noun* [C] a piece of equipment which is used to cause liquid, air or gas to move from one place to another: *a water/bicycle/fuel pump* ○ *a (UK) petrol/(US) gas pump*

pump /pʌmp/ *verb* **1** [T usually + adv or prep] to force liquid or gas to move somewhere: *Our latest machine can pump a hundred gallons a minute.* ○ *The new wine is pumped into storage tanks.* ○ *The heart pumps blood through the arteries/round the body.* **2** [T] *INFORMAL* to keep asking someone for information, especially in an indirect way: *She was pumping me for details of the new project.*
• **pump sb's hand** *INFORMAL* to SHAKE someone's hand (= hold their hand and move it up and own, especially in order to greet them)
• **pump iron** *INFORMAL* to lift heavy weights for exercise: *These days both men and women pump iron for fitness.*

pump SHOE *US* /pʌmp/ *noun* [C] (*UK* **court shoe**) a type of plain shoe with a raised heel and no fastenings which is worn by women

---

PHRASAL VERBS WITH **pump** ▼

▲ **pump sth into sth** *phrasal verb* to spend a lot of money trying to make something operate successfully: *They had been pumping money into the business for some years without seeing any results.*

▲ **pump sth out** REMOVE *phrasal verb* [M] to remove water or other liquid from something using a pump: *We took turns pumping out the boat.*

▲ **pump sth out** *phrasal verb* If someone's stomach is pumped out, a poisonous substance is removed from it by being sucked through a tube: *She had to go to hospital to have her stomach pumped out.*

▲ **pump sth out** PRODUCE *phrasal verb* [M] *INFORMAL DISAPPROVING* to produce words or loud music in a way that is repeated, forceful and continuous: *The government keeps pumping out the same old propaganda.* ○ *The car radio was pumping out music with a heavy beat.*

▲ **pump sth up** *phrasal verb* [M] to fill something with air using a pump: *Have you pumped up the balloons yet?* ○ *I must pump the tyres up on my bike.*

pump-action /'pʌmp.æk.ʃªn/ *adj* [before n] describes a device which operates by forcing something, especially air, in or out of an enclosed space or container: *a pump-action shotgun* ○ *a pump-action toilet*

pumpernickel /'pʌm.pə.nɪk.l̩/ Ⓤ /-pɚ-/ *noun* [U] a type of firm dark brown bread made from RYE (= a type of grain)

pumpkin /'pʌmp.kɪn/ *noun* [C or U] a large round vegetable with hard yellow or orange flesh: *pumpkin pie* ⊃See picture **Vegetables** on page Centre 2

pump priming *noun* [U] *SPECIALIZED* the activity of helping a business, programme, economy, etc. to develop by giving it money: *The government is awarding small, pump-priming grants to single mothers who are starting their own businesses.*

pun /pʌn/ *noun* [C] an amusing use of a word or phrase which has several meanings or which sounds like another word: *She made a couple of dreadful puns.* ○ *This is a well-known joke based on a pun: "What's black and white and red (= read) all over?" "A newspaper."*
pun /pʌn/ *verb* [I] to make a pun
punster /'pʌn.stər/ Ⓤ /-stɚ/ *noun* [C] a person who makes puns

punch HIT /pʌntʃ/ *noun* [C] a forceful hit with a fist: *She gave him a punch (UK) on/(US) in the nose.*
punch /pʌntʃ/ *verb* [T] **1** to hit someone or something with your fist: *He punched him in the stomach.* **2** *MAINLY US* to hit with your fingers the buttons on a telephone or the keys on a keyboard

• **punch sb's lights out** *INFORMAL* to hit someone repeatedly very hard
• **punch the clock** *US* to put a card into a special machine to record the times you arrive at and leave work: *After 17 years of punching the clock, he just disappeared one morning and was never heard from again.*

punch EFFECT /pʌntʃ/ *noun* [U] the power to be interesting and have a strong effect on people: *I felt the performance/speech/presentation lacked punch.*
punchy /'pʌn.tʃi/ *adj* expressing something effectively and with power: *a short punchy presentation/speech* ○ *The article is written in his usual punchy style.*

punch DRINK /pʌntʃ/ *noun* [C or U] a cold or hot drink made by mixing fruit juices, pieces of fruit and often wine or other alcoholic drinks

punch TOOL /pʌntʃ/ *noun* [C] a piece of equipment which cuts holes in a material by pushing a piece of metal through it: *a ticket punch* ○ *Have you seen the hole punch anywhere?*
punch /pʌntʃ/ *verb* [T] to make a hole in something with a special piece of equipment: *I was just punching holes in some sheets of paper.* ○ *This belt's too big – I'll have to punch an extra hole in it.*

Punch and Judy show /,pʌntʃ.ªnd'dʒuː.di.ʃəʊ/ Ⓤ /-ʃoʊ/ *noun* [C] a traditional children's entertainment in which a man, Mr Punch, argues with his wife, Judy. It was especially popular in the past as an entertainment in British towns by the sea in summer.

'punch ,ball *UK noun* [C] (*US* **punching bag**) an air-filled leather bag hung from a frame or fixed to a stand, used by boxers for training or exercise

'punch ,bowl *noun* [C] a large bowl in which punch is served

punch-drunk INJURED /'pʌntʃ.drʌŋk/ *adj* describes a boxer who behaves in a way that suggests his brain has been damaged as a result of being hit repeatedly on the head

punch-drunk TIRED /'pʌntʃ.drʌŋk/ *adj* tired and confused, especially after dealing with a difficult situation

'punch ,line , **punchline** *noun* [C] the last part of a story or a joke which explains the meaning of what has happened previously or makes it amusing

punch-up /'pʌntʃ.ʌp/ *noun* [C] *MAINLY UK INFORMAL* a fight: *There was a punch-up in the bar.*

punctilious /pʌŋk'tɪl.i.əs/ *adj* *FORMAL* very careful to behave correctly or to give attention to details: *He was always punctilious in his manners.* **punctiliously** /pʌŋk-'tɪl.i.ə.sli/ *adv* **punctiliousness** /pʌŋk'tɪl.i.ə.snəs/ *noun* [U]

punctual /'pʌŋk.tju.əl/ *adj* arriving, doing something or happening at the expected, correct time; not late: *a punctual start to the meeting* ○ *He's fairly punctual* (= He usually arrives on time). **punctually** /'pʌŋk.tju.ə.li/ *adv*: *The meeting started punctually at 10.00 a.m.* **punctuality** /,pʌŋk.tju'æl.ɪ.ti/ Ⓤ /-ə.ti/ *noun* [U] *Punctuality has never been his strong point.*

punctuate /'pʌŋk.tju.eɪt/ *verb* [T] *SLIGHTLY FORMAL* to happen or cause something to happen repeatedly while something else is happening; to interrupt something repeatedly: *The President spoke at length in a speech punctuated by applause.* ○ *He chatted freely, punctuating his remarks as often as possible with the interviewer's first name.* ⊃See also **punctuate** at **punctuation**.

punctuation /,pʌŋk.tju'eɪ.ʃªn/ *noun* [U] (the use of) special marks that you add to writing to separate phrases and sentences, to show that something is a question, etc: *His letter was completely without punctuation.*
punctuate /'pʌŋk.tjuː.eɪt/ Ⓤ /-tuː-/ *verb* [T] to add punctuation marks to written words so that people can see when a sentence starts and finishes, or that something is a question, etc. ⊃See also **punctuate**.

punctu'ation ,mark *noun* [C] a symbol used in punctuation: *Full stops/Periods, commas, semicolons, question marks and brackets are all different types of punctuation mark.*

puncture /'pʌŋk.tʃər/ Ⓤ /-tʃɚ/ *noun* [C] a small hole made by a sharp object, especially in a tyre: *My bike has had two punctures in the last three weeks.* ○ *I (= My car* tyre) **had** *a puncture when I was driving back from Keele.* ○ *She had a puncture wound in her arm, from a wasp sting.*

puncture /ˈpʌŋk.tʃəʳ/ ⓤ /-tʃɚ/ *verb* **1** [I or T] to make a small hole in something, or to get a small hole in something: *She had used a screwdriver to puncture two holes in the lid of a paint tin.* ○ *The knife went through his ribs and punctured his lung.* **2** [T] to suddenly make someone less confident or positive: *My positive mood was rather punctured by the news.*

pundit /ˈpʌn.dɪt/ *noun* [C] a person who knows a lot about a particular subject and is therefore often asked to give an opinion about it: *a political/foreign-policy/ sports pundit*

pungent /ˈpʌn.dʒ³nt/ *adj* **1** describes a very strong smell or taste, sometimes one that is unpleasantly strong: *the pungent whiff of a goat* ○ *I sat down to a cup of wonderfully pungent Turkish coffee.* **2** LITERARY describes speech or writing that is very strongly felt: *pungent criticism/commentary* **pungently** /ˈpʌn.dʒ³nt.li/ *adv* **pungency** /ˈpʌn.dʒ³nt.si/ *noun* [U] *The cheeses vary in pungency.*

punish /ˈpʌn.ɪʃ/ *verb* [T] **1** to cause someone who has done something wrong or committed a crime to suffer, by hurting them, forcing them to pay money, sending them to prison, etc: *Those responsible for these crimes must be brought to court and punished.* ○ *He punished the class by giving them extra work.* ○ *The oil company was found guilty on ten counts of pollution, and was punished with a $250 million fine.* ◆See also **punitive. 2** to punish anyone who commits a particular crime: *Drunken driving can be punished with a prison sentence.*

punishable /ˈpʌn.ɪ.ʃə.bl̩/ *adj* describes a crime that you can be punished for: *a punishable offence* ○ *Drug dealing is punishable by death in some countries.*

punishment /ˈpʌn.ɪʃ.mənt/ *noun* [C or U] when someone is punished: *Many people think that the death penalty is too severe a punishment for any crime.* ○ FORMAL *It was always our father who administered/meted out punishments.* ○ *Drink-driving is one case where severe punishment seems to work as a deterrent.*

punishing /ˈpʌn.ɪ.ʃɪŋ/ *adj* [before n] very difficult and making you feel tired: *Currently she has a punishing schedule of five presentations a day.*

punishing /ˈpʌn.ɪ.ʃɪŋ/ *noun* INFORMAL **take a punishing** to be damaged because of rough treatment: *My tyres took quite a punishing on the rough terrain.*

punishingly /ˈpʌn.ɪ.ʃɪŋ.li/ *adv*: *a punishingly heavy workload* (= a very large amount of work)

punishment /ˈpʌn.ɪʃ.mənt/ *noun* [U] rough treatment: *These trucks are designed to take a lot of punishment.*

punitive /ˈpjuː.nɪ.tɪv/ ⓤ /-t̬ɪv/ *adj* **1** FORMAL intended as a punishment: *punitive action* ○ *The UN has imposed punitive sanctions on the invading country.* ○ LEGAL *She is suing the newspaper for $5 million punitive damages claiming they knew the article about her was untrue.* **2** used to describe costs which are so high they are difficult to pay, and which are often used to punish someone or limit their activities: *The President has threatened to impose punitive import duties/tariffs on a range of foreign goods.* **punitively** /ˈpjuː.nɪ.tɪv.li/ ⓤ /-nə.t̬ɪv./ *adv*

punk CULTURE /pʌŋk/ *noun* **1** [U] a culture popular among young people, especially in the late 1970s, involving opposition to authority expressed through shocking behaviour, clothes and hair, and through fast loud music **2** [C] (ALSO **punk rocker**) a person who wears punk clothes and likes punk music **punk** /pʌŋk/ *adj* [before n] *a punk band* ○ *a punk hairstyle*

punk CRIMINAL /pʌŋk/ *noun* [C] MAINLY US SLANG a young man who fights and is involved in criminal activities: *Listen to me, you little punk – you do that again and I'm gonna break your neck.*

punk 'rock *noun* [U] a type of fast, loud, often offensive music that was originally popular among young people in the late 1970s

punnet /ˈpʌn.ɪt/ *noun* [C] UK a small square or rectangular box in which particular types of fruit are sold: *a punnet of strawberries/raspberries*

punster /ˈpʌn.stəʳ/ ⓤ /-stɚ/ *noun* [C] ◆See at **pun**.

punt MONEY /pʌnt/ *noun* [C] (ALSO **Irish pound**) the standard unit of money used in Ireland before they started using the euro

punt BOAT /pʌnt/ *noun* [C] a long narrow boat with a flat bottom and a square area at each end, which is moved by a person standing on one of the square areas and pushing a long pole against the bottom of the river **punt** /pʌnt/ *verb* [I or T] to travel in a punt: *We punted up the river.* ○ *It's a lovely afternoon – let's go punting.* **punter** /ˈpʌn.təʳ/ ⓤ /-t̬ɚ/ *noun* [C] a person who punts ◆See also **punter** CUSTOMER; **punter** GAMBLER.

punt KICK /pʌnt/ *verb* [T] **1** (in rugby or American football) to kick the ball after you have dropped it from your hands and before it touches the ground, or (in football) to kick the ball powerfully so that it goes a long way **2** US INFORMAL If you punt something, you decide not to do or include it: *We were running out of time, so we decided to punt the sightseeing and just go shopping.* **punt** /pʌnt/ *noun* [C] a way of kicking the ball in rugby or American football, by dropping it from your hands and kicking it before it hits the ground, or a powerful kick in football which causes the ball to go a long way

punter GAMBLER /ˈpʌn.təʳ/ ⓤ /-t̬ɚ/ *noun* [C] UK SPECIALIZED a person who makes a bet: *Bookmakers are offering punters odds of 6-1 on the horse Red Devil winning the race.* ◆See also **punter** at **punt** BOAT.

punter CUSTOMER /ˈpʌn.təʳ/ ⓤ /-t̬ɚ/ *noun* [C] UK INFORMAL **1** a customer; a user of services or buyer of goods: *Many hotels are offering discounts in an attempt to attract punters/pull in the punters.* **2** a person who uses the services of a prostitute

puny /ˈpjuː.ni/ *adj* small; weak; not effective: *a puny little man* ○ *My car only has a puny little engine.* ○ *The party's share of the vote rose from a puny 11% in the last election to 21% this time.*

pup /pʌp/ *noun* [C] the young of particular animals, or a PUPPY: *a seal pup* ○ *an otter pup*

pupa /ˈpjuː.pə/ *noun* [C] *plural* **pupas** or **pupae** an insect in the stage of development which happens before it is completely developed, during which it is contained in a COCOON (= a protective covering) and does not move: *a moth pupa* ○ *mosquito pupae* ◆See also **chrysalis**. **pupal** /ˈpjuː.p³l/ *adj*: *the pupal stage of development*

pupil STUDENT /ˈpjuː.p³l/ *noun* [C] **1** a person, especially a child at primary school, who is being taught: *a second-year pupil* ○ *a primary-school pupil* ○ *The school has over 400 pupils.* ○ *There is a very relaxed atmosphere between staff and pupils at the school.* ○ *Her school report described her as a very promising pupil.* **2** someone who is being taught a skill, especially such as painting or music, by an expert: *The painting is believed to be by a pupil of Titian.*

pupil EYE /ˈpjuː.p³l/ *noun* [C] the circular black area in the centre of your eye, through which light enters: *Pupils contract in bright light, and dilate in darkness.*

puppet /ˈpʌp.ɪt/ *noun* [C] **1** a toy in the shape of a person or animal that you can move with strings or by putting your hand inside: *We took the children to a puppet show/theatre.* **2** DISAPPROVING a person or group whose actions are controlled by someone else: *Western powers have been accused of trying to establish a puppet government/regime in the divided country.* **puppeteer** /ˌpʌp.ɪˈtɪəʳ/ ⓤ /-əˈtɪr/ *noun* [C] a person who entertains with puppets

puppy /ˈpʌp.i/ *noun* [C] (ALSO **pup**) a young dog: *Our dog has just had four puppies.* ○ *a dalmatian puppy*

puppy ˌfat UK *noun* [U] (US **baby fat**) fat which a child sometimes has, and which disappears as the child grows older: *He's a little overweight but it's just puppy fat.*

puppy ˌlove *noun* [U] romantic love which a young person feels for someone else, and which usually disappears as the young person becomes older

purchase BUY /ˈpɜː.tʃəs/ ⓤ /ˈpɝː-/ *verb* [T] FORMAL to buy: *Tickets must be purchased two weeks in advance.* ○ *Except under clearly defined circumstances, it is illegal in Britain for a company to purchase its own shares.* ○ *She purchased her first house with the money.*

purchase /ˈpɜː.tʃəs/ ⑤ /ˈpɝː-/ noun FORMAL **1** [C] something that you buy: *How do you wish to pay for your purchases?* ○ *a major purchase* **2** [C or U] the act of buying something: *New restrictions have been placed on the purchase of guns.* ○ *A house is the most expensive purchase that most people ever **make**.* ○ *No purchase is necessary for you to enter this competition.* ○ *This product may be frozen. If required, freeze on day of purchase.*

purchaser /ˈpɜː.tʃə.səʳ/ ⑤ /ˈpɝː.tʃə.sɚ/ noun [C] FORMAL the person who buys something: *We haven't been able to find a purchaser for our house yet.*

purchase HOLD /ˈpɜː.tʃəs/ ⑤ /ˈpɝː-/ noun [S or U] FORMAL a firm hold which allows someone or something to be pulled or lifted without sliding or falling: *Dancers use a special powder on their shoes to help them **get** a better purchase on the floor.*

ˈpurchasing ˌpower noun [U] **1** A person's purchasing power is their ability to buy goods: *The purchasing power of people living on investment income has fallen as interest rates have gone down.* **2** the value of money considered as the amount of goods it will buy: *The purchasing power of the average hourly wage has risen in the last five years.*

purdah /ˈpɜː.də/ ⑤ /ˈpɝː-/ noun [U] **1** (the condition of following) the custom, found in some Muslim and Hindu cultures, of women not allowing their faces to be seen by men who are not their relatives, either by staying in a special part of the house or by wearing a covering over their faces: *The women in the village live in (strict) purdah.* ○ *In this region women seldom venture out of purdah.* **2** the state of not seeing or speaking to anyone: *Jeff has gone into purdah while he's preparing for his exams.*

pure NOT MIXED /pjʊəʳ/ ⑤ /pjʊr/ adj **1** not mixed with anything else: *a pure cotton shirt* ○ *pure orange juice* ○ *pure English honey* ○ *a pure Arab horse* **2** describes a colour which is not mixed with any other colour: *a swan's pure white plumage* **3** describes a sound which is clear and perfect: *the pure vocal tones of the choirboy* **4** clean and free from harmful substances: *The mountain air was wonderfully pure.* ○ *Tap water is never chemically pure.* ✱ NOTE: The opposite is **impure**.

purify /ˈpjʊə.rɪ.faɪ/ ⑤ /ˈpjʊr-/ verb [T] to remove bad substances from something to make it pure: *Plants help to purify the air.* ○ *One of the functions of the kidneys is to purify the blood.* ○ *water-purifying tablets*

purification /ˌpjʊə.rɪ.fɪˈkeɪ.ʃᵊn/ ⑤ /ˌpjʊr-/ noun [U] the act of removing harmful substances from something: *a water purification plant* ○ *an air purification system*

purifier /ˈpjʊə.rɪ.faɪ.əʳ/ ⑤ /ˈpjʊr.ɪ.faɪ.ɚ/ noun [C] a machine or a substance which removes harmful substances from something: *a water purifier* ○ *an air purifier* ○ *In traditional medicine, certain herbs are used as blood purifiers.*

purity /ˈpjʊə.rɪ.ti/ ⑤ /ˈpjʊr.ə.ţi/ noun [U] **1** the state of not being mixed with anything else: *the atrocities carried out in the name of ethnic/racial purity* **2** when a sound is clear and perfect: *the purity of her voice* **3** when something is clean or free from harmful substances: *air/water purity*

pure MORALLY GOOD /pjʊəʳ/ ⑤ /pjʊr/ adj behaving in a way that is morally completely good, or not having sex: *I'm trying to think only pure thoughts.* ○ *He invited me up to his flat for coffee, but I didn't think that his motives were entirely pure.* ○ *In many cultures, it is considered important for a woman to keep herself pure* (= not to have sex) *until she marries.* ✱ NOTE: The opposite is **impure**.

● **be as pure as the driven snow** to be morally completely good: *How dare he criticize me for having an affair? He's not exactly as pure as the driven snow himself.*

purify /ˈpjʊə.rɪ.faɪ/ ⑤ /ˈpjʊr-/ verb [T] *One of the main teachings of Buddhism is that you should try to purify* (= remove immoral thoughts from) *your mind.*

purification /ˌpjʊə.rɪ.fɪˈkeɪ.ʃᵊn/ ⑤ /ˌpjʊr-/ noun [U] in some religions, the act of removing from a person, usually by a ceremony, the bad effects that they are suffering because they have broken a religious or moral law

purity /ˈpjʊə.rɪ.ti/ ⑤ /ˈpjʊr.ə.ţi/ noun [U] moral goodness or the state of not having sex: *the purity and innocence of*

children ○ *For Christians, the Virgin Mary is a symbol of purity.*

pure COMPLETE /pjʊəʳ/ ⑤ /pjʊr/ adj [before n] **1** complete; only: *It was pure coincidence/chance that we met.* ○ *This last month has been pure hell.* ○ *Her face had a look of pure delight.* ○ *The minister dismissed the newspaper reports as pure speculation.* **2** describes an area of study that is studied only for the purpose of developing theories about it, not for the purpose of using those theories in a practical way: *pure mathematics* ○ *pure economics*

● **pure and simple** used after a noun to mean 'and nothing else': *He is motivated by greed, pure and simple.*

purely /pjʊə.li/ ⑤ /pjʊr-/ adv only: *On a purely practical level, it is difficult to see how such proposals would work.* ○ *We made this decision purely for financial reasons.*

● **purely and simply** for only one reason or purpose: *They decided to close the museum purely and simply because it cost too much to run.*

purebred /ˈpjʊə.bred/ ⑤ /ˈpjʊr-/ adj (of an animal or type of animal) with parents which are both of the same breed: *purebred cattle* ○ *a purebred stallion* ⊃See also **thoroughbred**.

purée /ˈpjʊə.reɪ/ ⑤ /pjʊˈreɪ/ verb [T] to make fruit or vegetables into a thick smooth sauce by crushing them, usually in a machine: *Purée the strawberries in the liquidizer and add the lightly whipped cream.* ○ *The first solid food she gave her baby was puréed carrot.*

purée /ˈpjʊə.reɪ/ ⑤ /pjʊˈreɪ/ noun [C or U] a thick smooth sauce made by crushing fruit or vegetables: *apple purée* ○ *Add two tablespoonsful of tomato purée.*

purgative /ˈpɜː.gə.tɪv/ ⑤ /ˈpɝː.gə.ţɪv/ noun [C] a substance which makes you excrete the contents of your bowels: *Prunes can have a purgative effect.* ⊃See also **laxative**.

Purgatory /ˈpɜː.gə.tri/ ⑤ /ˈpɝː.gə.tɔːr.i/ noun [U] the place to which Roman Catholics believe that the spirits of dead people go and suffer for the evil acts that they did while they were alive, before they are able to go to heaven

purgatory /ˈpɜː.gə.tri/ ⑤ /ˈpɝː.gə.tɔːr.i/ noun [U] HUMOROUS an extremely unpleasant experience which causes suffering: *I've been on a diet for two weeks now, and it's purgatory!*

purge REMOVE PEOPLE /pɜːdʒ/ ⑤ /pɝːdʒ/ verb [T] to get rid of people from an organization because you do not agree with them: *Party leaders have undertaken to purge the party of extremists.* ○ *Hard-liners are expected to be purged from the administration.*

purge /pɜːdʒ/ ⑤ /pɝːdʒ/ noun [C] *Between 1934 and 1938, Stalin mounted a massive purge of* (= an act of forcefully removing unwanted members from) *the Communist Party, the government and the armed forces in the Soviet Union.*

purge REMOVE EVIL /pɜːdʒ/ ⑤ /pɝːdʒ/ verb [T] to make someone or something free of something evil or harmful: [R] *Roman Catholics go to confession to purge their souls/themselves (from/of sin).* ○ *The new state governor has promised to purge the police force of corruption.*

purifier /ˈpjʊə.rɪ.faɪ.əʳ/ ⑤ /ˈpjʊr.ɪ.faɪ.ɚ/ noun [C] ⊃See at **pure** NOT MIXED

purist /ˈpjʊə.rɪst/ ⑤ /ˈpjʊr.ɪst/ noun [C] someone who believes in and follows very traditional rules or ideas in a subject: *Although purists may object to split infinitives, like 'to boldly go', the fact is, they are commonly used.* ○ *Purists eat smoked salmon with nothing more than lemon and black pepper.* **purism** /ˈpjʊə.rɪ.zᵊm/ ⑤ /ˈpjʊr.-ɪ-/ noun [U]

puritan /ˈpjʊə.rɪ.tᵊn/ ⑤ /ˈpjʊr.ɪ.tᵊn/ noun [C] **1** someone who believes that self-control and hard work are important and that pleasure is wrong or unnecessary: *Despite his apparent liberal views, he's really something of a puritan/he has a puritan streak.* **2** Puritan a member of an English religious group in the 16th and 17th centuries which wanted to make church ceremonies simpler, and who believed that self-control and hard work were important and that pleasure was wrong or unnecessary: *During the seventeenth century,*

the Puritans destroyed many decorations in English churches.
puritanical /ˌpjʊə.rɪˈtæn.ɪ.kəl/ [US] /ˌpjʊr.ɪ-/ *adj* believing or involving the belief that self-control and hard work are important and that pleasure is wrong or unnecessary: *She is very puritanical about sex.* ○ *He rebelled against his puritanical upbringing.* **puritanically** /ˌpjʊə.rɪˈtæn.ɪ.kli/ [US] /ˌpjʊr.ɪ-/ *adv*
puritanism /ˈpjʊə.rɪ.tən.ɪ.zəm/ [US] /ˈpjʊr.ɪ.t̬ən-/ *noun* [U] **1** the belief that self-control and hard work are important and that pleasure is wrong or unnecessary **2 Puritanism** the beliefs and behaviour of a Puritan

purl /pɜːl/ [US] /pɝːl/ *noun* [U] a type of stitch which you make when you knit by putting the needle into the front of the first stitch on the other needle
purl /pɜːl/ [US] /pɝːl/ *verb* [I or T] to knit a purl stitch: *Knit one, purl one.*

purloin /pəˈlɔɪn/ [US] /pɚ-/ *verb* [T] *FORMAL OR HUMOROUS* to steal something: *I was using a pen that I'd purloined **from** the office.*

purple /ˈpɜː.pl̩/ [US] /ˈpɝː-/ *adj* **1** of a dark reddish blue colour: *purple plums* ○ *a dark purple bruise* **2 purple in the face/purple with rage** dark red in the face because of anger **3** *UK* describes a piece of writing which is complicated or sounds false because the writer has tried too hard to make the style interesting: *Despite occasional patches of purple **prose**, the book is mostly clear and incisive.*
purple /ˈpɜː.pl̩/ [US] /ˈpɝː-/ *noun* [C or U] a dark reddish blue colour: *She wore a dress of dark purple.* ○ *The evening sky was full of purples and reds.* **purpleness** /ˈpɜː.pl̩.nəs/ [US] /ˈpɝː-/ *noun* [U]
purplish /ˈpɜː.pl̩.ɪʃ/ /-plɪʃ/ [US] /ˈpɝː-/ *adj* almost purple in colour: *He has a purplish birthmark on his cheek.*

ˌPurple ˈHeart *noun* [C] an American medal given to soldiers who have been injured in war

purport [CLAIM] /pəˈpɔːt/ [US] /pɝːˈpɔːrt/ *verb* [+ *to* infinitive] *FORMAL* to pretend to be or to do something, especially in a way that is not easy to believe: *They purport **to** represent the wishes of the majority of parents at the school.* ○ *The study purports **to** show an increase in the incidence of the disease.* ○ *The tape recording purports **to** be of a conversation between the princess and a secret admirer.*

purport [GENERAL MEANING] /ˈpɜː.pɔːt/ [US] /ˈpɝː.pɔːrt/ *noun* [U] *FORMAL* the general meaning of someone's words or actions: *I didn't read it all but I think the purport of the letter was that he will not be returning for at least a year.*

purpose /ˈpɜː.pəs/ [US] /ˈpɝː-/ *noun* **1** [C] why you do something or why something exists: *The purpose **of** the research is to try and and find out more about the causes of the disease.* ○ *His only purpose **in life** seems to be to enjoy himself.* ○ *Her main/primary purpose **in** suing the newspaper for libel was to clear her name.* ○ *I came to Brighton **for/with** the **express** purpose **of** seeing you.* ○ *Letters whose **sole** purpose is to make a political point will not be published.* ○ *She had the operation entirely **for** cosmetic purposes.* ○ *a multi-purpose kitchen knife* ○ *I can see no useful purpose in continuing this conversation.* ○ *All my efforts were **to no** purpose* (= failed). ○ *He gave her a sum of money which she used **to good** purpose* (= well). **2** [U] determination or a feeling of having a reason for what you do: *I've always admired her for her strength of purpose.* ○ *Parenthood would give him **a sense of** purpose.* **3** [C] a need: *We haven't yet managed to find new premises that are suitable for our purposes.* ○ *The fabric I bought isn't exactly what I wanted, but it will **serve** my purposes* (= fulfil my needs).
• **on purpose** If you do something on purpose, you do it intentionally, not accidentally: *I didn't do it on purpose – it was an accident.*
• **serve a purpose** to have a use: *These small village shops serve a very useful purpose.*
purposeful /ˈpɜː.pəs.fəl/ [US] /ˈpɝː-/ *adj* showing that you know what you want to do: *He has a quiet, purposeful air.* **purposefully** /ˈpɜː.pə.sfəl.i/ [US] /ˈpɝː-/ *adv*: *He strode purposefully into the room.* **purposefulness** /ˈpɜː.pə.sfəl.nəs/ [US] /ˈpɝː-/ *noun* [U]
purposeless /ˈpɜː.pə.sləs/ [US] /ˈpɝː-/ *adj* done without a clear intention: *a purposeless existence* ○ *purposeless fighting* **purposelessly** /ˈpɜː.pə.slə.sli/ [US] /ˈpɝː-/ *adv* **purposelessness** /ˈpɜː.pə.slə.snəs/ [US] /ˈpɝː-/ *noun* [U]
purposely /ˈpɜː.pə.sli/ [US] /ˈpɝː-/ *adv* intentionally: *The trial has been purposely delayed.* ○ *I purposely avoid making train journeys during the rush hour.*

purpose-built /ˌpɜː.pəsˈbɪlt/ [US] /ˌpɝː-/ *adj* designed and built for a particular use: *The college was the first purpose-built teacher training college in the country.*

purr /pɜː/ [US] /pɝː/ *verb* [I] to make a quiet continuous soft sound: *The cat purred as I stroked its fur.* ○ *We could hear the sound of a lawnmower purring in the back garden.* ○ *A black limousine purred **up*** (= drove up making a quiet continuous soft sound) *outside the hotel.* ○ [+ speech] *"I love it when you stroke my back," she purred* (= said with pleasure). **purr** /pɜː/ [US] /pɝː/ *noun* [S] *I stroked the cat and it gave a low purr.* ○ *I heard the gentle purr **of** an engine outside the house.*

purse [MONEY CONTAINER] /pɜːs/ [US] /pɝːs/ *noun* [C] **1** *UK* a small container for money, usually used by a woman: *a leather purse* ➲Compare **wallet**. **2** *US FOR* **handbag**

purse [AMOUNT TO SPEND] /pɜːs/ [US] /pɝːs/ *noun* [C usually sing] the total amount of money which an organization or government has available for spending: *Having a lot of people out of work places a large drain on the **public** purse.*
• **the purse strings** the spending of money by a family, company or country: *A recent survey showed that in 53% of families, women **hold*** (= control) *the purse strings.*

purse [PRIZE] /pɜːs/ [US] /pɝːs/ *noun* [C] an amount of money which is offered as a prize in a sports competition: *The players in the golf tournament are competing for a purse **of** £525 000.*

purse [MOVE LIPS] /pɜːs/ [US] /pɝːs/ *verb* [T] to bring your lips tightly together so that they form a rounded shape, usually as an expression of disapproval: *"I don't approve of that kind of language," she said, pursing her lips.*

purser /ˈpɜː.səʳ/ [US] /ˈpɝː.sɚ/ *noun* [C] an officer on a ship who deals with the ship's accounts, or a person on a passenger ship or aircraft who is responsible for taking care of passengers

pursuant /pəˈsjuː.ənt/ [US] /pɚˈsuː-/ *adj* [after v] *FORMAL OR LEGAL* according to: *The fact that a person acted pursuant **to** an order of his government does not relieve him from responsibility under international law.*

pursue [FOLLOW] /pəˈsjuː/ [US] /pɚˈsuː/ *verb* [T] **1** to follow someone or something, usually to try to catch or kill them: *The car was pursued by helicopters.* ○ *The hunters spent hours pursuing their prey.* ○ *He was killed by the driver of a stolen car who was being **hotly** pursued by the police.* **2** to try very hard to persuade someone to accept a job: *The company has been pursuing Holton for some time, but so far he has rejected all their offers.* **3** to try to discover information about a subject: *We will not be pursuing this **matter** any further.* ○ *The police are currently pursuing several lines of inquiry into the case.* ○ *I don't think this idea is worth pursuing any further.* ○ *The press has pursued this story relentlessly.* **4** to try very hard to persuade someone to have a relationship with you: *He's been pursuing her for months and yet she's so clearly not interested.*
pursuer /pəˈsjuː.əʳ/ [US] /pɚˈsuː.ɚ/ *noun* [C] someone who is chasing you: *She made a sudden right turn off the road in order to escape her pursuers.* ○ *FIGURATIVE The team are ten points ahead of their closest pursuers in the league.*
pursuit /pəˈsjuːt/ [US] /pɚˈsuːt/ *noun* [C or U] when you follow someone or something to try to catch them: *Three people have been killed in high-speed pursuits by the police recently.* ○ *The robbers fled the scene of the crime, with the police **in** pursuit.*

pursue [ATTEMPT] /pəˈsjuː/ [US] /pɚˈsuː/ *verb* [T] If you pursue a plan, activity or situation, you try to do it or achieve it, usually over a long period of time: *He decided to pursue a career in television.* ○ *We need to decide soon what marketing strategy we should pursue for these new products.* ○ *Michael Evans is leaving the company to pursue his own business interests.* ○ *She is ruthless in pursuing her goals.*

P

pursuance /pə'sjuː.ənts/ ⓤ /pɚ'suː-/ *noun* [U] *FORMAL She has devoted herself to the pursuance **of** (= the act of trying to achieve) justice for her son.* ○ *In pursuance **of** his aims, he has decided to stand for parliament.*

pursuer /pə'sjuː.əʳ/ ⓤ /pɚ'suː.ɚ/ *noun* [C] *He described himself as a pursuer **of** (= someone who tries to achieve) truth and justice.*

pursuit /pə'sjuːt/ ⓤ /pɚ'suːt/ *noun* [U] *when you try to achieve a plan, activity or situation, usually over a long period of time: the pursuit of happiness* ○ *The company is ruthless **in** its pursuit **of** profit.* ○ *The union is on strike **in** pursuit **of** (= the act of trying to achieve) a 10% pay increase.*

pursuit /pə'sjuːt/ ⓤ /pɚ'suːt/ *noun* [C usually pl] *an activity that you spend time doing, usually when you are not working: I enjoy **outdoor** pursuits, like hiking and riding.* ○ *I don't have much opportunity for **leisure** pursuits these days.*

purvey /pə'veɪ/ ⓤ /pɚ-/ *verb* [T] *FORMAL to provide goods or services as a business, or to provide information: This company has purveyed clothing **to** the armed forces for generations.* ○ *The prime minister's speech was intended to purvey a message of optimism.*

purveyor /pə'veɪ.əʳ/ ⓤ /pɚ'veɪ.ɚ/ *noun* [C usually pl] *FORMAL purveyors **of** seafood* ○ *a purveyor **of** leather goods* ○ *UK Purveyors of Jams and Marmalades to Her Majesty the Queen*

purview /'pɜː.vjuː/ ⓤ /'pɝ-/ *noun* [U] *FORMAL the limit of someone's responsibility, interest or activity: This case falls **outside** the purview **of** this particular court.* ○ *Some of the bank's lending operations come **under/within** the purview of the deputy manager, and some are handled directly by the manager.*

pus /pʌs/ *noun* [U] *thick yellowish liquid that forms in and comes from an infected cut or injury in the body: a pus-filled wound*

push USE PRESSURE /pʊʃ/ *verb* [I or T] *to use physical pressure or force, especially with your hands, in order to move something into a different position, usually one that is further away from you: Can you help me move this table? You push and I'll pull.* ○ *The window sticks – you have to push **hard** to open it.* ○ *He helped me push my car off the road.* ○ *He pushed his plate away from him, refusing to eat any more.* ○ *She pushed her hair out of her eyes.* ○ *I tried to push the door open but it was stuck.* ○ *It isn't clear whether he fell off the balcony, or was pushed.* ○ *To turn the television on, you just push (= press) this button.* ○ *He pushed the money into my hand (= forcefully gave me the money). "Please take it," he said.* ○ *We pushed the boat **off** from (= moved the boat forward by using pressure against) the river bank.*

● **push the boat out** *UK INFORMAL to spend a lot of money on celebrating something: They really pushed the boat out for Annie's wedding.*

● **be pushing up (the) daisies** *HUMOROUS to be dead: I'll be pushing up the daisies long before it happens.*

● **push your luck** (*ALSO* **push it**) *to try too hard to get a particular result and risk losing what you have achieved: She's agreed to look after me on Saturday, but I think I'd be pushing my luck if I asked her to have charge of her the whole weekend.*

push /pʊʃ/ *noun* [C] *when you move someone or something by pressing them with your hands or body: Get on the swing and I'll **give** you a push.* ○ *I **gave** the door a hard push, but it still wouldn't open.* ○ *I can order all these goods **at** the push **of** a button (= by pushing a button).*

● **at a push** *UK If you can do something at a push, you can do it but it will be difficult: At a push I could be there by eight o'clock.*

● **if/when push comes to shove** *If something can be done if push comes to shove, it can be done if the situation becomes so bad that you have to do it: If push comes to shove, we can always sell the car.*

● **give sb the push** *UK INFORMAL* **1** *to tell someone to leave their job: I heard he'd been given the push.* **2** *to end a relationship with someone: Oh, give him the push – he's a loser.*

● **get the push** *UK INFORMAL* **1** *to be told to leave your job: Rick got the push a few weeks ago.* **2** *to be told by someone that your relationship with them has ended: She got the push from Martin last night.*

push MOVE FORCEFULLY /pʊʃ/ *verb* **1** [I or T; usually + adv or prep] *to move forcefully, especially in order to cause someone or something that is in your way to move, so that you can go through or past them: Stop pushing – wait your turn.* ○ *She pushed **through** the crowd.* ○ *I'm sorry – I didn't mean to push in front of you.* ○ *The minister pushed past the waiting journalists, refusing to speak to them.* ○ *In the final lap of the race, he managed to push (= move strongly) **ahead**.* ○ *Weeds push (= grow strongly) **up** through the cracks in the concrete.* ○ *They pushed (= forcefully made) their **way** to the front of the queue.* **2** [I usually + adv or prep] *When an army pushes in a particular direction, it advances there: The invading troops have pushed further into the north of the country.*

push /pʊʃ/ *noun* [C] *The army is continuing its push (= advance) towards the capital.*

push PERSUADE FORCEFULLY /pʊʃ/ *verb* [T] *to forcefully persuade or direct someone to do or achieve something: Her parents pushed her **into** marrying him.* ○ *The school manages to push most of its students **through** their exams.* ○ *If we want an answer from them by Friday, I think we're going to have to push them **for** it.* ○ [+ to infinitive] *We had to push them **to** accept our terms, but they finally agreed to the deal.* ○ [R] *You'll never be successful if you don't push yourself (= work) harder.*

push /pʊʃ/ *noun* [C] *a determined attempt to get an advantage over other companies in business: The company plans to **make** a big push into the European market next spring.* ○ [+ to infinitive] *The hotel is **making** a major push **to** attract customers.*

pushy /'pʊʃ.i/ *adj DISAPPROVING behaving in an unpleasant way by trying too much to get something or to make someone do something: a pushy salesman* **pushiness** /'pʊʃ.ɪ.nəs/ *noun* [U]

push ADVERTISE /pʊʃ/ *verb* [T] *INFORMAL to advertise something repeatedly in order to increase its sales: They're really pushing their new car.*

push /pʊʃ/ *noun* [S] *a lot of advertising: This film is unlikely to attract large audiences unless it **gets**/it is **given** a big push in the media.*

push SELL DRUGS /pʊʃ/ *verb* [T] *INFORMAL to sell illegal drugs: He was arrested for pushing drugs **to** schoolchildren.*

pusher /'pʊʃ.əʳ/ ⓤ /-ɚ/ *noun* [C] (*ALSO* **drug pusher**) *someone who sells illegal drugs*

PHRASAL VERBS WITH **push**   ▼

▲ **push sb about/around** *phrasal verb INFORMAL DISAPPROVING to tell someone what to do in a rude or threatening way: If you think you can push me around like that, you're mistaken.*

▲ **push ahead** *phrasal verb to continue with an activity in a determined or enthusiastic way, especially when it is difficult or tiring: They have decided to push ahead **with** the legal action.*

▲ **push along** *phrasal verb OLD-FASHIONED INFORMAL to leave: Anyway, I'd better be pushing along now.*

▲ **push sth aside** *phrasal verb* [M] *to decide to forget about or ignore something or someone: He claimed that he had been pushed aside (= not given a job) in favour of a younger person.*

▲ **push for sth** *phrasal verb to demand something repeatedly, or to take strong action to try to make it happen: Local residents are pushing for the road to be made safer.*

▲ **push (sth) forward** CONTINUE *phrasal verb* [M] *to continue doing something or making advances in something, with effort or enthusiasm: Their research has pushed forward the frontiers of knowledge.* ○ *An additional grant has enabled the team to push forward **with** research plans.*

▲ **push yourself forward** GET ATTENTION *phrasal verb to try to make other people notice and pay attention to you: She always seemed to be pushing herself forward and not giving anyone else a chance.*

▲ **push in** *phrasal verb* to rudely join a line of people who are waiting for something, by moving in front of some of the people who are already there: *I was waiting in the bus queue when two men pushed in in front of me.*
▲ **push off** [GO] *phrasal verb* SLANG used to rudely tell someone to go away: *He told me to push off.*
▲ **push off** [IN WATER] *phrasal verb* to push against the side of a pool, lake or river in order to move your body or a boat away from the side: *He pushed off **from** the side of the pool and swam slowly to the other side.*
▲ **push on** *phrasal verb* **1** to continue doing something, especially when this is difficult: *They are pushing on **with** their campaign for improved childcare facilities.* **2** to continue travelling somewhere: *"You've been driving for a long time – do you want to stop for a rest?" "No, we're nearly there – let's push on."*
▲ **push *sb* out** *phrasal verb* [M] to make someone leave a job or stop being involved in an activity by being unpleasant or unfair to them: *I felt I was being pushed out **of** the job.*
▲ **push *sb/sth* over** *phrasal verb* [M] to push someone or something so that they fall to the ground: *Daddy, Matthew pushed me over.*
▲ **push *sth* through** *phrasal verb* [M] to cause a plan or suggestion to be officially accepted or put into use: *We are trying to push this deal through as quickly as possible.* ○ *The president is trying to push through various tax reforms.*
▲ **push *(sb)* towards *sth*** *phrasal verb* to try to do or achieve something, or to make someone more likely to do or achieve something: *It is hoped that these measures will push the nation towards recovery.* ○ [+ v-ing] *New employment laws are expected to push more women towards voting Labour.*
▲ **push *sth* up/down** *phrasal verb* [M] to cause the amount, number or value of something to increase or decrease: *Rising demand tends to push prices up, and falling demand pushes them down.* ○ *The rise in interest rates has pushed up the value of my investments.*

pushbike /ˈpʊʃ.baɪk/ *noun* [C] UK OLD-FASHIONED a bicycle

push-button /ˈpʊʃ.bʌt.ᵊn/ Ⓤⓢ /-bʌt̬-/ *adj* [before n] describes an electronic object that you control by pushing buttons: *a push-button phone*

pushchair UK /ˈpʊʃ.tʃeəʳ/ Ⓤⓢ /-tʃer/ *noun* [C] (US **stroller**) a small, usually folding, chair on wheels which a baby or small child sits in and is pushed around in

pushed /pʊʃt/ *adj* **1** MAINLY UK **be pushed for time/money** to not have enough time or money: *I'm a bit pushed for money this month.* **2 be (hard) pushed to do *sth*** to find it difficult to do something: *We'll be hard pushed to get to Brighton by six o'clock.*

pushing /ˈpʊʃ.ɪŋ/ *adv* **be pushing fifty/sixty, etc.** to be almost fifty/sixty, etc. years old: *He looks great and yet he must be pushing sixty by now.*

pushover /ˈpʊʃ,əʊ.vəʳ/ Ⓤⓢ /-ˌoʊ.vɚ/ *noun* [C usually sing] INFORMAL something that is easy to do or to win, or someone who is easily persuaded or influenced or defeated: *The interview was an absolute pushover.* ○ *Jean will look after Harry, I'm quite sure – she's a pushover **for*** (= is easily persuaded to do things for) *babies.*

pushpin /ˈpʊʃ.pɪn/ *noun* [C] US a small pin with a small ball-shaped piece of plastic on one end, used especially for fixing notices, pictures etc. to a board or a wall

push-start /ˈpʊʃ.stɑːt/ Ⓤⓢ /-stɑːrt/ *verb* [T] (ALSO **bump-start**) to push your car in order to make the engine start
ˈpush ˌstart *noun* [C] (ALSO **bump start**)

push-up US /ˈpʊʃ.ʌp/ *noun* [C] (UK **press-up**) a physical exercise in which you lie flat with your face towards the floor and try to push up your body with your arms while keeping your legs and your back straight

pusillanimous /ˌpjuː.sɪˈlæn.ɪ.məs/ *adj* FORMAL weak and cowardly; frightened of taking risks: *He's too pusillanimous to stand up to his opponents.*
pusillanimity /ˌpjuː.sɪ.ləˈnɪm.ɪ.ti/ Ⓤⓢ /-ə.t̬i/ *noun* [U]
pusillanimously /ˌpjuː.sɪˈlæn.ɪ.mə.sli/ *adv*

puss /pʊs/ *noun* [C; often as form of address] INFORMAL a cat: *Here, puss.*

ˈpussy (ˌcat) [ANIMAL] *noun* [C] CHILD'S WORD a cat: *Look, Martha, a pussy cat!*

pussy [SEX] /ˈpʊs.i/ *noun* OFFENSIVE **1** [C] a woman's vagina **2** [U] sex with a woman

pussyfoot /ˈpʊs.i.fʊt/ *verb* [I] INFORMAL DISAPPROVING to avoid making a decision or expressing an opinion because you are uncertain or frightened about doing so: *Stop pussyfooting **around/about** and tell me what you really think.*

pussy willow /ˌpʊs.iˈwɪl.əʊ/ Ⓤⓢ /-oʊ/ *noun* [C or U] a tree which has small greyish furry flowers in the spring, or the flowers themselves

pustule /ˈpʌs.tjuːl/ *noun* [C] SPECIALIZED a small raised area on the skin which contains pus

put [MOVE] /pʊt/ *verb* [T + adv or prep] **putting, put, put** to move something or someone into the stated place, position or direction: *Where have you put the keys?* ○ *Put your clothes **in** the cupboard.* ○ *He put salt **into** the sugar bowl by mistake.* ○ *She put her bag **on** the table.* ○ *She put her hands **over** her eyes.* ○ *I put my arm **round** him to comfort him.* ○ *We always put the cat **out*** (= outside the house) *at night.* ○ *Every night, she puts **out** her clothes* (= takes them from where they are kept so that they are ready) *for the next day.* ○ *If we put the chairs a bit closer **together*** (= move them nearer to each other)*, we should be able to get another one round the table.* ○ *If you put **together*** (= mix) *yellow and blue paint you get green.* ○ *The prisoners were put **up against*** (= moved into a position next to) *a wall and shot.*
• **put together** said after a phrase which refers to a group of people or things to show that you are thinking of them as a group rather than separately: *She earns more than all the rest of us put together.* ○ *The population of the US is bigger than that of Britain, France and Germany put together.*
• **put it about** (ALSO **put *yourself* about**) UK INFORMAL to have sex with a lot of different people: *Have you been putting it about recently, then?*
• **put *yourself* in *sb's* place/position/shoes** to imagine how someone else feels in a difficult situation: *Put yourself in my place – what else could I have done?*
• **Put it there!** INFORMAL something that you say when you want someone to shake your hand to show that you have just made an agreement: *"So, do we have a deal?" "Sure, put it there."*
• **put *your* back into *sth*** to use a lot of physical effort to try to do something: *You could dig this plot in an afternoon if you really put your back into it.*
• **put your feet up** UK to relax, especially by sitting with your feet supported above the ground: *You go home and put your feet up, love.*
• **put the shot** to throw a heavy metal ball as far as possible in a sports competition: *He won the gold medal for putting the shot.*

put [WRITE] /pʊt/ *verb* [T + adv or prep] **putting, put, put** to write something: *She puts her name **in** all her books.* ○ *Put a cross **next to** the name of the candidate you want to vote for.* ○ *I've put the date of the party **down** in my diary.* ○ *He asked me to put my objections **(down) on paper**.* ○ *It was an interesting article but I wish they'd put **in** more information* (= included more information) *about the costs.*

put [EXPRESS] /pʊt/ *verb* [T usually + adv or prep] **putting, put, put** **1** to express something in words: *She wanted to tell him that she didn't want to see him any more, but she didn't know **how to** put **it**.* ○ *We're going to have to work very hard, but **as** Chris so succinctly put **it**, there's no gain without pain.* ○ *Why do you always have to put things so crudely?* ○ *Has everyone had a chance to put their point of view?* **2 put a price/value/figure on *sth*** to say what you think the price or value of something is: *The agent has put a price of £120 000 on our house.* ○ *You can't put a value on friendship* (= say what it is worth).
• **to put it bluntly/simply/briefly/mildly, etc.** used to describe the way you are expressing an event or opinion: *To put it bluntly, you're going to have to improve.* ○ *He was annoyed, to put it mildly* (= He was very annoyed).

put [CONDITION] /pʊt/ *verb* [T] **putting, put, put** to cause someone or something to be in the stated condition or situation: *Are you prepared to put your children **at risk**?* ○ *This puts me **in** a very difficult position.* ○ *What has* *put* you **in** *such a bad mood?* ○ *This election is a chance for the country to put a new government* **in** (= elect a new government). ○ *It's broken into so many pieces, it'll be impossible to put it* **back together** *again* (= repair it). ○ *Let's give her the chance to put her ideas into practice.* ○ *The terrorists were put on trial* (= Their case was judged in a law court) *six years after the bombing.* ○ *Wilson was put* **out** (**of** *the competition*) (= was defeated) *by Clarke in the second round.* ○ **[+ adj]** *How much did it cost to have the television put* **right** (= repaired)*?* ○ *I originally thought he was Australian, but he soon put me* **straight** (= corrected me) *and explained he was from New Zealand.* ○ *I know she's gone forever, but I just can't put her out of my mind/head* (= forget her). ○ *He's putting me under pressure to change my mind.*

- **put** *sb* **to** *sth* to cause someone to experience or do something: *Your generosity puts me to* **shame**. ○ *I've put the children to* **work** *clearing the snow from the path.* ○ *I hope we're not putting you to any* **inconvenience**.

put OPERATION /pʊt/ *verb* **[T usually + adv or prep]** putting, put, put to bring into operation; to cause to be used: *When the drugs failed to cure her, she put her* **faith/trust** *in herbal medicine.* ○ *The school puts a lot of* **emphasis on** *teaching children to read and write.* ○ *He's putting* **pressure on** *me to change my mind.* ○ *The events of the last few weeks have put a real* **strain on** *him.* ○ *In the story of Sleeping Beauty, the wicked fairy puts a* **spell/curse**/(US) **hex** *on the baby princess.* ○ *You know it was your fault, so don't try and put the* **blame on** *anyone else.* ○ *The government is expected to put a new* **tax on** *cars.* ○ *The new tax will put 8% on fuel prices* (= increase them by 8%). ○ *She's never put* **a bet/money on** *a race before.* ○ *He put everything he had* **into** (= He used all his abilities and strength in) *the final game.* ○ *The more you put* **into** *something, the more you get out of it* (= The harder you work at something, the more satisfying it is). ○ *They put* (= invested) *a lot of money* **into** *the family business.* ○ *The President is trying to put* **through** (= bring into operation) *reforms of the country's economic system.* ○ *They've got to put* **an end to/a stop to** *their fighting* (= to stop fighting).

- **put the squeeze on** *sb* (*US ALSO* **put the bite on** *sb*) *SLANG* to ask someone to give you money: *She put the squeeze on her mother for a hundred bucks.* ○ *The insurance company put the bite on me* **for** *a huge increase in my premium after I crashed the car.*

put JUDGE /pʊt/ *verb* **[T + adv or prep]** putting, put, put to judge something or someone in comparison with other similar things or people: *I'd put him* **among** *the top six tennis players of all time.* ○ *Drama critics have put her on a level/par with the great Shakespearean actresses.* ○ *He always puts the needs of his family* **first/last** (= they are the most/least important thing to him).

put SAIL /pʊt/ *verb* **[I + adv or prep]** putting, put, put to travel in a boat or ship across the sea: *Our mast broke, so we had to put* **about** (= turn round) *and return to port.* ○ *The ship put* **in at** (= stopped at) *Cape Town for fresh supplies.* ○ *We put* **to sea** (= began our sea journey) *at dawn.*

PHRASAL VERBS WITH **put** ▼

▲ **put** *sth* **about/around** *phrasal verb* **[M]** *INFORMAL* to tell a lot of people something that is not true: **[+ that]** *I'd like to know who put the rumour around* **that** *I'm pregnant.* ○ *Someone's been putting it about that Dan is leaving.*

▲ **put** *sth* **across/over** *sb* DECEIVE *phrasal verb INFORMAL* to cause a piece of false information to be believed by one or more people: *You didn't manage to put that story over on the tax people, did you?*

▲ **put** *sth* **across** EXPRESS *phrasal verb* **[M]** to express your ideas and opinions clearly so that people understand them easily: *It's an interesting idea and I thought he put it across well.*

▲ **put** *yourself* **across** *phrasal verb* to express your ideas and opinions clearly so that people understand them and realize what you are like as a person: *I don't think I managed to put myself across very well in my interview.*

▲ **put** *sth* **aside** SAVE *phrasal verb* **[M]** to save something, usually time or money, for a special purpose: *I put aside*

a little every month for a deposit on a house. ○ *He tries to put some time aside every evening to read to the kids.*

▲ **put** *sth* **aside** IGNORE *phrasal verb* **[M]** If you put a disagreement or problem aside, you ignore it temporarily so that it does not prevent you doing what you want to do: *Let's put our differences aside and make a fresh start.* ○ *Can we put that question aside for now, and come back to it later?*

▲ **put** *sth* **at** *sth phrasal verb* to guess or roughly calculate that something will cost a particular amount, or that something is a particular size, number or amount: *The value of the painting has been put at £1 million.* ○ *I'd put her at* (= guess that her age is) *about 35.*

▲ **put** *sth* **away** STORAGE PLACE *phrasal verb* **[M]** to put something in the place or container where it is usually kept: *Put your toys away now.*

▲ **put** *sb* **away** PLACE TO LIVE *phrasal verb* **[M]** *INFORMAL* to move someone into a place where people live and are cared for together, such as a mental hospital or old people's home: *In the past, people who suffered from schizophrenia were often put away.*

▲ **put** *sb* **away** PRISON *phrasal verb* **[M]** *SLANG* to send someone to prison: *After what he did, he deserves to be put away for life.*

▲ **put** *sth* **away** FOOD *phrasal verb* **[M]** *INFORMAL* to eat a large amount of food: *He put away a whole box of chocolates in one evening.*

▲ **put** *sth* **back** REPLACE *phrasal verb* **[M]** to return an object to where it was before it was moved: *Will you put the books back when you've finished with them?*

▲ **put** *sth* **back** DELAY *phrasal verb* **[M]** *UK* to delay a planned event: *We had to put the meeting back a week.*

▲ **put** *sth* **back** DRINK *phrasal verb* **[M]** *MAINLY UK INFORMAL* to drink something quickly, especially a large amount of alcohol: *He regularly puts back six pints a night – I don't know how he does it.*

▲ **put** *sth* **back** CLOCK *phrasal verb* **[M]** to adjust a clock or watch to make it show an earlier time, for example because you are now in a part of the world where the time is different

▲ **put** *sth* **before** *sb* IMPORTANCE to give more attention to one thing than another because you think it is more important: *I'd never put my work before my family.*

▲ **put** *sth* **before** *sb* TELL *phrasal verb* to formally tell or explain facts or ideas to a group of people in authority: *We've got to put our proposal before the committee.*

▲ **put** *sth* **behind** *you phrasal verb* If you put an unpleasant experience behind you, you stop thinking about it, so that it does not affect your life: *Like any divorce, it was a painful business but I've put it all behind me now.*

▲ **put** *sth* **by** *phrasal verb* **[M]** to save an amount of money to use later: *I try to put by a few pounds every week.*

▲ **put** *sth/sb* **down** STOP HOLDING *phrasal verb* **[M]** to put an object that you are holding onto the floor or onto another surface, or to stop carrying someone: *I put my bags down while we spoke.* ○ *Put me down, Daddy!* ➲See picture **Phrasal Verbs** on page Centre 9

- **not put** *sth* **down** If you cannot put a book down, you are unable to stop reading it until you reach the end: *It was so exciting from the first page I couldn't put it down.*

▲ **put** *sth* **down** TELEPHONE *phrasal verb* **[M]** If you put the telephone down, you place the RECEIVER back in the position you keep it in when it is not being used.

▲ **put** *sth* **down** PAY *phrasal verb* **[M]** to pay part of the cost and promise to pay the rest later: *I've put a deposit down on a new car.*

▲ **put** *sb* **down** INSULT *phrasal verb* **[M]** *INFORMAL* to make someone feel foolish or unimportant by criticizing them: *Why did you have to put me down in front of everybody like that?*

put-down /ˈpʊt.daʊn/ *noun* **[C]** *INFORMAL* an unkind remark that makes someone seem foolish: *One of the big put-downs of the American presidential election campaign was the comment that he was 'no Jack Kennedy'.*

▲ **put** *sb/sth* **down** NAME *phrasal verb* to write someone's name on a list or document, usually in order to in-

P

clude them in an event or activity: *Do you want me to put you down **for** the trip to London?* ○ [R] *I've put myself down **for** the office football team.* ○ *If you want to get your children into that school, you have to put their **names** down at birth.*

▲ **put *sth* down** [KILL] *phrasal verb* [M] to kill an animal that is old, ill or injured, to prevent it from suffering: *If a horse breaks its leg, it usually has to be put down.*

▲ **put *sth* down** [OPPOSITION] *phrasal verb* [M] to stop or limit an opposing political event or group: *Police used tear gas to put the **riot** down.* ○ *Thousands of troops were needed to put down the **uprising**.*

▲ **put down** [PRICE] *UK phrasal verb* [M] (*US AND UK ALSO* **bring down**) to reduce a price or a charge: *Shops are being forced to put their prices down in order to attract customers.* ○ *It's time that the government put down interest rates.*

▲ **put *sb* down** [BABY] *phrasal verb* to place and make a baby comfortable in the place where it sleeps: *I'd just put Jack down for his nap.*

▲ **put *(sth)* down *(somewhere)*** [AIRCRAFT] *phrasal verb* [M] When an aircraft puts down, it lands, and when pilots put down their aircraft, they land: *She put down safely in the corner of the airfield.*

▲ **put *sb* down *somewhere*** [VEHICLE] *phrasal verb* [M] *UK SLIGHTLY OLD-FASHIONED* to stop a vehicle and allow someone to get out of it or off it: *Ask the taxi driver to put you down outside the church.*

▲ **put *sb* down as *sth*** *phrasal verb* to think that someone is a particular type of person, especially when you do not know them very well: *I'd hate them to put me down as a snob.*

▲ **put *sb* down for *sth*** *phrasal verb* to make a record that someone has promised to pay a particular sum of money as part of a collection to help people in need: *Put me down for a £10 donation, and you can put my husband down for the same.*

▲ **put *sth* down to *sth*** *phrasal verb* to think that a problem or situation is caused by a particular thing: *I put the children's bad behaviour down to the fact that they were tired.*

• **put it down to experience** to decide that instead of being upset about something bad that has happened or that you have done, you will learn from it: *Okay, so you made a mistake – you just have to put it down to experience and carry on with your life.*

P

▲ **put *sth/sb* forward** [SUGGEST] *phrasal verb* [M] (*US* **put *sth/sb* forth**) to state an idea or opinion, or to suggest a plan or person, for other people to consider: *The **proposals** that you have put forward deserve serious consideration.* ○ *I wasn't convinced by any of the **arguments** that he put forward.* ○ *Many **suggestions** have been put forward, but a decision is unlikely until after next year's general election.* ○ *The peace **plan** put forward last August has been revived for the latest round of negotiations.* ○ [R] *She has decided to put her **name**/put her**self** forward **as** a candidate.*

▲ **put *sth* forward** [CHANGE CLOCK] *phrasal verb* [M] to adjust a clock or watch to make it show a later time, especially an hour later: *Most European countries put the clocks forward in the spring.*

▲ **put *sth* in** [EQUIPMENT] *phrasal verb* [M] to fix a large piece of equipment or system into a room or building, ready to be used: *I've just had central heating/a new kitchen put in.*

▲ **put *sth* in/put *sth* into *sth*** [EFFORT] *phrasal verb* [M] to spend a lot of time or effort doing something: *You've obviously put a lot of **work** in **on** your garden.* ○ *If I put in some extra hours* (= spend some extra hours working) *today, I can have some time off tomorrow.* ○ *We've put a lot of time and effort into mak**ing** the house look nice.*

▲ **put *sth* in** [OFFER] *phrasal verb* [M] to formally offer a particular thing for consideration: *I've put in an application to the college.* ○ *They've put in a bid for the company/a bid to buy the company.*

▲ **put *(sth)* in** [SAY] *phrasal verb* [M] to say something which adds to or interrupts what is already being said: [+ speech] *"But she's rather inexperienced for the job," put in Jane.*

▲ **put in for *sth*** *phrasal verb* to make an official request to have or do something: *I'm putting in for a job at the hospital.* ○ *Richard's finally put in for his driving test.*

▲ **put *sth* into *sth*** *phrasal verb* ➲See **put [sth] in**.

▲ **put *sth* off** [DELAY] *phrasal verb* [M] to decide or arrange to delay an event or activity until a later time or date: *The meeting has been put off **for** a week.* ○ [+ v-ing] *I can't put off go**ing** to the dentist any longer.*

▲ **put *sb* off** *phrasal verb* [M] to tell someone that you cannot see them or do something for them, or stop them from doing something, until a later time: *I really don't want to go out with Helen and Greg tonight – can't we put them off ?* ○ *He keeps asking me out, and I keep putting him off.*

• **Never put off until tomorrow what you can do today.** *SAYING* said to emphasize that you should not delay doing something if you can do it immediately

▲ **put *sb* off *(sth)*** [TAKE ATTENTION AWAY] *phrasal verb* to take someone's attention away from what they want to be doing or should be doing: *Once she's made up her mind to do something, nothing will put her off.* ○ *Could you be quiet please – I'm trying to concentrate and you're putting me off.* ○ *The sudden flash of the camera put the players off their game.*

• **put *sb* off *their* stride** (*UK ALSO* **put *sb* off *their* stroke**) to take someone's attention away from what they are doing, so that they stop doing it or do it wrong: *He interrupted mid-speech and it put me off my stride.*

▲ **put *sb* off *(sth/sb)*** [DISLIKE] *phrasal verb* to make someone dislike something or someone, or to discourage someone from doing something: *The smell of hospitals always puts me off.* ○ *You have to work long hours and that puts off a lot of people.* ○ *His attitude put me **right** off him.* ○ [+ v-ing] *Personally, I didn't enjoy the film, but don't let that put you off go**ing**.*

▲ **put *sth* on** [COVER BODY] *phrasal verb* [M] to cover part of the body with clothes, shoes, make-up or something similar: *Put your shoes on – we're going out.* ○ *He put on his jacket.* ○ *She puts face cream on every night.* ➲See picture **Phrasal Verbs** on page Centre 9

▲ **put *sth* on** [OPERATE] *phrasal verb* [M] *MAINLY UK* to make a device operate, or to cause a device to play something, such as a CD or video, by pressing a switch: *Could you put the light on?* ○ *Do you mind if I put the television/some music on?* ○ *Don't forgot to put the brake on.*

▲ **put *sth* on** [PRETEND] *phrasal verb* [M] to pretend to have a particular feeling or way of behaving which is not real or natural to you: *Why are you putting on that silly **voice**?* ○ *There's no need to put on that injured expression – you know you're in the wrong.* ○ *I can't tell whether he's really upset, or if he's just putting **it** on.*

▲ **put *sb* on** *phrasal verb MAINLY US INFORMAL* to try to deceive someone into believing something that is not true: *She said she was planning to give her house to a charity for the homeless but I thought she was putting me on.*

put-on /ˈpʊt.ɒn/ [US] /-ɑːn/ *noun* [C] *US INFORMAL* when a person tries to deceive someone into believing something that is not true: *She's not really angry – it's just a put-on.*

▲ **put *sth* on** [PRODUCE] *phrasal verb* [M] *MAINLY UK* to produce or provide something, especially for the benefit of other people or for a special purpose: *She put on a wonderful meal for us.* ○ *They've put on a late-night bus service for students.*

▲ **put *sth* on** [WEIGHT] *phrasal verb* [M] If people or animals put weight on, they become heavier: *I'd expected to put **weight** on when I gave up smoking, but I didn't.* ○ *He's put on 10 pounds in the last month.*

▲ **put *sb* onto *sth*** *phrasal verb* to introduce a person to something or someone that could benefit them: *David put me onto a wonderful vegetarian cookery book.* ○ *Can you put me onto* (= tell me where to find) *a good dentist?*

▲ **put *sth* out** [LIGHT] *phrasal verb* [M] to make a light stop shining by pressing a switch: *Did you put the lights out downstairs?* ○ *Put that torch out!*

▲ **put *sth* out** [STOP BURNING] *phrasal verb* [M] to make something that is burning, such as a fire or cigarette, stop burning: *Firefighters have been called to put out the*

***fire** in the city centre.* ○ *Would you mind putting your **cigarette** out, please?*

▲ **put *sb* out** [CAUSE TROUBLE] *phrasal verb* **1** [M] to cause trouble or extra work for someone: *Would it put you out if we came tomorrow instead of today?* **2** [M usually passive] to annoy or upset someone, often by what you do or say to them: *She was rather put out when they turned up two hours late for dinner.* ○ *He seemed a bit put out **at** not having been invited.*

▲ **put *yourself* out** [HELP] *phrasal verb* [R] to make an effort to do something to help somebody, even if it is inconvenient: *Brian's always willing to put himself out **for** other people.*

▲ **put *sth* out** [MOVE FORWARD] *phrasal verb* [M] to move forward part of your body, such as your hand or your tongue, from your body: *She put out her hand to shake mine.* ○ *Don't put your tongue out – it's rude.*

▲ **put *sth* out** [INJURE] *phrasal verb* INFORMAL to injure part of your body by causing it to be moved out of its correct position: *He put his knee out playing football.*

▲ **put *sth* out** [PRODUCE] *phrasal verb* [M] to produce something in large quantities, so that it can be sold: *They put out millions of pairs of shoes a year.*

▲ **put *sth* out** [INFORMATION] *phrasal verb* [M] to produce information and make it available for everyone to read or hear: *Police have put out a warning to people living in the area.*

▲ **put out** [HAVE SEX] *phrasal verb* US SLANG (especially of a woman) to have sex willingly: *I wasn't going to put out just because he'd paid for dinner.*

▲ **put *sth* out** [MAKE WRONG] *phrasal verb* [M] If a mistake puts out a set of mathematical calculations, it causes them to be wrong: *That one error put the figures out by several thousand pounds.*

▲ **put *sth* out** [WORK] *UK phrasal verb* [M] (*US USUALLY* **contract *sth* out**) If you put work out, you employ someone outside your organization to do it: *The council has put the job of street-cleaning out **to** a private firm.*

▲ **put *sth* over/across** *phrasal verb* [M] to express an idea clearly so that people understand it: *Did you feel that you managed to put over your point of view?* ○ *She's not very good at putting across her ideas.*

• **put one over on *sb*** INFORMAL to trick someone: *He'd tried to put one over on the tax office and got found out.*

▲ **put *sb* through *sth*** [BAD EXPERIENCE] *phrasal verb* to make someone experience something unpleasant or difficult: *I'm sorry to put you through this ordeal.*

▲ **put *sb* through** [TELEPHONE] *phrasal verb* to connect a person using a telephone to the person they want to speak to: *Could you put me through **to** customer services, please?*

▲ **put *sb* through *sth*** [EDUCATION] *phrasal verb* to pay for someone to study at school, college or university: *It's costing them a lot of money to put their children through school.* ○ [R] *She's putting herself through college.*

▲ **put *sth* to *sb*** *phrasal verb* **1** to suggest an idea or plan to someone so that they can consider it or discuss it: *"Shall we all go out for a pizza tonight?" "I don't know. I'll put **it** to Jim and see what he says."* ○ [+ **that**] FORMAL *I put **it** to you* (= I believe it to be true), *Ms Dawson, **that** you were in the building at the time of the murder.* **2** to ask someone a question: *I have a question I want to put to you.*

▲ **put *sth* together** [JOIN] *phrasal verb* [M] to put the parts of something in the correct places and join them to each other: *Model aeroplanes come in pieces which you have to put together.*

▲ **put *sth* together** [COLLECT] *phrasal verb* [M] to prepare a piece of work by collecting several ideas and suggestions and organizing them: *The management are putting together a **plan/proposal/package** to rescue the company.* ○ *It takes about three weeks to put the magazine together.*

▲ **put *sth* towards *sth*** *phrasal verb* to use an amount of money to pay part of the cost of something: *My grandma gave me some money to put towards a new coat.*

▲ **put *sth* up** [RAISE] *phrasal verb* [M] to raise something, or to fix something in a raised position: *Why don't you put up your hood/umbrella* (= raise it over your head)*?* ○ *I put my hand up to ask the teacher a question.* ○ *I put my hair up* (= fixed it into a position on the top of my head) *for the wedding.*

▲ **put *sth* up** [BUILD] *phrasal verb* [M] to build something: *They're planning to put a hotel up where the museum used to be.* ○ *We're going to put up a new fence around our garden.*

▲ **put *sth* up** [FIX] *phrasal verb* [M] to fix an object to a vertical surface: *We've put up some new curtains in the living room.* ○ *Posters advertising the concert have been put up all over the town.*

▲ **put *sth* up** [PRICE] *phrasal verb* [M] *MAINLY UK* to increase the price or value of something: *I see they've put up the price of fuel again.*

▲ **put *sth* up** [MONEY] *phrasal verb* [M] to provide or lend an amount of money for a particular purpose: *The money for the new hospital was put up by an anonymous donor.* ○ *His brother has agreed to put up **bail** for him.*

▲ **put up *sth*** [OPPOSITION] *phrasal verb* to show or express a particular type of opposition to something: *The villagers were unable to put up any **resistance** to the invading troops.* ○ *We're not going to let them build a road here without putting up a **fight**.*

▲ **put *sth/sb* up** [SUGGESTION] *phrasal verb* [M] to suggest an idea, or to make a person available, for consideration: *It was Bob who originally put up the idea of the exhibition.* ○ *Each party is allowed to put up one **candidate**.* ○ *William has been put up **as** a candidate for the committee.* ○ *Is Chris willing to be put up **for** election?*

▲ **put *sb* up** [PLACE TO STAY] *phrasal verb* [M] to provide someone with a place to stay temporarily: *Sally is putting me up **for** the weekend.*

▲ **put up** *phrasal verb MAINLY UK* to stay somewhere for the night: *We put up **at** a small hotel for the night.*

▲ **put *sb* up to *sth*** *phrasal verb* to encourage someone to do something, usually something wrong: *I think he was put up to it by his friends.*

▲ **put up with *sth/sb*** *phrasal verb* to accept or continue to accept an unpleasant situation or experience, or someone who behaves unpleasantly: *I can put up with the house being untidy, but I hate it if it's not clean.* ○ *He's so moody – I don't know why she puts up with him.* ○ *They have a lot to put up with* (= They have a lot of difficulties).

▲ **be put upon** *phrasal verb* [always passive] INFORMAL to be treated badly by someone who takes advantage of your wish to be helpful: *I'm fed up with being put upon by my boss all the time.*

put-upon /ˈpʊt.ə.pɒn/ [US] /ˈpʊt̬.ə.pɑːn/ *adj* INFORMAL having to do more than is fair in order to allow other people to get what they want in a situation: *I don't mind helping them, but I can't help **feeling** a bit put-upon.*

putative /ˈpjuː.tə.tɪv/ [US] /-t̬ə.t̬ɪv/ *adj* [before n] FORMAL generally thought to be or to exist, whether or not this is really true: *The putative leader of the terrorist organization was arrested by police in Birmingham yesterday.*

putatively /ˈpjuː.tə.tɪv.li/ [US] /-t̬ə.t̬ɪv-/ *adv*

putrefy /ˈpjuː.trɪ.faɪ/ *verb* [I] to decay, producing a strong unpleasant smell: *the smell of putrefying flesh* ○ *The body had putrefied beyond recognition.*

putrefaction /ˌpjuː.trɪˈfæk.ʃᵊn/ *noun* [U] FORMAL the state of decaying

putrid [DECAYED] /ˈpjuː.trɪd/ *adj* decayed and having an unpleasant smell: *the putrid body of a dead fox* ○ *What's that putrid **smell**?*

putrid [UNPLEASANT] /ˈpjuː.trɪd/ *adj* INFORMAL very unpleasant or unattractive: *a dress in a putrid shade of yellow*

putsch /pʊtʃ/ *noun* [C] an attempt to remove a government by force

putt /pʌt/ *verb* [I or T] to hit a golf ball gently across an area of short and even grass towards or into a hole: *Palmer putted the ball straight into the hole.* ○ *You need to use a special club for putting.*

putt /pʌt/ *noun* [C] *She won the competition with an impressive six-metre putt* (= a gentle hit across short grass which sends a ball towards or into a hole).

putter /ˈpʌt.əʳ/ [US] /ˈpʌt̬.ɚ/ *noun* [C] **1** a GOLF CLUB (= stick for hitting a golf ball) with a short handle and metal end which is specially designed for putting **2** someone who putts: *He's a good putter.*

putter RELAX US /ˈpʌt.ɚ/ UK /ˈpʌt.ə/ verb [I usually + adv or prep] (*UK* **potter**) to move about without hurrying and in a relaxed and pleasant way: *He really enjoys puttering around in the garden.* **putter** US /ˈpʌt.ɚ/ US /ˈpʌt.ə/ noun [S] (*UK* **potter**)

putter MAKE NOISE /ˈpʌt.ɚ/ US /ˈpʌt.ə/ verb [I] If a machine putters, it makes a low sound repeatedly, showing that it is working slowly

putting green noun [C usually sing] a small area of short grass on which people can gently hit golf balls into a series of holes for entertainment or to practise for a game of golf

putty /ˈpʌt.i/ US /ˈpʌt̬-/ noun [U] a soft oily clay-like substance which is used especially for fixing glass into window frames or for filling small holes in wood
• be (like) putty in sb's hands to be willing to do anything someone wants you to, because you like them so much

put-up job /ˈpʊt.ʌp.dʒɒb/ US /ˈpʊt.ʌp.dʒɑːb/ noun [C usually sing] INFORMAL an attempt to trick or deceive someone: *The scheme looked like a good investment, but it turned out that the whole thing was a put-up job.*

putz /pʌts/ noun [C] US SLANG a stupid person

puzzle /ˈpʌz.l/ verb [I + adv or prep; T] to cause someone to feel confused and slightly worried because they cannot understand something, or to think hard about something in order to understand it: *The findings of the survey puzzle me – they're not at all what I would have expected.* ○ [+ question word] *It puzzles me why she said that.* ○ *Management are still puzzling about/over how the accident could have happened.*

puzzle /ˈpʌz.l/ noun **1** [S] a situation which is difficult to understand: *Scientists have been trying to solve this puzzle for years.* **2** [C] a game or toy in which you have to fit separate pieces together, or a problem or question which you have to answer by using your skill or knowledge: *a jigsaw puzzle ○ a crossword puzzle ○ a puzzle book*

puzzled /ˈpʌz.ld/ adj confused because you do not understand something: *He had a puzzled look on his face.* ○ *I'm still puzzled as to why she said that.* ○ *I'm a bit puzzled that I haven't heard from Liz for so long.*

puzzlement /ˈpʌz.l.mənt/ noun [U] FORMAL a state of confusion because you do not understand something

puzzler /ˈpʌz.lɚ/ /-l.ɚ/ US /-lɚ/ noun [C] INFORMAL something that is difficult to explain or understand: *I don't know what happened to the money – it's a real puzzler.*

puzzling /ˈpʌz.l.ɪŋ/ /-l.ɪŋ/ adj difficult to explain or understand: *It's a rather puzzling film. ○ a puzzling situation*

PHRASAL VERBS WITH **puzzle** ▼

▲ **puzzle** *sth* **out** *phrasal verb* [M] to discover or understand something by thinking hard about it: [+ question word] *I still can't puzzle out how I managed to spend so much money last month.*

▲ **puzzle over** *sth* *phrasal verb* to try to solve a problem or understand a situation by thinking carefully about it: *Scientists are puzzling over the results of the research on the drug.*

PVC /ˌpiː.viːˈsiː/ noun [U] ABBREVIATION FOR POLYVINYL CHLORIDE (= a type of plastic which is used especially for making clothes, floor coverings and bags): *Are those trousers leather or PVC?*

p.w. /ˌpiːˈdʌb.l.juː/ UK ABBREVIATION FOR per week: *I am writing to inform you that your rent will be increased to £60 p.w. from October 1st.*

PWA /ˌpiː.dʌb.l.juːˈeɪ/ noun [C] ABBREVIATION FOR person with AIDS

PWR /ˌpiː.dʌb.l.juːˈɑː/ US /-ˈɑːr/ noun [C] SPECIALIZED ABBREVIATION FOR PRESSURIZED WATER REACTOR (= a device for producing nuclear power which uses water at high pressure to control the production of heat)

PX /ˌpiːˈeks/ noun [C] a shop at a place where American soldiers live and work

Pygmy, **Pigmy** /ˈpɪg.mi/ noun [C] **1** a member of one of several groups of very small people who live in central Africa: *Pygmies average about 1.5 metres in height.* **2** DISAPPROVING someone who is not important or who has little skill: *a political pygmy ○ an intellectual pygmy*

pygmy, **pigmy** /ˈpɪg.mi/ adj [before n] describes an animal or bird which is one of a type which is smaller than animals or birds of that type usually are: *a pygmy hippopotamus ○ a pygmy owl*

pyjamas /pɪˈdʒɑː.məz/ plural noun **1** MAINLY UK (US USUALLY **pajamas**) soft loose clothing which is worn in bed and consists of trousers and a type of shirt: *I need a new pair of pyjamas.* **2** loose trousers that are tied around the waist and worn by men and women in some Asian countries

pyjama MAINLY UK, US USUALLY **pajama** /pɪˈdʒɑː.mə/ adj [before n] *pyjama bottoms* (= trousers) ○ *a pyjama top*

pylon /ˈpaɪ.lɒn/ US /-lɑːn/ noun [C] **1** a tall steel structure to which wires carrying electricity are fixed so that they are safely held high above the ground: *electricity pylons* **2** a tall tower or post which shows where aircraft should land

PYO /ˌpiː.waɪˈəʊ/ US /-ˈoʊ/ ABBREVIATION FOR 'pick your own', used in signs outside farms where people can pick fruit and vegetables themselves and then pay for the amount they have picked: *PYO strawberries*

pyramid /ˈpɪr.ə.mɪd/ noun [C] **1** a solid object with a flat square base and four flat triangular sides which slope toward each other and meet to form a point at the top **2** **the Pyramids** stone structures in Egypt of a pyramid shape which were built in ancient times as places to bury important people, especially kings and queens **3** a pile of things which has the shape of a pyramid: *The acrobats formed a pyramid by standing on each other's shoulders.* ○ FIGURATIVE *Many organizations have a pyramid structure* (= there are fewer people at the top levels of them than there are at the bottom).

pyramidal /pɪˈræm.ɪ.dəl/ adj SPECIALIZED having a pyramid shape

pyramid scheme noun [C] US a way of deceiving investors in which money that a company receives from new customers is not invested for their benefit, but is used instead to pay debts owed to existing customers

pyramid selling noun [U] in business, when someone buys the right to sell a company's goods, and then sells the goods to other people. These people then sell the goods to other people.

pyre /paɪə/ US /paɪr/ noun [C] a large pile of wood on which a dead body is burnt in some parts of the world: *A traditional Indian custom used to involve widows burning themselves alive on their husbands' funeral pyres.*

Pyrex /ˈpaɪ.reks/ noun [U] TRADEMARK a type of glass that does not break when it is heated, so it is used for making containers that are used for cooking: *a Pyrex dish/bowl*

pyromania /ˌpaɪ.rəʊˈmeɪ.ni.ə/ US /-roʊ-/ noun [U] a mental illness in which a person feels an uncontrollable desire to start fires

pyromaniac /ˌpaɪ.rəʊˈmeɪ.ni.æk/ US /-roʊ-/ noun [C] someone who suffers from pyromania

pyrotechnics /ˌpaɪ.rəʊˈtek.nɪks/ US /-roʊ-/ plural noun **1** a public show of fireworks **2** a show of great skill, especially by a musician or someone giving a speech: *His verbal pyrotechnics could hold an audience spellbound.* **pyrotechnic** /ˌpaɪ.rəʊˈtek.nɪk/ US /-roʊ-/ adj [before n]

Pyrrhic victory /ˌpɪr.ɪkˈvɪk.tʳr.i/ US /-tɚ-/ noun [C usually sing] a victory which is not worth winning because the winner has lost so much in winning it: *She won the court case, but it was a Pyrrhic victory because she had to pay so much in legal fees.*

python /ˈpaɪ.θ³n/ US /-θɑːn/ noun [C] plural **pythons** or **python** a very large snake that kills animals for food by wrapping itself around them and crushing them

pzazz /pəˈzæz/ noun [U] INFORMAL **pizzazz**

Q

Q [LETTER] (*plural* **Q's** or **Qs**), **q** (*plural* **q's** or **qs**) /kjuː/ *noun* [C] the 17th letter of the English alphabet

Q [QUESTION], **q** *WRITTEN ABBREVIATION FOR* **question** ASKING

ˌQ and ˈA *adj* [before n] *MAINLY US ABBREVIATION FOR* question and answer: *The textbook has a Q and A section at the end of each chapter.*

QC /ˌkjuːˈsiː/ *noun* [C] *ABBREVIATION FOR* Queen's Counsel: a high-ranking British lawyer: *A QC is a senior barrister.* ○ *Charles Gordon, QC* ➲Compare **KC**.

QED /ˌkjuː.iːˈdiː/ *SPECIALIZED* written after an argument in mathematics to show that you have proven something that you wanted to prove

qt *WRITTEN ABBREVIATION FOR* **quart**

Q-Tip /ˈkjuː.tɪp/ *noun* [C] *US TRADEMARK FOR* **cotton bud**

qua /kwɑː/ *prep FORMAL* as a particular example of something, or the general idea of something: *Qua musician, he lacks skill, but his playing is lively and enthusiastic.*

quack [SOUND] /kwæk/ *verb* [I] to make the usual sound of a duck: *The ducks started quacking loudly when we threw them some bread.* **quack** /kwæk/ *noun* [C]

quack [DISHONEST PERSON] /kwæk/ *noun* [C] **1** *DISAPPROVING* a person who dishonestly pretends to have medical skills or knowledge **2** *UK INFORMAL OFTEN DISAPPROVING* a doctor: *Have you seen a quack about that cough?*

quackery /ˈkwæk.ər.i/ [US] /-ɚ-/ *noun* [U] *DISAPPROVING* medical methods that do not work and are only intended to make money

quad [PERSON] /kwɒd/ [US] /kwɑːd/ *noun* [C] *INFORMAL FOR* **quadruplet**

quad [SQUARE SPACE] /kwɒd/ [US] /kwɑːd/ *noun* [C] (*FORMAL* **quadrangle**) a square space outside, which has buildings on all four sides, especially in a school or college

ˈquad ˌbike *noun* [C] a motor vehicle similar to a motorcycle with four wheels

quadrant [PART OF CIRCLE] /ˈkwɒd.rənt/ [US] /ˈkwɑː.drənt/ *noun* [C] *SPECIALIZED* a quarter of a circle

quadrant [DEVICE] /ˈkwɒd.rənt/ [US] /ˈkwɑː.drənt/ *noun* [C] *SPECIALIZED* a device for measuring the height of stars in the sky which was used in the past for calculating directions when travelling across the sea

quadraphonic, *UK ALSO* **quadrophonic** /ˌkwɒd.rəˈfɒn.ɪk/ [US] /ˌkwɑː.drəˈfɑː.nɪk/ *adj* (of an electronic system of recording, playing or receiving sound) having sound coming from four different directions ➲Compare **mono** SOUND; **stereo**.

quadratic equation /kwɒdˌræt.ɪk.ɪˈkweɪ.ʒən/ [US] /-ˌræt̬-/ *noun* [C] an EQUATION (= mathematical statement) which includes an unknown value that is multiplied by itself only once, and which does not include an unknown value multiplied by itself more than once: *In the quadratic equation, $2y^2+3y=14$, $y=2$ or $y=-3\frac{3}{4}$.*

quadrilateral /ˌkwɒd.rɪˈlæt.ər.əl/ [US] /ˌkwɑː.drɪˈlæt̬-/ *noun* [C] *SPECIALIZED* a flat shape with four straight sides: *Squares and rectangles are quadrilaterals.*

quadriplegic, *AUS* **quadruplegic** /ˌkwɒd.rəˈpliː.dʒɪk/ [US] /ˌkwɑː.drə-/ *noun* [C] a person who is permanently unable to move any of their arms or legs, often because their spine has been injured

quadruped /ˈkwɒd.rʊ.ped/ [US] /ˈkwɑː.drə-/ *noun* [C] *SPECIALIZED* any animal that has four legs: *Horses, lions and dogs are quadrupeds, but humans are bipeds.* ➲Compare **biped**.

quadruple /kwɒdˈruː.pl̩/ [US] /kwɑːˈdruː-/ *verb* [I or T] to become four times as big, or to multiply a number or amount by four: *The number of students at the college has quadrupled in the last ten years.* ○ *We expect to quadruple our profits this year.*

quadruple /ˈkwɒd.rʊp.l̩/ [US] /kwɑːˈdruː.pl̩/ *adj, predeterminer*: *a quadruple measure* (= one four times as big as usual) ○ *We have had quadruple the number of applicants we expected.*

quadruplet /kwɒdˈruː.plət/ [US] /kwɑːˈdruː-/ *noun* [C] (*INFORMAL* **quad**) any of four children who are born to the same mother at the same time

quaff /kwɒf/ [US] /kwæf/ *verb* [I or T] *OLD-FASHIONED* to drink something quickly or in large amounts

quaffable /ˈkwɒf.ə.bl̩/ [US] /ˈkwæf-/ *adj HUMOROUS* If an alcoholic drink is quaffable, it is easy and pleasant to drink a lot of it: *This wine is very quaffable, isn't it?*

quagmire /ˈkwɒg.maɪər/ [US] /ˈkwæg.maɪr/ *noun* [C] **1** an area of soft wet ground which you sink into if you try and walk on it: *At the end of the match, the pitch was a real quagmire.* **2** a difficult and dangerous situation: *Since the coup, the country has sunk deeper into a quagmire of violence and lawlessness.*

quail [BIRD] /kweɪl/ *noun* [C or U] *plural* **quail** or **quails** a small brown bird which is shot for sport or food, or the meat of this bird: *Quails' eggs are considered to be a delicacy.*

quail [SHOW FEAR] /kweɪl/ *verb* [I] *LITERARY* to feel or show fear; to want to be able to move away from something because you fear it: *Charlie quailed* ***at*** *the sound of his mother's angry voice.* ○ *She quailed* ***before*** *her boss's anger.*

quaint /kweɪnt/ *adj* **1** attractive because of being unusual and especially old-fashioned: *a quaint old cottage* **2** Quaint can also be used to show that you do not approve of something, especially an opinion, belief or way of behaving, because it is strange or old-fashioned: *"What a quaint idea!" she said, laughing at him.* **quaintly** /ˈkweɪnt.li/ *adv* **quaintness** /ˈkweɪnt.nəs/ *noun* [U]

quake [SHAKE] /kweɪk/ *verb* [I] to shake because you are very frightened or very amused, or to feel or show great fear: *Every time I get on a plane, I quake* ***with fear.*** ○ *Charlie stood outside the head teacher's office, quaking* ***in*** *his* ***boots/shoes*** (= feeling very frightened). ○ *The play was so funny, we were all quaking* ***with laughter.***

quake [EARTH MOVEMENT] /kweɪk/ *noun* [C] *INFORMAL FOR* **earthquake**

Quaker /ˈkweɪ.kər/ [US] /-kɚ/ *noun* [C] (*ALSO* **Friend**) a member of a Christian group called the Society of Friends, which does not have formal ceremonies or a formal system of beliefs, and which is strongly opposed to violence and war **Quaker** /ˈkweɪ.kər/ [US] /-kɚ/ *adj*

qualify [FINISH TRAINING] /ˈkwɒl.ɪ.faɪ/ [US] /ˈkwɑː.lɪ-/ *verb* [I or T] to successfully finish a training course so that you are able to do a job; to have or achieve the necessary skills, etc: *She hopes to qualify* ***(as*** *a lawyer) at the end of the year.* ○ [+ obj + **to** infinitive] *This course qualifies you* ***to*** *teach in any secondary school.*

qualification /ˌkwɒl.ɪ.fɪˈkeɪ.ʃən/ [US] /ˌkwɑː.lɪ-/ *noun* **1** [C] an official record showing that you have finished a training course or have the necessary skills, etc: *You'll never get a good job if you don't have any qualifications.* ○ *Do you have any teaching/legal/medical/secretarial/academic qualifications?* **2** [C or U] an ability, characteristic or experience that makes you suitable for a particular job or activity: *Some nursing experience is a necessary qualification* ***for*** *this job.* ○ [+ **to** infinitive] *One of the qualifications you need* ***to*** *work here is a sense of humour!*

qualified /ˈkwɒl.ɪ.faɪd/ [US] /ˈkwɑː.lɪ-/ *adj* having finished a training course, or having particular skills, etc: *Tim is now a qualified architect.* ○ *What makes you think that you are qualified* ***for*** *this job?* ○ *I'm not qualified* ***to*** *give advice on such matters.*

qualify [GET INTO COMPETITION] /ˈkwɒl.ɪ.faɪ/ [US] /ˈkwɑː.lɪ-/ *verb* [I] to succeed in getting into a competition: *Nigeria was the first team to qualify* ***for*** *the World Cup.* ○ *England has to win tonight's qualifying match to go through to the next round of the competition.*

qualifier /ˈkwɒl.ɪ.faɪ.ər/ [US] /ˈkwɑː.lɪ.faɪ.ɚ/ *noun* [C] **1** a team or person who has won part of a competition and is therefore competing in the next part of it: *The qualifiers from the first round will go into the quarter final.* **2** a game from which the winner will go on to compete in the next part of a competition: *Belgium and Italy are playing in tonight's qualifier.*

qualify RIGHT /ˈkwɒl.ɪ.faɪ/ Ⓤ /ˈkwɑː.lɪ-/ *verb* [I or T] to have the legal right to have or do something because of the situation you are in, or to cause someone to have such a right: *She doesn't qualify **for** maternity leave because she hasn't been in her job long enough.* ○ *To qualify **for** the competition you need to be over 18.* ○ *Being a single parent qualifies you **for** extra benefits.* ○ [+ obj + to infinitive] FIGURATIVE *He thinks the fact that he's worked here longer than the rest of us qualifies him* (= gives him the right) **to** *tell us all what to do.*

qualify LIMIT /ˈkwɒl.ɪ.faɪ/ Ⓤ /ˈkwɑː.lɪ-/ *verb* [T] **1** to limit the strength or meaning of a statement: *I'd like to qualify my criticisms of the school's failings, by adding that it's a very happy place.* **2** SPECIALIZED In grammar, a word or phrase which qualifies another word or phrase limits its meaning and makes it less general: *In the sentence 'He walked quickly along the road', 'quickly' and 'along the road' qualify 'walked'.*

qualification /ˌkwɒl.ɪ.fɪˈkeɪ.ʃən/ Ⓤ /ˌkwɑː.lɪ-/ *noun* [C] a limitation: [+ that] *The doctor said I can leave hospital today, but with the qualification **that** I've got to come back every day to have the dressing changed.*

qualified /ˈkwɒl.ɪ.faɪd/ Ⓤ /ˈkwɑː.lɪ-/ *adj* limited: *There seems to be qualified support for the idea.*

qualifier /ˈkwɒl.ɪ.faɪ.əʳ/ Ⓤ /ˈkwɑː.lɪ.faɪ.ɚ/ *noun* [C] SPECIALIZED in grammar, a word or phrase which limits the meaning of another word or phrase, or makes it less general, such as an adjective or adverb

quality STANDARD /ˈkwɒl.ɪ.ti/ Ⓤ /ˈkwɑː.lə.t̬i/ *noun* **1** [C or U] how good or bad something is: *a shop advertising top quality electrical goods* ○ *The food was of such poor/low quality.* ○ *Their products are of very high quality.* ○ *I only buy good-quality wine.* ○ *The quality **of** the picture on our television isn't very good.* **2** [U] a high standard: *He's not interested in quality. All he cares about is making money.*

● **quality of life** the level of enjoyment, comfort and health in someone's life: *My quality of life has improved tremendously since I moved to the country.*

quality /ˈkwɒl.ɪ.ti/ Ⓤ /ˈkwɑː.lə.t̬i/ *adj* [before n] of a high standard: *This is a quality product.* ○ MAINLY UK *The story received little coverage in the quality **papers*** (= more serious newspapers).

qualitative /ˈkwɒl.ɪ.tə.tɪv/ Ⓤ /ˈkwɑː.lɪ.teɪ.t̬ɪv/ *adj* FORMAL relating to how good or bad something is: *Is there any qualitative difference between these two video recorders?*

quality CHARACTERISTIC /ˈkwɒl.ɪ.ti/ Ⓤ /ˈkwɑː.lə.t̬i/ *noun* [C] a characteristic or feature of someone or something: *leadership qualities* ○ *He has a lot of good qualities but being organized isn't one of them.* ○ [+ to infinitive] *I don't think he has the right qualities **to** be a teacher.* ○ *This cheese has a rather rubbery quality **to** it* (= it is like rubber).

qualitative /ˈkwɒl.ɪ.tə.tɪv/ Ⓤ /ˈkwɑː.lɪ.teɪ.t̬ɪv/ *adj* FORMAL relating to what something or someone is like: *There has been a qualitative change in the relationship between the public and the government.* ⊃Compare **quantitative** at **quantity**. **qualitatively** /ˈkwɒl.ɪ.tə.tɪv.li/ Ⓤ /ˈkwɑː.lɪ.teɪ.t̬ɪv-/ *adv*

quality conˌtrol *noun* [C or U] the process of looking at goods when they are being produced to make certain that all the goods are of the intended standard

quality ˌtime *noun* [U] time that you spend with someone, giving them your full attention because you value the relationship: *He makes sure he **spends** a few hours quality time with his children every day.*

qualm /kwɑːm/ *noun* [C usually pl] an uncomfortable feeling of doubt about whether you are doing the right thing: *She **had no** qualms **about** lying to the police.*

quandary /ˈkwɒn.dri/ Ⓤ /ˈkwɑːn-/ *noun* [C usually sing] a state of not being able to decide what to do about a situation in which you are involved: *I've had two job offers, and I'm **in a** real quandary **about/over** which one to accept.*

quango /ˈkwæŋ.ɡəʊ/ Ⓤ /-ɡoʊ/ *noun* [C] *plural* **quangos** OFTEN DISAPPROVING an organization which is established by a government to consider a subject of public importance, but which is independent from the government

quantify /ˈkwɒn.tɪ.faɪ/ Ⓤ /ˈkwɑːn.t̬ə-/ *verb* [T] to measure or judge the size or amount of something: *It's difficult to quantify how many people will be affected by the change in the law.*

quantifiable /ˈkwɒn.tɪ.faɪ.ə.bl̩/ Ⓤ /ˈkwɑːn.t̬ə-/ *adj* able to be measured: *The benefits of the new policy are not easily quantifiable.* **quantification** /ˌkwɒn.tɪ.fɪˈkeɪ.ʃən/ Ⓤ /ˌkwɑːn.t̬ə-/ *noun* [U]

quantifier /ˈkwɒn.tɪ.faɪ.əʳ/ Ⓤ /ˈkwɑːn.t̬ə.faɪ.ɚ/ *noun* [C] SPECIALIZED a word or phrase which is used before a noun to show the amount of it that is being considered: *'Some', 'many', 'a lot of' and 'a few' are examples of quantifiers.*

quantity /ˈkwɒn.tɪ.ti/ Ⓤ /ˈkwɑːn.t̬ə.t̬i/ *noun* **1** [C or U] the amount or number of something, especially that can be measured or is fixed: *Police found a **large/small** quantity **of** drugs in his possession.* ○ *We consumed **vast** quantities **of** food and drink that night.* ○ *The (**sheer**) quantity* (= large amount) ***of** equipment needed for the trip is staggering.* ○ *They are now developing ways to produce the vaccine **in** large quantities and cheaply.* ○ *This recipe is only for four, so I usually double the quantity if I'm cooking for my family.* ○ *It's quality not quantity that really counts.*

quantitative /ˈkwɒn.tɪ.tə.tɪv/ Ⓤ /ˈkwɑːn.t̬ə.teɪ.t̬ɪv/ *adj* SPECIALIZED relating to numbers or amounts: *quantitative analysis* ⊃Compare **qualitative** at **quality** CHARACTERISTIC. **quantitatively** /ˈkwɒn.tɪ.tə.tɪv.li/ Ⓤ /ˈkwɑːn.t̬ə.teɪ.t̬ɪv-/ *adv*

quantity surˌveyor *noun* [C] UK a person whose job is to calculate the cost of the materials and work needed for future building work

quantum /ˈkwɒn.təm/ Ⓤ /ˈkwɑːn.t̬əm/ *noun* [C] *plural* **quanta** SPECIALIZED the smallest amount or unit of something, especially energy: *quantum theory*

quantum ˈleap *noun* [C usually sing] a great improvement or important advance in something: *The appointment of a female director is a quantum leap for women's equality.*

quantum meˈchanics *plural noun* SPECIALIZED in physics, a theory that explains the behaviour of ELEMENTARY PARTICLES, both separately and in groups

quarantine /ˈkwɒr.ən.tiːn/ Ⓤ /ˈkwɔːr-/ *noun* [U] a period of time during which a person or animal that might have a disease is kept away from other people or animals so that the disease cannot spread: *The horse had to spend several months **in** quarantine when it reached Britain.* **quarantine** /ˈkwɒr.ən.tiːn/ Ⓤ /ˈkwɔːr-/ *verb* [T]

quark /kwɑːk/ Ⓤ /kwɑːrk/ *noun* [C] SPECIALIZED in physics, one of the most basic forms of matter that make up the heavier ELEMENTARY PARTICLES: *Atoms are made up of smaller particles – protons, neutrons and electrons – some of which are made up of even smaller ones, called quarks.*

quarrel /ˈkwɒr.əl/ Ⓤ /ˈkwɔːr-/ *noun* [C] an angry disagreement between two or more people or groups: *They **had a** bitter quarrel **about/over** some money three years ago and they haven't spoken to each other since.* ○ *We have no quarrel **with** the people of your country* (= We have no reason to disagree with or dislike them). ○ *They seem to have **patched up** their quarrel* (= finished their disagreement and started to be friendly). **quarrel** /ˈkwɒr.əl/ Ⓤ /ˈkwɔːr-/ *verb* [I] -ll- or US USUALLY -l- *What did you quarrel **about/over**?*

quarrelsome /ˈkwɒr.əl.səm/ Ⓤ /ˈkwɔːr-/ *adj* DISAPPROVING A quarrelsome person repeatedly argues with other people.

quarry HOLE /ˈkwɒr.i/ Ⓤ /ˈkwɔːr-/ *noun* [C] a large artificial hole in the ground where stone, sand, etc. is dug out of the ground for use as building material: *a granite/limestone/marble/slate quarry*

quarry /ˈkwɒr.i/ Ⓤ /ˈkwɔːr-/ *verb* [T] to dig stone, etc. from a quarry

quarry HUNTED /ˈkwɒr.i/ Ⓤ /ˈkwɔːr-/ *noun* [S] a person or animal being hunted or looked for: *The dogs pursued their quarry into an empty warehouse.*

quart /kwɔːt/ Ⓤ /kwɔːrt/ *noun* [C] (WRITTEN ABBREVIATION **qt**) a unit of measurement for liquids, equal to approximately 1.14 litres in Britain, or 0.95 litres in the US: *A* *quart is so called because it is a quarter of a gallon.*

quarter [FOURTH PART] /ˈkwɔː.təʳ/ [US] /ˈkwɑː.t̬ɚ/ *noun* [C] **1** one of four equal or almost equal parts of something; ¼: *He cut the orange into quarters.* ○ *Under a quarter **of** people questioned said that they were happily married.* ○ *My house is situated a mile and three-quarters from here.* **2 a quarter of an hour** 15 minutes: *I waited a quarter of an hour and then went home.* ○ *I was there three-quarters of an hour.* ○ *an hour and three-quarters* **3 a quarter to/**(US ALSO) ***of two/three/four, etc.*** 15 minutes before two/three/four, etc: *It was a quarter to six when I left.* **4 a quarter past/**(US ALSO) ***after two/three/four, etc.*** 15 minutes after two/three/four, etc: *I'll meet you at a quarter past five.* **5** one of four periods of time into which a year is divided for financial calculations, such as for profits or taxes: *There was a fall in unemployment in the second quarter of the year.* ○ *I get an electricity bill every quarter.* **6** one of four periods in a game of American football and other ball sports

quarter /ˈkwɔː.təʳ/ [US] /ˈkwɑː.t̬ɚ/ *verb* [T often passive] to cut something into four parts

quarterly /ˈkwɔː.tᵊl.i/ [US] /ˈkwɑː.t̬ɚ.li/ *adj, adv*: *a quarterly magazine* ○ *The magazine will be published quarterly* (= four times a year).

quarter [MONEY] /ˈkwɔː.təʳ/ [US] /ˈkwɑː.t̬ɚ/ *noun* [C] in the US and Canada, a coin worth 25 cents

quarter [AREA] /ˈkwɔː.təʳ/ [US] /ˈkwɑː.t̬ɚ/ *noun* [C] an area of a town where a particular group of people live or work or where a particular activity happens: *This is the bustling commercial quarter of the city.*

quarter [PERSON] /ˈkwɔː.təʳ/ [US] /ˈkwɑː.t̬ɚ/ *noun* [C] one or more people who provide help, information or a particular reaction to something but who are not usually named: *Help came from an unexpected quarter.* ○ *There is a feeling **in certain/some** quarters* (= Some people consider) *that a change is needed.*

quarter [FORGIVENESS] /ˈkwɔː.təʳ/ [US] /ˈkwɑː.t̬ɚ/ *noun* [U] LITERARY a show of kindness and forgiveness towards a person that you have defeated, especially in allowing them to live: *We can expect **no** quarter from our enemies.*

quarterback /ˈkwɔː.tə.bæk/ [US] /ˈkwɑː.t̬ɚ-/ *noun* [C] MAINLY US (in American football) the player who receives the ball at the start of every play and tries to move it along the field

quarterdeck /ˈkwɔː.tə.dek/ [US] /ˈkwɑː.t̬ɚ-/ *noun* [C] the highest part of the DECK at the back of a ship: *The quarterdeck is usually reserved for officers.*

quarterfinal /ˌkwɔː.təˈfaɪ.nəl/ [US] /ˌkwɑː.t̬ɚ-/ *noun* [C] any of the four games in a competition that decides which players or teams will play in the two SEMI-FINALS

ˈquarter ˌnote *noun* [C] US FOR **crotchet**

quarters /ˈkwɔː.təz/ [US] /ˈkwɑː.t̬ɚz/ *plural noun* a room or house that has been provided, especially for servants or soldiers and their families, to live in: *The army's **married** quarters are just outside the town.*

quarter /ˈkwɔː.təʳ/ [US] /ˈkwɑː.t̬ɚ/ *verb* [T usually passive + adv or prep] to send especially soldiers to live in a place: *The soldiers were quartered with* (= they lived with) *local villagers during the war.*

quartet /kwɔːˈtet/ [US] /kwɔːr-/ *group noun* [C] a group of four people who play musical instruments or sing as a group: *A string quartet was playing Mozart.* ○ *He has composed 14 quartets and 11 symphonies.*

quartet /kwɔːˈtet/ [US] /kwɔːr-/ *noun* [C] a piece of music written for four people

quartz /ˈkwɔːts/ [US] /ˈkwɔːrts/ *noun* [U] a hard colourless mineral substance, used in making electronic equipment and accurate watches and clocks

quasar /ˈkweɪ.zɑːʳ/ [US] /-zɑːr/ *noun* [C] SPECIALIZED the centre of a very distant GALAXY (= group of stars), producing large amounts of energy

quash [REFUSE] /kwɒʃ/ [US] /kwɑːʃ/ *verb* [T] to state officially that something, especially an earlier official decision, is no longer to be accepted: *His **conviction** was quashed in March 1986 after his counsel argued that the police evidence was a tissue of lies.*

quash [STOP] /kwɒʃ/ [US] /kwɑːʃ/ *verb* [T] to forcefully stop something that you do not want to happen: *The revolt was swiftly quashed by government troops.* ○ *The company moved quickly to quash **rumours/speculation** that it is losing money.*

quasi- /kweɪ.zaɪ-/ *prefix* used to show that something is almost, but not completely, the thing described: *The school uniform is quasi-military in style.*

quatrain /ˈkwɒt.reɪn/ [US] /ˈkwɑː.treɪn/ /-ˈ-/ *noun* [C] SPECIALIZED a group of four lines in a poem

quaver [SHAKE] /ˈkweɪ.vəʳ/ [US] /-vɚ/ *verb* [I] (of a person's voice) to sound shaky, especially because of emotion: *Her **voice** began to quaver and I thought she was going to cry.* **quaver** /ˈkweɪ.vəʳ/ [US] /-vɚ/ *noun* [S] *There was a quaver in her voice as she thanked her staff for all their support.* **quavery** /ˈkweɪ.vᵊr.i/ [US] /-vɚ-/ *adj*

quaver [MUSICAL NOTE] MAINLY UK /ˈkweɪ.vəʳ/ [US] /-vɚ/ *noun* [C] (US USUALLY **eighth note**) SPECIALIZED a musical note that is half as long as a CROTCHET

quay /kiː/ *noun* [C] a long structure, usually built of stone, where boats can be tied up to load and unload their goods

quayside /ˈkiː.saɪd/ *noun* [C usually sing] the edge of a QUAY, beside the water: *The animals were unloaded **on/at** the quayside.*

queasy /ˈkwiː.zi/ *adj* likely to vomit: *I started to **feel** queasy as soon as the boat left the harbour.* ○ *Just the thought of blood makes me queasy.* **queasily** /ˈkwiː.zɪ.li/ *adv* **queasiness** /ˈkwiː.zɪ.nəs/ *noun* [U]

queen [WOMAN] /kwiːn/ *noun* [C] **1** a woman who rules a country because she has been born into a royal family, or a woman who is married to a king: *How long did Queen Victoria **reign**?* ○ *The Queen is meeting the Prime Minister today.* **2** any woman who is considered to be the best at what she does: *She's the **reigning** queen **of** crime writers.* **3** the most powerful piece on the board in the game of CHESS **4** in a group of insects, a single large female that produces eggs: *a queen **bee*** ○ *a queen **ant*** ○ *a queen **wasp*** **5** in a set of playing cards, a card with a picture of a queen on it. It is usually worth less than a king.

queen [HOMOSEXUAL] /kwiːn/ *noun* [C] SLANG OFFENSIVE a homosexual man, especially an older man, whose manner is noticeable and artificial: *James is such an **old** queen.*

Queen Anne's lace /ˌkwiːn.ænzˈleɪs/ *noun* [U] MAINLY US **cow parsley**

ˌQueen ˈMother *noun* [C usually sing] the mother of the king or queen who is ruling

Queen's evidence /ˌkwiːnzˈev.ɪ.dᵊnts/ *noun* [U] LEGAL evidence from someone who has been accused of committing a crime, given against the people who were accused with them, in order to have their own punishment reduced ➲See also **King's evidence**; **state's evidence**.

• **turn Queen's evidence** to give evidence against someone else in this way

queenside /ˈkwiːn.saɪd/ *noun* [U] SPECIALIZED in the game of chess, the side of the board on which your queen is positioned at the start of the game **queenside** /ˈkwiːn.saɪd/ *adj*

queer [HOMOSEXUAL] /kwɪəʳ/ [US] /kwɪr/ *adj* OFFENSIVE (especially of a man) homosexual * Note: Homosexuals sometimes use this word in a way that is not offensive.

queer /kwɪəʳ/ [US] /kwɪr/ *noun* [C] OFFENSIVE a homosexual, especially a man

queer [STRANGE] /kwɪəʳ/ [US] /kwɪr/ *adj* OLD-FASHIONED strange, unusual or not expected: *What a queer thing to say!* ○ *I'm feeling rather queer* (= ill), *may I sit down?*

queer [SPOIL] /kwɪəʳ/ [US] /kwɪr/ *verb* UK INFORMAL **queer *sb's* pitch** to spoil a chance or an opportunity for someone, often on purpose: *If she asks Ian for a pay rise before I do, it will probably queer my pitch.*

ˈqueer ˌbashing *noun* [U] SLANG when people are physically attacked and hurt because they are homosexual

quell /kwel/ *verb* [T] to stop something, especially by using force: *Police in riot gear were called in to quell the **disturbances/unrest**.* ○ *This latest setback will have done nothing to quell the growing **doubts** about the future of the club.*

Q

quench /kwentʃ/ *verb* [T] **1** to satisfy your thirst by having a drink: *When it's hot, it's best to quench your **thirst** with water.* **2** *LITERARY* to cause a fire to stop burning with water: *The flames were quenched by heavy rain.* **3** to satisfy a need or desire: *Her thirst for knowledge will never be quenched.*

querulous /ˈkwer.jʊ.ləs/ *adj* often complaining, especially in a weak high voice: *He became increasingly dissatisfied and querulous in his old age.* **querulously** /ˈkwer.jʊ.lə.sli/ *adv*

query /ˈkwɪə.ri/ [US] /ˈkwɪr.i/ *noun* [C] a question, often expressing doubt about something or looking for an answer from an authority: *If you have any queries **about** your treatment, the doctor will **answer** them.*

query /ˈkwɪə.ri/ [US] /ˈkwɪr.i/ *verb* [T] to ask questions, especially in order to check if something is true: *A few students have queried their marks.* ○ [+ question word] *She queried **wh**ether three months was long enough.* ○ [+ speech] *"Any chance of a cup of tea?" he queried hopefully.*

quest /kwest/ *noun* [C] *LITERARY* a long search for something that is difficult to find, or an attempt to achieve something difficult: *Nothing will stop them **in** their quest **for** truth.* ○ *She went to India **on** a spiritual quest.* ○ [+ to infinitive] *She does aerobics four times a week in her quest **to** achieve the perfect body.*

question [ASKING] /ˈkwes.tʃən/ *noun* [C] **1** a sentence or phrase used to find out information: *The police **asked** me questions all day.* ○ *Why won't you **answer** my question?* ○ *"So where is the missing money?" **"That's a good** question."* (= I don't know the answer.) ○ *There will be a question-**and-answer session*** (= a period when people can ask questions) *at the end of the talk.* **2** in an exam, a problem that tests a person's knowledge or ability: ***Answer/Do** as many questions as you can in the allotted time.*

question /ˈkwes.tʃən/ *verb* [T] **1** to ask a person about something, especially officially: *Several men were questioned by police yesterday about the burglary.* ○ *68% of those questioned in the poll thought noise levels had increased.* **2** to express doubts about the value of something or whether something is true: *I questioned **the wisdom of** taking so many pills.* ○ [+ question word] *Two months ago, results from a European study questioned **wh**ether early treatment with the drug really improved survival.* ○ *She gave me a questioning look* (= as if she wanted an answer from me).

questionable /ˈkwes.tʃə.nə.bl̩/ *adj* [+ question word] not certain, or wrong in some way: ***It** is questionable **wh**ether this goal can be achieved.* ○ *Much of late-night television is of questionable **value/taste**.*

questioner /ˈkwes.tʃə.nəʳ/ [US] /-nɚ/ *noun* [C] a person who asks a question

questioning /ˈkwes.tʃə.nɪŋ/ *noun* [U] when the police ask someone questions about a crime: *Three suspects were **taken in for** questioning at Hereford police station.*

COMMON LEARNER ERROR

ask a question

Remember to use the verb **ask** with the noun **question**.

We weren't allowed to ask any questions.

~~*We weren't allowed to make any questions.*~~

question [PROBLEM] /ˈkwes.tʃən/ *noun* **1** [C] any matter that needs to be dealt with or considered: *This **raises** the question of teacher pay.* ○ *What are your views on the Northern Irish question?* **2** [U] doubt or uncertainty: *There's no question **about*** (= It is certain) *whose fault it is.* ○ *Whether children are reading fewer books is **open to** question* (= there is some doubt about it). ○ *Her loyalty is **beyond** question* (= There is no doubt about it). ○ *There's no question that he's guilty.*

• ***sb/sth* in question** *FORMAL* the person or thing that is being discussed: *I stayed at home on the night in question.*

• **be a question of *doing sth*** to be necessary to do a particular thing: *It's **simply/just** a question of working hard for a month and then you can relax.*

• **be out of the question** (*ALSO* **be no question of *(doing) sth***) to be an event which cannot possibly happen: *A trip to New Zealand is out of the question this year.* ○ *There's no question of agree**ing** to the demands.*

ˈquestion ˌmark *noun* [C] the ? punctuation mark that is put at the end of a phrase or sentence to show that it is a question

• **a question mark over *sth*** an expression used when doubt exists about a particular thing: *A question mark **hangs over** the future of the company.*

questionnaire /ˌkwes.tʃəˈneəʳ/ [US] /-ˈner/ *noun* [C] a list of questions that a number of people are asked so that information can be collected about something: *Visitors to the country have been asked to **fill in** a detailed questionnaire.*

ˈquestion ˌtag *noun* [C] a short phrase such as 'isn't it' or 'don't you' that is added to the end of a sentence to check information or to ask if someone agrees with you: *In the sentence, 'It's hot, isn't it?, 'isn't it' is a question tag.*

queue *UK* /kjuː/ *noun* [C] (*US* **line**) **1** a line of people, usually standing or in cars, waiting for something: *Are you **in** the queue **for** tickets?* ○ *There was a long queue of traffic stretching down the road.* ○ *If you want tickets you'll have to **join** the queue.* ○ *DISAPPROVING It makes me mad when someone **jumps the** queue* (= goes straight to the front). **2** a lot of people wanting something: *There's a queue of companies wanting to sell the product.*

ˌqueue (ˈup) *UK verb* [I] (*US* **line up**) **1** to wait in a line of people, often to buy something: *Dozens of people were queueing up **to** get tickets.* ○ *We had to queue for three hours to get in.* **2** *INFORMAL* to want very much to do something: [+ to infinitive] *There are thousands of young women queueing up to be models.*

ˈqueue-ˌjump *verb* [I] *UK* to unfairly go to the front of a queue

queue-jumping /ˈkjuːˌdʒʌm.pɪŋ/ *noun* [U] *UK* when you unfairly go to the front of a queue: *Hey, no queue-jumping!*

quibble /ˈkwɪb.l̩/ *verb* [I] *DISAPPROVING* to argue about, or say you disapprove of, something very small and unimportant: *There's no point quibbling **about/over** a couple of dollars.* **quibble** /ˈkwɪb.l̩/ *noun* [C]

quiche /kiːʃ/ *noun* [C] an open pastry case, filled with a mixture of eggs, cream and other savoury foods, which is baked and eaten hot or cold: *asparagus/broccoli quiche*

quick [FAST] /kwɪk/ *adj* **1** happening or done with great speed, or lasting only a short time: *It's a quick journey.* ○ *I had a quick coffee and left the house.* ○ *I only had time for a quick glance at the paper this morning.* ○ *He scored three goals in quick **succession*** (= happening one after the other in a short time). ○ *Could I have a quick **word*** (= speak to you for a short time)*?* **2 be quick to do *sth*** to do something immediately: *She was quick to point out that it wasn't her fault.* **3** describes someone who is clever and understands or notices things quickly: *She was quick **at** understand**ing** what we wanted her to do.* ○ *He has a quick mind.* ○ *Glyn's quick **thinking*** (= ability to solve problems with speed) *averted what could have been a disaster.* ➲See also **quick-witted**. **quick** /kwɪk/ *exclamation*: *Quick! Close the door before the cat comes in!* **quicken** /ˈkwɪk.ən/ *verb* [I or T] *This is music that will make your **pulse** quicken.* ○ *We'll have to quicken the **pace** if we want to keep up with him.* ○ *LITERARY Peter walked in the room and her heart quickened.* **quickly** /ˈkwɪk.li/ *adv*: *We'll have to walk quickly to get there on time.* ○ *Quickly now, you two, daddy's waiting in the car!*

quick [BODY PART] /kwɪk/ *noun* [U] the area of flesh under your nails: *He's bitten his nails **to the** quick.*

quickfire /ˈkwɪk.faɪəʳ/ [US] /-faɪr/ *adj* said or done very fast: *quickfire dialogue from the two comedians*

ˌquick ˈfix *noun* [C] *INFORMAL DISAPPROVING* something that seems to be a fast and easy solution to a problem but is in fact not very good or long-lasting: *People are still looking for the quick fix.* ○ *He warned against any quick-fix solutions.*

quickie /ˈkwɪk.i/ *noun* [C] *INFORMAL* something done or had quickly, especially sex or an alcoholic drink: *Shall we just **have** a quickie?* ○ *a quickie divorce*

ˈquick ˌone *noun INFORMAL* **have a quick one** to have a drink, usually an alcoholic drink, just before going somewhere else: *Do we have time for a quick one before the train arrives?*

quicksand /ˈkwɪk.sænd/ *noun* [U] deep wet sand that sucks in anyone trying to walk across it

quicksilver /ˈkwɪkˌsɪl.vəʳ/ [US] /-vɚ/ *noun OLD USE* **mercury** METAL

quickstep /ˈkwɪk.step/ *noun* [C] a dance with a lot of quick steps, or a piece of music for this

ˌquick ˈtemper *noun* **have a quick temper** to become angry very easily **quick-tempered** /ˌkwɪkˈtem.pəd/ [US] /-pɚd/ *adj*

quick-witted /ˌkwɪkˈwɪt.ɪd/ [US] /-ˌwɪt̬-/ *adj* able to reply in a clever or funny way without thinking for a long time

quid /kwɪd/ *noun* [C] *plural* **quid** *UK INFORMAL* a pound; £1: *Could you lend me twenty quid* (= £20)*, mate?*
• **be quids in** *UK INFORMAL* to be making a profit: *If this deal goes ahead, we'll be quids in.*

quid pro quo /ˌkwɪd.prəʊˈkwəʊ/ [US] /-proʊˈkwoʊ/ *noun* [C usually sing] *plural* **quid pro quos** *FORMAL* something that is given to a person in return for something they have done: *The government has promised food aid* ***as a*** *quid pro quo* ***for*** *the stopping of violence.*

quiescent /kwiˈes.ᵊnt/ *adj LITERARY* temporarily quiet and not active: *The political situation was now relatively quiescent.*

quiet /kwaɪət/ *adj* **1** making very little noise: *She spoke in a quiet voice so as not to wake him.* ○ *It's so quiet without the kids here.* ○ *Please be quiet* (= stop talking)*!* ○ *Could you* ***keep*** *quiet while I'm on the phone, please?* ✻ NOTE: Do not confuse with **quite**. **2** having little activity or excitement and few people: *a quiet, peaceful little village* ○ *It was a quiet wedding, with just a few friends and relations.* ○ *Business is quiet during the holidays.* **3** A quiet person is one who does not talk much: *He was a quiet, almost taciturn, young man.* **4 keep (sth) quiet** to try to stop other people from finding out about a fact: *She managed to keep the operation quiet for a while.* ○ *Davies kept quiet* ***about*** *the amount of money being spent.*
quietly /ˈkwaɪət.li/ *adv* without making much noise: *I slipped quietly out of the back door.* ○ *He is a quietly spoken, thoughtful man.*
quiet /kwaɪət/ *noun* [U] the state of being silent: *Let's have* ***some*** *quiet!* ○ *I go camping for some* ***peace and*** *quiet* (= absence of activity and excitement).
• **on the quiet** *INFORMAL* secretly: *His wife found out he'd been seeing someone on the quiet.*
quietness /ˈkwaɪət.nəs/ *noun* [U] almost no noise: *This luxury car offers comfort, quietness and speed.*

COMMON LEARNER ERROR

quiet or **quite?**

Be careful, these two words look similar, but they are spelled differently and have completely different meanings.

Quiet means 'making little or no noise'.

The house was very quiet without the children around.
~~*The house was very quite without the children around.*~~

In British English **quite** has two meanings, depending on how you say it. It can mean 'a little, but not very' if you put more stress on the word after **quite**.

It's quite (= not very) cold today.

If you use it with a word such as 'impossible', 'ridiculous' or 'exhausted' and if you put more stress on the word **quite** than on next word, this changes the meaning so that it means 'completely'.

I'm afraid that would be quite (= completely) impossible and I cannot agree to it.

In American English **quite** usually means 'very'.

---

quieten *UK* /ˈkwaɪə.tᵊn/ *verb* [I or T] (*US* **quiet**) to (cause to) become calmer or less noisy: *The barking dogs quietened* ***(down)*** *when they recognized me.*

quietism /ˈkwaɪə.tɪ.zᵊm/ *noun* [U] *FORMAL* the belief that it is best to accept things in life and not try to change them

quietude /ˈkwaɪə.tjuːd/ [US] /-tuːd/ *noun* [U] *FORMAL* calmness and peace: *In many of his poems the poet reflects on the quietude of the countryside.*

quiff *UK* /kwɪf/ *noun* [C] (*US* **pompadour**) a hairstyle, worn usually by men, in which the hair at the front of the head is brushed up

quill /kwɪl/ *noun* [C] any of the long sharp pointed hairs on the body of a PORCUPINE

ˈquill (ˌpen) *noun* [C] a pen made from a bird's feather, used in the past

quilt /kwɪlt/ *noun* [C] **1** a decorative cover for a bed **2** *UK* a **duvet**

quilted /ˈkwɪl.tɪd/ [US] /-t̬ɪd/ *adj* (especially of clothes) filled with thick soft material which is sewn in place: *She wore a quilted satin jacket.*

quince /kwɪnts/ *noun* [C or U] a hard fruit that looks like an apple and has a strong sweet smell: *quince jam*

quinine /ˈkwɪn.iːn/ [US] /ˈkwaɪ.naɪn/ *noun* [U] a drug used to treat fevers such as MALARIA

quintessential /ˌkwɪn.tɪˈsent.ʃᵊl/ [US] /-te-/ *adj FORMAL* being the most typical example or most important part of something: *Roasted garlic with sheep's milk cheese is the quintessential Corsican meal.*
quintessentially /ˌkwɪn.tɪˈsent.ʃᵊl.i/ [US] /-te-/ *adv FORMAL* typically
quintessence /kwɪnˈtes.ᵊnts/ *noun* [U] *FORMAL* the most typical example: *An American football game is* ***the*** *quintessence* ***of*** *machismo.*

quintet /kwɪnˈtet/ *group noun* [C] a group of five people who play musical instruments or sing as a group
quintet /kwɪnˈtet/ *noun* [C] a piece of music written for five people

quintuplet /kwɪnˈtuː.plət/ /ˈkwɪn.tjʊ-/ [US] /-ˈtuː.plɪt/ *noun* [C] (*ALSO* **quin**) any of five children born at the same time to the same mother

quip /kwɪp/ *noun* [C] an amusing and clever remark: *It was Oscar Wilde who* ***made*** *the famous quip about life mimicking art.* **quip** /kwɪp/ *verb* [I] **-pp-** *MAINLY US* [+ speech] *When asked earlier why he seemed to be so relaxed, Mr McCarthy quipped: "It's the drugs".*

quirk /kwɜːk/ [US] /kwɝːk/ *noun* [C] an unusual part of someone's personality or habit, or something that is strange and unexpected: *You have to get used to other people's quirks and foibles.* ○ *There is a quirk in the rules that allows you to invest money without paying tax.* ○ ***By*** *some strange quirk/****By*** *an odd quirk* ***of fate*** (= unexpectedly)*, we ended up on the same train.*
quirky /ˈkwɜː.ki/ [US] /ˈkwɝː-/ *adj* unusual in an attractive and interesting way: *He was tall and had a quirky, offbeat sense of humour.*

quisling /ˈkwɪz.lɪŋ/ *noun* [C] a person who helps the enemy army that has taken control of his or her country; a TRAITOR

quit /kwɪt/ *verb* [I or T] **quitting, quit, quit** to stop doing something or leave a job or a place: *Would you quit your job if you inherited lots of money?* ○ [+ v-ing] *I'm going to quit smoking.* ○ *Quit wasting my time!* ○ *Press Q to quit the program.*
quitter /ˈkwɪt.əʳ/ [US] /ˈkwɪt̬.ɚ/ *noun* [C] *DISAPPROVING* a person who gives up easily instead of finishing something: *I'm no quitter.*

quite [NOT VERY] /kwaɪt/ *adv, predeterminer UK* a little or a lot but not completely: *I'm quite tired but I can certainly walk a little further.* ○ *There was quite a lot of traffic today but yesterday was even busier.* ○ *He's quite attractive but not what I'd call gorgeous.* ⊃See Note **quiet or quite?** at **quiet**.

quite [COMPLETELY] /kwaɪt/ *adv* **1** completely: *The two situations are quite different.* ○ *Are you quite sure you want to go?* ○ *The colours almost match but not quite.* ○ *I enjoyed her new book though it's* ***not*** *quite as good as her last one.* ○ *Quite* ***honestly/frankly****, the thought of it terrified me.* ⊃See Note **quiet or quite?** at **quiet**. **2 not quite** used to express uncertainty: *I don't quite know what to say.* ○ *I didn't quite catch what he said.* **3** *UK* used to show agreement with someone's opinion: *"You'd think he could spare some money – he's not exactly poor." "Quite."* **4** *FORMAL* **quite the best/worst/etc.** used for emphasis: *It was quite the worst dinner I have ever had.*

quits /kwɪts/ *adj INFORMAL* **be quits** to not owe money to someone or to each other now: *I paid for the tickets and you bought dinner so we're quits, I reckon.* ○ *Am I quits with you now?*

quiver SHAKE /'kwɪv.əʳ/ US /-ɚ/ *verb* [I] to shake slightly, often because of strong emotion: *Lennie's bottom lip quivered and tears started in his eyes.* **quiver** /'kwɪv.əʳ/ US /-ɚ/ *noun* [C] *The opening bars of the music sent a quiver of excitement through the crowd.*

quiver CONTAINER /'kwɪv.əʳ/ US /-ɚ/ *noun* [C] a long thin container for carrying arrows

quixotic /kwɪk'sɒt.ɪk/ US /-'saː.t̬ɪk/ *adj LITERARY* having or showing ideas that are imaginative but not practical or likely to succeed: *This is a vast, exciting and some say quixotic project.* **quixotically** /kwɪk'sɒt.ɪ.kli/ US /-'saː.t̬ɪ-/ *adv*

quiz /kwɪz/ *noun* [C] *plural* **quizzes 1** a game or competition in which you answer questions: *a history/sport, etc. quiz* ○ *There are so many inane television quiz shows.* ○ *UK A lot of pubs have quiz nights once or twice a week.* **2** *MAINLY US* a short informal test: *US There was a pop* (= surprise) *quiz in history at school today.*

quiz /kwɪz/ *verb* [T] **-zz-** to ask someone questions about something: *She spent an hour being quizzed by journalists.*

quizzical /'kwɪz.ɪ.kəl/ *adj* seeming to ask a question without saying anything: *She gave me a quizzical look/glance/smile.* **quizzically** /'kwɪz.ɪ.kli/ *adv*

quoits /kɔɪts/ /kwɔɪts/ *noun* [U] a game in which you throw rings over a small post, often played on ships

quokka /'kwɒk.ə/ US /'kwɑː.kə/ *noun* [C] a small WALLABY (= an animal with a long tail and strong legs for jumping with) which in the past existed in great numbers in Western Australia

Quonset hut /'kwɒn.sɪt.hʌt/ US /'kwɑːn-/ *noun* [C] *US TRADEMARK FOR* **Nissen hut**

Quorn /kwɔːn/ US /kwɔːrn/ *noun* [U] *TRADEMARK* a substance made of vegetable protein that is used in cooking instead of meat

quorum /'kwɔː.rəm/ US /'kwɔːr.əm/ *noun* [S] *FORMAL* the smallest number of people needed to be present at a meeting before it can officially begin and before official decisions can be taken

quorate /'kwɔː.reɪt/ US /'kwɔːr.eɪt/ *adj FORMAL* having the necessary number of people present for decisions to be allowed to be made: *a quorate meeting*

quota /'kwəʊ.tə/ US /'kwoʊ.t̬ə/ *noun* [C] a fixed limited amount or number that is officially allowed: *The country now has a quota on immigration.* ○ *FIGURATIVE The class contains the usual quota* (= number) *of troublemakers.*

quo'tation ˌmarks *plural noun* (*UK ALSO* **inverted commas**, *INFORMAL* **quotes**) the " " punctuation marks that are put around a word or phrase to show that someone else has written or said it

quote SAY /kwəʊt/ US /kwoʊt/ *verb* [T] **1** to repeat the words that someone else has said or written: *He's always quoting from the Bible.* ○ *"If they're flexible", the official was quoted as saying.* ○ *She worked, to quote her daughter, "as if there was no tomorrow".* ○ *Can I quote you on that* (= Can I repeat to other people what you have just said)? **2** If you quote a fact or example, you refer to it in order to add emphasis to what you are saying: [+ two objects] *Quote me one organization that doesn't have some bad managers.*

● **quote...unquote** *INFORMAL* said to show that you are repeating someone else's words, especially if you do not agree with them: *She says they're, quote 'just good friends' unquote.*

quotes /kwəʊts/ US /kwoʊts/ *plural noun INFORMAL* **quotation marks**: *Put the title of the article in quotes.*

quotation /kwəʊ'teɪ.ʃᵊn/ US /kwoʊ-/ *noun* [C] (*INFORMAL* **quote**) a phrase or short piece of writing taken from a longer work of literature, poetry, etc. or what someone else has said: *At the beginning of the book there's a quotation from Abraham Lincoln.*

quote PRICE /kwəʊt/ US /kwoʊt/ *verb* [T] to give a price, especially one that will be charged for doing a piece of work: *The architect has quoted £3000 to build an extension.*

quotation /kwəʊ'teɪ.ʃᵊn/ US /kwoʊ-/ *noun* [C] (*INFORMAL* **quote**) the price that a person says they will charge to do a piece of work: *I asked several builders to give me a quote for the work.*

quoth /kwəʊθ/ US /kwoʊθ/ *verb* [T] *OLD USE OR HUMOROUS* said: *"Point taken, Kingers," quoth I.*

quotidian /kwəʊ'tɪd.i.ən/ US /kwoʊ-/ *adj FORMAL* ordinary; EVERYDAY: *Television has become part of our quotidian existence.*

quotient /'kwəʊ.ʃᵊnt/ US /'kwoʊ-/ *noun* [C] **1** a particular degree or amount of something: *This is a car with a high head-turning quotient* (= a lot of people turn to look at it). **2** *SPECIALIZED* the result of dividing one number by another

the Qur'an /ðə.kɒr'aːn/ US /-kə'raːn/ *noun* [S] the Koran

Q

R

R [LETTER] (*plural* **R's** or **Rs**), **r** (*plural* **r's** or **rs**) /ɑːʳ/ [US] /ɑːr/ *noun* [C] the 18th letter of the English alphabet

R [ROYAL PERSON] /ɑːʳ/ [US] /ɑːr/ *ABBREVIATION FOR Rex* (= king) or *Regina* (= queen), used after the name of a king or queen: *Elizabeth R*

R [DIRECTION] *adj, adv, noun* [U] *ABBREVIATION FOR* **right** DIRECTION: *R eye: 3.20/L eye: 3.25*

R [RIVER] *noun ABBREVIATION FOR* **river**, used in writing before or after the name of a river: *R Thames*

R [ROYAL] *adj WRITTEN ABBREVIATION FOR* **royal**, used in the names of organizations: *He's an RAF officer.*

R [FILM] /ɑːʳ/ [US] /ɑːr/ *adj US ABBREVIATION FOR* **restricted**; used to refer to a film that people under 17 years of age can see only if a parent or GUARDIAN is with them

rabbi /ˈræb.aɪ/ *noun* [C] a religious leader and teacher in the Jewish religion: *Rabbi Jonathan Sacks* ○ [as form of address] *Good morning, Rabbi.* **rabbinical** /rəˈbɪn.ɪ.kəl/ *adj: a rabbinical student/college*

rabbit [ANIMAL] /ˈræb.ɪt/ *noun* [C] a small animal with long ears and large front teeth, which moves by jumping on its long back legs ➲See also **bunny (rabbit)**.

rabbit /ˈræb.ɪt/ *verb* [I]

▲ **rabbit on** *phrasal verb UK INFORMAL DISAPPROVING* to continue talking about something which is not interesting to the listener: *He's always rabbiting on* ***about*** *his stamp collection.*

rabble /ˈræb.l̩/ *group noun* [C usually sing] *DISAPPROVING* a large noisy uncontrolled group of people: *The defeated army returned home as a demoralized rabble.* ○ *He views his opponents as a mindless rabble.*

• **the rabble** *DISAPPROVING* people of a low social position: *Her speech stirred the emotions of the rabble.*

rabble-rouser /ˈræb.l̩ˌraʊ.zəʳ/ [US] /-zɚ/ *noun* [C] a person who makes speeches that make people excited or angry, especially in a way that causes them to act as the person wants them to: *Johnson was unpopular with the management because he was a well-known rabble-rouser.* **rabble-rousing** /ˈræb.l̩ˌraʊ.zɪŋ/ *adj* [before n] *a rabble-rousing speech*

rabid /ˈræb.ɪd/ *adj MAINLY DISAPPROVING* having and expressing extreme and unreasonable feelings: *The attack is believed to have been carried out by a group of rabid anti-semites.* ○ *a rabid feminist* ➲See also **rabid** at **rabies**. **rabidly** /ˈræb.ɪd.li/ *adv*

rabies /ˈreɪ.biːz/ *noun* [U] (*SPECIALIZED* **hydrophobia**) a fatal disease of the nervous system of dogs and other animals, which can also cause death in humans who are bitten by a diseased animal: *Dogs, cats, foxes and bats can all* ***carry*** *rabies.*

rabid /ˈræb.ɪd/ *adj* suffering from rabies: *a rabid dog* ➲See also **rabid**.

the RAC /ðiˌɑː.reɪˈsiː/ [US] /-ˌɑːr.eɪ-/ *group noun* [S] *ABBREVIATION FOR* the Royal Automobile Club: a British organization which gives help and information to drivers who are members of it

raccoon, racoon /rækˈuːn/ *noun* [C] (*MAINLY US INFORMAL* **coon**) a small North American animal with black marks on its face and a long tail with black rings on it

race [COMPETITION] /reɪs/ *noun* [C] **1** a competition in which all the competitors try to be the fastest and to finish first: *Do you know who* ***won/lost*** *the race?* ○ *Let's* ***have*** *a swimming race.* ○ *They're taking part in a race* ***to*** *the top of Ben Nevis.* **2** an attempt to be the first to do or to get something: *Kieran and Andrew are in a race* ***for*** *promotion.* ○ [+ to infinitive] *Three newspapers are involved in a race* ***to*** *publish the story.* ○ *Another candidate has now* ***entered*** *the presidential race* (= attempt to be elected as president). ○ *Finishing this project by December is going to be a race* ***against time/the clock*** (= an attempt to finish fast within a time limit).

race /reɪs/ *verb* [I or T] to (cause to) compete in a race: *He has been racing for over ten years.* ○ *I used to race* ***(against)*** *him when we were boys.* ○ *He's racing three of his dogs on Saturday.*

racer /ˈreɪ.səʳ/ [US] /-sɚ/ *noun* [C] **1** a person or thing that races **2** a **racing bike**

races /ˈreɪ.sɪz/ *plural noun* a series of horse races in a particular place on one day: *He often has* ***a day at*** *the races.*

racing /ˈreɪ.sɪŋ/ *noun* [U] **1** competition in races: *I enjoy cycling, but I'm not interested in racing.* ○ *I like watching* ***horse/motor*** *racing on television.* **2** horse races

race [PEOPLE] /reɪs/ *noun* [C or U] a group, especially of people, with particular similar physical characteristics, who are considered as belonging to the same type, or the fact of belonging to such a group: *People of many different races were living side by side.* ○ *Discrimination on grounds of race will not be tolerated.* ○ *An increasing number of people in the country are of* ***mixed*** *race* (= with parents of different races).

race /reɪs/ *group noun* [C] a group of people who share the same language, history, characteristics, etc: *LITERARY The British are an island race.*

• **play the race card 1** *UK DISAPPROVING* to try to win an election by saying unfair things about people from another race **2** *US DISAPPROVING* to mention someone's race in order to influence the way people think about them

racial /ˈreɪ.ʃəl/ *adj* connected with a particular race or with various races: *They are members of a racial minority.* ○ *racial* ***discrimination/prejudice*** ○ *He had a vision of a society living in racial harmony.* **racially** /ˈreɪ.ʃəl.i/ *adv: Racially* ***motivated*** *assaults on Asians are increasing.*

race [HURRY] /reɪs/ *verb* [I or T; usually + adv or prep] to move or go fast: *He raced down the street.* ○ *The ambulance raced* (= quickly took) *the injured* ***to*** *a nearby hospital.* ○ *The summer seems to have raced* ***by*** (= passed very quickly). ○ *He raced the car engine* (= made it work faster than it needed to) *as he sat impatiently at the traffic lights.*

• **heart/mind/pulse races** If your heart/mind/pulse races it works extremely fast because of excitement, drugs, illness, etc: *She was hot and sweaty and had a racing heart.* ○ *A glimpse of his bare torso set my pulse racing.*

racecourse *MAINLY UK* /ˈreɪs.kɔːs/ [US] /-kɔːrs/ *noun* [C] (*MAINLY US* **racetrack**) a wide, usually circular, path with a grass surface, on which horses race, or the whole area in which this path is situated, including buildings

racehorse /ˈreɪs.hɔːs/ [US] /-hɔːrs/ *noun* [C] a horse bred and trained for racing

ˈrace ˌmeeting *UK noun* [C] (*US* **race meet**) a series of horse, car or running races that happen on one day in one place

ˌrace reˈlations *plural noun* the relationship between the members of different races: *We want to improve race relations in this area of town.*

racetrack /ˈreɪs.træk/ *noun* [C] **1** a path or road, usually circular and with a hard surface, on which runners, cars or bicycles, etc. race, or the whole area in which this path is situated, including buildings **2** *MAINLY US FOR* **racecourse**

racial /ˈreɪ.ʃəl/ *adj* ➲See at **race** PEOPLE.

racily /ˈreɪ.sɪ.li/ *adv* ➲See at **racy**.

raciness /ˈreɪ.sɪ.nəs/ *noun* [U] ➲See at **racy**.

ˈracing ˌbike *noun* [C] a bicycle designed for speed with a light frame and HANDLEBARS which curve downwards so that the rider's back is parallel to the ground

ˈracing ˌcar *noun* [C] a low car with a powerful engine and wide wheels which is designed for use in races ➲See picture **Cars and Trucks** on page Centre 13

ˈracing ˌdriver *noun* [C] a driver of a racing car

ˈracing ˌpigeon *noun* [C] a pigeon that takes part in races

ˌracing ˈstart *noun* [C usually sing] an advantage you have because you start more quickly than other people or things: *We* ***had*** *a racing start* ***over*** *our competitors.*

racism /ˈreɪ.sɪ.zəm/ *noun* [U] (*UK OLD-FASHIONED* **racialism**) *DISAPPROVING* the belief that people's qualities are influenced by their race and that the members of other races are not as good as the members of your own, or the resulting unfair treatment of members of other races: *The authorities are taking steps to combat/fight/ tackle racism in schools.* ○ *The report made it plain that* ***institutional*** *racism* (= racism in all parts of an organization) *is deep-rooted in this country.*

racist /'reɪ.sɪst/ *noun* [C] (*UK OLD-FASHIONED* **racialist**) *DISAPPROVING* someone who believes that other races are not as good as their own and therefore treats them unfairly: *Two of the killers are known to be racists.* **racist** /'reɪ.sɪst/ *adj*: *He furiously denied being racist.* ○ *They were the victims of a vicious racist attack.*

rack [FRAME] /ræk/ *noun* [C] **1** a frame or shelf, often formed of bars, which is used to hold things: *a vegetable rack* ○ *a plate rack* ○ *a luggage rack* **2** *US* (*UK* **frame**) a triangular frame used to arrange the balls at the start of a game of BILLIARDS, POOL, SNOOKER, etc.

rack [CAUSE PAIN] /ræk/ *verb* [T often passive] to cause physical or mental pain, or trouble, to someone or something: *Even at the end, when cancer racked his body, he was calm and cheerful.* ○ *The dog was already racked* ***by/ with*** *the pains of old age.* ○ *He was racked* ***by/with*** *doubts/guilt.*

• **rack** ***your*** **brains** to think very hard: *I've been racking my brains all day but I can't for the life of me remember her name.*

the rack *noun* [S] in the past, a device to which people were tied and which stretched their bodies by pulling their arms in one direction and their legs in the other direction, usually used as a way of forcing them to tell information

• **be on the rack** to be suffering great physical or mental pain

-racked /-rækt/ *suffix* showing or feeling the physical or mental pain, trouble, etc. mentioned: *a pain-racked gesture* ○ *a guilt-racked society*

racking /'ræk.ɪŋ/ *adj* very bad and very painful: *a racking cough/headache/toothache*

rack [MACHINE] /ræk/ *noun* [C] a bar with tooth-like parts along one edge which fits into a PINION (= a wheel with tooth-like parts), allowing change between circular and straight-line movement

rack [DECAY], *MAINLY US* **wrack** /ræk/ *noun* **rack and ruin** a bad state; decay: *The whole farm was* ***going to*** *rack and ruin.*

▲ **rack** ***sth*** **up** *phrasal verb* [M] **1** *MAINLY US INFORMAL* to gradually get more points, profits, etc.; to ACCUMULATE: *He has racked up 450 points in three months.* ○ *Astronomical profits/losses were racked up by airlines last year.* **2** to increase something such as a rent or price, especially by an amount that is considered to be too much: *Our landlord racked up the rent by 15% this year.*

racket [SPORT], **racquet** /'ræk.ɪt/ *noun* [C] a net fixed tightly to an oval frame with a long handle, used in various sports for hitting a ball: *a tennis/squash/ badminton racket*

racket [NOISE] /'ræk.ɪt/ *noun* [S] *INFORMAL* an unpleasant loud continuous noise: *They were* ***making*** *such a racket outside that I couldn't get to sleep.*

racket [CRIME] /'ræk.ɪt/ *noun* [C usually sing] **1** *INFORMAL* a dishonest or illegal activity that makes money: *They were jailed for* ***running*** *a protection/prostitution racket.* ➲See also **protection** at **protect**. **2** *DISAPPROVING* a way of making a large unfair profit: *Telephone chat lines are a real racket.* **racketeer** /ˌræk.ə'tɪəʳ/ [US] /-'tɪr/ *noun* [C] *DISAPPROVING* **racketeering** /ˌræk.ə'tɪə.rɪŋ/ [US] /-'tɪr.ɪŋ/ *noun* [U] *They have been accused of racketeering.*

raconteur /ˌræk.ɒn'tɜːʳ/ [US] /-ɑːn'tɝː/ *noun* [C] someone who tells amusing or interesting stories: *He was a brilliant raconteur.*

racoon /ræk'uːn/ *noun* [C] a **raccoon**

racy /'reɪ.si/ *adj* (of speech or writing) exciting, especially because of being about sex, or (of someone or something) having an exciting, interesting and attractive appearance, sometimes in a sexual way: *a racy story* ○ *a racy style* ○ *a racy advertisement* ○ *racy swimwear* ○ *She is trying to create a racier image for herself.* **racily** /'reɪ.sɪ.li/ *adv* **raciness** /'reɪ.sɪ.nəs/ *noun* [U]

rad /ræd/ *adj SLANG* extremely exciting or good: *a rad new computer game*

Rack

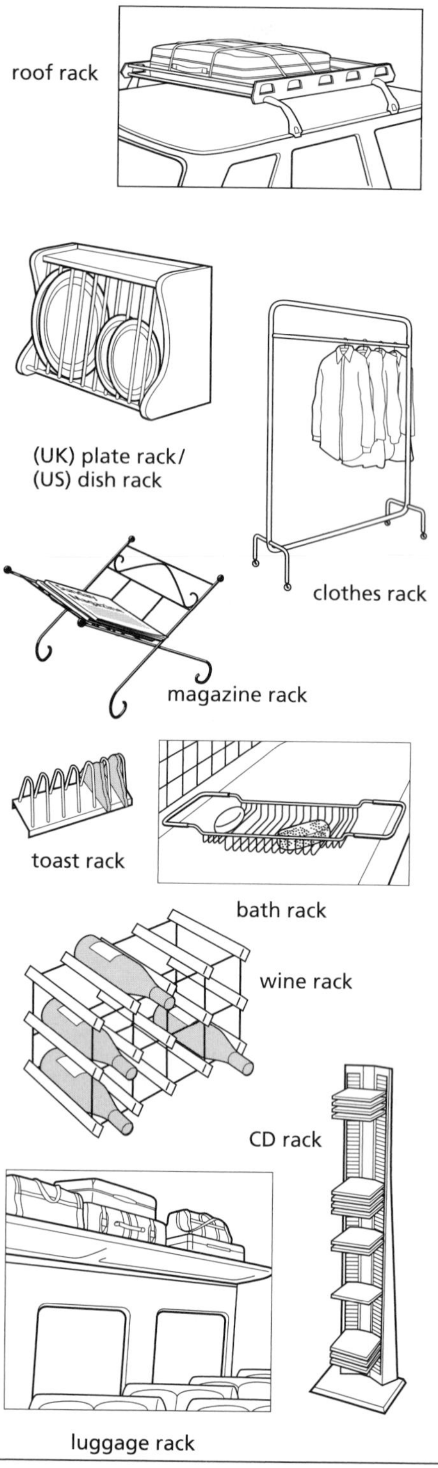
roof rack
(UK) plate rack/
(US) dish rack
clothes rack
magazine rack
toast rack
bath rack
wine rack
CD rack
luggage rack

R

radar /ˈreɪ.dɑːʳ/ [US] /-dɑːr/ *noun* [U] a system which uses radio waves to find the position of objects which cannot be seen: *Other vessels in the area show up on the ship's radar* ***(screen)***.

ˈradar ˌtrap *noun* [C] a system, using radar, which the police use to catch vehicles that are travelling too fast

raddled /ˈræd.l̩d/ *adj UK* looking tired or old

ˌradial (ˈtyre) *noun* [C] a tyre which has cords inside the rubber that go across the edge of the wheel at an angle of 90° rather than along it

radiant /ˈreɪ.di.ənt/ *adj* obviously very happy, or very beautiful: *He gave a radiant* ***smile*** *when he heard her news.* ➲See also **radiant** at **radiate** PRODUCE HEAT/LIGHT.

radiance /ˈreɪ.di.ənts/ *noun* [U] *He was struck by the radiance of her smile.*

radiate [PRODUCE HEAT/LIGHT] /ˈreɪ.di.eɪt/ *verb* [I or T] to produce heat and/or light, or (of heat or light) to be produced: *The planet Jupiter radiates twice as much heat from inside as it receives from the Sun.* ○ *A single beam of light radiated* ***from*** *the lighthouse.* **radiant** /ˈreɪ.di.ənt/ *adj* [before n] *a radiant heater* ○ *the radiant heat of the sun* ➲See also **radiant**.

radiance /ˈreɪ.di.ənts/ *noun* [U] *We basked in the radiance* (= brightness) *of the African sun.*

radiate [EXPRESS] /ˈreɪ.di.eɪt/ *verb* [I or T] to show an emotion or quality, or (of an emotion or quality) to be shown or felt: *He was radiating joy and happiness.* ○ *Enthusiasm was radiating* ***from*** *her.*

radiate [SPREAD] /ˈreɪ.di.eɪt/ *verb* [I + adv or prep] to spread out in all directions from a central point: *Flows of lava radiated* ***out from*** *the volcano's crater.* ○ *Just before the breeding season, these birds radiate outwards to warmer climates.*

radial /ˈreɪ.di.əl/ *adj* spreading out from a central point: *a radial road system* **radially** /ˈreɪ.di.ə.li/ *adv*

radiation /ˌreɪ.diˈeɪ.ʃən/ *noun* [U] **1** a form of energy that comes from a nuclear reaction and that can be very dangerous to health: *Many servicemen suffered radiation* ***sickness*** *after the early atomic tests.* **2** energy from heat or light that you cannot see: *microwave/ultraviolet/electromagnetic radiation*

radiator /ˈreɪ.di.eɪ.təʳ/ [US] /-t̬ɚ/ *noun* [C] a device, usually a container filled with water, that sends out heat, often as part of a heating or cooling system: *When we installed the central heating, we put a radiator in every room.* ○ *My car engine overheated because the water had leaked out of the radiator.*

radical [SUPPORTING CHANGE] /ˈræd.ɪ.kəl/ *adj* believing or expressing the belief that there should be great or extreme social or political change: *He was known as a radical reformer/thinker/politician.* ○ *These people have very radical views.*

radical /ˈræd.ɪ.kəl/ *noun* [C] a person who supports great social and political change: *She was a radical all her life.*

radicalism /ˈræd.ɪ.kəl.ɪ.zəm/ *noun* [U]

radical [EXTREMELY IMPORTANT] /ˈræd.ɪ.kəl/ *adj* relating to the most important parts of something or someone; complete or extreme: *We need to make some radical* ***changes*** *to our operating procedures.* ○ *She has had to undergo radical surgery* (= aimed at removing the cause of a disease). **radically** /ˈræd.ɪ.kli/ *adv*: *Barker introduced some radically new ideas.*

radicchio /ræˈdɪ.ki.əʊ/ [US] /-oʊ/ *noun* [U] a type of plant with purple or red leaves which are eaten raw in salads: *Radicchio has a slightly bitter flavour.*

radii /ˈreɪ.di.aɪ/ *plural of* **radius**

radio /ˈreɪ.di.əʊ/ [US] /-oʊ/ *noun plural* **radios** **1** [C] a piece of electronic equipment used for listening to radio broadcasts: *a car radio* ○ *I switched on the radio.* **2** [S or U] the programmes that you hear when you listen to the radio: *I heard a good programme* ***on the*** *radio last night.* ○ *I don't listen to radio much.* **3** [U] the system or work of broadcasting sound programmes for the public to listen to: *a local radio station* ○ *She's got some kind of job in radio.* **4** [C or U] a piece of electronic equipment that can send and receive spoken messages or signals, or the messages or signals that are sent or received: *We sent a message over the radio/by radio.* ○ *The children had radio-****controlled*** *toy cars for Christmas.*

radio /ˈreɪ.di.əʊ/ [US] /-oʊ/ *verb* [I or T] **radioing, radioed, radioed** to send a message to someone by radio: *We'll have to radio for more supplies.* ○ *They radioed their base for help.*

radioactivity /ˌreɪ.di.əʊ.ækˈtɪv.ɪ.ti/ [US] /-oʊ.ækˈtɪv.ə.t̬i/ *noun* [U] **1** the quality that some atoms have of producing energy, which can be very harmful to health **2** the energy produced by atoms in this way: *A dangerous amount of radioactivity was* ***released*** *into the environment last month.*

radioactive /ˌreɪ.di.əʊˈæk.tɪv/ [US] /-oʊ-/ *adj* possessing or producing the energy which comes from the breaking up of atoms: *Uranium is a radioactive material.* ○ *radioactive* ***waste***

ˌradio aˈlarm (ˌclock) *noun* [C] (*ALSO* **clock radio**) a radio which can be switched on by a clock at a particular time, usually to wake someone up

radiography /ˌreɪ.diˈɒg.rə.fi/ [US] /-ˈɑː.grə-/ *noun* [U] the use of RADIATION (= a form of energy), especially X-RAYS, either to produce a picture of the inside of people or objects, or for the treatment of disease

radiographer /ˌreɪ.diˈɒg.rə.fəʳ/ [US] /-ˈɑː.grə.fɚ/ *noun* [C] a person who operates a machine that uses RADIATION, especially X-RAYS, to take pictures of the inside of people or things, or for the treatment of disease

radiology /ˌreɪ.diˈɒl.ə.dʒi/ [US] /-ˈɑː.lə-/ *noun* [U] the scientific study of the medical use of RADIATION, especially X-RAYS

radiologist /ˌreɪ.diˈɒl.ə.dʒɪst/ [US] /-ˈɑː.lə-/ *noun* [C] a person who specializes in radiology

ˌradio ˈtelescope *noun* [C] a device for receiving, for scientific study, the ELECTROMAGNETIC waves sent out by objects in space such as stars

radiotherapy /ˌreɪ.di.əʊˈθer.ə.pi/ [US] /-oʊ-/ *noun* [U] the use of controlled amounts of RADIATION (= a form of energy), aimed at a particular part of the body, to treat disease

radish /ˈræd.ɪʃ/ *noun* [C] a small vegetable, usually red or white and round or finger-shaped, which grows underground and is usually eaten raw in salads ➲See picture **Vegetables** on page Centre 2

radium /ˈreɪ.di.əm/ *noun* [U] a radioactive element which is used in the treatment of some diseases, especially cancer

radius /ˈreɪ.di.əs/ *noun* [C] *plural* **radii** **1** (the length of) a straight line joining the centre of a circle to its edge or the centre of a sphere to its surface: *The radius of this wheel is 30 cm.* ○ *This wheel* ***has*** *a radius* ***of*** *30 cm.* **2** a distance: *The station, shopping centre and school lie within a one-mile radius of the house.*

the RAF /ðiˌɑː.reɪˈef/ [US] /-ˌɑːr.eɪ-/ /ðəˈræf/ *group noun* [S] *ABBREVIATION FOR* the Royal Air Force: the air force of the United Kingdom: *He was in the RAF for thirty years.* ➲See also **air force**.

Rafferty's rules /ˈræf.ə.tizˌruːlz/ [US] /-ɚ.t̬iz-/ *plural noun AUS SLANG* (especially used when referring to a competition or an organization which is not well organized) no rules

raffia /ˈræf.i.ə/ *noun* [U] long narrow pieces of pale-yellow dried leaf, especially from a type of palm tree, used as string or for making hats, containers, etc.

raffish /ˈræf.ɪʃ/ *adj* not following usual social standards of behaviour or appearance, especially in a careless and attractive way: *He has a certain raffish elegance.*

raffishness /ˈræf.ɪʃ.nəs/ *noun* [U]

raffle /ˈræf.l̩/ *noun* [C] an activity in which people buy numbered tickets, some of which are later chosen to win prizes, which is arranged in order to make money for a good social purpose: *a raffle ticket/prize* ○ *I have never won anything* ***in*** *a raffle.*

raffle /ˈræf.l̩/ *verb* [T] to offer something as a prize in a raffle: *We are going to raffle* ***off*** *a car for the hospital appeal.* ➲See also **draw** CHOOSE.

raft [FLOATING STRUCTURE] /rɑːft/ [US] /ræft/ *noun* [C] **1** a flat floating structure for travelling across water, often made of pieces of wood tied roughly together and moved along with a PADDLE (= pole with a flat end): *We lashed together anything that would float to make a raft.* **2** a fixed flat floating structure which swimmers can use to

R

land on or dive from **3** a small rubber or plastic boat that can be filled with air: *a rubber raft* ○ *an inflatable raft*

raft /rɑːft/ ⓤ /ræft/ *verb* [I or T] to travel or transport something on a raft: *They rafted their supplies down the river.* ○ *We rafted through the rapids.* ○ *Have you ever been white water rafting?*

raft MANY /rɑːft/ ⓤ /ræft/ *noun* [C] a large number or range; a lot: *a raft of data* ○ *We have designed a whole raft of measures to improve the transport system.*

rafter /ˈrɑːf.tər/ ⓤ /ˈræf.tər/ *noun* [C] any of the large sloping pieces of wood which support a roof

rag CLOTH /ræg/ *noun* [C] **1** a torn piece of old cloth: *I keep these rags for cleaning the car.* **2** *US FOR* **duster** ⊃See at **dust**.

rag JOKE /ræg/ *verb* [T] **-gg-** *OLD-FASHIONED INFORMAL* to say things which are amusing but a little unkind: *They ragged him about his girlfriend.*

rag NEWSPAPER /ræg/ *noun* [C] *INFORMAL* a newspaper or magazine which is considered to be of bad quality: *He had his picture taken for some local rag.*

rag COLLEGE EVENT /ræg/ *noun* [C] in Britain, a series of amusing events and activities organized by college students once a year to collect money for charity

rag MUSIC /ræg/ *noun* [C] a piece of RAGTIME music

ragamuffin /ˈræg.əˌmʌf.ɪn/ *noun* [C] *OLD-FASHIONED INFORMAL* a dirty untidy child in torn clothes

rag and 'bone ˌman *UK noun* [C] (*US* **ragman**) in the past, a man who went round the streets of a town to buy old clothes, furniture and other unwanted things cheaply

ragbag /ˈræg.bæg/ *noun* [C usually sing] a confused mixture of different types of things: *His book is just a ragbag of unsupported opinions.*

ˌrag 'doll *noun* [C] a soft child's toy, made from cloth, in the shape of a person

rage ANGER /reɪdʒ/ *noun* [C or U] (a period of) extreme or violent anger: *Her sudden towering rages were terrifying.* ○ *I was frightened because I had never seen him in such a rage before.* ○ *He flew into a fit of rage over the smallest mistake.*

-rage /-reɪdʒ/ *suffix* describes situations where people become extremely angry or violent: *road-rage* ○ *trolley-rage* ○ *air-rage*

● **be (all) the rage** *OLD-FASHIONED* to be very popular at a particular time: *Long hair for men was all the rage in the seventies.*

rage /reɪdʒ/ *verb* [I usually + adv or prep] **1** to speak very angrily to someone: *He raged at (= spoke angrily to) us for forgetting to order a replacement.* **2** to happen in a strong or violent way: *The storm raged outside.* ○ *A flu epidemic is raging in/through local schools.* ○ *The argument rages on (= continues strongly).*

raging /ˈreɪ.dʒɪŋ/ *adj* **1** very severe or extreme: *a raging toothache* ○ *a raging thirst* ○ *He's got a raging (= high) temperature.* ○ *a raging bore* **2** very strong or violent: *a raging temper* ○ *The rains had turned the stream into a raging torrent.*

rage EVENT /reɪdʒ/ *noun* [C usually sing] *AUS INFORMAL* an exciting or entertaining event involving a lot of activity: *The party was a rage.*

ragga /ˈræg.ə/ *noun* [U] a type of music which combines elements of REGGAE, RAP and dance music, mostly played by Afro-Caribbean people

ragged /ˈræg.ɪd/ *adj* **1** (of clothes) not in good condition; torn or uneven: *The children were wearing dirty ragged clothes.* ○ *This part of the coastline is rather ragged (= uneven).* **2** (of a person) untidy, dirty and wearing old torn clothes: *Two ragged children stood outside the station begging for money.* **3** (especially of an edge) uneven; rough and not smooth: *The leaves of this plant have ragged edges.* ○ *The patient's breathing was ragged (= not regular) and uneven.* ○ *A ragged (= not straight) line of people were waiting at the bus stop.* **4** not performing well, because of not being organized: *The team were rather ragged in the first half of the match, but improved in the second half.* **raggedly** /ˈræg.ɪd.li/ *adv* **raggedness** /ˈræg.ɪd.nəs/ *noun* [U]

raglan /ˈræg.lən/ *adj* (of a sleeve) sewn in two straight lines out from the neck to a point under the arm: *a sweater with raglan sleeves*

ragout /ˈræg.uː/ *noun* [C or U] a dish consisting of small pieces of meat or fish and vegetables cooked together

rags /rægz/ *plural noun* clothes that are old and torn: *an old man dressed in rags.* ○ *Their clothes were in rags (= torn).*

rags-to-riches /ˌrægz.tə.ˈrɪtʃ.ɪz/ *adj* [before n] used to describe what happens to a person who was poor but becomes rich: *She told a rags-to-riches story of a child brought up in poverty becoming the owner of a hotel chain.*

ragtag /ˈræg.tæg/ *adj* untidy and not similar or organized: *The village was guarded by a ragtag group of soldiers.* ○ *He arrived with a ragtag collection of friends.*

ragtime /ˈræg.taɪm/ *noun* [U] a type of popular music, developed by black musicians in North America in the early 1900s, with tunes that are not on regular beats

the 'rag ˌtrade *noun* [S] *INFORMAL* the clothes-making industry

raid /reɪd/ *noun* [C] **1** a short sudden attack, usually by a small group of people: *The commandos made/staged/ carried out a daring raid (on the enemy).* ○ *planes on a bombing raid* **2** when people enter a place by force in order to steal from it: *Millions of dollars were stolen in a bank raid last night.* **3** when the police enter a place suddenly in order to find someone or something: *The drugs were found during a police raid on the house.*

raid /reɪd/ *verb* [T] **1** to attack a place suddenly: *The nomads raided the enemy camp and captured over 100 camels.* **2** to enter a place illegally and usually violently and steal from it: *The post office was raided late at night.* **3** (of the police) to enter a place suddenly in order to find someone or something: *Police officers from the organized crime branch have raided solicitors' offices in central London.* **4** *INFORMAL* to take something from a place, usually secretly: *I caught Toby raiding the fridge.* **raider** /ˈreɪ.dər/ ⓤ /-də/ *noun* [C]

rail TRAINS /reɪl/ *noun* [C or U] the system of transport which uses trains, or one of the two metal bars fixed to the ground on which trains travel: *Environmentalists argue that more goods should be transported by rail.* ○ *A train left/went off the rails and crashed into the bank, killing several passengers.*

● **go off the rails** *INFORMAL* to start behaving in a way that is not generally acceptable, especially dishonestly or illegally: *He went off the rails in his first year at university.*

rail ROD /reɪl/ *noun* [C] a horizontal bar fixed in position, especially to a wall or to vertical posts, used to enclose something, as a support, or to hang things on: *Will spectators please stay behind the rail?* ○ *Hold onto the rail so that you don't fall.* ○ *The (clothes) rail in her wardrobe was crammed full of dresses.* ○ *He folded the towels neatly and hung them on the towel (UK) rail/(US) rack.*

rail COMPLAIN /reɪl/ *verb* [I + prep] *FORMAL* to complain angrily: *He railed against/at the injustices of the system.*

▲ **rail sth off** *phrasal verb* [M] to enclose something, especially using RAILINGS: *Part of the playing field had been railed off for use as a car park.*

railcard /ˈreɪl.kɑːd/ ⓤ /-kɑːrd/ *noun* [C] in Britain, a card which you can buy and then use to buy train tickets more cheaply: *a young person's railcard* ○ *a family railcard*

railing /ˈreɪ.lɪŋ/ *noun* [C usually pl] a vertical, usually metal or wooden post, which is used together with other such posts to form a fence: *Tourists pressed their faces against the palace railings.*

raillery /ˈreɪ.lºr.i/ ⓤ /-lə.i/ *noun* [U] *FORMAL* joking or laughing at someone in a friendly way

railroad TRAIN /ˈreɪl.rəʊd/ ⓤ /-roʊd/ *noun* [C] (*WRITTEN ABBREVIATION* **RR**) *US FOR* **railway**

railroad FORCE /ˈreɪl.rəʊd/ ⓤ /-roʊd/ *verb* [T usually + adv or prep] to force something to happen or force someone to do something, especially quickly or unfairly: *We were railroaded into signing the agreement.*

railway *UK* /ˈreɪl.weɪ/ *noun* [C] (*US* **railroad**) **1** the metal tracks on which trains run: *We live close to the railway*

Rail

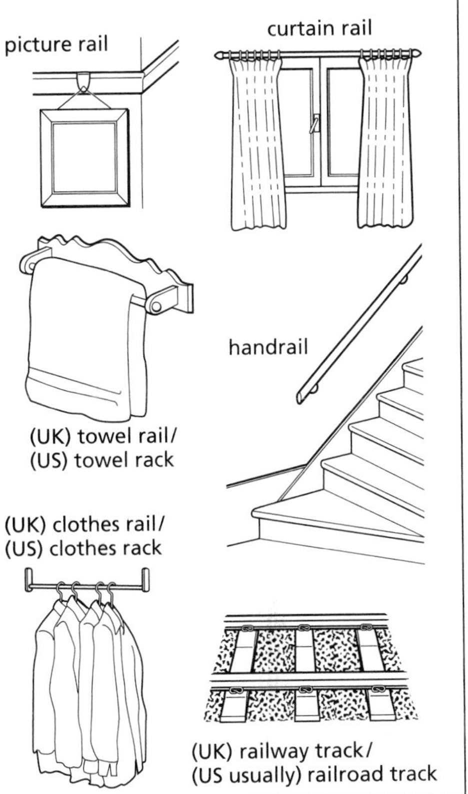
picture rail
curtain rail
handrail
(UK) towel rail/
(US) towel rack
(UK) clothes rail/
(US) clothes rack
(UK) railway track/
(US usually) railroad track

line. ○ *She travelled across Siberia on the Trans-Siberian railway.* **2** the system of tracks, stations, trains, etc: *a railway station/timetable/siding, etc.* ○ *Thomas Grant worked **on the** railway(s) for fifty years.*

raiment /ˈreɪ.mənt/ *noun* **[U]** *OLD USE* clothes

rain /reɪn/ *noun* **[U]** drops of water from clouds: *Rain is forecast for tomorrow.* ○ *Come inside out of **the** rain.* ○ *We had **heavy/light** rain all day.* ○ *We got caught in **pouring/torrential*** (= a lot of) *rain without either raincoats or umbrellas.* ○ *There will be **showers of** rain/rain **showers*** (= short periods of rain) *in the east.* ○ ***It looks like** rain* (= as if rain is going to fall).

• **come rain or shine** whatever happens: *Come rain or shine, I'll see you on Thursday.*

rain /reɪn/ *verb* **[I]** If it rains, water falls from the sky in small drops: *I think **it's** starting to rain.* ○ ***It's** raining **hard/heavily*** (= a large amount of rain is falling).

• **It never rains but it pours.** *UK* (*US* **When it rains, it pours.**) *SAYING* said when one bad thing happens, followed by a lot of other bad things, which make a bad situation worse

the rains *plural noun* the season of the year in tropical countries when there is a lot of rain: *Villagers are now waiting for the rains to **come** so that the rice will grow.* ○ *This is the third year in a row that the rains have failed.* **rainy** /ˈreɪ.ni/ *adj*: *We had three rainy days on holiday, but otherwise it was sunny.*

• **save/keep money for a rainy day** to save money for a time when it might be needed unexpectedly: *Luckily she had saved some money for a rainy day.*

PHRASAL VERBS WITH **rain** ▼

▲ **rain *(sth)* down** *phrasal verb* to fall in large amounts, or to direct something in large amounts, usually forcefully or violently: ***Bombs** rained down **on** the besieged city.* ○ *Her attacker rained down **blows** on her.*

▲ **rain *sth* off** *UK phrasal verb* (*US* **rain *sth* out**) If an event is rained off, it cannot start or continue because it is raining: *His hockey match was rained off.*

rainbow /ˈreɪn.bəʊ/ [US] /-boʊ/ *noun* **[C]** a many-coloured arch seen in the sky when rain is falling and the sun is shining: *The tropical butterfly's wings were shimmering with **all the colours of the** rainbow.*

ˈrain ˌcheck *noun* **[C]** *US* **1** a piece of paper that you are given by a shop when something which is advertised for sale at a certain price is not available. This piece of paper allows you to buy the item at the advertised price when it becomes available. **2** a ticket that allows you to see an event at a later time if bad weather stops that event from happening

• **take a rain check (on *sth*)** *INFORMAL* used to tell someone that you cannot accept their invitation now, but would like to do so at a later time: *Mind if I take a rain check on that drink? I've got to work late tonight.*

raincoat /ˈreɪŋ.kəʊt/ [US] /-koʊt/ *noun* **[C]** a waterproof coat worn for protection against rain: *a plastic raincoat*

raindrop /ˈreɪn.drɒp/ [US] /-drɑːp/ *noun* **[C]** a single drop of rain

rainfall /ˈreɪn.fɔːl/ [US] /-fɑːl/ *noun* **[U]** rain, or the amount of rain that falls: *Heavy rainfall ruined the match.* ○ *The average annual rainfall in this region: 750 mm.*

rainforest *MAINLY UK*, *MAINLY US* **rain forest** /ˈreɪn.fɒr.ɪst/ [US] /-fɔːr-/ *noun* **[C or U]** a forest in a tropical area which receives a lot of rain: *a **tropical** rainforest*

ˈrain ˌgauge *noun* **[C]** a device for measuring how much rain falls

rainstorm /ˈreɪn.stɔːm/ [US] /-stɔːrm/ *noun* **[C]** a weather condition with strong wind and heavy rain

ˈrain ˌwater *noun* **[U]** water that has fallen as rain, rather than water which has come from a TAP: *I collect rain water to water my plants.*

rainy /ˈreɪ.ni/ *adj* ➲See at **rain**.

raise [LIFT] /reɪz/ *verb* **[T]** **1** to lift something to a higher position: *Would all those in favour please raise their hands?* ○ *He raised the window and leaned out.* ○ *Mary Quant was the first fashion designer to raise hemlines.* ➲See Note **rise or raise?** at **rise** MOVE UP. **2** If you raise another player in a game of cards, you risk more money than that player has risked: *I'll raise you.* ○ **[+ two objects]** *I'll raise you $50.*

• **raise *your* hand to/against *sb*** to hit someone: *Never raise your hand to a child.*

• **raise (a few) eyebrows** to cause surprise or shock: *Jemma's miniskirt raised a few eyebrows at the board meeting.*

raise [INCREASE] /reɪz/ *verb* **[T]** to cause something to increase or become bigger, better, higher, etc: *The government plan to raise **taxes**.* ○ *I had to raise my **voice*** (= speak more loudly) *to make myself heard over the noise.* ○ *The inspector said that **standards** at the school had to be raised.* ○ *Our little chat has raised my **spirits*** (= made me feel happier).

raise [EXIST] /reɪz/ *verb* **[T]** to cause to exist: *Her answers raised **doubts/fears/suspicions** in my mind.* ○ *This discussion has raised many important **issues/problems**.* ○ *The announcement raised a **cheer/laugh**.* ○ *I want to raise* (= talk about) *two problems/questions **with** you.* ○ *I want to start my own business if I can raise* (= obtain) *the **money/cash/capital/funds**.* ○ *FORMAL The chapel was raised* (= built) *as a memorial to her son.*

-raiser /-reɪ.zəʳ/ [US] /-zɚ/ *suffix* a person or thing that causes the stated thing to exist or be obtained: *a money-raiser* ○ *These new taxes are designed to be a revenue-raiser.*

raise [DEVELOP] /reɪz/ *verb* **[T]** to take care of a person, or an animal or plant, until they are completely grown: *Her parents died when she was a baby and she was raised by her grandparents.* ○ *The lambs had to be raised **by hand*** (= fed artificial milk by people) *when their mother died.* ○ *The farmer raises* (= breeds) *chickens and pigs.* ○ *The soil around here isn't good enough for raising* (= growing) *crops.*

raise [STOP] /reɪz/ *verb* **[T]** *FORMAL* to end or stop: *They agreed to raise the trade embargo if three conditions were met.* ○ *After three weeks the siege was raised.*

raise COMMUNICATE /reɪz/ *verb* [T] to communicate with someone, especially by telephone or radio: *I've been trying to raise Jack/Tokyo all day.*

raise PAY /reɪz/ *noun* [C] *US FOR* **rise** (= increase in pay): *She asked the boss for a raise.*

raisin /ˈreɪ.zᵊn/ *noun* [C] a dried black grape

raison d'être /ˌrez.ɑːˈdet.rə/ (US) /ˌreɪ.zɑːn-/ *noun* [C usually sing] *plural* **raisons d'être** reason for existence: *Her job is her raison d'être.*

the Raj /ðəˈrɑːdʒ/ *noun* [S] the period of British rule in India: *the days of the Raj*

rajah /ˈrɑː.dʒə/ *noun* [C] a male Indian ruler ➲See also **rani**.

rake TOOL /reɪk/ *noun* [C] a garden tool with a long handle and long pointed metal parts sticking out in a row at the bottom, used for making the earth level or for gathering leaves, etc.

rake /reɪk/ *verb* [I or T] to use a rake to make earth level or to gather leaves: *In the autumn I rake **(up)** the dead leaves.* ○ *Rake **(over)** the soil before planting the seeds.*

rake MAN /reɪk/ *noun* [C] *OLD-FASHIONED* a man, especially one who is rich or with high social position, who lives in an immoral way, especially having sex with a lot of women **rakish** /ˈreɪ.kɪʃ/ *adj*: *He has a rakish air about him.* ➲See also **rakish**. **rakishness** /ˈreɪ.kɪʃ.nəs/ *noun* [U]

rake SLOPE /reɪk/ *noun* [C] a slope

raked /reɪkt/ *adj* sloping: *a steeply raked stage, sloping down towards the audience* ○ *raked wings* ○ *a raked mast*

rake SEARCH /reɪk/ *verb* [I + adv or prep] to search in a container by moving the contents around quickly: *He raked **about in** the drawer looking for his passport.* ○ *I've raked **through** the cupboard but I can't find my tennis racket.*

PHRASAL VERBS WITH **rake**

▲ **rake *sth* in** *phrasal verb* [M] to earn or obtain a large amount of money: *He rakes in over £100 000 a year.* ○ *She's really raking **it** in* (= making a lot of money).

▲ **rake *sth* out** *phrasal verb* [M] *UK* to look for something and find it, usually among various things you have stored: *I raked this old blanket out for camping.*

▲ **rake over *sth*** *phrasal verb* to keep talking or thinking about an unpleasant event or experience: *He keeps on raking over his divorce, when really he should be getting on with his life.*

▲ **rake *sth* up** TALK ABOUT *phrasal verb* [M] to talk again about a past event or experience which should be forgotten, because it upsets or annoys someone else: *She's always raking up the past/that old quarrel.*

▲ **rake *sth/sb* up** GET *phrasal verb* [M] to get the things or people you need, with difficulty or by looking in various places: *I'm trying to rake up some people to play football on Saturday – do you want to come along?*

rake-off /ˈreɪk.ɒf/ (US) /-ɑːf/ *noun* [C] *INFORMAL* a dishonest or illegal share in profits that is given to someone who has been involved in making the profits

rakish /ˈreɪ.kɪʃ/ *adj* confidently careless and informal: *He wore his hat at a rakish **angle**.* ➲See also **rakish** at **rake** MAN. **rakishly** /ˈreɪ.kɪʃ.li/ *adv*

rally MEETING /ˈræl.i/ *noun* [C] a public meeting of a large group of people, especially supporters of a particular opinion: *5000 people **held** an anti-nuclear rally.* ○ *an election/campaign rally*

rally SUPPORT /ˈræl.i/ *verb* [T] to (cause to) come together in order to provide support or make a shared effort: *Supporters/Opponents of the new shopping development are trying to rally local people **in favour of/against** it.* ○ *The prime minister has called on the public to rally **to/behind** the government.* ○ [+ obj + to infinitive] *The general rallied his forces **to** defend the town.* ○ *'Workers of the world unite' was their rallying **cry/call*** (= a phrase said to encourage support).

rally RACE /ˈræl.i/ *noun* [C] a car or motorcycle race, especially over long distances on public roads: *The French driver has taken the lead in the Paris-Dakar rally.*

rally SPORT /ˈræl.i/ *noun* [C] a continuous exchange of hits between players in tennis, SQUASH or BADMINTON

rally IMPROVE /ˈræl.i/ *verb* [I] to return to a better condition: *The nurse said my mother had rallied after a poor night.* ○ *The team played badly in the first half of the match but rallied in the second.* ○ *The pound rallied **against** the dollar in trading today.*

rally /ˈræl.i/ *noun* [C] improvement: *Share prices fell again today after yesterday's rally.*

▲ **rally round *(sb)*** *UK phrasal verb* (*US* **rally around *(sb)***) to help or support someone: *When I'm ill, my friends always rally round.*

ram HIT /ræm/ *verb* [I or T] **-mm-** to hit or push something with force: *Someone rammed **(into)** my car while it was parked outside my house.* ○ *He rammed the sweets/his pipe **into** his mouth.* ○ *I rammed **down** the soil around the fence post.* ○ *The prisoners who were being force-fed had tubes rammed **down** their throats.* ○ *She slammed the door and rammed **home** the bolt* (= closed it forcefully and completely).

▲ **ram *sth* into *sb*** *phrasal verb* to force someone to accept an idea, opinion or principle: *It's time someone rammed a bit of **sense** into you.*

• **ram *sth* home** to emphasize the importance of what you are saying in order to make certain people understand it: *He thumped the desk as he rammed his point home.*

• **ram *sth* down *sb's* throat** to force someone who disagrees with you to listen to your opinions: *For years I've had his political views rammed down my throat.*

ram /ræm/ *noun* [C] **1** (*ALSO* **battering ram**) a piece of equipment used to hit something and force it open or break it: *They used a ram to break down the door.* **2** a moving part in a machine which puts pressure or force on something

ram ANIMAL /ræm/ *noun* [C] an adult male sheep which can breed

RAM COMPUTER /ræm/ *noun* [U] *SPECIALIZED ABBREVIATION FOR* random access memory: a type of computer memory which can be searched in any order and changed as necessary ➲Compare **ROM**.

Ramadan /ˈræm.ə.dæn/ (US) /ˌræm.əˈdɑːn/ *noun* [U] the ninth month of the Muslim year, during which time Muslims have no food or drink during the day

ramble WALK /ˈræm.bl̩/ *verb* [I usually + adv or prep] to walk for pleasure, especially in the countryside: *I love to ramble **through** the fields and lanes in this part of the country.* ○ *Shall we **go** rambling tomorrow?*

ramble /ˈræm.bl̩/ *noun* [C] a long walk especially through the countryside: *We go for a ramble through the woods every Saturday.*

rambler /ˈræm.bləʳ/ (US) /-blɚ/ *noun* [C] a person who enjoys long walks in the countryside **rambling** /ˈræm.blɪŋ/ *noun* [U]

ramble TALK /ˈræm.bl̩/ *verb* [I] *DISAPPROVING* to talk or write in a confused way, often for a long time: *Sorry, I'm rambling **(on)** – let me get back to the point.*

rambling /ˈræm.blɪŋ/ *adj* too long and confused: *a long rambling speech*

ramblings /ˈræm.blɪŋz/ *plural noun* long and confused speech or writing

ramble SPREAD /ˈræm.bl̩/ *verb* [I] (especially of a plant) to go in many different directions: *An old clematis rambles **over** the garden wall.*

rambling /ˈræm.blɪŋ/ *adj* large and spreading out in many different directions: *a rambling rose* ○ *a rambling old house*

Rambo /ˈræm.bəʊ/ (US) /-boʊ/ *noun* [C] *plural* **Rambos** someone who uses, or threatens to use, strong and violent methods against their enemies: *The Americans responded, Rambo-**style**/Rambo-**like**, by threatening to attack immediately if their conditions were not met.*

rambunctious /ræmˈbʌŋk.ʃəs/ *adj* *MAINLY US* full of energy and difficult to control: *rambunctious children* ○ *a lively and rambunctious puppy*

ramekin /ˈræm.ə.kɪn/ *noun* [C] a small dish in which food for one person is baked and served

ramification /ˌræm.ɪ.fɪˈkeɪ.ʃᵊnz/ *noun* [C usually pl] the possible results of an action: *Have you considered all the ramifications **of** your suggestion?*

ramp /ræmp/ *noun* [C] **1** an artificial slope: *I pushed the wheelchair up the ramp and into the supermarket.* **2** *UK* a raised strip built into a road to make vehicles drive more slowly **3** *US FOR* **slip road**

ramp /ræmp/ *verb*

▲ **ramp** ***sth*** **up** *phrasal verb* **[M] 1** If a business ramps up its activity, it increases it: *The company announced plans to ramp up production to 10 000 units per month.* ○ *To stay competitive, they'll have to ramp up product development as well as cutting prices.* **2** to increase the speed, power or cost of something: *Announcement of the merger is expected to ramp up share prices over the next few days.* ○ *Mitsubishi has ramped up the speed of its new micro-controllers.*

rampage /ræmˈpeɪdʒ/ *verb* **[I]** to go through an area making a lot of noise and causing damage: *The demonstrators rampaged* ***through*** *the town, smashing windows and setting fire to cars.* ○ *Several villages were destroyed by rampaging soldiers.*

rampage /ˈræm.peɪdʒ/ *noun* **[C or U]** violent and usually wild behaviour: *Rioters* ***went on a/the*** *rampage through the city.*

rampant [INCREASING] /ˈræm.pənt/ *adj* (of something bad) getting worse quickly and in an uncontrolled way: *rampant corruption* ○ *Rampant inflation means that our wage increases soon become worth nothing.* ○ *He said that he had encountered rampant prejudice in his attempts to get a job.* ○ *Disease is rampant in the overcrowded city.*

rampant [STANDING] /ˈræm.pənt/ *adj* **[after n]** *SPECIALIZED* (of an animal represented on a COAT OF ARMS) standing on its back legs with its front legs raised: *a lion rampant*

rampart /ˈræm.pɑːt/ [US] /-pɑːrt/ *noun* **[C usually pl]** a large wall built round a town, castle, etc. to protect it

ram-raiding /ˈræm.reɪ.dɪŋ/ *noun* **[U]** when a car, usually a stolen car, is driven through the front window of a shop so that the contents of the shop can be stolen: *The police are increasing their efforts to prevent car thefts and subsequent ram-raiding.* **ram-raid** /ˈræm.reɪd/ *noun* **[C]** **ram-raider** /ˈræm.reɪ.dər/ [US] /-dɚ/ *noun* **[C]**

ramrod /ˈræm.rɒd/ [US] /-rɑːd/ *noun* **[C]** a long thin rod used for pushing explosives, bullets, etc. into old types of gun

• **(as) stiff/straight as a ramrod** very straight: *The old lady's back is still as straight as a ramrod.*

ramshackle /ˈræmˌʃæk.l̩/ *adj* **1** *DISAPPROVING* badly or untidily made and likely to break or fall down easily: *There's a ramshackle old shed at the bottom of the garden* **2** badly organised: *We need to reorganize this ramshackle system.*

ran /ræn/ *past simple of* **run**

ranch /rɑːntʃ/ [US] /ræntʃ/ *noun* **[C]** a very large farm on which animals are kept, especially in North and South America: *a cattle ranch* ○ *a sheep ranch* ○ *He went to work* ***on*** *a ranch.*

rancher /ˈrɑːn.tʃər/ [US] /ˈræn.tʃɚ/ *noun* **[C]** someone who owns or works on a ranch

ranching /ˈrɑːn.tʃɪŋ/ [US] /ˈræn-/ *noun* **[U]** the activity of keeping animals on a ranch

ˈranch ˌhouse *noun* **[C]** (*ALSO* **ranch-style house**) *US* a house which usually has only one level, and a roof that does not slope much, either in a city or on a ranch

rancid /ˈrænt.sɪd/ *adj* (of butter, oil, etc.) tasting or smelling unpleasant because not fresh

rancour *UK, US* **rancor** /ˈræŋ.kər/ [US] /-kɚ/ *noun* **[U]** *FORMAL* a feeling of hate and continuing anger about something in the past: *They cheated me, but I feel no rancour* ***towards/against*** *them.* **rancorous** /ˈræŋ.kər.əs/ [US] /-kɚ.əs/ *adj*: *a rancorous dispute*

rand /rænd/ *noun* **[C]** *plural* **rand** the standard unit of money used in South Africa

R & B /ˌɑːr.ənˈbiː/ [US] /ˌɑːr-/ *noun* **[U]** *ABBREVIATION FOR* **rhythm and blues**

ˌR and ˈD *noun* **[U]** *ABBREVIATION FOR* research and development: the part of a business that tries to find ways to improve existing products, and to develop new ones: *If we want to get ahead of our competitors, we ought to invest more in R and D.*

random /ˈræn.dəm/ *adj* happening, done or chosen by chance rather than according to a plan: *random checks/tests/attacks* ○ *We asked a random* ***sample/selection*** *of people what they thought.*

• **at random** without choosing intentionally; by chance: *The winning entry will be the first correct answer drawn at random.*

randomly /ˈræn.dəm.li/ *adv* in a random way: *The books were randomly arranged on the shelves.*

ˌrandom ˈbreath ˌtest *noun* **[C]** (*ABBREVIATION* **RBT**) *AUS* a test given by the police to drivers chosen by chance, to measure the amount of alcohol the drivers have in their blood

randy /ˈræn.di/ *adj INFORMAL* full of sexual desire **randiness** /ˈræn.dɪ.nəs/ *noun* **[U]**

ranee /ˈrɑː.niː/ /ˌ-ˈ-/ *noun* **[C]** a **rani**

rang /ræŋ/ *past simple of* **ring**

range [SET] /reɪndʒ/ *noun* **[C] 1** a set of similar things: *I offered her a range* ***of*** *options.* ○ *There is a* ***wide/whole*** *range of opinions on this issue.* **2** (*US ALSO* **line**) the goods made by one company or goods of one particular type that are sold in a shop: *We stock the* ***full*** *range* ***of*** *model railway accessories.* ○ *This jacket is part of our autumn/spring range.* **3** a group of hills or mountains: *a mountain range* ○ *the Pennine Range* ○ *We could see a low range* ***of*** *hills in the distance.*

range [LIMIT] /reɪndʒ/ *noun* **1 [S]** the amount, number or type of something between an upper and a lower limit: *The price range is* ***from*** *$100* ***to*** *$500.* ○ *The product is aimed at young people* ***in*** *the 18 – 25 age range.* ○ *The coat was* ***in/out of*** *my price range.* ○ *This type of work is* ***outside/beyond/out of*** *my range (****of*** *experience).* **2 [S or U]** the distance within which you can see, hear or hit someone: *The ship was* ***in/out of*** *range of our guns.* ○ *He was shot* ***at point blank/at close*** *range* (= from very near). **3 [S]** the period of time in the future within which something is planned or expected to happen: *long-range plans* ○ *short-/medium-/long-range weather forecasting* **4 [S]** the distance that a vehicle or aircraft can travel without having to stop for more fuel: *short-/medium-/long-range airliners* **5 [C]** all the musical notes that a singer can sing or a musical instrument is able to produce **range** /reɪndʒ/ *verb* **[I usually + adv or prep]** *Dress sizes range* ***from*** *petite* ***to*** *extra large.* ○ *Prices range* ***between*** *$50* ***and*** *$250.*

range [POSITION] /reɪndʒ/ *verb* **[T usually + adv or prep]** to position people or things together, especially in rows; to arrange: **[R]** *The crowd ranged itself along the route of the procession.* ○ *The troops were ranged in front of the commanding officer.*

range [MOVE] /reɪndʒ/ *verb* **[I usually + adv or prep] 1** to move or travel freely: *The hens range freely about/over the farm.* ○ *The walkers ranged through/over the hills all day.* **2** (of a piece of writing or speech) to deal with: *Our discussion ranged* ***over*** *many current issues.* ○ *The findings of a* ***wide****-ranging* (= including many subjects) *survey of young people's attitudes are published today.*

range [WEAPONS AREA] /reɪndʒ/ *noun* **[C]** an area where people can practise shooting or where bombs or other weapons can be tested: *The soldiers were practising on the* ***rifle/shooting*** *range.* ○ *The bomb was tested on a missile range in the desert.*

range [LAND] /reɪndʒ/ *noun* **[C]** *US* land for animals to feed on: *The cowboys were herding the cattle* ***on*** *the range.*

range [COOKER] /reɪndʒ/ *noun* **[C] 1** (*ALSO* **kichen range**) *UK* an old type of cooker, with one or more ovens and cooking surfaces, which is heated with wood or coal and is kept hot all the time **2** *US* a **cooker**

▲ **range against/with** ***sth/sb*** *phrasal verb* **[T often passive]** to join together as a group to oppose/support a particular idea, plan or group: *Politicians from all parties are ranged against the new law.* ○ **[R]** *She ranged herself with my opponents.*

ˈrange ˌfinder *noun* **[C]** an instrument which you use for measuring the distance of an object when you are shooting at it or taking a photograph of it

ranger /ˈreɪn.dʒər/ [US] /-dʒɚ/ *noun* **[C]** a person whose job is to protect a forest or natural park: *a forest ranger*

rani, ranee /ˈrɑː.niː/ /ˌ-ˈ-/ *noun* **[C]** a female Indian ruler or the wife of an Indian ruler

rank POSITION /ræŋk/ *noun* [C or U] **1** a position in an organization, such as the army, showing the importance of the person having it: *senior/high/junior/low rank* ○ *He has just been promoted to the rank of captain.* ○ *Ministers of Cabinet rank receive a higher salary than other ministers.* ○ *Having a large income is one of the advantages of rank* (= high position). **2** a particular position, higher or lower than others: *He's in the front/first rank of* (= one of the best) *international tennis players.* ○ *Consumer preferences were placed in rank order from 1 to 5.*

rank /ræŋk/ *verb* [I or T; usually + adv or prep] to have a position higher or lower than others, or to be considered to have such a position: *A captain ranks* (= has a position) *above a lieutenant.* ○ *My entry was ranked third in the flower show.* ○ *She ranked the bottles in order of size along the shelf.* ○ *In my opinion, he ranks among the theatre's greatest actors.* ○ *She said that 1989 must rank as* (= be) *the most remarkable year for change in Europe since 1848.*

ranking /'ræŋ.kɪŋ/ *noun* [C] a rank or level, for example in a competition: *Last year Wiseman rose from 266 to 35 in the tennis world rankings.* ○ *The city's housing costs were enough to earn it a ranking of 66th nationally.*

ranking /'ræŋ.kɪŋ/ *adj* [before n] US being the officer of highest rank present at a particular time: *General Steinberger was the ranking officer present at the meeting.*

ranks /ræŋks/ *plural noun* the membership of a group or organization: *Party ranks have swelled by nearly 300 000.* ○ *Marty has joined the ranks of the* (= become) *unemployed.* ○ *The party leadership seems to be losing support in the ranks.*

● **rise from/through the ranks** to be moved up from a low level position in an organization to a higher one: *He rose through the ranks to become a General.* ○ *He joined the company in 1998 and has been rising through the ranks ever since.*

rank ROW /ræŋk/ *noun* [C] **1** a row, especially of people or things standing side by side: *The front rank of the riot squad raised their shields.* ○ LITERARY *We could see nothing for miles but serried ranks* (= many close rows) *of fir trees.* **2** a place where taxis wait for passengers: *There were no taxis at the taxi/cab rank.*

rank EXTREME /ræŋk/ *adj* [before n] (especially of something bad) complete or extreme: *It was rank stupidity to drive so fast on an icy road.* ○ *The horse that won the race was a rank outsider.*

rank GROWN /ræŋk/ *adj* describes plants that grow too fast or too thickly, or an area covered by these: *The abandoned garden was rank with weeds.*

rank SMELL /ræŋk/ *adj* smelling strong and unpleasant: *His clothes were rank with sweat.*

,rank and 'file *group noun* the ordinary workers in a company or the ordinary members of an organization, and not the leaders: *The party's rank and file are beginning to question the prime minister's choice of advisers.* ○ *Most rank and file police officers rejected the new pay offer.*

rankle /'ræŋ.kl̩/ *verb* [I] to cause annoyance or anger which lasts a long time: *The unkind way in which his girlfriend left him still rankled with him long after.* ○ [+ that] *It still rankles that she got promoted, and I didn't.*

rank outsider /,ræŋk.aʊt'saɪ.də/ *noun* [C] someone who is not expected to win a race or competition: *He came from nowhere, this rank outsider, to beat a field of top-class athletes.*

ransack /'ræn.sæk/ *verb* [T] to search a place or container in a violent and careless way: *The burglars ransacked the house but found nothing valuable.* ○ *I ransacked the cupboard for my ski boots.*

ransom /'ræn.s³m/ *noun* [C or U] a large sum of money which is demanded in exchange for someone who has been taken prisoner, or sometimes for an animal: *a ransom demand/note* ○ *They demanded a huge ransom for the return of the little girl whom they had kidnapped.* ○ *The gang held the racehorse to/for ransom.*

● **hold sb to ransom** to force someone to do something by putting them in a situation where something bad will happen to them if they do not: *The government says it is being held to ransom by the actions of terrorist groups.*

ransom /'ræn.s³m/ *verb* [T] to pay money in order to set someone free: *Her father ransomed her for a million dollars.*

rant /rænt/ *verb* [I] to speak or shout in a loud, uncontrolled or angry way, often saying confused or foolish things: *He's always ranting (on) about the government.* ○ *I get fed up with my mother ranting and raving (about my clothes) all the time.*

rant /rænt/ *noun* [C] a long, angry and confused speech: *The minister's speech descended into a rant against his political opponents.* **ranting** /'ræn.tɪŋ/ US /-t̬ɪŋ/ *noun* [U] (ALSO **rantings**)

rap MUSIC /ræp/ *noun* [U] a type of popular music with a strong rhythm in which the words are spoken, not sung: *a rap artist/star*

rap /ræp/ *verb* [I] -pp- to perform rap

rap HIT /ræp/ *verb* -pp- **1** [I or T] to hit or say something suddenly and forcefully: *She rapped (on) the table to get everyone's attention.* ○ *The colonel rapped (out) an order to his men.* **2** [T] to criticize someone, especially officially: *The headline read 'Judge raps police'.*

● **rap sb over the knuckles** to speak officially to someone, in a severe or angry way, because you disapprove of their actions: *He was rapped over the knuckles by the management.*

rap /ræp/ *noun* [C] a sudden short noise, especially one made by hitting a hard surface: *There was a series of raps on the window.*

● **a rap on/over the knuckles** when you are spoken to severely or angrily because of something you have done or failed to do: *I got a rap on the knuckles for not finishing my essay on time.*

rap PUNISHMENT /ræp/ *noun* [C or U] MAINLY US SLANG an accusation of crime, or a punishment: *He always said he was jailed on a bum rap* (= false accusation). ○ *The police caught him, but somehow he managed to beat the rap* (= escape punishment). ○ *I'm not going to take the rap for you* (= be punished for something you did).

rap JUDGMENT /ræp/ *noun* [C] US SLANG a judgment or a reaction: *The new show got a bum/bad rap* (= was severely criticized) *in all the papers.*

rapacious /rə'peɪ.ʃəs/ *adj* FORMAL having or showing a strong desire to take things for yourself, usually using unfair methods or force: *a rapacious landlord/businessman* ○ *her rapacious appetite for fame* **rapaciously** /rə'peɪ.ʃə.sli/ *adv* **rapaciousness** /rə'peɪ.ʃə.snəs/ *noun* [U] **rapacity** /rə'pæs.ə.ti/ US /-t̬i/ *noun* [U]

rape FORCE /reɪp/ *verb* [I or T] to force someone to have sex when they are unwilling, using violence or threatening behaviour: *She was pulled from the car and raped.* ○ *It's difficult to understand what causes a man to rape.*

rape /reɪp/ *noun* **1** [C or U] (an example of) the crime of forcefully having sex with someone against their wish: *He had committed several rapes.* ○ *He was convicted of rape.* **2** [U] destruction of the natural world, often for profit: *The road builders were accused of the rape of the countryside.*

rapist /'reɪ.pɪst/ *noun* [C] a person who commits rape: *The police have caught the rapist.*

rape PLANT /reɪp/ *noun* [U] (ALSO **oilseed rape**) a plant with yellow flowers from which oil and animal food are produced

rapid /'ræp.ɪd/ *adj* fast or sudden: *The 1990s were a period of rapid change/growth.* ○ *I was startled by a rapid movement to my left.* ○ *His response to the accusation was rapid.* **rapidity** /rə'pɪd.ɪ.ti/ US /-ə.t̬i/ *noun* [U] FORMAL **rapidly** /'ræp.ɪd.li/ *adv*

rapid-fire /'ræp.ɪd.faɪə/ US /-faɪr/ *adj* [before n] describes questions or jokes which come very quickly one after another

rapids /'ræp.ɪdz/ *plural noun* a dangerous part of a river which flows very fast because it is steep and sometimes narrow: *They shot* (= travelled through) *the rapids in a canoe.*

,rapid 'transit *adj* [before n] describes a system of fast moving trains in the city

rapier /'reɪ.pi.ə/ US /-ɚ/ *noun* [C] a sword with a long thin blade

rapier /ˈreɪ.pi.əʳ/ [US] /-ɚ/ *adj* [before n] describes a statement or a sense of humour, etc. that is extremely clever and amusing: *He is renowned for his rapier(-like) wit.*

rappel /ræˈpel/ *verb* [I], *noun* [C] *US FOR* **abseil**

rapper /ˈræp.əʳ/ [US] /-ɚ/ *noun* [C] someone who performs rap music

rapport /ræˈpɔːʳ/ [US] /-ˈpɔːr/ *noun* [S or U] a good understanding of someone and an ability to communicate well with them: *We'd worked together for years and developed a* ***close/good*** *rapport.* ○ *She* ***has*** *an excellent rapport* ***with*** *her staff.*

rapprochement /ræˈprɒʃ.mɑ̃ŋ/ [US] /ˌræˌproʊʃˈmɑːn/ *noun* [C or U] *FORMAL* (an) agreement reached by opposing groups or people: *There are signs of (a) rapprochement* ***between*** *the warring factions.*

ˈrap ˌsheet *noun* [C] *US INFORMAL* an official police document which lists the crimes that a particular person has committed ➲Compare **charge sheet**.

rapt /ræpt/ *adj* **1** giving complete attention, or showing complete involvement, or (of attention) complete: *She sat with a rapt expression reading her book.* ○ *The children watched with rapt* ***attention***. **2** *AUS INFORMAL* **wrapped** (= extremely happy or excited)

rapture /ˈræp.tʃəʳ/ [US] /-tʃɚ/ *noun* [U] extreme pleasure and happiness or excitement: *He listened to the music with an expression of pure rapture on his face.* ○ *The prime minister's supporters greeted her speech with rapture.*

raptures /ˈræp.tʃəz/ [US] /-tʃɚz/ *plural noun* an expression of extreme pleasure and happiness or excitement: *She* ***went into*** *raptures at the news of her success.* ○ *She was* ***in*** *raptures about/over her first visit to Paris.* **rapturous** /ˈræp.tʃᵊr.əs/ [US] /-tʃɚ-/ *adj*: *The play was greeted with rapturous* ***applause***. **rapturously** /ˈræp.tʃᵊr.ə.sli/ [US] /-tʃɚ-/ *adv*

rare [NOT COMMON] /reəʳ/ [US] /rer/ *adj* **1** not common; very unusual: *a rare disease/species* ○ *The museum is full of rare and precious treasures.* ○ *a rare occasion/opportunity/visit/treat, etc.* ○ [+ to infinitive] ***It's*** *very rare* ***to*** *find these birds in England in winter.* **2** describes the atmosphere or air at the top of a mountain which contains less oxygen, making it harder to breathe ➲See also **rarefied**.

• **rare bird** unusual person: *He's that rare bird, a barman who doesn't drink alcohol.*

• **have a rare old time 1** *MAINLY UK OLD-FASHIONED* to enjoy yourself very much: *We went on a tour of the city's bars and had a rare old time.* **2** *UK OLD-FASHIONED* to have difficulty: *We had a rare old time trying to get tickets.*

rarely /ˈreə.li/ [US] /ˈrer-/ *adv* not often: *We rarely see each other now.* ○ *I rarely have time to read a newspaper.* ○ *FORMAL Rarely have I seen such a beautiful sunset.* ➲See also **seldom**.

rarity /ˈreə.rə.ti/ [US] /ˈrer.ə.t̬i/ *noun* [C or U] something that is very unusual, or the quality of being very unusual: *Men who do the cooking are* ***something of a*** *rarity.* ○ *Diamonds are valuable because of their rarity.*

rare [COOKED] /reəʳ/ [US] /rer/ *adj* (of meat) not cooked for very long; still red: *I'd like my steak rare, please.* ➲Compare **medium** VALUE.

rarefied /ˈreə.rɪ.faɪd/ [US] /ˈrer.ə-/ *adj* **1** (of air) with little oxygen **2** describes a place or situation which does not have any of the problems of ordinary life: *the rarefied atmosphere/circles of college life*

raring /ˈreə.rɪŋ/ [US] /ˈrer.ɪŋ/ **be raring to do *sth*** to be very enthusiastic about starting something: *I've bought all the paint for decorating the bedrooms and I'm raring to get started.* ○ *I had been preparing for the exam for a year and now I was raring* ***to go*** (= eager to start).

rascal /ˈrɑː.skᵊl/ [US] /ˈræs.kᵊl/ *noun* [C] **1** a person, especially a child or a man, who does things of which you disapprove, but whom you still like: *I caught those* ***little/young*** *rascals dressing up in my clothes.* ○ *What's that* ***old*** *rascal been up to now?* **2** *OLD USE* a dishonest person **rascally** /ˈrɑː.skᵊl.i/ [US] /ˈræs.kᵊl-/ *adj*

rash [WITHOUT THOUGHT] /ræʃ/ *adj* careless or unwise, without thought for what might happen or result: *That was a rash decision – you didn't think about the costs involved.* ○ [+ to infinitive] *I think* ***it*** *was a bit rash* ***of*** *them* ***to*** *get married when they'd only known each other for a few weeks.* **rashness** /ˈræʃ.nəs/ *noun* [U] ***In a moment of*** *rashness, I agreed to do a parachute jump for charity.* **rashly** /ˈræʃ.li/ *adv*

rash [SKIN CONDITION] /ræʃ/ *noun* [C or U] a lot of small red spots on skin: *I've got an* ***itchy*** *rash all over my chest.* ○ *He* ***came out/up in*** *a rash after he fell in a patch of nettles.* ○ *If you stay in the sun too long you'll get (a)* ***heat*** *rash.*

rash [LARGE NUMBER] /ræʃ/ *noun* **a rash of *sth*** a large number of unpleasant events of the same type: *There has been a rash of robberies/accidents/complaints in the last two months.*

rasher /ˈræʃ.əʳ/ [US] /-ɚ/ *noun* [C] a thin flat piece of BACON

rasp [TOOL] /rɑːsp/ [US] /ræsp/ *noun* [C] a tool with a rough blade, used for shaping wood or metal

rasp /rɑːsp/ [US] /ræsp/ *verb* [T] to rub something roughly: *The horse rasped my hand with his tongue as I fed him the apple.*

rasp [SOUND] /rɑːsp/ [US] /ræsp/ *noun* [S] a rough unpleasant noise, like metal being rubbed against metal: *There was* ***the*** *rasp* ***of*** *a bolt and the door suddenly opened.*

rasp /rɑːsp/ [US] /ræsp/ *verb* [I or T] to make a rough unpleasant sound, especially while breathing or speaking: *I heard his breath rasping in his chest.* ○ *The gunman rasped* ***(out)*** *an urgent order* (= gave it in an unpleasant-sounding voice) *to the other members of the gang.*

raspy /ˈrɑːsp.i/ [US] /ˈræsp-/ *adj* A raspy voice sounds unpleasantly rough.

raspberry [FRUIT] /ˈrɑːz.bᵊr.i/ [US] /ˈræz.ber-/ *noun* [C or U] a small soft red fruit, or the bush on which it grows: *raspberries and ice cream* ○ *raspberry jam* ➲See picture **Fruit** on page Centre 1

raspberry [SOUND] /ˈrɑːz.bᵊr.i/ [US] /ˈræz.ber-/ *noun* [C] *INFORMAL* a rude sound made by sticking the tongue out and blowing: *The boy turned and* ***blew*** *a raspberry at the teacher before running off.*

Rastafarian /ˌræs.təˈfeə.ri.ən/ [US] /-ˈfer.i-/ *noun* [C] (*INFORMAL* **Rasta**) a member of a religious group which originated in Jamaica and which worships Haile Selassie **Rastafarian** /ˌræs.təˈfeə.ri.ən/ [US] /-ˈfer.i-/ *adj* **Rastafarianism** /ˌræs.təˈfeə.ri.ə.nɪ.zᵊm/ [US] /-ˈfer.i-/ *noun* [U]

rat [ANIMAL] /ræt/ *noun* [C] a small RODENT, larger than a mouse, which has a long tail and is considered to be harmful: *Rats carry disease.* ○ *I think we've* ***got*** *rats* (= there are rats in our house).

rat [PERSON] /ræt/ *noun* [C] *INFORMAL* an unpleasant person who deceives others or is not loyal

▲ **rat on *sb/sth*** *phrasal verb SLANG DISAPPROVING* to be not loyal to someone, especially by giving away secret information about them, or to fail to do something that you said you would do: *He ratted on us.* ○ *They ratted on the deal.*

rat-arsed *UK* /ˈræt.ɑːst/ [US] /-ɑːrst/ *adj* (*US* **rat-assed**) *OFFENSIVE* extremely drunk: *I got completely rat-arsed at Kate's party.*

ratatouille /ˌræt.əˈtuː.i/ [US] /ˌræt̬-/ *noun* [U] a savoury dish made by cooking vegetables, such as tomatoes, AUBERGINES and PEPPERS, in liquid at a low heat

ratbag /ˈræt.bæg/ *noun* [C] *MAINLY UK INFORMAL* an unpleasant person

ratchet /ˈrætʃ.ɪt/ *noun* [C] a part of a machine which allows movement in one direction only. It is usually a wheel with teeth-like parts which either slide over or lock against the free end of a bar.

ratchet /ˈrætʃ.ɪt/ *verb*

▲ **ratchet *sth* up/down** *phrasal verb* [M] to increase/decrease something over a period of time: *The debate should ratchet up awareness of the problem.* ○ *The government was accused of ratcheting up pressure on the health services.* ○ *Costs have been ratcheted down by as much as 50% since 1999.*

rate [MEASURE] /reɪt/ *noun* [C] the speed at which something happens or changes, or the amount or number of times it happens or changes in a particular period: *Although she's recovering from her illness, her rate* ***of*** *progress is quite slow.* ○ *I told my assistants to work* ***at their own***

rate. ○ *The taxi was going* ***at*** *a tremendous rate.* ○ *the growth/inflation/mortality/unemployment, etc. rate* ○ *The drug has a high* ***success/failure*** *rate.* ➲See also **rate** at **rates**.

• **at a rate of knots** *UK* If someone does something at a rate of knots, they do it very quickly: *She got through her work at a rate of knots.*

• **at this rate** if the situation stays as it is: *At this rate, we won't be home till midnight.*

• **at any rate 1** whatever happens: *Well, I'm not going home on foot, at any rate.* **2** something you say to show that you are going to say something more exactly: *I don't think they liked my idea. At any rate, they weren't very enthusiastic about it.*

rate [PAYMENT] /reɪt/ *noun* [C] an amount or level of payment: *We agreed a rate with the painter before he started work.* ○ *What's the* ***going*** (= standard) *rate* ***for*** *this type of work?* ○ *Do you pay your mortgage on a* ***fixed*** *or* ***variable*** *rate?* ➲See also **rate** at **rates**.

rate [JUDGE] /reɪt/ *verb* [T] **1** to judge the value or character of someone or something: *How do you rate him* ***as*** *a footballer?* ○ *She is rated very* ***highly*** *by the people she works for.* ○ *INFORMAL "What do you think of her as a singer?" "I don't really rate her* (= I do not think that she is very good)." ○ *I rate cars* ***as*** *one of the worst polluters of the environment.* ○ [+ obj + n] *On a scale of one to ten, I'd rate his book a five.* ○ *Car crashes are so frequent that they don't rate* ***a mention*** (= are not considered to be worth reporting) *in the newspaper unless a lot of people are killed.* ➲See also **rate** at **rates**; **underrate**; **overrate**. **2 rate as *sth*** to be considered to be something of a particular quality: *That rates as the worst film I've ever seen.*

-rate /-reɪt/ *suffix*: *His suggestions are always* ***first****-rate* (= very good). ○ *This company produces* ***second/third****-rate* (= not very good) *goods.*

rating /ˈreɪ.tɪŋ/ [US] /-t̬ɪŋ/ *noun* [C or U] a measurement of how good or popular someone or something is: *The government's* ***popularity*** *rating sank to an all-time low.*

ratings /ˈreɪ.tɪŋz/ [US] /-t̬ɪŋz/ *plural noun* a list of television and radio programmes showing how popular they are: *Advertisers are interested in ratings.* ○ *The serial has fallen in* ***the*** *ratings this week.*

rateable value /ˌreɪ.tə.bl̩ˈvæl.juː/ [US] /-t̬ə-/ *noun* [C] an official value that was formerly given to a building in the UK, based partly on its size and type, which decided the amount of local tax that the owner should pay

ˌrate of exˈchange *noun* [C] the **exchange rate**

rates /reɪts/ *plural noun* a local tax paid in Australia, and in Britain in the past, by the owners of houses and other buildings

rate /reɪt/ *verb* [T] *UK* In Britain in the past, a building was rated to decide how much local tax the owner should pay.

R

rather [SMALL AMOUNT] /ˈrɑː.ðəʳ/ [US] /ˈræð.ɚ/ *adv* quite; to a slight degree: *It's rather cold today, isn't it?* ○ *That's rather* ***a*** *difficult book – here's an easier one for you.* ○ *The train was rather too crowded for a comfortable journey.* ○ *She answered the telephone rather sleepily.* ○ *I rather doubt I'll be able to come to your party.*

rather [VERY] /ˈrɑː.ðəʳ/ [US] /ˈræð.ɚ/ *adv, predeterminer* very; to a large degree: *Actually, I did rather well in my exams.* ○ *I've got rather a lot of work to do at the moment.*

rather [MORE EXACTLY] /ˈrɑː.ðəʳ/ [US] /ˈræð.ɚ/ *adv* **1** more accurately; more exactly: *She'll go to London on Thursday,* ***or*** *rather, she will if she has to.* ○ *He's my sister's friend really, rather* ***than*** *mine.* **2** used to express an opposite opinion: *The ending of the war is not a cause for celebration, but rather for regret that it ever happened.* ○ *No, I'm not tired. Rather the opposite in fact.*

rather [PREFERENCE] /ˈrɑː.ðəʳ/ [US] /ˈræð.ɚ/ *adv* **rather than** in preference to; instead of: *I think I'd like to stay at home this evening rather than go out.*

• **Rather *you* than *me*.** said by someone who does not want to do the thing that someone else is doing: *"I've got to have two teeth out next week." "Rather you than me."*

rather [YES] /ˌrɑːˈðɜːʳ/ [US] /ˌræðˈɝː/ *exclamation MAINLY UK OLD-FASHIONED* certainly; yes: *"Do you want to come out for dinner with us this evening?" "Rather!"*

ratify /ˈræt.ɪ.faɪ/ [US] /ˈræt̬.ə-/ *verb* [T] *FORMAL* (especially of governments or organizations) to make an agreement official: *Many countries have now ratified the UN convention on the rights of the child.* ○ *The decision will have to be ratified* (= approved) *by the executive board.* **ratification** /ˌræt.ɪ.fɪˈkeɪ.ʃən/ [US] /ˌræt̬.ə-/ *noun* [U]

ratio /ˈreɪ.ʃi.əʊ/ [US] /-oʊ/ *noun* [C] *plural* **ratios** the relationship between two groups or amounts, which expresses how much bigger one is than the other: *The ratio* ***of*** *men* ***to*** *women at the conference was ten to one/10:1.* ○ *The school is trying to improve its pupil-teacher ratio* (= the number of teachers compared with the number of students).

ration /ˈræʃ.ən/ *noun* [C] **1** a limited amount of something which one person is allowed to have, especially when there is not much of it available: *During the war, no one was allowed more than their ration* ***of*** *food, clothing and fuel.* **2** an amount of something that you would expect to have: *We've had more than our ration* ***of*** *problems recently.*

ration /ˈræʃ.ən/ *verb* [T] to limit the amount of a particular thing that someone is allowed to have: *Do you remember when petrol was rationed* ***to*** *five gallons a week?* ○ *My children would watch television all day long, but I ration it.*

rationing /ˈræʃ.ən.ɪŋ/ *noun* [U] a system of limiting the amount of something that each person is allowed to have: *fuel rationing*

rations /ˈræʃ.ənz/ *plural noun* the total amount of food that is given to someone to be eaten during a particular activity and in a particular period of time, especially that given to soldiers when they are fighting

▲ **ration *sth* out** *phrasal verb* [M] to divide something between a group of people so that each person gets a small amount: *Ann rationed out the cake* ***between*** *the children.*

rational /ˈræʃ.ən.əl/ *adj* showing clear thought or reason: *He was too upset to be rational.* ○ *a rational course of action/argument/explanation*

rationally /ˈræʃ.ən.əl.i/ *adv* in a way based on reason rather than emotions: *Rationally, he knows that she won't ever go back to him, but emotionally he can't accept it.*

rationale /ˌræʃ.əˈnɑːl/ [US] /-ˈnæl/ *noun* [C or U] *FORMAL* the reasons or intentions for a particular set of thoughts or actions: *I don't understand the rationale* ***behind*** *the council's housing policy.*

rationalism /ˈræʃ.ən.əl.ɪ.zəm/ *noun* [U] the belief or principle that actions and opinions should be based on reason rather than on emotion or religion **rationalist** /ˈræʃ.ən.əl.ɪst/ *adj* (*ALSO* **rationalistic**)

rationalist /ˈræʃ.ən.əl.ɪst/ *noun* [C] someone whose actions and decisions are based on reason rather than emotions or beliefs **rationality** /ˌræʃ.ənˈæl.ɪ.ti/ [US] /-ə.t̬i/ *noun* [U]

rationalize [EXPLAIN], *UK USUALLY* **-ise** /ˈræʃ.ən.əl.aɪz/ *verb* [T] to try to find reasons to explain your behaviour, decisions, etc: *She rationalized the expense by saying that the costly carpet she had bought would last longer than a cheaper one.* **rationalization**, *UK USUALLY* **-isation** /ˌræʃ.ən.əl.aɪˈzeɪ.ʃən/ *noun* [C or U]

rationalize [CHANGE], *UK USUALLY* **-ise** /ˈræʃ.ən.əl.aɪz/ *verb* [I or T] to make a company, way of working, etc. more effective, usually by combining or stopping particular activities, or (of a company, way of working, etc.) to become more effective in this way: *We rationalized the production system so that one operator could control all three machines.* ○ *The recession is forcing the company to rationalize.* **rationalization**, *UK USUALLY* **-isation** /ˌræʃ.ən.əl.aɪˈzeɪ.ʃən/ *noun* [C or U]

the ˈrat ˌrace *noun* [S] a way of life in modern society, characterized by people competing with each other for power and money: *He decided to get out of the rat race, and went to work on a farm.*

ˈrat ˌrun *noun* [C] *UK* a small road which is used by a lot of drivers who are trying to avoid traffic on larger roads: *The road through our village has become a rat run for commuters trying to avoid delays on the A14.*

rattle [SOUND] /ˈræt.l̩/ [US] /ˈræt̬-/ *noun* **1** [S] a sound similar to a series of quickly repeated knocks: *From across the town came the rattle* ***of*** *machine-gun fire.* **2** [C] a toy which makes a noise like a series of knocks: *The baby was waving around a plastic rattle.* **3** [C] a wooden device that when turned round and round produces a noise like a series of knocks **4** [C] the part of a RATTLESNAKE's tail that produces a noise

rattle /ˈræt.l̩/ [US] /ˈræt̬-/ *verb* [I or T] to (cause to) make a noise like a series of knocks: *The explosion rattled the cups on the table.* ○ *The dying man's voice rattled in his throat.* ○ [+ adv or prep] *The car rattled* ***over*** *the cobblestones.* ○ *My car engine is making a strange rattling noise.*

rattle [WORRY] /ˈræt.l̩/ [US] /ˈræt̬-/ *verb* [T] to worry someone or make someone nervous: *The creaking upstairs was starting to rattle me.*

PHRASAL VERBS WITH **rattle**

▲ **rattle *sth* off** *phrasal verb* [M] *INFORMAL* to say or read aloud very quickly a list of names or items, or something you have learned: *She rattled off the names of the people who were coming to the party.*

▲ **rattle on/away** *phrasal verb* to talk for a long time, especially about things that are not important: *She was on the phone for hours last night, just rattling on to her friends.*

▲ **rattle through *sth*** *phrasal verb INFORMAL* to do or say something very quickly: *I'm going to rattle through my work today so that I can go home early.* ○ *He rattled through the list of countries he had visited.*

rattlesnake /ˈræt.l̩.sneɪk/ [US] /ˈræt̬-/ *noun* [C] (*INFORMAL* **rattler**) a poisonous snake found in southern parts of the US which, when annoyed, produces a loud noise by shaking its tail

ratty /ˈræt.i/ [US] /ˈræt̬-/ *adj INFORMAL* easily annoyed; IRRITABLE: *She was a bit ratty with me this morning.*

raucous /ˈrɔː.kəs/ [US] /ˈrɑː-/ *adj* loud and unpleasant: *I heard the raucous call of the crows.* ○ *Raucous* ***laughter*** *came from the next room.* ○ *The party was becoming rather raucous.* **raucously** /ˈrɔː.kə.sli/ [US] /ˈrɑː-/ *adv* **raucousness** /ˈrɔː.kə.snəs/ [US] /ˈrɑː-/ *noun* [U]

raunchy /ˈrɔːn.tʃi/ [US] /ˈrɑːn-/ *adj* connected with sex in a very clear and obvious way: *a raunchy magazine/video* **raunchily** /ˈrɔːn.tʃɪ.li/ [US] /ˈrɑːn-/ *adv* **raunchiness** /ˈrɔːn.tʃɪ.nəs/ [US] /ˈrɑːn-/ *noun* [U]

ravage /ˈræv.ɪdʒ/ *verb* [T often passive] to cause great damage to something: *The area has been ravaged by drought/floods/war.*

ravages /ˈræv.ɪ.dʒɪz/ *plural noun* **the ravages of disease/time/war, etc.** the damage caused by disease/time/war, etc: *The ravages of the fire showed in the splintered woodwork and blistered paint of the houses.*

rave [SPEAK FOOLISHLY] /reɪv/ *verb* [I] to speak in an uncontrolled way, usually because you are upset or angry, or because you are ill: *He's always raving* ***(on) about*** *the government.* ○ *She was* ***ranting and*** *raving* ***about*** *some imagined insult.* ➲See also **raving**.

ravings /ˈreɪ.vɪŋz/ *plural noun* crazy meaningless statements: *The things he said are simply the ravings of a disturbed mind.*

rave [ENTHUSIASTIC] /reɪv/ *adj* [before n] *INFORMAL* admiring; giving praise: *The show has received rave* ***reviews/notices*** *in all the papers.*

rave /reɪv/ *verb* [I] *INFORMAL* to praise something greatly: *She raved* ***about/over*** *the clothes she had seen at the Paris fashion shows.* ➲See also **raving**.

rave [PARTY] /reɪv/ *noun* [C] *MAINLY UK INFORMAL* an event where young people dance to modern electronic music and sometimes take illegal drugs: *an all-night/open-air rave* ○ *rave music*

raver /ˈreɪ.vər/ [US] /-vɚ/ *noun* [C] someone who takes part in raves

raven [BIRD] /ˈreɪ.vən/ *noun* [C] the largest bird in the crow family, with shiny black feathers

raven [BLACK] /ˈreɪ.vən/ *adj* [before n] *LITERARY* (especially of hair) shiny black: *Her pale face was framed by raven locks.*

ravening /ˈræv.ən.ɪŋ/ *adj* **1** *LITERARY* (especially of wild animals) fiercely hunting for food: *ravening wolves* **2** describes a group of people who try to get what they want in a forceful way: *She said that she was tired of being pursued by ravening journalists.*

ravenous /ˈræv.ən.əs/ *adj* extremely hungry: *I'm ravenous – where's supper?* ○ *Growing boys have ravenous appetites.* **ravenously** /ˈræv.ən.ə.sli/ *adv*: *He looked ravenously at the buffet table.* ○ *I'm ravenously* ***hungry***.

ravine /rəˈviːn/ *noun* [C] a deep narrow valley with steep sides

raving /ˈreɪ.vɪŋ/ *adj* [before n], *adv INFORMAL* complete or extreme, or completely or extremely: *He must be a raving* ***idiot/lunatic***. ○ *Her last book was a raving bestseller/success.* ○ *She's no raving* ***beauty***. ○ *I think you're* ***(stark)*** *raving* ***mad*** *to agree to do all that extra work without being paid for it.*

ravings /ˈreɪ.vɪŋz/ *plural noun* ➲See at **rave** SPEAK FOOLISHLY.

ravioli /ˌræv.iˈəʊ.li/ [US] /-ˈoʊ-/ *noun* [U] small square cases of pasta filled with meat or cheese, which are cooked in boiling water

ravish [PLEASURE] /ˈræv.ɪʃ/ *verb* [T usually passive] *LITERARY* to give great pleasure to someone: *I was utterly ravished by the way she smiled.*

ravishing /ˈræv.ɪ.ʃɪŋ/ *adj* very beautiful: *She* ***looked*** *ravishing/She was a ravishing* ***sight*** *in her wedding dress.*

ravish [FORCE] /ˈræv.ɪʃ/ *verb* [T] *OLD USE* to force a woman to have sex against her wishes

raw [NOT COOKED] /rɔː/ [US] /rɑː/ *adj* (of food) not cooked: *raw fish*

raw [NOT PROCESSED] /rɔː/ [US] /rɑː/ *adj* **1** (of materials) not processed; in a natural state: *Oil is an important raw* ***material*** *which can be processed into many different products, including plastics.* ○ *They claimed that raw* ***sewage*** *was being pumped into the sea.* **2** describes information which has been collected but has not yet been studied in detail: *raw data/evidence/figures* **3** describes a person who is not trained or is without experience: *I would prefer not to leave this job to John while he's still a raw recruit/beginner.* **4** Feelings or qualities that are raw are those which are natural and which you do not or cannot control: *We were struck by the raw* ***energy/power*** *of the dancers' performances.* ○ *Her emotions are still a bit raw after her painful divorce.* **5** A piece of writing that is raw is one which does not try to hide anything about its subject: *His new play is a raw drama about family life.*

• **come the raw prawn** *AUS* to try to deceive someone, especially by pretending that you have no knowledge of something: *Don't come the raw prawn* ***with*** *me – you know very well what I'm talking about.*

• **in the raw 1** *INFORMAL* naked: *They sunbathed in the raw.* **2** in a plain and honest way, with nothing hidden: *The film really showed you prison life in the raw.*

rawness /ˈrɔː.nəs/ [US] /ˈrɑː-/ *noun* [U] the quality or fact of being raw

raw [PAINFUL] /rɔː/ [US] /rɑː/ *adj* **1** sore or painful because of being rubbed or damaged: *The shoe had rubbed a raw place on her heel.* **2** describes weather that is very cold: *a raw morning* ○ *a raw wind* ○ *The evening was cold and raw.*

• **a raw deal** bad or unfair treatment: *He said that many children in the city's schools were* ***getting/being given*** *a raw deal by being taught in classes that were too large.*

rawness /ˈrɔː.nəs/ [US] /ˈrɑː-/ *noun* [U] the quality of being raw

ˌraw siˈenna *noun* [U] a brownish yellow colour

ray [BEAM] /reɪ/ *noun* [C] **1** a narrow beam of light, heat, etc. travelling in a straight line from its place of origin: *A ray* ***of*** *sunshine shone through a gap in the clouds.* ○ *Light rays bend as they pass from air to water.* **2** a small amount: *There's still a ray* ***of hope*** *that the missing child will be found alive.*

• **ray of sunshine** a happy person who makes others feel happy, especially in a difficult situation: *We love looking after our grandchild. He's a ray of sunshine!*

ray [FISH] /reɪ/ *noun* [C] a large flat sea fish with a long narrow tail

ˈray ˌgun *noun* [C] in SCIENCE FICTION stories, a gun which produces rays that kill people or make them unable to move

Raynaud's disease /ˈreɪ.nəʊz.dɪˌziːz/ [US] /ˈreɪ.noʊz.dɪˌziːz/ *noun* [U] (*ALSO* **Raynaud's phenomenon**) a disease which affects the flow of blood in the fingers, toes, ears or nose, and can make them turn blue or white, and feel cold and painful

rayon /ˈreɪ.ɒn/ [US] /-ɑːn/ *noun* [U] a smooth cloth used to make clothes

raze /reɪz/ *verb* [T] to completely destroy a city, building, etc: *The town was razed **to the ground** in the bombing raid – not a building was left standing.*

razor /ˈreɪ.zəʳ/ [US] /-zɚ/ *noun* [C] a small device with a sharp blade for removing hair, especially from the face or legs: *Do you use an **electric** razor or the kind that you have to put a razor **blade** in?*

• **on a razor edge** in a very uncertain and dangerous situation: *Allegations of fraud have put the minister's career on a razor edge.*

razor /ˈreɪ.zəʳ/ [US] /-zɚ/ *verb* [T] to cut something such as hair using a razor: *My hairdresser always razors my fringe to give a soft effect.*

ˈrazor ˌblade *noun* [C] a thin flat piece of metal with a sharp edge for cutting that can be used in a razor

ˈrazor ˌknife *noun* [C] *US FOR* **Stanley knife**

razor-sharp [SHARP] /ˌreɪ.zəˈʃɑːp/ [US] /-zɚˈʃɑːrp/ *adj* extremely sharp: *These animals have razor-sharp teeth.*

razor-sharp [CLEVER] /ˌreɪ.zəˈʃɑːp/ [US] /-zɚˈʃɑːrp/ *adj* If you describe someone or someone's mind as razor-sharp, you mean that they think very clearly and quickly: *She's got a razor-sharp **mind**.*

razor-thin /ˌreɪ.zəˈθɪn/ [US] /-zɚ-/ *adj* describes a difference in amount which is very small: *The president won the election by a razor-thin **margin**.*

ˈrazor ˌwire *noun* [U] wire with pieces of sharp metal fixed across it, which is often arranged on top of walls, such as those surrounding a prison, to stop people climbing over the walls

razzle /ˈræz.l̩/ *noun UK INFORMAL* **on the razzle** enjoying yourself, visiting bars and dancing, etc: *I was **(out)** on the razzle last night, and I'm rather tired this morning.*

razzle-dazzle /ˌræz.l̩ˈdæz.l̩/ /ˈ--ˌ--/ *noun* [U] *MAINLY US* (confusion caused by) noisy and noticeable activity or very colourful appearance, intended to attract attention: *Amid all the razzle-dazzle of the party convention, it was easy to forget about the real political issues.*

razzmatazz /ˈræz.mə.tæz/ *noun* [U] (*ALSO* **razzamatazz**) noisy and noticeable activity, intended to attract attention: *The new car was launched with great razzmatazz: champagne, food, free gifts and dancers.*

R

RBT /ˌɑː.biːˈtiː/ [US] /ˌɑːr-/ *noun* [C] *AUS ABBREVIATION FOR* **random breath test**

RC /ˌɑːˈsiː/ [US] /ˌɑːr-/ *adj, noun* [C] *ABBREVIATION FOR* **Roman Catholic**

the RCMP /ðiˌɑː.siː.emˈpiː/ [US] /-ˌɑːr-/ *group noun* [S] *ABBREVIATION FOR* the Royal Canadian Mounted Police

Rd *WRITTEN ABBREVIATION FOR* road: *Shaftesbury Rd*

RDS /ˌɑː.diːˈes/ [US] /ˌɑːr-/ *noun* [U] *ABBREVIATION FOR* Radio Data System: a system for automatically finding the strongest signal for a radio station, and for providing information about it on an electronic screen

re /riː/ *prep FORMAL* (especially in business letters) about; on the subject of: *Re your communication of 15 February ...*

re- /riː-/ /ri-/ /rɪ-/ *prefix* **1** used to add the meaning 'do again', especially to verbs: *rebuild* ○ *remarry* ○ *reusable* **2** returning something to its original state: *reafforestation* (= planting new trees in an area where they were previously cut down).

're /ᵊr/ [US] /ɚ/ *short form of* are: *You're late.*

reach [ARRIVE] /riːtʃ/ *verb* [T] **1** to arrive at a place, especially after spending a long time or a lot of effort travelling: *We won't reach Miami till five or six o'clock.* ○ *They finally reached the coast after five weeks sailing.* ○ *News of his accident had only just reached us.* **2 reach a decision/agreement/conclusion, etc.** to make a decision/agreement, etc. about something: *She reached the conclusion that there was no more she could do.* ○ *We'll inform you when a decision has been reached.* ○ *The jury took four days to reach a verdict.*

COMMON LEARNER ERROR

reach

When **reach** means 'arrive somewhere' or 'get to a particular level' it is not normally followed by a preposition.

We finally reached the hotel just after midnight.

The project has now reached the final stage.

~~*The project has now reached to the final stage.*~~

reach [LEVEL] /riːtʃ/ *verb* [T] to get to a particular, especially high level, etc: *The temperature is expected to reach 30°C today.* ○ *He's just reached the grand old age of 95.* ○ *I've reached the **point** where I'm not going to put up with her criticisms of me any more.*

reach [STRETCH] /riːtʃ/ *verb* [I or T] **1** to stretch out your arm in order to get or touch something: *She's grown so tall that she can reach the door handle now.* ○ *He reached **for** the phone and knocked over a glass.* ○ *The child reached **down/out/over** and picked up the kitten.* ○ *He reached his hand **out** for the money.* ○ [+ two objects] *UK Can you reach me **(down)** that book?* **2** If an object reaches something, the top or bottom of it touches that thing: *The ladder won't quite reach the top of the wall.* ○ *She was wearing a dress that reached **(to)** her ankles.*

• **reach for the stars** to want or try to get something that is difficult or impossible to get

reach /riːtʃ/ *noun* **1** [U] Someone's reach is the distance within which they can stretch out their arm and touch something: *I like to keep a notebook and pencil **within (arm's)** reach.* ○ *The top shelf is **within/out of** (his) reach.* ○ *Make sure that you keep all dangerous substances **out of** the reach **of** the children.* **2** [U] the distance that can be travelled, especially easily: *We live **within (easy)** reach of the station.* **3** [S or U] the limit within which someone can achieve something: *An expensive trip like that would be completely **beyond/out of** (my) reach* (= I would not have enough money to pay for it). ○ *After years of saving, the car was at last **within** (her) reach* (= she had enough money to pay for it). **4** [S] the length of your arm when you stretch it out: *You've got quite a long reach – can you get that box down from the top shelf for me?* **5** [C usually sing] an act of stretching out your arm: *He made a sudden reach **for** his gun.*

• **a reach of the imagination** when you have to try very hard to imagine something: *It **takes** (quite) a reach of the imagination to believe that story.*

reach [COMMUNICATE] /riːtʃ/ *verb* **1** [T] to communicate with someone in a different place, especially by telephone or post: *The only way to reach them in the place where they're staying is **by** mail.* ○ *I've been trying to reach you on the phone all day.* **2** to understand and communicate with someone: *He's a strange child and his teachers find it difficult to reach him.*

▲ **reach out to *sb*** *phrasal verb* **1** *MAINLY US* to try to communicate with a person or a group of people, usually in order to help or involve them: *The new mayor is reaching out to the local community to involve them in his plans for the city.* **2** to offer help and support to someone: *She set up her charity to reach out to the thousands of homeless on the streets.*

reaches /ˈriː.tʃɪz/ *plural noun* **1** a part of a river or part of an area of land: *The expedition set out for the **upper** reaches **of** the Amazon.* ○ *There was little snow on the **lower** reaches of the ski run.* ○ *We know very little about the **farthest/outermost** reaches **of** the universe.* **2** the highest or lowest levels of an organization: *The news has shocked **the upper** reaches **of** the government.*

react /riˈækt/ *verb* [I] to act in a particular way as a direct result of something else: *She slapped him and called him names, but he didn't react.* ○ *The judge reacted angrily **to** the suggestion that it hadn't been a fair trial.* ○ *Many people react **(badly) to*** (= are made ill by) *penicillin.* ○ *SPECIALIZED Potassium reacts* (= changes when mixed) ***with** water.*

reactant /ri'æk.tᵊnt/ *noun* [C] *SPECIALIZED* a substance which is part of a chemical reaction

reaction /ri'æk.ʃᵊn/ *noun* **1** [C] behaviour, a feeling or an action that is a direct result of something else: *I love to watch people's reactions when I say who I am.* ○ *There has been an immediate/widespread/hostile reaction* ***against*** *the government's proposed tax increases.* ○ *Reactions* ***to*** *the proposal so far have been adverse/favourable/mixed.* ➲See also **reaction**. **2** [C usually sing] a type of behaviour or opinion that is produced or held with the intention of being different from something else: *Her left-wing views are a reaction* ***against*** *the conservatism of her parents.* **3** [C] an unpleasant effect resulting from eating particular things or taking particular drugs: *Some people* ***have*** *an* ***allergic*** *reaction* ***to*** *shellfish.* **4 chemical reaction** when two or more substances react with and change each other

reactions /ri'æk.ʃᵊnz/ *plural noun* someone's ability to act quickly when something happens: *You need to have quick reactions to play these computer games.*

▲ **react against *sth*** *phrasal verb* to intentionally do the opposite of what someone wants you to do because you do not like their rules or ideas: *He reacted against everything he had been taught.*

reaction /ri'æk.ʃᵊn/ *noun* [U] *DISAPPROVING* the belief or principle that there should be no social or political change, and the attempt to stop such change from happening: *We must not allow reaction to stand in the way of progress.*

reactionary /ri'æk.ʃᵊn.ᵊr.i/ [US] /-er-/ *noun* [C] *DISAPPROVING* a person who is opposed to political or social change or new ideas: *Reactionaries are preventing reforms.* ➲Compare **progressive** at **progress**. **reactionary** /ri'æk.ʃᵊn.ᵊr.i/ [US] /-er-/ *adj*: *Reactionary* ***forces/elements*** *in the industry are preventing its progress towards greater efficiency.*

reactivate /ri'æk.tɪ.veɪt/ *verb* [I or T] to bring or come back into action or use: *The police file was reactivated because of new evidence.* ○ *The virus can reactivate at any time.*

reactive /ri'æk.tɪv/ *adj* reacting to events or situations rather than acting first to change or prevent something: *Unfortunately, the police have dealt with the problem of car theft in a reactive rather than a proactive way.*

reactor /ri'æk.təʳ/ [US] /-tɚ/ *noun* [C] (*ALSO* **nuclear reactor**) a large device in which atoms are either divided or joined in order to produce power

read [UNDERSTAND] /riːd/ *verb* **read** /red/, **read** /red/ **1** [I or T] to obtain meaning by looking at words or symbols: *He spent a pleasant afternoon reading (the newspaper/a book).* ○ *I read* ***about*** *the family's success in the local paper.* ○ *It was too dark to read our map and we took a wrong turning.* ○ *Can you read music?* ○ *Your handwriting is so untidy I can't read it.* ○ [+ (that)] *I've read in the newspapers* ***(that)*** *there is a threat of war.* ○ *Put your plastic card in the slot, and the machine will read it and identify who you are.* ○ *Some children can read* (= have learnt the skill of reading) *by the age of four.* **2** [I or T] to say the words that are printed or written: *She read (the poem) slowly and quietly.* ○ [+ two objects] *Their teacher always reads them a story at the end of the day.* ○ *Children love to have stories read* ***(aloud/out) to*** *them.* **3** [T] to understand and give a particular meaning to written information, a statement, a situation, etc: *She missed the train because she read 18.30* ***as*** *8.30 p.m. instead of 6.30 p.m.* ○ *On page 19,* ***for*** *'Blitish', please read 'British'.* ○ *If I've read the situation correctly, we should have some agreement on the contract by the end of the week.* **4** [I or T] How you read a piece of writing, or how it reads, is how it seems when you read it: *The letter reads* ***as if/*** *(US ALSO, UK NOT STANDARD)* ***like*** *it was written in a hurry.* ○ *Her latest novel reads well* (= is written in an attractive way). **5** [T] (especially when communicating by radio), to hear and understand someone: *Do you read me?* ○ *I read you loud and clear.*

• **read *sb* to sleep** to read aloud to someone until they go to sleep: *Every night when I was a child my father used to read me to sleep.*

• **read between the lines** to try to understand someone's real feelings or intentions from what they say or write: *Reading between the lines, I'd say he isn't happy with the situation.*

• **read *sb's* lips** to follow the movements of someone's lips in order to understand what they are saying, especially if you are unable to hear them speak: *She read his lips across the busy conference hall – "Time to go".* ➲See also **lip-read**.

• **read my lips** *INFORMAL* a slightly rude way of telling someone to listen carefully to what you are saying: *Read my lips. No new taxes.*

• **read *sb's* mind** (*ALSO* **read *sb's* thoughts**) to know what someone is thinking without them telling you: *HUMOROUS "How about a drink, then? "Ah, you read my mind!"*

• **read *sb's* palm** to look at the lines on a person's hand as a way of trying to find out what will happen to them in the future: *In a tent an old gypsy woman was reading palms.*

• **read *(sb)* the riot act** to speak angrily to someone about something they have done and warn them that they will be punished if they do it again: *He'd put up with a lot of bad behaviour from his son and thought it was time to read him the riot act.*

• **read the runes** *UK LITERARY* to understand what will happen in the future, by looking at what is happening now: *He was the first of the Eastern leaders to read the runes and make political changes to stay in power.*

read /riːd/ *noun* [S] *UK* the act of reading something: *It's not brilliant but it's worth a read.* ○ *The book is a* ***good/ easy*** *etc. read.* ○ *INFORMAL Could I* ***have a*** *read* ***of*** (= Could I read) *your newspaper, if you've finished with it?*

read /red/ *adj*: *It's a* ***widely*** *read newspaper* (= it has many readers).

• **take *sth* as read** *UK* to accept that something is true without making sure that it is: *I just took it as read that anyone who applied for the course would have the necessary qualifications.*

readable /'riː.də.bl̩/ *adj* easy and enjoyable to read: *It is an excellent and* ***highly*** *readable account of the army today.*

-readable /-riː.də.bl̩/ *suffix* **machine/computer-readable** in a form which is able to be used by a computer: *Machine-readable passports will permit precise identity-checking.*

reader /'riː.dəʳ/ [US] /-dɚ/ *noun* [C] **1** someone who reads for pleasure, especially a person who reads a lot: *He's a* ***great/voracious*** *reader* (= reads many books). ○ *She's an* ***avid*** *reader* ***of*** *historical novels.* **2** a book designed and written for children who are learning to read **3** someone who reads a particular newspaper or magazine: *We asked our readers to write in and give us their views.* ○ *She described him as a typical Guardian reader.* **4** *SPECIALIZED* a teacher, at British universities, just under the rank of PROFESSOR: *Alan is a Reader* ***in*** *History at Dublin University.* **5** *SPECIALIZED* a person whose job is to advise a publishing company on whether or not a book should be published **6** a device that helps you to read very small writing, or a machine that can recognize printed material: *a microfilm/microfiche reader* ○ *an optical character reader*

readership /'riː.də.ʃɪp/ [US] /-dɚ-/ *group noun* [C] the group of people who regularly read a particular newspaper, magazine, etc: *The magazine has a readership* ***of*** *over 250 000.* ○ *It's a newspaper with a large right-wing readership.*

reading /'riː.dɪŋ/ *noun* **1** [U] the skill or activity of getting information from books: *Reading and tennis are my favourite pastimes.* ○ *The diaries* ***make good (bedtime)*** *reading* (= are good to read (in bed at night)). ○ *These books are* ***compulsory/required*** *reading for students of architecture.* **2** [C] an occasion when something written, especially a literary work, is spoken to an audience: *The society often arranges* ***poetry*** *readings and musical evenings.* **3** [C] In a parliament, a reading of a new law is one of the stages of discussion before it is approved: *The Housing Bill was* ***given*** *its second reading in Parliament today.* **4** [C] the way in which you understand something: *My reading* ***of*** *he situation is that John wanted any excuse to resign.*

read [STATE] /riːd/ *verb* [L] **read** /red/, **read** /red/ (of something written or printed) to have or give the stated informa-

R

tion or meaning: [+ speech] *The start of the American Constitution reads 'We, the people of the United States...'* ○ *The thermometer is reading 40°C in the shade.* **reading** /ˈriː.dɪŋ/ *noun* [C] *a thermometer reading*

read [STUDY] /riːd/ *verb* [I or T] **read** /red/, **read** /red/ *UK FORMAL* to study at university or to study for a specialized qualification: *They're both reading history at Cambridge.* ○ *LEGAL She's reading* ***for the Bar*** (= studying to become a type of lawyer called a barrister).

PHRASAL VERBS WITH **read**

▲ **read *sth* into *sth*** *phrasal verb* to believe that an action, remark or situation has a particular importance or meaning, often when this is not true: *Don't read too much into her leaving so suddenly – she probably just had a train to catch.*

▲ **read *sth* out** *phrasal verb* [M] to read something and say the words aloud so that other people can hear: *He read out the names of all the winners.*

▲ **read *sth* over/through** *phrasal verb* [M] to read something quickly from the beginning to the end, especially to find mistakes: *I read your proposal through last night and I think we'll agree to it.* ○ *Always read over your work when you've finished.*

▲ **read up (on/about) *sth*** *phrasal verb* [M] to spend time reading in order to find out information about something: *It's a good idea to read up on a company before going for an interview.*

readdress /ˌriː.əˈdres/ *verb* [T] to write a different address on an envelope because the person for whom it is intended has moved to another place: *We readdressed all his letters* ***to*** *Australia for years after he had emigrated.*

the readies /ðəˈred.iz/ *plural noun UK SLANG FOR* **money**: *I'm a bit short of the readies.*

ˈreading ˌknowledge *noun* [S or U] the ability to read a language, but not to speak it: *I've got a good reading knowledge* ***of*** *Spanish.*

ˈreading ˌlist *noun* [C] a list of books that students are expected to read as part of their course

ˈreading ˌroom *noun* [C] a room in a library, hotel or other building which is for people who want to read quietly and where conversation is not usually allowed

readjust /ˌriː.əˈdʒʌst/ *verb* [I or T] to change in order to fit a different situation, or to repair something slightly: *After living abroad for so long, he found it difficult to readjust* ***to*** *life at home.* ○ *The clock automatically readjusts when you enter a new time zone.* ○ *The machines were old and constantly needed readjusting.* **readjustment** /ˌriː.əˈdʒʌst.mənt/ *noun* [C]

read-out /ˈriːd.aʊt/ *noun* [C usually sing] information produced by electronic equipment, shown in print, on a screen or by sound: *I got the computer to give a read-out* ***of*** *the total figures.*

ready [PREPARED] /ˈred.i/ *adj* prepared and suitable for immediate activity: [+ to infinitive] *Are you ready* ***to*** *leave?* ○ *Are you ready* ***to*** *order, Madam?* ○ *Okay, Evie, ready* ***when you are*** (= I am ready to do what we have arranged). ○ *Dinner's ready!* ○ *Are you ready? Hurry up – we're late.* ○ *We're leaving at eight o'clock, so you've got half an hour to* ***get*** *ready.* ○ *The army are said to be ready* ***for*** *action.* ○ *The concert hall was* ***made/got*** *ready* (= prepared) **for** *the performance.*

• **at the ready** prepared for immediate use or action: *He stood by the phone, pencil at the ready.*

• **ready and waiting** waiting and prepared to act: *Secret information allowed the police to be ready and waiting when the robbers came out of the bank.*

• **be ready to do *sth*** **1** *INFORMAL* to be going to do something immediately: *I should think you're about ready to collapse after all that walking.* **2** to be willing to do something: *These men are ready to die for their country.*

• **ready to hand** *UK* close to you and therefore available for use when necessary: *The sheriff slept with his gun ready to hand under his pillow.*

• **Ready, steady, go!** *UK SAYING* said at the start of a race, especially one for children

• **ready-to-wear** (of clothes) produced in standard sizes and not made to fit a particular person

readily /ˈred.ɪ.li/ *adv* quickly, immediately, willingly or without any problem: *He readily agreed to help.* ○ *Larger sizes are readily available.*

readiness /ˈred.ɪ.nəs/ *noun* [U] willingness or a state of being prepared for something: [+ to infinitive] *The company has declared its readiness* ***to*** *fight a challenge in the courts.* ○ *The scaffolding has been put up* ***in*** *readiness* ***for*** *the repair work on the building.*

ready [QUICK] /ˈred.i/ *adj* [before n] *MAINLY APPROVING* quick with answers, jokes, solutions, etc: *He had a ready reply to every question.* ○ *He was charming, with a ready* ***wit*** (= the ability to quickly say clever and funny things).

ready-made /ˌred.iˈmeɪd/ *adj* bought or found in a finished form and available to use immediately: *a ready-made frozen meal* ○ *FIGURATIVE When she married Giles, she acquired a ready-made family – two teenage sons and a daughter.*

ˌready ˈmoney *noun* [U] *OLD-FASHIONED INFORMAL* money that is available to be spent immediately ➲See also **the readies**.

reaffirm /ˌriː.əˈfɜːm/ [US] /-ˈfɝːm/ *verb* [T] to give your support to a person, plan, idea, etc. for a second time; to strengthen: *The government yesterday reaffirmed its* ***commitment*** *to the current peace process.* ○ *These events reaffirm my* ***belief*** *in the need for better information.*

reafforest /ˌriː.əˈfɒr.ɪst/ [US] /-ˈfɔːr.ɪst/ *verb* [T] *UK FOR* **reforest**

reafforestation /ˌriː.əˌfɒr.ɪˈsteɪ.ʃᵊn/ [US] /-ˌfɔːr.ɪ-/ *noun* [U] *UK FOR* **reforestation** ➲See at **reforest**.

reagent /ˌriːˈeɪ.dʒənt/ *noun* [C] *SPECIALIZED* a substance which acts on another in a chemical reaction

real [NOT IMAGINARY] /rɪəl/ [US] /riː.əl/ *adj* **1** existing in fact; not imaginary: *Assuring the patient that she has a real and not imaginary problem is the first step.* ○ *There is a very real threat that he will lose his job.* **2 real earnings/income, etc.** the value of earnings, etc. after the effect of rising prices is considered: *Wages rose by 2.9% last year, but real earnings still fell by 1.3%.*

• **Get real!** *INFORMAL* used for telling someone that they should try to understand the true facts of a situation and not hope for what is impossible: *Get real! He's never going to give you the money.*

• **in real terms** existing in fact, despite what appears to be the situation: *A family man's earnings rose 5% in real terms after deducting income tax, insurance, child allowances, etc.*

realism /ˈrɪə.lɪ.zᵊm/ [US] /ˈriː.ə-/ *noun* [U] **1** a way of thinking and acting based on the facts of a situation and what appears to be possible, rather than on hopes for things which are unlikely to happen: *His decision not to expand the business shows his down-to-earth realism.* ➲Compare **idealism** at **ideal** PRINCIPLE. **2** *SPECIALIZED* paintings, films, books, etc. that try to represent life as it really is: *The anti-drugs adverts used hand-held camera techniques to add to the* ***gritty*** *realism of the situations.* **3** *SPECIALIZED* in science and philosophy, the belief that objects continue to exist in the world even when no one is there to see them

realist /ˈrɪə.lɪst/ [US] /ˈriː.ə-/ *noun* [C] **1** someone who hopes for or accepts only what seems possible or likely, and does not hope for or expect more: *I'm a realist – I knew there was no way I could win, so I swam for a good finish, for points.* **2** *SPECIALIZED* an artist, writer, etc. who represents life as it really is, rather than in an imagined way

realistic /ˌrɪəˈlɪs.tɪk/ [US] /ˌriː.ə-/ *adj* **1** accepting things as they are in fact and not basing decisions on unlikely hopes for the future: *Let's be realistic* ***(about*** *this) – I just can't afford to pay that much money.* ○ ***It*** *isn't realistic* ***to*** *expect people to work for so little money.* ➲See also **realpolitik**. **2** seeming to exist or be happening in fact: *The special effects were so realistic.*

realistically /ˌrɪəˈlɪs.tɪ.kli/ [US] /ˌriː.ə-/ *adv* **1** according to the facts and what is possible: *Realistically speaking, he hadn't a hope, but that didn't stop him trying.* **2** in a way that seems as if it exists: *He was made up very realistically to look like an old woman.*

reality /riˈæl.ɪ.ti/ [US] /-ə.t̬i/ *noun* **1** [S or U] the state of things as they are, rather than as they are imagined to be: *The reality* ***of*** *the situation is that unless we find some* *new funding soon, the youth centre will have to close.* ○ *He* **escaped from** *reality by going to the cinema every afternoon.* ○ *He seemed very young, but he was* **in** *reality* (= in fact) *older than all of us.* **2** [C] a fact: *The book confronts the harsh social and political realities of the world today.* ○ *Her childhood ambition* **became a** *reality* (= happened in fact) *when she was made a judge.*

realize, *UK USUALLY* **-ise** /ˈrɪə.laɪz/ [US] /ˈriː.ə-/ *verb* [T] **1** to cause something to be real or to exist or happen in fact: *Lots of money, a luxury house, a fast car – Danny had realized all his ambitions by the age of 25.* ○ *Ten years later her worst fears were realized.* ➲See also **realize**. **2** *LEGAL* **realize assets** to change property, etc. into money: *He had to realize all his assets to pay off his debts.*

realizable, *UK USUALLY* **-isable** /ˈrɪə.laɪ.zə.bl̩/ [US] /ˈriː.ə-/ *adj* able to be made real or changed into money: *He doubted whether the plan was realizable in practice.* ○ *realizable assets*

realization, *UK USUALLY* **-isation** /ˌrɪə.laɪˈzeɪ.ʃᵊn/ [US] /ˌriː.-ə-/ *noun* [S] *To win the Olympic gold medal was the realization of his life's dream.* ○ *Even the realization of all his assets* (= changing property into money) *would not be enough to prevent financial ruin.* ➲See also **realization** at **realize**.

really /ˈrɪə.li/ [US] /riː.ə-/ *adv* **1** in fact: *He isn't really angry – he's just pretending.* ○ *You don't really expect them to refuse, do you?* **2** used to express great certainty: *Thank you, but I really couldn't eat another thing.* ○ *He's really going to do it this time.*

real [NOT FALSE] /rɪəl/ [US] /riː.əl/ *adj* [before n] **1** not false; being what it appears to be; GENUINE: *real leather/fur* ○ *Is that a toy gun or* **the** *real* **thing?** **2** *UK APPROVING* (especially of foods) produced using traditional methods and without artificial substances: *The pub sells several kinds of real* **ale** (= traditional beer).

- **for real** *INFORMAL* real, not pretended: *I thought it was just a fire practice but apparently it was for real.*
- **Is he/she for real?** *INFORMAL* used when you think someone is ridiculous or very surprising

real [IMPORTANT] /rɪəl/ [US] /riː.əl/ *adj* [before n] the most important; the main: *The real difficulty was the language, because my children don't speak English.* ○ *Novelty value may be a part of it, but the real reason people like our paper is that it speaks the truth.*

real [VERY GREAT] /rɪəl/ [US] /riː.əl/ *adj* [before n] used to emphasize a noun: *He's a real gentleman.* ○ *She was a real help.* ○ *It's a real nuisance.*

real /rɪəl/ [US] /riː.əl/ *adv MAINLY US INFORMAL* very: *I like this homemade lemonade, it's real good!* ○ *It's real easy to do.*

really /ˈrɪə.li/ [US] /ˈriː.ə-/ *adv* very or very much: *She's really nice.* ○ *This room is really hot.* ○ *That's really interesting.* ○ *It's a really difficult decision.* ○ *"Did you like it?* **Not** *really* (= No)."

really /ˈrɪə.li/ [US] /ˈriː.ə-/ *exclamation* used to express interest, surprise or annoyance: *"I'm getting married to Fred." "Really? When?"* ○ *"She's agreed to do a parachute jump for charity." "Really? Do you think she'll do it?"* ○ *"He hasn't brought the book back." "Oh, really! That's the second time I've asked him!"*

ˈreal esˌtate *noun* [U] *MAINLY US* property in the form of land or buildings: *We're going to buy a piece of real estate.*

ˈreal estate ˌagent *noun* [C] *US FOR* **estate agent**

ˈreal estate ˌbroker *noun* [C] *AUS FOR* **estate agent**

realign /ˌriː.əˈlaɪn/ *verb* [T] to put something into a new or correct position: *She realigned the books along the edge of the shelf.* ○ [R] *Several politicians left the party and realigned themselves* **with** *the opposition.* **realignment** /ˌriː.əˈlaɪn.mənt/ *noun* [C or U] *This war will inevitably lead to a realignment* **of/within** *European politics.*

reˈality ˌcheck *noun* [C usually sing] an occasion that causes you to consider the facts about a situation and not your opinions, ideas or beliefs: *The recent failure of so many Internet businesses has provided a reality check for those who predicted huge profits.*

realize, *UK USUALLY* **-ise** /ˈrɪə.laɪz/ [US] /ˈriː.ə-/ *verb* [I or T] to understand a situation, sometimes suddenly: *They didn't realize the danger they were in.* ○ [+ (that)] *"Do you realize* **(that)** *this is the third time you've forgotten?" she said angrily.* ○ [+ question word] *I realize* **how** *difficult it's going to be, but we must try.* ○ *As he watched the TV drama, he* **suddenly** *realized* **(that)** *he'd seen it before.* ○ *"You're standing on my foot." "Sorry, I didn't realize."* ➲See also **realize** at **real** NOT IMAGINARY.

realization, *UK USUALLY* **-isation** /ˌrɪə.laɪˈzeɪ.ʃᵊn/ [US] /ˌriː.-ə-/ *noun* [C usually sing] [+ *that*] *The realization was* **dawning** (= They were starting to realize) **that** *this was a major disaster.*

ˌreal ˈlife *noun* [U] what happens in human situations rather than in a story, film, etc: **In** *real life the star of the film is a devoted husband and father.* ○ *The film is based on a real-life story.*

realm [AREA] /relm/ *noun* [C] an area of interest or activity: *Her interests are* **in** *the realm* **of** *practical politics.*

- **within the realms of possibility** possible: *A pay rise is not within the realms of possibility, I'm afraid.*

realm [COUNTRY] /relm/ *noun* [C] *FORMAL* a country ruled by a king or queen: *the defence of the realm* ○ *The matter was hotly debated in all the towns of the realm.*

the ˌreal McˈCoy *noun* [S] the original or best example of something: *The caviar was the real McCoy too – not the stuff we buy in the supermarket at home.*

realpolitik /reɪˈɑː.lpɒl.ɪ.tiːk/ [US] /-poʊ.lɪ-/ *noun* [U] practical politics, decided more by the immediate needs of the country, political party, etc., than by morals or principles

the ˌreal ˈthing *noun* [S] the original, best or most typical example of something: *It's a synthetic material which looks like the real thing.*

real-time /ˈrɪəl.taɪm/ [US] /ˈriː.əl-/ *adj* [before n] describes computing systems that are able to deal with and use new information immediately and therefore influence or direct the actions of the objects supplying that information

realtor /ˈrɪəl.təʳ/ [US] /ˈriː.əl.tɔːr/ *noun* [C] *US FOR* **estate agent**

realty /ˈrɪəl.ti/ [US] /ˈriː.əl.t̬i/ *noun* [U] *US FOR* **real estate**: *a realty agent* ○ *a realty company*

the ˌreal ˈworld *noun* [S] the set of situations most humans have to deal with in their lives, rather than what happens in stories, films, etc: *Christine, the play's bullying main character, wouldn't last a minute* **in** *the real world.*

ream /riːm/ *noun* **1** [C] *SPECIALIZED* 500 sheets of paper **2** [C usually pl] *INFORMAL* a lot of something, especially writing: *She's written reams* **of** *poetry.*

ream /riːm/ *verb*

▲ **ream *sb* (out)** *phrasal verb* [M] *US SLANG* to tell someone off severely because you strongly disapprove of their behaviour: *The boss reamed them out for sleeping on the job.*

reamer /ˈriː.məʳ/ [US] /-mɚ/ *noun* [C] *SPECIALIZED* a tool used to make holes larger or to an exact size

reap /riːp/ *verb* [I or T] to cut and collect a grain crop

- **reap the benefit/reward, etc.** to get the benefit, etc. that is the result of your own actions: *She studied every evening and reaped the benefit at exam time.* ○ *We sold them most of their modern weapons and now we are reaping the bitter harvest.*
- **reap what *you* have sown** to benefit or lose as a result of something you did in the past

reappear /ˌriː.əˈpɪəʳ/ [US] /-ˈpɪr/ *verb* [I] to appear again or return after a period of time: *Ten minutes later she reappeared from the storeroom holding the paint.* **reappearance** /ˌriː.əˈpɪə.rənts/ [US] /-ˈpɪr.ənts/ *noun* [C]

reapply [ASK] /ˌriː.əˈplaɪ/ *verb* [I] to officially ask again for something, for example for yourself to be considered for a job, especially by writing or sending in a form: *Mr Gubbay said yesterday that he will not be reapplying* **for** *the job.*

reapply [PUT ON] /ˌriː.əˈplaɪ/ *verb* [T] to put a substance on again: *She carefully reapplied her lipstick*

reapply [USE] /ˌriː.əˈplaɪ/ *verb* [T] to make use of something in a different way or use it for a different practical purpose: *to reapply principles/methods*

R

reappraise /ˌriː.əˈpreɪz/ *verb* [T] to examine and judge something or someone again
reappraisal /ˌriː.əˈpreɪ.zᵊl/ *noun* [C or U] when you reappraise something or someone: *He'd like to see a fundamental reappraisal **of** the way unions operate.*

rear [BACK] /rɪəʳ/ [US] /rɪr/ *adj* [before n] at the back of something: *There's a sticker on the rear door/window.* ○ *The horse had injured one of its rear legs.* ➲See also **rearguard**.
the rear *noun* [S] the back part of something: *We walked round to the rear of the house.* ○ *Two police motorcyclists **brought up** the rear* (= formed the last part) *of the demonstration.* ➲See also **rear (end)**.
rearmost /ˈrɪə.məʊst/ [US] /ˈrɪr.moʊst/ *adj* [before n] *FORMAL* furthest to the back or the last in a row: *the rearmost seats on the bus*

rear [CARE FOR] /rɪəʳ/ [US] /rɪr/ *verb* [T] to care for young animals or children until they are able to care for themselves: *Some women make a deliberate choice to rear a child alone.* ○ *He describes how these birds rear their young.* ➲See also **child-rearing**.

rear [RISE] /rɪəʳ/ [US] /rɪr/ *verb* [I or T] to rise up or to lift up: *The horse reared **(up)*** (= suddenly rose onto its back legs) *when it heard the gun shot.* ○ *The lion slowly reared its head* (= lifted it up) *and looked around.*
• **rear its (ugly) head** (of something unpleasant) to appear: *The familiar spectre of drought and famine has reared its ugly head again.*
▲ **rear above/over *sth/sb*** *phrasal verb LITERARY* to appear very tall and big in comparison with another thing or person: *The mountain reared above the village.*

ˌrear ˈadmiral *noun* [C] an officer of very high rank in the navy

ˌrear (ˈend) [BOTTOM] *noun* [C usually sing] *OLD-FASHIONED INFORMAL* a person's bottom

rear-end [ACCIDENT] /ˈrɪə.rend/ [US] /ˈrɪr.end/ *verb* [T] *US INFORMAL* to hit the back of one car with another in an accident: *My new car was rear-ended while it was parked outside the station.*

rearguard /ˈrɪə.gɑːd/ [US] /ˈrɪr.gɑːrd/ *noun* [C] the people who are the last in a row or group, especially in a military situation

ˈrearguard ˌaction *noun* [C or U] a final attempt to prevent something from happening: *The unions were determined to **fight** a rearguard action **against** the government's plans to strip them of their powers.*

ˌrear ˈlight *UK noun* [C] (*US* **tail light**) a red light at the back of a road vehicle that enables the vehicle to be seen in the dark ➲See picture **Car** on page Centre 12

rearm /ˌriːˈɑːm/ [US] /-ˈɑːrm/ *verb* [I or T] to supply yourself or others with new weapons, especially in order to become a strong military power again **rearmament** /riˈɑː.mə.mənt/ [US] /-ˈɑːr-/ *noun* [U]

rearrange /ˌriː.əˈreɪndʒ/ *verb* [T] to change the order, position or time of arrangements already made: *The new sofa was bigger than the old one, so they had to rearrange the rest of the furniture.* ○ *I'm busy tomorrow – could we rearrange the meeting **for** Monday* (= have it on Monday instead)*?* **rearrangement** /ˌriː.əˈreɪndʒ.mənt/ *noun* [C] *a rearrangement **of/to** our plans* ○ *As students of chemistry know, even small rearrangements **of** a molecule's structure can produce a compound that acts differently.* ○ *Going on a long trip always means lots of rearrangements **to** my schedule.*

ˌrear ˌview ˈmirror *noun* [C] a mirror which allows a driver to see what is happening behind their car ➲See picture **Car** on page Centre 12

ˌrear ˌwheel ˈdrive *noun* [U] If a car has rear-wheel drive, the engine provides power to the back wheels.

reason [EXPLANATION] /ˈriː.zᵊn/ *noun* [C or U] the cause of an event or situation or something which provides an excuse or explanation: *The reason **for** the disaster was engine failure, not human error.* ○ [+ question word] *The reason **why** grass is green was a mystery to the little boy.* ○ [+ (*that*)] *The reason **(that)** I'm ringing is to ask a favour.* ○ *NOT STANDARD The reason I walked out was **because** I was bored.* ○ [+ to infinitive] *The police **have (every good)** reason **to** believe that he is guilty.* ○ *She was furious, and **with** reason* (= with good cause). ○ ***For some reason/For** reasons **best known to himself*** (= For reasons no one else knows about) *he's decided to leave his job.*
• **by reason of** *FORMAL* because of: *He's always asked to these occasions by reason of his position.*

reason [JUDGMENT] /ˈriː.zᵊn/ *noun* [U] the ability of a healthy mind to think and make judgments, especially based on practical facts: *We humans believe that we are the only animals to have **the power of** reason.* ○ *MAINLY UK OLD-FASHIONED He **lost** his reason* (= became mentally ill) *when both his parents were killed in the crash.*
• **listen to reason** (*ALSO* **see reason**) to listen to good advice and be influenced by it: *Friends tried to persuade them to change their minds, but neither man would listen to reason.*
• **within reason** within the limits of what is acceptable and possible: *We can wear anything we like to the office, within reason.*
reason /ˈriː.zᵊn/ *verb* [T] to try to understand and to make judgments based on practical facts: [+ (*that*)] *Newton reasoned **(that)** there must be a force such as gravity, when an apple fell on his head.* ○ *I spent hours reasoning **out** the solution to the puzzle.*
reasonable /ˈriː.zᵊn.ə.bl̩/ *adj* **1** based on or using good judgment and therefore fair and practical: *If you tell him what happened, I'm sure he'll understand – he's a reasonable man.* ○ *He went free because the jury decided there was a reasonable **doubt** about his guilt.* **2** acceptable: *We had a reasonable journey.* ○ *We have a strong team and a reasonable chance of winning the game.* **3** not too expensive: *Tomatoes are very reasonable at this time of year.* **reasonableness** /ˈriː.zᵊn.ə.bl̩.nəs/ *noun* [U]
reasonably /ˈriː.zᵊn.ə.bli/ *adv* **1** using good judgement: *Stop shouting and let's discuss this reasonably.* **2** satisfactorily: *She writes reasonably good children's books.* ○ *I bought a reasonably priced* (= not expensive) *radio.* ○ *I did reasonably well at school but nowhere near as well as my sister or brother.*
reasoned /ˈriː.zᵊnd/ *adj* If an argument is (well) reasoned, it is clear and carefully considered.
reasoning /ˈriː.zᵊn.ɪŋ/ *noun* [U] the process of thinking about something in order to make a decision: *The reasoning **behind** her conclusion is impossible to fault.*
▲ **reason with *sb*** *phrasal verb* to try to persuade someone to act in a wise way or to change their behaviour or a decision, by giving them good reasons: [+ to infinitive] *The police reasoned with the hijackers **to** at least let the children go free.*
• **be no reasoning with *sb*** If there is no reasoning with someone, it is impossible to persuade them to change their opinions or actions by arguing with them: *She's absolutely determined to go and **there**'s just no reasoning with her.*

reassemble /ˌriː.əˈsem.bl̩/ *verb* **1** [I or T] to come together again, or bring something together again, in a single place: *After lunch, the class reassembled.* **2** [T] to make something again by joining its separate parts together: *Investigators have been reassembling the wreckage of the plane.*

reassess /ˌriː.əˈses/ *verb* [T] to think again about something in order to decide whether to change the way you feel about it or deal with it: *We need to reassess our values as a nation.* ○ *The customer services department is reassessing its procedures for handling customer complaints.* ○ *I've reassessed the situation and decided to stay.*

reassure /ˌriː.əˈʃɔːʳ/ [US] /-ˈʃʊr/ *verb* [T] to comfort someone and stop them from worrying: [+ to infinitive] *I was nervous on my first day at college, but I was reassured **to** see some friendly faces.* ○ [+ (*that*)] *He reassured me **(that)** my cheque would arrive soon.*
reassuring /ˌriː.əˈʃɔː.rɪŋ/ [US] /-ˈʃʊr.ɪŋ/ *adj* making you feel less worried: *He smiled at me in a reassuring way.*
reassuringly /ˌriː.əˈʃɔː.rɪŋ.li/ [US] /-ˈʃʊr.ɪŋ-/ *adv*: *"Don't worry," he said reassuringly. "Everything will be alright."*
reassurance /ˌriː.əˈʃɔː.rᵊnts/ [US] /-ˈʃʊr.ᵊnts/ *noun* [C or U] words of advice and comfort intended to make someone feel less worried: *I felt I couldn't cope with the situation and was in desperate need of some reassurance.* ○ *Despite*

R

her father's reassurances, she was still frightened of the dark.

rebate /ˈriː.beɪt/ *noun* [C] an amount of money which is returned to you, especially by the government, for example when you have paid too much tax: *a tax rebate*

rebel /ˈreb.ᵊl/ *noun* [C] a person who is opposed to the political system in their country and tries to change it using force, or a person who shows their disagreement with the ideas of people in authority or of society by behaving differently: *The rebels took over the capital and set up a new government.* ○ *He was a bit of a rebel when he was a teenager and dyed his hair pink and had his nose pierced.*

rebel /rɪˈbel/ *verb* [I] **-ll- 1** to fight against the government or to refuse to obey rules, etc: *The people rebelled* ***against*** *the harsh new government.* ○ *Jacob rebelled* ***against*** *his parents' plans for him and left school at the age of 16.* **2** to react against a feeling, action, plan, etc: *My poor sick stomach rebelled* ***at*** *the idea of any more food.*

rebellion /rɪˈbel.i.ən/ *noun* **1** [C or U] violent action organized by a group of people who are trying to change the political system in their country: *The government has brutally crushed the rebellion.* **2** [C] action against those in authority or against the rules or against normal and accepted ways of behaving: *a backbench rebellion* ***against*** *the new foreign policy* ○ *her teenage rebellion*

rebellious /rɪˈbel.i.əs/ *adj* **1** If a group of people are rebellious, they oppose the ideas of the people in authority and plan to change the system, often using force: *rebellious groups of southern tribespeople* **2** If someone is rebellious, they are difficult to control and do not behave in the way they are expected to: *Her teachers regard her as a rebellious, trouble-making girl.* **rebelliously** /rɪˈbel.i.ə.sli/ *adv* **rebelliousness** /rɪˈbel.i.ə.snəs/ *noun* [U]

rebirth /ˌriːˈbɜːθ/ [US] /-ˈbɝːθ/ *noun* [S or U] a new period of growth of something or an increase in popularity of something that was popular in the past: *English drama has enjoyed a rebirth since the 1950s with writers like John Osborne, Harold Pinter and Tom Stoppard.*

rebound /ˌriːˈbaʊnd/ *verb* [I] **1** to bounce back after hitting a hard surface **2** If one of your actions rebounds on you, it does not have its desired effect but has an unpleasant effect on you instead: *His continual demands for sympathy rebounded* ***on*** *him because his friends finally stopped listening.*

rebound /ˈriː.baʊnd/ *noun* [C or U] when something rebounds: *I hit the ball* ***on the*** *rebound* (= after it had hit the wall or ground once).

• **on the rebound** INFORMAL unhappy and confused because a close, romantic relationship of yours has recently finished: *Five months after Nick had left her, she married another man on the rebound.*

rebuff /rɪˈbʌf/ *verb* [T] FORMAL to refuse to accept a helpful suggestion or offer from someone, often by answering in an unfriendly way: *She rebuffed all suggestions that she should resign.* **rebuff** /rɪˈbʌf/ *noun* [C] *Her desperate request for help was met with a rebuff.*

rebuild /ˌriːˈbɪld/ *verb* [T] **rebuilt, rebuilt 1** to build something again that has been damaged or destroyed: *The cathedral was completely rebuilt in 1425 after it had been destroyed by fire.* **2** If you rebuild a system or organization, you develop it so that it works effectively: *Before the election, the party claimed it would rebuild the country's economy.* **3 rebuild *your* life** to try to return to the good situation that you were in before the unpleasant event happened to you: *Many people have difficulty in rebuilding their lives when they come out of prison.*

rebuke /rɪˈbjuːk/ *verb* [T] FORMAL to speak angrily to someone because you disapprove of what they have said or done: *I was rebuked by my manager* ***for*** *be****ing*** *late.* **rebuke** /rɪˈbjuːk/ *noun* [C or U] *He received a stern rebuke from the manager.*

rebut /rɪˈbʌt/ *verb* [T] **-tt-** FORMAL to argue that a statement or claim is not true: *She has rebutted charges that she has been involved in any financial malpractice.*

rebuttal /rɪˈbʌt.ᵊl/ [US] /-ˈbʌt̬-/ *noun* [C] FORMAL a statement which says that a claim or criticism is not true: *She issued a point-by-point rebuttal of the company's accusations.*

recalcitrant /rɪˈkæl.sɪ.trᵊnt/ *adj* FORMAL (of a person) unwilling to obey orders or to do what should be done, or (of an animal) refusing to be controlled **recalcitrance** /rɪˈkæl.sɪ.trᵊnts/ *noun* [U]

recall [REMEMBER] /rɪˈkɔːl/ [US] /ˈriː.kɑːl/ *verb* **1** [I or T] to bring the memory of a past event into your mind, and often to give a description of what you remember: *The old man recalled the city as it had been before the war.* ○ *"As I recall," he said with some irritation, "you still owe me £150."* ○ [+ (*that*)] *He recalled* ***(that)*** *he had sent the letter over a month ago.* ○ [+ question word] *Can you recall* ***what*** *happened last night?* ○ [+ v-*ing*] *She recalled see****ing*** *him outside the shop on the night of the robbery.* **2** [T] to cause you to think of a particular event, situation or style: *His paintings recall the style of Picasso.*

recall /rɪˈkɔːl/ [US] /ˈriː.kɑːl/ *noun* [U] the ability to remember things: *Old people often have astonishing* ***powers of*** *recall.* ○ *My brother has* ***total*** *recall* (= He can remember every detail of past events).

recall [CALL BACK] /rɪˈkɔːl/ [US] /ˈriː.kɑːl/ *verb* [T] to order the return of a person who belongs to an organization or of products made by a company: *The ambassador was recalled when war broke out.* ○ *The company recalled thousands of tins of baby food after a salmonella scare.* **recall** /rɪˈkɔːl/ [US] /ˈriː.kɑːl/ *noun* [C usually sing] *an emergency recall* ***of*** *Parliament* ○ *The company issued a recall* ***of*** *all their latest antibiotics.*

recant /rɪˈkænt/ *verb* [I or T] FORMAL to announce in public that your past beliefs or statements were wrong and that you no longer agree with them: *After a year spent in solitary confinement, he publicly recanted (his views).* **recantation** /ˌriː.kænˈteɪ.ʃᵊn/ *noun* [C or U]

recap /ˈriː.kæp/ /ˌ-ˈ-/ *verb* [I or T] **-pp-** to repeat the main points of an explanation or description: *Finally, the teacher recapped the main points of the lesson.* ○ *To recap, our main aim is to increase sales by 12% this year.* **recap** /ˈriː.kæp/ *noun* [S] *Could you give me a quick recap* ***on*** *what happened in the meeting?*

recapitulate /ˌriː.kəˈpɪt.jʊ.leɪt/ *verb* [T] FORMAL FOR **recap** **recapitulation** /ˌriː.kəˌpɪt.jʊˈleɪ.ʃᵊn/ *noun* [S] FORMAL FOR **recap**

recapture /ˌriːˈkæp.tʃəʳ/ [US] /-tʃɚ/ *verb* [T] **1** to take something into your possession again, especially by force: *The army recaptured the town* ***from*** *the rebels.* **2** If something recaptures a previous emotion or style, it makes you experience that emotion again or it repeats that style: *The film successfully recaptures the joyful style of the 1940s Hollywood musical.*

recast /ˌriːˈkɑːst/ [US] /-ˈkæst/ *verb* [T] **recast, recast** to change the form of something, or to change an actor in a play or film: *She recast her novel* ***as*** *a musical comedy.* ○ *In despair, the theatre director recast the leading role.*

recce /ˈrek.i/ *noun* [C] INFORMAL FOR **reconnaissance**

recede /rɪˈsiːd/ *verb* [I] to move further away into the distance, or to become less clear or less bright: *As the boat picked up speed, the coastline receded* ***into*** *the distance until finally it became invisible.* ○ *The painful memories gradually receded in her mind.*

reˌceding ˈhairline *noun* [C usually sing] If a man has a receding hairline, he is losing the hair from the front of his head.

receipt /rɪˈsiːt/ *noun* [C] (US ALSO **sales slip**) a piece of paper which proves that money, goods or information have been received: *Make sure you are given a receipt* ***for*** *everything you buy.* ➲See also **receipt** at **receive** GET.

receipts /rɪˈsiːts/ *plural noun* the amounts of money received during a particular period by a business: *The theatre's receipts* ***for*** *the winter were badly down.*

receive [GET] /rɪˈsiːv/ *verb* [T] **1** to get or be given something: *Did you receive my letter?* ○ *I received a phone call* ***from*** *your mother.* ○ *They received a visit* ***from*** *the police.* ○ *She died after receiving a blow to the head.* ○ *Members of Parliament received a 4.2% pay increase this year.* **2** (of a radio or television) to change signal into sounds and pictures ➲See also **reception** RADIO/TELEVISION. **3** to be able to hear someone's voice when they are communicating with you by radio: *I'm receiving you **loud and clear**.*

• **be at/on the receiving end** If you are at/on the receiving end of something unpleasant that someone does, you suffer because of it: *Sales assistants are often at the receiving end of verbal abuse from customers.*

receiver /rɪ'siː.vəʳ/ [US] /-vɚ/ *noun* [C] **1** (*ALSO* **telephone receiver**) the part of the telephone that you hold to your ear and mouth: *She picked up the receiver and dialled his number.* ➲See also **receiver**; **recipient**. **2** a piece of equipment that changes radio and television signals into sounds and pictures **3** *UK LEGAL* A receiver (of stolen goods) is a person who buys and sells property which they know has been stolen.

receipt /rɪ'siːt/ *noun* [U] *FORMAL* the act or state of receiving money or goods: *Goods will be delivered **on** receipt **of** payment* (= after the money is received). ○ *You have been **in** receipt **of** unemployment benefit for two months.* ➲See also **receipt**.

receive [WELCOME] /rɪ'siːv/ *verb* [T] **1** to formally welcome a visitor or guest: *She stood by the door to receive her guests as they arrived.* ➲See also **reception** WELCOME. **2** to react to something or someone in a particular way that shows how you feel about it or them: *The prime minister's speech was well/warmly/coldly, etc. received by the conference delegates.* **3** *FORMAL* **be received into *sth*** to be made a member of an organization: *He was received **into** the church.*

received /rɪ'siːvd/ *adj* [before n] *FORMAL* generally accepted as being right or correct because it is based on authority: *According to received **wisdom**, exposure to low level radioactivity is harmless.*

Re͵ceived Pronunci'ation *noun* [U] (*ABBREVIATION* **RP**) *UK SPECIALIZED* the standard way in which middle-class speakers of southern British English pronounce words

receiver /rɪ'siː.vəʳ/ [US] /-vɚ/ *noun* [C] (*UK ALSO* **official receiver**) a person who officially deals with the business matters of companies who cannot pay their debts: *The company went bankrupt and was **put into the hands of** the receivers.* ➲See also **receiver** at **receive** GET.

receivership /rɪ'siː.və.ʃɪp/ [US] /-vɚ-/ *noun* [U] when a company is controlled by the receiver because it has no money: *Since January over a hundred companies have been forced **into** receivership.*

recent /'riː.sᵊnt/ *adj* happening or starting from a short time ago: *Is that a recent photo?* ○ *Have you been following recent political events?* ○ *In recent times/years/months, etc. there has been an increase in the amount of violence on television.* **recently** /'riː.sᵊnt.li/ *adv*: *Have you seen any good films recently?* ○ *Until very recently he worked as a teacher and he still shudders at the memories.*

receptacle /rɪ'sep.tə.kl̩/ *noun* [C] *FORMAL* a container used for storing or putting objects in: *Householders are given four separate receptacles **for** their rubbish.*

reception [WELCOME] /rɪ'sep.ʃᵊn/ *noun* **1** [U] the act of welcoming someone or something: *The new hospital was ready for the reception **of** its first patients.* ➲See also **receive** WELCOME. **2** [C] a formal party at which important people are welcomed: *The President gave a reception for the visiting heads of state.* **3** [S] the way in which people react to something or someone: *Her first book got a wonderful/warm/frosty reception from the critics.*

reception [PLACE] /rɪ'sep.ʃᵊn/ *noun* [U] the place in a hotel or office building where people go when they first arrive: *Ask for me at reception.* ○ *I signed in at the reception **desk**.*

receptionist /rɪ'sep.ʃᵊn.ɪst/ *noun* [C] a person who works in a place such as a hotel, office or hospital, who welcomes and helps visitors and answers the telephone

reception [SCHOOL] /rɪ'sep.ʃᵊn/ *noun* [U] *UK OLD-FASHIONED* FOUNDATION (= the first year of INFANT school): *a reception class/teacher*

reception [RADIO/TELEVISION] /rɪ'sep.ʃᵊn/ *noun* [U] the degree to which radio or television sounds and pictures are clear: *We live on top of a hill and so we get excellent radio reception.* ➲See also **receive** GET.

re'ception ͵room *noun* [C] *UK FORMAL* (especially in descriptions of houses for sale) a room in a house where people can sit together: *The house has two reception rooms – a living room and a dining room.*

receptive /rɪ'sep.tɪv/ *adj* willing to listen to and accept new ideas and suggestions: *The government is not receptive **to** the idea of a Freedom of Information Act.* **receptiveness** /rɪ'sep.tɪv.nəs/ *noun* [U] (*ALSO* **receptivity**)

receptor /rɪ'sep.təʳ/ [US] /-tɚ/ *noun* [C] *SPECIALIZED* a nerve ending that reacts to a change, such as heat or cold, in the body by sending a message to the CENTRAL NERVOUS SYSTEM

recess [PAUSE] /rɪ'ses/ /'riː-/ *noun* **1** [C or U] a period of time in the year when the members of a parliament are not meeting **2** [U] *US* in school, a period of time between classes when children do not study

recess [SPACE] /rɪ'ses/ /'riː-/ *noun* [C] **1** a small area in a room which is formed by one part of a wall being set back further than other parts: *The room has a recess designed to hold bookshelves.* **2** a secret or hidden place: *Psychoanalysts aim to explore the **deepest/innermost** recesses of the mind.*

recessed /rɪ'sest/ *adj* built in a space in a wall

recession /rɪ'seʃ.ᵊn/ *noun* [C or U] a period when the economy of a country is not successful and conditions for business are bad: *The country is sliding into the depths of (a) recession.*

recessive /rɪ'ses.ɪv/ *adj SPECIALIZED* (of genes and the physical qualities they control) only appearing in a child if both parents supply the controlling gene

recharge /͵riː'tʃɑːdʒ/ [US] /-'tʃɑːrdʒ/ *verb* [I or T] to fill a battery with electricity so that it can work again

• **recharge *your* batteries** to have a period of rest and relaxation so that you feel energetic again: *She took a trip to the South of France to recharge her batteries.*

rechargeable /riː'tʃɑː.dʒə.bl̩/ [US] /-'tʃɑːr-/ *adj* able to be recharged: *a rechargeable battery*

recherché /rə'ʃeə.ʃeɪ/ [US] /-'ʃer-/ *adj FORMAL* very unusual and not generally known about and chosen with great care in order to make people admire your knowledge or style: *a recherché word/topic* ○ *a recherché menu*

recidivist /rɪ'sɪd.ɪ.vɪst/ *noun* [C] *SPECIALIZED* a criminal who continues to commit crimes even after they have been punished **recidivism** /rɪ'sɪd.ɪ.vɪ.zᵊm/ *noun* [U]

recipe /'res.ɪ.pi/ *noun* [C] a set of instructions telling you how to prepare and cook food, including a list of what food is needed for this: *For real Indian food, just follow these recipes.* ○ *Do you know a good recipe **for** wholemeal bread?*

• **be a recipe for disaster/trouble/success, etc.** to be very likely to become a disaster/success, etc: *All those children unsupervised sounds to me like a recipe for disaster.*

recipient /rɪ'sɪp.i.ənt/ *noun* [C] *FORMAL* a person who receives something: *This latest cut in government spending will affect income support recipients and their families.* ○ *He was a recipient **of** the Civilian Service Award.*

reciprocate /rɪ'sɪp.rə.keɪt/ *verb* **1** [I or T] *FORMAL* to share the same feelings as someone else, or to behave in the same way as someone else: *Sadly, my feelings for him were not reciprocated.* ○ *We invited them to dinner and a week later they reciprocated.* **2** *SPECIALIZED* If a part of a machine reciprocates, it moves backwards and forwards: *Some electric razors have reciprocating heads.*

reciprocal /rɪ'sɪp.rə.kᵊl/ *adj FORMAL* A reciprocal action or arrangement involves two people or groups of people who behave in the same way or agree to help each other and give each other advantages. **reciprocally** /rɪ'sɪp.rə.kli/ *adv* **reciprocation** /rɪ͵sɪp.rə'keɪ.ʃᵊn/ *noun* [U]

reciprocity /͵res.ɪ'prɒs.ɪ.ti/ [US] /-'prɑː.sə.t̬i/ *noun* [U] *FORMAL* behaviour in which two people or groups of people give each other help and advantages

recital /rɪ'saɪ.tᵊl/ [US] /-t̬ᵊl/ *noun* [C] **1** a performance of music or poetry, usually given by one person or a small group of people: *I went to a violin recital today.* ○ *He is **giving** a recital **of** Bach's sonatas.* **2** a detailed description of something or a list of things: *She gave us a long, boring recital **of** all her troubles.*

R

recite /rɪˈsaɪt/ *verb* [I or T] to say a piece of writing aloud from memory, or to publicly state a list of things: *She proudly recited the Oath of Allegiance.* ○ *The opposition party recited a long list of the government's failings.*

recitation /ˌres.ɪˈteɪ.ʃən/ *noun* [C] saying a piece of writing aloud from memory: *He gave a beautiful recitation of some poems by Blake.*

recitative /ˌres.ɪ.təˈtiːv/ *noun* [C or U] SPECIALIZED in opera, words that are sung as if they are being spoken

reckless /ˈrek.ləs/ *adj* doing something dangerous and not caring about the risks and the possible results: *He was found guilty of reckless **driving**.* **recklessly** /ˈrek.lə.sli/ *adv* **recklessness** /ˈrek.lə.snəs/ *noun* [U]

reckon THINK /ˈrek.ən/ *verb* [I] INFORMAL to think or believe: *I reckon it's going to rain.* ○ [+ (*that*)] *How much do you reckon (that) it's going to cost?* ○ *"Can you fix my car today?" "I reckon not/so (= probably not/probably)."*

reckon CONSIDER /ˈrek.ən/ *verb* [T] to consider or have the opinion that something is as stated: *I don't reckon much (UK) **to**/(US) **of** their chances of winning* (= I do not think they will win). ○ *She was widely reckoned **(to be)** the best actress of her generation.*

reckon CALCULATE /ˈrek.ən/ *verb* [T] MAINLY UK to calculate an amount: *Angela quickly reckoned the amount on her fingers.* ○ *The inflation rate is now reckoned **to be** 10%.*

reckoning /ˈrek.ən.ɪŋ/ *noun* [C or U] a calculation which you make: *By my reckoning, we should arrive in ten minutes.*

PHRASAL VERBS WITH **reckon** ▼

▲ **reckon** *sth* **in** *phrasal verb* [M] to include an amount in your calculations: *When you reckon in all my overtime, my total pay is quite good.*

▲ **reckon on** *sth* *phrasal verb* to feel that something is likely to happen and to make plans which depend upon it happening: [+ *v-ing*] *We're reckoning on having sales of 2000 cars a month.* ○ *I'm reckoning on your continued support.*

▲ **reckon** *sth* **up** *phrasal verb* [M] to calculate the total amount of something: *She can reckon up a bill faster than any calculator.*

▲ **reckon with** *sb/sth* *phrasal verb* INFORMAL to deal with a difficult or powerful person or thing: *If you harm her, you're going to have the police to reckon with.*

● **to be reckoned with** Someone or something to be reckoned with is difficult to deal with because they are strong or powerful: *Since the government limited their powers, the unions are no longer **a force** to be reckoned with* (= they are no longer very strong).

▲ **reckon without** *sth* *phrasal verb* UK to fail to think about something when you are making plans and therefore not be prepared to deal with it: *We'd expected a 2-hour drive but had reckoned without the rain.*

reclaim /rɪˈkleɪm/ *verb* [T] **1** to take back something that was yours: *You'll be able to reclaim the tax on all equipment that you buy.* ○ *I reclaimed my suitcase **from** the left luggage office.* **2** to make land, such as desert or flooded areas, suitable for farming or building **3** to treat waste materials in order to obtain useful materials, such as glass or paper, that can be used again

reclamation /ˌrek.ləˈmeɪ.ʃən/ *noun* [U] FORMAL **1** the attempt to make land suitable for building or farming **2** the treatment of waste materials to obtain useful materials from them

recline /rɪˈklaɪn/ *verb* FORMAL **1** [I or T] to lean or lie back with the upper part of your body in a nearly horizontal position: *She was reclining elegantly **on** the sofa.* ○ *He reclined his head **against/on** my shoulder.* **2** [T] If you recline a chair, you change the position of its back so that it is in a leaning position. **reclining** /rɪˈklaɪ.nɪŋ/ *adj* [before n] *The coach has air conditioning and reclining seats.*

recliner /rɪˈklaɪ.nər/ ⑩ /-nɚ/ *noun* [C] a chair in which you can lean back at different angles

recluse /rɪˈkluːs/ *noun* [C] a person who lives alone and avoids going outside or talking to other people: *He is a millionaire recluse who refuses to give interviews.* **reclusive** /rɪˈkluː.sɪv/ *adj*

recognize KNOW, UK USUALLY **-ise** /ˈrek.əg.naɪz/ *verb* [T] to know someone or something because you have seen, heard or experienced them before: *I hadn't seen her for 20 years, but I recognized her immediately.* ○ *"Do you recognize this song?"* ○ *Doctors are trained to recognize the symptoms of different diseases.*

recognizable, UK USUALLY **-isable** /ˈrek.əg.naɪ.zə.bl̩/ *adj* easy to recognize: *The Eiffel Tower in Paris is an instantly recognizable landmark.* **recognizably**, UK USUALLY **-isably** /ˈrek.əg.naɪ.zə.bli/ *adv*: *At seven weeks, an embryo is recognizably human.*

recognition /ˌrek.əgˈnɪʃ.ən/ *noun* [U] *When he returned to his home town after the war, he found it had **changed out of all/beyond all** recognition* (= it had changed so much that he no longer recognized it).

recognize ACCEPT, UK USUALLY **-ise** /ˈrek.əg.naɪz/ *verb* **1** [T] to accept that something is legal, true or important: *The international community has refused to recognize* (= officially accept the existence of) *the newly independent nation state.* ○ [+ (*that*)] *He sadly recognized **(that)** he would die childless.* ○ *You must recognize the seriousness of the problems we are facing.* **2** [T often passive] If a person's achievements are recognized, official appreciation is shown for them: *The Prime Minister recognized her services to her country by awarding her an MBE.*

recognized /ˈrek.əg.naɪzd/ *adj* If someone or something is recognized, it is generally accepted that they have a particular position or quality: *Professor Jones is a recognized authority on ancient Egypt.* ○ *Violence in schools is a recognized problem.*

recognition /ˌrek.əgˈnɪʃ.ən/ *noun* [U] **1** an acceptance that something is true or legal: *It's a new country, hoping for diplomatic recognition from the international community.* ○ [+ *that*] *There's a growing recognition **that** this country can no longer afford to be a nuclear power.* **2** If you are given recognition, people show appreciation of your achievements: *Ella complained that the company never gave her any recognition **for** her work.* ○ *He was presented with a gold watch **in** recognition **of** (= to show appreciation of) *his years as club secretary.*

recoil FEAR/DISGUST /rɪˈkɔɪl/ *verb* [I] **1** to move back because of fear or disgust: *He leant forward to kiss her and she recoiled in horror.* ○ *I recoiled **from** the smell and the filth.* **2** to refuse to accept an idea or principle, feeling strong disgust or disapproval: *She wondered how it would be to touch him and recoiled at the thought.*

recoil GUN /ˈriː.kɔɪl/ *noun* [U] the sudden backward movement that a gun makes when it is fired

recollect /ˌrek.əˈlekt/ *verb* [I or T] FORMAL to remember something: *Can you recollect his name?* ○ *As far as I can recollect, his name is Edward.* ○ [+ (*that*)] *She suddenly recollected **(that)** she had left her handbag in the restaurant.* ○ [+ question word] *Do you recollect **where** she went?* ○ [+ *v-ing*] *He does not recollect see**ing** where he went at the party.*

recollection /ˌrek.əˈlek.ʃən/ *noun* FORMAL **1** [C] a memory of something: *I have many pleasant recollections **of** the time we spent together.* **2** [U] the ability to remember things: *His powers of recollection are extraordinary.*

● **to the best of** *my* **recollection** from what my memory tells me: *To the best of my recollection I have never seen her before.*

recommend /ˌrek.əˈmend/ *verb* [T] to suggest that someone or something would be good or suitable for a particular job or purpose, or to suggest that a particular action should be done: *I can recommend the chicken in mushroom sauce – it's delicious.* ○ *She has been recommended **for** promotion.* ○ *The headmistress agreed to recommend the teachers' proposals **to** the school governors.* ○ [+ (*that*)] *The doctor recommended **(that)** I take more exercise.* ○ [+ *v-ing*] *I recommend writing your feelings down on paper.* ○ *The city **has much/little to** recommend it* (= It has a lot of/few pleasant qualities). **recommended** /ˌrek.əˈmen.dɪd/ *adj*: *It is dangerous to take more than the recommended dose of this medicine.* ○ *She is a **highly** recommended architect.*

recommendation /ˌrek.ə.menˈdeɪ.ʃən/ *noun* **1** [C or U] a suggestion that something is good or suitable for a particular purpose or job: *I bought this computer **on** John's recommendation* (= because John told me that it was good). ○ *I got the job* **on** *Sam's recommendation* (= because she told her employers that I was suitable for the job). **2** [C] advice telling someone what the best thing to do is: [+ *that*] *The report* **makes** *the recommendation* **that** *no more prisons should be built.*

COMMON LEARNER ERROR

recommend (spelling)

Many learners make mistakes when spelling this word. The correct spelling has 'c' and 'mm'. One way to remember this is that the word is made up of 're' + 'commend'.

I can recommend the mushroom curry – it's excellent.

recom,mended daily al'lowance *noun* [C usually sing] (*ABBREVIATION* **RDA**) the amount of a substance, such as a vitamin, that should be in your food every day

recompense /'rek.əm.pents/ *noun* [U] *FORMAL* a present given to someone to thank them for their help, or payment given to someone because of inconvenience or because of the loss of or damage to their property: *I received £500 from the local council* **in** *recompense* **for** *the damage to my garden.* **recompense** /'rek.ᵊm.pents/ *verb* [T] *The court awarded the women $100 000 each to recompense them* **for** *nine years of lost wages.*

recon /'riː.kɒn/ [US] /-kɑːn/ *noun* [C] *US INFORMAL FOR* **reconnaissance**

reconcile /'rek.ᵊn.saɪl/ *verb* [T] **1** to find a way in which two situations or beliefs that are opposed to each other can agree and exist together: *It is sometimes difficult to reconcile science and religion.* ○ *It's difficult to reconcile such different points of view.* ○ *How can you reconcile your fur coat* **and/with** *your love of animals?* **2 be reconciled** When two people are reconciled they become friendly again after they have argued: *They were finally reconciled* **with** *each other, after not speaking for nearly five years.*
reconciliation /,rek.ᵊn,sɪl.i'eɪ.ʃᵊn/ *noun* **1** [C or U] when two people or groups of people become friendly again after they have argued: *It took hours of negotiations to bring about a reconciliation* **between** *the two sides.* **2** [U] the process of making two opposite beliefs, ideas or situations agree
▲ **reconcile *yourself* to *sth*** *phrasal verb* to accept a situation or fact although you do not like it: *She must reconcile herself to the fact that she must do some work if she wants to pass her exams.*

recondite /'rek.ᵊn.daɪt/ *adj FORMAL* not known about by many people and difficult to understand: *We had to work from material that was both complex and recondite.*

recondition /,riː.kᵊn'dɪʃ.ᵊn/ *verb* [T] to repair a machine or piece of equipment and return it to good condition: *The shop sells reconditioned vacuum cleaners and washing machines.*

reconnaissance /rɪ'kɒn.ɪ.sᵊnts/ [US] /-'kɑː.nə-/ *noun* [U] (*UK INFORMAL* **recce**, *US INFORMAL* **recon**) *SPECIALIZED* the process of obtaining information about enemy forces or positions by sending out small groups of soldiers or by using aircraft, etc: **Aerial** *reconnaissance* **of** *the enemy position showed they were ready to attack.*

reconnoitre, *US USUALLY* **reconnoiter** /,rek.ə'nɔɪ.təʳ/ [US] /,riː.kə'nɔɪ.t̬ɚ/ *verb* [I or T] *SPECIALIZED* (of soldiers or military aircraft) to obtain information about an area or the size and position of enemy forces

reconsider /,riː.kᵊn'sɪd.əʳ/ [US] /-kɑːn'sɪd.ɚ/ *verb* [I or T] to think again about a decision or opinion and decide whether you want to change it: *He begged her to reconsider but she would not.* ○ *We have reconsidered your proposals and we have decided to go ahead with the deal.* **reconsideration** /,riː.kᵊn,sɪd.ə'reɪ.ʃᵊn/ [US] /-kɑːn-/ *noun* [U]

reconstitute /,riː'kɒn.stɪ.tjuːt/ [US] /-'kɑːn.stə.tuːt/ *verb* [T] **1** to change food that has been dried back into its original form by adding water: *The powdered milk/egg can be reconstituted by adding water.* **2** to change an organization so that it has a different form: *The Health Education Council has been reconstituted* **as** *the Health Education Authority.*

reconstruct /,riː.kᵊn'strʌkt/ *verb* [T] **1** to build or create again something that has been damaged or destroyed: *The post-war government had the enormous task of reconstructing the city.* **2** to change a system or organization completely, so that it works more effectively: *They were given the task of reconstructing the city's public transport system.* **3** If you reconstruct something that has happened in the past, you combine a lot of information in order to obtain a complete description of what happened: *The police tried to reconstruct the crime using the statements of witnesses and clues that they had found.*
reconstruction /,riː.kᵊn'strʌk.ʃᵊn/ *noun* **1** [U] the process of building or creating something again that has been damaged or destroyed: *Post-war economic reconstruction in the country must begin with the resumption of agricultural production.* **2** [C] an attempt to obtain a complete description of an event using the information available, or an attempt to repeat what happened during the event: *A dramatized reconstruction of the robbery was shown on television to try to make people remember any vital pieces of information that would help the police.* **reconstructive** /,riː.kᵊn'strʌk.tɪv/ *adj*: *After the accident, he underwent reconstructive* **surgery** *to rebuild his face.*

record [STORE INFORMATION] /rɪ'kɔːd/ [US] /-'kɔːrd/ *verb* [T] **1** to keep information for the future, by writing it down or storing it on a computer: *She records everything that happens to her in her diary.* ○ *Unemployment is likely to reach the highest total that has ever been recorded.* ○ [+ *that*] *In his journal, Captain Scott recorded* **that** *he and his companions were weakened by lack of food.* ○ *LEGAL The coroner recorded* (= decided) *a verdict of accidental death.* **2** If a device records a measurement, it shows that measurement: *The thermometer recorded a temperature of 30 degrees Celsius.*
record /'rek.ɔːd/ [US] /-ɚd/ *noun* **1** [C or U] a piece of information or a description of an event which is written on paper or stored on a computer: *The weather centre* **keeps** *a record* **of** *the weather.* ○ *This summer has been the hottest* **on** *record* (= the hottest summer known about). **2** [C] information about someone or something which is stored by the police or by a doctor: *A person's* **medical** *records are confidential.* ○ *He is well known to the police and has a long* **criminal** *record* (= a list kept by the police of his previous crimes). **3** [C] the facts that are known about a person or a company and the actions they have done in the past: *I won't fly with an airline that has a bad* **safety** *record* (= whose aircraft have often had accidents).
• **for the record** something that you say before you tell someone something important that you want them to remember: *And, just for the record, we were never any more than good friends.*
• **go on record** (*ALSO* **be on record**) If you go on record or if you are on record as saying something, you state it publicly and officially and it is written down.
• **off the record** If someone says something off the record, they do not want it to be publicly reported: *She made it clear that her comments were strictly off the record.*
• **set/put the record straight** to write or say something in order to make the true facts known: *She's decided to write her memoirs to set the record straight once and for all.*
recorded /rɪ'kɔː.dɪd/ [US] /-'kɔːr-/ *adj*: *The last recorded* (= known) *case of smallpox was in the 1970s.*

record [STORE ELECTRONICALLY] /rɪ'kɔːd/ [US] /-'kɔːrd/ *verb* [T] to store sounds or moving pictures using electronic equipment so that they can be heard or seen later: *Cliff Richard has recorded more number one hit songs than any other British pop star.* ○ *We recorded their wedding* **on** *video.* ○ *I tried to phone her, but all I got was a recorded message saying that she was away for the weekend.* ○ *Was the concert live or or was it recorded* (= made before being broadcast)*?*
record /'rek.ɔːd/ [US] /-ɚd/ *noun* [C] **1** a flat plastic disc on which music is recorded: *Would you like to listen to some records?* **2** a song or music which has been recorded and which is available for the public to buy: *The Beatles'*

first hit record was 'Love Me Do'.
recorder /rɪ'kɔː.dəʳ/ [US] /-'kɔːr.dɚ/ *noun* [C] a **cassette recorder**, a **tape recorder** or a **video recorder**
recording /rɪ'kɔː.dɪŋ/ [US] /-'kɔːr-/ *noun* **1** [C] a record, disc or tape on which you can hear speech or music or watch moving pictures: *I bought a recording **of** Maria Callas singing Verdi.* **2** [U] the process or business of putting sounds, especially music, onto records or magnetic tapes using electronic equipment: *a recording **studio***

record [BEST] /'rek.ɔːd/ [US] /-ɚd/ *noun* [C] the best or fastest ever done: *He ran the 100 metres in 9.79 seconds and **broke/smashed** the **world** record.* ○ *She **set/established** a new European record in the high jump.*
record /'rek.ɔːd/ [US] /-ɚd/ *adj* at a higher level than ever achieved before: *The long hot summer has led to a record harvest this year.* ○ *Inflation has reached record levels.* ○ *We finished the work **in** record **time*** (= faster than had ever been done before).

record-breaking /'rek.ɔːd,breɪ.kɪŋ/ [US] /-ɔːrd-/ *adj* [before n] better, bigger, longer, etc. than anything else before: *Company profits are rising and it looks as though this is going to be a record-breaking year.*

re,corded de'livery *UK noun* [C or U] (*US* **certified mail**) If a letter is sent by recorded delivery, the person who receives it must write their name in a book to show that they have received it.

recorder [INSTRUMENT] /rɪ'kɔː.dəʳ/ [US] /-'kɔːr.dɚ/ *noun* [C] a musical instrument consisting of a wooden or plastic tube which you blow down while covering holes with your fingers

recorder [JUDGE] /rɪ'kɔː.dəʳ/ [US] /-'kɔːr.dɚ/ *noun* [C] *UK* a judge

'record ,label *noun* [C] a company that records and sells music: *She's signed a three-album deal with a new record label.*

'record ,player *noun* [C] a machine on which records can be played

recount [DESCRIBE] /rɪ'kaʊnt/ *verb* [T] *FORMAL* to describe how something happened; to tell a story: *He recounted his adventures since he had left home.* ○ [+ question word] *He was fond of recounting **how** he had played for Manchester United when he was 19.*

re-count [COUNT AGAIN] /,riː'kaʊnt/ *verb* [T] to count something again
recount /'riː.kaʊnt/ *noun* [C] another count, especially of the number of votes in an election: *The Democrats demanded a recount but still lost by a few votes.*

recoup /rɪ'kuːp/ *verb* [T] to get back money that you have spent or lost: *It takes a while to recoup the initial **costs** of starting up a business.* ○ *The gambler recouped his **losses** in the next game.*

recourse /rɪ'kɔːs/ [US] /'riː.kɔːrs/ *noun* [U] *FORMAL* using something or someone as a way of obtaining help, especially in a difficult or dangerous situation: *It is hoped that the dispute will be settled **without** recourse **to** litigation.*

recover /rɪ'kʌv.əʳ/ [US] /-ɚ/ *verb* [I or T] to get back something lost, especially health, ability, possessions, etc: *It took her a long while to recover* (= become completely well again) ***from/after** her heart operation.* ○ *He never really recovered **from** the shock of his wife dying* (= He was never happy after his wife died). ○ *She went into a coma and died without recovering consciousness.* ○ [R] *She was astonished to see me, but she soon recovered her composure/herself* (= soon gave the appearance of being calm). ○ *It took a long time for the economy to recover* (= improve) ***after** the slump.* ○ *Police only recover* (= get back) *a very small percentage of stolen goods.* ○ *The initial outlay of setting up a company is considerable and it takes a while to recover those **costs*** (= get back what you have spent).
recovery /rɪ'kʌv.ᵊr.i/ [US] /-ɚ-/ *noun* [S or U] *Mira **made** a full/speedy, etc. recovery **from*** (= became well again after) *the operation.* ○ *At last the economy is showing **signs of** recovery* (= is starting to improve). ○ *The police arranged the recovery* (= the getting back) ***of** her body from the river.*

recreate /,riː.kri'eɪt/ *verb* [T] to make something exist or happen again: *They plan to recreate a typical English village in Japan.* ○ *Their work involves restoring and recreating wildlife habitats all across the country.*

recreation /,rek.ri'eɪ.ʃᵊn/ *noun* [C or U] (a way of) enjoying yourself when you are not working: *His favourite recreations are golf and playing Scrabble.* ○ *Emma's only **form of** recreation seems to be shopping.* **recreational** /,rek.ri'eɪ.ʃᵊn.ᵊl/ *adj*: *recreational activities/facilities/interests*

recre,ational 'vehicle *noun* [C] (*ABBREVIATION* **RV**) *US FOR* **motorhome**

recre'ation ,center *noun* [C] *US* a building which is open to the public where meetings are held, sports are played and there are activities available for young and old people

recre'ation ,ground *noun* [C] a piece of publicly owned land used for sports and games

recrimination /rɪ,krɪm.ɪ'neɪ.ʃᵊn/ *noun* [U] (*ALSO* **recriminations**) argument between people who are blaming each other: *The peace talks broke down and ended in **bitter** mutual recrimination(s).* **recriminatory** /rɪ'krɪm.ɪ.nə.tᵊr.i/ [US] /-ə.nə.tɔːr-/ *adj FORMAL*

recrudescence /,riː.kruː'des.ᵊnts/ *noun* [U] *FORMAL* a sudden new appearance and growth, especially of something dangerous and unpleasant: *There has been an unwelcome recrudescence **of** racist attacks.*

recruit /rɪ'kruːt/ *verb* [T] to persuade someone to work for a company or become a new member of an organization, especially the army: *Charities such as Oxfam are always trying to recruit volunteers to help in their work.* ○ *Even young boys are now being recruited **into** the army.* ○ *an army recruiting centre/officer*
recruit /rɪ'kruːt/ *noun* [C] a new member of an organization, especially the army: ***Raw** recruits* (= completely new soldiers) *were trained for six months and then sent to the war front.* **recruitment** /rɪ'kruːt.mənt/ *noun* [U] *The recession has forced a lot of companies to cut down on graduate recruitment.* ○ *It's all part of a recruitment **drive** intended to increase the party's falling numbers.*

rectal /'rek.tᵊl/ *adj SPECIALIZED* ➲See at **rectum**.

rectangle /'rek.tæŋ.gl̩/ *noun* [C] a flat shape with four 90° angles and four sides, with opposite sides of equal length
rectangular /rek'tæŋ.gjʊ.ləʳ/ [US] /-gjə.lɚ/ *adj* shaped like a rectangle

rectify [CORRECT] /'rek.tɪ.faɪ/ *verb* [T] **1** *SLIGHTLY FORMAL* to correct something or make something right: *I am determined to take whatever action is necessary to rectify the **situation**.* ○ *Every effort is made to rectify any **errors/mistakes** before the book is printed.* **2** *SPECIALIZED* in chemistry, to make a substance pure
rectification /,rek.tɪ.fɪ'keɪ.ʃᵊn/ *noun* [C or U] *FORMAL*

rectify [ELECTRIC CURRENT] /'rek.tɪ.faɪ/ *verb* [T] *SPECIALIZED* to change an electrical current from AC to DC
rectifier /'rek.tɪ.faɪ.əʳ/ [US] /-ɚ/ *noun* [C] *SPECIALIZED* an electronic device for changing AC to DC

rectilinear /,rek.tɪ'lɪn.i.əʳ/ [US] /-tə'lɪn.i.ɚ/ *adj FORMAL* moving in or formed from straight lines: *a rectilinear street plan*

rectitude /'rek.tɪ.tjuːd/ [US] /-tə.tuːd/ *noun* [U] *FORMAL* honesty and correct moral behaviour: *An austere man of unquestioned **moral** rectitude, Nava inspired deep devotion in those who worked for him.*

rector /'rek.təʳ/ [US] /-tɚ/ *noun* [C] **1** a priest in charge of a PARISH (= area) in the Church of England **2** an important official at some colleges in Scotland, elected by the students **3** *US* the person in charge of a university or school
rectory /'rek.tᵊr.i/ [US] /-tɚ-/ *noun* [C] the house in which a rector lives

rectum /'rek.təm/ *noun* [C] the lowest end of the bowels, down which excrement travels before leaving the body through the anus **rectal** /'rek.tᵊl/ *adj SPECIALIZED* **rectally** /'rek.tᵊl.i/ *adv*: *They took his temperature rectally.*

recumbent /rɪ'kʌm.bənt/ *adj LITERARY* lying down: *She looked at Timothy's recumbent **form** beside her.*

recuperate /rɪ'kjuː.pᵊr.eɪt/ [US] /-'kuː.pə.reɪt/ *verb* [I] *SLIGHTLY FORMAL* to become well again after an illness; to get back your strength, health, etc: *She spent a month in the country recuperating* **from/after** *the operation.* **recuperation** /rɪˌkjuː.pərˈeɪ.ʃ³n/ ⓤ /-ˌkuː.pəˈreɪ-/ *noun* [U] **recuperative** /rɪˈkjuː.p³r.ə.tɪv/ ⓤ /-ˈkuː.pɚ.ə.t̬ɪv/ *adj FORMAL* helping you to become well again after illness: *The doctor reminded her of the recuperative power of a good night's sleep.*

recur /rɪˈkɜːʳ/ ⓤ /-ˈkɜː-/ *verb* [I] -rr- to happen many times or to happen again: *The theme of freedom recurs throughout her writing.* ○ *If the pain/problem/trouble, etc. recurs, come and see me.* **recurring** /rɪˈkɜː.rɪŋ/ ⓤ /-ˈkɜː.-ɪŋ/ *adj* (*ALSO* **recurrent**) *The father-daughter relationship is a recurring theme in her novels.* ○ *For much of his life he suffered from recurring bouts of depression.* ○ *LeFanu suffered all his life from a recurrent nightmare that he was trapped in a falling house.* **recurrence** /rɪˈkʌr.³nts/ ⓤ /-ˈkɝː-/ *noun* [C or U] *The doctor told him to go to the hospital if there was a recurrence* **of** *his symptoms.*

reˌcurring ˈnumber *noun* [C] (*SPECIALIZED* **recurring decimal**) a number that repeats itself forever following a DECIMAL POINT, such as 3.3333...

recycle /ˌriːˈsaɪ.kl̩/ *verb* [T] to collect and treat rubbish to produce useful materials which can be used again: *The Japanese recycle more than half their waste paper.* **recyclable** /ˌriːˈsaɪ.klə.bl̩/ *adj* able to be recycled **recycled** /ˌriːˈsaɪ.kl̩d/ *adj* having been used before and then processed so that it can form a new product: *This newspaper is made of recycled* **paper.** **recycling** /ˌriːˈsaɪ.klɪŋ/ *noun* [U] when paper, glass, plastic, etc. is put through a process so that it can be used again: *ways to encourage recycling* ○ *a recycling centre*

red COLOUR /red/ *adj* **redder, reddest 1** of the colour of fresh blood: *red lipstick* ○ *The dress was bright red.* **2** describes hair which is an orange-brown colour **3** go/ **turn (bright) red** If you go/turn red, your face becomes red because you are angry or embarrassed: *Look, you've embarrassed him – he's gone bright red!* **4** If your eyes are red, the white part of your eyes and the skin around your eyes is red, because of crying, tiredness, too much alcohol, etc.
• **be like a red rag to a bull** *MAINLY UK* to be certain to produce an angry or violent reaction: *Don't tell him you're a vegetarian – it's like a red rag to a bull.*
• **not a red cent** *US INFORMAL* no money at all: *It turns out his paintings aren't worth a red cent.*
red /red/ *noun* [C or U] the colour of fresh blood: *She uses a lot of reds and pinks in her paintings.* ○ *I've always worn a lot of red.* ○ *She was dressed all* **in** *red.*
• **be in the red** *INFORMAL* If you or your bank account are in the red, you owe money to the bank. ⊃Compare **be in the black** at **black** DARK IN COLOUR.
reddish /ˈred.ɪʃ/ *adj* slightly red in colour: *Nicky's got reddish-blond hair.*
redden /ˈred.³n/ *verb* [I or T] If something reddens, it becomes or is made more red than it was: *His face reddened with embarrassment.* **redness** /ˈred.nəs/ *noun* [U] *Her scar healed, but the redness remained for a long time.*

Red POLITICAL /red/ *noun* [C] *MAINLY DISAPPROVING* a person who has SOCIALIST or communist political opinions **Red** /red/ *adj*

ˌred aˈlert *noun* [C] (the state of being ready to deal with) a sudden dangerous situation: *The army was* **on** **red alert** *against the possibility of an attack.*

the ˌRed ˈArmy *noun* [U] in the past, the SOVIET army

ˌred ˈblood ˌcell *noun* [C] (*SPECIALIZED* **red corpuscle**) any of the cells that carry oxygen around the body

red-blooded /ˌredˈblʌd.ɪd/ *adj* describes someone who seems full of confidence or sexual energy: *He says he's a red-blooded American male!*

redbrick /ˈred.brɪk/ /ˌ-ˈ-/ *adj* [before n] describes any of the British universities built in the late 19th and early 20th centuries in cities such as Liverpool and Manchester, and not one of the older ones such as Oxford or Cambridge: *Ben actually chose to go to a redbrick* **university** *because he didn't like the elitism of Oxford and Cambridge.* ⊃Compare **Oxbridge.**

ˌred ˈcard *noun* [C usually sing] in football, a small red card which is shown by the REFEREE (= the official who is responsible for making certain that the rules are followed) to a player who has not obeyed a rule and who is therefore not allowed to continue playing

the ˌred ˈcarpet *noun* [S] a long, red, floor covering that is put down for an important guest to walk on when they visit somewhere and receive a special official welcome, or a special welcome of this type: *We'll* **roll out the red carpet** *for the senator.* ○ *The minister was given the red carpet* **treatment.**

the ˌRed ˈCrescent *group noun* [S] an international organization in Muslim countries that takes care of people who are suffering because of war, hunger, disease, or other problems

the ˌRed ˈCross *group noun* [S] an international organization that takes care of people who are suffering because of war, hunger, disease or other problems: *The Red Cross is/are supplying medicine to the earthquake victims.*

redcurrant /ˈred.kʌr.³nt/ ⓤ /-ˌkɝː-/ *noun* [C] a very small round red edible fruit, or the bush which produces it: *redcurrant wine/jam/jelly*

ˌred ˈdeer *noun* [C] a deer with brown fur which changes to a different brown or brownish-red colour in summer

redecorate /ˌriːˈdek.ə.reɪt/ *verb* [I or T] *UK* to paint the inside of a house or put paper on the inside walls when this has been done previously: *We're redecorating the kitchen.* **redecoration** /ˌriː.dek.əˈreɪ.ʃ³n/ *noun* [C or U]

redeem IMPROVE /rɪˈdiːm/ *verb* [T] *FORMAL* to make something or someone seem less bad: *A poor game was redeemed in the second half by a couple of superb goals from Anthony Edwards.* ○ [R] *He was an hour late, but he redeemed himself in her eyes by giving her a huge bunch of flowers.* ○ *She took me to see a really dull film, the only* **redeeming feature** *of which* (= the only thing which prevented it from being completely bad) *was the soundtrack.* **redemption** /rɪˈdemp.ʃ³n/ *noun* **be beyond/past redemption** to be too bad to be improved or saved by anyone

redeem GET BACK /rɪˈdiːm/ *verb* [T] to get something back: *She managed to save enough money to redeem her jewellery* **from** *the pawn shop.*

redeem EXCHANGE /rɪˈdiːm/ *verb* **redeem a coupon/ voucher, etc.** to exchange a piece of paper representing a particular sum of money for that amount of money or for goods to this value

redeem FULFIL /rɪˈdiːm/ *verb* [T] *FORMAL* to fulfil a promise or pay back a debt: *The amount required to redeem the mortgage was £358 587.*

redeem RELIGION /rɪˈdiːm/ *verb* [T] (in Christianity) to free people from SIN OFFENCE: *"Jesus," said the priest, "saved and redeemed mankind by taking our sins upon himself."* **the Redeemer** /ðəˌrɪˈdiː.məʳ/ ⓤ /-mɚ/ *noun* [S] (in Christianity) Jesus Christ **redemption** /rɪˈdemp.ʃ³n/ *noun* [U] (especially in Christianity) when someone is saved from evil, suffering, etc. **redemptive** /rɪˈdemp.tɪv/ *adj FORMAL*

redeploy /ˌriː.dɪˈplɔɪ/ *verb* [T] to move employees, soldiers, equipment, etc. to a different place or use them in a more effective way **redeployment** /ˌriː.dɪˈplɔɪ.mənt/ *noun* [C or U] *the redeployment of troops*

redevelop /ˌriː.dɪˈvel.əp/ *verb* [T] to change an area of a town by replacing old buildings, roads, etc. with new ones **redevelopment** /ˌriː.dɪˈvel.əp.mənt/ *noun* [C or U]

red-eye /ˈred.aɪ/ *noun* [C] *MAINLY US INFORMAL* a flight taken at night: *We caught the red-eye from LA and got to New York at five this morning.*

ˌred ˈflag *noun* [C] **1** a flag used as a sign of danger: *You're not allowed to swim when the red flag is flying.* **2** a flag used as a symbol of REVOLUTION

ˌred ˈgiant *noun* [C] *SPECIALIZED* a very large cool star that gives out a reddish light

red-handed /ˌredˈhæn.dɪd/ *adj* **catch** *sb* **red-handed** to find someone in the act of doing something illegal

redhead /'red.hed/ noun [C] INFORMAL a person, especially a woman, whose hair is a colour between red, brown and orange

red 'herring noun [C] a fact, idea or subject that takes people's attention away from the central point being considered: *The police investigated many clues, but they were all red herrings.*

red-hot /ˌred'hɒt/ ⓤ /-'hɑːt/ adj **1** extremely hot **2** extreme; extremely new, exciting, etc: *red-hot news, straight from the war zone*

Red 'Indian noun [C] OFFENSIVE OLD-FASHIONED FOR a **Native American**

redirect /ˌriː.daɪ'rekt/ verb [T] to change the direction of something, especially to send a letter to a new address: *Resources must be redirected into the many under-funded areas of education.* ○ *Please redirect any **mail** that arrives for me to my address in Ottawa.*

rediscover /ˌriː.dɪ'skʌv.ər/ ⓤ /-ɚ/ verb [T] to find something or someone again after losing or forgetting about them for a long time: *Ashia Hansen rediscovered her best form with a morale-boosting win in the triple jump.* ○ *After her husband Ivor's death in 1976, she rediscovered the joys of bowling and golf.*

redistribute /ˌriː.dɪ'strɪb.juːt/ /-strɪ'bjuːt/ verb [T] to share out differently from before, especially in a fairer way: *As president he would redistribute the country's **wealth**.* **redistribution** /ˌriː.dɪ.strɪ'bjuː.ʃᵊn/ noun [U]

red-letter day /ˌred'let.ə.deɪ/ ⓤ /-'let̬.ɚ-/ noun [C usually sing] a special, happy and important day that you will always remember: *The day I first set foot in America was a red-letter day for me.*

red 'light noun [C] a red traffic signal that tells drivers to stop: *The police fined her for **driving through/jumping** a red light.*

red-light district /ˌred'laɪt.dɪs.trɪkt/ noun [C] a part of a city where people and businesses sell sex

red 'meat noun [U] meat from mammals, especially BEEF and LAMB: *My doctor advised me that eating red meat increased the risk of cancer.*

redneck /'red.nek/ noun [C] MAINLY US INFORMAL a poor white person without education, especially one living in the countryside in the southern US, who has PREJUDICED (= unfair and unreasonable) ideas and beliefs

redness /'red.nəs/ noun [U] ⊃See at red COLOUR.

redo /ˌriː'duː/ verb [T] **1** to do something again: *These new measurements mean that I'll have to redo the calculations.* **2** If you redo a room or a building, you paint it, put new furniture in it, etc. to make it more attractive or useful: *We spent £2000 redoing the kitchen.*

redolent /'red.ᵊl.ᵊnt/ adj [after v] LITERARY smelling strongly of something or having qualities (especially smells) that make you think of something else: *The album is a heartfelt cry, redolent of a time before radio and television.* ○ *The mountain air was redolent with the scent of pine needles.*

redouble /ˌriː'dʌb.l̩/ verb [T] to make something much more than before; to increase something: *The government, he said, must redouble their **efforts** to beat crime.*

redoubt /rɪ'daʊt/ noun [C] **1** FORMAL something which maintains or defends a belief or a way of life, especially one that is disappearing or threatened: *He described British public schools as, "the **last** redoubt of upper-class privilege".* **2** SPECIALIZED a small, often hidden, building in which soldiers can hide themselves while they are fighting

redoubtable /rɪ'daʊ.tə.bl̩/ ⓤ /-t̬ə-/ adj LITERARY OR HUMOROUS very strong, especially in character; producing respect and a little fear in others: *Tonight Villiers faces the most redoubtable opponent of his boxing career.*

red 'pepper noun **1** [C] the red ripe fruit of the CAPSICUM plant, eaten as a vegetable **2** [U] a red powder made from these fruits that gives a spicy taste to cooked food

redress /rɪ'dres/ verb [T] FORMAL to put right a wrong or give payment for a wrong that has been done: *Most managers, politicians and bosses are men – how can women **redress the balance** (= make the situation fairer and more equal)?*

redress /rɪ'dres/ noun [U] FORMAL money that someone has to pay to someone else because they have injured them or treated them badly: *He went to the industrial tribunal to seek redress for the way his employers had discriminated against him.*

redskin /'red.skɪn/ noun [C] OFFENSIVE OLD-FASHIONED FOR a **Native American**

red 'tape noun [U] DISAPPROVING official rules and processes that seem unnecessary and delay results: *We must **cut through** the red tape.*

reduce /rɪ'djuːs/ ⓤ /-'duːs/ verb [I or T] to make something smaller in size, amount, degree, importance, etc: *Do nuclear weapons really reduce the risk of war?* ○ *The plane reduced speed as it approached the airport.* ○ *My weight reduces when I stop eating sugar.* ○ *We bought a television that was reduced (**from** £500 **to** £350) in the sales.* ○ *To make a thicker sauce, reduce the ingredients by boiling for 5 minutes.* ○ *I reduced the problem **to** a few simple questions.* **reduction** /rɪ'dʌk.ʃᵊn/ noun [C or U] *a reduction **in** traffic* ○ *huge price reductions*

PHRASAL VERBS WITH **reduce** ▼

▲ **reduce** *sb* **to** *sth* PERSON phrasal verb **1** to make someone unhappy or cause them to be in a bad state or situation: *His comments reduced her to **tears** (= made her cry).* ○ *The sergeant was reduced **to the ranks** (= made an ordinary soldier) for his cowardice.* **2** If you are reduced to doing something, you are forced to do it because you have no other choice: *I'd run out of cigarettes and was reduced to smoking the butts left in the ashtrays.*

▲ **reduce** *sth* **to** *sth* STRUCTURE phrasal verb to cause something, especially a large structure, to be destroyed and broken into pieces: *Allied bombing reduced the city to **ruins/rubble**.*

re,duced 'circumstances plural noun OLD-FASHIONED a polite way to describe when someone is poorer than they once were: *She claims she is a duchess **living in** reduced circumstances.*

re,duced 'time noun [U] short time

re'dundancy ,payment noun [C] money that a company pays to workers who have lost their jobs because they are no longer needed

redundant NOT EMPLOYED /rɪ'dʌn.dᵊnt/ adj UK having lost your job because your employer no longer needs you: *To keep the company alive, half the workforce is being **made** redundant.* ○ FIGURATIVE *New technology often **makes** old skills and even whole communities redundant.* **redundancy** /rɪ'dʌn.dᵊnt.si/ noun [C or U] (AUS ALSO **retrenchment**) *The economic downturn has meant 10 000 redundancies in the North-East.* ○ *She took voluntary redundancy.*

redundant EXTRA /rɪ'dʌn.dᵊnt/ adj (especially of a word, phrase etc.) unnecessary because it is more than is needed: *In the sentence, "She is a single unmarried woman", the word "unmarried" is redundant.* **redundancy** /rɪ'dʌn.dᵊnt.si/ noun [U]

redwood /'red.wʊd/ noun [C or U] a CONIFEROUS tree of California that grows very tall, or the valuable wood of this tree

reed PLANT /riːd/ noun [C] (the hollow stem of) any of various types of tall stiff grass-like plants growing together in groups near water

reedy /'riː.di/ adj **1** describes a place where there are many reeds growing: *the reedy river banks* **2** DISAPPROVING describes a sound, especially a voice, that is thin and high and not pleasant to listen to

reed DEVICE /riːd/ noun [C] a thin piece of wood or metal which shakes very quickly to produce sound when a musician blows over it

'reed ,instrument noun [C] a musical instrument such as the CLARINET or OBOE, which produces sound when a musician blows on the REED

reef /riːf/ noun [C] a line of rocks or sand just above or just below the surface of the sea, often dangerous to ships: *a dangerous offshore reef* ○ *a **coral** reef*

reefer /'riː.fər/ ⓤ /-fɚ/ noun [C] OLD-FASHIONED INFORMAL a hand-rolled cigarette containing the drug CANNABIS

R

'reefer (ˌjacket) *noun* [C] a jacket made of thick material and often worn by sailors

'reef ˌknot *noun* [C] (*US ALSO* **square knot**) a type of strong knot that is tied twice and cannot easily be unfastened

reek /riːk/ *verb* [I] *INFORMAL* to have a strong unpleasant smell: *Her breath reeked **of** garlic.* **reek** /riːk/ *noun* [S] *The room was filled with the reek **of** stale beer and cigarettes.*

▲ **reek of *sth*** *phrasal verb* If an event or situation reeks of an unpleasant quality, it seems to be caused by or connected to that quality: *His promotion reeks of favouritism.*

reel [HOLDER] /rɪəl/ *noun* [C] a round wheel-shaped object on which sewing thread, fishing wire, film, etc. can be rolled, or the amount of thread, etc. stored on one of these

reel [MOVE] /rɪəl/ *verb* [I] **1** to walk moving from side to side, looking like you are going to fall: *At closing time he reeled out of the pub and fell down on the pavement.* ○ *She hit him so hard that he reeled backwards.* **2** If the place where you are reels, what you are looking at seems to go round and round in front of you: *A stone hit his head and the street reeled before his eyes.* **3** If you reel, or your mind or brain reels, you feel very confused or shocked and unable to act: *We were reeling **(in** amazement/shock/delight, etc.**) from/with** the news that we had won all that money.*

reel [DANCE] /rɪəl/ *noun* [C] a fast Scottish or Irish dance, or the music for this

PHRASAL VERBS WITH **reel**

▲ **reel *sth* in/out** *phrasal verb* [M] to pull in a rope or an object on the end of a rope by turning a wheel round and round, or to release something in the same way: *Slowly the fisherman reeled in his line, bringing the fish ashore.* ○ *The firemen reeled out the hoses from their fire engine.*

▲ **reel *sth* off** [LIST] *phrasal verb* [M] *INFORMAL* to say a long list of things quickly and without stopping: *The old man reeled off the names of his twenty-two grandchildren.*

▲ **reel *sth* off** [SPORT] *phrasal verb* [M] *US INFORMAL* to win several games or points one after the other in a sports competition

re-elect /ˌriː.ɪ'lekt/ *verb* [T] to elect someone again to a particular position

re-election /ˌriː.ɪ'lek.ʃən/ *noun* [C or U] when someone is elected again to the same position: *She's (UK) **standing for**/(US) **running for** re-election (= she is trying to be re-elected).*

re-enact, reenact /ˌriː.ɪ'nækt/ *verb* [T] If you re-enact an event, you try to make it happen again in exactly the same way that it happened the first time, often as an entertainment or as a way to help people remember certain facts about an event: *Police officers re-enacted the crime in an attempt to get witnesses to come forward.*

re-enactment /ˌriː.ɪ'nækt.mənt/ *noun* [C] an occasion in which people re-enact an event: *a re-enactment **of** the battle of Gettysburg*

ref [SPORT] /ref/ *noun* [C] *INFORMAL ABBREVIATION FOR* **referee** JUDGE

ref [BUSINESS] *noun* [C] *WRITTEN ABBREVIATION FOR* **reference**, see at **refer to** DESCRIBE and **refer to** DIRECT

refectory /rɪ'fek.tᵊr.i/ [US] /-tɚ-/ *noun* [C] *UK OLD USE* a large room in a monastery, college, school, etc. where meals are eaten

refer /rɪ'fɜːʳ/ [US] /-'fɝː/ *verb* **-rr-**

PHRASAL VERBS WITH **refer**

▲ **refer to *sb/sth*** [DESCRIBE] *phrasal verb* **1** to talk or write about someone or something, especially briefly: *In her autobiography she occasionally refers to her unhappy schooldays.* ○ *He always refers to the house **as** his "refuge".* **2** If writing or information refers to someone or something, it relates to that person or thing: *The new salary scale only refers to company managers and directors.*

reference /'ref.ᵊr.ənts/ [US] /-ɚ-/ *noun* [C or U] a mention of something: *Knowing what had happened, I avoided **making** any **reference to** (= mentioning) weddings.* ○ *FORMAL I am writing **with/in** reference **to** (= in connection with) your letter of 15 March.*

▲ **refer *sb* to *sth*** [DIRECT] *phrasal verb* to direct someone or something to a different place or person for information, help or action, often to a person or group with more knowledge or power: *My doctor referred me to a hospital specialist.* ○ *The High Court has referred the **case** to the Court of Appeal.*

referral /rɪ'fɜː.rəl/ [US] /-'fɝː.ᵊl/ *noun* [C or U] *The doctor gave him a referral **to** (= arranged for him to see) the consultant.*

reference /'ref.ᵊr.ənts/ [US] /-ɚ-/ *noun* [C] **1** a writer or a book, article, etc. that is mentioned in a piece of writing, showing you where the author found their information **2** (*ABBREVIATION* **ref**) in a business letter, a number that tells you who to speak to or where to look for more information: *In all future letters on this subject, please use/quote our reference JW/155/C/1991.*

▲ **refer (*sb*) to *sth*** [LOOK AT] *phrasal verb* to look at, or tell someone else to look at, a book or similar record in order to find information and help: *She spoke for an hour without once referring to her notes.* ○ *He referred to a history book to find out the dates of the French Revolution.* ○ *The reader is constantly referred **back** to the introduction.*

reference /'ref.ᵊr.ənts/ [US] /-ɚ-/ *noun* [U]

referee [JUDGE] /ˌref.ə'riː/ *noun* [C] **1** a person who is in charge of a game and who makes certain that the rules are followed: *Liverpool only lost the game because the referee was biased.* **2** a person or organization that helps to find a fair answer to a disagreement: *A senior judge is acting as referee in the pay dispute between the trade union and management.* **referee** /ˌref.ə'riː/ *verb* [I or T] *They had to ask one of the spectators to referee (the match).*

referee [SUPPORTER] *UK* /ˌref.ə'riː/ *noun* [C] (*ALSO* **reference**) a person who knows you and who is willing to describe and, usually, praise you, to support you when you are trying to get a job, etc: *She **gave** her college tutor **as** her referee to the interviewer.*

reference /'ref.ᵊr.ənts/ [US] /-ɚ-/ *noun* [C] a letter that is written by someone who knows you, to describe you and say if you are suitable for a job or course, etc: *My old headteacher said he would **write/give** me a glowing (= very good) reference.* ➲See also **reference** at **refer to** DESCRIBE; **refer to** DIRECT; **refer to** LOOK AT.

'reference ˌbook *noun* [C] a book of facts, such as a dictionary or an ENCYCLOPEDIA, which you look at to discover particular information

'reference ˌlibrary *noun* [C] (a place for looking at) a collection of books that must be read only where they are kept and not taken away

referendum (*plural* **referendums** or *FORMAL* **referenda**) /ˌref.ə'ren.dəm/ *noun* [C] (*FORMAL* **plebiscite**) a vote in which all the people in a country or an area are asked to give their opinion about or decide an important political or social question: *Is it more democratic to **hold a** referendum, rather than let the government alone decide?*

referral /rɪ'fɜː.rəl/ [US] /-'fɝː.ᵊl/ *noun* [C] ➲See at **refer to** DIRECT.

refill /'riː.fɪl/ *noun* [C] (a container holding) an amount of some material needed to fill up again an object which has become empty: *My pen seems to be running out of ink – I need a refill.* ○ *INFORMAL Chuck, you've nearly finished your drink – do you want a refill?* **refill** /ˌriː'fɪl/ *verb* [T] *He got up and refilled their **glasses**.*

refine /rɪ'faɪn/ *verb* [T] **1** to make something pure or improve something, especially by removing unwanted material: *Crude oil is industrially refined to purify it and separate out the different elements, such as benzene.* **2** to improve an idea, method, system, etc. by making small changes: *Engineers spent many months refining the software.*

refined /rɪ'faɪnd/ *adj* **1** A refined substance has been made pure by removing other substances from it: *refined foods such as white bread and white sugar* **2**

improved because of many small changes that have been made: *highly refined theories* **3** very polite and showing knowledge of social rules

refinement /rɪˈfaɪn.mənt/ *noun* **1** [U] the process of making a substance pure: *The refinement of raw opium yields other drugs, such as morphine.* **2** [C or U] a small change that improves something: *These refinements have increased the machine's accuracy by 25%.* ○ *Clearly, the hypothesis does need some refinement, in the light of these surprising results.* **3** [U] a quality of politeness and education: *She's the personification of culture and refinement.*

refinery /rɪˈfaɪ.nᵊr.i/ [US] /-nɚ-/ *noun* [C] a factory where raw substances such as oil or sugar are made pure: *There were two huge* ***oil*** *refineries on the coast.*

refit /ˌriːˈfɪt/ *verb* [I or T] **refitting, refitted** or *US ALSO* **refit, refitted** or *US ALSO* **refit** to put a ship back into good condition by repairing it or adding new parts: *The ship sailed into the dock to refit/to be refitted.* **refit** /ˈriː.fɪt/ *noun* [C]

reflate /ˌriːˈfleɪt/ *verb* [I or T] *SPECIALIZED* in economics, to increase the amount of money in use in a country's economy: *The government hopes to increase consumer demand and therefore industrial production by reflating (the economy).* **reflation** /ˌriːˈfleɪ.ʃᵊn/ *noun* [C or U] **reflationary** /ˌriːˈfleɪ.ʃᵊn.ᵊr.i/ [US] /-er-/ *adj*

reflect [RETURN] /rɪˈflekt/ *verb* [I or T] If a surface reflects light, heat, sound, or an image, it sends the light, etc. back and does not absorb it: *He saw himself reflected* ***in*** *the water/mirror/shop window.* ○ *The light reflected* ***off*** *the surface of the water.*

reflective /rɪˈflek.tɪv/ *adj* describes a surface which sends back most of the light that shines on it and which therefore can be seen easily

reflection /rɪˈflek.ʃᵊn/ *noun* [C or U] the image of something in a mirror or on any reflective surface: *In Greek mythology, Narcissus fell in love with his own reflection* ***in*** *a pool of water.* ○ *He put silver foil around the fire to increase heat reflection.*

reflector /rɪˈflek.təʳ/ *noun* [C] an object on a bicycle, car, or other vehicle which reflects light and is intended to show the vehicle's position to other road users

reflectors /rɪˈflek.təz/ [US] /-tɚz/ *plural noun US FOR* **cat's eyes**

reflect [SHOW] /rɪˈflekt/ *verb* [T] to show, express or be a sign of something: *The statistics reflect a change in people's spending habits.*

reflection /rɪˈflek.ʃᵊn/ *noun* [C usually sing] a sign or result of something: *The fact that soldiers are on the streets is a reflection* ***of*** *how terrified the government is.*

reflect [THINK] /rɪˈflekt/ *verb* [I] *FORMAL* to think carefully, especially about possibilities and opinions: *The manager demanded time to reflect (****on*** *what to do).* ○ [+ **that**] *She reflected* ***that*** *this was probably the last time she would see him.*

reflection /rɪˈflek.ʃᵊn/ *noun* [C or U] *FORMAL* serious and careful thought: ***On*** *reflection* (= After considering it), *I decided I had been wrong.* ○ *After thirty years as a judge, her reflections* ***on/about*** *justice were well worth listening to.*

reflective /rɪˈflek.tɪv/ *adj FORMAL* thinking carefully and quietly: *After hearing the news they sat in a quiet, reflective silence.* **reflectively** /rɪˈflek.tɪv.li/ *adv*

▲ **reflect on** ***sb/sth*** *phrasal verb* to affect other people's opinion of someone or something, especially in a bad way: *When one player behaves disgracefully, it reflects* ***(badly)*** *on the whole team.* ○ *The whole affair does not reflect well on the government.*

reflection /rɪˈflek.ʃᵊn/ *noun* **a reflection on** ***sb/sth*** something that makes other people have a particular opinion about someone or something, especially a bad opinion: *Low test scores are a sad reflection on our school system.*

reflex /ˈriː.fleks/ *noun* [C] an uncontrollable physical reaction to something: *I'm sorry I punched him, it was a reflex* ***action/response****.*

reflexes /ˈriː.flek.sɪz/ *plural noun* the ability to react quickly: *Fighter pilots need good/fast reflexes.*

reflexive /rɪˈflek.sɪv/ *adj* describes words that show that the person who does the action is also the person who is affected by it: *In the sentence, "She prides herself on doing a good job", "prides" is a reflexive* ***verb*** *and "herself" is a reflexive* ***pronoun****.*

reflexology /ˌriː.flekˈsɒl.ə.dʒi/ [US] /-ˈsɑː.lə-/ *noun* [U] a treatment in which your feet are rubbed and pressed in a special way in order to improve blood flow and help you relax

reforest /ˌriːˈfɒr.ɪst/ [US] /-ˈfɔːr-/ *verb* [T] (*MAINLY UK* **reafforest**) to plant trees on an area of land which has become bare or spoiled **reforestation** /ˌriː.fɒr.ɪˈsteɪ.ʃᵊn/ [US] /-fɔːr.ɪ-/ *noun* [U] *MAINLY US*

reform /rɪˈfɔːm/ [US] /-ˈfɔːrm/ *verb* [I or T] to make an improvement, especially by changing a person's behaviour or the structure of something: *Who will reform Britain's unfair electoral system?* ○ *For years I was an alcoholic, but I reformed when the doctors gave me six months to live.*

reform /rɪˈfɔːm/ [US] /-ˈfɔːrm/ *noun* [C or U] an improvement, especially in a person's behaviour or in the structure of something: *Some reforms* ***of/to*** *the system will be necessary.* ○ *The education system in Britain was crying out for reform.* **reformation** /ˌref.əˈmeɪ.ʃᵊn/ [US] /-ɚ-/ *noun* [C or U] *He's undergone something of a reformation – he's a changed man.*

reformed /rɪˈfɔːmd/ [US] /-ˈfɔːrmd/ *adj* [before n] (especially of a person) changed and improved because no longer doing something harmful: *a reformed alcoholic/criminal*

reformer /rɪˈfɔː.məʳ/ [US] /-ˈfɔːr.mɚ/ *noun* [C] someone who tries to improve a system or law by changing it: *a social reformer* **reformist** /rɪˈfɔː.mɪst/ [US] /-ˈfɔːr-/ *adj*: *a reformist, rather than a revolutionary approach to progress*

the Reformation *noun* [S] the 16th-century religious ideas and activity in Europe which were an attempt to change and improve the Catholic Church, and resulted in the establishment of the Protestant Churches

reˌformed ˈcharacter *noun* [C] someone who has changed and become a much better person: *He was in trouble with the police a lot when he was younger, but now he's a reformed character.*

refract /rɪˈfrækt/ *verb* [T] *SPECIALIZED* When water or glass, etc. refracts light or sound, etc., it causes it to change direction or to separate when it travels through it: *The glass prism refracted the white light* ***into*** *the colours of the rainbow.* **refraction** /rɪˈfræk.ʃᵊn/ *noun* [U]

refrain [NOT DO] /rɪˈfreɪn/ *verb* [I] *FORMAL* to avoid doing or stop yourself from doing something: *We refrained* ***from*** *talk****ing*** *until we knew that it was safe.* ○ *The sign on the wall said "Please refrain* ***from*** *smok****ing****."*

refrain [SONG] /rɪˈfreɪn/ *noun* [C] **1** a short part of a song or poem that is repeated, especially between the VERSES (= the separate parts) **2** a phrase that is often repeated: *'Every vote counts' is a familiar refrain in politics.*

refresh /rɪˈfreʃ/ *verb* **1** [T or R] to make someone less hot or tired: *It was such a hot night that I had a cold shower to refresh myself.* **2** [I or T] to make the most recent information on an Internet page appear, usually by CLICKING a button on the computer screen

• **refresh** ***sb's*** **memory** to help someone remember something: *I looked the word up in the dictionary to refresh my memory* ***of*** *its exact meaning.*

refreshed /rɪˈfreʃt/ *adj* less hot or tired: *I feel so refreshed after that cup of tea.* ○ *He felt refreshed* (= more energetic and relaxed) *after the holiday.*

refresher /rɪˈfreʃ.əʳ/ [US] /-ɚ/ *noun* [C] a course to practise and improve skills, especially because you have not used them for a long time: *I went on a refresher* ***course*** *on new techniques in design to bring myself up to date.*

refreshing /rɪˈfreʃ.ɪŋ/ *adj* **1** making you feel less hot or tired: *There's nothing more refreshing on a hot day than a cold beer.* **2** pleasantly different and interesting: *It's a refreshing* ***change*** *to see a losing team shaking hands and still smiling after a match.* **refreshingly** /rɪˈfreʃ.ɪŋ.li/ *adv*: *refreshingly cold water* ○ *FIGURATIVE a woman with refreshingly original ideas*

refreshment /rɪˈfreʃ.mənt/ *noun* [C or U] (*ALSO* **refreshments**) (small amounts of) food and drink: *He stopped at a bar for a little refreshment.* ○ ***Light*** *refreshments will be available at the back of the hall.*

refrigerate /rɪˈfrɪdʒ.ᵊr.eɪt/ [US] /-ɚ.eɪt/ *verb* [T] to make or keep something, especially food or drink, cold so that it

R

stays fresh, usually in a fridge: *Fresh orange juice should be refrigerated after opening and drunk within three days.* refrigeration /rɪˌfrɪdʒ.əˈreɪ.ʃən/ *noun* [U]

refrigerator /rɪˈfrɪdʒ.ʳr.eɪ.təʳ/ ⑩ /-ɚ.eɪ.t̬ɚ/ *noun* [C] *US, UK FORMAL FOR* **fridge** ⊃See picture **In the Kitchen** on page Centre 16

refrigerator-freezer /rɪˌfrɪdʒ.ʳr.eɪ.təˈfriː.zəʳ/ ⑩ /-ɚ.eɪ.t̬əˈfriː.zɚ/ *noun* [C] *US FOR* **fridge-freezer**

refuel /ˌriːˈfjʊəl/ *verb* [I or T] to put more fuel into an aircraft, ship, etc. so that it can continue its journey refuelling /ˌriːˈfjʊə.lɪŋ/ *noun* [U]

refuge /ˈref.juːdʒ/ *noun* [C or U] (a place which gives) protection or shelter from danger, trouble, unhappiness, etc: *These people are **seeking/taking** refuge **from** persecution.* ○ *The climbers slept in a mountain refuge.* ○ *The woman had fled from her violent husband to a **women's** refuge in Chelmsford.*

refugee /ˌref.jʊˈdʒiː/ *noun* [C] a person who has escaped from their own country for political, religious or economic reasons or because of a war: *Thousands of refugees fled across the border.*

refu'gee ˌcamp *noun* [C] a place where people who have escaped their own country can live, usually in bad conditions and only expecting to stay for a limited time

refund /ˈriː.fʌnd/ *noun* [C] an amount of money that is given back to you, especially because you are not happy with a product or service that you have bought: *I took the radio back to the shop and asked for/demanded/got/ was given a refund.*

refund /rɪˈfʌnd/ *verb* [T] to give someone a refund: *When I went on business to Peru, the office refunded my expenses.* ○ [+ two objects] *The holiday was cancelled so the travel agency had to refund everybody the price of the tickets.* refundable /rɪˈfʌn.də.bl̩/ *adj*

refurbish /ˌriːˈfɜː.bɪʃ/ ⑩ /-ˈfɝː-/ *verb* [T] *FORMAL* to make a building look new and bright again: *The developers refurbished the house inside and out.* refurbished /ˌriː-ˈfɜː.bɪʃt/ ⑩ /-ˈfɝː-/ *adj* [before n] refurbishment /ˌriː.ˈfɜː.bɪʃ.mənt/ ⑩ /-ˈfɝː-/ *noun* [C or U]

refuse SAY NO /rɪˈfjuːz/ *verb* [I or T] to say that you will not do or accept something: *He asked me to give him another loan, but I refused.* ○ *He's in trouble but he's refused all (my offers of) help.* ○ [+ to infinitive] *On cold mornings the car always refuses to start.* ○ [+ two objects] *The local council refused him planning permission to build an extra bedroom.*

refusal /rɪˈfjuː.zəl/ *noun* [C or U] when someone refuses to do or accept something: *Our request for permission to travel **met with/received** a **flat/point-blank** (= complete) refusal from the authorities.* ○ [+ to infinitive] *The government's refusal to see that the protection of the environment must be our first priority today is a great tragedy.*

refuse RUBBISH /ˈref.juːs/ *noun* [U] *FORMAL* unwanted waste material, especially material that is regularly thrown away from a house, factory, etc.; rubbish: *garden/kitchen refuse*

'refuse col,lector *noun* [C] *UK FORMAL FOR* **dustman**

'refuse ˌdump *noun* [C] a place where a town's rubbish is put

refute /rɪˈfjuːt/ *verb* [T] *FORMAL* to say or prove that a person, statement, opinion, etc. is wrong or false: *to refute a person/theory/argument/claim* refutation /ˌref.jʊˈteɪ.ʃən/ *noun* [C or U]

reg /redʒ/ *noun* [C] *INFORMAL FOR* **registration (number)**

regain /rɪˈgeɪn/ *verb* [T] **1** to take or get possession of something again: *The government has regained control of the capital **from** rebel forces.* ○ *She made an effort to regain her self-control.* **2** to reach or return to a place, especially after difficulty or danger: *The swimmers struggled to regain the shore.*

regal /ˈriː.gəl/ *adj* very special and suitable for a king or queen: *a regal manner* ○ *He made a regal entrance.* regally /ˈriː.gəl.i/ *adv*

regale /rɪˈgeɪl/ *verb*

▲ **regale sb with sth** *phrasal verb MAINLY HUMOROUS* to entertain someone with stories, jokes, etc: *The sailor regaled us all night with stories of his adventures.*

regalia /rɪˈgeɪ.li.ə/ *noun* [U] **1** official and traditional special clothes and decorations, especially those worn or carried on ceremonial occasions: *The queen's regalia at her coronation included her crown and sceptre.* **2** *INFORMAL HUMOROUS* any set of special clothes: *The biker was dressed **in full regalia**, with shiny black leather and lots of chains.*

regard /rɪˈgɑːd/ ⑩ /-ˈgɑːrd/ *verb* [T usually + adv or prep] **1** to consider or have an opinion about something or someone: *Local people regard this idea of a motorway through their village **with** horror.* ○ *Her parents always regarded her **as** the cleverest of their children.* **2** *FORMAL* to look carefully at something or someone: *The bird regarded me **with** suspicion as I walked up to its nest.*

• **as regards** *FORMAL* in connection with: *There is no problem as regards the financial arrangements.*

regard /rɪˈgɑːd/ ⑩ /-ˈgɑːrd/ *noun* [U] *FORMAL* respect or consideration for someone or something: *The company **holds** her **in high regard**.* ○ *He **has** no regard **for** other people's feelings.*

• **in/with regard to** *FORMAL* in connection with: *I am writing to you with regard to your letter of 15 March.*

• **in this/that regard** *FORMAL* in this particular way: *The union is the largest in the country and in this/that regard is best placed to serve its members.*

regarding /rɪˈgɑː.dɪŋ/ ⑩ /-ˈgɑːr-/ *prep FORMAL* about: *The company is being questioned regarding its employment policy.*

regardless /rɪˈgɑːd.ləs/ ⑩ /-ˈgɑːrd-/ *adv* despite; not being affected by something: *The plan for a new office tower went ahead regardless **of** local opposition.* ○ *She knew it was dangerous to visit him except at night, but she set out regardless **(of the risk)**.* ○ *This job is open to all, regardless **of** previous experience.*

regards /rɪˈgɑːdz/ ⑩ /-ˈgɑːrdz/ *plural noun FORMAL* greetings: *Please **give/send/convey** my regards to your mother if you see her.*

regatta /rɪˈgæt.ə/ ⑩ /-ˈgɑː.t̬ə/ *noun* [C] a sports event consisting of boat races

regenerate IMPROVE /rɪˈdʒen.ʳr.eɪt/ ⑩ /-ɚ.eɪt/ *verb* [T] to improve a place or system, especially by making it more active or successful regeneration /rɪˌdʒen.ʳr.eɪ.ʃən/ ⑩ /-ɚ-/ *noun* [U] *The council is committed to a programme of urban regeneration.* regenerative /rɪˈdʒen.ʳr.ə.tɪv/ ⑩ /-ɚ.ə.t̬ɪv/ *adj FORMAL*

regenerate GROW /rɪˈdʒen.ʳr.eɪt/ ⑩ /-ɚ.eɪt/ *verb* [I or T] *SPECIALIZED* to grow again: *Tissue regenerates after skin is scratched.* ○ *A lizard can regenerate its tail.* regeneration /rɪˌdʒen.ə.ˈreɪ.ʃən/ ⑩ /-ɚ-/ *noun* [U] regenerative /rɪˈdʒen.ʳr.ə.tɪv/ ⑩ /-ɚ.ə.t̬ɪv/ *adj SPECIALIZED*

regent /ˈriː.dʒənt/ *noun* [C] a person who rules a country only for a limited period, because the king or queen is absent or too young or too ill, etc. regent /ˈriː.dʒənt/ *adj* [after n] *George IV became **Prince** Regent in 1811, because of his father's insanity.*

regency /ˈriː.dʒənt.si/ *noun* [C], *adj* **1** a period of time when a country is ruled by a regent **2 Regency** the style of buildings, furniture, literature, etc. popular in Britain from 1811 to 1820

reggae /ˈreg.eɪ/ *noun* [U] a type of popular music from Jamaica, with a strong second and fourth beat

regicide /ˈredʒ.ɪ.saɪd/ *noun* [C or U] *FORMAL* a person who kills a king, or the act of killing a king

regime /reɪˈʒiːm/ *noun* [C] **1** *MAINLY DISAPPROVING* a particular government or a system or method of government: *The old corrupt, totalitarian regime was overthrown.* **2** a particular way of operating or organizing a business, etc: *The regime in this office is hard work and more hard work.* **3** a **regimen**

regimen /ˈredʒ.ɪ.mən/ *noun* [C] *FORMAL* any set of rules about food and exercise that someone follows, especially in order to improve their health: *After his heart attack the doctor put him on a strict regimen.*

regiment /ˈredʒ.ɪ.mənt/ *group noun* [C] a large group of soldiers, or (more generally) any large number of things or people: *Regiments are usually commanded by a colonel and are sometimes made up of soldiers from a particular city or part of the country.* regimental /ˌredʒ.ɪˈmen.tʳl/ ⑩ /-əˈmen.t̬ʳl/ *adj*: *a regimental tie/uniform*

regimented /ˈredʒ.ɪ.men.tɪd/ [US] /-ə.men.t̬ɪd/ *adj* too organized and controlled: *a regimented school/society/lifestyle*
regimentation /ˌredʒ.ɪ.menˈteɪ.ʃən/ [US] /-ə.mən-/ *noun* [U] DISAPPROVING extreme organization and control of people

region /ˈriː.dʒən/ *noun* [C] a particular area or part of the world, of the body, etc., or any of the large official areas into which a country is divided: *the semi-desert regions of Australia* ○ *the Birmingham region* ○ *He said he had sharp pains* ***in*** *the stomach region/the region of the stomach.*
• **in the region of** approximately: *They estimate that the temperature yesterday was (somewhere) in the region of -30°C.*
regional /ˈriː.dʒən.əl/ *adj* relating to or coming from a particular part of a country: *a regional accent/dialect/newspaper* **regionally** /ˈriː.dʒən.əl.i/ *adv*

regionalism /ˈriː.dʒən.əl.ɪ.zəm/ *noun* **1** [U] when you feel loyal to a particular part of a country and want it to have more political independence **2** [C] a phrase, custom, etc. that is used or found only in a particular part of a country or area

register [LIST] /ˈredʒ.ɪ.stər/ [US] /-stɚ/ *verb* [I or T] to put information, especially your name, into an official list or record: *I registered the car in my name.* ○ *Within two weeks of arrival all foreigners had to register* ***with*** *the local police.* ○ *Students have to register* ***for*** *the new course by the end of April.*
register /ˈredʒ.ɪ.stər/ [US] /-stɚ/ *noun* [C] **1** a book or record containing a list of names: *Guests write their names in the (hotel) register.* ○ *Is your name on the register* ***of*** *voters?* **2** a book used to record whether a child is present at school: *If a child is absent, the teacher notes it down in the (class) register.*
registered /ˈredʒ.ɪ.stəd/ [US] /-stɚd/ *adj* officially listed and accepted: *a registered nurse/charity/trademark*
registration /ˌredʒ.ɪˈstreɪ.ʃən/ *noun* [U] when a name or information is recorded on an official list: *With an election approaching, both political parties are encouraging voter registration.*
register /ˈredʒ.ɪ.stər/ [US] /-stɚ/ *noun* [U] in school, the period at the start of the morning and afternoon when a teacher records on an official list which children are present
registry /ˈredʒ.ɪ.stri/ *noun* [C] MAINLY UK a place where official records are kept: *a land/business/electoral registry*

register [SHOW] /ˈredʒ.ɪ.stər/ [US] /-stɚ/ *verb* [I or T] to record, show or express something: *The Geiger counter registered a dangerous level of radioactivity.* ○ *The earthquake was too small to register* ***on*** *the Richter scale.* ○ FORMAL *His face registered extreme disapproval of what he had witnessed.*

register [AWARE] /ˈredʒ.ɪ.stər/ [US] /-stɚ/ *verb* [I or T] INFORMAL If something registers, someone becomes aware of it and if someone registers something, they become aware of it: *I did mention the address but I'm not sure that it registered (****with*** *him).* ○ *I scarcely registered the fact that he was there.*

register [MAIL] /ˈredʒ.ɪ.stər/ [US] /-stɚ/ *verb* [T] When you register a letter or parcel, you send it using a special postal service, so that it will be dealt with in a special way and not be lost: *a registered letter*

register [RANGE] /ˈredʒ.ɪ.stər/ [US] /-stɚ/ *noun* [C] all the notes that a musical instrument or a person's voice can produce, from the highest to the lowest: *music written mainly for the* ***lower/higher*** *register of the clarinet*

register [LANGUAGE STYLE] /ˈredʒ.ɪ.stər/ [US] /-stɚ/ *noun* [C or U] SPECIALIZED the style of language, grammar and words used for particular situations: *People chatting at a party will usually be talking in (an) informal register.*

register [MONEY] /ˈredʒ.ɪ.stər/ [US] /-stɚ/ *noun* [C] US FOR **till** MONEY DRAWER: *a cash register*

ˌregistered ˈpost UK *noun* [U] (US **registered mail**) a special postal service that deals with letters and parcels in a special way and makes sure they do not get lost: *You'd better send the cheque* ***(by)*** *registered post.*

ˈregister ˌoffice *noun* [C] a **registry office**

registrar [KEEPING RECORDS] /ˌredʒ.ɪˈstrɑːr/ [US] /ˈredʒ.ɪ.strɑːr/ *noun* [C] **1** an official whose job is to keep official records, especially of births, deaths and marriages **2** at some colleges, an official in charge of exams, keeping records and admitting new students

registrar [DOCTOR] /ˌredʒ.ɪˈstrɑːr/ [US] /ˈredʒ.ɪ.strɑːr/ *noun* [C] UK a type of hospital doctor: *A hospital registrar is of a lower rank than a consultant.*

regiˈstration (ˌnumber) *noun* [C] (UK INFORMAL **reg**, US USUALLY **license plate number**) the official set of numbers and letters shown on the front and back of a road vehicle: *Police are looking for a small blue car with the registration number K17 EMW.*

ˈregistry ˌoffice *noun* [C] (ALSO **register office**) MAINLY UK a place where births, deaths and marriages are officially recorded and where you can get officially married, without a religious ceremony

regress /rɪˈgres/ *verb* [I] FORMAL to return to a previous and less advanced or worse state, condition or way of behaving: *She suffered brain damage from the car accident and regressed* ***to*** *the mental age of a five-year-old.* ➲Compare **progress**. **regression** /rɪˈgreʃ.ən/ *noun* [U]
regressive /rɪˈgres.ɪv/ *adj* FORMAL (of tax) lower on large amounts of money, so that the rich are less affected

regret /rɪˈgret/ *noun* [C or U] a feeling of sadness about something sad or wrong or about a mistake that you have made, and a wish that it could have been different and better: *I left school at 16, but I've had a great life and I* ***have no*** *regrets.* ○ *The manager expressed deep regret* ***at/for*** *the number of staff reductions.* ○ *We think,* ***much to our regret*** (= and we regret this very much)*, that we will not be able to visit you next year.*
regret /rɪˈgret/ *verb* [T] **-tt-** to feel regret: *Is there anything you've done in your life that you regret?* ○ [+ **v-ing**] *I have always regretted not hav****ing*** *studied harder at school.* ○ [+ (**that**)] FORMAL *The council regrets* ***(that)*** *the money to subsidise the youth club is no longer available.* ○ [+ **to infinitive**] FORMAL *British Airways regret* ***to*** *announce the cancellation of flight BA205 to Madrid.*
• **send (*sb*) *your* regrets** to send a polite message that you cannot go to a party, etc: *We did have an invitation, but we had to send Graham our regrets.*
regretful /rɪˈgret.fəl/ *adj* expressing regret: *a regretful goodbye/glance/smile* **regretfully** /rɪˈgret.fəl.i/ *adv*
regrettable /rɪˈgret.ə.bl̩/ [US] /-ˈgret̬-/ *adj* FORMAL making you feel sad and sorry about something: *a most/deeply regrettable mistake* **regrettably** /rɪˈgret.ə.bli/ [US] /-ˈgret̬-/ *adv*

regular [EVEN] /ˈreg.jʊ.lər/ [US] /-lɚ/ *adj* **1** existing or happening repeatedly in a fixed pattern, with equal or similar amounts of space or time between one and the next; even: *Her heartbeat was regular.* ○ *The gardeners planted the trees at regular intervals.* ○ *I suggest that we have regular meetings/meet* ***on a*** *regular* ***basis***. **2** If you say someone is regular, you mean they excrete the contents of their bowels frequently enough, or (of women) that their period is always at approximately the same time: *The doctor asked if I was regular/if my bowel movements were regular.*
• **(as) regular as clockwork** never late: *In this country the trains are regular as clockwork.* **regularly** /ˈreg.jʊ.lə.li/ [US] /-lɚ-/ *adv*: *The competitors set off at regularly spaced intervals.*

regular [OFTEN] /ˈreg.jʊ.lər/ [US] /-lɚ/ *adj* happening or doing something often: *a regular customer/churchgoer/reader/user* ○ *Top footballers make regular appearances on TV.* **regularity** /ˌreg.jʊˈlær.ə.ti/ [US] /-ˈler.ə.t̬i/ *noun* [U] *The same familiar faces reappear in the law courts* ***with*** *depressing regularity.* **regularly** /ˈreg.jʊ.lə.li/ [US] /-lɚ-/ *adv*: *Accidents regularly occur on this bend.*
regular /ˈreg.jʊ.lər/ [US] /-lɚ/ *noun* [C] someone who often goes to a particular event or place, such as a shop or restaurant: *He's one of the regulars at the Rose and Crown pub.*

regular [SIMILAR] /ˈreg.jʊ.lər/ [US] /-lɚ/ *adj* the same on both or all sides: *He's very handsome, with regular features and deep brown eyes.* ○ *A square is a regular quadrilateral.* **regularly** /ˈreg.jʊ.lə.li/ [US] /-lɚ-/ *adv*

regular [USUAL] /ˈreg.jʊ.ləʳ/ Ⓤⓢ /-lɚ/ *adj* **1** *US* usual or ordinary: *Her regular secretary was off sick for a week.* ○ *I couldn't see my regular dentist.* ○ *MAINLY US I bought a regular size tee-shirt, rather than extra large.* **2** *SPECIALIZED* describes a verb, noun or adjective which follows the usual rules in the structure of its various forms: *'To talk' is a regular verb but 'to be' is not.* **3** *US* **a regular guy** a normal man who is liked and trusted **4** **regular army/soldier, etc.** an army that exists all the time, or a soldier in such an army

regular /ˈreg.jʊ.ləʳ/ Ⓤⓢ /-lɚ/ *noun* **[C]** a soldier whose permanent job is being a soldier

regularize, *UK USUALLY* **-ise** /ˈreg.jʊ.lᵊr.aɪz/ Ⓤⓢ /-lɚ-/ *verb* **[T]** to change a situation or system so that it obeys laws or is based on reason: *The position of our formerly illegal workers has now been regularized* (= made legal and official). ○ *Some people want to regularize the English spelling system* (= change it so that all words follow the same rules for spelling). **regularization**, *UK USUALLY* **-isation** /ˌreg.jə.lə.raɪˈzeɪ.ʃᵊn/ *noun* **[U]**

regular [COMPLETE] /ˈreg.jʊ.ləʳ/ Ⓤⓢ /-lɚ/ *adj* **[before n]** *INFORMAL* real; complete: *The situation here now is becoming a regular disaster.* ○ *OLD-FASHIONED That child is a regular charmer/little nuisance.*

regulate /ˈreg.jʊ.leɪt/ *verb* **[T]** to control something, especially by making it work in a particular way: *You can regulate the temperature in the house by adjusting the thermostat.* ○ **[+ question word]** *Her mother strictly regulates* ***how*** *much TV she can watch.*

regulation /ˌreg.jʊˈleɪ.ʃᵊn/ *noun* **[C or U]** an official rule or the act of controlling: *safety/health/traffic/fire/security regulations* ○ *The correct procedure is laid down in the* ***rules and*** *regulations.* ○ *government regulation* ***of*** *inflation*

regulation /ˌreg.jʊˈleɪ.ʃᵊn/ *adj* usual; ordered by the rules: *businessmen in their regulation pin-stripe suits* ○ *It's regulation to wear suits at the office.*

regulator /ˈreg.jʊ.leɪ.təʳ/ Ⓤⓢ /-t̬ɚ/ *noun* **[C]** **1** a device used to control things such as the speed of a clock, the temperature in a room, etc. **2** an official who makes certain that the companies who operate a system, such as the national electricity supply, work effectively and fairly

regulatory /ˌreg.jʊˈleɪ.tᵊr.i/ Ⓤⓢ /ˈreg.jʊ.lə.tɔːr.i/ *adj* *FORMAL* controlling: *a regulatory body/organization*

regurgitate /rɪˈgɜː.dʒɪ.teɪt/ Ⓤⓢ /-ˈgɝː.dʒə-/ *verb* **1** **[I or T]** to bring back swallowed food into the mouth: *Owls regurgitate partly digested food to feed their young.* **2** **[T]** *DISAPPROVING* If you regurgitate facts, you just repeat what you have heard without thinking about it: *Many students simply regurgitate what they hear in lectures.*

rehab /ˈriː.hæb/ *noun* **[U]** *INFORMAL* the process of helping someone to stop taking drugs or alcohol: *She's just finished four months of rehab.* ○ *a rehab clinic* ○ *After his arrest in 1998, he checked himself into rehab to get over his heroin addiction.*

rehabilitate /ˌriː.həˈbɪl.ɪ.teɪt/ *verb* **[T]** to return someone or something to a good or healthy condition, state or way of living: *The prison service should try to rehabilitate prisoners so that they can lead normal lives when they leave prison.* ○ *Physiotherapy is part of rehabilitating accident victims.* ○ *After 20 years in official disgrace, she's been rehabilitated* (= given a positive public image again). **rehabilitation** /ˌriː.həˌbɪl.ɪˈteɪ.ʃᵊn/ *noun* **[U]** *a drug rehabilitation clinic* ○ *the rehabilitation of derelict buildings*

rehash /ˈriː.hæʃ/ *noun* **[C]** *INFORMAL DISAPPROVING* writing or speech that uses old ideas as if they were new: *His new book is just a rehash (***of*** *his previous ones).* **rehash** /ˌriːˈhæʃ/ *verb* **[T]** *Some students merely rehash what they've heard in lectures.*

rehearse /rɪˈhɜːs/ Ⓤⓢ /-ˈhɝːs/ *verb* **1** **[I or T]** to practise a play, a piece of music, etc. in order to prepare it for public performance: *The musicians rehearsed (the symphony) for the concert.* ○ *FIGURATIVE On her way to her interview she silently rehearsed what she would say.* **2** **[T]** *FORMAL* When someone rehearses a story or an argument, they repeat it with all the details: *These are arguments that I've heard rehearsed at meetings many times before.*

rehearsal /rɪˈhɜː.sᵊl/ Ⓤⓢ /-ˈhɝː-/ *noun* **[C or U]** a time when all the people involved in a play, dance, etc. practise in order to prepare for a performance: *They didn't have time for (a) rehearsal before the performance.* ○ *He's a producer with three plays* ***in*** *rehearsal.*

rehouse /ˌriːˈhaʊz/ *verb* **[T]** to move someone to a new and usually better place to live: *The local residents demanded to be rehoused.*

the Reich /ðəˈraɪk/ /ðəˈraɪx/ *noun* **[S]** (*ALSO* **the Third Reich**) Germany during the period of NAZI control from 1933 to 1945

reign /reɪn/ *verb* **[I]** **1** to be the king or queen of a country: *Queen Victoria reigned* ***over*** *Britain from 1837 to 1901.* **2** to be the main feeling or quality in a situation or person: *The bomb attacks produced a panic which reigned* ***over*** *the city.* ○ *Love reigned supreme in her heart.* **reign** /reɪn/ *noun* **[C]** *the reign of Henry VIII*

• **a reign of terror** a period of time when a ruler controls people in a violent and cruel way

reigning /ˈreɪ.nɪŋ/ *adj* **[before n]** the most recent winner of a competition: *She's the reigning* ***champion*** *at Wimbledon.*

reimburse /ˌriː.ɪmˈbɜːs/ Ⓤⓢ /-ˈbɝːs/ *verb* **[T]** *FORMAL* to pay back money to someone who has spent it for you or lost it because of you: *The airline reimbursed me* ***for*** *the amount they had overcharged me.* ○ *She was reimbursed by the gas company* ***for*** *the damage to her house.* **reimbursement** /ˌriː.ɪmˈbɜːs.mənt/ Ⓤⓢ /-ˈbɝː-/ *noun* **[C or U]**

rein /reɪn/ *noun* **[C usually pl]** **1** a long thin piece of material, especially leather, which helps you to control and direct a horse: *You pull on both reins to stop or slow a horse, but only the left rein to turn left.* ➲See picture **Sports** on page Centre 10 **2** *UK* a strap which is put around a small child's body or wrist and held at the other end by an adult so that the adult can stop the child running away: *I always put my son on reins when we go shopping.*

• **free rein** the freedom to do, say or feel what you want: *The young film-makers were* ***given*** *free rein* ***to*** *experiment with new themes and techniques.* ○ *He deliberately* ***gave*** *his emotions free rein as he played the sonata.*

• **keep a tight rein on *sb/sth*** (*ALSO* **keep *sb/sth* on a tight rein**) to have a lot of control over someone or something: *My father always kept us on a tight rein.*

rein /reɪn/ *verb*

PHRASAL VERBS WITH **rein**

▲ **rein *sth* in** [HORSE] *phrasal verb* **[M]** to make a horse go more slowly or stop by pulling on its REINS

▲ **rein *sth* in/back** [ACTIVITY] *phrasal verb* **[M]** to control an emotion, activity or situation to prevent it from becoming too powerful: *We tried to rein in our excitement and curiosity.* ○ *Reports today suggest consumers are already reining back spending.*

reincarnation /ˌriː.ɪn.kɑːˈneɪ.ʃᵊn/ Ⓤⓢ /-kɑːr-/ *noun* **1** **[U]** the belief that a dead person's spirit returns to life in another body: *Hindus and Buddhists believe in reincarnation.* **2** **[C]** a person or animal in whose body a dead person's spirit returns to life: *He believes he's a reincarnation* ***of*** *Julius Caesar.*

reincarnate /ˌriː.ɪn.kɑːˈneɪt/ Ⓤⓢ /-ˈkɑːr.neɪt/ *verb* **[T always passive]** If a dead person or animal is reincarnated as someone or something else, their spirit returns to life in that person or animal.

reindeer /ˈreɪn.dɪəʳ/ Ⓤⓢ /-dɪr/ *noun* **[C]** *plural* **reindeer** a type of deer with large horns, which lives in the northern parts of Europe, Asia and America: *Father Christmas travels in a sleigh pulled by reindeer.*

reinforce /ˌriː.ɪnˈfɔːs/ Ⓤⓢ /-ˈfɔːrs/ *verb* **[T]** **1** to make something stronger: *The pockets on my jeans are reinforced* ***with*** *double stitching.* **2** If something reinforces an idea or opinion, it provides more proof or support for it and makes it seem true: *The final technical report into the accident reinforces the findings of initial investigations.* ○ *His behaviour merely reinforced my dislike of him.* **3** to provide an army with more soldiers or weapons to make it stronger: *The garrison is to be reinforced* ***with/by*** *another two battalions of soldiers.*

reinforcement /,ri:.ɪn'fɔ:.smənt/ ⓤ /-'fɔ:r-/ *noun* [U] when something is made stronger: *The harbour walls need urgent reinforcement.*

reinforcements /,ri:.ɪn'fɔ:.smənts/ ⓤ /-'fɔ:r-/ *plural noun* soldiers sent to join an army to make it stronger

reinforced 'concrete *noun* [U] concrete that contains metal rods to make it stronger

reinstate /,ri:.ɪn'steɪt/ *verb* [T] FORMAL to give someone back their previous job or position, or to cause something to exist again: *A month after being unfairly dismissed, he was reinstated in his job.* ○ *The Supreme Court reinstated the death penalty in 1976.*

reinstatement /,ri:.ɪn'steɪt.mənt/ *noun* [U] FORMAL when someone is given back their job or when something exists again: *The union demanded the immediate reinstatement of all sacked workers.* ○ *Reinstatement of the tax would be a disaster.*

reinvent /,ri:.ɪn'vent/ *verb* [T] to produce something new that is based on something that already exists: *The story of Romeo and Juliet was reinvented as a Los Angeles gangster movie.*

• **reinvent the wheel** to waste time trying to create something that someone else has already created

reinvent *yourself* *verb* [R] to change your job and/or the way you look and behave so that you seem very different: *He's one of those sportsmen who reinvent themselves as TV presenters.*

reissue /,ri:'ɪʃ.u:/ *verb* [T] to print or produce something again: *The recording has been reissued to celebrate the conductor's 80th birthday.* **reissue** /,ri:'ɪʃ.u:/ *noun* [C]

reiterate /ri'ɪt.ər.eɪt/ ⓤ /-'ɪt̬.ɚ.eɪt/ *verb* [T] FORMAL to say something again, once or several times: *The government has reiterated its refusal to compromise with terrorists.* ○ [+ that] *She reiterated that she had never seen him before.* **reiteration** /ri,ɪt.ər'eɪ.ʃən/ ⓤ /-,ɪt̬.ə'reɪ-/ *noun* [C or U]

reject /rɪ'dʒekt/ *verb* [T] **1** to refuse to accept, use or believe something or someone: *The appeal was rejected by the High Court.* ○ *Coin-operated machines in England reject Irish money.* ○ *The prime minister rejected the suggestion that it was time for him to resign.* ○ *I applied for a job as a mechanic in a local garage, but I was rejected* (= I was not offered the job). ○ *The football coach rejected him for the first team* (= He was not offered a place in the team). **2** to not give someone the love and attention they want and are expecting from you: *When she was sent to boarding school, she felt as though her parents had rejected her.* **3** SPECIALIZED If your body rejects an organ that has been put in by an operation, it fails to accept it and tries to attack and destroy it.

reject /'ri:.dʒekt/ *noun* [C] **1** a product which is damaged or faulty **2** a person who has not been accepted by an organization or by society: *He considered himself as one of life's rejects.*

rejection /rɪ'dʒek.ʃən/ *noun* [C or U] when someone refuses to accept, use or believe someone or something: *The government's rejection of the plans is a setback for us.* ○ *I've applied for ten jobs, but all I've got is rejections/rejection letters.* ○ *He never asked her to marry him out of fear of rejection.*

'reject ,shop *noun* [C] a shop that sells damaged or faulty products that cannot be sold at the full price

rejig UK (-**gg**-) /,ri:'dʒɪg/ *verb* [T] (*US USUALLY* **rejigger**) INFORMAL to change and improve the arrangement of something: *We'll have to rejig the shed in order to get the extra chairs in.*

rejoice /rɪ'dʒɔɪs/ *verb* [I] FORMAL to feel or show great happiness about something: *Everyone rejoiced at the news of his safe return.* ○ *She rejoiced in her good fortune.* ○ [+ to infinitive] *I rejoiced to see that she had made such a quick recovery.*

rejoicing /rɪ'dʒɔɪ.sɪŋ/ *noun* [U] FORMAL when you feel or show great happiness about something: *There was much rejoicing at/over the good news.*

rejoin RETURN /,ri:'dʒɔɪn/ *verb* [T] to return to someone or something: *She rejoined her husband in Toronto, after her holiday in Paris.*

rejoin ANSWER QUICKLY /rɪ'dʒɔɪn/ *verb* [+ speech] FORMAL to give a quick answer to what someone has said, in an an-

gry or amusing way: *"No, I do not have time to help you," he rejoined impatiently.*

rejoinder /rɪ'dʒɔɪn.dər/ ⓤ /-dɚ/ *noun* [C] FORMAL a quick and often angry or amusing answer: *She always has a witty rejoinder to/for any question.*

rejuvenate /rɪ'dʒu:.vən.eɪt/ *verb* [T] **1** to make someone look or feel young and energetic again: *She felt rejuvenated by her fortnight in the Bahamas.* **2** to make an organization or system more effective, productive and modern by introducing new methods and ideas: *He has decided to rejuvenate the team by bringing in a lot of new, young players.* **rejuvenation** /rɪ,dʒu:.vən'eɪ.ʃən/ *noun* [U]

rekindle /,ri:'kɪn.dl̩/ *verb* [T] to make someone have a feeling that they had in the past: *The holiday was a last chance to rekindle their love.*

relapse /rɪ'læps/ *verb* [I] FORMAL to become ill or start behaving badly again, after making an improvement: *She managed to stop using drugs for a month, but then relapsed.* ○ *He looked happy for a brief while, before relapsing into silent misery.*

relapse /'ri:.læps/ *noun* [C] FORMAL If someone who is getting better after an illness has a relapse, they become ill again: *She was looking quite healthy on Friday, but she had/suffered a relapse over the weekend and was taken back into hospital.*

relate CONNECT /rɪ'leɪt/ *verb* [T] to find or show the connection between two or more things: *Researchers are trying to relate low exam results and/to/with large class sizes.*

related /rɪ'leɪ.tɪd/ ⓤ /-t̬ɪd/ *adj* **1** connected: *We discussed unemployment and related issues.* ○ *Experts believe that the large number of cancer cases in the area are directly related to the new nuclear power station.* **2** If people are related, they belong to the same family: *She claims she is related to royalty.* ○ *Jim and I are related by marriage.* **3** If different types of animal are related, they originate from the same type of animal: *The cat and the lion are related species.*

relation /rɪ'leɪ.ʃən/ *noun* **1** [U] the connection or similarity between two things: *The relation between the original book and this new film is very faint.* ○ *She bears no relation to* (= She is not similar to) *her brother.* ●See also **relations**. **2** [C] a member of your family: *The funeral was attended by friends and relations.* ○ *She's a relation by marriage because she married my cousin.*

relationship /rɪ'leɪ.ʃən.ʃɪp/ *noun* [C] **1** the way in which two things are connected: *Scientists have established the relationship between lung cancer and smoking.* **2** the way in which two or more people feel and behave towards each other: *He has a very good relationship with his uncle.* ●See also **relationship** at **relate** CONNECT. **3** a close romantic friendship between two people, which is often sexual: *Have you had any serious relationships in the past year?* **4** the family connection between people: *The judge asked the witness what the relationship was between her and the victim, and she replied, "He's my son."*

relative /'rel.ə.tɪv/ ⓤ /-t̬ɪv/ *adj* FORMAL **relative to** If something is relative to a particular subject, it is connected with it: *Are these documents relative to the discussion?*

relative /'rel.ə.tɪv/ ⓤ /-t̬ɪv/ *noun* [C] (*AUS INFORMAL* **rellie**) a member of your family: *I haven't got many blood relatives* (= people related to me by birth rather than by marriage). ○ *All her close/distant relatives came to the wedding.*

COMMON LEARNER ERROR

have a relationship with someone

Be careful to use the preposition 'with' in this expression.

I have a good relationship with my parents.

~~I have a good relationship to my parents.~~

---

relate TELL /rɪ'leɪt/ *verb* [T] FORMAL to tell a story or describe a series of events: *She related the events of the previous week to the police.* ○ [+ question word] *He relates how at the age of 23 he was interned in a prison camp.*

PHRASAL VERBS WITH **relate**

▲ **relate to** ***sb/sth*** [CONNECT] *phrasal verb* to be connected to, or to be about someone or something: *Chapter nine relates to the effects of inflation on consumers.*
▲ **relating to** ***sth*** connected with something: *Anything relating to maths is a complete mystery to me.*
• **in/with relation to** ***sth*** in connection with something: *She used the map to discover where she was in relation to her surroundings.*
▲ **relate to** ***sb*** [UNDERSTAND] *phrasal verb* to understand someone and be able to have a friendly relationship with them: *Many parents find it hard to relate to their children when they are teenagers.*
▲ **relate to** ***sth*** *phrasal verb* to understand a situation or someone's feelings because you have experienced a similar situation or similar feelings: *The culture that he describes is so different from mine that I sometimes find it hard to relate to.*

relations /rɪˈleɪ.ʃənz/ *plural noun* the way in which two people or groups of people feel and behave towards each other: *Relations* ***between*** *him and his new wife are rather strained.* ○ *FORMAL Britain* ***enjoys*** *friendly relations* ***with*** *Canada.* ➲See also **relation** at **relate** CONNECT.
• **have (sexual) relations (with** ***sb*****)** *FORMAL* to have sex or a sexual relationship with someone: *The couple had been having sexual relations for a year.*

relative /ˈrel.ə.tɪv/ [US] /-t̬ɪv/ *adj FORMAL* **1** being judged or measured in comparison with something else: *We weighed up the relative advantages of driving there or going by train.* ➲See also **relative** at **relate** CONNECT. **2** Relative can also mean that something is true to a particular degree when it is being compared with other things: *Since I got a job, I've been living in relative comfort* (= more comfort than before). **3 relative to** If something is relative to something else, it varies according to the speed or level of the other thing: *The amount of petrol a car uses is relative to its speed.*
relatively /ˈrel.ə.tɪv.li/ [US] /-t̬ɪv-/ *adv* **relatively good/bad, etc.** quite good/bad/etc. in comparison with other similar things or with what you expect: *He's a relatively good squash player.* ○ *There was relatively little violence.*
• **relatively speaking** said when you are judging one thing in comparison with other things: *Relatively speaking, it's a fairly poor country.*

ˌrelative ˈclause *noun* [C] *SPECIALIZED* part of a sentence which cannot exist independently and which describes a noun which comes before it in the main part of the sentence: *In the sentence 'The woman who I met was wearing a brown hat', 'who I met' is a relative clause.*

ˌrelative ˈdensity *noun* [C] *SPECIALIZED* the mass of a particular volume of a substance when compared with the mass of an equal volume of water at 4°C

ˌrelative huˈmidity *noun* [C] The relative humidity of the air is the amount of water that is present in the air compared to the greatest amount it would be possible for the air to hold at that temperature: *The relative humidity will be about 80% today.*

ˌrelative ˈpronoun *noun* [C] *SPECIALIZED* a pronoun such as *which, who* or *that* which is used to begin a RELATIVE CLAUSE: *In the sentence 'The woman who I met was wearing a brown hat', 'who' is a relative pronoun.*

relativity /ˌrel.əˈtɪv.ɪ.ti/ [US] /-ə.t̬i/ *noun* [U] *SPECIALIZED* either of two theories of physics giving the relationship between space, time and energy, especially for two objects moving in different ways

relax /rɪˈlæks/ *verb* **1** [I or T] to (cause someone to) become less active and more calm and happy, or to (cause a part of the body to) become less stiff: *After work she relaxed* ***with*** *a cup of tea and the newspaper.* ○ *A good massage will relax your tired muscles.* ○ *He relaxed his* ***grip*** *on my arm* (= He began to hold it less tightly). **2** [T] to make a rule or control less severe: *Two weeks after the police relaxed security at the airports, there was a bomb attack.*
• **relax** ***your*** **grip/hold** to start to control something less: *The Mafia has relaxed its grip on local businesses.*
relaxation /ˌriː.lækˈseɪ.ʃən/ *noun* **1** [U] the feeling of being relaxed: *I go fishing* ***for*** *relaxation.* **2** [C] a pleasant activity which makes you become calm and less worried: *Yoga is one of my favourite relaxations.* **3** [U] the act of making rules or the control of something less severe: *I cannot allow any relaxation* ***in/of*** *the rules.*
relaxed /rɪˈlækst/ *adj* **1** feeling happy and comfortable because nothing is worrying you: *She seemed relaxed and in control of the situation.* **2** A relaxed situation or place is comfortable and informal: *It's a very friendly bar with a nice relaxed atmosphere.* **3** If someone is relaxed about something, they are not worried about it: *My parents are fairly relaxed about me staying out late.*
relaxing /rɪˈlæk.sɪŋ/ *adj* making you feel relaxed: *a relaxing holiday* ○ *I find swimming so relaxing.*

relay [REPEAT] /riˈleɪ/ /ˈriː.leɪ/ *verb* [T] to repeat something you have heard, or to broadcast a signal, message or programme on television or radio: *I was told the news first and then I relayed it* ***to*** *the others.* ○ *TV pictures of the war were relayed around the world by satellite.*

relay [TEAM] /ˈriː.leɪ/ *noun* [C] a group of people who continue an activity that others from the same team or organization have been doing previously: *Relays of workers kept the machines going through the night.* ○ *After the landslide, volunteers worked* ***in*** *relays to rescue people buried under the rubble.*

relay [EQUIPMENT] /ˈriː.leɪ/ *noun* [C] a device that reacts to a small change in an electrical current by moving switches or other devices in an electrical circuit

ˈrelay (ˌrace) *noun* [C] a running or swimming race between two or more teams in which each person in the team runs or swims part of the race

release [MAKE FREE] /rɪˈliːs/ *verb* [T] **1** to give freedom or free movement to someone or something: *He was released* ***from*** *prison after serving two years of a five-year sentence.* ○ *She was arrested for shoplifting but was released* ***on bail*** (= after paying a sum of money to the law court). ○ *FIGURATIVE The operation released him from years of pain.* **2** to move a device from a fixed position to allow it to move freely: *He released the handbrake and the car jumped forwards.* **3** to fire a bomb or a missile, or to allow it to fall: *The plane released its bombs at 10 000 feet.* **4** to allow a substance to flow out from somewhere: *Coal power stations release sulphur dioxide* ***into*** *the atmosphere.* ○ *Hormones are released* ***from*** *glands* ***into*** *the bloodstream.* **5** to express a feeling which you have been trying not to show: *He punched the pillow in an effort to release his anger.*
release /rɪˈliːs/ *noun* **1** [S or U] when someone is allowed to leave prison, etc: *Her early release* ***from*** *prison led to a demonstration.* **2** [U] when something flows out from somewhere: *The accident caused the release* ***of*** *radioactivity* ***into*** *the atmosphere.* **3** [S or U] a feeling that you are free from something unpleasant: *I noticed a release* ***of*** *tension when he left the room.* ○ *After years of suffering, his death came as a merciful release.*

release [MAKE PUBLIC] /rɪˈliːs/ *verb* [T] **1** to allow something to be shown in public or to be available for use: *Police have released a picture of the man they want to question.* ○ *The minister has released a statement explaining the reasons for his resignation.* **2** If a company releases a film or musical recording, it allows the film to be shown in cinemas, or makes the musical recording available for the public to buy: *The band's latest album will be released next week.*
release /rɪˈliːs/ *noun* **1** [U] when something is shown in public or made available for use: *There are strict rules on the release* ***of*** *official information.* **2** [C] a written statement which gives information to be broadcast or published: *The Department of Transport has issued a* ***press*** *release about the proposals for the new motorway.* **3** [C] a musical recording which is made available for the public to buy: *Her latest release, a song about doomed love, she wrote herself.* **4 be** *(UK)* **on/***(US)* **in general release** If a film is on/in general release, it is available to be shown in cinemas: *The latest film from Disney goes on general release next month.*

relegate /ˈrel.ɪ.geɪt/ *verb* [T] **1** to put someone or something into a lower or less important rank or position: *She resigned when she was relegated* ***to*** *a desk job.* ○ *The story was relegated* ***to*** *the middle pages of the paper.* **2** *UK* If a football team is relegated, it is moved down to a lower division: *If Southampton lose again they may be relegated from the Premier League to the First Division.* ⊃Compare promote RAISE.

relegation /ˌrel.ɪˈɡeɪ.ʃᵊn/ *noun* [U] *UK* the act of moving a football team to a lower division: *Southampton face relegation if they lose again.*

relent /rɪˈlent/ *verb* [I] SLIGHTLY FORMAL to act in a less severe way towards someone and allow something that you had refused to allow before: *Her parents eventually relented and let her go to the party.* ○ *The security guard relented and let them through.*

relentless /rɪˈlent.ləs/ *adj* continuing in a severe or extreme way: *relentless criticism/pressure* ○ *relentless heat* **relentlessly** /rɪˈlent.lə.sli/ *adv*: *She has campaigned relentlessly for her husband's release from prison.*

relevant /ˈrel.ə.vᵊnt/ *adj* **1** connected with what is happening or being discussed: *Education should be relevant to the child's needs.* ○ *For further information, please refer to the relevant leaflet.* ○ *The point is highly relevant to this discussion.* ○ *I'm sorry but your personal wishes are not relevant* (= important) *in this case.* ∗ NOTE: The opposite is **irrelevant**. **2** correct or suitable for a particular purpose: *plans to make schooling more relevant to life beyond school*

relevance /ˈrel.ə.vᵊnts/ *noun* [U] (*ALSO* **relevancy**) the degree to which something is related or useful to what is happening or being talked about: *What relevance does that point have to the discussion?* ∗ NOTE: The opposite is **irrelevance**.

reliable /rɪˈlaɪə.bl̩/ *adj* Something or someone that is reliable can be trusted or believed because they work or behave well in the way you expect: *Is your watch reliable?* ○ *reliable information* ○ *Gideon is very reliable – if he says he'll do something, he'll do it.* ∗ NOTE: The opposite is **unreliable**. **reliability** /rɪˌlaɪəˈbɪl.ɪ.ti/ ⓤ /-ə.t̬i/ *noun* [U] *Rolls-Royce cars are famous for their quality and reliability.* **reliably** /rɪˈlaɪə.bli/ *adv*: *I am reliably informed that you have been talking about resigning from the company.*

reliance /rɪˈlaɪ.ənts/ *noun* [U] when you depend on or trust in something or someone: *The region's reliance on tourism is unwise.* ○ *You place too much reliance on her ideas and expertise.* **reliant** /rɪˈlaɪ.ənt/ *adj*: *He's completely reliant on his wheelchair to get about.* ⊃See also **self-reliant**.

relic /ˈrel.ɪk/ *noun* [C] **1** an object, tradition or system from the past which continues to exist: *During the dig, the archeological team found some relics from the Stone Age.* ○ *The country's employment system is a relic of the 1960s when jobs were scarce.* **2** a part of the body or something that belonged to a holy person: *These bones are the relics of a 12th-century saint.*

relief HELP /rɪˈliːf/ *noun* [C or U] food, money or services which provide help for people in need: *an international relief operation* ○ *relief agencies/supplies* ○ *Pop stars have raised millions of pounds for famine relief in Africa.* ○ *When the driver was taken ill, a relief* (= a new driver) *was sent to take his place.*
● **be on relief** *US INFORMAL* to be receiving money from the government because you are poor

relieve /rɪˈliːv/ *verb* [T] **1** to provide relief for a bad situation or for people in need: *emergency food aid to help relieve the famine* **2** to take the place of someone and continue doing their job or duties: *I'm on duty until 2 p.m. and then Peter is coming to relieve me.* **3** FORMAL to free a place that has been surrounded by an enemy army by military force: *An armoured battalion was sent to relieve the besieged town.*

relief HAPPINESS /rɪˈliːf/ *noun* [S or U] a feeling of happiness that something unpleasant has not happened or has ended: [+ to infinitive] *It was such a relief to hear that Marta was found safe and well.* ○ *After the exam, I felt an incredible sense of relief.* ○ *"James can't come tonight." "Well, that's a relief!"* ○ *to seek/find/provide relief from the heat/cold/pain/noise*

relieve /rɪˈliːv/ *verb* [T] **1** to make an unpleasant feeling, such as pain or worry, less strong: *She was given a shot of morphine to relieve the pain.* ○ *She relieved her boredom at home by learning how to type.* **2** to improve an unpleasant situation: *The council is considering banning*

vehicles from the town centre to relieve congestion.

relieved /rɪˈliːvd/ *adj* happy that something unpleasant has not happened or has ended: [+ to infinitive] *I'm so relieved to find you – I thought you'd already gone.* ○ *He was relieved to see Jeannie reach the other side of the river safely.* ○ [+ (that)] *I'm relieved (that) you didn't tell her.*

relief RAISED AREA /rɪˈliːf/ *noun* **1** [U] a method of raising shapes above a flat surface so that they appear to stand out slightly from it: *Coins have pictures on them in relief.* **2** [C] a sculpture made from a flat surface in which the forms are raised above the background: *stone/marble/bronze reliefs*
● **stand (out) in relief** to appear or show very clearly and noticeably: *The mountain stood out in sharp relief against the evening sky.*

re'lief ˌmap *noun* [C] a map that shows the hills, valleys and mountains of a particular area or country

re'lief ˌroad *noun* [C] *UK* a road that drivers can use to avoid driving on very busy main road

relieve yourself /rɪˈliːv/ *verb* [R] *POLITE PHRASE FOR* urinate: *He proceeded to relieve himself against a tree.*

PHRASAL VERBS WITH **relieve**   ▼

▲ **relieve sb of sth** OBJECT *phrasal verb* **1** FORMAL to take from a person something that they are carrying, in a helpful or polite way: *May I relieve you of that heavy bag?* **2** HUMOROUS to steal something from someone: *The pickpocket delicately relieved him of his wallet.*

▲ **relieve sb of sth** JOB *phrasal verb* [usually passive] FORMAL to dismiss someone from their job or position because they have done something wrong: *Following the scandal, he was relieved of his post as deputy finance minister.* ○ *The committee's chairperson is to be relieved of her duties.* ○ *The general was relieved of his command in 1941.*

religion /rɪˈlɪdʒ.ᵊn/ *noun* **1** [C or U] the belief in and worship of a god or gods, or any such system of belief and worship: *the Christian religion* **2** [C] INFORMAL an activity which someone is extremely enthusiastic about and does regularly: *Football is a religion for these people.*

religious /rɪˈlɪdʒ.əs/ *adj* **1** relating to religion: *religious education* **2** having a strong belief in a god or gods: *He's deeply religious and goes to church twice a week.*

religiously /rɪˈlɪdʒ.ə.sli/ *adv* **1** in ways or subjects relating to religion: *India is quite diverse, both politically and religiously.* **2** INFORMAL If you do something religiously, you do it regularly: *He visits his mother religiously every week.*

relinquish /rɪˈlɪŋ.kwɪʃ/ *verb* [T] FORMAL **1** to give up something such as a responsibility or claim: *He has relinquished his claim to the throne.* ○ *She relinquished control of the family investments to her son.* **2** to unwillingly stop holding or keeping something: *She relinquished her hold/grip on the steering wheel.*

relish ENJOY /ˈrel.ɪʃ/ *verb* [T] SLIGHTLY FORMAL **1** to like or enjoy something: *I always relish a challenge.* ○ [+ v-ing] *I don't relish telling her that her son has been arrested.* **2** If you relish the idea or thought of something, you feel pleasure that it is going to happen: *She's relishing the prospect of studying in Bologna for six months.*
relish /ˈrel.ɪʃ/ *noun* [U] SLIGHTLY FORMAL the enjoyment you get from doing something: *She ate her cake slowly and with relish.* ○ *I have no relish for hunting and killing animals.*

relish SAUCE /ˈrel.ɪʃ/ *noun* [C or U] a type of sauce which is eaten with food to add flavour to it: *tomato and onion relish* ○ *Would you like relish on your burger?*

relive /ˌriːˈlɪv/ *verb* [T] to remember clearly an experience that happened in the past: *Whenever I smell burning, I relive the final moments of the crash.*

rellie /ˈrel.i/ *noun* [C] (*ALSO* **rello**) *AUS INFORMAL FOR* a relative (= member of your family)

reload /ˌriːˈləʊd/ ⓤ /-ˈloʊd/ *verb* [I or T] to put more bullets in a gun: *to reload a gun/rifle/pistol* ○ *He reloaded and fired a second shot.*

relocate /ˌriːˈləʊˈkeɪt/ ⓤ /-ˈloʊ.keɪt/ *verb* [I or T] to (cause a person or company to) move to a new place: *The company has relocated to Liverpool.* ○ *My company* *relocated me **to** Paris.* **relocation** /ˌriː.ləʊˈkeɪ.ʃᵊn/ [US] /-ˈloʊ.keɪ-/ *noun* [U] *relocation costs*

reluctant /rɪˈlʌk.tᵊnt/ *adj* not very willing to do something and therefore slow to do it: [+ **to** infinitive] *I was having such a good time I was reluctant **to** leave.* ○ *Many parents feel reluctant **to** talk openly with their children.* ○ *She persuaded her reluctant husband to take a trip to Florida with her.* **reluctantly** /rɪˈlʌk.tᵊnt.li/ *adv*: *She reluctantly agreed to step down as managing director.*

reluctance /rɪˈlʌk.tᵊnts/ *noun* [S or U] an unwillingness to do something: *I accepted his resignation with great reluctance.* ○ [+ **to** infinitive] *Her reluctance **to** talk to the press was quite understandable.*

rely /rɪˈlaɪ/ *verb*

▲ **rely on *sb/sth*** *phrasal verb* **1** to need a particular thing or the help and support of someone or something in order to continue, to work correctly, or to succeed: [+ v-**ing**] *The success of this project relies on everyone mak**ing** an effort.* ○ *I rely on you **for** good advice.* ○ [+ **to** infinitive] *I'm relying on the garage **to** fix the car by tomorrow.* **2** to trust someone or something or to expect them to behave in a particular way: *British weather can never be relied on – it's always changing.* ○ [+ v-**ing**] *Don't rely on find**ing** me here when you get back* (= I might have gone).

remade /ˌriːˈmeɪd/ *past simple and past participle of* **remake**

remain /rɪˈmeɪn/ *verb* **1** [I or L] SLIGHTLY FORMAL to stay in the same place or in the same condition: *The doctor ordered him to remain in bed for a few days.* ○ *Most commentators expect the basic rate of tax to remain at 25%.* ○ [+ **to** infinitive] *A great many things remain **to** be done* (= have not yet been done). ○ *He remained silent.* ○ *It remains a secret.* ○ *The bank will remain open while renovations are carried out.* ➲See Note **rest, stay or remain?** at **rest** STOP. **2** [I] to continue to exist when other parts or other things no longer exist: *After the flood, nothing remained of the village.* ○ *Only a few hundred of these animals remain today.*

• **the fact remains** it is still true: *I know you're sorry now, but the fact remains **that** you hit your sister.*

• **it remains to be seen** it is not yet certain: *It remains to be seen **who** will win.*

the remainder *noun* [S] the part of something that is left after the other parts have gone, been used, or been taken away: *I ate most of it and gave the remainder to the dog.* ○ *It rained the first day but the remainder **of** the trip was lovely.* ➲See also **remainder**.

remainder /rɪˈmeɪn.dəʳ/ [US] /-dɚ/ *noun* [U] SPECIALIZED in mathematics, the amount that is left when one number cannot be exactly divided by another: *9 divided by 4 is 2, remainder 1.*

remaining /rɪˈmeɪ.nɪŋ/ *adj* [before n] continuing to exist or be left after other parts or things have been used or taken away: *Bernstein's two remaining lectures will take place on January 22 and 23.* ○ *Mix in half the butter and keep the remaining 50g for later.*

remains /rɪˈmeɪnz/ *plural noun* **1** pieces or parts of something which continue to exist when most of it has been used, destroyed or taken away: *The remains **of** lunch were still on the table.* ○ *We visited the remains **of** a 12th-century monastery.* **2** FORMAL **human/*sb's* remains** someone's dead body or the remaining parts of it: *Fifty years after he died, his remains were returned to his homeland.* ○ *Human remains were found in the woods.*

remainder /rɪˈmeɪn.dəʳ/ [US] /-dɚ/ *verb* [T] to sell a book cheaply because it has not sold well and no more copies of it will be produced: *His autobiography never sold very well and was soon remaindered.* ➲See also **the remainder** at REMAIN.

remake /ˌriːˈmeɪk/ *verb* [T] **remade, remade** to make a new film which has a story and title similar to an old one: *The French film 'trois hommes et un bébé' was remade in Hollywood **as** 'Three Men and a Baby'.* **remake** /ˈriː.meɪk/ *noun* [C] *Do you prefer **the** remake **of** 'King Kong' to the original?*

remand /rɪˈmɑːnd/ [US] /-ˈmænd/ *verb* [T often passive] LEGAL to send someone accused of committing a crime away from court until their trial begins: *He was remanded **on** theft charges.* ○ *The accused was remanded **in custody*** (= kept in prison before the trial began) *for a week.*

• **be remanded on bail** to be allowed to leave the law court after you have been accused of committing a crime to go to a particular place, usually your home, to wait until the trial begins, after paying a sum of money to the court which will not be given back if you do not appear at the trial

remand /rɪˈmɑːnd/ [US] /-ˈmænd/ *noun* [U] **1** LEGAL when someone is remanded **2** UK LEGAL **on remand** in prison until a court trial begins: *He was **held** on remand in Brixton prison for 18 months.*

reˈmand ˌcentre *noun* [C] UK a place where young people accused of committing a crime are sent to wait until their trial begins

remark /rɪˈmɑːk/ [US] /-ˈmɑːrk/ *verb* [T] to give a spoken statement of an opinion or thought: [+ **(that)**] *Dr Johnson once remarked **(that)** "When a man is tired of London, he is tired of life".* ○ [+ **that**] *He remarked **that** she was looking thin.* **remark** /rɪˈmɑːk/ [US] /-ˈmɑːrk/ *noun* [C] *Her remarks **on** the employment question led to a heated discussion.* ○ *The children **made/passed** rude remarks **about** the old man.*

remarkable /rɪˈmɑː.kə.bl̩/ [US] /-ˈmɑːr-/ *adj* unusual or special and therefore surprising and worth mentioning: *Nelson Mandela is a truly remarkable man.* ○ *Meeting you here in Rome is a remarkable coincidence.* ○ *The 20th century was remarkable **for** its inventions.*

remarkably /rɪˈmɑː.kə.bli/ [US] /-ˈmɑːr-/ *adv*: *It is a remarkably noisy and crowded city.* ○ *Remarkably* (= Surprisingly), *she wasn't hurt in the crash.*

▲ **remark on *sth*** *phrasal verb* to notice something and make a remark about it: *All his friends remarked on the change in him since his marriage.*

remarry /ˌriːˈmær.i/ [US] /-ˈmer-/ *verb* [I or T] to marry again: *After a lengthy and painful divorce, she vowed never to remarry.* ○ *Her mother died in childbirth, and her father remarried when she was a baby.* ○ *Richard Burton famously remarried Elizabeth Taylor.*

remaster /ˌriːˈmɑː.stəʳ/ [US] /-ˈmæs.tɚ/ *verb* [T often passive] to make a new MASTER (= a recording from which all copies are made) of an earlier recording, usually in order to produce copies with better sound quality: *The soundtrack of 'The Godfather' has been **digitally** remastered and transformed from mono to stereo.*

remedial /rɪˈmiː.di.əl/ *adj* UK describing or relating to teaching which is intended to help people who have difficulties in reading or writing: *remedial classes/courses* ○ *She is a teacher of remedial English.*

remedy /ˈrem.ə.di/ *noun* [C] **1** a successful way of curing an illness or dealing with a problem or difficulty: *an effective herbal remedy **for** headaches* ○ *The best remedy **for** grief is hard work.* **2** LEGAL **legal remedy** a way of solving a problem or instructing someone to make a payment for harm or damage they have caused, using a decision made in a court of law: *We have exhausted all possible legal remedies **for** this injustice.*

remedy /ˈrem.ə.di/ *verb* [T] FORMAL to do something to correct or improve something that is wrong: *This mistake must be remedied immediately.*

remedial /rɪˈmiː.di.əl/ *adj* FORMAL **1** describes an action which is intended to correct something that is wrong or to improve a bad situation: *to take urgent/immediate remedial **action*** ○ *The bill requires owners to undertake remedial **work** on dilapidated buildings.* **2** describes exercises which are intended to improve someone's health when they are ill

remember /rɪˈmem.bəʳ/ [US] /-bɚ/ *verb* **1** [I or T] to be able to bring back a piece of information into your mind, or to keep a piece of information in your memory: *"Where did you park the car?" "I can't remember."* ○ *I can remember people's faces, but not their names.* ○ [+ **(that)**] *She suddenly remembered **(that)** her keys were in her other bag.* ○ [+ v-**ing**] *I don't remember sign**ing** a contract.* ○ [+ question word] *Can you remember **what** her telephone number is?* ○ *I remember him **as*** (= I thought he was) *a rather annoying man.* ➲See Note **remind or remember?** at **remind**. **2 remember to *do sth*** to not forget to do something: *Did you remember to do the shopping?* **3 be remembered for *sth*** to be kept in people's memories because of a particular action or quality: *She will be remembered for her courage.* **4** [T] to hold a

R

special ceremony to honour a past event or someone who has died: *On November 11th, the British remember those who died in the two World Wars.* **5** [T] to give a present or a sum of money to someone you love or who has provided good service to you: *My Granny always remembers me* (= sends me a present) *on my birthday.* ○ *My cousin remembered me in her will.*

• **you remember** *INFORMAL* said when you are talking to someone about something that they used to be aware of but may have forgotten: *We went and had tea in the little café on Primrose Hill – you remember, the one next to the bookshop.*

remembrance /rɪˈmem.brᵊnts/ *noun FORMAL* **1** [U] when you remember and show respect for someone who has died or a past event: *A church service was held **in** remembrance **of** the victims.* **2** [C usually pl] a memory of something that happened in the past: *fond/sweet/personal remembrances*

COMMON LEARNER ERROR

remember or memory?

Remember is a verb. Use **remember** when you think about or bring thoughts into your mind about a person, place, or event from the past.

I can remember when I went on holiday to the seaside for the first time.

Memory is a noun. Use **memory** to talk about the person, place, or event from the past that you think about.

I have many good memories of when I was a child.

▲ **remember *sb* to *sb*** *phrasal verb SLIGHTLY FORMAL* to ask someone to say hello to another person for you: *Please remember me to your parents.*

Reˈmembrance ˌDay *noun* [C usually sing] (*ALSO* **Remembrance Sunday**) in Britain, November 11 or the closest Sunday to that date, when people honour those who were killed in wars, especially the two World Wars

remind /rɪˈmaɪnd/ *verb* [T] to make someone aware of something they have forgotten or might have forgotten: *Could you remind Paul **about** dinner on Saturday?* ○ [+ to infinitive] *Please remind me **to** post this letter.* ○ [+ (that)] *I rang Jill and reminded her **(that)** the conference had been cancelled.*

reminder /rɪˈmaɪn.dəʳ/ [US] /-dɚ/ *noun* [C] a written or spoken message which reminds someone to do something: *If he forgot to pay his rent, his landlady would send him a reminder.* ○ [+ to infinitive] *Mum sent me off with a final reminder **to** be back before 11pm.*

COMMON LEARNER ERROR

remind or remember?

If you **remember** a fact or something from the past, you keep it in your mind, or bring it back into your mind.

I can't remember the name of that film.
Did you remember to bring your passport?

When you **remind** someone to do something, you make them remember it.

Can you remind me to phone Anna tomorrow?
~~*Can you remember me to phone Anna tomorrow?*~~

▲ **remind *you* of *sth/sb*** *phrasal verb* to be similar to, and make you think of, something or someone else: *Your hair and eyes remind me of your mother.*

reminder /rɪˈmaɪn.dəʳ/ [US] /-dɚ/ *noun* **a reminder of *sb/sth*** a person or thing which makes you remember a particular person, event or situation: [+ question word] *Alison's story is a reminder of **how** vulnerable women can be in what is still essentially a man's world.*

reminisce /ˌrem.ɪˈnɪs/ *verb* [I] *FORMAL* to talk or write about past experiences which you remember with pleasure: *My grandfather used to reminisce **about** his years in the navy.*

reminiscence /ˌrem.ɪˈnɪs.ᵊnts/ *noun* [U] *FORMAL* the act of remembering events and experiences from the past

reminiscences /ˌrem.ɪˈnɪs.ᵊnt.sɪz/ *plural noun FORMAL* Your reminiscences are the experiences you remember from the past, often written in a book: *The novel contains endless reminiscences **of/about** the author's youth.*

reminiscent /ˌrem.ɪˈnɪs.ᵊnt/ *adj FORMAL* **reminiscent of *sb/sth*** making you remember a particular person, event or thing: *That song is so reminiscent of my adolescence.*

remiss /rɪˈmɪs/ *adj* [after v] *FORMAL* careless and not doing a duty well enough: *You have been remiss **in** your duties.* ○ [+ to infinitive] ***It** was remiss **of** me **to** forget to give you the message.*

remission [ILLNESS] /rɪˈmɪʃ.ᵊn/ *noun* [C or U] *FORMAL* a period of time when an illness is less severe: *Her cancer has been **in** remission for several years.* ➲See also **remission** at **remit** REDUCE.

remission [RELIGION] /rɪˈmɪʃ.ᵊn/ *noun* [U] *FORMAL* forgiveness for breaking religious laws or rules: *He believes that redemption is based on remission **of** sins.*

remit [REDUCE] /rɪˈmɪt/ *verb* [T] **-tt-** *UK LEGAL* to reduce a period of time that someone must spend in prison: *She has had part of her sentence remitted.* ○ *His prison sentence was remitted **to** two years.*

remission /rɪˈmɪʃ.ᵊn/ *noun* [U] *UK LEGAL* a reduction of the time that a person has to stay in prison: *He was given three months' remission for good behaviour.* ➲See also **remission** ILLNESS; **remission** RELIGION.

remit [SEND] /rɪˈmɪt/ *verb* [T] **-tt-** *FORMAL* **1** to send money to someone: *He worked as a builder in Chicago and remitted half his monthly wage **to** his family in the Philippines.* **2** to refer a matter to someone in authority to deal with: *She remitted the case **to** a new tribunal for reconsideration.*

remittance /rɪˈmɪt.ᵊnts/ [US] /-ˈmɪţ-/ *noun FORMAL* **1** [C] a sum of money which you send to someone: *She sends a small remittance home to her parents each month.* **2** [U] when you send payment to someone: *remittance advice/information*

remit [AREA] /ˈriː.mɪt/ *noun* [C usually sing] the area which a person or group of people in authority has responsibility for or control over: *The remit **of** this official inquiry is to investigate the reasons for the accident.*

remnant /ˈrem.nənt/ *noun* [C usually pl] a small piece or amount of something that is left from a larger original piece or amount: *the remnants **of** last night's meal* ○ *remnants **of** the city's former glory* ○ *a carpet remnant*

remodel /ˌriːˈmɒd.ᵊl/ [US] /-ˈmɑː.dᵊl/ *verb* [T] **-ll-** or *US USUALLY* **-l-** to give a new shape or form to something: *We've completely remodelled the kitchen.*

remonstrate /ˈrem.ᵊn.streɪt/ [US] /rɪˈmɑːnt-/ *verb* [I] *FORMAL* to complain to someone or about something: *I went to the boss to remonstrate **against** the new rules.* ○ *The barrister remonstrated **with** the judge **about** the amount of the fine.* **remonstrance** /rɪˈmɒnt.strᵊnts/ [US] /-ˈmɑːnt-/ *noun* [C or U]

remorse /rɪˈmɔːs/ [US] /-ˈmɔːrs/ *noun* [U] *FORMAL* a strong feeling of guilt and regret about something you have done: *He felt no remorse **for** the murders he had committed.* ○ *After the argument, she was **filled with** remorse.*

remorseful /rɪˈmɔː.sfᵊl/ [US] /-ˈmɔːr-/ *adj FORMAL* feeling regret and guilt **remorsefully** /rɪˈmɔː.sfᵊl.i/ [US] /-ˈmɔːr-/ *adv*

remorseless /rɪˈmɔː.sləs/ [US] /-ˈmɔːr-/ *adj FORMAL* **1** severe and showing no regret or guilt: *remorseless cruelty/violence* ○ *a remorseless judge* **2** never stopping or impossible to stop: *the hurricane's remorseless approach* ○ *remorseless pressure to succeed* **remorselessly** /rɪˈmɔː.slə.sli/ [US] /-ˈmɔːr-/ *adv*

remortgage /ˌriːˈmɔː.gɪdʒ/ [US] /-ˈmɔːr-/ *verb* [I or T] to arrange a second MORTGAGE (= an agreement with a bank or similar organization in which you borrow money to buy property), or increase the first mortgage, especially in order to obtain more money: *Robin decided to remortgage his house to pay off his debts.* **remortgage** /ˈriː.mɔː.gɪdʒ/ [US] /-mɔːr-/ *noun* [C] *The building society will arrange a remortgage for a fee of £100.*

remote /rɪˈməʊt/ [US] /-ˈmoʊt/ *adj* **1** far away in distance, time or relation: *remote galaxies* ○ *It happened in the remote **past**, so no one worries about it any more.* ○ *They take little interest in a conflict far from their homes and remote **from** their everyday problems.* **2** describes an area, house or village that is a long way from any towns or cities: *a remote mountain village* **3** slight: *a remote possibility* ○ *The chances of a visit by Martians to the Earth are remote.* **4** not very friendly or showing little interest in other people: *Her manner was remote and cool.*

• **not have the remotest idea** to not know at all: *"Who's that?" "I haven't the remotest idea."*

remotely /rɪˈməʊt.li/ [US] /-ˈmoʊt-/ *adv* **1** in a remote place: *a remotely situated farmhouse* **2** in a remote or very slight way: *I'm afraid we're not remotely interested in your proposal.* **remoteness** /rɪˈməʊt.nəs/ [US] /-ˈmoʊt-/ *noun* [U]

reˌmote conˈtrol *noun* [C or U] a system or device for controlling something such as a machine or vehicle from a distance, by using electrical or radio signals: *Have you seen the remote control for the TV anywhere?* ○ *The bomb was detonated **by** remote control.* **remote-controlled** /rɪˌməʊt.kənˈtrəʊld/ [US] /-ˌmoʊt.kənˈtroʊld/ *adj*: *a remote-controlled model aircraft*

remould /ˈriː.məʊld/ [US] /-moʊld/ *verb, noun* UK FOR **retread**

reˈmoval ˌvan UK *noun* [U] (US **moving van**) a vehicle used to transport furniture and other possessions when people move to a new home

remove [TAKE AWAY] /rɪˈmuːv/ *verb* [T] **1** to take something or someone away from somewhere, or off something: *The men came to remove the rubbish **from** the backyard.* ○ *This detergent will remove even old stains.* ○ *It got so hot that he removed his tie and jacket.* ○ *They decided to remove their son from the school.* **2** to make a negative feeling disappear: *Hearing your opinion has removed my last doubts/suspicions about her.* **removal** /rɪˈmuː.vəl/ *noun* [U] *stain removal* ○ *furniture removal*

remove /rɪˈmuːv/ *noun* [C] FORMAL a stage in a process or development: *We are **at one** remove **from*** (= very close to) *war.*

removable /rɪˈmuː.və.bl̩/ *adj* able to be removed: *This jacket has removable sleeves/a removable collar.*

removals /rɪˈmuː.vəlz/ *plural noun* the business of transporting furniture and other possessions when people move to a new home: *Does your firm do removals?*

removed /rɪˈmuːvd/ *adj* FORMAL **once/twice, etc. removed** describes a COUSIN (= a relative) separated from you by one, two, etc. GENERATIONS (= same family age groups): *She's my first cousin once removed.*

• **be far removed from *sth*** FORMAL to be very different from something: *It's a wonderful experience but it's far removed from reality.*

remover /rɪˈmuː.vəʳ/ [US] /-vɚ/ *noun* [C or U] **1** a substance which removes something: *Do you have any nail-varnish remover?* **2** **(furniture) remover**/(US) ***(furniture) mover***/(AUS) ***(furniture) removalist*** a person or company who helps people to move their furniture and other possessions when they move to a new home

remove [DISMISS] /rɪˈmuːv/ *verb* [T] FORMAL to force someone to leave an important job or a position of power because they have behaved badly or not in a way you approve of: *The company's shareholders have voted to remove the executive board.* ○ *Several opposition groups are fighting to remove the president **from power**.* ○ *She has been removed **from** her **post/position** as managing director.*

removal /rɪˈmuː.vəl/ *noun* [U] FORMAL when someone is forced to leave an important position or job: *There have been calls for the president's removal.*

remunerate /rɪˈmjuː.nəʳr.eɪt/ [US] /-nə.reɪt/ *verb* [T] FORMAL to pay someone for work or services: *He is poorly remunerated **for** all the work he does.* **remuneration** /rɪˌmjuː.nəʳˈeɪ.ʃəʳn/ [US] /-nəˈreɪ-/ *noun* [C or U] *They demanded adequate remuneration **for** their work.* ○ *In return for some caretaking duties, we are offering a free flat and a small remuneration.* ○ *a remuneration package*

remunerative /rɪˈmjuː.nəʳr.ə.tɪv/ [US] /-nə.reɪ.t̬ɪv/ *adj* FORMAL *a highly remunerative* (= well paid) *job* ○ *Charity work is not very remunerative.*

renaissance /rəˈneɪ.səʳnts/ [US] /ˈren.ə.sɑːnts/ *noun* [S] a new growth of activity or interest in something, especially art, literature or music: *Opera in Britain is enjoying a long-awaited renaissance.*

• **the Renaissance** the period of new growth of interest and activity in the areas of art, literature and ideas in Europe, especially northern Italy, during the 14th, 15th and 16th centuries: *Renaissance art/painting/architecture*

renal /ˈriː.nəʳl/ *adj* SPECIALIZED relating to the kidneys: *a renal unit* ○ *renal dialysis*

rename /ˌriːˈneɪm/ *verb* [T] to give something a new name: *You must rename the file before you save it.* ○ *The ship was sold, painted and renamed the 'Suez Star'.*

rend /rend/ *verb* [T] **rent** or US ALSO **rended, rent** or US ALSO **rended** OLD USE OR LITERARY to tear or break something violently: *With one stroke of his sword, he rent his enemy's helmet **in** two.* ○ [+ adj] *Firemen had to rend him **free*** (= pull him out) *of the burning car.* ○ FIGURATIVE *A terrifying scream rent the air.*

render [CAUSE] /ˈren.dəʳ/ [US] /-dɚ/ *verb* [T] FORMAL **1** to cause someone or something to be in a particular state: [+ adj] *His rudeness rendered me speechless.* ○ *New technology has rendered my old computer obsolete.* **2** to change words into a different language or form: *She is rendering the book **into** English from French.* **rendering** /ˈren.dəʳr.ɪŋ/ [US] /-dɚ-/ *noun* [C] *a new rendering of the Bible **into** modern English*

render [GIVE] /ˈren.dəʳ/ [US] /-dɚ/ *verb* [T] FORMAL to give something such as a service, a personal opinion or expression, or a performance of a song or poem, etc. to people: *The singers rendered the song with enthusiasm.* ○ *We see that freight railroads make good profits while rendering excellent **service**.*

rendering /ˈren.dəʳr.ɪŋ/ [US] /-dɚ-/ *noun* [C] (ALSO **rendition**) the way that something is performed, written, drawn, etc: *Her rendering **of** the song was delightful.*

render [BUILDING] /ˈren.dəʳ/ [US] /-dɚ/ *verb* [T] SPECIALIZED to put a first layer of plaster or cement on a wall **rendering** /ˈren.dəʳr.ɪŋ/ [US] /-dɚ-/ *noun* [U] *The rendering on two sides of the house needed to be removed.*

▲ **render *sth* down** *phrasal verb* **1** [M] SPECIALIZED to melt fat in order to make it purer **2** to prepare or treat the bodies of dead animals in order to take out the fat and other substances that can be used in other products: *to render down animal carcasses* **rendering** /ˈren.dəʳr.ɪŋ/ [US] /-dɚ-/ *noun* [U] *the rendering of beef products* ○ *a rendering plant*

rendezvous /ˈrɒn.deɪ.vuː/ [US] /ˈrɑːn-/ *noun* [C] *plural* **rendezvous** **1** an arrangement to meet someone, especially secretly, at a particular place and time, or the place itself: *We have a rendezvous **for** next week, don't we?* ○ *The lovers met at a secret rendezvous in the park.* **2** a place where a particular group of people often go or meet, by arrangement or habit: *This restaurant is a popular rendezvous **for** local artists.* **rendezvous** /ˈrɒn.deɪ.vuː/ [US] /ˈrɑːn-/ *verb* [I] *The police arranged to rendezvous **with** their informant at a disused warehouse.*

renegade /ˈren.ɪ.geɪd/ *noun* [C] FORMAL DISAPPROVING a person who has changed their feelings of support and duty from one political, religious, national, etc. group to a new one: *A band of renegades had captured the prince and were holding him to ransom.* **renegade** /ˈren.ɪ.geɪd/ *adj* [before n] *a renegade soldier/priest*

renege /rɪˈneɪg/ *verb* [I] FORMAL to fail to keep a promise or an agreement, etc: *If you renege **on** the deal now, I'll fight you in the courts.*

renew [REPEAT] /rɪˈnjuː/ [US] /-ˈnuː/ *verb* [T] to begin doing something again: *The kidnappers renewed their threats.* ○ *She renewed her efforts to escape.* **renewed** /rɪˈnjuːd/ [US] /-ˈnuːd/ *adj*: *renewed interest/enthusiasm*

renew [MAKE NEW] /rɪˈnjuː/ [US] /-ˈnuː/ *verb* [T] to increase the life of or replace something old: *Every year I renew my membership of the sports club.* ○ *I forgot to renew my season ticket.* ○ *I'll use this material to renew the chair covers.*

renewable /rɪˈnjuː.ə.bl̩/ [US] /-ˈnuː-/ *adj* **1** describes a form of energy that can be produced as quickly as it is used: *renewable energy sources such as wind and wave power* **2** If an official document is renewable, its use can be lengthened for an extra period of time: *a renewable passport/contract* **renewal** /rɪˈnjuː.əl/ [US] /-ˈnuː-/ *noun* [C or U] *Do you deal with season-ticket renewals here?*

ren,minbi yu'an *noun* [C] the **yuan**

rennet /'ren.ɪt/ *noun* [U] (*US ALSO* **rennin**) a substance used for thickening milk, especially to make cheese

renounce /rɪ'naʊnts/ *verb* [T] *FORMAL* to say formally or publicly that you no longer own, support, believe in or have a connection with something: *Her ex-husband renounced his* ***claim*** *to the family house.* ○ *Gandhi renounced the use of violence.* **renunciation** /rɪ,nʌnt.si'eɪ.ʃᵊn/ *noun* [S or U] *the renunciation* ***of*** *violence*

renovate /'ren.ə.veɪt/ *verb* [T] to repair and improve something, especially a building: *He renovates old houses and sells them at a profit.* **renovation** /,ren.ə'veɪ.ʃᵊn/ *noun* [C or U] *The museum is closed for renovation.* ○ *Extensive renovations were carried out on the property.*

renown /rɪ'naʊn/ *noun* [U] *FORMAL* the state of being famous: *a woman of great renown* ○ *Her renown spread across the country.* **renowned** /rɪ'naʊnd/ *adj*: *The region is renowned* ***for*** *its outstanding natural beauty.* ○ *Marco Polo is a renowned explorer/is renowned* ***as*** *an explorer.*

rent [PAYMENT] /rent/ *noun* [C or U] a fixed amount of money that you pay regularly for the use of a room, house, car, television, etc. that someone else owns: *I pay a higher rent/more rent than the other tenants because my room is bigger.* ○ *Rents here are ridiculously* ***high/low.***

• **for rent** offered by the owner for someone else to use in exchange for money

rent /rent/ *verb* [T] to pay or receive a fixed amount of money for the use of a room, house, car, television, etc: *I rented a car* ***from*** *a garage so that I could get about.* ○ [+ two objects] *The old lady rented us her spare bedroom* ***for*** *£55 a week.* ○ *My Dad has a cottage which he rents* ***(out) to*** *tourists.*

rental /'ren.tᵊl/ [US] /-t̬ᵊl/ *noun* [C or U] an arrangement to rent something, or the amount of money that you pay to rent something: *Property rental is quite expensive here.* ○ *Video and television rentals have decreased this year.* ○ *a car rental* ***company***

USAGE

rent or hire?

In British English you usually **rent** something for a long time.

I rent a 2-bedroom flat.

In British English you **hire** something for a short time.

We hired a car for the weekend.

In American English the word **rent** is used in both situations.

I rent a 2-bedroom apartment.
We rented a car for the weekend.

---

rent [TEAR] /rent/ *noun* [C] *MAINLY OLD USE* a large hole torn in a piece of material: *There was a large rent in his parachute.*

rent [TORN] /rent/ *past simple and past participle of* **rend**

rent-a- /ren.tə-/ *prefix UK DISAPPROVING* used when a person, thing or group of people seems to have been rented for a particular purpose and is not sincere: *Most of the people on the protest seemed to be rent-a-mob, not real supporters.* ○ *HUMOROUS Old rent-a-quote is always turning up on TV to give his opinions.*

'rent ,boy *noun* [C] *UK INFORMAL* a young male prostitute used by other men

rent-free /,rent'friː/ *adj, adv* If a house is rent-free or if you are living or staying rent-free, the owner is not asking for payment.

'rent ,strike *noun* [C] a refusal to pay rent, especially by all the people living in a particular house or houses

renunciation /rɪ,nʌnt.si'eɪ.ʃᵊn/ *noun* [S or U] ➲See at **renounce**.

reopen /,riː'əʊ.pᵊn/ [US] /-'oʊ-/ *verb* [I or T] **1** If a place or business, etc. reopens or is reopened, it begins to operate, or it becomes open for people to use, after being closed for a period of time: *The museum has reopened after nearly two years of reconstruction.* ○ *He hung a sign on the door of the shop which said it would reopen at 11.* **2** If a formal process or activity reopens or is reopened, it begins again or starts to be dealt with again after a period of time: *to reopen an enquiry/investigation* ○ *to reopen a debate/discussion* ○ *to reopen a legal case/file*

reorganize, *UK ALSO* **reorganise** /,riː'ɔː.gᵊn.aɪz/ [US] /-'ɔːr-/ *verb* [I or T] to organize something again in order to improve it: *I've reorganized my files so that I can easily find what I'm looking for.* ○ *The new managing director plans to completely reorganize this department.* **reorganization** /riː,ɔː.gᵊn.aɪ'zeɪ.ʃᵊn/ [US] /-,ɔːr-/ *noun* [C or U]: *the office reorganization*

rep [BUSINESS] /rep/ *noun* [C] *INFORMAL* a **sales rep**

rep [THEATRE] /rep/ *noun* [U] *INFORMAL FOR* **repertory**

repaid /rɪ'peɪd/ *past simple and past participle of* **repay**

repair /rɪ'peəʳ/ [US] /-'per/ *verb* [T] **1** to put something that is damaged, broken or not working correctly, back into good condition or make it work again: *to repair (the surface of) the road* ○ *to repair a roof after a storm* ○ *The garage said the car was so old it wasn't worth repairing.* ○ *I really must* ***get*** *my bike repair****ed*** *this weekend.* **2** If you repair something wrong or harmful that has been done, you do something to make it right: *to repair a broken friendship* ○ *Is it too late to repair the* ***damage*** *we have done to our planet?*

repair /rɪ'peəʳ/ [US] /-'per/ *noun* [C or U] when something is done to fix something that is broken or damaged: *My car is in the garage for repairs.* ○ *The repairs* ***to*** *the roof will be expensive.* ○ *The mechanic pointed out the repair* (= repaired place) *on the front of my car.*

• **under repair** being repaired: *This section of motorway will be under repair until January.*

• **in good/bad repair** (*ALSO* **in a good/bad, etc. state of repair**) in good/bad, etc. condition: *The house is in very good repair.*

repairable /rɪ'peə.rə.bl̩/ [US] /-'per.ə-/ *adj* able to be repaired

▲ **repair to *somewhere*** *phrasal verb FORMAL* to go to another place, usually in a group of people: *After dinner, we repaired to the lounge for coffee.*

reparation /,rep.ə'reɪ.ʃᵊn/ *noun* [C or U] *FORMAL* payment for harm or damage: *The company had to* ***make*** *reparation* ***to*** *those who suffered ill health as a result of chemical pollution.*

repartee /,rep.ɑː'tiː/ [US] /-ɑːr-/ *noun* [U] quick and usually amusing answers and remarks in conversation: *Oscar Wilde's plays are full of* ***witty*** *repartee.*

repast /rɪ'pɑːst/ [US] /-'pæst/ *noun* [C] *LITERARY* a meal: *Yet that simple repast was fit for a king.*

repatriate /,riː'pæt.ri.eɪt/ [US] /-'peɪ.tri-/ *verb* [T] to send or bring someone, or sometimes money or other property, back to their own country: *The government repatriated him because he had no visa.* **repatriation** /,riː.pæt.ri'eɪ.ʃᵊn/ [US] /rɪ,peɪ.tri-/ *noun* [U]

repay /rɪ'peɪ/ *verb* [T] **repaid, repaid** to pay back or to reward someone or something: *He had to sell his car to repay the bank loan.* ○ *She repaid the loan* ***to*** *her mother.* ○ [+ two objects] *She repaid her mother the loan.* ○ *How can I ever repay you* ***for*** *all your kindness?*

repayable /rɪ'peɪ.ə.bl̩/ *adj*: *The loan is repayable* (= must be repaid) *over six months.*

repayment /rɪ'peɪ.mənt/ *noun* [C or U] when you repay someone or something: *mortgage repayments* ○ *The bank demanded immediate repayment.*

repeal /rɪ'piːl/ *verb* [T] If a government repeals a law, it causes that law no longer to have any legal force. **repeal** /rɪ'piːl/ *noun* [S or U] *We're campaigning for a/the repeal* ***of*** *the abortion laws.*

repeat /rɪ'piːt/ *verb* **1** [T] to say or tell people something more than once: *Would you mind repeating what you just said?* ○ *Please don't repeat what I've just told you* ***to*** *anyone else.* ○ [+ that] *She repeated* ***that*** *she had no intention of standing for President.* **2** [I or T] to happen, or to do something, more than once: *The test must be repeated several times.* ○ *This is an offer never to be repeated.* ○ *Johnny had to repeat a year/class at school.* ○ [R] *Some historians think that history repeats itself.* **3** **repeat yourself** to say the same thing again, or the same things again and again: *His speech was dreadful – he just kept repeating himself.*

repeat /rɪ'piːt/ *noun* [C] **1** when something happens or is done more than once: *All this is a repeat/a repeat performance of what happened last year.* **2** a television or radio programme that is broadcast again: *There's*

R

nothing but repeats on television these days.
repeated /rɪˈpiː.tɪd/ [US] /-t̬ɪd/ *adj* happening again and again: *repeated attempts/mistakes/warnings*
repeatedly /rɪˈpiː.tɪd.li/ [US] /-t̬ɪd-/ *adv* many times: *He telephoned repeatedly, begging her to return.*
repetition /ˌrep.əˈtɪʃ.ᵊn/ *noun* [C or U] when you repeat something: *His books are full of repetition and useless information.*
▲ **repeat on *sb*** *phrasal verb* When food repeats on you, the taste of it comes up again into your mouth: *Cucumber always repeats on me.*

repel [FORCE AWAY] /rɪˈpel/ *verb* [T] **-ll- 1** to force something or someone to move away or stop attacking you: *This coat has a special surface that repels moisture.* ○ *FORMAL The defenders repelled the attack without losing any men.* **2** *SPECIALIZED* to have a MAGNETIC FIELD which pushes away something with a similar magnetic field: *Similar poles of magnets repel each other, and opposite poles attract.*
repellent /rɪˈpel.ᵊnt/ *noun* [C or U] a substance used to repel something: *insect/mosquito repellent*

repel [CAUSE STRONG DISLIKE] /rɪˈpel/ *verb* [T] **-ll-** People or things that repel you disgust you or make you feel strongly that you do not want to be near, see or think about them: *She was repelled by his ugliness.* ○ *Her arrogance repels many people.* **repellent** /rɪˈpel.ᵊnt/ *adj*: *repellent behaviour/beliefs* ○ *I find any cruelty to children utterly repellent.*

repent /rɪˈpent/ *verb* [I] *FORMAL* to be very sorry for something bad you have done in the past and wish that you had not done it: *He repented **(of** his sins) just hours before he died.* **repentance** /rɪˈpen.tᵊnts/ *noun* [U] *This was an extremely violent crime, for which the boy showed no repentance.*
repentant /rɪˈpen.tᵊnt/ *adj FORMAL* feeling sorry for something that you have done * NOTE: The opposite is **unrepentant**.

repercussion /ˌriː.pəˈkʌʃ.ᵊn/ [US] /-pɚ-/ *noun* [C usually pl] the effect that an action, event or decision has on something, especially a bad effect: *Any decrease in tourism could have serious repercussions for the local economy.* ○ *President Kennedy's assassination had far-reaching repercussions.*

repertoire /ˈrep.ə.twɑːʳ/ [US] /-ɚ.twɑːr/ *noun* [C] all the music or plays, etc. that you can do or perform or that you know: *The Royal Shakespeare Company also have many modern plays **in** their repertoire.* ○ *There is an extensive repertoire of music written for the flute.*

repertory /ˈrep.ə.tᵊr.i/ [US] /-ɚ.tɔːr-/ *noun* [U] (*INFORMAL* **rep**) the repeated performance of several plays one after the other by one company of actors: *a repertory company/group/theatre*
• **in repertory 1** If a play is in repertory, it is one of several different plays being performed on particular days by the same company of actors: *'Macbeth' is in repertory at the RSC.* **2** If an actor is in repertory, they are working with a repertory theatre group.

repetition /ˌrep.ɪˈtɪʃ.ᵊn/ *noun* [C or U] ⊃See at **repeat**.

repetitive /rɪˈpet.ə.tɪv/ [US] /-ˈpet̬.ə.t̬ɪv/ *adj* (*ALSO* **repetitious**) involving doing or saying the same thing several times, especially in a way that is boring: *a repetitive job/task* **repetitively** /rɪˈpet.ə.tɪv.li/ [US] /-ˈpet̬.ə.t̬ɪv-/ *adv*

reˌpetitive ˈstrain ˌinjury *noun* [U] (*ABBREVIATION* **RSI**) a painful medical condition which can cause damage to the hands, wrists, upper arms and backs especially of people who use computers and other forms of keyboard

rephrase /ˌriːˈfreɪz/ *verb* [T] to say or write something again in a different and usually clearer way: *Could you rephrase your question, please?*

replace [CHANGE FOR] /rɪˈpleɪs/ *verb* [T] **1** to take the place of something, or to put something or someone in the place of something or someone else: *The factory replaced most of its workers **with** robots.* ○ *Tourism has replaced agriculture as the nation's main industry.* **2** If you replace something broken, damaged or lost, you provide a new one: *I promised to replace the plate that I'd dropped.* **replacement** /rɪˈpleɪs.mənt/ *noun* [C or U] *The agency sent a replacement **for** the secretary who resigned.*
replaceable /rɪˈpleɪ.sə.bl̩/ *adj*: *Don't worry – all that stolen stuff is replaceable.*

replace [PUT BACK] /rɪˈpleɪs/ *verb* [T] to put something back where it was before: *The librarian replaced the books correctly on the shelves.*

replay [COMPETITION] /ˌriːˈpleɪ/ *verb* [T] to play a game, especially a football game, again that neither team won the first time **replay** /ˈriː.pleɪ/ *noun* [C] *The semi-final replay will be on Saturday.*

replay [RECORDING] /ˌriːˈpleɪ/ *verb* [T] to play something again, especially music or film recorded already: *The police replayed the video of the robbery in court.* **replay** /ˈriː.pleɪ/ *noun* [C] *a slow-motion replay*

replenish /rɪˈplen.ɪʃ/ *verb* [T] *FORMAL* to fill something up again: *Food stocks were replenished **by/with** imports from the USA.* ○ *Does your glass need replenishing?*
replenishment /rɪˈplen.ɪʃ.mənt/ *noun* [U]

replete /rɪˈpliːt/ *adj* [after v] *FORMAL* **1** full, especially with food: *After two helpings of dessert, Sergio was at last replete.* **2** well supplied: *This car has an engine replete **with** the latest technology.*

replica /ˈrep.lɪ.kə/ *noun* [C] an exact copy of an object: *The ship is an exact replica **of** the original Golden Hind.*
replicate /ˈrep.lɪ.keɪt/ *verb* **1** [T] *FORMAL* to make or do something again in exactly the same way: *Researchers tried many times to replicate the original experiment.* **2** [I or T] *SPECIALIZED* If organisms and genetic or other structures replicate, they make exact copies of themselves: *Chromosomes replicate before cells divide and multiply.* ○ [R] *Computer viruses replicate themselves and are passed along from user to user.* **replication** /ˌrep.lɪˈkeɪ.ʃᵊn/ *noun* [C or U] *FORMAL*

reply /rɪˈplaɪ/ *verb* [I] **1** to answer: [+ speech] *"Where are you going?" I asked. "Home," he replied.* ○ [+ that] *I replied **that** it was 12 o'clock.* ○ *I try to reply **to** letters the day I receive them.* **2** to react to an action by someone else: *She replied **to** the threats by going to the police.* ○ *Newport took an early lead before Bridgend replied **with** three tries in 14 minutes.*
reply /rɪˈplaɪ/ *noun* [C or U] an answer: *I asked why, but he **made/gave** no reply.* ○ *There were very few replies **to** our advertisement.* ○ ***In** reply **to** their questions, she just shrugged.*

reply-paid /rɪˌplaɪˈpeɪd/ *adj* [before n] *UK* A reply-paid envelope has had the cost of posting it already paid for, usually by the person it is addressed to.

report [TELL] /rɪˈpɔːt/ [US] /-ˈpɔːrt/ *verb* **1** [I or T] to give a description of something or information about it to someone: *We rang the insurance company to report the theft.* ○ *The assassination was reported in all the newspapers.* ○ *I want you to report **(to** me) **on** progress* (= on what you have done) *every Friday.* ○ [+ v-ing] *Spies reported **seeing** a build-up of soldiers.* ○ [+ obj + adj] *He was reported missing in action.* ○ *The inquiry reports* (= will officially make its results known) *next week.* **2 be reported to be/do *sth*** to be described by people as being or doing a particular thing although there is no real proof: *The storm is reported to have killed five people.* **3** [T] to make a complaint to a person in authority about something or someone: *My neighbours reported me **to** the police **for** firing my rifle in the garden.*
report /rɪˈpɔːt/ [US] /-ˈpɔːrt/ *noun* [C] **1** (*ALSO* **school report,** *US ALSO* **report card**) a teacher's written statement to the parents about a child's ability and performance at school **2** a description of an event or situation: *a news/weather report* ○ *a company's financial/annual report* ○ *I gave/made/submitted a report **of** the theft to the insurance company.* ○ *She sent in weekly reports **on** the situation.*
reports /rɪˈpɔːts/ [US] /-ˈpɔːrts/ *plural noun* stories for which you do not yet have real proof: *According to reports, ten pupils were expelled.* ○ *We're getting reports **of** a plane crash in Paris.*
reportage /ˌrep.ɔːˈtɑːʒ/ [US] /rɪˈpɔːr.t̬ɪdʒ/ *noun* [U] *FORMAL* the activity of, or style of, reporting events in newspapers or broadcasting them on television or radio
reported /rɪˈpɔː.tɪd/ [US] /-ˈpɔːr.t̬ɪd/ *adj*: *There has been a reported* (= unofficial news about a) *hijack in Tel Aviv this morning.*

R

reportedly /rɪˈpɔː.tɪd.li/ Ⓤ /-ˈpɔːr.tɪd-/ *adv*: *New York is reportedly* (= People say that New York is) *a very exciting place to live.*

reporter /rɪˈpɔː.tər/ Ⓤ /-ˈpɔːr.tər/ *noun* [C] a person whose job is to discover information about news events and describe them for a newspaper or magazine or for radio or television

report GO /rɪˈpɔːt/ Ⓤ /-ˈpɔːrt/ *verb* [I usually + adv or prep] to go to a place or a person and say that you are there: *I report for* (= am ready for and at) *work/duty at 8 a.m. every morning.*

report NOISE /rɪˈpɔːt/ Ⓤ /-ˈpɔːrt/ *noun* [C] FORMAL the loud noise of a shot: *We heard the loud/sharp report of a rifle.*

PHRASAL VERBS WITH **report**   ▼

▲ **report back** *phrasal verb* to bring information to someone in authority: *Find out their names and report back to me tomorrow.*

▲ **report to** *sb phrasal verb* Someone you report to at work is the person in authority over you who gives you tasks and checks that you do them: *You will report directly to the boss.*

re‚ported ‘speech *noun* [U] SPECIALIZED **indirect speech**

repose /rɪˈpəʊz/ Ⓤ /-ˈpoʊz/ *verb* [I usually + adv or prep] FORMAL to rest or lie: *She reposed on the sofa.*

repose /rɪˈpəʊz/ Ⓤ /-ˈpoʊz/ *noun* [U] FORMAL *Your face is so beautiful in repose* (= when resting).

repository /rɪˈpɒz.ɪ.t°r.i/ Ⓤ /-ˈpɑː.zɪ.tɔːr-/ *noun* **1** [C] FORMAL a place where things are stored and can be found **2** [C usually sing] a person who has, or a book that contains, a lot of information or detailed knowledge: *She's a repository of knowledge about our family history.*

repossess /ˌriː.pəˈzes/ *verb* [T] to take back possession of something, especially property that has not been completely paid for: *I couldn't make my mortgage repayments so the building society repossessed my house.*

repossession /ˌriː.pəˈzeʃ.°n/ *noun* [C or U] when someone repossesses something, or the thing that is repossessed: *house/mortgage repossessions*

reprehensible /ˌrep.rɪˈhent.sə.bl̩/ *adj* FORMAL If someone's behaviour is reprehensible, it is extremely bad or unacceptable: *reprehensible conduct/actions* **reprehensibly** /ˌrep.rɪˈhent.sɪ.bli/ *adv*

represent ACT FOR /ˌrep.rɪˈzent/ *verb* [T] **1** to speak, act or be present officially for another person or people: *They chose a famous barrister to represent them in court.* ○ *Union officials representing the teachers met the government today.* ○ *Women were well/poorly represented at the conference* (= there were many/few present). **2** to be the Member of Parliament, or of Congress, etc. for a particular area: *Mr Smythe represents Barnet.* **3** FORMAL to express or complain about something, to a person in authority: *We represented our grievances/demands to the boss.* **representation** /ˌrep.rɪ.zenˈteɪ.ʃ°n/ *noun* [U] *Can he afford legal representation?*

• **make representations/a representation to** *sb/sth* FORMAL to complain officially to a person or organization: *We made representations to the boss about the long working hours.*

representative /ˌrep.rɪˈzen.tə.tɪv/ Ⓤ /-tə.t̬ɪv/ *noun* [C] **1** someone who speaks or does something officially for another person or group of people: *The firm has two representatives in every European city.* **2** US someone who has been elected to the US House of Representatives **representative** /ˌrep.rɪˈzen.tə.tɪv/ Ⓤ /-tə.t̬ɪv/ *adj*: *a representative system of government*

represent DESCRIBE /ˌrep.rɪˈzent/ *verb* [T] **1** to show or describe something or someone: [+ v-*ing*] *The statue represents St George killing the dragon.* ○ *This new report represents the current situation in our schools.* ○ *He represents himself as an expert, but he knows nothing.* **2** to be a sign or symbol of something: *In this dictionary the word 'noun' is represented by the letter n.* ○ *To many people the Queen represents the former glory of Britain.* **representation** /ˌrep.rɪ.zenˈteɪ.ʃ°n/ *noun* [C or U] *This statue is a representation of Hercules.* ○ *He gave a talk on the representation of women in 19th-century art.*

representational /ˌrep.rɪ.zenˈteɪ.ʃ°n.°l/ *adj* showing things as they are normally seen: *representational art/pictures*

representative /ˌrep.rɪˈzen.tə.tɪv/ Ⓤ /-tə.t̬ɪv/ *adj* typical of, or the same as, others in a larger group of people or things: *Are your views/opinions representative of all the workers here?* ○ *a representative sample/cross-section/selection*

represent BE /ˌrep.rɪˈzent/ *verb* [L only + n] to be the result of something, or to be something: *This book represents ten years of thought and research.* ○ *The new offer represented an increase of 10% on the previous one.*

repress /rɪˈpres/ *verb* [T] **1** to not allow something, especially feelings, to be expressed: *He repressed a sudden desire to cry.* **2** to control what people do, especially by using force **repressed** /rɪˈprest/ *adj*: *repressed anger/sexuality* ○ *English people are notoriously repressed and don't talk about their feelings.*

repression /rɪˈpreʃ.°n/ *noun* [U] **1** when people are controlled severely, especially by force: *The political repression in this country is enforced by terror.* **2** the process and effect of keeping particular thoughts and desires out of your conscious mind in order to defend or protect it: *an attitude of unhealthy sexual repression*

repressive /rɪˈpres.ɪv/ *adj*: *a repressive* (= cruel) *military regime* ○ *sexually repressive* **repressiveness** /rɪˈpres.ɪv.nəs/ *noun* [U]

reprieve /rɪˈpriːv/ *noun* [C] **1** an official order that stops or delays the punishment, especially by death, of a prisoner: *He was sentenced to death but was granted a last-minute reprieve.* **2** an escape from a bad situation or experience: *The injection provided a temporary reprieve from the pain.*

reprieve /rɪˈpriːv/ *verb* [T] **1** to stop or delay the punishment, especially by death, of a prisoner **2** to provide something or someone with an escape from a bad situation or experience, especially to delay or stop plans to close or end something: *The threatened hospitals could now be reprieved.*

reprimand /ˈrep.rɪ.mɑːnd/ Ⓤ /-rə.mænd/ *verb* [T] FORMAL to express to someone your strong official disapproval of them: *She was reprimanded by her teacher for biting another girl.* **reprimand** /ˈrep.rɪ.mɑːnd/ Ⓤ /-rə.mænd/ *noun* [C] *His boss gave him a severe reprimand for being late.*

reprint /ˌriːˈprɪnt/ *verb* [I or T] to print a book again, or to be printed again: *The first edition sold out so we are reprinting it/it is reprinting.* **reprint** /ˈriː.prɪnt/ *noun* [C] when you reprint a book, or a book that has been reprinted

reprisal /rɪˈpraɪ.z°l/ *noun* [C or U] (an example of) activity against another person, especially as a punishment by military forces or a political group: *economic/military reprisals* ○ *They promised that individuals could live freely without fear of reprisal from the military.* ○ *The attack was in reprisal for the kidnapping of their leaders.*

reprise /rɪˈpriːz/ *noun* [C] SPECIALIZED a repeat of something or part of something, especially a piece of music

reproach /rɪˈprəʊtʃ/ Ⓤ /-ˈproʊtʃ/ *verb* [T] to criticize someone, especially for not being successful or not doing what is expected: *His mother reproached him for not eating all his dinner.* ○ [R] *You have nothing to reproach yourself for/with.* **reproach** /rɪˈprəʊtʃ/ Ⓤ /-ˈproʊtʃ/ *noun* [C or U] *The look of reproach on his face made her feel guilty.* ○ *Your reproaches are useless – what's done is done.*

• **be above/beyond reproach** to not deserve any blame: *Your behaviour today has been above reproach.*

• **be a reproach to** *sb/sth* to be something that should make a person or organization feel ashamed: *His immaculate garden was a reproach to all his less organized neighbours.*

reproachful /rɪˈprəʊtʃ.f°l/ Ⓤ /-ˈproʊtʃ-/ *adj* expressing reproach: *reproachful looks/words* **reproachfully** /rɪˈprəʊtʃ.f°l.i/ Ⓤ /-ˈproʊtʃ-/ *adv*: *He looked at me reproachfully.*

reprobate /ˈrep.rəʊ.beɪt/ Ⓤ /-rə-/ *noun* [C] FORMAL OR HUMOROUS a person of bad character and habits: *Every* *time I see you, you're drunk, you old reprobate.*

reprocess /ˌriːˈprəʊ.ses/ ⓤ /-ˈprɑː-/ *verb* [T] to put a material that has been used through another industrial process to change it so that it can be used again: *to reprocess nuclear waste* **reprocessing** /ˌriːˈprəʊ.ses.ɪŋ/ ⓤ /-ˈprɑː-/ *noun* [U] *waste/plutonium reprocessing* ○ *a reprocessing plant*

reproduce PRODUCE YOUNG /ˌriː.prəˈdjuːs/ ⓤ /-ˈduːs/ *verb* [I or T] When living things reproduce, they produce young: *These plants can reproduce sexually and asexually.* ○ [R] *Some creatures were better at surviving and reproducing themselves than others.*
reproduction /ˌriː.prəˈdʌk.ʃᵊn/ *noun* [U] the process of producing babies or young animals and plants: *human/ sexual reproduction* ○ *We are researching reproduction in elephants/the reproduction of elephants.* **reproductive** /ˌriː.prəˈdʌk.tɪv/ *adj*: *reproductive organs* ○ *reproductive behaviour*

reproduce COPY /ˌriː.prəˈdjuːs/ ⓤ /-ˈduːs/ *verb* **1** [I or T] to produce a copy of something, or to be copied in a production process: *His work was reproduced on posters, leaflets and magazines.* ○ *The said the printing was too faint to reproduce well.* **2** [T] to show or do something again: *The new design unfortunately reproduced some of the problems of the earlier model.*
reproduction /ˌriː.prəˈdʌk.ʃᵊn/ *noun* [C or U] a copy of something, especially a painting, or the process of copying something: *The book contains excellent colour reproductions of Monet's paintings.* ○ *This system has excellent sound reproduction.*

repro'duction 'furniture *noun* [U] copies of ANTIQUE furniture

reprove /rɪˈpruːv/ *verb* [T] FORMAL to tell someone that you disapprove of their wrong or foolish behaviour: *The teacher gently reproved the boys for not paying attention.* **reproving** /rɪˈpruː.vɪŋ/ *adj*: *She threw him an angry and reproving look/glance.* **reproof** /rɪˈpruːf/ *noun* [C or U] FORMAL *She got a sharp reproof for being late.* ○ *He picked up the broken vase without a word of reproof to his son.*

reptile /ˈrep.taɪl/ *noun* [C] an animal which produces eggs and uses the heat of the sun to keep its blood warm **reptilian** /repˈtɪl.i.ən/ *adj* **1** SPECIALIZED belonging to or like a reptile: *reptilian skin/eyes* **2** DISAPPROVING describes an unpleasantly strange and unfriendly person or type of behaviour: *He turned a cold, reptilian gaze on me.*

republic /rɪˈpʌb.lɪk/ *noun* [C] a country without a king or queen, usually governed by elected representatives of the people and a president: *the People's Republic of China*
republican /rɪˈpʌb.lɪ.kən/ *noun* [C] a supporter of government by elected representative of the people rather than government by a king
Republican /rɪˈpʌb.lɪ.kən/ *noun* [C] **1** a member of the REPUBLICAN PARTY in the US **2** a person who believes that Northern Ireland should become part of the Irish Republic
republican /rɪˈpʌb.lɪ.kən/ *adj* relating to a republic: *a republican system of government* **republicanism** /rɪˈpʌb.lɪ.kə.nɪ.zᵊm/ *noun* [U]

the Re'publican ,Party *group noun* [S] one of the two largest political parties in the USA

repudiate /rɪˈpjuː.di.eɪt/ *verb* [T] FORMAL to refuse to accept something or someone as true, good or reasonable: *He repudiated the allegation/charge/claim that he had tried to deceive them.* ○ *I utterly repudiate those remarks.* **repudiation** /rɪˌpjuː.diˈeɪ.ʃᵊn/ *noun* [U] *They were surprised by his sudden repudiation of all his former beliefs.*

repugnant /rɪˈpʌg.nənt/ *adj* FORMAL If behaviour or beliefs, etc. are repugnant, they are very unpleasant, causing a feeling of disgust: *a repugnant smell* ○ *I find your attitude towards these women quite repugnant.* ○ *The idea of cheating in an exam is morally repugnant to me.* **repugnance** /rɪˈpʌg.nənts/ *noun* [U] *The thought of eating meat fills me with repugnance.*

repulse PUSH AWAY /rɪˈpʌls/ *verb* [T] FORMAL to push away or refuse something or someone unwanted, especially to

successfully stop a physical attack against you: *The enemy attack was quickly repulsed.*
repulse /rɪˈpʌls/ *noun* [S or U] FORMAL OR OLD-FASHIONED when someone or something is repulsed
repulsion /rɪˈpʌl.ʃᵊn/ *noun* [U] SPECIALIZED the force in physics that pushes two objects apart: *magnetic repulsion*

repulse DISLIKE /rɪˈpʌls/ *verb* [T often passive] FORMAL If something repulses you, it causes you to have a strong feeling of dislike, disapproval or disgust: *The tourists were repulsed by the filthy conditions.*
repulsion /rɪˈpʌl.ʃᵊn/ *noun* [U] strong dislike or disgust: *to feel repulsion* ○ *A look of repulsion flashed across her face.*
repulsive /rɪˈpʌl.sɪv/ *adj* extremely unpleasant or unacceptable: *What a repulsive old man!* ○ *I think rats and snakes are repulsive.*

repurpose /ˌriːˈpɜː.pəs/ ⓤ /-ˈpɜː-/ *verb* [I or T] to find a new use for an idea, product or building: *The company's role is to repurpose print data for use on the Web.* ○ *Movie theaters are harder to repurpose than ordinary stores in a shopping mall.*

reputation /ˌrep.jʊˈteɪ.ʃᵊn/ *noun* [C usually sing; U] the opinion that people in general have about someone or something, or how much respect or admiration someone or something receives, based on past behaviour or character: *The company has a worldwide reputation for quality.* ○ *She has the reputation of being a good doctor.* ○ *His reputation was destroyed when he was caught stealing some money.* ○ *The hotel has a bad/good reputation.* ○ *He earned/established/gained/acquired a reputation as an entertaining speaker.*
● **by reputation** indirectly, by hearing what other people say: *The two men know each other only by reputation.*
reputable /ˈrep.jʊ.tə.bl̩/ *adj* having a good reputation and able to be trusted: *I insured my property with an established, reputable company.* * NOTE: The opposite is **disreputable**. **reputably** /ˈrep.jʊ.tə.bli/ ⓤ /-tə-/ *adv*
repute /rɪˈpjuːt/ *noun* FORMAL **ill/good, etc. repute** when someone or something has a bad/good, etc. reputation: *a place of ill repute*
● **hold sb in high/low repute** to respect someone greatly/ very little: *My father was held in high repute by his colleagues.*
reputed /rɪˈpjuː.tɪd/ ⓤ /-tɪd/ *adj* said to be the true situation although this is not known to be certain and may not be likely: *She is reputed to be 25 years younger than her husband.* ○ *They employed him because of his reputed skill in dealing with the press.*
reputedly /rɪˈpjuː.tɪd.li/ ⓤ /-tɪd/ *adv*: *He's reputedly (= is said to be) the strongest man in Britain.*

request /rɪˈkwest/ *noun* **1** [C or U] when you politely or officially ask for something: *They received hundreds of requests for more information.* ○ [+ to infinitive] *The boss refused our request to leave work early.* ○ *The clause was added to the contract at Carlos's request (= because Carlos asked for this).* ○ *An application form will be sent to you on request (= if you ask).* ⊃See Note **require or request?** at **require.** Compare **order** INSTRUCTION. **2** [C] a song or similar item which someone has asked to be included in a show or on the radio: *The next song is a request from/for Roz in Totteridge.* **request** /rɪˈkwest/ *verb* [T] FORMAL [+ that] *We requested that the next meeting be held on a Friday.* ○ [+ obj + to infinitive] *Visitors are requested not to walk on the grass.* ○ *I requested a taxi for 8 o'clock.*

requiem (mass) /ˌrek.wi.əmˈmæs/ *noun* [C] **1** a MASS (= Christian religious ceremony) at which people honour and pray for a dead person **2** a piece of music written for this ceremony: *Mozart's/Verdi's Requiem*

require /rɪˈkwaɪəʳ/ ⓤ /-ˈkwaɪr/ *verb* [T] to need or make necessary: *Please telephone this number if you require any further information.* ○ *Skiing at 80 miles per hour requires total concentration.* ○ [+ obj + to infinitive] *Bringing up children often requires you to put their needs first.* ○ *You are required by law to stop your car after an accident.* ○ [+ that] *The rules require that you bring only one guest to the dinner.* **requirement** /rɪˈkwaɪə.mənt/ ⓤ /-ˈkwaɪr-/ *noun* [C] *A good degree is a minimum require-*

ment ***for*** *many jobs.* ○ [+ that] *It is a legal requirement* ***that*** *you have insurance for your car.* ○ *Students who fail to* ***meet*** *the requirements (****of*** *the course) will fail.*

COMMON LEARNER ERROR

require or **request?**

The main meaning of **require** is 'need'.

Learning a language requires time and effort.

Request means 'ask for'.

I wrote a letter to request more information.

~~*I wrote a letter to require more information.*~~

requisite /ˈrek.wɪ.zɪt/ *adj* [before n] *FORMAL* necessary; needed for a particular purpose: *He lacked the requisite skills for the job.* ○ *The requisite* ***number*** *of countries have now ratified the convention.*
requisite /ˈrek.wɪ.zɪt/ *noun* [C usually pl] *FORMAL* an important necessary item: *A good book is a requisite* ***for*** *long journeys.* ○ *Self-esteem, self-judgment and self-will are said to be the three requisites* ***of*** *independence.*

requisition /ˌrek.wɪˈzɪʃ.ᵊn/ *verb* [T] to officially request or take: *The army requisitioned all the cars and trucks they could find.*
requisition /ˌrek.wɪˈzɪʃ.ᵊn/ *noun* [C or U] *The staff* ***made a*** *requisition* ***for*** (= sent a written request for) *new chairs and desks.*

requite /rɪˈkwaɪt/ *verb* [T] *FORMAL* to give or do something in return for something given to you or done for you: *Requited* ***love*** *is not enough to sustain a long-term relationship.*

reroute /ˌriːˈruːt/ [US] /-ˈraʊt/ *verb* [T] to change the route of something: *The plan entails rerouting traffic through a tunnel to create a vast pedestrian area around Al-Azhar.*

rerun /ˌriːˈrʌn/ *verb* [T] **rerunning, reran, rerun** to show a television programme, film, etc. again: *The James Bond films are always being rerun on television.*
rerun /ˈriː.rʌn/ *noun* **1** [C] a programme or film that has already been shown before on television: *This week's films are all reruns.* **2** [C usually sing] something that happens or is done again: *The Muslim RDR is demanding a rerun* ***of*** *last week's presidential poll.*

resat /ˌriːˈsæt/ *past simple and past participle of* **resit**

reschedule /ˌriːˈʃed.juːl/ [US] /-ˈskedʒ.uːl/ *verb* [T] **1** to agree a new and later date for something to happen: *I rescheduled my doctor's appointment* ***for*** *later in the week.* **2** *SPECIALIZED* to agree that money owed can be paid back at a later date: *Banks have rescheduled the* ***debts*** *of many Third-World countries .*

rescind /rɪˈsɪnd/ *verb* [T] *FORMAL* to make a law, agreement, order or decision no longer have any (legal) power: *The policy of charging air travellers for vegetarian meals proved unpopular and has already been rescinded.*

rescue /ˈres.kjuː/ *verb* [T] to help someone or something out of a dangerous, harmful or unpleasant situation: *The lifeboat rescued the sailors* ***from*** *the sinking boat.* ○ *The government has refused to rescue the company* ***from*** *bankruptcy.*
rescue /ˈres.kjuː/ *noun* [C or U] *Lifeboats carry out many rescues every month.* ○ *We huddled together on the cliff ledge, waiting for rescue.* ○ *I didn't know anybody at the party, but the hostess* ***came to*** *my rescue* (= helped me out of a difficult situation) *by introducing me to a few people.* **rescuer** /ˈres.kjuː.əʳ/ [US] /-ɚ/ *noun* [C] *Two of the rescuers died in a second earthquake.*

ˈRescue ˌRemedy *noun* [U] *TRADEMARK* an oil made from flowers which you can drink or rub onto your skin to help you relax when you feel anxious

research /rɪˈsɜːtʃ/ /ˈriː.sɜːtʃ/ [US] /ˈriː.sɝːtʃ/ *noun* [U] a detailed study of a subject, especially in order to discover (new) information or reach a (new) understanding: *scientific/medical research* ○ *a research student/assistant/laboratory* ○ *They are* ***carrying out/conducting/doing*** *some fascinating research* ***into/on*** *the language of dolphins.* **research** /rɪˈsɜːtʃ/ [US] /-ˈsɝːtʃ/ *verb* [I or T] *She's researching* ***into*** *possible cures for AIDS.* ○ *Journalists were frantically researching the new Prime Minister's background, family and interests.*
researcher /rɪˈsɜː.tʃəʳ/ [US] /-ˈsɝː.tʃɚ/ *noun* [C] *a television/political researcher*
researches /rɪˈsɜː.tʃɪz/ /ˈriː.sɜː-/ [US] /ˈriː.sɜːr-/ *plural noun*: *His researches* (= research) *in the field of disease prevention produced unexpected results.*

reˌsearch and deˈvelopment *noun* [U] (*ABBREVIATION* **R and D**) the part of a business that tries to find ways to improve existing products, and to develop new ones: *All our profits are re-invested in research and development.*

resell /ˌriːˈsel/ *verb* [T] to sell something which you previously bought: *He buys up run-down properties, fixes them up and resells them.*

resemble /rɪˈzem.bl̩/ *verb* [T] to look like or be like someone or something: *You resemble your mother very closely.* ○ *After the earthquake, the city resembled a battlefield.*
resemblance /rɪˈzem.blənts/ *noun* [C or U] *There was a clear* ***family*** *resemblance* ***between*** *all the brothers.* ○ *These prices* ***bear*** *no resemblance* ***to*** (= are completely different from) *the ones I saw printed in the newspaper.*

resent /rɪˈzent/ *verb* [T] to be angry about and to dislike being forced to accept something or someone annoying: *She bitterly resented her father's new wife.* ○ [+ v-ing] *He resents having to explain his work to other people.*
resentful /rɪˈzent.fᵊl/ *adj*: *a resentful look* ○ *She was resentful* ***of*** *anybody's attempts to interfere in her work.*
resentfully /rɪˈzent.fᵊl.i/ *adv* **resentfulness** /rɪˈzent.fᵊl.nəs/ *noun* [U] **resentment** /rɪˈzent.mənt/ *noun* [C or U] *He feels/harbours (a) deep resentment* ***against/towards*** *his parents for his miserable childhood.*

reservation /ˌrez.əˈveɪ.ʃᵊn/ [US] /-ɚ-/ *noun* [C usually pl; U] a doubt or feeling of not being able to agree with or accept something completely: *Workers and employees shared deep reservations* ***about*** *the wisdom of the government's plans for the industry.* ○ *He accepted my advice* ***without*** *reservation.* ➲See also **reservation** at **reserve** KEEP SEPARATE.
reserve /rɪˈzɜːv/ [US] /-ˈzɝːv/ *noun* [U] *FORMAL* when you have reservations about someone or something: *I can recommend him to you* ***without*** *reserve.* ➲See also **reserve** KEEP SEPARATE; **reserve** BEHAVIOUR.

reserve [KEEP SEPARATE] /rɪˈzɜːv/ [US] /-ˈzɝːv/ *verb* [T] **1** to keep something for a particular purpose or time: *I reserve Mondays* ***for*** *tidying my desk and answering letters.* ○ *These seats are reserved* ***for*** *the elderly and women with babies.* ○ *I reserve* ***judgment*** *on this issue* (= I won't give an opinion on it now) *until we have more information.* **2** If you reserve something such as a seat on an aircraft or a table at a restaurant, you arrange for it to be kept for your use: *I reserved a double room at the Lamb Hotel.* ○ [+ two objects] *If you get there early, reserve me a seat/reserve a seat* ***for*** *me.*
reservation /ˌrez.əˈveɪ.ʃᵊn/ [US] /-ɚ-/ *noun* **1** [C or U] when you arrange to have something such as a seat on an aircraft or a table at a restaurant kept for you: *I'd like to* ***make*** *a table reservation* ***for*** *two people* ***for*** *9 o'clock.* ○ *Please* ***confirm*** *your reservation in writing by Friday.* ➲See also **reservation**. **2** [C] an area of land made available for a particular group of people to live in: *The family lives* ***on*** *a Native American reservation.* **3** [C] (*ALSO* **reserve,** *US ALSO* **preserve**) an area of land in which wild animals are protected: *He's the chief warden of a big-game reservation.*
reserve /rɪˈzɜːv/ [US] /-ˈzɝːv/ *noun* **1** [C or U] when you keep something or a supply of something until it is needed, or a supply that you keep: *She keeps a little money* ***in*** *reserve* (= for use if and when needed). ○ *The librarian has put the book* ***on*** *reserve* ***for*** *me* (= will keep it for me when it becomes available). ○ *We still have a reserve of food/food reserves in case of emergency.* **2** [C] (*ALSO* **reservation,** *US ALSO* **preserve**) an area of land kept in its natural state, especially for wild animals to live in to be protected: *a nature/game/wildlife reserve* **3** [C] in sports, an extra player who is ready to play if needed: *We had two reserves in case anyone was injured.*
the reserves *plural noun* a group of people who are not permanently in the armed forces but are used only if needed: *They will call up the reserves.* **reserved** /rɪ-

R

ˈzɜːvd/ [US] /-ˈzɝːvd/ *adj*: *May I sit here, or is this seat/table reserved?*
reservist /rɪˈzɜː.vɪst/ [US] /-ˈzɝː-/ *noun* **[C]** a person who is trained as a soldier and is ready to fight in the army if needed

reserve [BEHAVIOUR] /rɪˈzɜːv/ [US] /-ˈzɝːv/ *noun* **[U]** the habit of not showing your feelings or thoughts: *I took her out for a drink and tried to break through her reserve.* **reserved** /rɪˈzɜːvd/ [US] /-ˈzɝːvd/ *adj*: *a quiet, reserved woman* ○ *The English have a reputation for being reserved.*

reˈserve (ˌprice) *noun* **[C usually sing]** the lowest amount of money the owners will accept for something being sold, especially at auction: *A rare Stradivarius violin failed to reach* (= no one offered to pay) *its reserve price when put up for auction on Tuesday.* ○ *We set/put a reserve **of** £50 **on** the picture.*

reservoir /ˈrez.ə.vwɑːʳ/ [US] /-ɚ.vwɑːr/ *noun* **[C]** **1** a place for storing liquid, especially a natural or artificial lake providing water for a city or other area **2** a large supply of something: *The universities constitute a reservoir **of** expert knowledge.*

resettle /ˌriːˈset.l̩/ [US] /-ˈset̬-/ *verb* **[I or T]** to (be helped or forced to) move to another place to live: *His family originally came from Ireland, but resettled **in** the US in the 19th century.* ○ *The US government forcibly resettled the Native Americans **in** reservations.* **resettlement** /ˌriːˈset.l̩.mənt/ [US] /-ˈset̬-/ *noun* **[U]** *the resettlement of refugees*

reshape /ˌriːˈʃeɪp/ *verb* **[T]** to shape something again or differently

reshuffle /ˈriːˌʃʌf.l̩/ *noun* **[C]** when the positions of people or things within a particular group are changed: *They expect a Cabinet reshuffle in the summer.* ○ *a government/management reshuffle* **reshuffle** /ˌriːˈʃʌf.l̩/ *verb* **[T]** *to reshuffle the deck/cards* ○ *The prime minister is expected to reshuffle his ministerial team next month.*

reside /rɪˈzaɪd/ *verb* **[I usually + adv or prep]** FORMAL to live, have your home or stay in a place: *The family now resides in southern France.*
residence /ˈrez.ɪ.dᵊnts/ *noun* **[C]** FORMAL a home: *the Governor's official residence*
• **in residence** FORMAL **1** officially staying or living somewhere: *The Queen is in residence at the Palace this week.* **2 author/poet/artist in residence** an author, poet or artist who is employed at a school or college, etc. for a short period
• **take up residence/residency *somewhere*** FORMAL to go to live somewhere: *She took up residence **in** Canada.* ○ *She took up permanent residency abroad.*
residency /ˈrez.ɪ.dᵊnt.si/ *noun* **[U]** FORMAL the fact of living in a place: *There is a residency requirement for obtaining citizenship.*
residential /ˌrez.ɪˈden.tʃᵊl/ *adj* **1** A residential road, area, etc. has only private houses, not offices and factories. **2** A residential job, position, course, etc. is one for which you live at the same place where you work or study. **3** relating to where you live or have lived: *You must satisfy the residential qualifications to get a work permit.*
▲ **reside in *sth/sb*** *phrasal verb* FORMAL If a power or quality resides in someone or something, they have that power or quality: *The power to sack employees resides in the Board of Directors.*

resident [PLACE] /ˈrez.ɪ.dᵊnt/ *noun* **[C]** a person who lives or has their home in a place: *a resident of the UK/Australia* ○ *The local residents were angry at the lack of parking spaces.* ○ *The hotel bar was only open to residents* (= to people staying at the hotel).
resident /ˈrez.ɪ.dᵊnt/ *adj* **1** living or staying in a place: *She's resident abroad/**in** Moscow.* **2** **[before n]** describes someone who has a special skill or quality in a group or organization: *She is the university's resident expert on Italian literature.* ○ HUMOROUS *Tony is the company's resident clown.*

resident [MEDICAL] /ˈrez.ɪ.dᵊnt/ *noun* **[C]** US a doctor who is still training, and who works in a hospital: *She's a first-year resident in oncology at Boston General Hospital.* ➲See also **houseman**.

residue /ˈrez.ɪ.djuː/ [US] /-ə.duː/ *noun* **[C usually sing]** **1** FORMAL the part that is left after the main part has gone or been taken away, or a substance that remains after a chemical process such as EVAPORATION: *She cut off the best meat and threw away the residue.* ○ *The white residue **in/on** the kettle is a result of minerals in the water.* **2** LEGAL the part of a dead person's money and property that is left after taxes, debts, etc. have been paid: *The residue (**of** the estate) went to her granddaughter.*
residual /rɪˈzɪd.ju.əl/ [US] /-ˈzɪdʒ-/ *adj* remaining after most of something has gone: *I still felt some residual bitterness ten years after my divorce.*

resign /rɪˈzaɪn/ *verb* **[I or T]** to give up a job or position by telling your employer that you are leaving: *He resigned **from** the company in order to take a more challenging job.* ○ *She resigned **as** director.* ○ *She resigned the directorship.* **resignation** /ˌrez.ɪɡˈneɪ.ʃᵊn/ *noun* **[C or U]** *There have been calls for his resignation.* ○ *I **handed in/gave in/sent in** my resignation this morning.*
▲ **resign *yourself* to *sth*** *verb* **[R]** to make yourself accept something that you do not like because you cannot change it: **[+ v-ing]** *He resigned himself to living alone.*
• **be resigned to *sth*** If you are resigned to something unpleasant, you calmly accept that it will happen: *She seems resigned to losing the race.*

resignation /ˌrez.ɪɡˈneɪ.ʃᵊn/ *noun* **[U]** when you accept something that you do not like because you cannot easily change it: *They received the news **with** resignation.* ➲See also **resignation** at **resign**. **resigned** /rɪˈzaɪnd/ *adj*: *a resigned look/expression/tone* **resignedly** /rɪˈzaɪn.ɪd.li/ *adv*: *"We're going to be late again," he said resignedly.*

resilient /rɪˈzɪl.i.ənt/ *adj* able to quickly return to a previous good condition: *This rubber ball is very resilient and immediately springs back into shape.* ○ *She's a resilient girl – she won't be unhappy for long.* **resilience** /rɪˈzɪl.i.ənts/ *noun* **[U]** (FORMAL **resiliency**)

resin /ˈrez.ɪn/ *noun* **[U]** a thick sticky substance that is produced by some trees and that becomes yellow and hard after it is collected, or any of various similar substances produced chemically for use in industry: *pine resin* **resinous** /ˈrez.ɪ.nəs/ *adj*

resist /rɪˈzɪst/ *verb* **1** **[I or T]** to fight against something or someone that is attacking you: *The soldiers resisted (the enemy attacks) for two days.* **2** **[T]** to refuse to accept or be changed by something: *The party leader resisted demands for his resignation.* ○ *He tried to run away from the police and was charged with resisting **arrest**.* ○ *The new hybrid crops are much better at resisting disease.* **3** **[T]** to stop yourself from doing something that you want to do: *I can never resist temptation/chocolate/the urge to laugh.* ○ **[+ v-ing]** *She couldn't resist laughing at him in those clothes.*
resistance /rɪˈzɪs.tᵊnts/ *noun* **1** **[U]** when something or someone resists: *resistance **to** disease* ○ *Government troops offered no resistance (**to** the rebels).* ○ *There's a lot of resistance* (= opposition) ***to** the idea of a united Europe.* **2** **[U]** a force which acts to stop the progress of something or make it slower: *The car's speed was reduced by **air/wind** resistance.* **3** **[C or U]** SPECIALIZED the degree to which a substance prevents the flow of an electric current through it: *Copper has (a) low resistance.* **4 the Resistance** an organization that secretly fights against an enemy that has taken control of its country
• **the path of least resistance** (UK USUALLY **the line of least resistance**) the easiest way to continue: *I **took** the path of least resistance and agreed with the others.*
resistant /rɪˈzɪs.tᵊnt/ *adj* **1** not wanting to accept something, especially changes or new ideas: *Why are you so resistant **to** change?* **2** not harmed or affected by something: *a stain-resistant carpet* ○ *a disease-resistant variety of tomato*
resistor /rɪˈzɪs.təʳ/ [US] /-tɚ/ *noun* **[C]** SPECIALIZED a part of an electrical circuit designed to produce a particular amount of resistance to the flow of current

resit /ˌriːˈsɪt/ *verb* **[T]** **resitting, resat, resat** MAINLY UK to take an exam again: *If you fail these exams, you can resit them next year.* **resit** /ˈriː.sɪt/ *noun* **[C]** *She's got to do resits **in** French and German.*

resolute /ˈrez.ə.luːt/ *adj* FORMAL determined in character, action or ideas: *Their resolute opposition to new working methods was difficult to overcome.* ○ *She's utterly resolute in her refusal to apologise.* **resolutely** /ˈrez.ə.luːt.li/ *adv*: *She resolutely refused to learn about computers.*

resolution /ˌrez.əˈluː.ʃən/ *noun* [U] (ALSO **resoluteness**) FORMAL APPROVING determination: *He showed great resolution in facing the robbers.*

resolution /ˌrez.əˈluː.ʃən/ *noun* [U] SPECIALIZED **1** when something separates or is separated into clearly different parts: *the resolution of oil into bitumen and tar* **2** the ability of a microscope, or a television or computer screen, to show things clearly and with a lot of detail: *a high/low resolution image* ⸺See also **resolution** at **resolve** SOLVE and **resolve** DECIDE.

resolve SOLVE /rɪˈzɒlv/ ⓤ /-ˈzɑːlv/ *verb* [T] to solve or end a problem or difficulty: *Have you resolved the problem of transport yet?* ○ *The couple resolved their differences and made an effort to get along.* **resolution** /ˌrez.əˈluː.ʃən/ *noun* [S or U] FORMAL *a successful resolution to the crisis*

resolve DECIDE /rɪˈzɒlv/ ⓤ /-ˈzɑːlv/ *verb* [I] FORMAL to make a decision formally or with determination: [+ that] *She resolved that she would never speak to him again.* ○ [+ adv or prep] *After hours of argument, they resolved against taking legal action.* ○ [+ to infinitive] *The company resolved to take no further action against the thieves.* ⸺See also **resolute**.

resolve /rɪˈzɒlv/ ⓤ /-ˈzɑːlv/ *noun* [U] FORMAL strong determination: *to weaken/strengthen/test someone's resolve*

resolved /rɪˈzɒlvd/ ⓤ /-ˈzɑːlvd/ *adj* [after v] FORMAL determined: [+ to infinitive] *He was resolved to ask her to marry him the next day.*

resolution /ˌrez.əˈluː.ʃən/ *noun* [C] **1** an official decision that is made after a group or organization have voted: *to approve/adopt a resolution* ○ [+ to infinitive] *The United Nations passed* (= voted to support) *a resolution to increase aid to the Third World.* **2** a promise to yourself to do or to not do something: [+ to infinitive] *I made a resolution to give up chocolate.*

▲ **resolve** *sth* **into** *sth phrasal verb* SPECIALIZED to separate something into different and definite parts: [R] *There was a blur of sound, which slowly resolved itself into different words.*

resonate /ˈrez.ᵊn.eɪt/ *verb* [I] **1** to produce, increase or fill with sound, by VIBRATING (= shaking) objects which are near: *His voice resonated in the empty church.* ○ *The noise of the bell resonated through the building.* ⸺Compare **resound**. **2** to be filled with a particular quality: *The building resonates with historic significance.* **3** to continue to have a powerful effect or value: *The significance of those great stories resonates down the centuries.* **4** If an experience or memory resonates, it makes you think of another similar one: *Her experiences resonate powerfully with me, living, as I do, in a similar family situation.*

resonance /ˈrez.ᵊn.ənts/ *noun* [C or U] *magnetic resonance* ○ *This poem has many resonances* (= connected thoughts and memories) *for me.*

resonant /ˈrez.ᵊn.ənt/ *adj* **1** clear and loud, or causing sounds to be clear and loud: *a deep, resonant voice* ○ *a resonant concert hall* ⸺See also **resound**. **2** making you think of a similar experience or memory: *We felt privileged to be the first group of Western visitors to enter the historic palace, resonant with past conflicts.*

resonator /ˈrez.ᵊn.eɪ.təʳ/ ⓤ /-t̬ɚ/ *noun* [C] SPECIALIZED a device, for example in a musical instrument, which makes sounds resonate

resort PLACE /rɪˈzɔːt/ ⓤ /-ˈzɔːrt/ *noun* [C] a place where many people go for rest, sport or another stated purpose: *a tourist resort* ○ *a (UK) holiday/(US) vacation resort* ○ *a seaside/beach resort* ○ *a ski resort* ⸺See also **resort to**.

resort ACTION /rɪˈzɔːt/ ⓤ /-ˈzɔːrt/ *noun* [U] when you have to do something because there is no other way of achieving something: *He got hold of the money legally, without resort to violence.*

• **be your last resort** to be the only person or thing that might be able to help you, when every other person or possibility has failed: *You have to help me – you're my last resort.*

resort /rɪˈzɔːt/ ⓤ /-ˈzɔːrt/ *verb*

▲ **resort to** *sth phrasal verb* to do something that you do not want to do because you cannot find any other way of achieving something: *I had to resort to violence/threats to get my money.* ○ [+ v-ing] *When she didn't answer the telephone, I resorted to standing outside her window and calling up to her.*

resound /rɪˈzaʊnd/ *verb* [I] to sound loudly or for a long time, or (of a place) to be filled with sound: *The noise of the fire alarm resounded through/throughout the building.* ○ *The concert hall resounded with cheers and applause.* ⸺See also **resonate**.

resounding /rɪˈzaʊn.dɪŋ/ *adj* [before n] **1** loud: *Supporters gave the team three resounding cheers.* **2** very great: *The plan was a resounding success/failure.* **resoundingly** /rɪˈzaʊn.dɪŋ.li/ *adv*

resource /rɪˈzɔːs/ /ˈriː.sɔːs/ ⓤ /ˈriː.sɔːrs/ *noun* [C usually pl] **1** a useful or valuable possession or quality of a country, organization or person: *The country's greatest resource is the dedication of its workers.* ○ *Britain's mineral resources include oil, coal and gas deposits.* **2** FORMAL FOR **resourcefulness**

• **have inner resources** to have the ability to help yourself manage or achieve something: *He can't cope with difficult situations on his own – he has no inner resources.*

resource /rɪˈzɔːs/ /ˈriː.sɔːs/ ⓤ /ˈriː.sɔːrs/ *verb* [T] to provide an organization or department with money or equipment: *The school must be properly resourced with musical instruments and audio equipment.* **resourced** /rɪˈzɔːst/ /ˈriː.sɔːst/ ⓤ /ˈriː.sɔːrst/ *adj*: *It is widely acknowledged that the welfare system is under-resourced.*

resourceful /rɪˈzɔː.sfᵊl/ ⓤ /-ˈsɔːr-/ *adj* APPROVING skilled at solving problems and making decisions on your own: *She's a very resourceful manager.* **resourcefully** /rɪˈzɔː.sfᵊl.i/ ⓤ /-ˈsɔːr-/ *adv*

resourcefulness /rɪˈzɔː.sfᵊl.nəs/ ⓤ /-ˈsɔːr-/ *noun* [U] (FORMAL **resource**) APPROVING the ability to make decisions and act on your own: *This film reveals their resourcefulness in overcoming appalling weather and treacherous terrain.*

respect ADMIRATION /rɪˈspekt/ *noun* [U] admiration felt or shown for someone or something that you believe has good ideas or qualities: *I have great/the greatest respect for his ideas, although I don't agree with them.* ○ *She is a formidable figure who commands a great deal of respect* (= who is greatly admired by others). ○ *New teachers have to earn/gain the respect of their students.* ⸺See also **self-respect**.

respect /rɪˈspekt/ *verb* [T] to feel or show admiration for someone or something that you believe has good ideas or qualities: *I deeply respect David for what he has achieved.*

respect yourself *verb* [R] to have pride in your own qualities or achievements

respected /rɪˈspek.tɪd/ *adj* admired by many people for your qualities or achievements: *a highly respected politician/doctor* ○ *the country's most respected daily newspaper* ○ *He is very well respected in the business world.*

respectful /rɪˈspekt.fᵊl/ *adj* showing admiration for someone or something: *"We're so pleased to meet you at last," he said in a respectful tone of voice.* ✳ NOTE: The opposite is **disrespectful**. **respectfully** /rɪˈspekt.fᵊl.i/ *adv*: *The audience clapped respectfully as she stood up to speak.*

respect HONOUR /rɪˈspekt/ *noun* [U] **1** politeness, honour and care shown towards someone or something that is considered important: *You really should treat your parents with more respect.* ○ *She has no respect for other people's property* (= She does not treat it carefully). **2** when you accept that something which is established or formally agreed is right or important and do not attempt to change it or harm it: *In their senseless killing of innocent people, the terrorists have shown their lack of respect for human life.* ○ *She grumbled that young people today have/show no respect for the law.* **3** when you accept that different customs or cultures are different from your own and behave towards them in a way which would not cause offence: *She teaches the students to* ***have*** *respect* ***for*** *different races and appreciate the diversity of other cultures.*

• **with (all due) respect** (*ALSO* **with (the greatest) respect**) used to express polite disagreement in a formal situation: *With all due respect, Minister, I cannot agree with your last statement.*

respect /rɪˈspekt/ *verb* [T] **1** to treat something or someone with kindness and care: *to respect someone's feelings* ○ *We should respect the environment and not pollute it.* **2** to accept the importance of someone's rights or customs and to do nothing that would harm them or cause them offence: *The agreement will respect the rights of both nations.* ○ *I would appreciate it if you would respect my* ***privacy***. **3** to accept that something which is established or formally agreed is right or important and not to attempt to change it or harm it: *The president pledged to respect the existing frontiers between the two countries.* **4** to think that it is important to obey a law or rule: *I was always taught to respect the law.*

• **respect** ***sb's*** **wishes** to do what someone has asked to have done: *His children respected his* ***last*** *wishes and held a simple funeral for him.*

respecter /rɪˈspek.təʳ/ [US] /-tɚ/ *noun* [C] *He is a great respecter* ***of*** *tradition* (= He thinks tradition is very important). ○ *Air pollution is* ***no*** *respecter* ***of*** *national frontiers* (= It is a problem in every country).

respectful /rɪˈspekt.fəl/ *adj* **1** showing politeness or honour to someone or something: *There was a respectful two-minute silence as we remembered the soldiers who had died in the war.* **2 be respectful of** ***sth*** to accept that something is important and not to try to change it or cause offence: *He taught his children to be respectful of other cultures.*

respectfully /rɪˈspekt.fəl.i/ *adv*: *When she was asked if she had any ambition to become prime minister, she respectfully* (= politely) *declined to answer the question.* ○ *As the body was carried through the crowd, people drew back respectfully* (= to show their respect).

• **Respectfully yours** a very formal and polite way of ending a letter

respects /rɪˈspekts/ *plural noun FORMAL* ***sb's*** **respects** polite formal greetings: *Please* ***convey/give*** *my respects* ***to*** *your parents.*

• **pay** ***your*** **respects** *FORMAL* **1** to visit someone in order to welcome them or talk to them: *We went to pay our respects* ***to*** *our new neighbours.* **2** (*ALSO* **pay** ***your*** **last respects**) to honour someone after their death, usually by going to their funeral: *Friends and relatives came to pay their last respects* ***to*** *Mr Clarke.*

respect [FEATURE] /rɪˈspekt/ *noun* [C] a particular feature or detail: *This proposal differs from the last one* ***in*** *many important respects/one important respect.* ○ ***In most*** *respects, the new film is better than the original.*

• **in respect of** ***sth*** (*ALSO* **with respect to** ***sth***) *FORMAL* in connection with something: *I am writing with respect to your letter of 15 June.*

respectable /rɪˈspek.tə.bl̩/ *adj* **1** considered to be socially acceptable because of your good character, appearance or behaviour: *a respectable young woman from a good family* ○ *This part of the city has become quite respectable in the last ten years.* ○ *I wore my boring, respectable suit to the interview.* **2** describes an amount or quality that it is large enough or of a good enough standard to be acceptable: *She earns a respectable salary.* ○ *The final score was a respectable 2:1.*

• **make** ***yourself*** **respectable** *HUMOROUS* to put on clothes so that you are in a suitable state to meet someone: *Could you wait for a few minutes while I make myself respectable?*

respectably /rɪˈspek.tə.bli/ *adv* **1** in a respectable way **2** in a way which achieves a reasonable result: *The car performs respectably on the motorway, although it is slightly noisy.* ○ *It is a small-budget film, but it has done respectably at the box office.* **respectability** /rɪˌspek.təˈbɪl.ɪ.ti/ [US] /-ə.t̬i/ *noun* [U] *an attempt to* ***gain*** *international respectability* ○ *The company operates out of modern offices and expensive hotel suites to create an air of respectability.*

respective /rɪˈspek.tɪv/ *adj* [before n] relating or belonging to each of the individual people or things you have just mentioned: *Everyone would go into the hall for assembly and then afterwards we'd go to our respective classes.* ○ *Clinton and Zedillo ordered their respective Cabinets to devise a common counter-drug strategy.*

respectively /rɪˈspek.tɪv.li/ *adv*: *In the 200 metres, Lizzy and Sarah came first and third respectively* (= Lizzy won the race and Sarah was third).

respiration /ˌres.pɪˈreɪ.ʃən/ *noun* [U] *FORMAL OR SPECIALIZED* breathing: *Her respiration was slow and difficult.* ○ *The diaphragm is the principal muscle of respiration.* ➲See also **artificial respiration**.

respirator /ˈres.pɪ.reɪ.təʳ/ [US] /-t̬ɚ/ *noun* [C] **1** artificial breathing equipment: *Doctors put the patient* ***on*** *a respirator.* **2** a device worn over the mouth and nose to prevent harmful substances from being breathed in: *The firefighters wore respirators to help them breathe in the smoke-filled house.* **respiratory** /rɪˈspɪr.ə.tri/ [US] /ˈres.pɚ.ə.tɔːr.i/ *adj* [before n] *FORMAL OR SPECIALIZED Smoking can cause respiratory diseases.*

respire /rɪˈspaɪəʳ/ [US] /-ˈspaɪr/ *verb* [I] *SPECIALIZED* to breathe

reˈspiratory ˌsystem *noun* [C usually sing] the organs which enable you to breathe

respite /ˈres.paɪt/ *noun FORMAL* **1** [U] a pause or rest from something difficult or unpleasant: *We worked for hours without respite.* **2** [S] a useful delay before something unpleasant happens: *Their teacher was away, so they had a day's respite before their essays were due.*

resplendent /rɪˈsplen.dənt/ *adj LITERARY* having a very bright or splendid appearance: *the queen's resplendent purple robes* ○ *I saw Anna at the other end of the room, resplendent* ***in*** *a red sequined cocktail dress.* **resplendently** /rɪˈsplen.dənt.li/ *adv* **resplendence** /rɪˈsplen.dənts/ *noun* [U]

respond /rɪˈspɒnd/ [US] /-ˈspɑːnd/ *verb* [I] **1** to say or do something as a reaction to something that has been said or done: [+ speech] *To every question, he responded "I don't know."* ○ *I asked her what the time was, but she didn't respond.* ○ *He responded* ***by*** *march****ing*** *off and slamming the door behind him.* ○ *How did she respond* ***to*** *the news?* ○ [+ that] *When the tax office wrote to me demanding unpaid income tax, I responded* ***that*** *I had been working abroad since 1998.* ○ *The police respond* ***to*** *emergencies* (= arrive and are ready to deal with emergencies) *in just a few minutes.* **2 respond to** ***sth*** If diseases or patients respond to treatment, the treatment begins to cure them: *It remains to be seen whether the cancer will respond to treatment.* ○ *For patients who do not respond to drug treatment, surgery is a possible option.*

respondent /rɪˈspɒn.dənt/ [US] /-ˈspɑːn-/ *noun* [C] **1** *SPECIALIZED* a person who answers a request for information: *In a recent opinion poll, a majority of respondents were against nuclear weapons.* **2** *LEGAL* in a court case, the person against whom a PETITION (= a formal letter to the court requesting a particular action) is made, especially in a DIVORCE case: *She divorced the respondent on the grounds of unreasonable behaviour.* ➲Compare **co-respondent**.

response /rɪˈspɒnts/ [US] /-ˈspɑːnts/ *noun* **1** [C or U] an answer or reaction: *Responses* ***to*** *our advertisement have been disappointing.* ○ *Her proposals met with an enthusiastic response.* ○ *I looked in her face for some response, but she just stared at me blankly.* ○ *Management have granted a 10% pay rise* ***in*** *response* ***to*** *union pressure.* **2** [C] any of the parts sung or said, in some religious ceremonies, by the people in answer to the parts said or sung by the priest

responsive /rɪˈspɒnt.sɪv/ [US] /-ˈspɑːnt-/ *adj* making a positive and quick reaction to something or someone: *a responsive engine* ○ *a responsive audience* ○ *She wasn't responsive* ***to*** *questioning.* ○ *The disease has proved responsive* ***to*** *the new treatment.* * NOTE: The opposite is **unresponsive**. **responsively** /rɪˈspɒnt.sɪv.li/ [US] /-ˈspɑːnt-/ *adv* **responsiveness** /rɪˈspɒnt.sɪv.nəs/ [US] /-ˈspɑːnt-/ *noun* [U]

responsible [BLAME] /rɪˈspɒnt.sɪ.bl/ [US] /-ˈspɑːnt-/ *adj* **be responsible for *sth/doing sth*** to be the person who caused something to happen, especially something bad: *Who is responsible for this terrible mess?* ○ *Last month's bad weather was responsible for the crop failure.*

• **hold *sb/sth* responsible** to blame someone or something: *He held me personally responsible whenever anything went wrong in the project.*

• **be responsible for *your* actions** to be in control of yourself so that you can fairly be blamed for your bad actions: *The defendant was depressed and therefore not fully responsible for her **own** actions.*

responsibility /rɪˌspɒnt.sɪˈbɪl.ɪ.ti/ [US] /-ˌspɑːnt.səˈbɪl.ə.t̬i/ *noun* [U] *Terrorists have **claimed** responsibility **for*** (= stated that they caused) *yesterday's bomb attack.* ○ *The minister **took/accepted** full responsibility **for*** (= admitted that he was to blame for) *the disaster and resigned.*

responsible [DUTY] /rɪˈspɒnt.sɪ.bl/ [US] /-ˈspɑːnt-/ *adj* **1 be responsible for *sb/sth/doing sth*** to have control and authority over something or someone and the duty of taking care of it or them: *Paul is directly responsible **for** the efficient running of the office.* ○ *Her department is responsible **for** overseeing the councils.* **2 be responsible to *sb/sth*** to be controlled by someone or something: *In Australia, the Prime Minister and the Cabinet of Ministers are responsible **to** the House of Representatives.*

responsibility /rɪˌspɒnt.sɪˈbɪl.ɪ.ti/ [US] /-ˌspɑːnt.səˈbɪl.ə.t̬i/ *noun* [C or U] **1** something that it is your job or duty to deal with: [+ to infinitive] *It's her responsibility **to** ensure the project finishes on time.* ○ *She takes her responsibilities as a nurse very seriously.* **2 have responsibility** to be in a position of authority over someone and to have a duty to make certain that particular things are done: *Who has responsibility here?* ○ *Jenny, you have responsibility **for** clearing up the room after the class.*

• **have a responsibility to *sb*** to have a duty to work for or help someone who is in a position of authority over you: *The company says it cannot cut its prices any more because it has a responsibility to its shareholders.*

responsible [GOOD JUDGMENT] /rɪˈspɒnt.sɪ.bl/ [US] /-ˈspɑːnt-/ *adj* **1** having good judgment and the ability to act correctly and make decisions on your own: *a hardworking and responsible employee* ○ *Let's stay calm and try to behave like responsible adults.* ○ *Many big companies are now becoming more responsible **about** the way they operate.* * NOTE: The opposite is **irresponsible**. **2** A responsible job or position involves making important decisions or doing important things. **responsibly** /rɪˈspɒnt.sɪ.bli/ [US] /-ˈspɑːnt-/ *adv*: *When he saw the crash, the young boy acted very responsibly and called the police.*

responsibility /rɪˌspɒnt.sɪˈbɪl.ɪ.ti/ [US] /-ˌspɑːnt.səˈbɪl.ə.t̬i/ *noun* [U] *He has no sense of responsibility.* ○ *The job **carries** a lot of responsibility* (= it involves making important decisions).

• **act/do sth on *your* own responsibility** *FORMAL* to act without being told to by someone in authority

rest [STOP] /rest/ *verb* [I or T] **1** to (cause someone or something to) stop doing a particular activity or stop being active for a period of time in order to relax and get back your strength: *The doctor told him that he should rest for a few days.* ○ *He looked away from the computer screen to rest his eyes.* ○ *She promised that she would not rest* (= would not stop looking) *until the murderer of her son was caught and imprisoned.* ➲See also **rest up**. **2** *INFORMAL* **be resting** to be an actor who does not have any work: *Over 90% of professional actors are resting at any given time.*

• **I rest my case.** (*ALSO* **My case rests.**) *LEGAL* said by lawyers in a law court when they have finished the explanation of their case

• **let *sth* rest** *INFORMAL* to not talk about or mention a particular subject: *After he had told his friends he was writing a novel, they wouldn't let the subject rest.*

• **rest in peace 1** said to express the hope that someone's spirit has found peace after they have died: *She was a decent and compassionate woman: **may** she rest in peace.* **2** (*WRITTEN ABBREVIATION* **RIP**) often written on a GRAVESTONE

rest /rest/ *noun* **1** [C or U] a period of time in which you relax, do not do anything active, or sleep: *After they had carried the piano up the stairs, they stopped for a rest.* ○ *The doctor prescribed some pills and told her to **get/have** a week's rest.* **2** [C] *SPECIALIZED* a period of silence between musical notes, or a symbol which represents this: *a minim rest*

• **at rest 1** describes someone or something that is not doing anything active, or not moving: *Her heartbeat is only 55 at rest.* **2** used in a polite or respectful way to say that someone is dead: *Your father was a very troubled man, but he's at rest now.*

• **come to rest** to stop, usually in a particular place: *The car hit the kerb, rolled over and came to rest in a ditch.*

• **give it a rest** *INFORMAL* said when you want someone stop talking about or doing something that is annoying you: *Oh, give it a rest, can't you?*

rested /ˈres.tɪd/ *adj* healthy and active after a period of relaxation: *I came back from my trip to California **feeling** rested and rejuvenated.*

restful /ˈrest.fəl/ *adj* describes something that produces a feeling of calmness and relaxation: *I love the restful sound of the wind in the trees.* **restfully** /ˈrest.fəl.i/ *adv*

restless /ˈrest.ləs/ *adj* unwilling or unable to stay still or to be quiet and calm, because you are worried or bored: *He's a restless type – he never stays in one country for long.* ○ *She spent a restless night* (= She did not sleep well), *tossing and turning.* **restlessly** /ˈrest.lə.sli/ *adv*: *She shifted restlessly in her chair.* **restlessness** /ˈrest.lə.snəs/ *noun* [U]

COMMON LEARNER ERROR

rest, stay or **remain?**

Rest means to relax or sleep because you are tired or ill.

The doctor told him to rest.

Stay means to continue to be in the same place, job, or particular state.

It was raining, so we stayed at home.
~~*It was raining, so we rested at home.*~~

Remain means to continue to be in the same state, or to continue to exist when everything or everyone else has gone.

He remained unconscious for a week after the accident.
After the earthquake, nothing remained of the village.

---

rest [SUPPORT] /rest/ *verb* [I or T; usually + adv or prep] to lie or lean on something, or to put something on something else so that its weight is supported: *She rested her head **on** my shoulder.* ○ *The bicycle was resting **against** the wall.*

• **rest on *your* laurels** to be satisfied with your achievements and not to make an effort to do anything else: *Just because you've got your degree doesn't mean you can rest on your laurels.*

rest /rest/ *noun* [C] an object which supports the weight of something: *I used a pile of books as a rest **for** my telescope.* ➲See also **headrest**; **armrest**.

rest [REMAIN] /rest/ *verb* [I] *FORMAL* to remain in a particular state or place: *We must talk to the council about the problem – the matter cannot be allowed to rest here* (= further action must be taken).

• **rest easy** (*ALSO* **rest assured**) used to tell someone not to worry and that you are in control of the situation: *"Rest assured, Mrs. Cooper" said the police officer. "We will find your son for you."*

the rest [OTHER PART] *group noun* [S] the other things, people or parts that remain or that have not been mentioned: *I've got two bright students, but the rest are average.* ○ *I'll keep a third of the money and the rest is for you.* ○ *Have you got anything planned for the rest **of** the day?*

• **for the rest** used when you have already mentioned the important parts of something and you now want to mention the other less important parts: *The salary in my new job is great, but (as) for the rest, I'm not impressed.*

• **(and) all the rest** *INFORMAL* used at the end of a phrase or list to refer to other things or people that belong to

R

the same set or group and that you have not had time to mention: *Bob, June and Alison and all the rest are coming to dinner tonight.*
• **the rest is history** everything which happened since then is well known: *The Beatles had their first hit record in 1962 and the rest is history.*

PHRASAL VERBS WITH **rest** ▼

▲ **rest on *sb/sth*** [EYES] *phrasal verb* If your eyes rest on something or someone when you are looking around an area, you start looking only at that particular object or person: *Her eyes rested on a small wooden box at the back of the shop.*
▲ **rest on/upon *sth*** [NECESSARY] *phrasal verb FORMAL* If something rests on a particular idea, belief or fact, it is based on it or needs it in order for it to be true: *Christianity rests on the belief that Jesus was the son of God.*
▲ **rest on/upon *sb/sth*** *phrasal verb FORMAL* to depend on someone or something: *Our success rests on an increase in sales.*
▲ **rest up** *phrasal verb US* to relax in order to have strength for something: *Why don't you take a nap to rest up **for** the party?*
▲ **rest with *sb*** *phrasal verb FORMAL* If a responsibility or decision rests with someone, they are responsible for it: *The authority to call an emergency meeting rests with the president.*
▲ **rest with *sb/sth*** *phrasal verb* to depend on someone or something: *Our hopes rest with you.*

restart /ˌriːˈstɑːt/ [US] /-ˈstɑːrt/ *verb* [I or T] to start something again: *Our car stalled and wouldn't restart.* ○ *Please restart your computer to complete installation.*

restate /ˌriːˈsteɪt/ *verb* [T] to say something again or in a different way: *He restated his belief that the sanctions need more time to work.* **restatement** /ˌriːˈsteɪt.mənt/ *noun* [C or U] *Her recent speech was merely a restatement **of** her widely publicised views.*

restaurant /ˈres.trɒnt/ [US] /-tə.rɑːnt/ *noun* [C] a place where meals are prepared and served to customers
restaurateur /ˌres.tər.əˈtɜːʳ/ [US] /-tɚ.əˈtɝː/ *noun* [C] *FORMAL* a person who owns and manages a restaurant

COMMON LEARNER ERROR

restaurant (spelling)

Be careful with the vowel combination in the middle of this word: 'au'

The Bengal Lancer is a wonderful restaurant.

ˈ**restaurant ˌcar** *noun* [C] (*MAINLY US* **dining car**) *UK* a carriage of a train in which passengers are served meals

ˈ**rest ˌhome** *noun* [C] a place where old people live and are cared for

resting place /ˈrest.ɪŋ.pleɪs/ *noun* [C usually sing] *FORMAL* a place where someone is buried: *His **last/final** resting place was in the churchyard in the village where he was born.*

restitution /ˌres.tɪˈtjuː.ʃən/ [US] /-ˈtuː-/ *noun* [U] **1** *FORMAL* the return of items stolen or lost: *They are demanding the restitution **of** ancient treasures that were removed from the country in the 16th century.* **2** *LEGAL* payment made for damage or loss: *The chemicals company promised to **make** full restitution **to** the victims **for** the injury to their health.*

restive /ˈres.tɪv/ *adj* unwilling to be controlled or be patient: *The audience was becoming restive as they waited for the performance to begin.* **restively** /ˈres.tɪv.li/ *adv* **restiveness** /ˈres.tɪv.nəs/ *noun* [U]

restore /rɪˈstɔːʳ/ [US] /-ˈstɔːr/ *verb* [T] **1** to return something or someone to an earlier good condition or position: *The badly neglected paintings have all been carefully restored.* ○ *After a week in bed, she was fully restored **to** health* (= she felt healthy again). ○ *The former leader was today restored **to** power in the first free elections for twenty years.* **2** If you restore a quality or ability that someone has not had for a long time, you make it possible for them to have that quality or ability again: *Doctors have restored his sight.* ○ *The government is trying to restore public confidence in its management of the economy.* **3** to bring back into use something that has been absent for a period of time: *Some people are in favour of restoring capital punishment for murderers.* **4** *FORMAL* to give something that has been lost or stolen back to the person it belongs to: *The painting was restored **to** its **rightful owner**.*
restoration /ˌres.təˈreɪ.ʃən/ [US] /-təˈreɪ-/ *noun* [C or U] **1** the act or process of returning something to its earlier good condition or position: *The first task following the disaster was the restoration **of** clean water supplies.* ○ *Restoration **work** on the Sistine Chapel ceiling is now complete.* ○ *A large majority of the population is demanding the restoration **of** the former government.* **2 the Restoration** the event in British history when Charles II was made King of Britain in 1660 after a period in which there was no king or queen
Restoration /ˌres.təˈreɪ.ʃən/ [US] /-təˈreɪ-/ *adj* [before n] belonging to or popular during THE RESTORATION: *Restoration comedy/architecture/art*
restorative /rɪˈstɒr.ə.tɪv/ [US] /-ˈstɔːr.ə.t̬ɪv/ *noun* [C] *OLD-FASHIONED* something which makes you feel better or more energetic if you are feeling tired or ill: *After a hard day at the office, a hot bath is a welcome restorative.*
restorative /rɪˈstɒr.ə.tɪv/ [US] /-ˈstɔːr.ə.t̬ɪv/ *adj FORMAL* *Ginseng is used as a restorative and preventive remedy.*
restorer /rɪˈstɔː.rəʳ/ [US] /-ˈstɔːr.ɚ/ *noun* [C] a person who restores buildings, furniture or paintings to their original condition: *She's a furniture restorer.*

restrain /rɪˈstreɪn/ *verb* [T] to control the actions or behaviour of someone by force, especially in order to stop them from doing something, or to limit the growth or force of something: *When he started fighting, it took four police officers to restrain him.* ○ [R] *She was so angry that she could hardly restrain **herself**.* ○ *You should try to restrain your ambitions and be more realistic.* ○ *Growth in car ownership could be restrained by increasing taxes.*
restrained /rɪˈstreɪnd/ *adj* **1** acting in a calm and controlled way: *I was expecting him to be furious but he was very restrained.* **2** controlled: *a more restrained policy on mortgage lending* ○ *The tone of his poetry is restrained and unemotional.*
restraint /rɪˈstreɪnt/ *noun* **1** [U] calm and controlled behaviour: *He showed admirable restraint, and refused to be provoked.* ○ *The security forces **exercised** (= used) great restraint by not responding to hostile attacks and threats.* **2** [C or U] something which limits the freedom of someone or something, or which prevents something from growing or increasing: *government spending restraints* ○ *Lack of space is the main restraint **on** the firm's expansion plans.* ○ *During the recession, the government opted for a policy of pay/wage restraint rather than a reduction in public investment.*
• **keep/place *sb* under restraint** to keep a violent person in a way that prevents them from moving freely: *The two prisoners were kept under restraint while they were transported between prisons.*

reˈstraining ˌorder *noun* [C] *LEGAL* a written instruction made by a court which forbids a particular action until a judge has make a decision about the matter: *She obtained a restraining order forbidding her partner from seeing their two children.*

restrict /rɪˈstrɪkt/ *verb* [T] to limit the movements or actions of someone, or to limit something and reduce its size or prevent it from increasing: *measures to restrict the sale of alcohol* ○ *The government has restricted freedom of movement into and out of the country.* ○ *Having small children really restricts your social life.* ➲See also **restrict to**.
restricted /rɪˈstrɪk.tɪd/ *adj* **1** limited, especially by official rules, laws, etc: *Building in this area of town is restricted.* ○ *Membership is restricted **to*** (= It is only for) *chief executive officers.* ○ *Our view of the stage was restricted* (= objects prevented us from seeing the whole stage). **2** describes an area which you need official permission to enter because the authorities want to keep it secret, or because it is considered dangerous: *Wellington Barracks is a restricted area and anyone who enters should have identification.* **3** describes a document which you need official permission to read because the authorities want to keep it secret **restric-**

tion /rɪˈstrɪk.ʃ ə n/ *noun* [C or U] *import/export/currency re-strictions* **speed/parking** *restrictions* ○ *At the turn of the century, Congress* **imposed/placed** *a height restriction of 13 storeys* **on** *all buildings in Washington.* ○ *The president urged other countries to* **lift** *the trade restrictions.*

restrictive /rɪˈstrɪk.tɪv/ *adj OFTEN DISAPPROVING* limiting the freedom of someone or preventing something from growing: *He is self-employed because he finds working for other people too restrictive.* ○ *The college is not able to expand because of restrictive planning laws.*
▲ **restrict** *yourself* **to** *sth phrasal verb* [R] to limit yourself to one particular thing or activity: *If I'm driving, I re-strict myself to one glass of wine.*

re,strictive 'practice *noun* [C] *UK SPECIALIZED* in industry or business, an action which limits the freedom of workers or employers: *Management accused the union of restrictive practices.*

re,strictive 'trade ,practice *noun* [C] *SPECIALIZED* a business agreement between companies which controls prices or the areas in which goods are sold, preventing fair competition from other companies

restroom /ˈrest.rʊm/ /-ruːm/ *noun* [C] *MAINLY US* a room with toilets that is in a public place, for example in a restaurant

restructure /ˌriːˈstrʌk.tʃ ə r/ /-tʃ ɚ / *verb* [T] to organize a company, business or system in a new way to make it operate more effectively: *The government restructured the coal industry before selling it to private owners.* **re-structuring** /ˌriːˈstrʌk.tʃ ə r.ɪŋ/ /-tʃ ɚ .ɪŋ/ *noun* [C or U] *The company underwent restructuring and 1500 workers lost their jobs.*

'**rest ,stop** *noun* [C] (*ALSO* **rest area**) *US* an area next to a road where people can park their vehicles, go to the toi-let, eat, etc.

result /rɪˈzʌlt/ *noun* **1** [C or U] something that happens or exists because of something else: *The road has been widened, but* **the** *result is just more traffic.* ○ *His broken leg is* **the** *direct result of his own carelessness.* ○ *I tried to repaint the kitchen walls* **with** *disastrous results.* ○ *To ensure* **good/the best** *results, use Italian tomatoes and fresh basil.* **2** [C] the information you get from something such as a scientific experiment or medical test: *The results of the opinion poll showed that most women supported this action.* **3** [C] the mark you receive after you have taken an exam or test: *I finished my exams yesterday, but I won't know/get the results until August.* **4** [C] the answer to a calculation in mathematics: *We used different methods of calculation, but we both* **got** *the same result.* **5** [C] the score or number of votes, showing the success or failure of the people involved, in a competitive activity such as a sports competition or an election: *the results of the local elections* ○ *the football results* ○ *We were expecting to win, so a draw was a dis-appointing result for us.* **6** [C] *UK INFORMAL* a win in a sports competition: *The team needs a result to go through to the semi-finals.* **7** [C usually pl] a good or pleas-ing effect: *We've spent a lot of money on advertising and we're beginning to see the results.* ○ *She's an excellent coach who knows how to* **get** *results.*
● **as a result of** *sth* because of something: *Profits have declined as a result of the recent drop in sales.*

result /rɪˈzʌlt/ *verb* [I] to happen or exist because some-thing else has happened: *Teachers were not fully pre-pared for the major changes in the exam system, and chaos resulted.*

resulting /rɪˈzʌl.tɪŋ/ *adj* [before n] (*FORMAL* **resultant**) caused by the event or situation which you have just mentioned: *The tape was left near a magnetic source, and the resulting damage was considerable.*

PHRASAL VERBS WITH **result** ▼

▲ **result from** *sth phrasal verb* If a situation or problem results from a particular event or activity, it is caused by it: *His difficulty in walking results from a childhood illness.*

▲ **result in** *sth phrasal verb* to cause a particular situa-tion to happen: *The fire resulted in damage to their property.* ○ [+ v-ing] *Icy road conditions in Teesdale resulted in two roads being closed.*

resume START AGAIN /rɪˈzjuːm/ /-ˈzuːm/ *verb FORMAL* **1** [I or T] If an activity resumes, or if you resume it, it starts again after a pause: *Normal services will be resumed in the spring.* ○ [+ v-ing] *He stopped to take a sip of water and then resumed speaking.* ○ *The talks are due to resume today.* **2** [T] If you resume a place or position which you have left for a period of time, you return to it: *to resume your post/job* ○ *Please resume your seats, as the performance will continue in two minutes.* **resumption** /rɪˈzʌmp.ʃ ə n/ *noun* [S or U] *The president called for an immediate ceasefire and* **a** *resumption* **of** *negotiations between the two sides.*

résumé LIST /ˈrez.juː.meɪ/ /ˈrez.ʊ-/ *noun* [C] **1** a short statement of the important details of something: *She gave us a brief résumé of the project so far.* **2** *US FOR* **CV**: *She sent her résumé to fifty companies, but didn't even get an interview.*

resurface COVER /ˌriːˈsɜː.fɪs/ /-ˈsɝː-/ *verb* [T] to put a new surface on a road: *Drivers will experience delays while stretches of the road are being resurfaced.*

resurface APPEAR /ˌriːˈsɜː.fɪs/ /-ˈsɝː-/ *verb* [I] **1** to rise to the surface of the water again: *When the divers did not resurface after an hour, three crew members dived down to look for them.* **2** to appear again after being lost, stolen or absent: *Please contact me if any of the stolen paintings resurface.* ○ *Jill resurfaced last week, after spending the past few months doing research in the library.* **3** If a memory resurfaces, you remember it again after you had forgotten about it: *Memories of his childhood resurfaced when he saw the photographs.*

resurgence /rɪˈsɜː.dʒ ə nts/ /-ˈsɝː-/ *noun* [S or U] *FORMAL* a new increase of activity or interest in a particular sub-ject or idea which had been forgotten for some time: *The creation of independent states has led to* **a** *resurgence* **of** *nationalism.* ○ *resurgence* **in** *demand/popularity/interest* **resurgent** /rɪˈsɜː.dʒ ə nt/ /-ˈsɝː-/ *adj FORMAL* increasing again, or becoming popular again: *resurgent inflation* ○ *Many people were critical of the resurgent militarism in the country.*

resurrect /ˌrez.ə rˈekt/ /-əˈrekt/ *verb* [T] **1** to bring someone back to life: *Almost all Christians believe that Jesus was resurrected* **from** *the dead.* **2** to bring back something into use or existence that had disappeared or ended: *Several members of the party have resurrected the idea of constitutional change.* ○ *She has been busily try-ing to resurrect her Hollywood career.*

resurrection /ˌrez.ə rˈek.ʃ ə n/ /-əˈrek-/ *noun* [U] when something that had disappeared or ended is brought back into use or existence
● **the Resurrection** In the Christian religion, the Resurrection is Jesus Christ's return to life on the third day after his death, or the return of all people to life at the end of the world.

resuscitate /rɪˈsʌs.ɪ.teɪt/ *verb* [T] to bring someone or something back to life or consciousness: *Her heart had stopped, but the doctors successfully resuscitated her.*
resuscitation /rɪˌsʌs.ɪˈteɪ.ʃ ə n/ *noun* [U] when someone or something is brought back to life or consciousness: *The patient suffered a cardiac arrest and died, despite an attempt at resuscitation.* ⇨See also **mouth-to-mouth (resuscitation)**

retail /ˈriː.teɪl/ *noun* [U] the activity of selling goods to the public, usually in small quantities: *The job is open to applicants with over two years' experience in retail.* ○ *The clothing company has six retail* **outlets** (= shops) *in south-eastern Australia.* ○ *$13 off the manufacturer's recommended retail* **price** ⇨Compare **wholesale** SELLING.

retail /ˈriː.teɪl/ *verb* [T] **1** to sell goods to the public in shops or by post: *The company makes and retails moderately priced sportswear.* **2** **retail at/for** *sth* to be sold at a particular price: *This model of computer is retailing at £650.* **retail** /ˈriː.teɪl/ *adv*: *It's much cheaper to buy wholesale than retail.*

retailer /ˈriː.teɪ.lə r/ /-lɚ/ *noun* [C] a person, shop or business that sells goods to the public: *a big electronics retailer*

,**retail 'price ,index** *noun* [S] (*ABBREVIATION* **RPI**) *UK* a measurement of the changes in the cost of basic goods and services ⇨Compare **consumer price index**.

R

ˈretail ˌtherapy *noun* [U] *HUMOROUS* when you buy special things for yourself in order to feel better when you are unhappy: *I needed a lot of retail therapy to help me get over my ex-boyfriend.*

retain /rɪˈteɪn/ *verb* [T] **1** *SLIGHTLY FORMAL* to keep or continue to have something: *She has lost her battle to retain control of the company.* ○ *He managed to retain his dignity throughout the performance.* ○ *She succeeded in retaining her lead in the second half of the race.* ○ *I have a good memory and am able to retain* (= remember) *facts easily.* **2** *SLIGHTLY FORMAL* If a substance retains something, such as heat or water, it continues to hold or contain it: *The sea retains the sun's warmth longer than the land.* **3** *LEGAL* to obtain the services of a lawyer by paying them in advance

retainer /rɪˈteɪ.nəʳ/ [US] /-nɚ/ *noun* [C] **1** *SPECIALIZED* an amount of money which you pay to someone in advance so that they will work for you when you need them to **2** *OLD USE* a servant who has usually been with the same family for a long time: *a faithful old retainer*

retention /rɪˈten.tʃᵊn/ *noun* [U] *SLIGHTLY FORMAL* the continued use, existence or possession of something or someone: *Two influential senators have argued for the retention of the unpopular tax.* ○ *The retention of old technology has slowed the company's growth.* ○ ***water/heat*** *retention*

retentive /rɪˈten.tɪv/ [US] /-t̬ɪv/ *adj SLIGHTLY FORMAL* If you have a retentive memory or brain, you can remember things easily. ➲See also **anally retentive**.

retake /ˌriːˈteɪk/ *verb* [T] **1** to take an exam again because you failed it the first time: *to retake your driving test/final exams* **2** to take something such as a place or position into your possession again, often by force, after losing possession of it: *In the battle to retake the village, over 150 soldiers were killed.* ○ *Finally, our team had a chance to retake the lead.* ○ *The junta tried to retake power in 1999.* **3** to take a photograph or film again

retake /ˈriː.teɪk/ *noun* [C] **1** an exam which you take again because you failed it the first time: *I'm doing my retakes next summer.* **2** a part of a film that must be photographed again to change or improve it: *It took seven retakes to get the scene exactly right.*

retaliate /rɪˈtæl.i.eɪt/ *verb* [I] to hurt someone or do something harmful to them because they have done or said something harmful to you: *If someone insults you, don't retaliate as it only makes the situation worse.* ○ *The demonstrators threw rocks at the police, who retaliated* ***by firing*** *blanks into the crowd.* ○ *The terrorists retaliated* ***against*** *the government* ***with*** *a bomb attack.*

retaliation /rɪˌtæl.iˈeɪ.ʃᵊn/ *noun* [U] *The bomb attack was* ***in*** *retaliation* ***for*** *the recent arrest of two well-known terrorists.*

retaliatory /rɪˈtæl.i.ə.tri/ [US] /-tɔːr.i/ *adj* describes an action that is harmful to someone who has done something to harm you: *retaliatory measures* ○ *He urged people not to resort to retaliatory violence.*

retard /rɪˈtɑːd/ [US] /-ˈtɑːrd/ *verb* [T] *FORMAL* to make something slower: *A rise in interest rates would severely retard economic* ***growth****.*

retardant /rɪˈtɑː.dᵊnt/ [US] /-ˈtɑːr-/ *noun* [C or U], *adj* (a substance) that makes the progress or growth of something slower: *Pot plants are commonly treated with (a) growth retardant so that they retain their shape.* ○ ***fire/flame*** *retardant furniture* (= furniture that does not burn easily)

retard /ˈriː.tɑːd/ [US] /-tɑːrd/ *noun* [C] *OFFENSIVE* a stupid or mentally slow person: *I'm not playing with him, he's a total retard.*

retarded /rɪˈtɑː.dɪd/ [US] /-ˈtɑːr-/ *adj OFFENSIVE OLD-FASHIONED* having had a slower mental development than other people of the same age: *mentally/emotionally retarded*

the retarded *plural noun OFFENSIVE OLD-FASHIONED* people with slow development, usually mental development: *The programme offers intermediate care for the* ***mentally*** *retarded.*

retardation /ˌriː.tɑːˈdeɪ.ʃᵊn/ [US] /-tɑːr-/ *noun* [U] *FORMAL* slow development, or development which is slower than it should be: *Severe iron deficiency can cause developmental delay and growth retardation.* * NOTE: **Retarded** and **retardation** are no longer used as specialized terms in the care of people with slow mental development, as they could sound offensive.

retch /retʃ/ *verb* [I] to react in a way as if you are vomiting: *The sight of blood makes him retch.*

retd *adj* [after n] **1** *WRITTEN ABBREVIATION FOR* **retired** ➲See at **retire** STOP WORKING. **2** *WRITTEN ABBREVIATION* used after someone's name to show that they are no longer in one of the armed forces: *The meeting will be chaired by Colonel E. Smith (retd).*

retention /rɪˈten.tʃᵊn/ *noun* [U] ➲See at **retain**.

rethink /ˌriːˈθɪŋk/ *verb* [I or T] **rethought, rethought** to think again about a plan, idea or system in order to change or improve it: *Her family's disapproval made her rethink her plans.* ○ [+ question word] *The European Commission is having to rethink* ***how*** *it can maintain farmers' incomes while cutting costs and excess production.* **rethink** /ˈriː.θɪŋk/ *noun* [S] *This new information means we should* ***have a*** *rethink.*

reticent /ˈret.ɪ.sᵊnt/ [US] /ˈret̬.ə-/ *adj FORMAL* unwilling to speak about your thoughts or feelings: *He is very reticent* ***about*** *his past.* ○ *Most of the students were reticent* ***about*** *answering questions.* **reticently** /ˈret.ɪ.sᵊnt.li/ [US] /ˈret̬.ə-/ *adv* **reticence** /ˈret.ɪ.sᵊnts/ [US] /ˈret̬.ə-/ *noun* [U] *His reticence* ***about*** *his past made them very suspicious.*

reticulation /rɪˌtɪk.jʊˈleɪ.ʃᵊn/ *noun* [C] *SPECIALIZED* a net-like pattern of lines and squares, or a structure of pipes or wires **reticulated** /rɪˈtɪk.jʊ.leɪ.tɪd/ [US] /-t̬ɪd/ *adj* (*ALSO* **reticulate**) *leaves with a reticulate vein structure* ○ *a reticulated pattern*

retina /ˈret.ɪ.nə/ [US] /ˈret̬.ᵊn.ə/ *noun* [C] *plural* **retinas** or **retinae** the area at the back of the eye that receives light and sends pictures of what the eye sees to the brain **retinal** /ˈret.ɪ.nəl/ [US] /ˈret̬.ᵊn.ᵊl/ *adj*: *The disease can result in retinal damage and loss of vision.*

retinue /ˈret.ɪ.njuː/ [US] /ˈret̬.ᵊn.uː/ *group noun* [C] a group of helpers and followers who travel with an important person: *The President travels with a large retinue of aides and bodyguards.*

retire [STOP WORKING] /rɪˈtaɪəʳ/ [US] /-ˈtaɪr/ *verb* **1** [I] to leave your job or stop working because of old age or ill health: *Since retiring* ***from*** *the company, she has done voluntary work for a charity.* ○ *He is due to retire* ***as*** *chief executive next year.* **2** [T often passive] If an employer retires an employee, they dismiss that person, usually at a time when they are near to the age at which they would normally stop working, or because they are ill: *Following the merger, he was retired with a generous pension.* **3** [I] to stop taking part in a race or competition because of illness or injury: *She retired* ***from*** *the competition after pulling a leg muscle.*

retired /rɪˈtaɪəd/ [US] /-ˈtaɪrd/ *adj* (*WRITTEN ABBREVIATION* **retd**) If someone is retired, they have stopped working: *Both my parents are retired.* ○ *He is a retired airline pilot.*

retiree /rɪˌtaɪəˈriː/ [US] /-ˈtaɪ.riː/ *noun* [C] *US* a person who has stopped working: *The neighborhood is a mixture of young couples, retirees and single professionals.*

retirement /rɪˈtaɪə.mənt/ [US] /-ˈtaɪr-/ *noun* **1** [C or U] when you leave your job and stop working, usually because you are old: *Many teachers over the age of 50 are* ***taking early*** *retirement.* ○ *What is the normal retirement* ***age*** *in this country?* **2** [U] the period in someone's life after they have stopped working because they reached a particular age: *We wish you a long and happy retirement.*

retiring /rɪˈtaɪə.rɪŋ/ [US] /-ˈtaɪr.ɪŋ/ *adj* [before n] describes someone who is planning to leave their job: *The match ended in disappointment for the retiring captain, Viv Richards.* ➲See also **retiring**.

retire [LEAVE A PLACE] /rɪˈtaɪəʳ/ [US] /-ˈtaɪr/ *verb* [I] **1** *FORMAL* to leave a room or group of people and go somewhere quiet or private: *After dinner our host said, "Shall we retire* ***to*** *the drawing room?"* **2** *FORMAL OR OLD-FASHIONED* to go to bed: *It had been a long day, so I retired early.*

retiring /rɪˈtaɪə.rɪŋ/ [US] /-ˈtaɪr.ɪŋ/ *adj FORMAL* unwilling to be noticed or to be with other people: *to be* ***shy and*** *retiring* ➲See also **retiring** at **retire** STOP WORKING.

retort /rɪˈtɔːt/ [US] /-ˈtɔːrt/ *verb* [T] to answer someone quickly in an angry or funny way: [+ speech] *"That doesn't concern you!" she retorted.*

retort /rɪˈtɔːt/ [US] /-ˈtɔːrt/ *noun* **[C]** a quick answer that is angry or funny: *"I'm going to tell him," said Max. "Just you try!" came the retort.*

retouch /ˌriːˈtʌtʃ/ *verb* **[T]** to make small changes to a picture, photograph, etc., especially in order to improve it: *We had the wedding photos retouched to make it seem like a sunny day.*

retrace /rɪˈtreɪs/ *verb* **[T]** to go back over something, for example a path or a series of past actions: *When he realised he had lost his keys, he retraced in his mind his movements that day.*
• **retrace *your* steps** to go back to a place in the same way that you came: *She walked straight past her office and then had to retrace her steps.*

retract /rɪˈtrækt/ *verb* FORMAL **1** **[T]** to take back an offer or statement, etc. or admit that a statement was false: *retract an invitation/confession/promise* ○ *When questioned on TV, the minister retracted his allegations.* **2** **[I or T]** to pull something back or in: *The wheels retract after the aircraft takes off.* ○ *The cat retracted its claws.* **retractable** /rɪˈtræk.tə.bl̩/ *adj*: *Cats have retractable claws.* **retraction** /rɪˈtræk.ʃən/ *noun* **[C]** *The newspaper printed a retraction for their previous error.*

retraining /ˌriːˈtreɪ.nɪŋ/ *noun* **[U]** when someone learns new skills so they can do a different job

retread /ˌriːˈtred/ *verb* **[T]** (UK ALSO **remould**) to put a new rubber surface on the outer part of a worn tyre: *Your tyres need retreading.* **retread** /ˈriː.tred/ *noun* **[C]** (UK ALSO **remould**) *Are those new tyres or retreads?*

retreat [POSITION] /rɪˈtriːt/ *verb* **[I often + adv or prep]** **1** to go away from a place or person in order to escape from fighting or danger: *Attacks by enemy aircraft forced the tanks to retreat (**from** the city).* ○ *When she came towards me shouting, I retreated (behind my desk).* **2** to go to a quiet safe place in order to avoid a difficult situation: *When he's done something wrong, he retreats to his bedroom.*
retreat /rɪˈtriːt/ *noun* **1** **[C usually sing; U]** a move back by soldiers or an army, either because they have been defeated or in order to avoid fighting: *the retreat **from** Dunkirk* ○ *Enemy soldiers are now **in** (full) retreat.* **2** **[C]** a private and safe place: *a country/mountain/lakeside retreat* **3** **[C or U]** a period of time used to pray and study quietly, or to think carefully, away from normal activities and duties: *We **went on** (a) retreat **at/to** a monastery in Wales.*

retreat [DECISION] /rɪˈtriːt/ to decide not to do something, or to stop believing something, because it causes too many problems: *The government is retreating **from** its promises.*
retreat /rɪˈtriːt/ *noun* **[C]** a change from previous beliefs or behaviour: *The professor's speech marked/signalled a retreat **from** his usual extreme views.*

retrench /rɪˈtrentʃ/ *verb* **[I]** FORMAL If governments, companies, etc. retrench, they start spending less money, or reducing costs: *The company had to retrench because of falling orders.*
retrenchment /rɪˈtrentʃ.mənt/ *noun* **[C or U]** when a government, etc. spends less or reduces costs

retrial /ˈriː.traɪəl/ *noun* **[C]** a new trial of a law case: *The discovery of new evidence forced a retrial.*

retribution /ˌret.rɪˈbjuː.ʃən/ *noun* **[U]** FORMAL deserved and severe punishment: *They fled because they feared retribution **for** the genocide.* ○ *She was asked whether a civilian government should **seek** retribution **against** military officers involved in human rights abuses.* ○ *Many saw her death as **divine** retribution* (= punishment by God) ***for** her crimes.* **retributive** /rɪˈtrɪb.jʊ.tɪv/ [US] /-t̬ɪv/ *adj* **[before n]** *retributive action/justice*

retrieve /rɪˈtriːv/ *verb* **[T]** to find and bring back something: *We taught our dog to retrieve a ball.* ○ *Computers are used to store and retrieve information efficiently.* **retrieval** /rɪˈtriː.vəl/ *noun* **[U]** *the storage and retrieval of information*

retriever /rɪˈtriː.vər/ [US] /-vɚ/ *noun* **[C]** a large dog with thick black or light brown fur

retro- [BACKWARDS] /ret.rəʊ-/ [US] /-roʊ-/ *prefix* going backwards

retro- [PAST] /ret.rəʊ-/ [US] /-roʊ-/ *prefix* looking at or copying the past: *retro-pop* (= popular music from the past)
retro /ˈret.rəʊ/ [US] /-roʊ/ *adj* similar to styles, fashions, etc. from the past: *retro clothes/music* ○ *a retro style*

retroactive /ˌret.rəʊˈæk.tɪv/ [US] /-roʊ-/ *adj* (ALSO **retrospective**) FORMAL If a law or decision, etc. is retroactive, it has effect from a date before it was approved: *the first British law to have retroactive effect* **retroactively** /ˌret.rəʊˈæk.tɪv.li/ [US] /-roʊ-/ *adv*

retrograde /ˈret.rəʊ.greɪd/ [US] /-rə-/ *adj* FORMAL returning to older and worse conditions, methods, ideas, etc: *He said it would be a retrograde **step** to remove single parent benefit.*

retrogress /ˌret.rəʊˈgres/ [US] /ˈret.rə.gres/ *verb* **[I]** FORMAL to return to an older and worse state **retrogression** /ˌret.rəʊˈgreʃ.ən/ [US] /-rə-/ *noun* **[U]** **retrogressive** /ˌret.rəʊˈgres.ɪv/ [US] /ˈret.rə.gres-/ *adj*: *retrogressive and disastrous policies*

retrospect /ˈret.rəʊ.spekt/ [US] /-rə-/ *noun* **in retrospect** thinking now about something in the past: *In retrospect, I think my marriage was doomed from the beginning.* ○ *I'm sure my university days seem happier in retrospect than they really were.* **retrospection** /ˌret.rəʊˈspek.ʃən/ [US] /-rə-/ *noun* **[U]** *a time/mood of retrospection*
retrospective /ˌret.rəʊˈspek.tɪv/ [US] /-rə-/ *adj* relating to or thinking about the past: *a retrospective album of solo Freddie Mercury tracks*
retrospective /ˌret.rəʊˈspek.tɪv/ [US] /-rə-/ *noun* **[C]** a show of the work an artist has done in their life so far: *a Hockney retrospective/a retrospective of Hockney's work*
retrospectively /ˌret.rəʊˈspek.tɪv.li/ [US] /-rə-/ *adv*: *Retrospectively, I can see where we went wrong.*

retrovirus /ˌret.rəʊˈvaɪ.rəs/ [US] /-rə-/ *noun* **[C]** a type of virus that includes some cancer viruses and HIV (= the virus that causes AIDS)

retsina /retˈsiː.nə/ *noun* **[U]** a Greek wine that tastes strongly of the RESIN of particular trees

return [GO BACK] /rɪˈtɜːn/ [US] /-ˈtɝːn/ *verb* **[I]** **1** to come or go back to a previous place: *Odysseus returned home/returned **to** his home after many years of travelling.* ○ *She left South Africa at the age of 15 and has never returned.* ○ **[+ to infinitive]** *David returned (**from** work) **to** find his house had burned down.* **2 return to sth** If people or things return to a previous condition, they go back to that condition: *Within a week, the situation had returned to normal.* **3 return to sth** If you return to an activity or subject, you start doing it or talking about it again: *Gandhi urged Indians to return to spinning their own yarn.* ○ *Every five minutes, he returned to the same subject.*
return /rɪˈtɜːn/ [US] /-ˈtɝːn/ *noun* **[S]** **1** when someone goes or comes back to a place where they were before: *The whole town came out to celebrate his return (**from** the war).* ○ ***On** her return, she went straight to the office.* ➲See also **return (ticket)**. **2** when you start to do or have something again: *Some environmentalists argue for a return **to** a pre-industrial society.* ○ *Most people have welcomed her return **to power/office**.* **return** /rɪˈtɜːn/ [US] /-ˈtɝːn/ *adj* **[before n]** *The return **journey** took longer because the train was rerouted.*

return [HAPPEN AGAIN] /rɪˈtɜːn/ [US] /-ˈtɝːn/ *verb* **[I]** to happen again: *You must go to the doctor if the pain returns.*
return /rɪˈtɜːn/ [US] /-ˈtɝːn/ *noun* **[S]** when something starts to happen or be used again: *Will we ever see the return **of**/a return **to** comfortable fashion clothes?*

return [PUT BACK] /rɪˈtɜːn/ [US] /-ˈtɝːn/ *verb* **[T]** **1** to send, take, give, put, etc. something back to where it came from: *The new TV broke so they returned it **to** the shop.* ○ *He returned two books he had borrowed from me in 1963.* ○ *She carefully returned the book **to** its place on the shelf.* **2** in sports such as tennis, to hit the ball back to your opponent
return /rɪˈtɜːn/ [US] /-ˈtɝːn/ *noun* **1** **[S]** when something is given back, put back, or sent back: *the return of the stolen goods* **2** **[C]** when you hit the ball back to your opponent in sports such as tennis
• **by return (of post)** UK (AUS ALSO **by return mail**) in the first post collection that leaves after you receive a letter: *She answered my letter by return.*

returns /rɪ'tɜːnz/ ⓤ /-'tɜːnz/ *plural noun* **1** goods that have been taken back to the shop where they were bought by customers because they are damaged or unsuitable **2** *US* the votes that are returned, or the results of the voting, in an election: *The **election** returns produced a confusing picture of gains and losses.* **returnable** /rɪ'tɜː.nə.bl̩/ ⓤ /-'tɜː-/ *adj*: *a returnable bottle*

return EXCHANGE /rɪ'tɜːn/ ⓤ /-'tɜːn/ *verb* [T] **1** to give, do or get something in exchange: *to return an invitation/greeting* ○ *I returned his stare.* ○ *I gave her a ride when her car broke down and now she is returning **the favour*** (= doing something to help me in exchange). ○ *The terrorists started shooting and the police returned **fire*** (= started shooting back). **2** to give a particular amount of profit in exchange for an investment: *My investments return a high rate of interest.*

return /rɪ'tɜːn/ ⓤ /-'tɜːn/ *noun* [C or U] **1** when something is given, done or received in exchange: *Several soldiers were wounded in the return **of** fire.* **2** the profit that you get from an investment: *The return **on** the money we invested was very low.*

● **in return** in exchange: *America helped the rebels in return **for** their promise to support democracy.*

return DECIDE /rɪ'tɜːn/ ⓤ /-'tɜːn/ *verb* **1** LEGAL **return a verdict/sentence** to decide and say whether you think someone is guilty or not guilty, or what punishment the person will be given in a law court: *The jury returned a verdict **of** not guilty.* **2** *UK* to elect someone to be a member of parliament, or to another political job

return COMPUTER /rɪ'tɜːn/ ⓤ /-'tɜːn/ *noun* [U] the key on a computer keyboard that you press in order to say that the words or numbers on the screen are correct, or that an instruction should be performed or in order to move down a line on the screen: *Press return/the return key twice to leave a blank line.*

re͵turn 'match *noun* [C] another game between the same teams or players: *We enjoyed the game so much that we arranged a return match for the next week.*

re͵turn ('ticket) *noun* [C] **1** *UK* (*US* **roundtrip ticket**) a ticket for travel to a place and back again: *May I have a return to Birmingham, please?* **2** *US* **return ticket** a ticket for the return part of a journey

reunify /riː'juː.nɪ.faɪ/ *verb* [T] to join together into one country, parts of a country that were divided **reunification** /͵riː.juː.nɪ.fɪ'keɪ.ʃ³n/ *noun* [U] when a country that was temporarily divided into smaller countries is joined together again as one country: *the reunification of Germany*

reunite /͵riː.juː'naɪt/ *verb* [T] to bring together again: *to reunite a divided family/country/world* ○ *Sarah was finally reunited **with** her children at the airport.* **reunion** /͵riː'juː.ni.ən/ ⓤ /-'njən/ *noun* [C] *to have a family reunion*

reuse /͵riː'juːz/ *verb* [T] to use something again: *To conserve resources, please reuse this carrier bag.* **reusable** /͵riː'juː.zə.bl̩/ *adj*: *reusable nappies/packaging*

Rev PRIEST *noun* [before n] (*UK ALSO* **Revd**) ABBREVIATION FOR **Reverend**

rev SPEED /rev/ *noun* [C usually pl] INFORMAL a **revolution** (= one complete turn of a part in an engine): *Keep the revs **up*** (= the engine parts turning quickly) *or the engine will stall.* ○ *a rev counter* ⊃See also **rpm**.

rev /rev/ *verb* [I or T] **-vv-** to increase the operating speed of an engine while the vehicle is not moving, usually to warm it to the correct temperature: *The noise of the car revving **(up)** woke the whole neighbourhood.*

revalue /͵riː'væl.juː/ *verb* [T] to change the value of something or to consider it again: *to revalue a currency* ○ *The company's assets are periodically revalued.*

revamp /͵riː'væmp/ *verb* [T] INFORMAL to change or arrange something again, in order to improve it: *We revamped all the management system, but the business is doing no better than it was before.* **revamp** /'riː.væmp/ *noun* [C usually sing] *The company has spent £5 million on a major revamp of its offices.*

Revd *noun* UK ABBREVIATION FOR **Reverend**

reveal /rɪ'viːl/ *verb* [T] **1** to make known or show something that is surprising or that was previously secret: *He was jailed for revealing secrets to the Russians.* ○ [+ that] *Her biography revealed **that** she was not as rich as*

everyone thought. ○ [+ question word] *He would not reveal **where** he had hidden her chocolate eggs.* **2** to allow something to be seen that, until then, had been hidden: *A gap in the clouds revealed the Atlantic far below.*

revealing /rɪ'viː.lɪŋ/ *adj* **1** describes clothes which show more of the body than is usual: *a revealing dress/shirt* **2** showing something that was not previously known or seen: *A joke can be very revealing **about/of** what someone's really thinking.* **revealingly** /rɪ'viː.lɪŋ.li/ *adv*

reveille /rɪ'væl.i/ ⓤ /'rev.ə.li/ *noun* [S or U] a musical signal played to wake up soldiers in the morning, or the time when it is played

revel /'rev.³l/ *verb* [I] **-ll-** or *US USUALLY* **-l-** LITERARY to dance, drink, sing, etc. at a party or in public, especially in a noisy way **reveller** *UK*, *US* **reveler** /'rev.³l.ə³/ ⓤ /-ə-/ *noun* [C] *On New Year's Eve, thousands of revellers fill Trafalgar Square.* **revelry** /'rev.³l.ri/ *noun* [C usually pl; U] LITERARY *Sounds of revelry came from next door.* ○ *The revelries next door kept me awake all night.*

▲ **revel in** *sth phrasal verb* LITERARY to get great pleasure from a situation or an activity: *She's revelling in her newly found freedom.* ○ *He revelled in his role as team manager.*

revelation /͵rev.ə'leɪ.ʃ³n/ *noun* [C or U] **1** when something is made known that was secret, or a fact that is made known: *a moment of revelation* ○ [+ that] *His wife divorced him after the revelation **that** he was having an affair.* ○ *Shocking revelations **about** their private life appeared in the papers.* **2** **come as/be a revelation** to be an extremely pleasant surprise: *This book came as a complete revelation **to** me.*

revenge /rɪ'vendʒ/ *noun* [U] harm done to someone as a punishment for harm that they have done to someone else: *She **took/got/exacted** (her) revenge **on** him for leaving her by smashing up his car.* ○ *He is believed to have been shot by a rival gang in revenge **for** the shootings last week.*

● **Revenge is sweet.** SAYING said when you feel satisfaction from harming someone who has harmed you

revenge /rɪ'vendʒ/ *verb* [T] to harm someone as a punishment for harm that they have done to you: *to revenge a death/defeat/injustice* ○ [R] *The red team revenged themselves **on** the blue team by winning the semi-final.*

revengeful /rɪ'vendʒ.f³l/ *adj* wanting revenge

revenue /'rev.³n.juː/ ⓤ /-ə.nuː/ *noun* [U] (*ALSO* **revenues**) the income that a government or company receives regularly: *Taxes provide most of the government's revenue.* ○ *Government revenues fell dramatically.*

reverberate /rɪ'vɜː.b³r.eɪt/ ⓤ /-'vɜː.bɚ.eɪt/ *verb* **1** [I] LITERARY If a loud deep sound reverberates, it continues to be heard around an area, so that the area seems to shake: *The narrow street reverberated **with/to** the sound of the workmen's drills.* **2** [I + adv or prep] If an event or idea reverberates somewhere, it has an effect on everyone or everything in a place or group: *News of the disaster reverberated **around** the organization.* ○ *The surge in US share prices reverberated **across** the globe.*

reverberation /rɪ͵vɜː.b³r'eɪ.ʃ³n/ ⓤ /-͵vɜː.bɚ'reɪ-/ *noun* [C usually pl; U] LITERARY *She felt the reverberation(s) in her chest and cursed the drilling outside.* ○ *This move is likely to **have** reverberations* (= effects) *throughout the health service.*

revere /rɪ'vɪə³/ ⓤ /-'vɪr/ *verb* [T] FORMAL to greatly respect and admire someone or something: *Nelson Mandela is revered **for** his brave fight against apartheid.* **reverence** /'rev.³r.³nts/ ⓤ /-ɚ.³nts/ *noun* [U] *She has/shows/feels great reverence **for** her professors.* **reverent** /'rev.³r.³nt/ ⓤ /-ɚ.³nt/ *adj*: *A reverent silence fell over the crowd.* ✻ NOTE: The opposite is **irreverent**. **reverently** /'rev.³r.³nt.li/ ⓤ /-ɚ.³nt-/ *adv*: *He laid the wreath reverently in front of the memorial.* **reverential** /͵rev.³r'ent.ʃ³l/ ⓤ /-ə'rent-/ *adj*: *He opened the ancient book with reverential care.* **reverentially** /͵rev.³r'ent.ʃ³l.i/ /-ə'rent-/

Reverend /'rev.³r.³nd/ /-³nd/ ⓤ /-ɚ.³nd/ *noun* (*WRITTEN ABBREVIATION* **Rev/Revd**) a title for a minister of the Christian church: *the Reverend H. Clark*

reverie /'rev.ªr.i/ ⓤ /-ɚ-/ noun [C or U] LITERARY (a state of having) pleasant dream-like thoughts: *He was lost in reverie until he suddenly heard someone behind him.*

reverse /rɪ'vɜːs/ ⓤ /-'vɝːs/ verb [I or T] to (cause something to) go backwards, or to change the direction, order, position, result, etc. of something to its opposite: MAINLY UK *She reversed (US USUALLY **backed**) (the car) into the parking space.* ○ *The new manager hoped to reverse the decline in the company's fortunes.* ○ *Now that you have a job and I don't, our situations are reversed.* ○ *The Court of Appeal reversed the earlier judgment and set him free.*

• **reverse the charges** (US ALSO **call collect**) to make a telephone call that is paid for by the person receiving it

reverse /rɪ'vɜːs/ ⓤ /-'vɝːs/ noun **1 the reverse** the opposite of what has been suggested: *The teachers say my son is slow, but I believe the reverse (is true).* **2 the reverse** the back of a coin, medal, etc: *The English £1 coin has a royal coat of arms on the reverse.* **3** [U] (ALSO **reverse gear**) the method of controlling a vehicle that makes it go backwards, you must put *the car in/into reverse (gear).* **4** [C] FORMAL a defeat or failure: *They suffered a serious military/political reverse.*

• **in reverse (order)** in the opposite order or way: *To stop the engine, you repeat the same procedures, but in reverse (order).*

• **go into reverse** If a situation goes into reverse, it becomes the opposite of what it was before: *The trend towards home ownership has gone into reverse.*

reversal /rɪ'vɜː.s³l/ ⓤ /-'vɝː-/ noun [C] **1** when something changes to its opposite: *He demanded a reversal of the previous decision/policy.* **2** a problem or failure: *We have suffered a couple of minor/temporary reversals.*

reversible /rɪ'vɜː.s³.bl/ ⓤ /-'vɝː-/ adj **1** If something is reversible, it can be changed back to what it was before. **2** describes clothes that can be worn so that the inside becomes the outside: *a reversible raincoat*

re,verse discrimi'nation noun [U] (UK ALSO **positive discrimination**) when an advantage is given to people who are typically thought to be treated unfairly, usually because of their race or sex

reversion /rɪ'vɜː.ʃ³n/ ⓤ /-'vɝː.ʒ³n/ noun [S or U] **1** FORMAL a change back to a previous and often worse condition: *The new procedures are being seen as a reversion to old, inefficient ways of working.* **2** LEGAL a return of something to its previous owner

revert /rɪ'vɜːt/ ⓤ /-'vɝːt/ verb

▲ **revert to sth** phrasal verb to return to doing, using, being or referring to something, usually something bad or less satisfactory: *Why does the conversation have to revert to money every five minutes?* ○ [+ v-ing] *When they divorced, she reverted to using her maiden name.*

▲ **revert to sb** phrasal verb LEGAL to become the property of a particular person again: *When I die, the house will revert to my sister.*

review /rɪ'vjuː/ verb [T] **1** to consider something in order to make changes to it, give an opinion on it or study it: *The committee is reviewing the current arrangement/situation.* ○ *Let's review (= talk about) what has happened so far.* ○ *He reviewed (= thought about) his options before making a final decision.* **2** If critics review a book, play, film, etc. they write their opinion of it: *I only go to see films that are reviewed favourably.* **3** When an important person reviews a large group of military forces, they formally visit and look at them: *The Queen reviewed the troops on her recent visit.* **4** US FOR **revise** STUDY

review /rɪ'vjuː/ noun **1** [C or U] when you consider something again in order to make changes to it, give an opinion of it or study it: *an annual review of company performance* ○ *a review of the year's top news stories* ○ *Salary levels are under review at the moment.* ○ *Your licence will come up for review every July.* **2** [C] a report in a newspaper, magazine, or programme that gives an opinion about a new book, film, etc: *Derek writes film/theatre/book reviews for the newspapers.* ○ *The play got excellent reviews when it was first seen.* **3** [C usually sing] a (part of a) newspaper or magazine that has articles on films, books, travel, famous people, etc: *Could you pass me the review (section of the paper), please?* **4** [C] a for-

mal military ceremony in which forces are reviewed by an important person: *Many diplomats attended a naval review to mark the anniversary of the end of the war.* **5** [C] a **revue 6** [C] US information or a practice exercise about a subject to be studied: *Their teacher distributed a review for the exam.*

reviewer /rɪ'vjuː.əʳ/ ⓤ /-ɚ/ noun [C] someone who writes articles expressing their opinion of a book, play, film, etc.

revile /rɪ'vaɪl/ verb [T] FORMAL to criticize someone strongly, or say unpleasant things to or about someone: *The judge was reviled in the newspapers for his opinions on rape.*

revise CHANGE /rɪ'vaɪz/ verb [T] to look at or consider again an idea, piece of writing, etc. in order to correct or improve it: *His helpfulness today has made me revise my original opinion/impression of him.* ○ *His publishers made him revise his manuscript three times.*

revised /rɪ'vaɪzd/ adj changed in some ways: *a revised edition of a book* **revision** /rɪ'vɪʒ.³n/ noun [C or U] *These proposals will need a lot of revision.* ○ *He was forced to make several revisions to his speech.*

revise STUDY UK /rɪ'vaɪz/ verb [I or T] (US **review**) to study again something you have already learned, in preparation for an exam: *We're revising (algebra) for the test tomorrow.* **revision** /rɪ'vɪʒ.³n/ noun [U] *She did no revision, but she still got a very high mark.*

revisionism /rɪ'vɪʒ.³n.ɪ.z³m/ noun [U] the questioning of, and attempts to change, the existing beliefs of a political or religious system, especially the Marxist political system **revisionist** /rɪ'vɪʒ.³n.ɪst/ noun [C] *revisionists within the Communist Party* **revisionist** /rɪ'vɪʒ.³n.ɪst/ adj: *revisionist ideas/history*

revitalize, UK USUALLY **-ise** /ˌriː'vaɪ.t³l.aɪz/ ⓤ /-t̬³l-/ verb [T] to give new life, energy, activity or success to something: *Japanese investment has revitalized this part of Britain.*

revive /rɪ'vaɪv/ verb [I or T] to come or bring something back to life, health, existence, or use: *to revive someone's hopes/confidence/fortunes* ○ *My plants revived as soon as I gave them some water.* ○ *A hot shower and a cup of tea will revive you.* ○ *Traditional skills are being revived by local craftsmen.*

revival /rɪ'vaɪ.v³l/ noun **1** [C or U] when something becomes more active or popular again: *Recently, there has been some revival of (interest in) ancient music.* ○ *An economic/artistic revival is sweeping the country.* **2** [C] a performance of a play which has not been seen for a long time: *We're staging a revival of a 1950s play.*

revivify /ˌriː'vɪv.ɪ.faɪ/ verb [T] FORMAL to give new energy and strength to an event or activity: *A leader with real charisma is needed to revivify the political party.*

revoke /rɪ'vəʊk/ ⓤ /-'voʊk/ verb [T] FORMAL to say officially that an agreement, permission, a law, etc. is no longer in effect: *The authorities have revoked their original decision to allow development of this rural area.* **revocation** /ˌrev.ə'keɪ.ʃ³n/ noun [C or U]

revolt FIGHT /rɪ'vəʊlt/ /-'vɒlt/ ⓤ /-'voʊlt/ verb [I] If a large number of people revolt, they refuse to be controlled or ruled, and take often violent action against authority: *The people revolted against foreign rule and established their own government.* **revolt** /rɪ'vəʊlt/ /-'vɒlt/ ⓤ /-'voʊlt/ noun [C or U] *Troops were called in to crush/put down the revolt.* ○ *The army is in revolt (against its commanders).* ⸦See also **revolution**.

revolt DISGUST /rɪ'vəʊlt/ /-'vɒlt/ ⓤ /-'voʊlt/ verb [T] to make someone feel unpleasantly shocked or disgusted: *We were revolted by the dirt and mess in her house.* ○ *It revolts me to know that the world spends so much money on arms when millions are dying of hunger.* ⸦See also **revulsion**.

revolting /rɪ'vəʊl.tɪŋ/ /-'vɒl-/ ⓤ /-'voʊl.t̬ɪŋ/ adj extremely unpleasant; disgusting: *a revolting smell of rotting cabbage* ○ *Picking your nose is a revolting habit.* **revoltingly** /rɪ'vəʊl.tɪŋ.li/ /-'vɒl-/ ⓤ /-'voʊl.t̬ɪŋ-/ adv

revolution POLITICS /ˌrev.ə'luː.ʃ³n/ noun [C or U] a change in the way a country is governed, usually to a different political system and often using violence or war: *The French Revolution changed France from a monarchy to a* *republic.* ○ *The country seems to be heading towards revolution.* ➔See also **revolution** at **revolve**.

revolutionary /ˌrev.əˈluː.ʃᵊn.ᵊr.i/ ⑩ /-er-/ *noun* [C] someone who tries to cause or take part in a revolution
revolutionary /ˌrev.əˈluː.ʃᵊn.ᵊr.i/ ⑩ /-er-/ *adj: a revolutionary leader/movement*

revolution [CHANGE] /ˌrev.əˈluː.ʃᵊn/ *noun* [C] a very important change in the way that people do things: *a technological revolution* ○ *Penicillin produced a revolution in medicine.* ➔See also **revolution** at **revolve**.
revolutionary /ˌrev.əˈluː.ʃᵊn.ᵊr.i/ ⑩ /-er-/ *adj* completely new and having a great effect: *Penicillin was a revolutionary drug.* ○ *The twentieth century brought about revolutionary changes in our lifestyles.*
revolutionize, UK USUALLY **-ise** /ˌrev.əˈluː.ʃᵊn.aɪz/ *verb* [T] to completely change something so that it is much better: *Newton's discoveries revolutionized physics.*

revolve /rɪˈvɒlv/ ⑩ /-ˈvɑːlv/ *verb* [I or T] to move or cause something to move round a central point or line: *The Earth revolves around the sun.* ○ *The gun turret revolved until the gun was aimed at the advancing soldiers.*
revolution /ˌrev.əˈluː.ʃᵊn/ *noun* 1 [S] a circular movement: *The revolution of the Earth around the sun was proposed by Copernicus.* ➔See also **revolution** CHANGE. 2 [C] one complete circular movement of something, for example a wheel: *Engine speed can be measured in revolutions per minute (ABBREVIATION rpm).*
revolving /rɪˈvɒl.vɪŋ/ ⑩ /-ˈvɑːl-/ *adj* [before n] describes something that revolves: *a revolving door*

▲ **revolve around/round sb/sth** *phrasal verb* to have someone or something as the main or most important interest or subject: *The conversation revolved around childcare problems.* ○ *His whole life revolves around football.*
● **think the (whole) world revolves around you** to think you are extremely important: *The trouble with John is he thinks the whole world revolves around him.*

revolver /rɪˈvɒl.vəʳ/ ⑩ /-ˈvɑːl.vɚ/ *noun* [C] a type of small gun held in one hand that can be fired several times without putting more bullets in it

re,volving 'door *noun* [C] a set of doors which you go through by pushing them round in a circle

revue /rɪˈvjuː/ *noun* [C] (ALSO **review**) a not very serious theatrical show with songs, dances, and jokes and short plays often about recent events

revulsion /rɪˈvʌl.ʃᵊn/ *noun* [U] a strong, often sudden, feeling that something is extremely unpleasant: *I turned away in revulsion when they showed a close-up of the operation.* ○ *She looked at him with revulsion.* ○ *He expressed his revulsion at/against/towards the whale hunting.* ➔See also **revolt** DISGUST.

reward /rɪˈwɔːd/ ⑩ /-ˈwɔːrd/ *noun* [C] 1 something given in exchange for good behaviour or good work, etc: *There's a reward for whoever finishes first.* ○ *The rewards of motherhood outweigh the anguish.* 2 an amount of money given to someone who helps the police or who helps to return stolen property to its owner: *The police offered a reward for any information about the robbery.*
reward /rɪˈwɔːd/ ⑩ /-ˈwɔːrd/ *verb* [T] to give someone a reward: *The company rewarded him for his years of service with a grand farewell party and several presents.* ○ SLIGHTLY FORMAL *All his hard work was rewarded (= was made worth it) when he saw his book in print.* ○ FORMAL *He rewarded their kindness with hostility and contempt.*
rewarding /rɪˈwɔː.dɪŋ/ ⑩ /-ˈwɔːr-/ *adj* giving a reward, especially by making you feel satisfied that you have done something important or useful, or done something well: *Is it a rewarding job?* ○ *Textbook writing can be an intellectually and financially rewarding activity.*

rewind /ˌriːˈwaɪnd/ *verb* [T] **rewound, rewound** to put a tape recording back to the beginning: *Will you rewind the tape so we can hear it again?* **rewind** /ˈriː.waɪnd/ *adj: a rewind button*

rewire /ˌriːˈwaɪəʳ/ ⑩ /-ˈwaɪr/ *verb* [T] to put a new system of electric wires into a building or machine: *You really should have the whole house rewired – the existing wiring isn't safe.*

reword /ˌriːˈwɜːd/ ⑩ /-ˈwɜːd/ *verb* [T] to write something again in different words: *She reworded sensitive areas of the report so that it wouldn't be so controversial.*

rework /ˌriːˈwɜːk/ ⑩ /-ˈwɜːk/ *verb* [T] to change a speech or a piece of writing in order to improve it or make it more suitable for a particular purpose: *She reworked her speech for a younger audience.* **reworking** /ˌriːˈwɜː.kɪŋ/ ⑩ /-ˈwɜː-/ *noun* [C] *His latest book is a reworking of material from his previous short stories.*

rewound /ˌriːˈwaʊnd/ *past simple and past participle of* **rewind**

rewrite /ˌriːˈraɪt/ *verb* [T] **rewrote, rewritten** to write something such as a book or speech again, in order to improve it or change it because new information is available: *The news of the revolt meant she had to rewrite her speech.* **rewrite** /ˈriː.raɪt/ *noun* [C] *The producer disliked the script and demanded a rewrite.*

rhapsody /ˈræp.sə.di/ *noun* [C] 1 SPECIALIZED a piece of music which has no formal structure and which expresses powerful feelings: *Rachmaninov's 'Rhapsody on a Theme of Paganini'* 2 FORMAL a speech or piece of writing that contains powerful feelings and enthusiasm
● **go into rhapsodies** to express very great enthusiasm and admiration for something: *She went into rhapsodies over/about the chocolate cake.*
rhapsodic /ræpˈsɒd.ɪk/ ⑩ /-ˈsɑːd-/ *adj* 1 in the form of a rhapsody, or expressing powerful feelings: *The slow movement is wonderfully moody and rhapsodic.* 2 FORMAL expressing great enthusiasm about something
rhapsodize, UK USUALLY **-ise** /ˈræp.sə.daɪz/ *verb* [I] FORMAL to express great enthusiasm for something: *He's always rhapsodizing about/over the joys of having children.*

rheostat /ˈriː.əʊ.stæt/ ⑩ /-oʊ-/ *noun* [C] SPECIALIZED a device used to control and vary the flow of electric current through a machine such as an electric light

rhesus factor /ˈriː.səs,fæk.təʳ/ ⑩ /ˈriː.səs,fæk.tɚ/ *noun* [S] (ABBREVIATION **Rh factor**) SPECIALIZED a substance in the red blood cells of most people which causes the production of ANTIBODIES in the blood: *People whose blood contains the rhesus factor are rhesus positive (Rh+) and those whose blood does not contain it are rhesus negative (Rh-).*

rhesus monkey /ˈriː.səs,mʌŋ.ki/ *noun* [C] a monkey from northern India

rhetoric /ˈret.ᵊr.ɪk/ ⑩ /ˈret.ɚ-/ *noun* [U] 1 speech or writing which is intended to be effective and persuasive: *How far the president will be able to translate his campaign rhetoric into action remains to be seen.* ○ *I was swayed by her rhetoric into donating all my savings to the charity.* 2 SPECIALIZED the study of the ways of using language effectively 3 DISAPPROVING clever language which sounds good but is not sincere or has no real meaning: *In reply to the question, he just produced a lot of empty (= meaningless) rhetoric.*
rhetorical /rɪˈtɒr.ɪ.kᵊl/ ⑩ /-ˈtɔːr.ɪ-/ *adj* describes speech or writing which is intended to seem important or persuasive: *repetition, that tedious rhetorical device*
rhetorically /rɪˈtɒr.ɪ.kli/ ⑩ /-ˈtɔːr.ɪ-/ *adv:* "*You want to know what courage is?*" *he asked rhetorically.*
rhetorician /ˌret.əˈrɪʃ.ᵊn/ ⑩ /ˌret-/ *noun* [C] 1 FORMAL a person who is good at speaking in public 2 SPECIALIZED a person who teaches the skill of speaking and writing in an effective and persuasive way: *Lucian was a famous Greek rhetorician.*

rhe,torical 'question *noun* [C] a question that is asked in order to make a statement and which does not expect an answer: *"Why do these things always happen to me?" is a rhetorical question.*

rheu,matic 'fever *noun* [U] a serious disease that causes fever, swelling of the joints, and possible heart damage

rheumatism /ˈruː.mə.tɪ.zᵊm/ *noun* [U] a medical condition that causes stiffness and pain in the joints or muscles of the body: *She suffers from rheumatism.* ○ *I can't play the piano any more because I have rheumatism in my fingers.* **rheumatic** /ruːˈmæt.ɪk/ ⑩ /-ˈmæt-/ *adj: She has a rheumatic hip.*

R

rheumatoid arthritis /ˌruː.mə.tɔɪd.ɑːˈθraɪ.tɪs/ [US] /-ɑːr-ˈθraɪ.t̬əs/ *noun* [U] a disease that causes stiffness, swelling and pain in the joints of the body

Rh factor *noun* [C usually sing] *WRITTEN ABBREVIATION FOR* **rhesus factor**

rhinestone /ˈraɪn.stəʊn/ [US] /-stoʊn/ *noun* [C] a bright colourless artificial jewel which looks like a diamond and can be sewn onto clothes

rhino /ˈraɪ.nəʊ/ [US] /-noʊ/ *noun* [C] a **rhinoceros**

rhinoceros (*plural* **rhinoceros** or **rhinoceroses**) /raɪˈnɒs.ər.-əs/ [US] /-ˈnɑː.sɚ-/ *noun* [C] (*INFORMAL* **rhino**) a very large thick-skinned animal from Africa or Asia, which has one or two horns on its nose: *a population of black/white rhinoceros* ➲See picture **Animals and Birds** on page Centre 4

rhizome /ˈraɪ.zəʊm/ [US] /-zoʊm/ *noun* [C] *SPECIALIZED* a stem of some plants which grows horizontally along or under the ground and which produces roots and leaves

rhododendron /ˌrəʊ.dəˈden.drən/ [US] /ˌroʊ-/ *noun* [C] a large evergreen bush with large usually bright pink, purple or white flowers: *a rhododendron bush*

rhombus /ˈrɒm.bəs/ [US] /ˈrɑːm-/ *noun* [C] *plural* **rhombuses** or **rhombi** *SPECIALIZED* a flat shape which has four sides that are all of equal length

rhubarb [FOOD] /ˈruː.bɑːb/ [US] /-bɑːrb/ *noun* [U] a plant which has long sour-tasting red and green stems that can be cooked and eaten as a fruit: *Have you ever eaten rhubarb crumble?*

rhubarb [SOUND] /ˈruː.bɑːb/ [US] /-bɑːrb/ *exclamation* a word which is repeated many times in order to produce the sound of people talking when the meaning of the word is not important: *We had to stand at the back of the stage saying "rhubarb, rhubarb" in the crowd scenes.*

rhyme /raɪm/ *verb* [I or T] Words which rhyme have the same last sound: *'Blue' and 'flew' rhyme.* ○ *Can you think of a word that rhymes* ***with*** *'orange'?*

rhyme /raɪm/ *noun* **1** [C] a word which has the same last sound as another word: *Can you think of a rhyme* ***for*** *'orange'?* **2** a short poem, especially for young children: *a book of rhymes and songs* ➲See also **nursery rhyme**. **3** [U] the use of rhymes in poetry: *This poem is her first attempt at rhyme.*

• **in rhyme** written as a poem so that the word at the end of a line has the same last sound as a word at the end of another line: *A lot of modern poetry is not written in rhyme.*

• **be no/without rhyme or reason** to be without any obvious reasonable explanation: *Government money was given out to some people and not to others, apparently without rhyme or reason.* ○ *There is no rhyme or reason* ***to*** *her behaviour.*

ˌrhyming ˈslang *noun* [U] slang which is used instead of a word or phrase and which rhymes with it: *In* ***Cockney*** *rhyming slang, you say 'apples and pears' to mean 'stairs'.*

rhythm /ˈrɪð.əm/ *noun* **1** [C or U] a strong pattern of sounds, words or musical notes which is used in music, poetry and dancing: *He beat out a jazz rhythm on the drums.* ○ *I've got no sense of rhythm, so I'm a terrible dancer.* **2** [C or U] a regular movement or pattern of movements: *She was lulled to sleep by the gentle rhythm of the boat in the water.* ○ *She hit the ball so hard that her opponent had no chance to establish any rhythm in her game.* **3** [C] a regular pattern of change, especially one which happens in nature: *the rhythm of the seasons* ○ *Breathing and sleeping are examples of* ***biological*** *rhythms in humans.*

rhythmic /ˈrɪð.mɪk/ *adj* (*ALSO* **rhythmical**) describes a sound with a regular movement or beat which is repeated: *the rhythmic sound of the train* **rhythmically** /ˈrɪð.mɪ.kli/ *adv*: *Try to breathe deeply and rhythmically.*

ˌrhythm and ˈblues *noun* [U] (*ALSO* **R & B**) a type of popular music of the 1940s and 1950s which has a strong beat

ˈrhythm ˌmethod *noun* [S] a way of preventing pregnancy, in which partners have sex on those days when the woman is unlikely to become pregnant

ˈrhythm ˌsection *noun* [C usually sing] the instruments in a dance or jazz group that give a strong beat to the music: *The drums and double bass usually form the rhythm section of a jazz group.*

rial /ˈraɪ.əl/ /riˈɑːl/ [US] /ˈriː.ɔːl/ *noun* [C] the standard unit of currency used in Iran, Oman and Yemen

rib [BONE] /rɪb/ *noun* **1** [C] a bone that curves round from your back to your chest: *My son broke a rib when he fell off a ladder.* ➲See picture **The Body** on page Centre 5 **2** [C or U] a piece of meat taken from this part of an animal: *He cooked rib of lamb for Sunday lunch.* ➲See also **spareribs**. **3** [C] one of the curved pieces of metal or wood which support the structure of a boat or roof

• **poke/dig *sb* in the ribs** to push your finger quickly into someone's chest, usually to make them notice something or to stop them from doing or saying something

rib [JOKE] /rɪb/ *verb* [T] **-bb-** *INFORMAL* to joke and laugh at someone in a friendly way about something: *His brothers ribbed him* ***about*** *his new girlfriend.* **ribbing** /ˈrɪb.ɪŋ/ *noun* [C usually sing] *They* ***gave*** *him a ribbing about his accent.* ➲See also **ribbing** at **rib** PATTERN.

rib [PATTERN] /rɪb/ *noun* [U] a method of knitting that makes a pattern of raised parallel lines **ribbed** /rɪbd/ *adj*: *Do you prefer plain or ribbed tights?*

ribbing /ˈrɪb.ɪŋ/ *noun* [U] a pattern of raised lines on a piece of woollen clothing: *He liked the ribbing on the cuffs of the sweater.* ➲See also **ribbing** at **rib** JOKE.

ribald /ˈrɪb.əld/ /ˈraɪ.bəld/ [US] /ˈraɪ.bɔːld/ *adj* *OLD-FASHIONED* describes language that refers to sex in a rude but humorous way: *He entertained us with ribald stories.*

ribaldry /ˈrɪb.əl.dri/ /ˈraɪ.bəl-/ [US] /ˈraɪ.bɔːl-/ *noun* [U] *OLD-FASHIONED* language that refers to sex in a rude but humorous way: *good-natured ribaldry*

ribbon /ˈrɪb.ən/ *noun* **1** [C or U] a long narrow strip of material used to tie things together or as a decoration: *Sandra often wears a ribbon in her hair.* ○ *He tied up the present with ribbon.* **2** *LITERARY* **a ribbon of *sth*** a long narrow piece of something: *A ribbon of road stretched ahead of us across the desert.* **3** [C] a small piece of coloured material given to someone in the armed forces to show appreciation for their brave actions **4** [C] *SPECIALIZED* the narrow strip of material that contains the ink for a typewriter: *My typewriter needs a new ribbon.*

• **in ribbons** torn into narrow strips: *Her coat was in ribbons.* ○ *His shirt hung in tattered ribbons.*

• **cut/tear *sth/sb* to/into ribbons** to destroy or badly damage something or someone by cutting or tearing them many times: *Our new kitten has torn the living room curtains to ribbons.* ○ *FIGURATIVE The attacking soldiers were cut to ribbons* (= killed) *by machine-gun fire.*

ˌribbon deˈvelopment *noun* [U] *UK* when long rows of buildings are built along main roads leading out of towns

ˈrib ˌcage *noun* [C usually sing] the structure of ribs that protects your heart and lungs in your chest

riboflavin /ˌraɪ.bəʊˈfleɪ.vɪn/ [US] /ˈraɪ.bə.fleɪ-/ *noun* [U] *SPECIALIZED* **vitamin B_2**

rib-tickling /ˈrɪb.tɪk.lɪŋ/ *adj* (*ALSO* **rib-ticklingly funny**) *INFORMAL* describes a story or joke which is very amusing

rice /raɪs/ *noun* [U] **1** the small seeds of a particular type of grass, which are cooked and eaten as food: *boiled/steamed/fried rice* ○ *long-grain rice* ○ *Do you prefer brown rice or white rice?* **2** a grass which produces these seeds and grows in warm wet places

ˈrice ˌpaddy *noun* [C] a field full of water in which rice is grown

ˈrice ˌpaper *noun* [U] thin edible paper that is used in cooking and in painting

ˌrice ˈpudding *noun* [U] a sweet dish made by cooking rice in milk and sugar

rich [MONEY] /rɪtʃ/ *adj* **1** having a lot of money or valuable possessions: *He's the third richest man in Britain.* ○ *They're one of the world's richest nations.* ○ *He is determined to* ***get*** *rich quickly.* **2** containing a large amount of a valuable natural substance such as coal, oil or wood: *The region is rich* ***in*** *minerals and coal deposits.* ○ *The country has vast oil reserves and rich deposits of other minerals.* **3** Rich land or soil contains a large

R

amount of substances which help plants to grow: *the richest arable land in the country* **4** A rich material is very beautiful and valuable: *She wore a velvet skirt and a rich brocade jacket.* **5** If the style of something such as a piece of furniture or a building is rich, it contains a lot of decoration: *The temple is noted for its rich carvings.* **6 rich in *sth*** containing a lot of something desirable: *Pineapple juice is rich in vitamins A and B.* ○ *The English language is rich in vocabulary.* **7** containing a lot of exciting events or experiences and therefore very interesting: *He has written a book about the island's rich **history**.* ○ *She had a rich and varied life and met many famous and exciting people.*

-rich /-rɪtʃ/ *suffix* containing a large amount of a valuable substance: *milk and other calcium-rich food* ○ *an oil-rich country*

the rich *plural noun* rich people considered together as a group: *The resort is frequented by the rich and famous.*

riches /ˈrɪtʃ.ɪz/ *plural noun* **1** a large amount of money or valuable possessions: *She donated a sizeable portion of her riches to children's charities.* **2** a large quantity of a valuable natural substance: *The country has great oil/ mineral riches.* ○ *They plundered the rainforest for its natural riches.*

richly /ˈrɪtʃ.li/ *adv* **1 richly decorated/furnished, etc.** having a lot of beautiful or expensive decoration, furniture, etc: *The facade of the church is richly decorated in green and white marble.* **2** in a very special or valuable way, or in a way that is greater than usual: *The cake takes two hours to cook, but your patience will be richly **rewarded**.* ○ *She finally obtained the recognition which she so richly **deserved**.*

richness /ˈrɪtʃ.nəs/ *noun* [U] when something has a lot of a particular quality or valuable substance: *We were impressed by the great richness of detail in her painting.* ➲See also **richness** at **rich** FOOD, **rich** COLOUR/SOUND.

rich [FOOD] /rɪtʃ/ *adj* If food is rich, it contains a large amount of oil, butter, eggs or cream: *This chocolate mousse is too rich for me.* ➲See also **richness** at **rich** MONEY; **rich** COLOUR/SOUND. **richness** /ˈrɪtʃ.nəs/ *noun* [U] *The richness of the food made him feel slightly ill.*

rich [COLOUR/SOUND] /rɪtʃ/ *adj* A rich colour, sound, smell or taste is strong in a pleasing or attractive way: *This lipstick gives long-lasting rich colour.* ○ *She produced a rich, deep tone from her clarinet.* ○ *The wine has a rich aromatic flavour.* **richness** /ˈrɪtʃ.nəs/ *noun* [U] *richness of flavour* ○ *It's a wonderful painting – I love the richness of the colours.* ➲See also **richness** at **rich** MONEY, **rich** FOOD.

rich [CRITICISM] /rɪtʃ/ *adj* [after v] used to describe someone's opinions when that person has the same bad qualities that they are criticizing: *The education minister's criticism of the new exam system seems rich, considering it was he who demanded the changes in the first place.* ○ *"He said I was looking rather fat." "**That's** a bit rich **coming from** him."*

the Richter scale /ðəˈrɪk.tə.skeɪl/ [US] /-t̬ɚ-/ *noun* [S] a system used to measure the strength of an earthquake: *The earthquake in Mexico City registered 7.1 on the Richter scale.*

rick [PILE] /rɪk/ *noun* [C] (ALSO **hayrick**) a large pile of straw or hay that has been built in a regular shape

rick [TWIST] /rɪk/ *verb* [T] *UK INFORMAL* to twist a part of your body and hurt it: *I ricked my neck while I was playing squash.*

rickets /ˈrɪk.ɪts/ *noun* [U] a disease which children who lack VITAMIN D can suffer from, in which the bones become soft and not shaped correctly

rickety /ˈrɪk.ɪ.ti/ [US] /-ə.t̬i/ *adj* in bad condition and therefore weak and likely to break: *Careful! That chair's a bit rickety.* ○ *She slowly climbed the rickety wooden steps.* ○ *FIGURATIVE The recession put a lot of strain on an already rickety economic system.*

rickshaw, ricksha /ˈrɪk.ʃɔː/ [US] /-ʃɑː/ *noun* [C] a small covered passenger vehicle with two wheels which is usually pulled by one person

ricochet /ˈrɪk.ə.ʃeɪ/ *verb* [I] If a ball or bullet ricochets, it hits a surface and bounces away from it at an angle: *The ball ricocheted **off** the goalkeeper and into the net.*

ricochet /ˈrɪk.ə.ʃeɪ/ *noun* [C] *He was hit by a ricochet from a stray bullet.*

ricotta /rɪˈkɒt.ə/ [US] /-ˈkɑː.t̬ə/ *noun* [U] a soft white Italian cheese which does not have a strong taste

rid /rɪd/ *adj* **1 be rid of *sth/sb*** to not now have an unwanted or unpleasant task, object or person: *I didn't enjoy marking those papers and I was glad to be rid of them.* **2 get rid of *sth*** to remove or throw away something unwanted: *That cream got rid of my skin rash.* ○ *I used weedkiller to get rid of the weeds in the garden.* **3 get rid of *sth*** to sell an old or unwanted possession: *Have you managed to get rid of your old Volvo yet?* **4 get rid of *sb*** to send away someone annoying or to persuade them to leave: *We got rid of our unwelcome guests by saying we had to go to bed.*

rid /rɪd/ *verb* **ridding, rid** or **ridded, rid** or **ridded**

▲ **rid *sb/sth* of *sth/sb*** *phrasal verb* to cause someone or something to be free of an unpleasant or harmful thing or person: *Our aim is to rid this government of corruption.*

riddance /ˈrɪd.ᵊnts/ *noun INFORMAL* **good riddance (to bad rubbish)** said when you are pleased that a bad or unwanted thing or person, or something of poor quality, has gone: *We've got rid of the old computer system, and good riddance to bad rubbish is what I say.*

ridden [RIDE] /ˈrɪd.ᵊn/ *past participle of* **ride**

-ridden [FULL OF] /-rɪd.ᵊn/ *suffix* full of something unpleasant or bad: *It is a superstition-ridden community.* ○ *She was guilt-ridden when she discovered that the business had failed because of her.*

riddle [QUESTION] /ˈrɪd.l̩/ *noun* **1** [C] a type of question which describes something in a difficult and confusing way, and which has a clever or amusing answer, often asked as a game: **2** [C usually sing] something which is confusing, or a problem which is difficult to solve: *Scientists may have **solved** the riddle **of** Saturn's rings.*

• **talk/speak in riddles** to say things in a confusing way

riddle [MAKE HOLES] /ˈrɪd.l̩/ *verb* [T] to make a lot of holes in something: *The anti-aircraft guns riddled the plane's wings **with** bullets.*

riddled /ˈrɪd.l̩d/ *adj* **riddled with holes** full of holes: *He wore an old jacket riddled with holes.*

• **be riddled with *sth*** If a plan or system, etc. is riddled with bad features, such as mistakes, it is full of them: *This article is riddled with errors.*

ride /raɪd/ *verb* [I or T] **rode, ridden 1** to sit on a horse or a bicycle and travel along on it controlling its movements: *I learned to ride a bike when I was six.* ○ *I ride my bicycle to work.* ○ *I ride to work **on** my bicycle.* ○ *The hunters came riding **by/past** on their horses.* ○ *He rides well/ badly* (= He can ride horses well/badly). ➲See Note **drive or ride?** at **drive** USE VEHICLE. **2** to travel in a vehicle, such as a car, bus or train: *MAINLY US We rode the train from Sydney to Perth.* ○ *He hasn't got a car so he rides to work **on** the bus.*

• **ride (on) a wave of *sth*** If you ride (on) a wave of a feeling, you benefit from it: *The Prime Minister is riding (on) a wave of popularity.*

• **let *sth* ride** *INFORMAL* to not take any action to stop something wrong or unpleasant, thinking that action may not be necessary or is not yet necessary: *Don't panic about the low sales – let it ride for a while till we see if business picks up.*

• **be riding for a fall** to be behaving in a way that is likely to lead you into trouble: *She spends far more than she earns and she's riding for a fall.*

• **be riding high** to be very successful: *riding high **in** the polls/charts*

• **ride roughshod over *sb/sth*** to do what you want without giving any attention to other people or their wishes: *They accused the government of riding roughshod over parliamentary procedure.*

ride /raɪd/ *noun* [C] **1** a journey on a horse or bicycle, or in a vehicle: *It's a short bus ride to the airport.* ○ *I went for a (horse) ride last Saturday.* ○ *Do you want to come for a ride **on** my motorbike?* **2** a free journey in a car to a place where you want to go: *He asked me for a ride into town.* **3** a machine in an amusement park which people travel in or are moved around by for entertainment: *My*

R

favourite ride is the Ferris wheel.

• **take** *sb* **for a ride** INFORMAL to deceive or cheat someone: *Be careful or he'll take you for a ride.*

rider /'raɪ.dəʳ/ ⓤ /-dɚ/ *noun* [C] a person who travels along on a horse or bicycle: *One of the riders was thrown off his horse.* ⊃See also **rider.** ⊃See picture **Sports** on page Centre 10 **riderless** /'raɪ.də.ləs/ ⓤ /-dɚ-/ *adj:* a *riderless horse*

riding /'raɪ.dɪŋ/ *noun* [U] the sport or activity of riding horses: *Have you ever been riding?* ○ *She goes riding on Saturdays.* ○ *riding boots and a riding hat*

PHRASAL VERBS WITH **ride** ▼

▲ **ride on** *sth/sb phrasal verb* When something important, such as your reputation or money, rides on a particular person or thing, it will be gained or achieved if that person or thing is successful: *The future of the company now rides on the new managing director.* ○ *I have a lot of money riding on that horse* (= I will win or lose a lot of money if that horse wins or loses the race).

▲ **ride** *sth* **out** *phrasal verb* [M] **1** to continue to exist during a difficult situation and until it ends, without serious harm: *Many companies did not manage to ride out the recession.* **2** If a ship rides out a period of bad weather, it continues to float during it, without serious damage: *The ship managed to ride out the storm.*

• **ride (out) the storm** to manage not to be destroyed, harmed or permanently affected by the difficult situation you experience: *The government seem confident that they'll ride out the storm.*

▲ **ride up** *phrasal verb* If an item of clothing rides up, it moves up out of position: *Your skirt has ridden up at the back.*

rider /'raɪ.dəʳ/ ⓤ /-dɚ/ *noun* [C] FORMAL a statement that is added to what has already been said or decided, or an addition to a government BILL (= a written plan for a law): *I should like to add a rider to the judgment of the court.* ⊃See also **rider** at **ride.**

ridge /rɪdʒ/ *noun* [C] **1** a long narrow raised part of a surface, especially a high edge along a mountain: *We walked along the narrow mountain ridge.* ○ FIGURATIVE *A ridge* (= narrow area) *of high pressure will bring good weather this afternoon.* **2** the part of a roof where the sloping sides join at the top

ridicule /'rɪd.ɪ.kjuːl/ *noun* [U] unkind words or actions that make someone or something look stupid or worthless: *She was treated with scorn and ridicule by her colleagues when she applied for the job.* ○ *He's become an object of ridicule* (= a person that everyone thinks is stupid and criticizes or laughs at).

• **hold** *sb/sth* **up to ridicule** to laugh unkindly and publicly at someone or something, or make them seem ridiculous: *Her plans were held up to ridicule.*

• **lay** *yourself* **open to ridicule** to make it easy for people to laugh unkindly at you: *You lay yourself open to ridicule wearing clothes like that.*

ridicule /'rɪd.ɪ.kjuːl/ *verb* [T] to laugh at someone in an unkind way: *She rarely spoke her mind out of fear of being ridiculed.* ○ *At the time he was ridiculed for his ideas.*

ridiculous /rɪ'dɪk.jʊ.ləs/ *adj* stupid or unreasonable and deserving to be laughed at: *Do I look ridiculous in this hat?* ○ *Don't be so ridiculous! I can't possibly afford to go on holiday.* ○ *It's ridiculous to expect a two-year-old to be able to read!* **ridiculously** /rɪ'dɪk.jʊ.lə.sli/ *adv:* *Hotel rooms in the city are ridiculously overpriced during the festival.*

riding /'raɪ.dɪŋ/ *noun* [U] ⊃See at **ride.**

'riding ,school *noun* [C] a place where you can learn to ride horses

rife /raɪf/ *adj* [after v] FORMAL **1** If something unpleasant is rife, it is very common or frequent: *Dysentery and malaria are rife in the refugee camps.* **2 rife with** *sth* full of something unpleasant: *The office was rife with rumours.*

riff /rɪf/ *noun* [C] in jazz or popular music, a tune which continues or appears regularly in a piece of music while other parts vary or are added: *The song is punctuated by long guitar riffs.*

riffle /'rɪf.l̩/ *verb* [T] (ALSO **riffle through**) to look quickly through the pages of a book, magazine, etc., or through a collection of things: *He riffled through the stack of papers on his desk.*

riff-raff /'rɪf.ræf/ *plural noun* DISAPPROVING people with a bad reputation or of a low social class: *She says that charging high prices will keep the riff-raff out.*

rifle GUN /'raɪ.fl̩/ *noun* [C] a type of gun with a long barrel, which is fired from the shoulder and is designed to be accurate at long distances

rifle SEARCH /'raɪ.fl̩/ *verb* [I or T] to search quickly through something, often in order to steal something: *The safe had been rifled and the diamonds were gone.* ○ *He rifled through the papers on the desk, but couldn't find the photographs.*

'rifle ,range *noun* [C] a place where you can practise shooting with a rifle

rift /rɪft/ *noun* [C] **1** a large crack in the ground or in rock: *The stream had cut a deep rift in the rock.* **2** a serious disagreement which separates two people who have been friends and stops their friendship continuing: *The marriage caused a rift between the brothers and they didn't speak to each other for ten years.*

'rift ,valley *noun* [C] a valley with steep sides formed by movements of the Earth's surface

rig DISHONESTLY ARRANGE /rɪg/ *verb* [T] **-gg-** to arrange dishonestly for the result of something, for example an election, to be changed: *Previous elections in the country have been rigged by the ruling party.*

• **rig the market** to make the price of shares go up or down in order to make a profit

rigging /'rɪg.ɪŋ/ *noun* [U] when a vote or result, etc. is rigged: *ballot rigging* ○ *Opposition parties have protested over alleged vote rigging in the election.* ⊃See also **rigging** at **rig** FIX IN PLACE.

rig FIX IN PLACE /rɪg/ *verb* [T] **-gg-** to fix a piece of equipment in place: *We rigged up a tent between two trees.* ○ *The sailors rigged the ship with new sails.*

rigging /'rɪg.ɪŋ/ *noun* [U] the ropes which support and control a ship's sails ⊃See also **rigging** at **rig** DISHONESTLY ARRANGE.

rig STRUCTURE /rɪg/ *noun* [C] a large structure which is used for removing oil or gas from the ground or the bottom of the sea: *Safety precautions on oil rigs are designed to cope with fires and small-scale explosions.*

rig TRUCK /rɪg/ *noun* [C] MAINLY US a truck consisting of two or more parts which bend where they are joined so that the vehicle can turn corners more easily

---

PHRASAL VERBS WITH **rig** ▼

▲ **rig** *sb* **out** *phrasal verb* [M] INFORMAL to put a particular type of clothing on someone: [R] *We rigged ourselves out in tracksuits and running shoes for the race.*

rig-out /'rɪg.aʊt/ *noun* [C] INFORMAL a set of clothes: *I want to get myself a new rig-out for the party.*

▲ **rig** *sth* **up** *phrasal verb* [M] to quickly make a piece of equipment from any materials you can find: *I rigged up a temporary radio aerial from a coat hanger.*

right CORRECT /raɪt/ *adj* **1** correct: *You got three answers right and two wrong.* ○ *I set the clock to the right time.* ○ *"Is that Ms Kramer?" "Yes, that's right."* ○ *Am I right in thinking* (= Is it true) *that you will be at the conference?* ○ *You're right to be annoyed – you've been treated very badly.* ○ *You must put matters right* (= make the situation better) *by telling the truth.* ⊃Compare **wrong** NOT CORRECT. See **correct or right?** at **correct. 2** If you are right about something or someone, you are correct in your judgment or statement about it or them: *You were right about Pete – he's a real troublemaker.*

• **be on the right track** to be doing something in a way that will bring good results: *These results suggest that we are on the right track.*

• **put/set** *sb* **right** INFORMAL to stop someone believing something which is not true, or to correct them by telling them the truth: *She thought she wouldn't have to work hard, but we soon put her right on that.* ⊃See also **put/set** sb **right** at **right** HEALTHY.

right /raɪt/ *adv* correctly: *Why does he never do anything right?*

right /raɪt/ *verb* [T] **1** FORMAL If you right a situation or a mistake, you make it better or correct it: *It's a terrible situation and we should right it as soon as possible.* **2** If a boat rights itself, it turns itself back to its correct position in the water: *The canoe will right itself if it capsizes.*

rightly /ˈraɪt.li/ *adv* in a correct or exact way: *Many people rightly believe that the war is a sham.* ○ *"What's the quickest way from here to the library?" "I don't rightly know."*

rights /raɪts/ *plural noun* **put/set sth to rights** to improve or correct something: *The company needs over a million dollars to set its finances to rights.*

USAGE

right or **true**?

Right is usually used to say something is correct or to agree with something someone has said.

He gave the right answer.

"That's right, they live in central London."

True is usually used to say that something is based on facts.

Is it true that she's leaving?

Everything I've told you is true.

---

right SUITABLE /raɪt/ *adj* **1** suitable or desirable, or as it should be: *He's the right person for the job.* ○ *I think you've made the right decision.* ○ *The temperature of the swimming pool was just right* (= exactly as I wanted it). ○ *That hat looks just right on you.* ○ *He thought the time was right to let his intentions be known.* ⊃Compare **wrong** NOT SUITABLE. **2** describes a person who is considered socially important or a place that is considered socially desirable: *She knows all the right people.* ○ *He likes to be seen in the right clubs and restaurants.*

● **the right way round/up** UK (US **the right way around/up**) in the correct position: *The lid has to go on the right way round or it won't fit.* ○ *Keep the bottle the right way up.*

● **in the right place at the right time** in the best position or place to take advantage of an opportunity: *The key to success is to be in the right place at the right time.*

right /raɪt/ *adv* **go right** If something goes right, it is successful or happens in a way that you hoped it would: *Things haven't been going right for me these past few months.*

right MORALLY ACCEPTABLE /raɪt/ *adj* [after v] considered fair or morally acceptable by most people: *I don't believe they should have put him in prison. It isn't right.* ○ [+ to infinitive] *It's not right to criticize someone behind their back.* ○ [+ that] *It is only* (= completely) *right that men and women should be paid the same for doing the same work.* ⊃Compare **wrong** IMMORAL.

right /raɪt/ *noun* **1** [U] what is considered to be morally good or acceptable: *Your conscience should tell you the difference between right and wrong.* **2** [C] the claim which a person or animal has to be treated in a fair, morally acceptable or legal way, or to have the things that are necessary for life: *She campaigned for women's rights during the 1960s.* ○ *Everyone has a right to education.* ○ *She has no more right to a company car than I have* (= She does not deserve one more than I do). ○ [+ to infinitive] *You're not my boss, so what right* (= authority) *have you got to criticize me?* ○ *You have every right* (= You have a good reason) *to complain.*

● **the rights and wrongs** the details of who or what is fair or unfair: *I don't care about the rights and wrongs of the matter – I just want you both to stop arguing.*

● **by rights** if the situation was fair: *By rights, it should be my turn next.*

● **by right of** because of: *She spoke first, by right of her position as director.*

● **in the right** If you are in the right, what you are doing is morally or legally correct.

● **in your own right** If someone has a position in their own right, they have earned it or obtained it by themselves and not because of anyone else: *She's a millionaire in her own right.*

● **within your rights** If you are within your rights to do something, you are legally allowed to do it: *I think I'm quite within my rights to demand a full refund.*

rightly /ˈraɪt.li/ *adv* **1** acting in a way that is suitable and acceptable: *They quite rightly complained to the manager.* **2 rightly or wrongly** used to mean that whether something is correct or not, it is a fact: *Rightly or wrongly, she has been given the post of managing director.*

rightness /ˈraɪt.nəs/ *noun* [U] moral or legal correctness: *He is convinced of the rightness of his actions.*

rightful /ˈraɪt.fᵊl/ *adj* A rightful position or claim is one which is morally or legally correct: *Don't forget that I am the rightful owner of this house.* **rightfully** /ˈraɪt.fᵊl.i/ *adv*: *The furniture rightfully belongs to you.*

rights /raɪts/ *plural noun* the legal authority over who may use a book or film: *He has acquired the **film** rights to the book* (= He is allowed to make a film of the book).

right DIRECTION /raɪt/ *adj, adv* on or towards the side of your body that is to the east when you are facing north: *Most people write with their right hand.* ○ *Turn/Go right* (= Turn into the road on the right side) *at the first traffic lights.* ○ US *I took/made/*(INFORMAL) *hung a right* (= turned into the next road on the right side) *after crossing the bridge.* ○ *In this photo, my wife is the woman standing on/to my right.* ⊃Compare **left** DIRECTION.

● **give your right arm** INFORMAL If you say that you would give your right arm to do or have something, you mean you would like it very much: *I would give my right arm to meet the President.*

● **right, left and centre** (US **right and left**) all the time or everywhere: *He spends money right, left and centre.*

right /raɪt/ *noun* [S] the right side: *English is written and read from left to right.* ○ *King's Avenue is the first right* (= the first road on the right side).

the right POLITICS, **the Right** *group noun* [S] political parties or people that have traditional opinions, and who believe in low taxes, private ownership of property and industry, and less help for the poor: *In Britain, the right was/were in power after 1979.* ○ *He's a man of the far* (= extreme) *right.* ⊃Compare **the left** POLITICS.

rightist /ˈraɪ.tɪst/ ⓤ /-t̬ɪst/ *adj* A rightist politician or government is one that supports the beliefs of the political right.

rightist /ˈraɪ.tɪst/ ⓤ /-t̬ɪst/ *noun* [C] a politician who supports the beliefs of the political right.

right HEALTHY /raɪt/ *adj* healthy, or working correctly: *Since eating that food last night, I haven't felt quite right.* ○ *Something isn't quite right **with** the brakes on your bike.*

● **be as right as rain** INFORMAL to be healthy, especially after having been ill for a period of time

● **be not in your right mind** to be not thinking clearly or to be mentally ill: *My poor old granny isn't in her right mind half the time.*

● **be not (quite) right in the head** INFORMAL to lack one or more of the mental abilities that most people have

● **put/set sb right** to make someone feel better: *A good night's sleep will soon put you right.* ⊃See also **put/set sb right** at **right** CORRECT.

right AGREEMENT /raɪt/ *exclamation* INFORMAL **1** used to express agreement with someone or to show that you have understood what someone has said: *"Johnny, you climb up first." "Right."* **2** said when you want to make a group of people notice you, especially so that you can start an activity: *Right, you lot. Could you all stop talking, and then we'll begin.* **3** said between parts of a story that you are telling, in order to make certain that people are paying attention and understanding: *"So there I was right, middle of the night, right, and this guy came up to me...*

● **Right you are** (ALSO **Right oh**) OLD-FASHIONED INFORMAL said to show that you understand and agree: *"Give me a shout when you're ready." "Right you are."*

● **too right** UK INFORMAL said when you agree completely: *"You can't do anything in this town if you haven't got any money." "Too right."*

right EXACTLY /raɪt/ *adv* **1** exactly or all the way: *I've got a pimple right on the end of my nose.* ○ *They built a row of hotels right along the sea-front.* **2** used for emphasis: *The car ran right* (= completely) *out of fuel.* ○ *She walked right* (= all the way) *past me without noticing me.*

○ *I'll be right back/I'll be right with you* (= I will return very soon).

• **right behind *sb*** If someone is right behind you, they give you their complete support: *My whole family are right behind me in this crisis.*

• **right away/now** immediately: *You'd better leave right now.*

• **right now** at the present time: *We're very busy right now.*

right /raɪt/ *adj* **[before n]** *INFORMAL* used for emphasizing when something is bad: *He's a right idiot.* ○ *His house is a right mess.*

• **a right one** *INFORMAL* someone or something that you think is very foolish: *"We've got a right one here, eh!"*

right [TITLE] /raɪt/ *adv* used as part of the title of particular people, such as bishops and some members of Parliament: *The committee will be chaired by the Right Honourable Sarah Bast, MP.*

ˈright ˌangle *noun* **[C]** an angle of 90°: *A square has four right angles.*

right-angled triangle *UK* /ˌraɪt.æŋ.gl̩dˈtraɪ.æŋ.gl̩/ *noun* **[C]** (*US* **right triangle**) a triangle which has one angle of 90°

righteous /ˈraɪ.tʃəs/ *adj FORMAL* morally correct: *He was regarded as a righteous and holy man.* ○ *The government has shown an outburst of righteous anger at the attack.* ➲See also **self-righteous**. **righteously** /ˈraɪ.tʃə.sli/ *adv* **righteousness** /ˈraɪ.tʃə.snəs/ *noun* **[U]**

ˌright ˈfield *noun* **[U]** the area of a baseball field beyond the BASES (= places to which players run) and between first and second base

rightful /ˈraɪt.fəl/ *adj* ➲See at **right** MORALLY ACCEPTABLE **rightfully** /ˈraɪt.fəl.i/ *adv*

right-hand /ˈraɪt.hænd/ *adj* **[before n]** on or to the right: *In North America, vehicles drive on the right-hand **side** of the road.*

ˌright-hand ˈdrive *adj* A right-hand drive vehicle has the controls on the right side, and the vehicle is intended to be driven on the left side of the road. **ˌright-hand ˈdrive** *noun* **[S]**

right-handed /ˌraɪtˈhæn.dɪd/ *adj* using your right hand to write with and do most things: *She's right-handed.*

right-hander /ˌraɪtˈhæn.dəʳ/ [US] /-dɚ/ *noun* **[C]** **1** *INFORMAL* someone who uses their right hand for writing and for doing most things **2** (*ALSO* **right**) a hit made with the right hand

ˌright-hand ˈman *noun* **[C usually sing]** Someone's right-hand man is their most trusted and important helper and supporter, especially at work.

rightly /ˈraɪt.li/ *adj* ➲See at **right** MORALLY ACCEPTABLE and **right** CORRECT

right-minded /ˌraɪtˈmaɪn.dɪd/ *adj* **[before n]** (*ALSO* **right-thinking**) *APPROVING* having beliefs or opinions that most people think are reasonable and sensible: *Every right-minded person is against terrorism.*

ˌright of ˈway [DRIVING] *noun* **[C or U]** the legal right to go first across a road, before other road users: *Pedestrians have right of way at this turning.*

ˌright of ˈway [WALKING] *noun* **[C]** a path or road over private land which people are legally allowed to walk along

ˌright ˈon [POLITICAL] *OFTEN DISAPPROVING* having beliefs that are characteristic of someone who supports the political LEFT

ˌright ˈon [YES] *exclamation OLD-FASHIONED SLANG* an expression of agreement or approval: *"D'you want to listen to some Jimi Hendrix?" "Right on."*

right-wing /ˌraɪtˈwɪŋ/ *adj* supporting the political right: *She's extremely right-wing.* **the ˌright ˈwing** *noun* **[S + sing or pl v]** *He's **on** the right wing of the party.*

right-winger /ˌraɪtˈwɪŋ.əʳ/ [US] /-ɚ/ *noun* **[C]** someone who supports the beliefs of the political right

rigid /ˈrɪdʒ.ɪd/ *adj* stiff or fixed; not able to be bent, moved, changed or persuaded: *a rigid steel and concrete structure* ○ *I was rigid **with*** (= stiff and unable to move because of) *fear.* ○ *DISAPPROVING We were disappointed that they insisted on such a rigid interpretation of the rules.* **rigidly** /ˈrɪdʒ.ɪd.li/ *adv MAINLY DISAPPROVING*

rigidity /rɪˈdʒɪd.ɪ.ti/ [US] /-ə.t̬i/ *noun* **[U]**

rigmarole, *US ALSO* **rigamarole** /ˈrɪg.mə.rəʊl/ [US] /-roʊl/ *noun* **[U]** *DISAPPROVING* a long set of actions or words without any real purpose: *The customs officials made us **go through the (whole)** rigmarole of opening up our bags for inspection.*

rigor mortis /ˌrɪg.əˈmɔː.tɪs/ [US] /-ɚˈmɔːr.t̬ɪs/ *noun* **[U]** *SPECIALIZED* the stiffness of the joints and muscles of a dead body: *Rigor mortis usually **sets in** between two and four hours after death.*

rigour [FORCEFULNESS] *UK, US* **rigor** /ˈrɪg.əʳ/ [US] /-ɚ/ *noun* **[U]** forcefulness or extremely strict obedience of rules: *They were punished with unusual rigour.* **rigours** *UK, US* **rigors** /ˈrɪg.əz/ [US] /-ɚz/ *plural noun*: *They survived the rigours* (= severe conditions) *of the winter.* **rigorous** /ˈrɪg.ər.əs/ [US] /ˈ-ɚ-/ *adj* **rigorously** /ˈrɪg.ər.ə.sli/ [US] /-ɚ-/ *adv*

rigour [CARE] *UK, US* **rigor** /ˈrɪg.əʳ/ [US] /-ɚ/ *noun* **[U]** *SLIGHTLY FORMAL APPROVING* when you look at or consider every part of something carefully to make certain that it is correct or safe: *Her arguments lacked intellectual rigour.* **rigorous** /ˈrɪg.ər.əs/ [US] /-ɚ-/ *adj APPROVING* careful to look at or consider every part of something to make certain it is correct or safe: *rigorous testing/checking/methods* **rigorously** /ˈrɪg.ər.ə.sli/ [US] /-ɚ-/ *adv*

rile /raɪl/ *verb* **[T]** *INFORMAL* to make angry: *Don't let her rile you.*

rim /rɪm/ *noun* **[C]** the outer, often curved or circular, edge of something: *The rim of the cup was chipped and broken.* ○ *My reading glasses have gold/plastic/wire rims.*

rim /rɪm/ *verb* **[T]** **-mm-** to be round or along the edge of something: *The glass was rimmed **with** sugar.* **rimless** /ˈrɪm.ləs/ *adj*: *He's got new rimless reading glasses.* **-rimmed** /-rɪmd/ *suffix*: *gold-rimmed glasses*

rind /raɪnd/ *noun* **[C or U]** the hard outer layer or covering of particular fruits and foods: *lemon/orange rind* ○ *bacon/cheese rind* ➲Compare **peel** FOOD.

Ring

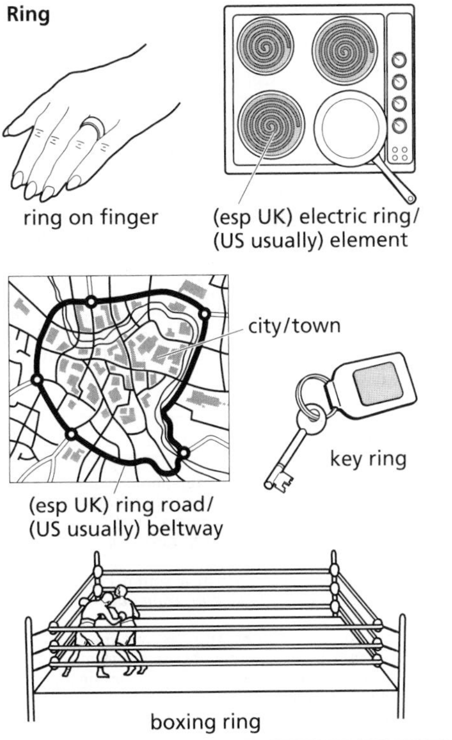
ring on finger
(esp UK) electric ring/
(US usually) element
city/town
key ring
(esp UK) ring road/
(US usually) beltway
boxing ring

ring [CIRCLE] /rɪŋ/ *noun* **[C]** **1** a circle of any material, or any group of things or people in a circular shape or arrangement: *The game involved throwing metal rings over a stick.* ○ *The children sat in a ring around the teacher.* **2** a circular piece of jewellery worn especially on your finger: *He bought her a diamond/emerald/etc. ring* (= a ring with a jewel fixed to it). **3** a group of people who help each other, often secretly and in a way which is to their advantage: *a drug ring* ○ *a spy ring* ➔See also **ringleader**. **4** (*US USUALLY* **element**) a circular piece of material often made of metal that can be heated in order to be used for cooking: *a gas ring* ○ *an electric ring* **5** an enclosed space where people perform or compete: *a boxing ring* ○ *The horses trotted round the ring.* ➔See also **ringside**. ➔See picture **Sports** on page Centre 10

ring /rɪŋz/ *plural noun* two round handles at the ends of two long ropes which hang from the ceiling and which are used in GYMNASTICS

• **run rings round** *sb* If someone runs rings round you, they are very much better, faster, or more successful at something than you are: *Our girls' hockey team have run rings round all their opponents this year.*

ring /rɪŋ/ *verb* [T] **ringed**, **ringed** **1** to surround something: *Armed police ringed the hijacked plane.* ○ *The harbour is dangerous – it's ringed by/with rocks and reefs.* **2** UK to draw a circle round something: *Students should ring the correct answers in pencil.* **3** to put a ring on something, especially an animal: *We ringed the birds* (= put rings around their legs) *so that we could identify them later.*

ring [TELEPHONE] *MAINLY UK* (**rang**, **rung**) /rɪŋ/ *verb* [I or T] (*US USUALLY* **call**) to make a telephone call to someone: *I ring home once a week to tell my parents I'm okay.* ○ *There's been an accident – can you ring for an ambulance?* ○ *The boss rang* (**in**) *to say he'll be back at 4.30.* ○ UK *I rang* **round** (= I called many) *airlines to find out the cheapest price.* ○ *Why don't you ring* (**up**) *Simon and ask him to the party?*

ring *MAINLY UK* /rɪŋ/ *noun* [S] (*US USUALLY AND UK ALSO* **call**) when you make a telephone call to someone: *I'll* **give** *you* **a** *ring tomorrow.*

ring [SOUND] /rɪŋ/ *verb* [I or T] **rang**, **rung** to (cause to) make the sound of a bell: *The doorbell/telephone rang.* ○ *Anne's alarm clock rang for half an hour before she woke.* ○ *I rang the bell but nobody came to the door.* ○ *My head is/My ears are still ringing* (= are full of a ringing noise) *from the sound of the military band.*

• **ring a bell** to sound familiar: *The name rang a bell but I couldn't remember where I had heard it before.*

• **ring the changes (on)** to do something in a different way in order to make it more interesting: *For variety, ring the changes on packed lunches using different types of bread and spicy fillings.*

• **ring true/false** to seem true/false: *Her explanations didn't ring true.*

ring /rɪŋ/ *noun* [C] the sound a bell makes: *There was a ring at the door.* ○ *He gave a ring at the door.*

• **ring of truth** If something has a ring of truth, it seems to be true: *This story* **has a/the** *ring of truth.*

• **familiar ring** If something has a familiar ring, you think you already know it, but you are not sure: *Her name had a familiar ring* **to it.**

PHRASAL VERBS WITH ring ▼

▲ **ring (sb) back** *phrasal verb* UK to telephone someone who rang you earlier or to telephone someone for a second time: *I'm a bit busy – can I ring you back later?*

▲ **ring off** *phrasal verb* UK to end a telephone conversation intentionally: *She said "No, thank you" and rang off hurriedly.*

▲ **ring out** *phrasal verb* When a sound rings out, it is loud and clear: *A cry of warning rang out.* ○ *A shot rang out.*

▲ **ring** *sth* **up** *phrasal verb* [M] to record the money that has been paid by a customer by pressing buttons on a CASH REGISTER: *I'm sorry, I've rung up the wrong amount.*

▲ **ring with** *sth* *phrasal verb* If a place rings with a sound, it is full of it: *The room rang with his screams.*

'ring ,binder *noun* [C] a piece of stiff folded cardboard with metal rings inside, used to keep loose pages in position

'ring ,finger *noun* [C] the finger nearest to your LITTLE FINGER. In many Western cultures, people often wear a ring on their ring finger to show that they are married or are planning to get married. ➔See **engagement ring**; **wedding ring**. ➔See picture **The Body** on page Centre 5

ring-in /'rɪŋ.ɪn/ *noun* [C] AUS INFORMAL a person included in an activity at a late stage

ringleader /'rɪŋ.liː.dəʳ/ US /-dɚ/ *noun* [C] the leader of a group of people who are doing something harmful or illegal

ringlet /'rɪŋ.lət/ US /-lɪt/ *noun* [C usually pl] a curled piece of long hair: *Her hair hung about her shoulders* **in** *ringlets.*

ring-pull UK /'rɪŋ.pʊl/ *noun* [C] (US **pull-tab**) a metal ring which must be lifted to open a closed metal container, especially of drink: *a ring-pull can*

'ring ,road *noun* [C] (US USUALLY **beltway**) UK a main road that goes around the edge of a town, allowing traffic to avoid the town centre

ringside /'rɪŋ.saɪd/ *noun* [S] the edge of an enclosed space where people compete or perform: *We managed to get ringside seats for the circus.*

ringtone /'rɪŋ.təʊn/ US /-toʊn/ *noun* [C] the sound that a telephone makes, especially when a MOBILE PHONE when someone is calling it: *My phone came with 20 optional ringtones.*

ringtoss /'rɪŋ.tɒs/ US /-tɑːs/ *noun* [U] US FOR **hoopla** GAME

ringworm /'rɪŋ.wɜːm/ US /-wɝːm/ *noun* [U] a disease that causes red rings on the skin

rink /rɪŋk/ *noun* [C] a large flat surface, of ice or other hard material, for SKATING (= a sport using special boots to move along), or the area or building which contains this: *an ice rink* ○ *a roller-skating rink*

rinky-dink /'rɪŋ.ki.dɪŋk/ *adj* US INFORMAL having little importance or influence, or old-fashioned or of poor quality: *Their family business is a rinky-dink operation.*

rinse /rɪnts/ *verb* [I or T] to use water to clean the soap or dirt from something: *First apply shampoo to hair and then rinse* **thoroughly.** ○ *There was no soap, so I just quickly rinsed my hands with water/*(UK ALSO) **under the tap.**

rinse /rɪnts/ *noun* **1** [C] when you use water to get rid of soap or dirt: *He* **gave** *the soapy dishes a rinse.* ○ *She* **gave** *the dirty towel a quick rinse.* **2** [C or U] a temporary colouring of or for the hair: *My grandmother has a blue rinse every month.*

▲ **rinse** *sth* **out** *phrasal verb* [M] to quickly wash the inside of something with clean water: *I'll just rinse these glasses out and leave them to dry.* ○ *She rinses out her mouth every morning to prevent bad breath.*

Rioja /riː'ɒ.kə/ US /-'ɑː-/ *noun* [C or U] a type of Spanish wine

riot /'raɪ.ət/ *noun* **1** [C] a noisy, violent, and uncontrolled public gathering: *Inner-city riots* **erupted** *when a young man was shot by police.* ○ *Police in riot* **gear** (= protective clothes and equipment) *lined up at the end of the street.* **2** [S] OLD-FASHIONED INFORMAL a very amusing or entertaining occasion or person: *"How was the party?" "It was great – we* **had** *a riot."* ○ *I met Mike's brother for the first time – he's a riot.*

• **a riot of colour** extremely colourful and bright: *Jim's rose garden is a riot of colour.*

riot /'raɪ.ət/ *verb* [I] to take part in a riot: *Students are rioting in the streets of the capital.* **rioter** /'raɪ.ə.təʳ/ US /-t̬ɚ/ *noun* [C] *Police and rioters clashed violently.* **rioting** /'raɪ.ə.tɪŋ/ US /-t̬ɪŋ/ *noun* [U] *The government is afraid of further serious rioting today.*

riotous /'raɪ.ə.təs/ US /-t̬əs/ *adj* very lively, loud and uncontrolled: *We went to a riotous party and danced all night.* ○ UK *Five students were arrested for riotous behaviour.* **riotously** /'raɪ.ə.tə.sli/ US /-t̬ə-/ *adv* **riotousness** /'raɪ.ə.tə.snəs/ US /-t̬ə-/ *noun* [U]

'riot po,lice *noun* [U] a special section of a police force trained to deal with noisy, violent groups

RIP [DEAD] /ˌɑː.raɪ'piː/ US /ˌɑːr.aɪ-/ *WRITTEN ABBREVIATION FOR* **rest in peace**, see at **rest**

rip [TEAR] /rɪp/ *verb* **-pp-** **1** [I or T] to pull apart; to tear or be torn violently and quickly: *His new trousers ripped when he bent down.* ○ *I ripped my shirt on a nail.* ○ [+ obj + adj] *She excitedly ripped the parcel* **open.** ○ *The wind ripped* *the flag **to/into shreds*** (= into little pieces). **2** [T + adv or prep] to remove something quickly, without being careful: *I wish the old fireplaces hadn't been ripped **out**.* ○ *We ripped **up** the carpets and laid a new wooden floor.* **rip** /rɪp/ *noun* [C] *Your sleeve has got a rip in it.*

PHRASAL VERBS WITH **rip**

▲ **rip *sb* off** [CHEAT] *phrasal verb* [M] INFORMAL to cheat someone by making them pay too much money for something: *Bob's tickets cost much less than ours – I think we've been ripped off.*

rip-off /ˈrɪp.ɒf/ [US] /-ɑːf/ *noun* [C usually sing] something that is not worth what you pay for it: *$300 for that shirt? – That's a complete rip-off.*

▲ **rip *sth* off** [REMOVE] *phrasal verb* [M] to remove something very quickly and carelessly: *They ripped off their clothes and ran into the sea.*

▲ **rip *sth/sb* off** [STEAL] *phrasal verb* [M] SLANG to steal something: *He rips stuff off from supermarkets to pay for his heroin.*

▲ **rip through *sth*** *phrasal verb* to move very powerfully through a place or building, destroying it quickly: *The explosion ripped through the hotel.* ○ *A hurricane ripped through the Caribbean.*

▲ **rip *sth* up** *phrasal verb* [M] to tear something into small pieces: *She ripped up his letters and burned the pieces.*

ripcord /ˈrɪp.kɔːd/ [US] /-kɔːrd/ *noun* [C] a cord that you pull to open a parachute

ripe /raɪp/ *adj* **1** (of fruit or crops) completely developed and ready to be collected or eaten: *Those bananas aren't ripe yet – they're still green.* **2** describes cheese which has developed a strong flavour: *This brie smells good and ripe.* **3** describes a smell which is strong and unpleasant: *There was a ripe smell from his socks.* **4** OLD-FASHIONED HUMOROUS describes language that is rude: *a ripe joke*

• **ripe for** developed to a suitable condition for something to happen: *The company is ripe for takeover.* ○ ***The time** is ripe* (= It is the right time) *for investing in new technology.*

• **ripe old age** APPROVING old age: *My grandmother died at the ripe old age **of** 92.*

ripen /ˈraɪ.pᵊn/ *verb* **1** [I or T] to (cause to) become ripe: *The summer sunshine ripened the melons.* ○ *These melons are ripening nicely.* **2** [I] to develop to a suitable condition for something to happen: *My plans are ripening – now all I need is official approval.* **ripeness** /ˈraɪp.nəs/ *noun* [U]

riposte /rɪˈpɒst/ [US] /-ˈpoʊst/ *noun* [C] a quick and clever remark, often made in answer to a criticism: *She made a sharp/witty/neat riposte.* **riposte** /rɪˈpɒst/ [US] /-ˈpoʊst/ *verb* [I or T]

ripple /ˈrɪp.l̩/ *noun* **1** [C] a small wave on the surface of water: *The stone she threw caused ripples to spread across the lake.* **2** [C] a sound or feeling that spreads through a person or group of people, gradually increasing and then decreasing: *A ripple **of laughter/applause/etc.** ran through the crowd.* ○ *A ripple **of excitement/unease/etc.** flowed up her spine.* ○ *News of the war hardly caused a ripple* (= people showed little interest). **3** [U] plain ice cream with thin wavy lines of other flavours in it: *raspberry ripple*

ripple /ˈrɪp.l̩/ *verb* [I or T] to (cause to) move in small waves: *The breeze rippled the water.* ○ *His muscles rippled under his skin.*

ˈripple efˌfect *noun* [C usually sing] when one event produces effects which spread and produce further effects, etc: *The bank crash has **had** a ripple effect **on** the whole community.*

rip-roaring /ˌrɪpˈrɔː.rɪŋ/ [US] /-ˈrɔːr.ɪŋ/ *adj* [before n] INFORMAL wild, noisy, and exciting: *The party was a rip-roaring, riotous **success**.*

rise [MOVE UP] /raɪz/ *verb* [I] **rose, risen 1** to move upwards: *The balloon rose gently **(up)** into the air.* ○ *At 6am we watched the sun rise* (= appear and move upwards in the sky). ○ *When you put yeast in bread and bake the bread, it rises* (= gets bigger). ○ *New buildings are rising* (= being built) *throughout the city.* ○ *The River Cam rises* (= first comes out of the ground) ***in/at** a place called Ashwell.* ○ FIGURATIVE *Murmurs of disapproval rose **from*** (= came from) *the crowd.* **2** to stand, especially after sitting: *She rose **from** her chair to welcome us.* ○ *He rose **to his feet** to deliver his speech.* **3** FORMAL to get out of bed: *My grandfather rises at 5 every morning to do his exercises.*

• **Rise and shine!** HUMOROUS said to tell someone to wake up and get out of bed: *Wakey wakey, rise and shine!*

• **rise from the dead/grave** to become alive again after having died

• **rise to fame** to become famous: *He rose to fame in the 90s as a TV presenter.*

• **rise to the bait** to accept an offer or suggestion that seems good but is really a trick: *They offered a good salary, but I didn't rise to the bait.*

• **rise to the occasion/challenge** to show that you can deal with a difficult situation successfully: *In the exam she rose to the occasion and wrote a brilliant essay.*

rise /raɪz/ *noun* [S] when someone or something becomes very famous, powerful or popular: *Her rapid rise **to** fame/power/popularity/etc. meant that she made many enemies.*

• **get a rise out of** (UK ALSO **take a rise out of**) to annoy: *Steve always manages to get a rise out of me with his racist jokes.*

riser /ˈraɪ.zəʳ/ [US] /-zɚ/ *noun* **early/late riser** a person who usually gets out of be early/late in the morning

rising /ˈraɪ.zɪŋ/ *prep* MAINLY UK about to become: *The school accepts children who are rising five years old.*

COMMON LEARNER ERROR

rise or raise?

Be careful not to confuse these two verbs. **Rise** means to increase or move up. This verb cannot be followed by an object.

The price of petrol is rising.
~~*The price of petrol is raising.*~~

Raise means to lift something to a higher position or to increase an amount or level. This verb must always be followed by an object.

The government has raised the price of petrol.
~~*The government has rised the price of petrol.*~~

rise [INCREASE] /raɪz/ *verb* [I] **rose, risen 1** to increase: *Inflation is rising at/by 2.1% a month.* ○ *The wind/storm is rising* (= beginning to get stronger). **2** When emotions etc. rise, they start to increase: *Tempers are rising* (= people are becoming angry). ○ *My spirits rise* (= I feel happier) *whenever I think of my friends.* ○ *She felt panic and terror rise **in** her whenever she thought of the future.* ○ *His voice rose* (= became louder or higher) *as he got angry.*

rise /raɪz/ *noun* [C] an increase: *a sudden temperature rise* ○ *a 5% rise **in** inflation* ○ *August has seen a large rise in the number of unemployed.*

• **give rise to** to cause: *International support has given rise to a new optimism in the company.*

• **on the rise** increasing: *Police say that youth crime is on the rise again.*

rise [BECOME HIGHER] /raɪz/ *verb* [I] **rose, risen** to become higher: *The ground rises over there.* ○ *The castle is built on rising ground* (= ground higher than areas around it). ○ *You can see the Alps rising* (= showing as a higher area) ***in** the distance/**above** the clouds.*

rise /raɪz/ *noun* [C] a small hill or slope: *The castle is built on a slight rise above the town.*

riser /ˈraɪ.zəʳ/ [US] /-zɚ/ *noun* [C] SPECIALIZED the vertical part of a step

risers /ˈraɪ.zəz/ [US] /-zɚz/ *plural noun* US a group of steps on which people sit or stand to see or be seen better

rise [BE OPPOSED TO] /raɪz/ *verb* [I usually + adv or prep] **rose, risen** (of a group of people) to begin to oppose or fight a bad government or ruler: *The people rose **(up) against** the oppressor/tyrant/dictator.*

rising /ˈraɪ.zɪŋ/ *noun* [C] an **uprising**

rise [STOP WORK] /raɪz/ *verb* [I] **rose, risen** FORMAL If parliament or a court rises, it stops work: *Parliament/The court rose at 6 pm.*

▲ **rise above *sth*** *phrasal verb* to not allow something bad to affect your behaviour or upset you: *He rose above his pain/bad luck/difficulties.*

R

risible /ˈrɪz.ə.bl̩/ *adj* FORMAL DISAPPROVING not impressive; ridiculous: *She's been making risible attempts to learn the trumpet.*

ˌrising ˈdamp *noun* [U] water that moves into the walls of buildings from the ground and damages them

ˌrising ˈstar *noun* [C] a person who is likely to be successful: *She's the rising star of the organization.*

risk /rɪsk/ *noun* **1** [C or U] the possibility of something bad happening: *In this business, the risks and the rewards are high.* ○ *There's a high risk **of** another accident happening in this fog.* ○ [(+ that)] *The risk **(that)** we might fail made us work twice as hard.* ○ [+ v-ing] *It's always a risk starting up a new business.* ○ *The company is quite a **good** risk* (= safe to lend money to). ○ *We want clean rivers and lakes, where you can swim without risk **to** your health.* ○ *It's a **low/high**-risk strategy* (= one that is safe/not safe). **2** [C] something bad that might happen: *This wire is a **safety/fire** risk.* ○ *His employers thought he was a **security** risk* (= he might tell their secrets to a competitor).

• **at risk** in a dangerous situation: *All houses within 100 metres of the seas are at risk **of** flooding.*

• **at the risk of doing *sth*** used before you say something that may seem offensive or stupid: *At the risk of seeming rude, I'm afraid I have to leave now.* ○ *At the risk of sounding stupid, how do I send this email?*

• **at *your* own risk** used to mean that you are responsible for any damage, loss or difficulty: *Owners are reminded that they leave their cars here at their own risk.*

• **run/take a risk** to do something you know might be dangerous: *Don't take any risks – just ring the police.*

• **run the risk of doing *sth*** to do something although something bad might happen because of it: *If you tell him the truth, you run the risk of hurting his feelings.*

risk /rɪsk/ *verb* [T] **1** to do something although there is a chance of a bad result: *"It's dangerous to cross here." "I'll just have to risk **it**."* ○ [+ v-ing] *He risked losing his house when his company went bankrupt.* **2** If you risk something important, you cause it to be in a dangerous situation where you might lose it: *I'm not risking my **life/** (INFORMAL) **neck** in that old car.* ○ *He risked **life and limb** to get the cat down from the tree.* ○ *She was prepared to risk everything **on** a last throw of the dice.* **risky** /ˈrɪs.ki/ *adj*: ***It's** risky **to** buy a car without some good advice.* **riskily** /ˈrɪs.ki.li/ *adv*

risotto /rɪˈzɒt.əʊ/ [US] /-ˈzɑː.t̬oʊ/ *noun* [C or U] *plural* **risottos** a dish of rice cooked together with vegetables, meat, etc.

risqué /rɪˈskeɪ/ *adj* (of jokes or stories) slightly rude or shocking, especially because about sex

rissole /ˈrɪs.əʊl/ [US] /-oʊl/ *noun* [C] a type of food made from meat or vegetables cut into small pieces and then pressed together and cooked in fat: *chicken/lentil rissoles*

rite /raɪt/ *noun* [C usually pl] (a usually religious ceremony with) a set of fixed words and actions: *funeral/marriage/fertility rites* ○ *You have to go through an initiation rite before you become a full member.*

ˌrite of ˈpassage *noun* [C] an official ceremony or informal activity which marks an important stage or occasion in a person's life, especially becoming an adult

ritual /ˈrɪt.ju.əl/ [US] /ˈrɪtʃ.u-/ *noun* [C or U] a set of fixed actions and sometimes words performed regularly, especially as part of a ceremony: *Coffee and the newspaper are part of my morning ritual.* ○ *The birds were performing a complex mating ritual.* **ritualistic** /ˌrɪt.ju.əˈlɪs.tɪk/ [US] /ˌrɪtʃ.u-/ *adj* **ritualistically** /ˌrɪt.ju.əˈlɪs.tɪ.kli/ [US] /ˌrɪtʃ.u-/ *adv*

ritzy /ˈrɪt.si/ *adj* OLD-FASHIONED INFORMAL expensive, fashionable, and luxurious: *That's a ritzy dress.*

rival /ˈraɪ.vəl/ *noun* [C] a person, group, etc. competing with others for the same thing or in the same area: *He beat his **closest/nearest** rival by 20 marks.* ○ *The companies produce rival versions of the toy.*

rival /ˈraɪ.vəl/ *verb* [T] **-ll-** or US USUALLY **-l-** to be as good, clever, beautiful, etc. as someone or something else: *No computer can rival a human brain **for/in** complexity.* ○ *The beauty of the country is only rivalled by* (= is equal to) *the violence of its politics.* **rivalry** /ˈraɪ.vəl.ri/ *noun* [C or U] *There's such rivalry **among/between** my three sons.* ○ *There's fierce rivalry **for** the job/**to** get the job.*

riven /ˈrɪv.ən/ *adj* [after v] LITERARY violently divided: *It was a community/nation/family riven **by** jealousy, hatred and bitterness.*

river /ˈrɪv.ər/ [US] /-ɚ/ *noun* [C] **1** a natural wide flow of fresh water across the land into the sea, a lake, or another river: *We sailed slowly down the river.* **2** (WRITTEN ABBREVIATION **R**) used usually before, sometimes after, the name of a river: *the River Thames*

• **up (the) river** in the opposite direction to the flow of water in the river: *We sailed up river.*

• **down (the) river** in the same direction as the flow of water in the river

• **rivers of *sth*** a large amount of a liquid: *Rivers of sweat ran down his back.* ○ FIGURATIVE *If there's a revolution, rivers of blood will flow.*

ˈriver ˌbank *noun* [C] (ALSO **bank**) the land at either edge of a river: *We sat on the river bank and had a picnic.*

river-bed /ˈrɪv.ə.bed/ *noun* [C] the ground over which a river usually flows: *a stony/muddy/dry river-bed*

ˈriver ˌboat *noun* [C] a large passenger boat which travels up and down a river

riverside /ˈrɪv.ə.saɪd/ [US] /-ɚ-/ *noun* [S] the land along the edges of a river: *a riverside restaurant*

rivet /ˈrɪv.ɪt/ *noun* [C] a metal pin used to fasten flat pieces of metal or other thick materials such as leather

rivet /ˈrɪv.ɪt/ *verb* [T] **1** to fasten together with a rivet: *Many parts of an aircraft are riveted **together**.* **2 be riveted** to not be able to stop looking at something because it is so interesting or frightening: *It was an amazing film – I was absolutely riveted.* ○ *His eyes were riveted **on** the television.* ○ *He pulled out a gun and I was riveted **to the spot*** (= so frightened that I could not move).

riveting /ˈrɪv.ɪ.tɪŋ/ [US] /-t̬ɪŋ/ *adj* extremely interesting: *It was a riveting story.*

riviera /rɪ.viˈeə.rə/ [US] /-ˈer.ə/ *noun* [C] an area of coast, especially one where there are holiday towns with beaches: *the French/Italian/Cornish riviera*

rivulet /ˈrɪv.jʊ.lət/ [US] /-lɪt/ *noun* [C] LITERARY a very small stream: FIGURATIVE *Rivulets of sweat/rain/blood ran down his face.*

riyal /riˈɑːl/ [US] /riːˈjɑːl/ *noun* [C] the standard unit of money used in Saudi Arabia and Qatar

RN /ˌɑːˈren/ [US] /ˌɑːrˈen/ *noun* [U] ABBREVIATION FOR Royal Navy: used especially after the names of naval officers: *Captain H. Doughty, RN*

RNA /ˌɑː.renˈeɪ/ [US] /ˌɑːr.en-/ *noun* [U] SPECIALIZED ABBREVIATION FOR ribonucleic acid: an important chemical present in all living cells

roach [FISH] /rəʊtʃ/ [US] /roʊtʃ/ *noun* [C] *plural* **roach** a European fish that lives in fresh water

roach [INSECT] /rəʊtʃ/ [US] /roʊtʃ/ *noun* [C] *plural* **roaches** US INFORMAL FOR **cockroach**

roach [CIGARETTE] /rəʊtʃ/ [US] /roʊtʃ/ *noun* [C] *plural* **roaches** SLANG the end part of a CANNABIS cigarette that you breathe the smoke through

road /rəʊd/ [US] /roʊd/ *noun* [C or U] a long hard surface built for vehicles to travel along: *We live on a busy/quiet road.* ○ *Be careful when you cross a main road.* ○ *There's a sweet shop on the other side of the road.* ○ *The road **from** here **to** Adelaide runs/goes through some beautiful countryside.* ○ *All roads **into/out of** the town were blocked by the snow.* ○ *I hate flying so I go everywhere **by** road or rail.* ○ *I live **in/on** Mill Road.* ○ *My address is 82 Mill Road.* ○ *Is this the Oxford road* (= the road that goes to Oxford)? ○ *Most road **accidents** are caused by people driving too fast.*

• **Get out of the road!** INFORMAL used to rudely tell someone to stop blocking the way

• **on the road 1** If a vehicle is on the road, it is working properly and can be legally used: *My car was in the garage for a week, but it's now back on the road.* **2** When you are on the road, you are driving or travelling, usually over a long distance: *After two days on the road, they reached the coast.* **3** If a group of actors or musicians are on the road, they are travelling to different places to perform: *Most rock groups spend two or three months a year on the road.*

• **be on the road to** *sth* INFORMAL to be likely to achieve something: *The doctors say she's on the road to recovery.*

• **come to the end of the road** to finish: *My relationship with Jeannie has come to the end of the road.*

• **one for the road** INFORMAL an alcoholic drink just before leaving: *Before I went home, she persuaded me to have one for the road.*

• **road to Damascus** Someone's road to Damascus is an experience they have which they consider to be very important and which changes their life.

• **All roads lead to Rome.** SAYING said to mean that all the methods of doing something will achieve the same result in the end

• **The road to hell is paved with good intentions.** SAYING said to emphasize that you must not simply intend to behave well but you must act according to your intentions, because you will have problems or be punished if you do not

roadblock /ˈrəʊd.blɒk/ ⓤ /ˈroʊd.blɑːk/ *noun* [C] a temporary structure put across a road to stop traffic: *Police put up/set up roadblocks on all roads out of the town in an effort to catch the bombers.*

ˈroad ˌhog *noun* [C] INFORMAL DISAPPROVING a selfish and dangerous driver

roadholding /ˈrəʊd.həʊl.dɪŋ/ ⓤ /ˈroʊd.hoʊl-/ *noun* [U] the degree to which a vehicle can travel quickly and safely on roads that are wet or have a lot of bends

roadhouse /ˈrəʊd.haʊs/ ⓤ /ˈroʊd-/ *noun* [C] MAINLY US OLD-FASHIONED a restaurant or bar on a main road leading out of a city

roadie /ˈrəʊ.di/ ⓤ /ˈroʊ-/ *noun* [C] INFORMAL someone who works for travelling entertainers, especially setting up and taking care of their equipment

ˈroad ˌkill *noun* [U] INFORMAL animals which are killed on roads by cars or other vehicles: *On average, two crocodiles a year end up as road kill on Florida's Highway 1.*

ˈroad ˌrage *noun* [U] anger or violence between drivers, often caused by difficult driving conditions: *Earlier today a man was arrested for attacking a motorist in a road rage incident.*

roadrunner /ˈrəʊdˌrʌn.əʳ/ ⓤ /ˈroʊdˌrʌn.ɚ/ *noun* [C] a bird from the southwestern United States and Mexico with a long tail and feathers which stand up on the top of its head, which runs very fast

ˈroad ˌsense *noun* [U] If you have good road sense, you have the ability to drive or walk carefully and safely through traffic.

roadshow /ˈrəʊd.ʃəʊ/ ⓤ /ˈroʊd.ʃoʊ/ *noun* [C] a group of people who travel around the country in order to give shows for public entertainment, or the show itself: *The roadshow is coming to town.*

roadside /ˈrəʊd.saɪd/ ⓤ /ˈroʊd-/ *noun* [S] the edge of a road: *The car pulled in at/by/on the roadside.* ○ *We stopped at a roadside café for lunch.*

roadster /ˈrəʊd.stəʳ/ ⓤ /ˈroʊd.stɚ/ *noun* [C] OLD-FASHIONED a car without a roof and with only two seats

ˈroad ˌtax *noun* [C or U] in Britain, a tax that you must pay on your vehicle before you are allowed to drive it on the roads

ˈroad ˌtest TEST OF CAR *noun* [C] If you give a car a road test, you drive it to test its safety or how well it works.

ˈroad ˌtest TEST OF DRIVER *noun* [C] US a test of a driver's ability to control a vehicle, which must be passed in order to obtain official permission to drive

ˈroad ˌtoll *noun* [C] AUS the number of people who have died in road accidents

ˈroad ˌtrip *noun* [C] US If someone, especially a sports team, takes a road trip, they travel to other places to play games against other teams or for business reasons.

roadway /ˈrəʊd.weɪ/ ⓤ /ˈroʊd-/ *noun* [S] the part of the road on which vehicles drive: *An overturned bus was blocking the roadway.*

roadworks UK /ˈrəʊd.wɜːks/ ⓤ /ˈroʊd.wɜːks/ *plural noun* (US **roadwork**) building or repair work on a road: *There are delays on the M4 because of roadworks.*

roadworthy /ˈrəʊdˌwɜː.ði/ ⓤ /ˈroʊdˌwɜː-/ *adj* (of a vehicle) in good enough condition to be driven without danger

roam /rəʊm/ ⓤ /roʊm/ *verb* [I + adv or prep; T] to move about or travel, especially without a clear idea of what you are going to do: *After the pubs close, gangs of youths roam the city streets.* ○ *She roamed around America for a year, working in bars and restaurants.*

roan /rəʊn/ ⓤ /roʊn/ *noun* [C] a horse which is red, black or brown with a few white hairs

roar /rɔːʳ/ ⓤ /rɔːr/ *verb* **1** [I] to make a long, loud, deep sound: *We could hear the lions roaring at the other end of the zoo.* **2** [I] If a vehicle or aircraft roars somewhere, it moves there very quickly making a lot of noise: *She looked up as a plane roared overhead.* ○ *The street was full of boys roaring up and down on their motorbikes.* **3** [T] to shout loudly: [+ speech] *"Stop that!" he roared.*

roar /rɔːʳ/ ⓤ /rɔːr/ *noun* [C or S] a loud, deep sound: *The lion let out a loud roar.* ○ *His apartment was on a main road and there was a constant roar of traffic from down below.*

roaring /ˈrɔː.rɪŋ/ ⓤ /ˈrɔːr.ɪŋ/ *adj* loud and powerful: *the roaring wind* ○ *a roaring fire*

• **roaring drunk** INFORMAL very drunk and noisy: *They came back from the pub roaring drunk.*

• **roaring success** INFORMAL something which is very successful: *The party was a roaring success.*

• **do a roaring trade** INFORMAL to sell a lot of goods very quickly: *It was a hot sunny day and the ice-cream sellers were doing a roaring trade.*

▲ **roar with** *sth phrasal verb* to express an emotion, such as laughter or anger, noisily: *She roared with laughter when she saw what he was wearing.*

roast COOK /rəʊst/ ⓤ /roʊst/ *verb* [I or T] **1** to cook food in an oven or over a fire: *Just roast the chicken in the oven and baste it in oil and lemon.* ○ FIGURATIVE *We lay on the beach and roasted* (= got very hot) *in the Mediterranean sun.* **2** to heat nuts or coffee beans so that they become drier and browner

roast /rəʊst/ ⓤ /roʊst/ *noun* [C] a large piece of roasted meat *roast* /rəʊst/ ⓤ /roʊst/ *adj* [before n] (ALSO **roasted**) *roast beef/chicken/potatoes* ○ *roasted red pepper sauce*

ˌroasting (ˈhot) *adj* very hot: *It was a roasting summer day.* ○ *I'm roasting!*

roast CRITICISE /rəʊst/ ⓤ /roʊst/ *verb* [T] INFORMAL to severely criticize or speak angrily to someone **roast**ing /ˈrəʊst/ ⓤ /ˈroʊst/ *noun* [C usually sing] *I got a roasting from Mum for being back late.*

rob /rɒb/ ⓤ /rɑːb/ *verb* [T] -bb- **1** to take money or property illegally from a place, organization or person, often using violence: *The terrorists financed themselves by robbing banks.* ○ *My wallet's gone! I've been robbed!* ○ *They robbed the company of £2 million.* **2** If someone is robbed of something they deserve or want, it is taken away from them: *A last-minute injury robbed me of my place on the team.*

• **rob Peter to pay Paul** to borrow money from one person to pay back money you borrowed from someone else

robber /ˈrɒb.əʳ/ ⓤ /ˈrɑː.bɚ/ *noun* [C] someone who steals: *The robbers shot a policeman before making their getaway.*

robbery /ˈrɒb.ᵊr.i/ ⓤ /ˈrɑː.bɚ-/ *noun* [C or U] the crime of stealing from somewhere or someone: *The gang admitted they had committed four recent bank robberies.* ○ *He is in prison for armed robbery.*

robe /rəʊb/ ⓤ /roʊb/ *noun* [C] **1** a long, loose-fitting piece of clothing worn especially on very formal occasions: *Judges wear black robes when they are in court.* **2** (ALSO **bathrobe**) MAINLY US a loose-fitting piece of clothing which is worn before or after a bath or on top of clothing that is worn in bed: *He wrapped a robe around himself before answering the door.*

robed /rəʊbd/ ⓤ /roʊbd/ *adj* FORMAL **robed in** to be dressed in a particular way: *The judges were robed in scarlet.*

robin /ˈrɒb.ɪn/ ⓤ /ˈrɑː.bɪn/ *noun* [C] (LITERARY **robin redbreast**) a small brown European bird with a red front, or a similar but slightly larger brown bird of North America: *Robins mostly appear in the winter and are*

R

commonly pictured on Christmas cards. ⊃See picture
Animals and Birds on page Centre 4

robot /ˈrəʊ.bɒt/ ⓤ /ˈroʊ.bɑːt/ *noun* [C] **1** a machine used
to perform jobs automatically, which is controlled by a
computer **2** *DISAPPROVING* someone who does things in a
very quick and effective way but never shows their emotions **3** a traffic light in South Africa

robotic /rəʊˈbɒt.ɪk/ ⓤ /roʊˈbɑː.t̬ɪk/ *adj* relating to or like
a robot

robotics /rəʊˈbɒt.ɪks/ ⓤ /roʊˈbɑː.t̬ɪks/ *noun* [U] the
science of making and using robots

robust /rəʊˈbʌst/ ⓤ /roʊ-/ *adj* (of a person or animal)
strong and healthy, or (of an object or system) strong
and unlikely to break or fail: *He looks robust and
healthy enough.* ○ *a robust pair of walking boots* ○ *a
robust economy*

robustly /rəˈbʌst.li/ *adv* If you do something robustly,
you do it in a determined way: *Some of his colleagues felt
he could have defended himself more robustly.* **robust-
ness** /rəˈbʌst.nəs/ *noun* [U]

rock STONE /rɒk/ ⓤ /rɑːk/ *noun* **1** [C or U] the dry solid part
of the Earth's surface, or any large piece of this which
sticks up out of the ground or the sea: *Mountains and
cliffs are formed from rock.* ○ *The boat struck a rock outside the bay and sank.* **2** [C] *US* a large piece of rock or
stone: *The demonstrators were hurling rocks at the
police.* **3** [C] *US SLANG FOR* a valuable stone used in
jewellery, especially a DIAMOND: *Have you seen the size of
the rock he gave her for their anniversary?*
● **be (caught) between a rock and a hard place** to be in a
very difficult situation and to have to make a hard decision
● **be (as) solid as a rock** to be very strong: *You'd think her
own marriage was solid as a rock.*

rocks /rɒks/ ⓤ /rɑːks/ *plural noun* a line of large stones
sticking up from the sea: *The storm forced the ship onto
the rocks.*
● **on the rocks 1** *INFORMAL* likely to fail soon: *I think their
marriage is on the rocks.* **2** If you have an alcoholic
drink on the rocks, you have it with lumps of ice: *I'll
have a whisky on the rocks, please.*
● **get your rocks off** *OFFENSIVE* to have sex

rocky /ˈrɒk.i/ ⓤ /ˈrɑː.ki/ *adj* made of rock and therefore
usually rough and difficult to travel along: *She
scrambled along the rocky path.* ⊃See also **rocky** at **rock**
MOVE.
● **rocky road** If you are on a rocky road, you are
experiencing a difficult period and have a lot of
problems: *Greenspan predicts a rocky road ahead for the
economy.*

rock MOVE /rɒk/ ⓤ /rɑːk/ *verb* **1** [I or T] to (cause someone
or something to) move backwards and forwards or from
side to side in a regular way: *He picked up the baby and
gently rocked her to sleep.* ○ *If you rock back on that
chair, you're going to break it.* **2** [T] If a person or place is
rocked by something such as an explosion, the force of
it makes the person or place shake: *The explosion, which
rocked the city, killed 300.* **3** [T] If an event rocks a group
of people or society, it causes feelings of shock: *The
managing director's resignation rocked the whole
company.*
● **rock the boat** *INFORMAL* If you rock the boat, you do or
say something that will upset people or cause problems:
*Don't rock the boat until the negotiations are finished,
okay!*

rocker /ˈrɒk.əʳ/ ⓤ /ˈrɑː.kɚ/ *noun* [C] **1** one of the two
curved pieces of wood under a ROCKING CHAIR that allow it
to move backwards and forwards ⊃See also **rocker** at
rock MUSIC. **2 rocking chair**
● **off your rocker** *INFORMAL* If you say that someone is off
their rocker, you mean that they are behaving in a very
strange or foolish way.

rocky /ˈrɒk.i/ ⓤ /ˈrɑː.ki/ *adj* **1** unable to balance very
well: *After two months in a hospital bed, I felt a bit rocky
on my feet.* ⊃See also **rocky** at **rock** STONE. **2** uncertain
and difficult and not likely to last long: *Their relationship got off to a rocky start.*

rock MUSIC /rɒk/ ⓤ /rɑːk/ *noun* [U] a type of popular music
with a strong loud beat which is usually played with
electric guitars and drums: *a rock group* ○ *a rock star*

rock /rɒk/ ⓤ /rɑːk/ *verb* *SLANG* **sb/sth rocks** used to
show that you like or approve of someone or something
a lot: *Dom says MP3 rocks.*

rocker /ˈrɒk.əʳ/ ⓤ /ˈrɑː.kɚ/ *noun* [C] **1** a singer of rock
music: *an ageing rocker* ⊃See also **rocker** at **rock** MOVE.
2 *US* a rock song or a person who really likes rock music
3 *OLD-FASHIONED* a young person, especially in Britain in
the 1950s, who wore leather clothes, rode a motorcycle
and listened to rock and roll music

rock 'bottom LOW *noun* [U] *INFORMAL* the lowest
possible level: *Confidence in the government is at rock
bottom.* ○ *Prices have reached rock bottom.* ○ *The prime
minister's opinion poll ratings have hit rock bottom.*

rock 'bottom UNHAPPY *noun* [U] *INFORMAL* the most unhappy that someone has ever been in their life: *Ian had
just left me and I was at rock bottom.* ○ *Alcoholics often
have to reach/hit rock bottom before they can recognise
that they have a problem.*

rock ˌcake *noun* [C] (*ALSO* **rock bun**) *UK* a small cake
with a rough surface, which is made with dried fruit

rock ˌcandy *noun* [C or U] *US* large, clear, hard lumps of
sugar, often on a string or a stick

rock ˌchick *noun* [C] *INFORMAL* a woman who likes rock
music and who dresses like a rock star

rockery *UK* /ˈrɒk.ᵊr.i/ ⓤ /ˈrɑː.kɚ-/ *noun* [C] (*US USUALLY* **rock
garden**) a garden or an area within a garden that has
plants growing between piles of stones

rocket DEVICE /ˈrɒk.ɪt/ ⓤ /ˈrɑː.kɪt/ *noun* [C] **1** a large
cylindrical object which moves very fast by forcing out
burning gases, and which is used for space travel or as a
weapon: *They launched a rocket to the planet Venus.*
○ *The rebels were firing anti-tank rockets.* **2** (*ALSO*
skyrocket) a type of firework that flies up into the air
before exploding
● **give sb a rocket** *UK INFORMAL* If someone gives you a
rocket, they criticize you severely: *Her Mum gave her a
rocket for tearing her new jeans.*

rocket /ˈrɒk.ɪt/ ⓤ /ˈrɑː.kɪt/ *verb* [I often + adv or prep] (*ALSO*
skyrocket) *INFORMAL* to rise extremely quickly or make
extremely quick progress towards success: *House prices
in the north are rocketing (up).* ○ *Their team rocketed to
the top of the League.* ○ *Sharon Stone rocketed to fame in
the film 'Basic Instinct'.*

rocket PLANT *UK* /ˈrɒk.ɪt/ ⓤ /ˈrɑː.kɪt/ *noun* [U] (*US* **arugula**)
a plant whose long green leaves are used in salads

rocket ˌscience *noun* [U] the scientific study of
rockets
● **it's not rocket science** *HUMOROUS* used to say that you do
not think that something is very difficult to do or to
understand: *Come on, it's only a crossword, it's not rocket
science.*

rocket ˌship *noun* [C] *US* a spacecraft which is powered
by a rocket

rock ˌface *noun* [C] an area of vertical surface on a
large rock or mountain: *The path down to the beach was
a precarious one, tiny steps hewn out of the sheer rock
face.*

rockfall /ˈrɒk.fɔːl/ ⓤ /ˈrɑːk.fɑːl/ *noun* [C] a mass of stones
that is falling or has already fallen: *The road was
blocked by a rockfall.*

rock ˌgarden *noun* [C] **rockery**

rock 'hard *adj* extremely hard: *I can't eat this cake –
it's rock hard.*

rocking ˌchair *noun* [C] (*ALSO* **rocker**) a chair built on
two pieces of curved wood so that it swings forwards
and backwards when you are sitting in it

rocking ˌhorse *noun* [C] a wooden toy horse that
children can make swing backwards and forwards when
they are sitting on it

rockmelon /ˈrɒk.mel.ən/ ⓤ /ˈrɑːk-/ *noun* [C] *AUS FOR*
cantaloupe

rock 'n' roll /ˌrɒk.ᵊnˈdᵊrəʊl/ ⓤ /ˌrɑːk.ᵊnˈdᵊroʊl/ *noun* [U]
(*ALSO* **rock and roll**) a style of popular dance music that
began in the 1950s in the United States and has a strong
loud beat and simple repeated tunes
● **be the new rock 'n' roll** *UK INFORMAL* If an activity is the
new rock 'n' roll, it has become very popular and many
people are doing it and talking about it.

rock ,pool noun [C] a small area of sea water contained by the rocks around it

rock ,salt noun [U] salt that is taken from the ground, not the sea

,rock 'solid adj not likely to move or break: *I've fixed the table – it's rock solid now.*

rococo /rəʊˈkəʊ.kəʊ/ ⓤ /rəˈkoʊ.koʊ/ adj relating to the highly decorated and detailed style in buildings, art and furniture that was popular in Europe in the 18th century **rococo** /rəʊˈkəʊ.kəʊ/ ⓤ /rəˈkoʊ.koʊ/ noun [U]

rod /rɒd/ ⓤ /rɑːd/ noun [C] a long thin pole made of wood or metal: *He was given a fishing rod for his birthday.* ○ *The concrete is strengthened with steel rods.*

● **make a rod for your own back** UK If you make a rod for your own back, you act in a way which creates more problems for yourself in the future: *By giving in to the terrorists' demands, the government will simply be making a rod for its own back.*

rode /rəʊd/ ⓤ /roʊd/ past simple of **ride**

rodent /ˈrəʊ.dᵊnt/ ⓤ /ˈroʊ-/ noun [C] any of various small mammals with large sharp front teeth, such as mice and rats

rodeo /rəʊˈdeɪ.əʊ/ ⓤ /ˈroʊ.di-/ noun [C] plural **rodeos** in North America, a sport and public entertainment in which cowboys show different skills by riding wild horses and catching cattle with ropes

roe /rəʊ/ ⓤ /roʊ/ noun [U] fish eggs, which are eaten as food

roe ,deer noun [C] plural **roe deer** a small European and Asian deer

roentgen /ˈrɒnt.gən/ ⓤ /ˈrent-/ noun [C] SPECIALIZED **röntgen**

roger ⌈UNDERSTOOD⌉ /ˈrɒdʒ.əʳ/ ⓤ /ˈrɑː.dʒɚ/ exclamation used in radio communications to mean that a message has been received and understood: *"You are clear to land." "Roger, I'm coming in to land now."*

roger ⌈HAVE SEX⌉ /ˈrɒdʒ.əʳ/ ⓤ /ˈrɑː.dʒɚ/ verb [T] UK OFFENSIVE OLD-FASHIONED to have sex with someone

rogue /rəʊg/ ⓤ /roʊg/ adj **1** behaving in ways that are not expected or not normal, often in a destructive way: *a rogue state* ○ *rogue cells* **2** [before n] SPECIALIZED A rogue animal is a fierce, dangerous animal that lives apart from the rest of its group.

rogue /rəʊg/ ⓤ /roʊg/ noun [C] **1** OLD-FASHIONED HUMOROUS a person who behaves badly but who you still like: *"Come here, you little rogue!" chuckled my uncle.* ○ *The women all think he's a loveable old rogue.* **2** OLD-FASHIONED a dishonest or immoral man

roguish /ˈrəʊ.gɪʃ/ ⓤ /ˈroʊ-/ adj (of a person) looking amused because of slightly bad behaviour: *His eyes were bright blue with a roguish twinkle in them.* **roguishly** /ˈrəʊ.gɪʃ.li/ ⓤ /ˈroʊ-/ adv **roguishness** /ˈrəʊ.gɪʃ.nəs/ ⓤ /ˈroʊ-/ noun [U]

rogues' gallery /ˌrəʊgzˈgæl.ᵊr.i/ ⓤ /ˌroʊgzˈgæl.ɚ-/ noun [C usually sing] a collection of photographs of criminals kept by the police: FIGURATIVE *He occupies a prominent position in the rogues' gallery of the financial world.*

,rogue 'trader noun [C] a STOCKBROKER (= someone who buys and sells shares for other people) who secretly loses a large amount of their employer's money after making a bad or illegal investment

role ⌈DUTY⌉ /rəʊl/ ⓤ /roʊl/ noun [C] the position or purpose that someone or something has in a situation, organization, society or relationship: *What is his role in this project?* ○ *Schools play an important role in society.* ○ *Six people have been put on trial for their role (= involvement) in the anti-government demonstrations.*

role ⌈REPRESENTATION⌉ /rəʊl/ ⓤ /roʊl/ noun [C] an actor's part in a film or play: *She's got a leading/supporting role in the school play.* ○ *She plays the role of a crooked lawyer.*

'role ,model noun [C] a person whom someone admires and whose behaviour they try to copy: *Sports stars are role models for thousands of youngsters.*

'role ,play noun [C or U] pretending to be someone else, especially as part of learning a new skill: *Role play is used in training courses, language-learning and psychotherapy.*

role re,versal noun [C usually sing] a situation in which two people exchange their usual duties or positions

roll ⌈MOVE⌉ /rəʊl/ ⓤ /roʊl/ verb **1** [I or T; usually + adv or prep] to (cause to) move somewhere by turning over and over or from side to side: *The vase rolled off the edge of the table and smashed.* ○ *The dog rolled over onto its back.* ○ *I rolled the wheel along the side of the road back to the car.* **2** [I or T; usually + adv or prep] to move somewhere easily and without sudden movements: *A tear rolled down his cheek.* ○ *A wave of cigarette smoke rolled towards me.* ○ *The piano's on wheels, so we can roll it into the room.* **3** [I] If an aircraft or a ship rolls, it leans to one side and then to the other because of the wind or waves. **4** [I] If a machine is rolling, it is operating: *Just as the television cameras started rolling, it began to pour down with rain.* **5** [T] If you roll your eyes, you move them so that you are looking up, to show that you consider someone or something stupid or foolish: *When he suggested they should buy a new car, she rolled her eyes in disbelief.*

● **a rolling stone (gathers no moss)** OLD-FASHIONED SAYING said to mean that a person who is always travelling and changing jobs has the advantage of having no responsibilities, but also has disadvantages such as having no permanent place to live: *Hal was a bit of a rolling stone before he married and settled down.*

● **rolling in it** (ALSO **rolling in money**) INFORMAL extremely rich: *If they can afford a yacht, they must be rolling in it.*

● **rolling in the aisles** INFORMAL laughing uncontrollably: *The comedian had the audience rolling in the aisles.*

● **Roll on the weekend/five o'clock!, etc.** UK INFORMAL said when you want time to go quickly because you are looking forward to something: *I can't wait to be finished with this project – roll on October!*

● **Roll up! Roll up!** UK OLD-FASHIONED said, especially in the past, by someone who wanted people to come and pay to look at something unusual or interesting: *"Roll up! Roll up! Come and see the amazing bearded lady!" shouted the circus man.*

● **roll with the punches** INFORMAL to be able to deal with a series of difficult situations

roll /rəʊl/ ⓤ /roʊl/ noun **1** [C] when something or someone rolls on the ground: *The dog went for a roll in the grass.* **2** [U] The roll of a ship or aircraft is its movement from side to side in the water or air.

● **be on a roll** INFORMAL to be having a successful or lucky period: *Pippa won five games in a row and it was obvious she was on a roll.*

roller /ˈrəʊ.ləʳ/ ⓤ /ˈroʊ.lɚ/ noun **1** [C] a tube-shaped object in a machine that turns over and over in order to carry things along or press them down or together: *As the hot metal passed between the huge rollers it was pressed into thin sheets.* ➲See also **roller** at **roll** SMOOTH. **2** [C usually pl] a tube-shaped device, often heated, that women use to curl their hair: *She answered the door with her rollers in.* **3** [C] a large, long wave on the sea

roll ⌈TURN OVER⌉ /rəʊl/ ⓤ /roʊl/ verb **1** [T usually + adv or prep] to (cause something to) turn over onto itself to form a cylinder or a sphere: *He rolled the clay into a ball in his hands.* ○ *As I got closer, the hedgehog rolled itself (up) into a ball.* **2** [T] to make a cigarette by wrapping a piece of paper around some tobacco **3** [I or T; + adv or prep] to fold over a piece of clothing or material to make it shorter: *We rolled back the carpet to see the floorboards.*

● **rolled into one** If someone or something has several qualities rolled into one, they have all of those qualities: *He is a father, sales manager, and athlete all rolled into one.*

roll /rəʊl/ ⓤ /roʊl/ noun [C] **1** a piece of film, paper or cloth that is rolled into the shape of a tube: *a roll of carpet* ○ *a toilet roll* (= roll of toilet paper) **2** If a person or animal has rolls of fat on their body, they are very fat: *The dog had rolls of fat along its neck.*

roll ⌈SMOOTH⌉ /rəʊl/ ⓤ /roʊl/ verb [T] to make something smooth and flat: [+ adj] *She borrowed a garden roller to roll the grass (flat).* ○ *When you have rolled (out) the pastry, place it in a pie dish.*

roller /ˈrəʊ.ləʳ/ ⓤ /ˈroʊ.lɚ/ noun [C] a heavy machine used to make surfaces smooth and flat: *The men used a roller to flatten the tarmac.* ➲See also **steamroller** VEHICLE; **roller** at **roll** MOVE.

roll [SOUND] /rəʊl/ [US] /roʊl/ *verb* **1** [I] to make a continuous repeated deep sound: *The drums rolled as the acrobat walked along the tightrope.* **2** [T] If you roll your r's, you pronounce them with your tongue moving quickly and repeatedly against the top of the mouth: *The Italians roll their r's.* **roll** /rəʊl/ [US] /roʊl/ *noun* [C usually sing] *a drum roll* ○ *a deafening roll of thunder*

roll [LIST] /rəʊl/ [US] /roʊl/ *noun* [C] an official list of names: *Is your name on the* ***electoral*** *roll* (= the list of people who can vote)?

• **take/call the roll** MAINLY US If you take/call the roll, you read aloud the names of all the people on the list to make certain that they are present: *The teacher called the roll to see if any students were absent.*

roll [BREAD] /rəʊl/ [US] /roʊl/ *noun* [C] (ALSO **bread roll**) a small loaf of bread for one person: *Would you like a roll and butter with your soup?* ○ UK *I bought a cheese roll (US cheese on a roll)* (= a small loaf of bread filled with cheese) *for lunch.*

PHRASAL VERBS WITH **roll** ▼

▲ **roll *sth* back** *phrasal verb* [M] to reduce the cost or price of something: *The furniture dealer is rolling back the prices on all beds for this week only.*

▲ **roll by** *phrasal verb* LITERARY If an amount of time rolls by, it passes: *The years rolled by, and I didn't see her again until she was married with two children.*

▲ **roll in** *phrasal verb* INFORMAL to arrive in great numbers or amounts: *Once our business gets started, the money will be rolling in.*

▲ **roll *(sth)* out** *phrasal verb* [M] to make a new product, service or system available for the first time: *The government plans to roll out a series of tax cuts over the next few years.*

▲ **roll *sth* up** [FOLD] *phrasal verb* [M] to fold something around itself to make the shape of a ball, or to fold cloth around itself to make a piece of clothing shorter: *Could you roll up that string for me?* ○ *I rolled up my sleeves and began to wash the dishes.*

• **roll up *your* sleeves** INFORMAL to prepare for hard work: *There's a lot of work to do, so roll up your sleeves and get busy.*

▲ **roll up** [ARRIVE] *phrasal verb* INFORMAL to arrive at a particular place or event, usually late: *They rolled up at the party two hours late and rather drunk.*

ˈroll ˌbar *noun* [C] a metal bar across the roof of a car, especially one used for racing, that protects the people inside if the car turns over

ˈroll ˌcall *noun* [C] If someone does a roll call, they read aloud the names of all the people on the list to make certain that they are present.

ˌrolled ˈgold *noun* [U] UK a piece of jewellery which is made of cheap metal covered with a thin layer of gold.

ˌrolled ˈoats *plural noun* oats that have had their outer covering removed and have been flattened

Rollerblade /ˈrəʊ.lə.bleɪd/ [US] /ˈroʊ.lɚ-/ *plural noun* (US ALSO **in-line skate**) TRADEMARK one of two boots with a single row of small wheels on the bottom which you wear in order to travel along quickly for enjoyment ↻See picture **Sports** on page Centre 10

ˈroller ˌblind UK *noun* [C] (US **window shade**) a piece of material fixed onto a wooden or metal roller that can be pulled down to cover a window

ˈroller ˌcoaster *noun* **1** [C] (ALSO **roller-coaster, rollercoaster**) an exciting entertainment in an amusement park, which is like a fast train that goes up and down very steep slopes and around very sudden bends **2** [S] a situation which changes from one extreme to another, or in which a person's feelings change from one extreme to another: *He was* ***on*** *an emotional roller coaster for a while when he lost his job.*

ˈroller ˌderby *noun* [C] US a race around a circular track between two teams of people on ROLLER SKATES

ˈroller ˌskate *noun* [C] a type of boot with four wheels on the bottom which you wear in order to travel along quickly for enjoyment **roller-skate** /ˈrəʊ.lə.skeɪt/ [US] /ˈroʊ.lɚ-/ *verb* [I] **ˈroller ˌskating** *noun* [U]

ˈroller ˌtowel *noun* [C] a piece of cloth joined at both ends which is fixed onto a wooden or metal roller and which you use for drying your hands

rollicking /ˈrɒl.ɪ.kɪŋ/ [US] /ˈrɑː-/ *adj* [before n] OLD-FASHIONED cheerful and energetic: *The play is described as 'a rollicking tale about love and lust'.*

rollicking /ˈrɒl.ɪ.kɪŋ/ [US] /ˈrɑː-/ *noun* [C usually sing] UK INFORMAL when someone tells you in a very angry way that you have done something wrong: *We* ***got*** *a rollicking from the coach at half time.*

rolling [GRADUAL] /ˈrəʊ.lɪŋ/ [US] /ˈroʊ-/ *adj* [before n] gradual: *The plan is for a rolling extension of the tax over the next ten years.*

rolling [HILL] /ˈrəʊ.lɪŋ/ [US] /ˈroʊ-/ *adj* [before n] (of hills) gently rising and falling: *The train journey took us through a valley past rolling hills.*

ˈrolling ˌmill *noun* [C] a factory or machine in which metal is rolled into flat pieces

ˈrolling ˌpin *noun* [C] a tube-shaped object that is used for making pastry flat and thin before cooking it

ˈrolling ˌstock *noun* [U] the engines and carriages that are used on a railway

rollmop /ˈrəʊl.mɒp/ [US] /ˈroʊl.mɑːp/ *noun* [C] UK a piece of HERRING with the bones removed that has been rolled up and preserved in vinegar

ˈroll ˌneck *noun* [C] UK **polo neck**

ˌroll of ˈhonour *noun* [C usually sing] (US ALSO **honor roll**) a list of people who should be remembered for their brave actions

roll-on /ˈrəʊl.ɒn/ [US] /ˈroʊl.ɑːn/ *noun* [C] a small container with a moving ball at the top which is used for storing and rubbing on DEODORANT (= a chemical substance that prevents or hides unpleasant body smells)

roll-on roll-off /ˌrəʊlɒnˌrəʊlˈɒf/ [US] /ˌroʊlɑːnˌroʊlˈɑːf/ *adj* [before n] (INFORMAL **ro-ro**) UK describes a ship built so that vehicles can drive on at one end and off at the other: *a roll-on roll-off ferry*

rollover /ˈrəʊl.əʊ.vəʳ/ [US] /ˈroʊl.oʊ.vɚ/ *noun* [C] when a prize has not been won in a competition and is added to the prize offered in the next competition: *a rollover week*

Rolls-Royce /ˌrəʊlzˈrɔɪs/ [US] /ˌroʊlz-/ *noun* [C] TRADEMARK a large and very expensive type of car made in the UK

• **Rolls-Royce** MAINLY UK **the Rolls-Royce of *sth*** the best type of that thing: *This model is the Rolls-Royce of lawnmowers.*

roll-top desk /ˌrəʊl.tɒpˈdesk/ [US] /ˌroʊl.tɑːp-/ *noun* [C] a type of writing table with a cover that you can push back or pull down

roll-up UK /ˈrəʊl.ʌp/ [US] /ˈroʊl-/ *noun* [C] (AUS **roll-your-own**) a cigarette which you make by wrapping a piece of paper around some tobacco

roly-poly /ˌrəʊ.liˈpəʊ.li/ [US] /ˌroʊ.liˈpoʊ-/ *adj* INFORMAL HUMOROUS (of a person) short and round: *He was a roly-poly little man.*

ˌroly-poly (ˈpudding) *noun* [C or U] UK a sweet dish made with thick pastry spread with jam, which is rolled up and cooked: *jam roly-poly*

ROM /rɒm/ [US] /rɑːm/ *noun* [U] SPECIALIZED ABBREVIATION FOR read only memory: a type of computer memory which holds information that can be used but not changed or added to ↻Compare **RAM** COMPUTER.

romaine /rəˈmeɪn/ *noun* [C] US FOR **cos (lettuce)**

Roman [CITY] /ˈrəʊ.mən/ [US] /ˈroʊ-/ *adj* **1** relating to the city of Rome and its empire in ancient times **2** relating to the modern city of Rome

Roman /ˈrəʊ.mən/ [US] /ˈroʊ-/ *noun* [C] **1** a person who lived in Rome or the Roman Empire in ancient times: *The Romans ruled over most of Europe.* **2** a person who lives in the modern city of Rome **Romano-** /rə.mɑː.nəʊ-/ [US] /-mæn.oʊ-/ *prefix*

roman [PRINT STYLE] /ˈrəʊ.mən/ [US] /ˈroʊ-/ *adj* describes the ordinary style of printed writing in which the letters are vertical **roman** /ˈrəʊ.mən/ [US] /ˈroʊ-/ *noun* [U] *In this book, definitions are printed* ***in*** *roman.*

ˌRoman ˈalphabet *noun* [U] (ALSO **Latin alphabet**) the alphabet used for writing most western European languages, including English

,Roman 'candle *noun* [C] a type of firework which produces brightly coloured stars when it explodes

,Roman 'Catholic *noun* [C] (*ALSO* **Catholic**) a member of the Roman Catholic Church ,Roman 'Catholic *adj* (*ALSO* **Catholic**)

the ,Roman ,Catholic 'Church *noun* [S] the part of the Christian religion which is ruled by the Pope in Rome ,Roman Ca'tholicism *noun* [U] the beliefs and activities of the Roman Catholic Church

romance LOVE /rəʊˈmæns/ /ˈrəʊ.mæns/ ⓤ /roʊˈmæns/ *noun* **1** [C] a close, usually short relationship of love between two people: *They got married last year after a* **whirlwind** (= very short and unexpected) *romance.* ○ *It was just a* **holiday** *romance.* ○ **Office** *romances are usually a bad idea.* **2** [U] when you feel love and sexual attraction for someone: *I felt as though all the romance had gone out of my marriage.* **3** [U] the feeling of excitement or mystery that you have from a particular experience or event: *He loves the romance* **of** *travelling on a steam train.* **4** [C] a story about love: *a historical romance* ○ *She loves reading romances.* **5** [C] a story of exciting events, especially one written or set in the past: *medieval romances*
romance /rəʊˈmæns/ /ˈrəʊ.mæns/ ⓤ /roʊˈmæns/ *verb* **1** [I] to tell stories that are not true, or to describe an event in a way that makes it sound better than it was **2** [T] *OLD-FASHIONED* to try to persuade someone to love you
romantic /rəʊˈmæn.tɪk/ ⓤ /roʊˈmæn.t̬ɪk/ *adj* **1** relating to love or a close loving relationship: *a romantic novel/comedy* ○ *You used to be so romantic, but now you never tell me that you love me.* ⊃See also **Romantic** at **Romanticism**. **2** exciting and mysterious and having a strong effect on your emotions: *We thought that Egypt was an incredibly romantic country.* **3** *SLIGHTLY DISAPPROVING* not practical and having a lot of ideas which are not related to real life: *She has a romantic idea of what it's like to be a struggling young artist.* romantic-ally /rəʊˈmæn.tɪk.li/ ⓤ /roʊˈmæn.t̬ɪ-/ *adv*
romantic /rəʊˈmæn.tɪk/ ⓤ /roʊˈmæn.t̬ɪk/ *noun* [C] *MAINLY DISAPPROVING* someone who is not practical and has ideas which are not related to real life: *You're a hopeless/incurable romantic.* ⊃See also **Romantic** at **Romanticism**.
romanticize, *UK USUALLY* -ise /rəʊˈmæn.tɪ.saɪz/ ⓤ /roʊˈmæn.t̬ə-/ *verb* [I] to talk about something in a way that makes it sound better than it really is, or to believe that something is better than it really is: *Stop romanticizing! Nothing's that perfect.*
romanticism /rəʊˈmæn.tɪ.sɪ.z³m/ ⓤ /roʊˈmæn.t̬ə-/ *noun* [U] a tendency to describe things in a way that makes them sound more exciting or mysterious than they really are ⊃See also **Romanticism**.

Romance LANGUAGE /rəʊˈmæns/ ⓤ /roʊ-/ *adj* [before n] *SPECIALIZED* (of a language) developed from Latin: *French, Italian and Spanish are all Romance languages.*

Romanesque /ˌrəʊ.məˈnesk/ ⓤ /ˌroʊ-/ *adj SPECIALIZED* relating to the style of building which was common in Western and Southern Europe from the 10th to the 12th centuries Romanesque /ˌrəʊ.məˈnesk/ ⓤ /ˌroʊ-/ *noun* [U]

Romanian /rəʊˈmeɪ.ni.ən/ ⓤ /roʊ-/ *adj* **1** from, belonging to or relating to Romania. Romanian *noun* [U] the language of Romania

,Roman 'law *noun* [U] *LEGAL* the system of laws of the ancient Romans, on which some modern legal systems are based

,Roman 'nose *noun* [C] a nose that is higher than usual at the top

,Roman 'numeral *noun* [C usually pl] any of the letters that the ancient Romans used to write numbers, for example I (= 1), II (= 2), III (= 3) ⊃Compare **Arabic numeral**.

Romanticism /rəʊˈmæn.tɪ.sɪ.z³m/ ⓤ /roʊˈmæn.t̬ə-/ *noun* [U] *SPECIALIZED* a style of art, music and literature that was common in Europe in the late 18th and early 19th centuries, which describes the beauty of nature and emphasizes the importance of human emotions ⊃See also **romanticism** at **romance** LOVE. Compare **Classicism**. Romantic /rəʊˈmæn.tɪk/ ⓤ /roʊˈmæn.t̬ɪk/ *adj, noun*

[C] *Beethoven, Schumann and Chopin were leading Romantic composers.* ⊃See also **romantic** at **romance** LOVE.

Romany /ˈrɒm.ə.ni/ ⓤ /ˈrɑː-/ *noun* [C or U] a GYPSY, or the language of the GYPSY people

Romeo /ˈrəʊ.mi.əʊ/ ⓤ /ˈroʊ.mi.oʊ/ *noun* [C] *plural* **Romeos** *HUMOROUS OR DISAPPROVING* a man who thinks he is attractive to women and has sexual relationships with many women

romp /rɒmp/ ⓤ /rɑːmp/ *verb* [I usually + adv or prep] to play in a rough, excited and noisy way: *The children romped happily around/about in the garden.*
● **romp home/in** *UK* to win easily: *She is riding the fastest horse and is certain to romp home.*
romp /rɒmp/ ⓤ /rɑːmp/ *noun* [C usually sing] an amusing, energetic and often sexual entertainment or situation: *The newspaper headline was 'Vicar Caught In Sex Romp'.*
▲ **romp through** *sth phrasal verb INFORMAL* to successfully do something, quickly and easily: *Rory expected to romp through the test and interviews.*

rompers /ˈrɒm.pəz/ ⓤ /ˈrɑːm.pɚz/ *plural noun* (*ALSO* **romper suit**) a single piece of clothing consisting of a top part and trousers worn by babies and very young children

rondo /ˈrɒn.dəʊ/ ⓤ /ˈrɑːn.doʊ/ *noun* [C] *plural* **rondos** *SPECIALIZED* a piece of music that repeats the main tune several times and often forms part of a longer piece

röntgen, roentgen /ˈrɒnt.gən/ ⓤ /ˈrent-/ *noun* [C] *SPECIALIZED* a unit of measurement for showing the amount of radiation received by a person over a period of time

roo /ruː/ *noun* [C] *plural* **roos** *AUS INFORMAL FOR* **kangaroo**

rood screen /ˈruːdˌskriːn/ *noun* [C] *SPECIALIZED* a decorative wooden or stone wall that in some Christian churches separates the area near the ALTAR from the other parts of the church

roof /ruːf/ *noun* [C] the covering that forms the top of a building, vehicle, etc: *The house has a sloping/flat/tiled/thatched/etc. roof.* ○ *Put the luggage* **on** *the roof of the car.* ○ *The roof* (= upper surface) *of the cave is 50 metres up.* ○ *This cake is so dry that it sticks to the roof* **of** *your mouth* (= upper surface of the mouth).
● **a roof over** *your* **head** a place to live: *She gave him enough money to get a roof over his head.*
● **under the same roof** in the same building: *I refuse to live under the same roof as that horrible man.*
● **go through the roof** to rise to a very high level: *Prices have gone through the roof.*
● **go through the roof** (*ALSO* **hit the roof**) *INFORMAL* to get very angry: *When I was expelled from school, my parents went through the roof.*
● **raise the roof** to play/sing very loudly and enthusiastically: *With their last, triumphant piece, the musicians raised the roof.*
roof /ruːf/ *verb* [T often passive] to put a roof on a building -roofed /-ruːft/ *suffix*: *a slate-roofed house*
roofer /ˈruː.fər/ ⓤ /-fɚ/ *noun* [C] a person whose job is to put new roofs on buildings or to repair damaged roofs
roofing /ˈruː.fɪŋ/ *noun* [U] material used for making roofs: *Slates, tiles and shingles are the commonest roofing materials.*
roofless /ˈruː.fləs/ *adj* without a roof: *a ruined and roofless church*
▲ **roof** *sth* **in/over** *phrasal verb* [M] to put a roof over a place or area: *The council has decided to roof over the open-air swimming pool.*

'roof ,garden *noun* [C] a garden on the roof of a building

'roof ,rack *noun* [C] a frame fixed on top of the roof of a vehicle, for carrying large objects

rooftop /ˈruːf.tɒp/ ⓤ /-tɑːp/ *noun* [C usually pl] the outside surface of the roof of a building: *a magnificent view of the rooftops* ○ *Police marksmen with rifles were stationed* **on** *the rooftops.*
● **shout/proclaim** *sth* **from the rooftops** to say something publicly: *I'm so in love I want to shout your name from the rooftops.*

R

rook [BIRD] /rʊk/ *noun* [C] a large black bird similar to a crow
rookery /ˈrʊk.ᵊr.i/ Ⓤⓢ /-ɚ-/ *noun* [C] several rooks' nests, high up in the branches of a group of trees
rook [GAME PIECE] /rʊk/ *noun* [C] (*INFORMAL* **castle**) in the game of chess, a piece that can move along any number of squares in straight lines parallel to the sides of the board
rook [CHEAT] /rʊk/ *verb* [T] *OLD-FASHIONED INFORMAL* to cheat someone out of some money
rookie /ˈrʊk.i/ *noun* [C] *MAINLY US INFORMAL* a person who is new to an organization or an activity: *These rookie cops don't know anything yet.*
room [PLACE] /ruːm/ /rʊm/ *noun* [C] **1** a part of the inside of a building that is separated from other parts by walls, floor and ceiling: *She's waiting for you in the conference room upstairs.* ○ *She's upstairs in her room* (= her private room, where she sleeps). ○ *FIGURATIVE The whole room* (= All the people in the room) *turned and looked at her.* **2** Room is also used as a combining form: *a bedroom* ○ *a bathroom* ○ *a dining-room* ○ *living-room* ○ *a hotel room* ○ *He booked a* ***single/double*** *room* (= a room for one person/two people in a hotel).
room /ruːm/ /rʊm/ *verb* [I usually + adv or prep] *US* to rent a room from someone, or share a rented room with someone: *At college he rooms* ***with*** *this guy from Nebraska.*
roomer /ˈruː.məʳ/ Ⓤⓢ /-mɚ/ *noun* [C] *US FOR* **lodger**
roomful /ˈruːm.fʊl/ *noun* [C usually sing] as many or as much as a room will hold: *a roomful* ***of*** *people/guests/boxes/etc.*
rooms /ruːmz/ /rʊmz/ *plural noun UK OLD-FASHIONED* a set of rented rooms, especially in a college or university
room [SPACE] /ruːm/ /rʊm/ *noun* [U] **1** the amount of space that someone or something needs: *That sofa would* ***take up*** *too much room in the flat.* ○ *James took the books off the little table to* ***make*** *room* ***for*** *the television.* ○ *He's fainted! Don't crowd him – give him room.* ○ *Is there (enough/any) room* ***for*** *me* ***in*** *the car?* ○ [+ to infinitive] *There's hardly room* ***to*** *move in here.* **2** opportunity for doing something: *I feel the company has little room* ***for*** *manoeuvre.*
• **room for doubt** a possibility of something being true: *There is little room for doubt about what happened.*
• **room for improvement** a possibility or hope that someone or something will improve: *Her writing is better but there is still room for improvement.*
• **no room for *sth*** If you say there is no room for a feeling or type of behaviour, you mean it is not acceptable: *In a small company like this, there is no room for lazy staff.*
• **There's no/not enough room to swing a cat.** *SAYING* said about a place or space that is very small
roomy /ˈruː.mi/ *adj APPROVING* If something such as a house or car is roomy, it has a lot of space inside it.
ˌroom and ˈboard *noun* [U] *US FOR* **board and lodging**
ˈrooming ˌhouse *noun* [C] *US FOR* **boarding house**
roommate /ˈrʊm.meɪt/ /ˈruːm-/ *noun* [C] **1** a person with whom you share a room for a period of time: *Jean was my roommate during our first year at university.* **2** *US* (*UK* **housemate,** *UK* **flatmate**) a person with whom you share an apartment or house: *Brian's moving out next month, so we're looking for another roommate to share our apartment.*
ˈroom ˌservice *noun* [U] In a hotel, room service is the serving of food and drink to customers in their room, or the people who do this work.
roost /ruːst/ *noun* [C] a place, such as a branch of a tree, where birds rest or sleep **roost** /ruːst/ *verb* [I]
• **come back/home to roost** to return to cause problems: *All his earlier mistakes are coming home to roost.*
rooster /ˈruː.stəʳ/ Ⓤⓢ /-stɚ/ *noun* [C] *US FOR* **cock** BIRD
root [PLANT PART] /ruːt/ *noun* [C] **1** the part of a plant which grows down into the earth to obtain water and food and which holds the plant firm in the ground **2** the part of a hair, tooth, or nail that is under the skin **3** the cause or origin of something bad: *We must* ***get to the root of*** (= discover the cause of) *this problem.* ○ *What* ***is/lies at*** *the root* ***of*** *the problem is their lack of interest.* ○ *The high crime rate has its roots* ***in*** *unemployment and poverty.* ○ *So what's the root* ***cause*** *of his anxiety?* **4** *SPECIALIZED* The root of a word is its most basic form, to which other parts, such as AFFIXES, can be added: *The root of the word 'sitting' is 'sit'.*
• **take root** If an idea, belief or system takes root somewhere, it starts to be accepted there: *Communism has never really taken root in England.*
• **root and branch** *UK* (*US* **roots and all**) completely: *Racism must be eliminated, root and branch.*
root /ruːt/ *verb* [I] to grow roots: *The trees failed to root and so died.*
-rooted /-ruː.tɪd/ Ⓤⓢ /-t̬ɪd/ *suffix* ➲See at **deep-seated**:
• **rooted to the spot** to be unable to move: *She was rooted to the spot with fear/amazement.*
rootless /ˈruːt.ləs/ *adj* describes a person without a home to return to **rootlessness** /ˈruːt.lə.snəs/ *noun* [U]
roots /ruːts/ *plural noun* origins: *The city of Tours can* ***trace*** *its roots* ***back to*** *Roman times.* ➲See also **grassroots.**
• **put down roots** If you put down roots in a place where you have moved to live, you make new friends and join in new activities there so that you feel it is your home.
root [MATHEMATICS] /ruːt/ *noun* [C] *SPECIALIZED* **1** a solution of some EQUATIONS (= mathematical statements) **2** A root **of** a particular number is another number which, when multiplied by itself one or more times, reaches that number: *The* ***square*** *root of 64 is 8, and the* ***cube*** *root of 64 is 4.*
root [LOOK] /ruːt/ *verb* [I usually + adv or prep] to look for something by turning things over: *She rooted* ***through/among*** *the papers on her desk.* ○ *The pigs rooted* ***for*** *acorns in the forest.*

PHRASAL VERBS WITH **root** ▼

▲ **root about/around** ***(somewhere)*** *phrasal verb INFORMAL* to search for something, especially by looking through other things: *She was rooting around* ***in*** *her drawer for a pencil.*
▲ **root for *sb*** *phrasal verb INFORMAL* to show support for someone who is in a competition or who is doing something difficult: *Most of the crowd were rooting for the home team.* ○ *Good luck! We're all rooting for you.*
▲ **root *sth/sb* out** [SEARCH FOR] *phrasal verb* [M] *INFORMAL* to search and find something or someone that is difficult to find: *I've rooted out an old pair of shoes that might fit you.*
▲ **root *sth/sb* out** [GET RID OF] *phrasal verb* [M] to find and remove a person or thing that is causing a problem: *Ms Campbell has been appointed to root out inefficiency in this company.*
▲ **root *sth* out/up** [PLANT] *phrasal verb* [M] to remove a whole plant, including the roots, from the ground: *I suggest you root out those weeds before they take hold.*

ˈroot ˌbeer *noun* [U] a fizzy brown drink without alcohol, that is flavoured with the roots of various plants
rootbound /ˈruːt.baʊnd/ *adj US FOR* **pot-bound**
ˈroot ˌcellar *noun* [C] *US* an area, often underground, for storing root crops and vegetables
ˈroot ˌcrop *noun* [C] a plant such as potatoes that is grown because its roots are eaten
rootstock /ˈruːt.stɒk/ Ⓤⓢ /-stɑːk/ *noun* [C] *SPECIALIZED* a stem to which part of another plant is joined so that both parts can grow together and benefit from a good feature of the stem
rope /rəʊp/ Ⓤⓢ /roʊp/ *noun* **1** [C or U] (a piece of) strong, thick cord made of long twisted fibres: *A sailor threw a rope ashore and we tied the boat to a post.* ○ *a* ***coil of*** *rope* ➲See picture **Sports** on page Centre 10 **2** [C] several of one type of object connected together on a string: *a rope* ***of*** *garlic* ○ *a rope* ***of*** *pearls*
ropes /rəʊps/ Ⓤⓢ /roʊps/ *plural noun* a fence made of rope enclosing an area: *The middleweight boxing champion had his opponent up against the ropes.*
• **on the ropes** *INFORMAL* doing badly and likely to fail: *I think the business is finally on the ropes.*
• **learn/know the ropes** to learn/know how to do a job or activity
• **show/teach *sb* the ropes** to show someone how to do a job or activity: *Lynn spent an afternoon showing the new girl the ropes.*

R

rope /rəʊp/ ⓤ /roʊp/ *verb* [T usually + adv or prep] to tie things together with rope: *I'll rope my horse **to** your car and pull you out of the ditch.* ○ *The climbers roped themselves **together**.*

PHRASAL VERBS WITH rope ▼

▲ **rope sb in** *phrasal verb* [M] INFORMAL to persuade someone to do something for you: *At the last minute, we roped in a couple of spectators to complete the team.*

▲ **rope sth/somewhere off** *phrasal verb* [M] to enclose an area or place with ropes in order to keep people out: *The police roped off the scene of the crime.*

rope 'bridge *noun* [C] a bridge made of long pieces of rope knotted together, and wooden boards for people to walk on, used especially in the past or for children's games

rope 'ladder *noun* [C] a ladder made of two long pieces of rope connected by short pieces of rope, metal, wood, etc.

ropey (ropier, ropiest), **ropy** /ˈrəʊ.pi/ ⓤ /ˈroʊ-/ *adj* MAINLY UK INFORMAL in bad condition or of low quality: *Your tyres look a bit ropey, don't they?* ○ *I usually feel rather ropey (= ill) the morning after a big party.*

rort /rɔːt/ ⓤ /rɔːrt/ *verb* [T] AUS INFORMAL to take unfair advantage of a public service for your own benefit: *Gary's been rorting the system, getting both a student allowance and unemployment benefit.*

rort /rɔːt/ ⓤ /rɔːrt/ *noun* [C] AUS INFORMAL a plan to take unfair advantage of a public service for your own benefit

rosary /ˈrəʊ.zᵊr.i/ ⓤ /ˈroʊ.zɚ-/ *noun* [C] a string of BEADS (= little decorative balls) used especially by Roman Catholics and Buddhists to count prayers, or the prayers themselves: *She was **saying** the rosary.*

rose RISE /rəʊz/ ⓤ /roʊz/ *past simple of* **rise**

rose PLANT /rəʊz/ ⓤ /roʊz/ *noun* [C] a garden plant with thorns on its stems and pleasant-smelling flowers, or a flower from this plant: *a rose bush* ○ *She sent him a bunch of red roses.* ➔See picture **Flowers and Plants** on page Centre 3

● **put the roses (back) into sb's cheeks** INFORMAL If something puts the roses back into your cheeks, it makes you look healthy, especially after an illness: *A brisk walk will put the roses back into your cheeks.*

● **coming up roses** If something is coming up roses, it is happening successfully.

● **not all roses** (ALSO **not a bed of roses**) If a situation is not all roses, there are unpleasant things to deal with as well as the pleasant ones: *Being in a relationship is not all roses, you know.*

rose COLOUR /rəʊz/ ⓤ /roʊz/ *adj, noun* [U] (having) a pink colour: *The houses were painted various shades of rose.*

● **look at/see sth through rose-coloured/tinted glasses** (UK ALSO **look at/see sth through rose-coloured/tinted spectacles**) to see only the pleasant things about a situation and not notice the things that are unpleasant: *She's always looked at life through rose-tinted glasses.*

rosy /ˈrəʊ.zi/ ⓤ /ˈroʊ-/ *adj* **1** having a pinkish-red colour: APPROVING *Your rosy **cheeks** always make you look so healthy.* ➔See **paint a bleak/gloomy/rosy, etc. picture of** at **paint.** **2** If a situation is described as rosy, it gives hope of success or happiness: *Our financial position is rosy.*

rose DEVICE /rəʊz/ ⓤ /roʊz/ *noun* [C] a circular device with small holes in it which is put on the end of a WATERING CAN (= a container used for pouring water on plants)

rosé WINE /ˈrəʊ.zeɪ/ ⓤ /roʊˈzeɪ/ *noun* [C or U] a pink wine

roseate /ˈrəʊ.zi.ət/ ⓤ /ˈroʊ.zi.ɪt/ *adj* LITERARY pink

rosebud /ˈrəʊz.bʌd/ ⓤ /ˈroʊz-/ *noun* [C] the beginning stage of a rose flower

'rose ,hip *noun* [C usually pl] a small round red fruit produced by a rose bush

rosella /rəʊˈzel.ə/ ⓤ /roʊ-/ *noun* [C] AUS one of the brightly-coloured parrots of eastern Australia

rosemary /ˈrəʊz.mə.ri/ ⓤ /ˈroʊz.mer.i/ *noun* [U] a bush whose leaves are used as flavouring in cooking and are used in some perfumes, or the leaves themselves

rosette /rəʊˈzet/ ⓤ /roʊ-/ *noun* [C] a flower-shaped decorative object cut into wood or stone, or one made of RIBBON (= narrow silk strips) worn as a sign that you support a particular team or political party or that you have won a race, etc: *The winning horse had a rosette fixed to its bridle.*

rose-water /ˈrəʊz.wɔː.tər/ ⓤ /ˈroʊz.wɑː.t̬ɚ/ *noun* [U] a liquid with a pleasant smell made from ROSES (= type of sweet-smelling flower), used on the skin as a perfume or to flavour food

,rose 'window *noun* [C] a round window, especially in a church, with coloured glass in it

rosewood /ˈrəʊz.wʊd/ ⓤ /ˈroʊz-/ *noun* [U] a hard dark-coloured wood used especially for making high-quality furniture

Rosh Hashana, Rosh Hashanah /ˌrɒʃ.hæʃˈɑː.nə/ ⓤ /ˌroʊʃ.həˈʃɑː.nə/ *noun* [U] the Jewish New Year festival, which is held in September

roster /ˈrɒs.tər/ ⓤ /ˈrɑː.stɚ/ *noun* [C] MAINLY US a list of people's names, often with the jobs they have been given to do: *If you look on the **duty** roster, you'll see when you're working.*

rostrum /ˈrɒs.trəm/ ⓤ /ˈrɑː.strəm/ *noun* [C] *plural* **rostrums** or **rostra** a small platform on which a person making a speech or a music CONDUCTOR (= leader) stands

rot /rɒt/ ⓤ /rɑːt/ *verb* [I or T] **-tt-** to (cause to) decay: *The fruit had been left to rot on the trees.* ○ *Rain has got in and rotted **(away)** the woodwork.* ○ *the smell of rotting fruit*

● **rot in jail/prison/etc.** to stay in prison/etc. for a very long time: *Ruben Carter was **left** to rot in jail for most of his life.*

rot /rɒt/ ⓤ /rɑːt/ *noun* [U] **1** decay: *Rot has got into the furniture.* **2** OLD-FASHIONED INFORMAL nonsense: *"Don't talk rot!"*

● **the rot sets in** INFORMAL (of a situation) to begin to go wrong: *The rot set in when his parents divorced and he started taking drugs.*

● **stop the rot** to take action against something bad, before it spreads and becomes worse: *We must try to stop the rot before the whole school is corrupted.*

rotten /ˈrɒt.ᵊn/ ⓤ /ˈrɑː.t̬ᵊn/ *adj* **1** decayed: *The room smelled of rotten vegetables.* **2** very bad: *rotten weather* ○ OLD-FASHIONED *It was rotten **of** you **to** leave without saying goodbye.*

rota MAINLY UK /ˈrəʊ.tə/ ⓤ /ˈroʊ.t̬ə/ *noun* [C] (US USUALLY **roster**) a list of things that have to be done and of the people who will do them: *a weekly rota*

rotate /rəʊˈteɪt/ ⓤ /ˈroʊ.teɪt/ *verb* **1** [I or T] to (cause to) turn in a circle, especially around a fixed point: *Rotate the handle by 180° to open the door.* ○ *The wheel rotates **around** an axle.* ○ *The satellite slowly rotates as it circles the earth.* **2** [T] If a job rotates or if a group of people rotate their jobs, the jobs are done at different times by different people. **3** [T] When farmers rotate crops, they regularly change which crops they grow in a particular field. **rotation** /rəʊˈteɪ.ʃᵊn/ ⓤ /roʊ-/ *noun* [C or U] *The earth completes 366 rotations **about** its axis in every leap year.* ○ *With this drill it's possible to adjust the speed of rotation.*

● **in rotation** one after the other, in a regular order: *There are ten employees and they do the various jobs in rotation.*

rotary /ˈrəʊ.tᵊr.i/ ⓤ /ˈroʊ.t̬ɚ-/ *adj* (of a machine) having a part that moves around in a circle: *a rotary engine/mower/pump*

rote learning /ˌrəʊtˈlɜː.nɪŋ/ ⓤ /ˌroʊtˈlɜː-/ *noun* [U] USUALLY DISAPPROVING learning something in order to be able to repeat it from memory, rather than in order to understand it

● **learn sth by rote** SLIGHTLY DISAPPROVING to learn something in order to be able to repeat it from memory, rather than in order to understand it: *She learned the equations by rote.*

ROTF, rotf INTERNET ABBREVIATION FOR rolling on the floor: used to show that you think something is amusing

ROTFL, rotfl (ALSO **ROFL**) INTERNET ABBREVIATION FOR rolling on the floor laughing: used to show that you think something is very amusing

R

ROTFLOL, **rotflol** *INTERNET ABBREVIATION FOR* rolling on the floor laughing out loud: used to show that you think something is extremely amusing

rotisserie /rəʊˈtɪs.ər.i/ [US] /roʊˈtɪs.ɚ-/ *noun* [C] (a shop or restaurant which contains) a device for cooking meat, especially chicken, by turning it round slowly near a flame or cooker

rotor /ˈrəʊ.təʳ/ [US] /ˈroʊ.t̬ɚ/ *noun* [C] a part of a machine that spins, especially the device supporting the spinning blades of a helicopter ➲See picture **Planes, Ships and Boats** on page Centre 14

rotten /ˈrɒt.ən/ [US] /ˈrɑː.tən/ *adj* ➲See at **rot**.

rotter /ˈrɒt.əʳ/ [US] /ˈrɑː.t̬ɚ/ *noun* [C] *MAINLY UK OLD-FASHIONED* someone who is very unpleasant or does very unpleasant things

rottweiler /ˈrɒtˌwaɪ.ləʳ/ /-ˌvaɪ-/ [US] /ˈrɑːtˌwaɪ.lɚ/ *noun* [C] a large, fierce and sometimes dangerous type of dog: *FIGURATIVE Jenkins is one of the new breed of political rottweilers in his party.*

rotund /rəʊˈtʌnd/ [US] /roʊ-/ *adj* (especially of a person) round or rounded in shape

rotunda /rəʊˈtʌn.də/ [US] /roʊ-/ *noun* [C] (part of) a building which is round in shape, and often has a DOME (= rounded roof) on top

rouble, **ruble** /ˈruː.bl̩/ *noun* [C] the standard unit of money used in Belarus, Russia and Tajikistan

rouge /ruːʒ/ *noun* [U] a red or pink powder put on the cheeks to make the face look more attractive

rough [UNEVEN] /rʌf/ *adj* **1** uneven or not smooth, often because of being in bad condition: *It was a rough mountain road, full of stones and huge holes.* **2** If a surface such as paper or skin is rough, it does not feel smooth when you touch it: *My hands get very rough in the cold.* **3** describes an alcoholic drink, especially wine, that tastes cheap and often strong **4** not very carefully or expensively made: *I made a rough table out of some old boxes.* **5** A rough voice or sound is hard and loud. **6** Rough ground is ground that is not used for any particular purpose and is uneven and full of wild plants. **7** If a machine sounds rough, it is making a noise because it is in bad condition.

• **rough and ready** produced quickly, with little preparation

the rough *noun* [S] in golf, an area of uneven ground with long grass: *My ball landed **in** the rough.*

• **take the rough with the smooth** to accept the unpleasant parts of a situation as well as the pleasant parts: *That's relationships for you – you have to take the rough with the smooth.*

roughen /ˈrʌf.ən/ *verb* [I or T] to (cause to) become less smooth

roughly /ˈrʌf.li/ *adv* without taking a lot of care to make something perfect: *Roughly chop the tomatoes and add to the onions.* **roughness** /ˈrʌf.nəs/ *noun* [U]

rough [NOT EXACT] /rʌf/ *adj* [before n] fairly correct but not exact or detailed; approximate: *The builder did a rough sketch of how the new stairs would look.* ○ *This is only a rough guess.* ○ *She made a rough estimate/calculation of the likely cost.* ○ *The tests are a rough **guide** to students' progress.*

• **in rough** simple and without details: *His first plans were drawn up in rough.*

• **rough and ready** simple but good enough: *rough and ready accommodation*

rough /rʌf/ *noun* [C] a first quick drawing of something

roughly /ˈrʌf.li/ *adv* approximately: *There has been an increase of roughly 2.25 million.* ○ *Roughly **speaking**, it's 2.25 million.* ○ *We have roughly similar tastes/roughly the same tastes.* **roughness** /ˈrʌf.nəs/ *noun* [U]

rough [VIOLENT] /rʌf/ *adj* dangerous or violent; not calm or gentle: *a rough area of town* ○ *The other boys were rough, always looking for a fight.* ○ *I'm always sea-sick if the water/wind/sea/weather is rough* (= stormy).

• **rough justice/luck** something that happens to you that is severe or unfair: *It seems like rough justice that he should lose his house as well as his wife.*

rough /rʌf/ *adv* forcefully or violently: *The Hull team had a bad reputation for playing rough.*

rough /rʌf/ *noun* [C] a violent person: *a gang of drunken young roughs*

• **rough and tumble 1** fighting between children that is not serious: *It was just a bit of rough and tumble.* **2** a busy activity which people do in a very forceful way: *She enjoys **the** rough and tumble **of** politics.* **roughly** /ˈrʌf.li/ *adv*: *He pushed the children roughly to one side.* ○ *"And what's going on here?" he said roughly.* **roughness** /ˈrʌf.nəs/ *noun* [U]

rough [DIFFICULT] /rʌf/ *adj* difficult or unpleasant: *He's had a rough time/month/year, what with the divorce and then his father dying.* ○ ***It** must be rough **to** have two kids and nowhere to live.*

rough /rʌf/ *adv* **live/sleep rough** to live outside not in a house, and sleep on the ground: *When we ran out of money, we slept rough for a week.*

rough /rʌf/ *verb INFORMAL* **rough it** to live temporarily in basic and uncomfortable conditions: *While the house was being decorated we roughed it in a tent.*

rough [ILL] /rʌf/ *adj* [after v] *UK* ill: *You look a bit rough – how much did you have to drink last night?*

rough /rʌf/ *verb*

PHRASAL VERBS WITH **rough** ▼

▲ **rough *sth* in** *phrasal verb* [M] If you rough a drawing in, you you draw the basic lines, without the detail.

▲ **rough *sth* out** *phrasal verb* [M] If you rough out a drawing, idea or plan, you draw or write the main parts of it without giving its details.

▲ **rough *sb* up** *phrasal verb* [M] *INFORMAL* to hit and kick someone, usually to frighten or threaten them

roughage /ˈrʌf.ɪdʒ/ *noun* [U] **fibre** FOOD

roughcast /ˈrʌf.kɑːst/ [US] /-kæst/ *noun* [U] *SPECIALIZED* a mixture of water, sand, lime and small stones which is used to cover the outside of buildings

ˌrough ˈcider *noun* [U] *AUS FOR* **cider**

ˌrough ˈdiamond *UK noun* [C] (*US* **diamond in the rough**) a person who is kinder and more pleasant than they seem to be from their appearance and manner

rough-hewn /ˌrʌfˈhjuːn/ *adj* describes a material, such as wood or stone, which has been shaped, but not given a smooth surface

roughhouse /ˈrʌf.haʊs/ *verb* [I or T] *US OR OLD-FASHIONED* to fight, often in a playful way: *A couple of boys were roughhousing (each other) in the park.*

roughhouse /ˈrʌf.haʊs/ *noun* [C usually sing] *US OR OLD-FASHIONED* a fight between many people, without weapons

roughneck /ˈrʌf.nek/ *noun* [C] **1** a worker on an OILRIG (= a large piece of equipment for getting oil from underground) **2** *MAINLY US INFORMAL* a person who is rough and rude, usually a man

ˈrough ˌpaper *noun* [U] *UK* paper which is used for the first versions of a drawing, piece of writing or calculation

ˌrough ˈtrade *noun* [U] *SLANG* male prostitutes who have sex with other men and who give the appearance of being from a poor social class: *He went to the docks to pick up a bit of rough trade.*

roulette /ruːˈlet/ *noun* [U] a game of chance in which a small ball is dropped onto a wheel that is spinning and the players guess in which hole it will finally stop

round [CIRCULAR] /raʊnd/ *adj* shaped like a ball or circle, or curved: *Tennis balls and oranges are round.* ○ *a round hole/stone/table/window* ○ *a round face* ○ *round eyes*

rounded /ˈraʊn.dɪd/ *adj* round or curved: *The little boy stared at the pregnant woman's rounded belly.*

round [COMPLETE] /raʊnd/ *adj* (of a number) whole or complete; given to the nearest 1, 10, 100, etc. and not as exact amounts: *2.8 to the nearest round **number** is 3.* ○ *"I've got 95 bottles here for you." "Could you make it a round hundred, please?"*

round [AROUND] *MAINLY UK* /raʊnd/ *prep, adv* (*US USUALLY* **around**) in a circular direction or position; around: *The Moon goes round the Earth.* ○ *We ran round (the outside of the house) to the back, looking for the dog.* ○ *The idea has been going round **and round** in my head all day* (= I can't stop thinking about it). ○ *When one engine stopped, we had to* ***turn*** *round* (= turn to face the opposite direction) *and fly home.* ➲See **theatre in the round**.

• **way round** a way of dealing with or avoiding a problem: *There's no way round this problem.*

• **right/wrong way round** facing the right/wrong way: *He put the wheel on the right/wrong way round.*

• **round about** approximately: *"We'll be at your house at round about 9 o'clock, okay?"*

round /raʊnd/ *verb* [T] to go around something: *Colin rounded the corner at high speed.*

round [IN ALL PARTS] *MAINLY UK* /raʊnd/ *prep, adv* (*US USUALLY* **around**) in every part of a place, or in various parts of a place: *The landlord showed me round (the house).* ○ *I had to go* ***all*** *round town to find a hotel that was open.* ○ *This virus has been going round (the school)* (= many people have had it).

round [SURROUNDING] *MAINLY UK* /raʊnd/ *prep, adv* (*US USUALLY* **around**) on all or some sides of something: *We sat round the fire.* ○ *The house has trees* ***all*** *round.* ○ *The pyramid is 50 metres high and 100 metres round (the base).* ○ *Everyone for a mile round* (= in the area) *heard the explosion.*

round [DIRECTION] *MAINLY UK* /raʊnd/ *prep, adv* (*US USUALLY* **around**) in a particular direction: *The garden is round the back (of the house).* ○ *I used to live round* (= near) *here when I was a child.* ○ *You must come round* ***(to*** *my house) sometime soon.* ○ *UK NOT STANDARD We're going round* (= to) *the pub for a quick drink.*

• **round the corner** very near here: *There's a great restaurant* ***just*** *round the corner.*

round [GROUP] /raʊnd/ *noun* [C] **1** a number of things or group of events: *Russia and America will hold another round* ***of*** *talks next month.* ○ *When we were young life was just one long round of parties/pleasure.* **2** drinks that you buy for a group of people: *It's your turn to buy a round.* **3** *UK* a single slice of toast, or a sandwich **4** *UK* (*US* **route**) a set of regular visits that you make to a number of places or people, especially in order to deliver products as part of your job: *He has a* ***milk/ paper*** *round.* **5** a part of a competition: *She was knocked out of the championship in the third round.* **6** one of the periods of time during a boxing or WRESTLING match when the competitors are fighting **7** a complete game in golf **8** *SPECIALIZED* a song for several singers, who begin singing one after the other at various points in the song

• **the daily round** *UK OLD-FASHIONED* the tasks you have to do every day: *I get exhausted just by the daily round.*

• **on *your* rounds** to be out on a regular visit: *The doctor's out on his rounds.*

• **make/do the rounds** to talk to a lot of people: *I've made/done the rounds of all the agents, but nobody has any tickets left.*

• **go the rounds** *UK* to go from person to person or place to place: *That story has gone the rounds in our office.*

• **round of applause** when people clap: *The singer got a big round of applause.*

round [BULLET] /raʊnd/ *noun* [C] a bullet or other single piece of AMMUNITION: *The soldiers had only twenty rounds left.*

PHRASAL VERBS WITH **round**

▲ **round *sth* down** *phrasal verb* [M] to reduce a number to the nearest whole or simple number

▲ **round *sth* off** [SHAPE] *phrasal verb* [M] to make something that is pointed or sharp into a smooth, curved shape by rubbing it: *He used a special machine to round off the corners of the old table.*

▲ **round *sth* off** [COMPLETE] *phrasal verb* [M] to complete an event or activity in a pleasant or satisfactory way: *To round off her education, her father sent her to a Swiss finishing school.* ○ *We rounded the meal off* ***with*** *a chocolate and rum cake.*

▲ **round on** If you round on someone or something, you suddenly turn and attack them: *The fox rounded on its pursuers.* ○ *FIGURATIVE The Prime Minister rounded on his critics with a very forceful speech.*

▲ **round *sth/sb* up** [GATHER] *phrasal verb* [M] to find and gather together a group of animals or people: *The cowboys rounded the cattle up.* ○ *I'll just go and round up Andrew and Patrick for the meeting.*

▲ **round *sth* up** [NUMBER] *phrasal verb* [M] to increase a number to the nearest whole or simple number

roundabout [CIRCULAR OBJECT] /ˈraʊnd.ə.baʊt/ *noun* [C] **1** *UK* (*US* **traffic circle**) a place where three or more roads join and traffic must go around a circular area in the middle, rather than straight across **2** *UK* (*US* **merry-go-round**) a flat round piece of equipment in play areas on which children sit or stand and are pushed round and round **3** *UK* a **merry-go-round** (= machine with animals or vehicles for children to ride at a fair)

roundabout [INDIRECT] /ˈraʊnd.ə.baʊt/ *adj* not in a simple, direct or quick way: *We took a roundabout* ***route*** *to avoid the accident.* ○ *He asked me, in a roundabout* ***way****, if he could have a salary increase.*

ˌround ˈbrackets *plural noun UK FOR* **parentheses**

roundel /ˈraʊn.dəl/ *noun* [C] a circular decoration, especially a coloured circle on a military aircraft that shows its nationality

rounders /ˈraʊn.dəz/ [US] /-dɚz/ *noun* [U] a British game similar to baseball, in which you try to hit a ball and you score a point if you run round all four sides of a large square area

round-eyed /ˌraʊndˈaɪd/ *adj* [after v] describes someone whose eyes are open very wide because they are surprised, shocked or frightened: *She was round-eyed* ***with*** *amazement/terror.*

roundly /ˈraʊnd.li/ *adv FORMAL* severely: *The government is being roundly criticized for its education policy.* ○ *The home team were roundly defeated.*

ˌround ˈrobin [LETTER] *noun* [C] *UK* a letter, usually of demands or complaints, which is signed by many people

ˌround ˈrobin [COMPETITION] *noun* [C] a competition in which all the players play against each other at least once

round-shouldered /ˌraʊndˈʃəʊl.dəd/ [US] /-ˈʃoʊl.dɚd/ *adj* having shoulders that curve down and forward: *He had become round-shouldered from years of sitting in front of a computer.*

round-table /ˌraʊndˈteɪ.bl̩/ *adj* [before n] A round-table discussion/meeting is one where people meet and talk in conditions of equality.

ˌround ˈtrip *noun* [C] If you make a round trip, you go on a journey and return to where you started from.

round-up /ˈraʊnd.ʌp/ *noun* [C] **1** a gathering together of people, cattle, things, etc: *The President ordered the round-up and imprisonment of all opposition politicians.* ➲See also **round** at **round** CIRCULAR, **round** AROUND. **2** a statement on the radio or television of the main items of news

roundworm /ˈraʊnd.wɜːm/ [US] /-wɝːm/ *noun* [C] any of various types of worm with a round body that can live in the bowels of people and some animals, and often cause disease

rouse /raʊz/ *verb* [T] to wake someone up or make someone more active or excited: *He roused himself* ***(from*** *a pleasant daydream) and got back to work.* ○ *The speaker attempted to rouse the crowd with a cry for action.*

rousing /ˈraʊ.zɪŋ/ *adj* making people feel excited and proud or ready to take action: *We sang a last rousing chorus of the national anthem.* ○ *She delivered a rousing speech full of anger and passion.*

roustabout *US* /ˈraʊst.ə.baʊt/ *noun* [C] (*AUS* **rouseabout**) a person whose job involves heavy unskilled work

rout /raʊt/ *verb* [T] *FORMAL* to defeat an enemy completely and force them to run away: *FIGURATIVE The Russian chess team have routed all the rest.*

rout /raʊt/ *noun* [C] defeat: *The battle/election was a complete and utter rout.*

▲ **rout *sb* out** *phrasal verb* [M] *US* to make someone come out of the place where they are: *His wife had to rout him out* ***of*** *the crowd.*

route /ruːt/ [US] /ruːt/ /raʊt/ *noun* [C] **1** a particular way or direction between places: *The route we had planned took us right across Greece.* ○ *I live* ***on*** *a bus route so I can easily get to work.* **2** a method of achieving something: *A college education is often the best route to a good job.* **3** *US*

(*UK* **round**) a set of regular visits that you make to a number of places or people, especially in order to deliver products as part of your job
• **Route** In the US, Route is used before the names of main roads between cities: *Route 66*
route /ruːt/ [US] /ruːt/ /raʊt/ *verb* [T usually + adv or prep] to send: *Deliveries are routed via/by way of London.*
ˈroute ˌmarch *noun* [C usually sing] a long, difficult and tiring walk, especially one done by soldiers as part of their training
routine /ruːˈtiːn/ *noun* **1** [C or U] a habitual or fixed way of doing things: *There's no* ***set/fixed*** *routine at work – every day is different.* ○ *He checks under the car for bombs as* ***a matter of*** *routine.* **2** [C] a regular series of movements, jokes or similar items used in a performance: *an* ***exercise/dance*** *routine* ○ *He went into his usual 'I'm the head of the family' routine* (= habitual way of speaking). **3** [C] *SPECIALIZED* a part of a computer program that does a particular operation
routine /ruːˈtiːn/ *adj*: *a routine* (= regular) *task/inspection/medical checkup* ○ *a routine* (= ordinary) *case of appendicitis* ○ *DISAPPROVING* *My job is so routine and boring – I hate it.*
routinely /ruːˈtiːn.li/ *adv*: *Health and safety rules are routinely* (= very often) *flouted/ignored on the building site.*
roux /ruː/ *noun* [C or U] *plural* **roux** a mixture made from equal amounts of fat and flour, used especially to thicken a sauce or soup
rove /rəʊv/ [US] /roʊv/ *verb* [I + adv or prep; T] *LITERARY* to move, travel or look around especially a large area: *His eye/gaze roved hungrily about the room.* ○ *He spent most of his life roving the world in search of his fortune.* **roving** /ˈrəʊ.vɪŋ/ [US] /ˈroʊ-/ *adj* [before n] *And now a live report from our roving reporter Martin Jackson.*
• **have a roving eye** *OLD-FASHIONED HUMOROUS* If you say that someone has a roving eye, you mean that they are always sexually interested in people other than their partner.
row [LINE] /rəʊ/ [US] /roʊ/ *noun* [C] **1** a line of things, people, animals, etc. arranged next to each other: *a row of houses/books/plants/people/horses* ○ *We had seats* ***in*** *the front/back row* ***of*** *the theatre.* **2** Row is also used in the names of some roads: *Prospect Row*
• **in a row** one after another without a break: *She's been voted Best Actress three years in a row.*

COMMON LEARNER ERROR

row
Remember to use the preposition 'in' when you say that something or someone is in a particular **row**.
We had seats in the back row.
~~*We had seats at the back row.*~~

row [ARGUMENT] /raʊ/ *noun MAINLY UK* **1** [C] a noisy argument or fight: *My parents often have rows, but my dad does most of the shouting.* ○ *What was a political row* ***over*** *government policy on Europe is fast becoming a diplomatic row* ***between*** *France and Britain.* **2** [S] loud noise: *I can't concentrate because of the row the builders are making.*
row /raʊ/ *verb* [I] *MAINLY UK INFORMAL* to argue, especially loudly: *My parents are always rowing* ***(about/over*** *money).*
row [MOVE THROUGH WATER] /rəʊ/ [US] /roʊ/ *verb* [I or T] to cause a boat to move through water by pushing against the water with oars: *The wind dropped, so we had to row (the boat) back home.* **rowing** /ˈrəʊ.ɪŋ/ [US] /ˈroʊ-/ *noun* [U] *I love rowing.* **row** /rəʊ/ [US] /roʊ/ *noun* [C usually sing] *They've gone for a row to the island.* **rower** /ˈrəʊ.əʳ/ [US] /ˈroʊ.ɚ/ *noun* [C]
rowan /ˈrəʊ.ən/ /ˈraʊ-/ [US] /ˈroʊ-/ *noun* [C] a small tree with small bright red fruit
rowdy /ˈraʊ.di/ *adj DISAPPROVING* noisy and possibly violent: *a rowdy party* ○ *rowdy behaviour* **rowdily** /ˈraʊ.dɪ.li/ *adv* **rowdiness** /ˈraʊ.dɪ.nəs/ *noun* [U]
ˈrow ˌhouse *US noun* [C] (*UK* **terraced house**) a house that is joined to the houses on either side of it by shared walls
ˈrowing ˌboat *UK noun* [C] (*US* **rowboat**) a small boat that is moved by pulling oars through the water ➲See picture **Planes, Ships and Boats** on page Centre 14
rowlock /ˈrɒl.ək/ /ˈrəʊ.lɒk/ [US] /ˈrɑː.lək/ /ˈroʊ.lɑːk/ *noun* [C] (*US* **oarlock**) a U-shaped device or hole on each side of a rowing-boat in which the oars are held
royal /ˈrɔɪ.əl/ *adj* **1** (*WRITTEN ABBREVIATION* **R**) belonging or connected to a king or queen or a member of their family: *the royal family* ○ *a royal visit* **2** good or excellent, as if intended for or typical of royalty: *The team was given a royal reception/welcome.* **3** *MAINLY US* big or great: *a royal pain/a royal mess*
royal /ˈrɔɪ.əl/ *noun* [C usually pl] *INFORMAL* a member of the royal family: *The press follow the royals everywhere.*
royalist /ˈrɔɪ.ə.lɪst/ *noun* [C] a person who supports a ruling king or queen or who believes that a king or queen should rule their country **royalist** /ˈrɔɪ.ə.lɪst/ *adj*: *royalist sympathies*
royalty /ˈrɔɪ.əl.ti/ [US] /-t̬i/ *group noun* [U] the people who belong to the family of a king and queen: *She believes she's related to royalty.* ➲See also **royalty**.
ˌroyal asˈsent *noun* [U] *UK SPECIALIZED* the official approval of a law by the British king or queen
ˌroyal ˈblue *noun* [U] a medium bright blue colour
ˌroyal ˈflush *noun* [C usually sing] in card games, a set of all the five highest cards in one suit
ˌRoyal ˈHighness *noun* **Her/His/Your Royal Highness** used when you are speaking about or to a royal person: *Thank you, Your Royal Highness.* ○ *His Royal Highness, Prince Andrew*
ˌroyal ˈpardon *noun* [C] an official order given by a king or queen to stop the punishment of a person accused of a crime ➲Compare **free pardon**.
ˌroyal preˈrogative *noun* [U] the special rights of the ruling king or queen
royalty /ˈrɔɪ.əl.ti/ [US] /-t̬i/ *noun* [C usually pl] a payment made to writers, people who have invented things, owners of property, etc. every time their books, devices, land, etc. are bought or used by others ➲See also **royalty** at **royal**.
RP /ˌɑːˈpiː/ [US] /ˌɑːr-/ *noun* [U] *ABBREVIATION FOR* **Received Pronunciation**
RPI /ˌɑː.piːˈaɪ/ [US] /ˌɑːr-/ *noun* [S] *UK ABBREVIATION FOR* **retail price index**
rpm /ˌɑː.piːˈem/ [US] /ˈɑːr-/ *ABBREVIATION FOR* revolutions per minute: used when stating the number of times something goes round during a minute
RR [TRAIN] /ˌɑːˈrɑːʳ/ [US] /ˌɑːrˈɑːr/ *US WRITTEN ABBREVIATION FOR* **railroad** TRAIN
RR [POST] /ˌɑːˈrɑːʳ/ [US] /ˌɑːrˈɑːr/ *US WRITTEN ABBREVIATION FOR* rural route: used in addresses in some areas in the US
RSI /ˌɑː.resˈaɪ/ [US] /ˌɑːr.es-/ *noun* [U] *ABBREVIATION FOR* **repetitive strain injury**
RSVP /ˌɑː.res.viːˈpiː/ [US] /ˌɑːr.es-/ used at the end of a written invitation to mean 'please answer': *RSVP by October 9th.*
Rt. Hon. /ˌraɪtˈɒn.ᵊr.ə.bl̩/ [US] /ˌraɪtˈɑː.nɚ-/ *ABBREVIATION FOR* Right Honourable: a title given to important British officials such as PRIVY COUNSELLORS and members of the government: *the Rt. Hon. Judith Smith MP*
rub /rʌb/ *verb* [I or T] **-bb-** to press or be pressed against something with a circular or up and down repeated movement: *She yawned and rubbed her eyes sleepily.* ○ *He rubbed* ***(at)*** *the stain on his trousers and made it worse.* ○ *We rubbed some polish* ***into*** *the surface of the wood.* ○ *She gently rubbed the ointment* ***in.*** ○ *First rub the baking tray well* ***with*** *butter.* ○ [+ obj + adj] *Alice rubbed the blackboard* ***clean*** *for the teacher.* ○ *Your cat keeps on rubbing itself* ***(up) against*** *my leg.* ○ *She was rubbing her hands* ***(together)*** *at the thought of winning.* ○ *The branches rubbed* ***against*** *each other in the wind.* ○ *The chair legs have rubbed holes in the carpet.* ○ *My new shoes are rubbing* ***(against/on*** *my toe) and now I've got blisters.* ○ *These marks will never rub* ***off*** (= be cleaned off). ○ *Alice rubbed the sums* ***off*** (= cleaned them off) *the blackboard for the teacher.*
• **rub shoulders (with)** (*US ALSO* **rub elbows (with)**) *INFORMAL* to meet and spend time with: *She claims that she rubs*

R

shoulders with royalty all the time.
• **rub** ***sb's*** **nose in it** to say or do things which make someone remember that they failed or got something wrong: *Sue failed her exam, so just to rub her nose in it, I put my certificate up on the wall.*
• **rub** ***sb*** **up the wrong way** *UK* (*US* **rub** ***sb*** **the wrong way**) to annoy someone without intending to: *As soon as they met they started to rub each other up the wrong way.*
rub /rʌb/ *noun* **[C]** when you rub something: *He **gave** her a good rub to dry it.*
• **the rub** *FORMAL* the particular problem that makes a situation difficult or impossible: *You can't get a job unless you have experience, but **there's** the rub, you can't get experience unless you have a job.*

PHRASAL VERBS WITH **rub**

▲ **rub along** *phrasal verb UK INFORMAL* If two people rub along, they work or live together in a satisfactory way: *My flat-mate and I rub along okay **together**.*
▲ **rub** ***sth*** **down** [SMOOTH] *phrasal verb* **[M]** to rub something with a rough cloth, brush or paper until its surface is smooth, or clean and shiny: *Rub the wood down **with** fine sandpaper till it is smooth.* ○ *We rubbed the walls down **with** soap and hot water.*
rub-down /ˈrʌb.daʊn/ *noun* **[S]** an act of cleaning and smoothing something, or of drying a person or animal: *a cold shower and a rub-down with a towel*
▲ **rub** ***sth/sb*** **down** [DRY] *phrasal verb* **[M]** to use a cloth to dry an animal or person: *I used a towel to rub the dog down after his bath.*
▲ **rub** ***sth*** **in** *phrasal verb* to talk to someone about something which you know they want to forget because they feel bad about it: *OK, I made a mistake, – you don't have to rub **it** in.*
▲ **rub off** *phrasal verb INFORMAL* If a quality or characteristic that someone has rubs off, other people begin to have it because they have been with that person and learnt it from them: *His enthusiasm is starting to rub off **on** the rest of us.*
▲ **rub** ***sth*** **out** [REMOVE MARK] *phrasal verb* **[M]** *UK* to remove writing or a mark from something by rubbing it with a piece of rubber or a cloth: *It's in pencil, so you can rub it out if you need to.*
▲ **rub** ***sb*** **out** [MURDER] *phrasal verb* **[M]** *US SLANG* to murder someone: *He was rubbed out by the Mafia.*

rubber [SUBSTANCE] /ˈrʌb.əʳ/ [US] /-ɚ/ *noun* **1 [U]** an elastic substance made either from the juice of particular tropical trees or artificially: *Tyres are almost always made of rubber.* **2 [C]** *UK* an **eraser** ➲See picture **In the Office** on page Centre 15 **3 [C]** *US SLANG FOR* **a condom**
rubbers /ˈrʌb.əz/ [US] /-ɚz/ *plural noun US OLD-FASHIONED FOR* **overshoes**
rubbery /ˈrʌb.ᵊr.i/ [US] /-ɚ-/ *adj* feeling or bending like rubber: *My legs felt all rubbery* (= weak) *after the race.*
rubber [GAME] /ˈrʌb.əʳ/ [US] /-ɚ/ *noun* **[C]** a series of three or five games between two teams, especially in card games or cricket: *We played a rubber of bridge.*
ˌrubber ˈband *noun* **[C]** (*ALSO* **elastic band**) a thin ring of rubber used for holding things together: *She put a rubber band around the box.*
ˌrubber ˈboot *noun* **[C]** *US FOR* **wellington (boot)** ➲See picture **Clothes** on page Centre 6
ˌrubber ˈdinghy *noun* **[C]** a small rubber boat which has air in it to keep its shape
rubbernecker /ˈrʌb.ə.nek.əʳ/ [US] /-ɚ.nek.ɚ/ *noun* **[C]** (*ALSO* **rubberneck**) *MAINLY US* a driver who drives more slowly to look at an accident, or a person who looks at something in a stupid way **rubbernecking** /ˈrʌb.ə.nek.ɪŋ/ [US] /-ɚ-/ *noun* **[U]**
ˈrubber ˌplant *noun* **[C]** a plant with dark green shiny leaves that comes originally from Asia
rubber-stamp [PRINTING] /ˌrʌb.əˈstæmp/ [US] /-ɚ-/ *noun* **[C usually sing]** a small device with raised letters made of rubber, that is used for printing the date, name of an organization, etc. on documents
rubber-stamp [APPROVE] /ˌrʌb.əˈstæmp/ [US] /-ɚ-/ *verb* **[T]** *DISAPPROVING* to officially approve a decision or plan without thinking about it: *The boss makes the decisions and the committee just rubber-stamps them.*
ˈrubber ˌtree *noun* **[C]** a type of tropical tree from which LATEX (= the liquid which is used to make rubber) is obtained
ˈrubbing ˌalcohol *noun* **[U]** *US FOR* **surgical spirit**
rubbish /ˈrʌb.ɪʃ/ *noun* **[U] 1** *MAINLY UK* (*MAINLY US* **garbage**, *US ALSO* **trash**) waste material or unwanted or worthless things: *I forgot to put the rubbish out for collection this morning.* ○ *Put the empty box in the rubbish **bin**.* ○ *Take the old furniture to the rubbish **dump**.* **2** *INFORMAL* something that you think is very low quality or not true: *The film was rubbish.* ○ *His ideas are **a load of (old)** rubbish.*
rubbish /ˈrʌb.ɪʃ/ *verb* **[T]** *UK INFORMAL* to criticize: *Why does everyone rubbish my ideas?*
rubbishy /ˈrʌb.ɪ.ʃi/ *adj MAINLY UK INFORMAL* very low quality: *a rubbishy film*
rubble /ˈrʌb.l̩/ *noun* **[U] 1** the piles of broken stone and bricks, etc. that are left when a building falls down or is destroyed: *The bomb **reduced** the house **to** rubble.* **2** small pieces of stone or rock used for building
rubella /ruːˈbel.ə/ *noun* **[U]** *SPECIALIZED* **German measles**
Rubicon /ˈruː.bɪ.kɒn/ /-kən/ [US] /-kɑːn/ *noun* **cross the Rubicon** to do something which you cannot later change and which will strongly influence future events: *Most EU states have crossed the Rubicon and adopted the euro.*
rubicund /ˈruː.bɪ.kənd/ [US] /-bə.kʌnd/ *adj LITERARY* having a red face
rubric /ˈruː.brɪk/ *noun* **[C]** *FORMAL* a set of instructions, etc., especially on an exam paper and usually printed in a different style or colour: *Read/Follow the rubric carefully.*
ruby /ˈruː.bi/ *noun* **[C]** a dark red jewel
ruched /ruːʃt/ *adj* (of cloth) in tight elastic folds: *elegant ruched curtains* ○ *a ruched collar*
ruck [CROWD] /rʌk/ *noun* **1 the ruck** ordinary people or things, that you consider boring: *Carter's brilliant second novel lifted her **out of** the ruck (of average writers).* **2 [C]** *SPECIALIZED* a group of players in rugby who are all together around the ball
ruck [FOLD] /rʌk/ *noun* **[C]** a fold
ruck /rʌk/ *verb*
▲ **ruck** ***(sth)*** **up** *phrasal verb* **[M]** If material rucks up, it gathers into a lump or folds, and if something rucks it up, it pushes the material into a lump or folds: *The blankets had rucked up around his feet.*
rucksack /ˈrʌk.sæk/ *noun* **[C]** (*US USUALLY* **backpack**) a large bag used to carry things on your back, used especially by walkers and climbers: *It's a frame rucksack with a belt and padded shoulder straps.*
ruckus /ˈrʌk.əs/ *noun* **[C usually sing]** *MAINLY US INFORMAL* a noisy situation or argument; a **rumpus**
ructions /ˈrʌk.ʃᵊnz/ *plural noun MAINLY UK INFORMAL* a noisy argument or angry complaint: *There'll be ructions if I'm not home by midnight.*
rudder /ˈrʌd.əʳ/ [US] /-ɚ/ *noun* **[C]** a flat piece of wood or metal at the back of a boat or aircraft, which is moved from side to side in order to control the direction of travel
rudderless /ˈrʌd.ə.ləs/ [US] /-ɚ-/ *adj* (of an organization) without anyone in control and therefore unable to take decisions
ruddy [COLOUR] /ˈrʌd.i/ *adj* red: *He was ruddy-cheeked from the walk in the cold.* ○ *Her face was ruddy and healthy-looking.*
ruddy [EXPRESSION] /ˈrʌd.i/ *adj* **[before n]**, *adv UK OLD-FASHIONED INFORMAL* used to avoid saying BLOODY to express anger or annoyance: *"Ruddy hell!"*
rude [NOT POLITE] /ruːd/ *adj* **1** not polite; offensive or embarrassing: *He's a very rude man.* ○ ***It's** rude not **to** say "Thank you" when you are given something.* ○ *He's got no manners – he's rude **to** everyone.* **2** relating to sex or going to the toilet: *He told a rude joke/story.* **rudely** /ˈruːd.li/ *adv*: *She rudely interrupted my speech.* **rudeness** /ˈruːd.nəs/ *noun* **[U]**
rude [SUDDEN] /ruːd/ *adj* **[before n]** sudden and unpleasant: *We had a rude **awakening*** (= unpleasant shock) *when we saw the amount of our phone bill.* **rudely** /ˈruːd.li/

R

adv: *The news rudely pushed her into the glare of worldwide publicity.*

rude [SIMPLE] /ruːd/ *adj* OLD USE OR LITERARY simply and roughly made: *We built a rude shelter from rocks on the beach.* **rudely** /ˈruːd.li/ *adv*

the rudiments /ðəˈruː.dɪ.mənts/ *plural noun* the simplest and most basic facts about a subject or activity: *It only took me an hour to learn/pick up the rudiments **of** skiing.*

rudimentary /ˌruː.dɪˈmen.tᵊr.i/ /-tri/ Ⓤⓢ /-tɚ-/ *adj* FORMAL **1** basic: *Her knowledge is still only rudimentary.* **2** describes methods, equipment, systems, etc. that are simple and not highly developed: SPECIALIZED *Some unusual fish have rudimentary legs.*

rue /ruː/ *verb* **[T]** **rueing** or **ruing**, **rued**, **rued** OLD USE OR LITERARY to feel sorry about an event and wish it had not happened; regret

• **rue the day** to regret something very much: *She'll rue the day **(that)** she bought that house.*

rueful /ˈruː.fᵊl/ *adj* LITERARY feeling sorry and full of regret: *He turned away with a rueful laugh.* **ruefully** /ˈruː.fᵊl.i/ *adv*

ruff /rʌf/ *noun* **[C]** a large stiff white collar with many folds, worn in Europe in the 16th and 17th centuries, or a circle of hair or feathers growing round the neck of a bird or animal

ruffian /ˈrʌf.i.ən/ *noun* **[C]** OLD-FASHIONED OR HUMOROUS a violent, wild and unpleasant person, usually a man

ruffle [MOVE] /ˈrʌf.l̩/ *verb* **1** **[T]** to make something that is smooth uneven: *She affectionately ruffled his hair with her hand as she passed.* ○ *The birds ruffled their feathers **(up)** in alarm.* **2** **[T often passive]** to annoy or upset someone, or to make them very nervous: *He's easily ruffled by criticism.*

• **ruffle *sb's* feathers** to upset or annoy someone: *She knows how to ruffle his feathers.*

ruffle [FOLD] /ˈrʌf.l̩/ *noun* **[C]** a series of small folds made in a piece of cloth or sewn onto it, as decoration

rug /rʌg/ *noun* **[C]** **1** a piece of thick heavy cloth smaller than a carpet, used for covering the floor or for decoration: *My dog loves lying on the rug in front of the fire.* **2** UK a soft cover that keeps you warm or comfortable **3** SLANG FOR **toupée**

rugby /ˈrʌg.bi/ *noun* **[U]** (FORMAL **rugby football**) a sport where two teams try to score points by carrying an oval ball across a particular line or kicking it over and between an H-shaped set of posts ➲See picture **Sports** on page Centre 10

ˌRugby ˈLeague *noun* **[U]** a form of rugby with 13 players in each team

ˌRugby ˈUnion *noun* **[U]** a form of rugby with 15 players in each team

R

rugged [UNEVEN] /ˈrʌg.ɪd/ *adj* (of land) uneven and wild; not easy to travel over: *rugged landscape/terrain/hills/cliffs*

rugged [STRONG] /ˈrʌg.ɪd/ *adj* **1** strong and simple; not delicate: *Jeeps are rugged vehicles, designed for rough conditions.* **2** describes a man's face that is strongly and attractively formed: *She fell for his rugged good looks.* **ruggedly** /ˈrʌg.ɪd.li/ *adv*

rugger /ˈrʌg.əʳ/ Ⓤⓢ /-ɚ/ *noun* **[U]** UK INFORMAL FOR **rugby**

ruin /ˈruː.ɪn/ *verb* **[T]** **1** to spoil or destroy severely or completely: *Huge modern hotels have ruined this once unspoilt coastline.* ○ *Her injury ruined her chances of winning the race.* **2** to cause a person or company to lose all their money or their reputation: *Cheap imported goods are ruining many businesses.* ○ *If there's a scandal I'll be ruined!*

ruin /ˈruː.ɪn/ *noun* **1** **[U]** when something is spoilt or destroyed: *The car accident meant the ruin **of** all her hopes.* ○ *They let the palace **fall into** ruin.* **2** **[U]** when a person or company loses all their money or their reputation: *Many companies are **on the edge/brink/verge of** ruin.* ○ *Alcohol was my ruin* (= the thing that spoiled my life). **3** **[C]** the broken parts that are left from an old building or town: *We visited a Roman ruin.* ○ *the ruins of the ancient city of Carthage*

• **be/lie in ruins** **1** (of a building or city) to be extremely badly damaged so that most of it has fallen down: *The town lay in ruins after years of bombing.* **2** to be in an extremely bad state: *The economy was in ruins after the war.*

ruined /ˈruː.ɪnd/ *adj* destroyed or spoilt: *an ancient ruined castle*

ruination /ˌruː.ɪˈneɪ.ʃᵊn/ *noun* **[U]** OLD-FASHIONED destruction: *Alcohol was the ruination **of** him.*

ruinous /ˈruː.ɪ.nəs/ *adj* causing great harm and destruction: *ten ruinous years of terrorism* **ruinously** /ˈruː.ɪ.nə.sli/ *adv*: *Having an accident without insurance can be ruinously expensive.*

rule [INSTRUCTION] /ruːl/ *noun* **[C usually pl]** an accepted principle or instruction that states the way things are or should be done, and tells you what you are allowed or are not allowed to do: *A referee must know all the rules of the game.* ○ *The first/most important rule in life is always to appear confident.* ○ *Before you start your own business you should be familiar with the government's rules **and regulations**.* ○ *You must **follow/obey/observe** the rules.* ○ *You must not **break** the rules.* ○ *In special cases the manager will **bend/stretch** the rules* (= allow the rules to be broken). ○ *You can trust Ruth because she always **plays (it) by/goes by/does things by** the rules* (= follows instructions, standards, or rules). ○ **[+ *to* infinitive]** *It's **against** the rules **(of/in** boxing) **to** hit below the belt.* ○ **[+ that]** *It's a club rule **that** new members must sing a song.*

• **rule of thumb** a practical and approximate way of doing or measuring something: *A good rule of thumb is that a portion of rice is two and a half handfuls.*

• **as a (general) rule** usually: *As a general rule, I only read detective novels.*

• **the rule** the usual situation: *In England, it often seems that rain is the rule all the year round.*

• **make it a rule** to act according to a principle: *I make it a rule not to eat fatty foods.*

• **Rules are made to be broken.** SAYING used to say that it is good and acceptable to disobey a rule

rule [CONTROL] /ruːl/ *verb* **[I or T]** **1** to control, or to be the person in charge of a country: *Most modern kings and queens rule (their countries) only in a formal way, without real power.* ○ *She rules her household **with an iron hand/fist*** (= severely). **2** to be the most important and controlling influence on someone: *Love ruled supreme in her heart.* ○ *The desperate desire to go to Moscow ruled their lives.*

• **rule OK** UK SLANG is the best: *The graffiti on the wall said 'Liverpool rules OK'.*

• **be ruled by *sb*** FORMAL to take the advice of someone: *If you're wise you'll be ruled by your father.*

• **rule the roost** to be the person who makes all the decisions in a group: *In that family it is the grandma who rules the roost.*

rule /ruːl/ *noun* **[U]** when a particular person or group is in control of a country: *The period of Fascist rule is one people try to forget.* ○ *We don't want one-party rule – we want rule **by** the people.* ➲See also **misrule**.

ruler /ˈruː.ləʳ/ Ⓤⓢ /-lɚ/ *noun* **[C]** the leader of a country: *The country was without a ruler after the queen died.*

ruling /ˈruː.lɪŋ/ *adj* **[before n]** being in control and making all the decisions: *The Communists are the ruling party at the moment.*

• **ruling passion** most important interest: *His ruling passion is music.*

rule [DECIDE] /ruːl/ *verb* **[I or T]** to decide officially: *Only the Appeal Court can rule **on** this point.* ○ *The judge ruled **for/in favour of/against** the defendant.* ○ **[+ that]** *The government has ruled **that** the refugees must be deported.* ○ **[+ obj + n or adj]** *The courts have ruled his brave action illegal.* ➲See also **overrule**.

ruling /ˈruː.lɪŋ/ *noun* **[C]** a decision: **[+ *that*]** *The court has made a final ruling **on** the case **that** the companies acted illegally.*

rule [DRAW] /ruːl/ *verb* **[T]** to draw a straight line using something that has a straight edge: *She ruled two red lines under the title.*

ruler /ˈruː.ləʳ/ Ⓤⓢ /-lɚ/ *noun* **[C]** (OLD-FASHIONED OR FORMAL **rule**) a long, narrow, flat piece of plastic, metal or wood with straight edges marked in centimetres or inches, or both. It is used for measuring things and for drawing straight lines. ➲See picture **In the Office** on page Centre 15

▲ **rule *sth or sb* out** *phrasal verb* **[M]** to decide or state that something is impossible or will not happen, or that something or someone is not suitable: *The police haven't yet ruled out murder.* ○ *I won't rule out a June election.* ○ *The police have not ruled him out **as** a suspect.*

▲ **rule *sth* out** *phrasal verb* **[M]** to prevent something from happening: *This recent wave of terrorism has ruled out any chance of peace talks.*

rule ˌbook *noun* **[C usually sing]** a book containing the official rules for an organization or activity

the ˌrule of ˈlaw *noun* **[S]** *FORMAL* a set of laws that people in a society must obey: *Everyone is subject to the rule of law.*

the ˈruling ˌclass *noun* **[S]** (*ALSO* **ruling classes**) the most powerful people in a country

rum [DRINK] /rʌm/ *noun* **[C or U]** a strong alcoholic drink made from the juice of the SUGAR CANE plant: *I'll have a (glass of) rum.*

rum [STRANGE] /rʌm/ *adj* **rummer, rummest** *UK OLD-FASHIONED* strange; PECULIAR: *She's a rum girl/lass/one.*

• **a rum do** a strange occasion

rumba, rhumba /ˈrʌm.bə/ *noun* **[C]** a type of dancing, originally from Cuba, or the music for this

rumble [SOUND] /ˈrʌm.bl̩/ *verb* **[I]** to make a continuous low sound: *Please excuse my stomach rumbling – I haven't eaten all day.* ○ *The tanks rumbled* (= moved slowly, making a continuous noise) *across the battlefield.* **rumble** /ˈrʌm.bl̩/ *noun* **[C]** *We could hear the rumble **of** distant guns/thunder.* **rumblings** /ˈrʌm.bl̩.ɪŋz/ /ˈ-blɪŋz/ *plural noun*: *rumblings **of** distant guns/thunder*

rumble [DISCOVER] /ˈrʌm.bl̩/ *verb* **[T usually passive]** *UK INFORMAL* to discover the true facts about someone or something secret and often illegal: *I'm afraid our little tax dodge has been rumbled.*

rumble [FIGHT] /ˈrʌm.bl̩/ *verb* **[I]** *AUS INFORMAL* to take part in a physical fight

rumbling /ˈrʌm.bl̩.ɪŋ/ /-blɪŋ/ *noun* **[C usually pl]** a sign of dissatisfaction: *There are rumblings **of** annoyance throughout the workforce.*

ruminate [THINK] /ˈruː.mɪ.neɪt/ *verb* **[I]** *FORMAL* to think carefully and for a long period about something: *She ruminated for weeks about whether to tell him or not.* **ruminative** /ˈruː.mɪ.nə.tɪv/ [US] /-neɪ.t̬ɪv/ *adj* *FORMAL* thinking carefully and for a long period

ruminate [EAT] /ˈruː.mɪ.neɪt/ *verb* **[I]** *SPECIALIZED* (of particular types of animal) to bring up food from the stomach and chew it again **ruminant** /ˈruː.mɪ.nənt/ *noun* **[C]**, *adj*: *Cows, sheep, and deer are ruminants/ruminant animals.*

rummage /ˈrʌm.ɪdʒ/ *verb* **[I + adv or prep]** to search for something by moving things around carelessly and looking into, under and behind them: *She rummaged **in/through** all the drawers, looking for a pen.* **rummage** /ˈrʌm.ɪdʒ/ *noun* **[S]** *I had a rummage **around/about** (the house), but I couldn't find my certificate anywhere.*

ˈrummage ˌsale *noun* **[C]** *US FOR* **jumble sale**

rummy /ˈrʌm.i/ *noun* **[U]** any of various card games in which two or more players try to collect cards which have the same value or whose numbers follow an ordered series

rumour *UK*, *US* **rumor** /ˈruː.məʳ/ [US] /-mɚ/ *noun* **[C or U]** an unofficial interesting story or piece of news that might be true or invented, which quickly spreads from person to person: *Rumours are **going round** (the school) **about** Mr Mason and his assistant.* ○ **[+ that]** *She's **circulating/spreading** rumours **that** the manager is going to resign.* ○ *I **heard a** rumour that she'd been seeing Luke Harrison*

• **rumour has it** people are saying: *Rumour has it **(that)** you're going to be the next managing director. Is it true?*

rumoured *UK*, *US* **rumored** /ˈruː.məd/ [US] /-mɚd/ *adj* describes a fact that people are talking about, which might be true or invented: *The rumoured stock market crash has yet to take place.* ○ **[+ to infinitive]** *The president is rumoured **to** be seriously ill.*

rumour-monger /ˈruː.məˌmʌŋ.gəʳ/ [US] /-mɚˌmʌŋ.gɚ/ *noun* **[C]** a person who spreads rumours

rump /rʌmp/ *noun* **[C]** **1** the back end of an animal **2** *HUMOROUS* a person's bottom **3** those few members of a group or organization who stay after the others have left or been forced out

rumple /ˈrʌm.pl̩/ *verb* **[T]** to make something become CREASED (= not smooth) or untidy: *You'll rumple your jacket if you don't hang it up properly.* **rumpled** /ˈrʌm.pl̩d/ *adj*: *a rumpled suit/sheet/bed* ○ *He hadn't brushed his hair and his clothes were rumpled.*

rumpus /ˈrʌm.pəs/ *noun* **[S]** *INFORMAL* a lot of noise, especially a loud and confused argument or complaint: *There was a real rumpus **going on** in the house next door last night.*

• **raise a rumpus** (*UK ALSO* **kick up a rumpus**) *INFORMAL* to make a forceful complaint: *You should raise a rumpus about the lack of safety routines here.*

ˈrumpus ˌroom *noun* **[C usually sing]** *US* a room in a house intended for games and entertainment

run [GO QUICKLY] /rʌn/ *verb* **running, ran, run** **1** **[I or T]** (of people and some animals) to move along, faster than walking, by taking quick steps in which each foot is lifted before the next foot touches the ground: **[+ to infinitive]** *The children had to run **to** keep up with their father.* ○ *I can run a mile in 5 minutes.* ○ *The sheep ran **away/off** in fright.* ○ *A little girl ran **up to*** (= came quickly beside) *me, crying for her daddy.* ○ *Are you running **against** each other or **against** the clock?* ○ *The first two races will be run **(off)*** (= will happen) *in 20 minutes.* **2** **[T]** If you run an animal in a race, you cause it to take part: *Thompson Stables are running three horses **in** the next race.* **3** **[I + adv or prep]** to go quickly or in a hurry: *Would you run round to the post office and get me some stamps?* ○ *You don't put on weight when you spend all day running round after small children.*

• **run *its* course** to develop and finish naturally: *The doctor's advice is to let the fever run its course.* ○ *I had to accept that the relationship had run its course.*

• **be running a fever** to be hotter than you should be because you are ill

• **run errands** to go out to buy or do something: *After school he runs errands **for** his father.*

• **run for *sth*** to run fast in order to get or avoid something: *I ran for the bus but it drove off.*

• **run a mile** *UK INFORMAL* to be extremely unwilling to be involved: *He'd run a mile if I asked him to marry me.*

• **run *yourself* into the ground** *INFORMAL* to make yourself very tired by working too much: *We ran ourselves into the ground to meet the July deadline.*

• **run on the spot** to move your legs as if running, while you stay in one place: *I run on the spot to warm up before I play football.*

• **run *sb* ragged** *INFORMAL* If you run someone ragged, you tire them out, usually by giving them too much work or work that is too demanding: *The kids have run me ragged this week – I'm glad they're going back to school tomorrow.*

• **run round in circles** *UK INFORMAL* to be very active but with few results: *Peter's been running round in circles since half his department resigned.*

• **run *sb/sth* to ground** (*UK ALSO* **run *sb/sth* to earth**) to find someone or something after a lot of searching and problems: *Detectives finally ran the terrorists to ground in an apartment building in Chicago.*

run /rʌn/ *noun* **[C]** when you move on your feet at a speed faster than walking, especially for exercise: *We go for/do a three-mile run every evening after work.* ○ *If you set off **at a** run* (= running), *you'll be exhausted later.*

• **the run of *sth*** the freedom to use something: *While she's away, I've got the run of her house.* ○ *So do you have the run of the garden?*

• **be on the run** **1** to be trying to avoid being caught, especially by the police: *After a month on the run, the prisoners were finally recaptured by the police.* **2** to hurry from one activity to another: *She's always on the run and never has time for a chat.*

• **on the run** while hurrying to go somewhere: *I eat breakfast on the run if I'm late for work.*

• **have a good run for *your* money** to have a good enough time: *I've achieved a lot in my life and I feel I've had a good run for my money.*

• **give *sb* a run for *their* money** to not allow someone to win easily: *We're going to give the other candidate a run for her money.*

runner /ˈrʌn.əʳ/ [US] /-ɚ/ *noun* [C] **1** someone who runs, especially in competitions: *a long-distance runner* ➲See also **runner-up**. **2** a horse running in a race **3** a person who works for someone by taking messages, collecting money, etc.

runners /ˈrʌn.əz/ [US] /-ɚz/ *plural noun AUS FOR* **plimsolls**

running /ˈrʌn.ɪŋ/ *noun* [U] *running shoes/shorts*

• **(go and) take a running jump** *UK INFORMAL* said to someone when you want them to go away and stop annoying you: *He kept following me around, so I just told him to go and take a running jump.*

run [TRAVEL] /rʌn/ *verb* [I or T; usually + adv or prep] **running, ran, run** to (cause to) travel, move or continue in a particular way: *Trains are still running, despite the snow.* ○ *A bus runs* (= goes on a particular route at particular times) *three times a day into town.* ○ *Skis are waxed on the bottom so that they run smoothly over the snow.* ○ *The route/railway/road runs* (= goes) ***across** the border/**into** Italy/**through** the mountains.* ○ *A climbing rose bush runs* (= grows) ***around** the front door.* ○ *There's a beautiful cornice running **around/round** all the ceilings.* ○ *The film runs* (= lasts) ***for** two hours.* ○ *The show/course/film runs* (= continues) ***for** another week.* ○ *A magazine subscription usually only runs* (= can be used) ***for** one year.* ○ *Buses are running an hour **late**, because of an earlier accident.* ○ *The truck's brakes failed and it ran* (= went) ***off** the road.* ○ *Trains run **on** rails* (= move along on top of them). ○ *Electricity is running **through*** (= moving along within) *this cable.* ○ *An angry muttering ran **through*** (= went through) *the crowd.* ○ *A shiver of fear ran **through** his (body).* ○ *She ran her finger **along/down** the page/list, looking for her name.* ○ *Could you run the tape/film/video **back/forwards**, please?* ○ *Could you possibly run me* (= take me in your car) ***home/to** the station?* ○ *He ran* (= pushed) *his fingers **through** his hair and looked up at me.*

• **run aground/ashore** (*ALSO* **run onto the rocks**) If a ship or boat runs aground/ashore, it hits the coast, sometimes becoming stuck there.

• **be running at *sth*** to be at the rate of something: *Inflation is running at 10%.*

• **run *sb* close** to be nearly as good, fast, etc. as someone else: *She got 90%, but Fred ran her close with 87%.*

• **run *your* eye over** to look quickly at the whole of something: *Can I have a copy of the article to run my eye over, before it's printed?*

• **run in the family** If a quality, ability, disease, etc. runs in the family, many members of the family have it: *Intelligence seems to run in that family.* ○ *We're all ambitious - it seems to run in the family.*

• **run in/through *your* head/mind** If something is running in/through your head/mind, you cannot stop thinking about it or singing it silently: *I've had that tune running in my head all day.*

• **run through *your* mind/head** to suddenly think of something: *It ran through my mind that I was being tricked by Charlie.*

• **run and run** to be performed successfully for a long period of time: *This show will run and run.*

run /rʌn/ *noun* [C] **1** a journey: *The number of aircraft on the New York-Moscow run is being increased.* ○ *OLD-FASHIONED Let's go for a run **(out)** in the car somewhere.* ○ *The plane swooped in on its bombing run.* **2** the period during which a play is performed: *The musical's London run was a disaster.* ○ *They're doing a run at the Donmar Warehouse.*

• **in the long run** at a time that is far away in the future: *It seems a lot of effort but I'm sure it's the best solution in the long run.*

• **in the short run** at a time that is near in the future: *It's not a long term solution, but it will save money in the short run.*

• **run of** A run of something is a continuous period during which it lasts or is repeated: *a run of successes/defeats/bad luck*

running /ˈrʌn.ɪŋ/ *adj* [after n] happening on a particular number of regular occasions: *You've been late three days running.* ○ *They won the trophy **for the** third **year** running.*

• **running battle** an argument that lasts over several different occasions: *I've had a running battle with the neighbours over whose responsibility that fence is.*

run [OPERATE] /rʌn/ *verb* **running, ran, run 1** [I or T] to (cause to) operate: *Keep clear of the machines while they're running.* ○ *The government took desperate measures to keep the economy running.* ○ *Do you know how to run this sort of machinery?* ○ *The mechanic asked me to run* (= switch on and allow to work) *the engine for a minute.* ○ *They had the new computer system **up and** running* (= working) *within an hour.* ○ *We've run the computer program, but nothing happens.* ○ *We're running* (= doing) *an experiment.* **2** [T] to be in control of: *He's been running a restaurant/his own company since he left school.* ○ *The local college runs* (= provides) *a course in self-defence.* ○ *a well-run/badly-run organization/business/course* **3** [T] If you run a car, you own one, drive it and pay for the costs: *I can't afford to run a car.* **4** [T] to organize the way you live or work: *Some people run their lives according to the movements of the stars.*

• **run the show** *INFORMAL* to be the leader, who is in control of a group of people doing something: *If you need help, ask Mark – he's running the show.*

running /ˈrʌn.ɪŋ/ *noun* [U] the activity of controlling or looking after something: *She has control of the day-to-day running of the business.*

• **make the running** *UK* to do the best and most work: *British companies have often made all the running in developing new ideas, but have then failed to market them successfully.*

run [FLOW] /rʌn/ *verb* [I or T] **running, ran, run** to (cause to) flow, produce liquid, or (especially of colours in clothes) to come out or spread: *I can feel trickles of sweat running **down** my neck.* ○ *Don't cry, or your make-up will run* (= become liquid and move down your face). ○ *The walls were running **with** damp.* ○ *The river runs **(down) to/into** the sea.* ○ *The hot tap is running cold* (= producing cold water)*!* ○ *I turned the tap on and ran some cold water **on** the burn.* ○ [+ two objects] *I'll run you a hot bath* (= fill a bath with water for you). ○ *My nose and eyes have been running all week because of hay fever.* ○ *I must have washed my dress at too high a temperature, because the colour has run.* ○ *If the first layer isn't dry before you add the next one, the colours will run **into** each other* (= mix). ○ *FIGURATIVE After 12 hours at her word processor, the words began to run **into** one another* (= seem mixed together).

• **running with blood** describes a place where a lot of fighting is happening and many people are being hurt or killed: *During the revolution **the streets** were running with blood.*

• **make *sb's* blood run cold** to make someone feel extremely shocked or frightened: *Reading about the murders made my blood run cold.*

run [BECOME] /rʌn/ *verb* [L only + adj] **running, ran, run** to be or become: *Differences between the two sides run **deep*** (= are serious). ○ *The river/reservoir/well ran **dry*** (= its supply of water finished). ○ *Supplies are running **low*** (= there's not much left). ○ *We're beginning to run **short of** money/Money is beginning to run **short*** (= there's not much left).

• **run high** If feelings are running high, people are angry or excited.

• **run wild** *DISAPPROVING* If someone, especially a child runs wild, they behave as they want to and no one controls them.

run [SHOW] /rʌn/ *verb* [T] **running, ran, run** to show something in a newspaper or magazine, on television, etc: *All the newspapers ran* (= printed) *stories about the new peace talks.* ○ *Channel 4 is running a series on the unfairness of the legal system.*

run [POLITICS] /rʌn/ *verb* [I] **running, ran, run** to compete as a CANDIDATE in an election: *Mrs Thatcher wanted to run a* *fourth time.* ○ *He's going to run against Smith/for President/for re-election.*

,in/,out of the 'running *noun* [U] having/not having a reasonable chance of winning: *Half the vote has been counted, and our candidate is still in the running.*

run TAKE /rʌn/ *verb* [T] running, ran, run to take guns or drugs illegally from one product to another: *He was arrested for running drugs across the border into America.* runner /'rʌn.əʳ/ *noun* [C] *a gun-runner*

run BUY /rʌn/ *noun* [C usually sing] when many people suddenly buy a particular product: *There's been a run on umbrellas because of all this rain.*

run SELL /rʌn/ *noun* [C usually sing] when many people suddenly sell a particular product: *A sudden run on the dollar has lowered its value.*

run ORDINARY /rʌn/ *noun* the general/usual run of sth the usual type of something: *Their food is the general run of hotel cooking.*

run AREA /rʌn/ *noun* [C] an area of ground of limited size for keeping animals: *a sheep/chicken/hen run*

run POINT /rʌn/ *noun* [C] in cricket and baseball, a single point, scored by running from one place to another: *England need 105 runs to win the game.* ○ *a home run*

run HOLE /rʌn/ *noun* [C] a long vertical hole in tights and stockings: *I've got a run in my tights from the nail on my chair.* run /rʌn/ *verb* [I] running, ran, run *Oh no, my tights have run!*

PHRASAL VERBS WITH **run** ▼

▲ **run across** *sb* *phrasal verb* INFORMAL to meet someone you know when you are not expecting to: *I ran across several old friends when I went back to my hometown.*

▲ **run across** *sth* *phrasal verb* INFORMAL to experience a problem when you are not expecting to: *We've run across a slight problem with the instruction manual.*

▲ **run after** *sb/sth* CHASE *phrasal verb* to chase someone or something that is moving away from you: *Why do dogs run after cats?* ○ *She ran after me to hand me some papers I'd dropped.*

▲ **run after** *sth* TRY TO ACHIEVE *phrasal verb* to try very hard to get or achieve something: *She has spent her life running after fame and fortune.*

▲ **run after** *sb* TRY TO START RELATIONSHIP *phrasal verb* INFORMAL DISAPPROVING to try to start a sexual relationship with someone: *He's always running after women.*

▲ **run against** *sb/sth* *phrasal verb* to oppose or have an effect that is not helpful towards someone or something: *Luck is really running against you tonight!* ○ *Public opinion is currently running against fox hunting.*

▲ **Run along!** *phrasal verb* OLD-FASHIONED said to children to tell them to go away: *Run along now, children!*

▲ **run around** *phrasal verb* to be very busy doing a lot of different things: *I'm exhausted – I've been running around all morning.*

▲ **run around after** *sb* *phrasal verb* INFORMAL to do a lot of things for someone else, especially when they should be able to do more for themselves: *I seem to spend most of my time running around after these kids.*

▲ **run around with** *sb* *phrasal verb* OLD-FASHIONED INFORMAL to spend a lot of time with someone: *She's running around with Micky and his friends these days.*

▲ **run away** LEAVE *phrasal verb* to leave a place or person secretly and suddenly: *He ran away from home when he was only 12.* ○ *Malcolm and my sister are planning to run away together to get married.* ●See picture **Phrasal Verbs** on page Centre 9

▲ **run away** AVOID *phrasal verb* to avoid dealing with a problem or difficult situation: *She accused him of running away from his responsibilities.*

▲ **run away with** *sb* RIDE *phrasal verb* If an animal or machine that someone is riding runs away with them, they lose control of it and it carries them away: *Her horse ran away with her.*

▲ **run away with** *sb* FEELING *phrasal verb* If a feeling or idea runs away with you, you cannot control it and it makes you behave stupidly: *Sometimes my imagination runs away with me and I convince myself that they are having an affair.*

▲ **run away with** *sth* WIN *phrasal verb* INFORMAL to win a competition or prize very easily: *She ran away with four first prizes.*

▲ **run** *sth* **by** *sb* *phrasal verb* INFORMAL to tell someone about something so that they can give their opinion about it: *Would you run your idea by me one more time?*

▲ **run** *sb/sth* **down** CRITICIZE *phrasal verb* [M] INFORMAL to criticize someone or something, often unfairly: *He's always running himself down.*

▲ **run** *(sth)* **down** REDUCE *phrasal verb* [M] UK to reduce a business or organization in size or importance, or to become reduced in this way: *They claim that the government is secretly running down the Youth Training Schemes.*

rundown /'rʌn.daʊn/ *noun* [S]

▲ **run** *sb/sth* **down** HIT *phrasal verb* [M] to hit and injure a person or animal with a vehicle, especially intentionally: *Two masked men on motorbikes tried to run me down.*

▲ **run** *sth* **down** SHIP *phrasal verb* [M] SPECIALIZED If a large ship runs down a smaller one, it hits it.

▲ **run** *(sth)* **down** LOSE POWER *phrasal verb* [M] If a machine or device such as a clock or battery runs down, it loses power, or if you run it down, you cause this to happen: *These batteries can be recharged when they run down.* ○ *You'll run the battery down if you leave your car lights on.*

▲ **run** *sb/sth* **down** FIND *phrasal verb* [M] to find someone or something after following or searching for them for a long time: *I finally ran Mr Green down in/to a house in the country.*

▲ **run** *sth* **in** USE CAREFULLY UK *phrasal verb* [M] (US **break** *sth* **in**) If you run in a vehicle, you use it carefully and slowly for a short time when it is new, so that you do not damage its engine.

▲ **run** *sb* **in** CATCH *phrasal verb* [M] OLD-FASHIONED If the police run someone in, they find them and take them to a police station.

▲ **run** *(sth)* **into** *sth/sb* HIT *phrasal verb* to drive a vehicle accidentally into an object or a person in another vehicle: *I had to brake suddenly, and the car behind ran into me.* ○ *He ran his motorbike into a tree.*

▲ **run into** *sb* MEET *phrasal verb* to meet someone you know when you are not expecting to: *Graham ran into someone he used to know at school the other day.*

▲ **run into** *sth* EXPERIENCE PROBLEMS *phrasal verb* If you run into problems, you begin to experience them: *We ran into bad weather/debt/trouble.*

▲ **run into** *sth* REACH *phrasal verb* to reach a particular cost or amount, as a total: *The repairs will probably run into thousands of pounds.*

▲ **run off** LEAVE *phrasal verb* to leave somewhere or someone suddenly: *You can't run off (home) now, just when I need you!* ○ *My wife has run off with another man.*

▲ **run** *sth* **off** PRINT *phrasal verb* [M] If you run off copies of something, you print them: [+ two objects] *Could you run me off five copies of this, please?*

▲ **run off with** *sth* *phrasal verb* INFORMAL to leave a place or person suddenly after having stolen something from them: *He ran off with $10 000 of the company's money.*

▲ **run on** *sth* POWER *phrasal verb* If a machine runs on a particular type or supply of power, it uses that power to work: *Some calculators run on solar power.*

▲ **run on** TIME *phrasal verb* **1** If an event runs on, it continues for longer than expected: *The game/speech/discussion ran on for hours.* **2** If time runs on, it seems to pass quickly: *Time's running on – let's get this job finished soon!*

▲ **run out** FINISH *phrasal verb* **1** to finish, use or sell all of something, so that there is none left: *I've run out of milk/money/ideas/patience.* ○ *"Have you got any milk?" "Sorry, I've run out."* **2** If a supply of something runs out, all of it has been used or it is completely finished: *The milk has run out.* ○ *My patience is beginning to run out.* **3** If a document or official agreement runs out, the period of time for which it lasts finishes: *My passport runs out next month – I must get it renewed.*

▲ **time is running out** used to say that there is not much time left in which to achieve something: *Time is* *running out for the men trapped under the rubble.*

● **run out of steam** to suddenly lose the energy or interest to continue doing what you are doing: *The peace talks seem to have run out of steam.*

▲ **run sb out** CRICKET *phrasal verb* [M] If you are run out in cricket, a player on the opposing team throws the ball at the WICKET you are running towards and hits it before you can reach it, and your turn as BATSMAN ends: *Their best batsman was run out for* (= having scored) *99.*

▲ **run out on sb/sth** *phrasal verb* to leave someone you are having a relationship with or something you are responsible for, without warning and usually causing problems: *She ran out on him two months ago, leaving him to look after their two children.*

▲ **run sb/sth over** HIT *phrasal verb* [M] If a vehicle or its driver runs over someone or something, the vehicle hits and drives over them: *I'm afraid we've just run a rabbit over.*

▲ **run over** FLOW OVER *phrasal verb* If liquid runs over, it flows over the edges of something, because there is too much of it: *The water/The bath is running over – quick, turn the taps off.*

▲ **run over (sth)** CONTINUE *phrasal verb* to continue beyond the expected finishing time: *I'm afraid we're starting to run over time, so could you make your speeches short please.*

▲ **run over/through sth** REPEAT *phrasal verb* to quickly say or practise something: *I'll just run over what's been said so far, for latecomers who missed the first speakers.* ○ *She quickly ran over her speech before going on-stage.* ○ *The director wants to run through the whole play this morning.*

run-through /ˈrʌn.θruː/ *noun* [C] when you perform or play something from beginning to end in order to practise it quickly: *We've got time for one more run-through before the concert.*

▲ **run over/through sth** EXPLAIN *phrasal verb* to examine a document or subject with someone in order to explain it or to get their help or their opinion on it: *I'd like to run over the main points of the article with you.* ○ *I'm really struggling with this maths – could you run through it with me later?*

▲ **run through sth** EXAMINE *phrasal verb* to look at, examine or deal with a set of things, especially quickly: *We ran through the list, but none of the machines seemed any good.* ○ *I'd like to run through these points/questions with you, if that's okay, because you've made several mistakes.*

▲ **run through sth** EXIST *phrasal verb* If a quality runs through something, it is in all parts of it: *Melancholy runs through all her stories.* ○ *Racism runs right through society.*

▲ **run through sth** USE UP *phrasal verb* to use up an amount of something quickly: *It took him just a few months to run through all the money his father left him.*

▲ **run sb/sth through** ATTACK *phrasal verb* LITERARY to push a sword or similar pointed weapon right into a person or animal: *He drew his sword and ran the villain through.*

▲ **run to sth** SIZE *phrasal verb* to reach a particular amount, level or size: *The new encyclopedia runs to several thousand pages.*

▲ **run to sth** MONEY *phrasal verb* to have enough money to buy something or (of an income, etc.) to be enough to buy something: *I can lend you £1000, but I can't run to more than that.* ○ *My salary won't run to foreign holidays.*

▲ **run to sth** ACTIVITY *phrasal verb* If your taste or skill runs to something, that is the type of thing that you enjoy or can manage to do: *I doubt if his musical taste runs to opera.* ○ *I'm afraid my cooking skills don't run to fancy cakes and desserts.*

▲ **run sth up** DEBT *phrasal verb* [M] If you run up a debt, you do things which cause you to owe a large amount of money: *She stayed two weeks at the hotel and ran up a bill which she couldn't pay.*

▲ **run sth up** MATERIAL *phrasal verb* [M] to quickly make an item such as a piece of clothing from material: [+ two objects] *I can run you up some curtains in a few hours, if you want.*

▲ **run sth up** VALUE *phrasal verb* [M] to make the price or value of something increase: *Heavy buying ran the price of stocks up higher than expected.*

▲ **run sth up** FLAG *phrasal verb* [M] UK to raise a flag into the air on a pole or mast: *They've run up a British flag on the roof.*

▲ **run up against sth** *phrasal verb* to experience an unexpected difficulty: *The community centre scheme has run up against strong local opposition.*

runabout /ˈrʌn.ə.baʊt/ *noun* [C] (ALSO **runaround**) INFORMAL a small car for short journeys

runaround /ˈrʌn.ə.raʊnd/ *noun* **give someone the runaround** to refuse to help someone, sending them to someone or somewhere else to get help: *I'm trying to get a new visa, but the embassy staff keep giving me the runaround.*

runaway /ˈrʌn.ə.weɪ/ *adj* out of control or escaped from somewhere: *A runaway bus/horse caused chaos on the streets.* ○ *a runaway child sleeping on the streets* ○ FIGURATIVE *Her first novel's runaway* (= surprisingly big) *success came as a great surprise.* **runaway** /ˈrʌn.ə.weɪ/ *noun* [C] *We're searching for a couple of runaways from the young offenders' institution.*

run-down REPORT /ˈrʌn.daʊn/ *noun* [S] a detailed report: *Here's a run-down on/of the activities of our ten biggest competitors.*

run-down CONDITION /ˌrʌnˈdaʊn/ *adj* **1** describes buildings or areas that are in very bad condition: *a run-down building/cemetery* **2** [after v] tired and not healthy, especially because of working too much: *My doctor said I was looking run-down and ought to take some time to rest.* ⊃See also **run-down**.

rune /ruːn/ *noun* [C] any of the letters of an ancient alphabet cut into stone or wood in the past by the people of northern Europe, or any similar mark with a secret or magic meaning **runic** /ˈruː.nɪk/ *adj*: *a runic letter/alphabet/message*

rung RING /rʌŋ/ *past participle of* ring

rung STEP /rʌŋ/ *noun* [C] any of the short bars that form the steps of a LADDER

● **be on the lowest/bottom rung of the ladder** to be at the lowest level of an organization: *I started my life on the bottom rung of the ladder in this company.*

run-in /ˈrʌn.ɪn/ *noun* [C] INFORMAL If you have a run-in with someone, you have a serious argument with them or you get into trouble with them: *I had a run-in with the boss/the law/the police yesterday.*

runner BLADE /ˈrʌn.əʳ/ US /-ɚ/ *noun* [C] one of two usually metal blades under a SLEDGE which allow it to move along easily

runner STEM /ˈrʌn.əʳ/ US /-ɚ/ *noun* [C] a long stem of a plant which grows along the ground in order to put down roots in a new place

runner 'bean UK *noun* [C usually pl] (US **string bean**) a bean with long green edible pods, or the plant from which these beans grow

runner-up /ˌrʌn.əˈrʌp/ US /-ɚˈʌp/ *noun* [C] *plural* **runners-up** a person who comes second in a race or competition

running /ˈrʌn.ɪŋ/ *noun, adj* ⊃See at **run** GO QUICKLY; **run** TRAVEL; **run** OPERATE; **run** POLITICS

running 'commentary *noun* [C] a description of an event, usually a sports event, given at the same time as it happens

running ,costs *plural noun* **1** the money you need to spend regularly to keep a system or organization functioning **2** the money you need to spend in order to maintain and use a vehicle

running ,mate *noun* [C] in the US, a political partner chosen for a politician who is trying to get elected: *If a candidate for president wins the election, his/her running mate becomes the vice president.*

running ,shoe *noun* [C] US FOR **trainer**

running ,sore *noun* [C] an injury that will not heal and keeps producing liquid

running ,stitch *noun* [U] a type of sewing stitch

running 'water *noun* [U] water supplied to a house by pipes: *Some of these older houses still don't have running water.*

runny /ˈrʌn.i/ *adj* **1** more liquid than usual: *The sauce looked runny so I added some more flour.* **2** If your nose is runny, it is producing more mucus than usual, usually because you are ill: *I've got a runny nose today.*

run-off /ˈrʌn.ɒf/ ⓤ /-ɑːf/ *noun* [C usually sing] an extra competition or election to decide the winner, because the leading competitors have finished equal: *In a run-off for the presidency of the assembly, Santos beat Gutierez.* ○ *a run-off race/election*

run-of-the-mill /ˌrʌn.əv.ðəˈmɪl/ *adj* ordinary and not special or exciting in any way: *He gave a fairly run-of-the-mill speech.*

the runs *plural noun* INFORMAL a condition of the bowels in which the contents are excreted too frequently and in a form which is too liquid; DIARRHOEA

runt /rʌnt/ *noun* [C] **1** the smallest and weakest animal of a group born at the same time to the same mother **2** INFORMAL a small or weak person whom you dislike

run-up /ˈrʌn.ʌp/ *noun* **1** [C] In some sports, a run-up is a period or distance of running that you do in order to be going fast enough to perform a particular action: *The longer and faster your run-up is, the higher you can jump.* **2** [S] MAINLY UK the final period of time before an important event: *Everyone is very busy during the run-up to publication.*

runway /ˈrʌn.weɪ/ *noun* [C] a long level piece of ground with a specially prepared smooth hard surface on which aircraft take off and land

rupee /ruːˈpiː/ ⓤ /ˈruː.piː/ *noun* [C] the standard unit of money used in India, Pakistan, Mauritius, Nepal, Sri Lanka and the Seychelles

rupiah /ruːˈpiː.ə/ *noun* [C] the standard unit of money used in Indonesia

rupture /ˈrʌp.tʃəʳ/ ⓤ /-tʃɚ/ *verb* [I or T] to (cause to) burst, break or tear: *His appendix ruptured and he had to be rushed to hospital.* ○ FIGURATIVE *This news has ruptured* (= violently ended) *the delicate peace between the rival groups.*

rupture *yourself verb* [R] If you rupture yourself, you break apart the wall of muscle which keeps your stomach and your bowels in place, usually by lifting something too heavy.

rupture /ˈrʌp.tʃəʳ/ ⓤ /-tʃɚ/ *noun* [C] **1** when something bursts, breaks or tears: *a rupture of the pipeline* ○ FIGURATIVE *a rupture* (= an end to a friendly relationship) *between the families* **2** when the wall of muscle holding the stomach and bowels in place inside the body is broken apart; HERNIA: *You're going to give yourself a rupture if you lift that.*

rural /ˈrʊə.rəl/ ⓤ /ˈrʊr.əl/ *adj* in, of or like the countryside: *The area is still very rural and undeveloped.* ⊃Compare **urban**.

ruse /ruːz/ *noun* [C] a trick intended to deceive someone

rush HURRY /rʌʃ/ *verb* **1** [I or T; usually + adv or prep] to (cause to) go or do something very quickly: *Whenever I see him, he seems to be rushing (about/around).* ○ *I rushed up the stairs/to the office/to find a phone.* ○ *When she turned it upside down the water rushed out.* ○ [+ to infinitive] *We shouldn't rush to blame them.* ○ *You can't rush a job like this.* ○ *The emergency legislation was rushed through Parliament in a morning.* ○ *Don't rush me!* ○ *The United Nations has rushed medical aid and food to the famine zone.* ○ *He rushed the children off to school so they wouldn't be late.* **2** [T] If a group of people rush an enemy or the place where an enemy is, they attack suddenly and all together: *We rushed the palace gates and killed the guards.* **3** [I] In American football, to rush is to carry the football forward across the place on the field where play begins. Also, a member of the opposite team rushes when they force their way to the back of the field quickly to catch the player carrying the football.

• **rush into** If you rush into something such as a job, you start doing it without having really decided if it is the right thing to do or having considered the best way to do it.

• **rush** *sb* **into (doing)** *sth* If someone rushes you into doing something, they forcefully persuade you to do it without giving you time to really decide.

rush /rʌʃ/ *noun* **1** [S] when you have to hurry or move somewhere quickly: *Slow down! What's the rush?* ○ *Why is it always such a rush to get ready in the mornings?* **2** [S] when a lot of things are happening or a lot of people are trying to do or get something: *There's always a rush to get the best seats.* ○ *I try to do my shopping before the Christmas rush.* ○ *There's been a rush for* (= sudden popular demand for) *tickets.* **3** [S] when something or someone suddenly moves somewhere quickly: *There was a rush of air as she opened the door.* ○ *They made a rush at him to get his gun.* **4** [S] a sudden strong emotion or physical feeling: *The memory of who he was came back to him with a rush.* ○ *I had my first cigarette for a year and felt a sudden rush (of dizziness).* **5** [S] a sudden movement of people to a certain area, usually because of some economic advantage: *the California gold rush* **6** [C] in American football, an attempt to run forwards carrying the ball, or an attempt to quickly reach and stop a player from the opposing team who is carrying the ball

rushed /rʌʃt/ *adj*: *Supper was rushed since the family had to go out that evening.*

rushing /ˈrʌʃ.ɪŋ/ *adj* fast moving: *I stretched out and listened to the sound of the rushing stream.*

rush PLANT /rʌʃ/ *noun* [C usually pl] a grass-like plant that grows in or near water and whose long thin hollow stems can be dried and made into floor coverings, containers, etc: *a rush mat*

▲ **rush** *sth* **out** *phrasal verb* [M] to very quickly produce something and make it available to sell: *When the war started, several publishers rushed out books on the conflict.*

'rush ,hour *noun* [C usually sing] the busy part of the day when towns and cities are crowded, either in the morning when people are travelling to work, or in the evening when people are travelling home: *rush hour traffic*

'rush ,job *noun* [C] a piece of work which is not as good as it could be, because you do it quickly: *The biography was a bit of a rush job.*

rusk /rʌsk/ *noun* [C] a type of very hard dry biscuit, eaten especially by babies

russet /ˈrʌs.ɪt/ *noun* [U], *adj* LITERARY reddish brown

Russian /ˈrʌʃ.ən/ *adj* from, belonging to or relating to Russia

Russian /ˈrʌʃ.ən/ *noun* [C] a person from Russia

,Russian rou'lette *noun* [U] a very dangerous game of chance where each player aims at their own head with a gun which has one bullet in it and five empty CHAMBERS (= spaces where bullets could go): FIGURATIVE *Doctors' refusal to take the issue seriously is **playing** Russian roulette **with*** (= taking unnecessary risks with) *ordinary citizens' health.*

rust /rʌst/ *noun* [U] **1** a reddish brown substance that forms on the surface of iron and steel as a result of decay caused by reacting with air and water: *patches of rust* **2** a reddish brown colour that looks like rust **3** any of various plant diseases that cause reddish brown spots

rust /rʌst/ *verb* [I or T] to become or cause something to become covered with rust: *Older cars will begin to rust.* ○ *Years of being left out in the rain had rusted the metal chairs.* ○ *The floor of the car had rusted away/through* (= been destroyed by rust), *so I was careful where I put my feet.*

rustic /ˈrʌs.tɪk/ *adj* simple and often rough in appearance; typical of the countryside: *a rustic bench/cabin* ○ *The property has a certain rustic charm.*
rusticity /rʌsˈtɪs.ɪ.ti/ ⓤ /-ṭɪs.ə.ṭi/ *noun* [U]

rustle NOISE /ˈrʌs.l̩/ *verb* [I or T] If things such as paper or leaves rustle, or if you rustle them, they move about and make a soft, dry sound: *The leaves rustled in the breeze.* ○ *He rustled his papers* (= noisily moved them about) *to hide his embarrassment.* **rustle** /ˈrʌs.l̩/ *noun* [S] **rustling** /ˈrʌs.l̩.ɪŋ/ /-lɪŋ/ *noun* [C or U] *I could hear (a) rustling in the bushes.* ○ *A small animal was making rustling noises among the leaves.*

rustle STEAL /ˈrʌs.l̩/ *verb* [T] MAINLY US to steal farm animals **rustler** /ˈrʌs.l̩.əʳ/ ⓤ /-lɚ/ *noun* [C] a person who steals farm animals

▲ **rustle** *sth* **up** *phrasal verb* [M] INFORMAL to make something quickly, usually a meal from the food that is available: *Give me a minute and I'll rustle something up for supper.*

rustproof /ˈrʌst.pruːf/ *adj* protected against RUST (= metal decay) **rustproof** /ˈrʌst.pruːf/ *verb* [T] *Painting steel is a good way to rustproof it.*

rusty METAL /ˈrʌs.ti/ *adj* covered with rust: *a rusty car/nail*

rusty NEED PRACTICE /ˈrʌs.ti/ *adj* If a skill you had is rusty, it is not now good because you have forgotten it: *My Italian is a bit rusty these days.*

rut HOLE /rʌt/ *noun* [C] a deep narrow mark made in soft ground especially by a wheel
• **in a rut** If a person, organization, etc. is in a rut, they have become too fixed in one particular type of job, activity, method, etc: *I've got to change jobs – after 15 years here I feel I'm (stuck) in a rut (= I'm bored).*

rut SEXUALLY ACTIVE PERIOD /rʌt/ *noun* [S] **1** the period of the year during which particular male animals, especially deer and sheep, are sexually active: *During the rut, stags can be seen fighting for females.* **2 in rut** (of particular male animals) sexually excited **rutting** /ˈrʌt.ɪŋ/ US /ˈrʌt̬-/ *adj*: *the rutting season*

rutabaga /ˌruː.təˈbeɪ.gə/ US /-t̬ə-/ *noun* [C] US FOR **swede** ➩See picture **Vegetables** on page Centre 2

ruthless /ˈruːθ.ləs/ *adj* without thinking or caring about any pain caused to others; cruel: *ruthless ambition* ○ *a ruthless dictator* ○ *Some people believe that to succeed in this world you have to be ruthless.* **ruthlessly** /ˈruːθ.lə-sli/ *adv* **ruthlessness** /ˈruːθ.lə.snəs/ *noun* [U]

rutted /ˈrʌt.ɪd/ US /ˈrʌt̬-/ *adj* If a surface is rutted, it has deep narrow marks in it made by wheels: *a deeply/badly rutted road*

RV /ˌɑːˈviː/ *noun* [C] ABBREVIATION FOR recreational vehicle: a MOTORHOME ➩See picture **Cars and Trucks** on page Centre 13

Rx US WRITTEN ABBREVIATION FOR **prescription** (= a piece of paper on which a doctor writes the details of the medicine or drugs that someone needs)

rye /raɪ/ *noun* [U] **1** a type of grain, the seeds of which are used to make flour or whisky or to feed animals: *rye bread* **2** whisky made with rye: *a glass of rye*

ˈrye ˌbread *noun* [U] dark brown bread made with rye

S

S [LETTER] *(plural* **S's**), **s** *(plural* **s's**) /es/ *noun* [C] the 19th letter of the English alphabet

S [SOUTH] *noun* [U], *adj* (*UK ALSO* **Sth**, *US ALSO* **So**) *WRITTEN ABBREVIATION FOR* south or SOUTHERN

S [SMALL] *adj WRITTEN ABBREVIATION FOR* **small** LIMITED, used to show the size of a piece of clothing

S [SATISFACTORY] *US WRITTEN ABBREVIATION FOR* **satisfactory**, when given as a mark for an exam or course

s (*ALSO* **sec**) *WRITTEN ABBREVIATION FOR* **second** TIME

-s /-s/ /-z/ *suffix* (*ALSO* **-es**) used to form the plural of nouns: *books* ○ *sandwiches*

-'s /-s/ /-z/ *suffix* **1** used to show that the following thing belongs to the person or thing named: *the cat's tail* ○ *Patricia's dress* ○ *today's paper* ○ *the children's shoes* * NOTE: *-'s* is used to form the possessive of singular nouns and of plural nouns which do not end in *-s*, and sometimes of names which end in *-s*. **2** the house belonging to the stated person: *The boys are at Alison's.* **3** *UK* the shop belonging to the stated person: *I got it at the greengrocer's.*

-s' /-s/ /-z/ *suffix* used to show that the following thing belongs to the people or things named: *the girls' books* ○ *employees' rights* * NOTE: *-s'* is used to form the possessive plural of most nouns.

's /-s/ /-z/ *short form of* **1** is: *It's in the cupboard.* **2** has: *She's gone home.* **3** *INFORMAL* (only used in spoken questions) does: *How's this thing work?* **4** (only used after 'let') us: *Let's go swimming this afternoon.*

the Sabbath /ðəˈsæb.əθ/ *noun* [S] the day of the week kept by some religious groups for rest and worship. The Sabbath is Sunday for most Christians, Saturday for Jews and Friday for Muslims: *to keep/break* (= follow/not follow the religious rules for) *the Sabbath*

sabbatical /səˈbæt.ɪ.kəl/ [US] /-ˈbæt̬-/ *noun* [C or U] a period of time when college or university teachers are allowed to stop their usual work in order to study or travel, usually while continuing to be paid: *to take/have a sabbatical* ○ *She's* ***on*** *sabbatical for six months.* ○ *sabbatical leave*

sable /ˈseɪ.bl̩/ *noun* [C or U] a small animal with thick warm fur, or the fur of this animal used for making clothes and artists' brushes

sabotage /ˈsæb.ə.tɑːʒ/ *verb* [T] **1** to damage or destroy equipment, weapons or buildings in order to prevent the success of an enemy or competitor: *The rebels had tried to sabotage the oil pipeline.* **2** to intentionally prevent the success of a plan or action: *This was a deliberate attempt to sabotage the ceasefire.* **sabotage** /ˈsæb.ə.tɑːʒ/ *noun* [U] *They began a campaign of industrial and economic sabotage.*

saboteur /ˌsæb.əˈtɜːʳ/ [US] /-ˈtɝː/ *noun* [C] a person who sabotages something

sabre *MAINLY UK, US USUALLY* **saber** /ˈseɪ.bəʳ/ [US] /-bɚ/ *noun* [C] **1** a heavy sword with a wide, usually curved blade, used in the past by soldiers on horses **2** a light pointed sword with one sharp edge used in the sport of FENCING

sabre-rattling /ˈseɪ.bəˌræt.l̩.ɪŋ/ [US] /-bɚˌræt̬-/ *noun* [U] *DISAPPROVING* talking and behaving in a way that threatens military action

sac /sæk/ *noun* [C] *SPECIALIZED* a part of a plant or animal which is like a bag and often contains liquid

saccharin /ˈsæk.ər.ɪn/ [US] /-ɚ-/ *noun* [U] a very sweet artificial substance which is used to replace sugar, especially by people who want to lose weight or who must not eat sugar: *saccharin tablets*

saccharine /ˈsæk.ər.iːn/ [US] /-ɚ-/ *adj DISAPPROVING* too sweet or too polite: *I don't trust her, with her saccharine smiles.* ○ *saccharine love songs*

sachet /ˈsæʃ.eɪ/ [US] /-ˈ-/ *noun* [C] a small closed container made of paper or plastic, containing a small amount of something, usually enough for only one occasion: *a free sachet of shampoo*

sack [BAG] /sæk/ *noun* [C] **1** a large bag made of strong cloth, paper or plastic, used to store large amounts of something: *The corn was stored in large sacks.* ○ *a sack* ***of*** (= one containing) *potatoes/coal/flour* ➲See also **haversack**; **knapsack**; **rucksack**. **2** *US* a paper or plastic bag used to carry items bought in a food shop: *a sack of groceries*

sackful /ˈsæk.fʊl/ *noun* [C] (*ALSO* **sackload**) the amount contained in a sack: *FIGURATIVE He got sackfuls* ***of*** (= very many) *letters from listeners following the show.*

the sack [BED] *noun* [S] *US INFORMAL* bed: *It's late – I'm going to* ***hit*** *the sack* (= go to bed). ○ *He came home and found Judy and Brad* ***in*** *the sack* (= in bed) *together.*

• **in the sack** *US INFORMAL* If someone is good/bad in the sack, they are sexually skilled/not sexually skilled.

sack [DISMISS] /sæk/ *verb* [T] to dismiss someone from a job, usually because they have done something wrong or badly, or sometimes as a way of saving the cost of employing them: *They sacked her* ***for*** *being late.* ○ *He* ***got*** *sacked from his last job.*

the sack *noun* [S] when someone is dismissed from their job: *They* ***gave*** *him the sack* ***for*** *being late.* ○ *Two workers* ***got*** *the sack* ***for*** *fighting in the warehouse.*

sacking /ˈsæk.ɪŋ/ *noun* [C] an act of stopping employing someone: *Mr Ali said the sackings would save the company about $40 million a year.* ➲See also at **sackcloth**

sack [STEAL] /sæk/ *verb* [T] to steal all the valuable things from a building, town, etc., and possibly destroy the building or town, usually during a war: *The invaders sacked every village they passed on their route.*

sack /sæk/ *noun* [S] ***The sack*** (= destruction) ***of*** *Rome by the Visigoths occurred in the 5th century.*

▲ **sack out** *phrasal verb US INFORMAL* to go to bed: *It's late – I'm going to sack out.*

sackcloth /ˈsæk.klɒθ/ [US] /-klɑːθ/ *noun* [U] (*ALSO* **sacking**) the thick rough material used to make SACKS (= large strong bags)

• **wear sackcloth and ashes** to show by your behaviour that you are very sorry for something you did that was wrong

ˈsack ˌlunch *noun* [C] *US FOR* **packed lunch**

ˈsack ˌrace *noun* [C usually sing] a race in which people jump along with both legs in a cloth sack that they hold up with their hands

sacrament /ˈsæk.rə.mənt/ *noun* **1** [C] an important religious ceremony in the Christian Church, such as BAPTISM or COMMUNION **2** [C usually sing] the holy bread and wine eaten at HOLY COMMUNION (= a religious ceremony)

sacramental /ˌsæk.rəˈmen.təl/ [US] /-t̬əl/ *adj*

sacred /ˈseɪ.krɪd/ *adj* **1** considered to be holy and deserving respect, especially because of a connection with a god: *sacred relics/temples* ○ *This area is sacred* ***to*** *the Apaches.* **2** connected with religion: *sacred music/writings* **3** considered too important to be changed: *His daily routine is absolutely sacred* ***to*** *him.* ○ *HUMOROUS The cricketers wore blue, not their usual white – is* ***nothing*** *sacred?* **sacredness** /ˈseɪ.krɪd.nəs/ *noun* [U]

ˌsacred ˈcow *noun* [C] *DISAPPROVING* a belief, custom, etc. that people support and do not question or criticize: *They did not dare to challenge the sacred cow of parliamentary democracy.*

sacrifice [KILL] /ˈsæk.rɪ.faɪs/ *verb* [I or T] to kill an animal or a person and offer them to a god or gods

• **be sacrificed on the altar of *sth*** *LITERARY* to be destroyed by an activity, system or belief that is bad but more important or more powerful: *Service and quality have been sacrificed on the altar of profit.*

sacrifice /ˈsæk.rɪ.faɪs/ *noun* [C or U] the act of killing an animal or person and offering them to a god or gods, or the animal, etc. that is offered: *The people offered a lamb on the altar as a sacrifice* ***for*** *their sins.*

sacrificial /ˌsæk.rɪˈfɪʃ.əl/ *adj* offered as a sacrifice: *The priest held up the head of the sacrificial goat.* **sacrificially** /ˌsæk.rɪˈfɪʃ.əl.i/ *adv*

sacrifice [GIVE UP] /ˈsæk.rɪ.faɪs/ *verb* [T] to give up something that is valuable to you in order to help another person: *Many women sacrifice interesting careers* ***for*** *their family.* **sacrifice** /ˈsæk.rɪ.faɪs/ *noun* [C or U] *We had*

to **make** sacrifices in order to pay for our children's education. ○ They cared for their disabled son for 27 years, **at** great personal sacrifice.
• **make the ultimate/supreme sacrifice** *FORMAL* to die while fighting for a principle

ˌsacrificial ˈlamb *noun* [C usually sing] someone or something which is given to people in authority and which is expected to be harmed or destroyed, especially in order to prevent other people or things from being harmed or destroyed: *We knew the department would be a sacrificial lamb when the time came to cut staff.*

sacrilege /ˈsæk.rɪ.lɪdʒ/ *noun* [S or U] (an act of) treating something holy or important without respect: [+ *to* infinitive] *Muslims consider it sacrilege **to** wear shoes inside a mosque.* ○ ***It** would be a sacrilege **to** put a neon sign on that beautiful old building.* **sacrilegious** /ˌsæk.rɪˈlɪdʒ.əs/ *adj*: *sacrilegious practices/acts* **sacrilegiously** /ˌsæk.rɪˈlɪdʒ.ə.sli/ *adv*

sacristy /ˈsæk.rɪ.sti/ *noun* [C] a **vestry**

sacrosanct /ˈsæk.rə.sæŋkt/ *adj MAINLY HUMOROUS* thought to be too important or too special to be changed: *I'm willing to help on any weekday, but I'm afraid my weekends are sacrosanct.*

sad [NOT HAPPY] /sæd/ *adj* **sadder, saddest 1** unhappy or sorry: *I've just received some very sad news.* ○ *She gave a rather sad smile.* ○ [+ (that)] *It's sad **(that)** the trip had to be cancelled.* ○ *I'm so sad **(that)** you can't come.* ○ [+ *to* infinitive] ***It**'s sad **to** see so many failures this year.* ○ *I was sad **to** hear that they'd split up.* **2** *HUMOROUS* If something looks sad, it looks worse than it should because it is not being cared for: *Give those flowers some water – they're looking a bit sad.*
• **sadder but wiser** If someone is sadder but wiser after a bad experience, they have suffered but they have also learned something from it.
sadly /ˈsæd.li/ *adv* in an unhappy way: *"He's gone away for six months," she said sadly.* **sadness** /ˈsæd.nəs/ *noun* [U] *Her sadness at her grandfather's death was obvious to us all.*
sadden /ˈsæd.ᵊn/ *verb* [T] to make someone sad: [+ *to* infinitive] ***It** saddens me **to** think that we'll never see her again.* ○ *We are **deeply** saddened by this devastating tragedy.*

sad [UNPLEASANT] /sæd/ *adj* [before n] **sadder, saddest** not satisfactory or pleasant: *The sad **fact/truth** is we can't afford to provide homes for all.* ○ *a very sad state of affairs*
• **sad to say** something you say when you are telling someone about something bad that happened: *Sad to say, the ring was never found.*
sadly /ˈsæd.li/ *adv* in a way that is unsatisfactory: *Sadly, the treatment doesn't work for all patients.* ○ *If you think she'll let you do that, you're sadly* (= completely) ***mistaken**.*

sad [BORING] /sæd/ *adj* **sadder, saddest** *UK SLANG* showing that you are not fashionable or interesting or have no friends: *You enjoy reading timetables? You sad man!*

SAD /ˌes.eɪˈdiː/ *noun* [U] *ABBREVIATION FOR* seasonal affective disorder: a medical condition in which a person lacks energy and enthusiasm during the winter because of the reduced period of natural light

saddle [SEAT] /ˈsæd.l̩/ *noun* [C] a seat, often made of leather, used on a horse, bicycle, motorcycle, etc: *He swung himself into the saddle and rode off.* ➲See also **sidesaddle**. ➲See picture **Sports** on page Centre 10
• **in the saddle 1** riding a horse **2** in charge or in control: *The chairman is back in the saddle after his heart attack.*
saddle /ˈsæd.l̩/ *verb* [T] to put a saddle on a horse: *She saddled **(up)** the horse for her friend.*
saddler /ˈsæd.ləʳ/ [US] /-lɚ/ *noun* [C] a person who makes, sells and repairs saddles and other leather objects for horses
saddlery /ˈsæd.lə.ri/ [US] /-lɚ.i/ *noun* [U] leather objects, such as saddles and BRIDLES, for horses

saddle [MEAT] /ˈsæd.l̩/ *noun* [C or U] a large piece of meat taken from the middle of the back of an animal: *saddle of lamb*
▲ **saddle *sb* with *sth*** *phrasal verb INFORMAL* to give someone a responsibility or problem which they do not want and which will cause them a lot of work or difficulty: *The company is saddled with **debt**.*

saddle-bag /ˈsæd.l̩bæg/ *noun* [C] a small bag which you fix to the back of your bicycle saddle, or one of a pair of bags you put over the back of a horse or over the back wheel of a bicycle or motorcycle

saddle-sore /ˈsæd.l̩.sɔːʳ/ [US] /-sɔːr/ *adj* having a sore bottom from sitting on a saddle for a long time

saddo /ˈsæd.əʊ/ [US] /-oʊ/ *noun* [C] *UK SLANG* someone, especially a man, who is not fashionable or interesting or has no friends: *So who says trainspotting is for saddos?*

sadism /ˈseɪ.dɪ.zᵊm/ [US] /ˈsæd.ɪ-/ *noun* [U] the obtaining of pleasure, sometimes sexual, from being cruel to or hurting another person
sadist /ˈseɪ.dɪst/ [US] /ˈsæd.ɪst/ *noun* [C] a person who obtains pleasure, sometimes sexual, by being cruel to or hurting another person **sadistic** /səˈdɪs.tɪk/ *adj*: *sadistic behaviour/pleasure* **sadistically** /səˈdɪs.tɪ.kli/ *adv*

sadomasochism /ˌseɪ.dəʊˈmæs.ə.kɪ.zᵊm/ [US] /ˌsæd.oʊ-/ *noun* [U] (*ABBREVIATION* **S&M**, *ABBREVIATION* **SM**) the obtaining of sexual pleasure from SADISM (= hurting other people) and from MASOCHISM (= being hurt)
sadomasochist /ˌseɪ.dəʊˈmæs.ə.kɪst/ [US] /ˌsæd.oʊ-/ *noun* [C] **sadomasochistic** /ˌseɪ.dəʊˌmæs.əˈkɪs.tɪk/ [US] /ˌsæd.oʊ-/ *adj*

sae *UK*, **SAE** /ˌes.eɪˈiː/ *noun* [C] (*US* **SASE**) *ABBREVIATION FOR* stamped addressed envelope or self-addressed envelope: an envelope with a stamp and your name and address on it, which you send inside another envelope to an organization when you want a reply: *Write to the above address, enclosing an sae.*

safari /səˈfɑː.ri/ [US] /-ˈfɑːr.i/ *noun* [C or U] an organized journey to look at, or sometimes hunt, wild animals, especially in Africa: *to go/be **on** safari*

saˈfari ˌjacket *noun* [C] a jacket made of light cloth with short sleeves, pockets on the chest and a belt

saˈfari ˌpark *noun* [C] a large enclosed park where wild animals are kept and can move freely, and can be watched by visitors driving through in their cars

saˈfari ˌsuit *noun* [C] a SAFARI JACKET with matching trousers or a matching skirt

safe [WITHOUT DANGER] /seɪf/ *adj* **1** not in danger or likely to be harmed: *In some cities you don't **feel** safe going out alone at night.* **2** not dangerous or likely to cause harm: *a safe play-area for children* ○ *a safe driver* ○ *That ladder doesn't look safe.* ○ *She wished us a safe journey.* ○ *Is this medicine safe **for** children?* ○ ***It**'s safe **to** cross the road now.* **3** not harmed or damaged: *She said that all the hostages were safe.* **4** describes things which do not involve any risk: *I think we should go for the safest option* (= the one that involves the least risks). ○ *He never usually remembers my birthday, so it's a safe **bet*** (= I am certain) *he'll forget again this time!* **5** If an official position in parliament is safe, it is likely to be won by the political party which has won it at previous elections: *a safe Conservative **seat***
• **as safe as houses** *UK* very safe
• **in safe hands** being cared for or dealt with by someone skilled: *Dr Bailey is doing the operation, so your wife is in safe hands.*
• **(just) to be on the safe side** being especially careful in order to avoid something unpleasant: *I'm sure it won't rain, but I'll take an umbrella (just) to be on the safe side* (= to be ready if it does rain).
• **safe and sound** completely safe and without injury or damage: *After three days lost in the mountains, all the climbers arrived home safe and sound.*
• ***your* secret's safe with *me*** used to say that you will not tell anyone what you have just been told: *"I'd appreciate it if you kept quiet about this." "Dont' worry - your secret's safe with me."*
safely /ˈseɪ.fli/ *adv* in a safe way: *We all arrived safely.* ○ *Drive safely* (= Do not take any risks)*!* ○ *Are the children safely fastened into their car seats?* ○ *I think we can safely* (= with no risk of being wrong) *say they won't find us now.*
safety /ˈseɪf.ti/ *noun* [U] a state in which or a place where you are safe and not in danger or at risk: ***For** your (comfort and) safety, we recommend you keep your*

S

seat belt loosely fastened during the flight. ○ *Journalists may enter the danger zone but unfortunately we cannot* ***guarantee/assure*** *their safety.* ○ *The crew of the ship were winched to safety by a rescue helicopter.* ○ *As the gunman opened fire, they all* ***ran/dived for*** *safety behind trees.* ○ *Police are* ***concerned for*** *the safety* ***of*** (= think that something bad might have happened to) *the five-year-old.* ○ *He was led to* ***a place of*** *safety* (= somewhere he would not be in danger, esp. of being found and harmed).

● **safety first** *SAYING* said to mean that it is best to avoid any unnecessary risks and to act so that you stay safe

● **There's safety in numbers.** *SAYING* said to emphasize that being part of a group makes you less likely to be harmed

USAGE

safety or **security**?

Safety is used to describe the state of being safe or to describe things that keep you safe.

Remember to wear your safety belt in the car.

Security means activities or people that protect you from harm, or that try to stop crime.

He works as a security guard.
airport security

safe [BOX] /seɪf/ *noun* **[C]** a strong box or cupboard with special locks where valuable things, especially money or jewels, are kept: *Thieves* ***broke into/cracked*** (= opened by force) *the safe and stole everything in it.*

safebreaker *UK* /ˈseɪfˌbreɪ.kəʳ/ [US] /-kɚ/ *noun* **[C]** (*US* **safe-cracker**) someone who opens SAFES using force and steals the valuable things from inside

safe-conduct /ˌseɪfˈkɒn.dʌkt/ [US] /-kɑːn-/ *noun* **[C or U]** official protection from harm while travelling through an area, or a document that gives this: *In exchange for the hostages, the terrorists demanded safe-conduct out of the country.*

ˈsafe deˌposit box *noun* **[C]** (*ALSO* **safety deposit box**) a strong box in a bank where you can keep money or valuable things

safeguard /ˈseɪf.ɡɑːd/ [US] /-ɡɑːrd/ *verb* **[T]** to protect something from harm: *The union safeguards the* ***interests*** *of all its members.* **safeguard** /ˈseɪf.ɡɑːd/ [US] /-ɡɑːrd/ *noun* **[C or U]** *The disk has built-in safeguards to prevent certain errors.*

▲ **safeguard against** ***sth*** to do things that you hope will stop something unpleasant from happening: *A good diet will safeguard against disease.*

ˌsafe ˈhaven *noun* **[C usually sing]** a place where you are protected from harm or danger: *As long as the UN soldiers were present, the city was regarded as a safe haven for the refugees.*

ˈsafe ˌhouse *noun* **[C]** a house where someone can hide or shelter

safekeeping /ˌseɪfˈkiː.pɪŋ/ *noun* **[U]** protection from harm or loss: *I left my watch with Helen* ***for*** *safekeeping while I swam.*

ˈsafe ˌperiod *noun* **[S]** the few days just before and during a woman's period when she is unlikely to become pregnant

ˌsafe ˈsex *noun* **[U]** the use of condoms or other methods of avoiding catching a disease, especially AIDS, from sexual contact with someone else: *It's to be hoped that they're* ***practising*** *safe sex.*

ˈsafety ˌbelt *noun* **[C]** a **seat belt**

ˈsafety ˌcatch *noun* **[C]** a small part on something dangerous, especially a machine or a gun, which prevents people from using it unintentionally

ˈsafety ˌcurtain *noun* **[C]** in a theatre, a curtain made of material which will not burn and which comes down between the stage and the part where people sit to prevent any possible fire from spreading

ˈsafety deˌposit box *noun* **[C]** a **safe deposit box**

ˈsafety ˌglass *noun* **[U]** a type of glass, used especially for car windows, that either stays in one piece in an accident, or breaks into small pieces which are not sharp

ˈsafety ˌglasses *plural noun* special pieces of strong glass or plastic in a frame which fits tightly to a person's face to protect their eyes from dangerous chemicals or machines

ˈsafety ˌmatch *noun* **[C]** a match that will only start burning if you rub it along a special surface on its box

ˈsafety ˌnet [NET] *noun* **[C]** a net put below people performing at a great height to catch them if they fall

ˈsafety ˌnet [HELP] *noun* **[C]** a system to help those who have serious problems and no other form of help: *The welfare state was set up to provide a safety net for the poor and needy.*

ˈsafety ˌpin *noun* **[C]** a pin used for fastening things, especially cloth, which has a round end into which the sharp point fits, so that it is covered and cannot stick into you

ˈsafety ˌrazor *noun* **[C]** a device for cutting hair on the face which has a blade that is partly covered, to prevent it from cutting the skin

ˈsafety ˌvalve [MACHINE] *noun* **[C]** a small part on a machine, which allows steam or gas to escape if the pressure inside becomes too high

ˈsafety ˌvalve [FEELINGS] *noun* **[C]** a way of getting rid of strong feelings without causing harm: *For many people who suffer from stress at work, sport is a vital safety valve.*

saffron [SPICE] /ˈsæf.rən/ *noun* **[U]** a dark yellow substance obtained from a flower and used as a spice to give colour and flavour to food: *saffron rice*

saffron [COLOUR] /ˈsæf.rən/ *adj, noun* **[U]** dark yellow

sag /sæɡ/ *verb* **[I]** **-gg-** **1** to drop down to a lower level in the middle: *The shelf sagged* ***under*** *the weight of the heavy books.* ○ *a sagging roof/floor/bed* **2** to become weaker: *The dollar held up well this morning but the pound sagged.*

sag /sæɡ/ *noun* **1** **[S or U]** where something has dropped down to a lower level: *a sag in the roof* **2** **[C usually sing]** a reduction in something: *a sag in sales*

saga /ˈsɑː.ɡə/ *noun* **[C]** **1** a long story about several past events or people, originally one told in the Middle Ages in Iceland or Norway: *a lengthy and compelling family saga* **2** a long complicated series of related usually negative events: *It was just another episode in an* ***on-going*** *saga* ***of*** *marriage problems.*

sagacious /səˈɡeɪ.ʃəs/ *adj FORMAL* having or showing understanding and the ability to make good judgments; wise: *a sagacious person/comment/choice* **sagaciously** /səˈɡeɪ.ʃə.sli/ *adv* **sagacity** /səˈɡæs.ɪ.ti/ [US] /-ə.t̬i/ *noun* **[U]**

sage [WISE] /seɪdʒ/ *adj LITERARY* wise, especially as a result of great experience: *sage advice* ○ *my sage old grandfather*

sage /seɪdʒ/ *noun* **[C]** *LITERARY OR HUMOROUS* a person, especially an old man, who is wise **sagely** /ˈseɪdʒ.li/ *adv LITERARY* *He nodded his head sagely.*

sage [PLANT] /seɪdʒ/ *noun* **[U]** a plant whose greyish green leaves are used as a herb to give flavour to some foods: *sage-and-onion stuffing*

ˌsage ˈgreen *adj, noun* **[U]** greyish-green

Sagittarius /ˌsædʒ.ɪˈteə.ri.əs/ [US] /-ˈter.i-/ *noun* **[C or U]** the ninth sign of the zodiac, relating to the period 22 November to 22 December and represented by a CENTAUR (= half human, half horse) shooting an arrow, or a person born during this period **Sagittarian** /ˌsædʒ.ɪˈteə.ri.ən/ [US] /-ˈter.i-/ *noun* **[C]**, *adj*

sago /ˈseɪ.ɡəʊ/ [US] /-ɡoʊ/ *noun* **[U]** small white grains that are obtained from part of the trunk of a particular tree and which are used in cooking: *sago pudding*

said [SAY] /sed/ *past simple and past participle of* **say**

said [ALREADY MENTIONED] /sed/ *adj* **[before n]** *LEGAL* used before the name of a person or thing you have already mentioned: ***The*** *said Joseph Brown was seen outside the house on the night of January 15th.*

sail [TRAVEL] /seɪl/ *verb* **1** **[I usually + adv or prep]** When a boat or a ship sails, it travels on the water: *The boat sailed along/down the coast.* ○ *As the battleship sailed by/past, everyone on deck waved.* ○ *The ship was sailing* ***to*** *China.* **2** **[I or T; usually + adv or prep]** to control a boat that has no engine and is pushed by the wind: *He sailed the dinghy*

S

up the river. ○ *She sailed around the world single-handed in her yacht.* **3** [I] When a ship sails, it starts its journey, and when people sail from a particular place or at a particular time, they start their journey in a ship: *Their ship sails **for** Bombay next Friday.*

• **sail against the wind** to be trying to achieve something that is unlikely to succeed because most people would oppose it: *He's sailing against the wind in his attempt to stop women using the club.*

• **sail close to the wind** to do something that is dangerous or only just legal or acceptable: *You were sailing a bit close to the wind there when you made those remarks about his wife.*

sail /seɪl/ *noun* [S] a journey in a boat or ship: *It's two days' sail/It's **a** two-day sail* (= a journey of two days by sea) *from here to the nearest island.*

sailing /ˈseɪ.lɪŋ/ *noun* **1** [U] the sport or activity of using boats with sails: *the sailing club* ○ *She loves to **go** sailing.* **2** [C] when a ship leaves a port: *There are frequent sailings from Dover.*

sailor /ˈseɪ.ləʳ/ [US] /-lɚ/ *noun* [C] **1** a person who works on a ship, especially one who is not an officer **2** a person who often takes part in the sport of using boats with sails **3 a good/bad sailor** someone who is rarely/often ill when they travel by boat

sail [MATERIAL] /seɪl/ *noun* [C] **1** a sheet of material fixed to a pole on a boat to catch the wind and make the boat move: *to hoist/lower the sails* ➲See picture **Planes, Ships and Boats** on page Centre 14 **2** On a WINDMILL, a sail is any of the wide blades which are turned by the wind in order to produce power.

• **set sail** to begin a boat journey: *We set sail **from** Kuwait.* ○ *They set sail **for** France.*

• **under sail** *LITERARY* travelling in a boat or ship with sails: *After ten hours under sail, they reached dry land.*

sail [MOVE QUICKLY] /seɪl/ *verb* [I + adv or prep] to move quickly, easily, and (of a person) confidently: *The ball went sailing **over** the garden fence.* ○ *He wasn't looking where he was going, and just sailed **straight into** her.* ○ *Manchester United sailed **on*** (= continued easily) ***to** victory in the final.*

▲ **sail through** *sth phrasal verb* to succeed very easily in something, especially a test or examination: *Rachel sailed through with a distinction in all exam papers.*

sailboard /ˈseɪl.bɔːd/ [US] /-bɔːrd/ *noun* [C] a **Windsurfer**

ˈsailing ˌboat *UK noun* [C] (*US* **sailboat**) a small boat with sails

ˈsailor ˌsuit *noun* [C] a set of clothes, especially for a child, in the style of a sailor's uniform, usually blue and white with a large collar at the back

saint /seɪnt/ /sᵊnt/ *noun* **1** [C] (*WRITTEN ABBREVIATION* **St**) (the title given to) a person who has received an official honour from the Christian, especially the Roman Catholic, Church for having lived in a good and holy way. The names of saints are sometimes used to name places and buildings: *Saint Peter* ○ *St Andrew's school* ○ *Saint Paul's Cathedral* **2** [C usually sing] a very good, kind person: *She must be a **real** saint to stay with him all these years.* ○ *He has **the patience of a** saint with those kids.*

sainted /ˈseɪn.tɪd/ [US] /-t̬ɪd/ *adj* [usually before n] given the title of saint by the church, or considered to be like a saint: *HUMOROUS And where is my sainted* (= extremely good) *little sister?* **sainthood** /ˈseɪnt.hʊd/ *noun* [U] **saintly** /ˈseɪnt.li/ *adj*: *Her saintly manner concealed a devious mind.* **saintliness** /ˈseɪnt.lɪ.nəs/ *noun* [U]

saint's day /ˈseɪnts‚deɪ/ *noun* [C] a day in the year when a particular saint is remembered and when people who have that saint's name often celebrate

sake [HELP] /seɪk/ *noun* **for the sake of *sb*/for *sb's* sake** in order to help or bring advantage to someone: *Please do it, for David's sake.* ○ *Their parents only stayed together for the sake of the children.* ○ *I hope for both our sakes that you're right!*

sake [REASON] /seɪk/ *noun* **for the sake of *sth*/for *sth's* sake** because of, or for the purpose of something: *Let's not disagree for the sake of* (= because of) *a few pounds.* ○ *Let's say, just for the sake of argument/for argument's sake* (= for the purpose of this discussion), *that prices rise by 3 per cent this year.* ○ *You're only arguing for the sake of arguing* (= because you like arguing).

sake [EMPHASIS] /seɪk/ *noun* **for goodness'/God's/Pete's/heaven's/etc. sake** used to emphasize requests or orders and when you are angry or have lost patience: *For goodness' sake don't let her know I told you!*

sake [DRINK], **saki** /ˈsɑː.ki/ *noun* [C or U] a Japanese alcoholic drink made from rice and usually drunk warm

salaam /səˈlɑːm/ *verb* [I or T] (especially in Muslim countries) to greet someone by bending low from the waist with the front of the right hand against the top of the face **salaam** /səˈlɑːm/ *noun* [C], *exclamation*

salable /ˈseɪ.lə.bl̩/ *adj MAINLY US FOR* **saleable**, see at **sale** SELL

salacious /səˈleɪ.ʃəs/ *adj DISAPPROVING* causing or showing a strong interest in sexual matters: *a salacious film/book/joke/comment* **salaciously** /səˈleɪ.ʃə.sli/ *adv* **salaciousness** /səˈleɪ.ʃə.snəs/ *noun* [U]

salad /ˈsæl.əd/ *noun* [C or U] **1** a mixture of raw vegetables, usually including lettuce, eaten either as a separate dish or with other food: ***Toss*** (= Mix) *the salad with a vinaigrette dressing.* ○ *Serve the risotto with a mixed salad.* ○ *a salad bowl* **2 cheese/egg, etc. salad** cheese, egg, etc. with salad **3** cooked or raw vegetables cut into very small pieces and often mixed with MAYONNAISE: *potato salad* ○ *rice/pasta salad*

• **in *your* salad days** *OLD-FASHIONED* when you were a young person and had little experience: *I met her in my salad days.*

ˈsalad ˌbar *noun* [C usually sing] a table where different prepared salads are served in a restaurant or shop

ˈsalad ˌcream *noun* [U] *UK* a thick, cream-coloured liquid, similar to MAYONNAISE but sweeter, which is eaten with salad

ˈsalad ˌdressing *noun* [U] a cold sauce made from oil and vinegar, which is added to salads to give flavour

salamander /ˈsæl.ə.mæn.dəʳ/ [US] /-dɚ/ *noun* [C] a small animal which looks like a lizard but has soft skin and lives both on land and in water

salami /səˈlɑː.mi/ *noun* [U] a large sausage made from meat and spices which has a strong taste and is usually eaten cold in slices

salary /ˈsæl.ᵊr.i/ [US] /-ɚ-/ *noun* [C or U] a fixed amount of money agreed every year as pay for an employee, usually paid directly into his or her bank account every month: *an **annual** salary of £20 000* ○ *His net **monthly** salary is £1500.* ○ *She's **on** quite a good/decent salary in her present job.* ○ *He **took a drop in*** (= accepted a lower) *salary when he changed jobs.* ○ *a 10% salary **increase*** ➲Compare **wage** MONEY.

salaried /ˈsæl.ᵊr.id/ [US] /-ɚ-/ *adj* being paid a salary: *salaried employees/workers/staff*

salaryman /ˈsæl.ᵊr.i.mæn/ [US] /-ɚ-/ *noun* [C] *plural* **salarymen** a Japanese businessman who works very long hours every day

sale [SELL] /seɪl/ *noun* **1** [C or U] an act of exchanging something for money: *The sale **of** cigarettes/alcohol is forbidden.* ○ *The building company get 10% commission on each house sale.* ○ *I haven't **made** a sale all morning.* ○ *They'll drop the price rather than **lose** the sale.* ➲See also **sell** MONEY. **2** [C] an occasion when things are sold, especially by an organization such as a school or church, in order to make money for the organization: *a charity/Christmas/book sale* **3** [C] an **auction**: *a sale of antique furniture* ○ *a cattle sale*

• **for sale** available to buy: *Is this painting for sale?* ○ *Our neighbours **put** their house **up** for sale* (= started to advertise that they want to sell it) *last week.*

• **on sale** *UK* available to buy in a shop: *On sale at record stores now.*

• **sale or return** a system by which goods are supplied to shops and can be returned if they are not sold within a particular period of time: *We can supply goods **on a** sale or return **basis**.*

sales /seɪlz/ *plural noun* the number of items sold: *Sales this year exceeded the total for the two previous years.* ➲See also **telesales**.

sales /seɪlz/ *group noun* [U] the department of a company that organizes and does the selling of the company's

S

products or services: *He works in Sales.* ○ *the sales department/manager*

saleable, MAINLY US **salable** /ˈseɪ.lə.bl̩/ *adj* easy to sell or suitable for selling: *saleable commodities* ○ *in saleable condition*

COMMON LEARNER ERROR

sale or **sales**?

Remember that when you are talking about an amount of something that is sold, you use the plural noun *sales*.

This could have a considerable effect on our sales in Poland.

~~This could have a considerable effect on our sale in Poland.~~

---

sale CHEAP PRICE /seɪl/ *noun* [C] an occasion when goods are sold at a lower price than usual: *a mid-season/end-of-season sale* ○ *a clearance/closing-down sale* ○ *I bought this in the January sales.* ○ *sale goods/prices*
 • **on sale** MAINLY US (UK USUALLY **in the sale**) reduced in price: *Can you tell me if this dress is in the sale?*

'sales as,sistant *noun* [C] UK a **shop assistant**

salesclerk /ˈseɪlz.klɑːk/ US /-klɜːk/ *noun* [C] US FOR **shop assistant**

'sales ,drive *noun* [C] a special effort to sell more than usual

'sales ,force *group noun* [C] all the employees of a company whose job is persuading customers to buy their company's products or services

salesman /ˈseɪlz.mən/ *noun* [C] a man whose job is selling things in a shop or directly to customers: *a car salesman* ○ *a travelling salesman* ○ *a door-to-door salesman*

salesmanship /ˈseɪlz.mən.ʃɪp/ *noun* [U] skill in selling: *Clever salesmanship can persuade you to buy things you don't really want.*

salesperson /ˈseɪlz.wʊm.ən/ *noun* [C] a person whose job is selling things in a shop or directly to customers: *a car/computer salesperson*

'sales ,pitch *noun* [S] a way of talking that is intended to persuade you to buy something: *He's got a good sales pitch.*

'sales ,rep *noun* [C] (FORMAL **sales representative**) someone who travels to different places trying to persuade people to buy their company's products or services

'sales ,slip *noun* [C] US a **receipt**

'sales ,talk *noun* [U] a way of talking that is intended to persuade you to buy something

'sales ,tax *noun* [C usually sing] US a tax paid by people when they buy goods or services ⊃See also **VAT**.

saleswoman /ˈseɪlz.wʊm.ən/ *noun* [C] a female SALESPERSON

salient /ˈseɪ.li.ənt/ *adj* FORMAL The salient facts about something or qualities of something are the most important things about them: *She began to summarize the salient **features/points** of the proposal.* ○ *The article presented the salient **facts** of the dispute clearly and concisely.*

saline /ˈseɪ.laɪn/ *noun* [U] SPECIALIZED a liquid mixture of salt and pure water, which helps to kill bacteria or can be used to replace liquid lost from the body: *a saline drip*

saline /ˈseɪ.laɪn/ *adj* SPECIALIZED containing or consisting of salt: *saline deposits/springs* ○ *saline solution* **salinity** /səˈlɪn.ɪ.ti/ US /-ə.t̬i/ *noun* [U] *You should test the salinity of the water.*

saliva /səˈlaɪ.və/ *noun* [U] the liquid produced in your mouth to keep the mouth wet and to help to prepare food for digestion **salivary** /səˈlaɪ.vᵊr.i/ US /-vɚ-/ *adj* [before n] SPECIALIZED *salivary glands*

salivate /ˈsæl.ɪ.veɪt/ *verb* [I] SPECIALIZED OR HUMOROUS to produce saliva: *The thought of all that delicious food made me salivate.*

sallow /ˈsæl.əʊ/ US /-oʊ/ *adj* (of white-skinned people) yellowish and looking unhealthy: *a sallow complexion/face* **sallowness** /ˈsæl.əʊ.nəs/ US /-oʊ-/ *noun* [U]

sally /ˈsæl.i/ *noun* [C] a sudden attack on an enemy, especially when they are surrounding you

sally /ˈsæl.i/ *verb* [I + adv or prep] to make a sally
 • **sally forth** OLD USE OR HUMOROUS to leave a safe place in a brave or confident way in order to do something

difficult: *The minister opened the door and sallied forth to face the angry crowd.*

the ,Sally 'Army *group noun* UK INFORMAL FOR **the Salvation Army**

salmon /ˈsæm.ən/ *noun* [C or U] *plural* **salmon** a medium-sized silvery fish which lives in the sea and swims up rivers to produce its eggs. Its pink flesh is valued as a food: *fresh/smoked/tinned salmon* ○ *salmon mousse/fishcakes* ○ *salmon fishing*

salmonella /ˌsæl.məˈnel.ə/ *noun* [U] **1** a type of bacteria that exists in several forms, some of which live in food and make the people who eat it ill: *salmonella poisoning* **2** the illness caused by this bacteria: *an outbreak of salmonella*

salmon-pink /ˌsæm.ənˈpɪŋk/ *adj*, *noun* [U] an orange-pink colour

salon SHOP /ˈsæl.ɒn/ US /səˈlɑːn/ *noun* [C] a shop where you can obtain a particular service, especially connected with beauty or fashion: *a beauty salon* ○ *a hairdressing/hair salon*

salon MEETING /ˈsæl.ɒn/ US /səˈlɑːn/ *noun* [C] LITERARY a meeting of writers, painters, etc., at the house of someone famous or important: *a literary salon in nineteenth-century Paris*

saloon CAR UK /səˈluːn/ *noun* [C] (US **sedan**) a car with seats for four or five people, two or four doors, and a separate section at the back for bags, boxes and cases: *a family saloon* ⊃See picture **Cars and Trucks** on page Centre 13

saloon BAR /səˈluːn/ *noun* [C] a public bar, especially in the past in the western United States

sa'loon ,bar *noun* [C] UK OLD-FASHIONED a bar in a pub or hotel which is more comfortable than the other bars, and in which you sometimes pay a little more for your drink ⊃Compare **public bar**.

salsa SAUCE /ˈsæl.sə/ US /ˈsɑːl-/ *noun* [C or U] a spicy sauce made from tomatoes, onions and CHILLIS (= small spicy red or green seed cases)

salsa MUSIC/DANCE /ˈsæl.sə/ US /ˈsɑːl-/ *noun* [S or U] a type of South American music with a strong beat, or a dance done to this music

salt FOOD /sɒlt/ US /sɑːlt/ *noun* [U] a common white substance found in sea water and in the ground, which is used especially to add flavour to food or to preserve it: *salt and pepper* ○ *Can you pass the salt please?* ○ *Add a **pinch of** (= small amount of) salt to the sauce.*
 • **be the salt of the earth** If you say that someone is the salt of the earth, you mean that they are a very good and honest person.
 • **take *sth* with a pinch of salt** UK (US **take *sth* with a grain of salt**) to not completely believe something that you are told, because you think it is unlikely to be true: *You have to take everything she says with a pinch of salt, she does tend to exaggerate.*

salt /sɒlt/ *verb* [T] to add salt to or put salt on something: *Don't forget to salt the potatoes.* ○ *When it's icy, the city salts the roads to thaw the ice.*

salt /sɒlt/ US /sɑːlt/ *adj* [before n] containing or preserved in salt: *salt water* ○ *salt beef/pork*

salted /ˈsɒl.tɪd/ US /ˈsɑːl.t̬ɪd/ *adj* containing or covered in salt: *salted peanuts* ○ *lightly salted butter*

salty /ˈsɒl.ti/ US /ˈsɑːl.t̬i/ *adj* tasting of salt: *This bacon is too salty for me.* **saltiness** /ˈsɒl.tɪ.nəs/ US /ˈsɑːl.t̬ɪ-/ *noun* [U]

salt CHEMICAL /sɒlt/ US /sɑːlt/ *noun* [C] SPECIALIZED a chemical substance which is a combination of a metal or a BASE with an acid: *Potassium nitrate and potassium chloride are potassium salts.*

SALT /sɒlt/ US /sɑːlt/ *noun* [U] ABBREVIATION FOR Strategic Arms Limitation Talks: a series of discussions between the US and the USSR that took place from 1969 to 1979 aimed to limit the number of nuclear weapons

▲ **salt *sth* away** *phrasal verb* [M] INFORMAL to save something, often money, secretly: *He salted away a fortune over the years and no one ever knew!*

salt-and-pepper /ˌsɒlt.ənˈpep.əʳ/ US /ˌsɑːlt.ənˈpep.ɚ/ *adj* [before n] US FOR **pepper-and-salt**

'salt ,cellar *noun* [C] (US **saltshaker**) a small container for salt, usually with one hole in the top

S

saltpetre *UK, US* **saltpeter** /ˌsɒltˈpiː.təʳ/ [US] /ˈsɑːltˌpiː.t̬ɚ/ *noun* **[U]** a salty-tasting white powder used to preserve meat and also used in the production of explosives and of substances which help plants grow better

ˈsalt ˌwater *noun* **[U]** sea water **saltwater** /ˈsɒltˌwɔː.təʳ/ [US] /ˈsɑːltˌwɔː.t̬ɚ/ *adj* **[before n]** *saltwater fish*

salubrious /səˈluː.bri.əs/ *adj* FORMAL describes a place that is pleasant, clean, and healthy to live in: *He doesn't live in a very salubrious part of town.*

salutary /ˈsæl.jʊ.tri/ [US] /-ter.i/ *adj* FORMAL causing improvement of behaviour or character: *a salutary experience* ○ *a salutary* ***reminder*** *of the dangers of mountain climbing*

salutation /ˌsæl.jʊˈteɪ.ʃᵊn/ *noun* **[C or U]** FORMAL a greeting in words or actions, or the words used at the beginning of a letter or speech

salute [SHOW RESPECT] /səˈluːt/ *verb* **[I or T]** (especially of people in the armed forces) to make a formal sign of respect to someone, especially by raising the right hand to the side of the head: *Whenever you see an officer, you must salute.* ○ *The soldiers saluted the colonel when he arrived.*

salute /səˈluːt/ *noun* **[C]** *The soldier* ***gave*** *a salute and the officer* ***returned*** *it.* ○ *Full military honours and a* ***21-gun*** *salute* (= 21 guns fired at the same time) *marked his funeral.*

• **take the salute** When a person of high rank takes the salute, they stand and watch while soldiers march past saluting them.

salute [PRAISE] /səˈluːt/ *verb* **[T]** FORMAL to honour or express admiration publicly for a person or an achievement: *On this memorable occasion we salute the wonderful work done by the association.* ○ *We salute you* ***for*** *your courage and determination.*

salvage /ˈsæl.vɪdʒ/ *verb* **[T] 1** to save goods from damage or destruction, especially from a ship that has sunk or been damaged or a building that has been damaged by fire or flooding: *gold coins salvaged from a shipwreck* ○ *After the fire, there wasn't much furniture left worth salvaging.* **2** to try to make a bad situation better: *It was a desperate attempt to salvage the* ***situation****.* ○ *After the fraud scandal he had to make great efforts to salvage his* ***reputation****.* **salvage** /ˈsæl.vɪdʒ/ *noun* **[U]** *They mounted a salvage* ***operation*** *after the fire.* **salvageable** /ˈsæl.vɪdʒ.ə.bl/ *adj*: *There is nothing that is salvageable in the building – we have lost everything.*

salvation /sælˈveɪ.ʃᵊn/ *noun* **1 [S or U]** (a way of) being saved from danger, loss or harm: *After the diagnosis, getting to know Mary was his salvation.* ○ *a marriage beyond salvation* **2 [U]** In the Christian religion, salvation of a person or their spirit is the state of being saved from evil and its effects by the death of Jesus Christ on a cross: *The Gospel message is one of personal salvation.*

the Salˌvation ˈArmy *group noun* **[S]** (*UK* INFORMAL **Sally Army**) an international Christian organization whose members have military-style ranks and uniforms, hold meetings with music, and work to help poor people: *a Salvation Army hostel for homeless men and women*

salve /sælv/ [US] /sæv/ *noun* OLD USE **1 [C or U]** an oily substance used to treat an injured, sore or dry place on your body; OINTMENT **2 [S]** something that makes you feel better about a difficult situation

salve /sælv/ [US] /sæv/ *verb* **salve** ***your*** **conscience** to do something so that you feel less guilty: *He salves his conscience by giving money to charity.*

salver /ˈsæl.vəʳ/ [US] /-vɚ/ *noun* **[C]** a large metal plate used to bring food, drinks or letters to people, especially in a formal situation: *a silver salver*

salvo /ˈsæl.vəʊ/ [US] /-voʊ/ *noun* **[C]** *plural* **salvos** or **salvoes** **1** a firing of several guns at the same time, either in a war or in a ceremony: *a salvo of guns/rockets* **2** a sudden loud sound made by many people at the same time: *Every joke the comedian made was greeted by a salvo of laughter from the audience.* **3** the first part of a speech or the first in a series of actions intended to obtain a particular result: *In his* ***opening*** *salvo the speaker fiercely attacked the Government's record on health care.*

SAM /sæm/ *noun* **[C]** ABBREVIATION FOR **surface-to-air missile**

Samaritan /səˈmær.ɪ.tᵊn/ [US] /-ˈmer.ɪ.t̬ᵊn/ *noun* **a good Samaritan** someone who gives help to people who need it

the Saˈmaritans *group noun* **[S]** in the UK, an organization you can telephone if you are very worried about something and need to talk to someone

Samaritan /səˈmær.ɪ.tᵊn/ [US] /-ˈmer.ɪ.t̬ᵊn/ *noun* **[C]** someone who works for the Samaritans: *He works as a Samaritan.*

samba /ˈsæm.bə/ *noun* **[C or U]** an energetic dance originally from Brazil, or music for this dance

same [EXACTLY LIKE] /seɪm/ *adj* **the same** exactly like another or each other: *My twin sister and I have got the same nose.* ○ *She was wearing* ***exactly*** *the same dress* ***as*** *I was.* ○ *Hilary's the same age* ***as*** *me.* ○ *She brought up her children in* ***just*** (= exactly) *the same* ***way*** *her mother did.* ⊃Compare **similar**.

• **by the same token** used to mean that something you are about to say is also true, for the same reasons as what has just been said: *I don't think that prices will go up but, by the same token, I don't see them going down either.*

• **it all amounts/comes to the same thing** used to mean that any of several different possible actions will produce the same result: *It doesn't matter whether you do it first or last – it all amounts to the same thing.*

• **same difference** NOT STANDARD said when you agree that what you said was not exactly correct, but you think the difference is unimportant: *"Did you see that bus?" "Actually it was a coach." "Same difference."*

the same *pronoun* **1** exactly alike: *People say I look* ***just*** *the same* ***as*** *my sister.* ○ *John thinks the same as I do – it's just too expensive.* **2** not changed: *After all these years you look* ***exactly*** *the same – you haven't changed a bit.* ○ *Charles is just the same* ***as*** *always.*

• **all the same** despite what has just been said: *It rained every day of our holiday – but we had a good time all the same.*

• **be all the same to** ***sb*** to not be important to someone which of several things is chosen: *I don't mind whether we eat now or this evening, it's all the same to me.* ○ *I'll have tea –* ***if*** *it's all the same to you.*

• **not the same** not as good: *You can make shortbread with margarine instead of butter, but it isn't the same.*

• **same again** INFORMAL said when you want another drink of the same type as you have just had: *"What are you having, David?" "Same again, please."*

• **same here** INFORMAL said when you agree with what has been said or you have experienced the same thing as they have: *"I thought that film was awful!" "Same here!"*

• **same to you** INFORMAL used as an answer to someone who has greeted or insulted you in order to wish the same thing to them: *"Have a good holiday." "Same to you* (= I hope you have a good holiday too)*!"*

the same *adv* in the same way: *We treat all our children the same.* ○ *I need some time to myself, the same* ***as*** *anybody else.*

sameness /ˈseɪm.nəs/ *noun* **[U]** the quality of being the same as or very similar to something else: *She was struck by the sameness of the houses.*

samey /ˈseɪ.mi/ *adj* UK INFORMAL DISAPPROVING not interesting because of being very similar: *His paintings all look a bit samey.*

same [NOT ANOTHER] /seɪm/ *adj* **[before n]** not another different place, time, situation, person or thing: *My brother and I sleep in* ***the*** *same room.* ○ *Rachel's still going out with* ***the*** *same boyfriend.* ○ ***That (very)*** *same day, he heard he'd passed his exam.* ○ *I would do* ***the*** *same* ***thing*** *again if I had the chance.* ○ *They eat at* ***the*** *same restaurant every week.* ○ *Shall we meet up at* ***the*** *same time tomorrow?*

• **at the same time** despite this: *No-one likes conflict, but at the same time we have to deal with this problem.*

• **be in the same boat** to be in the same unpleasant situation as other people: *She's always complaining that she doesn't have enough money, but we're all in the same boat.*

• **not in the same league** not nearly as good as something or someone else: *Her golf is brilliant – I'm not in the same league.*

• **It's the same old story.** INFORMAL said when talking about a bad situation has happened many times before: *It's the same old story – the rich get richer and the poor get poorer.*

• **one and the same** the same thing or person: *I was amazed to discover that Mary's husband and Jane's son are one and the same (person).*

the same *pronoun* **1** not another different thing or situation: *I'm hopeless at physics, and it's the same with chemistry – I get it all wrong.* **2** HUMOROUS not another different person: *"Was that Marion on the phone?" "The (very) same."*

same-sex /ˌseɪmˈseks/ *adj* A same-sex relationship, marriage, etc. is a romantic relationship between two men, or between two women.

samosa /səˈməʊ.sə/ US /-ˈmoʊ-/ *noun* [C] a small Indian triangular pastry case filled with vegetables or meat and spices and fried

samovar /ˈsæm.ə.vɑːʳ/ US /-vɑːr/ *noun* [C] a large metal container used, especially in Russia, to heat water for tea

sampan /ˈsæm.pæn/ *noun* [C] a small boat with a flat bottom used along the coasts and rivers of China and South East Asia

sample SMALL AMOUNT /ˈsɑːm.pl̩/ US /ˈsæm-/ *noun* [C] **1** a small amount of something that shows you what the rest is or should be like: *a free sample of shampoo* ○ *samples of carpet/curtain material* ○ *Please bring some samples of your work to the interview.* **2** a small amount of a substance that a doctor or scientist collects in order to examine it: *a blood/urine sample* **3** a group of people or things that is chosen out of a larger number and is questioned or tested in order to obtain information about the larger group: *a random sample of voters* ○ *a nationally representative sample of 200 schools*

sample /ˈsɑːm.pl̩/ US /ˈsæm-/ *verb* [T] **1** to taste a small amount of food or drink to decide whether you like it: *As the food looked so good, he decided to sample a little from each dish.* **2** to experience a place or an activity, often for the first time: *So you're going to sample the delights/pleasures of the new restaurant?*

sample MUSIC /ˈsɑːm.pl̩/ US /ˈsæm-/ *verb* [T] SPECIALIZED to record part of a song and use the recording to make a new piece of music: *This song has been heavily sampled.*

sample /ˈsɑːm.pl̩/ US /ˈsæm-/ *noun* [C] a small part of a song which has been recorded and used to make a new piece of music

sampler /ˈsɑːm.pləʳ/ US /ˈsæm.plɚ/ *noun* [C] SPECIALIZED a device which allows you to record parts of other people's songs and then use these parts to create new pieces of music

sampler /ˈsɑːm.pləʳ/ US /ˈsæm.plɚ/ *noun* [C] a piece of cloth with letters, words, pictures etc. stitched on it to show how well you can sew, made especially in the past and often then hung on the wall like a picture

samurai /ˈsæm.ʊ.raɪ/ US /-ʊr.aɪ/ *noun* [C] *plural* **samurai** or **samurais** a member of a military class of high social rank in the 11th to 19th century in Japan: *Samurai warriors*

sanatorium (*plural* **sanatoriums** or **sanatoria**) /ˌsæn.ə-ˈtɔː.ri.əm/ US /-ˈtɔːr.i-/ *noun* [C] (US ALSO **sanitarium**) a special type of hospital, usually in the countryside, where people can have treatment and rest, especially when getting better after a long illness

sanctify /ˈsæŋk.tɪ.faɪ/ *verb* [T] **1** FORMAL to make an event or place holy ⊃See also **sanctity**. **2** to make something socially or officially acceptable: *a practice sanctified by many years of tradition* **sanctification** /ˌsæŋk.tɪ.fɪˈkeɪ.ʃⁿn/ US /-t̬ɪ-/ *noun* [U] FORMAL

sanctimonious /ˌsæŋk.tɪˈməʊ.ni.əs/ US /-moʊ-/ *adj* FORMAL DISAPPROVING acting as if morally better than others: *sanctimonious religious leaders preaching about morality* **sanctimoniously** /ˌsæŋk.tɪˈməʊ.ni.ə.sli/ US /-moʊ-/ *adv* **sanctimoniousness** /ˌsæŋk.tɪˈməʊ.ni.ə.snəs/ US /-moʊ-/ *noun* [U]

sanction APPROVAL /ˈsæŋk.ʃⁿn/ *noun* [U] approval or permission, especially formal or legal: *They tried to get official sanction for the scheme.*

sanction /ˈsæŋk.ʃⁿn/ *verb* [T] to formally permit something: *The government was reluctant to sanction intervention in the crisis.*

sanction ORDER /ˈsæŋk.ʃⁿn/ *noun* **1** [C usually pl] an official order, such as the stopping of trade, which is taken against a country in order to make it obey international law: *Many nations have imposed sanctions on the country because of its attacks on its own people.* ○ *Trade/economic sanctions will only be lifted (= stopped) when the aggressor nation withdraws its troops.* **2** [C] a strong action taken in order to make people obey a law or rule, or a punishment given when they disobey: *Without realistic sanctions, some teachers have difficulty keeping order in the classroom.*

sanctity /ˈsæŋk.tɪ.ti/ US /-t̬ə.t̬i/ *noun* **1** **the sanctity of human life/marriage, etc.** when something is very important and deserves respect **2** [U] the quality of being holy: *the sanctity of a cemetery/tomb*

sanctuary /ˈsæŋk.tʃʊə.ri/ US /-tʃu.er.i/ *noun* **1** [C usually sing; U] protection or a safe place, especially for someone or something being chased or hunted: *Illegal immigrants found/sought/took sanctuary in a local church.* ○ *The chapel became a sanctuary for the refugees.* ○ FIGURATIVE *If I want some peace and quiet, I take sanctuary in my study.* **2** [C] a place where birds or animals can live and be protected, especially from hunters or dangerous conditions: *a wildlife/bird sanctuary* **3** [C] the most holy part of a religious building

sanctum /ˈsæŋk.təm/ *noun* **1** **inner sanctum** a private place or room where someone is never interrupted **2** [C] a holy place

sand SMALL GRAINS /sænd/ *noun* [U] a substance that is found on beaches and in deserts, which is made from very small grains of rock: *a grain of sand* ○ *The children played all day in/on the sand.* ○ *coarse/fine sand* ○ *Mix one part sand to three parts cement.*

sands /sændz/ *plural noun* large flat areas of sand beside the sea: *miles of golden sands*

sandy /ˈsæn.di/ *adj* **1** covered with sand or containing sand: *a lovely sandy beach* ○ *sandy soil* **2** describes hair which is a pale, brownish orange colour

sand MAKE SMOOTH /sænd/ *verb* [T] to make something smooth by rubbing it with something rough, especially SANDPAPER (= strong paper with sand fixed to it): *Sand the door (down) thoroughly before starting to paint.*

sander /ˈsæn.dəʳ/ US /-dɚ/ *noun* [C] (ALSO **sanding machine**) an electrical machine to which a sheet or disc of rough paper is attached with the purpose of rubbing other surfaces in order to make them smoother

sandal /ˈsæn.dⁿl/ *noun* [C] a light shoe, especially worn in warm weather, consisting of a bottom part held onto the foot by straps: *a pair of sandals* ○ *open-toed sandals* ⊃See picture **Clothes** on page Centre 6

sandalwood /ˈsæn.dⁿl.wʊd/ *noun* [U] the hard light-coloured wood of a tree that grows in southeast Asia and Australia, or the pleasant-smelling oil from this tree

sandbag /ˈsænd.bæg/ *noun* [C] a bag filled with sand which is used as a defence against flooding, explosions etc.

sandbag /ˈsænd.bæg/ *verb* [T] **-gg-** *They sandbagged (= put sandbags in front of) the doors to stop the water coming in.*

sandbank /ˈsænd.bæŋk/ *noun* [C] a raised area of sand below the surface of the sea or a river, which you can only see when the water level is low

sandbar /ˈsænd.bɑːʳ/ US /-bɑːr/ *noun* [C] a long raised area of sand below the surface of the water, especially where a river enters the sea, usually formed by moving currents

sandblast /ˈsænd.blɑːst/ US /-blæst/ *verb* [T] to clean or decorate stone, metal or glass with a machine that blows sand out at a high speed

sandcastle /ˈsænd.kɑː.sl̩/ US /-ˌkæs.l̩/ *noun* [C] a model castle of sand, usually made by children playing on the beach

'sand ˌdune *noun* [C] a hill of sand made by the wind on the coast or in a desert

the sandman /ðəˈsænd.mæn/ *noun* [S] *CHILD'S WORD* an imaginary man who sprinkles sand which makes children rub their eyes and fall asleep

sandpail /ˈsænd.peɪl/ *noun* [C] *US FOR* **bucket**

sandpaper /ˈsænd,peɪ.pəʳ/ [US] /-pɚ/ *noun* [U] strong paper with sand or a similar rough substance stuck to one side, used for rubbing a surface in order to make it smoother: *coarse/fine sandpaper* **sandpaper** /ˈsænd-ˌpeɪ.pəʳ/ [US] /-pɚ/ *verb* [T]

sandpit *UK* /ˈsænd.pɪt/ *noun* [C] (*US* **sandbox**) a hole in the ground, or a box, filled with sand in which children can play

sandstone /ˈsænd.stəʊn/ [US] /-stoʊn/ *noun* [U] a type of rock formed from sand

sandstorm /ˈsænd.stɔːm/ [US] /-stɔːrm/ *noun* [C] a strong wind in a desert carrying a large amount of sand

ˈsand ˌtrap *noun* [C] *US* a **bunker** GOLF

sandwich /ˈsænd.wɪdʒ/ [US] /-wɪtʃ/ *noun* [C] **1** two pieces of bread, sometimes spread with butter or MARGARINE, and with some other usually cold food between them: *a tuna/ham sandwich* ○ *a toasted sandwich* ○ *a sandwich bar/box* ○ *sandwich fillings* **2** a **sandwich (cake)**

sandwich /ˈsæn.wɪdʒ/ /-wɪtʃ/ *verb*

PHRASAL VERBS WITH **sandwich**

▲ **sandwich *sb/sth* between *sb/sth*** *phrasal verb* [usually passive] *INFORMAL* If you are sandwiched between two people or things, you are in a small space between them: *On the train I was sandwiched between two very large men.*

▲ **sandwich *sth* together** *phrasal verb* [M] to put a layer of something between two things which sticks them together: *I sandwiched the cakes together **with** chocolate butter cream.*

ˈsandwich ˌbar *noun* [C] *UK* a small shop where you can buy sandwiches, especially to eat during the working day

ˈsandwich ˌboard *noun* [C] a pair of connected boards which a person hangs over their shoulders and walks around with in public places to advertise something

ˈsandwich (ˌcake) *noun* [C] *UK* a cake consisting of two thin round layers with a filling such as cream between them: *a jam and cream sandwich* ○ *a Victoria sandwich*

ˈsandwich ˌcourse *noun* [C] *UK* a college course consisting of periods of study with periods of work between them so that students get practical experience

sandy /ˈsæn.di/ *adj* ➲See at **sand** SMALL GRAINS.

sane /seɪn/ *adj* having a healthy mind and not mentally ill, or showing good judgment and understanding: *In the doctor's opinion he was sane at the time of the murder.* ○ *HUMOROUS The only thing which **keeps** me sane after a hard day in the office is jogging!* ○ *It was a sane* (= sensible) *decision and one we all respected.*

sanity /ˈsæn.ɪ.ti/ [US] /-ə.t̬i/ *noun* [U] *He'd been behaving so strangely that they began to **doubt/question** his sanity.* ○ *Maybe Jenny can **bring some** sanity **into*** (= think and act with good judgment in) *this crazy situation.* ○ *to keep/preserve/retain your sanity*

sang /sæŋ/ *past simple of* **sing**

sangfroid /ˌsɒ̃ˈfwɑː/ [US] /ˌsɑːŋ-/ *noun* [U] *FORMAL* the ability to stay calm in a difficult or dangerous situation

sangria /sæŋˈgriː.ə/ [US] /sɑːn-/ *noun* [U] a cold Spanish drink made from red wine, fruit juice, fizzy water, and sometimes brandy

sanguine /ˈsæŋ.gwɪn/ *adj FORMAL* (of someone or their character) positive and hopeful: *They are less sanguine **about** the prospects for peace.* ➲See also **optimistic** at **optimism**.

sanitarium /ˌsæn.ɪˈteə.ri.əm/ [US] /-ˈter.i-/ *noun* [C] *plural* **sanitariums** or **sanitaria** *US FOR* **sanatorium**

sanitary /ˈsæn.ɪ.tri/ [US] /-ter.i/ *adj* **1** clean and not dangerous for the health, or protecting health by the removal of dirt and waste, especially human waste: *Cholera thrives in poor sanitary **conditions**.* ○ *There were only very basic sanitary facilities on the site.* ○ *His kitchen didn't look very sanitary* (= clean). **2** describes the items which are used by women during their period: *sanitary protection* ○ *disposable sanitary products*

ˈsanitary ˌfittings *UK plural noun* (*US* **bathroom fittings**) the items which are in a bathroom, such as a toilet, bath, etc.

ˈsanitary ˌtowel *UK noun* [C] (*US* **sanitary napkin,** *AUS* **sanitary pad**) a piece of soft, absorbent material worn by a woman between her legs during her period

sanitation /ˌsæn.ɪˈteɪ.ʃən/ *noun* [U] the systems for taking dirty water and other waste products away from buildings in order to protect people's health: *Many illnesses in these temporary refugee camps are the result of inadequate sanitation.*

saniˈtation ˌworker *noun* [C] *US FOR* **dustman**

sanitize [CLEAN], *UK USUALLY* **-ise** /ˈsæn.ɪ.taɪz/ *verb* [T] *MAINLY US* to make something completely clean and free from bacteria **sanitization**, *UK USUALLY* **-isation** /ˌsæn.ɪ.taɪˈzeɪ.ʃən/ *noun* [U]

sanitize [CHANGE], *UK USUALLY* **-ise** /ˈsæn.ɪ.taɪz/ *verb* [T] *DISAPPROVING* to change something in order to make it less strongly expressed, less harmful or less offensive: *The military wants to allow only a sanitized **report/version** of the incident to become public.* **sanitization**, *UK USUALLY* **-isation** /ˌsæn.ɪ.taɪˈzeɪ.ʃən/ *noun* [U]

sanity /ˈsæn.ɪ.ti/ [US] /-ə.t̬i/ *noun* [U] ➲See at **sane**.

sank /sæŋk/ *past simple of* **sink**

Santa Claus /ˈsæn.tə,klɔːz/ [US] /-t̬ə,klɑːz/ *noun* [S] (*INFORMAL* **Santa**) *CHILD'S WORD* the imaginary old man with long white hair and a beard and a red coat who is believed by children to bring them presents at Christmas, or a person who dresses as this character for children: *Go to sleep quickly or Santa Claus won't come!*

Santa's grotto /ˌsæn.təzˈgrɒt.əʊ/ [US] /-t̬əzˈgrɑː.t̬oʊ/ *noun* [S] a place where children can receive presents from a person dressed as Santa Claus

sap [WEAKEN] /sæp/ *verb* [T] **-pp-** to weaken someone or take away strength or an important quality from someone, especially over a long period of time: *Constant criticism saps you **of** your confidence.* ○ *Looking after her dying mother had sapped all her energy.* **sapping** /ˈsæp.ɪŋ/ *adj*: *sapping heat/humidity*

sap [LIQUID] /sæp/ *noun* [U] the liquid that carries food to all parts of a plant: *Maple syrup is obtained from the sap of the sugar maple tree.*

• **the sap is rising** *HUMOROUS* said to describe a feeling of increased interest in and energy for romance and sex

sap [PERSON] /sæp/ *noun* [C] *MAINLY US INFORMAL* a stupid person who can easily be tricked or persuaded to do something: *He's a sap **for*** (= He can easily be persuaded to buy) *any new machine.*

sappy /ˈsæp.i/ *adj US INFORMAL* describes something that is extremely emotional in an embarrassing way: *It's a sappy film – take some tissues when you see it.*

sapling /ˈsæp.lɪŋ/ *noun* [C] a young tree

Sapphic /ˈsæf.ɪk/ *adj LITERARY* relating to LESBIANS (= women who are sexually attracted to other women): *Sapphic love/passion*

sapphire /ˈsæf.aɪəʳ/ [US] /-aɪr/ *noun* [C or U] a transparent, usually bright blue, precious stone: *a sapphire ring/bracelet*

ˌsapphire (ˈblue) *adj, noun* [U] bright blue

sarcasm /ˈsɑː.kæz.əm/ [US] /ˈsɑːr-/ *noun* [U] the use of remarks which clearly mean the opposite of what they say, and which are made in order to hurt someone's feelings or to criticize something in an amusing way: *"You have been working hard," he said with **heavy** sarcasm, as he looked at the empty page.* ➲Compare **irony** FIGURATIVE SPEECH.

• **Sarcasm is the lowest form of wit/humour.** *SAYING* said to mean that sarcasm is very unkind

sarcastic /sɑːˈkæs.tɪk/ [US] /sɑːr-/ *adj* (*UK INFORMAL* **sarky**) using sarcasm: *a sarcastic comment/remark* ○ *Are you being sarcastic?* **sarcastically** /sɑːˈkæs.tɪ.kli/ [US] /sɑːr-/ *adv*: *"Thanks so much for your help," Tim said sarcastically.*

sarcoma /sɑːˈkəʊ.mə/ [US] /sɑːrˈkoʊ-/ *noun* [C or U] *plural* **sarcomas** or *FORMAL* **sarcomata** *SPECIALIZED* a type of cancer, or a cancerous lump, in the bones, muscles or joints

sarcophagus /sɑːˈkɒf.ə.gəs/ [US] /sɑːrˈkɑː.fə-/ *noun* [C] *plural* **sarcophaguses** or **sarcophagi** a stone coffin, which was used in ancient times and is often decorated

sardine /sɑːˈdiːn/ ⓤ /sɑːr-/ noun [C] a small sea fish which can be eaten: *a tin of sardines*

• **packed/squashed like sardines** If people are packed/squashed like sardines, they are positioned very close together so that they cannot move: *We were squashed like sardines in the rush-hour train going back to Edinburgh.*

sardonic /sɑːˈdɒn.ɪk/ ⓤ /sɑːrˈdɑː.nɪk/ adj showing a lack of respect in a humorous but unkind way, often because you think that you are too important to consider or discuss a matter: *a sardonic smile/look/comment* **sardonically** /sɑːˈdɒn.ɪ.kli/ ⓤ /sɑːrˈdɑː.nɪ-/ adv

sarge /sɑːdʒ/ ⓤ /sɑːrdʒ/ noun [S] INFORMAL FOR **sergeant**: [as form of address] *I'll be there straight away, sarge.*

sari, **saree** /ˈsɑː.ri/ ⓤ /ˈsɑːr.i/ noun [C] a dress, worn especially by Indian and Pakistani women, consisting of a very long piece of thin cloth wrapped around the body

sarky /ˈsɑː.ki/ ⓤ /ˈsɑːr-/ adj UK INFORMAL FOR **sarcastic**, see at **sarcasm**

sarnie /ˈsɑː.ni/ ⓤ /ˈsɑːr-/ noun [C] UK INFORMAL a **sandwich**

sarong /səˈrɒŋ/ ⓤ /-ˈrɑːŋ/ noun [C] a long piece of thin cloth which is worn wrapped around the waist ⊃See picture **Clothes** on page Centre 6

sarsaparilla /ˌsɑː.spəˈrɪl.ə/ ⓤ /ˌsæs.pə-/ noun [U] a plant with large roots and heart-shaped leaves which climbs up walls, or a drink which is flavoured with the root of this plant

sartorial /sɑːˈtɔː.ri.əl/ ⓤ /sɑːrˈtɔːr.i-/ adj [before n] FORMAL relating to the making of clothes, usually men's clothes, or to a way of dressing: *sartorial elegance* **sartorially** /sɑːˈtɔː.ri.ˈl.i/ ⓤ /sɑːrˈtɔːr.i-/ adv

the SAS /ˌðiˌes.eɪˈes/ group noun [S] ABBREVIATION FOR the Special Air Service: a part of the British Army that has been specially trained for secret or particularly dangerous military activities

SASE /ˌes.eɪˌesˈiː/ noun [C] (UK **sae**) US ABBREVIATION FOR self-addressed stamped envelope: an envelope with a stamp and your name and address on it, which you send inside another envelope to an organization when you want a reply: *Please enclose an SASE with your application.* ⊃Compare **sae**.

sash CLOTHING /sæʃ/ noun [C] a long narrow piece of cloth worn round the waist and fastened at the back, or a strip of cloth worn over the shoulder, which is often worn with a uniform at official ceremonies

sash WINDOW /sæʃ/ noun [C] a frame with a piece of glass in it which is used to make windows and doors

sashay /ˈsæʃ.eɪ/ ⓤ /-ˈ-/ verb [I + adv or prep] to walk confidently while moving your hips from side to side in a way that attracts attention: *She sashayed down the stairs and into the hall.*

sashimi /sæʃˈiː.mi/ noun [U] a Japanese dish consisting of small pieces of raw fish which are eaten with SOY SAUCE

sash **window** noun [C] a window which has two frames fixed one above the other that open by being moved up and down

Sasquatch /ˈsæs.kwɒtʃ/ ⓤ /-kwɑːtʃ/ noun [C] a **Bigfoot**

sass /sæs/ noun [U] MAINLY US INFORMAL talk or behaviour which is rude and lacking respect: *You just sit there and shut up – I don't want to hear any more of your sass.*

sass /sæs/ verb [T] MAINLY US INFORMAL to talk to someone in a rude way: *Don't you sass your father like that!*

sassy /ˈsæs.i/ adj MAINLY US INFORMAL **1** rude and lacking respect: *a sassy young girl* **2** fashionable, attractive or confident: *a sassy little black dress*

Sassenach /ˈsæs.ə.næk/ noun [C] SCOTTISH ENGLISH MAINLY DISAPPROVING an English person

sat SIT /sæt/ past simple and past participle of **sit**

Sat DAY OF THE WEEK WRITTEN ABBREVIATION FOR **Saturday**

SAT UK EDUCATION /ˌes.eɪˈtiː/ noun [C] ABBREVIATION FOR Standard Assessment Task: a test taken by children in England and Wales at the ages of 7, 11, 14, and 16 to find out the level of the NATIONAL CURRICULUM that they have reached: *SATs results*

SAT US EDUCATION /ˌes.eɪˈtiː/ noun [C] TRADEMARK ABBREVIATION FOR Scholastic Aptitude Test: a test taken in the US to measure students' abilities before entering college

Satan /ˈseɪ.tᵊn/ noun [U] FORMAL the name used by Christians and Jews for the DEVIL (= a powerful evil force and the enemy of God)

satanic /səˈtæn.ɪk/ adj **1** connected with worshipping Satan: *a satanic cult/practice/rite* **2** very evil: *He gave a satanic smile.*

Satanism /ˈseɪ.tᵊn.ɪ.zᵊm/ noun [U] the worship of Satan

Satanist /ˈseɪ.tᵊn.ɪst/ noun [C] a person who worships Satan

satchel /ˈsætʃ.ᵊl/ noun [C] a rectangular leather bag with a long strap, used especially in the past by children for carrying books to school

sated /ˈseɪ.tɪd/ ⓤ /-t̬ɪd/ adj FORMAL having had more of something than you can easily have at one time: *sated with drink/food*

satellite /ˈsæt.ᵊl.aɪt/ ⓤ /ˈsæt̬-/ noun [C] **1** an artificial object sent up into space to travel round the earth, used for collecting information or communicating by radio, television, etc: *The World Cup was transmitted around the world by satellite.* ○ *a spy/weather satellite* ○ *satellite television/TV* **2** a natural object moving round a larger object in space: *The moon is the satellite of the Earth.*

satellite dish noun [C] a round AERIAL for receiving television and radio signals broadcast from SATELLITES

satellite (state) noun [C] a country controlled by or dependent on a more powerful country ⊃See also **client state**.

sati /ˈsɑː.tiː/ noun [U] **suttee**

satiate /ˈseɪ.ʃi.eɪt/ verb [T often passive] FORMAL to completely satisfy yourself or a need, especially with food or pleasure, so that you could not have any more: *He drank greedily until his thirst was satiated.*

satin /ˈsæt.ɪn/ ⓤ /ˈsæt̬.ᵊn/ noun [U] a type of cloth, sometimes made of silk, which is smooth and shiny on one side but not on the other: *a cream satin dress*

satiny /ˈsæt.ɪ.ni/ ⓤ /ˈsæt̬.ᵊn.i/ adj smooth and soft

satin (finish) noun [S or U] a type of paint which is slightly shiny when it dries

satire /ˈsæt.aɪə/ ⓤ /-aɪr/ noun [C or U] a way of criticizing people or ideas in a humorous way, or a piece of writing or play which uses this style: *political satire* ○ *Her play was a biting/cruel satire on life in the 80s.* **satirical** /səˈtɪr.ɪ.kᵊl/ adj: *satirical cartoons/magazines*

satirist /ˈsæt.ɪ.rɪst/ ⓤ /ˈsæt̬.ɚ.ɪst/ noun [C] a person who writes satire

satirize, UK USUALLY -ise /ˈsæt.ɪ.raɪz/ ⓤ /ˈsæt̬.ə.raɪz/ verb [T] to use satire to show that people or ideas have bad qualities or are wrong

satisfaction /ˌsæt.ɪsˈfæk.ʃᵊn/ ⓤ /ˌsæt̬-/ noun **1** [C or U] a pleasant feeling which you get when you receive something you wanted, or when you have done something you wanted to do: *She looked at the finished painting with satisfaction.* ○ *She derived/obtained great satisfaction from/out of helping other people.* ○ *For me, job satisfaction is more important than the money.* ○ *She had the satisfaction of knowing that she'd done everything she could.* **2** [U] FORMAL when your complaint or problem is dealt with in a way you consider acceptable: *You've sold me a faulty product and I demand satisfaction (= you must return my money or give me a new product).* **3** [U] fulfilment of a need or desire: *the satisfaction of one's sexual desires*

• **to sb's satisfaction 1** in a way that a particular person can believe or accept: *The boy explained to the satisfaction of the court why he had lied.* **2** in a way that a particular person feels pleased or satisfied with: *He won't get paid until he completes the job to my satisfaction.*

satisfactory /ˌsæt.ɪsˈfæk.tᵊr.i/ ⓤ /ˌsæt̬.ɪsˈfæk.tɚ-/ adj good or good enough for a particular need or purpose: *The teachers seem to think his work is satisfactory.* ○ *We hope very much to find a satisfactory solution to the problem.* ○ *The result of the match was highly satisfactory (= very pleasing).* **satisfactorily** /ˌsæt.ɪsˈfæk.tᵊr.ᵊl.i/ ⓤ /ˌsæt̬.ɪsˈfæk.tɚ-/ adv: *I'm sure these problems can be satisfactorily resolved.*

S

satisfy [WANTING] /ˈsæt.ɪs.faɪ/ [US] /ˈsæt̬-/ *verb* [T] **1** to please someone by giving them what they want or need: *They have 31 flavours of ice-cream – enough to satisfy everyone!* ○ *Come on, satisfy my* ***curiosity*** (= tell me what I want to know), *what happened last night?* **2 satisfy conditions/needs/requirements** to have or provide something that is needed or wanted: *She satisfies all the requirements for the job.* ○ *There are three main conditions you must satisfy if you wish to be a member of the club.*

satisfied /ˈsæt.ɪs.faɪd/ [US] /ˈsæt̬-/ *adj* pleased because you have got what you wanted, or because something has happened in the way that you wanted: *Some people are never satisfied!* ○ *She finished her meal and gave a satisfied smile.* ○ *Are you satisfied* ***with*** *the new arrangement?*

satisfying /ˈsæt.ɪs.faɪ.ɪŋ/ [US] /ˈsæt̬-/ *adj* making you feel pleased by providing what you need or want: *a satisfying meal/result* ○ *It's an immensely satisfying job.* ○ ***It*** *is very satisfying* ***to*** *know that the project was a success.*

satisfy [BELIEVING] /ˈsæt.ɪs.faɪ/ [US] /ˈsæt̬-/ *verb* [T] to make someone believe that something is true: *His explanation satisfied the court.* ○ [R + (that)] *I satisfied myself* ***(that)*** *I had locked the door.* ○ *FORMAL The authorities were satisfied* ***of*** (= they accepted) *the seriousness of his situation.*

satisfied /ˈsæt.ɪs.faɪd/ [US] /ˈsæt̬-/ *adj* [after v; + (that)] If you are satisfied that something is true, you believe it: *The judge was satisfied* ***(that)*** *she was telling the truth.*

satsuma /ˌsætˈsuː.mə/ *noun* [C] a fruit like a small orange with skin that can be removed easily ➲See picture **Fruit** on page Centre 1

saturate [MAKE WET] /ˈsæt.jʊ.reɪt/ [US] /-jʊr.eɪt/ *verb* [T often passive] to make something or someone completely wet: *The grass had been saturated by overnight rain.* ○ *He had cut his leg badly, and his trousers were saturated* ***with/in*** *blood.*

saturated /ˈsæt.jʊ.reɪ.tɪd/ [US] /-jʊr.eɪ.t̬ɪd/ *adj* completely wet: *It's pouring down outside – I'm absolutely saturated!*

saturate [FILL] /ˈsæt.jʊ.reɪt/ [US] /-jʊr.eɪt/ *verb* [T] **1** to fill a thing or place completely so that no more can be added: *The police saturated* (= A large number of police officers were sent into) *the area in an attempt to find the missing child.* **2 saturate the market** to provide too much of a product so that there is more of this product available than there are people who want to buy it: *Since the US market has now been saturated, drug dealers are looking to Europe.* **saturation** /ˌsæt.jʊˈreɪ.ʃən/ [US] /-jʊr-/ *noun* [U] *market saturation*

saturate [FAT] /ˈsæt.jʊ.rət/ [US] /-jʊr-/ *noun* [C usually pl; U] **saturated fat** ➲Compare **polyunsaturate**.

ˌsaturated ˈfat *noun* [C or U] (*ALSO* **saturate**) a type of fat found in meat, eggs, milk, cheese, etc, which is thought to be bad for your health: *Butter and cream contain a lot of saturated fats.* ➲See also **polyunsaturated**.

ˌsaturated soˈlution *noun* [C] *SPECIALIZED* in chemistry, a SOLUTION (= a liquid containing a solid) in which as much solid as possible is dissolved

saturˈation ˌbombing *noun* [U] extremely heavy bombing

saturˈation ˌpoint *noun* **reach saturation point** to reach a stage where no more can be added, contained or accepted: *Demand for cars in the developed world will have reached saturation point within 20 years.*

Saturday /ˈsæt.ə.deɪ/ [US] /ˈsæt̬.ɚ-/ *noun* [C or U] (*WRITTEN ABBREVIATION* **Sat**) the day of the week after Friday and before Sunday: *He's leaving* ***on*** *Saturday.* ○ *Most football matches are played* ***on*** *Saturdays.* ○ *Joel was born* ***on a*** *Saturday.* ○ *last/next Saturday* ○ *I can't come* ***this*** *Saturday* (= the first one from now), *but I am free (UK) Saturday* ***week*** (= the second one from now). ○ *Saturday morning/afternoon/evening*

ˌSaturday night ˈspecial *noun* [C] *US INFORMAL* any small gun that is cheap, often bought illegally and used by criminals

Saturn /ˈsæt.ən/ [US] /ˈsæt̬.ɚn/ *noun* [S] the planet sixth in order of distance from the Sun, after Jupiter and before Uranus

Saturnalia /ˌsæt.əˈneɪ.li.ə/ [US] /ˌsæt̬.ɚ-/ *noun* [C] *plural* **Saturnalia** or **Saturnalias** **1** an ancient Roman celebration which happened on December 19th **2** *LITERARY* a party where people behave in an uncontrolled way

saturnine /ˈsæt.ə.naɪn/ [US] /ˈsæt̬.ɚ-/ *adj LITERARY* serious and unfriendly: *a saturnine character/look/frown*

satyr /ˈsæt.əʳ/ [US] /ˈsæt̬.ɚ/ *noun* [C] a god in Greek literature who is half man and half goat

sauce [THICK LIQUID] /sɔːs/ [US] /sɑːs/ *noun* **1** [C or U] a thick liquid eaten with food to add flavour: *a savoury/sweet sauce* ○ *tomato sauce* **2** [U] *US SLANG* alcohol: *Gran's been* ***on the*** *sauce again – she's passed out in the den.*

● **What's sauce for the goose is sauce for the gander.** *OLD-FASHIONED SAYING* said to emphasize that if one person is allowed to do something or to behave in a particular way, then another person must be allowed to do that thing or behave in that way, too

sauce [RUDENESS] /sɔːs/ [US] /sɑːs/ *noun* [U] *OLD-FASHIONED* remarks which are rude or which lack respect: *That's enough of your sauce, my girl!*

saucy /ˈsɔː.si/ [US] /ˈsɑː-/ *adj OLD-FASHIONED* rude and lacking respect, or referring to sex, especially in a humorous way: *a saucy remark/manner/look* ○ *a saucy postcard/magazine*

saucepan /ˈsɔː.spən/ [US] /ˈsɑː-/ *noun* [C] a deep round pan with straight sides, usually with a handle and a lid, used for cooking things over heat

saucer /ˈsɔː.səʳ/ [US] /ˈsɑː.sɚ/ *noun* [C] a small curved plate which you put a cup on: *a cup and saucer* ○ *She gave the cat a saucer* ***of*** *milk* (= a small amount of milk on a saucer).

sauerkraut /ˈsaʊə.kraʊt/ [US] /ˈsaʊr-/ *noun* [U] cabbage which has been cut into small pieces and preserved in vinegar

sauna /ˈsɔː.nə/ [US] /ˈsaʊ-/ *noun* [C] (a period of time spent in) a room or small building, often with wood fixed to the walls, which is heated to a high temperature, usually with steam: *have/go for/take a sauna*

saunter /ˈsɔːn.təʳ/ [US] /ˈsɑːn.t̬ɚ/ *verb* [I usually + adv or prep] to walk in a slow and relaxed way, often in no particular direction: *He sauntered* ***by,*** *looking very pleased with himself.* **saunter** /ˈsɔːn.təʳ/ [US] /ˈsɑːn.t̬ɚ/ *noun* [S]

sausage /ˈsɒs.ɪdʒ/ [US] /ˈsɑː.sɪdʒ/ *noun* [C or U] a thin tube-like case containing meat which has been cut into very small pieces and mixed with spices: *fried/grilled pork sausages* ○ *half a pound of garlic sausage*

● **not a sausage** *UK OLD-FASHIONED HUMOROUS* nothing: *"Did you find anything out?" "No, not a sausage."*

ˈsausage ˌdog *noun* [C] *UK INFORMAL* a DACHSHUND (= a small dog with a long body and short legs)

ˈsausage maˌchine *noun* [C] *UK DISAPPROVING* a system that deals with things or people as if they are all the same: *He claimed that the school was like a sausage machine, only interested in exam results.*

ˈsausage ˌmeat *noun* [U] the meat mixture used to make sausages

ˌsausage ˈroll *noun* [C] *UK* a tube of pastry filled with SAUSAGE MEAT

sauté /ˈsəʊ.teɪ/ /ˈsɔː-/ [US] /soʊˈteɪ/ /ˈsɔː-/ *verb* [T] to cook food in oil or fat over heat, usually until it is brown

sauté /ˈsəʊ.teɪ/ [US] /soʊˈteɪ/ *adj* [before n] *sauté potatoes*

savage /ˈsæv.ɪdʒ/ *adj* **1** extremely violent, wild or fierce: *a savage dog/beast* ○ *a brutal and savage* ***attack*** **2** very serious or cruel: *savage criticism* **3** very large and severe: *savage* ***cuts*** *in education spending*

savage /ˈsæv.ɪdʒ/ *verb* [T] If an animal savages someone, it attacks them violently and badly hurts them: *The child was savaged by a dog.*

savage /ˈsæv.ɪdʒ/ *noun* [C] *OFFENSIVE* a person whose way of life is at a very early stage of development: *Twelve thousand years ago, our ancestors were primitive savages living in caves.*

savagely /ˈsæv.ɪdʒ.li/ *adv* in a violent, cruel or very severe way

savagery /ˈsæv.ɪdʒ.ri/ *noun* [C or U] (acts of) violent cruelty

savannah, **savanna** /səˈvæn.ə/ *noun* [C or U] a large flat area of land covered with grass, usually with few trees, which is found in hot countries, especially in Africa

S

save [MAKE SAFE] /seɪv/ *verb* [T] to stop someone or something from being killed, injured or destroyed: *Wearing seat belts has saved many lives.* ○ *He fell in the river but his friend saved him **from** drown**ing**.* ○ *He had to borrow money to save his business.* ○ *He was desperately trying to save their failing marriage.* ○ *The former tennis champion was now serving to save the match* (= to win the next point so that the other player did not win the competition).

• **save *sb's* bacon/neck** *INFORMAL* to help someone avoid getting into trouble

• **save the day** to do something that prevents a likely defeat or failure: *Newcastle seemed to be heading for disaster until a late goal saved the day.*

• **can't do *sth* to save *your* life** *INFORMAL* said to mean that you are extremely bad at doing something: *I can't draw to save my life.*

• **save *sb's* life 1** to stop someone from being killed **2** *INFORMAL* to help someone escape from a difficult or unpleasant situation: *Thanks for helping me with that report – you saved my life!*

• **save *your* own skin/hide** *INFORMAL* to protect yourself from danger or difficulty, without trying to help other people

save [KEEP] /seɪv/ *verb* **1** [I or T] to keep something, especially money, for use in the future: *Tom's been saving his pocket money every week.* ○ *We're saving (up) **for** a new car.* ○ *I save all my old letters in case I want to read them again.* ○ *Save me a place at your table, will you?* **2** [T] to put information on a computer onto a computer disk

saver /ˈseɪ.vəʳ/ [US] /-vɚ/ *noun* [C] a person who saves money regularly

savings /ˈseɪ.vɪŋz/ *plural noun* the money which you keep in an account in a bank or similar financial organization: *He spent all his savings on an expensive car.*

save [NOT WASTE] /seɪv/ *verb* [I or T] to prevent time, money or effort being wasted or spent: *You'll save time if you take the car.* ○ [+ two objects] *Thanks for your help – it saved me a lot of work.* ○ [+ v-ing] *I'll lend you a bag for your trip – it'll save you buy**ing** one specially.* ○ *INFORMAL Can you save **it** for later* (= tell me your news later when I am less busy)*?*

• **save *your* breath** *INFORMAL* used to say that it is not worth talking to someone because they will not listen to you: *I don't know why I bother speaking to him – I might as well save my breath.*

-saver /-seɪ.vəʳ/ [US] /-vɚ/ *suffix* something that makes it possible for you to use less of the stated thing: *A washing machine is a great time-saver.* ○ *a money/energy saver*

-saving /-seɪ.vɪŋ/ *suffix* making it possible to use less of the stated thing: *a time-saving recipe* ○ *a money-saving offer* ○ *a labour-saving device*

saving /ˈseɪ.vɪŋ/ *noun* [C] an amount of money that you do not need to spend: *You can **make** huge savings* (= save a lot of money) *by buying food in bulk.*

save [SPORT] /seɪv/ *verb* [T] in football and similar games, to stop the ball from going into the goal when a player on the other team has kicked or hit it **save** /seɪv/ *noun* [C] *The goalkeeper **made** a great save in the last minute of the match.*

save [EXCEPT] /seɪv/ *prep* (*ALSO* **save for**) *FORMAL OR OLD-FASHIONED* but or except for: *They found all the lost documents save one.*

PHRASAL VERBS WITH **save** ▼

▲ **save on *sth*** *phrasal verb* to avoid using something so that you do not have to pay for it: *It was a warm winter, so we saved on electricity.*

▲ **save *(sth)* up** *phrasal verb* [M] to keep money so that you can buy something with it in the future: *It took me ages to save up enough money to go travelling.* ○ *She's saving up **for** a new bike.*

ˌsaving ˈgrace *noun* [S] a good quality that something or someone has which stops them from being completely bad: *The film's **(only/one)** saving grace is the excellent photography.*

ˈsavings acˌcount *noun* [C] an account in a bank or similar financial organization which earns interest ➲See also **current account**.

ˌsavings and ˈloan asˌsociation *noun* [C] *US FOR* **building society**

ˈsavings ˌbank *noun* [C] a bank which only offers accounts where your money earns interest

saviour /ˈseɪ.vjəʳ/ [US] /-vjɚ/ *noun* [C] **1** *UK* (*US* **savior**) a person who saves someone from danger or harm **2** **the/our Saviour** in the Christian religion, another word for **Jesus (Christ)**

savoir-faire /ˌsæv.wɑːˈfeəʳ/ [US] /-ˈfer/ *noun* [U] *FORMAL* the ability to do and say the right thing in any social situation: *She possesses **great** savoir-faire.*

savour *UK, US* **savor** /ˈseɪ.vəʳ/ [US] /-vɚ/ *verb* [T] to enjoy food or an experience slowly, in order to appreciate it as much as possible: *It was the first chocolate he'd tasted for over a year, so he savoured every mouthful.*

savour /ˈseɪ.vəʳ/ [US] /-vɚ/ *noun* [S or U] *LITERARY* **1** *UK* (*US* **savor**) pleasure and interest: *She felt that life had lost most of its savour.* **2** a smell or taste, especially a pleasant one

▲ **savour of *sth*** *phrasal verb* [never passive] *FORMAL* to possess particular characteristics or qualities that make people think of something, especially something unpleasant: *His behaviour does rather savour of hypocrisy.*

savoury *UK, US* **savory** /ˈseɪ.vᵊr.i/ [US] /-vɚ-/ *adj* **1** Savoury food is salty or spicy and not sweet in taste: *savoury dumplings/pancakes* **2** If you say that something is not savoury, you mean that it is not pleasant or socially acceptable: *That hotel doesn't have a very savoury reputation.*

savoy (cabbage) /səˌvɔɪˈkæb.ɪdʒ/ *noun* [C] a type of cabbage with curly leaves

savvy /ˈsæv.i/ *noun* [U] *INFORMAL* practical knowledge and ability: *She hasn't got much savvy.* ○ *business/political savvy*

saw [SEE] /sɔː/ [US] /sɑː/ *past simple of* **see**

saw [TOOL] /sɔː/ [US] /sɑː/ *noun* [C] a tool with a long or round blade and a row of sharp points along one edge, which is used for cutting hard materials, such as wood or metal: *a hand/power/chain/circular saw* ➲See also **fretsaw**; **hacksaw**; **jigsaw**.

saw /sɔː/ [US] /sɑː/ *verb* **sawed**, **sawn** or *MAINLY US* **sawed** **1** [I or T] to cut wood or other hard material using a saw: *They sawed the door in half.* ○ *He sawed through the pipe.* **2** [I + adv or prep] to move something backwards and forwards as if using a saw: *He was sawing **away** at his violin, making a terrible noise!*

PHRASAL VERBS WITH **saw** ▼

▲ **saw *sth* down** *phrasal verb* [M] to make something fall to the ground by cutting it with a saw

▲ **saw *sth* off** *phrasal verb* [M] to remove something by cutting it with a saw: *She sawed off the dead branches of the tree.*

▲ **saw *sth* up** *phrasal verb* [M] to cut something into smaller pieces using a saw: *I'll saw the logs up into smaller pieces.*

sawdust /ˈsɔː.dʌst/ [US] /ˈsɑː-/ *noun* [U] the dust and small pieces of wood which are produced when you cut wood with a saw

sawmill /ˈsɔː.mɪl/ [US] /ˈsɑː-/ *noun* [C] a factory where trees are cut up into pieces with machines

sawn-off shotgun *UK* /ˌsɔːn.ɒfˈʃɒt.gʌn/ [US] /ˌsɑːn.ɑːf-ˈʃɑːt-/ *noun* [C] (*US* **sawed-off shotgun**) a gun with most of the barrel cut off

sax /sæks/ *noun* [C] *INFORMAL FOR* **saxophone**: *alto/tenor sax* ○ *a sax player*

Saxon /ˈsæk.sᵊn/ *adj* relating to or belonging to a people who were originally from Germany and who came to live in Britain in the fifth and sixth centuries

saxophone /ˈsæk.sə.fəʊn/ [US] /-foʊn/ *noun* [C] (*INFORMAL* **sax**) a musical instrument made of metal which is played by blowing through a reed and pressing metal keys to produce notes

saxophonist /sækˈsɒf.ᵊn.ɪst/ [US] /-ˈsɑː.fᵊn-/ *noun* [C] (*INFORMAL* **sax player**) someone who plays the saxophone

S

say [SPEAK] /seɪ/ *verb* [T] **said, said** to pronounce words or sounds, to express a thought, opinion, or suggestion, or to state a fact or instruction: *Small children find it difficult to say long words.* ○ *She said **goodbye** to all her friends and left.* ○ *Ben never forgets to say "Please" and "Thank you".* ○ *"How do you say 'goodbye' in French?"* ○ *I'm sorry, what did you say?* ○ *Do you know what she said **to** him?* ○ *What did they say **about** the house?* ○ [+ speech] *"I'm going out this evening," she said.* ○ [+ (that)] *The doctors say **(that)** it will take him a few weeks to recover.* ○ [+ question word] *She didn't say **whether** she was coming.* ○ *Did she say* (= tell you) ***why** she wasn't coming?* ○ [+ to infinitive] *INFORMAL He said* (= told me) *to meet him here.* ○ *I've got **something** to say to you.* ○ *The offer was so good that I **couldn't** say **no*** (= couldn't refuse).

• **say goodbye to** *sth* to accept that you will not have something any more or that you will not get it: *If Europe fails to agree on this, we can say goodbye to any common foreign policy.*

• **You can't say fairer than that.** *UK INFORMAL* used to say that you think an offer or arrangement is good

• **I wouldn't say no** *INFORMAL* used to say that you would like something that is offered to you: *"Would you like another drink?" "I wouldn't say no."*

• **before you can say Jack Robinson** *OLD-FASHIONED INFORMAL* used to say that something happens very quickly: *Before you could say Jack Robinson, she'd jumped into the car and driven away.*

• **have a lot to say for *yourself*** *INFORMAL DISAPPROVING* to talk too much and seem to have a high opinion of yourself

• **have nothing to say for *yourself*** *INFORMAL* to not be willing to take part in conversations or express your opinions

• **What have you got to say for *yourself*?** used to ask someone to explain why they have done something bad: *Well, you've ruined my car – what have you got to say for yourself?*

• **having said that** despite what has just been said: *He forgets most things, but having said that, he always remembers my birthday.*

• **I'll say!** *INFORMAL* used to show that you agree very strongly with what has been said: *"Does he eat a lot?" "I'll say!"*

• **it goes without saying** used to mean that something is obvious: *Of course, it goes without saying **that** you'll be paid for the extra hours you work.*

• **not say boo 1** *US INFORMAL* to say nothing: *You didn't say boo to me about going to your mother's this weekend.* **2** *US* (*UK* **not say boo to a goose**) *INFORMAL* to be very nervous and easily frightened

• **not to say** and possibly even: *It would be unwise, not to say stupid, to leave your first job after only six months.*

• **say no more** said to show that you understand exactly what the other person is suggesting: *"I saw him coming out of her flat." "Say no more!"*

• **say this/that much for *sb/sth*** to say something good about someone or something considered to be bad: *I'll say this much for Kay, she always agrees to help whenever we ask her.*

• **say uncle** *US INFORMAL* to admit failure

• **say when** said when you are pouring a drink for someone and you want them to tell you when to stop pouring

• **say the word** used to tell someone that you will do what they want at the time when they ask you: *You only have to / Just say the word, and I'll come and help.*

• **That's not saying much.** used to show that you do not think what someone has said is special

• **that is to say ...** or more exactly: *Our friends, that is to say our son's friends, will meet us at the airport.*

• **there's something to be said for** (*ALSO* **there's a lot to be said for**) said to mean that something has advantages: *There's a lot to be said for living alone.*

• **there's little to be said for** *sth* said to mean that something has disadvantages: *Personally, I think there's little to be said for such a policy.*

• **to say the least** used to show that what you are describing is in fact much more serious or important than you have suggested: *It's going to be awkward, to say the least.*

• **to say nothing of ...** and in addition there is: *It would be an enormous amount of work, to say nothing of the cost.*

• **what *sb* says, goes** *INFORMAL* said to mean that you must do whatever a particular person says: *Around here, mate, what I say, goes!*

• **when all is said and done** said when you are about to tell someone the most important fact they should remember in a situation: *When all is said and done, you can only do your best.*

• **You can say that again!** used to show that you completely agree with what someone has said

• **You don't say!** *INFORMAL* used either to express surprise or lack of surprise in a humorous and slightly unkind way: *"He's lost his job." "You don't say!"*

• **You said it!** *INFORMAL* used to say that you agree with what has just been said: *"How stupid of me to lend him that money!" "You said it!"*

say /seɪ/ *noun* [S or U] (the right to give) an opinion about something: *Can't you keep quiet for a minute and let me **have** my say.* ○ *The judge usually has the final say.*

• **have a/some, etc. say in** *sth* to be involved in making a decision about something: *When he's 18, he'll begin to have a/some say in the running of the family business.* ○ *The staff had little/no say in the restructuring of the company.*

COMMON LEARNER ERROR

say or **tell**?

Say can refer to any type of speech.

"Good night," she said.
She said she was unhappy.
Jim said to meet him here.

Say is never followed directly by a person as an object: you must use *say* something **to** someone for this.

She said goodbye to me at the station.
~~She said me goodbye at the station.~~

Tell is used to report that someone has given information or an order. The verb **tell** is always followed by the person that the information or order is given to.

Simon told them all to stay inside the house.
Oscar told the boys a wonderful story about a giant.
~~Oscar told to the boys a wonderful story about a giant.~~

---

say [THINK] /seɪ/ *verb* **said, said 1** [I or T] to think or believe: [+ (that)] *People/They say **(that)** he's over 100.* ○ *"It's going to be a very hot summer." "So they say* (= That is what people believe)*."* ○ *She is a firm leader, too firm, **some might** say* (= some people believe that she is too firm)*.* **2** [I or T] to give (as) an opinion or suggestion about something: *"Who do you think will get the job?" "I'd rather not say."* ○ *What are you saying, exactly* (= What do you mean)*?* ○ [+ (that)] *We've been driving all day – I say **(that)** we start looking for a hotel now.* ○ *INFORMAL What do you say we* (= What do you think about the idea that we should) *sell the car?* **3** [T] to show what you think without using words: [+ (that)] *The look on his face said* (= showed) ***(that)** he knew what had happened.* **4** [T always passive] When something or someone is said to be a particular thing, that is what people think or believe about them: [+ (that)] *It is said **(that)** Latin is a difficult language to learn.* ○ [+ to be + n or adj] *He's said **to be** over 100.*

• **(let's) say** used to introduce a suggestion or possible example of something: *Try and finish the work by, let's say, Friday.* ○ *Say/Let's say* (= If we accept) ***(that)** the journey takes three hours, that means you'll arrive at 2 o'clock.*

• **Who can say?** no one knows: *"Is it possible?" "Who can say?"*

say [GIVE INFORMATION] /seɪ/ *verb* [T] **said, said** to give information in writing, numbers or signs: *My watch says 3 o'clock.* ○ *Can you read what that notice says?* ○ [+ (that)] *It says in the paper **(that)** they've found the man who did it.* ○ [+ to infinitive] *It says on the bottle **to** take three tablets a day.*

say [EXPRESSION] /seɪ/ *exclamation* used to express surprise or pleasure, or to attract attention to what you are about to say: *US Say, that's really good of you!* ○ *US Say, how about going out tonight?* ○ *UK OLD-FASHIONED OR HUMOROUS I say, what a splendid hat you're wearing!*

saying /ˈseɪ.ɪŋ/ *noun* **[C]** a well-known and wise statement, which often has a meaning that is different from the simple meanings of the words it contains: *As the saying* ***goes****, 'Don't count your chickens before they're hatched'.*

say-so [STATEMENT] /ˈseɪ.səʊ/ [US] /-soʊ/ *noun* **[S]** *INFORMAL* a statement made by someone without proof: *Don't just believe it* ***on*** *my say-so – find out for yourself.*

say-so [PERMISSION] /ˈseɪ.səʊ/ [US] /-soʊ/ *noun* **[S]** *INFORMAL* an instruction to do something, or permission given by someone to do something: *She's not allowed to do anything without her father's say-so.*

S-bend /ˈes.bend/ *noun* **[C usually sing]** a bend in a road which is in the shape of the letter S

scab [SKIN COVERING] /skæb/ *noun* **1 [C]** a rough surface made of dried blood which forms over a cut or broken skin while it is healing ➲Compare **scar**. **2 [U]** a plant or animal disease which causes rough areas on the skin
scabby /ˈskæb.i/ *adj*: *a scabby knee* ○ *scabby potatoes*

scab [WORKER] /skæb/ *noun* **[C]** *INFORMAL DISAPPROVING* an insulting word for a person who continues working while other people in the organization are on strike

scabbard /ˈskæb.əd/ [US] /-ɚd/ *noun* **[C]** a long thin cover for the blade of a sword, which is usually fixed to a belt

scabies /ˈskeɪ.biːz/ *noun* **[U]** a skin disease which causes your skin to become rough and uncomfortable

scabrous /ˈskeɪ.brəs/ *adj LITERARY* offensive or shocking, because describing or showing sex: *The book includes some memorably seedy characters and scabrous descriptions.*

scads /skædz/ *noun* **[C usually pl]** *US INFORMAL* a large number or amount: *He earns scads* ***of*** *money.*

scaffold /ˈskæf.əʊld/ [US] /-foʊld/ *noun* **[C] 1** a structure made of SCAFFOLDING for workers to stand on when they want to reach high parts of a building **2** a flat raised structure on which criminals are punished by having their heads cut off or by being hung with a rope around the neck until they die

scaffolding /ˈskæf.ᵊl.dɪŋ/ *noun* **[U]** a structure of metal poles and wooden boards put against a building for workers to stand on when they want to reach the higher parts of the building: *Scaffolding has been* ***erected*** *around the tower and repair work will start next week.*

scalawag /ˈskæl.ɪ.wæg/ *noun* **[C]** *US ALSO FOR* **scallywag**

scald /skɔːld/ [US] /skɑːld/ *verb* **[T] 1** to burn the skin with boiling liquid or steam: *I dropped a pan of boiling water and scalded my leg.* **2** to put something in boiling water or steam in order to make it completely clean: *Scald the needles to sterilize them.* **3** *SPECIALIZED* to heat a liquid until it almost boils: *Scald the milk and then add it to the egg and sugar mixture.*
scald /skɔːld/ [US] /skɑːld/ *noun* **[C]** an injury to the skin caused by boiling liquid or steam
scalding /ˈskɔːl.dɪŋ/ [US] /ˈskɑːl-/ *adj* **1** If a liquid is scalding, it is extremely hot: *scalding tea* ○ *scalding hot water* **2** If criticism is scalding, it is very strong or fierce.

scale [MEASURE] /skeɪl/ *noun* **1 [C]** a set of numbers, amounts etc., used to measure or compare the level of something: *the Centigrade/Fahrenheit scale* ○ *How would you rate his work* ***on a*** *scale* ***of*** *1 to 5?* ➲See also **scales**. **2 [C or U]** the relation between the real size of something and its size on a map, model or DIAGRAM: *a scale of 1:50 000* ○ *This map is* ***large*** *scale* (= things are shown in detail). ○ *Is the bridge drawn* ***to*** *scale* (= so that it shows the exact shape of the bridge, but much smaller)? ○ *He was building a scale* ***model*** *of Concorde.*

scale [SIZE] /skeɪl/ *noun* **[S or U]** the size or level of something, especially when this is large: *We don't yet know the scale of the problem.* ○ *Nuclear weapons cause destruction* ***on*** *a massive scale* (= cause a lot of destruction). ○ *My parents used to entertain friends* ***on a large/small*** *scale* (= they had large/small parties).
• **large/small-scale** describes an event or activity that is large/small in size: *a large-scale investigation*

scale [MUSIC] /skeɪl/ *noun* **[C]** a set of notes played or sung in order, going up or down: *the scale of G major* ○ *You must practise your scales every day.*

scale [SKIN] /skeɪl/ *noun* **[C usually pl]** one of the many very small flat pieces which cover the skin of fish, snakes etc.

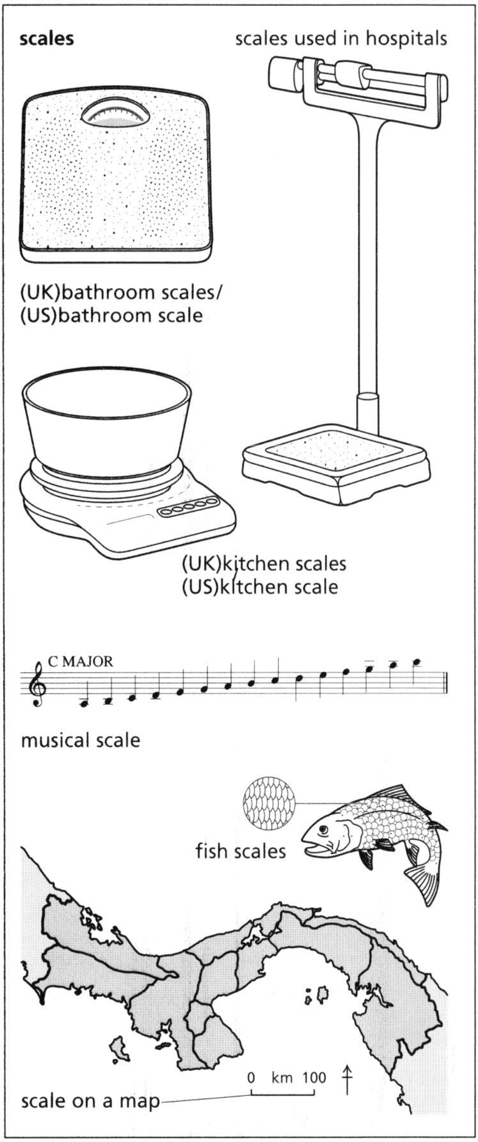
scales
scales used in hospitals
(UK)bathroom scales/
(US)bathroom scale
(UK)kitchen scales
(US)kitchen scale
C MAJOR
musical scale
fish scales
0 km 100
scale on a map

• **the scales fall from** ***sb's*** **eyes** *LITERARY* If the scales fall from your eyes, you suddenly know and understand the truth.
scaly /ˈskeɪ.li/ *adj* If skin is scaly, it has small hard dry areas which fall off in small pieces: *I get scaly patches on my scalp.* **scaliness** /ˈskeɪ.lɪ.nəs/ *noun* **[U]**

scale [COVERING] /skeɪl/ *noun* **[U]** (*UK ALSO* **limescale**) a hard white or grey layer of material which forms on the inside of pipes or containers that heat water **scaliness** /ˈskeɪ.lɪ.nəs/ *noun* **[U]** **scaly** /ˈskeɪ.li/ *adj*

scale [CLEAN TEETH] /skeɪl/ *verb* **[T]** *SPECIALIZED* to remove TARTAR (= hard white substance) and PLAQUE (= soft substance in which bacteria breed) from teeth: *The dentist scaled and polished my teeth last week.*

scale [CLIMB] /skeɪl/ *verb* **[T]** to climb up a steep surface, such as a wall or the side of a mountain, often using special equipment: *The prisoner scaled the high prison wall and ran off.*
• **scale the heights** If you scale the heights of a type of work, you are very successful in it: *At the age of 35, she had already scaled the heights* ***of*** *the acting profession.*

S

PHRASAL VERBS WITH **scale** ▼

▲ **scale** *sth* **down** *phrasal verb* [M] (*MAINLY US* **scale** *sth* **back**) to make something smaller than it was or smaller than it was planned to be: *A shortage of money has forced them to scale down the project.*

scaled-down /ˌskeɪld'daʊn/ *a scaled-down version/plan*

▲ **scale** *sth* **up** *phrasal verb* [M] to increase the size, amount or importance of something, usually an organization or process: *My company is scaling up its operations in the Middle East.*

scales /skeɪlz/ *plural noun* **1** *UK* (*US* **scale**) a device for weighing things or people: *kitchen/bathroom scales* ⊃See picture **In the Kitchen** on page Centre 16 **2** *UK* **a pair of scales** a weighing device with two containers attached to a metal bar which is free to move up and down about its fixed central point. An object of known weight is put in one container and the thing to be weighed is put in the other.

scallion /'skæl.i.ən/ *noun* [C] *US FOR* **spring onion** ⊃See picture **Vegetables** on page Centre 2

scallop /'skɒl.əp/ ⑩ /'skɑː.ləp/ *noun* [C] an edible sea creature which lives inside two joined flat round shells

scallywag, *US USUALLY* **scalawag** /'skæl.i.wæg/ *noun* [C] *INFORMAL HUMOROUS* someone, especially a child, who has behaved badly but who is still liked

scalp HEAD /skælp/ *noun* [C] **1** the skin on the top of a person's head where hair usually grows: *a dry/oily/itchy scalp* ○ *Some tribes used to collect scalps to prove how many of the enemy they had killed in battle.* **2** someone you defeat in a competition or election: *Although they are expected to take some important scalps in the election, they are unlikely to form the next government.*

• **be out for/after** *sb's* **scalp** to want to defeat or punish someone in some way, especially to make them lose their job: *He's made one mistake too many, and now they're out for his scalp.*

scalp /skælp/ *verb* [T] **1** to cut off the scalp of a dead enemy as a sign of victory **2** *HUMOROUS* to cut someone's hair very short

scalp SELL /skælp/ *verb* [T] *US INFORMAL* to buy things, such as theatre tickets, at the usual prices and then sell them, when they are difficult to obtain, at greatly increased prices **scalper** /'skæl.pə^r/ ⑩ /-pɚ/ *noun* [C] *A scalper offered me a $10 ticket for the final match for $70.*

scalpel /'skæl.p^əl/ *noun* [C] a very sharp knife that is used for cutting through skin and flesh during an operation

scam /skæm/ *noun* [C] *INFORMAL* an illegal plan for making money: *an insurance scam*

scamp /skæmp/ *noun* [C] *OLD-FASHIONED* a badly behaved but playful child

scamper /'skæm.pə^r/ ⑩ /-pɚ/ *verb* [I + adv or prep] When small children and animals scamper, they run with small quick steps, in a playful or frightened way: *The children scampered off into the garden.*

scampi /'skæm.pi/ *group noun* [U] large PRAWNS (= small edible sea animals) which are usually fried: *scampi and chips*

scan LOOK /skæn/ *verb* -nn- **1** [T] to look at something carefully, with the eyes or with a machine, in order to obtain information: *She anxiously scanned the faces of the men leaving the train.* ○ *Doug scanned the horizon for any sign of the boat.* **2** [I + adv or prep; T] to look through a text quickly in order to find a piece of information that you want or to get a general idea of what the text contains: *I scanned through the booklet but couldn't find the address.* ○ *Scan the newspaper article quickly and make a note of the main points.*

scan /skæn/ *noun* **1** [S] when you look at or through something carefully or quickly: *I gave the book a quick scan, and decided not to buy it.* **2** [C] a medical examination in which an image of the inside of the body is made using a special machine: *to do a brain scan* ○ *to have an ultrasound scan*

scanner /'skæn.ə^r/ ⑩ /-ɚ/ *noun* [C] a device for making images of the inside of the body or for reading information into a computer system: *an ultrasound scanner* ○ *bar code scanners* ⊃See picture **In the Office** on page Centre 15

scan FOLLOW A PATTERN /skæn/ *verb* [I] -nn- *SPECIALIZED* If a poem or part of a poem scans, it follows a pattern of regular beats: *This line doesn't scan – it's got too many syllables.*

scandal /'skæn.d^əl/ *noun* **1** [C or U] (an action or event that causes) a public feeling of shock and strong moral disapproval: *a financial/political/sex scandal* ○ *The affair caused/created a scandal in the office.* ○ *The scandal broke* (= became public knowledge) *right at the beginning of the Conservative Party Conference.* ○ *If there is the slightest suggestion/hint of scandal, the public will no longer trust us.* **2** [U] reports about actions or events that cause shock and disapproval: *Some magazines contain nothing but scandal and gossip.* ○ *to spread scandal* **3** [S] a situation that is extremely bad: [+ (that)] *It's a scandal that children could be treated in this way.*

scandalize, *UK USUALLY* **-ise** /'skæn.d^əl.aɪz/ *verb* [T often passive] If you are scandalized by someone's behaviour, you disapprove of it and are shocked by it because you think it is immoral: *The whole village was scandalized by her second marriage.*

scandalous /'skæn.d^əl.əs/ *adj*: *scandalous stories* ○ *It's scandalous* (= very annoying and upsetting) *that we do so little to prevent homelessness.*

scandalously /'skæn.d^əl.ə.sli/ *adv*: *scandalously* (= extremely and annoyingly) *expensive*

scandalmonger /'skæn.d^əlˌmʌŋ.gə^r/ ⑩ /-gɚ/ *noun* [C] *DISAPPROVING* a person who creates or spreads reports about actions and events that cause public shock and disapproval

Scandinavian /ˌskæn.dɪ'neɪ.vi.ən/ *noun* [C], *adj* (a person) coming from Sweden, Norway or Denmark, often also Iceland, Finland or the Faroe Islands

scansion /'ʃkæn.ʃ^ən/ *noun* [U] *SPECIALIZED* the rhythm of a line of poetry, or the process of examining the rhythm of a line of poetry

scant /skænt/ *adj* [before n] very little and not enough: *He pays scant attention to the needs of his children.* ○ *scant regard for the truth*

scanty /'skæn.ti/ ⑩ /-t̬i/ *adj* smaller in size or amount than is considered necessary or desirable: *scanty evidence/information*

scantily /'skæn.tɪ.li/ ⑩ /-t̬ɪ-/ *adv* **scantily clad/dressed, etc.** wearing very little clothing: *scantily clad dancers*

-scape /-skeɪp/ *suffix* used to form nouns referring to a wide view of a place, often one represented in a picture: *landscape* ○ *seascape* ○ *cityscape*

scapegoat /'skeɪp.gəʊt/ ⑩ /-goʊt/ *noun* [C] a person who is blamed for something that someone else has done: *The captain was made a scapegoat for the team's failure.*

scapula /'skæp.jʊ.lə/ *noun* [C] *SPECIALIZED FOR* **shoulder blade** ⊃See picture **The Body** on page Centre 5

scar /skɑː^r/ ⑩ /skɑːr/ *noun* [C] **1** a mark left on part of the body after an injury, such as a cut, has healed: *a prominent/noticeable/ugly scar* ○ *That burn will leave a nasty scar.* ○ *scar tissue* ⊃Compare **scab** SKIN COVERING. **2** a sign of damage to a person's mental state: *His early years in the refugee camp left a deep psychological scar.* **3** a sign of physical destruction in a place: *Every village bears the scars of war.*

scar /skɑː^r/ ⑩ /skɑːr/ *verb* [T often passive] -rr- *He was scarred as a result of the fire.* ○ *FIGURATIVE His experiences in the army left him scarred for life* (= had a serious mental effect on him for the rest of his life).

scarce /skeəs/ ⑩ /skers/ *adj* not easy to find or obtain: *Food and clean water were becoming scarce.* ○ *scarce resources*

• **make** *yourself* **scarce** *INFORMAL* to go away from a difficult situation in order to avoid trouble: *Dad's really angry with you, so you'd better make yourself scarce.*

scarcity /'skeə.sɪ.ti/ ⑩ /'sker.sə.t̬i/ *noun* [U] when something is not easy to find or obtain: *the scarcity of skilled workers*

scarcely ONLY JUST /'skeə.sli/ ⑩ /'sker-/ *adv* **1** (*LITERARY* **scarce**) only just or almost not: *I was scarcely able to* move my arm *after the accident.* ○ *I could scarcely* **believe** *it when she said she wanted to marry me.* **2** used to say that something happened immediately after something else happened: *I had scarcely sat down/Scarcely had I sat down to eat* **when** *the phone rang.*

scarcely NOT /'skeə.sli/ ⓤ /'sker-/ *adv* certainly not: *I'd scarcely have done it if I didn't think it was absolutely necessary.* ○ *He's only two – you can scarcely blame him for behaving badly.*

scare /skeə^r/ ⓤ /sker/ *verb* [I or T] to (cause to) feel frightened: *Sudden noises scare her.* ○ *She's very brave – she doesn't scare easily.* ○ *He scared me* **out of my wits** (= made me extremely frightened) *when he was driving so fast.* ○ *Meeting new people scares me* **stiff/to death** (= makes me extremely nervous and anxious). ○ *She scared* **the hell/life/living daylights out of** *me* (= frightened me very much) *when she crept up behind me and shouted in my ear.*

• **scare** *sb* **shitless** OFFENSIVE to make someone extremely frightened

scare /skeə^r/ ⓤ /sker/ *noun* **1** [S] a sudden feeling of fear or worry: *I* **got/had** *a scare* (= I was very worried) *when I looked at my bank statement this morning!* ○ *You* **gave** *us a real scare* (= frightened us) *when you fainted, you know.* **2** [C] when a subject receives a lot of public attention and worries many people, often unnecessarily: *a bomb/health scare* ○ *The government are accused of employing scare* **tactics** (= ways of frightening people in order to persuade them to do something). ○ *The press have been publishing scare* **stories** (= newspaper reports which make people feel unnecessarily worried) *about the mystery virus.*

scared /skeəd/ ⓤ /skerd/ *adj* frightened or worried: *He's scared* **of** *spiders.* ○ *I'm scared* **of** *tell*ing *her what really happened.* ○ *He's scared to tell her what really happened.* ○ *I was scared* (= very worried) **(that)** *you might not be there.* ○ *I was scared* **stiff** (= extremely frightened). ○ *She had a scared look on her face.*

scary, UK ALSO **scarey** /'skeə.ri/ ⓤ /'sker.i/ *adj* INFORMAL frightening: *a scary movie/story*

PHRASAL VERBS WITH scare ▼

▲ **scare** *sb/sth* **away/off** *phrasal verb* [M] to make a person or an animal so frightened that they go away: *Don't make too much noise or you'll scare away the birds.* ○ *She scared off her attacker by screaming.*

▲ **scare** *sb* **away/off** *phrasal verb* [M] to make someone so worried about doing something that they decide not to do it: *If you charge as much as that, you'll scare customers off.*

▲ **scare** *sb* **into** *doing sth phrasal verb* to persuade someone to do something by frightening them: *The two boys scared the old man into handing over his wallet.*

▲ **scare** *sth* **up** *phrasal verb* [M] US INFORMAL to find or obtain something despite difficulties or limited supplies: *There's hardly any food in the house, but I'll scare something up from these leftovers.*

scarecrow /'skeə.krəʊ/ ⓤ /'sker.kroʊ/ *noun* [C] a model of a person dressed in old clothes and put in a field of growing crops to frighten birds away

scaredy cat /'skeə.di.kæt/ ⓤ /'sker-/ *noun* [C] CHILD'S EXPRESSION someone, especially a child, who is easily frightened: *Come on, scaredy cat – it won't bite you!*

scaremonger /'skeə,mʌŋ.gə^r/ ⓤ /'sker,mʌŋ.gɚ/ *noun* [C] DISAPPROVING a person who spreads stories that cause public fear **scaremongering** /'skeə,mʌŋ.g^ər.ɪŋ/ ⓤ /'sker,mʌŋ.gɚ-/ *noun* [U]

scarf CLOTH /skɑːf/ ⓤ /skɑːrf/ *noun* [C] *plural* **scarves** or **scarfs** a strip, square or triangle of cloth, worn around the neck, head or shoulders to keep you warm or to make you look attractive: *a knitted/woollen/silk scarf* ⊃See picture **Clothes** on page Centre 6

scarf EAT /skɑːf/ ⓤ /skɑːrf/ *verb* [T] US FOR **scoff** EAT

scarlatina /,skɑː.lə'tiː.nə/ ⓤ /,skɑːr-/ *noun* [U] SPECIALIZED FOR **scarlet fever**

scarlet /'skɑː.lət/ ⓤ /'skɑːr-/ *noun* [U], *adj* bright red: *scarlet berries* ○ *He* **went** *scarlet with shame and embarrassment.*

scarlet 'fever *noun* [U] (SPECIALIZED **scarlatina**) an infectious illness of children which causes a sore throat, a high body temperature, and red spots on the skin

scarlet 'woman *noun* [C] OLD USE DISAPPROVING a woman who is considered to be immoral because she has sex with a lot of men

scarper /'skɑː.pə^r/ ⓤ /'skɑːr.pɚ/ *verb* [I] UK SLANG to leave very quickly, often to avoid getting into trouble: *The police are coming! We'd better scarper.*

scary /'skeə.ri/ ⓤ /'sker.i/ *adj*: See at **scare**.

scat GO AWAY /skæt/ *exclamation* INFORMAL said to an animal, especially a cat, or to a person to make them go away quickly

scat SINGING /skæt/ *noun* [U] a type of jazz singing that uses words with no meaning

scathing /'skeɪ.ðɪŋ/ *adj* severely and unkindly critical: *scathing criticism* ○ *He was very scathing* **about** *the report, saying it was inaccurate.* **scathingly** /'skeɪ.ðɪŋ.li/ *adv*: *She spoke scathingly of the poor standard of work done by her predecessor.*

scatological, UK ALSO **scatalogical** /,skæt.ə'lɒdʒ.ɪ.k^əl/ ⓤ /,skæt.ə'lɑː.dʒɪ-/ *adj* DISAPPROVING showing an extreme and unpleasant interest in excrement and sex: *scatological humour*

scatter MOVE /'skæt.ə^r/ ⓤ /'skæt.ɚ/ *verb* [I or T] to (cause to) move far apart in different directions: *The protesters scattered at the sound of gunshots.* ○ *The soldiers came in and scattered the crowd.*

• **be scattered to the four winds** LITERARY If a group of things or people are scattered to the four winds, they go or are sent to different places that are far away from each other: *It was the finest collection of paintings in Denmark, but during the last war it was broken up and scattered to the four winds.*

scattering /'skæt.^ər.ɪŋ/ ⓤ /'skæt.ɚ-/ *noun* [C usually sing] a small number or amount of things in a particular area: *a scattering of houses*

scatter COVER /'skæt.ə^r/ ⓤ /'skæt.ɚ/ *verb* [T usually + adv or prep] to cover a surface with things that are far apart and in no particular arrangement: *Scatter the powder* **around** *the plants.* ○ *I scattered grass seed all* **over** *the lawn.* ○ *I scattered the whole lawn* **with** *grass seed.*

scatterbrain /'skæt.ə.breɪn/ ⓤ /'skæt.ɚ-/ *noun* [C] a person who forgets things easily or does not think seriously about things: *I'm such a scatterbrain – I'm always leaving my umbrella behind.* **scatterbrained** /'skæt.ə.breɪnd/ ⓤ /'skæt.ɚ-/ *adj*

scattered /'skæt.əd/ ⓤ /'skæt.ɚd/ *adj* covering a wide area: *Toys and books were scattered* **about/around** *the room.* ○ *My family is scattered* **all over** *the world.* ○ *The forecast is for scattered showers* (= separate areas of rain) *tomorrow.*

scatty /'skæt.i/ ⓤ /'skæt-/ *adj* UK INFORMAL silly and often forgetting things: *a scatty child* ○ *scatty behaviour*

scavenge /'skæv.ɪndʒ/ *verb* [I or T] **1** to look for or obtain food or other objects in other people's rubbish: *The flood has left villagers and animals desperately scavenging* **for** *food.* ○ *We managed to scavenge a lot of furniture* **from** *the local rubbish dump.* **2** If a wild animal scavenges, it feeds on the flesh of dead decaying animals.

scavenger /'skæv.ɪn.dʒə^r/ ⓤ /-dʒɚ/ *noun* [C] a bird or animal which feeds on dead animals which it has not killed itself

scenario POSSIBLE EVENT /sɪ'nɑː.ri.əʊ/ ⓤ /sə'ner.i.oʊ/ *noun* [C] *plural* **scenarios** a description of possible actions or events in the future: *There are several possible scenarios.* ○ *a horrific/nightmare scenario such as a Third World War* ⊃See also **worst case scenario**.

scenario PLAN /sɪ'nɑː.ri.əʊ/ ⓤ /sə'ner.i.oʊ/ *noun* [C] *plural* **scenarios** a written plan of the characters and events in a play or movie

scene THEATRE/FILM /siːn/ *noun* [C] a part of a play or film in which the action stays in one place for a continuous period of time: *the funeral/wedding scene* ○ *nude/sex scenes* ○ *Juliet dies in Act IV, Scene iii.*

• **behind the scenes** If something happens behind the scenes, it happens without most people knowing about it, especially when something else is happening publicly: *A lot of hard work has been going on behind the scenes.*

● **set the scene 1** to describe a situation where something is about to happen: *First, let's set the scene – it was a dark, wet night with a strong wind blowing.* **2** to make something possible or likely to happen: *His resignation set the scene for a pre-election crisis.*

scene VIEW /siːn/ *noun* [C] a view or picture of a place, event, or activity: *Lowry painted street scenes.* ○ *scenes of everyday life* ○ FIGURATIVE *There were scenes of great joy as the hostages were re-united with their families.*

scene PLACE /siːn/ *noun* [C usually sing] a place where an unpleasant event has happened: *The police arrived to find a scene of horrifying destruction.* ○ *Evidence was found at the scene of the crime.*

● **be on the scene** to arrive: *I phoned the police and they were on the scene within minutes.*

scene AREA /siːn/ *noun* [S] a particular area of activity and all the people or things connected with it: *the pop/political/drugs/gay scene* ○ *Rap music arrived/came/appeared on the scene in the early 1980s.* ○ INFORMAL *I'd rather go to a jazz concert – I'm afraid opera isn't really my scene* (= is not the type of thing I like).

scene ARGUMENT /siːn/ *noun* [C] an expression of great anger or similar feelings, often between two people, or an occasion when this happens: *Please don't make a scene.* ○ *There was a terrible scene and Jayne ended up in tears.*

scenery COUNTRYSIDE /ˈsiː.nᵊr.i/ US /-nɚ-/ *noun* [U] the general appearance of natural surroundings, especially when these are beautiful: *beautiful/breathtaking/spectacular/ scenery* ○ *They stopped at the top of the hill to admire the scenery.*

● **blend into the scenery** to behave in the same way as people around you, so that you are not noticed

scenic /ˈsiː.nɪk/ *adj* having or allowing you to see beautiful natural features: *an area of outstanding scenic beauty* ○ *a scenic drive/railway* ○ *We took the scenic route home.*

scenery THEATRE /ˈsiː.nᵊr.i/ US /-nɚ-/ *noun* [U] the large painted pictures used on a theatre stage to represent the place where the action is

sceneshifter /ˈsiːn.ʃɪf.tər/ US /-tɚ/ *noun* [C] a person who changes the SCENERY in a theatre

scent /sent/ *noun* **1** [C] a pleasant natural smell: *the scent of roses* **2** [C] a smell produced by an animal which acts as a signal to other animals: *The hounds had lost the scent of the fox near the river.* **3** [C or U] a pleasant smelling liquid that people put on their skin; PERFUME: *a bottle of scent*

● **on the scent** close to discovering: *"We're on the scent of something big," said the police chief.*

● **throw/put sb off the scent** to give someone false or confusing information to prevent them from discovering something that you do not want them to know about

scent /sent/ *verb* [T] **1** If an animal scents something or someone, it knows they are there because it can smell them. **2** If a person scents something, they have a feeling that they are about to experience it: *Halfway through the match, the team could already scent victory.*

scented /ˈsen.tɪd/ US /-t̬ɪd/ *adj* having a pleasant strong smell: *scented notepaper* ○ *The air was scented with lavender.*

sceptic, US **skeptic** /ˈskep.tɪk/ *noun* [C] a person who doubts the truth or value of an idea or belief: *People say it can cure colds, but I'm a bit of a sceptic.* ○ *to convince the sceptics* **sceptical**, US **skeptical** /ˈskep.tɪ.kᵊl/ *adj* doubting that something is true or useful: *Many experts remain sceptical about/of his claims.* **sceptically**, US **skeptically** /ˈskep.tɪ.kli/ *adv* **scepticism**, US **skepticism** /ˈskep.tɪ.sɪ.zᵊm/ *noun* [U] *The company's environmental claims have been greeted/regarded/treated with scepticism by conservationists.*

sceptre UK /ˈsep.tər/ US /-tɚ/ *noun* [C] (US **scepter**) a decorated stick which is carried by a queen or king during some official ceremonies as a symbol of their authority

schadenfreude /ˈʃɑː.dᵊn.frɔɪ.də/ *noun* [U] a feeling of pleasure or satisfaction when something bad happens to someone else

schedule /ˈʃed.juːl/ US /ˈsked-/ *noun* [C] **1** a list of planned activities or things to be done showing the times or dates when they are intended to happen or be done: *a production schedule* ○ *a hectic/tight* (= very busy) *schedule* ○ *Everything went according to schedule* (= as planned). **2** US (UK **timetable**) a list of the times when events are planned to happen, especially the times when buses, trains and planes leave and arrive **3** FORMAL an official list of things: *a schedule of business expenses*

● **ahead of schedule** early: *We expect the building work to be completed ahead of schedule.*

● **on schedule** not early or late

● **fall behind schedule** to do less work than you planned to do by a particular point in time

schedule /ˈʃed.juːl/ US /ˈsked-/ *verb* [T often passive] to arrange that an event or activity will happen at a particular time: *The meeting has been scheduled for tomorrow afternoon.* ○ [+ to infinitive] *The train is scheduled to arrive at 8.45, but it's running twenty minutes late.* **scheduled** /ˈʃed.juːld/ US /ˈsked-/ *adj: This program will be broadcast half an hour later than the scheduled time.*

scheduler /ˈʃed.juː.lər/ US /ˈsked.juː.lɚ/ *noun* [C] a person who works for a broadcasting company putting the various programmes for the day, week, month, etc. into a particular order

scheduled 'flight *noun* [C] a regular flight organized by the company which owns the aircraft

schema /ˈskiː.mə/ *noun* [C] *plural* **schemata** SPECIALIZED a drawing that represents an idea or theory and makes it easier to understand

schematic /skɪˈmæt.ɪk/ US /-ˈmæt̬-/ *adj* showing the main form and features of something, usually in the form of a drawing, which helps people to understand it: *a schematic diagram/outline* **schematically** /skɪˈmæt.ɪ.kli/ US /-ˈmæt̬-/ *adv*

scheme /skiːm/ *noun* [C] **1** MAINLY UK an officially organized plan or system: *a training/housing/play scheme* ○ *a pension/savings scheme* ○ *There's a new scheme in our town for recycling plastic bottles.* ○ *Class sizes will increase under the new scheme.* **2** a plan for obtaining an advantage for yourself, especially by deceiving others: *He's got a hare-brained/crazy/daft scheme for getting rich before he's 20.*

● **the scheme of things** the way things are organized or happen in a particular situation, or the way someone wants them to be organized: *I was disappointed not to get the job, but it's not that important in the great/grand scheme of things* (= when all things are considered).

scheme /skiːm/ *verb* [I or T] DISAPPROVING to make clever secret plans which often deceive others: *All her ministers were scheming against her* ○ [+ to infinitive] *For months he had been scheming to prevent her from getting the top job.* **schemer** /ˈskiː.mər/ US /-mɚ/ *noun* [C] *He's a schemer who always finds a way of getting what he wants.* **scheming** /ˈskiː.mɪŋ/ *adj: a secretive and scheming politician*

scherzo /ˈskeət.səʊ/ US /ˈskert.soʊ/ *noun* [C] *plural* **scherzos** a fast and happy piece of music for instruments, often part of a longer piece

Schilling /ˈʃɪl.ɪŋ/ *noun* [C] the standard unit of money used in Austria before they started using the euro

schism /ˈskɪz.əm/ US /ˈsɪz-/ *noun* [C] a division into two groups caused by a disagreement about ideas, especially in a religious organization: *a schism in/within the Church*

schizo /ˈskɪt.səʊ/ US /-soʊ/ *noun* [C] *plural* **schizos** INFORMAL DISAPPROVING a person with very strange and usually violent or threatening behaviour: *He turns into a real schizo when he's had too much to drink.*

schizoid /ˈskɪt.sɔɪd/ *adj* SPECIALIZED suffering from or behaving as if suffering from SCHIZOPHRENIA: *a schizoid personality*

schizophrenia /ˌskɪt.səˈfriː.ni.ə/ *noun* [U] **1** a serious mental illness in which someone cannot understand what is real and what is imaginary: *paranoid schizophrenia* **2** *INFORMAL* behaviour in which a person appears to have two different personalities
schizophrenic /ˌskɪt.səˈfren.ɪk/ *noun* [C] someone who suffers from schizophrenia **schizophrenic** /ˌskɪt.səˈfren.ɪk/ *adj*: *schizophrenic patients/symptoms* **schizophrenically** /ˌskɪt.səˈfren.ɪ.kli/ *adv*

schlep (-pp-), **schlepp** /ʃlep/ *verb* [I or T; + adv or prep] *MAINLY US INFORMAL* to move yourself or an object with effort and difficulty: *Do I really have to schlep all that junk down to the cellar?*
schlep, schlepp /ʃlep/ *noun* [S] *MAINLY US INFORMAL* something that takes a lot of effort to do: *It's a real schlep getting it all home.*

schlock /ʃlɒk/ [US] /ʃlɑːk/ *noun* [U] *MAINLY US INFORMAL DISAPPROVING* goods or artistic works which are cheap or low in quality: *markets selling schlock* ○ *schlock TV shows* **schlocky** /ˈʃlɒk.i/ [US] /ˈʃlɑː.ki/ *adj*

schmaltz, schmalz /ʃmɒlts/ [US] /ʃmɑːlts/ *noun* [U] *INFORMAL DISAPPROVING* popular artistic works, such as music or writing, which are intended to cause strong sad or romantic feelings, but which lack any real artistic value: *Her second album was pure schmaltz.* **schmaltzy, schmalzy** /ˈʃmɒlt.si/ [US] /ˈʃmɑːlt-/ *adj*: *schmaltzy love songs*

schmooze /ʃmuːz/ *verb* [I] *INFORMAL* to talk informally with someone, especially in a way that is not sincere or to gain some advantage for yourself: *He spent the entire evening schmoozing **with** the senator.*

schmuck /ʃmʌk/ *noun* [C] *MAINLY US INFORMAL* a stupid or foolish person: *Her husband is such a schmuck!*

schnapps /ʃnæps/ *noun* [C or U] a colourless strong alcoholic drink made in eastern and northern parts of Europe, usually from grain, potato or fruit

schnitzel /ˈʃnɪt.səl/ *noun* [C or U] a thin slice of meat, usually VEAL (= young cow), which is covered in egg and very small pieces of bread before being fried

schnorkel /ˈʃnɔː.kəl/ [US] /ˈʃnɔːr-/ *noun* [C] *AUS FOR* **snorkel**

scholar /ˈskɒl.əʳ/ [US] /ˈskɑː.lɚ/ *noun* [C] **1** a person who studies a subject in great detail, especially at a university: *a classics/history scholar* ○ *Dr Miles was a **distinguished** scholar **of** Russian history.* **2** *INFORMAL* someone who is clever or good at learning by studying: *David's never been much of a scholar.*
scholarly /ˈskɒl.ə.li/ [US] /ˈskɑː.lɚ-/ *adj* **1** containing a serious detailed study of a subject: *a scholarly article/book/work/journal* **2** describes someone who studies a lot and knows a lot about what they study: *a scholarly young woman*
scholarship /ˈskɒl.ə.ʃɪp/ [US] /ˈskɑː.lɚ-/ *noun* **1** [U] serious, detailed study: *a work of great scholarship* **2** [C] an amount of money given by a school, college, university or other organization to pay for the studies of a person with great ability but little money: *He **got/won** a scholarship **to** Eton.* ○ *Paula went to the Royal College of Music **on** a scholarship.*

scholastic /skəˈlæs.tɪk/ *adj* relating to school and education: *scholastic achievements* **scholastically** /skəˈlæs.tɪ.kli/ *adv*

school [EDUCATION] /skuːl/ *noun* **1** [C or U] a place where children go to be educated: *a primary/secondary school* ○ *Milton Road School* ○ *They're building a new school in the village.* ○ *She drives the kids to school every morning.* ○ *UK I was **at** school **with*** (= I went to the same school at the same time as) *Luke's brother.* ○ *Is Emily **in** school today or is she still ill?* ○ *Which school do you **go to**/ (FORMAL) **attend**?* ○ *school meals/uniform* ○ *school buildings/fees* **2** [U] the period of your life during which you go to school, or the teaching and learning activities which happen at school: *British children **start/begin** school at the age of four or five.* ○ *What do you want to do when you **leave** school* (= finish studying at school)? ○ *I love/hate school.* ○ *US My sister **teaches** school* (= teaches children in a school) *in New York City.* **3** [U] the time during the day when children are studying in school: *before/after school* ○ *School starts at 9 a.m. and finishes at 3.30 p.m.* **4** [C or U] a part of a college or university specializing in a particular subject or group of subjects: *the School of Oriental and African Studies* ○ *She went to medical school in Edinburgh.* **5** [C] a place where people, especially adults, can study a particular subject either some of the time or all of the time: *a driving/dancing school* ○ *the London Business School* **6** [U] *US FOR* **university**: *We first met at **graduate** school* (= while doing a university course for a second or third degree).
school /skuːl/ *group noun* all the children and teachers at a school: *The whole school is/are delighted about Joel's success in the championships.*
• **school/university of life** all the good and bad experiences that you have in your life
• **school of hard knocks** If you learn something in the school of hard knocks, you learn it as a result of difficult or unpleasant experiences.
school /skuːl/ *verb FORMAL* **1** [T] to train a person or animal to do something: *It takes a lot of patience to school a dog/horse.* ○ [R + to infinitive] *You must school yourself **to** be tolerant.* **2** [T often passive] to teach a child: *Her children are **well** schooled **in** correct behaviour.*
schooling /ˈskuː.lɪŋ/ *noun* [U] education at school: *Jack didn't **receive** much **formal** schooling.*

school [GROUP] /skuːl/ *group noun* [C] a group of painters, writers, poets, etc. whose work is similar, especially similar to that of a particular leader: *the Flemish School* ○ *the Impressionist school **of** painting*

school [SEA ANIMALS] /skuːl/ *group noun* [C] a large number of fish or other sea animals swimming in a group: *a school of dolphins/whales*

schoolboy /ˈskuːl.bɔɪ/ *noun* [C] a boy who goes to school
schoolboy /ˈskuːl.bɔɪ/ *adj* [before n] childish: *I must say I find his schoolboy humour rather tiresome.*

schoolchild (*plural* **schoolchildren**) /ˈskuːl.tʃaɪld/ *noun* [C] (*INFORMAL* **schoolkid**) a child who goes to school: *We just sat there giggling like **naughty** schoolchildren.*

schooldays /ˈskuːl.deɪz/ *plural noun* the period of your life that you spend at school

schoolgirl /ˈskuːl.gɜːl/ [US] /-gɜːrl/ *noun* [C] a girl who goes to school

schoolhouse /ˈskuːl.haʊs/ *noun* [C] *MAINLY US* a building used as a school, especially in a village

school leaver /ˈskuːlˌliː.vəʳ/ [US] /-ˌliː.vɚ/ *noun* [C] *UK* a young person who is about to leave or has just left SECONDARY school (= a school for children aged 11 to 16 (or 18) years)

school-leaving age /ˈskuːlˌliː.vɪŋˌeɪdʒ/ *noun* [U] *UK* the lowest age at which a person can leave school

schoolmarm /ˈskuːl.mɑːm/ [US] /-mɑːrm/ *noun* [C] **1** *DISAPPROVING* a very formal and severe woman who likes to control other people and is easily shocked **2** *MAINLY US OLD-FASHIONED* a female school teacher
schoolmarmish /ˈskuːlˌmɑː.mɪʃ/ [US] /-ˌmɑːr-/ *adj DISAPPROVING* behaving like a schoolmarm: *Stop being so schoolmarmish and bossy.*

schoolmaster /ˈskuːlˌmɪs.trəs/ *noun* [C] *OLD-FASHIONED* a man who teaches children in a school

schoolmate /ˈskuːl.meɪt/ *noun* [C] a friend who is at the same school as you at the same time

schoolmistress /ˈskuːlˌmɪs.trəs/ *noun* [C] *OLD-FASHIONED* a woman who teaches children in a school

ˌschool of ˈthought *noun* [C] a set of ideas or opinions which a group of people share about a matter: *There are several schools of thought about how the universe began.*

ˈschool ˌrun *noun* [C usually sing] *UK* the time when parents drive their children to or from school: *Next week it's my turn to **do** the school run.*

schoolteacher /ˈskuːlˌtiː.tʃəʳ/ [US] /-tʃɚ/ *noun* [C] someone who teaches children in a school

schoolwork /ˈskuːl.wɜːk/ [US] /-wɝːk/ *noun* [U] studying done by a child at school or at home

schoolyard /ˈskuːl.jɑːd/ [US] /-jɑːrd/ *noun* [C] *MAINLY US* an outside area next to a school where children can play games or sport when they are not studying

schooner /ˈskuː.nəʳ/ [US] /-nɚ/ *noun* [C] a sailing ship with two or more masts and with its sails parallel to the length of the ship, rather than across it

S

schwa /ʃwɑː/ *noun* [C] the weak vowel sound in some syllables that are not emphasized, such as the first syllable of 'about' and the second syllable of 'given', or the ə symbol that represents this sound

sciatica /saɪˈæt.ɪ.kə/ [US] /-ˈæt̬-/ *noun* [U] pain in the lower part of the back and the back of the legs

science /saɪənts/ *noun* **1** [U] (knowledge obtained from) the systematic study of the structure and behaviour of the physical world, especially by observing, measuring and experimenting, and the development of theories to describe the results of these activities: *pure/applied science* ○ *recent developments in science and technology* ○ *Space travel is one of the marvels/wonders of modern science.* **2** [C or U] a particular subject that is studied using scientific methods: *physical sciences* ○ *Economics is not an* ***exact*** *science.* ○ *advances in* ***medical*** *science* **3** [U] the study of science: *a science graduate/teacher* ○ *a science course/lesson*

scientific /ˌsaɪənˈtɪf.ɪk/ *adj* **1** relating to science, or using the organized methods of science: *a scientific discovery/experiment/theory* ○ *scientific evidence/research* ○ *The project has attracted considerable criticism from* ***the*** *scientific* ***community*** (= from scientists). **2** careful and systematic: *We will have to adopt a more scientific* ***approach*** *in the future.* ○ *I try to arrange things in some kind of a system, but I'm not very scientific* ***about*** *it.* **scientifically** /ˌsaɪənˈtɪf.ɪ.kli/ *adv*: *scientifically proven*

scientist /ˈsaɪən.tɪst/ *noun* [C] an expert who studies or works in one of the sciences: *a research/nuclear scientist*

ˌscience ˈfiction *noun* [U] (*INFORMAL* **sci-fi**, *ALSO* **SF**) books, films or cartoons about an imagined future, especially about space travel or other planets: *a science-fiction novel/story*

ˈscience ˌpark *noun* [C] *MAINLY UK* an area, often started or supported by a college or university, where companies involved in scientific work and new technology are based

sci-fi /ˈsaɪ.faɪ/ *noun* [U] *INFORMAL FOR* **science fiction**

scimitar /ˈsɪm.ɪ.təʳ/ [US] /-t̬ɚ/ *noun* [C] a sword with a curved blade which is sharp only on its outer edge and which gets wider towards its pointed end

scintilla /sɪnˈtɪl.ə/ *noun FORMAL* **a scintilla of *sth*** the slightest amount of something: *There's* ***not*** *a scintilla of truth in what he says.*

scintillating /ˈsɪn.tɪ.leɪ.tɪŋ/ [US] /-t̬əl.eɪ.t̬ɪŋ/ *adj* interesting, exciting and clever: *scintillating wit/repartee/conversation* ○ *a scintillating personality/speech*

scion /ˈsaɪ.ən/ *noun* [C] *LITERARY* a young member of a rich and famous family: *He's the scion* ***of*** *a very wealthy newspaper-publishing family.*

scirocco /sɪˈrɒk.əʊ/ [US] /-ˈrɑː.koʊ/ *noun* [C] a **sirocco**

scissors /ˈsɪz.əz/ [US] /-ɚz/ *plural noun* a device used for cutting materials such as paper, cloth and hair, consisting of two sharp blades which are joined in the middle, and two handles with holes to put your fingers through: *a pair of scissors* ○ *Could you pass me the/those scissors, please.*

• **scissors and paste** *MAINLY DISAPPROVING* If something such as piece of writing is a scissors and paste job, it is not original, but is made up from parts of other people's work.

scissor /ˈsɪz.əʳ/ [US] /-ɚ/ *adj* [before n] relating to or like scissors: *a scissor blade*

sclerosis /skləˈrəʊ.sɪs/ [US] /-ˈroʊ-/ *noun* [U] *SPECIALIZED* a medical condition which causes a hardening of body tissue or organs, especially the arteries

sclerotic /skləˈrɒt.ɪk/ [US] /-ˈrɑː.t̬ɪk/ *adj SPECIALIZED sclerotic arteries* ○ *FIGURATIVE DISAPPROVING The tax cuts are designed to bring growth to a sclerotic* (= very slowly developing and not easily changed) *economy.*

scoff [LAUGH] /skɒf/ [US] /skɑːf/ *verb* [I] to laugh and speak about a person or idea in a way which shows that you think they are stupid or ridiculous: *The critics scoffed* ***at*** *his paintings.* ○ *Years ago people would have scoffed* ***at*** *the idea that cars would be built by robots.* **scoff** /skɒf/ [US] /skɑːf/ *noun* [C usually pl] *Despite the scoffs of her colleagues, the experiment was completely successful.*

scoffer /ˈskɒf.əʳ/ [US] /ˈskɑː.fɚ/ *noun* [C usually pl] *I was able to prove the scoffers wrong.*

scoff [EAT] /skɒf/ [US] /skɑːf/ *verb* [T] (*US ALSO* **scarf**) *INFORMAL* to eat something quickly and eagerly: *I baked a huge cake this morning, and the kids scoffed the lot.*

scold /skəʊld/ [US] /skoʊld/ *verb* [T] *OLD-FASHIONED* to tell off someone of whose behaviour you disapprove: *His mother scolded him* ***for*** *breaking her favourite vase.* **scolding** /ˈskəʊl.dɪŋ/ [US] /ˈskoʊl-/ *adj* **scolding** /ˈskəʊl.dɪŋ/ [US] /ˈskoʊl-/ *noun* [C] *He* ***gave*** *his son a scolding* ***for*** *coming home so late.*

sconce /skɒnts/ [US] /skɑːnts/ *noun* [C] *SPECIALIZED* a device which is fixed to a wall to hold electric lights or candles

scone /skɒn/ [US] /skɑːn/ *noun* [C] a small, usually round, bread-like cake made from flour, milk and a little fat: *tea and buttered scones*

scoop [TOOL] /skuːp/ *noun* [C] **1** a tool with a deep bowl-shaped end which is used to dig out and move a soft or powdery substance: *a measuring scoop* ○ *an ice-cream scoop* **2** the amount held by a scoop: *Just one scoop of mashed potato for me, please.*

scoop /skuːp/ *verb* [T] **1** to move something with a scoop or with something used as a scoop: *He scooped the sand into a bucket with his hands.* **2** to get a large number of votes or prizes: *The socialist party is expected to scoop* ***up*** *the majority of the working-class vote.*

• **scoop the pool** *UK INFORMAL* to win all the prizes that are available: *Cuba scooped the pool in the boxing at this year's Olympics.*

scoop [NEWS] /skuːp/ *noun* [C] a story or piece of news discovered and published by one newspaper before all the others: *The paper managed to secure a major scoop and broke the scandal to the world.*

scoop /skuːp/ *verb* [T] to be the first newspaper to discover and print an important news story: *Just as we were about to publish the story, we were scooped by a rival paper.*

PHRASAL VERBS WITH **scoop** ▼

▲ **scoop *sth* out** *phrasal verb* [M] to remove something that is inside something else with a spoon: *Cut the tomato in half and scoop out the seeds.*

▲ **scoop *sth/sb* up** *phrasal verb* [M] to lift something or someone with your hands or arms in a quick movement: *She scooped the children up and ran with them to safety.* ○ *I scooped up my belongings into my handbag.*

scoop-neck /ˌskuːpˈnek/ *adj* describes a piece of women's clothing which is cut low around the neck in a U-shape

scoot /skuːt/ *verb* **1** [I usually + adv or prep] *INFORMAL* to go quickly: *I'm scooting* ***off*** *to St Andrews for a few days' golf.* ○ *I'll have to scoot* (= leave quickly) *or I'll miss my train.* **2** [I + adv or prep] *US INFORMAL* to slide while sitting: *Scoot over and make room for your sister.*

scooter [TOY] /ˈskuː.təʳ/ [US] /-t̬ɚ/ *noun* [C] a child's vehicle with two or three small wheels joined to the bottom of a narrow board and a long vertical handle fixed to the front wheel. It is ridden by standing with one foot on the board and pushing against the ground with the other foot.

scooter [MOTORCYCLE] /ˈskuː.təʳ/ [US] /-t̬ɚ/ *noun* [C] a **motor scooter**

scope [RANGE] /skəʊp/ [US] /skoʊp/ *noun* [U] the range of a subject covered by a book, programme, discussion, class, etc: *I'm afraid that problem is* ***beyond/outside the*** *scope* ***of*** *my lecture.* ○ *Oil painting does not come* ***within the*** *scope* ***of*** *a course of this kind.* ○ *We would now like to* ***broaden/widen the*** *scope* ***of*** *the enquiry and look at more general matters.*

scope [OPPORTUNITY] /skəʊp/ [US] /skoʊp/ *noun* [U] the opportunity for doing something: *There is limited scope* ***for*** *further reductions in the workforce.*

-scope [TOOL] /-skəʊp/ [US] /-skoʊp/ *suffix* used to form nouns that refer to devices for looking at or discovering and measuring things: *a microscope* ○ *a telescope*

-scopic /-skɒp.ɪk/ [US] /-skɑː.pɪk/ *suffix* used to form adjectives: *a telescopic lens*

S

scope /skəʊp/ /skoʊp/ *verb*
▲ **scope** ***sth/sb*** **out** *phrasal verb* **[M]** *US INFORMAL* to look carefully to see if something or someone is interesting or attractive: *We scoped out the local shops and facilities to see if it would be a good place to rent a flat.*

scorch [BURN] /skɔːtʃ/ [US] /skɔːrtʃ/ *verb* **[I or T]** to (cause to) change colour with dry heat, or to burn slightly: *The iron was too hot and he scorched the shirt.* ○ *The surrounding buildings were scorched by the heat of the explosion.* **scorch** /skɔːtʃ/ [US] /skɔːrtʃ/ *noun* **[C]** *The fire left scorch* ***marks*** *halfway up the wall.*
scorched /skɔːtʃt/ [US] /skɔːrtʃt/ *adj* slightly burnt, or damaged by fire or heat: *The countryside was scorched after several weeks of hot sun.*
scorcher /ˈskɔː.tʃəʳ/ [US] /ˈskɔːr.tʃɚ/ *noun* **[C]** *INFORMAL* an extremely hot and sunny day
scorching /ˈskɔː.tʃɪŋ/ [US] /ˈskɔːr-/ *adj, adv* (*ALSO* **scorching hot**) very hot: *a scorching summer day* ○ *It was scorching* ***hot*** *inside the greenhouse.*

scorch [DRIVE FAST] /skɔːtʃ/ [US] /skɔːrtʃ/ *verb* **[I usually + adv or prep]** *OLD-FASHIONED INFORMAL* (especially of motorcycles and cars) to travel or be driven very fast: *The sports car scorched* ***past*** *and disappeared into the distance.*

scorched-earth policy /ˌskɔːtʃtˈɜːθˌpɒl.ə.si/ [US] /ˌskɔːrtʃtˈɝːθˌpɑː.lə-/ *noun* **[C usually sing]** when an army destroys everything in an area such as food, buildings or equipment which could be useful to an enemy

score [WIN] /skɔːʳ/ [US] /skɔːr/ *verb* **1 [I or T]** to win or obtain a point, goal etc. in a competitive activity, such as a sport or game, or in an exam: *Tennant scored (a* ***goal****) in the last minute of the match.* ○ *In American football, a touchdown scores* (= is worth) *six points.* ○ *She scored 18 out of 20 in the spelling test.* **2 [I or T]** to succeed in an activity or to achieve something: *She has certainly scored (****a success****) with her latest novel.* ○ *Nearly every bomb scored* ***a hit****.* ○ *You have a lot of patience – that's where you score* ***over*** (= are better than) *your opponents.* **3 [I]** *UK* to record the number of points won by competitors: **4 [T]** *US INFORMAL* to obtain something: *I managed to score a couple of tickets to the World Cup final.* **5 [I or T]** *SLANG* to obtain illegal drugs: *She tried to score some dope in a nightclub.* **6 [I]** *SLANG* If someone scores, they have sex with someone that they have usually just met: *Did you score last night, then?*
• **score (points) off/over** ***sb*** (*ALSO* **score points**) to make clever remarks in order to make someone look foolish: *He's always trying to score points over people and it's really irritating.*
score /skɔːʳ/ [US] /skɔːr/ *noun* **[C]** *plural* **scores** the number of points, goals, etc. achieved in a game or competition: *a high/low score* ○ *Have you heard the latest cricket score?* ○ *At half time, the score* ***stood at*** (= was) *two all.* ○ *The* ***final*** *score was 3-0.* ○ *Could you* ***keep*** (= record) *the score at this afternoon's match?*
• **What's the score?** *INFORMAL* used to ask someone about what is going to happen, especially when arrangements have been confused: *What's the score, then – are they coming?*
scoreless /ˈskɔː.ləs/ [US] /ˈskɔːr-/ *adj* In a scoreless game, no goals or points are scored: *After a scoreless first half, United went on to win 2-0.* ○ *a scoreless draw*
scorer /ˈskɔː.rəʳ/ [US] /ˈskɔːr.ɚ/ *noun* **[C]** **1** (*US USUALLY* **scorekeeper**) the person who records the score in a game **2** someone who scores a point or goal in a game

score [MUSICAL TEXT] /skɔːʳ/ [US] /skɔːr/ *noun* **[C]** *plural* **scores** **1** a piece of written music with the parts for all the instruments and voices arranged on separate lines: *an orchestral score* **2** the music written for a film, play, etc: *a film score* ○ *Rodgers wrote the score* ***for/of/to*** *'Oklahoma!'.*
score /skɔːʳ/ [US] /skɔːr/ *verb* **[T]** to write or adjust a piece of music for particular instruments or voices: *This piece is scored* ***for*** *strings and woodwind.*

score [MARK] /skɔːʳ/ [US] /skɔːr/ *verb* **[T]** to make a mark or cut on the surface of something hard with a pointed tool, or to draw a line through writing: *If you score the tile first, it will be easier to break.* ➲See also **underscore**.
▲ **score** ***sth*** **out/through** *phrasal verb* **[M]** to draw a line through a piece of writing: *He scored out two names on the list.*

score [ARGUMENT] /skɔːʳ/ [US] /skɔːr/ *noun* **[C]** *plural* **scores** an argument or disagreement that has existed for a long time: *It's time these* ***old*** *scores were forgotten.*
• **settle a score** to punish someone for something wrong which they did to you in the past, and which you cannot forgive: *Police believe the killer was a gang member settling a score with a rival gang.*

score [SUBJECT JUST MENTIONED] /skɔːʳ/ [US] /skɔːr/ **on this/that score** about the thing or subject which has just been mentioned: *I'll let you have the money, so there's nothing to worry about on that score.* ○ *"The team has great determination to win," declared the coach. "I've no doubts on that score."*

score [TWENTY] /skɔːʳ/ [US] /skɔːr/ *noun* **[C usually sing]** *plural* **score** *FORMAL* 20 or approximately 20: *He lived to be three score years and ten* (= until he was 70 years old).
• **by the score** in large numbers: *People are leaving the Nationalist Party by the score.*
scores /skɔːz/ [US] /skɔːrz/ *plural noun* a lot of things or people: *Benjamin received cards from scores* ***of*** *local well-wishers.*

scoreboard /ˈskɔː.bɔːd/ [US] /ˈskɔːr.bɔːrd/ *noun* **[C]** a large board on which the score of a game is shown

scorecard /ˈskɔː.kɑːd/ [US] /ˈskɔːr.kɑːrd/ *noun* **[C]** a small card for recording the score while watching or taking part in a game, race or competition

scoreline /ˈskɔː.laɪn/ [US] /ˈskɔːr-/ *noun* **[C]** the score achieved by the players in a game or competition: *The final scoreline was 5-3.*

scorn /skɔːn/ [US] /skɔːrn/ *noun* **[U]** a very great lack of respect for someone or something that you think is stupid or worthless: *She* ***has nothing but*** *scorn* ***for*** *the new generation of politicians.* ○ *Why do you always* ***pour/heap*** *scorn* ***on*** (= criticize severely and unfairly) *my suggestions?*
scorn /skɔːn/ [US] /skɔːrn/ *verb* **[T]** **1** to show scorn for someone or something: *So does he respect the press and media, or does he secretly scorn them?* ○ *You scorned all my suggestions.* **2** to refuse advice or an offer because you are too proud: *She scorned all my offers of help.*
scornful /ˈskɔːn.fəl/ [US] /ˈskɔːrn-/ *adj*: *a scornful look/remark/laugh/tone* ○ *They are openly scornful* ***of*** *the new plans.* **scornfully** /ˈskɔːn.fəl.i/ [US] /ˈskɔːrn-/ *adv*

Scorpio /ˈskɔː.pi.əʊ/ [US] /ˈskɔːr.pi.oʊ/ *noun* **[C or U]** *plural* **Scorpios** the eighth sign of the zodiac, relating to the period 23 October to 21 November and represented by a SCORPION, or a person born during this period, or a group of stars

scorpion /ˈskɔː.pi.ən/ [US] /ˈskɔːr-/ *noun* **[C]** a small insect-like creature which lives in hot dry areas of the world and has a long body and a curved tail with a poisonous sting

Scot /skɒt/ [US] /skɑːt/ *noun* **[C]** a person who comes from Scotland
the Scots *plural noun* the people of Scotland

Scotch [COUNTRY] /skɒtʃ/ [US] /skɑːtʃ/ *adj* (of products) of or from Scotland * NOTE: When referring to the people or language of Scotland, use **Scottish** or **Scots**.

Scotch [DRINK] /skɒtʃ/ [US] /skɑːtʃ/ *noun* **[C or U]** a type of WHISKY (= a strong alcoholic drink) made in Scotland: *a bottle of Scotch* ○ *I'll have a Scotch* (= a glass of Scotch).

scotch [PREVENT] /skɒtʃ/ [US] /skɑːtʃ/ *verb* **[T]** *SLIGHTLY FORMAL* to prevent something from being believed or being done: *She tried in vain to scotch the rumours.*

ˌScotch ˈbroth *noun* **[U]** a thick soup which usually contains beef, vegetables and barley

ˌScotch ˈegg *noun* **[C]** a boiled egg that has been covered with a mixture of crushed meat, spices and bread and then fried

ˌScotch ˈmist *noun* **[U]** a mixture of thin fog and light rain

ˌScotch ˈtape *noun* **[U]** *US TRADEMARK FOR* **Sellotape**

ˌScotch ˈterrier *noun* **[C]** a type of small active dog with short legs and rough fur

scot-free /ˌskɒtˈfriː/ [US] /ˌskɑːt-/ *adv* without receiving the deserved or expected punishment or without being harmed: *The court* ***let*** *her* ***off*** *scot-free.*

Scotland Yard /ˌskɒt.lənd'jɑːd/ [US] /ˌskɑːt.lənd'jɑːrd/ *group noun* [U] the main office of the London police force, or the officers who work there, especially those involved in solving serious crimes: *Scotland Yard have/has been **called in** to investigate the murder.*

Scots /skɒts/ [US] /skɑːts/ *adj, noun* [U] (*ALSO* **Scottish**) (of) the form of the English language that is spoken in Scotland: *a Scots accent* ○ *They still speak broad Scots even though they left Scotland twenty years ago.*

Scots /skɒts/ [US] /skɑːts/ *adj* (*ALSO* **Scottish**) of or from Scotland, used especially of people: *His wife is Scots.*

Scotsman /'skɒts.mən/ [US] /'skɑːts-/ *noun* [C] a man who comes from Scotland

Scotswoman /'skɒtsˌwʊm.ən/ [US] /'skɑːts-/ *noun* [C] a woman who comes from Scotland

Scottish /'skɒt.ɪʃ/ [US] /'skɑː.t̬ɪʃ/ *adj* (*ALSO* **Scots**) relating to Scotland: *Scottish dancing/music* ○ *the Scottish Highlands* ○ *Scots law*

scoundrel /'skaʊn.drəl/ *noun* [C] *OLD-FASHIONED OR HUMOROUS* a person, especially a man, who treats other people very badly and has no moral principles: *He was, she said, a heartless scoundrel who had stripped her of everything she owned.*

scour [CLEAN] /skaʊəʳ/ [US] /skaʊr/ *verb* [T] (*ALSO* **scour out**) to remove dirt from something by rubbing it hard with something rough: *You'll have to scour out those old cooking pots before you use them.* **scour** /skaʊəʳ/ [US] /skaʊr/ *noun* [U]

scourer *UK* /'skaʊə.rəʳ/ [US] /'skaʊr.ɚ/ *noun* [C] (*US* **scouring pad**) a small ball or rectangle of wire or stiff plastic netting which is used to clean dirt off surfaces

scour [SEARCH] /skaʊəʳ/ [US] /skaʊr/ *verb* [T] to search a place or thing very carefully in order to try to find something: *The police are scouring the countryside **for** the missing child.* ○ *I scoured the shops **for** a blue and white shirt, but I couldn't find one anywhere.*

▲ **scour *sth* out** *phrasal verb* [M] to make a hole by a movement that is repeated continuously over a long period of time: *The fast-moving water had scoured out a channel in the rock.*

scourge /skɜːdʒ/ [US] /skɝːdʒ/ *noun* [C usually sing] something or someone that causes great suffering or a lot of trouble: *the scourge **of** war* ○ *Aids has been described as the scourge **of** the modern world.*

Scouse /skaʊs/ *noun* [C] (*ALSO* **Scouser**) *UK INFORMAL* a person who comes from the Liverpool area, in northwest England

Scouse /skaʊs/ *noun* [U], *adj UK INFORMAL* (of) the form of English spoken by a person from Liverpool

scout [SOLDIER] /skaʊt/ *noun* [C] a person, especially a soldier, sent out to get information about where the enemy are and what they are doing

scout [SEARCH] /skaʊt/ *verb* [I or T; usually + adv or prep] to go to look in various places for something you want: *He's scouting **about/around for** somewhere better to live.* ○ *She's opened an office in Connecticut to scout **out*** (= discover information about) *the east coast housing market.*

ˌscout a'round/'round *noun* [S] *INFORMAL* a quick look around a place or area, especially in order to find something: *I had **a** quick scout around the house to check everything was okay.*

scout /skaʊt/ *noun* [C] a person employed to look for people with particular skills, especially in sport or entertainment: *a talent scout* ○ *Manchester United's chief scout spotted him when he was playing for his school football team.*

the Scouts *UK plural noun* (*US* **the Boy/Girl Scouts**) an international organization which encourages young people of all ages to take part in activities outside and to become responsible and independent ⊃Compare **the Guides**.

Scout /skaʊt/ *noun* [C] (*US ALSO* **Boy Scout**, *US ALSO* **Girl Scout**) a boy or girl who is a member of the Scouts: *a group of Scouts* ○ *a new Scout leader/troop*

'Scout ˌleader *noun* [C] (*US ALSO* **Scoutmaster**, *UK ALSO* **scouter**) the adult leader of a group of Scouts

scowl /skaʊl/ *verb* [I] to look at someone or something with a very annoyed expression: *The boy scowled **at** her and reluctantly followed her back into school.* **scowl** /skaʊl/ *noun* [C]

scrabble [MOVE QUICKLY] /'skræb.l̩/ *verb* [I + adv or prep] **1** to use your fingers to quickly find something that you cannot see: *He was scrabbling about **in** the sand searching for the ring.* **2** to try to obtain something quickly that is not easily available: *The government is scrabbling **around** for ways to raise revenue without putting up taxes.*

Scrabble [GAME] /'skræb.l̩/ *noun* [U] *TRADEMARK* a game played on a board covered in squares, in which players win points by creating words from letters with different values and connecting these words with ones already on the board

scraggly /'skræg.li/ *adj MAINLY US INFORMAL* growing in an untidy and irregular way: *long scraggly hair*

scraggy /'skræg.i/ *adj DISAPPROVING* very thin, especially so that the bones stick out: *He was wearing a high-necked pullover to hide his scraggy neck.*

scram /skræm/ *verb* [I] -mm- *INFORMAL* to go away quickly: *Get out of here! Go on, scram!* ✻ NOTE: This is usually used in the imperative form.

scramble [MOVE QUICKLY] /'skræm.bl̩/ *verb* **1** [I usually + adv or prep] to move or climb quickly but with difficulty, often using your hands to help you: *She scrambled **up** the steep hillside and **over** the rocks.* ○ *He scrambled **into** his clothes* (= put them on quickly) *and raced to fetch a doctor.* ○ *As the burning plane landed, the terrified passengers scrambled **for** the door* (= tried to reach the door quickly). **2** [I] to compete with other people for something there is very little of: [+ to infinitive] *People are scrambling **to** buy property before prices rise even further.*

scramble /'skræm.bl̩/ *noun* [S] **1** a climb which is difficult so that you have to use your hands to help you: *It was **a** real scramble to the top of the hillside.* **2** an act of hurrying: [+ to infinitive] *As soon as the plane landed there was **a** mad/wild scramble **to** get out.* **3** a hurried attempt to get something: *After the death of the dictator there was **an** unseemly scramble **for** power among the generals.*

scramble [CHANGE SIGNAL] /'skræm.bl̩/ *verb* [T] to change a radio or telephone signal so that it can only be understood using a special device

scrambler /'skræm.bləʳ/ [US] /-blɚ/ *noun* [C] an electronic device which scrambles radio or telephone messages

scramble [TAKE OFF] /'skræm.bl̩/ *verb* [I or T] *SPECIALIZED* to (cause a plane to) take off very quickly: *A helicopter was scrambled within minutes of the news.*

ˌscrambled 'eggs *plural noun* eggs mixed with a little milk and mixed again as they are being fried: *scrambled eggs on toast* **scramble** /'skræm.bl̩/ *verb* [T]

scrambling /'skræm.blɪŋ/ *noun* [U] **motocross**

scrap [THROW AWAY] /skræp/ *verb* [T] -pp- **1** to not continue with a system or plan: *They're considering scrapping the tax and raising the money in other ways.* ○ *We scrapped our **plans** for a trip to France.* **2** to get rid of something which is no longer useful or wanted, often using its parts in new ways: *Hundreds of nuclear weapons have been scrapped.*

scrap [METAL] /skræp/ *noun* [U] old cars and machines or pieces of metal, etc. that are not now needed but have parts that can be used to make other things: *scrap iron/metal* ○ *We've sold our old car **for** scrap.*

scrap [SMALL PIECE] /skræp/ *noun* [C] a small irregular piece of something or a small amount of information: *Have you got a scrap **of** paper I could write on?* ○ *I've read **every** scrap of information I can find on the subject.* ○ *There's **not a** scrap **of*** (= no) *evidence to suggest that he committed the crime.*

scraps /skræps/ *plural noun* small bits of food which have not been eaten and which are usually thrown away: *We give all our scraps to our cat.*

scrap [ARGUMENT] /skræp/ *noun* [C] a fight or argument, especially a quick noisy one about something unimportant: *A couple of kids were **having** a scrap in the street.* **scrap** /skræp/ *verb* [I] -pp-

scrappy /'skræp.i/ *adj US* describes a person who often wants to argue or fight

scrapbook /ˈskræp.bʊk/ *noun* [C] a book with empty pages where you can stick newspaper articles, pictures, etc. which you have collected and want to keep

scrape [REMOVE] /skreɪp/ *verb* [T] to remove an unwanted covering or a top layer from something, especially using a sharp edge or something rough: [+ obj + adj] *Scrape your boots clean before you come in.* ○ *We'll have to scrape the snow* ***off*** *the car before we go out in it.* ○ *Emily scraped* ***away*** *the dead leaves to reveal the tiny shoot of a new plant.*

• **scrape (the bottom of) the barrel** INFORMAL to use the worst people or things because that is all that is available: *Richard's in the team? – You really are scraping the barrel!*

scrape /skreɪp/ *noun* [C] INFORMAL a difficult or slightly dangerous situation which you cause by your own foolish behaviour: *She's always getting into silly scrapes – I do wish she'd think before she does things.* ○ *He had a couple of scrapes* ***with*** *the police and ended up in court.*

scraper /ˈskreɪ.pəʳ/ [US] /-pɚ/ *noun* [C] a tool for scraping: *Using a scraper to remove wallpaper can be very time-consuming.*

scrapings /ˈskreɪ.pɪŋz/ *plural noun* small pieces that are left on a surface or have been scraped off

scrape [RUB] /skreɪp/ *verb* [I or T; usually + adv or prep] to (cause to) rub against a surface so that slight damage or an unpleasant noise is produced: *Jackie fell over and scraped her knee (****on*** *the pavement).* ○ *I was woken up by the noise of branches scraping* ***against*** *my bedroom window.*

scrape /skreɪp/ *noun* [C or U] a slight injury or an unpleasant noise produced by rubbing against a surface: *"It's just a scrape," said the boy looking down at his bleeding knee.* ○ *I hate the scrape of chalk* ***on*** *a blackboard.*

scrape [SUCCEED] /skreɪp/ *verb* [I usually + adv or prep] to succeed in getting or achieving something, but only just or with great difficulty: *She scraped* ***into*** *university on very low grades.*

• **scrape home** UK to win by a very small amount in a competitive situation: *The reigning champion scraped home just 2.9 seconds ahead of his nearest rival.*

• **scrape a living** UK to only just earn enough money to provide yourself with food, clothing and a place to live: *He settled in Paris, where he scraped a living writing short stories and magazine articles.*

PHRASAL VERBS WITH **scrape**

▲ **scrape by/along** [LIVE] *phrasal verb* to manage to live when you do not have enough money and other necessary things: *He lost his job, so the family had to scrape along* ***on*** *£95 a week.*

▲ **scrape by/along** [GET RESULT] *phrasal verb* to manage with difficulty to get a successful result or to reach an acceptable standard: *I only learnt Spanish for a year but I can just scrape by in most situations.*

▲ **scrape through** ***(sth)*** *phrasal verb* to succeed in something but with a lot of difficulty: *He managed to scrape through his exam with 52%.*

▲ **scrape** ***sth/sb*** **together/up** *phrasal verb* [M] INFORMAL to manage with great difficulty to collect enough of something, especially money, or to find the things or people that you need: *I finally scraped together enough money for a flight home.* ○ *Do you think we can scrape up a team for the match on Saturday?*

ˈscrap ˌheap *noun* **1** [C] a pile of old, unwanted things, especially pieces of metal **2** [S] If an idea or person is on the scrap heap, people are no longer interested in them: *Some people believe that Communism has been* ***relegated/consigned to the*** *scrap heap* ***of history****.* ○ *Many top class players* ***end up on the*** *scrap heap after a short career.*

scrapie /ˈskreɪ.pi/ *noun* [U] a serious brain disease of sheep and goats which usually results in death

ˌscrap ˈpaper *noun* [U] (US ALSO **scratch paper**) loose sheets of paper, often already partly used, for writing notes on

scrappy /ˈskræp.i/ *adj* badly arranged or planned and consisting of parts which fit together badly: *I'm afraid your last essay was a very scrappy piece of work.*

scrappily /ˈskræp.ɪ.li/ *adv*

scratch [CUT] /skrætʃ/ *verb* **1** [I or T] to cut or damage a surface or your skin slightly with or on something sharp or rough: *We scratched the paintwork trying to get the bed into Martha's room.* ○ [R] *Be careful not to scratch yourself* ***on*** *the roses.* ○ *A few chickens were scratching* ***about/around*** (= searching with their beaks) *in the yard* ***for*** *grain.* **2** [T] If you scratch something on or off a surface, you add it or remove it by scratching: *People have been scratching their names* ***on*** *this rock for years.* ○ *I'm afraid I scratched some paint* ***off*** *the door as I was getting out of the car.* **3** [I] If an animal scratches, it rubs something with its claws: *The dog's scratching* ***at*** *the door – he wants to be let in.* **4** [T] to rub your skin with your nails: *He was scratching* ***(at)*** *his mosquito bites.* ○ *Hannah scratched her head thoughtfully.*

• **scratch beneath the surface** to look beyond what is obvious: *If you scratch beneath the surface you'll find she's really a very nice person.*

• **scratch** ***your*** **head** to think hard about something: *A lot of people must be scratching their heads about which way to vote.*

• **you scratch my back and I'll scratch yours** INFORMAL used to tell someone that if they help you, you will help them

scratch /skrætʃ/ *noun* **1** [C] a mark made by scratching: *Her legs were covered in scratches and bruises after her walk through the forest.* ○ *There was a scratch on the CD.* ○ *Amazingly, he survived the accident* ***without a*** *scratch* (= without suffering any injuries at all). **2** [S] when people or animals scratch themselves: *That dog is* ***having*** *a good scratch. It must have fleas.*

• **from scratch** from the beginning, without using anything that already exists: *Ben built the shed from scratch.*

• **up to scratch** reaching an acceptable standard: *Your last essay wasn't up to scratch/didn't* ***come*** *up to scratch.*

scratchy /ˈskrætʃ.i/ *adj* Scratchy clothes are rough and uncomfortable.

scratch [TEMPORARY] /skrætʃ/ *adj* UK **scratch team/side/orchestra** a group of people brought together in a hurry in order to play together on a particular occasion

scratch [REMOVE] /skrætʃ/ *verb* [I or T] to remove yourself or another person or an animal from a competition before the start: *The world champion scratched* ***from*** *the 800m after falling ill three hours earlier.* ○ *They scratched the horse* ***from*** *the race because she had become lame.*

▲ **scratch around for** ***sth*** *phrasal verb* INFORMAL to look for something that is very difficult to find because it is rare: *The editor of the local paper says he's really scratching around for stories this week.*

scratch-and-sniff /ˌskrætʃ.ənˈsnɪf/ *adj* [before n] A scratch-and-sniff picture is one which releases a smell if you rub it.

scratchcard, scratch card /ˈskrætʃ.kɑːd/ [US] /-kɑːrd/ *noun* [C] UK a small card that you can buy to try to win a prize and which has a covering that you rub off in order to see if you have winning numbers written on it: *a lottery scratchcard*

scratchpad /ˈskrætʃ.pæd/ *noun* [C] US a set of sheets of paper, joined along one edge, used for writing notes on

ˈscratch ˌpaper *noun* [U] US FOR **scrap paper**

scrawl /skrɔːl/ [US] /skrɑːl/ *verb* [T] to write something quickly, without trying to make your writing tidy or easy to read: *I scrawled a quick note* ***to*** *Judith and put it under her door.* ○ *Someone had scrawled graffiti* ***across*** *the wall.*

scrawl /skrɔːl/ [US] /skrɑːl/ *noun* [S] untidy writing that is difficult to read: *P.S. I hope you can decipher my scrawl!*

scrawny /ˈskrɔː.ni/ [US] /ˈskrɑː-/ *adj* unpleasantly thin, often with bones showing: *He came home after three months at college looking terribly scrawny.*

scream /skriːm/ *verb* **1** [I or T] to cry or say something loudly and usually on a high note, especially because of strong emotions such as fear or excitement or anger: *A spider landed on her pillow and she screamed.* ○ *Through the smoke, the rescuers could hear people screaming* ***for*** *help.* ○ *He was screaming* ***in/with*** *pain and begging for anaesthetic.* ○ *They screamed* ***with*** *laughter at her jokes.*

S

○ *Ken screamed **(out)** a warning telling people to get out of the way.* ○ *Mrs Brown screamed* (= shouted angrily) ***at** Joel **for** dropping the test-tube.* ○ *I've never found screaming **(and shouting)*** (= shouting angrily) ***at** my staff to be very effective.* ○ [+ speech] *"I wish you were dead!" she screamed* (= shouted angrily). ○ *I tried to apologize, but he just screamed **abuse/obscenities** at me.* ➲See Note **cry, scream or shout?** at **cry** SHOUT. **2** [I + adv or prep] If a vehicle screams, it moves very quickly making a loud high sound: *The cars screamed **round** the bend/**past** the spectators.* **3** [I] to make a loud high sound: *The ambulance raced round the corner with its tyres screaming.* **4** [I] (*ALSO* **scream out**) If a word or image screams (out), it gets attention because it is very big or impressive: *'Royal Plane Disaster!' screamed the newspaper headlines the next day.*

• **scream (out) for** to need very much: *This matter is screaming out for attention.*

• **scream *yourself* hoarse/silly** (*ALSO* **scream the place down**, *ALSO* **scream *your* head off**) to scream very loudly: *I screamed myself silly on the roller coaster.*

scream /skriːm/ *noun* [C] **1** a loud high sound you make when very frightened, excited or angry: *a scream **of** pain/rage/joy/laughter* ○ *No one heard their screams.* ○ *She **let out** a **piercing/shrill** scream.* **2** *INFORMAL* a person, thing or situation which is very amusing: *Jane's such a scream – her jokes have me in stitches.*

screamingly /ˈskriː.mɪŋ.li/ *adv INFORMAL* extremely: *She told me a screamingly **funny** story about the time she got stuck in an elevator.* ○ *The answer was suddenly screamingly **obvious** to me.*

scree /skriː/ *noun* [C or U] *SPECIALIZED* (an area on the side of a mountain covered with) large loose broken stones

screech /skriːtʃ/ *verb* [I] to make a unpleasant loud high noise: *She was screeching at him at the top of her voice.* ○ *He was screeching **with** pain/laughter.* ○ [+ speech] *"Don't you dare touch me!" she screeched.* ○ *The car screeched **to a halt/standstill*** (= stopped very suddenly, making a loud high noise). ○ *FIGURATIVE The economic recovery is likely to screech **to a halt/standstill*** (= stop very suddenly) *if taxes are increased.*

screech /skriːtʃ/ *noun* [C] a long loud high noise which is unpleasant to hear: *He **let out** a loud screech.* ○ *The truck stopped with a screech **of** brakes.*

screeds /skriːdz/ *plural noun* a large amount of writing: *She's written screeds **(and screeds)** on the subject, but hardly any of it is worth reading.*

screen [PICTURE] /skriːn/ *noun* **1** [C] a flat surface in a cinema or on a television or a computer system on which pictures or words are shown: *Our television has a 19-inch screen.* ○ *Coming to your screens* (= cinemas) *shortly, the amazing adventures of 'Robin Hood'.* ○ *Her ambition is to write for **the** screen* (= for television and films). ○ *Write the letter on the computer, then you can make changes easily **on** screen.* ➲See picture **In the Office** on page Centre 15 **2 the small screen** television: *He's made several films for the small screen.* **3 the big screen** cinema: *So this is your first appearance on the big screen?*

screen /skriːn/ *verb* [T] to show or broadcast a film or television programme: *The programme was not screened **on** British television.*

screening /ˈskriː.nɪŋ/ *noun* [C] a showing: *There will be three screenings of the film – at 3, 5 and 7 p.m.*

screen [EXAMINE] /skriːn/ *verb* [T] **1** to test or examine someone or something to discover if there is anything wrong with them: *All women over 50 will be screened **for** breast cancer.* ○ *Completely unsuitable candidates were screened **out*** (= tested and refused) *at the first interview.* **2 screen *your* calls** to delay your decision to speak to someone who is calling you on the telephone until you can discover who they are, either by listening to them leaving a message on your ANSWERING MACHINE or by seeing their telephone number displayed on your telephone: *I always screen my calls while I'm eating dinner.*

screening /ˈskriː.nɪŋ/ *noun* [C or U] *regular screening(s) **for** cervical cancer*

screen [SEPARATE] /skriːn/ *noun* [C] **1** a vertical structure which is used to separate one area from another, especially to hide something or to protect you from something unpleasant or dangerous: *The nurse pulled a screen around the bed so that the doctor could examine the patient in private.* ○ *A screen **of** trees at the bottom of the garden hid the ugly factory walls.* **2** *MAINLY US* an activity which is not dangerous or illegal but which is used to hide something which is: *That café's just a screen **for** their criminal activities.*

screen /skriːn/ *verb* [T] **1** to protect or hide: *She raised her hand to screen her eyes **from** the bright light.* **2** *MAINLY US* to protect someone by taking the blame yourself: *The husband says he's the murderer but we think it was his wife – he's just screening her.*

▲ **screen *sth* off** *phrasal verb* [M] to separate one area from another using a wall or other vertical structure: *We can screen off part of the room and use it as a temporary office.*

ˈscreen ˌdoor *noun* [C] *US* a door consisting of a wire net with very small holes stretched over a frame, which allows air but not insects to move through it

screenplay /ˈskriːn.pleɪ/ *noun* [C] the text for a film, including the words to be spoken by the actors and instructions for the cameras: *Who wrote/did the screenplay **for/of/to** the film 'Chariots of Fire'?*

ˈscreen ˌprinting *noun* [U] a method of printing by forcing ink through a pattern cut into a piece of cloth stretched across a frame

screensaver, **screen saver** /ˈskriːnˌseɪ.vəʳ/ [US] /-vɚ/ *noun* [C] on a computer, a program which protects the screen by automatically producing a moving image if the computer has not been used for a few minutes

screenwriter /ˈskriːnˌraɪ.təʳ/ [US] /-t̬ɚ/ *noun* [C] someone who writes the story for a film

screw [METAL OBJECT] /skruː/ *noun* [C] a thin pointed piece of metal with a raised edge twisting round along its length and a flat top with a cut in it, which is used to join things together, especially pieces of wood

• **have a screw loose** *INFORMAL* If you say that someone has a screw loose, you mean that they behave in a strange way and seem slightly mentally ill.

• **put/tighten the screws on *sb*** *INFORMAL* to use force or threats to make someone do what you want: *They put the screws on him until he paid up.*

screw /skruː/ *verb* [T usually + adv or prep] **1** to fasten something using a screw: *Screw this piece of wood **to** the wall.* ○ *Screw these two pieces **together**.* **2** to fasten something using an object similar to a screw: *We'll have to screw a hook **into** the wall.* **3** to fasten something by turning it or twisting it: *Screw the lid firmly **on** to the jar and shake well.* **4 screw in/together** If something screws in/together, it fits or fastens together by being turned: *This light bulb screws in.* ○ *The steel rods screw together.*

• **screw up *your* courage** to force yourself to be brave: *I screwed up my courage and went in to see the director.*

screw [TIGHT SHAPE] /skruː/ *verb* [T + adv or prep] **1** to tighten the muscles of your face or part of your face into a particular expression, especially one of disapproval or pain: *He screwed his eyes tight shut against the bright light.* ○ *The woman at the breakfast table screwed her mouth **into** a grimace.* **2** to twist and crush something, especially paper or cloth, roughly with your hands: *She screwed the bag **up** and threw it in the bin.* ○ *He screwed the letter **into** a ball and flung it away.*

screw [CHEAT] /skruː/ *verb* [T] *SLANG* to cheat or deceive someone: *It was only after we'd had the car for a few days that we realised we'd been screwed by the dealer.*

screw [HAVE SEX] /skruː/ *verb* [I or T] *OFFENSIVE* to have sex with someone: *They say he's screwing the boss's wife.*

• **Screw it/you/them, etc.!** *OFFENSIVE* used when expressing extreme anger or annoyance: *"Screw it!" he said. "If they won't give us the money, we'll just take it."* ○ *You don't like it? Well, screw you!*

screw /skruː/ *noun* [C] *OFFENSIVE* the act of sex, or a sexual partner: *I never feel like a screw when I wake up in the morning.* ○ *He's a really good screw.*

screw [PRISON GUARD] /skruː/ *noun* [C] *SLANG* (a word used especially by prisoners) a prison guard

S

PHRASAL VERBS WITH **screw** ▼

▲ **screw around** *phrasal verb* OFFENSIVE to have sex with a lot of people or with people other than your husband or wife

▲ **screw** *sth* **out of** *sb phrasal verb* UK INFORMAL to obtain something from someone by using force or threats: *We'll screw every last penny out of him.*

▲ **screw (sth) up** MISTAKE *phrasal verb* [M] INFORMAL to make a mistake, or to spoil something: *I reckon I screwed the chemistry exam up totally.*

▲ **screw** *you* **up** MAKE UNHAPPY *phrasal verb* [M] INFORMAL When bad experiences or people screw you up, they make you anxious and unhappy or they damage your personality: *It really screwed him up when he saw his friend get killed.*

,**screwed 'up** *adj* INFORMAL unhappy and anxious because of bad experiences: *He's been really screwed up since his wife died.*

screwball PERSON /ˈskruːˌbɔːl/ ⑩ /-bɑːl/ *noun* [C] MAINLY US INFORMAL a person who behaves in a strange and amusing way

screwball BALL /ˈskruːˌbɔːl/ ⑩ /-bɑːl/ *noun* [C] US a ball which is thrown during a baseball game so that it curves to one side

screwdriver /ˈskruːˌdraɪ.vəʳ/ ⑩ /-vɚ/ *noun* [C] a tool for turning screws, consisting of a handle joined to a metal rod shaped at one end to fit in the cut in the top of the screw

screws /skruːz/ *plural noun* **thumbscrew**

,**screw 'top** *noun* [C] a lid for a container which fastens by being turned '**screw-**,**top** *adj* (ALSO **screw-topped**) *a screw-top jar*

screwy /ˈskruː.i/ *adj* OLD-FASHIONED INFORMAL very strange, foolish or unusual: *Pat's always coming up with screwy ideas.*

scribble /ˈskrɪb.l̩/ *verb* [I] to write or draw something quickly or carelessly: *The baby's just scribbled all over my new dictionary!* ○ [+ two objects] *I'll just scribble Dad a note/scribble a note to Dad to say we're going out.*

scribble /ˈskrɪb.l̩/ *noun* [C or U] *What are all these scribbles doing on the wallpaper?* ○ *I hope you can read my scribble!*

scribbler /ˈskrɪb.ləʳ/ ⑩ /-lɚ/ *noun* [C] DISAPPROVING OR HUMOROUS a bad or unimportant writer of books or articles in newspapers or magazines

scribbly gum /ˈskrɪb.li.gʌm/ *noun* [C] AUS a type of eucalyptus tree whose smooth bark is marked by irregular patterns left by insects

scribe /skraɪb/ *noun* [C] **1** a person employed before the invention of printing to make copies of documents **2** in Biblical times, a teacher of religious law

scrimmage /ˈskrɪm.ɪdʒ/ *noun* [C] **1** a fight **2** US a practice game of American football

scrimp /skrɪmp/ *verb* [I] to save money by spending less than is necessary to reach an acceptable standard: *There is a risk that the debt-ridden airline that may be tempted to scrimp on maintenance or security.*

● **scrimp and save** If you scrimp and save, you manage to live on very little money in order to pay for something: *I've been scrimping and saving all year to pay for our holiday.*

script TEXT /skrɪpt/ *noun* [C] **1** the words of a film, play, broadcast or speech: *Bruce Robinson wrote the script for 'The Killing Fields'.* **2** AUS FOR **prescription** ⮑See at **prescribe** GIVE MEDICAL TREATMENT.

scripted /ˈskrɪp.tɪd/ *adj* A scripted speech or broadcast has been written before it is read or performed: *He read from a scripted speech and refused to answer any questions at all at the end of it.* ✳ NOTE: The opposite is **unscripted**.

script EXAM /skrɪpt/ *noun* [C] UK an answer paper written by a student in an exam

script WRITING /skrɪpt/ *noun* **1** [U] a set of letters used for writing a particular language: *Arabic/Cyrillic/Roman script* **2** [C or U] writing, especially when well-formed: *The invitation was written in beautiful italic script.*

scripture /ˈskrɪp.tʃəʳ/ ⑩ /-tʃɚ/ *noun* [C or U] the holy writings of a religion: *the Hindu/Buddhist/Muslim*

scriptures ○ *According to Holy Scripture* (= the Bible), *God created the world in six days.* **scriptural** /ˈskrɪp.tʃ³r.³l/ ⑩ /-tʃɚ-/ *adj* SPECIALIZED *scriptural texts/ passages*

scriptwriter /ˈskrɪptˌraɪ.təʳ/ ⑩ /-tɚ/ *noun* [C] a person who writes the words for films or radio or television broadcasts

scroll PAPER /skrəʊl/ ⑩ /skroʊl/ *noun* [C] **1** a long roll of paper or similar material with usually official writing on it: *The ancient Egyptians stored information on scrolls.* **2** a decoration that looks like a roll of paper: *The tops of the marble pillars were decorated with scrolls.*

scroll MOVE TEXT /skrəʊl/ ⑩ /skroʊl/ *verb* [I usually + adv or prep] to move text or other information on a computer screen in order to view a different part of it: *Scroll to the end of the document.*

scrooge /skruːdʒ/ *noun* [C] DISAPPROVING someone who spends as little money as possible and is not generous: *He's a mean old scrooge!*

scrotum /ˈskrəʊ.təm/ ⑩ /ˈskroʊ.t̬əm/ *noun* [C] *plural* **scrotums** or FORMAL **scrota** SPECIALIZED in most male mammals, a bag of skin near the penis which contains the testicles

scrounge /skraʊndʒ/ *verb* [I or T] INFORMAL to obtain things, especially money or food, by asking for them instead of buying them or working for them: *Peter never buys anything – he just scrounges (off his friends).*

scrounge /skraʊndʒ/ *noun* DISAPPROVING OR HUMOROUS **on the scrounge** Someone who is on the scrounge is asking people for things or for money. **scrounger** /ˈskraʊn.dʒəʳ/ ⑩ /-dʒɚ/ *noun* [C] DISAPPROVING *He thinks that people who receive state benefits are scroungers.*

▲ **scrounge around** *phrasal verb* US INFORMAL to look in different places or in a particular place where you might find something that you need: *She scrounged around in the tool box for a tack or nail to hang the notice up with.*

scrub CLEAN /skrʌb/ *verb* [I or T] **-bb-** to rub something hard in order to clean it, especially using a stiff brush, soap and water: *She scrubbed (at) the mark on the wall for ages, but it wouldn't come off.* ○ [+ obj + adj] *He scrubbed the old saucepan clean, and it looked as good as new.* **scrub** /skrʌb/ *noun* [S] *Children, give your hands a good scrub and come and get your dinner!*

scrub STOP (**-bb-**) /skrʌb/ *verb* [T] (US USUALLY **scratch**) INFORMAL to decide not to do something you had planned to do; cancel: *We had to scrub our plans when I lost my job.*

scrub PLANTS /skrʌb/ *noun* [U] (an area of land covered with) short trees and bushes, growing on dry earth of low quality **scrubby** /ˈskrʌb.i/ *adj*: *scrubby vegetation*

▲ **scrub up** *phrasal verb* If a doctor scrubs up, they wash their hands and arms very thoroughly before performing a medical operation.

'**scrubbing ,brush** *noun* [C] (US ALSO **scrub brush**) a stiff brush used for scrubbing floors

scruff NECK /skrʌf/ *noun* **by the scruff of** the/your **neck** by the skin at the back of the neck: *Cats carry their kittens by the scruff of the neck.* ○ *I took/grabbed him by the scruff of his neck and threw him out of the hall.*

scruff PERSON /skrʌf/ *noun* [C] UK INFORMAL a dirty and untidy person: *I feel a bit of a scruff in my jeans.*

scruffy /ˈskrʌf.i/ *adj* untidy and dirty: *They live in a rather scruffy part of town.* ○ *a small, scruffy-looking man* **scruffily** /ˈskrʌf.ɪ.li/ *adv*

scrum /skrʌm/ *noun* **1** [C] (ALSO **scrummage**) in the sport of rugby, a group of attacking players from each team who come together with their heads down and arms joined, and push against each other, trying to take control of the ball ⮑See picture **Sports** on page Centre 10 **2** [S] when a group of people push each other to get to a place or obtain something **scrummager** /ˈskrʌm.ɪ.dʒəʳ/ ⑩ /-dʒɚ/ *noun* [C]

scrumhalf /ˌskrʌmˈhɑːf/ ⑩ /-ˈhæf/ *noun* [C] *plural* **scrumhalves** a rugby player who throws the ball into the SCRUM

scrump /skrʌmp/ *verb* [T] UK OLD-FASHIONED INFORMAL to steal fruit such as apples from trees

scrumptious /ˈskrʌmp.ʃəs/ *adj* (*UK INFORMAL* **scrummy**) tasting extremely pleasant; DELICIOUS: *scrumptious cream cakes*

scrumpy /ˈskrʌm.pi/ *noun* [U] *UK* an alcoholic drink made from apples: *Scrumpy is a type of strong cider.*

scrunch [MAKE A NOISE] /skrʌntʃ/ *verb* [I or T] to make the noise produced by hard things being pressed together, or to press hard things together so that they make a noise: *The pebbles/gravel/snow scrunched beneath our feet.* ○ *We scrunched the pebbles/gravel/snow under our feet.*

scrunch [CRUSH] /skrʌntʃ/ *verb* [T] to crush material such as paper or cloth into a rough ball in the hand: *She scrunched the letter* ***up*** *and threw it in the bin.*
scrunchy, scrunchie /ˈskrʌn.tʃi/ *noun* [C] a piece of elastic covered in often brightly-coloured cloth which is used to hold long hair at the back of the head

scrunch [MAKE SMALL] /skrʌntʃ/ *verb* [I or T; + adv or prep] to make something or yourself smaller to fit into a small space: *The cat was hiding, scrunched* ***up*** *under the sofa.*

scrunch [FACE] /skrʌntʃ/ *verb* [I or T; usually + adv or prep] to make your face or part of your face into a tight shape in order to show an emotion, or to go into a tight shape which expresses an emotion: *He was red with anger and his face was all scrunched* ***up****.*

scruple /ˈskruː.pl̩/ *noun* [C or U] a feeling that prevents you from doing something that you think is morally wrong or makes you uncertain about doing it: *Robin Hood* ***had*** *no scruples* ***about*** *robbing the rich to give to the poor.* ○ *He is a man* ***without*** *scruple – he has no conscience.*
scruple /ˈskruː.pl̩/ *verb FORMAL* **not scruple to *do sth*** to not care that something you do is morally wrong or likely to have bad results: *He wouldn't scruple to cheat his own mother if there was money in it for him.*

scrupulous /ˈskruː.pjʊ.ləs/ *adj* extremely honest, or doing everything correctly and exactly as it should be done: *A scrupulous politician would not lie about her business interests.* ○ *The nurse told him to be scrupulous* (= extremely careful) ***about*** *keeping the wound clean.*
scrupulously /ˈskruː.pjʊ.lə.sli/ *adv*: *She is always scrupulously honest/fair.* ○ *A hospital must be kept scrupulously clean.*

scrutineer /ˌskruː.tɪˈnɪəʳ/ [US] /-t̬ənˈɪr/ *noun* [C] *UK* a person who counts votes in an election or who makes certain that the counting has been done correctly

scrutinize, *UK USUALLY* **-ise** /ˈskruː.tɪ.naɪz/ [US] /-t̬ən.aɪz/ *verb* [T] to examine something very carefully in order to discover information: *He scrutinized the men's faces carefully/closely, trying to work out who was lying.*
scrutiny /ˈskruː.tɪ.ni/ [US] /-t̬ən.i/ *noun* [U] the careful and detailed examination of something in order to obtain information about it: *The Government's record will* ***be subjected to/come under (close)*** *scrutiny in the weeks before the election.*

scuba diving /ˈskuː.bəˌdaɪ.vɪŋ/ *noun* [U] the sport of swimming under water with special breathing equipment **scuba diver** /ˈskuː.bəˌdaɪ.vəʳ/ [US] /-vɚ/ *noun* [C] *Two hundred scuba divers descended on the island to clean up the harbour.*

scud /skʌd/ *verb* [I usually + adv or prep] **-dd-** (especially of clouds and ships) to move quickly and without stopping in a straight line: *It was a windy day, and small white clouds were scudding* ***across*** *the blue sky.*

scuff /skʌf/ *verb* [T] to make a rough mark on a smooth surface, especially on a shoe or floor: *Please wear trainers in the gym, to avoid scuffing the floor.* ○ *Have you got anything for getting rid of scuff* ***marks*** *on shoes?* ○ *If you scuff your feet* (= pull your shoes along the ground as you walk) *like that, you'll ruin your shoes.*
scuffed /skʌft/ *adj*: *The book's a bit scuffed along the spine, but it was the only copy left in the shop.*

scuffle /ˈskʌf.l̩/ *noun* [C] a short and sudden fight, especially one involving a small number of people: *Two police officers were injured in scuffles with fans at Sunday's National Football League contest.* **scuffle** /ˈskʌf.l̩/ *verb* [I] *The youths scuffled* ***with*** *the policeman, then escaped down the lane.*

scullery /ˈskʌl.ər.i/ [US] /-ɚ-/ *noun* [C] especially in a large old house, a room next to the kitchen where pans are washed and vegetables are prepared for cooking

sculling /ˈskʌl.ɪŋ/ *noun* [U] the sport of rowing in a small narrow boat designed for one, two or four people, who use two small oars each, to move the boat

sculpture /ˈskʌlp.tʃəʳ/ [US] /-tʃɚ/ *noun* [C or U] the art of forming solid objects that represent a thing, person, idea, etc. out of a material such as wood, clay, metal or stone, or an object made in this way: *Tom teaches sculpture at the local art school.* ○ *The museum has several life-sized sculptures* ***of*** *people and animals.*
sculpt /skʌlpt/ *verb* **1** [I or T] to create solid objects that represent a thing, person, idea, etc. out of a material such as wood, clay, metal or stone: *Johnny sculpted an old man's head* ***out of*** *wood.* **2** [T] to form into a particular shape: *The dripping water had sculpted strange shapes* ***out of*** *the rocks/sculpted the rocks* ***into*** *strange shapes.*
sculptured /ˈskʌlp.tʃəd/ [US] /-tʃɚd/ *adj* **1** created as a sculpture: *a deer sculptured* ***in*** *wax* **2** describes a part of someone's body that has a strong smooth shape: *his beautifully sculptured features*
sculptural /ˈskʌlp.tʃə.rəl/ [US] /-tʃɚ-/ *adj SPECIALIZED Her delicate sculptural* ***pieces*** (= works of art) *are now selling in the USA, Europe and Japan.*
sculptor /ˈskʌlp.təʳ/ [US] /-tɚ/ *noun* [C] someone who creates sculptures: *Henry Moore, who died in 1986, is one of Britain's best-known sculptors.*

scum [DIRT] /skʌm/ *noun* [U] a layer of unpleasant or unwanted material that has formed on the top of a liquid: *The lake near the factory was covered with grey, foul-smelling scum.* **scummy** /ˈskʌm.i/ *adj*

scum [IMMORAL PERSON] /skʌm/ *noun* [C or U] *plural* **scum** *INFORMAL* a very bad or immoral person or group of people: *People who organize dog fights are scum in my opinion!* ○ *Those racist scum have been attacking Pakistanis.* ○ *His boss treats him* ***like*** *scum* (= very badly).
• **the scum of the earth** *INFORMAL* the worst type of people that can be imagined: *These men are the scum of the earth.*

scumbag /ˈskʌm.bæg/ *noun* [C] *OFFENSIVE* a very unpleasant person who has done something dishonest or immoral

scupper [SINK] /ˈskʌp.əʳ/ [US] /-ɚ/ *verb* [T] to sink your own ship on purpose

scupper [SPOIL] /ˈskʌp.əʳ/ [US] /-ɚ/ *verb* [T] to cause something such as a plan or an opportunity to fail: *Arriving late for the interview scuppered my* ***chances*** *of getting the job.*

scurf /skɜːf/ [US] /skɝːf/ *noun* [U] very small bits of dry dead skin which fall off the head; DANDRUFF

scurrilous /ˈskʌr.ɪ.ləs/ [US] /ˈskɝː-/ *adj FORMAL* expressing unfair or false criticism which is likely to damage someone's reputation: *a scurrilous remark/attack/article*
scurrilously /ˈskʌr.ɪ.lə.sli/ [US] /ˈskɝː-/ *adv*

scurry /ˈskʌr.i/ [US] /ˈskɝː-/ *verb* [I usually + adv or prep] to move quickly, with small short steps: *The mouse scurried* ***across*** *the floor.* ○ *The noise of the explosion* ***sent*** *the villagers scurry****ing*** *back into their homes.*
scurry /ˈskʌr.i/ [US] /ˈskɝː-/ *noun* [S]

scurvy /ˈskɜː.vi/ [US] /ˈskɝː-/ *noun* [U] an illness of the body tissues which is caused by a lack of VITAMIN C

scuttle [RUN] /ˈskʌt.l̩/ [US] /ˈskʌt̬-/ *verb* [I usually + adv or prep] to move quickly, with small short steps, especially in order to escape: *A crab scuttled* ***away*** *under a rock as we passed.* ○ *The children scuttled* ***off*** *as soon as the headmaster appeared.*

scuttle [SINK] /ˈskʌt.l̩/ [US] /ˈskʌt̬-/ *verb* [T] **1** to intentionally sink a ship, especially your own, in order to prevent it from being taken by an enemy **2** to stop something happening, or to cause a plan to fail

scuttle [CONTAINER] /ˈskʌt.l̩/ [US] /ˈskʌt̬-/ *noun* [C] a **coal scuttle**

scuttlebutt /ˈskʌt.l̩.bʌt/ [US] /ˈskʌt̬-/ *noun* [U] *US INFORMAL* news or information which may or may not be true: *Have you heard any scuttlebutt* ***about*** *the new boss?*

scuzzy /ˈskʌz.i/ *adj* INFORMAL (usually of people) unpleasant, dirty and probably unable to be trusted

scythe /saɪð/ *noun* [C] a tool with a long sharp curved blade and a long handle held in two hands, used especially to cut long grass ➲Compare **sickle**.

scythe /saɪð/ *verb* **1** [T] to cut using a scythe **2** [I + adv or prep] to move very quickly through a group of people or things: *The racing car left the track at 120 mph and scythed* ***through*** *the crowd of spectators, killing ten.*

SDI /ˌes.diːˈaɪ/ *noun* [U] (INFORMAL **Star Wars**) ABBREVIATION FOR Strategic Defense Initiative: a plan to defend the US from enemy nuclear weapons by destroying them in space

the SDLP /ðiˌes.diːˌelˈpiː/ *noun* [S] ABBREVIATION FOR the Social and Democratic Labour Party: a political party in N Ireland which supports union with the Republic of Ireland by peaceful methods

SE *noun* [U], *adj* ABBREVIATION FOR **southeast** or **southeastern**

sea /siː/ *noun* **1** [C or U] the salty water which covers a large part of the surface of the Earth, or a large area of salty water, smaller than an ocean, which is partly or completely surrounded by land: *the Mediterranean Sea* ○ *We went swimming* ***in the*** *sea.* ○ *The sea was* ***calm/smooth/choppy/rough*** *when we crossed the Channel.* ○ *The refugees were* ***at sea*** (= in a boat on the sea a long way from land) *for forty days before reaching land.* ○ *When we moved to the US, we sent our things* ***by*** *sea* (= in a ship). ○ *We spent a lovely week* ***by the sea*** (= on the coast) *this year.* ○ *Soon we had left the river estuary and were heading towards* ***the open*** *sea* (= the part of the sea a long way from land). **2** [C] one of the large flat areas on the moon which in the past were thought to be seas **3** **a sea of** ***sth*** a large amount or number of: *The teacher looked down and saw* ***a*** *sea of smiling faces.*

• **at sea** confused: *I'm all/completely at sea* ***with*** *the new coins.*

• **put (out) to sea** (of a ship) to leave a harbour and start a journey: *The boats will put (out) to sea on this evening's high tide.*

ˈsea aˌnemone *noun* [C] a soft, brightly coloured sea creature which looks like a flower and often lives on rocks under the water

the seabed /ðəˈsiː.bed/ *noun* [S] the solid surface of the Earth which lies under the sea: *The ship has been lying on the seabed for more than 50 years.*

seabird /ˈsiː.bɜːd/ [US] /-bɝːd/ *noun* [C] a bird that lives near the sea and obtains its food from it

seaboard /ˈsiː.bɔːd/ [US] /-bɔːrd/ *noun* [C usually sing] the long thin area of a country which is next to the sea; coast: *The company owns a chain of hotels* ***along/on*** *the Atlantic seaboard.*

seaborne /ˈsiː.bɔːn/ [US] /-bɔːrn/ *adj* carried in a ship: *seaborne trade/goods* ○ *seaborne missiles/troops/reinforcements*

ˌsea ˈbreeze *noun* [C] a light cool wind blowing from the sea onto the land

ˈsea ˌcaptain *noun* [C] a person in charge of a ship, especially one used for trading rather than for military purposes

ˈsea ˌchange *noun* [C] LITERARY a complete change: *There will have to be a sea change in people's attitudes if public transport is ever to replace the private car.*

ˈsea ˌdog *noun* [C] LITERARY OR HUMOROUS an old sailor with many years of experience at sea: *With his white beard and blue cap he looked like an* ***old*** *sea dog.*

seafaring /ˈsiːˌfeə.rɪŋ/ [US] /-ˌfer.ɪŋ/ *adj* [before n] LITERARY connected with travelling by sea: *a seafaring man* (= a sailor)

seafood /ˈsiː.fuːd/ *noun* [U] edible animals from the sea, especially fish or sea animals with shells

seafront /ˈsiː.frʌnt/ *noun* [C usually sing] (ALSO **front**) the part of a coastal town next to the beach, often with a wide road or path and a row of houses and shops facing the sea: *We rented a house* ***on*** *the seafront for the summer.* ○ *After dinner we went for a stroll* ***along*** *the seafront.*

seagoing /ˈsiːˌɡəʊ.ɪŋ/ [US] /-ˌɡoʊ-/ *adj* [before n] (of ships) built for use on journeys across the sea, not just for coastal and river journeys

seagull /ˈsiː.ɡʌl/ *noun* [C] (ALSO **gull**) a bird which lives near the sea and has short legs, long wings and white and grey feathers: *a flock of seagulls* ➲See picture **Animals and Birds** on page Centre 4

seahorse /ˈsiː.hɔːs/ [US] /-hɔːrs/ *noun* [C] a small fish which swims in a vertical position and has a head like that of a horse

seal [ANIMAL] /siːl/ *noun* [C] a large fish-eating mammal which lives partly in the sea and partly on land or ice

sealing /ˈsiː.lɪŋ/ *noun* [U] the hunting and killing of seals

seal [MARK] /siːl/ *noun* [C] an official mark on a document, sometimes made with wax, which shows that it is legal or has been officially approved: *The lawyer stamped the certificate with her seal.*

• **seal of approval** an official sign of approval: *The Government has* ***given*** *the proposal its seal of approval.*

• **set/put the seal on** to make the result of something certain: *The meeting set the seal on the negotiations.*

seal /siːl/ *verb* [T] to make an agreement more certain or to approve it formally: *The two leaders sealed their agreement* ***with*** *a handshake.*

seal [COVERING] /siːl/ *noun* [C] **1** something fixed around the edge of an opening to prevent liquid or gas flowing through it: *Clean the seal* ***on/around*** *the fridge door regularly so that it remains airtight.* **2** a thin piece of material such as paper or plastic that covers the opening of a container and has to be broken in order to open the container and use the contents

seal /siːl/ *verb* [T] **1** to close an entrance or container so that nothing can enter or leave it **2** to cover a surface with a special liquid to protect it: *This floor has just been sealed (****with*** *varnish), so don't walk on it!* **3** to close a letter or parcel by sticking the edges together: *Seal the package* ***(up)*** *with sticky tape.* ○ *He sealed* ***(down)*** *the* ***envelope*** *and put a stamp on it.*

• **seal *your* fate** If an action, event or situation seals your fate, nothing can stop some unpleasant thing happening to you: *From the moment she stepped into the busy road her fate was sealed.*

sealant /ˈsiː.lənt/ *noun* [C or U] a substance such as paint or polish that is painted onto a surface to protect it from other liquids from going into it, or is put in the space between two materials for the same reason

sealed /siːld/ *adj* closed: *The teacher opened the sealed envelope containing the exam papers.*

PHRASAL VERBS WITH **seal**

▲ **seal *sth* in** *phrasal verb* [M] to prevent a substance or quality from being lost from something during a process such as cooking: *Fry the meat quickly in hot oil to seal in the flavour/juices.*

▲ **seal *sth* off** *phrasal verb* [M] to prevent people from entering an area or building, often because it is dangerous: *Two more bombs have been discovered since the police sealed off the area.*

ˈsea ˌlane *noun* [C] a particular route across the sea regularly used by ships

ˌsealed ˈorders *plural noun* instructions given to a member of the armed forces which are not to be opened until a particular time

ˈsea ˌlegs *plural noun* a person's ability to keep their balance while walking on a moving ship and to not be ill

ˈsea ˌlevel *noun* [C] the average height of the sea where it meets the land: *The top of Mount Everest is 8848m* ***above*** *sea level.*

ˈsealing ˌwax *noun* [U] a type of wax which is used for making a seal because it melts easily and hardens quickly

ˈsea ˌlion *noun* [C] a large seal from the North Pacific Ocean which has large ears and can move on land

sealskin /ˈsiːl.skɪn/ *noun* [U] the skin or fur of a seal, especially when it is used for making clothing

seam [JOIN] /siːm/ *noun* [C] a line where two things join, especially a line of sewing joining two pieces of cloth or leather: *The bags we sell have very strong seams, so they* *will last for years.* ○ *My old coat is **coming/falling apart at the** seams* (= the stitches are coming out). ○ FIGURATIVE *Their marriage is **coming/falling apart at the** seams* (= likely to fail).

• **bursting at the seams** INFORMAL If a place is bursting at the seams, it has a very large number of people or things in it: *Now that they've got six children, their little house is bursting at the seams.*

seamed /siːmd/ *adj* LITERARY covered in lines: *The old man's face was seamed and wrinkled.* **seamless** /ˈsiːm.ləs/ *adj*: *seamless stockings/tights*

seam [LAYER] /siːm/ *noun* [C] a long thin layer of a substance such as coal which has formed between layers of other rocks

• **be a rich seam to mine** to be full of good material and ideas to use: *When she started writing novels, she found her time as a judge was a rich seam for her to mine.*

seaman /ˈsiː.mən/ *noun* [C] a sailor, especially one who is not an officer

seamanship /ˈsiː.mən.ʃɪp/ *noun* [U] skill in managing a ship

seamstress /ˈsiːm.strəs/ /ˈsem-/ *noun* [C] OLD-FASHIONED a woman whose job is sewing and making clothes

seamy /ˈsiː.mi/ *adj* (of a situation) unpleasant because of a connection with dishonesty, violence and illegal sex: *The film vividly portrays the seamy **side of life** in the London of the early 70s.*

séance /ˈseɪ.ɒs/ ⓤ /ˈseɪ.ɑːnts/ *noun* [C] a meeting where people try to talk with dead people: *They're **holding** a séance this evening.*

seaplane /ˈsiː.pleɪn/ *noun* [C] an aircraft that can take off from and land on water ➪See picture **Planes, Ships and Boats** on page Centre 14

seaport /ˈsiː.pɔːt/ ⓤ /-pɔːrt/ *noun* [C] (a city or town with) a port which can be used by ships

sear /sɪəʳ/ ⓤ /sɪr/ *verb* [T] **1** to burn the surface of something with sudden very strong heat: *The heat from the explosion seared their hands and faces.* **2** to fry a piece of meat quickly at a high temperature, in order to prevent liquid and flavour escaping from it **3** to have a strong unpleasant effect on someone's feelings or memories: *The disaster is indelibly seared **into** the villagers' memory.*

searing /ˈsɪə.rɪŋ/ ⓤ /ˈsɪr.ɪŋ/ *adj* **1** If something, such as a feeling or temperature, is described as searing, it is extreme: *A searing **pain** shot up her arm.* ○ *The race took place in the searing **heat**.* **2** (especially of a criticism or story) very powerful and emotional or critical: *The article is a searing attack on government mismanagement.* ○ *Her latest novel is a searing tale of love and hate.* **searingly** /ˈsɪə.rɪŋ.li/ ⓤ /ˈsɪr.ɪŋ-/ *adv*

search /sɜːtʃ/ ⓤ /sɝːtʃ/ *verb* **1** [I or T] to look somewhere carefully in order to find something: *The police searched the woods **for** the missing boy.* ○ *She searched his face **for** some sign of forgiveness, but it remained expressionless.* ○ *He searched **(in/through)** his pockets **for** some change.* ○ *I've searched **high and low** (= everywhere), but I can't find my birth certificate.* ○ *The detectives searched the house **from top to bottom** (= all over it), but they found no sign of the stolen goods.* ○ FIGURATIVE *She searched her **mind/memory** for the man's name, but she couldn't remember it.* ○ FIGURATIVE *People who are searching **after** inner peace sometimes turn to religion.* **2** [I] to try to find the answer to a problem: *Philosophers have searched for millennia but they haven't found the meaning of life.* **3** [T] A police officer who searches you or your possessions looks for something you might be hiding: *The men were searched **for** drugs and then released.*

• **Search me!** INFORMAL something that you say when you do not know the answer to a question: *"Where's Jack?" "Search me!"*

search /sɜːtʃ/ ⓤ /sɝːtʃ/ *noun* **1** [C] when you try to find someone or something: *After a long search, they eventually found the missing papers.* ○ *We're **doing** a computer search **for** all words beginning with 'high'.* ○ *The police **carried out/conducted/made** a thorough/exhaustive search **of** the premises, but they failed to find any drugs.* **2** [S] when you try to find an answer to a problem: *the search **for** happiness*

• **in search of** *sth* trying to find something: *She was shot by a sniper when she went out in search of firewood.*

searching /ˈsɜː.tʃɪŋ/ ⓤ /ˈsɝː-/ *adj* intended to find out the often hidden truth about something: *I think we need to ask some searching **questions** about how the money has been spent.* **searchingly** /ˈsɜː.tʃɪŋ.li/ ⓤ /ˈsɝː-/ *adv*

COMMON LEARNER ERROR

search or **search for**?

If you **search** a place or person, you look for something in that place or on that person:

The police searched the man/the house for weapons.

If you **search for** something or someone, you look for that thing or person.

The police searched for the stolen computers but they were never recovered.

~~The police searched the stolen computers but they were never recovered.~~

▲ **search** *sth/sb* **out** *phrasal verb* [M] to find something or someone after searching: *Despite the warm weather, we searched out some snow and went skiing.*

searchable /ˈsɜːtʃ.ə.bl̩/ ⓤ /ˈsɝːtʃ-/ *adj* If computer files are searchable, it is possible to search for words, numbers, and other information in those files: *a fully searchable database*

search ˌengine *noun* [C] a computer program which finds information on the Internet by looking for words which you have typed in

searchlight /ˈsɜːtʃ.laɪt/ ⓤ /ˈsɝːtʃ-/ *noun* [C] a light with a very bright beam that can be turned in any direction, used especially to guard prisons or to see the movements of enemy aircraft in the sky

search ˌparty *noun* [C] a group of people who look for someone who is lost: *A search party was **sent out** to look for the missing climbers.*

search ˌwarrant *noun* [C] an official document which gives police officers the authority to search a building for stolen property, illegal goods or information which might help to solve a crime

searing /ˈsɪə.rɪŋ/ ⓤ /ˈsɪr.ɪŋ/ *adj* ➪See at **sear**.

seascape /ˈsiː.skeɪp/ *noun* [C] a painting of a view of the sea

seashell /ˈsiː.ʃel/ *noun* [C] the empty shell of a small sea creature, often one found lying on the beach

the seashore /ðəˈsiː.ʃɔːʳ/ ⓤ /-ʃɔːr/ *noun* [S] the land along the edge of the sea: *As we walked along the seashore we saw several different sorts of seaweed and lots of tiny crabs.*

seasick /ˈsiː.sɪk/ *adj* vomiting or having the feeling you will vomit because of the movement of the ship you are travelling in: *I **was/felt** seasick, so I went up on deck for some fresh air.* **seasickness** /ˈsiː.sɪk.nəs/ *noun* [U]

the seaside /ðəˈsiː.saɪd/ *noun* [S] the area near the sea, especially where people spend their holidays and enjoy themselves: *Let's go to the seaside at the weekend!* ○ *a seaside holiday/hotel/resort*

season [PART OF YEAR] /ˈsiː.zⁿn/ *noun* [C] **1** one of the four periods of the year; spring, summer, autumn or winter **2** the period of the year when something that happens every year happens: *How long does the **dry/hurricane/monsoon/etc.** season last?* **3** the period of the year during which a particular sport is played: *The British football season begins in August and ends in May.* **4** UK a period when a set of programmes, plays or musical events are broadcast or seen: *There will be more documentaries and fewer quiz shows in the autumn season on TV.* ○ *There's a season (US **festival**) of 1960s French films at the Arts Cinema next month.* **5** the **(holiday/summer/tourist, etc.) season** the period when most people take their holidays, go to visit places or take part in an activity outside work: *Air fares are more expensive during the holiday season.*

• **in season 1** If fruit and vegetables are in season, they are being produced in the area and are available and ready to eat: *Fruit is cheaper when it's in season.* **2** at the time of year when many people want to travel or have a holiday: *Hotel rooms are more expensive in season.* **3** A

female animal that is in season is ready to have sex and able to become pregnant. **4** An animal that is in season can be hunted legally during a particular period of time.
• **out of season 1** If fruit and vegetables are out of season, they do not grow in the area during that time: *In Britain, tomatoes are out of season in winter.* **2** during the period when fewer people want to travel or have a holiday **3** during the period when it is not legal to hunt animals
• **the ˌseason of goodˈwill** the period around CHRISTMAS
seasonable /ˈsiː.zᵊn.ə.bl̩/ *adj* expected at or suitable for a particular time: *December brought some seasonable snow showers.*
seasonal /ˈsiː.zᵊn.ᵊl/ *adj* relating to or happening during a particular period in the year: *seasonal vegetables* ○ *seasonal farm work*
seasonally /ˈsiː.zᵊn.ᵊl.i/ *adv* relating to the particular season of the year: *Although total unemployment has decreased, the seasonally* ***adjusted*** *figure has risen slightly.*
season [FLAVOUR] /ˈsiː.zᵊn/ *verb* **[T]** to improve the flavour of savoury food by adding salt, herbs or spices when cooking or preparing it: *Drain the rice, stir in the salmon and season* ***to taste*** (= so that it has the taste you like).
seasoning /ˈsiː.zᵊn.ɪŋ/ *noun* **[C or U]** a substance that is added to savoury food to improve its flavour: *Taste the soup and adjust the seasoning, adding more salt or pepper as desired.*
season [HARDEN WOOD] /ˈsiː.zᵊn/ *verb* **[T]** to harden wood to make it ready for use, by drying it gradually
seasonal affective disorder /ˌsiː.zᵊn.ᵊl.əˈfek.tɪv.dɪˌsɔː.dəʳ/ [US] /-ˌsɔːr.dɚ/ *noun* **[U]** (*ABBREVIATION* **SAD**) a medical condition in which a person lacks energy and enthusiasm during the winter because of the reduced period of natural light
seasoned /ˈsiː.zᵊnd/ *adj* having a lot of experience of doing something and therefore knowing how to do it well: *a seasoned* ***traveller*** ○ *a seasoned* ***campaigner*** *for human rights*
Season's Greetings /ˌsiː.zᵊnzˈgriː.tɪŋz/ [US] /-t̬ɪŋz/ *sentence, plural noun* sometimes written on a Christmas card as a way of expressing a Christmas greeting, especially to someone who is not from a Christian culture
ˈseason ˌticket *noun* **[C]** a ticket which can be used many times within a limited period and is cheaper than paying separately for each use: *I have a season ticket* ***for*** *all Manchester United's games.*
seat [FURNITURE] /siːt/ *noun* **[C]** an item of furniture or part of a train, plane etc that has been designed for someone to sit on: *Chairs, stools, sofas and benches are different types of seat.* ○ *Please* ***have/take*** *a seat* (= sit down). ○ *A car usually has a* ***driver's*** *seat, a* ***front/passenger*** *seat and* ***back/rear*** *seats.* ○ *My ticket says 22D but there's already someone* ***in*** (= sitting on) *that seat.* ○ *Is this seat* ***free/taken*** (= Is anyone using it)*?* ○ *Would you* ***keep*** (= stop anyone else from sitting in) *my seat* ***(for*** *me) while I go to the buffet car?* ○ *FORMAL Please* ***keep*** *your seats* (= stay sitting down) *until asked to leave.* ○ *Could I* ***book/reserve*** *two seats* (= arrange for a seat to be officially kept for me) *for tomorrow evening's performance?* ➲See picture **Car** on page Centre 12
• **bums on seats** *UK* (*US* **fannies in the seats**) *INFORMAL* the number of people who have paid to watch a performance: *Lowering ticket prices should increase the number of bums on seats.*
-seat /-siːt/ *suffix* with enough seats for the particular number of people: *a 2000-seat theatre*
seat /siːt/ *verb* **1 [T + adv or prep]** to arrange for someone to have a particular seat: *The waiter greeted me with a big smile and seated us by the window.* **2 [R usually + adv or prep]** to sit somewhere: *"I'm so glad to see you!" she said, seating herself between Eleanor and Marianne.* **3 [T not continuous]** (of a building, room, table or vehicle) to have enough seats for: *The new concert hall seats 1500 people.*
seated /ˈsiː.tɪd/ [US] /-t̬ɪd/ *adj* sitting: *The woman seated opposite him refused to stop staring at him.* ○ *You are requested to* ***remain*** *seated during takeoff.* ○ *FORMAL Ladies and gentlemen, please* ***be*** *seated* (= please sit down).
-seater /-siː.təʳ/ [US] /-t̬ɚ/ *suffix* with enough seats for the particular number of people: *a 50 000-seater stadium*
seating /ˈsiː.tɪŋ/ [US] /-t̬ɪŋ/ *noun* **[U] 1** the seats which are provided in a place: *The car has seating* ***for*** *six.* **2** how or where people will sit: *Have you worked out the seating* ***arrangements/plan*** *for the wedding reception?*
seat [BOTTOM PART] /siːt/ *noun* **[C usually sing]** the part of an item of furniture or clothing on which a person sits: *I've spilt some coffee on the seat of the armchair.* ○ *The seat of those trousers looks rather tight, sir – Would you like to try a larger size?*
• **by the seat of** ***your*** **pants** If you do something by the seat of your pants, you do it using only your own experience and trusting your own judgment.
seat [OFFICIAL POSITION] /siːt/ *noun* **[C]** an official position as a politician or member of a group of people who control something: *She has a seat* ***on*** *the board of directors.* ○ *He is expected to* ***lose*** *his seat* ***on*** *the council in next month's elections.* ○ *She* ***won*** *her seat* ***in*** *Parliament in 1979.* ○ *He has a very* ***safe*** *seat* (= a seat that is very unlikely to be lost in an election).
seat [BASE] /siːt/ *noun* **[C]** a place which acts as a base or centre for an important activity: *The seat* ***of government*** *in the US is in Washington, DC.* ○ *St Petersburg was the seat* ***of*** *the Russian Revolution.*
• **ˌseat of ˈlearning** *FORMAL* a place where people are educated: *The Sorbonne is a world-famous seat of learning.*
ˈseat ˌbelt *noun* **[C]** (*ALSO* **safety belt**) a belt which fastens around someone travelling in a vehicle or aircraft, and which holds them in their seat in order to reduce the risk of them being injured in an accident: *Do you know how to* ***fasten/do up*** *your seat belt?* ○ *You must* ***wear*** *your seat belt.* ➲See picture **Car** on page Centre 12
ˈsea ˌurchin *noun* **[C]** a small edible sea animal which lives in water that is not very deep, and has a round shell that is covered with sharp points like needles
ˌsea ˈwall *noun* **[C]** a wall that protects land from being flooded or damaged by the sea or protects a port from the action of powerful waves
seaweed /ˈsiː.wiːd/ *noun* **[U]** a green, brown or dark red plant that grows in the sea or on land very close to the sea
seaworthy /ˈsiːˌwɜː.ði/ [US] /-ˌwɝː-/ *adj* (of a ship) in a condition that is good enough to travel safely on the sea
seaworthiness /ˈsiːˌwɜː.ðɪ.nəs/ [US] /-ˌwɝː-/ *noun* **[U]**
sebaceous gland /sɪˈbeɪ.ʃəsˌglænd/ *noun* **[C]** *SPECIALIZED* a very small organ in the skin which produces an oily substance that makes hair shiny and prevents skin from becoming dry
sec /sek/ *noun* **[C] 1** *WRITTEN ABBREVIATION FOR* **second** TIME **2** *INFORMAL* a very short period of time: *Would you mind waiting for me – I'll only be a couple of secs.*
secateurs *UK* /ˌsek.əˈtɜːz/ [US] /-ˈtɝːz/ *plural noun* (*US* **pruning shears**) a garden tool which has two short sharp blades and is used for cutting plant stems
secede /sɪˈsiːd/ *verb* **[I]** *FORMAL* to become independent of a country or area of government: *There is likely to be civil war if the region tries to secede* ***from*** *the south.*
secession /sesˈeʃ.ᵊn/ *noun* **[U]** **secessionist** /sesˈeʃ.ᵊn.ɪst/ *noun* **[C]**, *adj*
secluded /sɪˈkluː.dɪd/ *adj* quiet and private by being situated away from people, roads or buildings: *a secluded beach* ○ *a secluded house in the forest*
seclusion /sɪˈkluː.ʒᵊn/ *noun* **[U]** when someone is alone, away from other people: *He's been living* ***in*** *seclusion since he retired from acting.* ○ *In some societies women are kept* ***in*** *seclusion, so that they are hardly ever seen in public.* ○ *After being with a tour group all week I was glad to return to the seclusion* ***of*** *my own home.*
second [POSITION] /ˈsek.ᵊnd/ *determiner, pronoun, adj, adv* **1** immediately after the first and before any others: *Is Brian her first or second child?* ○ *This is the second of the four tests.* **2** the position in which a person finishes a race or competition if they finish immediately behind the winner: *Robertson won the race and Cameron* ***was/came/finished*** *second.* ○ *First prize is a fortnight in Barbados and second* ***prize*** *is a weekend in Rome.* ○ *In*

S

this business, money comes first and principles **come a very poor** *second* (= they are much less important). **3** Second is used to show that only one thing is better, bigger, etc. than the thing mentioned: *St Petersburg is Russia's second* **(biggest/largest)** *city.* ○ *Iraq's oil reserves are second* **only to** *Saudi Arabia's.* ○ *The conditions that these prisoners are kept in are second* **to none** (= better than all others). **4** another: *She is often described as the second Marilyn Monroe.* ○ *You really ought to make the most of the opportunity, because you won't get a second* **chance.** ○ *Richard and Liz have a second* **home** *in France.* ○ *Pay attention to what she's saying because she won't explain it a second* **time.** **5** happening only once out of every two possible times; ALTERNATE: *We've decided to hold the conference* **every second** *year.*

• **second best** not as good as the best and therefore less desirable: *She refuses to* **settle for** *second best – she strives for perfection.*

• **without a second thought** If you do something without a second thought, you do it immediately without having any doubts about it: *When I asked to borrow some money, she gave me £100 without a second thought.*

second /ˈsek.ənd/ *adv* (ALSO **secondly**) used for introducing the second reason, idea, etc: *There are two good reasons why we can't do it. First, we can't afford it, and second, we don't have time.*

second /ˈsek.ənd/ *noun* [C] (ALSO **second class degree**) *UK* a degree qualification immediately below the highest level you can obtain from a British university

secondly /ˈsek.ənd.li/ *adv* (ALSO **second**) used when stating the second of two or more reasons or pieces of information: *I want two things from my boss – firstly, a pay rise, and secondly, a longer contract.*

seconds /ˈsek.əndz/ *plural noun* INFORMAL an extra serving of food that is given after the first serving has been eaten: *Would anyone like seconds* **of** *ice cream?*

second TIME /ˈsek.ənd/ *noun* [C] **1** (ABBREVIATION **sec,** ABBREVIATION **s**) a short unit of time which is equal to a sixtieth of a minute: *There are sixty seconds in a minute.* ○ *These computers process millions of instructions* **per** *second.* ○ *The new system can trace a phone call in a* **fraction** *of a second.* **2** a very short period of time: *"Come on, hurry up!" "I'll* **just/only** *in a second – I've got to lock the back door."* ○ *Have you got a second, Paul? I'd like to have a word with you.* ○ *It won't take a second* (= It will be very quick). ○ *Wait* **a couple of/a few** *seconds before trying again.*

second SUPPORT /ˈsek.ənd/ *verb* [T] to make a formal statement of support for a suggestion made by someone else during a meeting so that there can be a discussion or vote: SPECIALIZED *The* **motion** *was proposed by the club's chairwoman and seconded by the secretary.* ○ *"I could do with a drink." "I'll second that* (= I agree with you)*!"*

seconder /ˈsek.ən.dəʳ/ ⓤ /-dəˈ/ *noun* [C] *There was no seconder for* (= person who was willing to second) *the motion so it could not be debated.*

second SEND /sɪˈkɒnd/ ⓤ /-ˈkɑːnd/ *verb* [T] *UK* to send an employee to work somewhere else temporarily, either to increase the number of workers or to replace other workers, or to exchange experience or skills: *During the dispute, many police officers were seconded* **from** *traffic duty* **to** *the prison service.* **secondment** /sɪˈkɒnd.mənt/ ⓤ /-ˈkɑːnd-/ *noun* [C or U] *His involvement with the project began when he was on (a) secondment* **from** *NASA* **to** *the European Space Agency.*

second MEASUREMENT /ˈsek.ənd/ *noun* [C] SPECIALIZED the smallest unit used for measuring an angle: *There are 3600 seconds in a degree.*

second DAMAGED PRODUCT /ˈsek.ənd/ *noun* [C] a product that is sold cheaply because it is damaged or not in perfect condition

second HELPER /ˈsek.ənd/ *noun* [C] a person who takes care of someone who is fighting in a boxing competition or, in the past, in a DUEL (= organized fight)

secondary LESS IMPORTANT /ˈsek.ən.dri/ ⓤ /-der.i/ *adj* less important than related things: *Her health is what matters – the cost of the treatment is of secondary importance.* ○ *The need for secrecy is secondary* **to** *the need to take immediate action.* **secondarily** /ˌsek.ənˈdeə.rɪ.li/ ⓤ /-ˈder.ɪ-/ *adv*

secondary EDUCATION /ˈsek.ən.dri/ ⓤ /-der.i/ *adj* [before n] relating to the education of children approximately between the ages of 11 and 18 years old: *The proposed reforms include making secondary* **education** *compulsory up to the age of 18.* ○ *Marcus has just started at secondary* **school.**

secondary COMING AFTER /ˈsek.ən.dri/ ⓤ /-der.i/ *adj* developing from something similar that existed earlier: *The drug is not very effective against AIDS, though it may be used to treat secondary viral* **infections.** ○ *You can't just rely on secondary* **sources** *for your research into her life history – you ought to look at primary sources such as her letters and diaries.*

second 'childhood *noun* [S] when someone starts to behave like a child, especially because of mental weakness caused by old age: *Her grandfather's in his second childhood and talks nonsense most of the time.*

second 'class *noun* [U] **1** the seats on a plane or in a train that are less good and less expensive than FIRST CLASS **2** a class of mail that is delivered less quickly than FIRST CLASS

second 'class *adj, adv* **1** relating to the less expensive way of travelling in a train, aircraft, etc., that most people use: *a second-class carriage/ticket* ○ *We always travel second class.* **2** relating to a particular class of mail: *second-class mail/postage* ○ *How much is a second-class stamp?* ○ *How much less would it cost to send it second class?*

second 'class *adj* **1** A second class university degree is a good degree but not the best possible. **2** less important than other people: *Women are still treated as second class citizens.*

the Second 'Coming *noun* [S] the return of Jesus Christ to Earth from heaven that Christians expect will happen one day

second 'cousin *noun* [C] any person who is a child of a cousin of your mother or father

second-degree burn /ˌsek.ənd.dɪˌgriːˈbɜːn/ ⓤ /-ˈbɜːn/ *noun* [C] a serious burn in which the skin develops BLISTERS ⊃Compare **first-degree burn**; **third-degree burn.**

the second 'floor *noun* [S] in British English, the floor of a building that is two floors above ground level, or in American English, the floor that is directly above ground level: *I live* **on** *the second floor.* ○ *a second-floor apartment*

second ('gear) *noun* [U] in a vehicle, the gear which combines power with limited speed and is used when increasing or reducing speed: *You'll have to* **change** **(down/up)** *into second.*

second-guess GUESS /ˌsek.əndˈges/ *verb* [T] to guess what someone will do in the future: *She's always trying to second-guess the boss.*

second-guess CRITICIZE /ˌsek.əndˈges/ *verb* [T] *US* to criticize someone's actions or an event after it has happened: *Of course it's easy to second-guess the management of the election campaign, but I do think serious mistakes were made.*

second-hand NOT NEW /ˌsek.əndˈhænd/ *adj, adv* not new; having been used in the past by someone else: *This bike is second-hand but it's still in good condition.* ○ *She buys all her clothes second-hand.*

second hand CLOCKS /ˈsek.ənd/ *noun* [C usually sing] a long thin pointer on some clocks and watches that shows how many seconds have passed

second 'honeymoon *noun* [C usually sing] HUMOROUS a holiday taken by a husband and wife who have been married for some time, especially in order to try to improve a relationship which is failing

second-in-command /ˌsek.ənd.ɪn.kəˈmɑːnd/ ⓤ /-ˈmænd/ *noun* [S] someone who is almost as important as the person in charge: *Well, if the manager isn't available I'd like to speak to the second-in-command.*

second 'language *noun* [C] a language that a person can speak which is not the first language they learnt naturally as a child: *German is my second language.*

second 'name *noun* [C] *UK* **surname** (= the name that you share with other members of your family)

second 'nature *noun* [U] If something is second nature to you, you are so familiar with it that you can do it easily without needing to think very much about it: *I used to hate computers, but using them is second nature to me now.*

second-rate /ˌsek.ənd'reɪt/ *adj* not very good: *a second-rate film*

second 'sight *noun* [U] an unusual ability that some people are thought to have that enables them to know without being told what will happen in the future or what is happening in a different place

second 'thought *noun* [C] If you do something without a second thought, you do it without first considering if you should do it or not: *She'll spend a hundred pounds on a dress without a second thought.*

• **have second thoughts** to change your opinion about something or start to doubt it: *You're not having second thoughts about getting married, are you?*

• **on second thoughts** UK (US **on second thought**) used when you want to change a decision you have made: *I'd like a cup of coffee, please – actually, on second thoughts, I'll have a beer.*

second 'wind *noun* [S] a return of strength or energy that makes it possible to continue in an activity that needs a lot of effort: *We started to feel we couldn't walk any further but when we saw the village in the distance we got a/our second wind.*

the ˌSecond ˌWorld 'War *noun* [S] **World War Two**

secret /'siː.krət/ *noun* **1** [C] a piece of information that is only known by one person or a few people and should not be told to others: *Why did you have to go and tell Bob about my illness? You just can't keep a secret, can you?* ○ *A close couple should have no secrets from each other.* ○ *Aren't you going to let me in on (= tell me) the secret?* ○ *There's no secret (= everyone knows) about his homosexuality.* ○ *She makes no secret of (= makes very clear) her dislike of her father.* ○ *That restaurant is one of the best-kept secrets in London.* **2** [C] a fact that is unknown about a subject: *the secrets of the universe* **3** [S] the particular knowledge and skills needed to do something very well: *So what's the secret of being a good cook?*

• **in secret 1** in a private place with no one else present and without other people knowing: *The negotiators were meeting in secret for several months before the peace agreement was made public.* **2** only in someone's thoughts, without telling other people: *He says he loathes her, but I think in secret he really likes her.*

secret /'siː.krət/ *adj* **1** If something is secret, other people are not allowed to know about it: *The President escaped through a secret passage underneath the parliament building.* ○ *We ought to keep these proposals secret from the chairman for the time being.* ○ *This is top (= extremely) secret information.* ○ *Do you think we'll manage to keep the surprise party secret from Mum until her birthday?* **2** [before n] describes someone who has a particular habit, hobby or feeling but does not tell or show other people that they do: *a secret drinker* ○ *a secret admirer*

secretive /'siː.krə.tɪv/ ⓤ /-t̬ɪv/ *adj* MAINLY DISAPPROVING People who are secretive hide their feelings, thoughts, intentions and actions from other people: *He's being very secretive about his new girlfriend.* **secretively** /'siː.krə.tɪv.li/ ⓤ /-t̬ɪv-/ *adv* **secretiveness** /'siː.krə.tɪv.-nəs/ ⓤ /-t̬ɪv-/ *noun* [U] **secretly** /'siː.krət.li/ *adv*: *She said she didn't care about it, but I believe she was secretly delighted.* ○ *He was convicted on the evidence of secretly recorded telephone conversations.*

secrecy /'siː.krə.si/ *noun* [U] The content of her report is **shrouded in** secrecy (= being kept secret). ○ *I'd love to tell you about it, but Martin's sworn me to secrecy (= made me promise not to tell anyone).* ○ *There has been strong criticism of the secrecy surrounding the negotiations.*

secret ad'mirer *noun* [C] HUMOROUS a person who likes another person but does not say so: *Who sent you those flowers – have you got a secret admirer?*

secret 'agent *noun* [C] a government employee whose job involves obtaining secret information about the governments of unfriendly foreign countries

secretary OFFICE /'sek.rə.tri/ ⓤ /-ter.i/ *noun* [C] someone who works in an office, writing letters, making telephone calls and arranging meetings for a person or for an organization: *My secretary will phone you to arrange a meeting.*

secretarial /ˌsek.rə'teə.ri.əl/ ⓤ /-'ter.i-/ *adj* relating to the work of a secretary: *a secretarial college* ○ *She's found some part-time secretarial work.*

secretary OFFICIAL /'sek.rə.tri/ ⓤ /-ter.i/ *noun* [C] an official who has responsibility for the general management of an organization: *The company secretary has written to all the shareholders to apologise for the mistake.*

secretariat /ˌsek.rə'teə.ri.ət/ ⓤ /-'ter.i-/ *group noun* [C] the office or people responsible for the management of an organization, particularly an international or political one

Secretary GOVERNMENT /'sek.rə.tri/ ⓤ /-ter.i/ *noun* [C] **1** UK a **Secretary of State**: *the Foreign Secretary* ○ *the Home Secretary* **2** US the head of a government department, chosen by the president and not a member of a law-making body: *the Secretary of Health and Human Services*

Secretary-General /ˌsek.rə.tri'dʒen.ər.əl/ ⓤ /-ter.i.dʒen.ɚ-/ *noun* [C] The Secretary-General of an organization is its most important official: *My moral duty as Secretary-General of the United Nations is to do everything possible to avoid war.*

Secretary of 'State *noun* [C] **1** (ALSO **Secretary**) in the UK, a Member of Parliament who is in charge of a government department: *She became Secretary of State for Education after spending three years as Environment Secretary.* ○ *Was the conference a success, Foreign Secretary?* **2** in the US, an important government official who has responsibility for establishing and maintaining relationships with the governments of other countries

secret 'ballot *noun* [C] a method of voting in which each person writes their choice on a piece of paper so that no one else knows how they have voted: *The election of the government is carried out by secret ballot.*

secrete PRODUCE /sɪ'kriːt/ *verb* [T] SPECIALIZED (of animals or plants or their cells) to produce and release a liquid: *Saliva is a liquid secreted by glands in or near the mouth.*

secretion /sɪ'kriː.ʃən/ *noun* [C or U] *The excessive secretion of gastric juices in the gut causes ulcers.* ○ *toxic secretions*

secrete HIDE /sɪ'kriːt/ *verb* [T] FORMAL to put something in a place where it is unlikely to be found: *He was arrested at the airport with a kilo of heroin secreted in his clothing.*

secretive /'siː.krə.tɪv/ ⓤ /-t̬ɪv/ *adj* ⊃See at **secret**.

secretly /'siː.krət.li/ *adv* ⊃See at **secret**.

secret po'lice *noun* [U] a police force which secretly gathers information about people who oppose the government and tries to weaken such opposition, often using illegal and violent methods

secret 'service *noun* [S] a government organization that is responsible for things such as the safety of important politicians and for preventing secret information being discovered by possible enemy countries

secret 'shopper *noun* [C] US someone employed to test the service in shops and businesses by pretending to be a normal customer; a **mystery shopper**

secret so'ciety *noun* [C] an organization which does not allow people who are not members to find out about its activities and customs

secret 'weapon *noun* [C] something or someone that no one knows about and that will give you an advantage over your competitors or enemies: *Johann was the bank robbers' secret weapon – he knew the secrets of the alarm system.*

sect /sekt/ *noun* [C] USUALLY DISAPPROVING a religious group which has developed from a larger religion and is considered to have extreme or unusual beliefs or customs: *When he was sixteen he ran away from home and joined a religious sect.*

sectarian /sek'teə.ri.ən/ ⓤ /-'ter.i-/ *noun* [C], *adj* MAINLY DISAPPROVING (a person) strongly supporting a particular religious group, especially in such a way as not to be

S

willing to accept other beliefs: *a sectarian murder* ○ *He called on terrorists on both sides of the sectarian divide to end the cycle of violence.* **sectarianism** /sek'teə.ri.ə.nɪ.-zᵊm/ ⓤ /-'ter.i-/ *noun* [U] DISAPPROVING

section PART /'sek.ʃᵊn/ *noun* [C] one of the parts that something is divided into: *the sports section of the newspaper* ○ *the tail section of an aircraft* ○ *Does the restaurant have a non-smoking section?* ○ *The poorest sections of the community have much worse health.* ○ *He was charged under section 17 of the Firearms Act* (= according to that part of the law).
sectional /'sek.ʃᵊn.ᵊl/ *adj* **1** US describes a piece of furniture that is made up of parts which can be arranged in various ways: *a sectional sofa* **2** Interests or aims that are sectional are limited to a particular group within an organization, society or country and do not consider other groups: *The national interest is more important than any sectional or personal interests.*

section CUT /'sek.ʃᵊn/ *noun* **1** [C or U] SPECIALIZED a cut made in part of the body in an operation **2** [C] SPECIALIZED a **caesarean (section) 3** [C] SPECIALIZED a very thin slice of a part of an animal, plant or other object made in order to see its structure: *Each section is mounted on a slide and examined under the microscope.* **4** [C] SPECIALIZED a drawing or model which shows the structure of something by cutting part of it away: *This vertical section of the soil shows four basic soil layers.* **5** [C] the shape of a flat surface that is produced when an object is cut into separate pieces
• **in section** showing what something would look like if the surface was cut away and you could see inside: *The first diagram is a view of the shop from the street, and the second shows it in section.*

sector ECONOMIC AREA /'sek.təʳ/ ⓤ /-tɚ/ *noun* [C] one of the areas into which the economic activity of a country is divided: *In the financial sector, banks and insurance companies have both lost a lot of money.* ○ *The new government's policy is to transfer state industries from the public sector to the private sector.*

sector CONTROLLED AREA /'sek.təʳ/ ⓤ /-tɚ/ *noun* [C] an area of land or sea that has been divided from other areas and is controlled by a particular country: *What is the total oil output from the British sector of the North Sea?*

secular /'sek.jʊ.ləʳ/ ⓤ /-jə.lɚ/ *adj* not having any connection with religion: *We live in an increasingly secular society, in which religion has less and less influence on our daily lives.* ○ *a secular education* ○ *a secular state*
secularism /'sek.jʊ.lᵊr.ɪ.zᵊm/ ⓤ /-jə.lɚ-/ *noun* [U] the belief that religion should not be involved with the ordinary social and political activities of a country
secularist /'sek.jʊ.lᵊr.ɪst/ ⓤ /-jə.lɚ-/ *noun* [C], *adj*
secularize, UK USUALLY **-ise** /'sek.jʊ.lᵊr.aɪz/ ⓤ /-jə.lə.raɪz/ *verb* [T] When something is secularized, religious influence, power or control is removed from it: *He claims that Western secularized society makes it difficult to live as a Christian.*

,**secular 'humanism** *noun* [U] a set of beliefs which emphasize the importance of reason and of individuals rather than religion ,**secular 'humanist** *noun* [C]

secure PROTECTED /sɪ'kjʊəʳ/ ⓤ /-'kjʊr/ *adj* (especially of objects, situations etc.) able to avoid being harmed by any risk, danger or threat: *Car manufacturers ought to produce vehicles which are more secure against theft.* ○ *Endangered species need to be kept secure from poachers.*
secure /sɪ'kjʊəʳ/ ⓤ /-'kjʊr/ *verb* [I or T] to make certain something is protected from danger or risk: *The building has only one main entrance and would be easy to secure (against/from intruders).* ○ *This form of investment is an excellent way of securing your children's financial future.*
securely /sɪ'kjʊə.li/ ⓤ /-'kjʊr-/ *adv*: *The door was securely fastened.* ○ *The offices were securely guarded.* ○ *This certificate is an important document, and should be kept securely* (= in a place where it cannot be lost or stolen).
security /sɪ'kjʊə.rɪ.ti/ ⓤ /-'kjʊr.ə.t̬i/ *noun* [U] protection of a person, building, organization or country against threats such as crime or attacks by foreign countries: *The station was closed for two hours because of a security*

alert. ○ *Thirty demonstrators were killed in clashes with the security forces over the weekend.* ○ *The tighter security measures/precautions include video cameras in the city centre.* ○ *The students were deported because they posed a threat to national security.* ○ *The proposed national identity card system would help to tighten security against fraud.* ○ *The most dangerous criminals are held in maximum-security prisons* (= prisons that are as difficult as possible to escape from). ➔See Note **safety or security?** at **safe** WITHOUT DANGER.
security /sɪ'kjʊə.rɪ.ti/ ⓤ /-'kjʊr.ə.t̬i/ *group noun* [U] the group of people responsible for protecting a building: *You'll need to notify security if you want to work late in the office.*

secure FIXED /sɪ'kjʊəʳ/ ⓤ /-'kjʊr/ *adj* **1** positioned or fixed firmly and correctly and therefore not likely to move, fall or break: *That ladder doesn't look very secure to me.* ○ *Check that all windows and doors are secure.* ○ *FIGURATIVE Her promotion has made her position in the company more secure.* ○ *FIGURATIVE The museum has been promised £22 million by the government, so its future is relatively secure.* **2** A secure place is one that it is difficult to get out of or escape from: *He killed the man just a month after his release from a secure mental hospital.*
secure /sɪ'kjʊəʳ/ ⓤ /-'kjʊr/ *verb* [T] to fasten one object firmly to another: *The gate won't stay open, so we'll have to secure it to that post.*
securely /sɪ'kjʊə.li/ ⓤ /-'kjʊr-/ *adv* positioned or fastened firmly and correctly and therefore not likely to move, fall or break: *Please ensure that your seat belts are fastened securely.* ○ *FIGURATIVE He has given up political power, but he remains securely in control of the army.*
security /sɪ'kjʊə.rɪ.ti/ ⓤ /-'kjʊr.ə.t̬i/ *noun* [U] when something is not likely to fail or be lost: *If it's a choice between higher pay and job security, I'd prefer to keep my job.* ○ *I'm on a temporary contract and have little financial security* (= little certainty of having enough money to live on).

secure OBTAIN /sɪ'kjʊəʳ/ ⓤ /-'kjʊr/ *verb* [T] FORMAL to get something, sometimes with difficulty: *He was disappointed by his failure to secure the top job with the bank.* ○ *The change in the law will make it harder for the police to secure convictions.*

secure CONFIDENT /sɪ'kjʊəʳ/ ⓤ /-'kjʊr/ *adj* having few worries or doubts about yourself and your personal relationships: *Children need to feel secure in order to do well at school.* **security** /sɪ'kjʊə.rɪ.ti/ ⓤ /-'kjʊr.ə.t̬i/ *noun* [U] *Most children need the security of a stable family life.*

secure FINANCIAL /sɪ'kjʊəʳ/ ⓤ /-'kjʊr/ *verb* [T] to make certain that money which has been lent will be paid back, by giving the person who lends the money the right to own property belonging to the person who borrows it, if the money is not paid back: *a secured loan* ○ *Her bank loan is secured against/by/on her house.*
security /sɪ'kjʊə.rɪ.ti/ ⓤ /-'kjʊr.ə.t̬i/ *noun* [U] *She used her shares in the company as security against a £23 million bank loan.* ○ *The hotel held onto our baggage as security while we went to the bank to get money to pay the bill.*

security /sɪ'kjʊə.rɪ.ti/ ⓤ /-'kjʊr.ə.t̬i/ *plural noun* SPECIALIZED investment in a company or in government debt which can be traded on the financial markets and which produces an income for the investor

se**'curity ,blanket** *noun* [C] a soft object such as a small piece of cloth or a toy which is very familiar to a baby or young child and makes it feel safe

se**'curity ,clearance** *noun* [C or U] official permission given to someone to enter a building or area, after making certain that they are not a threat

the Se**'curity ,Council** *noun* [S] a part of the United Nations whose purpose is to prevent war and maintain peace

se**'curity ,guard** *noun* [C] someone whose job involves preventing people going into places without permission, delivering and collecting large amounts of money, or protecting goods from being stolen

se**'curity ,risk** *noun* [C] something or someone likely to cause danger or difficulty: *The only reason she was con-*

S

sidered a security risk because her husband was a foreigner.

sedan /sɪˈdæn/ *noun* [C] *US FOR* **saloon** CAR ➲See picture **Cars and Trucks** on page Centre 13

se,dan 'chair *noun* [C] in the past, an enclosed seat for one person with horizontal poles at either side, designed to be lifted and carried by two people

sedate [CALM] /sɪˈdeɪt/ *adj* tending to avoid excitement or great activity and to be calm and relaxed: *The fight against a chemical storage site has transformed a normally sedate village into a battleground.* ○ *The speed limit in many areas is a sedate 55 mph.* **sedately** /sɪˈdeɪt.li/ *adv*

sedate [DRUG] /sɪˈdeɪt/ *verb* [T] to cause a person or animal to be very calm or go to sleep by giving them a drug: *When I saw him after the accident he was still in shock and was* ***heavily*** *sedated.* **sedation** /sɪˈdeɪ.ʃən/ *noun* [U] *She's* ***under*** *strong sedation and should not be disturbed.*
sedative /ˈsed.ə.tɪv/ [US] /-t̬ɪv/ *noun* [C] a drug used to calm a person or animal or to make them sleep

sedentary /ˈsed.ən.tri/ [US] /-ter.i/ *adj* involving little exercise or physical activity: *a sedentary job/occupation* ○ *My doctor says I should start playing sport because my* ***lifestyle*** *is too sedentary.*

sediment /ˈsed.ɪ.mənt/ *noun* [C or U] a soft substance that is like a wet powder and consists of very small pieces of a solid material which have fallen to the bottom of a liquid: *There was a brown sediment in the bottom of the bottle.*
sedimentary /ˌsed.ɪˈmen.tər.i/ [US] /-t̬ɚ.i/ *adj* (of rock) made from sediment left by the action of water, ice or wind: *sedimentary rock* **sedimentation** /ˌsed.ɪ.menˈteɪ.ʃən/ *noun* [U]

sedition /sɪˈdɪʃ.ən/ *noun* [U] *FORMAL* language or behaviour that is intended to persuade other people to oppose their government **seditious** /sɪˈdɪʃ.əs/ *adj*: *She was arrested after making a speech that the government considered to be seditious.*

seduce [PERSUADE] /sɪˈdjuːs/ [US] /-ˈduːs/ *verb* [T] to persuade someone to have sex with you, often someone younger than you, who has little experience of sex: *Pete lost his virginity at 15 when he was seduced by his best friend's mother.*
seducer /sɪˈdjuː.sər/ [US] /-ˈduː.sɚ/ *noun* [C] someone who seduces people: *The play tells the story of a fabulously wealthy woman who seeks revenge on her heartless seducer.*
seductress /sɪˈdʌk.trəs/ *noun* [C] a female seducer
seduction /sɪˈdʌk.ʃən/ *noun* [C or U] *The film depicts Charlotte's seduction by her boss.* **seductive** /sɪˈdʌk.tɪv/ *adj*: *It was a seductive black evening dress.* ○ *She gave him a seductive look.* **seductively** /sɪˈdʌk.tɪv.li/ *adv*
seductiveness /sɪˈdʌk.tɪv.nəs/ *noun* [U]

seduce [ATTRACT] /sɪˈdjuːs/ [US] /-ˈduːs/ *verb* [T usually passive] **1** to cause someone to do something that they would not usually consider doing by being very attractive and difficult to refuse: *I wouldn't normally have bought this, but I was seduced by the low price.* ○ *They were seduced* ***into buying*** *the washing machine by the offer of a free flight to the United States.* **2** If you are seduced by something, you like it because it seems attractive: *Almost every visitor to Edinburgh is seduced by its splendid architecture.*
seduction /sɪˈdʌk.ʃən/ *noun* [C usually pl] the attractive quality of something: *The seductions of life in a warm climate have led many Britons to live abroad, especially in Spain.*
seductive /sɪˈdʌk.tɪv/ *adj* making you want to do, have or believe something, because of seeming attractive: *Television confronts the viewer with a succession of glittering and seductive* ***images***. ○ *The* ***argument*** *that sanctions should be given more time to work is seductive but fatally flawed.* **seductively** /sɪˈdʌk.tɪv.li/ *adv*
seductiveness /sɪˈdʌk.tɪv.nəs/ *noun* [U]

see [USE EYES] /siː/ *verb* **seeing, saw, seen 1** [I or T] to be aware of what is around you by using your eyes: *Turn the light on so I can see.* ○ *"I* ***can*** *see you!"* ○ [+ (*that*)] *The teacher could see* ***(that)*** *the children had been fighting.* ○ [+ infinitive without *to*] *Jacqui saw the car drive up outside the police station.* ○ [+ v-*ing*] *From the window we could see the children play****ing*** *in the yard.* ○ [+ past participle] *His parents saw him award****ed*** *the winner's medal.* ○ *See* (= Look at) *p. 23 for prices and flight details.* ○ *See* ***over*** (= Look at the next page) *for further information.* ➲See Note **look, see or watch?** at **look** SEE. **2** [T] to watch a film, television programme, etc: *Did you see that documentary on Channel 4 last night?* **3** [T often passive] to be the time or place when something happens: *This summer has seen the end of water restrictions in the area thanks to a new reservoir.* **4** *HUMOROUS* **you ain't seen nothing yet** said to mean that more surprising or exciting things are likely to happen

• **have seen better days** to be old and in bad condition: *That jacket's seen better days. Why don't you get a new one?*

• **see *sth* coming** to expect something to happen: *No one else had expected the factory to close, but we saw it coming.*

• **not see *sb* for dust** *UK INFORMAL* when someone leaves quickly in order to avoid something: *If you let him know that Margaret's coming, you won't see him for dust.*

• **can't see further than the end of *your* nose** If someone can't see further than the end of their nose, they do not notice what is happening around them.

• **have to be seen to be believed** to exist, although it is difficult to believe: *The mess the burglars left behind had to be seen to be believed.*

• **see red** to become very angry: *People who don't finish a job really make me see red.*

• **see stars** If you see stars, you are partly unconscious because you have been hit on the head.

• **see the colour of *sb's* money** *INFORMAL* To see the colour of someone's money is to make certain that a person is going to pay for something: *"I'll have one of those." "Let's see the colour of your money first!"*

• **see the back of *sb/sth*** *UK* If you are pleased to see the back of something/someone, you are pleased that you no longer have to be involved with them: *The hotel staff were* ***glad*** *to see the back of such a difficult guest.*

• **see the last of something/someone** to not see something or someone again because they have gone away or are finished

• **seeing things** If you are seeing things, you are imagining that things are happening when they are not: *Didn't Marie come in just now? I must have been seeing things.*

• **wouldn't be seen dead** *INFORMAL* If someone wouldn't be seen dead in a particular place or doing a particular thing, they would never do it, usually because it would be too embarrassing: *I wouldn't be seen dead wear****ing*** *a dress like that.*

• **Seeing is believing.** *SAYING* said to mean that if you see something yourself you will believe it to exist or be true, despite the fact that it is extremely unusual or unexpected: *"I never thought Simon would get out of bed before lunchtime on a Saturday, but seeing is believing!"*

• **What you see is what you get.** *SAYING* said to show that there is nothing hidden ➲See also **WYSIWYG**.

see [UNDERSTAND] /siː/ *verb* [T] **seeing, saw, seen** to understand, know or be aware: [+ (*that*)] *I see* ***(that)*** *the social club is organising a theatre trip next month.* ○ [+ question word] *He can't see* ***what*** *difference it makes to come* (= He doesn't think it is important if he comes) *on Thursday instead of Friday.* ○ *They didn't see* ***the need/any need*** (= understand that it was important) *to notify their members of the changes in writing.* ○ *They only refused to help because they're too busy, but he seems to see more* ***in*** *it than that.* ○ *"I'm tired." "****So*** *I see – you've been yawning all afternoon."* ○ *The chairwoman thought the new scheme was a great improvement, but I couldn't see* ***it*** *myself* (= couldn't understand why it was thought to be good, or didn't agree). ○ *I was surprised that they couldn't see my point of view.* ○ *The government didn't want to* ***be*** *seen* ***to be*** *making concessions to terrorists.* ○ *After she read his book she started to see the issue* ***in another/a different/a new light*** (= differently).

• **can't see the wood for the trees** *UK* (*US* **can't see the forest for the trees**) to be unable to understand a situation clearly because you are too involved in it

S

• **see eye to eye** If two people see eye to eye, they agree with each other: *My sisters **don't** see eye to eye **with** me about the arrangements.*

• **see sense/reason** to be sensible and reasonable: *We talked to her for an hour, but we couldn't make her see sense.*

• **see the light** If you see the light you suddenly understand something you didn't understand before. ⊃See also **see the light of day** at see MEET.

• **see the point of** to understand the importance of or the reason for something: *They couldn't see the point of further training.*

• **see the joke** to understand something funny and find it funny yourself: *Everyone else laughed loudly but I didn't see the joke.*

• **you see** used when you hope someone else will understand what you are saying or asking: *Could you lend me £10? I need to do some shopping, you see.*

see CONSIDER /si:/ *verb* [T] seeing, saw, seen to consider or think about, especially to think about someone or something in a particular way, or to imagine someone doing a particular activity: *She didn't see herself **as** brave.* ○ *It was easy to see the gift **as** a sort of bribe.* ○ [+ obj + v-ing] *I can't see her accepting* (= I don't think she will accept) *the job in the present circumstances.* ○ *As I see **it/things/the situation**, we'll have to get extra help.* ○ *Try and see it my **way** – I'll be left without any help if you go to Edinburgh tomorrow.*

• **I/We'll (have to) see** used to say that you will make a decision about something later: *"Do you think there'll be time to stop for a meal?" "We'll see."*

• **we'll (soon) see about that** used when you are angry about something that you feel is unfair and that you intend to stop happening: *He wants to park his car on my lawn? Well, we'll soon see about that!*

• **Let me see/Let's see** used when you want to think for a moment about something: *"Do you know a shop that sells sports clothes?" "Let me see – I think there's one near the station."*

• **see fit** FORMAL If you see fit to do something, you think it is good or necessary to do it: *She saw fit to take her son away from the school.*

• **see *your* way (clear) to** to agree to do or allow something: *Could you see your way to letting us borrow the machine on Wednesday?*

see MEET /si:/ *verb* seeing, saw, seen **1** [I or T] to meet or come into contact with someone, or to visit a place: *We're seeing friends at the weekend.* ○ *I haven't seen Jerry **around** (= in the places I usually meet him) in the last few weeks.* ○ *No one has seen **much of** Daryl since he got married.* ○ *They see **a lot of** each other (= are often together) at weekends.* ○ *My mother is seeing the doctor again next week.* ○ *The children wanted to see the circus.* ○ *The agent said they could see the house* (UK ALSO see **round/through/**AUS USUALLY **over** the house) *at 3 p.m.* ⊃See Note **meet, see, visit or get to know?** at meet BECOME FAMILIAR WITH. **2** [T] to have a romantic relationship with someone: *How long has she been seeing him?*

• **See you (later)** INFORMAL goodbye

• **see a man about a dog** INFORMAL Someone might say they have to see a man about a dog when they don't want to tell you what they are really doing, especially when they are going to the toilet: *I've just got to see a man about a dog. I'll be back in a minute.*

• **not see hide nor hair of** INFORMAL to not see someone at all over a period of time: *I haven't seen hide nor hair of her since last Friday.*

• **see *sb* in hell before** MAINLY UK INFORMAL If you would see someone in hell before you would do something they have suggested, you are very determined not to do it: *I'd see her in hell before I'd agree to an arrangement like that.*

• **see life** to experience many different and often unexpected things: *As a volunteer on the childcare project, I really saw life.*

• **see the light of day** When something sees the light of day it appears for the first time.

see GO WITH /si:/ *verb* [T usually + adv or prep] seeing, saw, seen to take someone somewhere by going there with them: *He saw his visitors **to the door**.* ○ *Her friends saw her*

home. ○ *The security guard saw the protesters **off** the premises.*

• **see in the New Year** to not go to bed on 31 December until after 12 o'clock at night in order to celebrate the start of a new year

see TRY TO DISCOVER /si:/ *verb* [I + question word] seeing, saw, seen to try to discover: *Will you see **if** you can get anyone to help?* ○ *I'll see **what** I can do.*

see MAKE CERTAIN /si:/ *verb* [+ (that)] seeing, saw, seen to make certain that something happens: *See **(that)** you're ready by five, or there'll be trouble.* ○ *The receptionist said he'd see **(that)** she got the message.*

• **see *sb* right** UK INFORMAL To see someone right is to make certain that someone is helped or treated well: *Ask Mrs Martin at the desk over there about the invoices – she'll see you right.*

PHRASAL VERBS WITH see ▼

▲ **see about *sth*** *phrasal verb* INFORMAL to prepare for or deal with an action or event, or to arrange for something to be done: *It's getting late – I'd better see about lunch.* ○ [+ v-ing] *You should see about getting your hair cut.*

▲ **not see beyond *sth*** *phrasal verb* DISAPPROVING to have your attention fixed on something and therefore be unable to consider other things: *The government cannot see beyond next year's general election.*

▲ **see *sth* in *sb/sth*** *phrasal verb* to believe that someone or something has a particular quality: *We don't travel on bank holiday weekends – I just can't see the pleasure in it.*

• **not know what *sb* sees in *sb/sth*** to not understand why someone likes a particular person or thing: *He always so rude and lazy – I don't know what she sees in him.*

▲ **see *sb* off** SAY GOODBYE *phrasal verb* [M] to go to the place that someone is leaving from in order to say goodbye to them: *My parents saw me off at the airport.*

▲ **see *sb* off** GET RID OF *phrasal verb* [M] to send away an attacker or unwanted person, usually forcefully: *The caretaker ran out and saw off the boys who had been damaging the fence.*

▲ **see *sb/sth* off** *phrasal verb* [M] INFORMAL to defeat someone or something, or to deal with them effectively so that they can no longer cause harm: *England saw off Luxembourg 5-0.* ○ *He may not have seen off the challengers for the leadership of the party, but he has at least silenced them for a while.*

▲ **see *sth* out** WAIT *phrasal verb* [M] to wait or last until the end of a difficult event or situation: *The besieged town hasn't enough food to see the month out.* ○ *They saw out the storm in the best shelter they could find.*

▲ **see *sb* out** LEAVE *phrasal verb* (ALSO see *sb* to the door) to go to the door of a building or room with someone who does not live or work there, when they are leaving: *My secretary will see you out.*

▲ **see *yourself* out** *phrasal verb* [R] (ALSO see *yourself* to the door) to leave a building or room by yourself after visiting someone there: *It's ok – I'll see myself out.*

▲ **see *sb* through *sth*** HELP *phrasal verb* to help or support someone during a difficult period in their life: *He was a prisoner of war for five years, but his courage saw him through.* ○ *My brother's lent me £200 to see me through the next few weeks.*

▲ **see *sth* through** FINISH *phrasal verb* to continue doing a job or activity until it is finished, especially when it is difficult: *The course would take me three years to complete, but I was determined to see it through.*

▲ **see through *sb/sth*** NOT BELIEVE *phrasal verb* to be aware that someone is trying to deceive you to get an advantage, or that someone's behaviour is intended to deceive you, and to understand the truth about the situation: *They were very friendly, but I quickly saw through them.* ○ *She saw through his excuse at once.*

▲ **see to *sth/sb*** *phrasal verb* to deal with a person or task that needs to be dealt with or is waiting to be dealt with: *"These letters need posting." "I'll see to them later."* ○ *Mrs Chapman asked for some help with the orders – could you see to it?* ○ [+ that] *Please see to **it that** no-one comes in without identification.*

seed [PLANT] /siːd/ *noun* **1** [C or U] a small round or oval object produced by a plant and from which, when it is planted, a new plant can grow: ***Sow** the seeds* (= put them in the ground) *about 3 cm deep.* ○ *The chemical will stop all seeds from **sprouting*** (= starting to grow). ○ *The farmers grow these crops for seed* (= for planting to grow more crops, rather than for eating). ➲See picture **Fruit** on page Centre 1 **2** [C usually pl] the cause of a feeling or situation, or the early stages of it: *The seeds **of** friendship were sown early, and they remained lifelong companions.* ○ *He may be **sowing** the seeds **of** his own destruction in the long term by using violence against his own people.* **3** [U] *LITERARY* **semen**

• **go/run to seed 1** If a food plant goes or runs to seed, it produces flowers and seeds because it has not been picked early enough: *In hot weather lettuces can suddenly run to seed.* **2** If a person or place goes or runs to seed, their physical appearance becomes worse through lack of care: *After he retired, he really went to seed.*

seed /siːd/ *verb* **1** [I or T] to produce seeds: *The plants have seeded themselves* (= their seeds have fallen) *into the cracks between the paving stones.* **2** [T] (*ALSO* **deseed**) to remove the seeds from a fruit or vegetable: *Wash, seed and cut the pepper into small pieces.*

seeded /ˈsiː.dɪd/ *adj* **1** with the seeds removed: *Garnish with peeled, seeded and diced tomatoes.* **2** containing seeds **-seeded** /-siː.dɪd/ *suffix*: *The walnut is a hard-seeded fruit.*

seedless /ˈsiːd.ləs/ *adj* without seeds: *seedless grapes*

seedling /ˈsiːd.lɪŋ/ *noun* [C] a very young plant which has grown from a seed: ***Raise** the seedlings in the greenhouse, and transplant when the weather becomes warmer.*

seed [SPORT] /siːd/ *noun* [C] especially in tennis, a good player who is given a place on the list of those expected to win games in a particular competition because of the way they have played in the past: *Turner's opponent in the quarter-finals of the darts is the No. 1 seed.*

seed /siːd/ *verb* [T usually passive] to make a player a seed: [+ adj] *Jones, seeded second, has won her last ten matches.*
-seeded /-siː.dɪd/ *suffix*: *The 5th-seeded Browne crushed the defending champion.*

ˈseed ˌcorn *noun* [U] **1** grain which is kept for planting to produce new plants **2** something which is important because it is the starting point for future development: *Investment is the seed corn of economic progress.*

ˈseed ˌmoney *noun* [U] *US* money used to start a development or activity

ˈseed poˌtato *noun* [C] Seed potatoes are potatoes which are planted so that a plant will grow and more potatoes will be produced.

seedy /ˈsiː.di/ *adj* looking dirty or in bad condition and likely to be involved in immoral activities: *a seedy hotel* ○ *He didn't like the look of the seedy characters who were hanging around outside the bar.* **seediness** /ˈsiː.dɪ.nəs/ *noun* [U]

seeing-eye dog /ˌsiː.ɪŋˈaɪˌdɒg/ [US] /-ˌdɑːg/ *noun* [C] *US TRADEMARK FOR* **guide dog**

ˈseeing (that) *conjunction* (*INFORMAL* **seeing as,** *NOT STANDARD* **seeing as how**) considering or accepting the fact that; as: *We may as well go to the concert, seeing as we've already paid for the tickets.*

seek [SEARCH] /siːk/ *verb* [T] **sought, sought** *FORMAL* **1** to try to find or get something, especially something which is not a physical object: *"Are you actively seeking jobs?" she asked.* ○ *Hundreds of dissidents are seeking refuge/asylum in the US embassy.* **2** to ask for advice, help, approval, permission, etc: *Legal advice should be sought before you take any further action.* **seeker** /ˈsiː.kəʳ/ [US] /-kɚ/ *noun* [C] *asylum seekers* ○ *job-seekers* **-seeking** /-siː.kɪŋ/ *suffix*: *A lot of bad behaviour is **attention**-seeking on the part of mixed-up kids.*

seek [TRY] /siːk/ *verb* [I + *to* infinitive] **sought, sought** *FORMAL* to try or attempt: *They sought **to** reassure the public.*

▲ **seek *sb/sth* out** *phrasal verb* [M] *FORMAL* to look for someone or something, especially for a long time until you find them: *While he was at the library, Steve decided to seek out some information on accommodation in the area.*

seem /siːm/ *verb* [I + adv or prep; L] to give the effect of being; to be judged to be: *He's 16, but he often seems **(to be)** younger.* ○ *The children seemed **(as if/as though/like** they were) tired.* ○ *I suspect his claims are **not all** they seem – he tends to exaggerate.* ○ *Things are seldom **as/how/what** they seem.* ○ [+ *to* infinitive] *I seem **to** know more about him than anyone else.* ○ *They seem **to** be taking a long time to decide.* ○ [+ (that)] ***It** seems **(that)** she can't come.* ○ ***It** seems **to** me **(that)*** (= I think that) *he isn't the right person for the job.* ○ [+ (that)] *FORMAL* ***It would** seem **(that)** we need to be at the airport two hours before takeoff.* ○ ***There** seems **to** have been a mistake – my name isn't on the list.* ○ [after *so*] *"There's no reply – they've all gone home." "**So** it seems."* ○ *"Was a decision made?" "It seems **not/so**."*

seeming /ˈsiː.mɪŋ/ *adj* [before n] *FORMAL* appearing to be something, especially when this is not true: *He said, with seeming embarrassment, that he would have to cancel the meeting.*

seemingly /ˈsiː.mɪŋ.li/ *adv* **1** appearing to be something, especially when this is not true: *He remains confident and seemingly untroubled by his recent problems.* **2** according to the facts that you know: *The factory closure is seemingly inevitable.* ○ *Seemingly, she's gone off to live with another man.*

seemly /ˈsiːm.li/ *adj OLD USE* socially suitable and polite
* NOTE: The opposite is **unseemly**.

seen /siːn/ *past participle of* **see**

seep /siːp/ *verb* [I + adv or prep] to move or spread slowly out of a hole or through something: *Pesticides are seeping **out of** farmland and **into** the water supply.* ○ *FIGURATIVE Given the intense secrecy of the arms business, information only seeps **out** in company literature.*

seepage /ˈsiː.pɪdʒ/ *noun* [U] *Oil spills and seepage **from** refineries are common.*

seer /sɪəʳ/ [US] /sɪr/ *noun* [C] *LITERARY* a person who claims to be able to say what will happen in the future

seersucker /ˈsɪəˌsʌk.əʳ/ [US] /ˈsɪrˌsʌk.ɚ/ *noun* [U] a light cloth which has a pattern of raised and flat strips on it

seesaw /ˈsiː.sɔː/ [US] /-sɑː/ *noun* [C] (*US ALSO* **teeter-totter**) a long board that children play on. The board is balanced on a central point so that when a child sits on each end they can make the board go up and down by pushing off the ground with their feet.

seesaw /ˈsiː.sɔː/ [US] /-sɑː/ *verb* [I] to change repeatedly from one emotion, situation, etc. to another and then back again: *His mind seesawed between hope and despair all through those weeks.* **seesaw** /ˈsiː.sɔː/ [US] /-sɑː/ *adj* [before n] *The stock market's recent seesaw movements have made many investors nervous.*

seethe [FEEL ANGER] /siːð/ *verb* [I] to feel very angry but to be unable or unwilling to express it clearly: *The class positively seethed **with** indignation when Julia won the award.* ○ *By the end of the meeting he was seething.*
seething /ˈsiː.ðɪŋ/ *adj* [before n] *Their seething resentment led to angry jostling between team-mates.*

seethe [MOVE] /siːð/ *verb* [I] (of a large number or amount) to move about energetically in a small space: *The streets were seething* (= busy and crowded) ***with** tourists.* **seething** /ˈsiː.ðɪŋ/ *adj*: *A seething **mass** of children crowded around the tables.*

see-through /ˈsiː.θruː/ *adj* **1** describes a piece of clothing which is very thin and light, under which you can see other clothes or the body: *a see-through blouse* **2** transparent: *see-through partitions*

segment /ˈseg.mənt/ *noun* [C] any of the parts into which something (especially a circle or sphere) can be divided or into which it is naturally divided: *The salad was decorated with segments of orange.* ○ *People over the age of 85 make up the fastest-growing population segment.* ➲See picture **Fruit** on page Centre 1

segment /segˈment/ [US] /ˈ--/ *verb* [I or T] *SPECIALIZED* to divide something into different parts: *City Insurance segmented the market **into** three by issuing three types of policy.* **segmentation** /ˌseg.menˈteɪ.ʃᵊn/ *noun* [U]

segregate /ˈseg.rɪ.geɪt/ *verb* [T] **1** to keep one group of people apart from another and treat them differently,

S

especially because of race or sex: *a segregated school/society* ○ *Blacks were segregated **from** whites in every area of life.* **2** to keep one thing separate from another: *The systems will have to be able to segregate clients' money **from** the firm's own cash.* **segregation** /ˌseg.rɪˈgeɪ.ʃᵊn/ *noun* [U] *The system of **racial** segregation that used to exist in South Africa was called apartheid.*
segregated /ˈseg.rɪ.geɪ.tɪd/ [US] /-t̬ɪd/ *adj*: *segregated schools* ○ *The psychiatric section is segregated* (= separated) ***from** the rest of the prison.*

segue /ˈseg.weɪ/ *verb* [I] to move easily and without interruption from one piece of music, part of a story, subject or situation to another: *His performance of 'Alison' segued **into** a cover version of 'Tracks of My Tears'.* **segue** /ˈseg.weɪ/ *noun* [C usually sing]

seismic /ˈsaɪz.mɪk/ *adj* **1** [before n] relating to or caused by an earthquake: *seismic activity/waves* **2** having very great and damaging effects: *The news that the chairman would resign set off seismic waves in the business community.*

seismograph /ˈsaɪz.mə.grɑːf/ [US] /-græf/ *noun* [C] SPECIALIZED a piece of equipment which measures and records the strength of an earthquake

seismology /saɪzˈmɒl.ə.dʒi/ [US] /-ˈmɑː.lə-/ *noun* [U] the scientific study of the sudden violent movements of the Earth connected with earthquakes **seismologist** /saɪzˈmɒl.ə.dʒɪst/ [US] /-ˈmɑː.lə-/ *noun* [C]

seize /siːz/ *verb* **1** [T] to take something quickly and keep or hold it: *I seized his arm and made him turn to look at me.* ○ *He seized the **chance/opportunity** of a free flight **with both hands*** (= with eagerness or enthusiasm). **2** [T] to take using sudden force: *The rebels have seized ten soldiers to use as hostages.* ○ *Political instability helped the army to seize **power**.* ○ *Troops yesterday seized **control** of the broadcasting station.* **3** [T] If the police or other officials seize something, they take possession of it with legal authority: *Customs officers at Heathrow have seized 60 kilos of heroin.* **4** [usually passive] If a strong emotion or pain seizes you, you feel it suddenly: *I was suddenly seized **by/with** a feeling of great insecurity and loneliness.* **seizure** /ˈsiː.ʒəʳ/ [US] /-ʒɚ/ *noun* [C or U] *seizure of power/property/control* ○ *Seizures of illicit drugs have increased by 30% this year.*

PHRASAL VERBS WITH **seize**

▲ **seize on/upon *sth*** *phrasal verb* to use, accept or take advantage of something quickly or enthusiastically: *The story was seized on by the tabloid press, who printed it under huge headlines.*
▲ **seize up** *phrasal verb* INFORMAL to stop being able to move or work in the normal way: *The washing machine totally seized up on Thursday.* ○ *The traffic had seized up for miles because of the roadworks.*

seizure /ˈsiː.ʒəʳ/ [US] /-ʒɚ/ *noun* [C] **1** a very sudden attack of an illness involving unconsciousness or violent movement: *an epileptic seizure* **2** OLD USE a sudden failure of the heart: *His aunt died of a seizure.* ○ FIGURATIVE HUMOROUS *When I told her how much it cost she nearly had a seizure* (= she was very shocked).

S

seldom /ˈsel.dəm/ *adv* almost never: *Now that we have a baby, we seldom get the chance to go to the cinema.* ○ FORMAL *Seldom do we receive any apology when mistakes are made.*

select [CHOOSE] /sɪˈlekt/ *verb* [I or T] to choose a small number of things, or to choose by making careful decisions: *There was a choice of four prizes, and the winner could select one of them.* ○ *A mouse is a device which makes it easier to select different options **from** computer menus.* ○ *How do you select people **for** promotion?* ○ [+ obj + to infinitive] *He was selected **to** play for Australia at the age of only 18.* ○ FORMAL *The supermarket's policy is to select **out*** (= choose) *the best fruit and discard the rest.*
selection /sɪˈlek.ʃᵊn/ *noun* **1** [C or U] when someone or something is chosen: *the selection **process*** ○ *Success is achieved by the careful selection **of** projects.* ○ *The coach **made** her selection* (= chose who she wanted) ***for** the team.* **2** [C] a choice, range or variety of something: *Most schools would have **a** good selection **of** these books in their libraries.* ○ *The larger shops are able to stock **a** wider selection **of** goods.* **3** [C] an item or person which has been or will be chosen: *Their music was a mix of old stuff and selections **from** the new album.*
selective /sɪˈlek.tɪv/ *adj* intentionally choosing some things and not others: *As a teacher she was very selective, accepting only a small number of exceptionally gifted pupils.* ○ *He seemed to have a very selective recall of past events.* **selectively** /sɪˈlek.tɪv.li/ *adv* **selectivity** /ˌsɪl.ekˈtɪv.ɪ.ti/ [US] /səˌlekˈtɪv.ə.t̬i/ *noun* [U] (ALSO **selectiveness**)
selector /sɪˈlek.təʳ/ [US] /-tɚ/ *noun* [C] **1** a device that controls a piece of equipment: *a channel/gear/height selector* **2** UK a person who chooses a sports team: *His performance persuaded the selectors that he should be included in the team.*

select [BEST QUALITY] /sɪˈlekt/ *adj* of only the best type or highest quality, and usually small in size or amount: *It's a very select club – I've been trying unsuccessfully to join it for years.* ○ *These activities should be available to all pupils, not just a select **few**.* ○ *Hamilton lives in a very select part of London.*

seˌlect comˈmittee *noun* [C] a group of politicians, from different political parties, chosen to report and advise on a particular subject: *She is a member of the Commons Select Committee **on** education.*

seˌlective ˈservice *noun* [U] US the system in the US in which men aged 18-26 must put their names on an official list so that they can be called to join the army if there is a war ➲Compare **national service**.

self [PERSONALITY] /self/ *noun* [C or U] *plural* **selves** the set of someone's characteristics, such as personality and ability, which are not physical and make that person different from other people: *The hero of the film finally **finds** his **true** self.* ○ *When I saw them this afternoon they were more like their **old/normal** selves* (= as they were in the past). ○ *a sense of self*
● **Unto thine own self be true.** SAYING This means that you should only do what you think is right.

self [PERSONAL ADVANTAGE] /self/ *noun* [U] FORMAL DISAPPROVING interest only in your own advantage: *Her reply was typical of her constant regard for self.*
selfish /ˈsel.fɪʃ/ *adj* DISAPPROVING Someone who is selfish only thinks of their own advantage: *The judge told him: "Your attitude shows a selfish disregard for others."* **selfishly** /ˈsel.fɪʃ.li/ *adv* **selfishness** /ˈsel.fɪʃ.nəs/ *noun* [U]
selfless /ˈsel.fləs/ *adj* APPROVING Someone who is selfless only thinks of other people's advantage: *selfless devotion to duty* **selflessly** /ˈsel.flə.sli/ *adv* **selflessness** /ˈsel.flə.snəs/ *noun* [U]

self- [YOURSELF] /self-/ *prefix* of or by yourself or itself: *self-educated* ○ *a self-winding watch*

self-absorbed /ˌself.əbˈzɔːbd/ [US] /-ˈzɔːrbd/ *adj* USUALLY DISAPPROVING only interested in yourself and your own activities **self-absorption** /ˌself.əbˈzɔːp.ʃᵊn/ [US] /-ˈzɔːrp-/ *noun* [U] *Her self-absorption is total – she talks you to death about her health problems.*

self-addressed /ˌself.əˈdrest/ *adj* (especially of an envelope) addressed to the person who has sent it: *Send a self-addressed **envelope** for our free catalogue.* ➲See also **sae**; **SASE**.

self-appointed /ˌself.əˈpɔɪn.tɪd/ [US] /-t̬ɪd/ *adj* DISAPPROVING behaving as if you had responsibility or authority but without having been chosen by other people: *The newspaper has become the self-appointed guardian of public morals.*

self-assembly /ˌself.əˈsem.bli/ *adj, noun* [U] MAINLY UK designed to be made at home from a set of prepared parts by the person who buys it: *a self-assembly kitchen cabinet*

self-assertive /ˌself.əˈsɜː.tɪv/ [US] /-ˈsɝː.t̬ɪv/ *adj* giving your opinions in a powerful way so that other people will notice

self-assessment /ˌself.əˈses.mənt/ *noun* [C or U] a judgment, sometimes for official purposes, which you make about your abilities, principles or decisions

self-assured /ˌself.əˈʃɔːd/ [US] /ʃɝːd/ *adj* APPROVING having confidence in your own abilities: *The interview showed her as a self-assured and mature student.* **self-**

assurance /ˌself.əˈʃɔː.rənts/ ⓤ /-ˈʃɜː.ənts/ *noun* [U]

self-awareness /ˌself.əˈweə.nəs/ ⓤ /-ˈwer-/ *noun* [U] good knowledge and judgment about yourself **self-aware** /ˌself.əˈweəʳ/ ⓤ /-ˈwer/ *adj*

self-belief /ˌself.bɪˈliːf/ *noun* [U] trust in your own abilities

self-catering /ˌselfˈkeɪ.tᵊr.ɪŋ/ ⓤ /-t̬ɚ-/ *adj, noun* [U] UK (of a holiday) having a kitchen so that you can cook meals for yourself rather than having them provided for you: *self-catering apartments/accommodation* ○ *We chose self-catering rather than stay in a hotel.*

self-censorship /ˌselfˈsen.sə.ʃɪp/ ⓤ /-sɚ-/ *noun* [U] control of what you say or do in order to avoid annoying or offending others, but without being told officially that such control is necessary: *These writers knew that unless they practised a form of self-censorship, the authorities would persecute them.*

self-centred UK, US **self-centered** /ˌselfˈsen.təd/ ⓤ /-t̬ɚd/ *adj* DISAPPROVING only interested in yourself and your own activities: *Robert is a self-centred, ambitious and bigoted man.*

self-certification /ˌself.ˌsɜː.tɪ.fɪˈkeɪ.ʃᵊn/ ⓤ /-ˌsɜː.t̬ɪ-/ *noun* [U] UK FORMAL an official statement that you make about yourself, especially in connection with tax or illness: *You are able to notify up to eight days' illness by self-certification.*

self-confessed /ˌself.kənˈfest/ *adj* [before n] admitting to having a characteristic which is considered to be bad or not desirable: *He is a self-confessed **liar**.* ○ *a self-confessed gambler/alcoholic*

self-confident /ˌselfˈkɒn.fɪ.dᵊnt/ ⓤ /-ˈkɑːn-/ *adj* APPROVING behaving calmly because you have no doubts about your ability or knowledge: *At school he was popular and self-confident, and we weren't surprised at his later success.* **self-confidently** /ˌselfˈkɒn.fɪ.dᵊnt.li/ ⓤ /-ˈkɑːn-/ *adv* **self-confidence** /ˌselfˈkɒn.fɪ.dᵊnts/ ⓤ /-ˈkɑːn-/ *noun* [U]

self-congratulatory /ˌself.kənˌgrætˈjuˈleɪ.tᵊr.i/ ⓤ /-t̬ɚ-/ *adj* DISAPPROVING praising yourself or saying how well you have done something **self-congratulation** /ˌself.kənˌgrætˈjuˈleɪ.ʃᵊn/ *noun* [U]

self-conscious /ˌselfˈkɒn.ʃəs/ ⓤ /-ˈkɑːn-/ *adj* uncomfortably or unnaturally aware of yourself and your actions: *He looked uncomfortable, like a self-conscious adolescent who's gone to the wrong party.* **self-consciously** /ˌselfˈkɒn.ʃə.sli/ ⓤ /-ˈkɑːn-/ *adv* **self-consciousness** /ˌselfˈkɒn.ʃə.snəs/ ⓤ /-ˈkɑːn-/ *noun* [U]

self-contained /ˌself.kənˈteɪnd/ *adj* **1** containing or having everything that is needed within itself: *The government wants to encourage viable self-contained rural communities.* **2** describes someone who does not have a large number of relationships with other people or does not depend on others for support: *She's very self-contained and isn't at all worried about moving to a big city where she won't know anybody.*

self-contradictory /ˌself.ˌkɒn.trəˈdɪk.tᵊr.i/ ⓤ /-ˌkɑːn.trə-ˈdɪk.tɚ.i/ *adj* FORMAL expressing one thing which is the opposite of another thing that was already said; saying two things which cannot both be correct: *He is described as a Texas oil millionaire and environmentalist, which might appear to be self-contradictory.*

self-controlled /ˌself.kənˈtrəʊld/ ⓤ /-ˈtroʊld/ *adj* USUALLY APPROVING having strong control over your emotions and actions: *He's always seemed very self-controlled, so I was amazed by his sudden outburst in the office.* **self-control** /ˌself.kənˈtrəʊl/ ⓤ /-ˈtroʊl/ *noun* [U] *It took incredible self-control not to cry out with pain.*

self-deception /ˌself.dɪˈsep.ʃᵊn/ *noun* [U] when you hide the truth from yourself: *His claim to be an important and unjustly neglected painter is sheer self-deception – he's no good at all.*

self-declared /ˌself.dɪˈkleəd/ ⓤ /-ˈklerd/ *adj* [before n] stated or announced by yourself: *The self-declared guardians of law and order held a press conference.* ⸰See also **self-styled.**

self-defeating /ˌself.dɪˈfiː.tɪŋ/ ⓤ /-t̬ɪŋ/ *adj* describes something that causes or makes worse the problem it was designed to avoid or solve: *self-defeating regulations*

self-defence UK, US **self-defense** /ˌself.dɪˈfents/ *noun* [U] **1** protection of yourself, either by fighting or discussion: *He used the gun **in** self-defence.* ○ *In self-defence, I have to say that I only did what you asked me to do.* **2** the skill of fighting without weapons to protect yourself: *She goes to self-defence classes for women.*

self-delusion /ˌself.dɪˈluː.ʒᵊn/ *noun* [C or U] when you allow yourself to believe something that is not true: *It's self-delusion if he thinks he'll be offered a better contract.*

self-denial /ˌself.dɪˈnaɪ.əl/ *noun* [U] when you do not take or have something that you would like because you think it is good for you not to have it

self-deprecating /ˌselfˈdep.rɪ.keɪ.tɪŋ/ ⓤ /-t̬ɪŋ/ *adj* (ALSO **self-deprecatory**) FORMAL trying to make yourself, your abilities or your achievements seem less important: *a self-deprecating manner/remark* ○ *self-deprecating humour/jokes* **self-deprecatingly** /ˌselfˈdep.rɪ.keɪ.tɪŋ.-li/ ⓤ /-t̬ɪŋ-/ *adv* **self-deprecation** /ˌself.ˌdep.rɪˈkeɪ.ʃᵊn/ *noun* [U]

self-destruct /ˌself.dɪˈstrʌkt/ *verb* [I] **1** to be destroyed from within, especially in a way that is planned during the process of being made: *An investigation is underway after a missile self-destructed shortly after it was launched.* **2 (the/sb's) self-destruct button** a characteristic in a person that makes them likely to fail because of their own actions: *At least he reached the semi-final before hitting the self-destruct button.* **self-destruction** /ˌself.dɪˈstrʌk.ʃᵊn/ *noun* [U] **self-destructive** /ˌself.dɪˈstrʌk.tɪv/ *adj*: *He is rebellious, aggressive and at times self-destructive.*

self-determination /ˌself.dɪˌtɜː.mɪˈneɪ.ʃᵊn/ ⓤ /-ˌtɜː-/ *noun* [U] the ability or power to make decisions for yourself, especially the power of a nation to decide how it will be governed

self-discipline /ˌselfˈdɪs.ɪ.plɪn/ *noun* [U] APPROVING the ability to make yourself do things you know you should do even when you do not want to: *You need a lot of self-discipline when you're doing research work on your own.* **self-disciplined** /ˌselfˈdɪs.ɪ.plɪnd/ *adj*

self-discovery /ˌself.dɪˈskʌv.ᵊr.i/ ⓤ /-ɚ-/ *noun* [U] when you learn about yourself and your beliefs: *Her own **journey/voyage** of self-discovery started as she was recovering from a severe illness.*

self-doubt /ˌselfˈdaʊt/ *noun* [U] a lack of confidence in your abilities and decisions

self-drive /ˌselfˈdraɪv/ *adj, noun* [U] UK when you rent and drive a car yourself, rather than being driven by someone else: *a self-drive hire car* ○ *Self-drive is the best way to travel on the island.*

self-effacing /ˌself.ɪˈfeɪ.sɪŋ/ *adj* not making yourself noticeable; not trying to get the attention of other people; modest: *The captain was typically self-effacing when questioned about the team's successes, giving credit to the other players.* **self-effacingly** /ˌself.ɪˈfeɪ.sɪŋ.li/ *adv* **self-effacement** /ˌself.ɪˈfeɪ.smənt/ *noun* [U]

self-employed /ˌself.ɪmˈplɔɪd/ *adj* not working for an employer but finding work for yourself or having your own business: *a self-employed builder* ○ *Do you pay less tax if you're self-employed?* **self-employed** /ˌself.-ɪmˈplɔɪd/ *plural noun*: *They run an advice centre for **the** self-employed.* **self-employment** /ˌself.ɪmˈplɔɪ.mənt/ *noun* [U]

self-esteem /ˌself.ɪˈstiːm/ *noun* [U] belief and confidence in your own ability and value: *The compliments she received after the presentation boosted her self-esteem.*

self-evident /ˌselfˈev.ɪ.dᵊnt/ *adj* clear or obvious without needing any proof or explanation: *Solutions which seem self-evident **to** humans are often beyond the grasp of computers.* **self-evidently** /ˌselfˈev.ɪ.dᵊnt.li/ *adv*: *Any growth in unemployment is self-evidently a matter of extreme seriousness.*

self-explanatory /ˌself.ɪkˈsplæn.ə.tri/ ⓤ /-tɔːr.i/ *adj* easily understood from the information already given and not needing further explanation: *a self-explanatory list of instructions*

self-expression /ˌself.ɪkˈspreʃ.ᵊn/ *noun* [U] expression of your personality, emotions or ideas, especially through art, music or acting: *He regarded poetry as sentimental self-expression.*

S

self-financing /ˌselfˈfaɪ.nænt.sɪŋ/ *adj* paid for only by the money that an activity itself produces: *Fees will have to treble to make the courses self-financing.*

self-fulfilling /ˌself.fʊlˈfɪl.ɪŋ/ *adj* happening because it is expected to happen: *Pessimism is self-fulfilling – expect the worst and it happens.*

ˌself-fulˌfilling ˈprophecy *noun* [C] something that you cause to happen by saying and expecting that it will happen

self-fulfilment /ˌself.fʊlˈfɪl.mənt/ *noun* [U] a feeling of satisfaction that you have achieved what you wanted: *When the options are unemployment or a boring job, having babies can seem like the only means of self-fulfilment.* **self-fulfilled** /ˌself.fʊlˈfɪld/ *adj*

self-government /ˌselfˈgʌv.ən.mənt/ /-ᵊm-/ [US] /-ɚn-/ *noun* [U] the control of a country or an area by the people living there or the control of an organization by a group of people independent of central or local government: *The poll showed that 80% of the population supported regional self-government.* **self-governing** /ˌselfˈgʌv.ᵊn.ɪŋ/ [US] /-ɚ.nɪŋ/ *adj*: *self-governing trusts/schools*

self-help /ˌselfˈhelp/ *adj, noun* [U] the activity of providing what you need for yourself and others with similar experiences or difficulties without going to an official organization: [before n] *self-help groups* ○ *It is a group providing self-help for single parents.*

self-image /ˌselfˈɪm.ɪdʒ/ *noun* [C usually sing] the way a person feels about his or her personality, achievements and value to society: *Having a decent job contributes to a good self-image.*

self-importance /ˌself.ɪmˈpɔː.tᵊnts/ [US] /-ˈpɔːr.t̬ᵊnts/ *noun* [U] DISAPPROVING the belief that you are more important or have a higher value than other people: *He's a modest, mild-mannered man, without a trace of self-importance.* **self-important** /ˌself.ɪmˈpɔː.tᵊnt/ [US] /-ˈpɔːr.t̬ᵊnt/ *adj* **self-importantly** /ˌself.ɪmˈpɔː.tᵊnt.li/ [US] /-ˈpɔːr.t̬ᵊnt-/ *adv*

self-imposed /ˌself.ɪmˈpəʊzd/ [US] /-ˈpoʊzd/ *adj* decided by yourself, without being influenced or ordered by other people: *The end of the year was their self-imposed deadline for finishing the building work.* ○ *After the military coup, the family left for self-imposed* ***exile*** *in America.*

self-incrimination /ˌself.ɪn.krɪm.ɪˈneɪ.ʃᵊn/ *noun* [U] saying or doing something which shows that you are guilty of a crime: *A witness can legally refuse to give evidence to avoid self-incrimination.*

self-induced /ˌself.ɪnˈdjuːst/ [US] /-ˈduːst/ *adj* caused by yourself: *self-induced vomiting/hysteria*

self-indulgent /ˌself.ɪnˈdʌl.dʒᵊnt/ *adj* allowing yourself to have or do anything that you enjoy: *I know it's self-indulgent of me, but I'll just have another chocolate.* **self-indulgence** /ˌself.ɪnˈdʌl.dʒᵊnts/ *noun* [S or U]

self-inflicted /ˌself.ɪnˈflɪk.tɪd/ *adj* of something bad, done to yourself: *self-inflicted pain/damage*

self-interest /ˌselfˈɪn.tᵊr.est/ [US] /-t̬ɚ-/ *noun* [U] when you consider the advantage to yourself when making decisions, and act for your own benefit: *The company's donation was surely* ***motivated by*** *self-interest, as it attracted a lot of media attention.* **self-interested** /ˌselfˈɪn.tᵊr.es.tɪd/ [US] /-t̬ɚ-/ *adj*: *self-interested arguing*

selfish /ˈsel.fɪʃ/ *adj* ➲See at **self** PERSONAL ADVANTAGE.

selfless /ˈsel.fləs/ *adj* ➲See at **self** PERSONAL ADVANTAGE.

self-made /ˌselfˈmeɪd/ *adj* rich and successful as a result of your own work and not because of family wealth: *a self-made man/millionaire*

self-obsessed /ˌself.əbˈsest/ *adj* DISAPPROVING only interested in yourself and your own activities: *a self-obsessed teenager*

self-opinionated /ˌself.əˈpɪn.jə.neɪ.tɪd/ [US] /-t̬ɪd/ *adj* DISAPPROVING having and expressing very strong feelings and beliefs, and believing that your own ideas are the only correct ones

self-perpetuating /ˌself.pəˈpet.ju.eɪ.tɪŋ/ [US] /-pɚˈpet.juː.eɪ.t̬ɪŋ/ *adj* DISAPPROVING having a system which prevents change and produces new things which are very similar to the old ones: *The fighting between the different social groups has become a self-perpetuating spiral of death and hatred.*

self-pity /ˌselfˈpɪt.i/ [US] /-ˈpɪt̬-/ *noun* [U] DISAPPROVING sadness for yourself because you think you have a lot of problems or have suffered a lot: *He faced his illness bravely and without any hint of self-pity.* **self-pitying** /ˌselfˈpɪt.i.ɪŋ/ [US] /-ˈpɪt̬-/ *adj*

self-portrait /ˌselfˈpɔː.treɪt/ [US] /-ˈpɔːr.trɪt/ *noun* [C] a picture, photograph or piece of writing that you make of or about yourself

self-possession /ˌself.pəˈzeʃ.ᵊn/ *noun* [U] the characteristic of being calm and in control of your emotions at all times: *He looked surprised but soon recovered his self-possession.* **self-possessed** /ˌself.pəˈzest/ *adj*: *She is a confident and self-possessed public speaker.*

self-preservation /ˌselfˌprez.əˈveɪ.ʃᵊn/ [US] /-ɚ-/ *noun* [U] behaviour based on the characteristics or feelings which warn people or animals to protect themselves from difficulties or dangers: *It was his instinct for self-preservation that led him to abandon his former friends and transfer his allegiance to the new rulers.*

self-proclaimed /ˌself.prəˈkleɪmd/ *adj* MAINLY DISAPPROVING said or announced about yourself: *He's a self-proclaimed expert on national defence.*

self-professed /ˌself.prəˈfest/ *adj* said, announced or admitted about yourself: *a self-professed gambler* ○ *She's a self-professed supporter of prison reform.*

self-propelled /ˌself.prəˈpeld/ *adj* able to move by its own power: *self-propelled artillery/guns*

self-protection /ˌself.prəˈtek.ʃᵊn/ *noun* [U] keeping yourself safe from injury or damage: *They claimed that they needed the weapons for self-protection.*

self-raising flour UK /ˌself.reɪ.zɪŋˈflaʊəʳ/ [US] /-ˈflaʊɚ/ *noun* [U] (US **self-rising flour**) flour that contains a substance which makes cakes swell when they are cooked

self-referential /ˌself.ref.ᵊrˈent.ʃᵊl/ [US] /-əˈrent-/ *adj* A self-referential book, film, play, etc. contains a reference to itself, its author or other work by that author: *Modern television sitcoms are often ironic and self-referential.*

self-regulation /ˌself.reg.jʊˈleɪ.ʃᵊn/ *noun* [U] making certain yourself that you or your employees act according to the rules, rather than having this done by other people: *They favour the self-regulation of the industry, and strict codes of conduct have already been issued by the Advertising Association.* **self-regulating** /ˌselfˈreg.jʊ.leɪ.tɪŋ/ [US] /-t̬ɪŋ/ *adj* (ALSO **self-regulatory**) *a self-regulating body/organization*

self-reliant /ˌself.rɪˈlaɪ.ənt/ *adj* APPROVING not needing help or support from other people: *Lone parents have to be self-reliant, resilient and inventive.* **self-reliance** /ˌself.rɪˈlaɪ.ənts/ *noun* [U]

self-respect /ˌself.rɪˈspekt/ *noun* [U] respect for yourself which shows that you value yourself: *He felt what he was being asked to do took away his dignity and self-respect.* **self-respecting** /ˌself.rɪˈspek.tɪŋ/ *adj* [before n] *No self-respecting government would allow such atrocities to be carried out in its name.*

self-restraint /ˌself.rɪˈstreɪnt/ *noun* [U] control of your own actions: *He was angry but managed, with great self-restraint, to reply calmly.*

self-righteous /ˌselfˈraɪ.tʃəs/ *adj* DISAPPROVING believing that your ideas and behaviour are morally better than those of other people: *He's so self-righteous – you'd think he'd never done anything wrong in his life.* **self-righteously** /ˌselfˈraɪ.tʃə.sli/ *adv* **self-righteousness** /ˌselfˈraɪ.tʃə.snəs/ *noun* [U]

self-rule /ˌselfˈruːl/ *noun* [U] when a country, a part of a country or a nation chooses its own government and controls its own activities ➲See also **self-government**.

self-sacrifice /ˌselfˈsæk.rɪ.faɪs/ *noun* [U] APPROVING giving up what you want so that other people can have what they want: *People say this is a selfish society, but frankly I've seen too much kindness, self-sacrifice and generosity to believe that.* ○ *The job requires a lot of enthusiasm, dedication and self-sacrifice.* **self-sacrificing** /ˌselfˈsæk.rɪ.faɪ.sɪŋ/ *adj*

S

self-same /ˈself.seɪm/ *adj* **[before n]** exactly the same: *The self-same car has been parked outside three times this week.*

self-satisfied /ˌselfˈsæt.ɪs.faɪd/ [US] /-ˈsæt̬-/ *adj DISAPPROVING* very pleased with and not critical of yourself: *She was very smug and self-satisfied about getting the promotion.* **self-satisfaction** /ˌselfˌsæt.ɪsˈfæk.ʃən/ [US] /-ˌsæt̬-/ *noun* **[U]**

self-seeking /ˌselfˈsiː.kɪŋ/ *adj FORMAL DISAPPROVING* interested in your own advantage in everything that you do: *The army felt that the politicians of the day were just self-seeking opportunists.*

self-service /ˌselfˈsɜː.vɪs/ [US] /-ˈsɝː-/ *adj* especially in a shop or restaurant, not being served by an employee but collecting goods or food yourself: *a self-service salad bar* ○ *self-service (UK) petrol/(US) gas pumps*

self-serving /ˌselfˈsɜː.vɪŋ/ [US] /-ˈsɝː-/ *adj FORMAL DISAPPROVING* working or acting for your own advantage: *Politicians are seen as old-fashioned, corrupt and self-serving.*

self-starter /ˌselfˈstɑː.təʳ/ [US] /-ˈstɑːr.t̬ɚ/ *noun* **[C]** *APPROVING* a person who is able to work effectively without regularly needing to be told what to do: *The successful applicant for the position will be a well-motivated self-starter who has excellent communication skills.*

self-styled /ˈself.staɪld/ *adj* **[before n]** *USUALLY DISAPPROVING* given a name or title by yourself without any official reason for it: *The media appears to be full of self-styled 'experts' who are happy to give their views on subjects that they actually know very little about.*

self-sufficient /ˌself.səˈfɪʃ.ənt/ *adj* able to provide everything you need, especially food, for yourself without the help of other people: *The programme aims to make the country self-sufficient* ***in*** *food production and to cut energy imports.* **self-sufficiency** /ˌself.səˈfɪʃ.ənt.si/ *noun* **[U]**

self-supporting /ˌself.səˈpɔː.tɪŋ/ [US] /-ˈpɔːr.t̬ɪŋ/ *adj* earning or having enough money to pay for your activities without receiving financial help from other people: *The vast majority of students here are self-supporting.* ➲See also **self-financing**.

self-willed /ˌselfˈwɪld/ *adj DISAPPROVING* determined to base your actions on your own decisions without listening to advice from other people

self-worth /ˌselfˈwɜːθ/ [US] /-ˈwɝːθ/ *noun* **[U]** the value you give to your life and achievements: *Many people derive their self-worth from their work.*

sell [MONEY] /sel/ *verb* **[I or T] sold, sold** to give something to someone else in return for money: **[+ two objects]** *I sold him my car/I sold my car to him* ***for*** *£600.* ○ *We'll be selling the tickets* ***at/for*** *£50 each.* ○ *The stall sells drinks and snacks.* ○ *These baskets sell well* (= a lot of them are bought). ➲See also **sale** SELL.

• **sell *sb* down the river** *INFORMAL* to put someone in a difficult or dangerous situation by not acting as you had promised to act, usually in order to gain an advantage for yourself

• **sell *yourself/sth* short** to not value someone or something as much as they deserve to be valued: *Don't sell yourself short – you've got the skills and the experience.*

• **sell *your* soul (to the devil)** to be persuaded to do something, especially something bad, because of the money or other reward you will receive for doing it

• **sell *sb* a bill of goods** (*UK ALSO* **sell *sb* a pup**) to deceive someone into buying something which is worthless

seller /ˈsel.əʳ/ [US] /-ɚ/ *noun* **[C] 1** a person who is selling something: *flower/newspaper/souvenir sellers* ○ *Do you think the seller will accept £96,000 for the house?* **2** a product which a lot of people buy: *This car is our* ***biggest*** *seller at the moment.*

sell [PERSUADE] /sel/ *verb* **[T] sold, sold** to persuade someone that an idea or plan is a good one and likely to be successful: *My boss is very old-fashioned and I'm having a lot of trouble selling the idea of working at home occasionally.* ○ **[+ two objects]** *The chance of greater access to European markets would help sell the President the scheme/sell the scheme* ***to*** *the President.* ○ *She's really sold* ***on*** *the idea of buying a new car.*

PHRASAL VERBS WITH **sell**

▲ **sell *sth* off** *phrasal verb* **[M] 1** to charge a low price for something to encourage people to buy it: *They're selling off last year's stock at half price.* **2** to sell all or part of a business: *The company announced that it would be selling off its hotel business.*

sell-off /ˈsel.ɒf/ [US] /-ɑːf/ *noun* **[C] 1** a sale of an unwanted business at a low price to encourage someone to buy it **2** a sale of an investment, such as shares in a company, that causes its value to fall

▲ **sell out** [SELL ALL] *phrasal verb* **1** to sell all of the supply that you have of something: *We sold out* ***of*** *the T-shirts in the first couple of hours.* **2** If a supply of something sells out, there is no more of that thing to buy: *The first issue of the magazine sold out within two days.* **3 [often passive]** When a show or film sells out, all of the tickets for it are sold: *We couldn't get seats – the concert was sold out.*

sell-out /ˈsel.aʊt/ *noun* **[C usually sing]** a performance or sports event for which no more tickets are available, because it is so popular: *The concert was a sell-out.*

▲ **sell *(sb)* out** [BREAK PROMISE] *phrasal verb* **[M]** *INFORMAL* to not do what you have promised someone you will do or what you should do because you will get more advantages for yourself if you do something else: *French farmers feel they've been sold out by their government in the negotiations.* ○ *They've sold out* ***to*** *the road transport lobby* (= done what these people wanted).

sell-out /ˈsel.aʊt/ *noun* **[C usually sing]** *DISAPPROVING* when someone does not do what they have promised to do or what they should do: *Most of the workers see the union agreement as a sell-out.*

▲ **sell out** [SELL BUSINESS] *phrasal verb* to sell your business or part of your business: *They decided to sell out* ***to*** *their competitors.*

▲ **sell up** *phrasal verb UK* to sell your house or company in order to go somewhere else or do something else: *They sold up and retired to the West Country.*

sell-by date *UK* /ˈsel.baɪˌdeɪt/ *noun* **[C]** (*US* **pull date**) a date marked on a product such as food after which it should not be sold

ˈselling ˌpoint *noun* **[C]** a characteristic of a product which will persuade people to buy it: *Its best selling point is the price – it's the cheapest on the market.*

Sellotape *UK TRADEMARK* /ˈsel.ə.teɪp/ *noun* **[U]** (*US TRADEMARK* **Scotch tape**) a long thin strip of sticky and usually transparent material which is sold in a roll and is used for joining together things such as paper or card: *a roll of Sellotape* ○ *I stuck the note to the door* ***with*** *Sellotape.* **sellotape** *UK* /ˈsel.ə.teɪp/ *verb* **[T]** (*US* **Scotch-tape**) *When I got home, I found a mysterious message sellotaped* ***to*** *the front door.*

seltzer /ˈselt.səʳ/ [US] /-sɚ/ *noun* **[C or U]** *US FOR* fizzy MINERAL WATER

selves /selvz/ *plural of* **self** PERSONALITY

semantic /sɪˈmæn.tɪk/ [US] /-t̬ɪk/ *adj* connected with the meanings of words **semantically** /sɪˈmæn.tɪ.kli/ [US] /-t̬ɪk-/ *adv*

semantics /sɪˈmæn.tɪks/ [US] /-t̬ɪks/ *noun* **[U]** the study of meanings in a language: *Syntax describes the rules by which words can be combined into sentences, while semantics describes what they mean.*

semaphore /ˈsem.ə.fɔːʳ/ [US] /-fɔːr/ *noun* **[U]** a system of communication using two hand-held flags which are moved into different positions to represent different letters, numbers or symbols

semblance /ˈsem.bləns/ *noun* **[U]** *SLIGHTLY FORMAL* a situation or condition which is similar to what is wanted or expected, but is not exactly as desired: *The city has now returned to* ***some*** *semblance* ***of*** *normality after last night's celebrations.* ○ *He was executed without even* ***the*** *semblance* ***of*** *a fair trial.*

semen /ˈsiː.mən/ *noun* **[U]** a thick whitish liquid containing sperm which is produced by the sex organs of men and some male animals ➲See also **seminal** LIQUID.

semester /sɪˈmes.təʳ/ [US] /səˈmes.tɚ/ *noun* **[C]** one of the periods into which a year is divided at a college or university, especially in the US and Australia: *the first/*

second semester ○ *the spring/fall semester* ⊃Compare **term** TIME; **trimester**.

semi- HALF /ˈsem.i-/ /-ɪ-/ US /-ɪ/ /-i-/ /-aɪ-/ *prefix* half or partly: *semi-literate* ○ *semi-permanent* ○ *semi-skilled workers* ○ *a semi-autobiographical novel*

semi HOUSE /ˈsem.i/ *noun* [C] *plural* **semis** UK INFORMAL a house that is SEMI-DETACHED

semi VEHICLE /ˈsem.i/ *noun* [C] *plural* **semis** US INFORMAL an ARTICULATED truck ⊃See picture **Cars and Trucks** on page Centre 13

semi COMPETITION /ˈsem.i/ *noun* [C] *plural* **semis** INFORMAL FOR **semi-final**

semi-automatic /ˌsem.i.ɔːtəˈmæt.ɪk/ US /-ɑːˌtəˈmæt̬-/ *adj* partly automatic: *a semi-automatic gearbox/shotgun*

semibreve MAINLY UK /ˈsem.i.briːv/ *noun* [C] (US USUALLY **whole note**) SPECIALIZED a musical note with a time value equal to two MINIMS or four CROTCHETS

semicircle /ˈsem.iˌsɜː.kl̩/ US /-ˌsɜː-/ *noun* [C usually sing] half a circle: *We arranged the chairs in a semicircle.* **semi-circular** /ˌsem.iˈsɜː.kjʊ.lər/ US /-ˈsɜː.kjʊ.lə/ *adj*: *The chairs were placed in a semi-circular arrangement.*

semicolon /ˌsem.iˈkəʊ.lɒn/ US /ˈsem.iˌkoʊ.lən/ *noun* [C] the ; punctuation mark that is used in formal writing between two parts of a sentence, usually when each of the two parts could form grammatical sentences on their own. A semicolon can also separate the items in a list.

semiconductor /ˌsem.i.kənˈdʌk.tər/ US /-tə/ *noun* [C] a material, such as SILICON, which allows electricity to move through it more easily when its temperature increases, or an electronic device made from this material: *Semiconductors are used for making integrated circuits and computers.* **semiconducting** /ˈsem.i.kənˌdʌk.tɪŋ/ *adj* [before n]

semi-detached /ˌsem.i.dɪˈtætʃt/ *adj* UK A house that is semi-detached is one that is joined to another similar house on only one side: *They live in a semi-detached house.* ⊃Compare **detached** at **detach**.

semi-final /ˌsem.iˈfaɪ.nəl/ *noun* [C usually pl] (INFORMAL **semi**) one of the two games that are played to decide who will take part in the final game of a competition: *She's the youngest player ever to get through to/advance to a semi-final.*

seminal IMPORTANT /ˈsem.ɪ.nəl/ *adj* FORMAL containing important new ideas and being very influential on later work: *She wrote a seminal article on the subject while she was still a student.* ○ *He played a seminal role in the formation of the association.*

seminal LIQUID /ˈsem.ɪ.nəl/ *adj* [before n] SPECIALIZED connected with SEMEN: *seminal fluid*

seminar /ˈsem.ɪ.nɑːr/ US /-nɑːr/ *noun* [C] an occasion when a teacher or expert and a group of people meet to study and discuss something: *I attended practically every lecture and seminar when I was a student.* ○ *I'm giving a seminar on the latest developments in genetic engineering next week.* ○ *a seminar room* ⊃Compare **lecture**.

seminary /ˈsem.ɪ.nə.ri/ US /-ner.i/ *noun* [C] a college for training people to become priests

semiotics /ˌsem.iˈɒt.ɪks/ US /-ɑː.t̬ɪks/ *noun* [U] SPECIALIZED the study of signs and symbols, what they mean and how they are used **semiotic** /ˈsem.i.ɒt.ɪk/ US /-ˈɑː.t̬ɪk/ *adj* **semiotician** /ˌsem.i.əˈtɪʃ.ən/ *noun* [C] (ALSO **semiologist**)

semi-precious /ˌsem.iˈpreʃ.əs/ *adj* [before n] A semi-precious stone is one which is used for making jewellery but is not extremely valuable: *Jade and turquoise are semi-precious stones.*

semi-professional /ˌsem.i.prəˈfeʃ.ən.əl/ *adj* People who are semi-professional are paid for an activity which they take part in but which they do not do all the time: *semi-professional musicians/rugby players*

semiquaver MAINLY UK /ˈsem.iˌkweɪ.vər/ US /-və/ *noun* [C] (US USUALLY **sixteenth note**) a musical note which has a time value of half a QUAVER or one-sixteenth of a SEMIBREVE

semi-skilled /ˌsem.iˈskɪld/ *adj* having or needing only a small amount of training: *semi-skilled jobs/workers/labour*

semisweet chocolate /ˌsem.iˌswiːtˈtʃɒk.lət/ US /-ˈtʃɑːk-/ *noun* [U] US FOR **dark chocolate**

Semitic /sɪˈmɪt.ɪk/ US /səˈmɪt̬-/ *adj* **1** relating to the race of people that includes Arabs and Jews, or to their languages: *Hebrew and Arabic are Semitic languages.* ⊃See also **anti-Semitic** at **anti-Semitism**. **2** OLD USE Jewish **3** describes races such as the Babylonians and Phoenicians that existed in ancient times

semitone /ˈsem.i.təʊn/ US /-toʊn/ *noun* [C] (US ALSO **half step**, US ALSO **half tone**) the smallest difference in sound between two notes which are next to each other in the western musical scale

semolina /ˌsem.əˈliː.nə/ *noun* [U] a powder made from crushed wheat used for making pasta and, especially in Britain in the past, for making sweet dishes

Semtex /ˈsem.teks/ *noun* [U] TRADEMARK a powerful explosive, used especially to make illegal bombs

Sen. *noun* [before n] ABBREVIATION FOR **senator**, see at **the Senate**

the Senate POLITICS /ðəˈsen.ət/ *group noun* [S] the more important of the two groups of politicians who make laws in some countries such as the US, Australia and France: *the French/Australian Senate* ○ *The US Senate has 100 members.* ○ *The law has no chance of being passed by the Senate.*

senator /ˈsen.ə.tər/ US /-t̬ə/ *noun* [C] (WRITTEN ABBREVIATION **Sen.**) a politician who has been elected to a Senate: *Only two senators voted against the bill.* ○ [as form of address] *It's a pleasure to meet you, Senator.* **senatorial** /ˌsen.əˈtɔː.ri.əl/ US /-ˈtɔːr.i-/ *adj* MAINLY US *a senatorial candidate/committee*

the Senate EDUCATION /ðəˈsen.ət/ *group noun* [S] the group of people who control a college or university

send POST /send/ *verb* [T] **sent**, **sent** to cause something to go from one place to another, especially by post: [+ two objects] *I'll send her a letter/fax/parcel/postcard next week.* ○ *We'll send it by post/airmail/sea.* ○ *Could you send a reply to them as quickly as possible.* ○ *The news report was sent by satellite.* ○ *She sent a message with John to say that she couldn't come.* ○ *They sent her flowers for her birthday.* ○ *Maggie sends her love and hopes you'll feel better soon.*

• **send word** to send a message: *She sent word with her secretary that she would be unable to attend the meeting.* **sender** /ˈsen.dər/ US /-də/ *noun* [C] a person who sends something: *Postage stamps were introduced in Britain in 1840 as a way of showing that the sender had paid for the letter to be delivered.* ○ *The letter came back with 'return to sender – not known at this address' written on it.*

send CAUSE TO GO /send/ *verb* [T] **sent**, **sent** to cause or order someone to go and do something: [+ to infinitive] *We're sending the children to stay with my parents for a couple of weeks.* ○ *The commander has asked us to send reinforcements.* ○ *They've sent their son (away) to school in Scotland.* ○ *He was trying to explain but she became impatient and sent him away* (= told him to leave).

• **send sb packing** INFORMAL to ask someone to leave immediately: *There were some kids at the door asking for money but I sent them packing.*

• **send sb to Coventry** UK OLD-FASHIONED If a group of people send someone to Coventry, they refuse to speak to that person, usually as a punishment for having done something to upset the group.

send CAUSE TO HAPPEN /send/ *verb* [T] **sent**, **sent** to cause someone or something to do a particular thing, or to cause something to happen: *The explosion sent the crowd into a panic.* ○ *Watching the television always sends me to sleep.* ○ [+ adj] UK *His untidiness sends her crazy/mad/wild.* ○ [+ v-ing] *The announcement of the fall in profits sent the company's share price plummeting* (= caused it to go down a lot). ○ *The draught from the fan sent papers flying all over the room.*

• **send a signal to** to warn someone about something: *The rise in interest rates should send a signal to financial institutions that the government is serious about reducing inflation.*

▲ **send** *sth* **back** *phrasal verb* [M] to return something to the person who sent it to you, especially because it is damaged or not suitable: *I had to send the shirt back because it didn't fit me.*

▲ **send** *sb* **down** COLLEGE *phrasal verb* [M usually passive] *UK* to ask someone to leave a college or university without finishing their course because they have done something wrong: *She was sent down from Oxford for taking drugs.*

▲ **send** *sb* **down** PRISON *UK phrasal verb* [M usually passive] (*US* **send** *sb* **up**) *INFORMAL* to send someone to prison: *He was sent down for armed robbery.* ○ *She was sent down for three years.*

▲ **send for** *sb phrasal verb* to send someone a message asking them to come to see you: *Do you think we should send for a doctor?*

▲ **send (off/away) for/to** *sth phrasal verb* to write to an organization or place to ask them to send you something: *I've sent off for a catalogue.* ○ *We had to send off to Ireland for a replacement part.*

▲ **send** *sth* **in** GIVE *phrasal verb* [M] to send something to an organization: *The magazine asked its readers to send in their comments about the new style of presentation.*

▲ **send** *sth* **in** ORDER *phrasal verb* [M] to send soldiers, police, etc. to a place in order to deal with a dangerous situation: *UN troops were sent in as the situation got worse.*

▲ **send** *sth* **off** POST *phrasal verb* [M] to send a letter, document or parcel by post: *Have you sent off your application form yet?*

▲ **send** *sb* **off** SPORT *phrasal verb* [M] (*US* **eject**) *UK* to order a sports player to leave the playing area during a game because they have done something wrong: *He was sent off for swearing at the referee.*

▲ **send** *sth* **on** *phrasal verb* [M] to send something from someone's old address to their new one: *Paul's moved back to New York and he's asked me to send on his letters.*

▲ **send** *sth* **out** POST *phrasal verb* [M] to send something to a lot of different people, usually by post: *We sent out the wedding invitations about three weeks ago.*

▲ **send** *sth* **out** PRODUCE *phrasal verb* [M] to produce something in a way that causes it to spread out from a central point: *The equipment sent out a regular high-pitched signal.* ○ *The torch sends out a powerful beam of light.* ○ *It was a mild winter and by February the bushes were sending out new shoots.*

▲ **send out for** *sth phrasal verb* to ask for something to be delivered to you from another place, by using the telephone or sending a message: *There's not much to eat in the fridge. Should we send out for a pizza?*

▲ **send** *sb/sth* **up** *phrasal verb* [M] *UK INFORMAL* to make someone or something seem stupid by copying them in a funny way: *The show was very funny – they were sending up sports commentators.*

send-up /'send.ʌp/ *noun* [C] *INFORMAL* He does a brilliant send-up of the President.

send-off /'send.ɒf/ ⓤ /-ɑːf/ *noun* [C usually sing] an occasion at which people can express good wishes and say goodbye to someone who is leaving a place: *We'll have to give her a good send-off when she leaves the office.*

senile /'siː.naɪl/ ⓤ /'sen.aɪl/ *adj* showing a lack of mental ability because of old age, especially a lack of ability to think clearly and make decisions: *He spent many years caring for his senile mother.* ○ *I'm always losing my keys these days. I think I must be **going** senile.* **senility** /sɪ-'nɪl.ɪ.ti/ ⓤ /-ə.t̬i/ *noun* [U]

,**senile de'mentia** *noun* [U] *SPECIALIZED* a medical condition that causes a gradual worsening in the memory and other mental abilities of old people, leading them to behave in a confused manner

senior OLDER /'siː.ni.əʳ/ ⓤ /-njɚ/ *adj* **1** [before n] older: *Senior pupils are expected to set an example to the younger children.* ⊃Compare **junior** YOUNGER. **2** (*UK WRITTEN ABBREVIATION* **Snr**, *US WRITTEN ABBREVIATION* **Sr**.) used after a man's name to refer to the older of two people in the same family who have the same name: *Hello, may I speak to Ken Griffey senior, please?*

senior /'siː.ni.əʳ/ ⓤ /-njɚ/ *noun* **1** 20/30, etc. **years** *your* senior 20/30, etc. years older than you: *She married a man twenty years her senior.* ○ *She's my senior by three years* (= She is three years older than me). **2** [C] *US* a student in their final year of high school or university

seniority /,siː.ni'ɒr.ɪ.ti/ ⓤ /siː'njɔːr.ə.t̬i/ *noun* [U] the advantage that you get by working for a company for a long time: *In future, promotion will be based on merit not seniority.*

senior HIGH RANK /'siː.ni.əʳ/ ⓤ /-njɚ/ *adj* high or higher in rank: *senior management* ○ *a senior government minister* ○ *She's senior to me, so I have to do what she tells me.* ⊃Compare **junior** LOW RANK.

senior /'siː.ni.əʳ/ ⓤ /-njɚ/ *noun* [C] someone who is high or higher in rank: *It's important to impress your seniors if you want to be promoted.*

seniority /,siː.ni'ɒr.ɪ.ti/ ⓤ /siː'njɔːr.ə.t̬i/ *noun* [U] the state of being higher in rank than someone else: *I suppose I was impressed by his seniority.*

,**senior 'citizen** *noun* [C] (*US ALSO* **senior**) *POLITE WORD FOR* an old person: *Discounts are available for senior citizens.*

,**senior 'nursing ,officer** *UK noun* [C] (*US* **head nurse**, *UK OLD-FASHIONED* **matron**) the person in charge of all the nurses in a hospital

,**senior 'statesman/'states,woman** *noun* [C] an experienced politician who is usually no longer working in government ⊃See also **elder**.

sensation FEELING /sen'seɪ.ʃən/ *noun* **1** [C or U] the ability to feel something physically, especially by touching, or a physical feeling that results from this ability: *a burning sensation* ○ *I had no sensation of pain whatsoever.* ○ *The disease causes a loss of sensation in the fingers.* **2** [C usually sing] a general feeling caused by something that happens to you, especially a feeling which you cannot describe exactly: [+ (that)] *I had the odd sensation (that) someone was following me.* ○ *I can remember the first time I went sailing – it was a wonderful sensation.*

sensation EXCITEMENT /sen'seɪ.ʃən/ *noun* [S] something very exciting or interesting, or something which causes great excitement or interest: *Their affair **caused** a sensation.* ○ *The books have been a publishing sensation on both sides of the Atlantic.* ○ *The show was an overnight sensation* (= was very successful immediately).

sensational /sen'seɪ.ʃən.əl/ *adj* **1** *APPROVING* very good, exciting or unusual: *a sensational sports car/dress* ○ *She looks sensational* (= extremely attractive) *in her new dress.* **2** *DISAPPROVING* describes news reports and articles that are intended to excite or shock people rather than to be serious: *Some of the more sensational Japanese newspapers have given a lot of coverage to the scandal.*

sensationally /sen'seɪ.ʃən.əl.i/ *adv* **1** extremely; used to emphasize positive adjectives or adverbs: *sensationally popular/successful* ○ *The book sold sensationally well.* **2** in an extremely interesting or exciting way: *The show ended sensationally with fireworks.*

sensationalism /sen'seɪ.ʃən.əl.ɪ.zəm/ *noun* [U] *DISAPPROVING* when newspapers, TV, etc. intentionally present information in a way that is intended to excite or shock people: *The newspaper has been accused of sensationalism in its coverage of the murders.* **sensationalist** /sen-'seɪ.ʃən.əl.ɪst/ *adj* **sensationalize**, *UK USUALLY* -**ise** /sen-'seɪ.ʃən.əl.aɪz/ *verb* [T]

sense GOOD JUDGMENT /sents/ *noun* [U] the characteristic of having good judgment, especially when it is based on practical ideas or understanding: [+ to infinitive] *I hope they'll **have the (good)** sense/**have enough** sense to shut the windows before they leave.* ○ *It **makes (good)** sense to buy a large packet because it works out cheaper in the end.* ○ [+ v-ing] *There's no sense in waiting* (= It is not practical to wait) – *the next train isn't for two hours.* ○ *Where's/What's the sense* (= What is the advantage) *in paying someone when you could get a volunteer?* ○ *Planning so far ahead **makes no** sense* – *so many things will have changed by next year.*

senses /'sent.sɪz/ *plural noun*: *Have you **taken leave of** your senses* (= Have you lost your ability to make a good judgment)? ○ *It's time you **came to** your senses* (= started

S

to use your good judgment) *and realized that they are not going to help you.* ○ *The accident* ***brought*** *him* ***to*** *his senses* (= caused him to use his good judgment again) *and made him stop drinking.*

sensible /ˈsent.sɪ.bl̩/ *adj* **1** based on or acting on good judgment and practical ideas or understanding: *a sensible answer/approach/compromise/option* ○ *a sensible person* ○ *I think the sensible thing to do is phone before you go and ask for directions.* ○ ***It*** *would be sensible* ***to*** *take an umbrella.* * NOTE: The opposite is 'not sensible'. *Insensible* means 'unconscious'. **2** Sensible clothes or shoes are practical and suitable for the purpose they are needed for, rather than being attractive or fashionable: *It could be cold and wet so pack some sensible clothes.* **sensibly** /ˈsent.sɪ.bli/ *adv*: *The police praised motorists for driving sensibly in the appalling conditions.* ○ *She wasn't very sensibly dressed for hiking across the moors.*

senseless /ˈsent.sləs/ *adj* lacking good judgment, or lacking a good or useful purpose: *a senseless argument* ○ *senseless killings/violence/deaths* ➲See also **senseless** at **sense** ABILITY. **senselessly** /ˈsensləsli/ *adv*

COMMON LEARNER ERROR

sensible or **sensitive?**

Remember that **sensible** does not mean 'easily upset' or 'able to understand what people are feeling'. The word you need to express these two meanings is **sensitive**.

Don't criticize her too much. She's very sensitive.
He's very sensitive to other people's feelings.
~~*He's very sensible to other people's feelings.*~~

sense [ABILITY] /sents/ *noun* **1** [C] an ability to understand, recognize, value or react to something, especially any of the five physical abilities to see, hear, smell, taste and feel: *With her keen sense* ***of*** *smell, she could tell if you were a smoker from the other side of the room.* ○ *My cold is so bad I've* ***lost*** *my sense* ***of*** *smell/taste* (= I can't smell/taste anything). **2** [C or U] a general feeling or understanding: *Did you get any sense of how they might react?* ○ *The helicopters hovering overhead added to the sense* ***of*** *urgency.* **3 sense of fun** the ability to enjoy life and not be too serious: *Don't be angry – it was just a joke – where's your sense of fun?* **4 sense of humour** your ability to understand amusing things: *She* ***has*** *a really good sense of humour.* ○ *We* ***have*** *the same sense of humour.* ○ *Come on, lighten up! Where's your sense of humour?* **5** *UK* **sense of occasion** the feeling people have when there is a very important event or celebration: *The decorations, flowers and crowds gave the town a real sense of occasion.*

sense /sents/ *verb* [T] to be aware of something or experience it without being able to explain exactly how: *Although she said nothing, I could sense her anger* ○ *He sensed something was about to happen.* ○ [+ (that)] *He sensed* ***(that)*** *his guests were bored, although they were listening politely.* ○ [+ question word] *Could you sense* ***what*** *was likely to happen?*

senseless /ˈsent.sləs/ *adj* unconscious: *Panos was* ***beaten*** *senseless by the burglars.* ➲See also **senseless** at **sense** GOOD JUDGMENT.

sense [MEANING] /sents/ *noun* [C] one of the possible meanings of a word or phrase: *They are not immigrants, at least not in any sense that I understand.* ○ *The packaging is green – in both senses of the word* (= it is green in colour and it is good for the environment). ○ *Security defined* ***in the broad/broadest*** *sense* ***of*** *the term means getting at the root causes of trouble and helping to reduce regional conflicts.* ○ *This passage doesn't* ***make (any)*** *sense* (= the meaning is not clear). ○ *I've read the letter twice, but I can't* ***make (any)*** *sense* ***of*** *it* (= I can't understand it).

• **in every sense** in every way or feature: *It's a book which is, in every sense, about different ways of seeing the world.*

• **in a sense** (*ALSO* **in one sense**) thinking about something in one way, but not in every way: *She claims that the system is at fault and she's right, in a sense* (= she is partly right), *it could be improved.*

• **in no sense** not at all: *We are in no sense obliged to agree to this.*

ˈ**sense ˌorgan** *noun* [C] a part of the body which makes it possible to experience the physical characteristics of a situation: *Your ears, eyes, tongue, nose and skin are your sense organs.*

sensibility /ˌsent.sɪˈbɪl.ɪ.ti/ [US] /-səˈbɪl.ə.ţi/ *noun* [U] an awareness of or ability to decide about what is good or valuable, especially in connection with artistic or social activities: *literary/musical/artistic/theatrical/aesthetic sensibility* ○ *The author has applied* ***a*** *modern sensibility* (= way of understanding things) *to the social ideals of an earlier age.*

sensibilities /ˌsent.sɪˈbɪl.ɪ.tiz/ [US] /-səˈbɪl.ə.ţiz/ *plural noun* feelings: *In a multicultural society we need to show respect for the sensibilities* ***of*** *others.*

sensible /ˈsent.sɪ.bl̩/ *adj FORMAL* having an awareness or understanding of a situation: *He did not appear to be sensible* ***of*** *the difficulties that lay ahead.*

sensitive [KIND] /ˈsent.sɪ.tɪv/ [US] /-sə.ţɪv/ *adj* understanding what other people need, and being helpful and kind to them: *Representatives of the company claim their plan will be sensitive* ***to*** *local needs.* ○ *In the movie, he plays a concerned and sensitive father trying to bring up two teenage children on his own.* **sensitively** /ˈsent.sɪ.tɪv.li/ [US] /-sə.ţɪv-/ *adv*: *This is a very delicate situation and it needs to be handled sensitively.* **sensitiveness** /ˈsen.sɪ.tɪv.nəs/ [US] /-sə.ţɪv-/ *noun* [U] **sensitivity** /ˌsent.sɪˈtɪv.ɪ.ti/ [US] /-səˈtɪv.ə.ţi/ *noun* [C or U]

sensitize, *UK USUALLY* **-ise** /ˈsent.sɪ.taɪz/ *verb* [T] to make someone aware of something: *The association aims to sensitize employers* ***to*** *the problems faced by left-handed people in the workplace.*

sensitive [UPSET] /ˈsent.sɪ.tɪv/ [US] /-sə.ţɪv/ *adj* **1** easily upset by the things people say or do, or causing people to be upset, embarrassed or angry: *Her reply showed that she was very sensitive* ***to*** *criticism.* ○ *He was very sensitive* ***about*** *his scar and thought everyone was staring at him.* **2** A sensitive subject, situation, etc. needs to be dealt with carefully in order to avoid upsetting people: *Sex education and birth control are sensitive* ***issues.*** ○ *The stolen car contained military documents described as very sensitive.* **sensitiveness** /ˈsen.sɪ.tɪv.nəs/ [US] /-sə.ţɪv-/ *noun* [U] **sensitivity** /ˌsent.sɪˈtɪv.ɪ.ti/ [US] /-səˈtɪv.ə.ţi/ *noun* [U] *Such is the sensitivity of the information that only two people are allowed to know it.*

sensitive [REACTING EASILY] /ˈsent.sɪ.tɪv/ [US] /-sə.ţɪv/ *adj* **1** easily influenced, changed or damaged, especially by a physical activity or effect: *Some people's teeth are highly sensitive* ***to*** *cold.* ○ *sensitive* ***skin*** **2** Sensitive equipment is able to record small changes: *The patient's responses are recorded on a sensitive piece of equipment which gives extremely accurate readings.* **-sensitive** /-sent.sɪ.tɪv/ [US] /-sə.ţɪv/ *suffix*: *light-/heat-sensitive* **sensitivity** /ˌsent.sɪˈtɪv.ɪ.ti/ [US] /-səˈtɪv.ə.ţi/ *noun* [U] (*ALSO* **sensitiveness**) *One of the side effects of the drug is an increased sensitivity* ***to*** *sunlight.*

sensitize, *UK USUALLY* **-ise** /ˈsent.sɪ.taɪz/ *verb* [T] to make someone sensitive to something: *It seems very likely that air pollutants are sensitizing people so that they become allergic to pollen.*

sensor /ˈsent.sər/ [US] /-sɚ/ *noun* [C] a device which is used to record the presence of something or changes in something: *The security device has a heat sensor which detects the presence of people and animals.*

sensory /ˈsent.sər.i/ [US] /-sɚ-/ *adj* [before n] *SPECIALIZED* connected with the physical senses of touch, smell, taste, hearing and seeing

sensual /ˈsent.sjʊəl/ *adj* expressing or suggesting physical, especially sexual, pleasure or satisfaction: *sensual pleasure* ○ *a sensual mouth/voice* ○ *He is elegant, sensual, conscious of his body.* **sensuality** /ˌsent.sjuˈæl.ɪ.ti/ [US] /-ə.ţi/ *noun* [U] *She found his intense sensuality irresistible.*

sensuous /ˈsent.sjʊəs/ *adj* **1** giving or expressing pleasure through the physical senses, rather than pleasing the mind or the intelligence: *She luxuriated in the sensuous feel of the silk sheets.* **2** **sensual**: *He had a very*

sensuous mouth. **sensuously** /ˈsent.sjuəs.sli/ *adv*
sensuousness /ˈsent.sjuə.snəs/ *noun* [U]

sent /sent/ *past simple and past participle of* **send**

sentence PUNISHMENT /ˈsen.tənts/ *noun* [C] **1** a punishment given by a judge in court to a person or organization after they have been found guilty of doing something wrong: *He got a **heavy/light** sentence* (= He was severely/not severely punished). ○ *The offence **carries a jail/prison/life/5-year** sentence.* ○ *He was given a **non-custodial/suspended** sentence.* **2 pronounce sentence** (of a judge) to say officially what a punishment will be: *The judge will pronounce sentence **on** the defendant this afternoon.* **sentence** /ˈsen.tənts/ *verb* [T] LEGAL *He was sentenced **to** life imprisonment.*

sentence WORD GROUP /ˈsen.tənts/ *noun* [C] a group of words, usually containing a verb, which expresses a thought in the form of a statement, question, instruction or exclamation and starts with a capital letter when written: *He's very impatient and always interrupts me mid-sentence.* ○ *Your conclusion is good, but the final sentence is too long and complicated.*

sententious /senˈten.tʃəs/ *adj* FORMAL DISAPPROVING trying to appear wise, clever and important: *The document was sententious and pompous.* **sententiously** /senˈten.tʃə.sli/ *adv*

sentient /ˈsen.tʃənt/ /-tʃi.ənt/ *adj* FORMAL able to experience physical and possibly emotional feelings: *It is hard for a sentient person to understand how any parents could treat their child so badly.*

sentiment IDEA /ˈsen.tɪ.mənt/ /-t̬ə-/ *noun* [C or U] FORMAL a thought, opinion or idea based on a feeling about a situation, or a way of thinking about something: *Nationalist sentiment has increased in the area since the bombing.* ○ *I don't think she **shares** my sentiments.* ○ *His son was overwhelmed by the sentiments **of** love and support in the cards and letters he received.* ○ FORMAL *"It's a very bad situation." "My sentiments exactly* (= I completely agree)."

COMMON LEARNER ERROR

sentiments or **feelings**?

Feelings is the normal word used for talking about the way someone feels.

She couldn't find the words to express her feelings.
~~She couldn't find the words to express her sentiments.~~

Sentiments is a more formal word used especially for the way a person feels or thinks about a particular subject.

Many other people have expressed similar sentiments about the new plan.

---

sentiment FEELINGS /ˈsen.tɪ.mənt/ /-t̬ə-/ *noun* [U] OFTEN DISAPPROVING gentle feelings such as sympathy, love, etc., especially when considered to be foolish or not suitable: *The film is flawed by slightly treacly sentiment.*
sentimental /ˌsen.tɪˈmen.t̬əl/ /-t̬əˈmen.t̬əl/ *adj* **1** describes someone who is strongly influenced by emotional feelings, especially about happy memories of past events or relationships with other people, rather than by careful thought and judgment based on facts: *Why be sentimental **about** that old coat? There's no point in keeping it just because you were wearing it when you first met me.* ○ *It's a cheap ring but it has great sentimental **value** for me.* **2** DISAPPROVING too strongly influenced by emotional feelings: *silly sentimental songs/stories*
sentimentally /ˌsen.tɪˈmen.t̬əl.i/ /-t̬əˈmen.t̬əl-/ *adv*
sentimentalism /ˌsen.tɪˈmen.t̬əl.ɪ.zəm/ /-t̬əˈmen.t̬əl-/ *noun* [U] (ALSO **sentimentality**) FORMAL DISAPPROVING the tendency to be sentimental: *Caring for animals is not sentimentality – it reinforces our respect for life.*
sentimentalist /ˌsen.tɪˈmen.t̬əl.ɪst/ /-t̬əˈmen.t̬əl-/ *noun* [C] **sentimentalize**, UK USUALLY **-ise** /ˌsen.tɪˈmen.t̬əl.aɪz/ /-t̬əˈmen.t̬ə.laɪz/ *verb* [T] DISAPPROVING *Her book sentimentalizes parenthood and completely ignores the disadvantages of it.*

sentinel /ˈsen.tɪ.nəl/ /-t̬ɪ-/ *noun* [C] **1** OLD USE OR LITERARY a person employed to guard something; a **sentry**: *A policeman **stood** sentinel at the entrance.* **2** MAINLY US Sentinel is also used in the names of some

---

newspapers: *the Fort Lauderdale Sun-Sentinel*

sentry /ˈsen.tri/ *noun* [C] a soldier who guards a place, usually by standing at its entrance: *My squad were on sentry **duty** last night.*

'sentry ˌbox *noun* [C] a small shelter in which a sentry stands while guarding a place

separate /ˈsep.ər.ət/ /-ɚ-/ *adj* existing or happening independently or in a different physical space: *The art department and the main college are in two separate buildings.* ○ *I try to **keep** meat separate **from** other food in the fridge.* ○ *I have my public life and my private life, and as far as possible I try to **keep** them separate.* ○ *Three youths have been shot and killed in separate incidents this month.*
• **go your (own) separate ways** If two or more people go their separate ways, they stop being together: *In 1983 the group disbanded and went their separate ways.*
separate /ˈsep.ər.eɪt/ /-ə.reɪt/ *verb* **1** [I or T] to (cause to) divide into parts: *The north and south of the country are separated **by** a mountain range.* ○ *You can get a special device for separating egg whites **from** yolks.* ○ *The top and bottom sections are quite difficult to separate.* **2** [I or T] to make people move apart or into different places, or to move apart: *At school they always tried to separate Jane and me because we were troublemakers.* ○ *Somehow, in the rush to get out of the building, I got separated **from** my mother.* ○ *Perhaps we should separate now and meet up later.* **3** [T] to consider two people or things as different or not related: *You can't separate morality **from** politics.* **4** [I] If a liquid separates, it becomes two different liquids. **5** [I] to start to live in a different place from your husband or wife because the relationship has ended: *My parents separated when I was six and divorced a couple of years later.*
separable /ˈsep.ər.ə.bl̩/ /-ɚ-/ *adj* SLIGHTLY FORMAL able to be separated from each other ⊃Compare **inseparable**.
separately /ˈsep.ər.ət.li/ /-ɚ-/ *adv* not together: *Detectives interviewed the men separately over several days.* ○ *I tend to wear the jacket and skirt separately rather than as a suit.* ○ *I think we'd better deal with these two points separately.*
separates /ˈsep.ər.əts/ /-ɚ-/ *plural noun* pieces of women's clothing that are bought separately and not as part of a suit: *Ladies' separates are on the next floor, madam.*
separation /ˌsep.ərˈeɪ.ʃən/ /-əˈreɪ-/ *noun* **1** [U] when two or more people or things are separated: *During the war many couples had to endure long periods of separation* (= not being together). ○ *After many years the government finally abandoned its apartheid system of racial separation.* **2** [C or U] an arrangement, often legal, by which two married people stop living together as husband and wife: *Couples may agree to divorce each other after a separation.* ○ *They're considering separation as an option.*
separatism /ˈsep.ər.ə.tɪ.zəm/ /-ɚ.ə.t̬ɪ-/ *noun* [U] the belief held by a racial, religious or other group within a country that they should be independent and have their own government or in some way live apart from other people: *Basque separatism*
separatist /ˈsep.ər.ə.tɪst/ /-ɚ.ə.t̬ɪst/ *noun* [C] someone who is a member of a racial, religious or other group within a country and who believes that this group should be independent and have their own government or in some way live apart from other people

sepia /ˈsiː.pi.ə/ *adj* of the reddish brown colour of photographs in the past

sepsis /ˈsep.sɪs/ *noun* [U] SPECIALIZED a severe medical condition in which bacteria enter the blood after an operation or accident

September /sepˈtem.bər/ /-bɚ/ *noun* [C or U] (WRITTEN ABBREVIATION **Sept**) the ninth month of the year, after August and before October: *23(rd) September/September 23(rd)/23(rd) Sept/Sept 23(rd)* ○ *We're leaving for France **on** September the ninth/the ninth of September/(US) September ninth.* ○ *Claudia started school last September/is starting school **next** September.* ○ *My mother's birthday is **in** September.* ○ *We went to Greece two Septembers ago.*

septet /sep'tet/ *group noun* [C] seven people who play musical instruments or sing as a group, or a piece of music written for seven people

septic /'sep.tɪk/ *adj* infected by bacteria which produce pus: *I had my ears pierced and one of them **went** septic.*

septicaemia UK, US **septicemia** /ˌsep.tɪ'siː.mi.ə/ *noun* [U] SPECIALIZED a serious illness in which an infection spreads through the blood

septic 'tank *noun* [C] a large, especially underground, container in which excrement and urine are dissolved by the action of bacteria

septuagenarian /ˌsep.tjuə.dʒɪ'neə.ri.ən/ US /-tu.ə.dʒə-'ner.i-/ *noun* [C] a person who is between 70 and 79 years old

sepulchre, US ALSO **sepulcher** /'sep.ºl.kəʳ/ US /-kɚ/ *noun* [C] OLD USE a stone structure where someone is buried

sepulchral /sɪ'pʌl.krºl/ *adj* LITERARY suggesting death or places where the dead are buried: *The curtain rose to reveal a gloomy, sepulchral set for the play.*

sequel /'siː.kwºl/ *noun* [C] **1** a book, film or play which continues the story of a previous book etc: *I'm reading the sequel **to** 'Gone with the Wind'.* ⊃Compare **prequel**. **2** an event which happens after and is the result of an earlier event: *There was a dramatic sequel **to** last Thursday's scandalous revelations when the minister for trade suddenly announced his resignation.*

sequence [ORDERED SERIES] /'siː.kwənts/ *noun* [C or U] a series of related things or events, or the order in which they follow each other: *The first chapter describes the strange sequence **of events** that lead to his death.* ○ *Is there a particular sequence in which you have to perform these tasks?* ○ *For the sake of convenience the photographs are shown **in** chronological sequence (= in the order in which they were taken).*

sequencing /'siː.kwənt.sɪŋ/ *noun* [U] SPECIALIZED the process of deciding the correct order of things: *A common sign of dyslexia is that the sequencing of letters when spelling words may be incorrect.*

sequential /sɪ'kwen.ʃºl/ *adj* FORMAL following a particular order: *The publishers claim that the book constitutes 'the first sequential exposition of events and thus of the history of the revolution'.* **sequentially** /sɪ'kwen.ʃºl.i/ *adv*

sequence [FILM PART] /'siː.kwənts/ *noun* [C] a part of a film that shows a particular event or a related series of events: *The film's **opening** sequence is of a very unpleasant murder.*

sequester [TAKE] /sɪ'kwes.təʳ/ US /-tɚ/ *verb* [T] (ALSO **sequestrate**) LEGAL to take temporary possession of someone's property until they have paid back the money that they owe or until they have obeyed a court order **sequestration** /ˌsiː.kwes'treɪ.ʃºn/ *noun* [U]

sequester [KEEP SEPARATE] /sɪ'kwes.təʳ/ US /-tɚ/ *verb* [T] LEGAL to keep a jury together in a place so that they cannot discuss the case with other people or read or hear news reports about it **sequestration** /ˌsiː.kwes'treɪ.ʃºn/ *noun* [U]

sequestered /sɪ'kwes.təd/ US /-tɚd/ *adj* LITERARY describes a place that is peaceful because it is situated away from people: *I found a sequestered spot at the bottom of the garden and lay down with my book.*

sequin /'siː.kwɪn/ *noun* [C] a small shiny metal or plastic disc sewn onto clothes for decoration **sequined** /'siː.-kwɪnd/ *adj*: *a shimmering blue sequined dress*

sequoia /sɪ'kwɔɪə/ *noun* [C] a large Californian evergreen tree that can reach a height of more than 90 metres

sera /'sɪə.rə/ US /'sɪr.ə/ *plural of* **serum**

seraph /'ser.əf/ *noun* [C] *plural* **seraphim** or **seraphs** an ANGEL of the highest rank

seraphic /sə'ræf.ɪk/ *adj* LITERARY APPROVING beautiful in a way that suggests goodness and purity: *a seraphic smile* **seraphically** /sə'ræf.ɪ.kli/ *adv*

serenade /ˌser.ə'neɪd/ *verb* [T] to play a piece of music or sing for someone, especially for a woman while standing outside her house at night: *Romeo serenades Juliet in the moonlight.* ○ *Shoppers are serenaded with live piano music.*

serenade /ˌser.ə'neɪd/ *noun* [C] **1** a song or piece of music sung or played for someone **2** a piece of gentle classical music in several parts: *'Moonlight Serenade'*

serendipity /ˌser.ºn'dɪp.ɪ.ti/ US /-ə.t̬i/ *noun* [U] FORMAL the lucky tendency to find interesting or valuable things by chance **serendipitous** /ˌser.ºn'dɪp.ɪ.təs/ US /-t̬əs/ *adj*: *Reading should be an adventure, a personal experience full of serendipitous surprises.*

serene /sə'riːn/ *adj* peaceful and calm; troubled by nothing: *She has a lovely serene face.* **serenely** /sə'riːn.li/ *adv*: *She smiled serenely and said nothing.* **serenity** /sə-'ren.ɪ.ti/ US /-ə.t̬i/ *noun* [U] *I admired her serenity in the midst of so much chaos.*

serf /sɜːf/ US /sɜːf/ *noun* [C] a member of a low social class in medieval times who worked on the land and was the property of the person who owned that land **serfdom** /'sɜːf.dəm/ US /'sɜːf-/ *noun* [U] the state of being a serf or the system by which the land was farmed by serfs

serge /sɜːdʒ/ US /sɜːdʒ/ *noun* [U] a strong woollen cloth which is used especially to make jackets and coats

sergeant [SOLDIER] /'sɑː.dʒºnt/ US /'sɑːr-/ *noun* [C] (WRITTEN ABBREVIATION **Sgt**, INFORMAL **sarge**) a soldier of middle rank: *Sergeant Lewis* ○ [as form of address] *Dismiss the men, Sergeant.*

sergeant [POLICE OFFICER] /'sɑː.dʒºnt/ US /'sɑːr-/ *noun* [C] (WRITTEN ABBREVIATION **Sgt**, INFORMAL **sarge**) in Britain, a police officer whose rank is above CONSTABLE and below INSPECTOR, or in the US a police officer whose rank is below a CAPTAIN

sergeant 'major *noun* [C] a soldier of middle rank

serial [STORY] /'sɪə.ri.əl/ US /'sɪr.i-/ *noun* [C] a story on television or radio or in a newspaper, etc. which is broadcast or printed in separate parts: *Most of her novels have been made into **television** serials at some time.*

serialize, UK USUALLY **-ise** /'sɪə.ri.ə.laɪz/ US /'sɪr.i.ə.laɪz/ *verb* [T] If a book is serialized, it is made into a number of television or radio programmes or published in a newspaper or a magazine in parts: *The novel was serialized **for** TV back in the 1990s.* **serialization**, UK USUALLY **-isation** /ˌsɪə.ri.ºl.aɪ'zeɪ.ʃºn/ US /ˌsɪr.i.əl-/ *noun* [C or U]

serial [REPEATED] /'sɪə.ri.əl/ US /'sɪr.i-/ *adj* [before n] describes a person who repeatedly commits the same serious crime, often using the same method, or a serious crime that is committed repeatedly by one person: *She wrote a thriller about a brutal serial **killer**.* ○ *a serial rapist* ○ *serial murders/killings*

serial mo'nogamy *noun* [U] HUMOROUS the tendency to have a series of sexual relationships one after another, but never more than one at a time

serial ,number *noun* [C] one of a set of numbers that is put on items produced in large quantities, such as computers, televisions, paper money, etc. so that each has a different number and can be recognized

series [SET OF EVENTS] /'sɪə.riːz/ US /'sɪr.iːz/ *noun* [C] *plural* **series 1** a number of similar or related events or things, one following another: *There has been a series **of** sexual attacks on women in the area.* ○ *She gave a series **of** lectures at Warwick University last year on contemporary British writers.* **2** a number of games played by two teams: *The Yankees have a four-game series against the Orioles at home, after which they start a two-week road trip.*

• **in series** Parts of an electrical system that are in series are arranged in a single line so that the current flows through each part, one after another.

series [SET OF BROADCASTS] /'sɪə.riːz/ US /'sɪr.iːz/ *noun* [C] *plural* **series** a set of television or radio broadcasts on the same subject or using the same characters but in different situations: *The footballer Paul Gascoigne is to host a Channel 4 **television** series on soccer skills* ○ *a comedy series* ○ *I missed the second episode of the series so I don't know what's going on now.*

series [SET OF BOOKS] /'sɪə.riːz/ US /'sɪr.iːz/ *noun* [C] *plural* **series** a set of books published by the same company which deal with the same subject: *They do a series **on** architecture throughout the ages.*

serious BAD /ˈsɪə.ri.əs/ US /ˈsɪr.i-/ *adj* severe in effect; bad: *a serious illness* ○ *There were no reports of serious injuries.* ○ *The new tax regulations have landed some of the smaller companies in serious trouble.* ○ *Drugs have become a serious problem in a lot of schools.* ○ *This is a very serious offence.* ○ *He's been taken to hospital where his condition is described as serious but stable.* **seriously** /ˈsɪə.ri.ə.sli/ US /ˈsɪr.i-/ *adv: Badly cooked shellfish can make you seriously ill.* ○ *He wasn't seriously injured – he just got a few cuts and bruises.* **seriousness** /ˈsɪə.ri.ə.snəs/ US /ˈsɪr.i-/ *noun* [U] *I don't think he has any notion of the seriousness of the situation.*

serious NOT JOKING /ˈsɪə.ri.əs/ US /ˈsɪr.i-/ *adj* **1** not joking or intended to amuse: *Please don't laugh – I'm being serious.* ○ *He was wearing a very serious expression and I knew something was wrong.* ○ *On the surface it's a very funny novel but it does have a more serious underlying theme.* **2** A serious person is quiet, thinks carefully about things and does not laugh a lot: *I remember her as a very serious child.* **seriously** /ˈsɪə.ri.ə.sli/ US /ˈsɪr.i-/ *adv: Seriously now, did he really say that or are you just being silly?* ○ *You're not seriously thinking of leaving, are you?* **seriousness** /ˈsɪə.ri.ə.snəs/ US /ˈsɪr.i-/ *noun* [U] *In all seriousness now – joking aside – I do think there's a problem here that we've got to get sorted.*

serious NEEDING ATTENTION /ˈsɪə.ri.əs/ US /ˈsɪr.i-/ *adj* [before n] needing or deserving your complete attention: *That's an interesting job offer – I'd give it some serious consideration if I were you.* ○ *We've got some serious talking to do, you and me.* **seriously** /ˈsɪə.ri.ə.sli/ US /ˈsɪr.i-/ *adv* **take** *sb/sth* **seriously** to consider a person, subject or situation to be important or dangerous and worth your attention or respect: *The police have to take any terrorist threat seriously.* ○ *You don't take anything seriously, do you? It's all one big joke to you.* ○ *She's sick of being seen as a sex symbol and wants to be taken seriously as an actress.* ○ *These young actors take themselves so seriously!*

serious DETERMINED /ˈsɪə.ri.əs/ US /ˈsɪr.i-/ *adj* [after v] **1** determined to follow a particular plan of action: *Is she serious about going to live abroad?* **2** If two people who have a loving relationship are serious about each other they intend to stay with each other for a long time and possibly marry: *She's had a lot of boyfriends but Simon's the only one she's been serious about.*

serious EXTREME /ˈsɪə.ri.əs/ US /ˈsɪr.i-/ *adj* INFORMAL **1** extreme in degree or amount: *We did some fairly serious walking over the weekend.* ○ *I mean we're talking serious* (= a large amount of) *money, right?* **2** Serious can mean very good of its type: *This is a serious wine, Annabelle, you've just got to try some.* **seriously** /ˈsɪə.ri.ə.sli/ US /ˈsɪr.i-/ *adv* INFORMAL very: *They do some seriously good desserts there.* ○ *That boy is seriously stupid.*

sermon /ˈsɜː.mən/ US /ˈsɜː-/ *noun* [C] **1** a part of a Christian church ceremony in which a priest gives a talk on a religious or moral subject, often based on something written in the Bible: *The Reverend William Cronshaw delivered/preached the sermon.* ○ *Today's sermon was on the importance of compassion.* **2** DISAPPROVING a long talk in which someone advises other people how they should behave in order to be better people: *I really don't think it's a politician's job to go delivering sermons on public morality.*

sermonize, UK USUALLY **-ise** /ˈsɜː.mə.naɪz/ US /ˈsɜː-/ *verb* [I] DISAPPROVING to give a long talk to people, telling them how they should behave in order to be better people: *My grandmother's all right until she starts sermonizing and then she's unbearable.*

serotonin /ˌse.rəˈtəʊ.nɪn/ US /-ˈtoʊ-/ *noun* [U] a NEUROTRANSMITTER (= a chemical in the body which carries messages from the brain) which helps you feel relaxed and happy

serpent /ˈsɜː.pᵊnt/ US /ˈsɜː-/ *noun* [C] OLD USE a snake **serpentine** /ˈsɜː.pᵊn.taɪn/ US /ˈsɜː-/ *adj* LITERARY **1** curving and twisting like a snake: *We followed the serpentine course of the river.* **2** complicated and difficult to understand: *The film's serpentine plot was difficult to follow.*

serrated /səˈreɪ.tɪd/ US /-t̬ɪd/ *adj* having a row of sharp points along the edge: *You really need a knife with a*

serrated edge for cutting bread.

serried /ˈser.id/ *adj* LITERARY pressed closely together, usually in lines: *We flew over the city with its serried ranks of identical grey houses.*

serum /ˈsɪə.rəm/ US /ˈsɪr.əm/ *noun* [C or U] plural **serums** or **sera** the watery, colourless part of the blood, or this liquid taken from an animal and put into a human in order to fight an infection: *cholesterol levels in blood serum* ○ *an anti-venom serum*

servant /ˈsɜː.vᵊnt/ US /ˈsɜː-/ *noun* [C] a person who is employed in another person's house, doing jobs such as cooking and cleaning, especially in the past

service /ˈsɜː.vɪs/ US /ˈsɜː-/ *noun* OLD-FASHIONED **be in service** to be employed as a servant

serve DEAL WITH CUSTOMER /sɜːv/ US /sɜːv/ *verb* [T] in a shop, restaurant or hotel, to deal with a customer by taking their order, showing or selling them goods, etc: *Are you being served, madam?* ○ *That's the restaurant where they refused to serve Giles because he was so rude.*

service /ˈsɜː.vɪs/ US /ˈsɜː-/ *noun* [U] **1** the act of dealing with a customer in a shop, restaurant or hotel by taking their order, showing or selling them goods, etc.: *The only trouble with this café is that the service is so slow.* **2** an amount of money charged for serving a customer in a restaurant, which is often paid directly to the waiter: *There is a 10% service charge included in the bill.*

serve PROVIDE FOOD/DRINK /sɜːv/ US /sɜːv/ *verb* [I or T] to provide food or drinks: *Do they serve meals in the bar?* ○ *Breakfast is served in the restaurant between 7 and 9* ○ *We arrived at the hotel and were served with champagne and canapés.* ○ *All recipes in this book, unless otherwise stated, will serve* (= be enough for) *4 to 5 people.* ○ [+ obj + adj] *Serve the tarts hot with custard or whipped cream.*

server /ˈsɜː.vəʳ/ US /ˈsɜː.vɚ/ *noun* [C] a utensil that is used for serving food: *salad servers*

serving /ˈsɜː.vɪŋ/ US /ˈsɜː-/ *noun* [C] an amount of one type of food which is given to one person: *The quantities given in the recipe should be enough for four servings.*

serving /ˈsɜː.vɪŋ/ US /ˈsɜː-/ *adj* **serving dish/spoon, etc.** a utensil used for holding food before it is put onto plates, or for putting food onto plates

serve WORK /sɜːv/ US /sɜːv/ *verb* [I or T] to work for; to do your duty to: *He served in the army in India for twenty years.* ○ *She has served on the committee for the last fifteen years.* ○ *He served under Harold Wilson as Transport Minister.*

• **if my memory serves me right** if I remember correctly: *I think he was called Brian, if my memory serves me right.*

• **serve** *sb* **right** INFORMAL If you say that something bad serves someone right, you mean that they deserve it: *"He hit me!" "It serves you right. You shouldn't have been rude to him."*

servant /ˈsɜː.vᵊnt/ US /ˈsɜː-/ *noun* **public servant/servant of the state** a person who works for the government: *Public servants should be incorruptible.*

service /ˈsɜː.vɪs/ US /ˈsɜː-/ *noun* **1** [C] a government department that is responsible for a particular area of activity: *the diplomatic service* ○ *the security services* **2** [C or U] the time you spend working for an organization: *She was given the award for a lifetime of public service.* **3 in service** in use: *The battleship has been in service since 1965.*

• **be of service (to** *sb***)** to help someone: *"Thank you so much for that." "I'm glad to have been of service."*

• **do** *sb* **a service** FORMAL to do something to help someone: *You've done me a great service – thank you.*

services /ˈsɜː.vɪs.ɪz/ US /ˈsɜː-/ *plural noun* FORMAL the particular skills that someone has and can offer to others: *I may be needing the services of a surveyor soon, as I'm buying a house.*

serving /ˈsɜː.vɪŋ/ US /ˈsɜː-/ *adj* [before n] employed at the present time in a particular organization, especially the armed forces: *serving and retired military officers*

serve SPEND TIME /sɜːv/ US /sɜːv/ *verb* [T] to spend a period of time doing something: *He served four years in prison for robbery.* ○ *After he'd served his apprenticeship he found work overseas.*

S

• **serve time** to spend time in prison: *He's serving time for drugs offences.*

serve [HELP ACHIEVE] /sɜːv/ [US] /sɝːv/ *verb* [I or T] to help achieve something or to be useful as something: *The minister said she did not consider that a public enquiry would serve any useful* ***purpose***. ○ *The judge said that the fine would serve* ***as*** *a warning to other motorists who drove without due care.* ○ *In the absence of anything better the settee would serve* (= could be used) ***as*** *a bed for a couple of nights.* ○ [+ to infinitive] *Nothing serves* ***to*** *explain the violent fighting we have seen recently.* ○ *OLD-FASHIONED My umbrella will serve* ***for*** *a weapon.*

serve [PROVIDE SOMETHING NECESSARY] /sɜːv/ [US] /sɝːv/ *verb* [T] to provide with something that is needed: *London's hospitals, so says the report, are out of touch with the communities that they serve.*

service /ˈsɜː.vɪs/ [US] /ˈsɝː-/ *noun* **1** [C] a system or organization that provides for a basic public need: *the ambulance/health/postal/prison service* **2** [C or U] the operation of a system: *There isn't any railway service on Sundays.* ○ *We hope to be* ***operating*** *a normal service as soon as possible.*

services /ˈsɜː.vɪs.ɪz/ [US] /ˈsɝː-/ *plural noun UK* a place beside a large road at which fuel, food, drink and other items that people want on their journey are sold: *We stopped at the services to get petrol.*

serve [HIT BALL] /sɜːv/ [US] /sɝːv/ *verb* [I or T] in sports such as tennis, to hit the ball to the other player as a way of starting the game: *Whose turn is it to serve?* ○ *That's the third ace you've served this game.* **serve** /sɜːv/ [US] /sɝːv/ *noun* [C] (*ALSO* **service**) *It's your serve.* ○ *She's got a very fast service.*

serve [DELIVER DOCUMENT] /sɜːv/ [US] /sɝːv/ *verb* [T] *LEGAL* to deliver a legal document to someone, demanding that they go to a court of law or that they obey an order: *Less than two weeks ago Gough finally served* ***a writ on*** *Slater, claiming damages for alleged loss of royalties.* ○ *Each person served* ***with*** *a summons will be given six weeks before they have to appear in the Magistrates' Court.*

▲ **serve** ***(sth)*** **up/out** *phrasal verb* [M] to put food on plates for people to eat: *Come on everyone, I'm ready to serve up.* ○ *Jack, could you serve out the trifle?*

server /ˈsɜː.vəʳ/ [US] /ˈsɝː.vɚ/ *noun* [C] *SPECIALIZED* a central computer from which other computers obtain information: *a client/network/file server*

service [ARMED FORCES] /ˈsɜː.vɪs/ [US] /ˈsɝː-/ *noun* [C or U] (work in) the armed forces: *He joined the air force in 1964 and spent ten years* ***in*** *the service.* ○ *All men under thirty-five were told to report for* ***military*** *service within three days.* ○ *Service personnel are subject to the Official Secrets Act.*

• **on active service** fighting in a war: *He was the first member of his regiment to die while on active service.*

the services *plural noun* the army, navy and/or air force: *a career in the services*

serviceman /ˈsɜː.vɪs.mən/ [US] /ˈsɝː-/ *noun* [C] a man who belongs to the armed forces

servicewoman /ˈsɜː.vɪsˌwʊm.ən/ [US] /ˈsɜːr-/ *noun* [C] a woman who belongs to the armed forces

service [RELIGIOUS CEREMONY] /ˈsɜː.vɪs/ [US] /ˈsɝː-/ *noun* [C] a formal religious ceremony: *A* ***memorial*** *service is being* ***held*** *on Sunday for victims of the bomb explosion.*

service [REPAIR] /ˈsɜː.vɪs/ [US] /ˈsɝː-/ *verb* [T] to examine a machine and repair any faulty parts: *I'm taking the car in to have it serviced this afternoon.* **service** /ˈsɜː.vɪs/ [US] /ˈsɝː-/ *noun* [C] *MAINLY UK She took the car in for a service yesterday.* **servicing** /ˈsɜː.vɪs.ɪŋ/ [US] /ˈsɝː-/ *noun* [U] *MAINLY US Bryce has taken the car in for servicing.*

service [FOOD UTENSILS] /ˈsɜː.vɪs/ [US] /ˈsɝː-/ *noun* [C] a set of items such as plates, cups or other utensils that are used in providing and eating food: *a 24-piece dinner service* ○ *a tea service*

serviceable /ˈsɜː.vɪ.sə.bl̩/ [US] /ˈsɝː-/ *adj* suitable for the situation in which something is used; effective: *You're wearing some serviceable-looking footwear, Johnny.*

ˈservice ˌcharge *noun* [C] an amount of money added to the basic price of something to pay for the cost of dealing with the customer: *If you order the tickets by phone you have to pay a $2 service charge as well as $13.50 for each ticket.*

ˈservice ˌindustry *noun* [C] an industry that provides a service for people but does not result in the production of goods: *More than 70% of jobs in the borough are in service industries, ranging from hotels to banking.*

ˈservice ˌroad *noun* [C] a small road which is parallel to a bigger road and is used mainly by people travelling in the local area

ˈservice ˌstation *noun* [C] **1** **petrol station** **2** *UK* a place next to a motorway where you can buy petrol and food, and go to the toilet

serviette /ˌsɜː.viˈet/ [US] /ˌsɝː-/ *noun* [C] *UK OLD-FASHIONED OR CANADIAN ENGLISH* a square piece of cloth or paper used while you are eating for protecting your clothes or cleaning your mouth and fingers; a **napkin**

servile /ˈsɜː.vaɪl/ [US] /ˈsɝː.vəl/ *adj DISAPPROVING* too eager to serve and please someone else in a way that shows a lack of respect for yourself: *As a waiter you want to be pleasant to people without appearing totally servile.* **servility** /sɜːˈvɪl.ɪ.ti/ [US] /sɝːˈvɪl.ə.t̬i/ *noun* [U] *FORMAL DISAPPROVING She found the servility of the hotel staff embarrassing.*

servitude /ˈsɜː.vɪ.tjuːd/ [US] /ˈsɝː.vɪ.tuːd/ *noun* [U] *FORMAL* the state of being under the control of someone else and of having no freedom: *In the past, the majority of women were consigned to a lifetime of servitude and poverty.*

servomechanism /ˈsɜː.vəʊˌmek.ə.nɪ.zəm/ [US] /ˌsɝː.voʊˈmek-/ *noun* [C] (*ALSO* **servo**) *SPECIALIZED* a system that uses a small amount of power to control the power of a larger machine

servomotor /ˈsɜː.vəʊˌməʊ.təʳ/ [US] /ˈsɝː.voʊˌmoʊ.t̬ɚ/ *noun* [C] (*ALSO* **servo**) *SPECIALIZED* a motor which provides the power for a SERVOMECHANISM

sesame /ˈses.ə.mi/ *noun* [U] a herb grown for its small oval seeds and its oil: *sesame oil/seeds*

session [FORMAL MEETING] /ˈseʃ.ən/ *noun* [C or U] a formal meeting or series of meetings of an organization such as a parliament or a law court: *The* ***parliamentary*** *session is due to end on May 27th.* ○ *The UN Security Council met* ***in*** *emergency session to discuss the crisis.*

session [ACTIVITY] /ˈseʃ.ən/ *noun* [C] a period of time or meeting arranged for a particular activity: *The 21-year-old runner twisted his ankle in a* ***training*** *session last Friday.* ○ *As the European heads of state gathered, the press were allowed in for a* ***photo*** *session.* ○ *INFORMAL Rob and I had a* ***heavy*** *session last night* (= we drank a lot of alcohol).

session [COLLEGE PERIOD] /ˈseʃ.ən/ *noun* [C or U] *US AND SCOTTISH ENGLISH* at a college, any of the periods of time that a teaching year or day is divided into, or the teaching year itself: *The session begins on 1 October.* ○ *Access to these buildings is restricted when school is* ***in*** *session.*

set [POSITION] /set/ *verb* [T usually + adv or prep] **setting, set, set** **1** to put something in the stated place or position: *He set a vase of flowers on the table.* ○ *The campsite is set in the middle of a pine forest.* ○ *Our house is set back from the road.* **2** If a story, film, etc. is set in a particular time or place, the action in it happens in that time or place: *'West Side Story' is set* ***in*** *New York* ***in*** *the late 1950s.*

• **set** ***sb*** **to work** to give someone work to do: *I was set to work tidying the bookshelves.*

setting /ˈset.ɪŋ/ [US] /ˈset̬-/ *noun* [C usually sing] **1** the position of a house or other building: *Their cottage is in an idyllic rural setting.* **2** the time and the place in which the action of a book, film, play, etc. happens: *The play has its setting in a wartime prison camp.*

set [CONDITION] /set/ *verb* [T] **setting, set, set** **1** to cause something or someone to be in the stated condition or situation: *It is believed that the building was set* ***alight/ablaze/on fire*** *deliberately.* ○ *The new director has set a lot of changes* ***in motion*** *in our department.* ○ [+ adj] *After years in prison, the men who had wrongfully been found guilty of the bombing were finally set* ***free***. ○ *If I've made a mistake, then it's up to me to set it* ***right*** (= correct it). **2** **set** ***sb/sth*** **doing** ***sth*** to cause someone or something to start doing something: *His remarks set me thinking.* ○ *The thunderstorm set the radio crackling.*

S

• **not set the world on fire** to not be very exciting or successful: *He has a nice enough voice but he's not going to set the world on fire.*

set [GET READY] /set/ *verb* [T] **setting, set, set 1** to get something ready so that it comes into operation or can be used: [+ *to* infinitive] *The heating is set **to** come on at 5.00 p.m.* ○ *Have you set **up** the video recorder?* ○ *I usually set my watch **by** the time signal on the radio.* ○ *He set the alarm **for** 7.00 a.m.* ○ *Will you set the table* (= put plates and utensils on it ready for use), *please?* **2** to put furniture and other items on a stage so that it represents the time and the place in which the action of a play, film or television programme is going to happen: *During the interval the stage was set **for** the second act.*

• **set the scene/stage** (*ALSO* **the scene/stage *is* set**) used to mean that conditions have been made advantageous for something to happen, or that something is likely to happen: *This weekend's talks between the two leaders have set the scene **for** a peace agreement to be reached.* ○ *The stage looks set **for** a repeat of last year's final.*

set /set/ *adj* [after v] **1** ready and prepared: *Shall we go now – is everyone set?* ○ *Is everything **all** set for the party?* ○ *At the beginning of a race, the starter often says "On your marks, **get** set, go" or "Ready, **get** set, go".* ○ *We were just **getting** set **to** leave when Ben said he had something important to tell us.* **2** likely or in a suitable condition: *He looks set **to** become world champion again this year.*

set /set/ *noun* [C] the place where a film or play is performed or recorded, and the pictures, furniture etc. that are used: *a film set* ○ *a stage set* ○ *a set designer* ○ *They first met **on** the set of 'Star Wars'.*

setting /ˈset.ɪŋ/ [US] /ˈset̬-/ *noun* [C] **1** a position on the controls of a piece of equipment: *My hairdryer has three settings – high, medium and low.* ○ *You don't need to **adjust** the setting every time you take a photo.* **2** a **place setting**

set [ESTABLISH] /set/ *verb* [T] **setting, set, set** to establish or cause to exist: *The school has been criticized for failing to set high enough **standards** for its students.* ○ *The government has set new **limits** on public spending.* ○ *Lewis has set a new world **record**.* ○ *The court's decision has set a legal **precedent**.* ○ *Parents should set a good **example** to their children.* ○ *He's set himself the **goal/target** of making his first million by the time he's 30.*

set [FIX] /set/ *verb* **setting, set, set 1** [T] to fix or make certain: *Has a **date/time** been set for the meeting yet?* ○ *The **price** of the house has been set **at** £125,000.* **2 set into *sth*/be set with *sth*** If a precious stone is set in/into a piece of jewellery, or a piece of jewellery is set with a precious stone, the stone is fixed firmly to the piece of jewellery: *a gold tiepin with a diamond set into it* ○ *a brooch set with rubies and pearls* **3** [T] When a doctor sets a broken bone, he or she puts it into a fixed position so that it will heal. **4** [I] When a broken bone sets, it heals in a fixed position. **5** [T] If you have your hair set, you have it arranged while it is wet so that it will be fixed in a particular style when it is dry. **6** [T] If you set a part of your body, you tighten the muscles around it in order to show that you are determined about something: *"I'm never going back to him," she said, setting her **jaw** firmly.* ○ *His face was set in determination.* **7** [I] If a liquid or soft material sets, it becomes firm or hard: *Leave the jelly in the fridge to set.* ○ *Don't walk on the concrete until it has set.*

set /set/ *adj* **1** fixed or never changing: *My parents say I have to be home by a set time.* ○ *The restaurant does a set lunch* (= a meal which is offered at a fixed price, but with little or no choice about what you have to eat) *on Sundays.* ○ *The receptionist had a bright set smile on his face, but I could tell that he was bored.* ○ *My father has very set opinions/views on the matter.* **2 set expression/phrase** a phrase in which the words are always used in the same order

• **be (dead) set against *sth*** to be determined not to do something: *Why are you so set against going to college?* ○ *They are **dead** set against* (= strongly opposed to) *the plans to close the local hospital.*

• **be set on/upon *sth*** to be determined to do something: *She seems set on marrying him.*

• **be set fair** *UK OLD-FASHIONED* to be sunny and dry and not changing or expected to change

• **be set in *your* ways** to do the same things every day and to not want to change those habits: *As people get older, they often become set in their ways.*

set /set/ *noun* **1 the set of *sth*** the position in which you hold a part of your body: *I could tell from the set of his jaw that he was angry.* **2** [C] the act of having your hair set: *a **shampoo and** set*

setting /ˈset.ɪŋ/ [US] /ˈset̬-/ *noun* [C] the piece of metal in a ring, or other item of jewellery, into which a precious stone is fixed: *a single diamond in a plain gold setting*

set [GIVE WORK] *MAINLY UK* (**setting, set, set**) /set/ *verb* [T] (*US USUALLY* **assign**) to give or provide a piece of work or task for someone to do: *My science teacher always sets a lot of homework.* ○ *What books have been set for this term?* ○ [+ two objects] *We set the kids the task of clearing the snow from the front path.*

set /set/ *adj* [before n] *The students are reading 'Lord of the Flies' as one of their set **books/texts*** (= books that they have to study) *this year.*

set [MUSIC] /set/ *verb* [T] **setting, set, set** to write or provide music for a poem or other words so that they can be sung: *poems set **to music***

set [SUN] /set/ *verb* [I] **setting, set, set** (of the Sun, Moon or planets) to go down below the HORIZON (= the line at which the Earth seems to join the sky): *We sat on the beach and watched the sun set.* ○ *The setting sun cast long shadows across the lawn.* ➲See also **sunset** TIME; **sunset** SKY.

set [GROUP] /set/ *noun* [C] **1** a group of similar things that belong together in some way: *We bought Charles and Mandy a set **of** cutlery as a wedding present.* ○ *I always keep a tool set in the back of my car.* ○ *The doctor said that he hadn't seen this particular set **of** symptoms before.* ○ *We need to establish a new set **of** priorities.* **2** a number of items or pieces of equipment needed for a particular activity, especially playing a game: *a chess/train/chemistry set* **3** *SPECIALIZED* In mathematics, a set is a group of objects with stated characteristics.

set /set/ *group noun* [C] a group of people who have similar interests and ways of living: *the London set* ○ *She's got in with a very arty set.* ○ *The **smart** set is/are going to the Caprice restaurant this season.*

set [TELEVISION] /set/ *noun* [C] a television: *We need a new **television** set.* ○ *There is some interference on the signal – do not adjust your set.*

set [PART] /set/ *noun* [C] **1** a part of a game of tennis: *They won in **straight** sets* (= They won every set). **2** a musical performance which forms part of a concert, especially one of pop music or jazz: *The band's opening set lasted 45 minutes.*

PHRASAL VERBS WITH **set** ▼

▲ **set about *sth*** [START TO DO] *phrasal verb* to start to do or deal with something: [+ *v-ing*] *I've no idea how to set about chang**ing** a tyre on a car.* ○ *I tried to apologize, but I think I set about **it** the wrong way.*

▲ **set about *sb*** [ATTACK] *phrasal verb LITERARY* to attack someone: *Her attacker set about her **with** a knife.*

▲ **set *sb* against *sb*** [OPPOSITION] *phrasal verb* to cause one person to argue or fight with another person: *This war has set neighbour against neighbour.*

▲ **set *sth* against *sth*** [COMPARISON] *phrasal verb* to consider something in relation to another thing and compare their different qualities or effects: *You have to set the advantages of the scheme against the disadvantages.*

▲ **set *sth* against *sth*** [FINANCE] *phrasal verb* to use or record one item, especially the cost of something, in order to reduce or remove the effect of another: *The cost of business travel and entertainment can be set against **tax**.*

▲ **set *sth/sb* apart** *phrasal verb* If a quality or characteristic sets someone/something apart, it shows them to be different from, and usually better than, others of the same type: *What set her apart **from** the other candidates for the job was that she had a lot of original ideas.*

▲ **set** *sth* **aside** PURPOSE *phrasal verb* [M] to save something, usually money or time, for a special purpose: *He had some money in an account that he'd set aside for his kids.* ○ [+ *to* infinitive] *I set aside half an hour every evening to hear Erik read.*

▲ **set** *sth* **aside** LEGAL DECISION *phrasal verb* [M] If a judge or court sets aside a previous decision or judgment, they state that it does not now have any legal effect, usually because they consider it to have been wrong: *The Court of Appeal set aside his conviction.*

▲ **set** *sth* **aside** IGNORE *phrasal verb* **1** to decide that you will not be influenced by your own feelings or opinions because they are not important at a particular time: *In times of war people tend to set aside political differences.* **2** to ignore or not think about a particular fact or situation while considering a matter: *Setting aside the question of cost, what do you think of the idea in principle?*

▲ **set** *sb* **back (sth)** COST *phrasal verb* INFORMAL to cost someone a large amount of money: *Buying that suit must have set you back.* ○ *That new car looks as if it set you back a bit, Geoff.*

▲ **set** *sth/sb* **back** DELAY *phrasal verb* [M] to delay an event, process or person: *The opening of the new swimming pool has been set back by a few weeks.* ○ *A war would inevitably set back the process of reform.*

▲ **set** *sth* **back** REDUCE *phrasal verb* [M] to reduce something to a weaker or less advanced state: *This result has set back their chances of winning the competition.*

▲ **set** *sth* **down** WRITING *phrasal verb* [M often passive] to write or print something, especially to record it in a formal document: *The rules of the club are set down in the members' handbook.*

▲ **set** *sb* **down** PASSENGER *phrasal verb* [M] If a vehicle sets down a passenger, it stops so that the passenger can get out: *The taxi set us down a long way from our hotel, and we had to walk.*

▲ **set** *sth* **down** AIRCRAFT *phrasal verb* [M] to land an aircraft

▲ **set** *sth* **forth** *phrasal verb* [M] FORMAL FOR **set out** DETAILS

▲ **set in** *phrasal verb* When something unpleasant sets in, it begins and seems likely to continue in a serious way: *This rain looks as if it has set in for the rest of the day.* ○ *If you get bitten by a dog, you have to make sure the wound is properly cleaned, or an infection could set in.* ○ *Despair seems to have set in among the England team.*

▲ **set** *sth* **off** CAUSE *phrasal verb* [M] **1** to cause an activity or event, often a series of events, to begin or happen: *The court's initial verdict in the police officers' trial set off serious riots.* **2** to cause a loud noise or explosion, such as that made by a bomb or an ALARM (= a warning sound), to begin or happen: *Terrorists set off a bomb in the city centre.* ○ *Somebody set the alarm off on my car.*

▲ **set** *sb* **off** *phrasal verb* INFORMAL to cause someone to start doing something: [+ v-ing] *Every time I think about it, it sets me off laughing.* ○ *She's finally stopped crying – now don't set her off again.*

▲ **set** *sth* **off** MAKE NOTICEABLE *phrasal verb* [M] to make something look attractive by providing a CONTRAST (= attractive difference) to it: *The new yellow cushions nicely set off the pale green of the chair covers.*

▲ **set off/out** JOURNEY *phrasal verb* to start a journey: *What time will we have to set off for the station tomorrow?* ○ *Jenny set off down the road on her new bike.* ○ *They've just set off on a round-the-world cruise.* ➌See picture **Phrasal Verbs** on page Centre 9

▲ **set** *sb/sth* **on** *sb phrasal verb* [M] to make an animal or person attack someone: *The security guards set their dogs on the intruders.* ○ *If you do that again, I'll set my big brother on you!*

▲ **set on/upon** *sb phrasal verb* **1** [often passive] to attack someone: *He was set upon by a vicious dog.* **2** to surround or catch someone and prevent them from escaping: *As he left the theatre, the singer was set upon by fans desperate for autographs.*

▲ **set out** ACTIVITY *phrasal verb* to start an activity with a particular aim: *She set out with the aim of becoming the youngest ever winner of the championship.* ○ [+ *to* infinitive] *They set out to discover a cure for cancer.*

▲ **set out** JOURNEY *phrasal verb* to start a journey

▲ **set** *sth* **out** DETAILS *phrasal verb* [M] (FORMAL **set** *sth* **forth**) to give the details of something or to explain it, especially in writing, in a clear, organized way: *The management board has set out its goals/plans/proposals for the coming year.* ○ *Your contract will set out the terms and conditions of your employment.*

▲ **set** *sth* **out** ARRANGEMENT *phrasal verb* [M] to arrange something, usually a number of things, in an attractive or organized way: *The market was full of brightly coloured vegetables set out on stalls.* ○ *Every evening Michael sets out the breakfast things on the table, ready for the morning.*

▲ **set to** WORK *phrasal verb* to start working or dealing with something in an energetic and determined way: *If we all set to, we should be able to finish the job in a week.*

▲ **set to** FIGHT *phrasal verb* INFORMAL to begin to fight

set-to /ˈset.tuː/ /ˌ-ˈ-/ *noun* [C usually sing] INFORMAL a short argument or fight: *Dad had a bit of a set-to with the neighbours about their playing loud music all the time.*

▲ **set** *sth* **up** ARRANGE *phrasal verb* [M] to arrange for an event or activity to happen: *We need to set up a meeting to discuss the proposals.* ○ *The government has agreed to set up a public enquiry.*

set-up /ˈset.ʌp/ US /ˈseţ-/ *noun* [S] the way in which things are organized or arranged: *When I started my new job, it took me a while to get used to the set-up.* ○ *"Nice little set-up you've got here," he said as we showed him round the house.*

▲ **set** *sth* **up** START *phrasal verb* [M] to formally establish a new company, organization, system, way of working, etc: *A committee has been set up to organize social events in the college.* ○ *She plans to set up her own business.* ○ *They've set up a fund for victims of the earthquake.*

▲ **set** *sb* **up** *phrasal verb* [M] to establish someone or yourself in a business or position: *After he left college, his father set him up in the family business.* ○ [R] *She set herself up as an interior designer.*

▲ **set** *sth/sb* **up** PROVIDE *phrasal verb* [M] to provide someone or something with all the necessary things for a particular activity or period of time: *I think we're set up with everything we need for the journey.* ○ *We went on a shopping trip and got him all set up for the new term.*

▲ **set** *sb* **up** *phrasal verb* [M] **1** to provide the money that someone needs for an important task or activity which is expected to last a long time: *Winning the lottery has set them up for life.* **2** to provide someone with the energy or health that you need for a particular period of time: *A good breakfast really sets you up for the day.*

▲ **set (sth) up** PREPARE *phrasal verb* [M] to prepare something for use, especially by putting the different parts of it together: *We only had a couple of hours to set up before the exhibition opened.* ○ *I need one or two people to help me set up the equipment.*

▲ **set** *sb* **up** DECEIVE *phrasal verb* [M often passive] INFORMAL to trick someone in order to make them do something, or in order to make them seem guilty of something that they have not done: *They claimed that they weren't selling drugs, but that they'd been set up by the police.*

set-up /ˈset.ʌp/ US /ˈseţ-/ *noun* [C usually sing] *When drugs were found in her luggage, she claimed it was a set-up.*

▲ **set** *yourself* **up as** *sth phrasal verb* [R] OFTEN DISAPPROVING to claim to be a particular type of person: *He sets himself up as an expert on vegetable growing, but he doesn't seem to me to know much about it.*

set-aside /ˈset.ə.saɪd/ *noun* [U] when farmers are paid in order not to grow crops on areas of land, or land of this type

setback /ˈset.bæk/ *noun* [C] something that happens which delays or prevents a process from advancing: *Sally had been recovering well from her operation, but yesterday she experienced/suffered a setback.* ○ *There has been a slight/temporary setback in our plans.* ➌See also **set back**.

,set ˈpiece *noun* [C usually sing] part of a film, play, etc. which is exciting and attracts attention, but is often not a necessary part of the story

,set ˈpoint *noun* [C] If a tennis player has a set point, it means that if they win the next point, they will win the SET (= important part of a tennis competition).

setsquare UK /'set.skweə'/ US /-skwer/ noun [C] (ALSO **triangle**) a flat piece of metal or plastic in the shape of a triangle with one angle of 90°, which is used for drawing angles ⊃Compare **T-square**.

settee /set'i:/ noun [C] **1** a long soft seat with a back and usually with arms; a sofa **2** US a long wooden seat which has a back

setter /'set.ə'/ US /'set.ə/ noun [C] a long-haired dog, which is sometimes trained to help hunters find birds or animals to shoot. There are various types of setter: *an Irish setter* ○ *a red setter*

settle MAKE COMFORTABLE /'set.l/ US /'set-/ verb [I or T; usually + adv or prep] to relax into a comfortable position: *After dinner we settled in front of the television for the evening.* ○ *The dentist told her patient to settle back in the chair.* ○ [R] *He settled himself down with a newspaper, and waited for the train to arrive.*

settled /'set.ld/ US /'set-/ adj [after v] *Now that the children are settled at school* (= have become familiar with it and feel comfortable and happy there), *we don't really want to move again.* ○ *Although I worked there for over a year, I never really felt settled.*

settle QUIET /'set.l/ US /'set-/ verb [I or T] to become quiet and calm, or to make something or someone do this: *The weather is expected to settle towards the end of the week.* ○ *I'll call you back as soon as I've settled the children for the night.* ○ *Before a performance, she takes three deep breaths to settle her nerves.* ○ *We're very busy this week, but things should settle (down) a bit after the weekend.* ○ UK *Joe's parents are very worried about him because he doesn't seem to be able to settle to* (= to give his whole attention to) *anything.*

settled /'set.ld/ US /'set-/ adj: *It looks as if we are in for a settled spell* (= as if the weather will be calm) *this week.*

settle AGREE /'set.l/ US /'set-/ verb **1** [T] to reach a decision or an agreement about something, or to end a disagreement: *Good, that's all settled – you send out the invitations for the party, and I'll organize the food.* ○ [+ question word] *They haven't yet settled when the wedding is going to be.* ○ *"The tickets are £40 each." "Well, that settles that then – I can't afford that much."* ○ *I'd like to get this matter settled once and for all* (= reach a final decision on it). **2** [I or T] to arrange something: *The details of the contract have not yet been settled.* ○ *Our lawyer advised us that it would be better to settle out of court* (= reach an agreement in a legal case without it being decided in a court of law). ○ *It took months to settle* (= bring to an end) *the dispute/strike.* ○ *My father and I have agreed finally to settle our differences* (= stop arguing).

• **settle your affairs** FORMAL to decide what will happen to your possessions after your death, usually by making a legal document

• **settle an (old) score** (ALSO **settle (old) scores**) to harm someone because they have harmed you in the past: *The President used his speech to settle some old scores with his opponents.*

settlement /'set.l.mənt/ US /'set-/ noun **1** [C or U] an official agreement that finishes an argument: *It now seems unlikely that it will be possible to negotiate/reach a peaceful settlement of the conflict.* ○ *As part of their divorce settlement, Geoff agreed to let Polly keep the house.* **2** [C] an arrangement to end a disagreement involving a law having been broken, without taking it to a court of law, or an amount of money paid as part of such an arrangement: *They reached an out-of-court settlement.* ○ *The actor accepted a settlement of £100,000 from the newspaper.*

settle PAY /'set.l/ US /'set-/ verb [I or T] to pay, especially money owed or claimed: *Please settle your account/bill without further delay.* ○ *It took the insurance company months to settle my claim.* ○ FORMAL *Payment of your account is now overdue, and we must ask you to settle* (= pay the money you owe) *immediately.*

• **settle an account** to harm someone because they have harmed you in the past: *Police think that the killings may be a result of accounts being settled between local gangs.*

settlement /'set.l.mənt/ US /'set-/ noun [C or U] *The settlement of his debts took him several months.* ○ *I enclose a cheque in settlement of your claim.* ○ LEGAL *Her mother made a settlement on her* (= made a formal arrangement to give her money) *when she started college.*

settle LIVE /'set.l/ US /'set-/ verb **1** [I usually + adv or prep] to go and live somewhere, especially permanently: *After they got married, they settled in Brighton.* **2** [I or T; often passive] to arrive, especially from another country, in a new place and establish yourself, claiming the land as your own: *America was first settled by people who came across from Asia over 25,000 years ago.*

settled /'set.ld/ US /'set-/ adj: *After many years of travelling around, we're now enjoying a more settled life* (= we are living in one place).

settlement /'set.l.mənt/ US /'set-/ noun [C or U] *A large Roman settlement* (= a place where people lived during that period in history) *has been discovered just outside the town.* ○ *Many Native Americans were killed during the settlement of the American West by Europeans in the nineteenth century.*

settler /'set.lə'/ US /'set-/ noun [C] a person who arrives, especially from another country, in a new place and claims the land in order to live on it and farm it

settle MOVE LOWER /'set.l/ US /'set-/ verb to move to a lower level and stay there; to drop: *The house had been empty for years, and dust had settled on all the surfaces.* ○ *Do you think the snow will settle* (= remain on the ground and other surfaces without melting)? ○ *The contents of this packet may settle* (= fall towards the bottom of the container and so seem to be less).

settlement /'set.l.mənt/ US /'set-/ noun [U] the process of the slow sinking of a building or the ground

settle BE IN A CERTAIN STATE /'set.l/ US /'set-/ verb [I + adv or prep] to reach and remain at a certain level or in a certain state: *The pound rose slightly against the dollar today, then settled at $1.53.* ○ *A peaceful expression settled on her face.* ○ *After the recent riots, an uneasy calm has settled on the city.*

PHRASAL VERBS WITH **settle** ▼

▲ **settle down** FEEL COMFORTABLE phrasal verb (ALSO **settle into somewhere**) to become familiar with a place and to feel happy and confident in it: *She quickly settled down in her new house/job/school.*

▲ **settle down** NOT MOVE phrasal verb to start living in a place where you intend to stay for a long time, usually with your partner: *Eventually I'd like to settle down and have a family, but not yet.*

▲ **settle (sb) down** CALM phrasal verb to become quiet and calm, or to make someone become quiet and calm: *Come on children, stop chatting and settle down please!* ○ *They settled down on the sofa to watch the film.*

▲ **settle for sth** phrasal verb to accept or agree to something, or to decide to have something, although it is not exactly what you want or it is not the best: *They were hoping to sell their car for £2000, but settled for £1500.* ○ *He wants a full refund and he won't settle for anything less.* ○ *She never settles for second best.*

▲ **settle in** phrasal verb to become familiar with new surroundings, such as a new house, job or school, and to feel comfortable and happy there: *Once we've settled in, you must come round for dinner.*

▲ **settle sb in** phrasal verb [M] to help someone to become familiar with a new job or a new place where they will be living, working or staying: *The nurse will be with you soon – she's settling a new patient in at the moment.*

▲ **settle on sth** DECISION phrasal verb to agree on a decision: *Have you settled on a name for the baby?*

▲ **settle sth on sb** MONEY phrasal verb LEGAL to formally give money or property to someone: *When my uncle died, he settled £1000 a year on me.*

▲ **settle up** phrasal verb to pay someone the money that you owe them: *Would you like to settle up now, sir?* ○ *You buy the tickets and I'll settle up with you later.*

set-top box /ˌset.tɒp'bɒks/ US /-tɑːp'bɑːks/ noun [C] an electronic device that makes it possible to watch DIGITAL broadcasts on ordinary televisions

seven /'sev.ən/ determiner, pronoun, noun [C] (the number) 7: *five, six, seven, eight, nine* ○ *"How many grandchildren do you have now?" "I've got seven (grand-*

children)." ○ We're open seven days a week (= every day).

seventh /'sev.ᵊntθ/ determiner, pronoun, adj, adv, noun [S] 7th written as a word: It's **the** seventh (of May) today. ○ Our team was/came seventh.

seventh /'sev.ᵊntθ/ noun [C] one of seven equal parts of something

• **in seventh heaven** INFORMAL HUMOROUS extremely happy: Since they got married, they've been in seventh heaven.

seventeen /,sev.ᵊn'ti:n/ /'---/ determiner, pronoun, noun [C] (the number) 17: sixteen, seventeen, eighteen ○ There are seventeen days to go till my birthday. ○ "How old are you?" "I'm seventeen (years old)." ○ Is that a seventeen on the front of that bus?

seventeenth /,sev.ᵊn'ti:ntθ/ /'---/ determiner, pronoun, adj, adv, noun [S] 17th written as a word

Seventh-Day Adventist /,sev.ᵊntθ.deɪˈæd.ven.tɪst/ /-ᵊn-/ noun [C] a member of a Christian group which believes that Jesus Christ will return to the Earth soon, and which has Saturday as its day for worship

seventy /'sev.ᵊn.ti/ /-t̬i/ determiner, pronoun, noun [C] (the number) 70: sixty, seventy, eighty ○ This house was built seventy years ago. ○ There are seventy coming to the party. ○ There was a seventy on the door of our hotel room.

seventies /'sev.ᵊn.tiz/ /-t̬iz/ plural noun A person's seventies are the period in which they are aged between 70 and 79: He's very active considering he's **in** his seventies.

the seventies plural noun **1** the range of temperature between 70° and 79° Fahrenheit: The temperature is expected to be reach the seventies tomorrow. **2** the period of years between 70 and 79 in any century: Flared trousers and platform shoes were fashionable **in** the seventies (= between 1970 and 1979). **seventieth** /'sev.ᵊn.ti.əθ/ /-t̬i-/ determiner, pronoun, adj, adv, noun [S]

seventy-eight /,sev.ᵊn.ti'eɪt/ /-t̬i-/ noun [C] (ALSO **78**) an old-fashioned record which is played by being turned around 78 times every minute

seven-year itch /,sev.ᵊn.jɪə'rɪtʃ/ /-jɪr-/ noun [U] INFORMAL HUMOROUS If a married person has the seven-year itch, they are feeling dissatisfied with their marriage after seven years, and are considering having a sexual relationship with someone who is not their wife or husband.

sever /'sev.əʳ/ /-ɚ/ verb [T] **1** to break or separate, especially by cutting: The knife severed an artery and he bled to death. ○ Her foot was severed **from** her leg in a car accident. ○ Electricity cables have been severed by the storm. **2** to end a connection with someone or something: The US severed **diplomatic relations** with Cuba in 1961. ○ The company has severed its connection/links/relationship/ties with its previous partners.

severance /'sev.ᵊr.ᵊnts/ /-ɚ-/ noun [U] **1** money paid by an employer to an employee whose job the employer has had to bring to an end: The management have offered employees one week's severance **(pay)** for each six months they have worked at the company. ○ a severance agreement/deal/package **2** FORMAL the act of ending a connection, relationship, etc. or of being separated from a person, place, etc: The minister announced the severance **of** aid to the country. ○ The hardest thing to cope with was the severance **from** his family.

several SOME /'sev.ᵊr.ᵊl/ /-ɚ-/ determiner, pronoun some; an amount that is not exact but is fewer than many: I've seen 'Gone with the Wind' several times. ○ Several people have complained about the scheme. ○ Several of my friends are learning English at language schools in Cambridge.

several SEPARATE /'sev.ᵊr.ᵊl/ /-ɚ-/ adj [before n] FORMAL separate; different; RESPECTIVE: We are striving to reach an agreement which will satisfy the several interests of the parties concerned. **severally** /'sev.ᵊr.ᵊl.i/ /-ɚ-/ adv

severe VERY SERIOUS /sɪ'vɪəʳ/ /-'vɪr/ adj **1** causing very great pain, difficulty, anxiety, damage, etc.; very serious: a severe chest infection/a severe leg injury/severe toothache ○ This is a school for children with severe learning difficulties. ○ In parts of Africa there is a severe food/water shortage. ○ There is expected to be a severe

frost tonight. ○ Severe cutbacks in public spending have been announced. **2** extreme or very difficult: This will be a severe test of our strength. **severely** /sɪ'vɪə.li/ /-'vɪr-/ adv: Their daughter was severely injured in a car accident. ○ severely disabled/handicapped ○ Job opportunities are severely limited/restricted at the moment. **severity** /sɪ'ver.ɪ.ti/ /-ə.t̬i/ noun [U] Even the doctors were shocked by the severity **of** his injuries. ○ I don't think you quite understand the severity **of** our financial problems.

severe NOT KIND /sɪ'vɪəʳ/ /-'vɪr/ adj not kind or sympathetic; not willing to accept other people's mistakes or failures: The headteacher spoke in a severe voice. ○ The government is currently facing severe criticism. ○ There are severe penalties for failing to declare all your income to the tax authorities. **severely** /sɪ'vɪə.li/ /-'vɪr-/ adv: I was severely reprimanded by my boss. ○ "I will not allow that kind of behaviour in my class," the teacher said severely. **severity** /sɪ'ver.ɪ.ti/ /-ə.t̬i/ noun [U] He spoke with great severity. ○ The severity **of** the punishment should match the seriousness of the crime.

severe PLAIN /sɪ'vɪəʳ/ /-'vɪr/ adj OFTEN DISAPPROVING completely plain and without decoration: She wore a severe black dress, and plain black shoes. ○ I don't like these severe modern buildings. **severely** /sɪ'vɪə.li/ /-'vɪr/ adv: She dresses very severely. **severity** /sɪ'ver.ɪ.ti/ /-ə.t̬i/ noun [U]

sew /səʊ/ /soʊ/ verb sewed, sewn or sewed **1** [I or T] to join two pieces of cloth together by putting thread through them with a needle: My grandmother taught me to sew. ○ I made this skirt just by sewing two pieces of material **together**. ○ He sewed the badge neatly **onto** his uniform. **2** [T] to make a piece of clothing by joining pieces of cloth together by putting thread through them with a needle: She sews all her children's clothes. **3** [I or T] to use a needle and thread to join up the edges of a cut in the skin or other part of the body: The muscle layer needs to be sewn first. ○ His finger was cut off when he caught it in a machine, but the surgeon was able to sew it back **on**.

sewing /'səʊ.ɪŋ/ /'soʊ-/ noun [U] **1** a piece of cloth that is being or needs to be sewn: She put her sewing down. **2** the skill or activity of making or repairing clothes or other items made from cloth: I'm not very good at sewing.

PHRASAL VERBS WITH Phrasal verbs with **sew** ▼

▲ **sew** sth **up** REPAIR phrasal verb [M] to close or repair something by sewing the edges together: I've got to sew up that hole in your jeans. ○ A nurse will come and sew up that wound for you soon.

▲ **sew** sth **up** BE SUCCESSFUL phrasal verb INFORMAL **1** [usually passive] If you have a competition or game sewn up, you are certain you can win it or get control of it: The Democrats appear to have the election sewn up. **2** to complete all the arrangements for a successful business agreement: It's going to take another week or two to sew up this deal.

sewage ,works UK noun [C] (UK ALSO **sewage farm**, US **sewage treatment plant**) a place where sewage is treated so that it can be safely got rid of or changed into FERTILIZER

sewer /sʊəʳ/ /'suː.ɚ/ noun [C] **1** a large pipe, usually underground, which is used for carrying waste water and human waste, such as urine and excrement, away from buildings to a place where they can be safely got rid of: a sewer pipe ○ A complicated system of sewers runs under the city. **2 open sewer** a channel for carrying away waste water and waste from the human body which is above the ground and is not covered

sewage /'suː.ɪdʒ/ noun [U] **1** waste matter such as water or human urine or excrement: Some cities in the world do not have proper facilities for the disposal of sewage. ○ Raw/untreated sewage is being pumped into the sea, from where it pollutes our beaches. **2** the system of carrying away waste water and human waste from houses and other buildings through large underground pipes or passages

sewerage /'səʊ.rɪdʒ/ /'suː.ɚ.ɪdʒ/ noun [U] **sewage**

'sewing ma,chine *noun* [C] a machine which is used for joining together pieces of cloth, and which has a needle that is operated either by turning a handle, or by electricity

sex [MALE OR FEMALE] /seks/ *noun* **1** [U] the state of being either male or female: *What sex is your cat?* ○ *Some tests enable you to find out the sex **of** your baby before it's born.* ○ *It's illegal to discriminate against people on the basis of (their) sex.* ○ *She accused her employer of sex discrimination* (= of treating her unfairly because she was a woman). **2** [C] all males considered as a group, or all females considered as a group: *She seems to regard all **members of** the male sex as inferior.* ○ *Members of the **opposite** sex are not allowed in students' rooms overnight.*

sex /seks/ *verb* [T] SPECIALIZED to discover whether an animal is male or female: *How do you sex fish?*

sexless /'sek.sləs/ *adj* lacking sexual characteristics ➲Compare **neuter** REMOVE SEX ORGANS.

sexual /'sek.sjʊəl/ *adj* relating to being male or female: *Sexual equality will not be achieved until there is more provision for childcare.* ○ *Some steps have been taken towards ending sexual discrimination* (= treating people unfairly because of which sex they are).

sexually /'sek.sjʊə.li/ *adv*: *sexually stereotyped behaviour* (= behaviour which is considered to be typical of a male or a female)

sex [ACTIVITY] /seks/ *noun* [U] sexual activity involving the penis or vagina, especially when a man puts his penis into a woman's vagina: *Sex before/outside marriage is strongly disapproved of in some cultures.* ○ *She was complaining about all the sex and violence on television.* ○ *She'd been **having** sex **with** a colleague at work for years.* ○ *Most young people now receive sex **education** in school.* ○ ***extramarital/premarital** sex* ○ ***casual** sex* (= sex with someone you do not know) ○ ***unprotected** sex* (= sex without using a device to prevent spreading disease)

-sexed /-sekst/ *suffix*: *highly-sexed* (= having a large amount of sexual desire or interest)

sexual /'sek.sjʊəl/ *adj* **1** relating to the activity of sex: *Most people remember their first sexual experience.* ○ *a sexual relationship* ○ *sexual **assault/harassment*** ○ FORMAL *sexual **intercourse*** (= the act of having sex) ○ *sexual **orientation/preference*** (= whether someone chooses to have sex with men or women, or both) **2** relating to the reproduction of babies by the combining of a cell from a male with a cell from a female: *sexual reproduction*

sexuality /ˌsek.sju'æl.ɪ.ti/ [US] /-ə.ţi/ *noun* [U] someone's ability to experience or express sexual feelings: *She was uncomfortably aware of her son's developing sexuality.*

sexually /'sek.sjʊə.li/ *adv*: *She's fun to be with, but I don't find her sexually **attractive*** (= do not want to have sex with her).

sexy /'sek.si/ *adj* INFORMAL **1** sexually attractive: *He's very sexy.* ○ *a sexy smile* ○ *sexy underwear* **2** describes something that attracts a lot of interest and attention: *For most people grammar probably isn't a very sexy subject.* **sexily** /'sek.sɪ.li/ *adv*

sexless /'sek.sləs/ *adj* lacking sexual attractiveness: *I've always found her rather sexless.*

sexagenarian /ˌsek.sə.dʒɪ'neə.ri.ən/ [US] /-'ner.i-/ *noun* [C] a person who is between 60 and 69 years old

'sex ap,peal *noun* [U] sexual attractiveness

,sex ,change (oper'ation) *noun* [C] an operation which, together with hormone treatment, gives a man many of the characteristics of a woman, or a woman many of the characteristics a man

sexism /'sek.sɪ.zᵊm/ *noun* [U] DISAPPROVING (actions based on) the belief that the members of one sex are less intelligent, able, skilful, etc. than the members of the other sex, especially that women are less able than men: *The university has been accused of sexism because it has so few women professors.*

sexist /'sek.sɪst/ *adj* DISAPPROVING Sexist jokes or comments suggest that women are less able than men or refer to women's bodies, behaviour or feelings in a negative way: *sexist comments/jokes* **sexist** /'sek.sɪst/ *noun* [C]

'sex ,kitten *noun* [U] OLD-FASHIONED a sexually attractive young woman

'sex ,life *noun* [U] a person's sexual activities and relationships: *Many new parents find that having a baby seriously affects their sex life.*

sex-linked /'seks.lɪŋkt/ *adj* If something is sex-linked, it is found only among males or only among females: *Haemophilia is a sex-linked disease.*

,sex 'maniac *noun* [C] someone who always wants to have sex and thinks about it too much

'sex ,object *noun* [C] If you consider someone to be, or you treat someone like, a sex object, you are only interested in them sexually, and not as a person: *She wanted to be regarded as more than just a sex object.*

'sex of,fender *noun* [C] a person who commits a crime involving a sexual attack: *Some parents are demanding access to the sex offenders' **register*** (= a list, kept by the police, of all the people who have been found guilty in a court of a sexual offence).

sexologist /sek'sɒl.ə.dʒɪst/ [US] /-'sɑː.lə-ɪst/ *noun* [C] a person who studies human sexual behaviour

'sex ,organ *noun* [C] a part of the body involved in the production of babies, such as the vagina or penis

sexpot /'seks.pɒt/ [US] /-pɑːt/ *noun* [C] INFORMAL a woman who is sexually exciting or is very interested in sex. Some people, especially women, consider this offensive.

'sex ,shop *noun* [C] a shop that sells products connected with sexual activity, including magazines, clothing and equipment

sex-starved /'seks.stɑːvd/ [US] /-stɑːrvd/ *adj* having not had enough sex recently

'sex ,symbol *noun* [C] someone famous who is considered very sexually attractive by many people: *Marilyn Monroe is one of the cinema's most famous sex symbols.*

sextant /'sek.stᵊnt/ *noun* [C] a device used on a ship or aircraft for measuring angles, such as those between stars or that between the Sun and the Earth, in order to discover the exact position of the ship or aircraft

sextet /sek'stet/ *noun* [C] a group of six musicians or singers who play or sing together, or a piece of music for six players or singers: *a jazz sextet* ○ *a sextet **for** strings, oboe and flute*

'sex ,therapy *noun* [U] advice and/or training given by an expert to help people who have sexual problems **'sex ,therapist** *noun* [C]

sexton /'sek.stᵊn/ *noun* [C] a person whose job is to take care of a church building and its GRAVEYARD, and sometimes to ring the church bells

'sex ,tourism *noun* [U] when someone travels to another country for the purpose of paying to have sex, especially with children: *Several European governments have pledged to work together to crack down on child pornography and sex tourism.*

sextuplet /sek'stjuː.plɪt/ [US] /-'stuː-/ *noun* [C] any of six children born to the same mother at the same time

,sexual a'buse *noun* [U] the activity of having sex with a child or old person or someone who is mentally ill, against their wishes or without their agreement

sexuality /ˌsek.sju'æl.ɪ.ti/ [US] /-ə.ţi/ *noun* [U] ➲See at **sex** ACTIVITY.

,sexually trans,mitted dis'ease *noun* [C] (ABBREVIATION **STD**) a disease that people become infected with during sexual activity: *AIDS is a sexually transmitted disease.*

,sexual revo'lution *noun* [U] the change in people's ideas about sex which happened in many countries in the 1960s

'sex ,worker *noun* [C] POLITE WORD FOR a prostitute

sexy /'sek.si/ *adj* ➲See at **sex** ACTIVITY.

SF /ˌes'ef/ *noun* [U] ABBREVIATION FOR **science fiction**

SGML /ˌes.dʒiː.em'el/ *noun* [U] ABBREVIATION FOR standard generalized markup language: a system for organizing and marking parts of a computer document

Sgt *noun* [before n] WRITTEN ABBREVIATION FOR **sergeant**

sh, shh, ssh /ʃ/ /ʃː/ *exclamation* (ALSO **shush**) used to tell someone to be quiet: *Sh, you'll wake the baby!*

Shabbat /ʃæˈbæt/ *noun* [U] the Jewish day of rest and religious worship, celebrated on Saturday

shabby BAD CONDITION /ˈʃæb.i/ *adj* looking old and in bad condition because of long use or lack of care: *He wore a shabby old overcoat.* ○ *Her home is a rented one-bedroom flat in a shabby part of town.* ○ *The refugees were shabby* (= wore old clothes in bad condition) *and hungry.* **shabbily** /ˈʃæb.ɪ.li/ *adv*: *shabbily dressed* **shabbiness** /ˈʃæb.ɪ.nəs/ *noun* [U]

shabby NOT FAIR /ˈʃæb.i/ *adj* not honourable or fair; unacceptable: *She spoke out about the shabby way the case had been handled.* ○ *I felt the whole affair was a bit shabby.* **shabbily** /ˈʃæb.ɪ.li/ *adv*: *The hostages were shabbily treated when they came home.*

shack /ʃæk/ *noun* [C] a very simple and small building made from bits of wood, metal or other materials

shack /ʃæk/ *verb*
▲ **shack up** *phrasal verb* INFORMAL to start living in the same house as sexual partners without being married: *I hear Tony and Helen have shacked up together.* ○ *She's decided to shack up with her boyfriend.*
● **be shacked up** to be living with someone as a sexual partner when you are not married to them: *"Is Alan still living with Maria?" "No, he's shacked up with someone else now."*

shackles /ˈʃæk.lz/ *plural noun* **1** a pair of metal rings connected by a chain and fastened to a person's wrists or the bottom of their legs to prevent them from escaping: *The shackles had begun to cut into his ankles.* **2** something that prevents you from doing what you want to do: *The press, once heavily censored, has managed to shake off its shackles.*
shackle /ˈʃæk.l/ *verb* [T] If you are shackled by something, you are unable to do what you want to do because of this thing: *The government is shackled by its own debts.*

shade SLIGHT DARKNESS /ʃeɪd/ *noun* **1** [U] slight darkness caused by something blocking the direct light from the sun: *The sun was hot, and there were no trees to offer us shade.* ○ *The children played in/under the shade of a large beach umbrella.* ⊃See also **sunshade**. **2** [C] a covering that is put over an electric light in order to make it less bright: *The lamps all had matching purple shades.* **3** [U] (*ALSO* **shading**) SPECIALIZED the parts of a picture or painting that the artist has made slightly darker than the other parts: *A good artist can produce a very realistic effect using only light and shade.* **4** [C] US FOR roller blind
● **light and shade** variety in the character of a person or the quality of a thing: *The orchestra's playing brought out the light and shade in the music.*
● **put/leave sb in the shade** to be so good that another person or thing seems unimportant and not worth very much: *Although I thought I'd done well, my sister's exam results put mine in the shade.*
shade /ʃeɪd/ *verb* [T] to prevent direct light from shining on something: *I shaded my eyes from the glare of the sun.* ○ *The broad avenues are shaded by splendid trees.* **shaded** /ˈʃeɪd.ɪd/ *adj*: *Nothing will grow in the shaded part of the garden.* ○ *The shaded areas of the plans show where the houses will be built.*
shades /ʃeɪdz/ *plural noun* INFORMAL dark glasses: *She was wearing a black leather jacket and shades.*
shady /ˈʃeɪ.di/ *adj* **1** sheltered from direct light from the sun: *We sat on the shady grass for our picnic.* **2** INFORMAL dishonest or illegal: *They know some very shady characters.* ○ *He was involved in shady deals in the past.*

shade DEGREE /ʃeɪd/ *noun* [C] **1** a variety or degree of a colour: *Their kitchen is painted an unusual shade of yellow/an unusual yellow shade.* ○ *This hair colouring comes in several shades.* ○ *The room has been decorated in pastel shades* (= soft and light colours) *throughout.* **2** type or variation: *They are hoping to satisfy all shades of public opinion.* ○ *There are several shades of meaning in that sentence.*
● **a shade** slightly: *Don't you think those trousers are a shade too tight?* ○ *The journey took us a shade over/ under three hours.* ○ *Our new car cost us a shade more/ less than we were expecting it to.*

● **shades of grey** the possibility of uncertainty: *The film presents a straightforward choice between good and evil, with no shades of grey.*
shade /ʃeɪd/ *verb* [I usually + adv or prep] to gradually change into or become: *At sunset, the sky shaded from pink into dark red.* ○ *Their views shade into the policies of the extreme left of the party.*
▲ **shade sth in** *phrasal verb* [M] to make part of a picture darker

shades /ʃeɪdz/ *plural noun* INFORMAL **shades of 1** similarities with: *I fancied there were shades of socialism in the way the school was run.* **2** said to mean that something or someone makes you remember something or someone similar in the past: *In his speech he said – shades of Martin Luther King Jr. – that he had a dream.* ⊃See also **shades** at **shade** SLIGHT DARKNESS.

ˈshade ˌtree *noun* [C] US a tree that is planted to provide shade

shadow DARKNESS /ˈʃæd.əʊ/ US /-oʊ/ *noun* [C] **1** an area of darkness, caused by light being blocked by something, which usually has a similar shape to the object that is blocking the light and which appears to be joined to it: *The children were playing, jumping on each other's shadows.* ○ *Jamie followed his mother around all day like a shadow.* ○ *The sun shone through the leaves, casting/throwing shadows on the lawn.* ○ *This corner of the room is always in shadow* (= slight darkness). **2** a small dark area of skin under your eye: *She put on some make-up to cover the dark shadows under her eyes.*
● **cast a shadow over/on sth** LITERARY to spoil a good situation with something unpleasant: *Her father's illness had cast a shadow over the birth of her baby.*
● **be in/under sb's shadow** to always receive less attention than someone else: *She's always been under her sister's shadow.*
● **be in/under the shadow of sth 1** to be very close to a larger building or place: *They live in a charming house in the shadow of the cathedral.* **2** to be in a situation in which something unpleasant either seems likely to happen and to have a bad effect on your life, or is already having a bad effect on your life: *We are all living under the shadow of war.*
● **be a shadow of your former self** to have less health or strength, or less influence, than you did before: *He came home from hospital cured of the disease but a shadow of his former self.*
shadow /ˈʃæd.əʊ/ US /-oʊ/ *verb* [T] *We came across a glade shadowed* (= made slightly dark) *by large trees.*
the shadows *plural noun* an area of darkness in which people and things cannot be seen: *Someone jumped out of the shadows and grabbed her handbag.*
shadowy /ˈʃæd.əʊ.i/ US /-oʊ-/ *adj* **1** dark and full of shadows: *She was startled by a sudden movement in the shadowy hallway.* **2** describes someone or something about which little is known: *The English king, Arthur, is a somewhat shadowy figure who may not have even existed.* ○ *They are members of some shadowy extremist group.*

shadow FOLLOW /ˈʃæd.əʊ/ US /-oʊ/ *verb* [T] **1** to follow closely: *The police think that the robbers shadowed their victims for days before the crime.* ○ *The euro has closely shadowed the dollar.* **2** to follow someone else while they are at work in order to learn about that person's job: *Your first week in the job will be spent shadowing one of our more experienced employees.*
shadow /ˈʃæd.əʊ/ US /-oʊ/ *adj* [before n] UK used in the title of important politicians in the main opposition party: *the Shadow Foreign Secretary* ○ *the Shadow Cabinet*
shadow /ˈʃæd.əʊ/ US /-oʊ/ *noun* [C] **1** someone who follows another person everywhere: *"I think we have a shadow on our tail," muttered the detective.* ○ *Ever since he was able to walk, Stephen has been his older brother's shadow* (= has followed him and copied his actions). **2** a person, especially in industry, who follows someone else while they are at work in order to learn about that person's job

shadow [SMALL AMOUNT] /ˈʃæd.əʊ/ [US] /-oʊ/ *noun* [S] a small amount: *There isn't a shadow* ***of doubt*** *that you've made the right decision.*

shadow-box /ˈʃæd.əʊ.bɒks/ [US] /-oʊ.bɑːks/ *verb* [I] **1** to fight an imaginary enemy by hitting the air with your hands **2** to pretend to argue about or deal with a problem, often to avoid dealing with the most important problem: *The main political parties are merely shadow-boxing, instead of tackling the real economic problems facing this country.*

shaft [POLE] /ʃɑːft/ [US] /ʃæft/ *noun* [C] **1** a pole or rod which forms the handle of a tool or weapon: *the shaft* ***of*** *a golf club* **2** a rod which forms part of a machine such as an engine, and which turns in order to pass power on to the machine: *the drive shaft of a car* ○ *the propeller shaft of an aircraft* ➲See also **crankshaft**.

• **shaft of light** a beam of light: *A shaft of (sun)light came through the open door.*

shaft [PASSAGE] /ʃɑːft/ [US] /ʃæft/ *noun* [C] a long, either vertical or sloping, passage through a building or through the ground: *a (UK) lift/(US) elevator shaft* ○ *a ventilation/air shaft* ○ *a well shaft*

shaft [REMARK] /ʃɑːft/ [US] /ʃæft/ *noun* [C] LITERARY a clever remark, especially one that is intended as an attack on someone or something: *John came out with an unexpected shaft* ***of*** *wit/wisdom.*

shaft [TREAT UNFAIRLY] /ʃɑːft/ [US] /ʃæft/ *verb* [T] INFORMAL to cheat or trick someone in order to get money unfairly from them: *She was shafted by her agent over the film rights to her book.*

shag [HAVE SEX] /ʃæg/ *verb* [I or T] **-gg-** UK OFFENSIVE to have sex with someone

shag /ʃæg/ *noun* [C] UK OFFENSIVE an act of having sex, or a sexual partner

shag [LONG THREADS] /ʃæg/ *adj* [before n] (of a carpet) made of long thick threads: *shag* ***pile*** (= the soft surface of a carpet formed by cut threads)

shag [BIRD] /ʃæg/ *noun* [C] a large sea bird which has dark feathers, a long neck and body and a curved beak

• **like a shag on a rock** AUS SLANG completely alone

shag [EFFORT] /ʃæg/ *noun* [S] UK SLANG an activity which needs a lot of effort or causes inconvenience

• **can't be shagged** If you can't be shagged to do something, you do not have enough energy to do it.

ˌshagged (ˈout) *adj* [after v] UK OFFENSIVE extremely tired

shaggy /ˈʃæg.i/ *adj* having or covered with long, rough and untidy hair, or (of hair) long, rough and untidy: *a shaggy dog/pony* ○ *the shaggy coat of a sheep* ○ *a shaggy rug* **shagginess** /ˈʃæg.ɪ.nəs/ *noun* [U]

ˌshaggy ˈdog ˌstory *noun* [C] a long joke which has an intentionally silly or meaningless ending

Shah /ʃɑː/ *noun* [C] the title of a ruler of Iran in the past

shake [MOVE] /ʃeɪk/ *verb* **shook, shaken** **1** [T] to move backwards and forwards or up and down in quick, short movements, or to make something or someone do this: *A young boy climbed into the apple tree and shook the branches so that the fruit fell down.* ○ *Babies like toys that make a noise when they're shaken.* ○ *The explosion shook buildings for miles around.* ○ [+ obj + adj] *People in southern California were shaken awake by an earthquake.* ○ *She shook her hair* ***loose*** *from its ribbon.* ○ *Anna shook some powdered chocolate* ***over*** *her coffee.* ○ *Every time one of these big trucks goes through the village, all the houses shake.* ○ *The child's body was shaking* ***with*** *sobs.* **2** [I] If you are shaking, your body makes quick short movements, or you feel as if it is doing so, because you are frightened or nervous: *She was shaking as she opened the letter.* ○ *Her voice shook as she spoke about the person who attacked her.* ○ *I was shaking* ***in*** *my* ***shoes/boots*** (= very nervous) *about having to tell Dad what I'd done.* ○ *I was shaking* ***like a leaf/(UK) like a jelly*** (= very nervous) *before my exam.* **3** **shake *sb's* hand/shake *sb* by the hand** to hold someone's hand and move it up and down, especially when you meet them for the first time or when you make an agreement with them: *"Pleased to meet you," he said, shaking my hand.* ○ *The Princess was photographed shaking hands* ***with*** *AIDS victims.* ○ *It seems that we have a deal, so let's shake (hands)* ***on*** *it.* ○ *"Congratulations," she said, shaking the winner by the hand.* **4** **shake *your* head** to move your head from side to side, in order to express disagreement, sadness or that you do not want or believe something: *I asked Tim if he'd seen Jackie lately but he shook his head.* ○ *"That's incredible!" he said, shaking his head in disbelief.* **5** **shake *your* fist** to hold your hand up in the air with your fingers and thumb bent, and move it forcefully backwards and forwards, to show that you are angry: *He shook his fist at the driver who pulled out in front of him.*

• **more (...) than you can shake a stick at** INFORMAL a lot of: *There are more whisky distilleries in this part of Scotland than you can shake a stick at.*

• **shake a leg** OLD-FASHIONED INFORMAL used to tell someone to hurry or act more quickly: *Come on, Nick, shake a leg or we'll never be ready in time.*

shake /ʃeɪk/ *noun* [C] **1** when you shake something: *She* ***gave*** *the box a shake to see if there was anything inside it.* ○ *"No, no, no," he said with a shake* ***of*** *his head.* **2** INFORMAL a **milkshake**

• **in two shakes (of a lamb's tail)** (ALSO **a couple of shakes**) OLD-FASHIONED INFORMAL very soon: *I'll be with you in two shakes.*

shaker /ˈʃeɪ.kəʳ/ [US] /-kɚ/ *noun* [C] **1** a container with a tightly fitting lid in which liquids can be mixed together by moving the container quickly from side to side: *a cocktail shaker* **2** a container with holes in its lid from which a powdery substance can be put onto a surface by holding the container upside down and moving it up and down: *a salt/pepper shaker* **3** a container into which dice are put and moved quickly from side to side before being thrown onto a flat surface, usually during a game involving chance

shakes /ʃeɪks/ *plural noun* INFORMAL **the shakes** short quick movements from side to side that your body makes because you are ill, frightened or have drunk too much alcohol: *I watched her hands as she prepared coffee and she definintely* ***had*** *the shakes.*

shaky /ˈʃeɪ.ki/ *adj* moving with quick, short movements from side to side, not in a controlled way: *Soon after it was born, the calf got up and tried to stand on its shaky legs.* ○ *The child wrote her name in large shaky letters.* ○ *She's recovering well from her operation, but she's still a little shaky* ***on*** *her* ***feet.*** **shakily** /ˈʃeɪ.kɪ.li/ *adv*: *The old man stood up and walked shakily across the room.* **shakiness** /ˈʃeɪ.kɪ.nəs/ *noun* [U]

shake [UPSET] /ʃeɪk/ *verb* [T] **shook, shaken** to cause to feel upset and troubled: *The child seemed nervous and visibly shaken.* ○ *The news has shaken the whole country.*

shaky /ˈʃeɪ.ki/ *adj* upset: *The news left me feeling a little shaky.*

shake [WEAKEN] /ʃeɪk/ *verb* [T] **shook, shaken** to make less certain or firm or strong; to weaken: *What has happened has shaken the foundations of her belief.* ○ *After six defeats in a row, the team's confidence has been badly shaken.* ○ *This discovery may shake* ***(up)*** *traditional theories on how mountains are formed.*

shaky /ˈʃeɪ.ki/ *adj* not firm or strong: *The building's foundations are rather shaky, and it could collapse at any time.* ○ *The government is taking these steps to try to improve the country's shaky economy.* ○ *Their marriage looks pretty shaky to me.* ○ *I think you're on very shaky* ***ground*** *with that argument.* **shakily** /ˈʃeɪ.kɪ.li/ *adv* **shakiness** /ˈʃeɪ.kɪ.nəs/ *noun* [U]

shake [GET RID OF] /ʃeɪk/ *verb* [T] **shook, shaken** to get rid of or escape from something: *It's very difficult to shake the habit of a lifetime.* ○ *The company has so far been unable to shake* ***(off)*** *its reputation for being old-fashioned.*

PHRASAL VERBS WITH **shake** ▼

▲ **shake *sb* down** [THREATEN] *phrasal verb* [M] US INFORMAL to get money from someone by using threats or tricks

shakedown /ˈʃeɪk.daʊn/ *noun* [C]

▲ **shake *sb/somewhere* down** [SEARCH] *phrasal verb* [M] US INFORMAL to search a person or place thoroughly, usually in order to find things that are stolen or illegal: *We can't shake down the whole building, – only the suspect's apartment.*

S

shakedown /ˈʃeɪk.daʊn/ noun [C usually sing] *Two policemen gave his place a real shakedown.*

▲ **shake down** BECOME ORGANIZED *phrasal verb* INFORMAL to become satisfactorily or comfortably organized or established after a period of change: *Give the new arrangements time to shake down – I'm sure they'll be OK.*

shakedown /ˈʃeɪk.daʊn/ adj [before n] US *The new administration is still in the shakedown period.*

▲ **shake sth off** GET RID OF *phrasal verb* [M] INFORMAL to get rid of an illness: *I hope I can shake off this cold before the weekend.*

▲ **shake sb/sth off** GET AWAY FROM *phrasal verb* [M] **1** to get away from someone or something that will not stop following you: *He drove through the red lights in an attempt to shake off the police car that was chasing him.* **2** INFORMAL to beat an opponent, or to free yourself from someone or something that is limiting you: *I have no doubt that we will be able to shake off the challenge from our rivals.*

▲ **shake sth out** *phrasal verb* [M] to hold something such as a piece of cloth at one end and shake it up and down to get rid of dirt or folds: *I was on the back doorstep shaking out a rug.*

▲ **shake sb up** SHOCK *phrasal verb* If an unpleasant experience shakes someone up, it makes them feel shocked and upset: *I think she was quite shaken up by the accident.*

▲ **shake sth up** CHANGE *phrasal verb* [M] to cause large changes in something such as an organization, usually in order to make improvements: *Technological changes have shaken up many industries.* ○ *The first thing the new chairman of the company did was to shake up the management.* ○ *Several new players have been brought in to shake up the team.*

shake-up /ˈʃeɪk.ʌp/ noun [C usually sing] a large change in the way something is organized: *The company is undergoing a **radical** shake-up.* ○ *The arrival of the new baby caused a thorough shake-up **of** their family life.*

shakeout /ˈʃeɪk.aʊt/ noun [C usually sing] a situation in which people lose their jobs, or companies stop doing business, because of economic difficulties: *The shakeout in the labour market after Christmas usually makes January a bad month for unemployment.* ○ *There has been a shakeout of inefficient corporations.*

shale /ʃeɪl/ noun [U] a type of soft grey rock, usually formed from hardened clay, which breaks easily into thin layers

shall FUTURE STRONG /ʃæl/, WEAK /ʃ°l/ *modal verb* SLIGHTLY OLD-FASHIONED used instead of 'will' when the subject is 'I' or 'we': *If you do that one more time, I shall be very cross.* ○ *I shall never forget you.* ○ *Shall we be able to get this finished today, do you think?* ○ *I'm afraid I shall not/shan't be able to come to your party.* ○ FORMAL *I shall look forward to meeting you next week.* ○ *So we'll see you at the weekend, shall we* (= is that right)? ○ *We shall* (= intend to) *let you know as soon as there's any news.*

COMMON LEARNER ERROR

shall and will

Shall and will are both used to talk about what you are going to do in the future. Shall is usually used with 'I' or 'we' and is more formal than will. In speech, both shall and will are usually contracted to I'll, we'll, etc., so you cannot tell which verb is being used.

shall SUGGEST STRONG /ʃæl/, WEAK /ʃ°l/ *modal verb* used, with 'I' or 'we', to make a suggestion: *"I'm cold." "Shall I close this window?"* ○ *Shall we go out for dinner tonight?* ○ *Shall I pick the children up from school today?*

shall CERTAINLY WILL STRONG /ʃæl/, WEAK /ʃ°l/ *modal verb* used to say that something certainly will or must happen, or that you are determined that something will happen: *Don't worry, I shall be there to meet the train.* ○ FORMAL *The school rules state that no child shall be allowed out of the school during the day, unless accompanied by an adult.* ○ *You shall go to the ball, Cinderella.*

shallot /ʃəˈlɒt/ US /-ˈlɑːt/ noun [C or U] a type of small onion

shallow NOT DEEP /ˈʃæl.əʊ/ US /-oʊ/ adj **1** having only a short distance from the top to the bottom: *The stream was quite shallow so we were able to walk across it.* ○ *She told her children to stay in the shallow end (of the swimming pool).* ○ *Fry the onions in a shallow pan.* ○ *These beech trees have shallow roots* (= roots which do not go very deep into the ground). **2 shallow breathing** breathing in which you only take a small amount of air into your lungs with each breath **shallowly** /ˈʃæl.əʊ.li/ US /-oʊ-/ adv **shallowness** /ˈʃæl.əʊ.nəs/ US /-oʊ-/ noun [U] *Because of the shallowness of the water, we could see the fish in it very clearly.*

the shallows /ðəˈʃæl.əʊz/ US /-oʊz/ plural noun the shallow part of an area of water: *Alligators live **in** the shallows.*

shallow NOT SERIOUS /ˈʃæl.əʊ/ US /-oʊ/ adj DISAPPROVING not showing serious or careful thought: *I found the film rather shallow.* ○ *I think she found him physically quite attractive but a bit shallow.* **shallowly** /ˈʃæl.əʊ.li/ US /-oʊ-/ adv **shallowness** /ˈʃæl.əʊ.nəs/ US /-oʊ-/ noun [U] *The fine performances of the actors hide the shallowness of the play's script.*

shallow-fry /ˈʃæl.əʊ.fraɪ/ US /-oʊ-/ verb [T] to cook food in a small amount of oil or fat: *Shallow-fry the fish/bacon.*

shalom /ʃəˈlɒm/ US /-ˈlɑːm/ exclamation a form of greeting or a way of saying goodbye, used by Jewish people

shalt /ʃælt/ modal verb OLD USE **thou shalt** you shall

sham /ʃæm/ noun [C usually sing] DISAPPROVING something which is not what it seems to be and is intended to deceive people, or someone who pretends to be something they are not: *It turned out that he wasn't a real doctor at all – he was just a sham.* ○ *They claimed that the election had been fair, but really it was a sham.*

sham /ʃæm/ adj DISAPPROVING only pretending to be real; false: *They made a fortune through some sham property deal.* ○ *That jewellery looks sham to me.* ○ *She's trapped in a sham* (= not good or satisfying) *marriage.*

sham /ʃæm/ verb [I or T] -mm- DISAPPROVING to pretend: *He isn't really upset – he's just shamming.*

shaman /ˈʃeɪ.mən/ noun [C] in particular religions, a person who has special powers to control or influence good and evil SPIRITS (= beings which cannot be seen), which enables them to discover the cause of illness, bad luck, etc.

shamanism /ˈʃeɪ.mən.ɪ.z°m/ noun [U] a form of religion which includes a belief in the power of the shaman **shamanistic** /ˌʃeɪ.məˈnɪs.tɪk/ adj

shamble /ˈʃæm.bl/ verb [I + adv or prep] to walk slowly and awkwardly, without lifting your feet correctly: *Sick patients shambled along the hospital corridors.* ○ *He was a strange, shambling figure.*

shambles /ˈʃæm.blz/ noun [S] INFORMAL a state of confusion, bad organization or untidiness, or something which is in this state: *After the party, the house was a **total/complete** shambles.* ○ *Our economy is **in a** shambles.* ○ *The way these files are arranged is the biggest shambles I've ever seen.*

shambolic /ʃæmˈbɒl.ɪk/ US /-ˈbɑː.lɪk/ adj UK INFORMAL confused and badly organized: *Things are often a bit shambolic at the beginning of the school year.* ○ *Anna is far too shambolic to be able to run a business.* **shambolically** /ʃæmˈbɒl.ɪ.kli/ US /-ˈbɑː.lɪ-/ adv

shame BAD FEELING /ʃeɪm/ noun [U] **1** an uncomfortable feeling of guilt or of being ashamed because of your own or someone else's bad behaviour: *He said he felt no shame for what he had done.* ○ *The children **hung/bowed** their **heads** in shame.* ○ *The shame of the scandal was so great that he shot himself a few weeks later.* ○ *You can't go out dressed like that – **have** you **no** shame* (= don't you feel ashamed about being dressed like that)? **2** loss of honour and respect: *He thinks there's great shame in being out of work and unable to provide for his family.* ○ *In some societies, if a woman leaves her husband, it **brings** shame **on** her and her family.*

● **die of shame** INFORMAL to feel extremely ashamed: *If anyone found out that I took the money, I'd die of shame.*

● **put sb to shame** to make someone feel ashamed: *It puts me to shame that I still haven't replied to David's letter.*

● **to my shame** I feel ashamed because: *To my shame, I never wrote and thanked Mary for her present.*

• **shame on *you*** used to tell someone that they should feel sorry for something they did: *Shame on you **for** being so unkind.* ○ HUMOROUS *You mean you were in town and you didn't come and see us – shame on you!*

shame /ʃeɪm/ *exclamation* used to express disapproval of something that a public speaker is saying: *To cries of 'Shame!', the minister announced that taxes were being increased.*

shame /ʃeɪm/ *verb* [T] **1** to make someone feel ashamed, or to make someone or something lose honour and respect: *It shames me that I treated her so badly.* ○ *The behaviour of a few children has shamed the whole school.* **2 shame *sb* into/out of *sth*** to cause someone to do or not to do something by making them feel ashamed: [+ v-ing] *The number of people out of work has shamed the government into tak**ing** action to prevent further job losses.*

shameful /ˈʃeɪm.fᵊl/ *adj* DISAPPROVING deserving blame, or being a reason for feeling ashamed: *I couldn't see anything shameful in what I had done.* ○ *The crime figures are shameful.* ○ *The family kept their shameful secret for years.* **shamefully** /ˈʃeɪm.fᵊl.i/ *adv*: *Both of you have behaved shamefully.* ○ *The children had been shamefully neglected.* **shamefulness** /ˈʃeɪm.fᵊl.nəs/ *noun* [U]

shameless /ˈʃeɪm.ləs/ *adj* DISAPPROVING **1** not ashamed, especially about something generally considered unacceptable: *She is quite shameless **about** her ambition.* ○ *They seem to have a shameless disregard for truth.* **2** behaving in a way intended to attract sexual interest, without feeling ashamed about it: *She's a shameless **hussy**.* **shamelessly** /ˈʃeɪm.lə.sli/ *adv*: *The government has shamelessly abandoned its principles.* ○ *She's shamelessly having an affair with her friend's husband.* **shamelessness** /ˈʃeɪm.lə.snəs/ *noun* [U]

shame [BAD LUCK] /ʃeɪm/ *noun* [S] an unlucky situation: [+ that] ***It's a (great) shame that** the concert had to be cancelled.* ○ [+ to infinitive] *Have some more vegetables – **it** would be **a** shame **to** waste them.* ○ *"Douglas is having to miss the school concert because he's ill." "Oh, **what a** shame/**that's a** shame!"*

shame [COMPARE WELL] /ʃeɪm/ *verb* [T] to cause something not to seem of a high standard by comparison: *The school's examination results shame those of the other schools in the area.*

shame /ʃeɪm/ *noun* **put *sb/sth* to shame** to make someone or something seem not good by comparison: *Your cooking puts mine to shame.*

shamefaced /ˌʃeɪmˈfeɪst/ /ˈ--/ *adj* awkward and embarrassed or ashamed: *He looked somewhat shamefaced when he realized his mistake.* **shamefacedly** /ˌʃeɪmˈfeɪst.li/ /ˈ-ˌ--/ /-ˈfeɪ.sɪd-/ /ˈ-ˌ---/ *adv*

shammy (leather) /ˈʃæm.iˌleð.əʳ/ [US] /-ɚ/ *noun* [C or U] ➲See at **chamois**.

shampoo /ʃæmˈpuː/ *noun plural* **shampoos 1** [C or U] a soapy liquid used for washing hair, or for washing particular objects or materials: *an anti-dandruff shampoo* ○ *a carpet shampoo* ○ *Directions: wet hair, apply shampoo and massage into a rich lather.* **2** [C] an act of washing something, especially your hair, with shampoo: *My hair/The rug/The dog needs a shampoo.* ○ *She went to the hairdressers for a shampoo **and set**.*

shampoo /ʃæmˈpuː/ *verb* [T] **shampooing, shampooed, shampooed** to wash something with shampoo: *Duncan shampooed my hair and then Tracy cut it.*

shamrock /ˈʃæm.rɒk/ [US] /-rɑːk/ *noun* [C or U] a plant which has three round leaves arranged in a triangular pattern on each stem

shandy /ˈʃæn.di/ *noun* [C or U] MAINLY UK a drink made by mixing together beer and LEMONADE or sometimes GINGER ALE: *Two shandies* (= glasses of this drink), *please.*

shank [STRAIGHT PART] /ʃæŋk/ *noun* [C] a long thin straight part of particular objects, especially one which connects the end of a device or tool that you hold to the end of it which operates: *the shank **of** a screwdriver* ○ *the shank **of** a key/nail*

shank [LEG] /ʃæŋk/ *noun* [C] OLD-FASHIONED OR HUMOROUS the leg of a person or animal, especially the part below the knee

shan't /ʃɑːnt/ [US] /ʃænt/ *short form of* shall not: *I shan't be able to come to your party.* ○ *"Pick those books up immediately." "Shan't* (= I refuse to)*!"*

shanty [HOUSE] /ˈʃæn.ti/ [US] /-t̬i/ *noun* [C] a small house, usually made from pieces of wood, metal or cardboard, in which poor people live, especially on the edge of a city

shanty [SONG] /ˈʃæn.ti/ [US] /-t̬i/ *noun* [C] a song which sailors sang in the past while they were working on a ship

ˈshanty ˌtown *noun* [C] an area in or on the edge of a city, in which poor people live in small, very cheaply built houses

shape [FORM] /ʃeɪp/ *noun* **1** [C or U] the particular physical form or appearance of something: *Clay can be moulded into almost any shape.* ○ *These bricks are all different shapes.* ○ *Kim's birthday cake was **in the** shape **of** a train.* ○ *Our table is oval **in** shape.* ○ *My bicycle wheel has got bent **out of** shape.* ○ *This T-shirt has been washed so many times that it's **lost** its shape* (= has become loose and lost its form). **2** [C] an arrangement that is formed by joining lines together in a particular way or by the line or lines around its outer edge: *a round/square/circular/oblong shape* ○ *A triangle is a shape with three sides.* ○ *The children made patterns by sticking coloured shapes onto paper.* **3** [C] the physical form or appearance of a particular person or thing: *In the story, Faust is tempted by the Devil, who has **taken the** shape **of** a man.* ○ *Life on Earth **takes** many shapes.* **4** [C] a person or object that you cannot see clearly because it is too dark, or because the person or object is too far away: *I could see a dark shape in the street outside.*

• **all shapes and sizes** many different types: *We sell all shapes and sizes **of** teddy bear.* ○ *Cars **come in** all shapes and sizes.*

• **in any shape or form** of any type: *I'm opposed to war in any shape or form.*

• **in the shape of** in the form of; appearing as: *Luckily, help arrived in the shape of a police officer.*

• **take shape** to start to develop a more clear or certain form: *We watched the vase begin to take shape in the potter's hands.* ○ *Our ideas are beginning to take shape.*

shape /ʃeɪp/ *verb* [T] **1** to make something become a particular shape: *The skirt has been shaped so that it hangs loosely.* ○ *When you've made the dough, shape it **into** two loaves.* **2** SLIGHTLY FORMAL to make an object from a physical substance: *Early humans shaped tools **out of** stone.* **shaped** /ʃeɪpt/ *adj*: *an unusually shaped carrot* ○ *Jackie has a perfectly shaped figure.* ○ *The lenses of her sunglasses were shaped **like** hearts.*

-shaped /-ʃeɪpt/ *suffix* having a particular shape: *sunglasses with heart-shaped lenses* ○ *Our kitchen is L-shaped.*

shapeless /ˈʃeɪp.ləs/ *adj* without a clear form or structure: *My clay pot ended up as just a shapeless lump.* ○ *His ideas are interesting, but they're rather shapeless.* **shapelessly** /ˈʃeɪ.plə.sli/ *adv*: *Her clothes hung shapelessly* (= loosely and without fitting well) *on her.* **shapelessness** /ˈʃeɪ.plə.snəs/ *noun* [U]

shapely /ˈʃeɪ.pli/ *adj* APPROVING used to describe something that has an attractive form, especially a woman's body or parts of a woman's body: *shapely legs* **shapeliness** /ˈʃeɪ.plɪ.nəs/ *noun* [U]

shape [CHARACTER] /ʃeɪp/ *noun* [U] the way something is organized, or its general character or nature: *Technological developments have changed the shape **of** industry.* ○ *We need to change the whole shape **of** our campaign.*

• **the shape of things to come** the form or style that is likely to develop or be popular in the future: *I hope the fashions pictured in this magazine are not the shape of things to come.*

shape /ʃeɪp/ *verb* [T] to decide or influence the form of something, especially a belief or idea, or someone's character: *Many people are not able to shape their own destinies.* ○ *My relationship with my father played a major part in shaping my attitude towards men.* ○ *He was very influential in shaping the government's economic policy/strategy.*

shape CONDITION /ʃeɪp/ *noun* [U] **1** condition, or state of health: *He bought up businesses that were in bad/poor shape, and then sold them off bit by bit.* ○ *"How are you?" "Oh, I'm in great shape."* ○ *You're in no shape* (= not in a good enough state of health) *to go to work today.* **2** good structural or physical condition: *It's taken us five years to get our house into shape.* ○ *She runs six miles every day to help keep herself in shape.* ○ *I haven't had any exercise for weeks, and I'm really out of shape* (= not in good physical condition).

• **knock/lick sth/sb into shape** (*US USUALLY* **whip sth/sb into shape**) to take action to get something or someone into the good condition that you would like: *to knock the economy into shape* ○ *A better teacher would have licked him into shape.*

▲ **shape up** *phrasal verb* [usually continuous] *INFORMAL* **1** to develop: *How are your plans shaping up?* ○ *Things seem to be shaping up nicely.* ○ *Colin is shaping up quite well in his new job.* **2** to improve your behaviour or performance: *I've been told that if I don't shape up, I'll lose my job.*

• **Shape up or ship out!** *INFORMAL* said to tell someone that they must improve their performance or behaviour or they will have to leave

shard /ʃɑːd/ ⓤ /ʃɑːrd/ *noun* [C] a piece of a broken glass, cup, container or similar object: *Shards of glass have been cemented into the top of the wall to stop people climbing over.*

share PART /ʃeəʳ/ ⓤ /ʃer/ *noun* [C or U] a part of something that has been divided between several people, which belongs to, is owed to or has to be done by a particular person: *The total bill comes to £80, so our share is £20.* ○ *We must make sure that everyone gets equal shares of the food.* ○ *The party's share of the vote fell from 39% to 24%.* ○ *She's not doing her share of the work.* ○ *We must all accept some share of the responsibility.*

• **have your (fair) share of sth** to have a lot or more than enough of something bad: *We've certainly got our share of problems at the moment.* ○ *She's had her fair share of tragedies in her life.*

share /ʃeəʳ/ ⓤ /ʃer/ *verb* **1** [I or T] to have or use something at the same time as someone else: *She's very possessive about her toys and finds it hard to share.* ○ *Bill and I shared an office for years.* ○ *I share a house with four other people.* **2** [I or T] to divide food, money, goods, etc. and give part of it to someone else: *Will you share your sandwich with me?* ○ *Let's share the sweets (out) among/between everyone.* ○ *We should share (in) the reward.* **3** [I or T] If two or more people share an activity, they each do some of it: *Shall we share the driving?* ○ *We shared the preparation for the party between us, so it wasn't too much work.* **4** [I or T] If two or more people or things share a feeling, quality or experience, they both or all have the same feeling, quality or experience: *We share an interest in sailing.* ○ *All hospitals share some common characteristics.* ○ *I don't share your views/beliefs.* ○ *Management and the union both share in the responsibility for the crisis.* ○ *She knew that he was the person she wanted to share her life with.* **5** [T] to tell someone else about your thoughts, feelings, ideas, etc: *He's not very good at sharing his worries.* ○ *It's nice to have someone you can share your problems with.* ○ *Come on, Bob, share the joke (with us).*

• **share and share alike** used to encourage everyone to have an equal amount of something: *Don't keep all those chocolates to yourself – share and share alike.*

• **A problem shared is a problem halved.** *SAYING* used to say that if you tell someone about a problem, it is easier to deal with

shared /ʃeəd/ ⓤ /ʃerd/ *adj* owned, divided, felt or experienced by more than one person: *The company is in shared ownership.* ○ *She and her husband have many shared interests.* ○ *We talked about our shared experiences of India.*

share PART OF A BUSINESS /ʃeəʳ/ ⓤ /ʃer/ *noun* [C] one of the equal parts into which the ownership of a company is divided and which can be bought by members of the public: *The value of my shares has risen/fallen by 8%.* ○ *We've got some shares in British Telecom.* ○ *He invests in stocks and shares.* ○ *share prices*

sharecropper /ˈʃeəˌkrɒp.əʳ/ ⓤ /ˈʃerˌkrɑː.pɚ/ *noun* [C] *MAINLY US* a farmer who rents land and who gives part of his or her crop as rent **sharecropping** /ˈʃeəˌkrɒp.ɪŋ/ ⓤ /ˈʃerˌkrɑː.pɪŋ/ *noun* [U] *US*

shareholder /ˈʃeəˌhəʊl.dəʳ/ ⓤ /ˈʃerˌhoʊl.dɚ/ *noun* [C] (*MAINLY US* **stockholder**) a person who owns some of the equal parts into which the ownership of a company is divided: *Shareholders will be voting on the proposed merger of the companies next week.*

share-out /ˈʃeə.raʊt/ ⓤ /ˈʃer.aʊt/ *noun* [C usually sing] *UK* an act of dividing something between several people: *Everyone benefited from the share-out of the profits.*

shareware /ˈʃeə.weəʳ/ ⓤ /ˈʃer.wer/ *noun* [U] computer programs that you are allowed to use for a short period before you decide whether or not to buy them: *I've found a really good shareware text editor.*

sharia /ʃəˈriː.ə/ *noun* [U] (*ALSO* **shariah**) the holy laws of Islam, which cover all parts of a Muslim's life: *sharia law*

shark FISH /ʃɑːk/ ⓤ /ʃɑːrk/ *noun* [C] *plural* **shark** or **sharks** a large fish that has sharp teeth and a triangular FIN on its back which can sometimes be seen above the water: *a great white shark* ○ *a basking shark* ○ *The movie 'Jaws' is about a man-eating shark.*

shark PERSON /ʃɑːk/ ⓤ /ʃɑːrk/ *noun* [C] *plural* **shark** or **sharks** *INFORMAL DISAPPROVING* a dishonest person, especially one who persuades other people to pay too much money for something: *People who need a place to live can often find themselves at the mercy of local property sharks.*

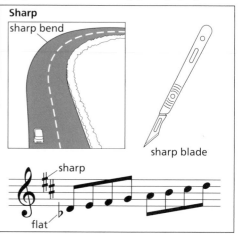

Sharp

sharp bend

sharp blade

sharp

flat

sharp ABLE TO CUT /ʃɑːp/ ⓤ /ʃɑːrp/ *adj* **1** having a thin edge or point which can cut something or make a hole in something: *a knife with a sharp edge/blade.* ○ *sharp teeth/claws/fingernails* ○ *The point of this pencil isn't sharp enough.* **2** producing or describing a quick strong pain that makes you feel like you have been cut: *She nudged me with a sharp elbow, to tell me to be quiet.* ○ *I have this sharp pain in my chest, doctor.* **3** describes a part of someone's face which is very pointed: *a thin face with a sharp nose* **4** If someone is sharp or makes a sharp statement, they speak or act in a severe and angry way, which can hurt other people: *He was rather sharp with me when I asked him to help.* ○ *The government's proposals came in for some sharp criticism.*

• **have a sharp tongue** (*ALSO* **be sharp-tongued**) to be someone who often speaks in a severe and critical way: *Jane has rather a sharp tongue, I'm afraid.*

sharpen /ˈʃɑː.pən/ ⓤ /ˈʃɑːr-/ *verb* [T] to make something sharp or sharper: *My pencil is blunt – I'll have to sharpen it.* ○ *FIGURATIVE The company is cutting production costs in an attempt to sharpen its competitive edge* (= in order to improve how competitive it is). ◑See also **sharpen.**

sharpener /ˈʃɑː.pən.əʳ/ ⓤ /ˈʃɑːr.pən.ɚ/ *noun* [C] a machine or tool for making things such as pencils or knives sharper: *a pencil/knife sharpener*

sharply /ˈʃɑː.pli/ ⓤ /ˈʃɑːr-/ *adv* **1** in a way which will cut or make a hole: *a sharply pointed nail* **2** severely and angrily: *a sharply-worded letter of complaint* ○ *He spoke sharply to his daughter.* ○ *The police have been sharply criticized for their handling of the affair.* **sharpness** /ˈʃɑːp.nəs/ ⓤ /ˈʃɑːrp-/ *noun* [U]

sharp TASTE /ʃɑːp/ ⓤ /ʃɑːrp/ *adj* acidic or sour in taste: *Lemons have a sharp taste.* ○ *This cheese is rather sharp.*

sharp SUDDEN /ʃɑːp/ ⓤ /ʃɑːrp/ *adj* happening suddenly, quickly and strongly: *a sharp drop in temperature* ○ *a sharp decline in the standard of living* ○ *a sharp rise/ increase in the number of cases of this illness* ○ *a sharp bend in the road* ○ *to suffer a sharp blow to the head* **sharp** /ʃɑːp/ ⓤ /ʃɑːrp/ *adv*: *After the church, turn sharp left/right.*

sharpish /ˈʃɑː.pɪʃ/ ⓤ /ˈʃɑːr-/ *adv* UK INFORMAL quickly: *We'd better get out of here pretty sharpish.* **sharply** /ˈʃɑː.pli/ ⓤ /ˈʃɑːr-/ *adv*: *Inflation has risen/fallen sharply.* ○ *His health improved/deteriorated sharply this week.* ○ *The road bends sharply to the left.* **sharpness** /ˈʃɑːp.nəs/ ⓤ /ˈʃɑːrp-/ *noun* [U]

sharp CLEAR /ʃɑːp/ ⓤ /ʃɑːrp/ *adj* clear; easy to see or understand: *This TV gives a very sharp picture.* ○ *The mountains stood in sharp contrast to the blue sky.* ○ *There is a sharp distinction between crimes which involve injury to people and those that don't.* ○ *It was a sharp reminder of how dangerous the world can be.*

sharpen /ˈʃɑː.pən/ ⓤ /ˈʃɑːr-/ *verb* [T] to make something clearer: *How do you sharpen the focus on this camera?* ⭘See also **sharpen**. **sharply** /ˈʃɑː.pli/ ⓤ /ˈʃɑːr-/ *adv*: *a sharply focused photograph* ○ *We have sharply differing views.* **sharpness** /ˈʃɑːp.nəs/ ⓤ /ˈʃɑːrp-/ *noun* [U] *the sharpness of a photograph/image*

sharp CLEVER /ʃɑːp/ ⓤ /ʃɑːrp/ *adj* MAINLY APPROVING clever or quick to notice things: *Bird-watchers need to have sharp ears and eyes.* ○ *She has a sharp eye for a bargain.* ○ *Our new director is very sharp.* ○ *She manages to combine a sharp mind/intellect with a sympathetic manner.* ○ *He was a man of sharp wit/sharp-witted man who always spoke his mind.* ○ *The play was full of sharp one-liners.* **sharpen** /ˈʃɑː.pən/ ⓤ /ˈʃɑːr-/ *verb* [T] *I went to university to sharpen my mind.* ○ *We'll need to sharpen our wits if we're going to defeat Jack's team.* ⭘See also **sharpen**. **sharply** /ˈʃɑː.pli/ ⓤ /ˈʃɑːr-/ *adv*: *Her ears are sharply attuned to her baby's cry.* **sharpness** /ˈʃɑːp.nəs/ ⓤ /ˈʃɑːrp-/ *noun* [U] *She has a remarkable sharpness of mind.*

sharp FASHIONABLE /ʃɑːp/ ⓤ /ʃɑːrp/ *adj* INFORMAL fashionable: *Tony is a very sharp dresser.* ○ *a sharp-suited business executive* **sharply** /ˈʃɑː.pli/ ⓤ /ˈʃɑːr-/ *adv*: *to be sharply dressed* **sharpness** /ˈʃɑːp.nəs/ ⓤ /ˈʃɑːrp-/ *noun* [U]

sharp MUSIC /ʃɑːp/ ⓤ /ʃɑːrp/ *adj, adv* higher than the correct or stated musical note: *The E string on my guitar is a bit sharp.* ○ *This concerto is in the key of C sharp (= the set of musical notes a SEMITONE higher than the one based on the note C).* ○ *to sing sharp* ⭘Compare **flat** MUSIC; **natural** MUSIC.
sharp /ʃɑːp/ ⓤ /ʃɑːrp/ *noun* [C] (a symbol for) a note that is a SEMITONE higher than the stated note **sharpen** /ˈʃɑː.pən/ ⓤ /ˈʃɑːr-/ *verb* [T] *You need to sharpen the A string on your violin.*

sharp EXACTLY /ʃɑːp/ ⓤ /ʃɑːrp/ *adv* exactly at the stated time: *The performance will start at 7.30 sharp.*

sharpen /ˈʃɑː.pən/ ⓤ /ˈʃɑːr-/ *verb* [T] **1** to make something stronger: *Recent changes have sharpened competition between the airlines.* ○ *The prison riots have sharpened the debate about how prisons should be run.* ⭘See also **sharpen** at **sharp** ABLE TO CUT; **sharp** CLEAR; **sharp** CLEVER. **2** to improve: *I hope this course will help me sharpen my computer skills.*
▲ **sharpen (sth) up** *phrasal verb* to perform better, or to improve the performance of something: *If the company doesn't sharpen up soon, it will go out of business.*
● **sharpen up your act** to improve your behaviour or performance: *He really needs to sharpen up his act a bit, or he'll never get to university.*

the ˈsharp ˌend *noun* [S] UK INFORMAL the part of an activity, such as a job, where the most problems are

likely to be found: *A job like hers would be much too demanding for me, but she enjoys being at the sharp end.*

sharp-eyed /ˌʃɑːpˈaɪd/ ⓤ /ˌʃɑːrp-/ *adj* very good at noticing things: *A sharp-eyed secretary noticed the mistake just in time.*

ˌsharp ˈpractice *noun* [U] a way of behaving, in business, that is dishonest but not illegal: *The building industry brought in rules to protect customers from sharp practice.*

sharpshooter /ˈʃɑːpˌʃuː.tə²/ ⓤ /ˈʃɑːrpˌʃuː.t̬ə/ *noun* [C] a person who is skilled at firing a gun and accurately hitting what they are aiming at

shat /ʃæt/ *past simple and past participle of* **shit**

shatter /ˈʃæt.ə²/ ⓤ /ˈʃæt̬.ə/ *verb* **1** [I or T] to (cause something to) break suddenly into very small pieces: *The glass shattered into a thousand tiny pieces.* ○ *His leg was shattered in the accident.* **2** [T] to end or severely damage something: *The book shattered all her illusions about the Romans.* ○ *Noisy motorbikes shattered the peace.*

shattered /ˈʃæt.əd/ ⓤ /ˈʃæt̬.əd/ *adj* **1** broken into very small pieces: *Shattered glass lay all over the road.* **2** extremely upset: *The family were shattered at the news of Annabel's suicide.*

-shattering /-ˌʃæt.ə².rɪŋ/ ⓤ /-ˌʃæt̬.ə-/ *suffix*: *a confidence-shattering defeat* (= one which destroys confidence) ⭘See also **earth-shattering**.

shattered /ˈʃæt.əd/ ⓤ /ˈʃæt̬.əd/ *adj* UK INFORMAL extremely tired: *By the time I got home, I was shattered.*

shattering /ˈʃæt.ə².rɪŋ/ ⓤ /ˈʃæt̬.ə-/ *adj* extremely tiring: *It was a shattering schedule – seven meetings in two days.*

shatterproof /ˈʃæt.ə.pruːf/ ⓤ /ˈʃæt̬.ə-/ *adj* Shatterproof glass or plastic, etc. is made so that it will not break into small pieces: *a shatterproof windscreen*

shave /ʃeɪv/ *verb* [I or T] to remove hair from the body, especially a man's face, by cutting it close to the skin with a RAZOR, so that the skin feels smooth: *John has to shave twice a day.* ○ *I always shave my legs in the bath.* ○ *Do you shave under your arms?* ○ *When my dad shaved his beard (off), he looked ten years younger.*
shave /ʃeɪv/ *noun* [C] the act of shaving, especially a man's face: *I need a shave.* ○ *He washed and had a shave.*

shaven /ˈʃeɪ.vən/ *adj* with the hair removed: *They all had shaven heads.*

shaver /ˈʃeɪ.və²/ ⓤ /-və/ *noun* [C] an electric device for shaving hair from someone's face or body ⭘Compare **razor**.

shaving /ˈʃeɪ.vɪŋ/ *adj* [before n] for using when you shave: *a shaving brush* ○ *shaving cream/foam*

shavings /ˈʃeɪ.vɪŋz/ *plural noun* small, very thin pieces of a hard substance: *The floor was covered in wood shavings.*

▲ **shave sth off/from sth** *phrasal verb* to cut a very thin piece from an object or surface: *She shaved a few millimetres off the bottom of the door, so that it would open more easily.*

▲ **shave sth off sth** *phrasal verb* (ALSO **shave sth by sth**) to reduce something by the stated amount: *The new high speed trains will shave 25 minutes off the journey time.* ○ *Our prices have been shaved by 5%!*

shawl /ʃɔːl/ ⓤ /ʃɑːl/ *noun* [C] a large piece of cloth worn especially by women or girls over their shoulders and/ or head

she STRONG /ʃiː/, WEAK /ʃi/ *pronoun* **1** used to refer to a woman, girl or female animal that has already been mentioned: *I asked my mother if she'd lend me some money, but she said no.* **2** used instead of 'it' to refer to something, especially a country, ship or vehicle, that has already been mentioned: *After India became independent, she chose to be a member of the Commonwealth.* ○ *Look at my new car – isn't she beautiful?*
she /ʃiː/ *noun* [C] a female: *Is this kitten a she or a he?*
she- /ʃiː-/ *prefix*: *a she-wolf* (= a female wolf)

s/he *pronoun* used in writing instead of 'she or he' to refer to a person whose sex is not known: *If any employee needs to take time off, s/he should contact the Personnel Department.* ⭘See also **they**.

sheaf /ʃiːf/ *noun* [C] *plural* **sheaves** a number of things, especially pieces of paper or plant stems,that are held or tied together: *A lawyer walked in carrying a whole sheaf **of** papers.* ○ *The corn was cut and tied in sheaves.*

shear [CUT] /ʃɪəʳ/ [US] /ʃɪr/ *verb* [T] **sheared, sheared** or **shorn 1** to cut the wool off a sheep: *The farmer taught her how to shear sheep.* **2** to cut the hair on a person's head close to the skin, especially without care: *He recalled the humiliation of having his hair shorn and exchanging his clothes for the prison uniform.* **3 be shorn of *sth*** to have something taken away from you: *The ex-President, although shorn of his official powers, still has a lot of influence.* **shearing** /ˈʃɪə.rɪŋ/ [US] /ˈʃɪr.ɪŋ/ *noun* [U] *sheep shearing*

shear [BREAK] /ʃɪəʳ/ [US] /ʃɪr/ *verb* [I] **sheared, sheared** or **shorn** SPECIALIZED If part of something, especially something made of metal, shears, it breaks into two pieces, usually because of a sideways force: *The old screws holding the engine casing had sheared **(off)**.*

shears /ʃɪəz/ [US] /ʃɪrz/ *plural noun* very large scissors: *gardening/dressmaking shears* ○ *They use electric shears for sheep shearing.*

sheath /ʃiːθ/ *noun* [C] **1** a close-fitting protective covering: *The cable has a copper wire surrounded by a plastic sheath.* ○ *The nerves are protected by thin sheaths of fatty tissue.* **2** a cover into which a knife or sword fits so that the blade cannot cut someone when it is not being used: *He drew the knife from its jewelled leather sheath.* **3** UK a **condom**

sheathe /ʃiːð/ *verb* [T] **1** to put a knife back inside its sheath **2** LITERARY to cover something in a thick or protective layer of a substance: *The landscape was sheathed **in** ice.*

sheathing /ˈʃiː.ðɪŋ/ *noun* [C or U] *The frame is covered by a glass and metal sheathing* (= protective cover).

ˈsheath ˌknife *noun* [C] a knife with a fixed blade

sheaves /ʃiːvz/ *plural of* **sheaf**

shebang /ʃɪˈbæŋ/ *noun* MAINLY US INFORMAL **the whole shebang** the whole of something, including everything that is connected with it: *The wedding's next week, but my parents are taking care of the whole shebang.*

shed [BUILDING] /ʃed/ *noun* [C] **1** a small building, usually made of wood, used for storing things: *a garden shed* ○ *a tool/bicycle shed* **2** a large simple building used for a particular activity: *the lambing shed*

shed [GET RID OF] /ʃed/ *verb* [T] **shedding, shed, shed 1** (often used in newspapers) to get rid of something you do not need or want: *900 jobs will be shed over the next few months.* ○ *Psychotherapy helped him to shed some of his insecurity/inhibitions.* ○ *I'm going on a diet to see if I can shed* (= become thinner by losing) *a few kilos.* **2** to lose a covering, such as leaves, hair or skin, because it falls off naturally, or to drop something in a natural or accidental way: *The trees shed their **leaves** in autumn.* ○ *They ran down to the sea, shedding clothes as they went.* ○ UK *A lorry had shed a load of gravel across the road.*

shed [PRODUCE] /ʃed/ *verb* **shed tears/blood/light, etc.** to produce tears, light, blood, etc: *She shed a few tears at her daughter's wedding.* ○ *So much blood has been shed* (= So many people have been badly hurt or killed) *in this war.*

she'd /ʃid/ /ʃiːd/ *short form* **1** she had: *She'd found the answer, at last.* **2** she would: *She'd be a great managing director, don't you think?*

shedload /ˈʃed.ləʊd/ [US] /-loʊd/ *noun* [C] UK INFORMAL a large amount: *The film has recently won **a** shedload **of** awards.* ○ *Shedloads **of** cash are needed to improve the failing health service.*

sheen /ʃiːn/ *noun* [S] APPROVING a bright smooth surface: *The conditioner gives the hair a beautiful soft sheen.*

sheep /ʃiːp/ *noun* [C] *plural* **sheep** a farm animal with thick wool, that eats grass and is kept for its wool, skin and meat: *The farmer has several large **flocks*** (= groups) *of long-haired sheep.* ○ *We heard sheep **bleating/baaing** in the field.* ➲See also **ewe**; **lamb**; **mutton**; **ram** ANIMAL.

• **be (like) sheep** DISAPPROVING If a group of people are (like) sheep, they all behave in the same way or all behave as they are told, and cannot or will not act independently.

• **separate/sort out the sheep from the goats** UK to make clear which people in a particular group are of a higher ability than the others: *The uphill stages of the race will really sort the sheep from the goats.*

ˈsheep ˌdip *noun* [C or U] a liquid in which sheep are washed in order to kill harmful insects living in their wool, or the container in which the liquid is put

sheepdog /ˈʃiːp.dɒg/ [US] /-dɑːg/ *noun* [C] a dog trained to help people control sheep and move them in the desired direction: *Two sheepdogs herded the sheep into pens.*

sheepish /ˈʃiː.pɪʃ/ *adj* embarrassed because you know that you have done something wrong or silly: *She gave me a sheepish smile and apologized.* **sheepishly** /ˈʃiː.pɪʃ.li/ *adv* **sheepishness** /ˈʃiː.pɪʃ.nəs/ *noun* [U]

sheepskin /ˈʃiːp.skɪn/ *noun* [C or U] the skin of a sheep with the wool still attached to it: *We've got a rug made from (a) sheepskin.* ○ *a sheepskin coat*

sheer [COMPLETE] /ʃɪəʳ/ [US] /ʃɪr/ *adj* [before n] used to emphasize how very great, important or powerful a quality or feeling is; nothing except: *The suggestion is sheer **nonsense**.* ○ *His success was due to sheer willpower/determination.* ○ *It was just sheer coincidence that we met.*

sheer [STEEP] /ʃɪəʳ/ [US] /ʃɪr/ *adj* extremely steep; almost vertical: *a sheer mountain side* ○ *a sheer drop of 100 metres* **sheer** /ʃɪəʳ/ [US] /ʃɪr/ *adv*

sheer [THIN] /ʃɪəʳ/ [US] /ʃɪr/ *adj* describes clothing or material which is so thin, light and delicate that you can see through it: *sheer nylon tights* ○ *She wore a dress of the sheerest silk.*

sheer [TURN] /ʃɪəʳ/ [US] /ʃɪr/ *verb* [I usually + adv or prep] to change direction suddenly: *I thought the boats were going to collide, but one sheered **off/away** at the last second.*

sheet /ʃiːt/ *noun* [C] **1** a large thin flat especially rectangular piece of something, especially a piece of cloth used for sleeping on: *I've put clean sheets on the bed.* ○ *a sheet **of** glass* ○ *They fixed a **polythene/plastic** sheet over the broken window.* **2** a piece of paper: *some sheets **of** wrapping paper* ○ *The application form was a single sheet **of paper**.* **3** a piece of paper with something printed on it: *The tourist office provides a weekly information sheet about things that are happening in the town.* **4 sheet of *sth*** a large wide mass of something such as fire or ice: *A sheet of **flame** shot up into the air immediately after the explosion.* ○ *A thick sheet of **ice** had formed over the water.*

sheets /ʃiːts/ *plural noun* a large quantity of rain or HAIL: *The rain was coming down **in** sheets.*

sheet /ʃiːt/ *verb* INFORMAL **be sheeting** to rain very hard: *We can't go out yet, it's sheeting **down** outside.* ○ *The rain was sheeting **against** the windows.*

sheeting /ˈʃiː.tɪŋ/ [US] /-t̬ɪŋ/ *noun* [U] thin material, especially cloth, plastic or metal

ˌsheet ˈlightning *noun* [U] lightning that lights up a large part of the sky

ˈsheet ˌmusic *noun* [U] music in its printed or written form, especially single sheets of paper not formed into a book

sheikh, sheik /ʃeɪk/ /ʃiːk/ *noun* [C] an Arab ruler or head of a tribe

sheikhdom /ˈʃeɪk.dəm/ /ˈʃiːk-/ *noun* [C] an area of land or a country ruled by a sheikh

sheila /ˈʃiː.lə/ *noun* [C] AUS SLANG a girl or a woman
✻ NOTE: Some people consider this offensive.

shekel /ˈʃek.əl/ *noun* [C] the standard unit of money used in Israel

shekels /ˈʃek.əlz/ *plural noun* SLANG HUMOROUS money

shelf /ʃelf/ *noun* [C] *plural* **shelves 1** a long flat board fixed horizontally, usually against a wall or inside a cupboard so that objects can be stored on it: *a glass shelf* ○ ***on** the top/bottom shelf* ○ *One wall had shelves from floor to ceiling, crammed with books.* ➲See also **bookshelf**. **2** SPECIALIZED a flat area of rock under water or on a cliff

• **off the shelf** If a product can be bought off the shelf, it does not need to be specially made or requested: *It's*

S

*often cheaper if you **buy** wallpaper off the shelf, rather than having to order it.* ○ *off-the-shelf goods/clothes*

• **on the shelf 1** not noticed or not used: *It's important to apply research in a practical way and not **leave** it on the shelf.* **2** *MAINLY UK INFORMAL* describes someone, usually a woman, who is not married and is considered too old for anyone to want to marry them: *In those days, if you hadn't married by the time you were 30, you were definitely on the shelf.*

• **remove *sth* from *your* shelves** When a shop removes something from its shelves, that product stops being available for sale there.

shelve /ʃelv/ *verb* [T] to put something onto shelves, or to fix shelves somewhere ➲See also **shelve** DELAY; **shelve** SLOPE.

shelving /ˈʃel.vɪŋ/ *noun* [U] shelves: *The carpenter put up some shelving in the living room.*

ˈshelf ˌlife *noun* [C usually sing] *plural* **shelf lives** the length of time that a product, especially food, can be kept in a shop before it becomes too old to be sold or used: *Fresh fruit has a very short shelf life.*

shell [COVERING] /ʃel/ *noun* **1** [C or U] the hard outer covering of something, especially nuts, eggs and some animals: *Brazil nuts have very hard shells.* ○ *A piece of shell fell into the cake mixture.* ○ *the shell of a snail/crab/tortoise* ○ *a shell necklace* (= a piece of jewellery made out of the shells of small sea animals) ➲See also **eggshell**; **nutshell**; **seashell**; **shellfish**. **2** [C] the basic outer structure of a building or vehicle, especially when the inner parts have been destroyed or taken or have not yet been made: *the shell **of** a burnt-out farmhouse*

• **come out of *your* shell** (*ALSO* **bring *sb* out of *their* shell**) If you come out of your shell, you become more interested in other people and more willing to talk and take part in social activities, and if someone brings you out of your shell, they cause you to do this: *Derek has really come out of his shell since he started working here.*

• **crawl/go/retreat/retire into *your* shell** to become less interested in other people and less willing to talk and take part in social activities: *The more they tried to get her to talk about her experiences, the further she retreated **back** into her shell.*

shell /ʃel/ *verb* [T] to remove peas, nuts, etc. from their shells or their natural protective covering

shell [EXPLOSIVE] /ʃel/ *noun* [C] a container, usually with a pointed end, which is filled with explosives and fired from a large gun: ***Artillery** and **mortar** shells were landing in the outskirts of the city.*

shell /ʃel/ *verb* [T] to fire shells at something: *They were under orders to shell the hospital and the town hall.*

shelling /ˈʃel.ɪŋ/ *noun* [U] *Shelling of enemy lines continued all day.*

▲ **shell *(sth)* out** *phrasal verb* [M] *INFORMAL* to pay or give money for something, usually unwillingly: *Having shelled out fifty pounds **for** the tickets, I wasn't going to miss the show.*

she'll /ʃɪl/ /ʃiːl/ *short form* she will: *She'll be here later.*

shellfish /ˈʃel.fɪʃ/ *noun* [C or U] *plural* **shellfish** sea creatures that live in shells and are eaten as food, or one of these creatures: *Lobsters, crabs, prawns and oysters are all shellfish.*

ˈshell ˌshock *noun* [U] mental illness caused by experiences of war: *He said many of the men who were shot for cowardice were in fact suffering from shell shock.*

shell-shocked /ˈʃel.ʃɒkt/ [US] /ʃɑːkt/ *adj* **1** suffering from shell shock: *I was treating shell-shocked soldiers.* **2** extremely tired and nervous or frightened, especially after an unpleasant and unexpected event, or extremely surprised: *After the crash, the passengers were shell-shocked but there were no serious injuries.* ○ *They were shell-shocked by the news.*

ˈshell ˌsuit *noun* [C] *UK* an informal loose top and trousers made of thin, light, smooth material with elastic at the wrist and ankle

shelter /ˈʃel.təʳ/ [US] /-t̬ɚ/ *noun* [C or U] (a building designed to give) protection from bad weather, danger or attack: *an air-raid shelter* ○ *They opened a shelter to provide temporary housing for the city's homeless.* ○ *The trees **gave/provided** some shelter **from** the rain.*

• **find/take shelter** to protect yourself from bad weather, danger or attack: *We took shelter for the night **in** an abandoned house.*

shelter /ˈʃel.təʳ/ [US] /-t̬ɚ/ *verb* **1** [I or T] to protect yourself, or another person or thing, from bad weather, danger or attack: *We were caught in a thunderstorm, without anywhere to shelter.* ○ *A group of us were sheltering **from** the rain under the trees.* **2** [T] to give someone a secret hiding place so that they will not be caught by the army, police, etc: *Local people risked their own lives to shelter resistance fighters **from** the army.*

sheltered /ˈʃel.təd/ [US] /-t̬ɚd/ *adj* protected from wind, rain or other bad weather: *We found a sheltered **spot*** (= place) *to have our picnic.*

• **have/lead a sheltered life** *DISAPPROVING* to have a life in which you are protected too much and experience very little danger, excitement or variety: *Until going to university, she had led a very sheltered life.*

ˌsheltered accommoˈdation *noun* [U] (*ALSO* **sheltered housing**) houses for old and ill people in a place where help can be given if it is needed: *She's just moved into sheltered accommodation.*

shelve [DELAY] /ʃelv/ *verb* [T] to not take action on something until a later time: *I've had to shelve my **plans** to buy a new car, because I can't afford it at the moment.*

shelve [SLOPE] /ʃelv/ *verb* [I] *SPECIALIZED* When a surface such as the bottom of the sea shelves, it slopes down gradually: *The sea bed shelves gently for several hundred metres.* ➲See also **shelf**.

shelves /ʃelvz/ *plural of* **shelf**

shenanigans /ʃɪˈnæn.ɪ.gənz/ *plural noun INFORMAL DISAPPROVING* secret or dishonest activities, usually of a complicated and amusing or interesting type: *More business/political shenanigans were exposed in the newspapers today.*

shepherd [JOB] /ˈʃep.əd/ [US] /-ɚd/ *noun* [C] a person whose job is to take care of sheep and move them from one place to another: *a shepherd boy*

shepherdess /ˈʃep.ə.des/ /ˌ--ˈ-/ [US] /-ɚ-/ *noun* [C] a female shepherd

shepherd /ˈʃep.əd/ [US] /-ɚd/ *verb* [T usually + adv or prep] *The dogs shepherded the sheep* (= made them move) *into the pens.*

shepherd [MOVE] /ˈʃep.əd/ [US] /-ɚd/ *verb* [T usually + adv or prep] to make a group of people move to where you want them to go, especially in a kind, helpful and careful way: *He shepherded the old people towards the dining room.*

shepherd's pie /ˌʃep.ədzˈpaɪ/ [US] /-ɚdz-/ *noun* [C or U] a dish consisting of a layer of small pieces of meat covered with a thick layer of MASHED POTATO

sherbet /ˈʃɜː.bət/ [US] /ˈʃɝː-/ *noun* [U] **1** *UK* an artificial fruit-flavoured powder eaten as a sweet or used to make a drink, especially for children **2** *US* **sorbet**

sheriff /ˈʃer.ɪf/ *noun* [C] **1** in the US, an official whose job is to be in charge of performing the orders of the law courts and making certain that the laws are obeyed within a particular county **2** in England and Wales, a person who represents the king or queen in a particular county, and who has mainly ceremonial duties **3** the most important judge of a county in Scotland

S

Sherpa /ˈʃɜː.pə/ [US] /ˈʃɝː-/ *noun* [C] a member of a Himalayan people who are skilled mountain climbers and who are often employed as guides by visiting climbers

sherry /ˈʃer.i/ *noun* [C or U] a type of strong wine, usually drunk before a meal, varying from a pale yellow to a brown colour: ***sweet/dry** sherry* ○ *Would you like a glass of sherry/some sherry?* ○ *Would you like a sherry* (= a glass of sherry)*?*

she's *STRONG* /ʃiːz/, *WEAK* /ʃiz/ *short form* **1** she is: *She's a writer.* **2** she has: *She's got the most elegant writing style.*

Shetland pony /ˌʃet.ləndˈpəʊ.ni/ [US] /-ˈpoʊ-/ *noun* [C] a very small rough-haired horse

Shia /ˈʃiː.ə/ *noun* [C] (*ALSO* **Shiite**) a member of the second largest religious movement within Islam, which is based on the belief that Ali, a member of Mohammed's family, and the teachers who came after him, were the true religious leaders

shiatsu /ʃi'æt.su/ [US] /-'ɑːt-/ *noun* [U] a treatment for pain or illness, originally from ancient Japan, in which particular places on the body are pressed

shibboleth /'ʃɪb.ᵊl.eθ/ *noun* [C] **1** FORMAL a belief or custom that is not now considered as important and correct as it was in the past: *They still cling to many of the old shibboleths **of** education.* **2** a word, phrase, custom, etc. only known to a particular group of people, which you can use to prove to them that you are a real member of that group

shield /ʃiːld/ *noun* [C] **1** in the past, a large flat object made of metal or leather that soldiers held in front of their bodies to protect themselves: **2** a large flat object made of strong plastic that policemen hold in front of their bodies to protect themselves: *The police held up their **riot** shields against the flying rocks and bricks.* **3** something or someone used as protection or providing protection: *The anti-personnel mines were laid as a **protective** shield around the town.* ○ *Anger can function as a shield **against*** (= a way of avoiding) *even more painful emotions of loss and hurt.* **4** a flat object with two straight sides, a rounded or pointed lower edge and usually a straight top edge, on which there is a COAT OF ARMS **5** an object shaped like a shield, which is given as a prize or used as a symbol or BADGE: *Our school won the county football shield this year.*

shield /ʃiːld/ *verb* [T] to protect someone or something: *She held her hand above her eyes to shield them **from** the sun.* ○ *They are accused of trying to shield the General **from** US federal investigators.*

shift [MOVE OR CHANGE] /ʃɪft/ *verb* **1** [I or T] to (cause something or someone to) move or change from one position or direction to another, especially slightly: *She shifted (her weight) uneasily **from** one foot **to** the other.* ○ *The wind is expected to shift (**to** the east) tomorrow.* ○ *Media attention has shifted recently **onto** environmental issues.* **2** [T] MAINLY US to move the gears of a vehicle into different positions in order to make it go faster or slower: *In cars that are automatics, you don't have to bother with shifting **gears**.*

• **shift *yourself*** If you shift yourself when you have a job to do, you hurry to do the job as quickly as possible: *Come on, there's work to be done – shift yourself.*

• **shift *(your)* ground** to change your opinion: *He's annoying to argue with because he keeps shifting his ground.*

shift /ʃɪft/ *noun* [C] a change in position or direction: *a shift **in** the wind/temperature* ○ *The shift **in** the balance of power in the region has had far-reaching consequences.* ○ *There has been a **dramatic** shift **in** public opinion **towards** peaceful negotiations.*

shifting /'ʃɪf.tɪŋ/ *adj* always changing or moving: *They lost their way in the shifting sands of the Sahara.*

shift [GET RID OF] /ʃɪft/ *verb* [T] UK INFORMAL to get rid of something unwanted, or to sell something: *Modern detergents will shift most stains.* ○ *The people at the toy shop expect to shift a lot of stock in the run-up to Christmas.*

▲ **shift for *yourself*** *phrasal verb* [R] OLD-FASHIONED to earn your own income or buy and cook your own food, etc: *He left home at 18 and had to shift for himself.*

shift [GROUP] /ʃɪft/ *group noun* [C] a group of workers who do a job for a period of time during the day or night, or the period of time itself: *As the **night** shift leave/leaves, the **day** shift arrive/arrives.* ○ *Are you on the **night** shift or the **day** shift* (= Do you work during the night period or the day period)*?*

shiftwork /'ʃɪft.wɜːk/ [US] /-wɝːk/ *noun* [U] when different groups of workers work somewhere at different times of the day and night: *The factory is run on shiftwork.* ○ *I hate shiftwork.*

shift [DRESS] /ʃɪft/ *noun* [C] a simple dress that hangs straight from the shoulders

'shift ˌkey *noun* [C] SPECIALIZED a key on a computer or a typewriter which you press at the same time as you press a letter key in order to produce a capital letter

shiftless /'ʃɪft.ləs/ *adj* DISAPPROVING lazy and lacking determination or a firm purpose: *He called the young people shiftless, lazy and good-for-nothing.*

shifty /'ʃɪf.ti/ *adj* looking or seeming dishonest: *He's got shifty eyes.* ○ *You're **looking** very shifty. What have you been up to?* ○ *There's a couple of shifty-**looking** people standing on the street corner.* **shiftily** /'ʃɪf.tɪ.li/ *adv* **shiftiness** /'ʃɪf.tɪ.nəs/ *noun* [U]

Shiite, Shi'ite /'ʃiː.aɪt/ *noun* [C] a **Shia**

shilling /'ʃɪl.ɪŋ/ *noun* [C] **1** a unit of money used in Britain until 1971, equal to 12 old pence or 5 new pence **2** the standard unit of money used in Kenya, Somalia, Tanzania and Uganda

shilly-shally /'ʃɪl.iˌʃæl.i/ /ˌ--'--/ *verb* [I] INFORMAL DISAPPROVING to spend too much time doing something or making a decision because you do not know what is the right thing to do: *Stop shilly-shallying and make a decision now!*

shimmer /'ʃɪm.əʳ/ [US] /-ɚ/ *verb* [I] to shine in such a way that the light seems to shake slightly and quickly: *She could see her reflection in the water, shimmering in the moonlight.*

shimmering /'ʃɪm.ᵊr.ɪŋ/ [US] /-ɚ-/ *adj* **1** shining unevenly, or seeming to move slightly: *We drove across the desert, through the shimmering heat haze.* **2** LITERARY attractive: *a shimmering new production of 'A Midsummer Night's Dream'*

shimmer /'ʃɪm.əʳ/ [US] /-ɚ/ *noun* [S] when something shimmers

shimmy /'ʃɪm.i/ *verb* [I] to do a dance in which you shake your hips and shoulders: *She shimmied across the dance floor.*

shin [BODY PART] /ʃɪn/ *noun* **1** [C] the front part of your leg between your knee and your foot: *She's got a nasty bruise on her shin.* ➲See picture **The Body** on page Centre 5 **2** [C or U] a joint of meat from the lower leg of a cow: *a shin of beef*

shin [CLIMB] (-nn-) /ʃɪn/ *verb* [I usually + adv or prep] (US ALSO **shinny**) to climb something such as a tree, using your hands and legs to move along quickly: *Several of us shinned **up** lampposts so that we could see over the crowd.*

shinbone /'ʃɪn.bəʊn/ [US] /-boʊn/ *noun* [C] (SPECIALIZED **tibia**) the bone at the front of your leg, between the knee and the foot ➲See picture **The Body** on page Centre 5

shindig /'ʃɪn.dɪg/ *noun* [C] **1** INFORMAL a noisy event or situation, especially a large, energetic party, celebration, etc: *Are you going to that shindig at the Town Hall tonight?* **2** MAINLY UK a noisy argument

shine /ʃaɪn/ *verb* **shone** or **shined**, **shone** or **shined** **1** [I] to send out or reflect light: *Is that light shining **in** your eyes?* ○ *The **sun** shone all afternoon.* ○ *He polished the brass till it shone.* **2 shine with *sth*** If a person's eyes or face shine with a quality, you can see that quality in them very strongly: *Her eyes shone with delight.* **3** [I or T] to point a light in a particular direction: *The policeman walked along the street, shining a torch into every car.* **4** [T] to make something bright by rubbing it: *Guy ironed his shirt and shined his **shoes** for the interview.* **5** [I] to be extremely good at an activity or skill, in an obvious way: *She's hopeless at languages, but she shines **at/in** science.*

shine /ʃaɪn/ *noun* [S or U] when something is bright from reflected light on its surface: *hair with body and shine* ○ *Wax polish gives a lovely shine to wood furniture.*

• **take a shine to *sb*** INFORMAL to like someone immediately: *I think he's taken a bit of a shine to you.*

shiner /'ʃaɪ.nəʳ/ [US] /-nɚ/ *noun* [C] INFORMAL a BLACK EYE (= an eye where the skin around it has gone dark because it has been hit): *I think you're going to have a real shiner there in the morning.* **shininess** /'ʃaɪ.nɪ.nəs/ *noun* [U]

shining /'ʃaɪ.nɪŋ/ *adj*: *a shining silver cup* ○ *She looked at him with shining* (= bright and happy) *eyes.* ○ *These pictures are shining* (= excellent) ***examples** of great photography.*

shiny /'ʃaɪ.ni/ *adj* A shiny surface is bright because it reflects light: *beautiful shiny hair* ○ *shiny black shoes* ○ *a shiny silver dollar*

▲ **shine out** *phrasal verb* **1** If people or things shine out, they are noticeable because they are very good: *The play has a very strong cast, but two actors in particular shine out.* **2** If a quality shines out of someone, it is strong and easy to see: *Her honesty and sincerity positively shine out.*

S

shingle STONES /ˈʃɪŋ.gl̩/ *noun* [U] small round stones that cover a beach or the ground by the edge of a river: *a shingle beach* ○ *I love the noise of the waves on the shingle.*

shingle PIECE /ˈʃɪŋ.gl̩/ *noun* [C] a thin flat TILE usually made of wood, that is fixed in rows to make a roof or wall covering

shingles /ˈʃɪŋ.gl̩z/ *noun* [U] a disease caused by a virus that infects particular nerves and that produces a line or lines of painful red spots, especially around the waist

shinny /ˈʃɪn.i/ *verb* [I] *US FOR* **shin** CLIMB.

Shinto /ˈʃɪn.təʊ/ ⑥ /-toʊ/ *noun* [U] (*ALSO* **Shintoism**) a Japanese religion in which people worship past members of their family and various gods that represent nature

ship BOAT /ʃɪp/ *noun* [C] a large boat for travelling on water, especially across the sea: *a sailing ship* ○ *a merchant/naval ship* ○ *They* **boarded** (= went on to) *a ship that was* **sailing** (= leaving) *the next day.* ➒See picture **Planes, Ships and Boats** on page Centre 14

ship /ʃɪp/ *verb* [T usually + adv or prep] -pp- to send something, usually a large object or a large quantity of objects or people, to a distant place: *We ship books* **out** *to New York every month.*

shipper /ˈʃɪp.əʳ/ ⑥ /-ɚ/ *noun* [C usually pl] a person or company whose job is to organize the sending of goods from one place to another: *wine shippers*

shipping /ˈʃɪp.ɪŋ/ *noun* [U] **1** ships considered as a group: *This stretch of water is heavily used by shipping.* **2** when goods are sent from one place to another, especially by ship: *The cost is $205 plus $3 for shipping.* ○ *The fruit is picked and artificially ripened before shipping.*

▲ **ship** *sb* **off** *phrasal verb* [M] *INFORMAL* to send someone away somewhere: *The children were shipped off to their grandparents' house for the holidays.*

-ship RANK /-ʃɪp/ *suffix* having the rank, position, skill or relationship of the stated type: *lordship* ○ *partnership* ○ *craftsmanship* ○ *friendship*

shipboard /ˈʃɪp.bɔːd/ ⑥ /-bɔːrd/ *adj* happening or used on a ship: *a shipboard romance* ○ *a shipboard transmitter*

shipbuilder /ˈʃɪp.bɪl.dəʳ/ ⑥ /-dɚ/ *noun* [C] a person or company that builds ships **shipbuilding** /ˈʃɪp.bɪl.dɪŋ/ *noun* [U] *industries such as shipbuilding, steel production and coalmining*

shipmate /ˈʃɪp.meɪt/ *noun* [C] A sailor's shipmate is another sailor who works on the same ship as they do.

shipment /ˈʃɪp.mənt/ *noun* [C or U] a large amount of goods sent together to a place, or the act of sending them: *A shipment* **of** *urgent medical supplies is expected to arrive very soon.*

shipping and **handling** *noun* [U] *US FOR* **postage and packing**

shipshape /ˈʃɪp.ʃeɪp/ *adj* *INFORMAL* tidy and with everything in its correct place: *The builders have gone, but it'll take a while to* **get** *things shipshape again.*

shipwreck /ˈʃɪp.rek/ *noun* [C or U] (*ALSO* **wreck**) an accident in which a ship is destroyed or sunk at sea, especially by hitting rocks, or a ship which has been destroyed or sunk in such an accident: *The danger of shipwreck is greater in fog.* ○ *There are many shipwrecks along this dangerous stretch of coast.* **shipwreck** /ˈʃɪp.rek/ *verb* [T usually passive] *They were shipwrecked* **off** *Scotland.* ○ *a shipwrecked sailor*

shipyard /ˈʃɪp.jɑːd/ ⑥ /-jɑːrd/ *noun* [C] a place where ships are built or repaired

shire /ʃaɪəʳ/ ⑥ /ʃaɪr/ *noun* [C] *UK OLD USE* a county, now used in combination in the names of many British counties: *Yorkshire* ○ *Oxfordshire*

the shires *plural noun* *UK* the central RURAL counties of England, such as Leicestershire, Nottinghamshire and Derbyshire

shire **horse** *noun* [C] a large strong English horse which has long hair covering its feet

shirk /ʃɜːk/ ⑥ /ʃɜːk/ *verb* [I or T] *DISAPPROVING* to avoid work, duties or responsibilities, especially if they are difficult or unpleasant: *If you shirk your* **responsibilities/duties** *now, the situation will just be*

that much harder to deal with next month. ○ *I shall not shirk* **from** *my obligations.*

shirker /ˈʃɜː.kəʳ/ ⑥ /ˈʃɜː.kɚ/ *noun* [C] someone who avoids something, especially work: *We have no room for shirkers in this office.*

shirt /ʃɜːt/ ⑥ /ʃɜːt/ *noun* [C] a piece of clothing worn, especially by men, on the upper part of the body, made of light cloth like cotton and usually having a collar and buttons at the front: *a striped/white shirt* ○ *a short-/long-sleeved shirt* ○ *You've spilled something down your shirt front.* ➒See also **nightshirt**; **sweatshirt**; **T-shirt**. ➒See picture **Clothes** on page Centre 6

● **keep** *your* **shirt on** (*UK ALSO* **keep** *your* **hair on**) *INFORMAL* said to tell someone to stop being so angry or upset: *Keep your shirt on! Your car isn't badly damaged!*

● **put** *your* **shirt on** *sth* *UK INFORMAL* to feel very certain that something will happen: *I'd put my shirt on the President being re-elected.*

● **the shirt off** *sb's* **back** *INFORMAL* the last thing that someone has left: *He's the kind of man who'd* **give** *you the shirt off his back.*

shirt-sleeve /ˈʃɜːt.sliːv/ ⑥ /ˈʃɜːt-/ *noun* [C] a sleeve of a shirt: *Susannah felt a hand tugging at her shirt-sleeve.* ○ *Jamie rolled up his shirt-sleeves and set to work.*

● **in shirt-sleeves** dressed informally without wearing anything, such as a jacket, over a shirt: *Because it was so hot, the men were all in their shirt-sleeves.*

shirt **tails** *plural noun* the part at the back of a shirt which comes down below the waist of the person wearing it: *He tucked his shirt tails into his trousers.*

shirty /ˈʃɜː.ti/ ⑥ /ˈʃɜː.ti/ *adj* *UK INFORMAL* annoyed or angry, especially in a rude way: *Don't get shirty* **with** *me - this is your fault, not mine.*

shish ke **bab** *noun* [C] a **kebab**

shit /ʃɪt/ *noun* **1** [U] *OFFENSIVE* the solid waste which is released from the bowels of a person or animal; excrement: *There's so much dog shit on the pavement.* ➒See also **bullshit**; **shite**. **2** [S] *OFFENSIVE* the act of releasing solid waste from the bowels: *I need to have/*(*US*) *take a shit.* **3** [C or U] *OFFENSIVE* someone or something you do not like, especially because they are unpleasant or of low quality: *She talks a* **load** *of shit.* ○ *The man's a complete shit.* **4** *OFFENSIVE* insults, criticism or unkind or unfair treatment: *Ben gets a lot of shit* **from** *his parents about the way he dresses.* ○ *Jackie doesn't* **take** (*any*) *shit* **from** *anyone* (= does not allow anyone to treat her badly). **5** *US OFFENSIVE* used in negatives to mean 'anything': *He doesn't know shit about what's going on.*

● **not give a shit** *OFFENSIVE* to not be interested in or worried about something or someone: *I don't give a shit what Nigel thinks.*

● **have/get** *your* **shit together** *MAINLY US OFFENSIVE* to be or become effective, organized and skilful: *One of these days I'll get my shit together.*

● **No shit!** *OFFENSIVE* an expression of surprise about information you have just heard: *"Richard's got the job in New York!" "No shit!"*

● **(the) shit hits the fan** (*ALSO* **the shit flies**) *OFFENSIVE* When the shit hits the fan or when the shit flies, a situation suddenly causes a lot of trouble for someone: *I don't want to be here when the shit hits the fan.*

● **the shit out of** *sb/sth* *OFFENSIVE* used to emphasize the degree of force of an action which you are describing: *His dad would* **beat/knock/kick** *the shit out of him if he disobeyed.* ○ *Don't creep up on me like that – you* **scared** *the shit out of me.*

shit /ʃɪt/ *verb* [I] **shitting**, **shit** or **shat** or **shitted**, **shit** or **shat** or **shitted** *OFFENSIVE* to excrete solid waste from the bowels: *That dog had better not shit in the house again!* ○ *MAINLY US I need to shit real bad.*

shit *yourself* *verb* [R] *OFFENSIVE* to be extremely frightened: *She was shitting herself, especially when he pulled out a gun.*

Shit! /ʃɪt/ *exclamation* *OFFENSIVE* used to express annoyance, anger, disgust or surprise: *Oh shit, we're going to be late!* ○ *Shit – the damn thing's broken!*

shitload /ˈʃɪt.ləʊd/ ⑥ /-loʊd/ *noun* *OFFENSIVE* **a shitload of** *sth* a lot of something: *He earns a shitload of money.*

the shits *plural noun* *OFFENSIVE* DIARRHOEA (= a medical condition in which the contents of the bowels are

S

excreted too often): *Something I ate has given me the shits.*

shitty /ˈʃɪt.i/ [US] /ˈʃɪt̬.i/ *adj OFFENSIVE* **1** unfair and unkind: *She's had really shitty treatment from the management.* **2** bad, difficult or unpleasant: *Jamie's had a shitty week at work.* ○ *Anna, if you're feeling shitty* (= ill), *just go home.*

▲ **shit on** ***sb*** *phrasal verb OFFENSIVE* to treat someone very badly and unkindly: *He was whinging that the boss had shat on him by not giving him a day off.*

shite /ʃaɪt/ *noun* **[C or U]** *UK OFFENSIVE* **shit**

shit-faced /ˈʃɪt.feɪst/ *adj OFFENSIVE* extremely drunk

shithead /ˈʃɪt.hed/ *noun* **[C]** *OFFENSIVE* a stupid, unpleasant and unpopular person: *That little shithead has screwed things up again.*

ˌshit ˈhot *adj UK OFFENSIVE* extremely good

ˈshit ˌstirrer *noun* **[C]** *OFFENSIVE* someone who makes trouble for other people, especially by making known facts that they would prefer to keep secret: *He didn't need to tell her that – he's just a shit-stirrer.*

shiver /ˈʃɪv.əʳ/ [US] /-ɚ/ *verb* **[I]** When people or animals shiver, they shake slightly because they feel cold, ill or frightened: *The poor dog – it's shivering!* ○ *He shivered* ***with*** *cold in his thin cotton shirt.* **shiver** /ˈʃɪv.əʳ/ [US] /-ɚ/ *noun* **[C]** *I felt/gave a shiver as I looked out at the dark expanse of sea.*

• **shiver (up and) down** ***your*** **spine** *INFORMAL* a frightened or excited feeling: *At its most terrifying, his writing* ***sends*** *shivers up and down my spine.* ○ *Whenever I hear that music, I feel a shiver down my spine.*

the shivers *plural noun* **1** when you shiver because you are ill: *She's aching and she's* ***got*** *the shivers, so I've sent her to bed.* **2** *INFORMAL* when you feel frightened of someone or something: *I don't like him – he* ***gives*** *me the shivers.*

shivery /ˈʃɪv.ᵊr.i/ [US] /-ɚ-/ *adj INFORMAL* shaking slightly because you feel cold, frightened or ill: *She's very hot and shivery, so I think she must have flu.*

shoal [FISH] /ʃəʊl/ [US] /ʃoʊl/ *group noun* **[C]** **1** a large number of fish swimming as a group: *We could see shoals of tiny fish darting about.* ○ *Piranhas often feed* ***in*** *shoals.* **2** *INFORMAL* a large number of things or people: *In the summer, tourists visit the city* ***in*** *shoals.*

shoal [RAISED AREA] /ʃəʊl/ [US] /ʃoʊl/ *noun* **[C]** *SPECIALIZED* a raised bank of sand or rocks under the surface of the water

shock [SURPRISE] /ʃɒk/ [US] /ʃɑːk/ *noun* **1** **[C or U]** (the emotional or physical reaction to) a sudden, unexpected and usually unpleasant event or experience: *Her mother's death* ***came as*** *a great shock – it was so unexpected.* ○ *It was such a loud crash – it* ***gave*** *me/I* ***got*** *quite a shock.* ○ ***It*** *was a shock* ***to*** *see her looking so ill.* ○ *I was* ***in (a state of)*** *shock for about two weeks after the accident.* ○ *UK The French suffered a shock* ***defeat*** (= completely unexpected defeat) *by the Italian side at the weekend.* **2** **[C]** an **electric shock**: *Ow! – I* ***got*** *a shock from that lamp!* **3** **[U]** a medical condition caused by severe injury, pain, loss of blood or fear which slows down the flow of blood around the body: *Several passengers from the wrecked vehicle were taken to hospital* ***suffering from*** *shock.*

• **a shock to the system** when something new or unusual feels difficult or unpleasant: *It's really hard getting back to work after three months off – it's quite a shock to the system.*

shock /ʃɒk/ [US] /ʃɑːk/ *verb* **[I or T]** to make someone feel upset or surprised: *The photographs of starving children shocked people* ***into*** *giving money.* ○ *The news of the accident shocked the family* ***deeply***. **shocked** /ʃɒkt/ [US] /ʃɑːkt/ *adj*: *After his announcement, there was a shocked silence.* ○ **[+ to infinitive]** *We were shocked* ***to*** *see smoke pouring out of the roof.*

shocking /ˈʃɒk.ɪŋ/ [US] /ˈʃɑː.kɪŋ/ *adj* extremely surprising: *The news came as a shocking blow.* ➲See also **shocking**; **shocking** at **shock** OFFEND. **shockingly** /ˈʃɒk.ɪŋ.li/ [US] /ˈʃɑː.kɪŋ-/ *adv*: *The restaurant charges shockingly high prices for its food.*

shock [OFFEND] /ʃɒk/ [US] /ʃɑːk/ *verb* **[I or T]** to offend or upset someone by doing or saying something which they consider is immoral or unacceptable: *The advertisements were designed to shock – that was the whole point of the campaign.* ○ **[+ obj + to infinitive]** *I think it shocks him* ***to*** *hear women talking about sex.* **shock** /ʃɒk/ [US] /ʃɑːk/ *noun* **[U]** *You should have seen the look of shock on her face when he started swearing!*

shockable /ˈʃɒk.ə.bl̩/ [US] /ˈʃɑː.kə-/ *adj*: *I have to be careful what I say to my mother – she's very shockable* (= easily offended).

shocker /ˈʃɒk.əʳ/ [US] /ˈʃɑː.kɚ/ *noun* **[C]** *INFORMAL* something that is likely to offend, especially something new or recently announced

shocking /ˈʃɒk.ɪŋ/ [US] /ˈʃɑː.kɪŋ/ *adj* offensive, upsetting or immoral: *The sex scenes in the book were considered very shocking at the time when it was published.* ○ *There are few crimes more truly shocking than the murder or abuse of children.* ➲See also **shocking**; **shocking** at **shock** SURPRISE. **shockingly** /ˈʃɒk.ɪŋ.li/ [US] /ˈʃɑː.kɪŋ-/ *adv*: *Stories of abused and battered children are shockingly familiar.*

shock [DAMAGING EFFECT] /ʃɒk/ [US] /ʃɑːk/ *noun* **[U]** the effect of one object violently hitting another, which might cause damage or a slight movement: *For running on hard roads, you need shoes with extra cushioning to* ***absorb*** (= reduce) *the shock.*

shock [HAIR] /ʃɒk/ [US] /ʃɑːk/ *noun* **[S]** a large and noticeable mass of hair: *She's got* ***a*** *shock* ***of*** *bright red hair.*

shock absorber /ˈʃɒk.əbˌzɔː.bəʳ/ [US] /ˈʃɑːk.əbˌzɔːr.bɚ/ *noun* **[C]** a device on a vehicle, especially a car or an aircraft, which reduces the effects of travelling over rough ground or helps it to land more smoothly

shocking /ˈʃɒk.ɪŋ/ [US] /ˈʃɑː.kɪŋ/ *adj MAINLY UK INFORMAL* extremely bad or unpleasant, or of very low quality: *What shocking weather!* ○ *My memory is shocking.* ➲See also **shocking** at **shock** SURPRISE, **shock** OFFEND. **shockingly** /ˈʃɒk.ɪŋ.li/ [US] /ˈʃɑː.kɪŋ-/ *adv*: *The service was shockingly* ***bad***.

ˌshocking ˈpink *adj, noun* **[U]** very bright pink

ˈshock ˌjock *noun* **[C]** *MAINLY US* a person whose job is to play music on a radio programme and who often says things that are not considered acceptable by most people during the programme: *Howard Stern is one of America's best known shock jocks.*

shockproof /ˈʃɒk.pruːf/ [US] /ˈʃɑːk-/ *adj* describes a watch or other device that is not easily damaged if hit or dropped

ˈshock ˌtactics *plural noun* If you use shock tactics, you do something unexpected in order to shock someone or to get an advantage over them.

ˈshock ˌtherapy *noun* **[U]** (*ALSO* **shock treatment**) the treatment of particular mental illnesses by sending electric currents through the brain

ˈshock ˌtroops *plural noun* soldiers who are specially trained for making sudden attacks

ˈshock ˌwave *noun* **[C]** **1** a sudden wave of increased pressure or temperature, caused by an explosion, an earthquake or an object moving faster than the speed of sound **2** a very strong reaction that spreads through a group of people when something surprising or bad happens: *The assassination of the president* ***sent*** *shock waves across the world.*

shod /ʃɒd/ [US] /ʃɑːd/ *past simple and past participle of* **shoe**

shoddy [BADLY MADE] /ˈʃɒd.i/ [US] /ˈʃɑː.di/ *adj DISAPPROVING* badly and carelessly made, using low quality materials: *shoddy goods* ○ *shoddy workmanship* **shoddily** /ˈʃɒd.ɪ.li/ [US] /ˈʃɑː.dɪ-/ *adv*: *These clothes are very shoddily made.* **shoddiness** /ˈʃɒd.ɪ.nəs/ [US] /ˈʃɑː.dɪ-/ *noun* **[U]**

shoddy [NOT RESPECTFUL] /ˈʃɒd.i/ [US] /ˈʃɑː.di/ *adj DISAPPROVING* showing a lack of respect, consideration and care: *They refused him sick pay when he was off ill, which is a shoddy way to treat an employee.* **shoddily** /ˈʃɒd.ɪ.li/ [US] /ˈʃɑː.dɪ-/ *adv*: *I've been treated very shoddily by the company.* **shoddiness** /ˈʃɒd.ɪ.nəs/ [US] /ˈʃɑː.dɪ-/ *noun* **[U]**

shoe /ʃuː/ *noun* **[C]** **1** one of a pair of coverings for your feet, usually made of a strong material such as leather, with a thick leather or plastic SOLE (= base), and usually a heel: *flat/high-heeled shoes* ○ *gym/tennis shoes* ○ *He* ***put on/took off*** *his new* ***pair of*** *shoes.* ○ *Hurry and* ***do***

S

up/lace up *your shoes.* ○ *a shoe shop* ➲See picture **Clothes** on page Centre 6 **2** a **horseshoe**

• **be in *sb's* shoes** INFORMAL to be in the situation, usually a bad or difficult situation, that another person is in: *I wouldn't like to be in Mike's shoes when the boss hears what he's done!*

• **if I were in your shoes** INFORMAL used when you want to tell someone what you would do in their situation: *If I were in your shoes, I think I'd write to her rather than try to explain over the phone.*

• **step into *sb's* shoes** (ALSO **fill *sb's* shoes**) to take someone's place, often by doing the job they have just left: *Who do you think will step into Sarah's shoes when she goes?*

shoe /ʃuː/ *verb* [T] **shoeing, shod** or US ALSO **shoed, shod** or US ALSO **shoed** If you shoe a horse, you nail a HORSESHOE (= a curved piece of metal) to one or each of its feet.

shoehorn /ˈʃuː.hɔːn/ [US] /-hɔːrn/ *noun* [C] a smooth curved piece of plastic or metal which you hold in the back of your shoe when putting it on, to help your foot slide into it

shoehorn /ˈʃuː.hɔːn/ [US] /-hɔːrn/ *verb* [T often passive] INFORMAL to fit something tightly in a particular place, often between two other things: *This tiny restaurant is shoehorned **between** two major banks.*

shoelace /ˈʃuː.leɪs/ *noun* [C usually pl] (ALSO **lace**, US ALSO **shoestring**) a thin cord or strip of leather used to fasten shoes: *My shoelaces came undone.* ○ ***Do/Tie up** your shoelaces, Rosie.*

shoestring /ˈʃuː.strɪŋ/ *noun* [C usually pl] US FOR **shoelace**

• **on a shoestring** INFORMAL If you do something on a shoestring, you do it with a very small amount of money: *The film was made on a shoestring.*

shoetree /ˈʃuː.triː/ *noun* [C] a piece of wood or metal shaped like the inside of a shoe, for putting inside a shoe to preserve its shape when it is not being worn

shone /ʃɒn/ [US] /ʃɑːn/ *past simple and past participle of* **shine**

shoo /ʃuː/ *exclamation* said to animals or children to make them go away: *"Shoo!" she shouted at the cat. "Get out of my garden!"*

shoo /ʃuː/ *verb* [T usually + adv or prep] **shooing, shooed, shooed** INFORMAL to make sounds and movements in order to send animals or children away: *Go and shoo that cat **away** before it catches a bird.*

shoo-in /ˈʃuː.ɪn/ *noun* [C usually sing] someone who is certain to win an election or a competition: *He's a shoo-in **for** the White House.* ○ *Manchester United's a shoo-in **to** win the title this season.*

shook /ʃʊk/ *past simple of* **shake**

shoot [WEAPON] /ʃuːt/ *verb* [I or T] **shot, shot** to fire a bullet or an arrow, or to hit, injure or kill a person or animal by firing a bullet or arrow at them: *If he's not armed, don't shoot.* ○ *The kids were shooting arrows **at** a target.* ○ *She was shot three times in the head.* ○ *He has a licence to shoot pheasants on the farmer's land.* ○ [+ obj + adj] *A policeman was shot **dead** in the city centre last night.* ○ *The troops were told to shoot **to kill**.*

• **shoot questions at *sb*** to ask someone a lot of questions very quickly, one after the other: *He shot questions at me so quickly that I didn't even have time to answer.*

• ***sb* should be shot** INFORMAL said when you think that someone's actions are extremely unreasonable: *They should be shot **for** selling drinks at that price!*

• **have shot *your* bolt** UK INFORMAL to have already achieved all that you have the power, ability or strength to do and to be unable to do more: *He started off the game well but seemed to have shot his bolt by half-time.*

• **shoot the breeze** US INFORMAL to talk with someone or a group of people about unimportant things: *We sat out on the porch, just shooting the breeze.*

• **shoot *sth/sb* down (in flames)** INFORMAL to refuse to accept someone's suggestion or idea and not give it any consideration

• **shoot a glance at *sb*** to look at someone quickly: *She shot him a glance as he entered the room.*

• **shoot *yourself* in the foot** to unintentionally do something which spoils a situation for yourself

• **shoot *your* mouth off** INFORMAL to talk too much in a loud and uncontrolled way: *It's just like Richard to go shooting his mouth off **about** other people's affairs.*

shoot /ʃuːt/ *noun* [C] an occasion on which a group of people go to an area of the countryside to shoot animals

-shooter /-ʃuː.təʳ/ [US] /-t̬ɚ/ *suffix* a type of gun, etc., or a person, that shoots: *a peashooter* ○ *a sharpshooter* ○ *a six-shooter*

shooting /ˈʃuː.tɪŋ/ [US] /-t̬ɪŋ/ *noun* **1** [U] when bullets are fired from guns or other weapons: *We heard some shooting in the night.* **2** [C] when someone is injured or killed by a bullet fired from a gun: *There have been a number of shootings in the capital this week.* **3** [U] the sport of shooting animals or birds: *pheasant/grouse shooting* ○ *He **goes** shooting most weekends.*

shot /ʃɒt/ [US] /ʃɑːt/ *noun* [C] **1** the action of firing a gun or another weapon: *He **fired** four shots at the car as it drove off.* **2 a good/poor shot** someone who is skilled/not skilled at aiming and firing a gun

• **like a shot** INFORMAL When someone does something like a shot, they do it extremely quickly and enthusiastically: *The moment I let go of the dog, she's off like a shot.*

• **a shot in the dark** INFORMAL an attempt to guess something when you have no information or knowledge about the subject and therefore cannot possibly know what the answer is

shoot [SPORT] /ʃuːt/ *verb* [I] **shot, shot** to try to score points for yourself or your team, in sports involving a ball, by kicking, hitting or throwing the ball towards the goal: *He shot from the middle of the field and still managed to score.* **shooter** /ˈʃuː.təʳ/ [US] /-t̬ɚ/ *noun* [C] *He's thought to be the best shooter in the league.*

shot /ʃɒt/ [US] /ʃɑːt/ *noun* [C] a kick, hit or throw of the ball which is intended to score points in cricket, football, tennis or golf: *And that was a great shot by Lineker!* ○ *Graf drove a forehand shot down the line to win the match.*

shoot [MOVE QUICKLY] /ʃuːt/ *verb* **shot, shot 1** [I usually + adv or prep] to move in a particular direction very quickly and directly: *She shot **past** me several metres before the finishing line.* ○ *He shot **out** of the office a minute ago – I think he was late for a meeting.* ○ *They were just shooting **off** to town so we didn't stop to speak.* ○ *Sylvester Stallone shot **to fame*** (= became famous suddenly) *with the film 'Rocky'.* **2** [T] to move through or past something quickly: INFORMAL *He shot three sets of **traffic lights*** (= went past them when they gave the signal to stop) *before the police caught him.* ○ *It was so exhilarating shooting **the rapids*** (= travelling through the part of a river where the water flows dangerously fast).

shoot [FILM] /ʃuːt/ *verb* [I or T] **shot, shot** to use a camera to record a film or take a photograph: *We shot four reels of film in Egypt.* ○ *The film was shot **on location** in Southern India.*

shoot /ʃuːt/ *noun* [C usually sing] when photographers take a series of photographs, usually of the same person or people in the same place: *We **did** a **fashion** shoot on the beach, with the girls modelling swimwear.*

shot /ʃɒt/ [US] /ʃɑːt/ *noun* [C] **1** a photograph: *I **got/took** some really good shots of the harbour at sunset.* **2** a short piece in a film in which there is a single action or a short series of actions

shoot [PLAY] /ʃuːt/ *verb* [T] **shot, shot** MAINLY US INFORMAL to play a game of POOL or CRAPS

shoot [DRUG] /ʃuːt/ *verb* [T] **shot, shot** SLANG to take an illegal drug by injecting yourself with it: *By the time he was sixteen, he was shooting heroin twice a day.*

shot /ʃɒt/ [US] /ʃɑːt/ *noun* INFORMAL **a shot of *sth*** the amount of a particular drug, whether medical or illegal, which is put into the body by a single injection: *The doctor **gave** him a shot of morphine.*

• **a shot in the arm** something which has a sudden and positive effect on something, providing encouragement and new activity: *Fresh investment would provide the shot in the arm that this industry so badly needs.*

shoot [PLANT] /ʃuːt/ *noun* [C] the first part of a plant to appear above the earth as it develops from a seed, or any new growth on an already existing plant: *Two weeks after we'd planted the seeds, little green shoots started to*

S

appear. ○ *FIGURATIVE The first green shoots* (= hopeful signs) *of economic recovery have started to appear.*

PHRASAL VERBS WITH **shoot**

▲ **shoot *sb* down** *phrasal verb* [M] to shoot and usually kill someone, showing no sympathy: *I saw Leonforte shoot him down like a dog in the street.*

▲ **shoot *sth* down** *phrasal verb* [M] to destroy an aircraft or make an aircraft, bird, etc. fall to the ground by shooting at it: *He was killed during the war when his plane was shot down.*

▲ **shoot for/at *sth*** *phrasal verb US* to try to do something: *It's worth taking chances when you're shooting at a chance of fame and wealth.*

• **shoot for the moon** *US* to ask for the best or the most you could hope for: *You might as well shoot for the moon and ask for a promotion as well as a raise.*

▲ **shoot out** *phrasal verb* If opposing groups or people armed with guns shoot it out, they shoot at each other until one of the groups or people is dead or defeated.

shoot-out /ˈʃuːt.aʊt/ [US] /ˈʃuːt̬-/ *noun* [C] a fight in which two people or two groups of people shoot at each other with guns

▲ **shoot through** *phrasal verb AUS INFORMAL* to leave a place very quickly, especially in order to avoid having to do something ➲See also **be shot through with** at **shot** WOVEN.

▲ **shoot up** [INCREASE] *phrasal verb INFORMAL* to grow in size, or increase in number or level, very quickly: *David has really shot up since I saw him last.* ○ *Prices shot up by 25%.*

▲ **shoot up** [DRUGS] *phrasal verb SLANG* to put illegal drugs into your blood using a special needle: *She saw a girl shooting up in the toilets.*

ˈshooting ˌgallery [GUNS] *noun* [C] an enclosed area in which people shoot guns at targets, either for entertainment or in order to improve their shooting skills

ˈshooting ˌgallery [DRUGS] *noun* [C] *US SLANG* a place where people go to inject illegal drugs: *Police raided a well-known shooting gallery on Thursday night.*

ˈshooting ˌpains *plural noun* sudden severe pains which move through the body: *I get shooting pains up my spine whenever I try to move.*

ˌshooting ˈstar *noun* [C] *INFORMAL FOR* **meteor**

ˈshooting ˌstick *noun* [C] a walking stick which has a sharp point to push into the ground at one end and a folded part that opens out to use as a seat at the other

shop [PLACE TO BUY THINGS] /ʃɒp/ [US] /ʃɑːp/ *noun* [C] **1** (*US USUALLY* **store**) a building, or a room in a building, where you can buy goods or obtain services: *a book/clothes/record/sweet shop* ○ *a barber's/betting shop* ○ *I need to go to the shops – I've got no food in the house.* **2** *UK* the act of shopping, especially of shopping for food and other things needed in the house: *I usually* ***do*** *the* ***weekly*** *shop on a Monday.*

• **be in the shops** to be available to buy: *His latest novel will be in the shops by Christmas.*

shop /ʃɒp/ [US] /ʃɑːp/ *verb* [I] **-pp-** to buy things in shops: *I like to shop* ***at*** *Harrods for clothes.* ○ *If I'm just shopping* ***for*** *food, I tend to go to the local supermarket.*

▲ **shop around** *phrasal verb* to compare the price and quality of the same or a similar item in different shops before you decide which one to buy: *When you're buying a flight, you should always shop around for the best deal.*

shopper /ˈʃɒp.əʳ/ [US] /ˈʃɑː.pɚ/ *noun* [C] a person who is buying things from a shop or a number of shops: *crowds of* ***Christmas*** *shoppers*

shopping /ˈʃɒp.ɪŋ/ [US] /ˈʃɑː.pɪŋ/ *noun* [U] **1** the activity of buying things from shops: *The store is open for late night shopping on Wednesdays.* ○ *I'm* ***going*** *shopping this afternoon.* ○ *My granddaughter* ***does*** *my weekly shopping for me.* ○ ***Christmas*** *shopping* **2** goods which you have bought from shops, especially food: *She had so many* ***bags of*** *shopping that she could hardly carry them.* ○ *I forgot my shopping* ***list***.

USAGE

shop or **store?**

In **American English** the usual word for shop is **store**.

He went to the store to buy some cookies.

In **British English** the word **store** is only used to mean a very large shop where you can buy many different things.

Harrods is a famous department store.

shop [WORK AREA] /ʃɒp/ [US] /ʃɑːp/ *noun* [C] a place where a particular type of thing is made or repaired: *He runs an auto-tyre repair shop.*

shop [BUSINESS] /ʃɒp/ [US] /ʃɑːp/ *noun INFORMAL* a business

• **set up shop** to start your own business: *She set up shop back in 1965 with a very small restaurant in the Kings Road.*

shop [GIVE INFORMATION] /ʃɒp/ [US] /ʃɑːp/ *verb* [T] **-pp-** *UK SLANG* to give the police information about a criminal: *His ex-wife shopped him* ***to*** *the police.*

ˈshop asˌsistant *UK noun* [C] (*US* **salesclerk**) someone who serves customers in a shop

the ˌshop ˈfloor *noun* [S] the ordinary workers in a factory, or the place where they work

• **on the shop floor** among the ordinary workers at a factory: *There is concern on the shop floor over job security.*

ˈshop ˌfront *noun* [C] (*US* **storefront**) the outside part of a shop which faces the street

shopkeeper /ˈʃɒpˌkiː.pəʳ/ [US] /ˈʃɑːpˌkiː.pɚ/ *noun* [C] (*US USUALLY* **storekeeper**) a person who owns and manages a small shop

shoplifting /ˈʃɒpˌlɪf.tɪŋ/ [US] /ˈʃɑːp-/ *noun* [U] the illegal act of taking goods from a shop without paying for them: *He was charged with shoplifting.* **shoplift** /ˈʃɒp.-lɪft/ [US] /ˈʃɑːp-/ *verb* [I] *He was caught shoplifting by a store detective.* **shoplifter** /ˈʃɒpˌlɪf.təʳ/ [US] /ˈʃɑːp-/ *noun* [C] *Shoplifters will be prosecuted.*

shopper /ˈʃɒp.əʳ/ [US] /ˈʃɑː.pɚ/ *noun* [C] ➲See at **shop** PLACE TO BUY THINGS.

shopping /ˈʃɒp.ɪŋ/ [US] /ˈʃɑː.pɪŋ/ *noun* [U] ➲See at **shop** PLACE TO BUY THINGS.

ˈshopping ˌbag *noun* [C] **1** (*US* **tote bag**) *UK* any bag intended to carry items bought in shops, especially one bought for this purpose and used many times **2** *US FOR* **carrier (bag)**

ˈshopping ˌcentre *UK, US* **shopping center** *noun* [C] a group of shops with a common area for cars to park, which usually provides goods and services for local people

ˈshopping ˌmall *noun* [C] (*ALSO* **mall**) *MAINLY US* a large usually enclosed shopping area where cars are not allowed

shopsoiled *UK* /ˈʃɒp.sɔɪld/ [US] /ˈʃɑːp-/ *adj* (*US* **shopworn**) If goods sold in shops are shopsoiled, they are slightly dirty or damaged and therefore reduced in price.

ˌshop ˈsteward *noun* [C] a worker elected by workers in a factory or business to represent them in discussions with the management

shopworn /ˈʃɒp.wɔːn/ [US] /ˈʃɑːp.wɔːrn/ *adj* **1** *US FOR* **shopsoiled** **2** *US* If a story or joke is shopworn, it is boring or not interesting because it is so familiar to people.

shore /ʃɔːʳ/ [US] /ʃɔːr/ *noun* [C or U] the land along the edge of a sea, lake or wide river: *You can walk for miles along the shore.* ○ *The boat was about a mile* ***from/off*** *(the) shore when the engine suddenly died.* ➲See also **onshore**; **offshore**.

shores /ʃɔːz/ [US] /ʃɔːrz/ *plural noun LITERARY* a country or continent with a coast: *In 1992, Britain played host to the first multi-racial South African team to visit these shores.*

• **on shore** on the land and not in a ship: *We waited until we were on shore before repairing the sails.*

shoreline /ˈʃɔː.laɪn/ [US] /ˈʃɔːr-/ *noun* [C usually sing] the edge of a sea, lake or wide river: *Oil from the wrecked tanker polluted more than 40 miles of the Normandy shoreline.*

shore /ʃɔːʳ/ [US] /ʃɔːr/ *verb*

PHRASAL VERBS WITH **shore**

▲ **shore *sth* up** [SUPPORT PHYSICALLY] *phrasal verb* [M] to stop a wall or a building from falling down by supporting it with building materials such as wood or metal: *Boundary walls have had to be shored up.*

▲ **shore** ***sth*** **up** [MAKE EFFECTIVE] *phrasal verb* [M] to strengthen or improve an organization, agreement or system that is not working effectively or that is likely to fail: *The new public relations manager has the difficult task of shoring up the company's troubled image.*

shorn /ʃɔːn/ [US] /ʃɔːrn/ *past participle of* **shear** CUT.

short [DISTANCE] /ʃɔːt/ [US] /ʃɔːrt/ *adj* **1** small in length, distance or height: *a short skirt* ○ *Her hair is much shorter than it used to be.* ○ *It's only a short walk to the station.* ○ *I'm quite short but my brother's very tall.* **2** describes a name that is used as a shorter form of a name: *Her name's Jo – it's short* ***for*** *Josephine.* ○ *Her name's Josephine, or Jo* ***for*** *short.*

• **draw/get the short straw** *INFORMAL* to have to do the least enjoyable of a range of duties, often because you have been chosen to do it: *Colin, I'm afraid you've drawn the short straw – you're cleaning out the toilets.*

short- /ʃɔːt-/ [US] /ʃɔːrt-/ *prefix* used with adjectives ending in -ed formed from nouns: *a short-haired dog* (= a dog with short hair) ○ *a short-sleeved shirt* (= a shirt with short sleeves)

shorten /ˈʃɔː.tᵊn/ [US] /ˈʃɔːr-/ *verb* [I or T] to become shorter or to make something shorter: *As you grow older, your spine shortens by about an inch.* ○ *I've asked him to shorten my grey trousers.* ○ *The name 'William' is often shortened* ***to*** *'Bill'.*

shortish /ˈʃɔː.tɪʃ/ [US] /ˈʃɔːr.t̬ɪʃ/ *adj* quite short: *She's got shortish black hair* ➲See also **shortish** at **short** TIME.

shortness /ˈʃɔːt.nəs/ [US] /ˈʃɔːrt-/ *noun* [U] ➲See also **shortness** at **short** TIME, **short** LACKING.

shorty /ˈʃɔː.ti/ [US] /ˈʃɔːr.t̬i/ *noun* [C] (*UK OFFENSIVE ALSO* **short-arse**) *INFORMAL* a short person: *That coat reaches your ankles, shorty!*

short [TIME] /ʃɔːt/ [US] /ʃɔːrt/ *adj* **1** being an amount of time which is less than average or usual: *a short film/visit* ○ *He's grown so much in such a short time.* ○ *I work much better if I take a short break every hour or so.* **2** describes books, letters and other examples of writing that do not contain many words and do not take much time to read: *It's a very short book – you'll read it in an hour.*

• **be caught/taken short** *UK INFORMAL* to suddenly and unexpectedly need to go to the toilet, especially when it is not convenient for you to do so

• **be short notice** to be very near the time when an event is expected to happen: *I will have to cancel this afternoon's class – I'm sorry it's such short notice.*

• **have a short memory** to forget things quickly

• **make short work of** ***sth*** *INFORMAL* to finish or deal with something quickly: *Well you certainly made short work of the chocolate cake! There's none left for your dad.*

• **short sharp shock** (describing or relating to) punishment that is quick and effective: *He's in favour of the short sharp shock* ***treatment*** *for young offenders.*

• **short and sweet** *INFORMAL* surprisingly short in a way that is pleasing: *This morning's lecture was short and sweet.*

short /ʃɔːt/ [US] /ʃɔːrt/ *noun* [C] a short film, especially one which is made for showing before the main film at a cinema

• **in short** used before describing something or someone in as few words and as directly as possible: *He's disorganized, inefficient, never there when you want him – in short, the man's hopeless.*

shortish /ˈʃɔː.tɪʃ/ [US] /ˈʃɔːr.t̬ɪʃ/ *adj* not long, but not very short: *"Is it a short film?" "Well, shortish."* ➲See also **shortish** at **short** DISTANCE.

shortly /ˈʃɔːt.li/ [US] /ʃɔːrt-/ *adv* **1** soon: *We will shortly be arriving in King's Cross Station.* **2 shortly after/before** ***sth*** a short time after or before something: *Shortly after you left, a man came into the office looking for you.* **shortness** /ˈʃɔːt.nəs/ [US] /ˈʃɔːrt-/ *noun* [U] *shortness of time* ➲See also **shortness** at **short** DISTANCE, **short** LACKING.

short [LACKING] /ʃɔːt/ [US] /ʃɔːrt/ *adj* lacking: *to be short* ***of*** *space/time* ○ *We're a bit short* ***of*** *coffee – I must get some more.* ○ *The bill comes to £85, but we're £15 short.* ○ *I'm a little short* (= I do not have much money) *this week - could you lend me ten dollars?*

• **short of breath** unable to breathe very well, for example because you have been running or doing some type of energetic exercise: *She's always short of breath when she climbs the stairs.*

• **be in short supply** to be few or not enough in number: *Computers are in rather short supply in this office.*

• **not be short of a bob or two** *UK INFORMAL* to be wealthy: *Did you see his car? He's not short of a bob or two!*

• **go short** *MAINLY UK* to lack something, especially when it is something you need in order to live: *My parents didn't have much money, but they made sure we didn't go short (***of*** anything).*

shortage /ˈʃɔː.tɪdʒ/ [US] /ˈʃɔːr.t̬ɪdʒ/ *noun* [C] when there is not enough of something: *There's a shortage* ***of*** *food and shelter in the refugee camps.* ○ *The long hot summer has led to serious water shortages.*

shortness /ˈʃɔːt.nəs/ [US] /ˈʃɔːrt-/ *noun* [U] *The disease may cause cold sweating, nausea, vomiting and shortness* ***of breath*** (= difficulties in breathing). ➲See also **shortness** at **short** DISTANCE, **short** TIME.

short [NOT PATIENT] /ʃɔːt/ [US] /ʃɔːrt/ *adj* [after v] saying little but showing a slight lack of patience or annoyance in the few words that you say: *I'm sorry if I was a bit short* ***with*** *you on the phone this morning.*

short [DRINK] /ʃɔːt/ [US] /ʃɔːrt/ *noun* [C] *UK INFORMAL* a drink of SPIRITS (= type of strong alcohol) without water or any other liquid added: *She only drinks shorts, never wine or beer.*

short [ELECTRICITY] /ʃɔːt/ [US] /ʃɔːrt/ *noun* [C], *verb* [I] *INFORMAL FOR* **short circuit**

short [EARLY] /ʃɔːt/ [US] /ʃɔːrt/ *adv* before the arranged or expected time or place: *We had to* ***cut*** *short our holiday* (= finish it early) *because Richard was ill.* ○ *We wanted to explain the plans fully, but the chairman* ***stopped*** *us short, as there were other important matters to discuss.*

shortage /ˈʃɔː.tɪdʒ/ [US] /ˈʃɔːr.t̬ɪdʒ/ *noun* [C] ➲See at **short** LACKING.

ˌshort ˌback and ˈsides *noun* [S] *OLD-FASHIONED* a hairstyle for men in which the hair is cut short at the back and sides, showing the ears

shortbread /ˈʃɔːt.bred/ [US] /ˈʃɔːrt-/ *noun* [U] (*ALSO* **shortcake**) a type of thick sweet biscuit which contains a lot of butter: *traditional Scottish shortbread*

shortcake /ˈʃɔːt.keɪk/ [US] /ˈʃɔːrt-/ *noun* **1** [U] **shortbread** **2** [C or U] *MAINLY US* a type of cake which is often served in layers with fruit and cream: *Do you like* ***strawberry*** *shortcake?*

short-change /ˌʃɔːtˈtʃeɪndʒ/ [US] /ˌʃɔːrt-/ *verb* [T] **1** to give someone back less money than they are owed when they are buying something from you: *I think I was short-changed in the pub last night, because I've only got £5 in my purse when I should have £10.* **2** to treat someone unfairly, by giving them less than they deserve: *Children who leave school unable to read and write properly are being tragically short-changed.*

ˌshort ˈcircuit *noun* [C] (*INFORMAL* **short**) a faulty electrical connection which causes the current to flow in the wrong direction, often having the effect of stopping the power supply **short-circuit** /ˌʃɔːtˈsɜː.kɪt/ [US] /ˌʃɔːrtˈsɝː-/ *verb* [I or T] (*INFORMAL* **short**) *If those two wires touch, the appliance will short-circuit and probably go up in flames.* ○ *The plumber's shorted the electric shower.*

shortcoming /ˈʃɔːtˌkʌm.ɪŋ/ [US] /ˈʃɔːrt-/ /ˌ-ˈ--/ *noun* [C usually pl] a fault or a failure to reach a particular standard: *Whatever his shortcomings as a husband, he was a good father to his children.* ○ *Like any political system, it has its shortcomings.*

shortcrust (pastry) /ˌʃɔːt.krʌstˈpeɪ.stri/ [US] /ˌʃɔːrt-/ *noun* [U] a type of soft pastry which breaks easily

shortcut /ˈʃɔːt.kʌt/ [US] /ˈʃɔːrt-/ *noun* [C] **1** (*UK ALSO* **short cut**) a route which leads from one place to another which is quicker and more direct than the usual route: *I know a shortcut* ***to*** *town through the back streets.* **2** (*UK ALSO* **short cut**) a quicker way of doing something in order to save time or effort **3** in computing, a quick way to start or use a computer program: *a shortcut key*

shortening /ˈʃɔː.tᵊn.ɪŋ/ [US] /ˈʃɔːrt.nɪŋ/ *noun* [U] *US* butter or other fat which is used in cooking, especially to make pastry soft and CRUMBLY (= easily broken)

shortfall /ˈʃɔːt.fɔːl/ [US] /ˈʃɔːrt.fɑːl/ *noun* [C] an amount which is less than the level that was expected or needed:

The drought caused serious shortfalls ***in*** *the food supply.*

shorthand /ˈʃɔːt.hænd/ [US] /ˈʃɔːrt-/ *noun* [U] (*ALSO* **stenography**) a system of fast writing which uses lines and simple signs to represent words and phrases: *Their conversations were taken down* ***in*** *shorthand by a secretary.*
• **shorthand for** ***sth*** a short simple phrase which is used instead of a longer and more complicated phrase

shorthanded /ˌʃɔːtˈhæn.dɪd/ [US] /ˌʃɔːrt-/ *adj* (*UK ALSO* **short-staffed**) If a company or organization is short-handed, it lacks the usual or necessary number of workers: *Some hospitals are so shorthanded that nurses and doctors are having to work twenty-hour shifts.*

ˌshorthand ˈtypist *noun* [C] *UK* someone who types and does shorthand as the main part of their job

short-haul /ˈʃɔːt.hɔːl/ [US] /ˈʃɔːrt.hɑːl/ *adj* [before n] travelling a short distance: *short-haul flights*

shortlist *UK, US* **short list** /ˈʃɔːt.lɪst/ [US] /ˈʃɔːrt-/ *noun* [C] a list of people who have been judged the most suitable for a job or prize, made from a longer list of people originally considered, and from which one person will be chosen: *We've* ***drawn up*** (= decided) *a shortlist for the job.* ○ *She's* ***on*** *the shortlist for a teaching post.* **shortlist** /ˈʃɔːt.lɪst/ [US] /ˈʃɔːrt-/ *verb* [T] *His latest novel has been shortlisted* ***for*** *the Booker prize.*

short-lived /ˌʃɔːtˈlɪvd/ [US] /ˌʃɔːrtˈlaɪvd/ /-ˈlɪvd/ *adj* If a feeling or experience is short-lived, it only lasts for a short time: *I had a few relationships at college, most of which were fairly short-lived.*

shortly /ˈʃɔːt.li/ [US] /ˈʃɔːrt-/ *adv* ➲See at **short** TIME.

shortness /ˈʃɔːt.nəs/ [US] /ˈʃɔːrt-/ *noun* [U] ➲See at **short** DISTANCE, **short** TIME, **short** LACKING.

short-range /ˌʃɔːtˈreɪndʒ/ [US] /ˌʃɔːrt-/ *adj* **1** reaching a short distance: *short-range missiles/weapons* **2** relating to a short time: *a short-range weather forecast*

shorts /ʃɔːts/ [US] /ʃɔːrts/ *plural noun* **1** trousers that end above the knee or reach the knee, which are often worn in hot weather or when playing a sport: *tennis shorts* ○ *She put on a* ***pair of*** *shorts and a T-shirt.* ➲See picture **Clothes** on page Centre 6 **2** *US* men's UNDERPANTS

short shrift /ˌʃɔːtˈʃrɪft/ [US] /ˌʃɔːrt-/ *noun* [U] If you get or are given short shrift by someone, you are treated without sympathy and given little attention: *He'll* ***get*** *short shrift from me if he starts complaining about money again, now that I know how much he earns!*
• **make short shrift of** ***sth*** to deal with or get rid of something quickly: *Arantxa Sanchez Vicario made short shrift of her opponent, allowing her only two games in a 6-0, 6-2 demolition.*

short-sighted [SIGHT] /ˌʃɔːtˈsaɪ.tɪd/ [US] /ˌʃɔːrtˈsaɪ.t̬ɪd/ *adj* (*US ALSO* **near-sighted**) describes someone who can only clearly see objects that are close to them **short-sightedness** /ˌʃɔːtˈsaɪ.tɪd.nəs/ [US] /ˌʃɔːrtˈsaɪ.t̬ɪd-/ *noun* [U] (*US ALSO* **near-sightedness**)

short-sighted [THOUGHT] /ˌʃɔːtˈsaɪ.tɪd/ [US] /ˌʃɔːrtˈsaɪ.t̬ɪd/ *adj DISAPPROVING* not thinking enough about how an action will affect the future: *It's very short-sighted of the government not to invest in technological research.*

short-staffed /ˌʃɔːtˈstɑːft/ [US] /ˌʃɔːrtˈstæft/ *adj UK FOR* **shorthanded**

ˌshort ˈstory *noun* [C] an invented story which is no more than about 10,000 words in length: *He published a book of short stories.*

short-tempered /ˌʃɔːtˈtem.pəd/ [US] /ˌʃɔːrtˈtem.pɚd/ *adj* If someone is short-tempered, they get angry easily, often for no good reason.

short-term /ˌʃɔːtˈtɜːm/ [US] /ˈʃɔːrt.tɜːrm/ *adj* **1** lasting a short time: *short-term memory* **2** relating to a short period of time: *a short-term weather forecast*

ˌshort ˈtime *noun* [U] (*ALSO* **reduced time**) when the people who work at a factory or in an office work fewer days or hours than usual for less money because there is not much work to do: *He's been put* ***on*** *short time because business is so quiet.*

ˈshort ˌwave *noun* [U] (*WRITTEN ABBREVIATION* **SW**) refers to radio waves of a length which is less than 60 metres

shorty /ˈʃɔː.ti/ [US] /ˈʃɔːr.t̬i/ *noun* [C] *INFORMAL* ➲See at **short** DISTANCE.

shot [SHOOT] /ʃɒt/ [US] /ʃɑːt/ *past simple and past participle of* **shoot**

shot [METAL BALL] /ʃɒt/ [US] /ʃɑːt/ *noun* **1** [C] a heavy metal ball thrown in a sports competition ➲See **shot put. 2** [U] a mass of small metal balls which are fired from a gun: *Shotgun cartridges contain* ***lead*** *shot.*

shot [ATTEMPT] /ʃɒt/ [US] /ʃɑːt/ *noun* [C usually sing] *INFORMAL* an attempt to do or achieve something that you have not done before: *I thought I'd* ***have*** *a shot* ***at*** *making my own wine.* ○ *I've never tried bowling before, but I thought I'd* ***give*** *it a shot.*
• **give** ***sth*** **your best shot** *INFORMAL* to do something as well as you can

shot [AMOUNT OF DRINK] /ʃɒt/ [US] /ʃɑːt/ *noun* [C] a small amount of an alcoholic drink: *a shot* ***of*** *whisky*

shot [FREE] /ʃɒt/ [US] /ʃɑːt/ *adj UK INFORMAL* **get/be shot of** ***sth*** to get rid of or free of something, or to leave something: *I can't wait to get shot of this office for a week.* ○ *I suspect he left home to get shot of that awful mother of his.*

shot [WOVEN] /ʃɒt/ [US] /ʃɑːt/ *adj* (of silk) woven in such a way that the colour appears to change depending on the angle at which the material is seen: *Her evening dress is made of green shot silk.*
• **be shot through with** ***sth*** to show or contain a particular emotion or quality in a noticeable way all the way through: *Her novel is shot through with a haunting lyricism.* ○ *The report was shot through with inaccuracies.* ➲See also **shoot through**.

shot [DESTROYED] /ʃɒt/ [US] /ʃɑːt/ *adj INFORMAL* no longer working or effective: *It's no good – these gears are shot.*

shotgun /ˈʃɒt.gʌn/ [US] /ˈʃɑːt-/ *noun* [C] a long gun which fires a large number of small metal bullets at one time, which is meant to be used for shooting birds and animals: *The robbers used a* (UK) ***sawn-off***/(US) ***sawed-off*** *shotgun in the raid.*

ˌshotgun ˈwedding *noun* [C] (*US ALSO* **shotgun marriage**) *OLD-FASHIONED INFORMAL* a marriage which is arranged very quickly and suddenly because the woman is pregnant

ˈshot ˌput *noun* [S] a sports competition in which a heavy metal ball is thrown from the shoulder as far as possible: *He's practising for* ***the*** *shot put.*
ˈshot ˌputter *noun* [C] a person who competes in the shot put

should [DUTY] *STRONG* /ʃʊd/, *WEAK* /ʃəd/ *modal verb* used to say or ask what is the correct or best thing to do: *If you're annoyed with him, you should tell him.* ○ *You should change trains at Peterborough if you're going to Newcastle.* ○ *"Should I apologize to him?" "Yes, I think you should."* ○ *You should be ashamed of yourselves.* ○ *This computer isn't working as it should.* ○ *There should be an investigation into the cause of the disaster.* ○ *He said that I should see a doctor.* ○ *I should* ***have*** *written to her but I haven't had time.* ○ *It's very kind of you, but you really shouldn't* ***have*** *bothered.* ○ *Where should* (= do you suggest that) *we meet tonight?* ○ *It's rather cold in here. Should I* (= Do you want me to) *turn the heating on?*
• **you should have seen/heard** ***sth/sb*** seeing or hearing something or someone would have interested or amused you very much: *You should have seen her – she was furious!*

should [PROBABLE] *STRONG* /ʃʊd/, *WEAK* /ʃəd/ *modal verb* used to show when something is likely or expected: *My dry cleaning should be ready this afternoon.* ○ *You should find this guidebook helpful.* ○ *I wonder what's happened to Annie. She should be* (= It was expected that she would be) *here by now.* ○ *"Could you have the report ready by Friday?" "Yes, I should think so* (= it is likely that it will be ready)*."* ○ *"Colleen wants to see us in her office immediately." "This should be good* (= This is likely to be interesting or amusing)*!"*
• **How should** ***I*** **know?** I cannot be expected to know: *"Where's Mikey?" "How should I know? He's hardly ever in the office these days."*
• **I should think not/so (too)!** said when you think what has been suggested is definitely not, or definitely is, the correct and expected thing: *"I bought her some flowers to*

S

say thank you." "I should think so ***too****." ○ "I don't like to drink more than one bottle of wine in an evening." "I should think not."*

• **I should be so lucky!** INFORMAL said when what you want is extremely unlikely to happen: *"You might win first prize." "I should be so lucky."*

should [POSSIBILITY] STRONG /ʃʊd/, WEAK /ʃəd/ *modal verb* **1** FORMAL used when referring to a possible event in the future: *If anyone should ask for me, I'll be in the manager's office.* ○ *Should you* (= If you) *ever need anything, please don't hesitate to contact me.* **2** used after 'that' and adjectives or nouns that show an opinion or feeling: *It's odd* ***that*** *she should think I would want to see her again.* ○ *It's so unfair* ***that*** *she should* ***have*** *died so young.* **3** used after 'that' to suggest that a situation possibly exists or might come into existence: *We agree* ***that*** *the money should be paid tomorrow.* **4** FORMAL used after 'so that' and 'in order that' to show purpose: *He took his umbrella so that he shouldn't get wet.* **5** FORMAL used after 'for fear that', 'in case' and 'lest': *He took his umbrella in case it should rain.*

should [SURPRISE] STRONG /ʃʊd/, WEAK /ʃəd/ *modal verb* used to express surprise in sentences that are in the form of questions: *I was just getting off the bus when who should I see* ***but*** *my old school friend Pat!*

should [WOULD] STRONG /ʃʊd/, WEAK /ʃəd/ *modal verb* MAINLY UK FORMAL used instead of 'would' when the subject is 'I' or 'we': *I should like a whisky before I go to bed.* ○ *I shouldn't expect you to pay, of course.*

should [ADVISE] STRONG /ʃʊd/, WEAK /ʃəd/ *modal verb* UK used after 'I' when giving advice: *I shouldn't worry about it if I were you.* ○ *I shouldn't* (= I advise you not to) *let it worry you.*

should [REASON] STRONG /ʃʊd/, WEAK /ʃəd/ *modal verb* used after 'why' when giving or asking the reason for something: *Why should anyone want to eat something so horrible?* ○ *Why shouldn't she buy it if she can afford it?*

shoulder [BODY PART] /ˈʃəʊl.dəʳ/ [US] /ˈʃoʊl.dɚ/ *noun* [C] **1** one of the two parts of the body at each side of the neck which join the arms to the rest of the body: *I rested my head on her shoulder.* ○ *Then she put her arm round my shoulder and gave me a kiss.* ○ *She* ***glanced*** *nervously* ***over*** *her shoulder to make sure no one else was listening.* ➲See picture **The Body** on page Centre 5 **2** the part of a bottle that curves out below its opening **3** US FOR **hard shoulder**

• **a shoulder to cry on** someone who is willing to listen to your problems and give you sympathy, emotional support and encouragement: *I wish you'd been here when my mother died and I* ***needed*** *a shoulder to cry on.*

• **shoulder to shoulder** If people are shoulder to shoulder, they are close together and next to each other: *The refugees were packed shoulder to shoulder on the boat.*

• **stand shoulder to shoulder with *sb*** to give someone or a group of people complete support during a difficult time

shoulder /ˈʃəʊl.dəʳ/ [US] /ˈʃoʊl.dɚ/ *verb* **1** [T] to put something on your shoulders to carry it: *Shouldering her pack, she strode off up the road.* **2** [T + adv or prep] to push something with one of your shoulders: *She was carrying two suitcases and had to shoulder the door open.* ○ *He shouldered his* ***way*** (= formed a way through by pushing with his shoulders) *to the front of the crowd to get a better look.* **-shouldered** /-ʃəʊl.dəd/ [US] /-ʃoʊl.dɚd/ *suffix: to be* ***broad/narrow****-shouldered*

shoulders /ˈʃəʊl.dəz/ [US] /ˈʃoʊl.dɚz/ *plural noun* **1** the top part of a person's back: *He was about six feet tall with* ***broad*** *shoulders.* ○ *"I don't know what to do about it," said Martha,* ***shrugging*** *her shoulders.* **2** the parts of a piece of clothing which cover the wearer's shoulders: *The shoulders look a bit tight. Do you want to try a larger size?* ○ *a jacket with* ***padded*** *shoulders*

shoulder [MEAT] /ˈʃəʊl.dəʳ/ [US] /ˈʃoʊl.dɚ/ *noun* [C or U] a piece of meat which includes the upper part of an animal's front leg: *I've bought a shoulder of* ***lamb*** *for Sunday lunch.*

shoulder [ACCEPT RESPONSIBILITY] /ˈʃəʊl.dəʳ/ [US] /ˈʃoʊl.dɚ/ *verb* **shoulder the blame/burden/responsibility/cost, etc.** to accept that you are responsible for something bad or difficult: *It is women who mainly shoulder responsibility for the care of elderly and disabled relatives.* ○ *Teachers cannot be expected to shoulder all the blame for poor exam results.*

shoulders /ˈʃəʊl.dəz/ [US] /ˈʃoʊl.dɚz/ *plural noun* **sb's shoulders** used to refer to the responsibility that someone has or feels for something: *A huge* ***burden*** *was* ***lifted*** *from my shoulders* (= I became much less worried and anxious) *when I told my parents about my problem.* ○ *Responsibility for the dispute* ***rests*** *squarely* ***on*** *the shoulders of the president.*

ˈshoulder ˌbag *noun* [C] a bag that hangs on a strap from the shoulder, especially one used for carrying small personal items

ˈshoulder ˌblade *noun* [C] (SPECIALIZED **scapula**) a large flat triangular bone on each side of your back below your shoulder, which helps to increase the range of movement of your arm ➲See picture **The Body** on page Centre 5

shoulder-length /ˈʃəʊl.dəˌleŋkθ/ [US] /ˈʃoʊl.dɚ-/ *adj* If your hair is shoulder-length, it goes down as far as your shoulders.

ˈshoulder ˌpad *noun* [C usually pl] a small piece of a soft material that is put into the shoulder of a piece of clothing to raise it or improve its shape

ˈshoulder ˌstrap *noun* [C] a narrow strip of material on a bag or a piece of clothing which hangs over the wearer's shoulder and holds the bag or clothing in position

shouldn't /ˈʃʊd.ᵊnt/ *short form of* should not: *You shouldn't do things like that.*

should've /ˈʃʊd.ᵊv/ *short form* should have: *You should've come to the party last night, Manya.*

shout [USE LOUD VOICE] /ʃaʊt/ *verb* **1** [I] to speak with a very loud voice, often as loud as possible, usually when you want to make yourself heard in noisy situations, or when the person you are talking to is a long way away or cannot hear very well: *There's no need to shout, I can hear perfectly well.* ○ [+ speech] *"I'll see you tomorrow," shouted Eleni* ***above*** *the noise of the helicopter.* ○ [+ that] *He shouted from the bottom of the garden* ***that*** *he'd be finished in about half an hour.* ➲See Note **cry, scream or shout?** at **cry** SHOUT. **2** [I or T] to express strong emotions, such as anger, fear or excitement, or to express strong opinions, in a loud voice: *Dad really shouted* ***at*** *me when I broke the window.* ○ *He shouted* ***abuse*** *at the judge after being sentenced to five years imprisonment.* ○ *The fans were screaming and shouting* ***out*** *the names of the band members.* ○ [+ to infinitive] *I shouted* ***at*** *him* ***to*** *put the gun down.* ○ [+ speech] *"Stop this childish nonsense at once!" he shouted furiously.* **3** [I] to try to attract attention in a loud voice: *I heard them shouting* ***for help****, but there was nothing I could do.* ○ FIGURATIVE *It's the charities that shout* ***loudest*** (= attract the most public attention) *that often get given the most money.*

• **something/nothing to shout about** INFORMAL something that makes/does not make you feel excited or pleased: *At last, a 5-0 victory gives England's supporters something to shout about.* ○ *The pay increase is nothing to shout about, but it's better than last year's.*

shout /ʃaʊt/ *noun* [C] when you say something very loudly or make a very loud sound with your voice: *Her speech was interrupted by* ***angry*** *shouts from the audience.*

• **give *sb* a shout** INFORMAL to tell someone: *Give me a shout* ***when*** *you've finished in the bathroom.*

shouting /ˈʃaʊ.tɪŋ/ [US] /-t̬ɪŋ/ *noun* [U] shouts: *We could hear shouting in the street outside.*

• **within shouting distance** very close: *We live within shouting distance* ***of*** *the station.*

▲ **shout *sb* down** *phrasal verb* [M] to prevent someone who is speaking at a meeting from being heard, by shouting: *She was shouted down when she tried to speak on the issue of abortion.*

shout [DRINKS] /ʃaʊt/ *noun* [C] UK INFORMAL a set of drinks for a group of people, or a particular person's turn to buy them: *Would you like another drink? It's my shout because you bought the last ones.*

ˈshouting ˌmatch *noun* [C] INFORMAL DISAPPROVING an argument which involves people shouting at each other because they have very strong opinions: *The meeting* *soon degenerated into a shouting match.*

shove PUSH /ʃʌv/ *verb* [I or T] to push someone or something forcefully: *She was jostled and shoved by an angry crowd as she left the court.* ○ *Just wait your turn – there's no need to shove.* ○ *Reporters **pushed and** shoved as they tried to get close to the princess.*

● **shove it** SLANG a rude expression showing a lack of respect for someone or for something that they have said: *When I told him he'd have to work harder, he said I could take the job and shove it.*

shove /ʃʌv/ *noun* [C] when you shove someone or something: *Would you help me **give** the piano a shove?*

shove PUT /ʃʌv/ *verb* [T + adv or prep] INFORMAL to put something somewhere in a hurried or careless way: *I'll just shove this laundry **in** the washer before we go out.* ○ *"Where should I put this suitcase?" "Shove it **down** there for the moment."* ○ *They can't just shove motorways anywhere they like, you know.*

shove MOVE BODY /ʃʌv/ *verb* [I + adv or prep] INFORMAL to move your body to make space for someone else: *Shove **over/along**, Lena, and make some room for me.* ○ UK *Why don't you shove **up** so that Brian can sit next to you?*

PHRASAL VERBS WITH **shove** ▼

▲ **shove** *sb* **around/about** *phrasal verb* **1** to push someone forcefully, in an unpleasant and threatening way: *The older boys at school are always shoving him around.* **2** INFORMAL to tell someone what to do, in a rude or threatening way: *Don't let them shove you around. You've got to stand up for your rights.*

▲ **Shove off!** GO AWAY *phrasal verb* INFORMAL used to tell someone angrily to go away: *Just shove off, will you?*

▲ **shove off** LEAVE LAND *phrasal verb* to leave land in a boat, usually by pushing against the land with your foot or an oar: *She jumped into the dinghy and shoved off.*

shovel /ˈʃʌv.ᵊl/ *noun* [C] **1** a tool consisting of a wide square metal or plastic blade, usually with slightly raised sides, fixed to a handle, for moving loose material such as sand, coal or snow **2** a similar part on a large machine, for picking up and holding loose material **3** (ALSO **shovelful**) the amount of something that can fit on a shovel: *Should I put another shovelful **of** coal on the fire?* **shovel** /ˈʃʌv.ᵊl/ *verb* [I or T] -**ll**- or US USUALLY -**l**- *Would you give me a hand shovelling the snow away from the garage door?*

● **shovel** *sth* **into** *your* **mouth** (ALSO **shovel** *sth* **down**) to put large quantities of food into your mouth very quickly: *He was sitting in front of the TV shovelling down a pizza.*

show MAKE SEEN /ʃəʊ/ US /ʃoʊ/ *verb* [T] showed, shown to make it possible for something to be seen: [+ two objects] *I must show you this new book I've just bought.* ○ *On this map, urban areas are shown **in** grey.* ○ *You ought to show that rash **to** your doctor.* ○ [+ obj + question word] *Why won't you show me **what** you've got in your hand?* ○ [+ obj + v-ing] *The secretly filmed video shows the prince and princess kiss**ing**.* ○ *These photographs show the **effects** of the chemical on the trees.* ○ *He began to show **signs** of recovery.* ○ *"I've got a Victorian gold coin here." "Have you? Show me (= Allow me to see it)."*

● **show** *your* **face** to appear somewhere when you are not expected to because you have done something bad: *How **dare** you show your face in here after saying all those dreadful things!*

● **show** *your* **hand** to permit people to know about intentions that you had previously kept secret: *Keep the names of the team secret – don't show your hand until the day of the match.*

● **that will show** *sb* INFORMAL said of an action which you intend as a punishment for someone who has done something wrong: *The next time she's late home, I'll throw her dinner away. That'll show her!*

● **have something/nothing to show for** *sth* If you have something/nothing to show for your work or effort, you have/have not gained any advantage from it: *I worked for two weeks, and fifty pounds was all I had to show for it.* ○ *I've been trying to write this essay all day and I've got nothing to show for it.*

show NOTICEABLE /ʃəʊ/ US /ʃoʊ/ *verb* [I] showed, shown to be easy to see or notice: *"Oh no, I've spilt red wine on my*

jacket!" "Don't worry, it doesn't show." ○ *Whatever she's thinking, she never lets it show.* ○ *I've painted over the graffiti twice, but it still shows **through**.* ○ *The drug does not show **up** in blood tests because it is effective in very small quantities.* ○ *When we moved in, the house hadn't been decorated for twenty years, and **it** showed.* ⊃See also **show up**.

● **show** *your* **age** to look as old as you really are: *Recently, he's really **starting** to show his age.*

show FAIL TO HIDE /ʃəʊ/ US /ʃoʊ/ *verb* [T] showed, shown to fail to hide, or to make it possible to be seen or known: *Your shirt's so thin that it shows your bra.* ○ *Light-coloured carpets show the dirt.* ○ [+ question word] *His failure in the exams shows **(up)** just how bad his teachers are.*

show MAKE AWARE /ʃəʊ/ US /ʃoʊ/ *verb* [T + obj + question word] showed, shown to make someone aware of something by directing their attention to it: *Can you show me **where** it hurts?* ○ *Show me **which** one you want.*

show LEAD /ʃəʊ/ US /ʃoʊ/ *verb* [T usually + adv or prep] showed, shown to take someone somewhere by going there with them: *Could you show Dr Sanchez into the living room?* ○ *The waiter showed us **to** our table.*

● **show** *sb* **the door** to make it obvious that you do not want someone to be present and that they should leave: *When I told my bank manager that I wanted to borrow £100,000, she showed me the door.*

show RECORD /ʃəʊ/ US /ʃoʊ/ *verb* [T] showed, shown to record or express a number or measurement: *The right-hand dial shows the temperature, and the left-hand one shows the air pressure.* ○ *The company showed a loss of £2 million last year.* ○ *The latest crime figures show a sharp rise in burglaries.*

show EXPLAIN /ʃəʊ/ US /ʃoʊ/ *verb* [T] showed, shown to explain something to someone, by doing it or by giving instructions or examples: [+ question word] *Can you show me **how** to set the video recorder?* ○ *This dictionary contains many examples that show **how** words are actually used.* ○ *Could you show me the **way** to the bus station?*

● **show** *(sb)* **the** *way* to do something original which others are likely to copy: *Sweden has shown the way **forward** on energy efficiency.*

show PROVE /ʃəʊ/ US /ʃoʊ/ *verb* [T] showed, shown to prove something or make the truth or existence of something known: [R] *She has shown herself **(to be)** a highly competent manager.* ○ *His diaries show him to have been an extremely insecure person.* ○ [+ (that)] *The diaries show **(that)** he was very insecure.* ○ *Show me **(that)** I can trust you.* ○ [+ question word] *Our research has shown (us) **how** little we know about this disease.*

show EXPRESS /ʃəʊ/ US /ʃoʊ/ *verb* [T] showed, shown to express ideas or feelings using actions or words: *He finds it difficult to show affection.* ○ *She showed enormous courage when she rescued him from the fire.* ○ [+ two objects] *You should show your parents more respect/show more respect to your parents.*

show /ʃəʊ/ US /ʃoʊ/ *noun* [C] **1** when you show a particular idea or feeling to others: *In an unexpected show **of** solidarity, the management and workers have joined forces to campaign against the closure of the factory.* ○ *Over 100 military vehicles paraded through the capital in a show of **strength**.* **2** a good/poor, etc. show an activity or piece of work which appears to be done with great, little, etc. effort: *She may not have won, but she certainly **put up** a good show.*

show ARRIVE /ʃəʊ/ US /ʃoʊ/ *verb* [I] showed, shown MAINLY US to **show up** ARRIVE.

show PUBLIC EVENT /ʃəʊ/ US /ʃoʊ/ *noun* [C] an event at which a group of related things are available for the public to look at: *a **fashion/flower** show* ○ *There were some amazing new cars at the **motor** show.* ○ *They put on a **retrospective** show **of** his work at the National Museum of American Art.* ⊃See also **airshow; peepshow; roadshow; showjumping; sideshow**.

● **on show** Something that is on show has been made available for the public to look at: *Her sculptures will be on show at the museum until the end of the month.*

show /ʃəʊ/ US /ʃoʊ/ showed, shown **1** [T] to make an artist's work available for the public to see: *Our aim is* *to make it easier for young unknown artists to show their work.* **2** [I or T] If a cinema or a television station shows a film or programme, or if a film or programme is showing somewhere, you can see it there: *It's the first time this film has been shown on British television.* ○ *Now showing at a cinema near you!*

showing /ˈʃəʊ.ɪŋ/ [US] /ˈʃoʊ-/ *noun* [C] an opportunity for the public to see something: *This is the film's first showing on British television.*

show [ENTERTAINMENT] /ʃəʊ/ [US] /ʃoʊ/ *noun* [C] a theatrical performance or a television or radio programme which is entertaining rather than serious: *a* ***radio/television/stage*** *show* ○ *a* ***quiz/game*** *show* ○ *Why don't we go to London on Saturday and* ***see*** *a show?* ○ *We had to raise £60,000 to* ***stage*** *the show.* ○ *We had a* ***puppet*** *show for Jamie's birthday party.* ➲See also **roadshow**.

• **The show must go on.** *SAYING* said to encourage someone to continue with what they are doing, even if they are experiencing difficulties

show [FALSE APPEARANCE] /ʃəʊ/ [US] /ʃoʊ/ *noun* [C] an appearance of something which is not really sincere or real: *Despite its public show* ***of*** *unity, the royal family had its share of disagreements just like any other.* ○ *They* ***put on*** *a show* ***of*** *be****ing*** *interested, but I don't think they really were.*

• **for show** Something that is for show has no practical value and is used only to improve the appearance of something else: *Do the lights on this cassette deck have any useful function or are they* ***just/only*** *for show?*

show [ACTIVITY] /ʃəʊ/ [US] /ʃoʊ/ *noun* [U] *INFORMAL* an activity, business or organization, considered in relation to who is managing it: *Who will* ***run*** *the show when Meg retires?* ○ *The wedding is their show – let them do it their way.*

• **get the/this show on the road** *INFORMAL* to begin an activity that has been planned: *Come on, let's get this show on the road or we'll be late.*

PHRASAL VERBS WITH **show**

▲ **show off** *phrasal verb* to behave in a way which is intended to attract attention or admiration, and which other people often find annoying: *She only bought that sports car to show off and prove she could afford one.* ○ *He's always showing off to his classmates.*

▲ **show** ***sth/sb*** **off** *phrasal verb* [M] to show something or someone you are proud of to other people, so that they will admire them: *She likes to wear short skirts to show off her legs.*

show-off /ˈʃəʊ.ɒf/ [US] /ˈʃoʊ.ɑːf/ *noun* [C] a person who shows off: *Jimena's such a show-off, she always wants to be the centre of attention.*

▲ **show** ***sb*** **out** *phrasal verb* [M] to go to the door of the building with someone who does not live or work there, when they are leaving: *If you'd like to come this way, I'll show you out.*

▲ **show** ***yourself*** **out** *phrasal verb* [R] to leave a building in which you do not live or work, without anyone going to the door with you: *Don't get up – I'll show myself out.*

▲ **show** ***sb*** **over** ***sth*** *phrasal verb UK* to lead someone around a place that they are visiting in a formal or official way, while telling them about it: *After lunch the VIPs will be shown over the new Arts Centre.*

▲ **show** ***sb*** **round/around** ***(sth)*** *phrasal verb* to go with someone to all parts, or the main parts, of a place that they have not visited before, so that they can see what it is like or learn about it: *Let me know when you're coming to Cambridge and I'll show you around.* ○ *A guide showed us round the exhibition.*

▲ **show up** [ARRIVE] *phrasal verb* (*MAINLY US* **show**) *INFORMAL* to arrive somewhere in order to join a group of people, especially late or unexpectedly: *I invited him for eight o'clock, but he didn't show up until nine-thirty.* ○ *We were expecting thirty people to come, but half of them never showed up.*

▲ **show** ***sb*** **up** [EMBARRASS] *phrasal verb* [M] to behave in a way which makes someone you are with feel ashamed or embarrassed: *I wish you wouldn't show me up in front of my parents by getting so drunk.*

show-and-tell /ˌʃəʊ.ənˈtel/ [US] /ˌʃoʊ-/ *noun* [U] a school activity for young children in which a child brings an object into the class and talks to the other children about it

ˈshow ˌbusiness *noun* [U] (*INFORMAL* **showbiz**) the entertainment business, especially the part which is considered to be popular but not very artistic or serious: *Stars of the entertainment world turned out to celebrate his 40th year* ***in*** *show business.* ○ *a charity dinner attended by a host of showbiz* ***personalities***

showcase [CONTAINER] /ˈʃəʊ.keɪs/ [US] /ˈʃoʊ-/ *noun* [C] a container with glass sides in which valuable or important objects are kept so that they can be looked at without being touched, damaged or stolen

showcase [OPPORTUNITY] /ˈʃəʊ.keɪs/ [US] /ˈʃoʊ-/ *noun* [C] a situation or event which makes it possible for the best features of something to be seen: *The Venice Film Festival has always been the showcase* ***of*** *Italian cinema.* ○ *The exhibition is an annual showcase* ***for*** *British design and innovation.*

showcase /ˈʃəʊ.keɪs/ [US] /ˈʃoʊ-/ *verb* [T] to show the best qualities or parts of something: *The main aim of the exhibition is to showcase British design.*

showdown /ˈʃəʊ.daʊn/ [US] /ˈʃoʊ-/ *noun* [C] an important argument which is intended to end a disagreement that has existed for a long time: *The President is preparing for a showdown* ***with*** *his advisers* ***over*** *his plans to reform the economy.* ○ *Millions of dollars were spent on lawyers in a courtroom showdown* ***between*** *the two companies.*

shower [RAIN] /ʃaʊəʳ/ [US] /ʃaʊr/ *noun* [C] a brief period of rain or snow: *showers of rain, hail and sleet* ○ *You're soaked! Did you get caught in the shower?* ○ *There will be* ***thundery/wintry*** *showers over many parts of the country.* ○ ***Snow*** *showers are expected at the end of the week.* **showery** /ˈʃaʊə.ri/ [US] /ˈʃaʊr.i/ *adj*: *showery weather*

shower [MASS] /ʃaʊəʳ/ [US] /ʃaʊr/ *noun* **a shower of** ***sth*** a lot of small objects or drops of liquid coming through the air: *There was a bang and a shower* ***of sparks.*** ○ *The pipe burst, sending out a shower* ***of*** *water.*

shower /ʃaʊəʳ/ [US] /ʃaʊr/ *verb* [I or T; usually + adv or prep] *I heard a massive explosion, and seconds later fragments of glass were showering* (= falling) *down on us.* ○ *She shook the bottle violently and showered us* ***with*** *champagne.* ➲See also **shower with**.

shower [WASHING DEVICE] /ʃaʊəʳ/ [US] /ʃaʊr/ *noun* [C] **1** a device which releases drops of water through a lot of very small holes and which you stand under to wash your whole body: *The shower is broken – you'll have to have a bath.* ○ *Many British homes have a shower* ***attachment*** *fixed to the bath taps.* ○ *a shower* ***curtain/cap*** **2** a wash using such a device: *Have I got time to (UK)* ***have****/(US)* ***take*** *a shower before we go out?* **3** a place, usually in a bathroom, where a shower is situated: *He's* ***in*** *the shower at the moment. Would you like him to phone you back?* **shower** /ʃaʊəʳ/ [US] /ʃaʊr/ *verb* [I] *I shower every morning.*

shower [PARTY] /ʃaʊəʳ/ [US] /ʃaʊr/ *noun* [C] *US* a party held for a woman just before she gets married or gives birth to a child, when she is given presents for her future home or baby: *I bought the cutest baby clothes to take to Jacey's* ***baby*** *shower.*

▲ **shower** ***sb*** **with** ***sth*** *phrasal verb* (*ALSO* **shower** ***sth*** **on** ***sb***) to give someone a lot of presents or praise: *She only sees her niece occasionally, so she showers her with* ***presents*** *when she does.* ○ *His boss showered him with* ***praise.***

ˈshower ˌgel *noun* [U] a type of thick liquid soap used for washing your body in the shower

showerproof *UK* /ˈʃaʊə.pruːf/ [US] /ˈʃaʊr-/ *adj* (*US* **water-repellent**) Showerproof clothing or material does not absorb water when it is raining lightly: *This coat isn't waterproof, but it is showerproof.*

showgirl /ˈʃəʊ.gɜːl/ [US] /ˈʃoʊ.gɝːl/ *noun* [C] a young woman who sings or dances in a musical theatrical entertainment

ˈshow ˌhome/ˌhouse *UK noun* [C] (*US* **model house**) a new house or apartment which has been decorated and filled with furniture to show possible buyers of similar homes what such a home might be like when people are living in it

showily /ˈʃəʊ.ɪ.li/ [US] /ˈʃoʊ-/ *adv* ➲See at **showy**.

showiness /ˈʃəʊ.ɪ.nəs/ [US] /ˈʃoʊ-/ *noun* [U] ➲See at **showy**.

showing /ʃəʊ.ɪŋ/ [US] /ʃoʊ-/ *noun* [C usually sing] the quality of someone's performance in a competitive activity: *She managed a* ***good/strong*** *showing in the world championship, but was knocked out in the semi-final.* ○ *She had a* ***dismal*** *showing in the opinion polls.*

showjumping /ˈʃəʊˌdʒʌm.pɪŋ/ [US] /ˈʃoʊ-/ *noun* [U] a sport which involves riding horses in competitions which test their ability to jump quickly over large objects such as walls and fences

showjumper /ˈʃəʊˌdʒʌm.pəʳ/ [US] /ˈʃoʊˌdʒʌm.pɚ/ *noun* [C] a rider or horse that takes part in show jumping

showman /ˈʃəʊ.mən/ [US] /ˈʃoʊ-/ *noun* [C] *MAINLY APPROVING* someone who is very good at entertaining people **showmanship** /ˈʃəʊ.mən.ʃɪp/ [US] /ˈʃoʊ-/ *noun* [U] *Muhammad Ali's showmanship in the ring shouldn't detract from his considerable skill.*

shown /ʃəʊn/ [US] /ʃoʊn/ *past participle of* **show**

ˌshow of ˈhands *noun* [S] a vote in which people raise one of their hands to show that they support a suggestion: *Her re-election to the committee was defeated* ***on*** *a show of hands.*

showpiece /ˈʃəʊ.piːs/ [US] /ˈʃoʊ-/ *noun* [C] an extremely good example of something, which deserves to be admired: *The hospital will be the new showpiece of the health service when it opens next year.*

showroom /ˈʃəʊ.rʊm/ /-ruːm/ [US] /ˈʃoʊ-/ *noun* [C] a large shop in which people are encouraged to look at the goods that are on sale before buying them: *a* ***car*** *showroom* ○ *Our complete range of carpets is on display in our showroom.*

showstopper /ˈʃəʊˌstɒp.əʳ/ [US] /ˈʃoʊˌstɑː.pɚ/ *noun* [C] *APPROVING* an item in a stage performance that the audience enjoy so much that their clapping and shouts of approval interrupt the performance **showstopping** /ˈʃəʊˌstɒp.ɪŋ/ [US] /ˈʃoʊˌstɑː.pɪŋ/ *adj* [before n] *a showstopping* ***performance***

ˈshow ˌtrial *noun* [C] a trial organized by a government in order to have an effect on public opinion and reduce political opposition, and not because it is interested in matters of justice

showy /ˈʃəʊ.i/ [US] /ˈʃoʊ-/ *adj DISAPPROVING* attracting a lot of attention by being very colourful or bright, but lacking any real beauty: *a showy production of a play* ○ *Her dress was too showy for such a formal occasion.* **showily** /ˈʃəʊ.ɪ.li/ [US] /ˈʃoʊ-/ *adv* **showiness** /ˈʃəʊ.ɪ.nəs/ [US] /ˈʃoʊ-/ *noun* [U]

shrank /ʃræŋk/ *past simple of* **shrink**

shrapnel /ˈʃræp.nᵊl/ *noun* [U] small pieces of metal that are scattered by a bomb or similar weapon when it explodes and are intended to injure people: *Twelve people were* ***hit*** *by shrapnel in the attack.* ○ *a shrapnel* ***wound***

S

shred [CUT] /ʃred/ *verb* [T] **-dd- 1** to cut or tear something roughly into thin strips: *Shred the lettuce and arrange it around the edge of the dish.* ○ *shredded carrot/paper* **2** to destroy a document by tearing it into strips: *He ordered his secretary to shred important documents when government inspectors started investigating his business affairs.*

shred /ʃred/ *noun* [C usually pl] a very small thin piece that has been torn from something: *Cut the radishes into shreds to garnish the plates*

• **in shreds 1** very badly torn: *My shirt was in shreds when I took it out of the washer.* **2** badly damaged: *The report has left the prison governor's reputation in shreds.*

• **tear/rip** ***sb/sth*** **to shreds 1** to fiercely criticize a person or something they do, think or say: *The critics tore his performance to shreds.* **2** to damage someone or something badly: *My trousers were torn to shreds when I fell off my bike.*

shredder /ˈʃred.əʳ/ [US] /-ɚ/ *noun* [C] a tool or machine that is used for cutting things into very small pieces: *a paper/document/vegetable shredder* ○ *Much of the documentary evidence against her had been put through the shredder before she was arrested.*

shred [SMALL AMOUNT] /ʃred/ *noun* [S] a very small amount of something: *There's still* ***a*** *shred* ***of*** *hope that a peace agreement can be reached.* ○ *There isn't* ***a*** *shred* ***of evidence*** *to support her accusation.*

shrew [ANIMAL] /ʃruː/ *noun* [C] an animal like a small mouse but with a longer pointed nose and small eyes

shrew [WOMAN] /ʃruː/ *noun* [C] *OLD-FASHIONED DISAPPROVING* an unpleasant woman who is easily annoyed and who argues a lot **shrewish** /ˈʃruː.ɪʃ/ *adj DISAPPROVING*

shrewd /ʃruːd/ *adj APPROVING* possessing or based on a clear understanding and good judgment of a situation, resulting in an advantage: [+ **to** infinitive] *He was shrewd* ***enough*** *not* ***to*** *take the job when there was the possibility of getting a better one a few months later.* ○ *She is a shrewd* ***politician*** *who wants to avoid offending the electorate unnecessarily.* ○ *It was a shrewd* ***move*** *to buy your house just before property prices started to rise.* **shrewdly** /ˈʃruːd.li/ *adv*: *She shrewdly predicted the stock market crash.* **shrewdness** /ˈʃruːd.nəs/ *noun* [U]

shriek /ʃriːk/ *noun* [C] a short, loud, high cry, especially one produced suddenly as an expression of a powerful emotion: *shrieks* ***of*** *delight* ○ *He suddenly let out a* ***piercing*** *shriek.* **shriek** /ʃriːk/ *verb* [I or T] *We shrieked* ***with laughter*** *when we realized how stupid we'd been.* ○ *I tried to apologize, but he just shrieked* ***abuse*** *at me.* ○ [+ speech] *"Don't you dare do that ever again!" she shrieked.*

shrill /ʃrɪl/ *adj* **1** having a loud and high sound that is unpleasant or painful to listen to: *She had a shrill high-pitched voice.* **2** *DISAPPROVING* describes a way of arguing or criticizing that seems too forceful: *He launched a shrill attack on the Prime Minister.* **shrilly** /ˈʃrɪl.li/ *adv* **shrillness** /ˈʃrɪl.nəs/ *noun* [U]

shrimp [ANIMAL] (*plural* **shrimps** or **shrimp**) /ʃrɪmp/ *noun* [C or U] (*UK ALSO* **prawn**) a small sea animal with a thin shell, ten legs and long tail, or its pink curved body eaten as food: *shrimp cocktail/paste*

shrimp [PERSON] /ʃrɪmp/ *noun* [C] *plural* **shrimps** *INFORMAL DISAPPROVING* an unusually short person

shrine /ʃraɪn/ *noun* [C] **1** a place for worship which is holy because of a connection with a holy person or object: *Islam's most sacred shrine is at Mecca in Saudi Arabia.* **2** a special place in which you remember and praise someone who has died, especially someone famous: *She's turned her bedroom into a shrine* ***to*** *the dead pop star and covered the walls with pictures of him.*

shrink [BECOME SMALLER] /ʃrɪŋk/ *verb* [I or T] **shrank**, **shrunk** to become smaller, or to make something smaller: *Your sweater will shrink if you wash it at too high a temperature.* ○ *The company's profits have shrunk* ***from*** *£5.5 million* ***to*** *£1.25 million.* ○ *The productivity improvements have shrunk our costs* ***by*** *25%.* ➲See also **shrunken**. **shrinkage** /ˈʃrɪŋ.kɪdʒ/ *noun* [U] *Synthetic fabrics are less susceptible to shrinkage than natural ones.*

shrink [BE FRIGHTENED] /ʃrɪŋk/ *verb* [I usually + adv or prep] **shrank**, **shrunk** *LITERARY* to move away from someone or something because you are frightened: *The child shrank behind the sofa as his father shouted at him.* ○ *When she was younger she would shrink* ***(away) from*** *me whenever I spoke to her.*

shrink [DOCTOR] /ʃrɪŋk/ *noun* [C] *INFORMAL* a **psychiatrist** or **psychoanalyst**: *I was so depressed that I ended up going to see a shrink.*

▲ **shrink from** ***sth*** *phrasal verb* to avoid doing something that is unpleasant or difficult: *We must not shrink from our responsibilities.* ○ [+ **v-ing**] *We will not shrink from using force.*

ˌshrinking ˈviolet *noun* [C] *INFORMAL* a person who is very shy or modest and does not like to attract attention: *She loves appearing on television and is* ***no*** *shrinking violet when it comes to expressing her views.*

shrink-wrap /ˈʃrɪŋk.ræp/ *noun* [U] a thin transparent plastic material which tightly covers the thing that it is wrapped around, used for protecting goods when they are being transported or sold **shrink-wrap** /ˈʃrɪŋk.ræp/ *verb* [T] *A lot of the fresh food sold in supermarkets is shrink-wrapped.*

shrivel /ˈʃrɪv.ᵊl/ *verb* **-ll-** or *US USUALLY* **-l- 1** [I or T] to become dry, smaller and covered with lines as if by crushing or folding, or to make something do this: *The* lack of rain has shrivelled the crops. ○ You ought to pick those lettuces before they shrivel **(up)** and die. **2** [I] to become much smaller than is desired: Profits are shrivelling as the recession gets worse. shrivelled /ˈʃrɪv.ᵊld/ adj: Those oranges were looking a bit old and shrivelled, so I threw them out.

shroud [CLOTH] /ʃraʊd/ noun [C] a cloth or long loose piece of clothing that is used to wrap a dead body before it is buried

shroud [HIDE] /ʃraʊd/ verb [T] to hide something by covering or surrounding it: Visitors have complained about the scaffolding that shrouds half the castle. ○ Suddenly all the lights went out and the house was shrouded **in** darkness. ○ The **mist** shrouding the valley had lifted by eight o'clock.

● **be shrouded in secrecy/mystery** to be a matter about which very little is known or understood: Her whereabouts have been shrouded in secrecy since she received the death threat.

shroud /ʃraʊd/ noun [C] **1** a layer of something which covers or surrounds something: Everything was covered in a thick shroud of dust. **2** a situation which prevents something from being known or understood: The truth about the accident remains hidden beneath a shroud **of** secrecy.

Shrove Tuesday /ˌʃrəʊvˈtjuːz.deɪ/ ⓊⓈ /ˌʃroʊvˈtuːz-/ noun [C or U] (UK ALSO **Pancake Day**) the day before the Christian period of LENT begins

shrub /ʃrʌb/ noun [C] a large plant with a rounded shape formed from many small branches growing either directly from the ground or from a hard woody stem, grown in gardens: She planted some roses and other *flowering* shrubs. ⊃See also **bush** PLANT.
shrubbery /ˈʃrʌb.ᵊr.i/ ⓊⓈ /-ɚ-/ noun **1** [C] a part of a garden where a lot of shrubs have been planted **2** [U] a group of shrubs

shrug /ʃrʌɡ/ verb [I or T] **-gg-** to raise your shoulders and then lower them in order to express a lack of knowledge or interest: "Where's Dad?" "How should I know?" replied my brother, shrugging. ○ He shrugged his **shoulders** as if to say that there was nothing he could do about it. ○ FIGURATIVE Thousands of people are starving to death while the world shrugs its shoulders (= shows no interest or care).
shrug /ʃrʌɡ/ noun [C] when you shrug your shoulders to express something: "I'm afraid there's nothing I can do about your problem," she said with a shrug. ○ "Well, I suppose we'll just have to do what he says," said Kim with a shrug **of** resignation.
▲ **shrug sth off** phrasal verb [M] to treat something as if it is not important or not a problem: The stock market shrugged off the economic gloom and rose by 1.5%. ○ You're a father and you can't simply shrug off your **responsibility** for your children.

shrunk /ʃrʌŋk/ past simple and past participle of **shrink** ⊃See also **preshrunk**.

shrunken /ˈʃrʌŋ.kən/ adj smaller than before, and less impressive: a shrunken old man ○ The company faces shrunken profits for the third year in succession. ⊃See also **shrink** BECOME SMALLER.

shtick /ʃtɪk/ noun [C usually sing] MAINLY US **1** (ALSO **schtick**) the type of humour typical of a COMEDIAN (= person whose job is to make people laugh): Pratfalls and other physical gags are typical of Carey's shtick. **2** a particular ability, talent or behaviour that someone has and which they are well known for

shuck /ʃʌk/ verb [T] US to remove the shell or natural covering from something that is eaten: to shuck corn/oysters
▲ **shuck sth off** phrasal verb [M] US **1** to remove an item of clothing, especially one that limits you: The lifeguard shucked off his sweatshirt. **2** to get rid of something that limits you or causes you problems: They seem to be able to just shuck off guilt.

shucks /ʃʌks/ exclamation US INFORMAL an expression of modesty, embarrassment, disappointment, regret or annoyance: "You played brilliantly in the concert." "Shucks, do you honestly think so?" ○ Shucks, I wish I

could have gone to the party with Jessica. ⊃See also **aw-shucks**.

shudder /ˈʃʌd.əʳ/ ⓊⓈ /-ɚ-/ verb [I] **1** to shake suddenly with very small movements because of a very unpleasant thought or feeling: The sight of so much blood made him shudder. ○ She shuddered **at the thought of** kissing him. **2** When something shudders, it shakes violently and quickly: I heard a massive explosion and the ground shuddered beneath me. ○ There was a screech of brakes and the bus shuddered **to a halt** (= shook violently and stopped).

● **shudder to a halt** If a system shudders to a halt, it suddenly stops working: The economy has shuddered to a halt because of the civil war.

● **I shudder to think** said when you are anxious about something unpleasant that might happen or might have happened: I shudder to think what my parents will say when I tell them I've failed my exams.
shudder /ˈʃʌd.əʳ/ ⓊⓈ /-ɚ-/ noun [C] when someone or something shudders: He gave a slight shudder as he considered how near he had come to death. ○ She recalled **with a** shudder how her boss had once tried to kiss her. ○ FIGURATIVE Britain's second biggest supermarket chain has **sent a** shudder **through** (= has had a strong effect on) its rivals by slashing its prices.

● **send shudders/a shudder down your spine** to cause you to feel extremely anxious or frightened: When I think of what might have happened in the accident, it sends shudders down my spine.

shuffle [MIX CARDS] /ˈʃʌf.l̩/ verb [I or T] to mix a set of playing cards without seeing their values before beginning a game, so that their order is unknown to any of the players: It's your turn to shuffle the cards. shuffle /ˈʃʌf.l̩/ noun [C] Make sure you give the cards a good shuffle before you deal.

shuffle [MOVE AROUND] /ˈʃʌf.l̩/ verb [T] to move similar things from one position or place to another, often to give an appearance of activity when nothing useful is being done: She shuffled her **papers** nervously on her desk. ○ Many prisoners have to be shuffled around police stations because of prison overcrowding.
shuffle /ˈʃʌf.l̩/ noun [C] **1** when things are moved around from one position to another: She gave her papers a quick shuffle. **2** MAINLY US a **reshuffle**

shuffle [WALK] /ˈʃʌf.l̩/ verb **1** [I + adv or prep; T] to walk by pulling your feet slowly along the ground rather than lifting them: I love shuffling **through** the fallen leaves. ○ He shuffled **into** the kitchen, leaning on his walking stick. ○ Don't shuffle your feet like that! Lift them properly. **2** [I usually + adv or prep; T] to move your feet or bottom around, while staying in the same place, especially because you are uncomfortable, nervous or embarrassed: The woman in front of me kept shuffling around in her seat all the way through the performance. ○ When I asked him where he'd been, he just looked at the ground and shuffled his feet. shuffle /ˈʃʌf.l̩/ noun [S] He's got arthritis and walks with a shuffle.

shufti, shufty /ˈʃʊf.ti/ noun UK OLD-FASHIONED INFORMAL **have/take a shufti** to look at something briefly: Can I have a shufti **at** your paper?

shun /ʃʌn/ verb [T] **-nn-** **1** to avoid something: She has shunned publicity since she retired from the theatre. **2** to ignore someone and not speak to them because you cannot accept their behaviour, beliefs, etc: After the trial he was shunned by friends and family alike.

shunt [TRAINS] /ʃʌnt/ verb [T] to move a train or carriage onto a different track in or near a station using a special railway engine designed for this purpose shunt /ʃʌnt/ noun [C usually sing]
shunter /ˈʃʌn.təʳ/ ⓊⓈ /-t̬ɚ/ noun [C] a small railway engine that is used for moving carriages around on the tracks rather than making journeys between stations

shunt [MOVE] /ʃʌnt/ verb [T usually + adv or prep] to move someone or something from one place to another, usually because they are not wanted and without consideration of any unpleasant effects: I spent most of my childhood being shunted **(about) between** my parents who had divorced when I was five. ○ He shunts his kids **off** to a camp every summer. ○ Viewers are fed up with their favourite sitcoms being shunted **to** later times to make

S

way for live football coverage.

shush /ʃʊʃ/ *exclamation INFORMAL* used to tell someone to be quiet: *Shush! I want to listen to the news.*

shush /ʃʊʃ/ *verb* [I or T] *INFORMAL* to (cause to) stop talking or making a noise: *I wish you children would shush and let me read the paper in peace.* ○ *He tried to shush the children.*

shut CLOSE /ʃʌt/ *verb* [I or T] shutting, shut, shut to (cause to) close something: *Please shut the gate.* ○ *I've got a surprise for you! Shut your eyes tightly and hold out your hand.* ○ *Mary shut her book and put it down on the table.* ○ *This window won't shut – it's jammed.*

• **shut your eyes to** to ignore something: *Until now the President has shut his eyes to the homelessness problem.*

• **shut your mouth/face** (*UK ALSO* **shut your gob**) *SLANG* a rude and angry way of telling someone to stop talking: *He told me to shut my mouth or there'd be trouble.* ○ *"You're a lazy slob!" "You shut your mouth* (= Don't talk to me like that)*!"*

shut /ʃʌt/ *adj* [after v] closed: *I suspected something was wrong when I noticed her curtains were still shut at lunchtime.* ○ *FIGURATIVE The government ought to have opened the door to Japanese investment instead of slamming it shut.* ⊃See **with your eyes shut** at **eye** ORGAN; **open-and-shut**.

shut STOP OPERATING /ʃʌt/ *verb* [I or T] shutting, shut, shut to (cause to) stop operating or being in service, either temporarily or permanently: *The shops shut at eight o'clock on Wednesday evenings.* ○ *It's such a shame they shut that factory* (down)*.*

PHRASAL VERBS WITH shut ▼

▲ **shut sb away** *phrasal verb* [M] to put a person in a place which they are not permitted or able to leave: *He was ten years old when he was shut away in an asylum for stealing an apple.*

▲ **shut sth away** *phrasal verb* to put something in a place where other people cannot see it or get it: *The diamonds are shut away in a bank vault somewhere.*

▲ **shut yourself away** *phrasal verb* [R] to go into a place that you are unwilling to leave and where you do not want to be interrupted by other people: *Andy shuts himself away in his studio for hours on end when he's recording a song.*

▲ **shut (sth) down** *phrasal verb* [M] If a business or a large piece of equipment shuts down or someone shuts it down, it stops operating: *The company plans to shut down four factories and cut 10,000 jobs.* ○ *The crew shut down the right-hand engine of the aircraft.*

shutdown /'ʃʌt.daʊn/ *noun* [C] when a business or large piece of equipment stops operating, usually for a temporary period: *It's just a regular maintenance shutdown.* ○ *The emergency shutdown procedure was activated.*

▲ **shut sb/sth in (sth)** PREVENT ESCAPE *phrasal verb* to prevent someone or something from leaving a place, usually by closing or fastening a door or gate: *The cat was shut in the garage all night.* ○ [R] *He was so upset that he shut himself in his bedroom and refused to come out.*

▲ **shut sth in sth** CATCH *phrasal verb* to trap part of your body or an object inside a device or container when it closes: *Steve was off work for a week after he shut his hand in the car door.*

▲ **shut (sth) off** MACHINE *phrasal verb* [M] If a machine or system shuts off, it stops operating, and if someone or something shuts it off, they stop it from operating: *The engine shuts off automatically when the desired speed is reached.*

▲ **shut sth off** SUPPLY *phrasal verb* [M] to stop the supply of something: *Did you remember to shut off the water and gas before you left the house?* ○ *Oil supplies have been shut off.*

▲ **shut sth off** AREA *phrasal verb* [M] to prevent something from being reached or seen: *The music room is shut off from the rest of the house by a soundproof partition.* ○ *A row of tall fir trees shuts off the view of the street in front.*

▲ **shut yourself off** PERSON *phrasal verb* [R] to stop speaking to other people or stop being involved with them:

When her husband died she seemed to shut herself off from her friends and family.

▲ **shut sb/sth out** PREVENT ENTRY *phrasal verb* to stop someone or something from entering or getting back inside a house or other building: *Don't forget to shut the cat out when you leave for work.* ○ *The wind blew the door closed behind me and now I'm shut out* (of the house)*.*

▲ **shut sb/sth out** NOT INCLUDE *phrasal verb* [M] to not include a person or organization in an activity: *Anna felt shut out of the conversation.* ○ *What are the chances of peace if we shut the terrorists out of negotiations?*

▲ **shut sb out** COMPETITOR *phrasal verb* [M] *US* to prevent your competitor in a sports competition from scoring any points: *She had shut out four of her first four Wimbledon opponents by identical 6-0, 6-0 scores.*

shutout /'ʃʌt.aʊt/ *US* /'ʃʌt̬-/ *noun* [C] *US* a situation in a sports competition in which a player or team wins without the other player or team scoring any points

▲ **shut sth out** THOUGHT/FEELING *phrasal verb* [M] to stop yourself thinking about something that upsets you or feeling something that hurts you: *She finds it impossible to shut out the memory of the accident.*

▲ **shut sth out** SOUND/LIGHT *phrasal verb* [M] to prevent a sound or light from being heard or seen: *The double glazing shuts out most of the traffic noise.* ○ *She pulled the duvet over her head to try to shut out the light.*

▲ **shut (sb) up** STOP TALKING *phrasal verb* [M] *INFORMAL* **1** to stop talking or making a noise, or to make someone do this: *I wish you'd shut up for a moment and listen to what the rest of us have to say.* ○ *Just shut up and get on with your work!* ○ *My dad never stops talking. It's impossible to shut him up!* ○ *FIGURATIVE If you breathe a single word to the police, we'll come round and shut you up for good* (= kill you). **2** to stop someone from talking about a particular subject or from complaining or asking for things: *The kids kept on about how hungry they were, so their father gave them some biscuits to shut them up.*

▲ **shut sb/sth up** KEEP IN *phrasal verb* [M] to keep a person or animal in an enclosed place: *She can't spend her whole life shut up in her office.*

▲ **shut (sth) up** CLOSE *phrasal verb* [M] *UK* to close a shop or other business for a period of time, usually when business is finished for the day: *By the time we got there, all the market traders were shutting up.*

• **shut up shop** *UK* (*MAINLY US* **close up shop**) to end an activity, usually a business activity, either temporarily or permanently: *Many companies are considering shutting up shop in this country and transferring production to low wage economies.*

shuteye /'ʃʌt.aɪ/ *US* /'ʃʌt̬-/ *noun* [U] *OLD-FASHIONED INFORMAL* sleep: *You look exhausted! Try to get some shuteye on the train.*

shutter PHOTOGRAPHY /'ʃʌt.ə^r/ *US* /'ʃʌt̬.ɚ/ *noun* [C] the part of a camera which opens temporarily to allow light to reach the film when a photograph is being taken

shutter WINDOW COVER /'ʃʌt.ə^r/ *US* /'ʃʌt̬.ɚ/ *noun* [C] **1** a wooden cover on the outside of a window which prevents light or heat from going into a room or heat from leaving it: *Shutters usually come in pairs and are hung like doors on hinges.* **2** a metal covering which protects the windows and entrance of a shop from thieves when it is closed **shuttered** /'ʃʌt.əd/ *US* /'ʃʌt̬.ɚd/ *adj*: *Shops are closed and shuttered on Sundays.*

shuttle VEHICLE /'ʃʌt.l̩/ *US* /'ʃʌt̬-/ *noun* [C] a vehicle or aircraft that travels regularly between two places: *To get across town, you can take the shuttle from Times Square to Grand Central.* ○ *The American (space) shuttle can be used many times to put payloads in space.*

shuttle /'ʃʌt.l̩/ *US* /'ʃʌt̬-/ *verb* [I or T; usually + adv or prep] to travel or take people regularly between the same two places: *A small train shuttles constantly between the concourse and the runways.*

shuttle THREAD /'ʃʌt.l̩/ *US* /'ʃʌt̬-/ *noun* [C] *SPECIALIZED* in weaving, a device which is used to carry the thread that goes across the cloth between the threads that go down the cloth

shuttlecock /ˈʃʌt.l̩.kɒk/ ⓤ /ˈʃʌt.l̩.kɑːk/ *noun* [C] (*INFORMAL* **shuttle**) a small light object with a rounded end to which real or artificial feathers are fixed and which is hit over the net in the game of BADMINTON

shuttle di‚plomacy *noun* [U] indirect discussions between two or more countries, in which someone travels between the different countries, talking to the governments involved, carrying messages and suggesting ways of dealing with problems

shy NERVOUS /ʃaɪ/ *adj* **shyer**, **shyest** nervous and un-comfortable with other people: *He was too shy to ask her to dance with him.* ○ *She gave a shy smile.* ○ *Children are often shy of/with people they don't know.* ○ *The deer were shy* (= unwilling to be near people) *and hid behind some trees.*
-shy /-ʃaɪ/ *suffix*: camera-shy (= not liking being photo-graphed) ○ *workshy* (= not liking work)
shyly /ˈʃaɪ.li/ *adv* in a shy way: *She smiled shyly at him.*
shyness /ˈʃaɪ.nəs/ *noun* [U] the condition of being shy: *His face went red with shyness when he walked into the crowded room.*

shy HORSES /ʃaɪ/ *verb* [I] (of a horse) to suddenly move sideways or backwards, especially because of fear: *The horse shied at the fence.* ○ *There's a lot of traffic on the road – I'm sure my horse is going to shy.*

shy THROW /ʃaɪ/ *verb* [T usually + adv or prep] *OLD-FASHIONED INFORMAL* to throw something suddenly, often in a side-ways movement: *Two small boys were shying stones at a tree.* **shy** /ʃaɪ/ *noun* [C]

shy LACKING /ʃaɪ/ *adj* [after n] less than; lacking: *We're only £100 shy of the total amount.*

▲ **shy away from** *sth phrasal verb* to avoid something that you dislike, fear or do not feel confident about: *I've never shied away from hard work.*

shyster /ˈʃaɪ.stəʳ/ ⓤ /-stɚ/ *noun* [C] *INFORMAL* a dishonest person, especially a lawyer or politician: *He's a real shyster.* ○ *What are those shyster politicians doing now?*

Siamese (cat) /ˌsaɪ.ə.miːzˈkæt/ *noun* [C] a short-haired cat with pale fur, but darker ears, tail and feet, and blue eyes

Siamese twins /ˌsaɪ.ə.miːzˈtwɪnz/ *plural noun SLIGHTLY OLD-FASHIONED* **conjoined twins**: (= two people with the same mother who were born at the same time, with some part of their bodies joined together)

sibling /ˈsɪb.lɪŋ/ *noun* [C] *FORMAL* a brother or sister: *I have four siblings: three brothers and a sister.* ○ *There was great sibling rivalry* (= competition) *between Peter and his brother.*

sibyl /ˈsɪb.ᵊl/ *noun* [C] *LITERARY* any of several women in the ancient world who were thought to be able to see into the future

sic /sɪk/ *adv* a word written in BRACKETS SYMBOL after a word that you have copied to show that you know it has been spelled or used wrongly: *The notice outside the cinema said 'Closed on Wedensday' (sic).*

sick ILL /sɪk/ *adj* physically or mentally ill; not well or healthy: *a sick child* ○ *a sick cow* ○ *My father has been off sick* (= not working because of illness) *for a long time.* ○ *Anyone who could hurt a child like that must be sick* (= mentally ill). ○ *The old woman fell/took/was taken sick* (= became ill) *while she was away and had to come home.* ○ *Sarah called in/reported sick* (= told her employer that she was unable to go to work because of illness). ○ *FIGURATIVE High rates of crime are considered by some people to be a sign of a sick society.* ➋See also **heartsick**; **homesick**; **lovesick**.
the sick *plural noun* people who are ill: *It's better for the sick to be cared for at home rather than in hospital.*
sicken /ˈsɪk.ᵊn/ *verb* [I] to become ill: *LITERARY The child sickened and died.* ○ *UK "You look feverish. Are you sick-ening for* (= about to become ill with) *something?"*
sickly /ˈsɪk.li/ *adj* weak, unhealthy and often ill: *a sickly child/plant* ○ *Her face was a sickly colour when she came out of the dentist's.*
sickness /ˈsɪk.nəs/ *noun* [U] the condition of being ill: *There's a lot of sickness around this winter.*

USAGE

sick, ill and **be sick**

In British English **ill** is the word that is usually used to mean 'not well'. In American English the word for this is **sick**.

He went home early because he was ill. (British English)
He went home early because he was sick. (American English).

In British English to **be sick** is to bring food up from the stomach. Another way of saying this is the word **vomit**, which is used both in British and American English.

The little boy in the back seat of the car was sick into a paper bag. (British English)

sick VOMIT /sɪk/ *adj* [after v] **1** feeling ill as if you are going to vomit: *Lucy felt sick the morning after the party.* ○ *If you eat any more of that cake, you'll make yourself sick.* ➋See also **airsick**; **carsick**; **seasick**. **2** be sick to vomit: *She was sick after she ate too much chocolate.*
● **sick as a dog** vomiting a lot: *I was sick as a dog after last night's meal.*
● **sick to your stomach** likely to vomit: *I'm (feeling) sick to my stomach.*
sick /sɪk/ *noun* [U] *UK INFORMAL* vomit: *a pool of sick on the floor*
sickly /ˈsɪk.li/ *adj DISAPPROVING* **1** causing a slight feeling of wanting to vomit: *A sickly smell of decaying fish came from the dirty river.* ○ *The chocolate cake was sickly sweet* (= too sweet). **2** emotional, in an embarrassing way: *His books are sometimes accused of sickly sentimentality.*
sickness /ˈsɪk.nəs/ *noun* [U] vomiting: *Drinking unclean water can cause diarrhoea and sickness.*

sick UNPLEASANT /sɪk/ *adj* [after v] *INFORMAL* causing or expressing unpleasant emotions: *I'm sick about/(UK) at/(US) over* (= unhappy about) *not getting that job.* ○ *It makes me sick* (= makes me very angry) *to see people wearing fur coats.* ○ *UK INFORMAL It's sick-making* (= very annoying) *that she's being paid so much for doing so little.* ○ *I'm sick (and tired/to death) of* (= very annoyed about) *the way you're behaving.* ○ *She was worried sick* (= very worried) *when her daughter didn't come home on time.* ○ *Joan was not amused by the sick* (= cruel or offensive) *joke her brother told.* ○ *I felt sick* (= felt shocked and disgusted) *when I heard about the prisoners being beaten.*
● **sick as a parrot** *UK HUMOROUS SLANG* very disappointed: *He was sick as a parrot when his team lost the match.*
● **sick at heart** *LITERARY* very unhappy: *David was sick at heart about having to leave his family behind.*
● **sick to your stomach** feeling very upset, worried or an-gry: *It makes me (feel) sick to my stomach when I remember my car accident.*
sicken /ˈsɪk.ᵊn/ *verb* [T] to cause someone to feel un-pleasant emotions, especially anger and shock: *The violence in the film sickened me.* ○ *He was sickened by/at the number of people who were hurt in the crash.*
sickening /ˈsɪk.ᵊn.ɪŋ/ *adj* **1** extremely unpleasant and causing you to feel shock and anger: *The slaves were treated with sickening cruelty.* ○ *There was a sickening thud when the child fell from the tree and hit the ground.* **2** annoying: *It's sickening that I can't go to the party.*
sickeningly /ˈsɪk.ᵊn.ɪŋ.li/ *adv*

sick /sɪk/ *verb*
▲ **sick** *sth* **up** *phrasal verb* [M] *UK INFORMAL* to vomit some-thing: *The baby sicked up some milk on his aunt's shoulder.*
sickbay /ˈsɪk.beɪ/ *noun* [C] a room with beds for people who are ill, especially on a ship or in a school
sickbed /ˈsɪk.bed/ *noun* [C] the bed of a person who is ill: *We visited my grandmother on her sickbed.*
‚sick 'building ‚syndrome *noun* [U] an unhealthy atmosphere in a building which may cause illness in workers: *Air conditioning can contribute to sick building syndrome.*
'sick ‚day *noun* [C] a day for which an employee will receive pay while absent from work because of illness
‚sick 'headache *noun* [C] a severe pain in the head, especially a MIGRAINE

sickie /ˈsɪk.i/ *noun* UK INFORMAL **throw a sickie** to say to your employer that you are ill when you are not so that you do not have to go to your place of work for a day: *I just didn't feel like work so I threw a sickie.*

sickle /ˈsɪk.l̩/ *noun* [C] a tool with a short handle and a curved blade, used for cutting grass and grain crops ➲Compare **scythe**.

ˈsick ˌleave *noun* [U] absence from work because of illness: *Mark is not in the office today. He broke his leg yesterday, so he's on/he's taken sick leave.*

sickle-cell anaemia, MAINLY US **sickle-cell anemia** /ˌsɪk.l̩.sel.əˈniː.mi.ə/ *noun* [U] a medical condition, given from parent to child and found especially in black people, in which the red blood cells are curved in shape, and which causes pain and fever

ˈsickness ˌbenefit *noun* [U] UK money paid by the government to someone who cannot work because of illness

sicko /ˈsɪk.əʊ/ [US] /-oʊ/ *noun* [C] *plural* **sickos** SLANG someone, especially a man, who is mentally ill or who performs unpleasant, often sexual, acts: *She's afraid of being attacked in the park by a sicko.* **sicko** /ˈsɪk.əʊ/ [US] /-oʊ/ *adj*

ˈsick ˌpay *noun* [U] money given by an employer to someone who cannot work because of illness

sickroom /ˈsɪk.rʊm/ /-ruːm/ *noun* [C] a room in which someone who is ill lies in bed

side [SURFACE] /saɪd/ *noun* [C] a flat outer surface of an object, especially one that is not the top, the bottom, the front or the back: *The names of ships are usually painted on their sides.* ○ *My room is at the side of the house.* ○ *Please write on one side of the paper only.* ○ *I've already written four sides* (= pages of writing) *for my essay.* ○ *Canadian coins have a picture of the Queen's head on one side.* ○ *Please use the side entrance.*

• **the other side of the coin** The other side of the coin is a different way of considering a situation, making it seem either better or worse than it did originally: *I like having a white car, but the other side of the coin is that it soon gets dirty.*

• **come down on one side of the fence or other** to make a decision between two opposing points of view: *The election is next week, so you'll have to come down on one side of the fence or other by then.*

side-on /ˌsaɪdˈɒn/ [US] /-ˈɑːn/ *adv, adj*: *The bus hit the car side-on* (= on its side). ○ *a side-on collision* **-sided** /-saɪ.dɪd/ *suffix*: *a steep-sided hill*

side [EDGE] /saɪd/ *noun* [C] an edge or border of something: *A square has four sides.* ○ *There are trees on both sides of the road.* ○ *They were surrounded **on all** sides/**on every** side by curious children.* **-sided** /-saɪ.dɪd/ *suffix*: *A square is a four-sided figure.*

side [NEXT TO] /saɪd/ *noun* [U] a place next to something: *I have a small table **at/by** the side of* (= next to) *my bed.* ○ *He stayed **at/by** her side* (= with her) *throughout her long illness.* ➲See also **alongside**; **aside** TO ONE SIDE; **beside**.

• **on the side 1** in addition to your main job: *He makes a little money on the side by cleaning windows in his spare time.* **2** secretly: *I think he has another woman on the side* (= a relationship with a woman who is not his wife). **3** MAINLY US (of food in a restaurant) served on another plate, or not on part of the meal: *I'd like a salad with the dressing on the side* (= with the dressing served separately from the salad), *please.* ○ *I'll have a omelette with fries on the side, please.*

• **put/lay *sth* on/to one side** to not use something, especially an amount of money, in order to keep it for later use: *We have put some money on one side for next year's summer holiday.*

• **put/leave *sth* on/to one side** to stop talking about a particular subject: *Can we leave the issue of pay on one side for the moment?*

• **side by side** next to each other: *The children sat side by side on the sofa watching television.*

• **take/lead *sb* on/to one side** to have a private talk with someone: *Bill's father took him to one side and told him to stop behaving so badly.*

side /saɪd/ *adj* [before n] *I'd like a side **dish**/*(MAINLY US) *side **order** of potatoes, please* (= some potatoes on a separate plate). ○ *We parked the car on a side **street/road*** (= a small road, especially one that joins on to a main road). ○ *I think that's a side **issue*** (= a subject which is separate from the main one) *which we should talk about later.*

side [PART] /saɪd/ *noun* **1** [C] a part of something, especially in relation to a real or imagined central line: *He likes to sleep on the right side of the bed.* ○ *In Britain, cars drive on the left side of the road.* ○ *There is no money **on** my mother's side **(of the family)**.* ○ *I could just see Joan **on the far/other** side **of** the room.* ○ *Children came running **from all** sides* (= from all directions). **2** [C usually sing] the part of the body from under the arm to the top of the leg: *I have a pain in my side.* **3** [C] UK a television station: *What side is 'Coronation Street' on?* **4** [C usually sing] half of an animal's body, considered as meat: *She bought a side of lamb from the butcher's shop.*

• **from side to side** from left to right and from right to left: *The curtains were swinging from side to side in the breeze.*

• **on the right/wrong side of the law** obeying/disobeying the law: *After coming out of prison, he tried to stay on the right side of the law.*

• **on the right/wrong side of *number*** looking younger/older than a particular age: *She looks to me as if she's on the wrong side of 50.*

• **the wrong/other side of the tracks** a part of a town that is considered poor and dangerous: *Her boyfriend came from the wrong side of the tracks.*

• **this side of** before reaching a particular age, date, place, etc: *I can't believe she's this side of 50.* ○ *We don't expect to see Gideon this side of Christmas.* ○ *This is the best pizza I've eaten this side of* (= anywhere other than) *Rome.* ○ *Parenting is the most rewarding thing I will do this side of **the grave*** (= in life).

• **on the large/small, etc. side** too large/small, etc. for a particular purpose: *This dress is rather on the large side **for** me.*

sideways /ˈsaɪd.weɪz/ *adv, adj* in a direction to the left or right, not forwards or backwards: *The fence is leaning sideways.* ○ *If you would move sideways to the left, I can get everyone in the picture.*

side [OPPOSING GROUP] /saɪd/ *group noun* [C] one of two or more opposing teams or groups: *This is a war which neither side can win.* ○ *Our side* (= team) *lost again on Saturday.* ○ *Whose/which side are you **on*** (= which team are you playing for/supporting)? ○ *Don't be angry with me – I'm **on** your side* (= I want to help you). ➲See **time is on** someone's **side** at **time** MINUTES/DAYS/YEARS.

• **have *sth* on *your* side** If you have something on your side, it gives you an advantage when you are trying to achieve something: *I thought I would get the job, but the other person who was being considered for it had experience on his side.*

• **take sides** to support one person or group rather than another, in an argument or war: *My mother never takes sides when my brother and I argue.*

• **take *sb's* side** to support someone in an argument: *My mother always take my father's side when I argue with him.*

side [OPINION] /saɪd/ *noun* [C] an opinion held in an argument; way of considering: *There are at least two sides **to** every question.* ○ *I've listened to your side **of the story**, but I still think you were wrong to do what you did.* **-sided** /-saɪ.dɪd/ *suffix*: *a many-sided question*

side [CHARACTER] /saɪd/ *noun* [C] a part of someone's character: *She seems quite fierce, but actually she has a gentle side.*

• **get on the right/wrong side of *sb*** to make someone pleased/annoyed with you: *As a teenager, Clare was always getting on the wrong side of her mother.*

• **keep on the right side of *sb*** to try to make certain that someone is pleased with you: *Paul kept on the right side of his teachers by doing masses of work.*

side /saɪd/ *verb*

▲ **side with *sb*** *phrasal verb* to support one person or group in an argument: *If ever there was any sort of argument, she'd always side with my father **against** me.*

S

sidearm /ˈsaɪd.ɑːm/ [US] /-ɑːrm/ *noun* [C] a weapon worn on the side of the body, especially a small gun or sword

sidebar /ˈsaɪd.bɑːʳ/ [US] /-bɑːr/ *noun* [C] *US* a short news story in a newspaper or magazine that relates to a longer main story, giving details or extra information

sideboard /ˈsaɪd.bɔːd/ [US] /-bɔːrd/ *noun* [C] a piece of furniture with a flat top and cupboards at the bottom, usually used for holding glasses, plates, etc.

sideburns /ˈsaɪd.bɜːnz/ [US] /-bɝːnz/ *plural noun* (*UK ALSO* **sideboards**) areas of hair grown down the sides of a man's face in front of the ears

sidecar /ˈsaɪd.kɑːʳ/ [US] /-kɑːr/ *noun* [C] a small one-wheeled vehicle fixed to the side of a motorcycle to hold a passenger

ˈside efˌfect *noun* [C] an unpleasant effect of a drug that happens in addition to the main effect: *Does this drug **have** any side effects?*

sidekick /ˈsaɪd.kɪk/ *noun* [C] *INFORMAL* a person who works with someone who is more important than they are: *I've been his sidekick for long enough – it's time I found myself something better to do.*

sidelight *UK* /ˈsaɪd.laɪt/ *noun* [C] (*US* **parking light**) either of the two smaller lights fixed on the front of a car ➲Compare **headlight**. ➲See picture **Car** on page Centre 12

sideline [JOB] /ˈsaɪd.laɪn/ *noun* [C] an activity that is additional to your main job: *Jim works in a bank, but teaches French in the evenings **as** a sideline.*

sideline [SPORT] /ˈsaɪd.laɪn/ *noun* [C] *MAINLY US* a line marking the side areas of play, especially for football: *The ball fell just **inside/on/outside** the sideline.*

• **on/from the sidelines** If you are on the sidelines or do something from the sidelines, you are not actively involved in something: *Our party has been on the **political** sidelines for too long – we must now work towards getting into power.* ○ *She could only **watch** from the sidelines as her brother's health deteriorated.*

sideline /ˈsaɪd.laɪn/ *verb* [T] **1** If a sports player is sidelined they are prevented from playing or competing, and can only watch: *Johnson has been sidelined through injury.* **2** to stop someone taking an active and important part in something: *The minister was sidelined after he criticized party policy.*

sidelong /ˈsaɪd.lɒŋ/ [US] /-lɑːŋ/ *adj* [before n], *adv* describes a short look at someone or something, moving your eyes to the side, and not looking directly: *He gave her a sidelong glance.* ○ *He glanced at her sidelong and smiled.*

ˈside mirˌror *noun* [C] *US FOR* **wing mirror** ➲See picture **Car** on page Centre 12

ˈside ˌplate *noun* [C] a small plate that you put your bread on when you are eating the main part of a meal

sidereal /saɪˈdɪə.ri.əl/ [US] /-ˈdɪr.i-/ *adj* [before n] *SPECIALIZED* of or calculated by the stars

siˈdereal ˌtime *noun* [U] *SPECIALIZED* time based on the movement of the Earth in relation to the stars

sidesaddle /ˈsaɪdˌsæd.l̩/ *noun* [C], *adv* (on) a saddle used especially in the past by women, on which the rider sits with both legs on the same side of the horse: *The Queen rode sidesaddle when she inspected the soldiers.*

sideshow /ˈsaɪd.ʃəʊ/ [US] /-ʃoʊ/ *noun* [C] **1** a small show or attraction in addition to the main entertainment: *Carol won a large soft toy at a sideshow at the fair.* **2** an event or subject which is connected to another event or subject, but which is considered to be much less important: *The media still regards women's sport as a sideshow to the main event.*

sidesplitting /ˈsaɪdˌsplɪt.ɪŋ/ [US] /-ˌsplɪt̬-/ *adj* extremely amusing: *a sidesplitting joke/story/film*

sidestep /ˈsaɪd.step/ *verb* [I or T] **-pp- 1** to step to the side in order to avoid something, especially being hit: *He sidestepped the blow/the tackle.* **2** to avoid talking about a subject, especially by starting to talk about something else: *The speaker sidestepped **the question** by saying that it would take him too long to answer it.*

sidestroke /ˈsaɪd.strəʊk/ [US] /-stroʊk/ *noun* [U] any of various ways of swimming lying on one side

sideswipe [REMARK] /ˈsaɪd.swaɪp/ *noun* [C] a remark attacking something or someone made while talking about something else: *During her lecture on her discoveries, she **made/took** several sideswipes **at** the management.*

sideswipe [HIT] /ˈsaɪd.swaɪp/ *verb* [T] to hit on the side: *The motorcycle turned the corner too quickly, and sideswiped a car coming towards it.* **sideswipe** /ˈsaɪd.swaɪp/ *noun* [C]

sidetrack /ˈsaɪd.træk/ *verb* [T usually passive] to direct a person's attention away from an activity or subject towards another one which is less important: *Ruth was looking for an envelope in a drawer when she was sidetracked by some old letters.* ○ *The students sidetracked their teacher **into** talking about her hobby.* ○ *I'm sorry I'm late – I **got** sidetracked.* **sidetrack** /ˈsaɪd.træk/ *noun* [C]

sidewalk /ˈsaɪd.wɔːk/ [US] /-wɑːk/ *noun* [C] *MAINLY US FOR* **pavement**

sideways /ˈsaɪd.weɪz/ *adv, adj* ➲See at **side** PART.

side-wheeler /ˈsaɪd.wiː.ləʳ/ [US] /-lɚ/ *noun* [C] *US FOR* **paddle steamer**

siding [MATERIAL] /ˈsaɪ.dɪŋ/ *noun* [U] *US* material which covers the surface of the outer walls of a building, usually in sloping layers: *vinyl/aluminum/wood siding*

siding [RAILWAY] /ˈsaɪ.dɪŋ/ *noun* [C] a short railway track connected to a main track, where carriages are kept when they are not being used

sidle /ˈsaɪ.dl̩/ *verb* [I usually + adv or prep] to walk towards or away from someone, trying not to be noticed: *Tim sidled **up/over to** the girl sitting at the bar and asked if he could buy her a drink.* ○ *She sidled **past** him, pretending that she had not seen him.*

SIDS /sɪdz/ *noun* [U] (*ALSO* **cot death**) *ABBREVIATION FOR* sudden infant death syndrome: a medical condition in which a baby dies suddenly while it is sleeping for no obvious reason

siege /siːdʒ/ *noun* [C or U] the surrounding of a place by an armed force in order to defeat those defending it: *The siege **of** Mafeking lasted for eight months.* ○ *The soldiers **laid** siege **to*** (= started a siege of) *the city.* ○ *The castle was **under** siege for months.* ○ *FIGURATIVE That whole weekend at Cannes Brigitte Bardot was **under** siege by photographers.* ➲See also **besiege**.

ˈsiege menˌtality *noun* [S] *DISAPPROVING* a feeling that makes you frightened of people around you, and causes you not to trust them: *Years of international isolation has led the country to develop a siege mentality.*

sienna /siˈen.ə/ *noun* [U] a type of earth which is used to colour paint

sierra /siˈeə.rə/ [US] /-ˈer.ə/ *noun* [C] a range of steep mountains, especially in North and South America and Spain

siesta /siˈes.tə/ *noun* [C] a rest or sleep taken after lunch, especially in hot countries

sieve /sɪv/ *noun* [C] a tool consisting of a wood, plastic or metal frame with a wire or plastic net fixed to it. You use it either to separate solids from a liquid, or you rub larger solids through it to make them smaller: *Pass the sauce through a sieve to remove any lumps.* ➲See picture **In the Kitchen** on page Centre 16

• **memory/mind like a sieve** If you have a memory/mind like a sieve, you forget things very easily.

sieve /sɪv/ *verb* [T] to put a liquid or powder through a sieve: *To make the pastry, sieve the flour and salt into a mixing bowl.*

sift [SEPARATE] /sɪft/ *verb* [T] to put flour, sugar, etc. through a SIEVE (= wire net shaped like a bowl) to break up large pieces: *When the cake is cooked, sift some icing sugar over the top of it.*

sifter /ˈsɪf.təʳ/ [US] /-tɚ/ *noun* [C] a container with many small holes in its lid for sifting powdery substances, usually foods: *a flour-sifter* ○ *a sugar-sifter.*

sift [EXAMINE] /sɪft/ *verb* [T] to make a close examination of all the parts of something in order to find something or to separate what is useful from what is not: *The police are sifting the evidence very carefully to try and find the guilty person.* ○ *After my father's death, I had to sift **through** all his papers.* ○ *The police are trying to sift **out** the genuine warnings **from** all the hoax calls they have received.*

sigh /saɪ/ *verb* [I] **1** to breathe out slowly and noisily, expressing tiredness, sadness, pleasure, boredom, etc: *She sighed deeply and sat down.* ○ [+ speech] *"I wish he was here," she sighed* (= she said with a sigh). **2** If the wind sighs, it makes a long, soft sound as it moves through trees: *I lay on my back, listening to the sound of the wind sighing in the trees.*

sigh /saɪ/ *noun* [C] a slow noisy breath: *He leaned back in his seat* ***with a*** *sigh.* ○ *"Ah, you're here," she said and* ***heaved/let out/gave*** *a sigh* ***of relief***.

sight [ABILITY TO SEE] /saɪt/ *noun* [U] the ability to see: *If your sight is poor, you should not drive a car.* ○ *The old woman has* ***lost*** *her sight* (= has become blind). ➲See also **eyesight**.

-sighted /-saɪ.tɪd/ (US) /-t̬ɪd/ *suffix* used when describing a particular way of seeing or thinking ➲See **clear-sighted**; **far-sighted**; **long-sighted**; **nearsighted**; **short-sighted**.

sighted /ˈsaɪ.tɪd/ (US) /-t̬ɪd/ *adj* FORMAL able to see

sightless /ˈsaɪt.ləs/ *adj* LITERARY unable to see

sight [VIEW] /saɪt/ *noun* [C or S or U] something that is in someone's view: *The flowers at the annual flower show were a beautiful sight.* ○ *You should always* ***keep*** *sight* ***of*** *your bags* (= have them where you can see them) *while you're at the airport.* ○ INFORMAL *You can't go out in those clothes – you look* ***a real*** *sight* (= look untidy or silly)*!* ○ *The child laughed* ***at the*** *sight* ***of*** (= when she saw) *the clockwork toy.* ○ FORMAL *The lawyer requested sight* ***of*** (= to see) *the papers.* ○ *I dare not let the children* ***out of*** *my sight* (= go where I cannot see them) *in this park.* ○ *The police officer was hidden* ***out of*** *sight* (= where he could not be seen) *behind a tree.* ○ *The castle came* ***into*** *sight* (= started to be able to be seen) *as we went round a bend in the road.* ○ *We're looking for a house which is* ***within*** *sight* ***of*** (= from which it is possible to see) *the mountains.* ○ FIGURATIVE *After three years of campaigning, the end is finally* ***in*** *sight* (= will happen soon) *for Jon.* ○ *I* ***caught*** *sight* ***of*** (= saw for a moment) *my former teacher while I was out shopping today, but she turned a corner and I* ***lost*** *sight of* (= could no longer see) *her.* ○ *"Do you know David Wilson?" "I haven't met him, but I know him* ***by*** *sight* (= I recognize him, but do not know him)*."* ○ INFORMAL *She hated/loathed* ***the*** *sight* ***of*** (= hated) *her former husband.* ○ INFORMAL *They used to be very good friends, but now they* ***can't bear/stand the*** *sight* ***of*** (= hate) *each other.* ○ *The question seemed easy* ***at first*** *sight* (= when they first saw it), *but when the students tried to answer it, they discovered how difficult it was.* ➲See **view or sight?** at **view** SIGHT.

• **the sights** places of interest, especially to visitors: *We spent a fortnight in Rome looking at all the sights.*

• **Get out of my sight!** INFORMAL an angry way of saying go away: *Get out of my sight, you idiot!*

• **out of sight 1** INFORMAL extremely expensive and more than you are able to spend: *The price of the house we like is out of sight.* **2** SLANG excellent: *The group's new record is out of sight!*

• **lose sight of** to forget about an important idea or fact because you are thinking too much about other things: *Some members of the peacekeeping force seem to have lost sight of the fact that they are there to help people.*

• **Out of sight, out of mind.** SAYING said to emphasize that when something or someone cannot be seen, it is easy to forget them

• **a sight for sore eyes** INFORMAL a way of saying that you are very pleased to see someone or that you think someone is very attractive: *You're a sight for sore eyes!*

• **sight unseen** without seeing something first: *I never buy anything sight unseen.*

sight /saɪt/ *verb* [T] to suddenly see something or someone: *After several days at sea, the sailors finally sighted land.*

sighting /ˈsaɪ.tɪŋ/ (US) /-t̬ɪŋ/ *noun* [C] when you see something or someone, especially that is rare or trying to hide: *This is the first sighting of this particularly rare bird in this country.*

sight [MUCH] /saɪt/ *noun* INFORMAL **a sight** a lot; much: *Food is* ***a*** *(darn/damn) sight* ***more*** *expensive than it used to be.* ○ *He's a sight better than he was yesterday.*

S

sight [GUN PART] /saɪt/ *noun* [C usually pl] a part of a gun or other device through which you look to help you aim at something: *Make sure you line up the sights before you fire the gun.*

• **set** ***your*** **sights on** to decide to achieve something: *Jenny has set her sights on winning the chess competition.*

• **lower** ***your*** **sights** to accept that you will only be able to get something less than you hoped for: *He had hoped to become a doctor, but he had to lower his sights after his disappointing exam results.*

sight-read /ˈsaɪt.riːd/ *verb* [I or T] to play or sing written music the first time you see it **sight-reader** /ˈsaɪtˌriː.dəʳ/ (US) /-dɚ/ *noun* [C] *She's an expert sight-reader.* **sight-reading** /ˈsaɪtˌriː.dɪŋ/ *noun* [U]

sightseeing /ˈsaɪtˌsiː.ɪŋ/ *noun* [U] the visiting of interesting places, especially by people on holiday: *We* ***did*** *a bit of sightseeing in Paris.* ○ *There was no time to* ***go*** *sightseeing in Rome.* **sightseer** /ˈsaɪtˌsiː.əʳ/ (US) /-ɚ/ *noun* [C]

COMMON LEARNER ERROR

sightseeing or **sight**

Sightseeing cannot be used to mean a place. If you are talking about the interesting or beautiful places which you can visit in a city or country, you say **sights** or **tourist attractions**.

We spent a week in Athens, seeing the sights.

~~*We spent a week in Athens, seeing the sightseeings.*~~

Sightseeing means the activity of visiting the interesting or beautiful places in a city or country.

We spent several days sightseeing in London.

sign [MARK] /saɪn/ *noun* [C] a written or printed mark which has a standard meaning: *+ and – are mathematical signs.* ○ *£ is the sign for the British pound.*

sign [NOTICE] /saɪn/ *noun* [C] a notice giving information, directions, a warning, etc: *a road sign* ○ *a shop sign*

sign [BODY MOVEMENT] /saɪn/ *noun* [C] a movement of the body which gives information or an instruction: *She pointed to her watch* ***as a*** *sign* ***that*** *it was getting late and she wanted to leave.* ○ *She* ***made/gave*** *a sign to her husband* ***to*** *stop talking.* ○ *The priest* ***made*** *the sign* ***of the cross*** (= made the shape of a cross by moving his hand between four points on his chest) *when he entered the church.* ➲See also **signal** ACTION.

sign /saɪn/ *verb* [I or T] **1** to give an order or information, or make a request, using hand and body movements: [+ to infinitive] *He signed* ***for/to*** *the waiter* ***to*** *bring him another drink.* ○ [+ that] *He signed* ***to*** *the waiter* ***that*** *he wanted another drink.* **2** to use SIGN LANGUAGE (= language used by people who cannot hear or talk)

sign [SHOWING] /saɪn/ *noun* [C] something showing that something else exists or might happen or exist in the future: *His inability to handle the situation is a sure sign* ***of*** *weakness.* ○ [+ that] *The fact that he's eating more is a sign* ***that*** *he's feeling better.* ○ *I've searched for my hat, but there's* ***no*** *sign* ***of*** *it anywhere* (= I can't find it). ○ *There was no sign* ***of life*** *in the building* (= there seemed to be no one in it). ○ *Billy's work at school has* ***shown*** *signs* ***of*** *improvement this year.* ○ ***There is every*** *sign* ***that/All the*** *signs* ***are that*** *the worst is over.* ➲See also **signal** SHOWING.

• **sign of the times** USUALLY DISAPPROVING something that is typical of the (bad) way things are now: *These riots in the north are a sign of the times.*

sign [WRITE] /saɪn/ *verb* **1** [I or T] to write your name, usually on a written or printed document, to show that you agree with its contents or have written or created it yourself: *to sign a letter/cheque/contract/lease/agreement* ○ *Sign here, please.* ○ *He signed his name at the end of the letter.* ○ [+ obj + n] *He signed himself 'Mark Taylor'.* ○ *She said the painting was by Picasso, but it wasn't signed.* **2** [T] in sport, to make a legal written agreement to employ a player: *The football club has just signed a new player.*

• **signed and sealed** (ALSO **signed, sealed and delivered**) completed and definite because all the necessary documents have been signed

• **sign on the dotted line** *INFORMAL* to agree to do something, especially by signing an agreement: *If you want to join the club, all you have to do is sign on the dotted line.*
• **sign *your* own death warrant** *INFORMAL* to do something that is harmful to your own position: *She signed her own death warrant by refusing to do what the boss demanded.*
signing /ˈsaɪ.nɪŋ/ *noun* [C] in sport, a player who has been bought by one team from another

PHRASAL VERBS WITH **sign**

▲ **sign *sth* away** *phrasal verb* [M] to give up your rights to something by signing a legal document: *Under the treaty, both sides will sign away a third of their nuclear weapons.*
▲ **sign for *sth*** [RECEIVE] *phrasal verb* to sign a form to show that you have received something: *I had to sign for the parcel when I collected it from the post office.*
▲ **sign for/with *sb*** [SPORT] *phrasal verb* to sign a formal agreement saying that you will play for a particular team
▲ **sign *(sb)* in** *phrasal verb* to sign your name or the name of someone who is visiting you in a book on arrival at a building such as an office or hotel: *New security measures require all visitors to sign in at reception and wear a visitor's badge.*
▲ **sign off** [FINANCIAL SUPPORT] *phrasal verb UK INFORMAL* to report to a government employment office that you now have a job and do not need to receive JOBSEEKER'S ALLOWANCE
▲ **sign off** [WORK] *phrasal verb US INFORMAL* to stop doing your work or a similar activity for a period of time: *As it's Friday, I think I'll sign off early today.*
▲ **sign *(sth)* off** [COMMUNICATION] *phrasal verb* to give a final message at the end of a letter or when communicating by radio, or at the end of a television or radio programme: *She signed off (her show) by wishing her listeners a Happy New Year.*
▲ **sign on** [FINANCIAL SUPPORT] *phrasal verb UK INFORMAL* to sign a form at a government office to say that you do not have a job and that you want to receive JOBSEEKER'S ALLOWANCE (= money paid by the government to unemployed people trying to find work)
▲ **sign on** *MAINLY US phrasal verb* (*UK* **sign up**) *INFORMAL* to agree to become involved in an organized activity: [+ *to* infinitive] *MAINLY US I've signed on to help at the school fair.*
▲ **sign on/up** [JOB] *phrasal verb UK INFORMAL* to sign a document saying that you will work for someone or do a particular job or activity: *She's signed on **with** a temp agency.* ○ *Julie has signed up **for** courses on English and French this year.*
▲ **sign *(sb)* out** *phrasal verb* to sign your name in a book on leaving a building such as an office or factory, or to write someone else's name in a book when they leave after visiting it: *Don't forget to sign out before you leave.*
▲ **sign *sth* out** *phrasal verb* [M] to record when you take something away, usually by signing your name in a book: *You have to sign books out when you borrow them from the library.*
▲ **sign *sth* over** *phrasal verb* [M] to give the legal rights to something or the ownership of something to someone else by formally signing a document: *Two years before her death she signed her property over **to** her two children.*
▲ **sign up** *phrasal verb* to agree to become involved in an organized activity: [+ *to* infinitive] *I've signed up **to** do the teas at the village fête.* ○ *She's signed up **for** evening classes at the community college.* ➲See also **sign on/up** JOB.

signal [ACTION] /ˈsɪg.nəl/ *noun* [C] **1** an action, movement or sound which gives information, a message, a warning or an order: *When she **gave** (them) the signal, they all cheered.* ○ [+ *that*] *The firework was a signal **that** the festival had started.* ○ [+ *to* infinitive] *The police officer **gave** us a signal **to** stop.* ○ *The signal **for** a race to start is often the firing of a gun.* **2** *US FOR* **indicator** See at **indicate** SIGNAL.
signal /ˈsɪg.nəl/ *verb* [I or T] -ll- or *US USUALLY* -l- to make a movement, sound, flash, etc. which gives information or tells people what to do: *Flashing lights on a parked car usually signal a warning (**to** other motorists).* ○ *He signalled left, and turned the lorry slowly.* ○ *He was signalling (*= giving a signal*) with a red flag.* ○ *She signalled **for** help.* ○ [+ *that*] *She signalled **to** the cars behind **that** they were going the wrong way.* ○ [+ obj + *to* infinitive] *The children's mother signalled them **to** be quiet.* ○ [+ *to* infinitive] *The children's mother signalled **to/for** them **to** be quiet.*

signal [SHOWING] /ˈsɪg.nəl/ *noun* [C] something which shows that something else exists or is likely to happen: *The poor result is a clear signal **of** his deteriorating confidence.* ○ *The changing colour of the leaves on the trees is a signal **that** it will soon be autumn.*
signal /ˈsɪg.nəl/ *verb* [T] -ll- or *US USUALLY* -l- to show that you intend or are ready to do something: [+ *that*] *The union has signalled **that** the workers will strike.* ○ *The union has signalled the workers' intention to strike.* ○ *The death of Chairman Mao signalled (*= marked*) the end of an era in Chinese history.*

signal [EQUIPMENT] /ˈsɪg.nəl/ *noun* [C] equipment, especially on the side of a railway or road, often with lights, which tells drivers whether they can go, must stop or should move more slowly: *a railway signal* ○ *a traffic signal* ○ *a road signal*

signal [WAVE] /ˈsɪg.nəl/ *noun* [C] a series of electrical or radio waves which are sent to a radio or television in order to produce a sound, picture or message

signal [IMPORTANT] /ˈsɪg.nəl/ *adj* [before n] *FORMAL* noticeable; not ordinary: *a signal success/failure*
signally /ˈsɪg.nə.li/ *adv FORMAL* noticeably: *The council is signally failing to keep the streets clean.*

ˈsignal ˌbox *UK noun* [C] (*US* **signal tower**) a building from which railway signals are operated

signalman /ˈsɪg.nəl.mən/ /-mæn/ *noun* [C] someone who operates a railway signal

signatory /ˈsɪg.nə.tri/ [US] /-tɔːr.i/ *noun* [C] a person, organization or country which has signed an agreement: *Most western European nations are signatories **to/of** the North Atlantic Treaty Organization.*

signature /ˈsɪg.nɪ.tʃəʳ/ [US] /-tʃɚ/ *noun* [C] your name written by yourself, always in the same way, usually to show that something has been written or agreed by you ➲Compare **autograph**.

ˈsignature ˌtune *noun* [C] a short tune used in broadcasting at the beginning and/or end of a particular programme or to mark the appearance of a particular performer

signet ring /ˈsɪg.nɪtˌrɪŋ/ *noun* [C] a finger ring with a flat piece at the front, which usually has a pattern cut into it

significant [IMPORTANT] /sɪgˈnɪf.ɪ.kənt/ *adj* important or noticeable: *There has been a significant increase in the number of women students in recent years.* ○ *The talks between the USA and the USSR were very significant **for** the relationship between the two countries.*
significance /sɪgˈnɪf.ɪ.kənts/ *noun* [U] importance: *The discovery of the new drug is **of** great significance **for/to** people suffering from heart problems.* **significantly** /sɪgˈnɪf.ɪ.kənt.li/ *adv*: *My piano playing has improved significantly since I've had a new teacher.*

significant [SPECIAL MEANING] /sɪgˈnɪf.ɪ.kənt/ *adj* having a special meaning: *She looked at him across the table and gave him a significant smile.* ○ *Do you think **it's** significant **that** he hasn't replied to my letter yet?*
significance /sɪgˈnɪf.ɪ.kənts/ *noun* [U] special meaning: *Do you think that look he gave you had any significance?*
significantly /sɪgˈnɪf.ɪ.kənt.li/ *adv* in a way that suggests a special meaning: *He said that he would be bringing a friend with him but, significantly, didn't say who it was.*

signification /ˌsɪg.nɪ.fɪˈkeɪ.ʃᵊn/ *noun* [C] *SPECIALIZED* the meaning (of a word)

signify [MEAN] /ˈsɪg.nɪ.faɪ/ *verb* [T] *FORMAL* to be a sign of something; to mean: *Nobody really knows what the marks on the ancient stones signify.* ○ [+ *that*] *The number 30 on a road sign signifies **that** the speed limit is 30 miles an hour.*

signify [MAKE KNOWN] /ˈsɪg.nɪ.faɪ/ *verb* [T] *FORMAL* to make something known; to show: *She signified her agreement by nodding her head.* ○ [+ (*that*)] *She signified **(that)** she was in agreement by nodding her head.*

[S]

signify BE IMPORTANT /'sɪg.nɪ.faɪ/ *verb* [I] FORMAL to have importance or to MATTER: *Don't worry about being late – it doesn't signify.*

'sign ˌlanguage *noun* [C] a system of hand and body movements representing words, which is used by and to people who cannot hear or talk, or the movements which people sometimes make when talking to someone whose language they do not speak

ˌsign of the 'Zodiac *noun* [C] in astrology, any of the twelve symbols which represent parts of the year: *"What sign are you?" "Gemini."*

signpost ROAD SIGN /'saɪn.pəʊst/ US /-poʊst/ *noun* [C] a pole at the side of a road, especially at a point where two or more roads meet, which gives information about routes and distances: *The signpost said 'London 18 miles'.*

signpost /'saɪn.pəʊst/ US /-poʊst/ *verb* [T usually passive] *The road wasn't very well signposted* (= provided with signposts). ○ *We found where we were going very easily, because it was signposted* (= the direction was shown by signposts) *all the way.*

signpost SHOW FUTURE /'saɪn.pəʊst/ US /-poʊst/ *noun* [C] something which shows what is going to happen, or what should happen, in the future: *This upturn in the country's economy is a splendid signpost to the future.*

Sikh /siːk/ *noun* [C] a member of the Indian religion which developed from Hinduism in the 16th century and is based on belief in a single god and on the teachings of Guru Nanak Sikh /siːk/ *adj*: *a Sikh temple* Sikhism /'siːk.ɪ.zᵊm/ *noun* [U]

silage /'saɪ.lɪdʒ/ *noun* [U] grass or other green plants that are cut and stored, without being dried first, to feed cattle in winter

silence QUIET /'saɪ.lənts/ *noun* [U] an absence of sound; complete quiet: *A loud crash of thunder broke the silence of the night.* ○ *Silence reigned* (= There was complete silence) *in the church.*

silent /'saɪ.lənt/ *adj* without any sound: *The empty house was completely silent.* silently /'saɪ.lənt.li/ *adv*

silence NO SPEAKING /'saɪ.lənts/ *noun* **1** [U] a state of not speaking or writing or making a noise: *The soldiers listened in silence as their captain gave the orders.* ○ *"Silence* (= Stop talking)!" *shouted the teacher.* ○ *My request for help was met with silence* (= I received no answer). ○ *Her silence on/about what had happened to her surprised everyone.* ○ *Their mother's angry words reduced the children to silence.* ○ *I don't expect to hear from her now, after three years' silence* (= three years in which she has not spoken or written to me). **2** [C] a period of time in which there is complete quiet or an absence of speaking: *Their conversation was punctuated by uncomfortable silences.*

● **Silence is golden.** SAYING said to mean it is often better to say nothing

silence /'saɪ.lənts/ *verb* [T] *The teacher raised his voice to silence the class* (= to make them stop talking). ○ *Her remark about his appearance completely silenced him* (= made him unable to answer). ○ FIGURATIVE *Al Capone silenced his opponents* (= prevented them from opposing him) *by killing them.* ○ FIGURATIVE *The enemy's guns were silenced* (= made to stop firing) *in a surprise attack.* silent /'saɪ.lənt/ *adj* without talking: *She whispered a silent prayer that her wounded brother would not die.* ○ *The police officer told the criminal that he had the right to remain silent.* ○ *The minister was silent on/about his plans for the future.* ○ *Arthur has always been the strong, silent type* (= a type of person, usually a man, who says very little). silently /'saɪ.lənt.li/ *adv*

silencer /'saɪ.lənt.səʳ/ US /-sɚ/ *noun* [C] **1** a piece of equipment that you use on a gun to reduce the sound of it firing **2** UK (US **muffler**) a part of a vehicle that reduces noise from the engine

ˌsilent 'film *noun* [C] (US ALSO **silent movie**) a film without any sound ➔Compare **talkie**.

ˌsilent 'letter *noun* [C] A silent letter in a word is one which is written but not pronounced, such as the 'b' in 'doubt'.

ˌsilent ma'jority *noun* [U] a large number of people who have not expressed an opinion about something: *A few people have spoken in favour of the plans to build a new car park, but I'm sure the silent majority are against it.*

ˌsilent 'partner *noun* [C usually sing] US FOR **sleeping partner**

silhouette /ˌsɪl.u'et/ *noun* [C or U] a dark shape seen against a light background: *The silhouette of the bare tree on the hill was clear against the winter sky.*

silhouetted /ˌsɪl.u'et.ɪd/ US /-eṯ-/ *adj* forming a silhouette: *The goats high up on the mountain were silhouetted against the snow.*

silica /'sɪl.ɪ.kə/ *noun* [U] a mineral which exists in various forms, including sand, QUARTZ and FLINT, and which is used to make glass and cement

silicate /'sɪl.ɪ.kət/ *noun* [C or U] any of a large number of common minerals formed of SILICA, oxygen and one or more other elements

silicon /'sɪl.ɪ.kən/ *noun* [U] a grey element, which is found combined with oxygen in a large number of common minerals, and which has unusual electrical characteristics

ˌsilicon 'chip *noun* [C] a small piece of silicon which is used in computers, CALCULATORS and other electronic machines

silicone /'sɪl.ɪ.kəʊn/ US /-koʊn/ *noun* [U] any of a number of compounds of SILICON that are used in making artificial rubber, paint, polish, varnish, etc.

'silicone ˌimplant *noun* [C] something used to replace or increase the size of body parts that can be seen: *a silicone breast implant*

silicosis /ˌsɪl.ɪ'kəʊ.sɪs/ US /-'koʊ-/ *noun* [U] a lung disease caused by breathing in SILICA dust, especially found among COAL MINERS and STONEMASONS

silk CLOTH /sɪlk/ *noun* [U] a delicate, soft type of cloth made from a thread produced by SILKWORMS, or the thread itself: *a silk dress* ○ *a silk shirt*

● **You can't make a silk purse out of a sow's ear.** SAYING used to mean that you can't make something good out of something that is naturally bad

silks /sɪlks/ *plural noun* the brightly coloured shirts worn by JOCKEYS (= people who ride horses in a race)

silken /'sɪl.kᵊn/ *adj* [usually before n] LITERARY soft, smooth and shiny like silk: *The princess in the fairy story had long silken hair.*

silky /'sɪl.ki/ *adj* USUALLY APPROVING soft and smooth, like silk: *Persian cats have long, silky fur.* ○ FIGURATIVE *The villain leans over and speaks to her in a silky persuasive voice.* silkiness /'sɪl.kɪ.nəs/ *noun* [U]

silk LAWYER /sɪlk/ *noun* [C] UK SPECIALIZED a high-ranking lawyer in the British legal system; a **QC**

● **take silk** UK SPECIALIZED to become a QC

ˌsilk ˌscreen ('printing) *noun* [U] a method of printing by forcing ink through a pattern cut into silk or other similar cloth, stretched across a frame

silkworm /'sɪlk.wɜːm/ US /-wɜːm/ *noun* [C] a type of CATERPILLAR (= a young worm-like form of an insect) which produces threads of silk from which it makes a COCOON (= a covering for its body)

sill /sɪl/ *noun* [C] a flat piece of wood, stone, etc. which forms the base of a window or door ➔See also **windowsill**.

silly /'sɪl.i/ *adj* showing a lack of thought or judgment; foolish: *Don't do that, you silly boy!* ○ *I made a silly mistake in the examination.* ○ *It was silly of you to go out in the hot sun without a hat.* ○ *I feel silly* (= embarrassed) *in this dress.*

● **drink/laugh, etc. yourself silly** to drink/laugh, etc. so much that you are unable to think clearly or behave with good judgment: *I laughed myself silly at his jokes.*

● **bore sb silly** to make someone feel very bored: *We were all bored silly by the play.*

● **silly billy** INFORMAL a silly person, especially a child.

silliness /'sɪl.ɪ.nəs/ *noun* [U] when someone or something is silly

'silly ˌseason *noun* [U] the time of year, usually in the summer, when newspapers are full of unimportant stories because there is no important, especially political, news

silo /ˈsaɪ.ləʊ/ (US) /-loʊ/ *noun* **[C]** *plural* **silos** **1** a large round tower on a farm for storing grain or winter food for cattle **2** a large underground place for storing and firing missiles

silt /sɪlt/ *noun* **[U]** sand or earth which is carried along by flowing water and then dropped, especially at a bend in a river or at a river's opening

silt /sɪlt/ *verb*

▲ **silt (sth) up** *phrasal verb* **[M]** to become blocked with silt, or to cause something to become blocked with silt: *The harbour silted up many years ago.*

silvan, sylvan /ˈsɪl.vən/ *adj* OLD USE OR LITERARY of or having woods

silver /ˈsɪl.vəʳ/ (US) /-vɚ/ *noun* **[C or U]** a valuable shiny white metal that is used for making utensils, jewellery, coins and decorative objects: *We gave Alison and Tom a dish made of* ***solid*** *silver as a wedding present.* ○ *Cleaning* ***the*** *silver* (= silver objects) *is a dirty job.* ○ *Shall we use* ***the*** *silver* (= utensils made of silver) *for dinner tonight?* ○ *I need some silver* (= coins made of silver or a metal of similar appearance) *for the ticket machine in the car park.* ➲See also **silver (medal)**.

silver /ˈsɪl.vəʳ/ (US) /-vɚ/ *adj* made of silver, or of the colour of silver: *a silver ring* ○ *My grandmother has silver hair.*

silver /ˈsɪl.vəʳ/ (US) /-vɚ/ *verb* **[T often passive]** to cover something, especially a window, with a thin layer of silver-coloured material in order to make a mirror

silvery /ˈsɪl.vᵊr.i/ (US) /-vɚ-/ *adj* LITERARY *The grass was silvery with frost.* ○ *We were woken early by the peal of silvery bells* (= those having a pleasant clear musical sound).

silver ˈbirch *noun* **[C]** a common type of BIRCH tree, which has a silver-coloured trunk and branches

silverfish /ˈsɪl.və.fɪʃ/ (US) /-vɚ-/ *noun* **[C]** *plural* **silverfish** or **silverfishes** a silvery-white insect without wings which lives inside buildings

silver ˈjubilee *noun* **[C usually sing]** a date that is exactly 25 years after the date of an important event

silver (ˈmedal) *noun* **[C or U]** a small disc of silver, or a metal that looks like silver, which is given to the person who comes second in a competition, especially in a sport: *Britain won a silver medal in the javelin.*

silver ˈpaper UK *noun* **[U]** (UK ALSO **silver foil**) shiny silver-coloured paper

silver ˈplate *noun* **[U]** objects made of metal with a thin covering of silver **silver-plated** /ˌsɪl.vəˈpleɪ.tɪd/ (US) /-vɚˈpleɪ.t̬ɪd/ *adj*

the ˌsilver ˈscreen *noun* **[S]** LITERARY the film industry: *the stars of the silver screen*

silverside /ˈsɪl.və.saɪd/ (US) /-vɚ-/ *noun* **[U]** UK part of a leg of beef

silversmith /ˈsɪl.və.smɪθ/ (US) /-vɚ-/ *noun* **[C]** a person who makes or sells silver objects

silver-tongued /ˌsɪl.vəˈtʌŋd/ (US) /-vɚ-/ *adj* LITERARY If you are silver-tongued, you speak in a way that charms or persuades people.

silverware /ˈsɪl.və.weəʳ/ (US) /-vɚ.wer/ *noun* **[U]** **1** objects, especially utensils, made of silver **2** US utensils made of steel or other materials

ˌsilver ˈwedding (anniˌversary) *noun* **[C]** the date exactly 25 years after the date of a marriage

sim card /ˈsɪm.kɑːd/ (US) /-kɑːrd/ *noun* **[C]** a plastic card in a MOBILE PHONE (= a telephone that you can carry with you) that contains your personal information and that allows you to use the phone

simian /ˈsɪm.i.ən/ *adj, noun* **[C]** FORMAL (of or like) a monkey

similar /ˈsɪm.ɪ.ləʳ/ (US) /-ə.lɚ/ *adj* looking or being almost, but not exactly, the same: *My father and I have similar views on politics.* ○ *I bought some new shoes which are very similar* ***to*** *a pair I had before.* ○ *Paul is very similar* ***in*** *appearance* ***to*** *his brother.* **similarity** /ˌsɪm.ɪˈlær.ɪ.ti/ (US) /-əˈler.ə.t̬i/ *noun* **[C or U]** *I can see the similarity* ***between*** *you and your mother.* ○ *The book bears several striking similarities* ***to*** *last year's bestseller.*

similarly /ˈsɪm.ɪ.lə.li/ (US) /-ə.lɚ-/ *adv*: *The children were similarly dressed.* ○ *Cars must stop at red traffic lights: similarly* (= in a similar way), *bicycles should stop too.*

simile /ˈsɪm.ɪ.li/ *noun* **[C or U]** (the use of) an expression comparing one thing with another, always including the words 'as' or 'like': *The lines 'She walks in beauty, like the night...' from Byron's poem contain a simile.*

simmer /ˈsɪm.əʳ/ (US) /-ɚ/ *verb* **1** **[I or T]** to cook something liquid, or something with liquid in it, at a temperature slightly below boiling: *Leave the vegetables to simmer for a few minutes.* **2** **[I]** If a disagreement or negative emotion simmers, it grows slowly stronger over a period of time and could become more serious at any moment: *The strike has been simmering for weeks.* ○ *She's been simmering* ***with*** *resentment ever since the meeting.*

simmer /ˈsɪm.əʳ/ (US) /-ɚ/ *noun* **[S]** *Bring the potatoes to a simmer.*

▲ **simmer down** *phrasal verb* INFORMAL to become less angry or excited about something: *Come on kids! Simmer down and get on with your work!*

simper /ˈsɪm.pəʳ/ (US) /-pɚ/ *verb* **[I]** to smile in a foolish or silly way: *She gave her teacher a simpering smile.*

simper /ˈsɪm.pəʳ/ (US) /-pɚ/ *noun* **[C]**

simple [PLAIN] /ˈsɪm.pl̩/ *adj* without decoration; plain: *I like simple food better than fancy dishes.* **simplicity** /sɪmˈplɪs.ɪ.ti/ (US) /-ə.t̬i/ *noun* **[U]** **simply** /ˈsɪm.pli/ *adv*

simple [EASY] /ˈsɪm.pl̩/ *adj* easy to understand or do; not difficult: *The instructions were written in simple English.* ○ ***It's*** *simple* ***to*** *find our house.* ○ *I want an explanation, but* ***keep/make it*** *simple.*

simplicity /sɪmˈplɪs.ɪ.ti/ (US) /-ə.t̬i/ *noun* **[U]** *The advantage of the plan is its simplicity.* ○ *The examination was simplicity* ***itself*** (= very easy).

simplify /ˈsɪm.plɪ.faɪ/ (US) /-plə-/ *verb* **[T]** to make something less complicated and therefore easier to do or understand: *the new simplified tax system* ○ *He tried to simplify the story for the younger audience.* **simplification** /ˌsɪm.plɪ.fɪˈkeɪ.ʃᵊn/ *noun* **[C or U]**

simplistic /sɪmˈplɪs.tɪk/ *adj* DISAPPROVING making something complicated seem simple by ignoring important parts of it: *They are taking a disgracefully simplistic point of view about the war.*

simply /ˈsɪm.pli/ *adv* in an easy way: *He explained it as simply as he could, but the class still didn't understand.*

simple [ONE PART] /ˈsɪm.pl̩/ *adj* **[before n]** having or made of only one or a few parts: *A hammer is a simple tool.* ○ *Simple forms of life have only one cell.*

simple [IMPORTANT] /ˈsɪm.pl̩/ *adj* **[before n]** used to describe the one important fact, truth, etc: *We didn't go swimming for the simple reason that the water was too cold.*

simply /ˈsɪm.pli/ *adv*: *I don't like my job – I simply* (= just) *do it for the money.* ○ *You look simply* (= really) *beautiful in that dress.* ○ *The hunger in parts of Africa is terrible – there's* ***(quite)*** *simply* (= without doubt) *no other word for it.*

simple [NATURAL] /ˈsɪm.pl̩/ *adj* USUALLY APPROVING ordinary; traditional or natural rather than modern and complicated: *He was just a simple fisherman.*

simplicity /sɪmˈplɪs.ɪ.ti/ (US) /-ə.t̬i/ *noun* **[U]** *The old people led a life of great simplicity* (= with few possessions and little money). **simply** /ˈsɪm.pli/ *adv*

simple [FOOLISH] /ˈsɪm.pl̩/ *adj* describes a person who does not have a normal level of intelligence: *He's a bit simple, I'm afraid.*

ˌsimple ˈfracture *noun* **[C]** a broken bone that has not cut through the surrounding flesh or skin ➲Compare **compound fracture**.

ˌsimple ˈinterest *noun* **[U]** money that is paid only on an original amount of money that has been borrowed or invested, and not on the additional money that the original sum earns ➲Compare **compound** COMBINATION.

simple-minded /ˌsɪm.pl̩ˈmaɪn.dɪd/ *adj* DISAPPROVING **1** describes a person who lacks the ability to reason and understand **2** describes an action or attitude that is based on a limited understanding of a situation

simpleton /ˈsɪm.pl̩.tᵊn/ *noun* **[C]** OLD-FASHIONED a person without the usual ability to reason and understand

simulacrum /ˌsɪm.jʊˈleɪ.krəm/ *noun* **[C]** *plural* **simulacrums** or **simulacra** FORMAL something that looks like or represents something else

simulate /ˈsɪm.jʊ.leɪt/ *verb* [T] to do or make something which looks real but is not real: *In cheap furniture, plastic is often used to simulate wood.* ○ *FORMAL Ruth simulated pleasure at seeing Simon, but really she wished he hadn't come.* ○ *Some driving teachers use computers to simulate* (= represent) *different road conditions for learners to practise on.* **simulated** /ˈsɪm.jʊ.leɪ.tɪd/ [US] /-t̬ɪd/ *adj*

simulation /ˌsɪm.jʊˈleɪ.ʃᵊn/ *noun* [C or U] *The manager prepared a computer simulation* (= a model of a problem or course of events) ***of** likely sales performance for the rest of the year.*

simulator /ˈsɪm.jʊ.leɪ.təʳ/ [US] /-t̬ɚ/ *noun* [C] *People learning to fly often practise on a **flight** simulator* (= piece of equipment which represents real conditions in an aircraft or spacecraft).

simulcast /ˈsɪm.ᵊl.kɑːst/ [US] /ˈsaɪ.mᵊl.kæst/ *noun* [C] *MAINLY US* a broadcast by a radio and a television station of the same programme at the same time

simultaneous /ˌsɪm.ᵊlˈteɪ.ni.əs/ [US] /ˌsaɪ.mᵊl-/ *adj* happening or being done at exactly the same time: *There were several simultaneous explosions in different cities.* **simultaneously** /ˌsɪm.ᵊlˈteɪ.ni.ə.sli/ [US] /ˌsaɪ.mᵊl-/ *adv*: *Two children answered the teacher's question simultaneously.* **simultaneousness** /ˌsɪm.ᵊlˈteɪ.ni.ə.snəs/ [US] /ˌsaɪ.mᵊl-/ *noun* [U] (*ALSO* **simultaneity**)

sin [OFFENCE] /sɪn/ *noun* [C or U] the offence of breaking, or the breaking of, a religious or moral law: *to **commit/confess** a sin* ○ *He thinks a lot about sin.* ○ [+ **to** infinitive] *INFORMAL I think **it's** a sin* (= is morally wrong) ***to** waste food, when so many people in the world are hungry.* ○ *HUMOROUS For my sins* (= As if it were a punishment), *I'm organizing the office party this year.*
• **as guilty/miserable/ugly as sin** *INFORMAL* very guilty/miserable/ugly

sin /sɪn/ *verb* [I] **-nn-** to break a religious or moral law

sinful /ˈsɪn.fᵊl/ *adj* **1** against the rules of a religion or morally wrong: *He confessed that he had sinful thoughts.* ○ *Buying that sports car was a sinful waste of money.* **2** *INFORMAL* describes something which is very pleasant, but very bad for you: *This cream cake is sinful!* **sinfully** /ˈsɪn.fᵊl.i/ *adv* **sinfulness** /ˈsɪn.fᵊl.nəs/ *noun* [U] **sinless** /ˈsɪn.ləs/ *adj* **sinner** /ˈsɪn.əʳ/ [US] /-ɚ/ *noun* [C]

sin [MATHEMATICS] /sɪn/ *WRITTEN ABBREVIATION FOR* **sine**

sin-bin /ˈsɪn.bɪn/ *noun* [C] *UK INFORMAL* in some sports, an area off the field where a player who has committed an act which is against the rules can be sent, for a stated length of time

since [TIME] /sɪnts/ *adv* from a particular time in the past until a later time, or until now: *Emma went to work in New York a year ago, and we haven't seen her since.* ○ *He started working for the company when he left school, and has been there **ever** since* (= and is still there). ○ *I've **long** since* (= long ago) *forgotten any Latin I ever learned.* **since** /sɪnts/ *prep*: *England have not won the World Cup in football since 1966.* **since** /sɪnts/ *conjunction*: *I've been very busy since I came back from holiday.*

since [BECAUSE] /sɪnts/ *conjunction* because; as: *Since we've got a few minutes to wait for the train, let's have a cup of coffee.*

sincere /sɪnˈsɪəʳ/ [US] /-ˈsɪr/ *adj* (of a person, feelings or behaviour) not pretending or lying; honest: *a sincere apology* ○ *He seems so sincere.* * NOTE: The opposite is **insincere**.

sincerely /sɪnˈsɪə.li/ [US] /-ˈsɪr-/ *adv* honestly and without pretending or lying: *I'm sincerely grateful.*
• **(Yours) sincerely** (*US ALSO* **Sincerely yours**) used to end a formal letter which is addressed to a particular person

sincerity /sɪnˈser.ɪ.ti/ [US] /-ə.t̬i/ *noun* [U] honesty: *The priest was a man of deep sincerity.*

sine /saɪn/ *noun* [C] (*WRITTEN ABBREVIATION* **sin**) *SPECIALIZED* (in a triangle that has one angle of 90°) the ratio of the length of the side opposite an angle less than 90° divided by the length of the HYPOTENUSE (= the side opposite the 90° angle) ➲Compare **cosine**; **tangent** TRIANGLE.

sinecure /ˈsɪn.ɪ.kjʊəʳ/ [US] /ˈsaɪ.nə.kjʊr/ *noun* [C] *DISAPPROVING* a position which involves little work, but for which the person is paid

sine qua non /ˌsɪn.i.kwɑːˈnəʊn/ [US] /ˌsɪn.eɪ.kwaˈnoʊn/ *noun* [S] *FORMAL* a necessary condition without which something is not possible: *An interest in children is a sine qua non **of** teaching.*

sinew /ˈsɪn.juː/ *noun* **1** [C] a TENDON (= strong cord in the body connecting a muscle to a bone) **2** [C usually pl] the parts of a structure or system that provide support and hold it together: *These steel posts form the sinews of the building.*

sinewy /ˈsɪn.juːi/ *adj*: *The fighter had a strong, sinewy body* (= a body with strong muscles and little fat).

sinful /ˈsɪn.fᵊl/ *adj* ➲See at **sin** OFFENCE.

sing [MAKE MUSIC] /sɪŋ/ *verb* [I or T] **sang**, **sung** to make musical sounds with the voice, usually a tune with words: *The children sang two songs by Schubert at the school concert.* ○ *We were woken early by the sound of the birds singing.* ○ *Your grandmother would like you to sing **for/to** her.* ○ [+ two objects] *Will you sing us a song/sing a song **to** us?* ○ *She sang her baby **to sleep** every night.* ○ *Pavarotti is singing Rodolfo* (= singing the part of Rodolfo) *in 'La Boheme' at La Scala this week.* ○ *Please sing (UK) **up**/(US) **out*** (= sing louder).
• **sing the praises of *sb/sth*** to praise someone or something: *The newspapers have been singing the praises of Italy's new star player.*

singer /ˈsɪŋ.əʳ/ [US] /-ɚ/ *noun* [C] a person who sings: *Kiri Te Kanawa is a famous singer from New Zealand.* **singing** /ˈsɪŋ.ɪŋ/ *noun* [U]

sing [RING] /sɪŋ/ *verb* [I] **sang**, **sung** to make or be filled with a (high) ringing sound: *A bullet sang **past** the top of the soldier's head.*

sing [SINGULAR] /sɪŋ/ *noun, adj ABBREVIATION FOR* singular

▲ **sing along** *phrasal verb* to sing a piece of music while someone else is singing or playing it: *The radio station played a Billy Joel song, and I found myself singing along **to** it.*

singalong /ˈsɪŋ.ə.lɒŋ/ [US] /-lɑːŋ/ *noun* [C] *US* a **singsong**

singe /sɪndʒ/ *verb* [I or T] **singeing** to burn slightly on the surface, without producing flames: *My jumper started to singe when I leaned over a burning candle.*

singe /sɪndʒ/ *noun* [C] a slight burn mark: *The hot iron left a singe (**mark**) on my dress.*

single [ONE] /ˈsɪŋ.gl̩/ *adj* [before n] one only: *He knocked his opponent down with a single blow.* ○ ***Not a** single person offered to help her.* ○ *You haven't been listening to a single word I've been saying.* ➲Compare **double** TWICE.

single /ˈsɪŋ.gl̩/ *verb* [I] A baseball player singles by hitting a ball that allows him to reach first base.

single /ˈsɪŋ.gl̩/ *noun* [C] **1** a record or CD which has only one main song on it: *Have you heard Michael Jackson's new single?* **2** in cricket, one run **3** in baseball, a hit which allows the player to reach first base **4** *UK* **single (ticket)** a ticket for a journey to a place, but not for the return: *May I have a single to London, please.* **5** a **single room**

singleness /ˈsiŋ.gl̩.nəs/ *noun* **singleness of mind/purpose** attention to one thing: *He showed great singleness of mind in dealing with the problem.*

singles /ˈsɪŋ.gl̩z/ *noun* [U] a game, especially in tennis, played between one player on one side and one on the other ➲Compare **doubles**.

singly /ˈsɪŋ.gli/ *adv* one at a time: *Doctors usually see their patients singly.*

single [SEPARATE] /ˈsɪŋ.gl̩/ *adj* [before n] considered on its own; separate from other things: *Patience is the single most important quality needed for this job.* ○ *She lost every single thing when her house burned down.*

single [NOT MARRIED] /ˈsɪŋ.gl̩/ *adj* not married, or not having a romantic relationship with someone: *a single woman/man/person* ○ *He's been single for so long now, I don't think he'll ever marry.* ○ *The number of single-parent **families** dependent on the state has risen enormously in recent years.*

singles /ˈsɪŋ.gl̩z/ *plural noun* people who are not married and do not have a romantic relationship with someone:

▲ **single *sb/sth* out** *phrasal verb* [M] to choose one person or thing from a group for special attention, especially criticism or praise: *It's not fair the way my sister is always singled out **for** special treatment.* ○ *Jamie was* *thrilled when the teacher singled out his poem and asked him to read it out.*

ˌsingle ˈbed *noun* [C] a bed for one person

single-breasted /ˌsɪŋ.gl̩ˈbres.tɪd/ *adj* [before n] describes a jacket or coat that fastens in the centre, with only one row of buttons: *a single-breasted coat/jacket/suit*

ˌsingle ˈcombat *noun* [U] fighting between two people, usually with weapons: *The two soldiers met* (= fought each other) ***in** single combat.*

ˌsingle ˈcream *noun* [U] (*US* **light cream**) *UK* a type of thin cream

single-decker /ˌsɪŋ.gl̩ˈdek.əʳ/ [US] /-ɚ/ *noun* [C] a bus or other vehicle which has only one level

ˌsingle ˈfile *noun* a way of walking with one person behind another: *The schoolchildren were told to walk **in** single file.*

single-handed /ˌsɪŋ.gl̩ˈhæn.dɪd/ *adj* without any help from anyone else: *Sir Francis Chichester was the first person to make a single-handed voyage round the world.* **single-handedly** /ˌsɪŋ.gl̩ˈhæn.dɪd.li/ *adv*

single-minded /ˌsɪŋ.gl̩ˈmaɪn.dɪd/ *adj* very determined to achieve something: *She had a single-minded will to win.* **single-mindedly** /ˌsɪŋ.gl̩ˈmaɪn.dɪd.li/ *adv* **single-mindedness** /ˌsɪŋ.gl̩ˈmaɪn.dɪd.nəs/ *noun* [U]

ˌsingle ˈroom *noun* [C] (*ALSO* **single**) a room in a hotel for one person: *I'd like a single room, please.*

ˈsingles ˌbar *noun* [C] a bar where single people go to meet other single people

single-sex /ˌsɪŋ.gl̩ˈseks/ *adj* [before n] describes a school that is for either girls or boys, but not both: *I went to a single-sex school.*

singlet /ˈsɪŋ.glət/ *noun* [C] *MAINLY UK* a piece of clothing without sleeves which is worn on the top part of the body under clothes, or for playing particular sports

singleton /ˈsɪŋ.gl̩.tᵊn/ *noun* [C] *HUMOROUS* a man or woman who does not have a romantic or sexual partner

singsong [MUSICAL VOICE] /ˈsɪŋ.sɒŋ/ [US] /-sɑːŋ/ *noun* [S] a voice rising and falling in level: *She spoke in **a** singsong.* **singsong** /ˈsɪŋ.sɒŋ/ [US] /-sɑːŋ/ *adj* [before n] *a singsong voice*

singsong [SINGING] *UK* /ˈsɪŋ.sɒŋ/ [US] /-sɑːŋ/ *noun* [C] (*US* **singalong**) the informal singing of songs by a group of people: *It's nice to have a good old-fashioned singsong now and again.*

singular [GRAMMAR] /ˈsɪŋ.gjʊ.ləʳ/ [US] /-lɚ/ *adj, noun* [S] the form of a word used when talking or writing about one thing: *a singular ending/form/noun/verb* ○ *The word 'woman' is singular.* ○ *The singular **of** 'children' is 'child'.* ○ *The word 'teeth' is plural – **in the** singular it's 'tooth'.*

singular [NOTICEABLE] /ˈsɪŋ.gjʊ.ləʳ/ [US] /-lɚ/ *adj* [before n] *FORMAL* of an unusual quality or standard; noticeable: *It was a building of singular grace and beauty.* ○ *He showed a singular lack of skill in painting.* **singularly** /ˈsɪŋ.gjʊ.lə.li/ [US] /-lɚ-/ *adv* to an unusual degree: *singularly beautiful* ○ *a singularly unattractive individual*

singular [STRANGE] /ˈsɪŋ.gjʊ.ləʳ/ [US] /-lɚ/ *adj FORMAL* unusual or strange; not ordinary **singularly** /ˈsɪŋ.gjʊ.lə.li/ [US] /-lɚ-/ *adv*

sinister /ˈsɪn.ɪ.stəʳ/ [US] /-stɚ/ *adj* making you feel that something bad or evil might happen: *The ruined house had a sinister appearance.* ○ *A sinister-looking man sat in the corner of the room.*

sink [GO DOWN BELOW] /sɪŋk/ *verb* [I or T] **sank** or *US ALSO* **sunk**, **sunk** to (cause something or someone to) go down below the surface or to the bottom of a liquid or soft substance: *The Titanic was a passenger ship which sank **(to the bottom of the ocean)** in 1912.* ○ *The legs of the garden chair sank **into** the soft ground.* ○ *Enemy aircraft sank two battleships.* ○ *The dog sank her teeth **into*** (= bit) *the ball and ran off with it.* ➲See also **sunken**.

• **sink or swim** If someone leaves you to sink or swim, they give you no help so that you succeed or fail completely by your own efforts: *My employer gave me no help when I started my new job – I was just **left to** sink or swim.*

• **sink like a stone** (*ALSO* **sink like a lead balloon**) to attract no support, attention or interest: *My suggestion that we all play tennis sank like a stone.*

• **sink without (a) trace** *INFORMAL* to be forgotten about completely, or to not attract any attention or interest: *Since his last book five years ago, he seems to have sunk without trace.* ○ *Her second symphony sank without a trace.*

sinker /ˈsɪŋ.kəʳ/ [US] /-kɚ/ *noun* [C] a weight fixed to a fishing net or line to keep it under the water

sink [FALL] /sɪŋk/ *verb* **sank** or *US ALSO* **sunk**, **sunk** **1** [I] to (cause something or someone to) fall or move to a lower level: *The sun glowed red as it sank slowly below the horizon.* ○ *Student numbers have sunk considerably this year.* ○ *INFORMAL We sank* (= drank) *a bottle of wine each last night.* ○ *The wounded soldier sank* (= fell) ***to** the ground.* ○ *He sank **into** deep despair* (= became very unhappy) *when he lost his job.* **2** [T] to hit a ball into a hole or pocket, especially in golf or snooker

• **sink to a whisper** to speak very quietly: *The child's voice sank to a whisper as she admitted that she had broken the window.*

• **spirits sink** (*ALSO* **heart sink**) to feel disappointed or to lose hope: *My heart sank when I realized we couldn't afford the new house.*

• **sinking feeling** a feeling that something bad is going to happen: *When I woke up this morning, I had a sinking feeling that it was going to be a difficult day.*

• **sinking fast** (of a person's health) getting much worse quickly so that death is likely: *Mrs Jones is sinking fast, and the doctor doesn't think she'll live much longer.*

• **sink to such a level/such depths** (*ALSO* **sink so low**) to do something so bad: *I can't believe you would sink so low as to snitch on your best friends.*

• **sunk in thought** *UK* thinking deeply: *Rodin's sculpture 'The Thinker' is of a man sitting with his head in his hand, sunk in thought.*

• **sink *your* differences** *UK* to forget your disagreements: *Paul and Mark agreed to sink their differences and be friends.*

sink [DIG] /sɪŋk/ *verb* [T] **sank** or *US ALSO* **sunk**, **sunk** to dig a hole in the ground, or to put something into a hole dug into the ground: *Sinking more wells is the best way of supplying the population with clean drinking water.* ○ *The first stage of building the fence is sinking the posts **into** the ground.* ➲See also **sunken**.

sink [FAILURE] /sɪŋk/ *verb* [T] **sank** or *US ALSO* **sunk**, **sunk** to cause something to fail or be in trouble: *This rain could sink our plans for the garden party.*

sink [BOWL] /sɪŋk/ *noun* [C] a bowl that is fixed to the wall in a kitchen or bathroom that you wash dishes or your hands, etc. in: *a bathroom/kitchen sink* ➲See picture **In the Kitchen** on page Centre 16

PHRASAL VERBS WITH **sink**

▲ **sink in** [IDEA] *phrasal verb INFORMAL* If an unpleasant or surprising fact or idea sinks in, you gradually start to believe it, understand it, or realize the effect it will have on you: *How many times do I have to tell you something before it sinks in?* ○ *His voice trailed off as the seriousness of his position sank in.*

▲ **sink in/sink into *sth*** [SUBSTANCE] *phrasal verb* If a liquid or soft substance sinks into something solid, it gradually passes into it through its surface: *You'd better wipe up that coffee you spilled on the carpet before it sinks in.*

▲ **sink into *sth*** [BODY] *phrasal verb* to slowly move your body into a sitting or lying position, in a relaxed or tired way: *I was so tired when I got home that all I wanted to do was sink into bed/an armchair/a hot bath.*

▲ **sink *sth* into *sth*** [MONEY] *phrasal verb* to spend a large amount of money on a business or other piece of work: *We sank all our money into my brother's business.*

ˈsinking ˌfund *noun* [C] *SPECIALIZED* money saved by a company or government for the payment of future debts

ˈsink ˌunit *noun* [C] a piece of kitchen furniture into which a sink is fitted

sinless /ˈsɪn.ləs/ *adj* ➲See at **sin** OFFENCE.

Sinn Fein /ˌʃɪnˈfeɪn/ *group noun* [U] an Irish political party that wants Northern Ireland to become part of the

S

Republic of Ireland: *Many people consider Sinn Fein to be the political wing of the IRA.*

Sino- /ˈsaɪ.nəʊ-/ US /-noʊ-/ *prefix* of or connected with China: *Sino-Cuban trade relations*

sinology /saɪˈnɒl.ə.dʒi/ US /-ˈnɑː.lə-/ *noun* [U] the study of Chinese language, literature, history, society, etc. **sinologist** /saɪˈnɒl.ə.dʒɪst/ US /-ˈnɑː.lə-/ *noun* [C]

ˈsin ˌtax *noun* [C usually sing] *US INFORMAL* a tax on items such as cigarettes, alcohol, gambling and other things which are considered unnecessary luxuries in life

sinuous /ˈsɪn.ju.əs/ *adj LITERARY* moving in a twisting, curving or indirect way, or having many curves: *He enjoyed watching the sinuous bodies of the dancers.* ○ *The walkers followed the sinuous path through the trees.* **sinuously** /ˈsɪn.ju.ə.sli/ *adv*

sinus /ˈsaɪ.nəs/ *noun* [C] any of the spaces inside the head that are connected to the back of the nose

sip /sɪp/ *verb* [I or T] **-pp-** to drink, taking only a very small amount at a time: *This tea is very hot, so sip it carefully.* ○ *She slowly sipped (at) her wine.* **sip** /sɪp/ *noun* [C]

siphon /ˈsaɪ.fən/ *noun* [C] **1** (*ALSO* **syphon**) a tube that is bent in the shape of an 'n', with each end in a separate container at two different levels, so that liquid can be pulled up into it from the higher container and go down through it into the lower container **2** a **soda siphon**

siphon, syphon /ˈsaɪ.fən/ *verb* [T usually + adv or prep] to remove liquid from a container using a siphon

▲ **siphon sth off** (*ALSO* **syphon sth off**) *phrasal verb* to dishonestly take money from an organization or other supply, and use it for a purpose for which it was not intended: *He lost his job when it was discovered that he had been siphoning off money from the company for his own use.*

sir MAN /sɜːʳ/ US /sɜː/ *noun* [as form of address] *FORMAL* **1** used as a formal and polite way of speaking to a man, especially one whom you are providing with a service or who is in a position of authority: *Would you like to see the menu, sir?* ○ *"Did you hear what I said?" "Yes, sir."* ⊃Compare **madam** WOMAN; **Miss** TITLE; **Ms. 2 Dear Sir** used to begin a formal letter to a man whose name you do not know. '**Dear Sirs**' is an old fashioned way of beginning a letter to a company. **3 Dear Sir or Madam,** used to begin a formal letter when you do not know whether the person you are writing to is a man or a woman

● **no sir** *US INFORMAL* certainly not: *I'm not going to ride the subway, no sir!*

Sir TITLE *STRONG* /sɜːʳ/ US /sɜː/, *WEAK* /səʳ/ US /sɚ/ *noun* used as the title of a knight, with a first name or with both first and family names, but never with just the family name: *Sir Walter (Scott)*

sire FATHER /saɪəʳ/ US /saɪr/ *noun* [C] a male parent of an animal, especially a horse

sire /saɪəʳ/ US /saɪr/ *verb* [T] to become the male parent of an animal or the father of a child: *The foal was sired by a cup-winning racehorse.* ○ *OLD USE OR HUMOROUS At the age of 70, he married a much younger woman and went on to sire two more children.*

sire KING /saɪəʳ/ US /saɪr/ *noun* [C] *OLD USE* used as a form of address to a king: *I will serve you always, sire.*

siren DEVICE /ˈsaɪə.rən/ US /ˈsaɪr.ən/ *noun* [C] a device for making a loud warning noise: *In big cities you hear police sirens all the time.* ○ *When the air raid siren went off people ran to their shelters.*

siren WOMAN /ˈsaɪə.rən/ US /ˈsaɪr.ən/ *noun* [C] **1** (in ancient Greek literature) one of the creatures who were half woman and half bird, whose beautiful singing encouraged sailors to sail into dangerous waters where they died **2** a woman who is considered to be very attractive, but also dangerous

sirloin (steak) /ˌsɜː.lɔɪnˈsteɪk/ US /ˌsɜː-/ *noun* [C or U] the best meat from the lower back of a cow

sirocco (*plural* **siroccos** or **sciroccos**), **scirocco** /sɪˈrɒk.əʊ/ US /-ˈrɑː.koʊ/ *noun* [C] a hot wind which blows from the Sahara Desert to southern Europe

sis /sɪs/ *noun* [C usually sing] *INFORMAL FOR* **sister**

sisal /ˈsaɪ.səl/ US /ˈsɪs.əl/ /ˈsaɪ-/ *noun* [U] (a tropical plant whose leaves produce) strong threads which are used for making rope and floor coverings

sissy /ˈsɪs.i/ *noun* [C] (*ALSO* **cissy**) *INFORMAL DISAPPROVING* a boy who other boys dislike and laugh at because they think he is weak or interested in activities girls usually like, or a person who is weak and cowardly: *Kevin is such a sissy.* ○ [as form of address] *Can't you climb that tree, you big sissy?* **sissy** /ˈsɪs.i/ *adj* (*ALSO* **cissy**)

sister FEMALE /ˈsɪs.təʳ/ US /-tɚ/ *noun* [C] **1** a girl or woman who has the same parents as another person: *Sophie and Emily are sisters.* ○ *Emily is Sophie's younger/little/older/big sister.* **2** a girl or woman who treats you in the kind way that a sister would: *Lynn's such a good friend – she's like a sister to me.* **3** a woman who shares an interest with you, especially that of improving women's rights: [as form of address] *"We must continue the fight, sisters!"* **4** *UK* a nurse who is in charge of a department of a hospital **5** a female member of a religious group, especially a nun **6** *US OLD-FASHIONED INFORMAL* used to address a woman: *OK, sister, move it!*

sisterhood /ˈsɪs.tə.hʊd/ US /-tɚ-/ *noun* [U] a strong feeling of companionship and support among women who are involved in action to improve women's rights

sisterhood /ˈsɪs.tə.hʊd/ US /-tɚ-/ *group noun* [C] a society of women living a religious life

the sisterhood *group noun* women involved in action to improve women's rights

sisterly /ˈsɪs.tə.li/ US /-tɚ.li/ *adj* feeling or behaving like a sister: *I felt quite sisterly towards him, but I couldn't marry him.*

sister IN SAME GROUP /ˈsɪs.təʳ/ US /-tɚ/ *adj* [before n] belonging to a group of similar and related things, such as businesses, usually owned or operated by the same person or organization: *our sister company in Australia* ○ *the US battleship Missouri and her sister ship, the Wisconsin*

sister-in-law /ˈsɪs.tə.rɪn.lɔː/ US /-tɚ.ɪn.lɑː/ *noun* [C] *plural* **sisters-in-law** the wife of your brother, or the sister of your husband or wife, or the wife of the brother of your husband or wife

sit BE SEATED /sɪt/ *verb* sitting, sat, sat **1** [I or T; usually + adv or prep] to (cause someone to) be in a position in which the lower part of the body is resting on a seat or other type of support, with the upper part of the body vertical: *to sit at a table/desk* ○ *to sit in an armchair* ○ *to sit on a chair/a horse/the ground* ○ *He came and sat (down) next to me.* ○ [R] *INFORMAL Sit yourself down and have a cup of tea.* ○ *The child's father sat her (down) on a chair.* **2** [I usually + adv or prep] to stay in one place for a long time and not be used: *The encyclopedia sits on my shelf at home, gathering dust.* **3** [I usually + adv or prep] to be in a particular position: *The village sits at/in the bottom of a valley.* **4** [I usually + adv or prep] (of clothes) to fit someone in a particular way: *That coat sits very well on you.* **5** [I usually + adv or prep] to be a model for a painter, photographer, etc: *Monet's wife sat for him many times.* **6** [I] (of an animal such as a dog) to move into a position with its back legs bent and its tail end on the ground: *We're trying to train our dog to sit.* **7** [I usually + adv or prep] If a bird sits on its eggs, it covers them with its body to keep them warm before they HATCH. **8** [I usually + adv or prep] to **babysit**

● **sit at the feet of sb** to be a very admiring student of someone important

● **sit in judgment on/over someone** *MAINLY DISAPPROVING* to make a judgment on someone especially when you have no right to do so: *I don't know why he thinks he can sit in judgment over us like that.*

● **sit on the fence** to delay making a decision: *You can't sit on the fence any longer – you have decide whose side you're on.*

● **sit on your arse** *UK* (*US* **sit on your ass**) *OFFENSIVE* to do nothing, especially when you should be doing something: *She just sits on her arse all day, while I do all the work.*

● **sit on your stomach** *INFORMAL* Food that sits on your stomach makes you feel uncomfortably full.

● **sit right/well (with sb)** to be something that you agree or are pleased with: *Their decision/answer didn't sit well with the Board of Directors.*

● **sit tight 1** to stay where you are: *You'd better sit tight and I'll call the doctor.* **2** *MAINLY UK* to refuse to change your mind: *My parents tried to persuade me not to go alone, but I sat tight.*

• **sitting duck** someone or something that is very easy for an enemy to shoot or attack: *With their bullets all gone, the soldiers were sitting ducks for the enemy.*

• **be sitting pretty** to be in a good situation, usually because you have a lot of money: *They bought their house while prices were low, so now they're sitting pretty.*

sitter /ˈsɪt.əʳ/ [US] /ˈsɪt̬.ɚ/ *noun* [C] **1** someone who is having their PORTRAIT (= picture of their face or body) painted **2** a **babysitter** ⊃See at **babysit**.

sitting /ˈsɪt.ɪŋ/ [US] /ˈsɪt̬-/ *noun* [C] **1** a period when a meal is served in a place like a hotel: *When the hotel is full, dinner is served in two sittings.* **2** a period spent by a model who is being painted, photographed, etc: *The portrait was finished after only three sittings.*

• **at/in one sitting** during one limited period of time, without stopping: *I enjoyed the book so much that I read it all in one sitting.*

sit [MEET] /sɪt/ *verb* [I] **sitting, sat, sat** to hold an official meeting of a parliament, court, etc: *The court will sit tomorrow morning.* ○ *As an MP, I see much less of my family when Parliament is sitting.*

sitting /ˈsɪt.ɪŋ/ [US] /ˈsɪt̬-/ *noun* [C] a meeting of a parliament, court, etc.

sit [BE A MEMBER] /sɪt/ *verb* [I] **sitting, sat, sat** to be a member of an official group: *I'm going to be sitting* ***on*** *the committee for one more year.* ○ *Our member of Congress has sat* ***for*** (= represented) *this town for years.* ○ *US All of the federal judges currently sitting* (= in office) *in Maryland hail from Baltimore.*

sit [EXAMINATION] /sɪt/ *verb* [T] **sitting, sat, sat** *MAINLY UK* to take an examination: *After I've sat my exams, I'm going on holiday.* ○ *AUS I sat* ***for*** *my exams today.*

PHRASAL VERBS WITH **sit** ▼

▲ **sit around** *phrasal verb* (*UK ALSO* **sit about**) *INFORMAL* to spend time sitting down and doing very little: *We sat around most of the evening, waiting for Jake and drinking beer.*

▲ **sit back** [COMFORTABLE] *phrasal verb* to sit comfortably with your back against the back of a chair

▲ **sit back** [WAITING] *phrasal verb INFORMAL* to wait for something to happen without making any effort to do anything yourself: *You can't just sit back* ***and*** *wait for job offers to come to you.*

▲ **sit by** *phrasal verb* to fail to take action to stop something wrong from happening: *I can't just sit by* ***and watch*** *you waste all our money.*

▲ **sit down** [NOT STAND] *phrasal verb* to move your body so that the lower part of it is resting on a seat or on the ground: *I sat down* ***on*** *the sofa next to Barbara.* ⊃See picture **Phrasal Verbs** on page Centre 9

sit-down /ˌsɪtˈdaʊn/ *noun* [S] *INFORMAL* a short period of sitting in order to rest: *You look tired. Why don't you come and have a sit-down for a few minutes.*

sit-down /ˈsɪt.daʊn/ *adj* [before n] describes a meal served to people who are sitting at a table: *We're having a sit-down meal at our wedding, rather than a buffet.*

▲ **sit down and do** ***sth*** [DISCUSS] *phrasal verb* to spend time discussing a problem in order to solve it or make a decision: *I think we should sit down and* ***talk*** *about this.*

sit-down /ˈsɪt.daʊn/ *adj* [before n] describes a strike in which workers refuse to leave their place of work until their employers have agreed to their demands: *The workers are holding a sit-down* ***strike***.

▲ **sit in** [COMPLAIN] *phrasal verb* to go as a group into a public building and refuse to leave or to allow normal activities to continue there until a situation that you are complaining about is changed

sit-in /ˈsɪt.ɪn/ [US] /ˈsɪt̬-/ *noun* [C] *Students staged a sit-in in the university offices as part of their protest campaign.*

▲ **sit in** [BE PRESENT] *phrasal verb* to be present in a meeting or class, watching it but not taking part in it: *There will be a school inspector sitting in* ***on*** *your class this morning.*

▲ **sit in for** ***sb*** *phrasal verb* to take the place of someone who would normally do a particular job or attend a particular meeting: *Mr Baker is ill today, so Miss Dixon is sitting in for him* ***(as*** *your teacher).*

▲ **sit on** ***sth*** [DELAY] *phrasal verb INFORMAL* to delay taking action about something: *The company has been sitting on my letter for weeks without dealing with my complaint.*

▲ **sit on** ***sth*** [KEEP SECRET] *phrasal verb INFORMAL MAINLY DISAPPROVING* to prevent people from knowing a piece of information: *The government will presumably sit on the report until after the election.*

▲ **sit on** ***sb*** [CONTROL] *phrasal verb INFORMAL* to force someone to be silent or not to do something: *The boss is going to sit on him to make sure he says nothing.*

▲ **sit** ***sth*** **out** [ACTIVITY] *phrasal verb* [M] to not take part in a physical activity such as a dance or a game, because you are tired or injured: *I'm feeling rather tired, so I think I'll sit out the next dance.*

▲ **sit** ***sth*** **out** [SITUATION] *phrasal verb* [M] to wait for an unpleasant situation or event to finish, without leaving or taking some other action: *The government is prepared to sit out the strike rather than agree to union demands.*

▲ **sit through** ***sth*** *phrasal verb* to stay until the end of an event such as a meeting or performance that is very long or boring: *We had to sit through two hours of speeches.*

▲ **sit under** ***sb*** *phrasal verb US* to receive teaching from someone: *He sat under the most influential teacher in his field.*

▲ **sit** ***(sb)*** **up** [NOT LYING DOWN] *phrasal verb* to move into a sitting position after you have been lying down, or to help someone else to do this: *Let me sit you up in the bed so you'll be more comfortable.*

▲ **sit up** *phrasal verb* to sit with a straight back: *How many times do I have to tell you children to sit up* ***straight?***

sit-up /ˈsɪt.ʌp/ [US] /ˈsɪt̬-/ *noun* [C] a type of exercise in which someone sits up from a lying position and which makes the stomach muscles stronger

▲ **sit up** [STAY AWAKE] *phrasal verb* to stay awake and not go to bed although it is late: [+ v-ing] *The book was so interesting that I sat up all night read****ing*** *it.* ○ *I'll be late tonight, so don't sit up* ***for*** (= wait for) *me.*

▲ **sit up** [NOTICE] *phrasal verb INFORMAL* to show interest or surprise: *The news that he was getting married really made her sit up.*

• **sit up and take notice** *INFORMAL* to show interest or surprise: *She sat up and took notice when she heard he was getting married.*

sitar /ˈsɪt.ɑːʳ/ [US] /sɪˈtɑːr/ *noun* [C] an Indian musical instrument with a round body, a long neck and two sets of strings

sitcom /ˈsɪt.kɒm/ [US] /-kɑːm/ *noun* [C or U] a **situation comedy**

site /saɪt/ *noun* [C] **1** a place where something is, was, or will be built, or where something happened, is happening, or will happen: *a building site* ○ *The council haven't yet chosen the site* ***for*** *the new hospital.* ○ *This is the site* ***of*** *the accident.* **2** a **website**

• **on site** inside a factory, office building, etc: *There are two restaurants on site.* ○ *The office complex has an on-site nursery.*

site /saɪt/ *verb* [T usually + adv or prep] *FORMAL* to exist or be built in a particular place: *The company head office is sited in Rome.*

ˌsitting ˈmember *noun* [C] *UK FORMAL* the person who is the MEMBER OF PARLIAMENT for an area at the present time

ˌsitting ˈroom *noun* [C] *UK FOR* **living room**

ˌsitting ˈtenant *noun* [C] a person with a legal right to stay in a property that they are renting: *We can't sell the house because we can't get rid of the sitting tenants.*

situate /ˈsɪt.ju.eɪt/ *verb* [T usually + adv or prep] *SLIGHTLY FORMAL* to put in a particular position: *They plan to situate the bus stop* ***at*** *the corner of the road.* ○ *To understand this issue, it must first be situated* ***in*** *its context.*

situated /ˈsɪt.ju.eɪ.tɪd/ [US] /-t̬ɪd/ *adj* [after v] *SLIGHTLY FORMAL* in a particular position: *The school is situated near to the station.* ○ [+ to infinitive] *With this new product, we are well situated* ***to*** *beat* (= we have a good chance of beating) *our competitors.* ○ *How are you situated* ***for*** *time* (= How much time do you have)?

situation /ˌsɪt.juˈeɪ.ʃən/ *noun* [C] **1** the set of things that are happening and the conditions that exist at a particular time and place: *the economic/political situation* ○ *Her news put me* ***in*** *a difficult situation.* ○ *"Would you get involved in a fight?" "It would* ***depend on the*** *situation."* ○ *I'll worry about it* ***if/when/as*** *the situation* ***arises*** (= if/when/as it happens). **2** *OLD USE* a job: *My sister has a good situation* ***as*** *a teacher in the local school.* **3** *FORMAL* the position of something, especially a town, building, etc: *The house's situation in the river valley is perfect.*

situˌation ˈcomedy *noun* [C or U] (*INFORMAL* **sitcom**) an amusing television or radio show in which the same characters appear in each programme in a different story

Situˌations ˈVacant *noun* [S or U] *UK* the part of a newspaper in which jobs are listed

SI unit /ˌesˈaɪˌjuː.nɪt/ *noun* [C] *SPECIALIZED* a unit of measurement that is part of a system used for scientific and technical work all over the world: *The SI unit of length is the metre.*

six /sɪks/ *determiner, pronoun, noun* [C] (the number) 6: *Look for a bus with a number six on the front of it.*

six /sɪks/ *noun* [C] in cricket, six points scored when the player hits the ball to the edge of the playing area without it touching the ground first: *The crowd cheered when Richards hit a six.*

• **at sixes and sevens** *INFORMAL* in a confused, badly organized or difficult situation: *We've been at sixes and sevens in the office this week.*

• **six of the best** *UK OLD-FASHIONED* a beating, usually of six hits with a stick

• **be six feet under** *HUMOROUS* to be dead and buried: *There's no point worrying about it – we'll both be six feet under by then.*

• **six of one and half a dozen of the other** *INFORMAL SAYING* said when you think that neither of two choices is better than the other: *"Shall we go by car or train?" "I don't know, it's six of one and half a dozen of the other."*

sixth /sɪksθ/ *determiner, pronoun, adj, adv, noun* [S] 6th written as a word: *I have to return my library books on* ***the*** *sixth (of July).* ○ *England* ***were/came*** *sixth in the 100 metres.*

sixth /sɪksθ/ *noun* [C] one of six equal parts: *Cut the cake into sixths.*

six-footer /ˌsɪksˈfʊt.əʳ/ [US] /-fʊt̬.ɚ/ *noun* [C] *INFORMAL* a person who is at least six feet (1.83 metres) tall

six-pack /ˈsɪks.pæk/ *noun* [C] **1** *INFORMAL* six containers, usually bottles or CANS, of a particular type of beer or other drink that are sold together as one unit **2** *HUMOROUS* the well-developed muscles of a man's stomach

sixpence /ˈsɪks.pənts/ *noun* [C or U] a small silver-coloured coin used in Britain until 1971 which was worth six old PENNIES, or this amount of money

sixpenny /ˈsɪks.pən.i/ *adj* [before n] worth or costing six pence: *a sixpenny bit*

six-shooter /ˈsɪks.ʃuː.təʳ/ [US] /-t̬ɚ/ *noun* [C] a small gun that holds six bullets

sixteen /ˌsɪkˈstiːn/ /ˈ--/ *determiner, pronoun, noun* [C] (the number) 16: *We've got sixteen (people) coming for lunch.* ○ *He bought her a birthday card with a big gold sixteen on the front.*

sixteenth /ˌsɪkˈstiːnθ/ /ˈ--/ *determiner, pronoun, adj, adv, noun* [S] 16th written as a word

sixˈteenth ˌnote *noun* [C] *US FOR* **semiquaver**

ˈsixth ˌform *noun* [C] in Britain, the part of a school for students aged 16-18: *The sixth-form students are preparing to take their A levels.*

ˈsixth ˌformer *noun* [C] a student in the sixth form

ˌsixth ˈsense *noun* [S] an ability which some people believe that they have which seems to give them information without using the five senses of sight, hearing, touch, smell or taste: *A sixth sense told me that the train was going to crash.*

sixty /ˈsɪk.sti/ *determiner, pronoun, noun* [C] (the number) 60: *There are sixty (people) coming to the wedding.* ○ *I want to buy a card with a sixty on it for my uncle.*

sixties /ˈsɪk.stiz/ *plural noun* A person's sixties are the period in which they are aged between 60 and 69: *Many people retire* ***in*** *their sixties.*

the ˈsixties *plural noun* **1** the range of temperature between 60° and 69° Fahrenheit: *The temperature is usually* ***in/around*** *the sixties at this time of year.* **2** the period of years between 60 and 69 in any century: *The Beatles made their first hit records* ***in*** *the sixties.*

sixtieth /ˈsɪk.sti.əθ/ *determiner, pronoun, adj, adv, noun* [S] 60th written as a word

size [AMOUNT] /saɪz/ *noun* [C or U] how large or small something or someone is: *We are concerned about the size of our debt.* ○ *Some kinds of trees grow to a huge size.* ○ *What is the size of that window?* ○ *The field was about ten acres* ***in*** *size.* ○ *He had a lump on his head the size* ***of*** (= the same size as) *an egg.* ○ *The baby is* ***a good*** *size* (= quite large). ○ *I was amazed at the size of their garden* (= It was very big).

• **that's about the size of it** *INFORMAL* used to show your agreement with someone who has said something correct: *"So you mean you won't come to the party with me?" "Yes, that's about the size of it."*

sizeable, sizable /ˈsaɪ.zə.bl̩/ *adj* large: *a sizeable amount/area/house*

-sized /-saɪzd/ *suffix*: *a good-sized* (= large) *garden* ○ *a child-sized chair* (= a chair of a size suitable for a child) ○ *a pocket-sized mobile phone* (= one small enough to fit into a pocket)

size [MEASURE] /saɪz/ *noun* [C] one of the standard measures according to which goods are made or sold: *a size 14 dress* ○ *Do these shoes come* (= Are they made) ***in*** *children's sizes?* ○ *What size are you?/What is your size?/What size do you* ***take?*** ○ *Would you like to* ***try*** *the coat* ***(on) for*** *size* (= see how well it fits you), *sir?* ○ *We'll need to get the carpet cut* ***to*** *size* (= cut so that it fits).

size [GLUE] /saɪz/ *noun* [U] *SPECIALIZED* a glue-like substance which gives stiffness and a hard shiny surface to cloth, paper, etc.

size /saɪz/ *verb* [T] to cover or treat cloth, paper, etc. with size

▲ **size** ***sth/sb*** **up** *phrasal verb* [M] to examine something or someone carefully and decide what you think about them: *We must size up the situation before we decide what to do.* ○ *The two cats walked in circles around each other, sizing each other up.*

sizzle /ˈsɪz.l̩/ *verb* [I] to make a sound like food cooking in hot fat: *The sausages are sizzling in the pan.*

sizzling /ˈsɪz.l̩.ɪŋ/ /-lɪŋ/ *adv* (*ALSO* **sizzling hot**) very hot: *It's a sizzling hot day today!*

sizzler /ˈsɪz.ləʳ/ [US] /-lɚ/ *noun* [C] *INFORMAL* a very hot day

Skate

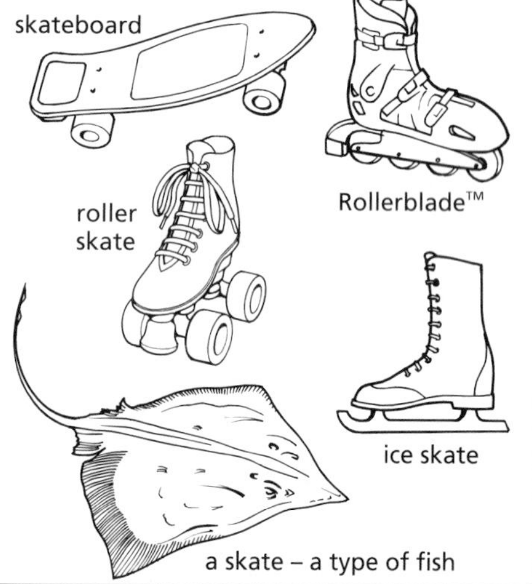
skateboard
Rollerblade™
roller skate
ice skate
a skate – a type of fish

skate [BOOT] /skeɪt/ *noun* [C] *plural* **skates** a special boot with a thin metal bar fixed to the bottom that you wear to move quickly on ice, or a boot with four small wheels fixed to the bottom so that you can move over a hard surface: *a pair of* ***ice*** *skates* ○ *a pair of* ***roller*** *skates*

• **get/put *your* skates on** *UK INFORMAL* used when you want to tell someone to hurry up: *Get your skates on, or we'll be late.*

skate /skeɪt/ *verb* **[I + adv or prep; T]** to move, or make a particular movement on a surface, using skates: *The ice on the river is thick enough to skate* ***on/across/over***. ○ *Shall we* ***go*** *skating tomorrow?*

• **be skating on thin ice** to be doing something risky or dangerous: *He's skating on thin ice by lying to the police.*

skater /ˈskeɪ.təʳ/ [US] /-t̬ɚ/ *noun* **[C]** a person on skates

skating /ˈskeɪ.tɪŋ/ [US] /-t̬ɪŋ/ *noun* **[U]** the activity or sport of moving on skates: *ice/roller skating* ○ *figure/speed skating*

skate [FISH] /skeɪt/ *noun* **[C or U]** *plural* **skate** or **skates** a large flat sea fish, which can be eaten as food

▲ **skate over/round/around *sth*** *phrasal verb* to avoid dealing completely with something or to fail to pay enough attention to it: *Providing homeless people with somewhere to stay when the weather is cold only skates round the problem, it doesn't solve it.* ○ *I didn't understand what the teacher said about prepositions, because she only skated over it.*

skateboard /ˈskeɪt.bɔːd/ [US] /-bɔːrd/ *noun* **[C]** a flat narrow board with two small wheels under each end, which a person stands on and moves forward by pushing one foot on the ground ➲See picture **Sports** on page Centre 10 **skateboarder** /ˈskeɪtˌbɔː.dəʳ/ [US] /-ˌbɔːr.dɚ/ *noun* **[C]**

skateboarding /ˈskeɪtˌbɔː.dɪŋ/ [US] /-ˌbɔːr-/ *noun* **[U]** the activity or sport of riding a skateboard ➲See picture **Sports** on page Centre 10

skating ˌrink *noun* **[C]** a specially prepared area for skating

skedaddle /skɪˈdæd.l̩/ *verb* **[I]** *INFORMAL* to run away quickly: *OK, children, skedaddle!*

skein [THREAD] /skeɪn/ *noun* **[C]** a length of wool or thread loosely wound into the shape of a ring

skein [BIRDS] /skeɪn/ *noun* **[C]** a large group of wild birds such as geese or ducks in flight

skeletal /ˈskel.ɪ.təl/ [US] /-t̬əl/ *adj* **1** of or like a SKELETON (= frame of bones): *Her body was skeletal* (= very thin). ○ *He suffered serious skeletal injuries in the accident.* **2** describes something that exists in its most basic form: *The newspaper report gave only a skeletal account of the debate.*

skeleton /ˈskel.ɪ.tən/ [US] /-t̬ən/ *noun* **[C]** **1** the frame of bones supporting a human or animal body: *We found an old sheep skeleton up on the cliffs.* ○ *FIGURATIVE Her long illness reduced her to a skeleton* (= made her very thin). ➲See picture **The Body** on page Centre 5 **2** the most basic form or structure of something: *The skeleton* ***of*** *my book is written/My book is* ***in*** *skeleton* ***form*** *– now I just have to add the details.*

• **skeleton in the/*your* cupboard/closet** an embarrassing secret: *Most families* ***have*** *one or two skeletons in the cupboard.*

ˈskeleton ˌkey *noun* **[C]** a key which will open several doors

ˈskeleton ˌservice *noun* **[S]** when something such as a transport system operates in an extremely limited way at certain times: *The local bus company only runs a skeleton service on Sundays.*

ˈskeleton ˌstaff *noun* **[S]** (*ALSO* **skeleton crew**) the smallest number of people needed for a business or organization to operate: *The hospital has a skeleton staff at weekends.*

skeptic /ˈskep.tɪk/ *noun* **[C]** *US FOR* **sceptic**

sketch [SIMPLE SHAPE/FORM] /sketʃ/ *noun* **[C]** **1** a simple, quickly-made drawing which does not have many details: *My mother made a (pencil) sketch* ***of*** *my brother reading a book.* **2** a short written or spoken story which does not have many details

sketch /sketʃ/ *verb* **[I or T]** to make a sketch of something: *The art students were told to sketch the landscape.* ○ *When I have some spare time, I like to sketch.* ○ *The artist has sketched* ***out*** *a design for the new school.*

sketcher /ˈsketʃ.əʳ/ [US] /-ɚ/ *noun* **[C]** someone who makes sketches

sketchy /ˈsketʃ.i/ *adj* containing few details: *So far we only have sketchy information about what caused the explosion.* **sketchily** /ˈsketʃ.ɪ.li/ *adv*

sketch [HUMOROUS PERFORMANCE] /sketʃ/ *noun* **[C]** a short humorous part of a longer show on stage, television or radio: *I thought the sketch about Queen Victoria was very funny.*

▲ **sketch *sth* out** *phrasal verb* to give a short description of something, containing few details: *She sketched out the plan in a few brief sentences.*

sketchpad /ˈsketʃ.pæd/ *noun* **[C]** (*ALSO* **sketchbook**) a number of sheets of plain paper fixed together for drawing on

skew /skjuː/ *verb* **[T]** to cause something to be not straight or exact; to twist or **distort**: *The company's results for this year are skewed because not all our customers have paid their bills.*

skew /skjuː/ *adj* **[after v]** not straight

skewer /skjʊəʳ/ [US] /ˈskjuː.ɚ/ *noun* **[C]** a long thin metal pin used for holding pieces of food, especially meat, together during cooking

skewer /skjʊəʳ/ [US] /ˈskjuː.ɚ/ *verb* **[T]** to put pieces of food, especially meat, on a skewer

skew-whiff /ˌskjuːˈwɪf/ *adj* **[after v]** *UK INFORMAL* sloping instead of straight; incorrectly positioned: *You've got your hat on skew-whiff.*

ski /skiː/ *noun* **[C]** *plural* **skis** one of a pair of long, flat narrow pieces of wood or plastic, which curve up at the front, and are fastened to boots so that the wearer can move quickly and easily over snow: *a pair of skis* ○ *ski boots* ○ *a ski club/resort*

ski /skiː/ *verb* **[I or T]** **skiing, skied, skied** to move over snow on skis: *He skied* ***down*** *the hill.* ○ *Shall we* ***go*** *skiing?*

skier /ˈskiː.əʳ/ [US] /-ɚ/ *noun* **[C]** a person who skis

skiing /ˈskiː.ɪŋ/ *noun* **[U]** the activity or sport of moving on skis: *a skiing trip/instructor* ➲See picture **Sports** on page Centre 10

skibob /ˈskiː.bɒb/ [US] /-bɑːb/ *noun* **[C]** a vehicle like a bicycle with skis instead of wheels, used for races

skid /skɪd/ *verb* **[I]** **-dd-** (especially of a vehicle) to slide along a surface so that you have no control: *Trevor's bus skidded* ***on*** *some ice and hit a tree.*

skid /skɪd/ *noun* **[C]** **1** an uncontrollable sliding movement: *She was riding too fast on a wet road, and the motorbike* ***went into a*** *skid.* **2** one of two long flat pieces under some aircraft such as helicopters, which help the aircraft to land

• **on skid row** *MAINLY US INFORMAL* poor, without a job or a place to live, and often drinking too much alcohol

• **on the skids** *INFORMAL* experiencing difficulties and unlikely to continue successfully: *Their marriage seems to be on the skids.*

• **put the skids under sth** *UK INFORMAL* to cause something such as a plan to fail: *Local residents have put the skids under plans to build a new shopping centre.*

ˈskid ˌmarks *plural noun* black marks made by the tyres of a car when it starts or stops moving very quickly: *There were skid marks on the road where a car had braked suddenly.*

skidpan /ˈskɪd.pæn/ *noun* **[C]** *UK* a specially prepared surface on which drivers can practise controlling skids

skiff /skɪf/ *noun* **[C]** a small light boat for rowing or sailing, usually used by only one person

skiffle /ˈskɪf.l̩/ *noun* **[U]** a type of music popular in the 1950s that is a mixture of jazz and FOLK music, in which players often perform on instruments they have made themselves

ˈski ˌjump *noun* **[S or U]** a competition in which people on skis move very fast down a specially made steep slope which turns up at the end, and jump off from the bottom of it, landing on a lower level

skilful *UK, US* **skillful** /ˈskɪl.fəl/ *adj* **1** good at doing something, especially because you have practised doing it: *Police officers have to be skilful drivers.* **2** done or made very well: *a skilful piece of playing on the clarinet*

skilfully *UK, US* **skillfully** /ˈskɪl.fəl.i/ *adv* with great skill

'ski ˌlift *noun* [C usually sing] a machine consisting of seats hanging down from a continuously moving wire, which carries people on skis to the top of slopes which they can then ski down

skill /skɪl/ *noun* [C or U] an ability to do an activity or job well, especially because you have practised it: *Ruth **had/possessed** great writing skills.* ○ *I have no skill **at/in** sewing.*

skilled /skɪld/ *adj* **1** having the abilities needed to do an activity or job well: *My mother is very skilled **at/in** dressmaking.* **2** Skilled work needs someone who has had special training to do it: *Nursing is a highly skilled job.*

skillet /'skɪl.ɪt/ *noun* [C] *US FOR* **frying pan**

skim [MOVE ABOVE] /skɪm/ *verb* **-mm- 1** [I or T] to move quickly just above a surface without touching it: *The birds skimmed **(across/along/over)** the tops of the waves.* **2** [T] *UK* (*US* **skip**) to throw a flat stone horizontally over water so that it touches and rises off the surface several times: *We watched a child skimming stones across the lake.*

skim [CONSIDER QUICKLY] /skɪm/ *verb* [I or T] **-mm-** to read or consider something quickly in order to understand the main points, without studying it in detail: *I've only skimmed **(through/over)** his letter; I haven't read it carefully yet.* ○ *We've only skimmed **the surface of*** (= considered a small part of) *the problem.*

skim [REMOVE] /skɪm/ *verb* [T] **-mm-** to remove something solid from the surface of a liquid: *Strain the cooking liquid and skim **off the fat**.*

▲ **skim *sb/sth* off** *phrasal verb* to choose the best people or things from a group: *We've skimmed off the six people who seem to be the most suitable for the job.*

ˌskimmed 'milk *UK noun* [U] (*US ALSO* **skim milk**) milk from which the cream has been removed

skimp /skɪmp/ *verb* [I or T] to not spend enough time or money on something, or to not use enough of something to do a job or activity properly: *Many old people skimp **on** food and heating in order to meet their bills.* ○ *When choosing an overseas package tour, do not skimp.*

skimpy /'skɪm.pi/ *adj* **1** *DISAPPROVING* not large enough: *a skimpy meal* **2** Skimpy clothing shows a lot of your body: *a skimpy dress*

skin /skɪn/ *noun* **1** [C or U] the natural outer layer which covers a person, animal, fruit, etc: *dark/fair/pale/tanned skin* ○ *skin cancer* ○ *Babies have soft skins.* ○ *Native Americans used to trade skins* (= the skins of animals that have been removed from the body, with or without the hair). ○ *a banana/potato skin* ➲See picture **Fruit** on page Centre 1 **2** [C or U] any outer covering: *The bullet pierced the skin of the aircraft.* **3** [S] a thin solid surface which forms on some liquids, such as paint, when they are left in the air, or others, such as heated milk, when they are left to cool **4** [C] *SPECIALIZED* the particular way that information is arranged and displayed on a computer screen: *Many electronic devices let you create your own skins.* **5 drenched/soaked/wet to the skin** extremely wet: *We had no umbrellas so we got soaked to the skin in the pouring rain.* **6 thin/thick skin** easily/not easily made unhappy by criticism: *I don't worry about what he says – I **have** a very thick skin.* ➲See also **thick-skinned**; **thin-skinned**.

• **by the skin of *your* teeth** If you do something by the skin of your teeth, you only just succeed in doing it: *He escaped from the secret police by the skin of his teeth.*

• **get under *sb's* skin** to annoy someone: *Jack really gets under my skin – he never buys anyone a drink.*

• **jump/leap out of *your* skin** to be extremely surprised by something: *The loud noise made me jump out of my skin.*

• **be no skin off *sb's* nose** (*US ALSO* **be no skin off *sb's* back/teeth**) used when you want to say that it makes no difference to you what someone else does or thinks: *It's no skin off my nose if you don't take my advice.*

• **be skin and bone(s)** to be extremely thin: *She was (just) skin and bone(s).*

skin /skɪn/ *verb* [T] **-nn-** to remove the skin of something: *The hunters skinned the deer they had killed.* ○ *I skinned my knee* (= hurt my knee by rubbing skin off it) *when I fell down the steps.*

• **skin *sb* alive** *INFORMAL HUMOROUS* to punish or tell someone off severely: *My mother will skin me alive for being so late home.*

skinless /'skɪn.ləs/ *adj* without a skin: *skinless, boneless fillets of fish* **-skin** /-skɪn/ *suffix*: *I've got an old sheepskin coat.* **-skinned** /-skɪnd/ *suffix*: *pale-skinned*

skin-deep /ˌskɪn'diːp/ *adj* not carefully considered or strongly felt: *After the first half-hour she realized that her new-found confidence was no more than skin-deep.*

skin-diving /'skɪnˌdaɪ.vɪŋ/ *noun* [U] swimming under water with only limited breathing equipment and without a special suit **skin-diver** /'skɪnˌdaɪ.vəʳ/ [US] /-vɚ/ *noun* [C]

'skin ˌflick *noun* [C] *US SLANG* a film that shows sexual acts in a way that is intended to cause sexual excitement but that would be considered unpleasant and offensive by many people: *It's a cheap movie house that only shows skin flicks.*

skinflint /'skɪn.flɪnt/ *noun* [C] *INFORMAL DISAPPROVING* a person who is unwilling to spend money: *He's a real skinflint.*

skinful /'skɪn.fʊl/ *noun* [S] *SLANG* an amount of alcohol that is enough to make a person drunk: *By ten o'clock he'd **had** a skinful.*

'skin ˌgraft *noun* [C] a piece of skin taken from one part of the body and used to replace damaged skin in another part

skinhead /'skɪn.hed/ *noun* [C] a young person, especially a man, who has very short hair or no hair and is part of a group, often a violent group ➲See picture **Hairstyles and Hats** on page Centre 8

skink /skɪŋk/ *noun* [C] a small lizard found in various hot parts of the world

skinny /'skɪn.i/ *adj MAINLY DISAPPROVING* very thin: *You should eat more, you're much too skinny.*

skinny-dip /'skɪn.i.dɪp/ *verb* [I] *INFORMAL* to swim while naked **skinny-dipping** /'skɪn.iˌdɪp.ɪŋ/ *noun* [U]

skint /skɪnt/ *adj* [after v] *UK SLANG* having no money: *I get paid each Friday, and by Tuesday I'm always skint.*

skin-tight /'skɪn.taɪt/ *adj* describes clothes that fit tightly around the body: *skin-tight jeans* ○ *a skin-tight dress*

skip [MOVE] /skɪp/ *verb* [I usually + adv or prep] **-pp-** to move lightly and quickly, making a small jump after each step: *She watched her little granddaughter skip **down** the path.* ○ *The lambs were skipping **about** in the field.*

skip /skɪp/ *noun* [C] a small light, dancing or jumping step: *She gave a little skip of joy.* ○ *a hop, skip and jump*

skip [JUMP] (**-pp-**) /skɪp/ *verb* [I] (*US* **jump rope, skip rope**) to jump lightly over a rope that is held in both your hands, or by two other people, and swung repeatedly under your legs and over your head as exercise or a game: *Sports players often train by skipping.* ○ *Several children were skipping in the playground.*

skip [LEAVE] /skɪp/ *verb* [I or T] **-pp-** to leave one thing or place, especially quickly, in order to go to another: *This part of the book isn't very interesting, so I'm going to skip **(over)** it.* ○ *The teacher kept skipping **from** one subject **to** another so it was difficult to follow what he was saying.* ○ *We're skipping **over/across/off*** (= making a quick journey) *to France for the day.* ○ *The police think that the bank robbers must have skipped* (= left) ***the country** by now.* ○ *She skipped **off/out*** (= left quickly and/or secretly) *without saying goodbye.*

skip [AVOID] /skɪp/ *verb* [T] **-pp-** *INFORMAL* to not do or not have something that you usually do or that you should do; to avoid: *I'm trying to lose weight, so I'm skipping* (= not eating) ***lunch** today.*

skip [CONTAINER] *UK* /skɪp/ *noun* [C] (*US TRADEMARK* **Dumpster**) a large metal container into which people put unwanted items or building or garden waste, and which is brought to and taken away from a place by a special truck when requested

'ski ˌpants *plural noun* tight trousers, usually for women, which are made from a material that stretches easily and are held firmly in place by an elastic strap worn under each foot

S

'ski ˌpole *noun* [C] (*UK ALSO* **ski stick**) one of two short pointed poles which are held one in each hand by people on skis to help them balance

skipper /'skɪp.əʳ/ [US] /-ɚ/ *noun* [C] the CAPTAIN of a ship or boat, a sports team, or an aircraft: *John is (the) skipper **of** the cricket team this year.* ○ [as form of address] *Ready to go, skipper.*
skipper /'skɪp.əʳ/ [US] /-ɚ/ *verb* [T] to be the CAPTAIN of a boat, team, aircraft, etc.

'skipping ˌrope *noun* [C] (*US ALSO* **jump rope**) a rope that is used for skipping (= jumping over)

skirmish /'skɜː.mɪʃ/ [US] /'skɝː-/ *noun* [C] **1** a fight between a small number of soldiers which is usually short and not planned, and which happens away from the main area of fighting in a war **2** a short argument: *There was a **short** skirmish **between** the political party leaders when the government announced it was to raise taxes.* **skirmish** /'skɜː.mɪʃ/ [US] /'skɝː-/ *verb* [I] **skirmisher** /'skɜː.mɪʃ.əʳ/ [US] /'skɝː.mɪʃ.ɚ/ *noun* [C]

skirt /skɜːt/ [US] /skɝːt/ *noun* [C] **1** a piece of clothing for women and girls that hangs from the waist and does not have legs: *a long/short skirt* ➲See picture **Clothes** on page Centre 6 **2** an outer covering or protective part on particular machines

skirt /skɜːt/ [US] /skɜːrt/ *verb* [T; I + prep] (*ALSO* **skirt around/round**) **1** to be on or move along the edge of something; to avoid: *Take the road which skirts (round) the village, not the one which goes through it.* **2** to avoid discussing a subject or problem, usually because there are difficulties that you do not want to deal with: *Though the government has promised to deal with drug abuse, it has been accused of skirting round the issue.*

skirting board *UK* /'skɜː.tɪŋ.bɔːd/ [US] /'skɝː.t̬ɪŋ.bɔːrd/ *noun* [C or U] (*US* **baseboard**) a piece of wood fixed along the bottom of a wall where it meets the floor

skit /skɪt/ *noun* [C] a short amusing play which makes a joke of something: *I thought the skit **on** politicians was really funny.*

skitter /'skɪt.əʳ/ [US] /'skɪt̬.ɚ/ *verb* [I usually + adv or prep] (especially of a small animal, bird or insect) to move very quickly and lightly: *When I lifted the log, there were lots of beetles skittering **about/around** under it.*

skittish /'skɪt.ɪʃ/ [US] /'skɪt̬-/ *adj* (of people and animals) nervous or easily frightened, or (of a person) not serious and likely to change their beliefs or opinions frequently: *My horse is rather skittish, so I have to keep him away from traffic.* ○ *Investors are skittish **about** the impact of an economic downturn.* ○ *Marilyn was a complete child, playful and skittish one moment, sulky and withdrawn the next.* **skittishly** /'skɪt.ɪʃ.li/ [US] /'skɪt̬-/ *adv* **skittishness** /'skɪt.ɪʃ.nəs/ [US] /'skɪt̬-/ *noun* [U]

skittle /'skɪt.l̩/ [US] /'skɪt̬-/ *noun* [C] one of a set of bottle-shaped objects which are knocked down with a ball as part of a game
skittles /'skɪt.l̩z/ [US] /'skɪt̬-/ *noun* [U] a game played especially in Britain in which players roll a ball at bottle-shaped objects to try to knock them down and score points

skive /skaɪv/ *verb* [I or T] *UK INFORMAL* to be absent from work or school without permission: *Tom and Mike have skived **(off)** school today to watch the football match.*
skiver /'skaɪ.vəʳ/ [US] /-vɚ/ *noun* [C] *UK INFORMAL* a person who is absent from work without permission

skivvies /'skɪv.iz/ *plural noun US INFORMAL* men's underwear

skivvy [SERVANT] /'skɪv.i/ *noun* [C] *UK INFORMAL* a person, in the past a female servant, who does the dirty and unpleasant jobs in a house, such as cleaning: *He treats me like a skivvy.*
skivvy /'skɪv.i/ *verb* [I] *UK INFORMAL* to do the dirty, unpleasant jobs in the house: *I'm not going to skivvy **for** you any more.*

skivvy [CLOTHING] /'skɪv.i/ *noun* [C] *AUS* a tight-fitting item of clothing, made of knitted cotton, with a high round collar

skol /skɒl/ [US] /skɑːl/ *verb* [T] **-ll-** *AUS INFORMAL* to drink something, especially beer, all at once without a pause

skua *UK* /'skjuː.ə/ *noun* [C] (*ALSO* **jaeger**) a type of large sea bird which lives in the north Atlantic and steals food from other birds

skulduggery *UK, US* **skullduggery** /ˌskʌl'dʌg.ᵊr.i/ [US] /-ɚ-/ *noun* [U] secret and dishonest behaviour

skulk /skʌlk/ *verb* [I usually + adv or prep] to hide or move around as if trying not to be seen, usually with bad intentions: *I thought I saw someone skulking **in** the bushes – perhaps we should call the police.*

skull /skʌl/ *noun* [C] the bones of the head, which surround the brain and give the head its shape: *The soldiers discovered a pile of human skulls and bones.* ➲See picture **The Body** on page Centre 5
• **get** ***sth*** **into** ***your*** **(thick) skull** *INFORMAL* to understand something with difficulty: *Has he got the truth into his thick skull yet?*

ˌskull and 'crossbones *noun* [S] a picture of a skull with two long bones crossing each other under it, which warns of death or danger, used in the past on PIRATE flags and now on containers or places containing dangerous substances or machinery

skullcap /'skʌl.kæp/ *noun* [C] a small round hat that fits closely on the top of the head, worn especially by religious Jewish men or high-ranking Roman Catholic priests

skunk /skʌŋk/ *noun* [C] a small black and white North American animal that makes a strong unpleasant smell as a defence when it is attacked

sky /skaɪ/ *noun* [S or U] the area above the Earth, in which clouds, the sun, etc. can be seen: *a blue/cloudy/dark sky* ○ *Can you see those birds high up **in** the sky?* ○ *We **looked up at/into** the sky at the sound of the plane.*
• **the sky's the limit** there is no limit: *The sky's the limit to what you can win in our competition.*
skies /skaɪz/ *plural noun* the sky in a particular state or place: *For weeks we had cloudless blue skies.* ○ *We're off to the sunny skies **of** Spain.*

sky-blue /ˌskaɪ'bluː/ *noun* [U], *adj* bright blue

skycap /'skaɪ.kæp/ *noun* [C] *US* a person who carries passengers' bags at an airport or receives them for loading onto an aircraft

skydiving /'skaɪˌdaɪ.vɪŋ/ *noun* [U] a sport in which a person jumps from an aircraft and falls for as long as possible before opening a parachute **skydiver** /'skaɪˌdaɪ.vəʳ/ [US] /-vɚ/ *noun* [C]

sky-high /ˌskaɪ'haɪ/ *adj, adv* describes a price or charge that is very high: *The price of oil **went** sky-high when war broke out.*

skylark /'skaɪ.lɑːk/ [US] /-lɑːrk/ *noun* [C] a **lark** BIRD.

skylight /'skaɪ.laɪt/ *noun* [C] a window built into a roof to allow light in: *Putting in a skylight made the attic seem big and bright.*

skyline /'skaɪ.laɪn/ *noun* [C usually sing] a shape or pattern made against the sky, especially by buildings: *You get a good view of the New York skyline from the Statue of Liberty.*

skyrocket /'skaɪˌrɒk.ɪt/ [US] /-ˌrɑː.kɪt/ *verb* [I] to rise extremely quickly or make extremely quick progress towards success; to **rocket**: *Housing prices have skyrocketed in recent months.*

skyscraper /'skaɪˌskreɪ.pəʳ/ [US] /-pɚ/ *noun* [C] a very tall modern building, usually in a city

skyward /'skaɪ.wəd/ [US] /-wɚd/ *adv, adj* (*ALSO* **skywards**) in the direction of the sky: *He raised his eyes slowly skyward.* ○ *FIGURATIVE At the news, share prices **shot** skyward* (= suddenly increased a lot).

slab /slæb/ *noun* [C] a thick, flat piece of a solid substance, such as stone, wood, metal, food, etc., which is usually square or rectangular: *a concrete/marble slab* ○ *He ate a whole slab **of** chocolate.*

slack [NOT TIGHT] /slæk/ *adj* not tight; loose: *These tent ropes are too slack – they need tightening.*
slacken /'slæk.ᵊn/ *verb* [I or T] to (cause to) loosen: *Slacken the reins or you'll hurt the horse's mouth.*
slack /slæk/ *noun* [U] when something is too loose: *There's too much slack in these ropes.* ○ *The men pulled on the ropes to **take up** the slack* (= to tighten them).

S

• **pick up/take up the slack** to do the work which someone else has stopped doing but which still needs to be done: *If Sue gets a job, Mick will have to take up the slack at home.*

slackly /'slæk.li/ *adv* not tightly **slackness** /'slæk.nəs/ *noun* [U]

slack NOT ACTIVE /slæk/ *adj* showing a lack of activity; not busy or happening in a positive way: *Business is always slack at this time of year.* ○ DISAPPROVING *Discipline in Mr Brown's class has become very slack recently.* ○ DISAPPROVING *The job is taking a long time because the workmen are so slack.*

slack /slæk/ *verb* [I] INFORMAL to work slower and with less effort than usual, or to go slower: *Everyone slacks off/up a bit at the end of the week.* ○ DISAPPROVING *You'll be in trouble if you're caught slacking on the job like that.* ○ *Slack off your speed as you approach the corner.*

slacken /'slæk.ᵊn/ *verb* [I or T] to (cause to) become slower or less active: *He stooped to pick it up, without slackening his pace* (= without walking more slowly). ○ *The pace of trading slackened during the winter months.* ○ *The management expects demand to slacken (off) in the New Year.* ○ *The car's speed slackened (off) as it went up a steep hill.* ○ *Most people slacken off/up at the end of a day's work.*

slacker /'slæk.əʳ/ US /-ɚ/ *noun* [C] INFORMAL DISAPPROVING a person who does not work hard enough: *Those slackers have gone home early again.*

slackness /'slæk.nəs/ *noun* [U] **1** when something is slower and less active than usual: *Low sales figures were partly because of normal mid-summer slackness in/of demand.* **2** DISAPPROVING when a person or organization is not working as well and as hard as they should: *The inspector criticized the slackness and incompetence of the staff.*

slack COAL /slæk/ *noun* [U] very small pieces and dust from coal

slack-jawed /ˌslæk'dʒɔːd/ US /-'dʒɑːd/ *adj* with your mouth open in surprise

slacks /slæks/ *plural noun* OLD-FASHIONED a pair of trousers, usually of a type that fit loosely

slag WASTE /slæg/ *noun* [U] waste material produced when coal is dug from the earth, or a substance produced by mixing chemicals with metal that has been heated until it is liquid in order to remove unwanted substances from it ⊃See also **slagheap**.

slag WOMAN /slæg/ *noun* [C] UK VERY INFORMAL DISAPPROVING a woman whose appearance and behaviour, especially sexual, are considered unacceptable

slag LIQUID /slæg/ *noun* [U] AUS INFORMAL FOR **spit**, see at **spit** FORCE OUT.

slag /slæg/ *verb* -gg-
▲ **slag sb off** *phrasal verb* [M] UK INFORMAL to criticize someone: *I hate the way Ian is always slagging people off behind their backs.*

slagheap /'slæg.hiːp/ *noun* [C] MAINLY UK a hill made from the waste material from a mine

slain /sleɪn/ *past participle of* **slay**

slake /sleɪk/ *verb* [T] LITERARY to satisfy a thirst or a desire: *After our long game of tennis, we slaked our thirst with a beer.* ○ *I don't think Dick will ever manage to slake his lust for power.*

slalom /'slɑː.ləm/ *noun* [C] a race for people on skis or in CANOES (= long light narrow boats) in which they have to follow a route that bends in and out between poles

slam /slæm/ *verb* -mm- **1** [I or T] to (cause to) move against a hard surface with force and usually a loud noise: *The wind made the door/window slam (shut).* ○ *Close the door carefully, don't slam it.* ○ *He slammed the brakes on* (= used them quickly and with force) *when a child ran in front of his car.* ○ *I had to stop suddenly, and the car behind slammed into the back of me.* **2** [T] INFORMAL to criticize: *Although the reviewers slammed the play, the audience loved it.*

slam /slæm/ *noun* [U] a sudden loud noise: *The door shut with a slam.*

slam dunk *noun* [C] a shot in basketball in which a player jumps up and pushes the ball down through the net

• **be a slam dunk** MAINLY US to be a certain winner: *Although he's a strong candidate, he's not a slam dunk.*

slam-dunk /'slæm.dʌŋk/ *verb* [T] (ALSO **dunk**) to jump up and force a basketball down through the net in order to score

the slammer /ðə'slæm.əʳ/ US /-ɚ/ *noun* [S] SLANG prison: *He's doing five to ten years in the slammer.*

slander /'slɑːn.dəʳ/ US /'slæn.dɚ/ *noun* [C or U] a false spoken statement about someone which damages their reputation, or the making of such a statement: *The doctor is suing his partner for slander.* ○ *She regarded his comment as a slander on her good reputation.* ⊃Compare **libel**.

slander /'slɑːn.dəʳ/ US /'slæn.dɚ/ *verb* [T] to damage someone's reputation by making a false spoken statement about them **slanderer** /'slɑːn.dᵊr.əʳ/ US /'slæn.dɚ.ɚ/ *noun* [C] **slanderous** /'slɑːn.dᵊr.əs/ US /'slæn.dɚ-/ *adj*: *a slanderous accusation/allegation/comment* **slanderously** /'slɑːn.dᵊr.ə.sli/ US /'slæn.dɚ-/ *adv*

slang INFORMAL LANGUAGE /slæŋ/ *noun* [U] very informal language that is usually spoken rather than written, used especially by particular groups of people: *army slang* ○ *a slang expression* ○ *'Chicken' is slang for someone who isn't very brave.*

slangy /'slæŋ.i/ *adj* INFORMAL *His language is very slangy* (= He uses a lot of slang expressions).

slang ATTACK /slæŋ/ *verb* [T] UK to attack with angry, uncontrolled language: *The football players started slanging each other in the middle of the game.*

slanging match *noun* [C] UK INFORMAL an argument in which both people use angry uncontrolled language and insult each other: *The politicians started a slanging match in the middle of the debate.*

slant /slɑːnt/ US /slænt/ *verb* **1** [I or T] to (cause to) lean in a diagonal position; to (cause to) slope: *Italic writing slants to the right.* ○ *The evening sun slanted through the narrow window.* **2** [T] OFTEN DISAPPROVING to present information in a particular way, especially showing one group of people, one side of an argument, etc. in such a positive or negative way that it is unfair: *The police claimed that reports in the media were slanted against/towards the defendant.*

slant /slɑːnt/ US /slænt/ *noun* **1** [U] a position that is sloping: *The house is built on/at a slant.* **2** [C usually sing] a particular way of showing or viewing something: *The book had a personal/political/sociological slant.*

slanted /'slɑːn.tɪd/ US /'slæn.t̬ɪd/ *adj* **1** sloping in one direction **2** DISAPPROVING showing information about one person, one side of an argument, etc. in such a positive or negative way that it is unfair: *Slanted media coverage is increasing public support for the war.*

slanting /'slɑːn.tɪŋ/ US /'slæn.t̬ɪŋ/ *adj* sloping in one direction: *Swiss chalets have steeply slanting roofs, so that snow does not settle on them.* **slantwise** /'slɑːnt.waɪz/ *adv* (US ALSO **slantways**)

slap HIT /slæp/ *noun* [C] **1** a quick hit with the flat part of the hand or other flat object: *She gave her son a slap for behaving badly.* **2** INFORMAL a slap in the face an action that insults or upsets someone: *It was a real slap in the face for him when she refused to go out to dinner with him.* **3** a slap on the back when someone hits you in a friendly way on the back in order to show praise for something you have done: *He's won – give him a slap on the back.* **4** INFORMAL a slap on the wrist a gentle warning or punishment: *The judge gave Minna a slap on the wrist for not wearing her seat belt.*

• **slap and tickle** UK INFORMAL HUMOROUS playful sexual behaviour: *I think there's a bit of slap and tickle going on in the back of that car over there.*

slap /slæp/ *verb* [T] -pp- to hit someone with the flat part of the hand or other flat object: *She slapped his face.* ○ *She slapped him across the face.* ○ INFORMAL *Her husband has been slapping her around* (= hitting her repeatedly), *but she's afraid to go to the police.* ○ *His friends slapped him on the back when he said he was getting married* (= hit him lightly on the back in a friendly way to express pleasure at what he had done). ○ *When her ideas were rejected, she slapped her report (down) on the table and stormed out of the meeting.*

slap [EXACTLY] /slæp/ *adv* (*UK ALSO* **slap-bang**) *INFORMAL* directly or right: *The football player kicked the ball slap into the middle of the net.* ➲See also **smack** EXACTLY.

PHRASAL VERBS WITH **slap**

▲ **slap *sb* down** *phrasal verb* [M] *USUALLY DISAPPROVING* to stop someone from talking or making suggestions, often in an unpleasant way: *I tried to suggest ways in which the plans could be improved, but he slapped me down.*
▲ **slap *sth* on** [SUBSTANCE] *phrasal verb* [M] to put or spread a substance over a surface very quickly or roughly: *We want to sell our house, so we've slapped some paint on the outside to make it look better.*
▲ **slap *sth* on/onto *(sth/sb)*** [UNPLEASANT ACTION] *phrasal verb* [M] *INFORMAL DISAPPROVING* When someone in authority slaps an unpleasant, difficult or extra thing on someone or something, they suddenly make them provide or accept it: *The government has slapped more tax on cigarettes.* ○ *The librarian slapped a fine on him for returning the books late.*

slapdash /ˈslæp.dæʃ/ *adj INFORMAL DISAPPROVING* done or made in a hurried and careless way: *He gets his work done quickly, but he's very slapdash.*
slaphappy /ˌslæpˈhæp.i/ *adj INFORMAL* happily careless and not thinking about the results of your actions: *He's slaphappy in his approach to rules and regulations.*
slaphead /ˈslæp.hed/ *noun* [C] *UK VERY INFORMAL* a person who is BALD (= has little or no hair on their head)
slapper /ˈslæpə/ *noun* [C] *UK OFFENSIVE* a woman who has sex with a lot of men: *She looked like a right **old** slapper.*
slapstick /ˈslæp.stɪk/ *noun* [U] a type of amusing acting in which the actors behave in a silly way, such as by throwing things, falling over, etc.
slap-up /ˈslæp.ʌp/ *adj* [before n] *UK INFORMAL* describes a meal that is unusually large and good: *We went for a slap-up meal on our wedding anniversary.*
slash [CUT] /slæʃ/ *verb* **1** [I or T] to cut with a sharp blade using a quick strong swinging action: *The museum was broken into last night and several paintings were slashed.* ○ *She tried to commit suicide by slashing her **wrists**.* ○ *We had to slash **(our way) through** the long grass to clear a path.* **2** [T] *INFORMAL* to greatly reduce something, such as money or jobs: *Prices have been slashed by 50%!*
slash /slæʃ/ *noun* [C] **1** a long, deep cut **2** a long swinging hit: *Ben took a wild slash **at** the ball and luckily managed to hit it.*
slasher /ˈslæʃ.əʳ/ [US] /-ɚ/ *noun* [C] *INFORMAL* a person who kills or injures people using a knife
slash [PUNCTUATION] /slæʃ/ *noun* [C] (*UK ALSO* **oblique (stroke)**) the / punctuation mark that can be used to separate letters, numbers or words: *You often write a slash between alternatives, for example, 'and/or'.*
slash [TOILET] /slæʃ/ *noun* [S] *UK SLANG* when you go to the toilet and urinate
ˈslasher ˌmovie *noun* [C] *MAINLY US INFORMAL* a film in which people, especially young women, are killed very violently with knives
slat /slæt/ *noun* [C] a thin narrow piece of wood, plastic or metal used to make floors, furniture, window coverings, etc: *The base of the bed was made of slats.*
slatted /ˈslæt.ɪd/ [US] /ˈslæt̬-/ *adj* made with slats: *slatted floors/doors/windows*
slate [ROCK] /sleɪt/ *noun* [C or U] a dark grey rock that can be easily divided into thin pieces, or a small thin piece of this used to cover a roof
slate /sleɪt/ *verb* [T] to cover a roof with slates
slate /sleɪt-/ *adj* of a colour similar to slate: *slate **grey*** ○ *slate **blue***
slate [FOR WRITING] /sleɪt/ *noun* [C] in the past, a small thin rectangular piece of SLATE ROCK, usually in a wooden frame, used for writing on, especially by children
• **on the slate** *UK INFORMAL* when the price of food or drink that a regular customer buys is recorded so that they can pay for it at another time: *Could you **put** these drinks on the slate?*
• **with the slate wiped clean** with your past mistakes or crimes forgotten

slate [CHOOSE] /sleɪt/ *verb* [T] *US* to be expected to happen in the future or to be expected to be or do something in the future: [+ *to* infinitive] *Geoff is slated **to** be the next captain of the football team.* ○ *The election is slated **for*** (= the chosen day is) *next Thursday.*
slate /sleɪt/ *noun* [C] *US* the group of people who are chosen by a particular party to take part in an election: *The senator has not got a full slate **of** delegates in New York.*
slate [CRITICIZE] /sleɪt/ *verb* [T] *UK INFORMAL* to attack by criticizing; to write or say that something is very bad: *Her last book was slated by the critics.*
slather /ˈslæð.əʳ/ [US] /-ɚ/ *verb* [T] to spread something thickly on something else: *She slathered lotion **on/all over** her body.* ○ *She slathered her toast **with** butter.*
slattern /ˈslæt.ən/ [US] /ˈslæt̬.ɚn/ *noun* [C] **1** *OLD USE DISAPPROVING* a dirty, untidy woman **2** *US VERY INFORMAL DISAPPROVING* a woman who has many sexual partners, for pleasure or payment **slatternly** /ˈslæt.ən.li/ [US] /ˈslæt̬.ɚn-/ *adv US VERY INFORMAL DISAPPROVING*
slaughter /ˈslɔː.təʳ/ [US] /ˈslɑː.t̬ɚ/ *noun* **1** [S or U] the killing of many people cruelly and unfairly, especially in a war: *Hardly anyone in the town escaped the slaughter when the rebels were defeated.* ○ *We must find ways of reducing the slaughter which takes place on our roads* (= death of many people in motor accidents) *every year.* **2** [U] the killing of animals for meat: *The geese are being fattened for slaughter.* ➲See also **slaughterhouse**. **3** [S] when one team is very easily defeated by the other: *Saturday's game was an absolute slaughter.*
slaughter /ˈslɔː.təʳ/ [US] /ˈslɑː.t̬ɚ/ *verb* [T] **1** to cruelly and unfairly kill a lot of people: *Thousands of people were slaughtered in the civil war.* **2** to kill an animal for meat: *The animals are slaughtered in abattoirs.* **3** to defeat someone very easily: *England slaughtered Germany 5-1 at football.*
slaughtered /ˈslɔː.təd/ [US] /ˈslɑː.t̬ɚd/ *adj UK INFORMAL* **get slaughtered** to get very drunk
slaughterhouse /ˈslɔː.tə.haʊs/ [US] /ˈslɑː.t̬ɚ-/ *noun* [C] *MAINLY US FOR* **abattoir**
Slav /slɑːv/ *noun* [C] a member of any of the Eastern European races of people who speak Slavic languages
Slav /slɑːv/ *adj* (*ALSO* **Slavic**)
slave /sleɪv/ *noun* [C] a person who is legally owned by someone else and has to work for them: *Black slaves used to work on the cotton plantations of the southern United States.* ○ *I'm tired of being **treated like a** slave!*
• **be a slave to *sth*** *DISAPPROVING* to be very influenced by something: *She's a slave to fashion.*
slave /sleɪv/ *verb* [I usually + adv or prep] *INFORMAL* to work very hard at something: *We slaved **away** all week **at** the report.* ○ *HUMOROUS I've been slaving **over a hot stove*** (= cooking) *all morning.* ➲See also **enslave**.
slaver /ˈsleɪ.vəʳ/ [US] /-vɚ/ *noun* [C] in the past, a ship used for carrying slaves, or a person who sold slaves ➲See also **slaver**.
slavery /ˈsleɪ.vᵊr.i/ [US] /-ɚ-/ *noun* [U] the activity of having slaves or the condition of being a slave: *Slavery still exists in many parts of the world.* ○ *Millions of Africans were **sold into** slavery between the 17th and 19th centuries.*
slavish /ˈsleɪ.vɪʃ/ *adj DISAPPROVING* showing complete obedience and no original thoughts or ideas: *a slavish devotion to duty* ○ *a slavish translation*
slavishly /ˈsleɪ.vɪʃ.li/ *adv* showing complete obedience; without any ideas of your own: *I followed the recipe slavishly.*
ˈslave ˌdriver *noun* [C] *INFORMAL DISAPPROVING* a person who makes other people work very hard: *My boss is a real slave driver.*
ˌslave ˈlabour *noun* [U] **1** work done by slaves **2** *INFORMAL DISAPPROVING* very hard work for which people are paid very little: *It's slave labour working in that office.*
slaver /ˈslæv.əʳ/ [US] /-ɚ/ *verb* [I] **1** (especially of an animal) to allow liquid to come out of the mouth, especially because of excitement or hunger: *The dog slavered **with** excitement when told it was time for a walk.* **2** *DISAPPROVING* to show great interest or excitement in someone or something, in a way that is un-

pleasant to other people: *Stop slavering **over** that guitar, Stephen!*

'slave ˌtrade *noun* [U] the buying and selling of slaves, especially of African people who were taken to North America from the 16th to the 19th centuries

slaw /slɔː/ ⓤ /slɑː/ *noun* [U] *US INFORMAL FOR* **coleslaw**

slay /sleɪ/ *verb* [T] **slew** or **slayed**, **slain 1** *UK OLD USE OR LITERARY* to kill in a violent way: *St George slew the **dragon**.* **2** (used especially in newspapers) to murder someone: *He was found slain in an alley two blocks from his apartment.*

slaying /'sleɪ.ɪŋ/ *noun* [C] *MAINLY US* a murder

sleazebag /'sliː.zbæg/ *noun* [C] (*US ALSO* **sleazeball/sleaze**) *INFORMAL* a person of low standards of honesty or morals

sleazy /'sliː.zi/ *adj* dirty, cheap or not socially acceptable, especially relating to moral or sexual matters: *This part of town is full of sleazy bars and restaurants.*

sleaze /sliːz/ *noun* **1** [U] activities, especially business or political, of a low moral standard: *The sleaze **factor** was the major reason for his electoral defeat.* **2** [C] *US* a **sleazebag**

sled /sled/ *noun* [C], *verb* [I or T] *US FOR* **sledge**

sledge *UK* /sledʒ/ *noun* [C] (*US* **sled**) an object used for travelling over snow and ice which has long narrow strips of wood or metal under it instead of wheels, and which is either a low frame, or (also **sleigh**) a carriage-like vehicle pulled by horses or dogs

sledge *UK* /sledʒ/ *verb* [I or T] (*US* **sled**) to ride or travel on snow using a sledge

sledgehammer /'sledʒˌhæm.əʳ/ ⓤ /-ɚ/ *noun* [C] **1** a large heavy hammer with a long handle, used for breaking stones or other heavy material, or for hitting posts into the ground, etc. **2** describes a way of behaving that is too forceful: *They accused the Prime Minister of using sledgehammer tactics.*

• **sledgehammer to crack a nut** *DISAPPROVING* If you use a sledgehammer to crack a nut you use much more force than is needed: *Fifty police officers to arrest two unarmed men is surely a case of **using** a sledgehammer to crack a nut.*

sleek /sliːk/ *adj* (especially of hair, clothes or shapes) smooth, shiny and lying close to the body, and therefore looking well cared for; not untidy and with no parts sticking out: *The cat had sleek fur.* ○ *Who owns that sleek black car parked outside your house?* ○ *DISAPPROVING He's one of those sleek* (= seeming rich and dishonest) *businessman types.* **sleekly** /'sliː.kli/ *adv* **sleekness** /'sliːk.nəs/ *noun* [U]

sleek /sliːk/ *verb*

▲ **sleek back/down** *phrasal verb* [M] to make something such as hair smooth, shiny and flat: *Before going to the party, he sleeked back his hair with hair cream.*

sleep ⟨RESTING STATE⟩ /sliːp/ *noun* **1** [U] the resting state in which the body is not active and the mind is unconscious: *I must **get** some sleep – I'm exhausted.* ○See also **sleepwalker**. **2** get/go to sleep to succeed in sleeping: *I couldn't get to sleep at all last night for worrying.* ○ *You'll find that your baby usually goes to sleep after a feed.* **3** [C] a period of sleeping: *You must be tired after all that driving – why don't you **have** a little sleep?* ○ *He **fell into a deep** sleep.*

• **go to sleep** *INFORMAL* If your arm or leg has gone to sleep, you cannot feel or control it, often because you have been sitting or lying for too long in a strange position.

• **put sth to sleep** to kill an animal that is very ill or very old so that it does not suffer any more

• **Go back to sleep!** *INFORMAL* used to tell someone off for not paying attention: *"Sorry, what did you say?" "Oh, go back to sleep!"*

sleep /sliːp/ *verb* **slept**, **slept 1** [I] to be in the state of rest when your eyes are closed, your body is not active, and your mind is unconscious: *I couldn't sleep because of all the noise next door.* ○ *I slept **late** on Sunday morning.* ○ *How can Jayne sleep **at night** with all those worries on her mind!* ○ *We had dinner with Ann and Charles and slept **the night** (with them)* (= at their home). ○See also **oversleep**; **sleepout**. **2** [T] If a vehicle, tent, etc. sleeps a particular number of people, it provides enough space

or beds for that number of people to be able to sleep in it: *The caravan sleeps four comfortably.* **3** *INFORMAL* **sleep like a log** to sleep very well: *I went to bed early and slept like a log.* **4 sleep on sth** to delay making a decision about something important until the next day so that you have time to consider it carefully: *"Can I sleep on it, and tell you my decision tomorrow?"* **5** *UK* **sleep rough** to sleep outside because you have no home and no money: *Hundreds of kids are sleeping rough on the streets of London.*

sleeper /'sliː.pəʳ/ ⓤ /-pɚ/ *noun* **1** a good/heavy/light sleeper someone who sleeps in the stated way: *I'm a light sleeper – the slightest noise wakes me.* ○ *You won't wake him – he's such a heavy sleeper.* ○See also **sleeper** SUDDEN ACTIVITY; **sleeper** RING; **sleeper** BLOCK. **2** a carriage in a train with beds for passengers to sleep in, or one of the beds in this carriage, or the type of train which has these carriages: *I'm travelling overnight so I've booked a sleeper.* ○ *The 11.45 to Glasgow is a sleeper.* **sleeping** /'sliː.pɪŋ/ *adj*: *She looked lovingly at the sleeping child.* ○See also **asleep**.

sleepless /'sliː.pləs/ *adj* **1** [before n] without any sleep: *I've spent so many sleepless **nights** worrying about him.* **2** [after v] not able to sleep: *Alone and sleepless, she stared miserably up at the ceiling.* **sleeplessness** /'sliː.pləs.nəs/ *noun* [U]

sleepy /'sliː.pi/ *adj* **1** tired and wanting to sleep ○See also **sleepyhead**. **2** A sleepy place is quiet and without much activity or excitement: *They retired to a sleepy little village in the west of Yorkshire.* **sleepily** /'sliː.pɪ.li/ *adv* **sleepiness** /'sliː.pɪ.nəs/ *noun* [U]

sleep ⟨SUBSTANCE⟩ /sliːp/ *noun* [U] *INFORMAL* a yellowish substance sometimes found in the corners of the eyes after sleeping

---

PHRASAL VERBS WITH **sleep** ▼

▲ **sleep around** *phrasal verb* *INFORMAL DISAPPROVING* to have sex with a lot of different people without having a close or long relationship with any of them

▲ **sleep in** *phrasal verb* *INFORMAL* to sleep until later in the morning than you usually do: *I usually sleep in at the weekends.*

▲ **sleep sth off** *phrasal verb* [M] If you sleep off something, especially a HANGOVER, you go to sleep so that you will feel better when you wake up.

▲ **sleep over** *phrasal verb* *INFORMAL* to sleep in someone else's home for a night: *If you don't want to catch a train home at that time of night, you're welcome to sleep over.*

sleep-over /'sliː.pˌəʊ.vəʳ/ ⓤ /-oʊ.vɚ/ *noun* [C] (a type of party) when a young person or a group of young people stay for the night at the house of a friend ○See also **slumber party**.

▲ **sleep through sth** *phrasal verb* If you sleep through a lot of noise or an activity, it does not wake you or keep you awake: *I never heard the storm last night – I must have slept through it.* ○ *I was so bored that I slept through the second half of the film.*

▲ **sleep together** *phrasal verb* *INFORMAL* If two people sleep together, they have sex: *I don't think they sleep together any more.*

▲ **sleep with sb** *phrasal verb* *INFORMAL* to have sex with someone: *He found out that his wife had been sleeping with his best friend.*

---

sleeper ⟨SUDDEN ACTIVITY⟩ /'sliː.pəʳ/ ⓤ /-pɚ/ *noun* [C] **1** a person or thing that is suddenly and surprisingly successful after a long period of not achieving anything **2** a SPY who only becomes active a long time after being put in place by an organization or country

sleeper ⟨RING⟩ /'sliː.pəʳ/ ⓤ /-pɚ/ *noun* [C] *UK* a small gold or silver ring which is worn in an ear which is PIERCED (= has a hole in it) to stop the hole from closing while other EARRINGS are not being worn ○See also **sleeper** at **sleep** RESTING STATE; **sleeper** BLOCK.

sleeper ⟨BLOCK⟩ /'sliː.pəʳ/ ⓤ /-pɚ/ *noun* [C] *UK* one of the heavy horizontal blocks that supports a railway track ○See also **sleeper** at **sleep** RESTING STATE; **sleeper** RING.

'sleeping ˌbag *noun* [C] a large thick bag for sleeping in, especially when you are camping

sleeping ,car *noun* [C] (*ALSO* **sleeper**) a railway carriage containing beds for passengers to sleep in

sleeping 'partner *UK noun* [C] (*US* **silent partner**) a partner in a company who does not take an active part in its management, especially one who provides some of the money

sleeping ,pill *noun* [C] (*ALSO* **sleeping tablet**) a pill which you take to help you to sleep better

sleeping po'liceman *noun* [C] *UK* a **speed bump**

sleeping ,sickness *noun* [U] an African disease which causes fever, severe lack of energy, weight loss and sometimes death

sleepout /'sli:p.aʊt/ *noun* [C] *AUS* a small building in a garden or an enclosed outside part of a house which is used for sleeping in

sleepwalker /'sli:p.wɔː.kər/ *US* /-ˌwɑː.kɚ/ *noun* [C] a person who gets out of bed and walks around while they are sleeping **sleepwalk** /'sli:p.wɔːk/ *US* /-wɑːk/ *verb* [I] **sleepwalking** /'sli:p.wɔː.kɪŋ/ *US* /-ˌwɑː-/ *noun* [U]

sleepyhead /'sli:.pi.hed/ *noun* [C] *INFORMAL* a person, especially a child, who is tired and looks as if they want to sleep: [as form of address] *Come on, sleepyhead, let's get you to bed.*

sleet /sli:t/ *noun* [U] wet, partly melted falling snow: *Driving snow and sleet brought more problems to the county's roads last night.* **sleet** /sli:t/ *verb* [I] *It's sleeting.* **sleety** /'sli:.ti/ *US* /-t̬i/ *adj: sleety rain*

sleeve /sli:v/ *noun* [C] (*ALSO* **arm**) the part of a piece of clothing that covers some or all of the arm: *short/long sleeves* ○ *The sleeves are too long for me.* ○ *You'd better roll your sleeves up or you'll get them dirty.*
• **have sth up your sleeve** *INFORMAL* to have secret plans or ideas: *If I know Mark he'll have one or two tricks up his sleeve.*

-sleeved /-sli:vd/ *suffix* having the length of sleeves mentioned: *a short/long-sleeved blouse*

sleeveless /'sli:v.ləs/ *adj* A piece of clothing which is sleeveless has no sleeves: *a sleeveless blouse/dress/jacket*

sleeve PROTECTIVE COVER /sli:v/ *noun* [C] **1** (*US* **jacket**) *UK* a protective cover: *Can you put the record back in its sleeve, please?* **2** a tube-shaped protective covering for a part of a machine

sleeve ,notes *UK plural noun* (*US* **liner notes**) information about a performer or a performance that is supplied with a sound recording: *According to the sleeve notes, she recorded all the songs at home in her attic.*

sleigh /sleɪ/ *noun* [C] a type of SLEDGE pulled by animals, especially horses or dogs

sleight of hand /ˌslaɪt.əv'hænd/ *noun* [U] **1** speed and skill of the hand when performing tricks: *Most of these conjuring tricks depend on sleight of hand.* **2** skilful hiding of the truth in order to gain an advantage: *By some statistical sleight of hand the government have produced figures showing that unemployment has recently fallen.*

slender /'slen.dər/ *US* /-dɚ/ *adj* **1** thin and delicate, often in a way that is attractive: *He put his hands around her slender waist.* ○ *The plant's leaves are long and slender.* **2** small in amount or degree: *a man of slender means* (= without much money) ○ *The chances of settling this dispute through talks seem increasingly slender.*

slenderize /'slen.dər.aɪz/ *US* /-dɚ-/ *verb* [I or T] *US* to become thinner or make something appear thinner: *We manufacture undergarments that tone and slenderize.* ○ *Wearing dark clothes from the waist down will help to slenderize your figure.* **slenderness** /'slen.də.nəs/ *US* /-dɚ-/ *noun* [U]

slept /slept/ *past simple and past participle of* **sleep**

sleuth /slu:θ/ *noun* [C] *OLD-FASHIONED OR HUMOROUS* someone whose job is to discover information about crimes and find out who is responsible for them; a **detective** **sleuthing** /'slu:.θɪŋ/ *noun* [U] *INFORMAL* A bit of sleuthing from our investigative reporter uncovered some interesting information on Mr Parkinson.

slew SLAY /slu:/ *past simple of* **slay**

slew LARGE AMOUNT /slu:/ *noun* [C usually sing] *US INFORMAL* a large amount or number: *Mr Savino has been charged*

with three murders as well as a *whole* slew *of* other crimes.

slew TURN ROUND /slu:/ *verb* [I or T; + adv or prep] to turn or be turned round suddenly and awkwardly: *The car hit a patch of ice and slewed around violently.* ○ *He slewed the van to the left to avoid the dog.*

slice PIECE /slaɪs/ *noun* **1** [C] a flat, often thin, piece of food that has been cut from a larger piece: *a slice of bread/cake* ○ *cucumber/lemon slices* ○ *Would you like another slice of ham/beef?* **2** [S] a part of something, such as an amount of money: *We agreed before we did the deal that we'd both take an equal slice of the profit.* ○ *The film presents us with a fascinating slice of history.* **3** [C] a kitchen utensil with a wide blade which is used for serving pieces of food: *a cake/fish slice*
• **a slice of life** A film, piece of literature or a play might be described as a slice of life if it describes or shows the ordinary details of real life.
• **a slice of the cake** *AUS INFORMAL* If you want a slice of the cake, you want a share of any money that is being made from an activity. ⊃See also **a piece/slice of the action** at **action** ACTIVITY.

slice /slaɪs/ *verb* **1** [T] to cut something into thin, flat pieces: *Slice the mushrooms thinly and fry in butter.* ○ [+ two objects] *Could you slice me a very thin piece of cake/slice a very thin piece of cake for me?* ⊃See picture **In the Kitchen** on page Centre 16 **2** [I + adv or prep] to easily cut into or through something with a sharp knife: *He screamed as the blade sliced into his leg.* ○ *FIGURATIVE She watched his slim strong body as it sliced effortlessly through the water.*
• **any way you slice it** (*ALSO* **no matter how you slice it**) *MAINLY US INFORMAL* in whatever way the matter is considered: *He shouldn't have hit her, any way you slice it.*

sliced /slaɪst/ *adj* cut into thin flat pieces: *sliced bread/ham/tomato*

slicer /'slaɪ.sər/ *US* /-sɚ/ *noun* [C] a machine or tool for slicing particular types of food: *an egg/bread/meat slicer*

slice HIT /slaɪs/ *verb* [T] **1** in the sports of golf and baseball, to hit a ball so that it goes to one side rather than straight in front: *Sara sliced the ball, sending it a hundred metres or so to the left.* **2** If you slice the ball in a game of tennis, you hit the bottom of the ball so that it does not bounce very high when it hits the ground.

slice /slaɪs/ *noun* [C] *That wonderful backhand slice of Ben's sends the ball where his opponent just can't reach it.*

▲ **slice sth off** *phrasal verb* [M] to remove an amount of something, or to move between or in something: *She sliced off a piece of sausage.* ○ *He accidentally sliced the top off his finger while he was cutting vegetables.* ○ *Amit won the race, slicing three seconds off his previous best time.*

slick SKILFUL /slɪk/ *adj* **1** operating or performing skilfully and effectively, without problems and without seeming to need effort: *Manilow gave the slick, polished performance that we've come to expect.* ○ *A slick pass from Eaves to Brinkworth set up the goal.* **2** *DISAPPROVING* skilful and effective but lacking sincerity or value: *It's precisely that sort of slick sales talk that I mistrust.*

slick OIL /slɪk/ *noun* [C] an **oil slick**

slick MAKE SMOOTH /slɪk/ *verb* [T usually + adv or prep] to cause hair to be smooth and close to the head by brushing it flat, often using a substance to make it stick: *He'd slicked his hair back with gel and he was wearing a new suit.*

slick MAGAZINE /slɪk/ *noun* [C] *US FOR* **glossy magazine**

slicker /'slɪk.ər/ *US* /-ɚ/ *noun* [C] a **city slicker**

slide MOVE /slaɪd/ *verb* [I or T] **slid**, **slid** to (cause to) move easily and without interruption over a surface: *When I was little I used to like sliding on the polished floor in my socks.* ○ *We've got one of those doors in the kitchen that slides open.* ○ *He slid the letter into his pocket while no one was looking.* ○ *sliding doors*

slide /slaɪd/ *noun* [C] **1** a sudden movement of a large mass of MUD (= wet earth) or rock down a hill: *a mud/rock slide* ⊃See also **landslide** FALLING EARTH. **2** a structure for children to play on which has a slope for them to slide down and usually a set of steps leading up to the

S

slope **3** a part that moves easily backwards and forwards on an instrument or machine: *the slide on a trombone*

slide [WORSEN] /slaɪd/ *verb* **[I]** **slid, slid** to go into a worse state, often through lack of control or care: *The dollar slid against other major currencies.* ○ *Car exports slid by 40% this year.* ○ *He was improving for a while, but I fear he's sliding **back** into his old habits.* ○ *I was doing really well with my diet, but I'm afraid I've **let it** slide* (= not tried as hard) *recently.* ➲See also **backslide**. **slide** /slaɪd/ *noun* **[C usually sing]** *The government must take measures, he said, to **halt** the country's slide **into** recession.*

slide [PHOTOGRAPHY] /slaɪd/ *noun* **[C]** (*SPECIALIZED* **transparency**) a small piece of photographic film in a frame which, when light is passed through it, shows a larger image on a screen or plain surface: *colour slides* ○ *a slide show*

slide [GLASS] /slaɪd/ *noun* **[C]** a small piece of glass on which you put something in order to look at it through a microscope

slide [HAIR] /slaɪd/ *noun* **[C]** *UK SHORT FOR* **hair slide**

'slide ˌrule *noun* **[C]** a long, narrow device for calculating numbers with a middle part which slides backwards and forwards

ˌsliding 'scale *noun* **[C usually sing]** a system in which the rate at which something is paid varies as a result of other conditions: *Charges are made on a sliding scale, which means that the amount you must pay increases with the level of your income.*

slight [SMALL IN AMOUNT] /slaɪt/ *adj* small in amount or degree: *a slight improvement* ○ *a slight incline* ○ *I've got a slight headache.* ○ *I haven't the slightest **idea** what he's talking about*

• **not in the slightest** not at all: *"Does it worry you?" "Not in the slightest."*

slightly /ˈslaɪt.li/ *adv* a little: *She's slightly taller than her sister.* ○ *I'm slightly upset that she forgot my birthday.*

slight [THIN] /slaɪt/ *adj* (of people) thin and delicate: *Like most long-distance runners she is very slight.*

slightly /ˈslaɪt.li/ *adv*: *He is small and slightly built* (= thin and delicate). **slightness** /ˈslaɪt.nəs/ *noun* **[U]**

slight [INSULT] /slaɪt/ *verb* **[T]** to insult someone by not paying them any attention or treating them as if they are not important: *I felt slighted when my boss thanked everyone but me for their hard work.*

slight /slaɪt/ *noun* **[C]** when a person fails to pay attention to someone or to treat them with the respect that they deserve: *I regarded her failure to acknowledge my greeting as a slight.* **slighted** /ˈslaɪ.tɪd/ [US] /-t̬ɪd/ *adj*: *I'm afraid I just didn't recognize him – I hope he didn't **feel** slighted.*

slim [THIN] /slɪm/ *adj* **slimmer, slimmest** *APPROVING* (especially of people) attractively thin: *slim hips/legs* ○ *She's got a lovely slim figure.* ○ *FIGURATIVE They've only a slim **chance** of winning* (= It's unlikely that they will win).

slim /slɪm/ *verb* **[I]** **-mm-** *UK* to try to get thinner by eating less food and taking more exercise: *You haven't got much lunch – are you slimming?*

slimmer /ˈslɪm.əʳ/ [US] /-ɚ/ *noun* **[C]** *UK* a person who is trying to get thinner by eating less and doing more exercise

slimming /ˈslɪm.ɪŋ/ *noun* **[U]** *UK* when someone is trying to become thinner by eating less food: *With all the diet-food and books on the market, slimming is big business these days.* ○ *slimming aids/clubs/magazines*

slimming /ˈslɪm.ɪŋ/ *adj* **1** *UK INFORMAL* describes food that you can eat without getting fat: *Have a salad – that's slimming.* **2** *US* making you look thinner: *Black is very slimming.* **slimness** /ˈslɪm.nəs/ *noun* **[U]**

PHRASAL VERBS WITH **slim** ▼

▲ **slim down** [THINNER] *phrasal verb* to become thinner: *He's really slimmed down over the last few months.*

▲ **slim *sth* down** [SMALLER] *phrasal verb* to reduce the size of something: *It is not our intention to slim down the workforce.*

Slim [DISEASE] /slɪm/ *noun* **[U]** *EAST AFRICAN ENGLISH FOR* **AIDS**

slime /slaɪm/ *noun* **[U]** a sticky liquid substance which i unpleasant to touch, such as the liquid produced by fis and snails and the greenish brown substance found nea water: *There was a revolting green slime in between th bathroom tiles.* ○ *You could see trails of slime where th slugs had been.*

slimy /ˈslaɪ.mi/ *adj* **1** covered in slime: *Although snake look slimy their skin is actually dry to the touch.* **2** *DIS APPROVING* If you describe a person or their manner a slimy, you mean that they appear to be friendly but in a way that you find unpleasant: *He was the very worst sor of slimy salesman.* **sliminess** /ˈslaɪ.mɪ.nəs/ *noun* **[U]**

'slime ˌball *noun* **[C usually sing]** *INFORMAL* a very un pleasant person whose friendly manner is not sincere *How can she go out with him? He's such a slime ball!*

slimline /ˈslɪm.laɪn/ *adj UK* (of liquid added to ar alcoholic drink to make it last longer) containing little or no sugar: *I'll have a gin and slimline **tonic**, please.*

ˌslim 'pickings *plural noun INFORMAL* lack of success in obtaining or achieving something: *Buyers who have waited for bargains at the end of the year will **find** slim pickings.*

sling [THROW] /slɪŋ/ *verb* **[T usually + adv or prep]** **slung, slung** **1** *INFORMAL* to throw or drop something carelessly: *Don't just sling your bag on the floor!* ○ *If any of the letters aren't interesting just sling them in the bin.* ○ *I'll just sling **together** a few things* (= put what I need to take with me in a bag) *and I'll be ready to go.* **2** *MAINLY UK INFORMAL* to throw or give something to someone: **[+ two objects]** *Sling me a pen, will you?*

• **sling *your* hook** *UK SLANG* to leave: *She told him to sling his hook.*

sling [HANG] /slɪŋ/ *verb* **[T usually + adv or prep]** **slung, slung** to hang something over something, especially in a careless way: *I usually sling my jacket **over** the back of my chair.*

sling [SUPPORTING DEVICE] /slɪŋ/ *noun* **[C]** **1** a device which uses a strap, piece of cloth or ropes for supporting, lifting or carrying objects: *The cylinder was lifted from the seabed **in** a sling.* **2** a device for supporting a broken or damaged arm in which the arm is held in front of the body in a piece of cloth which is tied around the neck: *I had my arm **in** a sling for six weeks.* **3** a bag-like device for carrying a baby which is tied to the front or the back of an adult's body **4** a simple weapon used mainly in the past in which a strap held at the ends was used for throwing stones

PHRASAL VERBS WITH **sling** ▼

▲ **sling *sb* out** [PERSON] *phrasal verb* **[M]** *MAINLY UK INFORMAL* to make someone leave a place because they have behaved badly: *She was slung out **of** college because she never did any work.*

▲ **sling *sth* out** [OBJECT] *phrasal verb* **[M]** *MAINLY UK INFORMAL* to get rid of something unwanted: *What about these old magazines? Shall I just sling them out?*

slingbacks /ˈslɪŋ.bæks/ *plural noun* women's shoes with a strap around the back of the heel instead of a full covering: *a pair of slingbacks* **slingback** /ˈslɪŋ.bæk/ *adj* **[before n]** *slingback sandals/shoes*

slingshot /ˈslɪŋ.ʃɒt/ [US] /-ʃɑːt/ *noun* **[C]** *US FOR* **catapult**

slink /slɪŋk/ *verb* **[I usually + adv or prep]** **slunk, slunk** to walk away from somewhere quietly so that you are not noticed: *I tried to slink out of the room so that nobody would see me go.* ○ *DISAPPROVING He usually slinks **off*** (= leaves) *at about 3.30.*

slinky /ˈslɪŋ.ki/ *adj* **1** (of women's clothes) made of delicate cloth and fitting the body closely in a way that is sexually attractive: *a slinky black dress* **2** *UK* (of music or dancing) slow and suggesting sex: *There's some very slinky dancing going on tonight!*

slip [SLIDE] /slɪp/ *verb* **[I]** **-pp-** to slide unintentionally: *She slipped on the ice.* ○ *Careful you don't slip – there's water on the floor.* ○ *The razor slipped while he was shaving and he cut himself.*

slippy /ˈslɪp.i/ *adj UK INFORMAL* describes a surface that causes you to slip easily because it is wet, smooth or oily: *Careful – I've just polished the floor and it's a bit slippy.* ➲See also **slippery**.

slip DO QUICKLY /slɪp/ *verb* [I or T; usually + adv or prep] **-pp-** to go somewhere or do something quickly, often so that you are not noticed: *Just slip out of the room while nobody's looking.* ○ *She slipped between the cool cotton sheets and was soon asleep.* ○ *He slipped a piece of paper into my hand with his address on it.* ○ [+ two objects] *If you slip the waiter some money/slip some money to the waiter he'll give you the best table.*

slip GET WORSE /slɪp/ *verb* [I] **-pp-** to go into a worse state, often because of lack of control or care: *Productivity in the factory has slipped quite noticeably in the last year.*

slippage /ˈslɪp.ɪdʒ/ *noun* [U] a reduction in the rate, amount or standard of something: *The party leader is said to be concerned at the slippage* (= loss of popularity) *in the recent opinion polls.*

slip PIECE OF PAPER /slɪp/ *noun* [C] a small piece of paper: *a slip of paper* ○ *If you want to order a book fill in the green slip.*

slip MISTAKE /slɪp/ *noun* [C] a small mistake: *She's made one or two slips – mainly spelling errors – but it's basically well written.*
● **slip of the tongue** when someone says something that they did not intend to say: *I called her new boyfriend by her previous boyfriend's name – it was just a slip of the tongue.*
● **There's many a slip twixt cup and lip.** SAYING said to emphasize that many bad things might happen before something is completed

slip UNDERWEAR /slɪp/ *noun* [C] a piece of underwear for a woman or girl which is like a dress or skirt

slip ESCAPE /slɪp/ *verb* [T] **-pp-** to get free from, leave or escape something: *The ship slipped its moorings.*
● **slip through the net** UK (US **slip through the cracks**) to escape a punishment or be missed by a system that should deal with or protect you: *Once again terrorists have slipped through the police net.* ○ *There are laws there to protect the mentally ill, but now and then some-one does slip through the net.*
● **slip through sb's fingers** If you allow an opportunity or a person to slip through your fingers, you lose it or them through lack of care or effort: *You're surely not going to let a job/man like that slip through your fingers!*
● **slip sb's memory/mind** to be forgotten: *I forgot I'd arranged to meet Richard last night – it completely slipped my mind.*

slip /slɪp/ *noun* INFORMAL **give sb the slip** to escape from someone

slip SMALL /slɪp/ *noun* OLD-FASHIONED **slip of a** small and thin, usually because of being young: *I knew her when she was a slip of a girl.*

PHRASAL VERBS WITH slip ▼

▲ **slip into** *sth phrasal verb* (ALSO **slip** *sth* **on**) to quickly put on a piece of clothing: *If you could wait two minutes, I'm just going to slip into a smarter dress.* ○ *You don't need to go into the changing rooms – just slip the jacket on over your sweater.*
slip-on /ˈslɪp.ɒn/ US /-ɑːn/ *noun* [C usually pl] shoes with no fastenings which can be quickly put on and taken off: *a pair of slip-ons* ○ *slip-on shoes*
▲ **slip out** *phrasal verb* If a remark slips out, you say it without intending to.
▲ **slip out of** *sth phrasal verb* (ALSO **slip** *sth* **off**) to quickly take off a piece of clothing: *Slip your shirt off and I'll listen to your heart.*
▲ **slip up** *phrasal verb* to make a mistake: *These figures don't make sense – have we slipped up somewhere?*
slip-up /ˈslɪp.ʌp/ *noun* [C] a mistake or something which goes wrong

slipcase /ˈslɪp.keɪs/ *noun* [C] a protective case for a book, usually made of cardboard, with one open end

slipcover /ˈslɪpˌkʌv.əʳ/ US /-ɚ/ *noun* [C] a cover for a chair or sofa

slipknot /ˈslɪp.nɒt/ US /-nɑːt/ *noun* [C] a knot that can easily be made tighter or looser by pulling one of its ends

slipped 'disc UK, US **slipped disk** *noun* [C] a medical condition in which one of the DISCS (= flat pieces of tissue between the bones in the back) slides out of its usual place, causing pain

slipper /ˈslɪp.əʳ/ US /-ɚ/ *noun* [C] a type of soft comfortable shoe for wearing inside the house: *a pair of slippers*

slippery /ˈslɪp.ᵊr.i/ US /-ɚ-/ *adj* **1** wet, smooth or oily so that it slides easily or causes something to slide: *slippery soap* ○ *a slippery floor* ○ *The road was wet and slippery.* **2** INFORMAL DISAPPROVING Someone who is slippery cannot be trusted: *He's as slippery as an eel – you can never get a straight answer out of him.* ○ *He's a slippery customer* (= person), *that Tim, I've never felt comfortable with him.*

slippery 'slope *noun* [U] a bad situation or habit which, after it has started, is likely to get very much worse: *You're on a slippery slope once you start lying about your age!*

slip ˌroad UK *noun* [C] (US **ramp**) a short road on which vehicles join or leave a motorway

slipshod /ˈslɪp.ʃɒd/ US /-ʃɑːd/ *adj* DISAPPROVING (especially of a piece of work) showing lack of care, effort and attention: *She complained that the solicitor's work had been slipshod.*

slipstream /ˈslɪp.striːm/ *noun* [C] a current of air behind a quickly moving object such as a car travelling extremely fast or an aircraft

slipway /ˈslɪp.weɪ/ *noun* [C] a sloping track used to move boats into or out of the water

slit /slɪt/ *verb* [T] **slitting, slit, slit** to make a long straight narrow cut in something: *He slit open the envelope with a knife.* ○ *She killed herself by slitting her wrists.* ○ *He was found the next day with his throat slit.* ○ *She was wearing one of those skirts that's slit up the front.*

slit /slɪt/ *noun* [C] a straight narrow cut or opening in something: *Make a small slit in each chicken breast and push in a piece of garlic.*

slither /ˈslɪð.əʳ/ US /-ɚ/ *verb* [I usually + adv or prep] (of bodies) to move easily and quickly across a surface while twisting or curving: *She watched the snake slither away.*

sliver /ˈslɪv.əʳ/ US /-ɚ/ *noun* [C] FORMAL a very small thin piece of something, usually broken off something larger: *a sliver of glass* ○ *Just a sliver of cake for me, please – I shouldn't really be having any.*

Sloane (ranger) /ˌsləʊnˈreɪn.dʒəʳ/ US /ˌsloʊnˈreɪn.dʒɚ/ *noun* [C] UK OLD-FASHIONED DISAPPROVING a young person from a high social class who lives usually in or near London, wears expensive, traditional clothes and speaks with an UPPER CLASS voice

slob /slɒb/ US /slɑːb/ *noun* [C] INFORMAL DISAPPROVING a lazy, untidy and often rude person: *He's a big fat slob of a man – I can't stand him.* **slobbish** /ˈslɒb.ɪʃ/ US /ˈslɑːbɪʃ/ *adj*

slob /slɒb/ US /slɑːb/ *verb*
▲ **slob around/about** *phrasal verb* INFORMAL DISAPPROVING to behave in a very lazy way, doing very little: *He won't get a job and just slobs around the house all day.*

slobber /ˈslɒb.əʳ/ US /ˈslɑːb.ɚ/ *verb* [I] DISAPPROVING to allow saliva or food to run out of the mouth
slobber /ˈslɒb.əʳ/ US /ˈslɑːb.ɚ/ *noun* [U] DISAPPROVING saliva or food which has run out of the mouth
slobbery /ˈslɒb.ᵊr.i/ US /ˈslɑːb.ɚ-/ *adj* DISAPPROVING a big slobbery (= wet) *kiss*
▲ **slobber over** *sb phrasal verb* INFORMAL DISAPPROVING to show too much admiration and liking for someone, in a way that shows a lack of control of yourself: *Ted was slobbering over the pretty new assistant in marketing.*

sloe /sləʊ/ US /sloʊ/ *noun* [C] a small bluish-black fruit which tastes sour

sloe 'gin *noun* [U] an alcoholic drink made from gin with sloes in it

slog WORK HARD /slɒg/ US /slɑːg/ *verb* **-gg- 1** [I usually + adv or prep] MAINLY UK INFORMAL to work hard over a long period, especially doing work that is difficult or boring: *I've been slogging away for days on this essay and I'm still not finished.* **2** [I + adv or prep] to travel or move with difficulty, for example through wet, sticky soil or snow, or when you are very tired: *Despite the rain, they slogged on for another six miles.*

S

slog /slɒg/ ⓤ /slɑːg/ *noun* [S] MAINLY UK INFORMAL a period of difficult or tiring effort: *The exams were **a** real **hard** slog but I'm glad I did them.* ○ *That last hill before the finishing-line was **a** long slog!*

slog HIT HARD /slɒg/ ⓤ /slɑːg/ *verb* [T] -gg- UK to hit a ball hard and often in an uncontrolled way

slog /slɒg/ ⓤ /slɑːg/ *noun* [C] UK INFORMAL a very hard, and often uncontrolled hit: *And that was a real slog from Kumar.*

slogan /ˈsləʊ.gən/ ⓤ /ˈsloʊ-/ *noun* [C] a short easily remembered phrase, especially one used to advertise an idea or a product: *an advertising slogan* ○ *a campaign slogan* **sloganeering** /ˌsləʊ.gəˈnɪə.rɪŋ/ ⓤ /ˌsloʊ.gəˈnɪr.ɪŋ/ *noun* [U] MAINLY US DISAPPROVING *Without a coherent set of policies to persuade the electorate, the Republicans have resorted to sloganeering and empty rhetoric.*

sloop /sluːp/ *noun* [C] a small sailing boat with one mast

slop /slɒp/ ⓤ /slɑːp/ *verb* [I or T; + adv or prep] -pp- to cause a liquid to flow over the edge of a container through lack of care or rough movements: *Careful, you've just slopped coffee all over the carpet!* ○ *Water slopped out of the bucket as he carried it up the stairs.* ⊃See also **slops**.

slop /slɒp/ ⓤ /slɑːp/ *noun* [U] INFORMAL DISAPPROVING food that is more liquid than it should be and is therefore unpleasant: *Have you tried the slop that they call curry in the canteen?* ⊃See also **slops**.

PHRASAL VERBS WITH **slop** ▼

▲ **slop about/around** *phrasal verb* [I] INFORMAL to relax and do very little: *Jeans are all right just for slopping around the house, but I don't wear them for work.*

▲ **slop out** *phrasal verb* UK When prisoners slop out, they empty the containers they use as toilets during the night in the rooms where they sleep.

slope /sləʊp/ ⓤ /sloʊp/ *noun* [C] **1** a surface which lies at an angle to the horizontal so that some points on it are higher than others: *The roof is at a slope (= at an angle to a horizontal surface) of 30°.* **2** (part of) the side of a hill or mountain: *a ski/mountain slope* ○ *Snow had settled on some of the higher slopes.* ○ *There's a very **steep** slope just before you reach the top of the mountain.* ○ *There are some nice **gentle** (= not steep) slopes that we can ski down.* **slope** /sləʊp/ ⓤ /sloʊp/ *verb* [I] *The path slopes **up/down** to the house.* ○ *Our school football pitch sloped at the south end, so one half of the game always had to be played uphill.* **sloping** /ˈsləʊ.pɪŋ/ ⓤ /ˈsloʊ-/ *adj*: *sloping handwriting/shoulders* ○ *The bedroom is in the roof so it's got a sloping ceiling.*

▲ **slope off** *phrasal verb* UK INFORMAL to leave somewhere quietly so that you are not noticed, usually to avoid work: *I saw you sloping off just after lunch yesterday!*

sloppy TOO WET /ˈslɒp.i/ ⓤ /ˈslɑː.pi/ *adj* INFORMAL DISAPPROVING (of a substance) more liquid than it should be, often in a way that is unpleasant: *The batter was a bit sloppy so I added some more flour.*

sloppy LACKING CARE /ˈslɒp.i/ ⓤ /ˈslɑː.pi/ *adj* **1** DISAPPROVING lacking care or effort: *Spelling mistakes always look sloppy in a formal letter.* ○ *Another sloppy pass like that might lose them the whole match.* **2** describes clothes which are large, loose and often untidy: *At home I tend to wear big sloppy jumpers and jeans.*

sloppily /ˈslɒp.ɪ.li/ ⓤ /ˈslɑː.pɪ-/ *adv* DISAPPROVING badly or carelessly: *a sloppily written letter* **sloppiness** /ˈslɒp.ɪ.nəs/ ⓤ /ˈslɑː.pɪ-/ *noun* [U]

sloppy EMOTIONAL /ˈslɒp.i/ ⓤ /ˈslɑː.pi/ *adj* INFORMAL DISAPPROVING expressing feelings of love in a way that is silly or embarrassing: *a sloppy love song*

slops /slɒps/ ⓤ /slɑːps/ *plural noun* (ALSO **slop**) liquid or wet food waste, especially that which is fed to animals: *We feed the slops to the pigs.* ○ *There's a tray under each tap to catch the beer slops.*

slosh /slɒʃ/ ⓤ /slɑːʃ/ *verb* [I or T; usually + adv or prep] INFORMAL (of a liquid) to move around noisily in the bottom of a container, or to cause liquid to move around in this way by making rough movements: *I could hear you sloshing around in the bath.* ○ *We sloshed through the puddles.* ○ INFORMAL *She sloshed (= poured without care) some more brandy into her glass.*

sloshed /slɒʃt/ ⓤ /slɑːʃt/ *adj* [after v] SLANG drunk: *He always **gets** sloshed at the annual office party.*

slot LONG HOLE /slɒt/ ⓤ /slɑːt/ *noun* [C] a long narrow hole, especially one for putting coins into or for fitting a separate piece into: *I put my money in the slot and pressed the button but nothing came out.* ○ *The holder has slots for 100 CDs.* **slot** /slɒt/ ⓤ /slɑːt/ *verb* [I or T; + adv or prep] -tt- *The legs of the chair are meant to slot **into** the holes at the back.* ○ *Do these two pieces slot **together**?* ○ *Slot piece A **into** piece B, taking care to keep the two pieces at right angles.*

slotted /ˈslɒt.ɪd/ ⓤ /ˈslɑː.t̬ɪd/ *adj* A slotted kitchen utensil or tool has long narrow holes in it: *a slotted spoon/spatula/screw*

slot AMOUNT OF TIME /slɒt/ ⓤ /slɑːt/ *noun* [C] an amount of time which is officially allowed for a single event in a planned order of activities or events: *The programme will occupy that half-hour slot before the nine o'clock news.*

▲ **slot** *sb/sth* **in** *phrasal verb* to find time to see someone or do something between various other arrangements that have already been made: *Doctor Meredith is busy this morning, but she might be able to slot you in around one o'clock.*

sloth NO EFFORT /sləʊθ/ ⓤ /sloʊθ/ *noun* [U] LITERARY unwillingness to work or make any effort: *The report criticizes the government's sloth in tackling environmental problems.*

slothful /ˈsləʊθ.fəl/ ⓤ /ˈsloʊθ-/ *adj* LITERARY lazy: *slothful adolescents*

sloth ANIMAL /sləʊθ/ ⓤ /sloʊθ/ *noun* [C] an animal that moves slowly and lives in trees: *Sloths live in Central and South America.*

slot ma,chine *noun* [C] (UK ALSO **fruit machine**, AUS ALSO **poker machine**) a machine that you try to win money from by putting coins into it and operating it, often by pressing a button or pulling a handle

slouch /slaʊtʃ/ *verb* [I] to stand, sit or walk with the shoulders hanging forward and the head bent slightly over so that you look tired and bored: *Straighten your back – try not to slouch.* ○ *A couple of boys were slouched over the table reading magazines.* ○ *A group of teenagers were slouching around outside the building.* **slouch** /slaʊtʃ/ *noun* [C usually sing] *He's developed a slouch from leaning over his books all day.*

● **be no slouch** INFORMAL If you say that someone is no slouch at a particular activity, you mean that they work hard at it and produce good results: *She's no slouch when it comes to organizing parties.*

slough SKIN /slʌf/ *verb* [T] (of some animals) to have a layer of skin come off: *Snakes slough their skin regularly.*

▲ **slough** *sth* **off** *phrasal verb* [M] **1** LITERARY to get rid of something or someone unwanted: *He seemed to want to slough off all his old acquaintances.* **2** SPECIALIZED When snakes and other reptiles slough off their skin, they get rid of an old, dead layer of skin.

slough SADNESS /slaʊ/ ⓤ /sluː/ /slaʊ/ *noun* [S] LITERARY a mental state of deep sadness and lack of hope: *She seems unable to pull herself out of this deep slough **of** self-pity.*

slough WET AREA /slaʊ/ ⓤ /sluː/ /slaʊ/ *noun* [C] an area of soft, wet land

slovenly /ˈslʌv.ən.li/ *adj* untidy and dirty: *a slovenly appearance* ○ *I'll have to improve my slovenly habits – my mother's coming to stay.* **slovenliness** /ˈslʌv.ən.li.nəs/ *noun* [U]

slow /sləʊ/ ⓤ /sloʊ/ *adj* **1** doing, moving or happening without much speed: *a slow runner/driver/reader* ○ *She's a very slow eater.* ○ *We're making slow but steady progress with the decorating.* ○ *The government was very slow **to** react to the problem.* ○ *Business is always slow during those months because everyone's on holiday.* ✳ NOTE: The opposite is **fast** or **quick**. **2** describes a film, book, play, etc. that lacks excitement and action: *His films are so slow they send me to sleep.* **3** A person might be described as slow if they are not very clever and do not understand or notice things quickly: *I feel so slow when I'm with Andrew – he's so much brighter than me.* ○ *I was a bit slow **off the mark/on the uptake** there – I* *didn't follow his reasoning at all.* ➲See also **slow-witted**. **4** If a clock or watch is slow, it shows a time that is earlier than the real time: *That clock is ten minutes slow.*

slow /sləʊ/ [US] /sloʊ/ *adv* at a slow speed: *I can't walk any slower.* ○ *slow-moving traffic* ○ *a slow-burning candle* ○ *MAINLY US He drives too slow!*

slow /sləʊ/ [US] /sloʊ/ *verb* **[I or T]** to reduce speed or activity, or to make something do this: *Business development has slowed in response to the recession.* ○ *Traffic slows* ***to a crawl*** (= goes so slowly it almost stops) *during rush hour.* ○ *The pilot was asked to slow his approach to the runway.* ➲See also **slow down**.

slowly /ˈsləʊ.li/ [US] /ˈsloʊ-/ *adv* at a slow speed: *Could you please speak more slowly?*

• **slowly but surely** carefully, in order to avoid problems: *Slowly but surely we made our way down the muddy hillside.*

▲ **slow** ***(sb/sth)*** **down/up** *phrasal verb* **[M]** to become slower, or to make someone or something become slower: *Slow down, you two, you're walking too fast!* ○ *If I run with Christina she tends to slow me down.* ○ *We slowed up when we saw the police.*

▲ **slow down** *phrasal verb* **[M]** to be less active and relax more: *The doctor has told him to slow down or he'll have a heart attack.*

ˌslow ˈburn [ACTIVITY] *noun* **[C usually sing]** *UK* a period of low activity: *Many workers have benefited from the new scheme, which allows careers to be put* ***on*** *a slow burn for months or years and then reactivated.*

ˌslow ˈburn [ANGER] *noun* **[C usually sing]** *US* a slow, controlled show of anger: *When angered, Ellen was given to spontaneous outbursts, while her partner Terry would* ***do*** *a slow burn.*

slowcoach *UK* /ˈsləʊ.kəʊtʃ/ [US] /ˈsloʊ.koʊtʃ/ *noun* **[C]** (*US* **slowpoke**) *INFORMAL* someone, especially a child, who is walking or doing something too slowly: **[as form of address]** *Come on, slowcoach, we haven't got all day you know!*

slowdown /ˈsləʊ.daʊn/ [US] /ˈsloʊ-/ *noun* **[C]** **1** a reduction in speed, activity or the rate that things are produced: *a worldwide economic slowdown* ○ *a slowdown* ***in*** *production* **2** *US FOR* **go-slow**

ˌslow ˈhandclap *noun* **[C usually sing]** *UK* a slow, regular clap, used by a crowd watching a performance, sports event, etc. to show their annoyance

ˌslow ˈmotion *noun* **[U]** a way of showing pictures from a film or television programme at a slower speed than normal: *They showed the goal* ***in*** *slow motion.*

slowpoke /ˈsləʊ.pəʊk/ [US] /ˈsloʊ.poʊk/ *noun* **[C]** *US FOR* **slowcoach**

slow-witted /ˌsləʊˈwɪt.ɪd/ [US] /ˌsloʊˈwɪṭ-/ *adj* not clever and therefore slow to notice or understand things

slowworm /ˈsləʊ.wɜːm/ [US] /ˈsloʊ.wɝːm/ *noun* **[C]** a small brownish-grey lizard with no legs, found in Europe

SLR (camera) /ˌes.elˌɑːˈkæm.rə/ [US] /-ˌɑːr-/ *noun* **[C]** *ABBREVIATION FOR* single-lens reflex (camera): a type of film camera in which the same lens (= special piece of glass) is used for looking at and recording an image

sludge /slʌdʒ/ *noun* **[U]** soft wet earth or a substance that looks like this: *We seemed to spend the last mile of the walk knee-deep in sludge.*

sludgy /ˈslʌdʒ.i/ *adj DISAPPROVING* soft, wet and very thick: *a thick, sludgy pudding*

slug [CREATURE] /slʌg/ *noun* **[C]** **1** a small, usually black or brown, creature with a long soft body and no arms or legs, like a snail but with no shell **2** *MAINLY US INFORMAL* a slow-moving, lazy person ➲See also **sluggish**.

slug [BULLET] /slʌg/ *noun* **[C]** *INFORMAL* a bullet: *The poor guy wound up with a slug in his stomach.*

slug [AMOUNT OF DRINK] /slʌg/ *noun* **[C]** *INFORMAL* an amount of drink, especially strong alcoholic drink, that you can swallow at one time: *I had a slug* ***of*** *vodka to give me courage.*

slug [HIT] /slʌg/ *verb* **[T]** **-gg-** **1** *INFORMAL* to hit someone hard with the fist: *She slugged him and he fell against the bar.* **2** *US* to hit a baseball hard

• **slug it out** If two people slug it out, they fight or argue fiercely until one of them wins.

slug [COIN] /slʌg/ *noun* **[C]** *US* a piece of metal used instead of a coin for putting in machines

sluggish /ˈslʌg.ɪʃ/ *adj* moving or operating more slowly than usual and with less energy or power: *A heavy lunch makes me sluggish in the afternoon.* ○ *Something is wrong with the car – the engine feels a bit sluggish.* ○ *The housing market has been very sluggish these past few years.* **sluggishly** /ˈslʌg.ɪʃ.li/ *adv* **sluggishness** /ˈslʌg.ɪʃ.nəs/ *noun* **[U]**

ˈslug ˌpellet *noun* **[C usually pl]** a small hard piece of a substance which is poisonous to SLUGS (= small garden creatures harmful to plants)

sluice /sluːs/ *noun* **[C]** (*ALSO* **sluiceway**) an artificial channel for carrying water, which has an opening at one end to control the flow of the water

sluice /sluːs/ *verb* **[I usually + adv or prep]** If water sluices out from somewhere, it flows in large amounts: *Water sluiced* ***out*** *from the pipes.*

▲ **sluice** ***sth*** **down/out** *phrasal verb* **[M]** to wash something with a large amount of running water: *We had to sluice out the garage to get rid of the smell of petrol.*

slum /slʌm/ *noun* **[C]** **1** a very poor and crowded area, especially of a city: *an inner-city slum* ○ *She was brought up in the slums of Lima.* **2** *INFORMAL DISAPPROVING* a very untidy or dirty place: *This flat would be an absolute slum if I wasn't here to clean it.*

slum /slʌm/ *verb INFORMAL* **slum it** to spend time in conditions which are much less good than the standard that you are used to: *We ran out of money on holiday and had to slum it in cheap hostels.*

slumber /ˈslʌm.bəʳ/ [US] /-bɚ/ *noun* **[C or U]** *LITERARY* sleep: *I fell into a gentle slumber.* ○ *I didn't want to rouse you from your slumbers.* ○ *FIGURATIVE Sharp cuts in interest rates have failed to bring the economy out of its slumber.*

slumber /ˈslʌm.bəʳ/ [US] /-bɚ/ *verb* **[I]** *LITERARY* to sleep

ˈslumber ˌparty *noun* **[C]** *US* a party when a group of children spend the night at one child's house ➲See also **sleep-over** at **sleep over**.

slump [REDUCE SUDDENLY] /slʌmp/ *verb* **[I]** (of prices, values or sales) to fall suddenly: *The value of property has slumped.* ○ *Car sales have slumped dramatically over the past year.*

slump /slʌmp/ *noun* **[C]** **1** a fall in the price, value, sales, etc. of something: *There's been a slump in the demand for new cars.* **2** a period when an industry or the economy is in a bad state and there is a lot of UNEMPLOYMENT: *an economic slump* ○ *The airline industry is currently* ***in a*** *slump.*

slump [SIT/FALL] /slʌmp/ *verb* **[I usually + adv or prep]** to sit or fall heavily and suddenly: *She slumped into the chair, exhausted.*

slumped /slʌmpt/ *adj* having your head low and shoulders forward: *He sat slumped* ***over*** *his desk, the picture of misery.*

slung /slʌŋ/ *past simple and past participle of* **sling**

slunk /slʌŋk/ *past simple and past participle of* **slink**

slur [PRONOUNCE BADLY] /slɜːʳ/ [US] /slɝː/ *verb* **[T]** **-rr-** to pronounce the sounds of a word in a way which is unclear, uncontrolled or wrong: *Her* ***speech*** *was slurred but she still denied she was drunk.* **slur** /slɜːʳ/ [US] /slɝː/ *noun* **[S]** *The drug affected her vision and made her speak with* ***a*** *slur.*

slur [CRITICISM] /slɜːʳ/ [US] /slɝː/ *noun* **[C]** a critical remark about someone which is likely to have a harmful effect on their reputation: *Her letter contained several outrageous slurs* ***against/on*** *her former colleagues.* ○ *His comments* ***cast*** *a slur* ***on*** *the integrity of his employees.* **slur** /slɜːʳ/ [US] /slɝː/ *verb* **[T]** **-rr-** *The report slurs both the teachers and pupils.*

slur [MUSIC] /slɜːʳ/ [US] /slɜːr/ *verb* **[T]** **-rr-** to sing or play notes in a smooth and connected manner

slur /slɜːʳ/ [US] /slɜːr/ *noun* **[C]** a curved line written over or under musical notes to show that they must be played in a smooth and connected manner

slurp /slɜːp/ [US] /slɝːp/ *verb* **1** **[I or T]** *INFORMAL* to drink a liquid noisily as a result of sucking air into the mouth

S

at the same time as the liquid: *Do try not to slurp.* ○ *I wish you wouldn't slurp your soup like that.* ○ *He slurped* ***down*** *his coffee.* **2** [I] *UK INFORMAL* When a thick liquid slurps, it makes loud noises: *The lava slurped and bubbled down the mountainside.* **slurp** /slɜːp/ [US] /slɝːp/ *noun* [C] *INFORMAL She paused to take a slurp* ***of*** *tea.*

slurry /ˈslʌr.i/ [US] /ˈslɝː-/ *noun* [U] a mixture of water and small pieces of a solid, especially such a mixture used in an industrial or farming process

slush [SNOW] /slʌʃ/ *noun* **1** [U] snow that is lying on the ground and has started to melt **2** [C or U] *MAINLY US* a thick drink made from crushed ice and a sweet liquid: *a cherry/cola slush*

slushy /ˈslʌʃ.i/ *adj* Slushy snow is partly melted.

slush [ROMANTIC LANGUAGE] /slʌʃ/ *noun* [U] language or writing that is too emotional and romantic and lacks any real importance or meaning **slushy** /ˈslʌʃ.i/ *adj*: *a slushy romantic novel*

ˈslush ˌfund *noun* [C] a sum of money that is kept for dishonest or illegal activities in politics or business: *He used his party's slush fund to buy votes in the election.*

slut [SEXUALLY ACTIVE WOMAN] /slʌt/ *noun* [C] *VERY INFORMAL DISAPPROVING* a woman who has sexual relationships with a lot of men without any emotional involvement

sluttish /ˈslʌt.ɪʃ/ [US] /ˈslʌt̬-/ *adj* (*ALSO* **slutty**)

slut [LAZY WOMAN] /slʌt/ *noun* [C] *UK VERY INFORMAL DISAPPROVING* a woman who is habitually untidy and lazy

sluttish /ˈslʌt.ɪʃ/ [US] /ˈslʌt̬-/ *adj* (*ALSO* **slutty**) *VERY INFORMAL DISAPPROVING*

sly /slaɪ/ *adj* **slyer, slyest 1** deceiving people in a clever way in order to get what you want: *He's a sly old devil – I wouldn't trust him with my money.* **2** [before n] seeming to know secrets: *"You'll find out eventually," said Mary with a sly* ***smile****.*

sly /slaɪ/ *noun* **on the sly** If you do something on the sly, you do it secretly because you should not be doing it: *He drives his mother's car on the sly while she's at work.*

slyly /ˈslaɪ.li/ *adv*: *She grinned slyly and refused to tell me where the money came from.* **slyness** /ˈslaɪ.nəs/ *noun* [U]

slyboots /ˈslaɪ.buːts/ *noun* [C] *plural* **slyboots** *UK OLD-FASHIONED INFORMAL* a person who avoids showing or telling other people what he or she is thinking or intending: [as form of address] ***You*** *old slyboots! Why didn't you tell us about your new girlfriend?*

ˈsly ˌgrog *noun* [U] *AUS INFORMAL* illegally sold alcoholic drink

S&M /ˌes.ənˈdem/ *noun* [U], *adj* *ABBREVIATION FOR* **sadomasochism** or **sadomasochistic**

smack [HIT FORCEFULLY] /smæk/ *verb* **1** [T] to hit someone or something forcefully with the flat inside part of your hand, producing a brief loud noise, especially as a way of punishing a child: *I never smack my children.* ○ *I'll smack your* ***bottom*** *if you don't behave yourself.* **2** [I or T; usually + adv or prep] to hit something hard against something else: *I smacked my head on the corner of the shelf.* ○ *She smacked her books* ***down*** *on the table and stormed out of the room.*

• **smack *your* lips** to close and open your mouth loudly to express a strong desire to eat something you like a lot: *"I adore chocolate cake," said Susannah, smacking her lips.*

smack /smæk/ *noun* [C] **1** a hit from someone's flat hand as a punishment: *You're going to get a smack* ***on*** *the bottom if you don't stop being such a naughty boy.* **2** *INFORMAL* a hit given with the fist: *I* ***gave*** *him a smack* ***on*** *the jaw.* **3** a brief loud noise: *She slammed her case down on the desk with a smack.* **4** *INFORMAL* a loud kiss: *a big smack* ***on*** *the lips*

smack [EXACTLY] /smæk/ *adv* (*UK ALSO* **smack-bang,** *US ALSO* **smack-dab**) exactly in a place: *She lives smack in the middle of London.*

smack [DIRECTLY] /smæk/ *adv* (*UK ALSO* **smack-bang,** *US ALSO* **smack-dab**) directly and forcefully, producing a brief loud noise: *I wasn't looking where I was going and walked smack into a lamppost.*

smack [DRUG] /smæk/ *noun* [U] *SLANG* heroin: *How long has she been* ***on*** *smack?*

▲ **smack of *sth*** *phrasal verb* If something smacks of an unpleasant quality, it seems to have that quality: *The whole affair smacks of mismanagement and incompetence.*

smacker [MONEY] /ˈsmæk.əʳ/ [US] /-ɚ/ *noun* [C usually pl] *SLANG* a pound or dollar: *It cost me fifty smackers to get that window fixed.*

smacker [KISS] /ˈsmæk.əʳ/ [US] /-ɚ/ *noun* [C] *INFORMAL* a loud or long kiss

smacker [LIPS] /ˈsmæk.əʳ/ [US] /-ɚ/ *noun* [C] *US* the lips or the outer part of the mouth: *a kiss* ***on*** *the smacker*

smackhead /ˈsmæk.hed/ *noun* [C] *UK INFORMAL* a person who regularly takes heroin

small [LIMITED] /smɔːl/ [US] /smɑːl/ *adj* limited in size or amount when compared with what is typical or average: *a small dog/house/car/country* ○ *I'd rather live in a small town than a big city.* ○ *Would you like a large or small cola with your burger?* ○ *Ella is the smallest girl in her class.* ○ *That jacket's too small* ***for*** *you.* ○ *He's small* ***for*** *his age.* ○ *Only a small* ***number*** *of applicants are successful.* ○ *The number of women in parliament is* ***pitifully*** (= extremely) *small.* ○ *Liqueurs are usually drunk* ***in*** *small* ***quantities****.*

• **grateful/thankful for small mercies** If someone should be grateful/thankful for small mercies, they should be grateful for something although it is not as good as they would like: *We've only raised a quarter of the money we needed, but I suppose we must be thankful for small mercies.*

• **a small fortune** *INFORMAL* a large sum of money: *You'll have to* ***spend*** *a small fortune in legal fees if you decide to sue for compensation.*

• **small wonder** used to mean that something is not surprising: *After five years with the company she hadn't been promoted – small wonder then* ***that*** *she decided to quit her job.*

• **It's a small world.** *SAYING* said to show your surprise that people or events in different places are connected: *So you know my old science teacher! Well, it's certainly a small world, isn't it?*

small /smɔːl/ [US] /smɑːl/ *adv* in a small size: *The instructions are printed so small I can hardly read them.*

small /smɔːl/ [US] /smɑːl/ *noun* **the small of *your* back** the middle of the lower back: *I have a pain* ***in*** *the small of my back.* ➲See picture **The Body** on page Centre 5

smallness /ˈsmɔːl.nəs/ [US] /ˈsmɑːl-/ *noun* [U] *The smallness* ***of*** *the city often surprises first-time visitors.*

COMMON LEARNER ERROR

small or **little?**

Small refers to size and is the usual opposite of 'big' or 'large'.

Could I have a hamburger and a small Coke please?
Our house is quite small.

Little refers to size but also expresses the speaker's feelings. For example, it can suggest that the speaker likes or dislikes something.

They live in a beautiful little village.
Rats are horrible little animals.

The comparative and superlative forms of **little** are not usually used in British English. Use **smaller** or **smallest** instead.

My car is smaller than yours.
~~*My car is littler than yours.*~~

small [YOUNG] /smɔːl/ [US] /smɑːl/ *adj* being a very young child that is older than a baby: *Looking after small children can be very tiring.*

small [LACKING IMPORTANCE] /smɔːl/ [US] /smɑːl/ *adj* not important or effective: *Talking to her makes me* ***feel*** *small.* ○ *He's always trying to make me* ***look*** *small in front of my boss.*

small [LIMITED ACTIVITY] /smɔːl/ [US] /smɑːl/ *adj* [before n] limited in the amount of an activity: *The government should give more help to small businessmen* (= people whose businesses are of a limited size). ○ *Chris is quite a small* ***eater*** *so he won't want much.* ○ *If you can help us in a small* ***way*** (= to a limited degree) *it would be greatly appreciated.*

small [LETTER SIZE] /smɔːl/ [US] /smɑːl/ *adj* **1** [before n] describes letters that are not capital letters: *The poet e. e. cummings wrote his name with small letters, not capital letters.* **2** *UK* A CONSERVATIVE with a small 'c' is someone who has traditional values, such as disliking change in society, rather than being a member or supporter of the CONSERVATIVE PARTY. We can use this structure with other words to say something is more general or less extreme than the usual meaning: *Management is all about politics with a small 'p'.*

ˈsmall ˌad *noun* [C] *UK* **classified ad**

ˈsmall ˌarms *plural noun* small light guns that are held and fired in one or both hands

ˌsmall ˈbeer *UK noun* [U] (*US* **small potatoes**) *INFORMAL* something that seems unimportant when compared to something else: *The insurance premium is small beer compared to what we'd have to pay if the house burnt down.*

ˌsmall ˈchange *noun* [U] **1** money that is in the form of coins of low value **2** something that is not considered to be expensive or important: *He spent $10 million on a race horse, but that's just small change to him.*

ˌsmall ˈclaims ˌcourt *noun* [C or U] a law court which deals with claims for small amounts of money, especially from people who believe that they have had money taken from them unfairly by a business

ˌsmallest ˈroom *noun* [U] *UK INFORMAL FOR* the **toilet** (= room with a toilet)

ˈsmall ˌfry *noun* [U] *INFORMAL* people or things that are not considered to be important: *They may be key players in their own company, but they're small fry in the industry itself.*

smallholding /ˈsmɔːlˌhəʊl.dɪŋ/ [US] /ˈsmɑːlˌhoʊl-/ *noun* [C] *UK* an area of land that is used for farming but which is much smaller than a typical farm

smallholder /ˈsmɔːlˌhəʊl.dəʳ/ [US] /ˈsmɑːlˌhoʊl.dɚ/ *noun* [C] *UK* someone who owns a smallholding

ˈsmall ˌhours *plural noun* the early hours of the morning, between twelve o'clock at night and the time when the sun rises: *She was up until* ***the*** *small hours of the morning trying to finish her essay.*

ˌsmall inˈtestine *noun* [C usually sing] the upper part of the bowels between the stomach and the LARGE INTESTINE

small-minded /ˌsmɔːlˈmaɪn.dɪd/ [US] /ˌsmɑːl-/ *adj DISAPPROVING* having fixed opinions and refusing to consider new or different ideas: *He has some very small-minded opinions about foreigners.* **small-mindedness** /ˌsmɔːlˈmaɪn.dɪd.nəs/ [US] /ˌsmɑːl-/ *noun* [U]

smallpox /ˈsmɔːl.pɒks/ [US] /ˈsmɑːl.pɑːks/ *noun* [U] an extremely infectious disease which causes a fever, spots on the skin and often death

ˈsmall ˌprint *UK noun* [U] (*US* **fine print**) text in a formal agreement which is printed smaller than the rest of the text, sometimes in the hope that it will not be noticed because it contains rules or information that will be disadvantageous to the person signing the agreement: *Don't sign anything until you've* ***read*** *the small print.*

smalls /smɔːlz/ [US] /smɑːlz/ *plural noun UK OLD-FASHIONED INFORMAL* underwear, especially when being washed or about to be washed: *Have you got any smalls that need washing?*

the ˈsmall ˌscreen *noun* [S] television, especially when compared with cinema: *Her new detective series will be her debut on the small screen.*

ˈsmall ˌtalk *noun* [U] conversation about unimportant things, often between people who do not know each other well: *I don't enjoy parties where I have to* ***make*** *small talk with complete strangers.*

small-time /ˈsmɔːl.taɪm/ [US] /ˈsmɑːl-/ *adj DISAPPROVING* not very successful or important: *a small-time crook* ○ *a small-time theatre* **small-timer** /ˈsmɔːl.taɪ.məʳ/ [US] /ˈsmɑːl.taɪ.mɚ/ *noun* [C] *The police are arresting the small-timers when they should be going for the ringleaders.*

small-town /ˈsmɔːl.taʊn/ [US] /ˈsmɑːl-/ *adj* [before n] describes small social groups where ordinary people live: *The film explores the life of small-town America in the 1930s.*

smarmy /ˈsmɑː.mi/ [US] /ˈsmɑːr-/ *adj INFORMAL DISAPPROVING* extremely polite, respectful or helpful in a way which is intended to be attractive but which does not seem sincere: *She was trying to be friendly, but she just seemed smarmy and insincere.* **smarm** /smɑːm/ [US] /smɑːrm/ *verb* [I or T] *He's always trying to smarm his way into a promotion.*

smart [STYLISH] /smɑːt/ [US] /smɑːrt/ *adj UK OR US OLD-FASHIONED* **1** having a clean, tidy and stylish appearance: *Guy* ***looks*** *very smart in his new suit, doesn't he?* ○ *I need a smart jacket for my interview.* ○ *She works in a very smart* ***new*** *office overlooking the River Cam.* **2** A place or event that is smart attracts fashionable, stylish or rich people: *a smart restaurant* ○ *We went to a very smart party on New Year's Eve.*

smartly /ˈsmɑːt.li/ [US] /ˈsmɑːrt-/ *adv UK OR US OLD-FASHIONED* in a fashionable and slightly formal way: *Paul's always very smartly* ***dressed.*** **smartness** /ˈsmɑːt.nəs/ [US] /ˈsmɑːrt-/ *noun* [U] *UK*

smart [CLEVER] /smɑːt/ [US] /smɑːrt/ *adj* intelligent, or able to think quickly or cleverly in difficult situations: *Gemma's teacher says she's one of the smartest kids in the class.* ○ *Why don't you fix it if you're so smart?* ○ *I'm not smart enough to understand computers.* ○ *He's smart enough to know he can't run the business without her.* ○ *Quitting that job was the smartest* ***move*** *I ever made.*

• **the smart money is on/says...** If the smart money is on something or says something, that thing is considered to be likely to happen: *The smart money says she'll win the world championship.*

smart [QUICK] /smɑːt/ [US] /smɑːrt/ *adj* [before n] done quickly with a lot of force or effort: *She gave him a smart smack on the bottom.* ○ *We'll have to work at a smart pace if we're going to finish on time.*

smartly /ˈsmɑːt.li/ [US] /ˈsmɑːrt-/ *adv* quickly or forcefully: *The good economic news caused share prices to rise smartly this afternoon.*

smart [STING] /smɑːt/ [US] /smɑːrt/ *verb* [I] **1** to cause someone to feel a stinging pain: *My eyes were smarting* ***from*** *the onions.* **2** to feel upset and angry because of failure or criticism: *The police are* ***still*** *smarting* ***from*** *their failure to prevent the robbery.*

smart alec, **smart aleck** /ˌsmɑːtˈæl.ɪk/ [US] /ˌsmɑːrt-/ *noun* [C] *INFORMAL* someone who tries to appear clever or who answers questions in a clever way that annoys other people

ˈsmart ˌarse *UK noun* [C] (*US* **smart ass**) *OFFENSIVE* someone who is always trying to seem more clever than other people in a way that is annoying: *I don't want some smart arse from the city telling me how to manage my farm.*

ˈsmart ˌbomb *noun* [C] a bomb which is directed to the object it is intended to hit by a television signal or a LASER

ˈsmart ˌcard *noun* [C] a small plastic card which is used to make payments and to store personal information and which can be read when connected to a computer system

ˈsmart ˌdrug *noun* [C usually pl] a drug which is designed to make you more intelligent or help you think more clearly

smarten /ˈsmɑː.tᵊn/ [US] /ˈsmɑːr-/ *verb*

▲ **smarten** ***(sb/sth)*** **up** *phrasal verb* [M] *MAINLY UK* to (cause to) become more clean, tidy and stylish: [R] *She's really smartened her****self*** *up since she left university.* ○ *You'll have to smarten up if you want to work in television.*

• **smarten up** ***your*** **act** *MAINLY UK* to make more effort: *Why are you always so late? You'll have to smarten up your act if you want to keep your job.*

the ˈsmart ˌmoney *noun* [U] money that is invested by experienced investors who know a lot about what they are doing: *The smart money is coming back into mortgages as the best investment now.*

ˌsmart ˈmouth *noun* [C usually sing] *US INFORMAL* If someone has or is a smart mouth, they speak to other people in a way that shows a lack of respect. **smart-mouthed** /ˌsmɑːtˈmaʊðd/ [US] /ˌsmɑːrt-/ *adj*: *a smart-mouthed little brat*

smarts /smɑːts/ [US] /smɑːrts/ *plural noun US INFORMAL* intelligence: *He's got* ***the*** *smarts to figure out what to do next.*

ˈsmart ˌset *noun* [U] *UK* people who are fashionable, rich and often artistic or well educated: *The nightclub is*

S

popular with Berlin's smart set.

smarty-pants /ˈsmɑː.ti.pænts/ [US] /ˈsmɑːr.t̬i-/ *noun* [C] *plural* **smarty-pants** *INFORMAL* someone who wants to appear to be clever: [as form of address] *Okay, smarty-pants, you tell me how to do it then.*

smash [BREAK NOISILY] /smæʃ/ *verb* [I or T] to cause something to break noisily into a lot of small pieces: *Rioters ran through the city centre smashing* ***windows*** *and looting shops.* ○ *She dropped her cup and watched it smash* ***to pieces/to smithereens*** *on the stone floor.*

smash /smæʃ/ *noun* [U] the sound of something being smashed: *I was woken by the smash of glass.*

smash [MOVE FORCEFULLY] /smæʃ/ *verb* **1** [I or T; + adv or prep] to cause something to move with great force against something hard, usually causing damage or injury: *Several boats were smashed against the rocks during the storm.* ○ *He tried to smash the door* ***down*** *to get to me.* ○ *The car was travelling very fast when it smashed* ***into*** *the tree.* ○ *He threatened to smash* ***my face in*** *if I didn't give him the money.* **2** [I or T] in tennis, to hit the ball down toward the ground quickly and forcefully

smash /smæʃ/ *noun* [C] **1** the sound of something smashing: *The cars collided with a loud smash.* **2** a **smash-up** **3** (in tennis) a powerful downward hit which sends the ball forcefully over the net

smash [DEFEAT] /smæʃ/ *verb* [T] to defeat someone or to destroy something completely: *The government said it would to whatever was necessary to smash the rebellion.*

smash [DO BETTER] /smæʃ/ *verb* [T] to do much better than the best or fastest result recorded previously: *Petersen smashed the 400m record* ***by*** *over half a second.*

smash [SUCCESSFUL FILM/SONG] /smæʃ/ *noun* [C] an extremely popular and successful song, play or film: *This CD contains all the latest smash* ***hits***. ○ *Her first movie was an international* ***box-office*** *smash.*

▲ **smash** ***sth*** **up** *phrasal verb* [M] to damage something in a violent and destructive way: *In the sixties he was famous for taking drugs and smashing up hotel rooms.*

smashed-up /ˈsmæʃt.ʌp/ *adj*: *a smashed-up car*

smash-and-grab raid /ˌsmæʃ.ənˈgræbˌreɪd/ *noun* [C] *UK* a crime in which thieves break the window of a shop and steal things before quickly escaping

smashed /smæʃt/ *adj* [after v] *SLANG* extremely drunk, or powerfully affected by illegal drugs

smashing /ˈsmæʃ.ɪŋ/ *adj MAINLY UK* extremely good, attractive, enjoyable or pleasant: *There's a smashing view from her office.* ○ *Jonathan would make a smashing dad.* ○ *He* ***looks*** *smashing in his dinner suit.*

smasher /ˈsmæʃ.əʳ/ [US] /-ɚ/ *noun* [C] *UK OLD-FASHIONED INFORMAL* someone who is very attractive

smash-up /ˈsmæʃ.ʌp/ *noun* [C usually sing] (*ALSO* **smash**) a road or train accident: *He hasn't driven since his smash-up two years ago.*

smattering /ˈsmæt.ər.ɪŋ/ [US] /ˈsmæt̬.ɚ-/ *noun* [C usually sing] a very small amount or number: *There's only a smattering* ***of*** *people who oppose the proposal.*

smear [SPREAD] /smɪəʳ/ [US] /smɪr/ *verb* [T usually + adv or prep] to spread a liquid or a thick substance over a surface: *The children had smeared peanut butter all* ***over*** *the sofa.* ○ *Can you explain why the front of your car is smeared* ***with*** *blood?* **smear** /smɪəʳ/ [US] /smɪr/ *noun* [C] *You'd look very stylish if it wasn't for that smear* ***of*** *ketchup on your shirt.*

smear [ACCUSATION] /smɪəʳ/ [US] /smɪr/ *noun* [C] an accusation which is unpleasant, unreasonable or unlikely to be true and which is made publicly with the intention of harming a person's reputation: *The prime minister has dismissed the allegations as smears and innuendo.* ○ *She claims she was the victim of a smear* ***campaign*** (= repeated attempts to damage her reputation). **smear** /smɪəʳ/ [US] /smɪr/ *verb* [T] *She decided to sue for libel after the newspaper smeared her private life.*

ˈsmear (ˌtest) *UK noun* [C] (*US* **pap smear**) a medical test in which cells from a woman's CERVIX (= entrance to the womb) are removed and examined to discover if there is any disease

smell [ABILITY] /smel/ *noun* [U] the ability to notice or discover the presence of a substance by using your nose: *Smell is one of the five senses.* ○ *Dogs have a very good* ***sense of*** *smell.*

smell /smel/ *verb* [I] **smelled** or *UK ALSO* **smelt**, **smelled** or *UK ALSO* **smelt** to have the ability to notice or discover the presence of a substance by using your nose: *Humans can't smell as well as dogs.* ○ *What I hate most about having a cold is not being able to smell.*

smell [CHARACTERISTIC] /smel/ *noun* [C] **1** the characteristic of something that can be recognized or noticed using the nose: *What's your favourite smell?* ○ *I love* ***the smell of*** *orange blossoms.* ○ *The marketplace was filled with delightful smells.* ○ *There's a* ***delicious*** *smell in here.* ○ *I wish we could get rid of that smell* (= bad smell) *in the bathroom.* **2** *LITERARY* **the smell of** the particular character or feeling that someone or something has: *She's still enjoying the* ***sweet*** *smell* (= pleasant experience) ***of success*** *after her victory in the world championships.*

smell /smel/ *verb* [I; L only + adj] **smelled** or *UK ALSO* **smelt**, **smelled** or *UK ALSO* **smelt** to have a particular quality that others can notice with their noses: *My hands smell (UK)* ***of****/(US)* ***like*** *onions.* ○ *That cake smells good.* ○ *There's something in the fridge that smells mouldy.* ○ *Your feet smell* (= have an unpleasant smell). *Why don't you wash them?*

• **come up/out smelling of roses** *UK* (*US* **come up/out smelling like roses**) to have people believe that you are good and honest after a difficult situation which could have made you seem bad or dishonest: *When the results of the fraud investigation were announced last week, the staff came up smelling of roses.* **-smelling** /-smel.ɪŋ/ *suffix*: ***sweet****-smelling flowers* ○ ***foul****-smelling rubbish*

smelly /ˈsmel.i/ *adj* having an unpleasant smell: *smelly feet* ➲See also **smell fishy** at **fishy**.

smell [DISCOVER] /smel/ *verb* [T] **smelled** or *UK ALSO* **smelt**, **smelled** or *UK ALSO* **smelt** **1** to notice or discover something using the nose: *Come and smell these flowers!* ○ *Can you smell something* ***burning****?* ○ [+ (that)] *Didn't you smell* ***(that)*** *the pie was burning?* ○ *I can smell something nasty in the bottom of the fridge.* **2** *INFORMAL* to know about or be aware of a situation without having to be told about it: *Brenda can smell* ***trouble*** *a mile off* (= a long time in advance).

• **smell blood** to recognize an opportunity to take advantage of someone who is in a difficult situation: *When she smells blood, you don't get a second chance.*

• **smell a rat** to recognize that something is not as it appears to be or that something dishonest is happening: *He's been working late with her every night this week – I smell a rat!*

smell /smel/ *noun* [S] *MAINLY UK* when you put your nose near something and breathe in so that you can discover its characteristics with your nose: *Have* ***a*** *smell* ***of*** *this perfume.*

▲ **smell** ***somewhere*** **out** *UK phrasal verb* [M] (*US* **smell** ***somewhere*** **up**) to fill a place with a smell, in an unpleasant way: *That aftershave of yours is smelling out the whole house.*

▲ **smell** ***sth/sb*** **out** *MAINLY UK phrasal verb* [M] (*US USUALLY* **sniff** ***sth/sb*** **out**) to discover where something or someone is by smelling: *At customs, dogs are used to smell out drugs in passengers' luggage.*

ˈsmelling ˌsalts *plural noun* a chemical with a strong smell which is put under the nose of people who have lost consciousness in order to bring them back to consciousness

smelt [SMELL] /smelt/ *UK past simple and past participle of* **smell**

smelt [OBTAIN METAL] /smelt/ *verb* [T] to obtain a metal from rock by heating it to a very high temperature, or to melt objects made from metal in order to use the metal to make something new

smelter /ˈsmel.təʳ/ [US] /-t̬ɚ/ *noun* [C] a factory or machine in which metal is smelted **smelting** /ˈsmel.tɪŋ/ [US] /-t̬ɪŋ/ *noun* [U]

smidge /smɪdʒ/ *noun* [C usually sing] **smidgen**

smidgen, smidgin, smidgeon /ˈsmɪdʒ.ɪn/ *noun* [S] *INFORMAL* a very small amount: *Could I have* ***a*** *smidgen more wine?* ○ *It was five years since I'd last seen him, but he hadn't changed a smidgeon.*

S

smile /smaɪl/ *noun* [C] a facial expression in which the ends of the mouth curve up slightly, often with the lips moving apart so that the teeth can be seen: *Amy had a **big/broad** smile **on** her face.* ○ *She has a nice smile.* ○ *He winked and **gave** me a smile.* ○ *It's nice to be able to **bring** a smile **to** people's faces* (= make people smile).
• **be all smiles** to look happy and friendly, especially when other people are not expecting you to: *She's never been very friendly, but she was all smiles when she asked me to help her with her homework.*

smile /smaɪl/ *verb* **1** [I or T] to make a happy or friendly expression in which the corners of your mouth curve up: *He smiled and shook my hand.* ○ *When he smiled **at** me I knew everything was all right.* ○ *Esme's so cheerful – she's always smiling.* ○ *I couldn't help smiling when I thought of how pleased she was going to be.* ○ *He smiled **politely** as Mary apologized for her drunken friends.* ○ *He smiled to himself as he thought about his new girlfriend.* ○ *He smiled the **smile** of a man who knew victory was within reach.* **2** [T] to express or say something with a smile: *He smiled his congratulations and left without another word.* ○ *"Don't you worry about a thing. Everything's going to be just fine," smiled Robin reassuringly.*

smiley /ˈsmaɪ.li/ *adj* **smilier**, **smiliest** INFORMAL A smiley person or someone who has a smiley face looks friendly and smiles a lot.

smiling /ˈsmaɪ.lɪŋ/ *adj* having a smile: *I really miss seeing their happy smiling faces.*

smilingly /ˈsmaɪ.lɪŋ.li/ *adv* If someone does something smilingly, they smile as they are doing it: *When I complained about how long we'd had to wait for our food, the bill was whisked away and smilingly returned without the service charge.*

COMMON LEARNER ERROR

smile at someone/something
Be careful to use the preposition 'at' after the verb **smile** if you are smiling in someone's direction.
She smiled at the little girl.
~~She smiled to the little girl.~~

▲ **smile on** *sth/sb phrasal verb* LITERARY to feel positive about something or someone, or to treat them in a very positive way: *The government began to smile on small businesses when it realized that they were the key to economic growth.* ○ FIGURATIVE *The gods smiled on us and we had brilliant sunshine throughout the day.*

smiley /ˈsmaɪ.li/ *noun* [C] an EMOTICON (= a sideways image of a face, consisting of keyboard symbols, which is used in emails to express emotions)

smirk /smɜːk/ ⑩ /smɝːk/ *noun* [C] DISAPPROVING a smile that expresses satisfaction or pleasure about having done something or knowing something which is not known by someone else: *"Maybe your husband does things that you don't know about," he said with a smirk.* ○ *"I told you it would end in disaster," said Polly with a self-satisfied smirk on her face.* **smirk** /smɜːk/ ⑩ /smɝːk/ *verb* [I or T] *I don't like the way he winks and smirks **at** me whenever he sees me.* ○ *He smirked his way through the interview.*

smite /smaɪt/ *verb* [T] **smote**, **smitten** LITERARY to hit someone forcefully or to have a sudden powerful or destructive effect on someone

smith /smɪθ/ *noun* [C], *suffix* someone who makes things out of metal, especially by heating and hammering it to shape it: *a goldsmith/silversmith* ➲See also **blacksmith**.

smithy /ˈsmɪð.i/ *noun* [C] a place where things are made out of metal, especially iron or steel, by heating and hammering

smithereens /ˌsmɪð. əˈriːnz/ ⑩ /-əˈriːnz/ *plural noun* INFORMAL a lot of very small broken pieces: *Our city was bombed **to** smithereens during the war.* ○ *So many films nowadays involve everyone and everything being **blown** to smithereens.*

smitten /ˈsmɪt.ən/ ⑩ /ˈsmɪt-/ *adj* [after v] having suddenly started to like or love something or someone very much: *The story's about a man smitten **with** love for his wife's cousin.* ○ *He was so smitten **by** her that he promised to move to Argentina to be near her.*

smock /smɒk/ ⑩ /smɑːk/ *noun* [C] a piece of clothing like a long shirt which is worn loosely over other clothing to protect it when working, or a piece of women's clothing that is similar to this: *an artist's smock*

smocking /ˈsmɒk.ɪŋ/ ⑩ /ˈsmɑː.kɪŋ/ *noun* [U] decoration on a piece of clothing consisting of cloth which has been gathered into tight folds that are held in position with decorative stitching

smog /smɒg/ ⑩ /smɑːg/ *noun* [S or U] air pollution, especially in cities, that is caused by a mixture of smoke, gases and chemicals: *Smog is a major problem in Athens.* ○ *As we flew into the airport, we could see a murky yellow smog hovering over the city.* **smoggy** /ˈsmɒg.i/ ⑩ /ˈsmɑː.gi/ *adj*: *Mexico City is one of the world's smoggiest capitals.*

smoke GREY GAS /sməʊk/ ⑩ /smoʊk/ *noun* [U] the grey, black or white mixture of gas and very small pieces of carbon that is produced when something burns: *cigarette smoke* ○ *a tiny smoke-**filled** pub* ○ *The fire produced a **pall** (= large mass) **of** smoke visible twenty miles away.* ○ *Plumes of smoke **billowed** from the chimney.* ○ *She leaned back thoughtfully and blew **a puff of** (= a small amount of) smoke into the air.*
• **There's no smoke without fire.** UK (US **Where there's smoke, there's fire.**) SAYING If unpleasant things are said about someone or something, there is probably a good reason for it: *She says the accusations are not true, but there's no smoke without fire.*
• **go up in smoke 1** Something that goes up in smoke fails to produce the desired result: *When the business went bankrupt, twenty years of hard work went up in smoke.* **2** to be destroyed by burning: *Because of the fire, hundreds of houses have gone up in smoke.*

smoke /sməʊk/ ⑩ /smoʊk/ *verb* [I] to produce smoke as a result of industrial activity or of something such as an electrical fault: *The skyline is dominated by smoking factory chimneys.* ○ *Suddenly the TV went blank and started smoking.*

smoked /sməʊkt/ ⑩ /smoʊkt/ *adj* [before n] describes glass or a window that has been darkened, as if by smoke: *She works in a modern office with smoked-glass windows.*

smokeless /ˈsməʊk.ləs/ ⑩ /ˈsmoʊk-/ *adj* **1** UK not causing or allowing smoke: *If you live in a smokeless **zone** you have to use smokeless **fuels** instead of coal.* **2** US **smokeless tobacco** tobacco which is chewed or put in the mouth

smoky (**smokier**, **smokiest**), **smokey** /ˈsməʊ.ki/ ⑩ /ˈsmoʊ-/ *adj* **1** If a place is smoky, there is a lot of smoke in it: *a smoky pub/restaurant* ○ *a smoky fire* **2** describes something which appears to be similar to smoke: *a smoky blue colour* ○ *This wine has a delicious smoky flavour.*

smoke BREATHE SMOKE /sməʊk/ ⑩ /smoʊk/ *verb* [I or T] to breathe smoke into the mouth and usually lungs from a cigarette, pipe, etc: *Do you mind if I smoke?* ○ *I used to smoke a (UK) packet/(US) pack of cigarettes a day.*

smoke /sməʊk/ ⑩ /smoʊk/ *noun* **1** [S] the act of smoking a cigarette: *I really enjoy **a** smoke at the end of a meal.* **2** [C] INFORMAL a cigarette: *Would you buy me some smokes while you're out?*

smoker /ˈsməʊ.kər/ ⑩ /ˈsmoʊ.kɚ/ *noun* [C] **1** someone who smokes tobacco regularly: *a cigarette/pipe smoker* ○ *Chris is a **light/heavy** smoker* (= smokes a little/a lot each day). **2** UK OLD-FASHIONED a train carriage in which people are allowed to smoke tobacco

smoking /ˈsməʊ.kɪŋ/ ⑩ /ˈsmoʊ-/ *noun* [U] when someone smokes a cigarette, pipe, etc., or when someone regularly does this: *Smoking is not permitted anywhere in this theatre.* ○ *The nicotine patches are designed to help people **give up/quit/stop** smoking.* ○ *Cigarette smoking kills thousands of people every year.* ○ *No smoking, please.* ○ *I avoid going to restaurants that don't have a (UK) **no**-smoking/(US) **non**-smoking area.*

smoke PRESERVE /sməʊk/ ⑩ /smoʊk/ *verb* [T] to preserve meat, fish or cheese using smoke from burning wood: *People in the Middle East, India and Egypt were salting, drying and smoking fish and meat 6000 years ago.* ○ *She had champagne and smoked **salmon** sandwiches at her birthday party.*

S

smoke [CITY] /sməʊk/ ⓤⓢ /smoʊk/ *noun UK INFORMAL* **the (big) smoke** any large city, especially London, Sydney or Melbourne: *He was a young lad of 16 when he first came to the big smoke.*

▲ **smoke** *sb/sth* **out** *phrasal verb* [M] If you smoke out an animal or person that is hiding, you force them to leave the place where they are by filling it with smoke: *FIGURATIVE The finance minister has promised a tougher approach to smoking out* (= finding) *tax dodgers.*

,**smoke and** '**mirrors** *plural noun MAINLY US* Something that is described as smoke and mirrors is intended to take attention away from an embarrassing or unpleasant situation: *Instead of cutting expenditure, the government's relying on smoke and mirrors to make it seem as though it's doing something.*

'**smoke** ,**bomb** *noun* [C] a device like a bomb which produces a lot of smoke instead of exploding

'**smoke de,tector** *noun* [C] a device that makes a loud noise when there is smoke present to tell people that there is a fire

smoke-filled room /,sməʊk.fild'ru:m/ ⓤⓢ /,smoʊk-/ *noun* [C] a place where powerful people, such as politicians, meet to have discussions and make agreements in secret: *The whole business stinks of political corruption and decisions made in smoke-filled rooms.*

smokescreen /'sməʊk.skri:n/ ⓤⓢ /'smoʊk-/ *noun* [C] **1** something which hides the truth about someone's intentions: *Instead of doing something about the problem, the council is hiding* **behind** *a smokescreen of bureaucracy.* **2** an artificial cloud of smoke that is used to hide the movements or positions of soldiers from the enemy

'**smoke** ,**signal** *noun* [C usually pl] **1** a message using smoke from a fire, which can be seen from a long distance **2** an indirect statement about someone's intentions: *The chancellor was* **sending out** *smoke signals about the new budget proposal.*

smokestack /'sməʊk.stæk/ ⓤⓢ /'smoʊk-/ *noun* [C] a tall vertical pipe which takes smoke or steam into the air from an engine powered by steam or from a factory

'**smokestack** ,**industry** *noun* [C] *MAINLY US* traditional industries that produce large machines or materials used in other industries and create a lot of pollution in doing so: *There's been a steady decline in smokestack industries such as shipbuilding and steel.*

,**smoking** '**gun** *noun* [C usually sing] information which proves who committed a crime: *The tape recordings provided prosecutors with the smoking gun they needed to prove he'd been involved in the conspiracy.*

'**smoking** ,**jacket** *noun* [C] *OLD-FASHIONED* a comfortable coat for a man that is made from a soft material and is worn when relaxing at home, traditionally when smoking

smolder /'sməʊl.dər/ ⓤⓢ /'smoʊl.dɚ/ *verb* [I] *US FOR* **smoulder**

smooch /smu:tʃ/ *verb* [I] **1** *INFORMAL* to kiss, hold and touch someone very affectionately: *Didn't I see you smooching* **with** *Mark at Kim's party?* **2** *UK* When two people are smooching, they are dancing slowly and very close together to slow romantic music: *The dance floor was full of middle-aged couples smooching* **to** *slushy ballads.*

smooch /smu:tʃ/ *noun* [C usually sing] **1** *INFORMAL* a kiss: *I was so embarrassed when I walked in on them* **having a** *smooch on the sofa.* **2** *UK* a slow, romantic dance: *Kate* **had a** *smooch with a very attractive young man at the Christmas party.*

smooth [REGULAR] /smu:ð/ *adj* having a surface or substance which is perfectly regular and has no holes, lumps or areas that rise or fall suddenly: *a smooth surface/texture/consistency* ○ *This custard is deliciously smooth and creamy.* ○ *Mix together the butter and sugar until smooth.* ○ *The road ahead was flat and smooth.* ○ *This cream will help to keep your* **skin** *smooth.*

● **as smooth as silk/a baby's bottom** extremely smooth: *Her skin was as smooth as silk.*

smooth /smu:ð/ *verb* [I or T] to move your hands across something in order to make it flat: *He straightened his tie nervously and smoothed* **(down)** *his hair.* **smooth-**

ness /'smu:ð.nəs/ *noun* [U] *I just love the smoothness of silk.*

smooth [NOT INTERRUPTED] /smu:ð/ *adj* happening without any sudden changes, interruption, inconvenience or difficulty: *We had a very smooth* **flight** *with no turbulence at all.* ○ *The car's improved suspension gives a much smoother* **ride** *than earlier models.* ○ *An efficient transport system is vital to the smooth* **running** *of a country's economy.*

smooth /smu:ð/ *verb* [T] to remove difficulties and make something easier to do or achieve: *We encourage parents to help smooth their children's* **way** *through school.* ○ *We must do more to smooth the country's* **path** *to democratic reform.*

smoothly /'smu:ð.li/ *adv* easily and without interruption or difficulty: *The road was blocked for two hours after the accident, but traffic is now* **flowing** *smoothly again.* ○ *Lead is added to fuel to make car engines* **run** *more smoothly.* ○ *The pregnancy's* **gone** *very smoothly so far.* ○ *If all goes smoothly, we should arrive by nine o'clock.* **smoothness** /'smu:ð.nəs/ *noun* [U]

smooth [TASTING PLEASANT] /smu:ð/ *adj* having a pleasant flavour which is not sour, acidic or bitter: *This coffee is incredibly smooth and rich.* **smoothness** /'smu:ð.nəs/ *noun* [U] *The wine possesses a smoothness and balanced depth which is rare at such a low price.*

smooth [INSINCERE] /smu:ð/ *adj* very polite, confident and persuasive in a way that is not sincere: *The foreign minister is so smooth that many of his colleagues distrust him.* ○ *In job interviews, the successful candidates tend to be the smooth* **talkers** *who know exactly how to make the right impression.*

smoothie, smoothy /'smu:.ði/ *noun* [C] *DISAPPROVING* a man who is very polite, confident and persuasive in a way that is not sincere: *He's such a smoothie – I just assumed he worked in sales.* ⇒See also **smoothie**.

smooth [RUB] /smu:ð/ *verb* [T + adv or prep] to cover the surface of something with a liquid, cream or wax, using gentle rubbing movements: *Pour some oil into the palm of your hand and then smooth it over your arms and neck.*

PHRASAL VERBS WITH **smooth** ▼

▲ **smooth** *sth* **away** *phrasal verb* [M] to remove the difficulties from something: *My mother was always there to smooth away my fears.*

▲ **smooth** *sth* **out** *phrasal verb* [M] to reduce the difficulties or changes in a process or situation: *By investing small amounts regularly, you can smooth out the effects of sudden rises and falls in the stock market.*

▲ **smooth** *sth* **over** *phrasal verb* [M] to make problems, difficulties or disagreements less serious or easier to solve, usually by talking to the people involved: *Would you like me to try to smooth* **things** *over between you and your parents?*

smoothie, smoothy /'smu:.ði/ *noun* [C] a thick cold drink made from fruit, ice and often YOGURT or ice cream, which is mixed together until smooth ⇒See also **smoothie** at **smooth** INSINCERE.

smorgasbord /'smɔ:.gəs.bɔ:d/ ⓤⓢ /'smɔ:r.gəs.bɔ:rd/ *noun* **1** [C] a mixture of many different hot and cold Scandinavian dishes which are arranged so that you can serve yourself **2** [C usually sing] a wide variety of something: *a smorgasbord* **of** *choices*

smote /sməʊt/ ⓤⓢ /smoʊt/ *past simple of* **smite**

smother [NOT DEVELOP] /'smʌð.ər/ ⓤⓢ /-ɚ-/ *verb* [T] **1** to prevent something from developing or growing freely: *The latest violence has smothered any remaining hopes for an early peace agreement.* **2** to give someone too much love and attention so that they feel they have lost their independence and freedom: *I think she broke off their engagement because she felt smothered by him.*

smother [NOT LIVE] /'smʌð.ər/ ⓤⓢ /-ɚ-/ *verb* [T] **1** to kill someone by covering their face so that they cannot breathe: *They threatened to smother the animals with plastic bags.* **2** to kill something by covering it and preventing it from receiving the substances and conditions it needs for life: *Snow soon smothered the last of the blooms.* ○ *FIGURATIVE I tried desperately to smother a* *sneeze* (= I tried not to sneeze) *during his speech.* **3** to stop a fire from burning by covering it with something which prevents air from reaching it: *I threw a blanket over the cooker to smother the flames.*

▲ **smother** *sth* **in/with** *sth phrasal verb* to cover something completely with a substance or objects: *She took a slice of chocolate cake and smothered it in cream.*

smoulder *UK,* *US* **smolder** /ˈsməʊl.dəʳ/ *US* /ˈsmoʊl.dɚ/ *verb* [I] **1** to burn slowly with smoke but without flames: *a smouldering fire* ○ *smouldering* **embers** ○ *The fire was started by a smouldering cigarette.* **2** If a problem or unpleasant situation smoulders, it continues to exist and may become worse at any time: *The dispute is* **still** *smouldering, five years after the negotiations began.* **3** If a strong emotion smoulders, it exists, but is prevented from being expressed: *She was smouldering* **with** *rage as she explained how her son had been killed.* **4** A person who smoulders has strong sexual or romantic feelings but does not express them: *He gazed at her with smouldering* **eyes**, *wishing she wasn't married.*

SMS /ˌes.em'es/ *noun* [U] *ABBREVIATION FOR* short message service: a system for sending text messages from one MOBILE PHONE (= a telephone that you can carry with you) to another

smudge /smʌdʒ/ *noun* [C] a mark with no particular shape that is caused, usually accidentally, by rubbing something such as ink or a dirty finger across a surface: *Her hands were covered in dust and she had a black smudge on her nose.* ○ *FIGURATIVE She said we were nearly there, but the island was still no more than a distant smudge on the horizon.*

smudge /smʌdʒ/ *verb* [I or T] If ink, paint, etc. smudges or if someone smudges it, it becomes dirty or not clear because someone or something has touched it: *She was crying and her mascara had smudged.*

smudged /smʌdʒd/ *adj* dirty or not clear: *The signature was smudged and impossible to decipher.* **smudging** /ˈsmʌdʒ.ɪŋ/ *noun* [U] **smudgy** /ˈsmʌdʒ.i/ *adj*

smug /smʌg/ *adj* **smugger**, **smuggest** *DISAPPROVING* too pleased or satisfied about something you have achieved or something you know: *a smug grin* ○ *She deserved her promotion, but I wish she wasn't so damned smug* **about** *it.* ○ *There was a hint of smug* **self-satisfaction** *in her voice.* ○ *He's been* **unbearably** *smug since he gave up smoking.*

smugly /ˈsmʌg.li/ *adv DISAPPROVING* in a way that shows too much satisfaction or confidence: *"I own three cars and two boats," he said smugly.* **smugness** /ˈsmʌg.nəs/ *noun* [U]

smuggle /ˈsmʌg.l̩/ *verb* [T usually + adv or prep] to take things or people to or from a place secretly and often illegally: *She was caught trying to smuggle 26 kilos of heroin* **out of/into** *the country.* ○ *They managed to smuggle a videotape of the captive journalists* **out** *of the prison.*

smuggler /ˈsmʌg.ləʳ/ *US* /-lɚ/ *noun* [C] someone who smuggles **smuggling** /ˈsmʌg.lɪŋ/ *noun* [U] *The murdered man is thought to have been involved in* **drug** *smuggling.*

smut *SEXUAL MATERIAL* /smʌt/ *noun* [U] *DISAPPROVING* magazines, books, pictures, films, jokes or conversations which offend some people because they relate to sex: *There's an awful lot of smut on television these days.* ○ *Patrick's conversations are always full of smut.*

smutty /ˈsmʌt.i/ *US* /ˈsmʌt̬-/ *adj DISAPPROVING* related to or containing smut: *I was really embarrassed by his smutty* **jokes.** **smuttiness** /ˈsmʌt.ɪ.nəs/ *US* /ˈsmʌt̬-/ *noun* [U]

smut *DIRT* /smʌt/ *noun* [C or U] dirt or ash that makes a mark on something

snack /snæk/ *noun* [C] a small amount of food that is eaten between meals, or a very small meal: *I had a huge lunch, so I'll only need a snack for dinner.* ○ *Fresh or dried fruit makes an ideal snack.* ○ *Many snack* **foods** *are high in salt, sugar and fat.* **snack** /snæk/ *verb* [I] *I've been snacking all day.* ○ *If you eat three good meals a day, you're less likely to snack* **on** *biscuits and crisps.*

'snack ˌbar *noun* [C] a small informal restaurant where small meals can be eaten or bought to take away

snaffle /ˈsnæf.l̩/ *verb* [I or T] *UK INFORMAL* to take something quickly for yourself, in a way that prevents someone else from having or using it: *Who's snaffled my pen? It was on my desk a moment ago.* ○ *Martha snaffled* (= ate) *all the peanuts before the party had even begun!* ○ *The company grew by snaffling* **up** *several smaller businesses.*

snafu /snæˈfuː/ *noun* [C] *US INFORMAL* a situation in which nothing has happened as planned: *The company isn't wholly to blame for the snafu.* ○ *A single snafu* (= serious mistake) *by an airline can leave a lasting impression on travelers.*

snag *PROBLEM* /snæg/ *noun* [C] *SLIGHTLY INFORMAL* a problem, difficulty or disadvantage: *We don't anticipate any snags* **in/with** *the negotiations.* ○ *The drug is very effective – the* **only** *snag is that it cannot be produced in large quantities.*

snag /snæg/ *verb* [I or T] **-gg-** *MAINLY US* to cause problems or difficulties for someone or something: *Financial problems have snagged the project for the past six months.* ○ *The negotiations have snagged* **on** *a dispute about who should chair them.*

snag *DAMAGE* /snæg/ *noun* [C] a tear, hole or loose fibre in a piece of clothing or cloth caused by a sharp or rough object: *This sweater's full of snags.*

snag /snæg/ *verb* [T] **-gg-** If you snag something, it becomes caught on a sharp object and tears: *Be careful not to snag your coat* **on** *the barbed wire.*

snag *OBTAIN* /snæg/ *verb* [T] **-gg-** *US INFORMAL* to obtain or catch something by acting quickly: *They'd have gone bust if they hadn't snagged that contract* **from** *their rivals.* ○ *The ball was hit well, but Silverman snagged it for the final out of the inning.*

snag *FOOD* /snæg/ *noun* [C] *AUS INFORMAL FOR* **sausage**

snail /sneɪl/ *noun* [C] a small creature with a soft wet body and a round shell, that moves very slowly and often eats garden plants

● **at a snail's pace** extremely slowly: *The roads were full of traffic and we were travelling at a snail's pace for two hours.*

'snail ˌmail *noun* [U] *INFORMAL HUMOROUS* letters or messages that are not sent by email, but by regular post: *We agreed the deal online, but we'll have to wait for snail mail to get the paperwork.*

snake *ANIMAL* /sneɪk/ *noun* [C] **1** a reptile with a long cylindrical body and no legs: *He's terrified of being* **bitten** *by a snake.* ○ *a snake bite* ○ *snake* **venom 2 a snake (in the grass)** an unpleasant person who cannot be trusted

snake *TWIST* /sneɪk/ *verb* [I usually + adv or prep] to move along a route that includes a lot of twists or bends: *The river snakes through some of the most spectacular countryside in France.* ○ *The queue for tickets snaked all the way around the block.*

● **snake** *your* **way** Something that snakes its way moves or is arranged in a twisting way: *A long queue had formed, snaking its way downstairs and out into the street.*

'snake ˌcharmer *noun* [C] an entertainer who seems to control the movements of snakes by playing music

ˌsnakes and 'ladders *UK plural noun* (*US* **chutes and ladders**) a children's game played on a board that has pictures of snakes and ladders

snaky /ˈsneɪ.ki/ *adj AUS INFORMAL* annoyed or angry

snap *BREAK* /snæp/ *verb* **-pp- 1** [I or T] to cause something which is thin to break suddenly and quickly with a cracking sound: *You'll snap that ruler if you bend it too far.* ○ *Some vandal's gone and snapped* **off** *my car aerial again.* **2** [I] to suddenly become unable to control a strong feeling, especially anger: *When she asked me to postpone my trip to help her move house, I just snapped* (= got angry).

snap /snæp/ *noun* **1** [C usually sing] a sudden loud sound like something breaking or closing: *She broke the stick over her knee with a loud snap.* **2** [C] *US FOR* **press stud**

snap *MOVE QUICKLY* /snæp/ *verb* **-pp- 1** [I or T; usually + adv or prep] to move into a position quickly, producing a brief noise as if breaking: *Tendons store elastic energy by stretching and then snapping* **back** *into shape like rubber* *bands.* ○ *Simply snap the pieces into place.* **2** [I + adv or prep] to quickly return to a previous place or condition: *After substantial losses last year, the company has snapped **back** to profitability* (= started making profits again).

• **snap *your* fingers** to a make a brief noise by pushing your second finger hard against your thumb and then releasing it suddenly so that it hits the base of your thumb: *He was snapping his fingers in time with the music.*

• **snap shut** If something snaps shut or is snapped shut, it closes quickly with a sudden sharp sound: *She snapped her book shut and got up to leave.* ○ *Her mouth snapped shut when she realized he'd heard everything she'd said about him.*

• **snap to it** *UK* (*US* **snap it up**) *INFORMAL* used to tell someone to do something more quickly: *We're leaving in five minutes so you'd better snap to it and finish your breakfast.*

snappy /'snæp.i/ *INFORMAL* **make it snappy** used to tell someone that you want them to do something immediately and to do it quickly: *I'd like my bill please, waiter, and make it snappy – I've already been waiting half an hour for it.* ⊃See also **snappy** STYLISH; **snappy** EFFECTIVE.

snap [ANIMAL] /snæp/ *verb* [I] **-pp-** If an animal snaps, it tries to bite someone: *The guard dog was snarling and snapping behind the fence.*

• **snap at *sb's* heels 1** If an animal is snapping at your heels, it is running behind you and trying to bite you. **2** to compete strongly with someone and have a chance of soon defeating or replacing them: *With so many younger women snapping at her heels, this year may be her last chance to win the championship.*

snap [SPEAK] /snæp/ *verb* [I or T] **-pp-** to say something suddenly in an angry way: *There's no need to snap **at** me – it's not my fault that you lost your wallet.* ○ [+ speech] *"Well, I hate you too!" she snapped.*

• **snap *sb's* head off** to answer someone in an unreasonably angry way: *There's no point trying to discuss anything with him if all he's going to do is snap your head off.*

snappish /'snæp.ɪʃ/ *adj* (*ALSO* **snappy**) easily annoyed and tending to speak in an angry way: *He's very snappish when he arrives at work in the morning.* **snappishly** /'snæp.ɪʃ.li/ *adv*: *"Of course I know what I'm doing!" she said, snappishly.*

snap [PHOTOGRAPH] /snæp/ *noun* [C] *UK INFORMAL* an informal photograph which is not particularly skilful or artistic: ***holiday** snaps* ○ *Did you **take** many snaps while you were away?*

snap /snæp/ *verb* [I or T] **-pp-** to take a lot of photographs quickly: *He was arrested for snapping photos of a military parade.* ○ *She's very pleased with her new camera and was snapping **away** the whole time we were abroad.*

snap [GAME] /snæp/ *noun* [U] a card game in which the players compete to call out the word 'snap' when they see two cards that have the same value: *a game of snap*

snap /snæp/ *exclamation* **1** 'Snap!' is what you say in the game of snap when two cards of the same value have been played. **2** *UK INFORMAL* something that you say when you notice that two things are the same: *Snap! We're wearing the same shirts!*

snap [SOMETHING EASY] /snæp/ *noun* [S] *US INFORMAL* something that can be done without any difficulty: *"Will you finish on time?" "Sure thing. It's **a** snap."* ○ *Talking to girls is a snap **for** him.*

snap [DONE SUDDENLY] /snæp/ *adj* [before n] done suddenly without allowing time for careful thought or preparation: *He always makes snap **decisions** and never thinks about their consequences.*

PHRASAL VERBS WITH **snap**

▲ **snap out of *sth*** *phrasal verb INFORMAL* to force yourself to stop feeling sad and upset: *He just can't snap out of the depression he's had since his wife died.* ○ *Now come on, snap out of **it**. Losing that money isn't the end of the world.*

▲ **snap *sth* up** *phrasal verb* [M] *INFORMAL* to buy or get something quickly and enthusiastically because it is cheap or exactly what you want: *The tickets for the concert were snapped up within three hours of going on sale.* ○ *The fall in property prices means that there are a lot of bargains waiting to be snapped up.*

▲ **snap *sb* up** *phrasal verb* [M] *INFORMAL* to immediately accept someone's offer to join your company or team because you want them very much: *She was snapped up by a large law firm.*

'snap ˌbean *noun* [C] *US FOR* **sugar (snap) pea**

snapdragon /'snæpˌdræg.ən/ *noun* [C] a garden plant with white, yellow, pink or red flowers whose petals are shaped like a pair of lips which open when they are pressed

'snap ˌfastener *noun* [C] *UK* a **press stud**

snapper /'snæp.əʳ/ [US] /-ɚ/ *noun* [C] an edible fish that lives in warm seas

snappy [STYLISH] /'snæp.i/ *adj INFORMAL APPROVING* (especially of a man's clothes or of his appearance) modern and stylish: *He's a snappy **dresser**.* ○ *That's a very snappy new suit you've got, Peter.* ⊃See also **snappy** at **snap** MOVE QUICKLY. **snappily** /'snæp.ɪ.li/ *adv*: *The sales team are usually fairly snappily dressed.*

snappy [EFFECTIVE] /'snæp.i/ *adj APPROVING* immediately effective in getting people's attention or communicating an idea: *The magazine will be launched in September with a snappy new design.* ○ *They're looking for a snappy slogan to communicate the campaign's message.* ⊃See also **make it snappy** at **snap** MOVE QUICKLY. **snappily** /'snæp.ɪ.li/ *adv*

snapshot /'snæp.ʃɒt/ [US] /-ʃɑːt/ *noun* [C] *INFORMAL* a photograph

snare /sneəʳ/ [US] /sner/ *noun* [C] **1** a device for catching small animals and birds, usually with a rope or wire which tightens around the animal **2** a trick or situation which deceives you or involves you in some problem of which you are not aware: *The legal system is full of snares for those who are not wary.*

snare /sneəʳ/ [US] /sner/ *verb* [T] to catch an animal using a snare: *We used to snare small birds such as sparrows and robins.* ○ *FIGURATIVE She grew up in the days when a woman's main aim was to snare a rich husband.*

'snare ˌdrum *noun* [C] (*ALSO* **side drum**) a drum with twisted wires stretched across the bottom which shake against it when it is hit

snarky /'snɑː.ki/ [US] /'snɑːr.ki/ *adj INFORMAL* criticizing someone in an annoyed way and trying to hurt their feelings: *There was some idiot at the back of the hall making snarky comments.*

snarl /snɑːl/ [US] /snɑːrl/ *verb* [I or T] (especially of dogs) to make a deep rough sound while showing the teeth, usually in anger or (of people) to speak or say something angrily and fiercely: *The dogs started to snarl **at** each other so I had to separate them.* ○ [+ speech] *"Go to hell!", he snarled.* **snarl** /snɑːl/ [US] /snɑːrl/ *noun* [C] *The dog gave a low snarl so I quickly drew my hand back.* ○ *"Take your hands off me!" she said with a snarl.*

ˌsnarled 'up *UK USUALLY adj* (*US USUALLY* **snarled**) describes a long line of traffic that is unable to travel forward because something is blocking the road: *The traffic was snarled up in both directions for two miles because of the accident.* **snarl-up** *UK USUALLY* /snɑːl.ʌp/ [US] /'snɑːrl-/ *noun* [C] (*US USUALLY* **snarl**)

snatch [TAKE QUICKLY] /snætʃ/ *verb* [T] **1** to take hold of something suddenly and roughly: *He snatched the photos out of my hand before I had a chance to look at them.* ○ *FIGURATIVE Running the best race of his career, Fletcher snatched* (= only just won) *the gold medal from the Canadian champion.* **2** to take something or someone away by force: *The six-year-old girl was snatched from a playground and her body was found two days later.* ○ *She had her purse snatched* (= stolen) *while she was in town.* **3** to do or get something quickly because you only have a short amount of time: *Perhaps you'll be able to snatch a couple of hours' sleep before dinner.*

• **snatch victory (from the jaws of defeat)** to win a surprising victory at the last moment possible, when it had previously seemed certain that you were going to lose

S

snatch /snætʃ/ *noun* [C] when someone tries to take something quickly and forcefully: *I felt someone behind me **make** a snatch at my bag.*
snatcher /ˈsnætʃ.əʳ/ [US] /-ɚ/ *noun* [C] *You have to watch out for bag/purse snatchers* (= people who steal bags/ PURSES).

snatch [BRIEF PART] /snætʃ/ *noun* [C] a brief part of something: *I tried to hear what they were saying, but I only managed to catch a few snatches **of** conversation.*

snatch [VAGINA] /snætʃ/ *noun* [C] OFFENSIVE FOR the **vagina**
▲ **snatch at *sth*** *phrasal verb* **1** to try to take hold of something: *A man snatched at my bag, but he didn't get it.* **2** UK to try to use an opportunity quickly before it disappears: *I was desperate to find a way out of teaching so when this job came along I snatched at it.*

snazzy /ˈsnæz.i/ *adj* INFORMAL APPROVING modern and stylish in a way that attracts attention: *Paula's wearing a very snazzy pair of shoes!* ○ *He designs snazzy new graphics for software packages.* **snazzily** /ˈsnæz.ɪ.li/ *adv*

sneak [MOVE SECRETLY] /sniːk/ *verb* [I or T; usually + adv or prep] **sneaked** or US ALSO **snuck**, **sneaked** or US ALSO **snuck** to go somewhere secretly, or to take someone or something somewhere secretly: *I managed to sneak **in** through the back door while she wasn't looking.* ○ *Jan hasn't got a ticket but I thought we might sneak her **in**.* ○ *I thought I'd sneak **up on** him* (= move close to him without him seeing) *and give him a surprise.*
sneaky /ˈsniː.ki/ *adj* doing things in a secret and unfair way: *a sneaky plan* **sneakily** /ˈsniː.kɪ.li/ *adv*: *I rather sneakily looked in her diary when she was out last night.*

sneak [TELL SECRETLY] /sniːk/ *verb* [I] **sneaked** or US ALSO **snuck**, **sneaked** or US ALSO **snuck** UK SLANG DISAPPROVING to secretly tell someone in authority, especially a teacher, that someone else has done something bad, often in order to cause trouble: *She was one of those dreadful children who was always sneaking **on** other kids in the class.*
sneak UK /sniːk/ *noun* [C] (US **snitch**, AUS **dobber**) SLANG DISAPPROVING a person who tells people in authority when someone else does something bad: *You told Mrs Cooper that it was me who tipped the paint over, didn't you – you nasty little sneak!*

sneaker /ˈsniː.kəʳ/ [US] /-kɚ/ *noun* [C] US a type of light comfortable shoe that is suitable for playing sports ➲See picture **Clothes** on page Centre 6

sneaking /ˈsniː.kɪŋ/ *adj* [before n] If you have a sneaking feeling about someone or something, you have that feeling, although you are not certain it is correct: *I've got a sneaking **feeling/suspicion** that we're going the wrong way.*

ˌ**sneak** ˈ**preview** *noun* [C] an opportunity to see (a part of) something new before the rest of the public see it

sneer /snɪəʳ/ [US] /snɪr/ *verb* [I or T] to talk about or look at someone or something in an unkind way that shows you do not respect or approve of them: *You may sneer, but a lot of people like this kind of music.* ○ *She'll probably sneer **at** my new shoes because they're not expensive.* ○ [+ speech] *"Is that the best you can do?" he sneered.*
sneer /snɪəʳ/ [US] /snɪr/ *noun* [C] DISAPPROVING an unkind facial expression which shows your lack of respect or approval of someone or something: *"How much did you say you earned last year – was it fifteen thousand?" she said with a sneer.*
sneering /ˈsnɪə.rɪŋ/ [US] /ˈsnɪr.ɪŋ/ *adj* DISAPPROVING rude and not showing respect: *I don't like that superior, sneering tone of his.* **sneeringly** /ˈsnɪə.rɪŋ.li/ [US] /ˈsnɪr.ɪŋ-/ *adv*

sneeze /sniːz/ *verb* [I] When you sneeze, air and often small drops of liquid suddenly come out of your nose and mouth in a way you cannot control: *Cats make him sneeze – I think he's allergic to the fur.*
• **not to be sneezed at** INFORMAL If you say that something, especially an amount of money, is not to be sneezed at, you mean that it is a large enough amount to be worth having: *Well, a 5% pay increase means an extra £700 a year which is not to be sneezed at!*
sneeze /sniːz/ *noun* [C] an act or sound of sneezing: *He's got all the classic symptoms of a cold – the coughs and sneezes and the sore throat.*

snick /snɪk/ *verb* [T] UK in sports, especially cricket, to hit the ball off the edge of the bat: *Carlton snicked the ball low and fast to Lynch's right.* **snick** /snɪk/ *noun* [C]

snicker /ˈsnɪk.əʳ/ [US] /-ɚ/ *verb* [I], *noun* [C] US FOR **snigger**

snide /snaɪd/ *adj* (especially of remarks) containing unpleasant and indirect criticism: *She made one or two snide **remarks** about their house which I thought was a bit unnecessary.*
snidely /ˈsnaɪd.li/ *adv* rudely and critically: *"Well, she's certainly better looking than her mother," she said snidely.* **snideness** /ˈsnaɪd.nəs/ *noun* [U]

sniff /snɪf/ *verb* **1** [I or T] to smell something by taking air in through your nose: *He sniffed his socks to see if they needed washing.* ○ *Dogs love sniffing each other.* ○ *She sniffed **at** her glass of wine before tasting it.* ○ *Dogs are sometimes used at airports to sniff **out*** (= find by smelling) *drugs in people's luggage.* ○ *He was expelled from school for sniffing **glue*** (= taking in the gas from glue because of the feelings of pleasure that this gives). **2** [I] to take air in quickly through your nose, usually to stop the liquid inside the nose from flowing out: *You were sniffing a lot – I presumed you had a cold.* **3** [T] to speak in an unpleasant way, showing that you have a low opinion of something: [+ speech] *"They didn't even serve wine at dinner!" she sniffed.*
sniff /snɪf/ *noun* [C] a quick breath in through the nose to smell something, or to stop liquid in the nose from coming out: *Have a sniff of this medicine – it smells revolting, doesn't it?* ○ *"I don't think much of that idea," she said with a sniff* (= an expression of a low opinion).
sniffer /ˈsnɪf.əʳ/ [US] /-ɚ/ *noun* [C] someone who sniffs chemicals for the feelings of pleasure it causes: *a **glue/ paint** sniffer.*
sniffy /ˈsnɪf.i/ *adj* INFORMAL showing disapproval and a low opinion: *She's a bit sniffy **about** my taste in music.*

PHRASAL VERBS WITH **sniff** ▼

▲ **sniff at *sth*** [DISAPPROVING] *phrasal verb* to show disapproval or a low opinion of something: *The men at City Hall, sniffing at anything too ideological, insist that big cuts are just not practical.*
• **not to be sniffed at** INFORMAL valuable or worth having: *A two million pound profit is not to be sniffed at.*
▲ **sniff at *sth*** [INTERESTED] *phrasal verb* (ALSO **sniff around (*sth*)**) to show that you are interested in something: *A few computer firms are sniffing at the project already.* ○ *Chief executive David Prosser said the takeover speculation was wrong and no one was sniffing around.*
▲ **sniff *sth* out** *phrasal verb* [M] to search for and discover something: *Her job is to go round the big fashion shows sniffing out talent for a modelling agency.*

ˈ**sniffer** ˌ**dog** *noun* [C] MAINLY UK INFORMAL a dog that is trained and used by the police or army to find hidden drugs or bombs by smelling them

sniffle /ˈsnɪf.l̩/ *verb* [I] (ALSO **snuffle**) to breathe in quickly and repeatedly through the nose, usually because you are crying or because you have a cold: *You're sniffling a lot today – have you got a cold?*
sniffle /ˈsnɪf.l̩/ *noun* [C] (ALSO **snuffle**) an act or sound of sniffling
• **a sniffle** (ALSO **the sniffles**) a slight cold which mainly affects your nose: *I had a cold a couple of weeks ago and it's left me with a bit of a sniffle.*

snifter [DRINK] /ˈsnɪf.təʳ/ [US] /-tɚ/ *noun* [C] OLD-FASHIONED INFORMAL a small drink of something alcoholic: *How about a snifter before dinner?*

snifter [GLASS] /ˈsnɪf.təʳ/ [US] /-tɚ/ *noun* [C] US a bowl-shaped glass which is narrower at the top and has a short stem, used for drinking brandy

snigger /ˈsnɪg.əʳ/ [US] /-ɚ/ *verb* [I] (US ALSO **snicker**) to laugh at someone or something childishly and often unkindly: *They spent half the time sniggering **at** the clothes people were wearing.* ○ *What are you two sniggering **at/about**?*
snigger /ˈsnɪg.əʳ/ [US] /-ɚ/ *noun* [C] *We were **having** a snigger at the bride who was rather large and dressed in a tight pale pink dress.*

snip [CUT] /snɪp/ *verb* [I or T] **-pp-** to cut something with scissors, usually with small quick cuts: *Have you seen the scissors? I want to snip **off** this loose thread.* ○ *I snipped **out** the article and gave it to her.*

S

snip /snɪp/ *noun* [C] a quick, short cut with scissors: *Give it a snip with the scissors.*

snip /snɪp/ *noun* UK INFORMAL HUMOROUS **the snip** a **vasectomy**

snip [CHEAP ITEM] /snɪp/ *noun* [S] UK INFORMAL **1** an item which is being sold cheaply, for less than you would expect: *The sunglasses are now available in major stores, **a** snip **at** £12 a pair.* **2** used humorously of an item which is extremely expensive: *"What did you say you got your dress for in the sale? – £350 reduced from £500?" "Yes, it was **a** snip!"*

snipe [SHOOT] /snaɪp/ *verb* [I] **1** to shoot at someone from a position where you cannot be seen: *The rebels have started sniping **at** civilians.* **2** to criticize someone unpleasantly: *The former minister has been making himself unpopular recently, sniping **at** his ex-colleagues.*

sniper /ˈsnaɪ.pəʳ/ [US] /-pɚ/ *noun* [C] someone who shoots at people from a place where they cannot be seen: *He was shot and fatally injured by a sniper.* ○ *Sniper fire has claimed countless lives these past few weeks.* **sniping** /ˈsnaɪ.pɪŋ/ *noun* [U]

snipe [BIRD] /snaɪp/ *noun* [C] *plural* **snipe** or **snipes** a bird with a long straight beak which lives near rivers and MARSHES (= low land that is wet and sometimes flooded)

snippet /ˈsnɪp.ɪt/ *noun* [C] INFORMAL a small and often interesting piece of news, information or conversation: *I heard an interesting snippet on the radio this morning.* ○ *I love listening to snippets **of** conversation in restaurants.*

snit /snɪt/ *noun* [C] US INFORMAL an angry mood: *He was **in** a snit this morning and I didn't dare approach him.*

snitch [TELL SECRETLY] /snɪtʃ/ *verb* [I] SLANG DISAPPROVING to secretly tell someone in authority that someone else has done something bad, often in order to cause trouble: *He snitched **to** my boss that I'd been making long-distance calls at work!* ○ *She's always snitching **on** someone.*
snitch /snɪtʃ/ *noun* [C] *You little snitch!*

snitch [STEAL] /snɪtʃ/ *verb* [T] INFORMAL to steal something: *"Where did you get that money?" "I snitched it **from** my dad when he wasn't looking."*

snivel /ˈsnɪv.əl/ *verb* [I] **-ll-** or US USUALLY **-l-** to cry slightly in a way that is weak and does not make other people feel sympathy for you: *He's sitting in his bedroom snivelling because he was told off for not doing his homework.*
snivelling, US USUALLY **sniveling** /ˈsnɪv.əl.ɪŋ/ *adj* OLD-FASHIONED INFORMAL used to describe someone whom you do not like because they are weak and unpleasant: *That snivelling creep/coward!*

snob /snɒb/ [US] /snɑːb/ *noun* [C] MAINLY DISAPPROVING a person who respects and likes only people who are of a high social class, and/or a person who has extremely high standards who is not satisfied by the things that ordinary people like: *He's a frightful snob – if you haven't been to the right school he probably won't even speak to you.* ○ *I'm afraid I'm a bit of a wine snob/a snob where wine is concerned.*
snobbish /ˈsnɒb.ɪʃ/ [US] /ˈsnɑː.bɪʃ/ *adj* (INFORMAL **snobby**) DISAPPROVING like a snob: *My brother is very snobbish **about** cars.*
snobbishly /ˈsnɒb.ɪʃ.li/ [US] /ˈsnɑː.bɪʃ-/ *adv* (ALSO **snobbily**) DISAPPROVING in a snobbish way
snobbery /ˈsnɒb.ər.i/ [US] /ˈsnɑː.bɚ-/ *noun* [U] (ALSO **snobbishness**) DISAPPROVING behaviour and opinions that are typical of a snob: *She accused me of snobbery because I sent my sons to a private school.*

snog /snɒg/ [US] /snɑːg/ *verb* [I or T] **-gg-** UK INFORMAL to kiss and hold a person in a sexual way: *I saw them snogging on the back seat of a bus.* ○ *I've never snogged **(with)** a man with a beard.* **snog** /snɒg/ [US] /snɑːg/ *noun* [C] *He caught us **having** a snog.*

snook /snuːk/ [US] /snʊk/ UK **cock a snook at *sb/sth*** ⊃See at **cock** SHOW LACK OF RESPECT.

snooker [GAME] /ˈsnuː.kəʳ/ [US] /-kɚ/ *noun* [U] a game played by two people in which CUES (= long thin poles) are used to hit 15 red balls and 6 balls of different colours into six holes around a cloth-covered table in a fixed order ⊃Compare **pool** GAME.

snooker [PREVENT] /ˈsnuː.kəʳ/ [US] /-kɚ/ *verb* [T] **1** UK to prevent someone from completing an intended plan of action: *We had intended to go driving around Scotland, but unless I can get my licence we're snookered.* **2** US to deceive or trick someone

snoop /snuːp/ *verb* [I usually + adv or prep] INFORMAL DISAPPROVING **1** to look around a place secretly, in order to discover things or find out information about someone or something: *People were sent out to snoop **on** rival businesses.* ○ *She's the sort of person you can imagine snooping **about/around** your room when you're not there.* **2** to try to find out about other people's private lives: *I don't mean to snoop, but is there something wrong?* ○ *Clara's husband is snooping **on** her because he thinks she is seeing another man.*
snoop /snuːp/ *noun* **1** [S] INFORMAL the act of snooping: *I think someone's been **having** a snoop around my office – I didn't leave that drawer open.* **2** [C] (ALSO **snooper**) INFORMAL DISAPPROVING someone who snoops: *He's such a snoop – he's always going through my mail.* ○ *Most journalists are snoopers by nature.*

snoot /snuːt/ *noun* [C] US SLANG a nose: *Keep your big snoot out of my business!*
• **stick *your* snoot in/into (*sth*)** US INFORMAL DISAPPROVING to try to discover things or influence events which are not really related to you to: *Stop sticking your snoot into other people's business!*

snooty /ˈsnuː.ti/ [US] /-t̬i/ *adj* INFORMAL behaving in an unfriendly way because you believe you are better than other people: *She was one of those really snooty sales assistants that you often find in expensive shops.* **snootily** /ˈsnuː.tɪ.li/ [US] /-t̬ɪ-/ *adv*

snooze /snuːz/ *verb* [I] INFORMAL to sleep lightly for a short while: *The dog's snoozing in front of the fire.*
snooze /snuːz/ *noun* [C] *I **had** a nice little snooze in the back of the car.*

ˈsnooze ˌbutton *noun* [C] a button on an ALARM CLOCK (= a clock for waking you up) that you press after it has woken you up, so that you can sleep for a few minutes more before being woken up again by the clock

snore /snɔːʳ/ [US] /snɔːr/ *verb* [I] to breathe in a very noisy way while you are sleeping: *Sometimes my husband snores so loudly, it keeps me awake at night.* ○ *Do you know any cures for snoring?*
snore /snɔːʳ/ [US] /snɔːr/ *noun* [C] a very noisy breath while you are sleeping: *I could hear loud snores coming from Jim's bedroom.* **snorer** /ˈsnɔː.rəʳ/ [US] /ˈsnɔːr.ɚ/ *noun* [C] *He's a terrible snorer.*

snorkel /ˈsnɔː.kəl/ [US] /ˈsnɔːr-/ *noun* [C] (AUS ALSO **schnorkel**) a tube that you hold in your mouth to help you breathe if you are swimming with your face under water
snorkelling UK, US **snorkeling** /ˈsnɔː.kəl.ɪŋ/ [US] /ˈsnɔːr-/ *noun* [U] the activity of swimming while using a snorkel: *We **went** snorkelling along the Great Barrier Reef.*

snort /snɔːt/ [US] /snɔːrt/ *verb* **1** [I] to make an explosive sound by forcing air quickly up or down the nose: *He did an impression of a horse snorting.* ○ *Camille snorts when she laughs.* ○ INFORMAL *By this time I was snorting **with** laughter* (= laughing a lot and loudly). **2** [T] to take an illegal drug by breathing it in through the nose: *People were snorting **cocaine** in the toilets.* **3** [T] to suddenly express strong feelings of annoyance, disapproval or dissatisfaction, either by speaking or in a sound that you make: *"And you call that a first class service?" snorted one indignant customer.*
snort /snɔːt/ [US] /snɔːrt/ *noun* [C] a loud sound made by forcing air through the nose: *The minister's speech drew loud snorts of derisive laughter.*

snot [MUCUS] /snɒt/ [US] /snɑːt/ *noun* [U] INFORMAL mucus produced in the nose
snotty /ˈsnɒt.i/ [US] /ˈsnɑː.t̬i/ *adj* INFORMAL covered with mucus from the nose: *You could have told me I had a snotty nose!* ○ *I don't want to use your snotty handkerchief!*

snot [PERSON] /snɒt/ [US] /snɑːt/ *noun* [C] US INFORMAL DISAPPROVING a person who behaves badly and whom you do not like: *Amber is such a snot!*
snotty /ˈsnɒt.i/ [US] /ˈsnɑː.t̬i/ *adj* US INFORMAL DISAPPROVING rude and behaving badly: *a snotty teenager* ○ *She was so snotty to me!*

S

snotty /ˈsnɒt.i/ ⓤ /ˈsnɑː.t̬i/ *adj UK INFORMAL DISAPPROVING* tending to behave rudely to other people in a way that shows that you believe yourself to be better than them: *The only difficult bit about working in a shop is when you get a snotty customer that you have to deal with.*

snout /snaʊt/ *noun* [C] **1** the nose and mouth which stick out from the face of some animals: *a pig's snout* **2** *SLANG FOR* a person's nose: *George has an enormous snout.*

snow [WEATHER] /snəʊ/ ⓤ /snoʊ/ *noun* **1** [U] the small soft white bits of ice which sometimes fall from the sky when it is cold, or the white layer on the ground and other surfaces which it forms: *Outside the snow began to fall.* ○ *Let's go and play in the snow!* ○ *A blanket of snow lay on the ground.* ○ *Her hair was jet-black, her lips ruby-red and her skin as white as snow.* **2** [C] a single fall of snow: *We haven't had many heavy snows this winter.*

snow /snəʊ/ ⓤ /snoʊ/ *verb* [I] If it snows, snow falls from the sky: *It's snowing.* ○ *It's starting to snow.* ○ *It had snowed overnight and a thick white layer covered the ground.*

• **be snowed in** to be unable to travel away from a place because of very heavy snow: *We were snowed in for four days last winter.*

• **be snowed under (with sth)** to have so much work that you have problems dealing with it all: *I'm absolutely snowed under with work at the moment.*

snowy /ˈsnəʊ.i/ ⓤ /ˈsnoʊ-/ *adj* full of or like snow: *We've had a very snowy winter this year.* ○ *I remember him as an old man with a snowy-white* (= pure white) *beard.*

snow [CHARM] /snəʊ/ ⓤ /snoʊ/ *verb* [T] *US INFORMAL* to deceive or trick someone by charming and persuasive talk or by giving them a lot of information: *She always snowing the bosses with statistics.*

snow [DRUG] /snəʊ/ ⓤ /snoʊ/ *noun* [U] *SLANG* **cocaine**

snowball /ˈsnəʊ.bɔːl/ ⓤ /ˈsnoʊ.bɑːl/ *noun* [C] a ball of snow pressed together in the hands, especially for throwing

• **not have a snowball's chance in hell** *INFORMAL* to have no chance of succeeding: *If he can't afford a good lawyer, he doesn't have a snowball's chance in hell of winning the case.*

snowball /ˈsnəʊ.bɔːl/ ⓤ /ˈsnoʊ.bɑːl/ *verb* [I] If a plan, problem, idea, etc. snowballs, it quickly grows bigger and more important: *I suggested a few drinks after work, and the whole thing snowballed into a company party.*

'snow ˌbank *noun* [C] *MAINLY US* a large pile of snow ⊃See also **snowdrift**.

'snow ˌblindness *noun* [U] a temporary loss of sight which is caused by the brightness of light reflected by large areas of snow or ice **snow-blind** /ˈsnəʊ.blaɪnd/ ⓤ /ˈsnoʊ-/ *adj*: *Halfway up the mountain I suddenly went snow-blind.*

snowboard /ˈsnəʊ.bɔːd/ ⓤ /ˈsnoʊ.bɔːrd/ *verb* [I] to slide on the snow by standing on a specially shaped board: *I'm learning to snowboard at the moment.* ○ *Snowboard parks are becoming more popular.*

snowboard /ˈsnəʊ.bɔːd/ ⓤ /ˈsnoʊ.bɔːrd/ *noun* [C] a specially shaped board that you stand on to slide down a snow-covered slope **snowboarder** /ˈsnəʊ.bɔː.də/ ⓤ /ˈsnoʊ.bɔːr.də-/ *noun* [C]

snowboarding /ˈsnəʊ.bɔː.dɪŋ/ ⓤ /ˈsnoʊ.bɔːr-/ *noun* [U] the activity or sport of moving over snow using a snowboard

snowbound /ˈsnəʊ.baʊnd/ ⓤ /ˈsnoʊ-/ *adj* (of vehicles or people) unable to travel because of heavy snow, or (of roads) not able to be travelled on or reached because of heavy snow: *Hundreds of vehicles have become snowbound and police are warning people not to travel on this stretch of the motorway.*

snow-capped /ˈsnəʊ.kæpt/ ⓤ /ˈsnoʊ-/ *adj* Snow-capped mountains and hills have snow on the top of them.

snowdrift /ˈsnəʊ.drɪft/ ⓤ /ˈsnoʊ-/ *noun* [C] a large pile of snow formed by the wind

snowdrop /ˈsnəʊ.drɒp/ ⓤ /ˈsnoʊ.drɑːp/ *noun* [C] a plant which produces small white bell-shaped flowers in the early spring ⊃See picture **Flowers and Plants** on page Centre 3

snowfall /ˈsnəʊ.fɔːl/ ⓤ /ˈsnoʊ.fɑːl/ *noun* [C or U] the amount of snow that falls in a particular area during a particular period, or a fall of snow: *The annual snowfall for this region is 30 centimetres.* ○ *Heavy snowfalls are predicted for tonight and tomorrow.*

snowflake /ˈsnəʊ.fleɪk/ ⓤ /ˈsnoʊ-/ *noun* [C] a small piece of snow

snow-job /ˈsnəʊ.dʒɒb/ ⓤ /ˈsnoʊ.dʒɑːb/ *noun* [C] *MAINLY US INFORMAL* an attempt to persuade someone to do something, especially by praising them and using charm: *My boss did a snow-job on me.*

snowline /ˈsnəʊ.laɪn/ ⓤ /ˈsnoʊ-/ *noun* **the snowline** the level on a mountain above which snow is found for most or all of the year: *above/below the snowline*

snowman /ˈsnəʊ.mæn/ ⓤ /ˈsnoʊ-/ *noun* [C] a model of a person made of snow, especially by children

snowmobile /ˈsnəʊ.mə.biːl/ ⓤ /ˈsnoʊ-/ *noun* [C] a small motor vehicle for travelling on snow and ice

'snow ˌpea *noun* [C] *US FOR* **mangetout**

snowplough [VEHICLE] *UK, US* **snowplow** /ˈsnəʊ.plaʊ/ ⓤ /ˈsnoʊ-/ *noun* [C] a vehicle or device for removing snow from roads or railways

snowplough [SPORT] *UK, US* **snowplow** /ˈsnəʊ.plaʊ/ ⓤ /ˈsnoʊ-/ *noun* [C usually sing] in skiing, a simple way of turning or stopping in which the points of the skis are turned toward each other

snowshoe /ˈsnəʊ.ʃuː/ ⓤ /ˈsnoʊ-/ *noun* [C] a flat frame with straps of material stretched across it which can be fixed to a boot to allow a person to walk on snow without sinking in

snowstorm /ˈsnəʊ.stɔːm/ ⓤ /ˈsnoʊ.stɔːrm/ *noun* [C] a heavy fall of snow which is blown by strong winds

snowsuit /ˈsnəʊ.suːt/ ⓤ /ˈsnoʊ-/ *noun* [C] an item of winter clothing for a child which is warm and covers most of the body

'snow ˌtyre *UK noun* [C] (*US* **snow tire**) a tyre with a pattern of raised lines which are thicker than usual in order to stop a vehicle from sliding on ice or snow

snow-white /ˌsnəʊˈwaɪt/ ⓤ /ˌsnoʊ-/ *adj* pure white: *snow-white hair/fur*

snowy /ˈsnəʊ.i/ ⓤ /ˈsnoʊ-/ *adj* ⊃See at **snow** WEATHER.

Snr *UK adj* [after n] (*US* **Sr**) *WRITTEN ABBREVIATION FOR* **senior** OLDER, used after a man's name to refer to the older of two people in the same family who have the same name

snub /snʌb/ *verb* [T] **-bb-** to insult someone by not giving them any attention or treating them as if they are not important: *I think she felt snubbed because Anthony hadn't bothered to introduce himself.* **snub** /snʌb/ *noun* [C] *I simply didn't recognize her and apparently she took it as a snub.*

snub ˌnose *noun* [C] a nose that is short and turns upwards at the end

snub-nosed /ˌsnʌbˈnəʊzd/ ⓤ /-ˈnoʊzd/ *adj* **1** describes a nose which is short and turns up at the end **2** describes a gun that has a very short barrel: *a snub-nosed revolver*

snuck /snʌk/ *MAINLY US* past simple and past participle of **sneak** MOVE SECRETLY.

snuff [POWDER] /snʌf/ *noun* [U] tobacco in the form of a powder for breathing into the nose: *Very few people take snuff nowadays.*

snuff [PUT OUT] /snʌf/ *verb* [T] to put out a flame, especially from a candle, usually by covering it with something: *One by one she snuffed the candles.*

• **snuff it** *MAINLY UK INFORMAL* to die

▲ **snuff sth out** *phrasal verb* [M] **1** *INFORMAL* to cause something to end suddenly: *The country has been able to celebrate the return of its independence so brutally snuffed out in 1940.* **2** to put out a flame, especially from a candle: *One by one she snuffed out the candles.*

▲ **snuff sb out** *phrasal verb* [M] *US SLANG* to kill someone

snuffle /ˈsnʌf.l̩/ *verb* [I], *noun* [C] **sniffle**

'snuff ˌmovie *noun* [C] (*UK ALSO* **snuff film**) *INFORMAL* a violent PORNOGRAPHIC film (= sex film) in which one of the actors or actresses is murdered

snug /snʌg/ *adj* **snugger**, **snuggest** **1** (of a person) feeling warm, comfortable and protected, or (of a place, especially a small place) giving feelings of warmth, comfort and protection: *We curled up in bed, all snug and warm,* *and listened to the storm outside.* ○ *I bet your feet are nice and snug in your fur-lined boots!* **2** fitting closely: *These shoes are a bit too snug – do you have them in a larger size?*

snugly /ˈsnʌg.li/ *adv*: *She's curled up snugly in the armchair, reading a book.* ○ *If we put the washing machine over there the fridge will **fit** snugly* (= closely) *into this space.*

snug /snʌg/ *noun* [C] (*ALSO* **snuggery**) *UK* a small room or enclosed area in a pub where only a few people can sit

snuggle /ˈsnʌg.l̩/ *verb* [I usually + adv or prep] to move yourself into a warm and comfortable position, especially one in which your body is against another person or covered by something: *The children snuggled **up** to their mother to get warm.* ○ *I was just snuggling **down** into my warm duvet when the telephone rang.*

so VERY /səʊ/ *US* /soʊ/ *adv* **1** very, extremely, or to such a degree: *The house is so beautiful.* ○ *Thank you for being so patient.* ○ *Don't be so stupid!* ○ *I didn't know she had so many children!* ○ *You can only do so much to help* (= There is a limit to how much you can help). ○ *UK INFORMAL She's **ever** so kind and nice.* ○ *I'm so tired **(that)** I could sleep in this chair!* ○ *I'm **not** so desperate **as to** agree to that.* ○ *The word itself is so rare **as to be** almost obsolete.* ○ *I've never been to so expensive **a** restaurant* (= such an expensive restaurant) *before.* **2** *MAINLY US NOT STANDARD* used before a noun or before 'not' to emphasize that something is being said: *Don't wear that – it's so last year* (= it was fashionable last year but not now). ○ *I'm sorry, but she is so **not** a size 10* (= she is very much larger than a size 10). **3** used at the end of a sentence to mean to a very great degree: *Is that why you hate him so?* ○ *You worry so!*

so SAME WAY /səʊ/ *US* /soʊ/ *adv* used usually before the verbs 'have', 'be' or 'do', and other AUXILIARY VERBS to express the meaning 'in the same way' or 'in a similar way': *"I've got an enormous amount of work to do." "So have I."* ○ *"I'm allergic to nuts." "So is my brother."* ○ *Neil left just after midnight and so did Roz.* ○ *Just **as** you like to have a night out with the lads, so I like to go out with the girls now and again.*

so SENTENCE BEGINNING /səʊ/ *US* /soʊ/ *conjunction* **1** used at the beginning of a sentence to connect it with something that has been said or has happened previously: *So, there I was standing at the edge of the road with only my underwear on ...* ○ *So, just to finish what I was saying earlier...* **2** used as a way of making certain that you or someone else understand something correctly, often when you are repeating the important points of a plan: *So we leave on the Thursday and get back the next Tuesday, is that right?* **3** used to refer to a discovery that you have just made: *So that's what he does when I'm not around!* **4** used as a brief pause, sometimes to emphasize what you are saying: *So, here we are again – just you and me.* **5** used before you introduce a subject of conversation that is of present interest, especially when you are asking a question: *So, who do you think is going to win the election?* **6** *INFORMAL* used to show that you agree with something that someone has just said, but you do not think that it is important: *So the car's expensive – well, I can afford it.*

• **So what?** *INFORMAL* used to mean 'it's not important' and 'I don't care': *So what if I'm 35 and I'm not married – I lead a perfectly fulfilling life!* ○ *"Andrew won't like it, you know." "So what? – I don't care what Andrew thinks!"*

so IN ORDER THAT /səʊ/ *US* /soʊ/ *conjunction, adv* used before you give an explanation for the action that you have just mentioned: [+ **(that)**] *I deliberately didn't have lunch so **(that)** I would be hungry tonight.* ○ *Leave the keys out so **(that)** I remember to take them with me.*

• **so as to** in order to: *I always keep fruit in the fridge so as to keep insects off it.*

so THEREFORE /səʊ/ *US* /soʊ/ *conjunction* and for that reason; therefore: *My knee started hurting so I stopped running.* ○ *I was lost so I bought a street map.*

• **so there** *INFORMAL HUMOROUS* used for emphasis, or to show that something is being done in opposition to someone else's wishes: *Mine's bigger than yours, so there!* ○ *No, I won't help you, so there!*

so MENTIONED EARLIER /səʊ/ *US* /soʊ/ *adv* **1** used to avoid repeating a phrase mentioned earlier: *"I hope they stay together." "I hope so too."* ○ *"Do you think he's upset?" "I don't think so."* ○ *James is coming tonight, or so he said.* **2** used to say that a situation mentioned earlier is correct or true: *"Is it true that we're not getting a pay increase this year?" "I'm afraid so."* ○ *"Anthony and Mia don't get on very well." "Is that so?"* ○ *"The forecast says it might rain." "If so we'll have the party inside."* **3** used to give certainty to a fact that has just been stated: *"My eyes are slightly different colours." "So they are."* ○ *"That's her brother – he looks like James Dean." "So he does."* **4** used instead of repeating an adjective that has already been mentioned: *She's quite reasonable to work with – more so than I was led to believe.* ○ *He's quite bright – well, certainly more so than his brother.* **5** *US CHILD'S WORD* used, especially by children, to argue against a negative statement: *"You didn't even see the movie." "I did so!"*

so IN THIS WAY /səʊ/ *US* /soʊ/ *adv* **1** in this way; like this: *The pillars, which are outside the building, are so placed in order to provide the maximum space inside.* ○ *I've so arranged my trip that I'll be home on Friday evening.* **2** used when you are showing how something is done: *Just fold this piece of paper back, so, and make a crease here.* ○ *Gently fold in the eggs **like** so.* **3** used when you are representing the size of something: *"How tall is he next to you?" "Oh, about so big," she said, indicating the level of her neck.* ○ *"The table that I liked best was about so wide," she said, holding her arms out a metre and a half.*

so TIDY /səʊ/ *US* /soʊ/ *adj* **just/exactly so** perfectly tidy and well arranged: *He's a perfectionist – everything has to be just so.*

soak MAKE WET /səʊk/ *US* /soʊk/ *verb* **1** [I + adv or prep; T] to make very wet, or (of liquid) to be absorbed in large amounts: *The wind had blown the rain in and soaked the carpet.* ○ *You'd better wipe up that red wine you've spilt before it soaks* (= is absorbed) ***into** the carpet.* ○ *Blood had soaked **through** both bandages.* **2** [I or T] to leave something in liquid, especially in order to clean it, soften it, or change its flavour: *You can usually soak **out** a stain.* ○ *Leave the beans **to** soak overnight./Let the beans soak overnight.* ○ *Soak the fruit **in** brandy for a few hours before you add it to the mixture.*

soak /səʊk/ *US* /soʊk/ *noun* [C] when something is put into a liquid for a long period of time: *Most dried beans need a soak before they're cooked.* ○ *Showers are all right but there's nothing like a good long soak in the bath.*

soaked /səʊkt/ *US* /soʊkt/ *adj* extremely wet: *I'm going to have to take these clothes off – I'm soaked **to the skin**!* ○ *My shoes are soaked **(through)**.* ○ *His T-shirt was soaked **in** sweat.*

soaking /ˈsəʊ.kɪŋ/ *US* /ˈsoʊ-/ *adj* completely wet: *It's so hot outside – I've only been walking ten minutes and my shirt is soaking **(wet)**!*

soak PERSON /səʊk/ *US* /soʊk/ *noun* [C] *OLD-FASHIONED INFORMAL* a person who is habitually drunk

---

PHRASAL VERBS WITH soak ▼

▲ **soak sth up** LIQUID *phrasal verb* [M] If a dry material or substance soaks up a liquid, it absorbs the liquid through its surface: *I tried to soak up most of the spilt milk with a cloth.*

▲ **soak sth up** EXPERIENCE *phrasal verb* [M] to enjoy the effects or experience of something as much as possible: *I love to lie on the beach and soak up **the sun**.* ○ *Just stroll around the bazaar and soak up **the atmosphere**.*

▲ **soak sth up** INFORMATION *phrasal verb* [M] *INFORMAL* to understand and remember information well: *Given the right environment, children are like sponges and will soak up information.*

▲ **soak sth up** SUPPLY *phrasal verb* [M] to use up all or most of a supply of something, especially a supply of money: *The repairs on our house soaked up all our savings.*

so-and-so PERSON NOT NAMED /ˈsəʊ.ənd.səʊ/ *US* /ˈsoʊ.ənd.soʊ/ *noun* [U] *INFORMAL* used instead of a particular name to refer to someone or something, especially when the real name is not important or you have forgotten it: *She always keeps me up to date with the latest gossip – you know, so-and-so from down the road is having a baby and so-and-so's just bought a car.*

so-and-so UNPLEASANT PERSON /ˈsəʊ.ənd.səʊ/ US /ˈsoʊ.ənd.soʊ/ *noun* [C] *INFORMAL* a polite way of referring to an unpleasant person: *Mr Baker was such a so-and-so – he didn't have a pleasant word to say about anyone!*

soap /səʊp/ US /soʊp/ *noun* [C or U] a substance used for washing the body which is usually hard, often has a pleasant smell, and produces a mass of bubbles when rubbed with water, or a piece of this: *a **bar** of soap* ○ *liquid soap* ○ *soap and water* ○ *a soap dish/dispenser* ○ *soap bubbles* ○ *She bought me a box of prettily coloured soaps.*

soap /səʊp/ US /soʊp/ *verb* [T] to put soap on something: *Have you soaped yourself all over, Alice?* ○ *Let me soap your back.*

soapy /ˈsəʊ.pi/ US /ˈsoʊ-/ *adj* containing or like soap: *I soaked it in some soapy water and the stains came out.* ○ *I used to think avocados tasted soapy when I was a child.*

soapbox /ˈsəʊp.bɒks/ US /ˈsoʊp.bɑːks/ *noun* [C] a rough wooden box or any raised temporary platform for people to stand on while making informal public speeches

● **get on *your* soapbox** *INFORMAL* to express your opinions about a particular subject forcefully: *She never misses the chance to get on her soapbox **about** government reform.*

soap flakes *plural noun* small flat pieces of soap used for washing clothes, especially by hand: *a box of soap flakes*

soap opera *noun* [C] (*INFORMAL* **soap**) a series of television or radio programmes about the lives and problems of a particular group of characters. The series continues over a long period and is broadcast (several times) every week.

soapstone /ˈsəʊp.stəʊn/ US /ˈsoʊp.stoʊn/ *noun* [U] a soft stone which feels slightly oily

soapsuds /ˈsəʊp.sʌdz/ US /ˈsoʊp-/ *plural noun* (*ALSO* **suds**) the mass of small bubbles that form on the surface of soapy water

soar RISE QUICKLY /sɔːʳ/ US /sɔːr/ *verb* **1** [I usually + adv or prep] to rise very quickly to a high level: *All night long fireworks soared into the sky.* ○ *Temperatures will soar into the eighties over the weekend say the weather forecasters.* ○ *House prices had soared a further twenty per cent.* **2** [T] to reach an impressive height: *The highest peak in the range soars 15,771 feet into the sky.* **soaring** /ˈsɔː.rɪŋ/ US /ˈsɔːr.ɪŋ/ *adj* *soaring property prices*

soar FLY /sɔːʳ/ US /sɔːr/ *verb* [I] (of a bird or aircraft) to rise high in the air while flying without moving the wings or using power: *She watched the gliders soaring effortlessly above her.*

sob /sɒb/ US /sɑːb/ *verb* [I] **-bb-** to cry noisily, taking in deep breaths: *I found her sobbing in the bedroom because she'd broken her favourite doll.* ○ *You're not going to help matters by lying there sobbing!*

● **sob *your* heart out** to cry very much

sob /sɒb/ US /sɑːb/ *noun* [C] an act or sound of sobbing: *I could hear her sobs from the next room.*

S.O.B. /ˌes.əʊ'biː/ US /-oʊ-/ *noun* [C usually sing] *ABBREVIATION FOR* **son of a bitch**

sober NOT DRUNK /ˈsəʊ.bəʳ/ US /ˈsoʊ.bɚ/ *adj* not drunk or affected by alcohol: *Are you sober enough to drive, Jim?* ○ *I'd had no wine all evening so I was **stone cold** (= completely) sober.*

sobriety /səˈbraɪ.ɪ.ti/ US /-ə.ti/ *noun* [U] *FORMAL* the state of being sober: *US The police said his car had been weaving all over the road, so they pulled him over and gave him a sobriety **test**.*

sober SERIOUS /ˈsəʊ.bəʳ/ US /ˈsoʊ.bɚ/ *adj* serious and calm: *In fact the whole wedding was a sober affair – no dancing, just people standing around in groups chatting politely.* ○ *Anthony was in a very sober mood – I scarcely heard him laugh all night.*

sober /ˈsəʊ.bəʳ/ US /ˈsoʊ.bɚ/ *verb* [I or T] to become more calm and serious, or to make someone do this: *News of the tragedy has sobered us.*

soberly /ˈsəʊ.bᵊl.i/ US /ˈsoʊ.bɚ.li/ *adv* seriously and reasonably: *She was dressed very soberly in a plain grey suit.*

sobering /ˈsəʊ.bᵊr.ɪŋ/ US /ˈsoʊ.bɚ-/ *adj* making you feel serious or think about serious matters: *a sobering thought* ○ *Surviving a car accident is a sobering experience.*

sobriety /səˈbraɪ.ɪ.ti/ US /-ə.ti/ *noun* [U] *FORMAL* seriousness: *We had the priest sitting at our table which instilled a little sobriety into the occasion.*

▲ **sober (sb) up** *phrasal verb* to become less drunk, or to make someone become less drunk: *I went for a walk to try to sober up.* ○ *Have a black coffee – that should sober you up!*

sobriquet, soubriquet /ˈsəʊ.brɪ.keɪ/ US /ˈsoʊ-/ *noun* [C] *FORMAL* a name given to someone or something which is not their real or official name; *NICKNAME*: *These charms have earned the television programme's presenter the sobriquet 'the thinking woman's crumpet'.*

sob story *noun* [C] *INFORMAL DISAPPROVING* a story or piece of information that someone tells you or writes about themselves which is intended to make you feel sad and sympathetic towards them: *She came out with some sob story about not having enough money to go and see her father who was ill.*

so-called /ˌsəʊˈkɔːld/ US /ˌsoʊˈkɑːld/ *adj* [before n] **1** used to show that you think a word that is used to describe someone or something is not suitable or not correct: *It was one of his so-called friends who supplied him with the drugs that killed him.* **2** used to introduce a new word or phrase which is not yet known by many people: *It isn't yet clear how destructive this so-called 'super virus' is.*

soccer /ˈsɒk.əʳ/ US /ˈsɑː.kɚ/ *noun* [U] (*UK ALSO* **football**) a game played between two teams of eleven people, where each team tries to win by kicking a ball into the other team's goal ➔See picture **Sports** on page Centre 10

social /ˈsəʊ.ʃᵊl/ US /ˈsoʊ-/ *adj* relating to activities in which you meet and spend time with other people and which happen during the time when you are not working: *I had an active social **life** when I was at college.* ○ *I'm a social drinker – I only drink when I'm with other people.* ○ *Most British schools organize social events for the students.* ○ *I've just become a member of the company's sports and social club.* ➔See also **social** at **society** PEOPLE. **socially** /ˈsəʊ.ʃᵊl.i/ US /ˈsoʊ-/ *adv*: *I chat to him at work now and then but I've never seen him socially.* ○ *Socially, she's a disaster – she's always offending someone or picking a fight.* ○ *Socially they're a great company to work for – I've never been to so many parties in my life.*

social /ˈsəʊ.ʃᵊl/ US /ˈsoʊ-/ *noun* [C] *OLD-FASHIONED* an occasion when the members of a group or organization meet informally to enjoy themselves: *a church social*

sociable /ˈsəʊ.ʃə.bl̩/ US /ˈsoʊ-/ *adj* *APPROVING* describes someone who likes to meet and spend time with other people: *Rob's very sociable – he likes his parties.* ○ *I had a headache and I wasn't feeling very sociable.* ✳ NOTE: The opposite is **unsociable**.

socialite /ˈsəʊ.ʃᵊl.aɪt/ US /ˈsoʊ.ʃə.laɪt/ *noun* [C] a person, usually of high social class, who is famous because they go to a lot of parties and social events which are reported in the newspapers: *a wealthy socialite*

socialize, *UK USUALLY* **-ise** /ˈsəʊ.ʃᵊl.aɪz/ US /ˈsoʊ.ʃə.laɪz/ *verb* [I] to spend the time, when you are not working, with friends or other people in order to enjoy yourself: *I tend not to socialize **with** my colleagues.* ○ *I hope Adrian's actually doing some work at college – he seems to spend all his time socializing!*

social climber *noun* [C] *DISAPPROVING* someone who tries to improve their social position by being very friendly to people from a higher social class

social conscience *noun* [U] If you have a social conscience, you worry about people who are poor, ill, old, etc. and try to help them.

Social Democrat *noun* [C] a member of the Social Democratic Party

Social Democratic Party *noun* [U] a political party which existed in Britain from 1981-1990

social engin'eering noun [U] the artificial controlling or changing of the groups within society

socialism /ˈsəʊ.ʃªl.ɪ.zªm/ ⑩ /ˈsoʊ-/ noun [U] the set of beliefs which states that all people are equal and should share equally in the wealth of the country, or the political systems based on these beliefs ⊃Compare **capitalism**; **communism**. **socialist** /ˈsəʊ.ʃªl.ɪst/ ⑩ /ˈsoʊ-/ adj, noun [C] socialist policies ○ He was a socialist all his life.

socialized 'medicine noun [U] US medical services provided or paid for by the government for anyone who needs them

social 'science noun [C or U] the study of society and the way people live

social se'curity noun [U] UK a system of payments made by the government to people who are ill, poor or who have no job: He's **on** social security.

Social Se'curity noun [U] US a system of payments made by the government to old people, people whose husbands or wives have died and people who are unable to work because they are ill

social 'services plural noun (ALSO **social service**) services provided by local or national government to help people who are old or ill or need support in their lives

social 'worker noun [U] a person who works for the social services or for a private organization providing help and support for people who need it **'social ,work** noun [U]

society PEOPLE /səˈsaɪ.ə.ti/ ⑩ /-ṭi/ noun **1** [C or U] a large group of people who live together in an organized way, making decisions about how to do things and sharing the work that needs to be done. All the people in a country, or in several similar countries, can be referred to as a society: a classless/multicultural/capitalist/ civilized society ○ These changes strike at the heart of British/American/modern society. ○ There's a danger that we will end up blaming innocent children for society's problems. ○ We must also consider the needs of the younger/older **members of** society. **2** [U] (ALSO **high society**) the part of society that consists of people who are rich, powerful and fashionable: a society hostess/ ball/function **3** [U] FORMAL the state of being together with other people: She prefers her own society (= likes to be alone).

social /ˈsəʊ.ʃªl/ ⑩ /ˈsoʊ-/ adj [before n] relating to society and living together in an organized way: social classes/ groups ○ social disorder/trends/change/equality/ justice/differences ○ Monkeys are highly social **animals**. ⊃See also **social**. **socially** /ˈsəʊ.ʃªl.i/ ⑩ /ˈsoʊ-/ adv: Drinking and driving is no longer socially acceptable. ○ Private education is often regarded as socially divisive.

socialize, UK USUALLY -**ise** /ˈsəʊ.ʃªl.aɪz/ ⑩ /ˈsoʊ.ʃə.laɪz/ verb [T] to train people or animals to behave in a way that others in the group think is suitable: Here at the special school we make every effort to socialize these young offenders. **socialization**, UK USUALLY -**isation** /ˌsəʊ.ʃªl.aɪˈzeɪ.ʃªn/ ⑩ /ˌsoʊ.ʃªl.ɪ-/ noun [U]

society ORGANIZATION /səˈsaɪ.ə.ti/ ⑩ /-ṭi/ noun [C] an organization to which people who share similar interests can belong: an amateur dramatic society ○ the Royal Society for the Protection of Birds

---

COMMON LEARNER ERROR

society or **company**?

Society is only used to mean an organization of people with similar interests.

the Edingsford Village Drama Society

Company is the correct word for a business organization which produces something, provides a service, etc.

I work for a large company.
~~I work for a large society.~~

---

socioeconomic /ˌsəʊ.si.əʊˌek.əˈnɒm.ɪk/ ⑩ /ˌsoʊ.si.oʊˌiː.-kəˈnɑː.mɪk/ adj related to the differences between groups of people caused mainly by their financial situation: socioeconomic groups/groupings ○ socioeconomic factors ○ College Board officials said the difficulties arise more from socioeconomic than from ethnic differences. **socioeconomically** /ˌsəʊ.si.əʊˌek.əˈnɒm.ɪ.kli/ ⑩ /ˌsoʊ.si.oʊˌiː.kəˈnɑː.mɪ-/ adv

sociology /ˌsəʊ.siˈɒl.ə.dʒi/ ⑩ /ˌsoʊ.siˈɑː.lə-/ noun [U] the study of the relationships between people living in groups, especially in industrial societies: She has a degree in sociology and politics. ○ He specializes in the sociology **of** education/law/the family.

sociological /ˌsəʊ.si.əˈlɒdʒ.ɪ.kªl/ ⑩ /ˌsoʊ.si.əˈlɑː.dʒɪ-/ adj related to or involving sociology: sociological theory/ research **sociologically** /ˌsəʊ.si.əˈlɒdʒ.ɪ.kli/ ⑩ /ˌsoʊ.si.ə-ˈlɑː.dʒɪ-/ adv

sociologist /ˌsəʊ.siˈɒl.ə.dʒɪst/ ⑩ /ˌsoʊ.siˈɑː.lə-/ noun [C] someone who studies or is an expert in sociology

sociopath /ˈsəʊ.si.əʊ.pæθ/ ⑩ /ˈsoʊ.si.ə-/ noun [C] a person who is completely unable or unwilling to behave in a way that is acceptable to society: I'm telling you he's a complete/total sociopath.

sock CLOTHES /sɒk/ ⑩ /sɑːk/ noun [C] plural **socks** or US ALSO **sox** a piece of clothing made from soft material which covers your bare foot and lower part of the leg: a pair of socks ○ nylon/woollen/cotton socks ○ thermal socks ○ ankle/knee socks ○ Put on your **shoes and** socks. ○ The little boy was wearing odd/(US USUALLY) **mismatched** socks (= socks of different colours). ⊃See picture **Clothes** on page Centre 6

● **Put a sock in it!** INFORMAL HUMOROUS used to tell someone to be quiet or stop making so much noise: Hey, put a sock in it, will you? I'm trying to work here.

sock HIT /sɒk/ ⑩ /sɑːk/ verb [T] **1** OLD-FASHIONED SLANG to hit someone with your fist: He socked the policeman **on** the jaw/**in** the eye. **2** US in baseball, to hit a ball very powerfully

● **get socked with sth** MAINLY US to suddenly receive a lot of something which causes you problems: If you don't pay your credit card bill on time, you'll get socked with a huge late fee.

sock /sɒk/ ⑩ /sɑːk/ noun [C usually sing] OLD-FASHIONED SLANG a powerful hit: a sock **on** the jaw

▲ **sock sth away** phrasal verb [M] US INFORMAL to save money by putting it in a bank or by investing it: He's socked away hundreds of dollars in a savings account over the last six months.

socket /ˈsɒk.ɪt/ ⑩ /ˈsɑː.kɪt/ noun [C] **1** the part of a piece of equipment, especially electrical equipment, into which another part fits: an electrical socket ○ a light socket ○ He had forgotten to plug the television into the **wall**/(UK) **mains** socket. ○ The air freshener plugs into a car's **lighter** socket. **2** a part of the body into which another part fits: a **tooth**/**eye** socket ○ a **ball-and**-socket joint like the hip joint

socket ,set noun [C] a set of metal tools of different sizes, which fix onto one handle and are used to fasten and unfasten nuts on pieces of equipment

sod UNPLEASANT /sɒd/ ⑩ /sɑːd/ noun [C] **1** UK OFFENSIVE something or someone considered unpleasant or difficult: Apparently he's a sod to work for. ○ What did you do that for, you stupid sod? ○ It was a sod of a car to repair. **2** UK OFFENSIVE used to show that you think that someone has done better than they should: He's won again – the lucky sod! **3** UK INFORMAL used to or about someone that you feel sympathy for: The poor old sod – I don't suppose he's got a home.

● **not care/give a sod** UK OFFENSIVE to not be worried about other people's opinions or actions: I'm leaving and I don't give a sod **(about)** what Margaret thinks. ○ She doesn't care a sod about her reputation.

sod /sɒd/ ⑩ /sɑːd/ exclamation (ALSO **Sod it!**) UK OFFENSIVE used to express annoyance: Oh sod it – I've left my glasses behind!

sodding /ˈsɒd.ɪŋ/ ⑩ /ˈsɑː.dɪŋ/ adj [before n] UK OFFENSIVE used to express annoyance: Stupid sodding thing, why won't it move?

sod GRASS /sɒd/ ⑩ /sɑːd/ noun [S] **1** SPECIALIZED a rectangular piece which has been cut from an area of grass: He worked fast, cutting and slicing the turf neatly, heaving the sod to one side. **2** LITERARY soil or earth: She sleeps beneath the sod (= She is dead and has been buried).

sod /sɒd/ [US] /sɑːd/ *verb*
▲ **sod off** *phrasal verb* [not continuous] *UK OFFENSIVE* to go away: *Oh sod off, you stupid git!* ○ *She told him to sod off.*

ˌ**sod ˈall** *noun UK OFFENSIVE* nothing: *Ann's just been chatting on the phone all morning – she's done sod all.*

ˈ**soda (ˌpop)** *noun* [C] *US* any type of sweet fizzy drink which is not alcoholic

ˈ**soda ˌsiphon** *noun* [C] a bottle for filling water with gas and forcing it out under pressure to use in drinks

ˈ**soda (ˌwater)** *noun* [C or U] (*US ALSO* **club soda**) a type of fizzy water, often mixed with alcoholic drinks

sodden /ˈsɒd.ᵊn/ [US] /ˈsɑː.dᵊn/ *adj* (of something which can absorb water) extremely wet: *The football pitch was absolutely sodden.* ○ *Her thin coat quickly became sodden.*

sodium /ˈsəʊ.di.əm/ [US] /ˈsoʊ-/ *noun* [U] a soft silver-white chemical element that is found in salt

sodium bicarbonate /ˌsəʊ.di.əm.baɪˈkɑː.bᵊn.ət/ [US] /ˌsoʊ.di.əm.baɪˈkɑːr-/ *noun* [U] *SPECIALIZED* **bicarbonate of soda**

ˌ**sodium ˈchloride** *noun* [U] *SPECIALIZED* salt

sodomy /ˈsɒd.ə.mi/ [US] /ˈsɑː.də-/ *noun* [U] *FORMAL OR LEGAL* the sexual act of putting the penis into a man's or woman's anus **sodomite** *noun* [C] *OLD USE* **sodomize**, *UK USUALLY* **-ise** /ˈsɒd.ə.maɪz/ [US] /ˈsɑː.də-/ *verb* [T]

Sod's law /ˌsɒdzˈlɔː/ [US] /ˌsɑːdzˈlɑː/ *noun* [U] *UK OFFENSIVE* **Murphy's law**

sofa /ˈsəʊ.fə/ [US] /ˈsoʊ-/ *noun* [C] (*UK ALSO* **settee**) a long soft seat with a back and usually arms, on which more than one person can sit at the same time

ˈ**sofa ˌbed** *noun* [C] a sofa which opens to form a bed

soft [NOT HARD] /sɒft/ [US] /sɑːft/ *adj* **1** not hard or firm: *soft ground* ○ *a soft pillow/mattress* ○ *soft cheese* ○ *I like chocolates with soft centres.* ○ *Soft* ***tissue****, such as flesh, allows X-rays through.* **2** describes things, especially parts of the body, which are not hard or rough and feel pleasant and smooth when touched: *soft lips/cheeks/skin/hair* ○ *soft leather* **3** *INFORMAL DISAPPROVING* Someone who is soft is not very healthy and strong: *Look at you! You need more exercise. You're* ***going/getting*** *soft.*
• **soft in the head** *UK INFORMAL* crazy or stupid: *Is the boss* ***going*** *soft in the head?*
soften /ˈsɒf.ᵊn/ [US] /ˈsɑː.fᵊn/ *verb* [I or T] to become soft, or to make something soft: *You can soften the butter by warming it gently.* ○ *These dried apples will soften* ***(up)*** *if you soak them in water.*
softener /ˈsɒf.ᵊn.əʳ/ [US] /ˈsɑː.fᵊn.ɚ/ *noun* [C or U] a substance used to make something soft: *(a) fabric softener*
softness /ˈsɒft.nəs/ [US] /ˈsɑːft-/ *noun* [U]

soft [GENTLE] /sɒft/ [US] /sɑːft/ *adj* **1** not forceful, loud or easily noticed: *a soft voice/sound* ○ *soft music/lighting* ○ *a soft glow* **2** *DISAPPROVING* not severe or forceful enough, especially in criticizing or punishing someone who has done something wrong: *She thinks I'm too soft* ***on*** *the kids when they misbehave.* ○ *The government can't be seen to be* ***taking a*** *soft* ***line*** (= not being severe enough) *with criminals.*
• **be soft on sb** *US* to love someone or like them very much: *I think Matt must be soft on Tammy.*
soften /ˈsɒf.ᵊn/ [US] /ˈsɑː.fᵊn/ *verb* [I or T] to become more gentle, or to make someone do this: *The news will upset him – we must think of a way to soften* ***the blow*** (= make the news less unpleasant for him). ○ *Would you say the government's stance on law and order has softened?*
softie, **softy** /ˈsɒf.ti/ [US] /ˈsɑːf-/ *noun* [C] *INFORMAL* a kind, gentle person who is not forceful, looks for the pleasant things in life and can be easily persuaded to do what you want them to
softly /ˈsɒft.li/ [US] /ˈsɑːft-/ *adv* gently: *She speaks softly but usually gets her own way.* **softness** /ˈsɒft.nəs/ [US] /ˈsɑːft-/ *noun* [U]

soft [EASY] /sɒft/ [US] /sɑːft/ *adj UK* not difficult: *He's got a pretty soft job – he hardly seems to do anything all day.*

soft [DRUGS] /sɒft/ [US] /sɑːft/ *adj* [before n] Soft drugs are illegal drugs that many people think are not dangerous.

softback /ˈsɒft.bæk/ [US] /ˈsɑːft-/ *adj, noun* [C] (*US USUALLY* **softcover**) (a book) with a bendable cover ➲Compare **hardback**; **paperback**.

softball /ˈsɒft.bɔːl/ [US] /ˈsɑːft.bɑːl/ *noun* [U] a game similar to baseball but played with a larger softer ball

ˌ**soft ˈdrink** *noun* [C] a cold, usually sweet, drink which does not contain alcohol

soften /sɒf.ᵊn/ [US] /ˈsɑː.fᵊn/ *verb*
▲ **soften *sb* up** *phrasal verb* [M] to do things that will please someone so that they will do what you want: *You're trying to soften me up so I'll drive you to Jodie's house, aren't you?*

ˌ**soft ˈfruit** *noun* [C or U] *MAINLY UK* a general name for small fruits such as STRAWBERRIES, RASPBERRIES and BLACKCURRANTS which do not have a thick skin

ˌ**soft ˈfurnishings** *UK plural noun* (*US* **soft goods**) a general name for curtains, furniture coverings and other items made of cloth which decorate a room: *Soft furnishings are on the third floor, sir.*

soft-hearted /ˌsɒftˈhɑː.tɪd/ [US] /ˌsɑːftˈhɑːr.t̬ɪd/ *adj* kind and often feeling sympathy for other people ➲Compare **hard-hearted**.

ˌ**soft ˈlanding** *noun* [C usually sing] when a person or vehicle comes down from the air to the ground without difficulty or damage

softly-softly /ˌsɒft.liˈsɒft.li/ [US] /ˌsɑːft.liˈsɑːft.li/ *adj UK* **softly-softly approach** If you take a softly-softly approach, you are try to solve a problem in a quiet and reasonable way.

ˌ**soft ˈoption** *noun* [C usually sing] *UK* the easiest of two or more possible choices: *The soft option is simply to say nothing for the moment.*

soft-pedal /ˌsɒftˈped.ᵊl/ [US] /ˌsɑːft-/ *verb* [I or T] to make something seem less important or less bad than it really is: *This is a rather sensitive issue – I think we'd better soft-pedal it for the moment.*

ˌ**soft ˈporn** *noun* [U] books and films showing sexual activity which are less extreme and less offensive than other material of the same type

ˌ**soft ˈsell** *noun* [S] a way of trying to sell something to someone by being gently persuasive: *The training brochure deliberately adopts a soft sell approach.*

soft-soap /ˌsɒftˈsəʊp/ [US] /ˌsɑːftˈsoʊp/ *verb* [T] *INFORMAL* to try to persuade someone to do what you want by saying pleasant things to them

soft-spoken /ˌsɒftˈspəʊ.kᵊn/ [US] /ˌsɑːftˈspoʊ-/ *adj* having a quiet pleasant voice

ˈ**soft ˌspot** *noun* **have a soft spot for *sb*** to feel a lot of affection for someone, often without knowing why: *She'd always had a soft spot for her younger nephew.*

ˌ**soft ˈtarget** *noun* [C] something that is easy to attack or obtain an advantage from: *Major tourist attractions are a soft target* ***for*** *pickpockets.*

ˈ**soft ˌtop** *noun* [C] a **convertible** ➲See at **convert**.

ˌ**soft ˈtouch** *noun* [C usually sing] someone who you can easily persuade to do what you want

ˌ**soft ˈtoy** *UK noun* [C] (*US* **stuffed animal**) a toy animal made from cloth and filled with a soft material so that it is pleasant to hold

software /ˈsɒft.weəʳ/ [US] /ˈsɑːft.wer/ *noun* [U] the instructions which control what a computer does; computer programs: *He's written a piece of software which calculates your tax returns for you.* ➲Compare **hardware** COMPUTER.

ˈ**software ˌpackage** *noun* [C] a computer program that is sold together with instructions on how to use it

ˌ**soft ˈwater** *noun* [U] water which does not contain chalk and allows soap to produce bubbles easily

softwood /ˈsɒft.wʊd/ [US] /ˈsɑːft-/ *noun* [C or U] wood from evergreen trees like PINE which grow quickly, or a tree of this type: *window frames made from softwood* ○ *A 200,000-acre forest site will be replanted with softwoods to supply the paper and pulp mill.* ➲Compare **hardwood**.

soggy /ˈsɒg.i/ [US] /ˈsɑː.gi/ *adj* (of things which can absorb water, especially food) unpleasantly wet and soft: *soggy ground* ○ *I hate it when cereal* ***goes*** *soggy.* **soggily** /ˈsɒg.ɪ.li/ [US] /ˈsɑː.gɪ-/ *adv* **sogginess** /ˈsɒg.ɪ.nəs/ [US] /ˈsɑː.gɪ-/ *noun* [U]

soil [EARTH] /sɔɪl/ *noun* **1** [C or U] the material on the surface of the ground in which plants grow; earth: *light/heavy/fertile soil* ○ *sandy or chalky soils* **2** [U] *LITERARY* a

S

country: *It was the first time we had set foot on foreign/French/American soil* (= gone to a foreign country/France/America). **3** *LITERARY* **the soil** the activity of farming: *The government is trying to encourage a return to the soil.*

soil [MAKE DIRTY] /sɔɪl/ *verb* **[T]** *FORMAL* to make something dirty, especially with excrement: *soiled diapers/nappies/sheets*

• **not soil *your* hands** *LITERARY* to not become involved in something unpleasant or bad: *These were top lawyers, the kind who wouldn't normally soil their hands with police work or criminal law.*

soiled /sɔɪld/ *adj* dirty: *soiled clothes*

'soil ˌscience *noun* **[U]** the scientific study of soils

soiree, soirée /ˈswɑː.reɪ/ Ⓤⓢ /swɑːˈreɪ/ *noun* **[C]** *FORMAL* an evening party, often with musical entertainment

sojourn /ˈsɒdʒ.ən/ Ⓤⓢ /ˈsoʊ.dʒɝːn/ *noun* **[C]** *LITERARY* a short period when a person stays in a particular place: *My sojourn **in** the youth hostel was thankfully short.*

sojourn /ˈsɒdʒ.ən/ Ⓤⓢ /ˈsoʊ.dʒɝːn/ *verb* **[I usually + adv or prep]**

solace /ˈsɒl.ɪs/ Ⓤⓢ /ˈsɑː.lɪs/ *noun* **[S or U]** *LITERARY* help and comfort when you are feeling sad or worried: *When his wife left him, he **found** solace **in** the bottle* (= drank alcohol). ○ *Music was a great solace to me during this period.*

solace /ˈsɒl.ɪs/ Ⓤⓢ /ˈsɑː.lɪs/ *verb* **[T]** *LITERARY* to give help and comfort to someone when they are feeling sad or worried

solar /ˈsəʊ.ləʳ/ Ⓤⓢ /ˈsoʊ.lɚ/ *adj* **[before n]** of or from the Sun, or using the energy from the Sun to produce electric power: *solar radiation* ○ *solar flares* ○ *a solar cell/panel* ○ *solar heating*

solarium /səˈleə.ri.əm/ Ⓤⓢ /soʊˈler.i-/ *noun* **[C]** *plural* **solariums** or **solaria 1** a room in which you can TAN (= make brown) your skin using either light from the Sun or special equipment **2** *US FOR* **conservatory** ROOM.

ˌsolar ˈpanel *noun* **[C]** a device that changes energy from the Sun into electricity: *Solar panels are used to power satellites.*

solar plexus /ˌsəʊ.ləˈplek.səs/ Ⓤⓢ /ˌsoʊ.lɚ-/ *noun* **[S]** the front part of the body below the chest: *a punch in **the** solar plexus*

the ˈsolar ˌsystem *noun* **[S]** the Sun and the group of planets which move around it

ˌsolar ˈyear *noun* **[C]** *SPECIALIZED* the time it takes for the Earth to go round the Sun, just over 365 days

sold /səʊld/ Ⓤⓢ /soʊld/ *past simple and past participle of* **sell**

solder /ˈsəʊl.dəʳ/ Ⓤⓢ /ˈsɑː.dɚ/ *noun* **[U]** a soft metal that is melted in order to join together pieces of metal so that they stick together when it cools and becomes hard again

solder /ˈsəʊl.dəʳ/ Ⓤⓢ /ˈsɑː.dɚ/ *verb* **[I or T]** to join pieces of metal together using solder

ˈsoldering ˌiron *noun* **[C]** a tool which you use for heating solder

soldier /ˈsəʊl.dʒəʳ/ Ⓤⓢ /ˈsoʊl.dʒɚ/ *noun* **[C]** a person who is in an army and wears its uniform, especially someone who fights when there is a war: *Soldiers were patrolling the streets.*

soldiering /ˈsəʊl.dʒəʳr.ɪŋ/ Ⓤⓢ /ˈsoʊl.dʒɚ-/ *noun* **[U]** the job of being a soldier: *a life of soldiering*

soldier /ˈsəʊl.dʒəʳ/ Ⓤⓢ /ˈsoʊl.dʒɚ/ *verb*

▲ **soldier on** *phrasal verb* to continue doing something although it is difficult: *I admired the way she soldiered on when her business ran into trouble.*

ˌsoldier of ˈfortune *noun* **[C]** *LITERARY* someone who fights for anyone who will pay, not necessarily for their own country

sole [ONLY] /səʊl/ Ⓤⓢ /soʊl/ *adj* **[before n] 1** being one only; single: *My sole objective is to make the information more widely available.* ○ *The sole **survivor** of the accident was found in the water after six hours.* **2** not shared with anyone else: *She has sole **responsibility** for the project.* ○ *I have sole charge of both children all day.*

solely /ˈsəʊl.li/ Ⓤⓢ /ˈsoʊl-/ *adv* only and not involving anyone or anything else: *I bought it solely for that purpose.* ○ *It seems he's not solely to blame for the accident.* ○ *The product's success cannot be attributable solely to the ads.*

sole [BOTTOM PART] /səʊl/ Ⓤⓢ /soʊl/ *noun* **[C]** *plural* **soles** the bottom part of a foot which touches the ground when you stand or walk, or the bottom part of a shoe which touches the ground, usually not including the heel: *a cut on the sole of her foot* ○ *shoes with rubber soles* **-soled** /-səʊld/ Ⓤⓢ /-soʊld/ *suffix*: *leather-soled shoes*

sole /səʊl/ Ⓤⓢ /soʊl/ *verb* **[T]** to put a new sole on a shoe

sole [FISH] /səʊl/ Ⓤⓢ /soʊl/ *noun* **[C]** *plural* **sole** one of a number of flat round fish which are eaten as food: *lemon sole* ○ *Dover sole*

solecism /ˈsɒl.ɪ.sɪ.zᵊm/ Ⓤⓢ /ˈsɑː.lə-/ *noun* **[C]** *FORMAL* **1** behaviour that is a social mistake or is not polite: *to commit a social solecism* **2** a grammatical mistake: *a grammatical solecism*

solemn /ˈsɒl.əm/ Ⓤⓢ /ˈsɑː.ləm/ *adj* **1** serious and without any amusement: *a solemn face/voice* ○ *solemn music* ○ *Everyone looked very solemn.* **2 solemn promise/commitment/undertaking, etc.** an agreement which you make in a serious way and expect to fulfil

solemnly /ˈsɒl.əm.li/ Ⓤⓢ /ˈsɑː.ləm-/ *adv*

solemnity /səˈlem.nɪ.ti/ Ⓤⓢ /-nə.t̬i/ *noun* **[U]** (*ALSO* **solemnness**) the quality of being serious: *the solemnity **of** a funeral service*

solemnities /səˈlem.nɪ.tiz/ Ⓤⓢ /-nə.t̬iz/ *plural noun* the ways of behaving or the activities which are considered suitable for a serious formal social ceremony, such as a funeral

solemnize, *UK USUALLY* **-ise** /ˈsɒl.əm.naɪz/ Ⓤⓢ /ˈsɑː.ləm-/ *verb SPECIALIZED* **solemnize a marriage** to perform the official marriage ceremony, especially as part of a religious ceremony in a church **solemnization**, *UK USUALLY* **-isation** /ˌsɒl.əm.naɪˈzeɪ.ʃᵊn/ Ⓤⓢ /ˌsɑː.ləm.nɪ-/ *noun* **[U]**

solicit /səˈlɪs.ɪt/ *verb* **1 [T]** *FORMAL* to ask someone for money, information or help: *to solicit donations for a charity* ○ *It is illegal for public officials to solicit gifts or money in exchange for favours.* **2 [I]** to offer sex for money, usually in a public place **solicitation** /səˌlɪs.ɪˈteɪ.ʃᵊn/ *noun* **[C or U]** *FORMAL*

soliciting /səˈlɪs.ɪ.tɪŋ/ Ⓤⓢ /-t̬ɪŋ/ *noun* **[U]** *LEGAL* when someone offers to have sex for money

solicitor /səˈlɪs.ɪ.təʳ/ Ⓤⓢ /-t̬ɚ/ *noun* **[C]** a type of lawyer in Britain and Australia who is trained to prepare cases and give advice on legal subjects and can represent people in lower courts: *a firm of solicitors* ➲See Note **lawyer, solicitor, barrister and attorney** at **lawyer**.

solicitous /səˈlɪs.ɪ.təs/ Ⓤⓢ /-t̬əs/ *adj FORMAL* showing care and helpful attention to someone: *He made a solicitous enquiry after her health.* **solicitously** /səˈlɪs.ɪ.tə.sli/ Ⓤⓢ /-t̬ə-/ *adv* **solicitude** /səˈlɪs.ɪ.tjuːd/ Ⓤⓢ /-tuːd/ *noun* **[U]** (*ALSO* **solicitousness**)

solid [HARD] /ˈsɒl.ɪd/ Ⓤⓢ /ˈsɑː.lɪd/ *adj* **1** hard or firm, keeping a clear shape: *solid ground* ○ *a solid object* ○ *a solid structure* **2** completely hard or firm all through an object, or without any spaces or holes: *solid rock* ○ *a solid oak table* ○ *solid doors/walls* ○ *a solid line of traffic* ○ *The lecture hall was **packed** solid (**with** students).* **3** describes a metal or a colour which is pure, and does not have anything else mixed together with it: *solid gold/silver candlesticks* ○ *a white rose on a solid blue background*

solid /ˈsɒl.ɪd/ Ⓤⓢ /ˈsɑː.lɪd/ *noun* **[C]** *SPECIALIZED* an object that has a height, width and length, and is not flat: *A cube and a pyramid are both solids.*

solidly /ˈsɒl.ɪd.li/ Ⓤⓢ /ˈsɑː.lɪd-/ *adv*: *The house seems very solidly* (= strongly and firmly) *built.* **solidity** /səˈlɪd.ɪ.ti/ Ⓤⓢ /-ə.t̬i/ *noun* **[U]** (*ALSO* **solidness**)

solid [NOT LIQUID/GAS] /ˈsɒl.ɪd/ Ⓤⓢ /ˈsɑː.lɪd/ *adj* **1** not liquid or gas: *Liquid and solid waste is collected in the tank.* ○ *Freeze the mixture for about 3 hours or so until solid.* **2** describes food which is not in liquid form, especially when given to babies or people who are ill: *That rice pudding was the first solid **food** he's eaten since his operation.*

solid /ˈsɒl.ɪd/ Ⓤⓢ /ˈsɑː.lɪd/ *noun* **1 [C]** a substance that is not liquid or gas **2 [C usually pl]** a food not in liquid form

S

solidify /sə'lɪd.ɪ.faɪ/ *verb* [I or T] to become solid or to make something solid: *Molten volcanic lava solidifies as it cools.* ○ *The chemical reaction solidifies the resin.* **solidification** /sə,lɪd.ɪ.fɪ'keɪ.ʃən/ *noun* [U] *a process of gradual solidification*

solidity /sə'lɪd.ɪ.ti/ [US] /-ə.ţi/ *noun* [U] the quality of being solid

solid [CERTAIN] /'sɒl.ɪd/ [US] /'sɑː.lɪd/ *adj* certain or safe; of a good standard; giving confidence or support: *This provided solid evidence that he committed the crime.* ○ *The drama course gives students a solid grounding in the basic techniques of acting.*

solidly /'sɒl.ɪd.li/ [US] /'sɑː.lɪd-/ *adv*: *The economy has been growing solidly for five years now.* ○ *My colleagues are solidly* ***behind*** *me* (= they support me) *on this issue.*

solidify /sə'lɪd.ɪ.faɪ/ *verb* [I or T] to become or make something become certain: *He solidified his commitment to the treaty, giving a forceful speech in favour of it.* ○ *Support for the policy is solidifying.*

solidity /sə'lɪd.ɪ.ti/ [US] /-ə.ţi/ *noun* [U] (*ALSO* **solidness**) certainty: *The agreement would give a new solidity to military cooperation between the two countries.*

solid [CONTINUOUS] /'sɒl.ɪd/ [US] /'sɑː.lɪd/ *adj* continuing for a period of time without stopping: *I slept for eleven solid hours.* ○ *The hotel was booked solid all of December.*

solidarity /,sɒl.ɪ'dær.ɪ.ti/ [US] /,sɑː.lɪ'der.ə.ţi/ *noun* [U] agreement between and support for the members of a group, especially a political group: *The situation raises important questions about solidarity among member states of the UN.* ○ *The lecturers joined the protest march to show solidarity* ***with*** *their students.*

,solid 'fuel *noun* [C or U] a solid substance such as coal or wood, rather than oil or gas:

solid-state /,sɒl.ɪd'steɪt/ [US] /,sɑː.lɪd-/ *adj* [before n] *SPECIALIZED* describes an electronic device in which the flow of electrical current is through solid material and not through a VACUUM (= space without air)

soliloquy /sə'lɪl.ə.kwi/ *noun* [C] *SPECIALIZED* a speech in a play which the character speaks to him- or herself or to the people watching rather than to the other characters: *Hamlet's soliloquy 'To be or not to be'*

solipsism /'sɒl.ɪp.sɪ.zəm/ [US] /'sɑː.lɪp-/ *noun* [U] *SPECIALIZED* the belief that only one's own experiences and existence can be known with certainty **solipsistic** /,sɒl.ɪp'sɪs.tɪk/ [US] /,sɑː.lɪp-/ *adj*

solitaire [JEWEL] /,sɒl.ɪ'teər/ /'---/ [US] /'sɑː.lə.ter/ *noun* [C] a single jewel which is part of a piece of jewellery, especially a ring, or the ring itself: *a solitaire diamond*

solitaire [CARDS] *US* /,sɒl.ɪ'teər/ /'---/ [US] /'sɑː.lə.ter/ *noun* [U] (*UK* **patience**) a game played with cards by one person

solitary /'sɒl.ɪ.tri/ [US] /'sɑː.lə.ter.i/ *adj* **1** A solitary person or thing is the only person or thing in a place: *On the hill, a solitary figure was busy chopping down trees.* ○ *In the distance was a solitary building.* ○ *He was a solitary child* (= He enjoyed being alone). **2** done alone: *solitary walks by the river* ○ *fishing and other solitary pastimes*

,solitary con'finement *noun* [U] when someone is kept in a room alone, usually in a prison

solitude /'sɒl.ɪ.tjuːd/ [US] /'sɑː.lə.tuːd/ *noun* [U] the situation of being alone without other people: *a life of solitude* ○ *After months of solitude at sea it felt strange to be in company.* ○ *It provides one with a chance to reflect on spiritual matters* ***in*** *solitude.*

solo /'səʊ.ləʊ/ [US] /'soʊ.loʊ/ *adj* [before n], *adv* alone; without other people: *a solo performance/flight* ○ *to sail/fly solo* ○ *He used to play with a group but now he's* ***going*** *solo/pursuing a solo career.*

solo /'səʊ.ləʊ/ [US] /'soʊ.loʊ/ *noun* [C] *plural* **solos** a musical performance done by one person alone, or a musical performance in which one person is given special attention: *a trumpet solo* ○ *Parker's solo on 'A Night in Tunisia' was so amazing that the pianist backing him simply stopped playing.*

soloist /'səʊ.ləʊ.ɪst/ [US] /'soʊ.loʊ-/ *noun* [C] a musician who performs a solo: *The soloist in the violin concerto was Yehudi Menuhin.*

solstice /'sɒl.stɪs/ [US] /'sɑːl-/ *noun* [C] either of the two occasions in the year when the Sun is directly above either the furthest point north or the furthest point south of the equator that it ever reaches. These are the times in the year, in the middle of the summer or winter, when there are the longest hours of day or night: *the* ***summer/winter*** *solstice* ➲Compare **equinox**.

solution /sə'luː.ʃən/ *noun* [C or U] *SPECIALIZED* a liquid into which a solid has been mixed and has dissolved: *an aqueous solution of salts* ○ *copper sulphate* ***in*** *solution* (= dissolved in water) ➲See also **solution** at **solve**.

soluble /'sɒl.jʊ.bl̩/ [US] /'sɑːl-/ *adj* able to be dissolved to form a solution: *soluble aspirins* ✻ NOTE: The opposite is **insoluble**. **solubility** /,sɒl.jʊ'bɪl.ɪ.ti/ [US] /,sɑːl.jə'bɪl.ə.ţi/ *noun* [U]

solve /sɒlv/ [US] /sɑːlv/ *verb* [T] to find an answer to a problem: *to solve a problem* ○ *to solve a mystery/puzzle* ○ *Just calm down – shouting won't solve anything!* ○ *This strategy could cause more problems than it solves.* ○ *Police are still no nearer to solving the crime.*

solution /sə'luː.ʃən/ *noun* [C] the answer to a problem: *There's no easy solution* ***to*** *this problem.* ○ *She just seems so unhappy and I don't know what the solution is.* ○ *When you finish doing the crossword, the solution is on the back page.* ○ *They help you talk through your problems but they don't give you any solutions.* ➲See also **solution**.

COMMON LEARNER ERROR

solution to a problem

Be careful to choose the correct preposition after **solution**.

This could be one solution to the problem.
~~*This could be one solution of the problem.*~~

solvable /'sɒl.və.bl̩/ [US] /'sɑːl-/ *adj* (*ALSO* **soluble**) able to be solved

solvent [HAVING MONEY] /'sɒl.vənt/ [US] /'sɑːl-/ *adj* (especially of companies) having enough money to pay all the money that is owed to other people: *Many insurance companies are under pressure to increase premiums to* ***stay*** *solvent.* ✻ NOTE: The opposite is **insolvent**. **solvency** /'sɒl.vənt.si/ [US] /'sɑːl-/ *noun* [U]

solvent [LIQUID] /'sɒl.vənt/ [US] /'sɑːl-/ *noun* [C] a liquid in which solids will dissolve ➲See also **dissolve** BE ABSORBED.

'solvent a,buse *noun* [U] *FORMAL* the habit of breathing in the dangerous gases produced by some types of glue to achieve an excited mental condition

sombre *UK, US* **somber** /'sɒm.bər/ [US] /'sɑːm.bɚ/ *adj* **1** serious, sad and without humour or amusement: *a sombre atmosphere/voice/face* ○ *The funeral was a sombre occasion.* ○ *I left them in a sombre mood.* **2** dark and plain: *He wore a sombre black suit.* **sombrely** *UK, US* **somberly** /'sɒm.bə.li/ [US] /'sɑːm.bɚ-/ *adv* **sombreness** *UK, US* **somberness** /'sɒm.bə.nəs/ [US] /'sɑːm.bɚ-/ *noun* [U]

sombrero /sɒm'breə.rəʊ/ [US] /sɑːm'brer.oʊ/ *noun* [C] *plural* **sombreros** a hat with a wide brim, worn especially by men in Mexico ➲See picture **Hairstyles and Hats** on page Centre 8

some [UNKNOWN AMOUNT] *STRONG* /sʌm/, *WEAK* /səm/ *determiner* an amount or number of something which is not stated or not known; a part of something: *There's some cake in the kitchen if you'd like it.* ○ *Here's some news you might be interested in.* ○ *We've been having some problems with our TV over the last few weeks.* ○ *Could you give me some idea of when the building work will finish?* ○ *I've got to do some* ***more*** *work before I can go out.*

some *STRONG* /sʌm/, *WEAK* /səm/ *pronoun* **1** an amount or number of something which is not stated or not known; a part of something: *If you need more paper then just take some.* ○ *"Would you like to have dinner with us?" "No thanks, I've already had some."* ○ *Some* ***of*** *you here have already met Imran.* ○ *Have some* ***of*** *this champagne – it's very good.* **2** some people: *Some have compared his work to Picasso's.*

• **and then some** *MAINLY US INFORMAL* and even more: *It looked like 20,000 people and then some at the demonstration.*

S

USAGE

some or **any?**

Some is used in positive sentences. **Any** is used in questions and negative sentences.

There are some flowers in the garden, but there aren't any trees.
Has he got any brothers or sisters?

Some is sometimes used in offers or requests, especially if you want to give something to someone.

Would you like some more cake?

The same rules are true for **something** and **anything**, **someone** and **anyone**, and **somewhere** and **anywhere**.

---

some [LARGE AMOUNT] *STRONG* /sʌm/, *WEAK* /səm/ *determiner* a large amount or number of something: *It'll be some time before we meet again.* ○ *It was some years later when they next met.* ○ *We discussed the problem at some length.*

some [PARTICULAR THING] *STRONG* /sʌm/, *WEAK* /səm/ *determiner* used to refer to a particular person or thing without stating exactly which one: *Some lucky person will win more than $1,000,000 in the competition.* ○ *Some idiot's locked the door!* ○ *There must be some way you can relieve the pain.*

• **some ... or other** refers to one of several possibilities when the exact one is not known or not stated: *They found the painting in some antique shop or other.*

some [ANNOYANCE] /sʌm/ *determiner INFORMAL* used before a noun, especially at the beginning of a sentence to show annoyance or disapproval, often by repeating a word which was not accurately used: *Some people just don't know when to shut up.* ○ *Some help you were! You sat on your backside most of the afternoon!* ○ *"A friend of mine sold me a radio that doesn't work." "Some friend!"*

some [EXCELLENT] /sʌm/ *determiner INFORMAL* used before a noun to show how good something or someone is: *Wow, that was some dinner!*

some [APPROXIMATELY] /sʌm/, *WEAK* /səm/ *adv* used before a number to mean approximately; about: *Some fifty tons of stone are taken from the quarry every day.* ○ *The water is some twenty to thirty metres beneath the ground.*

some [SMALL AMOUNT] *STRONG* /sʌm/, *WEAK* /səm/ *adv US INFORMAL* by a small amount or degree; a little: *She says she's feeling some better.* ○ *We could turn down the heat some if that would make you more comfortable.*

somebody /ˈsʌm.bə.di/ /-ˌbɒd.i/ [US] /-ˌbɑː.di/ *pronoun* **someone**

someday /ˈsʌm.deɪ/ *adv* at some time in the future which is not yet known or not stated: *Maybe someday you'll both meet again.* ○ *Someday soon you're going to have to make a decision.*

somehow /ˈsʌm.haʊ/ *adv* **1** (*US INFORMAL ALSO* **someway**) in a way or by some means which is not known or not stated: *It won't be easy, but we'll get across the river somehow.* **2** for a reason which is not clear: *I know what we're doing is legal, but somehow it doesn't feel right.*

someone /ˈsʌm.wʌn/ *pronoun* (*ALSO* **somebody**) used to refer to a single person when you do not know who they are or when it is not important who they are: *There's someone outside the house.* ○ *Someone must have seen what happened.* ○ *Eventually someone in the audience spoke.* ○ *You'll have to ask someone* ***else***. ○ *We'll need a software engineer* ***or*** *someone* (= a person with skill of or like the stated type) *on the project team.* * NOTE: This is not usually used in negatives and questions. ➲See Note **some or any?** at **some** UNKNOWN AMOUNT.

someplace /ˈsʌm.pleɪs/ *adv US FOR* **somewhere** PLACE: *They live someplace in the South.* ○ *If they don't like it here they can go someplace* ***else***.

somersault /ˈsʌm.ə.sɔːlt/ [US] /-ɚ.sɑːlt/ *noun* [C] a rolling movement or jump, either forwards or backwards, in which you turn over completely, with your body above your head, and finish with your head on top again: *She was so happy she* ***turned*** *three somersaults on the lawn.*
somersault /ˈsʌm.ə.sɔːlt/ [US] /-ɚ.sɑːlt/ *verb* [I] *The bus plunged down the embankment, somersaulted twice and finally landed on its side.*

something /ˈsʌm.θɪŋ/ *pronoun* **1** an object, situation, quality or action which is not exactly known or stated: *There's something sharp in my shoe.* ○ *Something in the cupboard smells odd.* ○ *We thought there must be something* ***wrong*** *because we hadn't heard from you.* ○ *There's something wrong with the engine – it's making strange noises.* ○ *Something's happened to upset him but we don't know what it is.* ○ *I heard something rather worrying at work this morning.* ○ *Is there something you'd like to say?* ○ *Don't just stand there,* ***do*** *something.* ○ ***There's*** *just something* ***odd*** *about him.* * NOTE: This is not usually used in negatives and questions. ➲See Note **some or any?** at **some** UNKNOWN AMOUNT. **2** a situation or an event for which you are grateful, especially because an unpleasant thing has also happened: *We were given five hundred pounds in compensation which isn't much but at least it's something.*

• **be (really) something** *INFORMAL* to be very special or admirable: *Imagine England winning the World Cup – now that would be something.*

• **have got something there** If you say that a person has got something there, you mean they have said or discovered an important or interesting thing.

• **have something going with** ***sb*** *INFORMAL* If you have something going with someone, you are involved in a sexual relationship with them: *Didn't he have something going with one of his students?*

• **or something (like that)** *INFORMAL* used to show that what you have just said is only an example or you are not certain about it: *She works for a bank or something.* ○ *Why don't you go to a movie or something?*

• **something for nothing** If someone gets something for nothing, they get something they want, such as money, without having to work or make any effort.

• **there's something in** used to admit that there is some value or truth in what someone does or says, although you do not completely approve of it: *I don't go along with all his theories but there's probably something in it.*

• **something like 96%/half, etc.** approximately, when talking about an amount or number: *Something like sixty percent of all married men will have an affair at some point in their marriage.* ○ *He paid something like ninety pounds for a T-shirt.*

• **something a little stronger** *HUMOROUS* a drink containing alcohol: *We have fruit juice but perhaps you'd like something a little stronger?*

• **be something of a** ***sth*** *INFORMAL* used to describe a person or thing in a way that is partly true but not completely or exactly: *It came as something of a surprise.* ○ *He has a reputation as something of a troublemaker.* ○ *I have a biology question for you – I gather you're something of an expert.*

• **be/have something to do with** *INFORMAL* to be related to something or a cause of something but not in a way that you know about or understand exactly: *I'm not sure what he does exactly – it's something to do with finance.* ○ *It might have something to do with the way it's made.*

-something /-sʌm.θɪŋ/ *suffix INFORMAL* used after a number like 20, 30, etc. to refer to the age of a person who is between 20 and 29, 30 and 39 years old, etc., or to a person who is of this age: *I'd guess she's thirty-something.* ○ *Most of these places are aimed at twenty-somethings.*

sometime [UNKNOWN TIME] /ˈsʌm.taɪm/ *adv* at a time in the future or the past which is not known or not stated: *sometime before June* ○ *We really should meet sometime soon to discuss the details.* ○ *sometime* ***in*** *the autumn*

sometime [NOT NOW] /ˈsʌm.taɪm/ *adj* **[before n]** *FORMAL* (especially of a job or position) in the past but not any longer: *The enquiry will be headed by Lord Jones, sometime editor of the 'Daily News'.*

sometimes /ˈsʌm.taɪmz/ *adv* on some occasions but not always or often: *Sometimes we take food with us and sometimes we buy food when we're there.* ○ *Sometimes it's best not to say anything.*

someway /ˈsʌm.weɪ/ *adv* (*ALSO* **someways**) *US INFORMAL FOR* **somehow**: *Don't worry – I'll get there someway.*

somewhat /ˈsʌm.wɒt/ [US] /-wɑːt/ *adv SLIGHTLY FORMAL* slightly: *The resort has changed somewhat over the last few years.* ○ *She's somewhat more confident than she used to be.* ○ *We were somewhat tired after our long walk.*

- **somewhat of** to some degree: *She was known for being somewhat of a strange character.*

somewhere PLACE /'sʌm.weəʳ/ US /-wer/ *adv* (*US ALSO* **someplace**) in or at a place having a position which is not stated or not known: *He was last heard of living somewhere on the south coast.* ○ *You must have put their letter somewhere!* ○ [+ **to** infinitive] *I'm looking for somewhere to eat/stay.* ○ *Can we go somewhere else to talk – it's very noisy here.* ○ *Wouldn't you like to go to Disneyland or somewhere (= or to a similar place)? * NOTE: This is not usually used in negatives and questions.* ⊃See Note **some or any?** at some UNKNOWN AMOUNT.
- **be getting somewhere** INFORMAL to be achieving something: *Right, that's the printer working. Now we're getting somewhere!*

somewhere APPROXIMATELY /'sʌm.weəʳ/ US /-wer/ *adv* **somewhere around/between, etc.** approximately; about: *Somewhere between 900 and 1100 minor crimes are reported in this city every week.* ○ *It will take us somewhere between three and four hours to get to Madrid.* ○ *The company's annual turnover is somewhere around £70.7 million.*

somnambulism /spm'næm.bjʊ.lɪ.zᵊm/ US /sɑːm-/ *noun* [U] SPECIALIZED the action, sometimes habitual, of a person walking around while they are sleeping **somnambulist** /spm'næm.bjʊ.lɪst/ US /sɑːm-/ *noun* [C]

somnolent /'spm.nəl.ənt/ US /'sɑːm-/ *adj* LITERARY almost sleeping, or causing sleep: *a somnolent summer's afternoon* ○ *the somnolent villages further north* **somnolence** /'spm.nəl.ənts/ US /'sɑːm-/ *noun* [U]

son /sʌn/ *noun* [C] **1** your male child: *This is our son Raja.* ○ *We have two sons and three daughters.* **2** used as an informal form of address by a man to a boy: *Come on, son, we haven't got all day.* **3** LITERARY **a son of somewhere** a man who was born in a particular place: *that notable son of Württemberg, Martin Brecht*

sonar /'səʊ.nɑːʳ/ US /'soʊ.nɑːr/ *noun* [U] equipment, especially on a ship, which uses sound waves to discover how deep the water is or the position of an object in the water, such as a group of fish

sonata /sə'nɑː.tə/ US /-t̬ə/ *noun* [C] a piece of music in three or four parts, either for a piano or for another instrument, such as a violin, sometimes also with a piano

son et lumière /ˌspn.eɪˌluːˈmi'eəʳ/ US /ˌsɑːn.eɪˌluːˈmi'er/ *noun* [C] an outside entertainment which uses sounds, lights and often a spoken story to tell the history of a place

song /spŋ/ US /sɑːŋ/ *noun* **1** [C] a usually short piece of music with words which are sung: *to sing a song* ○ *a love/folk/pop song* ⊃See also **swansong**. **2** [U] the act of singing, or singing when considered generally: *He was so happy he wanted to **burst/break into** song (= start singing).* **3** [C or U] the musical sound that a bird makes: *bird song* ○ *A thrush's song was the only sound to break the silence.*
- **for a song** INFORMAL very cheaply: *She bought the bed for a song at an auction.* ○ *Because the shop's closing down, most of the stock is **going** for a song (= being sold very cheaply).*
- **song and dance** MAINLY US INFORMAL a long and complicated statement or story, especially one which is not true
- **make a song and dance about sth** UK INFORMAL to make something seem more important than it really is so that everyone notices it: *I only asked her to move her car but she made such a song and dance about it.*

songbird /'spŋ.bɜːd/ US /'sɑːŋ.bɜːd/ *noun* [C] any of many different types of bird that make musical sounds

songbook /'spŋ.bʊk/ US /'sɑːŋ-/ *noun* [C] a book containing a collection of songs showing both their words and their music

songfest /'spŋ.fest/ US /'sɑːŋ-/ *noun* [C] US FOR **singsong** SINGING.

songster /'spŋ.stəʳ/ US /-stɚ/ *noun* [C] LITERARY **1** a skilled singer **2** a bird with a musical song

songstress /'spŋ.strəs/ *noun* [C] LITERARY a skilled female singer: *The city's most famous songstress, Gloria Estefan, grew up here after her parents fled communist-ruled Cuba.*

song thrush *noun* [C] a type of **thrush** BIRD

songwriter /'spŋˌraɪ.təʳ/ US /'sɑːŋˌraɪ.t̬ɚ/ *noun* [C] a person who writes the music and words of songs **songwriting** /'spŋˌraɪ.tɪŋ/ US /'sɑːŋˌraɪ.t̬ɪŋ/ *noun* [U]

sonic /'spn.ɪk/ US /'sɑː.nɪk/ *adj* SPECIALIZED of sound or the speed at which sound travels in air ⊃See also **supersonic**.

sonic 'boom *noun* [C usually sing] an explosive sound made by an aircraft, bullet, etc. travelling faster than the speed at which sound travels

son-in-law /'sʌn.ɪn.lɔː/ US /-lɑː/ *noun* [C] *plural* **sons-in-law** your daughter's husband

sonnet /'spn.ɪt/ US /'sɑː.nɪt/ *noun* [C] a poem that has 14 lines and a particular pattern of rhyme

sonny /'sʌn.i/ *noun* [S] OLD-FASHIONED a form of address used by an older person to a boy or a young man: *Look here, sonny, you've got a lot to learn!*

son of a 'bitch (*plural* **sons of bitches**) *noun* [C usually sing] (*ALSO* **sonofabitch**, *ABBREVIATION* **S.O.B.**) MAINLY US OFFENSIVE an unpleasant man: *What low-down son of a bitch took my clothes?* ○ *I'm going to beat that sonofabitch if it kills me!*

son of a 'gun *noun* [C] *plural* **sons of guns** US POLITE EXPRESSION FOR **son of a bitch**

sonogram /'spn.ə.græm/ US /'sɑː.nə-/ *noun* [C] SPECIALIZED an image, especially of a baby that is still inside the womb, which is produced by ULTRASOUND (= sound waves)

sonorous /'spn.ᵊr.əs/ US /'sɑː.nɚ-/ *adj* FORMAL having a deep pleasant sound: *a sonorous voice* **sonorously** /'spn.ᵊr.ə.sli/ US /'sɑː.nɚ-/ *adv*

sook /sʊk/ *noun* [C] AUS a shy or cowardly child or person

soon /suːn/ *adv* in or within a short time; before long; quickly: *She'll soon be here./She'll be here soon.* ○ *It will soon be impossible for foreigners to enter the country.* ○ *The sooner we leave, the sooner we'll get there.* ○ *Soon after agreeing to go, she realized she'd made a mistake.* ○ *How soon (= When) can we sign the contract?* ○ *"When would you like to meet?" "**The** sooner **the better**." ○ I couldn't get out of that place soon enough.*
- **as soon as** at the same time or a very short time after: *As soon as I saw her, I knew there was something wrong.*
- **as soon as possible** If you do something as soon as possible, you do it as quickly as you can: *We need the repairs done as soon as possible.*
- **no sooner ... than** used to show that one thing happens immediately after another thing: *No sooner had I started mowing the lawn than it started raining.*
- **no sooner said than done** used to say that you will do something immediately
- **sooner or later** used to say that you do not know exactly when something will happen, but you are certain that it will happen: *Sooner or later she's going to realize what a mistake she's made.*
- **would (just) as soon** (*ALSO* **would sooner**) If you would (just) as soon do something or would sooner do something, you would prefer to do it rather than something else which is possible: *"Would you like to go out for dinner?" "I'd just as soon stay in – I'm not feeling very well."*

soot /sʊt/ *noun* [U] a black powder made mainly of carbon which is produced when coal, wood, etc. is burnt: *It can be dangerous to let too much soot accumulate inside a chimney.* **sooty** /'sʊt.i/ US /'sʊt̬-/ *adj*

soothe REDUCE ANGER /suːð/ *verb* [T] to make someone feel calm or less worried: *to soothe a crying baby* **soothing** /'suː.ðɪŋ/ *adj* making you feel calm: *I put on some nice soothing music.* ○ *Her words had a soothing effect.* **soothingly** /'suː.ðɪŋ.li/ *adv*

soothe REDUCE PAIN /suːð/ *verb* [T] to make an injury less painful: *I had a long hot bath to soothe my aching muscles.* **soothing** /'suː.ðɪŋ/ *adj* making something less painful: *a soothing ointment*

soothsayer /'suːθˌseɪ.əʳ/ US /-ɚ/ *noun* [C] OLD USE a person who is believed to have the ability to know and tell what will happen in the future

sop /spp/ US /sɑːp/ *noun* [C usually sing] DISAPPROVING something unimportant or of little value which is offered to stop complaints or unhappiness: *Critics see the increase in defence spending as a sop* ***to*** *the armed forces rather than an improvement of national security.*

sop /sɒp/ [US] /sɑːp/ *verb*

▲ **sop** ***sth*** **up** *phrasal verb* [M] to absorb liquid into a piece of solid matter: *It's surprising how much milk the bread sops up.*

sophisticated /səˈfɪs.tɪ.keɪ.tɪd/ [US] /-t̬ɪd/ *adj* **1** having a good understanding of the way people behave and/or a good knowledge of culture and fashion: *She was slim, svelte and sophisticated.* ○ *I don't suppose I have any books that would suit your sophisticated tastes.* ○ *He was older than me and from London and I thought him very sophisticated.* **2** clever in a complicated way and therefore able to do complicated tasks: *I think a more sophisticated approach is needed to solve this problem.* ○ *These are among the most sophisticated weapons in the world.* **sophistication** /səˌfɪs.tɪˈkeɪ.ʃᵊn/ *noun* [U] *Her sophistication is evident from the way she dresses.* ○ *The sophistication of computers is increasing as their size decreases.*

sophisticate /səˈfɪs.tɪ.kət/ *noun* [C] *FORMAL* a person who is sophisticated

sophistry /ˈsɒf.ɪ.stri/ [US] /ˈsɑː.fɪ-/ *noun* [U] *FORMAL* the clever use of arguments which seem true but are really false in order to deceive people

sophism /ˈsɒf.ɪ.zᵊm/ [US] /ˈsɑː.fɪ-/ *noun* [C] *FORMAL* an argument which seems true but is really false and is used to deceive people

sophomore /ˈsɒf.ə.mɔːʳ/ [US] /ˈsɑː.fə.mɔːr/ *noun* [C] *US* a student studying in the second year of a course at a US college or HIGH SCHOOL (= a school for students aged 15 to 18)

sophomoric /ˌsɒf.əˈmɒr.ɪk/ [US] /ˌsɑː.fəˈmɔːr-/ *adj US* silly and childish: *a sophomoric sense of humour*

soporific /ˌsɒp.ᵊrˈɪf.ɪk/ [US] /ˌsɑː.pəˈrɪf-/ *adj* causing sleep or making a person want to sleep: *the soporific effect of the heat* **soporifically** /ˌsɒp.ᵊrˈɪf.ɪ.kli/ [US] /ˌsɑː.pəˈrɪf-/ *adv*

sopping /ˈsɒp.ɪŋ/ [US] /ˈsɑː.pɪŋ/ *adj INFORMAL* extremely wet: *The bottle had leaked in my bag and everything was sopping.* ○ *You're sopping* ***wet*** *– go and dry yourself and get changed.*

soppy /ˈsɒp.i/ [US] /ˈsɑː.pi/ *adj INFORMAL DISAPPROVING* showing or feeling too much of emotions such as love or sympathy, rather than being reasonable or practical: *a film with a soppy ending* ○ *That's one of the soppiest stories I've ever heard!* ○ *Some people are really soppy* ***about*** *their pets.* **soppily** /ˈsɒp.ɪ.li/ [US] /ˈsɑː.pɪ-/ *adv INFORMAL* **soppiness** /ˈsɒp.ɪ.nəs/ [US] /ˈsɑː.pɪ-/ *noun* [U]

soprano /səˈprɑː.nəʊ/ [US] /-ˈpræn.oʊ/ *noun* [C] *plural* **sopranos** a woman or girl with a voice which can sing the highest notes **soprano** /səˈprɑː.nəʊ/ [US] /-ˈpræn.oʊ/ *adj, adv*

sorbet /ˈsɔː.beɪ/ [US] /sɔːrˈbeɪ/ *noun* [C or U] (*US ALSO* **sherbet**) a frozen food made from fruit juice, water and sugar: *lemon sorbet*

sorcery /ˈsɔː.sᵊr.i/ [US] /ˈsɔːr.sɚ-/ *noun* [U] a type of magic in which SPIRITS (= beings that cannot be seen), especially evil ones, are used to make things happen: *It seems that some people still believe in sorcery and black magic.*

sorcerer /ˈsɔː.sᵊr.əʳ/ [US] /ˈsɔːr.sɚ.ɚ/ *noun* [C] in stories, a man who has magical powers and who uses them to harm other people

sorceress /ˈsɔː.sᵊr.əs/ [US] /ˈsɔːr.sɚ-/ *noun* [C] a female sorcerer

sordid [DIRTY] /ˈsɔː.dɪd/ [US] /ˈsɔːr-/ *adj* dirty and unpleasant: *There are lots of really sordid apartments in the city's poorer areas.* **sordidness** /ˈsɔː.dɪd.nəs/ [US] /ˈsɔːr-/ *noun* [U]

sordid [IMMORAL] /ˈsɔː.dɪd/ [US] /ˈsɔːr-/ *adj* immoral and shocking: *He told me he'd had an affair but he spared me the sordid* ***details.*** **sordidly** /ˈsɔː.dɪd.li/ [US] /ˈsɔːr-/ *adv* **sordidness** /ˈsɔː.dɪd.nəs/ [US] /ˈsɔːr-/ *noun* [U]

sore [PAINFUL] /sɔːʳ/ [US] /sɔːr/ *adj* painful and uncomfortable because of injury, infection or too much use: *All the dust has made my eyes sore.* ○ *I've got a sore* ***throat.*** ○ *My feet were sore with all the walking.*

● **stand/stick out like a sore thumb** *INFORMAL* If someone or something stands/sticks out like a sore thumb, everyone notices them because they are very different from the people or things around them: *Everyone else was in jeans and casual gear and I had my office clothes on – I stuck out like a sore thumb.*

sore /sɔːʳ/ [US] /sɔːr/ *noun* [C] a painful area on the surface of a body, especially an infected area: *The poor dog's back was covered with sores.* ➲See also **cold sore**. **soreness** /ˈsɔː.nəs/ [US] /ˈsɔːr-/ *noun* [U]

sore [ANGRY] /sɔːʳ/ [US] /sɔːr/ *adj US INFORMAL* angry because you feel you have been unfairly treated: *He accused me of being a sore* ***loser*** (= someone who does not accept defeat well).

sorehead /ˈsɔː.hed/ [US] /ˈsɔːr-/ *noun* [C] *US INFORMAL* a person who is easily made angry: *Don't be such a sorehead – it was only meant to be a joke.*

sorely /ˈsɔː.li/ [US] /ˈsɔːr-/ *adv FORMAL* extremely; very much: *I was sorely* ***tempted*** *to say exactly what I thought of his offer.* ○ *You'll be sorely missed by everyone here, and we wish you success in your new job.*

ˌsore ˈpoint *noun* [C usually sing] a subject that someone prefers not to talk about because it makes them angry or embarrassed: *"So how are your job applications going?" "Oh, it's a bit of a sore point, I'm afraid."*

sorghum /ˈsɔː.gəm/ [US] /ˈsɔːr-/ *noun* [U] a type of grain grown in hot countries

sorority /səˈrɒr.ɪ.ti/ [US] /-ˈrɔːr.ə.t̬i/ *noun* [C] a social organization for female students at some US colleges ➲Compare **fraternity**.

sorrel /ˈsɒr.ᵊl/ [US] /ˈsɔːr-/ *noun* [U] a plant with acidic-tasting leaves which are used in cooking and salads

sorrow /ˈsɒr.əʊ/ [US] /ˈsɔːr.oʊ/ *noun* [C or U] *FORMAL* (a cause of) a feeling of great sadness or regret: *The sorrow she felt* ***over/at*** *the death of her husband was almost too much to bear.* ○ *The sorrows of her earlier years gave way to joy in later life.*

sorrow /ˈsɒr.əʊ/ [US] /ˈsɔːr.oʊ/ *verb* [I usually + adv or prep] *FORMAL* *For years she sorrowed (= felt great sadness)* ***over*** *her missing son.*

sorrowful /ˈsɒr.əʊ.fᵊl/ [US] /ˈsɔːr.ə-/ *adj LITERARY* very sad: *With a sorrowful sigh she folded the letter and put it away.* **sorrowfully** /ˈsɒr.əʊ.fᵊl.i/ [US] /ˈsɔːr.ə-/ *adv*

sorry [SAD] /ˈsɒr.i/ [US] /ˈsɔːr-/ *adj* [after v] **1** feeling sadness, sympathy, or disappointment, especially because something unpleasant has happened or been done: *I'm just sorry* ***about*** *all the trouble I've caused her.* ○ *He'd really upset her and he didn't seem at all sorry.* ○ [+ (*that*)] *I'm sorry* ***(that)*** *you had such a difficult journey.* ○ [+ **to** infinitive] *We were both sorry* ***to hear*** *you've been ill again.* ○ *I* ***feel*** *so sorry* ***for*** *the children – it must be really hard for them.* **2** *DISAPPROVING* **feel sorry for yourself** to feel sad because you have a problem and you feel that it is not fair that you are suffering so much: *He sounded very sorry for himself on the telephone.*

● **I'm sorry to say** used to show that something which must be said causes sadness or disappointment: *I'm sorry to say* ***that*** *the project's funding has been cancelled.* ○ *Most people who start the course do, I'm sorry to say, give up within the first two weeks.*

sorry [REGRET] /ˈsɒr.i/ [US] /ˈsɔːr-/ *adj* [after v] used to say that you wish you had not done what you have done, especially when you want to be polite to someone you have done something bad to: *Oh, I'm sorry – I didn't see you there.* ○ *Tom, I'm so sorry* ***about*** *last night – it was all my fault.* ○ *I've* ***said*** *I'm sorry.* **Sorry!** /ˈsɒr.i/ [US] /ˈsɔːr-/ *exclamation*: *"That's my foot you're treading on." "Sorry!"*

sorry [REFUSAL OR DISAGREEMENT] /ˈsɒr.i/ [US] /ˈsɔːr-/ *adj* **I'm sorry** used to show politeness when expressing refusal or disagreement: *I'm sorry but I think you've made a mistake.* ○ *I'm sorry, I can't agree.*

sorry /ˈsɒr.i/ [US] /ˈsɔːr-/ *exclamation* **1** used to show politeness when expressing refusal or disagreement: *Sorry, you can't go in there.* **2** *MAINLY UK* used when politely asking someone to repeat something or when politely interrupting someone: *"He's late." "Sorry?" "I said he's late."* ○ *Sorry, could you just say that last sentence again please?*

sorry BAD CONDITION /'spr.i/ US /'sɔːr-/ adj **sorry sight/ state/tale** a bad condition or situation: *He was a sorry sight when he got home – soaking and covered in mud.* ○ *It's a sorry state of affairs when there isn't any food in the house.*

sort TYPE /sɔːt/ US /sɔːrt/ noun [C] **1** a group of things which are of the same type or which share similar qualities: *We both like the same sort of music.* ○ *I'm going to have a salad of some sort.* ○ *What sort of shoes will I need?* ○ *We saw all sorts* (= many types) *of animals in the park.* ○ *Many sorts of bacteria are resistant to penicillin.* ○ *This sort of camera is very expensive.* ○ *Plants of this sort need shady conditions.* **2** your **sort** the type of thing or person that you like: *Hmm, this is my sort of wine!* ○ *I'd have thought these black trousers were more your sort of thing.* ○ *I wouldn't have thought he was your sort* (= was the type of man you would be physically attracted to).
● **(and) that sort of thing** INFORMAL used to show that what you have just said is only an example from a much larger group of things: *They sell souvenirs, postcards, that sort of thing.*
● **of sorts** (ALSO **of a sort**) used to describe something which is not a typical or good example of something: *He managed to make a curtain of sorts out of an old sheet.*
● **be out of sorts** SLIGHTLY OLD-FASHIONED to be slightly ill or slightly unhappy: *I've been feeling tired and headachy and generally out of sorts.*
● **(a) sort of** INFORMAL used to describe something approximately: *It's a sort of pale orange colour.*
● **sort of** INFORMAL in some way or to some degree: *I was sort of hoping to leave early today.* ○ *It's sort of silly, but I'd like a copy of the photograph.*
● **It takes all sorts (to make a world).** SAYING said to emphasize that people have different characters, opinions and abilities, and that you should accept this

sort ORDER /sɔːt/ US /sɔːrt/ verb [I or T] to put a number of things in an order or to separate them into groups: *Paper, plastic and cans are sorted for recycling.* ○ *I'm going to sort these old books into those to be kept and those to be thrown away.* ○ *You can use the computer to sort the newspaper articles alphabetically, by date, or by subject.* ○ *She found the ring while sorting (through) some clothes.* ⊃See also **sort out** SEPARATE.

sort DEAL WITH /sɔːt/ US /sɔːrt/ verb [T] UK INFORMAL to deal with something by repairing or organizing it: *Can you sort the car by tomorrow?* ○ *We must get the phone sorted soon.* ○ *I must get this paperwork sorted before I go on holiday next week.*

sorted /'sɔː.tɪd/ US /'sɔːr.tɪd/ adj [after v], exclamation UK INFORMAL when something is correctly organized or repaired, or when someone has the things they need: *Debbie's sorted for Tuesday night because she's found a baby sitter.* ○ *"Have you spoken to Grant about the party?" "Sorted!"*

sort PERSON /sɔːt/ US /sɔːrt/ noun [C usually sing] SLIGHTLY OLD-FASHIONED a person having the stated or suggested character: *He seemed like a decent sort to me.*

PHRASAL VERBS WITH **sort** ▼

▲ **sort** *sb* **out** PUNISH *phrasal verb* [M] UK INFORMAL to punish or attack someone, usually to make them understand that they have behaved badly: *Has he been bothering you again – do you want me to sort him out?*
▲ **sort** *sth* **out** SEPARATE *phrasal verb* [M] to separate one type of things from a group of things: *Sort out any clothes you want to throw away and give them to me.*
▲ **sort** *sth/sb* **out** DEAL WITH *phrasal verb* [M] to deal satisfactorily or successfully with a problem, a situation, or a person who is having difficulties: *We've sorted out the computer system's initial problems.* ○ [+ question word] *It'll be difficult to sort out how much each person owes.* ○ *Most of the job involves sorting customers out who have queries.*

sort code noun [C] (ALSO **sorting code**) an official number used to refer to a particular bank

sortie /'sɔː.ti/ US /'sɔːr.ti/ noun [C] **1** a brief attack by a military force, such as a small group of soldiers or an aircraft, made against an enemy position: *A series of*

sorties was carried out at night by specially equipped aircraft. **2** a brief journey to somewhere you have not been before, often with a particular purpose: *It was our first sortie into the town centre.* **3** an attempt to do something: *This is the acclaimed historian John Taylor's first sortie into fiction.*

sorting office noun [C] a building where letters, parcels, etc. are taken after they have been posted and where they are then put into groups according to their addresses before being delivered

sort-out /'sɔːt.aʊt/ US /'sɔːrt-/ noun [C usually sing] UK INFORMAL when you put things in order or in their correct place: *I've had a sort-out in the bedroom – it's looking rather better.*

SOS /ˌes.əʊ'es/ US /-oʊ'-/ noun [S] a request for help, especially because of danger: *Within an hour of the ship transmitting an SOS (message/call), six boats had arrived and started a rescue operation.* ○ *The hospital sent out an SOS for extra blood supplies.*

so-so /ˌsəʊ'səʊ/ US /ˌsoʊ.soʊ/ adj, adv INFORMAL between average quality and low quality; not good or well: *a so-so performance* ○ *"How are you getting on with your new boss?" "So-so."*

sotto voce /ˌsɒt.əʊ'vəʊ.tʃeɪ/ US /ˌsɑː.toʊ'voʊ-/ adv, adj FORMAL (said) in a quiet voice so that only people near can hear: *The remark was uttered sotto voce.*

sou /suː/ noun [S] UK OLD-FASHIONED a very small amount of money: *I don't have a sou.*

soubriquet /'suː.brɪ.keɪ/ noun [C] FORMAL a **sobriquet**

soufflé /'suː.fleɪ/ US /su'fleɪ/ noun [C or U] a light food which has a lot of air in it, is made mainly from eggs, and can be either sweet or savoury: *a cheese soufflé* ○ *a lemon soufflé*

sought /sɔːt/ US /sɑːt/ past simple and past participle of **seek**

sought-after /'sɔːt.ɑːf.tə/ US /'sɑːt.æf.tɚ/ adj wanted by many people and usually of high quality or rare: *At the age of seventeen she is already one of Hollywood's most sought-after actresses.*

soul SPIRIT /səʊl/ US /soʊl/ noun [C] the spiritual part of a person which some people believe continues to exist in some form after their body has died, or the part of a person which is not physical and experiences deep feelings and emotions: *She suffered greatly while she was alive, so let us hope her soul is now at peace.*

soul DEEP FEELINGS /səʊl/ US /soʊl/ noun [U] the quality of a person or work of art which shows or produces deep good feelings: *If you can't enjoy this music you've got no soul.* ○ *For me her paintings somehow lack soul.*
soulful /'səʊl.fəl/ US /'soʊl-/ adj expressing deep feelings, often sadness: *a soulful performance/ballad* ○ *The dog looked at me with its big soulful brown eyes.* **soulfully** /'səʊl.fəl.i/ US /'soʊl-/ adv **soulfulness** /'səʊl.fəl.nəs/ US /'soʊl-/ noun [U]
soulless /'səʊl.ləs/ US /'soʊl-/ adj DISAPPROVING lacking any human influence or qualities: *a soulless building of grey concrete*

soul PERSON /səʊl/ US /soʊl/ noun [C] **1** a person of a stated type: *She's a happy little soul.* ○ *Some poor soul had fallen 500 metres to their death.* **2** not a soul no one: *By the time I arrived there wasn't a soul there.*

soul BLACK CULTURE /səʊl/ US /soʊl/ noun [U] US a deep understanding of and pride in the culture of black people **soul** /səʊl/ US /soʊl/ adj [before n] *soul food* **soulful** /'səʊl.fəl/ US /'soʊl-/ adj

soul-destroying /'səʊl.dɪˌstrɔɪ.ɪŋ/ US /'soʊl-/ adj MAINLY UK describes a job or other activity which is so boring that is makes you very unhappy: *Repetitive work can become soul-destroying after a while.*

soul mate noun [C] someone, usually your romantic or sexual partner, with whom you have a special relationship, and whom you know and love very much: *Later that year she met Adam and she knew instantly that they were soul mates.*

soul music noun [U] (ALSO **soul**) popular music which expresses deep feelings, originally performed by Black Americans: *Soul music is often an affirmation of, and a manifesto for, black dignity.*

soul-searching /ˈsəʊlˌsɜː.tʃɪŋ/ [US] /ˈsoʊlˌsɝː-/ *noun* [U] deep and careful consideration of inner thoughts, especially about a moral problem: *After much soul-searching, he decided it was wrong to vote in the elections.*

sound [NOISE] /saʊnd/ *noun* **1** [C or U] something that you can hear or that can be heard: *They could **hear** the sound of a bell tolling in the distance.* ○ *She stood completely still, not **making** a sound.* ○ *Suddenly we heard a loud knocking sound from the engine.* ○ *Sound can **travel** over very large distances in water.* **2** [U] the activity of recording and broadcasting sound such as from a performance of music or for a film: *a sound engineer/recording* **3** [U] the volume or quality of the sound of a television or film: *Could you **turn** the sound **down/up** on the TV.* **4** [C] the particular quality of the music which a musician or a group of musicians produce: *The band's sound is a distinctive mixture of funk and rap.*

sound /saʊnd/ *verb* [I or T] **1** to make a noise: *If the alarm sounds, leave the building immediately.* ○ *It sounds **like** a bird.* ○ *He sounds* (= speaks) *just **like** someone I used to work with.* ○ *Sounding the car's horn, she drove at high speed through the crowded streets.* ➲See **death knell**. **2** **sound the alarm** to cause a noise to be made or say or shout a message to warn people about something: *Quick, sound the alarm – there's a fire in the machine room!*

soundless /ˈsaʊnd.ləs/ *adj FORMAL* without sound: *Above the mountain, eagles circled in soundless flight.* **soundlessly** /ˈsaʊnd.lə.sli/ *adv*

sound [SEEM] /saʊnd/ *verb* **1** **sound good/interesting/strange, etc.** to seem good/interesting/strange, etc. from what is said or written: *Your job sounds really interesting.* ○ *I know **it** sounds silly, but I'll miss him when he's gone.* **2** **sound like/as if/as though** to seem like something, from what is said or written: *That sounds like a good idea.* ○ *It sounds like you've got a sore throat.* ○ ***It** sounds as if they had a good holiday.* ○ *You're going skiing with three friends? That sounds like fun.* **3** **sound angry/happy/rude, etc.** to seem angry/happy/rude, etc. when you speak: *He sounded very depressed when we spoke on the telephone yesterday.* ○ *At the press conference, he sounded at his most relaxed.*

sound /saʊnd/ *noun* **the sound of *sth*** how something seems to be, from what is said or written: *I like the sound of the beef in red wine sauce.* ○ ***By/From** the sound of **it** I don't think it was her fault.* ○ *So I'm going to be talking to over ninety people, am I? I don't like the sound of that!*

sound [GOOD CONDITION] /saʊnd/ *adj* not broken or damaged; healthy; in good condition: *It's an old building but it's still structurally sound.* ○ *Considering his age, his body is quite sound.* ○ *Was she **of** sound **mind*** (= not mentally ill) *at the time of the incident?*

• **be as sound as a bell** *UK INFORMAL* to be very healthy or in very good condition

soundness /ˈsaʊnd.nəs/ *noun* [U] the fact of being in good condition

sound [GOOD JUDGMENT] /saʊnd/ *adj* showing good judgment; able to be trusted: *She gave me some very sound **advice**.* ○ *Are these pesticides environmentally sound* (= will they not damage the environment)*?* ○ *Government bonds are a sound **investment** because they combine good profits and high security.* **soundness** /ˈsaʊnd.nəs/ *noun* [U]

sound [COMPLETE] /saʊnd/ *adj* complete: *How sound is her knowledge of the subject?*

soundly /ˈsaʊnd.li/ *adv* completely: *The committee soundly rejected all of the proposed changes.*

sound [SLEEP] /saʊnd/ *adj* [before n], *adv* (of sleep) deep and peaceful: *He was sound **asleep** within moments of getting into bed.* **soundly** /ˈsaʊnd.li/ *adv*: *I slept very soundly, thank you – the bed was really comfortable.*

sound [WATER PASSAGE] /saʊnd/ *noun* [C] a passage of sea connecting two larger areas of sea, or an area of sea mostly surrounded by land: *the Kalmar Sound*

sound [WATER DEPTH] /saʊnd/ *verb* [T] to measure the depth of a mass of water, such as the sea, usually by SONAR ➲See **echo sounder**.

soundings /ˈsaʊn.dɪŋz/ *plural noun* measurements that are taken of the depth of the water: *They **took** soundings and found that the water was 120 feet deep.*

• **make/take soundings** to ask questions in order to gather information or opinions: *Can you take some discreet soundings to see what her future plans are?*

PHRASAL VERBS WITH **sound** ▼

▲ **sound off** *phrasal verb INFORMAL* to express your opinions forcefully, especially without being asked for them: *He's always sounding off **about** how he thinks the country should be run.*

▲ **sound *sb* out** *phrasal verb* [M] to discover informally what someone thinks or intends to do about a particular thing, so that you can be prepared or take appropriate action: *Perhaps you could sound the chairwoman out before the meeting, to see which way she's going to vote?*

the ˈsound ˌbarrier *noun* [S] a large increase in the force opposing a moving object as its speed approaches the speed at which sound travels: *There is usually a sonic boom when an aircraft **breaks** the sound barrier.*

soundbite /ˈsaʊnd.baɪt/ *noun* [C] a short sentence or phrase that is easy to remember, often included in a speech made by a politician and repeated in newspapers and on television and radio: *Most politicians want to master the art of the soundbite.*

soundboard /ˈsaʊnd.bɔːd/ [US] /-bɔːrd/ *noun* [C] a thin sheet of wood on a musical instrument such as a guitar which the strings go over and which helps to produce the sound

ˈsound ˌcard *noun* [C] a CIRCUIT BOARD (= small piece of electronic equipment) inside a computer that enables it to record and play sounds

ˈsound ˌcheck *noun* [C] when someone tests the musical instruments and recording equipment at a music show, especially before the players come on stage, to make certain that everything is working and that the sound quality is good

ˈsound efˌfect *noun* [C usually pl] in a radio or television programme or a film, one of the sounds other than speech or music which are added to make it seem more exciting or real

ˈsounding ˌboard *noun* [C usually sing] a person or group of people that you use to test something such as a new idea or suggestion to see if they will accept it or if they think it will work

soundproof /ˈsaʊnd.pruːf/ *adj* (of a building or part of a building) not allowing sound to go through: *a soundproof room/wall/studio* **soundproof** /ˈsaʊnd.pruːf/ *verb* [T] *It was a well soundproofed building, so we didn't hear the traffic outside.* **soundproofing** /ˈsaʊndˌpruː.fɪŋ/ *noun* [U]

ˈsound ˌsystem *noun* [C] a piece or several pieces of electronic equipment which can be used to play music from recordings, radio broadcasts, etc.

soundtrack /ˈsaʊnd.træk/ *noun* [C] the sounds, especially the music, of a film, or a separate recording of this: *The best thing about the film is its soundtrack.*

ˌsound ˈwave *noun* [C] the form that sound takes when it passes through air, water, etc.

soup /suːp/ *noun* [C or U] a usually hot, liquid food made from vegetables, meat or fish: *chicken/oxtail/fish/tomato soup* ○ *Would you like **a bowl of** soup?*

• **be in the soup** *OLD-FASHIONED INFORMAL* to be in an unpleasant or difficult situation

soup /suːp/ *verb*

▲ **soup *sth* up** *phrasal verb* [M] *INFORMAL* to make something more powerful or more attractive by making changes to it, especially when it is old: *New circuit boards can be used to soup up existing machines.*

souped-up /ˌsuːptˈʌp/ *adj*: *a souped-up Mini*

soupçon /ˈsuːp.sɒ̃/ [US] /-sɑ̃ː/ *noun* [S] *MAINLY HUMOROUS* a very small amount: *"Milk in your coffee?" "Just a soupçon, please."* ○ *Do I detect a soupçon of sarcasm in what you just said?*

ˈsoup ˌkitchen *noun* [C] a place where free soup or other food is given to people with no money or no homes

ˈsoup ˌspoon *noun* [C] a rounded spoon used for eating soup

S

sour /saʊəʳ/ ⓤ /saʊr/ *adj* **1** having a sharp, sometimes unpleasant, taste or smell, like a lemon, and not sweet: *These plums are a bit sour.* **2** unfriendly or easily annoyed: *Overnight, it seemed, their relationship had turned sour.* ○ *She gave me a sour look.*
• **sour grapes** If you describe someone's attitude as sour grapes, you mean that they are angry because they have not got or achieved something that they wanted: *I don't think it's such a great job – and that's not just sour grapes because I didn't get it.*

sour /saʊəʳ/ ⓤ *noun* [C] MAINLY US a drink made from strong alcohol, lemon or lime juice, sugar and ice: *a whisky sour*

sour /saʊəʳ/ ⓤ /saʊr/ *verb* [I or T] **1** to turn sour or to make something turn sour: *Hot weather sours milk.* ○ *Milk sours in hot weather.* **2** to (cause to) become unpleasant or unfriendly: *Her whole attitude to life soured as a result of that experience.* ○ *This affair has soured relations between the two countries.* **sourly** /ˈsaʊə.li/ ⓤ /ˈsaʊr-/ *adv* **sourness** /ˈsaʊə.nəs/ ⓤ /ˈsaʊr-/ *noun* [U]

source /sɔːs/ ⓤ /sɔːrs/ *noun* [C] **1** the place something comes from or starts at, or the cause of something: *a source of heat/energy/light* ○ *a heat/energy/light source* ○ *Oranges are a good source of vitamin C.* ○ *Experts are trying to track down the source of the contamination in the water supply.* ○ *We walked up the river to its source in the hills.* ○ *Money is often a source of tension and disagreements in young married couples.* **2** someone or something that supplies information: *The journalist refused to reveal her sources* (= say who had given the information to her). ○ *According to Government sources* (= people in the Government) *many MPs are worried about this issue.* ○ *Always acknowledge your sources* (= say which books you have used) *at the end of an essay.*
• **at source** at the place where something comes from: *Tax is deducted from my income at source.*

source /sɔːs/ ⓤ /sɔːrs/ *verb* [T often passive] to get something from a particular place: *Where possible the produce used in our restaurant is sourced locally.*

sour cream *noun* [U] (*UK ALSO* **soured cream**) cream which is made sour by adding special bacteria

sourdough /ˈsaʊə.dəʊ/ ⓤ /ˈsaʊr.doʊ/ *noun* [U] a mixture of flour and water which is left to FERMENT (= change chemically) and then used to make bread: *sourdough bread*

sourpuss /ˈsaʊə.pʊs/ ⓤ /ˈsaʊr-/ *noun* [C] INFORMAL someone who always looks unhappy and annoyed

sousaphone /ˈsuː.zə.fəʊn/ ⓤ /-foʊn/ *noun* [C] a large TUBA (= metal musical instrument played by blowing) with tubes which go round the player's body, sometimes used in marching musical groups

souse /saʊs/ *verb* [T] to put something into a liquid, or to make something completely wet

soused /saʊst/ *adj* **1** (of fish) preserved in salty water or vinegar: *soused herring/mackerel* **2** OLD-FASHIONED INFORMAL drunk

south /saʊθ/ *noun* **1** [U] (*ALSO* **South**) (*WRITTEN ABBREVIATION* **S**, *UK ALSO* **Sth**, *US ALSO* **So**) the direction which goes towards the part of the Earth below the equator, opposite to the north, or the part of an area or country which is in this direction: *The points of the compass are North, South, East and West.* ○ *The best beaches are in the south (of the island).* ○ *We usually spend our holidays in the South of France.* ○ *Canberra is/lies to the south of Sydney.* **2 the South** the developing countries of the world, most of which are below the equator ⊃See also **the Third World**. **3 the South** the southern states of the middle and eastern part of the US: *The American Civil War was fought between the North and the South partly over the issue of slavery.*

south /saʊθ/ *adj* **1** (*ALSO* **South**) (*WRITTEN ABBREVIATION* **S**, *UK ALSO* **Sth**, *US ALSO* **So**) in or forming the south part of something: *South Africa* ○ *the South China Sea* ○ *These plants grow well on a south-facing wall.* **2 south wind** a wind coming from the south

south /saʊθ/ *adv* towards the south: *The Mississippi river flows south.* ○ *They drove south towards the coast.* ○ *He travelled due* (= directly) *south, towards the desert.*
• **down south** to or in the south of a country or region: *Alice got a job down south.*

southbound /ˈsaʊθ.baʊnd/ *adj, adv* going or leading towards the south: *southbound passengers/traffic* ○ *All southbound trains leave from platform one.*

southerly /ˈsʌð.ə.li/ ⓤ /-ɚ.li/ *adj* **1** towards or in the south: *We walked in a southerly direction.* ○ *Los Cristianos is the most southerly resort in Tenerife.* **2 southerly wind** a wind that comes from the south

southern, Southern /ˈsʌð.ən/ ⓤ /-ɚn/ *adj* (*WRITTEN ABBREVIATION* **S**, *US ALSO* **So**) in or from the south part of an area: *a southern route/bypass* ○ *the Southern Hemisphere*

southerner, Southerner /ˈsʌð.ə.nəʳ/ ⓤ /-ɚ.nɚ/ *noun* [C] a person who comes from the south of a country

southernmost /ˈsʌð.ən.məʊst/ ⓤ /-ɚn.moʊst/ *adj*: furthest towards the south of an area: *the southernmost tip of the island*

southward /ˈsaʊθ.wəd/ ⓤ /-wɚd/ *adj* towards the south: *We walked in a southward direction.*

southwards /ˈsaʊθ.wədz/ ⓤ /-wɚdz/ *adv* (*ALSO* **southward**) *They cycled southwards* (= towards the south) *towards the sea.*

South America *noun* [U] the continent that is to the south of North America, to the west of the Atlantic Ocean and to the east of the Pacific Ocean **South American** *adj*

southeast /ˌsaʊθˈiːst/ *noun* **1** [U] (*WRITTEN ABBREVIATION* **SE**) the direction which is between south and east: *We live in the southeast.* **2 the Southeast** an area of Britain around London which is considered to be wealthier than other parts of the country

southeast /ˌsaʊθˈiːst/ *adj, adv* (*WRITTEN ABBREVIATION* **SE**) in or towards the southeast: *Southeast Asia* ○ *The mountains are/lie southeast of the city.*

southeast /ˌsaʊθˈiːst/ *adj* **southeast wind** a wind that comes from the southeast

southeasterly /ˌsaʊθˈiː.stə.li/ ⓤ /-stɚ-/ *adj* towards the southeast: *The plane was flying in a southeasterly direction.*

southeastern /ˌsaʊθˈiː.stən/ ⓤ /-stɚn/ *adj* (*WRITTEN ABBREVIATION* **SE**) in or from the southeast: *The southeastern part of Britain is the most populated.*

southeastward /ˌsaʊθˈiːs.twəd/ ⓤ /-twɚd/ *adj* towards the southeast: *If we sail in a southeastward direction we'll reach land.* **southeastwards** /ˌsaʊθˈiːs.twədz/ ⓤ /-twɚdz/ *adv* (*ALSO* **southeastward**) *Looking southeastwards, they could see the distant mountains.*

the Southern Cross *noun* [S] the group of stars which points towards the South Pole and appears on the flags of Australia and New Zealand

southpaw /ˈsaʊθ.pɔː/ ⓤ /-pɑː/ *noun* [C] **1** *UK* a left-handed boxer **2** *US* a left-handed person, especially a left-handed pitcher in the sport of baseball

the South Pole *noun* [S] the point on the Earth's surface which is furthest south

southwest /ˌsaʊθˈwest/ *noun* **1** [U] (*WRITTEN ABBREVIATION* **SW**) the direction which is between south and west **2 the Southwest** the area in the southwest of Britain or of another country: *There will be rain in the Southwest.*

southwest /ˌsaʊθˈwest/ *adj, adv* (*WRITTEN ABBREVIATION* **SW**) in or towards the southwest: *I come from the southwest part of the island.* ○ *They moved southwest in an attempt to find better land.*

southwester /ˌsaʊθˈwes.təʳ/ ⓤ /-tɚ/ *noun* [C] (*ALSO* **sou'wester**) a strong wind coming from the southwest

southwesterly /ˌsaʊθˈwes.tə.li/ ⓤ /-tɚ-/ *adj* towards the southwest: *They were travelling in a southwesterly direction.*

southwestern /ˌsaʊθˈwes.tən/ ⓤ /-tɚn/ *adj* (*WRITTEN ABBREVIATION* **SW**) in or from the southwest: *The southwestern corner of Britain is the warmest.*

southwestward /ˌsaʊθˈwes.twəd/ ⓤ /-twɚd/ *adj* towards the southwest: *We sailed in a southwestward direction.* **southwestwards** /ˌsaʊθˈwes.twədz/ ⓤ /-twɚdz/ *adv* (*ALSO* **southwestward**) *They sailed southwestwards until they reached land.*

souvenir /ˌsuː.vənˈɪəʳ/ ⓤ /-vəˈnɪr/ *noun* [C] something you buy or keep to help you remember a holiday or special event: *He bought a model of a red London bus as a souvenir of his trip to London.* ○ *We brought back a few souvenirs from our holiday in Greece.*

S

COMMON LEARNER ERROR

souvenir

A **souvenir** is a thing, not a feeling. If you want to talk about a feeling or memory that you have about something in the past, you should use the noun **memory**.

~~*I have a lot of happy souvenirs of staying at my grandparents' house.*~~
I have a lot of happy memories of staying at my grandparents' house.

sou'wester /ˌsaʊˈwes.təʳ/ [US] /-tɚ/ *noun* [C] **1** a waterproof hat with a wide piece at the back to protect the neck, worn especially by sailors **2** a **southwester**

sovereign [RULER] /ˈsɒv.ᵊr.ɪn/ [US] /ˈsɑːv.rən/ *noun* [C] a king or queen, or the person with the highest power in a country

sovereign /ˈsɒv.ᵊr.ɪn/ [US] /ˈsɑːv.rən/ *adj* [before n] *Sovereign* (= The highest) *power is said to lie with the people in some countries, and with a ruler in others.* ○ *We must respect the rights of sovereign* (= completely independent) ***states/nations*** *to conduct their own affairs.*

sovereignty /ˈsɒv.rɪn.ti/ [US] /ˈsɑːv.rᵊn.ṭi/ *noun* [U] the power of a country to control its own government: *Talks are being held about who should* ***have*** *sovereignty* ***over*** *the island.*

sovereign [EXCELLENT] /ˈsɒv.ᵊr.ɪn/ [US] /ˈsɑːv.rən/ *adj* *OLD-FASHIONED OR FORMAL* **sovereign remedy** an extremely successful way of dealing with a problem: *Love is a sovereign remedy for unhappiness.*

sovereign [COIN] /ˈsɒv.ᵊr.ɪn/ [US] /ˈsɑːv.rən/ *noun* [C] a British gold coin which was in use in Britain from 1817 to 1914 and was worth £1

Soviet [NATIONALITY] /ˈsəʊ.vi.ət/ [US] /ˈsoʊ-/ *adj* (in the past) of the USSR: *the Soviet people*

Soviet /ˈsəʊ.vi.ət/ [US] /ˈsoʊ-/ *noun* *MAINLY US* **the Soviets** the people of the USSR

soviet [ORGANIZATION] /ˈsəʊ.vi.ət/ [US] /ˈsoʊ-/ *noun* [C] an elected group at any of several levels in Communist countries, especially (in the past) the USSR

sow [PLANT] /səʊ/ [US] /soʊ/ *verb* [I or T] **sowed, sown** or **sowed** to put seeds in or on the ground so that plants will grow: *Sow the* ***seeds*** *in pots.* ○ *We'll sow this field* ***with*** *barley.*

• **As ye sow, so shall ye reap.** *LITERARY SAYING* used to mean that the way you behave in life will affect the treatment you will receive from others

• **sow the seeds of *sth*** to do something that will cause an unpleasant situation in the future: *He's sowing the seeds of his own downfall.*

• **sow *your* wild oats** If a young man sows his wild oats he has a period of his life when he does a lot of exciting things and has a lot of sexual relationships.

sow [CAUSE] /səʊ/ [US] /soʊ/ *verb* [T] **sowed, sown** or **sowed** to cause a bad emotion or condition to begin somewhere, which will grow or continue: *Now that you've sown* ***doubts*** *in my mind, I'll never again be sure I can trust him.*

sow [ANIMAL] /saʊ/ *noun* [C] an adult female pig

ˈsoya ˌbean *noun* [C usually pl] (*MAINLY US* **soybean**) a small edible bean grown especially in Asia and the US, which is used as a food for people and animals

soya /ˈsɔɪ.ə/ *noun* [U] (*US* **soy**) soya beans as a crop

ˈsoya ˌmilk *UK noun* [U] (*US* **soy milk**) a white liquid made from soya beans which some people use instead of milk

ˌsoy ˈsauce *noun* [U] (*UK ALSO* **soya sauce**) a strong-tasting dark brown liquid made from FERMENTED soya beans and used especially in Chinese and Japanese cooking

sozzled /ˈsɒz.l̩d/ [US] /ˈsɑː.zl̩d/ *adj* [after v] *UK INFORMAL* very drunk

<sp?> *INTERNET ABBREVIATION FOR* spelling?: used after a word whose spelling you are not certain of

spa /spɑː/ *noun* [C] **1** a town where water comes out of the ground and people come to drink it or lie in it because they think it will improve their health: *Baden Baden in Germany and Bath in Britain are two of Europe's famous spa* ***towns.*** ○ *spa water* **2** *MAINLY US* a place where people go in order to become more healthy, by doing exercises, eating special food, etc: *Two weeks in a luxury spa can be yours just for answering a few simple questions.*

space [EMPTY PLACE] /speɪs/ *noun* **1** [C or U] an empty area which is available to be used: *Is there any space* ***for*** *my clothes in that cupboard?* ○ *I've got to* ***make*** *(some) space for Mark's things.* ○ *When the roads are wet, you've got to leave plenty of space* ***between*** *you and the car in front.* ○ *The blank space at the end of the form is for your name.* ○ *We found a* ***parking*** *space close to the museum.* ➲See also **airspace**. **2** [U] that which is around everything that exists and which is continuous in all directions: *He was absent-mindedly* ***staring/gazing into*** *space* (= looking, but seeing nothing). ○ *Virtual Reality aims to give us artificial worlds to explore, outside normal space and time.* **3 open space** land, especially in a town, which has no buildings on it: *What I like about Cambridge is that there's so much open space – there are parks and commons everywhere.* ○ *I love the* ***wide*** *open spaces* (= large areas of countryside) *of central Australia.*

• **in/within a short space of time** very soon: *Within a short space of time you could be speaking perfect English!*

• **in/within the space of six weeks/three hours, etc.** during a period of six weeks/three hours, etc: *It all happened in the space of ten minutes.*

space /speɪs/ *verb* [T] to arrange things or people so that there is some distance or time between them: *That page looks badly spaced* (= there is too much/too little distance between the lines or words). ○ *The flowers were spaced* ***(out)*** *evenly* (= planted at equal distances) *beside the path.* ○ *If you're in financial difficulty, we're happy to let you space* ***(out)*** *your payments* (= pay in smaller amounts over a longer period of time) ***over*** *two years.*

spacing /ˈspeɪ.sɪŋ/ *noun* [U] the amount of distance between lines or words, especially on a printed page: *single/double/triple spacing*

spacious /ˈspeɪ.ʃəs/ *adj APPROVING* large and with a lot of space: *a spacious house/living room* ○ *spacious accommodation* **spaciously** /ˈspeɪ.ʃə.sli/ *adv* **spaciousness** /ˈspeɪ.ʃə.snəs/ *noun* [U]

spatial /ˈspeɪ.ʃᵊl/ *adj* relating to the position, area and size of things: *This task is designed to test the child's spatial* ***awareness*** (= understanding of where things are in relation to other things). **spatially** /ˈspeɪ.ʃᵊl.i/ *adv*: *spatially aware*

space [BEYOND EARTH] /speɪs/ *noun* [U] the empty area outside the Earth's atmosphere, where the planets and the stars are: *space exploration/travel* ○ *a space rocket* ○ *Who was the first human being* ***in*** *space/the first to go* ***into*** *space?*

space-age /ˈspeɪs.eɪdʒ/ *adj* [before n] very modern: *space-age technology*

space bar /ˈspeɪs.bɑːʳ/ [US] /-bɑːr/ *noun* [C usually sing] on a computer keyboard or a typewriter, the long bar below the letter keys which you press in order to make a space between words

ˈspace caˌdet *noun* [C] *HUMOROUS* someone who behaves strangely: *She's a bit of a space cadet but she's nice enough.*

spacecraft /ˈspeɪs.krɑːft/ [US] /-kræft/ *noun* [C] *plural* **spacecraft** a vehicle used for travel in space: *a manned/unmanned spacecraft* (= with/without people inside)

ˌspaced ˈout *adj* [after v] (*ALSO* **spacey**) *SLANG* describes someone who is not completely aware of what is happening around them, often because of taking drugs or lack of sleep: *I hadn't slept for two days and was completely spaced out.*

spaceman /ˈspeɪs.mæn/ *noun* [C] **1** an astronaut **2** in stories, a creature from another planet: *to be abducted by spacemen*

ˈspace ˌprobe *noun* [C] a small spacecraft, with no one travelling in it, sent into space to make measurements and send back information to scientists on Earth

space-saving /ˈspeɪs.seɪ.vɪŋ/ *adj* [before n] describes a device, piece of furniture, etc. which takes up little room, for example a folding bed

spaceship /ˈspeɪs.ʃɪp/ *noun* [C] (especially in stories) a vehicle used for travel in space

S

ˈspace ˌshuttle *noun* **[C usually sing]** a vehicle in which people travel into space and back again, sometimes carrying a SATELLITE or other equipment into ORBIT (= a curved path through space)

ˈspace ˌstation *noun* **[C]** a vehicle in which people can travel round the Earth, outside its atmosphere, doing scientific tests

spacesuit /ˈspeɪs.sjuːt/ [US] /-suːt/ *noun* **[C]** a piece of clothing worn by a person who travels in space to protect the body when outside a spacecraft

space-time /ˌspeɪsˈtaɪm/ *noun* **[U]** *SPECIALIZED* a part of Einstein's Theory of Relativity, which adds the idea of time to those of height, depth and length

spacewalk /ˈspeɪs.wɔːk/ [US] /-wɑːk/ *noun* **[C]** an act of moving around in space outside a spacecraft but connected to it: *The crew are planning a four-hour spacewalk to carry out necessary repair work on the shuttle.*

spacey /ˈspeɪ.si/ *adj* **spaced out**

spacing /ˈspeɪ.sɪŋ/ *noun* **[U]** ➲See at **space** EMPTY PLACE.

spacious /ˈspeɪ.ʃəs/ *adj* ➲See at **space** EMPTY PLACE.

spade [TOOL] /speɪd/ *noun* **[C]** a tool used for digging especially earth or sand, with a long handle and a flat blade: *a garden spade* ○ *The kids took their* ***buckets and spades*** *to the beach.*

spade [CARD] /speɪd/ *noun* **[C]** a playing card with one or more black shapes like pointed leaves with short stems printed on it

spades /speɪdz/ *plural noun* one of the four suits in a set of playing cards: *the ace/Queen* ***of*** *spades*

• **in spades** *INFORMAL* in large amounts or to a very great degree: *I don't get colds very often but when I do I get them in spades.*

spade [PERSON] /speɪd/ *noun* **[C]** *OFFENSIVE OLD-FASHIONED* a black person

spadework /ˈspeɪd.wɜːk/ [US] /-wɝːk/ *noun* **[U]** *UK* hard, sometimes boring work done in preparation for something: *Now that the spadework's all been* ***done****, we can start to write the report itself.*

spaghetti /spəˈget.i/ [US] /-ˈgeṭ-/ *noun* **[U]** pasta made in the form of long, thin threads

spaghetti bolognese /spəˌget.i.bɒl.əˈneɪz/ [US] /-ˌgeṭ.i.boʊ.ləˈnjeɪz/ *noun* **[U]** (*INFORMAL* **spag bol**) *UK* a dish consisting of spaghetti with a tomato and meat sauce

spaˌghetti ˈwestern *noun* **[C]** a film about cowboys in the Wild West made cheaply in Europe, usually by an Italian DIRECTOR (= person in charge of making a film)

spake /speɪk/ *OLD USE OR HUMOROUS past simple of* **speak** SAY WORDS: *Thus spake the expert.*

spam [FOOD] /spæm/ *noun* **[U]** *TRADEMARK* a type of meat sold in metal containers, made mostly from PORK (= meat from a pig): *spam fritters*

spam [COMPUTING] /spæm/ *noun* **[U]** *INFORMAL DISAPPROVING* unwanted email, usually advertisements

spam /spæm/ *verb* **[T]** to send someone an advertisement by email that they do not want

spammer /ˈspæ.m.əʳ/ [US] /-ɚ/ *noun* **[C]** a person or company that sends spam

span [SPACE] /spæn/ *noun* **1** **[C usually sing]** the period of time that sometimes exists or happens: *He has a short* ***attention/concentration*** *span.* ○ *an average* ***life*** *span of seventy years* ○ ***Over a*** *span* ***of*** *just three years, the new government has transformed the country's economic prospects.* ➲See also **lifespan**; **wingspan**. **2** **[C]** the length of something from one end to the other: *huge wings with a span of over a metre* **3** **[C]** the area of a bridge, etc. between two supports: *The bridge crosses the river in a single span.*

span /spæn/ *verb* **[T]** **-nn-** **1** to exist or continue for a particular length of time: *Tennis has a history spanning several centuries.* ○ *Her acting career spanned almost six decades.* **2** If a bridge spans a river, it goes from one side to the other: *An old bridge spans the river just outside the town.*

span [SPIN] /spæn/ *past simple of* **spin**

span [CLEAN] /spæn/ *adj* **spick and span**, see at **spick** CLEAN.

Spandex /ˈspæn.deks/ *noun* **[U]** *TRADEMARK* a stretchy material used especially for making clothes fit tightly

spangle /ˈspæŋ.gl/ *noun* **[C]** a small piece of shiny metal or plastic, used especially in large amounts to decorate clothes; a **sequin**

spangly /ˈspæŋ.gḷd/ *adj* (*ALSO* **spangled**) covered with spangles: *a spangly top*

Spaniard /ˈspæn.jəd/ [US] /-jɚd/ *noun* **[C]** a person from Spain ➲See also **Spanish**.

spaniel /ˈspæn.jəl/ *noun* **[C]** a type of dog with long hair and long ears that hang down

Spanish /ˈspæn.ɪʃ/ *adj* from, belonging to or relating to Spain: *Are you Spanish?* ○ *Spanish literature* ○ *I met a Spanish person/some Spanish people yesterday.* ○ *Spanish customs/food/people*

Spanish /ˈspæn.ɪʃ/ *noun* **[U]** the language of Spain: *Do you speak Spanish?*

spank /spæŋk/ *verb* **[T]** **1** to hit a child with the hand, usually several times on the bottom as a punishment **2** to hit an adult on the bottom in order to get or give sexual pleasure **spanking** /ˈspæŋ.kɪŋ/ *noun* **[C or U]** (*ALSO* **spank**) *He needs a* ***good*** *spanking.*

spanking [FAST] /ˈspæŋ.kɪŋ/ *adj* **[before n]** *INFORMAL APPROVING* very quick: *They raced by at a spanking* ***pace****.*

spanking [VERY] /ˈspæŋ.kɪŋ/ *adv* *OLD-FASHIONED INFORMAL APPROVING* (used with some adjectives) very, completely: *a spanking* ***new*** *suit* ○ *spanking white sheets*

spanner *UK* /ˈspæn.əʳ/ [US] /-ɚ/ *noun* **[C]** (*US* **wrench**) a metal tool with a shaped end, used to turn nuts and bolts: *an open-ended/adjustable/ring spanner*

• **put/throw a spanner in the works** *UK* (*US* **throw a (monkey) wrench in the works**) to do something that prevents a plan or activity from succeeding: *The funding for the project was withdrawn so that really threw a spanner in the works.*

spar [FIGHT] /spɑːʳ/ [US] /spɑːr/ *verb* **[I]** **-rr-** **1** to practise boxing, without hitting hard **2** to argue: *Frank and Jill always spar* ***with*** *each other at meetings, but they're good friends really.*

spar [POLE] /spɑːʳ/ [US] /spɑːr/ *noun* **[C]** *SPECIALIZED* a strong pole, especially one used as a mast to hold the sail on a ship

spare [EXTRA] /speəʳ/ [US] /sper/ *adj* **1** If something is spare, it is available to use because it is extra: *a spare key/tyre* ○ *spare sheets and blankets* ○ *Have you got a spare pen?* ○ *We've got a spare* ***room*** *if you want to stay overnight with us.* ○ *Could I have a word with you when you've got a spare* ***moment/minute****?* ○ *UK INFORMAL "Do you want this cake?" "Yes, if it's* ***going*** *spare* (= if no one else wants it)*."* **2** **spare time** time when you are not working: *I like to do a bit of gardening* ***in*** *my spare time.*

spare /speəʳ/ [US] /sper/ *noun* **[C]** **1** an extra thing which is not being used and which can be used instead of a part which is broken, lost, etc. **2** a **spare (part)**

spare [THIN] /speəʳ/ [US] /sper/ *adj* *LITERARY* tall and thin: *He had the spare build of a runner.*

spare [SAVE] /speəʳ/ [US] /sper/ *verb* **[T]** to not hurt or destroy something or someone: *They asked him to spare the women and children.*

spare [AVOID] /speəʳ/ [US] /sper/ *verb* **[T + two objects]** to prevent someone from having to experience something unpleasant: *Luckily, I was spared the embarrassment of having to sing in front of everyone.* ○ *It was a nasty accident – but I'll spare you* (= I won't tell you) *the gruesome* ***details****.*

• **spare *sb's* blushes** *HUMOROUS* to avoid making someone feel embarrassed

spare [TRY HARD] /speəʳ/ [US] /sper/ *verb* **1** **spare no effort/expense** to use a lot of effort/EXPENSE (= money), etc. to do something: **[+ *to* infinitive]** *We will spare no effort* ***to*** *find out who did this.* ➲See also **no expense is spared** at **expense**. **2** *FORMAL* **not spare yourself** to try as hard as you can to achieve something: *She never spared herself in the pursuit of excellence.*

• **Spare the rod and spoil the child.** *OLD-FASHIONED SAYING* said to mean that if you do not punish a child when it does something wrong, it will not learn what is right

spare [GIVE] /speəʳ/ [US] /sper/ *verb* **[T]** **1** to give time, money or space to someone especially when it is difficult for you: **[+ two objects]** *Could you spare me £10?* ○ *I'd love to come, but I'm afraid I can't spare the time.* **2** **spare a**

thought for *sb* to think about someone who is in a difficult or unpleasant situation: *Spare a thought for me tomorrow, when you're lying on a beach, because I'll still be here in the office!*

• **to spare** left over or more than you need: *If you've got any wool to spare when you've finished the pullover, can you make me some gloves?* ○ *I caught the plane with only two minutes to spare.* ○ *There's no time/We've got no time to spare if we want to get the article written by tomorrow.*

sparing /ˈspeə.rɪŋ/ [US] /ˈsper.ɪŋ/ *adj* using very little of something: *Be sparing **with** the butter as we don't have much left.* ○ *He is sparing **with/in** his praise* (= praises people very little). **sparingly** /ˈspeə.rɪŋ.li/ [US] /ˈsper.ɪŋ-/ *adv*: *There wasn't enough coal during the war, so we had to use it sparingly.*

spare [ANNOYED] /speəʳ/ [US] /sper/ *adj* UK INFORMAL **go spare** to get very upset or angry: *She goes spare if I'm so much as five minutes late.*

ˌspare (ˈpart) *noun* [C usually pl] a piece that can be used to replace another similar piece in a car or other device

spare-part surgery UK /ˌspeəˈpɑːtˌsɜː.dʒəʳr.i/ [US] /ˌsperˈpɑːrtˌsɝː.dʒɚ-/ *noun* [U] (US **organ transplant surgery**) when a healthy organ such as a heart or lung is taken from a person who has just died and put into a living person to replace a diseased organ

spare ribs /ˈspeə.rɪbz/ [US] /ˈsper-/ *plural noun* pig's ribs with most of the meat cut off them, which are cooked and eaten: *barbecued spare ribs*

ˌspare ˈtyre UK *noun* [C usually sing] (US **spare tire**) HUMOROUS unwanted fat around your waist

spark [FIRE/ELECTRICITY] /spɑːk/ [US] /spɑːrk/ *noun* [C] **1** a very small bit of fire which flies out from something that is burning or which is made by rubbing two hard things together, or a flash of light made by electricity: *Sparks were flying out of the bonfire and blowing everywhere.* ○ *You can start a fire by rubbing two dry pieces of wood together until you produce a spark.* **2 spark of anger/inspiration/life, etc.** a very small amount of a particular emotion or quality in a person

• **sparks fly** If sparks fly between two or more people, they argue angrily: *When they get together in a meeting **the** sparks really fly.*

spark [CAUSE] /spɑːk/ [US] /spɑːrk/ *noun* [S] a first small event or problem which causes a much worse situation to develop: *That small incident was the spark that set off the street riots.*

spark /spɑːk/ [US] /spɑːrk/ *verb* [T] to cause the start of something, especially an argument or fighting: *This proposal will almost certainly spark another countrywide debate about how to organize the school system.* ○ *The recent interest rises have sparked new problems for the Government.* ○ *The visit of the all-white rugby team sparked **off*** (= caused the start of) *mass demonstrations.*

sparkle /ˈspɑː.kl̩/ [US] /ˈspɑːr-/ *verb* [I] **1** to shine brightly with a lot of small points of light: *The snow/sea sparkled in the sunlight.* **2** If a person or performance sparkles, they are energetic, interesting and exciting: *Alice is shy and quiet at parties, but her sister really sparkles!*

sparkle /ˈspɑː.kl̩/ [US] /ˈspɑːr-/ *noun* [U] **1** bright shine: *The radiant smile and the sparkle in her blue eyes were the clear signs of a woman still deeply in love.* **2** energy and interest: *Their latest performance of My Fair Lady really **lacked** sparkle.* ○ *The sparkle **went out of/left** her* (= She became unhappy) *after her husband died.*

sparkling /ˈspɑː.klɪŋ/ [US] /ˈspɑːr-/ *adj* **1** shining brightly: *sparkling white teeth* **2** energetic and interesting: *a sparkling performance* ○ *sparkling conversation/wit* **3** A sparkling drink is one which is fizzy: *Champagne is a sparkling wine.* ➲Compare **still** NOT MOVING.

sparkler /ˈspɑː.kləʳ/ [US] /ˈspɑːr.klɚ/ *noun* [C] **1** a firework which children can hold in their hands and which produces a lot of SPARKS as it burns **2** SLANG a jewel, especially a diamond

ˈspark ˌplug [ENGINE] *noun* [C] a device in an engine which produces an electrical SPARK which lights the fuel and makes the engine start

ˈspark ˌplug [PERSON] *noun* [C] US a person who gives energy to an activity involving others: *She's the spark plug of the team – the one who gets everyone else to give their all.*

sparky /ˈspɑː.ki/ [US] /ˈspɑːr-/ *adj* INFORMAL energetic, clever and enjoyable to be with

ˈsparring ˌpartner *noun* [C usually sing] **1** a person you practise boxing with **2** someone you have friendly arguments with

sparrow /ˈspær.əʊ/ [US] /ˈsper.oʊ/ *noun* [C] a small grey-brown bird which is especially common in towns ➲See picture **Animals and Birds** on page Centre 4

sparrowhawk /ˈspær.əʊ.hɔːk/ [US] /ˈsper.oʊ.hɑːk/ *noun* [C] a small HAWK (= a type of bird which catches and eats other birds or animals)

sparse /spɑːs/ [US] /spɑːrs/ *adj* small in numbers or amount, often scattered over a large area: *a sparse population/audience* ○ *sparse vegetation/woodland* ○ *a sparse beard* ○ *Information coming out of the disaster area is sparse.* **sparsely** /ˈspɑː.sli/ [US] /ˈspɑːr-/ *adv*: *sparsely furnished/populated* **sparseness** /ˈspɑː.snəs/ [US] /ˈspɑːr-/ *noun* [U] (ALSO **sparsity**)

spartan /ˈspɑː.tən/ [US] /ˈspɑːr-/ *adj* simple and severe with no comfort: *a spartan diet/meal* ○ *spartan living conditions* ○ *They lead a rather spartan life, with very few comforts and no luxuries.*

spasm /ˈspæz.ᵊm/ *noun* [C or U] **1** a sudden uncontrollable tightening of a muscle: *a muscle/muscular spasm* ○ MAINLY UK *My leg suddenly **went into** spasm.* **2 spasm of *sth*** a short period of something, especially something uncontrollable: *a spasm of guilt/coughing/laughing*

spasmodic /spæzˈmɒd.ɪk/ [US] /-ˈmɑː.dɪk/ *adj* happening suddenly for short periods of time and not in a regular way: *He made spasmodic attempts to clean up the house.*

spastic /ˈspæs.tɪk/ *adj* **1** OLD-FASHIONED suffering from CEREBRAL PALSY (= a condition of the body which makes it difficult to control the muscles) **2** INFORMAL an offensive way of saying 'stupid', used especially by children **spastic** /ˈspæs.tɪk/ *noun* [C]

spat [SPIT] /spæt/ *past simple and past participle of* **spit** FORCE OUT.

spat [ARGUMENT] /spæt/ *noun* [C] INFORMAL a short argument, usually about something unimportant: *She was **having a** spat **with** her brother **about** who did the washing up.*

spat [SHOE] /spæt/ *noun* [C usually pl] a piece of cloth or leather covering the ankle and part of the shoe and fastening on the side, worn in the past by men

spate /speɪt/ *noun* [C usually sing] an unusually large number of events, especially unwanted ones, happening at about the same time: *Police are investigating a spate **of** burglaries in the Kingsland Road area.*

• **in (full) spate** UK If a river is in (full) spate it has more water in it and is flowing faster than it usually does.

spatial /ˈspeɪ.ʃᵊl/ *adj* ➲See at **space** EMPTY PLACE.

spatter /ˈspæt.əʳ/ [US] /ˈspæt̬.ɚ/ *verb* [I or T] to scatter drops of liquid, etc. on a surface, or (of liquid) to fall, especially noisily, in small drops: *Two bikes raced by and spattered mud **over** our clothes.* ○ *The bikes spattered them **with** mud.* ○ *They could hear raindrops spattering **on** the roof of the caravan.* **spatter** /ˈspæt.əʳ/ [US] /ˈspæt̬.ɚ/ *noun* [C]

spattered /ˈspæt.əd/ [US] /ˈspæt̬.ɚd/ *adj* covered with small drops of a liquid: *a paint-spattered shirt* ○ *His clothes were spattered **with** blood.*

spatula /ˈspæt.jʊ.lə/ *noun* [C] **1** a cooking utensil with a wide flat blade which is not sharp, used especially for lifting food out of pans **2** UK (US **tongue depressor**) a small piece of wood used by a doctor to hold someone's tongue down in order to examine their mouth or throat

spawn [EGGS] /spɔːn/ [US] /spɑːn/ *noun* [U] the eggs of fish, frogs, etc. ➲See also **frogspawn**.

spawn /spɔːn/ [US] /spɑːn/ *verb* [I] *The frogs haven't spawned* (= produced eggs) *yet.*

spawn [START] /spɔːn/ [US] /spɑːn/ *verb* [T] to cause something new, or many new things, to grow or start suddenly: *The new economic freedom has spawned hundreds of new small businesses.* ○ *He death spawned countless films and books.*

S

'spawning ˌground *noun* [C usually sing] a place where fish leave their eggs for FERTILIZATION: *Salmon and sea trout use the upper river as a spawning ground.*

spay /speɪ/ *verb* [T] to remove the OVARIES of a female animal: *We're having the cat spayed.*

speak [SAY WORDS] /spiːk/ *verb* [I or T] **spoke, spoken 1** to say words, to use the voice, or to have a conversation with someone: *Would you mind speaking more slowly, please?* ○ *"Can I speak **to**/(MAINLY US) **with** Ian please?" "Speaking* (= This is Ian)." ○ *If he tells Julie what I said, I'll never speak **to** him again.* ○ FORMAL *She spoke **of** her sadness over her father's death.* ○ *She speaks very **highly of*** (= says good things about) *the new director.* ○ *I can certainly come but I can't speak **for** my wife* (= I can't tell you whether she can or not). ○ FORMAL *Who is going to speak **for*** (= represent in a court of law) *the accused?* ○ *He's old enough to speak **for himself*** (= to say what he thinks). ○ *I went with Ava – speaking **of*** (= on the subject of) *Ava, have you seen her new haircut?* ○ *We've been invited to Rachel and Jamie's wedding – speaking **of which**, did you know that they're moving to Ealing?* ○ *Speaking **as*** (= With my experience as) *a mother of four, I can tell you that children are exhausting.* ○ *Sue speaks **with an** American **accent**.* ○ *Why are you speaking **in a whisper*** (= very quietly)? ○ *For five whole minutes, neither of them spoke **a word*** (= they both said nothing). **2 broadly/historically/strictly, etc. speaking** talking from a particular point of view: *Historically speaking, the island is of great interest.* ○ *Generally speaking, it's quite a good school.* ○ *Strictly speaking* (= If I behave according to the rules), *I should report it to the police.* **3 speak to *sb*** to tell someone that they have done something wrong: *The manager promised that she would speak to the person responsible.*

• **speaks for itself** If something speaks for itself, it is clear and needs no further explanation: *The school's excellent record speaks for itself.*

• **speak for yourself** INFORMAL something you say to someone to tell them that the opinion that they have just expressed is not the same as your opinion: *"We had a really boring trip." "Speak for yourself! I had a wonderful time!"*

• **speak *your* mind** to say what you think about something very directly: *He's certainly not afraid to speak his mind.*

• **none to speak of** (ALSO **no *sth* to speak of**) very little of something: *"Did you get much rain while you were in Singapore?" "None to speak of."*

• **so to speak** used to explain that what you are saying is not to be understood exactly as stated: *In that relationship it's very much Lorna who wears the trousers, so to speak* (= Lorna makes all the important decisions).

• **be on speaking terms** (ALSO **know *sb* to speak to**) to know someone well enough to talk to them

• **not be on speaking terms** If you are not on speaking terms with someone you refuse to speak to them because you are angry with them: *They had a quarrel last night and now they're not on speaking terms **(with** each other).*

• **speak too soon** to say something which is quickly shown not to be true: *He won't be home for ages yet ... Oh, I spoke too soon – here he is now!*

speak [LANGUAGE] /spiːk/ *verb* [T] **spoke, spoken** to (be able to) talk in a language: *He speaks fluent French.* ○ *How many foreign languages do you speak?* ○ *I couldn't speak **a word of*** (= I did not know any) *Spanish when I got there.* ○ *I couldn't work out what language they were speaking.*

speaker /ˈspiː.kəʳ/ [US] /-kɚ/ *noun* [C] someone who speaks a particular language: *a French speaker* ○ *a **fluent** Russian speaker* ○ *non-English speakers*

-speaking /-spiː.kɪŋ/ *suffix* using the stated language: *a Spanish-speaking country*

-speak [SPECIAL LANGUAGE] /-spiːk/ *suffix* INFORMAL MAINLY DISAPPROVING used to form nouns, to mean the special language used in a particular subject area or business: *computerspeak* ○ *marketingspeak*

speak [FORMAL TALK] /spiːk/ *verb* [I] **spoke, spoken** to give a formal talk to a group of people: *Who is speaking in the debate tonight?* ○ *The Queen speaks **to** the nation on television every Christmas.* ○ *Janet is speaking **for** the motion* (= trying to persuade the people listening that the idea is good) *and Peter is speaking **against** (it)* (= trying to persuade them that it is bad).

speaker /ˈspiː.kəʳ/ [US] /-kɚ/ *noun* [C] a person who gives a speech at a public event: *a good **public** speaker* ○ *Please join with me in thanking our **guest** speaker tonight.* ○ *The Democrats have chosen the Texas state treasurer as the **keynote*** (= most important) *speaker at their convention.*

Speaker /ˈspiː.kəʳ/ [US] /-kɚ/ *noun* [C] the person who controls the way in which business is done in an organization which makes laws, such as a parliament: *He served for eight years as Speaker of the House of Representatives.* ○ [as form of address] *Mr Speaker, my honourable friend has failed to consider the consequences of his proposal.*

speak [SUGGEST] /spiːk/ *verb* [I + adv or prep; T] **spoke, spoken** LITERARY to show or express something without using words: *She was silent, but her eyes spoke her real feelings for him.* ○ *The whole robbery spoke **of*** (= made it seem that there had been) *inside knowledge on the part of the criminals.*

• **speak volumes** If something speaks volumes, it makes an opinion, characteristic or situation very clear without the use of words: *She said very little but her face spoke volumes.*

PHRASAL VERBS WITH **speak** ▼

▲ **speak out/up** *phrasal verb* to give your opinion about something in public, especially on a subject which you have strong feelings about: *If no one has the courage to speak out **against** the system, things will never improve.*

▲ **speak up** *phrasal verb* to speak in a louder voice so that people can hear you: *Could you speak up? We can't hear at the back.*

▲ **speak up for *sb/sth*** *phrasal verb* to support someone or something, especially by saying good things about them: *She has often spoken up for the rights of working mothers.*

speakeasy /ˈspiːkˌiː.zi/ *noun* [C] a place where alcohol was illegally sold and drunk in the US in the 1920s and 1930s

speaker /ˈspiː.kəʳ/ [US] /-kɚ/ *noun* [C] the part of a radio or television, or of a piece of electrical equipment for playing recorded sound, through which the sound is played. A speaker can be part of the radio, etc. or be separate from it: *There's no sound coming out of the right-hand speaker.* ⊃See also **speaker** at **speak** LANGUAGE; **speak** FORMAL TALK. ⊃See picture **In the Office** on page Centre 15

speakerphone /ˈspiː.kə.fəʊn/ [US] /-kɚ.foʊn/ *noun* [C] a telephone which you can use without having to hold any part of it in your hand

Speakers' Corner /ˌspiː.kəzˈkɔː.nəʳ/ [US] /-kɚzˈkɔːr.nɚ/ *noun* [S] a place in Hyde Park, in London, where people speak publicly about moral and political matters

spear /spɪəʳ/ [US] /spɪr/ *noun* [C] **1** a weapon consisting of a pole with a sharp, usually metal, point at one end, which is either thrown or held in the hand **2** a thin pointed stem or leaf: *asparagus spears*

spear /spɪəʳ/ [US] /spɪr/ *verb* [T] **1** to push or throw a spear into an animal: *They catch the fish by spearing them.* **2** to catch something on the end of a pointed tool or object: *He speared a meatball with his fork.*

'spear ˌcarrier *noun* [C] in the theatre, someone who has a small part, usually without any words to say

spearhead /ˈspɪə.hed/ [US] /ˈspɪr-/ *verb* [T] to lead something such as an attack or a course of action: *British troops spearheaded the invasion.* ○ *Joe Walker will be spearheading our new marketing initiative.*

spearhead /ˈspɪə.hed/ [US] /ˈspɪr-/ *noun* [C usually sing] *American troops formed the spearhead* (= were at the front) ***of** the attack.*

spearmint /ˈspɪə.mɪnt/ [US] /ˈspɪr-/ *noun* [U] a strong fresh-tasting flavouring, or the plant from which this flavouring comes: *spearmint chewing-gum/toothpaste*

spec [CHANCE] /spek/ *adj* INFORMAL **on spec** taking a chance, without any certainty that you will get what you want: *We just turned up at the airport on spec, hoping that we'd get tickets.* ○ *You could always send your*

S

CV to a few companies on spec.

spec [PLAN] /spek/ *noun* [C] *INFORMAL FOR* **specification**, see at **specify**: *We've had a spec* ***drawn up*** *for a new bathroom.*

'spec ˌbuilder *noun* [C] *MAINLY AUS* a person or company that builds houses to sell to anyone who will buy them rather than for a particular customer

special [NOT USUAL] /ˈspeʃ.əl/ *adj* **1** not ordinary or usual: *The car has a number of special safety features.* ○ *Is there anything special that you'd like to do today?* ○ *Passengers should tell the airline in advance if they have any special dietary needs.* ○ *I don't expect special treatment – I just want to be treated fairly.* ○ *Full details of the election results will be published in a special edition of tomorrow's newspaper.* ○ *I have a suit for special* ***occasions****.* ○ *There's a 50p-off special* ***offer*** *on cornflakes/(UK ALSO) Cornflakes are* ***on*** *special* ***offer*** (= They are being sold at a reduced price) *this week.* **2** unusually great or important, or having an extra quality: *Could I ask you a special favour?* ○ *I'm cooking something special for her birthday.*

special /ˈspeʃ.əl/ *noun* [C] **1** a television programme made for a particular reason or occasion and which is not part of a series: *a three-hour election night special* **2** *MAINLY US* a meal that is available in a restaurant on a particular day which is not usually available: *Today's specials are written on the board.* **3** *MAINLY US* a product that is being sold at a reduced price for a short period: *Today's specials include children's T-shirts and pants for only £2.99.*

speciality *UK* /ˌspeʃ.iˈæl.ɪ.ti/ [US] /-ə.t̬i/ *noun* [C] (*US* **specialty**) a product that is extremely good in a particular place: *Oysters are a* ***local*** *speciality/a speciality* ***of*** *the area.* ○ *Paella is a speciality* ***of the house*** (= a food that is unusually good in a particular restaurant).

specially /ˈspeʃ.əl.i/ *adv* (*ALSO* **especially**) extremely or particularly: *This is a specially good wine.* ○ *"Is there anything you want to do this evening?" "Not specially."* ○ *The children really liked the museum, specially the dinosaurs.*

special [PARTICULAR] /ˈspeʃ.əl/ *adj* [before n] having a particular purpose: *Firefighters use special breathing equipment in smoky buildings.* ○ *Some of the children have special educational needs.* ○ *You need special tyres on your car for snow.* ○ *She works as a special adviser to the President.*

specialism /ˈspeʃ.əl.ɪ.zəm/ *noun* **1** [C] *UK* (*US* **specialty**) a subject that someone knows a lot about: *His specialism is tax law.* **2** [U] limiting study or work to a few subjects: *I don't think too much specialism in schools is a good idea.*

specialist /ˈspeʃ.əl.ɪst/ *noun* [C] **1** someone who has a lot of experience, knowledge or skill in a particular subject: *a software specialist* ○ *She's a specialist* ***in*** *modern French literature.* ○ *specialist advice/help* **2** (*UK ALSO* **consultant**) a doctor who has special training in and knowledge of a particular area of medicine: *She's a specialist* ***in*** *childhood illnesses.* ○ *I've asked to be referred to a specialist about my back pain.* ○ *a leading cancer/eye specialist*

speciality /ˌspeʃ.iˈæl.ɪ.ti/ [US] /-ə.t̬i/ *noun* [C] **1** *UK* (*US* **specialty**) a subject that someone knows a lot about **2** *HUMOROUS* a particular thing that you regularly do or make: *Unkind remarks are one of his specialities.*

specialize, *UK USUALLY* **-ise** /ˈspeʃ.əl.aɪz/ [US] /-ə.laɪz/ *verb* [I] to spend most of your time studying one particular subject or doing one type of business: *She's hired a lawyer who specializes* ***in*** *divorce cases.* ○ *a restaurant that specializes* ***in*** *seafood* ○ *I enjoy working in general medicine, but I hope to be able to specialize in the future.*

specialization, *UK USUALLY* **-isation** /ˌspeʃ.əl.aɪˈzeɪ.ʃən/ *noun* [C or U] *In the course I'm taking, there's no opportunity for specialization* (= limiting my studying or work to one particular area) *until the final year.* ○ *The lawyer said that he was unable to help us because our case fell outside his specialization* (= his particular area of knowledge).

specialized, *UK USUALLY* **-ised** /ˈspeʃ.əl.aɪzd/ [US] /-ə.laɪzd/ *adj*: *Her job is very specialized* (= involves only one limited area). ○ *The hospital is unable to provide the highly specialized care needed by very sick babies.* ○ *specialized skills*

specially /ˈspeʃ.əl.i/ *adv* (*ALSO* **especially**) for a particular purpose: *I came here specially to see you.* ○ *She has a wheelchair that was specially made for her.* ○ *The opera 'Aida' was specially written for the opening of the Cairo opera house in 1871.*

COMMON LEARNER ERROR

specially or **especially?**

Sometimes these two words both mean 'for a particular purpose'.

I cooked this meal specially/especially for you.

Specially is often used before an adjective made from a past participle.

specially prepared/specially trained.
He uses a specially adapted wheelchair.

Especially is used to give emphasis to a person or thing. This word is usually used at the beginning of a phrase but not at the beginning of a sentence.

I like all kinds of films, especially horror films.
~~*Especially I like horror films.*~~

'Special ˌBranch *noun* [S or U] the department of the British police which deals with crimes such as TERRORISM that threaten the government of the UK

ˌspecial deˈlivery *noun* [U] the delivery of a letter or parcel which is much quicker, and more expensive than, normal delivery

ˌspecial efˈfect *noun* [C usually pl] an unusual piece of action in a film, or an entertainment on a stage, created by using particular equipment: *The film's special effects are amazing.*

ˌspecial ˈinterest ˌgroup *noun* [C] (*US ALSO* **special interests**) a group of people who have particular demands and who try to influence political decisions involving them: *Much of the pressure for changing the law has come from special interest groups.*

the ˌSpecial Oˈlympics *plural noun* a set of international sports competitions for people who have lower than usual mental or physical abilities

ˌspecial ˈpleading *noun* [U] the practice of arguing from a particular case in order to get an unfair advantage in a more general situation

'special ˌschool *noun* [C] a school for children who have physical difficulties or problems with learning

specialty /ˈspeʃ.əl.ti/ [US] /-t̬i/ *noun* [C] *US FOR* **speciality** or **specialism**, see at **special**.

species /ˈspiː.ʃiːz/ *noun* [C] *plural* **species** a set of animals or plants in which the members have similar characteristics to each other and can breed with each other: *Mountain gorillas are an* ***endangered*** *species.* ○ *Over a hundred species* ***of*** *insect are found in this area.* ○ *FIGURATIVE HUMOROUS Women film directors in Hollywood are a rare species.* ➲See also **subspecies**.

specific /spəˈsɪf.ɪk/ *adj* relating to one thing and not others; particular: *The virus attacks specific cells in the brain.* ○ *The money is intended to be used for specific purposes.* ○ *FORMAL The disease seems to be specific* ***to*** (= only found in) *certain types of plant.* ○ *Is there anything specific you want from the shops?* ➲See also **specific** at **specify**.

specifically /spəˈsɪf.ɪ.kli/ *adv* for a particular reason, purpose, etc: *These jeans are designed specifically* ***for*** *women.* ○ [+ to infinitive] *I bought it specifically* ***to*** *wear at the wedding.* ○ *We are aiming our campaign specifically at young people.*

speˌcific ˈgravity *noun* [U] *SPECIALIZED* the mass of a particular volume of a substance when compared with the mass of an equal volume of water at 4°C. A more modern term for this is RELATIVE DENSITY.

specify /ˈspes.ɪ.faɪ/ *verb* [T] to state or describe something clearly and exactly: *He said we should meet but didn't specify a time.* ○ *The peace treaty clearly specifies the terms for the withdrawal of troops.* ○ [+ question word] *The newspaper report did not specify* ***how*** *the men were killed.* ○ [+ (that)] *My contract specifies* ***(that)*** *I must give a month's notice if I leave my job.* ○ *The loan must be repaid within a specified period/by a specified date.*

specific /spə'sɪf.ɪk/ *adj* clear and exact: *No specific allegations have yet been made about the prison officers' behaviour.* ○ *Can you be more specific **about** where your back hurts?*

specifically /spə'sɪf.ɪ.kli/ *adv* clearly, exactly or in detail: *I specifically asked you not to be late.* ○ *The law specifically prohibits acts of this kind.* ○ *It specifically said/stated on the label that the jacket should be dry-cleaned only.*

specification /ˌspes.ɪ.fɪ'keɪ.ʃən/ *noun* [C or U] (*INFORMAL* **spec**) a detailed description of how something should be done, made, etc: *All products are made exactly **to** the customer's specifications.* ○ *A specification has been **drawn up** for the new military aircraft.* ○ *a job specification* ○ *The cars have been built **to** a **high** specification (= a high standard).*

specifics /spə'sɪf.ɪks/ *plural noun* exact details: *I can't comment on the specifics **of** the case.* ○ *The specifics of the plan still have to be worked out.*

specificity /ˌspes.ɪ'fɪs.ɪ.ti/ ⑩ /-ə.t̬i/ *noun* [U] *FORMAL* the quality of being specific

specimen /'spes.ə.mɪn/ *noun* [C] **1** something shown or examined as an example; a typical example: *He has a collection of rare insect specimens.* ○ *Museums will pay large amounts of money for good dinosaur fossil specimens.* ○ *Astronauts brought back specimens **of** moon rock.* **2** a small amount of blood or urine used for testing: *They **took** blood and urine specimens for analysis.*

specious /'spiː.ʃəs/ *adj FORMAL DISAPPROVING* seeming to be right or true, but really wrong or false: *a specious argument/claim* ○ *specious allegations/promises* **speciously** /'spiː.ʃə.sli/ *adv* **speciousness** /'spiː.ʃə.snəs/ *noun* [U]

speck /spek/ *noun* [C] a very small mark, piece or amount: *He'd been painting the door and there were specks of paint all over the floor.* ○ *There's not a speck of (= not any) **dust/dirt** in their house.* ○ *We could see a speck (= a small amount) **of** light at the end of the tunnel.*

speckle /'spek.l̩/ *noun* [C usually pl] a very small mark of a different colour from the surface on which it is found, and which is usually found with a large number of other marks of the same type: *A blackbird's egg is blue with brown speckles on it.*

speckled /'spek.l̩d/ *adj* covered with speckles: *a bird with a speckled breast*

spectacle [UNUSUAL EVENT] /'spek.tɪ.kl̩/ *noun* [C] an unusual or unexpected event or situation which attracts attention, interest or disapproval: *It was a strange spectacle to see the two former enemies shaking hands and slapping each other on the back.* ○ *We witnessed the extraordinary spectacle of an old lady climbing a tree to rescue her cat.*
• **make a spectacle of *yourself*** to do something that makes you look stupid and attracts other people's attention: *I wasn't going to make a spectacle of myself just to give you a laugh!*

spectacle [PUBLIC EVENT] /'spek.tɪ.kl̩/ *noun* [C or U] a splendid public event or show; a splendid appearance: *The carnival was a magnificent spectacle.* ○ *The television show was mere spectacle (= had a splendid appearance, but little value).*

spectacularly /spek'tæk.jʊ.lə.li/ ⑩ /-lɚ-/ *adv* in a very beautiful and impressive way: *At night, the city is spectacularly lit.*

spectacles /'spek.tɪ.kl̩z/ *plural noun* (*INFORMAL* **specs**) *SLIGHTLY OLD-FASHIONED* glasses: *a pair of spectacles* ○ *steel-rimmed spectacles* **spectacle** /'spek.tɪ.kl̩/ *adj* [before n] *a spectacle case*

spectacular [BEAUTIFUL] /spek'tæk.jʊ.lər/ ⑩ /-lɚ/ *adj* **1** very exciting to look at: *a spectacular view* ○ *He scored a spectacular goal in the second half.* ○ *There was a spectacular sunset last night.* **2** unusually great: *We've had spectacular success with the product.*

spectacularly /spek'tæk.jʊ.lə.li/ ⑩ /-lɚ-/ *adv* extremely: *spectacularly beautiful countryside* ○ *House prices have risen spectacularly.*

spectacular [SHOW] /spek'tæk.jʊ.lər/ ⑩ /-lɚ/ *noun* [C] an event or performance which is very exciting to watch and which involves a lot of people

spectator /spek'teɪ.tər/ ⑩ /-t̬ɚ/ *noun* [C] a person who watches an activity, especially a sports event, without taking part: *They won 4-0 in front of over 40,000 cheering spectators.*

spectate /spek'teɪt/ *verb* [I] to watch an activity, especially a sports event, without taking part

spec'tator ˌsport *noun* [C] a sport which people go to watch: *Football is certainly the biggest spectator sport in Britain.*

spectre UK, US **specter** /'spek.tər/ ⑩ /-t̬ɚ/ *noun* **1** the **spectre of *sth*** the idea of something unpleasant that might happen in the future: *The awful spectre of civil war looms over the country.* ○ *Drought and war have **raised** the spectre of food shortages for up to 24 million African people.* **2** [C] *LITERARY* a ghost

spectral /'spek.trəl/ *adj* coming from or seeming to be the spirit of a dead person: *a spectral figure/presence* ⊃See also **spectral** at **spectrum**.

spectrum /'spek.trəm/ *noun* [C] *plural* **spectra** or **spectrums 1** the set of colours into which a beam of light can be separated, or a range of waves, such as light waves or radio waves: *The colours of the spectrum – red, orange, yellow, green, blue, indigo and violet – can be seen in a rainbow.* **2** a range of opinions, feelings, etc: *He has support from across the whole **political** spectrum.* ○ *The group includes students from both ends of the **social** spectrum (= range of social classes).* ○ *A wide spectrum **of** opinion was represented at the meeting.*

spectral /'spek.trəl/ *adj SPECIALIZED* of the set of colours into which a beam of light can be separated: *spectral light* ⊃See also **spectral** at **spectre**.

speculate [GUESS] /'spek.jʊ.leɪt/ *verb* [I] to guess possible answers to a question when you do not have enough information to be certain: *I don't know why she did it – I'm just speculating.* ○ *A spokesperson declined to speculate **on** the cause of the train crash.* ○ *Journalists are speculating **about** whether interest rates will be cut.* ○ [+ that] *The newspapers have speculated **that** they will get married next year.*

speculation /ˌspek.jʊ'leɪ.ʃən/ *noun* [C or U] when you guess possible answers to a question without having enough information to be certain: *Rumours that they are about to marry have been dismissed as **pure** speculation.* ○ *Speculation **about** his future plans is rife.* ○ [+ that] *The Prime Minister's speech **fuelled/prompted** speculation **that** an election will be held later in the year.*

speculative /'spek.jʊ.lə.tɪv/ ⑩ /-t̬ɪv/ *adj* based on a guess and not on information: *The article was dismissed as highly speculative.* **speculatively** /'spek.jʊ.lə.tɪv.li/ ⑩ /-t̬ɪv-/ *adv*

speculate [TRADE] /'spek.jʊ.leɪt/ *verb* [I] to buy and sell in the hope that the value of what you buy will increase and that it can then be sold at a higher price in order to make a profit: *He made his money speculating **on** the London gold and silver markets.* ○ *The company has been speculating **in** property for years.*

speculation /ˌspek.jʊ'leɪ.ʃən/ *noun* [C or U] when people speculate in order to make a profit

speculative /'spek.jʊ.lə.tɪv/ ⑩ /-t̬ɪv/ *adj* bought or done in order to make a profit in the future: *The office block was built as a speculative venture.* **speculatively** /'spek.jʊ.lə.tɪv.li/ ⑩ /-t̬ɪv-/ *adv*

speculator /'spek.jʊ.leɪ.tər/ ⑩ /-t̬ɚ/ *noun* [C] a person who buys goods, property, money, etc. in the hope of selling them at a profit

speech [SAY WORDS] /spiːtʃ/ *noun* **1** [U] the ability to talk, the activity of talking, or a piece of spoken language: *Children usually develop speech in the second year of life.* ○ *People who suffer a stroke may experience a loss of speech.* **2** [U] the way a person talks: *His speech was slurred and I thought he was drunk.* **3** [U] the language used when talking: *Some expressions are used more **in** speech than in writing.* **4** [C] a set of words spoken in a play: *Do you know the words to Hamlet's famous speech at the beginning of Act III?*

speechless /'spiːtʃ.ləs/ *adj* unable to speak because you are so angry, shocked, surprised, etc: *The news **left us** speechless.* ○ *She was speechless **with** indignation.* **speechlessly** /'spiːtʃ.lə.sli/ *adv* **speechlessness** /'spiːtʃ.lə.snəs/ *noun* [U]

speech [FORMAL TALK] /spiːtʃ/ *noun* [C] a formal talk given usually to a large number of people on a special occasion: *I had to* ***give/make*** *a speech at my brother's wedding.* ○ *The Governor of New York* ***delivered*** *a rousing speech to the national convention.* ○ *He gave the* ***after-dinner*** *speech* (= a talk given after a formal evening meal at which a large number of people are present). ○ *Did you hear her* ***acceptance*** *speech at the Oscars ceremony?* ➲See also **speak** FORMAL TALK.

speechify /ˈspiː.tʃɪ.faɪ/ *verb* [I] *INFORMAL DISAPPROVING* to give a speech, especially in a boring way or in a way that shows you think you are important

COMMON LEARNER ERROR

make/give a speech

Be careful to choose the correct verb.

I have to make a speech.
~~*I have to do a speech.*~~
He gave a speech at the conference.
~~*He said a speech at the conference.*~~

ˈspeech ˌbubble *noun* [C] a round shape next to the head of a character in a cartoon inside which the character's words or thoughts are written

ˈspeech ˌday *noun* [C] a day each year in some British schools when prizes and formal talks are given

ˈspeech imˌpediment *noun* [C] a difficulty in speaking clearly, such as a LISP or STAMMER

ˌspeech ˈtherapy *noun* [U] the treatment of people who have difficulty speaking: *She needed speech therapy after she suffered severe head injuries in a car accident.* **ˌspeech ˈtherapist** *noun* [C] *A speech therapist helped him overcome his stammer.*

ˈspeech ˌwriter *noun* [C] a person whose job is to write formal speeches for somebody else, usually for politicians

speed [RATE OF MOVEMENT] /spiːd/ *noun* **1** [C or U] how fast something moves: *He was travelling* ***at a*** *speed* ***of*** *90 mph.* ○ *The car has a* ***top*** *speed* ***of*** *155 miles per hour.* ○ *You should* ***lower/reduce*** *your speed as you approach a junction.* ○ *On a clear, straight road you can* ***gather/pick up*** *speed.* ○ *He came off the road while driving his car round a bend at* ***high/breakneck*** *speed* (= very fast). ○ *There are speed* ***restrictions*** (= controls on how fast traffic is allowed to move) *on this part of the road.* ○ *an electric drill with two speeds* (= rates at which it turns) **2** [U] very fast movement: *I get a real thrill from speed.* ○ *He put on a sudden burst of speed.* ○ *Both cars were travelling* ***at*** *speed* (= very fast) *when the accident happened.* **3** [U] how fast something happens: *We were surprised at the speed* ***of*** *the response to our enquiry.* ○ *It was the speed at which it all happened that shocked me.* ○ *She got through her work* ***with*** *speed* (= quickly) *and efficiency.* **4 the speed of light/sound** the rate at which light/sound travels: *The speed of light is 300 million metres per second.* ○ *These planes travel at twice the speed of sound.* **5** [C] a gear: *a bicycle with ten speeds* ○ *a ten-speed bicycle* **6** [C] the rate at which a photographic film absorbs or reacts to light: *What speed film do I need for taking photographs indoors?* **7 shutter speed** the length of time for which part of a camera is open to allow light to reach the film when a photograph is being taken: *a high/low shutter speed*

• **up to speed** If you are up to speed with a subject or activity, you have all the latest information about it and are able to do it well: *We arranged for some home tutoring to* ***get*** *him up to speed with the other children in his class.* ○ *Before we start the meeting I'm going to* ***bring*** *you up to speed with the latest developments.*

speed /spiːd/ *verb* [I or T; usually + adv or prep] **sped** or **speeded**, **sped** or **speeded** **1** to (cause to) move, go or happen fast: *The train sped* ***along*** *at over 120 miles per hour.* ○ *The actress then sped* ***away/off*** *in a waiting car.* ○ *We sped* ***down*** *the ski slopes.* ○ *This year is speeding* ***by/past.*** ○ *Ambulances sped the injured people* (= moved them quickly) *away from the scene.* ○ *The best thing you can do to speed your recovery* (= make it quicker) *is to rest.* **2 be speeding** to be driving faster than you are legally allowed to do: *He was* ***caught*** *speeding.*

speeding /ˈspiː.dɪŋ/ *noun* [U] driving faster than is allowed in a particular area: *She was* ***fined for*** *speeding last month.*

speedy /ˈspiː.di/ *adj* quick: *He's a very speedy worker.* ○ *We need to take speedy action/make a speedy decision.* ○ *Everyone is hoping for a speedy* ***end*** *to the conflict* (= hoping that an end to it will happen quickly). ○ *We wished her a speedy* ***recovery*** *from her illness* (= that she would get better quickly). **speedily** /ˈspiː.dɪ.li/ *adv*: *The problem was speedily solved.* **speediness** /ˈspiː.dɪ.nəs/ *noun* [U]

speed [DRUG] /spiːd/ *noun* [U] *INFORMAL FOR* **amphetamine** (= a drug that makes the mind or body more active): *She was* ***on*** *speed at the time.*

▲ **speed** ***(sth)*** **up** *phrasal verb* [M] to happen or move faster, or to make something happen or move faster: *This drug may have the effect of speeding up your heart rate.* ○ *Can the job be speeded up in some way?* ○ *The tape speeded up towards the end.* ○ *I think you need to speed up a bit* (= drive faster) *– we're going to be late.* ○ *The economy shows signs of speeding up* (= increasing activity).

speed-up /ˈspiːd.ʌp/ *noun* [S] an increase in the rate of change or growth: *Measures should be taken to halt the speed-up* ***in*** *population growth.*

speedboat /ˈspiːd.bəʊt/ [US] /-boʊt/ *noun* [C] a small boat which has a powerful engine and which travels very fast

ˈspeed ˌbump *noun* [C] (*UK ALSO* **speed hump,** *UK ALSO* **sleeping policeman**) a small raised area built across a road to force people to drive more slowly: *Local residents are asking for speed bumps to be installed in their street.*

ˈspeed ˌcamera *noun* [C] a camera at the side of the road which takes pictures of cars that are going faster than is legally allowed

ˈspeed ˌdial *noun* [U] *MAINLY US* a feature on a telephone that enables you to ring a number by pressing only one button **ˈspeed ˌdial** *verb* [I or T]

ˈspeed ˌlimit *noun* [C] the fastest rate at which you are allowed to drive in a particular area: *a 50 mph speed limit* ○ *Slow down – you're* ***breaking*** *the speed limit.* ○ *Try not to go* ***over*** *the speed limit, Daniel.*

speedometer /spiːˈdɒm.ɪ.təʳ/ [US] /spɪˈdɑː.mə.t̬ɚ/ *noun* [C] (*UK INFORMAL* **speedo**) a device in a vehicle which shows how fast the vehicle is moving ➲See picture **Car** on page Centre 12

ˈspeed ˌskating *noun* [U] the sport of racing on ice, usually around an oval track

ˈspeed ˌtrap *noun* [C] a place on a road where the police use special hidden equipment to see whether drivers are going faster than is allowed in a particular area

speedway /ˈspiːd.weɪ/ *noun* [C or U] (a special racing track used for) the sport of racing special cars, or light motorcycles without brakes

speleology /ˌspiː.liˈɒl.ə.dʒi/ [US] /-ˈɑː.lə-/ *noun* [U] *SPECIALIZED* **1** the scientific study of caves **2** the sport of walking and climbing in caves

speleologist /ˌspiː.liˈɒl.ə.dʒɪst/ [US] /-ˈɑː.lə-/ *noun* [C] *SPECIALIZED* someone who studies caves, or who climbs in them for sport

spell [FORM WORDS] /spel/ *verb* [I or T] **spelled** or *UK ALSO* **spelt**, **spelled** or *UK ALSO* **spelt** to form a word or words with the letters in the correct order: *"How do you spell 'receive'?" "R E C E I V E."* ○ *Shakespeare did not always spell his own name the same way.* ○ *Our address is 1520 Main Street, Albuquerque – shall I spell that* ***(out)*** (= say in the correct order the letters that form the word) *for you?* ○ *I think it's important that children should be taught to spell* (= how to form words with the letters in the correct order).

• **N O spells no.** *SAYING* used as a reply to a request, to emphasize that when you said no previously you really meant it

speller /ˈspel.əʳ/ [US] /-ɚ/ *noun* **good/bad speller** someone who is good/bad at spelling

spelling /ˈspel.ɪŋ/ *noun* **1** [U] forming words with the correct letters in the correct order, or the ability to do this: *He's hopeless at spelling.* ○ *My computer has a pro-*

S

gram which corrects my spelling. ○ *Your essay is full of spelling* ***mistakes/errors.*** **2** [C] the way a particular word is spelt: *This dictionary includes both British and American spellings* ***of*** *words.*

spell [RESULT] /spel/ *verb* **spell disaster/trouble, etc.** to cause something bad to happen in the future: *The new regulations could spell disaster for small businesses.* ○ *This cold weather could spell trouble for gardeners.*

spell [PERIOD] /spel/ *noun* [C] **1** a period of time for which an activity or condition lasts continuously: *I lived in London* ***for*** *a spell.* ○ *She* ***had*** *a brief spell* ***as*** *captain of the team.* ○ *I keep having/getting* ***dizzy*** *spells* (= periods of feeling as if I'm spinning around). **2** a short period of a particular type of weather: *a spell of dry weather* ○ *The weather forecast is for dry, sunny spells.*

spell [MAGIC] /spel/ *noun* [C] spoken words which are thought to have magical power, or (the condition of being under) the influence or control of such words: *The witch* ***cast/put*** *a spell* ***on*** *the prince and he turned into a frog.* ○ *A beautiful girl would have to kiss him to* ***break*** (= stop) *the spell.* ○ *Sleeping Beauty lay* ***under*** *the wicked fairy's spell until the prince woke her with a kiss.*
• **be under *sb*'s spell** to be strongly attracted to someone and influenced by them

spell [DO INSTEAD] /spel/ *verb* [T] **spelled, spelled** *MAINLY US* to do something which someone else would usually be doing, especially in order to allow them to rest: *You've been driving for a while – do you want me to spell you?*
spell /spel/ *noun* [C] *US If we take spells* ***(with)*** *doing the painting, it won't seem like such hard work.*
▲ **spell *sth* out** *phrasal verb* [M] to explain something in a very clear way with details: *The government has so far refused to spell out its plans/policies.* ○ *INFORMAL What do you mean you don't understand – do I have to spell* ***it*** *out for you?*

spellbound /ˈspel.baʊnd/ *adj* having your attention completely held by something, so that you cannot think about anything else: *The children* ***listened*** *to the story spellbound.* ○ *He* ***held*** *his audience spellbound.*
spellbinding /ˈspelˌbaɪn.dɪŋ/ *adj* holding your attention completely: *He gave a spellbinding performance.*

ˈspell ˌcheck *verb* [T] to use a computer program which makes certain that the words in a document have the correct letters in the correct order **ˈspell ˌcheck** *noun* [C] *It's always a good idea to* ***run*** *a spell check once you've finished writing.*

spell-checker /ˈspeltʃek.əʳ/ [US] /-ɚ/ *noun* [C] a computer program which makes certain that the words in a document have the correct letters in the correct order: *After you've finished each chapter,* ***run*** *the spell-checker.*

ˈspelling ˌbee *noun* [C] *US* a competition in which the winner is the person or group who is able to form correctly the highest number of the words they are asked to form

spelunking *US* /spəˈlʌŋ.kɪŋ/ *noun* [U] (*UK* **potholing**) the sport of walking and climbing in caves: *Shall we* ***go*** *spelunking at the weekend?* **spelunker** *US* /spəˈlʌŋ.kəʳ/ [US] /-kɚ/ *noun* [C] (*UK* **potholer**)

spend [MONEY] /spend/ *verb* [I or T] **spent, spent** to give money as a payment for something: *How much did you spend?* ○ *I don't know how I managed to spend so much in the pub last night.* ○ *We spent* ***a fortune*** *when we were in New York.* ○ *She spends a lot of* ***money on*** *clothes.* ○ *We've just spent £1.9 million* ***on*** *improving our computer network.* ○ *We went on a spending* ***spree*** (= We bought a lot of things) *on Saturday.*
• **spend a penny** *UK OLD-FASHIONED POLITE EXPRESSION FOR* to urinate: *If you'll excuse me, I need to spend a penny.*
spend /spend/ *noun* [S] *UK INFORMAL* the amount of money that is spent on something: *The total spend* ***on*** *the project was almost a million pounds.*
spender /ˈspen.dəʳ/ [US] /-dɚ/ *noun* [C] someone who spends money: *Tourists are often* ***big*** *spenders* (= they buy a lot of things).
spending /ˈspen.dɪŋ/ *noun* [U] the money which is used for a particular purpose, especially by a government or organization: *government spending* ***on*** *health* ○ *spending cuts* ○ *Consumer spending has more than doubled in the last ten years.*

COMMON LEARNER ERROR

spend money/time on

Remember to use the preposition 'on' when you are talking about **spending** money or time on something.

Schools should spend more money on new technology.
~~*Schools should spend more money in new technology.*~~
You're spending too long on these tasks, Jon.
~~*You're spending too long for these tasks, Jon.*~~

spend [TIME] /spend/ *verb* [T] **spent, spent** to use time doing something or being somewhere: *I think we need to spend more* ***time*** *together.* ○ *I spent a lot of time clean****ing*** *that room.* ○ *I've spent years build****ing*** *up my collection.* ○ *I spent an hour at the station wait****ing*** *for the train.* ○ *How long do you spend* ***on*** *your homework?* ○ *My sister always spends ages in the bathroom.* ○ *We spent the weekend in London.* ○ *You can spend the night here if you like.*
• **spend the night together** (*ALSO* **spend the night with *sb***) *POLITE EXPRESSION FOR* to have sex with someone: *Did you spend the night together?*

spend [FORCE] /spend/ *verb* [T] **spent, spent** to use energy, effort, force, etc., especially until there is no more left: *For the past month he's been spending all his energy trying to find a job.* ○ *They continued firing until all their ammunition was spent* (= there was none of it left). ○ *The hurricane will probably have spent most of its force* (= most of its force will have gone) *by the time it reaches the northern parts of the country.* ○ *Her anger soon spent* ***itself*** (= stopped).
spent /spent/ *adj* **1** Something that is spent has been used so that it no longer has any power or effectiveness: *spent bullets/matches* ○ *After several defeats in a row, people are starting to say that the team is a spent* ***force.*** **2** *LITERARY* tired: *We arrived home spent after our long journey.*

ˈspending ˌmoney *noun* [U] money that you can spend for fun, entertainment, personal things, etc: *How much spending money are you taking on holiday?*

spendthrift /ˈspend.θrɪft/ *noun* [C] someone who spends a lot of money in a wasteful way **spendthrift** /ˈspend.θrɪft/ *adj* [before n]

spent /spent/ *past simple and past participle of* **spend**

sperm /spɜːm/ [US] /spɝːm/ *noun plural* **sperm** or **sperms** **1** [C] a reproductive cell produced by a male animal: *In human reproduction, one female egg is usually fertilized by one sperm.* **2** [U] *INFORMAL FOR* **semen** (= the thick, whitish, slightly sticky liquid that is produced by the male sex organs, and which contains sperm)

spermatozoon /ˌspɜː.mə.təˈzəʊ.ɒn/ [US] /ˌspɝː.mə.t̬əˈzoʊ.ɑːn/ *noun* [C] *plural* **spermatozoa** *SPECIALIZED FOR* **sperm**

ˈsperm ˌbank *noun* [C] a place in which human sperm is stored in order to be used by doctors to try to make women pregnant

ˈsperm ˌcount *noun* [C] the number of live male reproductive cells in a particular amount of the liquid in which they are contained: *He has a* ***low/high*** *sperm count.*

spermicide /ˈspɜː.mɪ.saɪd/ [US] /ˈspɝː-/ *noun* [C or U] a substance that kills sperm, used especially on condoms or by a woman before she has sex in order to stop herself becoming pregnant **spermicidal** /ˌspɜː.mɪˈsaɪ.dəl/ [US] /ˌspɝː-/ *adj*: *spermicidal jelly* ○ *spermicidal cream*

ˈsperm ˌwhale *noun* [C] a large whale with a very large long head

spew /spjuː/ *verb* [I or T; + adv or prep] If something spews liquid or gas or liquid or gas spews from something, it flows out in large amounts: *The volcano spewed a giant cloud of ash, dust and gases* ***into*** *the air.* ○ *The drains spew* ***(out)*** *millions of gallons of raw sewage* ***into*** *the river.* ○ *Paper came spewing from the computer printer.*
▲ **spew *(sth)* up** *phrasal verb* [M] *SLANG* to vomit: *I was spewing up all night after those mussels.*

SPF /ˌes.piːˈef/ *noun* [C] *ABBREVIATION FOR* sun protection factor: the letters on a bottle of SUNSCREEN (= substance which prevents the skin from burning in the sun) which show how effective the SUNSCREEN is

S

sphere ROUND OBJECT /sfɪəʳ/ ⑥ /sfɪr/ *noun* [C] an object shaped like a round ball: *Doctors have replaced the top of his hip bone with a metal sphere.*

spherical /'sfer.ɪ.kəl/ *adj* round, like a ball: *The Earth is not perfectly spherical.*

spheroid /'sfɪə.rɔɪd/ ⑥ /'sfɪr.ɔɪd/ *noun* [C] SPECIALIZED a solid object that is almost spherical: *The Earth is a spheroid.*

sphere AREA /sfɪəʳ/ ⑥ /sfɪr/ *noun* [C] a subject or area of knowledge, work, etc: *the political sphere* ○ *The minister said that the government planned to develop exchanges with other countries, particularly in cultural, scientific and economic spheres.*

sphincter /'sfɪŋk.təʳ/ ⑥ /-təʳ/ *noun* [C] SPECIALIZED a muscle that surrounds an opening in the body and can tighten to close it: *the anal sphincter* ○ *a sphincter muscle*

sphinx /sfɪŋks/ *noun* [C] *plural* **sphinx** or **sphinxes** **1** an ancient imaginary creature with a lion's body and a woman's head **2 the Sphinx** a large stone statue with a lion's body and a person's head, found in the desert near Cairo in Egypt

sphinx-like /'sfɪŋks.laɪk/ *adj* mysterious and not allowing people to know what you are thinking: *He sat silently with a sphinx-like smile on his face.*

spic, spick, spik /spɪk/ *noun* [C] US OFFENSIVE a person from a Spanish-speaking country

spice /spaɪs/ *noun* **1** [C or U] a substance made from a plant, which is used to give a special flavour to food: *Cinnamon, ginger and cloves are all spices.* ○ *Spices are widely used in Indian cooking.* **2** [S or U] something that makes something else more exciting and interesting: *A scandal or two adds a little spice to office life.*

spice /spaɪs/ *verb* [T] to use spice to add flavour to food or drink: *coffee spiced with cinnamon* ○ *a highly spiced curry*

spicy /'spaɪ.si/ *adj* **1** containing strong flavours from spice: *Do you like spicy food?* **2** exciting and interesting, especially because of being shocking or dealing with sexual matters: *a spicy novel* ○ *spicy details* **spiciness** /'spaɪ.sɪ.nəs/ *noun* [U]

▲ **spice** *sth* **up** *phrasal verb* [M] to add excitement or interest to a speech, story or performance: *He'd spiced up his speech with a few rude jokes.* ○ *It was one of those articles on how to spice up your sex life.*

spick CLEAN /spɪk/ *adj* INFORMAL **spick and span** (especially of a place) very clean and tidy: *Their house is always spick and span.* ○ *The council spends a lot of money keeping the town spick and span.*

spick PERSON /spɪk/ *noun* [C] OFFENSIVE a **spic**

spider /'spaɪ.dəʳ/ ⑥ /-dəʳ/ *noun* [C] a small insect-like creature with eight thin legs which catches other insects in a web (= a net made from sticky threads): *a spider's web*

spidery /'spaɪ.dʳr.i/ ⑥ /-dəʳ-/ *adj* consisting of thin dark bending lines, like a spider's legs: *spidery handwriting* ○ *a spidery pattern*

spider ˌmonkey *noun* [C] a small thin South American monkey which uses its long tail to help it to move around in the branches of trees

spider ˌplant *noun* [C] a plant commonly found in houses and offices and which has long flat thin green leaves with white lines

spider's web UK /'spaɪ.dəz.web/ ⑥ /-dəʳz-/ *noun* [C] (US **spiderweb**) a net-like structure of sticky silk threads made by a spider for catching insects

spiel /ʃpiːl/ *noun* [C] INFORMAL DISAPPROVING a speech, especially one which is long and spoken quickly and is intended to persuade the listener about something: *a sales spiel* ○ *They gave us a long spiel about why we needed to install double glazing in our house.*

spiff /spɪf/ *verb*

▲ **spiff** *sb/sth* **up** *phrasal verb* [M] US INFORMAL to make someone or something look more stylish, or cleaner and tidier: *He's really spiffed up his wardrobe since he started his new job.*

spiffy /'spɪf.i/ *adj* US INFORMAL stylish, attractive or pleasing: *a spiffy haircut/dresser*

spigot /'spɪg.ət/ *noun* [C] **1** a device used to control the flow of liquid from something such as a barrel **2** US a TAP, especially on the outside of a building

spik /spɪk/ *noun* [C] OFFENSIVE a **spic**

spike POINT /spaɪk/ *noun* [C] **1** a narrow thin shape with a sharp point at one end, or something, especially a piece of metal, with this shape: *There were large spikes on top of the railings to stop people climbing over them.* ○ *Some types of dinosaur had sharp spikes on their tails.* **2 spikes** a set of short pointed pieces of metal or plastic fixed to the bottom of shoes worn for particular sports, which stop the person wearing the shoes from sliding on the ground, or shoes with these pointed pieces

spike /spaɪk/ *verb* [T] to push a sharp point into something or someone: *She got badly spiked when one of the runners trod on her heel.*

spiked /spaɪkt/ *adj* with a sharp point or points: *spiked helmets*

spiky /'spaɪ.ki/ *adj* covered with spikes or having that appearance: *a spiky cactus* ○ *spiky leaves* ○ *spiky hair* ⊃See also **spiky**. ⊃See picture **Hairstyles and Hats** on page Centre 8

spike STOP /spaɪk/ *verb* [T] INFORMAL to decide not to publish an article in a newspaper: *The story was deemed too controversial and so they spiked it.*

● **spike** *sb's* **guns** to spoil someone's plans: *We wanted to build an extra room onto the side of our house, but our neighbours spiked our guns.*

spike MAKE STRONGER /spaɪk/ *verb* [T] to make a drink stronger by adding alcohol, or to add flavour or interest to something: *She claimed that someone had spiked her drink with whisky.* ○ *The pasta was served in a cream sauce spiked with black pepper.* ○ *His writing is spiked with humour.*

spike HIT /spaɪk/ *verb* [T] in the sport of VOLLEYBALL, to hit the ball so that it goes almost straight down on the other side of the net

ˌspike ˈheels *plural noun* MAINLY US STILETTO heels (= narrow, high heels on a woman's shoes)

spiky /'spaɪ.ki/ *adj* INFORMAL easily annoyed and not polite: *a spiky teenager* ⊃See also **spiky** at **spike** POINT.

spill /spɪl/ *verb* [I or T; usually + adv or prep] spilled or UK ALSO **spilt**, spilled or UK ALSO **spilt** to (cause to) flow, move, fall or spread over the edge or beyond the limits of something: *I spilt coffee on my silk shirt.* ○ *You've spilt something down your tie.* ○ *Let's see if I can pour the juice into the glass without spilling it.* ○ *He dropped a bag of sugar and it spilt all over the floor.* ○ *Crowds of football fans spilled onto the field at the end of the game.*

● **spill the beans** to tell people secret information: *So who spilt the beans about her affair with David?*

● **spill blood** LITERARY to kill or hurt people

spill /spɪl/ *noun* [C] an amount of something which has come out of a container: *a fuel spill on the road* ○ *Could you wipe up that spill, please?* ○ *In 1989, there was a massive oil spill in Alaska.*

● **take a spill** INFORMAL to fall off something, usually a bicycle or a horse

spillage /'spɪl.ɪdʒ/ *noun* [C or U] FORMAL a spill: *oil spillages*

PHRASAL VERBS WITH spill ▼

▲ **spill out** MOVE OUT *phrasal verb* **1** to flow or fall out of a container: *All the shopping had spilled out of my bag.* ○ *The contents of the truck spilled out across the road.* **2** If people spill out of a place, large numbers of them come out of it: *People were spilling out of the wine bar onto the street.*

▲ **spill** *(sth)* **out** EXPRESS *phrasal verb* to talk about or express an emotion freely: *All his resentment spilled out.* ○ *I listened quietly as she spilled out all her anger and despair.*

▲ **spill over** *phrasal verb* **1** If an activity or situation spills over, it begins to affect another situation or group of people, especially in an unpleasant or unwanted way: *I try not to let my work spill over into my life outside the office.* ○ *The conflict threatens to spill over into neighbouring regions.* **2** to continue for a longer time than expected: *The talks between the two leaders look* *likely to spill over **into** the weekend.*

spillover /'spɪləʊ.və^r/ ⓤ /-ˌoʊ.vɚ/ *noun* [C] MAINLY US **1** an amount of liquid which has become too much for the object that contains it and flows or spreads out: *The spillover from the adjacent river flooded the lower fields.* **2** the effects of an activity which have spread beyond what was originally intended: *We are now witnessing a spillover of the war into neighboring regions.*

spin TURN /spɪn/ *verb* [I or T] spinning, spun, spun or UK ALSO span **1** to (cause to) turn around and around, especially fast: *The Earth spins on its axis.* ○ *The roulette players silently watched the wheel spin **around/round**.* ○ *He was killed when his car hit a tree and spun off the road.* ○ *Spin the ball* (= Make it turn around and around as you throw it) *and it will change direction when it hits the ground.* **2 head/room spins** If your head or the room spins you feel as if it is turning around and around, and you cannot balance: *The room started spinning and I felt faint.*
• **spin out of control** If activities or events spin out of control they change very quickly and in an uncontrolled way: *The country's economy seemed to be spinning out of control.*
• **spin a coin** to make a coin turn around and around on its edge so that someone can guess which side will land facing upwards: *Let's spin a coin to decide who'll have the first turn.* ◐Compare **toss a coin** at **toss**.

spin /spɪn/ *noun* [C or U] the movement of something turning round very quickly: *I hit something on the road, which sent the car **into** a spin.* ○ *Suddenly, the plane went **into** a spin.* ○ *These clothes need another spin* (= to be turned round very fast in a machine to get water out of them) *– they're still very wet.* ○ *She put a lot of spin on the ball* (= threw or hit it in a way that made it spin).
• **in a spin** INFORMAL anxious and confused: *She's in a spin over the arrangements for the party.* ○ *News of the director's resignation sent/threw the management into a spin.*

spinner /'spɪn.ə^r/ ⓤ /-ɚ/ *noun* [C] in cricket, a BOWLER who makes the ball turn around and around as he or she throws it, or a ball that is BOWLED in that way: *a left-arm spinner*

spin MAKE THREAD /spɪn/ *verb* [I or T] spinning, spun, spun or UK ALSO span **1** to make thread by twisting fibres, or to produce something using thread: *The final stage of the production of cotton is when it is spun **into** thread.* ○ *Spiders spin webs.* **2 spin** *(sb)* **a story/tale/yarn** to tell a story, either to deceive someone or for entertainment: *He spun some tale about needing to take time off work because his mother was ill.* ○ [+ two objects] *They spun us a story about being in desperate need of money.*

spinner /'spɪn.ə^r/ ⓤ /-ɚ/ *noun* [C] a person who makes thread by twisting fibres

spin DECEIVING /spɪn/ *noun* [S or U] INFORMAL when an idea or situation is expressed or described in a clever way that makes it seem better than it really is, especially in politics: *They have tried to **put** a positive spin **on** the situation.* ○ *This report **puts** a different spin **on** the issue.*

spin DRIVE /spɪn/ *verb* [I + adv or prep] spinning, spun, spun or UK ALSO span INFORMAL (of a vehicle) to move quickly, or to move quickly in a vehicle: *We were spinning **along**, when suddenly one of our tyres burst.* ○ *Chris spun **past** in a flashy new car.*

spin /spɪn/ *noun* [C usually sing] OLD-FASHIONED INFORMAL a short journey in a car for pleasure: *Rupert took me **for a** spin in his new car.*

PHRASAL VERBS WITH **spin** ▼

▲ **spin** *sth* **off** PRODUCT *phrasal verb* [M] to produce a useful and unexpected result in addition to the intended result: *The American space program has spun off new commercial technologies.* ○ *Every new job that is created spins off three or four more in related fields.*

spin-off /'spɪn.ɒf/ ⓤ /-ɑːf/ *noun* [C] **1** a product that develops from another more important product: *The research has had spin-offs in the development of medical equipment.* **2** a programme or other show involving characters from a previous programme or film: *The stage show is a spin-off **from** a television programme.*

▲ **spin** *sth* **off** COMPANY *phrasal verb* [M] MAINLY US to form a separate company from part of an existing company: *The company is trying to spin off part of its business.*

▲ **spin** *sth* **out** *phrasal verb* [M] to make something such as an activity or story last longer than usual or necessary, or as long as possible: *Can we spin our holiday out for a few more days?* ○ *Somehow, she managed to spin her story out so that it took her the whole train journey to tell it.*

▲ **spin** *(sb)* **round** UK *phrasal verb* (US **spin** *(sb)* **around**) to quickly turn your own or someone else's body to face the opposite direction: *She spun round to see what had happened.*

spina bifida /ˌspaɪ.nəˈbɪf.ɪ.də/ *noun* [U] a serious condition in which part of the spine is not correctly developed at birth, leaving the nerves in the back without any protection

spinach /'spɪn.ɪtʃ/ *noun* [U] a vegetable which has wide dark green leaves which are eaten cooked or raw: *spinach lasagne/salad*

spinal column *noun* [C] the **spine** BONE.

spinal cord *noun* [C] the set of nerves inside the spine that connect the brain to other nerves in the body

spin bowler *noun* [C] a cricket player who BOWLS (= throws) the ball in such a way that it turns around and around and changes direction when it hits the ground

spinbowling /'spɪnˌbəʊ.lɪŋ/ ⓤ /-ˌboʊ-/ *noun* [U]

spindle /'spɪn.dl̩/ *noun* [C] a part of a machine around which something turns, or a rod onto which thread is twisted when it is spun

spindly /'spɪnd.li/ *adj* long or tall and thin, and looking weak: *spindly legs* ○ *a plant with a spindly stem*

spin doctor *noun* [C] MAINLY DISAPPROVING someone whose job is to make ideas, events, etc. seem better than they really are, especially in politics

spin-dryer, **spin-drier** /ˌspɪnˈdraɪ.ə^r/ ⓤ /-ɚ/ *noun* [C] UK a machine into which you put wet clothes, which turns them around and around very fast in order to get most of the water out of them ◐Compare **tumble dryer**.

spin-dry /ˌspɪnˈdraɪ/ *verb* [T] *The label says 'Do not spin-dry'.*

Spine

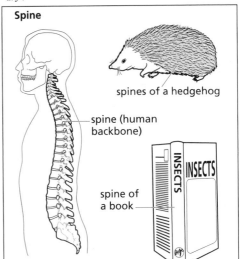

spines of a hedgehog

spine (human backbone)

INSECTS

spine of a book

---

spine BONE /spaɪn/ *noun* [C] the line of bones down the centre of the back that provides support for the body and protects the SPINAL CORD: *She injured her spine in a riding accident.* ○ FIGURATIVE *The Apennine mountains form the spine* (= central row of mountains) *of Italy.* ◐See picture **The Body** on page Centre 5

spinal /'spaɪ.n^əl/ *adj* of the spine: *a spinal injury*

spineless /'spaɪn.ləs/ *adj* DISAPPROVING describes someone who lacks determination and the willingness to take risks: *He was, she concluded, a spineless individual.*

spinelessly /'spaɪn.lə.sli/ *adv* **spinelessness** /'spaɪn.lə.-snəs/ *noun* [U]

spine POINT /spaɪn/ *noun* [C] a long sharp needle-like point growing out of an animal such as a HEDGEHOG or a plant such as a CACTUS

spiny /'spaɪ.ni/ *adj* covered with spines

spine BOOK PART /spaɪn/ *noun* [C] the narrow strip where the cover of a book is joined to the pages, usually with the title and writer's name printed on it

spine-chilling /'spaɪn,tʃɪl.ɪŋ/ *adj* (ALSO **spine-tingling**) very frightening: *He told them a spine-chilling ghost story.*

spine-tingling /'spaɪn,tɪŋ.lɪŋ/ *adj* very special and exciting: *Watching Christie win the Olympic hundred metres was one of those spine-tingling moments.*

spinifex /'spɪn.ɪ.feks/ *noun* [U] a grass with sharp spines which grows especially on sand hills in Australia

spinney /'spɪn.i/ *noun* [C] MAINLY UK a small wood; a **copse**

'**spinning ,top** *noun* [C] a toy with rounded sides, a flattened top, a vertical handle, and a point at the bottom, which turns round and round on the point when the handle is pushed and pulled up and down or twisted

'**spinning ,wheel** *noun* [C] a small machine used, especially in the past, at home for producing thread from fibres by turning them on a wheel operated by foot

spinster /'spɪn.stəʳ/ US /-stɚ/ *noun* [C] OLD-FASHIONED a woman who is not married, especially a woman who is no longer young and seems unlikely ever to marry

spiral /'spaɪə.rʲl/ US /'spaɪr.əl/ *noun* [C] **1** a shape made up of curves, each one above or wider than the one before: *A corkscrew is spiral-shaped.* **2 downward spiral** when a price, etc. is decreasing, or when a situation is getting worse and it is difficult to control because one bad event causes another: *This year's downward spiral of house prices has depressed the market.* ○ *We must avoid the downward spiral in which unemployment leads to homelessness and then to crime.* **spiral** /'spaɪə.rʲl/ US /'spaɪr.əl/ *adj* [before n] *a spiral staircase* ○ *a spiral galaxy*

spiral /'spaɪə.rʲl/ US /'spaɪr.əl/ *verb* [I usually + adv or prep] -ll- or US USUALLY -l- **1** to move in a spiral: *With one wing damaged, the model airplane spiralled downwards.* **2** If costs, prices, etc. spiral, they increase faster and faster: *Spiralling costs have squeezed profits.* **3 spiral downwards** (of prices, etc.) to get less, at a faster and faster rate

spiral-bound /'spaɪə.rʲl.baʊnd/ US /'spaɪr.əl-/ *adj* (of a book) having a spiral-shaped piece of metal or plastic holding its pages together

spire /spaɪəʳ/ US /spaɪr/ *noun* [C] a tall pointed structure on top of a building, especially on top of a church tower

spirit WAY OF FEELING /'spɪr.ɪt/ *noun* [S or U] **1** a particular way of thinking, feeling or behaving, especially a way that is typical of a particular group of people, an activity, a time or a place: *The players have a very strong team spirit* (= loyalty to each other). ○ *As rock musicians in the 1960s, they were very much part of the spirit of the age/times.* ○ *We acted in a spirit of cooperation.* **2 the spirit of a law/rule, etc.** the principle which a law/rule, etc. was created to strengthen, rather than the particular things it says you must or must not do: *They followed neither the spirit nor the letter of the law.*

• **enter/get into the spirit** to show enthusiasm and enjoyment: *They went to the tennis club a few times but never really got into the spirit of it.*

• **that's the spirit** used to approve or encourage someone's positive attitude or action: *"Come on, we can win this game." "That's the spirit."*

spirits /'spɪr.ɪts/ *plural noun* the way a person is feeling: *I've been in high/low spirits* (= feeling happy/sad) *lately.* ○ *Her spirits lifted/rose* (= She felt happier) *as she read the letter.* ○ *The negative reply dashed his spirits* (= made him unhappy).

-spirited /-spɪr.ɪ.tɪd/ US /-tɪd/ *suffix*: *low-spirited* (= sad) ○ *The children are rather high-spirited* (= excited and happy).

spirit NOT BODY /'spɪr.ɪt/ *noun* **1** [U] the characteristics of a person that are considered as being separate from the body, and which many religions believe continue to exist after the body dies: *Although he's now living in America, I feel he's with me in spirit* (= I feel he is present and is influencing me, in a way that is not physical). **2** [C] the form of a dead person, similar to a ghost, or the presence of a dead person which you can feel but not see: *an evil spirit* ○ *The spirits of long-dead warriors seemed to haunt the area.*

• **as/if/when/etc. the spirit moves sb** taking action only when you feel is the right time, not following a plan: *It's impossible to predict what he'll do – he just acts when the spirit moves him.*

• **The spirit is willing, but the flesh is weak.** HUMOROUS SAYING said when you would like to do something, but you do not have the time, skills or energy necessary to do it

spiritual /'spɪr.ɪ.tju.əl/ *adj* relating to deep feelings and beliefs, especially religious beliefs: *Traditional ways of life fulfilled both economic and spiritual needs.* **spiritually** /'spɪr.ɪ.tju.ə.li/ *adv*

spirituality /,spɪr.ɪ.tju'æl.ɪ.ti/ US /-ə.t̬i/ *noun* [U] APPROVING the quality of being concerned with deep, often religious, feelings and beliefs, rather than with the physical parts of life

spiritualism /'spɪr.ɪ.tju.ə.lɪ.zᵊm/ *noun* [U] the belief that living people can communicate with people who have died **spiritualist** /'spɪr.ɪ.tju.ə.lɪst/ *noun* [C] *A spiritualist had told her he could give her a message from her dead husband.*

spirit ENTHUSIASM /'spɪr.ɪt/ *noun* [U] APPROVING enthusiasm, energy or bravery: *The orchestra performed the Rite of Spring with great spirit.* ○ *The torture failed to break the prisoner's spirit.*

spirited /'spɪr.ɪ.tɪd/ US /-t̬ɪd/ *adj* APPROVING enthusiastic and determined: *The home team's spirited playing ensured them a comfortable victory.*

spiritless /'spɪr.ɪt.ləs/ *adj* DISAPPROVING lacking energy and enthusiasm: *It was rather a spiritless performance.*

spirit ALCOHOL /'spɪr.ɪt/ *noun* **1** [C or U] a strong alcoholic drink: *Vodka is a type of spirit.* ○ *Spirits are more expensive than beer, but they get you drunk faster.* **2** [U] Some types of spirit are alcoholic liquids used especially for cleaning, mixing with paint, etc: *Thin the paint with white spirit.*

spirit MOVE /'spɪr.ɪt/ *verb* **spirit sb or sth away/off/out, etc.** to move someone or something out of or away from a place secretly: *Somehow the prisoners managed to spirit news out to the world outside.*

'**spirit ,level** UK *noun* [C] (US **level**) a tool which contains a tube of liquid with an air bubble in it and shows whether a surface is level by the position of the bubble

spiritual /'spɪr.ɪ.tju.əl/ *noun* [C] (ALSO **negro spiritual**) a type of religious song, originally developed by African Americans in the US

,**spiritual 'home** *noun* [C usually sing] a place where you feel you belong, although you were not born there, because you have a lot in common with the people, the culture and the way of life

spit FORCE OUT /spɪt/ *verb* **spitting, spat** or US ALSO **spit, spat** or US ALSO **spit 1** [I or T] to force out the contents of the mouth, especially saliva: *Bob Ewell spat contemptuously right in the lawyer's face.* ○ *He spat the meat out in disgust.* ○ *They bought watermelons and ate them as they walked, spitting out the seeds.* **2** [I] If something hot, such as a fire, spits, it produces short sharp noises and throws out little bits.

• **spit blood/venom** (US ALSO **spit nails**, AUS ALSO **spit tacks**) to speak in an angry way, or to show anger: *I thought he was going to spit blood when he saw what had happened.*

• **in/within spitting distance** INFORMAL If something is in/within spitting distance, it is very close: *The house is within spitting distance of the sea.*

• **be the spitting image of** to look extremely similar to: *Josie is the spitting image of her granny at the same age.*

spit /spɪt/ *noun* [U] (FORMAL **spittle**, AUS INFORMAL **slag**) INFORMAL saliva, especially when it is outside the mouth: *She used a little spit on a tissue to wipe the mirror clean.*

• **the spit (and image) of** INFORMAL If someone is the spit (and image) of someone else, they look extremely similar to them: *The old man was the (dead) spit of Winston Churchill.*

• **spit and polish** *INFORMAL* careful cleaning and shining: *The car needs some spit and polish.*

spit [RAIN] /spɪt/ *verb* [I] **spitting** *INFORMAL* to rain very slightly: *If **it's** only spitting **(with rain)**, perhaps we don't need waterproofs.*

spit [ROD] /spɪt/ *noun* [C] a long thin rod put through a piece of food, especially meat, so that it can be cooked above a fire: *Roast the lamb **on** a spit.*

spit [LAND] /spɪt/ *noun* [C] a long, thin, flat beach which goes out into the sea

▲ **spit *sth* out** *phrasal verb* [M] to say something quickly and angrily: *He spat out an insult and marched out of the room.*

• **Spit it out!** *INFORMAL* used to tell someone to start speaking or to speak more quickly, when they are unwilling to speak or are speaking slowly: *Come on, spit it out, who told you about this?*

spitball /ˈspɪt.bɔːl/ [US] /-bɑːl/ *noun* [C] *US* a piece of paper that has been chewed and then rolled into a ball to be thrown or shot at someone

spite [HURT] /spaɪt/ *noun* [U] a feeling of anger towards someone that makes a person want to annoy, upset or hurt them, especially in a small way: *He's the sort of man who would let down the tyres on your car just **out of/from** spite.*

spite /spaɪt/ *verb* [T] to intentionally annoy, upset or hurt someone: *I almost think he died without making a will just to spite his family.* **spiteful** /ˈspaɪt.fəl/ *adj DISAPPROVING* **spitefully** /ˈspaɪt.fəl.i/ *adv* **spitefulness** /ˈspaɪt.fəl.nəs/ *noun* [U]

spite [DESPITE] /spaɪt/ *noun* **1 in spite of** (used before one fact that makes another fact surprising) despite: *In spite of his injury, Ricardo will play in Saturday's match.* **2 in spite of** *yourself* used when you do something which you do not intend to do and which you are trying not to do: *She started to laugh, in spite of her**self**.*

spittoon /spɪˈtuːn/ *noun* [C] (*US ALSO* **cuspidor**) especially in the past, a metal container on the floor in a public place for SPITTING (= forcing out the contents of your mouth) into

spiv /spɪv/ *noun* [C] *UK OLD-FASHIONED INFORMAL DISAPPROVING* a man, especially one who is well-dressed in a way that attracts attention, who makes money dishonestly

splash [LIQUID] /splæʃ/ *verb* (*UK INFORMAL ALSO* **splosh**) **1** [I or T; usually + adv or prep] If a liquid splashes or if you splash a liquid, it falls on or hits something or someone: *Water was splashing from a hole in the roof.* ○ *Unfortunately some paint splashed **onto** the rug.* ○ *She splashed her face with cold water.* ○ *She poured a large gin and splashed soda **into** it from a siphon.* **2** [I usually + adv or prep] to move in water so that drops of it go in all directions: *The kids were splashing **(about/around)** in the shallow end of the swimming pool.*

splash /splæʃ/ *noun* [C] **1** a small amount of a liquid which has fallen or been dropped: *There were several splashes of white paint on the carpet.* **2** the noise of something hitting or moving in water: *We heard a splash and then saw that Toni had fallen in the river.* **splash** /splæʃ/ *adv*: *The ball fell splash into the river.*

splash [SHOW] /splæʃ/ *verb* [T + adv or prep] to print or show something in a very noticeable way: *Several newspapers splashed colour pictures of Princess Diana **across** their front pages.*

splash /splæʃ/ *noun* [C] something or someone bright or very noticeable: *The little girl in her flowery dress provides the only splash **of colour** in the picture.*

• **make a splash** to become suddenly very successful or very well known: *Jodie Foster made quite a splash in the film 'Taxi Driver'.*

▲ **splash out *(sth)*** *phrasal verb UK* to spend a lot of money on buying things, especially items which are pleasant to have but which you do not need: *They splashed out £3000 **on** a holiday.* ➲See also **splurge**.

splash-down /ˈsplæʃ.daʊn/ *noun* [C usually sing; U] a landing by a spacecraft in the sea

ˈsplash ˌguard *noun* [C] *MAINLY US FOR* **mudflap**

splashy /ˈsplæʃ.i/ *adj US* unnecessarily expensive, exciting, etc: *Hollywood tends to make splashy films with lots of star actors.*

splat /splæt/ *noun* [U] *INFORMAL* the sound of something wet hitting a surface or of something hitting the surface of a liquid **splat** /splæt/ *adv*: *She fell, splat, into the water.*

splatter /ˈsplæt.əʳ/ [US] /ˈsplæt̬.ɚ/ *verb* [I or T] (especially of a thick liquid) to hit and cover a surface with small drops, or to cause this to happen: *The bike was splattered **with** mud.*

splay /spleɪ/ *verb* [I or T] to spread wide apart: *At one point the dancers flipped onto their backs and splayed their legs.* ○ *The petals splay **out** from the middle of the flower.*

spleen [ORGAN] /spliːn/ *noun* [C] an organ near the stomach which produces and cleans the body's blood

spleen [ANGER] /spliːn/ *noun* [U] *FORMAL* a feeling of anger and dissatisfaction: *MAINLY UK She threatened, in a **fit/burst of** spleen, to resign.* ○ *Shareholders used the conference as an opportunity to **vent** their spleen **on*** (= get angry with) *the Board of Directors.*

splendid /ˈsplen.dɪd/ *adj FORMAL* excellent, or beautiful and impressive: *We had splendid food/a splendid holiday/splendid weather.* ○ *You look splendid in that outfit.* ➲See also **resplendent**. **splendidly** /ˈsplen.dɪd.li/ *adv*

splendiferous /splenˈdɪf.ər.əs/ [US] /-ɚ-/ *adj HUMOROUS* splendid

splendour *UK, US* **splendor** /ˈsplen.dəʳ/ [US] /-dɚ/ *noun* [U] great beauty which attracts admiration and attention: *They bought a decaying 16th-century manor house and restored it to its original splendour.*

splendours *UK, MAINLY US* **splendors** /ˈsplen.dəz/ [US] /-dɚz/ *plural noun* the beautiful features or qualities of a place, etc: *So many writers have described the splendours **of** Venice.*

splice /splaɪs/ *verb* [T] to join two pieces of rope, film, etc. together at their ends in order to form one long piece: *Scientists have discovered how to splice pieces of DNA.*

• **get spliced** *OLD-FASHIONED INFORMAL* to get married

splice /splaɪs/ *noun* [C] a join between two pieces of something so that they form one long piece

spliff /splɪf/ *noun* [C] *SLANG* a hand-rolled cigarette containing the drug cannabis

▲ **spliff up** *phrasal verb SLANG* to make and light a cannabis cigarette

splint /splɪnt/ *noun* [C] a long flat object used as a support for a broken bone so that the bone stays in a particular position while it heals: *The doctor put a splint **on** the arm and bandaged it up.*

splinter /ˈsplɪn.təʳ/ [US] /-t̬ɚ/ *noun* [C] a small sharp broken piece of wood, glass, plastic or similar material: *The girl had got a splinter **(of** wood) in her toe.*

splinter /ˈsplɪn.təʳ/ [US] /-t̬ɚ/ *verb* [I] to break into small, sharp pieces: *The edges of the plastic cover had cracked and splintered.* ○ *FIGURATIVE The danger is that the Conservative Party may splinter **into** several smaller political parties.*

ˈsplinter ˌgroup *noun* [C] a group of people who have left a political party or other organization and formed a new separate organization: *The Socialist Workers' Party seemed to split into several splinter groups.*

split [DIVIDE] /splɪt/ *verb* **splitting, split, split 1** [I or T] to (cause to) divide into two or more parts, especially along a particular line: *The prize was split **between** Susan and Kate.* ○ *Split the aubergines **in** half and cover with breadcrumbs.* ○ *The teacher split the children **(up) into** three groups.* ○ *INFORMAL I'll split* (= share) *this croissant **with** you.* ○ *His trousers split when he tried to jump the fence.* ○ [+ obj + adj] *The woman had split her head **open*** (= got a long deep wound in her head) *when she was thrown off the horse.* **2** [I or T] If the people in an organization or group split, or if something splits them, they disagree and form smaller groups: *The childcare issue has split the employers' group.* ○ *The union executive has split **down the middle*** (= divided into two equal-sized groups who disagree with each other) *on what to do next.* ○ *A group of extremists split **(off) from** the Labour Party to form a new "Workers' Communist Party".* **3** [I] *OLD-FASHIONED INFORMAL* to leave a place

S

• **split hairs** *DISAPPROVING* to argue about whether unimportant details are correct
• **split *your* sides** to laugh a lot at something: *We nearly split our sides* ***laughing/with laughter*** *watching Paul trying to get the dog into the bicycle basket.*
• **split the difference** If you split the difference you agree on a number or amount that is exactly in the middle of the difference between two other numbers or amounts.
split /splɪt/ *noun* **[C]** **1** a long, thin hole in something where it has broken apart: *Rain was getting in through a split* ***in*** *the plastic sheeting.* **2** when a group of people divides into smaller groups because they disagree about something: *There is a widening split* ***between*** *senior managers and the rest of the workforce.* ○ *The tax issue has caused a split* ***in/within*** *the government.* ○ *There was a 70%, 25%, 5% split* ***in*** *the voting.*
the splits *UK plural noun* (*US* **split**) the action of sitting on the floor with your legs straight out and flat along the floor in opposite directions: *Can you* ***do*** *the splits?*
splitting /ˈsplɪt.ɪŋ/ [US] /ˈsplɪt̬-/ *adj* **splitting headache** a very severe pain that you feel in your head

split [TELL] /splɪt/ *verb* **[I]** **splitting, split, split** *UK OLD-FASHIONED INFORMAL* to tell other people secret and damaging information about someone: *They knew Josie wouldn't split* ***on*** *them* ***to*** *the teacher.*
▲ **split up** *phrasal verb INFORMAL* If two people split up, they end their relationship or marriage: *She split up* ***with*** *her boyfriend last week.*
split-up /ˈsplɪt.ʌp/ *noun* **[C usually sing]** *INFORMAL* when two people end their relationship

ˌsplit ˈend *noun* **[C usually pl]** a hair that has divided into several parts at its end: *Dry, brittle hair and split ends were the unfortunate consequence of years of dyeing it peroxide blond.*

ˌsplit inˈfinitive *noun* **[C]** *SPECIALIZED* a phrase in which an adverb or other word is put between "to" and an INFINITIVE. Some people consider split infinitives to be bad grammar, but they are becoming more acceptable: *'To quickly decide' is an example of a split infinitive.*

split-level /ˌsplɪtˈlev.əl/ *adj* A split-level building or room has floors at slightly different heights.

ˌsplit ˈpea *noun* **[C usually pl]** a dried pea that has been separated into its two halves, used especially in soups

ˌsplit personˈality *noun* **[C usually sing]** Someone with a split personality behaves so differently at different times that they seem to have more than one character.

ˈsplit ˌpin *noun* **[C]** a thin metal rod divided into two parts which open out in order to fasten parts of a machine

ˌsplit ˈsecond *noun* **[S]** a very short moment of time: *They brought out guns and for a split second nobody moved.* ○ *We had to make a split-second* (= very quick) *decision.*

splodge *MAINLY UK* /splɒdʒ/ [US] /splɑːdʒ/ *noun* **[C]** (*US USUALLY* **splotch**) *INFORMAL* an irregularly shaped mark or spot: *He put his hand on the bed, and left a splodge of blood on the bedspread.*

splosh /splɒʃ/ [US] /splɑːʃ/ *verb* **[I]**, *noun* **[C]** *MAINLY UK INFORMAL FOR* **splash** LIQUID.

splurge /splɜːdʒ/ [US] /splɝːdʒ/ *verb* **[I or T]** *INFORMAL* to spend a lot of money on buying goods, especially luxury goods; **splash out**: *I feel like splurging* ***(out) on*** *a new dress.* **splurge** /splɜːdʒ/ [US] /splɝːdʒ/ *noun* **[C]**

splutter /ˈsplʌt.əʳ/ [US] /ˈsplʌt̬.ɚ/ *verb* **[I]** (of a person) to speak in a quick and confused way, producing short unclear noises because of surprise, anger, etc., or (of a person or thing) to make a series of noises similar to this: *The old gentleman was spluttering* ***with*** *indignation.* ○ **[+ speech]** *"But, er ... when, um, ... how?" he spluttered.* ○ *She took too big a gulp of whisky and started to cough and splutter.* **splutter** /ˈsplʌt.əʳ/ [US] /ˈsplʌt̬.ɚ/ *noun* **[C]**

spoil [DESTROY] /spɔɪl/ *verb* **spoiled** or **spoilt, spoiled** or **spoilt** **1** **[T]** to destroy or reduce the pleasure, interest or beauty of something: *He tried not to let the bad news spoil his evening.* ○ *The oil spill has spoilt the whole beautiful coastline.* ○ *I haven't seen the film, so don't spoil it* ***for*** *me by telling me what happens.* ○ *You'll spoil your* ***appetite*** *for dinner if you have a cake now.* **2** **[I or T]** When food spoils or is spoilt, it is no longer good enough to eat: *The dessert will spoil if you don't keep it in the fridge.* **3** **[T]** *UK SPECIALIZED* to mark a BALLOT PAPER so that it cannot be officially counted as a vote: *Since she supported none of the candidates, she spoiled her ballot paper.*
• **be spoiling for a fight** to be very eager to fight or argue: *Local councillors are spoiling for a fight over plans to close two village schools.*
• **spoil *sb's* party** (*ALSO* **spoil the party for *sb***) to cause trouble for someone at a moment when they are enjoying a success
spoiler /ˈspɔɪ.ləʳ/ [US] /-lɚ/ *noun* **[C]** an newspaper article, television programme, etc. that is produced just before or at the same time as another similar one in order to take attention away from it ⊃See also **spoiler**.

spoil [TREAT WELL] /spɔɪl/ *verb* **[T]** **spoiled** or **spoilt, spoiled** or **spoilt** to treat someone very or too well, especially by being extremely generous: *When I'm feeling miserable I go shopping and spoil myself – a couple of new dresses always make me feel better.*
• **be spoilt for choice** to be unable to choose because there are so many possible good choices: *There's so much good theatre and cinema in London, really one is spoilt for choice.*

spoil [CHILD] /spɔɪl/ *verb* **[T]** **spoiled** or **spoilt, spoiled** or **spoilt** *DISAPPROVING* to allow a child to behave exactly as it wants to, usually so that it becomes selfish and lacking in care and respect for other people: *Mr Harvey, unable for once to do exactly as he wanted, sulked just like a spoilt* ***child.***

spoil [RUBBISH] /spɔɪl/ *noun* **[U]** earth, stones, etc. dug out from a hole in the ground: *a spoil heap*

spoiler /ˈspɔɪ.ləʳ/ [US] /-lɚ/ *noun* **[C]** a device on a car or aircraft which is positioned so that it stops the air from flowing around the vehicle in a smooth way and so helps to control it ⊃See also **spoiler** at **spoil** DESTROY.

spoils /spɔɪlz/ *plural noun FORMAL* goods, advantages, profits, etc. obtained by your actions or because of your position or situation: *The spoils* ***of victory/war*** *included mounds of treasure and armour.*

spoilsport /ˈspɔɪl.spɔːt/ [US] /-spɔːrt/ *noun* **[C]** *INFORMAL DISAPPROVING* a person who stops other people from enjoying themselves: *She did ask her dad if she could have a big party, but the old spoilsport refused.*

spoke [SPEAK] /spəʊk/ [US] /spoʊk/ *past simple of* **speak**

spoke [WHEEL PART] /spəʊk/ [US] /spoʊk/ *noun* **[C]** any of the rods that join the edge of a wheel to its centre, so giving the wheel its strength: *a bicycle spoke*
• **put a spoke in (*sb's*) wheel, etc.** *INFORMAL* to make it difficult for someone to achieve something they had planned to do: *His letter really put a spoke in our plans.*

spoken [SPEAK] /ˈspəʊ.kən/ [US] /ˈspoʊ-/ *past participle of* **speak**

-spoken [MANNER OF SPEECH] /-spəʊ.kən/ [US] /-spoʊ-/ *suffix* speaking in a particular way: *a softly-spoken young man* ○ *a well-spoken lady*

ˈspoken ˌfor *adj* **[after v]** **1** describes something that is not available because someone has already bought or claimed it: *Most of the best paintings in the exhibition were already spoken for.* **2** *OLD-FASHIONED* describes someone who is not available for a romantic relationship because they are already having one with someone else: *Both girls were spoken for.*

spokesman /ˈspəʊks.mən/ [US] /ˈspoʊks-/ *noun* **[C]** (*ALSO* **spokesperson**) someone who is chosen by a group or organization to speak officially to the public for them: *a government spokesperson*

spokeswoman /ˈspəʊksˌwʊm.ən/ [US] /ˈspoʊks-/ *noun* **[C]** a female spokesman: *a spokeswoman* ***for*** *the environmental group Greenpeace*

spondulicks, spondulix /spɒnˈduː.lɪks/ [US] /spɑːn-/ *plural noun OLD-FASHIONED INFORMAL HUMOROUS FOR* **money**

sponge [SUBSTANCE] /spʌndʒ/ *noun* **1** **[C]** a soft substance that is full of small holes and can absorb a lot of liquid, and is used for washing and cleaning **2** **[S]** when you rub something or someone with a wet sponge or cloth in order to clean them: *Give it* ***a*** *sponge* ***with*** *a damp cloth – that will remove the blood stains.*

S

sponge /spʌndʒ/ *verb* [T] (*ALSO* **sponge down**) to rub something or someone with a wet sponge or cloth, especially to clean them: *Most food stains will come off if you sponge the material with a little detergent.* ○ *The doctor told me to sponge Erik down with cold water in order to lower his temperature.*
spongy /ˈspʌn.dʒi/ *adj* soft and able to absorb or having already absorbed a lot of liquid, like a sponge

sponge [GET MONEY] /spʌndʒ/ *verb* [I or T] *DISAPPROVING* to get money, food, etc. from other people, especially in order to live without working: *There must be a growing realization among younger people that sponging* ***off*** *the state is no longer possible.* **sponger** /ˈspʌn.dʒəʳ/ [US] /-dʒɚ/ *noun* [C]

ˈsponge ˌbag *noun* [C] *UK* a small waterproof bag used for carrying your TOOTHBRUSH, FACECLOTH, soap, etc. when you are travelling

ˈsponge (ˌcake) *noun* [C or U] a soft cake made with eggs, sugar and flour but usually no fat

ˈsponge ˌrubber *noun* [U] *US FOR* **foam rubber**

sponsor /ˈspɒn.səʳ/ [US] /ˈspɑːn.sɚ/ *verb* [T] to support a person, organization or activity by giving money, encouragement or other help: *The team is sponsored by JVC, so the players wear the letters JVC on their shirts.* ○ *Eva said she was doing a ten-mile walk for charity and asked if I'd sponsor her* ***for*** *£1 a mile.* **sponsor** /ˈspɒn.səʳ/ [US] /ˈspɑːn.sɚ/ *noun* [C] *All the major theatres now have sponsors, especially* ***for*** *high-cost productions.* **sponsorship** /ˈspɒn.sə.ʃɪp/ [US] /ˈspɑːn.sɚ-/ *noun* [U] *The orchestra receives £2 million a year* ***in*** *sponsorship from various companies.*

spontaneous /spɒnˈteɪ.ni.əs/ [US] /spɑːn-/ *adj* happening or done in a natural, often sudden way, without any planning or without being forced: *His jokes seemed spontaneous, but were in fact carefully prepared beforehand.* ○ *APPROVING She's such a spontaneous, lively woman.* **spontaneously** /spɒnˈteɪ.ni.ə.sli/ [US] /spɑːn-/ *adv*: *The liquid spontaneously ignited.* **spontaneity** /ˌspɒn.təˈneɪ.ɪ.ti/ [US] /ˌspɑːn.t̬əˈneɪ.ə.t̬i/ *noun* [U] *APPROVING The script has a refreshing spontaneity and sparkle.*

sponˌtaneous comˈbustion *noun* [U] when something burns without any obvious cause

spoof [COPY] /spuːf/ *noun* [C] an amusing and ridiculous piece of writing, music, theatre, etc. that copies the style of an original work: *They did a spoof* ***on/of*** *the Nine O'Clock News.* ○ *It was a spoof cowboy film.*

spoof [DECEIVE] /spuːf/ *verb* [I or T] *US INFORMAL* to try to make someone believe in something that is not true, as a joke

spook [SPIRIT] /spuːk/ *noun* [C] *INFORMAL FOR* **ghost** SPIRIT: *The film was dreadful – all spooks and vampires.*
spook /spuːk/ *verb* [T] *MAINLY US* to frighten a person or animal: *Seeing the police car outside the house really spooked them.*
spooky /ˈspuː.ki/ *adj INFORMAL* strange and frightening: *It was a spooky coincidence.*

spook [PERSON] /spuːk/ *noun* [C] *US FOR* **spy** SECRET PERSON.

spool /spuːl/ *noun* [C] a tube-shaped object with top and bottom edges that stick out and around which a length of thread, wire, film, etc. is wrapped in order to store it: *a spool* ***of*** *cotton/film*

spoon /spuːn/ *noun* [C] **1** an object consisting of a round hollow part and a handle, used for mixing, serving and eating food **2** (used as a combining form): *a soup spoon* ○ *a teaspoon* **3** (*ALSO* **spoonful**) an amount held in a particular spoon: *a couple of spoons* ***of*** *sauce*
spoon /spuːn/ *verb* [T + adv or prep] to move something, especially food, using a spoon: *He spooned the mush* ***into*** *the baby's open mouth.* ○ *Spoon a little sauce* ***over*** *the fish.*
spoonful /ˈspuːn.fʊl/ *noun* [C] *plural* **spoonfuls** or **spoonsful** an amount held in a particular spoon: *a spoonful of mustard*

spoonerism /ˈspuː.nᵊr.ɪ.zᵊm/ [US] /-nɚ-/ *noun* [C] a mistake made when speaking in which the first sounds of two words are exchanged with each other to produce a not intended and usually amusing meaning: *The Reverend William Spooner used to produce spoonerisms such as 'a scoop of boy trouts', instead of what he had meant to say – 'a troop of boy scouts'.*

spoon-feed [FEED] /ˈspuːn.fiːd/ *verb* [T] to feed a baby or other person using a spoon

spoon-feed [PROVIDE INFORMATION] /ˈspuːn.fiːd/ *verb* [T] *DISAPPROVING* to give someone so much help or information that they do not need to try themselves: *By giving out printed sheets of facts and theories, the teachers spoon-fed us* ***with*** *what we needed for the exam.*

spoor /spɔːʳ/ [US] /spʊr/ *noun* [S] *SPECIALIZED* the marks left by a wild animal as it travels

sporadic /spəˈræd.ɪk/ *adj* happening irregularly; not regular or continuous: *sporadic gunfire* ○ *a sporadic electricity supply* ○ *More than 100 people have been killed this year in sporadic outbursts of ethnic violence.* **sporadically** /spəˈræd.ɪ.kli/ *adv*

spore /spɔːʳ/ [US] /spɔːr/ *noun* [C] a reproductive cell produced by some plants and simple organisms such as FERNS and MUSHROOMS

sporran /ˈspɒr.ᵊn/ [US] /ˈspɔːr.ən/ *noun* [C] a small bag usually made of fur worn in front of the KILT (= type of skirt) by a person wearing traditional Scottish clothes

sport [GAME] /spɔːt/ [US] /spɔːrt/ *noun* **1** [C] a game, competition or activity needing physical effort and skill that is played or done according to rules, for enjoyment and/or as a job: *Football, cricket and hockey are all team sports.* ○ *I enjoy winter sports like skiing and skating.* ➲See picture **Sports** on page Centre 10 **2** [U] *UK* all types of physical activity which people do to keep healthy or for enjoyment: *She used to* ***do/play*** *a lot of sport when she was younger.* **3** [U] *OLD-FASHIONED* fun or enjoyment
sporting /ˈspɔː.tɪŋ/ [US] /ˈspɔːr.t̬ɪŋ/ *adj* **1** relating to sports: *The Olympics is the biggest sporting* ***event*** *in the world.* **2** *OLD-FASHIONED* showing fairness and respect towards an opposing team or player
sports /spɔːts/ [US] /spɔːrts/ *adj* [before n] relating to sport: *sports equipment.* ○ *It's the school sports day on Monday.*
sportsman /ˈspɔːts.mən/ [US] /ˈspɔːrts-/ *noun* [C] **1** a man who plays sport, especially well **2** someone who plays sport in a way that shows respect and fairness towards the opposing player or team: *He'll be remembered both as a brilliant footballer and as a true sportsman.*
sportsmanlike /ˈspɔːts.mən.laɪk/ [US] /ˈspɔːrts-/ *adj* behaving in a fair and respectful way towards the opposing team or player when playing sport
sportsmanship /ˈspɔːts.mən.ʃɪp/ [US] /ˈspɔːrts-/ *noun* [U] when you behave in a fair and respectful way towards the opposing team or player when playing sport
sportsperson /ˈspɔːts.pɜː.sᵊn/ [US] /ˈspɔːrtsˌpɝː-/ *noun* [C] someone who plays sport, especially well: *He was voted Sportsperson of the Year.*
sportswoman /ˈspɔːtsˌwʊm.ən/ [US] /ˈspɔːrts-/ *noun* [C] a woman who plays sport, especially well: *a famous/keen/talented sportswoman*
sporty /ˈspɔː.ti/ [US] /ˈspɔːr.t̬i/ *adj* **1** describes someone who enjoys sport and is good at it: *Guy wasn't really the sporty type.* **2** describes clothes that are bright and informal, often looking like the type of clothes that you could wear for sports **3** A sporty car is a fast low car, often for two people only.

sport [PERSON] /spɔːt/ [US] /spɔːrt/ *noun* [C] **1** *OLD-FASHIONED INFORMAL* a pleasant, positive, generous person who does not complain about things they are asked to do or about games that they lose: *Oh, Douglas – be a* ***(good)*** *sport and give me a lift to the station.* ➲See also **spoilsport**. **2** *AUS* a friendly way of addressing a man or boy: [as form of address] *Hello sport – how are you?*

sport [WEAR] /spɔːt/ [US] /spɔːrt/ *verb* [T] to wear or be decorated with something: *Back in the 1960s he sported bell-bottom trousers, platform heels and hair down past his shoulders.* ○ *The front of the car sported a German flag.*

ˌsporting ˈchance *noun* [U] If there is a sporting chance that something good will happen it is possible that it will happen: *It's not definite that they'll accept our offer, but there's a sporting chance.*

ˈsports ˌcar *noun* [C] a fast low car, often for two people only ➲See picture **Cars and Trucks** on page Centre 13

S

sportscaster /ˈspɔːtsˌkɑː.stəʳ/ [US] /ˈspɔːrtsˌkæs.t̬ɚ/ *noun* [C] *MAINLY US* someone who appears on television or radio, giving information and news about sports events

ˈsports ˌjacket *noun* [C] a man's jacket made of TWEED (= thick woollen cloth)

sportswear /ˈspɔːts.weəʳ/ [US] /ˈspɔːrts.wer/ *noun* [U] (used especially in shops) clothes that are worn for sports or other physical activities

spot [CIRCLE] /spɒt/ [US] /spɑːt/ *noun* [C] **1** a small, usually round area of colour which is differently coloured or lighter or darker than the background: *He had a spot of grease on his tie.* **2** one of many spots, that form a pattern: *I wore that skirt with the green spots.* **3** *UK* a raised pinkish red circle on the skin which is temporary: *Teenagers often suffer a lot from spots.* **4** *MAINLY UK* a small amount: *I felt a few spots of rain.* ○ *Shall we stop for a spot of lunch?* ○ *I'm having a spot of* ***bother*** (= some trouble) *with one of my back teeth.*

spot /spɒt/ [US] /spɑːt/ *verb* [I] **-tt-** *UK* If someone says it's spotting (with rain) they mean that a few drops of rain are falling. **spotted** /ˈspɒt.ɪd/ [US] /ˈspɑː.t̬ɪd/ *adj*: *a spotted toad* ○ *She was wearing a black and white spotted dress.*

spotty /ˈspɒt.i/ [US] /ˈspɑː.t̬i/ *adj* **1** *UK* describes a person with spots on their skin: *I knew him when he was just a spotty youth.* **2** *US* (*UK* **patchy**) bad in some parts: *She has a fairly spotty work record.* ○ *Sales have picked up a little but they're still spotty.*

spot [SEE] /spɒt/ [US] /spɑːt/ *verb* [T] **-tt-** to see or notice someone or something, usually because you are looking hard: *I've just spotted Malcolm – he's over there, near the entrance.* ○ *If you spot any mistakes in the article just mark them with a pencil.* ○ [+ v-ing] *The police spotted him driv****ing*** *a stolen car.* ○ [+ question word] *I soon spotted* ***what*** *was wrong with the printer.* ○ [+ *that*] *The policewoman spotted* ***that*** *I hadn't got my seat belt on and signalled me to stop.*

• **well spotted** *UK* used to praise someone who has noticed something: *"I've just seen your glasses – they're under the table." "Ah, well spotted!"*

-spotter /-spɒt.əʳ/ [US] /-spɑː.t̬ɚ/ *suffix* describes a person whose job or interest is to notice people or things of the type mentioned: *a talent-spotter* ○ *UK a train-spotter* **-spotting** /-spɒt.ɪŋ/ [US] /-spɑː.t̬ɪŋ/ *suffix*: *talent-spotting*

spot [PLACE] /spɒt/ [US] /spɑːt/ *noun* [C] a particular place: *This looks like a nice spot for a picnic.*

• **on the spot 1** at the place where an event is happening or has recently happened: *The police were called and they were on the spot within three minutes.* **2** immediately: *You can be sacked on the spot for stealing.*

• **put** ***sb*** **on the spot** If you put someone on the spot you cause them embarrassment or difficulty by forcing them at that moment to answer a difficult question or make an important decision: *Mira rather put the boss on the spot by asking him when he was going to give us a pay-rise.*

S

spot [PART OF A SHOW] /spɒt/ [US] /spɑːt/ *noun* [C] a short length of time in a show which is given to a particular performer: *She's doing a regular five-minute spot on his show.*

ˈspot ˌcheck *noun* [C] a quick examination of a few members of a group instead of the whole group: *The police are doing spot checks* ***on*** *motorists to test alcohol levels.*

ˈspot ˌfine *noun* [C] a FINE (= money you have to pay as a punishment) that is given to you at the time of breaking the law

spotless [CLEAN] /ˈspɒt.ləs/ [US] /ˈspɑːt-/ *adj* extremely clean: *Her home is spotless.* **spotlessly** /ˈspɒt.lə.sli/ [US] /ˈspɑːt-/ *adv*: *The kitchen is spotlessly* ***clean****.*

spotless [GOOD] /ˈspɒt.ləs/ [US] /ˈspɑːt-/ *adj* **spotless character/record/reputation, etc.** a very good and honest character, etc: *She was young and pretty, with a spotless reputation.*

spotlight /ˈspɒt.laɪt/ [US] /ˈspɑːt-/ *noun* [C] **1** (*UK INFORMAL* **spot**) (a circle of strong light which is sent from) a lamp whose beam can be directed **2 in the spotlight** (of a person) receiving a lot of public attention: *The senator has been in the spotlight recently since the revelation of his tax frauds.*

spotlight /ˈspɒt.laɪt/ [US] /ˈspɑːt-/ *verb* [T] **spotlighted** or **spotlit, spotlighted** or **spotlit 1** to light something or someone with a spotlight: *The paintings in the alcove were spotlit from below.* **2** If something spotlights a particular situation, it directs public attention to it.

spot-on /ˌspɒtˈɒn/ [US] /ˌspɑːt̬ˈɑːn/ *adj* [after v] *UK INFORMAL* exact: *"How old do I reckon she is? I'd say thirty-eight." "Spot-on."*

ˌspotted ˈdick *noun* [C or U] *UK* a hot sweet dish, consisting of cake and dried fruit

ˌspotted ˈgum *noun* [C] *AUS* a tree that has a trunk that is pale with small darker areas

spot-welding /ˈspɒtˌwel.dɪŋ/ [US] /ˈspɑːt-/ *noun* [U] a way of joining together two pieces of wire or two flat pieces of metal by sending an electric current through small areas of them

spouse /spaʊs/ *noun* [C] *FORMAL OR LEGAL* a person's husband or wife: *In 60% of the households surveyed both spouses went out to work.*

spout [SPEAK] /spaʊt/ *verb* [T; I + adv or prep] *DISAPPROVING* to speak a lot, in a way that is boring or annoying for other people: *He spouts a load of pretentious nonsense and people are stupid enough to believe him!* ○ *I really don't want to listen to Mike spouting* ***on/off*** *all afternoon.*

spout [OPENING] /spaʊt/ *noun* [C] a tube-shaped opening which allows liquids to be poured out of a container

• **be up the spout** *UK SLANG* to be pregnant

• **up the spout** *UK SLANG* wasted or spoiled: *Peter lost his job so that was our holiday plans up the spout.*

spout [FLOW] /spaʊt/ *verb* [I + adv or prep; T] to flow or send out liquid or flames quickly and with force, in a straight line: *Flames spouted* ***(out)*** *from the oil wells.* ○ *The gash was spouting blood.* **spout** /spaʊt/ *noun* [C] *A spout of water shot out of the geyser.*

sprain /spreɪn/ *verb* [T] to cause an injury to a joint in the body by a sudden movement: *She sprained her ankle playing squash.* **sprain** /spreɪn/ *noun* [C] *He hasn't broken anything – it's just a bad sprain.*

sprang /spræŋ/ *past simple of* **spring**

sprat /spræt/ *noun* [C] a small edible fish which lives in the sea

sprawl [BODY] /sprɔːl/ [US] /sprɑːl/ *verb* [I] *DISAPPROVING* to spread the arms and legs out carelessly and untidily while sitting or lying down: *I knocked into her in the corridor and* ***sent*** *her sprawling* (= knocked her over). **sprawl** /sprɔːl/ [US] /sprɑːl/ *noun* [U] **sprawled** /sprɔːld/ [US] /sprɑːld/ *adj* [after v] *He was sprawled* ***(out) on*** *the floor.*

sprawl [CITY] /sprɔːl/ [US] /sprɑːl/ *verb* [I usually + adv or prep] *DISAPPROVING* (especially of a city) to cover a large area of land with buildings which have been added at different times so that it looks untidy: *The refugee camps sprawl across the landscape.* **sprawl** /sprɔːl/ [US] /sprɑːl/ *noun* [C usually sing] *the* ***urban*** *sprawl of South Florida* **sprawling** /ˈsprɔː.lɪŋ/ [US] /ˈsprɑː-/ *adj*: *sprawling suburbs*

spray [LIQUID] /spreɪ/ *noun* **1** [U] a mass of very small drops of liquid carried in the air: *Can you feel the spray from the sea/waterfall?* **2** [C] a liquid which is forced out of a special container under pressure so that it becomes a cloud-like mass of small liquid drops: *a quick spray of perfume/polish* **3** [C] a mass of small drops of liquid scattered onto plants and crops, etc. from a special piece of equipment, or the piece of equipment itself: *Farmers use a lot of* ***chemical*** *sprays on crops.* **spray** /spreɪ/ *verb* [I or T; usually + adv or prep] [R] *She sprayed herself* ***with*** *perfume.* ○ *Vandals had sprayed graffiti on the wall.* ○ *The pipe burst and water was spraying everywhere.* ○ *FIGURATIVE Rush hour commuters were sprayed* ***with bullets*** *by a gunman in a car.*

sprayer /ˈspreɪ.əʳ/ [US] /-ɚ/ *noun* [C] a device for sending out small drops of liquid, especially chemicals used in the garden

spray [FLOWERS] /spreɪ/ *noun* [C] a single small branch or stem with leaves and flowers on it: *All the wedding guests wore sprays of carnations.*

ˈspray ˌgun *noun* [C] a device which is held in the hand and used for sending out liquid such as paint in very small drops

spread /spred/ *verb* **[I or T]** **spread, spread** to (cause to) cover, reach or have an effect on a wider or increasing area: *The fire spread very rapidly because of the strong wind.* ○ *It started off as cancer of the liver but it spread **to** other areas of the body.* ○ *The redundancies are spread **across** the clothing, banking and building industries.* ○ *We spread the picnic rug **out** on the ground and sat down to eat.* ○ *The AIDS virus is spread* (= given to other people) *through contact with blood and other body fluids.* ○ *Are you spreading* (= telling a lot of people) ***gossip/rumours** again?* ○ *If we spread* (= divide) *the work between us, it won't seem so bad.* ○ *She spread her toast **with** a thick layer of butter./She spread a thick layer of butter **on** her toast.* ○ *It's a special sort of butter that spreads easily even when cold.* ○ *The suburbs spread **(out)** for miles to either side of the city.* ○ *Slowly a smile spread across her face.* ⊃See picture **In the Kitchen** on page Centre 16

• **spread *your* wings** to use your abilities for the first time in your life to do new and exciting things: *She'd been working for the same company for fifteen years and it was time to leave and spread her wings.*

• **spread the word** to communicate a message to a lot of people: *We've arranged a meeting for next Thursday so if you see anyone do spread the word.*

spread /spred/ *noun* **1** **[S]** when something moves to cover a larger area or affect a larger number of people: *The spread of AIDS in the last few years has been alarming.* **2** **[S]** the area or range covered by something: *The survey found **a** wide spread of opinion over the proposed new building.* **3** **[C]** a large article or advertisement covering one or more pages in a newspaper or magazine: *There's a double-page spread on the latest fashions.* **4** **[C or U]** a soft food for putting on bread and biscuits: *cheese/chocolate/fish spread* ○ *There's bread and various spreads for tea.* **5** **[C]** *US FOR* **ranch** **6** **[C]** *UK OLD-FASHIONED OR US* a meal, especially one for a special occasion with a lot of different dishes arranged on a table: *Sheila **laid on**/(UK ALSO) **put on*** (= made) *a lovely spread for us.*

PHRASAL VERBS WITH **spread**

▲ **spread out** *phrasal verb* If people spread out, they move from being close together in a group to being in different places across a larger area: *They spread out to search the whole area.*

▲ **spread *sth* over *sth*** *phrasal verb* to arrange for something to happen in stages during a period of time: *The course is spread over two years.* ○ *The repayments on the loan can be spread **out** over three years.*

spread-eagled /ˌspred'iː.gl̩d/ *adj* **[usually after v]** describes someone who is lying with their arms and legs stretched out: *William was lying spread-eagled on the grass, blind drunk.*

spreadsheet /'spred.ʃiːt/ *noun* **[C]** a computer program, used especially in business, which allows you to do financial calculations and plans

spree /spriː/ *noun* **[C]** a short period of doing a particular, usually enjoyable, activity much more than is usual: *I **went on** a drinking/shopping/spending spree on Saturday.* ○ *Twenty people were shot dead in the city making it the worst killing spree since the riots.*

sprig /sprɪg/ *noun* **[C]** a single small plant stem with leaves on it: *Garnish the dish with sprigs of parsley.*

sprightly /'spraɪt.li/ *adj* (especially of old people) energetic and in good health: *He's a sprightly old man of seventy-five.* **sprightliness** /'spraɪt.lɪ.nəs/ *noun* **[U]**

spring [MOVE QUICKLY] /sprɪŋ/ *verb* **[I usually + adv or prep]** **sprang** or *US ALSO* **sprung, sprung** to move quickly and suddenly towards a particular place: *I sprang out of bed to answer the door.* ○ *The organization is ready to spring **into action*** (= start taking action) *the moment it receives its funding.* ○ *He always springs **to** his **feet** when she walks in the room.* ○ *FIGURATIVE I noticed the way you sprang **to** his **defence** when Caroline started joking about his clothes.* ○ *The lid of the box sprang shut.*

• **spring to life** to suddenly become very active or busy: *After about 8 o'clock the city springs to life.*

• **spring to mind** to come quickly into your mind: *Say the word 'Australia' and a vision of beaches and blue seas immediately springs to mind.*

spring [APPEAR SUDDENLY] /sprɪŋ/ *verb* **[I usually + adv or prep]** **sprang** or *US ALSO* **sprung, sprung** to appear or start to exist suddenly: *Thousands of new businesses have sprung **up** in the past couple of years.* ○ *INFORMAL "Where did you spring **from**? – I didn't see you come in!"*

spring [SEASON] /sprɪŋ/ *noun* **[C or U]** the season of the year between winter and summer, lasting from March to June north of the equator, and from September to December south of the equator, when the weather becomes warmer, leaves and plants start to grow again and flowers appear: *spring flowers/weather* ○ *Many bulbs bloom **in (the)** spring.* ○ *Janet's coming over for a couple of weeks next spring.*

spring [CURVED METAL] /sprɪŋ/ *noun* **1** **[C]** a piece of curved or bent metal that can be pressed into a smaller space but then returns to its usual shape: *The children have jumped on the couch so much that they've ruined the springs.* **2** **[U]** something's ability to return to its usual shape after it has been pressed: *Over the years the mattress has lost its spring.*

• **a spring in *your* step** If you walk with or have a spring in your step, you walk energetically in a way that shows you are feeling happy and confident: *There's been a definite spring in his step ever since he met Joanna.*

springy /'sprɪŋ.i/ *adj* returning quickly to the usual shape, after being pulled, pushed, crushed, etc: *The turf feels very springy underfoot.*

sprung *UK* /sprʌŋ/ *adj* (*US* **spring**) (of furniture) using springs for internal support

spring [WATER] /sprɪŋ/ *noun* **[C]** (*ALSO* **springs**) a place where water naturally flows out from the ground: *bubbling/hot springs*

PHRASAL VERBS WITH **spring**

▲ **spring from *sth*** *phrasal verb* to come from or be a result of something: *His need to be liked obviously springs from a deep-rooted insecurity.*

▲ **spring *sth* on *sb*** *phrasal verb* to suddenly tell or ask someone something when they do not expect it: *I hope he's not going to spring any nasty surprises on us at the meeting this morning.*

springboard /'sprɪŋ.bɔːd/ [US] /-bɔːrd/ *noun* **[C]** **1** a flexible board which helps you to jump higher when jumping or diving into a swimming pool or when doing GYMNASTICS **2** something which provides you either with the opportunity to follow a particular plan of action, or the encouragement that is needed to make it successful: *The firm's director is confident that the new project will act as a springboard **for/to** further contracts.*

springbok /'sprɪŋ.bɒk/ [US] /-bɑːk/ *noun* **[C]** *plural* **springboks** or **springbok** an animal like a small deer that lives in southern Africa, is reddish brown with a white back end and can jump very high

ˌspring 'chicken *noun HUMOROUS* **be no spring chicken** to be no longer young

spring-clean /ˌsprɪŋ'kliːn/ *verb* **[T]** to clean all of a place, especially your house, very well, including parts you do not often clean **spring-clean** /ˌsprɪŋ'kliːn/ *noun* **[S]** *UK I gave the kitchen a spring-clean at the weekend.* **spring-cleaning** /ˌsprɪŋ'kliː.nɪŋ/ *noun* **[U]** *to do some spring-cleaning*

ˌspring 'greens *plural noun UK* the leaves of young cabbage plants, eaten as vegetables

ˌspring 'onion *UK noun* **[C]** (*US* **green onion**) a long thin green and white onion that is often eaten raw ⊃See picture **Vegetables** on page Centre 2

ˌspring 'roll *noun* **[C]** (*UK ALSO* **pancake roll**, *US ALSO* **egg roll**) a savoury Chinese pancake which is rolled up, filled with small pieces of vegetables and sometimes meat and fried

springtime /'sprɪŋ.taɪm/ *noun* **[U]** the season of spring: ***In (the)** springtime the woods are full of bluebells.*

sprinkle /'sprɪŋ.kl̩/ *verb* **[T]** to scatter a few bits or drops of something over a surface: *Sprinkle a few herbs **on** the pizza./Sprinkle the pizza **with** a few herbs.* ○ *FIGURATIVE The speech was liberally sprinkled with* (= contained

S

many) *jokes about the incident.*

sprinkle /ˈsprɪŋ.kl̩/ *noun* [C usually sing] (*US ALSO* **sprinkling**) a very light fall of rain or snow which lasts only a short time

sprinkler /ˈsprɪŋ.kl̩.əʳ/ [US] /-ɚ/ *noun* [C] **1** a piece of equipment for scattering water onto fires to put them out **2** a device with a lot of small holes which you put on the end of a HOSE in order to water plants, grass, etc.

sprinkling /ˈsprɪŋ.kl̩.ɪŋ/ *noun* [C usually sing] small bits or drops of something that are scattered over a surface: *Top each bowl with **a** generous sprinkling **of** fresh mint.* ○ *FIGURATIVE The audience were mainly women with **a** sprinkling* (= a small number) ***of** earnest-looking men.* ○ *FIGURATIVE Looking young for his forty years, he has just **a** sprinkling* (= a small number) ***of** grey hairs at the temples.*

sprint /sprɪnt/ *verb* [I] to run as fast as you can over a short distance, either in a race or because you are in a great hurry to get somewhere: *We had to sprint to catch the bus.*

sprint /sprɪnt/ *noun* **1** [C] a short and very fast race, such as the 100-metre race, or the last part of a longer running race which is run as fast as possible: *the 100-metre sprint* **2** [S] a very fast run that someone makes when they are in a great hurry to get somewhere: *He suddenly **broke into*** (= started) *a sprint.* **sprinter** /ˈsprɪn.təʳ/ [US] /-t̬ɚ/ *noun* [C] *Five years later and she's now a world-class sprinter.*

sprite /spraɪt/ *noun* [C] *LITERARY* a FAIRY (= small imaginary person with wings), especially one connected with water: *a sea/water sprite*

spritz /sprɪts/ *verb* [I] *US* to spray a mass of very small drops of liquid out of a container, usually by pressing a part of the container: *After you've applied your powder, spritz with a little mineral water.* **spritz** /sprɪts/ *noun* [C] *A quick spritz of scent and I'm ready.*

spritzer /ˈsprɪt.səʳ/ [US] /-sɚ/ *noun* [C] a drink made with white wine and especially SODA WATER (= fizzy water)

spritzig /ˈsprɪt.sɪg/ *adj AUS describes wine that is* slightly fizzy

sprocket (wheel) /ˈsprɒk.ɪt.wiːl/ [US] /ˈsprɑː.kɪt-/ *noun* [C] *SPECIALIZED* a device like a wheel with one or more rows of tooth-like parts sticking out which keeps a chain moving on a bicycle or pulls film, paper, etc. through a machine

sprog /sprɒg/ [US] /sprɑːg/ *noun* [C] *UK SLANG* a baby or young child: *She's got a couple of sprogs now.*

sprout /spraʊt/ *verb* **1** [I or T] to produce leaves, hair and other new developing parts, or (of leaves, hair and other developing parts) to begin to grow: *It takes about three days for the seeds to sprout.* ○ *Your hair is sticking up – it looks like you're sprouting horns!* **2** [I] (*ALSO* **sprout up**) *INFORMAL* If a large number of things sprout (up), they suddenly appear or begin to exist: *New factories have sprouted up everywhere.*

sprout /spraʊt/ *noun* [C] **1** a part of a plant that is just beginning to grow **2** *MAINLY UK* a **brussel sprout**

spruce [TREE] /spruːs/ *noun* [C or U] an evergreen tree with needle-like leaves, or the pale-coloured wood of this tree

spruce [TIDY] /spruːs/ *adj APPROVING* (of a person) tidy and clean in appearance: *He looked spruce and handsome in a clean white shirt.*

spruce /spruːs/ *verb*

▲ **spruce *sb/sth* up** *phrasal verb* [M] *INFORMAL* to make someone or something cleaner and tidier or to improve the way they appear generally: [R] *I thought I'd have a shave and generally spruce myself up for the interview.* ○ *They've employed an advertising agency to spruce up the company image.*

sprung /sprʌŋ/ *past participle of* **spring**

spry /spraɪ/ *adj* (especially of older people) active and able to move quickly and energetically: *He was amazingly spry for a man of almost 80.*

spud /spʌd/ *noun* [C] *INFORMAL* a potato

spun /spʌn/ *past simple and past participle of* **spin**

spunk [BRAVERY] /spʌŋk/ *noun* [U] *OLD-FASHIONED INFORMAL* bravery and determination **spunky** /ˈspʌŋ.ki/ *adj*

spunk [SEXUAL LIQUID] /spʌŋk/ *noun* [U] *OFFENSIVE* **semen** (= liquid sent out through the penis during sexual activity)

spunk [ATTRACTIVE MAN] /spʌŋk/ *noun* [C] *AUS INFORMAL* a sexually attractive man **spunky** /ˈspʌŋ.ki/ *adj*

spur [ENCOURAGE] /spɜːʳ/ [US] /spɝː/ *verb* [T] **-rr-** to encourage an activity or development or make it happen faster: *Rising consumer sales have the effect of spurring the economy **to** faster growth.* ○ *Spurred **(on)** by her early success, she went on to write four more novels in rapid succession.* **spur** /spɜːʳ/ [US] /spɝː/ *noun* [C] *The manager said that the team's win on Saturday would be a spur **to** even greater effort this season.*

spur [SHARP OBJECT] /spɜːʳ/ [US] /spɝː/ *noun* [C] a sharp, metal, wheel-shaped object which is fixed to the heel of boots worn by people riding horses and is used to encourage the horse to go faster

• **win/gain *your* spurs** to achieve something which proves that you are skilled in a particular type of activity and to therefore win the respect of other people: *He won his political spurs fighting hospital closures during his time as a local councillor in Bristol.*

• **spur-of-the-moment** *INFORMAL* describes a decision, action, etc. that is sudden and done without any planning: *We hadn't planned to go away – it was one of those spur-of-the-moment **decisions**.* ○ *We just jumped in a car **on the** spur of the moment and drove to the seaside.*

spur /spɜːʳ/ [US] /spɝː/ *verb* [T] **-rr-** to push spurs into the side of a horse to make it go faster: *He spurred his horse **on** and shouted "Faster! Faster!"*

spur [MOUNTAIN] /spɜːʳ/ [US] /spɝː/ *noun* [C] a high piece of land which sticks out from a mountain or a group of mountains

spurious /ˈspjʊə.ri.əs/ [US] /ˈspjʊr.i-/ *adj* false and not what it appears to be, or (of reasons and judgments) based on something that has not been correctly understood and therefore false: *Some of the arguments in favour of shutting the factory are questionable and others downright spurious.*

spurn /spɜːn/ [US] /spɝːn/ *verb* [T] *SLIGHTLY FORMAL* to refuse to accept something or someone because you feel that they are not worth having: *She spurned my offers of help.* ○ *Ellis plays the part of the young lover spurned by his mistress.*

spurt [LIQUID] /spɜːt/ [US] /spɝːt/ *verb* [I or T] to (cause to) flow out suddenly and with force, in a fast stream: *Blood was spurting out all over the place.* ○ *His arm was spurting blood where the vein had been severed.* **spurt** /spɜːt/ [US] /spɝːt/ *noun* [C] *The water came out **in** spurts.*

spurt [INCREASE] /spɜːt/ [US] /spɝːt/ *noun* [C] a sudden and brief period of increased activity, effort or speed: *There was a sudden spurt **of** activity in the housing market.* ○ *He tends to work **in** spurts.*

spurt /spɜːt/ [US] /spɝːt/ *verb* [I or T] *MAINLY US* to increase or grow very quickly, or to suddenly increase by a particular amount: *Shares of the jewellery-store chain spurted $6.*

sputter [SOUND] /ˈspʌt.əʳ/ [US] /ˈspʌt̬.ɚ/ *verb* [I or T] to make several quick explosive sounds: *The car sputtered once or twice and then stopped.* **sputter** /ˈspʌt.əʳ/ [US] /ˈspʌt̬.ɚ/ *noun* [C] *The engine wouldn't start – it **gave** one or two sputters but that was all.*

sputter [ACTIVITY] /ˈspʌt.əʳ/ [US] /ˈspʌt̬.ɚ/ *verb* [I] *LITERARY* If an activity sputters, it is weak and varied, and does not make people feel confident about it: *Russia's presidential campaign sputtered to an uneasy close on Monday.*

sputum /ˈspjuː.təm/ [US] /-t̬əm/ *noun* [U] *SPECIALIZED* liquid from the passages in your body which go to the lungs; **phlegm**

spy [SECRET PERSON] /spaɪ/ *noun* [C] a person who secretly gathers and reports information about the activities of another country or organization

spy /spaɪ/ *verb* [I] **1** to secretly gather and report information about the activities of another country or organization: *He was arrested for spying **on** missile sites.* **2** *INFORMAL* **spy out** to obtain knowledge secretly, especially of a place: *I generally like to spy out restaurants before I go to eat in them.*

• **spy out the land** If you spy out the land you try to obtain knowledge of something in advance: *We drove around the area where our new house is to spy out the land.*

S

spy [SEE] /spaɪ/ *verb* [T] *OLD-FASHIONED OR HUMOROUS* to see or notice someone or something usually when it involves looking hard: *I think I've just spied Andrew in the crowd.*
▲ **spy on sb/sth** *phrasal verb* to watch someone or something secretly, often in order to discover information about them: *He was spying on her through the keyhole.*

spyhole /ˈspaɪ.həʊl/ [US] /-hoʊl/ *noun* [C] *UK* a **peephole**

sq /skweəʳ/ [US] /skwer/ *adj* [before n] *WRITTEN ABBREVIATION FOR* **square**, in measurements of length; see at **square** SHAPE.

squab /skwɒb/ [US] /skwɑːb/ *noun* [U] *MAINLY US* a young PIGEON eaten as food

squabble /ˈskwɒb.l̩/ [US] /ˈskwɑː.bl̩/ *noun* [C] an argument over an unimportant matter: *Polly and Susie were* ***having*** *a squabble about who was going to hold the dog's lead.* **squabble** /ˈskwɒb.l̩/ [US] /ˈskwɑː.bl̩/ *verb* [I]

squad /skwɒd/ [US] /skwɑːd/ *group noun* [C] **1** a small group of people trained to work together as a unit: *An army bomb squad arrived and defused the bomb.* **2** a team in sports from which the players for a match are chosen: *Eight of their 24-man squad are injured.* **3** In the army a squad is a small group of soldiers, especially one gathered together for DRILL (= marching, etc.).
squaddie /ˈskwɒd.i/ [US] /ˈskwɑː.di/ *noun* [C] *UK SLANG* a low-ranking soldier

ˈsquad ˌcar *noun* [C] (*ALSO* **patrol car**) *UK OLD-FASHIONED OR US* a car used by police officers

squadron /ˈskwɒd.rᵊn/ [US] /ˈskwɑː.drən/ *group noun* [C] a unit of one of the armed forces, especially (in Britain) the air force or the navy

ˈsquadron ˌleader *noun* [C] an officer in the air force of the UK and some other countries

squalid [DIRTY] /ˈskwɒl.ɪd/ [US] /ˈskwɑː.lɪd/ *adj DISAPPROVING* (of places) extremely dirty and unpleasant, often because of lack of money: *Many prisons, even today, are overcrowded and squalid places.* **squalor** /ˈskwɒl.əʳ/ [US] /ˈskwɑː.lɚ/ *noun* [U] *It was a dirty, damp, smelly flat – the usual student squalor.*

squalid [IMMORAL] /ˈskwɒl.ɪd/ [US] /ˈskwɑː.lɪd/ *adj* (of situations and activities) immoral; involving sex and drugs, etc. in an unpleasant way: *It's the usual squalid rock star tale of drugs, sex and overdoses.* **squalor** /ˈskwɒl.əʳ/ [US] /ˈskwɑː.lɚ/ *noun* [U]

squall [STRONG WIND] /skwɔːl/ [US] /skwɑːl/ *noun* [C] a sudden strong wind or brief storm: *Violent squalls signalled the approach of the hurricane.* **squally** /ˈskwɔː.li/ [US] /ˈskwɑː-/ *adj*

squall [SHOUT] /skwɔːl/ [US] /skwɑːl/ *verb* [I] (especially of a baby) to make a loud sharp noise **squall** /skwɔːl/ [US] /skwɑːl/ *noun* [C]

squander /ˈskwɒn.dəʳ/ [US] /ˈskwɑːn.dɚ/ *verb* [T] to spend or use money or supplies in a wasteful way, or to waste opportunities by not using them to your advantage: *They'll quite happily squander a whole year's savings on two weeks in the sun.* ○ *Ireland squandered several chances, including a penalty that cost them the game.*

square [SHAPE] /skweəʳ/ [US] /skwer/ *noun* [C] **1** a flat shape with four sides of equal length and four angles of 90°: *First draw a square.* ○ *It's a square-shaped room.* **2** any square-shaped object: *When cooled, cut the chocolate brownies into squares.* **3** an area of approximately square-shaped land in a city or a town, often including the buildings that surround it: *Are they still living at 6 Eaton Square?* ○ *A band were playing* ***in*** *the town square.* **4** a marked space on a board used for playing games: *She moved her castle forward three squares.* **5** *US* a tool for drawing or testing a RIGHT ANGLE
● **go/be back to square one** *INFORMAL* to be forced to think of a new course of action because your first course of action failed: *The deal with the house fell through so I'm afraid we're back to square one.*
square /skweəʳ/ [US] /skwer/ *adj* **1** having the shape of a square: *The recipe recommends that you use a square cake tin.* ○ *He's got that square-jawed masculinity that a lot of women seem to find attractive.* **2** (*WRITTEN ABBREVIATION* **sq**, *SPECIALIZED* ²) used with units of measurement of length to express the total size of an area: *The floor is 3 metres wide by 5 metres long so its total area is 15 sq metres.* ○ *The city itself covers thirteen square miles.* ○ *SPECIALIZED Ensure that the exposed area is less than 2cm².* **3** Square is used immediately after measurements of length when expressing the length of the four sides of a square-shaped area: *So you want carpet for a room that's eight metres square* (= 8 metres long and 8 metres wide).
● **the Square Mile** *UK* **the City** ➲See at **the City** FINANCIAL CENTRE.
● **square peg (in a round hole)** *INFORMAL* a person whose character makes them unsuitable for the job or other position they are in: *He never quite fitted in when he was working here – he was always a bit of a square peg.*
square /skweəʳ/ [US] /skwer/ *verb* **square** ***your*** **shoulders** to pull your shoulders up and back because you feel determined to do something: *He squared his shoulders and took a deep breath before diving into the pool.*
● **square the circle** If you try to square the circle you try to do something which is very difficult or impossible.
squared /skweəd/ [US] /skwerd/ *adj*: *Squared paper* (= paper with squares printed on it) *is better for drawing graphs on.*

square [EQUAL] /skweəʳ/ [US] /skwer/ *adj INFORMAL* **1** equal or level: *Could you stand back from these shelves and tell me if they're square* (= level)*?* **2** **(all) square** If two people are all square one of them has paid off a debt to the other and neither now owes or is owed any money.
● **square the accounts/books** to make certain that you have paid and received all the money that you owed or that others owed you

square [BORING PERSON] /skweəʳ/ [US] /skwer/ *noun* [C] *OLD-FASHIONED INFORMAL* a boring person who does not like new and exciting ideas: *He's a bit of a square.* **square** /skweəʳ/ [US] /skwer/ *adj*: *Do you think my new haircut makes me look a bit square?*

square [MULTIPLY] /skweəʳ/ [US] /skwer/ *verb* [T] to multiply a number by itself: *10 squared equals a hundred.* ○ *4² means four squared, and equals 16.* **square** /skweəʳ/ [US] /skwer/ *noun* [C] *The square of 7 is 49.*

square [STRAIGHT] /skweəʳ/ [US] /skwer/ *adj* in a straight line
squarely /ˈskweə.li/ [US] /ˈskwer-/ *adv*: *She stood squarely, with her feet apart.*

PHRASAL VERBS WITH **square** ▼

▲ **square off** *phrasal verb US* to prepare to fight, compete or argue with someone: *The two giants in the fast-food industry are squaring off this month with the most aggressive advertising campaigns yet.*
▲ **square up** [FIGHT] *phrasal verb UK* to prepare to fight, compete or argue with someone: *The players squared up to each other and started shouting.*
▲ **square up** [PAY] *phrasal verb INFORMAL* to pay someone the money that you owe them: *If you pay for both tickets now, I'll square up* ***with*** *you later.*
▲ **square up to sb/sth** *UK phrasal verb* (*US* **face up to sb/sth**) to deal with a problem or difficult person bravely and with determination: *I thought she squared up to the situation admirably.*
▲ **square *(sth)* with *sth*** *phrasal verb* to match or agree with something, or to think that one thing is acceptable together with another thing: *Her story doesn't quite square with the evidence.* ○ *I don't think I could spend that much money on a jacket – I couldn't square it with my conscience* (= I would feel too guilty).

ˌsquare ˈbrackets *plural noun* the [ ] brackets that are shaped like two halves of a square

ˈsquare ˌdance *noun* [C] in the US, a traditional dance in which four pairs of dancers dance together

ˌsquare ˈdeal *noun* [C] *INFORMAL* a fair agreement: *I reckon we got a square deal on that car.*

square-eyed /ˌskweəˈraɪd/ [US] /ˌskwerˈaɪd/ *adj UK INFORMAL* If you say someone is or will go square-eyed, you mean they are watching too much television: *You'll* ***go*** *square-eyed if you sit in front of that TV any more!*

ˈsquare ˌknot *noun* [C] *US FOR* **reef knot**

squarely /ˈskweə.li/ [US] /ˈskwer/ *adv* (*ALSO* **square**) directly and with certainty: *She refused to come down squarely on either side of the argument.* ○ *She punched him square on the jaw.*

S

,square 'meal noun [C] a satisfying meal that fills you and provides you with all the different types of food that your body needs in order to stay healthy: *If you're only eating a chocolate bar for lunch, you need a good square meal in the evening.*

,square 'root noun [C] The square root of a particular number is the number that was multiplied by itself to reach that number: *The square root of 49 is 7.*

squash MAKE FLAT /skwɒʃ/ ⑩ /skwɑːʃ/ verb [T] to crush something into a flat shape: *He accidentally sat on her hat and squashed it.*
squashy /'skwɒʃ.i/ ⑩ /'skwɑː.ʃi/ adj soft and easy to crush: *I've bought some squashy pillows for the couch.*

squash PUSH /skwɒʃ/ ⑩ /skwɑːʃ/ verb [I or T; usually + adv or prep] to push a person or thing into a small space: *The room was so full you couldn't squash another person in.* ○ *If you all squashed up (= moved closer together), we could fit an extra person in the car.* ○ *He tried to squash his ripped jeans into the suitcase while his mother wasn't looking.* **squash** /skwɒʃ/ ⑩ /skwɑːʃ/ noun [S] *There are over two hundred people coming to the party so it might be a bit of a squash.*

squash END /skwɒʃ/ ⑩ /skwɑːʃ/ verb [T] to stop something from continuing to exist or happen, by forceful action: *Rumours of a possible takeover of the company were soon squashed by the management.*

squash SPORT /skwɒʃ/ ⑩ /skwɑːʃ/ noun [U] a game played between two or four people on a specially marked enclosed playing area which involves hitting a small rubber ball against a wall

squash DRINK /skwɒʃ/ ⑩ /skwɑːʃ/ noun [U] UK a drink which is made from water and sweetened fruit juice

squash VEGETABLE /skwɒʃ/ ⑩ /skwɑːʃ/ noun [C or U] MAINLY US a type of large vegetable with a hard skin and a lot of seeds at its centre which is very common in America ➲See picture **Vegetables** on page Centre 2

squat SIT /skwɒt/ ⑩ /skwɑːt/ verb [I] -tt- to position yourself close to the ground balancing on the front part of your feet with your legs bent under your body: *She squatted on the ground and warmed her hands by the fire.* ○ *He squatted down and examined the front wheel of his bike.* **squat** /skwɒt/ ⑩ /skwɑːt/ noun [C]

squat LIVE /skwɒt/ ⑩ /skwɑːt/ verb [I or T] -tt- to live in an empty building or area of land without the permission of the owner: *Their squatted (in) an old house in King's Cross when their money ran out.*
squat /skwɒt/ ⑩ /skwɑːt/ noun [C] the place that you live in when you are squatting: *They're living in a damp squat with no electricity.*
squatter /'skwɒt.əʳ/ ⑩ /'skwɑː.t̬ɚ/ noun [C] **1** a person who lives in an empty building without permission **2** AUS someone in the past who took land which did not officially belong to them in order to use it for farming

squat SHORT /skwɒt/ ⑩ /skwɑːt/ adj **squatter, squattest** short and wide, usually in an unattractive way: *a row of ugly squat houses* ○ *a heavily-built squat man*

squat ANYTHING /skwɒt/ ⑩ /skwɑːt/ noun [U] US SLANG anything: *She shouldn't talk – she doesn't know squat about it.* ○ *His opinion isn't worth squat.*

squat-thrust /'skwɒt.θrʌst/ ⑩ /'skwɑːt-/ noun [C] a type of physical exercise in which your hands are kept on the floor while your legs move from a position in which they are bent under the body to one in which they are straight out behind you

squattocracy /,skwɒt'ɒk.rə.si/ ⑩ /,skwɑː'tɑː.krə-/ noun [C or U] AUS the established and wealthy owners of large properties in the countryside

squaw /skwɔː/ ⑩ /skwɑː/ noun [C] OLD-FASHIONED a Native American woman, especially a wife. This word is now considered offensive by many people.

squawk /skwɔːk/ ⑩ /skwɑːk/ verb [I] **1** to make an unpleasantly loud sharp cry: *As the fox came into the yard, the chickens began squawking in alarm.* **2** INFORMAL DISAPPROVING to complain about something noisily: *Environmental groups have been squawking about the decision to build the motorway through a forest.* **squawk** /skwɔːk/ ⑩ /skwɑːk/ noun [C]

squeak SOUND /skwiːk/ verb [I] to make a short very high cry or sound: *The mice in the cupboard squeaked.* ○ *The*

door *squeaked as it swung back and forth on its rusty hinges.*
squeak /skwiːk/ noun [C] *She let out a squeak of fright at the sight of the spider.* ○ *If I hear one more squeak out of you (= if you say anything else), there'll be trouble!*
squeaky /'skwiː.ki/ adj
● **The squeaky wheel gets the grease.** US SAYING said to emphasize that attention is paid to those problems which are made most noticeable

squeak SUCCEED /skwiːk/ verb [I + adv or prep] US to only just succeed in something such as a test or competition: *He squeaked through the exam.*
squeaker /'skwiː.kəʳ/ ⑩ /-kɚ/ noun [C] US a competition or race which you only just win or lose: *The Buffalo Bills lost a squeaker to the Dallas Cowboys in the Super Bowl.*
squeaky /'skwiː.ki/ adj US *The president had a squeaky six-vote win (= he won by only six votes) in Congress.*

squeaky-clean /,skwiː.ki'kliːn/ adj INFORMAL **1** completely clean: *I love the squeaky-clean feel of my hair after I've washed it.* **2** Someone who is squeaky-clean is completely good and honest and never does anything bad: *Journalists have been trying to discover if the senator really is as squeaky-clean as he claims to be.*

squeal /skwiːl/ verb [I] **1** to make a long very high sound or cry: *We could hear the piglets squealing as we entered the farmyard.* ○ *The brakes squealed as the van rounded the corner.* ○ *The two children squealed with joy.* **2** INFORMAL to complain about something loudly: *The threat of further changes in the education system is making teachers squeal.* **3** SLANG DISAPPROVING to give information to the police about people you know who have committed a crime: *When he finds out who squealed on him, he's going to make them very sorry.* **squeal** /skwiːl/ noun [C] *Erik collapsed into giggles and squeals as Penny began tickling him.* ○ *The train ground to a halt with a squeal of brakes.*

squeamish /'skwiː.mɪʃ/ adj easily upset or shocked by things which you find unpleasant or which you do not approve of: *She's really squeamish and can't stand the sight of blood.* ○ *Many cooks are squeamish about putting live shellfish into boiling water.*
● **not for the squeamish** describes something that is unpleasant, and will upset people who are squeamish: *'The Silence of the Lambs' is an entertaining but violent movie and is not for the squeamish.*
squeamishly /'skwiː.mɪʃ.li/ adv in a way that shows how easily upset or shocked you are by something **squeamishness** /'skwiː.mɪʃ.nəs/ noun [U]

squeegee /'skwiː.dʒiː/ noun [C] a tool with a rubber blade and a short handle which is used for removing water from a surface such as a window or mirror after it has been washed **squeegee** /'skwiː.dʒiː/ verb [T]

squeeze PRESS TOGETHER /skwiːz/ verb [T] **1** to press something firmly, especially from all sides in order to change its shape, reduce its size or remove liquid from it: *Cut the lemon in half and squeeze the juice into the bowl.* ○ *As she waited to go into the exam, he squeezed her hand (= pressed it affectionately with his hand) and wished her good luck.* ○ *Once he had finished cleaning the floor, he squeezed the cloth out.* ○ *He reloaded the gun, took aim and then squeezed (= pulled back) the trigger.* ○ FIGURATIVE *The studio is using all sorts of marketing tricks to squeeze as much profit from the movie as they can.* **2** If you are squeezed by financial demands, they cause you financial problems: *Small businesses are being squeezed by heavy taxation.*
● **squeeze sb dry** If you squeeze someone dry, you obtain as much from them as possible: *When they got divorced, his wife squeezed him dry and took everything.*
squeeze /skwiːz/ noun **1** [C] when you press something firmly: *She gave the present a quick squeeze and tried to guess what was inside.* ○ *Garnish the fish with some fresh parsley and a squeeze of lemon.* **2** [C usually sing] a reduction or limit: *The squeeze on profits in the oil industry has led to thousands of redundancies.* ○ *The squeeze on local spending means that many services will have to be cut.* **3** [C usually sing] a period in which the supply of money is limited by the government because of economic difficulties: *The government has imposed a*

sharp ***credit*** *squeeze in an attempt to hold down inflation.*

squeezer /ˈskwiː.zəʳ/ [US] /-zɚ/ *noun* [C] a device which removes the juice from fruit by pressing it: *Have you got a* ***lemon*** *squeezer?*

squeeze [MOVE] /skwiːz/ *verb* [I + adv or prep] to get in, through, under, etc. with difficulty: *She squeezed* ***through*** *the crowd and found a seat at the front.* ○ *They managed to squeeze* ***under*** *the fence and get into the festival without paying.*

PHRASAL VERBS WITH **squeeze**

▲ **squeeze** ***(sb/sth)*** **in/squeeze** ***(sb/sth)*** **into** ***sth*** [SPACE] *phrasal verb* [M] to succeed in getting someone or something into a small space or object, often by pushing or forcing: *The car's quite full, but we could manage to squeeze another couple of people in.* ○ *I must have put on a lot of weight over Christmas because I can only just squeeze* ***into*** *my jeans.*

squeeze /skwiːz/ *noun* [S] *I can give you a lift, but it'll be a* ***tight*** *squeeze as I'm taking four other people as well.*

▲ **squeeze** ***sb/sth*** **in** [TIME] *phrasal verb* [M] to manage to do something or see someone in a short period of time or when you are very busy: *While we're in Australia, we're hoping to squeeze in a trip to the Barrier Reef.* ○ *I'm very busy this week but I could squeeze you in at 2.30 on Tuesday.*

▲ **squeeze** ***sth*** **out of** ***sb*** *phrasal verb* (ALSO **squeeze** ***sth*** **from** ***sb***) INFORMAL to obtain something, especially money or information, from someone using persuasion or force: *During the negotiations, the union managed to squeeze several concessions from the management.*

ˈsqueeze ˌbottle *noun* [C] US a plastic container whose contents can be forced out through a narrow hole at the top by pressing the sides of the bottle together

squeezebox /ˈskwiːz.bɒks/ [US] /-bɑːks/ *noun* [C] OLD-FASHIONED INFORMAL an **accordion**

squelch /skweltʃ/ *verb* **1** [I usually + adv or prep] to make a sucking sound like the one produced when you are walking on soft wet ground: *He got out of the car and squelched through the mud to open the gate.* **2** [T] US to quickly end something that is causing you problems: *A spokeswoman at the White House has squelched* ***rumors*** *about the president's ill-health.* **3** [T] US to silence someone by making a critical remark: *The senator thoroughly squelched the journalist who tried to interrupt him during his speech.* **squelch** /skweltʃ/ *noun* [C usually sing] *As the hikers walked down the path by the house, she could hear the squelch of their boots in the mud.* **squelchy** /ˈskwel.tʃi/ *adj*

squib /skwɪb/ *noun* [C] a small FIREWORK consisting of a tube filled with powder which makes a HISSING noise when it is lit

squid /skwɪd/ *noun* [C or U] *plural* **squid** a sea creature with a long body and ten arms situated around the mouth, or this animal eaten as food

squidgy /ˈskwɪdʒ.i/ *adj* UK INFORMAL soft and wet and changing shape easily when pressed: *Bread which has just come out of the oven is often still squidgy in the middle.*

squiffy /ˈskwɪf.i/ *adj* (US ALSO **squiffed**) INFORMAL OLD-FASHIONED slightly drunk: *"I've only had one glass of sherry and I feel squiffy already," she said.*

squiggle /ˈskwɪg.l̩/ *noun* [C] a short line that has been written or drawn and that curves and twists in an irregular way: *His signature was an illegible squiggle at the bottom of the page.* **squiggly** /ˈskwɪg.l̩.i/ *adj*

squinch /skwɪntʃ/ *verb* [T] US to squeeze together the features of the face or the muscles of the body: *He squinched* ***up*** *his face in a look that left no doubt about his displeasure.*

squint [WAY OF LOOKING] /skwɪnt/ *verb* [I] to partly close your eyes in order to see more clearly: *The sun was shining straight in her eyes which made her squint.*

squint /skwɪnt/ *noun* [C] INFORMAL, OLD-FASHIONED a quick look: *"The back wheel of my bike doesn't seem straight." "I'll* ***have/take*** *a squint at it if you like."*

squint [EYE CONDITION] /skwɪnt/ *noun* [C] a condition caused by a weakness of the eye muscles which makes the eyes look in different directions from each other: *As a child she wore thick glasses and* ***had*** *a bad squint.*

squire /skwaɪəʳ/ [US] /skwaɪr/ *noun* [C] **1** OLD USE in the past in England, a man who owned most of the land around a village **2** UK OLD-FASHIONED INFORMAL used as a friendly form of address by one man to another who might be of a higher social class: *"I don't know if all my luggage is going to fit in the back of the taxi." "Don't worry, squire, I'll get it in."*

squirm /skwɜːm/ [US] /skwɝːm/ *verb* [I] to move from side to side in an awkward way because of nervousness, embarrassment or pain: *Nobody spoke for at least five minutes and Rachel squirmed in her chair* ***with*** *embarrassment.* ○ *The fish squirmed on the ground for a few moments and then lay still.* **squirm** /skwɜːm/ [US] /skwɝːm/ *noun* [C]

squirrel /ˈskwɪr.əl/ [US] /ˈskwɝː-/ *noun* [C] a small furry animal with a long furry tail which climbs trees and feeds on nuts and seeds

squirrel /ˈskwɪr.əl/ [US] /ˈskwɝː-/ *verb*

▲ **squirrel** ***sth*** **away** *phrasal verb* [M] INFORMAL to hide or store something, especially money, in order to use it in the future: *As soon as I get paid, I squirrel some money away so I won't be tempted to spend it.*

squirt /skwɜːt/ [US] /skwɝːt/ *verb* **1** [I or T; usually + adv or prep] (to force a liquid) to flow out through a narrow opening in a fast stream: *He squirted some tomato sauce* ***on*** *his burger.* ○ *There was a leak in one of the pipes and water was squirting* ***out*** *all over the kitchen floor.* **2** [T] to hit someone or something with a liquid or gas: *She was squirting the neighbours with a water pistol.*

squirt /skwɜːt/ [US] /skwɝːt/ *noun* [C] **1** an amount of liquid or gas that is squirted out: *The door should stop squeaking once I've given it a few squirts of oil.* **2** OLD-FASHIONED a young or small person whom you consider to be unimportant and who has behaved rudely towards you: *I caught my neighbour's son writing graffiti on our wall, the little squirt.*

ˈsquirt ˌgun *noun* [C] US FOR a **water pistol**

squish /skwɪʃ/ *verb* [T] INFORMAL to crush something which is soft: *Don't sit on that bag – you'll squish the sandwiches.* **squish** /skwɪʃ/ *noun* [C] *As he walked along the path through the field, he could hear the squish of the damp ground beneath his boots.* **squishy** /ˈskwɪʃ.i/ *adj: a squishy banana*

Sr US *adj* [after n] (UK **Snr**) WRITTEN ABBREVIATION FOR **senior** OLDER, used after a man's name to refer to the older of two people in the same family who have the same name

SS /ˌesˈes/ *noun* ABBREVIATION FOR **steamship**

ssh /ʃː/ *exclamation* **sh**

St [HOLY PERSON] ABBREVIATION FOR **saint**: used only before personal names: *St Andrew*

St [ROAD], **St.** *noun* WRITTEN ABBREVIATION FOR **street**, used in writing after the name of a street: *My address is 19 East Norwood St.*

st [WEIGHT] WRITTEN ABBREVIATION FOR **stone** WEIGHT: *He weighs 12st 3lbs.*

stab /stæb/ *verb* **-bb- 1** [T] to injure someone with a sharp pointed object such as a knife: *She was stabbed several times* ***in*** *the chest.* ○ *He was jailed for fifteen years for stabbing his wife* ***to death.*** **2** [I or T] to make a short forceful pushing movement with a finger or a long thin object: *As she spoke she stabbed the air with her finger.* ○ *He stabbed* ***at*** *the meat with his fork.*

• **stab** ***sb*** **in the back** to do something harmful to someone who trusted you: *He had been lied to and stabbed in the back by people that he thought were his friends.* ➲See also **back-stabber**.

stab /stæb/ *noun* [C] **1** the act of pushing a knife into someone, or a wound caused by stabbing: *He was admitted to Middlesex Hospital with stab* ***wounds.*** **2** a sudden feeling, especially an unpleasant one such as pain: *She felt a stab* ***of*** *envy when she saw all the expensive presents Zoe had been given for Christmas.* **3** an action or remark that attacks someone's reputation: *Her criticism of the company's plans was a stab* ***at*** *the chairman himself.*

• **have/make a stab at** ***sth*** INFORMAL to attempt to do something although you are not likely to be very successful:

I'd never tried snorkelling before but I had a stab at it while I was in Greece.

stabbing /ˈstæb.ɪŋ/ *noun* [C] when someone stabs someone: *There have been a few stabbings in our neighbourhood.*

stabbing /ˈstæb.ɪŋ/ *adj* **stabbing pain** a sudden pain: *She was awoken by a* ***sharp*** *stabbing pain in her chest.*

stable [FIXED] /ˈsteɪ.bl̩/ *adj* **1** firmly fixed or not likely to move or change: *If the foundations of the house aren't stable, collapse is possible.* ○ *After several part-time jobs, he's now got a stable job in a bank.* ○ *The hospital said she was in a stable condition* (= not likely to get worse) *following the operation.* **2** describes someone who is mentally healthy: *She seems more stable these days.* **3** *SPECIALIZED* describes a substance that keeps the same chemical or atomic state

stability /stəˈbɪl.ɪ.ti/ [US] /-ə.t̬i/ *noun* [U] when something is not likely to move or change: *a period of political stability*

stabilize, *UK USUALLY* **-ise** /ˈsteɪ.bɪ.laɪz/ *verb* **1** [I] If something stabilizes, it becomes fixed or stops changing: *He suffered a second heart attack two days ago but his condition has now stabilized.* **2** [T] If you stabilize something, you cause it to become fixed or to stop changing: *The country's population has stabilized* ***at*** *1.6 billion.*

stabilizer, *UK USUALLY* **-iser** /ˈsteɪ.bɪ.laɪ.zəʳ/ [US] /-zɚ/ *noun* [C] **1** *UK* a method used to limit sudden changes in prices or to limit the level of production **2** *SPECIALIZED* a chemical which is added to something so that it stays in the same state **3** a device which helps an aircraft, ship or vehicle to balance

stabilisers *UK* /ˈsteɪ.bɪ.laɪ.zəz/ [US] /-zɚz/ *plural noun* (*US* **training wheels**) small wheels fixed to each side of the back wheel of a bicycle to prevent it falling over when a child is learning to ride it **stabilization**, *UK USUALLY* **-isation** /ˌsteɪ.bɪ.laɪˈzeɪ.ʃᵊn/ *noun* [U]

stable [BUILDING] /ˈsteɪ.bl̩/ *noun* [C] **1** a building in which horses are kept **2** a group of RACEHORSES that are owned or trained by one person **3** a group of people who perform a similar activity and who are trained by the same person or employed by the same organization: *During the 1950s, Sun Records' stable* ***of*** *singers included Elvis Presley, Johnny Cash and Jerry Lee Lewis.*

stable /ˈsteɪ.bl̩/ *verb* [T] to keep a horse in a stable

stabling /ˈsteɪ.bl̩.ɪŋ/ /ˈ-blɪŋ/ *noun* [U] a stable

ˈstable ˌboy *noun* [C] (*UK ALSO* **stable lad**) a young man who works in a stable and cares for the horses

stablemate /ˈsteɪ.bl̩meɪt/ *noun* [C] something that is similar to something else or is part of the same organisation as something else: *the Daily news and its stablemate The Weekly News*

staccato /stəˈkɑː.təʊ/ [US] /-t̬oʊ/ *adj, adv* **1** describes musical notes that are shortened and separate when played, or this way of playing music: *The music suddenly changed from a smooth melody to a staccato rhythm.* **2** describes a noise or way of speaking that consists of a series of short and separate sounds: *She gave staccato replies to every question.*

stack [PILE] /stæk/ *noun* [C] **1** a pile of things arranged one on top of another: *He chose a cartoon from the stack of videos on the shelf.* **2** *INFORMAL* a large amount: *Don't worry, we've got stacks of time.*

• **the stacks** a set of shelves in a library which are positioned close together so that a lot of books can be stored on them

stack /stæk/ *verb* [T] to arrange things in an ordered pile: *Once the last few people had left the hall, the caretaker began stacking* ***(up)*** *the chairs.*

• **stack the cards** *UK* (*US* **stack the deck**) to arrange something in a dishonest way in order to achieve the result you want

• **have the odds/cards stacked against** ***you*** to be very unlikely to succeed because you are not in an advantageous position

stack [ACCIDENT] /stæk/ *noun* [C] *AUS INFORMAL* a car accident, especially one that causes damage

PHRASAL VERBS WITH **stack** ▼

▲ **stack up** [COMPARE] *phrasal verb MAINLY US INFORMAL* to compare with another thing of a similar type: *The new model of this car just doesn't stack up* ***against*** *previous models* (= is not as good as previous models).

▲ **stack up** [AIRCRAFT] *phrasal verb* If aircraft are stacked up over an airport, they circle over the airport at different heights waiting to be told they can land.

stacked /stækt/ *adj* **1** covered or filled with a large amount of things: *The fridge is stacked with food.* **2** *US SLANG* (of a woman) having large breasts. This word is considered offensive by many women.

ˈstack ˌsystem *noun* [C] a set of electronic equipment to play recorded sound, the parts of which are put on top of each other

stack-up /ˈstæk.ʌp/ *noun* [C] *INFORMAL* a road accident involving a row of cars

stadium /ˈsteɪ.di.əm/ *noun* [C] *plural* **stadiums** or **stadia** a large enclosed area of land with rows of seats around the sides and often with no roof which is used for sports events and musical performances: *Thousands of football fans packed into the stadium to watch the match.*

staff [PEOPLE] /stɑːf/ [US] /stæf/ *group noun* [S] the group of people who work for an organization: *There is a good relationship between staff and pupils at the school.* ○ *The staff are not very happy about the latest pay increase.* ○ *There are over a hundred staff in the company.* ○ *He is* ***on*** (= a member of) *the editorial staff of the magazine.*

staff /stɑːf/ [US] /stæf/ *verb* [T] *Many charity shops in Britain are staffed* ***by/with*** *volunteers.*

COMMON LEARNER ERROR

staff or **a member of staff?**

Staff means the people who work for a shop, company, etc. **Staff** always refers to a group of people. If you want to refer to a single person, say **a member of staff**.

The company employs around 150 staff.
~~*The company employs around 150 staffs.*~~
Is there a member of staff who can speak Spanish?
~~*Is there a staff who can speak Spanish?*~~

staff [STICK] /stɑːf/ [US] /stæf/ *noun* [C] *FORMAL* **1** a long strong stick held in the hand which is used as a support when walking, as a weapon or as a symbol of authority **2** (*ALSO* **flagstaff**) a **flagpole**

• **the staff of life** *LITERARY* bread, considered as one of the most important foods we eat

staff /stɑːf/ [US] /stæf/ *noun* [C] *US FOR* a **stave**

staffer /ˈstɑːf.əʳ/ [US] /ˈstæf.ɚ/ *noun* [C] *MAINLY US* an employee, often of a political organization: *White House staffers briefed reporters before the president arrived.*

ˈstaff ˌnurse *noun* [C] *UK* a person who works in a hospital taking care of the ill and injured and whose rank is below that of a SISTER

ˈstaff ˌofficer *noun* [C] an army officer who helps the officer in charge to plan military activities

staffroom /ˈstɑːf.rʊm/ /-ruːm/ [US] /ˈstæf-/ *noun* [C] a room in a school which is for the use of the teachers when they are not teaching: *FIGURATIVE The government proposal to test 14-year-olds has been causing controversy in the staffroom* (= among teachers).

stag [ANIMAL] /stæg/ *noun* [C] *plural* **stags** or **stag** an adult male deer

• **go stag** *MAINLY US* If a man goes stag to an event, he goes without a partner.

stag [PERSON] /stæg/ *noun* [C] *plural* **stags** *UK* a person who buys shares in a company which is being sold to the public with the intention of selling them immediately for profit **stag** /stæg/ *verb* [I or T] **-gg-**

stage [PART] /steɪdʒ/ *noun* [C] **1** a part of an activity or a period of development: *The project is* ***in*** *its final stages and should be completed by August.* ○ *They did the last stage of their journey on foot.* ○ *Our marriage is going through a difficult stage at the moment.* ○ *Their youngest child is* ***at*** *the stage* ***where*** *she can say individual words but not full sentences.* ○ *I'm not tired at the moment but I will need a rest* ***at some*** *stage* (= at some time) *during the walk.* ○ *Andrew spends all his spare time playing with his computer but it's probably* ***just*** *a stage he's* ***going through*** (= a period of development that will end soon). **2** *SPECIALIZED* one of the separate parts of a rocket, each stage having its own engine: *Once its fuel supply runs*

S

out, each stage separates from the main part of the rocket and falls back to Earth.

• **in stages** If you do something in stages, you divide the activity into parts and complete each part separately: *We're decorating the house in stages so it won't be ready for another couple of months.*

COMMON LEARNER ERROR

stage

Stage cannot be used to mean a training course.

He did a course in web design.

~~He did a stage in web design.~~

---

stage [THEATRE] /steɪdʒ/ noun [C] **1** the area in a theatre which is often raised above ground level and on which actors or entertainers perform: *Hamlet is on stage for most of the act.* ○ *The orchestra went on/off stage to great applause.* ○ *The play is a stage adaptation of William Golding's novel.* ○ *The opera singer returns to the London stage* (= will perform again in London) *this summer.* **2** a particular area of public life: *The president was extremely popular on the world stage but was disliked in his own country.*

• **take the stage** to go onto the stage and start to perform

• **be on the stage** to be an actor: *Her daughter is an artist and her son is on the stage.*

• **go on the stage** to become an actor: *At the age of ten, he decided that he wanted to go on the stage.*

• **take centre stage** to be at the centre of attention: *She always likes to take centre stage in whatever she does.*

stage /steɪdʒ/ verb [T] **1** to arrange and perform a play or show: *The local drama group is staging a production of the musical 'Grease'.* **2** to organize an event: *Barcelona staged the Olympic Games in 1992.*

staging /'steɪdʒɪŋ/ noun [C] the performance of a play or show: *The production is a modern staging of the fairy tale 'Cinderella'.*

stagy, **stagey** /'steɪdʒi/ adj DISAPPROVING very theatrical and not very natural

stagecoach /'steɪdʒ.kəʊtʃ/ ⓤ /-koʊtʃ/ noun [C] (in the past) a covered vehicle pulled by horses that carried passengers and goods on regular routes

'stage di,rection noun [C] a description or instruction in the text of a play which explains how the play should be performed

,stage 'door noun [C] the door which is used by the actors and theatre workers when entering and leaving the theatre: *We stood by the stage door waiting to get the actors' autographs.*

'stage ,fright noun [U] Actors or performers who have stage fright are nervous because they are about to perform.

stagehand /'steɪdʒ.hænd/ noun [C] a person who is employed in a theatre to move the equipment on the stage

,stage 'left noun [U], adv the part of the stage to the left of the actors when they are facing the people watching the performance

stage-manage /'steɪdʒ.mæn.ɪdʒ/ verb [T] to arrange and control an event carefully in order to achieve the result you want: *Many people have become cynical about the stage-managed debates between politicians which regularly appear on television.*

'stage ,manager noun [C] the person who is responsible for the equipment and the use of the stage during a play or performance

'stage ,name noun [C] the name by which an actor or entertainer is publicly known and which is different from their real name: *David Bowie is the stage name of the singer David Jones.*

,stage 'right noun [U], adv the part of the stage to the right of the actors when they are facing the people watching the performance

stage-struck /'steɪdʒ.strʌk/ adj If you are stage-struck, you are extremely interested in the theatre and want to become an actor or actress.

,stage 'whisper noun [C] **1** If an actor says something in a stage whisper, it is intended to be heard by the people watching the play, and the other actors on the

stage pretend not to hear it. **2** If you say something in a stage whisper, you intend it to be heard by people other than the ones you are talking to.

stagflation /stæg'fleɪ.ʃ°n/ noun [U] an economic condition in which rising prices, high UNEMPLOYMENT and little or no economic growth are present

stagger [MOVE] /'stæg.əʳ/ ⓤ /-ɚ/ verb [I usually + adv or prep] to walk or move with a lack of balance as if you are going to fall: *After he was attacked, he managed to stagger to the phone and call for help.* ○ FIGURATIVE *The company is staggering under a $15 million debt and will almost certainly collapse by the end of the year.* **stagger** /'stæg.əʳ/ ⓤ /-ɚ/ noun [C usually sing] *He left the pub with a drunken stagger.*

stagger [SHOCK] /'stæg.əʳ/ ⓤ /-ɚ/ verb [T] to cause someone to feel shocked or surprised because of something unexpected or very unusual happening: *He staggered all his colleagues by suddenly announcing that he was leaving the company at the end of the month.* **staggered** /'stæg.əd/ ⓤ /-ɚd/ adj [after n] very shocked or surprised: *I was staggered at the prices.* **staggering** /'stæg.°r.ɪŋ/ ⓤ /-ɚ-/ adj very shocking and surprising: *It costs a staggering $50,000 per week to keep the museum open to the public.* **staggeringly** /'stæg.°r.ɪŋ.li/ ⓤ /-ɚ-/ adv: *staggeringly expensive*

stagger [ARRANGE] /'stæg.əʳ/ ⓤ /-ɚ/ verb [T] **1** to arrange, especially hours of work, holidays or events, so that they begin at different times from those of other people: *Some countries have staggered school holidays so that holiday resorts do not become overcrowded.* **2** If a race has a staggered start the competitors start at different times or in different positions.

,staggered 'junction noun [C] UK a place where several roads meet a main road at a slight distance apart so that they do not all come together at the same point

staging /'steɪdʒɪŋ/ noun [C] ⊃See at **stage** THEATRE.

'staging ,area noun [C] a place where soldiers and equipment are gathered together and prepared before military activity

'staging ,post noun [C] UK a place where stops are regularly made on long journeys: *Hong Kong is often used as a staging post on flights from Melbourne to London.* ○ FIGURATIVE *For people who have spent a long time in a mental hospital, a hostel acts as an important staging post* (= a place to stay temporarily) *between the hospital and a home of their own.*

stagnant [NOT FLOWING] /'stæg.nənt/ adj (of water or air) not flowing or moving, and smelling unpleasant: *a stagnant pond*

stagnant [NOT BUSY] /'stæg.nənt/ adj not growing or developing: *a stagnant economy*

stagnate /stæg'neɪt/ ⓤ /'stæg.neɪt/ verb [I] to stay the same and not grow or develop: *The electronics industry is showing signs of stagnating after 15 years of tremendous growth.* **stagnation** /stæg'neɪ.ʃ°n/ noun [U]

'stag ,night/,party UK noun [C] (US **bachelor party**, AUS **bucks party**) a party for a man who is going to get married, to which only his male friends are invited ⊃Compare **hen night**.

stagy /'steɪ.dʒi/ adj ⊃See at **stage** THEATRE.

staid /steɪd/ adj serious, boring and slightly old-fashioned: *In an attempt to change its staid image, the newspaper has created a new section aimed at younger readers.*

stain [MARK] /steɪn/ verb **1** [I or T] to leave a mark on something which is difficult to remove: *Tomato sauce stains terribly – it's really difficult to get it out of clothes.* ○ *While she was changing the wheel on her car, her coat had become stained with oil.* **2** [I] If a material stains, it absorbs substances easily causing it to become marked, or coloured by a chemical: *This carpet is ideal for the kitchen because it doesn't stain easily.* **3** [T] to change the colour of something using a chemical: *She stripped the floorboards in the living room and stained them dark brown.*

stain /steɪn/ noun [C] **1** a chemical for changing the colour of something **2** a dirty mark on something that is difficult to remove: *a blood/grass stain* ○ *You can*

S

remove a red wine stain from a carpet by sprinkling salt over it. **-stained** /-steind/ *suffix*: **tear**-*stained faces* ○ *a* **blood**-*stained blanket*

stain SPOIL /stein/ *verb* [T] LITERARY to permanently spoil something such as someone's reputation: *Several important politicians have had their reputations stained by this scandal.* ○ *The country's history is stained with the blood of* (= The country is guilty of killing) *millions of innocent men and women.* **stain** /stein/ *noun* [S] *His solicitor, William Jackson, said, "He leaves this court without a stain on his character."*

stained 'glass *noun* [U] glass which has been coloured and cut into various shapes to form pictures or patterns, used especially in church windows: *a stained glass window*

stainless steel /ˌsteɪn.ləsˈstiːl/ *noun* [U] a type of steel containing CHROMIUM, which does not chemically react with air or water and does not change its colour

stair /steəʳ/ ⑩ /ster/ *noun* **1** [C] one of the steps in a set of steps which lead from one level of a building to another: *The top stair creaked as she went upstairs and the noise woke up her mother.* **2** [S] OLD USE OR LITERARY a set of stairs: *He climbed the wooden stair and knocked on his grandfather's door.*

stairs /steəz/ ⑩ /sterz/ *plural noun* a set of steps which lead from one level of a building to another: *Go up the stairs and her office is on the right.* ○ *I had to climb a steep* **flight** (= set) *of stairs to her front door.* ○ *He stood at the* **foot** (= bottom) *of the stairs and called out, "Breakfast's ready!"*

• **below/above stairs** UK OLD USE In a large house, below stairs was the part of the house in which the servants worked and lived, and above stairs was the part in which the family of the owner of the house lived.

staircase /ˈsteə.keɪs/ ⑩ /ˈster-/ *noun* [C] a set of stairs inside a building usually with a bar fixed on the wall or onto vertical poles at the side for you to hold on to: *She descended the* **sweeping** (= long and wide) *staircase into the crowd of photographers and journalists.*

stairway /ˈsteə.weɪ/ ⑩ /ˈster-/ *noun* [C] a passage in a public place with a set of steps that leads from one level to another

stairwell /ˈsteə.wel/ ⑩ /ˈster-/ *noun* [C] a long vertical passage through a building around which a set of stairs is built

stake STICK /steɪk/ *noun* [C] a strong stick or metal bar with a pointed end: *The stakes are pushed or hammered into the ground and can be used for marking an area, supporting a plant or forming part of a fence.*

• **the stake** in the past, a wooden post to which people were tied before being burned to death as a punishment: *In medieval Europe, many women were accused of being witches and were* **burnt at the stake.**

• **go to the stake for** *sth* to defend an action, opinion or belief despite the risks that are involved: *She passionately believed that the company was being mismanaged and was prepared to go to the stake for her views.*

stake /steɪk/ *verb* [T] to hold up and support something by attaching it to stakes: *Tomato plants should be staked.*

• **stake a claim** If you stake a claim to something, you state that you have a right to it and that it should belong to you: *He marked the spot on his map where he had seen the gold and returned later that month to stake his claim.*

stake SHARE /steɪk/ *noun* [C] a share or a financial involvement in something such as a business: *He holds* (= owns) *a 40% stake in/of the company.*

• **have a stake in** If you have a stake in something which is important to you, you have a personal interest or involvement in it: *Employers have a stake in the training of their staff.*

stakeholder /ˈsteɪkˌhəʊl.dəʳ/ ⑩ /-ˌhoʊl.dɚ/ *noun* [C] **1** a person or group of people who own a share in a business **2** a person such as an employee, customer or CITIZEN who is involved with an organization, society, etc. and therefore has responsibilities towards it and an interest in its success

stake RISK /steɪk/ *noun* [C] the amount of money which you risk on the result of something such as a game or competition: *She spent two weeks in Las Vegas playing* **high**-*stakes blackjack at the casinos.*

the stakes *plural noun* **1** In an activity or competition, the stakes are the reward for the person who wins or succeeds in it: *The team is playing for enormous stakes – the chance to play in the final.* **2 the Stakes** a horse race in which the prize money is provided by all the owners of the horses which are competing in the race **3 the popularity, etc. stakes** a situation where someone is judged on how much of a particular quality they have: *The prime minister is not very high in the popularity stakes* (= he is not very popular) *at the moment.*

• **raise/up the stakes 1** to increase the prize or reward in a competition or any activity in which you are competing **2** to make a situation more urgent or more difficult to ignore: *The stowaways are trying to raise the stakes by refusing to eat until they are given money and aid.*

• **at stake** If something that is valuable is at stake, it is in a situation where it might be lost: *Thousands of lives will be at stake if emergency aid does not arrive in the city soon.*

stake /steɪk/ *verb* [T] to bet an amount of money: *At the roulette table, he staked $10,000 on number 21.*

stakeholder /ˈsteɪkˌhəʊl.dəʳ/ ⑩ /-ˌhoʊl.dɚ/ *noun* [C] a person who is in charge of the prize money given by people betting on the result of a game or competition and who gives it to the winner

PHRASAL VERBS WITH stake

▲ **stake** *sth* **on** *sth* *phrasal verb* to risk harming or losing something important if an action, decision or situation does not have the result you want or expect: *I think she'll be head of this company in five year's time – I'd stake my reputation on it.*

▲ **stake** *somewhere/sth* **out** CLAIM OWNERSHIP *phrasal verb* [M] **1** to mark the limits of an area or a piece of land with wooden sticks in order to claim ownership of it **2** to show other people that you claim ownership, control or use of a particular area in a physical way, for example by putting personal items there: *Each gang in the city has staked out its territory and defends it ruthlessly from other gangs.* ○ *They arrived several hours early for the concert and staked out a place at the front of the queue.*

▲ **stake** *sth* **out** WATCH *phrasal verb* [M] MAINLY US INFORMAL to watch a place continuously in order to catch criminals or to see a famous person: *The police staked out the hotel where the two terrorists were reported to be staying.*

stakeout /ˈsteɪk.aʊt/ *noun* [C] MAINLY US INFORMAL the continuous watching of a building or area, especially by the police

▲ **stake** *sth* **out** MAKE CLEAR *phrasal verb* [M] to establish or make clear your opinion or position on something: *Two of the president's chief advisors have staked out opposite positions on this issue.* ○ *New software companies are going to find it hard staking out a position in an already crowded market.*

▲ **stake** *sb* **to** *sth* *phrasal verb* US to provide someone with a particular thing or with what they need to obtain it: *The governor has promised to stake the city's homeless to what they need for a fresh start.*

stalactite /ˈstæl.ək.taɪt/ *noun* [C] a column of rock that hangs from the roof of a cave and which is formed over a very long period of time by drops of water containing lime falling from the roof of the cave

stalagmite /ˈstæl.əg.maɪt/ *noun* [C] a column of rock which rises from the floor of a cave which is formed over a very long period of time by drops of water containing lime falling from the roof of the cave

stale /steɪl/ *adj* **1** no longer new or fresh, usually as a result of being kept for too long: *The bread/biscuits/cake had* **gone** *stale.* ○ *The morning after the party, their apartment smelled of stale cigarette smoke.* **2** not fresh and new; boring because too familiar: *stale jokes/news* **3** describes someone who has lost interest in what they are doing because they are bored or are working too hard: *They had been working together for over five years and they had both become a little stale.* **staleness** /ˈsteɪl.nəs/ *noun* [U]

stalemate /ˈsteɪl.meɪt/ *noun* [C or U] **1** a situation in which neither group involved in an argument can win or get an advantage and no action can be taken: *Tomorrow's meeting between the two leaders is expected to* ***break*** *a diplomatic stalemate that has lasted for ten years.* ○ *Despite long discussions, the workers and the management remain* ***locked in*** *stalemate.* **2** in chess, a position in which one player is unable to move, but their king is not being attacked, which means that neither of the two players wins ➲Compare **checkmate**.

stalk [PLANT PART] /stɔːk/ [US] /stɑːk/ *noun* [C] **1** the main stem of a plant, or the narrow stem that joins leaves, flowers or fruit to the main stem of a plant: *She trimmed the stalks of the tulips before putting them in a vase.* **2** a narrow structure that supports a part of the body in some animals: *The eyes of shrimps are on movable stalks.*
• **eyes out on stalks** *UK HUMOROUS* If your eyes are out on stalks, they are wide open with surprise: *His eyes were out on stalks as he watched his neighbour drive past in a brand new Porsche.*

stalk [FOLLOW] /stɔːk/ [US] /stɑːk/ *verb* **1** [T] to follow an animal or person as closely as possible without being seen or heard, usually in order to catch or kill them: *The police had been stalking the woman for a week before they arrested her.* **2** [I or T] to illegally follow and watch someone, usually a woman, over a period of time: *He was arrested for stalking.* **3** [T] *LITERARY* If something unpleasant stalks a place, it appears there in a threatening way: *When night falls, danger stalks the streets of the city.*
stalker /ˈstɔː.kəʳ/ [US] /ˈstɑː.kɚ/ *noun* [C] a person who illegally follows and watches someone, especially a woman, over a period of time: *Several well-known women have been troubled by stalkers recently.*

stalk [WALK] /stɔːk/ [US] /stɑːk/ *verb* [I + adv or prep] to walk in an angry or proud way: *She refused to accept that she was wrong and stalked furiously* ***out of*** *the room.*

ˈstalking ˌhorse *noun* [C] If a group of politicians use someone who has no chance of winning as a stalking horse, they make that person compete for a position in order to divide the opposition or to take attention away from another person who they really want to win.

stall [SHOP] /stɔːl/ [US] /stɑːl/ *noun* [C] a large table or a small shop with an open front from which goods are sold in a public place: *In the village market, the stalls are piled high with local vegetables.*

stall [ENCLOSURE] /stɔːl/ [US] /stɑːl/ *noun* [C] **1** a small enclosure within a farm building in which there is space for one animal to be kept **2** a small area of a room which is separated from the main part of the room by walls or curtains: *There was one bathroom with a* ***shower*** *stall in the corner.*

stall [ENGINE] /stɔːl/ [US] /stɑːl/ *verb* [I or T] If an engine stalls, or if you stall it, it stops working suddenly and without you intending it to happen: *A car may stall due to the driver braking too suddenly.* ○ *I stalled the car twice during my driving test but still managed to pass.*

stall [DELAY] /stɔːl/ [US] /stɑːl/ *verb* **1** [I] to delay taking action or avoid giving an answer in order to have more time to make a decision or obtain an advantage: *She says she'll give me the money next week but I think she's just stalling* ***(for time)***. **2** [T] If you stall a person, you delay them or prevent them from doing something for a period of time: *I managed to stall him for a few days until I'd got enough money to pay back the loan.* ○ *MAINLY US The thief broke into the office while his accomplice stalled* ***off*** *the security guard.* **3** [T] If you stall an event, you delay it or prevent it from happening for a period of time: *Commandoes stalled the enemy attack by destroying three bridges.* ○ *Fears are growing that a tax increase may stall economic recovery.*

stallholder /ˈstɔːlˌhəʊl.dəʳ/ [US] /ˈstɑːlˌhoʊl.dɚ/ *noun* [C] *MAINLY UK* a person who rents or owns a stall in a market

stallion /ˈstæl.jən/ *noun* [C] an adult male horse which is used for breeding ➲Compare **mare**.

the stalls [CHURCH] *plural noun* the rows of fixed seats in a church which often have their sides and backs enclosed

the stalls [THEATRE] *UK plural noun* (*US* **the orchestra**) the seats on the main floor of a theatre or cinema, not at a higher level ➲Compare **the circle** UPPER FLOOR; **gallery** RAISED AREA.

stalwart [LOYAL] /ˈstɔːl.wət/ [US] /ˈstɑːl.wɚt/ *adj* loyal, especially for a long time; able to be trusted: *She has been a stalwart supporter of the party for many years.*
stalwart /ˈstɔːl.wət/ [US] /ˈstɑːl.wɚt/ *noun* [C] a person who has been loyal for a long time: *Let me introduce Bob, one of the club's stalwarts.* **stalwartly** /ˈstɔːl.wət.li/ [US] /ˈstɑːl.wɚt-/ *adv*

stalwart [STRONG] /ˈstɔːl.wət/ [US] /ˈstɑːl.wɚt/ *adj FORMAL* (especially of a person) physically strong

stamen /ˈsteɪ.mən/ *noun* [C] *plural* **stamens** or **stamina** *SPECIALIZED* the male reproductive part of a flower, consisting of a thin stem which holds an ANTHER

stamina /ˈstæm.ɪ.nə/ *noun* [U] the physical and/or mental strength to do something which might be difficult and which will take a long time: *The triathlon is a great test of stamina.*

stammer /ˈstæm.əʳ/ [US] /-ɚ/ *verb* [I or T] to speak or say something with unusual pauses or repeated sounds, either because of speech problems or because of fear and anxiety: [+ speech] *"Wh-when can we g-go?" she stammered.* ○ *He dialled 999 and stammered* ***(out)*** *his name and address.* ➲Compare **stutter** SPEAK. **stammer** /ˈstæm.əʳ/ [US] /-ɚ/ *noun* [C usually sing] *Robert* ***has*** *a bit of a stammer.*
stammerer /ˈstæm.ᵊr.əʳ/ [US] /-ɚ.ɚ/ *noun* [C] a person who stammers **stammeringly** /ˈstæm.ᵊr.ɪŋ.li/ [US] /-ɚ-/ *adv*

stamp [LETTER] /stæmp/ *noun* [C] **1** (*FORMAL* **postage stamp**) a small piece of paper with a picture or pattern on it which is stuck onto a letter or parcel before it is posted to show that postage has been paid for: *I stuck a 50p stamp on the envelope.* **2** *UK* A stamp is also a small piece of paper worth a particular amount of money which you can buy repeatedly as a way of paying for something over a period of time: *vehicle licence stamps*

stamp [FOOT] /stæmp/ *verb* [I or T] (*US ALSO* **stomp**) to put a foot down on the ground hard and quickly, making a loud noise, often to show anger: *The little boy was stamping his foot and refusing to take his medicine.* ○ *She stood by the road, stamping her feet to stay warm.* ○ *I wish those people upstairs would stop stamping* ***(about/around)***. ○ *Why did you stamp* ***on*** *that insect?* ➲Compare **stomp**. **stamp** /stæmp/ *noun* [C] *With a stamp of her foot she stormed out.*

stamp [MARK] /stæmp/ *noun* [C] a tool for putting a mark on an object either by printing on it or pushing into it, or the mark made in this way: *A date stamp inside the front cover of a library book shows when it should be returned.* **stamp** /stæmp/ *verb* [T] *It is necessary to stamp your passport.* ○ *Every carton of yoghurt is stamped* ***with*** *a sell-by date.*
• **stamped on *sb's* memory** If a particular event, etc. is stamped on someone's memory, the person will always remember it: *The awful sound of the crash will be stamped on her memory forever.*

stamp [QUALITY] /stæmp/ *noun* [U] a particular quality in something or someone, or a quality in something which shows it was done by a particular person or group of people: *Although this painting clearly bears the stamp* ***of*** *genius, we don't know who painted it.* ○ *Each manager has left his or her own stamp* ***on*** *the way the company has evolved.* **stamp** /stæmp/ *verb* [T] *Our new administrator seems to be trying to stamp her authority* ***on*** *every aspect of the department.*

PHRASAL VERBS WITH **stamp** ▼

▲ **stamp on *sth*** *phrasal verb* to use force to stop or prevent something that you consider to be wrong or harmful: *Any opposition to the new government was immediately stamped on by the army.*

▲ **stamp *sth* out** *phrasal verb* [M] to get rid of something that is wrong or harmful: *The new legislation is intended to stamp out child prostitution.*

S

ˌstamped adˌdressed ˈenvelope *noun* [C] (*ALSO* **sae**) an envelope with a stamp and your name and address on it, which you send inside another envelope to an organization when you want a reply

stampede /stæmˈpiːd/ *noun* [C] when many large animals or many people suddenly all move quickly and in an uncontrolled way, usually in the same direction at the same time, especially because of fear: *Two shoppers were injured in the stampede as shop doors opened on the first day of the sale.*

stampede /stæmˈpiːd/ *verb* [I or T] *A loud clap of thunder made the herd stampede.* ○ *FIGURATIVE No amount of pressure will stampede (= force) this committee into making hasty decisions.*

ˈstamping ˌground *noun* [C] *INFORMAL* a place or area which someone is very familiar with and which they like to spend time in: *Do you ever go back to any of our old stamping grounds?*

stance OPINION /stɑːnts/ ⓤ /stænts/ *noun* [C] a way of thinking about something, especially expressed in a publicly stated opinion: *The doctor's stance on the issue of abortion is well known.*

stance WAY OF STANDING /stɑːnts/ ⓤ /stænts/ *noun* [C] a particular way of standing: *Jenny took up a stance with her feet slightly apart, ready to catch the ball.*

stanch /stɑːntʃ/ *verb* [T] *US FOR* **staunch** STOP.

stanchion /ˈstɑːn.tʃ⁰n/ ⓤ /ˈstæn-/ *noun* [C] a fixed vertical bar or pole used as a support for something

stand VERTICAL /stænd/ *verb* [I or T] **stood**, **stood** to be in a vertical state or to put into a vertical state, especially (of a person or animal) by straightening the legs: *Granny says if she stands (up) for a long time her ankles hurt.* ○ *As a sign of politeness you should stand (up) when she comes in.* ○ *Stand still and be quiet!* ○ *After the earthquake not a single building was left standing in the village.* ○ *Stand the bottles on the table over there.* ⤷See picture **Phrasal Verbs** on page Centre 9

• **Stand and deliver!** said in the past by HIGHWAYMEN when they stopped a carriage on a road to demand items of value from the travellers

• **stand** *your* **ground** to refuse to be pushed backwards, or to maintain your beliefs in an argument: *The battalion stood its ground in the face of repeated attacks.* ○ *Clare stood her ground in the meeting and refused to be intimidated even when Michael got angry.*

• **stand on ceremony** to behave in a formal way: *Please sit down and make yourself comfortable, we don't stand on ceremony here.*

• **stand on** *your* **dignity** *USUALLY DISAPPROVING* to demand to be shown the respect which you think you deserve: *The Director didn't stand on her dignity; she helped clear up after the party.*

• **stand on** *your* **hands/head** to support yourself only on your hands, or only on your head and hands, with your feet as high as possible

• **standing on** *your* **head** *INFORMAL* If someone can do something standing on their head they can do it very easily: *It's the sort of program Andrew could write standing on his head.*

• **stand** *sth* **on** *its* **head** If something new stands something established on its head, then the truth of the established thing or the beliefs on which it is based are doubted: *New data has stood the traditional explanation of the island's origin on its head.*

• **stand on** *your* **own (two) feet** *INFORMAL* to be able to provide all of the things you need for living without help from anyone else: *She'll have to get a job and learn to stand on her own two feet sooner or later.*

• **stand or fall by** *sth* to depend completely on something for success

• **stand (up) and be counted** to make your opinions known even if doing so might cause you harm or difficulty: *Those who did have the courage to stand up and be counted were arrested and imprisoned.*

• **from a standing start** from not moving: *This car can reach 60mph from a standing start in less than six seconds.*

stand STATE /stænd/ *verb* [I; L only + adj] **stood**, **stood** to be in, cause to be in or get into a particular state or situation:

How do you think your chances stand (= are) of being offered the job? ○ *The national debt stands at fifty-five billion dollars.* ○ *The house stood empty for years.* ○ *Martina is currently standing second in the world listings.* ○ [+ to infinitive] *Our firm stands to lose (= will lose) a lot of money if the deal is unsuccessful.* ○ *We really can't allow the current situation to stand (= to exist in its current form).* ○ *Newton's laws of mechanics stood (= were thought to be completely true) for over two hundred years.* ○ *Mix one sachet of paste into two litres of water, then leave the mixture to stand (= do not touch it) for at least fifteen minutes before use.* ○ *It would be difficult for her to stand much lower/higher in my opinion (= for me to have a worse/better opinion of her) after the way she behaved at the party.* ○ *FORMAL You stand accused of murder, how do you plead?*

• **know where you stand** to know what your opinion or situation is: *I know where I stand on this issue – I'm against the war.* ○ *When we've paid all our debts we'll know where we stand.*

• **stand fast/firm** to be determined: *Stand firm on your decision and you're more likely to get the result you want.*

• **stand bail** to pay money temporarily to a court so that someone can be released from prison until the date of their trial: *She can't be released from police custody until someone stands bail for her.*

• **I stand corrected.** *FORMAL* used to admit that something you have said or done was wrong: *I stand corrected – the date of foundation was 1411, and not 1412 as I had written.*

• **stand** *sb* **in good stead** If an experience stands a person in good stead it is or will be of great use to them: *Getting some work experience now will stand you in good stead (for) when you apply for a permanent job.*

• **it stands to reason** said when something is obvious or clear from the facts: *If 20% of the Earth's population has 80% of its resources, then it stands to reason that 80% of the population has only 20% of the resources.*

• **stand trial** to be put on trial in a court of law: *Two other men are to stand trial next month for their part in the bombing.*

stand PLACE /stænd/ *verb* **stood**, **stood** **1** [I or T; usually + adv or prep] to be in, cause to be in or put into a particular place: *The room was empty except for a wardrobe standing in one corner.* ○ *Stand the paintings against the wall while we decide where to hang them.* ○ *The photograph shows the happy couple standing beside a banana tree.* **2** [I usually + adv or prep] Vehicles that are standing are waiting: *The train now standing at platform 8 is the 15.17 for Oxford.*

• **stand in the way of** *sth/sb* (*ALSO* **stand in** *sb's* **way**) to try to stop or prevent: *You know I won't stand in your way if you want to apply for a job abroad.*

stand ACCEPT /stænd/ *verb* [T usually in negatives] **stood**, **stood** to successfully accept or bear something which is unpleasant or difficult: *I can't stand her voice.* ○ *Our tent won't stand another storm like the last one.* ○ [+ v-ing] *I can't stand hearing her cry.*

• **stand the test of time** If something stands the test of time, it is still popular, strong, etc. after a long time: *Which songs from the last year will stand the test of time?*

• **can't stand the sight of** to hate: *Aunt Gloria can't stand the sight of cats because she was attacked by one when she was a child.*

stand SPORT /stænd/ *noun* [C] *UK* a large structure at a sports ground, usually with a sloping floor and sometimes a roof, where people either stand or sit to watch a sports event ⤷Compare **grandstand**.

stands /stændz/ *plural noun*: *Fighting broke out in the stands (= stand) five minutes before the end of the match.*

stand OPINION /stænd/ *noun* [C] an opinion, especially one which is public: *What's her stand on sexual equality?*

stand /stænd/ *verb* [I usually + adv or prep] **stood**, **stood** *How/Where does he stand (= What are his opinions) on foreign policy issues?*

• **from where** *sb* **stands** being in a particular position and having your particular experience, beliefs and responsibilities: *You can see why they refused her demand for a pay rise, but from where she stands it probably seemed perfectly reasonable to ask.*

stand [POLITICS] *UK* (**stood, stood**) /stænd/ *verb* [I] (*MAINLY US* **run**) to compete, especially in an election, for an official position: *The president has announced she does not intend to stand **for** re-election.*

stand [CHANCE OF SUCCESS] /stænd/ *verb* **stand a chance** to have a chance of success: *She stands a good chance **of** passing her exam if she works hard.*

stand [COURT] /stænd/ *noun* [C] *US FOR* **witness box**: *The witness **took** the stand* (= went to the place in a court where you stand and answer questions).

stand [SHOP] /stænd/ *noun* [C] a small shop or STALL or an area where products can be shown, usually outside or in a large public building, at which people can buy things or obtain information: *a hot dog stand* ○ *Over three thousand companies will have stands at this year's microelectronics exhibition.* ➲See also **newsstand**.

stand [FRAME] /stænd/ *noun* [C] a frame or piece of furniture for supporting or putting things on: *a music stand* ○ *a hatstand*

stand [HEIGHT] /stænd/ *verb* [L only + n] **stood, stood** to be a stated height: *Even without his shoes he stood over two metres tall.*

stand [OPPOSITION] /stænd/ *noun* [C usually sing] an act of opposition, especially in defence: *Environmental groups are **making a** stand **against** the new road through the valley.* ➲See also **stand out against**.

stand [BUY] /stænd/ *verb* [T + two objects] **stood, stood** to buy something, especially a meal or a drink, for someone: *I couldn't get to the bank, so could you stand me lunch?*

stand [PERFORMANCES] /stænd/ *noun* [C usually sing] *US* a particular number or period of performances: *The Orioles will be in town for a three-game stand against the Tigers.*

PHRASAL VERBS WITH **stand** ▼

▲ **stand about/around** *phrasal verb* to spend time standing somewhere and doing very little: *We stood around in the cold for about an hour, waiting for the demo to start.*

▲ **stand aside** *phrasal verb* **1** to leave a job or position so that someone else can have it instead: *It's time he stood aside and let a more qualified person do the job.* **2** *SLIGHTLY FORMAL* to step sideways to make a space for someone else: *Stand aside, please, so the doctor can get through.*

▲ **stand back** *phrasal verb* to move a short distance away from something or someone: *Please stand back – then all of you will be able to see what I'm doing.*

▲ **stand by** [BE READY] *phrasal verb* to be waiting and ready to do something or to help: *Cabin crew, please stand by **for** takeoff.* ➲See also **standby**.

▲ **stand by** [DO NOTHING] *phrasal verb* to allow something unpleasant to happen without doing anything to stop it: *We can't stand by while millions of people starve.* ➲See also **bystander**.

▲ **stand by *sb*** [SUPPORT] *phrasal verb* to continue to support or help someone who is in a difficult situation: *She has vowed to stand by her husband during his trial.*

▲ **stand by *sth*** *phrasal verb* **1** to continue doing what you said you would when you made a decision, agreement or promise: *Despite its financial problems, the company is standing by the no-redundancy agreement.* **2** to continue to believe that something you have said before is still true: *I stand by the statement I made earlier – there is no reason for the minister to resign.*

▲ **stand clear** *phrasal verb* to move a short distance away from something so that you are safe: *"Stand clear!" shouted the policewoman. "It might fall any minute."*

▲ **stand down** *phrasal verb UK* to give up your official job or position: *He's decided to stand down after fifteen years as managing director.*

▲ **stand for *sth*** [ACCEPT] *phrasal verb* If you will not stand for something, you will not accept a situation or a particular type of behaviour: *I wouldn't stand for that sort of behaviour from him, if I were you.*

▲ **stand for *sth*** [REPRESENT] *phrasal verb* **1** to support or represent a particular idea or set of ideas: *This party stands for low taxes and individual freedom.* **2** If one or more letters stand for a word or name, they are the first letter or letters of that word or name and they represent it: *'GMT' stands for Greenwich Mean Time.*

▲ **stand in** *phrasal verb* (*US USUALLY* **fill in**) to do the job that another person was going to do or usually does, or to take their place at an event, because they cannot be there: *Paula stood in **for** Jane, while Jane was on holiday.*

stand-in /ˈstænd.ɪn/ *noun* [C] a person who takes the place or does the job of another person for a short time, for example because the other person is ill or on holiday: *The lecturer didn't turn up, so we had to find a stand-in.*

▲ **stand out** [NOTICEABLE] *phrasal verb* to be very noticeable: *The black lettering really stands out on that orange background.*

▲ **stand out** [BETTER] *phrasal verb* to be much better than other similar things or people: *We had lots of good applicants for the job, but one stood out **from** the rest.*

standout /ˈstænd.aʊt/ *noun* [C] *US* an excellent or the best example of something: *While all the desserts are pretty good, the clear standout is the lemon pie.*

▲ **stand out against *sth/sb*** *phrasal verb* to openly oppose something or someone: *More and more people are standing out against what is a very unpopular piece of legislation.* ➲See also **stand** OPPOSITION.

▲ **stand over *sb*** *phrasal verb* to stand close to someone and watch what they are doing: *Don't stand over me all the time – it makes me nervous.*

▲ **stand together** *phrasal verb* If a group of people stand together on a particular matter, they agree strongly about it and take action together about it.

▲ **stand up** [GET PROOF] *phrasal verb* If an idea or some information stands up, it is proved to be true or correct: *Their evidence will never stand up in court.* ○ *Their argument won't stand up **to** detailed criticism* (= when it is studied critically).

▲ **stand *sb* up** [NOT MEET] *phrasal verb* [M] *INFORMAL* to intentionally fail to meet someone when you said you would, especially someone you were starting to have a romantic relationship with: *I don't know if I've been stood up or if she's just late – I'll wait another half hour.*

▲ **stand up for *sth/sb*** *phrasal verb* (*ALSO* **stick up for *sth/sb***) to defend or support a particular idea or a person who is being criticized or attacked: *It's high time we all stood up for our rights around here.* ○ [R] *Don't be bullied, learn to stand up for yourself and what you believe in.*

▲ **stand up to *sb/sth*** [DEFEND] *phrasal verb* to defend yourself against a powerful person or organization when they treat you unfairly: *He wasn't afraid to stand up to bullies.*

▲ **stand up to *sth*** [NOT CHANGE] *phrasal verb* to not be changed or damaged by something: *Will the lorries stand up to the journey over rough roads?*

stand-alone /ˈstænd.əˌləʊn/ [US] /-ˌloʊn/ *adj* [before n] Something, such as a computer or a business, which is stand-alone can operate on its own without needing help from another similar thing.

standard [USUAL] /ˈstæn.dəd/ [US] /-dɚd/ *adj* **1** usual rather than special, especially when thought of as being correct or acceptable: *White is the standard colour for this model of refrigerator.* ○ *These are standard **procedures** for handling radioactive waste.* ○ *The metre is the standard unit for measuring length in the SI system.* ○ *MAINLY UK Your new TV comes with a two year guarantee **as** standard.* ➲See also **substandard**. **2** Language described as standard is the form of that language which is considered acceptable and correct by most educated users of it: *Most announcers on the BBC speak standard **English**.* ○ *In Standard **American**, 'gotten' is used as a past participle of 'get'.* **3** [before n] A standard book or writer is the one that is most commonly read for information on a particular subject: *Her book is still a standard text in archaeology, even though it was written more than twenty years ago.*

standard /ˈstæn.dəd/ [US] /-dɚd/ *noun* **1** [C] a song or other piece of music which has been popular and often played over a long period of time **2** [C usually sing] a pattern or model that is generally accepted: *This program is an industry standard for computers.* **3** [C] *US* a car with gears that are changed by hand

S

standardize, UK USUALLY **-ise** /'stæn.də.daɪz/ US /-dɚ-/ verb [T] to make things of the same type all have the same basic features: *We standardize parts such as rear-view mirrors, so that one type will fit any model of car we make.* **standardization**, UK USUALLY **-isation** /ˌstæn.də.daɪˈzeɪ.ʃən/ US /-dɚ-/ noun [U]

standard QUALITY /'stæn.dəd/ US /-dɚd/ noun **1** [C or U] a level of quality: *This essay is not **of** an acceptable standard – do it again.* ○ *This piece of work is **below** standard/is not **up** to standard.* ○ *We have very high safety standards in this laboratory.* ○ *Not everyone judges success by the same standards – some people think happiness is more important than money.* ○ *Her technique became a standard against which all future methods were compared.* **2** [C usually plural] a moral rule which should be obeyed: *Most people agree that there are standards **(of behaviour)** which need to be upheld, but agreeing on them is rather more difficult.*

standard FLAG /'stæn.dəd/ US /-dɚd/ noun [C] a flag, especially a long narrow one ending with two long points: *the royal standard*

standard-bearer /'stæn.dəd,beə.rə'/ US /-dɚd,ber.ɚ/ noun [C] the person or thing that seems to lead a group of people having similar ideas or moral opinions: *Mr Everhart wants Caltech to be the standard-bearer for excellence in scientific research of all kinds.*

standard ,lamp UK noun [C] (US **floor lamp**) an electric light supported by a tall pole which is fixed to a base that rests on the floor of a room

standard of 'living (plural **standards of living**) noun [C usually sing] (ALSO **living standard**) the amount of wealth and comfort people have in a particular society: *The standard of living in many developing countries is low.* ⊃Compare **cost of living**.

standard 'operating ,procedure noun [U] (ABBREVIATION **SOP**) US the usual way of doing something: *Checking references before we lend money is standard operating procedure.*

standard ,time noun [U] In a country or a part of a country, standard time is the time which is officially used. ⊃Compare **Greenwich Mean Time**.

standby /'stænd.baɪ/ noun [C] plural **standbys** something which is always ready for use, especially if a regular one fails: *Board games are a good standby to keep the children amused if the weather is bad.* ○ *There are standby generators but these usually only have to work for a few hours a year during power cuts.*
● **on standby** When a person or a thing is on standby they are ready to be used if necessary: *Hospitals are on standby ready to deal with casualties being flown in from the crash site.*

standby (,ticket) noun [C] a cheap ticket sold just before a flight or a performance if there is a seat available

standing PERMANENT /'stæn.dɪŋ/ adj [before n] permanent, rather than formed or created when necessary: *a standing committee* ○ *You know you have a standing **invitation** to come and stay anytime you're in town.*

standing REPUTATION /'stæn.dɪŋ/ noun [U] reputation, rank or position in an area of activity, system or organization: *As a pathologist of considerable standing, his opinion will have a lot of influence.* ○ *A financial scandal would shake the Institute's standing **in** the international academic community.*

standing TIME /'stæn.dɪŋ/ noun [U] SLIGHTLY FORMAL the time for which something has existed: *One member, **of** twelve years' standing on the committee, resigned in protest at the changes.* ⊃See also **long-standing**.

standing 'joke noun [C usually sing] something which a particular group of people are familiar with and laugh about often, especially in an unkind way: *The fact that Debbie is always late has become a standing joke among her friends.*

standing 'order noun [C] UK an instruction to a bank to pay a particular amount of money at regular times from a person's bank account to another bank account ⊃Compare **direct debit**.

standing o'vation noun [C] when the people in an audience stand up to clap at the end of a performance or speech because they liked it very much: *She **received** a standing ovation at the end of her speech.*

standing ,room noun [U] space in a sports ground, theatre, bus, etc. where people can stand, especially if all of the seats have people sitting in them: *All the seats were gone, so there was standing room **only**.*

standoff /'stænd.ɒf/ US /-ɑːf/ noun [C] a situation in which agreement in an argument does not seem possible; STALEMATE

standoffish /ˌstændˈɒf.ɪʃ/ US /-ˈɑː.fɪʃ/ adj INFORMAL DISAPPROVING behaving in a slightly unfriendly and too formal way **standoffishly** /ˌstændˈɒf.ɪʃ.li/ US /-ˈɑː.fɪʃ-/ adv **standoffishness** /ˌstændˈɒf.ɪʃ.nəs/ US /-ˈɑː.fɪʃ-/ noun [U]

standpipe /'stænd.paɪp/ noun [C] a vertical pipe which is connected to a water supply and provides water to a public place such as a road

standpoint /'stænd.pɔɪnt/ noun [C] a set of beliefs and ideas from which opinions and decisions are formed: *"I have to put aside my emotions," he says, "and consider it from a professional standpoint."*

standstill /'stænd.stɪl/ noun [S] a condition in which all movement or activity has stopped: *The runaway bus eventually **came to a** standstill when it rolled into a muddy field.* ○ *Fighting and shortages have **brought** normal life **to a** virtual standstill in the city.*

stand-up /'stænd.ʌp/ adj [before n] describes comedy performed by a single person telling jokes: *stand-up comedy* ○ *a stand-up comedian*

stand-up /'stænd.ʌp/ noun [C] a person who performs stand-up comedy; a stand-up comedian

stank /stæŋk/ past simple of **stink**

Stanley knife /'stæn.li.naɪf/ noun [C] TRADEMARK a sharp knife with a short blade which can be replaced or put inside the handle if not being used

stanza /'stæn.zə/ noun [C] a group of lines of poetry forming a unit; **verse**

staple WIRE /'steɪ.pl/ noun [C] **1** a short thin piece of wire used to fasten sheets of paper together. It has sharp ends which are pushed through the paper and then bent flat by a special device. ⊃See picture **In the Office** on page Centre 15 **2** a U-shaped piece of metal with sharp ends which is hammered into a surface to hold something, such as a wire fence, in a particular position **staple** /'steɪ.pl/ verb [T] *Would you mind stapling the reports **together**?*

stapler /'steɪ.plə'/ US /-plɚ/ noun [C] a small device which you can hold in your hand or use on a table to push staples through pieces of paper ⊃See picture **In the Office** on page Centre 15

staple BASIC /'steɪ.pl/ adj [before n] basic or main; standard or regular: *The staple **diet** here is mutton, fish and boiled potatoes.* ○ *Prices of staple **foods** such as wheat and vegetables have also been increasing.* ○ *Her latest film is the staple offering of action and comedy which we have come to expect.*

staple /'steɪ.pl/ noun [C] SHORTAGES *mean that even staples* (= basic foods) *like bread are difficult to find.* ○ *Phosphate has been a staple* (= main product) **of** *this area for many years.* ○ *Romantic fiction and reference books are a staple **of** many public libraries.*

staple-gun /'steɪ.pl.ɡʌn/ noun [C] a tool which you hold in your hand and use to push staples into a surface

star OBJECT IN SPACE /stɑː'/ US /stɑːr/ noun [C] a very large ball of burning gas in space which is usually seen from Earth as a point of light in the sky at night: *Stars **twinkled** above them as they lay on the hill.* **starry** /'stɑː.ri/ US /'stɑː.ri/ adj: *a starry night/sky*
● **starry-eyed** If a person is starry-eyed they have lots of thoughts and opinions which are unreasonably positive, so they do not understand things as they really are: *It's easy to be starry-eyed about a place you've never been to.*

star SYMBOL /stɑː'/ US /stɑːr/ noun [C] **1** a symbol with four or more points: *star-shaped* ○ *How many stars* (= symbols showing quality) *has this restaurant got?* ○ *The teacher gave Atticus a gold star* (= paper symbol rewarding good work) *for his drawing.* ⊃See also **-star** RANK. **2** a symbol made of metal or cloth worn by particular officials to show their rank: *a sheriff's star* ○ *a four-star general* **3** an ASTERISK (= a symbol (*), like a star)

starred /stɑːd/ [US] /stɑːrd/ *adj* marked by an ASTERISK: *The starred items on the agenda are the most important.*

star [PERFORMER] /stɑːʳ/ [US] /stɑːr/ *noun* [C] a very famous, successful and important person, especially a performer such as a musician, actor or sports player: *a rock/movie/football star* ○ *Kids wanting to be stars come to Hollywood from all over America.* ➲See also **co-star**; **superstar**.

star /stɑːʳ/ [US] /stɑːr/ *verb* [I + prep; T] **-rr-** If a film, play, etc. stars someone, or if someone stars in a film, play, etc., they are the main person in it: *Ben Kingsley starred* ***in*** *the film 'Gandhi'.* ○ *Fowles's novel 'The French Lieutenant's Woman' was turned into a film starring Meryl Streep.*

stardom /ˈstɑː.dᵊm/ [US] /ˈstɑːr-/ *noun* [U] fame: *From childhood, Britney Spears seemed destined for stardom.*

starlet /ˈstɑː.lət/ [US] /ˈstɑːr-/ *noun* [C] OFTEN DISAPPROVING a young actress who hopes to be or is thought likely to be famous in the future

star [MAIN] /stɑːʳ/ [US] /stɑːr/ *adj* [before n] INFORMAL best or most important: *Natalie is, without a doubt, the star student in this year's ballet class.* ○ *This afternoon the prosecution will call its star witness.*

star [LUCK] /stɑːʳ/ [US] /stɑːr/ *noun* [C] INFORMAL any planet or other object in the sky thought of in astrology as influencing a person's luck: *She was* ***born under*** *a lucky/an unlucky star.* ➲See also **star sign**.

stars /stɑːz/ [US] /stɑːrz/ *plural noun* INFORMAL **horoscope**: *I always like to see what* ***the*** *stars say in the newspaper.*

-star [RANK] /-stɑːʳ/ [US] /-stɑːr/ *suffix* a ranking of quality, usually in numbers from one to five with one being the lowest: *A three-star hotel is better than a two-star.*

starred /stɑːd/ [US] /stɑːrd/ *adj*: *a starred restaurant* (= one good enough to be ranked)

starboard /ˈstɑː.bəd/ [US] /ˈstɑːr.bɚd/ *noun* [U] SPECIALIZED the right side of a ship or aircraft as you are facing forward ✻ NOTE: The opposite is **port**.

starch [FOOD] /stɑːtʃ/ [US] /stɑːrtʃ/ *noun* [U] a white substance which exists in large amounts in potatoes and particular grains such as rice: *Corn starch is used as a thickener in stews.* ➲Compare **carbohydrate**. **starchy** /ˈstɑː.tʃi/ [US] /ˈstɑːr-/ *adj*

starch [CLOTH] /stɑːtʃ/ [US] /stɑːrtʃ/ *noun* [U] a white substance obtained from potatoes and particular grains which is used to make cloth stiff

starch /stɑːtʃ/ [US] /stɑːrtʃ/ *verb* [T] *She wore a starched* (= very stiff) *white apron over her black dress.*

ˌstar ˈchamber *noun* [C] MAINLY UK FORMAL DISAPPROVING a court or other group which meets privately and makes judgments which can be severe

starchy /ˈstɑː.tʃi/ [US] /ˈstɑːr-/ *adj* INFORMAL DISAPPROVING behaving in a formal way and without humour: *Science museums have tried to shake off their somewhat starchy image by mounting exhibitions designed to draw in the crowds.* **starchily** /ˈstɑː.tʃɪ.li/ [US] /ˈstɑːr-/ *adv*

star-crossed /ˈstɑː.krɒst/ [US] /ˈstɑːr.krɑːst/ *adj* LITERARY unlucky: *star-crossed lovers*

stardust /ˈstɑː.dʌst/ [US] /ˈstɑːr-/ *noun* [U] LITERARY (something which causes) a pleasant dream-like or romantic feeling

stare /steəʳ/ [US] /ster/ *verb* [I or T] to look for a long time with the eyes wide open, especially when surprised, frightened or thinking: *Don't stare* ***at*** *people like that, it's rude.* ○ *Chuck sat quietly for hours staring into the distance, thinking of what might have been.* ○ *During the press conference, each boxer tried to stare the other* ***down***/(UK ALSO) ***out*** (= force the other to look away by continual staring).

• **be staring at** If you are staring at a bad situation or problem, you know you must experience it or deal with it very soon: *By late in the first half United were staring at a seven-goal deficit and almost certain defeat.*

• **stare *sb* in the face** INFORMAL If something stares someone in the face it is very easy to see or obvious: *The answer has been staring us in the face all along!*

stare /steəʳ/ [US] /ster/ *noun* [C] when you look at something or someone for a long time: *She gave him a long stare but didn't answer his question.* **staring** /ˈsteə.rɪŋ/ [US] /ˈster.ɪŋ/ *adj*: *In the darkness we could just make out the blank staring eyes of a child.*

starfish /ˈstɑː.fɪʃ/ [US] /ˈstɑːr-/ *noun* [C] *plural* **starfish** or **starfishes** a flat animal that lives in the sea and has five arms which grow from its body

stargazer /ˈstɑːˌgeɪ.zəʳ/ [US] /ˈstɑːrˌgeɪ.zɚ/ *noun* [C] INFORMAL a person who is involved in astronomy or astrology

stargazing /ˈstɑːˌgeɪ.zɪŋ/ [US] /ˈstɑːr-/ *noun* [U]

stark [BARE] /stɑːk/ [US] /stɑːrk/ *adj* bare, simple or obvious, especially without decoration or anything which is not necessary; severe or extreme: *It was a stark room with its white walls, and a bed and chair as the only furniture.* ○ *The stark* ***reality*** *is that we are operating at a huge loss.* ○ *In the suburbs the spacious houses stand in stark* ***contrast*** *to the slums of the city's poor.* **starkly** /ˈstɑː.kli/ [US] /ˈstɑːr-/ *adv* **starkness** /ˈstɑːk.nəs/ [US] /ˈstɑːrk-/ *noun* [U]

stark [COMPLETELY] /stɑːk/ [US] /stɑːrk/ *adv* completely or extremely: *The children were splashing in the river, stark* ***naked***/(US ALSO) ***buck naked***. ○ *I think he's stark* ***raving mad***/(UK ALSO) *stark* ***staring mad*** *to want to spend his holiday watching trains!* ➲See also **starkers**.

starkly /ˈstɑː.kli/ [US] /ˈstɑːr-/ *adv* very obviously and clearly: *Her later sensual works contrast starkly with the harsh earlier paintings.*

starkers /ˈstɑː.kəz/ [US] /ˈstɑːr.kɚz/ *adj* [after v] UK INFORMAL OFTEN HUMOROUS naked

starlet /ˈstɑː.lət/ [US] /ˈstɑːr-/ *noun* [C] ➲See at **star** PERFORMER.

starlight /ˈstɑː.laɪt/ [US] /ˈstɑːr-/ *noun* [U] the light produced by stars **starlit** /ˈstɑː.lɪt/ [US] /ˈstɑːr-/ *adj*: *a starlit night*

starling /ˈstɑː.lɪŋ/ [US] /ˈstɑːr-/ *noun* [C] a common bird with black or dark brown feathers which lives in large groups in many parts of the world

Star of David /ˌstɑː.rəvˈdeɪ.vɪd/ [US] /ˌstɑːr.əv-/ *noun* [C] a star with six points which represents Judaism

starry /ˈstɑː.ri/ [US] /ˈstɑːr.i/ *adj* ➲See at **star** OBJECT IN SPACE.

ˌStars and ˈStripes *noun* the US flag

ˈstar ˌsign *noun* [C] in astrology, any of the twelve symbols which represent parts of the ZODIAC: *"What's your star sign?" "I'm a Leo."*

Star-Spangled Banner /ˌstɑː.spæŋ.gḷdˈbæn.əʳ/ [US] /ˌstɑːr.spæŋ.gḷdˈbæn.ɚ/ *noun* the national ANTHEM (= song) of the US

starstruck /ˈstɑː.strʌk/ [US] /ˈstɑːr-/ *adj* OFTEN DISAPPROVING feeling great or too much respect for famous or important people, especially famous actors or performers: *It's the story of a starstruck young girl who goes to Hollywood to make her fortune.*

star-studded /ˈstɑːˌstʌd.ɪd/ [US] /ˈstɑːr-/ *adj* INFORMAL If a group of people, a film or a show is star-studded there are lots of famous people in it.

start [BEGIN] /stɑːt/ [US] /stɑːrt/ *verb* **1** to begin doing something: *When do you start your course/your new job?* ○ *We'll be starting (the session) at six o'clock.* ○ *Can you start* (= begin a new job) *on Monday?* ○ [+ v-ing] *They started building the house in January.* ○ [+ to infinitive] *I'd just started* ***to*** *write a letter when the phone rang.* **2** [I or T] (ALSO **start up**) If a business or other organization starts, or if someone starts one, it is created and starts to operate: *She started her own software company.* ○ *A lot of new restaurants have started up in the region.* **3** [I or T] to begin to happen or to make something begin to happen: *A new series of wildlife programmes has started on Monday evenings.* ○ *Police believe the fire was started by arsonists.* **4** [I or T] to begin a set of activities with the thing or person mentioned: *The speaker started* ***with*** *a description of her journey to China.* ○ *Give me your answers one by one, starting* ***with*** *Lucy.* ○ *You could start* ***by*** *weeding the flowerbeds.* ○ *He started his working life* ***as*** *an engineer but later became a teacher.* **5** [I] INFORMAL to begin to complain or be annoying in some way: *Don't start – we're not going and that's that!* ○ INFORMAL *"It would help if Richard did some work." "Oh,* ***don't get*** *me started on Richard!"* **6 get started** to begin: *When can we get started?* **7 start a family** to have your first child **8 start work** to begin being employed: *He started work at 16 in a local bakers.* **9 to start with** at the beginning, or as the first of several things: *We only knew two people*

[S]

in London to start with, but we soon made friends. ○ *To start with we need better computers – then we need more training.* ➲See also **for starters** at **start** BEGIN.

start /stɑːt/ [US] /stɑːrt/ *noun* **1** [S] the beginning of something: *We were doubtful about the product's usefulness* ***from*** *the start.* ○ *They announced the start* ***of*** *a new commercial venture.* ○ *The weather was good* ***at*** *the start* (= in the first part) *of the week.* ○ *The event* ***got off to*** *a shaky/poor start with the stage lights failing in the first few minutes.* **2** [C] when you begin doing something: *We need to* ***make*** *a start* ***on*** *(preparing) the brochure next week.*

• **from start to finish** including all of something, from the beginning to the end: *The whole course was a disaster from start to finish.*

• **for a start 1** *UK* first, or as the first in a set of things: *We'll take names and phone numbers for a start, then later on we can get more details.* ➲See also **for starters** at **start** BEGIN. **2** [C] *MAINLY UK* a small dish served as the first part of a meal: *We had soup/pâté/pasta as a starter.*

starter /ˈstɑː.təʳ/ [US] /ˈstɑːr.t̬ɚ/ *noun* [C] a person, animal or organization that is involved at the beginning of an activity, especially a race: *Of the ten starters* (= horses which started in the race), *two fell at the first fence.*

• **under starter's orders** ready for the signal to start a race

• **for starters** *INFORMAL* used to say that something is the first in a list of things: *Try this exercise for starters.* ○ *"Why did you decide not to go to the concert?" "Well, for starters, the tickets were ridiculously expensive."* ➲See also **for a start** at **start** BEGIN.

start [MOVE] /stɑːt/ [US] /stɑːrt/ *verb* [I usually + adv or prep] to begin at one point and then move to another, in distance or range: *The bus starts* ***at/from*** *the main depot.* ○ *We'll need to start* ***(off/out)*** *early because the journey takes six hours.* ○ *Tell me what happened – start* ***at the beginning.*** ○ *Ticket prices start* ***at/from*** *£20 and go up to £100.*

start [MOVE SUDDENLY] /stɑːt/ [US] /stɑːrt/ *verb* [I] to move your body suddenly because something has surprised or frightened you: *He started* ***at*** *the sound of the phone.*

start /stɑːt/ [US] /stɑːrt/ *noun* [S] when someone moves their body suddenly because something has surprised or frightened them: *He woke* ***with a*** *start.* ○ *She* ***gave a*** *start as I entered.*

start [WORK] /stɑːt/ [US] /stɑːrt/ *verb* [I or T] (*ALSO* **start up**) to (cause to) begin to work or operate: *I'm having trouble starting the car.* ○ *The engine won't start.*

PHRASAL VERBS WITH **start** ▼

▲ **start** ***(sth)*** **off** *phrasal verb* to begin by doing something, or to make something begin by doing something: *She started off the meeting with the monthly sales report.* ○ *I'd like to start off by thanking you all for coming today.*

▲ **start** ***sb*** **off** *phrasal verb* **1** to help someone to start an activity, especially a piece of work: *I'll start her off on some fairly basic stuff and see how she gets on.* **2** to make someone start to laugh, cry, or talk about something that they often talk about: *I could see Emma trying not to laugh and of course that started me off.*

▲ **start on** ***sth*** *phrasal verb* to start to deal with something, or to start to use something: *I'm just about to start on the cleaning.* ○ *Shall we start on the wine or wait till Colin gets here?*

▲ **start on at** ***sb*** *phrasal verb* to start complaining angrily to someone about something they have done: *She started on at him about the way he's always looking at other women.*

▲ **start out** *phrasal verb* to begin your life, or the part of your life when you work, in a particular way: *My dad started out* ***as*** *a sales assistant in a shop.*

▲ **start over** *US phrasal verb* (*UK* **start afresh**) to begin to do something again, sometimes in a different way: *We decided to abandon the first draft of the report and start over.* ○ *The agreement allows old expectations to be forgotten and everyone can start afresh.*

▲ **start (*sth*) up** [BUSINESS] *phrasal verb* If a business or other organization starts up, or if someone starts one up, it is created and starts to operate: *Many small businesses started up in the 1980s to cater to this growing market.* ○ *We ought to start up a drama group.*

start-up /ˈstɑːt.ʌp/ [US] /ˈstɑːrt-/ *noun* [C] a small business that has just been started: *Start-ups are very vulnerable in the business world.*

▲ **start (*sth*) up** [ENGINE] *phrasal verb* If a vehicle or engine starts up, or someone starts it up, it starts to work: *The car wouldn't start up this morning.*

ˈstarter ˌmotor *noun* [C] an electrical device which causes an engine to begin to operate

ˈstarting ˌdate *noun* [C] (*ALSO* **start date**) the planned day for the start of an important activity: *The starting date for the construction work is June 23rd.*

ˈstarting ˌline *noun* [C] a line drawn on the ground behind which competitors wait for a signal to begin a race

ˈstarting ˌpistol *noun* [C] a small gun that makes a loud noise instead of firing bullets and is used for starting races

ˈstarting ˌpoint *noun* [C usually sing] (*UK ALSO* **start point**) a place or position where something begins: *The starting point for the guided tour of the town is in the market square.* ○ *The committee emphasised that its report was only meant as a starting point* ***for*** *discussion.*

ˈstarting ˌprice *noun* [C] (*ABBREVIATION* **SP**) *UK* the amount of money offered just at the start of a race by a BOOKMAKER for a winning bet

ˈstarting ˌsalary *noun* [C] the amount of money received when starting a particular type of job for the first time: *My starting salary as a newly qualified teacher wasn't enough to support a family.*

ˈstarting ˌtime *noun* [C] (*ALSO* **start time**) the planned time for starting an official activity: *The starting time for our monthly meetings will be 6.30.*

startle /ˈstɑː.tl̩/ [US] /ˈstɑːr.t̬l̩/ *verb* [T] to do something unexpected which surprises and sometimes worries a person or animal: *She was concentrating on her book and his voice startled her.* ○ *The noise of the car startled the birds and the whole flock flew up into the air.* ○ *Her article on diet startled many people* ***into*** *changing their eating habits.* **startled** /ˈstɑː.tl̩d/ [US] /ˈstɑːr.t̬l̩d/ *adj*: *a startled expression*

startling /ˈstɑː.tl̩ɪŋ/ [US] /ˈstɑːr.t̬lɪŋ/ *adj* surprising and sometimes worrying: *startling results* ○ *He made some startling admissions about his past.* **startlingly** /ˈstɑː.tl̩.ɪŋ.li/ [US] /ˈstɑːr.t̬l̩-/ *adv*: *startlingly poor results*

ˌstar ˈturn *noun* [C usually sing] either the main performer in a film, play or other show, or an extremely good performance by someone

starˈvation ˌdiet *noun* [C] when you eat only a very small amount of food in order to lose weight quickly: *She* ***went on*** *a starvation diet and ended up in hospital.*

starve /stɑːv/ [US] /stɑːrv/ *verb* **1** [I or T] to (cause to) become very weak or die because there is not enough food to eat: *Whole communities starved* ***to death*** *during the long drought.* ○ *From talking to former prisoners in the camps, an obvious conclusion is that they have been starved.* **2** [T often passive] If you are starved of something necessary or good, you do not receive enough of it: *People starved* ***of*** *sleep start to lose their concentration and may hallucinate.*

starved /stɑːvd/ [US] /stɑːrvd/ *adj* **1** *MAINLY US INFORMAL* very hungry **2 half-starved** dangerously thin: *A lot of these fashion models look half-starved to me.*

starving /ˈstɑː.vɪŋ/ [US] /ˈstɑːr-/ *adj* **1** dying because of not having enough food: *The cats were neglected and starving.* **2** *INFORMAL* very hungry: *Isn't lunch ready yet? I'm starving.*

starvation /stɑːˈveɪ.ʃᵊn/ [US] /stɑːr-/ *noun* [U] a lack of food during a long period, often causing death: *Twenty million people* ***face*** *starvation unless a vast emergency aid programme is launched.* ○ *The animals had* ***died of*** *starvation.* ○ *FIGURATIVE They pay starvation* ***wages*** (= not enough money to live on).

starving /ˈstɑː.vɪŋ/ [US] /ˈstɑːr-/ *adj* [after v] *SCOTTISH ENGLISH AND NORTHERN ENGLISH* extremely cold: *Could you put the heating on? I'm starving!*

ˈStar ˌwars *plural noun INFORMAL FOR* **SDI**

S

stash /stæʃ/ *verb* [T] *INFORMAL* to store or hide something, especially a large amount: *The stolen pictures were stashed (away) in a London warehouse.* stash /stæʃ/ *noun* [C] *They discovered a stash of money hidden at the back of a drawer.*

stasis /'steɪ.sɪs/ *noun* [U] *FORMAL* a state which does not change: *She was bored – her life was in stasis.*

state CONDITION /steɪt/ *noun* [C] a condition or way of being that exists at a particular time: *The building was in a state of disrepair.* ○ *She was found wandering in a confused state (of mind).* ○ *Give me the keys – you're in no fit state to drive.* ○ *After the accident I was in a state of shock.* ○ *I came home to an unhappy state of affairs* (= situation). ○ *The kitchen was in its original state, with a 1920s sink and stove.*
• **be in/get into a state** *MAINLY UK* to become nervous and upset: *She got into a real state before her driving test.*

state COUNTRY /steɪt/ *noun* **1** [C or U] a country or its government: *The drought is worst in the central African states.* ○ *Britain is one of the member states of the European Union.* ○ *The government was determined to reduce the number of state-owned industries.* ○ *Some theatres receive a small amount of funding from the state.* ○ *FORMAL His diary included comments on affairs/matters of state* (= information about government activities). ⊃See **country, land, nation, or state?** at **country** POLITICAL UNIT. **2** [C] a part of a large country with its own government, such as in Germany, Australia or the US: *Alaska is the largest state in the US.* ○ *Representatives are elected from each state.*
• **in state** If a king, queen or government leader does something in state, they do it in a formal way as part of an official ceremony: *The Queen rode in state to the opening of Parliament.*
• **the States** *INFORMAL* used to refer to the United States of America

state /steɪt/ *adj* [before n] **1** provided, created or done by the state: *state education/industries* ○ *state legislature/law* ○ *state control* ○ *state funding/pensions/subsidies* **2** formal, official and ceremonial when referring to activities involving a representative of the government or leader of the country: *the state opening of Parliament* ○ *a state funeral*

statecraft /'steɪt.krɑːft/ ⑥ /-kræft/ *noun* [U] the skill of governing a country

statehood /'steɪt.hʊd/ *noun* [U] the condition of being a country or a part of a large country that has its own government: *The US-Mexican War of 1846-48 was sparked by a dispute over impending Texas statehood.*

stateless /'steɪt.ləs/ *adj* A stateless person has no country that they officially belong to.

stateside /'steɪt.saɪd/ *adj, adv* related to the US; in or towards the US: *a stateside job* ○ *Some girls dream of finding an American husband to transport them stateside* (= to the United States).

statewide /'steɪt.waɪd/ /ˌ-'-/ *adj*: *statewide* (= in every part of a state) *elections*

state EXPRESS /steɪt/ *verb* [T] *SLIGHTLY FORMAL* to say or write something, especially clearly and carefully: *Our warranty clearly states the limits of our liability.* ○ [+ (that)] *Union members stated (that) they were unhappy with the proposal.* ○ [+ question word] *Please state why you wish to apply for this grant.* ○ *Children in the stated* (= named) *areas were at risk from a lack of food, the report said.*

statement /'steɪt.mənt/ *noun* [C] **1** something that someone says or writes officially, or an action done to express an opinion: *The government is expected to issue a statement about the investigation to the press.* ○ *He produced a signed statement from the prisoner.* ○ *He threw paint over the fur coats because he wanted to make a statement about cruelty to animals.* ○ [+ that] *We were not surprised by their statement that the train services would be reduced.* **2** (*ALSO* **bank statement**) a piece of paper which shows the amounts of money paid into and taken out of your bank account during a particular period of time

State Department *noun* [S] the part of the US government which deals with foreign matters

state line *noun* [C usually sing] *US* a border between two US states

stately /'steɪt.li/ *adj* *SLIGHTLY FORMAL* formal and splendid in style and appearance: *The procession moved through the mountain village at a stately pace.* ○ *He always walked with a stately bearing.* **stateliness** /'steɪt.lɪ.nəs/ *noun* [U]

stately home *noun* [C] *UK* a large old house which usually has beautiful furniture, decorations and gardens

state occasion *noun* [C] an official formal occasion, which has traditional ceremonies connected with it, and at which important members of the government, royalty, etc. are present

state of emergency *noun* [C] a temporary system of rules to deal with an extremely dangerous or difficult situation: *After the floods the government declared a state of emergency.*

state-of-the-art *adj* very modern and using the most recent ideas and methods: *a state-of-the-art computer* ○ *The control panel uses all the newest technology and is considered state-of-the-art.*

state premier *noun* [C] the leader of an Australian state government

stateroom /'steɪt.rʊm/ /-ruːm/ *noun* [C] a large room, especially in a castle or PALACE, which is used for formal or important occasions: *the staterooms at Windsor Castle*

state school *UK noun* [C] (*US* **public school**) a school that is free to go to because the government provides the money for it

state's evidence /ˌsteɪts'ev.ɪ.dənts/ *noun* [U] *US FOR* **Queen's evidence** *or* **King's evidence**

statesman /'steɪts.mən/ *noun* [C] *APPROVING* an experienced politician, especially one who is respected for making good judgments

statesmanlike /'steɪts.mən.laɪk/ *adj* *APPROVING* having or showing the qualities of a statesman: *a statesmanlike speech* **statesmanship** /'steɪts.mən.ʃɪp/ *noun* [U]

state visit *noun* [C] an official formal visit by the leader of one country to another

static NOT MOVING /'stæt.ɪk/ ⑥ /'stæt̬-/ *adj* staying in one place without moving, or not changing for a long time: *Oil prices have remained static for the last few months.*

static ELECTRICITY /'stæt.ɪk/ ⑥ /'stæt̬-/ *noun* [U] **1** noise on a radio or television caused by electricity in the air: *There's so much static on this radio I can't hear what they're saying.* **2** (*ALSO* **static electricity**) an electrical charge which collects on the surface of objects made from some types of material when they are rubbed

station BUSES/TRAINS /'steɪ.ʃən/ *noun* [C] a building and the surrounding area where buses or trains stop for people to get on or off: *a train/rail station* ○ *a bus/coach station* ○ *UK a railway station* ○ *Our office is near the station.* ○ *We looked on our map to find the nearest* (*UK*) *underground/tube/*(*US*) *subway/metro station.*

USAGE

station or **stop**?

Station is used for trains.

I'll meet you at the station in an hour.
a railway station
an underground station

Stop or bus stop is used for buses.

I stood at the bus stop for over half an hour.
Get off at the third stop.

A bus station is a place where many buses start or end their journeys.

station BROADCASTING /'steɪ.ʃən/ *noun* [C] a company which sends out radio or television broadcasts: *a radio/television station* ○ *a commercial/foreign station* ○ *a pirate* (= illegal) *station* ○ *The reception is not very good – try to tune in to another station.*

station SERVICE /'steɪ.ʃən/ *noun* [C] **1** a building or place used for a particular service or type of work: *a* (*UK*) *petrol/*(*US*) *gas station* ○ *a police/fire station* ○ *a biological research station* **2** *MAINLY AUS* a large farm with animals in Australia and New Zealand: *a sheep station*

station [POSITION] /ˈsteɪ.ʃᵊn/ *verb* **[T + adv or prep]** to cause especially soldiers to be in a particular place to do a job: *I hear your son's in the army – where's he stationed?* ○ *The regiment was stationed* ***in*** *Singapore for several years.* ○ *Armed guards were stationed around the airport.*
station /ˈsteɪ.ʃᵊn/ *noun* **[C]** a particular position that someone has been ordered to move into or to stay in: *The police* ***took up*** *their stations at the edge of the road, holding back the crowd.*

stationary /ˈsteɪ.ʃᵊn.ᵊr.i/ [US] /-ʃə.ner-/ *adj* not moving, or not changing: *a stationary car/train* ○ *The traffic got slower and slower until it was stationary.* ○ *The rate of inflation has been stationary for several months.*

ˈ**station ˌbreak** *noun* **[C]** *US* a pause in a television or radio broadcast for the broadcasting station to give its name

stationery /ˈsteɪ.ʃᵊn.ᵊr.i/ [US] /-ʃə.ner-/ *noun* **[U]** **1** the items needed for writing, such as paper, pens, pencils and envelopes **2** good quality paper for writing letters on and matching envelopes
stationer /ˈsteɪ.ʃᵊn.əz/ [US] /-ɚz/ *noun* **[C]** a person or business that sells stationery
stationer's /ˈsteɪ.ʃᵊn.əz/ [US] /-ɚz/ *noun* **[C]** *UK* a shop which sells stationery: *You'll be able to get a tube of glue at the stationer's down the road.*

ˈ**station ˌhouse** *noun* **[C]** *US INFORMAL FOR* **police station** or **fire station**

stationmaster /ˈsteɪ.ʃᵊnˌmɑː.stəʳ/ [US] /-ˌmæs.tɚ/ *noun* **[C]** the person who is in charge of a railway station

ˈ**station ˌwagon** *noun* **[C]** *US FOR* **estate (car)** ➲See picture **Cars and Trucks** on page Centre 13

statistics /stəˈtɪs.tɪks/ *plural noun* (*INFORMAL* **stats**) information based on a study of the number of times something happens or is present, or other NUMERICAL facts: *Statistics* ***show/suggest*** *that women live longer than men.* ○ *According to* ***official*** *statistics, the Japanese work longer hours than workers in most other industrialized countries.*
statistics /stəˈtɪs.tɪks/ *noun* **[U]** the science of using information discovered from studying numbers
statistic /stəˈtɪs.tɪk/ *noun* **[C]** a fact in the form of a number that shows information about something: *The city's most shocking statistic is its high infant mortality rate.*
statistical /stəˈtɪs.tɪ.kᵊl/ *adj* relating to statistics: *statistical errors/evidence* **statistically** /stəˈtɪs.tɪ.kli/ *adv*: *Statistically speaking, you're more likely to die from a bee sting than win the lottery.*
statistician /ˌstæt.ɪˈstɪʃ.ᵊn/ *noun* **[C]** someone who studies or is an expert in statistics

statue /ˈstætʃ.uː/ *noun* **[C]** an object made from a hard material, especially stone or metal, to look like a person or animal: *a statue* ***of*** *a boy* ○ *They planned to* ***put up/erect*** *a statue* ***to*** *the President.*
statuette /ˌstætʃ.uˈet/ *noun* **[C]** a statue which is small enough to stand on a table or shelf
statuary /ˈstætʃ.u.ᵊr.i/ [US] /-er-/ *noun* **[U]** *FORMAL* statues: *a display of garden statuary*

statuesque /ˌstætʃ.uˈesk/ *adj* A statuesque woman is attractively tall and large.

stature [REPUTATION] /ˈstætʃ.əʳ/ [US] /-ɚ/ *noun* **[U]** the good reputation a person or organization has, based on their behaviour and ability: *an artist* ***of*** *great stature* ○ *His stature* ***as*** *an art critic was tremendous.* ○ *If the school continues to* ***gain in*** *stature, it will attract the necessary financial support.*

stature [HEIGHT] /ˈstætʃ.əʳ/ [US] /-ɚ/ *noun* **[C usually sing]** *SLIGHTLY FORMAL* (especially of people) height: *His red hair and short stature made him easy to recognize.*

status [OFFICIAL POSITION] /ˈsteɪ.təs/ [US] /-t̬əs/ *noun* **[U]** an official position, especially in a social group: *The association works to promote the status of retired people as useful members of the community.* ○ *There has been an increase in applications for refugee status.* ○ *The success of her book has given her unexpected celebrity status.* ○ *Applicants should have a degree or a qualification of equal status.*

status [RESPECT] /ˈsteɪ.təs/ [US] /-t̬əs/ *noun* **[U]** the amount of respect, admiration or importance given to a person, organization or object: *high/low status* ○ *As the daughter of the president, she enjoys high status among her peers.* ○ *The leaders were often more concerned with status and privilege than with the problems of the people.*

the status quo /ðəˌsteɪ.təsˈkwəʊ/ [US] /-t̬əsˈkwoʊ/ *noun* **[S]** the present situation: *Certain people always want to* ***maintain*** *the status quo.*

ˈ**status ˌsymbol** *noun* **[C]** any thing which people want to have because they think other people will admire them if they have it: *Among young people, this brand of designer clothing is the* ***ultimate*** *status symbol.*

statute /ˈstætʃ.uːt/ *noun* **[C or U]** a law which has been formally approved and written down
● **statute book** *UK* When a law is on or reaches the statute book, it has been formally approved and written down and can be used in a law court.
statutory /ˈstæt.jʊ.tᵊr.i/ [US] /-tɔːr-/ *adj* decided or controlled by law: *statutory obligations*

staunch [LOYAL] /stɔːntʃ/ [US] /stɑːntʃ/ *adj* always loyal in supporting a person, organization or set of beliefs or opinions: *a staunch friend and ally* ○ *He gained a reputation as being a staunch* ***defender/supporter*** *of civil rights.*
staunchly /ˈstɔːntʃ.li/ [US] /stɑːntʃ-/ *adv* strongly: *staunchly loyal/independent* **staunchness** /ˈstɔːntʃ.nəs/ [US] /ˈstɑːntʃ-/ *noun* **[U]**

staunch [STOP] /stɔːntʃ/ [US] /stɑːntʃ/ *verb* **[T]** (*US ALSO* **stanch**) to stop something happening, or to stop liquid, especially blood, from flowing out: *The country's asylum laws were amended to staunch the* ***flow/flood*** *of economic migrants.* ○ *Mike pressed hard on the wound and staunched the* ***flow*** *of blood.*

stave *UK* /steɪv/ *noun* **[C]** (*US* **staff**) the five lines and four spaces between them on which musical notes are written

stave /steɪv/ *verb*

PHRASAL VERBS WITH **stave**

▲ **stave *sth* in** *phrasal verb* **[M]** *MAINLY UK* to push or hit something such as a door or other surface so that it breaks and falls inward: *A couple of teenagers were trying to stave in our shed door.* ○ *The front of the ship was stove in where it had hit the rock.*
▲ **stave *sth/sb* off** *phrasal verb* **[M]** to stop something bad from happening, or to keep an unwanted situation or person away, usually temporarily: *We were hoping to stave off these difficult decisions until September.*

staves /steɪvz/ *plural of* **staff** STICK and **stave**

stay [NOT LEAVE] /steɪ/ *verb* **[I]** to not move away from or leave: *They need an assistant who is willing to stay* ***for*** *six months.* ○ *Stay* ***until*** *the rain has stopped.* ○ *Can you stay after work to play tennis?* ○ *Because of the snow, schools have been closed and children told to stay* ***at home***/(*MAINLY US*) *stay* ***home***. ➲See Note **rest, stay or remain?** at **rest** STOP.
● **stay put** to remain in the same place or position: *Just stay put with the cases, while I go and find a taxi.*
● **here to stay** If something is here to stay, it has stopped being unusual and has become generally used or accepted: *Fax machines are here to stay.*

stay [CONTINUE] /steɪ/ *verb* **[I usually + adv or prep; L]** to continue doing something, or to continue to be in a particular state: *Stay away from the edge of the cliff.* ○ *He's decided not to stay* ***in*** *teaching/medicine/the army.* ○ *The final figures showed that most departments had stayed within budget.* ○ *It was so warm we stayed* ***(out)*** *in the garden until ten that night.* ○ *Put a lid on the pan so the food will stay hot.* ○ *The shops stay open until 9 o'clock.* ○ *They stayed friends after their divorce.*
● **stay on the sidelines** If you stay on the sidelines you are not an important part of what is happening.
● **stay the course** to continue doing something until it is finished or until you achieve something you have planned to do: *She interviewed slimmers who had failed to stay the course to find out why they had given up.*
stayer /ˈsteɪ.əʳ/ [US] /-ɚ/ *noun* **[C]** a person or animal that continues to try hard rather than giving up: *The horse isn't very fast but it's a stayer and always finishes even the longest races.*

S

stay [LIVE] /steɪ/ *verb* [I] to live or be in a place for a short time as a visitor: *I stayed* ***in*** *Montreal for two weeks then flew home.* ○ *They said they'd stay* ***at/in*** *a hotel.* ○ *The children usually stay* ***with*** *their grandparents for a week in the summer.*

• **stay overnight** (*ALSO* **stay the night**) to sleep somewhere for one night: *We've arranged to stay overnight at my sister's house.*

stay /steɪ/ *noun* [C] a period of time that you spend in a place: *She planned a short stay* ***at/in*** *a hotel to celebrate their anniversary.* **stayer** /ˈsteɪ.əʳ/ [US] /-ɚ/ *noun* [C] *The longest stayers are the British, who visit Australia to see friends and relatives.*

COMMON LEARNER ERROR

stay at/in a place

If you want to talk about **staying at** a place, such as a hotel, remember to use the prepositions 'at' or 'in'.

I was really impressed by the hotel we were staying at.
~~*I was really impressed by the hotel we were staying.*~~

stay [STOP PUNISHMENT] /steɪ/ *noun LEGAL* **stay of execution/deportation, etc.** an order by a judge which stops a judgment being performed until new information can be considered

PHRASAL VERBS WITH **stay**

▲ **stay behind** *phrasal verb* to not leave a place when other people leave: *I stayed behind after class.*

▲ **stay in** *phrasal verb* to stay in your home: *Let's stay in tonight and watch a video.*

▲ **stay on** *phrasal verb* to continue to be in a place, job or school after the other people who were with you have left: *Gill decided to stay on at university to do further research.* ○ *We asked him to stay on* ***as*** *youth leader for another year.*

▲ **stay out** *phrasal verb* [usually + adv or prep] to not come home at night, or to go home late: *Our cat usually stays out at night.* ○ *My mum won't let me stay out* ***late.***

▲ **stay out of** ***sth*** *phrasal verb* to not become involved in an argument or discussion: *It's better to stay out of their arguments.* ○ *You don't know anything about this, so just stay out of* ***it!***

▲ **stay up** *phrasal verb* to go to bed later than usual: *We stayed up* ***(late)*** *to watch a film.*

stay-at-home /ˈsteɪ.ət,həʊm/ [US] /-,hoʊm/ *noun* [C] *INFORMAL DISAPPROVING* someone who does not like to go to parties or events outside the home and is considered boring

ˈstaying ˌpower *noun* [U] If someone has staying power they always manage to continue doing what they have to do until it is finished.

St Bernard /ˌseɪntˈbɜː.nəd/ /ˌsənt-/ [US] /ˌseɪnt.bɚˈnɑːrd/ *noun* [C] a very large strong dog used especially in Switzerland in the past to find people lost in the mountains

STD [DISEASE] /ˌes.tiːˈdiː/ *noun* [C] *ABBREVIATION FOR* **sexually transmitted disease**

std [USUAL] *adj WRITTEN ABBREVIATION FOR* **standard** USUAL.

STD [TELEPHONE] /ˌes.tiːˈdiː/ *noun* [U] *ABBREVIATION FOR* subscriber trunk dialling: a system in Britain and Australia by which people make telephone calls over long distances

stead [IN PLACE OF] /sted/ *noun FORMAL* **in sb's stead** in place of someone: *The marketing manager was ill and her deputy ran the meeting in her stead.*

stead [STATE] /sted/ *noun* **stand sb in good stead** ➲See at **stand** STATE.

steadfast /ˈsted.fɑːst/ /-fəst/ [US] /-fæst/ *adj APPROVING* staying the same for a long time and not changing quickly or unexpectedly: *a steadfast friend/ally* ○ *steadfast loyalty* ○ *The group* ***remained*** *steadfast* ***in*** *its support for the new system, even when it was criticized in the newspapers.*

steadfastly /ˈsted.fɑːst.li/ /-fəst-/ [US] /-fæst-/ *adv* strongly and without stopping: *She was steadfastly in support of women's rights.* **steadfastness** /ˈsted.fɑːst.nəs/ /-fəst-/ [US] /-fæst-/ *noun* [U]

steady [GRADUAL] /ˈsted.i/ *adj* happening in a smooth, gradual and regular way, not suddenly or unexpectedly: *The procession moved through the streets at a steady pace.* ○ *Orders for new ships are rising, after several years of steady decline.* ○ *Over the last 10 years he has produced a steady* ***flow/stream/trickle*** *of articles and papers.* ○ *Progress has been* ***slow but*** *steady.*

steadily /ˈsted.ɪ.li/ *adv* gradually: *Prices have risen steadily.* **steadiness** /ˈsted.ɪ.nəs/ *noun* [U]

steady [FIRM] /ˈsted.i/ *adj* fixed and not moving or changing suddenly: *I'll* ***hold*** *the boat steady while you climb in.* ○ *Most rental prices have* ***held*** *steady this year.* ○ *Young people assume that if you are in a steady* ***relationship****, you don't have to worry about HIV.*

steady /ˈsted.i/ *verb* [T] to make something stop shaking or moving: *He wobbled about on the bike and then steadied himself.* ○ *He steadied his rifle on the wall and fired.*

steady /ˈsted.i/ *adv OLD-FASHIONED* **go steady (with** ***sb*****)** to have a romantic relationship with one person for a long period: *She's been going steady with Mike for six months.*

steady [CONTROLLED] /ˈsted.i/ *adj* **1** under control: *a steady voice/look/gaze* ○ *You need steady* ***nerves*** *to drive in city traffic.* ○ *Painting these small details needs a steady* ***hand.*** **2** describes someone who can be trusted to show good judgment and act in a reasonable way: *a steady friend*

• **go steady on** ***sth*** *UK* (*US* **go easy on** ***sth***) *INFORMAL* to not use too much of something: *Go steady on the milk, Dan – that's our last bottle.*

• **Steady on!** *UK INFORMAL* used to tell someone that what they are saying is too extreme: *Steady on, Chris – she's nice but she's not that nice!*

steady /ˈsted.i/ *verb* [T] to become calm and controlled, or to make someone do this: *Some people say that a drink will steady your nerves.*

steadily /ˈsted.ɪ.li/ *adv* calmly and in a controlled way: *She returned his gaze steadily.* **steadiness** /ˈsted.ɪ.nəs/ *noun* [U]

steak /steɪk/ *noun* [C or U] a thick, flat piece of meat or fish, especially meat from a cow: ***T-bone/sirloin*** *steaks* ○ *salmon/turkey steaks* ○ *Shall we have steak for dinner?*

ˈsteak ˌhouse *noun* [C] a restaurant that specializes in serving steak

ˈsteak ˌknife *noun* [C] a sharp knife with small teeth-like parts along one edge which cuts meat easily

steak tartare /ˌsteɪk.tɑːˈtɑːʳ/ [US] /-tɑːrˈtɑːr/ *noun* [U] steak cut into very small pieces and eaten without being cooked

steal [TAKE AWAY] /stiːl/ *verb* [I or T] **stole, stolen 1** to take something without the permission or knowledge of the owner and keep it: *She admitted stealing the money* ***from*** *her employers.* ○ *The number of cars which are stolen every year has risen.* ○ *They were so poor they had to steal in order to eat.* **2** to do something quickly or without being noticed: *She stole* ***a glance*** *at her watch.* ○ *He stole* ***out*** *of the room while no one was looking.*

• **steal the limelight** to get more attention than anyone or anything else in a situation: *The experimental car certainly stole the limelight at the motor show.*

• **steal a march on** ***sb*** If you steal a march on someone, you get an advantage over them by acting before they do: *Our rival company managed to steal a march on us by bringing out their software three months ahead of ours.*

• **steal the show/scene** to be the most popular or the best part of an event or situation: *The child with the dog stole the show.*

• **steal** ***sb's*** **thunder** to do what someone else was going to do before they do it, especially if this takes success or praise away from them: *Sandy stole my thunder when she announced that she was pregnant two days before I'd planned to tell people about my pregnancy.*

steal [CHEAP] /stiːl/ *noun* [S] *MAINLY US INFORMAL* an item that has a very low price, or a price that is much lower than the original cost: *I picked up a new iron at the sale – it was a steal.*

stealth /stelθ/ *noun* [U] movement which is quiet and careful in order not to be seen or heard, or secret or indirect action: *These thieves operate **with** terrifying stealth – they can easily steal from the pockets of unsuspecting travellers.* ○ *It would seem that some politicians would prefer to **use** financial stealth rather than legislation to produce change.* ○ *The weapons had been acquired **by** stealth.* **stealthy** /'stel.θi/ *adj*: *stealthy footsteps* **stealthily** /'stel.θɪ.li/ *adv*

stealth 'bomber *noun* [C] (*ALSO* **stealth fighter**) an aircraft which cannot be seen on RADAR ⊃See picture **Planes, Ships and Boats** on page Centre 14

steam /stiːm/ *noun* [U] the hot gas that is produced when water boils: *Steam rose from the simmering stew.* ○ *steam turbines* ○ *a steam engine/locomotive* ○ *the age of steam* (= the period when steam provided power for railways and factories) ○ *The pump is driven **by** steam.*
• **let/blow off steam** to do or say something that helps you to get rid of strong feelings or energy: *He lifts weights after work to let off steam.*
• **get/pick up steam** to start working much more effectively: *After the first three months, the fundraising project really started to pick up steam.*
• **under your own steam** If you do something under your own steam, you do it without help: *Do you want a lift or will you get there under your own steam?*

steam /stiːm/ *verb* **1** [I] to move by steam power: *The train/ship steamed **out** of the station/harbour.* **2** [T] to cook food using steam: *steamed vegetables* **3** [T usually + adv or prep] to use steam to soften something, especially glue so that something can be removed: *Ross steamed **open** the envelope to see if it was a love letter.*
• **steamed up** when a person shows their anger, especially about something that other people do not think is important: *She got all steamed up **about** the books being left on the tables.*

steamy /'stiː.mi/ *adj* **1** filled with steam, or hot and wet like steam: *steamy summer weather* ○ *a steamy kitchen/bathroom* **2** *INFORMAL* sexually exciting or including a lot of sexual activity: *a steamy love scene* ○ *His new novel is advertised as his steamiest yet.*

steaming /'stiː.mɪŋ/ *adj* producing steam: *a steaming bowl of soup*

▲ **steam (sth) up** *phrasal verb* [M] If glass or something with a glass or similar surface steams up, it becomes covered with a thin layer of water caused by steam touching it, and if you steam it up, you cause this to happen: *The bathroom mirror steamed up during my shower.* ○ *Going into the warm room steamed my glasses up.*

steamboat /'stiːm.bəʊt/ ⑥ /-boʊt/ *noun* [C] a boat which moves by steam power

steamer [BOAT] /'stiː.məʳ/ ⑥ /-mɚ/ *noun* [C] a boat or ship which moves by steam power

steamer [CONTAINER] /'stiː.məʳ/ ⑥ /-mɚ/ *noun* [C] a container with holes in the bottom which is put over boiling water in order to cook food in steam, or a machine which cooks food with steam: *a rice steamer* ○ *a vegetable steamer*

'steam ,iron *noun* [C] an electrical iron that has water inside and produces steam to help make clothes smooth

steamroller [VEHICLE] /'stiːm,rəʊ.ləʳ/ ⑥ /-,roʊ.lɚ/ *noun* [C] a vehicle which moves forward on a large heavy wheel in order to make a road surface flat

steamroller [FORCE] /'stiːm,rəʊ.ləʳ/ ⑥ /-,roʊ.lɚ/ *verb* [T] *INFORMAL* to use great force either to make someone do something or on something to make it happen or be successful: *He steamrollered the plan **through** the committee.* ○ *I hate being steamrollered **into** do**ing** something I don't want to.*

steamroller /'stiːm,rəʊ.ləʳ/ ⑥ /-,roʊ.lɚ/ *noun* [C] *INFORMAL* a person who forces other people to agree with them and prevents any opposition

steamship /'stiːm.ʃɪp/ *noun* [C] a ship which moves by steam power

'steam ,shovel *noun* [C] *US FOR* **excavator** ⊃See at **excavate.**

steamy /'stiː.mi/ *adj* ⊃See at **steam.**

steed /stiːd/ *noun* [C] *LITERARY* a horse which is ridden: *a fine white steed*

steel [METAL] /stiːl/ *noun* [U] a strong metal which is a mixture of iron and carbon, and which is used for making things which need a strong structure, especially vehicles and buildings: *steel girders/rods/struts* ○ *a steel helmet* ○ *a steel-plated army truck*
steely /'stiː.li/ *adj* **1** like steel in colour: *steely grey* **2** very strong and determined: *steely eyes/nerves* ○ *steely determination* ○ *a steely look/stare*

steel yourself [PREPARE] *verb* [R] to force yourself to get ready to do something unpleasant or difficult: [+ to infinitive] *She steeled herself **to** jump out of the plane.*

'steel ,band *noun* [C] a group of musicians who play steel drums

'steel 'drum *noun* [C usually pl] a large oil container which has been made into a musical instrument and is played like a drum

'steel ,mill *noun* [C] a factory where steel is made

'steel 'wool *noun* [U] (*UK ALSO* **wire wool**) a thick layer of thin steel threads twisted together, small pieces of which can be used to rub a surface smooth

steelworks /'stiːl.wɜːks/ ⑥ /-wɝːks/ *group noun* [C] *plural* **steelworks** a factory where steel is made

steelworker /'stiːl.wɜːkəʳ/ ⑥ /-,wɝː.kɚ/ *noun* [C] a person who works in a factory making steel

steep [NOT GRADUAL] /stiːp/ *adj* **1** (of a slope) rising or falling at a sharp angle: *a steep slope* ○ *It's a steep **climb** to the top of the mountain, but the view is worth it.* ○ *The castle is set on a steep **hill/hillside**.* **2** A steep rise or fall is one which goes very quickly from low to high or from high to low: *There has been a steep **increase/rise** in prices.*
steepen /'stiː.pən/ *verb* **1** [I or T] to become steeper, or to make something do this: *The trail began to steepen near the top of the hill.* **2** [I] If something such as a cost steepens, it increases: *Our costs have steepened since we began this project.* **steeply** /'stiː.pli/ *adv*: *The beach slopes steeply down to the sea.* ○ *The value of the land has risen steeply.* **steepness** /'stiː.pnəs/ *noun* [U]

steep [TOO MUCH] /stiːp/ *adj INFORMAL* (especially of prices) too much, or more than is reasonable: *They are having to face very steep taxes.* ○ *We enjoyed our meal at the restaurant, but the bill was **a bit** steep.* ○ *The membership fees at the golf club are **pretty** steep.*

steep [MAKE WET] /stiːp/ *verb* [I or T] to cause to stay in a liquid, especially in order to become soft or clean or to improve flavour: *Leave the cloth to steep in the dye overnight.* ○ *We had pears steeped in red wine for dessert.*
• **steeped in blood** *LITERARY* describes a place where many people have died in a violent way, or a person responsible for the deaths of many people: *The castle's history is steeped in blood.*

▲ **steep sth/sb in sth** *phrasal verb* If something or someone is steeped in something, they are completely surrounded by or involved in it, or they know a lot about it: *The college is steeped in **history/tradition**.* ○ *These ancient scholars were steeped in poetry and painting, as well as maths and astronomy.*

steeple /'stiː.pl̩/ *noun* [C] a pointed structure on the top of a church tower, or the tower and the pointed structure considered as one unit: *a church steeple*

steeplechase /'stiː.pl̩.tʃeɪs/ *noun* [C] a long race in which horses or people have to jump over fences, bushes, etc., either across the countryside or, more usually, on a track

steeplejack /'stiː.pl̩.dʒæk/ *noun* [C] a person whose job is to climb high buildings in order to repair, paint, clean them, etc.

steer [DIRECT] /stɪəʳ/ ⑥ /stɪr/ *verb* **1** [I or T] to control the direction of a vehicle: *She carefully steered the car around the potholes.* ○ *This car is very easy to steer.* **2** [I or T] If a vehicle steers, it follows a particular route or direction: *The ship passed Land's End, then steered towards southern Ireland.* **3** [T usually + adv or prep] to take someone or something, or cause them to go, in the direction in which you want them to go: *She steered her guests into the dining room.* ○ *I'd like to steer our discussion **back to** our original topic.* ○ *The main task of the* *new government will be to steer the country* ***towards*** *democracy.*

• **steer a course/path** to take a series of actions, usually of a particular type, carefully and intentionally: *It will be difficult to steer a* ***middle*** *course* ***between*** *the competing claims of the two sides in the conflict.*

• **steer clear of** to avoid someone or something which seems unpleasant, risky or dangerous: *Her speech steered clear of controversial issues.* ○ *They warned their children to steer clear of drugs.*

steer [MALE COW] /stɪəʳ/ [US] /stɪr/ *noun* [C] a young male of the cattle family that has had its sex organs removed, and which is usually kept for meat

'steering ˌcolumn *noun* [C] the part of a vehicle that the STEERING WHEEL is attached to: *My car has an adjustable steering column.*

'steering comˌmittee *group noun* [C] a group of people who are chosen to direct the way something is dealt with

'steering ˌwheel *noun* [C] a wheel in a vehicle which the driver turns in order to make the vehicle go in a particular direction ➲See picture **Car** on page Centre 12

stein /staɪn/ *noun* [C] **1** a very large cup, usually made of clay and often decorated, which has a handle and a lid, and is used for drinking beer **2** *US FOR* **tankard**

stellar /'stel.əʳ/ [US] /-ɚ/ *adj* **1** of a star or stars: *a stellar explosion* ○ *stellar light* **2** *INFORMAL* describes people or their activities that are of an extremely high standard: *a stellar performance/player/team*

stem [CENTRAL PART] /stem/ *noun* [C] **1** a central part of something from which other parts can develop or grow, or which forms a support **2** the stick-like central part of a plant which grows above the ground and from which leaves and flowers grow, or a smaller thin part which grows from the central part and which supports the leaves and flowers: *flower stems* **3** the vertical part of a glass or similar container which supports the part into which you put liquid: *Champagne glasses usually have long stems.* **4** the part of a word that is left after you take off the part which changes when forming a plural, past tense, etc: *From the stem 'sav-' you get 'saves', 'saved', 'saving' and 'saver'.* **5** *US* the small part on the side of the watch which you turn to change the position of the pointers on the watch, or to make the watch operate **6** the main supporting structure at the front of a ship

• **from stem to stern** *US* from one end of something to the other: *We overhauled the car from stem to stern.*

-stemmed /-stemd/ *suffix* having the stated type of stem: *a thick-stemmed plant* ○ *a long-stemmed wine glass*

stem [STOP] /stem/ *verb* [T] **-mm- 1** to stop something unwanted from spreading or increasing: *These measures are designed to stem the rise of violent crime.* ○ *We must take action to stem the* ***tide*** *of resignations.* **2** to stop the flow of a liquid such as blood: *She tied a handkerchief around the wound to stem the* ***flow*** *of blood.*

▲ **stem from** ***sth*** *phrasal verb* to originate or develop as the result of something: *Her problems stem from her difficult childhood.* ○ *Their disagreement stemmed from a misunderstanding.*

'stem ˌcell *noun* [C] a cell, especially one taken from a person or animal in a very early stage of development, that can develop into any other type of cell

stench /stentʃ/ *noun* **1** [C usually sing] a strong unpleasant smell: *the stench* ***of*** *rotting fish/burning rubber/cigarette smoke* ○ *an* ***overpowering*** *stench* **2** [S] *LITERARY* a bad effect that follows an unpleasant event or situation and is noticeable for a long time: *For some time after the minister's resignation, the stench* ***of*** *scandal hung over the government.*

stencil /'stent.səl/ *noun* [C] **1** a piece of card, plastic, metal, etc. into which shapes have been cut, and which is used to draw or paint patterns onto a surface **2** a picture made by drawing or painting through the holes in such a piece of card, etc. onto a surface: *She did a stencil* ***of*** *a rainbow on her daughter's bedroom wall.*

stencil /'stent.səl/ *verb* [T] **-ll-** or *US USUALLY* **-l-** to draw or paint something using a stencil

stenographer /stə'nɒg.rə.fəʳ/ [US] /-'nɑː.grə.fɚ/ *noun* [C] (*US INFORMAL ALSO* **steno**) a **shorthand typist**

stenography /stə'nɒg.rə.fi/ [US] /-'nɑː.grə-/ *noun* [U] **shorthand**

stentorian /sten'tɔː.ri.ən/ [US] /-'tɔːr.i-/ *adj FORMAL* using a very loud voice, or (of a voice) very loud: *a stentorian preacher* ○ *Suddenly a stentorian* ***voice*** *boomed across the room.*

step [FOOT MOVEMENT] /step/ *noun* **1** [C] the act of lifting one foot and putting it down on a different part of the ground, such as when you walk or run: *Sophie* ***took*** *her first steps when she was eleven months old.* ○ *He rose to his feet and* ***took*** *a couple of steps* ***towards*** *her.* ○ ***With*** *every step, her feet hurt her more and more.* ○ *I* ***retraced*** *my steps, looking for my lost keys.* ➲See also **footstep**. **2** [C] the distance you cover when you take a step: *I'd only gone a few steps down the road when I realized I'd forgotten to lock the door.* **3** [U] the way in which you move your feet when you are walking or running which can sometimes show how you are feeling: *She walked out of the office with* ***a spring in*** *her step* (= in a way that showed she was happy). ○ *The driver told us to* ***mind/watch*** *our step* (= walk carefully) *as we got off the bus.* **4** [C] a particular movement that you make with your feet when you dance: *She's teaching me some basic* ***dance*** *steps.*

• **a few/couple of steps** *INFORMAL* a short distance: *The museum is just a few steps from the hotel.*

• **mind/watch *your* step** be careful about how you behave, or you will get into trouble: *You need to watch your step, young lady!*

• **in step 1** when you lift your feet off the ground and put them down again at the same time as other people: *The soldiers marched in step.* **2** describes opinions, ideas or ways of living that are the same as those of other people: *Television companies need to* ***keep*** *in step* ***with*** *public opinion.*

• **out of step 1** when you do not lift the same foot and put it down again at the same time as other people: *I'm no good at dancing – I always get hopelessly out of step.* **2** describes opinions, ideas or ways of living that are different from those of other people: *The Republicans are out of step* ***with*** *the country, Williams said.* ○ *He thinks that everyone is out of step except him.*

step /step/ *verb* [I + adv or prep] **-pp-** to move by lifting your foot and putting it down in a different place, or to put your foot on or in something: *She stepped* ***backwards*** *and fell over a chair.* ○ *They stepped* ***out*** *onto the balcony.* ○ *Be careful not to step* ***in*** *the mud.* ○ *Ow, you stepped* ***on*** *my foot!* ○ *MAINLY US I'm afraid Mr Taylor has just stepped* (= gone) ***out*** *for a few minutes, but I'll tell him you called.* ○ *FORMAL Would you care to step this way please, sir?*

• **step back (in time)** to go back into the past: *Visiting her house was like stepping back in time/stepping back 50 years.*

• **step into the breach** If you step into the breach, you do someone else's work when they are unable to do it: *Gill's sudden illness meant that Kathy had to step into the breach.*

• **step on it** *INFORMAL* used to tell someone to drive faster or to hurry: *Could you step on it? I'm late.*

• **step out of line** to behave in a way that is unacceptable or not expected: *Step out of line one more time Peters, and you're fired!*

step [STAGE] /step/ *noun* [C] **1** a stage in a process: *What's the next step in the programme?* ○ *We must stay one step* ***ahead*** *of our competitors.* ○ *Most people believe that the decision to cut interest rates was a step* ***in the right direction.*** ○ *Let's take things* ***a*** *step/****one*** *step* ***at a time*** (= slowly). ○ *Following the success of our products in Europe, our logical* ***next*** *step is to move into the American market.* **2** an action in a series of actions taken for a particular purpose: *The country is* ***taking*** *its first tentative steps towards democracy.* ○ *We need to* ***take*** *drastic steps* ***to*** *reduce pollution.* ○ *The President* ***took*** *the unusual step* ***of*** *altering his prepared speech in order to condemn the terrorist attack.*

• **a step forward** an improvement or development: *No one is sure whether this plan will work, but it's a step forward.*

S

• **a step backwards** (*ALSO* **a backward step**) going back to a worse or less developed state: *The changes that have been introduced are being seen as a step backwards.*
• **one step forward, two steps back** If you take one step forward, two steps back, you advance but then experience events which cause you to be further behind than you were when you made the advance.
• **step by step** dealing with one thing and then another thing in a fixed order: *step-by-step instructions* ○ *Don't worry – I'll go through the procedure with you step by step.*

step [SURFACE] /step/ *noun* [C] one of the surfaces that you walk on when you go up or down stairs: *a flight of steps* ○ *We had to* ***climb*** *some steps to reach the front door.* ○ *I asked them to leave the parcel on the* ***(front)*** *step* (= outside the door to the house). ○ *(UK)* ***Mind the*** *step/(US)* ***watch your*** *step as you leave the train.* ○ *It's difficult for people in wheelchairs to* ***negotiate*** (= move up and down) *steps.* ○ *One of the steps* ***on*** *the ladder is broken.*
steps /steps/ *plural noun UK* another word for **stepladder**: *kitchen steps* ○ *library steps*

step [MUSIC] /step/ *noun* [C] *US FOR* **tone** DIFFERENCE IN SOUND.

step- [RELATIONSHIP] /step-/ *prefix* being of the stated relationship to someone through the previous marriage of their husband or wife, or through their mother or father marrying again: *stepfather* ○ *stepmother* ○ *stepchildren*

PHRASAL VERBS WITH **step** ▼

▲ **step aside** [MAKE SPACE] *phrasal verb FORMAL* to step sideways to make a space for someone else: *Step aside, please – this lady needs a doctor.*
▲ **step aside/down** [LEAVE] *phrasal verb* to leave an important job or position, especially to allow someone else to take your place: *He has decided to step down* ***as*** *captain of the team.* ○ *He is unwilling to step aside* ***in favour of*** *a younger person.*
▲ **step back** *phrasal verb MAINLY UK* to temporarily stop being involved in an activity or situation in order to think about it in a new way: *Let's just step back* ***from*** *the problem and think about what we could do.*
▲ **step *sth* down** *phrasal verb* [M] to reduce the amount, supply or rate of something: *The doctor has said that I can start stepping down my medication in a few days' time.* ○ *This device is used for stepping down the* ***voltage***.
▲ **step forward** *phrasal verb* to offer to provide or do something, or to help with something: *No one has yet stepped forward* ***to*** *claim responsibility for the attack.* ○ *At the last minute another company stepped forward* ***with*** *a bid.*
▲ **step in** *phrasal verb* to become involved in a difficult situation or argument in order to help find a solution: [+ to infinitive] *An outside buyer has stepped in* ***to*** *save the company from going out of business.* ○ *When the leading actress broke her leg, Isobel stepped in and took over.*
▲ **step into *sth*** *phrasal verb UK INFORMAL* If you step into a job, you get it very easily: *He just stepped* ***straight*** *into a job as soon as he left college.*
▲ **step on *sb*** *phrasal verb INFORMAL* to treat someone unfairly or unkindly
▲ **step out on *sb*** *phrasal verb US INFORMAL* If you step out on your husband, wife or usual sexual partner, you have sexual relationships with people other than them.
▲ **step *sth* up** *phrasal verb* [M] to increase the size, amount or speed of a process that is intended to achieve something: *The police are stepping up their efforts to fight crime.* ○ *Following the bomb explosion, security has been stepped up at the airport.*

ˈstep aeˌrobics *noun* [U] (*ALSO* **step**) a type of exercise usually done to music in which you quickly step on and off a slightly raised surface

stepbrother /ˈstepˌbrʌð.əʳ/ [US] /-ðɚ/ *noun* [C] not your parents' son, but the son of a person one of your parents has married ➲Compare **half-brother**.

stepchild /ˈstep.tʃaɪld/ *noun* [C] *plural* **stepchildren** the child of your husband or wife from a previous marriage

stepdad /ˈstep.dæd/ *noun* [C] *US INFORMAL FOR* **stepfather**

stepdaughter /ˈstepˌdɔː.təʳ/ [US] /-ˌdɑː.t̬ɚ/ *noun* [C] the daughter of your husband or wife from a previous marriage

stepfather /ˈstepˌfɑː.ðəʳ/ [US] /-ðɚ/ *noun* [C] the man who is married to someone's mother but who is not their real father

stepladder /ˈstepˌlæd.əʳ/ [US] /-ɚ/ *noun* [C] (*UK ALSO* **steps**) a short, folding platform with steps: *I can't reach the top shelf unless I use a stepladder.*

stepmum *UK* /ˈstep.mʌm/ *noun* [C] (*US* **stepmom**) *INFORMAL FOR* **stepmother**

stepmother /ˈstepˌmʌð.əʳ/ [US] /-ɚ/ *noun* [C] the woman who is married to someone's father but who is not their real mother

step-parent /ˈstepˌpeə.rᵊnt/ [US] /-ˌper.ᵊnt/ *noun* [C] the man or woman who is married to someone's mother or father but who is not their real father or mother

steppe /step/ *noun* [C usually pl; U] a large area of land with grass but no trees, especially in southeastern Europe, Russia and northern Asia: *These people have lived for centuries on* ***the*** *Russian steppes.*

ˈstepping ˌstone [STONE] *noun* [C] one of a row of large flat stones on which you can walk in order to cross a stream or river that is not deep

ˈstepping ˌstone [STAGE OF ACHIEVEMENT] *noun* [S] an event or experience that helps you achieve something else: *I see this job just as a stepping stone* ***to*** *better things.*

stepsister /ˈstepˌsɪs.təʳ/ [US] /-tɚ/ *noun* [C] not your parents' daughter, but the daughter of a person one of your parents has married ➲Compare **half-sister**.

stepson /ˈstep.sʌn/ *noun* [C] the son of your husband or wife from a previous marriage

stereo /ˈster.i.əʊ/ [US] /-oʊ/ *noun* **1** [U] a way of recording or playing sound so that it is separated into two signals and produces more natural sound: *The concert will be broadcast* ***in*** *stereo.* **2** [C] a piece of electrical equipment for playing CDs and tapes, listening to the radio, etc. that sounds very natural because the sounds come out of two SPEAKERS (= parts for playing sound) **stereo** /ˈster.i.əʊ/ [US] /-oʊ/ *adj* (*FORMAL* **stereophonic**) *a stereo system* ➲Compare **mono** SOUND; **quadraphonic**.

stereotype /ˈster.i.ə.taɪp/ *noun* [C] *DISAPPROVING* a fixed idea that people have about what someone or something is like, especially an idea that is wrong: *racial/sexual stereotypes* ○ *He doesn't* ***conform to/fit/fill*** *the national stereotype* ***of*** *a Frenchman.* ○ *The characters in the book are just stereotypes.*
stereotype /ˈster.i.ə.taɪp/ *verb* [T] *DISAPPROVING* to have a fixed idea about what a particular type of person is like, especially an idea that is wrong: *The study claims that British advertising stereotypes women.* ○ *We tried not to give the children sexually stereotyped toys.*
stereotypical /ˌster.i.əˈtɪp.ɪ.kᵊl/ *adj DISAPPROVING* having the qualities that you expect a particular type of person to have: *Customers are tired of the stereotypical, fast-talking salesperson.* **stereotypically** /ˌster.i.əˈtɪp.ɪ.kli/ *adv*

sterile [UNABLE TO PRODUCE] /ˈster.aɪl/ [US] /-ᵊl/ *adj* **1** (of a living being) unable to produce young, or (of land) unable to produce plants or crops: *Mules are usually sterile.* ○ *One of the side effects of the drug could be to make men sterile.* **2** lacking in imagination or new ideas or energy: *a sterile argument*
sterility /stəˈrɪl.ɪ.ti/ [US] /-ə.t̬i/ *noun* [U] **1** (in animals and people) the condition of being unable to produce young, or (in plants) the condition of being unable to produce plants or crops **2** when you have no imagination, new ideas or energy: *Over a bottle of wine, we shared our despair over the emotional sterility* ***of*** *our marriages.*
sterilize, *UK USUALLY* **-ise** /ˈster.ɪ.laɪz/ *verb* [T] to perform a medical operation on someone in order to make them unable to have children: *After having five children, she decided to be sterilized.*
sterilization, *UK USUALLY* **-isation** /ˌster.ɪ.laɪˈzeɪ.ʃᵊn/ *noun* [U] the process of having a medical operation to make it impossible to have children: *My wife and I have discussed sterilization, but we haven't made a decision about it yet.*

S

sterile [CLEAN] /ˈster.aɪl/ [US] /-ᵊl/ *adj* completely clean and free from dirt and bacteria: *The operation must be carried out under sterile conditions.*

sterilization, *UK USUALLY* **-isation** /ˌster.ɪ.laɪˈzeɪ.ʃᵊn/ *noun* [U] the process of making something completely clean and free from bacteria: *The needles have been sent off for sterilization.*

sterilize, *UK USUALLY* **-ise** /ˈster.ɪ.laɪz/ *verb* [T] to make something completely clean and free from bacteria: *All equipment must be sterilized before use.*

sterilizer, *UK USUALLY* **-iser** /ˈster.ɪ.laɪ.zəʳ/ [US] /-zɚ/ *noun* [C] a machine for making things completely clean and free from bacteria

sterilizing, *UK USUALLY* **-ise** /ˈster.ɪ.laɪ.zɪŋ/ *adj* making something completely clean and free from bacteria: *I put my contact lenses in sterilizing* ***solution*** *every night.*

sterling [MONEY] /ˈstɜː.lɪŋ/ [US] /ˈstɝː-/ *noun* [U] British money: *The value of sterling increased against several other currencies yesterday.* ○ *If you buy things on the plane, you can either pay for them in* ***pounds*** *sterling* (= British pounds) *or in US dollars.*

sterling [METAL] /ˈstɜː.lɪŋ/ [US] /ˈstɝː-/ *adj* (of precious metal, especially silver) of a fixed standard of purity: *a sterling silver candlestick*

sterling [ADMIRABLE] /ˈstɜː.lɪŋ/ [US] /ˈstɝː-/ *adj APPROVING* of a very high standard, or admirable: *You've done a sterling job.* ○ *Everyone has made a sterling effort.*

stern [SEVERE] /stɜːn/ [US] /stɝːn/ *adj* **1** severe, or showing disapproval: *a stern look/warning/voice* ○ *She is her own sternest critic.* ○ *Journalists received a stern warning not to go anywhere near the battleship.* **2** If something, such as a job, is stern, it is difficult: *The President is facing the sternest test of his authority since he came to power five years ago.*

• **made of sterner stuff** If someone is described as being made of sterner stuff, they are very strong and determined: *I was ready to give up the fight, but Nicky was made of sterner stuff and wanted us to carry on.*

sternly /ˈstɜːn.li/ [US] /ˈstɝːn-/ *adv* in a way that shows disapproval: *"This kind of behaviour is not acceptable," said the teacher sternly.* **sternness** /ˈstɜːn.nəs/ [US] /ˈstɝːn-/ *noun* [U]

stern [SHIP PART] /stɜːn/ [US] /stɝːn/ *noun* [C] the back part of a ship or boat ➲Compare **bow** FRONT PART.

sternum /ˈstɜː.nəm/ [US] /ˈstɝː-/ *noun* [C] *plural* **sternums** or **sterna** *SPECIALIZED* a **breastbone** ➲See picture **The Body** on page Centre 5

steroid /ˈstɪə.rɔɪd/ /ˈster.ɔɪd/ [US] /ˈstɪr.ɔɪd/ *noun* [C] **1** one of a variety of chemical substances that is produced in the body **2** an artificial form of a natural chemical substance which is used for treating particular medical conditions: *I'm taking steroids/I'm* ***on*** *steroids for my asthma.* **3** a drug which increases the development of your muscles, sometimes taken illegally by people taking part in sports competitions

stethoscope /ˈsteθ.ə.skəʊp/ [US] /-skoʊp/ *noun* [C] a piece of medical equipment which doctors use to listen to your heart and lungs

Stetson /ˈstet.sᵊn/ *noun* [C] *TRADEMARK* a hat with a wide, curving lower edge, especially worn by cowboys ➲See picture **Hairstyles and Hats** on page Centre 8

stevedore /ˈstiː.və.dɔːʳ/ [US] /-dɔːr/ *noun* [C] a **docker**

stew /stjuː/ [US] /stuː/ *noun* [C or U] a type of food consisting usually of meat or fish and vegetables cooked slowly in a small amount of liquid: *lamb/bean/fish stew* ○ *She prepared a* ***hearty*** *stew for dinner.*

• **in a stew** *INFORMAL* If someone is in a stew, they are in a difficult situation which causes them to feel anxious or upset: *William is in a stew* ***about/over*** *the demand he received from the tax office.*

stew /stjuː/ [US] /stuː/ *verb* **1** [T] to cook meat, fish, vegetables or fruit slowly and gently in a little liquid **2** [I] *INFORMAL* to be angry: *You're not still stewing about what happened yesterday, are you?* **3** [I] *UK* to do nothing productive: *With jobs so scarce, many young people spend long hours with little to do but drink and stew.*

• **stew (in *your* own juice)** *INFORMAL* to think about or suffer the results of your own foolish actions, without anyone giving you any help

stewed /stjuːd/ [US] /stuːd/ *adj* **1** *UK* describes tea that has been kept too long before it is poured, and is therefore strong and bitter **2** *MAINLY US INFORMAL* drunk

steward /ˈstjuː.əd/ [US] /ˈstuː.ɚd/ *noun* [C] **1** a person whose job it is to organize a particular event, or to provide services to particular people, or to take care of a particular place: *Stewards will be inspecting the race track at 9.00.* ○ *If you need help at any time during the conference, one of the stewards will be pleased to help you.* **2** (*FEMALE* **stewardess**) a person who serves passengers on a ship or aircraft **3** *UK* a person who organizes the supply and serving of food at a CLUB: *He's the steward* ***of*** *the City of Wakefield's Working Men's Club.*

stewardship /ˈstjuː.əd.ʃɪp/ [US] /ˈstuː.ɚd-/ *noun* [U] Someone's stewardship of something is the way in which that person controls or organizes it: *The company has been very successful while it has been* ***under*** *the stewardship* ***of*** *Mr White.*

ˈstewing/ˈbraising ˌsteak *noun* [U] *UK* meat from cattle which is usually cut into small pieces and cooked slowly in liquid

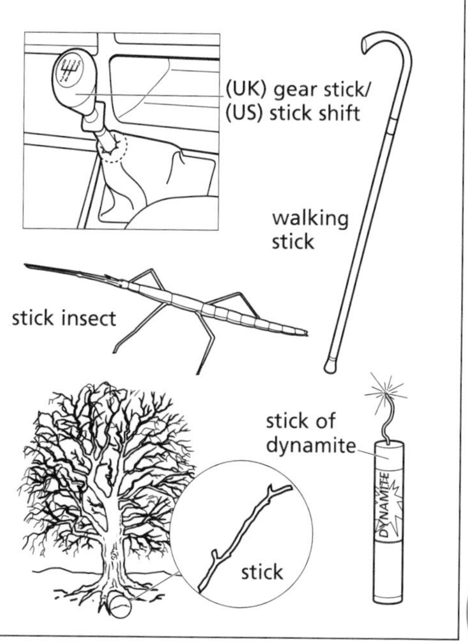

Stick

stick [THIN PIECE] /stɪk/ *noun* [C] **1** a thin piece of wood: *The old man was carrying a load of sticks.* ○ *Police said that the child had been beaten with a stick.* ○ *Find some dry sticks and we'll make a campfire.* ○ *A lollipop is a sweet on a stick* (= a short thin piece of wood, plastic or paper). **2** *MAINLY UK* a long, thin wooden pole that especially old or injured people use to help them walk: *a* ***walking*** *stick* ○ *At 84 he's still quite active, although he walks with the aid of a stick.* **3** a long thin piece of wood with a curved end used in playing hockey, or a long thin piece of wood with a triangular shaped net at one end used for playing LACROSSE, or a long thin piece of wood with a solid tube-shaped piece fixed horizontally to one end of it used for playing POLO: *a hockey/lacrosse/polo stick* **4** A stick **of** something is a long thin piece of it: *carrot/bread sticks* ○ *a stick of* ***celery/rhubarb/chewing gum/chalk/dynamite*** **5** *INFORMAL* a piece of furniture: *When they got married, they didn't have a stick* ***of furniture.***

• **a stick to beat *sb* with** *UK* something that you can use to criticize, influence or cause difficulty for someone or something you dislike or disapprove of: *The party has a*

S

number of sticks with which to beat the prime minister into submission.

• **take a stick to** to hit someone or something with a long thin piece of wood: *He said that when he was a boy, his father used to take a stick to him to punish him.*

• **up sticks** *UK* (*US* **pull up stakes**) *INFORMAL* to take all the things that you own and go and live in a different place: *This is the fourth time in five years that we've had to up sticks.*

• **Sticks and stones may break my bones, (but words can never hurt me).** *CHILD'S EXPRESSION SAYING* said in order to show to that people cannot be hurt by unpleasant things that are said to them

stick [CRITICISM] /stɪk/ *noun* [U] *UK INFORMAL* severe criticism: *I really **got/took** stick from my boss about being late for work again.* ○ *We **gave** him some stick for wearing that silly hat.*

stick [PUSH INTO] /stɪk/ *verb* [I or T; usually + adv or prep] **stuck, stuck** to push a pointed object into or through something, or (of a pointed object) to be pushed into or through something and stay there: *She stuck the needle **into** my arm.* ○ *We decided where to go for our holiday by closing our eyes and sticking a pin **in** the map.* ○ *A thorn stuck **in** her finger.* ○ *The metal springs were sticking **through** the mattress.*

stick [FIX] /stɪk/ *verb* **stuck, stuck 1** [I or T] to cause something to become fixed as if with glue or another similar substance: *I tried to stick the pieces together with some glue/tape.* ○ *He stuck **up** a notice on the board **with** pins.* ○ *This glue won't stick.* ○ *My car's stuck **in** the mud.* ○ *Stir the sauce so that it doesn't stick **to** the pan.* ○ *My book got wet and all the pages have stuck **together**.* ➲Compare **non-stick**; **stuck** FIXED. **2** [I] If a name sticks, it continues to be used: *Although her name is Clare, her little sister called her Lali, and somehow the name stuck.*

• **make *sth* stick** *INFORMAL* to show that a statement or accusation is true: *They've arrested him for fraud but they'll never make the **charges** stick.*

• **stick in *your* throat/craw** to make you angry: *It really sticks in my throat **that** I did all the work, and she's getting all the credit.*

• **stick in *your* mind/head/memory** *INFORMAL* to remember something

• **stick to *sb's* ribs** If you describe food as sticking to your ribs, you mean that it makes you feel like you have eaten a lot.

sticky /ˈstɪk.i/ *adj* **1** made of or covered with a substance that stays fixed to any surface it touches: *sticky tape* ○ *sticky fingers* ○ *The floor's still sticky where I spilled the juice.* ○ *The children's faces were sticky **with** chocolate.* **2** If the weather is sticky, it is very hot and the air feels wet. ➲See also **humid**. **3** *INFORMAL* difficult: *There were a few sticky moments during the meeting, but everything turned out all right in the end.* **4** *UK INFORMAL* unwilling to agree: *Their bank manager was sticky **about** lending them the money they wanted to borrow.*

• **have sticky fingers** *INFORMAL* to be likely to steal: *The last person we hired in the shop turned out to have sticky fingers.*

• **come to/meet a sticky end** *UK HUMOROUS* to die in an unpleasant way: *He comes to a sticky end halfway through the film.*

stickiness /ˈstɪk.ɪ.nəs/ *noun* [U] the quality of being sticky

stick [NOT CONTINUE] /stɪk/ *verb* [I] **stuck, stuck** In some card games, if you stick, you say that you do not want to be given any more cards.

stick [PUT] /stɪk/ *verb* [T usually + adv or prep] **stuck, stuck 1** *INFORMAL* to put something somewhere, especially in a not very careful way: *"Where shall I put these books?" "Oh, just stick them on the table for now."* ○ *She stuck her fingers in her ears so that she couldn't hear the noise.* ○ *I'll pay for lunch – I can stick it on my expenses.* **2** *OFFENSIVE* If you tell someone to stick something or where they can stick something, it means that you do not want to keep that thing: *"I've had enough of working here," she said, "You can stick your job!"*

• **stick *your* neck out** to take a risk

stick [BEAR] /stɪk/ *verb* [T] **stuck, stuck** *UK INFORMAL* to bear or accept something or someone unpleasant: *I don't think I can stick this job a day longer.* ○ [+ v-ing] *I don't know how you can stick living in this place.*

PHRASAL VERBS WITH **stick**

▲ **stick around** *phrasal verb INFORMAL* to stay somewhere for a period of time: *You go – I'll stick around here a bit longer.*

▲ **stick at *sth*** *UK phrasal verb* (*ALSO* **stick to/with *sth***) to continue trying hard to do something difficult: *You'll never learn to play the piano if you're not prepared to stick at it.*

▲ **stick by *sth/sb*** *phrasal verb* to continue to support something or someone, especially in a difficult situation: *We must stick by our decision.*

▲ **stick out** [GO BEYOND] *phrasal verb* to go beyond the surface or edge of something: *Paul's ears stick out a bit, don't they.* ○ *There was a handkerchief sticking out of his jacket pocket.*

▲ **stick out** [BE NOTICED] *phrasal verb INFORMAL* to be very easy to notice: *She certainly sticks out in a crowd.*

▲ **stick *(sth)* out** *phrasal verb* [M] to come forward from the rest of your body, or to make part of your body do this: *Mum, Lewis stuck out his tongue at me!* ○ *He stuck his arm out of the window and waved at us.* ○ *I wish my stomach didn't stick out so much.*

▲ **stick it out** [CONTINUE] *phrasal verb INFORMAL* to continue to the end of a difficult or unpleasant situation: *I know things are difficult at the moment, but if we just stick it out, I'm sure everything will be OK in the end.*

▲ **stick out for *sth*** *phrasal verb UK* to continue to demand or try to get something: *The unions have said that they are going to stick out for a 10% rise.*

▲ **stick to *sth*** *phrasal verb* **1** to limit yourself to doing or using one particular thing and not change to anything else: *Could you stick to the point, please?* ○ *We'd better stick to the main road, because the other roads are blocked with snow.* **2** If you stick to a law, rule or promise, you obey it or do what it states: *If you make a promise, you should stick to it.* **3** *US FOR* **stick at**

• **stick to *your* guns** To stick to your guns is to continue to have your beliefs or continue with a plan of action, even if other people disagree with you: *Despite harsh criticism, she's sticking to her guns **on** this issue.*

▲ **stick together** [SUPPORT] *phrasal verb INFORMAL* If people stick together, they support and help each other: *The country's Foreign Minister said that it was important for small nations to stick together.*

▲ **stick together** [CLOSE] *phrasal verb* If people stick together, they stay close to each other: *The two brothers always stick together at school.*

▲ **stick up** [GO UP] *phrasal verb* to point up above the surface of something and not lie flat: *When I get up in the morning, my hair is always sticking up.* ○ *There were some large rocks sticking up **out of** the water.*

▲ **stick *sth/sb* up** [STEAL] *phrasal verb* [M] *MAINLY US INFORMAL* to steal from a place or person, using a gun as a threat: *Did you hear that someone stuck up the post office last night?*

stick-up /ˈstɪk.ʌp/ *noun* [C] *OLD-FASHIONED INFORMAL* the act of threatening someone with a gun in order to steal from them: *Two men ran into the bank, shouting "This is a stick-up!"*

▲ **stick up for *sth/sb*** *phrasal verb INFORMAL* to support or defend someone or something, especially when they are being criticized: *I can stick up for myself.* ○ *It's sweet the way he sticks up for his little brother.*

▲ **stick with *sth/sb*** *phrasal verb INFORMAL* to continue doing something or using someone to do work for you, and not stopping or changing to something or someone else: *He said that he was going to stick with the traditions established by his grandfather.* ○ *He's a good car mechanic – I think we should stick with him.*

• **stick with it** to continue doing something although it is difficult: *Things are hard at the moment, but if we stick with it, they are bound to get better.*

sticker /ˈstɪk.əʳ/ [US] /-ɚ/ *noun* [C] a small piece of paper or plastic with a picture or writing on one side and glue or another similar substance on the other side, so that it will fasten to a surface: *a bumper/window sticker* ○ *Sophie's notebook is covered with stickers.* ○ *There were*

S

*two different **price** stickers on the shoes I wanted to buy.*

'**sticker** ,**price** *noun* [C] *US* the official price of something such as a car, given by its maker: *I got my truck for $2000 less than the sticker price.*

'**stick** ,**figure** *noun* [C] (*ALSO* **matchstick figure**) a simple picture of a person in which the head is drawn as a circle and the body, arms and legs are drawn as lines

'**sticking** ,**plaster** *UK noun* [C or U] (*US TRADEMARK* **Band-Aid**) a material that you can put over a small cut in the skin in order to protect it and keep it clean: *Timmy had sticking plasters on both knees.*

sticking-plaster *adj* [before n] *UK DISAPPROVING* dealing with a problem in a temporary and unsatisfactory way: *a sticking-plaster approach/solution/measure* ○ *sticking-plaster politics*

'**sticking** ,**point** *noun* [C] A sticking point in a discussion is a point on which it is not possible to reach an agreement: *Exactly how the land is to be divided up is the main sticking point of the peace talks.*

'**stick** ,**insect** *noun* [C] a large insect with a long thin body and legs: *She's as thin as a stick insect.*

stick-in-the-mud /'stɪk.ɪn.ðə,mʌd/ *noun* [C] *INFORMAL DISAPPROVING* someone who is old-fashioned, too serious and avoids enjoying themselves: *My dad's a real stick-in-the-mud.*

stickleback /'stɪk.l̩.bæk/ *noun* [C] a small fish which has sharp points along its back

stickler /'stɪk.ləʳ/ (*US* /-lɚ/ *noun* [C] *INFORMAL* a person who thinks that a particular type of behaviour is very important, and always follows it or tries to make other people follow it: *He's a stickler **for** detail/accuracy/efficiency.*

,**stick of** '**rock** *noun* [C] *UK* a long hard cylindrical sweet

stick-on /'stɪk.ɒn/ (*US* /-ɑːn/ *adj* [before n] describes something that has glue on one side of it, so that it can fix to a surface: *a stick-on label* ○ *I got some stick-on soles for my shoes, but they keep coming off.*

sticks /stɪks/ *plural noun INFORMAL DISAPPROVING* **the sticks** an area in the countryside which is far from a town or city: *I'm fed up with living **in** the sticks.* ○ *They live **out** in the sticks somewhere.*

'**stick** ,**shift** *noun* [C] *US FOR* gear lever

stick-to-it-iveness /stɪk'tuː.ɪt.ɪv.nəs/ *noun* [U] *US INFORMAL* the ability and determination to continue doing something despite difficulties

'**sticky** ,**tape** *noun* [U] *UK INFORMAL FOR* Sellotape

,**sticky** '**wicket** *noun* [C usually sing] *UK* a difficult situation: *This is something of a sticky wicket you've got us into.*

stiff FIRM /stɪf/ *adj* **1** firm or hard: *stiff cardboard* ○ *a stiff collar* ○ *His clothes were stiff with dried mud.* ○ *This hair spray has made my hair stiff.* ○ *Mix the powder and water into a stiff paste.* **2** not easily bent or moved: *The handle on this door is rather stiff.* ○ *The man's body was* **(as) stiff as a board** *when it was found in the snow.* **3** If you are stiff or part of your body is stiff, your muscles hurt when they are moved: *Sitting still at a computer terminal all day can give you a stiff neck.*

stiff /stɪf/ *noun* [C] *SLANG* a dead body: *They found a stiff in the river.*

stiffen /'stɪf.ən/ *verb* [I] to become firm or more difficult to bend: *Beat the cream until it begins to stiffen* (= become firm). ○ *His body stiffened in fear.*

stiffly /'stɪf.li/ *adv* straight and not bending: *The soldiers stood stiffly to attention.* **stiffness** /'stɪf.nəs/ *noun* [U]

stiffy /'stɪf.i/ *noun* [C] *UK OFFENSIVE* an ERECTION (= when a man's penis is harder and bigger than usual and points up): *to **get/have** a stiffy*

stiff NOT RELAXED /stɪf/ *adj* behaving in a way that is formal and not relaxed: *The general is a tall man with steel spectacles and a stiff, rather pompous **manner**.*

stiffen /'stɪf.ən/ *verb* [I] to become less relaxed and more formal: *She stiffened when her former husband walked into the room.*

stiffly /'stɪf.li/ *adv* in a way that is too formal: *"I don't think that it's anything to do with you," he said stiffly.*

stiffness /'stɪf.nəs/ *noun* [U] the quality of being very formal and not relaxed: *Her initial stiffness began to wear off as we got to know her.*

stiff SEVERE /stɪf/ *adj* **1** severe and difficult: *The athlete was given a stiff punishment for using drugs.* ○ *They are campaigning for stiffer penalties for people who drink and drive.* ○ *There has been stiff **opposition/resistance** to the proposed tax increases.* ○ *It's a stiff climb to the top of the hill.* ○ *Some college courses have stiffer entry requirements than others.* ○ *Both companies are worried about losing business in the face of stiff **competition**.* **2** a **stiff breeze/wind** a strong wind **3** a **stiff drink/ brandy/gin, etc.** an alcoholic drink that is very strong: *A stiff whisky – that's what I need.* **4** A stiff price is very expensive: *We had to pay a stiff membership fee to join the health club.*

stiffen /'stɪf.ən/ *verb* [I or T] to make something stronger or more difficult: *These events have stiffened our resolve to succeed.* ○ *Penalties for selling illegal drugs have been stiffened.* ○ *Stiffening competition in the market has led to a reduction in the company's profits this year.*

stiffly /'stɪf.li/ *adv* severely: *I wrote a stiffly-worded letter of complaint to the council.* **stiffness** /'stɪf.nəs/ *noun* [U] *Everyone was surprised at the stiffness **of** the sentence/ punishment/penalty/sanctions.*

stiff VERY MUCH /stɪf/ *adv* very much, or to a great degree: *I got **frozen** stiff* (= very cold) *waiting at the bus stop.* ○ *I was **scared** stiff when I heard someone moving around upstairs.*

stiff PERSON /stɪf/ *noun* [C] *US INFORMAL* a person of the type described: *a working stiff* ○ *you lucky stiff*

,**stiff** ,**upper** '**lip** *noun* [C usually sing] Someone who has a stiff upper lip does not show their feelings when they are upset: *He was taught at school to **keep** a stiff upper lip, whatever happens.*

stifle NO AIR /'staɪ.fl̩/ *verb* [I or T] to (cause to) be unable to breathe because of a lack of air: *He is said to have stifled his victim with a pillow.* ○ *We almost stifled in the heat of the city.*

stifling /'staɪ.fl̩.ɪŋ/ *adj* extremely hot and unpleasant: *I can't bear this stifling humidity.* ○ *Several hundred people were crammed into the stifling room.* **stiflingly** /'staɪ.fl̩.ɪŋ.li/-flɪŋ/ *adv: It's stiflingly hot in here.*

stifle PREVENT HAPPENING /'staɪ.fl̩/ *verb* [T] to prevent something from happening, being expressed or continuing: *She stifled a cough/yawn/scream/sneeze.* ○ *I don't know how I managed to stifle my anger.* ○ *We should be encouraging new ideas, not stifling them.* **stifling** /'staɪ.fl̩.- ɪŋ/ *adj: stifling bureaucracy*

stigma FEELING /'stɪg.mə/ *noun* [C usually sing; U] when people disapprove of something, especially when this is unfair: *There is no longer any stigma **to** being divorced.* ○ *Being an unmarried mother no longer **carries** the **social** stigma that it used to.*

stigmatize, *UK USUALLY* -**ise** /'stɪg.mə.taɪz/ *verb* [T often passive] to treat someone or something unfairly by disapproving of them: *People should not be stigmatized on the basis of race.*

stigma FLOWER PART /'stɪg.mə/ *noun* [C] the top of the central female part of a flower, where POLLEN is received

stigmata /'stɪg.mə.tə/ (*US* /stɪg'mɑː.t̬ə/ *plural noun* marks that appear on a person's body in the same places as those made on Jesus Christ's body when he was nailed to a cross

stile /staɪl/ *noun* [C] a set of usually two steps which you climb over in order to cross a fence or a wall, especially between fields

stiletto /stɪ'let.əʊ/ (*US* /-'let̬.oʊ/ *noun* [C] *plural* **stilettos** a woman's shoe with a narrow high heel: *She was wearing a short skirt and stilettos.* ○ *stiletto **heels***

still CONTINUING /stɪl/ *adv* continuing to happen or continuing to be done: *I'm still hungry.* ○ *I still haven't finished my essay.* ○ *There is still no news about the hostages.* ○ *Do you still work for the government?* ○ *Hope is fading that the missing child is still alive.* ○ *There's still time for us to get to the cinema before the film starts.*

still DESPITE /stɪl/ *adv* despite that: *You may not approve of what he did, but he's still your brother.* ○ *I know you don't like her, but you still don't have to be so rude to her.*

S

○ *Even though she hasn't really got the time, she still offered to help.*

still [GREATER DEGREE] /stɪl/ *adv* to an even greater degree or in an even greater amount: *The number of people killed in the explosion is likely to rise still higher.* ○ *The company is hoping to extend its market still further.* ○ *Still more snow fell overnight.* ○ *I'll meet you at the theatre. No,* ***better*** *still, let's meet in a pub and have a drink first.* ○ *I'm worried that his car has broken down, or* ***worse*** *still, that he's had an accident.* ○ *Why do you have to tell me still* (= even) *more lies?*

still [NOT MOVING] /stɪl/ *adj* **1** staying in the same position; not moving: *Children find it difficult to* ***sit/stand/stay*** *still for very long.* ○ *I can't brush your hair if you don't* ***keep/hold*** *still.* ○ *She sat perfectly still while I took her photograph.* ○ *The* ***air*** *was so still* (= There was so little wind) *that not even the leaves on the trees were moving.* ○ *She dived into the still* (= calm and not flowing) ***water*** *of the lake.* **2** *MAINLY UK* A still drink is one that is not fizzy: *Would you like still or sparkling water?*

• **Still waters run deep.** *SAYING* said about a person who says little, but who might in fact know a lot

still /stɪl/ *verb* **[T]** to make something stop moving or become more calm: *He tried to still the swaying of the hammock.* ○ *LITERARY She cuddled her baby to still its cries.*

still /stɪl/ *noun* **1 [C]** *SPECIALIZED* a photograph of a piece of action in a film **2 [U]** *LITERARY* when it is quiet and calm: *In the still* ***of the night****, nothing moved.* **stillness** /ˈstɪl.nəs/ *noun* **[U]**

still [EQUIPMENT] /stɪl/ *noun* **[C]** a piece of equipment used for making alcohol

stillbirth /ˈstɪl.bɜːθ/ (US) /-bɝːθ/ *noun* **[C]** the birth of a dead baby ➲Compare **abortion** at **abort** END PREGNANCY; **miscarriage**.

stillborn /ˌstɪlˈbɔːn/ (US) /-ˈbɔːrn/ /ˈ--/ *adj* **1** born dead: *a stillborn baby* ○ *The child was stillborn.* **2** If an idea or event is stillborn, it is unsuccessful or does not happen.

ˌstill ˈlife *noun* **[C or U]** *plural* **still lifes** a type of painting or drawing of an arrangement of objects that do not move, such as flowers, fruit, bowls, etc: *We went to an exhibition of 17th century Dutch still lifes.*

stilt /stɪlts/ *noun* **[C usually pl]** **1** one of a set of long pieces of wood or metal used to support a building so that it is above the ground or above water: *The houses are built* ***on*** *stilts to protect them from the annual floods.* **2** one of two long pieces of wood with supports for the feet which allow you to stand and walk high above the ground: *to walk* ***on*** *stilts*

stilted /ˈstɪl.tɪd/ (US) /-t̬ɪd/ *adj DISAPPROVING* (of a person's behaviour or way of speaking or writing) too formal and not smooth or natural: *He writes in a formal and rather stilted style.* ○ *The dialogue sounded stilted and unnatural, perhaps because of the translation from the original Russian.* **stiltedly** /ˈstɪl.tɪd.li/ (US) /-t̬ɪd-/ *adv*

Stilton /ˈstɪl.tᵊn/ *noun* **[U]** a white and blue English cheese with a strong flavour

stimulate /ˈstɪm.jʊ.leɪt/ *verb* **1 [T]** to encourage something to grow, develop or become active: *The government plans to cut taxes in order to stimulate the economy.* **2 [I or T]** to make someone excited and interested about something: *The film was intended to stimulate and amuse.* ○ **[+ obj + to infinitive]** *Good teachers should ask questions that stimulate students* ***to*** *think.* ○ *Erotic images are often more sexually stimulating to men than to women.* **3 [T]** *SPECIALIZED* to cause part of the body to function: *The drugs stimulate the damaged tissue* ***into*** *repairing itself.* ○ *Standing on your head is supposed to stimulate hair growth.*

stimulant /ˈstɪm.jʊ.lənt/ *noun* **[C]** **1** something which makes or causes something else to grow or develop: *Tourism has acted as a stimulant* ***to*** *the country's economy.* **2** a substance, such as a drug, which makes the mind or body more active: *Caffeine, which is found in coffee and tea, is a mild stimulant.*

stimulating /ˈstɪm.jʊ.leɪ.tɪŋ/ (US) /-t̬ɪŋ/ *adj* **1** If something is stimulating, it encourages new ideas: *a stimulating discussion* ○ *Universities have been asked to make their courses more attractive and stimulating.* **2** describes someone who makes you feel enthusiastic and full of ideas: *a really stimulating teacher* **3** If an activity is stimulating, it causes your body to be active: *Aerobics is one of the most stimulating forms of exercise.*

stimulation /ˌstɪm.jʊˈleɪ.ʃᵊn/ *noun* **[U]** when something causes someone or something to become more active or enthusiastic, or to develop or function: *While she was at home looking after her children, she felt deprived of* ***intellectual*** *stimulation.* ○ *SPECIALIZED Electric stimulation can help to heal fractured bones.*

stimulus /ˈstɪm.jʊ.ləs/ *noun* **[C]** *plural* **stimuli** **1** something that causes growth or activity: *Foreign investment has been a stimulus* ***to*** *the industry.* ○ *The book will provide a stimulus* ***to*** *research in this very important area.* **2** *SPECIALIZED* something which causes part of the body to react: *The tip of the tongue is sensitive to salt and sweet stimuli and the back of the tongue is sensitive to bitter stimuli.*

sting [HURT] /stɪŋ/ *verb* **[I or T]** **stung, stung** **1** If an insect, plant or animal stings, it produces a small but painful injury, usually with a poison, by brushing against the skin or making a very small hole under the skin: *Do all types of bee sting?* ○ *I got stung by a wasp yesterday.* ○ *I didn't see the nettles until I was stung by them.* **2** to cause sharp but usually temporary pain: *The soap/smoke/sweat stung my eyes.* ○ *This type of disinfectant doesn't sting, even if you put it on a fresh cut.* **3** If someone's hurtful remarks sting you, they make you feel upset and annoyed: *He was stung by her criticisms.* ○ *She knew he was right, but his words still stung.* ○ *She managed to give a stinging reply* (= an angry answer intended to upset), *before slamming down the phone.*

sting /stɪŋ/ *noun* **1 [C or S]** a sudden burning pain in your eyes, on your skin, etc., or the ability to cause such pain: *She had several bee stings.* ○ *the sting of salt in a wound* ○ *Some types of jellyfish have a powerful sting.* **2 [S]** the feeling of being upset by something: *the sting of defeat* **3 [C]** *UK* (*US* **stinger**) a pointed part of an insect, plant or animal that goes through a person's or animal's skin and leaves behind poison

• **have a sting in the/its tail** *UK* If something, such as a story or joke, has a sting in the/its tail, it has a surprising or unpleasant part which only becomes clear at the end.

• **take the sting out of** If something takes the sting out of an unpleasant situation, it makes it less unpleasant: *The new policy of shorter working hours will serve to take the sting out of the pay cut.*

sting [CHARGE] /stɪŋ/ *verb* **[T]** **stung, stung** *INFORMAL* to charge someone a surprisingly large amount of money for something: *The bank stung me* ***for*** *£50 in charges when I went overdrawn.*

sting /stɪŋ/ *noun* **[C]** *MAINLY US SLANG* **1** a clever and complicated act of stealing: *A bank employee was involved in the sting in which $5 million was stolen.* **2** a police action to catch criminals in which the police pretend to be criminals: *a sting operation*

ˈstinging ˌnettle *noun* **[C]** a wild plant which has leaves with very short hairs that sting

stingray /ˈstɪŋ.reɪ/ *noun* **[C]** a large flat round fish with a long tail that has poisonous points on it

stingy /ˈstɪn.dʒi/ *adj INFORMAL DISAPPROVING* unwilling to spend money: *He's really stingy and never buys the drinks when we go out.* ○ *The owners are so stingy – they've refused to pay for new carpets or even a bit of paint to brighten up the house.* **stinginess** /ˈstɪn.dʒɪ.nəs/ *noun* **[U]** *He blames government stinginess for the lack of money available to spend on new books in schools.*

stink [SMELL] /stɪŋk/ *verb* **[I]** **stank** or *US ALSO* **stunk**, **stunk** *INFORMAL* to smell very unpleasant: *Your feet stink!* ○ *The morning after the party, the whole house stank* ***of*** *beer and cigarettes.* ○ *He hadn't washed for over a week and stank* ***to high heaven*** (= greatly). ○ *The woman next to me sprayed on some perfume and* (UK) *stank* ***out****/*(US) *stunk* ***up*** *the whole shop* (= filled it with an unpleasant smell).

stink /stɪŋk/ *noun* **[C usually sing]** a strong unpleasant smell: *The stink* ***of*** *rotting seaweed was strong along the seashore.*

stinking /ˈstɪŋ.kɪŋ/ *adj* having a very unpleasant smell: *a pile of stinking rotten food*

S

stink [BE BAD] /stɪŋk/ *verb* [I] **stank** or *US ALSO* **stunk, stunk** *INFORMAL DISAPPROVING* to be extremely bad or unpleasant: *I think her whole attitude stinks.* ○ *His acting stinks but he looks good, so he's offered lots of movie roles.*
• **cause a stink** *INFORMAL* to cause trouble and make people angry: *The article about political corruption caused a real stink.*
• **create/kick up/raise a stink** *INFORMAL* to make a strong public complaint: *She created a stink* ***about*** *the lack of recycling facilities in the town.*
• **like stink** *UK INFORMAL* If someone works like stink, they work extremely hard.
stinker /ˈstɪŋ.kəʳ/ [US] /-kɚ/ *noun* [C] *OLD-FASHIONED INFORMAL* someone or something that is very unpleasant: *What a stinker that man is!* ○ *She'd had a real stinker* ***of a*** *day at work.*
stinking /ˈstɪŋ.kɪŋ/ *adj INFORMAL* describes something which is very unpleasant or bad: *I hate this stinking job!* ○ *She had a stinking* ***cold*** *and felt very sorry for herself.*
• **be stinking rich** to be extremely rich

ˈstink ˌbomb *noun* [C] a small device that gives off an extremely bad smell: *The two boys were caught letting off stink bombs in the school toilets.*

stint [PERIOD] /stɪnt/ *noun* [C] a fixed or limited period of time spent doing a particular job or activity: *He has just finished a stint of compulsory military service.* ○ *Perhaps her most productive period was her five-year stint as a foreign correspondent in New York.*

stint [LIMIT] /stɪnt/ *verb* [I or T; usually in negatives] to provide, take or use only a small amount of something: *The bride's parents did not stint* ***on*** *the champagne – there was plenty for everyone.* ○ *Don't stint yourself – take another slice of cake.* ➲See also **unstinting**.

stipend /ˈstaɪ.pend/ *noun* [C] **1** a fixed regular income: *an annual stipend* **2** the income paid to a priest in the UK
stipendiary /staɪˈpen.di.ᵊr.i/ [US] /-er-/ *adj UK* A stipendiary clergyman or magistrate receives a fixed income: *He was appointed as a stipendiary* ***priest*** *in the diocese of York.*

stipple /ˈstɪp.l̩/ *verb* [T] *SPECIALIZED* to draw or paint something using small spots or marks: *She tried to create the impression of strong sunlight by stippling the canvas in yellow and white.* ○ *FIGURATIVE The evening sky was stippled with a few wisps of low-lying clouds.*
stippled /ˈstɪp.l̩d/ *adj SPECIALIZED* drawn, painted or coloured using small spots or marks: *The divers saw tropical fish stippled in gold and black.*
stippling /ˈstɪp.l̩.ɪŋ/ /ˈstɪp.lɪŋ/ *noun* [U] *SPECIALIZED* when someone draws or paints using small spots or marks

stipulate /ˈstɪp.jʊ.leɪt/ *verb* [T] *FORMAL* to state exactly how something must be or must be done: *She agreed to buy the car, but stipulated racing tyres and a turbo-powered engine.* ○ [+ that] *The law stipulates* ***that*** *new cars must have seat belts for the driver and every passenger.* ○ [+ question word] *We have signed a contract which stipulates* ***when*** *the project must be completed.*
stipulation /ˌstɪp.jʊˈleɪ.ʃᵊn/ *noun* [C or U] *FORMAL* when someone says exactly how something must be done: *Is there any stipulation as regards qualifications?* ○ [+ that] *The only stipulation is* ***that*** *candidates must be over the age of 35.*

stir [MIX] /stɜːʳ/ [US] /stɝː/ *verb* [I or T] **-rr-** to mix a liquid or other substance by moving an object such as a spoon in a circular pattern: *Stir the sauce gently until it begins to boil.* ○ *Stir the egg yolks* ***into*** *the mixture.* ○ *She paused to stir some milk* ***into*** *her coffee.* ○ *Slowly add the flour, stirring until completely blended.*
stir /stɜːʳ/ [US] /stɝː/ *noun* [C usually sing] the act of stirring a liquid or other substance in order to mix it: *Could you* ***give*** *the soup a quick stir?*

stir [MOVE] /stɜːʳ/ [US] /stɝː/ *verb* **-rr- 1** [I or T] to cause something to move slightly: *A light breeze stirred the leaves lying on the path.* ○ *He stirred in his sleep as I kissed him.* **2** [T] If something stirs you, it makes you feel a strong emotion: *I was deeply stirred by her performance.* ○ [+ obj + to infinitive] *The speech stirred the crowd* ***to*** *take action.* **3** [I] *LITERARY* If an emotion stirs within you, you begin to feel it: *Hope stirred within her heart.*
• **stir (*yourself*)** to wake up or begin to move or take action: *Come on, stir yourselves, or you'll be late!* ○ *The alarm clock went off, but she didn't stir.*
• **stir the blood** (*ALSO* **stir *your* blood**) *LITERARY* If something stirs the blood, it excites you: *tales to stir the blood*
stir /stɜːʳ/ [US] /stɝː/ *noun* [U] *INFORMAL* a lot of interest or excitement: *The scandal* ***caused/created*** *quite a stir at the time.*
stirring /ˈstɜː.rɪŋ/ [US] /ˈstɝː.ɪŋ/ *noun* [C] the beginning of something, such as an emotion or thought: *She felt a faint stirring* ***of*** *envy when she heard that one of her colleagues had been promoted.*
stirring /ˈstɜː.rɪŋ/ [US] /ˈstɝː.ɪŋ/ *adj APPROVING* A stirring speech or song is one which produces strong positive emotions. **stirringly** /ˈstɜː.rɪŋ.li/ [US] /ˈstɝː.ɪŋ-/ *adv*

stir [CAUSE TROUBLE] /stɜːʳ/ [US] /stɝː/ *verb* [I] **-rr-** *UK INFORMAL DISAPPROVING* to cause trouble intentionally between other people, especially by telling false or secret information: *There's a lot of gossip about me going around. Have you been stirring?* ➲See also **stir up** EMOTION.
stirrer /ˈstɜː.rəʳ/ [US] /ˈstɝː.ɚ/ *noun* [C] *MAINLY UK INFORMAL DISAPPROVING* a person who intentionally causes trouble between other people: *He's such a stirrer!*

PHRASAL VERBS WITH **stir**

▲ **stir *sth* up** [EMOTION] *phrasal verb* [M] to cause an unpleasant emotion or problem to begin or grow: *The teacher told him to stop stirring up* ***trouble.*** ○ *The photographs stirred up some painful memories.*
▲ **stir *sth* up** [SUBSTANCE] *phrasal verb* [M] to cause a substance such as earth or dust to move and rise up: *The helicopter stirred up clouds of dust.*

stir-crazy /ˈstɜːˌkreɪ.zi/ [US] /ˈstɝː-/ /ˌ-ˈ--/ *adj INFORMAL* upset or angry because you have been prevented from going somewhere or doing something for a long time: *I've been laid up for two weeks with this broken leg and I'm beginning to* ***go*** *stir-crazy.*

stir-fry /ˈstɜː.fraɪ/ [US] /ˈstɝː-/ *verb* [I or T] to fry small pieces of meat, vegetables, etc. quickly while mixing them around: *Stir-fry the chicken for one minute, then add the vegetables.*
stir-fry /ˈstɜː.fraɪ/ [US] /ˈstɝː-/ *noun* [C or U] a method of frying food while mixing it quickly, or food cooked this way: *We're having a vegetable stir-fry for supper tonight.* ○ *I don't like stir-fry.*

stirrup /ˈstɪr.əp/ *noun* [C] one of a pair of D-shaped pieces of metal that hang from the side of a horse's saddle and which is used for resting your foot in when you are riding

stitch [THREAD] /stɪtʃ/ *noun* [C] **1** a piece of thread sewn in cloth, or the single movement of a needle and thread into and out of the cloth which produces this: *Secure the two pieces together with a couple of stitches.* **2** one of the small circles of wool that you make when you are knitting: *He* ***cast on/off*** *a stitch* (= added/removed a length of thread from the needle). ○ *I've* ***dropped*** *a stitch* (= lost a length of thread from the needle). **3** a particular type of stitch made in sewing or knitting, or the pattern which this produces: *a pearl/satin stitch* ○ *The bedspread was embroidered with cross-stitch.* **4** a length of special thread used to join the edges of a deep cut in the flesh: *Her head wounds needed 50 stitches.* ○ *He got hit with a broken bottle and needed five stitches* ***in*** *his cheek.* **5** *INFORMAL* **not a stitch** without any clothes: *I haven't got a stitch to wear* (= I have not got anything to wear) *for this party tonight.* ○ *She ran down the corridor to the bathroom without a stitch on* (= naked).
• **A stitch in time (saves nine).** *SAYING* said to mean that it is better to act or deal with problems immediately, because if action is delayed until later, things will get worse and the problems will take longer to deal with
stitch /stɪtʃ/ *verb* [I or T] to sew two things together, or to repair something by sewing: *This button needs to be stitched back* ***onto*** *my shirt.* ○ *Stitch the pieces* ***together*** *along the fold.* **stitching** /ˈstɪtʃ.ɪŋ/ *noun* [U] *The stitching along my coat hem is coming undone.*

stitch [PAIN] /stɪtʃ/ *noun* [C usually sing] a sharp pain in the side of your stomach or chest, often caused by not

S

breathing enough when running or laughing: *I **got** a stitch after running for the bus.*

• **in stitches** *INFORMAL* If a joke or an amusing story has you in stitches, it makes you laugh uncontrollably.

PHRASAL VERBS WITH **stitch**

▲ **stitch *sth* together** *phrasal verb* **[M]** *INFORMAL DISAPPROVING* to create or form something quickly or roughly: *Britain is likely to stitch together some sort of political deal to avoid a confrontation.*

▲ **stitch *sb* up** [NOT GUILTY] *phrasal verb* **[M]** *UK SLANG* to intentionally make someone look guilty of doing something which they did not do: *He claims he was stitched up by the police.*

stitch-up /ˈstɪtʃ.ʌp/ *noun* **[C usually sing]** *a police stitch-up*

▲ **stitch *sth/sb* up** [CUT] *phrasal verb* **[M]** to join the two sides of something with stitches, for example torn clothing or a deep cut, or to treat someone who has a deep cut by doing this: *I've ripped my trousers – can you stitch them up for me?* ○ *After giving birth, she was stitched up by a junior doctor.*

stoat /stəʊt/ [US] /stoʊt/ *noun* **[C]** a small thin furry animal which has brown fur in summer and white fur in winter

stock [SUPPLY] /stɒk/ [US] /stɑːk/ *noun* **1** **[C or U]** a supply of something for use or sale: *It is now halfway through winter and food stocks are already low.* ○ *The local shop has a good stock **of** postcards and guidebooks.* ○ *Much of the city's housing stock* (= the number of houses in the city) *is over 100 years old.* **2** **[U]** the total amount of goods or the amount of a particular type of goods available in a shop: *This shop sells its old stock at a very low prices.* ○ *We'll be getting our new stock **in** on Friday.* ○ *The new edition is **in/out of** stock* (= available/not available) *in major bookshops.*

• **put stock in *sth*** If you put stock in something that someone says or does, you have a high opinion of it: *He's been wrong several times before, so I don't put much stock in what he says anymore.*

• **take stock** To take stock (of something) is to think carefully about a situation or event and form an opinion about it, so that you can decide what to do: *After two years spent teaching abroad, she returned home for a month to take stock **of** her life.*

stock /stɒk/ [US] /stɑːk/ *verb* **[T]** **1** If a shop or factory stocks something, it keeps a supply of it: *Most supermarkets stock a wide range of wines.* **2** to fill something such as a cupboard or shelves with food or goods: *He has a Saturday job stocking shelves in the local supermarket.* ○ *I always stock **up** the fridge before my sister comes to stay.*

stockist /ˈstɒk.ɪst/ [US] /ˈstɑː.kɪst/ *noun* **[C]** *UK* a shop that sells a particular type of goods: *a health food stockist*

stocktaking /ˈstɒkˌteɪ.kɪŋ/ [US] /ˈstɑːk-/ *noun* **[U]** *UK* the counting of all the goods, materials, etc. kept in a place such as a shop

stock [MONEY] /stɒk/ [US] /stɑːk/ *noun* **1** **[U]** the amount of money which a company has through selling shares to people: *They own 20% of the company's stock.* **2** **[C or U]** part of the ownership of a company which people buy as an investment: *Stock **prices** fell yesterday in heavy trading.* ○ *She buys and sells stocks **and shares**.* **3** **[C or U]** *UK* money which people invest in the government and which produces a fixed rate of interest: *government stock(s)*

stockbroker /ˈstɒkˌbrəʊ.kəʳ/ [US] /ˈstɑːkˌbroʊ.kɚ/ *noun* **[C]** a person or company that buys and sells stocks and shares for other people **stockbroking** /ˈstɒkˌbrəʊ.kɪŋ/ [US] /ˈstɑːkˌbroʊ.kɪŋ/ *noun* **[U]**

stockholder /ˈstɒkˌhəʊl.dəʳ/ [US] /ˈstɑːkˌhoʊl.dɚ/ *noun* **[C]** *US FOR* **shareholder**

stock [LIQUID] /stɒk/ [US] /stɑːk/ *noun* **[U]** a liquid used to add flavour to food and which is made by boiling meat or fish bones or vegetables in water: *vegetable/beef/chicken stock*

stock [ANIMALS] /stɒk/ [US] /stɑːk/ *noun* **[U]** animals, such as cows or sheep, kept on a farm

stock [POPULARITY] /stɒk/ [US] /stɑːk/ *noun* **[U]** *FORMAL* the degree to which a person or organization is popular and respected: *At present, the Prime Minister's stock is **high/low**.*

stock [ORIGIN] /stɒk/ [US] /stɑːk/ *noun* **[U]** *SLIGHTLY FORMAL* the family or group from which a person or animal originates: *He's an American **of** Irish stock.* ○ *She's **of** peasant/noble stock.* ○ *Some of the animals will be kept as breeding stock.*

stock [HANDLE] /stɒk/ [US] /stɑːk/ *noun* **[C]** the support or handle of a tool, especially the triangular part of a gun that rests against your shoulder

stock [PLANT] /stɒk/ [US] /stɑːk/ *noun* **[C]** a garden plant with small pleasant-smelling, brightly-coloured flowers

stock [USUAL] /stɒk/ [US] /stɑːk/ *adj* (of an idea, expression or action) usual or typical, and used or done so many times that it is no longer original: *a stock phrase/response* ○ *"Don't worry – worse things happen at sea" is her stock expression for whenever anything goes wrong.*

▲ **stock up** *phrasal verb* to buy a large quantity of something: *During the emergency, people stocked up **on** essential items like candles, medicines and tins of food.*

stockade /stɒkˈeɪd/ [US] /stɑːˈkeɪd/ *noun* **[C]** a strong wooden fence built around an area to defend it against attack

ˈstockbroker ˌbelt *noun* **[C]** *UK* the area near London where many rich people live in large houses and from where they travel to work in the City (= the financial area of London)

stock car /ˈstɒk.kɑːʳ/ [US] /ˈstɑːk.kɑːr/ *noun* **[C]** an ordinary car that has been made stronger and faster so that it can be driven in special races

ˈstock conˌtrol *noun* **[U]** In a company or shop, stock control is the system of making certain that new supplies are ordered and that goods have not been stolen.

ˈstock ˌcube *noun* **[C]** (*US USUALLY* **bouillon cube**) a small block of dried flavouring which you dissolve in hot water before using it in some dishes such as soups

ˈstock exˌchange *noun* **[C usually sing]** (*ALSO* **stock market**) a place where parts of the ownership of companies are bought and sold, or the organization of people whose job is to do this buying or selling: *They bought some shares **on** the London stock exchange.* ○ *Stock markets around the world are reacting to news of the US president's announcement.*

stockily /ˈstɒk.ɪ.li/ [US] /ˈstɑː.kɪ-/ *adv* ➲See at **stocky**.

stockiness /ˈstɒk.ɪ.nəs/ [US] /ˈstɑː.kɪ-/ *noun* **[U]**

stocking /ˈstɒk.ɪŋ/ [US] /ˈstɑː.kɪŋ/ *noun* **[C]** one of a pair of tight-fitting coverings for the feet and legs made of light material and worn by women: ***nylon/silk** stockings.* ➲Compare **nylons** at **nylon**; **tights**. ➲See picture **Clothes** on page Centre 6

• **in *your* stocking(ed) feet** wearing only socks or stockings and not shoes: *Jerome stands 1m 75 in his stocking feet.*

ˈstocking ˌcap *noun* **[C]** *US* a close-fitting knitted cap with a long tail

stocking-filler *UK* /ˈstɒk.ɪŋˌfɪl.əʳ/ [US] /ˈstɑː.kɪŋˌfɪl.ɚ/ *noun* **[C]** (*US* **stocking-stuffer**) a small, usually cheap Christmas present

ˈstocking ˌmask *noun* **[C]** a stocking which thieves pull over their heads to hide their faces

stock-in-trade /ˌstɒk.ɪnˈtreɪd/ [US] /ˌstɑːk-/ *noun* **[U]** **1** the typical characteristics or behaviour of someone or something: *The song was perfect for the soft vocals that are her stock-in-trade.* **2** *OLD-FASHIONED* the tools and other objects that you need for your job

ˈstock ˌmarket *noun* **[C usually sing]** a **stock exchange**

stockpile /ˈstɒk.paɪl/ [US] /ˈstɑːk-/ *noun* **[C]** a large amount of food, goods or weapons which are kept ready for future use: *They have a stockpile of weapons and ammunition that will last several months.*

stockpile /ˈstɒk.paɪl/ [US] /ˈstɑːk-/ *verb* **[T]** to store a large supply of something for future use: *The rebels have been stockpiling weapons.*

stockroom /ˈstɒk.rʊm/ /-ruːm/ [US] /ˈstɑːk-/ *noun* **[C]** a room in a shop, factory or office which is used for storing a supply of goods or materials

'stock ,route noun [C] AUS a road on which traffic must stop so that cattle and sheep which are being moved from one place to another can go past

stocks /stɒks/ ⑩ /stɑːks/ plural noun (in Europe in the Middle Ages) a wooden frame which was fixed around someone's feet, hands and sometimes head, so that they were forced to sit or stand for a long time in public as a punishment

stock-still /ˌstɒkˈstɪl/ ⑩ /ˌstɑːk-/ adv without moving; completely still: On seeing us, the deer **stock-still** for a moment, then turned and retreated into the forest.

stocktaking /ˈstɒkˌteɪkɪŋ/ ⑩ /ˈstɑːk-/ noun [U] ⊃See at **stock** SUPPLY.

stocky /ˈstɒk.i/ ⑩ /ˈstɑː.ki/ adj describes a person, especially a man, whose body is wide across the shoulders and chest and who is short; THICKSET: The man was described as short and stocky and very strong. ⊃Compare **sturdy**. **stockily** /ˈstɒk.ɪ.li/ ⑩ /ˈstɑː.kɪ-/ adv: a stockily-built man **stockiness** /ˈstɒk.ɪ.nəs/ ⑩ /ˈstɑː.kɪ-/ noun [U]

stockyard /ˈstɒk.jɑːd/ ⑩ /ˈstɑːk.jɑːrd/ noun [C] a set of enclosures where farm animals are kept before being sold or killed

stodge /stɒdʒ/ ⑩ /stɑːdʒ/ noun [U] UK INFORMAL DISAPPROV-ING heavy food, such as potatoes, bread and rice, which contains too much starch and makes you feel very full

stodgy FOOD /ˈstɒdʒ.i/ ⑩ /ˈstɑː.dʒi/ adj UK INFORMAL DIS-APPROVING describes food which is heavy and unhealthy, sometimes in an unpleasant way: I've been eating too many stodgy puddings. **stodginess** /ˈstɒdʒ.ɪ.nəs/ ⑩ /ˈstɑː.dʒɪ-/ noun [U]

stodgy BORING /ˈstɒdʒ.i/ ⑩ /ˈstɑː.dʒi/ adj UK INFORMAL DIS-APPROVING boring, serious and formal: Neither company has succeeded in shedding its stodgy image. ○ Younger consumers, it is said, regard their products as stodgy and unfashionable. **stodginess** /ˈstɒdʒ.ɪ.nəs/ ⑩ /ˈstɑː.dʒɪ-/ noun [U]

stoic /ˈstəʊ.ɪk/ ⑩ /ˈstoʊ-/ adj (ALSO **stoical**) SLIGHTLY FOR-MAL determined not to complain or show your feelings, especially when something bad happens to you: She knew she must be in pain, despite her stoic attitude. ○ He showed a stoic resignation towards his fate. ○ Local people were stoical **about** the damage caused by the hurricane.

stoic /ˈstəʊ.ɪk/ ⑩ /ˈstoʊ-/ noun [C] SLIGHTLY FORMAL some-one who does not complain or show their emotions: My father is a stoic by nature and found it hard to express his grief when my mother died. **stoically** /ˈstəʊ.ɪ.kli/ ⑩ /ˈstoʊ-/ adv: She listened stoically as the guilty verdict was read out. ○ Stoically, and with great determination, the people set about rebuilding the village.

stoicism /ˈstəʊ.ɪ.sɪ.zᵊm/ ⑩ /ˈstoʊ-/ noun [U] SLIGHTLY FOR-MAL the quality of experiencing pain or trouble without complaining or showing your emotions: He endured the pain of his wounds with great stoicism.

stoke /stəʊk/ ⑩ /stoʊk/ verb [I or T] (ALSO **stoke up**) **1** to add fuel to a large enclosed fire and move the fuel around with a stick so that it burns well and produces a lot of heat: Once the fire had been stoked up, the room began to get warm. **2** to encourage bad ideas or feelings in a lot of people: He's been accused of stoking up racial hatred in the region. ○ Rumours of an emergency meeting of the finance ministers stoked the atmosphere of crisis.

stoker /ˈstəʊ.kəʳ/ ⑩ /ˈstoʊ.kɚ/ noun [C] a person whose job is adding fuel to a large enclosed fire

▲ **stoke up on/with** sth phrasal verb INFORMAL to eat a lot of a particular food in order to avoid feeling hungry or weak later: As it was a cold morning, she stoked up on bacon, eggs and beans on toast.

stole CLOTHING /stəʊl/ ⑩ /stoʊl/ noun [C] **1** FORMAL a long narrow piece of cloth or fur which is worn around the shoulders by women, usually on special occasions: a **mink** stole **2** SPECIALIZED a long narrow piece of cloth, especially silk, which is worn over the shoulders by some priests in the Christian Church during religious ceremonies

stole TOOK /stəʊl/ ⑩ /stoʊl/ past simple of **steal**

stolen /ˈstəʊ.lᵊn/ ⑩ /ˈstoʊ-/ past participle of **steal**

stolid /ˈstɒl.ɪd/ ⑩ /ˈstɑː.lɪd/ adj SLIGHTLY DISAPPROVING (of a person) calm and not showing emotion or excitement, or (of a thing) not interesting or attractive: He's a very stolid, serious man. ○ The college is a stolid-looking building with no lawn. **stolidly** /ˈstɒl.ɪd.li/ ⑩ /ˈstɑː.lɪd-/ adv

stomach /ˈstʌm.ək/ noun [C] plural **stomachs** an organ in the body where food is digested, or the soft front part of your body just below the chest: He was punched in the stomach. ○ The doctor asked him to lie down **on** his stomach. ○ The sight of blood always **churns/turns** my stomach (= makes me feel as if I am going to vomit). ○ She's got a very **delicate** stomach and doesn't eat spicy food. ○ I was hungry and my stomach had started **growling/rumbling** (= making noises). ○ He felt a knot of nervousness in the **pit** (= bottom) of his stomach. ○ I suggested that a cup of tea might **settle** (= calm) her stomach. ⊃See picture **The Body** on page Centre 5

• **not have the stomach for** sth (ALSO **have no stomach for** sth) to not feel brave or determined enough to do some-thing unpleasant: I didn't have the stomach for another fight.

• **have a strong stomach** to be able to smell, taste or see unpleasant things without feeling ill or upset: You need to have a very strong stomach to watch some of the surgery scenes.

stomach /ˈstʌm.ək/ verb [T usually in negatives] to be able to accept an unpleasant idea or watch something un-pleasant: He can't stomach the idea that Peter might be the next chairman. ○ She found the violence in the film **hard** to stomach.

'stomach ,ache noun [C or U] pain in your stomach: I ate too much and got a terrible stomach ache.

'stomach ,pump noun [C] a medical device with a long tube which is pushed down the throat to remove the contents of the stomach when someone has swallowed poison

stomp /stɒmp/ ⑩ /stɑːmp/ verb **1** [I usually + adv or prep] to walk with intentionally heavy steps, especially as a way of showing that you are annoyed: She stomped up the stairs and slammed her bedroom door. ○ He woke up in a bad mood and stomped off to the bathroom. **2** [I or T] US FOR **stamp** FOOT.

▲ **stomp on** sb/sth phrasal verb **1** MAINLY US to step down hard on someone or something: I stomped on his toes and ran away. **2** MAINLY US to treat someone or some-thing badly, or to defeat them: This is another example of the big companies joining together to stomp on small businesses.

stone ROCK /stəʊn/ ⑩ /stoʊn/ noun plural **stones** **1** [C or U] the hard solid substance found in the ground which is often used for building, or a piece of this: a stone wall/ floor ○ a flight of stone steps ○ a primitive stone axe ○ They cut enormous blocks of stone out of the hillside. ○ Some demonstrators were arrested for **throwing** stones at the police. **2** [C] a piece of hard material which can form in some organs in the body and cause severe pain: **kidney/gall** stones

• **a stone's throw** a very short distance: The cottage is just a stone's throw **from** the sea. ○ "Is your house far from here?" "No, it's only a stone's throw **away**."

• **not be set/carved in stone** UK (US **not be carved/etched in stone**) to not be fixed and to be able to be changed: These are just a few ideas – nothing is set in stone yet.

stone /stəʊn/ ⑩ /stoʊn/ verb [T] to throw stones at some-thing or someone: Rioters set up barricades and stoned police cars

• **stone** sb **to death** to kill someone as a punishment by throwing stones at them

• **stone the crows** UK OLD-FASHIONED (UK ALSO **stone me**) used as an expression of surprise: Well, stone the crows – it's five o'clock already!

stony /ˈstəʊ.ni/ ⑩ /ˈstoʊ-/ adj **1** describes ground that contains a lot of stones: The island has several small stony beaches which are usually deserted. **2** A stony expression or attitude is one which shows no sympathy or kindness: She gave me a stony glare as I walked into the room. ○ Most of her comments were met with a stony silence.

S

• **fall on stony ground** If a request or a piece of advice falls on stony ground, it is ignored or unpopular: *Her speech about the need for a peaceful solution to the crisis fell on stony ground.*

stone WEIGHT /stəʊn/ ⓤ /stoʊn/ *noun* [C] *plural* **stone** or **stones** (*WRITTEN ABBREVIATION* **st**) *UK* a unit of weight equal to 6.35 kilograms or 14 pounds, used especially when talking about a person's weight: *I weigh ten and a half stone.* ○ *She has **put on**/**lost** a stone (= is a stone heavier/lighter).*

stone JEWEL /stəʊn/ ⓤ /stoʊn/ *noun* [C] *plural* **stones** a small piece of a hard valuable substance, such as a diamond, which is found in the ground and used in jewellery: *a **precious**/**semi-precious** stone* ○ *The large central diamond is surrounded by eight smaller stones.*

stone SEED /stəʊn/ ⓤ /stoʊn/ *noun* [C] *plural* **stones** (*US ALSO* **pit**) a large hard seed inside some types of fruit: *Peaches, plums, dates, avocados and olives all contain stones.* ⟳Compare **pip** SEED. ⟳See picture **Fruit** on page Centre 1

stone /stəʊn/ ⓤ /stoʊn/ *verb* [T] (*US USUALLY* **pit**) to remove the stone from a fruit: *Could you stone the cherries for me?*

stoned /stəʊnd/ ⓤ /stoʊnd/ *adj* (*US USUALLY* **pitted**) with the stone removed: *stoned olives* ⟳See also **stoned**.

the 'Stone ,Age *noun* [S] the early period in human history when people made tools and weapons only out of stone: *a Stone Age settlement/site* ○ *FIGURATIVE My gran's TV looks **like something out of** the Stone Age (= very old-fashioned)!* ⟳Compare **the Bronze Age**; **the Iron Age**.

'stone ,age *adj INFORMAL* describes something which is very basic, simple and not well developed: *DISAPPROVING The organization is criticized for its surly service and stone age software.*

stone-cold /ˌstəʊnˈkəʊld/ ⓤ /ˌstoʊnˈkoʊld/ *adj* very or completely cold: *Your dinner's been on the table for over an hour and it's stone-cold.*

,stone-cold 'sober *adj* [after v] not having drunk any alcohol

stoned /stəʊnd/ ⓤ /stoʊnd/ *adj SLANG* experiencing the effects of a drug, such as CANNABIS: *They spent the evening **getting stoned**.* ⟳See also **stoned** at **stone** SEED.

stone-dead /ˌstəʊnˈded/ ⓤ /ˌstoʊn-/ *adj* [after v] dead: *By the time the paramedics got to him, he was stone-dead.*
• **kill sth stone-dead** to cause something to be completely unsuccessful or to stop completely: *One bad review can kill a film stone-dead.*

stone-deaf /ˌstəʊnˈdef/ ⓤ /ˌstoʊn-/ *adj* completely unable to hear anything: *She has been stone-deaf since birth.*

stonefish /ˈstəʊn.fɪʃ/ ⓤ /ˈstoʊn-/ *noun* [C] *plural* **stonefish** or **stonefishes** a tropical fish with a poisonous bite

stone-ground /ˈstəʊn.graʊnd/ ⓤ /ˈstoʊn-/ *adj* Flour that is stone-ground has been made by crushing grain between two large stones.

stonemason /ˈstəʊn.meɪ.sᵊn/ ⓤ /ˈstoʊn-/ *noun* [C] (*ALSO* **mason**) a person whose job it is to cut, prepare and use stone for building

stonewall /ˈstəʊn.wɔːl/ ⓤ /ˈstoʊn.wɑːl/ *verb* [I or T] to stop a discussion from developing by refusing to answer questions or by talking in such a way that you prevent other people from giving their opinions: *The interviewer accused the minister of stonewalling on the issue of tax increases.*

stoneware /ˈstəʊn.weəʳ/ ⓤ /ˈstoʊn.wer/ *noun* [U] plates, dishes, cups, etc. which are made from a special clay baked at a very high temperature

stonewashed /ˈstəʊn.wɒʃt/ ⓤ /ˈstoʊn.wɑːʃt/ *adj* (of a new piece of clothing, especially denim) washed together with small pieces of stone in order to make it lose some of its colour and look older: *stonewashed jeans*

stonework /ˈstəʊn.wɜːk/ ⓤ /ˈstoʊn.wɜːk/ *noun* [U] the parts of a building which are made of stone

stonkered /ˈstɒŋ.kəd/ ⓤ /ˈstɑːŋ.kɚd/ *adj UK SLANG* defeated or extremely tired: *I was completely stonkered after that game of squash.*

stonking /ˈstɒŋ.kɪŋ/ ⓤ /ˈstɑː.ŋ-/ *adj UK SLANG* used to emphasize how good something is: *We had a stonking good time at the party last night.*

stony /ˈstəʊ.ni/ ⓤ /ˈstoʊ-/ *adj* ⟳See at **stone** ROCK.

,stony 'broke *UK adj* [after v] (*US* **stone broke**) *INFORMAL* describes someone who has no money

stood /stʊd/ *past simple and past participle of* **stand**

stooge /stuːdʒ/ *noun* [C] *DISAPPROVING* **1** a person who is forced or paid by someone in authority to do an unpleasant or secret job for them: *The newly appointed mayor is widely regarded as a government stooge.* **2** an actor in an amusing show in the theatre or on television whose job is to allow the main actor to make him or her look foolish

stool SEAT /stuːl/ *noun* [C] a seat without any support for the back or arms: *a bar/kitchen/piano stool* ○ *a three-legged stool* ⟳See also **footstool**.

stool EXCRETION /stuːl/ *noun* [C] *SPECIALIZED* a piece of excrement: *He told the doctor he had been **passing** bloody stools.*

'stool ,pigeon *noun* [C] *SLANG DISAPPROVING* a person, often a criminal, who gives information in secret to the police so that they can catch other criminals

stoop BEND /stuːp/ *verb* [I] **1** to bend the top half of the body forward and down: *The doorway was so low that we had to stoop to go through it.* ○ *Something fell out of her coat pocket and she stooped **down** and picked it up.* **2** If someone stoops, their head and shoulders are always bent forwards and down: *He's over six feet tall, but the way he stoops makes him look shorter.*

stoop /stuːp/ *noun* [S] when someone stands or walks with their head and shoulders bent slightly forwards and down: *He is a tall man with a slight stoop.* **stooped** /stuːpt/ *adj*: *She is small and slightly stooped.*

stoop STEPS /stuːp/ *noun* [C] *US* a raised flat area in front of the door of a house, with steps leading up to it: *She got home to find the kids sitting on the stoop waiting for her.*

▲ **stoop to sth** *phrasal verb DISAPPROVING* to lower your moral standards by doing something which is unpleasant, dishonest or unfair: *I don't believe she would ever stoop to bribery or blackmail.* ○ [+ v-ing] *He was amazed that a reputable firm would stoop to selling the names of their clients to other companies.*

stop FINISH /stɒp/ ⓤ /stɑːp/ *verb* **-pp-** **1** [I or T] to finish doing something that you were doing: *Once I start eating chocolate, I can't stop.* ○ [+ v-ing] *Stop shouting – you're giving me a headache!* ○ *I couldn't stop laughing.* ○ *Stop it!/Stop that!* **2** [I or T] to not continue to operate: *My watch must have stopped.* ○ *The air conditioner has stopped working.* **3** [I or T] to not move anymore or to make someone or something not move anymore: *Stop the car, I want to get out!* ○ *I heard him shout "Stop, or I'll shoot!"* **4** [I + v-ing] to finish doing something that you do regularly or as a habit: *Apparently she's stopped drinking.* ○ *I stopped seeing him last year.* **5** [I] to pause in a journey or an activity for a short time: *Does this train stop **at** Finsbury Park?* ○ *Why don't you just stop somewhere and ask for directions?* ○ [+ to infinitive] *I stopped **to** pick up a letter that I'd dropped.*
• **stop at nothing sth** If you stop at nothing to achieve something, you are willing to do anything in order to achieve it, even if it involves danger, great effort or harming other people: *She'll stop at nothing to get her revenge.*
• **stop short of sth** If you stop short of doing or saying something, you decide not to do or say it although you almost do: *I stopped short of telling him the brutal truth, but only just.*

stop /stɒp/ ⓤ /stɑːp/ *noun* [C] **1** when you stop an activity or journey, or a period of time when you stop: *Please remain in your seat until the plane **comes to a complete stop**.* ○ *We'd have been here sooner, but we made several stops along the way.* ○ *At the beginning of the project there were a lot of stops **and starts**.* ⟳See also **doorstop**. **2** a place where vehicles, especially buses, stop in order to allow passengers to get off and on: *a bus stop* ○ *I'm getting off at the next stop.* ○ *Is this our stop (= where we must get off?)* ⟳See Note **station or stop?** at

station BUSES/TRAINS. **3** *UK SHORT FOR* **full stop**
• **put a stop to *sth*** to stop an unpleasant, unwanted activity or habit from continuing: *He used to smoke in bed when I first got to know him, but I soon put a stop to that!*
stoppage /ˈstɒp.ɪdʒ/ [US] /ˈstɑː.pɪdʒ/ *noun* [C] **1** a time when work is stopped because of a disagreement between workers and employers **2** *UK* (*US* **deduction**) an amount which is subtracted from the money that you are paid before you officially receive it: *Stoppages include things like tax, pension contributions and national insurance.* **-stopper** /-stɒp.əʳ/ [US] /-stɑː.pɚ/ *suffix*: *a conversation stopper* ○ *a crowd-stopper* ○ *a heart-stopper* ➲See also **showstopper**.

COMMON LEARNER ERROR

stop doing something or stop to do something?

Stop doing something means 'not continue with an activity'.

Suddenly, everyone stopped talking.
~~*Suddenly, everyone stopped to talk.*~~

Stop to do something means 'stop one activity so that you can do something else'.

We stopped to look at the map.

stop [PREVENT] /stɒp/ [US] /stɑːp/ *verb* [T] **-pp-** to prevent someone from doing something: *If she really wants to leave, I don't understand what's stopping her.* ○ [+ v-ing] *They've put barriers up to stop people **(from)** getting through.* ○ *Something must be done to stop the fighting.*
• **stop a cheque** *UK* (*US* **stop payment on a check**) to prevent your bank from dealing with a cheque which you have written, so that the money is not paid from your bank account
stop [STAY] /stɒp/ [US] /stɑːp/ *verb* [I] **-pp-** to stay in a place: *Are you coming with me or are you stopping here?* ○ *I can't stop – Malcolm's waiting for me outside.* ○ *UK Now that you're here, why don't you stop for some tea?* ○ *UK I've been out every night this week, so I thought I'd stop **in*** (= stay at home) *tonight.* ○ *UK We stopped **up*** (= did not go to bed) *until two o'clock last night watching the late film.*
stop [BLOCK] /stɒp/ [US] /stɑːp/ *verb* [T] **-pp-** to block a hole: *We stopped **(up)** the gap with some rags.*
stopper /ˈstɒp.əʳ/ [US] /ˈstɑː.pɚ/ *noun* [C] **1** an object which fits into the top of a bottle **2** *US FOR* **bung** CLOSING DEVICE.

PHRASAL VERBS WITH **stop** ▼

▲ **stop by *(somewhere)*** *phrasal verb* to visit someone briefly, usually on the way to another place: *I was passing your house, so I thought I'd stop by for a chat.*
▲ **stop in** *phrasal verb* **1** *INFORMAL* to visit a person or place for a short time, usually when you are going somewhere else: *I stopped in **at** work on the way home to check my mail.* **2** *UK INFORMAL* to stay at home, especially in the evening: *I've had my tea and I'm stopping in now.*
▲ **stop off *somewhere*** *phrasal verb* to visit or stay at a place briefly when you are going somewhere else: *I'll stop off **at** the shops on my way home and get some wine.* ○ *We're going to stop off **in** Paris for a couple of days before heading south.*
▲ **stop over** *phrasal verb* to stay at a place for one night or a few nights on the way to somewhere else or before returning home: *They're stopping over in Malaysia for a couple of nights on the way to Australia.* ○ *UK Come round for dinner one night and you can stop over* (*US* **stay over**).

stop-and-go /ˌstɒp.ənˈgəʊ/ [US] /ˌstɑː.p.ənˈgoʊ/ *adj US* A stop-and-go activity is one in which there are short periods of movement regularly interrupted by a lack of movement: *stop-and-go traffic on city streets*
stopcock /ˈstɒp.kɒk/ [US] /ˈstɑːp.kɑːk/ *noun* [C] a valve in a pipe which controls the flow of liquid through it
stopgap /ˈstɒp.gæp/ [US] /ˈstɑːp-/ *noun* [C] something intended for temporary use until something better or more suitable can be obtained: *Hostels are usually provided **as a** stopgap until the families can be housed in permanent accommodation.* ○ *We might have to employ someone temporarily as a stopgap **measure** until we can fill the post.*
stop-go /ˌstɒpˈgəʊ/ [US] /ˌstɑːpˈgoʊ/ *adj* [before n] *UK* describes a situation in which there are periods of development and activity quickly followed by periods without activity, especially in a country's economy: *The UK cannot afford another stop-go cycle of economic development.*
stoplight /ˈstɒp.laɪt/ [US] /ˈstɑːp-/ *noun* [C] *US FOR* **traffic light**
stopover *UK* /ˈstɒpˌəʊ.vəʳ/ [US] /ˈstɑːpˌoʊ.vɚ/ *noun* [C] (*US* **layover**) a brief stay in a place that you make while you are on a longer journey to somewhere else: *Our tickets to Australia include a stopover for two nights in Singapore.*
ˈ**stoppage** ˌ**time** *noun* [U] *UK* **injury time**
stopper /ˈstɒp.əʳ/ [US] /ˈstɑː.pɚ/ *noun* [C] ➲See at **stop** BLOCK.
ˌ**stop** ˈ**press** *noun* [U] *UK* Stop press refers to a particular space on the front or back page of a newspaper which contains very recent news which was added to the newspaper after the printing process had started.
ˈ**stop** ˌ**sign** *noun* [C] a sign on the road which tells drivers of vehicles to stop and not to continue until all other vehicles have gone past
stopwatch /ˈstɒp.wɒtʃ/ [US] /ˈstɑːp.wɑːtʃ/ *noun* [C] a watch that can be started and stopped in order to measure the exact time of an event, especially a sports event
ˈ**storage de**ˌ**vice** *noun* [C] a piece of computer equipment in which information and instructions can be kept
ˈ**storage** ˌ**heater** *noun* [C] *UK* an electric device for heating rooms which uses electricity during the hours when it is cheapest in order to store warmth for later use
store [SHOP] /stɔːʳ/ [US] /stɔːr/ *noun* [C] **1** *UK* a large shop where you can buy many different types of goods: *a department store* ○ *a DIY/furniture store* ➲See **shop or store?** at **shop** PLACE TO BUY THINGS. **2** *US* any type of shop: *a clothing/liquor store* ○ *a convenience store*
store [KEEP] /stɔːʳ/ [US] /stɔːr/ *verb* [T usually + adv or prep] to put or keep things in a special place for use in the future: *The data is stored **on** a hard disk and backed up on a floppy disk.* ○ *I stored my possessions **in** my mother's house while I was living in Spain.* ○ *I've stored my thick sweaters and jackets **(away)** until next winter.* ○ *Squirrels store **(up)** nuts for the winter.*
storage /ˈstɔː.rɪdʒ/ [US] /ˈstɔːr.ɪdʒ/ *noun* [U] **1** the putting and keeping of things in a special place for use in the future: *We've had to build some cupboards to give us more storage **space**.* **2 in storage** If items such as furniture are in storage, they are being kept safe in a special building while they are not needed.
store /stɔːʳ/ [US] /stɔːr/ *noun* [C] **1** an amount of something which is being kept for future use: *He's got an impressively large store **of** wine in his cellar.* ○ *Food stores are reported to be running dangerously low in the capital.* ○ *FIGURATIVE I'm afraid my great store of wit is rather depleted* (= I'm not able to be very amusing) *this evening.* **2** a building in which things are kept until they are needed: *a grain/weapons store*
• **in store** going to happen soon: *You never know what's in store **for** you.* ○ *There's a bit of a shock in store **for** him when he gets home tonight!*
store [IMPORTANCE] /stɔːʳ/ [US] /stɔːr/ *noun* [U] value or importance
• **set great/little, etc. store by *sth*** to consider something to be of great/little, etc. importance or value: *She's setting a lot of store by this job interview – I only hope she gets it.*
▲ **store *sth* up** *phrasal verb* [M] **1** to keep a lot of something in one place, to be used in the future: *We believe that he has been training an army and storing up arms.* **2** to remember things, usually so that you can tell people about them later: *I listen in to their conversations and store it all up to tell you later.*
• **store up trouble/problems** to act in a way that will make your problems much worse in the future: *If you don't deal with the problem now, you'll be storing up trouble **for yourself** in the future.*

S

store-bought *US* /ˈstɔː.bɔːt/ [US] /ˌstɔːr.bɑːt/ *adj* (*UK* **shop-bought**) describes food bought in a shop and not made at home: *Why use store-bought pastry when it's so easy to make your own?*

ˈstore ˌbrand *noun* **[U]** *US FOR* **own brand**

ˈstore ˌcard *noun* **[C]** a small plastic card which can be used as a method of payment at a particular shop, with the money being taken from you at a later date

ˈstore deˌtective *noun* **[C]** a person who works in a large shop, especially a DEPARTMENT STORE, watching the customers so that they do not steal goods

storefront /ˈstɔː.frʌnt/ [US] /ˈstɔːr-/ *noun* **[C]** (*UK* **shop front**) *US* the part of a shop which faces the road: *A number of storefronts were damaged in the riots.*

storehouse /ˈstɔː.haʊs/ [US] /ˈstɔːr-/ *noun* **[C]** *US FOR* **warehouse**

storekeeper /ˈstɔːˌkiː.pəʳ/ [US] /ˈstɔːrˌkiː.pɚ/ *noun* **[C]** *US FOR* **shopkeeper**

storeroom /ˈstɔː.rʊm/ /-ruːm/ [US] /ˈstɔːr-/ *noun* **[C]** a room for keeping items in while they are not being used

storey *UK, US* **story** /ˈstɔː.ri/ [US] /ˈstɔːr.i/ *noun* **[C]** a level of a building: *a three-storey house* ○ *Their new house has four storeys including the attic.* **storeyed** *UK, US* **storied** /ˈstɔː.rid/ [US] /ˈstɔːr.id/ *adj*: *It's a normal two-storeyed house.*

storied /ˈstɔː.rid/ [US] /ˈstɔːr.id/ *adj* **[before n]** *MAINLY US* often spoken of or written about; famous: *Theirs was the most storied romance in Hollywood.*

stork /stɔːk/ [US] /stɔːrk/ *noun* **[C]** a large white bird with very long legs which walks around in water to find its food

storm [VIOLENT WEATHER] /stɔːm/ [US] /stɔːrm/ *noun* **[C]** an extreme weather condition with very strong wind, heavy rain and often thunder and lightning: *A lot of trees were blown down in the recent storms.* ○ *They're still clearing up the storm damage.*
• **cook/dance/talk, etc. up a storm** *MAINLY US INFORMAL* to do something with a lot of energy and often skill: *Rob was in the kitchen cooking up a storm.* **-storm** /-stɔːm/ [US] /-stɔːrm/ *suffix*: *a rainstorm* ○ *a sandstorm* ○ *a snowstorm* ○ *a thunderstorm* ○ *a windstorm* **stormy** /ˈstɔː.mi/ [US] /ˈstɔːr-/ *adj*: *stormy* ***weather*** ○ *The sky was dark and stormy.*

storm [EMOTIONAL REACTION] /stɔːm/ [US] /stɔːrm/ *noun* **[C usually sing]** a very angry reaction from a lot of people: *There was a storm* ***of*** *protest when the new tax was announced.*
• **storm in a teacup** *UK* (*US* **tempest in a teapot**) a lot of unnecessary anger and anxiety about an unimportant matter
storm /stɔːm/ [US] /stɔːrm/ *verb* **[I or T] 1** *LITERARY* to express anger in a loud and often uncontrolled way: **[+ speech]** *"Get out and never come back!" he stormed.* **2 storm in/into/out** to enter or leave a place in a way that shows that you are angry: *He stormed out of the house, slamming the door as he went.*
stormy /ˈstɔː.mi/ [US] /ˈstɔːr-/ *adj* involving a lot of fierce argument and shouting: *a stormy debate* ○ *They had a passionate and often stormy relationship.*
stormily /ˈstɔː.mi.li/ [US] /ˈstɔːr-/ *adv* angrily

storm [ATTACK] /stɔːm/ [US] /stɔːrm/ *verb* **[T]** to attack a place or building by entering suddenly in great numbers: *The fortress was stormed by hundreds of soldiers.*
storm /stɔːm/ [US] /stɔːrm/ *noun* **take *sb/sth* by storm** to be suddenly extremely successful in a place or with a group of people: *Her performance has taken the London critics by storm.*

ˈstorm ˌcloud *noun* **[C usually sing]** a large dark cloud which brings rain or comes before a storm

ˈstorm ˌclouds *plural noun LITERARY* trouble, especially trouble that is going to happen soon: *Economic storm clouds are* ***gathering*** *over India.* ○ *The storm clouds* ***of war*** *seem to be looming over the east.*

ˈstorm ˌdoor/ˌwindow *noun* **[C]** *US* an extra door/window which is fitted to the usual door/window for protection in bad weather

ˈstorm ˌtrooper *noun* **[C]** a soldier in the private army of the Nazi political party in Germany before and during World War Two

story [DESCRIPTION] /ˈstɔː.ri/ [US] /ˈstɔːr.i/ *noun* **[C] 1** a description, either true or imagined, of a connected series of events: *Will you* ***read/tell*** *me a story, daddy?* ○ *Martha chose her favourite book of* ***bedtime*** *stories.* ○ *He writes* ***children's*** *stories.* ○ *I don't know if it's true but it's a good story* (= entertaining to listen to although probably not true). ○ *She gave me her version of what had happened, but it would be interesting to hear his* ***half/side of the*** *story* (= the events as described by him). ○ *Apparently his first words to her were "Will you marry me?"* ***or so*** *the story* ***goes*** (= that is what people say happened). **2** a report in a newspaper or on a news broadcast of something that has happened: *The main story in the papers today is the president's speech.* **3** a lie: *He* ***made up*** *some story about having to be at his aunt's wedding anniversary.*
• **It's/That's the story of my life.** *HUMOROUS* said when something bad happens to you that has happened to you many times before: *Honestly, it's the story of my life – I meet a totally gorgeous bloke and he's leaving for Australia the next day!*

story [LEVEL] /ˈstɔː.ri/ [US] /ˈstɔːr.i/ *noun* **[C]** *US FOR* **storey**

storyboard /ˈstɔː.ri.bɔːd/ [US] /ˈstɔːr.i.bɔːrd/ *noun* **[C]** (in films and television) a series of drawings or images showing the order of images planned for a film

storybook /ˈstɔː.ri.bʊk/ [US] /ˈstɔːr.i-/ *adj* **[before n]** (of real life situations) happy and pleasant in the way that situations in children's stories usually are: *If you're looking for a storybook romance, you're always going to be disappointed.*

ˈstory ˌline *noun* **[C]** (in a book, film, play, etc.) the PLOT (= the series of events which happen in it)

storyteller /ˈstɔː.riˌtel.əʳ/ [US] /ˈstɔːr.iˌtel.ɚ/ *noun* **[C]** a person who writes, tells or reads stories

stout [PERSON] /staʊt/ *adj* (especially of older people) quite fat and solid-looking, especially around the waist: *Mrs Blower was the rather stout lady with the glasses and the sensible shoes.*

stout [OBJECT] /staʊt/ *adj APPROVING* describes objects that are strongly made from thick, strong materials: *I've bought myself a pair of good stout boots for hiking.*
stoutly /ˈstaʊt.li/ *adv*: *stoutly-made boots*

stout [CHARACTER] /staʊt/ *adj* **[before n]** *LITERARY* strong and determined: *He needed a cool head, a stout* ***heart*** *and nerves of steel.*
stoutly /ˈstaʊt.li/ *adv* in a firm and determined way: *They have stoutly denied the recent rumours that there are problems with their marriage.*

stout [ALCOHOLIC DRINK] /staʊt/ *noun* **[U]** a dark bitter and slightly creamy type of beer

stouthearted /ˌstaʊtˈhɑː.tɪd/ [US] /-ˈhɑːr.t̬ɪd/ *adj OLD-FASHIONED LITERARY* brave and determined: *Even the most stouthearted of hikers would have had to turn back in this weather.*

stove /stəʊv/ [US] /stoʊv/ *noun* **[C] 1** a piece of equipment which burns fuel or uses electricity in order to heat a place **2** *MAINLY US* a cooker ➲See picture **In the Kitchen** on page Centre 16

stovetop /ˈstəʊv.tɒp/ [US] /ˈstoʊv.tɑːp/ *noun* **[C]** *US FOR* **hob**

stow /stəʊ/ [US] /stoʊ/ *verb* **[T]** to store something: *There's a big cupboard under the stairs for stowing toys.*
stowage /ˈstəʊ.ɪdʒ/ [US] /ˈstoʊ-/ *noun* **[U]** space for stowing things on a boat or plane

PHRASAL VERBS WITH **stow** ▼

▲ **stow away** [PERSON] *phrasal verb* to hide on a ship, aircraft or other vehicle in order to escape from a place or to travel without paying
stowaway /ˈstəʊ.əˌweɪ/ [US] /ˈstoʊ-/ *noun* **[C]** a person who hides on a ship, aircraft or other vehicle

▲ **stow *(sth)* away** [OBJECT] *phrasal verb* **[M]** to put something in a safe place so that it can be used in the future: *I think I'll stow the camping equipment away in the loft until next summer.*

straddle /ˈstræd.l̩/ *verb* **[T] 1** to sit or stand with your legs on either side of something: *He pulled on his helmet and straddled the motorbike.* **2** Something that straddles a line, such as a border or river, exists on each side of it or goes across it: *Our farm straddles the railway line.* **3** to combine different styles or subjects: *It's described as a new kind of dance music which straddles jazz and soul.* **4** MAINLY US DISAPPROVING to be unable to decide which of two opinions about a subject is better and so partly support both opinions: *It's not the first time this year that the president has been accused of straddling an* ***issue***.

strafe /streɪf/ *verb* [T] to attack an enemy by shooting from aircraft which are flying low in the sky

straggle /'stræg.l̩/ *verb* [I usually + adv or prep] to move or spread untidily and in small numbers or amounts: *I tie my hair up because I don't like it straggling down my back.* ○ *A year after the hurricane, tourists are beginning to straggle* (= come in small numbers) *back to the region.* **straggler** /'stræg.ləʳ/ (US) /-lɚ/ *noun* [C] a person or animal that is last in a group to do something or the last to get to or leave a place: *We watched the last of the stragglers come in, three hours after the first runner.* **straggly** /'stræg.li/ *adj* growing or spreading out in an untidy way: *He has a long, straggly grey beard.*

straight NOT CURVING /streɪt/ *adj, adv* continuing in one direction without bending or curving: *a straight line* ○ *She's got straight blonde hair.* ○ *Skirts this summer are long and straight.* ○ *Can't you see it? – it's straight* ***ahead*** *(of you)!* ○ *The dog seemed to be coming straight* ***at/for*** *me.* ○ *Go straight along this road and turn left at the traffic lights.* ➲See picture **Hairstyles and Hats** on page Centre 8

• **(as) straight as a die** extremely straight: *The road runs (as) straight as a die for fifty or so miles.* ➲See also **(as) straight as a die** at **straight** HONEST.

straighten /'streɪ.tᵊn/ (US) /-t̬ᵊn/ *verb* [I or T] to become straight or to make something become straight: *He straightened his tie.* ○ *Her hair is naturally curly but she always straightens it.* ○ *The road straightens* ***out*** *after a few miles.*

straight LEVEL /streɪt/ *adj* level and not sloping to either side: *This picture's not straight.* ○ *The shelf isn't straight – it sags in the middle.* **straighten** /'streɪ.tᵊn/ (US) /-t̬ᵊn/ *verb* [T] to make something level: *The picture fell while I was trying to straighten it.*

straight IMMEDIATELY /streɪt/ *adv* **1** without pausing or delaying: *I got home and went straight to bed.* ○ *Shall we go straight to the party or stop off at a pub first?* ○ *Time is short so I'll get straight* ***to the point*** (= explain the matter immediately). ➲See also **straightaway**. **2** MAINLY UK **straight away/off** immediately: *I knew straight away what you were thinking.* ○ *We don't need to go straight off – we can stay for a little while.*

straight TIDY /streɪt/ *adj* [after v] MAINLY UK tidy, or arranged in order: *It only took an hour to get the flat straight after the party.* ○ *Have you got a mirror? – I'll just put my* ***hair*** *straight.* **straighten** /'streɪ.tᵊn/ (US) /-t̬ᵊn/ *verb* [T] to make something tidy: *She stood up and straightened her clothes.* ○ *Pepe was careful to straighten his room before leaving.*

straight HONEST /streɪt/ *adj, adv* **1** honest: *Just be straight with her and tell her how you feel.* ○ INFORMAL ***Tell*** *me straight, would you rather we didn't go tonight?* ➲Compare **bent** DISHONEST. See also **straightforward** HONEST. **2 straight out** If you tell someone something straight out, you tell them directly and honestly, without trying to make what you are saying more pleasant: *I told her straight out that I didn't love her anymore.*

• **straight up** SLANG used to show that you are telling the truth: *You're a really attractive woman, straight up!* ○ *You're not telling me she's sixteen! Straight up?* (= Are you telling the truth)?

• **(as) straight as a die** completely honest: *She's as straight as a die, I can trust her to tell me what she's really thinking.* ➲See also **(as) straight as a die** at **straight** NOT CURVING.

straight PLAIN /streɪt/ *adj* plain and basic, or without anything added: *No tonic for me, please, I like my vodka straight.* ○ *Straight pasta is very bland – you need some kind of sauce to make it interesting.*

straight CLEAR /streɪt/ *adj* [before n] clear or not complicated: *It's a straight choice – either you leave him or you stay.* ○ *Let's* ***get this*** *straight – you're travelling to Frankfurt on Monday and Brussels on Tuesday, is that correct?* ➲See also **straightforward** SIMPLE. **straight** /streɪt/ *adv* clearly: *You know you've had too much to drink when you can't* ***see*** *straight.* ○ *I'm so tired I can't* ***think*** *straight any more.*

• **put/set someone straight** to make certain that someone knows the real facts about a situation: *Don't worry, I set him straight (****on*** *this matter).*

straight FOLLOWING EACH OTHER /streɪt/ *adj* [before n] following one after another without an interruption: *They're the only team to have won ten straight games this season.*

straight TRADITIONAL /streɪt/ *adj* INFORMAL traditional or serious: DISAPPROVING *He was a nice enough bloke, but he was so straight – I always felt I had to be on my best behaviour with him.* ○ *There's a lot of straight theatre at the festival as well as the newer, more experimental stuff.*

straight SEXUAL PREFERENCE /streɪt/ *adj* INFORMAL not homosexual **straight** /streɪt/ *noun* [C] INFORMAL a person who is not homosexual

straight NO DRUGS /streɪt/ *adj* INFORMAL not using illegal drugs or alcohol: *He's been straight for five months.*

straight SPORTS TRACK /streɪt/ *noun* [C] (US USUALLY **straightaway**) the straight part of a RACETRACK (= the track on which competitors race): *And the runners are just coming up to the* ***finishing*** *straight.*

straight NOT OWING MONEY /streɪt/ *adj* [after v] INFORMAL neither owing nor owed any money: *You bought the tickets, so if I pay for the taxi, we'll be straight.*

PHRASAL VERBS WITH **straighten**

▲ **straighten *sth* out** SITUATION *phrasal verb* [M] to solve a problem or to deal successfully with a confusing situation: *Once we get these problems straightened out, we should be all right.*

▲ **straighten *sb* out** PERSON *phrasal verb* [M] INFORMAL to improve someone's behaviour: *I thought that once he got a girlfriend that would straighten him out.*

▲ **straighten *sth* out** PLACE *phrasal verb* [M] to make something tidy or organized: *Could you straighten out these cupboards, please?*

▲ **straighten up** STAND STRAIGHT *phrasal verb* to stand straight after bending at the waist

▲ **straighten up** IMPROVE BEHAVIOUR *phrasal verb* US to behave well after behaving badly: *You'd better straighten up or else!*

▲ **straighten *sth* up** MAKE TIDY *phrasal verb* [M] to make a place tidy: *Mark and I managed to straighten up the house before our parents got home.*

straightaway IMMEDIATELY /ˌstreɪt.ə'weɪ/ (US) /ˌstreɪt̬-/ *adv* without pausing or delaying: *We don't have to go straightaway do we?*

straightaway SPORTS TRACK /ˌstreɪt.ə'weɪ/ (US) /ˌstreɪt̬-/ *noun* [C] US FOR a **straight** SPORTS TRACK.

ˌstraight 'face *noun* [C usually sing] a serious facial expression that you use when you do not want someone to know that you think something is funny: *Brian looked ridiculous in leather trousers, and I was desperately trying to* ***keep a straight face***. **straight-faced** /ˌstreɪt'feɪst/ *adj* without laughing or smiling: *We laughed, but Chris was straight-faced and seemed a little offended by the joke.*

straightforward SIMPLE /ˌstreɪt'fɔː.wəd/ (US) /-'fɔːr.wɚd/ *adj* easy to understand or simple: *Just follow the signs to Bradford – it's very straightforward.*

straightforward HONEST /ˌstreɪt'fɔː.wəd/ (US) /-'fɔːr.wɚd/ *adj* (of a person) honest and not tending to hide their opinions: *Roz is straightforward and let's you know what she's thinking.* **straightforwardly** /ˌstreɪt'fɔː.wəd.li/ (US) /-'fɔːr.wɚd-/ *adv*: *He explained quite straightforwardly that there wasn't enough work for us all.*

straightjacket /'streɪtˌdʒæk.ɪt/ *noun* [C] a **straitjacket**

'straight ˌman *noun* [C usually sing] In a comedy act between two men, the straight man is the more serious

S

of the two who is often made to look ridiculous by his partner.

strain [PRESSURE] /streɪn/ *noun* **1** [C usually sing or U] a force or influence that stretches, pulls or puts pressure on something, sometimes causing damage: *The hurricane **put** such a strain **on** the bridge that it collapsed.* ○ *As you get older, excess weight **puts** a lot of strain **on** the heart.* ○ *Their constant arguments were **putting** a strain **on** their marriage.* ○ *The recent decline in the dollar has **put a** bigger strain **on** the economic system.* ○ *Migration into the cities is **putting** a strain **on** already stretched resources.* ➲See also **eyestrain**. **2** [C] an injury to a muscle or similar soft part of the body caused by using that part too much: *a groin/hamstring strain* **3** [C or U] when you feel nervous and worried about something: *She's a lot better than she was but she's still not ready to face the **stresses and** strains of a job.* ○ *He's been **under** a lot of strain recently.*

strain /streɪn/ *verb* [I or T] to become stretched or to experience pressure, or to make something do or experience this: *I've put on such a lot of weight recently – this dress is straining at the seams.* ○ *I strained a muscle in my back playing squash.* ○ *Don't watch TV in the dark – you'll strain your **eyes**!* ○ [+ to infinitive] *FIGURATIVE I really had to strain* (= try very hard) ***to** reach those top notes.* ○ *FIGURATIVE I was straining **(my ears)*** (= listening hard) *to hear what they were saying.* ➲Compare **restrain**.

• **strain every nerve** to make the greatest possible effort: *She's straining every nerve to get the work finished on time.*

strained /streɪnd/ *adj* **1** If a relationship is strained, problems are spoiling that relationship: *Relations between the two countries have become strained* (= difficult) *recently.* **2** showing that someone is nervous or anxious: *She was looking strained and had dark circles beneath her eyes.* ○ *Jean felt uncomfortable but managed to force a strained smile.*

strain [SEPARATE] /streɪn/ *verb* [T] to separate liquid food from solid food, especially by pouring it through a utensil with small holes in it: *Could you strain the vegetables, please.* ○ *I usually strain the juice **off** the pineapple and use it in another recipe.*

strainer /ˈstreɪ.nəʳ/ [US] /-nɚ/ *noun* [C] a kitchen utensil with a lot of holes in it for separating liquid from solid: *a **tea** strainer*

strain [TYPE] /streɪn/ *noun* [C] **1** a particular type or quality: *A strain **of** puritanism runs through all her work.* **2** an animal or plant from a particular group whose characteristics are different in some way from others of the same group: *Scientists have discovered a new strain **of** the virus which is much more dangerous.*

strains /streɪnz/ *plural noun LITERARY* the sound of music being played or performed: *I could hear the strains **of** Mozart in the background.*

strait /streɪt/ *noun* [C usually pl] a narrow area of sea which connects two larger areas of sea: *the Straits of Gibraltar* ➲See also **straits**.

straitened /ˈstreɪ.tᵊnd/ *adj* [before n] *FORMAL* describes a situation which is difficult because there is much less money available to you than there was in the past: *With job losses and high interest rates, a lot of people are finding themselves in very straitened **circumstances** these days.*

straitjacket, **straightjacket** /ˈstreɪtˌdʒæk.ɪt/ *noun* [C usually sing] **1** a strong item of special clothing which ties the arms to the body and is used for limiting the movements of dangerous prisoners and mentally ill patients whose behaviour is violent: *Brody was locked in a padded cell and forced to wear a straitjacket.* **2** *DISAPPROVING* something that severely limits development or activity in a way that is damaging: *He refused to be fitted into any ideological straitjacket.*

straitlaced /ˌstreɪtˈleɪst/ [US] /ˈ--/ *adj DISAPPROVING* having old-fashioned and fixed morals, especially relating to sexual matters

straits /streɪts/ *plural noun* a difficult and troubled situation, especially because of financial problems: *So many companies are **in** such **dire/difficult** straits that their prices have come right down.* ➲See also **strait**.

S

strand [THREAD] /strænd/ *noun* [C] a thin thread of something, often one of a few twisted around each other to make a cord or rope: *a strand of cotton* ○ *She tucked a loose strand of hair behind her ears.*

strand [PART] /strænd/ *noun* [C] a part which combines with other parts to form a whole story, subject or situation: *There are so many different strands to the plot that it's quite hard to follow.*

strand [COAST] /strænd/ *noun* [C] *LITERARY* a **shore**

stranded /ˈstræn.dɪd/ *adj* unable to leave somewhere because of an inconvenience such as a lack of transport or money: *He **left** me stranded in town with no car and no money for a bus.* ○ *If the tide comes in, we'll be stranded on these rocks.*

strange [UNUSUAL] /streɪndʒ/ *adj* **1** unusual and unexpected, or difficult to understand: *He's got some very strange ideas about women!* ○ *You say the strangest things sometimes.* ○ *I had a strange feeling that we'd met before.* ○ ***It's** strange **that** tourists almost never visit this village.* ○ ***That's** strange – I'm sure I put my glasses in my bag and yet they're not there.* **2 feel strange** to feel uncomfortable and not normal or correct: *I hope that fish was all right – my stomach feels a bit strange.*

strangeness /ˈstreɪndʒ.nəs/ *noun* [U] the quality of being strange **strangely** /ˈstreɪndʒ.li/ *adv*: *She was strangely calm – I found it quite disturbing.*

• **strangely enough** used to remark that something is surprising but true: *Strangely enough, when it came to the exam I actually felt quite relaxed.*

COMMON LEARNER ERROR

strange or foreign?

Strange means unusual, unexpected, or not familiar. **Foreign** means coming from another country which is not your country.

There are a lot of foreign students in Cambridge.
~~*There are a lot of strange students in Cambridge.*~~

strange [NOT FAMILIAR] /streɪndʒ/ *adj* not known or familiar: *I don't usually accept lifts from strange men.* ○ *With so many strange faces around her, the baby started to cry.* ○ *I've never been here before either, so it's all strange **to** me too.* **strangeness** /ˈstreɪndʒ.nəs/ *noun* [U] *She was struck by the strangeness of her surroundings.*

stranger /ˈstreɪn.dʒəʳ/ [US] /-dʒɚ/ *noun* [C] **1** someone whom you do not know: *My mother always warned me not to talk to strangers.* ○ *I'd never met anyone at the party before – they were **complete** strangers.* ➲Do not confuse with **foreigner** (= a person from another country). **2** A stranger in a particular place is someone who has never been there before: *Do you know the way to St Peter's church or are you a stranger here too?*

• **hello stranger** *HUMOROUS* said to a person that you know but have not seen for a long time: *Hello stranger, I haven't seen you for weeks!*

• **be no stranger to *sth*** *FORMAL* to be familiar with a particular experience or activity: *He is no stranger to hard work.*

strangle /ˈstræŋ.gl̩/ *verb* [T] **1** to kill someone by pressing their throat so that they cannot breathe: *She had been strangled with her own scarf and her body dumped in the woods.* **2** *LITERARY* to stop something from developing: *For years, the organization was strangled by excessive bureaucracy.* ○ *There is a great deal of fear that the new restrictions might strangle the country's economy.*

strangled /ˈstræŋ.gl̩d/ *adj* [usually before n] *LITERARY* describes a weak, high, interrupted or not continuous sound made by an extremely frightened or anxious person: *It came again, a strangled **cry** from the room next door.*

strangler /ˈstræŋ.gləʳ/ [US] /-glɚ/ *noun* [C] a person who kills people by pressing their throats so that they cannot breathe: *The newspapers dubbed him 'the Boston Strangler'.*

strangulated /ˈstræŋ.gjʊ.leɪ.tɪd/ [US] /-t̬ɪd/ *adj* **1** *SPECIALIZED* describes an organ or other part inside the body which has become tightly pressed, blocking the flow of blood or air through it: *a strangulated hernia* **2** (*US ALSO* **strangled**) describes a sound that is not full or relaxed, but made when your throat is tight, for example because of fear or anger: *He let out a*

strangulated squeak of outrage.
strangulation /ˌstræŋ.gjʊˈleɪ.ʃᵊn/ *noun* [U] the action of killing someone by pressing their throat so that they cannot breathe, or the act of dying in this way: *The post-mortem showed that the boy had died from strangulation.*

stranglehold /ˈstræŋ.gl̩.həʊld/ [US] /-hoʊld/ *noun* [C usually sing] DISAPPROVING a position of complete control that prevents something from developing: *The two major companies have been **tightening** their stranglehold **on** the beer market.*

strap /stræp/ *noun* [C] **1** a narrow piece of leather or other strong material used for fastening something or giving support: *Could you help me fasten this strap around my suitcase?* **2** used with this meaning as a combining form: *a **watch** strap* ○ *shoes with **ankle** straps*
strap /stræp/ *verb* [T usually + adv or prep] -pp- to fasten something in position by fixing a narrow piece of leather or other strong material around it: *Are the kids strapped into their car seats?* ○ *We strapped the surfboard **to** the car roof.*
strapless /ˈstræp.ləs/ *adj* describes a piece of women's clothing, such as a dress or BRA (= item of underwear), which does not have pieces of material going over the shoulders: *a strapless taffeta evening gown*
strappy /ˈstræp.i/ *adj* INFORMAL having straps: *a pair of strappy **sandals***

PHRASAL VERBS WITH **strap**

▲ **strap *sb* in** *phrasal verb* to fasten a seat belt around someone in a car, aircraft or other vehicle, for safety purposes: *Are you kids strapped in back there?*
▲ **strap *sth* up** *UK phrasal verb* [M often passive] (*US* **tape *sth* up**) to wrap a leg, arm or other part of the body in a BANDAGE (= strip of material for wrapping around injuries): *He'd just injured himself playing football and his arm was strapped up.*

strapped /stræpt/ *adj* INFORMAL not having enough money: *I'd love to come to Malaysia with you, but I'm afraid I'm a bit strapped **(for cash)** at the moment.*

strapping /ˈstræp.ɪŋ/ *adj* [before n] INFORMAL MAINLY HUMOROUS describes someone who is tall and strong-looking: *A big strapping **lad** like you shouldn't have much difficulty lifting that!*

stratagem /ˈstræt.ə.dʒəm/ [US] /ˈstræt̬-/ *noun* [C or U] a carefully planned way of achieving or dealing with something, often involving a trick: *Her stratagem **for** dealing with her husband's infidelities was to ignore them.* ○ *He was a master of stratagem.*

strategy /ˈstræt.ə.dʒi/ [US] /ˈstræt̬-/ *noun* [C or U] a detailed plan for achieving success in situations such as war, politics, business, industry or sport, or the skill of planning for such situations: *The president held an emergency meeting to discuss military strategy with his defence commanders yesterday.* ○ *Their marketing strategy **for** the product involves obtaining as much free publicity as possible.* ○ [+ to infinitive] *We're working on new strategies **to** improve our share of the market.*
strategic /strəˈtiː.dʒɪk/ *adj* **1** helping to achieve a plan, for example in business or politics: *strategic planning* ○ *a strategic withdrawal/advance* ○ *Their bombs are always placed **in** strategic **positions** to cause as much chaos as possible.* **2** Strategic weapons, war or places provide military forces with an advantage: *There are plans to modernize the US strategic **forces**.* ○ *strategic arms reduction talks* **strategically** /strəˈtiː.dʒɪ.kli/ *adv*: *Her scarf was strategically **placed** to hide a tear in her shirt.* ○ *Central Asia is a fragile region, politically weak but strategically **important**.*
strategist /ˈstræt.ə.dʒɪst/ [US] /ˈstræt̬-/ *noun* [C] someone with a lot of skill and experience in planning, especially in military, political or business matters: *He's the president's chief **political** strategist.*

stratify /ˈstræt.ɪ.faɪ/ [US] /ˈstræt̬-/ *verb* [T] to arrange the different parts of something in separate layers or groups: *The sample of people questioned was drawn from the university's student register and stratified **by** age and gender.* **stratification** /ˌstræt.ɪ.fɪˈkeɪ.ʃᵊn/ [US] /ˌstræt̬-/ *noun* [U] FORMAL *The Prime Minister wants to reduce **social** stratification and make the country a classless society.*
stratum /ˈstrɑː.təm/ [US] /ˈstræt̬.əm/ *noun* [C] *plural* **strata** **1** one of the parts or layers into which something is separated: *The report shows that drugs have penetrated every stratum **of** American society.* **2** SPECIALIZED a layer of rock, earth or similar material: *The cliffs are characterized by remarkable zigzagging strata of shale, limestone and sandstone.*

the stratosphere /ðəˈstræt.ə.sfɪəʳ/ [US] /-ˈstræt̬.ə.sfɪr/ *noun* [S] the layer of gases surrounding the Earth at a height of between 15 and 50 kilometres, which is not affected by the weather and in which the temperature increases with height: *During the 1980s, the amount of ozone in the stratosphere above Europe decreased by about 8%.* ➲Compare **the ionosphere**.
• **go into the stratosphere** INFORMAL to go up to an extremely high level: *Property prices have gone into the stratosphere.*

straw [DRIED STEMS] /strɔː/ [US] /strɑː/ *noun* [U] the dried yellow stems of crops such as wheat, used as food for animals or as a layer on the ground for animals to lie on, and for making traditional objects: *a **bale** of straw* ○ *a straw basket/hat* ○ *straw-**coloured** hair*
• **clutch/grasp at straws** to be willing to try anything to improve a difficult or disadvantageous situation, even if it has little chance of success: *She offered to take a pay cut to keep her job, but she was just clutching at straws.*
• **the final/last straw** (ALSO **the straw that breaks the camel's back**) the last in a series of unpleasant events which finally makes you feel that you cannot continue to accept a bad situation: *Losing my job was bad enough, but being evicted from my house was the final straw.* ○ *She's always been rude to me, but it was the last straw when she started insulting my mother.*
• **straw in the wind** *UK* something that suggests what might happen: *She described the theatre's closure as "a straw in the wind" as companies faced up to the realities of life after the lottery.*

straw [TUBE] /strɔː/ [US] /strɑː/ *noun* [C] a thin tube made of plastic or waterproof paper that is used to suck liquid into the mouth: *Why don't you drink your milkshake **through** a straw?*

strawberry /ˈstrɔː.bᵊr.i/ [US] /ˈstrɑːˌber.i/ *noun* [C] a small juicy red fruit which has small brown seeds on its surface, or the plant with white flowers on which this fruit grows: *I thought we'd have strawberries **and cream** for dessert.* ○ *strawberry **jam*** ➲See picture **Fruit** on page Centre 1

ˌstrawberry ˈblonde *adj* describes hair which is a pale reddish yellow colour **ˌstrawberry ˈblonde** *noun* [C] *Who was that strawberry blonde in the red dress?*

ˈstrawberry ˌmark *noun* [C] a permanent dark red mark on a person's skin which has existed since birth

ˌstraw ˈboater *noun* [C] a stiff hat with a flat top and wide straight brim which is traditionally worn when travelling along a river in a boat to protect the wearer from the sun ➲See picture **Hairstyles and Hats** on page Centre 8

ˌstraw ˈman *noun* [C] (ALSO **man of straw**) MAINLY UK an argument, claim or opponent which is invented in order to defeat or create an argument: *The idea that national identity will be lost as a result of European integration is just a man of straw which he is wasting his time fighting.*

ˌstraw ˈpoll *noun* [C] an unofficial vote which is taken to discover what people think about an idea or problem or how they intend to vote in an election: *A straw poll **of** local inhabitants concluded that British tourists were the worst dressed and Italians the most stylish.*

stray /streɪ/ *verb* [I] **1** to travel along a route that was not originally intended, or to move beyond a limited area: *A herd of cattle had strayed into the road.* ○ *They got lost when they strayed **too far from** the footpath.* ○ *The ship strayed off course during the storm.* **2** to start thinking or talking about a different subject from the one you should be giving attention to: *I think we've strayed **too far from** our original plan.* ○ *Sorry – I've strayed from the **subject**.*

S

stray /streɪ/ *noun* **[C]** a pet that no longer has a home or cannot find its home: *a stray dog* ○ *"Who owns that cat?" "I don't know. I think it must be a stray."*

stray /streɪ/ *adj* **[before n]** Stray things have moved apart from similar things and are not in their expected or intended place: *There are still a few stray spots of paint on the window pane.* ○ *Several journalists have been killed or injured by stray* ***bullets*** *while reporting on the civil war.*

streak [MARK] /striːk/ *noun* **[C]** a long thin mark which is easily noticed because it is very different from the area surrounding it: *The window cleaner has left dirty streaks on the windows.* ○ *I dye my hair to hide my grey streaks.* ○ *Meteors produce streaks* ***of*** *light as they burn up in the Earth's atmosphere.*

• **like a streak of lightning** *INFORMAL* extremely quickly: *She grabbed the money and ran out of the shop like a streak of lightning.*

streak /striːk/ *verb* **be streaked** to have long thin noticeable lines of a different colour: *Doesn't Chris look good with her hair streaked?* ○ *Her clothes were streaked* ***with*** *mud.* ○ *White marble is frequently streaked* ***with*** *grey, black or green.* **streaky** /ˈstriː.ki/ *adj*: *This door needs another coat of paint – it's looking rather streaky.* ○ *UK Streaky* ***bacon*** *contains strips of fat.*

streak [CHARACTERISTIC] /striːk/ *noun* **[C]** an often unpleasant characteristic which is very different from other characteristics: *Her* ***stubborn*** *streak makes her very difficult to work with sometimes.* ○ *You need to have a* ***competitive*** *streak when you're working in marketing.*

streak [SHORT PERIOD] /striːk/ *noun* **[C]** a short period of good or bad luck: *I just hope my* ***lucky*** *streak continues until the world championships.* ○ *Their longest* ***losing*** *streak has been three games.* ○ *After winning a couple of bets, he thought he was* ***on*** *a winning streak.*

streak [MOVE FAST] /striːk/ *verb* **[I usually + adv or prep]** to move somewhere extremely quickly, usually in a straight line: *The motorbike streaked off* ***down*** *the street.* ○ *Did you see that bird streak* ***past*** *the window?*

streak [RUN NAKED] /striːk/ *verb* **[I]** to run naked through a public place in order to attract attention or to express strong disapproval of something **streaker** /ˈstriː.kəʳ/ [US] /-kɚ/ *noun* **[C]** *The match was interrupted when two streakers ran onto the field with a banner.*

▲ **streak ahead** *phrasal verb* to be much more successful than your competitors: *The study revealed that Asian youngsters are streaking ahead in the race to get into university.*

stream [SMALL RIVER] /striːm/ *noun* **[C]** **1** water that flows naturally along a fixed route formed by a channel cut into rock or earth, usually at ground level: *a* ***mountain*** *stream* ○ *underground streams* ○ *There's a lovely stream that* ***flows*** *through their garden.* **2** any current of water or liquid: *the level of cholesterol in your* ***blood*** *stream* **3** the direction in which water is moving: *She stopped rowing and let the boat float with the stream.*

stream [CONTINUOUS FLOW] /striːm/ *noun* **[C]** a continuous flow of things or people: *There has been a* ***steady*** *stream of phone calls from worried customers about the safety of the product.* ○ *I had a* ***constant*** *stream of visitors while I was ill.*

• **on stream** *UK* Something in industry or business that is on stream is being produced or is available for use: *The company's increased sales were primarily a result of new stores* ***coming*** *on stream.*

stream /striːm/ *verb* **1** **[I usually + adv or prep]** to flow somewhere or produce liquid, quickly and in large amounts without stopping: *There were* ***tears*** *streaming* ***down*** *his* ***face.*** ○ *One woman was carried from the scene of the accident with* ***blood*** *streaming* ***from*** *her head.* ○ *UK I've got a terrible cold and my nose has been streaming all week.* **2 stream in/out/through, etc.** to move continuously in one direction: *We were all very excited as we streamed* ***out of*** *our final exam.* ○ *Red Cross officials estimate that 20,000 refugees streamed* ***into*** *the city last week.* ○ *His hair streamed* ***out*** *behind him as he rode off.* **3** **[T]** to listen to or watch sound or video on a computer directly from the Internet rather than DOWNLOADING it and saving it first

streaming /ˈstriː.mɪŋ/ *noun* **[U]** when you listen to or watch sound or video directly from the Internet

stream [STUDENTS] *UK* /striːm/ *noun* **[C]** (*US* **track**) a group of school students with similar intelligence who are approximately the same age and are taught together: *I'm in the A stream for maths, and the B stream for English.* ○ *the top/bottom stream* **stream** *UK* /striːm/ *verb* **[T]** (*US* **track**) *We start to stream the children in the third form.* **streaming** *UK* /ˈstriː.mɪŋ/ *noun* **[U]** (*US* **tracking**) *Some people object to streaming because it gives an unfair advantage to intelligent children.*

streamer /ˈstriː.məʳ/ [US] /-mɚ/ *noun* **[C]** a long narrow strip of brightly coloured paper that is used as a decoration for special occasions such as parties: *We decorated the office with streamers for Paul's leaving party.*

streamline [SHAPE] /ˈstriːm.laɪn/ *verb* **[T]** to shape something so that it can move as effectively and quickly as possible through a liquid or gas: *Streamlining cars increases their fuel efficiency.* ○ *The bodies of dolphins are more streamlined than those of porpoises.*

streamline [IMPROVE] /ˈstriːm.laɪn/ *verb* **[T]** to improve the effectiveness of an organization such as a business or government, often by making the way activities are performed simpler: *The cost-cutting measures include streamlining administrative* ***procedures*** *in the company.* ○ *The government recently announced details of its plan to streamline the taxation system.* ○ *Streamlining management could save at least 10 percent in costs.*

ˌstream of ˈconsciousness *noun* **[U]** *SPECIALIZED* a literary style that is used to represent a character's continuous and random feelings and thoughts, using long continuous pieces of text without obvious organization or structure: *a stream-of-consciousness novel/style*

street /striːt/ *noun* **[C]** a road in a city, town or village which has buildings that are usually close together along one or both sides: *The streets were strewn with rubbish after the carnival.* ○ *a street map* ○ *Our daughter lives just* ***across*** *the street from us.* ○ *Diane's house is (UK)* ***in****/(US)* **on** *Cherrywood Street.* ○ *Builders jeer at us even when we're just* ***walking down the*** *street.* ○ *Be sure to look both ways when you* ***cross*** *the street.* ○ *The town's streets were* ***deserted*** *by dusk.* ○ *At five in the morning, there were still crowds of people* ***roaming*** *the streets.* ○ *I bought these sunglasses from a street* ***vendor*** *in Florence.*

• **the whole street** *INFORMAL* everyone living along a particular road: *Keep your voice down, we don't want the whole street to hear us!*

• **the streets are paved with gold** *LITERARY* said about a place where it is easy to get rich, or where people imagine that it is: *Many asylum seekers appear to be economic migrants, convinced that the streets of Europe are paved with gold.*

• **be streets ahead** *UK INFORMAL* to be much better or much more advanced than another thing or person: *The latest sales figures show that we're streets ahead* ***of*** *the competition.*

• **ˌman/ˌwoman/ˌperson in/on the ˈstreet** an ordinary, average person whose opinions are considered to be representative of most people: *To win the election he needs to appeal to the typical man in the street.*

• **on the streets** (*US ALSO* **on the street**) without a home: *Some of these people have been* ***living*** *on the streets for years.*

• **take to the streets** When people take to the streets, they express their opposition to something publicly and often violently: *Thousands of people have taken to the streets to protest against the military coup.*

• **be up *your* street** *UK* (*US* **be up *your* alley**) to be the type of thing that you are interested in or that you enjoy doing: *Carpentry isn't really up my street. I'd rather pay someone else to do it.* ○ *I've got a little job for you which is* ***right*** (= exactly) *up your street.*

streetcar /ˈstriːt.kɑːʳ/ [US] /-kɑːr/ *noun* **[C]** *US FOR* **tram**: *The cheapest way of seeing the city is to* ***take*** *a streetcar.*

street-cred /ˈstriːt.kred/ *noun* **[U]** (*ALSO* **street-credibility**) *UK* a quality that makes you likely to be accepted by ordinary young people who live in towns and cities because you have the same fashions, styles, interests, culture or opinions: *Many celebrities develop a working class accent to increase their street-credibility.* ○ *That*

S

jacket won't do much for your street-cred. It looks awful! **street-credible** /ˈstriːtˌkred.ɪ.bl̩/ *adj*

ˈstreet ˌfurniture *noun* [U] *UK SPECIALIZED* equipment such as lights, road signs and telephone boxes that is positioned at the side of a road for use by the public

streetlight /ˈstriːt.laɪt/ *noun* [C] (*ALSO* **streetlamp**) a light in or at the side of a road or public area which is usually supported on a tall post: *He crashed his car into a streetlight.*

ˈstreet ˌpeople *plural noun US* people who do not have a home and who often sleep outside in cities

ˈstreet ˌsmarts *plural noun US* the ability to manage or succeed in difficult or dangerous situations, especially in big towns or cities: *You haven't got the street smarts to last ten minutes in New York without getting ripped off.* **street-smart** /ˈstriːt.smɑːt/ [US] /-smɑːrt/ *adj US FOR* **streetwise**

ˈstreet ˌvalue *noun* [C usually sing; U] the price that is paid for something illegal, especially a drug, by the person who uses it: *Customs officers at Felixstowe discovered heroin with a street value **of** £6 million.*

streetwalker /ˈstriːtˌwɔː.kəʳ/ [US] /-ˌwɑː.kɚ/ *noun* [C] *OLD-FASHIONED* a PROSTITUTE who looks for customers outside in public places

streetwise /ˈstriːt.waɪz/ *adj* (*US ALSO* **street-smart**) able to deal successfully with dangerous or difficult situations in big towns or cities where poor people live or where there is a lot of crime: *McDonald was as streetwise as any of the criminals he had investigated.*

strength [EFFORT] /streŋθ/ *noun* **1** [U] the ability to do things that need a lot of physical or mental effort: *She had the strength and stamina to take the lead and win the gold medal.* ○ *Admitting you've made a mistake is a sign of strength, not weakness.* ○ *He showed great strength **of character** when he refused to accept the bribes.* ○ *We shall struggle on, **drawing** our strength from the courage of others.* ○ *Much of the country's military strength lies in its missile force.* **2** [C usually sing] the degree to which something is strong or powerful: *Opinion polls put the **combined** strength of the two ecology parties at 15% nationwide.* ○ *You can **gauge*** (= measure) *the strength of a democracy by the way it treats its minorities.*

• **Give me strength!** *MAINLY UK* an expression of amused annoyance and dissatisfaction about someone else's stupidity or inability to do something: *Oh, give me strength! Do you want me to do it for you?*

• **go from strength to strength** *MAINLY UK* to gradually become increasingly successful: *The firm's gone from strength to strength since the new factory was built.*

• **on the strength of *sth*** If you do something on the strength of something such as advice, you do it because you have been influenced by it or believe it: *I invested in the company on the strength of my brother's advice.*

strengthen /ˈstreŋ.θᵊn/ *verb* [I or T] to make something stronger or more effective, or to become stronger or more effective: *They have been strengthening their border defences in preparation for war.* ○ *His battle against cancer has strengthened his **belief** in God.* ○ *The accident strengthens the **case** for better safety measures at fairgrounds.* ○ *The bank loan has greatly strengthened our financial position.* ○ *The organization's aim is to strengthen the cultural ties between Britain and Germany.* ○ *The rise in US interest rates caused the dollar to strengthen* (= increase in value) ***against** all the Asian currencies.*

• **strengthen *sb's* hand** to give someone more power: *The police want tougher laws to strengthen their hand **against** drug traffickers.*

strength [GOOD FEATURE] /streŋθ/ *noun* [C] a good characteristic: *She's well aware of her strengths and weaknesses as an artist.* ○ *His greatest strengths are his determination and resilience.*

strength [NUMBER] /streŋθ/ *noun* [U] the number of people in a group: *What's the current strength **of** the Cambridgeshire police force?*

• **in strength** in large numbers: *Demonstrators arrived in strength to protest against the closure of the factory.*

• **below strength** *UK* If a group is below strength, it consists of fewer people or members than usual: *The office will be below strength in August when a lot of people will be away.*

• **at full strength** with the complete number of people who are usually in a group: *The staff cuts have meant that we haven't been **working** at full strength for over a year.*

strenuous /ˈstren.ju.əs/ *adj* needing or using a lot of physical or mental effort or energy: *He rarely does anything more strenuous than changing the channels on the television.* ○ *His doctor advised him not to take any strenuous **exercise**.* ○ *Strenuous **efforts** were made throughout the war to disguise the scale of civilian casualties.* **strenuously** /ˈstren.ju.ə.sli/ *adv*: *He strenuously **denies** all the allegations against him.* ○ *Most local residents strenuously **object** to the building proposals.*

ˌstrep ˈthroat *noun* [C or U] *MAINLY US* a severe infection of the throat

streptococcus (*plural* **streptococci**) /ˌstrep.təˈkɒk.əs/ [US] /-ˈkɑː.kəs/ *noun* [C] (*MAINLY US INFORMAL* **strep**) *SPECIALIZED* a bacterium, many types of which cause disease: *Tonsillitis is normally caused by infection with streptococci.* **streptococcal** /ˌstrep.təˈkɒk.l̩/ [US] /-ˈkɑː.kᵊl/ *adj*: *Pneumonia tends to be caused by streptococcal or viral infection.*

stress [WORRY] /stres/ *noun* [C or U] great worry caused by a difficult situation, or something which causes this condition: *People **under** a lot of stress may experience headaches, minor pains and sleeping difficulties.* ○ *Yoga is a very effective technique for **combating** stress.* ○ *the stresses **and strains** of the job* ○ *stress-**related** illness*
ˌstressed (ˈout) *adj* [after v] worried and anxious: *She's been **feeling** very stressed since she started her new job.* ○ *I was really stressed out before the exam.* **stressful** /ˈstres.fᵊl/ *adj*: *a stressful day/job* ○ *Police work is physically demanding and stressful.* ○ *She's very good at coping in stressful **situations**.*

stress [EMPHASIZE] /stres/ *verb* [T] to give emphasis or special importance to something: [+ (*that*)] *He is careful to stress **(that)** the laboratory's safety standards are the best in the country.* ○ *I'd just like to stress **the importance of** neatness and politeness in this job.* **stress** /stres/ *noun* [U] *During his speech, he **laid** particular stress on the freedom of the press.*

stress [PRONOUNCE] /stres/ *verb* [T] to pronounce a word or syllable with greater force than other words in the same sentence or other syllables in the same word, or to play a musical note with greater force than others in a group: *In the word 'engine', you should stress the first syllable.* **stress** /stres/ *noun* [C or U] *The meaning of a sentence often depends on stress and intonation.* ○ *When 'insert' is a verb, the stress is **on** the second syllable, but when it is a noun, the stress is **on** the first syllable.*

stress [FORCE] /stres/ *noun* [C or U] *SPECIALIZED* a force that acts in a way which tends to change the shape of an object: *Computers work out the stresses that such a craft will encounter in flight.* ○ *Jogging **puts** a lot of stress **on** your knee joints.* ○ *He needs to have an operation for a stress **fracture** in his foot.*

▲ **stress *sb* out** *phrasal verb* [M] to make someone feel very nervous and worried: *Interviews always stress me out.*

ˈstress ˌmark *noun* [C] a short vertical line which, when the pronunciation of a word is being shown, is printed before the syllable that receives the most stress or the second most stress in the word: *Stress marks above the line indicate **primary** stress, while those below the line show **secondary** stress.*

stretch [LENGTHEN] /stretʃ/ *verb* **1** [I or T] to (cause an elastic material to) become longer or wider than usual as a result of pulling at the edges: *an exercise to stretch the leg muscles* ○ *That elastic band will snap if you stretch it too far.* ○ *This substance stretches **to** any shape you want.* **2** [I] If a material stretches, it can become longer or wider when pulled and then return to its original size: *stretch **fabrics***
stretch /stretʃ/ *noun* [U] the degree to which an elastic material can be made longer or wider by pulling: *This*

S

fabric doesn't have much stretch in it, does it? **stretchy** /ˈstretʃ.i/ *adj*: *stretchy leggings* ○ *stretchy material*

stretch [GO BEYOND] /stretʃ/ *verb* [T] to go as far as or beyond the usual limit of something: *Many families' budgets are already stretched* ***to breaking point.*** ○ *We can't work any harder, Paul. We're already* ***fully*** *stretched.* ○ *This movie really stretches the patience of the audience* ***to the limit.*** ○ *We don't normally allow in people under 18, but I suppose we could stretch the* ***rules*** *for you as it's your birthday tomorrow.*

• **be stretching it** to be going beyond the truth: *She's very clever, but it's stretching it a bit* ***to*** *call her a genius.*

• **stretch a point** to make a claim which is not completely true, or to do something which goes beyond what is considered to be reasonable: *They claim to be the biggest company in the world, which is stretching a point, but it's true if you include their subsidiaries.*

• **stretch the truth** to say something which is not completely honest in order to make someone or something seem better than it really is: *He was accused of stretching the truth about how much he had helped in the project.*

• **by no stretch of the imagination** (*ALSO* **not by any stretch of the imagination**) used to describe things that are impossible to believe, even with a lot of effort: *By no stretch of the imagination could he be seriously described as an artist.*

stretch [REACH] /stretʃ/ *verb* **1** [T usually + adv or prep] to cause something to reach, often as far as possible, in a particular direction: *I tripped on a piece of wire that someone had stretched across the path.* ○ *She stretched out her* ***hand*** *and helped him from his chair.* **2** [I] to straighten your body or your arms or legs so that they are as long as possible, in order to exercise the joints after you have been in the same place or position for a long time: *"I'm so tired," she said, yawning and stretching.* ○ *It's a good idea to stretch before you take vigorous exercise.*

• **stretch *your* legs** to go for a walk, especially after sitting in the same position for a long time: *The car journey took three hours, including a couple of stops to stretch our legs.*

stretch /stretʃ/ *noun* [C usually sing] when someone or something stretches: *I always* ***have*** *a good stretch when I get up in the morning.*

stretch [SPREAD] /stretʃ/ *verb* [I usually + adv or prep] to spread over a large area or distance: *A huge cloud of dense smoke stretched* ***across*** *the horizon.* ○ *The Andes stretch* ***for*** *7250 km along the west coast of South America.* ○ *Unsettled weather will stretch* ***from*** *the middle Mississippi Valley* ***to*** *the southern Middle Atlantic States.* ○ *The refugee camps stretch* ***as far as the eye can see.***

stretch /stretʃ/ *noun* [C usually sing] **1** a continuous area of land or water: *This particular stretch* ***of*** *coast is especially popular with walkers.* ○ *Traffic is at a standstill* ***along*** *a five-****mile*** *stretch of the M11 just south of Cambridge.* ○ *Some very rare birds inhabit our stretch* ***of*** *the river.* **2** a stage in a race, or a part of a race track: *She looked certain to win as she entered the* ***final*** *stretch.* ○ *He fell as he galloped down the* ***home*** *stretch* (= towards the finish).

stretch [LONG TIME] /stretʃ/ *verb* [I usually + adv or prep] to spread over a long period of time: *The dispute stretches* ***back*** *over many years.* ○ *Although we were supposed to finish this month, it looks like the work will stretch well* ***into*** *next year.*

ˌ**stretch (ˈout)** *verb* [T] to make a process or task continue for a longer period of time than was originally planned: *I'd like to stretch my mortgage payments* ***out*** *over a longer period if possible.*

stretch /stretʃ/ *noun* [C usually sing] **1** a continuous period of time: *The elderly generally need far less rest than the young, and tend to sleep in several short stretches.* **2** *INFORMAL* a period of time that a criminal spends in prison: *Her brother's doing a ten-year stretch for armed robbery.*

• **at a stretch** *MAINLY UK* continuously or without any interruptions: *There's no way I could work* ***for*** *ten* ***hours*** *at a stretch.*

stretch [DO MORE] /stretʃ/ *verb* [T] If jobs or tasks stretch you, they make you learn new things which use your skill and experience more than you have done before: *My present job doesn't stretch me, so I'm looking for something more demanding.*

PHRASAL VERBS WITH **stretch** ▼

▲ **stretch *(yourself)* out** *phrasal verb* to lie with your legs and arms spread out in a relaxed way: *I just want to get home and stretch out on the sofa.*

▲ **stretch to *sth*** *phrasal verb UK INFORMAL* to manage to give or do a particular amount, often a larger amount than you might expect: *"How much money do you want to borrow?" "Could you stretch to £50?"*

stretcher /ˈstretʃ.əʳ/ [US] /-ɚ/ *noun* [C] a light frame made from two long poles with a cover of soft material stretched between them, used for carrying people who are ill, injured or dead: *She was carried off the track on a stretcher.*

stretcher /ˈstretʃ.əʳ/ *verb* [T + adv/prep] *UK* to carry someone on a stretcher: *Watson was stretchered* ***off*** *the pitch with a broken leg.*

stretcher-bearer /ˈstretʃ.əˌbeə.rəʳ/ [US] /-ɚˌber.ɚ/ *noun* [C] someone who carries a stretcher, with another person at its other end, particularly in a war or emergency

ˌ**stretch limouˈsine** *noun* [C] (*INFORMAL* **stretch limo**) a large luxurious car that has been specially lengthened to provide extra space or seats and is used by very rich, famous or important people

stretchmarks /ˈstretʃ.mɑːks/ [US] /-mɑːrks/ *plural noun* thin silvery lines or marks on the front or sides of the body of a woman who has given birth

strew /struː/ *verb* [T] **strewed, strewn** or **strewed** to scatter things untidily over a surface, or to be scattered untidily over a surface: *They marked the end of the war by strewing flowers over the graves of 18,000 soldiers.* ○ *Wine bottles and dirty dishes were strewn* ***across*** *the lawn.* ○ *The park was strewn* ***with*** *litter after the concert.*

strewth /struːθ/ *exclamation AUS INFORMAL AND UK OLD-FASHIONED* used to express surprise or disappointment: *Strewth, look at the size of that steak!*

striated /straɪˈeɪ.tɪd/ [US] /-t̬ɪd/ *adj SPECIALIZED* having long thin lines, marks or strips of colour: *The canyon walls were striated* ***with*** *colour.*

striation /straɪˈeɪ.ʃᵊn/ *noun* [C usually pl] *SPECIALIZED* a long thin line, mark or strip of colour: *What has caused the striations in this rock?*

strict /strɪkt/ *adj* **1** greatly limiting someone's freedom to behave as they wish, and likely to severely punish them if they disobey: *My parents were very strict* ***with*** *me when I was young.* ○ *Stricter* ***controls*** *on air pollution would help to reduce acid rain.* ○ *A strict* ***curfew*** *has been imposed from dusk till dawn.* ○ *We follow very strict* ***guidelines*** *on the use and storage of personal details on computers.* ○ *Do you think stricter gun* ***laws*** *would reduce the murder rate in the United States?* ○ *The drug should only be administered under strict medical* ***supervision.*** ○ *The negotiations took place in strict* (= total) ***secrecy.*** ➲See also **restrict**. **2** exactly correct: *a strict translation of the text* ○ *He would be found guilty under a strict* ***interpretation*** *of the law.* **3** describes someone who follows the rules and principles of a belief or way of living very carefully and exactly, or a belief or principle that is followed very carefully and exactly: *His parents were strict Catholics.* ○ *She's a strict* ***vegetarian*** *and refuses to eat any poultry or fish.*

• **in a strict sense** in the most limited meaning of a word, phrase, etc: *In a strict sense, frost refers simply to a temperature of zero degrees Celsius or less.*

• **in the strictest confidence** If you tell someone something in the strictest confidence, you expect them not to tell it to anyone else.

strictly /ˈstrɪkt.li/ *adv* **1** in a way that would bring severe punishment if disobeyed: *The speed limit is strictly* ***enforced*** *on urban roads.* ○ *The use of cameras in this museum is strictly* ***forbidden.*** **2** in a very limited or limiting way: *Should I mark this letter to your accountant 'strictly* ***confidential****'?* ○ *The proposed*

S

change in the law would make abortion illegal except for strictly ***defined*** *medical reasons.* ○ *This unrepeatable offer is only available for a strictly* ***limited*** *period.* **3** exactly or correctly: *I have acted strictly* ***in accordance with*** *the regulations at all times.* ○ *It is essential that the safety procedures are strictly* ***adhered to.*** ○ *Their salaries are not strictly* ***comparable*** (= cannot be directly compared) *because of the differences in UK and US tax rates.* ○ *Are all these questions strictly* (= really) ***necessary?***

• **strictly speaking** being completely accurate: *Strictly speaking, Great Britain consists of Scotland, Wales and England, and the United Kingdom consists of Great Britain and Northern Ireland.*

strictness /ˈstrɪkt.nəs/ *noun* **[U]** when someone or something greatly limits someone's freedom: *the increased strictness of the immigration rules*

stricture [CRITICISM] /ˈstrɪk.tʃəʳ/ [US] /-tʃɚ/ *noun* **[C]** *FORMAL* a statement of severe criticism or disapproval: *The strictures of the United Nations have failed to have any effect on the warring factions.*

stricture [LIMITATION] /ˈstrɪk.tʃəʳ/ [US] /-tʃɚ/ *noun* **[C]** *FORMAL* a severe moral or physical limitation: *religious/financial strictures* ○ *the Taliban's strictures* ***on*** *women's rights and education*

stride [WALK] /straɪd/ *verb* **[I usually + adv or prep] strode, strode, stridden** to walk somewhere quickly with long steps: *She strode* ***purposefully*** *up to the desk and demanded to speak to the manager.* ○ *He strode* ***across/into/out of*** *the room.*

stride /straɪd/ *noun* **[C]** a long step when walking or running: *She attributes her record-breaking speed to the length of her stride.*

• **not break *your* stride** to not stop walking or running at the same speed: *Without pausing for breath or breaking her stride, she pushed open the door of his private office.*

• **get into *your* stride** *MAINLY UK* (*US USUALLY* **hit *your* stride**) to become familiar with and confident at something you have recently started doing: *Let's wait until she's got into her stride before we ask her to negotiate that contract.*

• **put *sb* off *their* stride/stroke** *MAINLY UK* to take your attention away briefly from something you are doing, making it more difficult to do: *The slightest noise puts him off his stride when he's performing.*

• **take *sth* in *your* stride** *UK* (*US* **take *sth* in stride**) to deal with a problem or difficulty calmly and not to allow it to influence what you are doing: *When you become a politician, you soon learn to take criticism in your stride.*

stride [DEVELOPMENT] /straɪd/ *noun* **[C]** an important positive development: *The West* ***made*** *impressive strides* ***in*** *improving energy efficiency after the huge rises in oil prices during the seventies.* ○ *The group has made strides* ***to*** *expand internationally.*

strident [LOUD] /ˈstraɪ.dᵊnt/ *adj* describes a sound which is loud, unpleasant and rough: *People are put off by his strident voice.* **stridently** /ˈstraɪ.dᵊnt.li/ *adv* ➲See also **stridently** at **strident** FORCEFUL. **stridency** /ˈstraɪ.dᵊnt.si/ *noun* **[U]**

strident [FORCEFUL] /ˈstraɪ.dᵊnt/ *adj* expressing or expressed in forceful language which does not try to avoid upsetting other people: *a strident newspaper article* ○ *They are becoming increasingly strident in their criticism of government economic policy.* **stridently** /ˈstraɪ.dᵊnt.li/ *adv*: *She has always stridently denied the accusations against her.* ○ *He is stridently opposed to abortion.* **stridency** /ˈstraɪ.dᵊnt.si/ *noun* **[U]** *As the situation becomes more desperate, there is a growing stridency in the appeals for aid.*

strides /straɪdz/ *plural noun AUS INFORMAL* **trousers**: *a new* ***pair of*** *strides*

strife /straɪf/ *noun* **[U]** *FORMAL* violent or angry disagreement: *What are the prospects for overcoming the strife* ***between*** *the Christian minority and Muslim majority?* ○ *Twenty years of* ***civil*** *strife have left the country's economy in ruins.*

strike [HIT] /straɪk/ *verb* **struck, struck 1** **[I or T]** to hit or attack someone or something forcefully or violently: *Her car went out of control and struck an oncoming vehicle.* ○ *The police have warned the public that the killer could strike again.* ○ *The autopsy revealed that his murderer had struck him* ***on*** *the head with an iron bar.* ○ *Have you ever been struck* ***by*** *lightning?* ○ *My golf was terrible today – I just didn't strike the ball well.* **2** **[I or T]** When a clock strikes, its bells ring to show what the time is: *The clock was striking ten as we went into the church.* **3** **[I]** When a particular time strikes, a clock's bells ring to tell people what time it is: *Midnight had just struck when I went upstairs to bed.* **4** **[T]** If you strike a match, you cause it to burn by rubbing it against a hard rough surface: *She struck a match and lit another cigarette.* ○ *He lent down and struck a match* ***on*** *the sole of his boot.*

• **strike a blow against/at *sth*** to do something which harms something severely: *Her resignation has struck a blow against the company's plans for expansion.*

• **strike a blow for *sth*** to do something which supports or defends something: *The judge's ruling has struck a blow for racial equality.*

• **be struck dumb** to be so surprised by something that you cannot say anything: *We were struck dumb when she announced she was pregnant.*

• **strike fear/terror into *sb*** to make someone extremely frightened: *The brutal military regime has struck terror into the whole population.*

• **strike at the heart of *sth*** to damage something severely by attacking the most important part of it: *By its nature, terrorism is designed to strike at the heart of our democratic values.*

• **strike home** to hit the intended place or have the intended effect: *The laser guidance system dramatically increases the likelihood that the missile will strike home.* ○ *The government's message about the dangers of smoking seems to have struck home.*

• **strike while the iron is hot** to take advantage of an opportunity as soon as it exists, in case the opportunity goes away and does not return: *He doesn't often make such offers – I'd strike while the iron is hot if I were you.*

• **within striking distance 1** near: *We live within striking distance* ***of*** *both Baltimore and Washington.* **2** very near to obtaining or achieving something: *His victory in the Brazilian Grand Prix puts him within striking distance* ***of*** *the world championship.*

strike /straɪk/ *noun* **[C]** **1** when something hits or attacks with force: *Lightning conductors protect buildings and tall structures from* ***lightning*** *strikes.* ➲See also **strike force**. **2** a sudden brief military attack, particularly one by aircraft or missiles: *The United Nations has authorized the use of* ***air*** *strikes.* ○ *The violence is unlikely to stop without* ***military*** *strikes* ***against*** *terrorist bases.* ○ *Would you support a* ***nuclear*** *strike to bring an end to a war?* ○ *We have no intention of* ***launching*** *a* ***pre-emptive*** *strike, but we will retaliate if provoked.*

striker /ˈstraɪ.kəʳ/ [US] /-kɚ/ *noun* **[C]** a player in a game such as football whose main purpose is to try to score goals rather than to prevent the opposing team from scoring: *The club's new manager is a former England striker.* ○ *The 24-year-old striker scored 35 goals for Newcastle United last season.*

strike [CAUSE SUFFERING] /straɪk/ *verb* **[I or T] struck** or *MAINLY US* **stricken, struck** or *MAINLY US* **stricken** to cause a person or place to suffer severely from the effects of something very unpleasant that happens suddenly: *I've got a life insurance policy that will look after my family if* ***disaster*** *strikes.* ○ *The disease has struck the whole community, sometimes wiping out whole families.* ○ *They predict that a large* ***earthquake*** *will strike the east coast before the end of the decade.*

stricken /ˈstrɪk.ᵊn/ *adj LITERARY* suffering severely from the effects of something unpleasant: *All the oil from the stricken tanker has now leaked into the sea.* ○ *My country has been stricken* ***by*** *war for the past five years.* ○ *He has been stricken with* ***grief*** *since the death of his wife.* ○ *emergency aid for* ***famine****-stricken countries* ○ *a* ***poverty****-stricken area*

strike [STOP WORK] /straɪk/ *verb* **[I] struck, struck** to refuse to continue working because of an argument with an employer about working conditions, pay levels or job losses: *Democratization has brought workers* ***the right to*** *strike and join a trade union.* ○ *We're striking* ***for*** *a re-*

S

duction in the working week and improved safety standards.

strike /straɪk/ *noun* [C] *After last year's long and bitter strike, few people want further industrial action.* ○ *Most of the workers have ignored their union's* ***call*** *for strike* ***action****.* ○ *Some miners are* ***calling for*** *a nationwide strike in support of their sacked colleagues.* ○ *They have voted to stage* ***lightning/wildcat*** (= sudden and brief) *strikes in pursuit of their demands.* ○ *We've voted to* ***stage*** *a series of* ***one-day*** *strikes.* ○ *A* ***wave of*** *strikes swept the country.* ○ *The result of the strike* ***ballot*** *will be known tomorrow morning.*

• **go on strike** to start to strike: *All 2,500 employees* ***went*** *on strike in protest at the decision to close the factory.*

• **on strike** (*UK ALSO* **out on strike**) taking part in a strike: *The city's bus drivers have been on strike for three weeks.*

strikebound /ˈstraɪk.baʊnd/ *adj* describes a place that is closed or unable to operate because the people employed there are refusing to work: *The factory has been strike-bound for two months because of a pay dispute.*

strikebreaker /ˈstraɪkˌbreɪ.kəʳ/ [US] /-kɚ/ *noun* [C] someone who continues working during a strike or who takes the job of a worker who is involved in a strike: *Many strikebreakers were subjected to verbal and physical attacks.* **strikebreaking** /ˈstraɪkˌbreɪ.kɪŋ/ *noun* [U]

striker /ˈstraɪ.kəʳ/ [US] /-kɚ/ *noun* [C] someone who is involved in a strike: *Many people sympathize with the strikers.*

strike [REMOVE] /straɪk/ *verb* [T usually + adv or prep] **struck** or *MAINLY US* **stricken**, **struck** or *MAINLY US* **stricken** **1** *FORMAL* to remove something officially from a document: *Please strike my name* ***from*** *your mailing list immediately.* ○ *Several unreliable dealers have been struck* ***off*** *our list of authorized suppliers.* **2 strike camp** to take down your tents in preparation for leaving the place where you have been camping: *We woke up late and it was ten o'clock before we struck camp.*

strike [DISCOVER] /straɪk/ *verb* [T] **struck**, **struck** to discover a supply of oil, gas or gold underground: *The first person to strike* ***oil*** *in the US was Edwin Laurentine Drake.*

• **strike gold** *LITERARY* **1** to win a gold medal in a sports competition: *She is the favourite to strike gold in the 400 metres hurdles.* **2** to make large profits or to become rich: *A few lucky people have struck gold by investing in this company.*

• **strike it lucky** (*UK ALSO* **strike lucky**) to suddenly have a lot of unexpected luck: *What would you do if you struck it lucky in the national lottery?*

• **strike it rich** to become rich suddenly and unexpectedly: *His father struck it rich in the diamond business.*

strike /straɪk/ *noun* [C] when a valuable substance is discovered underground: *The population and settlement of Colorado expanded after the* ***gold*** *strike of 1858.*

strike [AGREE] /straɪk/ *verb* [T] **struck**, **struck** to reach or make an agreement: *Do you think the government should try to strike a* ***deal*** *with the terrorists?*

• **strike a balance** If you strike a balance between two things, you accept parts of both things in order to satisfy some of the demands of both sides in an argument, rather than all the demands of just one side: *It's a question of striking the right balance* ***between*** *quality and productivity.*

• **strike a chord** **1** If something strikes a chord, it causes people to approve of it or agree with it: *The party's policy on childcare facilities has struck a* ***responsive*** *chord* ***with*** *women voters.* ○ *Her speech struck a* ***sympathetic*** *chord* ***among*** *business leaders.* **2** If something strikes a chord, it causes people to remember something else because it is similar to it.

strike [CAUSE A FEELING] /straɪk/ *verb* [T] **struck** or *MAINLY US* **stricken**, **struck** or *MAINLY US* **stricken** to cause someone to have a feeling or idea about something: *Doesn't it strike you* ***as*** *rather* ***odd*** *that he never talks about his family?* ○ *I was immediately struck* ***by*** *the similarities between the two murders.* ○ *So how does my proposition strike you* (= What do you think of it)*?* ○ [+ (that)] ***It*** *strikes me* ***(that)*** *you'd be better off working for someone else.*

• **strike a note** to express and communicate a particular opinion or feeling about something: *I find it really difficult to strike* ***the right*** *note when I'm writing job applications.* ○ *At the end of her speech, she struck a note* ***of*** *warning about the risks involved in the project.*

strike [CAUSE TO THINK] /straɪk/ *verb* [T] **struck**, **struck** If a thought or idea strikes you, you suddenly think of it: [+ that] ***It****'s just struck me* ***that*** *I still owe you for the concert tickets.* ○ *Sitting at her desk, she was struck by the thought that there must be something more to life.*

strike [MOVE BODY] /straɪk/ *verb FORMAL* **strike a pose/attitude** to move your body into a particular position: *She may be 67, but Joan Collins can still strike a sexy pose.* ○ *Bainbridge pulled up his sagging trousers and struck the pose* ***of*** *a fearless sea captain.*

strike [MAKE COINS] /straɪk/ *verb* [T] **struck**, **struck** to make a metal disc-shaped object such as a coin with a machine that quickly presses a picture into a piece of metal: *When was the first pound* ***coin*** *struck?* ○ *A special medal has been struck to celebrate the end of the war.*

strike [BASEBALL] /straɪk/ *noun* [C] **1** a ball that has been thrown by the pitcher and not been hit successfully when it should have been: *A batter is out after three strikes.* **2** *US* a failure, mistake or disadvantage: *California's "three strikes and you're out" bill means that from now on criminals found guilty of three crimes are jailed for life.* ○ *One strike* ***against*** *him as a candidate is his perceived lack of charisma.*

PHRASAL VERBS WITH **strike** ▼

▲ **strike back** *phrasal verb* to attack someone who has attacked you

▲ **strike *sb* down** *phrasal verb* [M] If someone is struck down, they die suddenly or start to suffer from a serious illness: *It's a tragedy that these young people were struck down in their prime.* ○ *He was struck down* ***by*** *polio when he was a teenager.*

▲ **strike *sb* off *(sth)*** *phrasal verb* [M] *UK* If someone with a responsible job such as a doctor or lawyer is struck off, they are officially forbidden from continuing in that work because they have done something seriously wrong: *A solicitor who insulted two officials from the Law Society was struck off* ***for*** *abusive behaviour.*

▲ **strike on/upon *sth*** *phrasal verb* to discover or think of something: *She struck on the idea for her novel while she was travelling in Russia.*

▲ **strike out *(somewhere)*** [START] *phrasal verb* to start on a long or difficult journey in a determined way: *In heavy rain, we struck out across the field.* ○ *She struck out* ***for*** *the opposite bank.*

▲ **strike out** *phrasal verb* to start doing something new, independently of other people: *After working for her father for ten years, she felt it was time to strike out* ***on*** *her* ***own****.*

▲ **strike *(sb)* out** [BASEBALL] *phrasal verb* [M] to fail three times to hit the ball successfully in baseball and therefore to lose one of your team's chances to score, or to cause someone to do this: *The pitcher struck out all three batters in the ninth inning and saved the game.*

strikeout /ˈstraɪk.aʊt/ *noun* [C] the act of failing three times to hit the ball, or of making a BATTER (= person trying to hit the ball) do this: *He averaged 14 strikeouts per game last season.*

▲ **strike out** [FAIL] *phrasal verb US INFORMAL* to be unsuccessful: *I really struck out* ***with*** *her – she wouldn't even kiss me goodnight.*

▲ **strike *sth* out/through** [TEXT] *phrasal verb* [M] to draw a line through text in a document to show that it does not relate to you or is not correct: *Please strike out whichever option does not apply to you.*

▲ **strike up *(sth)*** [PLAY] *phrasal verb* to start to play or sing something: *When the applause had died down, a regimental band struck up the national anthem.*

▲ **strike up *sth*** [RELATE] *phrasal verb* to start a relationship or conversation with someone: *He gets really jealous if his girlfriend strikes up a* ***friendship*** *with another man.* ○ *It can be difficult to strike up a* ***conversation*** *with a complete stranger.*

S

'strike ,force *noun* [C] a group of people, especially soldiers or police officers, who are organized and trained to take strong sudden action to stop something harmful or unpleasant from continuing: *We need a multinational strike force to combat drug trafficking.*

'strike ,pay *noun* [U] money that is paid to people involved in a strike by their union from a sum of money saved specially for this purpose

striking /'straɪ.kɪŋ/ *adj* **1** very unusual or easily noticed, and therefore attracting a lot of attention: *She bears a striking resemblance to her mother.* ○ *There's a striking contrast between what he does and what he says he does.* ○ *St Peter's Church is a striking example of mission revival architecture.* ○ *There are striking similarities between the two cases.* ○ *Their production of Macbeth was the most visually striking performance I've ever seen.* **2** unusually attractive: *He's quite good-looking, but he's not as striking as his brother.* **strikingly** /'straɪ.kɪŋ.li/ *adv*: *Her latest novel is strikingly different from her earlier work.* ○ *They gave a strikingly original performance of the play.* ○ *Her husband is strikingly handsome.*

Strimmer UK TRADEMARK /'strɪm.ə^r/ US /-ɚ/ *noun* [C] (US TRADEMARK **Weed whacker**) an electric or mechanical tool that is held in the hand and is used for cutting grass in places that are difficult to reach with a larger machine

string CORD /strɪŋ/ *noun* [C or U] (a piece of) strong thin cord which is made by twisting very thin fibres together and which is used for fastening and tying things: *a parcel tied with string* ○ *a ball/piece of string* ○ *When you pull the strings, the puppet's arms and legs move.*
• **strings attached** If something such as an agreement has strings attached, it involves special demands or limitations: *Most of these so-called special offers come with strings attached.* ○ *The bank's agreed to lend me £1000, no strings attached.*
stringy /'strɪŋ.i/ *adj* similar to string: *These beans are rather stringy* (= hard and difficult to chew).

string MUSIC /strɪŋ/ *noun* [C] a thin wire or cord which is stretched across a musical instrument and is used to produce a range of notes which depend on its thickness, length and tightness: *A violin has four strings.* ○ *Guitar strings nowadays are made from steel or nylon.* ○ *You can pluck the strings on a guitar with your fingers or a plectrum.* ○ *a twelve-string guitar*
• **have another/more than one string to your bow** to have an additional interest or skill which you can use if your main one cannot be used: *I enjoy my work, but I'd like to have another string to my bow in case I lose my job.*
string /strɪŋ/ *adj* consisting of or relating to THE STRINGS: *the string section* ○ *a string quartet* ➔See also **stringed instrument**.
the strings *plural noun* the group of instruments which have strings which you pull or hit with your fingers or rub with a BOW to produce sound, or the players in a musical group who play these instruments: *I prefer his compositions for the strings.* ○ *He played the cello and joined the strings in the school orchestra.*
string /strɪŋ/ *verb* [T] strung, strung to put strings on something: *First you need to learn how to string and tune your guitar.*

string SPORT /strɪŋ/ *noun* [C] one of the thin plastic cords which are stretched between the sides of the frame of a RACKET used in sport
string /strɪŋ/ *verb* [T] strung, strung You ought to have your racket re-strung (= have new strings put on it) *before the competition.*

string SET /strɪŋ/ *noun* [C] a set of objects joined together in a row on a single cord or thread: *a string of beads/pearls* ○ *A string of onions hung from a beam in the kitchen.*
string /strɪŋ/ *verb* [T] strung, strung to put a string through a number of objects: *Would you help me string these beads?*

string SERIES /strɪŋ/ *noun* [C] a series of related things or events: *What do you think of the recent string of political scandals?* ○ *He had a string of top-twenty hits during the eighties.*

string COMPUTING /strɪŋ/ *noun* [C] SPECIALIZED a usually short piece of text consisting of letters, numbers or symbols which is used in computer processes such as searching through large amounts of information: *If you type in the search string 'ing', the computer will find all the words containing 'ing'.*

PHRASAL VERBS WITH **string**　　　　　　　▼

▲ **string sb along** *phrasal verb* [M] to deceive someone for a long time about what you are really intending to do: *She's been promising to pay back the money for six months, but I reckon she's just stringing me along.* ○ *He strung her along for years, saying he'd marry her and divorce his wife.*

▲ **string sth out** GROUP *phrasal verb* If a group of similar things or people are strung out, they are in a long line with spaces between each of them: *Most of Canada's population is strung out along its 5525-mile border with the United States.* ○ *The geese were strung out along the river bank.*

▲ **string sth out** ACTIVITY *phrasal verb* [M] to make an activity last longer than necessary: *I think the lawyer's just stringing out the case so that he'll earn more money.*

▲ **string sth together** *phrasal verb* [M] If you string words or sentences together, you manage to say something that other people can understand: *People tend to be very impressed if you can string together a couple of sentences in Japanese.*

▲ **string sb up** PUNISH *phrasal verb* [M] **1** INFORMAL to kill someone by hanging them by the neck from a rope, usually as a punishment for a crime: *He reckons they're too soft on mass murderers and says they ought to be strung up.* **2** INFORMAL to punish someone severely: *He ought to be strung up for what he said about his mother.*

▲ **string sth up** TIE *phrasal verb* [M] to tie or fix the ends of a long thin object to two points that are high up, allowing the rest of it to hang freely: *Let's string up a banner in the garden to welcome him home.*

,string 'bean *noun* [C] US FOR **runner bean**

stringed instrument /ˌstrɪŋd.ɪn.strə.mənt/ *noun* [C] (ALSO **string instrument**) a musical instrument with a set of strings which VIBRATE to produce sound when they are pulled, hit or rubbed with a BOW: *Guitars, pianos and cellos are different types of stringed instrument.*

stringent SEVERE /'strɪn.dʒənt/ *adj* having a very severe effect, or being extremely limiting: *The most stringent laws in the world are useless unless there is the will to enforce them.* ○ *We need to introduce more stringent security measures such as identity cards.* ○ *Stringent safety regulations were introduced after the accident.* **stringently** /'strɪn.dʒənt.li/ *adv*: *Fire regulations are stringently enforced in all our factories.* **stringency** /'strɪn.dʒ^ənt.si/ *noun* [U] *The stringency of the safety regulations threatens to put many manufacturers out of business.*

stringent LIMITING MONEY /'strɪn.dʒənt/ *adj* SPECIALIZED involving a lack of money that is available for borrowing which results from firm controls on the amount of money in an economy: *Already low living standards have been worsened by stringent economic reforms.* **stringency** /'strɪn.dʒ^ənt.si/ *noun* [U] *Greater financial stringency is needed to eradicate inflation from the economy.*

,string 'instrument *noun* [C] a **stringed instrument**

,string quar'tet *noun* [C] **1** a group of four instruments with strings that play together: *A string quartet consists of two violins, a viola and a cello.* **2** a piece of music written for such a group: *Joseph Haydn's works include 104 symphonies and 84 string quartets.*

strip REMOVE COVER /strɪp/ *verb* [T] -pp- to remove, pull or tear the covering or outer layer from something: *Because of the pollution, the trees are almost completely stripped of bark.* ○ *The paintwork was so bad that we decided to strip off all the paint and start again.* ○ [+ adj] *During the summer months, the sheep strip the mountains bare.*
stripper /'strɪp.ə^r/ US /-ɚ/ *noun* [C or U] a liquid chemical or an electric tool that is used for removing things such as paint: *a can of paint stripper* ○ *My new wallpaper stripper uses high-pressure steam to lift off the paper.*

strip [REMOVE CLOTHING] (-pp-) /strɪp/ *verb* [I or T] (*UK ALSO* **strip off**) to remove your clothing, or to remove all the clothing of someone else: *UK Suddenly he stripped off and ran into the sea.* ○ *It was so hot that we stripped* ***off*** *our shirts.* ○ [+ adj] *He was interrogated, stripped* ***naked*** *and then beaten.*
strip /strɪp/ *noun* [S] an entertainment in which the performer removes all his or her clothing: *He jumped up on the table and started to* ***do*** *a strip.*
stripper /ˈstrɪp.əʳ/ [US] /-ɚ/ *noun* [C] someone whose job is removing all their clothing to entertain other people: *We organized a male stripper for her 50th birthday party.*
strippagram, **strippergram** /ˈstrɪp.ə.græm/ [US] /ˈ-ɚ-/ *noun* [C] *UK* a surprise visit on a special occasion from a person who is paid to remove most or all of their clothes before giving someone a message from their friends or relatives: *They'd arranged a strippagram for Nigel's leaving party.*

strip [REMOVE PARTS] /strɪp/ *verb* [T] **-pp- 1** to remove parts of a machine, vehicle or engine in order to clean or repair it: *I've decided to strip* ***down*** *my motorbike and rebuild it.* **2** *MAINLY US* to remove the parts of a car, etc. in order to sell them

strip [PIECE] /strɪp/ *noun* [C] a long flat narrow piece: *a* ***narrow*** *strip* ***of*** *land* ○ *He didn't have a bandage, so he ripped up his shirt into* ***thin*** *strips.* ○ *Protect the* ***magnetic*** *strip on your credit card from scratches, heat, damp or other damage.*

strip [CLOTHING] /strɪp/ *noun* [C usually sing] *UK* the clothing worn by a football team which has the team's colours on it: *The team will be wearing its new strip at next Saturday's match.*

PHRASAL VERBS WITH **strip** ▼

▲ **strip *sth* away** *phrasal verb* [M] to gradually reduce something important or something that has existed for a long time: *Stripping away all the waffle, he said that no Conservative government would let Britain be drawn into a European superstate.*
▲ **strip *(down)* to *sth*** *phrasal verb* to remove everything except for a particular item of clothing or above a particular part of the body: *I had to strip down to my underwear for my medical examination.* ○ *He was stripped to the waist.*
▲ **strip *sb* of *sth*** *phrasal verb* to take something important, such as a title, away from someone as a punishment: *He was stripped of his knighthood after he was convicted of stealing from the company.*

ˌstrip carˈtoon *noun* [C] *UK* **comic strip**

ˈstrip ˌclub *noun* [C] (*INFORMAL* **strip joint**) A strip club or strip joint is a bar where the main entertainment is performers removing their clothes while dancing to music: *The city is notorious for its red light district and strip clubs.* ○ *She worked in a strip joint before she became a model.*

stripe [COLOURED STRIP] /straɪp/ *noun* [C] a strip on the surface of something which is a different colour from the surrounding surface: *The zebra is a wild African horse with black and white stripes.*
stripy (**stripier**, **stripiest**), **stripey** /ˈstraɪ.pi/ *adj* with stripes or a pattern of stripes: *He always wears stripy shirts with white collars.*
striped /straɪpt/ *adj* Something that is striped has stripes on it: *green and white striped* ***pyjamas*** ○ *Do you prefer plain or striped* ***shirts?***

stripe [MATERIAL] /straɪp/ *noun* [C] (*US ALSO* **bar**) a strip of material that is sewn onto the arm of a military uniform to show the rank of the person wearing it: *By the age of 25 he'd already got his third stripe and become a sergeant.*

ˈstrip ˌlight *UK noun* [C] (*US* **fluorescent light**) a FLUORESCENT electric light in the form of a thin glass tube, often with a protective plastic cover

ˈstrip ˌlighting *UK noun* [U] (*US* **fluorescent lighting**) one or more strip lights: *Strip lighting is very effective in offices, but it's too bright for the home.*

ˈstrip ˌmining *noun* [U] *US* a method of removing substances such as coal from the ground, which involves removing the top layer of earth instead of digging deep holes underground

ˌstrip ˈpoker *noun* [U] a card game in which players remove an item of clothing each time they lose

strip-search /ˈstrɪp.sɜːtʃ/ [US] /-sɝːtʃ/ *noun* [C] the removal of the clothes of a prisoner, or someone thought to have committed a crime, by a police officer or government official in order to find any illegal items, such as drugs, hidden in their clothing or on their body **strip-search** /ˈstrɪp.sɜːtʃ/ [US] /-sɝːtʃ/ *verb* [T] *We were stopped by customs officers at the airport and strip-searched for no apparent reason.*

striptease /ˈstrɪp.tiːz/ /ˌ-ˈ-/ *noun* [C or U] a form of entertainment in which a performer, usually a woman, takes off their clothes in a way which is sexually exciting to the people who are watching: *I'm not the sort of person who'd* ***do*** *a striptease.* ○ *a striptease* ***club/artist***

strive /straɪv/ *verb* [I] **strove** or **strived**, **striven** or **strived** to try very hard to do something or to make something happen, especially for a long time or against difficulties: [+ to infinitive] *Mr Roe has kindled expectations that he must now strive* ***to*** *live up to.* ○ *In her writing she strove* ***for*** *a balance between innovation and familiar prose forms.*

strobe (light) /ˈstrəʊb.laɪt/ [US] /ˈstroʊb-/ *noun* [C] a light which quickly flashes on and off: *The strobes and loud music in the club made her want to dance.*

strode /strəʊd/ [US] /stroʊd/ *past simple of* **stride** WALK.

stroke [TOUCH] /strəʊk/ [US] /stroʊk/ *verb* [T] to move a hand, another part of the body or an object gently over something, usually repeatedly and for pleasure: *Stroke the dog if you like, it won't bite.* ○ *She lovingly stroked Chris's face with the tips of her fingers.* **stroke** /strəʊk/ [US] /stroʊk/ *noun* [C] *Don't be frightened, just give the horse a stroke.*

stroke [ILLNESS] /strəʊk/ [US] /stroʊk/ *noun* [C] a sudden change in the blood supply to a part of the brain, which can cause a loss of the ability to move particular parts of the body: *She* ***suffered/had*** *a stroke which left her unable to speak.*

stroke [MARK] /strəʊk/ [US] /stroʊk/ *noun* [C] (a line or mark made by) a movement of a pen or pencil when writing or a brush when painting: *a brush stroke* ○ *With a few* ***bold*** *strokes, she signed her name.*

stroke [HIT] /strəʊk/ [US] /stroʊk/ *noun* [C] **1** an act of hitting a ball when playing a sport: *She returned the volley with a powerful stroke to win the game.* **2** *SLIGHTLY OLD-FASHIONED* an act of hitting someone with a weapon: *The punishment was twenty strokes of the lash.* **stroke** /strəʊk/ [US] /stroʊk/ *verb* [T] *The batsman stroked the ball effortlessly to the boundary.*

stroke [SWIMMING ACTION] /strəʊk/ [US] /stroʊk/ *noun* [C] (a particular movement which is usually repeated in) a method of swimming: *What's your best stroke when you're swimming?* ➲See also **backstroke**; **breaststroke**; **sidestroke**.

stroke [EVENT] /strəʊk/ [US] /stroʊk/ *noun* **a stroke of luck/genius, etc.** when something happens or succeeds suddenly by luck, intelligence, etc: *By a stroke of luck, someone else was walking along the path and heard my shouts for help.*

stroke [WORK] /strəʊk/ [US] /stroʊk/ *noun* [S] *INFORMAL* a small amount of work: *She's been gossiping and hasn't* ***done a*** *stroke* ***(of work)*** *all morning.*

stroke [ACTION] /strəʊk/ [US] /stroʊk/ *noun* [C] a quick forceful action: *Ending negotiations was seen as a* ***bold*** *stroke by many commentators.* ○ *By computerizing we could,* ***at a (single)/in one*** *stroke, improve efficiency and reduce costs.*

stroke [CLOCK SOUND] /strəʊk/ [US] /stroʊk/ *noun* [C] one of the sounds which some clocks make at particular times, especially by ringing a bell once for each number of the hour: *How many strokes did you count?*
• **at/on the stroke of *sth*** exactly at a particular time: *Fireworks started at the stroke of ten.*

stroke [SLOPING LINE] /strəʊk/ [US] /stroʊk/ *noun* [C] *UK* used in spoken English to mean an **oblique** DIAGONAL: *Please complete form D7/8* (= 'D seven stroke eight').

S

stroll /strəʊl/ ⓤ /stroʊl/ *verb* [I] to walk in a slow relaxed manner, especially for pleasure: *We could stroll into town if you like.* **stroll** /strəʊl/ ⓤ /stroʊl/ *noun* [C] *The whole family was enjoying a leisurely stroll in the sunshine.*

stroller /ˈstrəʊ.ləʳ/ ⓤ /ˈstroʊ.lɚ/ *noun* [C] **1** someone who strolls **2** MAINLY US FOR **pushchair**

strong NOT WEAK /strɒŋ/ ⓤ /strɑːŋ/ *adj* **1** powerful; having or using great force or control: *She must be very strong to carry such a weight on her back.* ○ *It is surely the duty of the stronger members in a society to help those who are weak.* ○ *My grandmother had a strong influence/effect on my early childhood.* ○ *Strong winds are forecast in the area for the next few days.* ○ *It's surprising what strong memories a photograph can produce.* **2** effective; of a good quality or level and likely to be successful: *We will need strong policies if our economic problems are to be solved.* ○ *I can give you stronger pain-killing drugs if these aren't strong enough.* ○ *Strong trading links exist between us and many South American countries.* **3** clever or good at doing things: *Without a doubt, she's the strongest candidate we've interviewed for the post.* ○ *As a guitarist, he's strong on* (= good at) *technique but perhaps lacks feeling in some pieces.*

strong /strɒŋ/ ⓤ /strɑːŋ/ *adv* INFORMAL **come on strong** to behave in a way which makes it clear that you are sexually interested in a particular person, or to behave towards another person in a way which many people think is too severe: *He's always coming on strong to me – I wish he'd stop.* ○ *You came on too strong then – she didn't do it deliberately.*

• **be going strong** to continue to exist and be successful or work well, after a long period: *After two hundred years, the town's theatre is still going strong.* ○ *His father is still going strong* (= alive and well) *at 94.*

strongly /ˈstrɒŋ.li/ ⓤ /ˈstrɑːŋ-/ *adv* very much or in a very serious way: *They strongly believe their children should make choices for themselves.* ○ *Many locals are strongly opposed to the development.*

strong NOTICEABLE /strɒŋ/ ⓤ /strɑːŋ/ *adj* If a taste, smell, etc. is strong, it is very noticeable or powerful: *A strong light was shining straight in my eyes.* ○ *There's a really strong smell of bleach in the corridor.* ○ *I don't like coffee/tea if it's too strong.* ○ *The room was decorated in very strong colours.* ○ *What a strong likeness there is between the brothers.*

strong DIFFICULT TO BREAK /strɒŋ/ ⓤ /strɑːŋ/ *adj* difficult to break, destroy or make ill, or able to support a heavy weight or force: *a strong box/chair* ○ *The window is made from very strong glass – it won't shatter.* ○ *He's never been very strong, and I'm afraid all the excitement was too much for him.* ○ *He had such a strong will to live – he simply refused to die.* ⊃See also **strength** EFFORT.

• **strong nerves** (ALSO **a strong stomach**) an ability to not be upset by unpleasant things: *You need a strong stomach to work in the accident department.*

strongly /ˈstrɒŋ.li/ ⓤ /ˈstrɑːŋ-/ *adv* in a way or form that is difficult to break: *Equipment will have to be strongly made to endure the weather conditions on the ice cap.*

strong DETERMINED /strɒŋ/ ⓤ /strɑːŋ/ *adj* difficult to argue with; firm and determined: *She has strong opinions about religion.* ○ *He has a strong personality, but don't let him bully you.* ○ *Most of the group have strong views on the subject of divorce.*

strong LIKELY /strɒŋ/ ⓤ /strɑːŋ/ *adj* very likely to happen: *There's a strong possibility/likelihood of finding the child within the next few hours.* ○ *The treatment's chances of success are stronger if it is started as soon as the disease is diagnosed.*

strong IN NUMBER /strɒŋ/ ⓤ /strɑːŋ/ *adj* [after n] having the stated number of people, members, etc: *Our social club is currently about eighty strong.* ⊃See also **strength** NUMBER.

strong-arm /ˈstrɒŋ.ɑːm/ ⓤ /ˈstrɑːŋ.ɑːrm/ *adj* DISAPPROVING **a strong-arm tactic/method** a method or a type of behaviour that involves using force and threats to make people do what you demand: *Police resorted to strong-arm tactics to break up the protest outside Cape Town's castle.*

strong-box /ˈstrɒŋ.bɒks/ ⓤ /ˈstrɑːŋ.bɑːks/ *noun* [C] MAINLY US a specially made box which is fastened with a lock and is very difficult to break, used to keep valuable items safe

stronghold /ˈstrɒŋ.həʊld/ ⓤ /ˈstrɑːŋ.hoʊld/ *noun* [C] **1** a building or position which is strongly defended: *a rebel stronghold* ○ *They captured the last stronghold of the presidential guard.* **2** a place or area where a particular belief or activity is common: *Rural areas have been traditionally thought of as a stronghold of old-fashioned attitudes.*

strong language *noun* [U] speech which states ideas forcefully and often contains swearing

strongman /ˈstrɒŋ.mæn/ ⓤ /ˈstrɑːŋ-/ *noun* [C] **1** a man who is employed or famous for his great physical strength: *If she talks to the police, Joey's strongmen will be paying her a visit.* **2** LITERARY a person who is very powerful and able to cause change, especially of a political type: *Haitian strongman Duvalier could feel his power slipping away.*

strong-minded /ˌstrɒŋˈmaɪn.dɪd/ ⓤ /ˌstrɑːŋ-/ *adj* If someone is strong-minded, they are determined and unwilling to change their opinions and beliefs: *You'll have to be strong-minded if you're going to push the changes through.*

strong point MAINLY UK *noun* [C] (MAINLY US **strong suit**) a particular skill or ability which a person has: *Tact is not her strong point, judging by the way she behaved.*

strongroom /ˈstrɒŋ.ruːm/ /-rʊm/ ⓤ /ˈstrɑːŋ-/ *noun* [C] a special room with strong walls and a strong door where valuable items can be kept safe: *the bank's strongroom*

strong-willed /ˌstrɒŋˈwɪld/ ⓤ /ˌstrɑːŋ-/ *adj* If you are strong-willed, you are determined to behave in a particular way although there might be good reasons for not doing so: *She's very strong-willed and if she's decided to leave school, nothing will stop her.*

strop /strɒp/ ⓤ /strɑːp/ *noun* [C] UK INFORMAL a bad mood, especially one in which a person will not do what they are asked and is unpleasant to other people: *Don't go in unless you have to – she's in a (real) strop.*

• **have a strop on** UK INFORMAL to be in a bad mood: *Why have you got such a strop on – what's happened?*

stroppy /ˈstrɒp.i/ ⓤ /ˈstrɑː.pi/ *adj* UK INFORMAL angry and unpleasant or rude to other people: *It's no use getting stroppy – I said no and I meant it!* **stroppily** /ˈstrɒp.ɪ.li/ ⓤ /ˈstrɑː.pɪ-/ *adv* **stroppiness** /ˈstrɒp.ɪ.nəs/ ⓤ /ˈstrɑː.pɪ-/ *noun* [U]

strove /strəʊv/ ⓤ /stroʊv/ *past simple of* **strive**

struck /strʌk/ *past simple and past participle of* **strike**

structure ARRANGEMENT /ˈstrʌk.tʃəʳ/ ⓤ /-tʃɚ/ *noun* [C or U] the way in which the parts of a system or object are arranged or organized, or a system arranged in this way: *the grammatical structure of a sentence* ○ *The structure of this protein is particularly complex.* ○ *They have a very old-fashioned management structure.* ○ *Some people like the sense of structure that a military lifestyle imposes.* **structural** /ˈstrʌk.tʃər.ᵊl/ ⓤ /-tʃɚ-/ *adj*: *The political reforms have led to major structural changes in the economy.* **structurally** /ˈstrʌk.tʃər.ᵊl.i/ ⓤ /-tʃɚ-/ *adv* **structure** /ˈstrʌk.tʃəʳ/ ⓤ /-tʃɚ/ *verb* [T] *We must carefully structure and rehearse each scene.* ○ *a well-structured argument*

structuralism /ˈstrʌk.tʃər.ᵊl.ɪ.zᵊm/ ⓤ /-tʃɚ-/ *noun* [U] SPECIALIZED a system of ideas used in the study of language, literature, art, ANTHROPOLOGY and SOCIOLOGY, which emphasizes the importance of the basic structures and relationships of that particular subject **structuralist** /ˈstrʌk.tʃər.ᵊl.ɪst/ ⓤ /-tʃɚ-/ *adj, noun* [C]

structure BUILDING /ˈstrʌk.tʃəʳ/ ⓤ /-tʃɚ/ *noun* [C] something which has been made or built from parts, especially a large building: *The proposed new office tower is a steel and glass structure 43 storeys high.* **structural** /ˈstrʌk.tʃər.ᵊl/ ⓤ /-tʃɚ-/ *adj* relating to the structure of a building or similar object: *Hundreds of houses in the typhoon's path suffered structural damage.* **structurally** /ˈstrʌk.tʃər.ᵊl.i/ ⓤ /-tʃɚ-/ *adv*: *Few buildings were left structurally safe after the earthquake.*

strudel /ˈstruː.dᵊl/ noun [C or U] a type of cake made from fruit which is wrapped in a thin layer of pastry and then baked: *(an) apple strudel*

struggle EFFORT /ˈstrʌg.l̩/ verb [I] **1** to experience difficulty and make a very great effort in order to do something: [+ *to* infinitive] *The dog had been struggling to get free of the wire noose.* ○ *I've been struggling to understand this article all afternoon.* ○ *Fish struggle for survival when the water level drops in the lake.* **2 struggle along/through/out, etc.** to move somewhere with great effort: *He struggled along the rough road holding his son.* ○ *By this time he'd managed to struggle out of bed.* **3** INFORMAL to be in danger of failing or being defeated: *After the first half, United were really struggling at 1-3 down.*

struggle /ˈstrʌg.l̩/ noun [C] *It was a terrible struggle for him to accept her death.* ○ *The people of this country will continue in their struggle for independence.* ○ [+ *to* infinitive] *She never gave up the struggle to have her son freed from prison.* ○ *It's going to be an uphill struggle* (= very difficult) *to get your ideas accepted.*

struggling /ˈstrʌg.lɪŋ/ adj unsuccessful but trying hard to succeed: *It's the story of a struggling artist who marries a rich woman.*

struggle FIGHT /ˈstrʌg.l̩/ verb **1** [I] to fight, especially with your hands: *He struggled with his attacker who then ran off.* **2** [I usually + adv or prep] to use a lot of effort to defeat someone, prevent something, or achieve something: *For years she struggled with/against the establishment to get her theories accepted.* **struggle** /ˈstrʌg.l̩/ noun [C] *a struggle with an armed robber* ○ *the struggle between good and evil* ○ *Clearly there will be a power struggle within the party.*

▲ **struggle on** phrasal verb to continue dealing with a difficult situation or to continue doing something difficult: *When Bobbie leaves, we'll have to struggle on until we find a replacement.*

strum /strʌm/ verb [I or T] -mm- to move your fingers across the strings of a guitar or similar instrument

strumpet /ˈstrʌm.pɪt/ noun [C] OLD USE a female prostitute

strung /strʌŋ/ past simple and past participle of string

strung 'out adj [after v] SLANG experiencing the strong effects of drugs such as HEROIN or COCAINE: *For most of her teenage years, she was strung out on crack.* ➔See also **string out**.

strung 'up adj [after v] UK INFORMAL nervous or anxious: *She always gets strung up before a performance.* ➔See also **string up**.

strut WALK /strʌt/ verb [I] -tt- to walk in a proud way trying to look important: *The boys strutted around trying to get the attention of a group of girls who were nearby.*
● **strut your stuff 1** INFORMAL MAINLY HUMOROUS to dance in a confident and usually sexually exciting way, especially trying to be noticed by other people: *Hey baby, why don't you get out on the floor and strut your stuff?* **2** INFORMAL to show your abilities: *Wimbledon is the opportunity for all the world's best tennis players to strut their stuff.*

strut ROD /strʌt/ noun [C] a strong rod, usually made from metal or wood, which helps to hold something such as a vehicle or building together

strychnine /ˈstrɪk.niːn/ noun [U] a very poisonous chemical sometimes given in very small amounts as a medicine

stub SHORT END /stʌb/ noun [C] the short part of something which is left after the main part has been used, especially a cigarette after it has been smoked or one of the small pieces of paper left in a book from which cheques or tickets have been torn
stubby /ˈstʌb.i/ adj short and thick: *He had rather unattractive stubby fingers.*

stub HURT /stʌb/ verb **stub your toe** to hurt your toe by accidentally hitting it against a hard object
▲ **stub sth out** phrasal verb [M] to stop a cigarette from burning by pressing the burning end against a hard surface

stubble /ˈstʌb.l̩/ noun [U] **1** the short hair which grows on a man's face if he has not cut the hair for a few days: *With the back of his hand, he rubbed the stubble on his chin.* **2** the short stems left after a crop such as wheat has been cut: *In the distance, a wisp of smoke rose from burning stubble.* **stubbly** /ˈstʌb.li/ adj

stubborn /ˈstʌb.ən/ ⓤ /-ɚn/ adj MAINLY DISAPPROVING **1** describes someone who is determined to do what they want and refuses to do anything else: *They have massive rows because they're both so stubborn.* **2** Things that are stubborn are difficult to move, change or deal with: *He was famed for his stubborn resistance and his refusal to accept defeat.* ○ *Stubborn stains can be removed using a small amount of detergent.*
● **be as stubborn as a mule** to be very stubborn
stubbornly /ˈstʌb.ən.li/ ⓤ /-ɚn-/ adv MAINLY DISAPPROVING *She stubbornly refused to sign the document.*
stubbornness /ˈstʌb.ən.nəs/ ⓤ /-ɚn-/ noun [U]

stucco /ˈstʌk.əʊ/ ⓤ /-oʊ/ noun [U] a type of plaster used for covering walls and ceilings, especially one which can be formed into decorative patterns **stuccoed** /ˈstʌk.əʊd/ ⓤ /-oʊd/ adj

stuck STICK /stʌk/ past simple and past participle of **stick**

stuck FIXED /stʌk/ adj **1** unable to move, or fixed in a particular position, place or way of thinking: *This door seems to be stuck – can you help me push it open?* ○ *Seven of us were stuck in the lift for over an hour.* ○ *I hate being stuck* (= having to be) *behind a desk – I'd rather work outside.* ➔See also **stick** FIX. **2** in a difficult situation, or unable to change or get away from a situation: *We'd be stuck if your sister hadn't offered to come round and look after the children tonight.* **3** not able to continue reading, answering questions, etc. because something is too difficult: *I'm really stuck – have you got any ideas how to answer these questions?* **4 be stuck with sb/sth** to have to deal with someone or something unpleasant because you have no choice or because no one else wants to: *We were stuck with him for the entire train journey!*
● **be stuck on sb/sth** OLD-FASHIONED INFORMAL to like a person or an idea very much: *Nick's really stuck on Maria – he doesn't talk about anything else.*
● **get stuck in** (ALSO **get stuck into sth**) UK INFORMAL to start doing something enthusiastically: *We showed them where the crates had to be moved to, and they got stuck in straightaway.* ○ *You really got stuck into your food* (= ate your food quickly) *– you must have been hungry.* ○ *Mum brought in the sandwiches and told us to get stuck in.*

stuck-up /ˌstʌkˈʌp/ ⓤ /ˈ--/ adj INFORMAL DISAPPROVING proud and considering yourself to be very important

stud HORSE /stʌd/ noun [C] a group of animals, especially high quality horses, kept for breeding: *David Grenfell runs a 170-acre stud farm in Co. Wexford, Ireland.*
● **put (out) to stud** SPECIALIZED kept for breeding: *The Derby winner Generous will be put to stud in Britain at the end of the season.*

stud MAN /stʌd/ noun [C] SLANG a man who is thought to have sex a lot and be good at it: *He thinks he's a real stud.*

stud DECORATION /stʌd/ noun [C usually pl] a small nail or piece of metal, with a large rounded top, that is hammered into or fixed to the surface of something, usually for decoration
studded /ˈstʌd.ɪd/ adj **1** made with metal studs hammered into the surface in a pattern: *a studded dog collar/leather jacket* **2** LITERARY **studded with sth** If something is studded with many objects of the same type, those objects are arranged regularly across it or across the surface of it: *a baked ham studded with cloves* ○ *Elaine looked up at the black, velvety sky studded with tiny, twinkling stars.*

stud JEWELLERY /stʌd/ noun [C] a small piece of metal jewellery that is put through a part of your body such as your ear or nose: *gold studs* ○ *a nose stud*

stud BOOT /stʌd/ noun [C] (US **cleat**) any of the small pointed objects which stick out from the bottom of some boots and shoes used in particular sports, especially football

stud FASTENER /stʌd/ noun [C] a fastener made from two small flat parts joined together by a short bar, used for clothing, especially in the past to fix collars onto shirts

student /'stjuː.dªnt/ ⓤ /'stuː-/ *noun* [C] **1** a person who is learning at a college or university, or sometimes at a school: *a law student* (= someone learning about law) ○ *a postgraduate student* ○ *a student teacher* (= a person training to become a teacher) ○ *He was a student at the University of Chicago.* **2** If someone is a student of a stated subject, they know about it and are interested in it, but have not necessarily studied it formally: *When you're a nurse, you get to be a bit of a student of* (= to know about) *human nature.*

,student 'loan *noun* [C] an agreement by which a student at a college or university borrows money from a bank to pay for their education and then pays the money back after they finish studying and start a job

,student 'union *noun* [C usually sing] (ALSO **students' union**) **1** an organization of students in a college or university which arranges social events and sometimes helps to provide health services and places to live **2** the building or part of a building specially used by students to meet socially

studio ARTIST'S ROOM /'stjuː.di.əʊ/ ⓤ /'stuː.di.oʊ/ *noun* [C] *plural* **studios 1** a room in which an artist works, especially a painter or photographer **2** a company making artistic or photographic products: *The firm grew to be one of Europe's foremost graphics studios.*

studio RECORDING AREA /'stjuː.di.əʊ/ ⓤ /'stuː.di.oʊ/ *noun* [C] *plural* **studios 1** a specially equipped room where television or radio programmes or music recordings are made: *She spent three months in the studio working on her latest album.* ○ *a studio audience* (= people who watch a programme while it is being made in the studio) **2** a building or place where films are made for the cinema, or a company which makes them: *Ealing Studios made some famous British comedies in the 40s and 50s.* **3** a room or building where dancing is taught or practised: *a dance studio*

studio HOME (*plural* **studios**) /'stjuː.di.əʊ/ ⓤ /'stuː.di.oʊ/ *noun* [C] (*UK ALSO* **studio flat**, *US* **studio apartment**) a small apartment designed to be lived in by one or two people, usually with one large room for sleeping and living in, a bathroom and possibly a separate kitchen

study LEARN /'stʌd.i/ *verb* [I or T] to learn about a subject, especially in an educational course or by reading books: *to study biology/chemistry* ○ *Next term we shall study plants and how they grow.* ○ *She's been studying for her doctorate for three years already.* ➲See Note **learn, teach** or **study?** at **learn**.

study /'stʌd.i/ *noun* **1** [U] when you learn about a subject, usually at school or university: *the study of English literature* **2** [C] a room, especially in a house, used for quiet work such as reading or writing

studies /'stʌd.iz/ *plural noun* **1** studying or work involving studying: *Adam doesn't spend enough time on his studies.* **2** used in the names of some educational subjects and courses: *the department of business/media studies*

studious /'stjuː.di.əs/ ⓤ /'stuː-/ *adj* describes someone who enjoys studying or spends a lot of time studying: *She was a studious child, happiest when reading.* **studiously** /'stjuː.di.ə.sli/ ⓤ /'stuː-/ *adv* **studiousness** /'stjuː.di.ə.snəs/ ⓤ /'stuː-/ *noun* [U]

▲ **study under** *sb phrasal verb* to be taught by someone: *As a young painter, he studied under Picasso.*

study EXAMINE /'stʌd.i/ *verb* [T] to examine something very carefully: *I want time to study this contract thoroughly before signing it.* ○ [+ question word] *Researchers have been studying how people under stress make decisions.*

study /'stʌd.i/ *noun* [C] **1** when someone examines a subject in detail in order to discover new information: *a five-year study of the relationship between wildlife and farming* ○ *Some studies have suggested a link between certain types of artificial sweetener and cancer.* **2** a drawing which an artist makes in order to test ideas before starting a painting of the same subject

studied /'stʌd.id/ *adj* very carefully and intentionally done, made or considered, rather than in a completely honest or sincere way: *After a pause, he gave a studied answer.* ○ *She listened to his remarks with studied indifference.*

studious /'stjuː.di.əs/ ⓤ /'stuː-/ *adj* [before n] *The report was obviously prepared with studious* (= very great) *care and attention.* **studiously** /'stjuː.di.ə.sli/ ⓤ /'stuː-/ *adv*: *They studiously avoided/ignored each other.* **studiousness** /'stjuː.di.ə.snəs/ ⓤ /'stuː-/ *noun* [U]

stuff SUBSTANCE /stʌf/ *noun* [U] **1** INFORMAL used to refer to a substance or a group of things or ideas, etc., often with a description of their general type or quality or saying who they belong to, without saying exactly what they are: *There's sticky stuff all over the chair.* ○ *We'll have to carry all our camping stuff.* ○ *Do you want help bringing your stuff* (= possessions) *in from the van?* ○ *All that stuff she has been saying about Lee is rubbish.* **2** LITERARY **the stuff of** *sth* something that a particular type of thing is made of or based on: *Her appetite for shopping became the stuff of legend.* ➲See also **stuff** NECESSARY.

• **do your stuff** INFORMAL to do what you should do or what is expected of you: *If all the members of the team do their stuff, we should win easily.*

• **stuff and nonsense** OLD-FASHIONED an expression used to show that you think something is not true and/or is silly

stuff EAT /stʌf/ *verb* INFORMAL **stuff yourself** to eat a lot: *They'd been stuffing themselves with snacks all afternoon, so they didn't want any dinner.*

• **stuff your face** INFORMAL to eat a lot: *I've been stuffing my face all morning.*

stuff FILL /stʌf/ *verb* [T] **1** to completely fill a container with something: *Stuff the cushion and then sew up the final seam.* ○ *Under her bed, they found a bag stuffed with money.* ➲See also **stuff** at **stuffing** FOOD. **2** INFORMAL to push something into a small space, often quickly or in a careless way: *This case is absolutely full – I can't stuff another thing into it.* **3** to fill the body of a dead animal with special material so that it looks as if it is still alive

• **stuff it/them/you, etc.** MAINLY UK SLANG used to show anger, disapproval or lack of obedience towards a situation, person or thing: *He's expecting us to work late, well stuff that/him!* ○ *"Shall we tidy up now?" "No, stuff it!"*

stuffed /stʌft/ *adj* **1** when something is filled with material in order to keep its shape: *a collection of stuffed birds* **2** [after v] INFORMAL (of a person) having eaten enough or too much: *"No more for me thanks – I'm stuffed."*

• **Get stuffed!** MAINLY UK VERY INFORMAL used to show annoyance, anger or disagreement: *"I'll give you ten quid for the car." "Get stuffed!"*

stuff NECESSARY /stʌf/ *noun* LITERARY **the stuff of** *sth* the most necessary, important or typical part of something: *A thwarted love affair is the (very) stuff of fiction.*

,stuffed 'animal *noun* [C] US FOR **soft toy**

,stuffed 'shirt *noun* [C] INFORMAL DISAPPROVING someone who behaves in a very formal and old-fashioned way and thinks that they are very important

stuffed-up /,stʌft'ʌp/ *adj* If you are stuffed-up, your nose is blocked with mucus, usually because you have a cold: *He sounds all stuffed-up – is he all right?*

stuffing MATERIAL /'stʌf.ɪŋ/ *noun* [U] material which is pushed inside something to make it firm

• **beat/kick/knock the stuffing out of** *sb* INFORMAL to hit or kick someone very severely: *The muggers really kicked the stuffing out of him.*

• **knock/take the stuffing out of** *sb/sth* INFORMAL to weaken someone or something severely: *Her illness has really knocked the stuffing out of her.*

stuffing FOOD /'stʌf.ɪŋ/ *noun* [U] a mixture of food, such as bread, onions and herbs, which is put inside something which is going to be eaten, such as a chicken or a vegetable, before cooking it: *sage-and-onion stuffing*

stuff /stʌf/ *verb* [T] to fill something with stuffing: *Stuff the turkey, then put it into a pre-heated oven.* **stuffed** /stʌft/ *adj*: *stuffed peppers*

stuffy FORMAL /'stʌf.i/ *adj* DISAPPROVING old-fashioned, formal and boring: *Sir William had the ability to conduct proceedings in a dignified manner without ever becoming stuffy.* ○ *He is trying to promote a less stuffy image of the Conservatives.* **stuffily** /'stʌf.ɪ.li/ *adv* **stuffiness** /'stʌf.ɪ.nəs/ *noun* [U]

S

stuffy WITHOUT AIR /'stʌf.i/ *adj DISAPPROVING* A stuffy a room or building is unpleasant because of a lack of fresh air: *a stuffy office* ○ *It's really hot and stuffy in here – let's open the window.* **stuffiness** /'stʌf.ɪ.nəs/ *noun* [U]

stultifying /'stʌl.tɪ.faɪ.ɪŋ/ ⓤ /-t̬ə-/ *adj FORMAL DISAPPROVING* preventing something or someone from developing into the best possible state: *These countries are trying to shake off the stultifying effects of several decades of state control.* **stultify** /'stʌl.tɪ.faɪ/ ⓤ /-t̬ə-/ *verb* [T] *She felt the repetitive exercises stultified her musical technique so she stopped doing them.* **stultifyingly** /'stʌl.tɪ.faɪ.ɪŋ.li/ ⓤ /-t̬ə-/ *adv: stultifyingly dull/boring*

stumble FALL /'stʌm.bl̩/ *verb* [I] to step awkwardly while walking or running and fall or begin to fall: *Running along the beach, she stumbled on a log and fell on the sand.* ○ *In the final straight Meyers stumbled, and although he didn't fall it was enough to lose him first place.*

stumble NOT CONTROLLED /'stʌm.bl̩/ *verb* [I usually + adv or prep] to walk in a way which does not seem controlled: *We could hear her stumbling about/around the bedroom in the dark.* ○ *He pulled on his clothes and stumbled into the kitchen.*

stumble PAUSE /'stʌm.bl̩/ *verb* [I] to make a mistake, such as repeating something or pausing for too long, while speaking or playing a piece of music: *When the poet stumbled over a line in the middle of a poem, someone in the audience corrected him.*

▲ **stumble across/on/upon** *sth/sb phrasal verb* to discover something by chance, or to meet someone by chance: *Workmen stumbled upon the mosaic while digging foundations for a new building.*

stumbling block *noun* [C] something which prevents action or agreement: *Lack of willingness to compromise on both sides is the main/major stumbling block to reaching a settlement.*

stump PART LEFT /stʌmp/ *noun* [C] the part of something such as tree, tooth, arm or leg which is left after most of it has been removed: *the stump of a tree* ○ *Her smile broadened to reveal two rows of brown stumps.* **stumpy** /'stʌm.pi/ *adj INFORMAL MAINLY DISAPPROVING* short and thick: *There was a large ring on each of her stumpy fingers.*

stump NO ANSWER /stʌmp/ *verb INFORMAL* **be stumped** to be unable to answer a question or solve a problem because it is too difficult: *I'm completely stumped – how did she manage to escape?* ○ *Scientists are stumped by this mystery virus.*

stump WALK /stʌmp/ *verb* [I usually + adv or prep] to stomp

stump POLITICS /stʌmp/ *verb* [T] *US* to travel around an area giving speeches and trying to get political support: *She remembers when her dad ran for governor and stumped the north of the state.*

▲ **stump up** *phrasal verb UK INFORMAL* to pay an amount or type of money for something, especially unwillingly: *It can be cheaper to stump up for a new washing machine than to get your old one repaired.* ○ *Chissano said Western governments should stump up the cash to fund land redistribution.*

stumps /stʌmps/ *plural noun* the three vertical wooden poles at which the ball is thrown in cricket **stump** /stʌmp/ *verb* [T usually passive] If the person hitting the ball in cricket is stumped, their turn to try scoring points is ended by a member of the other team knocking the BAILS off the stumps with the ball while they are outside a safe area.

stun SHOCK /stʌn/ *verb* [T] **-nn-** to shock or surprise someone very much: *News of the disaster stunned people throughout the world.* ○ *She was stunned by the amount of support she received from well-wishers.* **stunned** /stʌnd/ *adj: They stood in stunned silence beside the bodies.* ○ *I am stunned and saddened by this news.* **stunning** /'stʌn.ɪŋ/ *adj: All the ideas have a stunning simplicity.* ⊃See also **stunning**. **stunningly** /'stʌn.ɪŋ.li/ *adv: He's stunningly naive for a person of his age.*

stun MAKE UNCONSCIOUS /stʌn/ *verb* [T] **-nn-** to make a person or animal unconscious, or to cause them to lose the usual control of their mind, especially by hitting their head hard: *Stunned by the impact, he lay on the*

ground wondering what had happened. ○ *This injection stuns the rhinoceros, so we can examine it.*

stung /stʌŋ/ *past simple and past participle of* **sting**

stun gun *noun* [C] a device which produces a small electric shock in order to stop an animal or human from moving temporarily without harming them permanently

stunk /stʌŋk/ *past simple and past participle of* **stink**

stunning /'stʌn.ɪŋ/ *adj* extremely beautiful or attractive: *a stunning dress* ○ *a stunning view over the bay of Saint Tropez* ⊃See also **stunning** at **stun** SHOCK. **stunningly** /'stʌn.ɪŋ.li/ *adv: a stunningly beautiful/attractive woman*

stunner /'stʌn.əʳ/ ⓤ /-ɚ/ *noun* [C] *OLD-FASHIONED INFORMAL* a person or thing which is very beautiful, especially a woman: *The new administrator in accounts is a real stunner.*

stunt EXCITING ACTION /stʌnt/ *noun* [C] an exciting action, usually in a film, that is dangerous or appears dangerous and usually needs to be done by someone skilled: *It's a typical action film with plenty of spectacular stunts.* ○ *Tom Cruise has performed his own stunts for Mission Impossible 2, defying warnings from professionals.*

● **pull a stunt** *INFORMAL* to do something silly and risky: *What did you want to pull a stupid stunt like that for?*

stunt GET ATTENTION /stʌnt/ *noun* [C] *MAINLY DISAPPROVING* something that is done to get attention for the person or people responsible for it: *an advertising stunt* ○ *Their marriage was just a cheap publicity stunt.*

stunt PREVENT GROWTH /stʌnt/ *verb* [T] to prevent the growth or development of something from reaching its limit: *Drought has stunted (the growth of) this year's cereal crop.* ○ *When Freya was a baby we were advised that watching television would stunt her imagination.* **stunted** /'stʌn.tɪd/ ⓤ /-t̬ɪd/ *adj: A few stunted trees were the only vegetation visible.* ○ *children with stunted growth*

stunt man/woman *noun* [C] a man or woman who performs stunts, especially instead of an actor in a film or television programme

stupefy TIRE /'stjuː.pɪ.faɪ/ ⓤ /'stuː-/ *verb* [T] to make someone tired and unable to think clearly **stupefaction** /ˌstjuː.pɪˈfæk.ʃᵊn/ ⓤ /ˌstuː-/ *noun* [U] *FORMAL Because of the drugs, he was in a state of stupefaction by the time we found him.* **stupefied** /'stjuː.pɪ.faɪd/ ⓤ /'stuː-/ *adj: Stupefied by tiredness, she just sat in front of the fire.* **stupefying** /'stjuː.pɪ.faɪ.ɪŋ/ ⓤ /'stuː-/ *adj: stupefying heat/noise* **stupefyingly** /'stjuː.pɪ.faɪ.ɪŋ.li/ ⓤ /'stuː-/ *adv: stupefyingly dull/boring*

stupefy SURPRISE /'stjuː.pɪ.faɪ/ ⓤ /'stuː-/ *verb* [T] to surprise or shock someone very much **stupefaction** /ˌstjuː.pɪˈfæk.ʃᵊn/ ⓤ /ˌstuː-/ *noun* [U] *FORMAL To her parents' stupefaction, she announced her intention to leave the next day.* **stupefied** /'stjuː.pɪ.faɪd/ ⓤ /'stuː-/ *adj: We were so stupefied by the news that we all sat in silence for a long time.* **stupefying** /ˌstjuː.pɪˈfæk.ʃᵊn/ ⓤ /ˌstuː-/ *adj: stupefying arrogance* **stupefyingly** /'stjuː.pɪ.faɪ.ɪŋ.li/ ⓤ /'stuː-/ *adv: stupefyingly rich*

stupendous /stjuːˈpen.dəs/ ⓤ /stuː-/ *adj* very surprising, usually in a pleasing way, especially by being large in amount or size: *He ran up stupendous debts through his extravagant lifestyle.* ○ *Stupendous news! We've won £500 000!* **stupendously** /stjuːˈpen.də.sli/ ⓤ /stuː-/ *adv: Our charity appeal has been stupendously successful.*

stupid /'stjuː.pɪd/ ⓤ /'stuː-/ *adj* **1** foolish or unwise; lacking judgment or intelligence: *She was really stupid to quit her job like that.* ○ *Whose stupid idea was it to travel at night?* ○ *He now thinks that retiring early was a stupid thing to do.* ○ *How could you be so stupid?* **2** *INFORMAL* annoying, or causing a problem: *Have your stupid book back if it's so important to you.* ○ *I hate doing this stupid exercise, I just can't get it right.* **stupid** /'stjuː.pɪd/ ⓤ /'stuː-/ *noun* [as form of address] *INFORMAL Don't lock it, stupid!* **stupidity** /stjuːˈpɪd.ɪ.ti/ ⓤ /stuːˈpɪd.ə.t̬i/ *noun* [U] *a moment/act of stupidity* ○ *Her stupidity is beyond belief sometimes.* ○ *It was sheer stupidity to refuse at the price they were offering.* **stupidly** /'stjuː.pɪd.li/ ⓤ /'stuː-/ *adv: Sorry, I stupidly forgot to bring my copy of the* *report – could I look at yours?*

stupor /ˈstjuː.pəʳ/ ⑥ /ˈstuː.pɚ/ *noun* [C usually sing] a state in which a person is almost unconscious and their thoughts are very unclear: *He was lying under the table in a drunken stupor.*

sturdy /ˈstɜː.di/ ⑥ /ˈstɝː-/ *adj* **1** physically strong and solid or thick, and therefore unlikely to break or be hurt: *sturdy walking boots* ○ *a sturdy table* ○ *sturdy little legs* **2** [before n] LITERARY strong and determined: *They put up a sturdy defence of their proposal.* **sturdily** /ˈstɜː.dɪ.li/ ⑥ /ˈstɝː-/ *adv*: *We could see the boat was sturdily built/constructed.* **sturdiness** /ˈstɜː.dɪ.nəs/ ⑥ /ˈstɝː-/ *noun* [U]

sturgeon /ˈstɜː.dʒən/ ⑥ /ˈstɝː-/ *noun* [C] a type of fish which lives in northern parts of the world and is usually caught for its eggs, which are eaten as CAVIAR

stutter SPEAK /ˈstʌt.əʳ/ ⑥ /ˈstʌt.ɚ/ *verb* [I] to speak or say something, especially the first part of a word, with difficulty, for example pausing before it or repeating it several times: *She stutters a bit, so let her finish what she's saying.* ○ [+ speech] *"C-c-can we g-go now?" stuttered Jenkins.* ⊃Compare **stammer**. **stutter** /ˈstʌt.əʳ/ ⑥ /ˈstʌt.ɚ/ *noun* [C] *Toni's developed a slight stutter over the last few months.*

stutter WORK UNEVENLY /ˈstʌt.əʳ/ ⑥ /ˈstʌt.ɚ/ *verb* [I] to work or happen unevenly: *Suddenly the engine stuttered and then it stopped completely.*

sty STRUCTURE /staɪ/ *noun* [C] a **pigsty**

sty SWELLING, **stye** /staɪ/ *noun* [C] a small sore swelling on the edge of an eyelid

Stygian /ˈstɪdʒ.i.ən/ *adj* LITERARY extremely and unpleasantly dark: *Stygian gloom*

style WAY /staɪl/ *noun* [C or U] a way of doing something, especially one which is typical of a person, group of people, place or period: *Jones favours a dynamic, hands-on style of management.* ○ *His office is very utilitarian in style, with no decoration.*
● **be your style** INFORMAL to be the type of thing that you would do: *He wouldn't try to mislead you – it's not his style.*
-style /-staɪl/ *suffix* in the style mentioned: *Japanese-style management* ○ *antique-style furniture* **stylistic** /staɪˈlɪs.tɪk/ *adj*: *In their second album, the band tried to expand their stylistic range.* ○ *Notice the stylistic similarities in the work of these three sculptors.* **stylistically** /staɪˈlɪs.tɪ.kli/ *adv*: *stylistically diverse/similar*
stylized /ˈstaɪ.laɪzd/ *adj* (UK USUALLY **-ised**) If something is stylized, it is represented with an emphasis on a particular style, especially a style in which there are only a few simple details: *The rock drawings depict a variety of stylized human, bird and mythological figures and patterns.*

style HIGH QUALITY /staɪl/ *noun* [U] APPROVING high quality in appearance, design or behaviour: *That car's got real style, no surprise considering how much it cost.* ○ *When she decides to do something, she always does it in/with great style.* **stylish** /ˈstaɪ.lɪʃ/ *adj*: *The film's direction is subtle and stylish.* **stylishly** /ˈstaɪ.lɪʃ.li/ *adv*: *stylishly dressed* **stylishness** /ˈstaɪ.lɪʃ.nəs/ *noun* [U]

style DESIGN /staɪl/ *verb* [T] to shape or design something such as a person's hair or an object like a piece of clothing or furniture, especially so that it looks attractive: *You've had your hair styled – it really suits you.* ○ *This range of jackets is styled to look good whatever the occasion.*
styling /staɪl/ *noun* [U] used in the name of products or devices which are used for shaping a person's hair: *styling mousse/gel* ○ *a styling comb* **style** /staɪl/ *noun* [C] a formal style of hat ○ *Her hair was cut in a really nice style.* ⊃See also **hairstyle**.
stylist /ˈstaɪ.lɪst/ *noun* [C] **1** a person whose job is to shape or design something: *the latest exciting new car designed by our team of stylists* ○ *I've been going to the same (hair) stylist for years.* **2** a writer who is very careful in the way they style their work: *She's no stylist, but she writes very exciting stories.*
stylistics /staɪˈlɪs.tɪks/ *noun* [U] the systematic study of style used in language

style FASHION /staɪl/ *noun* [C or U] fashion, especially in clothing: *a style consultant* ○ *I read the fashion pages in the newspapers to keep up with the latest styles.* ○ *The classic black dress is always in style.*

style TITLE /staɪl/ *verb* [T] to give a title to a person or group: [+ n] *She styles herself 'Doctor' but she doesn't have a degree.* ⊃See also **self-styled**.

stylus /ˈstaɪ.ləs/ *noun* [C] a small pointed device on a RECORD PLAYER which picks up the sound signals stored on a record

stymie /ˈstaɪ.mi/ *verb* [T often passive] **stymieing** INFORMAL to prevent something from happening or someone from achieving a purpose: *In our search for evidence, we were stymied by the absence of any recent documents.*

Styrofoam /ˈstaɪ.rə.fəʊm/ ⑥ /-foʊm/ *noun* [U] US TRADE-MARK FOR **polystyrene**

suave /swɑːv/ *adj* describes a man who is very polite, charming and usually attractive, often in a way that is slightly false: *He's very suave and sophisticated.* **suavely** /ˈswɑːv.li/ *adv* **suavity** /ˈswɑː.vɪ.ti/ ⑥ /-və.t̬i/ *noun* [U]

sub MONEY /sʌb/ *noun* [C] UK INFORMAL FOR **subscription**: *Have you paid your tennis-club sub yet?* ⊃See at **subscribe**.

sub CHANGE /sʌb/ *noun* [C] UK AND US INFORMAL FOR **substitute**: *One of the players was injured during the match, so a sub was brought on.* **sub** /sʌb/ *verb* [I] -bb- *Diane subbed for Ted* (= did his job temporarily) *as anchor of the late-night news show.*

sub SHIP /sʌb/ *noun* [C] INFORMAL FOR **submarine**: *a nuclear sub*

sub BREAD /sʌb/ *noun* [C] US INFORMAL FOR **submarine sandwich**

sub- BELOW /sʌb-/ *prefix* under or below: *Winter weather brought sub-zero* (= less than 0 degrees) *temperatures to much of the country.*

sub- NOT QUITE /sʌb-/ *prefix* almost or nearly: *subhuman* ○ *subtropical*

sub- NOT EQUAL /sʌb-/ *prefix* less important or lower in rank: *a sublieutenant* ○ *a subordinate*

sub- SMALLER /sʌb-/ *prefix* a smaller part of a larger whole: *a subcontinent* ○ *a subcommittee meeting* ○ *to subdivide*

subaltern /ˈsʌb. əl.tən/ ⑥ /səˈbɔːl.tɚn/ *noun* [C] UK an army officer whose rank is lower than CAPTAIN

subaqua /ˌsʌbˈæk.wə/ *adj* [before n] UK relating to sports that involve swimming under water: *a subaqua club*

subatomic /ˌsʌb.əˈtɒm.ɪk/ ⑥ /-ˈtɑː.mɪk/ *adj* SPECIALIZED smaller than or within an atom: *a subatomic particle*

subcommittee /ˈsʌb.kə.mɪt.i/ ⑥ /-ˌmɪt̬-/ *noun* [C] a number of people chosen from a COMMITTEE (= a small group of people who represent a larger organization and make decisions for it) to study and report on a particular subject: *Several subcommittees will be set up to deal with specific environmental issues.*

subcompact /ˈsʌb.kəm.pækt/ *noun* [C] US a very small car: *I rent a subcompact when I'm travelling alone because it saves on gas.*

subconscious /ˌsʌbˈkɒn.ʃəs/ ⑥ /-ˈkɑːn-/ *noun* [S] the part of your mind which notices and remembers information when you are not actively trying to do so, and which influences your behaviour although you are not aware of it: *The memory was buried deep within my subconscious.* **subconscious** /ˌsʌbˈkɒn.ʃəs/ ⑥ /-ˈkɑːn-/ *adj* [before n] *subconscious thoughts/fears* ○ *Such memories exist only on/at the subconscious level.* ○ *Our subconscious mind registers things which our conscious mind is not aware of.* ⊃Compare **conscious**. **subconsciously** /ˌsʌbˈkɒn.ʃə.sli/ ⑥ /-ˈkɑːn-/ *adv*: *I think I must have known subconsciously that something was going on between them.*

subcontinent /ˌsʌbˈkɒn.tɪ.nənt/ ⑥ /ˈsʌb.kɑːn.t̬ən.ənt/ *noun* [C] a large area of land which is part of a continent, often referring to India, Pakistan and Bangladesh: *the Indian subcontinent* ○ *He has written a book about the history of railways in the subcontinent.*

subcontract /ˌsʌb.kənˈtrækt/ *verb* [T] to pay someone else to do part of a job that you have agreed to do: *Most* *of the bricklaying has been subcontracted (out) to a local builder.*

subcontractor /ˌsʌb.kənˈtræk.təʳ/ ⓤ /-t̬ɚ/ *noun* [C] a person or company that does part of a job which another person or company is responsible for

subculture /ˈsʌb.kʌl.tʃəʳ/ ⓤ /-tʃɚ/ *noun* [C] the way of life, customs and ideas of a particular group of people within a society, which are different from the rest of that society: *youth subcultures* ◦ *the gay subculture*

subcutaneous /ˌsʌb.kjuˈteɪ.ni.əs/ *adj SPECIALIZED* existing under the skin: *subcutaneous fat/muscle*

subdivide /ˌsʌb.dɪˈvaɪd/ *verb* [T] to divide something into smaller parts: *Each chapter is subdivided into smaller sections.*

subdivision /ˈsʌb.dɪˌvɪʒ.ᵊn/ /ˌ--ˈ--/ *noun* **1** [C or U] any of the parts into which something is divided, or the act of creating these: *Each category has several subdivisions.* ◦ *They agreed that subdivision of the house into apartments would be a good idea.* **2** [C] *US FOR* **housing estate**

subdue /səbˈdjuː/ ⓤ /-ˈduː/ *verb* [T] to reduce the force of something, or to prevent something from existing or developing: *The fire burned for eight hours before the fire crews could subdue it.* ◦ *He criticized the school for trying to subdue individual expression.*

subdued /səbˈdjuːd/ ⓤ /-ˈduːd/ *adj* **1** If a colour or light is subdued, it is not very bright: *subdued lighting* **2** If a noise is subdued, it is not loud: *subdued laughter/cheers* **3** If a person is subdued, they are not as happy as usual or they are unusually quiet: *He seemed a bit subdued at lunch – is he all right?*

subheading /ˈsʌb.hed.ɪŋ/ *noun* [C] a word, phrase or sentence which is used to introduce part of a text: *The subheadings are numbered within each chapter.*

subhuman /ˌsʌbˈhjuː.mən/ *adj DISAPPROVING* having or showing behaviour or characteristics which are much worse than those expected of ordinary people: *Their treatment of prisoners is subhuman.*

subject AREA OF STUDY /ˈsʌb.dʒekt/ *noun* [C] **1** the thing which is being discussed, considered or studied: *Our subject for discussion is homelessness.* ◦ *She has made a series of documentaries on the subject of family relationships.* ◦ *The guest lecturer took as her subject* (= decided to speak about) *'punishment and imprisonment in modern society'.* ◦ *The number of planes flying over the town has been the subject of* (= has caused) *concern since last summer.* **2** an area of knowledge which is studied in school, college or university: *My favourite subjects at school were history and geography.* ◦ *MAINLY UK Her subject* (= special area of study) *is low-temperature physics.*
• **change the subject** to start talking about a different subject: *I'd tried to explain the situation, but he just changed the subject.*

subject PERSON /ˈsʌb.dʒekt/ *noun* [C] a person who lives in or who has the right to live in a particular country, especially a country with a king or queen: *He is a British subject.* ◗Compare **citizen**.

subject GOVERN /səbˈdʒekt/ *verb* [T] to defeat people or a country and then control them against their wishes and limit their freedom: *The invaders quickly subjected the local tribes.* **subject** /ˈsʌb.dʒekt/ *adj* [before n] *subject peoples/states*
subjection /səbˈdʒek.ʃᵊn/ *noun* [U] *The book discusses the political subjection* (= control) *of the island by its larger neighbour.*

▲ **subject sb/sth to sth** *phrasal verb* [often passive] to make someone or something experience an unpleasant or worrying thing: *The inquiry found that they had been subjected to unfair treatment.* ◦ *I didn't want to subject him to such a long journey.*

subject HAVING /ˈsʌb.dʒekt/ *adj* **be subject to sth** to have or experience a particular thing, especially something unpleasant: *Cars are subject to a high domestic tax.* ◦ *In recent years, she has been subject to attacks of depression.*

subject DEPEND /ˈsʌb.dʒekt/ *adj* **subject to sth** depending on the stated thing happening: *We plan to go on Wednesday, subject to your approval.* ◦ *Moving all the books should not take long, subject to there being* (= if there are) *enough helpers.*

subject GRAMMAR /ˈsʌb.dʒekt/ *noun* [C] *SPECIALIZED* the person or thing which performs the action of a verb, or which is joined to a description by a verb: *'Bob' is the subject of the sentence 'Bob threw the ball'.* ◗Compare **object** GRAMMAR.

subjective /səbˈdʒek.tɪv/ *adj* influenced by or based on personal beliefs or feelings, rather than based on facts: *I think my husband is the most handsome man in the world, but I realize my judgment is rather subjective.* ◦ *More specific and less subjective criteria should be used in selecting people for promotion within the company.* ◗Compare **objective** FAIR OR REAL. **subjectively** /səbˈdʒek.tɪv.li/ *adv* **subjectivity** /ˌsʌb.dʒekˈtɪv.ɪ.ti/ ⓤ /-ə.t̬i/ *noun* [U] *There's always an element of subjectivity in decision-making.*

'subject ˌmatter *noun* [C] the things that are being talked or written about or used as the subject of a piece of art, etc: *The programme's subject matter was quite unsuitable for children.*

sub judice /ˌsʌbˈdʒuː.dɪ.si/ *adj* [after v] *LEGAL* being studied or decided in a law court at the present time: *In Britain, cases which are sub judice cannot be publicly discussed in the media.*

subjugate DEFEAT /ˈsʌb.dʒʊ.geɪt/ *verb* [T] *FORMAL* to defeat people or a country and rule them in a way which allows them no freedom **subjugation** /ˌsʌb.dʒʊˈgeɪ.ʃᵊn/ *noun* [U] *They are bravely resisting subjugation by their more powerful neighbours.*

subjugate CONTROL /ˈsʌb.dʒʊ.geɪt/ *verb* [T] *FORMAL* to treat yourself, your wishes or your beliefs as being less important than other people or their wishes or beliefs: [R] *She subjugated herself to her mother's needs.* ◦ *Journalists must subjugate personal political convictions to their professional commitment to fairness and balance.*

subjunctive /səbˈdʒʌŋk.tɪv/ *noun* [S] *SPECIALIZED* a set of forms of a verb, in some languages, that refer to actions which are possibilities rather than facts: *In the sentence 'I wish I were rich', the verb 'were' is in the subjunctive.*

sublet /ˌsʌbˈlet/ ⓤ /ˈ--/ *verb* [T] **subletting, sublet, sublet** to allow someone to rent all or part of a house or other building which you are renting from someone else: *Our rental contract states that we are not allowed to sublet the house.*

sublieutenant /ˌsʌb.lefˈten.ᵊnt/ ⓤ /-luː-/ *noun* [C] an officer of low rank in the British navy

sublimate /ˈsʌb.lɪ.meɪt/ *verb* [T] *SPECIALIZED* to express strong emotions or use energy by doing an activity, especially an activity which is considered socially acceptable: *Hostile feelings and violent responses often seem to be sublimated into sporting activities.* **sublimation** /ˌsʌb.lɪˈmeɪ.ʃᵊn/ *noun* [U]

sublime /səˈblaɪm/ *adj* **1** extremely good, beautiful or enjoyable: *sublime beauty* ◦ *The book contains sublime descriptive passages.* **2** very great: *He possesses sublime self-confidence.*
the sublime *noun* [S] something that is sublime: *A great deal of literature is only the obvious transformed into the sublime.*
• **from the sublime to the ridiculous** from something that is very good or very serious to something very bad or silly: *The dresses in the fashion show went/ranged from the sublime to the ridiculous.*
sublimely /səˈblaɪm.li/ *adv* extremely: *At times the writing is sublimely funny.* **sublimity** /səˈblɪm.ɪ.ti/ ⓤ /-ə.t̬i/ *noun* [U]

subliminal /ˌsʌbˈlɪm.ɪ.nᵊl/ *adj* **1** not recognized or understood by the conscious mind, but still having an influence on it: *The Prime Minister was interviewed in front of a factory to give the subliminal message that he was a man of the people.* **2** describes advertising that uses indirect ways of influencing people to be attracted to a product, such as using a picture of a farm to advertise food to suggest that it is fresh

submachine gun /ˌsʌb.məˈʃiːn.gʌn/ *noun* [C] a type of automatic gun which is light enough to be carried easily

submarine /ˌsʌb.məˈriːn/ /ˈ---/ *noun* [C] (*INFORMAL* **sub**) a ship which can travel under water: *a nuclear submarine* ◦ *a submarine base/commander* ◗See picture **Planes,**

Ships and Boats on page Centre 14
submarine /ˌsʌb.məˈriːn/ /ˈ---/ *adj* SPECIALIZED existing below the surface of the sea:
ˈsubmarine ˌsandwich *noun* [C] (INFORMAL **sub**) *US* a long thin loaf of bread filled with salad and cold meat or cheese
submerge /səbˈmɜːdʒ/ [US] /-ˈmɝːdʒ/ *verb* **1** [I or T] to go below the surface of the sea or a river or lake: *The submarine submerged when enemy planes were sighted.* ○ *She was taken to hospital after being submerged* ***in*** *an icy river for 45 minutes.* **2** [T] LITERARY to cover or hide something completely: *She has submerged her identity in the role of photographer's wife and muse.* **submersion** /səbˈmɜː.ʃən/ [US] /-ˈmɝː.ʒən-/ *noun* [U] *The fruit was preserved by submersion* ***in*** *alcohol.*
▲ **submerge *yourself* in *sth*** *phrasal verb* to put all your effort into doing a particular activity: *She is an actress who always tries to submerge herself completely in a role.*
submersible /səbˈmɜː.sɪ.bl̩/ [US] /-ˈmɝː-/ *noun* [C] SPECIALIZED a type of ship which can travel under water, especially one which operates without people being in it
submit [ALLOW] /səbˈmɪt/ *verb* [I or T] **-tt-** to allow another person or group to have power or authority over you, or to accept something unwillingly: *We protested about the changes for a long time, but in the end we had to submit.* ○ [R] *She decided to resign from the party rather than submit herself* ***to*** *the new rules.*
submission /səbˈmɪʃ.ən/ *noun* [U] when a person or group submits to someone or something: *They thought the country could be bombed* ***into*** *submission.* ○ *The teachers agreed to a special meeting,* ***in*** *submission* ***to*** *parents' demands.*
submissive /səbˈmɪs.ɪv/ *adj* describes someone who allows themselves to be controlled by other people: *He was looking for a quiet submissive wife who would obey his every word.* **submissively** /səbˈmɪs.ɪv.li/ *adv* **submissiveness** /səbˈmɪs.ɪv.nəs/ *noun* [U]
submit [GIVE] /səbˈmɪt/ *verb* **-tt- 1** [T] to give or offer something for a decision to be made by others: *You must submit your application before January 1st.* ○ *The developers submitted building plans* ***to*** *the council for approval.* **2** [T + that] FORMAL to suggest: *In conclusion, I submit* ***that*** *the proposal will not work without some major changes.*
submission /səbˈmɪʃ.ən/ *noun* [C or U] *No date has yet been set for the submission of applications.* ○ *The final deadline for submissions is February 21st.* ○ [+ that] FORMAL *The judge will hear the defence's submission* (= suggestion) ***that*** *the case be dismissed.*
subnormal /ˌsʌbˈnɔː.məl/ [US] /-ˈnɔːr-/ *adj* below an average or expected standard, especially of intelligence: *mentally subnormal* ○ *subnormal temperatures*
subordinate /səˈbɔː.dɪ.nət/ [US] /-ˈbɔːr-/ *adj* having a lower or less important position: *a subordinate role* ○ *subordinate status* ○ *The individual's needs are subordinate* ***to*** *those of the group.*
subordinate /səˈbɔː.dɪ.nət/ [US] /-ˈbɔːr-/ *noun* [C] a person who has a less important position than you in an organization: *He left the routine checks to one of his subordinates.*
subordinate /səˈbɔː.dɪ.neɪt/ [US] /-ˈbɔːr-/ *verb* [T] to put someone or something into a less important position: *Her personal life has been subordinated* ***to*** *her career.*
subordination /səˌbɔː.dɪˈneɪ.ʃən/ [US] /-ˌbɔːr-/ *noun* [U] *She claims that society is still characterized by male domination and female subordination.* ○ *subordination of high standards* ***to*** *quick results*
suˌbordinate ˈclause *noun* [C] SPECIALIZED in grammar, a clause which cannot form a separate sentence but which can form a sentence when joined with a main clause
subplot /ˈsʌb.plɒt/ [US] /-plɑːt/ *noun* [C] a part of the story of a book or play which develops separately from the main story
subpoena /səˈpiː.nə/ *verb* [T] LEGAL **1** to order someone to go to a court of law to answer questions: *A friend of the victim was subpoenaed* ***as*** *a witness by lawyers representing the accused.* ○ [+ to infinitive] *They were subpoenaed* ***to*** *testify before the judge.* **2** to order that documents must be produced in a court of law
subpoena /səˈpiː.nə/ *noun* [C] LEGAL a legal document ordering someone to appear in a court of law: *Subpoenas were issued to several government employees.*
subscribe /səbˈskraɪb/ *verb* [I or T] **1** to pay money to an organization in order to receive a product, use a service regularly or support the organization: *She subscribes* ***to*** *several women's magazines.* ○ *I subscribe £10 a month* ***to*** *the charity.* **2** SPECIALIZED to offer to buy something or pay an amount for something as part of your business activities: *Existing shareholders subscribed* ***to*** *only 49% of the new share issue.*
subscriber /səbˈskraɪ.bər/ [US] /-bɚ/ *noun* [C] someone who subscribes to a product, service or organization: *Cable television companies have launched major campaigns to increase their number of subscribers.*
subscription /səbˈskrɪp.ʃən/ *noun* [C] (INFORMAL **sub**) an amount of money that you pay regularly to receive a product or service or to be a member of an organization: *UK We bought our niece an* ***annual*** *subscription* ***to*** *the tennis club.* ○ *I decided to* ***take out*** (= pay for) *a subscription* ***to*** *a gardening magazine.*
▲ **subscribe to *sth*** *phrasal verb* to agree with or support an opinion, belief or theory: *Frank subscribed firmly to the belief that human kindness would overcome evil.*
subsection /ˈsʌbˌsek.ʃən/ *noun* [C] one of the smaller parts into which the main parts of a document or organization are divided: *Further details can be found in section 7 subsection 4 of the report.*
subsequent /ˈsʌb.sɪ.kwənt/ *adj* happening after something else: *The book discusses his illness and subsequent resignation from the government.* ○ *Those explosions must have been subsequent* ***to*** *our departure, because we didn't hear anything.* **subsequently** /ˈsʌb.sɪ.kwənt.li/ *adv*: *In 1982 he was arrested and subsequently convicted on drug trafficking charges.*
subservient /səbˈsɜː.vi.ənt/ [US] /-ˈsɝː-/ *adj* DISAPPROVING willing to do what other people want, or considering your wishes as less important than those of other people: *to adopt a subservient* ***role/position*** ○ *The government was accused of being subservient* ***to*** *the interests of the pro-Europe campaigners.* **subserviently** /səbˈsɜː.vi.ənt.li/ [US] /-ˈsɝː-/ *adv* **subservience** /səbˈsɜː.vi.ənts/ [US] /-ˈsɝː-/ *noun* [U]
subside /səbˈsaɪd/ *verb* [I] **1** If a condition subsides, it becomes less strong or extreme: *The police are hoping that the violence will soon subside.* ○ *As the pain in my foot subsided, I was able to walk the short distance to the car.* **2** If a building, land or water subsides, it goes down to a lower level: *There is a danger that many homes will subside because of the drought.* ○ *Eventually the flood waters began to subside.*
subsidence /səbˈsaɪ.dənts/ /ˈsəb.sɪ-/ *noun* [U] when land or buildings sink to a lower level: *The building had to be demolished because of subsidence.*
subsidiarity /ˌsʌb.sɪd.iˈær.ɪ.ti/ [US] /-er.ə.t̬i/ *noun* [U] SPECIALIZED the principle that decisions should always be taken at the lowest possible level or closest to where they will have their effect, for example in a local area rather than nationally
subsidiary /səbˈsɪd.i.ər.i/ [US] /-er-/ *adj* describes something less important than something else with which it is connected: *a subsidiary role/factor*
subsidiary /səbˈsɪd.i.ər.i/ [US] /-er-/ *noun* [C] a company which is owned by a larger company
subsidy /ˈsʌb.sɪ.di/ *noun* [C] money given as part of the cost of something, to help or encourage it to happen: *The company received a substantial government subsidy.* ○ *The government is planning to abolish subsidies* ***to*** *farmers.*
subsidize, UK USUALLY **-ise** /ˈsʌb.sɪ.daɪz/ *verb* [T] to pay part of the cost of something: *£50 would help to subsidize the training of an unemployed teenager.* ○ *The refugees live in subsidized housing provided by the authorities.* **subsidization**, UK USUALLY **-isation** /ˌsʌb.sɪ.daɪˈzeɪ.ʃən/ *noun* [U]
subsist /səbˈsɪst/ *verb* [I] FORMAL to obtain enough food or money to stay alive: *The prisoners were subsisting* ***on*** *a diet of bread and water.*

S

subsistence /səbˈsɪs.tᵊnts/ *noun* [U] FORMAL **1** what a person needs in order to stay alive: *The money is intended to provide a basic subsistence and should not be paid to someone who receives other income.* **2** producing enough food or earning enough money to keep yourself alive: *subsistence farming* ○ *The family were living* ***at*** *subsistence* ***level****.*

subsoil /ˈsʌb.sɔɪl/ *noun* [U] the layer of earth which is under the surface level ➲Compare **topsoil**.

subsonic /sʌbˈsɒn.ɪk/ [US] /-ˈsɑː.nɪk/ *adj* slower than the speed of sound

subspecies /ˈsʌbˌspiː.ʃiːz/ *noun* [C] *plural* **subspecies** SPECIALIZED a particular type within a species, the members of which are different in some clear ways from those of other types of the species

substance [MATERIAL] /ˈsʌb.stᵊnts/ *noun* [C or U] **1** material with particular physical characteristics: *an organic/chemical substance* ○ *What sort of substance could withstand those temperatures?* **2** FORMAL **illegal substance** an illegal drug

substance [IMPORTANCE] /ˈsʌb.stᵊnts/ *noun* [U] FORMAL importance, seriousness or relationship to real facts: *There is no substance* ***in/to*** *the allegation.* ○ *This new information* ***gives*** *substance* ***to*** *the stories we have heard.*

ˈsubstance aˌbuse *noun* [U] FORMAL the use of a drug to get pleasure, or to improve a person's performance of an activity, or because a person cannot stop using it

substandard /sʌbˈstæn.dəd/ [US] /-dɚd/ *adj* below a satisfactory standard: *substandard housing/accommodation* ○ *substandard work/goods*

substantial [LARGE] /səbˈstæn.ʃᵊl/ *adj* large in size, value or importance: *The findings show a substantial difference between the opinions of men and women.* ○ *She inherited a substantial fortune from her grandmother.* ○ *The first draft of his novel needed a substantial amount of rewriting.*

substantially /səbˈstæn.ʃᵊl.i/ *adv*: *The new rules will substantially* (= to a large degree) *change how we do things.*

substantial [GENERAL] /səbˈstæn.ʃᵊl/ *adj* [before n] FORMAL relating to the main or most important things being considered: *The committee were in substantial agreement* (= agreed about most of the things discussed).

substantially /səbˈstæn.ʃᵊl.i/ *adv* generally: *This model has a few extra fittings, but the two cars are substantially the same.*

substantiate /səbˈstæn.ʃi.eɪt/ *verb* [T] FORMAL to show something to be true, or to support a claim with facts: *We have evidence to substantiate the* ***allegations*** *against him.* ○ *Reports that children had been hurt have not been substantiated.*

substantiation /səbˌstæn.ʃiˈeɪ.ʃᵊn/ *noun* [U] FORMAL *The company produced receipts* ***in*** *substantiation* ***of*** (= to support) *its claim.*

substantive /səbˈstæn.tɪv/ [US] /-t̬ɪv/ *adj* FORMAL important, serious or related to real facts: *Substantive research on the subject needs to be carried out.* ○ *The documents are the first substantive information obtained by the investigators.*

substation /ˌsʌbˈsteɪ.ʃᵊn/ *noun* **electricity substation** a place which allows electricity to go from one part of the electricity production system to another

substitute /ˈsʌb.stɪ.tjuːt/ [US] /-tuːt/ *verb* [T] **1** to use something or someone instead of another thing or person: *You can substitute oil* ***for*** *butter in this recipe.* ○ *Dayton was substituted* ***for*** *Williams in the second half of the match.* **2 substitute for *sth*** to perform the same job as another thing or to take its place: *Gas-fired power stations will substitute for less efficient coal-fired equipment.*

substitute /ˈsʌb.stɪ.tjuːt/ [US] /-tuːt/ *noun* [C] **1** a thing or person that is used instead of another thing or person: *Tofu can be used as a meat substitute in vegetarian recipes.* ○ *Vitamins should not be used as a substitute* ***for*** *a healthy diet.* **2** (INFORMAL **sub**) in sports, a player who is used for part of a game instead of another player: *Johnson* ***came on*** *as a substitute towards the end of the match.* ○ *The manager* ***brought on*** (US ALSO **sent in**) *another substitute in the final minutes of the game.*
• **there is no substitute for *sth*** nothing is as good as the stated thing: *You can work from plans of a garden, but there's no substitute for visiting the site yourself.*

substitution /ˌsʌb.stɪˈtjuː.ʃᵊn/ [US] /-ˈtuː-/ *noun* [C or U] *It looks as though the coach is going to* ***make a*** *substitution* (= change one player for another in the game).

ˌsubstitute (ˈteacher) *noun* [C] (INFORMAL **sub**) US FOR **supply teacher**

substructure /ˈsʌbˌstrʌk.tʃəʳ/ [US] /-tʃɚ/ *noun* [C] a firm structure which supports something built on top of it: *The explosion damaged the bridge, but the substructure remained intact.*

subsume /səbˈsjuːm/ [US] /-ˈsuːm/ *verb* [T] FORMAL to include something or someone as part of a larger group: *Soldiers from many different countries have been subsumed* ***into*** *the United Nations peace-keeping force.* ○ *All the statistics have been subsumed* ***under*** *the general heading 'Facts and Figures'.*

subtenant /ˌsʌbˈten.ᵊnt/ *noun* [C] a person who rents a building from someone who is renting it from the owner

subterfuge /ˈsʌb.tə.fjuːdʒ/ [US] /-tɚ-/ *noun* [C or U] a trick or a dishonest way of achieving something: *It was clear that they must have obtained the information by subterfuge.*

subterranean /ˌsʌb.tᵊrˈeɪ.ni.ən/ [US] /-təˈreɪ-/ *adj* under the ground: *subterranean passages* ○ *a subterranean river*

subtext /ˈsʌb.tekst/ *noun* [C] a hidden or less obvious meaning: *The political subtext of her novel is a criticism of government interference in individual lives.*

subtitle /ˈsʌbˌtaɪ.tl̩/ [US] /-t̬l̩/ *noun* [C] a word, phrase or sentence which is used as the second part of a book title and is printed under the main title at the front of the book **subtitled** /ˈsʌbˌtaɪ.tl̩d/ [US] /-t̬l̩d/ *adj*

subtitles /ˈsʌbˌtaɪ.tl̩z/ [US] /-t̬l̩z/ *plural noun* words shown at the bottom of a film or television picture to explain what is being said: *The Chinese film was shown with English subtitles.* ○ *The evening news has subtitles for the deaf.* **subtitled** /ˈsʌbˌtaɪ.tl̩d/ [US] /-t̬l̩d/ *adj*: *a subtitled film/programme*

subtle /ˈsʌt.l̩/ [US] /ˈsʌt̬-/ *adj* APPROVING **1** not loud, bright, noticeable or obvious in any way: *The room was painted a subtle shade of pink.* ○ *The play's message is perhaps too subtle to be understood by young children.* **2** small but important: *There is a subtle difference between these two plans.* **3** achieved in a quiet way which does not attract attention to itself and which is therefore good or clever: *a subtle plan/suggestion* ○ *subtle questions*

subtly /ˈsʌt.l̩.i/ [US] /ˈsʌt̬-/ *adv*: *This discovery had subtly* ***changed/altered*** *the way I thought about myself.*

subtlety /ˈsʌt.l̩.ti/ [US] /ˈsʌt̬.l̩.t̬i/ *noun* APPROVING **1** [U] the quality of being subtle: *Listening to the interview, I was impressed by the subtlety of the questions.* **2** [C] a small but important detail: *All the subtleties of the music are conveyed in this new recording.*

subtotal /ˈsʌbˌtəʊ.tᵊl/ [US] /-ˌtoʊ.t̬ᵊl/ *noun* [C] the total of one set of numbers to which other numbers will be added: *You have to add the cost of postage to the subtotal.*

subtract /səbˈtrækt/ *verb* [T] to remove a number from another number: *Four subtracted* ***from*** *ten equals six.* ➲Compare **add**; **divide**; **multiply**.

subtraction /səbˈtræk.ʃᵊn/ *noun* [U] the process of removing one number from another: *The test involves simple calculations, such as addition and subtraction.*

subtropical /ˌsʌbˈtrɒp.ɪ.kᵊl/ [US] /-ˈtrɑː.pɪ-/ *adj* belonging to or relating to parts of the world that have very hot weather: *a subtropical climate* ○ *Subtropical regions are cooler than equatorial regions.*

suburb /ˈsʌb.ɜːb/ [US] /-ɝːb/ *noun* [C] an area on the edge of a large town or city where people who work in the town or city often live: *Box Hill is a suburb of Melbourne.* ○ *We drove from middle-class suburbs to a very poor inner-city area.*

the suburbs *plural noun* the outer area of a town, rather than the shopping and business centre in the middle: *The company decided to relocate to the suburbs because the rent was much cheaper.*

S

suburban /sə'bɜː.bən/ [US] /-'bɝː-/ *adj* **1** relating to a suburb: *suburban schools/housing* ○ *They live in suburban Washington.* **2** DISAPPROVING used to suggest that something is boring and lacks excitement: *suburban life*
suburbanite /sə'bɜː.bə.naɪt/ [US] /-'bɝː-/ *noun* [C] US a person who lives in the suburbs of a large town or city
suburbia /sə'bɜː.bi.ə/ [US] /-'bɝː-/ *noun* [U] MAINLY DISAPPROVING **1** the outer parts of a town, where there are houses, but no large shops, places of work or places of entertainment: *They live in a two-bedroomed house in the heart of suburbia.* **2** the way of life of people who live in the outer parts of a town: *He has written a book about middle-class suburbia.*

subvert /səb'vɜːt/ [US] /-'vɝːt/ *verb* [T] FORMAL to try to destroy or weaken something, especially an established political system: *The rebel army is attempting to subvert the government.* ○ *Our best intentions are sometimes subverted by our natural tendency to selfishness.* **subversive** /səb'vɜː.sɪv/ [US] /-'vɝː-/ *adj*: *subversive elements/groups in society* ○ *subversive ideas/influences* **subversively** /səb'vɜː.sɪv.li/ [US] /-'vɝː-/ *adv* **subversiveness** /səb'vɜː.sɪv.nəs/ [US] /-'vɝː-/ *noun* [U]
subversion /səb'vɜː.ʃən/ [US] /-'vɝː-/ *noun* [U] FORMAL when someone tries to destroy or weaken an established system or government: *He was found guilty of subversion and imprisoned.*

subway [UNDERGROUND PASSAGE] /'sʌb.weɪ/ *noun* [C] UK an underground passage which allows people on foot to cross a busy road

subway [UNDERGROUND RAILWAY] /'sʌb.weɪ/ *noun* [C] MAINLY US a railway system in which electric trains travel along passages below ground: *We took the subway uptown to Yankee Stadium.* ➲See Note **metro, subway or underground?** at **metro** RAILWAY.

succeed [ACHIEVE SOMETHING] /sək'siːd/ *verb* [I] If you succeed, you achieve something that you have been aiming for, and if a plan or piece of work succeeds, it has the desired results: *She's been trying to pass her driving test for six years and she's finally succeeded.* ○ *You need to be pretty tough to succeed **in** the property world.* ○ *The campaign has certainly succeeded **in** raising public awareness of the issue.* ○ HUMOROUS *Richard succeeded **in** offending* (= managed unintentionally to offend) *just about everybody in the room!*
success /sək'ses/ *noun* **1** [U] the achieving of desired results: *The success of almost any project depends largely on its manager.* ○ *I've been trying to persuade her to take on more staff, but so far **without** success.* ○ *I'm not **having** much success **in** communicating with him at the moment.* ○ *The success **rate** for this operation is very low.* **2** [C] something that achieves positive results: *Both films have been a big box-office success in this country.* ○ *She's determined to make a success of this project.* ○ *That salmon dish was a success, wasn't it?*
successful /sək'ses.fəl/ *adj* **1** achieving the desired results: *a successful operation* ○ *My second attempt at making flaky pastry was a bit more successful.* ○ *This year's harvest was one of the most successful since the record crop of 1985.* * NOTE: The opposite is **unsuccessful**. **2** having achieved a lot, become popular and/or made a lot of money: *a successful career* ○ *She runs a very successful computer business.* ○ *He's the author of several **hugely** successful children's books* (= books which have been bought by a lot of people). ○ *The Birmingham Royal Ballet has had a highly successful season.* * NOTE: The opposite is **unsuccessful**. **successfully** /sək'ses.fəl.i/ *adv*: *A number of patients have been successfully treated with the new drug.*

COMMON LEARNER ERROR

succeed

Remember that **succeed** is often followed by the preposition 'in' + doing sth. It is never followed by an infinitive.

Two prisoners succeeded in escaping.
~~*Two prisoners succeeded to escape.*~~

COMMON LEARNER ERROR

success

Be careful to choose the correct verb with this noun.

*The evening **was** a great success.*
*They tried for weeks but **had** little success.*
*They are determined to **make** a success of the scheme.*
~~*She reached success as a writer.*~~

succeed [FOLLOW] /sək'siːd/ *verb* **1** [I or T] to take an official job or position after someone else: *He succeeded his father **as** editor of the paper.* ○ *When the queen dies, her eldest son will succeed **to** the throne.* **2** to come after another person or thing in time: *In the weeks that succeeded, five more patients showed similar symptoms.* ○ *Almost from its beginnings, New York has produced succeeding generations of intellectuals.*
succession /sək'seʃ.ən/ *noun* **1** [S] a number of similar events or people that happen, exist, etc. after each other: *A succession **of** scandals and revelations has undermined the government over the past year.* ○ *Life was just an endless succession **of** parties and dinners.* **2 in succession** happening one after another: *She had her first three children in **rapid** succession.* ○ *This is the seventh year in succession that they've won the cup.* **3** [U] when someone takes an official position or job after someone else: *Divorce would not prevent the Prince of Wales's succession **to** the throne.* **successive** /sək'ses.ɪv/ *adj* [before n] *It was the team's fourth successive defeat.* ○ *He won the World Championship for the third successive year.* **successively** /sək'ses.ɪv.li/ *adv*: *Since the championship began in 1987, they have finished successively in ninth, seventh and fifth position.*
successor /sək'ses.əʳ/ [US] /-ɚ/ *noun* [C] someone or something that succeeds another person or thing: *Oxford Brookes University is seeking a successor **to** its vice-chancellor who retires this Easter.* ○ *This range of computers is very fast, but their successors will be even faster.*

suc'cess ˌstory *noun* [C] something or someone that achieves great success, often by making a lot of money: *Angela Black's biscuit company is a rare success story in these times of recession.*

succinct /sək'sɪŋkt/ *adj* APPROVING said in a clear and short way; expressing what needs to be said without unnecessary words: *Keep your letter succinct and to the point.* **succinctly** /sək'sɪŋkt.li/ *adv*: *I thought she expressed her feelings most succinctly in the meeting.* **succinctness** /sək'sɪŋkt.nəs/ *noun* [U]

succour UK, US **succor** /'sʌk.əʳ/ [US] /-ɚ/ *noun* [U] LITERARY help given to someone, especially someone who is suffering or in need: *Her organization **gave** succour and strength **to** those who had been emotionally damaged.*
succour UK, US **succor** /'sʌk.əʳ/ [US] /-ɚ/ *verb* [T] *to succour the poor, help the helpless, support the weak* ○ *Students should be encouraged, supported and succoured.*

succulent [JUICY] /'sʌk.jʊ.lənt/ *adj* APPROVING Succulent food is pleasantly juicy: *a succulent peach.* ○ *a big piece of succulent steak* **succulence** /'sʌk.jʊ.lənts/ *noun* [U] *The grilled chicken had a wonderful flavour and succulence.*

succulent [PLANT] /'sʌk.jʊ.lənt/ *noun* [C] SPECIALIZED a plant such as a CACTUS in which the leaves and stem are thick and can store a lot of water: *Succulents often have thick waxy cuticles to minimize water loss.*

succumb /sə'kʌm/ *verb* [I] FORMAL **1** to lose the determination to oppose something; to accept defeat: *The town finally succumbed last week after being pounded with heavy artillery for more than two months.* ○ *I'm afraid I succumbed **to** temptation and had a piece of cheesecake.* ○ *I felt sure it would only be a matter of time before he succumbed **to** my charms.* **2** to die or suffer badly from an illness: *Thousands of cows have succumbed **to** the disease in the past few months.*

such [SO GREAT] /sʌtʃ/ *predeterminer, determiner* used before a noun or noun phrase to add emphasis: *That's such a good film.* ○ *It seems like such a long way to drive for just one day.* ○ *Oh Richard, you're such an idiot!* ○ *Such cruelty really is beyond my comprehension.* ○ *I'd*

S

put on such a lot of weight **that** *I couldn't get into my trousers.*

such [OF THAT TYPE] /sʌtʃ/ *predeterminer, determiner, pronoun* of a particular or similar type: *Small companies such* **as** *ours are very vulnerable in a recession.* ○ *I'm looking for a cloth for cleaning silver. Do you have such* **a thing**? ○ *Present on this grand occasion were Andrew Davies, Melissa Peters and other such stars.* ○ *I tried to tell her in such* **a way that** *she wouldn't be offended.* ○ *He said it was an Edwardian washstand or* **some** *such thing – I can't remember exactly.* ○ OLD-FASHIONED INFORMAL *I just bought one or two things – bread and milk* **and** *such* (ALSO **suchlike**). ○ FORMAL *Our lunch was such* (= of a type) *that we don't really need an evening meal.*

• **such as** for example: *That sum of money is to cover costs such as travel and accommodation.*

• **there's no such thing/person (as)** used to say that something or someone does not exist: *Darling, Mummy's told you before, there's no such thing as ghosts!*

• **such is life** used to refer to an event that has happened and that you must accept, because you know that this is the way life is: *So here I am, without a girlfriend again. Oh well, such is life.*

• **such as it is** used to suggest that something you have referred to is of low quality or not enough: *You're welcome to borrow my tennis racket, such as it is.* ○ *Breakfast, such as it was, consisted of a plain roll and a cup of coffee.*

such [EXACTLY] /sʌtʃ/ *noun* **as such** in the true or exact meaning of the word or phrase: *There wasn't much vegetarian food as such, although there were several different types of cheese.* ○ *We don't have a secretary as such, but we do have a student who comes in to do a bit of filing.*

ˈsuch and ˌsuch *adj* INFORMAL used to refer to something which you do not want to name or say exactly: *If they tell you to arrive at such and such a time, just get there a couple of minutes early.*

suchlike /ˈsʌtʃ.laɪk/ /ˌ-ˈ-/ *determiner, pronoun* things of that type: *There's a shop in the hospital where they sell flowers and chocolates and suchlike.*

suck [PULL IN] /sʌk/ *verb* **1** [I or T] to pull in liquid or air through your mouth without using your teeth, or to move the tongue and muscles of the mouth around something inside your mouth, often in order to dissolve it: *She was sitting on the grass sucking lemonade through a straw.* ○ *I sucked my* **thumb** *until I was seven.* ○ *I tried sucking* **(on)** *a mint to stop myself coughing.* ○ *They used to give you sweets to suck* **on** *(*UK ALSO **at**) *in aeroplanes to stop your ears from going pop.* **2** [T + adv or prep] Something which sucks a liquid or an object in a particular direction pulls it with great force: *The waves came crashing over my head and I could feel myself being sucked under by the currents.* ○ FIGURATIVE *Continued rapid growth in consumer spending will suck* **in** (= encourage) *more imports.*

• **suck it and see** UK INFORMAL to try something to find out if it will be successful: *I'm not sure whether this paint is the right colour for the bedroom – we'll just have to suck it and see.*

suck /sʌk/ *noun* [C usually sing] when you suck something: *Can I have a suck of your lolly please?*

suck [BE BAD] /sʌk/ *verb* [I] MAINLY US SLANG If someone or something sucks, they are bad or unpleasant: *Man, this job sucks!* ○ *While my brother was sick, I had to do all of his chores and it sucked.*

PHRASAL VERBS WITH **suck** ▼

▲ **suck *sb/sth* in/suck *sb/sth* into *sth*** *phrasal verb* [M often passive] to cause someone or something to gradually become involved in an an unpleasant situation or harmful activity: *I really don't want any part in this whole argument, but I can feel myself being sucked into it.*

▲ **suck *sb* off** *phrasal verb* [M] OFFENSIVE to use the tongue, lips and mouth to excite someone's sexual organs to give them pleasure

▲ **suck up to *sb*** *phrasal verb* INFORMAL DISAPPROVING to try to make someone who is in authority approve of you by doing and saying things that will please them: *"Why do you think he offered to take all that work home?" "Ah, he's just sucking up to the boss."*

sucker [FOOLISH PERSON] /ˈsʌk.əʳ/ [US] /-ɚ/ *noun* [C] INFORMAL DISAPPROVING a person who believes everything they are told and is therefore easy to deceive: *You didn't actually believe him when he said he had a yacht, did you? Oh, Annie, you sucker!*

sucker [LIKING] /ˈsʌk.əʳ/ [US] /-ɚ/ *noun* INFORMAL **be a sucker for *sth*** to think that something is so persuasive or attractive that you cannot refuse it or judge its real value: *I have to confess I'm a bit of a sucker* **for** *musicals.*

sucker [THING OR PERSON] /ˈsʌk.əʳ/ [US] /-ɚ/ *noun* [C] US INFORMAL used to refer to a thing or person that is unpleasant or difficult: *I've been working on that paper for weeks and almost have the sucker finished.* ○ *He's a nasty little sucker, isn't he?*

sucker [STICKING DEVICE] /ˈsʌk.əʳ/ [US] /-ɚ/ *noun* [C] **1** something that helps an animal or object to stick to a surface: *The leech has a sucker at each end of its body.* **2** UK INFORMAL FOR **suction cup**

sucker [SWEET] /ˈsʌk.əʳ/ [US] /-ɚ/ *noun* [C] US INFORMAL FOR **lollipop**

sucker [PLANT PART] /ˈsʌk.əʳ/ [US] /-ɚ/ *noun* [C] SPECIALIZED a new growth on an existing plant that develops under the ground from the root or the main stem, or from the stem below a GRAFT (= part where a new plant has been joined on)

sucker /ˈsʌk.əʳ/ [US] /-ɚ/ *verb*

▲ **sucker *sb* into *sth*** *phrasal verb* US INFORMAL to persuade someone to do something by deceiving them: [+ v-ing] *We were suckered into doing the job for free.*

suckle /ˈsʌk.l̩/ *verb* [I or T] to feed a baby, especially a baby animal, with milk from the organ in the mother that produces milk, or (of a baby, especially a baby animal) to drink milk from the mother: *We watched the cow suckling her calves.* ○ *The puppies went back to their mother to suckle.*

suckling /ˈsʌk.lɪŋ/ /ˈ-l̩.ɪŋ/ *noun* [C], *adj* [before n] OLD-FASHIONED (an animal that is) still young enough to be drinking milk from its mother: *The main course of the feast was roast suckling pig.*

sucrose /ˈsuː.krəʊz/ [US] /-kroʊs/ *noun* [U] SPECIALIZED the type of sugar that exists naturally in most plants that grow on land

suction /ˈsʌk.ʃən/ *noun* [U] when air is removed from a space resulting in a lower pressure in that space, either causing liquid, gases or other substances to enter, or causing two surfaces to stick together: *a suction pump*

ˈsuction ˌcup *noun* [C] (UK ALSO **sucker**) a circular piece of rubber which sticks to surfaces when pressed against them

sudden /ˈsʌd.ən/ *adj* happening or done quickly and without warning: *Drop the gun, put your hands in the air, and don't make any sudden movements.* ○ *He had a sudden heart attack while he was on holiday.* ○ *First they announce their engagement and then they tell me Angie's pregnant – it's all a bit sudden really.*

• **all of a sudden** INFORMAL very quickly: *It seemed to happen all of a sudden – I felt dizzy and I just collapsed.*

suddenly /ˈsʌd.ən.li/ *adv* quickly and unexpectedly: *"Do you remember much about the accident?" "No, it all happened so suddenly."* ○ *I was just dozing off to sleep when suddenly I heard a scream from outside.* ○ *I suddenly realised what I'd said, but it was too late.*

suddenness /ˈsʌd.ən.nəs/ *noun* [U] *It was the suddenness of his illness that came as such a shock.*

suds /sʌdz/ *plural noun* **1** (ALSO **soapsuds**) the mass of small bubbles that form on the surface of soapy water **2** US a mass of small bubbles that forms on the surface of any liquid **3** US OLD-FASHIONED INFORMAL FOR **beer**

sudsy /ˈsʌd.zi/ *adj* US covered in soapy bubbles

sue /suː/ *verb* [I or T] to take legal action against a person or organization, especially by making a legal claim for money because of some harm that they have caused you: *He was so furious about the accusations in the letter that he threatened to sue.* ○ *She sued the paper* **for** (= in order to obtain) *damages after they wrongly described* *her as a prostitute.* ○ *She is suing her husband* ***for*** (= in order to obtain a) *divorce.*

suede /sweɪd/ *noun* [U] leather which is slightly rough to touch and is not shiny: *suede shoes*

suet /ˈsuː.ɪt/ *noun* [U] a type of hard fat used in cooking which is taken from around the kidneys of such animals as sheep and cows: *suet* ***pudding***

suffer [FEEL PAIN] /ˈsʌf.əʳ/ [US] /-ɚ/ *verb* [I] to experience physical or mental pain: *I think he suffered quite a lot when his wife left him.* ○ *She suffers terribly in the winter when it's cold and her joints get stiff.* ○ *She's been suffering* ***from*** (= been ill with) *cancer for two years.* ○ *Johnny suffers* ***from*** (= is often ill with) *asthma.* ○ *If you're not happy with it, you should complain. Don't just suffer* ***in silence*** (= without saying anything).
sufferer /ˈsʌf.ᵊr.əʳ/ [US] /-ɚ.ɚ/ *noun* [C] a person who has or frequently gets a particular illness: *Almost 50 per cent of cancer sufferers are treated successfully.* ○ *A new drug may give new hope to thousands of hay-fever sufferers.*
suffering /ˈsʌf.ᵊr.ɪŋ/ [US] /-ɚ-/ *noun* [C or U] when you experience physical or mental pain: *The war will cause widespread human suffering.*

suffer [EXPERIENCE] /ˈsʌf.əʳ/ [US] /-ɚ/ *verb* [I or T] to experience or show the effects of something bad: *The Democrats suffered a crushing defeat in the last election.* ○ *Twenty-five policemen suffered minor injuries during the protest.* ○ *The city suffered another* ***blow*** *last month with the closure of the local car factory.* ○ *If you will insist on eating three helpings of dessert, I'm afraid you'll have to suffer* ***the consequences!*** ○ [+ obj + v-*ing*] *I had to suffer her father moan****ing*** *for half an hour on the phone last night!* ○ *When you're working such long hours, it's inevitable that your marriage will start to suffer.* ○ *Like a lot of his films, it suffers* ***from*** *being a bit too long.*
• **not suffer fools gladly** to have very little patience with people whom you think are foolish or have stupid ideas: *He's not one to suffer fools gladly.*

sufferance /ˈsʌf.ᵊr.ᵊnts/ [US] /-ɚ-/ *noun* FORMAL **on sufferance** If a person stays in a particular place on sufferance, they are allowed but not wanted there: *He gave me a bed for a couple of nights but I felt I was there on sufferance.*

sufficient /səˈfɪʃ.ᵊnt/ *adj* enough for a particular purpose: *This recipe should be sufficient* ***for*** *five people.* ○ *It was thought that he'd committed the crime but there wasn't sufficient evidence* ***to*** *convict him.* * NOTE: The opposite is **insufficient**. **sufficiently** /səˈfɪʃ.ᵊnt.li/ *adv*: *McGeechan has not recovered sufficiently to play in the semi-final tomorrow.* ○ *The case was sufficiently serious to warrant investigation by the police.*
sufficiency /səˈfɪʃ.ᵊnt.si/ *noun* [S] FORMAL an amount of something that is enough for a particular purpose: *"More ham, Mr Fletcher?" "No thank you – it was delicious, but I've had* ***a*** *sufficiency* (= I have eaten enough)*."*
suffice /səˈfaɪs/ *verb* [I] FORMAL to be enough: *I'm taking four hundred pounds' worth of travellers' cheques – I think that should suffice.*
• **suffice (it) to say** it is enough to say: *Suffice (it) to say, Mike won't be going to Tina's birthday party after what he said about her to her boss.*

suffix /ˈsʌf.ɪks/ *noun* [C] a letter or group of letters added at the end of a word to make a new word: *The suffix '-ness' added to the end of the word 'sweet' forms the word 'sweetness', changing an adjective into a noun.*

suffocate [DIE] /ˈsʌf.ə.keɪt/ *verb* [I or T] to (cause someone to) die because of a lack of oxygen: *The report said that the victims had suffocated in the fumes.* ○ *She suffocated him by holding a pillow over his head until he stopped moving.*
suffocating /ˈsʌf.ə.keɪ.tɪŋ/ [US] /-t̬ɪŋ/ *adj* INFORMAL Something that is suffocating makes you feel uncomfortably hot or unable to breathe properly: *I've got to open the window – it's suffocating in here!* ○ *suffocating smoke/fumes* **suffocation** /ˌsʌf.əˈkeɪ.ʃᵊn/ *noun* [U]

suffocate [PREVENT] /ˈsʌf.ə.keɪt/ *verb* [I or T] to prevent something or someone from improving or developing in a positive way **suffocating** /ˈsʌf.ə.keɪ.tɪŋ/ [US] /-t̬ɪŋ/ *adj*: *It is a land of antiquated social rules and suffocating traditions.* ○ *The book tells the story of a woman escaping from a suffocating marriage.*

suffrage /ˈsʌf.rɪdʒ/ *noun* [U] the right to vote in an election, especially for representatives in a parliament or similar organization: *universal suffrage* (= the right of all adults to vote)
suffragette /ˌsʌf.rəˈdʒet/ *noun* [C] a woman in Britain, Australia and the United States in the early 20th century who was a member of a group that demanded the right of women to vote and that increased awareness of the matter with a series of public protests
suffragist /ˈsʌf.rə.dʒɪst/ *noun* [C] someone who supports suffrage, especially a supporter of the right of women to vote in the early 20th century

suffuse /səˈfjuːz/ *verb* [T often passive] LITERARY to spread through or over something completely: *His voice was low and suffused* ***with*** *passion.*

Sufi /ˈsuː.fi/ *noun* [C] a member of an Islamic religious group which tries to achieve unity with God by living a simple life and by praying and MEDITATING **Sufic** /ˈsuː.fɪk/ *adj* (ALSO **Sufi**) *He's a member of a Sufic order.* **Sufism** /ˈsuː.fɪ.zᵊm/ *noun* [U]

sugar /ˈʃʊg.əʳ/ [US] /-ɚ/ *noun* **1** [C or U] a sweet substance which is obtained especially from the plants SUGAR CANE and SUGAR BEET and used to sweeten food and drinks: *I don't take sugar in my coffee, thanks.* ○ *How many sugars* (= spoonfuls or lumps of sugar) *do you take in your tea?* **2** [C] SPECIALIZED A sugar is any of several types of simple CARBOHYDRATE that dissolves in water: *Glucose and lactose are sugars.* **3** [as form of address] MAINLY US an affectionate way of addressing someone that you know: *Hi, sugar, did you have a good day at school?*
sugar /ˈʃʊg.əʳ/ [US] /-ɚ/ *exclamation* POLITE WORD FOR **shit**, used when something annoying happens: *Oh sugar, I've just spilt coffee all down my jacket!*
• **sugar and spice** If you describe someone, especially a woman or a girl, as being sugar and spice, you mean that they are behaving in a kind and friendly way: *She could be* ***all*** *sugar and spice when she wanted to be.*
sugar /ˈʃʊg.əʳ/ [US] /-ɚ/ *verb* [T] to put sugar in something: *Oh, I forgot to sugar your coffee.*
sugary /ˈʃʊg.ᵊr.i/ [US] /-ɚ-/ *adj* **1** containing sugar: *all those sugary snacks that kids eat* **2** DISAPPROVING too good or kind or expressing feelings of love in a way that is not sincere: *It's that sugary smile of his that I can't bear – it makes me want to puke!*

ˈsugar ˌbeet *noun* [C or U] a plant from whose white root sugar can be obtained

ˈsugar ˌcane *noun* [U] a tropical plant from whose tall thick stems sugar can be obtained

sugar-coated [SWEET] /ˌʃʊg.əˈkəʊ.tɪd/ [US] /-ɚˈkoʊ.t̬ɪd/ *adj* (of foods or pills) covered with a thin layer of sugar

sugar-coated [DECEIVING] /ˌʃʊg.əˈkəʊ.tɪd/ [US] /-ɚˈkoʊ.t̬ɪd/ *adj* DISAPPROVING An announcement or promise that is sugar-coated is intended to seem positive or pleasant, although in fact it will result in something unpleasant or unacceptable. **ˈsugar ˌcoat** *verb* [T]

ˈsugar ˌdaddy *noun* [C] INFORMAL a rich and usually older man who buys presents for or gives money to a young person, especially a woman, usually in order to spend time with them or have a sexual relationship with them

sugar-free /ˌʃʊg.əˈfriː/ [US] /-ɚ-/ *adj* Sugar-free foods do not contain any sugar and are usually artificially sweetened: *sugar-free chewing-gum*

ˌsugar (ˌsnap) ˈpea UK *noun* [C usually pl] (US **snap bean**) a long, thin green pod eaten as a vegetable

suggest [MENTION] /səˈdʒest/ *verb* [T] to mention an idea, possible plan or action for other people to consider: *They were wondering where to hold the office party and I suggested the Italian restaurant near the station.* ○ FORMAL *Might I suggest a white wine with your salmon, sir?* ○ [+ (*that*)] *I suggest* ***(that)*** *we wait a while before we make any firm decisions.* ○ *Liz suggested* ***(that)*** *I try the shop on Mill Road.* ○ [+ v-*ing*] *I suggested putt****ing*** *the matter to the committee.* ○ [+ question word] *Can you suggest* ***where*** *I might find a chemist's?*
suggestion /səˈdʒes.tʃᵊn/ *noun* [C or U] *I don't know what to wear tonight – have you* ***got*** *any suggestions?* ○ *She*

S

made some very helpful suggestions but her boss ***rejected*** *them all.* ○ [+ that] *They didn't like my suggestion* ***that*** *we should all share the cost.* ○ *I have a few favourite restaurants that I tend to go back to, but I'm always* ***open to*** *new suggestions* (= willing to try new ones that people suggest). ○ *I went to the Park Street dentist's* ***at*** *Ann's suggestion* (= as a result of Ann suggesting it) *and I was really impressed.*

suggestible /sə'dʒes.tɪ.bl̩/ [US] /-tə-/ *adj* FORMAL DISAPPROVING describes someone who is easily influenced by other people's opinions: *The success of advertising proves that we are all* ***highly*** *suggestible.*

suggest [SHOW/EXPRESS] /sə'dʒest/ *verb* [T] to communicate or show an idea or feeling without stating it directly or giving proof: [+ (that)] *There's no absolute proof, but all the evidence suggests* ***(that)*** *he's guilty.* ○ *Are you suggesting* ***(that)*** *I look fat in these trousers?* ○ *Something about his manner suggested a lack of interest in what we were doing.*

suggestive /sə'dʒes.tɪv/ *adj* **1** often used to describe something that makes people think about sex: *Some of his lyrics are rather suggestive.* **2** FORMAL If something is suggestive of something else, it makes you think about it: *The amplified sounds are suggestive of dolphins chatting to each other under the sea.* **suggestively** /sə'dʒes.tɪv.li/ *adv*

suggest [PRODUCE AN IDEA] /sə'dʒest/ *verb* [T] SLIGHTLY FORMAL to produce an idea in the mind: *Does anything suggest* ***itself*** (= Have you got any ideas about what we should do)*?*

suicide [DEATH] /'suː.ɪ.saɪd/ *noun* [C or U] the act of killing yourself intentionally, or a person who has done this: *to* ***attempt/commit*** *suicide* ○ *The suicide rate among men between the ages of 16 and 25 has risen alarmingly.* ○ *Many suicides occur in prisons.* ➲Compare **manslaughter**; **murder**.

suicidal /ˌsuː.ɪ'saɪ.dᵊl/ *adj* **1** People who are suicidal want to kill themselves or are in a mental state in which it is likely that they will try to do so: *Pete was so depressed after his girlfriend left him that I actually thought he was suicidal.* **2** describes behaviour that is likely to result in death: *He took some suicidal risks.* **suicidally** /ˌsuː.ɪ'saɪ.dᵊ.li/ *adv*

suicide [DEFEAT] /'suː.ɪ.saɪd/ *noun* [U] any act which has the effect of causing your own defeat: [+ to infinitive] *As a leader he knows that it is political suicide* ***to*** *appear indecisive.*

suicidal /ˌsuː.ɪ'saɪ.dᵊl/ *adj* A suicidal act causes the defeat of the person who does it: *It would be suicidal for the Prime Minister to call an election at a time when he's so unpopular.* **suicidally** /ˌsuː.ɪ'saɪ.dᵊ.li/ *adv*

'suicide ˌbomber *noun* [C] a person who has a bomb hidden on their body and who kills themselves in the attempt to kill others

'suicide ˌpact *noun* [C] an agreement between two or more people to kill themselves together at the same time: *The leader of the religious sect and thirty of his followers killed themselves in a suicide pact last year.*

suit [BE CONVENIENT] /sjuːt/ [US] /suːt/ *verb* [T] to be convenient and cause the least difficulty for someone: *We could go now or this afternoon – whatever time suits you best.* ○ *"How about eight o'clock outside the cinema?" "That suits me* ***fine.****"*

• **suit *sb* (right) down to the ground** If something suits someone down to the ground, it suits them perfectly, usually because it is convenient for them: *Part-time work would suit me* ***right*** *down to the ground.*

• **Suit *yourself*!** INFORMAL an expression used either humorously or angrily to mean 'do what you want to do': *"I don't think I'll come to the party tonight." "All right, suit yourself!"*

suit [BE RIGHT] /sjuːt/ [US] /suːt/ *verb* [T] to be right for a particular person, situation or occasion: *Corn is grown a lot in this area – the soil seems to suit it very well.* ○ *The city lifestyle seems to suit her – she's certainly looking very well.*

suited /'sjuː.tɪd/ [US] /'suː.t̬ɪd/ *adj* **1** right for someone or something: *With her qualifications and experience, she would seem to be ideally suited* ***to/for*** *the job.* **2** If two people who have a relationship are suited, they have a good relationship which will probably last, often because they share a lot of interests: *They were never suited* ***(to each other)*** *from the start – they've got nothing in common.*

suitable /'sjuː.tə.bl̩/ [US] /'suː.t̬ə-/ *adj* acceptable or right for someone or something: *The film is suitable* ***for*** *children.* ○ *My mother doesn't like me wearing short skirts to church – she doesn't think they're suitable.* * NOTE: The opposite is **unsuitable**. **suitably** /'sjuː.tə.bli/ [US] /'suː.t̬ə-/ *adv* **suitability** /ˌsjuː.tə'bɪl.ɪ.ti/ [US] /ˌsuː.t̬ə'bɪl.ə.t̬i/ *noun* [U]

suit [LOOK ATTRACTIVE] /sjuːt/ [US] /suːt/ *verb* [T] (usually of a colour or style of clothes) to make someone look more attractive: *You should wear more red – it suits you.* ○ *Short skirts don't really suit me – I haven't got the legs for them.* ➲See Note **fit or suit?** at **fit** CORRECT SIZE.

suit [SET OF CLOTHES] /sjuːt/ [US] /suːt/ *noun* [C] **1** a jacket and trousers or a jacket and skirt that are made from the same material: *All the businessmen were wearing pinstripe suits.* ○ *She wore a dark blue suit.* ➲See picture **Clothes** on page Centre 6 **2** a set of clothes or a piece of clothing to be worn in a particular situation or while doing a particular activity: *a diving/protective/ski, etc. suit* ○ *a swimsuit* ○ *a spacesuit* ○ *a suit* ***of*** *armour*

suit [PERSON] /sjuːt/ [US] /suːt/ *noun* [C often pl] INFORMAL MAINLY DISAPPROVING a man who works in an office and wears a suit, especially a man with a high position in a company who is considered to lack human feelings and good ideas

suit [LEGAL PROBLEM] /sjuːt/ [US] /suːt/ *noun* [C] (ALSO **lawsuit**) a problem taken to a court of law, by an ordinary person or an organization rather than the police, for a legal decision: *He* ***brought****/*(MAINLY US) ***filed*** *a $12 million libel suit against the newspaper, claiming his professional reputation had been damaged by the paper's stories.* ○ *a malpractice/negligence/paternity suit*

suit [PLAYING CARDS] /sjuːt/ [US] /suːt/ *noun* [C] any of the four types of card in a set of playing cards, each having a different shape printed on it: *The four suits in a pack of cards are hearts, spades, clubs and diamonds.*

suitcase /'sjuːt.keɪs/ [US] /'suːt-/ *noun* [C] (UK ALSO **case**) a large rectangular case with a handle for carrying clothes and possessions while travelling: *Have you packed/unpacked your suitcase yet?*

suite [SET OF ROOMS] /swiːt/ *noun* [C] a set of connected rooms, especially in a hotel: *The singer was interviewed in his £1500 a night* ***hotel*** *suite.* ○ *They've got a whole suite* ***of*** *offices on the 34th floor.*

suite [SET OF FURNITURE] /swiːt/ *noun* [C] a set of furniture for one room, of matching design and colour: *We're having a new bathroom/bedroom suite fitted at the weekend.* ○ *I've just ordered a new three-piece suite for the living-room.*

suite [MUSIC] /swiːt/ *noun* [C] a piece of music with several parts, usually all in the same KEY

suitor /'sjuː.təʳ/ [US] /'suː.t̬ɚ/ *noun* [C] **1** LITERARY a man who wants to marry a particular woman: *It's the story of a young woman who can't make up her mind which of her many suitors she should marry.* **2** SPECIALIZED a person or company who wants to take control of another company: *PJH Corporation said it had been approached by two possible suitors who had submitted bids to buy the company.*

sulfur /'sʌl.fəʳ/ [US] /-fɚ/ *noun* [U] US FOR **sulphur**

sulk /sʌlk/ *verb* [I] DISAPPROVING to be silent and childishly refuse to smile or be pleasant to people because you are angry about something that they have done: *He's sulking in a corner somewhere because I wouldn't let him have a second bar of chocolate.* **sulk** /sʌlk/ *noun* [C] *If she doesn't get what she wants she* ***goes into a*** *sulk just like a child.* ○ *Jim's in one of his sulks again – just ignore him.* **sulky** /'sʌlk.i/ *adj*: *She brought along a couple of sulky looking kids who didn't say a word all evening.* **sulkiness** /'sʌlk.ɪ.nəs/ *noun* [U]

sullen /'sʌl.ən/ *adj* angry and unwilling to smile or be pleasant to people: *His daughters stared back at him with an expression of sullen resentment.* ○ LITERARY *She looked up at the sullen* (= dark and unpleasant) *sky and shuddered.* **sullenly** /'sʌl.ən.li/ *adv*: *She turned her back*

S

to him and stared sullenly out of the window. **sullen-ness** /ˈsʌl.ən.nəs/ *noun* [U]

sully /ˈsʌl.i/ *verb* [T] *FORMAL* **1** to spoil something or someone's perfect reputation or purity: *His reputation, he said, had been unfairly sullied by allegations, half-truths and innuendos.* **2** to make something dirty: *No speck of dirt had ever sullied his hands.*

sulphate, *MAINLY US* **sulfate** /ˈsʌl.feɪt/ *noun* [C or U] a chemical formed from SULPHUR, oxygen and another element

sulphide, *MAINLY US* **sulfide** /ˈsʌl.faɪd/ *noun* [C or U] a chemical formed from SULPHUR and another element

sulphur, *MAINLY US* **sulfur** /ˈsʌl.fəʳ/ ⓤ /-fɚ/ *noun* [U] a pale yellow element which exists in various physical forms. It burns with a blue flame and a strong smell and is used in medicine and industry. **sulphurous**, *MAINLY US* **sulfurous** /ˈsʌl.fʳr.əs/ ⓤ /-fɚ-/ *adj*

,**sulphur di'oxide** *noun* [U] a colourless gas which has a strong unpleasant smell and dissolves in water. It is used in various industrial processes and for preserving food, and causes serious air pollution.

sulphuric acid, *MAINLY US* **sulfuric acid** /sʌlˌfjʊə.rɪkˈæs.ɪd/ ⓤ /-ˌfjʊr.ɪk/ *noun* [U] a strong colourless acid

sultan /ˈsʌl.tən/ *noun* [C] a ruler, especially in the past, of some Muslim countries: *the Sultan of Brunei*

sultanate /ˈsʌl.tə.nət/ *noun* [C] a country ruled by a sultan

sultana *MAINLY UK* /sʌlˈtɑː.nə/ *noun* [C] (*MAINLY US* **golden raisin**) a dried white grape

sultry [WARM] /ˈsʌl.tri/ *adj* (of weather) uncomfortably warm and with air that is slightly wet **sultriness** /ˈsʌl.trɪ.nəs/ *noun* [U]

sultry [SEXY] /ˈsʌl.tri/ *adj* (especially of a woman's face or voice) sexually attractive in a way that suggests sexual desire: *She's the sultry blonde in that new chocolate commercial.* **sultriness** /ˈsʌl.trɪ.nəs/ *noun* [U]

sum [AMOUNT OF MONEY] /sʌm/ *noun* [C] an amount of money: *Huge sums of money are spent on national defence.* ○ *He'll get £500 from the company when he retires, which is a tidy* (= large) *sum.* ○ *HUMOROUS I worked for three whole weeks for which I received the princely* (= very low) *sum of $100.*

sum [CALCULATION] /sʌm/ *noun* [C] a calculation, especially a simple one, using such processes as adding, subtracting, multiplying or dividing: *I remember how much I hated doing sums when I was at school.*

• **get/have your sums right/wrong** *MAINLY UK* to calculate the cost of something correctly/wrongly: *I must confess that I got my sums wrong – the house extension is costing a lot more than I expected.*

sum [TOTAL] /sʌm/ *noun* [S] **1** the whole number or amount when two or more numbers or amounts have been added together: *The sum of thirteen and eight is twenty-one.* **2** *FORMAL* **in sum** considered as a whole: *The meeting was, in sum, a disaster.* **3** **the sum of sth** all of something: *I'm afraid that's the pitiful sum of my knowledge on the subject!*

sum /sʌm/ *verb* -mm-

PHRASAL VERBS WITH **sum** ▼

▲ **sum (sth/sb) up** [EXPRESS] *phrasal verb* [M] to describe or express briefly the important facts or characteristics about something or someone: *The best way of summing up the situation in our office is to say that it is 'absolute chaos'.* ○ *I'd just like to sum up by saying that it's been a tremendous pleasure to work with you.* ○ *He's a small man with a big ego – that about sums him up, doesn't it?*

▲ **sum sth/sb up** *phrasal verb* [M] An action or object which sums something/someone up represents the most typical qualities of that person or thing: *For me, her paintings sum up the restless spirit of America.*

▲ **sum sb/sth up** [OPINION] *phrasal verb* [M] to quickly form an opinion about someone or something: *She summed up the situation quickly and took charge.*

▲ **sum up** [TRIAL] *phrasal verb* When a judge sums up towards the end of a trial, he or she makes a speech to the jury telling them again of the main matters they should consider in the case.

summing-up /ˌsʌm.ɪŋˈʌp/ *noun* [C]

summarize, *UK USUALLY* -**ise** /ˈsʌm.ʳr.aɪz/ ⓤ /-ə.raɪz/ *verb* [I or T] to express the most important facts or ideas about something or someone in a short and clear form: *I'll just summarize the main points of the argument in a few words if I may.*

summary /ˈsʌm.ʳr.i/ ⓤ /-ɚ-/ *noun* [C] (*FORMAL* **summation**) a short clear description that gives the main facts or ideas about something: *At the end of the news, they often give you a summary of the main news stories.*

summary /ˈsʌm.ʳr.i/ ⓤ /-ɚ-/ *adj* [before n] done suddenly, without discussion or legal arrangements: *summary arrest/dismissal/execution* **summarily** /ˌsʌm.ˈer.ɪ.li/ *adv*

summat /ˈsʌm.ət/ *pronoun UK NOT STANDARD* something: *There's summat wrong with this machine.*

summer /ˈsʌm.əʳ/ ⓤ /-ɚ-/ *noun* [C or U] the season of the year between spring and autumn when the weather is warmest, lasting from June to September north of the equator and from December to March south of the equator: *We have breakfast on the balcony in (the) summer.* ○ *Last summer they went to Australia, and two summers ago they went to Brazil.* ○ *I love these warm summer nights.* ○ *It was a perfect summer's day.* ➔See also **Indian summer**.

summery /ˈsʌm.ʳr.i/ ⓤ /-ɚ-/ *adj* typical of or suitable for summer: *Clare walked by looking very summery in a pale blue sundress.*

summerhouse /ˈsʌm.ə.haʊs/ ⓤ /-ɚ-/ *noun* [C] **1** a small building in a garden used for sitting in during the summer **2** *US* a house at the beach or in the mountains that you live in for part or all of the summer

,**summer 'pudding** *noun* [C or U] *UK* a cold sweet dish consisting of several soft red and purple fruits, such as RASPBERRIES and BLACKBERRIES, enclosed in bread

'**summer ,school** *noun* [C] **1** an educational course that happens during the summer when other courses have finished **2** *US* one or more educational courses taken during the summer which replace courses that were missed or failed, or which make it possible for students to advance more quickly toward a degree or GRADUATION

summertime /ˈsʌm.ə.taɪm/ ⓤ /-ɚ-/ *noun* [U] the season of summer: *You should see the garden in (the) summertime – it's beautiful.*

summit [HIGHEST POINT] /ˈsʌm.ɪt/ *noun* [C] **1** the highest point of a mountain: *On this day in 1784, Dr Michel Paccard and Jacques Balmat reached the summit of Mont Blanc.* **2** **the summit** the highest, most successful or most important point in something: *I certainly haven't reached the summit of my career.*

summit [MEETING] /ˈsʌm.ɪt/ *noun* [C] an important formal meeting between leaders of governments from two or more countries: *a summit meeting* ○ *World leaders will meet next week for their annual economic summit.*

summon [ORDER] /ˈsʌm.ən/ *verb* [T] to order someone to come to or be present at a particular place, or to officially arrange a meeting of people: *General Rattigan summoned reinforcements to help resist the attack.* ○ *HUMOROUS I'm afraid I'll have to go – I'm being summoned by my wife.* ○ *On July 20th, the council was summoned to hear an emergency report on its finances.*

summons /ˈsʌm.ənz/ *noun* [C] **1** an order to come and see someone: *I sat outside the boss's office awaiting my summons.* **2** *LEGAL* an official demand to appear in a court of law: *Mr Clarke's insurance company had issued a summons for unpaid mortgage repayments.*

summon [GATHER STRENGTH] /ˈsʌm.ən/ *verb* [T] to gather your bravery or strength, especially with an effort: *It took me six months to summon (up) the courage to ask him out for a drink.*

sumo wrestling /ˌsuː.məʊˈres.lɪŋ/ ⓤ /-moʊ-/ *noun* [U] a style of WRESTLING (= a fighting sport), originally from Japan, in which each man tries to defeat the other either by pushing him outside of a marked ring or by forcing him to touch the ground with a part of his body other than the bottom part of the foot **sumo wrestler** /ˌsuː.məʊˈres.ləʳ/ ⓤ /-moʊˈres.lɚ/ *noun* [C]

sump /sʌmp/ *noun* [C] a hole or container, especially in the lower part of an engine, into which a liquid that is not needed can flow

S

sumptuous /ˈsʌmp.tju.əs/ *adj* luxurious and showing wealth: *The celebrity guests turned up dressed in sumptuous evening gowns.* **sumptuously** /ˈsʌmp.tju.ə.sli/ *adv*

,**sum** ˈ**total** *noun* [U] The sum total of something is the whole of it, or everything: *It's the sum total of what you eat over a long period that matters and not what you consume in a day.*

sun STAR /sʌn/ *noun* [S or U] the star that the Earth spins around, which provides light and heat for the Earth, or the light or heat that the Earth receives from this star: *The sun rises in the east and sets in the west.* ○ *The sun's rays are at their most powerful at midday.* ○ *I think I've had a bit too much sun today – I've got a headache.* ○ *Shall we go and sit out in the sun?* ○ *We thought we'd go out for a walk while the sun was shining.*
● **sun sets on** *sth* LITERARY If the sun sets on something, it ends: *It used to be said that Britain ruled an empire on which the sun would never set.*
● **think the sun shines out (of)** *sb's* **arse/backside** UK OFFENSIVE to love and admire someone so much that you do not think they have any bad qualities
● **everything under the sun** everything that exists or is possible: *I've tried everything under the sun on this stain, but I just can't get rid of it.*
sun *yourself* *verb* [R] to lie or sit somewhere where there is a lot of sun, especially in order to make your skin darker: *I sat on the balcony sunning myself.*
sunny /ˈsʌn.i/ *adj* **1** bright because of light from the sun: *We're having the party in the garden, so I'm praying it'll be sunny.* **2** describes someone who is usually happy and relaxed and does not tend to get anxious or angry: *She has a very sunny disposition.*
sunless /ˈsʌn.ləs/ *adj* LITERARY lacking sun: *It was a grey and sunless day and our spirits were low.*

Sun DAY OF THE WEEK *WRITTEN ABBREVIATION FOR* Sunday

sun-baked /ˈsʌn.beɪkt/ *adj* [before n] An area of land or a place that is sun-baked is very dry and obviously receives a lot of sun: *We strolled along the sun-baked streets of Naples.*

sunbathe /ˈsʌn.beɪð/ *verb* [I] to sit or lie in the sun in order to make your skin darker: *I like to sunbathe in the morning when the sun is not so hot.* **sunbathing** /ˈsʌn-ˌbeɪ.ðɪŋ/ *noun* [U]

sunbeam UK /ˈsʌn.biːm/ *noun* [C] (US **sunray**) a beam of light from the sun that you can see

sunbed UK /ˈsʌn.bed/ *noun* [C] (US **tanning bed**) a bed-like frame containing a device for producing light, which you lie on in order to make the skin go darker

sunbelt /ˈsʌn.belt/ *noun* **the Sunbelt** the southern part of the US: *The sunbelt stretches from Florida to southern California.*

sunblock /ˈsʌn.blɒk/ ⑥ /-blɑːk/ *noun* [U] **sunscreen**

sunburn /ˈsʌn.bɜːn/ ⑥ /-bɜːn/ *noun* [U] when your skin has become sore and red because you have spent too long in the strong heat of the sun ○Compare **suntan**.
sunburnt, sunburned /ˈsʌn.bɜːnt/ ⑥ /-bɜːnt/ *adj* describes the condition of skin that has become red and sore by being in the strong heat of the sun for too long, or that is very SUNTANNED: *When you go out in the hot sun, you should always put cream on your skin to avoid getting sunburnt.* ○ *Fishermen with sunburnt faces sat on the beach mending their nets.*

sundae /ˈsʌn.deɪ/ *noun* [C] a food made from ice cream, with pieces of fruit, nuts, cream, sweet sauce, etc. on top of it

Sunday /ˈsʌn.deɪ/ *noun* [C or U] (WRITTEN ABBREVIATION **Sun**) the day of the week after Saturday and before Monday, when most people in Western countries do not go to work: *They go to church on Sundays.* ○ *We're going to visit my aunt and uncle on Sunday* (= next Sunday). ○ UK INFORMAL OR US *What are you doing Sunday* (= next Sunday)? ○ *We arrive in Paris on the* (= a particular) *Sunday, and leave the following Wednesday.* ○ *In Britain, the traditional Sunday lunch consists of roast meat, potatoes and other vegetables.*

,**Sunday** ˈ**best** *noun* [U] *your* **Sunday best** your best clothes which you wear on special occasions

,**Sunday** ˈ**driver** *noun* [C] DISAPPROVING someone who drives unnecessarily slowly, often annoying other drivers

,**Sunday** ˈ**paper** *noun* [C] (UK ALSO **Sunday**) a newspaper that is sold on Sundays and is usually bigger than newspapers sold on other days, often having several parts

ˈ**Sunday** ,**school** *noun* [C usually sing] a class held on Sundays in which especially Christian children are given religious teaching

sundeck /ˈsʌn.dek/ *noun* [C] a part of a ship or a flat area beside or on the roof of a house where you can sit in order to enjoy the sun

sundial /ˈsʌn.daɪl/ *noun* [C] a device used outside, especially in the past, which consists of a thin piece of metal fixed to a flat surface marked with numbers, which shows the time by the metal making a dark line on the surface as the sun moves across the sky above it

sundown /ˈsʌn.daʊn/ *noun* [U not after *the*] the time in the evening when you last see the sun in the sky: *We left early, anxious to make it back to Florence before/by sundown.*

sun-drenched /ˈsʌn.drentʃt/ *adj* [before n] A place that is sun-drenched frequently receives a lot of sun: *We spent the entire holiday lying on the sun-drenched beaches at the south end of the island.*

sundress /ˈsʌn.dres/ *noun* [C] an informal dress without sleeves that is worn in hot weather

sun-dried /ˈsʌn.draɪd/ *adj* [before n] describes vegetables that have been dried by leaving them in the sun so that their flavour becomes much stronger: *sun-dried tomatoes*

sundry /ˈsʌn.dri/ *adj* [before n] FORMAL several different; various: *Sundry distant relatives, most of whom I hardly recognized, turned up for my brother's wedding.*
● **all and sundry** MAINLY UK INFORMAL everyone: *I don't want all and sundry knowing about our problems.*
● **various and sundry** MAINLY US INFORMAL many different: *He spent an hour telling me about various and sundry ideas he has for making money.*
sundries /ˈsʌn.driz/ *plural noun* various different small items which are considered together, usually because they are not important enough to be considered separately: *There's an item on the hotel bill for sundries.*

sunflower /ˈsʌnˌflaʊəʳ/ ⑥ /-ˌflaʊr/ *noun* [C] a plant usually having a very tall stem and a single large round flat yellow flower, with many long thin narrow petals close together ○See picture **Flowers and Plants** on page Centre 3

sung /sʌŋ/ *past participle of* **sing**

sunglasses /ˈsʌŋˌglɑː.sɪz/ ⑥ /ˈsʌŋˌglæs.ɪz/ *plural noun* (ALSO **dark glasses**, INFORMAL **shades**) dark glasses which you wear to protect your eyes from bright light from the sun: *a pair of sunglasses*

sun-god /ˈsʌŋ.gɒd/ ⑥ /-gɑːd/ *noun* [C] a god who represented the sun in some ancient religions

ˈ**sun** ,**hat** *noun* [C] a hat to protect your head from the sun

sunk /sʌŋk/ *past simple and past participle of* **sink**

sunken /ˈsʌŋ.kən/ *adj* **1** having fallen to the bottom of the sea: *They're diving for sunken treasure.* **2** at a lower level than the surrounding area: *It was a luxurious bathroom, with a sunken bath.* **3** (of eyes or cheeks) seeming to have fallen inward into the face, especially because of tiredness, illness or old age: *She looked old and thin with sunken cheeks and hollow eyes.*

sun-kissed /ˈsʌn.kɪst/ *adj* [before n] MAINLY HUMOROUS describes a place that receives a lot of sun, or a person whose appearance is attractive because they have recently been in the sun

sunlamp /ˈsʌn.læmp/ *noun* [C] a device which produces light which has similar effects to that of light from the sun, and which is used especially for making the skin darker: *She spends several hours a week under a sunlamp to keep her skin looking tanned.*

sunless /ˈsʌn.ləs/ *adj* ○See at **sun** STAR.

sunlight /ˈsʌn.laɪt/ *noun* [U] the light that comes from the sun: *a ray/beam/shaft/pool of sunlight* ○ *The morning/afternoon/evening sunlight shone through the* curtains. ○ *The lake sparkled* **in** *the bright/brilliant sun-light.*

sunlit /'sʌn.lɪt/ *adj* (of a room, etc.) receiving a lot of light from the sun: *a sunlit room/courtyard/patio*

Sunni /'sun.i/ *adj, noun* [C] (a member) of the largest Islamic religious group, which follows the teachings only of Mohammed, not those of any of the religious leaders who came after him: *a Sunni Muslim*

sunny /'sʌn.i/ *adj* ➔See at **sun** STAR.

sunray /'sʌn.reɪ/ *noun* [C] US FOR **sunbeam**

sunrise TIME /'sʌn.raɪz/ *noun* [U] (US INFORMAL ALSO **sun-up**) the time in the morning when the sun starts to rise in the sky: *They went out* **at** *sunrise to go bird-watching.* ○ *We have to leave before sun-up tomorrow.*

sunrise SKY /'sʌn.raɪz/ *noun* [C] the appearance of the sky when the sun starts to rise: *There was a beautiful sun-rise this morning.*

sunroof /'sʌn.ruːf/ *noun* [C] part of a roof of a car which can be opened to allow air and light from the sun to come in ➔See picture **Car** on page Centre 12

sunscreen /'sʌn.skriːn/ *noun* [C or U] (ALSO **sunblock**) a substance which you put on your skin to prevent it from being burnt by the sun

sunset TIME /'sʌn.set/ *noun* [U] the time in the evening when you last see the sun in the sky: *The fishermen set out* **at** *sunset for a night's fishing.*

● **ride/drive/walk, etc. (off) into the sunset** to begin a new happy life at the end of a story: *At the end of the film, the pair of them ride off into the sunset.*

sunset SKY /'sʌn.set/ *noun* [C] the appearance of the sky in the evening before the sun goes down: *We sat on the beach watching a spectacular sunset.*

sunshade /'sʌn.ʃeɪd/ *noun* [C] **1** an object similar to an UMBRELLA which you carry to protect yourself from light from the sun **2** (US ALSO **umbrella**) a larger folding frame of this type, which you put into the ground to form an area which is sheltered from the light of the sun **3** US FOR **awning**

sunshine LIGHT /'sʌn.ʃaɪn/ *noun* [U] the light and heat that come from the sun: *The children were out playing* **in** *the sunshine.*

sunshine PLEASURE /'sʌn.ʃaɪn/ *noun* [U] **1** INFORMAL happi-ness or pleasure: *Their grandchildren have* **brought** *sunshine into their lives.* **2** MAINLY UK INFORMAL used as a form of address, either in a friendly way, or to express unwillingness to accept another person's delays, bad behaviour, etc.: *Hello, sunshine!* ○ *Come on, sunshine, get a move on.*

sunspot /'sʌn.spɒt/ /-spɑːt/ *noun* [C] a dark spot on the surface of the sun which appears for a few days or weeks and then disappears

sunstroke /'sʌn.strəʊk/ /-stroʊk/ *noun* [U] an illness caused by spending too much time in strong heat and light from the sun: *Someone who is suffering from sun-stroke feels dizzy and has a high temperature, but does not sweat.*

suntan /'sʌn.tæn/ *noun* [C] (ALSO **tan**) when your skin has turned darker because you have been in the sun: *She's on the beach all day, trying to get a really deep suntan.* ➔Compare **sunburn**. **suntanned** /'sʌn.tænd/ *adj* (ALSO **tanned**) *suntanned arms*

suntrap /'sʌn.træp/ *noun* [C] UK a sheltered room, etc. that receives a lot of light and heat from the sun

sun-up /'sʌn.ʌp/ *noun* [U] US FOR **sunrise** TIME

sun visor *noun* [C] a flat piece at the top of the front window of a vehicle which protects the driver's eyes from strong sun ➔See picture **Car** on page Centre 12

sup /sʌp/ *verb* [I usually + adv or prep; T] **-pp-** MAINLY UK to drink or to eat: NORTHERN ENGLISH *He spends most of his evenings in the pub, supping beer.* ○ OLD-FASHIONED *They supped on/off cold meat.*

super EXCELLENT /'suː.pəʳ/ /-pɚ/ *adj* SLIGHTLY OLD-FASHIONED INFORMAL excellent; extremely good: *The Natural History Museum is a super place for kids.* ○ *"Did you enjoy the film?" "Yes, I thought it was super."*

super PERSON /'suː.pəʳ/ /-pɚ/ *noun* [C] UK INFORMAL FOR **superintendent**, see at **superintend**

super- MORE THAN USUAL /suː.pəʳ-/ /-pɚ-/ *prefix* larger, or more effective, or more powerful, or more successful than usual; very or more than usually: *a supercomputer* ○ *a supermodel* ○ *the super-rich* ○ *superfine stockings*

super- OVER /suː.pəʳ-/ /-pɚ-/ *prefix* over; above: *a superstructure*

superabundant /ˌsuː.pəʳr.əˈbʌn.dənt/ /-pɚ-/ *adj* exist-ing in very large amounts: *Grapes and olives are super-abundant in this part of France.* **superabundance** /ˌsuː.pəʳr.əˈbʌn.dənts/ /-pɚ-/ *noun* [S]

superannuated /ˌsuː.pəʳrˈæn.ju.eɪ.tɪd/ /-pɚˈæn.ju.eɪ.tɪd/ *adj* FORMAL old, and almost no longer suitable for work or use

superannuation MAINLY UK /ˌsuː.pəʳrˌæn.juˈeɪ.ʃən/ /-pɚ-/ *noun* [U] (AUS INFORMAL **super**) money which people pay while they are working, so that they will receive payment when they stop working when they are old, or the payment they receive when they stop working

superb /suːˈpɜːb/ /-ˈpɝːb/ *adj* of excellent quality; very great: *He is a superb dancer.* ○ *Taylor scored a superb goal at the end of the first half.* **superbly** /suːˈpɜː.bli/ /-ˈpɝː-/ *adv*: *The orchestra played superbly.*

Super Bowl *noun* [C usually sing] in the US, a game of American football played each year between the winners of the two football LEAGUES (= groups) in order to decide which is the best team in the country

supercharge /'suː.pə.tʃɑːdʒ/ /-pɚ.tʃɑːrdʒ/ *verb* [T] to make an engine more powerful by forcing in more air and fuel than usual

supercharger /'suː.pə.tʃɑː.dʒəʳ/ /-pɚ.tʃɑːr.dʒɚ/ *noun* [C] a device which produces more power in an engine by forcing more air into the part of it in which fuel burns

supercharged FAST /'suː.pə.tʃɑːdʒd/ /-pɚ.tʃɑːrdʒd/ *adj* INFORMAL very fast or energetic: *The economy has expanded at a supercharged pace.*

supercharged EMOTIONAL /'suː.pə.tʃɑːdʒd/ /-pɚ.tʃɑːrdʒd/ *adj* INFORMAL containing or expressing very strong emotions: *There was a supercharged atmo-sphere during the debate in the House of Commons last night.*

supercilious /ˌsuː.pəˈsɪl.i.əs/ /-pɚ-/ *adj* DISAPPROVING behaving as if or showing that you think that you are better than other people, and that their opinions, beliefs or ideas are not important: *He spoke in a haughty, super-cilious voice.* **superciliously** /ˌsuː.pəˈsɪl.i.ə.sli/ /-pɚ-/ *adv* **superciliousness** /ˌsuː.pəˈsɪl.i.ə.snəs/ /-pɚ-/ *noun* [U]

superconductor /'suː.pə.kən.dʌk.təʳ/ /-pɚ.kən.dʌk.tɚ/ *noun* [C] a substance, especially a metal, that allows an electrical current to move freely through it at a very low temperature **superconductivity** /ˌsuː.pə.kɒn.dʌkˈtɪv.ɪ.ti/ /-pɚ.kɑːn.dʌkˈtɪv.ə.ti/ *noun* [U]

superego /ˌsuː.pəˈriː.gəʊ/ /-pɚˈiː.goʊ/ *noun* [C] plural **superegos** SPECIALIZED in PSYCHOANALYSIS, the part of your mind which knows what is right and wrong according to the rules of the society in which you live, and which causes you to feel guilty when you do something wrong ➔Compare **ego**; **id**.

superficial NOT SERIOUS /ˌsuː.pəˈfɪʃ.ªl/ /-pɚ-/ *adj* DIS-APPROVING (of a person) never thinking about things that are serious or important: *He's fun to be with, but he's very superficial.* **superficiality** /ˌsuː.pəˌfɪʃ.iˈæl.ɪ.ti/ /-pɚˌfɪʃ.iˈæl.ə.ti/ *noun* [U]

superficial NOT COMPLETE /ˌsuː.pəˈfɪʃ.ªl/ /-pɚ-/ *adj* USU-ALLY DISAPPROVING not complete and involving only the most obvious things: *I thought that article was written at a very superficial level.* ○ *The documentary's treatment/ analysis of the issues was very superficial.* ○ *I only have a superficial (= slight) knowledge of French.* **superficially** /ˌsuː.pəˈfɪʃ.ªl.i/ /-pɚ-/ *adv*: *Religious education is poorly and superficially taught in most schools.* **superficiality** /ˌsuː.pəˌfɪʃ.iˈæl.ɪ.ti/ /-pɚˌfɪʃ.iˈæl.ə.ti/ *noun* [U]

superficial FALSE APPEARANCE /ˌsuː.pəˈfɪʃ.ªl/ /-pɚ-/ *adj* appearing to be real or important until you realise the truth: *There are superficial similarities between the two cars, but actually they're quite different in terms of performance.*

superficially /ˌsuː.pəˈfɪʃ.ªl.i/ /-pɚ-/ *adv*: *The job I've been offered is superficially (= seems to be) attractive/*

appealing, but I think I might find it boring after a while.

superficial ONLY ON SURFACE /ˌsuː.pəˈfɪʃ.ᵊl/ (US) /-pɚ-/ *adj* only on the surface of something: *superficial damage* ○ *The driver only received superficial injuries/cuts/ wounds.* **superficiality** /ˌsuː.pəˌfɪʃ.iˈæl.ɪ.ti/ (US) /-pɚˌfɪʃ.iˈæl.ə.t̬i/ *noun* [U] **superficially** /ˌsuː.pəˈfɪʃ.ᵊl.i/ (US) /-pɚ-/ *adv*

superfluous /suːˈpɜː.flu.əs/ (US) /-ˈpɝː-/ *adj* more than is needed or wanted: *The report was marred by a mass of superfluous detail.* **superfluity** /ˌsuː.pəˈfluː.ɪ.ti/ (US) /-pɚˈfluː.ə.t̬i/ *noun* [C] FORMAL *The new director has said that there is **a** superfluity **of** staff in the organization, and that cuts must be made.* **superfluously** /suːˈpɜː.flu.ə.sli/ (US) /-ˈpɝː-/ *adv* **superfluousness** /suːˈpɜː.flu.ə.snəs/ (US) /-ˈpɝː-/ *noun* [U]

superglue /ˈsuː.pə.gluː/ (US) /-pɚ-/ *noun* [U] TRADEMARK a very strong quick-drying glue

supergrass /ˈsuː.pə.grɑːs/ (US) /-pɚ.græs/ *noun* [C] UK a person, especially a criminal, who gives the police a lot of information about the activities of criminals, especially serious ones

superhighway /ˈsuː.pəˌhaɪ.weɪ/ (US) /-pɚ-/ *noun* [C] US a large, wide road on which traffic travels at high speed

superhuman /ˌsuː.pəˈhjuː.mən/ (US) /-pɚ-/ *adj* having more powers than, or seeming beyond the powers of, a human: *I'll never get all this work done in a week – I'm not superhuman!* ○ *Thanks to the superhuman efforts of local volunteers, aid is now getting through to the disaster areas.*

superimpose /ˌsuː.pə.rɪmˈpəʊz/ (US) /-pɚ.ɪmˈpoʊz/ *verb* [T] to put especially a picture, words, etc. on top of something else, especially another picture, words, etc., so that what is in the lower position can still be seen, heard, etc.: *The book cover had a picture of a dove superimposed **on** a battle scene.*

superintend /ˌsuː.pə.rɪnˈtend/ (US) /-pɚ.ɪn-/ *verb* [T] FORMAL to be in charge of something: *Her job is to superintend the production process.*

superintendent /ˌsuː.pə.rɪnˈten.dənt/ (US) /-pɚ.ɪn-/ *noun* [C] **1** a person who is in charge of work done in a particular department, office, etc., or who is responsible for keeping a building or place in good condition: *In the US, a school superintendent is in charge of the schools in a particular area.* ○ *We asked the superintendent (ALSO US INFORMAL **super**) to fix the broken window in our apartment.* **2** a British police officer of high rank

superior BETTER /suːˈpɪə.ri.əʳ/ (US) /-ˈpɪr.i.ɚ/ *adj* **1** better than average or better than other people or things of the same type: *This is clearly the work of a superior artist.* ○ *She was chosen for the job because she was the superior candidate.* ○ *For all babies, breastfeeding is far superior **to** bottlefeeding.* ○ *The government troops were superior **in** numbers* (= There were more of them). ➲Compare **inferior**. **2** DISAPPROVING describes someone who believes that they are better than other people and acts in such a way: *a superior manner/smile* ○ *I can't bear Amanda – she's so superior.*

superiority /suːˌpɪə.riˈɒr.ɪ.ti/ (US) /-ˌpɪr.iˈɔːr.ə.t̬i/ *noun* [U] **1** when someone or something is better: *The Australian team soon demonstrated their superiority **over** the opposition.* ➲Compare **inferiority** at **inferior**. **2** when you behave and think as if you are better than other people: *Her sense of superiority makes her very unpopular.*

superior HIGHER /suːˈpɪə.ri.əʳ/ (US) /-ˈpɪr.i.ɚ/ *noun* [C], *adj* (a person or group of people who are) higher in rank or social position than others: *I will pass your complaint on to my superiors.* ○ *The soldier was reported to his superior officer for failing in his duties.* **superiority** /suːˌpɪə.riˈɒr.ɪ.ti/ (US) /-ˌpɪr.iˈɔːr.ə.t̬i/ *noun* [U]

superlative GRAMMAR /suːˈpɜː.lə.tɪv/ (US) /-ˈpɝː.lə.t̬ɪv/ *noun* [C] the form of an adjective or adverb which expresses that the thing or person being described has more of the particular quality than anything or anyone else of the same type: *'Richest' is **the** superlative **of** 'rich'.* ○ *The magazine article contained so many superlatives that I found it hard to believe that what it was saying was true.* **superlative** /suːˈpɜː.lə.tɪv/ (US) /-ˈpɝː.lə.t̬ɪv/ *adj*

superlative BEST /suːˈpɜː.lə.tɪv/ (US) /-ˈpɝː.lə.t̬ɪv/ *adj* of the highest quality; the best: *We went to a superlative restaurant.*

superlatively /suːˈpɜː.lə.tɪv.li/ (US) /-ˈpɝː.lə.t̬ɪv-/ *adv* extremely: *The company has been superlatively successful this year.*

superman /ˈsuː.pə.mæn/ (US) /-pɚ-/ *noun* [C] a man who has greater strength, ability, intelligence, etc. than other men: *The film portrays Gandhi as a kind of superman.*

supermarket /ˈsuː.pəˌmɑː.kɪt/ (US) /-pɚˌmɑːr-/ *noun* [C] a large shop which sells most types of food and other goods needed in the home, in which people take from shelves the items they want to buy and pay for them as they leave

ˌsupermarket ˈtabloid *noun* [C] US a newspaper sold in SUPERMARKETS which contains reports about famous people's private lives, or other things that have happened which are often hard to believe

supermodel /ˈsuː.pəˌmɒd.ᵊl/ (US) /-pɚˌmɑː.dᵊl/ *noun* [C] a very famous MODEL (= person, especially a woman, whose job is to wear clothes to show them to possible buyers)

supernatural /ˌsuː.pəˈnætʃ.ᵊr.ᵊl/ (US) /-pɚˈnætʃ.ɚ-/ *adj* caused by forces that cannot be explained by science: *Ghosts and evil spirits are supernatural.* ○ *She is said to have supernatural **powers** and to be able to communicate with the dead.*

the superˈnatural *noun* [S] things that cannot be explained by science: *I don't believe in **the** supernatural.*

supernaturally /ˌsuː.pəˈnætʃ.ᵊr.ᵊl.i/ (US) /-pɚˈnætʃ.ɚ-/ *adv*

supernova /ˌsuː.pəˈnəʊ.və/ (US) /-pɚˈnoʊ-/ *noun* [C] *plural* **supernovas** or **supernovae** a star which has exploded, greatly increasing its brightness for a few months

superpower /ˈsuː.pəˌpaʊəʳ/ (US) /-pɚˌpaʊr/ *noun* [C] a country which has very great political and military power: *Since the disintegration of the USSR, there has been only one superpower – the USA.*

supersaver /ˈsuː.pəˌseɪ.vəʳ/ (US) /-pɚˌseɪ.vɚ/ *noun* [C] **1** a ticket for travel by aircraft, train, etc. for which you pay less, either by buying it in advance or because you make your journey during a less busy period: *a supersaver ticket* **2** UK any item which you buy at specially reduced price: *The supersavers on offer this week are baked beans, chocolate biscuits and cornflakes.*

superscript /ˈsuː.pə.skrɪpt/ (US) /-pɚ-/ *noun* [U], *adj* (a word, letter, number, or symbol) written or printed just above a word, letter, number or symbol, usually in a smaller size: *References to the notes are given **in** superscript.*

supersede /ˌsuː.pəˈsiːd/ (US) /-pɚ-/ *verb* [T] to replace something, especially something older or more old-fashioned: *Most of the old road – which stretched from Chicago to Los Angeles – has been superseded by the great Interstate highways.*

supersize /ˈsuː.pə.saɪz/ (US) /-pɚ-/ *adj* [before n] US describes the largest size of meal or drink available in a FAST FOOD RESTAURANT

supersize /ˈsuː.pə.saɪz/ (US) /-pɚ-/ *verb* [T] US to give a customer in a FAST FOOD RESTAURANT the largest size of meal or drink: *"A burger and a coke please." "Can I supersize it for you?"*

supersonic /ˌsuː.pəˈsɒn.ɪk/ (US) /-pɚˈsɑː.nɪk/ *adj* faster than the speed of sound: *a supersonic fighter plane*

superstar /ˈsuː.pə.stɑːʳ/ (US) /-pɚ.stɑːr/ *noun* [C] an extremely famous actor, singer, musician, sports player, etc.: *a rock superstar* **superstardom** /ˈsuː.pəˌstɑː.dᵊm/ (US) /-pɚˌstɑːr-/ *noun* [U]

superstate /ˈsuː.pə.steɪt/ (US) /-pɚ-/ *noun* [C] a large and powerful state formed when several smaller countries unite: *a European/Federal superstate*

superstition /ˌsuː.pəˈstɪʃ.ᵊn/ (US) /-pɚ-/ *noun* [C or U] belief which is not based on human reason or scientific knowledge, but is connected with old ideas about magic, etc.: *According to superstition, if you walk under a ladder it brings you bad luck.* ○ *I don't believe in the old superstition **that** the number 13 is unlucky.* **superstitious** /ˌsuː.pəˈstɪʃ.əs/ (US) /-pɚ-/ *adj*: *superstitious nonsense* ○ *Some people are superstitious **about** spilling salt on the*

S

table. **superstitiously** /ˌsuː.pəˈstɪʃ.ə.sli/ [US] /-pɚ-/ *adv*

superstore /ˈsuː.pə.stɔːʳ/ [US] /-pɚ.stɔːr/ *noun* [C] an extremely large shop which sells food and/or other goods usually for use in the home at cheaper prices than most other shops: *a DIY superstore* ○ *an out-of-town superstore*

superstructure /ˈsuː.pəˌstrʌk.tʃəʳ/ [US] /-pɚˌstrʌk.tʃɚ/ *noun* [C] **1** (of a building) the part above the ground: *The foundations are finished and work has now begun on building the superstructure of the new library.* **2** (of a ship) the part above the main DECK **3** the ideas and systems of a society or organization which develop from more basic ideas and systems: *According to Marxist theory, a society's superstructure is its legal, social, cultural and political institutions, which are based on its economic systems.*

supertanker /ˈsuː.pəˌtæŋ.kəʳ/ [US] /-pɚˌtæŋ.kɚ/ *noun* [C] a very large ship, which transports especially oil

supertitle /ˈsuː.pəˌtaɪ.tl̩/ [US] /-pɚˌtaɪ.tl̬/ *noun* [C] *US FOR* **surtitle**

supervise /ˈsuː.pə.vaɪz/ [US] /-pɚ-/ *verb* [I or T] to watch a person or activity to make certain that everything is done correctly, safely, etc: *The UN is supervising the distribution of aid by local agencies in the disaster area.* ○ *The children play while two teachers supervise* (= make certain that they behave correctly and are safe).

supervision /ˌsuː.pəˈvɪʒ.ən/ [US] /-pɚ-/ *noun* [U] when someone watches a person or activity and makes certain that everything is done correctly, safely, etc: *Students are not allowed to handle these chemicals unless they are* ***under*** *the supervision* ***of*** *a teacher.*

supervisor /ˈsuː.pə.vaɪ.zəʳ/ [US] /-pɚ.vaɪ.zɚ/ *noun* [C] **1** a person whose job is to supervise someone or something **2** in some colleges, a teacher with responsibility for a particular student **3** *US* A town or county supervisor is an elected official who manages local government services. **supervisory** /ˌsuː.pəˈvaɪ.zər.i/ [US] /-pɚˈvaɪ.zɚ-/ *adj*: *We need to employ more supervisory staff.*

superwoman /ˈsuː.pəˌwʊm.ən/ [US] /-pɚ-/ *noun* [C] a woman who has greater strength, ability, intelligence, etc. than other women: *She said that she was tired of being expected to be a superwoman.*

supine [BODY] /ˈsuː.paɪn/ /ˈsjuː-/ *adj FORMAL* (lying) flat on your back, looking up: *We walked along the beach, past the rows of supine bodies soaking up the sun.* ⊃Compare **prone** LYING DOWN. **supinely** /ˈsuː.paɪn.li/ /ˈsjuː-/ *adv*

supine [CHARACTER] /ˈsuː.paɪn/ /ˈsjuː-/ *adj DISAPPROVING* If you are supine, you are weak and you willingly accept the control of others: *The new director has introduced a series of changes against little opposition from the supine staff.* **supinely** /ˈsuː.paɪn.li/ /ˈsjuː-/ *adv*

supper /ˈsʌp.əʳ/ [US] /-ɚ/ *noun* [C or U] a main meal eaten in the evening, or a small meal eaten in the late evening: *We usually have tea at about 5.30 p.m., then supper before we go to bed.* ○ *Would you like to come to supper tonight?* ○ *They had an early supper before going to the theatre.*

supplant /səˈplɑːnt/ [US] /-ˈplænt/ *verb* [T] *SLIGHTLY FORMAL* to replace: *In most offices, the typewriter has now been supplanted by the computer.* ○ *Small children can often feel supplanted (in their parents' affections)* (= that their parents no longer like them as much) *when a new brother or sister is born.*

supple [BENDING] /ˈsʌp.l̩/ *adj* bending or able to be bent easily; not stiff: *I'm not supple enough* (= My body doesn't bend easily enough) *to be able to touch the floor with my hands while I'm standing up.* ○ *The gloves were made of very supple leather.* **suppleness** /ˈsʌp.l̩.nəs/ *noun* [U]

supple [CHANGEABLE] /ˈsʌp.l̩/ *adj LITERARY* able to change quickly and successfully to suit different conditions: *She has shown that she has a supple mind.* ○ *We need a more supple monetary policy.*

supplement /ˈsʌp.lɪ.mənt/ *noun* [C] **1** something which is added to something else in order to improve it or complete it; something extra: *The doctor said she should be taking vitamin supplements.* ○ *The money I get from teaching evening classes provides a supplement* ***to*** *my main income.* ○ *We paid a supplement* (= an extra amount of money) *so that we could have a cabin on board the ship.* **2** a part of a magazine or newspaper, either produced separately or as part of the magazine or newspaper: *The newspaper publishes a sports supplement every Monday.* **3** A supplement to a book is an additional part of it, either produced separately or included at the end of the book, which contains information that was not available when the book was first produced: *There is a supplement* ***to*** *the dictionary containing new words.*

supplement /ˈsʌp.lɪ.ment/ /ˌ--ˈ-/ *verb* [T] to add something to something to make it larger or better: *He supplements* (= adds to) *his income by working in a bar in the evening.* ○ *Some vegetarians like to supplement their diets* ***with*** *iron tablets.* **supplementary** /ˌsʌp.lɪˈmen.tər.i/ [US] /-t̬ɚ-/ *adj* (*US ALSO* **supplemental**) *a supplementary income*

supplementary /ˌsʌp.lɪˈmen.tər.i/ [US] /-t̬ɚ-/ *adj SPECIALIZED* If an angle is supplementary to another angle, it forms 180° when combined with it.

supplicant /ˈsʌp.lɪ.kənt/ *noun* [C] *FORMAL* a person who asks a god or someone who is in a position of power for something in an anxious way that shows that they do not think of themselves as very important **supplication** /ˌsʌp.lɪˈkeɪ.ʃən/ *noun* [U] *Inside the temple, worshippers were kneeling* ***in*** *supplication.*

supply /səˈplaɪ/ *verb* [T] to provide something that is wanted or needed, often in large quantities and over a long period of time: *Electrical power is supplied by underground cables.* ○ *Three people have been arrested for supplying arms* ***to*** *the terrorists.* ○ *The company has supplied the royal family* (= provided them with something they need) *for years.* ○ *At the beginning of term, students are supplied* ***with*** *a list of books that they are expected to read.*

supply /səˈplaɪ/ *noun* [C or U] **1** an amount of something that is available for use: *Whenever she goes out with her baby, she always takes a large supply* ***of*** *baby food with her.* ○ *In London, demand for cheap housing far outstrips supply* (= what is provided). **2 the gas/electricity, etc. supply** the system used for supplying gas/electricity, etc. to people: *Someone has turned off the electricity supply.* **3 in short supply** when there is little of something available: *Strawberries are in short supply at the moment.*

• **supply and demand** the idea that the price of goods and services depends on how much of something is being sold and how many people want to buy it

supplies /səˈplaɪz/ *plural noun* food or other items necessary for living: *The refugees are urgently in need of food and medical supplies.*

supplier /səˈplaɪ.əʳ/ [US] /-ɚ/ *noun* [C] a company, person, etc. that provides things that people want or need, especially over a long period of time: *They used to be a leading supplier* ***of*** *military equipment.* ○ *He said that he had got the drugs from his usual supplier* (= person who sells drugs illegally).

suppliers /səˈplaɪ.əz/ [US] /-ɚz/ *plural noun* a company which sells something: *I'll contact* ***the*** *suppliers and see if I can get the paint you want by Friday.*

sup'ply ˌteacher *UK noun* [C] (*US* **substitute teacher**) a teacher who replaces teachers who are absent from work

support [ENCOURAGE] /səˈpɔːt/ [US] /-ˈpɔːrt/ *verb* [T] **1** to agree with and give encouragement to someone or something because you want them to succeed: *My father supported the Labour Party all his life.* ○ *The majority of people in the town strongly support the plans to build a by-pass.* ○ *I think it's important to support local businesses by buying locally.* **2** (*US USUALLY* **root for**, *AUS* **barrack for**) *MAINLY UK* If you support a sports team or a sports player, you want them to win, and might show it by going to watch them play: *Which team do you support?*

support /səˈpɔːt/ [US] /-ˈpɔːrt/ *noun* [U] agreement with and encouragement for an idea, group or person: *Environmental groups are fast gaining support among young people.* ○ *We've succeeded in* ***drumming up*** *a lot of local support* ***for*** *our attempt to stop the hospital being closed.* ○ *I signed a petition* ***in*** *support* ***of*** *the campaign to end the marketing of baby milk in developing countries.*

S

supporter /səˈpɔː.tə^r/ US /-ˈpɔːr.t̬ɚ/ *noun* [C] **1** someone who supports a particular idea, group or person: *He is one of the Prime Minister's strongest supporters within industry.* **2** UK (US **fan**) someone who wants a particular team to win and might show it by going to watch them play: *Thousands of supporters have travelled to London for the cup final.*

supportive /səˈpɔː.tɪv/ US /-ˈpɔːr.t̬ɪv/ *adj* showing agreement and giving encouragement: *Doubts about the government's policies are being expressed even by people who have been supportive of the government in the past.*

support HELP /səˈpɔːt/ US /-ˈpɔːrt/ *verb* [T] to help someone emotionally or in a practical way: *Alcoholics Anonymous is a group which supports people who are trying to stop drinking too much alcohol.* ○ *My family has always supported me in whatever I've wanted to do.* support /səˈpɔːt/ US /-ˈpɔːrt/ *noun* [C or U] *Liz gave me a lot of support when I lost my job.* ○ *You've been a great support to my mum in this difficult time.*

supportive /səˈpɔː.tɪv/ US /-ˈpɔːr.t̬ɪv/ *adj* APPROVING giving help and encouragement: *Children with supportive parents often do better at school than those without.* **supportively** /səˈpɔː.tɪv.li/ US /-ˈpɔːr.t̬ɪv-/ *adv* **supportiveness** /səˈpɔː.tɪv.nəs/ US /-ˈpɔːr.t̬ɪv-/ *noun* [U]

support STOP FROM FALLING /səˈpɔːt/ US /-ˈpɔːrt/ *verb* [T] to hold something firmly or bear its weight, especially from below to stop it from falling: *The church dome is supported by/on marble pillars.* ○ *When babies first learn to stand, they hold on to something to support themselves* (= to stop themselves from falling). ○ *My ankle is rather weak, so I always put a bandage on it to support it when I play tennis.* ○ FIGURATIVE *The Bank of England has taken measures to support the pound* (= to stop it from being reduced in value).
support /səˈpɔːt/ US /-ˈpɔːrt/ *noun* **1** [C or U] something that holds something firmly or bears its weight, especially from below to stop it from falling: *The floor is held up by wooden supports.* ○ *I've hurt my wrist, so I've got it bandaged to give it some support.* **2** [C] a device worn to hold part of the body, especially a weak part, firmly in position: *Jim always wears a knee support when he goes running.*

support PROVIDE /səˈpɔːt/ US /-ˈpɔːrt/ *verb* [T] **1** to give a person the money they need in order to buy food and clothes and pay for somewhere to live: *He has a wife and four children to support.* **2** If you support an activity or a habit, you provide the money needed to pay for it: *The drug company is supporting cancer research.* ○ *I don't know how they manage to support their expensive lifestyle.* ○ *Some drug addicts turn to crime in order to support their habit.* **3** to provide the right conditions, such as enough food and water, for life: *The land is so poor here that it cannot support any crops.*
support /səˈpɔːt/ US /-ˈpɔːrt/ *noun* [U] *He is dependent on his father for support* (= for paying for food, a place to live, etc.).

support PROVE /səˈpɔːt/ US /-ˈpɔːrt/ *verb* [T] to help to show something to be true: *These figures support my argument.* ○ *You can't make a statement like that without any supporting documentation.* support /səˈpɔːt/ US /-ˈpɔːrt/ *noun* [U] *This new evidence lends support to the theory that she was murdered.* ○ *We had to send a doctor's report in support of our claim to the insurance company.* **supportable** /səˈpɔː.tə.bl̩/ US /-ˈpɔːr.t̬ə-/ *adj* FORMAL

support BEAR /səˈpɔːt/ US /-ˈpɔːrt/ *verb* [T] FORMAL to bear; to allow to happen: *The headteacher told the boys that he would not support that kind of behaviour.*

sup'port ˌgroup *noun* [C] a group of people who have had similar experiences, especially difficult ones, and who provide help to each other: *After their baby died, they joined a local support group.*

supporting /səˈpɔː.tɪŋ/ US /-ˈpɔːr.t̬ɪŋ/ *adj* a supporting **actor/part/role** not the most important actor/part/role in a film or play: *She had a small supporting part in the play.*

sup'port ˌnetwork *noun* [C] a group of people who provide emotional and practical help to someone in serious difficulty: *It's very hard for battered women to rebuild their lives without a good support network.*

suppose THINK LIKELY /səˈpəʊz/ US /-ˈpoʊz/ *verb* **1** [T] to think that something is likely to be true: [+ (*that*)] *I couldn't get any reply when I called Dan, so I suppose (that) he's gone out.* ○ *He found it a lot more difficult to get a job than he supposed it would be.* ○ [+ (*that*)] *Do you suppose (that) Gillian will marry him?* ○ *It is widely supposed (that) the minister will be forced to resign.* ○ [+ to infinitive] *We all supposed him to be German, but in fact he was Swiss.* ○ *Her new book is supposed to be* (= generally people think it is) *very good.* **2** [+ (*that*)] used in making polite requests: *I don't suppose (that) you could/I suppose you couldn't lend me £5 till tomorrow, could you?* **3** [+ (*that*)] used to show that you think something is so, although you wish that it were not: *I suppose (that) all the tickets will be sold by now.* **4** [+ (*that*)] used to express annoyance: *I suppose (that) you're going to be late again.* ○ *I suppose (that) you think that's funny. Well, I certainly don't.* **5** used to show unwillingness to agree: *"Can I go out tonight?" "Oh, I suppose so."* ○ [+ (*that*)] *I don't agree with it, but I suppose (that) it's for the best.*

supposed /səˈpəʊzd/ US /-ˈpoʊzd/ *adj* [before n] used to show that you do not believe that something or someone really is what many other people consider them to be: *a supposed genius* ○ *The costs of the scheme outweigh its supposed benefits.*

supposition /ˌsʌp.əˈzɪʃ.ᵊn/ *noun* [C or U] when someone believes something is true without any proof: *That article was based on pure supposition.* **supposedly** /səˈpəʊ.zɪd.li/ US /-ˈpoʊ-/ *adv*: *Well, the tickets are supposedly in the mail.*

suppose NEED /səˈpəʊz/ US /-ˈpoʊz/ *verb* [T] FORMAL to expect and need: *Investment of this kind supposes* (= would not be possible without) *an increase in the company's profits this year.* ⊃See also **presuppose**.

suppose /səˈpəʊz/ US /-ˈpoʊz/ *conjunction* (ALSO **supposing**) used at the beginning of a sentence or clause to mean 'what would happen if': *Suppose we miss the train – what will we do then?* ○ *We'd love to come and see you on Saturday, supposing* (= if) *I don't have to work that day.*

supposed DUTY /səˈpəʊzd/ US /-ˈpoʊzd/ *adj* be supposed to to have to; to have a duty or a responsibility to: *The children are supposed to be at school by 8.45 a.m.* ○ *What are you doing out of bed – you're supposed to be asleep.* ○ *You're not supposed* (= allowed) *to park here.*

supposed INTENDED /səˈpəʊzd/ US /-ˈpoʊzd/ *adj* be supposed to to be intended to: *These batteries are supposed to last for a year.* ○ *We were supposed to have gone away this week, but Debbie's ill so we couldn't go.* ○ *How am I supposed to* (= How can I) *find that much money by the end of the week?*

suppository /səˈpɒz.ɪ.tri/ US /-ˈpɑː.zə.tɔːr.i/ *noun* [C] a small solid pill which contains a drug and which is put inside the anus where it dissolves easily

suppress END BY FORCE /səˈpres/ *verb* [T] to end something by force: *The Hungarian uprising in 1956 was suppressed by the Soviet Union.* **suppression** /səˈpreʃ.ᵊn/ *noun* [U] *brutal police suppression of the riots*

suppress PREVENT /səˈpres/ *verb* [T] to prevent something from being seen or expressed or from operating: *She couldn't suppress her anger/annoyance/delight.* ○ *His feelings of resentment have been suppressed for years.* ○ *The government tried to suppress the book because of the information it contained about the security services.* ○ *The virus suppresses the body's immune system.* **suppression** /səˈpreʃ.ᵊn/ *noun* [U] *suppression of evidence/emotions/free speech, etc.*

suppressor /səˈpres.ə^r/ US /-ɚ/ *noun* [C] a thing or person that prevents something bad from happening: *Plastic is a good weed suppressor* (= a substance which stops them from growing).

suppurate /ˈsʌp.jʊ.reɪt/ *verb* [I] SPECIALIZED (of an injury, etc.) to form or give out a thick yellow liquid because of infection: *a suppurating sore/wound*

supranational /ˌsuː.prəˈnæʃ.ᵊn.ᵊl/ *adj* involving more than one country; having power or authority which is greater than that of single countries: *NATO is a supranational organization.*

supreme HIGHEST /suːˈpriːm/ *adj, adv* having the highest rank, level or importance: *the supreme commander of the armed forces* ○ *the Supreme Court* ○ *The present constitution gives supreme authority to the presidency.* ○ *From 1960 to 1970, Ayatollah Mohsen al-Hakim reigned supreme among the Shi'ites of Iraq, Iran and elsewhere.*

supremacy /suːˈprem.ə.si/ *noun* [U] the leading or controlling position: *The company has begun to challenge the supremacy of the current leading manufacturers in the textiles industry.* ○ *The allies have established air supremacy* (= military control of the sky).

supremacist /suːˈprem.ə.sɪst/ *noun* [C] MAINLY DISAPPROVING someone who believes that a particular type or group of people should lead or have control over other types or groups of people because they believe they are better: *a white supremacist*

supreme GREATEST /suːˈpriːm/ *adj* very great or best: *She was awarded a medal for showing supreme courage/bravery.* ○ *For me, dieting requires a supreme effort of will.*

supremely /suːˈpriːm.li/ *adv* extremely: *Wales are supremely confident of winning the match.*

supremacy /suːˈprem.ə.si/ *noun* [U] when someone or something is the best: *a struggle for supremacy* ○ *This victory clearly proves the supremacy of the West Indies in world cricket.*

the ˌSupreme ˈBeing *noun* [S] LITERARY a name for God

the Suˌpreme ˈCourt *noun* [S] the most important court of law in the US

supremo /suːˈpriː.məʊ/ ⓤ /-moʊ/ *noun* [C] *plural* **supremos** UK INFORMAL the person in charge of an organization or who is considered to have most skill and authority in a particular type of activity: *BBC supremo, Lord Reith* ○ *the entertainment supremo, Alan Partridge*

Supt *noun* [before n] ABBREVIATION FOR **superintendent**

surcharge /ˈsɜː.tʃɑːdʒ/ ⓤ /ˈsɜːr.tʃɑːrdʒ/ *noun* [C] a charge in addition to the usual amount paid for something, or the amount already paid: *A surcharge may be made for deliveries outside normal hours.*

surcharge /ˈsɜː.tʃɑːdʒ/ ⓤ /ˈsɜːr.tʃɑːrdʒ/ /,-'-/ *verb* [I or T] to charge an extra amount

sure /ʃɔːr/ ⓤ /ʃʊr/ *adj* **1** certain; without any doubt: *"What's wrong with him?" "I'm not really sure." ○ I'm sure (that) I left my keys on the table. ○ I feel absolutely sure (that) you've made the right decision.* ○ *It now seems sure (that) the election will result in another victory for the government.* ○ *Simon isn't sure whether/if he'll be able to come to the party or not.* ○ *Is there anything you're not sure of/about?* ○ *There is only one sure way* (= one way that can be trusted) *of finding out the truth.* ➔See also **cocksure**. **2 be sure of/about sb** to have confidence in and trust someone: *Henry has only been working for us for a short while, and we're not really sure about him yet.* ○ *You can always be sure of Kay.* **3 be sure of yourself** to be very or too confident: *She's become much more sure of herself since she got a job.* **4 be sure of sth** to be confident that something is true: *He said that he wasn't completely sure of his facts.* **5 be sure of getting/winning sth** to be certain to get or win something: *We arrived early, to be sure of getting a good seat.* ○ *A majority of Congress members wanted to put off an election until they could be sure of winning it.* **6 be sure to** to be certain to: *She's sure to win.* ○ *I want to go somewhere where we're sure to have good weather.* **7 make sure (that)** to look and/or take action to be certain that something happens, is true, etc: *Make sure you lock the door behind you when you go out.* **8** If you have a sure knowledge or understanding of something, you know or understand it very well: *I don't think he has a very sure understanding of the situation.*

● **sure thing** MAINLY US INFORMAL used to show agreement: *"Could you give me a lift home tonight?" "Sure thing!"*

● **to be sure** FORMAL certainly: *This is not his best book, to be sure, but it is still worth reading.*

sure /ʃɔːr/ ⓤ /ʃʊr/ *adv* INFORMAL certainly: *"Do you want to come swimming with us?" "Sure." ○ MAINLY US "Will you help me with this?" "Sure I will." ○ US I sure am hungry.*

● **(as) sure as eggs is eggs** UK OLD-FASHIONED for certain: *One day he'll realize that I was right, as sure as eggs is eggs.*

● **(as) sure as hell** SLANG used for emphasis: *There better be another way in – I'm sure as hell not climbing up all those steps.*

● **for sure** certain or certainly: *I know for sure that I won't be able to go to the party.* ○ *One thing's for sure – once the baby's born, your lives will never be the same again.*

● **sure enough** as expected: *He said he'd left the book on the desk, and sure enough, here it was.*

surely /ˈʃɔː.li/ ⓤ /ˈʃʊr-/ *adv* **1** used to express that you are certain or almost certain about something: *The fault surely lies in the design of the equipment.* ○ *US "May I sit here?" "Surely* (= Yes, certainly)." ○ *Without more food and medical supplies, these people will surely not survive.* **2** used to express surprise that something has happened or is going to happen: *Surely you don't expect me to believe that?* ○ *Surely you're not going out on a night like this?*

sureness /ˈʃɔː.nəs/ ⓤ /ˈʃʊr-/ *noun* [U] confidence and control: *We admired the sureness of the orchestra's playing.* ○ *She has an enviable sureness of touch* (= She deals with things confidently and well).

surefire /ˈʃɔː.faɪər/ ⓤ /ˈʃʊr.faɪr/ *adj* [before n] INFORMAL certain or likely, especially to succeed: *The film looks a surefire Oscar winner.* ○ *Running into the road like that is a surefire way to get hurt.*

surefooted NOT FALLING /ˈʃɔːˌfʊt.ɪd/ ⓤ /ˈʃʊrˌfʊt-/ *adj* able easily to walk on rough ground, without falling: *a surefooted goat/llama/mule* **surefootedly** /ˌʃɔːˈfʊt.ɪd.li/ ⓤ /ˌʃʊrˈfʊt-/ *adv* **surefootedness** /ˌʃɔːˈfʊt.ɪd.nəs/ ⓤ /ˌʃʊrˈfʊt-/ *noun* [U]

surefooted CONFIDENT /ˈʃɔːˌfʊt.ɪd/ ⓤ /ˈʃʊrˌfʊt-/ *adj* showing confidence and the ability to make good judgements in a difficult situation **surefootedly** /ˌʃɔːˈfʊt.ɪd.-li/ ⓤ /ˌʃʊrˈfʊt-/ *adv* **surefootedness** /ˌʃɔːˈfʊt.ɪd.nəs/ ⓤ /ˌʃʊrˈfʊt-/ *noun* [U]

surety /ˈʃɔː.rə.ti/ ⓤ /ˈʃʊr.ə.ti/ *noun* [C or U] LEGAL a person who accepts legal responsibility for another person's debt or behaviour, or (money given as) a promise that someone will do something that they have said they will do, such as pay a debt or appear in court: *Her brothers are acting as sureties for her.* ○ *No one has yet been found who is willing to stand* (= act as a) *surety for Mr Naylor.* ○ *What are you able to provide as a surety that you will repay the loan?*

surf WAVES /sɜːf/ ⓤ /sɜːrf/ *noun* [U] the tops of the waves on the sea when they approach the coast or hit against rocks: *We were almost deafened by the crash/roar of the surf.*

surf /sɜːf/ ⓤ /sɜːrf/ *verb* [I or T] to ride on a wave as it comes towards land, while standing or lying on a special board: *They go surfing every weekend.* ➔See also **bodysurf**; **windsurfing**.

surfer /ˈsɜː.fər/ ⓤ /ˈsɜːr.fɚ/ *noun* [C] a person who rides on a wave on a special board ➔See also **windsurfer**.

surfing /ˈsɜː.fɪŋ/ ⓤ /ˈsɜːr-/ *noun* [U] the sport of riding on a wave on a special board ➔See also **windsurfing**. ➔See picture **Sports** on page Centre 10

surf INTERNET /sɜːf/ ⓤ /sɜːrf/ *verb* [I or T] to spend time visiting a lot of WEBSITES: *Many towns and cities have cybercafes where you can surf the Internet/Net/Web.* **surfing** /ˈsɜː.fɪŋ/ ⓤ /ˈsɜːr.fɪŋ/ *noun* [U] *Internet surfing*

surface TOP /ˈsɜː.fɪs/ ⓤ /ˈsɜːr-/ *noun* [C] **1** the outer or top part or layer of something: *Tropical rain forests used to cover 10% of the Earth's surface.* ○ *The marble has a smooth, shiny surface.* ○ *Neil Armstrong was the first person to set foot on the surface of the moon.* **2** the top layer of a field or track on which sports are played: *The match will be played on an artificial/all-weather surface.* **3** the flat top part of a table, cupboard, etc: *a work surface* ○ *Don't put anything wet on a polished surface, or it will leave a mark.*

● **scratch/scrape the surface** to deal with only a very small part of a subject or a problem: *There's far more to be said – I've only had time to scratch the surface in this talk.* ○ *The amount of aid which has been offered is hardly going to scratch the surface of the problem.*

surface /ˈsɜː.fɪs/ ⓤ /ˈsɝː-/ *adj* working or operating on the top of the land or sea, rather than under the land or sea, or by air

surface /ˈsɜː.fɪs/ ⓤ /ˈsɝː-/ *verb* **1** [I] to rise to the surface of water: *The submarine surfaced a few miles off the coast.* **2** [T] to cover a road or other area with a hard surface

surface ADVICE /ˈsɜː.fɪs/ ⓤ /ˈsɝː-/ *noun* [S] The surface of a situation or person is what they appear to be, or the features they have which are not hidden or difficult to see: **On** the surface, this seems like a difficult problem, but in fact there's an easy solution to it. ○ **Beneath/Below/Under** the surface of contemporary West Indian life lurk memories of slavery. ○ Suddenly, all her anger **came/rose** to the surface (= became obvious).

surface /ˈsɜː.fɪs/ ⓤ /ˈsɝː-/ *adj* [before n] appearing in a particular way but not necessarily showing the truth: *his surface appearance of calm confidence*

surface KNOWN /ˈsɜː.fɪs/ ⓤ /ˈsɝː-/ *verb* [I] If a feeling or information surfaces, it becomes known: *Doubts are beginning to surface **about** whether the right decision has been made.* ○ A rumour has surfaced that the company is about to go out of business.

surface OUT OF BED /ˈsɜː.fɪs/ ⓤ /ˈsɝː-/ *verb* [I] INFORMAL to get out of bed: *He never surfaces until at least 11.00 a.m. on a Sunday.*

ˈsurface ˌmail *noun* [U] a way of sending letters, parcels, etc. by road, sea or train and not by aircraft, or items sent in this way: *I sent the parcel by surface mail.*

ˌsurface ˈtension *noun* [C] the natural force existing in a liquid which holds its surface together

surface-to-air missile /ˌsɜː.fɪs.təˌeəˈmɪs.aɪl/ ⓤ /ˌsɝː.fɪs.təˌerˈmɪs.ᵊl/ *noun* [C] (ABBREVIATION SAM) a missile that is fired from land or the sea towards aircraft or other missiles

surface-to-surface /ˌsɜː.fɪs.təˈsɜː.fɪs/ ⓤ /ˌsɝː.fɪs.təˈsɝː-/ *adj* (of a missile) fired from land or the sea towards a place on land or a ship

surfboard /ˈsɜːf.bɔːd/ ⓤ /ˈsɝːf.bɔːrd/ *noun* [C] a long narrow board made of wood or plastic which is used for riding on waves as they come in towards the beach ⊃See picture **Sports** on page Centre 10

surfeit /ˈsɜː.fɪt/ ⓤ /ˈsɝː-/ *noun* [C usually sing] FORMAL an amount which is too large, or is more than is needed: *The country has **a** surfeit **of** cheap labour.*

surge /sɜːdʒ/ ⓤ /sɝːdʒ/ *noun* [C] **1** a sudden and great increase: *An unexpected surge **in** electrical power caused the computer to crash.* ○ There has been a surge **in** house prices recently. ⊃See also **resurgence**. **2** a sudden and great movement forward: *At the end of the game, there was a surge **of** fans onto the field.* ○ A **tidal** surge (= sudden and great rise in the level of the sea) caused severe flooding in coastal areas. **3** a sudden increase of an emotion: *She was overwhelmed by a surge **of** remorse.*

surge /sɜːdʒ/ ⓤ /sɝːdʒ/ *verb* [I] **1** to increase suddenly and greatly: *The company's profits have surged.* **2** to move quickly and powerfully: *An angry crowd surged through the gates of the president's palace.* ○ A few metres before the end of the race, Jenkins surged **into the lead**. **3** (of an emotion) to develop strongly and quickly: *She felt a wave of resentment surging **(up)** inside her.*

surgeon /ˈsɜː.dʒᵊn/ ⓤ /ˈsɝː-/ *noun* [C] a doctor who is specially trained to perform medical operations

ˌSurgeon ˈGeneral *noun* [C usually sing] In the US, the Surgeon General is the person who is in charge of the public health service.

surgery MEDICAL OPERATION /ˈsɜː.dʒ³r.i/ ⓤ /ˈsɝː.dʒɚ-/ *noun* [U] the treatment of injuries or diseases in people or animals by cutting open the body and removing or repairing the damaged part: *The patient **had/underwent** surgery **on** his heart.* ○ He made a good recovery after surgery **to** remove a brain tumour.

surgical /ˈsɜː.dʒɪ.kᵊl/ ⓤ /ˈsɝː-/ *adj* **1** used for medical operations: *surgical supplies/instruments/gloves, etc.* **2** involved in performing medical operations: *surgical procedures/techniques/intervention* ○ *surgical staff* **3** (of clothing) worn in order to treat a particular medical condition: *a surgical shoe/collar/corset* **surgically** /ˈsɜː.dʒɪ.kli/ ⓤ /ˈsɝː-/ *adv*

surgery ADVICE /ˈsɜː.dʒ³r.i/ ⓤ /ˈsɝː.dʒɚ-/ *noun* UK **1** [C or U] a place where you can go to ask advice from or receive treatment from a doctor or dentist: *If you come to the surgery (US **office**) at 10.30, the doctor will see you then.* ○ On Saturday mornings, surgery (= the fixed period of opening of the place where you can go to see your doctor) is (US **office hours** are) from 9.00 to 12.00. **2** [C] the regular period of time when a person can visit their MEMBER OF PARLIAMENT to ask advice: *Our MP **holds a** weekly surgery on Friday mornings.*

ˌsurgical ˈspirit UK *noun* [U] (US **rubbing alcohol**) a liquid for cleaning medical equipment or a person's skin so that it is free from bacteria

ˌsurgical ˈstrike *noun* [C] a type of military attack which is made in an exact way on a particular place: *A surgical strike was carried out on the enemy's military headquarters.*

surly /ˈsɜː.li/ ⓤ /ˈsɝː-/ *adj* bad-tempered, unfriendly and not polite: *We were served by a very surly waiter.* ○ He gave me a surly look. **surliness** /ˈsɜː.lɪ.nəs/ ⓤ /ˈsɝː-/ *noun* [U]

surmise /ˈsə.maɪz/ ⓤ /sɚ-/ *verb* [T] FORMAL to guess something, without having much or any proof: *[+ **(that)**] The police surmise **(that)** the robbers have fled the country.*

surmise /ˈsə.maɪz/ ⓤ /sɚ-/ *noun* [C or U] FORMAL a guess: *My surmise turned out to be right.* ○ The article is **pure** surmise and innuendo.

surmount DEAL WITH /səˈmaʊnt/ ⓤ /sɚ-/ *verb* [T] FORMAL to deal successfully with a difficulty or problem: *They managed to surmount all opposition/objections to their plans.* ○ There are still a few technical problems/obstacles/hurdles to be surmounted before the product can be put on sale to the public. **surmountable** /səˈmaʊn.tə.b|/ ⓤ /sɚˈmaʊn.t̬ə-/ *adj*

surmount BE ON TOP /səˈmaʊnt/ ⓤ /sɚ-/ *verb* [T] FORMAL to be on top of something tall: *The central 12-foot column is surmounted by a bronze angel with outspread wings.*

surname /ˈsɜː.neɪm/ ⓤ /ˈsɝː-/ *noun* [C] (US USUALLY **last name**, UK ALSO **second name**) the name that you share with other members of your family; last name: *Her first name is Sarah but I don't know her surname.*

surpass /səˈpɑːs/ ⓤ /sɚˈpæs/ *verb* [T] FORMAL to do or be better than: *His time for the 100 metres surpassed the previous world record **by** one hundredth of a second.* ○ The book's success has surpassed everyone's expectations. ○ [R] The director has really surpassed himself (= done better than he has done before) **with** this new film.

surpassing /səˈpɑː.sɪŋ/ ⓤ /sɚˈpæs.ɪŋ/ *adj* [before n] LITERARY extremely great: *a face of surpassing loveliness*

surplice /ˈsɜː.plɪs/ ⓤ /ˈsɝː-/ *noun* [C] SPECIALIZED a white, loose piece of clothing, which is worn over other clothing during religious ceremonies by some Christian priests and members of groups who sing in churches

surplus /ˈsɜː.pləs/ ⓤ /ˈsɝː-/ *noun* [C or U], *adj* **1** (an amount which is) more than is needed: *The world is now producing large food surpluses.* ○ We are unlikely to produce any surplus this year. ○ The government has authorized the army to sell its surplus weapons. ○ UK The store is selling off stock that is surplus **to requirements** (= more than they need to have). **2** the amount of money you have left when you sell more than you buy, or spend less than you have: *a budget/trade surplus* ○ Fortunately the school's bank account is currently **in** surplus.

surprise /səˈpraɪz/ ⓤ /sɚ-/ *noun* [C or U] an unexpected event, or the feeling caused by something unexpected happening: *Don't tell Anne we've arranged a party for her – I want it to be a surprise.* ○ It was a lovely/nasty, etc. surprise to get home and find the letter. ○ Last night's heavy snow **came as** a complete surprise. ○ You're always **full of** surprises (= doing unexpected things). ○ I wish you wouldn't keep **springing** surprises **on** me (= telling me unexpected things or causing unexpected things to happen). ○ He looked at her **in/with** surprise. ○ **To** my great surprise, they agreed to all our demands. ○ They mounted a surprise attack at dawn. ○ My uncle paid us a surprise visit yesterday. ⊃Compare **shock** SURPRISE.

• **surprise, surprise 1** said when someone has done something or when something has happened in a way which you expected and which you do not approve of: *"I've for-*

gotten my keys again." "Surprise, surprise!" **2** *US* said when you are telling someone about a situation in which something unexpected and pleasant has happened: *I asked him if he wanted to come to dinner with my parents, and surprise, surprise, he said yes!*

surprise /səˈpraɪz/ [US] /sɚ-/ *verb* **[T]** **1** to make someone feel surprise: *The news surprised everyone.* ○ **[+ that]** *It doesn't surprise me* ***that*** *their parents don't want them to get married.* ○ **[+ to infinitive]** *It will not surprise anyone* ***to*** *learn that the offer has been rejected.* ○ **[+ question word]** *Janet was surprised* ***how*** *quickly the time passed.* **2** to find, catch or attack someone when they are not expecting it: *The robbers had just opened the safe when they were surprised by the police.* ○ **[+ v-ing]** *His mother surprised him help****ing*** *himself to her gin.*

surprised /səˈpraɪzd/ [US] /sɚ-/ *adj* feeling or showing surprise because something has happened that you did not expect: *We were very surprised* ***at*** *the result.* ○ *It's not like you to behave like this, Alice – I'm surprised* ***at*** *you* (= I feel disappointed with you)*!* ○ *I'm not surprised* ***(that)*** *he didn't keep his promise.* ○ *I'm surprised* ***to*** *see you here.* ○ *I've managed to fix your car for now, but* ***don't be*** *surprised* ***if*** *it breaks down again* (= it probably will stop working again). ○ *She looked at him with a surprised expression on her face.*

surprising /səˈpraɪ.zɪŋ/ [US] /sɚ-/ *adj* unexpected: *He gave a rather surprising answer.* ○ ***It's hardly/scarcely/not*** *surprising* ***(that)*** *you're putting on weight, considering how much you're eating.* ○ *I must say that* ***it's*** *surprising* ***to*** *find you agreeing with me for once.*

surprisingly /səˈpraɪ.zɪŋ.li/ [US] /sɚ-/ *adv* unexpectedly or unusually: *The restaurant turned out to be surprisingly cheap.* ○ *Not surprisingly, the jury found them both guilty.*

surreal /səˈrɪəl/ *adj* strange; not like reality; like a dream: *Driving through the total darkness was a slightly surreal experience.* ○ *Buñuel's films have a surreal quality.*

Surrealism /səˈrɪə.lɪ.zᵊm/ *noun* **[U]** *SPECIALIZED* a type of 20th century art and literature in which unusual or impossible things are shown happening **Surrealist** /səˈrɪə.lɪst/ *noun* **[C]**, *adj*

surrealistic /səˌrɪəˈlɪs.tɪk/ *adj* not like reality; very unusual or impossible

surrender [ACCEPT DEFEAT] /sᵊrˈen.dəʳ/ [US] /səˈren.dɚ/ *verb* **[I]** **1** to stop fighting and admit defeat: *They would rather die than surrender (***to*** *the invaders).* **2** If you surrender to an experience or emotion, you stop trying to prevent or control it: *I finally surrendered* ***to*** *temptation, and ate the last remaining chocolate.*

surrender /sᵊrˈen.dəʳ/ [US] /səˈren.dɚ/ *noun* **[C or U]** when you stop fighting and admit defeat: *The rebels are on the point of surrender.*

surrender [GIVE] /səˈren.dəʳ/ [US] /-dɚ/ *verb* **[T]** to give something that is yours to someone else because you have been forced to do so or because it is necessary to do so: *The police demanded that the gang surrender their weapons.* ○ *Neither side is willing to surrender any territory/any of their claims.*

surreptitious /ˌsʌr.əpˈtɪʃ.əs/ [US] /ˌsɝː-/ *adj* done secretly, without anyone seeing or knowing: *She seemed to be listening to what I was saying, but I couldn't help noticing her surreptitious glances at the clock.* **surreptitiously** /ˌsʌr.əpˈtɪʃ.ə.sli/ [US] /ˌsɝː-/ *adv*: *Joe surreptitiously had a look in the answer book.* **surreptitiousness** /ˌsʌr.əpˈtɪʃ.ə.snəs/ [US] /ˌsɝː-/ *noun* **[U]**

surrogate /ˈsʌr.ə.gət/ [US] /ˈsɝː-/ *adj* **[before n]** **1** replacing someone else or used instead of something else: *surrogate birth mother* ○ *Because she had no children of her own, her friend's son became a kind of surrogate child to her.* **2** **surrogate (mother)** a woman who has a baby for another woman who is unable to become pregnant or have a baby herself: *She has agreed to act as a surrogate* ***mother*** *for her sister.* **surrogate** /ˈsʌr.ə.gət/ [US] /ˈsɝː-/ *noun* **[C]** *For some people, reading travel books is a surrogate* ***for*** *actual travel.*

surrogacy /ˈsʌr.ə.gə.si/ [US] /ˈsɝː-/ *noun* **[U]** the action of a woman having a baby for another woman who is unable to do so herself

surround /səˈraʊnd/ *verb* **[T]** to be everywhere around something: *Snow-capped mountains surround the city.* ○ *Gwen sat at her desk, surrounded by books and papers.* ○ *Mystery still surrounds the exact circumstances of Stalin's death.* ○ *She said that she wanted to die surrounded by the people she loves* (= with them all present). ○ *Early this morning, armed police surrounded* (= moved into a position so that they were everywhere around) *a house which they thought contained an escaped prisoner.*

surround /səˈraʊnd/ *noun* **[C]** the area or border around something: *Our bath has a tiled surround.* **surrounding** /səˈraʊn.dɪŋ/ *adj* **[before n]** *A lot of the children at the school do not live in the town, but come in from the surrounding countryside.*

surroundings /səˈraʊn.dɪŋz/ *plural noun* **1** the place where someone or something is and the things that are in it: *Some butterflies* ***blend in with*** *their surroundings so that it's difficult to see them.* **2** the place where someone lives and the conditions they live in: *They live in very comfortable/pleasant/drab/bleak surroundings.*

surrounds /səˈraʊndz/ *plural noun US* the area that is near: *I don't think there are any video stores in the immediate surrounds.*

COMMON LEARNER ERROR

surroundings

Do not confuse the plural noun **surroundings** with the adjective **surrounding**.

It's much better to see animals in their natural surroundings.

~~*It's much better to see animals in their natural surrounding.*~~

surˌround ˈsound *noun* **[U]** a system for playing sounds, especially in cinemas, that uses three or more LOUDSPEAKERS so that the listener seems to be surrounded by the sound

surtax /ˈsɜː.tæks/ [US] /ˈsɝː-/ *noun* **[U]** an additional tax which is paid by people who earn more than a particular large amount, or an additional tax which is added to something which is already taxed: *a surtax on company profits*

surtitle /ˈsɜːˌtaɪ.tl̩/ [US] /ˈsɝːˌtaɪ.t̬l̩/ *noun* **[C]** (*US USUALLY* **supertitle**) a written form in the listener's own language of the words that are being sung in an opera, which are shown above the stage during a performance

surveillance /səˈveɪ.lənts/ [US] /sɚ-/ *noun* **[U]** the careful watching of a person or place, especially by the police or army, because of a crime that has happened or is expected: *The police have* ***kept*** *the nightclub* ***under*** *surveillance because of suspected illegal drug activity.* ○ *More banks are now installing surveillance* ***cameras***.

survey [QUESTIONS] /ˈsɜː.veɪ/ [US] /ˈsɝː-/ *noun* **[C]** an examination of opinions, behaviour, etc., made by asking people questions: *A recent survey* ***found/revealed/showed*** *that 58% of people did not know where their heart is.* ○ *to* ***conduct/carry out/do*** *a survey*

survey /ˈsɜː.veɪ/ [US] /ˈsɝː-/ *verb* **[T]** to ask people questions in order to find out about their opinions or behaviour: *The researchers surveyed the attitudes of 2500 college students.* ○ *Many of the listeners surveyed said that they were not satisfied with the station's programmes.*

survey [LOOK AT] /səˈveɪ/ [US] /ˈsɝː.veɪ/ *verb* **1** **[T]** *SLIGHTLY FORMAL* to look at or examine all of something, especially carefully: *He got out of the car to survey the damage.* ○ *She has written a book which surveys* (= describes in detail) *the history of feminism.* **2** **[T]** to measure an area of land, and to record the details of it, especially on a map: *Before the new railway was built, its route was carefully surveyed.* **3** **[T often passive]** *UK* (*US* **inspect**) If a building is surveyed, it is examined carefully by a specially trained person, in order to discover whether there is anything wrong with its structure.

• **lord/master/mistress/king/queen of all** ***you*** **survey** *HUMOROUS* If you are lord/master/mistress/king/queen of all you survey, you own or control the place in which you live or work.

survey /ˈsɜː.veɪ/ [US] /ˈsɝː-/ *noun* **[C]** **1** the measuring and recording of the details of an area of land: *a* ***geological*** *survey* **2** a description of the whole of a subject: *His new* book is a survey **of** European theatre in the nineteenth century. **3** UK (US **inspection**) an examination of the structure of a building by a specially trained person

surveyor /sə'veɪ.ə^r/ Ⓤ /sɚ'veɪ.ɚ/ noun [C] **1** a person whose job is to measure and record the details of areas of land **2** UK (US **structural engineer**) a person who is specially trained to examine buildings and discover whether there are any problems with their structure

sur'vival ˌkit noun [C] a small box containing items that you need in order to stay alive if you are in a difficult or dangerous situation in which you are unable to get help

sur'vival of the 'fittest noun [U] the principle that animals and plants suited to the conditions they live in are more likely to stay alive and produce other animals and plants than those which are not suited

survive /sə'vaɪv/ Ⓤ /sɚ-/ verb [I or T] **1** to continue to live or exist, especially after coming close to dying or being destroyed or after being in a difficult or threatening situation: *The baby was born with a heart problem and only survived for a few hours.* ○ *These plants cannot survive in very cold conditions.* ○ *None of Shakespeare's plays survives in its original manuscript form.* ○ *The family are struggling to survive on very little money.* ○ *The front passengers were lucky to survive the accident.* ○ *The prime minister succeeded in surviving the challenge to his authority.* ○ INFORMAL *"How are you?" "Oh, (I'm) surviving (= life is satisfactory, but not very good)."* **2** [T] to continue to live after someone, especially a member of your family, has died: *He is survived by his wife and four children.*

survivable /sə'vaɪ.və.bl̩/ Ⓤ /sɚ-/ adj FORMAL (of an accident or injury) very serious but not causing death

survival /sə'vaɪ.v^əl/ Ⓤ /sɚ-/ noun **1** [U] when a person, organization, etc. continues to live or exist: *The doctors told my wife I had a 50/50 chance of survival.* ○ *His main concern is to ensure his own political survival.* ○ *England are fighting for survival (= trying not to be defeated) in the match.* **2** [C] something that has continued to exist from a previous time: *Most of these traditions are survivals from earlier times.* **survival** /sə'vaɪ.v^əl/ Ⓤ /sɚ-/ adj: *We all have a strong survival instinct.* ○ *The survival rate for people who have this form of cancer is now more than 90%.*

surviving /sə'vaɪ.vɪŋ/ Ⓤ /sɚ-/ adj [before n] continuing to live or exist: *The rhinoceros is one of the world's oldest surviving species.* ○ *Her estate was divided between her three surviving children (= those who continued to live after her death).*

survivor /sə'vaɪ.və^r/ Ⓤ /sɚ'vaɪ.vɚ/ noun [C] **1** a person who continues to live, despite nearly dying: *He was the sole (= only) survivor of the plane crash.* ○ *She's a cancer survivor/a survivor of cancer.* **2** a person who is able to continue living their life successfully despite experiencing difficulties: *He's one of life's survivors.* **3** US A person's survivors are the members of his or her family who continue to live after he or she has died.

susceptible INFLUENCED /sə'sep.tɪ.bl̩/ adj **1** easily influenced or harmed by something: *She isn't very susceptible to flattery.* ○ *These plants are particularly susceptible to frost.* ○ *Among particularly susceptible children, the disease can develop very fast.* **2** describes someone who is easily emotionally influenced: *They persuade susceptible teenagers to part with their money.*

susceptibility /sə.sep.tɪ'bɪl.ɪ.ti/ Ⓤ /-ə.t̬i/ noun [U] when someone or something is easily influenced, harmed or infected

susceptibilities /sə.sep.tɪ'bɪl.ɪ.tiz/ Ⓤ /-ə.t̬iz/ plural noun FORMAL the feelings someone has which are likely to be hurt: *I didn't mean to offend/upset/hurt your susceptibilities.*

susceptible PROVIDED WITH /sə'sep.tɪ.bl̩/ adj [after v] FORMAL (especially of an idea or statement) able to be understood, proved, explained, etc. in a particular way: *Shakespeare's plays are susceptible to various interpretations.* ○ UK *The facts are susceptible of other explanations.*

sushi /'suː.ʃi/ noun [U] a type of Japanese food consisting of squares or balls of cold boiled rice, with small pieces of other food, especially raw fish on top

suspect THINK LIKELY /sə'spekt/ verb [T] to think or believe something to be true or probable: *So far, the police do not suspect foul play.* ○ [+ (that)] *We had no reason to suspect (that) he might try to kill himself.* ○ *"Do you think she'll have told them?" "I suspect not/so."*

suspected /sə'spek.tɪd/ adj: *He has a suspected broken leg.*

suspicion /sə'spɪʃ.^ən/ noun [C] a belief or idea that something may be true: [+ that] *I have a suspicion (= belief or idea) that he only asked me out because my brother persuaded him to.* ○ *She had a nagging/sneaking suspicion that she might have sent the letter to the wrong address.*

suspiciously /sə'spɪʃ.ə.sli/ adv: *She brushed away what looked suspiciously like (= looked as if it probably was) a tear.*

suspect THINK GUILTY /sə'spekt/ verb [T] to think that someone has committed a crime or done something wrong: *No one knows who killed her, but the police suspect her husband.* ○ *The police suspect him of carrying out two bomb attacks.* ○ *Three suspected terrorists have been arrested.*

suspect /'sʌs.pekt/ noun [C] a person believed to have committed a crime or done something wrong, or something believed to have caused something bad: *Police have issued a photograph of the suspect.* ○ *The prime suspect in the case committed suicide.* ○ *No one knows what caused the outbreak of food poisoning, but shellfish is the main suspect (= is thought to have caused it).*

• **the usual suspects** the people you would expect to be present somewhere or doing a particular thing: *"Who was at Adrian's party?" "Oh, Paula, Roz, Lucy and gang – the usual suspects."*

suspicion /sə'spɪʃ.^ən/ noun [C or U] a feeling or belief that someone has committed a crime or done something wrong: *"I'm arresting you on suspicion of illegally possessing drugs," said the police officer.* ○ MAINLY UK *She is under suspicion of murder.* ○ *In this particular case, they are above/beyond suspicion (= cannot be thought to be guilty).* ○ *His strange behaviour aroused/raised his neighbours' suspicions.*

suspicious /sə'spɪʃ.əs/ adj making you feel that something illegal is happening or that something is wrong: *Her behaviour was very suspicious (AUS INFORMAL suss).* ○ *The fire at the bank is being treated as suspicious.* ○ *It's a bit suspicious that no one knows where he was at the time of the murder.* ○ *There were some suspicious characters hanging around outside.* ○ *There's a suspicious-looking van parked at the end of the road.* ○ *His new book bears a suspicious resemblance to a book written by someone else (= His book is so similar to the other book that it seems as if he has copied it).*

suspiciously /sə'spɪʃ.ə.sli/ adv: *The officers noticed two men acting suspiciously (= as if they were doing something wrong) in a car.*

suspect DOUBT /sə'spekt/ verb [T] to not trust; to doubt: *I have no reason to suspect her honesty/loyalty.* ○ *We suspected his motives in making his offer.*

suspect /'sʌs.pekt/ adj possibly false or dangerous: *The study was carried out with such a small sample that its results are suspect.* ○ *A suspect parcel was found at the station.*

suspicion /sə'spɪʃ.^ən/ noun [C or U] doubt or lack of trust: *Since they discovered the truth about his background, his colleagues have regarded him with suspicion.* ○ *They feel that she harbours (= has) suspicions of their politics.*

suspicious /sə'spɪʃ.əs/ adj feeling lack of trust or doubt in someone or something: *His colleagues became suspicious (= thought that there was something wrong) when he did not appear at work, since he was always punctual.* ○ *They are deeply/highly (= very) suspicious of one another/of each other's motives.* ○ *My mother has a very suspicious nature (= does not trust people).*

suspiciously /sə'spɪʃ.ə.sli/ adv: *He looked at her suspiciously.* ○ *The children are suspiciously quiet (= are so quiet that they are probably doing something wrong).* ○ *His hair is suspiciously black (= looks darker than it should be, and is therefore probably not natural) for a man of his age.*

suspend STOP /sə'spend/ *verb* [T] **1** to stop or to cause to be not active, either temporarily or permanently: *The ferry service has been suspended for the day because of bad weather.* ○ *The President has suspended the constitution and assumed total power.* ○ *When you go to the theatre, you have to be willing to suspend* **disbelief** (= to act as if you believe that what you are seeing is real or true, although you know that it is not). ○ *I'm suspending* **judgment** (= not forming an opinion) *on the book I'm reading until I've finished it.* ○ LEGAL *Mr Young was given a six-month jail* **sentence** *suspended for two years* (= If he commits another crime within two years, he will have to go to prison for six months for his original crime).* **2** If someone is suspended from work, school, etc., they are temporarily not allowed to work, go to school or take part in an activity because they have done something wrong: *She was suspended from school for fighting.* ○ *He was suspended for four matches after arguing with the referee.*

suspension /sə'spen.ʃən/ *noun* **1** [U] when someone stops something happening, operating, etc. for a period of time: *The suspension of fighting is to take effect at 6 am on Monday.* ○ *There have been calls for the drug's immediate suspension, following reports that it has dangerous side effects.* ➜See also **suspension**. **2** [C or U] when a person is temporarily not allowed to work, go to school or take part in an activity, as a punishment: *The union is protesting about the suspension* **of** *a restaurant worker .* ○ *The footballer is likely to receive a three-match suspension following an incident in yesterday's game.*

suspend HANG /sə'spend/ *verb* [T usually + adv or prep] **1** to hang: *The builders worked on wooden platforms, suspended by ropes* **from** *the roof of the building.* ○ *It was very uncomfortable lying on the hospital bed with my legs suspended* **in the air.** **2** If small pieces of solid material are suspended in a gas or a liquid, they hang or float in the gas or liquid: *The drug is suspended* **in** *a saline solution.* ○ *A cloud of smoke was suspended* **in** *the air.*

suspension /sə'spen.ʃən/ *noun* [C] a liquid in which small pieces of solid are contained, but not dissolved: *a suspension of fine cornflour* **in** *corn oil* ➜See also **suspension**.

su,spended ani'mation *noun* [U] a state in which life in a body is temporarily slowed down or stopped: *Some animals, such as hedgehogs, exist in a state of suspended animation during the winter.* ○ FIGURATIVE *A cut in interest rates would lift the economy out of its current state of suspended animation.*

suspender UK /sə'spen.dəʳ/ US /-dɚ/ *noun* [C] (US **garter**) a fastener that holds up a woman's stockings

su'spender ,belt UK *noun* [C] (US **garter belt**) a piece of women's underwear worn round the waist, which has fasteners fixed to it for holding up stockings

suspenders /sə'spen.dəz/ US /-dɚz/ *plural noun* US FOR **braces**, see at **brace** SUPPORT

suspense /sə'spents/ *noun* [U] the feeling of excitement or anxiety which you have when you are waiting for something to happen and are uncertain about what it is going to be: *She kept him* **in** *suspense for several days before she said that she would marry him.* ○ *The suspense* **is killing** *me* (= I am extremely eager to know what is going to happen).* ○ *There is a gradual build-up of suspense throughout the film, until it comes to an unexpected ending.*

suspension /sə'spen.ʃən/ *noun* [U] equipment fixed to the wheels of a vehicle which reduces the uncomfortable effects of going over uneven road surfaces ➜See also **suspension** at **suspend**.

su'spension ,bridge *noun* [C] a bridge which is supported by strong steel ropes hung from a tower at each end of the bridge

suspicion /sə'spɪʃ.ʃən/ *noun* [S] a small amount: *He gave just* **a** *suspicion of a smile.* ○ *I have* **a** *suspicion of doubt about whether I should accept his invitation or not.* ➜See also **suspicion** at **suspect** THINK LIKELY, **suspect** THINK GUILTY and **suspect** DOUBT.

SUSS DISCOVER /sʌs/ *verb* [T] UK INFORMAL to realize, understand or discover: [+ *that*] *He never sussed (**out**) that they'd tricked him.* ○ *She thinks she's got me sussed (**out**)*

(= She thinks she understands me), *but she's wrong.* ○ *I'll visit the college and suss it* **out** *before I decide whether to apply or not.*

SUSS UNABLE TO BE TRUSTED /sʌs/ *adj* AUS INFORMAL FOR **suspicious**, see at **suspect** THINK GUILTY

sustain MAINTAIN /sə'steɪn/ *verb* [T] **1** to cause or allow something to continue for a period of time: *The economy looks set to sustain its growth into next year.* ○ *He seems to find it difficult to sustain relationships with women.* ○ US *The judge sustained* (= accepted) *the lawyer's objection.* **2** to keep alive: *The soil in this part of the world is not rich enough to sustain a large population.*

sustainable /sə'steɪ.nə.bl̩/ *adj* **1** able to continue over a period of time: *That sort of extreme diet is not sustainable over a long period.* **2** causing little or no damage to the environment and therefore able to continue for a long time: *A large international meeting was held with the aim of promoting sustainable* **development** *in all countries.* **sustainability** /sə,steɪ.nə'bɪl.ɪ.ti/ US /-ə.ti/ *noun* [U]

sustained /sə'steɪnd/ *adj* **1** continuing for a long time: *The president's speech was greeted with sustained applause.* **2** determined: *We must make a sustained effort to get this task finished this week.*

sustain SUFFER /sə'steɪn/ *verb* [T] FORMAL to suffer or experience, especially damage or loss: *She sustained multiple injuries in the accident.* ○ *Most buildings sustained only minimal damage in the earthquake.* ○ *The company has sustained heavy losses this year.*

sustain SUPPORT /sə'steɪn/ *verb* [T] to support emotionally: *She was sustained by the strength of her religious faith.* ○ *The love of my family and friends sustained me through my ordeal.*

sustenance FOOD /'sʌs.tɪ.nənts/ *noun* [U] FORMAL **1** food: *During this freezing weather, the food put out by householders is the only form of sustenance that the birds have.* **2** the ability of food to provide people and animals with what they need to make them strong and healthy: *A stick of celery does not provide much sustenance.*

sustenance SUPPORT /'sʌs.tɪ.nənts/ *noun* [U] FORMAL emotional or mental support: *When her husband died, she* **drew** *sustenance* **from**/*she* **found** *sustenance* **in** *her religious beliefs.*

suttee /'sʌt.iː/ *noun* [U] (ALSO **sati**) the Hindu custom, which is no longer legal, of a woman being burnt alive in the same fire as that in which her dead husband's body is burnt

suture /'suː.tʃəʳ/ US /-tʃɚ/ *noun* [C] SPECIALIZED a stitch used to sew up a cut in a person's body

suture /'suː.tʃəʳ/ US /-tʃɚ/ *verb* [T] SPECIALIZED to sew together a cut in a person's body

SUV /ˌes.juː'viː/ *noun* [C] MAINLY US WRITTEN ABBREVIATION FOR sports utility vehicle: a large car with an engine that supplies power to all four wheels, but that is usually used for ordinary driving ➜See picture **Cars and Trucks** on page Centre 13

svelte /svelt/ *adj* attractively thin, graceful and stylish

SW SOUTHWEST *noun* [U], *adj* ABBREVIATION FOR **southwest** or **southwestern**

SW RADIO *noun* [U] ABBREVIATION FOR **short wave**

swab MEDICINE /swɒb/ US /swɑːb/ *noun* [C] a small piece of soft material used for cleaning a cut or for taking a small amount of substance from a body, or the substance itself which can then be tested: *The nurse cleaned the cut on my leg with a swab.* ○ *"I'm just going to take a swab* **of** *your ear," said the doctor.* **swab** /swɒb/ US /swɑːb/ *verb* [T] **-bb-**

swab WASH /swɒb/ US /swɑːb/ *verb* [T] **-bb-** to wash a surface, especially the open flat areas of a ship, with a wet cloth or MOP

swaddle /'swɒd.l̩/ US /'swɑː.dl̩/ *verb* [T] OLD-FASHIONED to wrap a baby tightly in cloth: *Swaddling a baby tightly* **in** *a blanket can be a good way to stop it crying.*

swag STEAL /swæg/ *noun* [U] OLD-FASHIONED SLANG stolen goods: *The cartoon showed a picture of a robber carrying a bag with 'swag' written on it.*

swag POSSESSIONS /swæg/ *noun* [U] AUS OLD-FASHIONED possessions wrapped in a cloth and carried by a person who does not have a home or a job, but walks around from place to place

swagger /'swæg.ə^r/ ⓤ /-ɚ/ *verb* [I] to walk, especially with a swinging movement, in a way that shows that you are very confident and think that you are important, or to act in that way: *They swaggered into the room.* ○ *A group of young men swaggered **about** outside the bar.* ○ *His swaggering self-confidence irritates many people.*

swagger /'swæg.ə^r/ ⓤ /-ɚ/ *noun* [S or U] *He walked out of the room with **a** self-confident swagger.* ○ *Underneath all his swagger* (= way of acting that shows he is very confident and thinks that he is important), *he's actually quite nervous.* **swaggerer** /'swæg.ᵊr.ə^r/ ⓤ /-ɚ.ɚ/ *noun* [C]
swaggeringly /'swæg.ᵊr.ɪŋ.li/ ⓤ /-ɚ-/ *adv*

swallow THROAT /'swɒl.əʊ/ ⓤ /'swɑː.loʊ/ *verb* **1** [I or T] to cause food, drink, pills, etc. to move from your mouth into your stomach by using the muscles of your throat, or to use the muscles of your throat as if doing this: *My throat is so sore that it really hurts when I swallow.* ○ *He put a grape into his mouth and swallowed it **whole**.* **2** [I] to use the muscles of your throat, as if moving something from your mouth into your stomach, because you are nervous or frightened, or are about to say something: *He swallowed **hard** and said, "Dad, I've got something to tell you."*

swallow /'swɒl.əʊ/ ⓤ /'swɑː.loʊ/ *noun* [C] an act of using the muscles of your throat, or the amount of something you move into your stomach from your mouth by using the muscles of your throat: *He gave a swallow, then began speaking.* ○ *INFORMAL Just let me have a couple more swallows of my coffee, and I'll be ready.*

swallow TAKE AWAY /'swɒl.əʊ/ ⓤ /'swɑː.loʊ/ *verb* **1** [M] If something large swallows (up) another thing, it makes it disappear or stop existing separately by making it part of itself: *An increasing amount of the countryside is being swallowed **(up)** by the town.* ○ *Many small businesses have been swallowed **(up)** by large companies.* **2** [T] to use or take away a large part of something valuable: *Taxes have swallowed up nearly half of my pay increase.*

swallow ACCEPT /'swɒl.əʊ/ ⓤ /'swɑː.loʊ/ *verb* [T] *INFORMAL* to accept something without question or without expressing disagreement: *Not surprisingly, this excuse was too much for them to swallow.* ○ *He swallowed her story **whole**.* ○ *She swallowed his sales pitch line **hook, line and sinker*** (= believed it completely).
● **swallow the bait** If you swallow the bait, you completely accept something, especially an offer that is a trick or way of getting something from you.

swallow NOT EXPRESS /'swɒl.əʊ/ ⓤ /'swɑː.loʊ/ *verb* [T] to not express or show something: *She swallowed her disappointment, saying, "That's OK, it doesn't matter."* ○ *He was forced to swallow his **pride** and ask if he could have his old job back.*
● **swallow your words** to be forced to admit that something you have said has been shown to be wrong: *I had to swallow my words when the scheme turned out to be a great success.*

swallow BIRD /'swɒl.əʊ/ ⓤ /'swɑː.loʊ/ *noun* [C] a small bird with pointed wings and a tail with two points, which flies quickly and catches insects to eat as it flies ⊃See picture **Animals and Birds** on page Centre 4
● **One swallow doesn't make a summer.** *SAYING* used to say that because one good thing has happened, it is not therefore certain that a situation is going to improve

'**swallow** ,**dive** *UK noun* [C] (*US* **swan dive**) a dive in which you hold your arms out from your side until you are close to the water

swam /swæm/ *past simple of* **swim**

swami /'swɑː.mi/ *noun* [C] (the title of) a Hindu religious teacher

swamp WET LAND /swɒmp/ ⓤ /swɑːmp/ *noun* [C or U] (an area of) very wet soft land: *an alligator-infested swamp* ○ *The Everglades are an area of swamp in southern Florida.*
swampy /'swɒm.pi/ ⓤ /'swɑːm-/ *adj* describes land that is soft and very wet

swamp COVER /swɒmp/ ⓤ /swɑːmp/ *verb* [T] to cover a place or thing with a large amount of water: *High tides*

have swamped the coast. ○ *The boat was swamped **by** an enormous wave.*

swamp TOO MUCH/BIG /swɒmp/ ⓤ /swɑːmp/ *verb* **1** [T often passive] If something swamps a person, system or place, they receive more of it than they can easily deal with: *Foreign cars have swamped the UK market.* ○ *I'm swamped **with** work at the moment.* ○ *Don't let feelings of depression swamp you.* **2** [T] *INFORMAL* If clothes swamp you, they are much too big for you.

'**swamp** ,**gas** *noun* [C usually sing] a gas produced in a SWAMP (= an area of extremely wet ground) by decaying plants that are covered by water: *You could smell the swamp gas a mile off.*

swan BIRD /swɒn/ ⓤ /swɑːn/ *noun* [C] a large usually white bird with a long neck that lives on rivers and lakes

swan GO /swɒn/ ⓤ /swɑːn/ *verb* [I + adv or prep] **-nn-** *UK INFORMAL DISAPPROVING* to travel, move or behave in a relaxed way for pleasure and without caring that others may feel annoyed: *She swanned into the room, carrying a glass of wine, taking no notice of the fact that she'd kept us all waiting for hours.* ○ *He's been swanning **around** the States* (= travelling and not doing any work) *all summer.*

'**swan** ,**dive** *noun* [C] *US FOR* **swallow dive**

swank /swæŋk/ *verb* [I] *INFORMAL DISAPPROVING* to behave or speak too confidently because you think that you are very important, in order to attract other people's attention and admiration: *Just because you won, there's no need to swank.* ○ *People around here don't swank **about** their money.*

swank /swæŋk/ *noun* [U] *INFORMAL DISAPPROVING* behaviour that is too confident: *In spite of all his swank, he's never really achieved very much.*
swanky /'swæŋ.ki/ *adj* **1** *INFORMAL* very expensive and fashionable, in a way that is intended to attract people's attention and admiration: *We stayed in a swanky hotel.* **2** *DISAPPROVING* behaving too confidently: *I'm sick of his swanky talk.*

swansong /'swɒn.sɒŋ/ ⓤ /'swɑːn.sɑːŋ/ *noun* [S] a person's last piece of work, achievement, or performance: *This weekend's match was his swansong as the team's captain.*

swap (**-pp-**), *UK ALSO* **swop** (**-pp-**) /swɒp/ ⓤ /swɑːp/ *verb* [I or T] to give something and be given something else instead; to exchange: *When you've finished reading your book, and I've finished mine, shall we swap?* ○ *We swapped addresses **with** the people we met on holiday.* ○ *When he got a job in a bank, he had to swap his jeans and T-shirt **for** a suit* (= he had to wear formal clothes instead of informal ones). ○ [+ two objects] *I'll swap you my chocolate bar **for** your peanuts.* ○ *We spent the evening in the pub, swapping* (= telling each other) *stories/jokes.*
swap, *UK ALSO* **swop** /swɒp/ ⓤ /swɑːp/ *noun* [C] an exchange, or something that is going to be or has been exchanged: *I thought Simon's food looked nicer than mine, so we **did a** swap.* ○ *This comic is a swap* (= something that was exchanged) *that I got from Nick.*

'**swap** ,**meet** *noun* [C] *US FOR* **car boot sale**

swarm INSECTS /swɔːm/ ⓤ /swɔːrm/ *noun* [C] a large group of insects all moving together: *a swarm **of** bees/wasps/ants/locusts* ○ *The dead sheep was covered with swarms **of** flies.*
swarm /swɔːm/ ⓤ /swɔːrm/ *verb* [I] When insects swarm, they come together in a large group.

swarm PEOPLE /swɔːm/ ⓤ /swɔːrm/ *group noun* [C] a large group of people all moving together: *A swarm **of**/ Swarms of journalists followed the film star's car.*
swarm /swɔːm/ ⓤ /swɔːrm/ *verb* [I] When people swarm somewhere, they move there in a large group or in large numbers: *After the game, thousands of football fans swarmed onto the pitch.*
▲ **swarm with** *sth phrasal verb* If a place is swarming with people or things, there are large numbers of them moving around it: *The garden is swarming with wasps.* ○ *Something must be going on – the town is swarming with police.*

swarthy /ˈswɔː.ði/ [US] /ˈswɔːr-/ *adj* (of a person or their skin) dark-coloured: *a swarthy face/complexion* ○ *a swarthy fisherman*

swashbuckling /ˈswɒʃˌbʌk.lɪŋ/ [US] /ˈswɑːʃ-/ *adj* **[before n]** behaving in a brave and exciting way, especially like a fighter in the past: *a swashbuckling hero/pirate* ○ *The players displayed a swashbuckling confidence.*

swastika /ˈswɒs.tɪ.kə/ [US] /ˈswɑː.stɪ-/ *noun* **[C]** a symbol in the form of a cross with each of its arms bent at a 90° (degree) angle half way along, used in the 20th century as the symbol of the NAZI party

swat /swɒt/ [US] /swɑːt/ *verb* **[T]** **-tt-** to hit something, especially an insect, with a flat object or your hand: *I swatted the fly with a rolled-up newspaper.* ○ *He tried to swat the ball too hard, and missed it entirely.* ○ FIGURATIVE *These missiles are capable of swatting enemy planes with deadly accuracy.* **swat** /swɒt/ [US] /swɑːt/ *noun* **[C]** *He gave the mosquito a swat.*

swatch /swɒtʃ/ [US] /swɑːtʃ/ *noun* **[C]** a small piece of cloth used as an example of the colour and type of the cloth

swathe [AREA] /sweɪð/ *noun* **1** **[C]** (ALSO **swath**) a long strip or large area especially of land: *Huge swathes **of** rain forest are being cleared for farming and mining.* **2** **[S]** LITERARY a varied section or range: *These people represent a **broad/wide** swathe **of** public opinion.*

swathe [CLOTH] /sweɪð/ *verb* **[T]** to wrap round or cover with cloth: *He came out of the hospital swathed **in** bandages.* ○ **[R]** *I love to swathe* (= dress) *myself **in** silk.*
swathe /sweɪð/ *noun* **[C]** (ALSO **swath**) a long strip of cloth: *His head was wrapped in swathes **of** bandages.*

sway [MOVE] /sweɪ/ *verb* **1** **[I]** to move slowly from side to side: *The trees were swaying in the wind.* ○ *The movement of the ship caused the mast to sway **from side to side/backwards and forwards**.* ○ *A drunk was standing in the middle of the street, swaying uncertainly and trying hard to stay upright.* **2** **[T]** to cause something to move or change: *Recent developments have swayed the balance of power in the region.*

sway [PERSUADE] /sweɪ/ *verb* **[T]** to persuade someone to believe or do one thing rather than another: *Her speech failed to sway her colleagues **into** supporting the plan.*

sway [CONTROL] /sweɪ/ *noun* **[U]** FORMAL control or influence: *In the 1980s, the organization came **under the** sway **of*** (= became strongly influenced by) *Christian fundamentalism.* ○ *Her parents no longer seem to have much sway **over** her.*

swear [USE RUDE WORDS] /sweəʳ/ [US] /swer/ *verb* **[I]** **swore, sworn** to use words that are rude or offensive as a way of emphasizing what you mean or as a way of insulting someone or something: *It was a real shock, the first time I heard my mother swear.* ○ *When the taxi driver started to swear **at** him, he walked off.*
swearing /ˈsweə.rɪŋ/ [US] /ˈswer.ɪŋ/ *noun* **[U]** when someone uses rude or offensive language

swear [PROMISE] /sweəʳ/ [US] /swer/ *verb* **[I or T]** **swore, sworn** to state or promise that you are telling the truth or that you will do something or behave in a particular way: *I don't know anything about what happened, I swear **(it)**.* ○ **[+ (that)]** *You might find it difficult to believe, but I swear **(that)** the guy just came up to me and gave me the money.* ○ INFORMAL *She swore **blind*** (= promised definitely) ***(that)** she didn't know what had happened to the money.* ○ **[+ to infinitive]** *New gang members must swear **to** obey the gang leaders at all times.* ○ *In some countries, witnesses in court have to swear **on** the Bible.* ○ *I swore an **oath** to tell the truth, the whole truth and nothing but the truth.* ○ *A few of us knew what was going to happen, but we were sworn **to** secrecy* (= we were made to promise that we would keep it a secret). ○ *I think his birthday is on the 5th, but I wouldn't/couldn't swear **to** it* (= I am not completely certain about it).

PHRASAL VERBS WITH **swear**

▲ **swear by *sth*** *phrasal verb* **[not continuous]** INFORMAL to believe strongly that something is effective or useful: *My dad swears by these vitamin pills.*

▲ **swear *sb* in** *phrasal verb* **[M]** LEGAL When someone is sworn in, they make a formal promise to be honest or loyal, either because they are in a law court or because they are starting a new official job: *The next witness was sworn in.* ○ *William Jefferson Clinton was sworn in **as** the 42nd President of the United States of America.*
swearing-in /ˌsweə.rɪŋˈɪn/ [US] /ˌswer.ɪŋ-/ *noun* **[S]** *She had a good seat at the President's swearing-in ceremony.*

▲ **swear off *sth*** *phrasal verb* to make a decision to stop doing, using or being involved with something harmful, such as drugs or alcohol, or something that is not good or helpful: *After years of addiction, he swore off drugs completely.*

ˈswear ˌword *noun* **[C]** a rude or offensive word: *All swear words, even mild ones such as 'damn', were deleted from the text.*

sweat /swet/ *verb* **[I]** **1** to excrete a salty colourless liquid through the skin because you are hot, ill or frightened: *It was so hot when we arrived in Tripoli that we started to sweat as soon as we got off the plane.* ○ *The prisoners were sweating **with** fear.* ○ INFORMAL *I was so afraid, I was sweating **like a pig*** (= sweating a lot). **2** If something sweats, it produces drops of liquid on the outside: *The walls in older houses sometimes sweat **with** damp.*

• **make *sb* sweat** INFORMAL to make someone wait anxiously: *It seemed that the authorities had delayed the news just to make us sweat.*

• **sweat blood** (ALSO **sweat *your* guts out**) INFORMAL to make a great effort: *We sweated blood to get the work finished on time.* ○ *I've been sweating blood over this report.*

• **sweat bullets** US INFORMAL to be extremely anxious about something: *I was sweating bullets **over** this interview.*

sweat /swet/ *noun* **[U]** the salty colourless liquid that you excrete through your skin: *The dancers were **dripping with/pouring with** sweat after a morning's rehearsal.* ○ *By the time we'd climbed to the top of the hill, we were **covered in** sweat.* ○ *She wiped the **beads*** (= drops) ***of** sweat from her forehead.* ○ FIGURATIVE *The cathedral was built by human toil and sweat* (= effort).

• **get in a sweat** INFORMAL to worry: *He tends to get in a sweat **about** flying.*

• **no sweat** INFORMAL If you say that something is no sweat, you mean that it will not be difficult or cause problems: *"Can you fix my car for me?" "No sweat!"*

sweaty /ˈswet.i/ [US] /ˈswet̬-/ *adj* covered in sweat or smelling of sweat: *a sweaty face* ○ *sweaty clothes* ○ *We spent the evening in a sweaty pub* (= one that causes you to sweat).

PHRASAL VERBS WITH **sweat**

▲ **sweat it out** [WORRY] *phrasal verb* INFORMAL When you sweat it out, you wait nervously for an unpleasant situation to end or improve: *My exams finish next week, and then I'll be sweating it out for a month waiting for the results.*

▲ **sweat it out** [EXERCISE] *phrasal verb* INFORMAL When you sweat it out, you do hard physical exercise: *I like to sweat it out in the gym for a couple of hours every day.*

▲ **sweat over *sth*** *phrasal verb* to work very hard using or doing something: *She's been sweating over that essay all afternoon.* ○ *I've been sweating over **a hot stove*** (= cooking) *all morning.*

ˈsweat ˌband *noun* **[C]** a thin strip of material that someone doing sport or exercise wears round their head to stop sweat going into their eyes or wears round their wrists to stop sweat going onto their hands

sweated /ˈswet.ɪd/ [US] /ˈswet̬-/ *adj* **[before n]** DISAPPROVING involving workers who are paid very little and who work many hours in very bad conditions: *The textile industry still relies to some extent on sweated **labour**.*

sweater /ˈswet.əʳ/ [US] /ˈswet̬.ɚ/ *noun* **[C]** (UK ALSO **jumper**) a usually woollen piece of clothing with long sleeves which is worn on the upper part of the body: *Put a sweater on if you're cold.* ○ *a V-necked sweater* ➲Compare **cardigan**. * NOTE: In UK English, a **sweater** is pulled on over the head and has no front opening. In US English, a **sweater** can also have a front opening (usually with buttons). ➲See picture **Clothes** on page Centre 6

S

ˈsweat ˌgland *noun* [C usually pl] one of the small organs under the skin which produce sweat

sweats *US* /swets/ *plural noun* (*UK* **tracksuit**) a loose top and trousers, worn either by people who are training for a sport or exercising, or as informal clothing ➲See picture **Clothes** on page Centre 6

sweatshirt /ˈswet.ʃɜːt/ [US] /-ʃɝːt/ *noun* [C] a piece of informal clothing with long sleeves, usually made of thick cotton, worn on the upper part of the body: *She was dressed casually in jeans and a sweatshirt.* ➲See picture **Clothes** on page Centre 6

sweatshop /ˈswet.ʃɒp/ [US] /-ʃɑːp/ *noun* [C] *DISAPPROVING* a small factory where workers are paid very little and work many hours in very bad conditions: *sweatshop conditions*

ˈsweat ˌsuit *noun* [C] a **tracksuit**

swede *UK* /swiːd/ *noun* [C or U] (*US USUALLY* **rutabaga**) a round vegetable with dark yellow flesh and a brown or purple skin ➲See picture **Vegetables** on page Centre 2

Swedish /ˈswiː.dɪʃ/ *adj* from, belonging to or relating to Sweden

Swedish /ˈswiː.dɪʃ/ *noun* [U] the language of Sweden

sweep [CLEAN] /swiːp/ *verb* [T] **swept, swept** to clean especially a floor by using a brush to collect the dirt into one place from which it can be removed: *sweep the floor*

• **sweep *sth* under the carpet** *UK* (*US* **sweep *sth* under the rug**) to hide a problem or try to keep it secret instead of dealing with it: *The committee is being accused of sweeping financial problems under the carpet to avoid embarrassment.*

sweep /swiːp/ *noun* **1** [C usually sing] the act of sweeping something: *I've given the kitchen floor **a** sweep* (= I have swept it). **2** [C] *OLD-FASHIONED FOR* **chimney sweep**

sweeper /ˈswiː.pəʳ/ [US] /-pɚ/ *noun* [C] **1** someone or something that sweeps: *a carpet sweeper* (= a machine for cleaning carpets) ○ *a road sweeper* (= a person whose job is cleaning the roads) **2** In football, a sweeper is a player whose position is behind the other DEFENDERS (= players whose main aim is to stop points from being scored).

sweep [REMOVE] /swiːp/ *verb* [T usually + adv or prep] **swept, swept** to remove and/or take in a particular direction, especially in a fast and powerful way: *A large wave swept **away** half the sandcastle.* ○ *She swept the pile of papers and books **into** her bag.* ○ *The boat was swept **out to sea*** (= away from land) *by the tide.* ○ *Government troops swept **aside** the rebel forces* (= caused them to move away from the area in which they were).

• **sweep *sb* off *their* feet** to make someone become suddenly and completely in love with you: *The first time he met her, he was completely swept off his feet.*

sweep [MOVE] /swiːp/ *verb* **swept, swept 1** [I + adv or prep] to move, especially quickly and powerfully: *Everyone looked up as she swept **into** the room.* ○ *The fire swept* (= spread quickly) ***through** the house.* ○ *The National Party swept **into power*** (= easily won the election) *with a majority of almost 200.* **2** [T] to quickly spread through and influence an area: *A 1970s fashion revival is sweeping Europe.* **3** [T] to travel across all of an area, especially when looking for something: *American minesweepers are sweeping the Arabian sea.* **4** [I usually + adv or prep] If a road, river, range of mountains, set of steps, etc. sweeps in a particular direction, they follow a particular curved path: *The road sweeps down to the coast.*

sweep /swiːp/ *noun* [C] *With a sweep* (= horizontal movement) ***of** its tail, the alligator knocked her under the water.* ○ *A broad sweep* (= area) ***of** flat countryside stretched to the horizon in all directions.*

sweeping /ˈswiː.pɪŋ/ *adj* [before n] **1** affecting many things or people; large: *It is obvious that sweeping **changes** are needed in the legal system.* ○ *We need to make sweeping **cuts** to our budget.* **2** *DISAPPROVING* **sweeping statement/generalization** something that you say or write that is too general and that has not been carefully thought about: *Sweeping generalizations about this complex and difficult situation are not helpful.*

sweep [WIN] /swiːp/ *verb* [T] **swept, swept** *US INFORMAL* to win all the parts of a competition, or to win very easily: *The Yankees swept a four-game series **from** the Blue Jays.*

• **sweep the board** to win everything that is available: *Australia swept the board in the swimming, with gold medals in every race.*

sweep /swiːp/ *noun* **a clean sweep** when a player, team, etc. win everything that is available: *Romania **made** a clean sweep of the medals.*

sweeping /ˈswiː.pɪŋ/ *adj*: *The party have failed to win the sweeping* (= complete) *victory they expected.*

PHRASAL VERBS WITH **sweep** ▼

▲ **sweep *sb* along** *phrasal verb* [M often passive] If a feeling or someone's behaviour sweeps you along, it makes you feel very enthusiastic about an activity and very involved in it: *We were swept along by her eloquence.*

▲ **sweep *sth* aside** *phrasal verb* [M] to refuse to consider something or to treat it as important: *They swept his doubts and objections aside.*

sweeps /swiːps/ *plural noun US* a period of time when measurements of the number of people watching different television stations are made so that the cost of advertising on each station can be set

sweepstake /ˈswiː.p.steɪk/ *noun* [C] (*INFORMAL* **sweep**) a type of gambling, usually on a horse race, in which people pay a small amount of money and choose a particular horse. The person who chooses the winning horse receives all the money paid by everyone else.

sweet /swiːt/ *adj* **1** (especially of food or drink) having a taste similar to that of sugar; not bitter or salty: *The pineapple was sweet and juicy.* ○ *Do you want your pancakes sweet or savoury?* **2** If an emotion or event is sweet, it is very pleasant and satisfying: *She was enjoying the sweet **smell of success**.* **3** If a sound is sweet, it is pleasant and easy to like: *She has a sweet singing voice.* **4** (especially of something or someone small) charming and attractive: *They live in a sweet little house.* ○ *What a sweet baby!* **5** kind and pleasant: *I think Alex is really sweet.* ○ ***It** was sweet **of** you to help me.*

• **keep *sb* sweet** to try to keep someone satisfied and pleased with you: *We're allowing the French engineers to use our computers, to keep them sweet in case we need their help later on.*

• **be sweet on *sb*** *OLD-FASHIONED INFORMAL* to like someone very much in a romantic way: *She's still sweet on him after all this time!*

• **sweet fanny adams** (*ABBREVIATION* **sweet FA**) *OLD-FASHIONED SLANG* nothing: *And what does she know about it? Sweet Fanny Adams!*

sweet /swiːt/ *noun* **1** [C] *UK* (*US* **candy**) a small piece of sweet food, made of sugar: *She bought a packet of sweets to suck on the journey.* **2** [C] *US* any food with a lot of sugar in it **3** [C or U] *UK* sweet food eaten at the end of a meal: *There was only one sweet on the menu – chocolate cake with cream.*

• **my sweet** *OLD-FASHIONED* an affectionate form of address

sweetly /ˈswiːt.li/ *adv* in a charming way: *He smiled sweetly at her.* **sweetness** /ˈswiːt.nəs/ *noun* [U]

• **be (all) sweetness and light** to be very peaceful and friendly: *They'd had a big argument yesterday, but by this morning it was all sweetness and light again.*

sweet-and-sour /ˌswiːt.ənˈsaʊəʳ/ [US] /-ˈsaʊr/ *adj* [before n] describes food with a flavour that is both sweet and sour: *sweet-and-sour pork*

sweetbread /ˈswiːt.bred/ *noun* [C usually pl] the PANCREAS (= organ near the stomach) of a young sheep or cow, used as food

ˌsweet ˈchestnut *UK noun* [C] (*US* **chestnut**) a large tree with leaves divided into five parts and large round nuts that are cooked and eaten hot

sweetcorn /ˈswiːt.kɔːn/ [US] /-kɔːrn/ *noun* [U] (*US USUALLY* **corn**) the yellow seeds of a particular type of the maize plant, which is eaten as a vegetable ➲See picture **Vegetables** on page Centre 2

sweeten /ˈswiː.tᵊn/ *verb* [T] **1** to make something taste sweet: *The apple mixture can be sweetened **with** honey.* **2** to make something more attractive: *The management sweetened the deal by offering an extra 2% to staff on the lowest end of the pay scale.* **3** to make a person or a mood

S

happier or friendlier: *I think you should try to sweeten him **up** before you ask him for the loan.*

sweetener /ˈswiː.nəʳ/ [US] /-nɚ/ *noun* **1** [C or U] an artificial substance that has a similar taste to sugar, or a small pill made of this **2** [C] *MAINLY UK* a gift or money given to persuade someone to do something, especially in a way that is secret and often dishonest: *a financial sweetener*

sweetheart /ˈswiːt.hɑːt/ [US] /-hɑːrt/ *noun* [C] **1** a person you love, especially a person with whom you have a romantic relationship: *She eventually married her **childhood** sweetheart.* ○ [as form of address] *"Happy birthday, sweetheart," he said.* **2** a kind and generous person: *"Oh, you're a sweetheart," she said, when I placed the breakfast tray on her lap.*

sweetheart ˌdeal *noun* [C] an agreement that you make in which you get something that is to your advantage, especially by agreeing to give up something else

sweetie /ˈswiː.ti/ [US] /-t̬i/ *noun* **1** [C] *UK CHILD'S WORD* a sweet **2** [C] *INFORMAL* a very pleasant or kind person: *He's a real sweetie.* **3** *INFORMAL* an affectionate form of address

sweetmeat /ˈswiːt.miːt/ *noun* [C] *OLD-FASHIONED* a small piece of sweet food, made of or covered in sugar

sweet ˈnothings *plural noun HUMOROUS* romantic and loving talk: *They're the couple in the corner, **whispering/murmuring** sweet nothings to each other.*

sweet ˈpea *noun* [C] a climbing plant with pale-coloured sweet-smelling flowers

sweet ˈpepper *noun* [C] a **pepper** VEGETABLE

sweet poˈtato (*plural* **sweet potatoes**) *noun* [C] (*ALSO* **yam**) a pinkish brown or orange-coloured vegetable with yellow or white flesh and a sweet taste ➲See picture **Vegetables** on page Centre 2

sweet ˌshop *UK noun* [C] (*US* **candy store**) a shop which sells sweets, cigarettes and often newspapers

sweet-talk /ˈswiːt.tɔːk/ [US] /-tɑːk/ *verb* [T] *INFORMAL* to talk to someone in a pleasing or clever way in order to persuade them to do or believe something: *The salesman tried to sweet-talk me **into** buying a bigger car.* **ˈsweet ˌtalk** *noun* [U]

sweet ˈtooth *noun* [U] If you have a sweet tooth, you like eating sweet foods, especially sweets and chocolate.

swell [INCREASE] /swel/ *verb* **swelled, swollen** or **swelled 1** [I or T] to become larger and rounder than usual; to (cause to) increase in size or amount: *It was obvious she had broken her toe, because it immediately started to swell **(up)**.* ○ *Twenty-five employees have joined the union in this month alone, swelling its **ranks*** (= increasing its size) *to 110.* ○ *LITERARY His heart/breast swelled **with pride*** (= He felt very proud) *as he stood watching his son graduate.* **2** [I] If music swells, it becomes louder.
swell /swel/ *noun* [U] an increase in sound produced by a musical instrument or instruments
swelling /ˈswel.ɪŋ/ *noun* [C or U] a part of your body which has become bigger because of illness or injury: *Put your foot into cold water to help the swelling go down.*

swell [WAVE MOVEMENT] /swel/ *noun* [U] the slow up and down movement of the sea with large but smooth waves ➲See also **groundswell**.

swell [EXCELLENT] /swel/ *adj US OLD-FASHIONED INFORMAL* very good or pleasant: *That's a swell idea!*
swell /swel/ *adv US OLD-FASHIONED INFORMAL* very well: *Everything's going real swell.*

swelter /ˈswel.təʳ/ [US] /-t̬ɚ/ *verb* [I] (of a person) to feel very hot: *The soldiers were sweltering in their uniforms.*

sweltering /ˈswel.tᵊr.ɪŋ/ [US] /-t̬ɚ-/ *adj* extremely and uncomfortably hot: *In the summer, **it's** sweltering in the smaller classrooms.*

swept /swept/ *past simple and past participle of* **sweep**

swept-back /ˈswept.bæk/ /ˌ-ˈ-/ *adj* having a front edge which faces backwards at an angle: *a swept-back hairstyle* ○ *an aircraft with swept-back wings*

swerve /swɜːv/ [US] /swɝːv/ *verb* **1** [I] to change direction, especially suddenly: *The bus driver swerved to avoid hitting the cyclists.* ➲Compare **unswerving**. **2** If you do not swerve from a principle or certain actions, you continue to think or act as you did in the beginning: *She is one of those rare politicians whom one can trust not to swerve **from** policy and principle.* **swerve** /swɜːv/ [US] /swɝːv/ *noun* [C]

swift [QUICK] /swɪft/ *adj* happening or moving quickly or within a short time, especially in a smooth and easy way: *The local police took swift action against the squatters.* ○ *Thank you for your swift reply.* ○ *The gazelle is one of the swiftest and most graceful of animals.* **swiftly** /ˈswɪft.li/ *adv*: *Walking swiftly, he was at the station within ten minutes.* **swiftness** /ˈswɪft.nəs/ *noun* [U]

swift [BIRD] /swɪft/ *noun* [C] a small bird with curved pointed wings that can fly very fast

swig /swɪg/ *verb* [T] **-gg-** *INFORMAL* to drink, especially by swallowing large amounts in a series of single actions
swig /swɪg/ *noun* [C] *She **took** a swig of whisky, straight from the bottle.*

swill [MOVE LIQUID] /swɪl/ *verb* [T usually + adv or prep] to cause a liquid to flow around or over something, often in order to clean it: *The dentist handed me a glass of water to swill my mouth **out** with.* **swill** /swɪl/ *noun* [S] *Give the sink **a** quick swill to get it clean.*

swill [DRINK] /swɪl/ *verb* [T] *INFORMAL OFTEN DISAPPROVING* to drink especially alcohol quickly and in large amounts

swill [FOOD] /swɪl/ *noun* [U] *US FOR* **pigswill**

swim [MOVE IN WATER] /swɪm/ *verb* [I or T] **swimming, swam, swum 1** to move through water by moving the body or parts of the body: *We spent the day on the beach but it was too cold to **go** swimming.* ○ *Her ambition is to swim **(across)** the English Channel.* ○ *I swam two miles this morning.* **2** *DISAPPROVING* **be swimming in/with *sth*** If food is swimming in/with a liquid, it has too much of that liquid in it or on it: *The salad was swimming in oil.*
swim /swɪm/ *noun* [S] a time when you swim: *Shall we **go for/have** a swim this afternoon?* **swimmer** /ˈswɪm.əʳ/ [US] /-ɚ/ *noun* [C] *Oliver is a very **strong** swimmer.* **swimming** /ˈswɪm.ɪŋ/ *noun* [U] *The doctor recommended swimming as the best all-round exercise.* ➲See picture **Sports** on page Centre 10

swim [SEEM TO MOVE] /swɪm/ *verb* [I] **swimming, swam, swum** (of an object) to seem to move about: *Getting up too suddenly made the room swim before her eyes.*

swim [HEAD] /swɪm/ *noun* [I] If your head swims, you feel confused and are unable to think or see clearly: *After the second or third drink, my **head** began to swim.*

swimmers /ˈswɪm.əz/ [US] /-ɚz/ *plural noun AUS INFORMAL FOR* **swimming costume** or **swimming trunks**

ˈswimming ˌbaths *group noun* [C] *UK OLD-FASHIONED FOR* a public SWIMMING POOL

ˈswimming ˌcostume *noun* [C] *UK* a piece of clothing that women wear for swimming

swimmingly /ˈswɪm.ɪŋ.li/ *adv OLD-FASHIONED INFORMAL* successfully and without any problems: *Everything **went** swimmingly until Peter started talking about money.*

ˈswimming ˌpool *noun* [C] an artificially maintained area of water for swimming, or a building containing this: *an **indoor/outdoor** swimming pool*

ˈswimming ˌtrunks *plural noun MAINLY UK* a piece of men's clothing that is worn when swimming

swimsuit /ˈswɪm.sjuːt/ [US] /-suːt/ *noun* [C] a piece of clothing that you wear for swimming

swimwear /ˈswɪm.weəʳ/ [US] /-wer/ *noun* [U] clothes that you wear for swimming

swindle /ˈswɪn.dl̩/ *verb* [T] to obtain money dishonestly from someone by deceiving or cheating them: *They swindled local businesses **out of** thousands of pounds.*
swindle /ˈswɪn.dl̩/ *noun* [C] *Fraud-squad officers are investigating a £5.6 million swindle.* **swindler** /ˈswɪnd.ləʳ/ [US] /-lɚ/ *noun* [C]

swine [PERSON] /swaɪn/ *noun* [C] *plural* **swine** or **swines** *OLD-FASHIONED* a person whom you consider to be extremely unpleasant and unkind: *You **filthy** swine!* ○ *Her ex-husband sounds like an absolute swine.* **swinish** /ˈswaɪ.nɪʃ/ *adj*: *swinish behaviour*

S

swine [ANIMAL] /swaɪn/ *noun* [C] *plural* **swine** *OLD USE OR SPECIALIZED* a pig

ˈ**swine** ˌ**fever** *noun* [U] a serious disease of pigs

swing [MOVE SIDEWAYS] /swɪŋ/ *verb* **swung, swung 1** [I or T] to move easily and without interruption backwards and forwards or from one side to the other, especially from a fixed point, or to cause something or someone to do this: *He walked briskly along the path swinging his rolled-up umbrella.* ○ *The door swung open.* **2** [I] to change: *His* ***mood*** *swings* ***between*** *elation and despair.*

• **swing into action** to quickly start working: *The emergency services swung into action as soon as the news of the bomb explosion reached them.*

• **swing the balance** If something swings the balance, it is the thing which causes a particular situation to happen or a particular decision to be made instead of other situations or decisions which are possible: *This latest election promise might just swing the balance in the government's favour.*

swing /swɪŋ/ *noun* [C] **1** a swinging movement **2** an attempt to hit someone: *The drunk* ***took*** *a wild swing* ***at*** *Harry.* **3** a change: *He experiences severe* ***mood*** *swings* (= sudden changes from one extreme mood to another). ○ *The Democrats only need a 5% swing* (= need 5% of voters to change to supporting them) *to win this election.*

swing [SEAT] /swɪŋ/ *noun* [C] a seat joined by two ropes or chains to a metal bar or a tree, on which a child can sit and move backwards and forwards

• **What you lose on the swings you gain on the roundabouts.** (*ALSO* **It's swings and roundabouts.**) *UK SAYING* said to mean that the positive and negative results of a situation or action balance each other: *"The route through town would be shorter, but there'll be more traffic." "Well, it's just swings and roundabouts."*

swing [BE EXCITING] /swɪŋ/ *verb* [I] **swung, swung** *INFORMAL* to be exciting and enjoyable: *You need music to make a* ***party*** *swing.*

swing /swɪŋ/ *noun UK INFORMAL* **go with a swing** If an event, especially a party, goes with a swing, it is very exciting and successful: *The Festival always goes with a swing.*

• **get into the swing of it/things** *INFORMAL* to start to understand, enjoy and be active in something: *I hadn't worked in an office for several years, so it took me a while to get back into the swing of it.*

swinging /ˈswɪŋ.ɪŋ/ *adj OLD-FASHIONED INFORMAL* exciting and fashionable: *It's a nostalgia trip back into the youth culture of the swinging 60s.*

swing [MUSIC] /swɪŋ/ *verb* [I or T] **swung, swung** (of music, especially jazz) to have a strong exciting rhythm with notes of uneven length, or (of musicians) to play especially jazz in this way

swing /swɪŋ/ *noun* [U] a type of dance music that was popular in the 1930s and 1940s

swing [ARRANGE] /swɪŋ/ *verb* [T] **swung, swung** *INFORMAL* to arrange for something to happen, by persuading people and often by acting slightly dishonestly: *If you want an interview with Pedro, I could probably swing* ***it*** *(****for*** *you).*

swing [BE PUNISHED] /swɪŋ/ *verb UK INFORMAL* **swing for it** to be punished severely for something that has happened: *If there's an error in the calculations, you know who'll swing for it!*

PHRASAL VERBS WITH **swing**

▲ **swing at *sb*** *phrasal verb* to try to hit someone

▲ **swing for *sb*** *phrasal verb UK OLD-FASHIONED INFORMAL* to hit someone

▲ **swing *(sth/sb)* round** *UK phrasal verb* [M] (*US* **swing *(sth/sb)* around**) to turn round quickly, or to turn something or someone round quickly: *She heard a sudden noise behind her, and swung round to look behind her.*

ˈ**swing** ˌ**bridge** *noun* [C usually sing] a bridge that can be turned to a position that is at 90° to its usual position, so that ships can go through

ˌ**swing** ˈ**door** *UK noun* [C] (*US* **swinging door**) a door that can swing open in both directions

swingeing /ˈswɪn.dʒɪŋ/ *adj UK FORMAL* extreme and having a serious and unpleasant effect: *We are going to have to make swingeing* ***cuts*** *in the budget.*

swinger /ˈswɪŋ.əʳ/ [US] /-ɚ/ *noun* [C] *OLD-FASHIONED SLANG* either a person who dresses in a fashionable way and who goes to lots of parties and nightclubs, or someone who is willing to have sex often with many different people

swinish /ˈswaɪ.nɪʃ/ *adj* ➲See at **swine** PERSON.

swipe [HIT] /swaɪp/ *verb* [I or T; usually + adv or prep] to hit or try to hit something, especially with a sideways movement: *She opened the window and swiped* ***at*** *the flies with a rolled-up newspaper to make them go out.* ○ *She swiped him* ***round*** *the head.* ○ *MAINLY US The car swiped the garage door as he pulled out.* ➲See also **sideswipe** HIT.

swipe /swaɪp/ *noun* [C] *Edwin* ***took*** *a swipe* ***at*** *the ball and missed.*

swipe [CRITICISM] /swaɪp/ *noun* [C usually sing] a criticism of someone or something, or an attempt to damage or annoy them: *In a recent interview, she* ***takes*** *a swipe* ***at*** *the theatre management.*

swipe [STEAL] /swaɪp/ *verb* [T] *INFORMAL* to steal: *Okay, who's swiped my keys?*

swipe [MOVE] /swaɪp/ *verb* [T] to move a card containing information stored on a magnetic strip through a device that reads this information

ˈ**swipe** ˌ**card** *noun* [C] a plastic card that you slide through a machine in order to be allowed into a building, pay for something, etc.

swirl /swɜːl/ [US] /swɝːl/ *verb* [I or T; usually + adv or prep] to (cause to) move quickly with a twisting circular movement: *Swirl a little oil* ***around*** *the frying pan.* ○ *The fog swirled thickly* ***around*** *us.* **swirl** /swɜːl/ [US] /swɝːl/ *noun* [C] *The truck went by in a swirl of dust.*

swish [MOVE] /swɪʃ/ *verb* [I or T] to (cause to) move quickly through the air making a soft sound: *I heard the rope swish through the air.* ○ *The horses swished their tails to get rid of the flies hovering around them.* **swish** /swɪʃ/ *noun* [C] *With a swish of the curtains, the stage was revealed.*

swish [FASHIONABLE] /swɪʃ/ *adj INFORMAL* fashionable or luxurious: *a swish hotel*

swish [LIKE A WOMAN] /swɪʃ/ *noun* [C] *US SLANG DISAPPROVING* a man who behaves or appears in a way that is generally considered more suited to a woman, and who lacks traditional male qualities **swishy** /ˈswɪʃ.i/ *adj*

Swiss roll *UK* /ˌswɪsˈrəʊl/ [US] /-ˈroʊl/ *noun* [C] (*US* **jelly roll**) a cake which has been spread with cream, jam or chocolate and then rolled into a cylindrical shape

switch [DEVICE] /swɪtʃ/ *noun* [C] a small device, usually pushed up or down with your finger, that controls and turns on or off an electric current: *a light switch*

switch /swɪtʃ/ *verb* [T; I usually + adv or prep] to use a switch to change a device from one state or type of operation to another: *switch the TV* ***off/on***

switches /ˈswɪtʃ.ɪz/ *plural noun US FOR* **points** RAILWAY

switch [CHANGE] /swɪtʃ/ *verb* [T; I usually + adv or prep] to change suddenly or completely, especially from one thing to another, or to exchange by replacing one person or thing with another: *She started studying English at college, but switched* ***to*** *Business Studies in her second year.* ○ *In 1971, Britain switched* ***over*** (= changed completely) ***to*** *a decimal currency.* ○ *After the bank robbery, the gang switched cars* (= left one car and got into another). **switch** /swɪtʃ/ *noun* [C]

PHRASAL VERBS WITH **switch**

▲ **switch off** *phrasal verb INFORMAL* to stop giving your attention to someone or something: *If he gets bored, he just switches off and looks out the window.*

▲ **switch *sth* on** *phrasal verb USUALLY DISAPPROVING* If someone switches on a particular emotion or behaviour, they suddenly start to feel or behave in that way, but usually not sincerely: *When a customer walks in, she switches on the charm.*

switchback /ˈswɪtʃ.bæk/ *noun* [C] a path, road or railway which bends sharply from one direction to almost the opposite direction as it goes up and down steep slopes

switchblade /ˈswɪtʃ.bleɪd/ *noun US FOR* **flick knife**

switchboard /ˈswɪtʃ.bɔːd/ [US] /-bɔːrd/ *noun* **[C]** a piece of equipment which is used to direct all the telephone calls made to and from a particular building or area: *Tearful fans* ***jammed*** *the radio station's switchboard after the singer's death* (= so many people rang that all the telephones were busy).

ˈswitchboard ˌoperator *noun* **[C]** a person whose job is to receive telephone calls and connect them to other numbers

switched-on /ˌswɪtʃtˈɒn/ [US] /-ˈɑːn/ *adj* OLD-FASHIONED INFORMAL quick to know about or be involved with the most recent fashions and ideas

swivel /ˈswɪv.əl/ *verb* **[I or T] -ll-** or *US USUALLY* **-l-** to (cause to) turn round a central point in order to face in another direction: *She swivelled* ***round*** *to look out of the window.* ○ *The ostrich swivelled its head in our direction.* **swivel** /ˈswɪv.əl/ *adj* **[before n]** *a swivel chair* ○ *a swivel lamp*

swizz, swiz /swɪz/ *noun* **[S]** *UK OLD-FASHIONED INFORMAL* something that is disappointing or unfair: *"There's only half as much in the new packets. "****What a*** *swizz!"*

swizzle stick /ˈswɪz.l̩ˌstɪk/ *noun* **[C]** a small glass or plastic rod for mixing drinks

swollen [INCREASE] /ˈswəʊ.lən/ [US] /ˈswoʊ-/ *past participle of* **swell** INCREASE

swollen [LARGER] /ˈswəʊ.lən/ [US] /ˈswoʊ-/ *adj* larger than usual: *a bruised, swollen face* ○ *The stream is swollen because of the heavy rain.*

ˌswollen ˈhead *noun* **[C usually sing]** (*US USUALLY ALSO* **swelled head**) *INFORMAL DISAPPROVING* If someone has a swollen head, they think they are more intelligent and more important than they really are: *Don't compliment him any more, or he'll* ***get*** *a swollen head.* ➲Compare **big-head**. **swollen-headed** /ˌswəʊ.lənˈhed.ɪd/ [US] /ˌswoʊ-/ *adj*

swoon /swuːn/ *verb* **[I] 1** to feel a lot of pleasure, love, etc. because of something or someone: *The audience swooned* ***with*** *delight.* **2** *OLD-FASHIONED LITERARY* to **faint** LOSE CONSCIOUSNESS

swoon /swuːn/ *noun* **[C]** *OLD-FASHIONED LITERARY* a **faint** (= sudden loss of consciousness)

swoop /swuːp/ *verb* **[I] 1** to move very quickly and easily through the air, especially down from a height in order to attack: *The eagle swooped* ***down*** *to snatch a young rabbit.* **2** *INFORMAL* to make a sudden attack on a place or group of people in order to surround and catch them: *Undercover police swooped* ***on*** *three houses in Bristol at 5 a.m. this morning.* **swoop** /swuːp/ *noun* **[C]**

swoosh /swuːʃ/ *verb* **[I]** *INFORMAL* to make the sound of fast-moving air **swoosh** /swuːʃ/ *noun* **[C]**

swop /swɒp/ [US] /swɑːp/ *verb* **[I or T] -pp-** *MAINLY UK FOR* **swap**

sword /sɔːd/ [US] /sɔːrd/ *noun* **[C]** a weapon with a long sharp metal blade and a handle, used especially in the past

• **put** *sb* **to the sword** *LITERARY* to kill someone: *Thousands of innocents were put to the sword.*

• **sword of Damocles** If you have a sword of Damocles hanging over you/your head, something bad seems very likely to happen to you: *Government threats to cut the budget by 50% are hanging over the Opera House* ***like a*** *sword of Damocles.*

• **beat/turn swords into ploughshares** *LITERARY* to change to a peaceful way of life and spend money on peaceful things rather than weapons

swordfish /ˈsɔːd.fɪʃ/ [US] /ˈsɔːrd-/ *noun* **[C or U]** *plural* **swordfish** or **swordfishes** a large long fish with a very long pointed beak-like part at the front of its head, often eaten as food

swordsman /ˈsɔːdz.mən/ [US] /ˈsɔːrdz-/ *noun* **[C]** a person skilled in fighting with a sword

swordsmanship /ˈsɔːdz.mən.ʃɪp/ [US] /ˈsɔːrdz-/ *noun* **[U]** the skill of fighting with a sword

swore /swɔːr/ [US] /swɔːr/ *past simple of* **swear**

sworn [SWEAR] /swɔːn/ [US] /swɔːrn/ *past participle of* **swear**

sworn [OFFICIALLY STATED] /swɔːn/ [US] /swɔːrn/ *adj* **[before n]** formally and officially stated as being true: *a sworn testimony*

ˌsworn ˈenemy *noun* **[C]** Sworn enemies are people who will always hate each other.

swot /swɒt/ [US] /swɑːt/ *verb* **[I] -tt-** *UK INFORMAL OR CHILD'S WORD* to study hard, usually by reading about or learning something, especially before taking an exam

swot /swɒt/ [US] /swɑːt/ *noun* **[C]** *UK INFORMAL DISAPPROVING* someone, usually a child, who studies very hard

▲ **swot up** ***(sth)*** *phrasal verb UK INFORMAL OR CHILD'S WORD* to learn as much as you can about a subject, especially before an examination: *She's at home, swotting up* ***on*** *her maths.*

SWOT /swɒt/ [US] /swɑːt/ *noun* **[U]** *ABBREVIATION FOR* strengths, weaknesses, opportunities, threats: a way of considering all the good and bad features of a business situation or a company

swum /swʌm/ *past participle of* **swim**

swung /swʌŋ/ *past simple and past participle of* **swing**

sybarite /ˈsɪb.ər.aɪt/ [US] /-ə.raɪt/ *noun* **[C]** *FORMAL* a person who loves luxury and pleasure ➲Compare **hedonist** at **hedonism**. **sybaritic** /ˌsɪb.ərˈɪt.ɪk/ [US] /-əˈrɪt̬-/ *adj*

sycamore /ˈsɪk.ə.mɔːr/ [US] /-mɔːr/ *noun* **[C]** a tree with leaves divided into five parts and seeds that spin slowly to the ground when they fall

sycophantic /ˌsɪk.əˈfæn.tɪk/ *adj FORMAL DISAPPROVING* (of a person or of behaviour) praising people in authority in a way that is not sincere, usually in order to get some advantage from them: *There was sycophantic laughter from the audience at every one of his terrible jokes.* **sycophant** /ˈsɪk.ə.fænt/ *noun* **[C]** *The Prime Minister is surrounded by sycophants.* **sycophancy** /ˈsɪk.ə.fənt.si/ *noun* **[U]**

syllable /ˈsɪl.ə.bl̩/ *noun* **[C]** a single unit of speech, either a whole word or one of the parts into which a word can be separated, usually containing a vowel ➲See also **disyllabic**; **monosyllabic**; **polysyllabic**. **syllabic** /sɪˈlæb.ɪk/ *adj SPECIALIZED*

syllabub /ˈsɪl.ə.bʌb/ *noun* **[U]** a sweet cold dish consisting of thickened cream mixed with sugar, white wine and sometimes the colourless part of an egg

syllabus /ˈsɪl.ə.bəs/ *noun* **[C]** *plural* **syllabuses** or **syllabi** (a plan showing) the subjects or books to be studied in a particular course, especially a course which leads to an examination: *Which novels are* ***on*** *the syllabus this year?* ➲Compare **curriculum**.

syllogism /ˈsɪl.ə.dʒɪ.zəm/ *noun* **[C]** *SPECIALIZED* (in philosophy) a process of LOGIC in which two general statements lead to a more particular statement **syllogistic** /ˌsɪl.əˈdʒɪs.tɪk/ *adj*

sylphlike /ˈsɪlf.laɪk/ *adj USUALLY HUMOROUS* (of a woman or girl) attractively thin and delicate

symbiosis /ˌsɪm.baɪˈəʊ.sɪs/ [US] /-ˈoʊ-/ *noun* **[U] 1** *SPECIALIZED* a relationship between two types of animals or plants in which each provides for the other the conditions necessary for its continued existence **2** a relationship between people or organizations that depend on each other equally **symbiotic** /ˌsɪm.baɪˈɒt.ɪk/ [US] /-ˈɑː.t̬ɪk/ *adj SPECIALIZED a symbiotic relationship* **symbiotically** /ˌsɪm.baɪˈɒt.ɪ.kli/ [US] /-ɑː.t̬ɪ-/ *adv*

symbol /ˈsɪm.bəl/ *noun* **[C] 1** a sign, shape or object which is used to represent something else: *A heart shape is the symbol of love.* ○ *The wheel in the Indian flag is a symbol* ***of*** *peace.* ➲Compare **emblem**. **2** something that is used to represent a quality or idea: *Water, a symbol* ***of*** *life, recurs as an image throughout her poems.* **3** a number, letter or sign used in mathematics, music, science, etc.: *The symbol* ***for*** *oxygen is* O_2. **4** An object can be described as a symbol of something else if it seems to represent it because it is connected with it in a lot of people's minds: *The private jet is a symbol* ***of*** *wealth.*

symbolic /sɪmˈbɒl.ɪk/ [US] /-ˈbɑː.lɪk/ *adj* (*ALSO* **symbolical**) **1** representing something else: *The skull at the bottom of the picture is symbolic* ***of*** *death.* **2** describes an action that expresses or seems to express an intention or feeling, but which has little practical influence on a situation: *Five hundred troops were sent in, more as a symbolic* ***gesture*** *than as a real threat.* **symbolically** /sɪmˈbɒl.ɪ.kli/ [US] /-ˈbɑː.lɪ-/ *adv*

symbolism /ˈsɪm.bəl.ɪ.zəm/ *noun* [U] **1** the use of symbols in art, literature, films etc. to represent ideas: *Religious symbolism is very characteristic of the paintings of this period.* **2** *SPECIALIZED* a type of art and literature which originated in the late 19th century and which tries to express ideas or states of mind rather than represent reality, using the power of words and images ➲Compare **Naturalism** at **nature** LIFE; **realism** at **real** NOT IMAGINARY; **Expressionism**. **symbolist** /ˈsɪm.bəl.ɪst/ *adj SPECIALIZED symbolist poets*
symbolist /ˈsɪm.bəl.ɪst/ *noun* [C] *SPECIALIZED* a writer or an artist connected with symbolism

symbolize, *UK USUALLY* **-ise** /ˈsɪm.bəl.aɪz/ [US] /-bə.laɪz/ *verb* [T] to represent something: *The lighting of the Olympic torch symbolizes peace and friendship among the nations of the world.*

symmetry /ˈsɪm.ə.tri/ *noun* [U] **1** the quality of having parts that match each other, especially in a way that is attractive, or similarity of shape or contents: *The design of the house had a* ***pleasing*** *symmetry, its oblong shape being picked up in its elongated windows.* ➲Compare **asymmetry** at **asymmetric**. **2** *SPECIALIZED* in mathematics, the quality of having two parts that match exactly, either when one half is like an image of the other half in a mirror, or when one part can take the place of another if it is turned 90° or 180° **symmetrical** /sɪˈmet.rɪ.kəl/ *adj* (*ALSO* **symmetric**) **symmetrically** /sɪˈmet.rɪ.kli/ *adv*

sympathy [UNDERSTANDING] /ˈsɪm.pə.θi/ *noun* [U] (an expression of) understanding and care for someone else's suffering: *The president has sent a message of sympathy to the relatives of the dead soldiers.* ○ *I don't have much sympathy* ***for*** *her – I think she's brought her troubles on herself.* ➲Compare **empathy**.
sympathetic /ˌsɪm.pəˈθet.ɪk/ [US] /-ˈθeţ-/ *adj* **1** describes someone who shows, especially by what they say, that they understand and care about someone's suffering: *He suffers from back trouble too, so he was very sympathetic* ***about*** *my problem.* ○ *She just needed someone who would* ***lend a*** *sympathetic* ***ear*** *to her* (= listen to her in a kind and understanding way) *once in a while.* * NOTE: The opposite is **unsympathetic**. **2** If a character in a book or film is sympathetic, they are described or shown in such a way that you are able to understand their feelings and the reasons for their actions, and so you like them: *She comes across as a more sympathetic character in the film.*
sympathetically /ˌsɪm.pəˈθet.ɪ.kli/ [US] /-ˈθeţ-/ *adv*: *She listened sympathetically, nodding her head now and again.*
sympathies /ˈsɪm.pə.θiz/ *plural noun FORMAL* **offer/send *your* sympathies** to express your sadness to someone because a relative or friend of theirs has recently died: *I went along to the funeral in order to offer my sympathies.*
sympathize, *UK USUALLY* **-ise** /ˈsɪm.pə.θaɪz/ *verb* [I] to understand and care about someone's problems: *I know what it's like to have migraines, so I do sympathize (****with*** *you).*

COMMON LEARNER ERROR

sympathetic

Be careful not to use **sympathetic** when you simply want to say that someone is **nice**, **friendly**, or **kind**. Remember that if you say someone is **sympathetic**, you mean that they understand your problems.

I explained to the teacher that I had been ill, but she wasn't sympathetic at all.
~~*I met some very sympathetic people while I was in London.*~~
I met some very nice people while I was in London.

---

sympathy [SUPPORT] /ˈsɪm.pə.θi/ *noun* [U] support and agreement: *I must confess I have some sympathy* ***with*** *his views.*
• **come out in sympathy with *sb*** to stop working in order to show your support for other workers who are ON STRIKE: *The railway workers came out in sympathy with the miners.*
sympathetic /ˌsɪm.pəˈθet.ɪk/ [US] /-ˈθeţ-/ *adj* agreeing with or supporting: *The Labour party are supposed to be sympathetic* ***to/towards*** *the unions.* ○ *Did he give your proposal/complaints a sympathetic* ***hearing****?*
sympathies /ˈsɪm.pə.θiz/ *plural noun*: *Of those people questioned, 93% said their sympathies were* ***with*** (= they supported) *the teachers.* ○ *He is known to have right-wing sympathies.*
sympathize, *UK USUALLY* **-ise** /ˈsɪm.pə.θaɪz/ *verb* [I] *I sympathize* ***with*** (= support) *the general aims of the party, but on this particular issue I'm afraid I disagree.*
sympathizer, *UK USUALLY* **-iser** /ˈsɪm.pə.θaɪ.zəʳ/ [US] /-zɚ/ *noun* [C] a person who supports a political organization or believes in a set of ideas: *He had been a known IRA sympathizer.*

ˈsympathy ˌvote *noun* [S] *UK INFORMAL* an occasion when a lot of people vote for or support a particular person because he or she has suffered recently: *He won the award, but some suspected it was a sympathy vote following his struggle with cancer.*

symphony /ˈsɪmp.fə.ni/ *noun* [C] a long piece of music for an orchestra, usually with four MOVEMENTS (= parts): *Mahler's 9th symphony* **symphonic** /sɪmˈfɒn.ɪk/ [US] /-ˈfɑː.nɪk/ *adj*

symposium /sɪmˈpəʊ.zi.əm/ [US] /-ˈpoʊ-/ *noun* [C] *plural* **symposiums** or **symposia** *FORMAL* an occasion at which people who have great knowledge of a particular subject meet in order to discuss a matter of interest: *a symposium* ***on*** *European cinema*

symptom /ˈsɪmp.təm/ *noun* [C] **1** any feeling of illness or physical or mental change which is caused by a particular disease: *He's complaining of all the usual flu symptoms – a high temperature, headache and so on.* ○ *He's been HIV-positive for six years, but just recently he's started to* ***develop*** *the symptoms of AIDS.* **2** any single problem which is caused by and shows a more serious and general problem: *It's her feeling that the recent outbreaks of violence are a symptom of the dissatisfaction that is currently affecting our society.*
symptomatic /ˌsɪmp.təˈmæt.ɪk/ [US] /-ˈmæţ-/ *adj* If something bad is symptomatic of something else, it is caused by the other thing and is proof that it exists: *Jealousy within a relationship is usually symptomatic* ***of*** *low self-esteem in one of the partners.*

synagogue /ˈsɪn.ə.gɒg/ [US] /-gɑːg/ *noun* [C] a building in which Jewish people worship and study their religion

synapse /ˈsaɪ.næps/ *noun* [C] *SPECIALIZED* the point at which electrical signals move from one nerve cell to another **synaptic** /saɪˈnæp.tɪk/ *adj*

sync, synch /sɪŋk/ *noun* [U] *INFORMAL FOR* **synchronization**, see at **synchronize**: *He's putting himself forward as a president whose ideas are* ***in*** *sync* ***with*** (= are suited to and show an understanding of) *a nation demanding change.*
• **in/out of sync** If two things are in/out of sync, they reach the same or related stage at the same time/at different times.

synchronicity /ˌsɪŋ.krəˈnɪs.ɪ.ti/ [US] /-ə.ţi/ *noun* [U] *SPECIALIZED* the happening by chance of two or more related or similar events at the same time

synchronize, *UK USUALLY* **-ise** /ˈsɪŋ.krə.naɪz/ *verb* **1** [I or T] to (cause to) happen at the same time: *The show was designed so that the lights synchronized* ***with*** *the music.* **2** [T] When people synchronize their watches, they make sure that all their watches show the same time: *We'd better synchronize our watches if we all want to be there at the same time.* **synchronization**, *UK USUALLY* **-isation** /ˌsɪŋ.krə.naɪˈzeɪ.ʃən/ *noun* [U]

ˌsynchronized ˈswimming *noun* [U] a sport in which a group of people make graceful dance-like movements in the water at the same time

syncopated /ˈsɪŋ.kə.peɪ.tɪd/ [US] /-ţɪd/ *adj* (of a tune) having a rhythm in which strong notes are not on the beat: *syncopated jazz rhythms* **syncopation** /ˌsɪŋ.kəˈpeɪ.ʃən/ *noun* [U]

syndicate /ˈsɪn.dɪ.kət/ *group noun* [C] a group of people or companies who join together in order to share the cost of a particular business operation for which a large amount of money is needed: *A syndicate* ***of*** *banks is/are financing the deal.* ➲See also **syndicate** at **syndicated**.
syndicate /ˈsɪn.dɪ.keɪt/ *verb* [T] **syndication** /ˌsɪn.dɪˈkeɪ.ʃən/ *noun* [U]

syndicated /ˈsɪn.dɪ.keɪ.tɪd/ [US] /-t̬ɪd/ *adj* **1** (of articles and photographs) sold to several different newspapers and magazines for publishing **2** *MAINLY US* (of television or radio programmes) sold to several different broadcasting organizations **syndicate** /ˈsɪn.dɪ.keɪt/ *verb* [T]

syndicate /ˈsɪn.dɪ.kət/ *noun* [C] an organization that supplies articles and photographs to different newspapers and magazines for publishing **syndication** /ˌsɪn.dɪˈkeɪ.ʃən/ *noun* [U]

syndrome /ˈsɪn.drəʊm/ [US] /-droʊm/ *noun* **1** [C] a combination of medical problems that commonly go together, which might show the existence of a particular disease or mental condition ➲See also **Down's syndrome**. **2** [U] used in the names of various illnesses: *irritable bowel syndrome* **3** [C] a type of negative behaviour or mental state that is typical of a person in a particular situation: *It's a classic case of the bored-housewife syndrome – she's got nothing to do all day except drink and go shopping.*

synergy /ˈsɪn.ə.dʒi/ [US] /-ɚ-/ *noun* [U] (*ALSO* **synergism**) *SPECIALIZED* the combined power of a group of things when they are working together which is greater than the total power achieved by each working separately: *Team work at its best results in a synergy that can be very productive.*

synod /ˈsɪn.əd/ /-ɒd/ *noun* [C] *SPECIALIZED* a regular meeting of church members for the discussion of religious matters

synonym /ˈsɪn.ə.nɪm/ *noun* [C] a word or phrase which has the same or nearly the same meaning as another word or phrase in the same language: *The words 'small' and 'little' are synonyms.* ➲Compare **antonym**.

synonymous /sɪˈnɒn.ɪ.məs/ [US] /-ˈnɑː.nə-/ *adj* **1** having the same meaning: *The words 'annoyed' and 'irritated' are more or less synonymous.* **2** If you say that one thing is synonymous with another, you mean that the two things are so closely connected in most people's minds that one suggests the other: *Oscar Wilde's name is synonymous* ***with*** *wit.*

synopsis /sɪˈnɒp.sɪs/ [US] /-ˈnɑːp-/ *noun* [C] *plural* **synopses** a brief description of the contents of something such as a film or book

syntax /ˈsɪn.tæks/ *noun* [U] *SPECIALIZED* the grammatical arrangement of words in a sentence **syntactic** /sɪnˈtæk.tɪk/ *adj* **syntactically** /sɪnˈtæk.tɪ.kli/ *adv*

synthesis [CHEMICAL PRODUCTION] /ˈsɪn.θə.sɪs/ *noun* [U] *SPECIALIZED* the production of a substance from simpler materials after a chemical reaction ➲See also **photosynthesis**. **synthetically** /sɪnˈθet.ɪ.kli/ [US] /-ˈθet̬-/ *adv*

synthesize, *UK USUALLY* **-ise** /ˈsɪn.θə.saɪz/ *verb* [T] *SPECIALIZED There are many vitamins that the body cannot synthesize* (= produce) *itself.*

synthesis [MIX] /ˈsɪn.θə.sɪs/ *noun* [C] *plural* **syntheses** *FORMAL* the mixing of different ideas, influences or things to make a whole which is different or new: *He describes his latest record as 'a synthesis of African and Latin rhythms'.*

synthesizer, *UK USUALLY* **-iser** /ˈsɪn.θə.saɪ.zəʳ/ [US] /-zɚ/ *noun* [C] an electronic keyboard instrument which can reproduce and combine a large range of recorded sounds, often in order to copy other musical instruments or voices

synthetic /sɪnˈθet.ɪk/ [US] /-ˈθet̬-/ *adj* **1** describes products that are made from artificial substances, often copying a natural product: *synthetic fibres* **2** *DISAPPROVING* false or artificial: *She criticized the synthetic charm of television presenters.*

syphilis /ˈsɪf.ɪ.lɪs/ *noun* [U] a VENEREAL DISEASE (= disease caught during sexual activity with an infected person) which spreads slowly from the sex organs to all parts of the body

syphon /ˈsaɪ.fən/ *noun* [C] a **siphon**

syringe /sɪˈrɪndʒ/ *noun* [C] a hollow cylindrical piece of equipment which is used for sucking liquid out of, or pushing liquid into something, especially one with a needle which can be put under the skin and used to inject drugs, remove small amounts of blood, etc.

syringe /sɪˈrɪndʒ/ *verb* [T] to clean the inside of the ears by pushing water into them and then sucking it out of them using a syringe

syrup /ˈsɪr.əp/ *noun* [U] **1** a very sweet, thick, light-coloured liquid made by dissolving sugar in water ➲Compare **treacle**. **2** a type of sweet liquid medicine: *cough syrup*

syrupy /ˈsɪr.əp.i/ *adj* **1** thick and sweet **2** *DISAPPROVING* too good or kind or expressing feelings of love in a way which is not sincere: *syrupy love songs*

system [SET] /ˈsɪs.təm/ *noun* [C] **1** a set of connected items or devices which operate together: *a central-heating system* **2** a set of computer equipment and programs used together for a particular purpose: *The system keeps crashing and no one is able to figure out why.* **3** a set of organs or structures in the body which have a particular purpose: *the immune system* ○ *the nervous system* **4** the way that the body works, especially the way that it digests and excretes: *A run in the morning is good for the system – it wakes the body up and gets everything going.*

• **get *sth* out of *your* system** *INFORMAL* If you get something out of your system, you get rid of a desire or emotion, especially a negative one, by allowing yourself to express it: *I had a really good shout at him this morning and got it out of my system.*

systemic /sɪˈstem.ɪk/ *adj* **1** *SPECIALIZED* A systemic drug, disease or poison reaches and has an effect on the whole of a body or a plant and not just one part of it. **2** *FORMAL* A systemic problem or change is a basic one, experienced by the whole of an organization or a country and not just particular parts of it: *The current recession is the result of a systemic change within the structure of the country's economy.*

system [METHOD] /ˈsɪs.təm/ *noun* **1** [C] a way of doing things: *We'll have to work out a proper filing system.* ○ ***Under*** *our education system, you're supposed to be able to choose the type of schooling that your child receives.* ○ *The legal system* ***operates*** *very differently in the US and Britain.* **2** [C] a particular method of counting, measuring or weighing things: *the metric system of measuring and weighing* **3** [U] *APPROVING* the intentional and organized use of a system: *There doesn't seem to be any system to the books on these shelves – they're certainly not in alphabetical order.*

• **the system** *DISAPPROVING* unfair laws and rules that prevent people from being able to improve their situation: *He has his own ways of* ***beating*** *the system, making sure that he has good relationships with influential people.*

systematic /ˌsɪs.təˈmæt.ɪk/ [US] /-ˈmæt̬-/ *adj* using a fixed and organized plan: *APPROVING We've got to be a bit more systematic in the way that we approach this task.* ○ *DISAPPROVING We're hearing reports of the systematic rape and torture of prisoners.* **systematically** /ˌsɪs.təˈmæt.ɪ.kli/ [US] /-ˈmæt̬-/ *adv*

systematize, *UK USUALLY* **-ise** /ˈsɪs.tə.mə.taɪz/ *verb* [T] *SPECIALIZED* to plan a system for something **systematization**, *UK USUALLY* **-isation** /ˌsɪs.tə.mə.taɪˈzeɪ.ʃən/ *noun* [U]

ˈsystems ˌanalyst *noun* [C] a person who examines complicated industrial and business operations in order to find ways of improving them, especially by the introduction of computer programs and equipment **ˈsystems aˌnalysis** *noun* [U]

S

T

T (*plural* **T's** or **Ts**), **t** (*plural* **t's** or **ts**), /tiː/ *noun* [C] the 20th letter of the English alphabet

ta /tɑː/ *exclamation* UK INFORMAL thank you

tab /tæb/ *noun* [C] **1** a small piece of paper, metal, etc. that is fixed to something larger and is used for giving information, fastening, opening, etc: *Make a file for these documents and write 'finance' on the tab.* ○ *Insert Tab A into Slot A and glue, before standing the model upright.* **2** US (UK **ringpull**) the small piece of metal, often joined to a ring, which is pulled off or pushed into the top of a can to open it **3** UK NORTHERN ENGLISH a cigarette **4** (ALSO **tab of acid**) INFORMAL a small piece of paper containing the drug LSD

the tab /ðə'tæb/ *noun* [S] MAINLY US INFORMAL the total money charged in a restaurant or hotel for food, drinks, etc: *He kindly offered to* ***pick up*** *the tab* (= pay).

• **keep tabs on** ***sth/sb*** to watch something or someone carefully: *I like to keep tabs on my bank account so that I don't overdraw.*

tabasco (sauce) /tə,bæs.kəʊ'sɔːs/ [US] /-koʊ'sɑːs/ *noun* [U] TRADEMARK a red sauce with a hot taste which is used on food for flavouring

tabby /'tæb.i/ *noun* [C], *adj* (a cat) having dark coloured marks on grey or brown fur

tabernacle /'tæb.ə,næk.l̩/ [US] /-ɚ-/ *noun* [C] **1** OLD USE a place of worship **2** SPECIALIZED in a Roman Catholic church, the box in which holy bread and wine are kept

table [FURNITURE] /'teɪ.bl̩/ *noun* [C] a flat surface, usually supported by four legs, used for putting things on

table /'teɪ.bl̩/ *group noun* the people sitting at a table: *There was a really noisy table behind us celebrating someone's birthday.*

• **lay/set the table** to put a cloth, knives and forks, etc. on the table in preparation for a meal: *Could you lay the table* ***for*** *lunch, please?*

• **on the table** If a plan or suggestion has been put/laid on the table, it has been made available for people to hear, read or discuss.

• **under the table** If something is done under the table, it is a secret, hidden action: *They offered him money under the table to change his mind.*

table [DISCUSS] /'teɪ.bl̩/ *verb* [T] **1** UK to suggest something for discussion: *An amendment to the proposal was tabled by Mrs James.* **2** US to delay discussion of a subject: *The suggestion was tabled for discussion at a later date.*

table [INFORMATION] /'teɪ.bl̩/ *noun* [C] **1** an arrangement of facts and numbers in rows or blocks, especially in printed material **2** a **multiplication table**

• **table of contents** a list of the information that is contained in a book **tabular** /'tæb.jʊ.ləʳ/ [US] /-lɚ/ *adj* [before n] FORMAL **tabulate** /'tæb.jʊ.leɪt/ *verb* [T]

tableau /'tæb.ləʊ/ [US] /-loʊ/ *noun* [C] *plural* **tableaux** or **tableaus** an arrangement of people who do not move or speak, especially on a stage, who represent a view of life, an event, etc.

tablecloth, UK ALSO **table cloth** /'teɪ.bl̩.klɒθ/ [US] /-klɑːθ/ *noun* [C] a large piece of material which covers a table during a meal and protects or decorates it

table d'hôte /,tɑː.blə'dəʊt/ [US] /-bl̩'doʊt/ *noun* [U] food that is served in a restaurant as a complete meal at a fixed price but with little choice of dishes ➲Compare **à la carte**.

'table ,lamp *noun* [C] a small electric light which is used on a table

'table ,linen *noun* [U] the TABLECLOTHS and NAPKINS that are put on a table for a meal

'table ,manners *plural noun* the way you eat your food, or the socially acceptable way to eat your food, especially when eating a meal with others: *Your table manners are appalling – don't you know how to use a knife and fork?* ○ *Don't they teach you table manners at school?*

'table ,mat *noun* [C] a small cover which protects a table against heat damage from food containers or plates

tablespoon /'teɪ.bl̩.spuːn/ *noun* [C] (WRITTEN ABBREVIATION **tbsp**) (the amount held by) a large spoon used for measuring or serving food: *3 tablespoons of sugar* ➲Compare **dessertspoon**; **teaspoon**.

tablespoonful (*plural* **tablespoonsful** or **tablespoonfuls**) /'teɪ.bl̩,spuːn.fʊl/ *noun* [C] (WRITTEN ABBREVIATION **tbsp**) *Sprinkle a tablespoonful* (= the amount a tablespoon can hold) *of grated cheese over the pasta.*

tablet [MEDICINE] /'tæb.lət/ *noun* [C] a small solid piece of medicine: *a sleeping tablet* ○ *a vitamin tablet*

tablet [BLOCK] /'tæb.lət/ *noun* [C] a thin flat often square piece of a hard material such as wood, stone or metal: *The poem was engraved on a tablet of stone.* ○ UK *a tablet of soap*

'table ,tennis *noun* [U] a game which is played on a large table where two or four players hit a ball over a low net ➲See picture **Sports** on page Centre 10

tableware /'teɪ.bl̩.weəʳ/ [US] /-wer/ *noun* [U] FORMAL the knives, forks, spoons, plates, glasses, etc. used for meals

'table ,wine *noun* [C or U] a wine which is not very expensive and is of average quality

tabloid /'tæb.lɔɪd/ *noun* [C], *adj* a type of popular newspaper with small pages which has many pictures and short simple reports: *the tabloid press* ○ *a tabloid newspaper*

taboo /tə'buː/ *noun* [C], *adj plural* **taboos** (an action or word) avoided for religious or social reasons: *In this society there is a taboo* ***on/against*** *any sort of public display of affection.* ○ *For some people, death is a taboo subject.*

tachograph /'tæk.ə.græf/ /-grɑːf/ [US] /-græf/ *noun* [C] a machine inside a vehicle such as a truck which records speed, distance travelled and stopping periods, and which is used to control the driver's legal hours of work

tachometer /tæk'ɒm.ɪ.təʳ/ [US] /-'ɑː.mɪ.t̬ɚ/ *noun* [C] (INFORMAL **rev counter**) a device for measuring the rate at which something turns

tacit /'tæs.ɪt/ *adj* understood without being expressed directly: *tacit agreement/approval/support* **tacitly** /'tæs.ɪt.li/ *adv*

taciturn /'tæs.ɪ.tɜːn/ [US] /-ə.tɝːn/ *adj* saying little, especially habitually: *He's a reserved, taciturn person.*

tack [NAIL] /tæk/ *noun* [C] a small sharp nail with a flat end

tack /tæk/ *verb* [T] to fasten something to a place with tacks

▲ **tack** ***sth*** **on** *phrasal verb* [M] INFORMAL to add something that you had not planned to add, often without much preparation or thought: *At the last minute, they tacked on a couple of extra visits* ***to*** *my schedule.*

tack [SAIL] /tæk/ *noun* [C] the direction or distance which a boat moves at an angle to the direction of the wind, so that the boat receives the wind on its sails: *The ship was* ***on*** *the starboard tack.* **tack** /tæk/ *verb* [I usually + adv or prep]

tack [SEW] /tæk/ *verb* [I or T] (US ALSO **baste**) to sew with a long loose stitch which holds two pieces of material together until they are stitched more effectively

tack /tæk/ *noun* [C] a long loose stitch **tacking** /'tæk.ɪŋ/ *noun* [U]

tack [RIDING EQUIPMENT] /tæk/ *noun* [U] all the objects which the rider of a horse needs, including saddles and BRIDLES

tackle [SPORT] /'tæk.l̩/ *verb* [T] (especially in football or hockey) to try to take the ball from a player in the other team, or (in rugby or American football) to do this by taking hold of the player and causing them to fall **tackle** /'tæk.l̩/ *noun* [C]

tackle [DEAL WITH] /'tæk.l̩/ *verb* [T] to try to deal with something or someone: *There are many ways of tackling this problem.* ○ *I tackled him* ***about*** *his careless work and frequent absences.*

tackle [EQUIPMENT] /'tæk.l̩/ *noun* [U] all the objects needed for a particular activity: *fishing tackle*

tackle [SEXUAL ORGANS] /'tæk.l̩/ *noun* [U] (ALSO **wedding tackle**) UK SLANG the male sexual organs

T

tacky [STICKY] /ˈtæk.i/ *adj* sticky; (especially of paint or glue) not completely dry **tackiness** /ˈtæk.ɪ.nəs/ *noun* [U]

tacky [LOW QUALITY] /ˈtæk.i/ *adj* INFORMAL DISAPPROVING of cheap quality or in bad style: *The shop sold tacky souvenirs and ornaments.* **tackiness** /ˈtæk.ɪ.nəs/ *noun* [U]

taco /ˈtæk.əʊ/ [US] /ˈtɑː.koʊ/ *noun* [C] *plural* **tacos** a hard, folded TORTILLA (= thin flat bread) filled with meat, cheese, etc. and hot spicy sauce

tact /tækt/ *noun* [U] the ability to say or do the right thing without making anyone unhappy or angry: *He's never had much tact and people don't like his blunt manner.*

tactful /ˈtækt.fəl/ *adj* careful not to say or do anything that could upset someone: *Mentioning his baldness wasn't very tactful.* **tactfully** /ˈtækt.fəl.i/ *adv*

tactic /ˈtæk.tɪk/ *noun* [C usually pl] a planned way of doing something: *These bomb attacks represent a change of tactics by the terrorists.*

tactical /ˈtæk.tɪ.kəl/ *adj* **1** relating to tactics or done in order to achieve something: *It was a tactical vote.* **2** describes weapons that are for use over short distances and, especially in the case of nuclear weapons, have a local effect only **tactically** /ˈtæk.tɪ.kli/ *adv*

tactician /tækˈtɪʃ.ən/ *noun* [C] someone who is skilled in using tactics

ˌtactical ˈvoting *noun* [U] when people vote for a political party that they do not usually support in order to prevent another party from winning **ˌtactical ˈvote** *noun* [C]

tactics /ˈtæk.tɪks/ *plural noun* the arrangement and use of soldiers and equipment in war

tactile /ˈtæk.taɪl/ [US] /-təl/ *adj* **1** related to touch **2** If something is tactile, it has a surface which is pleasant or attractive to touch: *Her paintings have a very tactile quality.* **3** describes someone who touches other people a lot

tactless /ˈtækt.ləs/ *adj* not careful about saying or doing something that could upset someone: *It was rather tactless of you to invite his ex-girlfriend.* **tactlessly** /ˈtækt.lə.sli/ *adv* **tactlessness** /ˈtækt.lə.snəs/ *noun* [U]

tad /tæd/ *noun* INFORMAL **a tad** a little, slightly: *The fish was OK, but the chips were a tad greasy.*

tadpole /ˈtæd.pəʊl/ [US] /-poʊl/ *noun* [C] a small black creature with a large head and long tail which lives in water and develops into a frog or TOAD

taffeta /ˈtæf.ə.tə/ [US] /-ɪ.t̬ə/ *noun* [U] a stiff, shiny cloth made from silk or artificial material, used especially for dresses to be worn at special events: *a taffeta ball gown*

Taffy /ˈtæf.i/ *noun* [C] (ALSO **Taff**) UK OFFENSIVE a Welshman

TAFN, tafn INTERNET ABBREVIATION FOR that's all for now: used at the end of an email or when you finish taking part in a discussion in a CHAT ROOM

tag [SMALL PART] /tæg/ *noun* [C] a small piece of paper, cloth or metal, on which there is information, fixed onto something larger: *a **price** tag*

tag /tæg/ *verb* [T] **-gg- 1** to put a tag on something **2** SPECIALIZED to mark computer information so that you can process it later

PHRASAL VERBS WITH **tag**

▲ **tag along** *phrasal verb* INFORMAL to go somewhere with a person or group, usually when they have not asked you to go with them: *I don't know her, she just tagged along **with** us.*

▲ **tag *sth* on** *phrasal verb* (ALSO **tag *sth* onto *sth***) to add something to what you have said or written at a later time: *Tag on a couple of paragraphs about recent events.*

tag [GAME] /tæg/ *noun* [U] a game played by two or more children in which one child chases the others and tries to touch one of them. This child then becomes the one who does the chasing.

tag [GRAMMAR] /tæg/ *noun* [C] a phrase such as 'he is' or 'isn't it?', added on to a sentence for emphasis, or to turn it into a question, usually to get agreement or to check information

tagliatelle /ˌtæl.jəˈtel.i/ [US] /ˌtɑːl-/ *noun* [U] a type of pasta shaped into long thin flat pieces

t'ai chi /ˌtaɪˈtʃiː/ *noun* [U] a form of exercise involving slow movements of muscles, originally practised in China

tail [ANIMAL] /teɪl/ *noun* [C] a part of an animal's body, sticking out from the base of the back, or something similar in shape or position: *The dog wagged its tail excitedly.*

• **tail wagging the dog** when a large group has to do something to satisfy a small group

• **leave/go off, etc. with *your* tail between *your* legs** to leave, feeling ashamed and embarrassed because you have failed or made a mistake: *The losing team went off with their tails between their legs.*

-tailed /-teɪld/ *suffix* having a tail of the type mentioned: *a furry-tailed animal*

tail [FOLLOW] /teɪl/ *verb* [T] to follow and watch someone very closely, especially in order to get information secretly: *That car has been tailing me for the last 10 minutes.*

tail /teɪl/ *noun* [C] INFORMAL someone who follows another person to discover where the other person goes to, who they speak to, what they do, etc.

• **be on *sb's* tail** to follow someone closely: *That driver's been on my tail for miles.*

PHRASAL VERBS WITH **tail**

▲ **tail back** *phrasal verb* UK If traffic tails back, it forms a long line and moves very slowly or stops: *There is traffic tailing back along the motorway for ten miles because of road repairs.*

▲ **tail off** *phrasal verb* to decrease in amount or become lower in level: *His voice tailed off as he drifted into sleep.* ○ *The profits tailed off after a few years.*

tailback /ˈteɪl.bæk/ *noun* [C] MAINLY UK a line of vehicles that have stopped or are moving only very slowly, because of an accident or other problem on the road in front of them: *Yesterday there was a four-mile tailback on the main road into the city after a crash involving a truck and a car.*

tailboard /ˈteɪl.bɔːd/ [US] /-bɔːrd/ *noun* [C] (US **tailgate**) the door or board at the back of a vehicle which can be lowered for loading

tailcoat /ˈteɪl.kəʊt/ [US] /-koʊt/ *noun* [C] (ALSO **tails**) an old-fashioned type of man's coat, waist-length at the front and with the lower half of the back divided into two pieces, now only worn on very formal occasions

the ˌtail ˈend *noun* [S] the final part: *I only saw the tail end **of** the TV news.* ○ *She was at the head of the queue but I was at the tail end.*

tailgate /ˈteɪl.geɪt/ *verb* [I or T] MAINLY US DISAPPROVING to drive too closely behind the vehicle in front **tailgating** /ˈteɪl.geɪ.tɪŋ/ [US] /-t̬ɪŋ/ *noun* [U]

ˈtail ˌlight *noun* [C] US a **rear light** ⊃See picture **Car** on page Centre 12

tailor [CLOTHES MAKER] /ˈteɪ.ləʳ/ [US] /-lɚ/ *noun* [C] someone whose job is to adjust, repair and make clothes, especially someone who makes jackets, trousers, coats, etc. for men

tailored /ˈteɪ.ləd/ [US] /-lɚd/ *adj*: *a tailored* (= close-fitting) *suit*

tailor [MAKE SPECIALLY] /ˈteɪ.ləʳ/ [US] /-lɚ/ *verb* [T] to make or prepare something following particular instructions

tailor-made /ˌteɪ.ləˈmeɪd/ [US] /-lɚ-/ *adj* specially made for a particular purpose: *a tailor-made package/product/course*

• **be tailor-made for *sth*** to have all the right skills and abilities for a particular task: *It sounds as though you're tailor-made for the job.*

tailpipe /ˈteɪl.paɪp/ *noun* [C] US FOR **exhaust pipe** ⊃See picture **Car** on page Centre 12

tails [COIN SIDE] /teɪlz/ *noun* [U] the side of a coin which does not have a picture of someone's head on it

tails [JACKET] /teɪlz/ *plural noun* a **tailcoat**

tailspin /ˈteɪl.spɪn/ *noun* **1** [C usually sing] when a plane turns round and round as it falls quickly towards the ground **2** [S] when something starts to fail or lose value and gets more and more out of control: *Share prices **went into a** tailspin when the President resigned.*

T

ˈtail ˌwind *noun* [C] a wind blowing from behind a vehicle

taint /teɪnt/ *verb* [T] to spoil something, especially food or blood, by adding a harmful substance, or to spoil people's opinion of someone: *His reputation was permanently tainted by the financial scandal.* **taint** /teɪnt/ *noun* [C usually sing; U] *The enquiry cleared him of any taint* ***of*** *suspicion/dishonesty.*

take [REMOVE] /teɪk/ *verb* [T] **took, taken 1** to remove something, especially without permission: *Has anything been taken* (= stolen)*?* ○ *Here's your pen, I took it by mistake.* ○ *All possessions had been taken* ***from*** *her.* **2** to subtract a number: *If you take 4* ***from*** *12 you get 8.*

take [MOVE] /teɪk/ *verb* [T] **took, taken** to move something or someone from one place to another: *The weather forecast said rain, so take your umbrella (****with*** *you) when you go out.* ○ *The suitcases were taken* ***to*** *Madrid by mistake.* ○ *Take the book up/down to the third floor of the library.* ○ [+ two objects] *I suggested that he should take her some chocolates/take some chocolates* ***to*** *her* (= bring them to her as a present). ➲See Note **bring or take?** at **bring** TOWARDS PLACE.

take [ACCEPT] /teɪk/ *verb* [T] **took, taken 1** to accept or have: *Do they take credit cards here?* ○ *Do you take milk in your tea?* ○ *Take this medicine three times a day.* ○ *This container will take* (= has room for) *six litres.* ○ *Which newspaper do you take* (= regularly buy)*?* ○ *We're taking the bomb threats very* ***seriously****.* ○ *He continually abuses her, and she just sits there and takes it.* ○ *If you think I'm going to take that* ***lying down*** (= accept it without complaining)*, you're very much mistaken.* ○ *I take* ***the****/your* ***point*** (= accept the argument)*, but I still don't think you should have gone.* **2** used when you want to mention something as a particular example of what you are talking about: *I've been very busy recently. Take last week, I had meetings on four evenings.* **3 take to be/take for** If you take someone or something to be something, or if you take them for something, you accept or believe that they are that thing: [+ *to* infinitive] *These creatures are generally taken to be descended from primitive fishes.* ○ *I could have taken him for* (= believed that he was) *your brother.* ○ *I'm not going to forge his signature for you! What do* ***you*** *take* ***me*** *for?* (= You should not believe I could do a thing like that.)

• **can't take *sth*** to not be able to deal with an unpleasant situation: *I can't take it* ***any more****. I'm leaving.*

• **point taken** used to say you accept what someone has said

• **if you take my meaning** *UK* used to say that you have left out information or your opinion from what you have just said, but that you expect the person listening to understand it anyway: *Let's just say we had 'problems', if you take my meaning.*

• **I take it** (*ALSO* **can take it**) said if you think that what you say is likely to be true, although it is not proved: *You'll be staying the night, I take it.* ○ *So we can take it you've resigned?*

• **take it from me** (*ALSO* **take *my* word for it**) accept that what I say is true, because I know or have experienced it: *It won't work – take it from me.*

• **take it or leave it** accept or refuse the offer completely: *That's my final offer – you can take it or leave it.*

• **can take it or leave it** said about something that you quite like, but that you do not love or need strongly: *My sister's absolutely crazy about chocolate whereas I can take it or leave it.*

• **take part** to be involved in an activity with other people: *She doesn't usually take part* ***in*** *any of the class activities.*

• **Take that!** *INFORMAL* said as someone hits someone else, especially in humorous films or cartoons

• **will not take no for an answer** to not allow someone to refuse what you have offered: *I've told Steve I'm not interested, but he keeps asking me out – he won't take no for an answer.*

• **take up office** to start an official job: *The minister took up office in December.*

taker /ˈteɪ.kəʳ/ [US] /-kɚ/ *noun* **few/no/not many takers** few/no/not many people interested in what has been offered: *I put an advert in the paper to sell my bike but I haven't had any takers.*

COMMON LEARNER ERROR

take part or **take place?**

If someone **takes part in** something, they join other people in doing it.

All the children took part in the competition.

If something **takes place**, it happens.

The festival takes place every summer in the castle gardens.

---

take [HOLD] /teɪk/ *verb* [T] **took, taken** to move in order to hold something in the hand(s): *Can you take this bag while I open the door?* ○ *He took my arm and led me outside.* ○ *Take an egg and break it into the bowl.* ○ *He took* ***hold of*** *the plant's root and pulled.*

take [CATCH] /teɪk/ *verb* [T] **took, taken** to get possession of something or someone: *Rebels ambushed the train and took several prisoners.* ○ *The Liberals need just 200 more votes to take the seat from Labour.* ○ *Centre-left parties look set to take* ***power****.* ○ *Adam, I'd like you to take* ***control*** *of the aircraft now.*

take [GO WITH] /teɪk/ *verb* [T] **took, taken 1** to go somewhere with someone, often paying for them or being responsible for them: *We're taking the children* ***to*** *the zoo on Saturday.* ○ [+ *to* infinitive] *I took my elderly parents* ***to*** *look at some new houses.* ○ [+ v-*ing*] *Will you take me swimming tomorrow?* **2** to show someone how to get to somewhere by going there with them: *Let me take you* ***to*** *your room.* **3** to go to a social event with someone: *Who's taking you* ***to*** *the dance?*

take [NEED] /teɪk/ *verb* **took, taken 1** [T] to need: *Parachuting takes a lot of nerve.* ○ *I take a size five in shoes.* ○ *Transitive verbs take a direct object.* ○ [+ v-*ing*] *His story took* ***some*** *believ****ing*** (= was difficult to believe). **2** [L only + n] If something takes a particular time, that period is needed in order to complete it: *The cooking process only takes ten minutes.* ○ [+ *to* infinitive] *How long does this paint take* ***to*** *dry?* ○ [(+ obj) + n] ***It*** *took (us) all day* ***to*** *drive home.*

• **not take long** to act or happen over a short period of time: *I'm just going to the shops – I won't take long.*

• **take time** to need a long time: *Broken bones always take time to mend.*

• **take the time** to make the effort to do something: *She didn't even take the time* ***to*** *wish me good morning.*

• **take *your* time 1** said to mean that you can spend as much time as you need in doing something, or that you should slow down **2** *DISAPPROVING* to do something too slowly: *The builders are really taking their time.*

take [ACT] /teɪk/ *verb* [T] **took, taken 1** to do or perform: *The Archbishop took our service of thanksgiving.* ○ *Shelley is taking* (= studying) *economics at university.* ○ *UK Mr Marshall takes us* ***for*** (= teaches us) *physics.* **2** used with many nouns to make a verb phrase that is equal in meaning to the related verb: *I think we'll take a break* (= we'll stop for a break) *there.* ○ *If you're tired you should take a rest* (= you should rest). ○ *I always like to take a walk* (= to walk) *after lunch.*

• **take one (thing) at a time** to do or deal with one thing before starting to do or deal with another: *There are a few problems, but let's take one thing at a time.*

take [REACTION] /teɪk/ *verb* [T] **took, taken** to have or come to have a particular feeling or opinion: *He doesn't take any* ***interest in*** *his children.* ○ *Don't take any* ***notice of*** *the cameras.* ○ *She takes* ***offence*** *too easily.* ○ *They took* ***pity on*** *the stray cat and fed it.* ○ *I take* ***the view that*** *fuel should be heavily taxed to reduce road use.*

• **take *sb* unawares** (*ALSO* **take *sb* by surprise**) to surprise someone: *The sudden noise took her unawares.*

take [MONEY] /teɪk/ *verb* [T] **took, taken** to receive money from sales or as payment for entrance to an event: *The show took $100 000 in its first week.* ➲See also **takings**.

take /teɪk/ *noun* [U] *The box office take* (= money received from payments) *was huge for the new show.*

• **on the take** *US* trying to profit in a personal and usually financial way from a situation: *I honestly don't trust him*

– *he always seems to be on the take.* ➲Compare **be on the make** at **make** PRODUCE.

take [WRITE] /teɪk/ *verb* [T] **took, taken** to write: *I hope you're all taking notes.*

take [TRANSPORT] /teɪk/ *verb* [T] **took, taken** to travel somewhere by using a particular form of transport or a particular vehicle, route, etc: *I always take the train – it's less hassle than a car.* ○ *She took the 10.30 flight to Edinburgh.* ○ *If you take the road on the left, you'll come to the post office.*

take [PERFORM WELL] /teɪk/ *verb* [I] **took, taken** to work or perform as expected: *These new plants haven't taken – they don't like this dry soil.*

take [FILM] /teɪk/ *noun* [C] the filming of a SCENE (= small part of a film): *This scene of the film needed ten takes before we felt it was right.*

PHRASAL VERBS WITH **take**

▲ **take *sb* aback** *phrasal verb* to surprise or shock someone so much that they do not know how to behave for a short time: *I was a little taken aback at the directness of the question.* ○ *The news really took us aback.*

▲ **take after *sb*** *phrasal verb* to be similar to an older member of your family in appearance or character: *He takes after his mother/his mother's side of the family.*

▲ **take against *sb*** *phrasal verb UK* to begin to dislike someone: *I think she took against me when I got the promotion she wanted.*

▲ **take *sth* apart** [SEPARATE] to separate something into its different parts: *We took the engine apart to see what the problem was.*

▲ **take *sb* apart** [DEFEAT] *phrasal verb* [M] *INFORMAL* to defeat someone very easily in a sport: *He took their defence apart, scoring three goals in the first twenty minutes.*

▲ **take *sth* away** [REMOVE] *phrasal verb* [M] to remove something: *Take these chairs away – we don't need them.* ○ *Supermarkets are taking business away* ***from*** *small local shops.*

▲ **take *sth* away** [SUBTRACT] *phrasal verb* [M] to subtract a number: *Four take away two is two.* ○ *If you take 4 away* ***from*** *12 you get 8.*

▲ **take *sth* back** [SOMETHING BOUGHT] *phrasal verb* [M] to return something you have bought to a shop: *Is it too small? Take it back and get a refund.*

▲ **take *sb* back** [PARTNER] *phrasal verb* [M] to permit a partner who previously left your home because of a disagreement or another relationship to come back to live with you: *His wife said she would never take him back.*

▲ **take *sth* back** [STATEMENT] *phrasal verb* [M] to admit that something you said was wrong: *All right, I take* ***it all*** *back. It wasn't your fault.*

▲ **take *sb* back** [MEMORY] *phrasal verb* If something takes you back, it makes you remember a period or an event: *That piece of music really took me back (****to*** *my schooldays).*

▲ **take *sth* down** [WRITE] *phrasal verb* [M] to write something that another person has just said: *He took down my address and phone number and said he'd phone back.*

▲ **take *sth* down** [REMOVE] *phrasal verb* [M] to remove something that is on a wall or something that is temporary, or to remove a structure by separating its different parts: *I've taken the pictures down.*

▲ **take *sth* from *sb*** *phrasal verb* [often passive] If you take words, information or ideas from another person or piece of work, you use or develop them in some way: *The plot is taken from Shakespeare.*

▲ **take *sth* in** [UNDERSTAND] *phrasal verb* [M] to understand completely the meaning or importance of something: *I had to read the letter twice before I could take it all in.* ○ *It was an interesting exhibition, but there was too much to take in at once.*

▲ **take *sth* in** [INCLUDE] *phrasal verb* [M] to include something: *The new town takes in three former villages.*

▲ **take *sth* in** [WATCH] *phrasal verb* [M] *MAINLY US* to go to watch a film or performance, or to visit a place such as a museum: *I thought we might get something to eat and then take in a movie.*

▲ **take *sb* in** [DECEIVE] *phrasal verb* [M often passive] to cause someone to believe something which is not true, or to trick or deceive someone: *I can't believe she was taken in by him.*

▲ **take *sb* in** [CARE FOR] *phrasal verb* [M] to take care of someone and provide a place in your home for them: *Several families take in foreign students.*

▲ **take *sth* in** [CLOTHES] *phrasal verb* [M] to make a piece of clothing narrower, by changing the position of some of the stitching joining it together: *I'll have to take this dress in* ***at*** *the waist – it's too big.*

▲ **take *sth* in** [WORK] *phrasal verb* [M] to do paid work for other people, such as washing or sewing, in your home: *She supported her family by taking in laundry.*

▲ **take *sb* in** [POLICE] *phrasal verb* If the police take you in, they take you to the police station: *Detectives on the murder inquiry have taken in a new suspect for questioning.*

▲ **take *sth* off** [REMOVE] *phrasal verb* [M] to remove something, especially clothes: *He took off his clothes and got into the bath.* ○ *After the poisoning scare, the product was taken off the shelves/the market* (= removed from sale). ➲See picture **Phrasal Verbs** on page Centre 9

▲ **take off** [FLY] *phrasal verb* If an aircraft, bird or insect takes off, it leaves the ground and begins to fly: *The plane took off at 8.30 a.m.* ➲See picture **Phrasal Verbs** on page Centre 9

take-off /ˈteɪk.ɒf/ [US] /-ɑːf/ *noun* [C] *Night take-offs and landings are banned at this airport.*

▲ **take *sth* off** [NOT WORK] *phrasal verb* [M] to spend time away from your work: *He took off two weeks in September.*

▲ **take off** [SUCCEED] *phrasal verb* to suddenly start to be successful or popular: *Her singing career had just begun to take off.*

▲ **take off** [LEAVE] *phrasal verb INFORMAL* to suddenly leave somewhere, usually without telling anyone that you are going: *When he saw me, he took off in the other direction.*

▲ **take *sb* off** [COPY] *phrasal verb* [M] *UK INFORMAL* to copy the way a particular person speaks or behaves, or the way something is done, usually in order to amuse others: *She's really good at taking people off.* ➲Compare **impersonate**.

take-off /ˈteɪk.ɒf/ [US] /-ɑːf/ *noun* [C] *It was the best take-off* ***of*** *the Prime Minister that I have ever seen.*

▲ **take *sth* on** [ACCEPT] *phrasal verb* [M] to accept a particular job or responsibility: *She took too much on and made herself ill.*

▲ **take *sb* on** [EMPLOY] *phrasal verb* [M] to employ someone: *She was taken on* ***as a*** *laboratory assistant.*

▲ **take *sb* on** [FIGHT] *phrasal verb* [M] to compete against or fight someone: *The Government took on the unions and won.*

▲ **take *sth* on** [BEGIN] *phrasal verb* [M] to begin to have a particular quality: *Her voice took on a troubled tone.*

▲ **take *sth* out** [REMOVE] *phrasal verb* [M] to remove something from somewhere: *I've had a tooth taken out.*

• **take it out of *sb*** (*ALSO* **take a lot out of *sb***) to make someone very tired: *Digging in the garden certainly takes it out of me these days.*

▲ **take *sb* out** [GO WITH] *phrasal verb* [M] to go somewhere and do something with someone, usually something you plan and pay for: *Dad's taking the whole family out* ***to*** *the cinema.* ○ *Our boss took us out* ***for*** *a meal.*

▲ **take *sb/sth* out** [DESTROY] *phrasal verb* [M] *SLANG* to kill someone or destroy something: *The soldiers said that they were trying to take out the snipers.*

▲ **take *sb* out of *themselves*** *phrasal verb UK* to change someone's mood and stop them from thinking about what was making them unhappy

▲ **take *sth* out on *sb*** *phrasal verb* [M] to treat someone badly because you are upset or angry, even though they have done nothing wrong: *I know you've had a bad day, but there's no need to take it out on me!*

▲ **take *(sth)* over** [START DOING] *phrasal verb* [M] to start doing a job or being responsible for something that another person did or had responsibility for before: *He took over* ***from*** *the previous headmaster in February.* ○ *She took over* ***as*** *manager two weeks ago.* ○ *Colin Lamb has taken over responsibility for this project.*

▲ **take *(sth)* over** [GET CONTROL] *phrasal verb* [M] to get control of a company by buying most of its SHARES (= the

T

equal parts into which the ownership of the company is divided): *The company he works for has recently been taken over.*
takeover /ˈteɪkˌəʊ.vəʳ/ [US] /-ˌoʊ.vɚ/ *noun* [C] *They were involved in a takeover last year.*
• **make a takeover bid for *sth*** to try to obtain control of something: *The company made a takeover bid for a rival firm.*
▲ **take *sb* round *(sth/somewhere)*** *phrasal verb* to walk through a building or visit a place with someone, showing them the most interesting or important parts: *You will be taken round the museum by one of the guides.*
▲ **take *sb* through *sth*** *phrasal verb* to explain something to someone: *I'll take you through it one more time, then you can try it yourself.*
▲ **take to *sb/sth*** [LIKE] *phrasal verb* to start to like someone or something: *His wife took to her new neighbours at once.* ○ *She's taken to tennis* ***like a duck to water*** (= she likes it and is good at it).
▲ **take to *sth*** [DO] *phrasal verb* to start doing something habitually: *She was so depressed she took to drink.* ○ [+ v-ing] *He's taken to staying out very late.*
▲ **take to *somewhere*** [GO] *phrasal verb* to go somewhere, usually because you are in a difficult or dangerous situation: *The refugees took to the hills for safety.*
▲ **take *sth* up** [START] *phrasal verb* [M] to start doing a particular job or activity: *He's taken up the post of supervisor.* ○ [+ v-ing] *Have you ever thought of taking up acting?* ○ *Ian took up* (= continued) *the story where Sue had left off.*
▲ **take *sth* up** [FILL] *phrasal verb* [M] to fill an amount of space or time: *This desk takes up too much room.* ○ *Too much of this report is taken up* ***with*** *out-of-date figures.*
▲ **take *sth* up** [DISCUSS] *phrasal verb* [M] to discuss something or deal with something: *The school took the matter up* ***with*** *the police.* ○ UK *I'd like to take you up* ***on*** *your sales figures for June.* ○ *A leading law firm took up his case.*
▲ **take *sth* up** [CLOTHING] *phrasal verb* to shorten a piece of clothing, such as a skirt or trousers
▲ **take *sb* up on *sth*** *phrasal verb* to accept an offer that someone has made: *Could I take you up on that offer of a lift, Rob?*
▲ **take up with *sb*** *phrasal verb* to become friendly or start a relationship with someone, especially someone who might have a bad influence on you: *She's taken up with a strange crowd of people.*

takeaway UK /ˈteɪk.ə.weɪ/ *noun* [C] (US **takeout**) a meal cooked and bought at a shop or restaurant but taken somewhere else, often home, to be eaten, or the shop or restaurant itself: *a Chinese takeaway*

take-home pay /ˈteɪk.həʊmˌpeɪ/ [US] /-hoʊm-/ *noun* [U] the amount of earnings that you have left after tax, etc.

taken [TAKE] /ˈteɪ.kᵊn/ *past participle of* **take**

taken [GIVING RESPECT] /ˈteɪ.kᵊn/ *adj* **taken with/by *sth*** believing something to be deserving of respect or admiration: *The committee was very taken with your proposals.*

takeout /ˈteɪk.aʊt/ *noun* [C or U] US **takeaway**

take-up /ˈteɪk.ʌp/ *noun* [S] how much people start to use or accept a service, or sometimes a product, that has become available to them: *We are calling for government action to improve the take-up of state benefits.*

takings /ˈteɪ.kɪŋz/ *plural noun* all the money that a business gets from selling things: *Our takings were down this week because the weather was so bad.*

talcum powder /ˈtæl.kəmˌpaʊ.dəʳ/ [US] /-dɚ/ *noun* [C or U] (ALSO **talc**) a powder, usually having a pleasant smell, put on the skin to make it feel smooth or to help it stay dry

tale /teɪl/ *noun* [C] a story, especially one which might be invented or difficult to believe: *He* ***told*** *some fascinating tales about his life in India.* ○ *She told me/invented/concocted a tale about missing the bus to explain her lateness.*
• **tale of woe** a report of the bad things that have happened: *I asked how he was and he gave me a real tale of woe.*

the Taliban /ðəˈtæl.ɪ.bæn/ *noun* [S] a Muslim political and military organization, with very traditional ideas about society and women, who took power in Afghanistan in the 1990s

talent /ˈtæl.ᵊnt/ *noun* **1** [C or U] (someone who has) a natural ability to be good at something, especially without being taught: *Her talent* ***for*** *music showed at an early age.* ○ *His artistic talents were wasted in his boring job.* **2** [U] UK SLANG MAINLY HUMOROUS people who are sexually attractive: *There was plenty of talent at the party last night.* **talented** /ˈtæl.ᵊn.tɪd/ [US] /-t̬ɪd/ *adj*: *a talented footballer/pianist* **talentless** /ˈtæl.ᵊnt.ləs/ *adj*

ˈtalent ˌcontest *noun* [C] an event in which people compete to show who is the most skilled, especially at being entertaining

ˈtalent ˌscout *noun* [C] someone who looks for people who have the skills they want, especially in entertainment or sport

talisman /ˈtæl.ɪz.mən/ *noun* [C] *plural* **talismans** an object believed to bring good luck or to keep its owner safe from harm

talk /tɔːk/ [US] /tɑːk/ *verb* [I] to say words aloud; to speak to someone: *We were just talking* ***about*** *Simon's new girlfriend.* ○ *My little girl has just started to talk.* ○ *She talks* ***to*** *her mother on the phone every week.*
• **talk business/politics, etc.** to discuss a particular subject: *Whenever they're together, they talk politics.*
• **talk about ...** INFORMAL used to emphasize that something is very noticeable in the stated way: *What a film – talk about boring!*
• **talk a blue streak** US INFORMAL to talk quickly and without stopping: *He talked a blue streak all through breakfast.*
• **talk dirty** INFORMAL to describe sexual acts to another person using rude words
• **talk *sb's* head off** INFORMAL to talk to someone for a long time, usually loudly: *She talked my head off.*
• **talk the hind leg(s) off a donkey** UK INFORMAL to talk without stopping for a long time
• **talk nonsense** (UK ALSO **talk rubbish**) to talk without making sense: *Is it just me or was she talking nonsense in the meeting?*
• **talking of *sb/sth*** (ALSO **speaking of *sb/sth***) while we are talking about a particular person or thing: *Talking of John, I saw a friend of his last week.*
• **talk sense** to speak in a reasonable way: *Why don't you talk sense!*
• **talk shop** to talk about your job with those you work with when not at work: *Even at a party they have to talk shop!*
• **talk through *your* hat** INFORMAL to talk about something without understanding what you are talking about: *Nothing of what he said made sense – he was talking through his hat.*
• **talk turkey** US INFORMAL to discuss something honestly and directly
• **Look who's talking!** (ALSO **You're a fine one to talk!**, ALSO **You can/can't talk!**, US ALSO **You should talk!**) INFORMAL something you say when someone criticises you for something that they do themselves: *I'm lazy? You're a fine one to talk!*
• **give *sb* something to talk about** (UK **set *sb* talking**) to provide someone with an interesting subject to discuss: *Our new car will give the neighbours something to talk about.*

talk /tɔːk/ [US] /tɑːk/ *noun* **1** [C] a conversation between two people, often about a particular subject: *I asked him to* ***have*** *a talk* ***with*** *his mother* ***about*** *his plan.* **2** [C] when someone speaks to a group of people about a particular subject: *He* ***gave*** *a talk* ***about/on*** *his visit to America.* **3** [U] when people talk about what might happen or be true, or the subject people are talking about: *Talk won't get us anywhere.* ○ ***The*** *talk/Her talk was all about the wedding.*
• **be the talk of *somewhere*** to be what people are discussing in a particular place: *Her behaviour is the talk of the neighbourhood/office.*
• **be the talk of the town** to be what everyone is talking about: *The new statue in the park is the talk of the town.*
• **all talk (and no action)** (ALSO **just talk**) used to mean that someone talks about doing something, but never does it:

She's all talk when it comes to doing something about the problem.
talker /ˈtɔː.kəʳ/ (US) /ˈtɑː.kɚ/ *noun* [C] a person who talks a lot, too much or in a particular way: *I'm afraid he's more of a talker than a doer, which is why he never finishes anything.* ○ *What a talker your mum is – I couldn't get off the phone!*
talks /tɔːks/ (US) /tɑːks/ *plural noun* serious and formal discussions on an important subject usually intended to produce decisions or agreements: *Talks were* ***held*** *in Madrid* ***about*** *the fuel crisis.*

COMMON LEARNER ERROR

talking about something

When you are **talking about** a particular subject, remember to use the preposition 'about'.

I didn't know what to talk about.
~~*I didn't know what to talk.*~~

COMMON LEARNER ERROR

speak a language or **talk a language?**

Remember that you **speak** a language. You do not **talk** it.

She speaks excellent French.
~~*She talks excellent French.*~~

PHRASAL VERBS WITH **talk**

▲ **talk at** ***sb*** *phrasal verb* to speak to someone without listening to them or allowing them to speak: *What discussion? You weren't talking to me, you were talking at me!*
▲ **talk back** *phrasal verb* If a child talks back, they reply rudely to someone they should be polite to: *Children who talk back are regarded as cheeky and disrespectful.*
▲ **talk** ***sth*** **down** [REDUCE] *phrasal verb* [M] to talk about something in a way that makes it seem less important or less serious than it really is: *He began his lecture by talking down the initiatives of a rival company.*
▲ **talk** ***sb*** **down** [PREVENT] *phrasal verb* [M] to speak loudly or without stopping to prevent someone else from speaking: *I tried to explain, but he just talked me down.*
▲ **talk** ***sb*** **down** [PERSUADE] *phrasal verb* [M] to persuade someone who is threatening to kill themselves not to jump from a high place: *The policeman talked the girl down after she had been on the roof for two hours.*
▲ **talk down to** ***sb*** *phrasal verb* to talk to someone as if they were less intelligent than you or not important: *I wish politicians wouldn't talk down to us as if we were idiots.*
▲ **talk** ***sb*** **into** ***sth*** *phrasal verb* to persuade someone to do something: *He's against the idea, but I think I can talk him into* ***it***.
▲ **talk** ***sth*** **out** *phrasal verb* [M] to discuss something such as a problem or plan completely in order to find a solution or an agreement: *If you two don't talk out the differences between you, it'll be very difficult for you to continue working together.*
▲ **talk** ***sb*** **out of** ***sth*** *phrasal verb* to persuade someone not to do something: [+ v-*ing*] *With some difficulty, he was able to talk his way out of pay****ing*** *the fine.*
▲ **talk** ***sth*** **over** *phrasal verb* [M] to discuss a problem or situation with someone, often to find out their opinion or to get advice before making a decision about it: *I'd like to talk it over* ***with*** *my wife first.*
▲ **talk** ***sb*** **round** [PERSUADE] *phrasal verb* UK to persuade someone to agree with you or to do what you want them to do: *She's not keen on the idea but we think we can talk her round.*
▲ **talk round/around** ***sth*** [SPEAK INDIRECTLY] *phrasal verb* to avoid speaking directly about something: *I felt that he just talked round the subject and didn't tackle the main issues.*
▲ **talk** ***sth*** **up** *phrasal verb* [M] to speak with enthusiasm about something: *If we talk up the event, people will surely come.*

talkative /ˈtɔː.kə.tɪv/ (US) /ˈtɑː.kə.t̬ɪv/ *adj* talking a lot: *She's a lively, talkative person.*

talkback /ˈtɔːk.bæk/ (US) /ˈtɑːk-/ *noun* [C] AUS a radio programme in which listeners use telephones to take part
talkie /ˈtɔː.ki/ (US) /ˈtɑː-/ *noun* [C] OLD USE a cinema film with speech and sound made during the period when most films were silent ➲Compare **silent film**.
ˌtalking ˈbook *noun* [C] a spoken recording of a book, used especially by blind people
ˈtalking ˌpoint *noun* [C] something which encourages discussion
talking-to /ˈtɔː.kɪŋ.tuː/ (US) /ˈtɑː-/ *noun* [C usually sing] INFORMAL a severe talk with someone who has done something wrong: *I* ***gave*** *her a good talking-to* ***about*** *doing her homework on time.*
ˈtalk ˌshow *noun* [C] US a radio or television programme on which famous guests are asked questions about themselves, or members of the public discuss a particular subject: *Radio talk shows have been besieged with callers expressing outrage on the subject.*
tall /tɔːl/ (US) /tɑːl/ *adj* of more than average height, or of a particular height: *a tall girl* ○ *a tall building* ○ *He's six feet tall.* ○ *She's much taller* ***than*** *me.*
• **stand/walk tall** to act with pride and confidence: *You'd have more chance of success if you'd stand tall.*
• **be a tall order** to be something which is difficult to do: *Getting the essay done on time will be a tall order.*
tallish /ˈtɔː.lɪʃ/ (US) /ˈtɑː-/ *adj* quite tall: *He's tallish, with fair hair and glasses.* **tallness** /ˈtɔːl.nəs/ (US) /ˈtɑːl-/ *noun* [U]
tallow /ˈtæl.əʊ/ (US) /-oʊ/ *noun* [U] fat from animals which is used for making soap and, especially in the past, candles
ˌtall ˈstory *noun* [C usually sing] a story or fact which is difficult to believe: *After dinner she told me a tall story about her pet.*
tally [AGREE] /ˈtæl.i/ *verb* [I] to match or agree with something else: *Our figures don't tally – you've made it twenty pounds more than me.* ○ *Your plans don't tally* ***with*** *mine.*
tally [COUNT] /ˈtæl.i/ *noun* [C usually sing] SLIGHTLY OLD-FASHIONED a record or count of a number of items: *Will you* ***keep a*** *tally* ***of*** *the number of customers going in and out?*
▲ **tally (*sth*) up** *phrasal verb* [M] SLIGHTLY OLD-FASHIONED INFORMAL to calculate something: *If the game's over I'll tally up.*
tally-ho /ˌtæl.iˈhəʊ/ (US) /-ˈhoʊ/ *exclamation* a shout made by a hunter who sees a fox
tally-room /ˈtæl.iˌruːm/ /-ˌrʊm/ *noun* [C usually sing] AUS a room in which votes are collected after an election
the Talmud /ðəˈtæl.mʊd/ (US) /-ˈtɑːl-/ *noun* [S] the collection of ancient Jewish laws and tradition for religious and social matters **Talmudic** /tælˈmʊd.ɪk/ (US) /tɑːl-/ *adj*
talon /ˈtæl.ən/ *noun* [C] a sharp nail on the foot of a bird which it uses when hunting animals
tamarind /ˈtæm.ᵊr.ɪnd/ (US) /-ɚ.ɪnd/ *noun* [C or U] (fruit of) a type of tropical tree
tambourine /ˌtæm.bəˈriːn/ *noun* [C] a small musical instrument, consisting of a circular wooden frame with metal discs loosely fixed to it and sometimes having plastic stretched across one side of it, which is shaken or hit with the hand
tame [NOT FIERCE] /teɪm/ *adj* (especially of animals) not wild or fierce, either naturally or because of training or long involvement with humans: *After a few months contact the monkeys became very tame.*
tame /teɪm/ *verb* [T] **1** to make a wild animal tame **2** to control something fierce or powerful: *He'll need to tame his temper if he wants to succeed.* **tameable** /ˈteɪ.mə.bl̩/ *adj*
tamer /ˈteɪ.məʳ/ (US) /-mɚ/ *noun* [C] someone who tames something that is wild, especially an animal: *a lion-tamer*
tame [NOT EXCITING] /teɪm/ *adj* DISAPPROVING not interesting or exciting: *It was a tame film in comparison to some that she's made.*
tamp /tæmp/ *verb* [T] to press something such as earth or tobacco down firmly
Tampax /ˈtæm.pæks/ *noun* [C] TRADEMARK a type of TAMPON

tamper /'tæm.pəʳ/ ⓤ /-pɚ/ *verb*
▲ **tamper with** *sth phrasal verb* to touch or make changes to something which you should not, usually without enough knowledge of how it works or when you are trying to damage it: *I could see at once that the lock had been tampered with.*

tampon /'tæm.pɒn/ ⓤ /-pɑːn/ *noun* [C] a small cylinder of cotton or other material which a woman puts in her vagina to absorb blood during her period

tan COLOUR /tæn/ *noun* [C] (*ALSO* **suntan**) when your skin is brown from being in the sun: *a deep tan* **tan** /tæn/ *verb* [I or T] -**nn**- *Her skin tans very quickly in the summer.* ○ *Tanned workmen were sitting around the dock.*
tan /tæn/ *noun* [U], *adj* (a) pale, yellowish brown

tan LEATHER /tæn/ *verb* [T] -**nn**- to change animal skin into leather using special chemicals such as TANNIN
• **tan sb's hide** (*UK ALSO* **tan the hide off** *sb*) to beat someone: *I'll tan his hide if I catch him.*
tanner /'tæn.əʳ/ ⓤ /-ɚ/ *noun* [C] a person who tans leather

tan TRIANGLE /tæn/ *WRITTEN ABBREVIATION FOR* **tangent** TRIANGLE

tandem /'tæn.dəm/ *noun* [C] a bicycle made for two people who sit one behind the other **tandem** /'tæn.dəm/ *adv*: *riding tandem*
• **in tandem 1** at the same time: *The heart and lungs will be transplanted in tandem.* **2** If two pieces of equipment, people, etc. are working 'in tandem' they are working together, especially well or closely: *I want these two groups to work/operate in tandem on this project.*

tandoori /tæn'dʊə.ri/ ⓤ /tɑːn'dʊr.i/ *noun* [U] a particular Indian method of cooking food in a clay cooker: *tandoori chicken*

tang /tæŋ/ *noun* [S] a strong sharp taste or smell: *the tang of the sea air*
tangy /'tæŋ.i/ *adj* A tangy flavour is pleasantly strong and sharp: *a deliciously tangy lemon tart*

tangent CIRCLE /'tæn.dʒ³nt/ *noun* [C] a straight line which touches but does not cut into a curve
• **go/fly off at a tangent** *UK* (*US* **go off on a tangent**) to suddenly start talking or thinking about a completely new subject: *It's hard to get a firm decision out of him – he's always going off at a tangent.* **tangential** /tæn-'dʒen.tʃ³l/ *adj*

tangent TRIANGLE /'tæn.dʒ³nt/ *noun* [C] (*WRITTEN ABBREVIATION* **tan**) *SPECIALIZED* (in a triangle that has one angle of 90°) the ratio of the length of the side opposite an angle less than 90° divided by the length of the shorter of the two sides that are next to the angle ⊃Compare **cosine**; **sine**.

tangerine /ˌtæn.dʒəˈriːn/ ⓤ /'---/ *noun* [C] a fruit like a small orange with a loose skin
tangerine /ˌtæn.dʒəˈriːn/ ⓤ /'---/ *noun* [U], *adj* (a) dark orange colour

tangible /'tæn.dʒə.bl̩/ *adj* real or not imaginary; able to be shown, touched or experienced: *We need tangible evidence if we're going to take legal action.* ○ *Other tangible benefits include an increase in salary and shorter working hours.* **tangibly** /'tæn.dʒə.bli/ *adv*

tangle /'tæŋ.gl̩/ *noun* [C] an untidy mass of things that are not in a state of order, or a state of confusion or difficulty: *a tangle of wires* **tangle** /'tæŋ.gl̩/ *verb* [I or T] ⊃See also **entangle**. **tangled** /'tæŋ.gl̩d/ *adj*: *tangled string*
▲ **tangle with** *sb phrasal verb INFORMAL* to become involved in an argument, usually by arguing or fighting with them: *He was a self-opinionated, overbearing tyrant, and he was the last man she should want to tangle with.*

tango /'tæŋ.gəʊ/ ⓤ /-goʊ/ *noun* [C] *plural* **tangos** an energetic dance of South American origin for two people, or the music for this dance **tango** /'tæŋ.gəʊ/ ⓤ /-goʊ/ *verb* [I] **tangoed, tangoed**

tangy /'tæŋ.i/ *adj* ⊃See at **tang**.

tank CONTAINER /tæŋk/ *noun* [C] a container which holds liquid or gas: *a water tank* ○ *a fuel/petrol tank*
tankful /'tæŋk.fʊl/ *noun* [C] the amount that can be held by a tank

tank VEHICLE /tæŋk/ *noun* [C] a large military fighting vehicle built to protect those inside it from attack,

which is driven by wheels which turn inside moving metal belts

tankard /'tæŋ.kəd/ ⓤ /-kɚd/ *noun* [C] a large usually metal drinking cup with sloping sides and a handle and sometimes a lid, mainly used for drinking beer

tanked up /ˌtæŋktˈʌp/ *adj INFORMAL* drunk

tanker /'tæŋ.kəʳ/ ⓤ /-kɚ/ *noun* [C] a ship or vehicle which is built to carry liquid or gas: *an oil tanker* ⊃See pictures **Cars and Trucks** on page Centre 13, **Planes, Ships and Boats** on page Centre 14

tankini /ˌtæŋˈkiːni/ *noun* [C] a two-piece SWIMMING COSTUME for women in which the top part covers the whole of the chest and a large part of the back

tank top *noun* [C] a piece of clothing that covers the upper part of the body but not the arms, and usually has a U-shaped opening at the neck

tannery /'tæn.³r.i/ ⓤ /-ɚ-/ *noun* [C] the place where leather is made

tannin /'tæn.ɪn/ *noun* [C or U] (*ALSO* **tannic acid**) (one of) a group of chemicals which are found in plant cells, especially in leaves, bark, and fruit which is not ripe

Tannoy /'tæn.ɔɪ/ *noun* [C *usually sing*] *UK TRADEMARK* a system of equipment which is used for making speech loud enough for a large number of people to hear, especially in order to give information

tantalize, *UK USUALLY* -**ise** /'tæn.t³l.aɪz/ ⓤ /-t̬ə.laɪz/ *verb* [T] to excite or attract someone by an offer or a suggestion of something which is, in fact, unlikely to happen
tantalizing, *UK USUALLY* **tantalising** /'tæn.tə.laɪ.zɪŋ/ ⓤ /-t̬ə-/ *adj* describes something that causes desire and excitement in you, but which is unlikely to provide a way of satisfying that desire: *I caught a tantalizing glimpse of the sparkling blue sea through the trees.* **tantalizingly**, *UK USUALLY* **tantalisingly** /'tæn.tə.laɪ.zɪŋ.li/ ⓤ /-t̬ə-/ *adv*

tantamount /'tæn.tə.maʊnt/ ⓤ /-t̬ə-/ *adj SLIGHTLY FORMAL* **tantamount to** being almost the same or having the same effect as, usually something bad: *Her refusal to answer was tantamount to an admission of guilt.*

tantrum /'tæn.trəm/ *noun* [C] a sudden period of uncontrolled childish anger: *Johnny had/threw a tantrum in the shop because I wouldn't buy him any sweets.* ○ *If she doesn't get her own way she has temper tantrums.*

Taoiseach /'tiː.ʃək/ *noun* [C] the leader of the government of the Republic of Ireland

Taoism, **Daoism** /'taʊ.ɪ.z³m/ ⓤ /'daʊ.ɪ-/ *noun* [U] a religion developed originally in ancient China which emphasizes a simple and natural life **Taoist** /'taʊ.ɪst/ *adj, noun* [C] *a Taoist temple* ○ *Taoist philosophy*

tap DEVICE /tæp/ *noun* [C] **1** *UK* (*US* **faucet**) a device that controls the flow of liquid, especially water, from a pipe: *the hot/cold tap* ○ *turn the tap on/off* ⊃See picture **In the Kitchen** on page Centre 16 **2** *UK* a device that controls the flow of gas from a pipe
• **on tap 1** describes beer which is served from a barrel through a tap **2** available for use at any time: *Working in a library as I do, I have all this information on tap.*

tap HIT /tæp/ *verb* [I or T] -**pp**- to hit something gently, and often repeatedly, especially making short sharp noises: *The branches tapped against the window.* ○ *I could hear him tapping his fingers on the desk.* ○ *I was tapping my feet (= hitting the floor gently with my feet) to the music.* ○ *Someone tapped me on the shoulder.* **tap** /tæp/ *noun* [C]

tap OBTAIN /tæp/ *verb* [T] -**pp**- to obtain or make use of something: *For more than a century, Eastern cities have expanded their water supplies by tapping ever more remote sources.* ○ *There is a rich vein of literary talent here just waiting to be tapped (into) by publishers.*
▲ **tap sb for** *sth phrasal verb OLD-FASHIONED INFORMAL* to get money from someone: *I might be able to tap my father for a loan.*

tap TELEPHONE /tæp/ *verb* [T] -**pp**- to use a small device fixed to a telephone in order to listen secretly to what people are saying: *He suspected that his telephone had been tapped.* **tap** /tæp/ *noun* [C] *He claims that he knew nothing of government phone taps on journalists during those years.*

tapas /'tæp.əs/ *plural noun* small amounts of Spanish food that are served, especially with alcoholic drinks, in Spanish bars and restaurants: *a tapas **bar***

tap (,**dancing**) *noun* [U] a type of dance in which the rhythm is marked by the noise of the dancer's shoes on the floor: *I did tap classes as well as ballet.* '**tap** ,**dance** *noun* [C or U] '**tap** ,**dancer** *noun* [C]

tape STRIP /teɪp/ *noun* [C or U] a long narrow strip of material which is sometimes sticky on one side: *UK sticky tape*
• **the (finishing) tape** a tape stretched across the finishing line of a race which the winner breaks as they finish ⊃See picture **Sports** on page Centre 10
tape /teɪp/ *verb* [T] to use strips of sticky material, especially to fix two things together or to fasten a parcel: *She taped a note to the door.*

tape RECORD /teɪp/ *noun* [C or U] thin plastic in a long narrow strip with a magnetic covering which allows sounds or sounds and pictures to be recorded and played again, or a CASSETTE, especially one on which sound is (to be) recorded: *magnetic tape* ○ *I've got that film **on** tape* (= recorded) *if you want to borrow it.* ○ *If you give me a **blank** tape I'll record it for you.*
tape /teɪp/ *verb* [T] to record something on tape
• **have *sb* taped** (*ALSO* **have** *sb* **on tape**) *UK INFORMAL* to know about and be able to deal with a person or situation

'**tape** ,**deck** *noun* [C] a machine which is used for playing and recording sound, often as a part of a set of electronic equipment on which music is played

'**tape** ,**measure** *noun* [C] a strip of plastic or bendable metal with measurements marked on it which is used for measuring ⊃Compare **ruler** at **rule** DRAW.

taper BECOME NARROW /'teɪ.pə^r/ US /-pə-/ *verb* [I or T] to become gradually narrower at one end, or to make something do this: *Turn left where the road tapers (off) into a track.* **tapering** /'teɪ.pə.rɪŋ/ US /-pə-/ *adj*
▲ **taper off** *phrasal verb* to become gradually smaller or less frequent: *Her voice tapered off as she realized everyone was listening.* ○ *Sales have gradually tapered off.*

taper CANDLE /'teɪ.pə^r/ US /-pə-/ *noun* [C] a very thin candle, or a long thin piece of string covered in wax or a very thin strip of wood used especially in the past for lighting candles, fires, etc.

'**tape re,corder** *noun* [C] a machine which is used for playing and recording sound, usually one which is light and small enough to be carried

tapestry /'tæp.ɪ.stri/ *noun* [C] a piece of cloth whose pattern or picture is created by sewing or weaving different coloured threads onto a special type of strong cloth

tapeworm /'teɪp.wɜːm/ US /-wɜːm/ *noun* [C] a long flat PARASITE (= organism which lives in another from which it obtains its food) which lives inside the bowels of humans and other animals

tapioca /,tæp.i'əʊ.kə/ US /-'oʊ-/ *noun* [U] small hard pieces of the dried and crushed root of the CASSAVA plant, usually cooked with milk and sugar to make a sweet food: *tapioca pudding*

tappet /'tæp.ɪt/ *noun* [C] a part of a machine which causes another part to move by hitting it

'**tap** ,**water** *noun* [U] the water which comes out of the taps in a building, which are usually connected to the main supply of the local water system

tar /tɑː^r/ US /tɑːr/ *noun* [U] **1** a black substance, sticky when hot, used especially for making roads **2** one of the poisonous substances found in tobacco: *a low tar cigarette*
• **beat/knock/whale the tar out of *sb*** *US INFORMAL* to hit someone forcefully and repeatedly: *The boxer knocked the tar out of his opponent.*
tar /tɑː^r/ US /tɑːr/ *verb* [T] **-rr-** to put tar on a surface
• **tar and feather *sb*** to cover someone in tar and feathers as a punishment
• **tar *sb* with the same brush** to think that someone has the same bad qualities as another person: *Because they worked so closely in the same department, John was tarred with the same brush as Tim.*

taramasalata /,tær.ə.mə.sə'lɑː.tə/ US /,tɑːr.ə.mə.sə-'lɑː.t̬ə/ *noun* [U] a pale pink food, originally from Greece, which is made mainly from a mixture of fish eggs, bread and oil

tarantula /tə'ræn.tjʊ.lə/ *noun* [C] any of various large hairy spiders, some of which have a poisonous bite

tardy /'tɑː.di/ US /'tɑːr-/ *adj FORMAL* slow or late in happening or arriving: *Dinner was somewhat delayed on account of David's rather tardy arrival.* **tardiness** /'tɑː.dɪ.nəs/ US /'tɑːr-/ *noun* [U]

target OBJECT FIRED AT /'tɑː.gɪt/ US /'tɑːr-/ *noun* [C] an object fired at during shooting practice, often a circle with a pattern of rings, or any object or place at which bullets, bombs, etc. are aimed: *I had four shots but I didn't even **hit** the target.* ○ *Any major airport or station is potentially a **terrorist** target.* ⊃See picture **Sports** on page Centre 10
• **on target** If you are on target with a piece of work, you are advancing well and likely to achieve what you planned. **target** /'tɑː.gɪt/ US /'tɑːr-/ *verb* [T] *It is hoped that civilians will not be targeted during the war.*

target PERSON/GROUP /'tɑː.gɪt/ US /'tɑːr-/ *noun* [C usually sing] **1** a person or a particular group of people at whom something is directed, or for whom it is intended: *The target audience **for** the TV series are young people aged 13 to 18.* **2** one or more people who are criticized or laughed at, or who experience unpleasant treatment from others: *Recently she has been the target **of** a series of obscene phone calls.*
target /'tɑː.gɪt/ US /'tɑːr-/ *verb* [T] to direct advertising, criticism or a product at someone: *The paper is targeted specifically **at** young people.*

target AIM /'tɑː.gɪt/ US /'tɑːr-/ *noun* [C] a level or situation which you intend to achieve: *The government's target of 3.5% annual growth seems easily attainable.*

'**target** ,**language** *noun* [C usually sing] *SPECIALIZED* a language that you are changing spoken or written words into

tariff /'tær.ɪf/ *noun* [C] a charge or list of charges either for services or on goods entering a country

tarmac /'tɑː.mæk/ US /'tɑːr-/ *noun* [S or U] (*ALSO* **tarmacadam**) *TRADEMARK* (an area of) black material used for building roads, etc., which consists of TAR mixed with small stones
the tarmac *noun* [S or U] an area covered in tarmac, especially the area in an airport where aircraft land and take off **tarmac** /'tɑː.mæk/ US /'tɑːr-/ *verb* [T] **tarmacking, tarmacked, tarmacked** *UK*

tarn /tɑːn/ US /tɑːrn/ *noun* [C] a small mountain lake

tarnish METAL /'tɑː.nɪʃ/ US /'tɑːr-/ *verb* [I or T] to make or (especially of metal) become less bright or a different colour **tarnished** /'tɑː.nɪʃt/ US /'tɑːr-/ *adj*

tarnish REPUTATION /'tɑː.nɪʃ/ US /'tɑːr-/ *verb* [T] to spoil the reputation of someone or something: *By this time a series of scandals had severely tarnished the leader's image/reputation.* **tarnished** /'tɑː.nɪʃt/ US /'tɑːr-/ *adj*

taro /'tær.əʊ/ US /-oʊ/ *noun* [C] *plural* **taros** a tropical plant which has a root that is cooked and eaten

tarot /'tær.əʊ/ US /-oʊ/ *noun* [S or U] a set of 78 cards, used for trying to find out what will happen to someone in the future

tarpaulin /tɑː'pɔː.lɪn/ US /tɑːr'pɑː-/ *noun* [C or U] (*US USUALLY* **tarp**) (a large piece of) heavy waterproof cloth used as a covering

tarragon /'tær.ə.gən/ US /-gɑːn/ *noun* [U] a plant with whitish flowers whose narrow leaves are used in cooking as a herb which has a taste similar to LIQUORICE

tarry /'tær.i/ *verb* [I] *OLD USE* to stay somewhere for longer than expected and delay leaving

tart FOOD /tɑːt/ US /tɑːrt/ *noun* [C or U] an open pastry case with a filling, usually of something sweet such as fruit: *apple/strawberry/custard tart*

tart SOUR /tɑːt/ US /tɑːrt/ *adj* (especially of fruit) tasting sour or acidic: *You might need some sugar on the rhubarb – it's a bit tart.* **tartness** /'tɑːt.nəs/ US /'tɑːrt-/ *noun* [U]

tart BEHAVIOUR /tɑːt/ US /tɑːrt/ *adj* (especially of a way of speaking) quick or sharp and unpleasant: *a tart* *remark/comment/reply* **tartly** /ˈtɑːt.li/ [US] /ˈtɑːrt-/ *adv*: *'You don't seem to appreciate the situation,' she said tartly.* **tartness** /ˈtɑːt.nəs/ [US] /ˈtɑːrt-/ *noun* [U]

tart [WOMAN] /tɑːt/ [US] /tɑːrt/ *noun* [C] **1** *VERY INFORMAL DISAPPROVING* a woman who intentionally wears the type of clothes and make-up that attract sexual attention in a way that is too obvious **2** *OLD-FASHIONED SLANG* a female PROSTITUTE

tarty /ˈtɑː.ti/ [US] /ˈtɑːr.ţi/ *adj INFORMAL DISAPPROVING* intentionally attracting sexual attention in a way that is too obvious: *I always think short skirts and high heels look a bit tarty.*

tart /tɑːt/ [US] /tɑːrt/ *verb*

PHRASAL VERBS WITH **tart**

▲ **tart *yourself* up** [PERSON] *phrasal verb* [R] *UK INFORMAL DISAPPROVING OR HUMOROUS* to try to make yourself look more attractive by putting on make-up, jewellery and fashionable clothes: *She's still in the bathroom, tarting herself up.*

▲ **tart *sth* up** [THING] *phrasal verb UK INFORMAL OFTEN DISAPPROVING* to make something look more attractive or decorative, usually by making very quick or very obvious changes: *He made his money by tarting up slum houses and selling them at a huge profit.*

tartan /ˈtɑː.tᵊn/ [US] /ˈtɑːr.ţᵊn/ *noun* [C or U] a pattern of different coloured straight lines crossing each other at 90 degree angles, or a cloth with this pattern: *a tartan kilt*

tartar [SUBSTANCE] /ˈtɑː.təʳ/ [US] /ˈtɑːr.ţɚ/ *noun* [U] a hard substance which forms on the teeth

tartar [PERSON] /ˈtɑː.təʳ/ [US] /ˈtɑːr.ţɚ/ *noun* [C] *OLD-FASHIONED DISAPPROVING* a person with a fierce, severe manner

tartaric acid /tɑːˌtær.ɪkˈæs.ɪd/ [US] /tɑːr-/ *noun* [U] an acidic substance which is found in many plants and fruits and is used to make CREAM OF TARTAR

ˈtartar ˌsauce *noun* [U] a cold white sauce containing small pieces of herbs and vegetables, usually eaten with fish

task [WORK] /tɑːsk/ [US] /tæsk/ *noun* [C] a piece of work to be done, especially one done regularly, unwillingly or with difficulty: *We usually ask interviewees to **perform** a few simple tasks on the computer just to test their aptitude.* ○ *The government now faces the **daunting** task of restructuring the entire health service.*

task /tɑːsk/ [US] /tæsk/ *verb* [T usually passive] to give someone a task: *We have been tasked **with** setting up camps for refugees.*

task [SPEAK ANGRILY] /tɑːsk/ [US] /tæsk/ *noun* **take *sb* to task** to criticize or speak angrily to someone for something that they have done wrong: *She took her assistant to task **for/over** her carelessness.*

ˈtask ˌforce, **taskforce** *noun* [C usually sing] a group of people who are brought together to do a particular job, or a large military group who have a military aim to achieve: *Retired teachers have formed a task force to help schools in Poland.*

tassel /ˈtæs.ᵊl/ *noun* [C] a group of short threads or cords held together at one end, which is used as a hanging decoration on hats, curtains, furniture, etc. **tasselled**, *US USUALLY* **tasseled** /ˈtæs.ᵊld/ *adj*

taste [FLAVOUR] /teɪst/ *noun* **1** [C or U] the flavour of something, or the ability of a person or animal to recognize different flavours: *I love the taste **of** garlic.* ○ *I didn't like red wine before but I **acquired** a taste **for** it* (= started to like it as I became familiar with it) *while I was living in France.* ○ *Olives are perhaps an **acquired** taste* (= you only like them after you have become familiar with their taste). ➲See also **aftertaste**. **2** [S] a small amount of food: *Have a taste of the sauce and tell me if it needs salt.*

taste /teɪst/ *verb* [T] **1** to put food or drink in your mouth to find out what flavour it has: *Taste this sauce and tell me if it needs seasoning.* ○ *Whatever's this? I've never tasted anything like it.* **2 taste good/bad/sweet, etc.** to have a particular flavour: *This sauce tastes strange.* ○ *The bread tastes **of** onions.* ○ *This coffee tastes **like** dishwater!*

taster /ˈteɪ.stəʳ/ [US] /-stɚ/ *noun* [C] a person who tastes food or drink as a job: *a **wine**-taster* **-tasting** /-teɪ.stɪŋ/ *suffix*: *sweet-tasting* ○ *foul-tasting*

taste [EXPERIENCE] /teɪst/ *noun* [S] a brief experience of something: *I **had** a taste **of** office work during the summer and that was quite enough.*

taste /teɪst/ *verb* [T] to experience something briefly: *Once you've tasted luxury it's very hard to settle for anything else.*

taster /ˈteɪ.stəʳ/ [US] /-stɚ/ *noun* [C] a small amount or brief experience of something which is intended either to make you understand what it is like or to make you want more of it

taste [JUDGMENT] /teɪst/ *noun* **1** [C or U] a person's appreciation of and liking for particular things: *I've never really cared much for flash new cars – old vintage cars are more **to** my taste* (= what I like). **2** [U] *APPROVING* a person's ability to judge and appreciate what is good or suitable, especially relating to such matters as art, style, beauty and behaviour: *He **has** the most awful taste so you can probably imagine what his house looks like.* ○ *His taste **in** clothes leaves a little to be desired.* ○ *He told a joke about death that I thought was **in** rather **poor** taste considering that Steve's father had just died.*

tastes /teɪsts/ *plural noun* the things a person likes: *I'm afraid I **have** expensive tastes* (= I like expensive things).

ˈtaste ˌbuds *plural noun* a group of cells, found especially on the tongue, which allow different tastes to be recognized

tasteful /ˈteɪst.fᵊl/ *adj* attractive and chosen for style and quality: *It's very tasteful, their house, but I can't help thinking it lacks a little character.* **tastefully** /ˈteɪst.fᵊl.i/ *adv*: *tastefully decorated*

tasteless /ˈteɪst.ləs/ *adj* **1** ugly and lacking in style **2** likely to upset someone: *tasteless jokes* **3** having no flavour **tastelessly** /ˈteɪst.lə.sli/ *adv*

tasty /ˈteɪ.sti/ *adj* **1** describes food which has a strong and very pleasant flavour: *This soup is very tasty.* **2** *INFORMAL* describes someone who is very sexually attractive

tat /tæt/ *noun* [U] *INFORMAL* anything which looks cheap, is of low quality or in bad condition: *Like most souvenir shops, it sells a lot of old tat.*

ta-ta /təˈtɑː/ /tætˈɑː/ [US] /tɑːˈtɑː/ *exclamation UK INFORMAL* goodbye

tatters /ˈtæt.əz/ [US] /ˈtæţ.ɚz/ *plural noun* **1 in tatters** (especially of cloth) badly torn: *Her clothes were old and in tatters.* **2 in tatters** badly damaged or completely spoiled: *After the newspaper story appeared his reputation was in tatters.* **tattered** /ˈtæt.əd/ [US] /ˈtæţ.ɚd/ *adj*

tattle /ˈtæt.l̩/ [US] /ˈtæţ-/ *noun* ➲See **tittle-tattle**.

tattletale /ˈtæt.l̩.teɪl/ [US] /ˈtæţ-/ *noun* [C] *US FOR* **tell-tale**

tattoo [DECORATION] /təˈtuː/ /tætˈuː/ *noun* [C] *plural* **tattoos** a permanent image, pattern or word on the skin which is created by using needles to put colours under the skin

tattoo /təˈtuː/ /tætˈuː/ *verb* [T] **tattooed** **tattooed** /təˈtuːd/ /tætˈuːd/ *adj*

tattooist /təˈtuː.ɪst/ /tætˈuː.ɪst/ *noun* [C] (*ALSO* **tattoo artist**) someone whose job is putting tattoos on people

tattoo [MILITARY SHOW] /təˈtuː/ /tætˈuː/ *noun* [C] *plural* **tattoos** an outside show, with several military performances especially of marching and music

tatty /ˈtæt.i/ [US] /ˈtæţ-/ *adj* old and in bad condition: *You are going to change out of those tatty **old** jeans, aren't you?*

taught /tɔːt/ [US] /tɑːt/ *past simple and past participle of* **teach**

taunt /tɔːnt/ [US] /tɑːnt/ *verb* [T] to intentionally annoy and upset someone by making unkind remarks to them, laughing at them, etc: *The other children used to taunt him in the playground because he was fat and wore glasses.* **taunt** /tɔːnt/ [US] /tɑːnt/ *noun* [C] *The protesters shouted taunts at the police.*

Taurus /ˈtɔː.rəs/ [US] /ˈtɔːr.əs/ *noun* [C or U] the second sign of the zodiac relating to the period 21 April to 22 May, represented by a bull, or a person born during this period

T

taut /tɔːt/ ⓤ /tɑːt/ adj **1** tight or completely stretched: *a taut rope* ○ *He kept his eyes on the road ahead, his face taut with concentration.* ⊃Compare **slack** NOT TIGHT. **2** LITERARY tense and excited or nervous: *His latest film was described in today's paper as a taut thriller.* ○ *There was a taut edge to Niall's voice.* **3** LITERARY describes writing or speech which is controlled, clear and brief: *taut prose* **tauten** /'tɔːtⁿn/ ⓤ /'tɑː-/ verb [I or T] *The muscles in his face suddenly tautened.* **tautly** /'tɔːt.li/ ⓤ /'tɑːt-/ adv **tautness** /'tɔːt.nəs/ ⓤ /'tɑːt-/ noun [U]

tautology /tɔː'tɒl.ə.dʒi/ ⓤ /tɑː'tɑː.lə-/ noun [C or U] the unnecessary and usually unintentional use of two words to express one meaning **tautological** /ˌtɔː.təˈlɒdʒ.ɪ.kⁿl/ ⓤ /ˌtɑː.təˈlɑː.dʒɪ-/ adj **tautologically** /ˌtɔː.təˈlɒdʒ.ɪ.kli/ ⓤ /ˌtɑː.təˈlɑː.dʒɪ-/ adv

tavern /'tæv.ⁿn/ ⓤ /-ɚn/ noun [C] OLD USE a place where alcohol is sold and drunk

tawdry /'tɔː.dri/ ⓤ /'tɑː-/ adj looking bright and attractive but in fact cheap and of low quality **tawdriness** /'tɔː.drɪ.nəs/ ⓤ /'tɑː-/ noun [U]

tawny /'tɔː.ni/ ⓤ /'tɑː-/ adj of a light yellowish brown colour, like that of a lion

tax MONEY /tæks/ noun [C or U] (an amount of) money paid to the government, which is based on your income or of the cost of goods or services you have bought: *They're putting up the tax **on** cigarettes.* ○ *Tax **cuts** (= reductions in taxes) are always popular.* ○ *What do you earn **before/after** tax (= before/after you have paid tax on the money you earn)?*
tax /tæks/ verb [T] to make someone pay a tax: *Husbands and wives may be taxed independently/together.* **taxable** /'tæk.sə.bl̩/ adj: *taxable income*

tax NEED EFFORT /tæks/ verb [T] to need a lot of effort, either physical or mental: *He only has to read a short report – it shouldn't tax him unduly.*

tax alˌlowance noun [C usually sing] the amount of income on which you do not have to pay tax

taxation /tæk'seɪ.ʃⁿn/ noun [U] the system of taxing people

tax aˌvoidance noun [U] the reduction, by legal methods, of the amount of tax that a person or company pays

tax ˌcredit noun [C] a sum of money that is taken off the amount of tax you must pay

tax-deductible /ˌtæks.dɪ'dʌk.tɪ.bl̩/ ⓤ /-tə-/ adj If a sum that you spend is tax-deductible, it can be taken away from the total amount of income you must pay tax on.

tax ˌdisc noun [C] a small round sign which you put in the corner of the front window of your car or other vehicle to show that you have paid the tax to use it

tax eˌvasion noun [U] ways of illegally paying less tax than you should

tax ˌexile noun [C] a rich person who has moved to another place where taxes are lower than in their own country: *The island is a haven for tax exiles.*

tax-free /ˌtæks'friː/ adj If something is tax-free, you do not pay tax on it.

tax ˌhaven noun [C] a place where people pay less tax than they would pay if they lived in their own country

taxi VEHICLE /'tæk.si/ noun [C] (ALSO **taxicab**, ALSO **cab**) a car with a driver whom you pay to take you somewhere: *I took a taxi from the station to the hotel.* ○ *a taxi **driver***

taxi MOVE /'tæk.si/ verb [I] **taxiing**, **taxied**, **taxied** (of an aircraft) to move slowly on the ground

taxicab /'tæk.si.kæb/ noun [C] a **taxi** VEHICLE

taxidermy /'tæk.sɪ.dɜː.mi/ ⓤ /-dɚ-/ noun [U] the activity of cleaning, preserving and filling the skins of dead animals with special material to make them look as if they are still alive
taxidermist /'tæk.sɪ.dɜː.mɪst/ ⓤ /-dɚ-/ noun [C] a person whose job is taxidermy

taxing /'tæk.sɪŋ/ adj difficult or needing a lot of thought or effort: *I like a bit of light reading when I'm on holiday – nothing too taxing.*

taxi ˌrank UK noun [C] (US **cab stand**) a place where taxis wait for customers

taxiway /'tæk.si.weɪ/ noun [C] a long path which aircraft travel along in order to get to or return from a RUNWAY (= place where aircraft take off and land)

the taxman /ðə'tæks.mæn/ noun [S] the government department that is responsible for collecting taxes

taxonomy /tæk'spn.ə.mi/ ⓤ /-'sɑː.nə-/ noun [C or U] SPECIALIZED a system for naming and organizing things, especially plants and animals, into groups which share similar qualities **taxonomic** /ˌtæk.sə'nɒm.ɪk/ ⓤ /-'nɑː.mɪk/ adj: *a taxonomic group/system*

taxpayer /'tæks.peɪ.ⁿr/ ⓤ /-ɚ/ noun [C] a person who pays tax
the 'tax.payer noun [S] all the people who pay tax to the government

tax reˌlief noun [U] the system of allowing someone not to pay tax on a part of their income

tax reˌturn noun [C] a form that a self-employed person must fill in to give information about how much they have earned in a year

tax ˌshelter noun [C] a financial arrangement by which investments can be made without paying tax

tax ˌyear noun [C] **financial year**

TB /ˌtiː'biː/ noun [U] ABBREVIATION FOR **tuberculosis**

T-bone (steak) /ˌtiː.bəʊn'steɪk/ ⓤ /-boʊn-/ noun [C] a piece of thickly-cut beef which has a T-shaped bone in it

tbsp WRITTEN ABBREVIATION FOR **tablespoonful**, see at **tablespoon**

T-cell /'tiː.sel/ noun [C] a type of white blood cell that helps protect the body against diseases such as viruses, infections or cancer

tea DRINK /tiː/ noun [C or U] (a drink made by pouring hot water onto) dried and cut leaves and sometimes flowers, especially the leaves of the tea plant: *China/Indian tea* ○ *jasmine/herbal tea* ○ *iced/lemon tea* ○ *I'd love a **cup of** tea, please.* ○ *Tea **and biscuits** will be provided at 11 o'clock.* ○ *Two teas (= cups of tea), please.* ○ *How do you like your tea – **strong** or **weak**?* ○ *I'm not much of a tea **drinker**.* ○ *We sat in the shade of a tree, **sipping** tea and eating scones.* ○ UK INFORMAL *How about a **nice cup of** tea? That'll make you feel better.* ○ *"Shall I pour the tea?" "No, let it **brew** (= get stronger) a while."*

● **would not do** *sth* **for all the tea in China** OLD-FASHIONED used to say that nothing could persuade you to do something: *I wouldn't take that job for all the tea in China.*

● **tea and sympathy** OLD-FASHIONED kindness and sympathy that you show to someone who is upset: *It's time for action, not just tea and sympathy.*

tea MEAL /tiː/ noun [C or U] **1** NORTHERN ENGLISH a meal that is eaten in the early evening and is usually cooked **2** a small meal eaten in the late afternoon, usually including cake and a cup of tea

tea ˌbag noun [C] a small paper bag filled with enough tea leaves to make tea for one person

tea ˌball noun [C] MAINLY US a small wire ball which is filled with tea leaves and put into hot water to make tea

tea ˌbreak noun [C] UK a short rest from working, usually spent drinking tea or something similar: *We had a chat in our tea break.*

tea ˌcaddy noun [C] a container to keep tea leaves in

teacake /'tiː.keɪk/ noun [C] UK a small round sweet cake containing dried fruit, which is often cut open, heated and eaten with butter: *toasted teacakes*

teach /tiːtʃ/ verb [I or T] **taught**, **taught 1** to give someone knowledge or to instruct or train someone: *She taught English **to** foreign students.* ○ [+ to infinitive] *Who taught you **to** cook?* ⊃See Note **learn, teach** or **study?** at **learn**. **2** US **teach school** to be a teacher in a school: *Ever since she was a child her dream has been to teach school.*

● **teach** *sb* **a lesson** A person or experience that teaches you a lesson improves your future behaviour by making you experience the bad effects of your actions: *Having my car stolen really taught me a lesson – I'll never leave it unlocked again.* ○ *She decided to teach the boy a lesson.*

● **that'll teach** *sb* If someone says that they or an unpleasant experience will teach you (not) to do something, they mean that they will stop you from doing it in future by making you experience the bad effects of your action: *So Roger spent the night in a freezing garage, did he? That'll teach him **to** (= show him that he should not) go out without his house keys!*

T

teaching /ˈtiː.tʃɪŋ/ *noun* **[U]** *He's always wanted to go into teaching* (= have a job as a teacher). ➲See also **teachings**.

teacher /ˈtiː.tʃəʳ/ [US] /-tʃɚ/ *noun* **[C]** someone whose job is to teach in a school or college

teacher's pet /ˌtiː.tʃəzˈpet/ [US] /-tʃɚz-/ *noun* **[C]** *DISAPPROVING* a student in a class who is liked best by the teacher and therefore treated better than the other students

teacher-training college *UK* /ˌtiː.tʃəˈtreɪ.nɪŋˌkɒl.ɪdʒ/ [US] /-tʃɚˈtreɪ.nɪŋˌkɑː.lɪdʒ/ *noun* **[C]** (*US* **teacher's college,** *AUS* **teachers college**) a college which trains teachers

ˈ**tea ˌchest** *noun* **[C]** a large wooden box used first for storing tea and after that for other things, especially when someone is moving from one house to another

teach-in /ˈtiː.tʃɪn/ *noun* **[C]** *OLD-FASHIONED* a meeting for discussion on a subject of public interest, often held among college students

teachings /ˈtiː.tʃɪŋz/ *plural noun* moral, religious or political opinions, especially of a famous leader: *Christ's teachings*

ˈ**tea ˌcloth** *noun* **[C]** *UK* **tea towel**

ˈ**tea ˌcosy** *noun* **[C]** a thick covering, like a hat, which is put on a TEAPOT to keep the tea warm

teacup /ˈtiː.kʌp/ *noun* **[C]** a cup with a handle from which tea is drunk

ˈ**tea ˌgarden** *noun* **[C]** *UK* either an outside restaurant where drinks and small meals are served, or a tea PLANTATION (= large area of land where tea plants are grown)

tea-house /ˈtiː.haʊs/ *noun* **[C]** in China and Japan, a small building in which tea is served

teak /tiːk/ *noun* **[U]** (the wood of) a type of large tropical tree: *a teak forest* ○ *teak furniture*

teakettle /ˈtiːˌket.l̩/ [US] /-ˌket̬-/ *noun* *US* See **ass over teakettle**, at **arse**.

teal /tiːl/ *noun* **[C]** a small wild duck

team /tiːm/ *group noun* **[C]** **1** a number of people or animals who do something, together as a group: *a basketball/hockey/netball team* ○ *a team* ***of*** *investigators* **2** used in a number of phrases which refer to people working together as a group in order to achieve something: *It was a real team* ***effort*** *– everyone contributed something to the success of the project.* ○ *Only good team* ***work*** *will enable us to get the job done on time.*

team /tiːm/ *verb*

▲ **team up** *phrasal verb* to join another person, or form a group with other people, in order to do something together: *They teamed up for a charity performance in July.*

team-mate /ˈtiːm.meɪt/ *noun* **[C]** a player on the same team

ˈ**team ˌplayer** *noun* **[C]** someone who is good at working closely with other people: *London company requires a team player committed to quality management.*

teamster /ˈtiːm.stəʳ/ [US] /-stɚ/ *noun* **[C]** *US* someone who drives a truck as a job

teamwork /ˈtiːm.wɜːk/ [US] /-wɝːk/ *noun* **[U]** when a group of people work well together: *Brilliant teamwork and old fashioned grit got the team a last minute point.* ○ *Her determination, teamwork skills and leadership capabilities convinced us that she was perfect for the job.*

ˈ**tea ˌparty** *noun* **[C]** an occasion when people meet in the afternoon to drink tea and eat a small amount of food

teapot /ˈtiː.pɒt/ [US] /-pɑːt/ *noun* **[C]** a container for making and serving tea with a handle and a shaped opening for pouring ➲See picture **In the Kitchen** on page Centre 16

tear [CRY] /tɪəʳ/ [US] /tɪr/ *noun* **[C usually pl]** a drop of salty liquid which flows from the eye, as a result of strong emotion, especially unhappiness, or pain: *tears* ***of*** *remorse/regret/happiness/joy/laughter* ○ *Did you notice the tears* ***in*** *his* ***eyes*** *when he talked about Diane?* ○ *Why do arguments with you always* ***reduce*** *me* ***to*** *tears* (= make me cry)*?* ○ *I won't* ***shed (any)*** *tears* (= I will not be unhappy) *when he goes, I can tell you!*

• **burst into tears** to suddenly start to cry

• **in tears** crying: *I found him in tears in his bedroom.*

tearful /ˈtɪə.fəl/ [US] /ˈtɪr-/ *adj*: *After a tearful farewell at the station, we went our separate ways.* ○ *Katy's always a bit tearful* (= She tends to cry) *when it's time to go back to school.* **tearfully** /ˈtɪə.fəl.i/ [US] /ˈtɪr-/ *adv* **tearfulness** /ˈtɪə.fəl.nəs/ [US] /ˈtɪr-/ *noun* **[U]**

tear [SEPARATE] /teəʳ/ [US] /ter/ *verb* **[I or T] tore, torn** to pull or be pulled apart, or to pull pieces off: *You have to be very careful with books this old because the paper tends to tear very easily.* ○ *I tore my skirt on the chair as I stood up.* ○ *A couple of pages had been torn* ***out of/from*** *the book.*

• **tear a strip off *sb*** (*ALSO* **tear *sb* off a strip**) *UK INFORMAL* to criticize someone in a forceful way

• **tear *your* hair out** If you tear your hair out over a problem, you are feeling a lot of anxiety over it: *She's been tearing her hair out* ***over*** *the final chapter of her novel for the last month.*

• **tear *sb's* heart out** to make someone very sad: *The thought of those poor, hungry children is tearing my heart out.*

tear /teəʳ/ [US] /ter/ *noun* **[C]** a hole in a piece of paper, cloth or other material, where it has been torn

tear [HURRY] /teəʳ/ [US] /ter/ *verb* **[I + adv or prep] tore, torn** *INFORMAL* to move very quickly: *He went tearing along the road after the bus.*

• **be in a tearing hurry** *UK OLD-FASHIONED* to be going somewhere very quickly, usually because you are late

PHRASAL VERBS WITH **tear** ▼

▲ **tear *sth* apart** [BREAK] *phrasal verb* to pull something so violently that it breaks into two or more pieces: *A dog can tear a rabbit apart in seconds.*

▲ **tear *sth* apart** [DIVIDE] *phrasal verb* **[M]** to make a group of people that was united, such as a country, family or political party, argue or fight with each other by dividing it into two or more parts: *Ethnic rivalries threaten to tear this country apart.* ○ **[R]** *He resigned, depressed at the way that the party was tearing itself apart.*

▲ **tear *sth* apart** [DESTROY] *phrasal verb* to destroy a building or room: *The blast had torn the building apart.*

▲ **tear *sb/sth* apart** [CRITICIZE] *phrasal verb* to criticize something or someone severely: *The speaker was applauded as he tore apart the prime minister's policies.*

▲ **tear *sb* apart** [UPSET] *phrasal verb* *INFORMAL* to make someone very unhappy: *Seeing the children suffer really tears me apart.*

▲ **tear *sb* away** *phrasal verb* to make someone stop doing something that they enjoy, usually because they have to go somewhere or do something else: *I'll bring Tim, if I can tear him away* ***from*** *the football.* ○ **[R]** *You could come to the party with us. That's if you can tear yourself away* ***from*** *that new boyfriend of yours!*

▲ **tear *sth* down** *phrasal verb* **[M]** to intentionally destroy a building or other structure because it is not being used or it is not wanted any more: *They're going to tear down the old hospital and build a new one.*

▲ **tear into *sb*** *phrasal verb* *INFORMAL* to criticize someone or something very strongly: *Unfortunately, if he doesn't agree with you, he tends to tear into you.*

▲ **tear off** [LEAVE] *phrasal verb* *INFORMAL* to leave very quickly: *He got in his car and tore off down the road.*

▲ **tear *sth* off** [REMOVE] *phrasal verb* **[M]** to remove your clothes quickly and carelessly: *I tore my sweaty clothes off and jumped into the shower.*

▲ **tear *sth* up** [PAPER] *phrasal verb* **[M]** to tear paper into a lot of small pieces: *He tore the letter up and threw it away.*

▲ **tear *sth* up** [AGREEMENT] *phrasal verb* **[M]** If you tear up an agreement, you refuse to accept it or be controlled by it any more: *She tore up the contract and walked out.*

tearaway /ˈteə.rə.weɪ/ [US] /ˈter.ə-/ *noun* **[C]** *UK INFORMAL* a young person, usually male, who behaves in an uncontrolled way and is often causing trouble: *He was a real tearaway at school – he was always in trouble with teachers or with the police.*

teardrop /ˈtɪə.drɒp/ [US] /ˈtɪr.drɑːp/ *noun* **[C]** a single tear

ˈ**tear ˌgas** *noun* **[U]** a gas used by some police and armed forces to control crowds of people. It hurts the eyes and makes them produce tears

tear jerker /'tɪəˌdʒɜː.kəʳ/ ⓤ /'tɪrˌdʒɜː.kɚ/ noun [C] INFOR-
MAL a book, film, play, etc. which has a sad story that is
intended to make people cry or be sad: *I'd recommend
that you take a pile of tissues with you when you see that
film – it's a **real** tear jerker!*

tea ˌroom noun [C] (ALSO **tea shop**) UK a small restaurant where drinks and small meals, such as tea and
cakes, are served

tease /tiːz/ verb [I or T] to laugh at someone or say unkind
things about them, either because you are joking or
because you want to upset them: *I used to hate being
teased **about** my red hair when I was at school.* ○ *I was
only teasing, I didn't mean to upset you.*

tease /tiːz/ noun [C] **1** someone who is always teasing
people: *Johnny, don't be such a tease – leave your sister
alone!* **2** SLANG DISAPPROVING someone who enjoys causing sexual excitement and interest in people with whom
she or he does not intend to have sex

PHRASAL VERBS WITH **tease** ▼

▲ **tease** *sth* **out** OBTAIN INFORMATION phrasal verb [M] to try
to obtain information or understand a meaning that is
hidden or unclear: *It took me a while to tease the truth
out **of** him.*

▲ **tease** *sth* **out** SEPARATE phrasal verb [M] to use your
fingers to gradually separate and straighten hairs or
threads that are stuck together: *While it was still wet, I
gently teased out the tangled knots in Rosie's hair.*

teaser /'tiː.zəʳ/ ⓤ /-zɚ/ noun [C] a **brainteaser**

tea ˌset noun [C] (ALSO **tea service**) a set of small plates,
cups, etc., with a matching design, for serving tea and
small amounts of food such as cakes and sandwiches

teaspoon /'tiː.spuːn/ noun [C] a small spoon used to STIR
(= mix) tea or coffee in a cup ➾Compare **dessertspoon**;
tablespoon.
teaspoonful (plural **teaspoonsful** or **teaspoonfuls**)
/'tiː.spuːn.fʊl/ noun [C] (WRITTEN ABBREVIATION **tsp**) the
amount a teaspoon can hold

tea ˌstrainer noun [C] an object that is used to collect
the tea leaves when tea is poured through it into a cup

teat ANIMAL /tiːt/ noun [C] a part of a female mammal's
body through which milk passes to her babies

teat BOTTLE /tiːt/ UK (US **nipple**) a piece of rubber
or SILICONE for feeding a baby from a bottle

teatime /'tiː.taɪm/ noun [C usually sing] the time in the
afternoon when some people eat a small meal

tea ˌtowel noun [C] (UK ALSO **tea cloth**, US **dishtowel**) a
cloth used for drying plates, knives, forks, etc., after you
have washed them

tea ˌtray noun [C] a small TRAY (= flat surface for carrying especially food and drink)

tea ˌtrolley noun [C] (MAINLY US **tea wagon/cart**) UK a
small table on wheels, sometimes with an upper and a
lower shelf, for serving drinks and food

tech /tek/ adj, noun [U] ABBREVIATION FOR **technical** or
technology

techie /'tek.i/ noun [C] INFORMAL someone who has an
expert knowledge of or is very enthusiastic about
technology, usually computers

technical /'tek.nɪ.kəl/ adj **1** relating to the knowledge,
machines or methods used in science and industry: *a
few technical **problems*** ➾See also **technical** at
technique. **2** relating to the knowledge and methods of
a particular subject or job: *Personally, I found some
parts of the book a little too technical to follow.* **3** relating
to practical skills and methods that are used in a
particular activity: *In her performance as the Snow
Queen she showed great technical brilliance.* **technically** /'tek.nɪ.kli/ adv: *technically advanced weapons*

technicality /ˌtek.nɪ'kæl.ə.ti/ ⓤ /-nə'kæl.ə.ṭi/ noun [C] a
detail or small matter: *He was disqualified from the
competition **on a** technicality.*

ˌtechnical supˈport noun [U] an advice service
provided, usually over the telephone, to help people who
have problems using a computer: *We had to make five
calls to technical support just to get the new computer
working.*

technician /tek'nɪʃ.ən/ noun [C] a worker trained with
special skills, especially in science or ENGINEERING: *a
laboratory technician*

Technicolor /'tek.nɪˌkʌl.əʳ/ ⓤ /-ɚ/ noun [U] TRADEMARK a
special process for making cinema films in colour
technicolor US, UK **technicolour** /'tek.nɪ.kʌl.əʳ/ ⓤ /-ɚ/
adj having a lot of bright colours
● **in glorious technicolor** US, UK **in glorious technicolour** very
or too brightly coloured: *Her room was painted in
glorious technicolour.*

technique /tek'niːk/ noun [C or U] a way of doing an
activity which needs skill: *We have developed a new
technique **for** detecting errors in the manufacturing
process.* ○ *She's a wonderfully creative dancer but she
doesn't have the technique of a truly great performer.*
➾See also **technical**.
technician /tek'nɪʃ.ən/ noun [C] a person whose
technique is very good

COMMON LEARNER ERROR

technique or **technical**?

A **technique** is a particular way of doing an activity. Do not confuse
with **technical** which is an adjective usually describing the knowledge,
machines or methods used in science or industry.

It's a college maths book and it includes a lot of technical terms.
~~It's a college maths book and it includes a lot of technique terms.~~

technology /tek'nɒl.ə.dʒi/ ⓤ /-'nɑː.lə-/ noun [C or U] (the
study and knowledge of) the practical, especially industrial, use of scientific discoveries: *computer technology* ○ ***Modern** technology is amazing, isn't it?* ○ *What
this country needs is a long-term policy for investment in
science and **technology**.* ➾See also **technology**.
technological /ˌtek.nə'lɒdʒ.ɪ.kəl/ ⓤ /-'lɑː.dʒɪ-/ adj:
*Technological **advances** in computing and telecommunications will reduce the need for many people to
travel to work.* **technologically** /'tek.nə'lɒdʒ.ɪ.kli/ ⓤ /-
'lɑː.dʒɪ-/ adv

technologist /tek'nɒl.ə.dʒɪst/ ⓤ /-'nɑː.lə-/ noun [C] someone who works with a particular technology

teddy /'ted.i/ noun [C] a piece of women's underwear for
the upper body

ˈteddy (ˌbear) noun [C] a soft toy bear

ˈteddy ˌboy noun [C] (INFORMAL **ted**) a young British
man, especially in the 1950s, who typically dressed in
narrow trousers, a long loose jacket and shoes with
thick soles

tedious /'tiː.di.əs/ adj boring: *a tedious job.* ○ *The
trouble is I find most forms of exercise so tedious.*
tediously /'tiː.di.ə.sli/ adv **tediousness** /'tiː.di.ə.snəs/
noun [U]

tedium /'tiː.di.əm/ noun [U] boredom: *Soldiers often say
that the worst thing about fighting is not the moments of
terror, but all the hours of tedium in between.*

tee /tiː/ noun [C] a short plastic stick with a cup-shaped
top on which a golf ball is put to be hit, or the area
where this is used to start the play for each hole
tee /tiː/ verb

PHRASAL VERBS WITH **tee** ▼

▲ **tee** *sb* **off** MAKE ANGRY phrasal verb [M] US INFORMAL to
make someone angry: *It really tees me off when she
doesn't listen to me.*

▲ **tee off** HIT BALL phrasal verb to hit a golf ball off the
tee, or to begin a game of golf by doing this: *We'll tee off
at 10 o'clock.*

▲ **tee** *(sth)* **up** phrasal verb [M] to put a golf ball on the tee
in preparation for playing

teem /tiːm/ verb [I] (ALSO **teem down**) UK to rain heavily:
It's been teeming down all day. ○ *It's teeming **with** rain.*
▲ **teem with** *sth* phrasal verb to contain large numbers
of animals or people: *The mall was teeming with shoppers that Saturday.* **teeming** /'tiː.mɪŋ/ adj: *the teeming
metropolis*

teenager /'tiːnˌeɪ.dʒəʳ/ ⓤ /-dʒɚ/ noun [C] (INFORMAL **teen**)
a young person between 13 and 19 years old: *The
magazine is aimed at teenagers and young adults.*

teenage /'tiːn.eɪdʒ/ *adj* [before n] (ALSO **teenaged**) *a teenage nephew*

teens /tiːnz/ *plural noun* **in your teens** aged between 13 and 19: *Both my daughters are in their teens.* ○ *He's in his early/mid/late teens.*

teenybopper /'tiː.ni.bɒp.əʳ/ US /-,bɑː.pɚ/ *noun* [C] INFORMAL a TEENAGER (= a person aged between 13 and 19 years old), especially a girl, who eagerly follows the most recent fashion, music, and other interests of her age group

teeny (weeny) /,tiː.ni'wiː.ni/ *adj* INFORMAL very small: *Just a teeny weeny slice of cake for me, please – I'm supposed to be on a diet.*

teepee /'tiː.piː/ *noun* [C] ANOTHER SPELLING OF **tepee**

'tee ,shirt *noun* [C] a **T-shirt**

teeter /'tiː.təʳ/ US /-t̬ɚ/ *verb* [I usually + adv or prep] to appear to be about to fall while moving or standing: *Delia was teetering around in five-inch heels.*
• **teeter on the brink/edge of** *sth* If something is teetering on the brink/edge of a bad situation, it is likely that the situation will happen soon: *What we are seeing now is a country teetering on the brink of civil war.*

teeter-totter /,tiː.tə'tɒt.əʳ/ US /-t̬ɚ'tɑː.t̬ɚ/ *noun* [C] US FOR **seesaw**

teeth TOOTH /tiːθ/ *plural of* **tooth** ⊃See picture **The Body** on page Centre 5

teeth POWER /tiːθ/ *plural noun* effective force or power: *This committee can make recommendations but it has no real teeth.*

teeth AGAINST /tiːθ/ *plural noun* **in the teeth of** *sth* If something happens or is done in the teeth of difficulties, the difficulties cause problems but do not stop it: *The road was built in the teeth of fierce opposition from the public.*

teethe /tiːð/ *verb* [I] If a baby or small child is teething, its first teeth are growing, usually causing it pain: *My sister was up most of the night with her baby who's teething.*

'teething ,troubles *plural noun* UK problems which happen in the early stages of doing something new: *There were the usual teething troubles at the start of the project, but that's to be expected.*

teetotal /,tiː'təʊ.t̬ᵊl/ US /-'toʊ.t̬ᵊl/ *adj* never drinking alcohol or opposed to the drinking of alcohol **teetotaller** UK, US USUALLY **teetotaler** /,tiː'təʊ.t̬ᵊl.əʳ/ US /-'toʊ.t̬ᵊl.ɚ/ *noun* [C]

TEFL /'tef.l̩/ *noun* ABBREVIATION FOR teaching English as a foreign language

Teflon /'tef.lɒn/ US /-lɑːn/ *noun* [U] TRADEMARK a plastic that is very smooth and does not react chemically with other substances. It is used in industry and as a surface for cooking pans so that food does not stick to the pan.

tel. *noun* (ALSO **tel. no.**) WRITTEN ABBREVIATION FOR telephone number

tele- /tel.ɪ-/ US /tel.ə-/ *prefix* over a long distance, done by telephone, or on or for television

telecommunications /,tel.ɪ.kə,mjuː.nɪ'keɪ.ʃᵊnz/ US /-ə-/ *plural noun* (INFORMAL **telecoms**) the sending and receiving of messages over distance, especially by telephone, radio and television: *the telecommunications industry*

telecommuting /,tel.ɪ.kə'mjuː.tɪŋ/ US /-t̬ɪŋ/ *noun* [U] **teleworking telecommute** /,tel.ɪ.kə'mjuːt/ *verb* [I] to **telework telecommuter** /,tel.ɪ.kə'mjuː.təʳ/ US /-t̬ɚ/ *noun* [C] a **teleworker**

telecoms /'tel.ɪ.kɒmz/ US /-kɑːmz/ *group noun* [U] short for **telecommunications**

teleconference /,tel.ɪ'kɒn.fᵊr.ᵊnts/ US /-'kɑːn.fɚ-/ *noun* [C] a meeting involving people who are in different places, but who are connected by video and computers **teleconferencing** /,tel.ɪ'kɒn.fᵊr.ᵊnt.sɪŋ/ US /-'kɑːn.fɚ-/ *noun* [U] *Medical researchers in many countries exchange information through email and video teleconferencing*

telecottage /'tel.ɪ,kɒt.ɪdʒ/ US /-,kɑː.t̬ɪ-/ *noun* [C] an office, usually in a village, equipped with computers and electronic communications equipment for use by individuals and businesses in the area

telecottaging /'tel.ɪ,kɒt.ɪ.dʒɪŋ/ US /-,kɑː.t̬ɪ-/ *noun* [U] when someone works from a telecottage

telegenic /,tel.ɪ'dʒen.ɪk/ US /-ə-/ *adj* APPROVING (especially of a person) appearing attractive on television: *With their new youthful and telegenic leader, the Labour party looks set to woo the voters.*

telegram /'tel.ɪ.græm/ *noun* [C] (US ALSO **wire**) (especially in the past) a piece of paper with a message sent by TELEGRAPH

telegramese /,tel.ɪ.græm'iːz/ US /-ə-/ *noun* [U] (ALSO **telegraphese**) a style of writing which leaves out unimportant words **telegrammatic** /,tel.ɪ.grə'mæt.ɪk/ US /-ə.grə'mæt̬-/ *adj*

telegraph /'tel.ɪ.grɑːf/ /-græf/ US /-ə-/ *noun* [U] (especially in the past) a method of sending and receiving messages by electrical or radio signals, or the special equipment used for this purpose: *The news came by telegraph.* **telegraph** /'tel.ɪ.grɑːf/ /-græf/ US /-ə-/ *verb* [T] *The story was immediately telegraphed to New York.*

'telegraph ,pole UK *noun* [C] (US **telephone pole**) a tall wooden pole to which telephone wires are fixed

telemarketing /'tel.ɪ,mɑː.kɪ.tɪŋ/ US /-ə,mɑːr.kə.t̬ɪŋ/ *noun* [U] MAINLY US FOR **telesales**

Telemessage UK /'tel.ɪ,mes.ɪdʒ/ *noun* [C] (US **Mailgram**) TRADEMARK a message sent by telephone or TELEX and delivered in printed form

telemetry /tɪ'lemɪtri/ *noun* [U] SPECIALIZED the science or process of gathering information about objects which are far away and sending the information somewhere electronically

teleology /,tiː.li'ɒl.ə.dʒi/ US /-'ɑː.lə-/ *noun* [U] SPECIALIZED (in philosophy) the belief that everything has a special purpose or use **teleological** /,tiː.li.ə'lɒdʒ.ɪ.kᵊl/ US /-'lɑː.dʒɪ-/ *adj: a teleological argument*

telepathy /tə'lep.ə.θi/ *noun* [U] the ability to know what is in someone else's mind or communicate with them mentally, without using words or other physical signals **telepathic** /,tel.ɪ'pæθ.ɪk/ US /-ə-/ *adj*

telephone /'tel.ɪ.fəʊn/ US /-ə.foʊn/ *noun* [C or U] a **phone telephone** /'tel.ɪ.fəʊn/ US /-ə.foʊn/ *verb* [I or T] to use a phone

---

COMMON LEARNER ERROR

telephone and **phone**

Telephone and phone mean the same thing, but we usually use phone for both the noun and the verb.

I'll phone you this evening.
Can I use your phone, please?

When the phone rings or when you want to make a phone call, you **pick** it **up**.

I picked up the phone and dialled his number.

When you finish a phone call, you **put** the phone **down** or you **hang up**.

Don't hang up – I can explain everything!
She thanked him and put the phone down.
~~She thanked him and hung up the phone.~~

'telephone ,booth *noun* [C] US a **phone box**

'telephone ,box *noun* [C] UK a **phone box**

'telephone di,rectory *noun* [C] (INFORMAL **phone book**) a large book containing all the telephone numbers for a particular area, organization, etc.

'telephone ex,change *noun* [C] the building which contains the equipment for connecting telephone calls

'telephone ,kiosk *noun* [C] UK a **phone box**

telephonist /tə'lef.ᵊn.ɪst/ *noun* [C] UK a **switchboard operator**

telephoto lens /,tel.ɪ,fəʊ.təʊ'lenz/ US /-ə,foʊ.t̬oʊ-/ *noun* [C] a camera lens that makes distant objects look nearer and larger when they are photographed

teleport /'tel.ɪ.pɔːt/ US /-ə.pɔːrt/ *verb* [I or T] to (cause to) travel by an imaginary immediate form of transport that uses special technology or special mental powers

teleprinter /'tel.ɪ,prɪn.təʳ/ US /-t̬ɚ/ *noun* [C] (MAINLY US **teletypewriter**) a type of electric printer for sending and receiving messages down a telephone line ⊃See also **telex**.

TelePrompter /ˈtel.ɪˌprɒmp.təʳ/ [US] /-ˌprɑːmp.tɚ/ *noun* [C] *US TRADEMARK FOR* **Autocue**

telesales /ˈtel.ɪ.seɪlz/ *noun* [U] (*US* **telemarketing**) the advertising or selling of goods or services by telephone

telescope [DEVICE] /ˈtel.ɪ.skəʊp/ [US] /-ə.skoʊp/ *noun* [C] a cylindrical device for making distant objects look nearer and larger, using a combination of lenses, or lenses and curved mirrors **telescopic** /ˌtel.ɪˈskɒp.ɪk/ [US] /-əˈskɑː.pɪk/ *adj*: *a telescopic lens*

telescope [SHORTEN] /ˈtel.ɪ.skəʊp/ [US] /-ə.skoʊp/ *verb* [I or T] to make or become shorter by reducing the length of the parts: *We had to telescope five visits into two days.*

Teletext /ˈtel.ɪ.tekst/ [US] /-ə-/ *noun* [U] *TRADEMARK* a system for giving written information on many subjects (such as news and sports results) by television

telethon /ˈtel.ɪ.θɒn/ [US] /-ə.θɑːn/ *noun* [C usually sing] a television show, usually several hours long, whose purpose is to make money for charity

televangelism /ˌtel.ɪˈvæn.dʒə.lɪ.zᵊm/ *noun* [U] (especially in the US) the activity of PREACHING (= giving religious speeches) on television in order to persuade people to become Christians and give their money to religious organizations **televangelist** /ˌtel.ɪˈvæn.dʒə.lɪst/ *noun* [C]

televise /ˈtel.ɪ.vaɪz/ [US] /-ə-/ *verb* [T] to show or broadcast on television: *The match will be televised* ***live*** (= shown as it is being played) *on BBC Scotland.* **televised** /ˈtel.ɪ.vaɪzd/ [US] /ˈ-ə-/ *adj*

television /ˈtel.ɪ.vɪʒ.ᵊn/ /ˌ--ˈ--/ [US] /-ə-/ *noun* [C or U] (*ALSO* **TV**, *UK INFORMAL* **telly**) a box-like device with a screen which receives electrical signals and changes them into moving images and sound, or the method or business of sending images and sound by electrical signals: *a colour/black-and-white television* ○ *Could you turn the television down?* ○ *It's one of the few television* ***programmes*** *that I always make a point of watching.* ○ *Is there anything interesting* ***on*** *television tonight?* ○ *Clare has worked* ***in*** *television since she left college.* ○ *Your problem is that you* ***watch*** *too much television.*

televisual /ˌtel.ɪˈvɪʒ.u.əl/ [US] /-ə-/ *adj MAINLY UK* relating to television: *the televisual age* ○ *an interesting televisual experience*

COMMON LEARNER ERROR

on television

Be careful to say **on television** when you are talking about the programmes that you watch.

What's on television tonight?
~~*What's in television tonight?*~~

COMMON LEARNER ERROR

watch television

Be careful to choose the correct verb with television. You **watch television**. You do not **look television**.

Most children watch too much television.
~~*Most children look too much television.*~~

teleworking /ˈtel.ɪˌwɜː.kɪŋ/ [US] /-əˌwɝː-/ *noun* [U] (*ALSO* **telecommuting**) working at home, while communicating with your office by telephone, FAX or computer **telework** /ˈtel.ɪ.wɜːk/ [US] /-ə.wɝːk/ *verb* [I] (*ALSO* **telecommute**) **teleworker** /ˈtel.ɪˌwɜː.kəʳ/ [US] /-əˌwɝː.kɚ/ *noun* [C] (*ALSO* **telecommuter**)

telex /ˈtel.eks/ *noun* [C or U] a method of sending written messages down a telephone line from one TELEPRINTER to another, the machine which does this, or the message itself: *The details were sent* ***by*** *telex.* **telex** /ˈtel.eks/ *verb* [I or T] [+ two objects] *We telexed him the news at once.*

tell [SPEAK] /tel/ *verb* [I or T] **told, told** to say something to someone, often giving them information or instructions: *Tell me* ***about*** *your holiday then.* ○ [+ two objects] *Can you tell me the way to the station?* ○ *FORMAL He told us* ***of*** *his extraordinary childhood.* ○ [+ (*that*)] *Did you tell anyone* ***(that)*** *you were coming to see me?* ○ [+ speech] *"I'm leaving you," she told him.* ○ [+ to infinitive] *I told her* ***to*** *go home.* ➲See Note **say or tell?** at **say** SPEAK. See also **telltale**.

• **tell a lie/lies** to say something/things that are not true: *She's always telling lies.*

• **tell the truth** to speak honestly: *How do you know she's telling the truth?*

• **to tell (you) the truth** to be honest: *To tell (you) the truth, I didn't understand a word of what he was saying.*

• **I told *you* so!** *INFORMAL* said when something bad happens after you warned someone that it would happen

• **tell the time** to be able to understand a clock: *My daughter has just learned to tell the time.*

• **tell tales** *DISAPPROVING* If someone, usually a child, tells tales, they tell someone such as a teacher about something bad that someone else has done: *Your classmates won't trust you if you're always telling tales, Alvin.*

• **tell *sb's* fortune** (*ALSO* **tell fortunes**) to say what will happen in someone's future: *At the fair, there was a lady who told your fortune.*

• **Tell me another!** *UK INFORMAL* (*US INFORMAL* **Tell me another one!**) used to say that you don't believe what someone has told you: *"I worked all day yesterday." "Oh yeah, tell me another!"*

• **You're telling me!** *INFORMAL* used to say that you strongly agree with what someone has just said: *"Stephen's in such a bad mood today." "You're telling me!"*

• **tell it like it is** *INFORMAL* to tell the facts without hiding anything

COMMON LEARNER ERROR

telling someone **about** something

Remember to use the preposition 'about' in the phrase **tell** someone **about** something.

Tell me about your trip – where did you go?
~~*Tell me your trip – where did you go?*~~

tell [KNOW] /tel/ *verb* [I or T] **told, told** to know, recognize or be certain: *"He's Dutch." "How can you tell?"* ○ [+ (*that*)] *I could tell* ***(that)*** *you were unhappy.*

• **tell the difference** to notice a difference in quality between two things: *This coffee is about half the price of that one and yet you really can't tell the difference.*

• **there is no telling** there is no way of knowing: *There is no telling* ***what*** *the future will hold for them.*

• **you never can tell** (*ALSO* **you can never tell**) said to mean that you can never know or be certain: *Who knows what will happen to Peter and me in the future – you can never tell.*

tell [HAVE AN EFFECT] /tel/ *verb* [I] **told, told** to have an effect: *She's been under a lot of stress recently and it's starting to tell.*

PHRASAL VERBS WITH **tell**

▲ **tell against *sb/sth*** *phrasal verb UK FORMAL* to make someone or something more likely to fail: *His reputation as a troublemaker told against him when he tried to change his job.*

▲ **tell *sth/sb* apart** *phrasal verb* to be able to see the difference between two very similar things or people: *As babies, the twins were so alike that I just couldn't tell them apart.*

▲ **tell *sb* off** *phrasal verb* [M] to speak angrily at someone because they have done something wrong: *The teacher told me off* ***for*** *swearing.* ➲See picture **Phrasal Verbs** on page Centre 9

telling-off /ˌtel.ɪŋˈɒf/ [US] /-ˈɑːf/ *noun* [C usually sing] *plural* **tellings-off** *He* ***gave*** *me a* ***good*** *telling-off* ***for*** *forgetting the meeting.*

▲ **tell on *sb*** [INFORM] *phrasal verb INFORMAL* to give information about someone, usually something bad that they have said or done, especially to a person in authority

▲ **tell on *sb*** [AFFECT BADLY] *phrasal verb* to have a bad effect on someone's health or behaviour: *A succession of late nights had begun to tell on him and his work was suffering.*

teller /ˈtel.əʳ/ [US] /-ɚ/ *noun* [C] **1** a person who counts votes at an election **2** *US, AUS* a person employed in a bank to receive and pay out money

T

telling /ˈtel.ɪŋ/ *adj* showing the truth about a situation or showing what someone really thinks: *a telling comment*

telltale [EVIDENCE] /ˈtel.teɪl/ *adj* **[before n]** allowing a secret to become known: *She found lipstick on his shirts – the telltale* ***sign*** *that he was having an affair.*

tell-tale [PERSON] /ˈtel.teɪl/ *noun* **[C]** (*US USUALLY* **tattletale**, *AUS* **dobber**) *DISAPPROVING* a person, especially a child, who secretly tells someone in authority, especially a teacher, that someone else has done something bad, often in order to cause trouble

telly /ˈtel.i/ *noun* **[C or U]** *UK INFORMAL FOR* **television**: *What's* ***on*** *telly tonight?*

temerity /təˈmer.ɪ.ti/ [US] /-ə.t̬i/ *noun* **[U]** *FORMAL DISAPPROVING* a willingness to do or say something that shocks or upsets other people: **[+ to infinitive]** *She* ***had the*** *temerity* ***to*** *call me a liar.*

temp /temp/ *noun* **[C]** *INFORMAL* a person employed to work for a short period, especially in an office while another person is absent or when there is extra work **temp** /temp/ *verb* **[I]** *I decided to temp for a while so that I could try different kinds of jobs.*

temper [BEHAVIOUR] /ˈtem.pəʳ/ [US] /-pɚ/ *noun* **[C]** when someone becomes angry very quickly: *She* ***has*** *a real temper.* ○ *He's got a really bad temper.*

• **keep *your* temper** to succeed in staying calm and not becoming angry: *I found it hard to keep my temper with so many things going wrong.*

• **lose *your* temper** to suddenly become angry: *The children behaved so badly that I lost my temper.*

• **be in a bad/foul, etc. temper** to be feeling angry: *I'd avoid her if I were you – she's in a foul temper.*

• **tempers get frayed** If you say that tempers are getting (rather) frayed, you mean that people are getting angry with each other.

-tempered /-tem.pəd/ [US] /-pɚd/ *suffix* having or showing the stated type of temper: *even-tempered* ○ *bad-tempered*

temper [REDUCE] /ˈtem.pəʳ/ [US] /-pɚ/ *verb* **[T]** *FORMAL* to make something less strong, extreme, etc: *My enthusiasm for the venture was somewhat tempered by my knowledge of the work that would be involved.* ○ *I learnt to temper my criticism.*

temper [METAL] /ˈtem.pəʳ/ [US] /-pɚ/ *verb* **[T]** to heat and then cool a metal in order to make it hard: *tempered steel*

tempera /ˈtem.pᵊr.ə/ [US] /-pɚ.ə/ *noun* **[U]** *SPECIALIZED* a method of painting with colours which are mixed with egg and water

temperament /ˈtem.pᵊr.ə.mənt/ /-prə.mənt/ [US] /-pɚ.ə-/ *noun* **[C or U]** the part of your character that affects your moods and the way you behave: *a fiery temperament*

temperamental /ˌtem.pᵊr.əˈmen.tᵊl/ /-prə-/ [US] /-pɚ.əˈmen.t̬ᵊl/ *adj* **1** describes someone whose mood tends to change very suddenly: *Be careful how you approach her – she's very temperamental.* **2** *INFORMAL* describes a machine that sometimes works and sometimes does not: *You have to treat our video recorder very carefully – it's rather temperamental.* **3** caused by your own character and feelings: *There are definitely temperamental similarities between the brothers.* **temperamentally** /ˌtem.pᵊr.əˈmen.tᵊl.i/ /-prə-/ [US] /-pɚ.əˈmen.t̬ᵊl-/ *adv*

temperance /ˈtem.pᵊr.ᵊnts/ /-prənts/ [US] /-pɚ.ᵊnts/ *noun* **[U]** *FORMAL* **1** control of your own behaviour, such as not drinking or eating too much **2** the habit of not drinking alcohol because you believe it is dangerous or wrong

temperate [WEATHER] /ˈtem.pᵊr.ət/ /-prət/ [US] /-pɚ.ət/ *adj* **1** (of weather conditions) neither very hot nor very cold: *a temperate* ***climate*** **2** describes plants that grow naturally in places where the weather is neither very hot nor very cold

temperate [BEHAVIOUR] /ˈtem.pᵊr.ət/ /-prət/ [US] /-pɚ.ət/ *adj* *FORMAL* If someone's behaviour is temperate, it is calm and controlled. * NOTE: The opposite is **intemperate**.

temperature /ˈtem.prə.tʃəʳ/ [US] /-pɚ.ə.tʃɚ/ *noun* **1** **[C or U]** the measured amount of heat in a place or in the body: *Preheat the oven to a temperature of 200 degrees Celsius.* ○ *There has been a sudden rise in temperature over the past few days* (= The weather has become warmer). ○ *The doctor examined him and* ***took*** *his temperature* (= measured it). **2** **[U]** If you say that the temperature in a particular situation is rising, you mean that it is likely to become violent because people have become angry: *The temperature of the discussion started to rise as each side added its own arguments.*

• **run/have a temperature** to have a higher body temperature than normal and to be ill

tempest /ˈtem.pɪst/ *noun* **[C]** *LITERARY* a violent storm **tempestuous** /temˈpes.tju.əs/ *adj*

tempestuous /temˈpes.tju.əs/ *adj* If something such as a relationship or time is tempestuous, it is full of strong emotions: *They got divorced in 1992 after a tempestuous marriage.* **tempestuously** /temˈpes.tju.ə.sli/ *adv*

template /ˈtem.pleɪt/ *noun* **[C]** **1** a pattern made of metal, plastic or paper, which is used for making many copies of a shape or to help cut material accurately **2** a system that helps you arrange information on a computer screen

temple [BUILDING] /ˈtem.pl̩/ *noun* **[C]** a building used for the worship of a god or gods in some religions

temple [BODY PART] /ˈtem.pl̩/ *noun* **[C often pl]** the flat area on each side of your head in front of the top of your ear

tempo /ˈtem.pəʊ/ [US] /-poʊ/ *noun plural* **tempos** or *SPECIALIZED* **tempi** **1** **[C]** the speed at which an event happens: *We're going to have to* ***up*** *the tempo* (= work faster) *if we're to finish on time.* **2** **[C or U]** *SPECIALIZED* the speed at which a piece of music is played: *a change* ***in*** *tempo*

temporal /ˈtem.pᵊr.ᵊl/ [US] /-pɚ.əl/ *adj* *FORMAL* relating to practical matters or material things, rather than spiritual ones

temporary /ˈtem.pᵊr.ᵊr.i/ /-prᵊr-/ [US] /-pə.rer.i/ *adj* not lasting or needed for very long: *The ceasefire will only provide a temporary solution to the current military crisis.* ○ *temporary staff* ➲Compare **permanent**. **temporarily** /ˈtem.pᵊr.er.ɪ.li/ [US] /-pə.rer-/ *adv*: *This office is closed temporarily for redecoration.*

temporize, *UK USUALLY* **-ise** /ˈtem.pᵊr.aɪz/ [US] /-pə.raɪz/ *verb* **[I]** *FORMAL* to delay making a decision or stating your opinion in order to obtain an advantage

tempt /tempt/ *verb* **[T]** to make someone want to have or do something, especially something that is unnecessary or wrong: *The offer of a free car stereo tempted her* ***into*** ***buying*** *a new car.* ○ **[+ to infinitive]** *They tempted him* ***to*** *join the company* ***by*** *offer****ing*** *him a large salary and a company car.*

• **be tempted** to want something or to want to do something: *"Did you apply for that job?" "Well, I was very tempted but in the end I decided not to."* ○ *I was* ***sorely*** (= very) *tempted* ***to*** *resign after my boss was so rude to me.*

• **tempt fate/providence** If you tempt fate/providence by doing something, you take a foolish risk by doing it and depend too much on your good luck: *You're tempting fate by riding your bike without wearing a cycle helmet.*

temptation /tempˈteɪ.ʃᵊn/ *noun* **1** **[C or U]** the desire to do or have something which you know you should not do or have: **[+ to infinitive]** *As a young actress, she managed to* ***resist*** *the temptation* ***to*** *move to Hollywood.* **2** **[C]** something that makes you want to do or have something that you know you should not: *He knew it was wrong to steal, but the money just lying there was too great a temptation.*

tempting /ˈtemp.tɪŋ/ *adj* If something is tempting, you want to do or have it: *a tempting offer* ○ *That pie looks very tempting.* ○ **[+ to infinitive]** *It's tempting* ***to*** *blame television for the increase in crime.* **temptingly** /ˈtemp.tɪŋ.li/ *adv*

temptress /ˈtemp.trɪs/ *noun* **[C]** *LITERARY OR HUMOROUS* a woman who tries to sexually attract men

ten /ten/ *determiner, pronoun, noun* the number 10

• **ten to one** If you say ten to one that something will or will not happen, you mean it is very likely that it will or will not happen: *Ten to one he won't be there tonight.*

tenth /tentθ/ *determiner, pronoun, adj, adv, noun* **[S]** 10th written as a word: *This is his tenth year of working for the company.* ○ *He was tenth in the batting order/He batted tenth.* ○ *My birthday is on* ***the*** *tenth (of May).*

tenth /tentθ/ *noun* **[C]** one of ten equal parts of something: *He receives a tenth of the profits.*

tenable /ˈten.ə.bl̩/ *adj* (of an opinion or position) able to be defended successfully or held for a particular period of time: *His theory is no longer tenable in light of the recent discoveries.* ○ *The university fellowship is tenable **for*** (= lasts for) *three years.*

tenacious /təˈneɪ.ʃəs/ *adj* holding tightly onto something, or keeping an opinion in a determined way: *The baby took my finger in its tenacious little fist.* ○ *There has been tenacious local opposition to the new airport.* **tenaciously** /təˈneɪ.ʃə.sli/ *adv*
tenacity /təˈnæs.ə.ti/ [US] /-t̬i/ *noun* [U] the determination to continue what you are doing

tenant /ˈten.ənt/ *noun* [C] a person who pays rent for the use of land or a building
tenancy /ˈten.ənt.si/ *noun* **1** [C or U] the right to use land or live in a building in exchange for rent **2** [C] the period of time for which you have the right to use a building or piece of land: *a two-year tenancy*

Ten Comˈmandments *plural noun* in the Bible, the rules of behaviour which God gave to Israel through Moses

tend [BE LIKELY] /tend/ *verb* [I] to be likely to behave in a particular way or have a particular characteristic: [+ *to* infinitive] *We tend **to** get cold winters and warm, dry summers in this part of the country.*

tend [CARE] /tend/ *verb* [T] FORMAL to care for something or someone: *He carefully tended his sunflower plants all summer.* ○ *The nurse gently tended the patient's cuts and bruises.*
▲ **tend to *sb/sth*** *phrasal verb* to deal with the problems or needs of a person or thing: *Would you mind waiting? I'm tending to another customer at the moment.* ○ *Nurses tended to the injured.*

tendency /ˈten.dənt.si/ *noun* [C] **1** a likelihood to behave in a particular way or to like a particular thing: [+ *to* infinitive] *His tendency **to** exaggerate is well known.* **2** If there is a tendency for something to happen, it is likely to happen or it often happens: *There is a tendency **for** unemployment to rise in the summer.* **3** If there is a tendency to do something, it starts to happen more often or starts to increase: [+ *to* infinitive] *There is a growing tendency **to** regard money more highly than quality of life.*

tendentious /tenˈden.tʃəs/ *adj* FORMAL (of speech or writing) expressing or supporting a particular opinion which many other people disagree with **tendentiously** /tenˈden.tʃə.sli/ *adv* **tendentiousness** /tenˈden.tʃə.snəs/ *noun* [U]

tender [GENTLE] /ˈten.dəʳ/ [US] /-dɚ/ *adj* gentle, caring or sympathetic: *a tender look/smile* ○ *What you need is some tender **loving care**.* **tenderly** /ˈten.dəl.i/ [US] /-dɚ.li/ *adv* **tenderness** /ˈten.də.nəs/ [US] /-dɚ-/ *noun* [U]

tender [PAINFUL] /ˈten.dəʳ/ [US] /-dɚ/ *adj* (of part of the body) painful, sore or uncomfortable when touched: *My arm was very tender after the injection.* **tenderness** /ˈten.də.nəs/ [US] /-dɚ-/ *noun* [U]

tender [SOFT] /ˈten.dəʳ/ [US] /-dɚ/ *adj* **1** (of meat or vegetables) easy to cut or chew: *My steak was beautifully tender.* **2** describes plants which are easily damaged by cold weather

tender [YOUNG] /ˈten.dəʳ/ [US] /-dɚ/ *adj* LITERARY young: *He was sent off to boarding school **at** the tender **age of** seven.*

tender [OFFER] /ˈten.dəʳ/ [US] /-dɚ/ *noun* [C] **1** a written or formal offer to supply goods or do a job for an agreed price: *The council has **invited** tenders for the building contract.* **2** SPECIALIZED a written offer to buy or sell shares in a company
• **put *sth* out to tender** UK If you put work out to tender, you ask people to make offers to do it: *Education departments in all the prisons are being put out to tender.*
tender /ˈten.dəʳ/ [US] /-dɚ/ *verb* **1** [I] If you tender for a job, you make a formal offer to do it for a stated price: *Five companies have tendered **for** the hospital contract.* **2** [I] SPECIALIZED If you tender for something such as shares, you make a formal offer to buy them for a stated price. **3** [T] FORMAL to give or offer something: *Please tender the exact fare.* ○ *The health minister has tendered her **resignation*** (= has offered to leave her job).

tender [CONTAINER] /ˈten.dəʳ/ [US] /-dɚ/ *noun* [C] SPECIALIZED a vehicle used for transporting water, wood or coal, especially one which is pulled behind a railway engine or used by the fire service, or a small boat used for transporting people or goods between a larger boat and the coast

tender-hearted /ˌten.dəˈhɑː.tɪd/ [US] /-dɚˈhɑːr.t̬ɪd/ *adj* very kind and sympathetic

tenderize, UK USUALLY **-ise** /ˈten.dər.aɪz/ [US] /-də.raɪz/ *verb* [T] to make meat easy to cut or chew by beating it or preparing it in a particular way

tenderloin /ˈten.də.lɔɪn/ [US] /-dɚ-/ *noun* [U] a strip of meat taken from the lower back of cows or pigs, which is not fatty and is easy to cut or chew

tendon /ˈten.dən/ *noun* [C] a strong cord in the body connecting a muscle to a bone

tendril /ˈten.drəl/ *noun* [C] a thin, stem-like part of a climbing plant which holds on to walls or other plants for support

tenement /ˈten.ə.mənt/ *noun* [C] a large building divided into apartments, usually in a poor area of a city

tenet /ˈten.ɪt/ *noun* [C] FORMAL one of the principles on which a belief or theory is based: *It is a tenet of contemporary psychology that an individual's mental health is supported by having good social networks.*

ten-four /ˌtenˈfɔːʳ/ [US] /-ˈfɔːr/ *exclamation* (ALSO **10-4**) MAINLY US said to mean that a message has been received

tenner /ˈten.əʳ/ [US] /-ɚ/ *noun* [C] UK INFORMAL ten pounds, or a note worth ten pounds ➲See also **fiver**.

tennis /ˈten.ɪs/ *noun* [U] a game played between two or four people on a specially marked playing area which involves hitting a small ball across a central net ➲See picture **Sports** on page Centre 10

ˌtennis ˈelbow *noun* [U] a painful swelling near the elbow which is caused by frequent twisting of the hand and arm

ˈtennis ˌshoe *noun* [C] a sports shoe with a rubber bottom and a top made of leather or strong cotton

tenon /ˈten.ən/ *noun* [C] SPECIALIZED the end of a piece of wood which is shaped to fit into a MORTISE (= an opening) in another piece of wood to form a joint

ˈtenon ˌsaw UK *noun* [C] (US **back saw**) a small tool with a sharp thin blade and a strong metal back

tenor [MUSIC] /ˈten.əʳ/ [US] /-ɚ/ *noun* [C] a male singer with a high voice, or (especially in combinations) a musical instrument which has the same range of notes as the tenor singing voice: *a tenor saxophone*

tenor [CHARACTER] /ˈten.əʳ/ [US] /-ɚ/ *noun* [U] FORMAL the general meaning, character or pattern of something: *What was the general tenor **of** his speech?*

ˌtenpin ˈbowling *noun* [U] (US **tenpins**) **bowling**, see at **bowl** ROLL

tense [STRETCHED] /tents/ *adj* (of your body or part of the body) stretched tight and stiff
tense /tents/ *verb* [I or T] (ALSO **tense up**) If you or your muscles tense, your muscles become stiff and tight because you are frightened or are preparing yourself to do something: *Don't tense your shoulders, just relax.* ○ *I could feel myself tense up as he touched my neck.* **tensely** /ˈtent.sli/ *adv* **tenseness** /ˈtent.snəs/ *noun* [U]
tension /ˈtent.ʃən/ *noun* [U] The tension of a wire or rope is the degree to which it is stretched.

tense [NERVOUS] /tents/ *adj* **1** nervous and anxious and unable to relax: *She was very tense as she waited for the interview.* **2** If a situation is tense, it causes feelings of anxiety: *There were some tense moments in the second half of the game.*
• **tensed up** very nervous and worried and unable to relax because of something that is going to happen: *You seem very tensed up. Are you still waiting for that phone call?*
tensely /ˈtent.sli/ *adv* in a way that is nervous or anxious

tense [VERB FORM] /tents/ *noun* [C] any of the forms of a verb which show the time at which an action happened

tensile /ˈten.saɪl/ [US] /-sɪl/ *adj* FORMAL If a material is tensile, it can be stretched.

T

ˌtensile ˈstrength *noun* [U] *SPECIALIZED* The tensile strength of a material such as wire, rope or stone is its ability to support a load without breaking.

tension /ˈten.ʃᵊn/ *noun* **1** [U] a feeling of nervousness before an important or difficult event: *You could feel the tension in the room as we waited for our exam results.* ➲See also **tension** at **tense** STRETCHED. **2** [C usually pl; U] a feeling of fear or anger between two groups of people who do not trust each other: *ethnic/racial tension* ○ *There are growing tensions betweeen the two countries.*

tent /tent/ *noun* [C] a shelter made of cloth, which you can fold up and carry with you and which is supported by poles and ropes

tentacle /ˈten.tə.kl̩/ [US] /-t̬ə-/ *noun* [C] one of the long thin arm-like parts of some sea creatures, which are used for feeling and holding things, catching food or moving

tentative /ˈten.tə.tɪv/ [US] /-t̬ə.t̬ɪv/ *adj* (of a plan or idea) not certain or agreed, or (of a suggestion or action) said or done in a careful but uncertain way because you do not know if you are right: *I have made tentative plans to take a trip to Seattle in July.*
tentatively /ˈten.tə.tɪv.li/ [US] /-t̬ə.t̬ɪv-/ *adv* If you do or say something tentatively, you do or say it in an uncertain way. **tentativeness** /ˈten.tə.tɪv.nəs/ [US] /-t̬ə.t̬ɪv-/ *noun* [U]

tenterhooks /ˈten.tə.hʊks/ [US] /-t̬ɚ-/ *plural noun* **on tenterhooks** worried or anxious about something that is going to happen: *We were **on** tenterhooks all morning waiting for the telephone to ring.*

tenth /tentθ/ *pronoun, noun, determiner, adv* ➲See at **ten**.

tenuous /ˈten.ju.əs/ *adj* A tenuous connection, idea or situation is weak and possibly does not exist: *We were only able to make a tenuous connection between the two robberies.* **tenuously** /ˈten.ju.əs.li/ *adv*

tenure /ˈten.jəʳ/ /-jʊəʳ/ [US] /-jɚ/ /-jʊr/ *noun* [U] *FORMAL* **1** the legal possession of land, a job or an official public position, or the period of time during which you possess it: *During his tenure as dean, he had a real influence on the students.* **2** the right to remain permanently in a job: *She is one of the few lecturers in this department who **have** tenure.*

tepee, teepee, tipi /ˈtiː.piː/ *noun* [C] a type of tent in the shape of a cone made from animal skins which is the typical shelter of some Native Americans

tepid /ˈtep.ɪd/ *adj* **1** (of liquid) not very warm **2** describes a reaction which is not enthusiastic: *I got a tepid response to my suggestion that we should start work earlier.*

tequila /təˈkiː.lə/ *noun* [C or U] a strong alcoholic drink originally from Mexico

teˌquila ˈslammer *noun* [C] a drink consisting of tequila mixed with a sweet fizzy drink, which is shaken and then drunk very quickly

tercentenary *MAINLY UK* /ˌtɜː.senˈtiː.nᵊr.i/ /-ˈten.ᵊr-/ [US] /tɚˈsen.tᵊn.er-/ *noun* [C] (*MAINLY US* **tercentennial**) the day or year which is 300 years after an important event

term [TIME] /tɜːm/ [US] /tɝːm/ *noun* **1** [C] the fixed period of time which something lasts for: *He received a prison term **for** drunk driving.* ○ *The Government's term of office* (= The period in which they have power) *expires at the end of the year.* ➲See also **terms**. **2** [C] *MAINLY UK* (*US USUALLY* **semester, quarter**) one of the periods into which a year is divided at school, college or university: *In Britain, the spring term starts in January and ends just before Easter.* ○ *We're very busy in term-**time*** (= during the term). **3** [C] *FORMAL* the period of time which a legal agreement lasts for: *The lease on our house is near the end of its term.* **4** [U] *SPECIALIZED* the end of a pregnancy when a baby is expected to be born: *Her last pregnancy went **to** term* (= The baby was born after the expected number of weeks). ○ *a full-term pregnancy*
• **in the long/medium/short term** for a long, medium or short period of time in the future: *Taking this decision will cost us more in the short term, but will be beneficial in the long term.*
-term /-tɜːm/ [US] /-tɝːm/ *suffix* **long/medium/short-term** lasting a long/medium/short time: *The project will have long-term benefits.*

term [DESCRIPTION] /tɜːm/ [US] /tɝːm/ *noun* [C] a word or expression used in relation to a particular subject, often to describe something official or technical: *'Without let or hindrance' is a legal term which means 'freely'.* ○ *a term **of endearment*** (= a kind or friendly name to call someone) ○ *a term **of abuse*** (= an unkind or unpleasant name to call someone)
term /tɜːm/ [US] /tɝːm/ *verb* [T] to give something a name or to describe it with a particular expression: *Technically, a horse which is smaller than 1.5 metres at the shoulder is termed a pony.*
terms /tɜːmz/ [US] /tɝːmz/ *plural noun* **in strong, etc. terms** using language which clearly shows your feelings: *He complained in the strongest terms.* ○ *She spoke of his achievements in **glowing** terms* (= in a very approving way).
• **in no uncertain terms** in a very clear way: *She told him what she thought of his behaviour in no uncertain terms* (= She made her disapproval very clear).

termagant /ˈtɜː.mə.gᵊnt/ [US] /ˈtɝː-/ *noun* [C] *DISAPPROVING* a woman who argues noisily to obtain or achieve what she wants

terminal [DEATH] /ˈtɜː.mɪ.nəl/ [US] /ˈtɝː-/ *adj* **1** (of a disease or illness) leading gradually to death: *She has terminal cancer.* **2** A terminal patient is one who is seriously ill and will die soon. **3** extreme, when referring to something unpleasant or negative: *He has nothing to do all day and is suffering from terminal **boredom**.* ○ *She claims that the shipbuilding industry is in terminal **decline**.* **terminally** /ˈtɜː.mɪ.nə.li/ [US] /ˈtɝː-/ *adv*: *a terminally ill child*

terminal [BUILDING] /ˈtɜː.mɪ.nəl/ [US] /ˈtɝː-/ *noun* [C] the area or building at a station, airport or port which is used by passengers leaving or arriving by train, aircraft or ship: *Your flight to Perth will leave from Terminal 4.*

terminal [COMPUTER] /ˈtɜː.mɪ.nəl/ [US] /ˈtɝː-/ *noun* [C] a piece of equipment consisting of a keyboard and screen, which is used for communicating with the part of a computing system that deals with information

terminal [ELECTRICITY] /ˈtɜː.mɪ.nəl/ [US] /ˈtɝː-/ *noun* [C] the point at which a connection can be made in an electric circuit

terminate /ˈtɜː.mɪ.neɪt/ [US] /ˈtɝː-/ *verb* [I or T] *FORMAL* to (cause something to) end or stop: *They terminated my contract in October.* ○ *This train will terminate at the next stop – passengers who wish to continue should change trains.* **termination** /ˌtɜː.mɪˈneɪ.ʃᵊn/ [US] /ˌtɝː-/ *noun* [U]

termination /ˌtɜː.mɪˈneɪ.ʃᵊn/ [US] /ˌtɝː-/ *noun* [C] *SPECIALIZED* the intentional ending of a pregnancy, usually by a medical operation **terminate** /ˈtɜː.mɪ.neɪt/ [US] /ˈtɝː-/ *verb* [T] *FORMAL*

terminology /ˌtɜː.mɪˈnɒl.ə.dʒi/ [US] /ˌtɝː.mɪˈnɑː.lə-/ *noun* [C or U] special words or expressions used in relation to a particular subject or activity: *scientific terminology* ➲Compare **jargon**. **terminological** /ˌtɜː.mɪ.nəˈlɒdʒ.ɪ.kᵊl/ [US] /ˌtɝː.mɪ.nəˈlɑː.dʒɪ-/ *adj* **terminologically** /ˌtɜː.mɪ.nəˈlɒdʒ.ɪ.kli/ [US] /ˌtɝː.mɪ.nəˈlɑː.dʒɪ-/ *adv*

ˈterm inˌsurance *noun* [U] a type of insurance which lasts for a limited time period ➲Compare **life insurance**.

terminus /ˈtɜː.mɪ.nəs/ [US] /ˈtɝː-/ *noun* [C] *plural* **terminuses** or **termini** the last stop or the station at the end of a bus or railway route

termite /ˈtɜː.maɪt/ [US] /ˈtɝː-/ *noun* [C] (*ALSO* **white ant**) a small white tropical insect which eats wood

term-paper /ˈtɜːmˌpeɪ.pəʳ/ [US] /ˈtɜːrmˌpeɪ.pɚ/ *noun* [C] *US* the main report written by a student for a particular class or subject in the middle of each school term

terms [RULES] /tɜːmz/ [US] /tɝːmz/ *plural noun* the conditions which control an agreement, arrangement or activity: *terms **of** employment* ○ ***Under the** terms **of** their contract, employees must give 3 months' notice if they leave.*
• **on easy terms** If you buy something on easy terms, you pay for it over a period of time.
• **come to terms with *sth*** to gradually accept a sad situation, often the death of someone you love: *I think he's still coming to terms with the death of his wife.*

• **in sb's terms** according to someone's opinion or way of considering a situation: *Of course, a 200-year-old building is very old in American terms.*
• **on your own terms** If you do something on your own terms, you decide the conditions under which you will do it, because you are in a position of power.
• **on equal terms** (*ALSO* **on the same terms**) having the same rights, treatment, etc: *British and overseas companies will compete for the government contract on equal terms.*
• **on good/bad terms** If two people are on good/bad terms, they have a good/bad relationship with one another: *I've always been on good terms* ***with*** *my neighbours.*
• **terms of reference** *FORMAL* the matters to which a study or report is limited

terms [DESCRIBING] *plural noun* **in terms of/in ... terms** used to describe which particular area of a subject you are discussing: *In financial terms, the project was not a success.* ○ *In terms of money, I was better off in my last job.*

tern /tɜːn/ Ⓤⓢ /tɝːn/ *noun* **[C]** a small black and white sea bird with long pointed wings and a divided tail

terrace [GROUND] /ˈter.əs/ *noun* **[C]** **1** a flat raised area **2** a flat area of stone or grass outside a house, where people sit and sometimes eat **3** one of several narrow strips of land which are built like steps on the slope of a hill and which are used for growing crops on
terrace /ˈter.əs/ *verb* **[T]** to build narrow strips of land on a slope so that people can plant crops there
the terraces *plural noun UK SPECIALIZED* wide steps on which people stand to watch a football match

terrace [HOUSE] /ˈter.əs/ *noun* **[C]** *UK* a row of often small houses joined together along their side walls **terraced** /ˈter.ɪst/ *adj* (*ALSO* **terrace**) *a terraced* ***house***

terracotta /ˌter.əˈkɒt.ə/ Ⓤⓢ /-ˈkɑː.t̬ə/ *noun* **[U]** **1** hard, baked reddish-brown clay: *Our kitchen tiles are made from terracotta.* ○ *The courtyard was full of exotic plants in terracotta pots.* **2** a reddish-brown colour: *I've painted my bedroom terracotta.*

terra firma /ˌter.əˈfɜː.mə/ Ⓤⓢ /-ˈfɝː-/ *noun* **[U]** *USUALLY HUMOROUS* dry land, when compared with the sea or air: *It was good to get back on terra firma again after that awful sea crossing.*

terrain /təˈreɪn/ *noun* **[U]** an area of land, when considering its natural features: *The car handles particularly well on rough terrain.*

terrapin /ˈter.ə.pɪn/ *noun* **[C]** *plural* **terrapin** or **terrapins** a type of small North American TURTLE which lives in warm rivers and lakes

terrestrial /təˈres.tri.əl/ *adj* **1** *FORMAL* relating to the planet Earth ➲Compare **extraterrestrial**. **2** *SPECIALIZED* (of animals) living on the land rather than in the sea or air **3** *FORMAL* describes television channels which are broadcast from stations on the ground and do not use SATELLITES

terrible [UNPLEASANT] /ˈter.ə.bl̩/ *adj* very unpleasant or serious or of low quality: *The weather was terrible.* ○ *We have just received some terrible news.*
terribly /ˈter.ə.bli/ *adv* very badly: *I slept terribly last night.*

terrible [VERY GREAT] /ˈter.ə.bl̩/ *adj INFORMAL* used to emphasize the great degree of something: *This project is a terrible waste of money.* ○ *She's a terrible nuisance.*
terribly /ˈter.ə.bli/ *adv INFORMAL* very: *I'm terribly pleased to hear that you've got a job.* ○ *She was terribly sorry not to have seen you last Saturday.*

ˌterrible ˈtwins *plural noun UK INFORMAL* two people who behave in a way which attracts attention

terrier /ˈter.i.əʳ/ Ⓤⓢ /-ɚ/ *noun* **[C]** a breed of small active dog, originally used for hunting and chasing animals into or out of their underground holes

terrific [VERY GOOD] /təˈrɪf.ɪk/ *adj INFORMAL* very good: *a terrific opportunity* ○ *You look terrific!* **terrifically** /təˈrɪf.ɪ.kli/ *adv*

terrific [VERY GREAT] /təˈrɪf.ɪk/ *adj INFORMAL* used to emphasize the great amount or degree of something: *The police car drove past at a terrific speed.* **terrifically** /təˈrɪf.ɪ.kli/ *adv*

terrified /ˈter.ə.faɪd/ *adj* very frightened: *He huddled in the corner like a terrified child.* ○ *I'm terrified* ***of*** *the dark.* ○ *She's terrified* ***(that)*** *her mother might find out her secret.*

terrify /ˈter.ə.faɪ/ *verb* **[T]** to frighten someone very much: *The idea of parachuting out of a plane terrifies me.*

terrifying /ˈter.ə.faɪ.ɪŋ/ *adj* very frightening: *a terrifying experience/ordeal* **terrifyingly** /ˈter.ə.faɪ.ɪŋ.li/ *adv*

terrine /təˈriːn/ *noun* **1** **[C or U]** a savoury dish made of small pieces of cooked meat, fish or vegetables which have been pressed into a rectangular shape, and which is eaten cold **2** **[C]** the type of cooking dish in which a terrine is made

the ˌTerritorial ˈArmy *noun* **[S]** *UK* a group of men and women who, without payment and during the time when they are not working, are trained as soldiers
territorial /ˌter.ɪˈtɔː.ri.əl/ Ⓤⓢ /-ˈtɔːr.i-/ *noun* **[C]** a member of the Territorial Army

ˌterritorial ˈwaters *plural noun* the area of sea near a country's coast and under its legal control

territory /ˈter.ɪ.tᵊr.i/ /-tri/ Ⓤⓢ /-tɔːr.i/ *noun* **[C or U]** (an area of) land or sometimes sea, which is considered as belonging to or connected with a particular country or person: *He was shot down in enemy territory.* ○ *The UN is sending aid to the* ***occupied*** *territories.* ○ *The robin keeps other birds off that part of the garden – that's his territory* (= the area he tries to control). ○ *The director is back* ***on*** *familiar territory* (= a familiar subject) *with his latest film.*
• **go/come with the territory** to be an expected fact or result of a particular situation or position: *The public attention that famous people get just goes with the territory.*
territorial /ˌter.ɪˈtɔː.ri.əl/ Ⓤⓢ /-ˈtɔːr.i-/ *adj* relating to territory: *a territorial dispute* ○ *Some animals and birds are territorial* (= they mark out areas which they defend against others).

terror /ˈter.əʳ/ Ⓤⓢ /-ɚ/ *noun* **1** **[C or U]** (violent action which causes) extreme fear: *They fled from the city* ***in*** *terror.* ○ *There was* ***sheer/abject*** *terror in her eyes when he came back into the room.* ○ *Lots of people have* ***a*** *terror* ***of*** *spiders.* ○ *What he said* ***struck*** *terror in my heart* (= made me very frightened). ○ *The separatists started a* ***campaign of*** *terror* (= violent action causing fear) *to get independence.* ○ *Heights* ***have/hold*** *no terrors for me* (= do not frighten me). **2** **[C]** someone, especially a child, who behaves badly and is difficult to control: *My brother is a little terror.*
• **in terror of your life** frightened that you will be killed

terrorism /ˈter.ə.rɪ.zᵊm/ Ⓤⓢ /-ɚ.ɪ-/ *noun* **[U]** (threats of) violent action for political purposes: *Governments must cooperate if they are to fight/combat international terrorism.* ○ *The bomb explosion was one of the worst* ***acts of*** *terrorism that Italy has experienced in recent years.*
terrorist /ˈter.ə.rɪst/ Ⓤⓢ /-ɚ.ɪst/ *noun* **[C]** *Several terrorists have been killed by their own bombs.* ○ *There has been an increase in terrorist attacks.* ○ *The government has said that it will not be intimidated by terrorist threats.*

terrorize, *UK USUALLY* **-ise** /ˈter.ə.raɪz/ *verb* **[T]** to make someone feel very frightened by threatening to kill or hurt them: *Street gangs have been terrorizing the neighbourhood.*

terror-stricken /ˈter.əˌstrɪk.ᵊn/ Ⓤⓢ /-ɚ-/ *adj* extremely frightened

terry /ˈter.i/ *noun* **[U]** (*UK ALSO* **terry towelling,** *US ALSO* **terry cloth**) a type of thick cotton cloth with short threads on each side, used especially for making TOWELS (= thick cloths used for drying)

terse /tɜːs/ Ⓤⓢ /tɝːs/ *adj* using few words, sometimes in a way that seems rude or unfriendly: *"Are you feeling any better?" "No," was the terse* ***reply***. **tersely** /ˈtɜː.sli/ Ⓤⓢ /ˈtɝː-/ *adv* **terseness** /ˈtɜː.snəs/ Ⓤⓢ /ˈtɝː-/ *noun* **[U]**

tertiary [THIRD] /ˈtɜː.ʃᵊr.i/ Ⓤⓢ /ˈtɝː.ʃi.er-/ *adj FORMAL* relating to a third level or stage

tertiary [EDUCATION] /ˈtɜː.ʃᵊr.i/ Ⓤⓢ /ˈtɝː.ʃi.er-/ *adj* **[before n]** *UK* relating to education in colleges and universities: *tertiary education*

tertiary [SERVICE] /ˈtɜː.ʃᵊr.i/ Ⓤⓢ /ˈtɝː.ʃi.er-/ *adj* **[before n]** *SPECIALIZED* describes an industry that provides a

T

service and is not involved with obtaining the materials with which products are made, or with making products

Terylene /ˈter.ə.liːn/ *noun* [U] *UK TRADEMARK* (cloth made from) an artificial fibre

TESL /ˈtes.l̩/ *noun* [U] *ABBREVIATION FOR* teaching English as a second language

TESOL /ˈtiː.sɒl/ [US] /-sɑːl/ *noun* [U] *ABBREVIATION FOR* teaching English to speakers of other languages

TESSA /ˈtes.ə/ *noun* [C] *ABBREVIATION FOR* Tax Exempt Special Savings Account: a British savings account, replaced by the ISA in 1999, in which no tax was paid if the investment was kept for five years

tessellate, *US ALSO* **tesselate** /ˈtes.ᵊl.eɪt/ *verb* [I] *SPECIALIZED* (of shapes) to fit together in a pattern with no spaces in between

tessellated, *US ALSO* **tesselated** /ˈtes.ᵊl.eɪ.tɪd/ [US] /-t̬ɪd/ *adj SPECIALIZED* A tessellated floor is one made from small pieces of coloured stone fitted together to make a pattern or picture. **tessellation**, *US ALSO* **tesselation** /ˌtes.ᵊlˈeɪ.ʃᵊn/ *noun* [C or U]

test /test/ *noun* [C] **1** a way of discovering, by questions or practical activities, what someone knows, or what someone or something can do or is like: *The class are **doing/having** a spelling test today.* ○ *She had to **take/do/sit** an aptitude test before she got the job.* **2** a medical examination of part of your body in order to find out how healthy it is or what is wrong with it: *a blood/urine test* ○ *an eye test* ○ *a pregnancy test* ○ *The doctors have **done** some tests to try and find out what's wrong with her.* **3** an act of using something to find out whether it is working correctly or how effective it is: *The new missiles are currently **undergoing** tests.* **4** a situation which shows how good something is: *Driving on that icy road was a real test **of** my skill.*

• **put *sth* to the test** to find out how good something is: *Her constant questions really put my patience to the test!*

test /test/ *verb* [T] **1** to do something in order to discover if something is safe, works correctly, etc., or if something is present: *The manufacturers are currently testing the new engine.* ○ *They tested her blood **for** signs of the infection.* **2** to give someone a set of questions, in order to measure their knowledge or ability: *Will you test me **on** the chemical formulae I've been learning?* **3** If a situation tests someone, it proves how good, strong, etc. they are: *That lecture really tested my powers of endurance, it was so boring.* **4** to do a medical examination of part of someone's body or of a particular physical ability

• **test the water(s)** to find out what people's opinions of something are before you ask them to do something

tester /ˈtes.təʳ/ [US] /-tɚ/ *noun* [C] **1** a person or a machine which tests something **2** a small container of a product which you can try in order to see if you like it

▲ **test *sth* out** *phrasal verb* [M] to test something, especially a theory or an idea, to find out how it works in a practical situation or how people react to it: *The students tested out their cost-cutting ideas in several companies.*

testament /ˈtes.tə.mənt/ *noun* [C or U] *FORMAL* proof: *The detail of her wildlife paintings is (a) testament **to** (= proof of) her powers of observation.*

testate /ˈtes.teɪt/ *adj FORMAL* (of a person) having left a will ＊ NOTE: The opposite is **intestate**.

ˈtest ˌban *noun* [C] an agreement between countries to stop the practice of exploding nuclear weapons in order to examine their effectiveness: *a test ban treaty*

ˈtest ˌcard *noun* [C] (*US* **test pattern**) *UK* a picture or pattern that is broadcast so that the quality of the television picture received can be examined and improved if necessary by adjusting the controls on the equipment

ˈtest ˌcase *noun* [C] a case in a court of law which establishes principles in relation to which other similar cases are considered in the future

ˈtest ˌdrive *noun* [C] an act of driving a car that you are considering buying, in order to see if you like it

testicle /ˈtes.tɪ.kl̩/ *noun* [C] (*SPECIALIZED* **testis**) either of the two round male sex organs which produce sperm and are enclosed in the SCROTUM (= bag of skin) below and behind the penis

testify /ˈtes.tɪ.faɪ/ *verb* [I or T] to speak seriously about something, especially in a court of law; to give or provide evidence: [+ **that**] *He testified **that** he had seen the man leaving the building around the time of the murder.*

testimonial /ˌtes.tɪˈməʊ.ni.əl/ [US] /-ˈmoʊ-/ *noun* [C] **1** a statement about the character or qualities of someone or something **2** *FORMAL OR OLD-FASHIONED* a formal written description of someone's character and qualities given by a previous employer

testiˈmonial ˌmatch *noun* [C] a match played to honour and make money for a famous player

testimony /ˈtes.tɪ.mᵊn.i/ [US] /-moʊ.ni/ *noun* [C or U] *FORMAL* (an example of) spoken or written statements that something is true, especially those given in a court of law: *Some doubts have been expressed about his testimony.*

• **be (a) testimony to *sth*** *FORMAL* to be clear evidence of something: *The reports are testimony to the many hours of research completed by this committee.*

testing /ˈtes.tɪŋ/ *adj MAINLY UK* difficult: *These are very testing **times** for our family.* ○ *To complete 77 laps of the testing Hungaroring circuit is a challenge for any racing driver.*

testis /ˈtes.tɪs/ *noun* [C] *plural* **testes** *SPECIALIZED* a **testicle**

ˈtest (ˌmatch) *noun* [C] a game of cricket or rugby played by the national teams of two countries

testosterone /ˌtesˈtɒs.tᵊr.əʊn/ [US] /-ˈtɑː.stɚ.oʊn/ *noun* [U] a male hormone that causes a stage of growth in older boys and change in their reproductive organs

ˈtest ˌpilot *noun* [C] someone whose job is to fly new aircraft in order to make certain that they are effective

ˈtest ˌtube *noun* [C] a small glass tube, with one closed, rounded end, which is used in scientific experiments

ˌtest tube ˈbaby *noun* [C] a baby which developed from an egg and a sperm which were joined outside the body and then placed in the mother to grow

testy /ˈtes.ti/ *adj* easily annoyed and lacking patience: *a testy old man* ○ *testy comments* **testily** /ˈtes.tɪ.li/ *adv* **testiness** /ˈtes.tɪ.nəs/ *noun* [U]

tetanus /ˈtet.ᵊn.əs/ *noun* [U] (*OLD-FASHIONED INFORMAL* **lockjaw**) a serious disease caused by bacteria entering the human body through small cuts, causing the muscles, especially around the mouth, to tighten and stop working

tetchy /ˈtetʃ.i/ *adj* easily made angry, unhappy or upset: *Be careful what you say to Anna – she's in a rather tetchy mood.* **tetchily** /ˈtetʃ.ɪ.li/ *adv* **tetchiness** /ˈtetʃ.ɪ.nəs/ *noun* [U]

tête-à-tête /ˌteɪt.əˈteɪt/ *noun* [C] an informal private conversation between two people, especially friends: *We must **have** a tête-à-tête sometime.*

tête-à-tête /ˌteɪt.əˈteɪt/ *adv* in private with only two people together: *We dined tête-à-tête.*

tether /ˈteð.əʳ/ [US] /-ɚ/ *noun* [C] a rope or chain used to tie especially an animal to a post or other fixed place, usually so that it can move freely within a small area

• **at the end of *your* tether** having no strength or patience left: *By 6 o'clock after a busy day I'm at the end of my tether.* **tether** /ˈteð.əʳ/ [US] /-ɚ/ *verb* [T] **tethered** /ˈteð.əd/ [US] /-ɚd/ *adj*

Teutonic /tjuːˈtɒn.ɪk/ [US] /tuːˈtɑː.nɪk/ *adj* of, or thought to be typical of, the groups of people in northwestern Europe of German origin: *a Teutonic language* ○ *Teutonic features*

Tex-Mex /ˌteksˈmeks/ *adj* referring to the Mexican-American culture existing in Texas and the south-western United States

text [WRITING] /tekst/ *noun* **1** [U] the written words in a book, magazine, etc., not the pictures: *The book has 100 pages of closely printed text.* **2** **the text of *sth*** the exact words of a speech, etc: *Can we see the full text of your speech before Tuesday?* **3** [C] a book or piece of writing that you study as part of a course: *'Ulysses' is a **set** text for the exam.* **4** [C] a sentence or reference from the Bible which a priest reads aloud in church and talks about

textual /ˈteks.tju.əl/ [US] /-tʃu-/ *adj* **1** relating to written or printed material **2** related to the way in which something has been written: *textual analysis*

text [SEND] /tekst/ *verb* [T] to **text message**

textbook [BOOK] /ˈtekst.bʊk/ *noun* [C] a book that contains detailed information about a subject for people who are studying that subject: *a science textbook*

textbook [TYPICAL] /ˈtekst.bʊk/ *adj* [before n] (of an example of something) extremely good, or thought to be usual or typical: *That was a textbook goal from Taylor.* ○ *It was a textbook* ***example*** *of how to deal with the problem.*

textile /ˈtek.staɪl/ *noun* [C] a cloth woven by hand or machine: *the textile* ***industry***

text ˌmessage *noun* [C] a written message, usually containing words that have been shortened, sent from one MOBILE PHONE or PAGER to another

ˈtext ˌmessage *verb* [I or T] (*ALSO* **text**) to send someone a text message: *Why don't you text all your friends and invite them to the party too?* **ˈtext ˌmessaging** *noun* [U] *Text messaging is all the rage among teenagers.*

texture /ˈteks.tʃəʳ/ [US] /-tʃɚ/ *noun* **1** [C or U] the quality of something that can be decided by touch; the degree to which something is rough or smooth, or soft or hard: *a smooth/rough/coarse texture* ○ *This artificial fabric has the texture of silk.* **2** [U] the character of a piece of writing or music: *The writing has a rich texture.*

textured /ˈteks.tʃəd/ [US] /-tʃɚd/ *adj* describes something that has a surface that is not smooth but has a raised pattern on it: *textured wallpaper*

-textured /-teks.tʃəd/ [US] /-tʃɚd/ *suffix* having a texture of the stated type: *coarse-textured*

thalidomide /θəˈlɪd.ə.maɪd/ *noun* [U] a drug which was once used to help people relax or sleep, and which was found to cause damage to babies inside the womb, especially by stopping the development of their arms and legs, when it was taken by their mothers

than *STRONG* /ðæn/ *WEAK* /ðən/ *prep, conjunction* **1** used to join two parts of a comparison: *My son is a lot taller than my daughter.* ○ *You always walk faster than I do!* ○ *You're earlier than usual.* **2** used with 'more' or 'less' to compare numbers or amounts: *I spent more than I intended to.* ○ *It cost less than I expected.*

thank /θæŋk/ *verb* [T] to express to someone that you are pleased about or appreciate something that they have done: *He thanked me* ***for*** *taking him home.*

• **thank *sb* for *sth*** If you thank someone for something, you mean that they are responsible or to blame for it: *You can thank John for the mess we're in.*

• **have *sb* to thank** If you have someone to thank for something, they are responsible or to blame for it: *You have John to thank for this problem.*

• **I'll thank you to do *sth*** *FORMAL* used to ask someone, in an annoyed way, to do something: *I'll thank you to leave my private papers alone.*

• **thank God/goodness/heaven(s), etc.** said to express happiness that something bad has been avoided or has finished: *Thank God you found the key.* ○ *I managed to catch the train, thank goodness.*

• **thank *your* lucky stars** to be very grateful for something: *She thanked her lucky stars that she had taken out insurance, when she was involved in an accident on holiday.*

• **won't thank *you* for doing *sth*** If someone won't thank you for doing something, they will not be pleased if you do it: *She won't thank you for telling everyone how old she is.*

thanks /θæŋks/ *plural noun* **1** grateful and appreciative feelings: *They expressed their thanks to the organisers.* ○ *He wrote a letter of thanks to the hospital.* ○ *Let us* ***give*** *thanks to God.* **2** *INFORMAL* **thank you**: *"Shall I do that for you?" "No, thanks."*

• **thanks for nothing** (*ALSO* **thanks a bunch**, *ALSO* **thanks a lot**) used to show you are annoyed when someone has done something you are unhappy about or has failed to help you in some way: *"I told Dad you'd love to wash his car." "Thanks a lot."* ○ *Thanks a lot for supporting me* (= You did not support me).

• **thanks to *sb/sth*** because of someone or something: *It's thanks to Sandy that I heard about the job.* ○ *DISAPPROVING The baby is awake thanks to your shouting.*

• **no thanks to *sb*** despite: *It's no thanks to you that I arrived on time.*

thankful /ˈθæŋk.fəl/ *adj* pleased or grateful for something: [+ that] *I was thankful* ***that*** *the meeting didn't last long, because I had a train to catch.* **thankfulness** /ˈθæŋk.fəl.nəs/ *noun* [U]

thankfully /ˈθæŋk.fəl.i/ *adv* used, usually at the beginning of a sentence, to show you are pleased or grateful about something: *Thankfully, nobody was hurt.*

thankless /ˈθæŋ.kləs/ *adj* describes a piece of work which is difficult or unpleasant, and for which people do not thank you: *Keeping the children's rooms tidy is a thankless* ***task/job.***

thanksgiving /ˌθæŋksˈgɪv.ɪŋ/ *noun* [U] when you say or show that you are grateful, especially to God

ˌThanksˈgiving (ˌDay) *noun* [C or U] a public holiday and celebration, held on the fourth Thursday of November in the US and on the second Monday of October in Canada, to remember the thanks that the people who first came from Europe gave to God when they gathered crops for the first time in their new country

ˈthank ˌyou *noun* [C usually sing], *exclamation* something that you say or do in order to show that you are grateful for something: *I'd like to say a* ***big*** *thank you* ***to*** *everyone for all their help.* ○ *He wrote a thank-you* ***note/letter*** *to his granny to thank her for the birthday present she sent him.* ○ *That was a delicious lunch, thank you.* ○ *"Here's your coffee." "Thank you* ***very much (indeed).****"* ○ *Thank you* ***for*** *my birthday present.*

ˈthank ˌyou *exclamation*, **1** said when you are answering a polite question or remark: *"How are you?" "I'm fine, thank you."* ○ *"You look very nice in that dress." "Thank you* ***very much.****"* **2** said to politely accept or refuse something that has been offered to you: *"Would you like some more cake?" "Yes, I will have a small piece, thank you."* ○ *"Do you need any help?" "No, thank you."* **3** said to show your disapproval of something: *I don't want to hear that kind of language, thank you* ***(very much).***

that [SOMETHING NOT HERE] /ðæt/ *determiner, pronoun plural* **those** used to refer to a person, object, idea, etc. which is separated from the speaker by space or time: *I've never liked that cousin of hers.* ○ *Who's that? Is that the girl you told me about?* ○ *How much are those shoes?* ○ *FORMAL His handwriting is like that* (= the writing) ***of*** *a much younger child.*

that *STRONG* /ðæt/, *WEAK* /ðət/ *pronoun plural* **those** **1** used to make a connection with an earlier statement: *My usual train was cancelled. That's why I'm so late.* ○ *Lucy has just ruined her new dress. That's children* ***for you*** (= Such behaviour is typical of children). **2** used to express a reaction to something: *I didn't know she'd been so ill. That's terrible.* ○ *Turn the engine on, then put the car in gear. That's* ***right*** (= you are doing it correctly). ○ *Smile for the camera. That's* ***more like it*** (= that smile is better than before).

that /ðæt/ *determiner plural* **those** used to refer to something which has been mentioned or was involved earlier, or to something with which the listener will be familiar: *Where's that pen* (= the one I was using earlier) *gone?* ○ *She lives in that house by the bus station* (= you know which one I mean).

• **that's it 1** used to say that something has ended: *Well, that's it, we've finished – we can go home now.* ○ *That's it! I'm not putting up with any more of her rudeness.* **2** used to say that something is correct: *You switch the computer on at the back. That's it.*

• **... at that** *INFORMAL* in addition to that: *It's too expensive, and probably out-of-date at that.*

• **that's that** (*ALSO* **that was that**) an expression that shows that something has ended: *I won't agree to it and that's that* (= I won't discuss it any longer).

• **that is (to say)** said when you want to give further details or be more exact about something: *I'll meet you in the city, that is, I will if the trains are running.*

• **That will do.** said to mean that you do not want any more of something: *"More peas?" "No, that'll do, thank you."* ○ *That will do, Charles. I don't want to see any more of that kind of behaviour.*

• **That's life.** *SAYING* said when something bad has happened that you cannot change

T

USAGE

this/these or that/those?

Use **this** or **these** to talk about people and things that are close to the speaker in space or time.

This is Sarah, who will be working with us for a few months.
Do you like these earrings I'm wearing?

Use **that** or **those** to talk about people and things which are further away from the speaker in space or time.

That girl over there is called Sarah.
I liked those earrings you wore last night.

that [INTRODUCING A CLAUSE] *STRONG* /ðæt/, *WEAK* /ðət/ *conjunction* used to introduce a clause which reports something or gives further information, although it can often be omitted: *She said (that) she'd collect it for me after work.* ○ *Is it true (that) she's gone back to teaching?* ○ *We'll be there at about 7.30,* ***provided/providing*** *(that) there's a suitable train.* ○ *It was* ***so*** *dark (that) I couldn't see anything.*

that [USED TO REFER] *STRONG* /ðæt/ *WEAK* /ðət/ *pronoun plural* **those** used as the subject or object of a verb to show which person or thing you are referring to, or to add information about a person or thing just mentioned. It is used for both people and things. It can often be omitted: *I can't find the books (that) I got from the library.* ○ *Is this the train that stops at Cambridge?* ○ *Have you been to the restaurant that's just opened in town?* ↄSee Note **which, who or that?** at **which** USED TO REFER.

that [AS MUCH] /ðæt/ *adv* as much as suggested: *She's too young to walk that far.* ○ *It wasn't* ***(all)*** *that* (= very) *good.*

thatch /θætʃ/ *verb* [T] to make a roof for a building with straw or reeds

thatch /θætʃ/ *noun* [U] **1** straw or reeds used to make roofs **2 thatch of hair** a mass of thick or untidy hair

thatched /θætʃt/ *adj*: *They live in a thatched* ***cottage****/a cottage with a thatched* ***roof****.*

thatcher /ˈθætʃ.əʳ/ [US] /-ɚ/ *noun* [C] a person whose job is thatching roofs

thaw [BECOME NOT FROZEN] /θɔː/ [US] /θɑː/ *verb* [I or T] to (cause to) change from a solid, frozen state to a liquid or soft one, because of an increase in temperature: *Allow the meat to thaw properly before cooking it.* ○ *The sun came out and thawed the ice.* ○ ***It's*** *beginning to thaw* (= The weather is warm enough for snow and ice to melt). ↄCompare **freeze**.

the thaw *noun* [S] a period of warmer weather when snow and ice begin to melt: *The thaw has* ***set in*** *early this year.*

▲ **thaw out** *phrasal verb* If you thaw out, you gradually get warm again after being very cold: *I'm only just beginning to thaw out after taking the dogs out this morning.*

thaw [BECOME FRIENDLY] /θɔː/ [US] /θɑː/ *verb* [I] to become friendlier or more relaxed: *The report shows that* ***relations*** *between the two enemies may be thawing.*

thaw /θɔː/ [US] /θɑː/ *noun* [S] an increase in friendliness: *There are signs of* ***a*** *thaw in relations between the two countries.*

the [PARTICULAR] *STRONG* /ðiː/, *WEAK* /ðə/, *BEFORE VOWELS* /ði/ *determiner* **1** used before nouns to refer to things or people when a listener or reader knows which particular things or people are being referred to, especially because they have already been mentioned or because what is happening makes it clear: *I just bought a new shirt and some new shoes. The shirt was quite expensive, but the shoes weren't.* ○ *Please would you pass the salt.* ○ *I'll pick you up at the station.* **2** used before some nouns that refer to place when you want to mention that type of place, without showing exactly which example of the place you mean: *We spent all day at the beach.* ○ *Shall we go to the movies this evening?* ○ *I must go to the bank and change some money.* **3** used before noun phrases in which the range of meaning of the noun is limited in some way: *I really enjoyed the book I've just finished reading.* ○ *Do you like the other students in your class?* **4** used to refer to things or people when only one exists at any one time: *What will happen in the future?* ○ *After I leave college, I want to travel round the world.* ○ *They live in the north of Spain.* ○ *Ed Koch was for many years the mayor of New York.* ○ *When we went to Paris, we went up the Eiffel Tower.* **5** used before superlatives and other words, such as 'first' or 'only' or numbers showing something's position in a list, which refer to only one thing or person: *That was one of the best films I've ever seen.* ○ *What's the highest mountain in Europe?* ○ *I shall never forget the first time we met.* ○ *You're the fifth person to ask me that question.* **6** used to say that the particular person or thing being mentioned is the best, most famous, etc. In this use, 'the' is usually given strong pronunciation: *Harry's Bar is the place to go.* ○ *You don't mean you met the Richard Gere, do you?* **7** used before some adjectives to turn the adjectives into nouns which refer to one particular person or thing described by the adjective: *It seems that the deceased* (= this particular dead person) *had no living relatives.* ○ *I suppose we'll just have to wait for the inevitable* (= the particular thing that is certain to happen). **8** used before some adjectives to turn the adjectives into nouns which refer to people or things in general that can be described by the adjective: *She lives in a special home for the elderly.* ○ *The French were defeated at Waterloo in 1815.* **9** used before a singular noun to refer to all the things or people represented by that noun: *The panda is becoming an increasingly rare animal.* ○ *The car is responsible for causing a lot of damage to our environment.* **10** used before a family name to refer to two people who are married or to a whole family: *The Jacksons are coming to lunch on Saturday.* **11** used before some nouns referring to musical instruments or dances to mean the type of instrument or dance in general: *Nico is learning to play the piano.* ○ *Can you do the waltz?* **12** used before a noun to represent the activity connected with that noun: *I've got to go under the surgeon's knife* (= have a medical operation) *next week.* ○ *It's not a good idea to spend more than three hours at the wheel* (= driving a vehicle) *without a break.* **13** used before numbers that refer to periods of ten years: *the sixties* **14** used before each of two comparative adjectives or adverbs when you want to show how one amount gets bigger or smaller in relation to the other: *The sooner I get this piece of work finished, the sooner I can go home.* **15** used before comparative adjectives or adverbs when you want to show that someone or something has become more or less of a particular state: *She doesn't seem to be any the worse* ***for*** *her bad experience.* **16** used for emphasis when you are expressing a strong opinion about someone or something: *André's got a new job, the lucky devil.*

the [YOUR] *STRONG* /ðiː/, *WEAK* /ðə/, *BEFORE VOWELS* /ði/ *determiner* used instead of a possessive adjective such as your, her or my: *He held his daughter by the arm.* ○ *I can't remember where I parked the* (= my) *car.*

the [ENOUGH] *STRONG* /ðiː/, *WEAK* /ðə/, *BEFORE VOWELS* /ði/ *determiner* enough: *I'd like to go out this evening, but I don't think I've got the energy.* ○ [+ **to** infinitive] *I haven't got the time* ***to*** *talk to you now.*

the [EACH] *STRONG* /ðiː/, *WEAK* /ðə/, *BEFORE VOWELS* /ði/ *determiner* each; every: *It does 30 miles to the gallon.*

theater /ˈθɪə.təʳ/ [US] /ˈθiː.ə.t̬ɚ/ *noun* [C] *US FOR* **1** theatre **2** (*ALSO* **movie theater**) a cinema

theatre [BUILDING] /ˈθɪə.təʳ/ /θiˈet.əʳ/ [US] /ˈθiː.ə.t̬ɚ/ *noun* [C] **1** *UK* (*US* **theater**) a building, room or outside structure with rows of seats, each row usually higher than the one in front, from which people can watch a performance or other activity: *the Lyceum Theatre* ○ *a lecture theatre* **2** *UK* **operating theatre**

theatre [PERFORMING ARTS] *UK, US* **theater** /ˈθɪə.təʳ/ /θiˈet.əʳ/ [US] /ˈθiː.ə.t̬ɚ/ *noun* [U] (the writing or performance of) plays, musicals or opera, written to be performed in public: *His latest play has delighted theatre* ***audiences*** *and theatre* ***critics*** *alike.* ○ *She made her career* ***in the*** *theatre.* **theatrical** /θiˈæt.rɪ.kəl/ *adj*: *theatrical make-up* **theatricality** /θiˌæt.rɪˈkæl.ɪ.ti/ [US] /-ə.t̬i/ *noun* [U] **theatrically** /θiˈæt.rɪ.kli/ *adv*

theatricals /θiˈæt.rɪ.kəlz/ *plural noun* stage performances by people who are not trained or paid to act, but who practise and perform in the time when they

T

are not working: *amateur theatricals*

theatre BEHAVIOUR *UK, US* **theater** /ˈθɪə.tər/ /ˈθiːˈet.ər/ *US* /ˈθiː.ə.t̬ər/ *noun* [U] insincere behaviour intended just to produce a particular effect or to attract attention: *Her tears were **pure** theatre.*

theatrical /θiˈæt.rɪ.kəl/ *adj* describes behaviour that is insincere and too extreme and that is intended to attract attention: *a theatrical gesture* **theatricality** /θiˌæt.rɪˈkæl.ɪ.ti/ *US* /-ə.t̬i/ *noun* [U]

theatre MILITARY *UK, US* **theater** /ˈθɪə.tər/ /ˈθiːˈet.ər/ *US* /ˈθiː.ə.t̬ər/ *noun* [C] an area or place in which important military events happen: *a theatre of war*

theatregoer /ˈθɪə.təˌɡəʊ.ər/ /ˈθiːˈet.ə-/ *US* /ˈθiː.ə.t̬əˌɡoʊ.ə-/ *noun* [C] (*US USUALLY* **theatergoer**) someone who regularly goes to the theatre

theatre in the ˈround *noun* [C or U] a theatre where people sit on all sides of the performers, not just in front of them. It is also a type of performance which tries to involve the people watching.

thee /ðiː/ *pronoun OLD USE* you; object form of THOU; used when speaking to one person: *With this ring, I thee wed.*

theft /θeft/ *noun* [C or U] (the act of) dishonestly taking something which belongs to someone else and keeping it: *Unfortunately, we have had several thefts in the building recently.* ⊃ *Shoplifting is theft.* ⊃See also **thief.**

their /ðeər/ *US* /ðer/ *determiner* **1** of or belonging to them: *He gave them their coats.* **2** used to refer to one person in order to avoid saying 'his or her': *One of the students has left their book behind.*

theirs /ðeəz/ *US* /ðerz/ *pronoun* of or belonging to them: *I think she's a relation of theirs.*

theism /ˈθiː.ɪ.zəm/ *noun* [U] the belief that there is only one god, who is completely separate from those things (the Earth, people, etc.) he has created, rather than being part of them ⊃Compare **atheism** at **atheist;** **deism.**

them THOSE PEOPLE/THINGS *STRONG* /ðem/, *WEAK* /ðəm/ *pronoun* **1** the object form of 'they' used after a verb or preposition: *I've lost my keys. I can't find them anywhere.* ○ *It's them. They've arrived early.* **2** used to refer to one person whose sex is unknown instead of saying 'him or her': *When each passenger arrives, we ask them to fill in a form.*

● **them and us** *INFORMAL* used when describing disagreements or differences especially between different social groups: *If parents are encouraged to be involved in school, there is less chance of a them-and-us situation developing.* ○ *The senior staff have their own restaurant. – It's definitely a case of them and us.*

them THOSE *STRONG* /ðem/ *determiner NOT STANDARD FOR* **those:** *Who gave you them sweets?*

theme /θiːm/ *noun* [C] **1** the main subject of a talk, book, film, etc. or a short, simple tune on which a piece of music is based: *The theme of loss runs through most of his novels.* **2** a song or tune which is played several times in a film, etc. and which is therefore remembered as belonging to that film: *a theme song/tune* **thematic** /θɪˈmæt.ɪk/ *US* /θiːˈmæt̬-/ *adj*: *In her study, the author has adopted a thematic* (= based on different subjects) *rather than a chronological approach to the French Revolution.*

ˈtheme ˌpark *noun* [C] (*US ALSO* **amusement park**) a large permanent area for public entertainment, with amusing activities and big machines to ride on or play games on, restaurants, etc., all connected with a single subject

themselves /ðəmˈselvz/ *pronoun* reflexive form of 'they', sometimes used for emphasis: *Did they enjoy themselves at the theatre?* ○ *They asked themselves where they had gone wrong.* ○ *FORMAL They themselves had no knowledge of what was happening.* ○ *They collected the evidence **(all by)** themselves* (= without help). ○ *They **had** the whole campsite **to themselves*** (= They were alone and did not have to share it with anyone). ○ *These facts are unimportant **in themselves*** (= when considered alone), *but if you put them together, they may mean more.*

● **be yourself** to act in your usual manner: *I wish people would just be themselves instead of trying to seem important.*

● **keep (yourself) to yourself** If you keep (yourself) to yourself, you do not socialize with other people: *Our neighbours keep (themselves) to themselves.*

then TIME /ðen/ *adv, adj* [before n] (at) that time (in the past or in the future): *I was working in the city then.* ○ *FORMAL I wanted to live in the city, but my then husband* (= the man who was my husband at that time) *preferred the country.* ○ *Give it to me next week – I won't have time to read it before/until then.* ○ *I'll phone you tomorrow – I should have the details by then.*

● **from then on** from that time: *She had a car accident a year ago and suffered from back pain from then on.*

● **then and there** (*ALSO* **there and then**) immediately: *I suggested he phone his mother and he did it there and then.*

then NEXT /ðen/ *adv* next or after that: *Let me finish this job, then we'll go.* ○ *Give her the letter to read, then she'll understand.*

then IN ADDITIONAL /ðen/ *adv* in addition: *This is the standard model, then there's the deluxe version which costs more.*

● **but then (again)** but when you think about the matter more or in another way: *I agree she types accurately, but then again, she's very slow.*

then RESULT /ðen/ *adv* as a result; in that case; also used as a way of joining a statement to an earlier piece of conversation: *Have a rest now, then you won't be so tired this evening.* ○ *You'll be selling your house, then?*

thence /ðents/ *adv OLD-FASHIONED OR FORMAL* from there: *We travelled to my parents' home and thence to my sister's.*

thenceforth /ˌðentsˈfɔːθ/ *US* /-ˈfɔːrθ/ *adv* (*ALSO* **thenceforward**) *OLD-FASHIONED OR FORMAL* after that; from that time forward: *The property was known thenceforth as The Manor.*

theocracy /θiˈɒk.rə.si/ *US* /-ˈɑː.krə-/ *noun* **1** [C] a country that is ruled by religious leaders **2** [U] when a country is ruled by religious leaders **theocratic** /ˌθiː.əʊˈkræt.ɪk/ /ˌ-əˈkræt̬-/ *adj*

theology /θiˈɒl.ə.dʒi/ /US /-ˈɑː.lə-/ *noun* [C or U] the study of religion and religious belief, or a set of beliefs about a particular religion **theologian** /ˌθiː.əˈləʊ.dʒən/ *US* /-ˈloʊ-/ *noun* [C] a student of theology **theological** /ˌθiː.əˈlɒdʒ.ɪ.kəl/ *US* /-ˈlɑː.dʒɪ-/ *adj* **theologically** /ˌθiː.əˈlɒdʒ.ɪ.kli/ *US* /-ˈlɑː.dʒɪ-/ *adv*

theorem /ˈθɪə.rəm/ *US* /ˈθiː.ə-.əm/ *noun* [C] *SPECIALIZED* (especially in mathematics) a formal statement that can be shown to be true by reasoning: *a mathematical theorem*

theoretical /θɪəˈret.ɪ.kəl/ *US* /ˌθiː.əˈret̬-/ *adj* **1** based on the ideas that relate to a subject, not the practical uses of that subject: *theoretical physics* **2** related to an explanation that has not been proved

theoretically /θɪəˈret.ɪ.kli/ *US* /ˌθiː.əˈret̬-/ *adv* in a way that obeys some rules but is not likely: *It is theoretically possible.*

theoˌretical possiˈbility *noun* [C] something which could, but is unlikely to, be or be true according to the known facts

theorist /ˈθɪə.rɪst/ *US* /ˈθiː.ə-.ɪst/ *noun* [C] someone who develops ideas about the explanation for events: *a political theorist*

theorize, *UK USUALLY* **-ise** /ˈθɪə.raɪz/ *US* /ˈθɪr.aɪz/ *verb* [I] to develop a set of ideas about something: *It's easy to theorize **about** what might have happened.*

theory /ˈθɪə.ri/ *US* /ˈθɪr.i/ *noun* [C or U] a formal statement of the rules on which a subject of study is based or of ideas which are suggested to explain a fact or event or, more generally, an opinion or explanation: *economic theory* ○ *scientific theory* ○ *Darwin's theory **of** evolution* ○ *He **has** a theory **that** the hole was caused by a meteorite.*

● **in theory** If something is possible in theory, it should be possible, but often it does not happen in that way: *In theory, the journey ought to take three hours, but in practice it usually takes four because of roadworks.*

therapeutic /ˌθer.əˈpjuː.tɪk/ *US* /-t̬ɪk/ *adj* causing someone to feel happier and more relaxed or to be more healthy: *I find gardening very therapeutic.*

therapy /'θer.ə.pi/ *noun* [C or U] a treatment which helps someone feel better, grow stronger, etc., especially after an illness: *occupational therapy* ○ *speech therapy* ○ *group therapy* ○ *Joining a club can be **a** therapy **for** loneliness.*
therapist /'θer.ə.pɪst/ *noun* [C] a speech therapist ○ *I'm seeing my therapist on Friday morning.*

there PLACE /ðeəʳ/ ⓤ /ðer/ *adv* (to, at or in) that place: *Put the chair there.* ○ *The museum is closed today. We'll go there tomorrow.* ○ *There's that book you were looking for.* ○ *I'll have to stop you there, we've run out of time.* ○ *I've left the boxes over/out/under there.*
• **there and back** adding together the distance or time to and from a particular place: *It was 20 miles there and back.*
• **get there 1** to arrive somewhere: *We'll never get there in time.* **2** INFORMAL to succeed: *Try again, you'll get there in the end.*
• **be there for** *sb* to be available to provide help and support for someone: *We haven't always been close, but she was there for me when I needed her.* ○ *Best friends are always there for each other in times of trouble.*

there INTRODUCING A SENTENCE /ðeəʳ/ ⓤ /ðer/ *adv* **1** used to introduce sentences, especially before the verbs *be*, *seem* and *appear*: *There's someone on the phone for you.* ○ *There's no doubt who is the best candidate.* ○ *NOT STANDARD There's* (= There are) *lives at stake and we can't afford to take any risks.* ○ *There appeared/seemed to be some difficulty in fixing a date for the meeting.* **2** LITERARY used to begin some children's stories written in a traditional style: *There once was/lived a poor widow who had a beautiful daughter.*
• **There's a good boy/girl/dog!** used to show approval or encouragement: *Tie your shoelaces, there's a good girl!*
• **there you are 1** (INFORMAL **there you go**) used when giving something to someone, usually after a request for the item, such as giving someone goods that they have bought **2** used to mean 'I told you so': *There you are, I knew you'd forget if you didn't write it down.*
• **there you go** used to express acceptance of something unlucky: *We didn't win the competition, but there you go – we can always try again next year.*
• **there** *you* **go again** a way of emphasizing that an action is often repeated: *There they go again, making trouble.*

there SYMPATHY/SATISFACTION /ðeəʳ/ ⓤ /ðer/ *exclamation* used to express sympathy or satisfaction: *There, I've made it work at last.*
• **there, there** (ALSO **there now**) something you say to comfort someone, especially a child: *There, there, don't cry.*

thereabouts /'ðeə.rə.baʊts/ ⓤ /,--'-/ ⓤ /'ðer.ə.baʊts/ *adv* approximately: *He's lived in Norwich for 40 years, or thereabouts.*

thereafter /,ðeə'rɑːf.təʳ/ ⓤ /,ðer'æf.tɚ/ *adv* FORMAL continuing on from a particular point in time, especially after something else has stopped happening: *He left the priesthood in 1970 and settled in the Washington area shortly thereafter* (= soon after that).

thereby /,ðeə'baɪ/ ⓤ /,ðer-/ *adv* FORMAL OR OLD-FASHIONED as a result of this action: *Diets that are high in saturated fat and cholesterol tend to clog up our arteries, thereby reducing the blood flow to our hearts and brains.*

therefore /'ðeə.fɔːʳ/ ⓤ /'ðer.fɔːr/ *adv* for that reason: *We were unable to get funding and therefore had to abandon the project.*

therein /,ðeə'rɪn/ ⓤ /,ðer'ɪn/ *adv* OLD-FASHIONED FORMAL in or into a particular place, thing, etc: *It is a thrilling tale of a haunted house and the ghosts therein.*
• **therein lies** in what has just been mentioned we see the reason or explanation for (a particular situation, quality or problem): *Her book is simply a collection of memories, told without conceit or self-absorption – and therein lies its power.*

thereof /,ðeə'rɒv/ ⓤ /,ðer'ɑːv/ *adv* FORMAL of or about the thing just mentioned: *Please refer to the Regulations and in particular Articles 99 and 100 thereof.*

thermal /'θɜː.məl/ ⓤ /'θɜː-/ *adj* [before n] SPECIALIZED connected with heat: *thermal **conductivity*** (= ability of a substance to carry heat) ○ *It was the Romans who first recognised the medicinal benefits of Hungary's thermal*

springs (= ones which produce hot water). **thermally** /'θɜː.mə.li/ ⓤ /'θɜː-/ *adv*
thermal /'θɜː.məl/ ⓤ /'θɜː-/ *noun* [C] SPECIALIZED a large column of hot air rising from the ground

,**thermal 'imaging** *noun* [U] the use of special electronic equipment, in conditions in which it is difficult to see, to create a picture based on the heat produced by a person or object

thermals /'θɜː.məlz/ ⓤ /'θɜː-/ *plural noun* INFORMAL FOR **thermal underwear**

,**thermal 'underwear** *noun* [U] (INFORMAL **thermals**) underwear that has been specially designed to keep you warm

thermo- /'θɜː.məʊ-/ ⓤ /'θɜː.moʊ-/ *prefix* connected with heat or temperature: *a thermo-nuclear device*

thermodynamics /,θɜː.məʊ.daɪ'næm.ɪks/ ⓤ /,θɜː.moʊ-/ *noun* [U] SPECIALIZED the area of physics connected with the action of heat and other types of energy, and the relationship between them **thermodynamic** /,θɜː.məʊ.daɪ'næm.ɪk/ ⓤ /,θɜː.moʊ-/ *adj* [before n]

thermometer /θə'mɒm.ɪ.təʳ/ ⓤ /θɚ'mɑː.mə.tɚ/ *noun* [C] a device used for measuring temperature, especially of the air or in a person's body

Thermos /'θɜː.məs/ ⓤ /'θɜː-/ *noun* [C] (UK ALSO **Thermos flask**, US ALSO **Thermos bottle**) TRADEMARK a **vacuum flask**

thermostat /'θɜː.mə.stæt/ ⓤ /'θɜː-/ *noun* [C] a device which keeps a building, engine, etc. within a usually limited temperature range by automatically switching the supply of heat on and off: *a central heating thermostat*

thesaurus /θɪ'sɔː.rəs/ ⓤ /-'sɔːr.əs/ *noun* [C] *plural* **thesauruses** or FORMAL **thesauri** a type of dictionary in which words with similar meanings are grouped together

these /ðiːz/ *determiner*, *pronoun*, *plural of* **this** THING REFERRED TO

thesis /'θiː.sɪs/ *noun* [C] *plural* **theses 1** a long piece of writing on a particular subject, especially one that is done for a higher college or university degree: *a doctoral thesis* (= for a PhD) **2** FORMAL the main idea, opinion or theory of a person, group, piece of writing or speech: *Their main thesis was that war was inevitable.*

thespian /'θes.pi.ən/ *adj* FORMAL connected with acting and the theatre
thespian /'θes.pi.ən/ *noun* [C] FORMAL an actor

they /ðeɪ/ *pronoun* **1** used as the subject of a verb to refer to people, animals or things already mentioned or, more generally, to a group of people not clearly described: *I've known the Browns for a long time. They're very pleasant people.* ○ *Where are my glasses? They were on the table just now.* ○ *They* (= People who know) *say things will be better in the new year.* **2** used to avoid saying 'he or she': *"There's someone on the phone for you." "What do they want?"*

they'd /ðeɪd/ *short form* **1** they had: *They'd had three bottles of wine of wine and were very drunk.* **2** they would: *They'd love to see 'Jurassic Park'.*

they'll /ðeɪl/ *short form* they will: *They'll be here any minute, if their train's on time.*

they're /ðeəʳ/ ⓤ /ðer/ *short form* they are: *They're so in love.*

they've /ðeɪv/ *short form* they have: *They've really made a mess of things now.*

thiamine /'θaɪ.ə.miːn/ /-mɪn/ *noun* [U] SPECIALIZED **vitamin B$_1$**

thick NOT THIN /θɪk/ *adj* having a large distance between two sides: *a thick rope* ○ *a thick layer of dust* ○ *She picked up a thick volume and began to read out loud.* ○ *The walls are two metres thick.* ○ *a thick* (= made of thick material) *sweater/coat* **thickly** /'θɪk.li/ *adv*
thickness /'θɪk.nəs/ *noun* [C or U] *The thickness of the mulch will prevent weeds growing around the shrubs.* ○ *Put several thicknesses* (= layers) *of newspaper on the table before you start painting.*

thick CLOSE TOGETHER /θɪk/ *adj* **1** growing close together and in large amounts: *thick forest* ○ *thick dark hair* **2** difficult to see through: *Thick, black smoke was pouring out of the chimney.*

- **be (as) thick as thieves** INFORMAL to be very close friends and share secrets, etc: *I'm sure she tells Ruth everything we say – they're as thick as thieves, those two.*

- **thick on the ground** MAINLY UK INFORMAL existing in large numbers: *Female engineers are not too thick on the ground.*

thicken /ˈθɪk.ᵊn/ *verb* [I or T] to (cause to) become thicker: *The smoke thickened rapidly.*

thick [NOT FLOWING] /θɪk/ *adj* (of a liquid) not flowing easily: *thick soup ○ a thick sauce ○ thick paint* ∗ NOTE: The opposite is **thin** or **runny**. **thicken** /ˈθɪk.ᵊn/ *verb* [I or T] *Thicken the sauce with a little flour.*

thickener /ˈθɪk.ᵊn.əʳ/ Ⓤ /-ɚ/ *noun* [C or U] (ALSO **thickening**) a substance which is used to make a liquid thicker: *Cornflour can be used as a thickener in sauces.*

thick [STUPID] /θɪk/ *adj* INFORMAL stupid: *I told you not to touch that – are you deaf or just thick?*

- **(as) thick as two short planks** SLANG very stupid: *He's a very skilled footballer but he's as thick as two short planks.*

thicket /ˈθɪk.ɪt/ *noun* [C] an area of trees and bushes growing closely together

thicko /ˈθɪk.əʊ/ Ⓤ /-oʊ/ *noun* [C] *plural* **thickos** INFORMAL a stupid person

thickset /ˌθɪkˈset/ *adj* describes a person, especially a man, whose body is wide across the shoulders and chest and who is short; **stocky**: *A thickset young man appeared in the doorway.*

thick-skinned /ˌθɪkˈskɪnd/ *adj* Someone who is thick-skinned does not appear to be easily hurt by criticism: *You do need to be thick-skinned to survive as a politician here.*

thief /θiːf/ *noun* [C] *plural* **thieves** a person who steals: *A post office was broken into last night, and the thieves got away with £120 000.* ➎See also **theft**.

- **like a thief in the night** secretly or unexpectedly and without being seen

- **It takes a thief to catch a thief.** SAYING used to mean that one dishonest person can guess what another dishonest person might do **thieving** /ˈθiː.vɪŋ/ *adj* [before n] INFORMAL *Those thieving kids tried to steal my car.*

thieving /ˈθiː.vɪŋ/ *noun* [U] FORMAL stealing: *His was a life of thieving and cheating.*

thigh /θaɪ/ *noun* [C] the part of a person's leg above the knee ➎See picture **The Body** on page Centre 5

thimble /ˈθɪm.bl̩/ *noun* [C] a small cover, usually made of metal or plastic, worn to protect the finger which pushes the needle when sewing

thimbleful /ˈθɪm.bl̩.fʊl/ *noun* [C] INFORMAL a very small amount of liquid: *He poured a thimbleful of whisky into the glass.*

thin [NOT THICK] /θɪn/ *adj* **thinner**, **thinnest** having a small distance between two opposite sides: *a thin book ○ thin black lines ○ a thin jacket* (= made from thin material)

- **thin end of the wedge** UK the start of a harmful development: *Identity cards for football supporters could be the thin end of the wedge – soon everyone might have to carry identification.*

thinly /ˈθɪn.li/ *adv* made or done so that something is not thick: *thinly-sliced ham* **thinness** /ˈθɪn.nəs/ *noun* [U]

▲ **thin down** *phrasal verb* INFORMAL If you thin down, you become less fat: *He's thinned down a lot since I last saw him.*

thin [NOT FAT] /θɪn/ *adj* **thinner**, **thinnest** (of the body) with little flesh on the bones: *Did you notice how thin her wrists were? ○ Thin, hungry dogs roamed the streets.* **thinness** /ˈθɪn.nəs/ *noun* [U] *The author discusses why female beauty has become linked to thinness.*

thin [TRANSPARENT] /θɪn/ *adj* **thinner**, **thinnest** not difficult to see through: *thin mist/cloud* ∗ NOTE: The opposite is **thick**. **thinly** /ˈθɪn.li/ *adv* **thinness** /ˈθɪn.nəs/ *noun* [U] *the thinness of his hair*

thin [FEW] /θɪn/ *adj* **thinner**, **thinnest** having only a small number of people or a small amount of something: *Attendance at the meeting was rather thin.*

- **be thin on the ground** UK to exist only in small numbers or amounts: *Shops which will deliver goods are thin on the ground these days.*

- **be thin on top** INFORMAL to have lost some of the hair on your head: *He's a bit thin on top nowadays, isn't he?*

- **disappear/vanish into thin air** to disappear suddenly and completely

- **out of thin air** from nothing: *I can't come up with £10000 out of thin air – it'll take a while to find that kind of money.*

thin ('out) *verb* [I or T] When a crowd or a group thins (out), it becomes fewer in number, and when you thin (out) a group of plants or other things, you remove some to make them fewer: *The traffic will thin out after the rush hour.* **thinly** /ˈθɪn.li/ *adv*

thin [FLOWING EASILY] /θɪn/ *adj* **thinner**, **thinnest** (of a liquid) flowing easily: *a thin soup*

thin /θɪn/ *verb* [T] **-nn-** to make a substance less thick, often by adding a liquid to it: *Thin the sauce down with a little stock.*

thinner /ˈθɪn.əʳ/ Ⓤ /-ɚ/ *noun* [U] a substance added especially to paint to make it flow more easily: *paint thinner*

thin [WEAK] /θɪn/ *adj* **thinner**, **thinnest** weak or of poor quality: *a thin excuse ○ a thin disguise ○ a thin smile*

- **a thin time (of it)** to have bad or unhappy experiences: *He's been having a thin time (of it) since his accident.*

thine /ðaɪn/ *determiner* OLD USE your; used before a vowel sound instead of THY; used when speaking to one person: *thine eyes*

thine /ðaɪn/ *pronoun* OLD USE yours; used when speaking to one person

thing [OBJECT] /θɪŋ/ *noun* [C] used to refer to an approximate way to an object or to avoid naming it: *What's that thing over there? ○ There are some nice things in the shops this summer. ○ I don't eat sweet things* (= sweet food). ○ *How does this damn thing work?*

things /θɪŋz/ *plural noun* **1** your possessions or a particular set of your possessions: *All their things were destroyed in the fire. ○ Bring your swimming things if the weather's nice.* **2** a particular set of objects: *Let me help you clear away the tea things* (= cups, plates, etc. that are used for having tea).

thing [IDEA/EVENT] /θɪŋ/ *noun* [C] **1** used to refer in an approximate way to an idea, subject, event, action, etc: *That was an unkind thing to say. ○ I've got so many things to do I don't know where to start. ○ Your information is correct but you left out one thing. ○ "What's the matter?" "It's this insurance thing. I'm really worried about it."* **2 the thing** the exact fact, object, idea, event, etc: *Your letter has told me precisely the thing I needed to know.*

- **what with one thing and another** INFORMAL You say what with one thing and another when you want explain that the reason you have failed to do something is because you have been very busy: *What with one thing and another, I forgot to phone you yesterday.*

- **be one thing after another** (ALSO **be one thing after the other**) You say that it is one thing after another/the other when many things are happening in a short time: *I've been so busy today. It's been one thing after another.*

- **it's a good thing** INFORMAL If it's a good thing that something happened, it is lucky that it happened: *It's a good thing (that) we booked our tickets early.*

- **a close/near thing** UK (MAINLY US **a close call**) something which almost happened: *The car just missed the child but it was a very close thing.*

- **be on to a good thing** INFORMAL to have an easy and pleasant life or job in which it is not necessary to work hard: *He's on to a good thing, he has free accommodation in return for answering the phone when the family are out.*

- **do your own thing** INFORMAL to do what you want without caring what anyone else thinks of you

- **have a thing about sth/sb** INFORMAL to like or dislike something or someone very much: *Ben's got a thing about Triumph motorbikes – he's got three of them. ○ She's got a thing about spiders – she won't touch them.*

- **make a big thing (out) of sth** INFORMAL to give something too much importance: *I want a party, but I don't want to make a big thing of it.*

- **one thing leads to another** If one thing leads to another, there is a series of events in which each event was caused by the previous one: *At first, we were just dancing together, but one thing led to another, and I ended up in bed with him.*

• **the thing is 1** INFORMAL used to introduce a subject for discussion: *The thing is, my parents like me to be home by 10 o'clock.* **2** used to emphasize the importance of what you are saying: *The thing is to be watchful even when you think your child is safe.*

things /θɪŋz/ *plural noun* used to refer to the general situation: *Things have been going very well recently.*

• **(just) one of those things** INFORMAL said to mean that there was no way of planning to avoid something: *The road was blocked, so we missed the meeting – it was just one of those things.*

• **be hearing/imagining/seeing things** INFORMAL to think you are experiencing something which is not really happening: *I'm sure I saw my glasses on this table, but they're not here now. I must have been seeing things.*

• **things that go bump in the night** HUMOROUS used to describe anything unknown which might be frightening, especially a noise

• **all things considered** Someone might say that something is good all things considered to mean it was generally good although the situation was not perfect: *I think the party was great, all things considered – I mean we didn't have much time to prepare and no help, but it still went well.*

• **How are things (with you)?** INFORMAL FOR How are you?

• **the way things are** (*ALSO* **as things stand**) in the present situation: *The way things are, I'll never have this ready by June.*

• **take things easy** to relax and not work too hard: *My doctor's told me to take things easy for a while.*

thing PERSON/ANIMAL /θɪŋ/ *noun* [C] used after an adjective to refer to a person or animal with affection or sympathy: *The poor things were kept in small cages without room to move.* ○ [as form of address] *You lucky thing winning a car.*

thingy /ˈθɪŋ.i/ *noun* [S] INFORMAL sometimes used if you can't remember someone's or something's name: *Ask thingy over there, he'll know.*

thing ANYTHING /θɪŋ/ *noun* [U] used instead of 'anything', 'everything', 'something' or 'nothing' for emphasis: *Don't worry about a thing* (= anything). *I'll take care of it all.*

• **not a (single) thing** not anything: *After the guests had gone, there wasn't a thing left to eat.*

• **not have a thing to wear** (*ALSO* **have nothing to wear**) HUMOROUS to have no clothes that are suitable for an occasion: *I'm going to a wedding on Saturday and I don't have a thing to wear.*

• **there isn't a thing you can do** you cannot do anything: *He broke his promise and there wasn't a thing we could do about it.*

• **all things being equal** if everything happens as expected: *All things being equal, I'll be at home on Tuesday.*

• **all things to all men/people** If you try to be all things to all men/people, you try to do things which will please everyone.

• **in all things** in every situation or subject: *Be true to yourself in all things.*

• **above all (things)** more than everything else: *I value my freedom above all things.*

• **one/a thing** something: *One thing you'll have to agree to is working in the evenings.* ○ *I went by plane, a thing I hardly ever do.*

• **a thing or two** some matters, facts or information: *I'm having trouble paying attention – I have a thing or two on my mind.* ○ *Why don't you ask Andrew about it? He knows a thing or two about* (= has some knowledge of) *computers.* ○ *She thinks she knows everything about raising children, but I could tell her a thing or two* (= some information she does not know).

• **does things to you** INFORMAL Something or someone that does things to you has a strong, usually enjoyable, effect on you: *That music really does things to me.*

• **for one thing** used to introduce a reason for something: *"Why won't you come to New York with me?" "For one*

thing, I don't like flying, and for another, I can't afford it."

• **and another thing** used to introduce one more in a series of arguments or complaints: *And another thing, why didn't you tell me you were going out?*

• **a thing of the past** something which no longer happens: *Giving up your seat to an older person seems to be a thing of the past.*

• **If it's not one thing it's another.** SAYING used when bad things keep happening to you

thing NOUN PHRASES /θɪŋ/ *noun* **the ... thing** used to make noun phrases with particular adjectives and adverbs: *The first thing (to do) is to write your name at the top of the page.*

• **the done thing** MAINLY UK (*US USUALLY* **the thing to do**) what you are expected to do in a social situation: *Don't forget to shake hands – it's the done thing, you know.*

• **not the done thing** MAINLY UK (*US USUALLY* **not the thing to do**) not socially acceptable: *Smoking during a meal is not the done thing.*

• **the last thing you want/need, etc.** something that you certainly do not want or need, etc.: *Go home? That's the last thing I want to do!*

• **the (latest) thing** something which is very new and fashionable: *Biodegradable plastic is the latest thing.*

• **the same thing** the same: *Training isn't the same thing as education.*

• **the real thing** something which is not false or a copy: *The fire alarm goes off accidentally so often that when it's the real thing* (= when it really does happen) *nobody will take any notice.*

• **just the thing** (*ALSO* **the very thing**) exactly what is needed: *A week's rest would be just the thing for her.*

• **the whole thing** everything that has been planned or discussed: *Let's call the whole thing off.* ○ *I want to forget the whole thing.*

thingamabob /ˈθɪŋ.ə.mə.bɒb/ ⑩ /-bɑːb/ *noun* [C] (*ALSO* **thingamajig,** UK *ALSO* **thingummy**) INFORMAL a word used, especially in spoken English, when the name of an object has been forgotten: *I need one of those red thingamabobs for this – have you got one?* ⊃See also **thingy** at **thing** PERSON/ANIMAL.

think CONSIDER /θɪŋk/ *verb* [I or T] thought, thought to believe something or have an opinion or idea: [+ (*that*)] *I think (that) I've met you before.* ○ *I don't think Emma will get the job.* ○ *"Do you think (that) you could get me some stamps while you're in town?"* ○ *I think (that) I'll go swimming after lunch.* ○ [+ n or adj] *Salmon used to be thought expensive/thought a luxury.* ○ [+ to infinitive] *He was thought to have boarded the plane in New York.* ○ *What did you think of the film? ○ What do you think about this latest government scheme?* ○ *I'm thinking about buying a new car.*

• **I thought as much** used to say that you are not surprised by what someone has said or done: *"I came to ask you a favour." "I thought as much."*

• **Who would have thought (it)?** used to say that you are very surprised something has happened: *So, Adrian is going out with Emma, is he? Who would have thought it?*

• **I can't think** I do not know: *I can't think why she hasn't phoned.*

• **couldn't think** did not know: *She couldn't think what to do next.*

• **think again** to form a new opinion about something or decide to change your decision on it, often after learning more about it: *When the children are misbehaving, it makes me think again about having a large family.*

• **think better of sth** to decide that something is not a good idea: *Originally we were going to buy John's old car, but we thought better of it.*

• **think not** a formal way of disagreeing or saying no: *"Will you be going tonight James?" "I think not."*

• **think nothing of sth** to consider that an activity is easy and not unusual: *When I was younger, I thought nothing of cycling 50 miles in a day.*

• **think big** to have plans to be very successful or powerful: *You need to think big if you want to succeed.*

• **to sb's way of thinking** in a particular person's opinion: *To my way of thinking, the plan should never have been approved.*

COMMON LEARNER ERROR

think about or **think of**?

Think about someone or something means to have thoughts in your mind about a person or thing, or to consider them.

I was thinking about my mother.
I thought about the question before answering.
~~I thought the question before answering.~~

What do you think of/about? is also used when asking someone to give their opinion.

What do you think of/about the colour?
~~What do you think the colour?~~

Think of doing something means to consider the possibility of doing something.

We are thinking of having a party.
~~We are thinking to have a party.~~

---

think REASON /θɪŋk/ *verb* [I] **thought, thought** to use the brain to plan something, solve a problem, make a decision, etc: *What are you thinking, Peter?* ○ *He just does these things without thinking and he gets himself into such a mess.* ○ *You think too much – that's your problem.* ○ *I'm sorry I forgot to mention your name. I just **wasn't** thinking.*
• **think long and hard** (*ALSO* **think twice**) to think very carefully about something: *I should think long and hard before you make any important decisions.*
• **think aloud** to automatically say what you are thinking: *"What did you say?" "Oh, nothing, I was just thinking aloud."*
• **think on** *your* **feet** to make a quick decision or give an answer quickly: *I'd never heard about the firm before, so I had to think on my feet.*
• **not be thinking straight** to not be thinking clearly or using good judgment: *I'm sorry, that was a stupid thing to do – I wasn't thinking straight.*

think /θɪŋk/ *noun* **have a think** to consider something for some time: *Let me have a think **about** it before I decide.* ○ *Have a think over the weekend and tell me what you've decided.*

think REMEMBER /θɪŋk/ *verb* [I usually + adv or prep] **thought, thought** to remember or imagine: *I was just thinking **about** you when you phoned.* ○ *She was so busy she didn't have to tell me about it.*

PHRASAL VERBS WITH **think** ▼

▲ **think back** *phrasal verb* to remember something that happened in the past: *It might help you to understand Elaine if you think back **to** when you were her age.*
▲ **think for** *yourself* *phrasal verb* [R] to make your own decisions and form your own opinions, without depending on other people: *It's no good asking me all the time, Anna – you're going to have to learn to think for yourself.*
▲ **think of** *sth* IDEA *phrasal verb* to produce a new idea or plan: *We'll have to think of a pretty good excuse for being late.*
▲ **think of** *sth/sb* OPINION *phrasal verb* If you think of something or someone in a particular way, you have that opinion about them: *I think of him **as** someone who will always help me.* ○ *What do you think of* (= do you like) *my new dress?*
▲ **think highly/well/a lot, etc. of** *sb* (*ALSO* **think the world of** *sb*) to have a good opinion of someone or something: *She thinks very highly of her boss.*
• **not think much of** *sb/sth* to have a low opinion of someone or something: *I don't think much of hav**ing** to work on Saturdays.*
▲ **think of/about** *sb/sth* IMAGINE *phrasal verb* to remember or imagine someone or something: *I thought of you immediately when they said they wanted someone who could speak English.* ○ *He was thinking about the time he spent in the army.*
▲ **think** *sth* **out** *phrasal verb* [M] to consider all the possible details of something: *The scheme was well thought out.*
▲ **think** *sth* **over** *phrasal verb* [M] to consider an idea or plan carefully before making a decision: *I'll think it over and give you an answer next week.*

▲ **think** *sth* **through** *phrasal verb* [M] to carefully consider the possible results of doing something: *I need some time to think it through – I don't want to make any sudden decisions.*
▲ **think** *sth* **up** *phrasal verb* to produce a new idea or plan: *I don't want to go tonight but I can't think up a good excuse.*

thinker /'θɪŋ.kər/ ⓤ /-kɚ/ *noun* [C] someone who considers important subjects or produces new ideas: *a political/religious thinker* ○ *He was known for being an original thinker.*

thinking /'θɪŋ.kɪŋ/ *noun* [U] **1** when you use your mind to consider something: *I'll have to **do** some thinking about how best to arrange the books.* **2** someone's ideas or opinions: *What's the thinking **behind** the decision to combine the two departments?* ○ *The book discusses the impact of Christian thinking on western society.*
• **put** *your* **thinking cap on** to think seriously about something: *I'm in need of some interesting suggestions so if you can put your thinking cap on I'd be grateful.*

thinking /'θɪŋ.kɪŋ/ *adj* [before n] describes people who use their minds to consider things carefully: *All thinking people realise that we must stop wasting our natural resources.*
• **the thinking woman's/man's crumpet** *UK HUMOROUS* a way of describing a man or a woman who is popular with the opposite sex because they are intelligent as well as being physically attractive: *Paxman is surely the ultimate thinking woman's crumpet.*

'**think ,tank** *group noun* [C usually sing] a group of specialists brought together, usually by a government, to develop ideas on a particular subject and to make suggestions for action

thin-skinned /ˌθɪn'skɪnd/ *adj* easily hurt by criticism or easily made unhappy

third /θɜːd/ ⓤ /θɝːd/ *pronoun, noun, determiner, adv* **1** [S] 3rd written as a word: *the third road on the right* ○ *the third time* ○ *"What's the date today?" "It's **the** third."* ○ *He cut the cake into thirds* (= three equal parts). **2** [C] a degree qualification from a British university that is below a 2:2
• **the third degree** *INFORMAL* serious questioning and/or rough treatment to get information: *I got the third degree when I got home last night.*

thirdly /'θɜːd.li/ ⓤ /'θɝːd-/ *adv* used in order to introduce the third thing in a list: *There are three factors to take into account: firstly cost, secondly time, and thirdly staff.*

third-degree burn /ˌθɜːd.dɪˌgriː'bɜːn/ ⓤ /ˌθɝːd.dɪˌgriː-'bɝːn/ *noun* [C] a very serious burn in which the flesh is destroyed ⊃Compare **first-degree burn**; **second-degree burn**.

,**third 'generation** *adj* (*ABBREVIATION* **3G**) describes technology that is new and improved, especially MOBILE PHONES on which you can use the Internet, watch television, etc.

,**third 'party** *noun* [C usually sing] *LEGAL* a third person or organization less directly involved in a matter than the main people or organizations that are involved

third-party insurance /ˌθɜːd.pɑːrˌti.ɪn'ʃɔː.rənts/ ⓤ /ˌθɝːd.pɑːrˌti.ɪn'ʃɔːr.ənts/ *noun* [U] insurance that will pay money to a person or group damaged in some way by the person or group who have this insurance

,**third-'rate** *adj* of low quality: *I don't want to work for some third-rate company.*

the ,Third 'Way *noun* [S] politics in which the development of business is balanced with the needs of society: *Tony Blair claims that New Labour is the Third Way between capitalism and socialism.*

the ,Third 'World *noun* [S] the countries of Africa, Latin America and Asia which have less developed industries: *She does a lot of work in the Third World.* ○ *a Third-World country/economy*

thirst NEED FOR DRINK /θɜːst/ ⓤ /θɝːst/ *noun* [S or U] a need for something to drink: *Hundreds of refugees collapsed from hunger and thirst.* ○ *I've got a terrible thirst after all that running.* ○ *I woke up with a thumping headache and a **raging** (= extreme) thirst.*

thirsty /ˈθɜː.sti/ [US] /ˈθɝː-/ *adj* needing to drink: *I felt/was hot and thirsty after my game of squash.* **thirstily** /ˈθɜː.stɪ.li/ [US] /ˈθɝː-/ *adv*

thirst [DESIRE] /θɜːst/ [US] /θɝːst/ *noun* [U] *LITERARY* a strong desire: *He's always had **a thirst for** adventure.*

thirsty /ˈθɜː.sti/ [US] /ˈθɝː-/ *adj LITERARY* Someone who is thirsty for power/knowledge, etc. wants to have it very much.

thirst /θɜːst/ [US] /θɝːst/ *verb*

▲ **thirst after/for *sth*** *phrasal verb LITERARY* to feel very strongly that you want and need a particular thing: *to be thirsting for justice/truth/adventure*

thirst-quenching /ˈθɜːstˌkwen.tʃɪŋ/ [US] /ˈθɝːst-/ *adj* describes a drink that stops you feeling thirsty

ˌthirsty ˈwork *noun* [U] *INFORMAL* hard physical work that makes you thirsty: *Sawing wood is thirsty work.*

thirteen /θɜːˈtiːn/ [US] /θɝː-/ *determiner, pronoun, noun* the number 13

thirteenth /θɜːˈtiːntθ/ [US] /θɝː-/ *determiner, pronoun, adj, adv, noun* 13th written as a word

thirty /ˈθɜː.ti/ [US] /ˈθɝː.t̬i/ *determiner, pronoun, noun* the number 30

thirties /ˈθɜː.tiz/ [US] /ˈθɝː.t̬iz/ *plural noun* A person's thirties are the period in which they are aged between 30 and 39: *My brother is **in** his thirties.*

the thirties *plural noun* **1** the range of temperature between 30° and 39°: *The temperature is expected to be **in** the thirties tomorrow.* **2** the period of years between 30 and 39 in any century: *My family fled Germany in the thirties.*

thirtieth /ˈθɜː.ti.əθ/ [US] /ˈθɝː.t̬i-/ *determiner, pronoun, adj, adv, noun* 30th written as a word

this [THING REFERRED TO] /ðɪs/ *determiner, pronoun plural* **these** used for a person, object, idea, etc. to show which one is referred to: *Can you sign this form here for me?* ○ *These books are too heavy for me to carry.* ○ *INFORMAL We met this girl* (= the girl I am going to tell you about) *in the hotel.* ○ *This is the one I want.* ○ *What's this? Is this what you're looking for?* ○ *What's this I hear about your moving to Scotland?* ➲See Note **this/these or that/those?** at **that** SOMETHING NOT HERE.

• **by this time** (*ALSO* **before this**) already: *I thought you'd have finished by this time.*

• **this and that** (*ALSO* **this, that and the other**) *INFORMAL* various things: *"What were you talking about?" "Oh, this and that."*

this [AS MUCH] /ðɪs/ *adv* as much as shown or to a particular degree: *It was only about this high off the ground.* ○ *She has never been this late for school before.*

thistle /ˈθɪs.l̩/ *noun* [C] a wild plant with sharp points on the leaves and, typically, purple flowers: *The thistle is the national emblem of Scotland.* ➲See picture **Flowers and Plants** on page Centre 3

thistledown /ˈθɪs.l̩.daʊn/ *noun* [U] the mass of thin soft white threads which are joined to THISTLE seeds and which help them to be blown through the air

thither /ˈðɪð.əʳ/ [US] /-ɚ/ *adv OLD USE* to that place, in that direction

thong /θɒŋ/ [US] /θɑːŋ/ *noun* [C] **1** a narrow piece of especially leather used to fasten something or as part of a whip **2** a piece of underwear or the bottom part of a BIKINI with a very narrow part at the back which does not cover the bottom **3** *US FOR* **flip-flop**

thorax /ˈθɔː.ræks/ [US] /ˈθɔːr.æks/ *noun* [C] *plural* **thoraces** or **thoraxes** *SPECIALIZED* **1** in humans and animals, the middle part of the body below the neck and above the waist **2** in insects, the middle part of the body, between the head and the ABDOMEN (= end part) **thoracic** /θɔːˈræs.ɪk/ *adj*

thorn /θɔːn/ [US] /θɔːrn/ *noun* [C] a small sharp pointed growth on the stem of a plant

• **thorn in *your* flesh/side** a person or thing that continually annoys you or causes you pain: *A relentless campaigner, he was a thorn in the government's side for a number of years.*

thorny /ˈθɔː.ni/ [US] /ˈθɔːr-/ *adj* having thorns

thorny /ˈθɔː.ni/ [US] /ˈθɔːr-/ *adj* [before n] describes a problem or subject that is difficult to deal with: *He has now raised the thorny **issue of** taxation within the European Union.*

thorough [CAREFUL] /ˈθʌr.ə/ [US] /ˈθɝː-/ /-oʊ/ *adj* detailed and careful: *a thorough revision of the manuscript* ○ *They did a thorough search of the area but found nothing.* **thoroughly** /ˈθʌr.ə.li/ [US] /ˈθɝː-/ /-oʊ/ *adv*: *We went through the report thoroughly but the information we wanted wasn't given anywhere.* **thoroughness** /ˈθʌr.ə.nəs/ [US] /ˈθɝː-/ /-oʊ/ *noun* [U]

thorough [COMPLETE] /ˈθʌr.ə/ [US] /ˈθɝː-/ /-oʊ/ *adj*: complete, very great, very much: *It was a thorough waste of time.* **thoroughly** /ˈθʌr.ə.li/ [US] /ˈθɝː-/ /-oʊ/ *adv*: *I thoroughly enjoyed the performance.*

thoroughbred /ˈθʌr.ə.bred/ [US] /ˈθɝː-/ /-oʊ/ *noun* [C], *adj* (a horse) with parents which are of the same breed and have good qualities: *a thoroughbred racehorse*

thoroughfare /ˈθʌr.ə.feəʳ/ [US] /ˈθɝː.ə.fer/ /-oʊ/ *noun* [C] *FORMAL* a main road for public use or a passage through somewhere

• **no thoroughfare** On road signs, no thoroughfare means no entry.

thoroughgoing /ˌθʌr.əˈgəʊ.ɪŋ/ /ˈ--ˌ--/ [US] /ˌθɝː.əˈgoʊ-/ /-oʊ/ *adj FORMAL* complete, detailed, careful: *a thoroughgoing reform of the economy*

those /ðəʊz/ [US] /ðoʊz/ *determiner, pronoun, plural of* **that** SOMETHING NOT HERE; **that** USED TO REFER

thou [YOU] /ðaʊ/ *pronoun OLD USE* you; used when speaking to one person

thou [THOUSAND] /θaʊ/ *noun* [C] *plural* **thou** *INFORMAL FOR* thousand, especially when referring to an amount of money: *"How much do you reckon it cost him?" "About thirty thou."*

though /ðəʊ/ [US] /ðoʊ/ *conjunction* **1** despite the fact that: *She hasn't phoned, **even** though she said she would.* **2** but: *They're coming next week, though I don't know which day.*

• **as though** as if: *You look as though you've had a bad time!*

though /ðəʊ/ [US] /ðoʊ/ *adv* despite this: *We were at school together. I haven't seen her for years though.*

thought [THINK] /θɔːt/ [US] /θɑːt/ *past simple and past participle of* **think**

thought [THINKING] /θɔːt/ [US] /θɑːt/ *noun* [C or U] the act of thinking about or considering something, an idea or opinion, or a set of ideas about a particular subject: *Ask me again tomorrow. I'll have to **give** it some thought.* ○ *She doesn't **give** any thought **to** her appearance.* ○ *Let me have your thoughts **on** that report by Friday.* ○ ***Spare a** thought **for*** (= Think about) *all those without shelter on a cold night like this.* ○ *He's the author of a book on the history of European thought.* ○ *You sent her a card? That was a kind thought.*

• **the thought crosses *sb's* mind** If the thought of (doing) something crosses someone's mind, they think about it briefly: *The thought had crossed my mind **that** I might need some help with the project.*

• **that's a thought** that's a good idea: *"Shall we go on Thursday instead of Friday?" "That's a thought."*

• **with no thought for *sth*** not thinking about a particular thing: *With no thought for his own safety, he rushed towards the burning car.*

thoughtful /ˈθɔːt.fəl/ [US] /ˈθɑːt-/ *adj* **1** carefully considering things: *He has a thoughtful approach to his work.* **2** quiet because you are thinking about something: *You look thoughtful.* **3** kind and always thinking about how you can help other people: *Thank you for phoning when I was ill – it was very thoughtful of you.* ○ *She's a very thoughtful person.* ∗ NOTE: The opposite is **thoughtless**. **thoughtfully** /ˈθɔːt.fəl.i/ [US] /ˈθɑːt-/ *adv*: *He gazed thoughtfully into the distance.* ○ *There were sandwiches, thoughtfully provided by his wife.* **thoughtfulness** /ˈθɔːt.fəl.nəs/ [US] /ˈθɑːt-/ *noun* [U]

thoughtless /ˈθɔːt.ləs/ [US] /ˈθɑːt-/ *adj* not considering how your actions or words may upset someone: *It was thoughtless not to phone and say you'd be late.* ○ *She's not intentionally unkind – she's just a little thoughtless sometimes.* **thoughtlessly** /ˈθɔːt.lə.sli/ [US] /ˈθɑːt-/ *adv* **thoughtlessness** /ˈθɔːt.lə.snəs/ [US] /ˈθɑːt-/ *noun* [U]

thought-out /ˌθɔːtˈaʊt/ [US] /ˈθɑːt-/ *adj* [after v] If something is carefully/well/badly thought-out, it is carefully/well/badly planned: *To me the whole scheme* *seems to be badly thought-out.*

thought-provoking /ˌθɔːt.prəˈvəʊk.ɪŋ/ [US] /ˈθɑːt.prə-ˈvoʊk-/ *adj* making you think a lot about a subject: *a thought-provoking book/film*

thousand /ˈθaʊ.zənd/ *determiner, pronoun, noun* the number 1000 **thousandth** /ˈθaʊ.zəndθ/ *determiner, pronoun, adj, adv, noun*

COMMON LEARNER ERROR

thousand or **thousands?**

If you are using **thousand** to describe an exact number, use the singular form. Only use it in the plural form to refer to a large number that is not exact.

The stadium holds thirty thousand people.
~~*The stadium holds thirty thousands people.*~~
Her paintings cost thousands.

thrash [HIT] /θræʃ/ *verb* [T] to hit a person or animal hard many times as a punishment: *He thrashed the horse with his whip.*

thrash [MOVE] /θræʃ/ *verb* [I] to move from side to side in a violent or uncontrolled way: *He was screaming and thrashing* ***around*** *on the floor.*

thrash [DEFEAT] /θræʃ/ *verb* [T] *INFORMAL* to defeat someone thoroughly in a game or sports competition: *We thrashed the visiting team 6-0.*

▲ **thrash *sth* out** *phrasal verb* [M] *INFORMAL* to discuss a problem in detail until you reach an agreement or find a solution: *If we've got an important decision to make, we sometimes spend a whole day thrashing it out in a meeting.*

ˌthrash ˈmetal *noun* [U] a very fast type of HEAVY METAL music, that also has some features of PUNK ROCK

thread [FIBRE] /θred/ *noun* **1** [C or U] (a length of) a very thin fibre: *needle and thread* ○ *loose threads* **2** [C] a long thin line of something such as light or smoke: *A thin thread* ***of*** *light made its way through the curtains.* **3** [C] The thread of a book, discussion, speech etc. is its story or the way that it develops, one part connecting with another: *One of the main threads of the film is the development of the relationship between the boy and his uncle.* ○ *Unfortunately my attention wandered for a moment and I* ***lost*** *the thread of* (= forgot) *what I was saying.*

thread [PUT THROUGH] /θred/ *verb* [T] to put something long and thin such as string or thread through a narrow hole or into a small space: *to thread a* ***needle*** ○ *The sari had gold strands threaded through the material.*

● **thread *your* way through/between, etc.** to move carefully through a crowded space, changing direction in order to avoid people or things: *She threaded her way through the crowded market place.*

thread [SCREW] /θred/ *noun* [C] a continuous raised line, such as the one which goes around the outside of a screw or bolt or the inside of a hole

threadbare [THIN] /ˈθred.beəʳ/ [US] /-ber/ *adj* describes material or clothes that have become thin or damaged because they have been used a lot: *a threadbare coat*

threadbare [WEAK] /ˈθred.beəʳ/ [US] /-ber/ *adj* A threadbare excuse, argument or idea lacks strength and no longer impresses people because it is old or has been used too much: *a threadbare excuse*

threat /θret/ *noun* [C] a suggestion that something unpleasant or violent will happen, especially if a particular action or order is not followed: [+ **to** infinitive] *She* ***carried out*** *her threat* ***to*** *throw away any clothes that were left on the floor.* ○ *The threat* ***of*** *jail failed to deter him from petty crime.* ○ *Drunken drivers* ***pose*** *a serious threat* (= cause a lot of harm) ***to*** *other road users.* ○ *He says he'll tell the authorities but it's just an* ***empty*** *threat* (= it will not happen).

● **be under threat of *sth*** to be in a situation where people are threatening you with something bad or unpleasant: *She left the country under threat of arrest if she returned.*

threatening /ˈθret.ən.ɪŋ/ /-nɪŋ-/ *adj* expressing a threat of something unpleasant or violent: *threatening behaviour* **threateningly** /ˈθret.ən.ɪŋ.li/ /-nɪŋ-/ *adv*

threaten /ˈθret.ən/ *verb* **1** [T] to tell someone that you will kill or hurt them, or cause problems for them if they do not do what you want: *They threatened the shopkeeper* ***with*** *a gun.* ○ [+ **to** infinitive] *They threatened* ***to*** *kill him unless he did as they asked.* **2** [I] If something bad threatens to happen, it is likely to happen: *Look at those clouds! There's a storm threatening.* **3** [T] to be likely to cause harm or damage to something or someone: *Changing patterns of agriculture are threatening the countryside.*

three /θriː/ *determiner, pronoun, noun* the number 3

● **the three Rs** *INFORMAL* used to refer to the basic areas of education: reading, writing and mathematics

three-dimensional /ˌθriː.daɪˈmentʃən.əl/ *adj* (*ABBREVIATION* **3-D**) having or appearing to have three DIMENSIONS (= length, width, and height) and therefore looking real: *The picture had a three-dimensional* ***effect.***

three-legged race /ˌθriːˈleg.ɪdˌreɪs/ *noun* [C] a race in which the right leg of one person is tied to the left leg of another person, and the two people run together as if they had three legs

three-line whip /ˌθriː.laɪnˈwɪp/ *noun* [C usually sing] In Britain, a three-line whip is an instruction given to Members of Parliament by the leaders of their party telling them they must vote in the way that the party wants them to on a particular subject.

threepence /ˈθrʌp.ənts/ *noun* [U] *OLD USE* a small thick brass coin used in Britain until 1971, or an earlier silver-coloured coin, which was worth three old PENNIES, or this amount of money

threepenny /ˈθrəp.ni/ *adj* [before n] *OLD USE* worth or costing three old pennies: *a threepenny* ***bit***

three-piece suit /ˌθriː.piːsˈsjuːt/ [US] /-suːt/ *noun* [C] a matching jacket, trousers and WAISTCOAT (= a top without sleeves which is worn over a shirt), especially for men

three-piece suite *UK* /ˌθriː.piːsˈswiːt/ *noun* [C] (*US* **living room suite**) a sofa with two matching chairs

three-ply /ˈθriː.plaɪ/ *adj, noun* [U] **1** (wood, TISSUES, TOILET PAPER, etc.) made of three layers joined together **2** (wool) having three threads woven together to make one

three-point turn /ˌθriː.pɔɪntˈtɜːn/ [US] /-ˈtɝːn/ *noun* [C] a method of turning a car round to face the other direction by moving forwards across the road, then backwards in the opposite direction across the road and then forwards again

three-quarter length /ˌθriː.kwɔː.təˈleŋkθ/ [US] /-kwɑː.t̬ɚ-/ *adj* A three-quarter length coat is between the length of a jacket and a coat.

ˌthree ˈquarters *determiner* three fourths of something

threesome /ˈθriː.səm/ *noun* [C] *INFORMAL* three people as a group

three-star /ˌθriːˈstɑːʳ/ [US] /-ˈstɑːr/ *adj* Something such as service or a hotel that is three-star is of good quality.

three-wheeler /ˌθriːˈwiː.ləʳ/ [US] /-lɚ/ *noun* [C] a vehicle with three wheels

thresh /θreʃ/ *verb* [I or T] (*ALSO* **thrash**) to remove the seeds of crop plants by hitting them, using either a machine or a hand tool

threshold [ENTRANCE] /ˈθreʃ.həʊld/ [US] /-hoʊld/ *noun* [C] the floor of entrance to a building or room

● **on the threshold of *sth*** at the start of a new and important time or development: *We are on the threshold of a new era in European relations.*

threshold [LEVEL] /ˈθreʃ.həʊld/ [US] /-hoʊld/ *noun* [C usually sing] the level or point at which you start to experience something, or at which something starts to happen: *I have a* ***low/high*** *boredom threshold* (= I do/don't feel bored easily). ○ *His secretary earns £268 a month, well below the threshold for paying tax.*

threw /θruː/ *past participle of* **throw**

thrice /θraɪs/ *adv OLD USE* three times

thrift [AVOIDING WASTE] /θrɪft/ *noun* [U] the careful use of money, especially by avoiding waste **thrifty** /ˈθrɪf.ti/ *adj*: *They have plenty of money now, but they still tend to be thrifty.* **thriftily** /ˈθrɪf.tɪ.li/ *adv* **thriftiness** /ˈθrɪf.tɪ.nəs/ *noun* [U]

T

thrift [PLANT] /θrɪft/ *noun* **[U]** a small plant with, typically, pink flowers on long stems which often grows wild on cliffs by the sea

ˈthrift ˌshop *noun* **[C]** *US* a shop which sells clothes and other goods that people no longer want, in order to raise money for people who are ill or have no food, homes, etc.

thrill /θrɪl/ *noun* **[C]** a feeling of extreme excitement, usually caused by something pleasant: *the thrill of winning a competition* ○ *So why do people still go hunting – is it the thrill of the chase?* ○ *It* ***gave*** *me a real thrill to see her again after so many years.* ○ *The video shows the thrills* ***and spills*** (= excitement and accidents) *of motor racing.*
thrill /θrɪl/ *verb* **[I or T]** *Ballesteros thrilled the golf world with his performance.*
thrilled /θrɪld/ *adj* extremely pleased: **[+ *that*]** *I was thrilled* ***that*** *so many people turned up to the party.*
• **thrilled to bits** *INFORMAL* extremely pleased: *She was thrilled to bits with her present.*

thriller /ˈθrɪl.əʳ/ [US] /-ɚ/ *noun* **[C]** a book, play or film which has an exciting story, often about solving a crime: *It's described here as a taut, psychological thriller.*

thrilling /ˈθrɪl.ɪŋ/ *adj* extremely exciting: *The book is a thrilling adventure story.*

thrive /θraɪv/ *verb* **[I]** **thrived** or *US ALSO* **throve**, **thrived** or *US ALSO* **thriven** to grow, develop or be successful: *His business thrived in the years before the war.* ○ *She seems to thrive* ***on*** *stress.* **thriving** /ˈθraɪ.vɪŋ/ *adj*: *a thriving economy*

throat /θrəʊt/ [US] /θroʊt/ *noun* **[C]** the front of the neck, or the space inside the neck down which food and air can go: *A fish bone got* ***stuck in*** *my throat.* ○ *a* ***sore*** *throat* ○ *He* ***cleared*** *his throat* (= coughed so he could speak more clearly) *and started speaking.*
• **at each other's throats** If two people are at each other's throats, they are arguing angrily: *Those two are always at each other's throats.*
• **force/ram *sth* down *sb's* throat** to force someone to listen to opinions and ideas and to try to get them to accept them: *I can't bear it when someone starts ramming their views down your throat.*
-throated /-θrəʊ.tɪd/ [US] /-θroʊ.t̬ɪd/ *suffix* of or with a particular type of throat: *a red-throated bird* (= a bird with a red throat) ○ *a* ***full****-throated* (= loud) *roar*
throaty /ˈθrəʊ.ti/ [US] /ˈθroʊ.t̬i/ *adj* describes a sound which is low and rough: *a throaty voice/laugh/cough*
throatily /ˈθrəʊ.tɪ.li/ [US] /ˈθroʊ.t̬ɪ-/ *adv* **throatiness** /ˈθrəʊ.tɪ.nəs/ [US] /ˈθroʊ.t̬ɪ-/ *noun* **[U]**

throb /θrɒb/ [US] /θrɑːb/ *verb* **[I]** **-bb- 1** to produce a strong, regular beat: *Both records have a good throbbing bass which is great to dance to.* ➲See also **heartthrob**. **2** If a part of your body throbs, you feel pain in it in a series of regular beats: *His* ***head*** *throbbed, and his body ached.* ○ *The throbbing pain in his leg was becoming unbearable.* **throb** /θrɒb/ [US] /θrɑːb/ *noun* **[S]** *the throb of the engine*

throes /θrəʊz/ [US] /θroʊz/ *plural noun* **in the throes of *sth*** experiencing or doing something which is difficult, unpleasant or painful: *The country is presently in the throes of the worst recession since the second world war.* ○ *He's in the throes of a mid-life crisis which makes him rather difficult to live with.* ➲See also **death throes**.

T

thrombosis /θrɒmˈbəʊ.sɪs/ [US] /θrɑːmˈboʊ-/ *noun* **[C]** *plural* **thromboses** a blockage preventing the flow of blood in the body caused by a CLOT (= half solid lump) of blood

throne /θrəʊn/ [US] /θroʊn/ *noun* **[C]** the special chair used by a ruler, especially a king or queen
the throne *noun* **[S]** the state of being a ruler: *Elizabeth II* ***ascended/came to*** *the throne* (= became queen of Britain) *when her father died.* ○ *Queen Victoria was* ***on*** *the throne* (= was queen) *at that time.* ○ *Charles is* ***next in line to*** *the throne* (= will become king next).

throng /θrɒŋ/ [US] /θrɑːŋ/ *group noun* **[C]** a crowd or large group of people: *A huge throng had gathered round the speaker.*
throng /θrɒŋ/ [US] /θrɑːŋ/ *verb* **[I + adv or prep; T]** to be or go somewhere in very large numbers: *Crowds thronged the market place.* ○ *The narrow streets were thronged* ***with*** *summer visitors.* ○ **[+ *to* infinitive]** *Thousands of people thronged* ***to*** *see the exhibition while it was in London.*

throttle [CONTROL] /ˈθrɒt.l̩/ [US] /ˈθrɑː.t̬l̩/ *noun* **[C]** a valve which allows more or less fuel to go into an engine and so changes the power with which the engine operates
• **at full/half throttle** at full/half speed or power: *He's working at full throttle* (= as hard as he can) *to get the job finished.* ○ *The captain of the boat had his engines at full throttle.*
▲ **throttle *(sth)* back/down** *phrasal verb* **[M]** to reduce speed, or to reduce the power and speed being produced by an engine: *The pilot throttled back (the engines) as he came in to land.*

throttle [THROAT] /ˈθrɒt.l̩/ [US] /ˈθrɑː.t̬l̩/ *verb* **[T] 1** to press someone's throat very tightly so that they cannot breathe: *INFORMAL Sometimes he annoys me so much that I could throttle him.* **2** to prevent something from succeeding: *The reduction in funds is throttling the development of new programmes.*

through [PLACE], *US NOT STANDARD* **thru** /θruː/ *prep, adv* from one end or side of something to the other: *They walked slowly through the woods.* ○ *The boy waded through the water to reach his boat.* ○ *He struggled through the crowd till he reached the front.* ○ *How long the journey takes will depend on how long it takes to* ***get*** *through the traffic.* ○ *Her words kept running through my mind/head* (= I kept hearing her words in my imagination). ○ *We drove through the tunnel.* ○ *I saw him drive through* ***a red light*** (= he did not stop at the red traffic light). ○ *I'll put you through* (= connect you by telephone) *(to the sales department).*
• **through and through** completely: *My mother is Irish through and through.*

through [FINISHED] /θruː/ *adj* to have finished using or doing something: *I've got some work to do but I should be through in an hour if you can wait.* ○ *Are you through* ***with*** *that atlas?*

through [TIME] /θruː/ *prep, adv* from the beginning to the end of a period of time: *It rained* ***all/right*** *through June and into the first half of July.* ○ *We sat through two lectures and then left.* ○ *She had just enough energy to* ***get*** *through the day.* ○ *US She works Monday through Thursday* (= from Monday to Thursday).

through [RESULT] /θruː/ *prep* as a result of: *The company lost the order through production delays.*

through [USING] /θruː/ *prep* by; using: *I got my car through my brother who works in a garage.* ○ *We sold the bike through advertising in the local paper.*

through [SUCCESSFUL] /θruː/ *adj* **be through (to *sth*)** to achieve success in an exam, etc: *"Has she heard about her entrance exams yet?" "Yes, she's through."* ○ *She's through to the next round of interviews.*

throughout /θruːˈaʊt/ *prep, adv* in every part, or during the whole period of time: *People throughout the country are out of work.* ○ *He yawned throughout the performance.* ○ *The school has been repainted throughout.*

throughput /ˈθruː.pʊt/ *noun* **[U]** an amount of work, etc. done in a particular period of time: *We need to improve our throughput because demand is high at present.*

ˈthrough ˌroute *noun* **[C]** a road which avoids a town centre

ˈthrough ˌtraffic *noun* **[U]** traffic which does not want to stop in a town

throve /θrəʊv/ [US] /θroʊv/ *US past simple and past participle of* **thrive**

throw [SEND THROUGH AIR] /θrəʊ/ [US] /θroʊ/ *verb* **[I or T]** **threw, thrown** to send something through the air with force, especially by a sudden movement of the arm: *My friend threw the* ***ball*** *back over the fence.* ○ *The coat was thrown over the back of the chair.* ○ **[R]** *She threw herself into a chair, exhausted.* ○ *The rider was thrown as the horse jumped the fence.* ○ *He threw* ***a punch*** *at* (= hit) *his attacker.*
• **throw the baby out with the bath-water** to lose valuable ideas or things in your attempt to get rid of what is not wanted
• **throw *sth* back in *sb's* face** to say unkind things about someone's behaviour in the past during an argument:

She threw all his failures back in his face.

• **throw the book at** *sb* to severely punish someone: *After the accident, the safety inspector threw the book at the company directors.*

• **throw caution to the wind/winds** to do something without worrying about the risk or negative results: *I threw caution to the wind and bought the most expensive one.*

• **throw cold water on** *sth* to be negative about someone's ideas or plans: *You're always throwing cold water on my suggestions.*

• **throw in the towel/sponge** to admit defeat

• **throw a glance/look** to look quickly or suddenly: *The boy threw a frightened look in the direction of the house.*

• **throw good money after bad** to waste money by spending more money on something that you have already spent money on and which is no good: *Trying to fix that old car would just be throwing good money after bad.*

• **throw** *(your)* **money/cash around** INFORMAL DISAPPROVING to spend money, especially in an obvious and careless way, on things that are not necessary: *He lost his job, but still seems to have plenty of money to throw around.*

• **throw money at** *sth* to spend a lot of money on trying to solve a problem: *We won't solve this problem by throwing money at it.*

• **throw** *yourself* **into** *sth* to do something actively and enthusiastically: *She's thrown herself into this new job.*

• **throw up** *your* **hands in horror/despair** to show that you are shocked or that you disagree strongly with something: *They threw up their hands in horror at his suggestion.*

• **throw** *your* **voice** to make something which is not real, such as a toy, seem to be speaking

• **throw** *your* **weight around/about** to act as if you have a lot of power or authority

throw MOVE QUICKLY /θrəʊ/ ⓤ /θroʊ/ *verb* [T] threw, thrown to (cause to) move/act quickly or carelessly: *She threw* **back** *her hair.* ○ *David threw* **open** *the window to get some air.*

throw CONFUSE /θrəʊ/ ⓤ /θroʊ/ *verb* [T] threw, thrown to confuse or shock someone or cause difficulty for them: *I wasn't expecting a visitor. I was really thrown.* ○ *The news of the coup threw them into into a state of panic.*

• **throw** *sb* **off balance** to confuse or upset someone for a short time by saying or doing something that they are not expecting: *The question threw him off balance for a moment.*

throw PARTY /θrəʊ/ ⓤ /θroʊ/ *verb* **throw a party** to have a party: *Janet threw a party for Jack's fiftieth birthday.*

throw ANGER /θrəʊ/ ⓤ /θroʊ/ *verb* **throw a fit/tantrum**/*(UK INFORMAL)* **wobbly** to experience and show a strong feeling of anger, especially suddenly: *My mother threw a fit when she saw what a mess we'd made of her kitchen.*

throw SHAPE /θrəʊ/ ⓤ /θroʊ/ *verb* [T] threw, thrown SPECIALIZED to shape CLAY on a special round table that spins

throw EACH ITEM /θrəʊ/ ⓤ /θroʊ/ *noun* INFORMAL **a throw** used to mean each item or for each time: *We could get a coffee in there but they charge two quid a throw which is a real rip-off.*

PHRASAL VERBS WITH **throw** ▼

▲ **throw** *yourself* **at** *sb phrasal verb* [R] INFORMAL DISAPPROVING to make it very obvious to someone that you want a sexual relationship with them: *I don't know what it is about John, but women just seem to throw themselves at him.*

▲ **throw** *sth* **away/out** GET RID OF *phrasal verb* [M] to get rid of something that you do not want any more: *So when are you going to throw away those old magazines of yours?*

▲ **throw** *sth* **away** WASTE *phrasal verb* [M] to waste a skill or opportunity: *You've spent three years studying – don't throw it all away.*

▲ **throw** *sth* **in** *phrasal verb* [M] If a person or business selling goods throws something in, they provide it for free when you buy something else from them: *When I bought my new glasses, they threw in a free pair of prescription sunglasses.*

▲ **throw** *sth* **off** CLOTHES *phrasal verb* [M] If you throw off your clothes, you take them off quickly and carelessly: *They threw off their clothes and jumped in the sea.*

▲ **throw** *sth/sb* **off** ESCAPE *phrasal verb* [M] to escape from something or someone following you: *They threw the police off the scent by travelling on false passports.*

▲ **throw** *sth* **off** COLD *phrasal verb* [M] to stop suffering from a cold or other minor illness: *I can't seem to throw off this cold.*

▲ **throw** *sth* **open** OBJECT *phrasal verb* [M] to open something which was closed, usually suddenly and completely: *She drew back the curtains and threw open all the windows.*

▲ **throw** *sth* **open** EVENT *phrasal verb* [M] to allow people to enter or become involved in an event: *The competition has been thrown open to the public.*

▲ **throw** *sth* **out** NOT ACCEPT *phrasal verb* [M] If people in authority throw out a plan, idea, case, etc. they refuse to accept or use it: *The case was thrown out by the courts due to lack of evidence.*

▲ **throw** *sb* **out** FORCE TO LEAVE *phrasal verb* [M] to force someone to leave a college, school, house or organization: *She was thrown out of college for not attending lectures.* ○ *They had a big row and she threw him out (= made him leave the house).*

▲ **throw** *sb* **over** *phrasal verb* [M] INFORMAL to finish a relationship with someone and start one with another person: *She threw him over* **for** *a richer man.*

▲ **throw** *sth* **together** MAKE *phrasal verb* [M] INFORMAL to make something quickly without special care or preparation: *I had to throw a meal together at the last minute.*

▲ **throw** *sb* **together** MEET *phrasal verb* If two people are thrown together, they meet each other in a way that was not planned, or events cause them to meet unexpectedly: *We were thrown together by chance at a conference.*

▲ **throw** *(sth)* **up** VOMIT *phrasal verb* [M] INFORMAL to vomit: *I spent the night throwing up.* ○ *He threw up his breakfast all over the back seat of the car.*

▲ **throw** *sth* **up** JOB *phrasal verb* [M] UK INFORMAL If you throw up your job, you choose to leave it or stop doing it: *He's thrown up his job and gone off to Africa to work for a children's charity.*

▲ **throw** *sth* **up** IDEA *phrasal verb* [M] to produce new problems or ideas: *The meeting threw up some interesting ideas.*

throwaway /ˈθrəʊ.ə.weɪ/ ⓤ /ˈθroʊ-/ *adj* [before n] **1** made to be destroyed after use: *throwaway cups and plates* ○ *We live in a throwaway society.* **2 throwaway comment/line/remark** something which someone says without thinking carefully and which is not intended to be serious

throwback /ˈθrəʊ.bæk/ ⓤ /ˈθroʊ-/ *noun* [C usually sing] a person or thing that is similar to an earlier type: *He's an unappealing throwback* **to** *the days of '80s City slickers.* ○ *In some ways the new applet technology is a throwback* **to** *the old pre-PC days.*

thru /θruː/ *prep* US NOT STANDARD through

thrush BIRD /θrʌʃ/ *noun* [C] (ALSO **song thrush**) a brown bird with a pale breast with spots on it which is known for its singing

thrush DISEASE /θrʌʃ/ *noun* [U] an infection of the vagina or mouth

thrust PUSH /θrʌst/ *verb* [I or T; usually + adv or prep] thrust, thrust to push suddenly and strongly: *She thrust the money into his hand.* ○ *They thrust a microphone in front of me and fired questions at me.* ○ *She thrust the papers* **at** *me (= towards me).* ○ *The bodyguards thrust past the crowd to get at the cameraman.*

thrust /θrʌst/ *noun* **1** [C] a strong push **2** [U] SPECIALIZED the driving force produced by, for example, an aircraft engine

▲ **thrust** *sth* **on/upon** *sb phrasal verb* [often passive] to force someone to accept or deal with something: *Fatherhood had been thrust on him.*

thrust IDEA /θrʌst/ *noun* [S] the main idea, subject or opinion that is discussed or written about: *The **main** thrust* **of** *her argument was that women are compromised by the demands of childcare.*

T

thud /θʌd/ *noun* [C] the sound that is made when something heavy falls or hits something else: *The boy fell to the ground with a thud.* ○ *I could hear the thud of horses' hooves down the track.* **thud** /θʌd/ *verb* [I] **-dd-**

thug /θʌg/ *noun* [C] a man who acts violently, especially to commit a crime: *Some thugs smashed his windows.* **thuggish** /'θʌg.ɪʃ/ *adj* INFORMAL *a thuggish looking youth with a shaven head and tattoos on his arms*

thumb /θʌm/ *noun* [C] the short thick finger on the side of your hand which makes it possible to hold and pick things up easily ➲See picture **The Body** on page Centre 5

• **thumbs down** INFORMAL used to show disapproval of something: *They've **given** our plan the thumbs down (= They have disagreed with our plan).*

• **thumbs up** INFORMAL used to show approval of something: *So it's the thumbs up for Brighton's latest night club.*

• **all (fingers and) thumbs** INFORMAL to be very awkward with your hands: *Can you untangle this thread for me? I'm all thumbs today.*

• **under sb's thumb** to be under someone's control: *He's got the committee firmly under his thumb – they agree to whatever he asks.*

thumb /θʌm/ *verb* INFORMAL **thumb a lift** to stand near the edge of a road and hold out your hand with the thumb raised as a signal for a vehicle to stop and take you somewhere: *We thumbed a lift **to** London.*

• **thumb your nose at sb/sth** to show a lack of respect: *He has thumbed his nose at authority all his life.*

▲ **thumb through sth** *phrasal verb* to turn the pages of a book, magazine, or a document quickly and only read small parts of it: *"Have you read the report?" "Well, I thumbed through it quickly on the train."*

thumbnail FINGER /'θʌm.neɪl/ *noun* [C] the nail on the thumb

thumbnail PICTURE /'θʌm.neɪl/ *noun* [C] a small picture of an image or page on a computer screen

,**thumbnail 'sketch** *noun* [C] a short description mentioning only the most important features

thumbscrew /'θʌm.skruː/ *noun* [C] (ALSO **screws**) a device used especially in the past to TORTURE people (= cause them great pain) by crushing their thumbs

thumbtack /'θʌm.tæk/ *noun* [C] US FOR **drawing pin**

thump /θʌmp/ *verb* [T] **1** to hit someone with your FIST (= closed hand), or to hit something and cause a noise: *He thumped him in the face.* ○ *He thumped **on** the door but nobody came.* **2 heart thumps** If your heart thumps, it beats more strongly and quickly than usual, because of exercise, fear or excitement: *She stood outside his room, her heart thumping.* **3 head thumps** If your head is thumping, you can feel pain in strong beats in your head: *When I woke up my mouth was dry and my head was thumping.*

thump /θʌmp/ *noun* [C] *If he does that again I'm going to **give** him a thump (= hit him with my closed hand).* ○ *She fell to the floor with a thump (= the sound of something heavy falling).*

thumping /'θʌm.pɪŋ/ *adj* INFORMAL **thumping headache** a pain in the head which is felt in strong beats

thumping /'θʌm.pɪŋ/ *adj* [before n], *adv* INFORMAL very big or impressive: *a thumping defeat/victory* ○ *I'm not carrying that thumping **great** thing around with me!* ○ *They won by a thumping majority.*

thunder /'θʌn.dər/ ⑩ /-dɚ/ *noun* **1** [U] the sudden loud noise which comes from the sky especially during a storm: *a **clap** of thunder* ○ *thunder **and lightning** 2* [S] continuous loud noise: *I couldn't hear what he was saying over the thunder **of** the waterfall.*

thunder /'θʌn.dər/ ⑩ /-dɚ/ *verb* **1** [I] When it thunders, a loud noise comes from the sky: *The sky grew dark and it started to thunder.* **2** [I + adv or prep] to move, making a lot of noise: *The train thundered past, shaking the whole house.* **3** [I] to shout angrily: [+ speech] *"I never want to see you here again!" he thundered.*

thundering /'θʌn.dər.ɪŋ/ ⑩ /-dɚ.ɪŋ/ *noun* [U] *We could hear the thundering (= continuous loud noise) **of** the guns all night.* **thundery** /'θʌn.dər.i/ ⑩ /-dɚ.i/ *adj*: *thundery weather*

thunderbolt /'θʌn.də.bəʊlt/ ⑩ /-dɚ.boʊlt/ *noun* **1** [C] a flash of lightning and the sound of thunder together **2** [S] an announcement, event or idea that is completely unexpected or shocking: *He dropped a thunderbolt on us this morning, when he told us that we were closing down.*

thunderclap /'θʌn.də.klæp/ ⑩ /-dɚ-/ *noun* [C] a single loud sound of thunder

thundercloud /'θʌn.də.klaʊd/ ⑩ /-dɚ-/ *noun* [C usually pl] a large dark cloud which produces thunder and lightning

thunderous /'θʌn.dər.əs/ ⑩ /-dɚ.əs/ *adj* [before n] extremely loud: *thunderous applause* ○ *a thunderous reception*

thunderstorm /'θʌn.də.stɔːm/ ⑩ /-dɚ.stɔːrm/ *noun* [C] a storm with thunder and lightning and usually heavy rain

thunderstruck /'θʌn.də.strʌk/ ⑩ /-dɚ-/ *adj* [after v] very surprised: *Ruth was thunderstruck when he presented her with an engagement ring.*

thundery /'θʌn.dər.i/ ⑩ /-dɚ.i/ *adj* ➲See at **thunder**.

Thur (ALSO **Thurs**) WRITTEN ABBREVIATION FOR Thursday

Thursday /'θɜːz.deɪ/ ⑩ /'θɜːz-/ *noun* [C or U] (WRITTEN ABBREVIATION **Thur/Thurs**) the day of the week after Wednesday and before Friday

thus /ðʌs/ *adv* FORMAL **1** in this way: *Bend from the waist, thus.* **2** with this result: *They planned to reduce staff and thus to cut costs.*

• **thus far** as far as this or until now: *We haven't had any problems thus far.*

thwack /θwæk/ *noun* [C] the short loud sound of something like a stick hitting a surface: *I heard the thwack of the whip against the horse's side.*

thwack /θwæk/ *verb* [T] to hit something, making a short loud sound

thwart /θwɔːt/ ⑩ /θwɔːrt/ *verb* [T] to stop something from happening or someone from doing something: *My holiday plans have been thwarted by the strike.*

THX, thx INTERNET ABBREVIATION FOR thanks

thy /ðaɪ/ *determiner* OLD USE your; used when speaking to one person

thyme /taɪm/ *noun* [U] a herb used in cooking

thyroid (gland) /'θaɪə.rɔɪd,glænd/ ⑩ /'θaɪ-/ *noun* [C] a GLAND (= an organ) in the front of the neck which is involved in controlling the way the body develops and works

thyself /ðaɪ'self/ *pronoun* OLD USE yourself; reflexive form or strong form of THOU; used when speaking to one person

TIA, tia INTERNET ABBREVIATION FOR thanks in advance: used in an e-mail when you ask somebody for information or want them to do something for you

tiara /ti'ɑː.rə/ ⑩ /-'er.ə/ *noun* [C] a piece of metal in the shape of half a circle decorated with jewels which is worn on the head by a woman, especially a queen, etc., at very formal social occasions

tibia /'tɪb.i.ə/ *noun* [C] *plural* **tibiae** or **tibias** SPECIALIZED a shinbone (= the bone which can be felt at the front of the lower leg) ➲See picture **The Body** on page Centre 5

tic /tɪk/ *noun* [C] a sudden and uncontrolled small movement, especially of the face, especially because of a nervous illness

tick SOUND /tɪk/ *verb* [I] When a clock or watch ticks, it makes a sound every second.

• **what makes sb tick** If you know what makes someone tick, you understand why they behave the way they do.

tick /tɪk/ *noun* [C] the sound clocks and watches make every second

tick SHORT TIME /tɪk/ *noun* [C] UK INFORMAL a very short time: *Hold on/Hang on a tick – I'm not quite ready.* ○ *I'll be with you in a tick/in two ticks.*

tick MARK MAINLY UK /tɪk/ *noun* [C] (US USUALLY **check**) a mark (✓) that shows that something is correct or has been done: *Put a tick by/against the names of the people who have accepted the invitation.*

tick MAINLY UK /tɪk/ *verb* [T] (US USUALLY **check**) to mark something with a tick: *Tick (off) each item on the list as you complete it.*

PHRASAL VERBS WITH **tick**

▲ **tick away/by** *phrasal verb* If time ticks away/by, it goes past: *With the final seconds ticking away, Milan scored a goal.*

▲ **tick *sb* off** [SPEAK SEVERELY] *phrasal verb* [M] *UK INFORMAL* to speak severely to and criticize someone who has done something wrong: *I had to tick him off for being late again.*

▲ **tick *sb* off** [ANNOY] *phrasal verb* [M] *US INFORMAL* to annoy someone: *It really ticks me off when she doesn't keep her promises.*

▲ **tick over** [ACTIVITY] *phrasal verb* If a business, job or system is ticking over, it continues to work but makes little progress: *I'll be able to **keep** things ticking over in the office until you get back.*

▲ **tick over** [ENGINE] *phrasal verb* If the engine of a vehicle is ticking over, the engine is operating slowly although the vehicle is not moving: *I've left the car with the engine ticking over.*

tick [PAYING LATER] /tɪk/ *noun UK OLD-FASHIONED INFORMAL* **on tick** If you buy something on tick, you pay for it later.

tick [ANIMAL] /tɪk/ *noun* [C] a very small creature like an insect which lives on and sucks the blood of other animals

ticker /ˈtɪk.əʳ/ [US] /-ɚ/ *noun* [C] *INFORMAL* a heart

ticker-tape parade /ˈtɪk.ə.teɪp.pəˌreɪd/ [US] /-ɚ-/ *noun* [C] *US* a special celebration in which someone who is being honoured for achieving something very important walks or drives along streets in a city and small pieces of paper are thrown over them from the windows of tall buildings

ticket [PROOF OF PAYMENT] /ˈtɪk.ɪt/ *noun* [C] a small piece of paper or card given to someone, usually to show that they have paid for an item or activity: *a concert ticket* ○ *a train/bus/plane ticket* ○ *a lottery/raffle ticket* ○ *a ticket office* ○ *a ticket collector*

• **just the ticket** *SLIGHTLY OLD-FASHIONED INFORMAL* very suitable and exactly what is needed

ticketing /ˈtɪk.ɪ.tɪŋ/ [US] /-t̬ɪŋ/ *noun* [U] the production or selling of tickets: *Electronic ticketing now allows customers to buy airline seats over the phone.*

ticket [PRICE CARD] /ˈtɪk.ɪt/ *noun* [C] **1** a piece of card or paper which is put on an item to show its size or price: *a **price** ticket* **2** a note telling you that you must pay some money as a punishment for not obeying a rule or law: *a parking ticket* **3** *UK* the range of ideas and plans that someone supports when they are in an election: *She's standing on an education ticket.* **4** *US* the group of people representing a particular political party in an election: *the Republican/Democratic ticket*

ˌticking ˈoff *noun* [S] *MAINLY UK INFORMAL* severe criticism because you have done something wrong: *I **gave** her a real ticking off yesterday.*

tickle [RUB SKIN] /ˈtɪk.l̩/ *verb* **1** [T] to touch someone lightly with your fingers, making them slightly uncomfortable and often making them laugh: *Stop! You're tickling me!* ○ *I tickled her feet and she laughed.* **2** [I or T] If a part of the body tickles, or if something tickles it, it feels slightly uncomfortable and you want to rub it: *My nose is tickling, I think I'm going to sneeze.*

• **tickle *your* fancy** *INFORMAL* If something tickles your fancy, you like it and want to have it: *Does anything on the menu tickle your fancy?*

tickle /ˈtɪk.l̩/ *noun* **1 give *sb* a tickle** to tickle someone **2** [S] an unpleasant feeling in your throat which makes you want to cough

tickle [PLEASE] /ˈtɪk.l̩/ *verb* [T often passive] *INFORMAL* If something tickles you, it amuses or pleases you: *OLD-FASHIONED I was tickled **pink*** (= very pleased) *to hear the news.*

ticklish [SKIN] /ˈtɪk.l̩.ɪʃ/ /-lɪʃ/ *adj* If someone is ticklish, they quickly feel uncomfortable when someone lightly touches their skin to make them laugh.

ticklish [DIFFICULT] /ˈtɪk.l̩.ɪʃ/ /-lɪʃ/ *adj* describes a situation that needs to be dealt with carefully: *This leaves me with the ticklish job of explaining to Debbie that she is not invited.*

tick-tack-toe /ˌtɪk.tækˈtəʊ/ [US] /-ˈtoʊ/ *noun* [U] *US FOR* **noughts and crosses**

ˈtidal ˌwave *noun* [C] **1** an extremely large wave caused by movement of the earth under the sea, often caused by an EARTHQUAKE (= when the Earth shakes) **2** a sudden large number of things: *a tidal wave **of** complaints*

tidbit /ˈtɪd.bɪt/ *noun* [C] *US FOR* **titbit**

tiddler /ˈtɪd.l̩.əʳ/ /-ləʳ/ [US] /-l̩.ɚ/ [US] /ˈ-lɚ/ *noun* [C] *INFORMAL* **1** something very small, especially a fish **2** a child

tiddly [SMALL] /ˈtɪd.l̩.i/ /-li/ *adj INFORMAL* extremely small: *All you ate was a tiddly little piece of cake.*

tiddly [DRUNK] /ˈtɪd.l̩.i/ /-li/ *adj UK OLD-FASHIONED INFORMAL* slightly drunk

tiddlywinks /ˈtɪd.l̩.i.wɪŋks/ /-li-/ *noun* [U] a game in which players try to get small plastic discs into a cup by pressing one piece against another to make it fly through the air

tiddlywink /ˈtɪd.l̩.i.wɪŋk/ /-li-/ *noun* [C] one of the pieces used in the game of tiddlywinks

tide [SEA] /taɪd/ *noun* [C] the rise and fall of the sea that happens twice every day: *high/low tide* ○ *the tide is **out/in***

• **go/swim with the tide** to follow what everyone else is doing: *I thought I'd just swim with the tide and leave when everyone else does.*

• **go/swim against the tide** to not follow what everyone else is doing

tidal /ˈtaɪ.dᵊl/ *adj* relating to the tide: *a tidal river*

tide [CHANGE] /taɪd/ *noun* [S] *LITERARY* a noticeable change in a situation or increase in a particular type of behaviour: *We must look for ways of **stemming*** (= stopping) *the rising tide **of** protest.*

-tide [TIME] /-taɪd/ *suffix OLD USE* a period of time: *Yuletide*

tide /taɪd/ *verb*

▲ **tide *sb* over *(sth)*** *phrasal verb* to help someone to work or operate normally through a difficult period, usually by lending them money: *Can you lend me some money to tide me over till the weekend?* ○ *Have another piece of cake. It'll tide you over till supper.*

tidemark /ˈtaɪd.mɑːk/ [US] /-mɑːrk/ *noun* [C] **1** (*ALSO* **high water mark**) a line of waste left on a beach which marks the highest point the sea reaches **2** *UK* a dirty mark around a bath or sink, left by the water

tide-table /ˈtaɪdˌteɪ.bl̩/ *noun* [C] a list of the times at which the tide in a particular place is high for each day

tidings /ˈtaɪ.dɪŋz/ *plural noun OLD USE* news: *tidings of great joy*

tidy [ORDERED] /ˈtaɪ.di/ *adj* having everything ordered and arranged in the right place, or liking to keep things like this: *The house was clean and tidy.* ○ *My flatmate isn't very tidy.* ○ ***neat and** tidy* ○ *a tidy solution*

tidy /ˈtaɪ.di/ *verb* [I or T] to make a place or a collection of things tidy: *Tidy **(up)** these papers before you leave, please.* ○ *I'm tired of asking you to tidy your room **(up)**.* ○ *Have you tidied **up** yet, kids?*

tidy /ˈtaɪ.di/ *noun* **a desk/car/sink, etc. tidy** a small container for a few items, that enables you to keep your desk, car, etc. tidy ➲See picture **In the Office** on page Centre 15 **tidily** /ˈtaɪ.dɪ.li/ *adv*: *Put your clothes away tidily.* **tidiness** /ˈtaɪ.dɪ.nəs/ *noun* [U] **tidy-up** /ˌtaɪ.diˈʌp/ *noun* [S] *Let's have/do a quick tidy-up before mum gets home.*

▲ **tidy *sth* away** *phrasal verb* [M] to put things back in drawers, cupboards and other places where they are kept, after you have used them: *The children were expected to tidy away their toys before bedtime.*

tidy [LARGE] /ˈtaɪ.di/ *adj* [before n] *INFORMAL* (of amounts of money) large: *His business deals make him a tidy sum/profit.*

tie [FASTEN] /taɪ/ *verb* [I or T] **tying, tied, tied 1** to fasten together two ends of a piece of string or other long thin material, or to (cause to) hold together with a long, thin piece of string, material, etc: *Could you tie this piece of string for me?* ○ *This skirt ties at the waist.* ○ *She tied the ribbon tightly **in** a bow/knot.* ○ *I tie my hair **back** when it's hot.* ○ *Tie **(up)** your shoelaces, or you'll trip over.* **2 be tied to** If you are tied to a job, place or person, you are forced to stay with them: *I felt tied to the job while I had a mortgage to pay.*

• **tied to *your* mother's/wife's apron strings** *DISAPPROVING* If you say that someone, especially a man, is tied to his

T

mother's/wife's apron strings, it means that he is strongly influenced and controlled by that person: *George never comes out with the rest of us – he's tied to Martha's/his wife's apron strings.*

• **tie the knot** to get married: *So when are you two going to tie the knot?*

• **tie *sb* (up) in knots** to confuse someone: *The Director of Studies tied me up in knots by asking tricky questions.*

tie /taɪ/ *noun* **[C] 1** (*US ALSO* **necktie**) a long thin piece of material that is worn under a shirt collar, especially by men, and tied in a knot at the front: *He always wears a jacket and tie to work.* ➲See picture **Clothes** on page Centre 6 **2** any piece of string, plastic, metal, etc. which is used to fasten or hold together something: *Can you see the ties for the rubbish bags in the cupboard?*

tie [RELATE] /taɪ/ *verb* **[T] tying, tied, tied** to relate to or connect to: *Is the allergy tied **to** dairy products, for example?* ○ *Can you tie his behaviour **up with** anything that's happened recently?*

ties /taɪz/ *plural noun* the friendly feelings that people have for other people, or special connections with places: *Family ties are weaker if you move a long way away.* ○ *I no longer feel any ties **with** my home town.* ○ *He urged governments worldwide to break **diplomatic** ties with the new regime.*

tie [FINISH EQUAL] /taɪ/ *verb* **[I] tying, tied, tied** to finish at the same time or score the same number of points, etc. in a competition as someone or something else: *Jane and I tied (**for** first place) in the spelling test.* ○ *We tied **with** a team from the south in the championships.*

tie /taɪ/ *noun* **[C]** when two or more people finish at the same time or score the same number of points: *It's a tie **for** first place.* ○ *They have changed the scoring system because there have been too many ties.*

PHRASAL VERBS WITH **tie** ▼

▲ **tie *sb* down** [NOT FREE] *phrasal verb* **[M often passive]** *INFORMAL* to limit someone's freedom: *He's tied down **by** having to work every Saturday.* ○ *We'd like to travel more, but having children at school really ties us down.*

▲ **tie *sb* down** [NOT CLEAR] *phrasal verb* **[M]** *INFORMAL* to make someone give you a clear decision: *I'll try to tie her down **on** her plans.*

▲ **tie *(sth)* in** *phrasal verb* **[M]** When ideas or statements tie in, they agree or are closely connected, and if you tie them in, you make them agree or connect closely: *I can't quite tie in what he said today **with** what he told me last week.*

▲ **tie *(sth)* in with *sth*** *phrasal verb* **[M]** to plan an event or activity so that it combines with or happens at the same time as another, or to be planned in this way: *We're trying to tie our holiday in with Simon's lecture tour.*

▲ **tie *sb* up** [FASTENED] *phrasal verb* **[M]** to make a person unable to move by tying a rope or something similar around their body or part of their body: *The burglars had tied him up (**to** the bed).*

▲ **tie *sth* up** *phrasal verb* **[M]** to fasten something together using string, rope or something similar: *Could you tie up the parcel for me?*

▲ **tie *sb* up** [NOT AVAILABLE] *phrasal verb* When someone is tied up, they are busy or are prevented from doing something, such as speaking to someone or going somewhere, because they are involved in another event or activity: *I'm afraid we can't meet till Wednesday – I'm tied up on Monday and Tuesday.* ○ *Mrs Moran is tied up **in** a meeting at the moment, but I'll ask her to call you later.*

▲ **tie *sth* up** *phrasal verb* to cause something, often money or possessions, not to be available for use: *All my money is tied up **in** property.* ○ *He tied up the printer all morning, printing out his reports.*

tie-breaker /ˈtaɪˌbreɪ.kəʳ/ [US] /-kɚ/ *noun* **[C]** (*UK ALSO* **tie-break**) extra play at the end of a game when both teams have the same points, to decide who is the winner

ˌtied ˈcottage *noun* **[C]** (*ALSO* **tied house**) *UK* a house owned by your employer that you can live in for as long as you are employed in a particular job

ˌtied ˈhouse *noun* **[C]** *UK* a pub which is owned by a particular beer company and which only sells that company's products ➲Compare **free house**.

tie-dye /ˈtaɪ.daɪ/ *verb* **[T] tie-dyeing** to colour cloth by tying it in knots so that when it is put in a dye the tied areas absorb less colour and produce circular patterns when unfastened: *There are pictures of us in the sixties wearing flares and tie-dyed T-shirts.*

tiepin /ˈtaɪ.pɪn/ *noun* **[C]** a small thin often decorative piece of metal used to hold the two parts of a tie together

tier /tɪəʳ/ [US] /tɪr/ *noun* **[C]** one of several layers or levels: *We sat in one of the upper tiers of the football stands.* ○ *My wedding cake had four tiers, each supported by small pillars.* ○ *I don't understand why you think we need yet another tier of management.* **tier** /tɪəʳ/ [US] /tɪr/ *verb* **[T]** *The seats in the theatre were steeply tiered.* **-tiered** /-tɪəd/ [US] /-tɪrd/ *suffix*: *a two-tiered structure* ○ *a three-tiered cake*

tie-up /ˈtaɪ.ʌp/ *noun* **[C] 1** *MAINLY UK* a connection or agreement that joins two things or organizations: *Cambridge University Press arranged a tie-up **with** the German publisher Klett.* **2** *US* a temporary problem that delays progress, such as too much traffic on the road: *I missed my flight because of a tie-up on the interstate.*

tiff /tɪf/ *noun* **[C]** *INFORMAL* a slight argument: *Have you two **had** a **lovers'** tiff?*

tiger /ˈtaɪ.gəʳ/ [US] /-gɚ/ *noun* **[C]** (*FEMALE ALSO* **tigress**) a large wild animal of the cat family with yellowish orange fur with black lines which lives in parts of Asia ➲See picture **Animals and Birds** on page Centre 4

tight [FIRMLY TOGETHER] /taɪt/ *adj, adv* (held or kept together) firmly or closely: *I can't untie the knot – it's too tight.* ○ *This lid is on very tight.* ○ *The people stood talking in tight groups.* ○ *Hold on tight when we go round this corner.* ○ *Check that windows and doors are shut tight* (= completely closed) *before you leave.* ○ *The plastic cover was stretched tight* (= stretched as much as it could be) *across the tank.* ➲See also **airtight**; **watertight**.

tight /taɪt/ *adj* **1** If you have a tight feeling in your chest you have an uncomfortable feeling of pressure, caused by illness, fear, etc. **2** Controls or rules that are tight are ones which severely limit what can happen. **3** If time or money is tight, there isn't enough of it: *I'm sorry I can't stop, time's really tight.* ○ *They're raising three kids on one small salary so money is very tight.* **4** Clothes or shoes that are tight fit the body too closely and are uncomfortable: *That jacket's too tight – you want a bigger size.*

• **be in a tight corner/spot** to be in a difficult situation

tightly /ˈtaɪt.li/ *adv* firmly or closely: *The baby was clutching his dummy tightly in his grubby fist.* ○ *Many commuters are forced to stand, tightly packed in, like sardines.* **tightness** /ˈtaɪt.nəs/ *noun* **[U]**

tighten /ˈtaɪ.tᵊn/ *verb* **[I or T]** to become tighter or to make something become tighter, firmer or less easy to move: *Tighten the straps so they don't rub.* ○ *As he struggled, the ropes tightened even more.*

• **tighten the net** (especially of the police) to become closer to catching someone, especially a criminal: *The police are tightening the net **around** the smugglers.*

• **tighten *your* belt** to spend less money than you did before because you have less money: *I've had to tighten my belt since I stopped working full-time.*

PHRASAL VERBS WITH **tighten** ▼

▲ **tighten *sth* up** [TIGHTER] *phrasal verb* **[M]** to make something become tighter, firmer or less easy to move: *Now tighten up the screws.*

▲ **tighten *(sth)* up** [STRONGER] *phrasal verb* **[M]** to make a rule, system, or law stronger and more difficult to avoid or ignore: *Are there any plans to tighten up **on** advertising controls?*

tight [DRUNK] /taɪt/ *adj OLD-FASHIONED INFORMAL* having had too much alcohol; drunk: *Jim, you're tight!*

tight-fisted /ˌtaɪtˈfɪs.tɪd/ *adj* (*ALSO* **tight**) *INFORMAL DISAPPROVING* unwilling to spend money: *Don't imagine Gillian'll buy you a drink – she's too tight-fisted.*

tight-lipped /ˌtaɪtˈlɪpt/ *adj* If someone is tight-lipped they are pressing their lips together to avoid showing anger or they are refusing to speak about something:

He's been very tight-lipped about what happened at the meeting.

tightrope /ˈtaɪt.rəʊp/ [US] /-roʊp/ *noun* [C] a tightly stretched wire or rope fixed high above the ground, which skilled people walk across, especially in order to entertain others: *One of the acrobats who **walked** the tightrope at the circus did it blindfolded.*

• **walk/tread a tightrope** If you walk/tread a tightrope, you have to deal with a difficult situation, especially one involving making a decision between two opposing plans of action: *Many manufacturers have to walk a tightrope **between** pricing their goods too high and not selling them, and pricing them low and losing money.*

tights /taɪts/ *plural noun* **1** *UK* (*US* **pantyhose**) a piece of clothing made of thin stretchy material which covers the legs and lower part of the body below the waist, and which is worn by women and girls: *She bought a new **pair of** tights.* ○ *Oh no, I've got a ladder/run/hole in my tights.* ➲See picture **Clothes** on page Centre 6 **2** the same type of clothing made from thicker material and worn by dancers and people doing physical exercises for health

tight ˈturn *noun* [C] (*ALSO* **tight bend**) a sudden sharp turn

tightwad /ˈtaɪt.wɒd/ [US] /-wɑːd/ *noun* [C] *US SLANG DISAPPROVING* a person who is not willing to spend money: *There's no point in asking Joe to pay for it – he's a real tightwad.*

tigress /ˈtaɪ.grəs/ *noun* [C] **1** a female TIGER **2** a woman who is behaving very fiercely: *Jean can be a real tigress if she feels criticised.*

tike /taɪk/ *noun* [C] **tyke**

tilde /ˈtɪl.də/ *noun* [C] (used when writing some languages) a ~ mark made above a letter, especially n, to show that the letter has a special sound

tile /taɪl/ *noun* [C] a thin, usually square or rectangular, piece of baked clay, plastic, etc. used for covering roofs, floors, walls, etc: *roof tiles* ○ *floor tiles* ○ *ceramic tiles* ○ *carpet tiles*

• **be/go out on the tiles** *UK INFORMAL* to enjoy yourself at night by going out to DISCOS, parties or bars: *I was out on the tiles last night and I've got such a headache this morning.*

tile /taɪl/ *verb* [T] to cover a wall or floor with tiles: *We're going to tile the bathroom.*

tiled /taɪld/ *adj* (of a surface) covered with tiles: *The kitchen has a tiled floor.*

tiler /ˈtaɪ.ləʳ/ [US] /-lɚ/ *noun* [C] a person who fixes tiles to a surface: *Can you recommend a good tiler?*

till [UNTIL] /tɪl/ *prep, conjunction* up to (the time that); until: *We waited till half past six for you.* ○ ***Up** till 1918, women in Britain were not allowed to vote.* ○ *How long is it till your baby is due?*

till [MONEY DRAWER] /tɪl/ *noun* [C] (*US USUALLY* **register**) *MAINLY UK* the drawer in a CASH REGISTER (= a machine which records sales in a shop, and in which money is kept) or the CASH REGISTER itself: *Next time you have the till open, could you give me some change?* ○ *I think these items have been **rung up** wrongly **on** the till.*

till [PREPARE LAND] /tɪl/ *verb* [T] to prepare and use land for growing crops: *This piece of land has been tilled for hundreds of years.*

tiller /ˈtɪl.əʳ/ [US] /-ɚ/ *noun* [C] a long handle fixed to and used to turn a RUDDER (= blade at the back of a boat used to control the boat's direction)

tilt [SLOPE] /tɪlt/ *verb* [I or T] to (cause to) move into a sloping position: *He tilted his chair backwards and put his feet up on his desk.* ○ *Anna looked up at him with her head tilted to one side.* ○ *The front seats of the car tilt.*

• **tilt the balance/scales** If something tilts the balance, it is the thing which causes a particular situation to happen or a particular decision to be made when other situations or decisions are possible: *This latest election promise might just tilt the balance in the government's favour.*

tilt /tɪlt/ *noun* [C usually sing] when something is in a sloping position or when something moves in a particular direction, especially up or down: *She wore her hat **at a** tilt.* ○ *FIGURATIVE There has been a tilt **to/towards/away from** the socialists among some groups of young people.*

tilt [FIGHT] /tɪlt/ *verb INFORMAL* **tilt at windmills** to fight enemies who do not really exist

timber /ˈtɪm.bəʳ/ [US] /-bɚ/ *noun* **1** [U] trees that are grown so that the wood from them can be used for building: *a timber forest* ○ *These trees are being grown for timber.* **2** [U] *UK* (*US* **lumber**) wood used for building: *a timber merchant* **3** [C] a long piece of wood used for building, especially houses and ships: *roof timbers* ○ *a timber-framed building*

timber /ˈtɪm.bəʳ/ [US] /-bɚ/ *exclamation* shouted when a tree which has been cut is about to fall

timberline /ˈtɪm.bə.laɪn/ [US] /-bɚ-/ *noun* [U] *US FOR* **tree-line**

timbre /ˈtæm.bəʳ/ [US] /-bɚ/ *noun* [U] a quality of sound which makes voices or musical instruments different from each other: *He has a wonderful singing voice, with a rich timbre and resonant tone.*

time [MINUTES/DAYS/YEARS] /taɪm/ *noun* [U] that part of existence which is measured in seconds, minutes, hours, days, weeks, months, years, etc., or this process considered as a whole: *He wants to **spend** more time with his family.* ○ *Time **passes** so quickly when you're enjoying yourself.* ○ *She grew more and more fascinated by the subject as time **went on/by**.* ○ *The curtains have faded **over/with** time* (= as years have gone past). ○ *You'll forget her **in** time* (= in the future). ○ *Over the course of time* (= as years have gone past), *holes have formed in the rock.* ○ *I only worked there for a short **period of** time.* ○ *I'd like to visit them all but time **is short*** (= there is little time left). ➲See Note **hour or time?** at **hour**.

• **time stands still** When time stands still, everything around you seems to stop: *I saw the car coming straight towards me, and for a moment time stood still.*

• **for all time** *LITERARY* always: *I will love you for all time.*

• **a matter/question of time** used when you think that something will happen at some point in the near future: *If you carry on driving like that, it'll only be a matter of time before you have an accident.*

• **of all time** that has ever lived or existed: *She's been called the greatest opera singer of all time.*

• **time is on *sb's* side** (*ALSO* **have time on *your* side**) If you say that time is on your side, or that you have time on your side, you mean that you do not have to do quickly whatever it is that you want or have to do: *We don't have to make a final decision till next week, so time is on our side.*

• **(only) time will/can tell** used to say that the truth or a result will only be known in the future after events have happened: *Only time will tell whether we made the right decision.*

• **Time and tide wait for no man.** *UK LITERARY SAYING* said to emphasize that people cannot stop the passing of time, and therefore should not delay doing things

• **Time's a great healer.** (*ALSO* **Time heals (all wounds).**) *SAYING* said to mean that a painful or difficult situation will seem less bad as time passes

• **Time flies.** *SAYING* used to mean that time passes very and surprisingly quickly: *Time flies when you're having fun.*

• **Time is money.** *SAYING* said to emphasize that you should not waste time, because you could be using it to earn money

• **Time is of the essence.** *FORMAL SAYING* said to encourage someone to hurry

• **Time hangs heavy.** *SAYING* said when minutes, hours, weeks, etc. seem to go past very slowly: *Time hangs heavy in prison.*

timeless /ˈtaɪm.ləs/ *adj* describes something that does not change as the years go past: *The city has a timeless quality as if it had existed forever.* **timelessly** /ˈtaɪm.lə.sli/ *adv* **timelessness** /ˈtaɪm.lə.snəs/ *noun* [U]

time [PERIOD] /taɪm/ *noun* **1** [U] a particular period of seconds, minutes, hours, days, weeks, months, years, etc. for which something has been happening, or which is needed for something, or which is available for something: *I enjoyed my course at first, but **after a** time I got bored with it.* ○ *They stayed with us **for a short** time.* ○ *That was the best restaurant I've been to **for/in a long** time* (= a long period has gone past since I went to such

T

a good restaurant). ○ *It was* **some** *time* **ago** *that I last heard from her.* ○ *We're going on holiday in* **two weeks' time** (= after two weeks have gone past). ○ **During her time** (= While she was) *in office, the Prime Minister introduced a large number of changes.* ○ *When Paula was ill, I took her some magazines to help her* **pass the time** (= to try to make the hours, etc. feel as if they were going past less slowly).* ○ *If you'd* **taken** *more time* **with/over** (= spent more hours doing) *this essay, you could have done it much better.* ○ *It* **takes a** *long time* (= many hours are needed) *to get from London to Sydney.* ○ *We'd* **save** *time on our journey* (= It would be quicker) *if we went by train.* ○ *What do you like doing in your* **spare/free** *time* (= the time when you're not working)? ○ *I don't know how you* **find** *time to do all the things you do.* ○ *I thought we'd* **give** *her a bit more time* (= allow her more time) *to get the job done.* ⊃See Note **hour or time?** at **hour. 2 have time** If you have got time, you have enough time to do something: *We haven't got much time before the train leaves.* ○ *Have you got time* **for** *a quick drink after work?* ○ *I'd like to learn to sail, but I haven't* **the** *time* (= I am too busy). ○ [+ **to** infinitive] *I haven't got time* **to** *go to the shops today.* **3** [C or U] Your time in a race is the number of minutes, hours, etc. you take to complete it: *Her time* **for** *the marathon was just under three hours.* ○ *He won the 100 metres in* **record** *time.* **4 have/take time off** to stop work, in order to do something else: *I asked my boss if I could have some time off* **(from** *work)* *to go to the dentist.*

• **all the time** continuously: *I wish you'd stop criticizing me all the time.*

• **all the time in the world** a large number of minutes, hours, etc. available: *The doctor made me feel as if she had all the time in the world to listen to my problems.*

• **be (all) out of time** MAINLY US INFORMAL to not have enough minutes, etc. available: *I'd like to continue this discussion but we're all out of time.*

• **be pressed for time** to be in a hurry: *I'd love to stop and chat but I'm rather pressed for time.*

• **do time** INFORMAL to spend a period of weeks, months, years, etc. in prison: *It's not always easy to find a job after you've done time.*

• **for a time** for a short period: *For a time, we all thought that Sheila and Frank would get married.*

• **for the time being** for a limited period: *Leave the ironing for the time being – I'll do it later.*

• **have a lot of time for sb** INFORMAL to like someone and be interested in them: *She's really nice – I have a lot of time for Helen.*

• **have no time for sb** to disapprove of someone and not want to be involved with them: *I've got no time for people who are always complaining.*

• **have time to kill** to have nothing to do for a particular period: *We've got some time to kill before our train arrives – shall we have a drink?*

• **time on your hands** to have nothing to do: *Now that her children are all at school, Mary has found that she has time on her hands, so she is taking a college course.*

• **in no time** (ALSO **in next to no time**) very quickly or very soon: *The children ate their dinner in no time.* ○ *We'll be home in next to no time.*

• **no time to lose** If you say there is or that you have no time to lose, it means that you must do quickly whatever it is that you want to do: *Come on, there's no time to lose, we must get home before John finds out where we've been.*

• **run out of time** to not have enough hours, etc. available to finish something you are trying to do: *She ran out of time and didn't finish the last question.*

• **time's up** INFORMAL there are no more minutes, hours, etc. available: *OK everyone, time's up for this week – see you all again at next week's class.*

• **waste time** to not make good use of the hours, etc. that you have available: *If you'd got on with your work instead of wasting time chatting, you'd be finished by now.*

time /taɪm/ *verb* [T] to measure how long it takes for something to happen or for someone to do something: *Will you time me to see how long it takes me to swim a length?*

-time /-taɪm/ *suffix*: *springtime* (= the spring period) ○ *Christmas-time* ○ *daytime* ○ *night-time*

timeless /'taɪm.ləs/ *adj* having a value that is not limited to a particular period but will last forever: *a timeless book/play/film/classic* ○ *timeless values/ questions* ○ *Rothko's paintings have a timeless quality.* **timelessly** /'taɪm.lə.sli/ *adv* **timelessness** /'taɪm.lə.snəs/ *noun* [U]

time PARTICULAR POINT /taɪm/ *noun* **1** [C or S or U] a particular point in the day, as expressed in hours and minutes or shown on a clock, or a particular point in the day, week, month or year, etc: *"What's the time?"* *"It's ten o'clock."* ○ *What time is it?* ○ *What time do you finish work?* ○ *Have you got* **the** *time* **(on** *you)* (= Do you know what time it is)? ○ *He's teaching his daughter to* **tell** *the time* (= to recognize what time it is by looking at a clock). ○ *Did you find out the times of the trains to London* (= the particular points in the day at which they leave)? ○ *The estimated time of arrival/departure of this flight is 11.15.* ○ *Oh dear, is that the* **(right)** *time* (= Is it that late)? ○ *The kitchen clock is* **gaining/losing** *time* (= is showing a particular point in the day that is increasingly later or earlier than the real one). ○ *My watch has never* **kept** *very good time* (= been correct in showing what particular point in the day it is). ○ *We always have dinner* **at the same** *time every day.* ○ *I was exhausted by* **the** *time* (= when) *I got home.* ○ *"What would be the best time of day for us to deliver the table?" "Oh, any time will be OK."* ○ *Today's temperatures will be normal for the time of year* (= will be as they are expected to be at this particular point in the year). ○ *Just think,* **this** *time* (= at the same particular point during) *next week we'll be in Mauritius.* ○ *We regret that* **at the present** *time* (US ALSO **at this time**) (= for now, although it is hoped not in the future) *we are unable to supply the goods you ordered.* ○ *The time is fast* **drawing near/approaching** *when* (= it will soon be the particular point at which) *we'll have to make a decision one way or the other.* ⊃See Note **hour or time?** at **hour. 2** [U] the system of recording hours used in different parts of the world: *Greenwich Mean Time* ○ *daylight saving time*

• **ahead of time** MAINLY US in advance: *Let's meet for lunch. I'll call you ahead of time to fix up exactly when and where.*

• **at all times** continuously: *When you're at the airport, you should make sure you have your luggage with you at all times.*

• **at any time** ever: *Parking is not allowed here at any time.*

• **at (any) one time** (ALSO **at a time,** ALSO **at any given time**) at or during any particular point or moment in the day: *Only a certain number of people are allowed in the building at any one time.* ○ *I'm sorry, but I'm too busy to help you now – I can only do one thing at a time.*

• **at your time of life** at a person's present age: *At his time of life, he ought to be taking things easy.*

• **at the time** at the particular point when something was thought of or done: *It seemed like a good idea at the time.*

• **not give sb the time of day** If someone will not give you the time of day, they are unfriendly and refuse to speak to you: *We had an argument with our neighbours, and now they won't even give us the time of day.*

time /taɪm/ *verb* [T] to decide that something will happen at a particular time: [+ **to** infinitive] *We timed our trip to coincide with my cousin's wedding.*

time SUITABLE POINT /taɪm/ *noun* **1** [S or U] a particular point of the day, week, month, year, etc. that is suitable for a particular activity, or at which something is expected to happen: *holiday time* ○ *party time* ○ *Put your toys away now, it's time for bed.* ○ *It's time* **(that)** *I was leaving.* ○ [+ **to** infinitive] *Is it time to go home yet?* ○ *When would be* **a** *good time for me to call you?* ○ *This is not the time* (= not a suitable moment) *to be thinking about buying a house.* ○ *This is no time* (= not a suitable moment) *to change your mind.* ○ *I feel that the time has* **come** (= now is a suitable moment) *for me to move on.* ○ *The repairs to the road were finished two weeks* **ahead of** *time* (= sooner than was expected). ○ *Why is it that the trains never run* **on** *time* (= make their journeys in the expected number of hours, etc.)? ○ *She's grown old* *before* her time (= sooner than she might have been expected to have done). ⊃See Note **hour or time?** at **hour**. **2** [U] the particular point in the day at which people who are drinking in a bar in Britain have to finish their drinks and leave: *"Time, please," called the landlord.* ○ *Is it time already?*

• **There's a time and a place (for everything).** SAYING said when someone is behaving in a way which you do not think is suitable for the situation they are in

• **There's no time like the present.** SAYING said to encourage someone to take action immediately instead of waiting

• **about time** (ALSO **high time**) INFORMAL If it is about time/high time that someone did something, it should have been done sooner or a long time ago: *It's about time (that) the school improved its meals service.* ○ *It is high time for Europe to take responsibility for its own defence.*

• **about time (too)** (ALSO **not before time**) INFORMAL said when someone does something or something happens that you think should have been done or have happened much sooner: *"So Ben's finally found a job." "Yes, and about time too."*

• **ahead of** *your* **time** (UK ALSO **before** *your* **time**) having new ideas, opinions or ways of living long before most other people do

• **in time** early enough: *I got home just in time – it's starting to rain.* ○ *If we don't hurry up, we won't be in time to catch the train.* ○ *We arrived in good time* (= We arrived early) *for the start of the match.*

• **bang/dead/right on time** INFORMAL happening or done at the particular moment that it was expected to happen or be done: *The bus arrived dead on time.*

• **the time is ripe** If you say that the time is ripe, you mean that it is a suitable point for a particular activity: *I'm waiting till the time is ripe before I tell my parents that I failed my exams.*

time /taɪm/ *verb* [T] to arrange something so that it happens at an exactly suitable time: *If you time your departure carefully, you should be able to miss the worst of the traffic.* ○ *She won the game with a brilliantly timed shot* (= one played at exactly the right moment).

timely /'taɪm.li/ *adj* happening at a suitable moment: *Your letter came as a timely reminder that we need to arrange a meeting.* ○ *The change in the exchange rate provided a timely boost to the company's falling profits.*
timeliness /'taɪm.lɪ.nəs/ *noun* [U]

timing /'taɪ.mɪŋ/ *noun* [U] **1** the time when something happens: *"Have we arrived too early?" "No, your timing is perfect – dinner is almost ready."* ○ *The bomb contained a timing device set to make it go off at rush hour.* **2** the ability to do something at exactly the right time: *To be a good tennis player, you have to have good timing.*

time OCCASION /taɪm/ *noun* [C] an occasion or period, or the experience connected with it: *The last time we went to Paris, it rained every day.* ○ *Every time/Each time I ask you to do something, you always say you're too busy.* ○ *They go swimming three or four times a week.* ○ *There are times when I wish I didn't live where I do.* ○ *The (UK) four-times/(US) four-time champion* (= the person who had been the winner on four occasions in the past) *was unexpectedly defeated in the second round of the competition.* ○ *If I'd known at the time* (= then) *that she was his former wife, I'd never have said what I did.* ○ *Sometimes I enjoy my English lessons, but at other times* (= on other occasions) *I find them really boring.* ○ *For the* **umpteenth/hundredth/thousandth** *time,* (= I've told you on many occasions to) *stop hitting your sister.* ○ *Did you* **have** *a* **bad/good** *time* (= an unenjoyable/enjoyable experience) *at the conference?* ○ *She had an* **easy/hard** *time of it* (= a comfortable/uncomfortable experience) *with the birth of her second baby.*

• **at times** sometimes: *You can be really annoying at times, you know.*

• **from time to time** sometimes but not often: *From time to time I still think of her.*

• **give** *sb* **a hard time** INFORMAL to make things difficult or unpleasant for someone: *Her kids always give her a hard time when she takes them shopping.* ○ *My mother gave me a really hard time* (= was angry with me) *about staying out late.*

• **time after time** again and again: *Time after time she gets herself involved in relationships with unsuitable men.*

• **time and (time) again** very often: *I've told you time and time again – make sure you look before you cross the road.*

• **the time of** *your* **life** an extremely enjoyable experience: *We had the time of our lives at Ali's party.*

• **the times** UK on many occasions: *The times I've told you, ask before you borrow my clothes.*

time HISTORICAL PERIOD /taɪm/ *noun* [C] (ALSO **times**) a period in history: *Charles Dickens' novel "A Tale of Two Cities" is set at the time* **of** *the French Revolution.* ○ *In/ During medieval times, women thought to be witches were burnt at the stake.* ○ *In times gone by, all crops were harvested by hand.* ○ *Times* **were hard** (= The conditions of life were uncomfortable) *when I was a boy.* ○ *He is widely regarded as one of the best writers of* **modern/ our** *times* (= the present or very recent past). ○ *I never thought it would happen* **in** *my time* (= before I died). ○ *We sat and talked about* **old** *times* (= things that had happened to us in the past.)

• **at one time** in the past: *At one time, George Eliot lived here.*

• **before** *your* **time** If something or someone is before your time, they happened or existed before you were born or were old enough to remember them: *I don't remember The Beatles – they were before my time.*

• **behind the times** If someone or something is behind the times, they are old-fashioned.

• **change with/keep up with/move with the times** to change your ideas, opinions or way of living or working to make them modern: *I don't really like working on a computer, but you have to move with the times, I suppose.*

• **time was** said to mean that there was a period in the past when something used to happen or be true: *Time was (when) you could buy a loaf of bread for sixpence.*

• **Times are changing.** SAYING said to emphasize that society is very different from the way it was in the past

time MUSIC /taɪm/ *noun* [U] the number of beats in a BAR of music, or the speed at which a piece of music is intended to be played: *This piece is written* **in** *4/4 time.* ○ *Small children often have difficulty singing* **in** *time* **with** *the music* (= at the same speed at which the music is being played). ○ *It seemed to me as if the violins were playing* **out** *of time* (= at a different speed from the other instruments playing the same piece of music). ○ *to* **beat** *time* (= to make a regular series of sounds or movements at the same speed as a piece of music is intended to be played). ○ *Watching the conductor will help you to* **keep** *time* (= to play the music at the speed at which it is intended to be played).

timing /'taɪ.mɪŋ/ *noun* [U] the ability to play all the notes in a piece of music at the correct speed: *My singing teacher says I must try and improve my timing.*

time and a 'half *noun* [U] the usual pay for a job with half the usual pay added on to it

time-and-motion study /ˌtaɪm.ən d'məʊ.ʃ°nˌstʌd.i/ US /-'moʊ-/ *noun* [C usually sing] a study of work methods, especially in industry or business, in order to find the most effective way of operating

'time ˌbomb BOMB *noun* [C usually sing] a bomb which contains a device that makes it explode at a particular point in the day

'time ˌbomb DIFFICULT SITUATION *noun* [C] a situation which is likely to become difficult to deal with or control: *By ignoring the wishes of their employees, the managers are* **setting/creating** *a time bomb for themselves.* ○ *The prison governors are* **sitting on** *a time bomb* (= are having to deal with a bad situation that is likely to become difficult to deal with or control).

'time ˌcapsule *noun* [C] a container which is filled with objects considered to be typical of the present period in history and then buried, so that it can be dug up and studied in a future period

'time ˌclock *noun* [C] a clock which employees use to record the particular point in the day at which they arrive at and leave work

time-consuming /ˈtaɪm.kənˌsjuː.mɪŋ/ ⓤ /-ˌsuː-/ *adj* describes a task that takes a lot of time to do: *Producing a dictionary is a very time-consuming job.*

ˌtimed ˈticket *noun* [C] a ticket which allows you to go into a place, such as a famous building which the public is able to visit, at a particular time

ˈtime ˌframe *noun* [C] a period of days, weeks, months, etc. within which an activity is intended to happen: *Have you set a time frame for completing the job?* ○ *The government plans to introduce these changes in/within a fairly long/short time frame.*

time-honoured /ˈtaɪmˌɒn.əd/ ⓤ /-ˌɑː.nɚd/ *adj* [before n] A time-honoured tradition, practice, or method is respected because it has been done or used in the same way for many years: HUMOROUS *The developers dealt with the problem in the time-honoured fashion/way, burying the industrial waste in landfill sites.*

timekeeper /ˈtaɪmˌkiː.pər/ ⓤ /-pɚ/ *noun* [C] **1** an object or person that records (an amount of) time: *There's no point in having a clock which looks attractive if it isn't a good timekeeper* (= if it doesn't record the time correctly). **2** a person who records the amount of time that people taking part in a race or competition take to finish the race or competition, or the amount of time that people at work spend working on their jobs **3** a **good/bad timekeeper** a person who usually arrives on time/late for something, especially work
timekeeping /ˈtaɪmˌkiː.pɪŋ/ *noun* [U] the ability to arrive at a place at the time expected

ˈtime ˌlag *noun* [C usually sing] a period between two related events: *There's a time lag of about a week between having the blood test and getting the results.*

time-lapse /ˈtaɪm.læps/ *adj* [before n] describes a method of filming very slow actions by taking a series of single pictures over a period of time and then putting them together to show the action happening very quickly: *time-lapse photography* ○ *a time-lapse camera/sequence*

ˈtime ˌlimit *noun* [C usually sing] the greatest length of time someone is allowed to spend doing something: *We've set a time limit of ten minutes for each child's turn on the trampoline.* ○ *There's a 30-minute time limit on Internet use in the library.*

ˈtime maˌchine *noun* [C usually sing] (especially in stories and films) a machine in which people can travel into the past or the future

time-out SPORT /ˌtaɪmˈaʊt/ *noun* [C usually sing] a short period during a game in some sports when the players stop playing in order to rest, plan what they are going to do next, etc: *The coach called a time-out to discuss strategy.*

time-out STOP ARGUING /ˌtaɪmˈaʊt/ *exclamation, noun US* used to tell people to stop what they are doing, especially when they are having a disagreement: *OK, time-out, everyone, let's all quiet down and talk about this calmly.*

timepiece /ˈtaɪm.piːs/ *noun* [C] OLD-FASHIONED OR FORMAL a clock or watch

timer /ˈtaɪ.mər/ ⓤ /-mɚ/ *noun* [C] **1** a device which records when a particular number of minutes, hours, etc. have gone past: *He set the timer on the oven to/for 20 minutes* (= to record when 20 minutes had gone past). **2** (UK ALSO **time switch**) a device on a machine which causes the machine to start or stop working at a particular point in the day

time-release /ˈtaɪm.rɪˌliːs/ *adj* (ALSO **timed-release**) (of a pill) releasing its contents gradually during the day

times HISTORY /taɪmz/ *plural noun* another word for **time**
HISTORICAL PERIOD

times MULTIPLIED /taɪmz/ *prep* multiplied by: *Two times two equals four (2 x 2 = 4).* ○ *The area of a rectangle is its height times its width.*

times AMOUNT /taɪmz/ *predeterminer, adv* (used to show the difference in amount of two things, by multiplying one of them by the stated number): *She earns five times as much as I do./She earns five times more than I do.* ○ *My foot swelled up to three times the normal size when it was stung by a wasp.*
● **ten/fifty/a hundred times better** INFORMAL much better: *This piece of work is ten times better than the last piece you did.*

timesaving /ˈtaɪmˌseɪ.vɪŋ/ *adj* reducing the amount of time needed for doing something: *Washing machines and vacuum cleaners are timesaving devices.*

timescale /ˈtaɪm.skeɪl/ *noun* [C] the period of time over which something happens: *Police officers are trying to construct the timescale of events leading up to the murder.* ○ *What's the timescale for this* (= How long will it take)?

timeserver /ˈtaɪmˌsɜː.vər/ ⓤ /-ˌsɜːː.vɚ/ *noun* [C] DIS-APPROVING **1** a person who does not work very hard at their job, and who is just waiting until they reach the age at which they can stop work **2** someone who changes their ideas and opinions in order to make them more like those that are held by people in power, especially because they believe it will be to their advantage
timeserving /ˈtaɪmˌsɜː.vɪŋ/ ⓤ /-ˌsɜːː-/ *noun* [U] *timeserving politicians*

timeshare /ˈtaɪm.ʃeər/ ⓤ /-ʃer/ *noun* **1** [C] a holiday house or apartment which is owned by several different people, each of whom is able to use it for a particular period of the year: *We've bought a timeshare in Spain.* ○ *timeshare holiday/property/developments* **2** [U] (ALSO **time-sharing**) the activity of owning and using a time-share

time-sharing /ˈtaɪmˌʃeə.rɪŋ/ ⓤ /-ˌʃer-/ *noun* [U] the use of a central computer by several other smaller computers connected to it

ˈtime ˌsheet *noun* [C] (US ALSO **time card**) a piece of paper on which an employee records the number of hours they have worked

ˈtime ˌsignal *noun* [C usually sing] a signal which is broadcast on the radio at an exact time, for example one o'clock, to show accurately what the time is

ˈtime ˌsignature *noun* [C] a symbol, usually in the form of two numbers, one above the other, written at the beginning of a piece of music to show how many beats there are in each BAR

ˈtime ˌswitch *noun* [C] UK a **timer**

timetable UK /ˈtaɪmˌteɪ.bl̩/ *noun* [C] (US **schedule**) **1** a list of the times when events are planned to happen, especially the times when buses, trains and planes leave and arrive: *Do you have a Birmingham to London train timetable that I could borrow?* ○ *The timetable for our trip to Paris includes visits to Notre Dame, the Eiffel Tower and the Louvre.* ○ *Here is the timetable of events for the day.* ○ *I've got a very busy timetable next week* (= I have a lot of activities planned). **2** a list of the times when classes in school happen: *The first lesson on the timetable for Monday morning is history.*
timetable UK /ˈtaɪmˌteɪ.bl̩/ *verb* [T usually passive] (US **schedule**) to plan when something is going to happen: [+ to infinitive] *We are timetabled to go to the British Museum on Thursday and the Tower of London on Friday.* ○ *The lecture is timetabled for 5.00 p.m.*

time-tested /ˈtaɪmˌtes.tɪd/ *adj* MAINLY US describes something, for example a method, that has been used for a long period and has been proved to work well: *The school uses old, time-tested techniques for teaching children to read.*

ˈtime ˌtravel *noun* [U] the theoretical process of travelling into the past or the future

ˈtime ˌwarp *noun* [C usually sing] a theoretical change in the measurement of time in which people and events from one part of history are imagined as existing in another part: FIGURATIVE *He's living in a time warp* (= He is old-fashioned).

timeworn /ˈtaɪm.wɔːn/ ⓤ /-wɔːrn/ *adj* (no longer of interest or value because of) having been used a lot over a long period of time: *a timeworn expression/excuse* ○ *a timeworn path*

ˈtime ˌzone *noun* [C] one of 24 equal parts into which the world is divided. In any place within each part, the particular point in the day is the same, and is an hour in front of or behind that in the parts on either side: *If you go from New York to London, you cross five time zones.*

timid /ˈtɪm.ɪd/ *adj* shy and nervous; lacking confidence; easily frightened: *Lucy is a rather timid child.* ○ *My horse is a bit timid and is easily frightened by traffic.*

timidly /ˈtɪm.ɪd.li/ *adv*: *"Um, excuse me," he said timidly.* **timidity** /tɪˈmɪd.ɪ.ti/ [US] /-ə.t̬i/ *noun* [U]

timing /ˈtaɪ.mɪŋ/ *noun* [U] ➲See at **time** SUITABLE POINT, **time** MUSIC.

timorous /ˈtɪm.ᵊr.əs/ [US] /-ɚ.əs/ *adj* LITERARY nervous and lacking confidence; TIMID **timorously** /ˈtɪm.ᵊr.ə.sli/ [US] /-ɚ-/ *adv* **timorousness** /ˈtɪm.ᵊr.ə.snəs/ [US] /ˈ-ɚ-/ *noun* [U]

timpani /ˈtɪm.pə.ni/ *plural noun* a set of KETTLEDRUMS (= large metal drums with round bottoms) played in an orchestra
timpanist /ˈtɪm.pə.nɪst/ *noun* [C] a person who plays the timpani

tin /tɪn/ *noun* **1** [U] a silvery-coloured metal, often combined with other metals or used to cover and protect other metals **2** [C] UK (UK ALSO AND US **can**) a closed cylindrical metal container in which food is sold: *a tin **of** beans* ○ *piles of soup tins* **3** [C] UK (US **cookie jar**) a metal container with a lid used for keeping cakes or biscuits: *a biscuit tin* **4** [C] UK (US **can**) a cylindrical metal container with a lid used for keeping liquid substances such as paint: *a tin **of** paint* **5** [C] UK (US **pan**) a metal container without a lid used for cooking food in the oven: *Put both cake tins in the oven for half an hour.* **6** [C] UK (US **can**) the contents of a tin, or the amount of something a tin contains: *The children ate two tins **of** beans.* ○ *We used four tins **of** paint when we painted the ceiling.*
tinned UK /tɪnd/ *adj* (US **canned**) Something, especially food, which is tinned is put in a tin in order to preserve it: *I don't like tinned tomatoes/spaghetti/milk.*
tinny /ˈtɪn.i/ *adj* **1** describes a sound which is of low quality or like metal being hit: *a tinny piano* ○ *a tinny recording* **2** INFORMAL DISAPPROVING If something made of metal is tinny, it is not strong and not of good quality: *a cheap tinny toy car*

tincture /ˈtɪŋk.tʃəʳ/ [US] /-tʃɚ/ *noun* [C or U] a medicine which consists of a mixture of alcohol and a small amount of a drug: *a/some tincture **of** iodine/myrrh*

tinder /ˈtɪn.dəʳ/ [US] /-dɚ/ *noun* [U] small pieces of something dry that burns easily and which can be used for lighting fires: *We used some dry grass and dead twigs as tinder to light the camp fire.* ○ *The grass is tinder-**dry*** (= so dry that it will burn easily), *so there's a risk of fire.*

tinderbox /ˈtɪn.də.bɒks/ [US] /-dɚ.bɑːks/ *noun* [C] a dangerous and uncontrolled situation in which violence is likely to happen: *The racial tension in the area makes it a tinderbox ready to ignite.*

ˌtin ˈfoil *noun* [U] shiny metallic material, as thin as paper, which is used especially for wrapping food in order to store it or cook it

ting /tɪŋ/ *adv, noun* [C] (with) a clear high ringing sound: *The bell on the hotel receptionist's desk **went** ting when I pressed it.*

ting-a-ling /ˌtɪŋ.əˈlɪŋ/ *exclamation* (MAINLY US **ding-a-ling**) said, especially by children, to represent the sound of a bell

tinge /tɪndʒ/ *noun* [C] a very slight amount of a colour or of a feeling: *His hair is starting to show tinges **of** grey.* ○ *I have a tinge **of** regret that I didn't accept her offer.*
tinge /tɪndʒd/ *verb* [T usually passive] to contain a slight amount of: *Her joy at the birth of her son was tinged **with** sadness that her father had not lived to see him.*
tinged /tɪndʒd/ *adj*: *Her dark hair is now tinged **with** grey.*

tingle /ˈtɪŋ.gl/ *verb* [I] **1** to have a feeling as if a lot of sharp points are being put quickly and lightly into your body: *My toes and fingers are tingling **with** the cold.* ○ *There's a line in that poem that makes my **spine** tingle every time I read it.* **2** When you tingle with an emotion, such as excitement or fear, you feel it very strongly: *She tingled **with** fear as she entered the dark alleyway.*
tingle /ˈtɪŋ.gl̩/ *noun* [C] *There's a slight tingle in my wrists.* ○ *She stroked his head, sending tingles down his spine.*
tingly /ˈtɪŋ.gl̩.i/ /-gli/ *adj* causing a feeling as if a lot of sharp points are being put quickly and lightly into your body: *My massage had left me with a pleasant tingly sensation.*

ˌtin ˈgod ALSO **little tin god** *noun* [C] LITERARY DISAPPROVING someone who behaves as if they are more important or powerful than they really are

ˌtin ˈhat *noun* [C] INFORMAL a protective metal hat worn by soldiers

tinker [MAKE CHANGES] /ˈtɪŋ.kəʳ/ [US] /-kɚ/ *verb* [I usually + adv or prep] to make small unimportant changes to something, especially in an attempt to repair or improve it: *He spends every weekend tinkering **(about) with** his car.* ○ *I wish the government would stop tinkering **with** the health service.* ➲Compare **fiddle** MOVE ABOUT.
tinker /ˈtɪŋ.kəʳ/ [US] /-kɚ/ *noun* **1** [S] UK when you make small changes to something: *I'll just have **a** tinker **with** the television and see if I can get it to work.* **2** [C] especially in the past, a person who travels from place to place, repairing pans or other metal containers
• **not give a tinker's cuss** UK (US **not give a tinker's damn**) OLD-FASHIONED INFORMAL to not be interested in or worried about something or someone: *I couldn't give a tinker's damn **about** what they think.*

tinker [CHILD] /ˈtɪŋ.kəʳ/ [US] /-kɚ/ *noun* [C] UK OLD-FASHIONED INFORMAL a child who behaves badly: [as form of address] *You tinker, Nicky, you shouldn't have done that.* ○ *Don't be such a tinker.*

tinkle [SOUND] /ˈtɪŋ.kl̩/ *noun* [C] a light ringing sound: *In the distance we heard the **silvery** tinkle of a stream.*
• **give *sb* a tinkle** OLD-FASHIONED INFORMAL to make a telephone call to someone: *I'll give you a tinkle some time next week.*
tinkle /ˈtɪŋ.kl̩/ *verb* [I] to make a light ringing sound: *Some small old-fashioned shops still have a bell which tinkles when you push the door open.*

tinkle [TOILET] /ˈtɪŋ.kl̩/ *noun* [C] INFORMAL OR CHILD'S WORD an act of URINATION **tinkle** /ˈtɪŋ.kl̩/ *verb* [I]

tinned /tɪnd/ *adj* ➲See at **tin**.

tinnitus /ˈtɪn.ɪ.təs/ [US] /-t̬əs/ *noun* [U] SPECIALIZED a condition of the ear in which the person suffering from it hears noises such as ringing

tinny /ˈtɪn.i/ *adj* ➲See at **tin**.

ˈtin ˌopener UK *noun* [C] (MAINLY US **can opener**) a device for opening closed cylindrical metal containers of food ➲See picture **In the Kitchen** on page Centre 16

ˌTin ˌPan ˈAlley *noun* [S] INFORMAL the people who write, perform and produce popular music, especially in the first half of the 20th century

tinplate /ˈtɪn.pleɪt/ *noun* [U] thin sheets of iron or steel covered with a thin layer of TIN **tinplated** /ˌtɪnˈpleɪ.tɪd/ [US] /-t̬ɪd/ *adj*

tinpot /ˈtɪn.pɒt/ [US] /-pɑːt/ *adj* [before n] INFORMAL DISAPPROVING unimportant, or having little value: *a tinpot dictator*

tinsel /ˈtɪnt.sᵊl/ *noun* [U] **1** long pieces of thin shiny material used as decoration, especially at Christmas: *a Christmas tree decorated with tinsel* **2** DISAPPROVING something, especially the entertainment business or someone's way of living, that seems exciting and attractive, but is really of low quality or value: *The show was all tinsel and glitter.* **tinselly** /ˈtɪnt.sᵊl.i/ *adj*

tint /tɪnt/ *noun* [C] **1** a small amount of a colour: *The paint we're using for the bathroom is white with a yellow tint.* ○ *The evening sky was deep pink, with tints **of** purple and red in it.* **2** a small amount of DYE, especially used on the hair, or the act of using such a substance: *She's had blonde tints put in her hair.* ○ *I'm going to the hairdresser's for a tint.*
tint /tɪnt/ *verb* [T] to slightly change the colour of something
tinted /ˈtɪn.tɪd/ [US] /-t̬ɪd/ *adj* [before n] (of glass) with colour added: *Tinted **glasses*** (= glasses with slightly darkened lenses) *are good for driving in bright sunlight.* ○ *The President arrived at the airport in a car with tinted **windows*** (= windows with darkened glass so that people cannot see into the car).

ˌtin ˈwhistle *noun* [C] a small musical instrument consisting of a thin metal tube which the player blows down. The tube has holes in it, which are covered or left open in order to play different notes.

tiny /ˈtaɪ.ni/ *adj* extremely small: *a tiny flower* ○ *a tiny helping of food* ○ *a tiny baby* ○ *a tiny **bit** late*

-tion /-ʃᵊn/ *suffix* ➲See at **-ion** ACTION.

tip [END] /tɪp/ *noun* [C] **1** the usually pointed end of something, especially something which is long and thin: *We had asparagus tips for dinner.* ○ *If I stand **on** the tips **of** my toes, I can just reach the top shelf.* ○ *The Keys are coral islands off the southern tip **of** Florida.* ○ *There's paint **on** the tip **of** your nose.* **2** a small part fitted to the end of something, especially something which is long and thin: *a walking cane with a metal tip* ○ *the filter tip of a cigarette*

• **be on the tip of *your* tongue** If something that you want to say is on the tip of your tongue, you think you know it and that you will be able to remember it very soon: *Her name is on the tip of my tongue.*

• **tip of the iceberg** a small noticeable part of a problem, the total size of which is really much greater: *These small local protests are just the tip of the iceberg.*

tip /tɪp/ *verb* [T usually passive] **-pp-** to cover the end of something pointed with a liquid, a colour, etc: *The giraffe was killed with a spear that had been tipped **with** poison.* **-tipped** /-tɪpt/ *suffix*: *steel-tipped boots*

tip [INFORMATION] /tɪp/ *noun* [C] a useful piece of information, especially about how to do something or about the likely winner of a race or competition: *gardening/cooking/sewing tips* ○ *She **gave** me a useful/helpful/valuable/practical tip **about/for** growing tomatoes.* ○ *Our racing correspondent has the following tips **for** the 3.15 and the 3.45 at Newmarket* (= thinks that particular horses will be the winners in those races). ○ *I've got a **hot** tip **for** you* (= I can tell you about a particular likely winner of a race or competition, or give you a valuable piece of information).

tip /tɪp/ *verb* [often passive] **-pp-** *MAINLY UK* to say that someone is likely to be successful or achieve something: *He is being tipped **as** the next Prime Minister.* ○ [+ *to* infinitive] *Davis is being tipped **to** win the championship.*

• **tip *sb* the wink** (*ALSO* **tip the wink to *sb***) *UK INFORMAL* to give someone a piece of secret or private information that might be of benefit to them: *Thanks for tipping me the wink **about** those cheap tickets, Bill.*

• **tip *your* hand** *US* If you tip your hand, you say what you are going to do or what you believe: *Despite weeks of media speculation, the president refused to tip his hand about his plans for re-election.*

tip [RUBBISH] *UK* /tɪp/ *noun* [C] (*MAINLY US* **dump**) a place where especially large pieces of rubbish can be taken and left: *a rubbish/waste tip* ○ *We need to take this old carpet to the tip.* ○ *UK INFORMAL This room is a complete/absolute/real tip* (= is very untidy) *– tidy it up at once.*

tip *UK* (**-pp-**) /tɪp/ *verb* [I or T; usually + adv or prep] (*US ALSO* **dump**) *A lot of waste is being tipped into the sea.* ○ *The sign by the side of the road said "No tipping".*

tip [POUR] /tɪp/ *verb* [T usually + adv or prep] **-pp-** *UK* to pour a substance from one container into another or onto a surface: *She tipped the contents of her purse out onto the table.* ○ *He tipped his breakfast cereal into a bowl.* ○ *The child picked up the box and tipped the toys **out** all over the floor.*

• **tipping (it) down** *UK INFORMAL* when a lot of rain is falling: *We won't be able to go to the beach today – **it's** tipping it down.*

tip [ONE SIDE HIGHER] /tɪp/ *verb* **-pp- 1** [I or T] to (cause to) move so that one side is higher than another side: *The table tipped and all our drinks fell on the floor.* ○ *If you put too many books on one end of the shelf, it'll tip **up**.* ○ *Don't tip your chair **back** like that, you'll fall.* **2** [I] If something tips over from something into something else, it stops being the first thing, and becomes the second: *At various points in the play, the action tips **over** from comedy **into** farce* (= stops being amusing and becomes ridiculous).

• **tip the scales** (*ALSO* **tip the balance**) If something tips the scales it is the thing which causes a particular situation to happen or a particular decision to be made, when other situations or decisions are possible: *The teams were evenly matched until two quick goals from Robson tipped the balance **in favour of** England.* ○ *She was a good candidate, but her lack of computer skills tipped the scales **against** her.*

• **tip the scales at** to weigh: *The baby tipped the scales at 3.75 kgs.*

tip [PAYMENT] /tɪp/ *noun* [C] a small amount of money given to someone who has provided you with a service, in addition to the official payment and for their personal use: *a 15% tip* ○ *He **gave** the porter a tip.* ○ *We don't need to **leave** a tip **for** the waiter, because there's a service charge included in the bill.* **tip** /tɪp/ *verb* [I or T] **-pp-** *The taxi driver was so rude to her that she didn't tip him.* ○ [+ two objects] *They tipped the waiter £5.*

PHRASAL VERBS WITH **tip**

▲ **tip *sb* off** *phrasal verb* [M] to warn someone secretly about something that will happen, so that they can take action or prevent it from happening: [+ *that*] *Somebody must have tipped the burglars off **that** the house would be empty.* ○ *The robber was caught when someone tipped off the police.*

tip-off /ˈtɪp.ɒf/ [US] /-ɑːf/ *noun* [C usually sing] *INFORMAL* a secret warning or piece of secret information: *Acting on a tip-off, the police arrested the drug dealers.* ○ *Following a tip-off from a friend, we sold all our shares in the company.*

▲ **tip *(sth/sb)* over** *phrasal verb* [M] to (cause to) fall over onto one side: *Be careful not to tip that cup of coffee over.*

ˈtipper ˌtruck/ˌlorry /ˈtɪp.ə-/ [US] /-ɚ-/ *noun* [C] *UK* a **dumper truck**

Tipp-Ex *UK TRADEMARK* /ˈtɪp.eks/ *noun* [U] (*US TRADEMARK* **Wite-Out**) a white liquid used for painting over mistakes in a piece of writing

tipple /ˈtɪp.l̩/ *noun* [C] *INFORMAL* an alcoholic drink: *What's your tipple* (= What alcoholic drink do you usually drink)*?*

tippler /ˈtɪp.l̩.əʳ/ /-ləʳ/ [US] /-l̩.ɚ/ /-lɚ/ *noun* [C] *INFORMAL* someone who often drinks alcohol

tipster /ˈtɪp.stəʳ/ [US] /-stɚ/ *noun* [C] a person who gives information to people, usually in exchange for money, especially about the likely winner of a race or competition, or who gives information to an official organization especially about someone who has done something wrong: *All the tipsters were wrong about the gold medal winner.* ○ *An anonymous tipster has leaked confidential government information to the press.*

tipsy /ˈtɪp.si/ *adj INFORMAL* slightly drunk: *Auntie Pat is getting a little tipsy again.* **tipsily** /ˈtɪp.sɪ.li/ *adv* **tipsiness** /ˈtɪp.sɪ.nəs/ *noun* [U]

tiptoe /ˈtɪp.təʊ/ [US] /-toʊ/ *noun* **on tiptoe(s)** on your toes with the heel of your foot lifted off the ground: *The children stood on tiptoe in order to pick the apples from the tree.* ○ *They walked across the room on tiptoe so as not to waken the baby.* **tiptoe** /ˈtɪp.təʊ/ [US] /-toʊ/ *verb* [I usually + adv or prep] *He waited until his daughter was asleep, then tiptoed quietly out of the room.*

▲ **tiptoe round/around *sth/sb*** *phrasal verb INFORMAL* to avoid dealing with a difficult subject, problem or person: *Guy keeps tiptoeing round the problem, instead of confronting it.*

tip-top /ˈtɪp.tɒp/ [US] /-tɑːp/ *adj INFORMAL* excellent; perfect: *I try and keep in tip-top **shape** by exercising every day.* ○ *Even though our house is in tip-top **condition**, we're having problems selling it.* ○ *The hotel we stayed in was absolutely tip-top.*

tirade /taɪˈreɪd/ /tɪ-/ [US] /ˈtaɪ.reɪd/ *noun* [C] a long angry speech expressing strong disapproval: *She launched into an **angry/furious** tirade **about** how she had been unfairly treated.* ○ *In a furious tirade **of** abuse, the opposition spokesperson demanded the minister's resignation.*

tire [LOSE ENERGY] /taɪəʳ/ [US] /taɪr/ *verb* [I or T] to begin to feel as if you have no energy and want to rest or go to sleep, or to make someone feel this way: *She's been leading throughout the race, but it now looks as if she's tiring.* ○ *Even doing the garden tires me these days.*

tired /taɪəd/ [US] /taɪrd/ *adj* **1** in need of rest or sleep: *I was so tired when I got home from work last night that I had a quick nap.* ○ *My legs are tired.* ○ *She spoke in a tired voice.* **2** *DISAPPROVING* describes people, ideas or subjects that are not interesting because they are very familiar: *It's always the same tired **old** faces at these meetings.*

• **tired and emotional** *UK HUMOROUS OR POLITE EXPRESSION FOR* **drunk** (= having had too much alcohol)

tiredly /ˈtaɪəd.li/ ⓤ /ˈtaɪrd-/ *adv* feeling or showing a need to rest or sleep

tiredness /ˈtaɪəd.nəs/ ⓤ /ˈtaɪrd-/ *noun* [U] a feeling of needing to rest or sleep: *He said that it was tiredness that led him to make the mistake.* ○ *I was overtaken by a sudden wave of tiredness.*

tireless /ˈtaɪə.ləs/ ⓤ /ˈtaɪr-/ *adj* working energetically and continuously: *Tony is a tireless worker.* ○ *The prisoner's family is conducting a tireless campaign for his release.* ○ *The police have been tireless **in** their search for the child's killer.* **tirelessly** /ˈtaɪə.lə.sli/ ⓤ /ˈtaɪr-/ *adv*: *Sylvia Pankhurst campaigned tirelessly for votes for women.*

tiring /ˈtaɪə.rɪŋ/ ⓤ /ˈtaɪ-/ *adj* making you feel tired: *I've had a very tiring day.* ○ *Looking after the kids is extremely tiring.*

PHRASAL VERBS WITH **tire** ▼

▲ **tire of** *sth/sb phrasal verb* **1** to become bored with someone or something, or to stop enjoying an activity: *This is the kind of toy that children will soon tire of.* ○ *He **never** tires of* (= He enjoys) *playing games on his computer.* **2** **be tired of** *sth/sb* to be bored with an activity or person: *I'm so tired of doing the same job, day after day.* ○ *Don't you **get** tired of quarrelling all the time?* ○ *I'm **sick and** tired of you telling me what to do all the time.*

▲ **tire of** *sth phrasal verb* to be annoyed by something

▲ **tire** *sb* **out** *phrasal verb* [T] to make someone very tired: *Let the kids run around in the garden and that'll soon tire them out.*

tired '**out** *adj* [after v] very much in need of rest or sleep: *We were all really tired out after our long journey.*

COMMON LEARNER ERROR

tired of or **tired from**?

If you are **tired of** something or **tired of doing** something, you are bored or annoyed by it.

I'm tired of hearing his awful jokes.

If you are **tired from** something, you want to rest because of it.

He was tired from the long journey.

~~He was tired of the the long journey.~~

---

tire WHEEL /taɪəʳ/ ⓤ /taɪɚ/ *noun* [C] US FOR **tyre** ⊃See picture **Car** on page Centre 12

tiresome /ˈtaɪə.səm/ ⓤ /ˈtaɪr-/ *adj* boring or annoying; causing a lack of patience: *I find it very tiresome doing the same job day after day.* ○ *He has the tiresome habit of finishing your sentences for you.* **tiresomely** /ˈtaɪə.səm.-li/ ⓤ /ˈtaɪr-/ *adv*: *a tiresomely repetitive speech* ○ *a tiresomely long wait*

tisane /tɪˈzæn/ *noun* [C or U] (ALSO **herbal tea**) (a) drink made by pouring boiling water onto particular types of dried or fresh flowers or leaves

tissue PAPER /ˈtɪʃ.uː/ /ˈtɪs.juː/ *noun* [C or U] soft paper which is used for cleaning, especially your nose, and is thrown away after use, or a small rectangular piece of this: *She handed me a tissue just as I sneezed.* ○ *I always keep a box of tissues in the car.* ○ *He used a piece of tissue to clean his sunglasses.* ⊃Compare **handkerchief**.

'**tissue** (,**paper**) *noun* [U] thin light paper used especially for wrapping delicate things: *The shop assistant wrapped the vase carefully in tissue paper.*

tissue CELLS /ˈtɪʃ.uː/ /ˈtɪs.juː/ *noun* [U] a group of connected cells in an animal or plant that are similar to each other, have the same purpose and form the stated part of the animal or plant: *human tissue* ○ *plant tissue* ○ *brain/lung/muscle/fat tissue* ○ *His face is covered with scar tissue where he was badly burned.*

tit BIRD /tɪt/ *noun* [C] a common small bird found in the northern half of the world

tit BREAST /tɪt/ *noun* [C] OFFENSIVE a woman's breast: *He says he likes women with big tits.*

● **get on** *sb's* **tits** UK OFFENSIVE to annoy someone: *Stop it, Joe, you're really getting on my tits.*

tit PERSON /tɪt/ *noun* [C] UK SLANG a stupid person. This word is considered offensive by some people: *Why did you do that, you stupid great tit?*

---

titan /ˈtaɪ.tᵊn/ *noun* [C] LITERARY a person who is very important, powerful, strong, big, clever, etc: *an intellectual titan* ○ *The final will be a **clash of the** titans.* ○ *The soft drink titans* (= big companies who produce these drinks) *are struggling for control of the market.*

titanic /taɪˈtæn.ɪk/ *adj* extremely powerful, strong, important or large: *titanic mountains* ○ *a titanic battle/performance/struggle*

titanium /tɪˈteɪ.ni.əm/ /taɪ-/ *noun* [U] a light strong white metallic element

titbit, US USUALLY **tidbit** /ˈtɪt.bɪt/ *noun* [C] a small piece of interesting information, or a small item of pleasant-tasting food: *Our guide gave us some interesting titbits **about** the history of the castle.* ○ *This magazine is full of juicy titbits* (= small pieces of interesting information, especially about other people's private lives). ○ *Grandma always has a few titbits for the children if they're visiting at lunchtime.*

titchy /ˈtɪtʃ.i/ *adj* UK CHILD'S WORD extremely small: *We've got a great big car, and you've only got a titchy little one.*

titch /tɪtʃ/ *noun* [C] UK a small person, especially a child: *I don't need to take any notice of a titch like you.* ○ [as form of address] *Come on, titch.*

,**tit for** '**tat** *noun* [U] DISAPPROVING actions done intentionally to punish other people because they have done something unpleasant to you: *I noticed she didn't send me a card – I think it was tit for tat because I forgot her birthday last year.* ○ *Recent months have seen a pattern of tit-for-tat killings between the two sides.*

titian /ˈtɪʃ.ᵊn/ *adj* LITERARY (of hair) reddish gold in colour

titillate /ˈtɪt.ɪ.leɪt/ *verb* [I or T] to excite intentionally but only a little, usually with sexual images or descriptions: *So many adverts nowadays are designed to titillate.* ○ HUMOROUS *Carter's biography is only spoiled by the fact that he refuses to titillate* (= interest) *his readers with any gossip.*

titillating /ˈtɪt.ɪ.leɪ.tɪŋ/ ⓤ /-t̬ɪŋ/ *adj*: *The photos, which include some mildly titillating semi-nude shots of the actress, will be on display for a week.* ○ HUMOROUS *It seems that people can't resist titillating* (= interesting and shocking) *headlines, especially if they concern the Royal family.* **titillation** /ˌtɪt.ɪˈleɪ.ʃᵊn/ *noun* [U]

titivate /ˈtɪt.ɪ.veɪt/ ⓤ /ˈtɪt̬.ə-/ *verb* [I or T] INFORMAL to improve the small details of someone's appearance by arranging their hair, putting on make-up, etc.

title NAME /ˈtaɪ.tl/ ⓤ /-t̬l/ *noun* [C] **1** the name of a film, book, painting, piece of music, etc: *The title **of** Evelyn Waugh's first novel was 'Decline and Fall'.* ○ *And this next record is the title **track** on the album 'The Red Shoes'* (= the piece of music and the record are both called 'The Red Shoes'). ⊃See also **subtitle**; **surtitle**. **2** SPECIALIZED a book: *Last year we published over a hundred new titles.*

titled /ˈtaɪ.tld/ ⓤ /-t̬ld/ *adj* [after v] with the title of: *Reed wrote a novel about de Sade titled 'When the Whip Comes Down'.*

title PERSON /ˈtaɪ.tl/ ⓤ /-t̬l/ *noun* [C] a word which is used before someone's name, stating their social rank, qualifications, position in an organization, sex, etc: *What's her title – is she Professor or just Doctor?* ○ *He will retain the honorary title **of** non-executive chairman.* ○ *What's your **job** title now – are you managing director?*

titled /ˈtaɪ.tld/ ⓤ /-t̬ld/ *adj* A person who is titled has a special word, such as SIR or LADY, before their own name, showing that they have a high social rank: *one of his titled friends*

title SPORTS PRIZE /ˈtaɪ.tl/ ⓤ /-t̬l/ *noun* [C] the position you get by beating all other competitors in a sports competition: *Hendry won the world snooker title after a tense 35-frame final.*

title LEGAL RIGHT /ˈtaɪ.tl/ ⓤ /-t̬l/ *noun* [U] SPECIALIZED the legal right to own a piece of land or a building: *If you wish to sell the property, you will first have to prove your title **to** it.*

'**title** ,**deed** *noun* [C usually pl] a document which states and proves a person's legal right to own a piece of land or a building

titleholder /ˈtaɪ.tl̩ˌhəʊl.dəʳ/ [US] /-tl̩ˌhoʊl.dɚ/ *noun* [C] a person who is in the position of having beaten all other competitors in a sports competition: *The field includes Portugal's Rosa Mota, the Olympic, world and European titleholder.*

ˈtitle ˌpage *noun* [C usually sing] a page at the front of a book on which you find the name of the book, the writer and the PUBLISHER (= the company that printed the book)

ˈtitle ˌrole *noun* [C usually sing] A title role in a play or film is the character referred to in its name, usually the main part: *She is currently to be seen at the National Theatre playing the title role in Pam Gems' play 'Queen Christina'.*

titles /ˈtaɪ.tl̩z/ [US] /-tl̩z/ *plural noun* (*ALSO* **credits**) the information given at the end or beginning of a film or television programme, stating the names of the people who acted in it or were involved in its production

titter /ˈtɪt.əʳ/ [US] /ˈtɪt.ɚ/ *verb* [I] to laugh nervously, often at something that you feel you should not be laughing at: *A couple of the younger teachers tittered at his smutty jokes.* **titter** /ˈtɪt.əʳ/ [US] /ˈtɪt.ɚ/ *noun* [C] *The love scene raised a few titters from a party of schoolboys.*

tittle-tattle /ˈtɪt.l̩ˌtæt.l̩/ [US] /ˈtɪt.l̩ˌtæt-/ *noun* [U] *OLD-FASHIONED INFORMAL* talk about other people's lives that is usually unkind, disapproving or not true; GOSSIP

titty /ˈtɪt.i/ [US] /ˈtɪt-/ *noun* [C] *INFORMAL* a **tit** BREAST

titular /ˈtɪt.jʊ.ləʳ/ [US] /ˈtɪtʃ.ə.lɚ/ *adj* [before n] having the title of a position but not the responsibilities, duties or power; in name only: *It is already agreed that Mr Alfonso Escamez will be the titular head of the new bank.*

tizzy /ˈtɪz.i/ *noun* [S] (*UK ALSO* **tizz**) *INFORMAL* a temporary state of anxiety and confusion: *She got herself **in a** real tizzy because she couldn't find her car keys and she thought they'd been stolen.*

T-junction *UK* /ˈtiːˌdʒʌŋk.ʃᵊn/ *noun* [C] (*US* **intersection**) a place where one road meets another without crossing it, forming the shape of a letter T

TNT /ˌtiː.enˈtiː/ *noun* [U] a powerful yellow explosive substance

to [INFINITIVE] *STRONG* /tuː/, *WEAK* /tʊ, tu, tə/ [US] /tə, tə, tu/ *prep* **1** used before a verb to show that it is in the infinitive **2** used after some verbs, especially when the action described in the infinitive will happen later: *She agreed to help.* ○ *I'll have to tell him.* ○ *Sadly she didn't live to see her grandchildren.* **3** used after many verbs of agreeing, needing and wanting: *I need to eat something first.* ○ *I'd love to live in New York.* ○ *That child ought to be in bed.* **4** used instead of repeating a verb clause: *"Are you going tonight?" "I'm certainly hoping to."* **5** used in phrases where there are reported orders and requests: *He told me to wait.* ○ *Did anyone ask Daniel to book the room?* **6** used after some adjectives: *It's not likely to happen.* ○ *Three months is **too** long to wait.* ○ *She's not strong **enough** to go walking up mountains.* **7** used after some nouns: *He has this enviable ability to ignore everything that's unpleasant in life.* ○ *This will be my second attempt to make flaky pastry.* **8** A clause containing *to* + *infinitive* can be used as a subject of a sentence: *To go overseas on your own is very brave.* ○ *My plan was to get it all arranged before I told anyone.* **9** used after question words: *I don't know what to do.* ○ *Can you tell me how to get there?* **10** used with an infinitive to express use or purpose: *I'm going there to see my sister.* ○ *This tool is used to make holes in leather.* ○ *To make this cake, you'll need 2 eggs, 175 g sugar and 175 g flour.* ○ *He works to get paid, not because he enjoys it.* **11** You can introduce a clause with a phrase containing *to* + *infinitive*: *To be honest* (= Speaking honestly), *Elaine, I prefer you in the grey shirt.* ○ *To be quite truthful with you, Betty, I never really liked the man.* **12** used with an infinitive after 'there is' or 'there are' and a noun: *There's an awful lot of work to be done.*

• **to be going on with** *UK* To be going on with means in order to continue with the present activity or situation: *Do we have enough paint to be going on with, or should I get some more while I'm out?*

to [FUTURE] *STRONG* /tuː/, *WEAK* /tʊ, tu, tə/ [US] /tə, tə, tu/ *prep* **1** used before an infinitive, usually with 'be', to form the future tense: *The government announced today that it is to cut funding for the arts for next year.* ➲See also **to-be**. **2** used in this pattern to say what someone should do or to give an order: *You're not to* (= You must not) *bite your nails like that.* **3** Newspapers often use to + *infinitive* without 'be' in their HEADLINES (= titles of articles) when reporting planned future events: *France to send troops in.*

to [SHOWING DIRECTION] *STRONG* /tuː/, *WEAK* /tʊ, tu, tə/ [US] /tə, tə, tu/ *prep* in the direction of: *We're going to town on the bus, okay?* ○ *We went to Prague last year.* ○ *I asked someone the way to the town centre.* ○ *You can walk **from** here to the station in under ten minutes.* ○ *I've asked Helen and Ben to dinner* (= invited them to come and eat dinner with me) *next week.* ○ *We received another invitation to a wedding this morning.* ○ *I had my back to them, so I couldn't see what they were doing.* ○ *She walked **over** to the window.* ○ *He went **up** to a complete stranger and started talking.* ○ *You've got your sweater on **back** to **front*** (= with the back of the sweater on the chest).

to [AGAINST] *STRONG* /tuː/, *WEAK* /tʊ, tu, tə/ [US] /tə, tə, tu/ *prep* against or very near: *Stand back to back.* ○ *They were dancing cheek to cheek.*

to [RECEIVING] *STRONG* /tuː/, *WEAK* /tʊ, tu, tə/ [US] /tə, tə, tu/ *prep* **1** used for showing who receives something or who experiences an action: *I lent my bike to my brother.* ○ *I told that to Glyn and he was horrified.* ○ *Who's the letter addressed to?* **2** With many verbs that have two objects, 'to' can be used before the INDIRECT OBJECT: *Give me that gun./Give that gun to me.*

to [IN CONNECTION WITH] *STRONG* /tuː/, *WEAK* /tʊ, tu, tə/ [US] /tə, tə, tu/ *prep* in connection with: *What was their response to your query?* ○ *She was so rude to me.* ○ *There's a funny side to everything.*

to [COMPARED WITH] *STRONG* /tuː/, *WEAK* /tʊ, tu, tə/ [US] /tə, tə, tu/ *prep* **1** compared with: *She's earning a reasonable wage, but **nothing** to what she could if she was in the private sector.* ○ *Paul beat me by three games to two* (= He won three and I won two). ○ *He was old enough to be her father – she looked about thirty to his sixty.* **2** used to show the position of something or someone in comparison with something or someone else: *John's standing to the left of Adrian in the photo.* ○ *The Yorkshire Dales are twenty miles to the north of the city.*

to [UNTIL] *STRONG* /tuː/, *WEAK* /tʊ, tu, tə/ [US] /tə, tə, tu/ *prep* **1** until a particular time, state or level is reached: *It's only two weeks to Christmas.* ○ *Unemployment has risen to almost eight million.* ○ *He drank himself to death.* ○ *She nursed me back to health.* **2** used when saying the time, to mean before the stated hour: *It's twenty to six.* **3** used to suggest an extreme state: *Look at your shirt – it's torn to shreds!* ○ *She was thrilled to bits.* ○ *I was bored to tears.*

to [CAUSING] *STRONG* /tuː/, *WEAK* /tʊ, tu, tə/ [US] /tə, tə, tu/ *prep* causing a particular feeling in a particular person: *That's when I learned, to my horror, that she was coming here.*

to [CONSIDERED BY] *STRONG* /tuː/, *WEAK* /tʊ, tu, tə/ [US] /tə, tə, tu/ *prep* considered by: *I realize it may sound strange to you.* ○ *I mean, fifty pounds is nothing to him* (= he would not consider it a large amount). ○ *INFORMAL "I hear you've been going out with Sally." "Well, **what's it** to you?* (= It should not interest you, and you have no right to ask about it).*"*

to [SERVING] *STRONG* /tuː/, *WEAK* /tʊ, tu, tə/ [US] /tə, tə, tu/ *prep* serving: *As a personal trainer to the rich and famous, he earns over a million dollars a year.*

to [MATCHING] *STRONG* /tuː/, *WEAK* /tʊ, tu, tə/ [US] /tə, tə, tu/ *prep* **1** matching or belonging to: *He's given me the keys to his car – the fool!* ○ *I've lost the trousers to this jacket.* **2** having as a characteristic feature: *She has a mean side to her.* ○ *There is a very moral tone to this book.*

to [IN HONOUR OF] *STRONG* /tuː/, *WEAK* /tʊ, tu, tə/ [US] /tə, tə, tu/ *prep* in honour or memory of: *I proposed a toast to the bride and the groom.* ○ *The record is dedicated to her mother, who died recently.*

to [FOR EACH] *STRONG* /tuː/, *WEAK* /tʊ, tu, tə/ [US] /tə, tə, tu/ *prep* for each; PER: *How many francs are there to the pound?* ○ *This car does about fifty miles to the gallon.* ○ *If we go swimming together I do six lengths to her twelve.*

T

to AT THE SAME TIME AS *STRONG* /tuː/, *WEAK* /tʊ, tu, tə/ US /tə, tə, tu/ *prep* at the same time as music or other sound: *I like exercising to music.* ○ *He left the stage to the sound of booing.*

to BETWEEN *STRONG* /tuː/, *WEAK* /tʊ, tu, tə/ US /tə, tə, tu/ *prep* used in phrases which show a range: *There must have been thirty to thirty-five* (= a number between 30 and 35) *people there.*

to POSITIVE *STRONG* /tuː/, *WEAK* /tʊ, tu, tə/ US /tə, tə, tu/ *prep* relating to a positive reaction or result: *Is the room to your **liking**, madam?* ○ *I think being present at the meeting would be to your **advantage**.*

to CLOSED /tuː/ *adv* into a closed position: *I'll just push the door to.*

toad /təʊd/ US /toʊd/ *noun* [C] **1** a small brownish green animal, similar to a frog, which has big eyes and long back legs for swimming and jumping: *Toads have dryer, lumpier skins than frogs and spend less time in the water.* **2** *INFORMAL* an extremely unpleasant man, especially one who is physically very unattractive: [as form of address] *You lying toad!*

toad-in-the-hole /ˌtəʊd.ɪn.ðəˈhəʊl/ US /ˌtoʊd.ɪn.ðəˈhoʊl/ *noun* [U] *UK* a savoury food, consisting of sausages cooked in a mixture of eggs, milk and flour

toadstool /ˈtəʊd.stuːl/ US /ˈtoʊd-/ *noun* [C] a poisonous fungus with a round top and a narrow stem ⊃Compare **mushroom**.

toady /ˈtəʊ.di/ US /ˈtoʊ-/ *noun* [C] *DISAPPROVING* a person who praises and is artificially pleasant to people in authority, usually in order to get some advantage from them **toady** /ˈtəʊ.di/ US /ˈtoʊ-/ *verb* [I] *She was always toadying **to** the boss, but she didn't get a promotion out of it!*

to and fro *adv, adj* [before n] in one direction and then in the opposite direction, a repeated number of times: *I was disturbed by all the people walking to and fro outside the office.* ○ *She was gazing out the window, rocking rhythmically to and fro.*

to-ing and fro-ing /ˌtuː.ɪŋ.əndˈfrəʊ.ɪŋ/ US /-ˈfroʊ-/ *noun* [U] **1** repeated movement from one place to another: *Inevitably, when both parents have custody of the child, there's a lot of to-ing and fro-ing between them for the child concerned.* **2** (*ALSO* **to-ings and fro-ings**) varied and frequent discussions and activities: *The legal to-ings and fro-ings could delay the start of the trial for up to six months.*

toast BREAD /təʊst/ US /toʊst/ *noun* [U] sliced bread made warm, crisp and brown by being put near a high heat: *a **slice of** toast* ○ *I have toast **and** marmalade for breakfast.* ○ *I'm having beans **on** toast for supper.*

toast /təʊst/ US /toʊst/ *verb* [T] **1** to make bread or other food warm, crisp and brown by putting it near a high heat: *Do you want this bread toasted?* ○ *Can I have a toasted **sandwich**, please?* **2** *INFORMAL* to warm yourself or part of your body: *He's just toasting his feet by the fire.*

toaster /ˈtəʊ.stər/ US /ˈtoʊ.stɚ/ *noun* [C] an electric device for making toast ⊃See picture **In the Kitchen** on page Centre 16

toasty, toastie /ˈtəʊ.sti/ US /ˈtoʊ-/ *noun* [C] *UK* a sandwich that has been toasted: *a cheese/ham/tuna toasty*

toast DRINK /təʊst/ US /toʊst/ *noun* [C] an expression of good wishes or respect for someone which involves holding up and then drinking from a glass of alcohol, especially wine, after a short speech: *Now, if you'd all please raise your glasses, I'd like to **propose** a toast to the bride and groom.* ○ *Champagne corks popped as the guests **drank** a toast **to** the happy couple.*

● **the toast of** *OLD-FASHIONED* The toast of a particular place is a person who is very much admired there for something they have recently done: *Not so long ago Viviana was a little-known actress playing in a provincial theatre – these days she's the toast of New York/**the town**.*

toast /təʊst/ US /toʊst/ *verb* [T] to hold up your glass and then drink as an expression of good wishes or respect: *We toasted the happy couple.*

toasting fork *noun* [C] a fork with a long handle used for holding slices of bread near a fire to make toast

toast rack *noun* [C] a device for serving pieces of toast which supports them vertically

toasty /ˈtəʊ.sti/ US /ˈtoʊ-/ *adj* comfortably and pleasantly warm: *My feet feel so warm and toasty in the new slippers.*

tobacco /təˈbæk.əʊ/ US /-oʊ/ *noun* [U] a substance which is smoked in cigarettes, pipes, etc., which is prepared from the dried leaves of a particular plant: *Twenty-eight per cent of people asked thought that the advertising of tobacco* (= tobacco and products made from it, such as cigarettes) *and alcohol should be banned.*

tobacconist /təˈbæk.ən.ɪst/ *noun* [C] a person who is in charge of a shop where tobacco, cigarettes, etc. are sold

to-be /-tə.biː/ *suffix* in the near future: *a bride-to-be* ○ *mothers-to-be*

toboggan /təˈbɒg.ən/ US /-ˈbɑː.gən/ *noun* [C] an object used for sliding over snow and ice which consists of a low frame on which a person or people sit **toboggan** /təˈbɒg.ən/ US /-ˈbɑː.gən/ *verb* [I] *We could **go** tobogganing on Primrose Hill.*

tocopherol /tɒˈkɒ.fə.rɒl/ US /-ˈkɑː.fɚ.ɑːl/ *noun* [U] *SPECIALIZED* **vitamin E**

tod /tɒd/ US /tɑːd/ *noun* *UK OLD-FASHIONED INFORMAL* **on your tod** alone: *Are you on your tod tonight – where's your missus?*

today /təˈdeɪ/ *adv, noun* **1** (on) the present day: *What's the date today?* ○ *He's going to ring you at some point today.* ○ *Today is even hotter than yesterday!* ○ *Is that today's paper?* ○ *He left today, which is a Tuesday, so he should be back today **week**/a **week** today* (= on the Tuesday of next week). **2** used more generally to mean the present time: *Today, people are much more concerned about their health than they were in the past.* ○ *With today's technology almost anything seems possible.* ○ *The youth **of** today don't know how lucky they are.*

toddle /ˈtɒd.l̩/ US /ˈtɑː.dl̩/ *verb* [I] **1** (especially of a young child) to walk with short steps, trying to keep the body balanced: *I watched my 2-year-old nephew toddling around after his puppy.* **2** *INFORMAL* to walk, especially in sentences which state the place that you are going to: *I'm just toddling **off/round** to the shops.*

toddler /ˈtɒd.lər/ US /ˈtɑː.dlɚ/ *noun* [C] a young child, especially one who is learning or has recently learned to walk

to-do /təˈduː/ *noun* [S] *INFORMAL* difficulty or trouble, usually which is more than the situation deserves: *What a to-do that was, getting my passport renewed at the consulate!*

toe BODY PART /təʊ/ US /toʊ/ *noun* [C] **1** any of the five separate parts at the end of the foot: *your big toe* (= your largest toe) ○ *your little toe* (= your smallest toe) ○ *I **stubbed*** (= knocked) *my toe on the edge of a bed.* ⊃See picture **The Body** on page Centre 5 **2** the part of a sock, shoe or other foot covering that goes over the toes

● **on your toes** Someone or something that keeps you on your toes forces you to continue directing all your attention and energy to what you are doing: *I work with people who are half my age so that **keeps** me on my toes.*

● **tread/step on sb's toes** If you tread/step on someone's toes you say or do something that upsets or annoys them, especially by involving yourself in matters that are their responsibility.

-toed /-təʊd/ US /-toʊd/ *suffix*: *open-toed sandals* ○ *the two-toed* (= having two toes) *sloth*

toe OBEY /təʊ/ US /toʊ/ *verb* **toe the line** to do what you are ordered or expected to do: *Ministers who wouldn't toe the **party** line were swiftly got rid of.*

toe cap *noun* [C] a hard protective covering for the toe end of a shoe or boot: *metal toe caps*

toe-curling /ˈtəʊ.kɜː.lɪŋ/ US /ˈtoʊ.kɚ-/ *adj* (*ALSO* **toes curl**) *UK INFORMAL* making you feel extremely embarrassed and ashamed for someone else: *I saw the worst comedy act I've ever seen last night – it was absolutely toe-curling!*

TOEFL /ˈtəʊ.fl̩/ US /ˈtoʊ-/ *noun* [U] *TRADEMARK ABBREVIATION FOR* test of English as a foreign language: an exam of English for speakers of other languages

toehold /ˈtəʊ.həʊld/ US /ˈtoʊ.hoʊld/ *noun* [C] **1** a small hole or surface on a rock which is just big enough for a climber to put the end of his or her foot in or on: *I searched desperately for a toehold in the rock face.* **2** a strong first position from which further advances can be made: *Insurance is a very difficult market to* ***get*** *a toe-hold* ***in****.*

toenail /ˈtəʊ.neɪl/ [US] /ˈtoʊ-/ *noun* **[C]** the hard slightly curved part that covers and protects the end of a toe: *She was cutting/painting her toenails.*

toerag /ˈtəʊ.ræg/ [US] /ˈtoʊ-/ *noun* **[C]** *UK INFORMAL* an extremely unpleasant person

toff /tɒf/ [US] /tɑːf/ *noun* **[C]** *UK OLD-FASHIONED* a rich person from a high social class: *Gone are the days when champagne-drinking was just for toffs.*

toffee /ˈtɒf.i/ [US] /ˈtɑː.fi/ *noun* **[C or U]** a hard, chewy, often brown sweet that is made from sugar boiled with butter

• **for toffee** *UK INFORMAL* If you say that someone cannot do something for toffee you mean that they are extremely bad at it: *He can't paint for toffee!*

ˈ**toffee ˌapple** *noun* **[C]** an apple covered with a sticky layer of toffee and held on a stick

toffee-nosed /ˈtɒf.i.nəʊzd/ [US] /ˈtɑː.fi.noʊzd/ *adj UK INFORMAL DISAPPROVING* People who are toffee-nosed consider themselves to be better than other people, especially than people of a lower social class: *He's a toffee-nosed git – take no notice of him!*

tofu /ˈtəʊ.fuː/ [US] /ˈtoʊ-/ *noun* **[U]** (*ALSO* **bean curd**) a soft pale food which has very little flavour but is high in protein, and which is made from the seed of the Asian SOYA bean plant

tog [UNIT] /tɒg/ [US] /tɑːg/ *noun* **[C]** *UK* a unit of measurement showing the degree of warmth of a bed cover, especially a duvet

tog [DRESS] /tɒg/ [US] /tɒːg/ *verb* **be/get (*yourself*) togged up/out** *INFORMAL* to dress yourself in clothes that are specially for a particular occasion or activity: *We got (ourselves) togged up in walking gear for the hike.* ○ *They were* ***all*** *togged out* ***in*** *dinner jackets and ball gowns.*

toga /ˈtəʊ.gə/ [US] /ˈtoʊ-/ *noun* **[C]** a piece of clothing worn by people in ancient Rome, consisting of a long piece of cloth wrapped around the body and hanging loosely from the shoulders

together [WITH EACH OTHER] /təˈgeð.əʳ/ [US] /-ɚ/ *adv* **1** with each other: *We used to go to aerobics together.* ○ *We worked together on a project a couple of years back.* ○ *Could you add these figures together for me?* ○ *You mix all the dry ingredients together before you add the milk.* ○ *I like both flavours separately but I don't like them together.* ○ *You could stick that back together* (= join the separate parts to each other) *with a bit of glue.* ○ *She said, "Never trust a man whose eyes are so* ***close*** *together!"* ○ *The waiter asked if we were* ***all*** *together so I explained that we were two separate parties.* ○ *We should* ***get*** *together* (= meet each other socially) *some time and have a drink.* ➲See also **altogether**. **2** If two people are described as together, they have a close romantic and often sexual relationship with each other: *Mira and Ellis have been together now for almost five years.*

• **get (it) together** *INFORMAL* If two people get (it) together they start a sexual relationship with each other: *We'd seen each other once or twice in a group, but we didn't really get it together till Rachel's party.* ➲See also **get it together** at **together** ORGANIZED.

togetherness /təˈgeð.ə.nəs/ [US] /-ɚ-/ *noun* **[U]** the pleasant feeling of being united with other people in friendship and understanding: *War had given to the community a greater sense of togetherness.*

together [AT THE SAME TIME] /təˈgeð.əʳ/ [US] /-ɚ/ *adv* at the same time: *Everyone seemed to arrive together.* ○ *We can deal with the next two items on the list together.*

together [COMBINED] /təˈgeð.əʳ/ [US] /-ɚ/ *adv* combined: *Together they must earn over eighty thousand dollars a year.* ○ *She's got more sense than the rest of you* ***put*** *together.*

together [IN ONE PLACE] /təˈgeð.əʳ/ [US] /-ɚ/ *adv* in one place: *I'll just gather my things together and then we can go.*

together [AND ALSO] /təˈgeð.əʳ/ [US] /-ɚ/ *adv* **together with** in addition to; and also: *The money that I owe you for the telephone together with the rent equals £300.* ○ *That bottle of champagne together with those chocolates will make a nice present.*

together [ORGANIZED] /təˈgeð.əʳ/ [US] /-ɚ/ *adj INFORMAL APPROVING* organized, confident of your abilities and able to use them to achieve what you want: *He's strikes me as a fairly together sort of a guy.*

• **get it together** to get something organized: *We were going to do something more ambitious over Christmas this year but we never got it together.* ➲See also **get (it) together** at **together** WITH EACH OTHER.

toggle [COMPUTER SWITCH] /ˈtɒg.l̩/ [US] /ˈtɑː.gl̩/ *noun* **[C]** a key or button on a computer which is pressed to turn a feature on and then off: *Select the function you require by pointing to the toggle* (= image of a button on the screen) *with the mouse and then clicking.*

toggle /ˈtɒg.l̩/ [US] /ˈtɑː.gl̩/ *verb* **[I or T]** to switch a feature on a computer on and off by pressing the same button or key: *Use this key to toggle* ***between*** *the two typefaces.* ○ *By toggling this key, you can switch the italics on and off.*

toggle [FASTENER] /ˈtɒg.l̩/ [US] /ˈtɑː.gl̩/ *noun* **[C]** a small bar of wood or plastic which acts as a fastener by being put through a hole or LOOP

togs /tɒgz/ [US] /tɑːgz/ *plural noun* **1** *INFORMAL* clothes: *Get your togs on, love, then we can go.* **2** *AUS INFORMAL FOR* **swimming costume** or **swimming trunks**

toil /tɔɪl/ *noun* **[U]** hard work, especially that which is physically tiring: *Lindi has achieved her comfortable life only after years of* ***hard*** *toil.* ○ *HUMOROUS Well, after a day's toil in the office I like to relax a little.*

toil /tɔɪl/ *verb* **[I]** **1** to work hard: *England's cricketers have been toiling in the 100-degree heat over the past week.* ○ *I was relaxing in the bath, having toiled* ***away*** *in the garden all afternoon.* **2** to move in a particular direction, slowly and with great effort: *I was toiling up the hill with four heavy bags when he took pity on me.*

toilet [CONTAINER] /ˈtɔɪ.lət/ *noun* **[C]** **1** a bowl-shaped device with a seat which you sit on or stand near when emptying the body of urine or excrement, or another device used for this purpose: *I was* ***on*** (= using) *the toilet when the phone rang.* ○ *Don't forget to* ***flush*** *the toilet.* ○ *Excuse me, Miss Lewis, I* ***need/want*** *(to go to) the toilet.* ○ *The toilet* ***seat*** *was cracked and there was no paper.* **2** *UK* (*US* **bathroom**) a room with a toilet in it: *Someone's in the toilet.*

• **go to the toilet** To go to the toilet is to empty the body of urine or excrement, usually using a toilet to do so: *It's going to be a long journey, kids, so if you want to go to the toilet do so now.*

toilets *UK* /ˈtɔɪ.ləts/ *plural noun* (*US* **restroom,** *US ALSO* **ladies'/men's room**) a room or small building in a public place in which there are several toilets: *Do you know where the ladies' toilets are?*

USAGE

toilet

Toilet is the most general word. In British English the informal word **loo** is often used. In American English **bathroom** is often used to mean toilet, especially in the home.

In public places toilets are usually called **the ladies** or **the gents** in British English and the **men's room, ladies' room,** or **restroom** in American English.

The **lavatory** is a slightly formal word for toilet, and **WC** is only used in British English. **WC** is usually only used in advertisments describing houses, hotels, etc.

---

toilet [WASHING] /ˈtɔɪ.lət/ *noun* **[U]** *OLD-FASHIONED FORMAL* the process of washing and dressing yourself: *Virginia had spent longer than usual* ***over*** *her toilet that evening, with pleasing results.*

toiletries /ˈtɔɪ.lə.triz/ *plural noun* items and substances that you use in washing yourself and preventing the body from smelling unpleasant: *Women's toiletries are at the other end of the shop, madam.*

ˈ**toilet ˌbag** *noun* **[C]** a bag in which you put things for keeping yourself clean and tidy, especially when you are travelling

T

'toilet ˌbrush *noun* [C] a brush with a long handle that is used to clean the inside of a toilet

'toilet ˌpaper *noun* [U] soft, absorbent paper, usually in a long roll, used to clean your bottom when you have emptied your body of excrement

'toilet ˌroll *noun* [C] UK a long, narrow length of toilet paper, rolled around a cardboard cylinder

'toilet ˌsoap *noun* [C or U] sweet-smelling soap that is intended for washing the body

'toilet ˌtissue *noun* [U] **toilet paper**

toilet-trained /'tɔɪ.lət.treɪnd/ *adj* **potty-trained**

'toilet ˌwater *noun* [C or U] a weak perfume

token [SYMBOL] /'təʊ.kən/ [US] /'toʊ-/ *noun* [C] a thing that you give or an action that you take which expresses your feelings or intentions, although it might have little practical effect: ***As a token of** our gratitude for all that you have done, we would like to accept this small gift.* ○ *It doesn't have to be a big present – it's just a token really.*

token /'təʊ.kən/ [US] /'toʊ-/ *adj* [before n] **1** used to describe actions which although small or limited in their practical effect, have a symbolic importance: *The troops in front of us either surrendered or offered only token* (= not much) *resistance.* ○ *They were the only country to argue for even token recognition of the Baltic states' independence.* **2** DISAPPROVING describes something which is done to prevent other people complaining, although it is not sincerely meant and has no real effect: *The truth is that they appoint no more than a token number of women to managerial jobs.*

tokenism /'təʊ.kən.ɪ.zəm/ [US] /'toʊ-/ *noun* [U] DISAPPROVING actions which are the result of pretending to give advantage to those groups in society who are often treated unfairly, in order to give the appearance of fairness

token [PAPER WORTH MONEY] UK /'təʊ.kən/ [US] /'toʊ-/ *noun* [C] (US **gift certificate**) a piece of paper with a particular amount of money printed on it which can be exchanged in a shop for goods of that value: *a £20 **book/gift/record** token*

token [DISC] /'təʊ.kən/ [US] /'toʊ-/ *noun* [C] a round metal or plastic disc which is used instead of money in some machines

told /təʊld/ [US] /toʊld/ *past simple and past participle of* **tell**

• **all told** as a complete total: *There were 550 people at the festival all told.*

tolerable /'tɒl.ər.ə.bl/ [US] /'tɑː.lɚ-/ *adj* of a quality that is acceptable, although certainly not good: *At their best the conditions in these prisons are scarcely tolerable.* ○ *For me it's friendships that make life tolerable.*

tolerably /'tɒl.ər.ə.bli/ [US] /'tɑː.lɚ-/ *adv* FORMAL to a limited degree or quite: *I play the piano tolerably **well**, though I have no particular talent for it.* ○ *The play is tolerably amusing, but it is let down by the actors' weak performances.*

tolerance [ACCEPTANCE] /'tɒl.ər.ənts/ [US] /'tɑː.lɚ-/ *noun* [U] (FORMAL **toleration**) willingness to accept behaviour and beliefs which are different from your own, although you might not agree with or approve of them: *This period in history is not noted for its **religious** tolerance.* ○ *Some members of the party would like to see it develop a greater tolerance **of/towards** contrary points of view.* **tolerant** /'tɒl.ər.ənt/ [US] /'tɑː.lɚ-/ *adj*: *The present government is even less tolerant **of** dissent.* ○ *On the continent people are more tolerant **of** children in public places.* **tolerantly** /'tɒl.ər.ənt.li/ [US] /'tɑː.lɚ-/ *adv*: *I would tell my grandmother about all the crazy things I'd been doing and she would just smile tolerantly.*

tolerate /'tɒl.ər.eɪt/ [US] /'tɑː.lə.reɪt/ *verb* [T] to accept behaviour and beliefs which are different from your own, although you might not agree with or approve of them: *I will not tolerate that sort of behaviour in my class.* ○ [+ v-ing] *I won't tolerate ly**ing**.*

tolerance [ABILITY TO BEAR] /'tɒl.ər.ənts/ [US] /'tɑː.lɚ-/ *noun* [U] **1** the ability to bear something unpleasant or annoying, or to continue existing despite disadvantageous conditions: *My tolerance **of** heat is considerably greater after having lived in the Far East for a couple of years.* **2** SPECIALIZED an animal's or plant's ability not to be harmed by a drug or poison over a long period of time: *a greater tolerance **of/to** the drug* **tolerant** /'tɒl.ər.ənt/ [US] /'tɑː.lɚ-/ *adj*: *I think men are less tolerant **of** stress than women.* ○ SPECIALIZED *Compared to other plants, rye is more tolerant **of** drought.*

tolerate /'tɒl.ər.eɪt/ [US] /'tɑː.lə.reɪt/ *verb* [T] to bear something unpleasant or annoying, or to continue existing despite disadvantageous conditions: *It seems these ants can tolerate temperatures which would kill other species.*

tolerance [VARIATION] /'tɒl.ər.ənts/ [US] /'tɑː.lɚ-/ *noun* [U] SPECIALIZED the amount by which a measurement or calculation might vary and still be acceptable

toll [CHARGE] /təʊl/ [US] /toʊl/ *noun* [C] **1** a small amount of money that you have to pay to use a road, cross a bridge, etc: *He's just got a job collecting tolls at the start of the motorway.* **2** US the money a long-distance telephone call costs: *Is Bayonne a toll **call*** (= a more expensive telephone call) *from New York?*

toll [SUFFERING] /təʊl/ [US] /toʊl/ *noun* [U] suffering, deaths or damage: *Independent sources say that the **death** toll from the earthquake runs into thousands.*

• **take its/their/a toll** If something takes its/their/a toll, it causes suffering, deaths or damage: *The problems of the past few months have taken their toll **on** her health and there are shadows beneath her eyes.* ○ *The deepening recession has also taken its toll in the south of the country, where unemployment is rife.*

toll [RING] /təʊl/ [US] /toʊl/ *verb* [I or T] to (cause a large bell to) ring slowly and repeatedly: *In the distance, a church bell tolled the hour* (= announced the time by ringing).

toll-free /ˌtəʊl'friː/ [US] /ˌtoʊl-/ *adj* US A toll-free telephone call is free for the person making the call.

tollgate /'təʊl.geɪt/ [US] /'toʊl-/ *noun* [C] (US USUALLY **tollbooth**) a gate at the start of a road or bridge at which you pay an amount of money in order to be allowed to use the road or bridge

tollhouse /'təʊl.haʊs/ [US] /'toʊl-/ *noun* [C] especially in the past, a small house at a TOLLGATE, in which the person who collects the money lives

tomahawk /'tɒm.ə.hɔːk/ [US] /'tɑː.mə.hɑːk/ *noun* [C] a small fighting axe used by Native Americans

tomato /tə'mɑː.təʊ/ [US] /-'meɪ.t̬oʊ/ *noun* [C or U] *plural* **tomatoes** a round red sharp-tasting fruit with a lot of seeds which is eaten cooked or raw as a savoury food ➲See picture **Vegetables** on page Centre 2

toˌmato 'ketchup *noun* [U] a sweet red tomato sauce, eaten cold and usually poured from a bottle

tomb /tuːm/ *noun* [C] a large stone structure or underground room where someone, especially an important person, is buried

tombola /tɒm'bəʊ.lə/ [US] /tɑːm'boʊ-/ *noun* [C] UK a game in which numbered tickets are bought from a spinning cylindrical container and small prizes are won when the numbers on the tickets are the same as the numbers on the prizes: *I won a bottle of port **on** the tombola at the fair.*

tomboy /'tɒm.bɔɪ/ [US] /'tɑːm-/ *noun* [C] a girl who acts and dresses like a boy, liking noisy, physical activities

tombstone /'tuːm.stəʊn/ [US] /-stoʊn/ *noun* [C] a **gravestone**

tomcat /'tɒm.kæt/ [US] /'tɑːm-/ *noun* [C] a male cat

Tom, Dick and/or Harry /ˌtɒmˌdɪk.ənd'hær.i/ [US] /ˌtɑːmˌdɪk.ənd'her-/ *noun* [S] DISAPPROVING an ordinary person/all ordinary people: *You'd better get a qualified electrician to sort this out – you don't want **any** Tom, Dick or Harry messing around with your electrics.*

tome /təʊm/ [US] /toʊm/ *noun* [C] USUALLY HUMOROUS a large heavy book: *She's written several **weighty** tomes on the subject.*

tomfoolery /ˌtɒm'fuː.lər.i/ [US] /ˌtɑːm'fuː.lɚ-/ *noun* [U] OLD-FASHIONED foolish, often playful, behaviour

tommy gun /'tɒm.i.gʌn/ [US] /'tɑː.mi-/ *noun* [C] a light MACHINE GUN (= quick firing gun) held in the hand

tomorrow /tə'mɒr.əʊ/ [US] /-'mɔːr.oʊ/ *adv, noun* [U] **1** (on) the day after today: *I've arranged to see Rachel tomorrow night.* ○ *Oh, leave it till tomorrow.* ○ *Is John coming to tomorrow's meeting?* ○ *He left today, which is Tuesday,*

T

and he'll be back tomorrow **week** (= the Wednesday of next week). **2** used more generally to mean the future: *Today's problem child may be tomorrow's criminal.* ○ *We make sacrifices now to give our children a better tomorrow.*

• **like there is/was no tomorrow** INFORMAL If someone does something like there is/was no tomorrow, they do it very fast, in large amounts and without thinking carefully: *After his win on the football pools, he began spending money like there was no tomorrow.*

tom-tom /ˈtɒm.tɒm/ ⓤ /ˈtɑːm.tɑːm/ *noun* [C] a drum which is usually beaten with the hands

ton WEIGHT (*plural* **tons** *or* **ton**) /tʌn/ *noun* [C] **1** (SPECIALIZED **metric ton**, SPECIALIZED **tonne**) a unit of weight equal to 1000 kg **2** (SPECIALIZED **long ton**) a unit of weight equal to 1016 kg **3** (SPECIALIZED **short ton**) a unit of weight equal to 907 kg

• **like a ton of bricks** very strongly or forcefully: *If father finds out what you've been doing, he'll* **come down on** (= punish) *you like a ton of bricks!*

tons /tʌnz/ *plural noun* INFORMAL an extremely large amount: *We've got tons* **of** *food left over from the party.*

ton SPEED /tʌn/ *noun* UK OLD-FASHIONED INFORMAL **do a ton** to drive at 100 miles per hour

tone VOICE EXPRESSION /təʊn/ ⓤ /toʊn/ *noun* [U] a quality in the voice which expresses the speaker's feelings or thoughts, often towards the person being addressed: *I tried to use a sympathetic tone of voice.* ○ *Don't speak to me in that tone of voice* (= angrily), *young lady!* ○ *It wasn't so much what she said that annoyed me – it was her tone.*

tones /təʊnz/ ⓤ /toʊnz/ *plural noun* LITERARY the quality of someone's voice: *She recounted the story to me* **in** *shocked tones* (= in a shocked voice). ○ *For more than half a century, the reassuring tones of BBC newscasters have informed British television viewers about world events.*

toneless /ˈtəʊn.ləs/ ⓤ /ˈtoʊn-/ *adj* LITERARY (of a voice) not expressing any emotion **tonelessly** /ˈtəʊn.ləs.li/ ⓤ /ˈtoʊn-/ *adv*

tone GENERAL MOOD /təʊn/ ⓤ /toʊn/ *noun* [S] the general mood or main qualities of something: *I didn't like the jokey tone of the article – I thought it inappropriate.* ○ *Trust you to* **lower** *the tone of the evening by telling vulgar jokes, Martin! ○ Well, I thought it might* **raise** *the moral tone of the evening if I invited a vicar to the party.* ○ *He was in a very bad mood when he arrived, and that* **set** *the tone* **for** *the whole meeting.* -**toned** /-təʊnd/ ⓤ /-toʊnd/ *suffix*

tone COLOUR VARIETY /təʊn/ ⓤ /toʊn/ *noun* [C] a form or degree of a colour: *warm tones of brown and yellow*

tone TIGHTNESS /təʊn/ ⓤ /toʊn/ *noun* [U] the healthy tightness of the body, especially the muscles: *After you've had a baby you lose the* **muscle** *tone in your stomach.*

toned /təʊnd/ ⓤ /toʊnd/ *adj* (of a body) firm and strong

tone /təʊn/ ⓤ /toʊn/ *verb* [T] (ALSO **tone up**) If you tone a part of the body you make it firmer and stronger, usually by taking physical exercise: *This is a good exercise for toning up the thighs.*

toner /ˈtəʊ.nəʳ/ ⓤ /ˈtoʊ.nɚ/ *noun* [C or U] a substance that you put on your face after you have cleaned it to make the skin feel firm

tone DIFFERENCE IN SOUND /təʊn/ ⓤ /toʊn/ *noun* [C] (US ALSO **step**) the largest difference in sound between two notes which are next to each other in the western musical scale: *The interval from G to A is a* **whole** *tone.*

tonal /ˈtəʊ.nᵊl/ ⓤ /ˈtoʊ-/ *adj* SPECIALIZED Tonal music is music that is based on MAJOR and MINOR KEYS (= sets of notes).

tone MUSICAL QUALITY /təʊn/ ⓤ /toʊn/ *noun* [C or U] the quality of sound of a musical instrument or singing voice: *the beautiful rich tones of his tenor voice* **tonal** /ˈtəʊ.nᵊl/ ⓤ /ˈtoʊ-/ *adj* SPECIALIZED

tone TELEPHONE NOISE /təʊn/ ⓤ /toʊn/ *noun* [C] one of the sounds that you hear on a telephone line when you pick up the RECEIVER: *I've called him several times but I keep getting the engaged tone.* ○ *Please wait until you hear the* (UK) *dialling/*(US) *dial tone* (= the sound that a telephone

makes when it is ready to be used) *before inserting your money.*

PHRASAL VERBS WITH **tone** ▼

▲ **tone** *sth* **down** *phrasal verb* [M] to make something less forceful or offensive, usually a piece of writing or a speech: *Some of the* **language** *in the original play has been toned down for the television version.*

▲ **tone in** *phrasal verb* When colours tone in, they match and looks pleasant together: *The green of your scarf tones in* **with** *your shoes.*

tone-deaf /ˌtəʊnˈdef/ ⓤ /ˌtoʊn-/ *adj* Someone who is tone-deaf is not able to recognize different notes or sing tunes accurately.

ˈtone ˌlanguage *noun* [C] SPECIALIZED a language in which the same series of sounds can represent different meanings, depending on how high or low they are spoken: *Chinese is a tone language.*

tongs /tɒŋz/ ⓤ /tɑːŋz/ *plural noun* a device used for picking up objects, consisting of two long pieces joined at one end and pressed together at the other end in order to hold an object between them: *coal tongs*

tongue MOUTH PART /tʌŋ/ *noun* **1** [C] the large soft piece of flesh in the mouth which you can move and which you use for tasting, speaking, etc: *I burnt my tongue on some soup last night.* ⊃See picture **The Body** on page Centre 5 **2** [U] the tongue of an animal, used as food **3** [C] a part of an object which is tongue-shaped, especially the piece of material which is under the LACES in a shoe

• **get** *your* **tongue round/around** *sth* to pronounce a difficult word or phrase: *It's one language that I have real difficulty getting my tongue round.*

• **loosen** *sb's* **tongue** to make someone speak very honestly: *A few whiskies should loosen his tongue.*

• **stick/put** *your* **tongue out** to make a rude sign by putting the tongue outside the mouth: *An old man was staring at her so she stuck her tongue out* **at** *him.*

• **tongues wagging** INFORMAL If what someone says or does starts tongues wagging, it causes other people to start talking and guessing things about their private lives: *Do you think if we leave the party together it will* **set/start** *tongues wagging? ○ They tried to keep their affair secret, but it wasn't long before tongues began to wag.*

• **tongue in cheek** (ALSO **with** *your* **tongue in** *your* **cheek**) if you say something tongue in cheek, you intend it to be understood as a joke, although you might appear to be serious: *He said that he was America's greatest lover, although I suspect it was tongue in cheek.* **tongue-in-cheek** /ˌtʌŋ.ɪnˈtʃiːk/ *adj: Her latest play is a firmly tongue-in-cheek look at the world of advertising.*

tongue LANGUAGE /tʌŋ/ *noun* [C] LITERARY a language: *immigrants struggling to learn a foreign tongue* ○ *an ancient tongue*

tongue STYLE OF EXPRESSION /tʌŋ/ *noun* [U] a person's way of expressing their ideas and feelings: *She is a prolific writer with critical views and a* **sharp** (= severe and critical) *tongue.*

-tongued /-tʌŋd/ *suffix: Coleman plays the part of the* **sharp***-tongued* (= severe and critical) *lawyer.* ○ *He was younger than her, in his forties, and had a* **silver***-tongued charm* (= said charming things).

tongue-lashing /ˈtʌŋˌlæʃ.ɪŋ/ *noun* [C] If you give someone a tongue-lashing, you speak angrily to them about something that they have done wrong.

tongue-tied /ˈtʌŋ.taɪd/ *adj* If you get tongue-tied, you find it difficult to express yourself, usually because you are nervous.

ˈtongue ˌtwister *noun* [C] a sentence or phrase that is intended to be difficult to say, especially when repeated quickly and often: *'She sells seashells on the seashore' is a well-known tongue twister.*

tonic /ˈtɒn.ɪk/ ⓤ /ˈtɑː.nɪk/ *noun* **1** [C] a liquid medicine which has the general effect of making you feel better rather than treating a particular health problem that you might have **2** [S] INFORMAL something that makes you feel stronger or happier: *The magazine is lively and interesting – the pictures alone are a tonic.*

tonic (ˌwater) *noun* [C or U] fizzy water with a bitter taste which can be drunk on its own or added to alcoholic drinks: *Two gin and tonics, please.*

tonight /təˈnaɪt/ *adv, noun* [U] (during) the night of the present day: *Tonight will be my first opportunity to meet her.* ○ *Tonight's meeting will take place in the main school hall.*

tonnage /ˈtʌn.ɪdʒ/ *noun* [U] the size of a ship or the weight of goods that a ship is able to carry

tonne (*plural* **tonnes** or **tonne**) /tʌn/ *noun* [C] (ALSO **metric ton**) 1000 kilograms: *Oil deliveries will fall 2.5 million tonnes short of demand this year.* ○ *a 7554-tonne ocean liner*

tonsil /ˈtɒnt.s^{ə}lz/ [US] /ˈtɑːnt-/ *noun* [C usually pl] one of two small soft organs at the back of the mouth

tonsillitis /ˌtɒnt.sɪˈlaɪ.təs/ [US] /ˌtɑːnt.sɪˈlaɪ.t̬əs/ *noun* [U] a painful infection of the tonsils

tonsure /ˈtɒn.tʃə^{r}/ [US] /ˈtɑːnt.ʃɚ/ *noun* [C] the top back part of a MONK'S head from which a circle of hair has been removed

too [MORE] /tuː/ *adv* more than is needed or wanted; more than is suitable or enough: *I'm too fat.* ○ *I can't reach the shelf – it's **(a bit)** too high.* ○ *There were **(far)** too many people for such a small room.* ○ *It's too difficult **(for** me) **to** explain.* ○ FORMAL *It was too expensive **a** desk **for** a child's room.* ○ *It's **(all)** too much* (= more than I can deal with) – *I can't bear it.*

• **all too** used before an adjective to emphasize a negative meaning: *The holidays flew by all too quickly.*

• **only too** used before an adjective to emphasize a positive meaning: *"Would you like to make a donation?" "I'd be only too pleased."*

• **too bad** INFORMAL If you say something is too bad, you can mean either that you are sympathetic about someone else's problem, or that you are not. The difference is in what is being talked about and the way that you say it: *It's too bad that you can't come to see Mark in his school play.* ○ *"I can't come on Friday." "That's too bad – I've already bought the tickets so you'll still have to pay."*

• **in too deep** too involved in a difficult situation

• **too good to miss** If you say that something is too good to miss, you mean that it is a very good opportunity and that people should see it, do it, etc: *Henri's latest show is simply too good to miss.*

• **too good to be true** so good that it is hard to believe, or seeming very good but not real: *Her new job sounds too good to be true.* ○ *I'm not surprised the offer wasn't genuine, it **sounded** too good to be true.*

• **too little too late** not happening early enough or in a strong enough way to stop a bad situation getting worse: *Officials admit that the re-planting of the hillsides only started five years ago and seems to be **a** classic **case of** too little too late.*

• **too much of a good thing** when something pleasant becomes unpleasant because you have or do too much of it: *You can **have** too much of a good thing.*

• **too much like hard work** describes an activity that you do not want to do because it needs a lot of effort: *I don't like gardening – it's too much like hard work.*

too [VERY] /tuː/ *adv* very, or completely: *He wasn't too **pleased/happy** when I told him about the mistake.* ○ *My mother hasn't been too **well** recently.* ○ FORMAL *Thank you, you're too **kind**.*

too [ALSO] /tuː/ *adv* **1** (especially at the end of a sentence) in addition, also: *I'd like to come too.* ○ INFORMAL *"I love chocolate." "Me too."* **2** used to show surprise: *It's a wonderful picture of light shining through trees – and by a child too!* ➲Compare **well** IN ADDITION; **moreover**; **what's more** at **what** THAT WHICH.

too [CERTAINLY] /tuː/ *adv* US INFORMAL used to emphasize a positive answer to a negative statement: *"I'm not going to school today." "You are too!"*

took /tʊk/ *past simple of* **take**

tool [EQUIPMENT] /tuːl/ *noun* [C] **1** a piece of equipment which you use with your hands to make or repair something: *power tools* ○ *machine tools* **2** something that helps you to do a particular activity: *A free low-interest credit card can be a **useful** budgeting tool.* **3** DISAPPROVING someone whose decisions and actions are unfairly controlled by others: *The President was widely regarded as the tool **of** the military.*

• **tool of the trade** A tool of the trade is something you need to use to do your job: *For the modern sales executive, a car phone is one of the tools of the trade.*

tooled /tuːld/ *adj* Something, especially a piece of leather, which is tooled is marked with decorative patterns using a special tool: *a tooled leather belt*

tool [PENIS] /tuːl/ *noun* [C] OFFENSIVE a penis

ˈtool ˌbox *noun* [C usually sing] a container in which you keep and carry small tools, especially those used in the house or for repairing a car

ˌtooled ˈup *adj* [after v] SLANG carrying a weapon, especially a gun

ˈtool ˌkit *noun* [C] a set of tools

ˈtool ˌshed *noun* [C] a small building in which tools and garden equipment are kept

toot /tuːt/ *verb* [I or T] to make a short sound or series of short sounds, especially with the HORN of a car as a warning: *The driver tooted (her horn).* **toot** /tuːt/ *noun* [C] *The waiting taxi **gave** a toot **on** its horn.*

tooth [MOUTH] /tuːθ/ *noun* [C] *plural* **teeth** one of the hard white objects in the mouth, which are used for biting and chewing: *a broken/missing tooth* ○ *front/back teeth* ○ ***false** teeth* ○ ***Brush/Clean** your teeth thoroughly morning and night.* ○ *I had to have a tooth **out*** (US ***pulled***) (= removed). ➲See also **eyetooth**.

• **get *your* teeth into *sth*** To get your teeth into something is to deal with something or become involved in something with great energy and enthusiasm: *I'm so bored at work, I wish they'd give me something I could really get my teeth into.*

• **set *sb's* teeth on edge** If something, especially a noise, sets your teeth on edge it annoys you very much: *That DJ's voice really sets my teeth on edge.*

• **fight tooth and nail** to try very hard to get something you want: *We fought tooth and nail to get the route of the new road changed.*

-toothed /-tuːθt/ *suffix* with the teeth described: *gap-toothed* (= with a space between the top two front teeth)

toothless /ˈtuːθ.ləs/ *adj* **1** having no teeth: *an ugly toothless old hag* **2** describes an organization or a rule that has no power: *This well-intentioned but toothless law will do nothing to improve the situation.*

toothy /ˈtuː.θi/ *adj* showing a lot of teeth when you smile: *He gave me a toothy **grin**.*

tooth [POINT] /tuːθ/ *noun* [C usually pl] *plural* **teeth** any of the row of points which stick out from the edge of a tool or piece of equipment, such as a comb, saw, or zip ➲See also **fine-tooth comb**.

toothache /ˈtuːθ.eɪk/ *noun* [C or U] (a) pain caused by something being wrong with one of your teeth: *I've got terrible toothache.*

toothbrush /ˈtuːθ.brʌʃ/ *noun* [C] a small brush with a long handle which you use to clean your teeth

ˈtooth ˌfairy *noun* [C] an imaginary being whom children believe takes away a BABY TOOTH which has come out and leaves them money instead

toothpaste /ˈtuːθ.peɪst/ *noun* [U] a thick creamy substance which you put onto a TOOTHBRUSH to clean your teeth: *a tube of toothpaste*

toothpick /ˈtuːθ.pɪk/ *noun* [C] a small thin pointed stick of wood, plastic or metal which can be used for removing pieces of food from between the teeth, especially after a meal

toothsome /ˈtuːθ.səm/ *adj* (especially of food) attractive or pleasant

toothy /ˈtuː.θi/ *adj* ➲See at **tooth** MOUTH.

tootle /ˈtuː.tl̩/ [US] /-t̬l̩/ *verb* [I usually + adv or prep] INFORMAL to go, especially to drive, slowly: *The car in front was just tootling along through the beautiful scenery.*

tootsie [FOOT], **tootsy** /ˈtʊt.si/ *noun* [C] CHILD'S WORD a toe or a foot: *Don't get your tootsies cold.*

tootsie [WOMAN] /ˈtʊt.si/ *noun* [C] (ALSO **toots**) MAINLY US INFORMAL a woman: [as form of address] *See you later, toots. I'll be home around eight.*

T

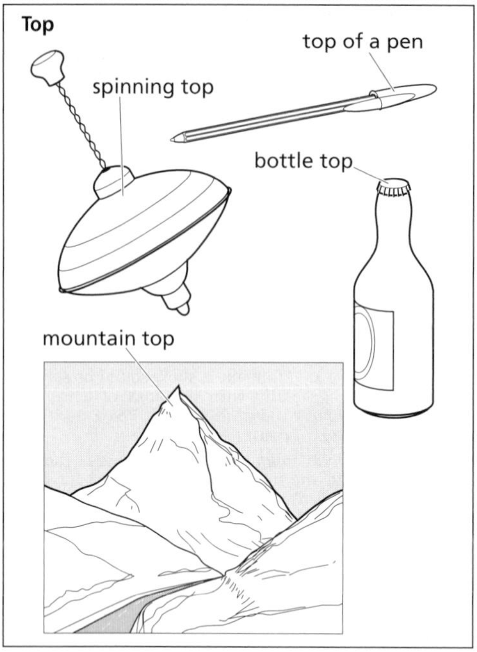

top [HIGHEST PART] /tɒp/ [US] /tɑːp/ *noun* [C] **1** the highest place or part: *She waited for me* ***at*** *the top* ***of*** *the stairs.* ○ *There were flags* ***on*** *the tops* ***of*** *many of the buildings.* ○ *There was a pile of books* ***on*** *top* ***of*** (= on) *the table.* ➲See also **clifftop**; **hilltop**; **mountaintop**; **rooftop**; **the treetops**. Compare **bottom** LOWEST PART; **summit** HIGHEST POINT. ✻ NOTE: The opposite is **bottom**. **2** the flat upper surface of something: *The top of the table/desk was badly scratched.*

• **be on top of *sth*** *INFORMAL* to be able to control a situation or deal with it

• **from top to bottom** If you search, paint, etc. a building from top to bottom, you search, paint, etc. all parts of it: *They cleaned the house from top to bottom.*

• **from top to toe** (*ALSO* **from head to foot**) (of the clothes a person is wearing, etc.) all in the same style, colour, etc: *A woman came into the room dressed in red from top to toe.*

• **on top of *sth*** in addition to something, especially something unpleasant: *We missed the train, and on top of that we had to wait for two hours for the next one.*

• **on top of the world** extremely happy: *She was feeling on top of the world.*

• **off the top of *your* head** from the knowledge you have in your memory: *"What's the capital of Mauritania?" "I couldn't tell you off the top of my head, but I could go and look it up."*

• **over the top** (*ABBREVIATION* **OTT**) *UK INFORMAL* too extreme and not suitable, or demanding too much attention or effort, especially in an uncontrolled way: *I thought the decorations were* ***way*** (= very) *over the top.* ○ *The speech was a bit OTT.* ○ *I think he realised he'd* ***gone*** *over the top with the seating arrangements.*

• **at the top of *your* voice** extremely loudly: *She shouted his name at the top of her voice.*

top /tɒp/ [US] /tɑːp/ *adj* [before n] at the highest part of something: *There's a dirty mark on the top left-hand corner of the photo.* ○ *The offices are on the top floor of the building.* ○ *He was standing on the top rung of a ladder.*

top /tɒp/ [US] /tɑːp/ *verb* [T] **-pp- 1** to be the most important, best, most successful, etc: *The record topped* ***the charts*** (= sold the largest number of recordings) *for five weeks.* ○ *She topped* ***the bill*** (= was the most important act in the show). ➲See also **topping**. **2** (*ALSO* **top off**) to be on the upper surface of something, especially as a decoration: *The dessert was topped off* ***with*** *cream and pieces of fruit.*

• **top and tail** to cut off the hard parts at each end of a fruit or vegetable when you prepare it for cooking: *Top and tail the beans.*

topmost /ˈtɒp.məʊst/ [US] /ˈtɑːp.moʊst/ *adj* [before n] highest: *We couldn't reach the apples on the topmost branches.*

topping /ˈtɒp.ɪŋ/ [US] /ˈtɑː.pɪŋ/ *noun* [C or U] a substance, especially a sauce, cream or pieces of food, which is put on top of other food to give extra flavour and to make it look attractive: *pizza topping* ○ *a topping of toasted almonds*

top [UPPER PART] /tɒp/ [US] /tɑːp/ *adj* [before n] in the part nearest to the highest part; in the upper part: *The top few steps were damaged and broken.*

top /tɒp/ [US] /tɑːp/ *noun* [C] any piece of light clothing worn on the part of the body above the waist: *a skimpy top* ○ *a pyjama top* ○ *I need a top to go with these trousers.*

topless /ˈtɒp.ləs/ [US] /ˈtɑː.pləs/ *adj, adv* describes someone, usually a woman, wearing nothing on the upper part of their body, or something connected with this way of dressing: *topless dancers/bars/sunbathing* ○ *Many women now* **go** *topless on European beaches.*

top [BEST] /tɒp/ [US] /tɑːp/ *adj, adv* **1** (in the position of being) most important or successful; best: *So what would be your top choice for a holiday?* ○ *As a chess player he's among the top 10% in the country.* **2 be/come top** to be the student with the best results: *She came top* ***of the class*** *in English.* ○ *Sam was top* ***at/in*** *Science.* **3** Top people, organizations or activities are the most important or successful ones: *top athletes/executives* ○ *top jobs* ○ *top universities*

top- /tɒp-/ [US] /tɑːp-/ *prefix* used with many different words to mean 'best': *a top-class athlete* ○ *top-ranking officers*

• **at top speed** as fast as possible: *The train thundered through the station at top speed.*

• **on top form** *UK* (*US* **in top form**) feeling or doing things as well as possible: *Paul's back on top form after his illness.*

the top /tɒp/ [US] /tɑːp/ *noun* [S] the most important position in a group or organization: *At forty, he was* ***at*** *the top* ***of*** *his profession.* ○ *Life* ***at*** *the top is stressful.*

top /tɒp/ [US] /tɑːp/ *verb* [T] **-pp-** to do, pay, etc. more or better than anyone else: *"They've offered me £1000." "I'm afraid we can't top that."* ○ *She topped my suggestion* ***with*** *an even better one of her own.*

top [EXCELLENT] /tɒp/ [US] /tɑːp/ *adj, exclamation UK INFORMAL* excellent: *"How was your party?" "Top, mate."* ○ *"You coming, then?" "Yeah, top!"*

the tops /ðəˈtɒps/ [US] /-ˈtɑːps/ *noun* [S] *OLD-FASHIONED* the best: *You're the tops, Linda!*

top [LID] /tɒp/ [US] /tɑːp/ *noun* [C] the cover or lid used to close a container or pen: *a screw-on top* ○ *a bottle top* ○ *a pen top*

top [TOY] /tɒp/ [US] /tɑːp/ *noun* [C] a **spinning top**

top *yourself* [KILL] *verb* [R] *UK SLANG* to kill yourself

PHRASAL VERBS WITH **top** ▼

▲ **top *sth* off** *phrasal verb* [M] to finish something in an enjoyable or successful way: *She topped off her performance* ***with*** *a dazzling encore.*

▲ **top *sth* up** [LIQUID] *UK phrasal verb* [M] (*US* **top *sth* off**) to add liquid in order to fill to the top a container which is already partly full: *Shall I top up your drink?* ○ *Mix together some lemon juice and sugar, then top it up* ***with*** *water.*

▲ **top *sb* up** *phrasal verb* [M] *INFORMAL* to put more drink into someone's glass or cup: *Your glass is nearly empty. Let me top you up.*

top-up /ˈtɒp.ʌp/ [US] /ˈtɑːp-/ *noun* [C] *Have you finished your coffee – would you like a top-up?*

▲ **top *sth* up** [MONEY] *phrasal verb* [M] to add more of something, especially money, to an existing amount to create the total you need: *Students are able to take out loans to top up their grants.* ○ *This is the easiest way to top up your mobile phone card.* ○ *top-up fees/payments*

top-up /ˈtɒp.ʌp/ [US] /ˈtɑːp-/ *noun* [C] *The bank agreed to lend me a top-up of £500.*

topaz /ˈtəʊ.pæz/ [US] /ˈtoʊ-/ *noun* [C or U] a transparent yellow precious stone used in jewellery

T

ˌtop ˈbrass *group noun* [U] the people with the highest positions of authority, especially in the armed forces

topcoat /ˈtɒp.kəʊt/ [US] /ˈtɑːp.koʊt/ *noun* [C or U] a final layer of paint put onto a surface over another layer, or the type of paint used to do this ⊃Compare **undercoat**.

ˌtop ˈdog *noun* [C usually sing] *INFORMAL* a person who has achieved a position of authority

top-down /ˌtɒpˈdaʊn/ [US] /ˈtɑːp-/ *adj* [before n] describes a situation in which decisions are made by a few people in authority rather than by the people who are affected by the decisions: *a top-down approach/strategy*

topee /ˈtəʊ.piː/ [US] /ˈtoʊ-/ *noun* [C] (*ALSO* **topi**) a **pith helmet**

top-flight /ˌtɒpˈflaɪt/ [US] /ˌtɑːp-/ *adj* [before n] highest in standard or quality: *He's one of our top-flight engineers.*

ˌtop ˈhat *noun* [C] (*INFORMAL* **topper**) a tall black or grey hat worn by men on some formal occasions ⊃See picture **Hairstyles and Hats** on page Centre 8

top-heavy /ˌtɒpˈhev.i/ [US] /ˌtɑːp-/ *adj* [after v] If something is top-heavy, it has more weight in the higher part than in the lower part and will not balance correctly: *The main reason the ship capsized was that it was top-heavy.* ○ *FIGURATIVE If they sacked a hundred senior managers, they would be less top-heavy.*

topiary /ˈtəʊ.pjər.i/ [US] /ˈtoʊ.pi.er-/ *noun* [U] *SPECIALIZED* the art of cutting bushes into attractive shapes, especially of animals and birds

topic /ˈtɒp.ɪk/ [US] /ˈtɑː.pɪk/ *noun* [C] a subject which is discussed, written about or studied: *Our discussion ranged over various topics, such as acid rain and the hole in the ozone layer.*

topical [HAPPENING NOW] /ˈtɒp.ɪ.kəl/ [US] /ˈtɑː.pɪ-/ *adj* of interest at the present time; relating to things which are happening at present: *a topical joke* ○ *The discussion focused on topical issues in medicine.* **topicality** /ˌtɒp.ɪˈkæl.ə.ti/ [US] /ˌtɑː.pɪˈkæl.ə.t̬i/ *noun* [U] **topically** /ˈtɒp.ɪ.kli/ [US] /ˈtɑː.pɪ-/ *adv*

topical [MEDICINE] /ˈtɒp.ɪ.kəl/ [US] /ˈtɑː.pɪ-/ *adj SPECIALIZED* describes a medical product which is used on the outside of the body: *This lotion is for topical application only.*

topknot /ˈtɒp.nɒt/ [US] /ˈtɑːp.nɑːt/ *noun* [C] long hair tied up onto the top part of the back of the head

topless /ˈtɒp.ləs/ [US] /ˈtɑː.pləs/ *adj, adv* ⊃See at **top** UPPER PART.

top-level /ˌtɒpˈlev.əl/ *adj* [before n] describes an activity in which the most important people in an organization or country take part: *top-level talks/negotiations/discussions*

topmost /ˈtɒp.məʊst/ [US] /ˈtɑːp.moʊst/ *adj* [before n] ⊃See at **top** HIGHEST PART.

top-notch /ˌtɒpˈnɒtʃ/ [US] /ˌtɑːpˈnɑːtʃ/ *adj INFORMAL* excellent: *That restaurant's really top-notch.*

topography /təˈpɒg.rə.fi/ [US] /təˈpɑː.grə-/ *noun* [U] *SPECIALIZED* the physical appearance of the natural features of an area of land, especially the shape of its surface **topographical** /ˌtɒp.əʊˈgræf.ɪ.kəl/ [US] /ˌtɑː.pə-/ *adj* **topographically** /ˌtɒp.əʊˈgræf.ɪ.kli/ [US] /ˌtɑː.pə-/ *adv* **topographer** /təˈpɒg.rə.fər/ [US] /təˈpɑː.grə.fɚ/ *noun* [C]

topper /ˈtɒp.ər/ [US] /ˈtɑː.pɚ/ *noun INFORMAL FOR* **top hat**

topple /ˈtɒp.l̩/ [US] /ˈtɑː.pl̩/ *verb* **1** [I or T] to (cause to) lose balance and fall down: *The statue of the dictator was toppled* ***(over)*** *by the crowds.* ○ *The tree toppled and fell.* **2** [T] to force a leader or government out of power: *The church was prominently involved in the struggle that toppled the dictatorship.*

ˌtop ˈsecret *adj* (*ALSO* **top security**) (of information) extremely secret and not to be told to anyone outside a particular group of people: *a top-security military research project* ○ *These papers are top secret.*

top-security /ˌtɒp.sɪˈkjʊə.rɪ.ti/ [US] /ˌtɑːp.sɪˈkjʊr.ə.t̬i/ *adj* [before n] describes a prison or hospital that has a very high level of security because it contains dangerous people

topsoil /ˈtɒp.sɔɪl/ [US] /ˈtɑːp-/ *noun* [U] (the earth which forms) the top layer of ground in which plants grow ⊃Compare **subsoil**.

topspin /ˈtɒp.spɪn/ [US] /ˈtɑːp-/ *noun* [U] a forward turning movement of a ball as it travels through the air

topsy-turvy /ˌtɒp.siˈtɜː.vi/ [US] /ˌtɑːp.siˈtɝː-/ *adj, adv INFORMAL* (in a state of being) confused, not well organized or giving importance to unexpected things; upside down: *The government's topsy-turvy priorities mean that spending on education remains low.*

ˌtop ˈten *noun* [C usually sing] **1** the set of ten records that have been bought by the largest numbers of people in the previous week: *The record has been* ***in*** *the Top Ten for three weeks.* **2** the ten most popular items in a group of similar things: *'Casablanca' is one of my top ten films.*

the Torah /ðəˈtɔː.rə/ [US] /-ˈtɔːr.ə/ *noun* [S] the holy book of the Jews

torch /tɔːtʃ/ [US] /tɔːrtʃ/ *noun* **1** [C] *UK* (*US* **flashlight**) a small light which is held in the hand and usually powered by batteries: *She* ***flashed/shone*** *the torch into the dark room.* **2** [C] a thick stick with material which burns tied to the top of it in order to give light: *a flaming/blazing torch* ○ *LITERARY Many buildings were* ***put to the*** *torch* (= burned intentionally) *during the riots.* **3** [S] *APPROVING* used as a symbol of a political movement or idea that has an important positive influence: *We must not let* ***the*** *burning torch* ***of*** *socialism go out.*

torch /tɔːtʃ/ [US] /tɔːrtʃ/ *verb* [T] to burn a building or other large thing, intentionally and usually illegally: *They smashed a side door to get in and then torched the warehouse when they had taken what they wanted.*

torchlight /ˈtɔːtʃ.laɪt/ [US] /ˈtɔːrtʃ-/ *noun* [U] the light from a TORCH: *I saw the blade of an open knife shine in his hand* ***in*** *the torchlight.*

torchlight /ˈtɔːtʃ.laɪt/ [US] /ˈtɔːrtʃ-/ *adj* [before n] (*ALSO* **torchlit**) describes an event that is lit by burning TORCHES: *a torchlight/torchlit procession*

tore /tɔːr/ [US] /tɔːr/ *past simple of* **tear**

toreador /ˈtɒr.i.ə.dɔːr/ [US] /ˈtɔːr.i.ə.dɔːr/ *noun* [C] a person, usually a man, who takes part in a BULLFIGHT riding a horse ⊃Compare **matador**; **picador**.

torment /ˈtɔː.ment/ [US] /ˈtɔːr-/ *noun* **1** [U] great mental suffering and unhappiness, or great physical pain: *The family said they had* ***endured*** *years of torment and abuse at the hands of the neighbours.* ○ *Waiting for the result of the medical tests was sheer torment.* ○ *He spent the night* ***in*** *torment, trying to decide what was the best thing to do.* **2** [C] something or someone that causes great suffering or annoyance: *The tax forms were an annual torment* ***to*** *him.*

torments /ˈtɔː.ments/ [US] /ˈtɔːr-/ *plural noun: Nothing can describe the torments* (= torment) *we* ***went through*** *while we were waiting for news.*

torment /tɔːˈment/ [US] /tɔːr-/ *verb* [T] to cause a person or animal to suffer: *The animals are tormented mercilessly by flies and mosquitoes.* ○ *The camera focused on a group of women whose faces were tormented* ***by/with*** (= showed that they were suffering) *grief.* ○ *It tormented me* (= caused me to worry) *all day – did I remember to lock the door when I left the house?* **tormentor** /tɔːˈmen.tər/ [US] /tɔːrˈmen.t̬ɚ/ *noun* [C]

torn /tɔːn/ [US] /tɔːrn/ *past participle of* **tear**

• **torn between** If you are torn between two possibilities, you find it very difficult to choose between them.

tornado (*plural* **tornados** or **tornadoes**) /tɔːˈneɪ.dəʊ/ [US] /tɔːrˈneɪ.doʊ/ *noun* [C] (*US INFORMAL ALSO* **twister**) a strong dangerous wind which forms itself into an upside-down spinning cone and is able to destroy buildings as it moves across the ground

torpedo /tɔːˈpiː.dəʊ/ [US] /tɔːrˈpiː.doʊ/ *noun* [C or U] *plural* **torpedoes** a long thin bomb which travels under water in order to destroy the ship at which it is aimed

torpedo /tɔːˈpiː.dəʊ/ [US] /tɔːrˈpiː.doʊ/ *verb* [T] **torpedoing, torpedoed, torpedoed** **1** to use a torpedo to destroy something **2** *INFORMAL* to destroy: *He accused them of trying to torpedo the peace process.*

torpid /ˈtɔː.pɪd/ [US] /ˈtɔːr-/ *adj FORMAL* not active; moving or thinking slowly, especially as a result of being lazy or feeling like you want to sleep: *If you have a sudden loss of cabin pressure at 20000 feet, passengers will become torpid and then lose consciousness.* **torpidly** /ˈtɔː.pɪd.li/ [US] /ˈtɔːr-/ *adv*

torpor /ˈtɔː.pəʳ/ [US] /ˈtɔːr.pɚ/ *noun* [U] (*ALSO* **torpidity**) **1** *FORMAL* lack of activity **2** *SPECIALIZED* the state of reduced activity that some animals experience during the winter

torque /tɔːk/ [US] /tɔːrk/ *noun* [U] *SPECIALIZED* a force which causes something to ROTATE (= turn in a circle)

torrent /ˈtɒr.ənt/ [US] /ˈtɔːr-/ *noun* **1** [S] a sudden large or too large amount, especially one which seems to be uncontrollable: *He let out **a** torrent **of** abuse/angry words.* ○ *They are worried that the flow/trickle/stream of tourists could swell into **an** unmanageable torrent if there are no controls.* **2** [C] a large amount of fast-moving water: *Heavy rainfall turned the river into a rushing/raging torrent.*

torrents /ˈtɒr.ənts/ [US] /ˈtɔːr-/ *plural noun* large amounts: *torrents of rain* ○ *The rain came down/fell **in** torrents.* ○ *We have received torrents of letters/requests/criticism.*

torrential /təˈren.tʃəl/ [US] /tɔːˈrent.ʃəl/ *adj* used to refer to very heavy rain: *torrential rain* ○ *a torrential downpour/storm*

torrid [WEATHER] /ˈtɒr.ɪd/ [US] /ˈtɔːr.ɪd/ *adj FORMAL* extremely hot: *the torrid heat of August*

torrid [EMOTIONS] /ˈtɒr.ɪd/ [US] /ˈtɔːr.ɪd/ *adj* involving strong emotions, especially those of sexual love: *a torrid romance*

• **a torrid time** *UK* a period when you experience a lot of problems

torsion /ˈtɔː.ʃən/ [US] /ˈtɔːr-/ *noun* [U] *SPECIALIZED* the act of twisting, the force which causes twisting, or the state of being twisted

torso /ˈtɔː.səʊ/ [US] /ˈtɔːr.soʊ/ *noun* [C] *plural* **torsos** the human body considered without head, arms or legs, or a statue representing this: *The air bag in the steering wheel will protect the head and torso.* ○ *a famous marble torso*

torte /ˈtɔːt/ [US] /tɔːrt/ *noun* [C] a round flat sweet cake, often with cream and fruit on top of or inside it: *chocolate/almond/blackcurrant torte*

tortilla /tɔːˈtiː.ə/ [US] /tɔːrˈtiː.jə/ *noun* **1** [C] a type of thin round Mexican bread made from maize flour and eggs **2** [C or U] a thick Spanish OMELETTE (= flat, round food made by frying eggs that have been mixed together) with potato and sometimes onion in it

torˈtilla ˌchip *noun* [C usually pl] a small fried piece of tortilla, often eaten with a spicy sauce

tortoise /ˈtɔː.təs/ [US] /ˈtɔːr.t̬əs/ *noun* [C] an animal with a thick, hard shell that it can move its head and legs into for protection. It eats plants, moves very slowly and sleeps during the winter.

tortoiseshell /ˈtɔː.təʃ.ʃel/ [US] /ˈtɔːr.t̬əs-/ *noun* [U] the hard shell of a TURTLE which is yellow, orange and brown and which is used to make decorative items, or an artificial substance made to look like this: *glasses with tortoiseshell frames*

ˌtortoiseshell ˈbutterfly *noun* [C] a type of butterfly with yellow, orange and brown marks on its wings

tortuous /ˈtɔː.tʃu.əs/ [US] /ˈtɔːr-/ *adj* with many turns and changes of direction; not direct or simple: *He took a tortuous **route** through back streets.* ○ *The path to peace seems at last to be clear, although it may be a long and tortuous one.* **tortuously** /ˈtɔː.tʃu.ə.sli/ [US] /ˈtɔːr-/ *adv* **tortuousness** /ˈtɔː.tʃu.ə.snəs/ [US] /ˈtɔːr-/ *noun* [U]

torture /ˈtɔː.tʃəʳ/ [US] /ˈtɔːr.tʃɚ/ *noun* **1** [U] the act of causing great physical or mental pain in order to persuade someone to do something or to give information, or as an act of cruelty to a person or animal: *Half of the prisoners died after torture and starvation.* ○ *He revealed the secret **under** torture.* **2** [C or U] *INFORMAL* a very unpleasant experience: *The rush-hour traffic was **sheer** torture as usual.*

torture /ˈtɔː.tʃəʳ/ [US] /ˈtɔːr.tʃɚ/ *verb* [T] **1** to cause great physical or mental pain to someone intentionally: *It is claimed that the officers tortured a man **to death** in 1983 in a city police station.* **2** to cause mental pain: [R] *He tortured himself for years **with** the thought that he could have stopped the boy from running into the road.*

tortured /ˈtɔː.tʃəd/ [US] /ˈtɔːr.tʃɚd/ *adj* involving suffering and difficulty: *the country's tortured past* ○ *the tortured history of race relations* **torturer** /ˈtɔː.tʃər.əʳ/ [US] /ˈtɔːr.tʃɚ.ɚ/ *noun* [C]

Tory /ˈtɔː.ri/ [US] /ˈtɔːr.i/ *noun* [C], *adj* (a member) of the British Conservative Party: ***The** Tories (= the Tory party) have dropped in the opinion poll ratings.* **Toryism** /ˈtɔː.ri.ɪ.zəm/ [US] /ˈtɔːr.i-/ *noun* [U]

tosh /tɒʃ/ [US] /tɑːʃ/ *noun* [U] *OLD-FASHIONED INFORMAL* nonsense: *It's just a lot of tosh.*

toss /tɒs/ [US] /tɑːs/ *verb* **1** [T usually + adv or prep] to throw something carelessly: *He glanced at the letter and then tossed it into the bin.* ○ *The bull tossed him up into the air.* ○ [+ two objects] *Andrew tossed him the ball.* **2** [T] If you toss your hair or a part of your body you move it up and back suddenly: *She tossed her head in annoyance.* ○ *She tossed back her hair.* **3** [T] When you toss food you shake or mix small pieces of it together with a sauce or DRESSING: *a tossed salad* ○ *carrots tossed **in** butter* **4** *UK* **toss a pancake** to quickly and suddenly lift the pan in which a PANCAKE (= thin, flat round cake) is cooking so that the pancake goes up into the air and turns over before falling back into the pan

• **toss and turn** to move about from side to side or turn a lot in bed, especially because you cannot sleep: *I was tossing and turning all night.*

• **toss a coin** (*ALSO* **toss *sb* for *sth***) to throw a coin up into the air and guess which side will land facing up, as a way of making a decision: *"I'll toss you for it – heads or tails?"* ○ *Let's toss a coin to see who'll go first.*

toss /tɒs/ [US] /tɑːs/ *noun* [C] a sudden quick movement: *"I don't care," she replied with a toss of her head.*

• **win/lose the toss** If you win/lose the toss you guess correctly/wrongly which side of a coin will be facing up when it lands on the ground after being thrown.

• **not give/care a toss** *UK VERY INFORMAL* to not be worried at all by something: *I don't give a toss what he thinks.*

PHRASAL VERBS WITH **toss** ▼

▲ **toss *sth* about/around** *phrasal verb* [M] *INFORMAL* If you toss ideas, suggestions or phrases about, you mention them and discuss them with other people.

▲ **toss *sth* aside** *phrasal verb* [M] *LITERARY* to throw away or get rid of something

▲ **toss *sth* away** *phrasal verb* [M] *INFORMAL* to spend or lose something carelessly: *That much money is not to be tossed away lightly.*

▲ **toss *sth* off** [DO QUICKLY] *phrasal verb* [M] *INFORMAL* to do something quickly, especially in a careless way or with little effort: *She tossed off a reply to the letter before she left for the meeting.*

▲ **toss *(sb)* off** [SEXUALLY EXCITE] *phrasal verb UK OFFENSIVE* to give someone sexual pleasure by rubbing their sex organs, or to do this to yourself: [R] *Is that your idea of a sex-life – tossing off over porn mags?*

tosser /ˈtɒs.əʳ/ [US] /ˈtɑː.sɚ/ *noun* [C] *UK OFFENSIVE* a stupid or unpleasant person: *Barry's such a tosser.*

toss-up /ˈtɒs.ʌp/ [US] /ˈtɑːs-/ *noun* [C] *INFORMAL* If you describe a situation as a toss-up, you mean that either of two possibilities is equally likely: *It's **a** toss-up **between** Angela and Moira for the editor's job.*

tot [CHILD] /tɒt/ [US] /tɑːt/ *noun* [C] *INFORMAL* a young child: *These are good strong toys for **tiny** tots.*

tot [DRINK] /tɒt/ [US] /tɑːt/ *noun* [C] a small drink of alcohol: *He poured them each a generous tot **of** whisky/rum.*

tot /tɒt/ [US] /tɑːt/ *verb*

▲ **tot (*sth*) up** *phrasal verb* [M] *INFORMAL* to add up numbers or amounts of something, or to have a particular number or amount as a total when added up: *She quickly totted up our bill and added an amount for the waiter.* ○ *That tots up **to** £20.*

total [AMOUNT] /ˈtəʊ.təl/ [US] /ˈtoʊ.t̬əl/ *noun* [C] the amount obtained when several smaller amounts are added together: *At that time of day, cars with only one occupant accounted for almost 80% of the total.* ○ ***A** total **of** 21 horses were entered for the race.* ○ *We made £700 **in** total, over three days of trading.*

total /ˈtəʊ.təl/ [US] /ˈtoʊ.t̬əl/ *adj* [before n] including everything: *the total cost* ○ *Total losses after all charges were $800.*

total /ˈtəʊ.təl/ [US] /ˈtoʊ.t̬əl/ *verb* [L only + n; T] **-ll-** or *US USUALLY* **-l-** to have as a complete amount, or to calculate this: *This is the eighth volume in the series, which totals*

T

21 volumes in all. ○ *We totalled* ***(up)*** *the money we had each earned, and then shared it equally among the three of us.*
totality /təʊ'tæl.ə.ti/ [US] /toʊ'tæl.ə.t̬i/ *noun* [U] *FORMAL* the whole of something: *We need to consider this very serious issue* ***in its*** *totality.*
total [VERY GREAT] /'təʊ.təl/ [US] /'toʊ.t̬əl/ *adj* very great or of the largest degree possible: *total secrecy* ○ *a total disregard for their feelings* ○ *total silence* ○ *The organization of the event was a total shambles* (= very bad). ○ *The collapse, when it came, was total.* **totally** /'təʊ.təl.i/ [US] /'toʊ.t̬əl-/ *adv*: *Her second husband is totally different from Mark.* ○ *I totally agree with you.*
totalitarian /təʊ,tæl.ɪ'teə.ri.ən/ [US] /toʊ,tæl.ə'ter.i-/ *adj DISAPPROVING* of or being a political system in which those in power have complete control and do not allow people freely to oppose them: *a totalitarian regime/state* **totalitarianism** /təʊ,tæl.ɪ'teə.ri.ə.nɪ.zəm/ [US] /toʊ,tæl.ə'ter.i-/ *noun* [U]
tote [CARRY] /təʊt/ [US] /toʊt/ *verb* [T] *INFORMAL* to carry something, especially something heavy or awkward: *She usually toted the baby* ***around*** *in a backpack.* ○ *The building was surrounded with bodyguards toting sub-machine* ***guns***. ○ ***Gun****-toting security men were posted at all the entrances.*
tote [RACING] /təʊt/ [US] /toʊt/ *noun SPECIALIZED* **the tote** a system of putting bets on horses or dogs in a race
'tote ,bag *noun* [C] *US* a large strong bag
totem /'təʊ.təm/ [US] /'toʊ.t̬əm/ *noun* [C] an object which is respected by a group of people, especially for religious reasons: *Television could be seen as a totem of modern society.* **totemic** /təʊ'tem.ɪk/ [US] /toʊ-/ *adj*
'totem ,pole *noun* [C] a tall wooden pole with symbols cut or painted on it, which is part of the tradition of the Native Americans of the west coast of Canada and the northern USA
toto /'təʊ.təʊ/ [US] /'toʊ.t̬oʊ/ *noun* [U] ➲See **in toto**.
totter /'tɒt.ər/ [US] /'tɑː.t̬ɚ/ *verb* [I] **1** to walk in a shaky way that looks as if you are about to fall: *She tottered unsteadily down the stairs in her high-heeled shoes.* ➲Compare **stagger** MOVE; **teeter**. **2** to move shakily from side to side: *Several tall piles of books tottered and fell.* **3** (of a company, government, etc.) to become weaker and less likely to carry on existing: *The industry has tottered from crisis to crisis now for two years.* **tottering** /'tɒt.ər.ɪŋ/ [US] /'tɑː.t̬ɚ-/ *adj*: *She walked slowly with tottering steps.* ○ *It was the last decision of a tottering government.* **tottery** /'tɒt.ər.i/ [US] /'tɑː.t̬ɚ-/ *adj*: *a tottery old man*
totty, tottie /'tɒt.i/ [US] /'tɑː.t̬i/ *noun* [U] *UK SLANG* sexually attractive people: *Any totty around last night?*
toucan /'tuː.kən/ [US] /-kæn/ *noun* [C] a South American bird that has a brightly coloured beak
touch [MOVE HAND] /tʌtʃ/ *verb* **1** [I or T] to move especially the hand or another part of the body lightly onto and off something or someone: *That paint is wet – don't touch (it).* ○ *He touched the girl* ***on*** *the arm to get her attention.* ○ *The child touched the worm* ***with*** *a twig.* ○ *FIGURATIVE The setting sun touched the trees* ***with*** *red* (= made them appear red for a short time). **2** [T] *INFORMAL* If you say you do not touch a food or drink, you mean that you never eat or drink it: *No thanks, I never touch chocolate/alcohol.* ○ *Honestly, I haven't touched* ***a drop*** (= drunk any alcohol) *all night.*
• **wouldn't touch** ***sth*** **with a barge pole** *UK* (*US ALSO* **wouldn't touch** ***sth*** **with a ten-foot pole**) *INFORMAL* used to mean that you certainly do not want to buy something or be involved with something
• **touch-and-go** *INFORMAL* describes a situation which is uncertain: *The doctor says that it's touch-and-go* ***whether*** *Mary will be okay.*
• **touch/strike/hit a (raw) nerve** to upset someone: *The newspaper article touched a raw nerve – people still resent the closure of the local school.*
• **touch wood** *UK* (*US* **knock on wood**) *INFORMAL* said in order to avoid bad luck, either when you mention good luck that you have had in the past or when you mention hopes you have for the future: *The deal will be agreed on Wednesday, touch wood.*

touch /tʌtʃ/ *noun* **1** [U] the ability to know what something is like by feeling it with the fingers: *the sense of touch* ○ *I found the right coin in the dark* ***by*** *touch.* **2** [C usually sing] a quick light movement of one thing, especially a hand, onto and off another thing: *I felt a cold touch on my arm.* ○ *At a/the touch* ***of*** *a button, the door opened.*
• **to the touch** (*ALSO* **to** ***your*** **touch**) used after an adjective to express how something feels when you put your hand on it: *The material was soft to the touch.*
touch [CLOSE TOGETHER] /tʌtʃ/ *verb* **1** [I or T] (of two or more things) to be so close together that there is no space between; to be in contact: *He fell asleep as soon as his head touched the pillow.* ○ *She pushed the two bookcases together until they touched/were touching.* **2** [T] (usually used in negative sentences) to reach the standard of someone or something: *Her novels* ***can't*** *touch* (= are not as good as) *those of her sister.* ○ ***There's no one to*** *touch him* ***as*** *an illustrator of children's books.*
touch /tʌtʃ/ *noun* **1 be/get/keep, etc. in touch** to communicate or continue to communicate with someone by using a telephone or writing to them: *Are you still in touch with any of your old school friends?* ○ *No, Jane and I never kept in touch after college.* ○ *We're in close touch with our office in Spain.* **2 lose touch** to stop communicating with someone, usually because they do not live near you now: *We lost touch over the years.*
• **be in/out of touch** If you are in touch/out of touch with a subject, activity or situation, your knowledge about it is recent/not recent: *He's not really in touch with what young people are interested in.* ○ *I didn't look at a newspaper all the time I was on holiday, so I'm completely out of touch.*
touch [INFLUENCE] /tʌtʃ/ *verb* [T] to influence someone or something emotionally, or cause feelings of sympathy in someone: *Tragedy touched their lives when their son was 16.* ○ *The TV report about the children's work for charity touched thousands of people's hearts.*
touched /tʌtʃt/ *adj* [after v] grateful for something kind that someone has done: *I was very touched by all the cards my friends sent me when I was in hospital.* ○ [+ that] *He was touched* ***that*** *you remembered his birthday.* ➲See also **touched**.
touching /'tʌtʃ.ɪŋ/ *adj* making you feel sadness, sympathy, etc: *a touching story* ○ *The way she looked after her little sister was really touching.* **touchingly** /'tʌtʃ.ɪŋ.li/ *adv*
touch [ABILITY] /tʌtʃ/ *noun* [U] an ability to do things in the stated, especially positive, way: *He has a deft touch with tricky painting jobs.* ○ *She gave the job her own special/magic/professional/personal touch.* ○ *I admire her lightness/sureness of touch as a cook.* ○ *He used to be a good writer but I think he's* ***losing*** *his touch.*
touch [SMALL AMOUNT] /tʌtʃ/ *noun* **1** [S] a small amount: *"Would you like milk?" "Just* ***a*** *touch."* ○ *There was a touch* ***of*** *irony/humour in her voice.* **2** [C] *INFORMAL* To show that an illness is not too serious, you can say you have had a touch of it: *I've had a touch of flu/hay fever.* **3** [C] a small addition or detail which makes something better: *The speech had several comic touches.* ○ *Using a sailing ship as the company badge was a touch* ***of genius*** (= a good/clever idea or action). ○ *The flowers on the table provided the* ***finishing*** *touch.*
• **a touch** slightly: *The weather has turned a touch too cold for my liking.*
touch [SPORT] /tʌtʃ/ *noun* [U] the area outside either of the long edges of the space on which football and similar games are played: *Playing for safety, he kicked the ball* ***into*** *touch.* ➲See also **touchline**.

PHRASAL VERBS WITH **touch**

▲ **touch down** *phrasal verb* When an aircraft touches down, it lands. ➲See also **touchdown** LANDING.
▲ **touch** ***sth*** **off** *phrasal verb* [M] to cause a violent or difficult series of events to suddenly begin: *The plans for a new airport have touched off a storm of protest.*
▲ **touch on/upon** ***sth*** *phrasal verb* to mention a subject briefly when speaking or writing about another subject: *The talk was about educational opportunities for adults, and the speaker also touched upon sources of finance.*

T

▲ **touch** *sth* **up** IMPROVE *phrasal verb* [M] to improve something by making small changes or additions: *She touched up her lipstick and brushed her hair.* ○ *We thought the photo had probably been touched up, because he looked so much younger in it.*

▲ **touch** *sb* **up** TOUCH SEXUALLY *UK phrasal verb* [M] (*US* **feel** *sb* **up**) INFORMAL to touch someone's body in a sexual way without their permission: *She claimed that he had tried to touch her up.*

touchdown LANDING /ˈtʌtʃ.daʊn/ *noun* [C] the landing of an aircraft or of some types of spacecraft: *One of the plane's tyres burst on touchdown.* ⊃See also **touch down**.

touchdown FOOTBALL /ˈtʌtʃ.daʊn/ *noun* [C] **1** (in rugby) the act of scoring points by putting the ball down on the ground behind the other team's goal posts **2** (in American football) the act of scoring points by carrying the ball across the other team's goal line or throwing the ball so that it is caught by a member of your team who is across the other team's goal line

touché /tuːˈʃeɪ/ *exclamation* used to admit that someone has made a good point against you in an argument or discussion: *"You say we should support British industries, but you always drink French wines." "Touché."*

touched /tʌtʃt/ *adj* [after v] OLD-FASHIONED INFORMAL behaving in an unusual and strange way: *You must think I'm a bit touched, hanging around in graveyards.* ⊃See also **touched** at **touch** INFLUENCE.

,**touch 'football** *noun* [U] *US* an informal type of football in which play stops if a player puts their hand onto the person who has the ball

touching /ˈtʌtʃ.ɪŋ/ *adj* ⊃See at **touch** INFLUENCE.

touchline *UK* /ˈtʌtʃ.laɪn/ *noun* [C] (*US* **sideline**) one of the two lines marking the long edges of the area in which particular games, such as football, are played: *She spends her Saturday afternoons standing on the touchline, watching her boyfriend play rugby.*

touchpaper /ˈtʌtʃˌpeɪ.pəʳ/ ⓤ /-pɚ/ *noun* [C] a small piece of paper on one end of a firework, which you light in order to start the firework burning: *The instructions on the fireworks said "Light the blue touchpaper, and stand well clear."*

touchstone /ˈtʌtʃ.stəʊn/ ⓤ /-stoʊn/ *noun* [C] an established standard or principle by which something is judged: *Until relatively recently, the Japanese car industry was the touchstone of international success.*

Touch-Tone /ˈtʌtʃ.təʊn/ ⓤ /-toʊn/ *adj* TRADEMARK describes a telephone which produces different sounds when the different buttons with numbers on them are pressed: *You can call your bank and perform a transaction using a Touch-Tone phone.*

touch-type /ˈtʌtʃ.taɪp/ *verb* [I] to use a keyboard without looking at the keys

touchy /ˈtʌtʃ.i/ *adj* **1** easily offended or upset: *You have to be careful what you say to Kevin – he's rather touchy.* ○ *She's very touchy about the fact that her husband has been married before.* **2** needing to be dealt with carefully: *This is a touchy subject/issue/point, so we'd better avoid it.* **touchily** /ˈtʌtʃ.ɪ.li/ *adv* **touchiness** /ˈtʌtʃ.ɪ.nəs/ *noun* [U] *Everyone is aware of the touchiness of the situation* (= that it needs to be dealt with carefully).

touchy-feely /ˌtʌtʃ.iˈfiː.li/ *adj* INFORMAL caring and physically affectionate, especially by touching and holding people more than is usual, often in a way that makes other people uncomfortable: *a touchy-feely approach/style* ○ *She's one of those touchy-feely people, always putting her hand on your arm while she's talking to you.*

tough STRONG /tʌf/ *adj* **1** strong; not easily broken or weakened or defeated: *These toys are made from tough plastic.* ○ *Children's shoes need to be tough.* ○ *You have to be tough to be successful in politics.* ○ INFORMAL *Their lawyer is a real tough customer/nut* (= person). **2** strong and determined: *Tough new safety standards have been introduced for cars.* ○ *There have been calls for tougher controls/restrictions on what newspapers are allowed to print.* ○ *After some tough bargaining, we finally agreed on a deal.* ○ *I think it's time the police got tougher on/with* (= treated more severely) *people who*

drink and drive. ○ *The government is continuing to take a tough line on terrorism.* **3** describes food that is difficult to cut or eat: *This steak is very tough.* ○ *These apples have tough skins.*

● (**as**) **tough as old boots** very strong, and not easily weakened: *He might be in his eighties but he's tough as old boots, that man.*

● (**as**) **tough as old boots** (*US ALSO* (**as**) **tough as shoe leather**) INFORMAL describes food that is very difficult to cut or eat

toughen /ˈtʌf.ᵊn/ *verb* [T] to make something or someone tough, strong, or stronger: *The UN announced its intentions to toughen sanctions still further.* ○ *The government wants to toughen (up) the existing drug laws/controls.* ○ *His time in the army certainly toughened him up.* ○ *Car windows are usually made from toughened glass.*

toughly /ˈtʌf.li/ *adv* (= strongly) *made.* ○ *The newspaper published a toughly worded article about racist behaviour.* **toughness** /ˈtʌf.nəs/ *noun* [U] *She has a reputation for toughness* (= being strong and determined).

tough DIFFICULT /tʌf/ *adj* difficult to do or to deal with: *They've had an exceptionally tough life.* ○ *They will be a tough team to beat.* ○ *The company is going through a tough time at the moment.* ○ *We've had to make some very tough decisions.* ○ *My boss has given me a tough job/assignment.* ○ *Many homeless people are facing a tough winter.*

● **It's tough at the top.** HUMOROUS SAYING used to mean that people in important positions have a lot of advantages and get a lot of benefits: *"The managing director always flies first class." "It's tough at the top, isn't it?"*

toughie, toughy /ˈtʌf.i/ *noun* [C] INFORMAL a difficult question or problem: *That last question was a real toughie.* **toughly** /ˈtʌf.li/ *adv* *We live in a toughly competitive world.* **toughness** /ˈtʌf.nəs/ *noun* [U] *They can't face the toughness of the competition.*

tough VIOLENT /tʌf/ *adj* likely to be violent or to contain violence; not kind or pleasant: *a tough neighbourhood* ○ *Many of the country's toughest criminals are held in this prison.*

tough /tʌf/ *noun* [C] (*ALSO* **toughie**) MAINLY US OR OLD-FASHIONED INFORMAL a violent person: *Bands of armed toughs roamed the city.* ⊃See also **toughie** at **tough** DIFFICULT.

tough UNLUCKY /tʌf/ *adj* INFORMAL **1** unlucky: *"I've been told I've got to work late today because I'm very behind on my work." "Oh, tough luck!"/(UK) "Oh, that's a bit tough!"* ○ *It's tough on Geoff that he's going to miss the party.* **2** sometimes used to show that you have no sympathy for someone's problems or difficulties: *"I haven't got any money left." "Well, (that's just) tough – you shouldn't have spent it all on cigarettes."*

● **tough luck** INFORMAL (OFFENSIVE **tough shit**) said to show that you have no sympathy for someone's problems or difficulties: *"They lost a lot of money on their investment." "Tough luck – they should have been more careful."*

tough /tʌf/ *verb*

▲ **tough** *sth* **out** *phrasal verb* [M] INFORMAL to deal with a difficult period or situation without becoming any less certain or determined in your plans or opinions: *It's a difficult situation, but if we can just tough it out, things are bound to get better soon.*

,**tough 'love** [U] when people intentionally do not show too much kindness to a person who has a problem so that the person will start to solve their own problem

toupée /ˈtuː.peɪ/ ⓤ /-ˈ-/ *noun* [C] a piece of artificial hair worn by a man to cover part of his head where there is no hair

tour /tʊəʳ/ /tɔːʳ/ ⓤ /tʊr/ *noun* **1** [C] a visit to a place or area, especially one during which you look round the place or area and learn about it: *We went on a guided tour of/(UK ALSO) round the cathedral/museum/factory.* ○ *A bus took us on a sightseeing tour of the city.* ○ *a tour guide* **2** [C] a journey made for pleasure, especially as a holiday, visiting several different places in an area: *a cycling tour of Provence* ○ *They've just come back from a tour of/(UK ALSO) round Devon and Cornwall.* ○ *Tour operators* (= companies which arrange holidays for people) *have reported a drop in bookings.* **3** [C or U] a

T

planned visit to several places in a country or area made for a special purpose, such as by a politician, sports team or group of entertainers: *a lecture/concert tour* ○ *The Queen is* ***making*** *a two-week tour* ***of*** *Australia.* ○ *She is performing in Birmingham tonight, on the third* ***leg of*** (= stage of) *her* ***nationwide*** *tour.* ○ *The England cricket team is currently* ***on*** *tour in Pakistan.*

tour /tʊəʳ/ /tɔːʳ/ [US] /tʊr/ *verb* **1** [I or T] to go on a tour somewhere: [+ prep] *We spent a month touring* ***(around/round/in)*** *Kenya.* ○ *The New Zealand team will be touring* ***(in)*** *Europe this winter.* ○ *The President toured US military bases yesterday.* ○ *The band are currently touring to promote their new album.* **2** [T] If a play tours a particular area, it is performed in several places there: *The play will be performed first in London, and will then tour the rest of the country.* **touring** /ˈtʊə.rɪŋ/ /ˈtɔː.rɪŋ/ [US] /ˈtʊr.ɪŋ/ *adj* [before n] *a touring opera* ***company***

ˌtour de ˈforce *noun* [S] an achievement or performance which shows great skill and attracts admiration: *a technical/musical/political tour de force* ○ *The painting/book/film is a tour de force.*

Tourette's syndrome /tʊəˈrets,sɪn.drəʊm/ [US] /tʊˈrets-ˌsɪn.droʊm/ *noun* [U] a rare illness of the brain in which the sufferer swears, makes noises and moves in a way that they cannot control

tourism /ˈtʊə.rɪ.zᵊm/ /ˈtɔː-/ [US] /ˈtʊr.ɪ-/ *noun* [U] the business of providing services such as transport, places to stay or entertainment for people who are on holiday: *Tourism is Venice's main industry.* ○ *These beautiful old towns have remained relatively untouched by tourism.*

tourist /ˈtʊə.rɪst/ /ˈtɔː-/ [US] /ˈtʊr.ɪst/ *noun* [C] **1** someone who visits a place for pleasure and interest, usually while they are on holiday: *Millions of tourists visit Rome every year.* ○ *Hordes* (= very large groups) *of tourists flock to the Mediterranean each year.* ○ *Disneyworld is one of Florida's major tourist* ***attractions.*** ○ *The island is very busy during the tourist* ***season.*** **2** *UK* a member of a sports team who is travelling from place to place in a foreign country, playing games: *The West Indies easily defeated the tourists.*

touristy /ˈtʊə.rɪ.sti/ /ˈtɔː-/ [US] /ˈtʊr.ɪ-/ *adj* DISAPPROVING describes a place which is unattractive because a lot of tourists visit it and it is full of things for them to buy and do: *This used to be an attractive seaside town, but now it's become very touristy.*

ˈtourist ˌclass *noun* [U] the ordinary travelling conditions passengers on a plane or ship get when they buy the cheapest tickets

ˈtourist ˌoffice *noun* [C] an office that supplies information to people who are visiting an area for pleasure or interest: *The local tourist* ***information*** *office provides a free map of the region.*

ˈtourist ˌtrap *noun* [C] DISAPPROVING a crowded place which provides entertainment and things to buy for tourists, often at high prices

tournament /ˈtʊə.nə.mənt/ /ˈtɔː-/ [US] /ˈtɝː-/ *noun* [C] (*US* ALSO **tourney**) a competition for teams or individual players in which a series of games is played, and the winners of each game play against each other until only one winner is left: *a tennis/chess/golf tournament* ○ *They were defeated in the first* ***round of*** *the tournament.*

tourniquet /ˈtʊə.nɪ.keɪ/ /ˈtɔː-/ [US] /ˈtɝː.nɪ.kɪt/ *noun* [C] a strip of cloth which is tied tightly round an injured arm or leg to stop it bleeding: *If it continues to bleed, you may have to* ***apply*** *a tourniquet* ***to*** *the limb.*

ˌtour (of ˈduty) *noun* [C] a period of time which someone, especially a soldier or an official, spends working in a foreign country: *The soldiers have just completed a six-month tour* ***in*** *the Philippines.*

tousled /ˈtaʊ.zḷd/ *adj* describing or having hair that looks untidy, as if it has been rubbed: *Naomi stood in front of them, her face flushed, her* ***hair*** *tousled.* ○ *He came to breakfast, all tousled, in last night's clothes.*

tout [MAKE KNOWN] /taʊt/ *verb* **1** [T] to advertise, make known or praise something or someone repeatedly, especially as a way of encouraging their sale, popularity or development: *As an education minister, she has been touting these ideas for some time.* ○ *He is being widely touted* ***as*** *the next leader of the Social Democratic party.* ○ *Several insurance companies are now touting their* ***services/wares*** *on local radio.* **2** [I] to repeatedly try to persuade people to buy your goods or services: *There were hundreds of taxis at the airport, all touting* ***for*** *business/custom.*

tout [SELL UNOFFICIALLY] *UK* /taʊt/ *verb* [T] (*US* **scalp**) DISAPPROVING to sell tickets for something such as a sports game or theatre performance unofficially, usually at a much higher price than the official price: *£30 seats for the match were being touted* ***for*** *£500.*

tout *UK* /taʊt/ *noun* [C] (*US* **scalper**) DISAPPROVING a person who touts tickets: *Britain's best-known* ***ticket*** *tout once boasted that he could get you tickets for anything.*

tow /təʊ/ [US] /toʊ/ *verb* [T] to pull a car, boat, etc. along, using a rope or a chain attached to another vehicle or boat: *You shouldn't drive fast when your car is towing a caravan.* ○ *The road was closed while the vehicles that had been involved in the accident were towed* ***away/off.*** ○ *The damaged boat was towed to safety.* ➲See also **tow *sth* away**.

tow /təʊ/ [US] /toʊ/ *noun* **give *sb/sth* a tow** to pull someone's vehicle using a rope or chain attached to your vehicle: *When my car broke down, a police car gave me a tow to the nearest garage.*

• **on tow** *UK* (*US* **in tow,** *AUS* ALSO **under tow**) being pulled along: *The car in front of us is on tow – that's why we're going so slowly.* ○ *The damaged boat drifted for days before it was finally* ***taken*** *in tow.*

• **in tow** INFORMAL If you go somewhere with a particular person in tow, they are with you: *She arrived at the party, with a tall, silver-haired man in tow.*

▲ **tow *sth* away** *phrasal verb* [often passive] to lift a vehicle that has been parked illegally onto an official truck and take it to a place from which you have to pay to collect it: *You're not allowed to park here – your car will be towed* ***away.***

towards [MOVEMENT] *MAINLY UK* /təˈwɔːdz/ [US] /tʊˈwɔːrdz/ *prep* (*MAINLY US* **toward**) in the direction of, or closer to someone or something: *She stood up and walked towards him.* ○ *He leaned towards his wife and whispered, "Can we go home soon?"* ○ *She kept glancing towards the telephone.* ○ *The country seems to be drifting towards war.* ○ *There is a trend towards healthier eating among all sectors of the population.*

towards [RELATION] *MAINLY UK* /təˈwɔːdz/ [US] /tʊˈwɔːrdz/ *prep* (*MAINLY US* **toward**) in relation to something or someone: *They've always been very friendly towards me.* ○ *There has been a change in government policy towards energy efficiency.* ○ *He feels a lot of anger/hostility/antagonism/animosity towards his father.* ○ *A lot of people think that most newspapers are biased towards one particular political party.*

towards [POSITION] *MAINLY UK* /təˈwɔːdz/ [US] /tʊˈwɔːrdz/ *prep* (*MAINLY US* **toward**) near to, just before or around a time or place: *Our seats were towards the back of the theatre.* ○ *I often get hungry towards the middle of the morning.* ○ *We're getting towards winter and it's getting dark earlier.*

towards [PURPOSE] /təˈwɔːdz/ [US] /tʊˈwɔːrdz/ *prep* (*MAINLY US* **toward**) *MAINLY UK* for the purpose of buying or achieving something: *I'm saving up to buy a car, and Dad has given me some money towards it.* ○ *Would you like to make a contribution* (= give some money) *towards a present for Linda?* ○ *The work that students do during the term counts towards their final grade.*

tow-away /ˈtəʊ.ə.weɪ/ [US] /ˈtoʊ-/ *noun* [C usually sing] an act of a car being officially removed from a place where it has been illegally left: *I couldn't find a parking meter, so I decided to park illegally and risk a tow-away.* ○ *This part of town is a tow-away* ***area/zone*** (= one in which cars left illegally will be removed).

ˈtow ˌbar *noun* [C] a bar fixed to the back of a car which is used for pulling a CARAVAN or TRAILER

towel /taʊəl/ *noun* [C] a piece of cloth or paper used for drying someone or something that is wet: *She came downstairs after her shower, wrapped in a towel.* ○ *The*

T

school provides ***paper*** *towels for the children to dry their hands on.*

• **throw/chuck in the towel** to stop trying to do something because you have become aware that you cannot succeed: *Three of the original five candidates for the Democratic presidential nomination have now thrown in the towel.*

towel /taʊəl/ *verb* [T] **-ll-** or *US USUALLY* **-l-** to rub something with a towel to dry it: [+ adj] *She towelled her hair dry.* ○ [R] *After our swim, we quickly towelled ourselves* ***down*** *and then went to play tennis.*

towelling, *US USUALLY* **toweling** /ˈtaʊə.lɪŋ/ [US] /ˈtaʊə-/ *noun* [U] a soft thick cloth used especially for making towels or clothing: *a towelling bath robe* ○ *towelling socks*

towelette /ˌtaʊəˈlet/ *noun* [C] a small square of wet paper, used especially for cleaning your face and hands with when there is no water available: *On the plane, the flight attendant brings you a towelette after your meal.*

ˈtowel ˌrail *UK noun* [C] (*US* **towel rack**) a horizontal bar on the wall, or a frame with a horizontal bar, used to hang towels on: *We have a heated towel rail in our bathroom.*

tower [STRUCTURE] /taʊəʳ/ [US] /taʊɚ/ *noun* [C] **1** a tall narrow structure, often square or circular, which either forms part of a building or stands alone: *the Eiffel tower* ○ *There's a clock on the* ***church*** *tower.* ○ *He works in an* ***office*** *tower in downtown San Francisco.* **2** a tall, usually metal structure used for broadcasting: *a radio/transmission tower*

• **a tower of strength** a person who gives you help and support when you are in a difficult situation: *Polly was a tower of strength* ***to*** *me when I was ill.*

tower [BE TALL] /taʊəʳ/ [US] /taʊɚ/ *verb* [I usually + adv or prep] to be very tall or large, usually in an impressive way: *We turned the corner and there was the cathedral, towering in front of us.* ➲See also **tower above/over**.

towering /ˈtaʊə.rɪŋ/ [US] /ˈtaʊɚ.ɪŋ/ *adj* **1** *LITERARY* very high and impressive: *the towering walls of the Acropolis* **2** very great: *a towering figure in the British art world* ○ *Laurence Olivier's Othello was a towering performance.*

PHRASAL VERBS WITH **tower** ▼

▲ **tower above/over** ***sb/sth*** *phrasal verb* to be very tall in comparison with someone or something else: *Canary Wharf towers above the Dockland area of London.* ○ *Although he's only 12, David towers over his mother.*

▲ **tower above/over** ***sth*** *phrasal verb* to be much bigger and more successful that another thing of the same type: *One computer manufacturer towers above all the rest.*

ˈtower ˌblock *UK noun* [C] (*US* **high-rise**) a tall building divided into apartments or offices

town /taʊn/ *noun* **1** [C or U] a place where people live and work, containing many houses, shops, places of work, places of entertainment, etc., and usually larger than a village but smaller than a city: *a seaside/industrial town* ○ *a fishing/mining town* ○ *They live in a sleepy provincial town.* ○ *He was born in the small town* ***of*** *Castleford, in Yorkshire.* ○ *We stayed in the best hotel* ***in*** *town.* ○ *the main road* ***into/out of*** *town* ➲See also **downtown**; **home town**; **uptown**. **2 the town** a town or city, rather than the countryside: *I've always lived in the town.* **3** [U] *MAINLY US* the place where you live or work: *I'm leaving town for a few days.* ○ *Barbara is* ***out of*** *town on business this week.* **4** [S or U] the part of a town where the main shops are: *I'm going* ***into/to*** *town at lunchtime to do some shopping.* ○ *I met Charles while I was* ***in*** *town.* **5** [U] the most important city or town in a country or area: *We went* ***up to*** *town to see a play.* ○ *Many people go* ***into*** *town* (= New York) *from New Jersey on weekends.*

town /taʊn/ *group noun* [C] the people who live in the town: *The* ***whole*** *town is/are hoping that their football team will win the final tomorrow.*

• **go to town** to do something in a detailed and enthusiastic way, especially by spending a lot of money: *They've really gone to town* ***on*** *their wedding.*

• **on the town** enjoying yourself by going to places of entertainment in a town or city: *I was* ***out*** *on the town/I had* ***a night*** *on the town last night, and I'm exhausted!*

ˌtown ˈcouncil *noun* [C] the local government of a town: *Mr Dunn has been a* ***member of*** *the town council for many years.* **ˌtown ˈcouncillor** *noun* [C]

ˌtown ˈhall *noun* [C] a building in which local government officials and employees work and have meetings

ˈtown ˌhouse *noun* [C] *UK* a house in a town or city, usually a comfortable, expensive one in a fashionable area: *a beautiful four-storey town house*

townhouse /ˈtaʊn.haʊs/ *noun* [C] *US* a house which is joined to another house

townie /ˈtaʊ.ni/ *noun* [C] **1** (*ALSO* **towny**) *INFORMAL DISAPPROVING* a person who lives in a town where there is a college but who is not involved with the college **2** *UK* (*US* **city slicker**) a person who lives in a town, and has no experience of or knowledge about living in the countryside: *A couple of townies walked into the village pub, looking very out of place in their smart suits.*

ˌtown ˈmeeting *noun* [C] *US* a gathering of the people who live or pay taxes in a town, for the purpose of governing the town

ˌtown ˈplanning *noun* [U] the planning of the way in which towns and cities are built in order to make them pleasant to live in: *He studied town planning at college.* **ˌtown ˈplanner** *noun* [C] *The town planners made a real mess of the riverside area during the 1960s.*

township /ˈtaʊn.ʃɪp/ *noun* [C] **1** a South African town where only blacks lived during APARTHEID: *a black township* ○ *the township* ***of*** *Soweto* ○ *township music* **2** in the US and Canada, a unit of local government consisting of a town and the area surrounding it: *the township* ***of*** *Dulce, New Mexico* ○ *Princeton Township*

townspeople /ˈtaʊnzˌpiː.pl̩/ *plural noun* (*ALSO* **townsfolk**) **1** people who live in a particular town, considered as a group: *The townspeople have raised $9 million for a new museum.* **2** people who live in towns rather than in the countryside

towpath /ˈtəʊ.pɑːθ/ [US] /ˈtoʊ.pæθ/ *noun* [C] a path which goes along the side of a river or a canal, and which was used in the past by horses pulling boats: *We walked* ***along*** *the towpath.*

towrope /ˈtəʊ.rəʊp/ [US] /ˈtoʊ.roʊp/ *noun* [C] a rope or chain which a vehicle uses to pull another vehicle

ˈtow ˌtruck *noun* [C] (*UK ALSO* **breakdown truck**) a truck with special equipment for pulling a vehicle that is not working to a place where it can be repaired ➲See picture **Cars and Trucks** on page Centre 13

toxaemia, *MAINLY US* **toxemia** /tɒkˈsiː.mi.ə/ [US] /tɑːk-/ *noun* [U] *SPECIALIZED* the condition of having a poisonous substance or substances in your blood

toxic /ˈtɒk.sɪk/ [US] /ˈtɑːk-/ *adj* poisonous: *toxic waste/chemicals/effluent* **toxicity** /tɒkˈsɪs.ɪ.ti/ [US] /tɑːkˈsɪs.ə.t̬i/ *noun* [U] *Tests of the chemical have shown that it has a high level of toxicity.* ○ *The toxicity* ***of*** *the drug severely limits its use.*

toxicology /ˌtɒk.sɪˈkɒl.ə.dʒi/ [US] /ˌtɑːk.sɪˈkɑː.lə-/ *noun* [U] the scientific study of the characteristics and effects of poisons

toxicologist /ˌtɒk.sɪˈkɒl.ə.dʒɪst/ [US] /ˌtɑːk.sɪˈkɑː.lə-/ *noun* [C] a person who studies or knows a lot about poisons

toxin /ˈtɒk.sɪn/ [US] /ˈtɑːk-/ *noun* [C] a poisonous substance, especially one which is produced by bacteria and which causes disease

toy [GAME] /tɔɪ/ *noun* [C] **1** an object for children to play with: *a cuddly/soft/stuffed toy* ○ *a clockwork/wind-up toy* ○ *a toy train/farm/soldier* ○ *UK toy bricks (US blocks)* ○ *Put your toys away now – it's time for bed.* ○ *Leave daddy's camera alone – it isn't a toy!* **2** an object which is used by an adult for amusement rather than for serious use: *His latest toy is a mobile phone.* ○ *She has several* ***executive*** *toys on her desk.*

toy [SMALL] /tɔɪ/ *adj* [before n] belonging or relating to a very small breed of dog that is kept as a pet: *a toy poodle/spaniel*

toy /tɔɪ/ *verb*

PHRASAL VERBS WITH **toy** ▼

▲ **toy with** ***sth*** [CONSIDER] *phrasal verb* to consider something or doing something, but not in a very serious way, and without making a decision: *We're toying with **the idea** of going to Peru next year.*

▲ **toy with *sb/sth*** *phrasal verb* OLD-FASHIONED to not care seriously about someone or about their feelings, especially during a romantic friendship

▲ **toy with *sth*** [TOUCH] *phrasal verb* to touch an object or move it around with your hand, without any purpose but while thinking about something else: *She just toyed with her salad.* ○ *He toyed nervously with a button on his jacket as he was speaking.*

'toy ˌboy, toyboy *noun* [C] INFORMAL a young man who is an older woman's lover or partner: *Pam turned up at the Hampsons' party with her new toy boy.*

TPTB, tptb INTERNET ABBREVIATION FOR the powers that be: used when you are referring to people who have authority and control: *If it were up to me, I'd say yes, but I'll have to check with TPTB.*

trace [FIND] /treɪs/ *verb* [T] **1** to find someone or something that was lost: *The police are trying to trace the mother of a newborn baby found abandoned outside a hospital.* ○ *Attempts to trace **the whereabouts of** a man seen leaving the scene of the crime have so far been unsuccessful.* ○ *Their missing daughter was finally traced **to*** (= found in) *Manchester.* **2** to find the origin of something: *The phone company were unable to trace the call.* ○ *No one has yet been able to trace the source of the rumour.* **3** to discover the cause or origin of something by examining the way in which it has developed: *The outbreak of food poisoning was traced **to** some contaminated shellfish.* ○ *The practice of giving eggs at Easter can be traced **back to** festivals in ancient China.* ○ *Rivalries between the gangs can be traced **back to*** (= first happened in) *the 1950s in some black and Hispanic neighbourhoods.* **4** to describe the way in which something has developed: *The film traces the events leading up to the Russian Revolution in 1917.*

trace /treɪs/ *noun* **1** [C or U] a sign that something has happened or existed: *He attempted to cover up all the traces **of** his crime.* ○ *When she moved out, she **left** no trace **of** having been there.* ○ *My wallet has been missing for several days and I can't find any trace **of** it.* ○ *He seems to have vanished **without** (a) trace* (= No one knows where he is). **2** [C] an act of finding information about something electronically, or the record of the information found in this way: *The phone company **put** a trace on the call.*

traceable /'treɪ.sə.bl̩/ *adj* possible to trace: *In theory, most telephone calls should be traceable.* ○ *His medical problems were shown to be traceable **to*** (= to have been caused by) *his having been exposed to dangerous chemicals.*

trace [DRAW] /treɪs/ *verb* [T] **1** to copy a drawing or pattern, etc. by drawing over its lines through a thin piece of transparent paper: *Did you draw this picture yourself, or did you trace it?* ○ *She learnt to write her name by tracing **out** the letters.* **2** to draw a shape by showing the main or outer lines: *The child was tracing patterns **in/on** the sand with a stick.*

tracing /'treɪ.sɪŋ/ *noun* [C] a copy of a drawing or pattern made by drawing over it through a piece of thin transparent paper: *He made a tracing **of** the picture.*

trace [SLIGHT AMOUNT] /treɪs/ *noun* [C] a very slight amount: *Traces **of** drugs were found in his blood.* ○ *There is just a trace **of** grey in his hair.* ○ *She speaks English without the slightest trace **of** an accent.* ○ *There was the faintest trace **of** a smile on her lips.* ○ *"How wonderful!" she said, without any trace **of** sarcasm.*

'trace ˌelement *noun* [C] one of several types of simple chemical substance that is necessary for healthy growth and development, and which exists in animals and plants in small amounts

tracer /'treɪ.səʳ/ Ⓤⓢ /-sɚ/ *noun* [C] a bullet which leaves a line of flame or smoke behind it when it is fired, so that you can see the direction it has taken: *Tracer **bullets** streaked through the sky.* ○ *The sky was bright with tracer **fire**.*

trachea /trə'kiː.ə/ Ⓤⓢ /'treɪ.ki.ə/ *noun* [C] SPECIALIZED **windpipe**

'tracing ˌpaper *noun* [U] thin transparent paper which you use for copying a picture by putting it on top of the picture and drawing over its lines

track [PATH] /træk/ *noun* **1** [C] a path or rough road which is made of earth rather than having a surface covered with stone or other material: *The house is at the end of a dirt/an unmade track.* **2** [C or U] the pair of long metal bars fixed on the ground at an equal distance from each other, along which trains travel: *a 10-mile stretch of track* ○ *Passengers are requested not to walk across the tracks.* **3** [C or U] the direction in which someone's job or education develops: *She was a lawyer, but then she changed track completely and became a doctor.*

• **get off the track** to start talking about something that is not part of what you should be talking about: *I think we're getting off the track here – we're supposed to be discussing our advertising campaign.*

• **on track** making progress and likely to succeed: *They're on track **to** make record profits.*

track [MARKS] /træk/ *noun* [C usually pl] **1** a mark or line of marks left on the ground or on another surface by an animal, person or vehicle which has moved over it, showing the direction they moved in: *Police found tyre tracks in the mud.* ○ *The hunters followed the tracks **of** the deer for hours.* ○ *The burglars were careful not to **leave** any tracks behind them.* **2** the direction which something has taken or will take through the air: *People living in the track **of** the hurricane have been advised to leave their homes until it has passed.* **3** the way in which a thought or idea has developed or might develop: *I found it difficult to follow the track **of** his argument.*

• **be on the track of *sb/sth*** to be examining marks or pieces of information which show where a person or animal has gone, in order to catch them: *The police are on the track of the killer.*

• **in *your* tracks** in the exact place where you are standing: *He fell dead in his tracks.* ○ *A sudden loud scream **stopped** me **(dead)** in my tracks* (= caused me suddenly to stop what I was doing).

• **keep track** to make certain that you know what is happening or has happened to someone or something: *My sister has had so many different jobs, I find it hard to keep track (**of** what she's doing).* ➲Compare **lose track** at **lose** NOT HAVE.

• **make tracks** INFORMAL to leave somewhere to go home: *It's getting late, Jim – I think we should make tracks.*

track /træk/ *verb* **1** [T] to follow a person or animal by looking for proof that they have been somewhere, or by using electronic equipment: *It's difficult to track an animal over stony ground.* ○ *The military use radar satellites to track targets through clouds and at night.* ○ *The terrorists were tracked **to*** (= found in) *Amsterdam.* ➲See also **backtrack**; **sidetrack**. **2** [T] to record the progress or development of something over a period: *The study tracked the careers of 1226 doctors who trained at the University of Michigan Medical School.* **3** [I] If a television or film camera tracks in a particular direction, it moves along while it is filming: *The film ends with a long tracking **shot** around the deserted house.* **4** [I] SPECIALIZED If a moving part of a recording machine tracks, it gets into the correct position for operating: *Our VCR tracks automatically.*

tracker /'træk.əʳ/ Ⓤⓢ /-ɚ/ *noun* [C] a person who is able to find animals or people by following the marks they leave on the ground as they move over it: *An Aboriginal tracker led them to the place where the plane had crashed.*

track [SPORT] /træk/ *noun* **1** [C] a type of path or road, often in the shape of a ring, which has been specially designed and built for sports events, particularly racing: *an all-weather track* ○ *a dog/horse track* ○ *The runners are now on their final lap of the track.* ➲See also **racetrack**. **2** [U] US a sport in which people compete with each other by running a race on a specially prepared circular path: *With the exception of Jonathan Edwards, Britain had no chance of striking gold on track **and field**.* ○ *a track event*

track [MUSIC] /træk/ *noun* [C] **1** one of several songs or pieces of music on a CD or other musical recording: *The album includes four previously unreleased tracks.* ➲See also **soundtrack**. **2** a part of a magnetic strip onto

T

which sound can be recorded, with several tracks on one magnetic strip: *When a piece of music is recorded, each instrument is recorded separately on a 24- or 48-track tape.*

▲ **track** ***sth/sb*** **down** *phrasal verb* [M] to find something or someone after looking for them in a lot of different places: *He finally managed to track down the book he wanted.*

ˌtrack and ˈfield *noun* [U] (*ALSO* **track**) *US FOR* **athletics** ➲See at **athlete**. ➲See picture **Sports** on page Centre 10

ˈtracker ˌdog *noun* [C] a dog specially trained to help the police find people they are looking for, using their sense of smell: *The body was found after an extensive search by police with tracker dogs.*

ˈtrack eˌvent *noun* [C] a sports event in which people compete with each other by running a race on a specially prepared circular path ➲See also **field event**.

ˈtracking ˌstation *noun* [C] a place where electrical waves are used to follow the direction of objects, such as spacecraft, in space

ˈtrack ˌmeet *noun* [C] *US* a sports competition between two or more teams, involving various different running races and jumping and throwing events

ˈtrack ˌrecord *noun* [C usually sing] all the achievements or failures that someone or something has had in the past: *The school has an impressive/strong track record in getting its students through examinations.*

tracksuit *UK* /ˈtræk.sjuːt/ [US] /-suːt/ *noun* [C] *US* **sweats** a loose top and trousers, worn either by people who are training for a sport or exercising, or as informal clothing ➲See picture **Clothes** on page Centre 6

tract [WRITING] /trækt/ *noun* [C] a short piece of writing, especially on a religious or political subject, which is intended to influence other people's opinions: *a moral/religious/socialist tract* ○ *Have you read John Milton's tracts* ***on*** *divorce?*

tract [LAND] /trækt/ *noun* [C] **1** a large area of land: *The house is surrounded by* ***vast*** *tracts* ***of*** *woodland.* **2** *US* a measured area of land that is used for a particular purpose, such as building houses or digging for oil: *The new company headquarters will be built on a 132-acre tract in Irving.*

tract [TUBE] /trækt/ *noun* [C] a system of connected tubes and organs in the body of a person or an animal, which has a particular purpose: *the* ***urinary/respiratory/digestive*** *tract*

tractable /ˈtræk.tə.bl̩/ *adj FORMAL* easily dealt with, controlled or persuaded: *The problem turned out to be rather less tractable than I had expected.* **tractability** /ˌtræk.təˈbɪl.ɪ.ti/ [US] /-ə.t̬i/ *noun* [U]

ˈtract ˌhouse *noun* [C] *US* one of a large number of very similar-looking houses built on a single area of land

traction [HOLDING] /ˈtræk.ʃən/ *noun* [U] the ability of a wheel or tyre to hold the ground without sliding: *In deep snow, people should use snow tyres on their vehicles to give them better traction.*

traction [PULLING] /ˈtræk.ʃən/ *noun* [U] *SPECIALIZED* **1** the pulling of a heavy load over a surface, or the power used in this: *steam traction* **2** a form of medical treatment which involves using special equipment to pull gently an injured part of the body, especially an arm or leg, for a long period of time: *After her hip operation poor Mira was* ***in/on*** *traction for six weeks.*

T

ˈtraction ˌengine *noun* [C] a large heavy vehicle, operated by steam power, used especially in the past for pulling heavy loads along roads

tractor /ˈtræk.təʳ/ [US] /-tɚ/ *noun* [C] a motor vehicle with large back wheels and thick tyres, which is used on farms for pulling machinery ➲See picture **Cars and Trucks** on page Centre 13

tractor-trailer /ˌtræk.təˈtreɪ.ləʳ/ [US] /-tɚˈtreɪ.lɚ/ *noun* [C] *US FOR* **juggernaut** VEHICLE

trad /træd/ *noun* [U] *UK* **trad (jazz)**

trade [BUYING AND SELLING] /treɪd/ *noun* [U] **1** the activity of buying and selling, or exchanging, goods and/or services between people or countries: *The country's trade* ***in*** *manufactured goods has expanded in the last ten years.* ○ *Seventy per cent of the country's trade is* ***with*** *Europe.* ○ *The two countries have signed a trade* ***agreement*** *for one year only.* ○ *The UK trade* ***deficit*** *widened/narrowed last month.* ○ *The chemical industry has a large and growing trade* ***surplus.*** **2** business activity: *Since the supermarket opened, many small local shops have lost up to 50% of their trade.* ○ *In hot weather, shops do a* ***roaring/brisk*** *trade* ***in*** (= selling a lot of) *cold drinks and ice creams.*

trade /treɪd/ *verb* **1** [I or T; usually + adv or prep] to buy and sell goods or services, especially between countries: *For centuries, Native Americans traded* ***with*** *European settlers.* ○ *The company has been trading* ***in*** *oil for many years.* ○ *The two countries have become close trading* ***partners.*** ○ *Our books are traded right across Asia.* ➲See also **horsetrade**. **2** [I or T] to be bought and sold, or to buy and sell shares, on the STOCK EXCHANGE: *On London's Stock Exchange, 18.5 million* ***shares*** *were traded yesterday.* ○ *Shares in the company traded* ***actively.*** **3** [T] to exchange something, or to stop using or doing something and start using or doing something else instead: *The children traded comics.* ○ [+ two objects] *I'll trade you some of my chocolate* ***for*** *some of your ice cream.* ○ *I wouldn't trade you* ***for*** *the world* (= I do not want a different partner). ➲See also **trade in**. **4** [T] If people trade statements of a particular type, they say or tell them to each other: *We sat around the dinner table, trading stories.* ○ *The two politicians didn't really discuss the issues, they just traded insults.*

trader /ˈtreɪ.dəʳ/ [US] /-dɚ/ *noun* [C] **1** a person who buys and sells things: *a wool/sugar trader* ○ *His father is a* ***market*** *trader, selling fruit and vegetables.* **2** a person who buys and sells company shares or money: *a stock/currency/futures trader* ○ *He is a well-known trader on the floor of the New York Stock Exchange.*

trading /ˈtreɪ.dɪŋ/ *noun* [U] **1** when goods and/or services are bought and sold: *She doesn't approve of* ***Sunday*** *trading* (= shops being open on Sunday). **2** the buying and selling of shares and money: *The stock market moved ahead slightly in active trading today.* ➲See also **insider dealing**.

PHRASAL VERBS WITH **trade** ▼

▲ **trade** ***sth*** **in** *phrasal verb* [M] to give something you own as part of your payment for something you buy, especially a new type of the same item: *He recently traded in his Jeep* ***for*** *a red Mercedes.*

▲ **trade on** ***sth*** *phrasal verb* to use something, especially a characteristic, for your own advantage and usually in an unfair way: *People are always trading on his generosity.* ○ *This kind of advertising trades on people's fears.* ○ *He trades on his good looks.*

▲ **trade up/down** *phrasal verb* to buy something, usually a house or car, that is of higher or lower value than the one you already have: *My car is costing me too much to run, so I'm going to trade down* ***to*** *a cheaper model.*

trade [BUSINESS] /treɪd/ *noun* **1** [C] a particular business or industry: *the* ***building/catering/tourist*** *trade* ○ *the* ***book/car/fur*** *trade* ○ *He worked* ***in*** *the same trade all his life.* **2** **the trade** the people who work in a particular business or industry or in the same one: *People who work* ***in*** *the trade can buy their books at a discount.* ○ *The company only supplies its goods to the (building/catering) trade, not direct to the public.* **3** [C or U] a job, especially one which needs special skill and which involves working with your hands: *After she left school, she went to college to learn a trade.* ○ *He's a carpenter* ***by*** *trade.*

trade /treɪd/ *adj* **trade publication/journal/magazine/paper** a newspaper, etc. produced for people working in a particular business or industry: *a steel industry trade journal*

ˈtrade ˌbalance *noun* [C usually sing] a country's BALANCE OF TRADE ➲See **balance of payments**.

ˈtrade ˌfair *noun* [C] (*US ALSO* **trade show**) a large gathering at which companies show and sell their products and try to increase their business

ˈtrade ˌfigures *plural noun* A country's trade figures are a record of how much the country has paid for goods which it has bought from other countries, compared with how much it has been paid for goods which it has sold to other countries: *The last set of trade figures showed exceptionally strong export growth.*

trade-in /ˈtreɪd.ɪn/ *noun* [C] a method of buying something new by giving an item you own as part of the payment for it: *We got a good trade-in* ***price*** *for our old television.*

trademark [PRODUCT] /ˈtreɪd.mɑːk/ [US] /-mɑːrk/ *noun* [C] a name or a symbol which is put on a product to show that it is made by a particular producer and which cannot be legally used by any other producer: *Velcro is a* ***registered*** *trademark.*

trademark [TYPICAL] /ˈtreɪd.mɑːk/ [US] /-mɑːrk/ *noun* [C] something particularly noticeable that a person typically has or does: *He was wearing one of the brightly coloured ties that are his trademark.* ○ *She gave one of her trademark smiles.*

ˈtrade ˌname *noun* [C] a **brand name**

trade-off /ˈtreɪd.ɒf/ [US] /-ɑːf/ *noun* **1** [C] a situation in which you balance two opposing situations or qualities: *There is a trade-off* ***between*** *doing the job accurately and doing it quickly.* ○ *She said that she'd had to make a trade-off* ***between*** *her job and her family.* **2** [C usually sing] a situation in which you accept something bad in order to have something good: *For some car buyers, lack of space is an acceptable trade-off* ***for*** *a sporty design.*

ˈtrade ˌprice *UK noun* [C] (*US* **wholesale**) the price at which goods are sold to shops by the people who produce them, rather than the price which the customer usually pays in the shop: *I bought my coat direct from the factory* ***at*** *trade price.*

ˈtrade ˌroute *noun* [C] a route, often covering a long distance, that people buying and selling goods habitually used in the past

ˈtrade ˌschool *US noun* [C] (*AUS* **technical school**) a school where students learn skills which involve working with their hands: *At trade school, he learned to be an auto mechanic.*

ˌtrade ˈsecret *noun* [C] **1** a piece of information about a product that is known only to the particular company that makes it: *The exact ingredients of Coca Cola are a trade secret.* **2** *INFORMAL* a piece of information that you are not willing to tell anyone: *My aunt won't tell anyone her age – she says that it's a trade secret.*

tradesman /ˈtreɪdz.mən/ *noun* [C] **1** *MAINLY UK* someone who buys and sells goods, especially someone who owns a shop: *Local tradesmen are objecting to plans for big new out-of-town shopping centre.* **2** someone who works in a trade which needs skill at using your hands, usually in the building industry

tradespeople /ˈtreɪdzˌpiː.pl̩/ *plural noun* people who buy and sell goods, especially people who own a shop

ˌtrade ˈunion *UK noun* [C] (*UK ALSO* **trades union**, *US* **labor union**) an organization that represents the people who work in a particular industry, protects their rights, and discusses their pay and working conditions with employers: *The government's proposals have been strongly criticized by the trade unions.* ○ *The rally was organized by local trade union officials.* ➲See also **the TUC**. **trade unionism** /ˌtreɪdˈjuː.ni.ᵊn.ɪ.zᵊm/ *noun* [U] **trade unionist** /ˌtreɪdˈjuː.ni.ᵊn.ɪst/ *noun* [C]

ˈtrading esˌtate *noun* [C] *UK* an **industrial estate**

ˈtrading ˌpost *noun* [C] a small place, especially in the past, far from other places in which people live, where goods can be bought and sold or exchanged: *New York was originally a Dutch trading post.*

tradition /trəˈdɪʃ.ᵊn/ *noun* [C or U] a belief, principle or way of acting which people in a particular society or group have continued to follow for a long time, or all of these in a particular society or group: *Fireworks have long been an American tradition on the Fourth of July.* ○ *Switzerland has a* ***long*** *tradition* ***of*** *neutrality.* ○ [+ that] *There's a tradition* ***in*** *our office* ***that*** *when it's somebody's birthday, they bring in a cake for us all to share.* ○ *We decided to* ***break with*** *tradition (= not behave as usual) this year and go away for Christmas.* ○ *According to tradition, a headless ghost walks through the corridors of the house at night.*

• **in the tradition of *sb/sth*** having characteristics similar to a particular person or thing: *His paintings are in the tradition of those of Bacon and Spencer.*

traditional /trəˈdɪʃ.ᵊn.ᵊl/ /-ˈdɪʃ.nᵊl/ *adj* following or belonging to the customs or ways of behaving that have continued in a group of people or society for a long time without changing: *The villagers retain a strong attachment to their traditional values/customs/beliefs.* ○ *The school uses a combination of modern and traditional methods for teaching reading.* ○ *The dancers were wearing traditional Hungarian dress/costume.* ○ *She's very traditional (in her ideas and opinions).* **traditionally** /trəˈdɪʃ.ᵊn.ᵊl.i/ /-ˈdɪʃ.nᵊl-/ *adv*: *Quaker meetings are traditionally held in silence.* ○ *Traditionally, the company's main markets have been Britain and the US.*

traditionalism /trəˈdɪʃ.ᵊn.ᵊl.ɪ.zᵊm/ /-nᵊl-/ *noun* [U] the belief in, or act of following, traditional ideas and ways of doing things: *The building's design is an interesting blend of traditionalism and modernism.*

traditionalist /trəˈdɪʃ.ᵊn.ᵊl.ɪst/ /-nᵊl-/ *noun* [C] someone who believes in and follows traditional ideas: *Religious traditionalists objected to theories of evolution being taught in schools.* **traditionalist** /trəˈdɪʃ.ᵊn.ᵊl.ɪst/ /-nᵊl-/ *adj*: *She holds traditionalist Muslim views.* ○ *This production of 'Swan Lake' is in traditionalist style.*

ˌtrad (ˈjazz) *UK noun* [U] (*US* **dixieland**) a type of jazz, which was first played in the 1920s, in which the players invent the music as they play it

traduce /trəˈdjuːs/ /-ˈdʒuːs/ [US] /-ˈduːs/ *verb* [T] *FORMAL* to strongly criticize someone, especially in a way that harms their reputation

traffic [VEHICLES] /ˈtræf.ɪk/ *noun* [U] **1** the amount of vehicles moving along roads, or the amount of aircraft, trains or ships moving along a route: *There was* ***heavy/a lot of*** *traffic on the roads this morning.* ○ *We got* ***stuck in*** *traffic for several hours.* ○ *New measures have been introduced to try and ease traffic* ***congestion*** *in the city.* ○ *Five people were injured in a traffic* ***accident*** (= one involving vehicles). ○ ***Air*** *traffic has increased 30% in the last decade.* **2** people or goods transported by road, air, train or ship, as a business: *The airline halved its overseas service because of a sharp reduction in traffic.* ○ *Environmental groups want more* ***passenger*** *and* ***freight*** *traffic moved off the roads and onto trains.*

traffic [TRADE] /ˈtræf.ɪk/ *noun* [U] illegal trade: *to cut down the traffic* ***in drugs****/the* ***drug*** *traffic* ○ *Police are looking for ways of curbing the traffic* ***in*** *guns.* **traffic** /ˈtræf.ɪk/ *verb* [I] **trafficking, trafficked, trafficked** *They were arrested for trafficking* ***in*** *the eggs of protected species of birds.* **trafficking** /ˈtræf.ɪ.kɪŋ/ *noun* [U] *arms/drugs trafficking* **trafficker** /ˈtræf.ɪ.kəʳ/ [US] /-kɚ/ *noun* a person who trades in illegal goods, particularly drugs: ***drug*** *traffickers* ○ *an international* ***arms*** *trafficker*

ˈtraffic ˌcalming *noun* [U] *UK* when raised areas, small ROUNDABOUTS or other similar structures are built onto roads, usually roads where there are houses, so that vehicles are forced to move more slowly along them: *Local residents are demanding that traffic-calming* ***measures*** *are introduced to reduce the number of accidents on the road.*

ˈtraffic ˌcircle *noun* [C] *US FOR* **roundabout** CIRCULAR OBJECT

ˈtraffic ˌcone *noun* [C] a cone-shaped, usually red and white or yellow object used to keep vehicles away from an area of road temporarily, usually because repairs are being done to it: *One lane of the road was closed off by traffic cones.*

ˈtraffic ˌisland *noun* [C] **1** (*ALSO* **island**) a raised area in the middle of a road where people who are crossing the road can wait safely for traffic to go past **2** *US FOR* **central reservation**

ˈtraffic ˌjam *noun* [C] a large number of vehicles close together and unable to move or moving very slowly: *Roadworks have caused traffic jams throughout the city centre.* ○ *I was* ***stuck in*** *a traffic jam for an hour yesterday.*

ˈtraffic ˌlight *noun* [C usually pl] one of a set of red, yellow and green lights which control the movement of vehicles at a point where two or more roads join: *The*

T

police pulled him over for failing to stop at a red traffic light. ○ *Turn left at the traffic lights.* ○ *The traffic lights turned green as we approached the junction.*

ˈtraffic ˌwarden *noun* [C] *UK* someone whose job is to make certain that people do not leave their cars in illegal places: *A traffic warden gave me a ticket for parking on a double yellow line.*

tragedy /ˈtrædʒ.ə.di/ *noun* [C or U] **1** a very sad event or situation, especially one involving death or suffering, or a play or literature about death or suffering: *The pilot averted a tragedy when he succeeded in preventing the plane from crashing.* ○ *Hitler's invasion of Poland led to the tragedy **of** the Second World War.* ○ *His life was touched by hardship and **personal** tragedy.* ○ *They had only recently arrived in London when tragedy **struck** – their son was killed in a traffic accident.* ○ [+ (that)] *It's a tragedy **(that)** so many young people are unable to find jobs.* **2** a play about death or suffering with a sad end, or this type of play generally: *Shakespeare's tragedies include 'Hamlet', 'King Lear' and 'Othello'.* ○ *In Greek tragedy, the role of the chorus is to express the audience's reactions to what is happening in the play.*

tragic /ˈtrædʒ.ɪk/ *adj* **1** very sad, often involving death and suffering: *His friends were deeply shocked and saddened by the tragic **news** of his death.* ○ *The bomb explosion resulted in a tragic loss of life.* ○ *Hospital authorities admitted that a tragic mistake/error had taken place.* ○ ***It** is tragic **that** the theatre has had to close.* **2** belonging or relating to literature about death or suffering: *During his acting career, he has played all Shakespeare's great tragic heroes.* **tragically** /ˈtrædʒ.ɪ.kli/ *adv*: *She died tragically young.* ○ *Tragically, the side-effects of the drug were not discovered until many people had been seriously damaged by it.*

tragicomedy /ˌtrædʒ.ɪˈkɒm.ə.di/ [US] /-ˈkɑː.mə-/ *noun* [C or U] a (type of) play or story which is both sad and amusing **tragicomic** /ˌtrædʒ.ɪˈkɒm.ɪk/ [US] /-ˈkɑː.mɪk/ *adj*

trail [PATH] /treɪl/ *noun* **1** [C] a path through the countryside, often made or used for a particular purpose: *a forest/mountain trail* **2** [C] the smell or series of marks left by a person, animal or thing as it moves along: *The dogs are specially trained to **follow** the trail left by the fox.* ○ *He **left a** trail **of** muddy footprints behind him.* **3** [S] various pieces of information which together show where someone you are searching for has gone: *The police admit that the thieves have **left** no trail for them to follow up.*

• **be on the trail of *sb/sth*** to be searching for someone or something by examining information you find about where they went: *The three men went to the Bahamas, on the trail of a sunken 17th-century galleon full of treasure.*

trail /treɪl/ *verb* [T] to follow the trail of someone or something

trail [COME AFTER] /treɪl/ *verb* **1** [I or T; usually + adv or prep] to (allow something to) move slowly along the ground or through the air or water, after someone or something: *Katherine, your skirt's trailing **in** the mud!* ○ *As the boat moved along, he trailed his hand **in** the water.* **2 be trailing** to be losing to your competitor in a competition: *The Swiss team are trailing **by** 6 points.* ○ *The Nationalist Party is trailing **(behind)** the Liberals in the opinion polls.* **3** [I usually + adv or prep] to move slowly and without energy or enthusiasm: *The delegates trailed **back** into the conference room for the afternoon session.* ○ *After a mile or two the youngest children were trailing **behind**.*

trailing /ˈtreɪ.lɪŋ/ *adj* [before n] describes plants that grow along the ground or over the surface of something: *a trailing rose*

▲ **trail away/off** *phrasal verb* When a person's voice or a similar sound trails away/off, it becomes quieter and less confident and then stops completely: *His voice trailed off as he saw the look on her face.*

ˈtrail ˌblazer *noun* [C] the first person to do something or go somewhere, who shows that it is also possible for other people: *Orville and Wilbur Wright were aviation trail blazers.*

trailer [VEHICLE] /ˈtreɪ.ləʳ/ [US] /-lɚ/ *noun* [C] **1** a vehicle without an engine, often in the form of a flat frame or a container, which is pulled by another vehicle: *The car was **pulling** a trailer with motorcycle on it.* **2** the separate back part of a large truck **3** *US FOR* **caravan** (= wheeled vehicle for living or travelling in)

trailer [ADVERTISEMENT] /ˈtreɪ.ləʳ/ [US] /-lɚ/ *noun* [C] an advertisement for a film, or television or radio programme, consisting of brief parts from it: *I saw a trailer **for** the latest Spielberg film and thought it looked quite interesting.*

ˈtrailer ˌpark *noun* [C] *US FOR* **caravan site**

train [VEHICLE] /treɪn/ *noun* [C] a railway engine connected to carriages for carrying people or wheeled containers for carrying goods: *a goods/freight/passenger train* ○ *the train to/from Bristol* ○ *a train journey/station* ○ *Did you come **by** train?* ○ *She **caught/took** the train to Edinburgh.* ○ *Hurry up, or we'll **miss*** (= arrive too late for) *the train.*

train [PREPARE] /treɪn/ *verb* [I or T] to prepare or be prepared for a job, activity or sport, by learning skills and/or by mental or physical exercise: *She trained **as** a pilot.* ○ [+ to infinitive] *Isn't Michael training **to** be a lawyer?* ○ [R + to infinitive] *I've had to train myself **to** be more assertive at work.* ○ *She trained hard **for** the race, sometimes running as much as 60 miles a week.* ○ *HUMOROUS I'm trying to train my boyfriend **to** do the occasional bit of housework.* **trained** /treɪnd/ *adj*: *I didn't realize Philippa was a trained nurse.* ○ *Are you trained **in** the use of this equipment?* ○ *HUMOROUS "Did I hear you say your children cleared up after the party?" "Oh yes, I've got them **well**-trained!"*

trainee /ˌtreɪˈniː/ *noun* [C] a person who is learning and practising the skills of a particular job: *a trainee dentist/electrician*

trainer /ˈtreɪ.nəʳ/ [US] /-nɚ/ *noun* [C] a person who teaches skills to people or animals and prepares them for a job, activity or sport: *They showed pictures of the horse and its trainer* (= the person who prepared it for its races). ○ *A lot of wealthy people have their own **personal** trainer* (= a person they employ to help them exercise). ➲See also **trainer**.

training /ˈtreɪ.nɪŋ/ *noun* [U] the process of learning the skills you need to do a particular job or activity: *a training course* ○ *a teacher-training college* ○ *New staff **have/receive** a week's training **in** how to use the computers.*

• **be in training for *sth*** to exercise a lot and eat particular food in order to prepare yourself for a competition

• **be good training for *sth*** to be a useful experience that will be helpful when doing a particular thing in the future: *His experience as a teacher was good training for parenthood.*

train [AIM] /treɪn/ *verb* [T usually + adv or prep] *FORMAL* to aim or point a gun, camera, light, etc. at someone or something: *With five guns suddenly trained **on** him, he was understandably nervous.*

train [DIRECT GROWTH] /treɪn/ *verb* [T] to direct the growth of a plant in a particular direction by cutting it and tying it: *The vines were trained **over** an arch, providing shade as well as fruit.*

train [SERIES] /treɪn/ *noun* **1 train of thought/events** a series of connected thoughts or events: *What amazing train of thought led you from Napoleon to global warming?* ○ *The book describes the train of events that led up to the assassination.* **2** [C] a line of animals, people or things moving along together: *a wagon train* ○ *a mule/camel train*

• **put/set *sth* in train** *FORMAL* to start a process: *The reform process was put in train in 1985, by the Liberal government.*

train [PART OF DRESS] /treɪn/ *noun* [C] the part of a long dress that spreads out onto the floor behind: *an elaborate wedding dress with a long train*

trainer *UK* /ˈtreɪ.nəʳ/ [US] /-nɚ/ *noun* [C] (*UK ALSO* **training shoe**, *US* **running shoe**) a type of light comfortable shoe that is suitable for playing sport ➲See picture **Clothes** on page Centre 6

ˈtrain ˌset *noun* [C] a toy train, together with the equipment, toy houses, etc. that go with it

trainspotting /ˈtreɪnˌspɒt.ɪŋ/ [US] /-ˌspɑː.t̬ɪŋ/ *noun* [U] *UK* the activity of watching trains and writing down the numbers that each railway engine has **trainspotter**

/ˈtreɪnˌspɒt.əʳ/ [US] /-ˌspɑːt̬.ɚ/ *noun* [C]

traipse /treɪps/ *verb* [I usually + adv or prep] INFORMAL to walk from one place to another, often feeling tired or bored: *I spent the day traipsing* ***round*** *the shops, but found nothing suitable for her.* ○ *It was awful having the builders traipsing* ***through*** *our home every day.*

trait /treɪt/ *noun* [C] a particular characteristic that can produce a particular type of behaviour: *His sense of humour is one of his better traits.* ○ *Arrogance is a very unattractive* ***personality/character*** *trait.*

traitor /ˈtreɪ.təʳ/ [US] /-t̬ɚ/ *noun* [C] DISAPPROVING a person who is not loyal or stops being loyal to their own country, social class, beliefs, etc: *The leaders of the rebellion were hanged as traitors.* ○ *The Chinese Communist Party* ***branded*** (= called) *Mr Gorbachev 'a traitor* ***to*** *socialism'.* **traitorous** /ˈtreɪ.tᵊr.əs/ [US] /-t̬ɚ-/ *adj* FORMAL DISAPPROVING

trajectory /trəˈdʒek.tᵊr.i/ /-tri/ [US] /-tɚ.i/ *noun* [C] SPECIALIZED the curved path that an object follows after it has been thrown or fired into the air: *the trajectory of a bullet/missile*

• **be on an upward/downward trajectory** to be getting higher or lower: *The Government is now claiming that inflation is on a downward trajectory.*

tram UK /træm/ *noun* [C] (US USUALLY **streetcar,** US ALSO **trolley**) an electric vehicle that transports people, usually in cities, and goes along metal tracks in the road

tramlines [TRACK] /ˈtræm.laɪnz/ *plural noun* two metal tracks set in the road, along which a tram goes

tramlines [SPORT] /ˈtræm.laɪnz/ *plural noun* UK two parallel painted lines along the edge of the playing area used in tennis and BADMINTON: *In doubles, the ball is not out if it lands between the tramlines.*

tramp [WALK] /træmp/ *verb* [I usually + adv or prep; T] to walk, especially long distances or with heavy steps: *to tramp* ***through*** *the forest/undergrowth* ○ *We spent a week tramping the streets of Rome, looking for movie locations.*

tramp /træmp/ *noun* **1** [S] the sound of people all walking together with heavy steps: *The streets echoed with the tramp* ***of*** *soldiers' feet.* **2** [C] a long walk: *The girls* ***went for*** *a tramp* ***through*** *the countryside.*

tramp [POOR PERSON] /træmp/ *noun* [C] a person with no home, job or money who travels around and asks for money from other people

tramp [WOMAN] /træmp/ *noun* [C] US VERY INFORMAL DISAPPROVING a woman who has sex often, with a lot of different partners

trample /ˈtræm.pl/ *verb* [I or T; usually + prep] **1** to step heavily on something or someone, causing damage or injury: *Somebody trampled* ***all over*** *my flowerbeds in the night!* ○ *Eight people were trampled* ***to death*** (= killed) *when the stadium collapsed and the crowd rushed out onto the football pitch.* **2** to act without any respect for someone or something: *She accused the government of trampling* ***on*** *the needs and rights of the ordinary citizen.* ○ *He argues that the Congress and President Clinton trampled the constitutional rights of legal immigrants in the new welfare reform law.*

trampoline /ˈtræm.pᵊl.iːn/ /ˌ--ˈ-/ [US] /ˈ---/ *noun* [C] a piece of sports equipment which you use for jumping on, consisting of a piece of stretchy material joined by springs to a frame **trampolining** /ˈtræm.pᵊl.iː.nɪŋ/ /ˌ--ˈ--/ [US] /ˈ---/ *noun* [U] *Rebecca's main hobby is trampolining.*

trance [MENTAL CONDITION] /trɑːnts/ [US] /trænts/ *noun* [C] a temporary mental condition in which someone is not completely aware of and/or not in control of themselves and of what is happening to them: *First she* ***goes/falls into*** *a deep trance and then the spirit voices start to speak through her.* ○ *When a hypnotist* ***puts*** *you* ***in(to)*** *a trance, you no longer have conscious control of yourself.* ○ *He sat staring out of the window as if* ***in*** *a trance.*

trance [MUSIC] /trænts/ *noun* [U] fast, electronic dance music with a regular beat, keyboards, but usually no singing

tranquil /ˈtræŋ.kwɪl/ [US] /ˈtræn-/ *adj* calm and peaceful and without noise, violence, anxiety, etc: *She stared at the tranquil surface of the water.* ○ *The hotel is in a tranquil rural setting.* ○ *A spasm of pain crossed his normally tranquil features.* **tranquilly** /ˈtræŋ.kwɪ.li/ [US] /ˈtræn-/ *adv* **tranquillity,** US USUALLY **tranquility** /træŋˈkwɪl.ɪ.ti/ [US] /trænˈkwɪl.ə.t̬i/ *noun* [U] *living in* ***peace and tranquillity*** ○ *I love the tranquillity of the countryside.*

tranquillize, US USUALLY **tranquilize,** UK USUALLY **-ise** /ˈtræŋ.kwɪ.laɪz/ [US] /ˈtræn-/ *verb* [T] to make an animal or person become unconscious or calm, especially with a drug: *a tranquillizing drug* ○ *The dogs were tranquillized with a dart gun and taken to a shelter.*

tranquillizer, US USUALLY **tranquilizer,** UK USUALLY **-iser** /ˈtræŋ.kwɪ.laɪ.zəʳ/ [US] /ˈtræn.kwɪ.laɪ.zɚ/ *noun* [C] a drug used to make a person or animal calmer: *She was* ***on*** *tranquillizers for a long time after her son died.*

trans- [ACROSS] /træns-/ /trænz-/ *prefix* across: *a trans-Atlantic flight* ○ *the trans-Alaskan pipeline*

trans- [CHANGED] /træns-/ /trænz-/ *prefix* having changed from one thing to another: *Kate has transformed* (= completely changed the appearance of) *that house since she moved in.* ○ *She is a transsexual* (= She has changed from being a man to a woman).

transact /trænˈzækt/ *verb* [T] FORMAL to do and complete a business activity: *The sale was transacted in conditions of the greatest secrecy.* **transaction** /trænˈzæk.ʃᵊn/ *noun* [C or U] *a business transaction* ○ *Each transaction at the foreign exchange counter seems to take forever.* ○ *We need to monitor the transaction of smaller deals.*

transatlantic /ˌtræn.zətˈlæn.tɪk/ [US] /-zætˈlæn.t̬ɪk/ *adj* crossing the Atlantic ocean, or relating to countries on both sides of the Atlantic Ocean: *transatlantic flights/routes* ○ *a transatlantic telephone call*

transcend /trænˈsend/ *verb* [T] FORMAL to go beyond, rise above or be more important or better than something, especially a limit: *The best films are those which transcend national or cultural barriers.* ○ *The underlying message of the film is that love transcends everything else.* **transcendence** /trænˈsen.dᵊnts/ *noun* [U]

transcendent /trænˈsen.dᵊnt/ *adj* FORMAL greater, better, more important, or going beyond or above all others: *transcendent power/beauty/love* ○ *He describes seeing Stanley Matthews play football as one of the transcendent* ***moments*** *of his life.*

transcendental /ˌtræn.senˈden.tᵊl/ [US] /-t̬ᵊl/ *adj* FORMAL describes an experience, event, object or idea that is extremely special and unusual and cannot be understood in ordinary ways: *a transcendental vision of the nature of God*

ˌtranscendental mediˈtation *noun* [U] a method of calming the mind and becoming relaxed by silently repeating a special word or series of words many times

transcontinental /ˌtrænz.kɒn.tɪˈnen.tᵊl/ /ˌtræns-/ [US] /-kɑːn-/ *adj* crossing a continent: *The transcontinental railway goes from New York in the east to San Francisco in the west.*

transcribe [RECORD] /trænˈskraɪb/ *verb* [T] to record something written, spoken or played by writing it down: *Tape recordings of conversations are transcribed by typists and entered into the database.*

transcript /ˈtræn.skrɪpt/ *noun* [C] an exact written copy of something: *Mysteriously, the transcript* ***of*** *what was said at the trial went missing.*

transcription /trænˈskrɪp.ʃᵊn/ *noun* [U] the process of transcribing something

transcribe [CHANGE] /trænˈskraɪb/ *verb* [T] to change a piece of writing or music into another form, for example into a different writing system or into music for different instruments: *Transcribing the Ethiopian text* ***into*** *the English alphabet was their first task.* ○ *The quintet had been transcribed* ***for*** *clarinet and piano.*

transcription /trænˈskrɪp.ʃᵊn/ *noun* [C] a written representation of words or music: *This is a* ***phonetic transcription of*** *the conversations that were recorded on tape.*

transept /ˈtræn.sept/ *noun* [C] either of the two side parts of a cross-shaped church that are at an angle of 90 degrees to the main part

transfer [MOVE] /trænsˈfɜːʳ/ [US] /ˈtræns.fɝː/ *verb* **-rr- 1** [T] to move someone or something from one place, vehicle, person or group to another: *He has been transferred* ***to*** *a psychiatric hospital.* ○ *She transferred her gun* ***from*** *its shoulder holster* ***to*** *her handbag.* ○ *We were transferred*

T

from one bus **into** *another.* ○ *Police are investigating how £20 million was illegally transferred* ***from/out of*** *the Trust's bank account.* ○ *The aim is to transfer* ***power/control/responsibility to*** *self-governing regional councils.* ○ *I'll be upstairs, so could you transfer my phone calls* (= arrange that I can receive them) ***up*** *there please?* **2** [I or T; usually + adv or prep] to change to a different job, team, place of work, etc., or to make someone do this: *After a year he transferred* ***to*** *University College, Dublin.* ○ *Some very high-profile British players have transferred* ***to*** *clubs abroad.* ○ *He threatened to give up football if his club didn't transfer him* (= sell him to another team). **3** [T] to make something the legal property of another person: *She transferred the house* ***to*** *her daughter before she died.*

transfer /ˈtræns.fɜːʳ/ [US] /-fɝː/ *noun* **1** [C or U] when something or someone moves or is moved from one place, position, etc. to another: *the transfer of information* ○ *Black's transfer* ***to*** *an Italian football club came as a shock to Coventry supporters.* ○ *The official transfer* ***of*** *ownership will take a few days to complete.* **2** [C] a player who has moved from one sports team to another: *They've a new transfer* ***from*** *Tottenham playing for them.* **3** [C] *US* a ticket which allows a passenger to change routes or to change from one bus or train to another

transference /trænsˈfɜː.rənts/ [US] /ˈtræns.fɚ.ənts/ *noun* [U] *FORMAL* the process of moving something or someone from one place, position, etc. to another: *UN observers were there to ensure the smooth transference of power.* **transferable** /trænsˈfɜː.rə.bl̩/ [US] /-ˈfɝː.ə-/ *adj*: *The tickets were marked 'Not Transferable'.*

transfer [PATTERN] /ˈtræns.fɜːʳ/ [US] /-fɝː/ *noun* [C] a picture or pattern which can be fixed to a surface by pressing it against the surface and then rubbing or heating it: *The kids bought transfers and ironed them onto their T-shirts.* ➲Compare **decal**.

ˈtransfer ˌfee *noun* [C] *UK* the amount of money which a sports team pays in order to buy a new player from another team: *The transfer fee for Darren Brinkworth was £500,000.*

ˈtransfer ˌlist *noun* [C usually sing] *UK* a football or rugby team's list of players that are available to be sold: *The club's top goalkeeper is on the transfer list.*

transfigure /trænsˈfɪg.əʳ/ [US] /-jɚ/ *verb* [T] *FORMAL* to change the appearance of a person or thing very noticeably, usually in a very positive and often spiritual way: *As she gazed down at the baby, her face was transfigured* ***with*** *tenderness.* ○ *The assassination somehow transfigured Kennedy* ***into*** *a modern American saint.* **transfiguration** /ˌtræns.fɪ.gəˈreɪ.ʃən/[US] /-fɪg.-jəˈreɪ-/ *noun* [U]

transfix /trænsˈfɪks/ *verb* [T] *LITERARY* to make a person or animal seem unable to move or stop looking at something because they are so interested, surprised or frightened, usually because their interest in or fear of something is so strong: *The conference delegates were transfixed by her speech.* **transfixed** /trænsˈfɪkst/ *adj*: *Rabbits transfixed in the glare of car headlights are common victims on the roads.*

transform /trænsˈfɔːm/ [US] /-ˈfɔːrm/ *verb* [T] to change completely the appearance or character of something or someone, especially so that they are improved: *The reorganization will transform the British entertainment industry.* ○ [R] *Whenever a camera was pointed at her, Marilyn would instantly transform herself* ***into*** *a radiant star.* **transformation** /ˌtræns.fəˈmeɪ.ʃən/ [US] /-fɚ-/ *noun* [C or U] *Local people have mixed feelings about the planned transformation of their town* ***into*** *a regional capital.* ○ *I'd never seen Carlo in smart evening clothes before – it was quite a transformation.*

transformer /trænsˈfɔː.məʳ/ [US] /-ˌfɔːr.mɚ/ *noun* [C] *SPECIALIZED* a device which changes the VOLTAGE or other characteristic of electrical energy as it moves from one circuit to another: *You may need a transformer if you want to run a personal stereo off mains electricity.*

transfusion /trænsˈfjuː.ʒən/ *noun* [C or U] **1** the process of adding an amount of blood to the body of a person or animal, or the amount of blood itself: *She suffered kidney failure and needed a* ***blood*** *transfusion.* **2 transfusion of** ***sth*** when a new quantity of something powerful, effective or important is put into an organization, group or place: *a transfusion of talent/energy/enthusiasm/money*

transgenic /trænsˈdʒen.ɪk/ *adj SPECIALIZED* describes an animal or plant that contains one or more genes that have been added from another type of plant or animal

transgress /trænzˈgres/ *verb* [I or T] *FORMAL* to break a law or moral rule: *Those are the rules, and anyone who transgresses will be severely punished.* **transgression** /trænzˈgreʃ.ən/ *noun* [C or U] *Who is supposed to have* ***committed*** *these transgressions?*

transgressor /trænzˈgres.əʳ/ [US] /-ˈgres.ɚ/ *noun* [C] *The system seems to be designed to punish the transgressor* (= the person breaking the rules) *rather than help his victim.*

transient /ˈtræn.zi.ənt/ [US] /-ʃənt/ *adj FORMAL* lasting for only a short time; temporary: *A glass of whisky has only a transient warming effect.* ○ *The city has a large transient population* (= many people who are living in it only temporarily).

transient /ˈtræn.zi.ənt/ [US] /-ʃənt/ *noun* [C] *MAINLY US FORMAL* someone who lives only temporarily in a place: *It's an organization set up to provide money and help for transients.* **transience** /ˈtræn.zi.ənts/ [US] /-ʃənts/ *noun* [U] *FORMAL the transience of human existence/fame*

transistor /trænˈzɪs.təʳ/ [US] /-ˈzɪs.tɚ/ *noun* [C] **1** a small electrical device containing a SEMICONDUCTOR, used in televisions, radios, etc. to control or increase an electric current **2** (*ALSO* **transistor radio, trannie**) a small radio containing transistors, used especially in the past

transistorized, *UK USUALLY* **-ised** /trænˈzɪs.tər.aɪzd/ [US] /-tə.raɪzd/ *adj* describes a device that uses transistors rather than valves: *transistorized amplifiers*

transit [MOVEMENT] /ˈtræn.zɪt/ *noun* [U] the movement of goods or people from one place to another: *It is possible to make an insurance claim for any goods lost or damaged* ***in*** *transit.* ○ *The question is whether road transit is cheaper than rail.* ○ *a* ***rapid****-transit train*

Transit [VEHICLE] /ˈtræn.zɪt/ *noun* [C] *TRADEMARK* a type of road vehicle used especially for carrying goods: *He was seen driving a white Transit* ***van*** *near Leeds.*

ˈtransit ˌcamp *noun* [C] a place where REFUGEES stay in tents or other temporary structures when they have nowhere to live permanently

transition /trænˈzɪʃ.ən/ *noun* [C or U] a change from one form or type to another, or the process by which this happens: *The health-care system is* ***in*** *transition at the moment.* ○ *There will be an interim government to oversee the transition* ***to*** *democracy.* **transitional** /trænˈzɪʃ.ən.əl/ *adj*: *a transitional government* ○ *Eastern Slavonia is to revert to Croatian government rule next year after a transitional* ***period*** *under U.N. administration.*

transitive /ˈtræn.sə.tɪv/ /-zə-/ [US] /-t̬ɪv/ *adj SPECIALIZED* (of a verb) having or needing an object: *In this dictionary, transitive verbs, such as 'put', are marked [T].* ➲Compare **ditransitive**; **intransitive**.

transitive /ˈtræn.sə.tɪv/ /-zə-/ [US] /-t̬ɪv/ *noun* [C] *SPECIALIZED* a transitive verb **transitively** /ˈtræn.sə.tɪv.li/ /-zə-/ [US] /-t̬ɪv-/ *adv*: *Can 'cry' be used transitively?* **transitivity** /ˌtræn.səˈtɪv.ɪ.ti/ /-zə-/ [US] /-ə.t̬i/ *noun* [U]

transitory /ˈtræn.zɪ.tri/ /-tər.i/ [US] /-tɔː.ri/ *adj FORMAL* lasting for only a short time: *the transitory nature of life*

translate /trænsˈleɪt/ /trænz-/ *verb* [I or T] **1** to change words into a different language: *We were asked to translate a list of sentences.* ○ *She works for the EU, translating* ***from*** *English* ***into*** *French.* ➲Compare **interpret** BETWEEN LANGUAGES. **2** to change something into a new form, especially to turn a plan into reality: *So how does this theory translate* ***into*** *practical policy?* ○ *The ways of working that he had learnt at college did not translate* ***well*** (= were not suitable) ***to*** *the world of business.* **3 translate** ***sth*** **as** ***sth*** to decide that words, behaviour or actions mean a particular thing: *He mumbled something which I translated as agreement.*

translation /trænsˈleɪ.ʃən/ /trænz-/ *noun* [C or U] *The children do one French translation a week.* ○ *A* ***literal*** *translation* ***of*** *'euthanasia' would be 'good death'.* ○ *The*

English version is boring – perhaps it has lost something in translation (= is not as good as the original).

● **in translation** changed into someone's own language, not in the original language: *She reads Proust in translation.*

translator /trænsˈleɪ.tə^r/ /trænz-/ US /-t̬ɚ/ *noun* [C] a person whose job is changing words, especially written words, into a different language ✪Compare **interpreter** at **interpret** BETWEEN LANGUAGES.

transliterate /trænzˈlɪt.^ər.eɪt/ US /trænsˈlɪt̬.ə.reɪt/ *verb* [T] SPECIALIZED to write a word or letter in a different alphabet: *On the road signs, the Greek place names have been transliterated into the Latin alphabet.* **transliteration** /ˌtrænz.lɪ.t^əˈreɪ.ʃ^ən/ US /ˌtrænsˌlɪt̬.ə-/ *noun* [C or U]

translucent /trænzˈluː.s^ənt/ US /træns-/ *adj* OFTEN APPROVING If an object or a substance is translucent, it is almost transparent, allowing some light through it in an attractive way: *translucent plastic/glass* ○ *This china is so fine and delicate that it's translucent.* ○ *Delia's skin has a translucent quality.* ✪Compare **opaque**; **transparent**. **translucence** /trænzˈluː.s^ənts/ US /træns-/ *noun* [U]

transmit /trænzˈmɪt/ US /træns-/ *verb* -tt- **1** [I or T] to broadcast something, or to send out or carry signals using radio, television, etc: *Radio Seven transmits on 201 medium wave* (= uses those particular radio waves to broadcast on). ○ *The information is transmitted electronically to the central computer.* **2** [T] to pass something from one person or place to another: *a sexually transmitted disease* ○ *Cholera is transmitted through contaminated water.* ○ *Some diseases are transmitted from one generation to the next.* ○ [R] *Somehow your panic and fear transmits itself to the horse that you're riding.*

transmission /trænzˈmɪʃ.^ən/ US /træns-/ *noun* **1** [C or U] the process of broadcasting something by radio, television, etc., or something which is broadcast: *We apologize for the interruption to our transmissions this afternoon.* **2** [U] the process of passing something from one person or place to another: *the transmission of disease* **3** [C or U] the machinery that brings the power produced by the engine to the wheels of a vehicle: *automatic transmission* ○ *The car had a faulty transmission.*

transmitter /trænzˈmɪt.ə^r/ US /trænsˈmɪt̬.ɚ/ *noun* [C] a piece of equipment for broadcasting radio or television signals: *a TV/radio transmitter*

transmogrify /trænzˈmɒg.rɪ.faɪ/ US /trænsˈmɑː.grə-/ *verb* [I or T] HUMOROUS to change or be changed completely: *Almost overnight, that sweet little child had transmogrified into an anti-social monster.* **transmogrification** /ˌtrænz.mɒg.rɪ.fɪˈkeɪ.ʃ^ən/ US /trænsˌmɑː.grə-/ *noun* [C or U]

transmute /trænzˈmjuːt/ US /træns-/ *verb* [I or T; usually + adv or prep] FORMAL to change something completely, especially into something different and better: *A few centuries ago alchemists thought they could transmute lead into gold.* ○ SPECIALIZED *Plutonium transmutes into/to uranium when it is processed in a nuclear reactor.* **transmutation** /ˌtrænz.mjuːˈteɪ.ʃ^ən/ US /ˌtræns-/ *noun* [C or U]

transnational /ˌtrænzˈnæʃ.^ən.^əl/ *adj* involving several nations: *transnational corporations/companies* ○ *transnational crime/issues*

transom /ˈtræn.səm/ *noun* [C] **1** SPECIALIZED a horizontal bar of stone or wood across a window, or separating the top of a window or door from a small window above **2** (*ALSO* **transom window**) US FOR **fanlight**

transparent /trænˈspær.^ənt/ US /trænˈsper-/ *adj* **1** If a substance or object is transparent, you can see through it very clearly: *Grow the bulbs in a transparent plastic box, so the children can see the roots growing.* ○ *Her blouse was practically transparent!* ✪Compare **opaque**; **translucent**. **2** clear and easy to understand or recognize: *I think we should try to make the instructions more transparent.*

transparency /trænˈspær.^ənt.si/ US /-ˈsper-/ *noun* **1** [U] the characteristic of being easy to see through: *The old-fashioned type of plastic lacked transparency.* **2** [C] SPECIALIZED a photograph or picture printed on plastic which you can see on a screen by shining a light through it

transpire BECOME KNOWN /trænˈspaɪə^r/ US /-ˈspaɪɚ/ *verb* [I] FORMAL If it transpires that something has happened, this previously secret or unknown fact becomes known: [+ *that*] *It may yet transpire that ministers knew more than they are admitting at the moment.* ○ *As it later transpired, she had known him at school.*

transpire HAPPEN /trænˈspaɪə^r/ US /-ˈspaɪɚ/ *verb* [I] FORMAL to happen: *No one is willing to predict what may transpire at the peace conference.*

transpire LOSE WATER /trænˈspaɪə^r/ US /-ˈspaɪɚ/ *verb* [I or T] SPECIALIZED If a body or plant transpires, it loses water through its surface or skin. **transpiration** /ˌtræn.spɪˈreɪ.ʃ^ən/ *noun* [U]

transplant /trænˈsplɑːnt/ US /-ˈsplænt/ *verb* [I or T; usually + adv or prep] to move something, or to be moved, from one place or person to another: *The plants should be grown indoors until spring, when they can be transplanted outside.* ○ *Doctors transplanted a monkey's heart into a two-year old child* (= removed the child's faulty heart and put a monkey's heart in its place). ✪Compare **implant** OBJECT.

transplant /ˈtrænsplɑːnt/ US /-ˈsplænt/ *noun* **1** [C or U] when something is transplanted, especially an operation in which a new organ is put into someone's body: *a liver/kidney transplant* ○ *transplant surgery* ○ *He had a heart transplant* (= Doctors gave him a different, healthier heart instead of his old one). **2** [C] something, especially a new organ, that has been transplanted: *His body accepted/rejected the transplant.* **transplantation** /ˌtræn.splɑːnˈteɪ.ʃ^ən/ US /-splæn-/ *noun* [U] *Transplantation of organs from living donors raises ethical issues.*

transponder /trænˈspɒn.də^r/ US /-ˈspɑːn.dɚ/ *noun* [C] SPECIALIZED an electronic device that gives out a radio signal when it receives a similar signal telling it to: *Aircraft are required by law to carry transponders, so that they can be identified.*

transport GOODS/PEOPLE /trænˈspɔːt/ US /-ˈspɔːrt/ *verb* [T] **1** to take goods or people from one place to another: *The pipeline was constructed to transport oil across Alaska to ports on the coast.* ○ *Such heavy items are expensive to transport (by plane).* **2** (in the past) to send a criminal to a country far away, to live, as a punishment: *162,000 convicts were transported to Australia from 1788 to 1868.*

transport /ˈtræn.spɔːt/ US /-spɔːrt/ *noun* [U] **1** when people or goods are moved from one place to another: *the transport of live animals* ○ *The company will arrange transport from the airport.* **2** UK (US **transportation**) a system of vehicles, such as buses, trains, aircraft, etc. for getting from one place to another: *the Department of Transport* ○ *investment in public transport* (= buses, trains, etc. available for everyone to use) ○ *Do you have your own transport* (= vehicle)? ○ *Bicycles are a cheap and efficient form of transport.*

transportation /ˌtræn.spɔːˈteɪ.ʃ^ən/ US /-spɚ-/ *noun* [U] **1** when people or goods are moved from one place to another: *In the past, British convicts could be sentenced to transportation (to Australia).* **2** US (UK **transport**) a vehicle or system of vehicles, such as buses, trains, etc. for getting from one place to another: *In Los Angeles many companies encourage their employees to use alternative means of transportation, rather than the car.*

transporter /trænˈspɔː.tə^r/ US /-ˈspɔːr.t̬ɚ/ *noun* [C] a long vehicle used for moving several large objects such as cars from one place to another: *a car transporter*

transport FEELING /trænˈspɔːt/ US /-ˈspɔːrt/ *verb* [T] LITERARY If something transports you to a different time or place, it makes you feel as if you are in it: *The film transported us back to the New York of the 1950s.*

transport /ˈtræn.spɔːt/ US /-ˈspɔːrt/ *noun* LITERARY **in transports (of delight)** extremely pleased or happy

ˈtransport ˌcafé UK *noun* [C] (US **truck stop**) a cheap restaurant next to a main road, used mainly by truck drivers

ˈtransport ˌplane *noun* [C] an aircraft used especially for taking soldiers or military supplies from one place to another ✪See picture **Planes, Ships and Boats** on page Centre 14

'transport ,ship noun [C] a ship used especially for taking soldiers or military supplies from one place to another

transpose /træn'spəʊz/ ⓤ /-'spoʊz/ verb [T] **1** FORMAL SPECIALIZED to change something from one position to another, or to exchange the positions of two things: *In their latest production they have reworked 'King Lear', transposing it to pre-colonial Africa.* ○ *The confusion was caused when two numbers were accidentally transposed by a Social Security clerk.* **2** SPECIALIZED to play or write a piece of music in a different KEY (= set of musical notes based on a particular note) from the one used originally: *The pianist transposed the song into C.* **transposition** /ˌtræn.spə'zɪʃ.ᵊn/ noun [C or U]

transsexual /trænz'sek.sjʊəl/ /-sju.əl/ ⓤ /-ʃu.əl/ noun [C] **1** a person, especially a man, who feels that they should have been the opposite sex, and therefore behaves and dresses like a member of that sex **2** a person who has had a medical operation to change their sex

transubstantiation /ˌtræn.səb,stæn.tʃi'eɪ.ʃᵊn/ noun [U] SPECIALIZED the belief, especially by Roman Catholics, that during MASS (= a religious ceremony) bread and wine are changed into the body and blood of Jesus Christ

transverse /trænz'vɜːs/ ⓤ /træns'vɜːrs/ adj SPECIALIZED in a position or direction that is at an angle of 90° to something else: *The main roof beams are given extra support by the smaller transverse beams.*

transvestite /trænz'ves.taɪt/ ⓤ /træns-/ noun [C] a person, especially a man, who wears the clothes of the opposite sex, often for sexual pleasure ⊃Compare **transsexual.** **transvestism** /trænz'ves.tɪ.zᵊm/ ⓤ /træns-/ noun [U] FORMAL

trap CATCHING DEVICE /træp/ noun **1** [C] a device or hole for catching animals or people and preventing their escape: *The fox got its foot caught in a trap.* **2** [S] a dangerous or unpleasant situation which you have got into and from which it is difficult or impossible to escape: *The under-cover agents went to the rendezvous knowing that it might be a trap.* ○ *She's too clever to fall into the trap of doing any unpaid work.*

trap /træp/ verb [T] -pp- **1** to catch an animal in a trap: *She survived in the forest by eating berries and trapping small animals and birds.* **2** to keep something such as heat or water in one place, especially because it is useful: *A greenhouse stays warm because the glass traps the heat of the sun.* **3 be trapped** If someone or something is trapped, they are unable to move or escape from a place or situation: *The two men died when they were trapped in a burning building.* ○ *Fire officers used cutting equipment to free his legs, which were trapped under a steel beam.* ○ FIGURATIVE *Jack left the job after ten years because he was beginning to feel trapped.* **4 be trapped into (doing) sth** to be forced or tricked into doing something that you do not want to do: *In his book, Holden speculates that Shakespeare was an unfaithful husband who was trapped into marriage.* ○ *She had been trapped into saying something she did not mean.*

trapper /'træp.əʳ/ ⓤ /-ɚ/ noun [C] a person who traps wild animals, usually to sell their fur: *a fur trapper*

trap MOUTH /træp/ noun [C] SLANG a mouth: *Oh, shut your trap* (= stop talking) – *I'm bored of listening to you!* ○ *I've told him it's a secret and he's to keep his trap shut* (= not say anything about it).

trap VEHICLE /træp/ noun [C] a light carriage with two wheels pulled by a horse, used especially in the past

trapdoor /'træp.dɔːʳ/ ⓤ /-dɔːr/ noun [C] a small door in a ceiling or floor: *There's a trapdoor into the attic.*

trapeze /trə'piːz/ noun [C] a short bar hanging high up in the air from two ropes, which ACROBATS use to perform special swinging movements: *A glamorous couple performed on the flying trapeze.* ○ *trapeze artists*

trapezium UK (plural **trapeziums** or **trapezia**) /trə'piː.zi.əm/ noun [C] (US **trapezoid**) SPECIALIZED a flat four-sided shape, where two of the sides are parallel

trapezoid UK /'træp.ɪ.zɔɪd/ noun [C] (US **trapezium**) SPECIALIZED a shape with four sides of different lengths, none of which are parallel

trappings /'træp.ɪŋz/ plural noun all the things that are part of or typical of a particular job, situation or event: *He enjoyed the trappings of power, such as a chauffeur-driven car and bodyguards.* ○ *The demonstration had all the trappings of a typical 1960s peace demo.*

Trappist (monk) /ˌtræp.ɪst'mʌŋk/ noun [C] a member of a Roman Catholic organization with very extreme rules, such as no talking

trapshooting /'træp,ʃuː.tɪŋ/ ⓤ /-t̬ɪŋ/ noun [U] the sport of shooting at CLAY PIGEONS (= round flat clay objects that are thrown into the air)

trash /træʃ/ noun [U] **1** INFORMAL something that is worth-less and of low quality: *I can't believe that someone of his intelligence can read such trash!* ○ *There's only trash on the television tonight.* **2** US FOR rubbish: *The trash really stinks – why don't you take it out?*

trash /træʃ/ group noun [U] US INFORMAL an insulting way of referring to a group of people you consider worthless: *We don't have anything to do with the people in the apartment below us – they're trash.*

• **talk trash 1** INFORMAL to say things that do not have a lot of meaning: *There are too many radio shows featuring idiots who call in and talk trash all day.* **2** US INFORMAL to criticize other people, especially unfairly or cruelly

trash /træʃ/ verb [T] INFORMAL **1** to throw away, destroy or severely damage something: *I simply trash that sort of mail.* ○ *The guys got angry and trashed the bar.* **2** to criticize something or someone severely: *The boss completely trashed her work, in front of everyone.*

trashy /'træʃ.i/ adj INFORMAL worthless and of low quality: *Why do so many people watch such ridiculous trashy programmes?*

'trash ,bag noun [C] US FOR dustbin bag/liner

'trash ,can noun [C] US FOR dustbin ⊃See picture **In the Office** on page Centre 15

'trash can ,liner noun [C] US FOR dustbin bag/liner

trauma /'trɔː.mə/ /'trɑʊ-/ ⓤ /'trɑː-/ noun [C or U] **1** severe emotional shock and pain caused by an extremely upsetting experience: *the trauma of marriage breakdown* ○ *He had psychotherapy to help him deal with his child-hood traumas.* **2** SPECIALIZED a severe injury, usually caused by a violent attack or an accident

traumatic /trɔː'mæt.ɪk/ /trɑʊ-/ ⓤ /trɑː'mæt̬-/ adj **1** If an experience is traumatic, it causes you severe emotional shock and upset: *Some of the most disturbed children had witnessed really traumatic things, such as rape and murder.* **2** INFORMAL frightening and causing anxiety: *Don't you find exams traumatic?* **traumatically** /trɔː-'mæt.ɪ.kli/ /trɑʊ-/ ⓤ /trɑː'mæt̬-/ adv **traumatize,** UK USU-ALLY **traumatise** /'trɔː.mə.taɪz/ /'trɑʊ-/ ⓤ /'trɑː-/ verb [T usually passive] *She was completely traumatized by the death of her mother.*

traumatized, UK USUALLY **-ised** /'trɔː.mə.taɪzd/ /'trɑʊ-/ ⓤ /'trɑː-/ adj very shocked and upset for a long time: *The whole experience left him traumatized.*

travails /'træv.eɪlz/ /trə'veɪlz/ plural noun OLD-FASHIONED OR LITERARY the difficulties that are experienced as part of a particular situation: *The travails of the British car industry are seldom out of the news.*

travel /'træv.ᵊl/ verb -ll- or US USUALLY -l- **1** [I or T] to make a journey, usually over a long distance: *After leaving school, she spent a year travelling, mostly in Africa and Asia.* ○ *I travel to work by train.* ○ *He travelled over 100 miles to be at the wedding.* ○ *As a young man he had travelled* (= been to many parts of) *the world.* **2** [I] to move or go from one place to another: *Supersonic planes can travel faster than the speed of sound.* **3** [I] If something such as food travels well/badly, it does/does not stay in good condition if it is moved long distances: *They say that real Yorkshire beers don't travel well.* **4** INFORMAL **really travel** to move very fast: *We were doing 90mph, so that other car that passed us must have been really travelling!* ○ *That bike can really travel!*

• **travel light** to make a journey without taking a lot of heavy things with you: *I always try to travel light.*

travel /'træv.ᵊl/ noun [U] the activity of travelling: *air/space travel* ○ *business travel* ○ *We share a love of* *literature, food and travel.* ○ *I heard on the travel* ***news*** *that there'd been an accident.*

travelled, *US USUALLY* **traveled** /ˈtræv.ᵊld/ *adj* **1 well-/much-/little-travelled** describes a journey or route that many/few people travel on **2 well-/widely-travelled** describes people who have visited many countries: *They're a well-travelled couple.*

traveller, *US USUALLY* **traveler** /ˈtræv.ᵊl.əʳ/ /-ləʳ/ [US] /-ᵊl.ɚ/ *noun* **[C] 1** someone who travels: *This hotel is for serious travellers, rather than tourists on two-week package holidays.* **2** *UK* a **New Age traveller** or **gypsy** **travelling**, *US USUALLY* **traveling** /ˈtræv.ᵊl.ɪŋ/ /-lɪŋ/ *noun* **[U]** *I love the work but I hate the travelling that's involved.* **travelling**, *US USUALLY* **traveling** /ˈtræv.ᵊl.ɪŋ/ /-lɪŋ/ *adj* **[before n]** *a travelling opera company/circus*

travels /ˈtræv.ᵊlz/ *plural noun* journeys: *a record of her travels* ***in/around*** *the Far East*

COMMON LEARNER ERROR

travel, journey or **trip?**

The noun **travel** is a general word which means the activity of travelling.

Air travel has become much cheaper.

Use **journey** to talk about when you travel from one place to another.

He fell asleep during the train journey.
Did you have a good journey?
~~*Did you have a good travel?*~~

A **trip** is a journey in which you visit a place for a short time and come back again.

a business trip
a 3-day trip to Spain

ˈtravel ˌagent *noun* **[C]** a person or company that arranges tickets, hotel rooms, etc. for people going on holiday or making a journey

ˈtravel ˌagency *noun* **[C]** a company or shop that makes travel arrangements for people

traveller's cheque /ˈtræv.ᵊl.əzˌtʃek/ [US] /-ɚz-/ *noun* **[C]** (*US* **traveler's check**) *UK* a piece of paper that you buy from a bank or a travel company and that you can use as money or exchange for the local money of the country you visit

ˌtravelling ˈsalesman *noun* **[C]** *OLD-FASHIONED* a **sales rep**

travelogue, *US ALSO* **travelog** /ˈtræv.ᵊl.ɒg/ [US] /-ə.lɑːg/ *noun* **[C]** a film or book about travelling to or in a particular place: *Peter Jackson's latest book 'Africa' is part travelogue, part memoir.*

ˈtravel ˌsickness *noun* **[U]** (*ALSO* **motion sickness**) a feeling of illness, especially of needing to vomit, which some people get in a moving vehicle

traverse /trəˈvɜːs/ [US] /-ˈvɝːs/ *verb* **[T]** *FORMAL* to move or travel through an area: *Stanley traversed the continent from west to east.* ○ *Bounded on the east by Lake Winnebago, the county is traversed by the Wolf and Fox rivers.*

travesty /ˈtræv.ə.sti/ *noun* **[C]** *SLIGHTLY FORMAL* something which fails to represent the values and qualities that it is intended to represent, in a way that is shocking or offensive: *Their production of 'Macbeth' was quite the worst I've ever seen – it was a travesty.* ○ *Langdale described the court ruling as a travesty* ***of justice.*** ➲Compare **parody**.

trawl [FISH] /trɔːl/ [US] /trɑːl/ *verb* **[T]** to pull a large cone-shaped net through the sea at a deep level behind a special boat in order to catch fish: *They trawl these waters* ***for*** *cod.*

ˈtrawl (ˌnet) *noun* **[C]** a large cone-shaped net used for trawling the water for fish

trawler /ˈtrɔː.ləʳ/ [US] /ˈtrɑː.lɚ/ *noun* **[C]** a large boat that uses a wide cone-shaped net to catch fish ➲See picture **Planes, Ships and Boats** on page Centre 14

trawl [SEARCH] /trɔːl/ [US] /trɑːl/ *verb* **[I or T; usually + adv or prep]** to search among a large number or a great variety of places in order to find people or information you want: *The newspaper had trawled its files* ***for*** *photos of the new minister.* ○ *You need to trawl* ***through*** *a lot of data to get results that are valid.*

trawl /trɔːl/ [US] /trɑːl/ *noun* **[C]** *We* ***did*** *a wide trawl* (= searched among a lot of people) *to find the right person to play the part.*

tray /treɪ/ *noun* **[C] 1** a flat object, usually with raised edges, used for carrying food and drinks: *She was carrying a tray* ***of*** *drinks.* **2** *MAINLY UK* a flat open container with raised edges which you put on your desk for keeping papers in: *She put the letter in your* ***in****-tray.* ○ *I don't know where I put that article – it must be in the bottom of my tray.* ➲See also **ashtray**. ➲See picture **In the Office** on page Centre 15

treacherous [DANGEROUS] /ˈtretʃ.ᵊr.əs/ [US] /-ɚ-/ *adj* If the ground or sea is treacherous, it is extremely dangerous, especially because of bad weather conditions: *Snow and ice have left many roads treacherous, and motorists are warned to drive slowly.*

treacherous [NOT LOYAL] /ˈtretʃ.ᵊr.əs/ [US] /-ɚ-/ *adj MAINLY OLD USE* A person who is treacherous deceives someone who trusts them, or lacks loyalty: *Vargas plays the part of treacherous aristocrat who betrays his king and country.* ○ *I feel a bit treacherous* ***to*** *my own sex if I ever make general criticisms of women.* **treachery** /ˈtretʃ.ᵊr.i/ [US] /-ɚ-/ *noun* **[U]** *FORMAL* *Corley said she was standing down as leader because of the treachery of her own colleagues.*

treacle /ˈtriː.kl̩/ *noun* **[U]** *UK* **1** (*ALSO* **black treacle**) a sweet dark thick liquid which is used in cooking sweet dishes and sweets: *treacle toffee* ➲Compare **syrup**. **2 golden syrup**: *treacle tart*

treacly /ˈtriː.kl̩.i/ /-kli/ *adj* **1** dark and sticky, like treacle: *He'd coated the shelves with a thick treacly varnish.* **2** *DISAPPROVING* too pleasant or kind, or expressing feelings of love in a false way: *The film is spoilt by a slightly treacly sentimentality.*

tread [STEP] /tred/ *verb* **[I or T; usually + adv or prep]** **trod** or *US ALSO* **treaded, trodden** or *US ALSO* **trod 1** *MAINLY UK* to put your foot on something or to press something down with your foot: *I kept treading* ***on*** *his toes when we were dancing.* ○ *Yuck! Look what I've just trodden* ***in****!* ○ *A load of food had been trodden* ***into*** *the carpet.* ○ *Before the days of automation, they used to tread* ***grapes*** *to make wine.* **2** *LITERARY* to walk: *He trod heavily and reluctantly up the stairs.* ○ *I sometimes see him flash past in his sports car as I tread* ***my weary way*** (= walk in a tired way) *to work.*

• **tread carefully/gently/lightly** to speak or behave carefully to avoid upsetting or causing offence to anyone: *The government know they have to tread carefully on this issue.*

• **tread the boards** *OLD-FASHIONED OR HUMOROUS* to act in plays: *It's three years now since you've trodden the boards, Ken – how does it feel to be back?*

• **tread water 1** to float vertically in the water by moving the legs and the arms up and down **2 be treading water** to not be advancing in any way: *I think she feels that she's just treading water in that job.*

tread /tred/ *noun* **1 [S]** the sound that your feet make on the ground as you walk: *Then I heard someone's tread on the stairs.* **2** the horizontal part of a step on which you put your foot

tread [PATTERN ON TYRE] /tred/ *noun* **[C or U]** the pattern of raised lines on a tyre which prevents a vehicle from sliding on the road: *The tread on your tyres is very worn.*

treadle /ˈtred.l̩/ *noun* **[C]** a part of a machine which, when operated by the foot, gives the power to turn a wheel in the machine: *My grandmother still uses her old treadle sewing machine.*

treadmill /ˈtred.mɪl/ *noun* **1 [S]** any type of repeated work which is boring and tiring and seems to have no positive effect and no end: *There were days when child-rearing seemed like an endless treadmill of feeding, washing and nappy-changing.* **2 [C]** an exercise machine which consists of a moving strip or two step-like parts on which you walk without moving forward **3 [C]** a wide wheel turned by the weight of people climbing on steps around its edge, used in the past to provide power for machines or, more usually, as a punishment for prisoners

treason /'triː.zᵊn/ *noun* [U] (the crime of) lack of loyalty to your country, especially by helping its enemies or attempting to defeat its government: *Guy Fawkes was executed for treason after he took part in a plot to blow up the British Parliament building.* **treasonable** /'triː.zᵊn.ə.bl̩/ *adj* (*ALSO* **treasonous**) *FORMAL a treasonable offence* ○ *treasonable activities*

treasure /'treʒ.əʳ/ [US] /-ɚ/ *noun* **1** [U] wealth, usually in the form of a store of precious metals, precious stones or money: *Stories about pirates often include a search for* ***buried*** *treasure.* ○ *When they opened up the tomb they found treasure beyond their wildest dreams.* **2** [C] *INFORMAL* someone who is very helpful and valuable to you: *I don't know what I'd have done without Lizzie when I was ill – she was an absolute treasure.* **3** *MAINLY UK OLD-FASHIONED INFORMAL* an affectionate way of addressing someone, especially a child: *Come on, treasure, let's go and see Granny.*

treasure /'treʒ.əʳ/ [US] /-ɚ/ *verb* [T] to take great care of something because you love it or consider it very valuable: *I shall always treasure those* ***memories*** *of her.* ○ *This pen that my grandfather gave me is one of my most treasured* ***possessions****.*

treasures /'treʒ.əz/ [US] /-ɚz/ *plural noun* very valuable things, especially pieces of art: *stolen* ***art*** *treasures* ○ *The museum houses many priceless treasures.*

'treasure ˌhunt *noun* [C] a game in which the players are given a series of CLUES (= pieces of information) to direct them to a hidden prize

treasurer /'treʒ.ᵊr.əʳ/ [US] /-ɚ.ɚ/ *noun* [C] a person who is responsible for an organization's money

treasure trove /'treʒ.əˌtrəʊv/ [US] /-ɚˌtroʊv/ *noun* [C or U] **1** a large amount of money or a large number of valuable metals, stones or other objects found hidden somewhere and seeming to belong to no one: *A Roman soldier's pay, found by a metal detector enthusiast in Norfolk, has been* ***declared*** *treasure trove at an inquest in Diss.* **2 a treasure trove of *sth*** a place that is full of something good: *a treasure trove of information* ○ *Though small, this museum is a veritable treasure trove of history.*

the Treasury /ðə'treʒ.ᵊr.i/ [US] /-ɚ-/ *noun* [S] the government department, in Britain and various other countries, which is responsible for financial matters such as spending and tax ⊃Compare **the Exchequer**.

treat [DEAL WITH] /triːt/ *verb* [T usually + adv or prep] to behave towards someone or deal with something in a particular way: *My parents treated us all the same when we were kids.* ○ *He treated his wife very badly.* ○ *It's wrong to treat animals* ***as if*** *they had no feelings.* ○ *I treat remarks like that* ***with*** *the contempt that they deserve.*

• **treat *sb* like dirt** to treat someone extremely badly: *For years I allowed him to treat me like dirt.*

• **treat *sb* like royalty** to treat someone extremely well: *The staff in the hotel treated us like royalty.*

treatment /'triːt.mənt/ *noun* **1** [U] the way you deal with or behave towards someone or something: *Peter gets* ***special*** *treatment because he knows the boss.* **2** [C or U] the way something is considered and examined: *The same subject matter gets a very different treatment by Chris Wilson in his latest novel.*

treat [GIVE MEDICAL CARE] /triːt/ *verb* [T] to use drugs, exercises, etc. to cure a person of a disease or heal an injury: *He is being treated* ***for*** *a rare skin disease.* ○ *Western medicine tends to treat* ***the symptoms*** *and not the cause.*

treatment /'triːt.mənt/ *noun* [C or U] *free* ***dental*** *treatment* ○ *Perhaps it's time to try a new course of treatment.* ○ *This disease doesn't generally* ***respond to*** (= improve as a result of) *treatment.* ○ *There are various treatments* ***for*** *this complaint.*

treat [SPECIAL EXPERIENCE] /triːt/ *noun* [C] a special and enjoyable occasion or experience: *We're going to Italy for the weekend – it's my* ***birthday*** *treat.* ○ *As a* ***special*** *treat, I'll take you to my favourite tea-shop.*

treat [PAY FOR] /triːt/ *verb* [T] to buy or pay for something for another person: *Put your money away – I'm going to treat you* (***to*** *this).* ○ *I'm going to treat* ***myself to*** (= buy for myself) *a new pair of sandals.*

treat /triːt/ *noun* [U] *No, you paid for dinner last time – this is* ***my*** *treat* (= I will pay).

treat [PUT ON] /triːt/ *verb* [T] to put a special substance on material such as wood, cloth, metal, etc. or put it through a special process, in order to protect it from damage or decay: *The material has been treated* ***with*** *resin to make it waterproof.*

treat [VERY WELL] /triːt/ *noun UK INFORMAL* **a treat** very well; with good results: *To prevent red wine from staining, put some salt on it – it* ***works*** *a treat.* ○ *That soup* ***went down*** *a treat* (= tasted very good)*!* ○ *I polished that old desk of grandma's and it* ***came up*** *a treat* (= its appearance improved).

treatise /'triː.tɪs/ [US] /-t̬ɪs/ *noun* [C] a formal piece of writing that considers and examines a particular subject: *a six-volume treatise* ***on*** *trademark law*

treaty /'triː.ti/ [US] /-t̬i/ *noun* [C] a written agreement between two or more countries formally approved and signed by their leaders: *a* ***peace*** *treaty* ○ *the treaty* ***on*** *European union* ○ [+ to infinitive] *We've* ***signed/concluded*** *a treaty* ***with*** *neighbouring states* ***to*** *limit emissions of harmful gases.*

treble [THREE TIMES] /'treb.l̩/ *predeterminer* three times greater in amount, number or size: *He earns almost treble the amount that I do.*

treble /'treb.l̩/ *verb* [I or T] to increase three times in size or amount, or to make something do this: *The price of property has almost trebled in the last ten years.*

treble [MUSIC] /'treb.l̩/ *adj* [before n], *adv* being or relating to a boy's voice which sings the highest notes, or an instrument that plays the highest notes: *a treble voice* ○ *He sings treble.*

treble /'treb.l̩/ *noun* [C] someone with a treble voice: *This part is for a* ***boy*** *treble.* ⊃Compare **soprano**.

ˌtreble 'clef *noun* [C usually sing] (*ALSO* **G clef**) a sign on a STAVE (= the five lines on which music is written) which shows that the notes are above MIDDLE C (= the C near the middle of a piano keyboard)

tree /triː/ *noun* [C] **1** a tall plant which has a wooden trunk and branches that grow from its upper part: *a plum/apple/chestnut tree* ○ *We sat under a tree for shade.* **2** another type of tall plant, without a wooden trunk: *palm trees*

'tree ˌfern *noun* [C] a large tropical FERN (= plant with feathery leaves) with a trunk-like stem

'tree ˌhouse *noun* [C] a small building, platform, or shelter built among the branches of a tree: *I spent hours in our tree house when I was a kid.*

treeline /'triː.laɪn/ *noun* [U] (*ALSO* **timberline**) the height above sea level or the distance south or north of the equator beyond which trees do not grow

tree-lined /'triː.laɪnd/ *adj* A tree-lined road has trees on both sides of it.

the treetops /ðə'triː.tɒpz/ [US] /-tɑːpz/ *plural noun* the upper branches of a group of trees: *Monkeys were playing* ***in*** *the treetops.*

trek /trek/ *verb* [I usually + adv or prep] **-kk-** to walk a long distance, usually over land such as hills, mountains or forests: *We spent the day trekking through forests and over mountains.* ○ *INFORMAL I trekked* (= walked a long and tiring distance) *all the way into town to meet him and he didn't even turn up.*

trek /trek/ *noun* [C] *We did an eight hour trek yesterday.* ○ *INFORMAL You can walk to town from here, but it's a bit of a trek* (= it's a long distance to walk).

trellis /'trel.ɪs/ *noun* [C] a light frame made of bars of wood or metal crossed over each other, fixed to a wall for plants to grow up

tremble /'trem.bl̩/ *verb* [I] to shake slightly, usually because you are cold, frightened, or very emotional: *When he came out of the water, he was trembling* ***with*** *cold.* ○ *Her* ***bottom lip*** *trembled and tears welled up in her eyes.* ○ *His* ***voice*** *started to tremble and I thought he was going to cry.*

• **tremble to think** If you say that you tremble to think about a possible future event, you are worried or frightened about it: *I tremble to think what will happen when he finds out.*

T

tremble /'trem.bl/ *noun* [U] when something or someone trembles: *There was a slight tremble in her voice as she recalled her husband.*

tremendous /trɪ'men.dəs/ *adj* very great in amount or level, or extremely good: *They were making the most tremendous amount of noise last night.* ○ *She's been a tremendous* (= very great) *help to me over the last few months.* ○ *You won? That's tremendous!* **tremendously** /trɪ'men.də.sli/ *adv*: *We all enjoyed ourselves tremendously.*

tremolo /'trem.əl.əʊ/ [US] /-ə.loʊ/ *noun* [C] *plural* **tremolos** *SPECIALIZED* when singing or playing an instrument, a shaking sound which is achieved by repeating the same note extremely quickly or by playing two notes very quickly, one after the other ➲Compare **vibrato**.

tremor /'trem.əʳ/ [US] /-ɚ/ *noun* [C] **1** a slight shaking movement in a person's body, especially because of nervousness or excitement: *The disease mostly affects people over 50, causing paralysis and uncontrollable tremors.* ○ *There was a slight tremor in her voice.* ○ *FIGURATIVE A tremor **of** excitement went through the audience as he came on stage.* **2** a slight earthquake: *The tremor was centered just south of San Francisco and was felt as far as 200 miles away.*

tremulous /'trem.jʊ.ləs/ *adj LITERARY* If a person's voice or a part of their body is tremulous, it is shaking slightly: *He watched her tremulous hand reach for the teacup.* ○ *In a tremulous **voice** she whispered: " Who are you people?"* **tremulously** /'trem.jʊ.lə.sli/ *adv*

trench /trentʃ/ *noun* **1** [C] a narrow channel which is dug into the ground: *A workman was killed when the sides of the trench he was working in collapsed.* **2** [C usually pl] a deep channel dug by soldiers and used as a place from which they can attack the enemy while being hidden: ***the** trenches of World War I* ○ *trench **warfare*** ➲Compare **foxhole**.

trenchant /'tren.tʃənt/ *adj SLIGHTLY FORMAL* severe, expressing strong criticism or forceful opinions: *His most trenchant **criticism** is reserved for the party leader, whom he describes as 'the most incompetent and ineffectual the party has known.'* ○ *Dorothy Parker's writing is characterized by a trenchant wit and sophistication.* **trenchantly** /'tren.tʃənt.li/ *adv* **trenchancy** /'tren.tʃənt.si/ *noun* [U]

'trench ˌcoat *noun* [C] a long loose coat with a belt, usually made from waterproof material and similar in style to a military coat

trencher /'trent.ʃəʳ/ [US] /-ʃɚ/ *noun* [C] **1** *AUS FOR* **mortarboard** **2** in the past, a flat wooden dish used to serve food

trend /trend/ *noun* [C] **1** a general development or change in a situation or in the way that people are behaving: *Surveys show a trend **away from** home-ownership and towards rented accommodation.* ○ *There's been a **downward/upward** trend in sales in the last few years.* **2** a new development in clothing, make-up, etc: *Whatever the latest **fashion** trend, you can be sure Nicki will be wearing it.* ○ *The trend at the moment is **towards** a more natural and less made-up look.*

trendy /'tren.di/ *adj INFORMAL* modern and influenced by the most recent fashions or ideas: *trendy clothes* ○ *a trendy nightclub* ○ *He writes for some trendy magazine for the under-30s.*

trendy /'tren.di/ *noun* [C] *INFORMAL MAINLY DISAPPROVING* a person who is very influenced by the most recent ideas and fashions: *This is where all the North London trendies go for a night out.*

trendsetter /'trendˌset.əʳ/ [US] /-ˌset̬.ɚ/ *noun* [C] a person, organization, etc. that starts new fashions, especially in clothes: *They are not only the world's biggest fast-food chain, but also the industry's trendsetter.*

trendspotter /'trendˌspɒt.əʳ/ [US] /-ˌspɑː.t̬ɚ/ *noun* [C] a person who notices and reports on new fashions, ideas or activities that are becoming popular: *Trendspotter Faith Starr believes a revolution is going on in the world of conferencing.*

trepidation /ˌtrep.ɪ'deɪ.ʃən/ *noun* [U] *FORMAL* fear or anxiety about what is going to happen: *We view future developments **with** some trepidation.*

trespass [BREAK LAW] /'tres.pəs/ [US] /-pæs/ *verb* [I] to go onto someone's land or enter their building without permission: *I hope this is a public footpath and we're not trespassing **on** someone's land.* **trespass** /'tres.pəs/ [US] /-pæs/ *noun* [C or U] **trespasser** /'tres.pə.səʳ/ [US] /-pæs.ɚ/ *noun* [C] *Can't you read the sign? It says 'Trespassers will be prosecuted!'*

trespass [IMMORAL ACTION] /'tres.pəs/ [US] /-pæs/ *noun* [C] *OLD USE* an offence in which you break a moral or religious law: *Forgive us our trespasses.* **trespass** /'tres.pəs/ [US] /-pæs/ *verb* [I]

▲ **trespass on/upon *sth*** *phrasal verb FORMAL* to take unfair advantage of a good quality in someone's character: *They said we should stay another night, but I didn't want to trespass on their hospitality.*

tresses /'tres.ɪz/ *plural noun LITERARY* a woman's hair, especially long hair: *Her black tresses lay around her on the pillow.*

trestle /'tres.l/ *noun* [C] **1** a supporting structure for a table, consisting of a flat piece of wood supported at each end by two pairs of sloping legs **2** *SPECIALIZED* a set of sloping supports holding a horizontal structure, used especially for railway bridges

'trestle ˌtable *noun* [C] a table which consists of a board supported by a trestle

trews /truːz/ *plural noun HUMOROUS* trousers: *a pair of **tartan** trews*

triad /'traɪ.æd/ *noun* **1** [C] a secret Chinese organization involved in illegal activities such as selling drugs **2** [S] *LITERARY* three related things that form a group: *the classic triad **of** the visual arts: architecture, painting and sculpture*

trial [LEGAL PROCESS] /traɪəl/ *noun* [C or U] the hearing of statements and showing of objects, etc. in a court of law to judge whether a person is guilty of a crime or to decide a case or a legal matter: *trial proceedings* ○ *Trial **by jury** is a fundamental right.* ○ *It was a very complicated trial that went on for months.* ○ *She's **going on/standing** trial **for** fraud.* ➲See also **try** LAW.

trial [TEST] /traɪəl/ *noun* [C or U] a test, usually over a limited period of time, to discover how effective or suitable something or someone is: *They're doing **clinical** trials on a new drug.* ○ *They've employed her for a six-month trial **(period)**.* ○ *MAINLY UK You can buy any of their garden equipment **on** trial/(US USUALLY) **on a** trial **basis**, and if you don't like it you can give it back.*

trial /traɪəl/ *verb* [T] **-ll-** or **-l-** *We're trialing* (= testing) *the new drug in several hospitals.*

trial [PROBLEM] /traɪəl/ *noun* [C] a person or thing that is annoying and causes a lot of problems: *She was a real trial **to** her parents when she was younger.* ○ *The book is all about the trials of growing up.*

● **trials and tribulations** *LITERARY OR HUMOROUS* troubles and events that cause suffering: *the trials and tribulations of marriage*

ˌtrial and 'error *noun* a way of achieving an aim or solving a problem by trying a number of different methods and learning from the mistakes that you make: *There's no instant way of finding a cure – it's just a **process of** trial and error.*

ˌtrial 'run *noun* [C] a practical test of something new or unknown to discover its effectiveness: *We're holding a tournament in the new ice-hockey stadium, as a trial run for next year's Winter Olympics.*

triangle /'traɪ.æŋ.gl/ *noun* [C] **1** a flat shape with three straight sides: *an equilateral/isosceles triangle* **2** anything which has three straight sides: *Which earrings did you buy in the end – the triangles or the circles?* **3** a musical instrument consisting of a thin metal bar bent into a triangle shape which is hit with a metal bar to make a sound **4** *US FOR* **setsquare** **triangular** /traɪ'æŋ.gjʊ.ləʳ/ [US] /-lɚ/ *adj*: *a triangular plot of land* ○ *The play is performed on a triangular stage.*

triangulation /traɪˌæŋ.gjʊ'leɪ.ʃən/ *noun* [U] *SPECIALIZED* the division of a map or plan into triangles for measurement purposes, or the calculation of positions and distances using this method

triathlon /traɪ'æθ.lɒn/ [US] /-lɑːn/ *noun* [C] a competition in which the people competing must swim, ride a bicycle and run particular distances without stopping between events

tribe /traɪb/ *group noun* [C] **1** a group of people, often of related families, who live together, sharing the same language, culture and history, especially those who do not live in towns or cities: *a tribe of Amazonian Indians* ○ *the Masai tribe* **2** INFORMAL a large family or other group that someone belongs to: *We've invited Carol's sisters and brothers and their spouses and children – the whole Cassidy tribe.*

tribal /ˈtraɪ.bᵊl/ *adj* relating to a tribe: *tribal dress/leaders* ○ INFORMAL FIGURATIVE *The fierce tribal* ***loyalty*** *among soccer supporters leads to violence between opposing fans.*

tribalism /ˈtraɪ.bᵊl.ɪ.zᵊm/ *noun* [U] the state of existing as a tribe, or a very strong feeling of loyalty to your tribe

tribesman /ˈtraɪbz.mən/ *noun* [C] a man who belongs to a tribe **tribespeople** /ˈtraɪbzˌpiː.pl̩/ *plural noun*

tribeswoman /ˈtraɪbzˌwʊm.ən/ *noun* [C] a woman who belongs to a tribe

tribulation /ˌtrɪb.jʊˈleɪ.ʃᵊn/ *noun* [C or U] FORMAL a problem or difficulty ➲See **trials and tribulations** at **trial** PROBLEM.

tribunal /traɪˈbjuː.nəl/ *noun* [C] a special court or group of people who are officially chosen, especially by the government, to examine (legal) problems of a particular type: *a war-crimes tribunal* ○ *She took her case to an immigration appeals tribunal.*

tributary /ˈtrɪb.jʊ.tᵊr.i/ /-tri/ [US] /-ter.i/ *noun* [C] a river or stream that flows into a larger river or a lake: *the Indre, a lesser tributary* ***of*** *the Loire*

tribute [RESPECTFUL ACTION] /ˈtrɪb.juːt/ *noun* [C] something that you say, write or give which shows your respect and admiration for someone, especially on a formal occasion: *Tributes have been pouring in from all over the world for the famous actor who died yesterday.* ○ *For wedding bouquets,* ***floral*** *tributes* (= flowers sent to someone's funeral) *and all your flower needs, call Mandy's Florists.*

• **pay tribute to *sb/sth*** to praise someone or something: *The minister paid tribute to the men who had fought the blaze.*

tribute [BENEFICIAL EFFECT] /ˈtrɪb.juːt/ *noun* **be a tribute to *sth/sb*** to show clearly how good, strong or effective something or someone is: *I've never known a 5-year-old as well-behaved as your son – he's a tribute* ***to*** *you!* ○ *It is a tribute to his determination over his 22 years that he has achieved where so many before him have failed.*

ˈtribute ˌband *noun* [C] a group of musicians who play the music of a famous pop group and pretend to be that group: *a Beatles tribute band*

trice /traɪs/ *noun* INFORMAL **in a trice** in a very short time: *Jim had the wheel mended in a trice.*

triceps /ˈtraɪ.seps/ *noun* [C] *plural* **triceps** or **tricepses** the large muscle at the back of the upper arm ➲Compare **biceps**.

trick [ACT OF DECEIVING] /trɪk/ *noun* [C] an action which is intended to deceive, either as a way of cheating someone, or as a joke or form of entertainment: *She* ***played*** *a really nasty trick* ***on*** *me – she put syrup in my shampoo bottle!* ○ *My niece was showing me all the tricks that she's learned to* ***do*** *with her new magic set.* ○ *It's a bit of trick* ***photography*** *– she's meant to look like she's walking on water.*

• **be a trick of the light** to be a visual effect caused by the light, making something appear different: *For a moment I thought you had a patch of grey hairs, but it's just a trick of the light.*

• **How's tricks?** INFORMAL FOR How are you?: *"Hi, how's tricks?" "Oh, fine, how are you doing?"*

trick /trɪk/ *verb* [T] to deceive someone, often as a part of a plan: *Dean tricked the old lady* ***into*** *giving him eight hundred pounds, claiming that he would invest it for her.*

trickery /ˈtrɪk.ᵊr.i/ [US] /-ɚ-/ *noun* [U] DISAPPROVING *The government, he said, had resorted to political trickery in their attempts to retain power.*

trickster /ˈtrɪk.stəʳ/ [US] /-stɚ/ *noun* [C] DISAPPROVING a person who deceives people: *a confidence trickster*

tricky /ˈtrɪk.i/ *adj* likely to deceive people ➲See also **tricky**.

trick [METHOD] /trɪk/ *noun* [C] an effective or quick way of doing something: *What's the trick* ***of*** *getting this to chair to fold up?* ○ *On page 21, twenty tricks to speed up your beauty routine.*

• **do the trick** INFORMAL If something does the trick, it has the necessary or desired effect: *This sauce needs a bit of flavour – I know, some lemon juice* ***should/ought to*** *do the trick.*

• **every trick in the book** every possible way: *I've tried every trick in the book to seduce him and still no luck!*

• **trick of the trade** a clever method used by people who are experienced in a particular type of work or activity: *Newspapers often improve photographs before they print them – it's one of the tricks of the trade.*

trick [WEAK] /trɪk/ *adj* [before n] US describes a part of the body, especially a joint, that sometimes feels weak suddenly and unexpectedly: *I've got a trick ankle which gives me problems if I do much running.*

trickle [LIQUID] /ˈtrɪk.l̩/ *verb* **trickle down/from/out of, etc.** If liquid trickles somewhere, it flows slowly and without force in a thin line: *Blood trickled out of the corner of his mouth.* ○ *Oil was trickling from a tiny hole in the tank.* **trickle** /ˈtrɪk.l̩/ *noun* [C] *A trickle of melted butter made its way down his chin.*

trickle [SMALL NUMBER] /ˈtrɪk.l̩/ *verb* **trickle in/out/back, etc.** to arrive or move somewhere slowly and gradually, in small numbers: *Gradually people trickled back into the theatre for the second half.*

trickle /ˈtrɪk.l̩/ *noun* [S] a very small number of people or things arriving or leaving somewhere: *We usually only get a trickle of customers in the shop in the mornings.*

trickle-down /ˌtrɪk.l̩ˈdaʊn/ *adj* [before n] describes a situation in which something that starts in the high parts of a system spreads to the whole of the system: *The supposed trickle-down* ***effect*** *of lower taxes for the rich has not yet resulted in greater prosperity for society as a whole.*

ˌtrick or ˈtreat *noun* [U] when children dress up in frightening or strange clothes on HALLOWEEN (= 31st October), especially in America and Canada, and visit people's homes to demand sweets or a small amount of money

• **go trick or treating** If children go trick or treating, they visit people's houses on Halloween to ask for sweets.

ˌtrick ˈquestion *noun* [C] a question which makes you believe you should answer it in one way, when the question you are really meant to answer is hidden within it

tricky /ˈtrɪk.i/ *adj* If a piece of work or problem is tricky, it is difficult to deal with and needs careful attention or skill: *Those bird models are quite tricky* ***to*** *make, aren't they?* ○ *I'm in a bit of a tricky situation really – whatever I do I'll offend someone.* ➲See also **tricky** at **trick** ACT OF DECEIVING.

tricolour UK, US **tricolor** /ˈtrɪk.ᵊl.əʳ/ [US] /ˈtraɪˌkʌl.ɚ/ *noun* [C] a flag which is divided into three equal parts of different colour: *the French tricolour*

tricycle /ˈtraɪ.sɪ.kl̩/ *noun* [C] (ALSO **trike**) a CYCLE (= vehicle powered by the rider's legs) with two wheels at the back and one at the front, used especially by young children

trident [LARGE FORK] /ˈtraɪ.dᵊnt/ *noun* [C] a weapon used in the past consisting of a pole with three sharp metal points on the end: *Neptune's trident*

Trident [EXPLOSIVE WEAPON] /ˈtraɪ.dᵊnt/ *noun* [C or U] a type of BALLISTIC MISSILE (= explosive weapon) which is sent from under the sea, whose explosive front ends can be aimed separately: *a Trident missile/submarine* ○ *The navy plans to move its Tridents.*

tried /traɪd/ *past simple and past participle of* **try**

triennial /traɪˈen.i.əl/ *adj* happening every three years: *the party's triennial congress*

trier /ˈtraɪ.əʳ/ [US] /-ɚ/ *noun* [C] ➲See at **try** ATTEMPT.

trifle [SWEET DISH] /ˈtraɪ.fl̩/ *noun* [C or U] a sweet cold dish consisting of a layer of fruit and SPONGE (= cake), a layer of CUSTARD (= thick sweet yellow sauce) and a top layer of cream: *a sherry trifle*

trifle [UNIMPORTANT THING] /ˈtraɪ.fl̩/ *noun* [C] **1** FORMAL a matter or item of little value or importance: *I brought a* *few trifles back from India – bits of jewellery and material mainly.* **2 a trifle** slightly: *I'm a trifle confused about the arrangements for tonight.*

trifling /ˈtraɪ.fl̩.ɪŋ/ /-flɪŋ/ *adj* FORMAL A trifling matter or amount of money is small or unimportant: *It was such a trifling sum of money to argue about!*

trifle /ˈtraɪ.fl̩/ *verb*

▲ **trifle with** ***sb/sth*** *phrasal verb* FORMAL OR OLD-FASHIONED to treat someone or something carelessly or without respect: *He trifled with her* ***affections*** (= feelings). ○ *As you know, Caroline O'Neill is not a woman to be trifled with.*

trigger [GUN PART] /ˈtrɪg.əʳ/ [US] /-ɚ/ *noun* [C] a part of a gun which causes the gun to fire when pressed: *It's not clear who actually* ***pulled*** *the trigger.*

trigger [START] /ˈtrɪg.əʳ/ [US] /-ɚ/ *verb* [T] to cause something bad to start: *Some people find that certain foods trigger their headaches.* ○ *The racial killings at the weekend have triggered* ***off*** *a wave of protests throughout the country.*

trigger /ˈtrɪg.əʳ/ [US] /-ɚ/ *noun* [C usually sing] *There are fears that the incident may be a trigger for* (= cause) *further violence in the capital.*

trigger-happy /ˈtrɪg.əˌhæp.i/ [US] /-ɚ-/ *adj* **1** INFORMAL describes someone who tends to use his or her gun a lot, shooting with very little reason: *Their police are worryingly trigger-happy.* **2** DISAPPROVING ready to use violence or force immediately, without careful consideration

trigonometry /ˌtrɪg.əˈnɒm.ə.tri/ [US] /-ˈnɑː.mə-/ *noun* [U] (INFORMAL **trig**) a type of mathematics that deals with the relationship between the angles and sides of triangles, used in measuring the height of buildings, mountains etc: *Trigonometry concerns the functions of angles, such as sine, cosine and tangent.*

trike /traɪk/ *noun* [C] INFORMAL a **tricycle**

trilby /ˈtrɪl.bi/ *noun* [C] MAINLY UK a man's hat made of FELT (= thick firm cloth), with a deep fold along its top ➲See picture **Hairstyles and Hats** on page Centre 8

trilingual /ˌtraɪˈlɪŋ.gwəl/ *adj* able to speak three languages ➲Compare **bilingual**.

trill [BIRD SONG] /trɪl/ *verb* [I] **1** When birds trill, they sing a series of quickly repeated high notes. **2** LITERARY to speak in a very high voice: [+ speech] *"Tea is ready," trilled Daphne.* **trill** /trɪl/ *noun* [C] *We heard the familiar trill of the lark.*

trill [MUSICAL EFFECT] /trɪl/ *noun* [C] SPECIALIZED (the effect achieved by) the fast playing of a note and the note above or below it, one after the other

trillion /ˈtrɪl.jən/ *determiner, noun* [C], *pronoun plural* **trillion** or **trillions** **1** the number 1 000 000 000 000 **2** INFORMAL an extremely large number: *I've never seen so many birds – there were trillions of them!* **trillionth** /ˈtrɪl.jənθ/ *determiner, noun* [C], *pronoun*

trilogy /ˈtrɪl.ə.dʒi/ *noun* [C] a series of three books or plays written about the same situation or characters, forming a continuous story

trim [CUT] /trɪm/ *verb* [T] **-mm-** to make something tidier or more level by cutting a small amount off it: *to trim the hedge* ○ *My hair needs trimming.* ○ *Trim* ***off*** *the leafy ends of the vegetable before cooking.* **trim** /trɪm/ *noun* [S] *I asked the hairdresser for* ***a*** *trim.* ○ *Just* ***give*** *the ends* ***a*** *trim, please.*

trim /trɪm/ *adj* **trimmer, trimmest** tidy and well-ordered: *trim lawns and neat flower beds*

trimmer /ˈtrɪm.əʳ/ [US] /-ɚ/ *noun* [C] a device used for making something tidier or more level by cutting a small amount off it: *a hedge trimmer*

trimmings /ˈtrɪm.ɪŋz/ *plural noun* small pieces that have been cut from something larger to make it tidier: *I always save the* ***hedge*** *trimmings for the compost heap.*

trim [REDUCE] /trɪm/ *verb* [T] **-mm-** to reduce the amount or size of something: *They're trying to trim their costs, so staff who leave are not being replaced.*

trim [THIN] /trɪm/ *adj* **trimmer, trimmest** APPROVING thin in an attractive and healthy way: *You're looking very trim – have you lost weight?*

trim [PREPARED] /trɪm/ *noun* INFORMAL **in trim** physically prepared and ready, or in good condition: *Are you in trim* ***for*** *the run on Sunday?*

trim [MATERIAL] /trɪm/ *noun* [C or U] **trimming**

trimaran /ˈtraɪ.mə.ræn/ *noun* [C] a small fast sailing boat which has a central HULL (= floating part) that is joined to two other smaller hulls, one at each side

trimester /trɪˈmes.təʳ/ /traɪ-/ [US] /traɪˈmes.t̬ɚ/ *noun* [C] **1** a three-month period **2** any of the three three-month periods that a human pregnancy is divided into: *The second trimester is generally the easiest part of a pregnancy.* **3** US any of the three-month periods into which the school or college year is sometimes divided: *Many students arrange internships or work-study placements during the second trimester.* ➲Compare **semester**.

trimmed /trɪmd/ *adj* [after v] If clothes and other cloth items are trimmed, they are decorated, especially around the edges: *She was wearing a black suit trimmed* ***with*** *white.*

trimming /ˈtrɪm.ɪŋ/ *noun* [C or U] (ALSO **trim**) (a piece of) decorative material added around the edge of something: *I want a plain black jumper with no fancy trimmings.* ○ *I wore my red jacket with the black trim.*

trimmings /ˈtrɪm.ɪŋz/ *plural noun* **1** additional things which complete or improve the appearance of something: *a big wedding celebration* ***with all the*** *trimmings* ○ *the traditional trimmings* ***of*** *fame/success* **2** the vegetables and other things that are eaten with the main item of food: *I'll have the turkey* ***with all the*** *trimmings, please.*

trinity /ˈtrɪn.ɪ.ti/ *noun* [C usually sing] LITERARY a group of three things or people: *British culture now appears to revolve around the* ***unholy*** *trinity of sport, shopping and sex.* ○ *Above all Amenabar worships the trinity* ***of*** *Hitchcock, Kubrick and Spielberg.*

the (ˌHoly) ˈTrinity *noun* [S] LITERARY in Christianity, the existence of one God in three forms, the Father, the Son and the Holy Spirit

trinket /ˈtrɪŋ.kɪt/ *noun* [C] a small decorative object, or an item of jewellery that is cheap or of low quality: *She always returns from vacation with a few souvenirs, even if they're only* ***cheap*** *trinkets.*

trio /ˈtriː.əʊ/ [US] /-oʊ/ *group noun* [C] *plural* **trios** **1** a group of three people or things: *There was disappointment for our trio* ***of*** *200 metre runners, all of whom failed to reach the final.* **2** a group of three musicians or singers who perform together: *Many* ***jazz*** *trios consist of a piano, guitar and double bass.*

trio /ˈtriː.əʊ/ [US] /-oʊ/ *noun* [C] *plural* **trios** a piece of music that has been written to be performed by three people: *The final item in today's programme is Beethoven's Trio in B flat, Opus 11.*

trip [LOSE BALANCE] /trɪp/ *verb* [I or T] **-pp-** to lose your balance after knocking your foot against something when you are walking or running, or to cause someone to do this: *He tripped and fell over, grazing his knee.* ○ *That cable is dangerous. Someone might trip* ***over*** *it.* ○ *He was sent off for deliberately tripping Robson when he was about to score a goal.* **trip** /trɪp/ *noun* [C] *She broke her ankle when she had a nasty trip on the stairs.*

trip [JOURNEY] /trɪp/ *noun* [C] a journey in which you go somewhere, usually for a short time, and come back again: *The trip* ***from*** *York* ***to*** *Newcastle takes about an hour by train.* ○ *Do you want to go* ***on*** *the school trip to France this year?* ○ *I thought we might hire a motorboat and* ***take*** *a trip* ***round/around*** *the bay.* ○ MAINLY UK *We can't afford another trip* ***abroad*** *this year.* ○ *It's a 10-mile trip from the airport to the city centre.* ○ *She's away on a* ***business*** *trip and won't be back until next week.* ○ *I was thinking we might go on a* ***shopping*** *trip to Oxford on Saturday.* ➲See Note **travel, journey or trip?** at **travel**.

tripper /ˈtrɪp.əʳ/ [US] /-ɚ/ *noun* [C] MAINLY UK someone who visits a place briefly, often with a large group of other people: *Thousands of* ***day*** *trippers flock to resorts on the south coast.* ○ *The café was full of* ***coach*** *trippers.*

trip [MOVE] /trɪp/ *verb* [I usually + adv or prep] **-pp-** to move with quick gentle steps: *She looked stunning as she tripped* ***down*** *the stairs in her ball gown.*

• **trip off the tongue** Something that trips off the tongue is easy to say or pronounce: *The new company will need to have a name that trips off the tongue and is easy to remember.*

trip [SWITCH] /trɪp/ *verb* [T] **-pp-** to move a switch that operates an electrical system, or to cause such a system to start or stop working by moving a switch: *A special system prevents the circuitry being tripped accidentally by a power surge or lightning strike.*

trip [EXPERIENCE] /trɪp/ *verb* [I] **-pp-** *SLANG* to experience the effects of taking an illegal drug which causes the user to see, hear or feel things that do not exist: *When I was a student I spent a lot of time tripping **out on** LSD.*

trip /trɪp/ *noun* [C] **1** *SLANG* when you trip as a result of taking an illegal drug: *If you take this stuff when you're depressed, you'll **have** a really **bad** trip.* **2** *DISAPPROVING* **guilt/power/ego trip** when you experience a particular feeling strongly and noticeably over a period of time: *She's been **on** a real **power** trip since she became the office manager.* ○ *I suffer from the classic working mother's **guilt** trip.*

PHRASAL VERBS WITH **trip** ▼

▲ **trip** *(sb)* **up** [FALL] *phrasal verb* [M] to fall because you hit your foot on something, or to make someone fall by putting your foot in front of their foot: *I'm terribly sorry. I didn't mean to trip you up.* ○ *She tripped up on the rug.*

▲ **trip** *(sb)* **up** [FAIL] *phrasal verb INFORMAL* to make a mistake, or to cause someone to make a mistake: *The exam went quite well, except at the end when I tripped up **on** the final question.* ○ *At the interview, they were trying to trip me up all the way through.*

tripartite /ˌtraɪˈpɑː.taɪt/ ⓊⓈ /-pɑːr.taɪt/ *adj FORMAL* involving three people or organizations, or existing in three parts: *The minister is to hold tripartite meetings with the oil and car industries to discuss ways of reducing pollution.* ○ *A tripartite agreement brought together government, industry and trade unions in an effort to reduce unemployment.*

tripe [FOOD] /traɪp/ *noun* [U] the covering of the inside of the stomach of an animal, such as a cow or sheep, used for food: *stewed tripe*

tripe [STUPID IDEAS] /traɪp/ *noun* [U] *INFORMAL* ideas, suggestions or writing that are stupid, silly or have little value: *She said my last essay was complete tripe.* ○ *People **talk a lot of** tripe about fashion.*

triple /ˈtrɪp.l̩/ *adj* **1** having three parts of the same type, or happening three times: *Her trainer is a triple Olympic **champion**.* ○ *There's a triple **bill** of Hitchcock films (= three films) on at the cinema next Sunday.* **2 triple** *sth* three times as large as something: *The number of one-parent U.S. households reached 10.1 million in 1991, **nearly** triple that of 1971.*

triple /ˈtrɪp.l̩/ *verb* [I or T] to increase three times in size or amount, or to make something do this: *We have tripled our output over the past two years.* ○ *The workforce has tripled **in size** since the new factory opened.*

the ˈ**triple** ˌ**jump** *noun* [S] a sports event in which the competitor jumps from one foot and lands on it, then jumps from one foot and lands on the other, and finally jumps with both feet: *She's the European triple jump champion.* ˈ**triple** ˌ**jumper** *noun* [C]

triplet /ˈtrɪp.lət/ *noun* [C] one of three children born to the same mother at the same time: *I was amazed when my doctor told me I was going to have triplets.*

triplicate /ˈtrɪp.lɪ.kət/ *adj* [before n] *FORMAL* existing in three parts that are exactly the same

• **in triplicate** When a document is prepared or written in triplicate, two exact copies of it are made also: *The application has to be completed in triplicate, with the original being kept by the bank and the copies going to the customer and the tax office.*

tripod /ˈtraɪ.pɒd/ ⓊⓈ /-pɑːd/ *noun* [C] a support with three legs for a piece of equipment such as a camera: *For photographs requiring long exposure times, your camera should be **mounted on** a tripod.*

triptych /ˈtrɪp.tɪk/ *noun* [C] *SPECIALIZED* a piece of art made of three paintings connected to each other in a way that allows the two outer ones to fold in towards

the larger central one: *A medieval triptych hung above the altar.*

tripwire /ˈtrɪp.waɪəʳ/ ⓊⓈ /-waɪr/ *noun* [C] a wire stretched low above the ground which operates an explosive device, a gun or a device for catching animals when it is touched by the foot of a person or animal

trite /traɪt/ *adj DISAPPROVING* expressed too frequently to be interesting or seem sincere: *His lyrics about love and peace are too trite for me to take them seriously.* ○ *I know it will **sound** trite, but I've loved being part of this club.* **tritely** /ˈtraɪt.li/ *adv* **triteness** /ˈtraɪt.nəs/ *noun* [U]

triumph /ˈtraɪ.əmpf/ *noun* [C or U] a very great success, achievement or victory, or a feeling of great satisfaction or pleasure caused by this: *The book celebrates the hostages' remarkable triumph **over** appalling adversity.* ○ *The signing of the agreement was a **personal** triumph for the Prime Minister.* ○ *It was the Republican Party's third **election** triumph in a row.* ○ *The eradication of smallpox by vaccination was one of medicine's greatest triumphs.* ○ *The constitutional changes were **hailed as** a triumph **for** democracy.* ○ *The match ended in triumph for the French team.* ○ *He **returned in** triumph from the sales with a half-price stereo system.* **triumph** /ˈtraɪ.əmpf/ *verb* [I] *I believe that sooner or later good must triumph **over** evil.* ○ *The Democrats once again triumphed in recent elections.*

triumphal /traɪˈʌm.fəl/ *adj* describes something that celebrates a great victory or success: *Shortly after his triumphal **entry** into Havana in January 1959, Castro spoke on television for seven hours without a break.* ○ *Her popularity has declined since her triumphal **return** from exile two years ago.*

triumphalism /traɪˈʌm.fəl.ɪ.z³m/ *noun* [U] *DISAPPROVING* when you obtain pleasure and satisfaction from the defeat of someone else: *There wasn't a hint of triumphalism in her acceptance speech at the awards ceremony.* **triumphalist** /traɪˈʌm.fəl.ɪst/ *adj, noun* [C] *a triumphalist victory parade*

triumphant /traɪˈʌm.fənt/ *adj* having achieved a great victory or success, or feeling very happy and proud because of such an achievement: *It seemed as though the whole city had turned out for their team's triumphant homecoming.* ○ *She emerged triumphant from the court after all the charges against her were dropped because of a lack of evidence.* ○ *She made a triumphant **return** to the stage after several years working in television.* **triumphantly** /traɪˈʌm.fənt.li/ *adv*: *Bob triumphantly announced his promotion.*

triumvirate /traɪˈʌm.vɪ.rət/ *noun* [C] *FORMAL* a group of three people who are in control of an activity or organization: *The shape of post-war Europe was decided in Potsdam in 1945 by the Allied triumvirate of Churchill, Truman and Stalin.*

trivet /ˈtrɪv.ɪt/ *noun* [C] *SPECIALIZED* a metal stand which you put on a table to protect its surface from hot dishes or pans

trivia /ˈtrɪv.i.ə/ *plural noun* unimportant details or information: *She has an encyclopedic knowledge of pop trivia.* ○ *I'm fascinated by the trivia of everyday life.*

trivial /ˈtrɪv.i.əl/ *adj* **1** having little value or importance: *I don't know why he gets so upset about something that is **utterly** trivial.* ○ *Sexual harassment in the workplace is not a trivial **matter**.* **2** describes a problem that is easy to solve: *Getting computers to understand human language is not a trivial problem.*

triviality /ˌtrɪv.iˈæl.ə.ti/ ⓊⓈ /-t̬i/ *noun* **1** [C usually pl] something that is unimportant: *I'm a busy man – don't bother me with trivialities.* **2** [U] lack of importance: *The prison sentence seemed rather harsh, considering the triviality of the offence.*

trivialize, *UK USUALLY* **-ise** /ˈtrɪv.i.ə.laɪz/ *verb* [T] *DISAPPROVING* to make something seem less important than it really is: *I don't want to trivialise the problem, but I do think there are more important matters to discuss.*

trod /trɒd/ ⓊⓈ /trɑːd/ *past simple and past participle of* **tread**: *It really hurt when Mark trod on my foot.*

trodden /ˈtrɒd.³n/ ⓊⓈ /ˈtrɑː.d³n/ *past participle of* **tread**: *The manufacturers claim the truck is strong enough to survive being trodden **on** by an elephant.*

T

troglodyte /ˈtrɒg.lə.daɪt/ ⓤ /ˈtrɑː.glə-/ *noun* [C] *SPECIALIZED* a person who lives in a cave: *Most people associate troglodytes with prehistoric times, but troglodyte communities still exist in Tunisia and China.*

troika /ˈtrɔɪ.kə/ *noun* [C] *FORMAL* a group of three people, especially government officials: *She is a member of the president's troika of close advisers.*

Trojan horse /ˌtrəʊ.dʒən ˈhɔːs/ ⓤ /ˌtroʊ.dʒən ˈhɔːrs/ *noun* [S] *LITERARY* a person or thing that joins and deceives a group or organization in order to attack it from the inside: *Older supporters have accused the new leadership of being a Trojan horse that will try to destroy the party from the inside.*

troll [CREATURE] /trəʊl/ /trɒl/ ⓤ /troʊl/ *noun* [C] an imaginary, either very large or very small creature in traditional Scandinavian stories, that has magical powers and lives in mountains or caves

troll [SEARCH] /trəʊl/ /trɒl/ ⓤ /troʊl/ *verb* [I or T] *MAINLY US* to search among a large number or a great variety of places in order to find people or information you want: *They are trolling the Internet for new customers.*

troll [COMPUTING] /trəʊl/ /trɒl/ ⓤ /troʊl/ *verb* [I or T] to leave an intentionally annoying message on a part of the Internet in order to get attention or cause trouble: *His hobby is trolling for newbies.* **troll** /trəʊl/ /trɒl/ ⓤ /troʊl/ *noun* [C] *A well-constructed troll will provoke irate or confused responses from flamers and newbies.*

trolley [FOR CARRYING] *UK* (*plural* **trolleys** or **trollies**) /ˈtrɒl.i/ ⓤ /ˈtrɑː.li/ *noun* [C] (*US* **cart**) **1** a small vehicle with two or four wheels that you push or pull to transport large or heavy objects on: *a shopping trolley* ○ *The hospital is so overcrowded that some patients are being treated on trolleys in the corridors.* ○ *Why will supermarket trolleys never move in the direction that you push them in?* **2** a table on four small wheels with one or more shelves under it which is used for serving food or drinks: *Betty almost ran me over with her tea trolley as I was walking into the office!* ○ *Every thirty minutes or so the flight attendant would wheel the drinks trolley down the aisle.*

● **off your trolley** *UK INFORMAL* behaving in an extremely unusual way or doing something very silly: *Anyone who saw us doing this would think we were off our trolleys.* ○ *Have you gone completely off your trolley? You'll never get away with it!*

trolley [VEHICLE] (*plural* **trolleys** or **trollies**) /ˈtrɒl.i/ ⓤ /ˈtrɑː.li/ *noun* [C] (*ALSO* **trolleycar**) *US FOR* **tram**: *You can catch the number 47 trolley from the train station.*

trolleybus /ˈtrɒl.i.bʌs/ ⓤ /ˈtrɑː.li-/ *noun* [C] a public transport vehicle with rubber tyres which travels along ordinary roads in towns and is powered by electricity that is collected from a wire above the road: *The trolleybus does not run on tracks.*

trolleyed /ˈtrɒl.id/ ⓤ /ˈtrɑː.lid/ *adj* [after v] *INFORMAL* extremely drunk

trollop /ˈtrɒl.əp/ ⓤ /ˈtrɑː.ləp/ *noun* [C] *OLD-FASHIONED OR HUMOROUS DISAPPROVING* a woman who has had a lot of sexual relationships without any emotional involvement: *That woman's a real trollop. Every time I see her she's with a different man.*

trombone /trɒmˈbəʊn/ ⓤ /trɑːmˈboʊn/ *noun* [C] a large, brass, musical instrument that you play by blowing into it and sliding a U-shaped tube in and out to change the length and produce different notes: *The main orchestral brass instruments are the horn, trumpet, trombone, and tuba.*

trombonist /trɒmˈbəʊ.nɪst/ ⓤ /trɑːmˈboʊ-/ *noun* [C] someone who plays a trombone: *My cousin is a jazz trombonist.*

troop [GROUP] /truːp/ *noun* [C] **1** a group of soldiers, especially ones who fight in strong military vehicles or on horses: *the King's Troop of the Royal Horse Artillery* **2** an organized group of young people who are Scouts: *We've got a troop of Scouts camping in one of our fields this weekend.*

trooper /ˈtruː.pəʳ/ ⓤ /-pɚ/ *noun* [C] **1** a soldier who belongs to the lowest rank in the part of an army that fights in strong military vehicles or on horses **2** *US* a police officer in one of the forces of the 50 political areas

of the United States: *state troopers* ○ *Troopers are called out in emergencies or dangerous situations.*

● **swear like a trooper** to swear a lot: *He was extremely drunk and swearing like a trooper.*

troop [WALK] /truːp/ *verb* **1** [I usually + adv or prep] to walk somewhere in a large group, usually with one person behind another: *The little boys trooped after him across the playing fields.* ○ *The Norwich fans gave their team a loud cheer as they trooped off the field.* ○ *None of us knew what to expect as we trooped into her office.* **2** [I] *INFORMAL HUMOROUS* to travel somewhere as a group, especially when told to: *I suppose head office expects us all to troop down to London for this meeting.*

● **the trooping of the colour** *UK* a ceremony in which a military flag is carried in public with the soldiers that it represents marching behind it: *We watched the trooping of the colour live from Horse Guards Parade.*

troop carrier *noun* [C] a vehicle, ship or aircraft that has been designed for transporting a lot of soldiers: *an armoured troop carrier*

troops /truːps/ *plural noun* soldiers on duty in a large group: *Traditionally, United Nations troops have been deployed only in a peacekeeping role.* ○ *The major powers have said they will not send in ground troops (= soldiers who fight on land).* ○ *In 1988, about 220 000 American troops were stationed in Western Europe.* ○ *All troops will be withdrawn by the end of the year.*

troop /truːp/ *adj* [before n] *Satellite photographs provide us with a lot of information about their troop movements.*

troopship /ˈtruːp.ʃɪp/ *noun* [C] a ship that is used for transporting large numbers of soldiers, especially one that was previously used for trading

trophy /ˈtrəʊ.fi/ ⓤ /ˈtroʊ-/ *noun* [C] **1** a prize, such as a gold or silver cup, which is given to the winner of a competition or race, and often returned after a year to be given to the winner of the competition in the following year: *He's an excellent snooker player, but he's never won a major trophy.* ○ *The Duchess of Kent will be presenting the trophies.* **2** something used as a symbol of success from hunting or war: *That stuffed pike above the fireplace is Pat's trophy from a fishing holiday in Scotland.*

trophy wife/girlfriend *noun* [C] *DISAPPROVING* a young attractive woman who is the partner of a rich and successful older man and acts as a symbol of his social position

tropic /ˈtrɒp.ɪk/ ⓤ /ˈtrɑː.pɪk/ *noun* [C] one of the two imaginary lines around the Earth at approximately 23.5 degrees north and 23.5 degrees south of the Equator

the tropics *plural noun* the hottest area of the Earth, between the Tropic of Cancer and the Tropic of Capricorn: *She's a botanist and spent several years researching in the tropics.*

tropical /ˈtrɒp.ɪ.kᵊl/ ⓤ /ˈtrɑː.pɪ-/ *adj* **1** from or relating to the area between the two tropics: *tropical fish* ○ *a tropical island/region/climate* ○ *Leprosy is one of the few tropical diseases which could be eradicated early in the 21st century.* ○ *She specialises in tropical medicine (= the treatment of diseases from the tropical areas of the world).* ○ *The Amazon river basin contains the world's largest tropical rainforest.* ○ *The hurricane was downgraded to a tropical storm when its speed dropped to 70mph.* ●See also **subtropical.** **2** *INFORMAL* extremely hot and feeling wet: *The weather was positively tropical last summer.*

the Tropic of Cancer *noun* [S] the northern tropic

the Tropic of Capricorn *noun* [S] the southern tropic

trot [RUN] /trɒt/ ⓤ /trɑːt/ *noun* **1** [S] a way in which a four-legged animal moves which is faster than walking, in which a front leg and the back leg on the opposite side move together: *He climbed onto his horse and set off at a relaxed trot down the lane.* **2** [C] a slow run by a human: *The team warmed up for the match with a trot around the pitch.* **trot** /trɒt/ ⓤ /trɑːt/ *verb* [I usually + adv or prep] **-tt-** *We were trotting along the lane when a car suddenly appeared from nowhere and almost made me fall off my pony.* ○ *The dog trotted down the path to greet* *me.* ➲Compare **canter**; **gallop**.

trot [HURRY] /trɒt/ [US] /trɑːt/ *verb* **-tt-** **1** [I usually + adv or prep] *INFORMAL* When people trot somewhere, they go there in a quick or busy way: *She left her purse on the counter, so I had to trot* ***down*** *the street after her.* ○ *"I'm in a bit of a rush. I'll give you a ring," said James, and* ***off*** *he trotted.* ○ *Although she retired from politics five years ago, she still trots around the globe, giving speeches and meeting world leaders.* ➲See also **globetrotter**. **2** [I + adv or prep] *INFORMAL* to speak or do something too quickly: *She was rather nervous and trotted* ***through*** *her speech a bit too quickly.*

• **a (quick/brisk) trot through** ***sth*** *INFORMAL* when you examine or explain the whole of a subject, method or piece of work quickly without stopping or getting slower: *In this book, John Pemble takes a* ***brisk*** *trot through the history and mysteries of Venice.*

• **on the trot** *UK INFORMAL* If you do things on the trot, you do them directly after each other without pausing: *They won three games on the trot.* ○ *She worked 30 hours on the trot to get the job finished on time.*

PHRASAL VERBS WITH **trot** ▼

▲ **trot** ***sth*** **out** *phrasal verb* [M] *DISAPPROVING* to state an idea, opinion or fact, especially one that has been stated often before or one that is foolish: *You trot out that argument whenever I try to discuss this matter with you.* ○ *Whenever I ask him why his essay's late, he just trots out the same* ***old*** *excuses.*

▲ **trot** ***sb*** **out** *phrasal verb* [M often passive] *DISAPPROVING* to send someone out to represent or defend your idea or opinion in public, in a boring and familiar way: *Whenever the President is in difficulties, her spokesman is trotted out to face the press.*

troth /trəʊθ/ [US] /troʊθ/ *noun* [U] ➲See **plight your troth** at **plight** MARRY.

the trots /ðəˈtrɒts/ [US] /-ˈtrɑːts/ *plural noun INFORMAL* **diarrhoea** (= a condition in which the contents of the bowels are emptied too often): *to get/have the trots* ○ *That prawn curry gave me the trots.*

trotter /ˈtrɒt.əʳ/ [US] /ˈtrɑː.t̬ɚ/ *noun* [C usually pl] a pig's foot used for food: *a dish of pigs' trotters*

troubadour /ˈtruː.bə.dɔːʳ/ [US] /-dɔːr/ *noun* [C] a male poet and singer who travelled around southern France and northern Italy between the 11th and 13th centuries entertaining wealthy people

trouble [DIFFICULTIES] /ˈtrʌb.l̩/ *noun* **1** [C or U] problems or difficulties: *The form was terribly complicated and I* ***had*** *a lot of trouble* ***with*** *it.* ○ *Their problems seem to be over for the moment, but there could be more trouble* ***ahead.*** ○ *The trouble* ***started/began when*** *my father came to live with us.* ○ [+ v-ing] *Parents often* ***have*** *trouble* ***finding*** *restaurants that welcome young children.* ○ *You'll only be* ***storing up*** *trouble* ***for*** *the future if you don't go to the dentist now.* ○ *I should get it finished over the weekend without* ***too much*** *trouble.* ○ *She thought her troubles would be over once she'd got divorced.* ○ *My Christmas shopping is* ***the least of*** *my troubles at the moment – I haven't even got enough money to pay the rent.* ○ *Most of the current troubles stem* (= originate) *from our new computer system.* **2** [U] a characteristic of someone or something that is considered a disadvantage or problem: *Ron's trouble is that he's too impatient.* ○ ***The*** *trouble* ***with*** *this carpet is that it gets dirty very easily.* ○ *It's a brilliant idea.* ***The only*** *trouble* ***is that*** *we don't know how much it will cost.* **3** [U] problems or difficulties caused by something failing to operate as it should: *The plane developed* ***engine*** *trouble shortly after takeoff.* ○ *They have a good reputation for building reliable trouble-****free*** *cars.* ○ *Her* ***knee*** *trouble is expected to keep her out of the game for the rest of the season.* **4** [U] problems in the form of arguments, fighting or violence: *Listen, I don't want any trouble in here, so please just finish your drink and leave.* ○ *You can only go to the match if you promise to leave* ***at the first sign of*** *trouble.* ○ *My little brother's always trying to* ***stir up*** (= create) *trouble* ***between*** *me and my boyfriend.* **5** [U] a situation in which you experience problems, usually because of something you have done wrong or badly: *He's never* ***been in*** *trouble* ***with*** *his teachers before.* ○ *She'll be in* ***big*** *trouble if she crashes Sam's car.* ○ *He got into* ***financial*** *trouble after his divorce.* ○ *I hope you won't* ***get into*** *trouble because of what I said to your dad.* ○ *The camp is a great way of getting kids off the street and* ***keeping*** *them* ***out of*** *trouble.* ○ *I hope I haven't* ***landed*** *you* ***in*** *trouble with your boss.* ○ *The marriage* ***ran into*** *trouble because of her husband's heavy drinking.* ○ *The company will be in* ***serious/real*** *trouble if we lose this contract.* ○ *He's* ***stayed out of*** *trouble since he was released from jail last year.*

• **be asking for trouble** to be likely to cause problems or difficulties for yourself: *Giving him such a powerful car when he's only just learned to drive is asking for trouble.*

• **spell trouble** to suggest that there may be problems in the future: *The latest opinion polls spell trouble* ***for*** *the government.*

• **get** ***sb*** **into trouble** *OLD-FASHIONED* If a man gets a woman or girl who is not married into trouble, he makes her pregnant: *When he got his girlfriend into trouble, they had to choose between marriage and an abortion.*

trouble /ˈtrʌb.l̩/ *verb* [T often passive] to cause someone to have a problem or difficulties: *He has been troubled by a knee injury for most of the season.* **troubled** /ˈtrʌb.l̩d/ *adj*: *The survival package involves selling off the unprofitable parts of the troubled* ***company.*** ○ *This troubled* ***region*** *has had more than its fair share of wars over the centuries.* ○ *In these troubled* ***times,*** *it makes a change to hear some good news.*

troublesome /ˈtrʌb.l̩.səm/ *adj* causing a lot of problems or worries for someone: *Her hip has been troublesome for quite a while, and she'll probably need surgery on it.* ○ *The negotiations have* ***proven*** *more troublesome than any of us expected.*

COMMON LEARNER ERROR

trouble or problem?

Problem means 'a situation that causes difficulties and that needs to be dealt with'. You can talk about **a problem** or **problems**.

Tell me what the problem is.
There's a problem with the engine.
He's having a few problems at work.

Trouble means 'problems, difficulties, or worries' and is used to talk about problems in a more general way. **Trouble** is almost always uncountable so do not use the determiner 'a' before it.

We had some trouble while we were on holiday.
He helped me when I was in trouble.
I had trouble with the car last night.
~~*I had a trouble with the car last night.*~~

Troubles is used in a small number of particular phrases to talk about all of the problems that someone has or that a country/organization has. You should not use **troubles** unless you are sure that it is correct.

~~*The report outlines the troubles caused by unemployment.*~~
The report outlines the problems caused by unemployment.

trouble [INCONVENIENCE] /ˈtrʌb.l̩/ *noun* [U] inconvenience or effort: *I didn't mean to* ***cause*** *you any trouble.* ○ *"I'd love some more tea, if it isn't too much trouble." "Oh, it's* ***no*** *trouble* ***at all."*** ○ *I don't want to* ***put*** *you* ***to*** *any trouble* (= create any work for you). ○ [+ to infinitive] *If you* ***took the*** *trouble* ***to*** *listen to what I was saying, you'd know what I was talking about.* ○ *They* ***went to a lot of*** *trouble* (= made a lot of effort) ***for*** *their dinner party, but half the guests didn't bother to turn up.* ○ *It's annoying, but I don't think I'll* ***go to the*** *trouble* ***of*** *making an official complaint.*

• **more trouble than it's worth** (*ALSO* **not worth the trouble**) *INFORMAL* If something is more trouble than it's worth or is not worth the trouble, it is not important or useful enough to make an effort doing it: ***It's*** *more trouble than it's worth* ***to*** *take it back to the shop and ask for a replacement.* ○ *It's not* ***worth the*** *trouble* ***(of)*** *applying for that job. You've no chance of getting it.*

trouble /ˈtrʌb.l̩/ *verb* [T] *SLIGHTLY FORMAL* to cause someone a small amount of inconvenience or effort: *May I trouble you* ***for*** (= Please could you give me) *some more wine, please?* ○ [+ obj + to infinitive] *Could I trouble you* ***to*** *open that window? I'm afraid I can't reach it.* ○ [R] *Let's not trouble ourselves* (= make the effort to think) ***about***

the precise details at the moment.

trouble [WORRY] /ˈtrʌb.l̩/ *verb* **[T]** to cause someone to be worried or anxious: *What's troubling you, dear? You look ever so worried.* ○ FORMAL *Many of us are deeply troubled* ***by*** *the chairman's decision.* ○ **[+ (that)]** ***It*** *troubles me* ***(that)*** *you didn't discuss your problems with me earlier.* **troubling** /ˈtrʌb.lɪŋ/ *adj*: *Some troubling* ***questions*** *remain about the legal status of frozen embryos.* **troublingly** /ˈtrʌb.lɪŋ.li/ *adv*

troublemaker /ˈtrʌb.l̩ˌmeɪ.kəʳ/ Ⓤⓢ /-kɚ/ *noun* **[C]** someone who intentionally causes problems for other people, especially people who are in a position of power or authority: *I was worried that I would be regarded as a troublemaker if I complained about the safety standards in the factory.*

troubleshooter /ˈtrʌb.l̩ˌʃuː.təʳ/ Ⓤⓢ /-t̬ɚ/ *noun* **[C]** someone whose job is to discover why something does not work effectively and make suggestions about how to improve it: *A troubleshooter is being appointed to make the prison service more efficient.* **troubleshooting** /ˈtrʌb.l̩ˌʃuː.tɪŋ/ Ⓤⓢ /-t̬ɪŋ/ *noun* **[U]** *The instruction manual includes a section on troubleshooting to help you with any simple problems you might have with the television.*

ˈtrouble ˌspot *noun* **[C]** a place where trouble, especially political violence, happens regularly: *There is increasing demand for the United Nations to intervene in trouble spots throughout the world.*

trough [CONTAINER] /trɒf/ Ⓤⓢ /trɑːf/ *noun* **[C] 1** a long narrow container without a lid that usually holds water or food for farm animals: *cows at the feeding trough* **2 the trough** a supply of money or other advantage which people eagerly and sometimes dishonestly take a share of: *The council had been handing out grants indiscriminately, and people were hurrying to get their* ***snouts in the*** *trough.*

trough [LOW POINT] /trɒf/ Ⓤⓢ /trɑːf/ *noun* **[C] 1** a low point in a regular series of high and low points: *Investing small amounts regularly is a good way of smoothing out the* ***peaks and*** *troughs of the stock market.* **2** SPECIALIZED in the study of weather patterns, a long area of low air pressure between two areas of high air pressure: *A trough* ***of low pressure*** *over hilly areas will bring heavy thunderstorms overnight.*

trounce /traʊnts/ *verb* **[T]** INFORMAL to defeat a competitor by a large amount: *France trounced Germany* ***by*** *five goals to one in the qualifying match.* ○ *She trounced her rivals in the election.*

trouncing /ˈtraʊnt.sɪŋ/ *noun* **[C usually sing]** INFORMAL a serious defeat: *the party's trouncing* (= serious defeat) *in the local elections* ○ *Major changes are expected in the England team following their 3-0 trouncing last Saturday.*

troupe /truːp/ *group noun* **[C]** a group of performers such as singers or dancers who work and travel together: *She joined a* ***dance*** *troupe and travelled all over Europe.* ○ *A troupe of* ***dancers*** *from Beijing is one of the leading attractions in the festival.*

trouper /ˈtruː.pəʳ/ Ⓤⓢ /-pɚ/ *noun* **[C] 1** a successful entertainer who has had a lot of experience **2** APPROVING anyone with a lot of experience who can be depended on and does not complain: *Good old Edna – she's a* ***real*** *trouper to do the washing-up without even being asked!* ○ *He took his disappointment* ***like a*** *trouper.*

ˈtrouser ˌpress *noun* **[C]** a device for making or keeping trousers smooth by pressing them between two boards

trousers /ˈtraʊ.zəz/ Ⓤⓢ /-zɚz/ *plural noun* (US USUALLY ALSO **pants**) a piece of clothing that covers the lower part of the body from the waist to the feet, consisting of two cylindrical parts, one for each leg, which are joined at the top: *I need a new* ***pair of*** *trousers to go with this jacket.* ○ *Why aren't you* ***wearing*** *any trousers, David?* ➲See picture **Clothes** on page Centre 6 **trouser** /ˈtraʊ.zəʳ/ Ⓤⓢ /-zɚ/ *adj* **[before n]** (US USUALLY **pants**) *"Just look at this scar," said Brian proudly, rolling up his trouser* ***leg***.

ˈtrouser ˌsuit UK *noun* **[C]** (US **pantsuit**) a matching jacket and pair of trousers that is worn by women on formal occasions: *She's bought a very smart trouser suit for her job interviews.*

trousseau /ˈtruː.səʊ/ Ⓤⓢ /-soʊ/ *noun* **[C]** OLD-FASHIONED a collection of personal possessions, such as clothes, that a woman takes to her new home when she gets married

trout [FISH] /traʊt/ *noun plural* **trout** or **trouts 1 [C or U]** a fish that is a popular food, especially a brown type that lives in rivers and lakes or a silver type that lives in the sea but returns to rivers to reproduce: *Thousands of young salmon and trout have been killed by the pollution.* ○ *Loch Leven is famous for its trout* ***fishing***. **2 [U]** the flesh of this fish eaten as food: *I love smoked trout, don't you?*

trout [PERSON] /traʊt/ *noun* **[C]** *plural* **trouts** UK INFORMAL an old unattractive person, especially a woman: *She's a miserable* ***old*** *trout who complains about everything.*

trowel /traʊəl/ *noun* **[C] 1** a small tool consisting of a flat metal blade joined to a handle, used for spreading building materials such as cement **2** a small tool with a curved pointed metal blade, used in the garden for digging small holes and removing small plants from the earth

truant /ˈtruː.ənt/ *noun* **[C]** a child who is regularly absent from school without permission: *Police reports showed that the vast majority of crime committed by children was carried out by truants.*

truant /ˈtruː.ənt/ *verb* **[I]** MAINLY UK Children who truant are regularly absent from school, usually while pretending to their parents that they have gone to school: *You'll fail all your exams if you carry on truanting.* **truancy** /ˈtruː.ənt.si/ *noun* **[U]** (UK ALSO **truanting**) *My daughter's school has very good exam results and hardly any truancy.* ○ *Truanting was a serious problem in a fifth of the schools surveyed.*

• **play truant** (US USUALLY ALSO **play hooky**) to be regularly absent from school without permission: *Most parents are horrified when they discover their children have been playing truant* ***from school***.

truce /truːs/ *noun* **[C]** a brief interruption in a war or argument, or an agreement to stop fighting or arguing for a period of time: *After years of rivalry, the two companies have* (UK) ***agreed***/(US) ***agreed to*** *a truce.* ○ *We've got to spend the weekend together, so we might as well* ***call*** (= have) *a truce.* ○ *Following last month's riots, the two big gangs in Los Angeles have finally* ***declared*** *a truce, ending years of bloodshed.* ○ *The fragile truce* ***between*** *the two sides is not expected to last long.*

truck [VEHICLE] /trʌk/ *noun* **[C] 1** (UK ALSO **lorry**) a large road vehicle which is used for transporting large amounts of goods: *The road was completely blocked by an overturned truck.* ○ *a truck driver* ➲See also **dumper truck**. ➲See picture **Cars and Trucks** on page Centre 13 **2** UK (US **car**) a part of a train that is used for carrying goods or animals: *Hundreds of refugees were herded into* ***cattle*** *trucks for the gruelling ten-hour journey.*

truck /trʌk/ *verb* **[T usually + adv or prep]** MAINLY US to transport something somewhere in a truck: *Most of the aid is being trucked into the city, although some is arriving by boat.*

• **keep on trucking** INFORMAL to continue to do something that that is ordinary and boring: *"How's work going?" "Oh, okay. I just keep on trucking."*

trucker UK AND US /ˈtrʌk.əʳ/ Ⓤⓢ /-ɚ/ *noun* **[C]** (AUS **truckie**) someone whose job is driving trucks **trucking** US /ˈtrʌk.ɪŋ/ *noun* **[U]** (UK **road haulage**) *The railroads have lost a lot of business to trucking* ***companies***.

truckload /ˈtrʌk.ləʊd/ Ⓤⓢ /-loʊd/ *noun* **[C]** the amount of something that can be carried by a truck: *Truckloads* ***of*** *rice have been brought in to the areas affected by drought.* ○ *Donations of food and medicines have been arriving* ***by*** *the truckload all week.*

truck [INVOLVEMENT] /trʌk/ *noun* INFORMAL **have no truck with** ***sth/sb*** to refuse to become involved with something or someone because you do not approve of them

ˈtruck ˌfarm *noun* **[C]** US a small farm where fruit and vegetables are grown for selling to the public: *We buy all our produce from the local truck farm.* **ˈtruck ˌfarmer** *noun* **[C]** *The floods have had a severe effect on the livelihoods of truck farmers in the area.*

ˈtruck ˌstop *noun* **[C]** US an area next to an important road with a restaurant, fuel and repair services, where

T

the main customers are truck drivers wanting to eat and drink cheaply

truculent /ˈtrʌk.jʊ.lənt/ *adj* unpleasant and tending to argue a lot: *a truculent teenager* ○ *I found him truculent and unpleasant.* **truculently** /ˈtrʌk.jʊ.lənt.li/ *adv* **truculence** /ˈtrʌk.jʊ.lənts/ *noun* [U]

trudge /trʌdʒ/ *verb* [I usually + adv or prep] to walk slowly with a lot of effort, especially over a difficult surface or while carrying something heavy: *We trudged back up the hill.* ○ *I'd had to trudge* ***through*** *the snow to get there.*
trudge /trʌdʒ/ *noun* [S] a long tiring walk: *We came back from our trudge across the moor wet and tired.*
▲ **trudge through** ***sth*** *phrasal verb* HUMOROUS to do work or a particular task slowly and with effort or difficulty: *I spent the whole weekend trudging through this report, and I still haven't finished reading it.*

true [NOT FALSE] /truː/ *adj* (especially of facts or statements) right and not wrong; correct: [+ that] *Is* ***it*** *true* ***that*** *Lucy and Mark are getting married?* ○ *The allegations,* ***if*** *true, could lead to her resignation.* ○ *Her story is only* ***partly*** *true.* ○ *Would* ***it*** *be true* ***to say*** *that you've never liked Jim?* ○ *I suspect she gave a true* ***picture*** (= accurate description) *of what had happened.* ○ *I don't believe these exam results are a true* ***reflection*** *of your abilities.* ○ *The movie is based on the true* ***story*** *of a London gangster.* ○ *She has since admitted that her earlier statement was not* ***strictly*** (= completely) *true.* ○ *It used to be very cheap but that's no longer true* (= that situation does not now exist). ○ *Alcohol should be consumed in moderation, and this is particularly true* ***for*** *pregnant women.* ○ *Parents of young children often become depressed, and* ***this is*** *especially true* ***of*** *single parents.* ➲See also **truth**. See Note **right or true?** at **right** CORRECT.
• **ring true** If something someone says or writes rings true, it seems to be true: *Something about his explanation didn't quite ring true.*
truism /ˈtruː.ɪ.zᵊm/ *noun* [C] a statement which is so obviously true that it is almost not worth saying: *As far as health is concerned, it's a truism that prevention is better than cure.*
truly /ˈtruː.li/ *adv* used to emphasize that what you are saying is true: *At this time of year the river is a truly beautiful sight.* ○ *She was a truly great actress.* ○ *This is a truly remarkable achievement.* ○ *It was a truly terrifying experience.*

true [REAL] /truː/ *adj* [before n] being what exists, rather than what was thought, intended or claimed: *true love* ○ *a true friend* ○ *There cannot be true democracy without reform of the electoral system.* ○ *The true* ***horror*** *of the accident did not become clear until the following morning.*
• **come true** If a hope, wish or desire comes true, it happens although it was unlikely that it would: *I'd always dreamt of owning my own house, but I never thought it would come true.* ○ *After all the problems I'd had getting pregnant, Oliver's birth was a* ***dream*** *come true.*
• **so ... it's not true** MAINLY UK used to emphasize an adjective: *Julie's brother's so handsome it's not true.*
truly /ˈtruː.li/ *adv* really existing; in fact: *These will be the first truly democratic elections in the country's history.* ○ *It's hard to obtain truly independent financial advice.* ○ *This is a desperate situation which requires a truly radical solution.*

true [SINCERE] /truː/ *adj* sincere or loyal, and likely to continue to be so in difficult situations: *There are few true believers in communism left in the party.* ○ *She has vowed to remain true* ***to*** *the president whatever happens.* ○ *He said he'd repay the money the next day, and true* ***to*** *his* ***word*** (= as he had promised), *he gave it all back to me the following morning.*
• **be true to** ***yourself*** to behave according to your beliefs and do what you think is right
• **true to form/type** Someone who does something true to form or type behaves as other people would have expected from previous experience: *True to form, when it came to his turn to buy the drinks, he said he'd left his wallet at home.*
truly /ˈtruː.li/ *adv* FORMAL sincerely: *Truly I could not have done this without you.* ○ *He truly* ***believes*** *he can cure himself by willpower alone.*
• **yours truly** MAINLY US used to end a letter: *I look forward to hearing from you. Yours truly, Taylor Champinski.*

true [HAVING NECESSARY QUALITIES] /truː/ *adj* [before n] possessing all the characteristics necessary to be accurately described as something: *Only true deer have antlers.* ○ FORMAL *It was said that the portrait was a very true* ***likeness*** *of her* (= looked very much like her). ○ *In true Hollywood* ***style*** (= In a way that is typical of Hollywood), *she's had four marriages and three facelifts.*
truly /ˈtruː.li/ *adv* in an exact way: *Mushrooms aren't truly vegetables, but many people think they are.*

true [ACCURATE] /truː/ *adj* [after v] fitted or positioned accurately: *None of the drawers were true.*
true /truː/ *adv*: *Make sure you hit the nails in true* (= straight and without moving to either side).
true /truː/ *noun* **be out of true** to not be in the correct position or to be slightly bent out of the correct shape: *This door won't shut properly. I think the frame must be out of true.*

true-blue /ˌtruːˈbluː/ *adj* completely loyal to a person or belief: *They want control of the company to remain in true-blue hands.*

true-life story /ˌtruː.laɪfˈstɔː.ri/ [US] /-ˈstɔːr.i/ *noun* [C] a story that is based on real rather than imaginary events

truelove /ˈtruː.lʌv/ *noun* [C] LITERARY a person who is loved by someone more than anyone else in the world

ˌtrue ˈnorth *noun* [U] the direction towards the top of the Earth along an imaginary line at an angle of 90° to the Equator: *True north runs parallel to the earth's axis.*

true-to-life /ˌtruː.təˈlaɪf/ *adj* showing things and people as they really are, or seeming to be real: *She was saying how true-to-life the characters in the film were.*

truffle [RARE FOOD] /ˈtrʌf.l̩/ *noun* [C] an edible type of fungus which grows underground and is expensive because it is very rare: *The Dordogne region's gastronomic specialities include truffles and foie gras.*

truffle [CHOCOLATE] /ˈtrʌf.l̩/ *noun* [C] a small round chocolate which is soft and creamy: *rum truffles*

ˈtrump ˌcard *noun* [C usually sing] an advantage that makes you more likely to succeed than other people, especially something that other people do not know about: *Anthea was about to* ***play*** *her trump card – without her signature none of the money could be released.*

trumpet [INSTRUMENT] /ˈtrʌm.pɪt/ *noun* [C] a brass musical instrument consisting of a metal tube with one narrow end, into which the player blows, and one wide end. Three buttons are pressed in order to change notes.
trumpeter /ˈtrʌm.pɪtəʳ/ *noun* [C] a musician who plays a trumpet: *a jazz trumpeter*

trumpet [ANIMAL CALL] /ˈtrʌm.pɪt/ *verb* [I] (of a large animal, especially an elephant) to produce a loud call: *We could hear the elephants trumpeting in the distance.*

trumpet [ANNOUNCE] /ˈtrʌm.pɪt/ *verb* [T] MAINLY DISAPPROVING to announce or state something proudly to a lot of people: *The museum has been* ***loudly*** *trumpeting its reputation as one of the finest in the world.* ○ *Their* ***much****-trumpeted price cuts affect only 5% of the goods that they sell.*

trumps /trʌmps/ *plural noun* one of the four groups in a set of playing cards which has been chosen to have the highest value during a particular game or part of a game: *Diamonds are trumps.*
• **turn/come up trumps** UK to complete an activity successfully or to produce a good result, especially when you were not expected to: *John's uncle came up trumps, finding us a place to stay at the last minute.*
trump /trʌmp/ *noun* [C] a card that belongs to the group of cards that has been chosen to have the highest value in a particular game: *I played a trump.* ○ *Luckily, I* ***drew*** *a trump.*
• **no trump(s)** when all four groups of cards have equal value in a game of BRIDGE
trump /trʌmp/ *verb* [T] **1** If you trump another player's card, you beat it with a card that belongs to the group of cards that has been chosen to have the highest value in the game you are playing. **2** to beat someone or some-

T

thing by doing or producing something better: *Their million-pound bid for the company was trumped at the last moment by an offer for almost twice as much from their main competitor.*

▲ **trump** *sth* **up** *phrasal verb* [M] to create a false accusation against someone in order to have an excuse for punishing them

trumped-up /ˌtrʌmpt'ʌp/ *adj* [before n] *She was imprisoned on trumped-up corruption* **charges**.

truncate /trʌŋ'keɪt/ *verb* [T] to make something shorter or briefer, especially by removing the end of it: *Television coverage of the match was truncated by a technical fault.* **truncated** /trʌŋ'keɪ.tɪd/ ⑤ /-t̬ɪd/ *adj* **truncation** /trʌŋ'keɪ.ʃ³n/ *noun* [U]

truncheon UK /'trʌnt.ʃ³n/ *noun* [C] (US **nightstick**) a thick heavy stick used as a weapon by police officers

trundle /'trʌn.dl̩/ *verb* **1** [I or T; usually + adv or prep] (to cause something) to move slowly and unevenly on wheels: *She trundled the wheelbarrow down the garden.* ○ *Hundreds of trucks full of fruit and vegetables trundle across the border each day.* **2** [I + adv or prep] INFORMAL DISAPPROVING to develop or operate slowly: *The negotiations have been trundling* **on** *for months and there's still no end in sight.*

▲ **trundle** *sth* **out** *phrasal verb* [M] INFORMAL to produce in a boring way something that has often been seen or used before: *They seem to trundle out the same old films every Christmas.*

trundle ˌ**bed** US *noun* [C] (UK **truckle bed**) a low bed on wheels which is stored under an ordinary bed ready for use by visitors

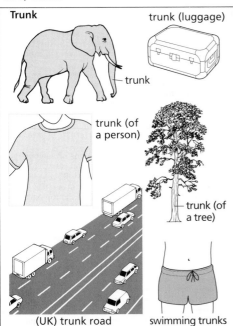

Trunk

trunk (luggage)

trunk

trunk (of a person)

trunk (of a tree)

(UK) trunk road

swimming trunks

trunk MAIN PART /trʌŋk/ *noun* [C] **1** the thick main stem of a tree, from which its branches grow **2** the main part of a person's body, not including the head, legs or arms: *He's got a thick trunk.*

trunk NOSE /trʌŋk/ *noun* [C] an elephant's nose which is long, shaped like a tube and can bend easily ⊃See picture **Animals and Birds** on page Centre 4

trunk CASE /trʌŋk/ *noun* [C] a large strong case that is used for storing clothes and personal possessions, often when travelling or going to live in a new place

trunk CAR US /trʌŋk/ *noun* [C] (UK **boot**) a covered space at the back of a car, for storing things in: *I always keep a blanket and a toolkit in the trunk for emergencies.* ○ *Her husband's dismembered body was later discovered in the*

trunk of her car. ⊃See picture **Car** on page Centre 12

'**trunk** ˌ**road** *noun* [C] UK an important road for travelling long distances at high speed, which is suitable for large vehicles and a lot of traffic

trunks /trʌŋks/ *plural noun* [C] (UK ALSO **swimming trunks**) a piece of men's clothing that covers the hips and bottom and the top part of the legs and is worn when swimming ⊃See picture **Clothes** on page Centre 6

truss TIE /trʌs/ *verb* [T] **1** (ALSO **truss up**) to tie the arms and legs of someone together tightly and roughly with rope to prevent them from moving or escaping: *Police said the couple had been trussed up and robbed before being shot.* **2** to prepare a bird for cooking by tying its wings and legs to its body

truss DEVICE /trʌs/ *noun* [C] a device for holding an organ of the body, especially part of the intestine, in its correct position after it has moved because of an injury

truss SUPPORT /trʌs/ *noun* [C] SPECIALIZED a support for a roof or bridge that is usually made of stone or brick

trust BELIEVE /trʌst/ *verb* [I or T] to have belief or confidence in the honesty, goodness, skill or safety of a person, organization or thing: *My sister warned me not to trust him.* ○ *Trust me – I know about these things.* ○ *Trust your instincts and do what you think is right.* ○ *I don't trust air travel – it's unnatural.* ○ [+ obj + to infinitive] *I trust him* **to** *make the right decision.* ○ *That man is* **not** **to be** *trusted.* ○ *I wouldn't trust him* **with** *my car.* ○ SLIGHTLY FORMAL *Sometimes you simply have to trust* **in** *the goodness of human nature.* ○ *However much you plan an expedition like this, you still have to trust* **to luck** *to a certain extent.*

● **Trust** *sb* (**to do** *sth*)! MAINLY UK INFORMAL used to say that it is typical of someone to do something stupid: *Trust Chris to leave the tickets at home!*

● **I wouldn't trust** *sb* **as far as I could throw them.** INFORMAL something that you say which means you do not trust someone at all: *He's very charming but I wouldn't trust him as far as I could throw him.*

trust /trʌst/ *noun* [U] the belief that you can trust someone or something: *a relationship based on trust and understanding* ○ *We were obviously wrong to* **put** *our* **trust** **in** *her.* ○ *He's in* **a position of** *trust* (= a position with responsibilities, especially to the public).

● **take** *sth* **on trust** to believe that something is true although you have no proof

trusting /'trʌs.tɪŋ/ *adj* (ALSO **trustful**) always believing that other people are good or honest and will not harm or deceive you: *The child gave a lovely trusting smile.* ○ *You shouldn't be so trusting – people take advantage of you.*

trusty /'trʌs.ti/ *adj* [before n] MAINLY HUMOROUS able to be trusted, especially because of having been owned and used for a long time: *I did the entire three hundred miles on my own – just me and my trusty bike.*

trust ARRANGEMENT /trʌst/ *noun* [C] **1** a legal arrangement in which a person or organization controls property and/or money for the benefit of another person or organization: *Under the terms of the trust he receives interest on the money, but he cannot get at the money itself.* ○ *The money that her father left her is being* **held/kept in trust** (= being controlled) *for her until she's 30.* **2** an organization which controls property and/or money for the benefit of another person: *He works for a charitable trust.* ○ *Housing trusts help to provide houses for people who are not well off.* **3** US used in the name of some banks: *Morgan Guaranty Trust*

trustee /ˌtrʌs'tiː/ *noun* [C] a person, often one of a group, who controls property and/or money for the benefit of another person or an organization: *the museum's board of trustees*

trusteeship /ˌtrʌs'tiː.ʃɪp/ *noun* [C or U] the position or responsibility of a trustee

trust HOPE /trʌst/ *verb* [I] FORMAL to hope and expect that something is true: [+ (that)] *I trust (that) you slept well?* ○ *The meeting went well, I trust.*

'**trust** ˌ**fund** *noun* [C] an amount of money which is being controlled for the benefit of a person or organization by another person or organization: *There are some* *tax advantages in setting up a trust fund for each of your children.*

trustworthy /ˈtrʌstˌwɜː.ði/ [US] /-ˌwɝː-/ *adj* able to be trusted **trustworthiness** /ˈtrʌstˌwɜː.ðɪ.nəs/ [US] /-ˌwɝː-/ *noun* [U]

truth /truːθ/ *noun* **1** [U] the quality of being true: *There would seem to be some truth* ***in*** *what she says.* ○ *There is no truth* ***in*** *the reports of his resignation.* ○ *You cannot question the truth* ***of*** *his alibi.* ○ *And yet what he says contains at least* ***a grain of*** (= a small amount of) *truth.* **2 the truth** the real facts about a situation, event or person: *But was he* ***telling*** *the truth?* ○ *I don't suppose we'll ever know the truth* ***about*** *what happened that day.* ○ ***To tell (you)*** *the truth* (= Speaking honestly) *I'm quite pleased he's not coming.* **3** [C] *FORMAL* a fact or principle which is thought to be true by most people: *It would seem to be a general truth that nothing is as straightforward as it at first seems.* ○ *The entire system of belief is based on a few simple truths.*

• **in truth** *FORMAL* used to show or emphasize that something is true: *In truth we feared for her safety although we didn't let it be known.*

• **Truth is stranger than fiction.** *SAYING* said when you want to emphasize that real events or things are sometimes stranger than imaginary ones

• **Truth will out.** *UK SAYING* said to show that you believe the truth will always be discovered

truthful /ˈtruːθ.fəl/ *adj* honest and not containing or telling any lies: *The public has a right to expect truthful answers from politicians.* ○ *Are you being quite truthful* ***with*** *me?* **truthfully** /ˈtruːθ.fəl.i/ *adv*: *I answered her questions truthfully.* **truthfulness** /ˈtruːθ.fəl.nəs/ *noun* [U]

try [ATTEMPT] /traɪ/ *verb* [I or T] to attempt to do something: *Keep trying and you'll find a job eventually.* ○ *If I don't get into the academy this year, I'll try* ***again*** *next year.* ○ *I've tried really* ***hard*** *but I can't persuade him to come.* ○ *I'm trying my* ***best/hardest****, but I just can't do it.* ○ [+ to infinitive] *I tried* ***to*** *open the window.* ○ [+ v-ing] *Perhaps you should try gett****ing*** *up* (= You should get up) *earlier in the mornings.*

• **try it on** *UK INFORMAL* to deceive someone or behave badly, especially in order to discover how much of your bad behaviour will be permitted: *He's not really ill – he's just trying it on.* ○ *The kids often try it on* ***with*** *a new babysitter.*

• **try *your* hand at *sth*** to try doing something for the first time: *I might try my hand at a bit of Indian cookery.*

try /traɪ/ *noun* [C usually sing] an attempt to do something: *They might just have a place left on the course – why don't you* ***give it/have*** *a try?* ○ *This will be her third try* ***at*** *jumping the bar.* ○ *You could ask him if he's willing – it's* ***worth a*** *try.*

trier /ˈtraɪ.əʳ/ [US] /-ɚ/ *noun* [C] *APPROVING* someone who tries hard to succeed in what they do, even if they fail: *She's a real trier, I'll give her that.*

try [TEST] /traɪ/ *verb* [T] to test something to see if it is suitable or useful or if it works: *I tried that recipe you gave me last night.* ○ *I'm afraid we don't sell newspapers – have you tried the shop on the corner?* ○ [+ v-ing] *Try us****ing*** *a different shampoo.* ○ *I thought I might try parachut****ing****.* ○ *I've forgotten my door-keys – we'd better try the window* (= test it to see if it is open).

• **try *sth* for size** *UK* (*US* **try *sth* on for size**) to test something or to think about an idea in order to decide whether it works or whether you can use it

• **try *your* luck** to try to achieve something although you know you might not succeed: *He'd always wanted to act and in 1959 came to London to try his luck on the stage.*

tried /traɪd/ *adj* **tried and tested/trusted** used many times before and proved to be successful: *I'll give you my mother's tried and tested recipe for wholemeal bread.*

try [LAW] /traɪ/ *verb* [T] to examine a person accused of committing a crime in a court of law by asking them questions and considering known facts, and then decide if they are guilty: *Because of security implications the officers were tried in secret.* ○ *They are being tried* ***for*** *murder.* ➲See also **trial** LEGAL PROCESS.

try [WORRY] /traɪ/ *verb* [T] to worry or annoy someone or upset a person's patience with many, often slight, difficulties: *The demands of the job have tried him* ***sorely****.* ○ *He's been trying my* ***patience*** *all morning with his constant questions.* ○ *Her endless demands would try* ***the patience of a saint*** (= are very annoying).

trying /ˈtraɪ.ɪŋ/ *adj* annoying and difficult: *I've had a very trying day at work.* ○ *He can be rather trying at times.*

try [SPORT] /traɪ/ *noun* [C] (in the game of rugby) the act of a player putting the ball on the ground behind the opposing team's goal line, which scores points for the player's team

PHRASAL VERBS WITH **try**

▲ **try for *sth*** *phrasal verb* to attempt to get something: *Are you going to try for that job in the sales department?*

▲ **try *sth* on** *phrasal verb* [M] to put on a piece of clothing to discover if it fits you or if you like it: *Try on the shoes to see if they fit.* ○ *What a lovely dress – why don't you try it on* ***for size*** (= to discover whether it fits)*?*

▲ **try *sth* out** *phrasal verb* [M] to use something to discover if it works or if you like it: *Don't forget to try out the equipment before setting up the experiment.*

▲ **try out for *sth*** *phrasal verb US* to compete for a position in a sports team or a part in a play: *Luke's trying out for the college football team.*

try-out /ˈtraɪ.aʊt/ *noun* [C] *INFORMAL* a test to see how useful or effective something or someone is: *After a try-out in Bath, the play is due to open in Edinburgh next month.* ○ *The try-outs* ***for*** *the team will be next weekend.*

tryst /trɪst/ *noun* [C] *OLD USE OR HUMOROUS* a meeting between two lovers, especially a secret one

tsar [RULER] *UK,* **tzar**, *US* **czar** /zɑːʳ/ [US] /zɑːr/ *noun* [C] (until 1917) the male Russian ruler: *Tsar Nicholas I*

tsarina *UK, US* **czarina** /zɑːˈriː.nə/ [US] /zɑːrˈiː-/ *noun* [C] (until 1917) the wife of a tsar or the female Russian ruler

tsarist *UK, US* **czarist** /ˈzɑː.rɪst/ [US] /ˈzɑːr.ɪst/ *adj, noun*: *the tsarist empire* ○ *Tsarist Russia*

tsar [OFFICIAL] *UK,* **tzar**, *US* **czar** /zɑːʳ/ [US] /zɑːr/ *noun* [C] a person who has been given special powers by the government to deal with a particular matter: *The government has appointed a drugs tsar to co-ordinate the fight against drug abuse.*

tsar [LEADER] *UK, US* **czar** /zɑːʳ/ [US] /zɑːr/ *noun* [C] a powerful person in business or politics: *a group of publishing tsars*

tsetse fly /ˈtet.siˌflaɪ/ *noun* [C or U] one of various types of African fly which feed on blood and can give serious diseases to the person or animal they bite

T-shirt /ˈtiː.ʃɜːt/ [US] /-ʃɝːt/ *noun* [C] (*ALSO* **tee shirt**) a simple piece of clothing which covers the top part of the body and which has no collar and usually short sleeves: *She was wearing jeans and a T-shirt.* ➲See picture **Clothes** on page Centre 6

tsk /tɪsk/ *exclamation* (*ALSO* **tsk tsk**) *OLD-FASHIONED* **tut**

tsp *WRITTEN ABBREVIATION FOR* **teaspoonful**, see at **teaspoon**: *Add one tsp each of ground cumin and ground coriander.*

T-square /ˈtiː.skweəʳ/ [US] /-skwer/ *noun* [C] a long flat T-shaped piece of wood, metal or plastic, which is used to draw parallel lines ➲Compare **setsquare**.

tsunami /tsuːˈnɑː.mi/ *noun* [C] *MAINLY US* an extremely large wave caused by movement of the earth under the sea, often caused by an EARTHQUAKE (= when the Earth shakes)

TTFN, ttfn *INTERNET ABBREVIATION FOR* ta-ta for now: a way of saying goodbye at the end of an email

tub [CONTAINER] /tʌb/ *noun* [C] **1** a large round container with a flat base and an open top: *Outside was a stone patio with tubs of flowering plants.* ○ *We've got a tub for compost at the bottom of our garden.* **2** a small plastic container with a lid, used for storing food: *a tub of ice cream/margarine*

tub [BATH] /tʌb/ *noun* [C] *US FOR* **bath**: *It's good to sink into a hot tub at the end of a hard day's work.*

tuba /ˈtjuː.bə/ [US] /ˈtuː-/ *noun* [C] a brass musical instrument consisting of a long bent metal tube which the player blows into, producing low notes

T

ubby /ˈtʌb.i/ *adj* INFORMAL (of a person) fat: *Our chef was a genial, slightly tubby man.*

ube [PIPE] /tjuːb/ [US] /tuːb/ *noun* **[C]** **1** a long hollow cylinder made from plastic, metal, rubber or glass, especially used for moving or containing liquids or gases: *Gases produced in the reaction pass through this tube and can then be collected.* **2** in biology, any hollow cylindrical structure in the body that carries air or liquid: *the bronchial tubes* **3** AUS INFORMAL a CAN or bottle of beer: *a tube of lager*

• **go down the tubes** INFORMAL to fail completely: *If business doesn't pick up soon, the company will go down the tubes.*

tubing /ˈtjuː.bɪŋ/ [US] /ˈtuː-/ *noun* **[U]** material in the form of a tube: *Rubber tubing can perish after a few years.*

tubular /ˈtjuː.bjʊ.ləʳ/ [US] /ˈtuː.bjə.lɚ/ *adj* made in or having the shape of a tube: *tubular steel*

tube [CONTAINER] /tjuːb/ [US] /tuːb/ *noun* **[C]** a long thin container made of soft metal or plastic, which is closed at one end and has a small hole at the other, usually with a cover, and which is used for storing thick liquids: *a tube of toothpaste*

the Tube [RAILWAY] *noun* **[S]** UK INFORMAL London's underground train system: *I got the Tube to Camden Town.* ○ *I go to work* ***on*** *the Tube.* ○ *a Tube station*

the tube [TELEVISION] *noun* **[S]** MAINLY US the television: *What's on the tube this weekend?*

tuber /ˈtjuː.bəʳ/ [US] /ˈtuː.bɚ/ *noun* **[C]** a swollen underground stem or root of a plant from which new plants can grow, as in the potato **tuberous** /ˈtjuː.bə.rəs/ [US] /ˈtuː.bɚ.əs/ *adj*

tuberculosis /tjuːˌbɜː.kjʊˈləʊ.sɪs/ [US] /tuːˌbɝː.kjəˈloʊ-/ *noun* **[U]** (ABBREVIATION **TB**) a serious disease which is infectious and can attack many parts of a person's body, especially their lungs **tubercular** /tjuːˈbɜː.kjʊ.ləʳ/ [US] /tuːˈbɝː.kjə.lɚ/ *adj*

tub-thumping /ˈtʌbˌθʌm.pɪŋ/ *adj* **[before n]** INFORMAL DISAPPROVING describes a style of speaking which is forceful or violent: *a tub-thumping speech/campaigner*

the TUC /ðəˌtiː.juːˈsiː/ *noun* **[S]** ABBREVIATION FOR the Trades Union Congress: an organization for British TRADE UNIONS which has a large meeting every year

tuck [TIDY] /tʌk/ *verb* **[T usually + adv or prep]** to push a loose end of a piece of clothing or material into a particular place or position, especially to make it tidy or comfortable: *Should I tuck my shirt* ***into*** *my trousers?* ○ *He tucked the bottom of the sheet* ***under*** *the mattress.*

tuck [STORE SAFELY] /tʌk/ *verb* **[T usually + adv or prep]** to put something into a safe or convenient place: *Tuck your gloves* ***in*** *your pocket so that you don't lose them.* ○ *She had a doll tucked* ***under*** *her arm.* ○ *Eventually I found the certificate tucked* ***under*** *a pile of old letters.* ○ *Tuck your chair* ***in*** (= put it so that the seat of it is under the table) *so that no one trips over it.*

PHRASAL VERBS WITH **tuck**

▲ **tuck *sth* away** *phrasal verb* **[M]** to put something in a private, safe place: *Grandma always kept a bit of money tucked away in case there was an emergency.*

▲ **tuck *sb* in** [PUT TO BED] *phrasal verb* **[M]** (UK ALSO **tuck *sb* up**) to make someone comfortable in their bed, especially a child, by arranging the covers round them: *Daddy, if I go to bed now will you tuck me in?* ○ *The children are safely tucked up in bed.*

▲ **tuck in/tuck into *sth*** [EAT] *phrasal verb* INFORMAL to start eating something eagerly: *Judging by the way they tucked into their dinner, they must have been very hungry.* ○ *There's plenty of food, so please tuck in.*

tuck [FOLD] /tʌk/ *noun* **[C]** **1** a narrow fold sewn into something, especially a piece of material, either for decoration or to change its shape **2** an operation to remove unwanted fat from a part of the body: *a tummy tuck*

tuck *verb* **[T usually + adv or prep]** to hold part of your body in a particular position: *Stand up straight, tuck your tummy* ***in*** *and tuck your bottom* ***under.*** ○ *She sat with her legs tucked* ***under*** *her.*

tuck [HIDDEN] /tʌk/ *verb* **be tucked away/along, etc.** to be in a place which is hidden or where few people go: *Tucked along/down this alley are some beautiful timber-framed houses.* ○ *A group of tiny brick houses is tucked away behind the factory.*

tuck [FOOD] /tʌk/ *noun* **[U]** UK OLD-FASHIONED CHILD'S WORD food, especially sweets and cakes: *a tuck shop* ➲See also **tucker**.

tucker /ˈtʌk.əʳ/ [US] /-ɚ/ *noun* **[U]** AUS INFORMAL food: *a tucker bag*

Tue (ALSO **Tues**) WRITTEN ABBREVIATION FOR Tuesday

Tuesday /ˈtjuːz.deɪ/ [US] /ˈtuːz-/ *noun* **[C or U]** (WRITTEN ABBREVIATION **Tue/Tues**) the day of the week after Monday and before Wednesday: *We'll meet at eight* ***on*** *Tuesday.* ○ *We meet every Tuesday.* ○ *Tuesday afternoon* ○ *The twenty-ninth is a Tuesday, isn't it?*

tuft /tʌft/ *noun* **[C]** a number of short pieces of especially hair or grass which closely grow together or are held together near the base: *He had a few tufts* ***of*** *hair on his chin, but you could hardly call it a beard.*

tufted /ˈtʌf.tɪd/ *adj* with a tuft: *the tufted duck*

tug [PULL] /tʌg/ *verb* **[I or T] -gg-** to pull something quickly and usually with a lot of force: *Tom tugged* ***at*** *his mother's arm.* **tug** /tʌg/ *noun* **[C]** *Feeling a tug at his sleeve, he turned to see Joe beside him.*

tug [BOAT] /tʌg/ *noun* **[C]** (ALSO **tugboat**) a boat with a powerful engine which can change direction easily and is used to pull large ships into and out of port

tug-of-love /ˌtʌg.əvˈlʌv/ *noun* **[S]** UK INFORMAL used, especially in newspapers, to refer to a situation in which one of the separated parents of a child takes care of the child but the other parent claims that right, or a situation in which a child is being taken care of by people other than the child's parents but the parents claim that right: *a tug-of-love battle*

tug-of-war /ˌtʌg.əvˈwɔːʳ/ [US] /-ˈwɔːr/ *noun* **[C usually sing]** a type of sport in which two teams show their strength by pulling against each other at the opposite ends of a rope, and each team tries to pull the other over a line on the ground

tuition /tjuːˈɪʃ.ᵊn/ [US] /ˈtuː-/ *noun* **[U]** **1** MAINLY UK teaching, especially when given to a small group or one person, such as in a college or university: *All students receive tuition* ***in*** *logic and metaphysics.* ○ *tuition* ***fees*** **2** MAINLY US the money paid for this type of teaching: *Few can afford the tuition of $12 000 a term.*

tulip /ˈtjuː.lɪp/ [US] /ˈtuː-/ *noun* **[C]** a plant which has a large brightly coloured bell-shaped flower on a stem and which grows from a BULB, or the flower itself ➲See picture **Flowers and Plants** on page Centre 3

tulle /tjuːl/ [US] /tuːl/ *noun* **[U]** a light net-like cloth of silk or similar material which is used on dresses, or to decorate hats, or for particular types of VEIL

tumble /ˈtʌm.bl̩/ *verb* **[I]** **1** to fall quickly and without control: *I lost my footing and tumbled* ***down*** *the stairs.* ○ *At any moment the whole building could tumble* ***down.*** ○ *He lost his balance and tumbled* ***over.*** ➲See also **tumbledown**. **2** to fall greatly in value in a short time: *Share prices tumbled yesterday.* **3** to move in an uncontrolled way, as if falling or likely to fall: *An excited group of children tumbled* ***out*** *of school/the bus.*

tumble /ˈtʌm.bl̩/ *noun* **[C]** when someone falls: *She* ***had*** *a nasty tumble on her way to work and grazed her arm.*

• **take a tumble** to fall suddenly to a lower level: *Company profits took a tumble last year, a spokesperson said, because of investment in new machinery.*

▲ **tumble to *sth*** *phrasal verb* UK OLD-FASHIONED INFORMAL to suddenly understand something: *I think he's tumbled to our plan.*

tumbledown /ˈtʌm.bl̩.daʊn/ *adj* **[before n]** (of a building) in a very bad condition, especially in a state of decay: *a tumbledown cottage*

ˈ**tumble** ˌ**dryer** UK, **tumble drier** *noun* **[C]** (US **dryer**) a machine which dries wet clothes by turning them in hot air ➲Compare **spin-dryer**.

tumbler /ˈtʌm.bləʳ/ [US] /-blɚ/ *noun* **[C]** a drinking container which does not have a handle or a stem

tumbleweed /ˈtʌm.bl̩.wiːd/ *noun* **[U]** a bush-like plant of North America and Australia which breaks near the ground when it dies and is then rolled about in large balls by the wind

tumescent /tjuːˈmes.ᵊnt/ ⑩ /tuː-/ *adj* SPECIALIZED (especially of parts of the body) swollen or becoming swollen: *a tumescent penis* **tumescence** /tjuːˈmes.ᵊnts/ ⑩ /tuː-/ *noun* [U]

tummy /ˈtʌm.i/ *noun* [C] INFORMAL OR CHILD'S WORD the stomach, or the lower front part of the body: *a tummy ache*

ˈtummy ˌbutton *noun* [C] UK INFORMAL FOR **navel**

tumour UK, US **tumor** /ˈtjuː.məʳ/ ⑩ /ˈtuː.mɚ/ *noun* [C] a mass of diseased cells which might become a lump or cause illness: *They found a **malignant** tumour in her breast.* ○ *a benign tumour* ○ *a brain tumour*

tumult /ˈtjuː.mʌlt/ ⑩ /ˈtuː-/ *noun* [C or U] FORMAL a loud noise, especially that produced by an excited crowd, or a state of confusion, change or uncertainty: *You couldn't hear her speak over the tumult from the screaming fans.* ○ *From every direction, people were running and shouting and falling over each other in a tumult **of** confusion.* ○ *The financial markets are **in** tumult.*

tumultuous /tjuːˈmʌl.tjʊəs/ ⑩ /tuː-/ *adj* very loud, or full of confusion, change or uncertainty: *Dame Joan appeared to tumultuous **applause** and a standing ovation.* ○ *After the tumultuous events of 1990, Eastern Europe was completely transformed.* **tumultuously** /tjuːˈmʌl.tjʊə.sli/ ⑩ /tuː-/ *adv*

tuna /ˈtjuː.nə/ ⑩ /ˈtuː-/ *noun* [C or U] *plural* **tuna** or **tunas** a large fish which lives in warm seas, or its flesh eaten as food: *shoals of tuna* ○ *a can of tuna (fish)*

tundra /ˈtʌn.drə/ *noun* [U] (part of) the very large area of land in Northern Asia, North America and Northern Europe where, because it is cold, trees do not grow and earth below the surface is permanently frozen: *Reindeer roam the tundra in large herds.* ○ *Few plants grow in tundra regions.*

tune MUSICAL NOTES /tjuːn/ ⑩ /tuːn/ *noun* [C] a series of musical notes, especially one which is pleasant and easy to remember; a MELODY: *He was humming a tune as he dried the dishes.* ○ *a theme tune* ○ *That's a very **catchy** (= easy to remember) tune.*

tuneful /ˈtjuːn.fᵊl/ ⑩ /ˈtuːn-/ *adj* with a pleasant tune: *The first track on the album is surprisingly tuneful.* **tunefully** /ˈtjuːn.fᵊl.i/ ⑩ /ˈtuːn-/ *adv* **tunefulness** /ˈtjuːn.fᵊl.nəs/ ⑩ /ˈtuːn-/ *noun* [U]

tuneless /ˈtjuːn.ləs/ ⑩ /ˈtuːn-/ *adj* having no tune and unpleasant: *tuneless whistling* **tunelessly** /ˈtjuːn.lə.sli/ ⑩ /ˈtuːn-/ *adv*: *She sang rather tunelessly.*

tune INSTRUMENT /tjuːn/ ⑩ /tuːn/ *verb* [T] to change a part of a musical instrument so that the instrument produces the correct sounds when played: *Get into the habit of tuning your guitar every day before you practise.* ○ *She tuned **(up)** her violin before the concert.*

tune /tjuːn/ ⑩ /tuːn/ *noun* **1 in tune** singing or playing the right notes **2 out of tune** singing or playing the wrong notes: *I'm afraid the piano is out of tune.*

tuning /ˈtjuː.nɪŋ/ ⑩ /ˈtuː-/ *noun* [U] the way an instrument is tuned: *The tuning on this piano is awful.*

tune UNDERSTANDING /tjuːn/ ⑩ /tuːn/ **be in/out of tune with sb/sth** If you are in tune with people or ideas, you understand or agree with them, and if you are out of tune with them, you do not: *Much of his success comes from being in tune with what his customers want.* ○ *Her theories were out of tune with the scientific thinking of the time.*

tune RADIO /tjuːn/ ⑩ /tuːn/ *verb* [T] to move the controls on a radio or television, etc. so that it receives programmes broadcast from a particular station: *Press this button and the video will automatically tune itself **to** the next channel.* ○ *His radio is constantly tuned **to** KROQ-FM, the local rock station.*

tuner /ˈtjuː.nəʳ/ ⑩ /ˈtuː.nɚ/ *noun* [C] **1** the part of a radio or television which allows you to choose the broadcasting station you want to listen to or watch **2** a radio which is part of a MUSIC SYSTEM

tune ENGINE /tjuːn/ ⑩ /tuːn/ *verb* [T] to change the setting of particular parts of an engine, especially slightly, so that it works as well as possible: *The **engine** certainly needs tuning but there's nothing wrong with the car.* ○ *Could you tune **(up)** the **engine** for me, please?* **tune-up** /ˈtjuːn.ʌp/ ⑩ /ˈtuːn-/ *noun* [C usually sing] (UK ALSO **tune**)

The engine needs a tune-up, and can you give the car a good service as well?

PHRASAL VERBS WITH **tune** ▼

▲ **tune in** TV/RADIO *phrasal verb* to watch or listen to a particular television or radio programme or station: *Be sure to tune in **to** next week's show.* ○ *Millions of viewers tune in every weekday for 'News at Night'.*

▲ **tune in** UNDERSTANDING *phrasal verb* **be tuned in** to have a good understanding of what is happening in a situation or what other people are thinking: *She just doesn't seem to be tuned in to her students' needs.*

▲ **tune (sb/sth) out** *phrasal verb* US INFORMAL to ignore someone or not give your attention to something or to what is happening around you: *He talks such garbage that I just tune him out.*

▲ **tune (sth) up** *phrasal verb* If musicians who are preparing to play tune up their instruments, they adjust them so that they produce the correct notes: *After the orchestra had tuned up, the conductor walked on to the stage.* ○ *He began to tune up his violin.*

tune AMOUNT /tjuːn/ ⑩ /tuːn/ *noun* **to the tune of** to the stated amount: *The City Council had financed the new building to the tune of over 4 million pounds.*

tungsten /ˈtʌŋ.stən/ *noun* [U] a hard metallic element: *tungsten steel* ○ *The filaments of light bulbs are made from tungsten wire.*

tunic /ˈtjuː.nɪk/ *noun* [C] a piece of clothing which fits loosely over a person's body, reaches to the waist or knees, and often has no sleeves: *a soldier's tunic*

ˈtuning ˌfork *noun* [C] a metal object in the form of a small bar which is divided into two for about half of its length, and which, when hit gently, produces a particular note. It is used when tuning musical instruments

ˈtuning ˌpeg *noun* [C] (ALSO **tuning pin**) a short wooden or metal stick with a flat rounded end that is turned to make the strings on a musical instrument tighter or looser

tunnel /ˈtʌn.ᵊl/ *noun* [C] a long passage under or through the earth, especially one made by people: *The train went into the tunnel.*

tunnel /ˈtʌn.ᵊl/ *verb* [I or T] **-ll-** or US USUALLY **-l-** to dig a tunnel: *The decision has not yet been made whether to tunnel **under** the river or build a bridge over it.* ○ *The alternative is to tunnel a route through the mountain.* ○ *He was trapped in a collapsed building but managed to tunnel his **way** out.* **tunneller** UK, US **tunneler** /ˈtʌn.ᵊl.əʳ/ ⑩ /-ɚ/ *noun* [C]

ˌtunnel ˈvision SEEING *noun* [U] a medical condition which causes someone to only see things which are directly in front of them

ˌtunnel ˈvision THINKING *noun* [U] DISAPPROVING when someone considers only one part of a problem or situation, or holds a single opinion rather than having a more general understanding

tuppence /ˈtʌp.ᵊnts/ *noun* [U] (ALSO **twopence**) INFORMAL two old or new British pence

● **not care/give tuppence** UK OLD-FASHIONED to not care about something or someone in any way

tuppenny /ˈtʌp.ᵊn.i/ /-ni/ *adj* [before n] (ALSO **twopenny**) OLD-FASHIONED INFORMAL costing two pence

Tupperware /ˈtʌp.ə.weəʳ/ ⑩ /-ɚ.wer/ *noun* [U] TRADE-MARK plastic containers, usually for storing food, and usually having lids which fit tightly

tuque /tuːk/ *noun* [C] CANADIAN ENGLISH FOR **bobble hat**

turban /ˈtɜː.bən/ ⑩ /ˈtɜː-/ *noun* [C] a head covering for a man, worn especially by Sikhs, Muslims and Hindus, and made from a long piece of cloth which is wrapped around the top of the head many times ⊃See picture **Hairstyles and Hats** on page Centre 8 **turbaned** /ˈtɜː.bənd/ ⑩ /ˈtɜː-/ *adj*: *a turbaned man*

turbid /ˈtɜː.bɪd/ ⑩ /ˈtɜː-/ *adj* FORMAL (of a liquid) not transparent because a lot of small pieces of matter are held in it: *Several different species of fish inhabit these turbid shallow waters.* **turbidity** /tɜːˈbɪd.ɪ.ti/ ⑩ /tɜː-ˈbɪd.ə.t̬i/ *noun* [U]

turbine /ˈtɜː.baɪn/ [US] /ˈtɝː-/ *noun* [C] a type of machine through which liquid or gas flows and turns a special wheel with blades in order to produce power: *a steam turbine* ○ *a turbine engine*

turbocharger /ˈtɜː.bəʊˌtʃɑː.dʒəʳ/ [US] /ˈtɝː.boʊˌtʃɑːr.dʒɚ/ *noun* [C] a small TURBINE turned by the waste gases from an engine which pushes the fuel and air mixture into the engine at a higher pressure, so increasing the power produced by the engine **turbocharged** /ˈtɜː.bəʊ.tʃɑːdʒd/ [US] /ˈtɝː.boʊ.tʃɑːrdʒd/ *adj*: *a turbocharged engine*

turbofan /ˈtɜː.bəʊ.fæn/ [US] /ˈtɝː.boʊ-/ *noun* [C] a TURBINE used as an engine, especially for an aircraft, which provides some force for movement from the gas that it pushes out, and some by turning a large special wheel with blades which also pushes air out, or an aircraft powered by this type of engine

turbojet /ˈtɜː.bəʊ.dʒet/ [US] /ˈtɝː.boʊ-/ *noun* [C] a TURBINE used as an engine, especially for an aircraft, which provides a forward force for movement from the gas it pushes out, or an aircraft powered by this type of engine

turboprop /ˈtɜː.bəʊ.prɒp/ [US] /ˈtɝː.boʊ.prɑːp/ *noun* [C] a TURBINE used as an aircraft engine which provides most force for movement by turning a PROPELLER, or an aircraft powered by this type of engine

turbot /ˈtɜː.bət/ [US] /ˈtɝː-/ *noun* [C or U] *plural* **turbot** or **turbots** a fish with a flat body which lives near to the coast in European seas, or its flesh eaten as food

turbulence /ˈtɜː.bjʊ.lənts/ [US] /ˈtɝː.bjə-/ *noun* [U] **1** a state of confusion and lack of order: *The era was characterized by political and cultural turbulence.* ○ *There are signs of turbulence ahead for the economy.* **2** strong sudden movements within air or water: *We might be experiencing some turbulence on this flight due to an approaching electrical storm.*

turbulent /ˈtɜː.bjʊ.lənt/ [US] /ˈtɝː.bjə-/ *adj* **1** involving a lot of sudden changes, arguments or violence: *a turbulent marriage* ○ *This has been a turbulent week for the government.* **2** Turbulent air or water moves very strongly and suddenly: *The sea was too turbulent for us to be able to take the boat out.*

turd /tɜːd/ [US] /tɝːd/ *noun* [C] *OFFENSIVE* **1** a piece of solid excrement: *dog turds on the pavement* **2** a rude word for someone who you think is unpleasant: *I'm not doing business with that little turd.*

tureen /tjʊˈriːn/ [US] /tə-/ *noun* [C] a large bowl, usually with a lid, from which soup or vegetables are served

turf [GRASS] /tɜːf/ [US] /tɝːf/ *noun* [C or U] *plural* **turfs** or *MAINLY UK* **turves** the surface layer of land on which grass is growing, consisting of the grass and the earth in which its roots grow, or a piece of this which is cut from the ground and is usually rectangular

the turf *noun* [S] the sport of horse racing

turf /tɜːf/ [US] /tɝːf/ *verb* [T] to cover a piece of land with turf

PHRASAL VERBS WITH **turf**

▲ **turf *sth* out** [OBJECT] *phrasal verb* [M] *UK INFORMAL* to get rid of a number of things or something large that you do not want: *I turfed out a load of old shoes last week.*

▲ **turf *sb* out** [PERSON] *phrasal verb* [M] *MAINLY UK INFORMAL* to force someone to leave a place or an organization: *She'll be turfed out **of** the study group if she carries on being disruptive.*

turf [AREA] /tɜːf/ [US] /tɝːf/ *noun* [U] **1** *INFORMAL* a subject in which a person or group has a lot of knowledge or influence: *Antiques are very much her turf.* **2** *MAINLY US INFORMAL* the area which a group considers its own: *Judges feel that the courtroom is their private turf.* ○ *The gymnastics team won the championship on home turf.*

ˈturf acˌcountant *noun* [C] *UK FORMAL* a **bookmaker**

ˈturf ˌwar *noun* [C] a fight or an argument to decide who controls an area or an activity

turgid [TOO SERIOUS] /ˈtɜː.dʒɪd/ [US] /ˈtɝː-/ *adj FORMAL* (of speech, writing, style, etc.) too serious about its subject matter; boring: *a couple of pages of turgid prose*

turgidity /tɜːˈdʒɪd.ɪ.ti/ [US] /tɝːˈdʒɪd.ə.t̬i/ *noun* [U]

turgidly /ˈtɜː.dʒɪd.li/ [US] /ˈtɝː-/ *adv*

turgid [NOT FLOWING] /ˈtɜː.dʒɪd/ [US] /ˈtɝː-/ *adj FORMAL* (of water) not flowing easily: *The river rolled darkly brown and turgid.*

turgid [SWOLLEN] /ˈtɜː.dʒɪd/ [US] /ˈtɝː-/ *adj SPECIALIZED* (of an organ or living tissue) swollen **turgidity** /tɜːˈdʒɪd.ɪ.ti/ [US] /tɝːˈdʒɪd.ə.t̬i/ *noun* [U]

turkey [BIRD] /ˈtɜː.ki/ [US] /ˈtɝː-/ *noun* [C or U] a large bird grown for its meat on farms, or its flesh used as food: *(a) roast turkey* ○ *a wild turkey*

turkey [FAILURE] /ˈtɜː.ki/ [US] /ˈtɝː-/ *noun* [C] **1** *MAINLY US INFORMAL* something that fails badly: *His last film was a complete turkey.* **2** *US INFORMAL* a stupid or silly person: *What did you do that for, you turkey?*

Turkish bath /ˌtɜː.kɪʃˈbɑːθ/ [US] /ˌtɝː.kɪʃˈbæθ/ *noun* [C] a health treatment in which you sit in a room full of steam and are then MASSAGED (= rubbed) and washed, or a building in which this treatment is available ➲Compare **sauna**.

Turkish delight /ˌtɜː.kɪʃ.dɪˈlaɪt/ [US] /ˌtɝː-/ *noun* [U] a soft type of sweet, usually in the form of square pink pieces covered with powdered sugar

turmeric /ˈtɜː.mᵊr.ɪk/ [US] /ˈtɝː.mɚ-/ *noun* [U] a yellow powder which is used as a spice to flavour particular foods, especially CURRY, and give them a yellow colour. It is made from the root of an Asian plant.

turmoil /ˈtɜː.mɔɪl/ [US] /ˈtɝː-/ *noun* [S or U] a state of confusion, uncertainty or lack of order: *The country is in a state of political turmoil.* ○ *The whole region is **in** turmoil.* ○ *The Stock Exchange is **in** turmoil following a huge wave of selling.*

turn [GO ROUND] /tɜːn/ [US] /tɝːn/ *verb* **1** [I or T] to (cause to) move in a circle round a fixed point or line: *The Earth turns **on** its axis once every 24 hours.* ○ *She turned **on** her toes, holding out her skirt.* ○ *The wheels started to turn **(round)**.* ○ *Turn the steering wheel as quickly as you can.* ○ *She turned the door knob and quietly opened the door.* ○ *Slowly, I turned the door handle.* **2** [T] *SPECIALIZED* to shape a piece of wood while it is fixed to a machine which spins it: *a turned bowl*

turn /tɜːn/ [US] /tɝːn/ *noun* [C] when you cause something to move in a circle round a fixed point: *Give the screw a couple of turns to make sure it's tight.*

• **a turn of the screw** an action which makes a bad situation worse, especially in order to force someone to do something: *Each letter from my bank manager is another turn of the screw.*

turn [CHANGE DIRECTION] /tɜːn/ [US] /tɝːn/ *verb* [I or T] to (cause to) change the direction in which you are facing or moving: *Turn right at the traffic lights.* ○ *The path **twists and** turns for the next half mile.* ○ *We have to turn down/into/up the next road on the right.* ○ *Plants tend to turn towards the source of light.* ○ *She turned to face him.* ○ *He turned **round** and waved to us.* ○ *He turned **on his heel*** (= turned quickly to face the opposite direction) *and left the room.* ○ *The person on my left turned **to** me and whispered "Not another speech!".* ○ *His wife tried to speak to him, but he turned his back (**on** her)/turned away (from her)* (= moved himself round and away from her to show his anger). ○ *At about three o'clock, **the tide** started to turn* (= the sea started to come closer to or move away from the beach). ○ *He turned his head to me to listen.* ○ *I'll just turn the car **round** and go back the way we've come.* ○ *We watched until the car had turned* (= gone round) *the corner.* ○ *The army turned their guns **on*** (= pointed them at and started to shoot at) *the protesters.* ○ *She can turn* (= perform) *a **somersault**.*

• **turn *your* back on *sth*** (*ALSO* **turn away from *sth***) to stop being involved in something: *Spain cannot afford to turn its back on tourism.*

• **turn *your* back on *sb*** to refuse to help someone: *Surely you won't turn your back on them?*

• **turn the corner** If something or someone turns the corner, their situation starts to improve after a difficult period: *After nine months of poor sales we've finally turned the corner.*

• **turn a blind eye** to ignore something that you know is wrong: *Management often turn a blind eye **to** bullying in the workplace.*

T

• **turn a deaf ear** to ignore someone when they complain or ask for something: *In the past they've tended to turn a deaf ear to such requests.*

• **not turn a hair** to not show any emotion when you are told something bad or when something bad happens: *I was expecting him to be horrified when he heard the cost but he didn't turn a hair.*

• **turn *your* hand to *sth*** If you say that someone could turn their hand to an activity or skill, you mean they could do it well although they have no experience of it: *Stella's very talented – she could turn her hand to anything.*

• **turn *sth* on *its* head** to cause something to be the opposite of what it was before: *These new findings turn the accepted theories on their head.*

• **turn the other cheek** to not do anything to hurt someone who has hurt you: *Neither nation is renowned for turning the other cheek.*

• **turn over a new leaf** to start behaving in a better way: *Apparently he's turned over a new leaf and he's not smoking any more.*

• **turn the tables on *sb*** to change a situation so that you now have an advantage over someone who previously had an advantage over you: *She turned the tables on her rival with allegations of corruption.*

• **turn tail** to turn around and run away, usually because you are frightened: *As soon as they saw we had guns, they turned tail and ran away.*

• **turn *your* nose up** to not accept something because you do not think it is good enough for you: *They turned their noses up at the only hotel that was available.*

• **turn *sth* upside down** to search everywhere for something, sometimes leaving the place very untidy: *I turned the apartment upside down but I couldn't find those photos.*

turn /tɜːn/ ⓤ /tɝːn/ *noun* [C] **1** a change in the direction in which you are moving or facing: *We got as far as the school, and there we had to **make** a right turn.* ○ *The path was full of **twists and** turns.* **2** **the turn of *sth*** the point at which something changes or moves in a different direction: *the turn of the tide* ○ *She was born around the turn of the century* (= around 1900/2000, etc.).

• **at every turn** If something unpleasant happens at every turn, it happens every time you try to do something: *They do their best to frustrate my efforts at every turn.*

• **on the turn** Something which is on the turn is about to change direction: *The tide is on the turn.*

turning /'tɜːnɪŋ/ ⓤ /'tɝː-/ *noun* [C] a place, especially a road, track or path, where you can leave the road you are on: *Take the third turning on the left after the traffic lights.*

turn CHANGE POSITION /tɜːn/ ⓤ /tɝːn/ *verb* [I or T] to move, or to move an object or page, so that a different side or surface is on the top: *Now turn the page, please, and start work on Exercise 2.* ○ *She turned the vase **over** to look for the price.* ○ *He turned **over** two or three pages.* ○ *She put out the light, turned **over** (= rolled in order to face in another direction) and went to sleep.* ○ *Now turn **to** (= open the book at) page 23.*

turn BECOME /tɜːn/ ⓤ /tɝːn/ *verb* [L; I or T usually + adv or prep] **1** to (cause to) become, change into or come to be something: *The weather has suddenly turned cold.* ○ *When I refused to pay, he turned nasty.* ○ *She turned pale and started to shiver.* ○ *The mood of the meeting turned solemn when the extent of the problem became known.* ○ *The companies worked well together for a time, but eventually the relationship turned sour* (= became bad). ○ *Keele, pop star turned business tycoon, has launched a new range of cosmetics.* ○ *The dry weather turned the soil **into/to** concrete.* ○ *By the end of September, the leaves have started to turn* (= become brown). ○ *Her attitude turned **from** politely interested **to** enthusiastic during the course of our conversation.* **2** **turn 16/50/9 o'clock, etc.** to become a particular age or time: *She turned 18 last year.* ○ *It's just turned 10 o'clock.*

turn /tɜːn/ ⓤ /tɝːn/ *noun* **take a ... turn** to develop in a particular way: *The situation took a nasty turn and the police were called.* ○ *Events took an unexpected turn when her mother suddenly arrived.*

• **take a turn for the better/worse** to suddenly become better or worse: *Their relationship took a turn for the worse when he lost his job.*

turn SWITCH /tɜːn/ ⓤ /tɝːn/ *verb* [I or T; usually + adv or prep] to use a control to switch a piece of equipment or a power or water supply on or off, or to increase or reduce what it is producing: *Turn **off/out** the light.* ○ *Who turned the telly **on**?* ○ *I asked him to turn **down** the heating.* ○ *Turn the sound **up** – I can't hear what they're saying.* ○ *This sort of heater turns **off** (= can be switched off) at the mains.* ⊃See picture **Phrasal Verbs** on page Centre 9

• **turn the clock back** If you try to turn the clock back, you want things to be the way they were in the past.

turn OPPORTUNITY /tɜːn/ ⓤ /tɝːn/ *noun* [C] an opportunity or a duty to do something at a particular time or in a particular order, before or after other people: *Is it my turn yet?* ○ [+ to infinitive] *I waited so long for my turn to see the careers adviser that I missed my train.* ○ *It's your turn **to** do the washing up!* ○ *In this game if you give the wrong answer you have to **miss** a turn.* ⊃Compare **go** OPPORTUNITY.

• **take turns** (MAINLY UK **take it in turn(s)**) When a number of people take turns, they do the same thing one after the other: *We take turns **to** answer the phone.*

• **in turn** (ALSO **by turns**) one after the other in an agreed order: *Each of us collects the mail in turn.*

• **speak/talk out of turn** to say something which you should not have said: *I'm sorry if I've spoken out of turn, but I thought everyone had already been told.*

turn ACTION /tɜːn/ ⓤ /tɝːn/ *noun* **good turn** an action that helps someone: *That's my good turn for the day!* ○ *You **did** me a good turn warning me that Abigail was going to be there.*

• **One good turn deserves another.** SAYING said when you do a helpful or kind act for someone who has done something good for you

turn PERFORMANCE /tɜːn/ ⓤ /tɝːn/ *noun* [C] a stage act or performance: *The first couple of turns were children singing and dancing.*

turn ILLNESS /tɜːn/ ⓤ /tɝːn/ *noun* [C] OLD-FASHIONED INFORMAL a slight illness, a strange feeling, or a nervous shock: *After the accident I started having funny turns.* ○ *It **gave** me quite **a** turn to see him after all these years.*

turn /tɜːn/ ⓤ /tɝːn/ *verb* [I or T] INFORMAL If your stomach turns or something turns your stomach, you feel as if you are going to vomit: *Just the smell makes my stomach turn.* ○ *It turned my stomach to look at the pictures.*

turn COOKED /tɜːn/ ⓤ /tɝːn/ *noun* OLD-FASHIONED **cooked/done to a turn** cooked for exactly the right amount of time: *The beef was done to a turn.*

PHRASAL VERBS WITH **turn**   ▼

▲ **turn (sb) against** *sb/sth phrasal verb* to start not to like or agree with someone or something, or to make someone do this: *After six years of fighting public opinion has turned against the war.* ○ *The girl's natural father claimed that her stepfather was turning her against him.*

▲ **turn *sth* around/round** *phrasal verb* [M] to change an unsuccessful business, plan or system so that it becomes successful: *The new management team turned the ailing company around in under six months.*

turnaround /'tɜːn.ə.raʊnd/ ⓤ /'tɝːn-/ *noun* [S] (UK ALSO **turnround**) **1** when a business, plan or system suddenly becomes successful: *The chairman, Tony Bramall, was responsible for the turnaround in the company's fortunes.* **2** any change from one thing to its opposite: *What a turnaround – at halftime they were losing 3-0, but in the end they won 4-3.*

▲ **turn *sb* away** NOT ALLOW IN *phrasal verb* [M] to not allow someone to enter a place: *They turned us away at the entrance because we hadn't got tickets.*

▲ **turn away** NOT LOOK *phrasal verb* to move your face so you are not looking at something: *When they show an operation on TV, I have to turn away.*

▲ **turn (sb) back** *phrasal verb* to return in the direction you have come from, or to make someone do this: *We're lost – we'll have to turn back.*

▲ **turn *sth/sb* down** *phrasal verb* [M] to refuse an offer or request: *He offered her a trip to Australia but she turned* it/him down. ○ *He turned down the job because it involved too much travelling.*

▲ **turn** *sth* **in** RETURN *phrasal verb* [M] to return something to an organization or a person in authority: *Please turn your old parking permits in at the end of the week.* ○ *Thousands of weapons were turned in during the national gun amnesty.*

▲ **turn** *sth* **in** PRODUCE *phrasal verb* [M] to produce results, usually good results: *Both companies turn in pre-tax profits of over 5.5 million annually.*

▲ **turn** *sb* **in** GO TO POLICE *phrasal verb* [M] to take a criminal to the police, or to go to them yourself to admit a crime: [R] *The hit-and-run driver turned himself in **to** the police the day after the accident.*

▲ **turn in** BED *phrasal verb* INFORMAL to go to bed: *I usually turn in at about midnight.*

▲ **turn** *(sb/sth)* **into** *sb/sth* to change and become someone or something different, or to make someone or something do this: *The council was hoping to turn a children's home into a residence for adolescent girls.* ○ *The town turned **from** a small seaside resort into a major commercial centre when oil was discovered.*

▲ **turn off** *(sth)* ROAD *phrasal verb* to leave the road you are travelling on and travel along another one: *Turn off the motorway at the next exit.*

▲ **turn** *sb* **off** FEELING *phrasal verb* INFORMAL to stop someone feeling interested or excited, especially sexually: *I should think the smell of her breath would turn any man off.*

▲ **turn** *sth* **on** SHOW *phrasal verb* [M] to start to show a particular quality: *He can really turn on **the charm** when he wants to.*

▲ **turn on** *sb* ATTACK *phrasal verb* to attack or criticize someone suddenly and unexpectedly: *Suddenly she just turned on me and accused me of undermining her.*

▲ **turn on** *sth* DEPEND *phrasal verb* If something turns on something else, it depends on it or is decided by it: *The success of the talks turns on **whether** both sides are willing to make some concessions.*

▲ **turn** *sb* **on** EXCITE *phrasal verb* INFORMAL to interest or excite you, especially sexually: *Short men really turn me on.* ○ *"In my spare time I make models out of matchsticks." "Oh well, **whatever** turns you on, I suppose (= That would not interest or excite me)."*

▲ **turn out** HAPPEN *phrasal verb* **1** to happen in a particular way or to have a particular result, especially an unexpected one: *As events turned out, we were right to have decided to leave early.* ○ *How did the recipe turn out?* **2** to be known or discovered finally and surprisingly: [+ to infinitive] *The truth turned out **to** be stranger than we had expected.* ○ [+ that] *It turns out **that** she had known him when they were children.*

▲ **turn** *sth* **out** PRODUCE *phrasal verb* [M] to produce or make something, often quickly or in large amounts: *They turn out thousands of these games every week.*

▲ **turn** *sth* **out** GO *phrasal verb* If people turn out for an event, they go to be there or to watch: *Thousands of people turned out to welcome the England team home.* ➔Compare **turn up** APPEAR.

turnout /ˈtɜːn.aʊt/ ⓤ /ˈtɜːn-/ *noun* [C] the number of people who are present at an event, especially the number who go to vote at an election: *Good weather on polling day should ensure a good turnout.*

▲ **turn** *sth* **out** EMPTY *phrasal verb* [M] If you turn out a container or the things in it, you empty it completely: *We turned out all the cupboards and drawers and found things we hadn't seen for years.*

▲ **turn** *sb* **out** REMOVE *phrasal verb* [M] to force someone to leave: *He was turned out **of** his flat because he couldn't pay the rent.*

▲ **turn** *sb* **out** DRESS *phrasal verb* **be beautifully/well, etc. turned out** to be beautifully/well, etc. dressed: *She's always beautifully turned out.*

▲ **turn** *(sth)* **over** TELEVISION *phrasal verb* UK to change to a different television station: *This programme's boring — shall I turn over to BBC?*

▲ **turn over** *sth* PRODUCE *phrasal verb* If a business turns over a particular amount of money, it produces that amount from its business activities during a stated

period: *The profits are not high, but the company turns over a large sum every year.*

turnover /ˈtɜːn.əʊ.vəʳ/ ⓤ /ˈtɜːn.oʊ.vɚ/ *noun* [C or U] the amount of business that a company does in a period of time: *Large supermarkets have **high** turnovers (= their goods sell very quickly).* ○ *The business has an annual turnover of £50 000.*

▲ **turn** *sth* **over** USE *phrasal verb* [M] to use or allow something to be used for a different purpose: *Grants are being offered to farmers who agree to turn over their land **to** woodland and forests.*

turnover /ˈtɜːn.əʊ.vəʳ/ ⓤ /ˈtɜːn.oʊ.vɚ/ *noun* [S or U] the rate at which employees leave a company and are replaced by new people: *The large number of temporary contracts resulted in a high turnover of staff.* ○ US *They've had a lot of turnover at the factory recently.*

▲ **turn** *sth* **over** THINK *phrasal verb* to think about something for a period of time: *His father had been turning the idea over **in his mind** for some time.*

▲ **turn** *somewhere/sth* **over** STEAL FROM *phrasal verb* [M] INFORMAL to steal something from a place or to search it, making it very untidy or causing damage: *Did you hear Paul's flat got turned over last week?*

▲ **turn** *sth* **over to** *sb* *phrasal verb* [M] to give something to someone in authority or someone who has a legal right to it, or to give someone legal responsibility for something: *They turned the videos over to the police.* ○ *All documents are to be turned over to the court.* ➔See also **turn in** RETURN.

▲ **turn** *sb* **over to** *sb* *phrasal verb* [M] to take a criminal to the police or other authority: *He was working here illegally and was terrified that his boss would turn him over to the police.*

▲ **turn to** *sb/sth* ASK FOR HELP *phrasal verb* to ask a person or organization for help or support: *Without someone to turn to **for** advice, making the most appropriate choice can be difficult.* ○ *Her family lived a long way away, and she had **no one to** turn to.*

▲ **turn to** *sth* *phrasal verb* to start to do or use something bad, especially because you are unhappy: *She turned to drugs after the break-up of her marriage.*

▲ **turn** *(sth)* **to** *sth* CHANGE SUBJECT *phrasal verb* If someone turns to a particular subject or they turn their thoughts or attention to it, they begin to speak, think or write about it: *I'd like us now to turn our **attention** to next year's budget.* ○ *We're now going to turn to an issue that concerns us all – racism.*

▲ **turn up** *(somewhere)* APPEAR *phrasal verb* [M] INFORMAL to arrive or appear somewhere, usually unexpectedly or in way that was not planned: *Do you think many people will turn up?* ○ *She turned up at my house late one night.*

▲ **turn up** *phrasal verb* If something that you have been looking for turns up, you find it unexpectedly: *The missing letter eventually turned up inside a book.*

● **turn up like a bad penny** OLD-FASHIONED to arrive at a place or event where you are not wanted

▲ **turn up** HAPPEN *phrasal verb* INFORMAL If a better situation or an opportunity to do something turns up, it happens or becomes available unexpectedly or in a way that was not planned: *Don't worry about it – something will turn up, you'll see.* ○ *This job turned up just when I needed it.*

● **turn-up for the book(s)** UK (US **one for the books**) a surprising or unexpected event: *Well, that's a turn-up for the books – I never thought he'd get the job.*

▲ **turn** *sth* **up** FOLD *phrasal verb* [M] to make a piece of clothing or part of a piece of clothing shorter, by folding the material and sewing it into position: *You could always turn the sleeves up.*

turn-up MAINLY UK /ˈtɜːn.ʌp/ ⓤ /ˈtɜːn-/ *noun* [C] (US USUALLY **cuff**) a piece of material at the bottom of a trouser leg which is folded back: *trouser turn-ups*

▲ **turn** *sth* **up** DISCOVER *phrasal verb* [M] INFORMAL to discover something, especially information, after a lot of searching: *See what you can turn up about the family in the files.*

turnabout /ˈtɜːn.ə.baʊt/ ⓤ /ˈtɜːn-/ *noun* [C] a complete change from one situation or condition to its opposite: *What accounts for the dramatic turnabout **in** Britain's international trading performance?*

turnaround /ˈtɜːn.ə.raʊnd/ [US] /ˈtɝːn-/ *noun* [U] (*UK USUALLY* **turnround**) the amount of time taken for something to happen after a vehicle, an instruction or an order for goods arrives at a place: *We'll have to improve the turnround – 3 days is too long.* ○ *Turnround* ***time*** *for the information is some four days and the average cost £12.* ➲See also **turn *sth* around**.

turncoat /ˈtɜːŋ.kəʊt/ [US] /ˈtɝːn-/ *noun* [C] *DISAPPROVING* a person who changes from one opinion to an opposite one in a way which shows they are not loyal to people who share the original opinion

ˈturning ˌcircle *noun* [C usually sing] (*US USUALLY* **turning radius**) the amount of space a vehicle needs in order to go round in a complete circle

ˈturning ˌpoint *noun* [C usually sing] the time at which a situation starts to change in an important way: *ASH, the anti-smoking group, called the new regulations a turning point in the campaign against smoking.* ○ *The turning point in her political career came when she was chosen to fight a crucial by-election.*

turnip /ˈtɜː.nɪp/ [US] /ˈtɝː-/ *noun* [C] a rounded white root which is eaten cooked as a vegetable, or the plant which produces it ➲See picture **Vegetables** on page Centre 2

turnkey /ˈtɜːn.kiː/ [US] /ˈtɝːn-/ *adj* [before n] (of a piece of equipment) ready for immediate use by the person who is buying or renting it: *More and more manufacturers are offering to tailor-make a turnkey system from their own components.*

ˌturn of eˈvents *noun* [C usually sing] a change in a situation: *an unexpected/strange/dramatic turn of events*

turn-off [ROAD] /ˈtɜːn.ɒf/ [US] /ˈtɝːn.ɑːf/ *noun* [C] a road which leaves another road to go in a different direction: *It's 4 km to the turn-off* ***for*** *Norwich/the Norwich turn-off.* ➲See also **turn off** ROAD.

turn-off [DISLIKE] /ˈtɜːn.ɒf/ [US] /ˈtɝːn.ɑːf/ *noun* [C usually sing] *INFORMAL* something which you dislike or which you do not find interesting or sexually exciting: *This system may provide a powerful tool for adults who find computers a turn-off yet need to learn to use them.* ○ *Hairy backs are for me the ultimate turn-off.* ➲See also **turn off** FEELING.

ˌturn of ˈmind *noun* [S] a characteristic tendency or way of thinking: *His natural supporters are the urban poor, and educated people of a liberal turn of mind.*

ˌturn of ˈphrase *noun* [C usually sing] **1** a way of saying something: *'Significant other' meaning 'partner' – now that's an interesting turn of phrase.* **2** the ability to express yourself well: *She has a nice turn of phrase which should serve her well in journalism.*

turn-on /ˈtɜːn.ɒn/ [US] /ˈtɝːn.ɑːn/ *noun* [C] *INFORMAL* something which you find exciting, especially sexually: *The smell of leather on a man is a real turn-on.* See also **turn *sb* on** EXCITE.

turnout /ˈtɜːn.aʊt/ [US] /ˈtɝːn-/ *noun* [C] ➲See at **turn out** GO.

turnover /ˈtɜːnˌəʊ.vəʳ/ [US] /ˈtɝːnˌoʊ.vɚ/ *noun* [C] a small cake made from a folded piece of pastry with fruit inside: *an apple turnover*

turnpike /ˈtɜːn.paɪk/ [US] /ˈtɝːn-/ *noun* [C] (*INFORMAL* **pike**) *US* a motorway which you usually have to pay to use: *the New Jersey Turnpike*

ˈturn ˌsignal *noun* [C] *US FOR* **indicator** ➲See at **indicate** SIGNAL. ➲See picture **Car** on page Centre 12

turnstile /ˈtɜːn.staɪl/ [US] /ˈtɝːn-/ *noun* [C] a device which controls the way into or out of a building, room or area of land, especially one which you have to pay to enter. It is a post with a number of short poles sticking out from it which have to be pushed round as each person walks through the entrance: *The number of spectators going through the turnstiles is up on last season.*

turntable /ˈtɜːnˌteɪ.bl̩/ [US] /ˈtɝːn-/ *noun* [C] **1** a circular surface on a RECORD PLAYER on which the record is played **2** a circular surface on which a railway engine is turned around

turpentine /ˈtɜː.pᵊn.taɪn/ [US] /ˈtɝː-/ *noun* [U] (*INFORMAL* **turps**) a colourless liquid with a strong smell which burns easily. It is sometimes used in products for removing paint from brushes.

turpitude /ˈtɜː.pɪ.tjuːd/ [US] /ˈtɝː.pɪ.tuːd/ *noun* [U] *FORMAL* evil: *acts/crimes of* ***moral*** *turpitude*

turquoise /ˈtɜː.kwɔɪz/ [US] /ˈtɝː-/ *noun* [C or U] a bluish green precious stone which is often used in jewellery **turquoise** /ˈtɜː.kwɔɪz/ [US] /ˈtɝː-/ *adj* bluish green in colour: *the clear turquoise water of the bay*

turret [TOWER] /ˈtʌr.ət/ *noun* [C] a small circular tower which is part of a castle or a large building **turreted** /ˈtʌr.ɪ.tɪd/ [US] /-ə.t̬ɪd/ *adj* with turrets

turret [GUN PART] /ˈtʌr.ət/ *noun* [C] a part of a military vehicle which contains a large gun or guns and which can move to face any direction

turtle /ˈtɜː.tl̩/ [US] /ˈtɝː.t̬l̩/ *noun* [C] *plural* **turtles** or **turtle** an animal which lives in or near water and has a thick shell covering its body into which it can move its head and legs for protection

turtledove /ˌtɜː.tl̩ˈdʌv/ [US] /ˌtɝː.t̬l̩-/ *noun* [C] a small pale brown bird which makes a soft pleasant sound

turtleneck /ˈtɜː.tl̩.nek/ [US] /ˈtɝː.t̬l̩-/ *noun* [C] **1** *US FOR* **polo neck 2** *UK* (*US* **mock turtleneck**) a high round collar that does not fold over on itself, or a jumper with this type of collar: *a turtleneck sweater*

turves /tɜːvz/ [US] /tɝːvz/ *plural of* **turf** GRASS

tush [STUPID] /tʊʃ/ *exclamation OLD USE* used to say that something is stupid or not true

tush [BOTTOM] /tʊʃ/ *noun* [C] *US SLANG* the part of your body that you sit on; bottom: *I slipped on the ice and landed right on my tush!*

tusk /tʌsk/ *noun* [C] either of the two long pointed teeth which stick out from the mouth of some animals such as elephants ➲See picture **Animals and Birds** on page Centre 4

tussle [DISAGREE] /ˈtʌs.l̩/ *verb* [I] to have difficult disagreements or fierce arguments: *During his twelve years in Congress he has tussled* ***with*** *the chemical, drug and power companies on behalf of the ordinary person's right to breathe clean air.* ○ *The residents are still tussling* ***over*** *the ever-scarcer street parking.* **tussle** /ˈtʌs.l̩/ *noun* [C] *a boardroom/bureaucratic/legal tussle* ○ *There followed a long tussle* ***for*** *custody of the children.*

▲ **tussle with *sth*** *phrasal verb INFORMAL* to try hard to understand or deal with a difficult idea or problem: *It's an idea that I've been tussling with for quite a while.*

tussle [FIGHT] /ˈtʌs.l̩/ *verb* [I] to fight with another person using your arms and body: *The boys started to tussle in the corridor.* **tussle** /ˈtʌs.l̩/ *noun* [C usually sing] *From the state of his clothes and hair, he had been* ***in a*** *tussle.*

tut /tʌt/ *exclamation* (*ALSO* **tut tut**) a written representation of the sound made to show you disapprove of something, or a word said twice in a humorous way to suggest disapproval: *Tut, it's raining – I'm going to get soaked.* ○ *You're late again – tut tut!* **tut** /tʌt/ *verb* [I] **-tt-** *He walked off, tutting to himself.* ○ [+ speech] *"Still not out of bed?" she tutted* (= said in disapproving way).

tutelage /ˈtjuː.tɪ.lɪdʒ/ [US] /ˈtuː.t̬ᵊl.ɪdʒ/ *noun* [U] *FORMAL* help, advice or teaching about how to do something: ***Under the*** *tutelage* ***of*** *Professor Roberts, the 900 delegates assessed and discussed the social market economy.*

tutor /ˈtjuː.təʳ/ [US] /ˈtuː.t̬ɚ/ *noun* [C] a teacher who works with one student or a small group, either at a British college or university or in the home of a child: *His tutor encouraged him to read widely in philosophy.* ○ *During my illness I was taught by a series of* ***home*** *tutors.* **tutor** /ˈtjuː.təʳ/ [US] /ˈtuː.t̬ɚ/ *verb* [T] *Children are routinely tutored for hours after school.*

tutorial /tjuːˈtɔː.ri.əl/ [US] /tuːˈtɔːr.i-/ *noun* [C] a period of study with a tutor involving one student or a small group

tutu /ˈtuː.tuː/ *noun* [C] a very short skirt made of many layers of very thin stiff material, which is worn by female ballet dancers

tu-whit tu-whoo /tʊˌwɪt.tʊˈwuː/ *exclamation* a written representation of the sound made by an OWL

tuxedo (*plural* **tuxedos**) /tʌkˈsiː.dəʊ/ [US] /-doʊ/ *noun* [C] (*INFORMAL* **tux**) *MAINLY US FOR* **dinner jacket**

TV /ˌtiːˈviː/ *noun* [C or U] *ABBREVIATION FOR* television: *We ate* ***in front of*** (= while watching) *the TV.* ○ *What's* ***on*** *TV* tonight? ○ *You **watch** too much TV!* ○ *TV personalities*

TV 'dinner *noun* [C] a meal which you buy already prepared from a shop and which only needs to be heated before being eaten, especially while watching TV

twaddle /ˈtwɒd.l̩/ ⓤ /ˈtwɑː.d̩l/ *noun* [U] INFORMAL speech or writing which is foolish or not true; nonsense: *She dismissed the findings as **utter** twaddle/**a load of old** twaddle.*

twain /tweɪn/ *noun* OLD USE two

twang SOUND /twæŋ/ *verb* [I or T] to make a noise like that of a tight string being sharply pulled and released: *He twanged the guitar string/his braces.* ○ *The springs twanged.* **twang** /twæŋ/ *noun* [C] *We heard a twang as the cable broke.*

twang VOICE /twæŋ/ *noun* [C usually sing] a quality of the human voice, produced by air passing out through the nose as you speak: *a nasal/southern twang*

twat VAGINA /twæt/ *noun* [C] OFFENSIVE the outer female sex organ; the vagina

twat PERSON /twæt/ *noun* [C] UK OFFENSIVE a stupid or unpleasant person

tweak /twiːk/ *verb* [T] **1** to pull and twist with a small sudden movement: *Standing in front of the mirror she tweaked a strand of hair into place.* **2** to change slightly, especially in order to make more correct, effective, or suitable: *The software is pretty much there – it just needs a little tweaking.* ○ *You just need to tweak the last paragraph and then it's done.* **tweak** /twiːk/ *noun* [C]

twee /twiː/ *adj* MAINLY UK INFORMAL DISAPPROVING artificially attractive or too perfect: *The village has escaped all modern developments, yet without becoming twee or 'preserved'.*

tweed /twiːd/ *noun* [C or U] a thick material woven from wool of several different colours: *a tweed jacket* ○ *a tweed skirt and sensible shoes*

tweeds /twiːdz/ *plural noun* clothes made from tweed, especially a jacket and matching trousers/skirt: *He wore tweeds and smoked a pipe.*

tweedy /ˈtwiː.di/ *adj* **1** of or like tweed: *a tweedy sports jacket* **2** describes the life of wealthy people with homes in the countryside and an interest in sports like hunting: *We met a tweedy man walking a couple of dogs.*

tweet /twiːt/ *noun* [C] INFORMAL the short weak sound made by a young bird **tweet** /twiːt/ *verb* [I] *We could hear the baby birds tweeting.*

tweezers /ˈtwiː.zəz/ ⓤ /-zɚz/ *plural noun* (US ALSO **tweezer**) a small piece of equipment made of two narrow strips of metal joined at one end. It is used to pull out hairs or to pick up small objects by pressing the two strips of metal together with the fingers: *a pair of tweezers* ○ *eyebrow tweezers*

twelfth 'man *noun* [U] UK in a cricket team, a RESERVE (= extra player)

Twelfth 'Night *noun* the sixth of January, twelve days after Christmas

twelve /twelv/ *determiner, pronoun, noun* (the number) 12: *ten, eleven, twelve, thirteen* ○ *a twelve-seater minibus* ⊃See also **dozen**.

twelfth /twelfθ/ *determiner, pronoun, adj, adv, noun* 12th written as a word

twenty /ˈtwen.ti/ ⓤ /-t̬i/ *determiner, pronoun, noun* (the number) 20: *nineteen, twenty, twenty-one* ○ *space for twenty people* ⊃See also **score** TWENTY.

twenties /ˈtwen.tiz/ ⓤ /-t̬iz/ *plural noun* A person's twenties are the period in which they are aged between 20 and 29: *I'd guess she's **in** her twenties.*

the twenties *plural noun* **1** the range of temperature between 20° and 29°: *The temperature is expected to be **in** the twenties tomorrow.* **2** the period of years between 20 and 29 in any century: *She was born **in** the twenties.*

twentieth /ˈtwen.ti.əθ/ ⓤ /-t̬i-/ *determiner, pronoun, adj, adv, noun* 20th written as a word

twenty-first (birthday) /ˌtwen.ti.fɜːst'bɜːθ.deɪ/ ⓤ /-t̬i.fɝːst'bɝːθ-/ *noun* [C usually sing] the day on which a person reaches the age of 21 and is traditionally said, in Western societies, to become an adult

twenty-four-hour clock /ˌtwen.ti.fɔːˌraʊə'klɒk/ ⓤ /-t̬i.fɔːrˌaʊr'klɑːk/ *noun* [U] the **24-hour clock**

twenty-four seven /ˌtwen.ti.fɔː'sev.ən/ ⓤ /-t̬i.fɔːr/ *adv, adj* (ALSO **24/7**) INFORMAL 24 hours a day, 7 days a week; all the time: *a football website updated 24/7* ○ *Having a kid is a 24/7 job.*

twenty-twenty vision /ˌtwen.ti,twen.ti'vɪʒ.ən/ ⓤ /-t̬i,twen.t̬i-/ *noun* [U] (ALSO **20/20 vision**) perfect sight, especially as measured by a standard test

twerp, twirp /twɜːp/ ⓤ /twɝːp/ *noun* [C] OLD-FASHIONED INFORMAL a stupid person

twice /twaɪs/ *predeterminer, adv* two times: *I've already asked him twice.* ○ *The post comes twice daily* (= two times every day). ○ *There are twice as many houses in this area as there used to be.* ○ *The state is at least twice as big as England.* ○ *He's twice her size* (= much bigger than she is).

twiddle /ˈtwɪd.l̩/ *verb* [I or T] to move something repeatedly between your fingers, especially without any purpose: *She was twiddling **(with)** a pencil/her hair.* ○ *Twiddle **a dial/knob** on a radio in Britain and you may hear more voices speaking crackly French or German than English.*

● **twiddle your thumbs** to do nothing for a period of time, usually while you are waiting for something to happen: *I arrived early for the meeting so I was twiddling my thumbs for half an hour.*

twiddle /ˈtwɪd.l̩/ *noun* [C] an act of turning something with the fingers: *At the twiddle of a knob the operators can focus on a tiny amount of airspace or scan the whole area.*

twiddly /ˈtwɪd.l̩.i/ /-li/ *adj* INFORMAL curly or decorative, especially in an unnecessary way: *The frame has twiddly **bits** at the corners which get very dusty.*

twig BRANCH /twɪg/ *noun* [C] a small thin branch of a tree or bush, especially one removed from the tree or bush and without any leaves: *We collected dry twigs to start the fire.*

twig UNDERSTAND /twɪg/ *verb* [I or T] -gg- INFORMAL to suddenly realize something: [+ question word] *Then he twigged what I meant.* ○ *She's six months pregnant and he still hasn't twigged.*

twilight EVENING /ˈtwaɪ.laɪt/ *noun* [U] the period just before it becomes completely dark in the evening: *I could make out a dark figure in **the** twilight.* **twilit** /ˈtwaɪ.lɪt/ *adj* LITERARY *a twilit street/room*

twilight FINAL PART /ˈtwaɪ.laɪt/ *noun* LITERARY **the twilight of sth** the final part of a period: *I knew him when he was in the twilight of his career.*

● **twilight years** the last years of someone's life: *Old people often rely on pets for comfort and companionship in their twilight years.*

twilight UNCLEAR /ˈtwaɪ.laɪt/ *adj* LITERARY used to describe a way of life which is characterized by uncertainty and difficult or slightly illegal situations, and which is on the edge of normal society: *The remaining inhabitants of this once-prosperous market town have got used to a twilight **existence**.* ○ *Leaving a secure job for the twilight **world** of pop music was perhaps a mistake.*

● **twilight zone** an area where two different ways of life or states of existence meet: *the twilight zone **between** life and death*

twill /twɪl/ *noun* [U] a strong cotton cloth which has raised diagonal lines on the surface

twin /twɪn/ *noun* [C] **1** either of two children born to the same mother on the same occasion: *My sister has twin sons.* ○ *a twin sister* **2** one of two very similar things: *The two countries are often regarded as economic twins.*

twin /twɪn/ *adj* [before n] **1** used to describe two similar things that are a pair: *twin towers* ○ *a car with twin exhausts* **2** existing at the same time: *his twin obsessions – women and cars*

twin /twɪn/ *verb* UK **be twinned with** If a town in one country is twinned with a town in another country, the two towns have a special relationship: *Cambridge is twinned with Heidelberg.*

twin 'bed *noun* [C] one of a pair of two beds which are each big enough for one person **twin-bedded** /ˌtwɪn'bed.ɪd/ *adj*: *I'd like to book one twin-bedded room and one double room.*

twine [WRAP] /twaɪn/ *verb* [I or T; usually + adv or prep] to wrap round an object several times: *The vine twines* ***round/up*** *the pole.* ○ *Twine the different coloured threads* ***together***. ➲See also **entwine**; **intertwine**. **twining** /ˈtwaɪ.nɪŋ/ *adj*: *a twining plant*

twine [STRING] /twaɪn/ *noun* [U] strong string made of two or more lengths of string twisted together: *a ball of twine* ○ *garden twine*

twinge /twɪndʒ/ *noun* [C] a sudden short feeling of physical or mental pain: *I* ***felt a*** *twinge in my knee.* ○ *He was feeling twinges from a calf injury after 20 minutes of the game.* ○ *I admit I felt* ***a*** *twinge* ***of*** *guilt as we left.*

twinkle /ˈtwɪŋ.kl̩/ *verb* [I] (of light or a shiny surface) to shine repeatedly strongly then weakly, as if flashing on and off very quickly: *The lights of the town twinkled in the distance.* ○ *The stars twinkled in the clear sky.* ○ *His brown eyes twinkled behind the gold-rimmed glasses.* **twinkle** /ˈtwɪŋ.kl̩/ *noun* [S] *the twinkle of the stars/lights/diamonds* ○ *He was holding the phone with a mischievous twinkle* ***in*** *his* ***eye***.

• **when** ***sb*** **was a (mere) twinkle in** ***their*** **father's eye** *HUMOROUS* at a time before someone was born

twinkling /ˈtwɪŋ.kl̩.ɪŋ/ /-klɪŋ/ *noun* [S] *OLD-FASHIONED* a very short time: *I shall be there* ***in a*** *twinkling.*

• **in the twinkling of an eye** If something happens in the twinkling of an eye, it happens very quickly: *Microprocessors do the calculations in the twinkling of an eye.*

ˈ**twin** ˌ**set** *noun* [C] a woman's jumper and CARDIGAN which have the same colour or pattern and are worn together: *She always wore a twin set* ***and pearls***.

ˌ**twin** ˈ**town** *UK noun* [C] (*US* **sister city**) a town or city which shares planned activities and visits with a similar town in another country: *Cambridge and Heidelberg are twin towns.*

twirl /twɜːl/ [US] /twɝːl/ *verb* [I or T; usually + adv or prep] to (cause to) give a sudden quick turn or set of turns in a circle: *She danced and twirled across the room.* ○ *He twirled the ribbon round the stick.* ○ *He twirled his* ***umbrella*** *as he walked.* ○ *She twirled her baton high in the air as she led the parade.* **twirl** /twɜːl/ [US] /twɝːl/ *noun* [C] *She did a twirl* (= turned quickly round) *in her new skirt.* **twirler** /ˈtwɜː.ləʳ/ [US] /ˈtwɝː.lɚ/ *noun* [C] (*ALSO* **majorette**) *US* a girl who marches as part of a group while spinning a BATON (= short metal stick) or throwing it in the air and then catching it **twirling** /ˈtwɜː.lɪŋ/ [US] /twɝː-/ *noun* [U] *US* the action or skill of spinning a BATON **twirly** /ˈtwɜː.li/ [US] /ˈtwɝː-/ *adj INFORMAL* with turns or curls: *a twirly moustache* ○ *twirly writing*

twirp /twɜːp/ [US] /twɝːp/ *noun* [C] a **twerp**

twist [TURN] /twɪst/ *verb* **1** [I or T] to turn something, especially repeatedly, or to turn or wrap one thing around another: *The path twists* ***and turns*** *for over a mile.* ○ *She sat there nervously twisting the ring around on her finger.* ○ *She twisted her head (round) so she could see what was happening.* ○ *Twist the rope tightly round that post over there.* **2** [T] If you twist a part of your body, such as your ankle, you injure it by suddenly turning it: *She slipped on the ice and twisted her knee.*

• **twist** ***sb's*** **arm** to persuade someone to do something they do not want to do: *I didn't want to go but Linda twisted my arm.*

• **twist** ***sb*** **around/round** ***your*** **little finger** to be able to persuade someone to do anything you want, usually because they like you so much: *He'd do anything for you. You've got him twisted around your little finger.*

twist /twɪst/ *noun* [C] **1** when you twist something: *She gave the cap another twist to make sure it was tight.* ○ *an Elvis-style twist of the hips* **2** the shape of or a piece of something which has been twisted: *a twist* ***of*** *hair* ○ *a twist* ***of*** *lemon* **3** a tight bend: *a path with many twists* ***and turns*** **4 the twist** a dance in which people stay in one place and twist their bodies from side to side to music

• **be/go round the twist** (*ALSO* **send** ***sb*** **round the twist**) *OLD-FASHIONED* to be, become or make someone else become angry or unable to behave in a reasonable way: *If I'd stayed there any longer, I'd have gone round the twist.*

twisted /ˈtwɪs.tɪd/ *adj* bent so that the original shape is changed or destroyed: *a twisted tree trunk* ○ *a twisted ankle* ○ *twisted metal* ➲See also **twisted**.

twisty /ˈtwɪs.ti/ *adj INFORMAL* describes a road with many turns

twist [CHANGE] /twɪst/ *verb* [T] *DISAPPROVING* to change information so that it gives the message you want it to give, especially in a way that is dishonest: *This report shows how she twisted the truth to claim successes where none, in fact, existed.* ○ *You're twisting my words – that's not what I said at all.*

twist /twɪst/ *noun* [C] **1** a change in the way in which something happens: *The story* ***took*** *a surprise twist today with media reports that the doctor had resigned.* ○ *The incident was the* ***latest*** *twist in the continuing saga of fraud and high scandal in banks and stockbroking firms.* ○ *But for a cruel twist* ***of fate/fortune***, *he could now be running his own business.* ○ *There's an unexpected twist* ***in/to*** *the plot towards the end of the film.* **2** a complicated situation or plan of action: *the twists* ***and turns*** *of fate* ○ *It has proved very difficult to unravel the twists* ***and turns*** *and contradictions of the evidence.*

twisted /ˈtwɪs.tɪd/ *adj* strange and slightly unpleasant or cruel: *The letter was clearly the product of a twisted* ***mind***. ○ *The experience had left her* ***bitter and*** *twisted.* ➲See also **twisted** at **twist** TURN.

twister /ˈtwɪs.təʳ/ *noun* [C] *US INFORMAL* a **tornado** or a **whirlwind**

twist-tie /ˈtwɪst.taɪ/ *noun* [C] *MAINLY US* a short piece of wire covered in plastic or paper which is used to fasten a plastic bag

twit /twɪt/ *noun* [C] *INFORMAL* a stupid person: *He's such a twit!* ○ *You stupid twit!*

twitch [UNCONTROLLED MOVEMENT] /twɪtʃ/ *verb* [I or T] (to cause) to make a sudden small movement with a part of the body, usually unintentionally: *He tried to suppress a smile but felt the corner of his mouth twitch.* ○ *She twitched her nose like a rabbit.* **twitch** /twɪtʃ/ *noun* [C] *I've got a twitch at the corner of my eye – can you see it?* **twitchy** /ˈtwɪtʃ.i/ *adj* nervous and anxious, sometimes showing this through sudden movements or movements which do not appear smooth or relaxed: *On camera he appears twitchy and ill at ease.* ○ *The president is reportedly getting twitchy about the recent fall in his popularity.*

twitch [PULL] /twɪtʃ/ *verb* [T] to give something a sudden light pull: *You'll feel something twitch the line when you get a fish.* **twitch** /twɪtʃ/ *noun* [C]

twitter /ˈtwɪt.əʳ/ [US] /ˈtwɪt̬.ɚ/ *verb* [I] **1** (of a bird) to make a series of short high sounds: *I was woken up in the early hours by a bird twittering just outside my window.* **2** to talk quickly and nervously in a high voice, saying very little of importance or interest: *She comes in here when I'm trying to work and just twitters on about nothing.* **twitter** /ˈtwɪt.əʳ/ [US] /ˈtwɪt̬.ɚ/ *noun* [C]

twixt /twɪkst/ *prep OLD USE OR LITERARY* between

two /tuː/ *determiner, pronoun, noun* (the number) 2: *They've got two houses.* ○ *I spent two years in Ethiopia.* ○ *It's two o'clock.* ○ *He'll be two (years old) in February.*

• **(There's) no two ways about it.** something that you say in order to emphasize that something is true: *She was the meanest person I've ever met – no two ways about it.*

• ***your*** **two cents worth** *US INFORMAL* your spoken opinion on a particular matter: *I thought I'd just* ***throw in*** (= add) *my two cents worth.*

• **put two and two together** *INFORMAL* to guess the truth about a situation from what you have seen or heard: *"How did you know they were having an affair?" "I'd seen them out together a couple of times so I just put two and two together."*

• **put two and two together and make five** *INFORMAL HUMOROUS* to understand a particular situation wrongly, often in a way which is more shocking or exciting than the truth: *"Why ever did she think you were pregnant?" "I was sick once or twice and I suppose she just put two and two together and made five."*

• **be in two minds** *UK* (*US* **be of two minds**) to be unable to decide about something: *I was in two minds whether or not to come this morning.*

T

• **be two of a kind** If two people are two of a kind, they are very similar: *"Patrick and Glyn got on really well, didn't they?" "Yes, well they're two of a kind."*
• **That makes two of us.** something that you say to tell someone that you are in the same unpleasant situation, or have the same negative feelings as them: *"I have absolutely no idea what's going on." "That makes two of us!"*
• **Two can play at that game.** *INFORMAL* something that you say when you intend to harm someone in the same way as they have harmed you: *Well, when I found out that my husband had been having an affair I thought two can play at that game!*
• **It takes two to tango.** *SAYING* said when you want to emphasize that both people involved in a difficult situation must accept the blame, or that an activity needs two people who are willing to take part for it to happen: *She may want to argue, but it takes two to tango and I won't stoop to her level.*
• **Two's company, three's a crowd.** *SAYING* said when two people are relaxed and enjoying each other's company but another person would make them feel less comfortable

ˌtwo ˈbits *noun* [C] *US INFORMAL* 25 cents
two-bit /ˈtuː.bɪt/ *adj* [before n] *US INFORMAL DISAPPROVING* worth very little, or very unimportant: *He plays a two-bit Chicago gangster in the play.*

two-dimensional [SHAPE] /ˌtuː.daɪˈment.ʃən.əl/ *adj* flat, having width and length but not depth

two-dimensional [TOO SIMPLE] /ˌtuː.daɪˈment.ʃən.əl/ *adj DISAPPROVING* A person or story which is two-dimensional is too simple, showing a lack of deep, serious thought and understanding: *I didn't believe in any of the characters in the book – they were somehow two-dimensional.*

two-edged [BLADE] /ˌtuːˈedʒd/ *adj* having two sharp edges for cutting: *a two-edged sword*

two-edged [TWO MEANINGS] /ˌtuːˈedʒd/ *adj* A two-edged remark can be understood in two very different ways, one of them positive and one of them negative: *"That was amazingly generous of you!" "Well, that was a two-edged comment – are you saying I'm usually mean?"*

two-faced /ˌtuːˈfeɪst/ *adj DISAPPROVING* describes someone who is not sincere, saying unpleasant things about you to other people while seeming to be pleasant when they are with you: *I don't trust her – I suspect she's a bit two-faced.*

ˌtwo ˈfingers *plural noun UK* in Britain, a sign that is considered rude, and which is made by holding your hand up with your palm facing towards you, and your first and second fingers held in a V shape: *She drove past and* ***stuck** two fingers* ***up at** him.*

two-handed /ˌtuːˈhæn.dɪd/ *adj* Something which is two-handed needs or involves the use of both hands at the same time: *a two-handed saw* ○ *My tennis is really improving – I've got a formidable two-handed backhand.*

two-hander /ˌtuːˈhæn.dəʳ/ [US] /-dɚ/ *noun* [C] *UK* a play written for two actors

twopence /ˈtʌp.ənts/ *noun* **tuppence** **twopenny** /ˈtʌp.ən.i/ /-ni/ *adj* [before n] **tupenny**

two-piece /ˈtuːˌpiːs/ *noun* [C usually sing] a set of clothes which consists of two separate matching parts, especially a woman's clothes for swimming, or a man's matching jacket and trousers

two-ply /ˈtuːˌplaɪ/ *noun* [U] Two-ply material, wood or wool consists of two layers or two sets of thread for added thickness or strength.

two-seater /ˌtuːˈsiː.təʳ/ [US] /-t̬ɚ/ *noun* [C] a car which has seats for only two people

twosome /ˈtuː.səm/ *noun* [C] two people considered together: *Zoe and I were inseparable as kids – my mother used to call us the terrible twosome.*

two-time /ˈtuː.taɪm/ *verb* [T] *INFORMAL* To two-time someone that you are having a relationship with is to deceive them by having a secret sexual relationship with someone else at the same time: *I finished with him when I found out he was two-timing me.*
two-timer /ˈtuːˌtaɪ.məʳ/ [US] /-mɚ/ *noun* [C] *INFORMAL* a person who deceives their partner by having a secret sexual relationship with someone else

two-tone /ˈtuː.təʊn/ [US] /-toʊn/ *adj* Clothes or shoes that are two-tone are two different colours or are a lighter and a darker variety of the same colour.

two-up, two-down /tuːˌʌp.tuːˈdaʊn/ *noun* [C] *UK INFORMAL* a small, two-storey house with just two main rooms on the ground floor and two bedrooms on the top floor: *a modest two-up, two-down*

two-way [DIRECTION] /ˈtuː.weɪ/ *adj* [before n] moving or allowing movement in both directions: *a two-way street*

two-way [RADIO] /ˈtuː.weɪ/ *adj* [before n] describes radios that can both send out and receive signals

two-way [RELATIONSHIP] /ˈtuː.weɪ/ *adj* describes a situation that involves two people or two groups of people working together to achieve a shared aim: *Negotiations are a two-way thing – both sides have to come to a compromise.* ○ *Remember, friendships are a* ***two-way street*** (= both people have to make an effort).

ˌtwo-way ˈmirror *noun* [C] a mirror that can be used in the usual way from one side but is transparent from the other side and can therefore be used to watch people without them knowing

tycoon /taɪˈkuːn/ *noun* [C] a person who has succeeded in business or industry and has become very wealthy and powerful: *a business/property/shipping tycoon*

tyke, tike /taɪk/ *noun* [C] **1** *UK INFORMAL* a child who is badly behaved in a playful way: *Come here, you cheeky little tyke!* **2** *INFORMAL* a young child

Tylenol /ˈtaɪ.lə.nɒl/ [US] /-nɑːl/ *noun* [C or U] *US TRADEMARK* a common drug in the US which reduces pain: *I was taking Tylenol for my arthritis.*

type [GROUP] /taɪp/ *noun* [C] **1** a particular group of people or things which shares similar characteristics and forms a smaller division of a larger set: *There were so many different types* ***of*** *bread that I didn't know which to buy.* ○ *What type* ***of*** *clothes does she wear?* ○ *It was dark so I didn't notice what type* ***of*** *car it was.* ○ *He's the type* ***of*** *man you could take home to your mother.* ○ *He's very attractive, if you like the blond athletic type.* ○ *They sell dried flowers and baskets and that type* ***of thing.*** ○ *We have a range of moisturizers for all different skin types.* ○ *She was young and she was wearing student-type clothes so I assumed she was studying here.* ○ *He took me to a pub in Soho full of actor types speaking at the tops of their voices.* **2** *SPECIALIZED* a person who seems to represent a particular group of people, having all the qualities that you usually connect with that group: *He doesn't use fully rounded characters in his plays – he uses types.* **3 be sb's type** to be the type of person that someone thinks is attractive: *He's a nice enough guy – he's just not my type.* ○ *I'd have thought Ben was more your type.*

typical /ˈtɪp.ɪ.kəl/ *adj* **1** showing all the characteristics that you would usually expect from a particular group of things: *I must look like the typical tourist with my shorts and my camera.* ○ *This sort of hot and spicy food is very typical* ***of*** *the food in the south of the country.* ○ *Typical symptoms would include severe headaches, vomiting and dizziness.* **2** *DISAPPROVING* showing all the bad characteristics that you expect from someone or something, often in a way that is annoying: *It's just typical* ***of*** *Ian to spend all that money on the equipment and then lose interest half way through the course.* ○ *"He phoned in at the last minute to say he wasn't coming." "Typical!"*

typically /ˈtɪp.ɪ.kli/ *adv* **1** showing all the characteristics that you would expect from the stated person, thing or group: *She has that reserve and slight coldness of manner which is typically English.* ○ *Paul, in typically rude fashion, told him he was talking rubbish.* **2** used when you are giving an average or usual example of a particular thing: *Typically, a doctor will see about thirty patients a day.* ○ *Tickets for such events will typically cost around thirty dollars.*

typify /ˈtɪp.ɪ.faɪ/ *verb* **1** Something which typifies a particular group of things shows all the characteristics that you would usually expect from it: *With her cropped hair and and her mannish clothes, she typifies the sort of feminist often feared by men.* **2** to be characteristic of

T

something: *His latest book reflects the old preoccupations with sex and religion that typify much of his work.*

COMMON LEARNER ERROR

typical or **formal?**

Typical (having all the qualities that something usually has) does not mean the same as **formal** (serious and correct).

The document was written in formal language.

~~*The document was written in typical language.*~~

type [WRITE] /taɪp/ *verb* **[I or T]** to write using a machine, either a computer keyboard or a typewriter: *She asked me to type a couple of letters.* ○ *He can type very quickly.* ○ *I was typing* ***away*** *into the early hours of the morning just to get the thing finished.* **typing** /ˈtaɪ.pɪŋ/ *noun* **[U]** *It's the usual boring secretarial job – a bit of typing and some filing.* ○ *a typing error*

typist /ˈtaɪ.pɪst/ *noun* **[C]** a person who is employed to type letters, reports and other documents

type [PRINTED LETTERS] /taɪp/ *noun* **[C or U]** (*SPECIALIZED* **typeface**) the style and size of printed letters used in a piece of printed writing such as in a newspaper, book or article: *Use bold type for your headings.* ○ *The software allows you to choose from over twenty sorts of typeface.*

PHRASAL VERBS WITH **type**

▲ **type** ***sth*** **in** *phrasal verb* **[M]** If you type an instruction or piece of information in, you press the necessary letters, numbers or other keys on your computer keyboard: *Type in your password.*

▲ **type** ***sth*** **up** *phrasal verb* **[M]** to make a typed copy of a piece of text that is written by hand: *Could you type up the minutes from the meeting, please?*

typecast /ˈtaɪp.kɑːst/ [US] /-kæst/ *verb* **[T]** **typecast, typecast** to always give an actor the same type of character to play, usually because he or she is physically suited to that type of part: *She soon found herself typecast* ***as*** *a dizzy blonde.*

typescript /ˈtaɪp.skrɪpt/ *noun* **[C]** a typed copy of a piece of writing such as a book

typewriter /ˈtaɪpˌraɪ.təʳ/ [US] /-tɚ/ *noun* **[C]** a machine with keys that you press to produce letters and numbers on paper: *He still uses an old typewriter.* **typewritten** /ˈtaɪpˌrɪt.ᵊn/ [US] /-ˌrɪt̬-/ *adj*: *a typewritten memo*

typhoid (fever) /ˌtaɪ.fɔɪdˈfiː.vəʳ/ [US] /-vɚ/ *noun* **[U]** an infectious disease spread by dirty water and food, causing a high body temperature, red spots on the upper body, severe pains in the bowels and sometimes death

typhoon /taɪˈfuːn/ *noun* **[C]** a violent wind which has a circular movement, found in the West Pacific Ocean: *The 169 000-ton vessel went down during a typhoon in the South China Sea.*

typhus /ˈtaɪ.fəs/ *noun* **[U]** an infectious disease spread by LICE (= small insects which live on the body), causing a high body temperature, severe pains in the head and purple spots on the body

typical /ˈtɪp.ɪ.kᵊl/ *adj* ➲See at **type** GROUP.

typify /ˈtɪp.ɪ.faɪ/ *verb* ➲See at **type** GROUP.

typist /ˈtaɪ.pɪst/ *noun* **[C]** ➲See at **type** WRITE.

typo /ˈtaɪ.pəʊ/ [US] /-poʊ/ *noun* **[C]** a small mistake in a text made when it was typed or printed

typography /taɪˈpɒg.rə.fi/ [US] /-ˈpɑː.grə-/ *noun* **[U]** the style, size and arrangement of the letters in a piece of printing **typographical** /ˌtaɪ.pəʊˈgræf.ɪ.kᵊl/ [US] /-poʊ-/ *adj* (*ALSO* **typographic**) *a typographical* ***error***

tyrannosaurus /tɪˌræn.əˈsɔː.rəs/ /taɪ-/ [US] /-ˈsɔːr.əs/ *noun* **[C]** (*ALSO* **tyrannosaur**) a fierce DINOSAUR with large, powerful back legs, small front legs and a long tail

tyranny /ˈtɪr.ᵊn.i/ *noun* **[U]** **1** government by a ruler or small group of people who have unlimited power over the people in their country or state and use it unfairly and cruelly: *This, the president promised us, was a war against tyranny.* **2** when a situation or person controls how you are able to live, in an unfair way: *Women, the play seems to suggest, must resist* ***the*** *tyranny* ***of*** *domesticity.* **tyrannical** /tɪˈræn.ɪ.kᵊl/ *adj*: *a tyrannical leader/regime/political system* ○ *In the end she left home just to escape the tyrannical rule of her mother.*

tyrannically /tɪˈræn.ɪ.kli/ *adv*

tyrannize, *UK USUALLY* **-ise** /ˈtɪr.ᵊn.aɪz/ *verb* **[T]** to treat someone cruelly, controlling everything that they do: *He was one of those school bullies who tyrannized the whole playground.*

tyrant /ˈtaɪə.rᵊnt/ [US] /ˈtaɪ-/ *noun* **[C]** a ruler who has unlimited power over other people, and uses it unfairly and cruelly: *Tamir, one of several sons of the exiled ruler, vowed he would liberate his country from the tyrant.* ○ *FIGURATIVE HUMOROUS Overnight my boss seems to have turned into a tyrant.*

tyre *UK, US* **tire** /taɪəʳ/ [US] /taɪr/ *noun* **[C]** a thick rubber ring, often filled with air, which is fitted around the outer edge of the wheel of a vehicle, allowing the vehicle to stick to the road surface and to travel over the ground more easily: *I've got a* ***flat*** *tyre* (= the air has gone out of it). ○ *He was driving along the motorway when his tyre burst.* ○ *I keep a* ***spare*** *tyre in the back of the car.* ➲See picture **Car** on page Centre 12

tyro /ˈtaɪ.rəʊ/ [US] /-roʊ/ *noun* **[C]** *plural* **tyros** a person who is new to an activity: *I look forward to seeing this young tyro's next ballet.*

tzar /zɑːʳ/ [US] /zɑːr/ *noun* **[C]** a **tsar**

tzetze fly /ˈtet.siˌflaɪ/ *noun* **[C or U]** a **tsetse fly**

T

U

U LETTER (*plural* **U's**), **u** (*plural* **u's**) /juː/ *noun* [C] the 21st letter of the English alphabet

U FILM *UK* (*plural* **U's**) /juː/ *adj, noun* [C] (*US* **G**) used to refer to a film that is considered suitable for children of any age

U COLLEGE /juː/ *noun* [U] *US WRITTEN ABBREVIATION FOR* **university**: *She goes to Kansas U/Sydney U.*

the UAE /ðə.juː.eɪˈiː/ *noun* [S] *ABBREVIATION FOR* the United Arab Emirates

U-bend /ˈjuː.bend/ *noun* [C] a U-shaped piece of pipe, especially one fixed under a toilet or sink, which holds water in its lower part and prevents unpleasant gases from getting out

über-, uber- /ˈuː.bəʳ/ ⓤ /-bɚ-/ *adj HUMOROUS* used before nouns to mean 'extreme' or 'extremely good/successful': *über-model, Giselle* ○ *über-billionaire*

ubiquitous /juːˈbɪk.wɪ.təs/ ⓤ /-wə.təs/ *adj FORMAL OR HUMOROUS* seeming to be in all places: *Leather is very much in fashion this season, as of course is **the** ubiquitous denim.* ○ *The Swedes are not alone in finding their language under pressure from **the** ubiquitous spread of English.* ○ *The radio, that most ubiquitous of consumer-electronic appliances, is about to enter a new age.* **ubiquitously** /juːˈbɪk.wɪ.tə.sli/ ⓤ /-wə.tə-/ *adv* everywhere

ubiquity /juːˈbɪk.wɪ.ti/ ⓤ /-wə.ti/ *noun* [U] *FORMAL* the ubiquity of fast-food outlets (= the fact that they are found everywhere)

U-boat /ˈjuː.bəʊt/ ⓤ /-boʊt/ *noun* [C] a German SUBMARINE, used especially in World Wars I and II

udder /ˈʌd.əʳ/ ⓤ /-ɚ/ *noun* [C] the milk-producing organ of a cow, sheep or other animal, that hangs like a bag between the legs

UFO /juː.efˈəʊ/ ⓤ /-ˈoʊ/ *noun* [C] *ABBREVIATION FOR* unidentified flying object: an object seen in the sky which is thought to be a spacecraft from another planet: *Several UFO sightings have been reported in the Pennine foothills.*

ugh /ʊx/ /ɜː/ *exclamation* used to express a strong feeling of disgust at something very unpleasant: *Ugh, I've got something horrible on the bottom of my shoe!* ○ *Ugh, I'm not eating that!*

ugly VERY UNATTRACTIVE /ˈʌg.li/ *adj* extremely unattractive: *I find a lot of modern architecture very ugly.* ○ *Yesterday in town I saw the ugliest baby I've ever seen in my life.* ○ *I feel really fat and ugly today.* ○ *He was a really unpleasant man and **as ugly as sin** (= very ugly).* **ugliness** /ˈʌg.lɪ.nəs/ *noun* [U] *the ugliness of the buildings*

ugly THREATENING /ˈʌg.li/ *adj* unpleasant and threatening or violent: *There were ugly scenes outside the stadium.* ○ *The demonstration turned ugly when a group of protesters started to throw bottles at the police.* **ugliness** /ˈʌg.lɪ.nəs/ *noun* [U]

ugly 'duckling *noun* [C] someone or something that is ugly and not successful when young or new but that will later become beautiful or successful

uh /ɜː/ /ʌ/ *exclamation* a written representation of the sound that people sometimes make when they are thinking what to say next: *It's not too far – it's about, uh, five miles from here.*

UHF /juː.eɪtʃˈef/ *noun* [U] *ABBREVIATION FOR* ultrahigh frequency: radio waves between 300 MHz and 3000 MHz ◗ Compare **VHF**.

uh-huh /ʌˈhʌ/ /ˈʌ.hʌ/ *exclamation INFORMAL* a written representation of the sound that people sometimes make in order to give certainty to, agree with or show understanding of something that has just been said: *"Did you hear what I just said?" "Uh-huh."* ○ *"You know that strange guy we saw yesterday?" "Uh-huh."* ○ *"I'll be back a little late because I'm going via town." "Uh-huh."*

uh-oh /ʌˈʌˈoʊ/ ⓤ /-ˈoʊ/ *exclamation INFORMAL* a written representation of the sound that people make when they discover that they have made a mistake or done some-

thing wrong: *Uh-oh, I think I just locked my keys in the car.*

UHT /juː.eɪtʃˈtiː/ *adj* [before n] *UK ABBREVIATION FOR* ultra heat treated: describes milk that has been heated to a very high temperature so that it will last for a long time if it is kept in a container that has not been opened, or a product made from this: *UHT milk/cream* **UHT** /juː.eɪtʃˈtiː/ *noun* [U] *a pint of UHT*

uh-uh /ˈʌ̃.ʌ̃/ *exclamation MAINLY US INFORMAL* a written representation of the sound that people sometimes make to give a negative answer: *"You didn't have time to go to the store?" "Uh-uh, no chance."*

the UK /ðə.juːˈkeɪ/ *noun* [S] *ABBREVIATION FOR* the United Kingdom: the country of Great Britain and Northern Ireland: *When were you last in the UK then?* **UK** /juːˈkeɪ/ *adj* [before n] *the UK ambassador to Sweden*

ukelele, ukulele /juː.kəˈleɪ.li/ *noun* [C] a small guitar or BANJO with four strings: *George Formby made the ukelele famous in his films in the 1940s.*

ulcer /ˈʌl.səʳ/ ⓤ /-sɚ/ *noun* [C] a break in the skin or on the surface of an organ inside the body, which does not heal naturally: *a mouth/stomach ulcer*

ulcerated /ˈʌl.sʳ.eɪ.tɪd/ ⓤ /-sɚ.eɪ.tɪd/ *adj* describes skin which is covered in ulcers: *She had lain in bed for so long that her shoulder blades had become ulcerated.* **ulceration** /ʌl.sʳˈeɪ.ʃʳn/ ⓤ /-səˈreɪ-/ *noun* [U] **ulcerous** /ˈʌl.sʳ.əs/ ⓤ /-sɚ-/ *adj*

ulterior /ʌlˈtɪə.ri.əʳ/ ⓤ /-ˈtɪr.i-/ *adj* **ulterior motive/reason/purpose, etc.** a secret purpose or reason for doing something: *He claims he just wants to help Lisa but I suspect he has an ulterior motive.*

ultimate /ˈʌl.tɪ.mət/ ⓤ /-tə-/ *adj* [before n] most extreme or important because either the original or final, or the best or worst: *Of course the ultimate responsibility for the present conflict without doubt lies with the aggressor.* ○ *The ultimate decision about who to employ lies with Andrew.* ○ *Infidelity is the ultimate betrayal.* ○ *the ultimate luxury cruiser*

ultimate /ˈʌl.tɪ.mət/ ⓤ /-tə-/ *noun* **the ultimate in sth** the best or most extreme example of something: *It describes the hotel as 'the ultimate in luxury'.* ○ *I mean, tackling six men single-handedly – that really is the ultimate in stupidity!*

ultimately /ˈʌl.tɪ.mət.li/ ⓤ /-tə-/ *adv* **1** finally, after a series of things have happened: *Everything will ultimately depend on what is said at the meeting with the directors next week.* ○ *Ultimately, of course, he'd like to have his own business but that won't be for some time.* **2** used to emphasize the most important fact in a situation: *Ultimately, he'll have to decide.*

ultimatum /ʌl.tɪˈmeɪ.təm/ ⓤ /-təˈmeɪ.təm/ *noun* [C] *plural* **ultimatums** or **ultimata** a threat in which a person or group of people are warned that if they do not do a particular thing, something unpleasant will happen to them. It is usually the last and most extreme in a series of actions taken to bring about a particular result: *He **gave** her an ultimatum – she could either stop seeing Peter and come back to him or it was divorce.* ○ *On Wednesday night the UN **issued** its toughest ultimatum to date, demanding that all troops withdraw from the city.*

ultra- /ˈʌl.trə-/ *prefix* extreme or extremely: *ultra-expensive* ○ *ultra-modern architecture* ○ *ultra-sensitive* ○ *an ultra-short haircut*

ultramarine /ʌl.trə.məˈriːn/ *noun* [U], *adj* (of) a bright blue colour

ultrasonic /ʌl.trəˈsɒn.ɪk/ ⓤ /-ˈsɑː.nɪk/ *adj* describes sound which is too high for people to hear

ultrasound /ˈʌl.trə.saʊnd/ *noun* **1** [U] special sound waves used in such processes as examining organs inside the body and directing the path of SUBMARINES: *They'll use ultrasound to monitor her ovaries to see if they're responding to the treatment.* ○ *ultrasound scanning/imaging* **2** [C] an ultrasound SCAN

ultraviolet /ʌl.trəˈvaɪə.lət/ *adj* (*ABBREVIATION* **UV**) describes light that has a WAVELENGTH which is beyond the VIOLET (= light purple) end of the range of colours that can be seen by human beings. Light of this type causes the skin to become darker in the sun.

U

um /əm/ *exclamation* a written representation of a sound that people make when they are pausing or deciding what to say next: *"What do you think of this jacket?" "Um, I don't know if I like the colour."* ○ *"So what did you talk about?" "Um, I don't remember, I suppose work mainly."*

umbilical cord /ʌmˈbɪl.ɪ.kəl̩kɔːd/ [US] /-ˌkɔːrd/ *noun* [C usually sing] the long tube-like structure which connects a baby which has not yet been born to its mother's PLACENTA (= the organ which provides it with food and oxygen): *He asked the nurse if he could cut his son's umbilical cord.*

umbrage /ˈʌm.brɪdʒ/ *noun* SLIGHTLY FORMAL **take umbrage** to feel upset or annoyed, usually because you feel that someone has been rude or shown a lack of respect to you: *You don't think she'll take umbrage if she isn't invited to the wedding, do you?*

umbrella [DEVICE] /ʌmˈbrel.ə/ *noun* [C] a device for protection against the rain which consists of a stick with a folding, material-covered frame at one end and usually a handle at the other, or a similar, often larger, device used for protection against the sun: *I felt a few spots of rain so I put my umbrella up.* ○ *I left another umbrella on the bus yesterday.* ○ *a folding umbrella*

umbrella [GROUP] /ʌmˈbrel.ə/ *noun* [C] something which includes or represents a group or range of similar things: *Mr. Hughes's agency is one of 980 community agencies **under the** umbrella **of** the National Community Action Foundation (NCAF) in Washington, D.C.* ○ *Donations should be sent to the Disaster Emergency Committee, an umbrella **organization** for UK based aid agencies.* ○ *Existentialism was really an umbrella **term** to lump together the works of several philosophers and writers.*

umlaut /ˈʊm.laʊt/ *noun* [C] a mark put over a vowel in some languages, such as German, to show that the pronunciation of the vowel is changed: *The German word 'Gebäude', which means 'building', has an umlaut over the 'a'.*

umpire /ˈʌm.paɪəʳ/ [US] /-paɪr/ *noun* [C] a person who is present at a sports competition in order to make certain that the rules of that particular game are obeyed and to make judgments about whether particular actions are acceptable: *a cricket/tennis umpire* **umpire** /ˈʌm.paɪəʳ/ [US] /-paɪr/ *verb* [T] *Starmers has been chosen to umpire the next cricket test match.*

umpteen /ʌmpˈtiːn/ /ˈ--/ *determiner, pronoun* INFORMAL very many; a lot (of): *We've been there umpteen times and she still can't remember the way.* **umpteenth** /ʌmpˈtiːnθ/ /ˈ--/ *determiner*: *I drank my umpteenth cup of coffee.* ○ *For the umpteenth time, Anthony, knives and forks go in the middle drawer!*

un- /ʌn-/ *prefix* used to add the meaning 'not', 'lacking' or 'the opposite of' before adjectives, adverbs, verbs and nouns: *unrealistic* ○ *unhappily* ○ *unscrew* ○ *unfairness*

'un /ən/ *noun* [C] NOT STANDARD one: *Mira'll fit in the back of the car – she's only a little 'un!*

the ˌU'N *group noun* [S] ABBREVIATION FOR the United Nations: an international organization that was established in 1945 to maintain world peace: *The UN has decided to impose sanctions.* **UN** /ˌjuːˈen/ *adj* [before n] *the UN Security Council* ○ *UN troops*

unabashed /ˌʌn.əˈbæʃt/ *adj* without any worry about possible criticism or embarrassment: *She is to this day unabashed in her patriotism.* ○ *He is an unabashed capitalist.* ➲Compare **abashed**.

unabated /ˌʌn.əˈbeɪ.tɪd/ [US] /-t̬ɪd/ *adj* [usually after v] FORMAL without weakening in strength or force: *The fighting **continued** unabated throughout the night.* ➲Compare **abate**.

unable /ʌnˈeɪ.bl̩/ *adj* **be unable to do *sth*** to not be able to do something: *We were unable to contact him at the time.*

unabridged /ˌʌn.əˈbrɪdʒd/ *adj* An unabridged book, speech or article is in its original form and has not been made shorter.

unacceptable /ˌʌn.əkˈsep.tə.bl̩/ *adj* too bad to be accepted, approved of or allowed to continue: *The unions have described the latest pay offer as unacceptable.* ○ *The taking of hostages, said the minister, was totally unacceptable under any circumstances.* ○ *The report found what it described as 'unacceptable levels of air pollution' in several major cities.*

• **the unacceptable face of *sth*** UK the bad side to a particular system or set of beliefs: *The paper showed a picture of homeless people sleeping on the streets with the caption underneath 'the unacceptable face of capitalism'.*

unacceptably /ˌʌn.əkˈsep.tə.bli/ *adv* in a way that cannot be accepted, approved of or allowed to continue: *unacceptably high risks*

unaccompanied /ˌʌn.əˈkʌm.pən.id/ *adj* **1** not having anyone with you when you go somewhere: *To everyone's great surprise, the princess arrived at the ball unaccompanied.* **2** describes music produced by a singer or by someone playing a musical instrument without anyone else singing or playing at the same time: *She sang the first three verses with a piano and the last verse unaccompanied.*

unaccountable [NOT RESPONSIBLE] /ˌʌn.əˈkaʊn.tə.bl̩/ [US] /-t̬ə-/ *adj* **be unaccountable to *sb/sth*** to not be expected to explain or provide a reason to a particular person or organization for your actions: *When Knight became leader, the council was run by a clique of officers largely unaccountable to the elected members.*

unaccountable [SURPRISING] /ˌʌn.əˈkaʊn.tə.bl̩/ [US] /-t̬ə-/ *adj* [often before n] not able to be explained or understood: *For some unaccountable **reason**, he keeps his wallet in his underwear drawer.* **unaccountably** /ˌʌn.əˈkaʊn.tə.bli/ [US] /-t̬ə-/ *adv*: *I felt unaccountably happy this morning as I left the house.*

unaccustomed /ˌʌn.əˈkʌs.təmd/ *adj* **1** [after v] not ACCUSTOMED: *The weather presented a particular challenge, especially for American servicemen unaccustomed **to** subarctic conditions.* **2** [usually before n] not usual: *The Olympic and world champion finished in the unaccustomed position of fourth.*

unadulterated /ˌʌn.əˈdʌl.tər.eɪ.tɪd/ [US] /-tə.reɪ.t̬ɪd/ *adj* **1** not spoilt or made weaker by the addition of other substances; pure: *People injecting drugs can never be sure that they're using unadulterated substances.* **2** [before n] complete: *I've never heard such unadulterated nonsense in my life!*

unaffected [NOT CHANGED] /ˌʌn.əˈfek.tɪd/ *adj* not influenced, harmed or interrupted in any way: *The west of the city was largely unaffected **by** the bombing.* ○ *It is hoped that train services on the main lines will be unaffected **by** today's industrial action.*

unaffected [SINCERE] /ˌʌn.əˈfek.tɪd/ *adj* APPROVING natural and sincere in your behaviour: *For someone who has spent forty years in show business she remains remarkably unaffected by it all.* **unaffectedly** /ˌʌn.əˈfek.tɪd.li/ *adv*

unaided /ˌʌnˈeɪ.dɪd/ *adj, adv* without any help from anyone else; independently: *Since his accident, he hasn't been able to walk unaided.* ○ *The two explorers attempted an unaided walk across the South Pole.*

unalienable /ʌnˈeɪ.li.ə.nə.bl̩/ *adj* **inalienable**

unalloyed /ˌʌn.əˈlɔɪd/ *adj* LITERARY (especially of a positive feeling) not spoilt by any amount of negative feeling; pure: *Spending time with one's family is never an unalloyed pleasure* (= There are bad things about it too). ○ *We had the perfect holiday – two weeks of unalloyed bliss.*

unambiguous /ˌʌn.æmˈbɪg.ju.əs/ *adj* expressed in a way which makes it completely clear what is meant: *The minister said she would give a clear and unambiguous **statement** on the future of the coal industry at the earliest possible opportunity.* **unambiguously** /ˌʌn.æmˈbɪg.ju.ə.sli/ *adv*

un-American /ˌʌn.əˈmer.ɪ.kən/ *adj* US DISAPPROVING guilty of activities, behaviour or beliefs that show opposition or a lack of loyalty to the US and its political system: *From 1940 to 1943, he was general counsel of the House committee investigating un-American **activities**.*

unanimous /juːˈnæn.ɪ.məs/ *adj* If a group of people are unanimous, they all agree about one particular matter or vote the same way, and if a decision or judgment is unanimous, it is formed or supported by everyone in a group: *The jury returned a unanimous* ***verdict*** *of guilty after a short deliberation.* ○ *After a lengthy discussion we reached a unanimous* ***decision*** *on the proposal.* ○ *The new format has unanimous support and could be introduced next season.* **unanimously** /juːˈnæn.ɪ.mə.sli/ *adv*: *All four proposals to the committee were unanimously approved.*

unanimity /ˌjuː.nəˈnɪm.ɪ.ti/ [US] /-ə.t̬i/ *noun* [U] *FORMAL* the state of being unanimous

unannounced [UNEXPECTED] /ˌʌn.əˈnaʊntst/ *adj, adv* If a person's arrival somewhere is unannounced, it is sudden and unexpected: *She appeared unannounced and took control of the meeting.*

unannounced [NOT PUBLICLY KNOWN] /ˌʌn.əˈnaʊntst/ *adj* not made publicly known: *The Texan singer will be supported by two other bands, as yet unannounced.*

unanswerable [CLEARLY TRUE] /ʌnˈɑːnt.sᵊr.ə.bl̩/ [US] /-ˈænt.sɚ-/ *adj FORMAL* If an argument or claim is unanswerable, people cannot disagree with it because it is so clearly true: *In economic terms the need to reduce inflation is unanswerable.*

unanswerable [WITHOUT AN ANSWER] /ʌnˈɑːnt.sᵊr.ə.bl̩/ [US] /-ˈænt.sɚ-/ *adj* (of a question) without an answer: *As to how long this war will last, it's an unanswerable question.*

unanswered /ʌnˈɑːnt.səd/ [US] /-ˈænt.sɚd/ *adj* not answered or explained: *Suspicions were first aroused after questions from local residents remained unanswered.*

unappealing /ˌʌn.əˈpiː.lɪŋ/ *adj* not attractive or interesting

unappreciative /ˌʌn.əˈpriː.ʃi.ə.tɪv/ [US] /-t̬ɪv/ *adj* not showing that you understand how good something is, or not grateful for something

unapproachable /ˌʌn.əˈprəʊ.tʃə.bl̩/ [US] /-ˈproʊ-/ *adj* Someone who is unapproachable has an unfriendly and slightly frightening manner which tends to discourage other people from speaking to them: *As a boss I found him rather unapproachable.*

unarguable /ʌnˈɑːg.ju.ə.bl̩/ [US] /-ˈɑːrg-/ *adj* not able to be argued

unarmed /ʌnˈɑːmd/ [US] /-ˈɑːrmd/ *adj* not armed

unashamed /ˌʌn.əˈʃeɪmd/ *adj* not ashamed; without hiding behaviour or opinions that other people might consider unacceptable: *Afterwards he spent five minutes with the President of whom he is an unashamed admirer.* ○ *We then checked into the hotel for a weekend of unashamed luxury.* **unashamedly** /ˌʌn.əˈʃeɪ.mɪd.li/ *adv*: *The school's headmistress is unashamedly traditional and refuses to allow the girls to wear trousers.*

unassuming /ˌʌn.əˈsjuː.mɪŋ/ [US] /-ˈsuː-/ *adj APPROVING* Someone who is unassuming is quiet and shows no desire for attention or admiration: *He was shy and unassuming and not at all how you expect an actor to be.*

unattached [NOT MARRIED] /ˌʌn.əˈtætʃt/ *adj* not married or not having a relationship with anyone; single: *He's thirty-two, he's gorgeous, he's got his own house and, what's more, he's unattached.*

unattached [NOT CONNECTED] /ˌʌn.əˈtætʃt/ *adj* not connected: *Please enclose your signed cheque and payment slip unattached and unfolded.*

unattainable /ˌʌn.əˈteɪ.nə.bl̩/ *adj* not achievable: *an unattainable ideal* ○ *Some economists think that full employment in Europe is an unattainable* ***goal****.*

unattended /ˌʌn.əˈten.dɪd/ *adj* not being watched or taken care of: *Please do not leave your luggage unattended.* ○ *According to the report, most accidents occur when young children are left unattended in the home.*

unattractive /ˌʌn.əˈtræk.tɪv/ *adj* **1** unpleasant to look at: *This is modern architecture at its most unattractive.* ○ *He was short and overweight and generally fairly unattractive.* **2** having no good or positive features: *The options were decidedly unattractive.* **unattractively** /ˌʌn.əˈtræk.tɪv.li/ *adv*

unauthorized, *UK ALSO* **-ised** /ʌnˈɔː.θə.raɪzd/ [US] /-ˈɑː-/ *adj* [before n] without someone's official permission to do something or be in a particular place: *No admittance to unauthorized personnel.* ○ *This unauthorized biography of the Princess has sold over 10 000 copies in its first week in print.*

unavailable /ˌʌn.əˈveɪ.lə.bl̩/ *adj* **1** [after v] If someone is unavailable, they are not able to talk to people or meet people, usually because they are doing other things: *The Minister accused of misleading parliament was unavailable* ***for comment*** *last night.* **2** If something is unavailable, you cannot get it or use it: *This information was previously unavailable to the public.*

unavailing /ˌʌn.əˈveɪ.lɪŋ/ *adj FORMAL OR LITERARY* When an attempt to do something is unavailing, it is unsuccessful or has no positive effect: *Diplomatic efforts at peace-making have so far proved unavailing.*

unavoidable /ˌʌn.əˈvɔɪ.də.bl̩/ *adj* impossible to avoid **unavoidably** /ˌʌn.əˈvɔɪ.də.bli/ *adv*

unaware /ˌʌn.əˈweəʳ/ [US] /-ˈwer/ *adj* [after v] not aware: [+ that] *He was unaware* ***that*** *the police were watching him.* ○ *I was quite unaware* ***of*** *the problem.*

unawares /ˌʌn.əˈweəz/ [US] /-ˈwerz/ *adv* suddenly and unexpectedly without any warning: *The overnight invasion* ***took*** *the military experts unawares.* ○ *The prime minster seemed to have been* ***caught*** *unawares by* (= was not expecting) *this sudden attack of criticism* .

unbalanced [NOT FIRM] /ʌnˈbæl.əntst/ *adj* not firm but likely to fall or change position suddenly

unbalance /ʌnˈbæl.ənts/ *verb* [T] to cause something or someone to be unbalanced: *The result was to further unbalance the monetary-fiscal policy mix and to push up the pound.*

unbalanced [MENTALLY ILL] /ʌnˈbæl.əntst/ *adj* mentally ill: *His relatives have said he became unbalanced after the death of his father.*

unbalance /ʌnˈbæl.ənts/ *verb* [T] to make someone mentally ill, especially temporarily

unbalanced [NOT FAIR] /ʌnˈbæl.əntst/ *adj* not fair or equal; false: *unbalanced reporting* ○ *He gave an unbalanced* ***view*** *of the situation.*

unbalance /ʌnˈbæl.ənts/ *verb* [T] to make something unfair or not equal

unbalanced [FOOD] /ʌnˈbæl.əntst/ *adj* not consisting of a combination of the correct types and amounts of food: *an unbalanced diet* ○ *There should always be variety in the cooking methods – too much deep frying or wok cooking makes an unbalanced meal.*

unbearable /ʌnˈbeə.rə.bl̩/ [US] /-ˈber.ə-/ *adj* too painful or unpleasant for you to continue to experience: *All I remember of childbirth was the unbearable pain and the relief when it was all over.* ○ *The atmosphere at work at the moment is quite unbearable.* ○ *The heat was unbearable.* **unbearably** /ʌnˈbeə.rə.bli/ [US] /-ˈber.ə-/ *adv*: *The sun was almost unbearably hot today.*

unbeatable /ʌnˈbiː.tə.bl̩/ [US] /-t̬ə-/ *adj APPROVING* unable to be defeated or improved because of excellent quality: *The 23-year-old US tennis star looks unbeatable this season.* ○ *For good pizzas at a reasonable price they're unbeatable.*

unbeaten /ʌnˈbiː.tᵊn/ *adj* in sports, having won every game: *Manchester United remain unbeaten this season so far.*

unbecoming /ˌʌn.bɪˈkʌm.ɪŋ/ *adj* **1** *FORMAL* describes clothes that do not look attractive on a particular person **2** describes behaviour that is not appropriate or not acceptable: *Any officer who is convicted of conduct unbecoming* ***(to)*** *an officer shall be court-martialled.*

unbeknown /ˌʌn.bɪˈnəʊn/ [US] /-ˈnoʊn/ *adv* (*ALSO* **unbeknownst**) *FORMAL* **unbeknown/unbeknownst to sb** without a particular person knowing: *Unbeknown to me, he'd gone and rented out the apartment in my absence.*

unbelievable [SURPRISING] /ˌʌn.bɪˈliː.və.bl̩/ *adj* extremely surprising: *She eats an unbelievable amount of food.* ○ *You've had such bad luck it's unbelievable.* ○ *You should see her wardrobe – it's unbelievable – she's got about fifty pairs of shoes.* **unbelievably** /ˌʌn.bɪˈliː.və.bli/ *adv*: *He works unbelievably hard.* ○ *It was still an unbelievably stupid thing to do.*

unbelievable [UNLIKELY] /ˌʌn.bɪˈliː.və.bl̩/ *adj* unable to be believed because unlikely: *I found most of the characters in the play totally unbelievable.*

unbeliever /ˌʌn.bɪˈliː.vəʳ/ [US] /-vɚ/ *noun* [C] a person who does not have any religious beliefs: *Most church schools are open to unbelievers.*

unbend /ʌnˈbend/ *verb* [I] **unbent, unbent** to relax and become less formal and serious in your manner: *I'd hoped that after a glass or two of wine she might unbend a little.*

unbending /ʌnˈben.dɪŋ/ *adj FORMAL* describes someone who tends to make fixed judgments and decisions which they are unwilling to change: *He has earned a reputation as a stern and unbending politician.*

unbiased /ʌnˈbaɪəst/ *adj* able to judge fairly because you are not influenced by your own opinions: *unbiased advice* ○ *an unbiased opinion*

unbidden /ʌnˈbɪd.ᵊn/ *adj* [usually after v] *LITERARY* not invited or wanted: *At night images would come unbidden into her mind.*

unbleached /ʌnˈbliːtʃt/ *adj* describes flour or material that is not made white artificially by the use of chemicals: *an unbleached cotton duvet* ○ *I buy unbleached flour from the local health food store.*

unblemished /ʌnˈblem.ɪʃt/ *adj* describes a reputation, character, etc. that has no faults and is not spoiled in any way: *For six years his championship record was unblemished.*

unborn /ʌnˈbɔːn/ [US] /-ˈbɔːrn/ *adj* not yet born; in the mother's womb: *the protection of the unborn child*

unbounded /ʌnˈbaʊn.dɪd/ *adj* describes a positive feeling which is very great and seems to have no limits: *her unbounded enthusiasm for her subject*

unbreakable /ʌnˈbreɪ.kə.bl̩/ *adj* impossible to break: *unbreakable glass/plastic*

unbridled /ʌnˈbraɪ.dl̩d/ *adj* [usually before n] not controlled or limited: *unbridled ambition/enthusiasm/lust*

unbroken /ʌnˈbrəʊ.kᵊn/ [US] /-ˈbroʊ-/ *adj* continuous and with no pauses: *The Giants winning streak remained unbroken for an impressive nineteen games.*

unbuckle /ʌnˈbʌk.l̩/ *verb* [T] to unfasten a shoe, belt, etc. by releasing its BUCKLE (= metal fastener)

unburden /ʌnˈbɜː.dᵊn/ [US] /-ˈbɝː-/ *verb* **unburden *yourself*** to free yourself of something that is worrying you, by talking about it to someone: *He'll unburden himself to anyone who'll listen.*

uncalled-for /ʌnˈkɔːld.fɔːʳ/ [US] /-fɔːr/ *adj DISAPPROVING* describes a criticism, insult, remark or action that is unfair, rude or hurtful and therefore considered to be unnecessary: *an uncalled-for remark* ○ *There's no need to make personal remarks – that was quite uncalled-for.*

uncanny /ʌnˈkæn.i/ *adj* strange or mysterious; difficult or impossible to explain: *an uncanny resemblance* **uncannily** /ʌnˈkæn.ɪ.li/ *adv*: *Her predictions turned out to be uncannily accurate.*

uncared for /ʌŋˈkeəd.fɔː/ [US] /-ˈkerd.fɔːr/ *adj* not taken care of well enough: *He looked unwashed and uncared for.*

uncaring /ʌnˈkeə.rɪŋ/ [US] /-ˈker.ɪŋ/ *adj DISAPPROVING* not worrying about other people's troubles or doing anything to help them: *The bishop criticized the government for its "callous, uncaring attitude" to the homeless and the unemployed.*

unceasing /ʌnˈsiː.sɪŋ/ *adj FORMAL* continuing and unlikely to stop or become less: *The authors are grateful for the unceasing support of the editors in London and New York.* **unceasingly** /ʌnˈsiː.sɪŋ.li/ *adv*

unceremonious /ʌnˌser.ɪˈməʊ.ni.əs/ [US] /-ˈmoʊ-/ *adj FORMAL* done in a rude, sudden or informal way: *an unceremonious refusal* **unceremoniously** /ʌnˌser.ɪˈməʊ.ni.ə.sli/ [US] /-ˈmoʊ-/ *adv*: *He was unceremoniously removed from the list of members, for gross misconduct.*

uncertain /ʌnˈsɜː.tᵊn/ [US] /-ˈsɝː-/ *adj* **1** not knowing what to do or believe, or not able to decide about something: [+ question word] *She's uncertain* ***whether*** *to go to New Zealand or not.* ○ *Bridie was uncertain* ***about*** *meeting him.* **2** not known or fixed, or not completely certain: *New arrivals face an uncertain* ***future***. ○ *The political outlook is* ***still*** *uncertain.* **uncertainly** /ʌnˈsɜː.tᵊn.li/ [US] /-ˈsɝː-/ *adv* **uncertainty** /ʌnˈsɜː.tᵊn.ti/ [US] /-ˈsɝː.tᵊn.t̬i/ *noun* [C or U] *Nothing is ever decided, and all the uncertainty is very bad for staff morale.* ○ *Life is full of uncertainties.*

unchallenged /ʌnˈtʃæl.ɪndʒd/ *adj* accepted without being questioned or criticized: *We can't allow her comments to* ***go*** *unchallenged.*

unchanged /ʌnˈtʃeɪndʒd/ *adj* [usually after v] staying the same: *The area has remained virtually unchanged in fifty years.*

uncharacteristic /ˌʌnˌkær.ɪk.təˈrɪs.tɪk/ [US] /-ˌker-/ *adj* not typical **uncharacteristically** /ˌʌnˌkær.ɪk.təˈrɪs.tɪk.li/ [US] /-ˌker-/ *adv*

uncharitable /ʌnˈtʃær.ɪ.tə.bl̩/ [US] /-ˈtʃer.ə.t̬ə-/ *adj* unkind and unfair: *The uncharitable explanation is that she's too afraid to ask.* **uncharitably** /ʌnˈtʃær.ɪ.tə.bli/ [US] /-ˈter.ə.t̬ə-/ *adv*

uncharted /ʌnˈtʃɑː.tɪd/ [US] /-ˈtʃɑːr.t̬ɪd/ *adj LITERARY* An uncharted place or situation is completely new and therefore has never been described before: *Nuclear fusion has taken physicists into uncharted* ***seas/territory/waters*** (= a new and unknown area).

unchecked /ʌnˈtʃekt/ *adj* describes something harmful that is continuing or increasing without or despite any limits or attempts to prevent it: *If present trends* ***go/continue*** *unchecked there will be a major epidemic of heart disease in the next five years.* ○ *The war raged on, unchecked* ***by*** *the UN's efforts to stop it.*

uncivil /ʌnˈsɪv.ᵊl/ *adj FORMAL* not polite: *He was most uncivil* ***to*** *your father – called him an old fool.* ➲See also **incivility**. **uncivilly** /ʌnˈsɪv.ɪ.li/ *adv*

uncivilized, *UK USUALLY* **-ised** /ʌnˈsɪv.ɪ.laɪzd/ *adj* not CIVILIZED, especially below the usual standards of Western society: *Conditions in these inner-city housing estates can be pretty uncivilized.*
• **uncivilized hour** *UK INFORMAL* a very early or very late time in the day: *Sorry to phone you at such an uncivilized hour.*

uncle /ˈʌŋ.kl̩/ *noun* [C] the brother of someone's mother or father, or the husband of someone's aunt: *I've got several uncles and aunts.* ○ *We invited my Uncle Steve round.* ○ [as form of address] *Did you bring me a present, Uncle Jack?*

unclean /ʌnˈkliːn/ *adj* **1** not clean and therefore likely to cause disease: *The health risk from drinking unclean water is considerable.* **2** *FORMAL* not clean or pure, or morally bad, as described by the rules of a religion: *Jews and Muslims consider pigs unclean.*

unclear /ʌnˈklɪəʳ/ [US] /-ˈklɪr/ *adj* **1** not obvious or easy to see or know: *The ownership of the painting remains unclear.* ○ [+ question word] *It's unclear* ***what*** *actually happened that night.* ○ *It's unclear* ***whether*** *he arrived before or after the shot was fired.* **2** If you are unclear about something, you are not certain about it: *I'm unclear about a couple of points in your proposal – could you go over them again?* ○ *I'm unclear* ***(as to) whether*** *we're meant to stay here or not.* **unclearly** /ʌnˈklɪə.li/ [US] /-ˈklɪr-/ *adv*

ˌUncle ˈSam /ˌʌŋ.kl̩ˈsæm/ *noun* [S not after *the*] *INFORMAL* the United States of America, or its government, sometimes represented, especially in political cartoons, by an image of a tall thin man with a white beard and a tall hat

ˌUncle ˈTom /ˌʌŋ.kl̩ˈtɒm/ [US] /-ˈtɑːm/ *noun* [C usually sing] *OFFENSIVE DISAPPROVING* a black person who is considered to be too eager to agree with white people or too willing to be treated in a way that is not equal to white people

uncomfortable /ʌnˈkʌmpf.tə.bl̩/ [US] /-ˈkʌmp.fɚ.t̬ə-/ *adj* **1** not feeling comfortable and pleasant, or not making you feel comfortable and pleasant: *I've eaten so much, I'm really quite uncomfortable.* ○ *These shoes are really uncomfortable.* **2** slightly embarrassed, or making you feel slightly embarrassed: *an uncomfortable silence* **uncomfortably** /ʌnˈkʌmpf.tə.bli/ [US] /-ˈkʌmp.fɚ.t̬ə-/ *adv*: *I was warm but not uncomfortably so.*

uncommitted /ˌʌn.kəˈmɪt.ɪd/ [US] /-ˈmɪt̬-/ *adj* having made no promise to support any particular group, plan, belief or action: *Twenty-five senators have admitted they are still uncommitted* ***on*** *the taxation question.*

uncommon [NOT FREQUENT] /ʌnˈkɒm.ən/ [US] /-ˈkɑː.mən/ *adj* not seen, happening or experienced often: *Accidents due*

U

to failure of safety equipment are uncommon nowadays. ○ It's not uncommon for people to become ill when they travel.

uncommon [EXTREME] /ʌnˈkɒm.ən/ ⓤ -ˈkɑː.mən/ adj OLD-FASHIONED FORMAL describes a quality, especially a human quality, that is unusually large in amount or degree: a woman of uncommon beauty

uncommonly /ʌnˈkɒm.ən.li/ ⓤ -ˈkɑː.mən-/ adv OLD-FASHIONED FORMAL extremely: She was uncommonly brave too.

uncommunicative /ˌʌn.kəˈmjuː.nɪ.kə.tɪv/ adj not willing to talk: He had a headache and was rather uncommunicative.

uncomplaining /ˌʌn.kəmˈpleɪ.nɪŋ/ adj APPROVING willing to do boring or difficult work without complaining or becoming angry: The work is boring, but he's cheerful and uncomplaining. **uncomplainingly** /ˌʌn.kəmˈpleɪ.nɪŋ.li/ adv

uncomplimentary /ʌnˌkɒm.plɪˈmen.tʰr.i/ ⓤ -ˌkɑːm.-pləˈmen.tɚ-/ adj rudely critical: She had some very uncomplimentary things to say about Stephen.

uncompromising /ʌnˈkɒm.prə.maɪ.zɪŋ/ ⓤ -ˈkɑːm-/ adj If people or their beliefs are uncompromising, they are fixed and do not change, especially when faced with opposition: The city council has taken an uncompromising stand against the proposals for the new building. **uncompromisingly** /ʌnˈkɒm.prə.maɪ.zɪŋ.li/ ⓤ -ˈkɑːm-/ adv

unconcerned /ˌʌn.kənˈsɜːnd/ ⓤ -ˈsɜːnd/ adj not worried or not interested, especially when you should be worried or interested: The baby seemed quite unconcerned by the noise. ○ Are you as unconcerned about the situation as you appear? **unconcernedly** /ˌʌn.kənˈsɜː.nɪd.li/ ⓤ -ˈsɜːr-/ adv

unconditional /ˌʌn.kənˈdɪʃ.ʰn.ʰl/ adj complete and not limited in any way: the unconditional love that one has for one's child ○ unconditional surrender ○ We demand the immediate and unconditional release of all political prisoners. **unconditionally** /ˌʌn.kənˈdɪʃ.ʰn.ʰl.i/ adv

unconfirmed /ˌʌn.kənˈfɜːmd/ ⓤ -ˈfɜːmd/ adj If facts are unconfirmed, it is not certain if they are true: According to unconfirmed **reports**, two people were killed in the riots last night.

unconnected /ˌʌn.kəˈnek.tɪd/ adj not connected; not related: It's no longer possible to argue that crime is unconnected **with** unemployment. ○ A series of apparently unconnected events led to his resignation.

unconscionable /ʌnˈkɒn.tʃʰn.ə.bl̩/ ⓤ -ˈkɑːn-/ adj FORMAL DISAPPROVING An unconscionable size, amount, or length of time is too great and is unacceptable: They had both drunk an unconscionable quantity of red wine the previous night. **unconscionably** /ʌnˈkɒn.tʃʰn.ə.bli/ ⓤ -ˈkɑːn-/ adv

unconscious /ʌnˈkɒn.tʃəs/ ⓤ -ˈkɑːn-/ adj 1 in the state of having lost consciousness, especially as the result of a head injury: She was hit on the head by a stone and **knocked** unconscious. 2 An unconscious thought or feeling is one that you do not know you have: my unconscious desire to impress him

unconscious /ʌnˈkɒn.tʃəs/ ⓤ -ˈkɑːn-/ noun **the unconscious** the part of your mind that contains feelings and thoughts that you do not know about, and that influences the way you behave **unconsciously** /ʌn-ˈkɒn.tʃə.sli/ ⓤ -ˈkɑːn-/ adv **unconsciousness** /ʌn-ˈkɒn.tʃə.snəs/ ⓤ -ˈkɑːn-/ noun [U]

unconsidered /ˌʌn.kənˈsɪd.əd/ ⓤ -ɚd/ adj FORMAL (of an action or remark) not carefully thought about

unconstitutional /ˌʌn.kɒn.stɪˈtjuː.ʃʰn.ʰl/ ⓤ -ˌkɑːn.stɪ-ˈtuː-/ adj not allowed by the CONSTITUTION (= set of rules for government) of a country or organization: Such a change in the law would be unconstitutional. **unconstitutionally** /ˌʌn.kɒn.stɪˈtjuː.ʃʰn.ʰl.i/ ⓤ -ˌkɑːn.stɪˈtuː-/ adv

uncontrollable /ˌʌn.kənˈtrəʊ.lə.bl̩/ ⓤ -ˈtroʊ-/ adj too strong or violent to be controlled: I was suddenly overcome with an uncontrollable desire to hit him. **uncontrollably** /ˌʌn.kənˈtrəʊ.lə.bli/ ⓤ -ˈtroʊ-/ adv: I arrived home to find him **sobbing** uncontrollably on the doorstep. **uncontrolled** /ˌʌn.kənˈtrəʊld/ ⓤ -ˈtroʊld/ adj: uncontrolled aggression

unconventional /ˌʌn.kənˈven.tʃʰn.ʰl/ adj different from what is usual or from the way most people do things: an unconventional childhood/lifestyle/marriage **unconventionally** /ˌʌn.kənˈven.tʃʰn.ʰl.i/ adv

unconvincing /ˌʌn.kənˈvɪn.tsɪŋ/ adj If an explanation or story is unconvincing, it does not sound or seem true or real: They produced some rather unconvincing explanations for the system failure. ○ The dialogue was unconvincing, partly because it was American actors trying to speak London English. **unconvincingly** /ˌʌn.kən-ˈvɪnt.sɪŋ.li/ adv

uncooperative /ˌʌn.kəʊˈɒp.ʰr.ə.tɪv/ ⓤ -koʊˈɑː.pɚ.ə.t̬ɪv/ adj not willing to work with or be helpful to other people: I found him rude and uncooperative. **uncooperatively** /ˌʌn.kəʊˈɒp.ʰr.ə.tɪv.li/ ⓤ -koʊˈɑː.-pɚ.ə.t̬ɪv-/ adv **uncooperativeness** /ˌʌn.kəʊˈɒp.ʰr.ə.tɪv.-nəs/ ⓤ -koʊˈɑː.pɚ.ə.t̬ɪv-/ noun [U]

uncoordinated /ˌʌn.kəʊˈɔː.dɪn.eɪ.tɪd/ ⓤ -koʊ-ˈɔːr.dɪ.neɪ.t̬ɪd/ adj with different parts failing to work or move well together: The marketing campaign was an uncoordinated effort by several different departments. ○ She was clumsy and uncoordinated as a girl.

uncork /ʌnˈkɔːk/ ⓤ -ˈkɔːrk/ verb [T] to open a bottle by pulling out its CORK (= cylindrical piece of soft wood used to close it): "Who's for some more wine?" asked Polly, uncorking another bottle.

uncountable /ʌnˈkaʊn.tə.bl̩/ ⓤ -t̬ə-/ adj SPECIALIZED describes a noun that you can have more or less of but that you cannot count or have many of: Words like 'electricity', 'blood' and 'happiness' are uncountable – you cannot say 'two electricities', 'a lot of bloods' or 'many happinesses' – and they are marked [U] in this dictionary. ⊃Compare **countable** at count NUMBER.

uncouple /ʌnˈkʌp.l̩/ verb [T] to separate two things that are joined together: The engine had been uncoupled **from** the rest of the train.

uncouth /ʌnˈkuːθ/ adj DISAPPROVING behaving in a rude, unpleasant way: She found him loud-mouthed and uncouth.

uncover /ʌnˈkʌv.əʳ/ ⓤ -ɚ/ verb [T] 1 to discover something secret or hidden or remove something covering something else: The investigation uncovered evidence of a large-scale illegal trade in wild birds. ○ The biography is an attempt to uncover the inner man. 2 to find something buried under the ground by removing the earth on top of it: Digging in her garden, she uncovered a hoard of gold dating back to the 9th century.

uncritical /ʌnˈkrɪt.ɪ.kʰl/ ⓤ -ˈkrɪt̬-/ adj OFTEN DISAPPROVING accepting something too easily, because of being unwilling or unable to criticize: an adoring, uncritical audience **uncritically** /ʌnˈkrɪt.ɪ.kli/ ⓤ -ˈkrɪt̬-/ adv

uncrowned /ˌʌnˈkraʊnd/ adj **uncrowned king/queen** a man or woman who is considered to be the best, the most famous or the most powerful in a particular area of life, especially when they do not have an official rank or title: Django Reinhardt, **the** uncrowned king **of** jazz guitarists

uncrushable /ˌʌnˈkrʌʃ.ə.bl̩/ adj describes cloth or clothing made of an artificial fibre and designed to stay free of unwanted folds: an uncrushable hat

unctuous /ˈʌŋk.tju.əs/ adj FORMAL DISAPPROVING describes people or behaviour expressing too much praise, interest, friendliness, etc., in a way that is false and unpleasant: his unctuous manner/voice/smile

uncut /ʌnˈkʌt/ adj complete and in its original form: the original, uncut version of a film ○ Uncut diamonds are worth less than those that have been cut and shaped.

undated /ʌnˈdeɪ.tɪd/ ⓤ -t̬ɪd/ adj An undated document has no date on it: The cheque/letter was undated.

undaunted /ʌnˈdɔːn.tɪd/ ⓤ -ˈdɑːn.t̬ɪd/ adj [after v] still determined and enthusiastic, despite problems or lack of success: Undaunted **by** the cold and the rain, people danced until 2am. ○ The team **remain** undaunted, despite three defeats in a row.

undecided /ˌʌn.dɪˈsaɪ.dɪd/ adj 1 If you are undecided, you have not yet made a decision or judgment about something: Are you still undecided **about** the job in Brussels? ○ 54% of voters were in favour, 30% against, and the rest were undecided. 2 not decided or finished:

The whole question is still undecided.

undefeated /ˌʌn.dɪˈfiː.tɪd/ [US] /-t̬ɪd/ *adj* in sports, having won every game: *Despite losing key players to injury, the team managed to remain undefeated in the final weeks of the season.*

undefinable /ˌʌn.dɪˈfaɪ.nə.bl̩/ *adj US FOR* **indefinable**

undeniable /ˌʌn.dɪˈnaɪ.ə.bl̩/ *adj* certainly true: *an undeniable fact* ○ *a woman of undeniable brilliance* **undeniably** /ˌʌn.dɪˈnaɪ.ə.bli/ *adv*: *She is undeniably good at her job.*

under [LOWER POSITION] /ˈʌn.dəʳ/ [US] /-dɚ/ *prep* **1** in or to a position below or lower than something else, often so that one thing covers the other: *He hid under the bed.* ○ *In AD 79 the city of Pompei was buried under a layer of ash seven metres deep.* ○ *She put the thermometer under my tongue.* ○ *She was holding a file under her arm* (= between her upper arm and the side of her chest). ○ *They stood under a tree* (= below its branches) *to avoid getting wet.* **2** If a book, article, or piece of information is under a particular title, you can find it below or following that title in a list, book, library, etc: *Books on Cecil Beaton will probably be under Art or Photography rather than Drama.* ○ *Trifle? That* ***comes*** *under Puddings and Desserts.*

under /ˈʌn.dəʳ/ [US] /-dɚ/ *adv* below the surface of something: *Because I'm a bad swimmer, I often go under and swallow a lot of water.*

• **go under** *INFORMAL* If a company goes under, it is unsuccessful and has to stop doing business: *Thousands of companies went under during the recession.*

under [LESS THAN] /ˈʌn.dəʳ/ [US] /-dɚ/ *prep* less than: *All items cost/are under a pound.* ○ *The discount applies only to children under* ***(the age of)*** *ten* (= younger than ten). ○ *If you get under 50%, you've failed the exam.* ✱ NOTE: The opposite is **over**.

under- /ʌn.dəʳ-/ [US] /-dɚ-/ *prefix* used before a word to mean 'not enough' or 'not done as well or as much as is necessary': *These potatoes are undercooked.* ○ *We're all overworked and underpaid.* ○ *His boss says he's underperforming* (= not doing as well as he should) *at work.* ➲Compare **over-** at **over** MORE THAN.

under [EXPERIENCING] /ˈʌn.dəʳ/ [US] /-dɚ/ *prep* **1** happening during, as a result of or according to a particular situation, event, rule, etc: *The work was completed under very difficult conditions.* ○ *Now that the deadline is approaching we all feel under pressure.* ○ *The chair broke under his weight* (= because he was too heavy for it). ○ *Under the present rules, you can buy ten litres of wine.* **2 under attack/consideration/discussion, etc.** in the process of being attacked, considered, discussed, etc: *The town is under* ***fire*** (= is being attacked) *from the air.* ○ *The proposals are now under* ***consideration*** *by the Board of Governors.* ○ *The situation is still not under* ***control***. **3** *UK* **under sedation/the doctor, etc.** treated in the way mentioned or by the medical person mentioned: *The patient is being kept under heavy sedation.* ○ *She'll have to go under anaesthetic for the operation.* ○ *OLD-FASHIONED She's been under the doctor for a viral infection.* **4 be under an impression/belief** to believe something, often wrongly: *He was under the mistaken belief that I was in charge.*

• **be/fall under** ***sb's*** **influence/spell** to be affected by somebody in a strong and often negative way: *She fell under his spell when he was her tutor at university.*

under [CONTROL] /ˈʌn.dəʳ/ [US] /-dɚ/ *prep* **1** controlled or governed by a particular person, organization or force: *He's a Colonel, with hundreds of soldiers under him* (= obeying his orders). ○ *I wonder what Britain was like under the Romans* (= during the time when the Romans controlled Britain). ○ *People born under* (= during the period of) *the star sign Pisces are supposed to be dreamy and artistic.* **2 be under orders** to be ordered to do something: *They're under strict orders not to discuss the situation.* ○ *He's under* ***doctor's*** *orders* (= has been told by a doctor) *to cut down on fatty food and to drink no alcohol for at least six months.*

under [NAME] /ˈʌn.dəʳ/ [US] /-dɚ/ *prep* using a particular name, especially one that is not your real name: *He writes under* ***the name (of)*** *John le Carré.* ○ *For his own safety, he has to operate under a false name/an alias.*

underachieve /ˌʌn.də.rəˈtʃiːv/ [US] /-dɚ.ə-/ *verb* [I] to do less well than you could or should: *Like a lot of boys his age, he's underachieving.* **underachiever** /ˌʌn.də.rəˈtʃiː.vəʳ/ [US] /-dɚ.əˈtʃiː.vɚ/ *noun* [C]

underage /ˌʌn.dəˈreɪdʒ/ [US] /-dɚˈeɪdʒ/ *adj* younger than the lowest age at which a particular activity is legally or usually allowed: *There are laws against underage sex and underage drinking.*

underarm [TOP OF ARM] /ˈʌn.də.rɑːm/ [US] /-dɚ.ɑːrm/ *adj* [before n] of or for use in the ARMPIT (= hollow place under the arm where the arm joins the body): *underarm deodorants/hair*

underarm [THROW] /ˈʌn.də.rɑːm/ [US] /-dɚ.ɑːrm/ *adj, adv* (*US ALSO* **underhand**) (done by) moving the arm below shoulder level: *underarm bowling* ○ *He bowled underarm for the younger children.* ✱ NOTE: The opposite is **overarm**.

underbelly /ˈʌn.dəˌbel.i/ [US] /-dɚ-/ *noun* [S] *LITERARY* the weakest or most unpleasant part of something which is most likely to fail or be easily defeated: *a film* ***exposing*** *the sordid underbelly of modern urban society* ○ *Small businesses are the* ***soft*** *underbelly* (= weakest parts) *of the British economy, and they need as much government support as possible.*

underbrush /ˈʌn.dəˌbrʌʃ/ [US] /-dɚ-/ *noun* [U] *US* **undergrowth** (= bushes, etc. growing under trees in a forest)

undercarriage /ˈʌn.dəˌkær.ɪdʒ/ [US] /-dɚˌker-/ *noun* [C] *UK* the set of wheels and other parts which support a plane when it is on the ground and make it possible to take off and land

undercharge /ˌʌn.dəˈtʃɑːdʒ/ [US] /-dɚˈtʃɑːrdʒ/ *verb* [I or T] to charge someone less than the correct price for something: *The sales assistant made a mistake and undercharged me* ***by*** *£2.* ✱ NOTE: The opposite is **overcharge**.

underclass /ˈʌn.də.klɑːs/ [US] /-dɚ.klæs/ *noun* [C usually sing] a group of people with a lower social and economic position than any of the other classes of society: *The long-term unemployed now constitute a sort of underclass.*

underclothes /ˈʌn.də.kləʊðz/ [US] /-dɚ.kloʊðz/ *plural noun* (*ALSO* **underclothing**) *FORMAL FOR* **underwear**

undercoat /ˈʌn.də.kəʊt/ [US] /-dɚ.koʊt/ *noun* [C or U] a first layer of paint that is put on a surface in order to improve the appearance of the final one, or the paint used for this: *Those red walls will probably need two undercoats.* ➲Compare **topcoat**.

undercook /ˌʌn.dəˈkʊk/ [US] /-dɚ-/ *verb* [T often passive] to not cook something enough **undercooked** /ˌʌn.dəˈkʊkt/ [US] /-dɚ-/ *adj*: *People can become infected after eating raw or undercooked* ***meat***.

undercover /ˌʌn.dəˈkʌv.əʳ/ [US] /-dɚˈkʌv.ɚ/ *adj* [before n] working secretly using a false appearance in order to get information for the police or government: *an undercover police operation* ○ *an undercover detective* **undercover** /ˌʌn.dəˈkʌv.əʳ/ [US] /-dɚˈkʌv.ɚ/ *adv*: *He was working undercover at the time almost certainly for the British Secret Service.*

undercurrent /ˈʌn.dəˌkʌr.ᵊnt/ [US] /-dɚˌkɝː-/ *noun* [C] an emotion, belief, or characteristic of a situation that is hidden and usually negative or dangerous but that has an indirect effect: *undercurrents of racism/anxiety/violence* ○ *Beneath the smooth surface of day-to-day political life, one senses powerful and dangerous undercurrents.*

undercut [CHARGE LESS THAN] /ˌʌn.dəˈkʌt/ [US] /-dɚ-/ *verb* [T] **undercutting, undercut, undercut** to charge less than a competitor: *Big supermarkets can undercut all rivals, especially small high-street shops.* ○ *They claim to undercut their competitors* ***by*** *at least 5%.*

undercut [WEAKEN] /ˌʌn.dəˈkʌt/ [US] /-dɚ-/ *verb* [T] **undercutting, undercut, undercut** to weaken or damage something or to cause it to fail; UNDERMINE: *He suspected it was an attempt to undercut his authority.*

underdeveloped /ˌʌn.də.dɪˈvel.əpt/ [US] /-dɚ-/ *adj* (especially of a country) without modern industry or modern services that provide transport, health care, etc: *an underdeveloped country* ○ *It's in the poorer, underdeveloped eastern region of the country that the biggest problems exist.*

U

underdog /ˈʌn.də.dɒg/ [US] /-dɚ.dɑːg/ *noun* **1 the underdog** a person or group of people with less power, money, etc. than the rest of society: *As a politician, her sympathy was always for the underdog in society.* **2** [C usually sing] in a competition, the person or team considered to be the weakest and the least likely to win

underdone /ˌʌn.dəˈdʌn/ [US] /-dɚ-/ *adj* describes food, especially meat, that is cooked for only a short time, or for less time than is necessary: *I like my steak underdone.* ○ *These potatoes are underdone – I'll put them back in the oven.*

underdressed /ˌʌn.dəˈdrest/ [US] /-dɚ-/ *adj* wearing clothes that are not attractive enough or formal enough for a particular occasion: *Everyone else was in smart suits and I felt a bit underdressed.*

underestimate /ˌʌn.dəˈres.tɪ.meɪt/ [US] /-dɚˈes-/ *verb* **1** [I or T] to fail to guess or understand the real cost, size, difficulty, etc. of something: *Originally the builders gave me a price of £2000, but now they say they underestimated and it's going to be at least £3000.* ○ *One shouldn't underestimate the difficulties of getting all the political parties to the conference table.* * NOTE: The opposite is **overestimate**. **2** [T] to fail to understand how strong, skilful, intelligent or determined someone, especially a competitor is: *Never underestimate your opponent!* **underestimate** /ˌʌn.dəˈres.tɪ.mət/ [US] /-dɚˈes-/ *noun* [C] *Clearly £25 was a serious underestimate.*

underexpose /ˌʌn.də.rɪkˈspəʊz/ [US] /-dɚ.ɪkˈspoʊz/ *verb* [T] to give too little light to a piece of photographic film when taking a photograph

underfloor /ˌʌn.dəˈflɔːʳ/ [US] /-dɚˈflɔːr/ *adj* [before n] MAINLY UK under the surface of a floor: *an underfloor heating system*

underfoot /ˌʌn.dəˈfʊt/ [US] /-dɚ-/ *adv* under your feet as you walk; on the ground: *The grass was cool and pleasant underfoot.* ○ *Many people were **trampled/crushed** underfoot when the police tried to break up the demonstration.*

underfunded /ˌʌn.dəˈfʌn.dɪd/ [US] /-dɚ-/ *adj* If an organization is underfunded, it does not receive a large enough income: *The government does not admit that the Hospital Service is underfunded.*

undergarment /ˈʌn.dəˌgɑː.mənt/ [US] /-dɚˌgɑːr-/ *noun* [C] FORMAL an item of underwear

undergo /ˌʌn.dəˈgəʊ/ [US] /-dɚˈgoʊ/ *verb* [T] **undergoing, underwent, undergone** to experience something which is unpleasant or which involves a change: *She underwent an operation on a tumour in her left lung last year.* ○ *Cinema in Britain is undergoing a revival of popularity.*

undergraduate /ˌʌn.dəˈgræd.ju.ət/ [US] /-dɚ-/ *noun* [C] a student who is studying for their first degree at college or university ➲Compare **graduate** PERSON.

underground [BELOW EARTH] *adj.* /ˈʌn.də.graʊnd/ [US] /-dɚ-/ *adv.* /ˌ--ˈ-/ below the surface of the earth; below ground: *an underground cave/passage/cable* ○ *Moles live underground.*

the ˈunderground [TRANSPORT] *noun* [S] (ALSO **the Tube**) UK a railway system in which electric trains travel along passages below ground: ***the** London Underground* ○ *They went **on the** Underground.* ➲See Note **metro, subway or underground?** at **metro** RAILWAY.

underground [PEOPLE] /ˈʌn.də.graʊnd/ [US] /-dɚ-/ *noun* [U] people in a society who are trying new and often shocking or illegal ways of living or forms of art: *In Britain and the USA in the 1970s, **the** underground was a powerful subversive force.*

the ˈunderground *group noun* [S] a group of people who secretly fight against the government: *He was a member of **the** underground, harassing the invading army.*

underground *adj.* /ˈʌn.də.graʊnd/ [US] /-dɚ-/ *adv.* /ˌ--ˈ-/ describes an activity that is secret and usually illegal: *an underground newspaper/movement* ○ *The Communist Party was forced (to **go**) underground, and its leaders went into hiding.*

undergrowth /ˈʌn.də.grəʊθ/ [US] /-dɚ.groʊθ/ *noun* [U] a mass of bushes, small trees and plants growing under the trees of a wood or forest: *Police discovered the body hidden in thick undergrowth.*

underhand [SECRETIVE] /ˌʌn.dəˈhænd/ [US] /-dɚ-/ *adj* (US USUALLY **underhanded**) DISAPPROVING done secretly, and sometimes dishonestly, in order to achieve an advantage: *What really angered her was the dirty underhand way they had tricked her.*

underhand [THROW] /ˈʌn.də.hænd/ [US] /-dɚ-/ *adj, adv* US FOR **underarm** THROW

underlay /ˈʌn.də.leɪ/ [US] /-dɚ.leɪ/ *noun* [U] UK thick material put between a carpet and the floor for extra comfort and to protect the carpet

underlie /ˌʌn.dəˈlaɪ/ [US] /-dɚ-/ *verb* [T] **underlying, underlay, underlain** to be a hidden cause of or strong influence on something: *Psychological problems very often underlie apparently physical disorders.*

underlying /ˌʌn.dəˈlaɪ.ɪŋ/ [US] /-dɚ-/ *adj* [before n] real but not immediately obvious: *And what might be the underlying significance of these supposedly random acts of violence?*

underline /ˌʌn.dəˈlaɪn/ [US] /-dɚ-/ *verb* [T] (ALSO **underscore**) **1** to draw a line under a word, especially in order to show its importance: *All the technical words have been underlined **in** red.* **2** to emphasize: *She put the figures up on the board to underline the seriousness of the situation.* ○ *To underline their disgust, the crowd started throwing bottles at the stage.*

underling /ˈʌn.dəl.ɪŋ/ [US] /-dɚ.lɪŋ/ *noun* [C] DISAPPROVING a person of low rank and little authority who works for someone more important: *She surrounded herself with underlings who were too afraid of her to ever answer back.*

undermanned /ˌʌn.dəˈmænd/ [US] /-dɚ-/ *adj* **understaffed**

undermentioned /ˌʌn.dəˈmen.tʃənd/ [US] /-dɚ-/ *adj* [before n] FORMAL used to refer to information that can be found in a later part of the same text: *The undermentioned staff all wish to join the union.* ➲Compare **abovementioned**.

undermine /ˌʌn.dəˈmaɪn/ [US] /-dɚ-/ *verb* [T] to make someone less confident, less powerful or less likely to succeed, or to make something weaker, often gradually: *The President has accused two cabinet ministers of working secretly to undermine his position/him.* ○ *Criticism just undermines their confidence.*

underneath /ˌʌn.dəˈniːθ/ [US] /-dɚ-/ *prep, adv* under or below: *The tunnel goes right underneath the city.* ○ *They found a bomb underneath the car.* ○ *Underneath that shy exterior, she's actually a very warm person.* ○ *He was wearing a garish T-shirt underneath his shirt.*

the underneath *noun* [S] the lower part or the bottom surface of something: *Bake for half an hour – the top should be crisp, and the underneath moist and succulent.* ○ *She found the key taped to the underneath of the table, as always.*

undernourished /ˌʌn.dəˈnʌr.ɪʃt/ [US] /-dɚˈnɝː-/ *adj* not eating enough food to maintain good health: *Many of the children are undernourished and suffering from serious diseases.*

underpants /ˈʌn.də.pænts/ [US] /-dɚ-/ *plural noun* (UK ALSO **pants**) a piece of underwear covering the area between the waist and the tops of the legs: *a pair of underpants* * NOTE: In British English, **underpants** usually refers to men's and boys' underwear. The word for girls' and women's underwear is **pants** or **knickers**. In American English **underpants** refers to the underwear worn by both men and women. In addition, underwear worn by women can be called **panties**. ➲See picture **Clothes** on page Centre 6

underpass /ˈʌn.də.pɑːs/ [US] /-dɚ.pæs/ *noun* [C] (UK **subway**) a road or path that goes under something such as a busy road, allowing vehicles or people to go from one side to the other

underpay /ˌʌn.dəˈpeɪ/ [US] /-dɚ-/ *verb* [T] **underpaid, underpaid** to pay someone too little for the work they do

underpaid /ˌʌn.dəˈpeɪd/ [US] /-dɚ-/ *adj*: *They're ridiculously underpaid, especially as the work is so dangerous.*

underpin /ˌʌn.dəˈpɪn/ [US] /-dɚ-/ *verb* [T] **-nn-** to give support, strength or a basic structure to something: *He presented the figures to underpin his argument.* ○ *Gradually the laws that underpinned* (= formed part of the basic structure of) *apartheid were abolished.* ○ SPECIALIZED

U

When restoring the building, the first priority was to underpin the exterior walls by adding wooden supports along the foundations. **underpinning** /ˈʌn.də,pɪn.ɪŋ/ [US] /-dɚ-/ *noun* [C or U] *After a while, we found ourselves questioning the spiritual and philosophical underpinning of the American way of life.*

underplay /,ʌn.dəˈpleɪ/ [US] /-dɚ-/ *verb* [T] to make something such as a dangerous situation seem less important or dangerous than it really is: *While not wanting to underplay the seriousness of the situation, I have to say that it is not as bad as people seem to think.*

underprivileged /,ʌn.dəˈprɪv.ɪ.lɪdʒd/ [US] /-dɚ-/ *adj* lacking the money, possessions, education, opportunities, etc. that the average person has: *Children from an underprivileged family background are statistically more likely to become involved in crime.*

the underprivileged *plural noun* POLITE EXPRESSION FOR poor people: *The charity raises money for holidays for the underprivileged.*

underrate /,ʌn.dəˈreɪt/ *verb* [T] to fail to understand how skilful, important, etc. someone or something is: *The company has consistently underrated the importance of a well-trained workforce.* **underrated** /,ʌn.dəˈreɪ.tɪd/ [US] /-t̬ɪd/ *adj*: *In my opinion, fennel is an underrated vegetable – few people realize how delicious it is.*

underscore /,ʌn.dəˈskɔːʳ/ [US] /-dɚˈskɔːr/ *verb* [T] to **underline**

undersea /,ʌn.dəˈsiː/ [US] /-dɚ-/ *adj* [before n] below the surface of the sea: *undersea exploration*

under-secretary /,ʌn.dəˈsek.rə.tri/ [US] /-dɚˈsek.rə.ter.i/ *noun* [C] a person who works for and has a slightly lower rank than the SECRETARY (= person in charge) of a government department: *She's Under-Secretary of State for Foreign Affairs.*

undersell [LOW PRICE] /,ʌn.dəˈsel/ [US] /-dɚ-/ *verb* [T] **undersold, undersold** to sell goods at a price lower than a competitor: *A big supermarket can usually undersell a small local store.*

undersell [BE MODEST] /,ʌn.dəˈsel/ [US] /-dɚ-/ *verb* [T] **undersold, undersold** to not give someone, especially yourself, or something the praise they deserve: [R] *Don't undersell yourself – you've got a lot to offer a company.*

undershirt /ˈʌn.də.ʃɜːt/ [US] /-dɚ.ʃɝːt/ *noun* [C] US FOR **vest** ➲See picture **Clothes** on page Centre 6

underside /ˈʌn.də.saɪd/ [US] /-dɚ-/ *noun* [C usually sing] the side of something that is usually nearest the ground: *The car had turned over in the ditch, and its underside was covered in oil and mud.*

the undersigned /ði,ʌn.dəˈsaɪnd/ [US] /-dɚ-/ *plural noun* FORMAL the people whose signatures appear below in the text, usually at the end of a formal letter: *We, the undersigned, strongly object to the closure of St. Mary's Hospital: Jack James (Dr), Philippa Curry (Dr), Hugh Edwards.*

undersized /,ʌn.dəˈsaɪzd/ [US] /ˈʌn.dɚ-/ *adj* (ALSO **undersize**) smaller than average, or smaller than the correct size: *an undersized, malnourished boy*

understaffed /,ʌn.dəˈstɑːft/ [US] /-dɚˈstæft/ *adj* (ALSO **undermanned**) If a shop, business or organization is understaffed, it does not have enough employees: *The school was overcrowded and desperately understaffed.* * NOTE: The opposite is **overstaffed**.

understand [KNOW] /,ʌn.dəˈstænd/ [US] /-dɚ-/ *verb* [I or T] **understood, understood 1** to know the meaning of something that someone says: *She explained the whole idea again, but I still didn't understand.* ○ *Is there anyone here who understands Arabic?* ○ *I think he was phoning from a pub – it was so noisy I couldn't understand* (= recognize) *a word he said.* **2 understand sb to mean sth** to think, especially incorrectly, that someone means a particular thing: *When he said 3 o'clock, I understood him to mean in the afternoon.* **3** to know why or how something happens or works: [+ question word] *We still don't fully understand how the brain works.* **4** to know how someone feels or why they behave in a particular way: *My wife doesn't understand me.* ○ *Sometimes I don't understand James.* ○ [+ question word] *You don't understand **what** it's like/**how** it feels to have to beg on the streets.* **5 understand one another/each other** When two people understand one another, they both know what the other means and wants and they have an agreement: *Both sides must try to understand one another, to recognise each others' rights, feelings and beliefs.* ➲See also **understanding** AGREEMENT.

• **make *yourself* understood** to communicate effectively: *Since they spoke only Swahili, we used signs and gestures to make ourselves understood.*

understandable /,ʌn.dəˈstæn.də.bl̩/ [US] /-dɚ-/ *adj* **1** easy to understand: *You've got to put the facts into a form that's understandable **to** everyone.* **2** You say that something, for example someone's behaviour, is understandable, if you feel that it is usual and not strange or difficult to understand: *Their refusal to cooperate is perfectly/completely understandable, considering the circumstances.* **understandably** /,ʌn.dəˈstæn.də.bli/ [US] /-dɚ-/ *adv*

understand [BE AWARE] /,ʌn.dəˈstænd/ [US] /-dɚ-/ *verb* **understood, understood** FORMAL **1** [T] to know or become aware of something because you have been told it: [+ (that)] *I understand **(that)** you are interested in borrowing some money from us.* ○ [+ that] *The Director had **given** her **to** understand* (= told her) ***that** she would be promoted.* ○ [+ obj + to infinitive] *A secret buyer is understood **to** have paid £1 million for the three pictures* (= there is unofficial news that this has happened). **2** [I or T] used when making certain that someone knows what you mean and that they will do as you want: *I don't want you to see that boy again. Understand?/Do you understand?/Is that understood?*

• **it is understood** used to refer to something such as a rule that everyone knows and accepts: *In the library it is understood **that** loud talking is not permissible.*

understanding [KNOWLEDGE] /,ʌn.dəˈstæn.dɪŋ/ [US] /-dɚ-/ *noun* [U] knowledge about a subject, situation, etc. or about how something works: *She doesn't have any understanding **of** politics/human nature/what it takes to be a good manager.* ○ *My understanding **of** the agreement* (= What I think it means) *is that they will pay £50 000 over two years.*

understanding [SYMPATHY] /,ʌn.dəˈstæn.dɪŋ/ [US] /-dɚ-/ *noun* [S or U] a positive, truthful, sympathetic relationship between two people or groups: *For peace to exist in the region there needs to be a much improved understanding **between** all the parties concerned.*

understanding /,ʌn.dəˈstæn.dɪŋ/ [US] /-dɚ-/ *adj* APPROVING describes someone who has the ability to know how someone else is feeling or what their situation is, and can forgive them if they do something wrong: *He had expected her to be horrified, but she was actually very understanding.*

understanding [AGREEMENT] /,ʌn.dəˈstæn.dɪŋ/ [US] /-dɚ-/ *noun* [C] an informal agreement between people: *It took several hours of discussion before they could **come to/reach** an understanding.*

• **on the understanding (that)** If you do something on the understanding that something else can or will happen, you do it because someone else has promised that it can or will: *We bought the cupboard on the understanding that we could return it if it wasn't suitable.*

understate /,ʌn.dəˈsteɪt/ [US] /-dɚ-/ *verb* [T] to state or describe something in a way that makes it seem less important, serious, bad, etc. than it really is: *She believes the research understates the amount of discrimination women suffer.*

understated /,ʌn.dəˈsteɪ.tɪd/ [US] /-dɚˈsteɪ.t̬ɪd/ *adj*: APPROVING *He's very elegant, in an understated* (= not too obvious) *way.* **understatement** /,ʌn.dəˈsteɪt.mənt/ [US] /-dɚ-/ *noun* [S or U] *To say that her resignation was a shock would be an understatement – it caused panic.* ○ *That New York City is not a peaceful place to live is **the** understatement **of the** year/month/century.*

understudy /ˈʌn.də,stʌd.i/ [US] /-dɚ-/ *noun* [C] an actor who learns the parts of other actors in a play, so that he or she can replace them if necessary, for example because they are ill **understudy** /ˈʌn.də,stʌd.i/ [US] /-dɚ-/ *verb* [T]

undertake [DO] /,ʌn.dəˈteɪk/ [US] /-dɚ-/ *verb* [T] **undertook, undertaken** SLIGHTLY FORMAL to do or begin to do something, especially something that will take a long time or

be difficult: *Students are required to undertake simple experiments.*
undertaking /ˌʌn.dəˈteɪ.kɪŋ/ [US] /-dɚ-/ *noun* [C] a job, business or piece of work: *The construction of the tunnel is a large and complex undertaking.*

undertake [PROMISE] /ˌʌn.dəˈteɪk/ [US] /-dɚ-/ *verb* [T] **undertook, undertaken** *FORMAL* to promise that you will do something: [+ **to** infinitive] *She undertook not* ***to*** *publish the names of the people involved.* ○ [+ **that**] *The government undertook* ***that*** *the buildings would not be redeveloped.*
undertaking /ˌʌn.dəˈteɪ.kɪŋ/ [US] /-dɚ-/ *noun* [C] *FORMAL* a formal promise: [+ **that**] *FORMAL The manager* ***gave*** *a written undertaking* ***that*** *no one would lose their job.*

undertaker /ˈʌn.dəˌteɪ.kəʳ/ [US] /-dɚˌteɪ.kɚ/ *noun* [C] (*US ALSO* **mortician**) a person whose job is to prepare dead bodies that are going to be buried or CREMATED (= burned) and to organize funerals

undertone [CHARACTERISTIC] /ˈʌn.də.təʊn/ [US] /-dɚ.toʊn/ *noun* [C] a particular but not obvious characteristic that a piece of writing or speech, an event or a situation has: *I thought her speech had slightly sinister undertones.* ○ *It was a comedy act with an undertone* ***of*** *cruelty.*

undertone [QUIET VOICE] /ˈʌn.də.təʊn/ [US] /-dɚ.toʊn/ *noun* **in an undertone** in a very quiet voice: *Freddie muttered something to me in an undertone.*

undertow /ˈʌn.də.təʊ/ [US] /-dɚ.toʊ/ *noun* [C usually sing] a strong current flowing under water in a different direction to the way the water on the surface is moving, especially the strong current that flows under water away from the land at the same time as a wave hits the beach

underused /ˌʌn.dəˈjuːzd/ [US] /-dɚ-/ *adj* not used as much as it could or should be: *Since the main hospital was built, the local clinics have been rather underused.*

undervalue /ˌʌn.dəˈvæl.juː/ [US] /-dɚ-/ *verb* [T] to consider someone or something as less valuable or important than they really are: *The company had undervalued the building* ***by*** *£20 000.* ○ *He felt undervalued and underpaid.*

underwater /ˌʌn.dəˈwɔː.təʳ/ [US] /-dɚˈwɑː.t̬ɚ/ *adj, adv* under the surface of the water, especially under the surface of the sea: *an underwater camera* (= a camera that you can use under water) ○ *Some species of turtle can remain underwater for 24 hours.*

underway, under way /ˌʌn.dəˈweɪ/ [US] /-dɚ-/ *adj* [after v] **1** If something is underway, it is happening now: *Economic recovery is* ***already*** *underway.* **2 get underway** to begin: *The film festival gets underway on 11th July.*

underwear /ˈʌn.də.weəʳ/ [US] /-dɚ.wer/ *noun* [U] clothes worn next to the skin, under other clothes

underweight /ˌʌn.dəˈweɪt/ [US] /-dɚ-/ *adj* Underweight people weigh too little and are too thin: *According to the hospital chart he's four kilos underweight.* ✻ NOTE: The opposite is **overweight**.

underwent /ˌʌn.dəˈwent/ [US] /-dɚ-/ *past simple of* **undergo**

underwhelmed /ˌʌn.dəˈwelmd/ [US] /-dɚ-/ *adj HUMOROUS* feeling no excitement about or admiration for something or someone: *I get the feeling that the staff are distinctly underwhelmed by John's latest proposal.*

underwired /ˌʌn.dəˈwaɪəd/ [US] /-dɚˈwaɪrd/ *adj* describes women's clothing made with a piece of wire under the breasts for additional support: *an underwired bra/bodice/top*

underworld [CRIME] /ˈʌn.də.wɜːld/ [US] /-dɚ.wɝːld/ *noun* [S] the part of society consisting of criminal organizations and activities

the underworld [IN STORIES] *noun* [S] in Greek mythology, a place under the earth where the SOULS of the dead go; **hades**

underwrite /ˌʌn.dəˈraɪt/ /ˈ---/ *verb* [T] **underwrote, underwritten 1** If a bank or other organization underwrites an activity, it gives it financial support and takes responsibility for paying any costs if it fails. **2** *SPECIALIZED* If a company underwrites an INSURANCE POLICY, someone's property, etc., they have an agreement to pay out money in cases of damage or loss. **underwriter** /ˈʌn.dəˌraɪ.təʳ/ [US] /-dəˌraɪ.t̬ɚ/ *noun* [C]

undesirable /ˌʌn.dɪˈzaɪə.rə.bl̩/ [US] /-ˈzaɪr.ə-/ *adj DISAPPROVING* not wanted, approved of or popular: *Houses near industrial sites often do not sell so quickly because they are regarded as undesirable.*
undesirables /ˌʌn.dɪˈzaɪə.rə.bl̩z/ [US] /-ˈzaɪr.ə-/ *plural noun OFTEN HUMOROUS* people whose behaviour or appearance makes them unacceptable in society or at a particular occasion: *There are guards on the door to keep out (the) undesirables.*

undeveloped /ˌʌn.dɪˈvel.əpt/ *adj* An undeveloped place or piece of land has not been built on or used for farming.

undid /ʌnˈdɪd/ *past simple of* **undo**

undies /ˈʌn.diz/ *plural noun INFORMAL* **underwear**

undisclosed /ˌʌn.dɪsˈkləʊzd/ [US] /-ˈkloʊzd/ *adj* If official information is undisclosed, it is secret: *The meeting is taking place at an undisclosed location.*

undisguised /ˌʌn.dɪsˈgaɪzd/ *adj* describes a feeling that is clearly shown or expressed, when it is usually kept hidden: *She looked at him with undisguised contempt.*

undisputed /ˌʌn.dɪˈspjuː.tɪd/ [US] /-t̬ɪd/ *adj* If something is undisputed, everyone agrees about it: *an undisputed fact* ○ *the undisputed champion/winner*

undisturbed /ˌʌn.dɪˈstɜːbd/ [US] /-ˈstɝːbd/ *adj* not interrupted or changed in any way: *eight hours of undisturbed sleep*

undivided /ˌʌn.dɪˈvaɪ.dɪd/ *adj* **1** existing as a whole, not in separate parts **2 undivided attention** complete attention: *If you just wait till I've finished this bit of work you will* ***have****/I will* ***give*** *you my undivided attention.*

undo [UNFASTEN] /ʌnˈduː/ *verb* [T] **undoing, undid, undone** to unfasten something that is fastened or tied: *Can someone help me to undo my seat belt?* **undone** /ʌnˈdʌn/ *adj*: *Why didn't you tell me my zip was undone!* ○ *Damn, my shoe-laces have* ***come*** *undone again.* ➲See also **undone**.

undo [REMOVE EFFECTS] /ʌnˈduː/ *verb* [T] **undoing, undid, undone** to remove the good or bad effects of an action or several actions: *I did a really tough aerobics class and then went out for a meal and undid* ***(all) the good work!*** ○ *It's very difficult to undo* ***the damage*** *that's caused by inadequate parenting in a child's early years.*

undoing /ʌnˈduː.ɪŋ/ *noun* [S] *FORMAL* the cause of someone's failure, or of their loss of power or wealth: *Greed has been* ***the*** *undoing* ***of*** *many a businessman.*

undone /ʌnˈdʌn/ *adj OLD USE* **be undone** to be without hope for the future, having experienced great disappointment, loss of money, etc. ➲See also **undone** at **undo** UNFASTEN.

undoubted /ʌnˈdaʊ.tɪd/ [US] /-t̬ɪd/ *adj* [usually before n] not questioned or doubted; accepted as the truth: *She is the undoubted star of British ballet.* **undoubtedly** /ʌnˈdaʊ.tɪd.li/ [US] /-t̬ɪd-/ *adv*: *She was undoubtedly the best candidate.*

undreamed of, undreamt of /ʌnˈdrempt.əv/ /--ˈdriːmd-/ *adj* describes wealth, success or progress that is better or greater than anyone would think possible: *We in the West enjoy a standard of living undreamed of by the majority of people in the world.* ○ [before n] *These two lads from a remote village in Norway have enjoyed undreamed-of success with their first album.*

undress /ʌnˈdres/ *verb* [I or T] to remove your clothes or remove the clothes from someone else: *Could you undress the kids for bed, Steve?* ○ *He undressed and got into the bath.*
• **undress** ***sb*** **with** ***your*** **eyes** *INFORMAL* to look at someone's body with strong, and often unpleasant, sexual desire
undress /ʌnˈdres/ *noun FORMAL OR HUMOROUS* **in a state of undress** not wearing many or any clothes: *He came to the door in a state of undress.* **undressed** /ʌnˈdrest/ *adj*: [rarely before n] *You two kids* ***get*** *undressed, and I'll run the bath.*

undue /ʌnˈdjuː/ [US] /-ˈduː/ *adj* [before n] *FORMAL* to a level which is more than is necessary, acceptable or reasonable: *Such a high increase will impose an undue burden on the local tax payer.* **unduly** /ʌnˈdjuː.li/ [US] /-ˈduː-/ *adv*: *There's no need to be unduly* ***pessimistic*** *about the situation.*

undulating /ˈʌn.djʊ.leɪ.tɪŋ/ [US] /-t̬ɪŋ/ *adj FORMAL* **1** describing or having small hills and slopes that look like waves: *undulating roads* ○ *I love the gently undulating hills of the Dales.* **2** moving gently up and down: *undulating waves* **undulate** /ˈʌn.djʊ.leɪt/ *verb* [I]

undying /ʌnˈdaɪ.ɪŋ/ *adj* [before n] *LITERARY* Undying feelings or beliefs are permanent and never end: *He pledged undying love/loyalty.*

unearned income /ʌnˌɜːndˈɪn.kʌm/ [US] /-ˌɝːnd-/ *noun* [U] money that you obtain from investments and property that you own, instead of earning by working

unearth /ʌnˈɜːθ/ [US] /-ˈɝːθ/ *verb* [T] **1** to discover something in the ground: *Building at the site was halted after human remains were unearthed earlier this month.* **2** to discover proof or some other information, especially after careful searching: *A private detective has apparently unearthed some fresh evidence.*

unearthly [INCONVENIENT] /ʌnˈɜːθ.li/ [US] /-ˈɝːθ-/ *adj INFORMAL* describes a time that is very inconvenient because it is too early in the morning or too late at night: *I was woken up **at some** unearthly **hour** of the morning by someone knocking on my door.*

unearthly [STRANGE] /ʌnˈɜːθ.li/ [US] /-ˈɝːθ-/ *adj* strange in a mysterious and sometimes frightening way: *Cats' cries have an unearthly quality.*

uneasy /ʌnˈiː.zi/ *adj* **1** If you are uneasy, you are slightly anxious or uncomfortable about a particular situation: *I feel a bit uneasy **about** asking her to do me such a big favour.* **2** describes a situation or condition that makes people slightly anxious, often because it may not continue successfully: *Who can predict how long this uneasy peace between the two countries will last?* ○ *She has a rather uneasy relationship with her mother-in-law.* **uneasily** /ʌnˈiː.zɪ.li/ *adv*

uneasiness /ʌnˈiː.zɪ.nəs/ *noun* [U] (*ALSO* **unease**) anxiety: ***Growing** unease **at** the prospect of an election is causing fierce arguments within the party.*

uneconomic /ʌnˌiː.kəˈnɒm.ɪk/ /-ˌek.ə-/ [US] /-ˈnɑː.mɪk/ *adj* (*ALSO* **uneconomical**) **1** describes businesses and industries that are not making enough profit or are losing money: *The minister maintained that the coal mines were uneconomic and would have to be closed.* **2** describes processes or activities that are wasteful and tend to result in a loss of money

unedifying /ʌnˈed.ɪ.faɪ.ɪŋ/ *adj FORMAL* unpleasant and causing people to feel no respect: *We were treated to the unedifying **spectacle** of two cabinet ministers fighting over a seat.*

uneducated /ʌnˈed.jʊ.keɪ.tɪd/ [US] /-t̬ɪd/ *adj* having received little or no education

unemployed /ˌʌn.ɪmˈplɔɪd/ *adj* not having a job that provides money: *He's been unemployed for over a year.*

unemployed /ˌʌn.ɪmˈplɔɪd/ *plural noun* people who do not have a job that provides money: *There are now over four million unemployed in this country.* ○ *Tickets are £10 or £5 for **the** unemployed.*

unemployment /ˌʌn.ɪmˈplɔɪ.mənt/ *noun* [U] **1** the number of people who do not have a job which provides money: *Unemployment has **fallen/risen** again for the third consecutive month.* **2** the state of being unemployed

unemˈployment ˌbenefit *UK noun* [U] (*US* **unemployment benefits**) *OLD-FASHIONED FOR* **Jobseeker's Allowance**

unemˈployment (compenˌsation) *noun* [U] (*ALSO* **unemployment insurance**) *US FOR* **Jobseeker's Allowance**

unending /ʌnˈen.dɪŋ/ *adj SLIGHTLY FORMAL* describes activities or events, especially unpleasant ones, when they seem to continue for ever: *Motherhood seemed to her an unending cycle of cooking, washing and cleaning.*

unendurable /ˌʌn.ɪnˈdjʊə.rə.bl̩/ [US] /-ˈdʊr.ə-/ *adj FORMAL* If a situation or experience is unendurable, it is so unpleasant or painful that it is almost impossible to bear: *unendurable pain/suspense*

unenforceable /ˌʌn.ɪnˈfɔː.sə.bl̩/ [US] /-ˈfɔːr-/ *adj* If a rule or law is unenforceable, it is impossible to force people to obey it.

unenviable /ʌnˈen.vi.ə.bl̩/ *adj* describes a duty or necessary action that is unpleasant or difficult: *I had the unenviable **task** of cleaning up after the party.*

unequal [NOT THE SAME] /ʌnˈiː.kwəl/ *adj FORMAL* different in size, level, amount, etc: *She cut two slices of noticeably unequal size.* **unequally** /ʌnˈiː.kwə.li/ *adv*

unequal [UNFAIR] /ʌnˈiː.kwəl/ *adj* not treating everyone the same; unfair: *Until women are paid as much as men, they will be competing on unequal terms.* ○ *They have a rather unequal relationship.* **unequally** /ʌnˈiː.kwə.li/ *adv*

unequal [UNABLE] /ʌnˈiː.kwəl/ *adj FORMAL* **be unequal to *sth*** to lack the necessary ability, power or qualities to achieve something: *He tried to cheer her up but found himself unequal to **the task**.*

unequalled, *US USUALLY* **unequaled** /ʌnˈiː.kwəld/ *adj SLIGHTLY FORMAL* better or more extreme than any other: *Though small, this restaurant offers a range of fish dishes unequalled anywhere else in London.*

unequivocal /ˌʌn.ɪˈkwɪv.ə.kəl/ *adj* total, or expressed in a clear and certain way: *The Prime Minister, he said, had the party's unequivocal support.* ○ *The church has been unequivocal in its condemnation of the violence.* **unequivocally** /ˌʌn.ɪˈkwɪv.ə.kli/ *adv*

unerring /ʌnˈɜː.rɪŋ/ [US] /-ˈer.ɪŋ/ *adj* **1** never failing to hit a target **2** always accurate in judgment or ability: *He has an unerring talent for writing catchy melodies.* **unerringly** /ʌnˈɜː.rɪŋ.li/ [US] /-ˈer.ɪŋ-/ *adv*

UNESCO, **Unesco** /juːˈnes.kəʊ/ [US] /-koʊ/ *group noun* [U] *ABBREVIATION FOR* United Nations Educational, Scientific and Cultural Organization: a department of the United Nations which aims to encourage peace between countries through education, science and culture

unethical /ˌʌnˈeθ.ɪ.kəl/ *adj* not ETHICAL, see at **ethic**

uneven [NOT EVEN] /ʌnˈiː.vən/ *adj* not level, equal, flat or continous: *Take care when you walk on that path – the paving stones are rather uneven.* ○ *There is an uneven distribution of wealth across the country from the north to the south.* ○ *The contest was very uneven – the other team was far stronger than us.* **unevenly** /ʌnˈiː.vən.li/ *adv*: *The two boxers were unevenly matched.* **unevenness** /ʌnˈiː.vən.nəs/ *noun* [U]

uneven [NOT GOOD] /ˌʌnˈiː.vən/ *adj* varying in quality; often used to avoid saying bad: *Your work has been rather uneven this term, Matthew.* **unevenly** /ˌʌnˈiː.vən.li/ *adv* **unevenness** /ˌʌnˈiː.vən.nəs/ *noun* [U]

unˌeven ˈbars *plural noun US FOR* **asymmetric bars**

uneventful /ˌʌn.ɪˈvent.fəl/ *adj* not EVENTFUL, see at **event** **uneventfully** /ˌʌn.ɪˈvent.fəl.i/ *adv*

unexceptionable /ˌʌn.ɪkˈsep.ʃən.ə.bl̩/ *adj FORMAL* not bad; having nothing that anyone could criticize or disapprove of: *an unexceptionable speech*

unexceptional /ˌʌn.ɪkˈsep.ʃən.əl/ *adj* ordinary, not EXCEPTIONAL: *He was a hard-working, if unexceptional, student.*

unexpected /ˌʌn.ɪkˈspek.tɪd/ *adj* not expected: *Well, fancy seeing you here! This really was an unexpected **pleasure**!* **unexpectedly** /ˌʌn.ɪkˈspek.tɪd.li/ [US] /-t̬ɪd-/ *adv*

unexplained /ʌn.ɪkˈspleɪnd/ *adj* describes events, behaviour, etc. for which people do not know or understand the reason: *an unexplained death/noise* ○ *He was shot dead earlier this year in unexplained **circumstances**.*

unexplored [PLACE] /ʌn.ɪkˈsplɔːd/ [US] /-ˈsplɔːrd/ *adj* describes a place where people have not been to find out what is there: *unexplored territory*

unexplored [PLAN] /ʌn.ɪkˈsplɔːd/ [US] /-ˈsplɔːrd/ *adj* describes a plan, idea or subject that has not been examined to find out what it involves: *The subject of alternative medical care for older people has been entirely unexplored.*

unexpurgated /ʌnˈek.spə.geɪ.tɪd/ [US] /-spɚ.geɪ.t̬ɪd/ *adj* describes a book, article, film, etc. that is complete and contains everything, including parts considered likely to cause offence

unfailing /ʌnˈfeɪ.lɪŋ/ *adj* describes a positive quality of someone's character when it shows itself at all times: *One of the good things about Inga is that you can always rely on her unfailing enthusiasm.* **unfailingly** /ʌnˈfeɪ.lɪŋ.li/ *adv*: *She's unfailingly cheerful no matter what the circumstances.*

unfair /ʌnˈfeəʳ/ [US] /-ˈfer/ *adj* not treating people in an equal way, or not morally right: *an unfair system* ○ *It's unfair to blame Roger.* **unfairly** /ʌnˈfeə.li/ [US] /-ˈfer-/ *adv* **unfairness** /ʌnˈfeə.nəs/ [US] /-ˈfer-/ *noun* [U]

unfaithful /ʌnˈfeɪθ.fəl/ *adj* having a sexual relationship or experience with a person who is not your husband, wife or usual sexual partner: *If a man was unfaithful **to** me I'd leave him no matter what the circumstances.* **unfaithfulness** /ʌnˈfeɪθ.fəl.nəs/ *noun* [U]

unfaltering /ʌnˈfɒl.tər.ɪŋ/ [US] /-ˈfɑːl.t̬ɚ-/ *adj* not FALTERING, see at **falter**

unfamiliar /ʌn.fəˈmɪl.i.əʳ/ [US] /-jɚ/ *adj* **1** not known to you: *I noticed several unfamiliar faces in the meeting room.* ○ *His name was unfamiliar **to** me.* **2 be unfamiliar with *sth*** to not have any knowledge or experience of something: *Many older people are unfamiliar with computers.*

unfashionable /ʌnˈfæʃ.ən.ə.bl̩/ *adj* not modern or popular: *They paid less for the house because it was in an unfashionable part of town.*

unfasten /ʌnˈfɑː.sən/ [US] /-ˈfæs-/ *verb* [I or T] to release or open something that is fixed or closed: *I can't unfasten this button/belt.* ○ *This blouse unfastens* (= can be unfastened) *at the back.*

unfathomable /ʌnˈfæð.ə.mə.bl̩/ *adj* SLIGHTLY FORMAL impossible to understand: *For some unfathomable reason they built the toilet next to the kitchen.* **unfathomably** /ʌnˈfæð.ə.mə.bli/ *adv* FORMAL

unfavourable UK, US **unfavorable** /ʌnˈfeɪ.vər.ə.bl̩/ [US] /-vɚ-/ *adj* not FAVOURABLE, see at **favour** SUPPORT **unfavourably** /ʌnˈfeɪ.vər.ə.bli/ [US] /-vɚ-/ *adv*

unfazed /ʌnˈfeɪzd/ *adj* INFORMAL not surprised or worried: *She seems unfazed by her sudden success and fame.*

unfeasible /ʌnˈfiː.zɪ.bl̩/ *adj* not FEASIBLE **unfeasibly** /ʌnˈfiː.zɪ.bli/ *adv*

unfeeling /ʌnˈfiː.lɪŋ/ *adj* DISAPPROVING not feeling sympathy for other people's suffering: *She accused me of being unfeeling because I didn't cry at the end of the film.*

unfettered /ʌnˈfet.əd/ [US] /-ˈfet̬.ɚd/ *adj* FORMAL not limited by rules or any other controlling influence: *In writing poetry, one is unfettered **by** the normal rules of sentence structure.*

unfinished /ʌnˈfɪn.ɪʃt/ *adj* **1** not completed **2 unfinished business** a matter, especially a disagreement, that is not yet decided or agreed: *I still have some unfinished business **with** you.*

unfit /ʌnˈfɪt/ *adj* not FIT, see **fit** HEALTHY, **fit** SUIT: *The building was declared unfit for human habitation.* ○ *I used to take plenty of exercise, but now I'm terribly unfit.*

unflagging /ʌnˈflæg.ɪŋ/ *adj* describes a quality, such as energy, interest or enthusiasm, when it never weakens: *He thanked Tony for his unflagging energy and support.*

unflappable /ʌnˈflæp.ə.bl̩/ *adj* not tending to get anxious, nervous or angry even in difficult situations: *She's totally unflappable – you have to be when working in such a highly-pressured environment.*

unflattering /ʌnˈflæt.ər.ɪŋ/ [US] /-ˈflæt̬.ɚ-/ *adj* making someone look less attractive or seem worse than they usually do: *an unflattering photo/dress/colour* ○ *The book portrays her in a most unflattering **light**.*

unflinching /ʌnˈflɪn.tʃɪŋ/ *adj* not frightened of or trying to avoid danger or unpleasantness: *It is a brave and unflinching account of prison life.*

unfold [DEVELOP] /ʌnˈfəʊld/ [US] /-ˈfoʊld/ *verb* **1** [I] If a situation or story unfolds, it develops or becomes clear to other people: *Like a lot of people, I've watched the **events** of the last few days unfold on TV.* ○ *As the plot unfolds, you gradually realise that all your initial assumptions were wrong.* **2** [T] FORMAL to tell someone about something, especially a plan, and explain it in detail: *I've arranged a lunch with him next Thursday at which I intend to unfold my proposal.*

unfold [OPEN] /ʌnˈfəʊld/ [US] /-ˈfoʊld/ *verb* [T] to open or spread out something that has been folded: *If we unfold the table we can fit eight people around it.* ○ *He watched her expression as she unfolded the letter.*

unforeseen /ˌʌn.fəˈsiːn/ [US] /-fɚ-/ *adj* unexpected: *Due to unforeseen **circumstances** the cost of the improvements has risen by twenty per cent.* ○ *Unless there are any unforeseen problems the whole project should be finished by the spring.*

unforgettable /ˌʌn.fəˈget.ə.bl̩/ [US] /-fɚˈget̬-/ *adj* An unforgettable experience has such a strong effect or influence on you that you cannot forget it. **unforgettably** /ˌʌn.fəˈget.ə.bli/ [US] /-fɚˈget̬-/ *adv*

unfortunate [UNLUCKY] /ʌnˈfɔː.tʃən.ət/ [US] /-ˈfɔːr-/ *adj* unlucky or having bad effects: *She has inherited her father's large nose, which is very unfortunate.* ○ ***It** was just unfortunate (that) he phoned exactly as our guests were arriving.*

unfortunate /ʌnˈfɔː.tʃən.ət/ [US] /-ˈfɔːr-/ *noun* [C] FORMAL OR HUMOROUS an unlucky person who is in a bad situation: *He was one of the **poor** unfortunates who invested in the company and now finds himself a few thousand pounds poorer.* **unfortunately** /ʌnˈfɔː.tʃən.ət.li/ [US] /-ˈfɔːr-/ *adv*: *Unfortunately, I didn't have my credit card with me or I'd certainly have bought it.*

unfortunate [UNSUITABLE] /ʌnˈfɔː.tʃən.ət/ [US] /-ˈfɔːr-/ *adj* FORMAL (of remarks or behaviour) unsuitable in a way which could cause embarrassment or offence: *The housing director's remark that 'the homeless could do more to help themselves' was unfortunate to say the least.*

unfounded /ʌnˈfaʊn.dɪd/ *adj* describes a claim or piece of news that is not based on fact: *I'm pleased to see that our fears about the weather **proved** totally unfounded.*

unfriendly /ʌnˈfrend.li/ *adj* showing dislike and lack of sympathy; not friendly **unfriendliness** /ʌnˈfrend.lɪ.nəs/ *noun* [U]

unfulfilled /ˌʌn.fʊlˈfɪld/ *adj* **1** If a wish, hope, promise, etc. is unfulfilled, it has not happened or been achieved: *an unfulfilled ambition/dream* **2** unhappy because you think you should be achieving more in your life

unfurl /ʌnˈfɜːl/ [US] /-ˈfɝːl/ *verb* [I or T] If a flag, sail or BANNER unfurls, it becomes open from a rolled position, and if you unfurl a flag, etc., you make it do this: *The demonstrators unfurled a large banner.*

unfurnished /ʌnˈfɜː.nɪʃt/ [US] /-ˈfɝː-/ *adj* describes a room, house or other building without furniture in it: *unfurnished accommodation*

ungainly /ʌnˈgeɪn.li/ *adj* awkward and without grace in movement: *Ducks are ungainly on land.*

unglamorous /ʌnˈglæm.ər.əs/ *adj* not GLAMOROUS (= especially attractive and exciting): *unglamorous work/surroundings*

unglued /ʌnˈgluːd/ *adj* US INFORMAL **come unglued** to experience difficulties and fail: *When the secret arrangements came unglued, the president was revealed to have ordered the burglary.*

ungodly /ʌnˈgɒd.li/ [US] /-ˈgɑːd-/ *adj* [before n] INFORMAL extreme or unacceptable: *I had to get up at some ungodly **hour** in the morning to take her to the airport.*

ungovernable /ʌnˈgʌv.ən.ə.bl̩/ [US] /-ɚ.nə-/ *adj* unable to be governed or controlled

ungrammatical /ˌʌn.grəˈmæt.ɪ.kəl/ [US] /-ˈmæt̬-/ *adj* not GRAMMATICAL, see at **grammar**

ungrateful /ʌnˈgreɪt.fəl/ *adj* not GRATEFUL

unguarded /ʌnˈgɑː.dɪd/ [US] /-ˈgɑːr-/ *adj* **1** not guarded or protected: *You shouldn't leave your bag unguarded in a pub like that.* **2** If you make an unguarded remark or say something in an unguarded moment, you tell someone something that you would usually keep secret, sometimes in a way that shows bad judgment: *In an unguarded moment, I said that I didn't trust Carlo.*

unhappy /ʌnˈhæp.i/ *adj* sad or not satisfied **unhappily** /ʌnˈhæp.ɪ.li/ *adv* **unhappiness** /ʌnˈhæp.ɪ.nəs/ *noun* [U]

unharmed /ʌnˈhɑːmd/ [US] /-ˈhɑːrmd/ *adj* [after v] not hurt or damaged: *Both children escaped unharmed from the burning building.*

unhealthy /ʌnˈhel.θi/ *adj* not HEALTHY, see at **health** **unhealthily** /ʌnˈhel.θɪ.li/ *adv*

unheard /ʌnˈhɜːd/ [US] /-ˈhɝːd/ *adj* **go unheard** to not be listened to or considered: *We complained but as usual our voices went unheard.*

U

unheard-of /ʌnˈhɜːd.ɒv/ ⓤ /-ˈhɜːd.ɑːv/ adj surprising or shocking because not known about or previously experienced: *It was not all that long ago that it was almost unheard-of for an unmarried couple to live together.*

unhelpful /ʌnˈhelp.fəl/ adj **1** not improving a difficult situation: *The instructions were badly written and unhelpful.* ○ *I don't need any more of your unhelpful advice!* **2** not wanting to help someone, in a way that seems unfriendly: *The shop assistant was rude and unhelpful.*

unhinged /ʌnˈhɪndʒd/ adj MAINLY HUMOROUS mentally ill: *I sometimes think that your mother is a little unhinged.* **unhinge** /ʌnˈhɪndʒ/ verb [T]

unholy CAUSING HARM /ʌnˈhəʊ.li/ ⓤ /-ˈhoʊ-/ adj describes a combination of things when it is very bad, harmful or unpleasant: *Religious fanatics have formed an unholy **alliance** with right wing groups.* ○ *There was a smell emanating from the fridge – an unholy **combination of** over-ripe cheese and unwrapped fish.*

unholy EXTREME /ʌnˈhəʊ.li/ ⓤ /-ˈhoʊ-/ adj [before n] INFORMAL extreme and unacceptable: *an unholy mess/row/ noise*

unhurt /ʌnˈhɜːt/ ⓤ /-ˈhɜːt/ adj not harmed

uni- ONE /juː.ni-/ prefix having or consisting of only one: *unilateral* ○ *unisex*

uni COLLEGE /ˈjuː.ni/ noun [C] AUS AND UK INFORMAL FOR **university**: *Which uni was she at?*

UNICEF /ˈjuː.nɪ.sef/ group noun [U] ABBREVIATION FOR United Nations Children's Fund: a department of the United Nations whose aim is improving children's health and education, particularly in poor countries

unicorn /ˈjuː.nɪ.kɔːn/ ⓤ /-kɔːrn/ noun [C] an imaginary white horse-like creature with a single horn growing from the front of its head

unicycle /ˈjuː.nɪˌsaɪ.kl̩/ noun [C] a vehicle like a bicycle with only one wheel

unidentified /ˌʌn.aɪˈden.tɪ.faɪd/ ⓤ /-t̬ə-/ adj whose name is not known or is being kept secret: *Police are investigating the death of an unidentified man whose body was found in Crackley Woods yesterday.* ○ *The airline is currently having merger talks with an unidentified rival.* ⊃See also **UFO**.

uniform CLOTHES /ˈjuː.nɪ.fɔːm/ ⓤ /-fɔːrm/ noun [C] **1** a particular set of clothes which has to be worn by the members of the same organization or group of people: *military/school uniform* ○ *a nurse's uniform* ○ *I love a man **in** uniform!* **2** a type of clothes that are connected with any group of people: *Photographs show him wearing the scruffy T-shirt and jeans that were the student's uniform of the time.* **uniformed** /ˈjuː.nɪ.fɔːmd/ ⓤ /-fɔːrmd/ adj: *uniformed officers/police/soldiers* ⊃Compare **mufti**.

uniform SAME /ˈjuː.nɪ.fɔːm/ ⓤ /-fɔːrm/ adj the same; not varying or different in any way: *As in so many offices that you see, the walls and furniture are a uniform grey.* ○ *Small businesses are demanding that they receive uniform treatment from the banks.* **uniformly** /ˈjuː.nɪ.fɔːm.li/ ⓤ /-fɔːrm-/ adv: *Critics were uniformly enthusiastic about the production.* **uniformity** /ˌjuː.nɪˈfɔː.mɪ.ti/ ⓤ /-ˈfɔːr.mə.t̬i/ noun [U]

unify /ˈjuː.nɪ.faɪ/ verb [T] to bring together; combine: *If the new leader does manage to unify his warring party it will be quite an achievement.* **unified** /ˈjuː.nɪ.faɪd/ adj **unification** /ˌjuː.nɪ.fɪˈkeɪ.ʃən/ noun [U] *the unification of East and West Germany*

unilateral /ˌjuː.nɪˈlæt.ər.əl/ ⓤ /-ˈlæt̬.ɚ-/ adj involving only one group or country: *The party leader has actually declared her support for unilateral nuclear **disarmament** (= giving up her country's nuclear weapons without first waiting for other countries to do the same).* ⊃Compare **bilateral**; **multilateral**. **unilaterally** /ˌjuː.nɪˈlæt.ər.əl.i/ ⓤ /-ˈlæt̬.ɚ-/ adv **unilateralism** /ˌjuː.nɪˈlæt.ər.əl.ɪ.zəm/ ⓤ /-ˈlæt̬.ɚ-/ noun [U] **unilateralist** /ˌjuː.nɪˈlæt.ər.əl.ɪst/ ⓤ /-ˈlæt̬.ɚ-/ noun [C]

unimaginable /ˌʌn.ɪˈmædʒ.ɪ.nə.bl̩/ adj describes something that is difficult to imagine because it is so bad, good, big, etc: *unimaginable pain/wealth* **unimaginably** /ˌʌn.ɪˈmædʒ.ɪ.nə.bli/ adv

unimaginative /ˌʌn.ɪˈmædʒ.ɪ.nə.tɪv/ ⓤ /-t̬ɪv/ adj not IMAGINATIVE, see at **imagine**

unimpeachable /ˌʌn.ɪmˈpiː.tʃə.bl̩/ adj FORMAL APPROVING describes a personal quality of honesty and morality that is so complete that it cannot be doubted or criticized: *Lord Fletcher, said the Bishop, was a man of unimpeachable integrity and character.*

unimportant /ˌʌn.ɪmˈpɔː.tənt/ ⓤ /-ˈpɔːr-/ adj not **important**: *Staffing is still a **relatively** unimportant issue compared to the other problems that we're encountering.*

unimpressed /ˌʌn.ɪmˈprest/ adj [after v] not IMPRESSED (= made to feel admiration or respect): *They looked the house over, but they seemed unimpressed (**by** it).* **unimpressive** /ˌʌn.ɪmˈpres.ɪv/ adj

uninformed /ˌʌn.ɪnˈfɔːmd/ ⓤ /-ˈfɔːrmd/ adj not INFORMED, see at **inform**: *Individuals and businesses appear woefully uninformed about this aspect of the information age.*

uninhabitable /ˌʌn.ɪnˈhæb.ɪ.tə.bl̩/ ⓤ /-t̬ə-/ adj not HABITABLE: *If there's no roof then the house is uninhabitable.*

uninhabited /ˌʌn.ɪnˈhæb.ɪ.tɪd/ ⓤ /-t̬ɪd/ adj describes a place with no people living in it: *an uninhabited island*

uninhibited /ˌʌn.ɪnˈhɪb.ɪ.tɪd/ ⓤ /-t̬ɪd/ adj APPROVING free and natural, without embarrassment or too much control: *The students we spoke to were surprisingly uninhibited in talking about sex.* ○ *We watched two hours of glorious, uninhibited football.* ○ *She gave a loud uninhibited laugh.*

the ˌuniˈnitiated plural noun MAINLY HUMOROUS people who are without knowledge or experience of a particular subject or activity: *Michelle, for the uninitiated, is the central female character in ITV's latest comedy series.* **uninitiated** /ˌʌn.ɪˈnɪʃ.i.eɪ.tɪd/ ⓤ /-t̬ɪd/ adj

uninjured /ʌnˈɪn.dʒəd/ ⓤ /-dʒɚd/ adj not injured: *The driver of the car was shocked but uninjured.*

uninspired /ˌʌn.ɪnˈspaɪəd/ ⓤ /-ˈspaɪrd/ adj not exciting or interesting: *an uninspired performance*

uninspiring /ˌʌn.ɪnˈspaɪə.rɪŋ/ ⓤ /-ˈspaɪr.ɪŋ/ adj not making you feel excited or interested: *The menu looked fairly uninspiring.*

uninstall /ˌʌn.ɪnˈstɔːl/ ⓤ /-ˈstɑːl/ verb [T] to remove a computer program from a computer: *The program ran so slowly, I had to uninstall it.* ○ *To uninstall this demo, double-click the Add/Remove icon.* **uninstall** /ˌʌn.ɪnˈstɔːl/ ⓤ /-ˈstɑːl/ adj [before n] describes a computer program which removes other programs from a computer: *There is still a lot of software that comes without an uninstall **program**.*

unintelligible /ˌʌn.ɪnˈtel.ɪ.dʒə.bl̩/ adj not INTELLIGIBLE: *He muttered something unintelligible.*

unintended /ˌʌn.ɪnˈten.dɪd/ adj not INTENDED (= planned): *The group argues that many of the proposed reforms will have unintended **consequences**.*

unintentional /ˌʌn.ɪnˈten.tʃən.əl/ adj not INTENTIONAL, see at **intend** **unintentionally** /ˌʌn.ɪnˈten.tʃən.əl.i/ adv

uninterested /ʌnˈɪn.tər.es.tɪd/ ⓤ /-t̬ɚ-/ adj not INTERESTED, see at **interest** INVOLVEMENT

uninteresting /ʌnˈɪn.tər.es.tɪŋ/ ⓤ /-t̬ɚ-/ adj not interesting

uninterrupted /ʌnˌɪn.tərˈʌp.tɪd/ ⓤ /-t̬əˈrʌp-/ adj (especially of a period of time) continuous: *The present government has had eight uninterrupted years in office.* **uninterruptedly** /ʌnˌɪn.tərˈʌp.tɪd.li/ ⓤ /-t̬əˈrʌp-/ adv

uninviting /ˌʌn.ɪnˈvaɪ.tɪŋ/ ⓤ /-t̬ɪŋ/ adj (especially of a place) not attractive

union JOINING /ˈjuː.ni.ən/ noun [S or U] the act or the state of being joined together: *Meanwhile the debate on European political and monetary union continues.* ○ *FORMAL OR OLD USE She believes that the union (= marriage) of man and woman in holy matrimony is for ever.*

union WORKERS /ˈjuː.ni.ən/ group noun [C] a **trade union**: *the electricians' union*

unionize, UK USUALLY **-ise** /ˈjuː.ni.ən.aɪz/ verb [T] to organize workers to become members of a union: *They're about to launch a campaign to unionize workers at all major discount supermarkets in the area.*

○ *unionized employees/labour/workers* unionization, *UK USUALLY* -isation /ˌjuː.ni.ᵊn.aɪˈzeɪ.ʃᵊn/ *noun* [U]

,Union 'Jack *noun* [C usually sing] (*ALSO* **Union flag**) the red, white and blue flag of the United Kingdom: *The Chinese anthem was played after the Union Jack was lowered in Hong Kong for the last time.*

unique /juˈniːk/ *adj* being the only existing one of its type or, more generally, unusual or special in some way: *Each person's genetic code is unique except in the case of identical twins.* ○ *I'd recognise your handwriting anywhere – it's unique.* ○ *Do not miss this unique opportunity to buy all six pans at half the recommended price.* ○ *As many as 100 species of fish, some unique **to** (= only found in) these waters, may have been affected by the pollution.* uniquely /juˈniː.kli/ *adv* uniqueness /juˈniːk.nəs/ *noun* [U]

COMMON LEARNER ERROR

unique

Unique describes something that is special or unusual because only one example of it exists. If something is not special or important but only one of it exists, you should use the adjective **only**.

~~It is the unique bus which goes to the airport.~~
It is the only bus which goes to the airport.

---

unisex /ˈjuː.ni.seks/ *adj* intended for use by both males and females: *unisex clothes* ○ *a unisex hairdresser's*

unison /ˈjuː.ni.sᵊn/ *noun* **in unison** together; at the same time: *Try to sing in unison if you can.*

unit MEASUREMENT /ˈjuː.nit/ *noun* [C] **1** a standard measure which is used to express amounts: *A centimetre is a unit of length.* ○ *The standard unit of currency in the US is the dollar.* **2** *UK* a standard measure of alcohol: *Experts say that women should not drink more than 14 units of alcohol a week.*

unit PEOPLE /ˈjuː.nit/ *group noun* [C] a group of people living or working together, especially for a particular purpose: *the traditional family unit* ○ *Dr Nussbaum is director of the Civil Liberties Research Unit at King's College, London.* ○ *Both soldiers spent two weeks in training before being allowed to rejoin their unit* (= the particular part of the army to which they belonged).

unit SEPARATE PART /ˈjuː.nit/ *noun* [C] **1** a single item or a separate part of something larger: *The first year of the course is divided into four units.* ○ *Each unit of the course book focuses on a different grammar point.* **2** a piece of furniture or equipment which is intended to be fitted as a part of a set of similar or matching pieces: *kitchen/shelf/sink units* **3** a small machine or part of a machine which has a particular purpose: *the central processing unit of a computer* ○ *a waste-disposal unit* **4** *SPECIALIZED* a single complete item of the type that a business sells **5** *US* a single apartment in a bigger building: *a multiple-unit dwelling* ○ *a public housing unit*

unit HOSPITAL DEPARTMENT /ˈjuː.nit/ *noun* [C] a department in a hospital for the treatment of people with similar illnesses or conditions: *She's in the burns/paediatric/psychiatric unit.*

unit SINGLE NUMBER /ˈjuː.nit/ *noun* [C] **1** any whole number less than ten: *Tens go in the left-hand column and units in the right.* **2** *SPECIALIZED* the number 1

Unitarian /ˌjuː.niˈteə.ri.ən/ ⑱ /-ˈter.i-/ *noun* (a member of) a division of the Christian church which does not believe in THE TRINITY Unitarian /ˌjuː.niˈteə.rian/ ⑱ /-ˈter.-i-/ *adj: a Unitarian church/minister*

unitary /ˈjuː.ni.tri/ ⑱ /-ter.i/ *adj UK* of a system of local government in the UK in which official power is given to one organization which deals with all matters in a local area instead of to several organizations which each deal with only a few matters: *Wales will be divided into 21 unitary **authorities** instead of eight counties and 37 districts.*

unite /juˈnaɪt/ /juː-/ *verb* [I or T] to join together as a group, or to make people join together as a group; to combine: *If the opposition groups manage to unite, they may command over 55% of the vote.* ○ *If ever a dance company could unite the differing worlds of rock and ballet, the Joffrey Ballet is it.* ⊃See also **reunite**.

united /juˈnaɪ.tɪd/ /juː-/ /-tɪd/ *adj* **1** joined together as a group: *Factions previously at war with one another are now united against the common enemy.* ○ *The whole village was united **in** their grief.* ○ *It has seen the first film festival to take place in a united Germany.* ⊃See also **the UK**. **2** If people are united, they all agree about something: *On that issue, we're united.* **3 a united front** an appearance of agreement: *The party's main failing has been their inability to **present** a united front to the people.*

unity /ˈjuː.ni.ti/ ⑱ /-nə.t̬i/ *noun* [U] the state of being joined together or in agreement: *European political and economic unity* ○ *a call for national unity*

the U,nited 'Kingdom *noun* [S] (*ABBREVIATION* **the UK**) the country that consists of England, Scotland, Wales and Northern Ireland

the U,nited 'Nations *group noun* [S] (*ABBREVIATION* **the UN**) an international organization that was established in 1945 and aims to solve world problems in a peaceful way

,unit 'trust *UK noun* [C] (*US* **mutual fund**) an organization which sells shares to the public and invests the money obtained in a range of different businesses

universal /ˌjuː.niˈvɜː.sᵊl/ ⑱ /-ˈvɜː-/ *adj* existing everywhere or involving everyone: *a universal truth* ○ *Food, like sex, is a subject of almost universal interest.* ○ *The new reforms have not met with universal approval within the government.* universally /ˌjuː.niˈvɜː.sᵊl.i/ ⑱ /-ˈvɜː-/ *adv* universality /ˌjuː.ni.vɜːˈsæl.ɪ.ti/ ⑱ /-vɜːˈsæl.ə.t̬i/ *noun* [U] *FORMAL*

,universal 'joint *noun* [C] a joint in a machine or engine which connects two parts and allows movement in all directions

universe /ˈjuː.ni.vɜːs/ ⑱ /-vɜːs/ *noun* [S] **1** everything that exists, especially all physical matter, including all the stars, planets, GALAXIES, etc. in space: *Is there intelligent life elsewhere in the universe?* **2** the world, or the world that you are familiar with: *The characters in his novels inhabit a bleak and hopeless universe.* ○ *His family is his whole universe* (= everything that is important to him).

university /ˌjuː.niˈvɜː.sɪ.ti/ ⑱ /-ˈvɜː.sə.t̬i/ *noun* [C] a college or collection of colleges at which people study for a degree: *Which university did you **go to**/were you **at** (= did you study at)?* ○ *She teaches at the University of Connecticut.* ○ *a university campus/course/lecturer*

unjust /ʌnˈdʒʌst/ *adj DISAPPROVING* not fair unjustly /ʌnˈdʒʌst.li/ *adv*

unjustifiable /ʌnˌdʒʌs.tɪˈfaɪ.ə.bl̩/ *adj* unacceptable and wrong because without any good or fair reason: *His behaviour was unjustifiable.* ○ *unjustifiable expense* unjustifiably /ʌnˈdʒʌs.tɪ.faɪ.ə.bli/ *adv DISAPPROVING*

unjustified /ʌnˈdʒʌs.tɪ.faɪd/ *adj DISAPPROVING* wrong and/or not deserved: *The defendant had supreme and, as it turned out, unjustified, confidence in his own judgment.*

unkempt /ʌnˈkempt/ *adj DISAPPROVING* untidy; not cared for: *an unkempt lawn*

unkind /ʌnˈkaɪnd/ *adj* slightly cruel: *an unkind remark* ○ *It was unkind of you to take his rattle away.* unkindly /ʌnˈkaɪnd.li/ *adv* unkindness /ʌnˈkaɪnd.nəs/ *noun* [U]

unknowing /ʌnˈnəʊ.ɪŋ/ ⑱ /-ˈnoʊ-/ *adj LITERARY* not aware of a particular situation or problem: *He took secret pictures of his unknowing victims.* unknowingly /ʌnˈnəʊ.ɪŋ.li/ ⑱ /-ˈnoʊ-/ *adv*

unknown /ʌnˈnəʊn/ ⑱ /-ˈnoʊn/ *adj* not known or familiar: *The exact number of people carrying the virus is unknown.* ○ *As recently as six months ago her name was almost unknown in Britain.* ○ *Unknown **to** me, she'd organized a party for my birthday.*

unknown /ʌnˈnəʊn/ ⑱ /-ˈnoʊn/ *noun* **1** [S] what is not familiar or known: *Racism is in some ways just a fear of the unknown.* **2** [C] a person, especially a performer or sports player, who is not famous: *For her latest film she deliberately chose a cast of unknowns.* **3** [C] *MAINLY US* something that cannot be guessed at or calculated because so little is known about it: *It's the big unknowns that make insurance companies uneasy.*

U

ˌunknown ˈquantity *noun* [C usually sing] a person or a thing whose abilities, powers or effects are not yet known: *The third candidate for the party leadership is a relatively unknown quantity.*

unlawful /ʌnˈlɔː.fəl/ [US] /-ˈlɑː-/ *adj* not allowed by law: *unlawful possession of guns* **unlawfully** /ʌnˈlɔː.fəl.i/ [US] /-ˈlɑː-/ *adv*

unleaded /ʌnˈled.ɪd/ *adj* describes a type of petrol or other substance that does not contain lead: *Does your car use unleaded petrol?*
unleaded /ʌnˈled.ɪd/ *noun* [U] unleaded petrol: *They cut 2p per litre off the price of unleaded.*

unlearn /ʌnˈlɜːn/ [US] /-ˈlɝːn/ *verb* [T] to make an effort to forget your usual way of doing something so that you can learn a new and sometimes better way: *I've had to unlearn the way I played guitar since I started taking formal lessons.*

unleash /ʌnˈliːʃ/ *verb* [T] to release suddenly a strong, uncontrollable and usually destructive force: *At worst, nuclear war could be unleashed.* ○ *Rachel's arrival on the scene had unleashed passions in him that he could scarcely control.*

unleavened /ʌnˈlev.ənd/ *adj* describes bread or similar food that is made without yeast and therefore flat

unless /ənˈles/ *conjunction* except if: *You can't get a job unless you've got experience* (= you can only get a job if you have experience). ○ *Unless you call me to say you're not coming, I'll see you at the theatre* (= I will see you there if you do not call to say you are not coming).

unlicensed /ʌnˈlaɪ.səntst/ *adj* not having a LICENCE (= a document giving legal permission) to do something, for example to sell alcohol, or use or own something, for example a gun: *an unlicensed restaurant*

unlike [DIFFERENT FROM] /ʌnˈlaɪk/ *prep* different from: *Dan's actually quite nice, unlike his father.* ○ *Unlike you, I'm not a great dancer.*

unlike [NOT TYPICAL] /ʌnˈlaɪk/ *prep* not typical or characteristic of: *It's unlike you to be quiet – is something wrong?*

unlikely /ʌnˈlaɪ.kli/ *adj* not LIKELY: [+ (*that*)] ***It's pretty unlikely (that) they'll turn up now*** *– it's nearly ten o'clock.* ○ *He seems an unlikely-looking policeman* (= He is not what I expect a policeman to look like).

unlimited /ʌnˈlɪm.ɪ.tɪd/ [US] /-t̬ɪd/ *adj* not limited; having a greatest possible amount, number or level: *Passes are available for one month's unlimited travel within Europe.* ○ *Demand for health care appears virtually unlimited.*

unlisted /ʌnˈlɪs.tɪd/ *adj* **1** not included in a list of STOCK EXCHANGE company prices: *unlisted securities/shares* **2** *US* not included in the public list of telephone numbers belonging to the customers of a telephone company: *Doctors most often have unlisted home phone numbers to protect their privacy.*

unload [REMOVE] /ʌnˈləʊd/ [US] /-ˈloʊd/ *verb* [I or T] to remove the contents of something, especially a load of goods from a vehicle, the bullets from a gun or the film from a camera: *We watched a ship unloading (sacks of flour).*

unload [TELL] /ʌnˈləʊd/ [US] /-ˈloʊd/ *verb* **1** [I or T] *INFORMAL* to tell someone about your worries, problems, etc: *I'm afraid I've been unloading my worries* ***on*** *poor Ann here.* **2** [I] *US INFORMAL* to express strong emotions such as anger freely to another person

unlock /ʌnˈlɒk/ [US] /-ˈlɑːk/ *verb* [T] **1** to open something, especially a door which is LOCKED (= fastened with a lock), using a key or an electronic device: *I keep worrying that I've left the garage door unlocked.* **2 unlock the mystery/secret of *sth*** to discover important new facts about something: *A chemical has been discovered that may be the key to unlocking the mysteries of Parkinson's disease.* **3 unlock the imagination** to make the imagination more active, producing interesting ideas and images: *One of poetry's functions is to somehow unlock the imagination.*

unlooked-for /ʌnˈlʊkt.fɔːr/ [US] /-fɔːr/ *adj* unexpected: *unlooked-for joy*

unloved /ʌnˈlʌvd/ *adj FORMAL* not loved: *He found himself alone and unloved.*
unlovable /ʌnˈlʌv.ə.bl̩/ *adj* not easy to love

unlucky /ʌnˈlʌk.i/ *adj* [often + *to* infinitive] not LUCKY: *The couple were unlucky* ***enough to*** *be in the hotel when the terrorist group struck.* **unluckily** /ʌnˈlʌk.ɪ.li/ *adv*

unmade /ʌnˈmeɪd/ *adj* If a bed is unmade, its sheets and covers are still untidy from having been slept in.

unmanageable /ʌnˈmæn.ɪ.dʒə.bl̩/ *adj* impossible to deal with or manage: *74 per cent of teachers found the paperwork was unmanageable.* ○ *Within weeks, a difficult boy had become unmanageable.*

unmanned /ʌnˈmænd/ *adj* describes a spacecraft, or a place where military guards work, that has no people present to operate or be in charge of it: *an unmanned mission to the planet Mars*

unmarked /ʌnˈmɑːkt/ [US] /-ˈmɑːrkt/ *adj* having no signs or marks showing what something is: *an unmarked police car* ○ *She died penniless and was buried in an unmarked grave.*

unmarried /ʌnˈmær.ɪd/ [US] /-ˈmer-/ *adj* not MARRIED, see at **marry**: *an unmarried mother* ○ *Their youngest son is still unmarried.*

unmask /ʌnˈmɑːsk/ [US] /-ˈmæsk/ *verb* [T] to show the bad, and previously hidden, truth about someone or something: *The conspirators were unmasked and summarily shot.*

unmatched /ʌnˈmætʃt/ *adj FORMAL* having no equal; better than any other of the same type: *For years they have enjoyed a standard of living unmatched* ***by*** *any other country in Europe.*

unmentionable /ʌnˈmen.tʃən.ə.bl̩/ *adj* shocking and embarrassing and therefore forbidden or disapproved of as a subject of conversation: *What's the matter with him – or is it some unmentionable disease that he doesn't like people to know about?*

unmentionables /ʌnˈmen.tʃən.ə.bl̩z/ *plural noun OLD-FASHIONED OR HUMOROUS* underwear

unmindful /ʌnˈmaɪnd.fəl/ *adj FORMAL* **unmindful of *sth*** not remembering, noticing or being careful about something

unmissable /ʌnˈmɪs.ə.bl̩/ *adj INFORMAL* An unmissable film or play, etc. is so good that it must be seen: *It's fairly entertaining as films go, but I wouldn't describe it as unmissable.*

unmistakable /ˌʌn.mɪˈsteɪ.kə.bl̩/ *adj* not likely to be confused with something else: *There was an unmistakable smell of incense in the air.* **unmistakably** /ˌʌn.mɪˈsteɪ.kə.bli/ *adv*

unmitigated /ʌnˈmɪt.ɪ.geɪ.tɪd/ [US] /-ˈmɪt̬.ə.geɪ.t̬ɪd/ *adj* [usually before n] complete, often describing something bad or unsuccessful that has no good or positive points: *The whole venture has been an unmitigated* ***disaster****.*

unmoved /ʌnˈmuːvd/ *adj* [after v] not feeling any emotion: *Both men appeared unmoved as the judge read out their sentence.*

unnamed /ʌnˈneɪmd/ *adj* An unnamed person or thing is talked about, but their name is not known or mentioned: *The article quoted an unnamed source from the White House.*

unnatural /ʌnˈnætʃ.ər.əl/ [US] /-ɚ-/ *adj* not NATURAL, see at **nature** LIFE **unnaturally** /ʌnˈnætʃ.ər.əl.i/ [US] /-ɚ-/ *adv*

unnecessary /ʌnˈnes.ə.ser.i/ *adj* **1** not needed or wanted, or more than is needed or wanted: *I found a lot of the violence in the film totally unnecessary.* ○ *The idea is to kill the animal as quickly as possible without causing unnecessary suffering.* **2** describes an offensive remark or action that could have been avoided: *He just humiliated her in front of everyone – it was so unnecessary.* **unnecessarily** /ʌnˈnes.ə.ser.ɪ.li/ *adv*: *Of course we don't want to alarm people unnecessarily, but they should be alerted to potential dangers.*

unnerve /ʌnˈnɜːv/ [US] /-ˈnɝːv/ *verb* [T] to make someone feel less confident and slightly frightened: *I think it unnerved me to be interviewed by so many people.* **unnerving** /ʌnˈnɜː.vɪŋ/ [US] /-ˈnɝː-/ *adj*: *Meeting a twin brother I didn't know I had was an unnerving experience.* **unnervingly** /ʌnˈnɜː.vɪŋ.li/ [US] /-ˈnɝː-/ *adv*

unnoticed /ʌnˈnəʊ.tɪst/ [US] /-ˈnoʊ.t̬ɪst/ *adj, adv* without being seen or noticed: *We managed to slip away un-*

U

noticed. ○ *His rude comments are not likely to* **go** *unnoticed.*

unobtrusive /ˌʌn.əbˈtruː.sɪv/ *adj APPROVING* not noticeable; seeming to fit in well with the background: *Make-up this season is unobtrusive and natural-looking.* **unobtrusively** /ˌʌn.əbˈtruː.sɪv.li/ *adv* **unobtrusiveness** /ˌʌn.əbˈtruː.sɪv.nəs/ *noun* [U]

unofficial /ˌʌn.əˈfɪʃ.ʲl/ *adj* not OFFICIAL, see at **office** *RESPONSIBILITY: unofficial estimates/figures/reports* **unofficially** /ˌʌn.əˈfɪʃ.ʲl.i/ *adv*

unoriginal /ˌʌn.əˈrɪdʒ.ɪ.nəl/ *adj* the same as a lot of other things and therefore not interesting or special

unorthodox /ʌnˈɔː.θə.dɒks/ ⓤ /-ˈɔːr.θə.dɑːks/ *adj* different from what is usual or expected in behaviour, ideas, methods, etc: *Steiner was recognized as an original if unorthodox thinker.*

unpack REMOVE /ʌnˈpæk/ *verb* [I or T] to remove things from a SUITCASE, bag or box: *I haven't even had time to unpack (my bag/clothes).*

unpack EXPLAIN /ʌnˈpæk/ *verb* [T] to explain or to make a meaning clearer: *He read the agreed statement to the group and then began to unpack it for them.*

unpaid /ʌnˈpeɪd/ *adj* **1** describes a debt, tax, etc. that has not been paid: *$50 000 in unpaid taxes* **2** describes work that you do without getting any money for it: *unpaid work/employment*

unpalatable /ʌnˈpæl.ə.tə.bl̩/ ⓤ /-t̬ə-/ *adj FORMAL* **1** describes a fact or idea that is unpleasant or shocking and therefore difficult to accept: *the unpalatable truth/facts about the war* **2** describes food that is unpleasant to taste or eat

unparalleled /ʌnˈpær.ʲl.eld/ ⓤ /-ˈper-/ *adj FORMAL* having no equal; better or greater than any other: *They enjoyed success on a scale unparalleled by any previous pop group.*

unpick /ʌnˈpɪk/ *verb* [T] **1** to cut or remove the stitches from a line of sewing **2** If you unpick a difficult subject, you separate and examine its different parts carefully: *As long as two years ago, Mandelson tried to unpick the reasons for the disaster.* **3** to gradually destroy or remove the good effects of what someone has done or created: *The former leader now has to watch his successor unpicking much of what he strived so hard to achieve.*

unplaced /ʌnˈpleɪst/ *adj* in horse racing, not one of the first three horses to finish a race: *The sole British runner, White Knight, was unplaced.*

unplanned /ʌnˈplænd/ *adj* not planned or expected: *an unplanned pregnancy*

unplayable SPORT /ʌnˈpleɪ.ə.bl̩/ *adj* **1** describes a ball that is hit or thrown so hard or skilfully that it is impossible to hit **2** describes an area of ground usually used for sports, that cannot be played on, especially because of bad weather conditions

unplayable MUSIC /ʌnˈpleɪ.ə.bl̩/ *adj* describes a piece of music that is too difficult to perform

unpleasant /ʌnˈplez.ʲnt/ *adj* **1** not enjoyable or PLEASANT: *an unpleasant surprise* ○ *the unpleasant truth* **2** [usually after v] rude and angry: *The waiter got quite unpleasant with us.* **unpleasantly** /ʌnˈplez.ʲnt.li/ *adv* **unpleasantness** /ʌnˈplez.ʲnt.nəs/ *noun* [C or U]

unplugged /ʌnˈplʌgd/ *adj, adv* describes musicians performing without electric instruments and without AMPLIFICATION (= electronic equipment that makes sound louder)

unpopular /ʌnˈpɒp.jʊ.lə/ ⓤ /-ˈpɑː.pjə.lɚ/ *adj* not liked by many people: *Night flights from the airport are deeply unpopular.* ○ *The government is becoming increasingly unpopular.* **unpopularity** /ˌʌn.pɒp.jʊˈlær.ɪ.ti/ ⓤ /-ˈpɑː.pjʊˈler.ə.t̬i/ *noun* [U]

unprecedented /ʌnˈpres.ɪ.den.tɪd/ ⓤ /-t̬ɪd/ *adj* never having happened or existed in the past: *This century has witnessed environmental destruction* **on an** *unprecedented* **scale.**

unpredictable /ˌʌn.prɪˈdɪk.tə.bl̩/ *adj* tending to change suddenly and without reason and therefore not able to be PREDICTED (= judged in advance) or depended on: *The weather there can be a bit unpredictable – one minute it's*

blue skies and the next minute it's pouring down. ○ *The hours in this job are very unpredictable – you sometimes have to work late at very short notice.* **unpredictably** /ˌʌn.prɪˈdɪk.tə.bli/ *adv* **unpredictability** /ˌʌn.prɪˌdɪk.təˈbɪl.ɪ.ti/ ⓤ /-ə.t̬i/ *noun* [U]

unprepared /ˌʌn.prɪˈpeəd/ ⓤ /-ˈperd/ *adj* not prepared; not ready: *He was completely/totally/wholly unprepared for what he saw.* ○ *The extreme cold weather* **caught** *them unprepared.*

unpretentious /ˌʌn.prɪˈten.ʃəs/ *adj APPROVING* not PRETENTIOUS: *The food is delicious and unpretentious.*

unprincipled /ʌnˈprɪnt.sɪ.pl̩d/ *adj* having or showing no moral rules or standards of good behaviour

unprintable /ʌnˈprɪn.tə.bl̩/ ⓤ /-t̬ə-/ *adj* containing swear words or other offensive language and therefore not acceptable in printed form, for example in a newspaper: *The taxi driver entertained us with unprintable observations/remarks/views about government ministers all the way to the airport.*

unprofessional /ˌʌn.prəˈfeʃ.ʲn.ʲl/ *adj* not showing the standard of behaviour or skills that are expected of a person in a skilled job: *Doctor Rivers was charged with gross negligence, unprofessional conduct and improper use of dangerous drugs.* **unprofessionally** /ˌʌn.prəˈfeʃ.ʲn.ʲl.i/ *adv*

unprofitable /ʌnˈprɒf.ɪ.tə.bl̩/ ⓤ /-ˈprɑː.fɪ.t̬ə-/ *adj* not making a profit: *Rural railway lines risk being axed because they are unprofitable.*

unpromising /ʌnˈprɒm.ɪ.sɪŋ/ ⓤ /-ˈprɑː.mɪ-/ *adj* not PROMISING, see at **promise**: *It was a rather unpromising start to the holiday.*

unprompted /ʌnˈprɒmp.tɪd/ ⓤ /-ˈprɑːmp-/ *adj* without being told to say or do something: *Jim was remarkably charming this evening – he even said, unprompted, how nice Margot looked in her dress.*

unpronounceable /ˌʌn.prəˈnaʊnt.sə.bl̩/ *adj* difficult to say or (of something written) difficult to know how to say: *She's got some unpronounceable name which seems to be all consonants.*

unprotected /ˌʌn.prəˈtek.tɪd/ *adj* **1** not protected and therefore able to be harmed or damaged: *Water and other liquids can stained unprotected wood surfaces.* ○ *Although some marine mammals are protected by environmental laws, many remain unprotected.* ○ *The lack of a shell leaves the larvae unprotected against predators.* **2 unprotected sex** sexual activity without a condom

unprovoked /ˌʌn.prəˈvəʊkt/ ⓤ /-ˈvoʊkt/ *adj* describes an unpleasant action or remark when it has not been caused by anything and is therefore unfair: *an unprovoked* **attack** *on her character*

unpublished /ʌnˈpʌb.lɪʃt/ *adj* written but not yet published: *After his death, his daughter found an unpublished manuscript among his papers.* ○ *a collection of unpublished poems*

unpunished /ʌnˈpʌn.ɪʃt/ *adj* [after v] not punished: *If a referee allows a foul like that to* **go** *unpunished he's asking for trouble.*

unputdownable /ˌʌn.pʊtˈdaʊ.nə.bl̩/ *adj INFORMAL* describes a book that is so exciting that you do not want to stop reading it: *"Was it a good read?" "Oh, totally unputdownable – I finished it in two days."*

unqualified PERSON /ʌnˈkwɒl.ɪ.faɪd/ ⓤ /-ˈkwɑː.lɪ-/ *adj* An unqualified person lacks the qualifications needed for a particular job.

unqualified COMPLETE /ʌnˈkwɒl.ɪ.faɪd/ ⓤ /ˈkwɑː.lɪ-/ *adj* not limited in any way; to the largest degree possible: *We achieved a lot but I wouldn't say that the project has been an unqualified* **success.** ○ *The proposal has the unqualified* **support** *of the entire committee.*

unquestionable /ʌnˈkwes.tʃə.nə.bl̩/ *adj* obvious and impossible to doubt ⊃Compare **questionable** at **question** ASKING. **unquestionably** /ʌnˈkwes.tʃə.nə.bli/ *adv*

unquestioned /ʌnˈkwes.tʃənd/ *adj* accepted as true or right by everyone, or trusted and respected by everyone: *He's the unquestioned leader in his field (= no one would say that he is not the leader).*

unquestioning /ʌnˈkwes.tʃə.nɪŋ/ *adj MAINLY DISAPPROVING* Unquestioning obedience or acceptance is total, and given without consideration, opposition or doubt: *Like all tyrannical leaders, he demanded unquestioning obedience from his followers.* **unquestioningly** /ʌnˈkwes.tʃə.nɪŋ.li/ *adv*

unquiet /ʌnˈkwaɪət/ *adj* LITERARY troubled and anxious; not peaceful or calm: *One can only hope that his unquiet spirit found some peace in the grave.*

unquote /ʌnˈkwəʊt/ [US] /-ˈkwoʊt/ ➲See **quote, unquote**, at **quote** SAY.

unravel /ʌnˈræv.əl/ *verb* **-ll-** or US USUALLY **-l-** **1** [I or T] If a piece of woollen or woven cloth, a knot, or a mass of thread unravels, it separates into a single thread, and if you unravel it, you separate it into a single thread: *You'd better mend that hole before the whole sweater starts to unravel.* ○ *I had to unravel one of the sleeves because I realised I'd knitted it too small.* **2** [I or T] If you unravel a mysterious, unknown or complicated subject, you make it known or understood, and if it unravels, it become known or understood: *We've got a long way to go before we unravel the secrets of genetics.* **3** [I; T usually passive] If a process or achievement that was slow and complicated unravels or is unravelled, it is destroyed: *As talks between the leaders broke down, several months of careful diplomacy were unravelled.*

unreadable /ʌnˈriː.də.bl̩/ *adj* **1** too boring, complicated or badly written to be worth reading: *I found James Joyce's 'Ulysses' totally unreadable.* **2 illegible** (= impossible to read because unclear or untidy): *completely unreadable handwriting*

unreal [IMAGINARY] /ʌnˈrɪəl/ [US] /-ˈriːl/ *adj* as if imagined; strange and dream-like: *The whole bizarre evening had an unreal quality to it.* **unreality** /ˌʌn.riˈæl.ɪ.ti/ [US] /-ə.t̬i/ *noun* [U] *There was an air of unreality about the visit, as if I'd stepped into another world for two weeks.*

unreal [SURPRISING] /ʌnˈrɪəl/ [US] /-ˈriːl/ *adj* SLANG extremely or surprisingly good: *He gave you £5000? Man, that's unreal!*

unrealistic /ˌʌn.rɪəˈlɪs.tɪk/ [US] /-riː.ə-/ *adj* having a wrong idea of what is likely to happen or of what you can really do; not based on facts: *I think these sales forecasts are unrealistic, considering how slow sales are at present.* ○ [+ to infinitive] ***It's** unrealistic **to** expect an answer before next week.* **unrealistically** /ʌn.rɪəˈlɪs.tɪ.kli/ [US] /ʌn.riː.ə-/ *adv*

unreasonable /ʌnˈriː.zən.ə.bl̩/ *adj* not fair or acceptable: *unreasonable demands* ○ [+ to infinitive] ***It** seems unreasonable **to** expect one person to do both jobs.* **unreasonably** /ʌnˈriː.zən.ə.bli/ *adv*

unreasoning /ʌnˈriː.zən.ɪŋ/ *adj* FORMAL describes feelings or beliefs that are not based on reason or judgment: *unreasoning hatred*

unreconstructed /ˌʌn.riː.kənˈstrʌk.tɪd/ *adj* OFTEN HUMOROUS having opinions or behaving in a way not considered to be modern or politically acceptable in modern times: *She describes herself as an unreconstructed feminist.*

unrefined /ˌʌn.rɪˈfaɪnd/ *adj* not REFINED, see at **refine**

unregulated /ʌnˈreg.jʊ.leɪ.tɪd/ [US] /-t̬ɪd/ *adj* describes a type of business or activity which is not controlled and directed by fixed rules or laws: *Parents have the right to expect information to guide them through a growing, yet unregulated **market (place)**.*

unrelated /ˌʌn.rɪˈleɪ.tɪd/ [US] /-t̬ɪd/ *adj* having no connection: *Police said his death was unrelated **to** the attack.*

unrelenting /ˌʌn.rɪˈlen.tɪŋ/ [US] /-t̬ɪŋ/ *adj* FORMAL extremely determined; never weakening in effort or admitting defeat: *She will be remembered as an unrelenting opponent of racial discrimination.* **unrelentingly** /ˌʌn.rɪˈlen.tɪŋ.li/ [US] /-t̬ɪŋ-/ *adv*

unreliable /ˌʌn.rɪˈlaɪə.bl̩/ *adj* not RELIABLE

unrelieved /ˌʌn.rɪˈliːvd/ *adj* [usually before n] FORMAL When a bad situation or emotion is unrelieved, it is continuous and never improves, not even for a short period: *She held the family together through years of unrelieved poverty.* **unrelievedly** /ˌʌn.rɪˈliː.vɪd.li/ *adv*

unremarkable /ˌʌn.rɪˈmɑː.kə.bl̩/ [US] /-ˈmɑːr-/ *adj* ordinary and not interesting: *an unremarkable town*

unremitting /ˌʌn.rɪˈmɪt.ɪŋ/ [US] /-ˈmɪt̬-/ *adj* FORMAL never stopping, weakening in effort or failing: *Our thanks are due to Bob Lawrence whose unremitting labours have ensured the success of the whole scheme.* **unremittingly** /ˌʌn.rɪˈmɪt.ɪŋ.li/ [US] /-ˈmɪt̬-/ *adv*

unrepeatable [EVENTS] /ˌʌn.rɪˈpiː.tə.bl̩/ [US] /-t̬ə-/ *adj* [usually before n] describes an event, price, etc. that cannot happen again: *an unrepeatable offer/opportunity* ○ *an unrepeatable experience*

unrepeatable [WORDS] /ˌʌn.rɪˈpiː.tə.bl̩/ [US] /-t̬ə-/ *adj* describes a word or remark used by another person which was too rude or too difficult for you to say what it was: *an unrepeatable joke/name*

unrepentant /ˌʌn.rɪˈpen.tənt/ *adj* not REPENTANT, see at **repent**

unrepresentative /ˌʌn.rep.rɪˈzen.tə.tɪv/ [US] /-t̬ə.t̬ɪv/ *adj* not REPRESENTATIVE, see at **represent** ACT FOR, **represent** DESCRIBE

unrequited /ˌʌn.rɪˈkwaɪ.tɪd/ [US] /-t̬ɪd/ *adj* FORMAL OR HUMOROUS If love that you feel for someone is unrequited, it is not felt in the same way by the other person: *It's just another poem on the pain of unrequited **love**.*

unreserved /ˌʌn.rɪˈzɜːvd/ [US] /-ˈzɝːvd/ *adj* FORMAL without any doubts or feeling uncertain; total: *He was a good strong leader, she said, who deserved his party's unreserved support.* **unreservedly** /ˌʌn.rɪˈzɜː.vɪd.li/ [US] /-ˈzɝː-/ *adv*: *The paper's editor has **apologized** unreservedly to the senator.*

unresolved /ˌʌn.rɪˈzɒlvd/ [US] /-ˈzɑːlvd/ *adj* FORMAL If a problem or difficulty is unresolved, it is not solved or ended: *The question of contracts **remains** unresolved.*

unresponsive /ˌʌn.rɪˈspɒnt.sɪv/ [US] /-ˈspɑːnt-/ *adj* not RESPONSIVE, see at **respond**

unrest /ʌnˈrest/ *noun* [U] disagreements or fighting between different groups of people: *It is feared that the civil unrest we are now witnessing in this country could lead to full-scale civil war.*

unrestrained /ˌʌn.rɪˈstreɪnd/ *adj* not limited or controlled: *unrestrained joy/anger/criticism*

unrivalled, US USUALLY **unrivaled** /ʌnˈraɪ.vəld/ *adj* having no equal; better than any other of the same type: *The museum boasts an unrivalled collection of French porcelain.*

unroll /ʌnˈrəʊl/ [US] /-ˈroʊl/ *verb* [I or T] to open and become flat from a rolled position, or to cause something to do this: *She unrolled the most beautiful carpet.*

unruffled /ʌnˈrʌf.l̩d/ *adj* calm; not nervous or worried, usually despite a difficult situation: *For a man in imminent danger of losing his job, he appeared quite unruffled.*

unruly /ʌnˈruː.li/ *adj* **1** Unruly people are difficult to control and tend not to obey rules: *an unruly class of adolescents* **2** Unruly hair is difficult to keep tidy, tending to stick up or out: *an unruly mop of black hair* **unruliness** /ʌnˈruː.lɪ.nəs/ *noun* [U]

unsaddle /ʌnˈsæd.l̩/ *verb* [T] to take the saddle off a horse or to cause someone riding a horse to fall off

unsafe [IN DANGER] /ʌnˈseɪf/ *adj* not safe

unsafe [LAW] /ʌnˈseɪf/ *adj* UK LEGAL describes a decision that someone is guilty which can be APPEALED against (= considered again) in court: *an unsafe conviction/verdict*

unsaid /ʌnˈsed/ *adj* [after v] not said, although thought of or felt: *I know she's put on weight, Michael, but some things are **better left** unsaid!* ➲See also **unspoken**.

unsanitary /ˌʌnˈsæn.ɪ.tri/ [US] /-ter.i/ *adj* (UK ALSO **insanitary**) dirty or unhealthy and therefore likely to cause disease: *unsanitary toilets* ○ *unsanitary living conditions*

unsatisfactory /ʌnˌsæt.ɪsˈfæk.tər.i/ [US] /-ˌsæt̬.ɪsˈfæk.tɚ-/ *adj* not satisfactory

unsatisfying /ʌnˈsæt.ɪs.faɪ.ɪŋ/ [US] /-ˈsæt̬-/ *adj* not satisfying

unsavoury UK, US **unsavory** /ʌnˈseɪ.vər.i/ [US] /-vɚ-/ *adj* unpleasant, or morally offensive: *unsavoury sexual practices* ○ *an unsavoury reputation*

unscathed /ʌnˈskeɪðd/ *adj* [after v] without injuries or damage being caused: *Her husband died in the accident but she, amazingly, escaped unscathed.*

U

unscientific /ˌʌn.saɪən'tɪf.ɪk/ adj DISAPPROVING not obeying scientific methods or principles: *an unscientific account/claim/method*

unscramble /ʌn'skræm.bl̩/ verb [T] to discover the meaning of information given in a secret or complicated way; to **decode**: *You need a decoding device to unscramble some of the signals sent out by satellite and cable TV.*

unscrew LID /ʌn'skruː/ verb [T] to take the lid or top off something by twisting it round: *I can't unscrew the top of this jar – it's really tight.*

unscrew SCREWS /ʌn'skruː/ verb [T] to remove something by taking the screws out of it

unscripted /ʌn'skrɪp.tɪd/ adj not SCRIPTED, see at **script** TEXT

unscrupulous /ʌn'skruː.pjʊ.ləs/ adj DISAPPROVING behaving in a way that is dishonest or unfair in order to get what you want: *an unscrupulous financial adviser*

unseasonable /ʌn'siː.zˀn.ə.bl̩/ adj (ALSO **unseasonal**) FORMAL describes weather that is not usual or suitable for the time of year: *When you're used to snow in January, warm sunny weather feels unseasonable.* **unseasonably** /ʌn'siː.zˀn.ə.bli/ adv (ALSO **unseasonally**) *unseasonably warm weather*

unseat POLITICIAN /ʌn'siːt/ verb [T] to remove someone from power, especially as a result of an election: *The opposition candidate failed by only 39 votes to unseat the cabinet minister.*

unseat RIDER /ʌn'siːt/ verb [T] If a horse unseats its rider, it throws them from its back.

unseeded /ʌn'siː.dɪd/ adj not SEEDED in a tennis competition

unseeing /ʌn'siː.ɪŋ/ adj LITERARY (especially of eyes) not seeing or noticing anything, although able to see: *Bored out of its mind, the monkey stares out of the cage with unseeing eyes.*

unseemly /ʌn'siːm.li/ adj FORMAL not SEEMLY (= socially suitable and polite) **unseemliness** /ʌn'siːm.lɪ.nəs/ noun [U]

unseen /ʌn'siːn/ adj not seen or not able to be seen: *She found the side-door open and slipped into the house unseen.* ○ *Unseen birds sang in the trees above us.*

unselfish /ʌn'sel.fɪʃ/ adj not SELFISH, see at **self** PERSONAL ADVANTAGE **unselfishly** /ʌn'sel.fɪʃ.li/ adv **unselfishness** /ʌn'sel.fɪʃ.nəs/ noun [U]

unsettled CHANGEABLE /ʌn'set.l̩d/ ⓤ /-'set̬-/ adj tending to change suddenly; not calm or having a regular pattern: *a period of unsettled weather* ○ *an unsettled political climate*
unsettling /ʌn'set.l̩ɪŋ/ ⓤ /-'set̬-/ adj causing change ⊃See also **unsettling** at **unsettled** ANXIOUS. **unsettle** /ʌn'set.l̩/ ⓤ /-'set̬-/ verb [T] *The airline's decision to cut air fares is likely to unsettle the market.*

unsettled ANXIOUS /ʌn'set.l̩d/ ⓤ /-'set̬-/ adj anxious and worried; unable to relax: *Children tend to get unsettled if you keep on changing their routine.*
unsettling /ʌn'set.l̩ɪŋ/ ⓤ /-'set̬-/ adj causing anxiety: *One of the film's many unsettling images is of a child playing with her father's gun.* **unsettle** /ʌn'set.l̩/ ⓤ /-'set̬-/ verb [T] *Even the most experienced of West Indian batsmen was unsettled by the sheer speed of this bowler.*

unshakeable, **unshakable** /ʌn'ʃeɪ.kə.bl̩/ adj If someone's trust or belief is unshakeable, it is firm and cannot be weakened or destroyed: *She was blessed with an unshakeable belief in her own abilities.*

unshaven /ʌn'ʃeɪ.vˀn/ adj not having had the hair removed: *a unshaven chin/man*

unsightly /ʌn'saɪt.li/ adj SLIGHTLY FORMAL unattractive; ugly: *He had undone the buttons of his shirt, exposing an unsightly expanse of white flesh.*

unskilled /ʌn'skɪld/ adj Unskilled people have no particular work skills, and unskilled work does not need any particular skills: *unskilled workers* ○ *unskilled labour/work/jobs*

unsliced /ʌn'slaɪst/ adj not SLICED, see at **slice** PIECE: *unsliced bread*

unsmiling /ʌn'smaɪ.lɪŋ/ adj not smiling: *Cabinet members were tight-lipped and unsmiling as they* emerged from Downing Street.

unsociable /ʌn'səʊ.ʃə.bl̩/ ⓤ /-'soʊ-/ adj not liking to meet people or to spend time with them

unsocial /ʌn'səʊ.ʃˀl/ ⓤ /-'soʊ-/ adj UK happening during the days of the week or hours of the day when most people do not have to work: *I don't want to work unsocial hours.*

unsold /ʌn'səʊld/ ⓤ /-'soʊld/ adj not sold: *stocks of unsold goods*

unsolicited /ˌʌn.sə'lɪs.ɪ.tɪd/ ⓤ /-t̬ɪd/ adj not requested: *unsolicited advice*

unsolved /ˌʌn'zɒlvd/ ⓤ /-'zuːlvd/ adj that has not been solved: *an unsolved mystery*

unsophisticated /ˌʌn.sə'fɪs.tɪ.keɪ.tɪd/ ⓤ /-t̬ɪd/ adj not SOPHISTICATED

unsound NOT ACCEPTABLE /ʌn'saʊnd/ adj If a person's activities or judgement are unsound, they are not good enough, acceptable or able to be trusted: *unsound accounting practices* ○ *unsound police evidence*

unsound WEAK /ʌn'saʊnd/ adj If a building or other structure is unsound, it is in bad condition and likely to fall down or fail: *The bridge is one of several said to be structurally unsound.*

unsparing HIDING NOTHING /ʌn'speə.rɪŋ/ ⓤ /-'sper.ɪŋ/ adj showing no kindness and no desire to hide the unpleasant truth: *The documentary went through all the graphic details of the operation in unsparing detail.*

unsparing GENEROUS /ʌn'speə.rɪŋ/ ⓤ /-'sper.ɪŋ/ adj FORMAL extremely generous with money, time, help, etc: *Last of all, our thanks go to the caterers who have been unsparing in their efforts to make this afternoon such a success.*

unspeakable /ʌn'spiː.kə.bl̩/ adj too bad or shocking to be expressed in words: *unspeakable crimes* ○ *No report can convey the unspeakable suffering that this war has caused.* ○ *The stench coming from the toilets was quite unspeakable.* **unspeakably** /ʌn'spiː.kə.bli/ adv

unspecified /ʌn'spes.ɪ.faɪd/ adj If something is unspecified, you are not told what it is: *The court awarded her an unspecified amount of money.*

unspoiled /ʌn'spɔɪld/ ⓤ /-'spɔɪlt/ adj (UK ALSO **unspoilt**) An unspoiled place is beautiful because it has not been changed or damaged by people: *an island with clean, unspoiled beaches*

unspoken /ʌn'spəʊ.kˀn/ ⓤ /-'spoʊ-/ adj not spoken, although thought of or felt: *unspoken doubts/fears* ○ *There's an unspoken assumption in the department that Sue will take over the post when Ian leaves.*

unsporting /ʌn'spɔː.tɪŋ/ ⓤ /-'spɔːr.t̬ɪŋ/ adj not SPORTING, see at **sport** GAME

unstable /ʌn'steɪ.bl̩/ adj **1** not solid and firm and therefore not strong, safe or likely to last: *That chair looks a bit unstable to me.* ○ *It is a poor and politically unstable society.* **2** describes someone who suffers from sudden and extreme changes in their mental and emotional state: *emotionally unstable*

unsteady /ʌn'sted.i/ adj moving slightly from side to side, as if you might fall: *She's been in bed with the flu and she's still a bit unsteady on her feet.* **unsteadily** /ʌn'sted.ɪ.li/ adv

unstinting /ʌn'stɪn.tɪŋ/ ⓤ /-t̬ɪŋ/ adj FORMAL extremely generous with time, money, praise, help, etc: *unstinting support/generosity* ○ *She was quite unstinting in her praise.*

unstoppable /ʌn'stɒp.ə.bl̩/ ⓤ /-'stɑː.pə-/ adj unable to be stopped or prevented from developing: *The band has enjoyed a seemingly unstoppable rise in popularity.*

unstuck NOT STUCK /ʌn'stʌk/ adj [after v] no longer stuck: *The sticky tape on the parcel came unstuck and the whole thing came undone.*

unstuck FAIL /ʌn'stʌk/ adj INFORMAL **come unstuck** to experience difficulties and fail: *It was in the third round of the championships that they came unstuck.*

unsuccessful /ˌʌn.sək'ses.fˀl/ adj not SUCCESSFUL, see at **succeed** ACHIEVE SOMETHING **unsuccessfully** /ˌʌn.sək-'ses.fˀl.i/ adv

U

unsuitable /ʌnˈsjuː.tə.bl̩/ [US] /-ˈsuː.t̬ə-/ *adj* not SUITABLE, see at **suit** BE RIGHT **unsuitably** /ˌʌnˈsjuː.tə.bli/ [US] /-ˈsuː.t̬ə-/ *adv*

unsuited /ʌnˈsjuː.tɪd/ [US] /-ˈsuː.t̬ɪd/ *adj* not right for someone or something, usually in character: *Liberman realised Kurt was unsuited* ***to*** *office life, but offered him a contract anyway.* ○ *She was simply swept off her feet when she met him. But they were completely unsuited.*

unsung /ˌʌnˈsʌŋ/ *adj* not noticed or praised for hard work, bravery or great achievements: *an unsung hero/heroine* ○ *Many of her achievements* ***went unsung*** *until after her death.*

unsupported [OPINION] /ˌʌn.səˈpɔː.tɪd/ [US] /-ˈpɔːr.t̬ɪd/ *adj* If someone's opinions or statements are unsupported, they do not have any proof or evidence to show that they are true: *unsupported allegations* ○ *Most of the report consists of generalized observations, unsupported* ***by*** *dates, names and times.*

unsupported [PERSON] /ˌʌn.səˈpɔː.tɪd/ [US] /-ˈpɔːr.t̬ɪd/ *adj* not receiving any help or encouragement from other people: *He made several attempts to reach the North Pole unsupported.*

unsupported [STRUCTURE] /ˌʌn.səˈpɔː.tɪd/ [US] /-ˈpɔːr.t̬ɪd/ *adj* describes a structure or object that does not use any other object or person to support its weight, especially from below to stop it from falling: *to stand unsupported* ○ *the largest unsupported marble dome in the world*

unsure /ʌnˈʃɔːʳ/ [US] /-ˈʃʊr/ *adj* **1** not certain or having doubts: *I'm a bit unsure* ***about*** *what to do next – can you help me?* **2 unsure of *yourself*** without confidence in yourself: *As a new teacher I was very unsure of myself when I was in front of a class.*

unsuspected /ˌʌn.səˈspek.tɪd/ *adj* not known or thought to exist: *an unsuspected talent/complication/problem/illness*

unsuspecting /ˌʌn.səˈspek.tɪŋ/ *adj* trusting; not aware of any danger or harm: *The killer lured his unsuspecting victims back to his apartment.*

unswerving /ʌnˈswɜː.vɪŋ/ [US] /-ˈswɝː-/ *adj* If someone's trust or belief is unswerving, it is always strong and never weakens: *unswerving loyalty/devotion/support/faith*

unsympathetic /ˌʌn.sɪm.pəˈθet.ɪk/ [US] /-ˈθet̬-/ *adj* not sympathetic

untangle /ʌnˈtæŋ.gl̩/ *verb* [T] **1** to remove the knots from an untidy mass of string, wire, etc. and separate the different threads **2** to make a complicated subject or problem, or its different parts clear and able to be understood: *It took years to untangle the legal complexities of the case.*

untapped /ʌnˈtæpt/ *adj* If a supply of something valuable is untapped, it is not yet used or taken advantage of: *untapped assets/resources/markets/talent*

untenable /ʌnˈten.ə.bl̩/ *adj* FORMAL **1** describes a theory or argument that cannot be supported or defended against criticism **2** describes a situation that cannot continue as it is: *If three people in four no longer support the government, isn't this an untenable situation?*

unthinkable /ʌnˈθɪŋ.kə.bl̩/ *adj* too shocking or unlikely to be imagined as possible: *You can't imagine what it would be like to have your child die – it's quite unthinkable.*
• **the unthinkable** an unthinkable event or situation: *The unthinkable had happened – his secret activities had been discovered by the press.*

unthinking /ʌnˈθɪŋ.kɪŋ/ *adj* FORMAL MAINLY DISAPPROVING not based on serious thought or an examination of the information: *What annoys me about these people is their unthinking hostility to anything foreign or unfamiliar.* **unthinkingly** /ʌnˈθɪŋ.kɪŋ.li/ *adv*: *I really didn't mean to offend her – I just said it unthinkingly.*

untidy /ʌnˈtaɪ.di/ *adj* not tidy: *an untidy room* ○ *She's really untidy at home.* **untidily** /ʌnˈtaɪ.dɪ.li/ *adv* **untidiness** /ʌnˈtaɪ.dɪ.nəs/ *noun* [U]

untie /ʌnˈtaɪ/ *verb* [T] **untying, untied, untied** to unfasten a knot or something tied

until [TIME] /ᵊnˈtɪl/ /ˈʌn-/ *prep, conjunction* (ALSO **till**) **1** up to (the time that): *I was up until three o'clock trying to get it finished!* ○ *Hadn't we better wait until Antony's here?* **2 not until** not before a particular time or event: *We didn't eat till past midnight.* ○ *Once he starts a decorating job he won't stop until it's finished.* ○ *Don't move until I tell you.*

until [DISTANCE] /ᵊnˈtɪl/ /ˈʌn-/ *prep, conjunction* (ALSO **till**) as far as: *You should stay on the train until Manchester and then change.*

untimely /ʌnˈtaɪm.li/ *adj* FORMAL describes something bad that happens unexpectedly early or at a time which is not suitable: *It was this passion for fast cars that led to his untimely* ***death*** *at the age of 43.*

untiring /ʌnˈtaɪə.rɪŋ/ [US] /-ˈtaɪr.ɪŋ/ *adj* If someone has untiring energy, interest or enthusiasm, it never weakens.

unto /ˈʌn.tuː/ /-tu/ /-tə/ *prep* OLD USE to: *And the Lord spake unto* (= spoke to) *him.*

untold /ʌnˈtəʊld/ [US] /-ˈtoʊld/ /ˈ--/ *adj* so great in amount or level that it can not be measured or expressed in words: *untold riches* ○ *Words alone cannot convey the untold* ***misery*** *endured by people in these refugee camps.*

untouchable [SOCIAL CLASS] /ʌnˈtʌtʃ.ə.bl̩/ *noun* [C] a member of the lowest social group in Indian society

untouchable [PROTECTED] /ʌnˈtʌtʃ.ə.bl̩/ *adj* not able to be punished, criticized or changed in any way: *We've got to change the present system in which high court judges are regarded as somehow untouchable.*

untouchable [NOT DEFEATED] /ʌnˈtʌtʃ.ə.bl̩/ *adj* not able to be defeated or equalled: *Coventry City have proved untouchable this season – they've just won their sixth consecutive game.*

untouched /ʌnˈtʌtʃt/ *adj* **1** not changed or spoilt in any way: *Most of the east coast remains mercifully untouched by tourism.* **2** If food is untouched, it has not been eaten: *She took a few spoonfuls of soup but left her main course untouched.*

untoward /ˌʌn.tʊˈwɔːd/ [US] /-ˈtə.wɔːrd/ *adj* unexpected and inconvenient or unpleasant: *Unless anything untoward happens we should arrive just before midday.*

untrained /ʌnˈtreɪnd/ *adj* **1** never having been taught the skills for a particular job: *untrained staff* **2 to the untrained eye** to someone without the skill or knowledge to judge what they see: *To the untrained eye, most fake diamonds look real.*

untrammelled, US USUALLY **untrammeled** /ʌnˈtræm.ᵊld/ *adj* FORMAL not limited by rules or any other controlling influence: *Self-governing schools are untrammelled by education authority rules.*

untreated /ʌnˈtriː.tɪd/ [US] /-t̬ɪd/ *adj* **1** describes a substance that is not cleaned and has not had special substances added to protect it or make it safe to use: *untreated water/sewage/waste* ○ *untreated timber* **2** describes illnesses, injuries, people or animals that do not receive medical treatment: *untreated illness/disease/depression* ○ *It is a form of anaemia which is nearly always fatal if left untreated.*

untrue /ʌnˈtruː/ *adj* not true; false

untruth /ʌnˈtruːθ/ *noun* **1** [C] a statement that is not true: *It's not the first time that the paper has been in trouble for printing untruths about people's private lives.* **2** [U] when something is not true: *The untruth of this statement was immediately clear to me.*

untutored /ʌnˈtjuː.təd/ [US] /-ˈtuː.t̬ɚd/ *adj* FORMAL **1** having no knowledge of or education in a particular subject **2 to *the/my, etc.* untutored eye** if or because you are/I am, etc. an untutored person: *You see, to my untutored eye that just looks like a load of random brush strokes and yet it's a very valuable painting.*

untypical /ʌnˈtɪp.ɪ.kᵊl/ *adj* not typical: *Her angry outburst was untypical; she's usually very quiet woman.* ○ *It is* ***not*** *untypical* ***of*** *girls of her age to be concerned about their appearance.*

unusable, **unuseable** /ʌnˈjuː.zə.bl̩/ *adj* describes something that cannot be used, especially because it is broken or not safe: *The normal supply of water has turned brown and unusable.* ○ *The virus deletes files and corrupts essential core microchips leaving computers unusable.*

unused [NOT USED] /ʌnˈjuːzd/ *adj* not being used at present, or never having been used: *You might as well take your father's car – there's no point in having it sit there unused in the garage.*

unused [NOT FAMILIAR] /ʌnˈjuːst/ *adj* **be unused to *sth*** to not be familiar with a particular habit or experience: *If you're unused to exercise, your joints may ache the next day.* ○ *I'm unused to getting up so early.*

unusual /ʌnˈjuː.ʒu.əl/ *adj* different from others of the same type in a way that is surprising, interesting or attractive: *"Do you like the new settee?" "Very much, it's most unusual."* ○ [+ to infinitive] ***It's** unusual **to** have adult conversation like that with such a young child.* ○ *I was actually on time, which is unusual for me.*
unusually /ʌnˈjuː.ʒu.ə.li/ *adv*: *He was unusually polite* (= more polite than usual).

unutterable /ʌnˈʌt.ər.ə.bl̩/ [US] /-ˈʌt̬.ɚ-/ *adj* FORMAL too bad to be expressed in words; extreme: *After an afternoon of unutterable boredom I was finally allowed to leave.*
unutterably /ʌnˈʌt.ər.ə.bli/ [US] /-ˈʌt̬.ɚ-/ *adv* FORMAL extremely: *She came home exhausted and unutterably sad.*

unvarnished /ʌnˈvɑː.nɪʃt/ [US] /-ˈvɑːr-/ *adj* [before n] describes a statement that is expressed in a plain and truthful way: *It's a bit optimistic to expect a politician to tell you the unvarnished **truth**.*

unveil /ʌnˈveɪl/ *verb* [T] **1** to remove a curtain-like covering from a new statue, etc. at a formal ceremony in order to show the opening or completion of a new building or work of art: *The memorial to those who had died in the war was unveiled in 1948 by the Queen.* **2** If you unveil something new, you show it or it make known for the first time: *A new government policy on forests is due to be unveiled in April.*

the unwaged *plural noun* UK unemployed people: *The entrance fee is six pounds, two pounds for the unwaged.*
unwaged /ʌnˈweɪdʒd/ *adj*

unwanted /ʌnˈwɒn.tɪd/ [US] /-ˈwɑːn.t̬ɪd/ *adj* not WANTED, see at **want** DESIRE

unwarranted /ʌnˈwɒr.ən.tɪd/ [US] /-ˈwɔːr.ən.t̬ɪd/ *adj* FORMAL lacking a good reason and therefore annoying or unfair: *People need to be protected against such unwarranted intrusions into their private lives by journalists.*

unwary /ʌnˈweə.ri/ [US] /-ˈwer.i/ *adj* not aware of or careful about possible risks and dangers: *Meanwhile, the cowboy trader is free to carry on ripping off unwary customers.* ○ *A range of tax and technical issues can trip up **the** unwary* (= unwary people).

unwashed /ʌnˈwɒʃt/ [US] /-ˈwɑːʃt/ *adj* not washed

unwelcome /ʌnˈwel.kəm/ *adj* not wanted: *There was more unwelcome news waiting for me at the office.* ○ *an unwelcome visitor*
unwelcoming /ʌnˈwel.kəm.ɪŋ/ *adj* not making a guest or visitor feel happy, comfortable or wanted: *The house was dusty, damp and unwelcoming.*

unwell /ʌnˈwel/ *adj* [after v] not well; ill: *I hear you've been unwell recently.*

unwieldy [DIFFICULT TO MOVE] /ʌnˈwiːl.di/ *adj* An unwieldy object is difficult to move or handle because it is heavy, large or a strange shape: *A piano is a very unwieldy item to get down a flight of stairs.*

unwieldy [NOT EFFECTIVE] /ʌnˈwiːl.di/ *adj* An unwieldy system is slow and not effective, usually because it is too big, badly organized or involves too many different organizations or people: *One disadvantage for the bank is that its huge size – over 15 000 staff – makes it unwieldy and slow-moving.*

unwilling /ʌnˈwɪl.ɪŋ/ *adj* not willing: *an unwilling helper* **unwillingly** /ʌnˈwɪl.ɪŋ.li/ *adv* **unwillingness** /ʌnˈwɪl.ɪŋ.nəs/ *noun* [U] *her unwillingness to help*

unwind [UNFASTEN] /ʌnˈwaɪnd/ *verb* [I or T] **unwound, unwound** If you unwind something that is wrapped around an object, you unfasten it, and if it unwinds, it becomes unfastened: *In a nearby medical tent, a US Army doctor gently unwinds Metruk's bandage.*

unwind [RELAX] (**unwound, unwound**) /ʌnˈwaɪnd/ *verb* [I] (ALSO **wind down**) to relax and allow your mind to be free from anxiety after a period of work or some other activity that has made you anxious: *A glass of wine in the evening helps me to unwind after work.*

unwise /ʌnˈwaɪz/ *adj* stupid and likely to cause problems **unwisely** /ʌnˈwaɪz.li/ *adv*

unwitting /ʌnˈwɪt.ɪŋ/ [US] /-ˈwɪt̬-/ *adj* [before n] FORMAL without knowing or planning: *The two women claimed they were the unwitting victims of a drugs dealer who planted a large quantity of heroin in their luggage.* **unwittingly** /ʌnˈwɪt.ɪŋ.li/ [US] /-ˈwɪt̬-/ *adv*: *I regret any anxiety or concern which I may, unwittingly, have caused.*

unwonted /ʌnˈwəʊn.tɪd/ [US] /-ˈwɑːn.t̬ɪd/ *adj* [before n] FORMAL unusual; rarely experienced or shown: *He sprang to the telephone with unwonted eagerness.*

unworkable /ʌnˈwɜː.kə.bl̩/ [US] /-ˈwɝː-/ *adj* describes a plan that is not practical or that you cannot really do successfully: *To be honest, I think the scheme is completely unworkable.*

unwrap /ʌnˈræp/ *verb* [T] to remove the paper or other covering from something: *Aren't you going to unwrap your presents?*

unwritten /ʌnˈrɪt.ən/ [US] /-ˈrɪt̬-/ *adj* **1** describes something that does not exist in a written or printed form: *an unwritten constitution* **2** describes a rule or law which does not exist officially but which people generally accept and obey: *There's an unwritten **rule** that you don't wear jeans to work.*

unyielding /ʌnˈjiːl.dɪŋ/ *adj* **1** completely unwilling to change a decision, opinion, demand, etc: *Korea is unyielding in its demands for a new treaty.* **2 rigid** (= not able to be bent or moved)

unzip /ʌnˈzɪp/ *verb* [T] **-pp- 1** to open something by using a zip: *He unzipped his suitcase.* **2** to return a computer file to its original size after it has been ZIPPED (= reduced in size so that it can be easily sent or stored)

up [HIGHER] /ʌp/ *adv* **1** towards a higher position; towards a higher value, number or level: *Put those books up on the top shelf.* ○ *A gravel road leads through the jungle and up into the Andes.* ○ *Pushing the number of unit sales up every quarter can't be continued indefinitely.* ○ *The water was up **to**/had come up **to** the level of the windows.* **2** out of the ground: *He spent the afternoon digging carrots up.*
• **up and down** from a higher to a lower position repeatedly: *My little daughter started **jumping** up and down with rage when she heard she couldn't go.*
• **up with *sth*** OLD-FASHIONED INFORMAL shouted or written on notices to show support: *Up with freedom!*
up /ʌp/ *prep* to or in a higher level or position: *We followed her up the stairs to a large meeting room.*
up /ʌp/ *adj* **1** moving up: *an up escalator* ➲See also **upper** HIGHER. **2** If a level or amount is up, it has increased: *The cost of car insurance is up, but not very much.* ○ *Last year the company's turnover was $240 billion, up 3% **on*** (= compared with) *the previous year.* **3** If someone's long hair is up, it is arranged on the top or back of their head: *You look lovely with your **hair** up.*
• **on the up and up** MAINLY US INFORMAL describes someone who is honest and can be trusted ➲Compare **on the up and up** at **up** IMPROVE.
up /ʌp/ *verb* [T] **-pp-** INFORMAL to increase something such as a price: *We won't be able to make a profit on the deal without upping the sale price.* ○ *It looks like tax rates are going to be upped again.*

up [VERTICAL] /ʌp/ *adv* in or into a vertical position: *Would you stand up for a moment? I want to see how tall you are.* ➲Compare **down** LOWER POSITION.
up /ʌp/ *verb* INFORMAL **up and ...** used with another verb to emphasize that someone left a place or did something in a sudden and possibly unexpected way: *After dinner they just upped and **left/went** without saying goodbye.*

up [TOP] /ʌp/ *adv* in a high position; at the top: *Our boardroom is up on the twenty-third floor.* ○ *You can tell which **way** up the crates have to be because they all say 'TOP'.* ➲Compare **down** LOWER LEVEL.
up /ʌp/ *prep* at the top of: *You'll find a dusty attic up these stairs.* ○ *If you want Fred, he's up that ladder.*

- **Up yours!** *OFFENSIVE* used to show that you very much dislike someone

up ALONG /ʌp/ *prep* (further) along: *The car shot off up the road at high speed.* ○ *They live just up the road.*

,up and 'down along the surface of something first in one direction and then in the opposite direction, usually repeatedly: *He was running up and down the path, shouting.*

up NEAR /ʌp/ *adv* very near: *Carrying a gun, he walked up to the cashier and demanded money.* ○ *A limousine drew up (= parked) outside the hotel.*

up INCREASE /ʌp/ *adv* to a greater degree; in order to increase: *The fire heats the room up (= makes it warmer) within minutes.* ○ *Grandma always turns the TV up really loud because she can't hear very well.* ○ *Try not to get worked up (= increasingly excited or angry), I'm sure we can sort the problem out.*

up OUT OF BED /ʌp/ *adv, adj* [after v] not in bed: *It's time to get up now!* ○ *Oh, I've been up all night, finishing my essay.*

- **be up and about/around** *INFORMAL* to be able to get out of bed and move around again after a period of illness, because your health has improved enough

up EXIST /ʌp/ *adv* into existence, view or consideration: *Originally the charity was set up to help orphans in urban areas.* ○ *Sorry darling, something unexpected has come up (= has happened) at the office, and I'll be home late.* ○ *Coming up (= Happening next) after the break, we have a man who claims he can communicate with fish.* ○ *Would this be a good time to bring up the issue of salary?*

up /ʌp/ *adj* [after v] used when talking or asking about what is happening: *Everyone was talking in whispers, and I could tell something was up (= something unusual was happening).* ○ *What's up (= What is happening or what is wrong)?*

up EQUAL /ʌp/ *adv* so as to be equal in quality, knowledge or achievement: *She couldn't go to school for a few weeks because of illness, but she'll be able to catch up (with her lessons) quickly.* ○ *So much scientific research is being performed that it's virtually impossible to keep up (with all the new developments).* ○ *US INFORMAL Kate and I were both playing well, and after ten minutes the score was 6-up (= 6 points each).*

- **be up there with sb** *INFORMAL* to match someone else in ability or in a particular skill: *As a composer, he was up there with the best.*

- **up to (doing) sth 1** good enough for a particular activity: *He wants to compete at international level, but frankly I don't think he's up to it.* **2** strong enough for a particular activity: *It was a serious fall – it'll be a while before you feel up to walking again.*

up TOGETHER /ʌp/ *adv* in a state of being together with other similar things: *You've got half an hour to gather up anything you'll need for the journey.* ○ *Add up the column of figures in your head and then tell me what the sum is.*

up TIGHTLY /ʌp/ *adv* tightly or firmly in order to keep something safe or in position: *Can you do my shoelaces up for me?* ○ *Tie up the top of the bag so the rubbish doesn't fall out.* ○ *You'd better wrap up (= wear warm clothes) – it's cold outside.*

up IN OPERATION /ʌp/ *adj* [after v] When a system, computer or similar machine is up, it is operating, especially in its usual way: *Andy, do you know when the network will be up again?* ✻ NOTE: The opposite is **down**.

- **up and running** If something, especially a system or a machine, is up and running, it is operating: *The engineer soon got the air-conditioning up and running again.*

up SMALLER /ʌp/ *adv* broken or cut into smaller pieces; made smaller in area: *He cut the letter up into a hundred pieces.* ○ *She folded the newspaper up and put it in her bag.* ○ *The car blew up (= exploded) when flames reached its fuel tank.*

up AGE /ʌp/ *adv* to a greater age: *No one said that growing up would be easy or painless.* ○ *Many single parents struggle to bring their children up on a low income.*

up FINISHED /ʌp/ *adj* [after v] When a period of time is up, it is finished: *When the two hours were up nobody had answered all of the questions.* ○ *Your time is up - it's someone else's turn on the training equipment now.*

up INTENDED /ʌp/ *adj* **1 up for sth** intended, suggested or being considered for something: *That house at the end of our road is up for sale again.* ○ *Are you really up for promotion?* **2** *INFORMAL* **up for (doing) sth** willing to do or take part in an activity: *I'm up for organizing the meeting if nobody else wants to do it.*

up /ʌp/ *adv* for consideration, or as a suggestion: *How many candidates will your party be putting up (= offering for election) at the elections next week?*

up IMPROVE /ʌp/ *adv* into an improved position or state: *By lap 26, Senna had moved up into second position.* ○ *Stein had a bad start to the race, but by the ninth lap she was up with the leaders.* ⊃Compare **down** LOWER LEVEL.

- **up and down** sometimes happy and sometimes sad: *She's been very up and down since her husband went into hospital.*

- **on the up and up** *UK* continually improving: *Her career has been on the up and up since she moved into sales.* ⊃Compare **on the up and up** at **up** HIGHER.

up ROAD /ʌp/ *adj* [after v] *UK* When a road is up, it is being repaired and so is unsuitable for use: *The council has got the road up because of a broken sewer.*

up TRIAL /ʌp/ *adj* [after v] on trial in a court: *If he doesn't pay the fine soon, he'll be up before the magistrate.* ○ *Max is up for armed robbery.*

up END /ʌp/ *adv* to an end, finish or state of completion: *Finish up the old packet of biscuits before you open a new one.* ○ *Crime won't help – you'll end up in prison.* ○ *I'd like to round up the meeting by thanking all those who were able to attend at such short notice.*

up NORTH /ʌp/ *adv* towards the north or towards a more important place, especially a city: *On Tuesday she'll be travelling up to Newcastle from Birmingham.* ○ *She comes up from her village about once a month on the train.*

- **up and down** *somewhere* everywhere in a particular area: *Cinemas up and down the country are reporting huge audiences for the film.*

up /ʌp/ *adj* [before n] *UK OLD-FASHIONED* What time does the next up train (= train going to an important place such as a capital city) leave?

up ORIGIN /ʌp/ *prep* towards the starting point of something, especially a river or stream: *Rowing up (the) river against the current was very hard work.* ⊃See also **upriver; upstream**.

up TO /ʌp/ *prep* *UK NOT STANDARD* to or at: *Are you going up the club tonight?* ⊃Compare **down** TO.

up- /ʌp-/ *prefix* higher or improved: *uphill* ○ *uplift*

up-and-coming /ˌʌp.ənd'kʌm.ɪŋ/ *adj* [usually before n] likely to achieve success soon or in the near future: *Playing the role of Tanya is Sylvia Roberts, one of our up-and-coming young actresses.*

up-and-down /ˌʌp.ən'daʊn/ *adj* sometimes successful and sometimes unsuccessful

up-and-over /ˌʌp.ənd'əʊ.vəʳ/ ⓤ /-'oʊ.vɚ/ *adj* [before n] *MAINLY UK* describes a door that opens by being lifted and then sliding into a horizontal position as it rises

upbeat /ʌp'biːt/ /'--/ *adj* *INFORMAL* full of hope, happiness and good feelings: *Live music and a parade set an upbeat mood for the official opening.* ✻ NOTE: The opposite is **downbeat**.

upbraid /ʌp'breɪd/ *verb* [T] *FORMAL* to forcefully or angrily tell someone they should not have done a particular thing and criticize them for having done it: *In newspaper articles she consistently upbraided those in authority who overstepped their limits.*

upbringing /'ʌp,brɪŋ.ɪŋ/ *noun* [C usually sing] the way in which someone is treated and educated when they are young, especially by their parents, particularly in relation to the effect which this has on how they behave and make moral decisions: *Is it right to say all the crimes he committed were simply the result of his upbringing?* ⊃See also **bring up** CARE FOR.

upcoming *MAINLY US* /'ʌp,kʌm.ɪŋ/ *adj* [before n] (*UK USUALLY* **forthcoming**) happening soon: *Tickets are selling well for the group's upcoming concert tour.*

update /ʌp'deɪt/ *verb* [T] **1** to make something more modern or suitable for use now by adding new information or changing its design: *an updated version of the* *software* **2** to give someone the most recent information: *We'll update you* **on** *this news story throughout the day.*

update /ˈʌp.deɪt/ *noun* [C] **1** when you update something or someone with new information: *Jo's just doing an update* **on** *the mailing list.* ○ *I'll need regular updates* **on** *your progress.* **2** a new form of something which existed at an earlier time: *It's an update* **of** *an old 60's movie.*

upend /ʌpˈend/ *verb* [T] to push or move something so that the part which usually touches the ground does so no longer: *She upended the chessboard halfway through the game because she was losing.*

upfront /ʌpˈfrʌnt/ *adj* [after v] speaking or behaving in a way which makes intentions and beliefs clear: *She's very upfront* **about** *why she wants the job – she'd earn a lot more money.* ➲See also **up front** at **front** PLACE.

upgrade /ʌpˈgreɪd/ *verb* [T] to improve the quality or usefulness of something, such as a machine or a computer program, or give a person a more important job or state that their job is more important than it was in the past: *It's quite simple to upgrade the indexing software.* ○ *Congratulations, I hear you've been upgraded* **to** *divisional manager.* * NOTE: The opposite is **downgrade**.

upgrade /ˈʌp.greɪd/ *noun* [C] *a hardware upgrade* ○ *The upgrade to version 5.0 costs $395.*

upheaval /ʌpˈhiː.vəl/ *noun* [C or U] (a) great change, especially causing or involving much difficulty, activity or trouble: *Yesterday's coup brought further upheaval to a country already struggling with famine.* ○ *It would cause a tremendous upheaval to install a different computer system.*

uphill /ˌʌpˈhɪl/ *adj, adv* **1** leading to a higher place on a slope: *an uphill climb* ○ *running uphill* ➲Compare **downhill**. **2** needing a large amount of effort: *It'll be an uphill* **struggle/battle/fight** *to get the new proposals accepted.* ➲Compare **downhill**.

uphold /ʌpˈhəʊld/ [US] /-ˈhoʊld/ *verb* [T] **upheld**, **upheld** to defend or maintain a principle or law, or to state that a decision which has already been made, especially a legal one, is correct: *As a police officer you are expected to uphold the law whether you agree with it or not.* ○ *Judge Davis upheld the county court's decision.*

upholder /ʌpˈhəʊl.dəʳ/ [US] /-ˈhoʊl.dɚ/ *noun* [C]

upholster /ʌpˈhəʊl.stəʳ/ [US] /-ˈhoʊl.stɚ/ *verb* [T] to cover a chair or other type of seat with suitable cloth and fill it with suitable substance **upholstered** /ʌpˈhəʊl.stəd/ [US] /-ˈhoʊl.stɚd/ *adj*: *a nicely upholstered sofa* **upholsterer** /ʌpˈhəʊl.stᵊr.əʳ/ [US] /-ˈhoʊl.stɚ.ɚ/ *noun* [C]

upholstery /ʌpˈhəʊl.stᵊr.i/ [US] /-ˈhoʊl.stɚ-/ *noun* [U] **1** the cloth used for covering a seat and/or the substance used for filling it: *an old sofa with faded green upholstery* **2** the activity of upholstering objects

upkeep /ˈʌp.kiːp/ *noun* [U] the cost or process of keeping something, such as a building, in good condition: *The upkeep* **of** *larger old properties is very expensive.* ○ *Council employees are responsible for the upkeep* **of** *the gardens.*

upland /ˈʌp.lənd/ *adj* describes an area of land that is situated high up, such as on a hill or mountain: *The whole plateau comprises one vast upland plain.*

uplands /ˈʌp.ləndz/ *plural noun* high areas of land

uplift [IMPROVEMENT] /ˈʌp.lɪft/ *noun* [U] SLIGHTLY FORMAL improvement of a person's moral or spiritual condition: *We are counting on your speech, bishop, to give some moral uplift to the delegates.* **uplifting** /ʌpˈlɪf.tɪŋ/ *adj*: *For me it was a marvellously uplifting performance/experience.*

uplift [RAISE] /ʌpˈlɪft/ *verb* [T] SPECIALIZED to raise something to a higher position

uplift /ˈʌp.lɪft/ *noun* [U] support for a woman's breasts that is provided by her clothes

uplifted /ʌpˈlɪf.tɪd/ *adj* SLIGHTLY FORMAL *With uplifted* (= stretching up) *arms, he ran towards them.*

uplift [COLLECT] /ʌpˈlɪft/ *verb* [T] SCOTTISH ENGLISH to collect goods or people from one place, in order to take them to another: *Coaches will set down and uplift passengers only as directed by the police in the streets mentioned.*

upload /ʌpˈləʊd/ [US] /-ˈloʊd/ *verb* [T] to copy or move programs or information to a larger computer system or to the Internet ➲Compare **download**.

upload /ˈʌp.ləʊd/ [US] /-loʊd/ *noun* [C] a computer program or information that can be uploaded

upmarket /ˌʌpˈmɑː.kɪt/ [US] /ˈʌp.mɑːr-/ *adj, adv* (MAINLY US **upscale**) describes goods and products that are of very high quality and intended to be bought by people who are quite rich: *an upmarket brand name* ○ *Many garment exporters want to move upmarket.* ➲Compare **downmarket**.

upon /əˈpɒn/ [US] /-ˈpɑːn/ *prep* **1** FORMAL on: *Upon her head she wore a black velvet hat.* ○ *You can never place enough emphasis upon the importance of safety.* ○ *Upon your arrival* (= As soon as you arrive), *please report to the reception desk.* **2** SLIGHTLY FORMAL **be upon** *you* to be something that you will experience or have to deal with soon: *Another couple of weeks and the holidays will be upon us.*

upper [HIGHER] /ˈʌp.əʳ/ [US] /-ɚ/ *adj* [before n] at a higher position or level than something else, or being the top part of something: *The office block's upper floors were being repainted.* ○ *If the infection is not checked it will probably spread to the upper body.* * NOTE: The opposite is **lower**.

upper /ˈʌp.əʳ/ [US] /-ɚ/ *noun* [C] the top part of a shoe which covers a person's foot and to which the heel and the sole are fixed: *These shoes have leather uppers and synthetic soles.*

• **be on** *your* **uppers** OLD-FASHIONED INFORMAL to be very poor

upper [DRUG] /ˈʌp.əʳ/ [US] /-ɚ/ *noun* [C] INFORMAL a drug which causes a person taking it to feel very active and excited * NOTE: The opposite is **downer**.

ˌupper ˈcase *noun* [U] SPECIALIZED If letters are in upper case, they are written as capitals: *upper-case letters* ➲Compare **lower case**.

ˌupper ˈclass *group noun* [S] (ALSO **the upper classes**) a social group consisting of the people who have the highest social rank and who are usually rich: *The upper classes usually send their children to expensive private schools.* ➲Compare **lower class**; **middle class**; **working class**. **upper-class** /ˌʌp.əˈklɑːs/ [US] /-ɚˈklæs/ *adj*: *She comes from a very upper-class family.*

the ˌupper ˈhand *noun* [S] If you have the upper hand, you have more power than anyone else and so have control: *After hours of fierce negotiations, the president* **gained/got/had** *the upper hand.*

ˌupper ˈhouse *noun* [C usually sing] (ALSO **upper chamber**) one of the two parts that some parliaments are divided into, usually the one with less political power: *In the UK, the upper house is the House of Lords.* ○ *The upper house of the US Congress is the Senate.* ➲Compare **lower house**.

uppermost /ˈʌp.ə.məʊst/ [US] /-ɚ.moʊst/ *adj, adv* in the highest position or having the most importance: *The office block's uppermost floors were engulfed with flames.* ○ *Store the canisters with their lids uppermost.* ○ *What's uppermost* **in** *your* **mind** *just before a race?*

uppity /ˈʌp.ɪ.ti/ [US] /-ə.t̬i/ *adj* INFORMAL DISAPPROVING describes a person who behaves in an unpleasant way because they think that they are more important than they really are: *He* **got/became** *very uppity when his fashion designs were criticized.*

upright [STRAIGHT] /ˈʌp.raɪt/ *adj* **1** straight up or vertical: *Please return your seat to an upright position and fasten your belt.* **2** describes something which is taller than it is wide: *an upright freezer/vacuum cleaner*

upright /ˈʌp.raɪt/ *adv* vertical and as straight as possible: *to sit/stand upright* ○ *The sound of breaking glass made her sit* **bolt** *upright* (= sit with her back straight).

upright /ˈʌp.raɪt/ *noun* [C] **1** a vertical part of something that supports other parts: *Firmly secure the two uprights to opposite walls in the alcove and then slot the shelves in between them.* **2** UK INFORMAL FOR **goalpost**

upright [MORAL] /ˈʌp.raɪt/ *adj* APPROVING honest, responsible and moral: *She behaved as any upright* **citizen** *would have under the circumstances.* **uprightly** /ˈʌp.raɪt.li/ *adv* **uprightness** /ˈʌp.raɪt.nəs/ *noun* [U]

ˌupright (piˈano) *noun* [C] a piano in which the strings are vertical ➲Compare **grand piano**.

U

uprising /ˈʌp,raɪ.zɪŋ/ *noun* [C] (*ALSO* **rising**) an act of opposition, sometimes using violence, by many people in one area of a country against those who are in power: *Following a determined resistance in the east, there was eventually a* ***popular*** *uprising in the capital.*

upriver /,ʌpˈrɪv.əʳ/ [US] /-ɚ/ *adv, adj* [before n] towards the place where a river starts: *We paddled upriver for a couple of hours.*

uproar /ˈʌp.rɔːʳ/ [US] /-rɔːr/ *noun* [S or U] when a lot of people complain about something angrily: *The book* ***caused*** *an uproar in France.* ○ *The whole hall was* ***in*** *uproar after the announcement.*

uproarious /ʌpˈrɔː.ri.əs/ [US] /-ˈrɔːr.i-/ *adj* **1** extremely noisy and confused: *an uproarious debate* **2** extremely amusing: *It's a very amusing play with an uproarious final act.* **uproariously** /ʌpˈrɔː.ri.ə.sli/ [US] /-ˈrɔːr.i-/ *adv: They laughed uproariously.*

uproot [PLANT] /ʌpˈruːt/ *verb* [T] to pull a plant including its roots out of the ground: *Hundreds of mature trees were uprooted in the storm.*

uproot [PERSON] /ʌpˈruːt/ *verb* [T] to remove a person from their home or usual surroundings: *The war has uprooted nearly two-thirds of the country's population.*

,ups and ˈdowns *plural noun* If someone or something experiences ups and downs, a mixture of good and bad things happens to them: *Like most married couples we've had our ups and downs, but life's like that.*

upscale /ˈʌp.skeɪl/ *adj US FOR* **upmarket**

upset [WORRY] /ʌpˈset/ *verb* [T] **upsetting, upset, upset** to make someone worried, unhappy or angry: *It still upsets him when he thinks about the accident.* ○ [R] *Don't upset your****self*** *by thinking about what might have been.* **upset** /ʌpˈset/ *adj* [after v] *Don't get upset* ***about*** *the dress – there's only a little stain on it.* ○ [+ to infinitive] *She was very upset* ***to*** *hear that the holiday had been cancelled.* ○ [+ that] *He was very upset* ***that*** *you didn't reply to his letters.* **upsetting** /ʌpˈset.ɪŋ/ [US] /-ˈset̬-/ *adj: Seeing her again would be an upsetting experience after so many years.*

upset [CHANGE] /ʌpˈset/ *verb* [T] **upsetting, upset, upset** to change the usual or expected state or order of something, especially in a way which stops it from happening or working: *Any mechanical problems would upset our plans of driving across the desert.*

upset /ˈʌp.set/ *noun* **1** [U] confusion and problems: *How much upset will the new monitoring procedures cause?* **2** [C] when someone beats the team or player that was expected to win: *It would be quite an upset if the favourite didn't win.*

upset [KNOCK] /ʌpˈset/ *verb* [T] **upsetting, upset, upset** to push or knock something out of its usual position, usually accidentally, especially causing it to fall: *Our dog upset the picnic table, spilling food everywhere.*

• **upset the apple cart** to cause trouble, especially by spoiling someone's plans

upset [ILLNESS] /ˈʌp.set/ *noun* [C] *INFORMAL* a slight illness of the stomach: *Melanie's got a* ***stomach/tummy*** *upset so she won't be going to school today.* **upset** /ʌpˈset/ *adj: I've got an upset* ***stomach/tummy*** *– serves me right for eating so much.* **upset** /ʌpˈset/ *verb* [T] **upsetting, upset, upset** *He can't eat grapes – they upset him/his stomach.*

the upshot /ðiˈʌp.ʃɒt/ [US] /-ʃɑːt/ *noun* [S] something which happens as a result of other actions, events or decisions: *The upshot* ***of*** *the discussions is that there will be no redundancies.*

upside /ˈʌp.saɪd/ *noun* [S] the advantage of a situation: *It's annoying that we can't travel until Thursday, but the upside is that the fare's cheaper then.* ➲Compare **downside**.

,upside ˈdown *adv, adj* having the part which is usually at the top turned to be at the bottom: ***Turn*** *the jar upside down and shake it.* ○ *The plane was flying upside down at high speed.*

• **turn upside down** to (cause something to) change completely and in a bad way: *Another poor harvest could turn the country's economy upside down.* ○ *Their lives were turned upside down when their son was arrested.*

upstage [STEAL ATTENTION] /ʌpˈsteɪdʒ/ *verb* [T] to take people's attention away from someone and make them listen to or look at you instead: *Most supporting bands tend to be youngsters, and rarely upstage the star.*

upstage [THEATRE AREA] /ʌpˈsteɪdʒ/ /ˈ--/ *adv, adj* [before n] towards or at the part of a theatre stage that is furthest from the people watching the performance: *He looks upstage to where the body is lying.* ✱ NOTE: The opposite is **downstage**.

upstairs /ʌpˈsteəz/ [US] /-ˈsterz/ *adv, adj* [before n] towards or on the highest floor or floors of a building: *an upstairs landing/window* ○ *He heard glass breaking and ran upstairs to see what had caused it.* ✱ NOTE: The opposite is **downstairs**. **upstairs** /ʌpˈsteəz/ [US] /-ˈsterz/ *noun* [S] *Sadly,* ***the*** *upstairs of the house was gutted by fire.*

upstanding /ʌpˈstæn.dɪŋ/ *adj SLIGHTLY FORMAL* behaving in a good and moral way: *She is regarded as an upstanding* ***citizen*** *in the local community.*

upstart /ˈʌp.stɑːt/ [US] /-stɑːrt/ *noun* [C] *DISAPPROVING* a person, especially a young one, who has suddenly got power or an important position and takes advantage of this in an unpleasant way

upstate /ˈʌp.steɪt/ *adj* [before n], *adv US* towards or of the northern parts of a state in the US, especially those which are far from cities where a lot of people live: *upstate New York* ○ *We're going upstate for our vacation.*

upstream /,ʌpˈstriːm/ *adj* [before n], *adv* (moving) on a river or stream towards its origin: *Salmon swim upstream against very strong currents to reach their breeding areas.* ✱ NOTE: The opposite is **downstream**.

upsurge /ˈʌp.sɜːdʒ/ [US] /-sɝːdʒ/ *noun* [C] a sudden and usually large increase in something: *An upsurge* ***of/in*** *violence in the district has been linked to increased unemployment.*

upswing /ˈʌp.swɪŋ/ *noun* [C] an increase or improvement: *Many analysts are predicting an upswing* ***in*** *the economy.*

uptake /ˈʌp.teɪk/ *noun* **1** [S or U] *SPECIALIZED* the rate or act of taking something in: *Plants in their growth stage generally exhibit an increased uptake* ***of*** *nutrients.* **2** [U] *UK* the rate or act of accepting something: *There is a 90% uptake* ***of*** *vaccination in this country.* ○ *Uptake* ***of*** *places on the training course has been disappointing.*

• **be quick/slow on the uptake** *INFORMAL* If someone is quick/slow on the uptake they understand things easily/with difficulty: *He's a bit slow on the uptake, so you may have to repeat the instructions a few times.*

up-tempo /,ʌpˈtem.pəʊ/ [US] /-poʊ/ *adj, adv* describes music that is played at a fast beat

uptight /,ʌpˈtaɪt/ *adj INFORMAL* worried or nervous and not able to relax: *Don't get uptight* ***about*** *the exam – just do your best.*

ˈup ,to [LESS THAN] *adv* used to say that something is less than or equal to but not more than a stated value, number or level: *Up to two hundred people were on board the ship.* ○ *We can teach dancers up to intermediate level here.*

ˈup ,to [UNTIL] *prep* (*ALSO* **up until**) until: *Up to yesterday, we had no idea where the child was.*

ˈup ,to [RESPONSIBILITY] *prep* **be up to *sb*** to be the responsibility of someone: *It's up to the manager to make the final decision.*

ˈup ,to [DOING] *prep INFORMAL* **be up to *sth*** to be doing something, often something bad or illegal, usually secretly: *She's up to* ***no good*** (= doing something bad or forbidden) *– you can always tell because she stays in her room.* ○ *He looks very suspicious hanging around by the bins – I'm sure he's up to* ***something***.

up-to-date /,ʌp.təˈdeɪt/ *adj* modern, recent, or containing the latest information: *Great trouble is taken to keep our database up-to-date.* ➲See also **update**.

up-to-the-minute /,ʌp.tə.ðəˈmɪn.ɪt/ *adj* most recent; containing the most recent information: *Now we're going live to our reporter in Washington for up-to-the-minute news on the crisis.*

uptown /,ʌpˈtaʊn/ *adj* [before n], *adv US* in or towards the northern part of a city or town, especially if there is not much business or industry there: *We could walk uptown or we could take the train.* ○ *I can get lunch in Chinatown for half of what it costs uptown.* ➲Compare **downtown**.

upturn /ˈʌp.tɜːn/ [US] /-tɝːn/ *noun* [C] (especially in economics) an improvement or advantageous change to a higher level or value: *Investors should not expect a sharp upturn **in** the economy.* ✻ NOTE: The opposite is **down-turn**.

upturned /ˌʌpˈtɜːnd/ [US] /-ˈtɜːrnd/ *adj* pointing or looking up, or having the part which is usually at the bottom turned to be at the top: *An upturned boat on the beach provided shelter.*

upward /ˈʌp.wəd/ [US] /-wɚd/ *adj* moving towards a higher position, level or value: *With an upward trend in inflation, you expect prices to rise.* ✻ NOTE: The opposite is **downward**. **upwards** /ˈʌp.wədz/ [US] /-wɚdz/ *adv* (US USUALLY **upward**) *She turned her face upwards to the midday sun.* ○ *The cost of completion has been revised upwards again due to inflation.* ✻ NOTE: The opposite is **downwards**.

upwardly mobile /ˌʌp.wəd.liˈməʊ.baɪl/ [US] /-wɚd.liˈmoʊ.bəl/ *adj* moving or able to move to a higher social class, for example by becoming more wealthy: *The meeting attracted upwardly mobile professional and political women.* **ˌupward moˈbility** *noun* [U]

ˈupward(s) ˌof *prep* If you say something is upward(s) of a number or value, you mean it is at least the stated amount and probably more: *Upwards of fifty thousand people assembled in the main square.*

upwind /ˌʌpˈwɪnd/ *adj* [before n], *adv* in the direction from which the wind is blowing: *Stay upwind **of** the fumes if you can.* ✻ NOTE: The opposite is **downwind**.

uranium /jʊˈreɪ.ni.əm/ *noun* [U] a heavy metal which is radioactive and is used in the production of nuclear power and in some types of nuclear weapon

Uranus /ˈjʊə.rᵊn.əs/ /jʊˈreɪ.nəs/ [US] /ˈjʊr-/ /jʊˈreɪ-/ *noun* [S] the planet seventh in order of distance from the Sun, after Saturn and before Neptune

urban /ˈɜː.bᵊn/ [US] /ˈɝː-/ *adj* [before n] of or in a city or town: *urban development* ○ *urban decay* ⊃Compare **rural**.

urbanize, UK USUALLY **-ise** /ˈɜː.bᵊn.aɪz/ [US] /ˈɝː-/ *verb* [T] to build houses, offices, etc. in an area of countryside so that it becomes a town **urbanized** /ˈɜː.bᵊn.aɪzd/ [US] /ˈɝː-/ *adj*: *The UK is a highly urbanized country.*

urbanization, UK USUALLY **-isation** /ˌɜː.bᵊn.aɪˈzeɪ.ʃᵊn/ [US] /ˌɝː-/ *noun* [U] the process by which more and more people leave the countryside to live in cities

urbane /ɜːˈbeɪn/ [US] /ɝː-/ *adj* APPROVING (especially of a man) confident, comfortable and polite in social situations: *John Herschel was an urbane, kindly and generous man.* **urbanely** /ɜːˈbeɪn.li/ [US] /ɝː-/ *adv* **urbanity** /ɜːˈbæn.ɪ.ti/ [US] /ɝːˈbæn.ə.t̬i/ *noun* [U]

ˌurban ˈjungle *noun* [C usually sing] DISAPPROVING city life, especially the unpleasant parts of it: *Traffic noise, pollution, huge concrete buildings – how can people survive in the urban jungle?*

urchin /ˈɜː.tʃɪn/ [US] /ˈɝː-/ *noun* [C] OLD-FASHIONED OR HUMOROUS a small child, especially one who behaves badly and is dirty or untidily dressed: *a street urchin*

Urdu /ˈʊə.duː/ /ˈɜː.duː/ [US] /ˈɜː-/ /ˈʊr-/ *noun* [U] the official language of Pakistan, which is also spoken by many people in India

urethra /jʊəˈriː.θrə/ [US] /juː-/ *noun* [C] *plural* **urethras** or SPECIALIZED **urethrae** the tube in most mammals which carries urine from the bladder out of the body. In males it also carries sperm.

urge [DESIRE] /ɜːdʒ/ [US] /ɝːdʒ/ *noun* [C] a strong desire, especially one which is difficult or impossible to control: *The two of them seem unable to control their sexual urges.* ○ [+ **to** infinitive] *The urge **to** steal is very strong in many of the young men we look after here.*

urge [ADVISE] /ɜːdʒ/ [US] /ɝːdʒ/ *verb* [I or T] to strongly advise or try to persuade someone to do a particular thing: [+ **to** infinitive] *Lawyers will urge the parents **to** take further legal action.* ○ [+ **that**] *Investigators urged **that** safety procedures at the site should be improved.* ○ *Police urged continued vigilance in the fight against crime.* ○ *The dogs are urged **into** fighting more fiercely by loud shouts from the crowd.* ○ *We shall continue to urge **for** leniency to be shown to these prisoners.* **urging** /ˈɜː.dʒɪŋ/ [US] /ˈɝː-/ *noun* [C or U] *He was happy to comply without any further urging from me.* ○ *It was only because of Alison's urgings that he sold the house.*

▲ **urge *sb* on** *phrasal verb* [M] to encourage someone to do or achieve something: *The crowd was cheering and urging her on all through the race.*

urgent [IMPORTANT] /ˈɜː.dʒᵊnt/ [US] /ˈɝː-/ *adj* needing attention very soon, especially before anything else, because important: *He's got to sign that paper – will you tell him it's urgent?* ○ *The most urgent thing in a fire is to make sure everyone is out of the building.* ○ *Many people are **in** urgent **need of** food and water.* **urgency** /ˈɜː.dʒᵊnt.si/ [US] /ˈɝː-/ *noun* [U] *It now is a matter of urgency that aid reaches the famine area.* **urgently** /ˈɜː.dʒᵊnt.li/ [US] /ˈɝː-/ *adv*: *Help is urgently needed.*

urgent [CONTINUALLY TRYING] /ˈɜː.dʒᵊnt/ [US] /ˈɝː-/ *adj* FORMAL (especially of a person's actions) continual and determined in trying to get or do something: *His urgent pleas of innocence made no difference to the judge's decision.* **urgency** /ˈɜː.dʒᵊnt.si/ [US] /ˈɜːr-/ *noun* [U] **urgently** /ˈɜː.dʒᵊnt.li/ [US] /ˈɝː-/ *adv*

uric /ˈjʊə.rɪk/ [US] /ˈjʊr.ɪk/ *adj* [before n] SPECIALIZED of urine: *uric acid*

urinal /jʊˈraɪ.nᵊl/ [US] /ˈjʊr.ᵊn.ᵊl/ *noun* [C] a device, usually fitted to a wall, into which men or boys can urinate, or a building which contains one or more of these devices

urinary /ˈjʊə.rɪ.nᵊr.i/ [US] /ˈjʊr.ɪ.ner-/ *adj* relating to urine or to the parts of the body which produce and carry urine: *urinary tract infections*

urinate /ˈjʊə.rɪ.neɪt/ [US] /ˈjʊr.ɪ-/ *verb* [I] to excrete urine from the body **urination** /ˌjʊə.rɪˈneɪ.ʃᵊn/ [US] /ˌjʊr.ɪ-/ *noun* [U]

urine /ˈjʊə.rɪn/ [US] /ˈjʊr.ɪn/ *noun* [U] the yellowish liquid waste which is released from the body when you go to the toilet

URL /ˌjuː.ɑːrˈel/ [US] /ˌjuː.ɑːrˈel/ *noun* [C] ABBREVIATION FOR uniform resource locator: a website address

urn /ɜːn/ [US] /ɝːn/ *noun* [C] **1** a container, especially a large round one on a stem, which is used for decorative purposes in a garden, or one which has a lid and is used for holding a dead person's ASHES (= the powder that is left after a dead body has been burned) **2** a large cylindrical metal container with a lid which is used for holding a large amount of drink such as tea or coffee and keeping it hot: *a tea urn*

us [GROUP] STRONG /ʌs/, WEAK /əs/ *pronoun* (used as the object of a verb or a preposition) me and at least one other person: *Thank you for driving us to the station.* ○ *Many of us in the editorial department disagree with the changes that are happening.*

us [ME] STRONG /ʌs/, WEAK /əs/ *pronoun* UK NOT STANDARD (especially used in spoken English) me: *Give us a light, mate.* ○ *Give us it here and I'll see if I can mend it.*

us [OUR] STRONG /ʌs/, WEAK /əs/ *determiner* NOT STANDARD NORTHERN ENGLISH our: *Where've you parked us car?*

the US /ðəˌjuːˈes/ [AMERICA] *noun* [S] ABBREVIATION FOR the United States: *A new study of education in the US has just been published.* ○ *When did you become a US citizen?*

the USA /ðəˌjuː.esˈeɪ/ *noun* [S] ABBREVIATION FOR the United States of America

the USAF /ðəˌjuː.es.eɪˈef/ *noun* [S] ABBREVIATION FOR the United States Air Force

use [PURPOSE] /juːz/ *verb* [T] **used**, **used** to put something such as a tool, skill or building to a particular purpose: *This glass has been used – please fetch me a clean one.* ○ [+ **to** infinitive] *Use scissors **to** cut the shapes out.* ○ *Going on the expedition gives me a chance to use all the training I've had.* ○ *The old hospital isn't used anymore.* ○ *These lights are used **for** illuminating the playing area.* ○ *To use military force **against** the protesters would be unacceptable.* ○ INFORMAL *I could use* (= I would like) *some help putting these decorations up if you're not too busy.*

• **use *your* head** (UK OLD-FASHIONED INFORMAL **use *your* loaf**) used to tell someone in a slightly angry way that they should think more carefully about what they are doing: *Why didn't you use your head and cover the furniture before you started painting?*

use /juːs/ *noun* **1** [C or U] a purpose for which something is used: *A food processor has a variety of uses in the kitchen.* ○ *Don't throw that cloth away, you'll find a use*

U

for it one day. ○ *No, I don't want to buy a boat – I have no use **for** one!* **2** [U] when you use something, or when something is being used: *You should be able to **put** your experience in electronics **to (good)** use in your new job.* ○ *Don't touch the machine when it's **in** use.* ○ *Sorry but the escalator is **out of*** (US USUALLY **not in**) *use* (= not operating). ○ *Traditional farming methods are **going out of/coming into** use* (= used less and less/more and more) *in many areas.*

• **be (of) no use** to not be useful, helpful or possible: *His advice turned out to be no use at all.* ○ ***There** is no use **(in)** argu**ing** any more.* ○ ***It** is no use try**ing*** (= There is no purpose in trying) *to escape – no one ever gets out of here.* ○ ***It's** no use* (= I cannot succeed) *– I just can't get this lid off.*

• **be (of) (any/some) use** to be useful: *Perhaps his advice will be of use to you when you're older.*

• **make use of *sth*** to use something that is available: *We might as well make use of the hotel's facilities.*

• **the use of *sth*** permission to use something, or the ability to use something: *They said we could **have** the use of their flat at the coast whenever they weren't there.* ○ *She hurt her arm in the fall and **lost** the use of her fingers temporarily.*

• **What's the use of...?** (ALSO **What use is...?**) used to tell someone to stop worrying because worrying will not help: *Try not to get depressed – after all, what's the use of worrying?*

usable /ˈjuː.zə.bl̩/ *adj* can be used: *The specific software is also usable in other areas of research.*

usage /ˈjuː.sɪdʒ/ *noun* **1** [C or U] the way a particular word in a language, or a language in general, is used: *a guide to common English usage* ○ *The earliest recorded usage of the word is in the twelfth century.* **2** [U] the way something is treated or used: *Sports equipment is designed to withstand hard usage.*

useful /ˈjuːs.fəl/ *adj* effective; helping you to do or achieve something: *A good knife is probably one of the most useful things you can have in a kitchen.* ○ *Do the exercises serve any useful purpose?*

• **come in useful** UK to be useful and help someone to do or achieve something: *You should keep that paint – it might come in useful one day.*

• **make *yourself* useful** a way of telling someone to start being helpful: *Now you're here you might as well make yourself useful – there's a lot of clearing up to do.*

usefully /ˈjuːs.fəl.i/ *adv* in an effective or helpful way: *We could usefully spend the free time sightseeing.*

usefulness /ˈjuːs.fəl.nəs/ *noun* [U] *Some people think this system of education has **outlived** its usefulness* (= is no longer useful).

useless /ˈjuː.sləs/ *adj* of no use; not working or not achieving what is needed: *Without fuel, the vehicles will become useless **for** moving supplies.* ○ [+ to infinitive] ***It's** useless **to** speculate without more information.* ○ *She's very good at methodical work, but useless when there's a lot of pressure.* ○ INFORMAL *You're absolutely useless* (= not able to act effectively) *– can't you even go to the shops without getting lost!* **uselessly** /ˈjuː.slə.sli/ *adv* **uselessness** /ˈjuː.slə.snəs/ *noun* [U]

user /ˈjuː.zəʳ/ [US] /-zɚ/ *noun* [C] someone who uses a product, machine or service: *Unemployed people are the main users of this advice centre.* ○ *drug users*

U

use [REDUCE] /juːz/ *verb* [T] **used, used** to reduce the amount of or finish something, by eating it, burning it, writing on it or changing it chemically; to **consume**: *We've used **(up)** nearly all of the bread – will you buy some more?* ○ *Does she still use drugs?* ○ *Don't worry if you use the polish **up*** (= finish it) *– I'm going shopping tomorrow.*

use /juːs/ *noun* [C or U] *Building a dam would be a use **of** financial resources which this country cannot afford.* ○ *There has been some increase in **the** use **of** casual labour over recent years.*

▲ **use *sth* up** *phrasal verb* [M] to finish a supply of something: *Don't use up all the milk, we need some for breakfast.* ○ *The Earth's resources are being used up at an alarming rate.*

use [TAKE ADVANTAGE] /juːz/ *verb* [T] **used, used** USUALLY DISAPPROVING to take advantage of a person or situation; to **exploit** *He's just using you – he'll steal your ideas and then take the credit for them himself.* ○ *It might be possible to use their mistake to help us get what we want.* ○ *Within the relationship he feels **ill*** (= badly) *used most of the time.*

usage /ˈjuː.sɪdʒ/ *noun* [U] FORMAL the bad and unfair way someone treats you: *Many had complained about the usage they'd received at his hands.*

used [IN THE PAST] /juːst/ *verb* **1 used to** used to show that a particular thing always happened or was true in the past, especially if it no longer happens or is no longer true: *She used to live in Glasgow.* ○ *She used to love cats but one attacked her and she doesn't like them anymore.* ○ *You don't come and see me like you used to.* ○ NOT STANDARD *He did used to work there, didn't he?* **2 used to** forms negatives and questions in the same way as modal AUXILIARY VERBS: *When we were younger, we used not to be allowed to drink coffee.*

use /juːs/ *verb* **use to** In negative sentences and questions, 'use *to*' replaces 'used to' when it follows 'did' or 'didn't': *Did he use to be the doctor in 'Star Trek'?* ○ *We didn't use to go out much in the winter months.*

COMMON LEARNER ERROR

used to or **be used to?**

Used to + verb is for talking about a situation or regular activity in the past.

My dad used to smoke when he was younger.
I used to live in Italy, but now I live in England.

When you make **used to + verb** into a question or negative using the verb 'do', the correct form is **use to**.

My dad didn't use to smoke.
Where did you use to live?
~~*Where did you used to live?*~~

The expression **be used to** something/do**ing** something is for talking about something which you have done or experienced a lot before.

I don't mind the heat. I'm used to hot weather.
He's not used to working long hours.
~~*He's not use to working long hours.*~~

---

used [NOT NEW] /juːzd/ *adj* that has already been put to the purpose it was intended for; not new: *a used airline ticket* ○ *The blackmailers demanded to be paid in used £20 notes.* ○ *I could only afford a used car* (= one that has already been owned by others).

used [FAMILIAR] /juːzd/ *adj* **be used to *sth/sb*** to be familiar with something or someone: *We're used to tourists here – we get thousands every year.* ○ [+ v-ing] *She was not used to speak**ing** Cantonese.* ○ *Eventually you'll **get/become** used to the smells of the laboratory.*

user-friendly /ˌjuː.zəˈfrend.li/ [US] /-zɚ-/ *adj* If something, especially something related to a computer, is user-friendly, it is simple for people to use: *a user-friendly interface/printer* ○ *a user-friendly instruction manual* **user-friendliness** /ˌjuː.zəˈfrend.lɪ.nəs/ [US] /-zɚ-/ *noun* [U]

username /ˈjuː.zə.neɪm/ [US] /-zɚ-/ *noun* [C] (ALSO **user ID**) a name or other word that you sometimes need to type in together with a PASSWORD before you are allowed to use a computer or the Internet: *Please enter your username and password.*

usher /ˈʌʃ.əʳ/ [US] /-ɚ/ *verb* [T usually + adv or prep] to show someone where they should go, or to make someone go where you want them to go: *She ushered us **into** her office and offered us a coffee.* ○ *Officials quickly ushered the protesters **out** of the hall.*

usher /ˈʌʃ.əʳ/ [US] /-ɚ/ *noun* [C] a man who shows people where they should sit, especially at a formal event such as a WEDDING or at a theatre or cinema

▲ **usher *sth* in** *phrasal verb* [M] to be at the start of a new period, especially when important changes or new things happen, or to cause important changes to start happening: *Yesterday's match between Arsenal and Spurs ushered in the start of the new football season.* ○ *Banksie threw a huge party to usher in* (= celebrate) *the New Year.* ○ *The legislation should usher in a host of new opportunities for school leavers.*

usherette /ˌʌʃ.əˈret/ *noun* [C] a woman who works in a theatre or cinema, whose job is to show people to their seats and to sell sweets and drinks

the USN /ˌðəˌjuːˈesˈen/ *noun* [S] *ABBREVIATION FOR* the United States Navy

USP /ˌjuːesˈpiː/ *noun* [C] *ABBREVIATION FOR* unique selling proposition: a feature of a product that makes it different from and better than other similar products and that can be emphasized in advertisements for the product

USS /ˌjuːesˈes/ *ABBREVIATION FOR* United States Ship: used before the names of ships in the US navy: *He was a radio technician aboard the USS Missouri.*

the USSR /ˌðəˌjuːesesˈɑːʳ/ Ⓤ /-ˈɑːr/ *noun* [S] *ABBREVIATION FOR* the Union of Soviet Socialist Republics

usu. *ABBREVIATION FOR* usually

usual /ˈjuːʒu.əl/ *adj* normal; happening, done or used most often: *I went to bed at my usual time.* ○ *There was more rainfall **than** usual this summer in the mountain areas.* ○ *You'll find the cutlery in its usual place.* ○ *Terry was, **as** usual, slow to respond.* ○ *This shop is open for business **as** usual despite the shortages.*

usual /ˈjuːʒu.əl/ *noun* [S] *INFORMAL* Someone's usual is the drink, especially an alcoholic one, which they most often have, for example when they are in a bar: *A gin and tonic for my dad, and I'll have **the/my** usual.*

usually /ˈjuːʒu.ə.li/ *adv* in the way that most often happens: *He usually gets home about 6 o'clock.* ○ *I usually just have a sandwich for lunch.* ○ *Is your friend usually so rude?* ○ *Usually we go to France in August.* ○ *"Does this shop open on Sundays?" "Usually."*

usurp /juːˈzɜːp/ /-ˈsɜːp/ Ⓤ /-ˈzɝːp/ /-ˈsɝːp/ *verb* [T] *SLIGHTLY FORMAL* to take control or a position of power, especially without having the right to: *The powers of local councils are being usurped by central government.* **usurper** /juːˈzɜːpəʳ/ /-ˈsɜː-/ Ⓤ /-ˈzɝː.pɚ/ /-ˈsɝːr-/ *noun* [C]

usury /ˈjuː.zju.ri/ Ⓤ /-ʒɚ.i/ *noun* [U] *FORMAL DISAPPROVING* the activity of lending someone money with the agreement that they will pay back a very much larger amount of money later

utensil /juːˈten.sɪl/ *noun* [C] a tool with a particular use, especially in a kitchen or house: *In the drawer was a selection of **kitchen** utensils – spoons, spatulas, knives and whisks.*

uterus /ˈjuː.tʳr.əs/ Ⓤ /-t̬ɚ-/ *noun* [C] *plural* **uteri** or **uteruses** *SPECIALIZED* a womb **uterine** /ˈjuː.tʳr.aɪn/ Ⓤ /-t̬ə.raɪn/ *adj* ➩See also **IUD.**

utilitarian /ˌjuː.tɪ.lɪˈteə.ri.ən/ Ⓤ /-ˈter.i-/ *adj* designed to be useful rather than decorative: *Like many factories it's a very ugly utilitarian building.*

utilitarianism /ˌjuː.tɪ.lɪˈteə.ri.ə.nɪ.zᵊm/ Ⓤ /-ter.i-/ *noun* [U] the system of thought which states that the best action or decision in a particular situation is the one which most benefits the most people

utility /juːˈtɪl.ɪ.ti/ Ⓤ /-ə.t̬i/ *noun* **1** [U] *FORMAL* the useful-ness of something, especially in a practical way **2** [C] *SLIGHTLY FORMAL* a service which is used by the public, such as an electricity or gas supply or a train service: *utility bills*

utilize, *UK USUALLY* **-ise** /ˈjuː.tɪ.laɪz/ Ⓤ /-t̬ᵊl.aɪz/ *verb* [T] *FORMAL* to use something in an effective way: *The vitamins come in a form that is easily utilized by the body.* **utilizable**, *UK USUALLY* **-isable** /ˈjuː.tɪ.laɪ.zə.bl̩/ Ⓤ /-t̬ᵊl.aɪ-/ *adj* **utilization**, *UK USUALLY* **-isation** /ˌjuː.tɪ.laɪˈzeɪ.ʃᵊn/ Ⓤ /-t̬ᵊl.ɪ-/ *noun* [U] *Sensible utilization of the world's resources is a priority.*

u'tility ˌroom *noun* [C] a room, especially in a house, where large pieces of useful equipment such as a washing machine can be kept and where things can be stored

utmost /ˈʌt.məʊst/ Ⓤ /-moʊst/ *adj* [before n] (*FORMAL* **uttermost**) used to emphasize how important or serious something is: *a matter of the utmost importance* ○ *The situation needs to be handled **with the** utmost care.* **utmost** /ˈʌt.məʊst/ Ⓤ /-moʊst/ *noun* [S] (*ALSO* **uttermost**) *The new model of the car offers **the** utmost **in** power and performance.*

● **do/try your utmost** to do something as well as you can by making a great effort: *She did her utmost **to** finish on time.*

utopia /juːˈtəʊ.pi.ə/ Ⓤ /-ˈtoʊ-/ *noun* [C or U] (the idea of) a perfect society in which everyone works well with each other and is happy **utopian** /juːˈtəʊ.pi.ən/ Ⓤ /-ˈtoʊ-/ *adj*: *a utopian vision* ○ *utopian aims*

utter COMPLETE /ˈʌt.əʳ/ Ⓤ /ˈʌt.ɚ/ *adj* [before n] complete or extreme: *utter confusion/misery/chaos* ○ *utter nonsense/rubbish/drivel* ○ *The meeting was a **complete and** utter waste of time.* ○ *Lying back in the hot bath was utter bliss.* **utterly** /ˈʌt.ᵊl.i/ Ⓤ /ˈʌt.ɚ.li/ *adv*: *What an utterly stupid thing to do!*

utter SPEAK /ˈʌt.əʳ/ Ⓤ /ˈʌt.ɚ/ *verb* [T] *SLIGHTLY FORMAL* to say something or to make a sound with your voice: *She sat through the whole meeting without uttering a word.* **utterance** /ˈʌt.ᵊr.ᵊnts/ Ⓤ /ˈʌt.ɚ-/ *noun* [C] **1** *FORMAL* something that someone says: *The senator's weekend utterances were promptly rebutted by three of his colleagues on Monday.* **2** *LITERARY* **give utterance to** *sth* to express your ideas or feelings in spoken words: *She has one great fear to which she will never give utterance.*

U-turn /ˈjuː.tɜːn/ Ⓤ /-tɝːn/ *noun* [C] (*US INFORMAL* **U-ie**) **1** a turn made by a car in order to go back in the direction from which it has come: *It is illegal to **do/make** a U-turn on a motorway.* **2** *MAINLY DISAPPROVING* a complete change from one opinion or plan of action to an opposite one: *The Prime Minister **did/made** a quick U-turn in response to all the adverse publicity.*

Uzi /ˈuː.zi/ *noun* [C] *TRADEMARK* (the name of the maker of) a type of MACHINE GUN (= automatic gun) which fires many bullets in a very short time

U

V

V LETTER (*plural* **V's** or **Vs**), **v** (*plural* **v's** or **vs**) /viː/ *noun* [C] the 22nd letter of the English alphabet

V NUMBER, **v** /viː/ *noun* [C] the sign used in the Roman system for the number 5

v AGAINST /viː/ *prep* (*ALSO* **vs**) **1** ABBREVIATION FOR **versus**: *I need to consider the advantages v the disadvantages.* **2** used to show who is competing in a game: *Sunderland United v Worthing* **3** used to show the two sides involved in a court case: *the 1973 Supreme Court decision, Roe v Wade*

v. VERY *adv* WRITTEN ABBREVIATION FOR **very** EXTREMELY: *The teacher wrote 'v. good' on my essay.*

V VERB *noun* [U] WRITTEN ABBREVIATION FOR **verb**

vac PERIOD /væk/ *noun* [C] UK INFORMAL FOR **vacation** PERIOD: *Have you managed to get a job for the **long** (= summer) vac?*

vac EQUIPMENT /væk/ *noun* **1** [C] INFORMAL FOR **vacuum (cleaner) 2** [S] UK INFORMAL an act of cleaning something with a **vacuum cleaner**: *Could you give the bedrooms a vac?*

vacant EMPTY /ˈveɪ.kənt/ *adj* **1** not filled or OCCUPIED; available to be used: *The hospital has no vacant beds.* ⊃Compare **engaged** IN USE. **2** A vacant job is one that no one is doing and is therefore available for someone new to do: *When the post **fell** (= became) vacant, Dennis Bass was appointed to fill it.*
vacancy /ˈveɪ.kənt.si/ *noun* [C] **1** a space or place which is available to be used: *We wanted to book a hotel room in July but there were no vacancies.* ○ *The dentist can't see you today but she has a vacancy tomorrow morning.* ○ *There are still some vacancies **for** students in science and engineering courses, but the vacancies in humanities have **been filled**.* **2** a job that no one is doing and is therefore available for someone new to do: *There is a vacancy for a shop assistant on Saturdays.*

vacant NOT INTERESTED /ˈveɪ.kənt/ *adj* showing no interest or activity: *She had a vacant **look/expression** on her face.* **vacantly** /ˈveɪ.kənt.li/ *adv*: *She **gazed/stared** vacantly into space/ahead.*

vacant pos'session *noun* [U] UK SPECIALIZED when someone who buys a house or property is allowed to use it immediately without anyone else still living in it or using it

vacate /vəˈkeɪt/ /ˈveɪ-/ *verb* [T] FORMAL to leave a room, building, chair, etc. so that it is available for other people: *Hotel guests are requested to vacate their rooms by twelve noon.* ○ *Denis vacates his post/job at the end of the week.*

vacation HOLIDAY /veɪˈkeɪ.ʃən/ *noun* [C or U] US a holiday, especially when you are travelling away from home for pleasure: *We're taking a vacation in June.* ○ *They went to Europe **on** vacation.* ○ *I've still got some vacation left before the end of the year.* **vacation** /veɪˈkeɪ.ʃən/ *verb* [I] *Remember that time we were vacationing **in** Vermont?*
vacationer /veɪˈkeɪ.ʃən.əʳ/ ⓤ /-ɚ/ *noun* [C] US FOR **holidaymaker**

vacation PERIOD /veɪˈkeɪ.ʃən/ *noun* [C] (UK INFORMAL **vac**) MAINLY US a period of the year when schools or colleges are closed, or when law courts do not operate: *the Christmas/Easter/summer/long vacation*

vaccine /ˈvæk.siːn/ *noun* [C or U] a substance which contains a harmless form of a virus or BACTERIUM (= extremely small organism), and which is given to a person or animal to prevent them from getting the disease which the virus or bacterium causes: *This vaccine protects against some kinds of the bacteria which cause meningitis.*
vaccinate /ˈvæk.sɪ.neɪt/ *verb* [T] to give someone a vaccine, usually by injection, to prevent them from getting a disease: *The children were vaccinated **against** the major childhood diseases.* ⊃See also **inoculate**; **immunize** at **immune**. **vaccination** /ˌvæk.sɪˈneɪ.ʃən/

noun [C or U] *All the children have received two vaccinations **against** measles.*

vacillate /ˈvæs.ɪ.leɪt/ *verb* [I] DISAPPROVING to be uncertain what to do, or to change frequently between two opinions: *Her mood vacillated **between** hope and despair.* **vacillation** /ˌvæs.ɪˈleɪ.ʃən/ *noun* [C or U]

vacuous /ˈvæk.ju.əs/ *adj* FORMAL not expressing or showing intelligent thought or purpose: *a vacuous remark/question/expression/smile* **vacuously** /ˈvæk.ju.ə.sli/ *adv* **vacuousness** /ˈvæk.ju.ə.snəs/ *noun* [U] (ALSO **vacuity**)

vacuum /ˈvæk.juːm/ *noun* **1** a space from which most or all of the air, gas or other material has been removed or is not present **2** [S] a lack of something: *The withdrawal of troops from the area has created a security vacuum which will need to be **filled**.* **3 in a vacuum** kept separate from other people and activities: *No artist works in a vacuum – we are all of us influenced by others.* **vacuum** /ˈvæk.juːm/ *verb* [I or T] (UK ALSO **hoover**) to use a vacuum cleaner to collect dust, dirt, etc: *Vacuum **(up)** the cake crumbs, would you?*

'vacuum ˌcleaner *noun* [C] (UK ALSO TRADEMARK **Hoover**, INFORMAL **vac**) a machine which cleans floors and other surfaces by sucking up dust and dirt

'vacuum ˌflask *noun* [C] (US **vacuum bottle**) a container that keeps hot liquids hot, or cold liquids cold, and usually has a lid that is used as a cup ⊃See also **flask** HOT DRINKS.

vacuum-packed /ˈvæk.juːmˌpækt/ /ˌ--ˈ-/ *adj* Something, especially food, which is vacuum-packed is in a soft container from which the air has been removed so that the contents can be stored longer.

'vacuum ˌpump *noun* [C] a piece of equipment for removing air or gas from a container, creating a vacuum inside

vagabond /ˈvæg.ə.bɒnd/ ⓤ /-bɑːnd/ *noun* [C] OLD USE OR LITERARY a person who has no home and usually no job, and who travels from place to place: *They live a vagabond life/existence, travelling around in a caravan.* ⊃Compare **vagrant**.

vagaries /ˈveɪ.gəˈr.iz/ ⓤ /-gɚ-/ *plural noun* FORMAL unexpected and uncontrollable events or changes which have an influence on a situation: *The success of the event will be determined by **the** vagaries **of the weather**.* ○ *She had her own style and was not influenced by **the** vagaries **of fashion**.*

vagina /vəˈdʒaɪ.nə/ *noun* [C] the part of a woman or other female mammal's body which connects her outer sex organs to her womb **vaginal** /vəˈdʒaɪ.nəl/ *adj*: *vaginal intercourse* **vaginally** /vəˈdʒaɪ.nəl.i/ *adv*

vagrant /ˈveɪ.grənt/ *noun* [C] FORMAL OR LEGAL a person who is poor and does not have a home or job; a **tramp**: *The town has shelters and food handouts for vagrants.* **vagrancy** /ˈveɪ.grənt.si/ *noun* [U] *Most European countries have abandoned laws that make vagrancy a crime.*

vague /veɪg/ *adj* **1** not clearly expressed, known, described or decided: *I do have a vague memory of meeting her many years ago.* ○ *The patient had complained of vague pains and backache.* **2** not clear in shape, or not clearly seen: *Through the mist I could just make out a vague figure.* **3** describes someone who is not able to think clearly, or who, sometimes as a way of hiding what they really think, does not express their opinions clearly: *My aunt is incredibly vague – she can never remember where she's left things.* ○ *Their report is **studiously** vague (= intentionally not exact) on future economic prospects.* **vaguely** /ˈveɪ.gli/ *adv*: *I vaguely remembered having met her before.* **vagueness** /ˈveɪg.nəs/ *noun* [U]

vain UNSUCCESSFUL /veɪn/ *adj* unsuccessful or useless; of no value: *The doctors gave him more powerful drugs in the vain **hope** that he might recover.* ○ FORMAL *It was vain **to** pretend to himself that he was not disappointed.*
• **in vain** unsuccessful or useless: *I tried in vain to start a conversation.* ○ *All the police's efforts to find him were in vain.*
vainly /ˈveɪn.li/ *adv* unsuccessfully: *He tried vainly to make them listen.*

vain [SELFISH] /veɪn/ *adj* too interested in your own appearance or achievements: *He was very vain* ***about*** *his hair and his clothes.*
vanity /ˈvæn.ɪ.ti/ [US] /-ə.t̬i/ *noun* **1** [U] DISAPPROVING when you are too interested in your appearance or achievements: *He wants the job purely for reasons of vanity and ambition.* **2** [C] US FOR **dressing table**

valance /ˈvæl.ənts/ *noun* [C] **1** a short piece of gathered material which hangs down especially around the base of a bed **2** US a **pelmet**

vale /veɪl/ *noun* [C] **1** used in the name of some valleys: *the Vale of Evesham* **2** OLD-FASHIONED OR LITERARY a valley: *a cloud that floats on high o'er hills and vales*
• **this vale of tears** LITERARY This vale of tears is the world we live in, seen as sad and difficult.

valediction /ˌvæl.əˈdɪk.ʃən/ *noun* [C or U] FORMAL the act of saying goodbye, especially formally, or a formal speech in which someone says goodbye

valedictorian /ˌvæl.ə.dɪkˈtɔː.ri.ən/ [US] /-ˈtɔːr.i-/ *noun* [C] US a student, usually one who has been the most successful in a particular class, who makes a speech at a special ceremony at the end of a school year

valedictory /ˌvæl.əˈdɪk.tᵊr.i/ [US] /-tɚ-/ *adj* FORMAL relating to saying goodbye, especially formally: *a valedictory speech*

valentine /ˈvæl.ən.taɪn/ *noun* [C] someone you love or would like to have a romantic relationship with, to whom you send a VALENTINE CARD: *The message on the card said 'Be my Valentine'.*

ˈvalentine (ˌcard) *noun* [C] a decorative card which you send, usually without your name on it, on 14 February (Valentine's Day) to someone you love: *Did you get any valentines?* ○ *Most of the valentine cards either had hearts on them or were very rude.*

Valentine's Day /ˈvæl.ən.taɪnz,deɪ/ *noun* [C or U] 14 February, a day when you give a valentine card to someone you have a romantic relationship with or would like a romantic relationship with

valet /ˈvæl.eɪ/ [US] /vəˈleɪ/ *noun* [C] **1** someone in a hotel who cleans clothes **2** US someone at a hotel or restaurant who puts your car in a parking space for you **3** the personal male servant of a wealthy man, especially in the past
valet /ˈvæl.eɪ/ /-ɪt/ [US] /vəˈleɪ/ /-ɪt/ *verb* [T] UK to clean, especially the inside of, something: *There's a service which will valet your* ***car*** *for you while it is parked at the airport.*

ˈvalet ˌparking *noun* [U] the service offered by a restaurant, hotel, etc. of putting your car in a parking space

ˈvalet ˌservice *noun* [U] the service of cleaning clothes offered by a hotel to people staying there

valiant /ˈvæl.i.ənt/ *adj* very brave or bravely determined, especially when things are difficult or the situation gives no cause for hope: *The company has made a valiant* ***effort/attempt*** *in the last two years to make itself more efficient.* **valiantly** /ˈvæl.i.ənt.li/ *adv*

valid /ˈvæl.ɪd/ *adj* **1** based on truth or reason; able to be accepted: *a valid argument/criticism/reason* ○ *My way of thinking might be different from yours, but it's equally valid.* ➲Compare **invalid** NOT CORRECT. **2** A ticket or other document is valid if it is based on or used according to a set of official conditions which often include a time limit: *My passport is valid for another two years.* **3** having legal force: *Is this contract/ticket/agreement still valid?*
validate /ˈvæl.ɪ.deɪt/ *verb* [T] to make something officially acceptable or approved, especially after examining it: *It is a one-year course validated by London's City University.* ○ *The data is validated automatically by the computer after it has been entered.* **validation** /ˌvæl.ɪˈdeɪ.ʃən/ *noun* [U] *External validation of the teachers' assessments is recommended.* **validity** /vəˈlɪd.ɪ.ti/ [US] /vəˈlɪd.ə.t̬i/ *noun* [U] *This research seems to* ***give/lend*** *some validity* ***to*** *the theory that the drug might cause cancer.* **validly** /ˈvæl.ɪd.li/ *adv*

Valium /ˈvæl.i.əm/ *noun* [C or U] TRADEMARK a drug which makes you calm and helps you to stop worrying, or a pill containing this: *She was* ***on*** (= using) *Valium for a few months after the accident.* ○ *to take a couple of Valium*

valley /ˈvæl.i/ *noun* [C] an area of low land between hills or mountains, often with a river running through it: *the Nile Valley* ○ *the Thames valley* ○ *There was snow on the hill tops but not in the valley.*

valour UK, US **valor** /ˈvæl.əʳ/ [US] /-ɚ/ *noun* [U] FORMAL great bravery: *He was promoted to the rank of major in recognition of his valour during the battle.*

value [IMPORTANCE] /ˈvæl.juː/ *noun* **1** [S or U] the importance or worth of something for someone: *For them, the house's main value lay in its quiet country location.* ○ *They are known to* ***place/put/set a*** *high value* ***on*** *good presentation.* **2** [U] how useful or important something is: *The photos are* ***of*** *immense historical value.* ○ *His contribution was of little or no* ***practical*** *value.* ○ *The necklace had great* ***sentimental*** *value.* ○ *It has* ***novelty*** *value because I've never done anything like it before.*
valuable /ˈvæl.jʊ.bl̩/ *adj* Valuable information, advice, etc. is very helpful or important: *He was able to provide the police with some valuable information.* ○ *Parents gave the school valuable support in its case for getting its facilities improved.* * NOTE: The opposite is **useless** or **worthless. Invaluable** means 'extremely useful'.
valueless /ˈvæl.jʊ.ləs/ *adj* not important or helpful: *His comments were so general as to be nearly valueless.*
value /ˈvæl.juː/ *verb* [T] to consider something important: *I've always valued her advice.*
valued /ˈvæl.juːd/ *adj* FORMAL useful and important: *a valued member of staff*
values /ˈvæl.juːz/ *plural noun* the beliefs people have about what is right and wrong and what is most important in life, which control their behaviour: *family/moral/traditional values*

value [MONEY] /ˈvæl.juː/ *noun* [C or U] the amount of money which can be received for something: *She had already sold everything* ***of*** *value that she possessed.* ○ *What is the value* ***of*** *the prize?* ○ *The value* ***of*** *the pound* ***fell*** *against other European currencies yesterday.* ○ *Property values have fallen since the plans for the airport were published.* ○ *I thought the offer was* ***good*** *value* ***(for money)****/(US ALSO)* ***a good*** *value* (= a lot was offered for the amount of money paid).
valuable /ˈvæl.jʊ.bl̩/ *adj* worth a lot of money: *These antiques are both beautiful and extremely valuable.* ○ *This is losing valuable business for the company.* * NOTE: The opposite is **worthless. Invaluable** means 'extremely useful'.
valuables /ˈvæl.jʊ.bl̩z/ *plural noun* small objects, especially jewellery, which might be sold for a lot of money
valueless /ˈvæl.jʊ.ləs/ *adj* not worth any money: *We thought the chair was an antique worth a lot of money, but it turned out to be a valueless replica.*
value UK /ˈvæl.juː/ *verb* [T] (US **appraise**) to give a judgment about how much money something might be sold for: *He valued the painting* ***at*** *$2000.* ○ *The insurance company said I should have my jewellery valued.*
valuer UK /ˈvæl.juː.əʳ/ [US] /-ɚ/ *noun* [C] (US **appraiser**) a person whose job is to say how much something is worth
valuation /ˌvæl.juˈeɪ.ʃən/ *noun* [C or U] the act of deciding how much money something might be sold for or the amount of money decided on: *You can receive a home loan of up to 95% of the official valuation of the property.*

ˈvalue ˌjudgment *noun* [C] a statement of how good or bad you think an idea or action is: *People often* ***make*** *value judgments about things without considering them carefully.*

valve /vælv/ *noun* [C] **1** a device which opens and closes to control the flow of liquids or gases, or a similar structure in the heart and the veins, which controls the flow of blood: *The valve failed to* ***open/close.*** ○ *It was a weak* ***heart*** *valve that caused her death.* **2** part of a musical instrument such as a TRUMPET which changes the sound by controlling the flow of air

vamp /væmp/ *noun* [C] a woman who is conscious of and makes use of her attractiveness to men in order to get what she wants **vampish** /ˈvæm.pɪʃ/ *adj*: *vampish behaviour*

V

vamp /væmp/ *verb*
▲ **vamp *sth* up** *phrasal verb* [M] to make something more exciting: *The dress is simple and elegant, but you could vamp it up for evening wear with some stunning jewellery.*

vampire /ˈvæm.paɪəʳ/ [US] /-paɪr/ *noun* [C] (in stories) a dead person who comes back to life and sucks blood from other people at night: *The most famous vampire is Count Dracula of Transylvania in the story written by Bram Stoker.*

ˈvampire ˌbat *noun* [C] a small Central and South American flying animal which sucks blood from other animals

van [VEHICLE] /væn/ *noun* [C] **1** a medium-sized road vehicle used especially for carrying goods and which often has no windows in the sides of the back half: *a delivery van* ○ *a Transit van* ○ *a van driver* ➲See picture **Cars and Trucks** on page Centre 13 **2** *US* a medium-sized vehicle with windows all round, used for carrying more people than an ordinary car

van [FRONT] /væn/ *noun UK FORMAL* **in the van of *sth*** at the front, or in the most advanced position, of something: *The United States is in the van of the quest to establish contact with beings from the beyond.* ➲See also **the vanguard**.

vandal /ˈvæn.dəl/ *noun* [C] a person who intentionally damages property belonging to other people: *Vandals smashed windows and overturned cars in the downtown shopping district.*
vandalism /ˈvæn.dəl.ɪ.zəm/ *noun* [U] **1** the crime of intentionally damaging property belonging to other people: *Beset by drug problems, prostitution, violence and vandalism, this is one of the most unpleasant areas in the city.* ○ *These schools are known to be vulnerable to vandalism.* **2** any activity that is considered to be damaging or destroying something that was good: *Cutting down the old forest was **an act of** vandalism.* ○ *The advertising industry's use of classic songs is vandalism of popular culture, he said.*
vandalize, *UK USUALLY* **-ise** /ˈvæn.dəl.aɪz/ *verb* [T] to intentionally damage property belonging to other people: *When I got back, my car had been vandalized.* ○ *They are the type of teenagers likely to vandalize phone boxes.*

vane /veɪn/ *noun* [C] a flat narrow part of a FAN, PROPELLER, etc. which turns because of the pressure of air or liquid against it

the vanguard /ðəˈvæn.gɑːd/ [US] /-gɑːrd/ *noun* [S] **1** the part of an army or navy that leads an attack on an enemy ➲Compare **rearguard**. **2** a group of people who lead the development of new ideas, or a leading position in the development of something: *He is **in** the vanguard **of** economic reform.* ➲See also **the forefront**.

vanilla /vəˈnɪl.ə/ *noun* [U] a substance made from the seeds of a tropical plant, which is used to give flavour to sweet foods: *vanilla essence/extract* ○ *vanilla ice cream/yoghurt* ○ *a vanilla milkshake* ○ *Add two teaspoons of vanilla and stir.* ○ *Keeping a vanilla (UK)* ***pod/(US) bean*** (= seed container) *in your sugar jar will add a delicate flavour.*

vanish /ˈvæn.ɪʃ/ *verb* [I] to disappear or stop being present or existing, especially in a sudden, surprising way: *The child vanished while on her way home from school.* ○ *We rushed out of the shop in hot pursuit, but the thief had vanished **into thin air*** (= had completely disappeared). ○ *Cheap rural housing is vanishing in the south of the country.*
vanished /ˈvæn.ɪʃt/ *adj* not now present or existing: *The temple ruins are a distant reminder of a vanished empire.*
vanishing /ˈvæn.ɪʃ.ɪŋ/ *adj* beginning to disappear: *They expressed worry about the district's current budget crisis and its vanishing middle-class work force.*

vanity /ˈvæn.ɪ.ti/ [US] /-ə.t̬i/ *noun* **1** ➲See at **vain** SELFISH. **2** [C] *US FOR* **vanity unit**

ˈvanity ˌplates *plural noun US* NUMBER PLATES on a vehicle which have particular numbers or letters on them that the vehicle's owner has specially chosen and paid to have

ˈvanity ˌpress *noun* [C] a publishing company where writers pay to have their books produced

vanity unit /ˈvæn.ɪ.tiˌjuː.nɪt/ [US] /-ə.t̬i-/ *noun* [C] *UK* a small cupboard which stands on the floor in a bathroom and has a WASHBASIN (= fixed bowl-shaped container for water) in the top

vanquish /ˈvæŋ.kwɪʃ/ *verb* [T] *LITERARY* to defeat an opponent, especially in war: *Napoleon was vanquished at the battle of Waterloo in 1815.* ○ *The vanquished army surrendered their weapons.*

vantage point [PLACE] /ˈvɑːn.tɪdʒˌpɔɪnt/ [US] /ˈvæn.t̬ɪdʒ-/ *noun* [C] a place, especially a high place, which provides a good clear view of an area: ***From** our lofty vantage point, we could see the city spread out below us.*

vantage point [OPINION] /ˈvɑːn.tɪdʒˌpɔɪnt/ [US] /ˈvæn.t̬ɪdʒ-/ *noun* [C usually sing] *SLIGHTLY FORMAL* a particular personal way of thinking or set of opinions: *The documentary contains a first-hand description of political life in Havana **from** the vantage point **of** a senior bureaucrat.*

vapid /ˈvæp.ɪd/ *adj FORMAL* lacking intelligence or imagination: *a vapid television programme* **vapidity** /væpˈɪd.ɪ.ti/ [US] /-ə.t̬i/ *noun* [U] *the spiritual vapidity of Western materialism*

vapour *UK, US* **vapor** /ˈveɪ.pəʳ/ [US] /-pɚ/ *noun* [C or U] gas or extremely small drops of liquid which result from the heating of a liquid or solid: *The hollow glass tank contains hot mercury vapour.* ○ *Poisonous vapours burst out of the factory during the accident, causing several hundred deaths.*
vaporize, *UK USUALLY* **-ise** /ˈveɪ.pər.aɪz/ [US] /-pɚ.aɪz/ *verb* [I or T] to turn, or cause something to turn, from a solid or liquid state into gas: *During surgery, doctors sometimes use a laser beam to vaporize tiny blood vessels.* ○ *Most meteorites striking the Earth vaporize instantly.*

the vapours *UK, US* **the vapors** *plural noun OLD USE* when someone suddenly feels ill and weak, usually because of a shock

ˈvapour ˌtrail *UK, US* **vapor trail** *noun* [C] water vapour that looks like a line of white smoke behind an aircraft as it flies

vapourware, *US* **vaporware** /ˈveɪ.pə.weəʳ/ [US] /-pɚ.wer/ *noun* [U] *HUMOROUS* a computer program which is advertised but which is not yet or is never made available

variable /ˈveə.ri.ə.bl/ [US] /ˈver.i-/ *adj* likely to change frequently: *a variable interest rate* ○ *British weather is perhaps at its most variable in the spring.*
variable /ˈveə.ri.ə.bl/ [US] /ˈver.i-/ *noun* [C] *SPECIALIZED* a number, amount or situation which can change: *The variables in the equation are X, Y and Z.* ○ *The data was analysed according to neighbourhoods, but other key variables like credit rating, job history, savings and marital status were ignored altogether.* **variability** /ˌveə.ri.əˈbɪl.ɪ.ti/ [US] /ˌver.i.əˈbɪl.ə.t̬i/ *noun* [U]

variance /ˈveə.ri.ənts/ [US] /ˈver.i-/ *noun* **1** [C or U] *SLIGHTLY FORMAL* when two or more things are different, or the amount or number by which they are different: *There has been some unusual variance in temperature this month.* ○ *I could detect subtle variances in fragrance as we strolled through the garden.* **2** [C] *US LEGAL* official permission to do something which is not normally permitted: *We had to get **a (zoning)** variance before we could build the extension on our house.*
• **be at variance with *sb/sth*** to be in disagreement with someone or something, or to be different from them: *Young people's reactions to world events are often at variance with those of their parents.* ○ *Most heavy metal fans are under 20 – this is at variance with the age of the bands themselves, who are often over 40.*

variant /ˈveə.ri.ənt/ [US] /ˈver.i-/ *noun* [C] something which is slightly different from other similar things: *There are many colas on the market now, all variants **on** the original drink.* ○ *There are four variants **of** malaria, all transmitted to humans by a particular family of mosquitoes.* **variant** /ˈveə.ri.ənt/ [US] /ˈver.i-/ *adj*: *a variant form* ○ *Words spelt with 'ae', such as 'encyclopaedia', have a variant **spelling** with 'e', as in 'encyclopedia'.*

variation /ˌveə.riˈeɪ.ʃən/ [US] /ˌver.i-/ *noun* **1** ➲See **vary** CHANGE; **vary** DIFFERENT. **2** [C] *SPECIALIZED* one of several short tunes which are based on the same simple tune,

V

but are different from it and from the others: *symphonic variations*

varicose vein /ˈvær.ɪ.kəʊsˈveɪn/ ⓤ /ˌver.ɪ.koʊs-/ *noun* [C usually pl] a swollen and often painful vein, especially in the legs: *Pregnant women often get varicose veins.*

varied /ˈveə.rɪd/ ⓤ /ˈver.ɪd/ *adj* containing or changing between several different things or types: *a varied group of people* ○ *a lengthy and varied career* ○ *With its varied climate, the country attracts both winter and summer sports enthusiasts.* ➲See **vary**.

variegated /ˈveə.rɪ.ɡeɪ.tɪd/ ⓤ /ˈver.i.ə.ɡeɪ.t̬ɪd/ *adj* having a pattern of different colours or marks: *variegated leaves* ○ *a variegated plant* **variegation** /ˌveə.rɪˈɡeɪ.ʃᵊn/ ⓤ /ˌver.i.ə-/ *noun* [U]

variety CHANGE /vəˈraɪə.ti/ ⓤ /-t̬i/ *noun* [U] the characteristic of frequently changing and being different: *When preparing meals, you need to think about variety and taste as well as nutritional value.* ○ *Sexual reproduction serves to create genetic variety.* ○ *Work on the production line is monotonous and lacks variety.*

• **Variety is the spice of life.** SAYING said to emphasize that doing many different things, or frequently changing what you do, makes life interesting

variety TYPE /vəˈraɪə.ti/ ⓤ /-t̬i/ *noun* **1** [C] a different type of something: *The article was about the different varieties of Spanish spoken in South America.* ○ *This variety of rose is especially hardy and drought-resistant.* ○ *Our supermarket stocks apples in several different varieties.* **2** [S] many different types of things or people: *She does a variety of fitness activities.* ○ *The equipment could be used for a variety of educational purposes.* ○ *Manufacturers need large sales to justify offering a big variety in export markets.*

variety ENTERTAINMENT /vəˈraɪə.ti/ ⓤ /-t̬i/ *noun* [U] a type of entertainment which includes several separate short performances, such as singing, dancing, magic tricks and telling jokes: *a variety show*

var'iety ,store *noun* [C] US a shop which sells many different things, usually at low prices

various /ˈveə.ri.əs/ ⓤ /ˈver.i-/ *adj* many different: *We had various problems on our journey, including a puncture.* ○ *The author gave various reasons for having written the book.* ○ *Girardo was out of action with various injuries for most of last season.* ○ *Various people whom we weren't expecting turned up at the meeting.*

variously /ˈveə.ri.ə.sli/ ⓤ /ˈver.i-/ *adv* in several different ways, at several different times, or by several different people: *It is one of a new class of electronic products variously called 'personal communicators' or 'personal digital assistants'.* ○ *The number of cases this year of salmonella poisoning has been variously put at 26, 46, 49 or 51.*

varnish /ˈvɑː.nɪʃ/ ⓤ /ˈvɑːr-/ *noun* [C or U] a liquid which is painted onto wood or paintings to protect the surface, or the hard shiny surface it produces when it dries: *Polyurethane varnish provides a tough, scratch-resistant finish.* ○ *Dyes and stains offer no surface protection for the wood, which requires a final coat of (clear) varnish.* ○ *The varnish had been deliberately scratched.*
varnish /ˈvɑː.nɪʃ/ ⓤ /ˈvɑːr-/ *verb* [T] **1** to put varnish on a surface: *They decided to spend the weekend varnishing their boat.* **2** UK to use NAIL VARNISH
varnished /ˈvɑː.nɪʃt/ ⓤ /ˈvɑːr-/ *adj* covered with varnish: *a varnished surface* ○ *varnished wood*

varsity /ˈvɑː.sɪ.ti/ ⓤ /ˈvɑːr.sə.t̬i/ *adj* [before n] US describes sports teams at schools or colleges which are at the most skilled level of play: *He was a member of the varsity baseball team.*

vary CHANGE /ˈveə.ri/ ⓤ /ˈver.i/ *verb* [I or T] to change or cause something to change in amount or level, especially from one occasion to another: *My taste in classical music varies greatly/widely, but I usually prefer Mozart or Brahms.* ○ *Some people give a regular monthly donation while others vary the amount they give.*
variation /ˌveə.riˈeɪ.ʃᵊn/ ⓤ /ˌver.i-/ *noun* [C or U] a change in amount or level: *Unemployment rates among white-collar workers show much less regional variation than corresponding rates among blue-collar workers.* ○ *The medical tests showed some variation in the baby's heart*

rate. ○ *global temperature variations over the last 140 years*

vary DIFFERENT /ˈveə.ri/ ⓤ /ˈver.i/ *verb* [I or T] If things of the same type vary, they are different from each other, and if you vary them, you cause them to be different from each other: *Salary scales vary between states/from state to state/according to state/with each state.* ○ *The samples varied in quality but were generally acceptable.*
variation /ˌveə.riˈeɪ.ʃᵊn/ ⓤ /ˌver.i-/ *noun* [C] something that is slightly different from the usual form or arrangement: *There are wide variations in the way pensioners have benefited from the system.* ○ *The films she makes are all variations on the same theme.*

vascular /ˈvæs.kju.ləʳ/ ⓤ /-lɚ/ *adj* SPECIALIZED relating to the tubes which carry blood or liquids in animals and plants: *the vascular system* ○ *vascular disease* ○ *a vascular surgeon*

vase /vɑːz/ ⓤ /veɪs/ *noun* [C] a container for holding flowers or for decoration: *a vase of flowers*

vasectomy /vəˈsek.tə.mi/ *noun* [C or U] the medical operation of cutting the tubes through which a man's sperm move, in order to make him unable to make a woman pregnant

Vaseline /ˈvæs.ə.liːn/ *noun* [U] TRADEMARK a soft yellow or white oily substance which is used especially on the skin to protect it or on surfaces to LUBRICATE them (= stop them sticking together)

vast /vɑːst/ ⓤ /væst/ *adj* extremely big: *A vast audience watched the broadcast.* ○ *The amount of detail the book contains is vast.* ○ *The people who have taken our advice have saved themselves vast amounts/sums of money.* ○ *The vast majority of pupils attend state-funded schools.* **vastly** /ˈvɑːst.li/ ⓤ /ˈvæst.li/ *adv: vastly different* ○ *vastly superior* ○ *vastly improved*

vat /væt/ *noun* [C] a large container used for mixing or storing liquid substances, especially in a factory: *a vat of wine/oil*

VAT, Vat /ˌviː.eɪˈtiː/ ⓤ /væt/ *noun* [U] value-added tax (= a type of tax in European countries which is paid by the person who buys goods and services)
VATable /ˈvæt.ə.bᵊl/ ⓤ /ˈvæt̬-/ *adj* UK describes goods on which VAT has to be paid: *The rich spend more than the poor on VATable goods.*

the Vatican /ðəˈvæt.ɪ.kən/ ⓤ /-ˈvæt̬-/ *noun* [S] **1** the Pope or the officials who represent the Pope: *The Vatican released a statement condemning the recent terrorist attacks.* ○ *The information was given by a Vatican official.* **2** the main offices of the Catholic Church in Rome, which includes the building where the Pope lives: *No tour of Rome is complete without a visit to the Vatican/the Vatican city.*

vaudeville US /ˈvɔː.də.vɪl/ ⓤ /ˈvoʊd.vɪl/ *noun* [U] (UK music hall) a type of theatre entertainment in the 1800s and early 1900s which included music, dancing and jokes

vault ARCH /vɒlt/ ⓤ /vɑːlt/ *noun* [C] a type of arch which supports a roof or ceiling, especially in a church or public building, or a ceiling or roof supported by several of these arches
vaulted /ˈvɒl.tɪd/ ⓤ /ˈvɑːl.t̬ɪd/ *adj* related to or having a vault: *a vaulted ceiling* ○ *a vaulted room*
vaulting /ˈvɒl.tɪŋ/ ⓤ /ˈvɑːl.t̬ɪŋ/ *noun* [U] arches which support a ceiling or room: *After the explosion nothing of the walls or vaulting remained intact.*

vault ROOM /vɒlt/ ⓤ /vɑːlt/ *noun* [C] **1** (UK ALSO **vaults**) a room, especially in a bank, with thick walls and a strong door, which is used to store money or valuable things in safe conditions: *a bank vault* ○ *She entered the vault with an armed guard.* **2** a room under a church or a small building in a CEMETERY where dead bodies are buried: *She was buried in the family vault.*

vault JUMP /vɒlt/ ⓤ /vɑːlt/ *verb* **1** [I usually + adv or prep; T] to jump over something by first putting your hands on it or by using a pole: *He vaulted over the gate.* ○ *She vaulted the wall and kept running.* ○ SPECIALIZED *He has vaulted 6.02m in indoor competitions this year.* ➲See also **the pole vault. 2** [T] FORMAL to move someone or something suddenly to a much more important position: *Last week's changes vaulted the general to the top, over the* *heads of several of his seniors.*

ˌvaulting amˈbition *noun* [U] *DISAPPROVING* a desire to achieve an important and powerful position and a belief that this is more important than anything else: *He sacrificed his marriage to his vaulting political ambition.*

vaunted /ˈvɔːn.tɪd/ [US] /ˈvɑːn.t̬ɪd/ *adj FORMAL* praised frequently in a way that is considered to be more than acceptable or reasonable: *His **(much)** vaunted new scheme has been shown to have serious weaknesses.*

VC /ˌviːˈsiː/ *noun* [C usually sing] *UK ABBREVIATION FOR* Victoria Cross: a medal which is the highest honour for bravery that can be given to a British soldier, or a soldier who has received this medal: *My grandfather was awarded **the** VC.*

VCR /ˌviː.siːˈɑːʳ/ [US] /-ˈɑːr/ *noun* [C] a **video cassette recorder** (= a machine that you use to record and play television programmes or films on video)

VD /ˌviːˈdiː/ *noun* [U] *ABBREVIATION FOR* **venereal disease**

VDT /ˌviː.diːˈtiː/ *noun* [C] *US ABBREVIATION FOR* video display terminal: a piece of equipment with a screen on which information from a computer can be shown

VDU /ˌviː.diːˈjuː/ *noun* [C] *UK ABBREVIATION FOR* visual display unit: a piece of equipment with a screen on which information from a computer can be shown

've /-v/ /-əv/ *short form of* have: *I've been waiting for ages.*

veal /viːl/ *noun* [U] meat from a very young cow

vector [CALCULATION] /ˈvek.təʳ/ [US] /-tɚ/ *noun* [C] *SPECIALIZED* something physical such as a force which has size and direction

vector [ANIMAL] /ˈvek.təʳ/ [US] /-tɚ/ *noun* [C] *SPECIALIZED* an insect or animal which carries a disease from one animal or plant to another: *Mosquitoes are the vectors **of** malaria.*

Veda /ˈveɪ.də/ *noun* [C] one or all of the holy books of writings of Hinduism **Vedic** /ˈveɪ.dɪk/ *adj*

Vedanta /vɪˈdæn.tə/ *noun* [U] one of the main systems of Hindu thought

veep /viːp/ *noun* [C] *US INFORMAL* a **vice president**

veer /vɪəʳ/ [US] /vɪr/ *verb* [I + adv or prep] to change direction: *All of a sudden, the car veered **off** the road.* ○ *Moments before crashing, the jet was seen veering sharply **to** the right.* ○ *Three men were feared dead last night after a helicopter veered **off course** into an oil platform.* ○ *Our talk soon veered **onto** the subject of football.*

veg /vedʒ/ *noun* [U], *plural noun UK INFORMAL* vegetables: *a fruit and veg stall* ○ *He still prefers the old-fashioned British meal of meat and two veg.*

veg /vedʒ/ *verb*

▲ **veg out** *phrasal verb INFORMAL* to relax and spend time doing very little: *I'm exhausted – I think I'll just go home and veg out in front of the TV tonight.*

vegan /ˈviː.gən/ *noun* [C] a person who does not eat or use any animal products, such as meat, fish, eggs, cheese or leather: *Vegans get all the protein they need from nuts, seeds, beans and cereals.* ➲Compare **vegetarian**. **vegan** /ˈviː.gən/ *adj*: *a vegan diet* ○ *She decided to **turn** vegan after watching a documentary about how poultry is raised.*

vegeburger /ˈvedʒ.ɪˌbɜː.gəʳ/ [US] /-ˌbɝː.gɚ/ *noun* [C] *UK FOR* **veggieburger**

vegetable /ˈvedʒ.tə.bl̩/ *noun* **1** [C] (*US INFORMAL* **veggie**) a plant, root, seed, or pod that is used as food, particularly in savoury dishes: *fresh/frozen vegetables* ○ *vegetable soup/stew/curry* ○ *fruit and vegetables* ○ *The potato is the most popular vegetable in Britain.* ○ *In the winter we tend to eat more **root** vegetables, such as carrots and parsnips.* ○ ***Raw** vegetables contain more potassium than **cooked** ones.* ○ *a vegetable knife* ➲Compare **fruit** PLANT PART. ➲See picture **Vegetables** on page Centre 2 **2** [C usually sing] *INFORMAL* a person who does not do anything or has no interest in doing anything: *Sitting at home all day in front of the TV slowly turned her into a vegetable.* **3** [C usually sing] *OFFENSIVE* a person who is unable to think or move correctly because of severe brain damage

vegetable /ˈvedʒ.tə.bl̩/ *adj* made or obtained from a plant, or growing in the form of a plant: *vegetable matter/dye* ○ *First think of an object and tell us if it is animal, vegetable or mineral.*

ˈvegetable ˌoil *noun* [C or U] cooking oil made from plants

vegetarian /ˌvedʒ.ɪˈteə.ri.ən/ [US] /-ˈter.i-/ *noun* [C] (*UK INFORMAL* **veggie**) a person who does not eat meat for health or religious reasons or because they want to avoid cruelty to animals: *Of the four million people who have become vegetarians in Britain, nearly two-thirds are women.* ➲Compare **vegan**. **vegetarian** /ˌvedʒ.ɪˈteə.ri.ən/ [US] /-ˈter.i-/ *adj* (*INFORMAL* **veggie**) *vegetarian cooking/food* ○ *a vegetarian dish/meal* ○ *a vegetarian restaurant* ○ *She's recently gone/become vegetarian.* **vegetarianism** /ˌvedʒ.ɪˈteə.ri.ə.nɪ.zᵊm/ [US] /-ˈter.i-/ *noun* [U] *Vegetarianism is very popular among young people in Britain, especially among teenage girls.*

vegetate /ˈvedʒ.ɪ.teɪt/ *verb* [I] to live in a way that lacks physical and mental activity: *A report has shown that children spend too much time vegetating in front of the TV.*

vegetative /ˈvedʒ.ɪ.te.tɪv/ [US] /-ə.teɪ.t̬ɪv/ *adj SPECIALIZED* alive but showing no brain activity

vegetation /ˌvedʒ.ɪˈteɪ.ʃᵊn/ *noun* [U] plants in general or plants which are found in a particular area: *The railway track will have to be cleared of vegetation if it is to be used again.* ○ *Much of the region's native vegetation has been damaged by developers who are building hotels along the coast.*

veggie /ˈvedʒ.i/ *noun* [C], *adj* (*ALSO* **veggy**) *UK INFORMAL* (a) **vegetarian**

veggie /ˈvedʒ.i/ *noun* [C] *US INFORMAL* a vegetable

veggieburger, *UK ALSO* **vegeburger** /ˈvedʒ.iˌbɜː.gəʳ/ [US] /-ˌbɝː.gɚ/ *noun* [C] a type of savoury food made by pressing together small pieces of vegetables, seeds, nuts and grains into a flat round shape

vehement /ˈviː.ə.mənt/ *adj* expressing strong feelings, or characterized by strong feelings or great energy or force: *Despite vehement opposition from his family, he quit school and became an actor.* ○ *Both men were vehement **in** their denial of the charges against them.* ○ *They launched a vehement attack on the government's handling of environmental issues.*

vehemently /ˈviː.ə.mənt.li/ *adv* in a strong and emotional way: *The president has vehemently **denied** having an extra-marital affair.* **vehemence** /ˈviː.ə.mənts/ *noun* [U] *She argued **with** such vehemence against the proposal that they decided to abandon it.*

vehicle [MACHINE] /ˈviː.ɪ.kl̩/ *noun* [C] *FORMAL* a machine usually with wheels and an engine, which is used for transporting people or goods on land, particularly on roads: *A truck driver died last night when his vehicle overturned.* ○ ***Road** vehicles include cars, buses and trucks.* ○ *Tractors are **farm** vehicles.* ○ *The number of thefts of **motor** vehicles rose by a third last year.* **vehicular** /vɪˈhɪk.jʊ.ləʳ/ [US] /viːˈhɪk.jʊ.lɚ/ *adj*: *The cottage has no vehicular access but can be reached by a short walk across the moor.*

vehicle [METHOD] /ˈviː.ɪ.kl̩/ *noun* [C usually sing] **1** a way of achieving, producing or expressing something: *The conference was seen as an ideal vehicle **for** increased cooperation between the member states.* ○ *Corporate America has embraced the Web as a new vehicle for advertising.* **2** a show, film, exhibition, etc. that is used to show the special skills or qualities of one particular performer or artist: *The play seems to be little more than a vehicle for its director and star.*

veil [MATERIAL] /veɪl/ *noun* [C] a piece of thin material worn by women to cover the face or head: *After the ceremony, the bride **lifted** up her veil to kiss her husband.* ○ *The women wore black veils which covered all but their eyes.*

• **take the veil** A Christian woman who takes the veil becomes a nun.

• **take/adopt the veil** A Muslim woman who takes or adopts the veil decides to wear traditional Muslim clothing.

veil /veɪl/ *verb* [T often passive] to cover something, especially the face or body, with a veil: *In some societies, women are expected to be veiled when they go out in public.*

veil [UNCLEAR EFFECT] /veɪl/ *noun* [S] *LITERARY* **1** a thin covering of something, which you can see through, but not very clearly: *The view over the lake was obscured by a veil **of** mist that hung in the air.* **2** something that prevents you from knowing what is happening: *The government has been urged to **lift** the veil **of secrecy** surrounding the minister's unexpected resignation.* **3 draw a veil over *sth*** to not talk any more about a subject because it could cause trouble or embarrassment: *I think we should draw a veil over everything that happened at the party, don't you?*
veil /veɪl/ *verb* [T] to hide or cover something so that you cannot see it clearly: *Thick fog veiled the city.*
veiled /veɪld/ *adj* describes words or ways of behaving which are not direct or expressed clearly: *a veiled reference/threat/warning* ○ *a **thinly** veiled **attack** on his abilities as a leader*

vein [TUBE] /veɪn/ *noun* [C] **1** a tube that carries blood to the heart from the other parts of the body **2** the frame of a leaf or an insect's wing
veined /veɪnd/ *adj* with many veins, or marked with lines that look like veins: *A thin, veined hand lay on the coverlet.* ○ *veined cheese/marble* **-veined** /-veɪnd/ *suffix*

vein [LAYER] /veɪn/ *noun* **1** [C] a narrow layer of a substance which forms in or fills a crack in rock: *A **rich** vein **of** iron ore was found in the hillside.* **2** [S] a particular quality or characteristic: *A vein **of** satirical anger runs through all his work.* ○ *In its bid to be elected, the party is attempting to **tap*** (= use) *an underlying vein **of** nationalism in the country.*

vein [MOOD] /veɪn/ *noun* [S or U] a style or a temporary mood: *The opening scene is very violent, and the rest of the film continues **in (a)** similar vein.* ○ *After laughing over the photo, they began to talk **in (a)** more serious vein about the damaging effect it could have on his career.*

Velcro /ˈvel.krəʊ/ Ⓤⓢ /-kroʊ/ *noun* [U] *TRADEMARK* material that consists of two pieces of cloth that stick together, used to fasten clothes

veld, **veldt** /velt/ *noun* [S] flat open country with few trees, which is characteristic of parts of southern Africa

vellum /ˈvel.əm/ *noun* [U] **1** a thick, cream-coloured, very high-quality writing paper **2** a material used in the past for writing on or for covering a book, made from the skins of young animals, especially cows or sheep

velocity /vəˈlɒs.ɪ.ti/ Ⓤⓢ /-ˈlɑː.sə.t̬i/ *noun* [C or U] *FORMAL* the speed at which an object is travelling: *Light travels at the highest achievable velocity in the universe.* ○ *He always used **high** velocity lead bullets in his rifle.*

velour, **velours** /vəˈlʊəʳ/ Ⓤⓢ /-ˈlʊr/ *noun* [U] a material similar to VELVET that has a soft surface and which is used for clothes and for covering furniture

velvet [CLOTH] /ˈvel.vɪt/ *noun* [U] a cloth usually woven from silk or cotton with a thick soft furry surface: *Her skin was **as soft as** velvet.* **velvet** /ˈvel.vɪt/: *adj*: *a velvet dress* ○ *velvet curtains/cushions*

velvet [QUALITY] /ˈvel.vɪt/ *adj* (*ALSO* **velvety**) *LITERARY* describes something that has a beautiful soft, smooth quality or appearance, usually something dark or deep: *under a wonderful velvet **sky*** ○ *His velvety **brown** eyes had been his passport to fame.*

venal /ˈviː.nəl/ *adj FORMAL* **1** A venal person is willing to behave in a dishonest or immoral way in exchange for money: *a venal ruler* * NOTE: Do not confuse with **venial**. **2** A venal activity is done in order to obtain money: *a venal regime* ○ *They are accused of being involved in venal practices.* **venality** /viːˈnæl.ɪ.ti/ Ⓤⓢ /vɪˈnæl.ə.t̬i/ *noun* [U]

vendetta /venˈdet.ə/ Ⓤⓢ /-ˈdet̬-/ *noun* [C] a long and violent argument between people or families in which one group tries to harm the other in order to punish them for things that have happened in the past: *He saw himself as the victim of a personal vendetta being **waged** by his political enemies.*

vending /ˈven.dɪŋ/ *noun* [U] *FORMAL* the selling of goods: *He had his street vending licence taken away.*
vendor /ˈven.dəʳ/ Ⓤⓢ /-dɚ/ *noun* [C] someone who is selling something: *For the past few months she's been working as a **street** vendor, selling fruit and veg.* ○ *LEGAL The vendor of the house wants to exchange contracts this week.*

ˈvending maˌchine *noun* [C] (*UK* **slot machine**) a machine from which you can buy small items such as cigarettes, drinks and sweets by putting coins into it: *The vending machine in the office **dispenses** really tasteless coffee.*

veneer /vəˈnɪəʳ/ Ⓤⓢ /-ˈnɪr/ *noun* **1** [C or U] a thin layer of decorative wood or plastic used to cover a cheaper material: *The wardrobe is made of chipboard with a pine veneer.* **2** [S] something which hides something unpleasant or unwanted: *She managed to hide her corrupt dealings under a veneer **of respectability**.* **veneered** /vəˈnɪəd/ Ⓤⓢ /-ˈnɪrd/ *adj*: *a veneered bookcase/surface/table*

venerable /ˈven.ər.ə.bl̩/ *adj* **1** *FORMAL* deserving respect because of age, high position or religious or historical importance: *a venerable tradition/company/family* **2** *INFORMAL MAINLY HUMOROUS* describes something that has been in use, or someone who has been involved in something, for a long time: *In recent years there has been a noticeable decline in such venerable British **institutions** as afternoon tea and the Sunday roast.*
Venerable /ˈven.ər.ə.bl̩/ *adj* **1 the Venerable** used as a title for an ARCHDEACON in the Church of England **2** used as a title for a person who is considered holy by the Roman Catholic Church but who has not yet been made a saint **3** used as a title for a monk in Buddhism

venerate /ˈven.ər.eɪt/ Ⓤⓢ /-ɚ.eɪt/ *verb* [T] *FORMAL* to honour or greatly respect a person or thing: *Robert Burns is Scotland's most venerated poet.* **veneration** /ˌven.ərˈeɪ.ʃən/ Ⓤⓢ /-ɚˈeɪ-/ *noun* [U] *Gandhi became an object of widespread veneration because of his unceasing struggle for freedom and equality.*

venereal /vəˈnɪə.ri.əl/ Ⓤⓢ /-ˈnɪr.i-/ *adj* caused or spread by sexual activity with another person: *a venereal infection*

veˈnereal diˌsease *noun* [C or U] (*ABBREVIATION* **VD**) *OLD-FASHIONED* a disease that is spread through sexual activity with an infected person; **sexually transmitted disease**

venereology /vəˌnɪə.ri.ˈɒl.ə.dʒi/ Ⓤⓢ /-ˌnɪr.iˈɑː.lə-/ *noun* [U] the part of medical science that involves studying and treating diseases that are spread through sexual activity **venereological** /vəˌnɪə.ri.əˈlɒdʒ.ɪ.kəl/ Ⓤⓢ /-ˌnɪr.i.əˈlɑː.dʒɪ-/ *adj* **venereologist** /vəˌnɪə.riˈɒl.ə.dʒɪst/ Ⓤⓢ /-ˌnɪr.iˈɑː.lə-/ *noun* [C]

venetian blind /vəˌniː.ʃənˈblaɪnd/ *noun* [C] a cover for a window made of thin horizontal pieces of wood, plastic or metal, which can be moved in order to vary the amount of light that is allowed in

vengeance /ˈven.dʒənts/ *noun* [U] the punishing of someone for harming you or your friends or family, or the desire for such punishment to happen: *On the day after the terrorist attack, the overall mood in the town was one of vengeance.* ○ *As he cradled his daughter's lifeless body in his arms, he **swore (to take)** vengeance **on** her killers.*
• **with a vengeance** with great force or extreme energy: *He's been working with a vengeance over the past few weeks to make up for lost time.* ○ *Flared trousers are **back** with a vengeance* (= very popular again) *this summer.*

vengeful /ˈvendʒ.fəl/ *adj FORMAL* expressing a strong desire to punish someone who has harmed you or your family or friends: *She sprayed red paint all over his car in one last vengeful act before leaving him for good.* **vengefully** /ˈvendʒ.fəl.i/ *adv* **vengefulness** /ˈvendʒ.fəl.nəs/ *noun* [U]

venial /ˈviː.ni.əl/ *adj FORMAL* describes a wrong action that is not serious and therefore easy to forgive: *a venial sin/error* * NOTE: Do not confuse with **venal**.

venison /ˈven.ɪ.sən/ *noun* [U] meat that comes from a deer

Venn diagram /ˌvenˈdaɪ.ə.græm/ *noun* [C] *SPECIALIZED* a mathematical plan consisting of OVERLAPPING circles which show how items that belong to mathematical sets relate to each other

venom [POISON] /ˈven.əm/ *noun* [U] a poisonous liquid which some snakes, insects, etc. produce when biting or stinging **venomous** /ˈven.ə.məs/ *adj*: *a venomous snake*

V

venom HATRED /'venəm/ *noun* [U] LITERARY the expression of feelings of hatred or extreme anger: *He was shocked at the sheer venom of her reply.*
venomous /'ven.ə.məs/ *adj* full of anger or hate: *Ms Brown has launched a venomous attack against the newspaper.* **venomously** /'ven.ə.mə.sli/ *adv*

venous /'vi:.nəs/ *adj* SPECIALIZED of or relating to the veins: *venous blood* ○ *the venous system* ⊃See also **intravenous**.

vent OPENING /vent/ *noun* [C] **1** a small opening which allows air, smoke or gas to enter or leave an enclosed space: *If you have a gas fire in a room, you should have some kind of outside vent.* **2** a cut in the bottom of a piece of clothing to allow the person wearing it to move more easily: *The skirt is long and straight with two side vents.*

vent EXPRESS FEELINGS /vent/ *verb* [T] to express a negative emotion in a forceful and often unfair way: *Please don't shout – there's no need to vent your frustration/anger/ rage/spleen on me.*

vent /vent/ *noun* **give vent to sth** to express a negative emotion in a forceful and often unfair way: *The meeting will be an opportunity for everyone to give vent to their feelings.*

ventilate PROVIDE AIR /'ven.tɪ.leɪt/ US /-t̬ə.l.eɪt/ *verb* [T] to cause fresh air to enter and move around an enclosed space: *I work in a very well-/poorly-ventilated building.* **ventilation** /ˌven.tɪ'leɪ.ʃən/ US /-t̬ə.l'eɪ-/ *noun* [U] *Her tiny attic room had poor ventilation and in summer it became unbearably stuffy.* ○ *a ventilation system* **ventilator** /'ven.tɪ.leɪ.tər/ US /-t̬ə.l.eɪ.t̬ə-/ *noun* [C] **1** an opening or a device that allows fresh air to come into an enclosed space **2** a machine that helps people breathe correctly by allowing air to flow in and out of their lungs: *He was brought into intensive care shortly after the crash and immediately put on a ventilator.*

ventilate MAKE KNOWN /'ven.tɪ.leɪt/ US /-t̬ə.l.eɪt/ *verb* [T] FORMAL to state an opinion or mention a subject so that it can be discussed by others: *She used the meeting to ventilate all her grievances.*

ventral /'ven.trəl/ *adj* [before n] SPECIALIZED of, on or near the UNDERSIDE of an animal ⊃Compare **dorsal**.

ventricle /'ven.trɪ.kl̩/ *noun* [C] SPECIALIZED either of two small hollow spaces, one in each side of the heart, which force blood into the tubes leading from the heart to the other parts of the body

ventriloquism /ven'trɪl.ə.kwɪ.zᵊm/ *noun* [U] the ability to speak without moving your lips so that your voice seems to be coming from someone or something else, usually as a way of entertaining people **ventriloquist** /ven'trɪl.ə.kwɪst/ *noun* [C]

ventriloquist's dummy /ven,trɪl.ə.kwɪsts'dʌm.i/ *noun* [C] a toy in the shape of a small person that ventriloquists operate, so that it seems to be alive

venture BUSINESS /'ven.tʃər/ US /-tʃə-/ *noun* [C] a new activity, usually in business, which involves risk or uncertainty: *She advised us to look abroad for more lucrative business ventures.* ○ *There are many joint ventures between American and Japanese companies.*

venture RISK /'ven.tʃər/ US /-tʃə-/ *verb* [I usually + adv or prep; T] FORMAL to risk going somewhere or doing something that might be dangerous or unpleasant, or to risk saying something that might be criticized: *She rarely ventured outside, except when she went to stock up on groceries at the corner shop.* ○ *As we set off into the forest, we felt as though we were venturing (forth) into the unknown.* ○ *She tentatively ventured the opinion that the project would be too expensive to complete, but the boss ignored her.*

• **Nothing ventured, nothing gained.** SAYING You have to take a risk in order to obtain something advantageous.

▲ **venture on/upon** sth *phrasal verb* FORMAL to try to do something difficult or dangerous: *The wind was so strong that when we did finally venture on a walk, we were nearly swept away.*

'venture ˌcapital *noun* [U] money that is invested or is available for investment in a new company, especially a risky one: *They'll need to raise £1 million in venture capital if they're to get the business off the*

ground. **'venture ˌcapitalist** *noun* [C]

venturesome /'ven.tʃə.səm/ US /-tʃə-/ *adj* FORMAL describes a person who is willing to take risks, or an action or behaviour that is risky: *He has become more venturesome this season with dress designs that incorporate a variety of ethnic influences.*

venue /'ven.ju:/ *noun* [C] **1** the place where a public event or meeting happens: *The hotel is an ideal venue for conferences and business meetings.* ○ *The stadium has been specifically designed as a venue for European Cup matches.* **2** US SPECIALIZED the city or county in which a trial happens

Venus /'vi:.nəs/ *noun* [U] the planet second in order of distance from the Sun, after Mercury and before the Earth. It is the nearest planet to the Earth.

Venus flytrap /ˌvi:.nəs'flaɪ.træp/ *noun* [C] a plant which feeds on insects and catches them by quickly closing its leaves when their surface is touched so that the insects cannot escape

veracity /və'ræs.ɪ.ti/ US /və'æs.ə.t̬i/ *noun* [U] FORMAL the quality of being true, honest or accurate: *Doubts were cast on the veracity of her alibi after three people claimed to have seen her at the scene of the robbery.*

veranda, **verandah** /və'ræn.də/ *noun* [C] (US ALSO **porch**) a raised, covered and sometimes partly enclosed area, often made of wood, on the front or side of a building: *Every evening we sat on the veranda watching the sun go down.*

verb /vɜːb/ US /vɜːb/ *noun* [C] a word or phrase that describes an action, condition or experience: *The words 'run', 'keep' and 'feel' are all verbs.*

verbal SPOKEN /'vɜː.bəl/ US /'vɜː-/ *adj* spoken rather than written: *a verbal agreement/description/explanation* ○ *Airport officials received a stream of verbal abuse from angry passengers whose flights had been delayed.* **verbally** /'vɜː.bəl.i/ US /'vɜː-/ *adv*

verbal WORDS /'vɜː.bəl/ US /'vɜː-/ *adj* relating to words: *It can sometimes be difficult to give a verbal description of things like colours and sounds.*

ˌverbal diar'rhoea *noun* INFORMAL HUMOROUS **have verbal diarrhoea** to talk continuously or too much

verbalize, UK USUALLY -**ise** /'vɜː.bəl.aɪz/ US /'vɜː.bə.laɪz/ *verb* [I or T] FORMAL to express ideas, opinions or emotions in words: *He found it hard to verbalize his feelings towards his son.*

verbatim /vɜː'beɪ.tɪm/ US /vɜː'beɪ.t̬əm/ *adv* using exactly the same words as were originally used: *She had an amazing memory and could recall verbatim quite complex conversations.* **verbatim** /vɜː'beɪ.tɪm/ US /'vɜː-'beɪ.t̬əm/ *adj* [before n] *a verbatim account*

verbiage /'vɜː.bi.ɪdʒ/ US /'vɜː-/ *noun* [U] FORMAL DISAPPROVING language which is very complicated and which contains a lot of unnecessary words: *His explanation was wrapped up in so much technical verbiage that I simply couldn't understand it.*

verbose /vɜː'bəʊs/ US /vɜː'boʊs/ *adj* FORMAL DISAPPROVING using or containing more words than are necessary: *a verbose explanation/report/speech/style* ○ *He was a notoriously verbose after-dinner speaker.* **verbosely** /vɜː'bəʊs.li/ US /vɜː'boʊs-/ *adv* **verbosity** /vɜː'bɒs.ɪ.ti/ US /vɜː'bɑː.sə.t̬i/ *noun* [U]

verdant /'vɜː.dᵊnt/ US /'vɜː-/ *adj* LITERARY covered with healthy green plants or grass: *Much of the region's verdant countryside has been destroyed in the hurricane.*

verdict /'vɜː.dɪkt/ US /'vɜː-/ *noun* [C] an opinion or decision made after judging the facts that are given, especially one made at the end of a trial: *The jury reached/ returned a unanimous verdict of (not) guilty.* ○ *Voters gave their verdict on the government's economic record last night by voting overwhelmingly for the opposition.* ⊃See also **open verdict**.

verdigris /'vɜː.dɪ.grɪs/ US /'vɜː-/ *noun* [U] a blue-green layer that forms on copper, brass or BRONZE

verdure /'vɜː.djər/ US /'vɜː.dʒə-/ *noun* [U] LITERARY (the green colour of) fresh healthy plants

verge /vɜːdʒ/ US /vɜːdʒ/ *noun* [C] **1** the edge or border of something: *They set up camp on the verge of the desert.* **2** UK (US **shoulder**) the strip of land which borders a road or

path: *She left her car by the side of the road and walked along the **grass** verge to the emergency phone.*
• **on the verge (of)** (ALSO **to the verge of**) If you are on the verge of something or come to the verge of something, you are very near to experiencing it: *on the verge of collapse/success/tears/death/disaster/war* ○ *Her husband's violent and abusive behaviour **drove** her to the verge of despair.*

verge /vɜːdʒ/ ⑥ /vɜːrdʒ/ *verb*
▲ **verge on sth** *phrasal verb* to be almost a particular state, quality or feeling, especially one that is very bad or very good: *At times, his performance verged on brilliance, but at others it was only ordinary.*

verger /ˈvɜː.dʒəʳ/ ⑥ /ˈvɜːr.dʒɚ/ *noun* [C] an official in some Christian churches who takes care of the inside of a church and performs some simple duties during church ceremonies

verify /ˈver.ɪ.faɪ/ *verb* [T] to prove that something exists or is true, or to make certain that something is correct: *Are you able to verify your account/allegation/report/theory?* ○ *These figures are surprisingly high and they'll have to be verified.* ○ [+ **(that)**] *Under interrogation, she verified (that) the tapes were authentic.*
verifiable /ˈver.ɪ.faɪ.ə.bl̩/ *adj* able to be proved: *Throughout the trial, he didn't produce a single verifiable fact.* **verification** /ˌver.ɪ.fɪˈkeɪ.ʃⁿn/ *noun* [U]

verily /ˈver.ɪ.li/ *adv* OLD USE in a completely truthful way

verisimilitude /ˌver.ɪ.sɪˈmɪl.ɪ.tjuːd/ ⑥ /-tuːd/ *noun* [U] FORMAL the quality of seeming true or of having the appearance of reality: *She has included photographs in the book to lend verisimilitude to the story.*

veritable /ˈver.ɪ.tə.bl̩/ ⑥ /-ə.tə-/ *adj* [before n] used to describe something as another, more exciting, interesting or unusual thing, as a way of emphasizing its character: *My garden had become **a** veritable jungle by the time I came back from holiday.* ○ *The normally sober menswear department is set to become **a** veritable kaleidoscope of colour this season.* **veritably** /ˈver.ɪ.tə.bli/ ⑥ /-ə.tə-/ *adv*

verity /ˈver.ɪ.ti/ ⑥ /-ə.t̬i/ *noun* FORMAL **1** [U] the quality of being true: *In the film, he plays a spy whose mission is to confirm the verity of a secret military document.* **2** [C] a belief, idea or principle that is generally accepted as being true: *She has spent her life in a search for eternal/scientific/universal verities.*

vermicelli /ˌvɜː.mɪˈtʃel.i/ ⑥ /ˌvɜːr-/ *noun* [U] **1** pasta made in long very thin threads, cooked in boiling water; a type of very thin SPAGHETTI **2** UK extremely small pieces of chocolate used for decorating cakes

vermilion, **vermillion** /vəˈmɪl.i.ən/ ⑥ /vɚˈmɪl.jən/ *adj, noun* [C or U] (of) a bright red colour: *She was wearing a jacket of bright vermilion.*

vermin /ˈvɜː.mɪn/ ⑥ /ˈvɜːr-/ *plural noun* **1** small animals and insects that can be harmful and which are difficult to control when they appear in large numbers: *Flies, lice, rats, foxes and cockroaches can all be described as vermin.* **2** OFFENSIVE DISAPPROVING people who are unpleasant and harmful to society: *He thought all terrorists were vermin and that prison was too good for them.*
verminous /ˈvɜː.mɪ.nəs/ ⑥ /ˈvɜːr-/ *adj* FORMAL covered with insects: *an old verminous blanket*

vermouth /vəˈmuːθ/ ⑥ /-məθ/ ⑥ /vɚ-/ *noun* [U] a strongly alcoholic red or white wine flavoured with herbs and spices

vernacular /vəˈnæk.jʊ.ləʳ/ ⑥ /vɚˈnæk.jə.lɚ/ *noun* [C usually sing] **1** the form of a language that a regional or other group of speakers use naturally, especially in informal situations: *The French I learned at school is very different from the local vernacular of the village where I'm now living.* ○ *Many Roman Catholics regret the replacing of the Latin mass by **the** vernacular.* **2** SPECIALIZED in architecture, a local style in which ordinary houses are built **3** SPECIALIZED dance, music, art, etc. that is in a style liked or performed by ordinary people **vernacular** /vəˈnæk.jʊ.ləʳ/ ⑥ /vɚˈnæk.jə.lɚ/ *adj*: *His lively vernacular style goes down well with younger viewers.* ○ *old stone vernacular buildings*

vernal /ˈvɜː.nⁿl/ ⑥ /ˈvɜːr-/ *adj* [before n] LITERARY relating to or happening in the spring

vernal ˈequinox *noun* [C usually sing] the time in the spring when the sun crosses the equator, and when night and day are of equal length

verruca /vəˈruː.kə/ ⑥ /vəˈruː-/ *noun* [C] *plural* **verrucas** or **verrucae** a small hard infectious growth on the skin, usually on the bottom of the foot

versatile /ˈvɜː.sə.taɪl/ ⑥ /ˈvɜːr.sə.t̬ⁿl/ *adj* APPROVING able to change easily from one activity to another or able to be used for many different purposes: *He's a very versatile young actor who's as happy in horror films as he is in TV comedies.* ○ *A leather jacket is a timeless and versatile garment that can be worn in all seasons.* **versatility** /ˌvɜː.səˈtɪl.ɪ.ti/ ⑥ /ˌvɜːr.səˈtɪl.ə.t̬i/ *noun* [U]

verse /vɜːs/ ⑥ /vɜːrs/ *noun* **1** [U] writing which is arranged in short lines with a regular rhythm; poetry: *comic/light/satirical verse* ○ *Shakespeare wrote mostly **in** verse.* **2** [C] one of the parts into which a poem or song is divided: *Each verse was sung as a solo and then everyone joined in on the chorus.* **3** [C] one of the series of short parts into which the writing of a holy book is divided: *She recited a verse from the Bible/the Koran.*

versed /vɜːst/ ⑥ /vɜːrst/ *adj* FORMAL **be versed in sth** to know a lot about a particular subject or be experienced in a particular skill: *I'm not sufficiently versed in computers to understand what you're saying.*

version /ˈvɜː.ʃⁿn/ /-ʒⁿn/ ⑥ /ˈvɜːr-/ *noun* [C] a particular form of something which varies slightly from other forms of the same thing: *The **official** version of events is that the police were attacked and were just trying to defend themselves.* ○ *You can make a reduced fat version **of** the cheesecake by using cottage cheese instead of cream cheese.* ○ *An English-language version **of** the book is planned for the autumn.* ○ *The TV series is a watered-down version **of** the movie, especially designed for family viewing.*

versus /ˈvɜː.səs/ ⑥ /ˈvɜːr-/ *prep* **1** (WRITTEN ABBREVIATION **v, vs**) used to say that one team or person is competing against another: *Tomorrow's game is Newcastle versus Arsenal.* **2** (WRITTEN ABBREVIATION **v, vs**) used in legal cases to show who a person is fighting against: *Abortion was legalized nationally in the United States following the Roe versus Wade case.* **3** used to compare two things or ideas, especially when you have to choose between them: *private education versus state education*

vertebra /ˈvɜː.tɪ.brə/ ⑥ /ˈvɜːr-/ *noun* [C] *plural* **vertebrae** SPECIALIZED one of the small bones that form the spine **vertebral** /ˈvɜː.tɪ.brⁿl/ ⑥ /ˈvɜːr.t̬ə-/ *adj*: *The vertebral **column** surrounds and protects the spinal cord.*

vertebrate /ˈvɜː.tɪ.brət/ ⑥ /ˈvɜːr.t̬ə-/ *adj* SPECIALIZED having a spine
vertebrate /ˈvɜː.tɪ.brət/ ⑥ /ˈvɜːr.t̬ə-/ *noun* [C] SPECIALIZED an animal that has a spine: *Birds, fish, mammals, amphibians and reptiles are all vertebrates.* ⊃Compare **invertebrate**.

vertex /ˈvɜː.teks/ ⑥ /ˈvɜːr.t̬eks/ *noun* [C] *plural* **vertexes** or **vertices** SPECIALIZED **1** (in mathematics) the point where two lines meet to form an angle, or the point that is opposite the base of a shape: *the vertex of a triangle/cone/pyramid* **2** the highest point of something

vertical /ˈvɜː.tɪ.kⁿl/ ⑥ /ˈvɜːr.t̬ə-/ *adj* standing or pointing straight up or at an angle of 90° to a horizontal surface or line: *vertical lines/stripes* ○ *She looked over the cliff and found she was standing at the edge of a vertical drop.* ⊃Compare **horizontal**.
vertical /ˈvɜː.tɪ.kⁿl/ ⑥ /ˈvɜːr.t̬ə-/ *noun* [C usually sing] a vertical line, surface or position: *The multi-spoked steel structure will be raised to **the** vertical.* **vertically** /ˈvɜː.tɪ.kli/ ⑥ /ˈvɜːr.t̬ə-/ *adv*: *A wall of rock towered vertically up on one side of the mountain path.*

vertical ˈblind *noun* [C] a cover for a window made of vertical strips of stiff cloth which can be moved in order to vary the amount of light that is allowed in

vertical inteˈgration *noun* [U] SPECIALIZED a process in business where a company buys another company that supplies it with goods or that buys goods from it in order to control all the processes of production

vertical ˈtake-off *noun* [C] when an aircraft rises straight up off the ground

V

vertigo /'vɜː.tɪ.gəʊ/ ⓤ /'vɜː.t̬ə.goʊ/ *noun* [U] a feeling of spinning round and being unable to balance, caused by looking down from a height: *She can't stand heights and has always **suffered from** vertigo.*

vertiginous /vɜː'tɪdʒ.ɪ.nəs/ ⓤ /vɚ-/ *adj FORMAL* causing or experiencing the feeling that everything is spinning round: *The two skyscrapers were connected by a vertiginous walkway.*

verve /vɜːv/ ⓤ /vɜːv/ *noun* [U] great energy and enthusiasm: *She delivered her speech **with** tremendous wit and verve.*

very EXTREMELY /'ver.i/ *adv* **1** (used to add emphasis to an adjective or adverb) to a great degree or extremely: *The situation is very serious.* ○ *We're very, very sorry about what's happened.* ○ *Think about it very carefully before deciding.* ○ ***How** very childish of her to refuse to speak to me!* ○ *"Are you tired?" "No, not very."* ○ *Thank you very **much**.* ○ *"Did you enjoy the play?" "Very **much so** (= Yes)."* ○ *I **can't** very well (= It would not be right for me to) say sorry when I didn't do anything wrong.* **2** used to add force to a superlative adjective or to the adjectives 'own' or 'same': *This is **the** very **best** chocolate cake I've ever tasted.* ○ *She always leaves her homework to **the** very **last** moment.* ○ *We now have our very **own** post office in the village.* ○ *This is **the** very **same** (= exactly the same) place we sat in the last time we came.*

• **all very well/fine/good** You say that something is all very well/fine/good if it seems good by itself but you think that there are problems connected with it: *It's all very well to want to get rich quickly, **but** don't expect any sympathy from me if things go wrong.*

• **very good** *UK OLD-FASHIONED* a way of saying yes to someone who is in a higher position or rank than you: *"Higgins, you may go now." "Very good, sir."*

• **very well** *FORMAL* a way of saying yes to someone or of agreeing to do what they ask: *"Can't I stay for five minutes longer?" "Oh, very well."*

very EXACT /'ver.i/ *adj* [before n] (used to add emphasis to a noun) exact or particular: *This is the very book I've been looking for all month.* ○ *You're the very person we need for the job.* ○ *The letter was sent on Monday from Manchester and arrived in London the very **same/next** day.* ○ *The very **idea/thought** of having her friends to stay fills me with dread.*

• **be the very thing** to be exactly what is needed: *Why not take garlic? It's the very thing **for** preventing colds.*

very FURTHEST POINT /'ver.i/ *adj* [before n] used to describe or emphasize the furthest point of something: *He found the piece of paper he had lost at **the** very **bottom** of the pile.* ○ *We were at **the** very **end** of the queue and so didn't manage to get any tickets.*

Very 'Reverend *adj* [before n] used as a title of respect for particular important church officials

vespers /'ves.pəz/ ⓤ /-pɚz/ *noun* [U] the evening ceremony in some Christian churches

vessel SHIP /'ves.ºl/ *noun* [C] *FORMAL* a large boat or a ship: *a cargo/fishing/naval/patrol/sailing/supply vessel*

vessel CONTAINER /'ves.ºl/ *noun* [C] **1** *FORMAL* a curved container which is used to hold liquid: *The remains of some Roman earthenware vessels were found during the dig.* **2** *LITERARY* a person who possesses a particular quality or who is used for a particular purpose: *As a young and spirited politician, he seems a worthy vessel for the nation's hopes.*

vessel TUBE /'ves.ºl/ *noun* [C] a tube that carries liquids such as blood through the body: *A heart attack is caused by the **blood** vessels that supply the blood to the heart muscle getting blocked.*

vest /vest/ *noun* [C] **1** *UK* (*US* **undershirt**, *AUS* **singlet**) a type of underwear, often with no sleeves, which covers the upper part of the body and which is worn for extra warmth: *a cotton/woollen/string vest* ○ *She always wore a long-sleeved **thermal** vest in winter.* ⊃See picture **Clothes** on page Centre 6 **2** (*ALSO* **vest top**) *UK* a shirt without sleeves, usually made out of cotton, which is worn in the summer or for sport: *The cyclists were all dressed in tight lycra shorts and **the** official team vest.* ○ *He wore a vest top and a pair of luminous shorts to the*

beach party. **3** *US FOR* **waistcoat** ⊃See picture **Clothes** on page Centre 6

vest /vest/ *verb*

▲ **be vested in** *sb/sth phrasal verb* (*ALSO* **be vested with** *sth*) *FORMAL* If power or authority is vested in someone or something, or if they are vested with power or authority, it is officially given to them: *Control has been vested in local authorities.* ○ *He has been vested with the **power/authority** to implement whatever changes he sees fit.*

vested interest /ˌves.tɪd'ɪn.tºr.est/ ⓤ /-tɚ-/ *noun* [C] a strong personal interest in something because you could benefit from it: *As both a teacher and parent, she **had** a vested interest **in** seeing the school remain open.*

vested interests /ˌves.tɪd'ɪn.tºr.ests/ ⓤ /-tɚ-/ *plural noun OFTEN DISAPPROVING* people or organizations who have a financial or personal interest in a business, company or existing system: *A compromise has to be reached between all the powerful vested interests before any restoration work in the city can take place.*

vestibule /'ves.tɪ.bjuːl/ *noun* [C] **1** *FORMAL* a small room just inside the outer door of a public building where you can leave your coat, etc: *I'll wait for you in the vestibule.* **2** *US* a small enclosed area on the front of a house; a **porch**

vestige /'ves.tɪdʒ/ *noun* [C] *FORMAL* a still existing small part or amount of something larger, stronger or more important that existed in the past but does not exist now: *These old buildings are the **last** vestiges of a colonial past.* ○ *There is now no vestige **of** hope that the missing children will be found alive.*

vestigial /ves'tɪdʒ.i.əl/ *adj* **1** [before n] being a small remaining part or amount **2** *SPECIALIZED* describes something, especially a part of the body, that has not developed completely, or has stopped being used and has almost disappeared: *a vestigial organ/limb/tail* **vestigially** /ves'tɪdʒ.i.ə.li/ *adv*

vestments /'vest.mənts/ *plural noun* the special clothes worn by priests during church ceremonies

vestry /'ves.tri/ *noun* [C] (*ALSO* **sacristy**) a room in a church, especially one in which priests and the group of people who sing in church put on the special clothes they wear for church ceremonies, and in which items used in church ceremonies are sometimes kept

vet ANIMAL DOCTOR /vet/ *noun* [C] **1** (*UK FORMAL* **veterinary surgeon**, *US FORMAL* **veterinarian**) a person with a medical degree trained to take care of the health of animals: *The farmer called the vet out to treat a sick cow.* **2** (*UK ALSO* **vet's**) the office where a vet works: *We took our cat to the vet's for its annual cat flu injection.*

vet EXAMINE /vet/ *verb* [T] **-tt-** to examine something or someone carefully to make certain that they are acceptable or suitable: *During the war, the government vetted all news reports before they were published.* ○ *The bank carefully vets everyone who applies for an account.*

vet ARMED FORCES /vet/ *noun* [C] *US INFORMAL FOR* **veteran** (= a person who has served in the armed forces)

veteran /'vet.ºr.ºn/ ⓤ /'vet̬.ɚ-/ *noun* [C] **1** a person who has had a lot of experience of a particular activity: *a 20-year veteran **of** the New York Police Department* **2** (*US INFORMAL* **vet**) someone who has been in the armed forces during a war: *a Vietnam veteran* ○ *The ceremony was attended by many of the surviving veterans **of** World War II.*

veteran /'vet.ºr.ºn/ ⓤ /'vet̬.ɚ-/ *adj* [before n] **1** having been involved in a particular activity for a long time: *She's also a veteran campaigner for human rights.* **2** *UK* old: *He collects veteran **cars** (= cars made before 1905).* ⊃Compare **vintage** HIGH QUALITY

'Veterans ˌDay *noun* [C or U] a legal holiday on November 11th in the US and Canada, when people honour members of their countries' armed forces who have fought in wars

veterinarian /ˌvet.ºr.ɪ'neə.ri.ən/ ⓤ /-'ner.i-/ *noun* [C] *US FORMAL FOR* **vet** ANIMAL DOCTOR

veterinary /'vet.ºr.ɪ.nºr.i/ ⓤ /-ner-/ *adj* [before n] connected with taking care of the health of animals: *veterinary medicine*

ˈveterinary ˌsurgeon *noun* [C] *UK FORMAL FOR* **vet** ANIMAL DOCTOR

veto /ˈviː.təʊ/ (US) /-t̬oʊ/ *noun* [C or U] *plural* **vetoes** (a) refusal to allow something to be done: *The Ministry of Defence has the power of veto* **over** *all British arms exports.* ○ *In theory the British government could use its veto to block this proposal.* ○ *The Senate voted to override the President's veto* **of** *the proposed measures.* ○ *MAINLY UK Mum has* **put** *a veto* **on** *our watching television for more than two hours an evening.*

veto /ˈviː.təʊ/ (US) /-t̬oʊ/ *verb* [T] **vetoing, vetoed, vetoed** to refuse to allow something: *In 1961, President De Gaulle vetoed Britain's entry into the Common Market.* ○ [+ v-ing] *My boss vetoed my tak**ing** any more time off this year.*

vex /veks/ *verb* [T] *OLD-FASHIONED* to cause difficulty to someone, or to cause someone to feel angry, annoyed or upset: *This issue looks likely to continue to vex the government.*

vexation /vekˈseɪ.ʃən/ *noun OLD-FASHIONED* **1** [U] worry or annoyance: *After several unsuccessful attempts to start his car, he swore in vexation.* **2** [C] something that is worrying or annoying

vexatious /vekˈseɪ.ʃəs/ *adj OLD-FASHIONED* difficult to deal with and causing a lot of annoyance, worry or argument: *This settlement will resolve one of the most vexatious* (= difficult) *problems in the field of industrial relations.* **vexatiously** /vekˈseɪ.ʃə.sli/ *adv*

vexed /vekst/ *adj* [before n] difficult to deal with and causing a lot of disagreement and argument: *The government has to deal with the vexed* **question** *of how to reduce spending.*

VHF /ˌviː.eɪtʃˈef/ *noun* [U] *ABBREVIATION FOR* very high frequency: radio waves between 30 to 300 MHz: *a VHF radio/transmitter/frequency* ➲Compare **UHF**.

VHS /ˌviː.eɪtʃˈes/ *noun* [U] *TRADEMARK ABBREVIATION FOR* Video Home System: the standard system for video recorders used at home

via /vaɪə/ /ˈviː.ə/ *prep* through; using: *The London-Addis flight goes via Rome.* ○ *Reports are coming in via satellite.* ○ *I only found out about it via my sister.*

viable /ˈvaɪ.ə.bl̩/ *adj* **1** able to work as intended or able to succeed: *In order to make the company viable, it will unfortunately be necessary to reduce staffing levels.* ○ *Solar power is now a viable alternative to oil-fired water heaters.* ○ *I am afraid your plan is not commercially/economically/financially/politically viable.* **2** *SPECIALIZED* able to continue to exist as or develop into a living being: *There is a continuing debate about the age at which a human fetus can be considered viable.* **viability** /ˌvaɪ.əˈbɪl.ɪ.ti/ (US) /-ə.t̬i/ *noun* [U] *Rising costs are threatening the viability* **of** *many businesses.* ○ *SPECIALIZED As the world population of Hawaiian geese has shrunk to very small numbers, the bird's continuing viability is in doubt.* **viably** /ˈvaɪ.ə.bli/ *adv*

viaduct /ˈvaɪə.dʌkt/ *noun* [C] a long high bridge, usually held up by many arches, which carries a railway or a road over a valley: *a railway viaduct*

Viagra /vaɪˈæg.rə/ *noun* [U] *TRADEMARK* a drug for treating men who are IMPOTENT (= who cannot have sex because their penis cannot become or stay hard)

vial /vaɪl/ *noun* [C] a **phial**

vibes [FEELING] /vaɪbz/ *plural noun INFORMAL* the general mood a person or place seems to have and the way they make you feel: *I didn't like the place – it had bad vibes.*

vibes [INSTRUMENT] /vaɪbz/ *plural noun INFORMAL FOR* **vibraphone**

vibrant /ˈvaɪ.brənt/ *adj* **1** energetic, exciting and full of enthusiasm: *a vibrant young performer* ○ *a vibrant personality* ○ *a vibrant city* ○ *The hope is that this area will develop into a vibrant commercial centre.* **2** describes colour or light that is bright and strong: *He always uses vibrant colours in his paintings.* **vibrantly** /ˈvaɪ.brənt.li/ *adv* **vibrancy** /ˈvaɪ.brənt.si/ *noun* [U] *No one can fail to be struck by the vibrancy* **of** *New York.*

vibraphone /ˈvaɪ.brə.fəʊn/ (US) /-foʊn/ *noun* [C] (*INFORMAL* **vibes**) a musical instrument consisting of a set of metal bars in a frame which have electrical devices fixed to them so that when they are hit they produce notes which shake slightly

vibrate /vaɪˈbreɪt/ *verb* [I or T] to shake slightly and quickly, or to cause something to do this, in a way that is felt rather than seen or heard: *The whole station seemed to vibrate as the express train rushed through.* ○ *His voice vibrated* **with** *anger.* **vibration** /vaɪˈbreɪ.ʃən/ *noun* [C or U] *Vibrations were felt hundreds of miles from the centre of the earthquake.* ○ *Aircraft manufacturers want to reduce vibration for the sake of safety.*

vibrator /vaɪˈbreɪ.təʳ/ (US) /-t̬ɚ/ *noun* [C] a device which shakes slightly and quickly and which is held against the body in order to give sexual pleasure

vibrato /vɪˈbrɑː.təʊ/ (US) /-t̬oʊ/ *noun* [C or U] *plural* **vibratos** *SPECIALIZED* (a) repeated slight shaking in a musical note, either when played on an instrument or sung, which gives a fuller sound to the note ➲Compare **tremolo**.

vicar /ˈvɪk.əʳ/ (US) /-ɚ/ *noun* [C] a priest in the Church of England who is in charge of a church and the religious needs of people in a particular area: *We were married by our local vicar.* ○ [as form of address] *Good evening, Vicar!*

vicarage /ˈvɪk.ᵊr.ɪdʒ/ (US) /-ɚ-/ *noun* [C] the house in which a VICAR lives

vicarious /vɪˈkeə.ri.əs/ (US) /-ˈker.i-/ *adj* [before n] experienced as a result of watching, listening to or reading about the activities of other people, rather than by doing the activities yourself: *They get a vicarious thrill from watching motor racing.* **vicariously** /vɪˈkeə.ri.ə.sli/ (US) /-ˈker.i-/ *adv* **vicariousness** /vɪˈkeə.ri.ə.snəs/ (US) /-ˈker.i-/ *noun* [U]

ˌVicar of ˈChrist *noun* [S] a title sometimes given to the Pope

vice [MORAL FAULT] /vaɪs/ *noun* **1** [C or U] (a) moral fault or weakness in someone's character: *Greed, pride, envy, dishonesty and lust are considered to be vices.* ○ *MAINLY HUMOROUS My one real vice* (= bad habit) *is chocolate.* **2** [U] illegal and immoral activities, especially involving illegal sex, drugs, etc: *The chief of police said that he was committed to wiping out vice in the city.*

vice [TOOL] *MAINLY UK, US USUALLY* **vise** /vaɪs/ *noun* [C] a tool with two parts which can be moved together by tightening a screw so that an object can be held firmly between them while it is being worked on: *Vices are often used to hold pieces of wood that are being cut or smoothed.* ○ *Her hand tightened like a vice around his arm.*

vice- [TITLE] /vaɪs-/ *prefix* used as part of the title of particular positions. The person who holds one of these positions is next below in authority to the person who holds the full position and can act for them: *the vice captain of the team* ○ *a vice admiral*

vice-chancellor /ˌvaɪsˈtʃɑːnt.sᵊl.əʳ/ (US) /-ˈtʃænt.sᵊl.ɚ/ *noun* [C] **1** *UK* the person in charge of a British college or university **2** *US* the person in charge of some parts of a college or university in the US

vice-like /ˈvaɪs.laɪk/ *adj* (*US USUALLY* **vise-like**) very tight: *He holds his tennis racket* **in/with** *a vice-like* **grip**.

ˌvice ˈpresident *noun* [C] **1** (*US WRITTEN ABBREVIATION* **VP**, *US INFORMAL* **veep**) the person who has the position immediately below the president in some countries, and who is responsible for the president's duties if he or she is unable to do them: *Vice President Cheney* **2** *US* the person who is responsible for a large important part of a company or organization: *She's vice president of sales and marketing.*

ˈvice ˌring *group noun* [C] a group of people involved in immoral illegal activities, especially illegal sex or drugs: *It's thought that the pornographic films are being distributed by an international vice ring.*

viceroy /ˈvaɪs.rɔɪ/ *noun* [C] a representative of a king or queen who rules for them in another country

ˈvice ˌsquad *group noun* [C] a special group of police officers whose job is to stop crimes that involve sex and drugs

vice versa /ˌvaɪsˈvɜː.sə/ (US) /ˌvaɪ.səˈvɝː-/ *adv* used to state that what you have just said is also true in the opposite order: *He doesn't trust her, and vice versa* (= she also doesn't trust him).

vicinity /vɪˈsɪn.ɪ.ti/ (US) /vəˈsɪn.ə.t̬i/ *noun* [S] the immediately surrounding area: *There are several hotels* ***in the immediate*** *vicinity* ***of*** *the station.*

V

• **in the vicinity of** approximately: *The team is believed to have paid in the vicinity of £3 million for Domingo.*

vicious /ˈvɪʃ.əs/ *adj* **1** describes people or actions that show an intention or desire to hurt someone or something very badly: *a vicious thug* ○ *a vicious dog* ○ *The police said that this was one of the most vicious attacks they'd ever seen.* ○ *He gave her a vicious look.* **2** describes an object, condition or remark that causes great physical or emotional pain: *a large collection of vicious medieval torture instruments* ○ *I've got a vicious headache.* ○ *Make sure you wrap up warmly – there's a vicious* (= extremely strong and unpleasant) *wind out there.* ○ *a vicious lie/accusation/rumour* **viciously** /ˈvɪʃ.ə.sli/ *adv* **viciousness** /ˈvɪʃ.ə.snəs/ *noun* [U]

ˌ**vicious ˈcircle** *noun* [S] a continuing unpleasant situation, created when one problem causes another problem which then makes the first problem worse: *Many people get **caught/trapped in** a vicious circle of dieting and weight gain.*

vicissitudes /vɪˈsɪs.ɪ.tjuːdz/ [US] /-tuːdz/ *plural noun* FORMAL changes which happen at different times during the life or development of someone or something, especially those which result in conditions being worse: *You could say that losing your job is just one of the vicissitudes **of** life.*

victim /ˈvɪk.tɪm/ *noun* [C] someone or something which has been hurt, damaged or killed or has suffered, either because of the actions of someone or something else, or because of illness or chance: *to provide financial aid to hurricane/flood, etc. victims* ○ *victims of crime* ○ *The children are the innocent/helpless victims **of** the fighting.* ○ *The new drug might help save the lives of cancer victims.* ○ *We appear to have been the victims **of** a cruel practical joke.* ○ *Our local hospital has become the latest victim **of** the cuts in government spending.*

• **be a victim of *your* own success** to have problems because of your success: *The school has become a victim of its own success as parents with children who have special needs now actively seek it out.*

• **fall victim to *sth*** to be hurt, damaged or killed because of something or someone: *In 1948, Gandhi fell victim to a member of a Hindu gang.* ○ *The company has fallen victim to increased competition.*

victimize, UK USUALLY **-ise** /ˈvɪk.tɪ.maɪz/ *verb* [T] to treat someone in an intentionally unfair way, especially because of their race, sex or beliefs: *He claimed he'd been victimized by the police.* ○ *Nixon felt that he was being victimized by the media.* **victimization**, UK USUALLY **-isation** /ˌvɪk.tɪ.maɪˈzeɪ.ʃən/ *noun* [U]

victimless /ˈvɪk.tɪm.ləs/ *adj* In a victimless crime no one suffers directly, sometimes because the people affected by the crime have agreed to take part in it: *Stock market fraud is sometimes regarded as a victimless crime.*

ˌ**victim supˈport** *noun* [U] UK the practice of providing emotional and practical help for people who suffer because of a crime, or an organization that provides this: *a victim support group/scheme* ○ *The police put me in touch with Victim Support.*

Victorian /vɪkˈtɔː.ri.ən/ [US] /-ˈtɔːr.i-/ *adj* **1** belonging to, made in or living in the time when Queen Victoria was queen of Britain (1837-1901): *a Victorian terraced house* ○ *Charles Dickens is one of the best-known Victorian novelists.* **2** describes morals, opinions, ways of living and beliefs, including special emphasis on self-control, hard work, loyalty and strong religious belief, thought to have been common when Queen Victoria was queen of Britain: *Victorian values* **3** AUS from or belonging or relating to the state of Victoria

Victorian /vɪkˈtɔː.ri.ən/ [US] /-ˈtɔːr.i-/ *noun* [C] a person who was alive while Queen Victoria was queen of Britain

victory /ˈvɪk.tər.i/ [US] /-tɚ-/ *noun* [C or U] when you win a game, competition, election, war, etc: *The Redskins opened the season by **scoring** a resounding/stunning/impressive 25-3 victory **against/over** Detroit.* ○ *Grant **won/achieved/gained** a comfortable/easy victory **against/over** Cooper in yesterday's match.* ○ *This result is a triumphant victory **for** democracy.* ➲See also **Pyrrhic victory**. * NOTE: The opposite is **defeat**.

• **be a victory for common sense** to be a very reasonable result in a particular situation: *There is no doubt that the court's decision is a victory for common sense.*

victor /ˈvɪk.təʳ/ [US] /-tɚ/ *noun* [C] the winner of a game, competition, election, war, etc: *The victor **in/of** the 1960 US Presidential election was John F. Kennedy.*

victorious /vɪkˈtɔː.ri.əs/ [US] /-ˈtɔːr.i-/ *adj*: *The victorious team* (= The team who won) *were loudly cheered by their fans.* ○ *The German player **emerged** victorious after a long five-hour match.* **victoriously** /vɪkˈtɔː.ri.ə.sli/ [US] /-ˈtɔːr.i-/ *adv*

victuals /ˈvɪt.əlz/ [US] /ˈvɪt̬-/ *plural noun* OLD-FASHIONED OR HUMOROUS food and drink: *"I can't bear to see good victuals wasted," said Martha.*

video [TAPE] (*plural* **videos**) /ˈvɪd.i.əʊ/ [US] /-oʊ/ *noun* **1** [C or U] (ALSO **videotape**) (a) recording of moving pictures and sound that has been made on a long narrow strip of magnetic material inside a rectangular plastic container, and which can be played on a special machine so that it can be watched on television: *Ed came over last night to watch the video **of** the football match that I'd **recorded**.* ○ *We had a video made **of** our wedding.* ○ *'Spiderman' is now available **on** video.* ➲See also **tape** RECORD. **2** [C] (ALSO **music video**) a short film made to advertise a popular song

video (**videoing**, **videoed**, **videoed**) /ˈvɪd.i.əʊ/ [US] /-oʊ/ *verb* [T] (ALSO **tape**) to record a programme from the television onto a video, or to use a video camera to film an event: *There's a play on TV tonight that I'd like to video.* ○ *We videoed the school concert.*

video /ˈvɪd.i.əʊ/ [US] /-oʊ/ *adj* **1** using video: *a video recording* **2** SPECIALIZED connected with or used in the showing of moving pictures by television: *video frequencies*

video [MACHINE] /ˈvɪd.i.əʊ/ [US] /-oʊ/ *noun* [C] *plural* **videos** UK FOR **video (cassette) recorder**

ˈ**video arˌcade** *noun* [C] a place equipped with machines which play video games when you put money into them

ˈ**video ˌcamera** *noun* [C] a camera which records moving pictures and sound onto a video: *Many shops have video cameras fixed to their walls or ceilings for security reasons.* ➲Compare **camcorder**.

ˈ**video ˌcard** *noun* [C] a CIRCUIT BOARD (= small piece of electronic equipment) inside a computer that enables it to receive and show moving images

ˌ**video casˈsette** *noun* [C] a **video** TAPE

ˌ**video (casˈsette) reˌcorder** *noun* [C] (US USUALLY **VCR**, UK INFORMAL **video**) a machine that you use to record and play television programmes or films on video: *Don't forget to set the video before you go out.*

video conferencing /ˈvɪd.i.əʊˌkɒn.fər.ənt.sɪŋ/ [US] /-oʊˌkɑːn.fɚ-/ *noun* [U] when two or more people who are in different parts of the world can talk to each other and see each other on television screens

ˈ**video ˌdisc** *noun* [C] a large disc, on which moving pictures and sound have been recorded and which can be played on a television

ˈ**video ˌgame** *noun* [C] a game in which the player controls moving pictures on a screen by pressing buttons

ˈ**video ˌmonitor** *noun* [C] US a device with a screen on which moving pictures can be shown

ˌ**video ˈnasty** *noun* [C] UK a video of a film containing extremely unpleasant and offensive violence and sex

ˈ**video reˌcorder** *noun* [C] a **video (cassette) recorder**

videotape /ˈvɪd.i.əʊ.teɪp/ [US] /-oʊ-/ *noun* [C or U] (a) **video** TAPE

videotape /ˈvɪd.i.əʊ.teɪp/ [US] /-oʊ-/ *verb* [T] to record a film, television programme or event on videotape

vie /vaɪ/ *verb* [I] **vying**, **vied**, **vied** to compete with other people to achieve or obtain something: *Six candidates are currently vying **for** the Democratic presidential nomination.* ○ *The two older children tend to vie **with** the younger one **for** their mother's attention.* ○ [+ to infinitive] *The two groups of scientists are vying **to** get funding for their research projects.*

view [OPINION] /vjuː/ *noun* [C] **1** an opinion or belief or idea, or a way of thinking about something: *Do you have any views **about/on** what we should do now?* ○ ***In** my*

V

view, her criticisms were completely justified. ○ [+ **that**] *It's my view* ***that*** *the price is much too high.* ○ *Many people* ***have/hold/share/take*** *the view* ***that*** *children should not be smacked.* ○ *Everyone will have a chance to* ***make*** *their views* ***known*** *at the meeting.* ○ *We had a friendly* ***exchange of*** *views* (= discussion). ○ *I* ***take*** *a very* ***dim/poor*** *view* ***of*** *this kind of behaviour* (= think that this type of behaviour is unacceptable). **2 world view** a way of thinking about the world: *Our world view is quite different from that of writers in the fourth century BC.*

• **in view of *sth*** because of a particular thing, or taking a particular fact into consideration: *In view of what you've said, I think we should reconsider our proposed course of action.*

• **with a view to *doing sth*** with the aim of doing something: *These measures have been taken with a view to increasing the company's profits.*

view /vjuː/ *verb* [T] to have a particular opinion or way of thinking about someone or something: *The journalist asked the minister how he viewed recent events.* ○ *She is viewed* ***as*** *a strong candidate for the job.* ○ *We view these latest developments* ***with*** *concern/suspicion/satisfaction.* ○ *If we view the problem* ***from*** *a different* ***angle***, *a solution may become more obvious.* ○ *How do you view your prospects/chances* (= What do you consider your chances to be) *in tomorrow's race?*

view [SIGHT] /vjuː/ *noun* **1** [C or U] what you can see from a particular place, or the ability to see from a particular place: *The view* ***from*** *the top of the mountain is breathtaking/magnificent/spectacular.* ○ *The rooftop restaurant* ***affords*** *a panoramic view* (= allows you to see a wide area) *across the bay.* ○ *Don't stand in front of me – you're* ***blocking/obstructing*** *my view* ***of*** *the stage.* ○ *The cloud lifted, and the tops of the mountains suddenly* ***came into*** *view* (= could be seen). ○ *She turned a corner, and disappeared* ***from*** *view/****out of*** *view.* **2** [C] a picture of a particular place: *He paints rural views* (= pictures of the countryside).

• **in view** *UK* close enough to be seen: *I always make sure I keep the children in view whenever we're in a public place.*

• **on view** If something is on view, it is arranged so that it can be seen by the public: *The plans for the new road will soon be on view* ***to*** *the public in the library.*

viewing /ˈvjuː.ɪŋ/ *noun* [C] (*UK ALSO* **view**) an occasion for a special look at an exhibition, film, etc: *We've been invited to a* ***private*** *viewing, before the exhibition opens.*

view /vjuː/ *verb* [I or T] **1** to watch something: *There's a special area at the airport where you can view aircraft taking off and landing.* ○ *Viewing* ***figures*** (= the number of people watching programmes) *for the show were very low.* **2** to look at something in a complete or careful way: *I haven't had a chance to actually view the house yet.* ○ *The extent of the flooding can only be fully appreciated when viewed from the air.*

viewer /ˈvjuː.ər/ [US] /-ɚ/ *noun* [C] **1** a person who watches something, especially television: *Millions of viewers will be glued to their sets for this match.* **2** a device for looking at SLIDES (= photographs on small pieces of film)

COMMON LEARNER ERROR

view or **sight?**

When you use this word to talk about things that you can see, **view** means a wide range of things you can see, such as a part of the countryside or a city, or how well you can see something. A **view** is usually pleasant.

We had a wonderful view of the mountains from the aircraft.
~~*We had a wonderful sight of the mountains from the aircraft.*~~

Sight means something particular that you can see, or the ability to see.

The garden is a beautiful sight in spring.
The sight of blood makes me feel sick.
~~*The view of blood makes me feel sick.*~~
He lost his sight in an accident.
~~*He lost his view in an accident.*~~

viewfinder /ˈvjuːˌfaɪn.dər/ [US] /-dɚ/ *noun* [C] the part of a camera that you look through to see what it is that you are taking a photograph of

viewpoint [VIEW] *UK* /ˈvjuː.pɔɪnt/ *noun* [C] (*US* **overlook**, *AUS* **lookout**) a place from where a person can look at something, especially at an area of natural beauty: *The viewpoint by the side of the road gave us a stunning panorama of the whole valley.*

viewpoint [OPINION] /ˈvjuː.pɔɪnt/ *noun* [C] a **point of view**

vigil /ˈvɪdʒ.ɪl/ *noun* [C or U] (an act of) staying awake, especially at night, in order to be with an ill person, or to express especially political disagreement, or to pray: *His parents* ***kept*** *vigil beside his bed for weeks before he died.* ○ *Supporters of the peace movement* ***held*** *an all-night candlelit vigil outside the cathedral.*

vigilant /ˈvɪdʒ.ɪ.lənt/ *adj* always being careful to notice things, especially possible danger: *Following the bomb scare at the airport, the staff have been warned to be extra vigilant.* **vigilantly** /ˈvɪdʒ.ɪ.lənt.li/ *adv*

vigilance /ˈvɪdʒ.ɪ.lənts/ *noun* [U] more careful attention, especially in order to notice possible danger: *The police said that it was thanks to the vigilance* ***of*** *a neighbour that the fire was discovered before it could spread.*

vigilante /ˌvɪdʒ.ɪˈlæn.ti/ [US] /-ˈlæn.t̬i/ *noun* [C] a person who tries in an unofficial way to prevent crime, or to catch and punish someone who has committed a crime, especially because they do not think that official organizations, such as the police, are controlling crime effectively. Vigilantes usually join together to form groups. **vigilantism** /ˌvɪdʒ.ɪˈlæn.tɪ.zəm/ [US] /-t̬ɪ-/ *noun* [U]

vignette /vɪˈnjet/ *noun* [C] a short piece of writing, music, acting, etc. which clearly expresses the typical characteristics of something or someone: *She wrote several vignettes* ***of*** *small-town life.*

vigour *UK*, *US* **vigor** /ˈvɪg.ər/ [US] /-ɚ/ *noun* [U] **1** strength, energy or enthusiasm: *They set about their work* ***with*** *youthful vigour and enthusiasm.* **2** strength of thought, opinion, expression, etc: *His book is written* ***with*** *considerable vigour.*

vigorous /ˈvɪg.ər.əs/ [US] /-ɚ-/ *adj* **1** very forceful or energetic: *a vigorous debate* ○ *There has been vigorous opposition to the proposals for a new road.* ○ *He takes plenty of vigorous exercise.* **2** healthy and strong: *Cutting the bush back in the autumn will help promote vigorous growth in the spring.* **vigorously** /ˈvɪg.ər.ə.sli/ [US] /-ɚ-/ *adv*

Viking /ˈvaɪ.kɪŋ/ *noun* [C] a person belonging to a race of Scandinavian people who travelled by sea and attacked parts of northern and southern Europe between the 8th and the 11th centuries, often staying to live in places they travelled to

vile /vaɪl/ *adj* **1** unpleasant, immoral and unacceptable: *This vile policy of ethnic cleansing must be stopped.* **2** *INFORMAL* extremely unpleasant: *This cheese smells vile.* ○ *He's in a vile mood/temper today.* **vilely** /ˈvaɪl.li/ *adv*

vileness /ˈvaɪl.nəs/ *noun* [U]

vilify /ˈvɪl.ɪ.faɪ/ *verb* [T] *FORMAL* to say or write unpleasant things about someone or something, in order to cause other people to have a bad opinion of them: *He was vilified by the press* ***as*** *a monster of perversity.* **vilification** /ˌvɪl.ɪ.fɪˈkeɪ.ʃən/ *noun* [U]

villa /ˈvɪl.ə/ *noun* [C] a house usually in the countryside or near the sea, particularly in southern Europe, and often one which people can rent for a holiday: *They have a villa in Spain.*

village /ˈvɪl.ɪdʒ/ *noun* [C] a group of houses and other buildings, such as a church, a school and some shops, which is smaller than a town, usually in the countryside: *a fishing village* ○ *a mountain village* ○ *a village shop* ○ *a village green* (= an area of grass in the middle of a village) ○ *Many people come from the outlying/surrounding villages to work in the town.*

village /ˈvɪl.ɪdʒ/ *group noun* [C usually sing] all the people who live in a village: *The village is/are campaigning for a by-pass to be built.*

villager /ˈvɪl.ɪ.dʒər/ [US] /-dʒɚ/ *noun* [C] a person who lives in a village

villain /ˈvɪl.ən/ *noun* **1** [C] a bad person who harms other people or breaks the law: *Some people believe that Richard III did not murder his nephews and was not the villain he is generally thought to have been.* ○ *He's either a hero or a villain, depending on your point of view.* **2** [C]

UK INFORMAL a criminal: *Bert's just a small-time villain.* **3** [C] a character in a book, play, film, etc. who harms other people: *He made his reputation as an actor playing villains.* **4** [C usually sing] *INFORMAL* something or someone considered harmful or dangerous: *We've always been told that cholesterol, in foods like eggs, was a major cause of heart disease but, actually, saturated fat is the worst villain.*

• **villain of the piece** *INFORMAL* The villain of the piece is someone or something which is seen as being the cause of trouble on a particular occasion: *When the minister was forced to resign, the press was generally seen as the villain of the piece.*

villainous /ˈvɪl.ə.nəs/ *adj* [before n] describes a person or an action that is evil: *a villainous dictator* **villainy** /ˈvɪl.ə.ni/ *noun* [U]

vim /vɪm/ *noun* [U] *OLD-FASHIONED* energy and enthusiasm: *At 87, Minna's still full of vim* ***and vigour****.*

vinaigrette /ˌvɪn.ɪˈgret/ *noun* [U] (*UK ALSO* **French dressing**) a cold sauce made from oil and vinegar, which is used especially on salad

vindicate /ˈvɪn.dɪ.keɪt/ *verb* [T] **1** to prove that what someone said or did was right or true, after other people thought it was wrong: *The decision to include Morris in the team was completely vindicated when he scored three goals.* ○ *The investigation vindicated her complaint about the newspaper.* **2** to prove that someone is free from guilt or blame, after other people blamed them: [R] *They said they welcomed the trial as a chance to vindicate them****selves****.* **vindication** /ˌvɪn.dɪˈkeɪ.ʃən/ *noun* [S or U] *The army's victory is being seen as (a) vindication* ***of*** *their tactics.*

vindictive /vɪnˈdɪk.tɪv/ *adj DISAPPROVING* having or showing a desire to harm someone because you think that they have harmed you; unwilling to forgive: *In the film 'Cape Fear', a lawyer's family is threatened by a vindictive former prisoner.* **vindictively** /vɪnˈdɪk.tɪv.li/ *adv* **vindictiveness** /vɪnˈdɪk.tɪv.nəs/ *noun* [U]

vine /vaɪn/ *noun* [C] **1** (*ALSO* **grapevine**) the climbing plant which produces grapes as its fruit ➲See also **vineyard**. **2** any type of plant which climbs or grows along the ground and which has woody twisting stems: *Ivy is a type of vine.*

vinegar /ˈvɪn.ɪ.gəʳ/ [US] /-gɚ/ *noun* [U] a sharp-tasting liquid, made especially from sour wine, MALT or CIDER, which is used for flavouring or preserving food: *wine vinegar* ○ *Would you like* ***oil and*** *vinegar on your salad?*

vinegary /ˈvɪn.ɪ.gᵊr.i/ [US] /-gɚ-/ *adj* **1** tasting of vinegar **2** very critical or angry and unpleasant

vineyard /ˈvɪn.jɑːd/ [US] /-jɚd/ *noun* [C] a piece of land on which VINES (= plants which produce grapes) are grown

vino /ˈviː.nəʊ/ [US] /-noʊ/ *noun* [U] *INFORMAL FOR* **wine**: *Would you like a drop more vino?*

vintage [WINE] /ˈvɪn.tɪdʒ/ [US] /-t̬ɪdʒ/ *noun* **1** [C] the wine made in a particular year, or a particular year in which wine has been made: *The 1983 vintage was one of the best.* ○ *What vintage is this wine* (= In what year was it made)*?* **2** [U] *LITERARY* a group of things which were produced, or a group of people who were active, during the same particular period: *He is undoubtedly England's best captain* ***of recent*** *vintage.*

vintage /ˈvɪn.tɪdʒ/ [US] /-t̬ɪdʒ/ *adj* [before n] describes wine of high quality that was made in a particular year, and which can be kept for several years in order to improve it: *vintage champagne/port/claret*

vintage [HIGH QUALITY] /ˈvɪn.tɪdʒ/ [US] /-t̬ɪdʒ/ *adj* of high quality and lasting value, or showing the best and most typical characteristics of a particular type of thing, especially from the past: *a vintage aircraft* ○ *a vintage comic book* ○ *This film is vintage* (= has the best characteristics typical of films made by) *Disney.*

ˌvintage ˈcar *noun* [C] *UK* a car made between 1919 and 1930

vintner /ˈvɪnt.nəʳ/ [US] /-nɚ/ *noun* [C] a person whose job it is to buy and sell wine

vinyl /ˈvaɪ.nᵊl/ *noun* [U] strong plastic which can be bent, and which is used for making floor coverings, furniture, clothing, etc. or (in the past) records

viola /vaɪˈəʊ.lə/ [US] /-ˈoʊ-/ *noun* [C] a wooden musical instrument with four strings, which is held against the neck and played by moving a BOW across the strings. It is slightly larger than the violin.

violate /ˈvaɪə.leɪt/ *verb* [T] **1** to break or act against something, especially a law, agreement, principle or something that should be treated with respect: *They were charged with violating federal law.* ○ *It seems that the planes deliberately violated the cease-fire agreement.* ○ *The doctor has been accused of violating professional ethics.* **2** to go, especially forcefully, into a place or situation which should be treated with respect and in which you are not wanted or not expected to be: *The fishermen claimed that ships from another country had violated their territorial waters.* ○ *Questions of this kind violate my privacy and I am not willing to answer them.* **3** *FORMAL* **rape** FORCE: *She said that she had been treated so roughly by the hospital staff that she felt violated.*

violation /ˌvaɪəˈleɪ.ʃən/ *noun* [C or U] *He claimed that the way he'd been treated was a gross violation* ***of*** *his civil/constitutional/human rights.* ○ *The takeover of the embassy constitutes a flagrant/blatant violation* ***of*** *international law.* ○ *It was clear that they had not acted* ***in*** *violation* ***of*** *the rules.* **violator** /ˈvaɪə.leɪ.təʳ/ [US] /-t̬ɚ/ *noun* [C]

violence /ˈvaɪə.lᵊnts/ *noun* [U] **1** actions or words which are intended to hurt people: *It seems that the attack was a gratuitous/random/mindless* ***act of*** *violence.* ○ *The recent* ***outbreak/eruption*** *of racial violence in the area is very troubling.* ○ *The report documents the staggering amount of domestic violence* ***against*** *women.* **2** extreme force: *We were all surprised at the violence* ***of*** *his anger/rage.* ○ *The storm turned out to be one of unexpected violence.*

violent /ˈvaɪə.lᵊnt/ *adj* **1** using force to hurt or attack: *He shouts a lot but I don't think he's ever been physically violent towards her.* **2** describes a situation or event in which people are hurt or killed: *a violent crime* ○ *There was a violent clash/confrontation between rival supporters after the match.* ○ *The more violent scenes in the film were cut when it was shown on television.* ○ *Her family are still trying to come to terms with her violent* ***death*** (= death caused suddenly and unexpectedly by the use of physical force, especially murder). **3** sudden and powerful: *He has a violent temper.* ○ *a violent thunderstorm* ○ *The speaker launched into a violent attack* (= spoke forcefully against) *the government's policies.* **4** [before n] describes a colour which is extremely or unpleasantly bright: *She was wearing a violent pink sweater and orange trousers.*

violently /ˈvaɪə.lᵊnt.li/ *adv* **1** in a forceful way that causes people to be hurt: *He claimed to have been violently assaulted while in detention.* **2** strongly or extremely: *She violently disagreed with what we said.* ○ *He was violently sick.*

violet [COLOUR] /ˈvaɪə.lət/ *noun* [U], *adj* (having) a bluish purple colour

violet [PLANT] /ˈvaɪə.lət/ *noun* [C] a small plant with pleasant-smelling purple, blue or white flowers

violin /ˌvaɪəˈlɪn/ *noun* [C] a wooden musical instrument with four strings which is held against the neck and played by moving a BOW across the strings

violinist /ˌvaɪəˈlɪn.ɪst/ *noun* [C] a person who plays a violin

violoncello /ˌvaɪə.lənˈtʃel.əʊ/ [US] /-oʊ/ *noun* [C] *plural* **violoncellos** *FORMAL* a **cello**

VIP /ˌviː.aɪˈpiː/ *noun* [C] a very important person; a person who is treated better than ordinary people because they are famous or influential in some way: *They were in the VIP* ***lounge*** *at the airport.* ○ *We were given the full VIP* ***treatment****.*

viper /ˈvaɪ.pəʳ/ [US] /-pɚ/ *noun* [C] **1** a small poisonous snake **2** *LITERARY* a very unpleasant person whom you cannot trust: *When I started my new job, I didn't realize that I was walking into* ***a nest of*** *vipers.*

virago /vɪˈrɑː.gəʊ/ [US] /-ˈgoʊ/ *noun* [C] *plural* **viragos** or **viragoes** *OLD-FASHIONED* a fierce, unpleasant woman who shouts a lot

viral /ˈvaɪə.rᵊl/ [US] /ˈvaɪ-/ *adj* ➲See at **virus** SMALL ORGANISM.

virgin PERSON /'vɜː.dʒɪn/ ⑥ /'vɝː-/ *noun* [C] **1** someone who has never had sex: *She remained a virgin till she was over thirty.* ○ *D'you think he's still a virgin?* **2** *HUMOROUS* a person with no experience of a particular activity

virgin /'vɜː.dʒɪn/ ⑥ /'vɝː-/ *adj* **1** [before n] never having had sex: *a virgin bride* **2** [usually before n] *LITERARY* pure and not spoilt, especially when describing something white: *a virgin sheet of paper* (= one not written on) **virginal** /'vɜː.dʒɪ.nᵊl/ ⑥ /'vɝː-/ *adj: virginal innocence/ modesty/purity* **virginity** /vəˈdʒɪn.ɪ.ti/ ⑥ /vɝˈdʒɪn.ə.t̬i/ *noun* [U] *She lost her virginity at the age of sixteen to the boy next door.*

virgin PLACE/PRODUCT /'vɜː.dʒɪn/ ⑥ /'vɝː-/ *adj* **1** describes a forest or an area of land which has not yet been cultivated or used by people: *The railway is being extended into areas of virgin forest.* **2** describes oil, especially OLIVE OIL, which is obtained directly from pressing the fruit, rather than by using heat: *extra virgin olive oil*

● **virgin territory** a completely new area of activity: *The BBC is moving into virgin territory by producing comic programmes of this type.*

virginia creeper /vəˈdʒɪn.jəˈkriː.pə/ ⑥ /vɝˌdʒɪn.jəˈkriː.pɚ/ *noun* [C or U] (*US ALSO* **woodbine**) a VINE (= climbing plant) often grown on walls, the leaves of which become dark red in autumn

Virgo /'vɜː.gəʊ/ ⑥ /'vɝː.goʊ/ *noun* [C or U] *plural* **Virgos** the sixth sign of the zodiac, relating to the period 23 August to 22 September, represented by a young woman, or a person born during this period

Virgoan /vɜːˈgəʊ.ən/ ⑥ /vɝːˈgoʊ-/ *noun* [C], *adj* relating to, or (a person) born in, the period between 23 August and 22 September: *Perfectionism is a Virgoan trait.*

virile MASCULINE /'vɪr.aɪl/ ⑥ /-ᵊl/ *adj* *APPROVING* describes a man, especially a young man, full of sexual strength and energy in a way that is considered attractive: *She likes her men young and virile.* **virility** /vɪˈrɪl.ɪ.ti/ ⑥ /vəˈrɪl.ə.t̬i/ *noun* [U] *APPROVING* masculine sexual strength or qualities: *There was no doubting his virility.*

virile POWER /'vɪr.aɪl/ ⑥ /-ᵊl/ *adj* *LITERARY APPROVING* powerful, strong and energetic: *In this role, Durante is able to give full expression to that wonderfully virile voice.* **virility** /vɪˈrɪl.ɪ.ti/ ⑥ /vəˈrɪl.ə.t̬i/ *noun* [U] *APPROVING* strength or power: *If a country's foreign trade is a measure of its economic virility, this country looks sadly impotent.*

virology /vaɪəˈrɒl.ə.dʒi/ ⑥ /vaɪˈrɑː.lə-/ *noun* [U] the scientific study of viruses and the diseases that they cause

virtual /'vɜː.tju.əl/ ⑥ /'vɝː-/ *adj* **1** [before n] almost a particular thing or quality: *Ten years of incompetent government had brought about the virtual collapse of the country's economy.* ○ *War in the region now looks like a virtual certainty.* **2** describes something that can be done or seen using a computer and therefore without going anywhere or talking to anyone: *virtual shopping/ banking*

virtually /'vɜː.tju.ə.li/ ⑥ /'vɝː-/ *adv* almost: *Their twins are virtually identical.* ○ *That wine stain on my shirt has virtually disappeared.*

virtual reˈality *noun* [U] a set of images and sounds produced by a computer, which seem to represent a place or a situation that a person can experience or take part in

virtue GOODNESS /'vɜː.tjuː/ ⑥ /'vɝː-/ *noun* [C or U] a good moral quality in a person, or the general quality of goodness in people: *Patience is a virtue.* ⊃Compare **vice** MORAL FAULT.

virtuous /'vɜː.tju.əs/ ⑥ /'vɝː-/ *adj* **1** having good moral qualities and behaviour: *He described them as a virtuous and hard-working people.* **2** *DISAPPROVING* describes a person who thinks himself or herself morally better than other people: *I'm convinced he only does that charity work so that he can feel virtuous.* **virtuously** /'vɜː.tju.ə.sli/ ⑥ /'vɝː-/ *adv*

virtue ADVANTAGE /'vɜː.tjuː/ ⑥ /'vɝː-/ *noun* [C or U] (an) advantage or benefit: *It always looks odd to see an actress on TV extolling* (= praising) *the virtues of washing-up liquid.* ○ *Would there be any virtue in taking an earlier train?*

● **make a virtue (out) of** *sth* to use something, especially a bad situation, to your advantage: *I had a couple of months to spare between jobs so I thought I'd make a virtue of necessity by acquiring a few new skills.*

virtue BECAUSE OF /'vɜː.tjuː/ ⑥ /'vɝː-/ *noun* *FORMAL* **by virtue of** because of; as a result of: *She succeeded by virtue of her tenacity rather than her talent.*

virtuoso /ˌvɜː.tjuˈəʊ.səʊ/ ⑥ /ˌvɝː.tʃuˈoʊ.soʊ/ *noun* [C] *plural* **virtuosos** or **virtuosi** a person who is extremely skilled at something, especially at playing an instrument or performing: *Famous mainly for his wonderful voice, Cole was also a virtuoso on the piano.*

virtuoso /ˌvɜː.tjuˈəʊ.səʊ/ ⑥ /ˌvɝː.tʃuˈoʊ.soʊ/ *adj* [before n] extremely skilled: *The Times critic described her dancing as 'a virtuoso performance of quite dazzling accomplishment'.* **virtuosity** /ˌvɜː.tjuˈɒs.ɪ.ti/ ⑥ /ˌvɝː.tʃuˈɑː.sə.t̬i/ *noun* [U] *FORMAL*

virulent /'vɪr.jʊ.lᵊnt/ *adj* **1** describes a dangerous disease or poison which very quickly spreads or has an effect: *A particularly virulent strain of flu has recently claimed a number of lives in the US.* **2** *FORMAL* full of hate and fierce opposition: *She is a virulent critic of US foreign policy.*

virulence /'vɪr.jʊ.lᵊnts/ *noun* [U] **1** the danger and speed of spreading of a disease: *The virulence of the disease is causing great concern in medical circles.* **2** *FORMAL* strength of hatred and opposition: *We are witnessing racism of a virulence that we haven't seen in Europe since the 1940s.*

virus SMALL ORGANISM /'vaɪə.rəs/ ⑥ /'vaɪ-/ *noun* [C] **1** an extremely small organism which causes disease in humans, animals and plants: *a chicken pox/flu/herpes/ mumps virus* ○ *Evidence suggested that the AIDS virus was spreading very quickly among the heterosexual community.* **2** a disease caused by a virus: *I don't know exactly what's wrong with her – I think it's some sort of virus.* **viral** /'vaɪə.rᵊl/ ⑥ /'vaɪ-/ *adj: The continuing search for drugs to combat viral infections presents modern medicine with one of its greatest challenges in the twenty-first century.*

virus COMPUTER PROBLEM /'vaɪə.rəs/ ⑥ /'vaɪ-/ *noun* [C] a computer program or part of a computer program which can make copies of itself and is intended to prevent the computer from working normally

visa /'viː.zə/ *noun* [C] an official mark made in a PASSPORT which allows you to enter or leave a particular country: *We travelled to Argentina on a tourist visa.*

visage /'vɪz.ɪdʒ/ *noun* [C] *LITERARY* the face

vis-a-vis /ˌviːz.əˈviː/ *prep* *FORMAL* **1** in relation to: *I've got to speak to James Lewis vis-a-vis the arrangements for Thursday.* **2** in comparison with: *The decline in the power of local authorities vis-a-vis central government is worrying.*

viscera /'vɪs.ᵊr.ə/ ⑥ /-ɚ-/ *plural noun* *SPECIALIZED* the large organs inside the body, including the heart, stomach, lungs and intestines **visceral** /'vɪs.ᵊr.ᵊl/ ⑥ /-ɚ-/ *adj*

visceral /'vɪs.ᵊr.ᵊl/ ⑥ /-ɚ-/ *adj* *LITERARY* based on deep feeling and emotional reactions rather than on reason or thought: *visceral hatred/excitement* ○ *His approach to acting is visceral rather than intellectual.*

viscose /'vɪs.kəʊs/ ⑥ /-koʊs/ *noun* [U] a smooth material similar to silk but made from plant substances

viscount /'vaɪ.kaʊnt/ *noun* [C] (the title of) a British man of high social rank, between an EARL and a BARON

viscountess /ˌvaɪ.kaʊnˈtes/ *noun* [C] a woman who has the rank of viscount, or a woman who is married to a viscount

viscous /'vɪs.kəs/ *adj* *SPECIALIZED* describes a liquid that is thick and sticky and does not flow easily **viscosity** /vɪˈskɒs.ɪ.ti/ ⑥ /-ˈskɑː.sə.t̬i/ *noun* [U]

vise /vaɪs/ *noun* [C] *US FOR* **vice** TOOL

visible /'vɪz.ɪ.bl/ *adj* **1** able to be seen: *You should wear something light-coloured when you're cycling at night so* *that you're more visible.* ○ *The writing on the tombstone was* ***barely*** *visible.* ○ *There are few visible* ***signs*** *of the illness that kept her in hospital for so long.* ○ *The comet should be visible* ***to the naked eye.*** **2** able or tending to attract public attention and be noticed: *In a very short period of time, she has become a* ***highly*** *visible national leader.*

visibly /ˈvɪz.ɪ.bli/ *adv* in a way that can be noticed; obviously: *The Princess, visibly moved, kept her head bowed during the ceremony.*

visibility /ˌvɪz.ɪˈbɪl.ɪ.ti/ [US] /-ə.t̬i/ *noun* [U] **1** how clearly objects can be seen, or how far you can see clearly, usually because of the weather conditions: *Mist is still causing* ***poor*** *visibility – down to five metres in parts of the south-east.* **2** the degree to which something is seen by the public: *The increasing visibility of the nation's poor and homeless has forced the government into taking action.*

vision [ABILITY] /ˈvɪʒ.ᵊn/ *noun* [U] the ability to see: *She has very little vision in her left eye.*

vision [MENTAL IMAGE] /ˈvɪʒ.ᵊn/ *noun* [C] **1** an idea or mental image of something: *We see in his novels his sinister, almost apocalyptic, vision* ***of*** *the future.* ○ *Johnny was late home and, as usual, I* ***had*** *visions* ***of*** *him lying dead in some alley.* **2** an experience in which you see things which do not exist physically, when your mind is affected powerfully by something such as deep religious thought or drugs or mental illness: *She* ***had*** *visions in which the angel Gabriel appeared to her.*

visionary /ˈvɪʒ.ᵊn.ri/ [US] /-er.i/ *noun* [C] a person who has a religious or spiritual experience in which they see a holy person who is not living or they see a holy event that cannot be explained scientifically **visionary** /ˈvɪʒ.ᵊn.ri/ [US] /-er.i/ *adj*

vision [VIEW OF THE FUTURE] /ˈvɪʒ.ᵊn/ *noun* [U] the ability to imagine how a country, society, industry, etc. could develop in the future and to plan in a suitable way: *He didn't have the mental agility or vision required for a senior politician.* ○ *The new theatre company director is a person of great artistic vision.*

visionary /ˈvɪʒ.ᵊn.ri/ [US] /-er.i/ *noun* [C] a person who possesses the ability to imagine how a country, society, industry, etc. will develop in the future and to plan in a suitable way **visionary** /ˈvɪʒ.ᵊn.ri/ [US] /-er.i/ *adj*: *a visionary author* ○ *visionary thinking*

vision [BEAUTIFUL SIGHT] /ˈvɪʒ.ᵊn/ *noun* [S] *LITERARY OR HUMOROUS* (used when referring to a person) a beautiful and splendid sight: *And that vision* ***of loveliness*** *over there is my wife, Sandra.* ○ *She emerged from the bedroom, a vision* ***in*** *cream silk.*

visit /ˈvɪz.ɪt/ *verb* **1** [I or T] to go to a place in order to look at it, or to a person in order to spend time with them: *We visited a few galleries while we were in Prague.* ○ *Will you visit me when I'm in hospital?* ○ *When did you last visit the dentist/doctor?* ➲See Note **meet, see, visit or get to know?** at **meet** BECOME FAMILIAR WITH. **2** [T] to go to a WEB SITE on the Internet

visit /ˈvɪz.ɪt/ *noun* [C] when you visit a place or person: *I think I'll* ***pay*** *a visit* ***to*** *the hairdresser's while I'm in town.* ○ *We had a visit from the school inspector last week.* ○ *I can't stop for a cup of tea – this is just a* ***flying*** (= very short) *visit.*

visitation /ˌvɪz.ɪˈteɪ.ʃᵊn/ *noun* **1** [C] an official visit from someone important: *HUMOROUS We're awaiting a visitation from the inspector.* ○ *On May 13, 1917 three young shepherd children reported a visitation* ***from*** *the Virgin Mary.* **2** [U] *US* when a DIVORCED (= previously but no longer married) parent may spend time with the child(ren) he or she no longer lives with, at agreed times and under agreed conditions: *The mother agreed to visitation* ***rights*** *for the boys' father.* **3** [C] *FORMAL* an event which is considered to be a message or a punishment from God

visitor /ˈvɪz.ɪ.təʳ/ [US] /-t̬ɚ/ *noun* [C] **1** someone who visits a person or place: *Ben, you've got some visitors to see you.* **2** someone who accesses a WEB SITE on the Internet

PHRASAL VERBS WITH **visit** ▼

▲ **visit** ***sth*** **on/upon** ***sb*** *phrasal verb OLD USE OR FORMAL* to cause damage to a place or to harm a person: *He left in 1983, horrified by the devastation that warfare and famine had visited on his homeland.*

▲ **visit with** ***sb*** *phrasal verb US* to spend time talking with or staying with someone you know: *I was hoping to visit with Katie while I was in town.*

ˈvisiting ˌhours *plural noun* the times when you are allowed to go and spend time with someone who is in a hospital, prison, etc: *Visiting hours are between 6.00 and 9.00 p.m.*

visitors' book /ˈvɪz.ɪ.təz,bʊk/ [US] /-t̬ɚz-/ *noun* [C] a book sometimes found in a hotel or a place of interest in which people who are visiting are asked to write their name, address and anything they would like to say about the quality of what they have experienced in the place

visor /ˈvaɪ.zəʳ/ [US] /-zɚ/ *noun* [C] a part of a helmet which can be lowered to cover the face, or a curved piece of stiff material which is worn above the eyes to give protection from strong light from the sun

vista /ˈvɪs.tə/ *noun* [C] **1** *LITERARY* a view, especially a splendid view from a high position: *After a hard climb, we were rewarded by a picture-postcard vista* ***of*** *rolling hills under a deep blue summer sky.* **2** a possible future action or event that you can imagine: *As leader, he* ***opened up*** *exciting vistas of global co-operation.*

visual /ˈvɪʒ.u.əl/ *adj* relating to seeing: *visual stimulus/impact/abilities* ➲See also **VDU**. **visually** /ˈvɪʒ.u.ə.li/ *adv*: *Guide dogs open up the lives of the blind or visually* ***impaired.*** ○ *Books for children have to be visually very exciting.*

visualize, *UK USUALLY* **-ise** /ˈvɪʒ.u.ᵊl.aɪz/ *verb* [T] to form a picture of someone or something in your mind, in order to imagine or remember them: *I was so surprised when he turned up – I'd visualized someone much older.* **visualization**, *UK USUALLY* **-isation** /ˌvɪʒ.u.ᵊl.aɪˈzeɪ.ʃᵊn/ *noun* [U] *FORMAL*

ˌvisual ˈaid *noun* [C] something that you are shown, such as a picture, film or map, in order to help you understand or remember information

the ˌvisual ˈarts *plural noun* the arts of painting and sculpture, rather than literature and music

vital /ˈvaɪ.tᵊl/ [US] /-t̬ᵊl/ *adj* necessary for the success or continued existence of something; extremely important: *A strong opposition is vital* ***to*** *a healthy democracy.* ○ *She had found out some information of vital* ***importance.*** ○ *The kidney plays a vital* ***role/part*** *in the removal of waste products from the blood.* ○ [+ that] ***It's*** *absolutely vital* ***that*** *you do exactly as I say.* ○ [+ to infinitive] ***It*** *is vital* ***to*** *get medical supplies to the area as soon as possible.* ➲See also **vital** at **vitality**. **vitally** /ˈvaɪ.tᵊl.i/ [US] /-t̬ᵊl-/ *adv*: *It's not vitally* ***important*** *that we get extra funding for the project but it would help.*

vitality /vaɪˈtæl.ɪ.ti/ [US] /-ə.t̬i/ *noun* [U] *APPROVING* energy and strength: *According to the packet, these vitamin pills will restore lost vitality.*

vital /ˈvaɪ.tᵊl/ [US] /-t̬ᵊl/ *adj* **1** *FORMAL APPROVING* energetic: *He had never felt so vital and full of life.* **2** *FORMAL* relating to life

ˌvital ˈorgans *plural noun* the main organs inside the body, such as the heart, lungs and brain, which are necessary for existence

ˌvital staˈtistics [OFFICIAL FACTS] *plural noun* a group of official facts which show such things as the number of births, deaths and marriages in a particular country, area, etc.

ˌvital staˈtistics [WOMAN'S BODY] *plural noun UK OLD-FASHIONED HUMOROUS* the measurements of a woman's breasts, waist and hips

vitamin /ˈvɪt.ə.mɪn/ [US] /ˈvaɪ.t̬ə-/ *noun* [C] any of a group of natural substances which are necessary in small amounts for the growth and good health of the body: *a vitamin pill* ○ *Oranges are full of vitamin C.*

ˌvitamin ˈA *noun* [U] (*SPECIALIZED* **retinol**) a vitamin found in foods such as butter, egg yolk, milk and fish-liver oils, or formed in the body from the CAROTENE in green leafy or orange vegetables, important for normal growth, healthy skin, and the ability to see well, especially at night

vitamin B_1 /ˌvɪt.ə.mɪn,biːˈwʌn/ [US] /ˌvaɪ.t̬ə-/ *noun* [U] (*SPECIALIZED* **thiamine**) a vitamin found in foods such as

V

whole grains, brown rice, nuts and liver, important for the production of energy from sugar and starch in the body and helping the heart, muscles and NERVOUS SYSTEM to work well

vitamin B₂ /ˌvɪt.ə.mɪnˌbiːˈtuː/ US /ˌvaɪ.tə-/ noun [U] (SPECIALIZED **riboflavin**) a vitamin found in foods such as liver, milk, cheese, yeast and whole grains, important for the production of energy in the cells and for the production of particular hormones

vitamin B₆ /ˌvɪt.ə.mɪnˌbiːˈsɪks/ US /ˌvaɪ.tə-/ noun [U] a vitamin found in foods such as liver, yeast, fish and BANANAS, important in chemical processes in the body, and for keeping the skin, digestion and NERVOUS SYSTEM healthy

vitamin B₁₂ /ˌvɪt.ə.mɪnˌbiːˈtwelv/ US /ˌvaɪ.tə-/ noun [U] a vitamin found in foods such as liver, kidney, eggs, fish and milk, important for a healthy NERVOUS SYSTEM, normal growth and the production of red blood cells

vitamin 'B ˌcomplex group noun a group of vitamins which dissolve in water and are found in food

vitamin 'C noun [U] (SPECIALIZED **ascorbic acid**) a vitamin found in foods such as CITRUS fruit, green leafy vegetables, tomatoes and potatoes, important for healthy bones, joints, teeth and gums, and for fighting infection

vitamin 'D noun [U] any of a group of vitamins found in foods such as liver, oily fish and egg yolk, important for healthy bones and teeth

vitamin 'E noun [U] (SPECIALIZED **tocopherol**) a vitamin found in foods such as vegetable oils, whole grains, green leafy vegetables and fish, important for healthy blood and cells

vitamin 'K noun [U] a vitamin found in foods such as green leafy vegetables, liver, vegetable oils and egg yolk, important for healthy blood

vitiate /ˈvɪʃ.i.eɪt/ verb [T] FORMAL to destroy or weaken something: He said that American military power should never again be vitiated by political concerns.

viticulture /ˈvɪt.ɪˌkʌl.tʃəʳ/ US /-ˌtɪˌkʌl.tʃɚ/ noun [U] SPECIALIZED the growing of grapes, or the science or study of this

vitreous /ˈvɪt.ri.əs/ adj made of or similar to glass: vitreous china/enamel

vitriol /ˈvɪt.ri.əl/ noun [U] fierce hate and anger expressed through severe criticism: He is a writer who has often been criticized by the press but never before with such vitriol. **vitriolic** /ˌvɪt.riˈɒl.ɪk/ US /-ˈɑː.lɪk/ adj: He launched a vitriolic **attack** on the prime minister, accusing him of shielding corrupt friends. **vitriolically** /ˌvɪt.riˈɒl.ɪ.kli/ US /-ˈɑː.lɪ-/ adv

vitro /ˈviː.trəʊ/ US /-troʊ/ noun ⊃See **in vitro**.

vituperative /vaɪˈtjuː.pʳr.ə.tɪv/ US /-ˈtuː.pə.reɪ.tɪv/ adj FORMAL A vituperative spoken or written attack is full of angry accusations: Miss Snowden yesterday launched a vituperative attack on her ex-boss and former lover. **vituperation** /vaɪˌtjuː.pʳrˈeɪ.ʃn/ US /-ˌtuː.pəˈreɪ-/ noun [U]

viva EXAMINATION /ˈvaɪ.və/ noun [C] (ALSO **viva voce**) SPECIALIZED a spoken examination for a college qualification

viva APPROVAL /ˈviː.və/ exclamation MAINLY US used to express approval or good wishes: Throngs of his supporters were shouting "Viva, Ollie, viva!"

vivacious /vɪˈveɪ.ʃəs/ adj APPROVING A vivacious person, especially a woman or girl, is attractively energetic and enthusiastic: He brought along his wife, a vivacious blonde, some twenty years his junior. **vivaciously** /vɪˈveɪ.ʃə.sli/ adv **vivacity** /vɪˈvæs.ɪ.ti/ US /-ə.t̬i/ noun [U]

vivid /ˈvɪv.ɪd/ adj **1** Vivid descriptions, memories, etc. produce very clear, powerful and detailed images in the mind: He gave a very vivid and often shocking account/description of his time in prison. ○ He's one of those people with a very vivid **imagination** – every time he hears a noise he's convinced it's someone breaking in. **2** very brightly coloured: She was wearing a vivid pink shirt. **vividly** /ˈvɪv.ɪd.li/ adv: I vividly remember my first day at school. **vividness** /ˈvɪv.ɪd.nəs/ noun [U]

viviparous /vɪˈvɪp.ʳr.əs/ US /-ɚ-/ adj SPECIALIZED giving birth to young that have already developed inside the mother's body rather than producing eggs

vivisection /ˌvɪv.ɪˈsek.ʃn/ noun [U] the cutting up or other use of living animals in tests which are intended to increase human knowledge of human diseases and the effects of using particular drugs

vivisectionist /ˌvɪv.ɪˈsek.ʃn.ɪst/ noun [C] a person who is involved in the activity of, or believes in the use of, vivisection

vixen /ˈvɪk.sⁿn/ noun [C] **1** a female fox **2** OLD-FASHIONED an unpleasant woman

viz /vɪz/ adv OLD-FASHIONED used, especially in written English, when you want to give more detail or be more exact about something you have just written: We both shared the same ambition, viz, to make a lot of money and to retire at 40.

V-neck /ˈviː.nek/ noun [C] a V-shaped opening for your neck on a piece of clothing, or a piece of clothing with this opening: I'm going to wear my black dress with the V-neck. ○ a V-neck jumper **V-necked** /ˌviːˈnekt/ adj: a V-necked dress

vocab /ˈvəʊ.kæb/ US /ˈvoʊ-/ noun [U] INFORMAL **vocabulary**

vocabulary /vəˈkæb.jʊ.lʳr.i/ US /voʊˈkæb.jə.ler.i/ noun **1** [C] all the words known and used by a particular person: a **wide/limited** vocabulary ○ By the age of two a child will have a vocabulary of about two hundred words. **2** [C or U] all the words which exist in a particular language or subject: Every week our French teacher gives us a list of vocabulary (= words) to learn. ○ Computing, like any subject, has its own vocabulary.

• **not be in** sb's **vocabulary** HUMOROUS You say that a particular quality is not in your vocabulary if you never show it or experience it: Did you say 'tact'? The word isn't in his vocabulary!

vocal OF THE VOICE /ˈvəʊ.kⁿl/ US /ˈvoʊ-/ adj relating to or produced by the voice, either in singing or speaking: a piece of vocal music ○ The six principal roles in this opera have an average vocal **range** of two octaves.

vocal /ˈvəʊ.kⁿl/ US /ˈvoʊ-/ noun [C usually pl] the singing in a piece of popular music: The vocals are shared by two members of the band. ○ Is that Tamsin Palmer **on** vocals (= singing)? **vocally** /ˈvəʊ.kⁿl.i/ US /ˈvoʊ-/ adv

vocalist /ˈvəʊ.kⁿl.ɪst/ US /ˈvoʊ-/ noun [C] a person who sings, especially with a group who play popular music: She won the Grammy Award for Best Female Vocalist in 1976.

vocalize /ˈvəʊ.kə.laɪz/ US /ˈvoʊ-/ verb [T] to express feelings or ideas in words: Most patients find it very difficult to vocalize feelings of shame.

vocal OFTEN HEARD /ˈvəʊ.kⁿl/ US /ˈvoʊ-/ adj often expressing opinions and complaints in speech: He had always been a very vocal **critic** of the president. ○ During these years, suffrage demands by women became increasingly vocal and difficult to ignore. **vocally** /ˈvəʊ.kⁿl.i/ US /ˈvoʊ-/ adv

'vocal ˌcords plural noun (ALSO **vocal chords**) a pair of folds at the upper end of the throat whose edges move quickly backwards and forwards and produce sound when air from the lungs moves over them

vocation /vəʊˈkeɪ.ʃⁿn/ US /voʊ-/ noun [C or U] a type of work that you feel you are suited to doing and to which you should give all your time and energy, or the feeling of suitability itself: I feel I've **found/missed** my true vocation. ○ "We need teachers who regard their profession as a vocation, not just a job," said the Minister. ○ To work in medicine, you should **have** a vocation (= feeling of suitability) **for** it.

vocational /vəʊˈkeɪ.ʃⁿn.ⁿl/ US /voʊ-/ adj providing skills and education that prepare you for a job: The Swedes regard vocational **training** as a part of a youngster's education. **vocationally** /vəʊˈkeɪ.ʃⁿn.ⁿl.i/ US /voʊ-/ adv

vociferous /vəˈsɪf.ʳr.əs/ US /-ɚ-/ adj Vociferous people express their opinions and complaints loudly and repeatedly in speech, and vociferous demands, etc. are made repeatedly and loudly: Local activist groups have become increasingly vociferous as the volume of traffic passing through the village has grown. ○ A vociferous **opponent** of gay rights, he is well-known for his right-wing views. **vociferously** /vəˈsɪf.ʳr.ə.sli/ US /-ɚ-/ adv

vodka /ˈvɒd.kə/ ⓤ /ˈvɑːd-/ *noun* [C or U] a colourless strong alcoholic drink made especially from grain or potatoes: *"What would you like to drink?" "Vodka and tonic please."* ○ *This is my third vodka* (= glass of vodka).

vogue /vəʊɡ/ ⓤ /voʊɡ/ *noun* [S or U] a fashion or general liking, especially one which is temporary: *In the 1920s, short hair for women became* **the** *vogue.* ○ *The postwar vogue for tearing down buildings virtually destroyed the city's architecture.* ○ *The short hemline is very much in vogue* (= fashionable) *this spring.* ○ *"Community" is one of the vogue words of the new government.*

voice SOUNDS /vɔɪs/ *noun* [C] the sounds that are made when people speak or sing: *She has a loud/quiet/soft voice.* ○ *a low-pitched/high-pitched voice* ○ *a booming/breathy/clear/deep/fruity/gravelly/husky/squeaky voice* ○ *a baritone/soprano singing voice* ○ *You could tell from her voice that she wasn't pleased.* ○ *"I don't know what you mean," said Fran in a quavering voice.* ○ *She lowered her voice to a whisper.* ○ *You'll have to raise your voice* (= speak louder) *if you want to be heard in here.* ○ *I've got a cold and I think I'm losing my voice* (= becoming unable to speak). ○ *He's at that age when his voice is breaking* (= changing from a boy's to a man's). ○ *She's done a lot of work with voice-activated computers.*

• **with one voice** FORMAL If a group of people express an opinion or decide something with one voice, they all agree: *The committee decided with one voice to accept the proposal.*

• **voice within you** your CONSCIENCE (= the part of you which tells you when you are doing something immoral): *Suddenly this voice within her told her to stop being so stupid.*

-voiced /-vɔɪst/ *suffix* having the type of voice mentioned: *I took my loud-voiced friend, Roz, with me to the party.*

voice OPINION /vɔɪs/ *noun* **1** [C often sing; U] (the right to) an expression of opinion: *There was only one dissenting voice during the discussion.* ○ *Unfortunately a strike was the only way to make our voices heard.* ○ *The committee represents the voice of the students.* ○ *Developing countries are demanding a stronger voice* (= right to express opinions) *in the debate.* **2** [S] an important quality or opinion which someone expresses, or the person who is able to express it: *She just won't listen to the voice of reason.* ○ *I wouldn't work for Peter if I were you – this is the voice of experience talking!*

• **give voice to** sth to express your thoughts or feelings in words: *I always had doubts about the scheme but I never gave voice to them.*

voice /vɔɪs/ *verb* [T] to say what you think about a particular subject, especially to express a doubt, complaint, etc. that you have about it: *I have on several occasions voiced my objections to the plan to management.*

voiceless /ˈvɔɪ.sləs/ *adj* LITERARY describes a group of people who lack the power or the legal right to express their opinions: *A committed socialist, he upheld the rights of the voiceless and the underprivileged.*

voice box *noun* [C usually sing] a **larynx**

voice mail *noun* [U] an electronic telephone answering system used especially by organizations and mobile phone users

voice-over /ˈvɔɪs.əʊ.vəʳ/ ⓤ /-oʊ.vɚ/ *noun* [C] on a television programme or film, the spoken words of a person that you cannot see: *Famous actors often provide voice-overs for adverts.*

void EMPTY SPACE /vɔɪd/ *noun* **1** [C usually sing] a large hole or empty space: *She stood at the edge of the chasm and stared into the void.* ○ *Before Einstein, space was regarded as a formless void.* **2** [S] a feeling of unhappiness because someone or something is missing: *They tried to describe their attempts to fill the void left by their son's death.*

void UNACCEPTABLE /vɔɪd/ *adj* having no legal authority and therefore unacceptable: *The lawyers declared the contract (null and) void.* ⊃See also **null and void.**

void /vɔɪd/ *verb* [T] to remove the legal force from something such as a legal agreement

void WITHOUT /vɔɪd/ *adj* LITERARY **void of** without; lacking in: *He's completely void of charm so far as I can see.*

voila /ˌvwɑːˈlɑː/ *exclamation* used when showing to other people something that you have just made or obtained and are pleased with: *Corn tortillas can be cut into strips, fried until golden, and sprinkled with salt – voila! tortilla chips.*

vol. WRITTEN ABBREVIATION FOR **volume**

volatile /ˈvɒl.ə.taɪl/ ⓤ /ˈvɑː.lə.t̬ᵊl/ *adj* **1** likely to change suddenly and unexpectedly or to suddenly become violent or angry: *Food and fuel prices are very volatile in a war situation.* ○ *The situation was made more volatile by the fact that people had been drinking a lot of alcohol.* ○ *He had a rather volatile temper and was never easy to live with.* **2** A volatile liquid or solid substance will change easily into a gas. **volatility** /ˌvɒl.əˈtɪl.ɪ.ti/ ⓤ /ˌvɑː.ləˈtɪl.ə.t̬i/ *noun* [U]

vol-au-vent /ˈvɒl.ə.vɒ̃/ ⓤ /ˌvɔː.loʊˈvɑ̃/ *noun* [C] a small, light, cup-shaped pastry case with a savoury sauce filling: *chicken/mushroom/prawn vol-au-vents*

volcano /vɒlˈkeɪ.nəʊ/ ⓤ /vɑːlˈkeɪ.noʊ/ *noun* [C] *plural* **volcanoes** or **volcanos** a mountain with a large circular hole at the top through which LAVA (= hot liquid rock), gases, steam and dust are or have been forced out: *an extinct/dormant volcano* ○ *an active volcano* ○ *Erupting volcanoes discharge massive quantities of dust into the stratosphere.* **volcanic** /vɒlˈkæn.ɪk/ ⓤ /vɑːl-/ *adj: volcanic ash/activity/rock*

vole /vəʊl/ ⓤ /voʊl/ *noun* [C] a small mouse-like animal with a thick body, short tail and small ears

volition /vəˈlɪʃ.ᵊn/ *noun* [U] FORMAL the power to make your own decisions: *The Minister wished it to be known that he had left the cabinet (out) of his own volition* (= it was his decision).

volley BULLETS /ˈvɒl.i/ ⓤ /ˈvɑː.li/ *noun* [C] a large number of bullets (seeming to be) fired at the same time: *Even as the funeral took place, guerrillas hidden nearby fired/let off a fresh volley of machine-gun fire.*

volley LOT /ˈvɒl.i/ ⓤ /ˈvɑː.li/ *noun* [C usually sing] a lot of similar things that are said or produced, or that happen, quickly one after the other: *I'm afraid my proposal was met with a volley of criticisms.*

volley SPORTS SHOT /ˈvɒl.i/ ⓤ /ˈvɑː.li/ *noun* [C] (in sports) a kick or hit in which a player returns a moving ball before it touches the ground: *That was a marvellous backhand volley.* ⊃See Note **basket or basketball?** at **basket. volley** /ˈvɒl.i/ ⓤ /ˈvɑː.li/ *verb* [I or T]

volleyball /ˈvɒl.i.bɔːl/ ⓤ /ˈvɑː.li.bɑːl/ *noun* [U] a game in which two teams use their hands to hit a large ball backwards and forwards over a high net without allowing the ball to touch the ground

volt /vɒlt/ ⓤ /voʊlt/ *noun* [C] the standard unit used to measure how strongly an electrical current is sent around an electrical system: *Electricity in Britain is 240 volts, AC.*

voltage /ˈvɒl.tɪdʒ/ ⓤ /ˈvoʊl.tɪdʒ/ *noun* [C or U] the force of an electric current, measured in volts: *high/low voltages*

volte-face /ˌvɒltˈfæs/ ⓤ /ˌvoʊlt-/ *noun* [C usually sing] *plural* **volte-face** LITERARY a sudden change from one set of beliefs or plan of action to the opposite: *In 1986 he made a very public and dramatic political volte-face from Left to Right.*

voluble /ˈvɒl.jʊ.bl̩/ ⓤ /ˈvɑːl-/ *adj* FORMAL **1** speaking a lot, with confidence and enthusiasm: *Many see Parker as the obvious leader, whose voluble style works well on TV.* **2** expressed in many words: *It's not often that one hears such voluble praise for this government.* **volubly** /ˈvɒl.jʊ.bli/ ⓤ /ˈvɑːl-/ *adv*

volume AMOUNT /ˈvɒl.juːm/ ⓤ /ˈvɑːl-/ *noun* **1** [C or U] the amount of space that is enclosed within an object or solid shape: *Which of these bottles do you think has the greater volume?* **2** [U] the number or amount of something in general: *It's the sheer volume of traffic in the city that is causing the problems.*

volume SOUND LEVEL /ˈvɒl.juːm/ ⓤ /ˈvɑːl-/ *noun* [U] the level of sound produced by a television, radio, etc., or the switch or other device controlling this: *Could you turn the volume down, please, I'm trying to sleep.* ○ *I'll* *turn it up if you tell me which is the volume* (= switch).

volume [BOOK] /ˈvɒl.juːm/ [US] /ˈvɑːl-/ *noun* [C] **1** one in a set of related books: *Now 'Realms Of Strife', his second volume **of** memoirs, is available too.* **2** FORMAL a book: *While still an undergraduate, his first slim volume 'Fighting Terms' enjoyed a considerable success.*

voluminous /vəˈluː.mɪ.nəs/ *adj* FORMAL **1** A voluminous piece of clothing is large and consists of a lot of cloth: *Her voluminous silk dress billowed out behind her.* **2** A voluminous piece of writing is long and detailed: *Have you read McClelland's voluminous account of his life and work?*

voluntary /ˈvɒl.ən.tri/ [US] /ˈvɑː.lən.ter.i/ *adj* **1** done, made or given willingly, without being forced or paid to do it: *They chose to take voluntary redundancy.* ○ *She does voluntary work for the Red Cross two days a week.* **2** describes an organization that is controlled and supported by people who give their time and money to it without being paid, and that exists to help other people: *The hospital has asked various voluntary organizations to help raise money for the new operating theatre.*
voluntarily /ˈvɒl.ən.trəl.i/ [US] /ˈvɑː.lən.ter.əl-/ *adv*

volunteer /ˌvɒl.ənˈtɪəʳ/ [US] /ˌvɑː.lənˈtɪr/ *noun* [C] a person who does something, especially helping other people, willingly and without being forced or paid to do it: *The Health clinic is relying on volunteers to run the office and answer the telephones.* ○ *Since it would be a highly dangerous mission, the Lieutenant asked for volunteers.* ○ *It's a volunteer army with no paid professionals.* ➲Compare **conscript**.

volunteer /ˌvɒl.ənˈtɪəʳ/ [US] /ˌvɑː.lənˈtɪr/ *verb* **1** [I or T] to offer to do something that you do not have to do, often without having been asked to do it and/or without expecting payment: [+ *to* infinitive] *During the emergency many staff volunteered **to** work through the weekend.* ○ *I volunteered myself **for** the post of Health and Safety Representative.* ○ *My mates volunteered me **to** do the talking.* ○ *He volunteered **for** the army* (= He became a member although he was not forced to by law). **2** [T] to give information without being asked: *If I were you, I wouldn't volunteer any details of what happened.* ○ [+ speech] *"I saw her going out of the main entrance at about half past two," he volunteered.*

voluptuous /vəˈlʌp.tju.əs/ *adj* **1** describes a woman who has a soft, curved, sexually attractive body: *a voluptuous body/mouth/figure* **2** LITERARY describes an experience or object that gives you a lot of pleasure because it feels extremely soft and comfortable or it sounds or looks extremely beautiful: *such voluptuous pleasure* ○ *I sank into the bed's voluptuous warmth.*
voluptuously /vəˈlʌp.tju.ə.sli/ *adv* LITERARY
voluptuousness /vəˈlʌp.tju.ə.snəs/ *noun* [U]

vomit /ˈvɒm.ɪt/ [US] /ˈvɑː.mɪt/ *verb* [I or T] to empty the contents of the stomach through the mouth: *He came home drunk and vomited all over the kitchen floor.* ○ *She was vomiting **(up)** blood.* **vomit** /ˈvɒm.ɪt/ [US] /ˈvɑː.mɪt/ *noun* [U]

voodoo /ˈvuː.duː/ *noun* [U] **1** a type of religion involving magic and the worship of SPIRITS (= beings which cannot be seen), especially common in Haiti **2** INFORMAL bad luck: *They felt as if there was some sort of voodoo **on** the band, because everything just went wrong.*

voracious /vəˈreɪ.ʃəs/ *adj* very eager for something, especially a lot of food: *He has a voracious **appetite*** (= he eats a lot). ○ *He's a voracious reader of historical novels* (= He reads a lot of them eagerly and quickly).
voraciously /vəˈreɪ.ʃə.sli/ *adv* **voraciousness** /vəˈreɪ.ʃə.snəs/ *noun* [U]

vortex /ˈvɔː.teks/ [US] /ˈvɔːr.t̬eks/ *noun plural* **vortexes** or **vortices** **1** [C] SPECIALIZED a mass of air or water that spins around very fast and pulls objects into its empty centre **2** [C usually sing] LITERARY a dangerous or destructive situation in which you become more and more involved without being able to escape: *I was **sucked into** a vortex **of** despair.*

vote /vəʊt/ [US] /voʊt/ *verb* [I or T] to express your choice or opinion, especially by officially marking a paper or by raising your hand or speaking in a meeting: *She was too young to vote **in** the national election.* ○ *The committee voted **on** the proposal, and accepted it unanimously.* ○ *Did you vote **for** or **against** the motion?* ○ *Over 55% voted Liberal.* ○ [+ *to* infinitive] *A majority of staff voted **to** accept the offer of an 8% pay rise.* ○ [+ (*that*)] *I vote **(that)** we* (= It is my opinion that we should) *go to the cinema first and eat afterwards.* ○ [+ obj + n] *The evening was voted a tremendous success* (= This was most people's opinion). ○ *It was the younger members who voted Smith **onto** the committee* (= Smith joined because he was the choice of the younger members). ○ *The Republican Party was voted **into/out of office*** (= was chosen in an election to become/stop being the government).
• **vote with *your* feet** If you vote with your feet, you leave an organization or stop supporting, using or buying something, and change to a new organization, service, or product: *When the price of skiing in the mountain resorts doubled, tourists voted with their feet and just stopped going.*

vote /vəʊt/ [US] /voʊt/ *noun* **1** [C] when someone shows their choice or opinion in an election or meeting by writing a cross on an official piece of paper or putting their hand up: *The suggestion was approved, with 25 votes in favour, and 7 against.* ○ *She **cast** her vote* (= voted) *for the Communist Party.* **2** [C usually sing] a way of making a decision by asking a group of people to vote: *We called a meeting in order to **take/hold** a vote **on** the issue.*

the vote *noun* [S] **1** the total number of votes given or received in an election: *The Green Party **got/took** 25% of the vote.* ○ *They are trying to capture the working-class vote* (= to persuade those people to vote for them). **2** when someone is officially allowed to vote: *In some countries women still don't **have** the vote.*
• **put *sth* to the/a vote** to vote on something: *The proposal was read out and then put to the vote.*

voter /ˈvəʊ.təʳ/ [US] /ˈvoʊ.t̬ɚ/ *noun* [C] a person who votes or who has a legal right to vote, especially in an election: *Of course, tax cuts are usually popular with (the) voters.* ○ *Are you a Labour voter?*

voting /ˈvəʊ.tɪŋ/ [US] /-t̬ɪŋ/ *noun* [U] when people choose someone or something in an election: *Voting was brisk in spite of the bad weather.* ○ *Pollsters asked people their voting intentions.*

PHRASAL VERBS WITH **vote** ▼

▲ **vote *sth* down** *phrasal verb* [M] to defeat something such as a law or plan by voting against it: *The proposal to build a new road through the forest was voted down by the local council.*

▲ **vote *sth* through** *phrasal verb* [M] to accept and make possible something such as a law or plan by voting for it: *The committee voted through a proposal to cut the defence budget.*

vote-getter /ˈvəʊtˌget.əʳ/ [US] /ˈvoʊtˌget̬.ɚ/ *noun* [C usually sing] US something that will win votes because it is popular with the voters: *Her stance on taxation could be a big vote-getter in this election.*

ˌvote of ˈconfidence *noun* [C usually sing] **1** FORMAL when the members of a parliament or other organization are asked to say that they support the people in authority and agree with their actions: *The government **held** a vote of confidence and lost/won it.* **2** a sign that you are pleased with the quality of something or what someone has done or produced: *I think the fact that so many of you are here tonight is a vote of confidence **in** the quality of our local performers.*

ˌvote of ˌno ˈconfidence *noun* [C usually sing] when the members of a parliament or other organization are asked to say that they do not support the people in authority and that they disagree with their actions

ˌvote of ˈthanks *noun* [C usually sing] when someone formally and publicly thanks a person or organization for something they have done: *The new Chairperson stood up and **proposed*** (= said) *a vote of thanks **to** the retiring Chair **for** all her hard work.*

ˈvoting maˌchine *noun* [C] MAINLY US a machine used to automatically record and count votes in an election

votive /ˈvəʊ.tɪv/ [US] /ˈvoʊ.t̬ɪv/ *adj* SPECIALIZED given or done to honour and thank a god: *votive offerings*

vouch /vaʊtʃ/ *verb* [T + *that*] to be able from your knowledge or experience to say that something is true: *As a medical examiner I* ***can*** *vouch from experience* ***that*** *his death was accidental.*

▲ **vouch for *sth/sb*** *phrasal verb* to say that you know from experience that something is true or good, or that someone is honest and has a good character: *Patricia has checked the reports and can vouch for the accuracy of the information.*

voucher /ˈvaʊ.tʃəʳ/ [US] /-tʃɚ/ *noun* [C] *UK* a piece of paper that can be used to pay for particular goods or services or that allows you to pay less than the usual price for them: *The voucher is valid between July and December and entitles you to 10% off all overseas flights.*

vouchsafe /ˌvaʊtʃˈseɪf/ *verb* [T] *FORMAL* to tell or give something to someone: *He vouchsafed the information that the meeting had been postponed.*

vow /vaʊ/ *verb* [T] to make a determined decision or promise to do something: [+ (*that*)] *The guerillas vowed* ***(that)*** *they would overthrow the government.* ○ [+ *to* infinitive] *After the awful meals we had last Christmas, I vowed* ***to*** *do more of the cooking myself.*

vow /vaʊ/ *noun* [C] a serious promise or decision: [+ *to* infinitive] *She* ***took/made*** *a vow never to lend money to anyone again.*

vowel /vaʊəl/ *noun* [C] **1** a speech sound produced by human beings when the breath flows out through the mouth without being blocked by the teeth, tongue or lips: *A* ***short*** *vowel is a short sound as in the word 'cup'.* ○ *A* ***long*** *vowel is a long sound as in the word 'shoe'.* ➲Compare **consonant**. **2** a letter that represents a sound produced in this way: *The vowels in English are a, e, i, o and u.*

vox pop /ˌvɒksˈpɒp/ [US] /ˌvɑːksˈpɑːp/ *noun UK INFORMAL* **1** [U] the opinions of people recorded talking informally in public places **2** [C] a broadcast for radio or television in which people going past in a public place are asked their opinion on a particular subject

voyage /ˈvɔɪ.ɪdʒ/ *noun* [C] a long journey, especially by ship: *He was a young sailor* ***on*** *his first sea voyage.* ○ *FIGURATIVE The first year of a loving relationship is a voyage* (= period) ***of*** *discovery.*

voyage /ˈvɔɪ.ɪdʒ/ *verb* [I] *OLD USE OR LITERARY* to travel: *In their little boat they planned to voyage* ***to*** *distant lands.*

voyager /ˈvɔɪ.ɪ.dʒəʳ/ [US] /-dʒɚ/ *noun* [C] a person who goes on a long and sometimes dangerous voyage: *Those voyagers who first ventured into space certainly showed courage.*

voyeur /vwɑːˈjɜːʳ/ [US] /-ˈjɝː/ *noun* [C] *DISAPPROVING* a person who gets sexual pleasure from secretly watching other people in sexual situations, or (more generally) a person who watches other people's private lives: *I felt like a voyeur visiting the war zone and seeing badly injured people being dragged from their bomb-shattered homes.* **voyeurism** /ˈvwɑː.jɜː.rɪ.zᵊm/ [US] /-jɝː-/ *noun* [U] **voyeuristic** /ˌvwɑː.jɜːˈrɪ.stɪk/ [US] /-jəˈrɪs.tɪk/ *adj*

VP /ˌviːˈpiː/ *US WRITTEN ABBREVIATION FOR* **Vice President**

vroom /vruːm/ /vrʊm/ *exclamation INFORMAL* a written representation of the sound of a car engine at high speed

vs *prep WRITTEN ABBREVIATION FOR* **versus**

V-shaped /ˈviː.ʃeɪpt/ *adj* shaped like a V

V-sign /ˈviː.saɪn/ *noun* [C] **1** *UK* a sign meaning victory or peace that is made by holding up the first two fingers of one hand in the shape of a V, while the thumb and other fingers are folded down and face out ➲See also **peace sign**. **2** (*ALSO* **two fingers**) *UK OFFENSIVE* a similar sign, made with the back of the hand facing out, used for expressing extreme dislike or anger towards someone: *The driver shouted rudely at the cyclist and* ***gave*** *her a/the V-sign.*

vulcanized, *UK USUALLY* **-ised** /ˈvʌl.kə.naɪzd/ *adj* Vulcanized rubber has been made stronger by a chemical process.

vulgar [NOT SUITABLE] /ˈvʌl.gəʳ/ [US] /-gɚ/ *adj DISAPPROVING* not suitable, simple, graceful or beautiful; common or not in the style preferred by the upper classes of society: *a vulgar patterned shirt* ○ *I've no idea how much the clothes cost because there was nothing so vulgar as a price tag in evidence.* ○ *Isn't it rather vulgar to talk about how much money you earn?* **vulgarity** /vʌlˈgær.ɪ.ti/ [US] /-ə.t̬i/ *noun* [U] **vulgarly** /ˈvʌl.gᵊl.i/ [US] /-gɚ.li/ *adv*

vulgar [RUDE] /ˈvʌl.gəʳ/ [US] /-gɚ/ *adj DISAPPROVING* rude and likely to upset or anger people, especially by referring to sex and the body in an unpleasant way: *It was an extremely vulgar joke.* **vulgarity** /vʌlˈgær.ɪ.ti/ [US] /-ə.t̬i/ *noun* [U] **vulgarly** /ˈvʌl.gᵊl.i/ [US] /-gɚ.li/ *adv*

vulnerable /ˈvʌl.nᵊr.ə.bl̩/ /ˈvʌn.rə-/ [US] /ˈvʌl.nɚ.ə-/ *adj* able to be easily physically, emotionally, or mentally hurt, influenced or attacked: *I felt very vulnerable, standing there without any clothes on.* ○ *It is on economic policy that the government is most vulnerable.* ○ *Tourists are more vulnerable* ***to*** *attack, because they do not know which areas of the city to avoid.* **vulnerability** /ˌvʌl.nᵊr.əˈbɪl.ɪ.ti/ /ˌvʌn.rə-/ [US] /ˌvʌl.nɚ.əˈbɪl.ə.t̬i/ *noun* [U]

vulture /ˈvʌl.tʃəʳ/ [US] /-tʃɚ/ *noun* [C] **1** a large bird with almost no feathers on its head or neck, that eats the flesh of dead animals **2** *DISAPPROVING* a person or organization that is eager to gain an advantage from other people's difficulties or problems: *When a company is in crisis like this, the vultures are always hovering.*

vulva /ˈvʌl.və/ *noun* [C] *plural* **vulvas** or **vulvae** the parts of the female sex organs which are outside the body, between the legs

vying /ˈvaɪ.ɪŋ/ *present participle of* **vie**

W

W [LETTER] *(plural* **W's** or **Ws**), **w** *(plural* **w's** or **ws**) /ˈdʌb.l̩.juː/ *noun* [C] the 23rd letter of the English alphabet

W [WEST] *noun, adj* WRITTEN ABBREVIATION FOR **1** [U] **west**: *W Africa* **2 western**

W [ELECTRICITY] *WRITTEN ABBREVIATION FOR* **watt**

wacko /ˈwæk.əʊ/ [US] /-oʊ/ *noun* [C] *plural* **wackos** MAINLY US INFORMAL a person whose behaviour is strange and different from that of most people; an **eccentric**

wacky /ˈwæk.i/ *adj* INFORMAL unusual in a pleasing and exciting or silly way: *He decided to become a clown to join the wacky world of the circus.* **wackiness** /ˈwæk.ɪ.nəs/ *noun* [U]

wad /wɒd/ [US] /wɑːd/ *noun* [C] a number of especially flat and/or small objects pressed tightly together: *a wad of banknotes* ○ *a wad of gum* ○ *She used a wad* (= a mass) *of tissues to wipe away the blood.*

wadding /ˈwɒd.ɪŋ/ [US] /ˈwɑː.dɪŋ/ *noun* [U] any soft material used for filling a space, especially in order to protect something or to give something shape: *The chandelier arrived in a big box, tightly packed around in wadding.*

waddle /ˈwɒd.l̩/ [US] /ˈwɑː.dl̩/ *verb* [I usually + adv or prep] (usually of a person or animal with short legs and a fat body) to walk with short steps, swinging the body from one side to the other **waddle** /ˈwɒd.l̩/ [US] /ˈwɑː.dl̩/ *noun* [C]

waddy /ˈwɒd.i/ [US] /ˈwɑː.di/ *noun* [C] AUS a heavy stick

wade /weɪd/ *verb* **1** [I usually + adv or prep; T] to walk through water with difficulty because of the pressure of the water against your legs: *The river was full but we managed to wade* ***across***. ○ *We waded a shallow river.* **2** US FOR **paddle** WALK

wader /ˈweɪ.dəʳ/ [US] /-dɚ/ *noun* [C] a bird with long legs and a long neck, that lives near water and eats fish

waders /ˈweɪ.dəz/ [US] /-dɚz/ *plural noun* rubber boots that cover the whole leg to keep a person dry in water: *The fishermen put on their waders.*

PHRASAL VERBS WITH **wade**

▲ **wade in** *phrasal verb* to start to do or say something in a forceful way, often without thinking about it carefully: *Even when she knows nothing about it, she wades in* ***with*** *her opinion.* ○ *When the crowd started throwing stones, the police waded in* ***with*** *tear gas.*

▲ **wade into** ***sth*** *phrasal verb* to become involved in a difficult situation, often without thinking about it carefully

▲ **wade through** ***sth*** *phrasal verb* INFORMAL to spend a lot of time and effort doing something boring or difficult, especially reading a lot of information: *We had to wade through pages of legal jargon before we could sign the contract.*

wadge /wɒdʒ/ [US] /wɑːdʒ/ *noun* [C] UK INFORMAL a **wodge**

wadi /ˈwɒd.i/ [US] /ˈwɑː.di/ *noun* [C] SPECIALIZED a valley which has a river that is usually dry except when it has rained, common in desert areas of North Africa and Southwest Asia

wading ˌpool *noun* [C] US FOR **paddling pool**

wafer /ˈweɪ.fəʳ/ [US] /-fɚ/ *noun* [C] **1** a very thin dry biscuit which is often sweet and flavoured **2** SPECIALIZED a very thin round piece of dry bread which the priest gives to people to eat during HOLY COMMUNION

wafer ˈbiscuit *noun* [C] a light sweet biscuit slightly thicker than a wafer with a creamy filling

wafer-thin /ˌweɪ.fəˈθɪn/ [US] /-fɚ-/ *adj* extremely thin: *The rooms were divided only by a wafer-thin partition.*

waffle [TALK] /ˈwɒf.l̩/ [US] /ˈwɑː.fl̩/ *verb* [I] DISAPPROVING to talk or write a lot without giving any useful information or any clear answers: *If you don't know the answer, it's no good just waffling* ***(on)*** *for pages and pages.* **waffle** /ˈwɒf.l̩/ [US] /ˈwɑː.fl̩/ *noun* [U] *"What did he say?" "Oh, it was a load of waffle – nothing important at all."*

waffle [CAKE] /ˈwɒf.l̩/ [US] /ˈwɑː.fl̩/ *noun* [C] a thin light cake, the surface of which is formed into a pattern of raised squares, eaten especially in the US and Canada

waft /wɒft/ [US] /wɑːft/ *verb* [I or T; usually + adv or prep] LITERARY to (cause to) move gently through the air: *A gentle breeze wafted the scent of roses in through the open window.* ○ *The sound of a flute wafted down the stairs.*

wag [MOVE] /wæg/ *verb* [I or T] **-gg-** (especially of a tail or finger) to move from side to side or up and down, especially quickly and repeatedly, or to cause this to happen: *The little dog's tail wagged in delight.* ○ *He wagged his finger sternly at the two boys.* **wag** /wæg/ *noun* [C usually sing] *With a single wag of her finger she managed to convey her total disapproval.*

wag [HUMOROUS PERSON] /wæg/ *noun* [C] OLD-FASHIONED INFORMAL a humorous person who likes to make jokes **waggish** /ˈwæg.ɪʃ/ *adj*

wage [MONEY] /weɪdʒ/ *noun* [S] a fixed amount of money that is paid, usually every week, to an employee, especially one who does work that needs physical skills or strength, rather than a job needing a college education: *a very low/high wage* ○ *an hourly/daily/weekly/annual wage* ○ *He gets/earns/is paid a good wage, because he works for a fair employer.* ➲Compare **income**; **salary**.

wages /ˈweɪ.dʒɪz/ *plural noun* a wage: *The smaller shops pay very low wages.*

wage [FIGHT] /weɪdʒ/ *verb* [T] SLIGHTLY FORMAL to fight a war or organize a series of activities in order to achieve something: *Surely the President needs Congress' permission to wage war* ***on*** *another country?* ○ *They've been waging a long campaign to change the law.*

ˈwage ˌearner *noun* [C] a person who works at a job for money

ˈwage ˌfreeze *noun* [C usually sing] when a company or government fixes the amount paid to workers and will not allow any increases

ˈwage ˌpacket UK *noun* [C usually sing] (US **paycheck**) UK the money that you earn, especially when it is given to you in notes and coins in an envelope: *cash a monthly/weekly wage packet* ○ *She got £25 in cash* ***in*** *her first wage packet.*

wager /ˈweɪ.dʒəʳ/ [US] /-dʒɚ/ *noun* [C] an amount of money that you risk in the hope of winning more, by trying to guess something uncertain, or the agreement that you make to take this risk; a bet: *She put a* ***cash*** *wager of £50* ***on*** *the biggest horse race of the year.* ○ *He tried to eat 50 hard-boiled eggs,* ***for*** *a wager.*

wager /ˈweɪ.dʒəʳ/ [US] /-dʒɚ/ *verb* **1** [I or T] to bet: [+ two objects + *(that)*] *I'll wager you £5* ***that*** *they'll get there first.* **2** [I] OLD-FASHIONED used to say that you are certain that something is true or will happen in the future: [+ *(that)*] *I'd wager* ***(that)*** *she's interested in you.*

waggle /ˈwæg.l̩/ *verb* [I or T] to (cause to) move quickly up and down or from side to side: *One of his party tricks is to waggle his* ***ears***.

wagon, UK ALSO **waggon** /ˈwæg.ən/ *noun* [C] **1** a vehicle with four wheels, usually pulled by horses or oxen, used for transporting heavy goods, especially in the past: *The first white settlers journeyed across America in* ***covered*** *wagons.* ➲See also **bandwagon**; **station wagon**; **Welcome Wagon**. **2** UK (US **freight car**) a large wheeled container for transporting goods, that is pulled by a train: *a* ***goods*** *wagon*

• **on the wagon** INFORMAL If you are on the wagon, you have decided not to drink any alcohol for a period of time: *He was on the wagon for ten years, when he was living in Connecticut.*

• **fall off the wagon** INFORMAL to start drinking alcohol, after a period when you have drunk none: *When her husband died, she fell off the wagon.*

wagon-lit /ˌvæg.ɔ̃nˈliː/ *noun* [U] UK a **sleeping car**

ˈwagon ˌtrain *noun* [C] a long line of wagons pulled by horses or oxen, used by people in the 19th century who were travelling to the western US with their possessions in order to live there

waif /weɪf/ *noun* [C] LITERARY a child or animal without a home or enough food and care, usually thin and dirty in appearance

• **waifs and strays** UK people with no homes: *Her house is always full of waifs and strays.*

waif-like /ˈweɪf.laɪk/ *adj* very thin and delicate in appearance: *waif-like supermodels*

wail /weɪl/ *verb* **1** [I or T] MAINLY DISAPPROVING to make a long, high cry, usually because of pain or sadness: *The women gathered around the coffin and began to wail, as was the custom in the region.* ○ [+ speech] *"My finger hurts," wailed the child.* **2** [I] INFORMAL to complain loudly or strongly: [+ that] *Business people wailed that their trade would be ruined.* **wail** /weɪl/ *noun* [C] *a wail of anguish* ○ *the wail of the police sirens*

waist /weɪst/ *noun* [C] **1** the part of the body above and slightly narrower than the hips: *a small/narrow/tiny/large/thick waist* ○ *These trousers are a bit tight around my waist.* ⊃See picture **The Body** on page Centre 5 **2** the part of a piece of clothing that goes around or covers the area between the hips and the ribs: *The skirt had an elasticated waist.*

waisted /ˈweɪs.tɪd/ *adj* (of a piece of clothing) narrow at the waist: *This particular jacket is rather waisted.* **-waisted** /-weɪs.tɪd/ *suffix: a slim-waisted boy* ○ *a high-waisted pair of trousers*

waistband /ˈweɪst.bænd/ *noun* [C] a strip of material that forms the waist of a pair of trousers or a skirt: *He had a gun tucked into the waistband of his trousers.*

waistcoat UK /ˈweɪst.kəʊt/ ⑨ /-koʊt/ /ˈwes.kət/ *noun* [C] (US **vest**) a piece of clothing that covers the upper body but not the arms and usually has buttons down the front, worn over a shirt ⊃See picture **Clothes** on page Centre 6

waistline /ˈweɪst.laɪn/ *noun* [C] an imaginary line going round the narrowest part of your waist: *a bulging/expanding waistline* ○ *She started jogging twice a week to try to reduce her waistline.*

ˈwaist ˌpack *noun* [C] US FOR **bumbag**

wait /weɪt/ *verb* [I] **1** to allow time to go by, especially while staying in one place without doing very much, until someone comes, until something that you are expecting happens or until you can do something: *I waited for her in the corridor, while she went in to see the doctor.* ○ *The dentist kept me waiting for ages.* ○ [+ to infinitive] *There were a lot of people waiting to use the telephone.* ⊃See Note **attend or wait/expect?** at **attend** BE PRESENT. **2** to be done or to happen at a later time: *The meeting will have to wait until tomorrow, because I'm too busy now.* ○ *The paperwork can't wait until tomorrow* (= is urgent and must be done now).

• **can't wait** (ALSO **can hardly wait**) to be very excited about something and eager to do or experience it: *I can't wait to see you.*

• **(just) you wait** used as a way of threatening someone: *Just you wait, Maria, till I get my hands on you!*

• **wait till/until ...** said when you are excited about seeing another person's reaction to something special or unusual: *Wait till you see what Rachel's wearing!* ○ *Wait till he hears the news.*

• **No Waiting** UK (US **No Standing**) used on signs to mean vehicles are not allowed to park, even for short periods of time: *The sign by the side of the road said 'No Waiting'.*

• **wait a minute/moment/second** said in order to interrupt someone, or to get their attention or when you have suddenly thought of something important: *Now, wait a moment – I don't agree with that.* ○ *Wait a minute – I've just had an idea.*

• **wait and see** to wait to discover what will happen: *No decision will be made until next year, so you'll just have to wait and see.*

• **wait for it** UK INFORMAL **1** to not start until the correct moment: *Wait for it! I haven't said 'go' yet.* **2** You say 'wait for it' to show that you are about to say something surprising, amusing or difficult to believe: *The new soap opera will be screened, wait for it, five times each day.*

• **wait in the wings** If someone or something is waiting in the wings, they are not yet active or important, but are ready or likely to be so soon: *The team has several talented young players waiting in the wings.*

• **wait at table(s)** UK (US **wait on table(s)**) to serve meals to people in a restaurant, as your job

• **wait your turn** to wait until it is really your turn to do or get something: *If people were more polite, they would wait their turn.*

wait /weɪt/ *noun* [S] when you stay in one place until someone comes, or something happens, or until you can do something: *We had a three-hour wait before we could see the doctor.* ○ *The long wait for the doctor/to see the doctor really made me anxious.*

• **lie in wait** to hide, ready to attack: *The gunmen were lying in wait when Mr Predit came out of the hotel.*

COMMON LEARNER ERROR

wait for

Remember to use the preposition 'for' when you are talking about waiting for someone or something.

We're still waiting for the results of the test.
~~We're still waiting the results of the test.~~
I'll wait for you outside.
~~I'll wait you outside.~~

COMMON LEARNER ERROR

wait or expect?

When you **wait**, you allow time to go by, especially while staying in one place, until a person or thing arrives or is ready.

I waited twenty minutes for the bus.
She's waiting for her exam results.

When you **expect** something, you think that it will happen.

I'm expecting the bus to arrive in about 5 minutes.
She expected to do well in the exam.
~~She waited to do well in the exam.~~

PHRASAL VERBS WITH **wait** ▼

▲ **wait around** *phrasal verb* (UK ALSO **wait about**) to stay in a place and do nothing while you wait for someone to arrive or something to happen: *We spent the whole day waiting around for something exciting to happen, but nothing did.*

▲ **wait behind** *phrasal verb* to stay in a place after all the other people have left: *The teacher made us wait behind after class.*

▲ **wait for sb/sth** PREPARED *phrasal verb* If someone is waiting for someone or something, they are expecting them and prepared to deal with them: *When the thieves left the building, the police were waiting for them.*

▲ **wait for sb** *phrasal verb* If something is waiting for you, it has been left or prepared for you to collect, use, enjoy or deal with when you arrive: *An envelope was waiting for me when I got home.* ○ *Uma had a cup of tea waiting for me, along with a plate of biscuits.*

▲ **wait sth for sb** DELAYED *phrasal verb* US to delay serving a meal until someone arrives: *Don't wait dinner for me – I'll be home late.*

▲ **wait in** *phrasal verb* UK to stay at home because you are expecting someone or something to arrive, or someone to telephone you: *I waited in for the plumber all morning, but he didn't turn up.*

▲ **wait on sb/sth** SERVE *phrasal verb* MAINLY US to serve food and drink, especially to customers in a restaurant: *The staff who waited on us at dinner were excellent.* ○ *She waited on tables* (= served meals as a job) *to earn some extra money.*

▲ **wait on sb** DO EVERYTHING *phrasal verb* to do everything for someone so that they do not have to do anything for themselves: *While she was pregnant, her husband waited on her hand and foot* (= did everything for her).

▲ **wait on sth** WAIT *phrasal verb* FORMAL to wait until you know the result of an activity before doing or deciding something: *The lawyers are waiting on the jury's verdict.*

▲ **wait sth out** *phrasal verb* [M] US to wait until something unpleasant has ended: *I'd rather wait out the storm than drive home immediately.*

▲ **wait up** *phrasal verb* to not go to bed at night because you are expecting someone to arrive: *I'll be home after midnight, so don't wait up for me.*

W

waiter /ˈweɪ.təʳ/ ⓤ /-t̬ɚ/ noun [C] a man whose job is to bring the food to customers at their tables in a restaurant

ˈwaiting ˌgame noun when you delay taking any action, so that you can watch how a situation develops and see what it is best for you to do: *In a contest like this, the stronger side can afford to play a waiting game.*

ˈwaiting ˌlist noun [C usually sing] a list of people who have asked for something which is not immediately available but which they will or might be able to receive in the future: *The hospital has a 2-year waiting list for minor operations.* ○ *I'm afraid the course is full, but I can put you on the waiting list, in case someone else cancels.*

ˈwaiting ˌroom noun [C] a room in a place where people can sit and rest while waiting, as in a railway station or a doctor's office

waitress /ˈweɪ.trəs/ noun [C] a woman whose job is to bring the food to customers at their tables in a restaurant

waive /weɪv/ verb [T] FORMAL to not demand something you have a right to, or not cause a rule to be obeyed: *The bank manager waived the charge* (= said we didn't have to pay)*, as we were old and valued customers.* ○ *If the government waives* (= removes) *the time limit, many more applications will come in.* ○ *He persuaded the delegates to waive* (= give up) *their objections.*

waiver /ˈweɪ.vəʳ/ ⓤ /-vɚ/ noun [C] an agreement that you do not have to pay or obey something: *We had to sign a waiver, giving up any rights to the land in the future.*

wake STOP SLEEPING (woke or waked, woken or waked or US ALSO woke) /weɪk/ verb [I or T] (ALSO wake up) to (cause someone to) become awake and conscious after sleeping: *Did you wake at all during the night?* ○ *Please wake me early tomorrow.* ○ *I woke up with a headache.* ○ *Jane's hand on my shoulder woke me out of/from a bad dream.*

wakeful /ˈweɪk.fəl/ adj FORMAL *We spent a wakeful night* (= We did not sleep very much) *worrying about where he was.* ○ *I felt wakeful* (= awake and aware) *and alert.*

wakefulness /ˈweɪk.fəl.nəs/ noun [U]

waken /ˈweɪ.kən/ verb [I or T] FORMAL to (cause to) wake from sleep: *I shook him but he didn't waken.* ○ *Waken me at 7, would you?*

wakey wakey /ˌweɪ.kiˈweɪ.ki/ exclamation HUMOROUS said to someone in order to wake them up from sleep: *Gloria knocked on the door and shouted "Wakey wakey!"*

waking /ˈweɪ.kɪŋ/ adj [before n] describes a period of time or an experience during which you are awake: *Children are in school for 15 per cent of their waking hours/life between birth and the age of 16.* ○ *She seems to spend every waking moment/minute/hour* (= all her available time) *at the piano.*

waking /ˈweɪ.kɪŋ/ noun [U] when you are awake: *For a moment, between waking and sleeping, he couldn't understand where he was.*

PHRASAL VERBS WITH **wake** ▼

▲ **wake (sb) up** STOP SLEEPING phrasal verb [M] to (cause to) become conscious after sleeping: *Come on, wake up – breakfast is ready.* ○ *He woke himself up with his own snoring!* ⊃See picture **Phrasal Verbs** on page Centre 9

▲ **wake (sb) up** REACT phrasal verb [M] to start to react to a situation after a period in which you have done very little, or to make someone start to react to a situation: *Companies need to wake up and take notice of the public's increasing concern with the environment.*

● **wake up and smell the coffee** INFORMAL used to tell someone that they are wrong about a particular situation and that they must realize what is really happening

● **Wake up!** something you say to tell someone to listen or to become involved when they have not been listening or paying attention: *Wake up, Daniel! It's your turn.*

wake-up call /ˈweɪk.ʌp.kɔːl/ ⓤ /-ˌkɑːl/ noun [C] If something that happens is a wake-up call, it should make you realise that you need to take action to change a situation: *The poor turnout for the election will hopefully be a wake-up call to the government.*

▲ **wake up to sth** phrasal verb to become aware of a situation or problem: *Governments are finally waking up to the fact that the environment should be cleaned up.*

wake WATER /weɪk/ noun [C] the waves that a moving ship or object leaves behind: *The wake spread out in a v-shape behind the ship.*

● **leave sth in your wake** to go somewhere new, leaving problems, confusion, etc. behind you, that you have caused: *The soldiers rampaged through the town centre, leaving chaos in their wake.*

● **in the wake of** If something happens in the wake of something else, it happens after and often because of it: *Airport security was extra tight in the wake of yesterday's bomb attacks.*

wake FUNERAL /weɪk/ noun [C] a gathering of the family and friends of a dead person in order to look at the dead body the night before it is buried, or a gathering held after a dead person has been buried, at which their family and friends drink and talk about the person's life

walk /wɔːk/ ⓤ /wɑːk/ verb **1** [I or T] to move along by putting one foot in front of the other, allowing each foot to touch the ground before lifting the next: *I walked home.* ○ *A cat was walking along the top of the fence.* ○ *He walks two kilometres to work every morning.* ⊃See also **jaywalk**; **sleepwalk** at **sleepwalker**. **2** [T] To walk someone to a particular place is to walk with them until they have reached it, usually because you are being friendly or polite, wish to protect them from danger, or to show them the way: *He offered to walk her home/to the station.* **3** [T] to take an animal, especially a dog, for a walk: *She walks the dog for an hour every afternoon.* **4** [T] UK INFORMAL to pass or win something, such as an examination or game, easily: *She'll walk the interview – the job is practically hers already.* **5** **a walking disaster/encyclopedia, etc.** someone who seems to be a human form of disaster/encyclopedia, etc: *You've broken another pair of glasses? – Oh, you're a walking disaster!*

● **walk all over sb** To walk all over someone is to treat them very badly or defeat them very easily: *If you don't want to work at the weekend, say so – don't let the boss walk all over you.*

● **walk on air** to feel extremely excited or happy: *After the delivery of her baby, she was walking on air.*

● **walk on eggs/eggshells** If you are walking on eggs/eggshells, you are being very careful not to offend someone or do anything wrong: *When my mother is staying at our house, I feel like I'm walking on eggshells.*

● **walk right into sth** If you walk right into something, you are caught or tricked by it because you did not know what was happening: *We set a trap and they walked right into it.*

walk /wɔːk/ ⓤ /wɑːk/ noun **1** [C] a journey that you make by walking, often for enjoyment: *He went for/took a walk around the block, to get some air.* ○ *They went on a ten-mile walk to raise money for charity.* ○ *Every afternoon she takes her Grandad out for a walk.* ⊃See also **boardwalk**; **catwalk**; **crosswalk**; **sidewalk**; **spacewalk**. **2** [C] a path or route where people can walk for enjoyment: *Do you know any nice walks around here?* **3** [S] a way of walking: *He's got a strange waddling sort of walk.* **4** [S] walking speed: *She slowed the horses to a walk.*

● **a short/five-minute/ten-minute walk** a journey that takes a short time/five minutes/ten minutes, etc. when you walk: *The station is only a five-minute walk away.*

● **walk of life** When people talk about walk(s) of life they are referring to different types of jobs and different levels of society: *We've got lawyers in this club, and builders and hairdressers – people from all (different) walks of life.*

walker /ˈwɔː.kəʳ/ ⓤ /ˈwɑː.kɚ/ noun [C] **1** a person who walks, especially for exercise or enjoyment: *She's a very fast/slow walker.* ○ *They've been keen walkers ever since they read about the benefits of exercise.* **2** US FOR **Zimmer frame**

walking /ˈwɔː.kɪŋ/ ⓤ /ˈwɑː-/ noun [U] **1** the activity of going for a walk, especially for pleasure in the countryside: *We're going walking in Wales for a week.* ○ *a pair of walking/hiking boots* ○ *a walking stick* **2** the sport of fast long-distance walking

W

COMMON LEARNER ERROR

walk or **go on foot**?

The expression **go on foot** means **walk**, usually when you are describing how you get somewhere.

How do you get to school? I go on foot/I walk.

PHRASAL VERBS WITH **walk** ▼

▲ **walk away** DIFFICULT SITUATION *phrasal verb* DISAPPROVING to stop being involved in a situation because it is difficult to deal with or does not give you any advantages: *You can't just walk away from a marriage at the first sign of a problem.*

▲ **walk away** ACCIDENT *phrasal verb* to escape an accident without being badly hurt: *She overturned the car, but walked away from it without a scratch.*

▲ **walk away with** *sth phrasal verb* to win a prize or competition very easily: *He walked away with all three gold medals.*

▲ **walk in on** *sb phrasal verb* to go into a room and see what someone is doing, when they did not want to be seen: *She walked in on me when I was getting undressed.*

▲ **walk into** *sth phrasal verb* to get a job very easily: *She walked straight into a well-paid job after leaving university.*

▲ **walk off** *(somewhere)* LEAVE *phrasal verb* to leave a place because you are angry or dissatisfied about something: *She threatened to walk off the film set because of the conditions.* ○ *He refused to discuss it and just walked off in a huff.*

▲ **walk** *sth* **off** CURE *phrasal verb* [M] to go for a walk in order to get rid of an illness, often a headache, or the feeling of having eaten too much: *I'm going out to walk off this headache.* ○ *Let's go to the park and walk off all that lunch.*

▲ **walk off with** *sth* WIN *phrasal verb* to win something easily: *She walked off with the top prize.*

▲ **walk off with** *sth* STEAL *phrasal verb* to steal something or take something without asking permission: *Who's walked off with my cup?*

▲ **walk out** LEAVE *phrasal verb* to leave an event such as a meeting or performance because you are angry or disapprove of something: *All the parents walked out (of the meeting) in protest.*

▲ **walk out** STOP WORK *phrasal verb* to stop working or leave your job because of a disagreement with your employer: *Workers are threatening to walk out.* ○See also **walkout**.

▲ **walk out** END RELATIONSHIP *phrasal verb* to suddenly leave your husband, wife or partner and end your relationship with them: *He walked out on his wife and two kids.*

▲ **walk** *sb* **through** *sth phrasal verb* US to slowly and carefully explain something to someone or show someone how to do something: *She walked me through the six-page document.* ○ *He'll walk you through the procedure.*

walkabout /ˈwɔː.kə.baʊt/ ⓤ /ˈwɑː-/ *noun* [C] MAINLY UK INFORMAL an occasion when an important person walks around a public place, meeting and talking to members of the public: *The princess went on a walkabout in the town centre.*

● **go walkabout** INFORMAL HUMOROUS If you say that an object has gone walkabout you mean that it is missing, often because someone has taken it: *My pen was here this morning but it seems to have gone walkabout.*

walkaway /ˈwɔː.kə.weɪ/ *noun* [C] US FOR **walkover** EASILY WON GAME

walkies /ˈwɔː.kiz/ ⓤ /ˈwɑː-/ *exclamation, plural noun* UK INFORMAL said to a dog to tell it that it is time for a walk: *Walkies, Shem, come on, walkies!*

walkie-talkie /ˌwɔː.kiˈtɔː.ki/ ⓤ /ˌwɑː.kiˈtɑː-/ *noun* [C] a small radio held in the hand which is used for both sending and receiving messages: *The policeman was speaking to HQ on his walkie-talkie.*

walk-in STORAGE /ˈwɔː.kɪn/ ⓤ /ˈwɑː.k-/ *adj* [before n] describes a storage space that is large enough for a person to enter and walk around in: *a walk-in wardrobe* ○ US *a walk-in closet* ○ AUS *a walk-in cupboard*

walk-in NOT ARRANGED BEFORE /ˈwɔː.kɪn/ ⓤ /ˈwɑː.k-/ *adj* [before n] MAINLY US describes a place that you can go to without having already made an arrangement: *It's a walk-in dental clinic – the sign outside said 'Walk-in patients welcome'.*

ˈwalking ˌframe *noun* [C] UK **Zimmer frame**

ˈwalking ˌpapers *plural noun* US FOR **marching orders**

Walkman (*plural* **Walkmans**) /ˈwɔːk.mən/ ⓤ /ˈwɑːk-/ *noun* [C] (ALSO **personal stereo**) TRADEMARK a small CASSETTE PLAYER, sometimes with radio, with small HEADPHONES

walk-on (part) /ˈwɔːk.ɒn.pɑːt/ ⓤ /ˈwɑːk.ɑːn.pɑːrt/ *noun* [C] A walk-on (part) in a play is a very small part in which the actor is on the stage very briefly and speaks very few or no words.

walkout /ˈwɔːk.aʊt/ ⓤ /ˈwɑː-/ *noun* [C] the act of leaving an official meeting as a group in order to show disapproval, or of leaving a place of work to start a strike: *Senior union workers staged (= had) a walkout this afternoon at the annual conference over the proposed changes in funding.* ○See also **walk out**.

walkover EASILY WON GAME /ˈwɔː.k,əʊ.vər/ ⓤ /ˈwɑː.k,oʊ.vɚ-/ *noun* [C] (US ALSO **walkaway**) INFORMAL a game or sports event that is won very easily by one side or one person: *The semi-final should be a walkover for France.* ○See also **walk all over** *sb* at **walk**.

walkover WIN WITHOUT PLAYING /ˈwɔː.k,əʊ.vər/ ⓤ /ˈwɑːk-,oʊ.vɚ/ *noun* [C] the act of winning one stage of a competition without having to compete in it because the person that you should be playing against is no longer taking part

walk-up /ˈwɔːk.ʌp/ ⓤ /ˈwɑːk-/ *noun* [C] US a building with several floors and no LIFT (= a device for going from one floor to another), or an apartment or office in such a building

walkway /ˈwɔː.kweɪ/ ⓤ /ˈwɑː-/ *noun* [C] a passage or path, especially one which is covered or raised above the ground

wall /wɔːl/ ⓤ /wɑːl/ *noun* **1** [C] a vertical structure, often made of stone or brick, that divides or encloses something: *The walls in this apartment are so thin you can hear just about every word the neighbours say.* ○ *The walls look a bit bare – can't we put some pictures up?* ○ *We had to climb over a ten-foot wall to get into the garden.* ○ *The Berlin Wall came down in 1989.* **2** [C] any outer part of a hollow structure in the body: *the wall of the womb/stomach* ○ *an artery wall* **3** [C] a mass of people or things formed in such a way that you cannot get through or past them: *The demonstrators formed a solid wall to stop the police from getting past them.* **4** [S] LITERARY a large, powerful, usually fast-moving mass of something: *After the rains, the houses were washed away by a wall of mud/water.* **5** [S] a way of feeling or behaving that completely prevents two groups of people from communicating with or understanding each other: *There is a wall of mistrust between the two groups.*

● **go to the wall** If a company goes to the wall it is destroyed financially: *After nine months of massive losses the company finally went to the wall.*

● **off the wall** surprising and unusual: *an off-the-wall joke* ○ *off-the-wall leisure pursuits*

● **drive** *sb* **up the wall** to make someone extremely angry: *My flat-mate is driving me up the wall at the moment.*

● **wall-to-wall 1** (especially of carpet) covering the whole floor: *a wall-to-wall carpet* **2** continuous or happening very often or everywhere around you: *I went away to college thinking it would be wall-to-wall parties and all the freedom I wanted.*

● **Walls have ears.** SAYING something you say to warn someone that it is not safe to speak at that particular time because other people might be listening

wall /wɔːl/ ⓤ /wɑːl/ *verb*

PHRASAL VERBS WITH **wall** ▼

▲ **wall** *sth* **off** *phrasal verb* [M] to build a wall around a place: *They've walled off the electric sub-station for safety reasons.*

▲ **wall** *sth* **up** *phrasal verb* [M] to fill up a space in a wall with brick or stone: *When we built the extension we had to wall up an old window.*

W

walled /wɔːld/ [US] /wɑːld/ *adj* surrounded by a wall: *Why not visit the beautiful walled city of York?*

wallaby /ˈwɒl.ə.bi/ [US] /ˈwɑː.lə-/ *noun* [C] an animal found in Australia and New Guinea which is like a small KANGAROO, and has strong back legs for jumping with and a long tail

wallah, walla /ˈwɒl.ə/ [US] /ˈwɑː.lə/ *noun* [C] *UK INFORMAL* a person who has a particular duty: *I made the tea yesterday so it's Mira's turn to be tea wallah this afternoon.*

wallet /ˈwɒl.ɪt/ [US] /ˈwɑː.lɪt/ *noun* [C] **1** (*US ALSO* **billfold**) a small folding case for carrying paper money, CREDIT CARDS and other flat objects, used especially by men: *He pulled out a big fat wallet stuffed with bank notes.* ➲Compare **purse** MONEY CONTAINER. **2** a large flat case that is made of card and used for holding documents

wallflower [PLANT] /ˈwɔːlˌflaʊəʳ/ [US] /ˈwɑːlˌflaʊr/ *noun* [C] a pleasant smelling garden plant that has yellow, orange or brown flowers which grow in groups

wallflower [SHY PERSON] /ˈwɔːlˌflaʊəʳ/ [US] /ˈwɑːlˌflaʊr/ *noun* [C] *INFORMAL* a shy person, especially a girl or woman, who is frightened to involve herself in social activities and does not attract much interest or attention: *Sooner or later someone would take pity on the poor wallflower and ask her to dance.*

ˈwall ˌhanging *noun* [C] a large piece of material or sewing which is hung on a wall as a decoration

wallop /ˈwɒl.əp/ [US] /ˈwɑː.ləp/ *verb* [T] *INFORMAL* to hit someone hard, especially with the flat part of the hand or with something held in the hand, or to defeat someone easily, especially in sports: *She walloped him across the back of the head.* ○ *"How did your tennis match go last night?" "Oh, I was walloped again."* **wallop** /ˈwɒl.əp/ [US] /ˈwɑː.ləp/ *noun* [C] *My mother* ***gave*** *me such a wallop when she eventually found me.*

walloping /ˈwɒl.ə.pɪŋ/ [US] /ˈwɑː.lə-/ *noun* [S] *INFORMAL* when someone is severely punished by being hit: *I* ***got*** *such a walloping from my father when he came home.*

walloping /ˈwɒl.ə.pɪŋ/ [US] /ˈwɑː.lə-/ *adj* [before n] *INFORMAL HUMOROUS* very big or great: *He cut me a walloping* ***(great)*** *slice of cake.*

wallow /ˈwɒl.əʊ/ [US] /ˈwɑː.loʊ/ *verb* [I] (especially of particular animals) to lie or roll about slowly in deep wet earth, sand or water: *Watching her husband relaxing in the shallow waters she was reminded of a hippopotamus wallowing* ***in*** *mud.* **wallow** /ˈwɒl.əʊ/ [US] /ˈwɑː.loʊ/ *noun* [C usually sing] *INFORMAL He likes a good wallow in the bath.*

PHRASAL VERBS WITH **wallow**

▲ **wallow in** ***sth*** [ENJOY] *phrasal verb* to allow yourself to enjoy something completely: *My idea of a holiday is to book myself into a five-star hotel and just wallow in the luxury for a week.*

▲ **wallow in** ***sth*** [REMAIN UNHAPPY] *phrasal verb DISAPPROVING* to remain in an unhappy emotional state without trying to get out of it, as if you are enjoying it or trying to get sympathy from other people: *I wish she'd do something to help herself instead of just wallowing in self-pity!*

wallpaper /ˈwɔːlˌpeɪ.pəʳ/ [US] /ˈwɑːlˌpeɪ.pɚ/ *noun* [C or U] a thick, often decorative, paper used for covering the walls and sometimes ceilings of a room: *a* ***roll*** *of wallpaper* ○ *We thought we'd* ***put up/hang*** *some wallpaper in the children's bedroom to make it brighter.* ○ *I saw a wallpaper today that would be just right for the bathroom.* ○ *We'll need some wallpaper* ***paste*** *and a big brush.* **wallpaper** /ˈwɔːlˌpeɪ.pəʳ/ [US] /ˈwɑːlˌpeɪ.pɚ/ *verb* [T] *We've wallpapered the bedrooms but we've decided to paint the living room.*

ˈwallpaper ˌmusic *noun* [U] *UK FOR* **Muzak**

ˈWall ˌStreet *noun* [U] a street in New York which represents the financial centre of the US: *On Wall Street today, the Dow Jones rose 55 points following good economic figures.*

wally /ˈwɒl.i/ [US] /ˈwɑː.li/ *noun* [C] *UK INFORMAL* a silly or useless person: *I'll look a right wally in these shorts!*

walnut /ˈwɔːl.nʌt/ [US] /ˈwɑːl-/ *noun* [C or U] a slightly bitter-tasting nut with a series of folds in it and a hard shell, or (the expensive light brown wood from) the tree that produces these nuts

walrus /ˈwɔːl.rəs/ [US] /ˈwɑːl-/ *noun* [C] *plural* **walruses** or **walrus** a mammal which lives in the sea and on beaches in the Arctic. It is similar to a seal but larger, with two tusks and long hairs growing near its mouth.

ˌwalrus mousˈtache *noun* [C] a moustache which is long and hangs down at both sides of the mouth

waltz [DANCE] /wɒlts/ [US] /wɑːlts/ *noun* [C] a formal dance in which two people holding each other move around a large room, turning as they go and repeating a movement of three steps, or a piece of music with three beats in a BAR written for this style of dancing
waltz /wɒlts/ [US] /wɑːlts/ *verb* [I] to dance a waltz

waltz [WALK] /wɒlts/ [US] /wɑːlts/ *verb* [I usually + adv or prep] *INFORMAL* to walk somewhere quickly and confidently, often in a way that annoys other people: *You can't just waltz* ***into*** *my bedroom without knocking – it's private!* ○ *My idiot wife has gone and waltzed* ***off with*** *my car keys and left me without any means of transport!*

▲ **waltz through** ***sth*** *phrasal verb INFORMAL* to complete something such as a test easily and successfully: *He waltzed through the first two rounds of the competition.*

wan /wɒn/ [US] /wɑːn/ *adj* **wanner, wannest** *LITERARY* (of a person's face) paler than usual and tired-looking **wanly** /ˈwɒn.li/ [US] /wɑːn-/ *adv*

wand /wɒnd/ [US] /wɑːnd/ *noun* [C] a special thin stick waved by a person who is performing magic tricks: *The fairy godmother* ***waved*** *her magic wand over the cabbages and they turned into horses.*

wander [WALK] /ˈwɒn.dəʳ/ [US] /ˈwɑːn.dɚ/ *verb* [I or T] to walk around slowly in a relaxed way or without any clear purpose or direction: *We spent the morning wandering* ***around*** *the old part of the city.* ○ *She was found several hours later, wandering* ***the streets****, lost.* ○ *He was here a moment ago but he's wandered* ***off*** *somewhere.* **wander** /ˈwɒn.dəʳ/ [US] /ˈwɑːn.dɚ/ *noun* [C usually sing] *INFORMAL While you're in your meeting I can* ***go for/have/take*** *a wander around the city.*

wanderings /ˈwɒn.dᵊr.ɪŋz/ [US] /ˈwɑːn.dɚ-/ *plural noun* time spent travelling around or going from one place or country to another: *After all her wanderings she had come back home to stay.* ○ *HUMOROUS If you see Alan* ***in/on your*** *wanderings, will you tell him he's wanted in the office?*

wander [SUBJECT] /ˈwɒn.dəʳ/ [US] /ˈwɑːn.dɚ/ *verb* [I] **1** to start talking about a different subject from the one you were originally discussing: *We've wandered* ***off/from the point*** *somewhat.* **2** If your mind or your thoughts wander, you stop thinking about the subject that you should be giving your attention to and start thinking about other matters: *Halfway through the meeting my* ***mind*** *started to wander.* **3** If you say that an old person's mind is beginning to wander, you mean that they are starting to get very confused because of their age: *Her* ***mind*** *is beginning to wander and she doesn't always know who I am.* **wanderings** /ˈwɒn.dᵊr.ɪŋz/ [US] /ˈwɑːn.dɚ-/ *plural noun: imaginative wanderings*

wanderlust /ˈwɒn.də.lʌst/ [US] /ˈwɑːn.dɚ-/ *noun* [U] the desire to travel far away and to many different places: *In July wanderlust takes over the whole nation.*

wane /weɪn/ *verb* [I] **1** to weaken in strength or influence: *By the late seventies the band's popularity was beginning to wane.* ➲Compare **wax** APPEAR LARGER. **2** *FORMAL* The moon wanes when it gradually appears less and less round, after the FULL MOON.
wane /weɪn/ *noun* **on the wane** (of power, popularity, etc.) becoming less strong: *There are signs that support for the party is on the wane.*

wangle /ˈwæŋ.gl/ *verb* [T] *INFORMAL* to succeed in obtaining or doing something by persuading someone or by being clever in some way: *I'll be so jealous if you manage to wangle an invitation to his house.* ○ *He's only been here two months and already he's managed to wangle* ***his way into*** *the biggest property company in London.* ○ *If I can think of some excuse to wangle* ***my way out of*** *going tonight I will do!*

wank /wæŋk/ *verb* [I] *UK OFFENSIVE* to **masturbate** (= excite your own or someone else's sex organs by hand)

W

wank /wæŋk/ *noun* [C usually sing] *to* ***have*** *a wank*
wanker /ˈwæŋ.kəʳ/ [US] /-kɚ/ *noun* [C] *UK OFFENSIVE* **1** a very stupid, unpleasant or useless person, usually a man: *They're all a bunch of wankers!* **2** less commonly, a person who MASTURBATES

wanly /ˈwɒn.li/ [US] /wɑːn-/ *adv* ➲See at **wan**.

wanna /ˈwɒn.ə/ [US] /ˈwɑː.nə/ *verb* [T] *NOT STANDARD* 'want to' or 'want a': [+ infinitive without *to*] *D'you wanna go now?* ○ *I wanna hamburger, Mom.*

wannabe, wannabee /ˈwɒn.ə.bi/ [US] /ˈwɑː.nə-/ *noun* [C] *INFORMAL DISAPPROVING* a person who is trying to achieve success or fame, usually unsuccessfully: *The bar is frequented by wannabe actresses and film directors.*

want [DESIRE] /wɒnt/ [US] /wɑːnt/ *verb* [T] **1** to desire a particular thing or plan of action. 'Want' is not used in polite requests in British English: *I want some chocolate.* ○ *She wants a word with you.* ○ *He's everything you'd ever want in a man – bright, funny and attractive.* ○ [+ *to* infinitive] *What do you want* ***to*** *eat?* ○ [+ obj + *to* infinitive] *Do you want me* ***to*** *take you to the station?* ○ [+ obj + past participle] *This letter – do you want it sent first class?* ○ [+ obj + adj] *Do you want this pie hot?* ○ [+ obj + v-*ing*] *I don't want a load of traffic go****ing*** *past my house all night, waking me up.* ○ *You wait – by next year she'll be wanting a bigger house!* ➲Compare **like** WANT. **2** to wish or need someone to be present: *Am I wanted at the meeting tomorrow?* ○ *He is wanted by the police* (= The police are searching for him). **3** *INFORMAL* **want in/out of** to want to start or stop being involved in something: *I want out of the whole venture before it's too late.*
wanted /ˈwɒn.tɪd/ [US] /ˈwɑːn.t̬ɪd/ *adj*: *She was a much wanted baby* (= her parents wanted to have her). ○ *He's a wanted man* (= the police are searching for him).

COMMON LEARNER ERROR

want something/someone **to do** something

Remember to use the infinitive in this expression. You cannot say 'that' after **want**.

I just want him to enjoy himself.
~~*I just want that he enjoy himself.*~~
They don't want the school holidays to end.
~~*They don't want that the school holidays end.*~~

want [NEED] /wɒnt/ [US] /wɑːnt/ *verb* [T] **1** to need something: *Do you think this soup wants a bit of salt?* ○ [+ v-*ing*] *The wine is in the fridge – it just wants cool****ing*** *for a couple of minutes.* ○ *If you ask me that child wants a good slap!* **2 want to** used in giving advice to mean that someone should do something: *You want to tell him now, before it's too late.*
• **not/never want for anything** *FORMAL* to have all the basic things you need to lead a satisfactory life: *As children we never wanted for anything – my grandmother made sure of that.*
want /wɒnt/ *noun* **in want of** needing: *He appeared tired and in want of a shave.*
wants /wɒnts/ *plural noun FORMAL* needs: *Our wants are few.*

want [LACK] /wɒnt/ [US] /wɑːnt/ *noun* [U] a lack of something: ***For*** *want* ***of*** *anything better to do I watched television for a while.* ○ *If we fail it won't be* ***for*** *want* ***of*** *trying* (= We have tried even if we fail).
wanting /ˈwɒn.tɪŋ/ [US] /ˈwɑːn.t̬ɪŋ/ *adj FORMAL* lacking: *I think she's perhaps a little wanting* ***in*** *charm.*
• **tried and found wanting** tried and discovered to be not effective: *This government's policies, said the speaker, have been tried and found wanting.*

ˈwant ˌad *noun* [C] *US FOR* **classified ad**

wanton [WITHOUT CARE] /ˈwɒn.tən/ [US] /ˈwɑːn.tᵊn/ *adj FORMAL* (of something bad, such as damage, cruelty, waste) extreme and showing complete lack of care: *wanton destruction of human life* ○ *a wanton disregard for safety* ○ *wanton extravagance* **wantonly** /ˈwɒn.tən.li/ [US] /ˈwɑːn.tᵊn-/ *adv*

wanton [SEXUAL] /ˈwɒn.tən/ [US] /ˈwɑːn.tᵊn/ *adj OLD USE OR HUMOROUS* (of a woman) behaving or appearing in a very sexual way **wantonly** /ˈwɒn.tən.li/ [US] /ˈwɑːn.tᵊn-/ *adv* **wantonness** /ˈwɒn.tən.nəs/ [US] /ˈwɑːn.tᵊn-/ *noun* [U]

WAP /wæp/ *noun* [U] *ABBREVIATION FOR* Wireless Applicaton Protocol: a system which allows you to use the Internet using a type of MOBILE PHONE (= a telephone that you can carry with you)

war /wɔːʳ/ [US] /wɔːr/ *noun* [C or U] **1** armed fighting between two or more countries or groups, or a particular example of this: *nuclear war* ○ *a war film/grave/hero/poet* ○ *If this country* ***goes to*** (= starts to fight in a) *war we will have to face the fact that many people will die.* ○ *Britain and France* ***declared*** *war* ***on*** *Germany in 1939 as a result of the invasion of Poland.* ○ *War* ***broke out*** *between the two countries after a border dispute.* ○ *They've been* ***at*** *war for the last five years.* ○ *He died in World War 1/the Vietnam war.* **2 war of attrition** a war which is fought over a long period and only ends when one side has neither the soldiers and equipment nor the determination left to continue fighting **3 war of nerves** a situation, often before a competition or BATTLE, in which two opposing sides attempt to frighten or discourage each other by making threats or by showing how strong or clever they are **4** any situation in which there is fierce competition between opposing sides or a great fight against something harmful: *The past few months have witnessed a* ***price*** *war between leading supermarkets.* ○ *The government are to step up their attempt to* ***wage*** *war* ***against/on*** *drugs.*
• **war clouds** (*ALSO* **clouds of war**) If someone says that war clouds are gathering over a particular country, they mean that a war seems increasingly likely there: *It was the 1930s and war clouds were gathering on the horizon in Europe.*
• **be in the wars** *UK INFORMAL* to have injuries to many different parts of the body: *You've got a cut on your arm as well, you poor thing. You really have been in the wars!*

warble /ˈwɔː.bl̩/ [US] /ˈwɔːr-/ *verb* [I] **1** (of a bird) to sing pleasantly **2** *HUMOROUS* to sing, especially in a high voice: *Was that you I heard warbling in the bathroom this morning?*
warbler /ˈwɔː.bləʳ/ [US] /ˈwɔːr.blɚ/ *noun* [C] a small bird that lives in trees and sings

ˈwar ˌbride *noun* [C] a girl or woman who, during a war, marries a member of the armed forces from a different country

ˈwar ˌcrime *noun* [C] a crime committed during a war which breaks the accepted international rules of war: *Genocide is a war crime.*
ˈwar ˌcriminal *noun* [C] someone who commits war crimes: *He was a Nazi war criminal.*

ˈwar ˌcry *noun* [C usually sing] (*ALSO* **battle cry**) a phrase or word shouted by people as they start to fight, which is intended to give them the strength and desire to fight harder: *FIGURATIVE The phrase 'burn your bra!' was the feminists' war cry of the 1970s.*

ward [HOSPITAL] /wɔːd/ [US] /wɔːrd/ *noun* [C] **1** one of the parts or large rooms into which a hospital is divided, for treating people with a similar type of condition: *a geriatric/maternity/psychiatric ward* **2** *US* one of the parts into which a prison is divided

ward [CITY AREA] /wɔːd/ [US] /wɔːrd/ *noun* [C] (in many countries) one of the areas into which a city, town or village is divided, having its own elected political representative or its own organizations for managing services

ward [CHILD] /wɔːd/ [US] /wɔːrd/ *noun* [C] *LEGAL* a person, especially a child, who is legally put under the protection of a court of law or a GUARDIAN: *The girl was made a ward* ***of court*** *to stop her father taking her out of the country.*

-ward [TOWARDS] /-wəd/ [US] /-wɚd/ *suffix* towards the stated place or direction: *At least we're homeward bound.*
-wards /-wədz/ [US] /-wɚdz/ *suffix*: *Take a couple of steps backwards/forwards.*

USAGE

-ward or **-wards?**

Generally, adjectives are formed using **-ward** and adverbs are formed using **-wards**.

an eastward journey
moving slowly backwards

W

The **-ward** form of the adverb is also possible, especially in American and Australian English.

---

ward /wɔːd/ ⓤ /wɔːrd/ *verb*
▲ **ward** *sth* **off** *phrasal verb* [M] to prevent something unpleasant from harming or approaching you: *In the winter I take vitamin C to ward off colds.* ◦ *She was given a magic charm to ward off evil spirits.*

'**war ,dance** *noun* [C] a ceremonial dance, performed by some TRIBAL people, either before they fight or after a victory

warden MANAGER OF BUILDING /'wɔː.dºn/ ⓤ /'wɔːr-/ *noun* [C] **1** a person who is in charge of (the people in) a particular building: *She's the warden of a home for mentally handicapped people.* **2** UK the head of a college: *He's the warden of Wadham College, Oxford.* **3** US the person in charge of a prison: *a prison warden*

warden OFFICIAL /'wɔː.dºn/ ⓤ /'wɔːr-/ *noun* [C] a person whose job is to make certain that members of the public obey particular rules: *a dog warden* ◦ *a park warden* ◦ *a traffic warden*

warder MALE /'wɔː.dəʳ/ ⓤ /'wɔːr.dɚ/ *noun* [C] (FEMALE OLD-FASHIONED ALSO **wardress**) UK a person who is in charge of people in prison

wardrobe /'wɔː.drəʊb/ ⓤ /'wɔːr.droʊb/ *noun* **1** [C or U] a tall cupboard in which you hang your clothes, or all of the clothes that a person owns: *She was showing me her new built-in/*(UK) *fitted wardrobes.* ◦ *I sometimes feel that my summer wardrobe is rather lacking* (= I don't have many clothes for summer). **2** [U] a department in a theatre, film company, etc. who are in charge of the clothes that the actors wear on stage, making certain that they are clean, repairing them and sometimes making them: *He's in charge of wardrobe at the local amateur theatre.*

-ware /-weəʳ/ ⓤ /-wer/ *suffix* used, often in shops, to refer to items of the same material or type, especially items used in cooking and serving food: *tableware* ◦ *the kitchenware department*

warehouse UK /'weə.haʊs/ ⓤ /'wer-/ *noun* [C] (US **storehouse**) a large building for storing items before they are sold, used or sent out to shops, or a large shop selling a large number of a particular items at a cheap rate: *The goods have been sitting in a warehouse for months because a strike has prevented distribution.* ◦ *We bought both sofas from a big furniture warehouse that's just off the motorway.*

wares /weəz/ ⓤ /werz/ *plural noun* **1** small items for selling, in a market or on the street but not usually in a shop: *Some displayed their wares on stalls, while others had just spread them out on the pavement.* **2** INFORMAL a company's products: *The company must do more to promote their wares overseas.*

warfare /'wɔː.feəʳ/ ⓤ /'wɔːr.fer/ *noun* [U] the activity of fighting a war, often including the weapons and methods that are used: *guerrilla/naval/nuclear/trench warfare*

warfarin /'wɔː.fºr.ɪn/ ⓤ /'wɔːr.fɚ-/ *noun* [U] TRADEMARK a substance which is used to kill rats and is also used in a slightly different form as a medical treatment in order to prevent blood from CLOTTING (= becoming solid)

'**war ,game** *noun* [C] a pretend military BATTLE which is performed only for the purpose of training

warhead /'wɔː.hed/ ⓤ /'wɔːr-/ *noun* [C] the front end of a bomb or missile that contains explosives: *a conventional/nuclear warhead*

warhorse PERSON /'wɔː.hɔːs/ ⓤ /'wɔːr.hɔːrs/ *noun* [C] INFORMAL an old and experienced politician, soldier or athlete, especially one who is still active: *Manchester City football club's old warhorse, still fighting fit at 36, was sent off for fouling after half an hour.*

warhorse ESTABLISHED SHOW /'wɔː.hɔːs/ ⓤ /'wɔːr.hɔːrs/ *noun* [C usually sing] OFTEN DISAPPROVING a piece of music, television show, play or other performed work which has often been performed or shown and is very famous: *I don't understand why a ballet company can't perform fresh new material instead of just bringing out the same old warhorses year after year.*

warily /'weə.rɪ.li/ ⓤ /'wer.ɪ-/ *adv* ⊃See at **wary**.

warlike /'wɔː.laɪk/ ⓤ /'wɔːr-/ *adj* FORMAL often involved in and eager to start wars: *It has often been said, perhaps unfairly, that they are a warlike nation/people.*

warlord /'wɔː.lɔːd/ ⓤ /'wɔːr.lɔːrd/ *noun* [C] MAINLY DISAPPROVING a military leader who controls a country or, more frequently, an area within a country

warm HIGH TEMPERATURE /wɔːm/ ⓤ /wɔːrm/ *adj* **1** having or producing a comfortably high temperature, although not hot: *Are you warm enough or do you want the fire on?* ◦ *I've got my hands in my pockets to keep them warm.* **2** describes clothes and covers made of a material that keeps you warm: *I don't have a warm winter coat.* ◦ *Those gloves look nice and warm.* **3** A warm colour is one which is based on or contains a colour such as red, yellow or orange which suggests warmth.

warm /wɔːm/ ⓤ /wɔːrm/ *verb* [I or T] to (cause to) become warm: *You're so cold – come and warm your hands by the fire.* ◦ *Your supper's just warming through in the oven.* ◦ *We can warm (up) the room quite quickly with this electric fire.*

the warm *noun* [S] UK a warm place: *It's cold standing out there – come into the warm.*

warming /'wɔː.mɪŋ/ ⓤ /'wɔːr-/ *adj* APPROVING describes a type of food or drink that makes you feel warm: *Have a nice warming bowl of soup.* **warmly** /'wɔːm.li/ ⓤ /'wɔːrm-/ *adv*: *You're not dressed warmly enough – put a sweater on.* **warmth** /wɔːmpθ/ ⓤ /wɔːrmpθ/ *noun* [U] *I've put a T-shirt on under my sweater for extra warmth.*

warm FRIENDLY /wɔːm/ ⓤ /wɔːrm/ *adj* friendly and affectionate: *They're a very warm family.* ◦ *He has a lovely warm smile.* ◦ *I'd like to give a warm welcome to our guests this evening.* **warmly** /'wɔːm.li/ ⓤ /'wɔːrm-/ *adv*: *He shook my hand warmly.* **warmth** /wɔːmpθ/ ⓤ /wɔːrmpθ/ *noun* [U]

warm NEAR /wɔːm/ ⓤ /wɔːrm/ *adj* [after v] INFORMAL (especially in children's games) near to guessing a correct answer or to discovering a hidden object: *You're getting warmer!*

PHRASAL VERBS WITH **warm** ▼

▲ **warm** *sth* **over** *phrasal verb* [M] US DISAPPROVING to use an idea that has been used before or to discuss a subject that has already been discussed before: *Voters are bored with politicians warming over old policies.*
warmed-over /,wɔːmd'əʊ.vəʳ/ ⓤ /,wɔːrmd'oʊ.vɚ/ *adj* [before n] *These commercials are just warmed-over imitations of earlier TV ads.*

▲ **warm to** *sb* PERSON *phrasal verb* to start to like someone: *I wasn't sure about Sarah at first, but I warmed to her after we'd been out together a few times.*

▲ **warm to** *sth* IDEA *phrasal verb* If you warm to an idea, you start to become interested in or enthusiastic about it: *Unfortunately, I had to leave just as the speaker was warming to his theme.*

▲ **warm** (*sb/sth*) **up** HEAT *phrasal verb* [M] to become warmer or to make someone or something warmer: *The house soon warms up with the heating on.* ◦ *I'll just warm up the engine while you're getting your coats on.*

▲ **warm** *sth* **up** *phrasal verb* [M] to heat food that has already been cooked: *I might just warm up the leftovers from yesterday's meal in the microwave.*

▲ **warm up** EVENT *phrasal verb* INFORMAL If an event warms up, it starts to become more interesting, lively or exciting: *The party was only just starting to warm up as I left.*

▲ **warm up** EXERCISE *phrasal verb* to prepare yourself for a physical activity by doing some gentle exercises and stretches: *If you don't warm up before taking exercise, you risk injuring yourself.*
warm-up /'wɔːm.ʌp/ ⓤ /'wɔːrm-/ *noun* [C] *A warm-up is important before a run so as not to strain any muscles.* ◦ *Let's do a few warm-up exercises.*

warm-blooded /,wɔːm'blʌd.ɪd/ ⓤ /'wɔːrm-/ *adj* having a body temperature which stays the same and does not change with the temperature of the surroundings: *Birds and mammals are warm-blooded.* ⊃Compare **cold-blooded**.

ˈwar meˌmorial *noun* [C] a large structure, made especially of stone, which is built in honour of those people who died in a particular war

warm-hearted /ˌwɔːmˈhɑː.tɪd/ [US] /ˌwɔːrmˈhɑːr.t̬ɪd/ *adj* kind and affectionate: *She's a good warm-hearted woman.*

warmonger /ˈwɔːˌmʌŋ.gəʳ/ [US] /ˈwɔːrˌmʌŋ.gɚ/ *noun* [C] *DISAPPROVING* a politician or other leader who is often encouraging a country to go to war **warmongering** /ˈwɔːˌmʌŋ.gᵊr.ɪŋ/ [US] /ˈwɔːr.mʌŋ.gɚ-/ *noun* [U] *The president was accused of warmongering.*

warn /wɔːn/ [US] /wɔːrn/ *verb* [I or T] to make someone aware of a possible danger or problem, especially one in the future: [+ obj + *to* infinitive] *We were warned not **to** eat the fish which might give us a slight stomach upset.* ○ [+ obj + (*that*)] *Have you warned them **(that)** there will be an extra person for dinner?* ○ *I was warned **against/off** going to the east coast because it was so full of tourists.* ○ *There were signs warning **of** fog as soon as we got onto the motorway.* ○ *This particular curry is extremely hot – **be** warned!* ○ *Put that ball down and come over here, Laura – I'm warning you* (= I will punish you if you do not)*!*

warning /ˈwɔː.nɪŋ/ [US] /ˈwɔːr-/ *noun* [C or U] **1** something that makes you aware of a possible danger or problem, especially one in the future: *Completely without warning he turned up on my doorstep with all four children!* ○ *There's a warning on the cigarette packet that says 'Tobacco seriously damages health'.* ○ *I'm not surprised you feel ill – **let it be a** warning to you!* ○ *Just a **word of** warning – restaurants in this area can be very expensive.* ○ *FORMAL The government have today **issued** a warning about the dangers of sunbathing.* ○ *They can't dismiss you just like that – they have to **give** you a **written** warning first.* ○ *The police fired warning **shots** but the protesters took no notice.* **2 warning sign** a physical condition that shows the presence of a disease: *The warning signs **of** the illness are respiratory problems and dizziness.*

• **hear warning bells** (*ALSO* **warning bells start to ring/sound**) used to describe when people see signs that something bad has started or is going to happen: *For me, the warning bells started to ring when she stopped eating properly and lost all that weight.*

warp [BEND] /wɔːp/ [US] /wɔːrp/ *verb* [I or T] (especially of wood) to become damaged by bending or twisting, usually as a result of the presence of water or heat, or (of water or heat) to cause this to happen: *Left in the garage where it was damp, the wooden frame had warped.* ○ *If I put the shelves near the radiator, the heat might warp them.* **warped** /wɔːpt/ [US] /wɔːrpt/ *adj*: *Have you noticed how warped these shelves are?*

warp [STRANGE] /wɔːp/ [US] /wɔːrp/ *verb* [T] to make a person or their behaviour strange, in an unpleasant or harmful way: *Prison warps people. Had it warped Kelley enough that he would kill a stranger?*

warped /wɔːpt/ [US] /wɔːrpt/ *adj*: *DISAPPROVING OR HUMOROUS* strange and unpleasant: *I suppose I shouldn't be laughing about death – perhaps I've got a warped **mind/sense of humour**!*

the warp [THREADS] *noun* [S] *SPECIALIZED* the threads that go along the length of a piece of cloth or a LOOM (= a device for weaving) ➲Compare **the weft**.

ˈwar ˌpaint [PAINT] *noun* [U] a paint used by some TRIBAL people to decorate the face and body before fighting

ˈwar ˌpaint [MAKE-UP] *noun* [U] *HUMOROUS* make-up

warpath /ˈwɔː.pɑːθ/ [US] /ˈwɔːr.pæθ/ *noun INFORMAL MAINLY HUMOROUS* **on the warpath** angry and likely to argue or punish: *If there was one thing she couldn't face in the morning it was her mother on the warpath.*

warrant [MAKE NECESSARY] /ˈwɒr.ᵊnt/ [US] /ˈwɔːr-/ *verb* [T] to make a particular activity necessary: *Obviously what she did was wrong, but I don't think it warranted quite such severe punishment.* ○ *It's a relatively simple task that really doesn't warrant a great deal of time being spent on it.* ➲See also **unwarranted**.

warrant [DOCUMENT] /ˈwɒr.ᵊnt/ [US] /ˈwɔːr-/ *noun* [C] an official document, signed by a judge or other person in authority, which gives the police permission to search someone's home, arrest a person or take some other action: *a search warrant* ○ *Judge La Riva had issued an arrest warrant/a warrant **for** his arrest.*

warrant [PROMISE] /ˈwɒr.ᵊnt/ [US] /ˈwɔːr-/ *verb* [T] *OLD-FASHIONED* to say that you are certain about something

ˈwarrant ˌofficer *noun* [C] a rank in the armed forces, between a COMMISSIONED OFFICER and an NCO: *Warrant Officer First Class*

warranty /ˈwɒr.ᵊn.ti/ [US] /ˈwɔːr.ᵊn.t̬i/ *noun* [C] a written promise from a company to repair or replace a product that develops a fault within a fixed period of time, or to do a piece of work again if it is not satisfactory; a **guarantee**: *The warranty **covers** the car mechanically for a year, with unlimited mileage.*

warren /ˈwɒr.ᵊn/ [US] /ˈwɔːr-/ *noun* [C] (*ALSO* **rabbit warren**) **1** a series of connecting underground passages and holes in which rabbits live **2** *MAINLY DISAPPROVING* a very crowded and confusing building or part of a city in which it is easy to get lost: *They live on a great concrete warren of a housing estate.*

warring /ˈwɔː.rɪŋ/ [US] /ˈwɔːr.ɪŋ/ *adj* [before n] describes countries or groups of people that are at war with each other or who are arguing fiercely with each other: *The Labour Party, he said, had disintegrated into warring **factions**.*

warrior /ˈwɒr.i.əʳ/ [US] /ˈwɔːr.i.ɚ/ *noun* [C] a soldier, usually one who has both experience and skill in fighting, especially in the past: *a Samurai warrior* ○ *a warrior king/nation*

warship /ˈwɔː.ʃɪp/ [US] /ˈwɔːr-/ *noun* [C] a ship equipped with guns, for use in war ➲See picture **Planes, Ships and Boats** on page Centre 14

wart /wɔːt/ [US] /wɔːrt/ *noun* [C] a small hard lump which grows on the skin, often on the face and hands

• **warts and all** *INFORMAL* A warts and all description or representation of a person is one that includes all the bad qualities in that person's character and makes no attempt to hide them: *He tried to paint the president as he really was, warts and all.*

warty /ˈwɔː.ti/ [US] /ˈwɔːr.t̬i/ *adj* having warts

warthog /ˈwɔːt.hɒg/ [US] /ˈwɔːrt.hɑːg/ *noun* [C] an African wild pig with a large head, tusks and little lumps on the male's face that look like WARTS

wartime /ˈwɔː.taɪm/ [US] /ˈwɔːr-/ *noun* [U] a period of time during which a war is being fought: ***In** wartime, food is often scarce.* ○ *The film is set in wartime England.* * NOTE: The opposite is **peacetime**.

war-torn /ˈwɔː.tɔːn/ [US] /ˈwɔːr.tɔːrn/ *adj* severely damaged by a long war, especially between different groups from the same country: *It is a long-term task to rebuild the infrastructure of a war-torn country such as Angola.*

wary /ˈweə.ri/ [US] /ˈwer.i/ *adj* not completely trusting or certain about something or someone: *I'm a bit wary **of/about** giving people my address when I don't know them very well.* **warily** /ˈweə.rɪ.li/ [US] /ˈwer.ɪ-/ *adv* **wariness** /ˈweə.rɪ.nəs/ [US] /ˈwer.ɪ-/ *noun* [U]

was *STRONG* /wɒz/ [US] /wɑːz/, *WEAK* /wəz/ *past simple of* **be**

wasabi /ˈwæs.æb.i/ *noun* [U] Japanese MUSTARD (= spicy sauce)

wash [CLEAN] /wɒʃ/ [US] /wɑːʃ/ *verb* **1** [T] to clean something using water: *wash your hair/hands* ○ *wash the car/clothes/floor* ○ *These sheets need washing.* ○ *I'll wash the bottle **out*** (= clean its inside) *and use it again.* **2** [I] (*US ALSO* **wash up**) to clean yourself, or a part of yourself, with water and usually soap: *I'd like to wash before dinner.*

• **wash well** If a particular material or piece of clothing washes well, it is not damaged or spoilt by repeated washing.

• **wash *your* dirty linen in public** *DISAPPROVING* People who wash their dirty linen in public discuss, or allow to be discussed in public, matters which should be kept private.

• **wash *your* hands of *sth*** If you wash your hands of something that you were previously responsible for, you intentionally stop being involved in it or connected with it in any way: *She couldn't wait to wash her hands of the whole project.*

W

• **wash *your* mouth out** Someone who has used a swear word might be told, humorously, to wash their mouth out (with soap, soapy water, etc.).

a wash *noun* [S] when you wash something or a part of your body: *Those curtains need a* **good** (= careful) *wash.* ○ *Erik needed a* **good** *wash after playing in the garden all day.*

• **have a wash** to wash your body or a part of it: *I need to have a wash before dinner.*

• **do a wash** to clean clothes, sheets, etc., usually in a washing machine: *Are you doing a wash tonight?*

the wash *noun* [S] **1** all the clothes, sheets, etc. that are washed together, especially in a washing machine: *Can I* **put** *this shirt* **in (with)** *the white wash?* ○ *"Where's my pink shirt?" "It's* **in** *the wash"* (= being washed or in a pile of clothes that is going to be washed). **2** *US FOR* **washing**

washable /ˈwɒʃ.ə.bl̩/ [US] /ˈwɑː.ʃə-/ *adj* able to be washed in a washing machine without being damaged: *I never buy clothes that aren't* **machine***-washable.*

washer /ˈwɒʃ.əʳ/ [US] /ˈwɑː.ʃɚ/ *noun* [C] a **washing machine**

washing /ˈwɒʃ.ɪŋ/ [US] /ˈwɑː.ʃɪŋ/ *noun* [U] **1** (*US ALSO* **the wash**) the act of washing clothes: **Doing** *the washing is such a bore!* **2** (*US ALSO* **wash**) clothes, sheets, etc. that need to be or have just been washed: *I* **do** *the washing and then I* **hang/peg** *it* **out** *in the garden.*

wash [FLOW] /wɒʃ/ [US] /wɑːʃ/ *verb* [I usually + adv or prep] **1** *LITERARY* If water washes somewhere, it flows there, usually repeatedly: *She stood on the shore and let the water wash* **over** *her tired feet.* **2 wash *sb/sth* up/ashore/overboard** (of the sea) to carry something or someone to or away from a place: *Overnight the sea had washed up a lot of rubbish.* ○ *More than 400 dead dolphins had been washed ashore.* ○ *A Spanish crew member had been washed overboard* (= carried off a ship into the sea by the force of the water) *in the storm.*

• **wash (with) *sb*** *INFORMAL* If an excuse or argument won't wash (with someone), they are unlikely to believe or accept it.

wash /wɒʃ/ [US] /wɑːʃ/ *noun* [U] *LITERARY* (the sound made) when the sea moves against land, etc: *Outside the flat, she could hear the gentle wash of the waves on the beach.*

wash [THIN LAYER] /wɒʃ/ [US] /wɑːʃ/ *noun* [C] a thin layer of water or watery paint, especially one which is brushed lightly over a painting to make the lines softer: *a blue wash/ a wash* **of** *blue* ○ *Just before the paint dries, I give it a light wash.*

wash [EVEN SITUATION] /wɒʃ/ [US] /wɑːʃ/ *noun* [C usually sing] *US* an event or situation in which positive and negative things balance each other: *If pollution controls are enforced here, the factories will move to where they're allowed to pollute, so it'll be a wash as far as clear air goes.*

PHRASAL VERBS WITH **wash**

▲ **wash *sth* away** *phrasal verb* [M] If water or rain washes something away, it removes it or carries it away: *The blood on the pavement had been washed away by the rain overnight.*

▲ **wash *sth* down** [CLEAN] *phrasal verb* [M] to clean a large object or surface with a liquid: *He washed the car down with soapy water.*

▲ **wash *sth* down** [EAT] *phrasal verb* [M] *INFORMAL* to eat food or swallow medicine with a drink that helps or improves it: *Supper was fresh salmon and vegetables, washed down* **with** *a bottle of white wine.*

▲ **wash *(sth)* out** [REMOVE] *phrasal verb* [M] If a colour or dirty mark washes out, or if you wash it out, it disappears when you wash it: *Do you think these stains will wash out?*

▲ **wash *sth* out** [PREVENT] *phrasal verb* [usually passive] If an event or sports competition is washed out, it is prevented from happening or stopped early because of heavy rain: *The men's semi-finals in the tennis were washed out this morning.*

ˈwash ˌout *noun* [C]

▲ **wash *(sth)* up** [PLATES] *phrasal verb* [M] to clean the plates, pans, and other things that you have used for cooking and eating: *He washed up his mug and put it back on the shelf.* ➲See picture **Phrasal Verbs** on page Centre 9

washing-up *UK* /ˌwɒʃ.ɪŋˈʌp/ [US] /ˌwɑːʃ-/ *noun* [U] (*US* **dishes**) the act of cleaning plates, pans, glasses, knives, forks, etc. after a meal, or the items needing to be washed: *You* **do** *the washing-up and I'll do the drying.* ○ *There's an enormous pile of washing-up in the sink.*

▲ **wash up** [HANDS] *phrasal verb US* to wash your hands, especially before a meal: *Go and wash up – your dinner's ready.*

washbasin /ˈwɒʃˌbeɪ.sᵊn/ [US] /ˈwɑːʃ-/ *noun* [C] (*US* **sink**) *UK* a bowl that is fixed to the wall in a bathroom or near a toilet, in which you wash your hands, face, etc. and which has pipes to supply and carry away water

washcloth /ˈwɒʃ.klɒθ/ [US] /ˈwɑːʃ.klɑːθ/ *noun* [C] *US FOR* **facecloth**

washed-out [NOT BRIGHT] /ˌwɒʃtˈaʊt/ [US] /ˌwɑːʃt-/ *adj* [before n] describes cloth that has become less bright as a result of frequent washing: *She was wearing an old washed-out T-shirt and jeans.*

washed-out [TIRED] /ˌwɒʃtˈaʊt/ [US] /ˌwɑːʃt-/ *adj* [after v] feeling or looking very tired: *I have to wear a bit of make-up in the winter or I look completely washed-out.*

washed-up /ˌwɒʃtˈʌp/ [US] /ˌwɑːʃt-/ *adj* [after v] If you are washed-up, the job for which you are trained is finished and you have no further chances of success in the future: *The tragedy of being a dancer is that you're* **all** *washed-up by the time you're thirty-five.*

washer /ˈwɒʃ.əʳ/ [US] /ˈwɑː.ʃɚ/ *noun* [C] a flat ring of metal, rubber or plastic which is put especially between a screw or bolt and a surface in order to improve the connection between them or between joined pipes to seal their connection

washer-dryer /ˌwɒʃ.əˈdraɪ.əʳ/ ʃ /ˌwɑː.ʃɚˈdraɪ.ɚ/ *noun* [C] a large electric machine for washing and drying clothes

ˈwashing maˌchine *noun* [C] a machine for washing clothes, sheets and other cloth items: *a front/top-loading washing machine* ○ *Could you empty/load the washing machine, please?* ➲See picture **In the Kitchen** on page Centre 16

ˈwashing ˌpowder/ˌliquid *UK noun* [C or U] (*US* **laundry detergent**) a DETERGENT in the form of a powder or liquid which is used for washing clothes and other cloth items

ˌwashing-ˈup ˌliquid *UK noun* [U] (*US* **dish liquid**) a thick liquid DETERGENT which is added to hot water when washing pans, knives and forks, etc.

washout /ˈwɒʃ.aʊt/ [US] /ˈwɑː.ʃaʊt/ *noun* [C usually sing] *INFORMAL* a complete failure: *The last party was a bit of a washout – hardly anyone turned up.*

washroom /ˈwɒʃ.rʊm/ /-ruːm/ [US] /ˈwɑːʃ-/ *noun* [C] *US OLD-FASHIONED FOR* **toilet** (= room with a toilet in it)

washstand /ˈwɒʃ.stænd/ [US] /ˈwɑːʃ-/ *noun* [C] a small table for holding a container of water for washing, used especially in the past

wasn't /ˈwɒz.ᵊnt/ [US] /ˈwɑː.zᵊnt/ *short form of* was not: *It was you who told me that, wasn't it?*

wasp [INSECT] /wɒsp/ [US] /wɑːsp/ *noun* [C] a black and yellow flying insect which can sting you: *There's a wasps'* **nest** *in that old tree.* ○ *a wasp* **sting**

WASP [PERSON], **Wasp** /wɒsp/ [US] /wɑːsp/ *noun* [C] *MAINLY US DISAPPROVING* White Anglo-Saxon Protestant (= a white American whose family originally came from northern Europe, and is therefore part of a group often considered the most influential and wealthy in American society): *My mother comes from an old WASP family which has been in this country for 350 years.* **WASPy** /ˈwɒs.pi/ [US] /ˈwɑː.spi/ *adj* (*ALSO* **WASPish,** *ALSO* **Waspish**)

waspish /ˈwɒs.pɪʃ/ [US] /ˈwɑː.spɪʃ/ *adj DISAPPROVING* likely to make sharp, slightly cruel remarks; having a slightly angry and unpleasant manner: *She had a waspish tongue which could hurt.*

waste [BAD USE] /weɪst/ *noun* [S or U] **1** an unnecessary or wrong use of money, substances, time, energy, abilities, etc: *That meeting achieved absolutely nothing – it was* **a** *complete waste* **of time.** ○ *She's been unemployed for two years and it's such* **a** *waste* **of** *her talents.* ○ *My mother couldn't bear waste – she always made us eat everything* *on our plates.* **2 waste ground/land** an area of ground in or near a city which is not built on, cultivated or used in any way: *His body had been dumped in an area of waste land just outside the city.*

• **go to waste** to not be used, eaten, etc: *"Go on, finish off this tart, Paul." "Well, it seems a shame to let it go to waste."*

• **waste of space** *INFORMAL* a useless person: *He's a total waste of space, that man.*

waste /weɪst/ *verb* [T] to use too much of something or use something badly when there is a limited amount of it: *You waste a lot of water by having a bath instead of a shower. Come on, let's get started – we've wasted enough* ***time*** *already.* ○ *Don't waste your* ***money*** *on me, love, keep it for yourself.* **wasted** /ˈweɪ.stɪd/ *adj*: *He wasn't in when I got there, so it was a completely wasted journey.* ➲See also **wasted** THIN; **wasted** DRUNK.

• **wasted on *sb*** If you say that something is wasted on someone, you mean that it is too clever or its quality is too high for them and they will not understand its true value: *I'm not going to serve that good coffee to Chris and Melanie – it would be wasted on them.*

• **waste *your* breath** If you waste your breath, you spend time and energy trying to give advice which is ignored: *Honestly, you're wasting your breath – he doesn't want to hear what anyone else has got to say.*

• **not waste words** If someone does not waste words, they talk only about what is important using as few words as possible: *He explained the whole system in about 30 seconds – he doesn't waste words, does he?*

• **Waste not, want not.** *SAYING* said to advise someone not to waste anything, because they might need it in the future

wastage /ˈweɪ.stɪdʒ/ *noun* [U] **1** the amount that is wasted: *Water companies have got to cut down on wastage.* **2** *UK FOR* **natural wastage 3** *UK* (*US* **attrition**) the people who leave an educational or training course before it has finished: *The wastage rates on the degree courses are a cause for concern.* **wasteful** /ˈweɪst.fəl/ *adj* *DISAPPROVING* *It's wasteful the way you throw so much food away!* **wastefully** /ˈweɪst.fəl.i/ *adv*

waster /ˈweɪ.stə^r/ [US] /-stɚ/ *noun* [C] **1** *INFORMAL DISAPPROVING* a person or thing who wastes something: *He's a time waster.* ○ *This project is nothing but a money waster.* **2** *UK INFORMAL DISAPPROVING* a person who does nothing positive with their life, making no use of their abilities or the opportunities that are offered them: *There were the usual bunch of wasters hanging round the bar.*

▲ **waste away** *phrasal verb* to gradually get thinner and weaker, in a way that is unhealthy: *You get thinner every time I see you, Sara – you're wasting away!*

waste [UNWANTED MATTER] /weɪst/ *noun* [C or U] unwanted matter or material of any type, often that which is left after useful substances or parts have been removed: *Britain produces 20 million tonnes of household waste each year.* ○ *He opposes any kind of nuclear waste being dumped at sea.* ○ *Every day, 30 million gallons of untreated human waste* (= excrement) *flow from Ciudad Juarez into the Rio Grande.* ○ *Oil spills are common, as is the dumping of toxic industrial wastes.* ○ *The Japanese recycle more than half of their waste* ***paper****.*

waste [KILL] /weɪst/ *verb* [T] *US SLANG* to kill someone

wastebasket *US* /ˈweɪstˌbɑː.skɪt/ [US] /-ˌbæs.kɪt/ *noun* [C] (*UK* **wastepaper basket**) an open container which stands on the floor inside buildings and is used for putting rubbish in, especially paper

wasted [THIN] /ˈweɪs.tɪd/ *adj* very thin and weak as a result of illness or lack of food: *Underneath the hospital blankets I could see the outline of her poor wasted* ***body****.* ➲See also **wasted** at **waste** BAD USE.

wasted [DRUNK] /ˈweɪ.stɪd/ *adj MAINLY US SLANG* very drunk or ill from drugs: *He was too wasted to drive.* ○ *Paula was completely wasted after only one drink.* ➲See also **wasted** at **waste** BAD USE.

ˈwaste disˌposal *UK noun* [C] (*US* **garbage disposal**) an electrical machine connected to a kitchen sink which cuts up food waste so that it will flow easily through the pipes

wasteland /ˈweɪst.lænd/ *noun* **1** [C or U] an empty area of land, especially in or near a city, which is not cultivated or built on, or used in any way: *The car was dumped in a stretch of wasteland in the south of the city.* **2** [S] *LITERARY DISAPPROVING* a place, time or situation containing nothing positive or productive, or completely lacking a particular quality or activity: *This new surge of interest in religion is perhaps a reaction to the* ***spiritual*** *wasteland of the 1980s.*

wasteˈpaper ˌbasket *UK noun* [C] (*US* **wastebasket**) an open container which stands on the floor inside buildings and is used for putting rubbish in, especially paper: *Most of the letters they receive end up in the wastepaper basket.*

ˈwaste ˌproduct *noun* [C] a substance of no value or use which is made during a process in which something useful is produced: *Cadmium is a toxic waste product of the electronics industry.*

wastes /weɪsts/ *plural noun* large areas of land that are not cultivated and have few living animals or plants: *the Arctic wastes of northern Siberia*

ˈwasting diˌsease *noun* [C usually sing] a disease that causes the sufferer to gradually become very thin and weak: *She suffers from a little-known* ***muscle****-wasting disease.*

wastrel /ˈweɪ.strəl/ *noun* [C] *LITERARY* a person who does nothing positive with their life, making no use of their abilities or the opportunities that are offered them

watch [SMALL CLOCK] /wɒtʃ/ [US] /wɑːtʃ/ *noun* [C] a small clock which is worn on a strap around the wrist or, sometimes, connected to a piece of clothing by a chain: *My watch seems to have stopped – it says 10:15 but I'm sure it must be later.* ○ *He glanced nervously* ***at*** *his watch.*

watch [LOOK AT] /wɒtʃ/ [US] /wɑːtʃ/ *verb* **1** [I or T] to look at something for a period of time, especially something that is changing or moving: *I had dinner and watched TV for a couple of hours.* ○ *He spent the entire afternoon watching a cricket match.* ○ [+ obj + infinitive without *to*] *I watched him get into a taxi.* ○ *I got the feeling I was being watched.* ○ [+ obj + v-*ing*] *I sit by the window and watch people walk****ing*** *past.* ○ [+ question word] *Just watch* ***how*** *he slides that ball in past the goalkeeper.* ○ *Bonner watched helplessly as the ball sneaked in at the near post.* ○ *She'll pretend that she hasn't seen us – you watch.* ➲See Note **look, see or watch?** at **look** SEE. **2** [T] to stay with something or someone such as a child for a short time to make certain that they are safe: *If you want me to watch the kids for a couple of hours while you go out, just let me know.* ○ *Could you watch my bags for me, while I go to the toilet?*

• **watch the clock** *DISAPPROVING* to frequently notice the time and wish that it was later, especially when you are doing work that you do not like

• **watch the world go by** to look at people as they go past: *I love sitting in outdoor cafes watching the world go by.*

• **watch this space** If someone says watch this space, they mean that there will very soon be an exciting change in their situation.

• **watch paint dry** *INFORMAL HUMOROUS* used to refer to an activity that you consider extremely boring: *"So you don't want to watch the football?" "To be honest I would rather watch paint dry".*

watch /wɒtʃ/ [US] /wɑːtʃ/ *noun* **1** [S or U] when you watch or give attention to something or someone, especially to make certain nothing bad happens: *Once your name has been linked with a drug offence, the police* ***keep*** *a close watch* ***on*** *you.* ○ *The soldiers slept at night, except for one who stayed awake* ***on*** *watch/to* ***keep*** *watch.* **2** [S] a person or group of soldiers or guards whose duty is to protect a person, place or thing from danger or attack **3** [C] a fixed period of time during which a person or a group of soldiers or guards has the duty of protecting and warning of danger

• **a watch out** when you stay aware and look for someone or something: ***Keep*** *a watch out* ***for*** *Nicki and Steve – they should be here somewhere.*

watchable /ˈwɒtʃ.ə.bl/ [US] /ˈwɑː.tʃə-/ *adj INFORMAL APPROVING* describes a television programme or film that

W

is entertaining: *It's not the most profound series I've ever seen but it's very watchable.*

watchful /ˈwɒtʃ.fəl/ [US] /ˈwɑːtʃ-/ *adj* paying careful attention and ready to deal with problems: ***Under the** watchful **eye of** their mother, the two boys played on the shore.* ○ *She **keeps a** watchful **eye on** her husband to see that he behaves himself.* **watchfully** /ˈwɒtʃ.fəl.i/ [US] /ˈwɑːtʃ-/ *adv*: *Slowly and watchfully they walked around the perimeter of the clearing.* **watchfulness** /ˈwɒtʃ.fəl.nəs/ [US] /ˈwɑːtʃ-/ *noun* [U]

-watcher /-wɒtʃ.ər/ [US] /-wɑː.tʃɚ/ *suffix* a person who is interested in and enjoys watching a particular thing: *Royal-watchers have once again been speculating on the health of the princess.*

watcher /ˈwɒtʃ.əʳ/ [US] /ˈwɑː.tʃɚ/ *noun* [C] a television or film viewer: *The new channel is certainly good news for the movie watcher.*

watch [BE CAREFUL] /wɒtʃ/ [US] /wɑːtʃ/ *verb* [T] to be careful of something: *I have to watch my **weight*** (= be careful not to become too heavy) *now I'm not doing so much sport.* ○ *Watch your language* (= Do not use rude words) *in front of ladies, young man!* ○ [+ (that)] *Watch **(that)** you don't get glue on your fingers, won't you?* ○ [+ question word] *Watch **what** you're doing with that knife, Jim, it's sharp.* ○ *You want to* (= You should) *watch him – he's a bit of a strange character.*

• **watch it** *INFORMAL* used to tell someone to be careful: *Watch it, you nearly knocked my head off with that plank!*

• **watch *your* back** to be careful of the people around you, making certain that they do nothing to harm you: *I have to watch my back at work – there are a lot of people who would like my job.*

• **watch *your* step** to be very careful about how you behave: *He'll have to watch his step if he wants to keep that job of his!*

PHRASAL VERBS WITH **watch** ▼

▲ **watch out** *phrasal verb* used to warn someone of danger or an accident that seems likely to happen: *"Watch out!" he shouted, but it was too late – she had knocked the whole tray of drinks on the floor.*

▲ **watch out for *sb/sth*** *phrasal verb* to be careful to notice someone or something interesting: *Watch out for his latest movie, which comes out next month.*

▲ **watch over *sb*** *phrasal verb* to protect someone and make certain that they are safe: *The prince has two bodyguards watching over him every hour of the day.*

watchdog [ORGANIZATION] /ˈwɒtʃ.dɒg/ [US] /ˈwɑːtʃ.dɑːg/ *noun* [C] a person or organization responsible for making certain that companies maintain particular standards and do not act illegally: *The Countryside Commission was set up as the government's official watchdog **on** conservation.*

watchdog [DOG] /ˈwɒtʃ.dɒg/ [US] /ˈwɑːtʃ.dɑːg/ *noun* [C] *US FOR* **guard dog**

watchman /ˈwɒtʃ.mən/ [US] /ˈwɑːtʃ-/ *noun* [C] a person who is employed to guard a building or several buildings

watchstrap *MAINLY UK* /ˈwɒtʃ.stræp/ [US] /ˈwɑːtʃ-/ *noun* [C] (*US* **watchband**) a strip of leather or other material or a metal chain which fastens a watch onto your wrist

watchtower /ˈwɒtʃˌtaʊəʳ/ [US] /ˈwɑːtʃˌtaʊr/ *noun* [C] a tower built especially around the edges of prisons and army camps, the top of which provides a good position from which to see anyone who is approaching

watchword /ˈwɒtʃ.wɜːd/ [US] /ˈwɑːtʃ.wɝːd/ *noun* [C usually sing] (a word or phrase which represents) the main ideas or principles directing the way that someone behaves or the way that something is done: *And remember, let caution be your watchword.*

water /ˈwɔː.təʳ/ [US] /ˈwɑː.t̬ɚ/ *noun* [U] **1** a clear liquid, without colour or taste, which falls from the sky as rain and is necessary for animal and plant life: *a bottle/drink/glass of water* ○ *bottled/mineral/tap water* ○ *hot/cold water* ○ *Can I have a **drop** of water in my whiskey, please?* ○ *Is the water hot enough for a bath?* ○ *The human body is about 50% water.* **2** an area of water, such as the sea, a lake or a swimming pool: *The water's much warmer today – are you coming for a swim?* ○ *I like swimming but I don't like getting my head **under*** (= in) *water.* ○ *Dad, I swam a whole length of the pool **under** water* (= with the whole head and body below the surface of the water)*!* **3** the level of an area of water: *High water this morning at Portsmouth is at 11.17 a.m.*

-water /wɔː.təʳ/ [US] /-wɑː.t̬ɚ/ *suffix* used to form adjectives: *freshwater fish* ○ *a saltwater lagoon*

• **water off a duck's back** *MAINLY DISAPPROVING* criticisms of or warnings to a particular person that have no effect on that person: *I've told him that he's heading for trouble, but he doesn't listen – it's just water off a duck's back.*

• **water under the bridge** problems that someone has had in the past that they do not worry about because they happened a long time ago and cannot now be changed: *Yes, we did have our disagreements but that's water under the bridge now.*

water /ˈwɔː.təʳ/ [US] /ˈwɑː.t̬ɚ/ *verb* **1** [T] to pour water on to plants or the soil that they are growing in: *I've asked my neighbour to water the plants while I'm away.* **2** [T] to give an animal water to drink: *The horses had been fed and watered.* **3** [I] When your eyes water, they produce tears but not because you are unhappy: *How do you stop your eyes from watering when you're cutting up onions?* **4** [I] If your mouth waters, it produces a lot of saliva, usually because you can see or smell some food that you would like to eat: *Ooh, the smell of that bread is making my mouth water!*

waters /ˈwɔː.təz/ [US] /ˈwɑː.t̬ɚz/ *plural noun* **1** the area of sea near to and belonging to a particular country: *St Lucia depends on its clean coastal waters because fishing and tourism provide much of its income.* **2** the water contained in a particular lake, river or section of sea: *In the shallow waters of the Gulf of Mexico, oil rigs attract shoals of fish, and fishermen too.* **3** *UK* (*US* **water**) the liquid that surrounds a baby inside a pregnant woman's womb: *At 3 a.m. her waters broke, and the baby was born soon after.* **4 murky/uncharted waters** a situation which is not familiar and which may be dangerous: *In the last two chapters of the book, she **enters** the murky waters of male sexuality.* ○ *After the Wall Street crash, the American economy **moved into** uncharted waters.*

the waters *plural noun OLD USE* water from a spring, especially when used for drinking or swimming in, in order to improve the health: *People used to come to this city to **take*** (= drink and swim in) *the waters.*

watery /ˈwɔː.tər.i/ [US] /ˈwɑː.t̬ɚ.i/ *adj* **1** *DISAPPROVING* (of food or drink) containing too much water and therefore weak in taste: *watery soup/coffee* **2** pale or weak in colour or strength: *The sun shed its thin watery **light** over the sea.*

• **watery grave** *LITERARY* death by DROWNING (= dying because you can not breathe under water): *It was off the coast of Italy that Shelley **went to** his watery grave.*

PHRASAL VERBS WITH **water** ▼

▲ **water *sth* down** [DRINK] *phrasal verb* [M] to add water to a drink, usually an alcoholic drink, in order to make it less strong

▲ **water *sth* down** [OPINION] *phrasal verb* [M] to intentionally make an idea or opinion less extreme or forceful, usually so that other people will accept it: *The party has watered down its socialist ideals in order to appeal to the centre ground.*

ˌwatered ˈdown *adj* [before n] *They have returned with a watered down and more acceptable version of the proposal.*

ˈwater ˌbed *noun* [C] a bed which is filled with water

ˈwater ˌbill *noun* [C] a regular charge which is made to people for the use of their local water supply

ˈwater ˌbird *noun* [C] any bird that lives near or on water

ˈwater ˌbiscuit *noun* [C] a thin hard biscuit, which is often eaten with cheese

waterborne /ˈwɔː.tə.bɔːn/ [US] /ˈwɑː.t̬ɚ.bɔːrn/ *adj* carried by or through water: *The disease, causing extreme stomach upsets, is caused by a waterborne parasite.*

ˈwater ˌbottle *noun* [C] a container for carrying drinking water on a journey

'water ,buffalo *noun* [C or U] a large cow-like Asian animal with horns that curve backwards, which is often used for pulling farming tools

'water ,butt UK *noun* [C] (US **rain barrel**, AUS **water tank**) a large container for collecting rain which can then be used to water plants

'water ,cannon *noun* [U] a device which sends out a powerful stream of water and is used in order to scatter large groups of people: *Police used water cannon to break up the demonstration.*

'water ,closet *noun* [C usually sing] UK OLD-FASHIONED FOR a **WC**

watercolour UK, US **watercolor** /ˈwɔː.tə.kʌl.əʳ/ US /ˈwɑː.t̬ɚ.kʌl.ɚ/ *noun* [C or U] a paint which is mixed with water and used to create pictures, or a picture which has been done with this type of paint: *Generally, I prefer painting with watercolours.* ○ *He's done some lovely watercolours.*

water-cooled /ˌwɔː.tə.ˈkuːld/ US /ˌwɑː.t̬ɚ-/ *adj* If something such as an engine is water-cooled, it is surrounded by water to keep it at the correct operating temperature.

'water ,cooler *noun* [C] a machine for cooling and providing drinking water, usually in an office or other public place ⊃See picture **In the Office** on page Centre 15

watercourse /ˈwɔː.tə.kɔːs/ US /ˈwɑː.t̬ɚ.kɔːrs/ *noun* [C] a stream of water such as a river or canal, or the channel along which it flows

watercress /ˈwɔː.tə.kres/ US /ˈwɑː.t̬ɚ-/ *noun* [U] a plant which grows in water, whose hot-tasting green leaves are used as food, often eaten raw in salads

waterfall /ˈwɔː.tə.fɔːl/ US /ˈwɑː.t̬ɚ.fɑːl/ *noun* [C] water, especially from a river or stream, dropping from a higher to a lower point, sometimes from a great height

'water ,filter *noun* [C] a device for removing unwanted substances such as bacteria or harmful chemicals from drinking water

'water ,fountain *noun* [C] a device, usually in a public place, which supplies water for drinking

waterfowl /ˈwɔː.tə.faʊl/ US /ˈwɑː.t̬ɚ-/ *noun* [C or U] *plural* **waterfowl** any bird that spends much of its life on or around a river or lake, especially one which is shot for food or sport

waterfront /ˈwɔː.tə.frʌnt/ US /ˈwɑː.t̬ɚ-/ *noun* [C usually sing] a part of a town which is next to an area of water such as a river or the sea: *She owns a popular tourist restaurant on the town's waterfront.*

waterhole /ˈwɔː.tə.həʊl/ US /ˈwɑː.t̬ɚ.hoʊl/ *noun* [C] a small pool of water in a dry area where animals go to drink

'water ,ice *noun* [C] UK OLD-FASHIONED FOR **sorbet**

'watering ,can *noun* [C] a container for water with a handle and a long tube used for pouring water onto garden plants

'watering ,hole *noun* [C] HUMOROUS a pub or bar where people go to drink alcohol

'water ,jump *noun* [C] an area of water with a fence before it, which people or horses jump over in a competition

'water ,lily *noun* [C] a plant whose large flat leaves and cup-shaped petals float on the surface of lakes and ponds

the waterline /ðəˈwɔː.tə.laɪn/ US /-ˈwɑː.t̬ɚ-/ *noun* [S] SPECIALIZED the level that the water reaches on the side of a ship

waterlogged /ˈwɔː.tə.lɒgd/ US /ˈwɑː.t̬ɚ.lɑːgd/ *adj* (of land) full of water and almost covered by a layer of it, or (of a boat) full of water and therefore unable to keep moving or floating: *Unfortunately the game was cancelled because of a waterlogged (UK) pitch/(US) field.*

'water ,main *noun* [C usually pl] the main underground pipe in a system of pipes supplying water to an area

watermark PAPER /ˈwɔː.tə.mɑːk/ US /ˈwɑː.t̬ɚ.mɑːrk/ *noun* [C] a mark which is made on some types of paper during its production which can only be seen if it is held against the light

watermark RIVER/SEA /ˈwɔː.tə.mɑːk/ US /ˈwɑː.t̬ɚ.mɑːrk/ *noun* [C] a mark showing the highest or lowest level that a river or the sea reaches

'water ,meadow *noun* [C] a field which floods with water from a river when there is a lot of rain

watermelon /ˈwɔː.tə.mel.ən/ US /ˈwɑː.t̬ɚ-/ *noun* [C or U] a large round or oval-shaped fruit with dark green skin, sweet watery pink flesh and a lot of black seeds ⊃See picture **Fruit** on page Centre 1

watermill /ˈwɔː.tə.mɪl/ US /ˈwɑː.t̬ɚ-/ *noun* [C] a MILL (= a machine which produces flour) whose power is provided by a large wheel which is turned by moving water, especially a river

'water ,park *noun* [C] MAINLY US a large area containing several different pools with equipment and activities for swimmers, which visitors pay to use

'water ,pistol *noun* [C] (US ALSO **squirt gun**) a toy gun with which you can send out a stream of water to hit people or things

'water ,polo *noun* [U] a game played in water in which two teams of swimmers try to get the ball into the other team's goal

waterpower /ˈwɔː.tə.paʊəʳ/ US /ˈwɑː.t̬ɚ.paʊr/ *noun* [U] power that is obtained from water flowing from one level to a lower level

waterproof /ˈwɔː.tə.pruːf/ US /ˈwɑː.t̬ɚ-/ *adj* not allowing water to go through: *Canvas boots are all right but they're not as waterproof as leather.*

waterproof /ˈwɔː.tə.pruːf/ US /ˈwɑː.t̬ɚ-/ *noun* [C] MAINLY UK a coat or other item of clothing which keeps you dry because it does not allow water in

waterproof /ˈwɔː.tə.pruːf/ US /ˈwɑː.t̬ɚ-/ *verb* [T] to put a special substance on the surface of something which will prevent water from going through it

water-repellent /ˈwɔː.tə.rɪ.pel.ᵊnt/ US /ˈwɑː.t̬ɚ-/ *adj* **showerproof**

watershed BIG CHANGE /ˈwɔː.tə.ʃed/ US /ˈwɑː.t̬ɚ-/ *noun* [S] an event or period which is important because it represents a big change in how people do or think about something: *The year 1969 was a watershed in her life – she changed her career and changed her partner.*

watershed HIGH GROUND /ˈwɔː.tə.ʃed/ US /ˈwɑː.t̬ɚ-/ *noun* [C] SPECIALIZED an area of high ground from which water flows down to a river

the 'watershed TELEVISION *noun* [S] UK in Britain, the time in the evening, usually 9 p.m., when television programmes which are not suitable for children may start to be shown

the waterside /ðəˈwɔː.tə.saɪd/ US /-ˈwɑː.t̬ɚ-/ *noun* [S] an area of land beside a river, lake or sea: *They're building a new sports complex on the waterside.* ○ *a waterside café*

'water ,skiing *noun* [U] a sport in which you are pulled along the surface of the water by a boat, while balancing on a pair of skis

'water ,softener *noun* [C] a substance or device that removes chemicals such as CALCIUM from water

water-soluble /ˈwɔː.tə.sɒl.jə.bl̩/ US /ˈwɑː.t̬ɚ.sɑːl-/ *adj* A water-soluble substance can dissolve in water: *Are these tablets water-soluble?*

'water ,sports *plural noun* sports which take place on or in water: *Popular water sports include swimming, surfing and water-skiing.*

waterspout /ˈwɔː.tə.spaʊt/ US /ˈwɑː.t̬ɚ-/ *noun* [C] MAINLY US a TORNADO (= violently spinning column of air) filled with water which forms over the sea

'water sup,ply *noun* [C usually sing] the water that is provided and treated for a particular area

'water ,table *noun* [C usually sing] the level below the surface of the ground at which you start to find water

'water ,taxi *noun* [C] a small boat on a river or other area of water, which is operated by a person whom you pay to take you where you want to go

watertight NO WATER /ˈwɔː.tə.taɪt/ US /ˈwɑː.t̬ɚ-/ *adj* having no openings to allow the entry of water: *They're doing some repairs on the church to make the roof more watertight.*

watertight NO DOUBTS /ˈwɔː.tə.taɪt/ US /ˈwɑː.t̬ɚ-/ *adj* (of a theory, plan or agreement) formed very carefully in every detail so that there is no doubt or uncertainty: *This book is designed to be provocative rather than a watertight piece of economic analysis.*

water ˌtower *noun* [C] a device to provide water pressure by positioning a large container for water on top of a tower-like structure

water ˌvapour *noun* [U] water in the form of a gas resulting from heating water or ice

waterway /ˈwɔː.tə.weɪ/ [US] /ˈwɑː.t̬ɚ-/ *noun* [C] a narrow area of water, such as a river or canal, which ships or boats can sail along

waterwheel /ˈwɔː.tə.wiːl/ [US] /ˈwɑː.t̬ɚ-/ *noun* [C] a large wheel which is turned round by flowing water and used to provide the power for machinery

waterwings /ˈwɔː.tə.wɪŋz/ [US] /ˈwɑː.t̬ɚ-/ *plural noun* (*UK* **armband**) hollow ring-shaped pieces of plastic filled with air, which children who cannot swim wear on their arms in water to help them float

waterworks /ˈwɔː.tə.wɜːks/ [US] /ˈwɑː.t̬ɚ.wɝːks/ *plural noun* **1** a system of buildings and pipes in which a public supply of water is stored and treated and from which it is sent out **2** *UK POLITE WORD* the parts of the body that deal with the removal of urine: *The doctor asked if I'd had any problems with my waterworks.*

• **turn on the waterworks** *OLD-FASHIONED DISAPPROVING* to start crying, especially too much or in way that does not seem necessary or real: *You can turn on the waterworks all you like – I'm not going to change my mind!*

watery /ˈwɔː.tᵊr.i/ [US] /ˈwɑː.t̬ɚ.i/ *adj* ➲See at **water**.

watt /wɒt/ [US] /wɑːt/ *noun* [C] (*WRITTEN ABBREVIATION* **W**) the standard measure of electrical power: *Do you want 60-watt light bulbs for this room?* **wattage** /ˈwɒt.ɪdʒ/ [US] /ˈwɑː.t̬ɪdʒ/ *noun* [U] *For lower wattage ovens, heating time must be increased.*

wattle and daub /ˌwɒt.l̩.ᵊndˈdɔːb/ [US] /ˌwɑːt̬.l̩.ᵊndˈdɑːb/ *noun* [U] a mixture of sticks, earth and clay, which is used in some parts of the world as a building material: *The walls of timber-framed houses were often made of wattle and daub.* ○ *a wattle-and-daub hut*

wave [HAND MOVEMENT] /weɪv/ *verb* [I or T] **1** to raise your hand and move it from side to side as a way of greeting someone, telling them to do something or adding emphasis to an expression: *I waved* ***to/at*** *him from the window but he didn't see me.* ○ *I was waving my hand madly but he never once looked in my direction.* ○ *She was so annoyed she wouldn't even wave us* ***goodbye****/wave goodbye* ***to*** *us.* ○ *She waves her hands* ***about/around*** *a lot when she's talking.* **2 wave *sb* away/on, etc.** to make a movement with your hand which tells someone to move in a particular direction: *You'll have to wait till the policeman waves this line of traffic on.* ○ *You can't just wave me away as if I were a child!*

• **wave/say goodbye to *sth*** *INFORMAL HUMOROUS* to accept that you will no longer have something you value or that you will not get something you hoped to receive: *Well, if you've argued with senior management you can wave goodbye to any chances of promotion!*

wave /weɪv/ *noun* [C] when you raise your hand and move it from side to side as a way of greeting someone, etc: ***Give*** *Grandpa a wave goodbye, Alice, you won't see him till next week.*

PHRASAL VERBS WITH **wave**

▲ **wave *sth* aside** *phrasal verb* [M] to refuse to consider what someone says: *She waved aside all my objections.*

▲ **wave *sb/sth* down** *phrasal verb* [M] to make a driver stop their vehicle by waving your arms up and down: *If a car comes along, wave it down.*

▲ **wave *sb* off** *phrasal verb* [M] to wave to someone as they leave a place in order to say goodbye: *We went to the station to wave her off.*

wave [MOVE REPEATEDLY] /weɪv/ *verb* [I or T] to move from side to side, or to make something move like this while holding it in the hand: *The corn waved gently in the summer breeze.* ○ *A crowd of football fans ran down the street waving banners and scarves.* ○ *He seems to just think I can wave a magic wand and everything will be all right.*

wave [WATER] /weɪv/ *noun* [C] a raised line of water which moves across the surface of an area of water, especially the sea: *At night, I listened to the sound of the waves* ***breaking/crashing*** *against the shore.*

• **make waves** *INFORMAL* to be very active so that other people notice you, often in a way that intentionally causes trouble: *If a member of the Cabinet started making waves, the prime minister simply got rid of them.*

wave [HAIR CURVES] /weɪv/ *noun* [C] a series of slight curves in a person's hair: *Your hair has a natural wave whereas mine's just straight and boring.* ➲See also **wavy**. Compare **curl**. **wave** /weɪv/ *verb* [I or T] *If she leaves her hair to dry on its own, it just waves naturally.*

wave [ENERGY] /weɪv/ *noun* [C] the pattern in which some types of energy, such as sound, light and heat are spread or carried: *radio waves* ➲See also **brainwave**.

wave [STRONG FEELING] /weɪv/ *noun* [C] A wave of an emotion or feeling is a sudden strong feeling which gets stronger as it spreads: *A wave* ***of*** *panic swept through the crowd and people started running.*

wave [LARGE NUMBER] /weɪv/ *noun* [C] **1** an unusually large number of events of a similar, often bad, type, happening within the same period: *a crime wave* ○ *In the 1970s, the country came close to collapse as it was swept by a wave* ***of*** *strikes.* **2 a new/second, etc. wave of *sth*** an activity which is happening again or is being repeated after a pause: *A new wave of job losses is expected this year.*

• **wave after/upon wave** *LITERARY* large quantities or groups of something, one after another: *Allied planes launched wave after wave of air attacks on the city.*

waveband /ˈweɪv.bænd/ *noun* [C] a set of radio waves of similar length which are used for broadcasting radio programmes

wavelength /ˈweɪv.leŋkθ/ *noun* [C] the distance between two waves of energy, or the length of the radio wave used by a particular radio station for broadcasting programmes: *I don't know which wavelength the station is* ***on*** *– is it on long wave?*

• **be on the same wavelength** (of two or more people) to think in a similar way and to understand each other well: *I can't seem to get on with him – we're just not on the same wavelength.*

waver /ˈweɪ.vəʳ/ [US] /-vɚ/ *verb* [I] **1** to lose strength, determination or purpose, especially temporarily: *I'm afraid my concentration began to waver as lunch approached.* ○ *He has never wavered* ***in*** *his support for the leader.* **2** If you waver between two possibilities, you can not decide which of them to choose or you keep choosing one way and then the other: *"What are you having?" "Er, I'm wavering* ***between*** *the fish soup and the mushroom tart."* **wavering** /ˈweɪ.vᵊr.ɪŋ/ [US] /-vɚ-/ *adj*: *It's the party's last attempt to persuade some of the nation's wavering voters to support them.*

wavy /ˈweɪ.vi/ *adj* having a series of curves: *Sarah's got lovely wavy blond hair.* ➲See picture **Hairstyles and Hats** on page Centre 8

wax [SUBSTANCE] /wæks/ *noun* [U] **1** a solid fatty substance that softens and melts when warm: *She watched the wax as it dripped down the side of the candle.* ➲See also **beeswax**. **2** the soft yellowish substance inside your ears

wax /wæks/ *verb* [T] to put a thin layer of wax on the surface of something, either to make it waterproof or to improve its appearance: *I've waxed the floor so I'm afraid it's a bit slippery.* **waxed** /wækst/ *adj*: *a waxed jacket*

waxen /ˈwæk.sᵊn/ *adj LITERARY* describes a face that has pale shiny skin and does not look healthy: *a waxen complexion*

waxy /ˈwæk.si/ *adj* slightly shiny; looking like wax

wax [APPEAR LARGER] /wæks/ *verb* [I] *FORMAL* When the moon waxes, it gradually appears larger and rounder each day.

• **wax and wane** to grow stronger and then weaker again: *His commitment to democracy and free markets has waxed and waned with his political fortunes.*

wax [SPEAK/WRITE] /wæks/ *OLD USE OR FORMAL* **wax lyrical/eloquent, etc.** to speak or write in the stated way: *My mother, a Spaniard, always used to wax lyrical about the lemon trees in the family garden.*

ˌwaxed ˈpaper *noun* [U] a type of paper which has a thin layer of wax on it and is used for wrapping food

waxhead /ˈwæks.hed/ *noun* [C] *AUS INFORMAL* someone who SURFS on waves

waxwork /ˈwæks.wɜːk/ [US] /-wɝːk/ *noun* [C] a wax model of a person

waxworks /ˈwæks.wɜːks/ [US] /-wɝːks/ *plural noun* a place where there are a lot of wax models of famous people for the public to look at

way [ROUTE] /weɪ/ *noun* [C] **1** a route, direction or path: *Do you know the way* ***to*** *the train station?* ○ *I've only been living in Madrid for a couple of weeks so I don't really know my way* ***around*** *it yet.* ○ *We'll have to stop for fuel* ***on the*** *way to the airport.* ○ *Can you* ***find*** *your own way* ***out of*** *the building?* ○ *It's getting late – we should* ***make*** *our way* (= go) *home soon.* ○ *He* ***elbowed/pushed*** *his way* (= hit/pushed people so that he could go past them) *to the front of the crowd.* ○ *The coach stopped for us to eat lunch but within half an hour we were* ***on*** *our way/* ***under*** *way* (= travelling) *again.* ○ *There's no way* ***through*** *the centre of town in a vehicle – it's for pedestrians only.* ○ *You'll have to go* ***by*** *way* ***of*** (= travel through) *Copenhagen if you want to go to Southern Sweden from here.* ○ *Many people have* ***lost*** *their way* (= become lost) *in the forest.* ○ *Only a local person could* ***find*** *their way* ***through*** *the maze of narrow streets.* **2** **Way** used in the names of some roads: *Our offices are at 17 King's Way.* **3** used to talk about the direction in which something is facing: *"Which way does the room face?" "North."* ○ *Which way* ***up*** *should this box be* (= Which side should be on top)*?* ○ *The numbers are the wrong way* ***round*** *– it should be 71, not 17.*

• **talk your way into/out of** ***sth*** *INFORMAL* to persuade people that you should do something/not do something by the reasons you give: *He talked his way into the job.* ○ *You might be able to talk your way out of most things but you still have to clean the dishes!*

• **by the way** used to introduce a new subject for consideration or to give further information: *I think we've discussed everything we need to – by the way, what time is it?* ○ *Oh, by the way, my name's Julie.*

• **go out of** ***your*** **way** to try very hard to do something, especially for someone else: *They really went out of their way* ***to*** *make us feel welcome by giving us the best room in the house.*

• **go** ***your*** **own way** When people or groups of people choose to go their own ways, they decide to live or work without continuing their previous personal or business relationship: *After a couple of years together, we realized we weren't suited to one another and decided to go our own ways.*

• **be out of the way** If a place or a building is out of the way, it is a long distance from where most people live: *It's a very beautiful village but it's a bit out of the way.*

• **way/direction the wind blows** If a person tries to discover which way the wind blows/is blowing, they try to discover information about a situation, especially other people's opinions, before they take action: *I think I'll* ***see*** *which way the wind is blowing before I vote at the board meeting.*

• **The way to a man's heart is through his stomach.** *HUMOROUS SAYING* said to mean that a woman can gain a man's affection by cooking him good meals

COMMON LEARNER ERROR

way or **journey?**

Way refers only to the route that you take to get from one place to another.

Is there another way out of here?
I must get a paper on my way home.

To talk more generally about the length of the route or the time it takes, use the word **journey**.

a car/train/long journey

way [DISTANCE] /weɪ/ *noun* [S] (*US* **ways**) distance or a period of time: *We walked* ***a long*** *way yesterday.* ○ *The holidays seem like they're* ***a long*** *way* ***off.*** ○ *FIGURATIVE There were people of every political belief at university, ranging* ***all the*** *way from communists to fascists.*

• **give way to** ***sth*** (*ALSO* **make way for** ***sth***) to be replaced by something, especially because it is better, cheaper, easier, etc: *In some areas, modern intensive farming is giving way to the re-introduction of traditional methods.*

• **all the way to** ***sth*** as far as someone or something at a high level in a process or structure: *I'll take my complaint all the way to the managing director if I have to.*

• **be on the way to** ***sth*** to be close to doing something: *I'm* ***well*** *on the way to complet****ing*** *the report.*

• **work** ***your*** **way up/to the top** to advance in a process or structure: *He started as an office junior and worked his way up through the company to become a director.*

way [POSSIBILITY] /weɪ/ *noun* [C or U] a particular choice, opinion, belief or action, especially from among several possibilities: *I like the way you've had your hair done.* ○ ***In some/many*** *ways it would be better if we met on Monday rather than Wednesday.* ○ ***In a*** *way* (= Partly)*, I would prefer it if they didn't come because it would mean extra work.* ○ *He might have to resign or he might be demoted, but* ***either*** *way, his career is effectively over.* ○ *They don't write songs* ***the*** *way* (= as) *they used to.*

• **all the way** as much as possible or completely: *If you want to take it up with the boss, I'll support you all the way.*

• **go all the way** *INFORMAL* to have sex, especially after a period of kissing and touching: *Did you go all the way, last night?*

• **have it both ways** to benefit from two opposing things: *You* ***can't*** *have it both ways – you either work longer and get paid more or have more leisure time and get paid less.*

• **no way** *INFORMAL* **1** used to tell someone that something is impossible: *I'm sorry but* ***there's*** *no way we can help you.* ○ *No way will she agree to you leaving early.* **2** **No way!** used to say 'no' in a forceful way: *"Go on, lend me your bike." "No way!"*

• **wouldn't have it any other way** If a person says they wouldn't have something any other way, they mean they would not change any of it, especially despite connected difficulties: *It's never going to be easy having kids but I wouldn't have it any other way.*

way [WANT] /weɪ/ *noun* [S] *INFORMAL* If someone gets or has their way, what they want happens: *If she doesn't* ***get/ have*** *her* ***(own)*** *way, she sulks like a four-year old.*

• **go** ***your*** **own (sweet) way** to do what you want without considering other people: *It doesn't matter how much good advice I give Cathy, she always goes her own sweet way.*

way [MANNER] /weɪ/ *noun* [S] the manner in which someone behaves or thinks, or in which something happens: *Don't be alarmed – it's just his way.* ○ *He looked at me* ***in*** *a sinister way.* ○ ***It's*** *amazing* ***the*** *way she manages to stay so calm.* ○ *The way he was shouting, you'd have thought he was badly hurt.* ○ ***To*** *my way of thinking, they shouldn't be building so many roads.* ○ *It's* ***always the*** *way at work – either I've got nothing to do or I'm rushed off my feet!*

ways /weɪz/ *plural noun* types of behaviour: *Over the years we've got used to his funny little ways.*

• **way of life** the manner in which a person lives: *Sleeping in doorways, begging for food and money – it's not a very enviable way of life.*

way [METHOD] /weɪ/ *noun* [C] an action that can produce the result you want; a method: *There are many ways* ***of*** *solv****ing*** *the problem.* ○ [+ **to** infinitive] *That's not the way* ***to*** *do it – let me show you.* ○ *That method hasn't worked, so let's try your way.*

• **by way of** as a type of: *He sent me some flowers by way of an apology.*

• **find a way** to discover how to achieve or deal with something: *Finding a way* ***through*** *the legislation is impossible without expert advice.*

• **point the way** to show how something can be done better in the future: *Recent medical discoveries are already pointing the way* ***to*** *more efficient vaccines.*

• **ways and means** The ways and means of achieving something are the methods and other things needed to make it happen: *With computer technology, even people working on their own have the ways and means to produce professional-looking documents.*

COMMON LEARNER ERROR

way or **method/means of**?

Way in this sense is used on its own or followed by the structures + to do [something] or of + -ing.

You can travel there in a number of ways.
What's the best way of travelling there?
What's the best way to travel there?

Use **method of** or **means of** before a noun.

What method of transport do you use?
We had no means of communication.

way FREE SPACE /weɪ/ noun [S] the space needed for a particular movement or action: *"Sorry, am I in your way? I'll move."* ○ *I couldn't see the stage because there was a pillar in the way* (= between me and the stage). ○ *Please make way so the ambulance can get by.* ○ *The best thing you can do if you're near to a tornado is get out of its way.* ○ FIGURATIVE *She's determined to succeed and she won't let anything get/stand in her way* (= prevent her).

way CONDITION /weɪ/ noun [S] the bad condition or state of someone or something, especially the state of a person's health: *He's been in a bad way* (= very ill) *ever since the operation.*

way EMPHASIS /weɪ/ adv INFORMAL used to emphasize degree or separation, especially in space or time: *After the third lap, she was way behind the other runners.* ○ *She spends way too much money on clothes.*

way PLACE /weɪ/ adv SLIGHTLY OLD-FASHIONED in the direction of: *I think they live Birmingham way.*

waylay /ˌweɪˈleɪ/ verb [T] **waylaid**, **waylaid** to wait for and then stop someone, especially either to attack them or talk to them: *A man on his way to deposit $120 000 in a bank was waylaid by two men who punched him and snatched his bag yesterday.* ○ *I meant to leave earlier but I was waylaid on the way out of a meeting by my manager.*

way-out /ˌweɪˈaʊt/ adj OLD-FASHIONED INFORMAL unusual, especially because very modern in style: *A lot of experimental theatre is too way-out for me.*

ways DISTANCE /weɪz/ noun [U] US FOR **way** DISTANCE

-ways MANNER /-weɪz/ suffix (used in adverbs) in the stated direction or manner: *edgeways* ○ *lengthways*

wayside /ˈweɪsaɪd/ noun **fall by the wayside** ⊃See at **fall** ACCIDENT.

'way ˌstation noun [C] US a place where people can stop when travelling from one place to another

wayward /ˈweɪwəd/ ⑩ /-wəd/ adj OLD-FASHIONED (especially of a person's behaviour) changeable, selfish and difficult to control **waywardness** /ˈweɪwədnəs/ ⑩ /-wəd-/ noun [U]

WC /ˌdʌb.l.juːˈsiː/ noun [C] UK ABBREVIATION FOR water closet: a toilet, or a room containing a toilet: *The wooden staircase leads to three bedrooms, the bathroom, and a separate WC.* ✳ NOTE: This word is usually used on signs in public places or in advertisements.

we GROUP STRONG /wiː/, WEAK /wɪ/ pronoun **1** (used as the subject of a verb) the speaker and at least one other person when considered together or as a group: *Can we all go to the swimming pool this afternoon?* ○ *If you don't hurry up, we'll be late.* **2** used by a speaker or a writer to refer to the listener(s) or reader and the person speaking or writing: *Perhaps we could move on to discuss the next item on the agenda.*

we ALL PEOPLE STRONG /wiː/, WEAK /wɪ/ pronoun (used as the subject of a verb) all people, especially when considered as a group: *This planet on which we all live should be cherished and not exploited.*

we YOU STRONG /wiː/, WEAK /wɪ/ pronoun INFORMAL (used as the subject of a verb, when talking to children or ill people) you: *Now we don't want to be late for school, do we?* ○ *"How are we this morning Mrs Flanagan?" said the doctor.*

we I STRONG /wiː/, WEAK /wɪ/ pronoun FORMAL (used by a queen or king when speaking officially) I

weak NOT STRONG /wiːk/ adj **1** not strong; not strong enough to work, last, succeed, persuade or be effective: *It's*

not surprising you feel weak if you haven't eaten properly for days. ○ *The electromagnetic field strength becomes weaker as you move further away from high voltage cables.* ○ *He was a weak king surrounded by corrupt advisers.* ○ *Any evidence that exists to support the hypothesis is fairly weak.* ○ *He gave the weakest of excuses when asked why he was late.* **2** describes a drink that contains a lot of water compared to its other contents, so that it does not have a strong flavour: *I can't stand weak coffee/tea.*

● **weak at the knees** If you go weak at the knees, you lose your strength and feel you are going to fall over, usually because of seeing or talking about either someone you are very attracted to or because of something unpleasant or frightening: *The thought of kissing him made me go weak at the knees.*

weaken /ˈwiː.kᵊn/ verb [I or T] to (cause to) become less strong, powerful or determined: *You could see the poor dog weakening daily as the disease spread through its body.* ○ *Another defeat in parliament would seriously weaken the president's ability to govern.* ○ *We know that prolonged exposure to vibration can weaken aircraft components.* ○ *She's weakening – ask her some more questions and see if she confesses.* **weakly** /ˈwiː.kli/ adv: *"The pain seems to have eased a little with these new tablets," he said weakly.*

weakness /ˈwiːk.nəs/ noun **1** [U] when someone or something is not strong or powerful: *Any change of policy will be interpreted as a sign of weakness.* **2** [C] a particular part or quality of someone or something that is not good or effective: *There are definite weaknesses in their security arrangements.* ○ *His main weakness as a manager is his inability to delegate.* **3** **weakness for** a strong liking, usually for something which might have unpleasant or unwanted effects: *My diet would be fine if only I didn't have this weakness for sweet things.*

weak BELOW STANDARD /wiːk/ adj below standard; not good enough, especially in ability, skill or quality: *He was always weak at/in languages but strong at/in science.* ○ *Our quiz team is a bit weak on sport.* ○ *In the end I think the film was spoilt by a weak story line.* **weakness** /ˈwiːk.nəs/ noun [C] *The later novels show none of the weaknesses of his earlier work.*

the ˈweaker ˌsex noun [U] used to refer to women in general: considered offensive by many people

weak-kneed /ˌwiːkˈniːd/ adj [after v] **1** INFORMAL DISAPPROVING not brave or determined enough to defend your beliefs against others: *Instead of defending traditional values, the church frequently seems weak-kneed and irresolute.* **2** made to feel weak and likely to fall by emotion: *She stood dazed and weak-kneed beside the coffin.*

weakling /ˈwiːk.lɪŋ/ noun [C] DISAPPROVING someone who is weak, either physically or in character: *It would need more than a few exercises to turn a seven-stone weakling into a heavyweight boxer.*

weak ˈlink noun [C usually sing] a weak part, especially the weakest part of something: *They're a fairly good team – their only weak link is a relatively inexperienced goalkeeper.* ○ *A chain can only be as strong as its weakest link, so we must look at the least committed country to see if the alliance will hold.*

weak-minded /ˌwiːkˈmaɪn.dɪd/ adj lacking determination or stupid

weak ˌspot noun [C] a weak part in something: *Targeting the opponent's weak spots is a typical technique in politics.*

weak-willed /ˌwiːkˈwɪld/ adj lacking the determination that is needed to continue with a difficult course of action: *My diets are never successful – I'm just too weak-willed.*

weal /wiːl/ noun [C] a raised mark on the skin caused by being hit or injured in some other way: *His back was covered with weals where he had been repeatedly beaten.*

wealth MONEY /welθ/ noun [U] a large amount of money or valuable possessions that someone has: *During a successful business career, she accumulated a great amount of wealth.*

wealthy /ˈwel.θi/ *adj* rich: *He's a very wealthy man.* ○ *With their natural resources, they are potentially a very wealthy country.*
the wealthy *plural noun* rich people

wealth [LARGE AMOUNT] /welθ/ *noun* **[S]** a large amount of something good: *Jim has* ***a*** *wealth* ***of*** *teaching experience.* ○ *Russia has* ***a*** *wealth* ***of*** *coal and timber.*

wean /wiːn/ *verb* **[T]** to cause a baby or young animal to stop feeding on its mother's milk and to start eating other food, especially solid food, instead: *The studies were carried out on calves that had been weaned at 5 weeks of age.* **weaning** /ˈwiː.nɪŋ/ *noun* **[U]** *A lot of mothers find early weaning from breast milk more convenient.*

PHRASAL VERBS WITH **wean**

▲ **wean *sb* off *sth*** *phrasal verb* (*US ALSO* **wean *sb* from *sth***) to make someone gradually stop using something that is bad for them: *It's difficult to wean an addict off cocaine once they're hooked.* ○ *The whole scheme is intended to wean people off welfare dependency.*
▲ **wean *sb* on *sth/sb*** *phrasal verb* **[usually passive]** If someone is weaned on something or someone, they have learned about and been influenced by them when they were young: *This generation has been weaned on computer games.*

weapon /ˈwep.ən/ *noun* **[C]** any object used in fighting or war, such as a gun, bomb, sword, etc: *a lethal weapon* ○ *chemical/nuclear/biological weapons* ○ *The youths were dragged from their car and searched for weapons.*
• **weapons of mass destruction** weapons that can kill thousands or millions of pople over a large area
weaponry /ˈwep.ən.ri/ *noun* **[U]** weapons in general: *nuclear/conventional weaponry* ○ *All hi-tech weaponry demands frequent servicing to ensure accuracy.*

wear [ON BODY] /weəʳ/ [US] /wer/ *verb* **[T] wore, worn 1** to have clothing, jewellery, etc. on your body: *Tracey is wearing a simple black dress.* ○ *What are you wearing* ***to*** *Caroline's wedding?* ○ *Some musicians don't like to wear rings when they're playing.* ○ *He wears glasses for reading.* ○ *She wears very little makeup.* **2** to show a particular emotion on your face: *The minister wore a confident smile throughout the interview.* **3** to arrange your hair in a particular way: *When she's working she wears her hair* ***in*** *a ponytail.* ○ *You should wear your hair* ***up*** (= so that it does not hang down) *more often – it suits you.*
• **wear *your* heart on *your* sleeve** to make your feelings and emotions obvious rather than hiding them
• **wear the trousers** (*US* **wear the pants**) *INFORMAL* (especially of a woman) to be the person in a relationship who is in control and who makes decisions for both people: *Brian may seem bossy, but I'll tell you it's Lisa that really wears the trousers in that relationship.*
wearable /ˈweə.rə.bl̩/ [US] /ˈwer.ə-/ *adj* Clothes that are wearable are easy to wear because they are comfortable, acceptable in most social situations and look attractive in combination with other clothes: *Unlike a lot of women's fashion magazines, it features clothes that are both affordable and wearable.*
wearer /ˈweə.rəʳ/ [US] /ˈwer.ɚ/ *noun* **[C]** the person wearing something: *In medieval times the sapphire was believed to offer protection to its wearer.* ○ *Clothes, of course, say a lot about the wearer.*

wear [CLOTHES] /weəʳ/ [US] /wer/ *noun* **[U]** (*ALSO* **-wear**) clothes suitable for a particular use or clothes of a particular type: *casual wear* ○ *leisure wear* ○ *knitwear*

wear [WEAKEN] /weəʳ/ [US] /wer/ *verb* **[I] wore, worn** to become weaker, damaged or thinner because of continuous use: *I'm very fond of this shirt but it's starting to wear at the collar.* ○ *The wheel bearings have worn over the years, which is what's causing the noise.*
• **wear thin** *INFORMAL* If something such as a joke wears thin, it becomes boring or annoying or stops being amusing or effective, because it has been seen, heard or used too much: *"Tony, the joke is beginning to wear thin now and a lot of us have had enough."* ○ *Her standard excuse for being late was beginning to wear thin.*
wear /weəʳ/ [US] /wer/ *noun* **[U]** the amount or type of use an item has had or can be expected to have, especially before showing damage: *I've had a lot of wear* ***out of*** *these boots – I've had them for five years.* ○ *I've only worn the shirt a couple of times and it's already showing* ***signs of*** *wear* (= damage).

wear [MAKE A HOLE] /weəʳ/ [US] /wer/ *verb* **[T usually + adv or prep] wore, worn** to produce something such as a hole or loss of material by continuous use, rubbing or movement: *I always seem to wear* ***a hole*** *in the left elbow of my sweaters.* ○ *Over many years, flowing water wore deep grooves* ***into*** *the rock.* ○ *Wind and water slowly wore* ***down*** *the mountain's jagged edges.*

wear [PERMIT] /weəʳ/ [US] /wer/ *verb* **[T] wore, worn** *UK OLD-FASHIONED INFORMAL* to permit or accept something: *I'd ask my boss for some time off but I don't think she'd wear* ***it.*** * NOTE: This is usually used in questions and negatives.

PHRASAL VERBS WITH **wear**

▲ **wear *(sth)* away** *phrasal verb* **[M]** to become thin and disappear after repeated use or rubbing, or to cause something to become thin and disappear in this way: *In some diseases, the protective layer in a joint wears away.*
▲ **wear *sb* down** *phrasal verb* **[M]** to make someone feel tired and less able to deal successfully with a situation: *Both sides are trying to wear the other down by being obstinate in the negotiations.* ○ *All the stress and extra travel is beginning to wear him down.*
▲ **wear off** *phrasal verb* If a feeling or the effect of something wears off, it gradually disappears: *Most patients find that the numbness from the injection wears off after about an hour.*
▲ **wear on** *phrasal verb* If a period of time wears on, it seems to pass very slowly: *She felt less confident about completing the course as the week wore on.*
▲ **wear *sb* out** [TIRE] *phrasal verb* **[M]** to make someone extremely tired: *Walking around a museum all day really wears you out.*
▲ **wear *(sth)* out** [DAMAGE] *phrasal verb* **[M]** to use something so much that it is damaged and cannot be used any more, or to become damaged in this way: *Moving parts in engines wear out much more quickly than stationary parts.*

ˌwear and ˈtear *noun* **[U]** the damage which happens to an object in ordinary use during a period: *Seat covers on trains* ***take*** *a lot of wear and tear.*
wearing /ˈweə.rɪŋ/ [US] /ˈwer.ɪŋ/ *adj* tiring: *Looking after three children all day is very wearing.*
wearisome /ˈwɪə.rɪ.sᵊm/ [US] /ˈwɪr.ɪ-/ *adj FORMAL* causing a person to be tired and/or bored: *Simple repetitive tasks can be very wearisome.*

weary /ˈwɪə.ri/ [US] /ˈwɪr.i/ *adj* **1** very tired, especially after working hard for a long time: *I think he's a little weary after his long journey.* ○ *Here, sit down and rest your weary legs.* **2 weary of** bored with something because you have experienced too much of it: *I've been going out with the same people to the same clubs for years and I've just* ***grown*** *weary of it.*
weary /ˈwɪə.ri/ [US] /ˈwɪr.i/ *verb FORMAL* **1 [T]** to make someone feel tired: *Children weary me all day with their constant inquiries and demands.* **2 [I]** to start to feel that something or someone is boring: *Some people never seem to weary* ***of*** *eating the same type of food every day.*
wearily /ˈwɪə.rɪ.li/ [US] /ˈwɪr.ɪ-/ *adv*: *I dragged myself wearily out of bed at five o'clock this morning.* **weariness** /ˈwɪə.rɪ.nəs/ [US] /ˈwɪr.ɪ-/ *noun* **[U]**
wearying /ˈwɪə.ri.ɪŋ/ [US] /ˈwɪr.i-/ *adj* tiring: *a long wearying journey*

weasel /ˈwiː.zᵊl/ *noun* **[C]** a small mammal with reddish brown fur and a long body, which can kill other small animals such as mice and birds for food

weasel /ˈwiː.zᵊl/ *verb*
▲ **weasel out of *sth*** *phrasal verb MAINLY US INFORMAL* to avoid doing something that you have agreed to do, especially by being dishonest: *Although they had signed the contract they tried to weasel out of the deal later.*

ˈweasel ˌwords *plural noun INFORMAL* something that someone says either to avoid answering a question clearly or to make someone believe something that is not true

weather [AIR CONDITIONS] /ˈweð.əʳ/ [US] /-ɚ/ *noun* [U] the conditions in the air above the Earth such as wind, rain or temperature, especially at a particular time over a particular area: *bad/good/cold/dry/hot/stormy/warm/wet/etc. weather* ○ *The weather in the hills can change very quickly, so take suitable clothing.* ○ *We're going to have a picnic, weather* ***permitting*** (= if the weather is good enough).
• **in all weathers** If something is done in all weathers, it is done in every type of weather: *He's a real enthusiast – he goes fishing in all weathers.*
• **be/feel under the weather** *INFORMAL* to be or feel ill: *I'm feeling a bit under the weather – I think I've caught a cold.*
weather /ˈweð.əʳ/ [US] /-ɚ/ *verb* [I or T] to change in colour or form over a period of time because of the effects of sun, wind or other weather conditions: *Rock is weathered by the action of ice and changes in temperature.* ○ *The paint on the outside walls has weathered* ***badly*** (= has changed and been damaged by the weather). **weathered** /ˈweð.əd/ [US] /-ɚd/ *adj*: *weathered stone/tiles*

weather [DEAL WITH] /ˈweð.əʳ/ [US] /-ɚ/ *verb* [T] to deal successfully with a difficult situation or a problem: *As a small new company they did well to weather the recession.*
• **weather the storm** If someone or something weathers the storm, they successfully deal with a very difficult problem: *In the next few days we shall see if the ambassador can weather the political storm caused by his ill-advised remarks.*

weather-beaten /ˈweðəˌbiː.tᵊn/ [US] /-ɚˌbiː.t̬ᵊn/ *adj* describes something, such as skin or a building material, that has been marked or damaged by the weather: *a weather-beaten face* (= a face which is brown and has many deep lines) ○ *ancient weather-beaten columns*

weatherboarding /ˈweð.əˌbɔː.dɪŋ/ [US] /-ɚˌbɔːr-/ *noun* [U] a set of boards fixed across the bottom of a door to stop water from entering a building

weathercock /ˈweð.ə.kɒk/ [US] /-ɚ.kɑːk/ *noun* [C] a type of WEATHER VANE (= device for showing which way the wind is blowing) in the shape of a chicken

ˈweather ˌforecast *noun* [C] a statement of what the weather is likely to be for the next day or few days, usually broadcast on television or radio or printed in a newspaper
ˈweather ˌforecaster *noun* [C] **1** someone who scientifically studies weather conditions and says what the weather is likely to be in the future **2** a **weatherman** or **weathergirl**

weathergirl, **weather girl** /ˈweð.ə.gɜːl/ [US] /-ɚ.gɝːl/ *noun* [C] *INFORMAL* a woman on a television or radio programme who gives a WEATHER FORECAST

weatherman, **weather man** /ˈweð.ə.mæn/ [US] /-ɚ-/ *noun* [C] a man on a television or radio programme who gives a WEATHER FORECAST

weatherproof /ˈweð.ə.pruːf/ [US] /-ɚ-/ *adj* not allowing wind or rain to go through: *a weatherproof tent/coat* ➲Compare **waterproof**.

ˈweather ˌstation *noun* [C] a building or place where information is gathered about local weather conditions

ˈweather ˌvane *noun* [C] a pointer with a flat blade at one end which is put on top of a high building and turns round in the wind to show which way it is blowing from

weave [MAKE CLOTH] /wiːv/ *verb* [I or T] **wove** or *US ALSO* **weaved, woven** or *US ALSO* **weaved** to make cloth by repeatedly crossing a single thread through two sets of long threads on a LOOM (= special frame): *This type of wool is woven* ***into*** *fabric which will make jackets.*
weave /wiːv/ *noun* [C usually sing] the way in which cloth has been woven, for example with the threads pulled firmly together, or the pattern produced by this process: *a tight weave* ○ *a striped/traditional weave* **weaver** /ˈwiː.vəʳ/ [US] /-vɚ/ *noun* [C] *Textile weavers receive low wages in the rural areas.* **weaving** /ˈwiː.vɪŋ/ *noun* [U] *There has been increasing automation of spinning and weaving.*

weave [TWIST] /wiːv/ *verb* [T] **wove** or *US ALSO* **weaved, woven** or *US ALSO* **weaved 1** to twist long objects together, or to make something by doing this: *We were shown how to roughly weave ferns and grass* ***together*** *to make a temporary shelter.* ○ *It takes great skill to weave a basket* ***from/out of*** *rushes.* **2** *LITERARY* to form something from several different things or to combine several different things, in a complicated or skilled way: *The biography is woven* ***from*** *the many accounts which exist of things she did.* **weaver** /ˈwiː.vəʳ/ [US] /-vɚ/ *noun* [C] *basket weavers* **weaving** /ˈwiː.vɪŋ/ *noun* [U]

weave [MOVE QUICKLY] /wiːv/ *verb* [I usually + adv or prep] **weaved, weaved** to go or make a path by moving quickly and changing direction often, especially to avoid hitting things: *To escape from police officers he weaved* ***through/between/in and out of*** *stationary traffic on a bicycle.*
• **get weaving** *UK OLD-FASHIONED INFORMAL* If you tell someone to get weaving, you either want them to start something or to hurry what they are doing: *We'd better get weaving – we've got a lot to do today.*

web [NET] /web/ *noun* [C] a fixed net used to catch insects, which is made by a spider from the sticky thread that its body produces: *a spider's web* ○ *We watched a spider* ***spin*** *a web between three tall grass stems.* ○ *FIGURATIVE Those involved in the fraud created an* ***intricate*** *web of trading companies to hide their activities.* ➲See also **cobweb**.

web [SKIN] /web/ *noun* [C] the skin connecting the toes of some birds and other animals living by or on water which helps them when swimming **webbed** /webd/ *adj*: *webbed toes/feet*

the Web [INTERNET] *noun* [S] the system of connected documents on the Internet, which often contain colour pictures, video and sound, and which can be searched for information about a particular subject: *Jane's been* ***surfing*** *the Web all morning.*

webbing /ˈweb.ɪŋ/ *noun* [U] fibre woven into strong strips, used to make belts and straps and to support springs in furniture

ˈweb ˌbrowser, **browser** *noun* [C] a computer program that enables you to read information on the Internet

web cam, **webcam** /ˈweb.kæm/ *noun* [C] a camera which records moving pictures and sound and allows these to be broadcast on the Internet as they happen ➲See picture **In the Office** on page Centre 15

webcast /ˈweb.kɑːst/ [US] /-kæst/ *noun* [C] a broadcast made on the Internet: *Click here to join our live webcast Current Consumer Issues.*

ˈweb ˌdesigner *noun* [C] a person who designs WEB SITES

web-footed /ˌwebˈfʊtɪd/ [US] /-ˌfʊt̬-/ *adj* (*ALSO* **web-toed**) (of an animal) having feet with webs

webmaster /ˈwebˌmɑː.stəʳ/ [US] /-ˌmæs.tɚ/ *noun* [C] a person who is responsible for creating a WEBSITE and making certain that it contains the most recent information and is working properly: *If you have any problems with this site, contact the webmaster.*

web page, **webpage** /ˈweb.peɪdʒ/ *noun* [C] (*ALSO* **page**) a page of information on the Internet about a particular subject, that forms (a part of) a WEB SITE: *A website may have many different web pages for you to click on and explore.*

website, **web site** /ˈweb.saɪt/ *noun* [C] (*ALSO* **site**) a set of pages of information on the Internet about a particular subject, which have been published by the same person or organization, and often contain colour pictures, video and sound: *For more information about other Cambridge titles,* ***visit*** *our website* ***at*** *www.cambridge.org*

wed /wed/ *verb* [I or T] **wed, wedded** or **wed, wedded** or **wed** *LITERARY* (used especially in newspapers) to marry someone: *The couple eventually wed after an eighteen year engagement.* ➲See also **newlywed**. **wedded** /ˈwed.ɪd/ *adj* [before n] *your lawful wedded husband/wife* ○ *Elaine and Ian have been living in wedded* ***bliss*** *for almost half a year now.* ➲See also **wedded**.

we'd *STRONG* /wiːd/, *WEAK* /wid/ *short form of* **1** we had: *We'd better be more careful in the future.* **2** we would: *We'd be grateful for an answer.*

Wed *WRITTEN ABBREVIATION FOR* **Wednesday**

wedded /ˈwed.ɪd/ *adj* **wedded to** believing firmly in an idea or theory and unwilling to change that belief: *The Social Democrats are still wedded to the concepts of high taxation and regulation.*

wedding /ˈwed.ɪŋ/ *noun* [C] a marriage ceremony and any celebrations such as a meal or a party which follow it: *a wedding cake/dress/invitation/present/reception* ○ *Do you know the date of Caroline and Matthew's wedding?* ○ *It was their twenty-fifth wedding anniversary last week.*

ˈwedding ˌband *noun* [C] a **wedding ring**

ˈwedding ˌlist *noun* [C usually sing] a record of all the items which two people who are soon to be married would like to receive as presents, often kept at a particular shop

ˈwedding reˌception *noun* [C] (*ALSO* **reception**) a partyto celebrate the marriage ceremony of two people: *The wedding will be held at St Martin's Church and the wedding reception at Crathorne Hotel.*

ˈwedding ˌring *noun* [C] (*US ALSO* **wedding band**) a ring, usually made of gold, worn by a person to show that they are married

wedge /wedʒ/ *noun* [C] **1** a piece of metal, wood, rubber, etc. with a pointed edge at one end and a wide edge at the other, which is either pushed between two objects to keep them still or forced into something to break pieces off it: *Push a wedge under the door to keep it open while we're carrying the boxes in.* ○ *Pieces of stone can be split off by forcing wedges* ***between*** *the layers.* **2** a triangular-shaped piece, especially of food: *Auntie Ann put a huge wedge of fruit cake on my plate.* ○ *a wedge of cheese*

wedge /wedʒ/ *verb* [T] [+ adj] *Find something to wedge the window* ***open/closed*** *with.* ○ *I was standing waiting for a bus, wedged* ***between*** (= fixed between and unable to move away from) *two old ladies and their bags of shopping.*

wedlock /ˈwed.lɒk/ [US] /-lɑːk/ *noun* [U] *OLD USE OR HUMOROUS* the state of being married

Wednesday /ˈwenz.deɪ/ *noun* [C or U] (*WRITTEN ABBREVIATION* **Wed**) the day of the week after Tuesday and before Thursday: *Did you say the meeting is* ***on*** *Wednesday?* ○ *The restaurant is always closed* ***on*** *Wednesdays.* ○ *Wednesday would be a good day for us to go running.*

wee [SMALL] /wiː/ *adj* [before n] *SCOTTISH ENGLISH OR INFORMAL* small; little: *There's a wee cottage inside the grounds.* ○ *Would you care for a wee* ***bit*** *more to eat?*

wee [URINATE] /wiː/ *verb* [I] (*ALSO* **wee-wee**) *INFORMAL OR CHILD'S WORD* to urinate: *Daddy, I want to wee!* **wee** /wiː/ *noun* **1** [C usually sing] (*ALSO* **wee-wee**) *INFORMAL* *"God, I need a wee!" she said.* ○ *CHILD'S WORD* *Do you* ***need/want (to do) a*** *wee-wee before we go out?* **2** [U] urine

weed [PLANT] /wiːd/ *noun* **1** [C] any wild plant which grows in an unwanted place, especially in a garden or field where it prevents the cultivated plants from growing freely **2** [U] *OLD-FASHIONED SLANG* **cannabis** **3** [U] *UK OLD-FASHIONED INFORMAL* **tobacco**

weed /wiːd/ *verb* [I or T] to remove wild plants from a place where they are unwanted: *I've been weeding (the vegetable garden).* **weeding** /ˈwiː.dɪŋ/ *noun* [U] *There's plenty of weeding to* ***do*** *now that the growing season's started.* **weedy** /ˈwiː.di/ *adj*: *a weedy pavement*

weed [PERSON] /wiːd/ *noun* [C] *UK INFORMAL DISAPPROVING* someone who is thin and physically weak or who is weak in character: *He looks like a real weed in those shorts.*

▲ **weed *sth/sb* out** *phrasal verb* [M] to get rid of unwanted things or people from a group: *The first round of interviews only really serves to weed out the very weakest of applicants.*

weedkiller /ˈwiːdˌkɪl.əʳ/ [US] /-ɚ/ *noun* [C or U] (a) chemical used for killing weeds

ˈWeed ˌWhacker *US TRADEMARK noun* [C] (*UK TRADEMARK* **Strimmer**) an electric tool that is held in the hand and is used for cutting grass in places that are difficult to reach

weedy /ˈwiː.di/ *adj UK INFORMAL DISAPPROVING* describes a person who is thin and physically weak: *a weedy child*

week /wiːk/ *noun* [C] **1** a period of seven days, especially either from Monday to Sunday or from Sunday to Saturday: *last/this/next week* ○ *We go to the cinema about once a week.* ○ *Will you be going to next week's class?* ○ *It usually takes about four weeks to get the forms processed.* ○ *Don't do anything strenuous for a week* ***or two.*** ○ *It'll be weeks* (= several weeks) *before the flood damage is cleared up.* **2** the five days from Monday to Friday, which are the usual working period for many people: *We're usually too tired to do much socializing during the week.* **3** one week after the day mentioned: *The first performance of the play is a week* ***today/tomorrow.*** ○ *Our holiday starts a week* ***on*** *Saturday.* ○ *She has to go back to see the doctor Friday week.* **4** one week before the day mentioned: *The problems with the TV started a week* ***last*** *Monday.* ○ *It was his birthday a week* ***ago this*** *Friday.* **5** the amount of hours spent working during a week or the number of days on which a person works: *A lot of farm labourers* ***work*** *a six-day week.*

• **week by week** each week during a period of time: *We could see his health deteriorate week by week.*

• **of the week** A thing or person of the week is one that has been chosen as the best in a particular week: *Book of the Week: Dog Breeds by A J Barker and H A Barker.*

• **week after week** (*ALSO* **week in, week out**) regularly or continuously for many weeks: *I go to aerobics three times a week, week in, week out.*

weekly /ˈwiː.kli/ *adj, adv* happening once a week or every week: *a weekly magazine/report* ○ *a twice-weekly meeting* ○ *The fire alarm has a weekly test/is tested weekly.*

weekly /ˈwiː.kli/ *noun* [C] a newspaper or magazine which is published once every week

weekday /ˈwiːk.deɪ/ *noun* [C] any day of the week except Sunday and usually Saturday: *On weekdays I'm usually in bed by ten o'clock.*

weekend /ˌwiːkˈend/ /ˈ--/ *noun* [C] **1** Saturday and Sunday, or Friday evening until Sunday night; the part of the week in which many people living in the West do not go to work: *Have you got anything planned for* ***the*** *weekend?* ○ *This/Next weekend we're going to see some friends.* **2** a holiday or a visit taken at a weekend: *How much would a weekend for two in Amsterdam cost?* ○ *They've got a weekend cottage in Sussex.*

• **at the weekend** *UK* (*US* **on the weekend**) on Saturday or Sunday, or on both Saturday and Sunday: *What did you do at the weekend?* ○ *We go out once in a while after work and on the weekend.*

• **at weekends** *UK* (*US* **on (the) weekends**) between Friday evening and Sunday night, or on Saturdays and Sundays: *They usually go windsurfing at weekends.*

weeknight /ˈwiːk.naɪt/ *noun* [C] the evening or night of any day of the week except Sunday and usually Saturday

weeny /ˈwiː.ni/ *adj INFORMAL* extremely small: *All right, I'll have a slice of cake then – but just a weeny bit.*

weep [CRY] /wiːp/ *verb* [I or T] **wept, wept** *LITERARY* to cry tears: *People in the street wept* ***with*** *joy when peace was announced.* ○ *She wept* ***buckets*** (= cried a lot) *when Paul left.* **weep** /wiːp/ *noun* [S] *It might help you to* ***have a*** *good weep.*

weepy /ˈwiː.pi/ *adj* sad and likely to cry: *I'd just waved Peter off at the airport and was feeling a bit weepy.*

weepy, weepie /ˈwiː.pi/ *noun* [C] *INFORMAL* a film or a book which makes people want to cry because it is sad: *If I were you, I'd take some tissues to the cinema – it's a real weepy.*

weep [INJURY] /wiːp/ *verb* [I] **wept, wept** (of an injury) to produce liquid such as pus: *The sore is still weeping a lot so you'll have to change the dressing once a day.*

weeping willow /ˌwiː.pɪŋˈwɪl.əʊ/ [US] /-oʊ/ *noun* [C] a type of WILLOW tree that has long, thin branches which hang down

weevil /ˈwiː.vᵊl/ *noun* [C] any of various beetles which destroy crops such as grains and cotton

the weft /ðəˈweft/ *noun* [S] *SPECIALIZED* the threads that go across the length of a piece of cloth or a LOOM (= special frame for weaving) ⮌Compare **the warp** THREADS.

weigh [HEAVINESS] /weɪ/ *verb* [L only + n; T] to have a heaviness of a stated amount, or to measure the heaviness of an object: *Yesterday a satellite weighing 15 tonnes was*

W

successfully placed in orbit. ○ [R] *She weighs herself every week on the scales in the bathroom.* ○ *Your luggage must be weighed before it is put on the aircraft.*
• **weigh a ton** *INFORMAL* to be very heavy: *What on earth have you got in this bag, Elaine? It weighs a ton!*
weight /weɪt/ *noun* **1** [C or U] the amount that something or someone weighs: *What weight can this lorry safely carry?* ○ *There was a slight decrease **in** his weight after a week of dieting.* **2** [C] a piece of metal of known heaviness which can be used to measure the heaviness of other objects **3** [C] any object which is heavy: *Try not to lift heavy weights.* ○ *I lift weights twice a week at the gym.*
• **be/take a weight off *your* mind** to enable you to stop worrying about a particular thing: *It's a great weight off my mind **to** know that the building is finally finished.* ○ *It was a weight off my mind know**ing** that our finances were taken care of.*
• **take the weight off *your* feet/legs** If you take the weight off your feet/legs, you sit down, especially after standing or walking for a long time: *You must be exhausted after all that shopping – why don't you take the weight off your feet!*
weight /weɪt/ *verb* [T] to attach something heavy to something: *Paper tablecloths need to be weighted **down** or they tend to blow away in the wind.*
weighty /ˈweɪ.ti/ [US] /-t̬i/ *adj* heavy: *I don't want to carry this bag around all afternoon – it's quite weighty.*

weigh [INFLUENCE] /weɪ/ *verb* [I usually + adv or prep] (of something such as a fact or an event) to have an influence or be important: *Easy access to a railway network weighed heavily **with** us when we chose a site for the new factory.*
weight /weɪt/ *noun* [U] respect, influence, trust or importance: *Her experience does give her opinions quite a bit of weight.* ○ *After he was voted out of power, few people **attached** much weight **to** what he said.* ○ *Radical views don't **carry** much weight anymore.*
weighted /ˈweɪ.tɪd/ [US] /-t̬ɪd/ prepared and structured in a way that is likely to produce a particular effect, usually an advantage, rather than any other: *The system of benefits is weighted **in favour of** those who have children.*
weighty /ˈweɪ.ti/ [US] /-t̬i/ *adj* describes a subject, book or piece of work that is important or serious: *weighty matters/issues*

weigh [CONSIDER] /weɪ/ *verb* [T] to carefully consider, especially by comparing facts or possibilities, in order to make a decision: *Only when we have weighed all the factors involved can we decide when would be the best time to start.* ○ *Economic benefits must be carefully weighed **against** the possible dangers of handling radioactive waste.* ➲Compare **outweigh**.
• **weigh *your* words** (*ALSO* **weigh each word**) to carefully think about everything you are going to say before you say it: *He gave evidence to the court, weighing each word as he spoke.*

weigh [SHIP] /weɪ/ *verb* **weigh anchor** to lift the ANCHOR (= a heavy metal object) of a ship from under the water so that it can move freely

PHRASAL VERBS WITH **weigh**

▲ **weigh *sb/sth* down** [LOAD] *phrasal verb* [M usually passive] If someone or something is weighed down with something, they are carrying a lot of or too much of it: *Weighed down **with** supplies, they found the steep path difficult to climb.*
▲ **weigh *sb* down** [WORRY] *phrasal verb* [M usually passive] to make a person feel worried and unhappy because of problems, responsibilities and duties: *I thought she looked somehow older, weighed down **by** all her new responsibilities.* ○ *Too much responsibility when too young can weigh down **on** a child.*
▲ **weigh in** [SPORT] *phrasal verb* to be officially weighed before competing in a sport, especially boxing or horse racing: *Tyson weighed in **at** 245 lbs for the fight.*
▲ **weigh in** [DISCUSSION] *phrasal verb INFORMAL* to become involved in an argument or discussion in a forceful way: *Several leading architects weighed in **with** criticisms regarding the design of the new museum.*
▲ **weigh on *sb/sth*** *phrasal verb* If a problem or responsibility weighs on you, it makes you worried or unhappy: *He's under huge pressure at work and it's really weighing on him.* ○ *She knew she had treated him badly and it weighed **heavily** on her mind for a long time.*
▲ **weigh *sth* out** *phrasal verb* [M] to measure an amount of something: *Will you weigh out two kilograms of flour for me please?*
▲ **weigh *sth* up** [SITUATION] *phrasal verb* [M] to think carefully about the advantages or disadvantages of a situation before making a decision: *I'm weighing up my options before I decide to apply for the job.*
▲ **weigh *sb* up** [CHARACTER] *phrasal verb* [M] to form an opinion about a situation or someone's abilities and character by careful consideration: *I weighed up my chances of escape, and decided to wait for a better moment.* ○ *When you're a detective you learn to weigh people up quickly.*

weighbridge /ˈweɪ.brɪdʒ/ *noun* [C] a machine for weighing vehicles and their loads, that you drive onto

weighting /ˈweɪ.tɪŋ/ [US] /-t̬ɪŋ/ *noun UK* **1** [U] an increase in an amount, especially extra money paid to someone because they work in an area where it is expensive to live: *Do they pay London weighting?* **2** [C or U] a value which is given to a number or a group of numbers to show how important they are when compared with each other: *When the final marks are calculated greater weighting is given to the practical tests than to the written work.*

weightless /ˈweɪt.ləs/ *adj* having or appearing to have no weight: *There is a lot of interest in carrying out experiments in the weightless conditions which are experienced aboard space stations.* **weightlessly** /ˈweɪt.lə.sli/ *adv* **weightlessness** /ˈweɪt.lə.snəs/ *noun* [U]

weightlifting /ˈweɪtˌlɪf.tɪŋ/ *noun* [U] the activity of lifting heavy objects either as a sport or for exercise
weightlifter /ˈweɪtˌlɪf.təʳ/ *noun* [C]

ˈweight ˌtraining *noun* [U] the activity of lifting heavy objects for exercise, especially to improve the strength of muscles and the appearance of the body: *I **do/go** weight training in a gym during the week.* ➲Compare **bodybuilding**; **weightlifting**.

weir /wɪəʳ/ [US] /wɪr/ *noun* [C] a wall built under the water across a river, over which the water flows from one level to another in a controlled way

weird /wɪəd/ [US] /wɪrd/ *adj* very strange and unusual, unexpected or not natural: *He was sitting alone by a window with a weird contraption on the bench in front of him.* ○ *Her boyfriend's a bit weird but she's all right.* ○ *That's weird – I thought I'd left my keys on the table but they're not there.* ○ *There is nothing to rival the weird **and wonderful** things that come out on the streets at carnival time.* **weirdly** /ˈwɪəd.li/ [US] /ˈwɪrd-/ *adv* **weirdness** /ˈwɪəd.nəs/ [US] /ˈwɪrd-/ *noun* [U]
weirdo /ˈwɪə.dəʊ/ [US] /ˈwɪr.doʊ/ *noun* [C] *plural* **weirdos** *INFORMAL DISAPPROVING* a person who behaves strangely: *What did he mean by that? Weirdo!*

welch /weltʃ/ *verb* [I] (*ALSO* **welsh**) *INFORMAL DISAPPROVING* to avoid doing something you have promised to do, especially not to pay a debt: *Their competitors' behaviour gave them a great opportunity to welch **on** their promises.*

welcome [MEET] /ˈwel.kəm/ *verb* [T] to meet and speak to someone in a friendly way when they come to the place where you are: *The visitors to the College were **warmly** welcomed by the Warden.* ○ *Browning stood at the door, welcoming newcomers with a large smile and a pat on the arm.* ○ *Please welcome* (= Please clap for) *our guest of honour, George Taylor.*
welcome /ˈwel.kəm/ *noun* [C or U] **1** when someone is met and spoken to in a friendly way when they arrive in a place: *They were **given a warm*** (= very friendly) *welcome.* ○ *The opposition leader returned to a **hero's/heroine's** welcome after seven years in exile.* ○ *She referred to his previous visit in her **speech of** welcome/welcome **speech**.* **2** **outstay/overstay *your* welcome** to stay too long: *I left after two days – I didn't want to overstay my welcome.*
welcome /ˈwel.kəm/ *exclamation* said as a greeting to someone arriving at a place: *Welcome – please come in.*

○ Welcome **home/back** – we've missed you! ○ Welcome **to** Cambridge.

welcome /'wel.kəm/ adj If someone is welcome, you are pleased when they visit you: *Come and see us whenever you're in town – you're always welcome/you'll always be welcome.* ○ *Out in the desert the traveller is a welcome* **guest**.

• make *sb* welcome to show someone that you are pleased that they are with you: *The restaurant made the children very welcome.*

welcoming /'wel.kəm.ɪŋ/ adj friendly or making you feel welcome: *She gave everyone a welcoming smile.*

welcome SUPPORT /'wel.kəm/ verb [T] to be pleased about and encourage or support something: *The new appointment has been widely welcomed.* **welcome** /'wel.kəm/ noun [S] *Their supporters* **gave** *the decision a guarded/cautious welcome.* **welcome** /'wel.kəm/ adj: *The holiday was a welcome* **change/break/relief.** ○ *She offered him the welcome* **chance/opportunity** *to do something different.*

• you're welcome said as a polite answer when someone thanks you for doing something: *"It was very kind of you to help." "You're welcome."*

• be welcome to INFORMAL If someone is welcome to someone or something, they can have it or do it, especially because it is not valued by anyone else: *You're welcome to it – I can never get it to work properly.* ○ *If they want to change the rules, they are welcome to try.*

'welcome ,**mat** noun [C] a small piece of strong material with 'Welcome' written on it which is put on the floor by the door to greet people as they come in: FIGURATIVE *A new immigration law means the US will be* **dusting off the** *welcome mat for (= will be ready to welcome) famous people who want to live in the country.* ○ FIGURATIVE *We had better* **put the** *welcome mat* **out** *(= be ready to welcome), if your mother is coming to visit.*

'Welcome ,**Wagon** noun [U] US TRADEMARK an organization which gives information about businesses and services in a town to people who have recently moved there: FIGURATIVE *She likes to* **roll out** *the welcome wagon* **for** *(= greet and be friendly to) everyone who moves onto the block.*

weld JOIN METAL /weld/ verb [T] to join two pieces of metal together permanently by melting the parts that touch: *Iron spikes have been welded* **(on) to** *the railings around the embassy.*

weld /weld/ noun [C] a joint made by welding

welder /'wel.də^r/ US /-dɚ/ noun [C] a person whose job is welding

welding /'wel.dɪŋ/ noun [U] the activity of joining metal parts together

weld JOIN PEOPLE /weld/ verb [T] to make separate people into a group who can work together successfully: *He is a born leader, who welded a collection of gifted individualists* **into** *a real team.*

welfare HEALTH AND HAPPINESS /'wel.feə^r/ US /-fer/ noun [U] physical and mental health and happiness, especially of a person: *The police are very concerned for the welfare* **of** *the missing child.* ○ *These organizations have fought very hard for the rights and welfare* **of** *immigrants.* ○ *Scientists have to consider the balance between human health and animal welfare as they push forward the frontiers of research.*

welfare HELP /'wel.feə^r/ US /-fer/ noun [U] **1** help given, especially by the state or an organization, to people who need it, especially because they do not have enough money: *This national fund pays for welfare* **benefits** *such as unemployment and sickness pay.* ○ UK *After her month's sick leave, she was summoned to see the company's welfare* **officer.** **2** US on welfare receiving financial help from the state because you are poor or have not been employed for a long time

,**welfare 'state** noun [C usually sing] a system of taxation which allows the government of a country to provide social services such as health care, UNEMPLOYMENT pay, etc. to people who need them

well HEALTHY /wel/ adj [usually after v] better, best healthy; not ill: *He hasn't been too well lately.* ○ *When she came home from school she really didn't* **look** *well.* ○ *I'm sorry*

you're ill – I hope you **get** well soon. ○ *They sent a get well card.*

wellness /'wel.nəs/ noun [U] US the state of being healthy

well EXCLAMATION /wel/ exclamation used to introduce something you are going to say, often to show surprise, doubt, slight disagreement or annoyance, or to continue a story: *Well, what shall we do now?* ○ *Well now/then, how are we going to arrange things?* ○ *"Who was that?" "Well, I'm afraid I can't remember her name."* ○ *"He's decided to give up his job and move to the north with her." "Well, well – that's what love does for you."* ○ *Well, really, how thoughtless of him!* ○ *Well? What did you do next?* ○ *Well, after that we went camping in the mountains.* ○ *Well/Oh well, it doesn't matter – I can always buy another one.* ○ *Very well, if you insist I'll meet him next week.*

well IN A GOOD WAY /wel/ adv better, best in a good way, to a high or satisfactory standard: *The documentary presented both sides of the problem very well.* ○ *The concert was well enough advertised but ticket sales were poor.* ○ *a well-cut suit* ○ *a well-paid job* ○ *Her points were well* **put** *(= expressed in a good or clever way).* ○ *His point about the need to reduce waste was well* **taken** *(= it was accepted as a good criticism).* ○ *They took two hours to discuss the plans and considered it time well* **spent** *(= had been a useful discussion).* ○ *I can't do it* **as well as** *Marie can.*

• well done used as a way of praising someone and saying that you are pleased about and approve of something they have done: *"I passed my exam." "Well done!"* ⊃See also **well-done**.

• well out of *sth* UK INFORMAL lucky not to be involved: *"Did I tell you the company went bust the month after I left?" "Really? Oh, you're well out of* **that!"**

well TO A GREAT DEGREE /wel/ adv better, best **1** very much, to a great degree or completely: *Knead the dough well, then divide it into four pieces.* ○ *He could well imagine how much his promise was going to cost him.* ○ *I can't catch the bus – there are no buses after midnight, as you well know.* ○ *He's plays the piano well* **enough** *(= to a satisfactory standard).* **2** used to emphasize some prepositions: *The results are well* **above/below** *what we expected.* ○ *Keep well* **away from** *the edge of the cliff.* ○ *It cost well* **over** *£100.* ○ *Stand well clear of the doors!* **3** used to emphasize some adjectives: *The police are well* **aware** *of the situation.* ○ *The museum is well* **worth** *a visit.* ○ *Some machines look more like cheap, plastic toys –* **leave** *these well* **alone.** **4** UK SLANG very: *The film was well* **good.** ○ *Watch out for those two – they're well* **hard** *(= strong and willing to use violence).*

• well and truly completely: *The party was well and truly over when he arrived.*

• well away UK INFORMAL completely involved in what you are doing, or drunk: *He was soon well away on (= talking a lot about) his favourite subject of steam train conservation.* ○ *After five pints of lager and a couple of whiskeys I was well away.*

• well in (with) (US in well with) UK INFORMAL to have a good relationship with someone in which they like you and from which you benefit: *He's well in with the boss, these days.*

• all very well (ALSO all well and good) If something is all very well, it is quite useful or good in some situations but not excellent and not useful or good in every situation: *Electric heating is all very well until there's a power cut.*

well REASONABLY /wel/ adv better, best with good reason: *She might well be the best person to ask.* ○ *I* **can't very** *well (= It would not be acceptable to) refuse their kind offer.*

• be just as well (MAINLY UK be as well) to be a good thing to do, or to be a lucky thing to happen or be done: *It's just as well you're not here – you wouldn't like the noise.* ○ *He left at three, which was just as well or he'd have missed the train.* ○ *It* **would** *be as well to check the small print.* ⊃See also **well** IN ADDITION.

well HOLE /wel/ noun [C] a deep hole in the ground from which water, oil or gas can be obtained ⊃See also **stairwell**.

W

well IN ADDITION /wel/ *adv* **as well (as)** in addition (to): *Invite Emlyn – and Simon as well.* ○ *I want to visit Andrew as well as Martin.* ⊃See also **be just as well** at **well** REASONABLY.

well SURFACE /wel/ *verb* [I usually + adv or prep] (of liquid) to appear on the surface of something or come slowly out from somewhere: *Dirty water welled (up) out of the damaged pipe.* ○ *As she read the letter tears welled up in her eyes.* ○ FIGURATIVE *Conflicting emotions welled up in his heart.*

we'll STRONG /wiːl/, WEAK /wil/ we will: *We'll do better next time, I'm sure.*

well-adjusted /ˌwel.əˈdʒʌs.tɪd/ *adj* describes a person who behaves sensibly and reasonably and whose behaviour is not difficult or strange: *His family could not understand how this quiet, well-adjusted man could have been driven to this terrible deed.*

well-advised /ˌwel.ədˈvaɪzd/ *adj* [after v] FORMAL showing good judgment: [+ *to* infinitive] *You would be well-advised to book in advance.*

well-appointed /ˌwel.əˈpɔɪn.tɪd/ US /-t̬ɪd/ *adj* FORMAL having a good supply of comfortable or necessary furniture and attractive decorations: *The hotel has spacious, well-appointed public rooms and bedrooms.*

well-argued /ˌwelˈɑː.gjuːd/ US /-ˈɑːr-/ *adj* described or requested in a persuasive and clever way: *She presented a well-argued case for the banning of smoking in public places.*

well-attended /ˌwel.əˈten.dɪd/ *adj* describes an event where many people are present: *The information was given at an unusually well-attended press conference yesterday.*

well-balanced /ˌwelˈbæl.əntst/ *adj* **1** containing a mixture of ideas, people, etc. with each one being represented equally or fairly: *a well-balanced article* ○ *a well-balanced team* **2** describes a group of foods which together provide a good range of the things you need to stay healthy: *a well-balanced meal/diet* **3** describes someone who is calm and reasonable and who shows good judgment: *Do these nurseries produce the happy, well-balanced children that teachers and parents say they do?*

well-behaved /ˌwel.bɪˈheɪvd/ *adj* APPROVING behaving in a way that is accepted as correct: *a well-behaved child*

well-being /ˌwelˈbiː.ɪŋ/ *noun* [U] (ALSO **wellbeing**) the state of feeling healthy and happy: *People doing yoga benefit from an increased feeling of well-being.*

well-bred /ˌwelˈbred/ *adj* **1** speaking or behaving in a way that is generally considered correct and polite: *A television announcer with a well-bred voice was reading the news.* **2** OLD-FASHIONED coming from a family that has a high social position: *a well-bred young English woman*

well-brought-up /ˌwel.brɔːˈtʌp/ US /-brɑːˈt̬ʌp/ *adj* APPROVING describes people, especially children, who are polite and who act in a quiet and pleasant way, because they have been taught this behaviour at home: *Some children were well brought up, despite family breakdown, he admitted.*

well-built /ˌwelˈbɪlt/ *adj* **1** describes a person who is large and strong **2** UK POLITE WORD FOR **fat** BIG **3** US having a strong, attractive body: *I was always a trim, well-built guy until I turned forty.*

well-chosen /ˌwelˈtʃəʊ.zən/ US /-ˈtʃoʊ-/ *adj* carefully chosen: *These debates have made a successful series, mostly because of well-chosen speakers and lively topics.*
● **a few well-chosen words** a short speech: *He introduced the visitors with a few well-chosen words.*

well-connected /ˌwel.kəˈnek.tɪd/ *adj* having friends or family members who are important or powerful people: *She was born in 1940 into a very well-connected family.*

well-defined /ˌwel.dɪˈfaɪnd/ *adj* clearly expressed, explained or described: *We were not expecting Mr Levy to give us a clear or well-defined answer.* ○ *Scientists follow several well-defined steps in investigating unexpected outbreaks of disease.*

well-developed /ˌwel.dɪˈvel.əpt/ *adj* having grown or increased in a positive way: *The less well-developed areas of Europe are much less attractive as investment*

prospects than the major centres. ○ *She is a physically well-developed teenager with the emotional and mental level of a four-year-old.*

well-disposed /ˌwel.dɪˈspəʊzd/ US /-ˈspoʊzd/ *adj* friendly and helpful: *If you've got a good feeling about yourself, you are more likely to feel well-disposed to/ towards other people.*

well-documented /ˌwelˈdɒk.jʊ.men.tɪd/ US /-ˈdɑː.kjʊ.men.t̬ɪd/ *adj* having been frequently recorded: *The medicinal values of garlic are well-documented.*

well-done /ˌwelˈdʌn/ *adj* describes meat that is cooked all the way through and not just on the outside: *"How would you like your steak?" "Well-done."* ⊃See also **well done** at **well** IN A GOOD WAY.

well-dressed /ˌwelˈdrest/ *adj* wearing attractive and stylish clothes

well-earned /ˌwelˈɜːnd/ US /-ˈɜːnd/ /ˈ--/ *adj* UK deserved because of what you have done or experienced: *Liz won't be at work next week – she's having a well-earned break/rest/holiday.*

well-educated /ˌwelˈed.jʊ.keɪ.tɪd/ US /-t̬ɪd/ *adj* having had a good education: *well-educated and highly motivated workers*

well-endowed /ˌwel.ɪnˈdaʊd/ *adj* **1** having a lot of something, especially money or possessions: *It is a very well-endowed college.* ○ *The city is well-endowed with modern medical facilities.* **2** HUMOROUS APPROVING (of a man) having large sexual organs, or (of a woman) having large breasts: *He's very well-endowed!*

well e'stablished *adj* having a recognized position, or being generally known about: *The rules, though not written down, are fairly well established.* ○ *World Music is now well established and popular with mass audiences and mainstream companies.*

well-fed /ˌwelˈfed/ *adj* having a lot to eat: *It should be possible to be warm and well-fed, and to enjoy all the good things of life, while respecting the needs of the planet.*

well-founded /ˌwelˈfaʊn.dɪd/ *adj* based on facts: *He had to show that he had a well-founded fear of persecution on religious or political grounds to qualify as a refugee.*

well-groomed /ˌwelˈgruːmd/ *adj* having a tidy and pleasant appearance that is produced with care: *He is the sort of well-groomed man you expect to inhabit an executive-size corporate office.*

well-grounded /ˌwelˈgraʊn.dɪd/ *adj* being based on or having a good knowledge of facts: *The young players all seemed very well grounded in the rich history of the music they were performing.* ○ *The claim must be well grounded in fact.* ○ *a well-grounded criticism*

well-heeled /ˌwelˈhiːld/ *adj* INFORMAL rich: *His family was very well-heeled.*

well-heeled /ˌwelˈhiːld/ *plural noun* rich people: *The shop attracted a loyal following among the well-heeled.*

wellie, welly /ˈwel.i/ *noun* [C] UK INFORMAL FOR **wellington (boot)**

well-informed /ˌwel.ɪnˈfɔːmd/ US /-ˈfɔːrmd/ *adj* having a lot of knowledge or information about a particular subject or things in general: *He was well-informed and shrewd, with good, calm judgment.* ○ *How well-informed is the customer about the range, quality and cost of the products on offer?*

wellington (boot) UK /ˌwel.ɪŋ.tənˈbuːt/ *noun* [C usually pl] (US **rubber boot**, AUS AND US OLD-FASHIONED **gumboot**) a waterproof boot that reaches almost to the knees: *He left his muddy wellingtons outside the back door.* ⊃See picture **Clothes** on page Centre 6

well-intentioned /ˌwel.ɪnˈten.ʃənd/ *adj* wanting to have good effects, but sometimes having bad effects which were not expected: *Well-intentioned development projects can have unintended negative effects on population control.* ⊃See also **well-meaning**.

well-kept TIDY /ˌwelˈkept/ *adj* clean, tidy and cared for: *Saunders said his guest was astonished to find pleasant public parks, nice streets and well-kept houses.*

W

well-kept [HIDDEN] /ˌwelˈkept/ *adj* A well-kept secret has not been told or shown to anyone: *The details of the new car were a well-kept **secret**.*

ˌwell ˈknown *adj* known or recognized by many people: *Her views on the subject are already well known.* ○ *It is well known **that** he never gives interviews.* ○ *The restaurant is well known **for** its friendly atmosphere and excellent service.* ○ *a well-known local artist* ○ *a well-known face/voice*

well-liked /ˌwelˈlaɪkt/ *adj* liked by many people: *A colleague described him as well-liked and respected by all.*

well-mannered /ˌwelˈmæn.əd/ [US] /-ɚd/ *adj* behaving in a pleasant and polite way: *The other visitors were too well-mannered to complain.*

well-matched /ˌwelˈmætʃt/ *adj* similar or equal (to something): *At the start of the competition the three teams looked extremely well matched.* ○ *Her skills are well-matched **to** the job.*

well-meaning /ˌwelˈmiː.nɪŋ/ *adj* wanting to have a good effect, but not always achieving one: *I know he's well-meaning, but I wish he'd leave us alone.* **well-meant** /ˌwelˈment/ *adj*: *a well-meant suggestion*

wellness /ˈwel.nəs/ *noun* [U] ➲See at **well** HEALTHY.

well-nigh /ˌwelˈnaɪ/ *adv* almost or very nearly: *With no help, finishing the job in a day was well-nigh **impossible**.*

well-off [RICH] /ˌwelˈɒf/ [US] /-ˈɑːf/ *adj* rich: *Her family was very well-off.*

• **know when *you* are well off** If you do not know when you are well off, you do not understand that your present situation is good compared with other people's or with what it might be like: *She's always complaining about her car – she doesn't know when she's well off* (= she's lucky to have a car even if it's bad)*!*

well-off /ˌwelˈɒf/ [US] /-ˈɑːf/ *plural noun* rich people: *It is a resort that clearly caters for **the** well-off.*

ˌwell ˈoff [HAVING A LOT] *adj* **[after v]** having a lot of or a number of: *The city is well off **for** parks and gardens.*

well-oiled [DRUNK] /ˌwelˈɔɪld/ *adj* SLANG drunk

well-oiled [EFFECTIVE] /ˌwelˈɔɪld/ *adj* working easily and effectively: *a well-oiled political machine*

well-preserved /ˌwel.prɪˈzɜːvd/ [US] /-ˈzɝːvd/ *adj* **1** (especially of something old) kept in good condition: *It was a pretty town with a picturesque harbour and well-preserved buildings.* **2** OFTEN HUMOROUS (of an older person) not looking as old as they really are: *Most female models have to retire around the age of 25, whereas a well-preserved man can go on working into his forties.*

well-qualified /ˌwelˈkwɒl.ɪ.faɪd/ [US] /-ˈkwɑː.lɪ-/ *adj* **[+ *to* infinitive]** having suitable experience or formal qualifications: *Ken has more than 10 years of experience in photography behind him, so he is well qualified **to** offer advice.* ○ *He seems well qualified **for** the job.*

well-read /ˌwelˈred/ *adj* describes someone who has obtained a lot of information on different subjects by reading

well-rounded /ˌwelˈraʊn.dɪd/ *adj* involving or having experience in a wide range of ideas or activities: *It's a well-rounded article which is fair to both sides of the dispute.* ○ *She describes herself as a "well-rounded person" who works hard but has a varied social life.*

well-spoken /ˌwelˈspəʊ.kən/ [US] /-ˈspoʊ-/ *adj* APPROVING having a pleasant and polite way of speaking which is considered socially acceptable: *The two men who called at the house were well-spoken and had a reassuring manner.*

wellspring /ˈwel.sprɪŋ/ *noun* [S] LITERARY the place something comes from or starts at, or the cause of something; the **source**: *the wellspring of the creative spirit*

well-thought-of /ˌwelˈθɔː.tɒv/ [US] /-ˈθɑː.t̬ɑːv/ *adj* considered by other people as good; admired and approved of: *He was efficient at his job and well-thought-of by everyone.* ○ *It's a well-thought-of school.*

ˌwell thought ˈout *adj* planned in an effective way: *The training schedule wasn't very well thought out.* ○ *a well thought out scheme for traffic control*

well-thumbed /ˌwelˈθʌmd/ *adj* A well-thumbed book/copy/magazine is one whose slightly damaged appearance shows that it has been used many times.

well-timed /ˌwelˈtaɪmd/ *adj* happening or caused to happen at a suitable or effective time: *A well-timed joke stopped the disagreement developing into something more serious.*

well-to-do /ˌwel.təˈduː/ *adj* rich: *well-to-do families*

well-tried /ˌwelˈtraɪd/ *adj* used many times before and known to be effective: *a well-tried recipe*

well-trodden /ˌwelˈtrɒd.ən/ [US] /-ˈtrɑː.dən/ *adj* **[before n]** **1** much used or visited: *We followed the well-trodden tourist **route** from Paris to Chartres.* **2** describes a set of actions that many people have done or a subject that many people have dealt with previously: *The survey showed that people become managers by well-trodden **paths**.*

well-turned /ˌwelˈtɜːnd/ [US] /-ˈtɝːnd/ *adj* cleverly expressed: *a well-turned phrase*

well-versed /ˌwelˈvɜːst/ [US] /-ˈvɝːst/ *adj* knowing a lot about something: *He was well-versed **in** modern history.*

well-wisher /ˈwelˌwɪʃ.əʳ/ [US] /-ɚ/ *noun* [C] a person who encourages or supports you: *He was clutching the award he had just won for Best Newcomer, surrounded by fans and well-wishers.*

ˌwell ˈwoman/ˈman ˌclinic *noun* [C] a place that provide tests and advice relating particularly to the health of women/men, or a fixed period when it is open: *There's a well woman clinic at the health centre on Wednesday afternoons.*

well-worn /ˌwelˈwɔːn/ [US] /-ˈwɔːrn/ *adj* **1** describes clothes that have been worn frequently and are becoming old: *a well-worn sports jacket* **2** used very often or too often: *Ecology can be written about without relying on well-worn examples such as tropical rain forests.*

welly /ˈwel.i/ *noun* [C] MAINLY UK INFORMAL FOR **wellington (boot)**

welsh /weltʃ/ *verb* [I] to **welch**

Welsh rarebit /ˌwelʃˈreə.bɪt/ [US] /-ˈrer-/ *noun* [U] (ALSO **Welsh rabbit**) a piece of toast with cheese on it which is heated until the cheese melts

welt /welt/ *noun* [C] a raised, red area of skin caused by being hit or by cuts healing

welter /ˈwel.təʳ/ [US] /-t̬ɚ/ *noun* [S] a large and especially badly organized number of things: *We are reducing the company's welter **of** development projects and will streamline sales and marketing.*

welterweight /ˈwel.tə.weɪt/ [US] /-t̬ɚ-/ *noun* [C] a boxer whose body weight is between LIGHTWEIGHT and MIDDLEWEIGHT

wench /wentʃ/ *noun* [C] OLD USE a young woman

wend /wend/ *verb* **wend *your* way** to move slowly and indirectly: *The thieves then wended their way through the dark back streets to the docks.*

ˈWendy ˌhouse *noun* [C] UK a toy house or PLAYHOUSE

went /went/ *past simple of* **go**

wept /wept/ *past simple and past participle of* **weep**

were STRONG /wɜːʳ/ [US] /wɝː/, WEAK /wəʳ/ [US] /wɚ/ *past simple of* **be**

we're /wɪəʳ/ [US] /wɪr/ *short form* we are: *We're here, Diane.*

weren't /wɜːnt/ [US] /wɝːnt/ *short form of* were not: *Weren't we lucky with the weather?*

werewolf /ˈwɪə.wʊlf/ /ˈweə-/ [US] /ˈwɪr-/ /ˈwer-/ *noun* [C] *plural* **werewolves** someone who, in stories, changes into a wolf at the time of the FULL MOON (= when the moon is a complete circle)

west [DIRECTION], **West** /west/ *noun* [U] (WRITTEN ABBREVIATION **W**) the direction in which the sun goes down in the evening, opposite to the east, or the part of an area or country which is in this direction: *The points of the compass are North, South, East and West.* ○ *The sun rises **in the** east and sets **in the** west.* ○ *Most of the country will be dry tomorrow, but **the** west will have some rain.* ○ *America **is/lies to the** west of Britain.*

• **the West** In the US, the West is the part of the country west of the Mississippi river which only became developed in the late 1800s: *the Wild West*

west /west/ *adj* **1** (ALSO **West**) (WRITTEN ABBREVIATION **W**) in or towards the west: *West Africa* ○ *the west coast of*

Ireland ○ *Ireland is west* ***of*** *Britain.* **2** A west wind is a wind coming from the west.

west /west/ *adv*: *Go* ***due*** (= directly) *west until you see a lake.* ○ *The balcony* ***faces*** *west.*

• **go west** *UK INFORMAL* If something goes west, it is lost, damaged or spoilt in some way: *I couldn't get a ticket – that's my last chance to see the show gone west.*

• **out west** *US* to or in the west of the US: *Travis moved out west after college.*

westbound /ˈwest.baʊnd/ *adj* [before n], *adv* going or leading towards the west: *The accident occurred in the westbound lanes of the M25.* ○ *The worst areas for traffic were westbound between the Beltway and Nutley Street.*

westerly /ˈwes.tᵊl.i/ [US] /-tɚ.li/ *adj* **1** towards the west: *We travelled in a westerly direction.* **2** west: *So far, only the westerly part of the site has been developed.* **3** Westerly winds are winds from the west. **western, Western** /ˈwes.tən/ [US] /-tɚn/ *adj* (*WRITTEN ABBREVIATION* **W**) *western Europe* ○ *California and other western states*

western /ˈwes.tən/ [US] /-tɚn/ *noun* [C] (*UK ALSO* **cowboy film**, *US ALSO* **cowboy movie**) a film based on invented stories about life in the west of the US in the past

westernmost /ˈwes.tən.məʊst/ [US] /-tɚn.moʊst/ *adj* furthest west: *Ouessant is the westernmost point of France.*

westward /ˈwest.wəd/ [US] /-wɚd/ *adj* towards the west: *The westward advance of the road repairs is being held up by protesters.*

westwards /ˈwest.wədz/ [US] /-wɚdz/ *adv* (*ALSO* **westward**) towards the west: *The boat drifted westwards in the prevailing winds.*

the West [COUNTRIES] *noun* [S] North America, those countries in Europe which did not have communist governments before the 1990s, and some other parts of the world: *East-West relations* ○ *There has been concern* ***in/throughout*** *the West about the effects of this measure.*

western /ˈwes.tən/ [US] /-tɚn/ *adj*: *western opinion/culture* ○ *a Western-educated engineer* ○ *western medicine*

westerner, Westerner /ˈwes.tə.nəʳ/ [US] /-tɚ.nɚ/ *noun* [C] someone who is from a country in North America or western Europe: *Some of the Buddhists came from Sri Lanka, South-East Asia and East, while others were Westerners by birth and upbringing.*

westernize, *UK ALSO* **-ise** /ˈwes.tən.aɪz/ [US] /-tɚ.naɪz/ *verb* [T] to cause the ideas and ways of doing things which are common in North America and most of Europe to be used and accepted by someone or something in or from another part of the world **westernization**, *UK ALSO* **-isation** /ˌwes.tᵊn.aɪˈzeɪ.ʃᵊn/ [US] /-tɚ.naɪ-/ *noun* [U]

westernized, *UK ALSO* **-ised** /ˈwes.tən.aɪzd/ [US] /-tɚ.naɪzd/ *adj* having a culture like North America and western Europe: *As the political emphasis shifts, Bulgaria will inevitably become more westernized.*

the ˌWest ˈCoast *noun* [S] the area of the Pacific coast in the US which includes California: *They're moving to the West Coast.* ○ *West Coast companies*

the ˈWest ˌCountry *noun* [S] the area in the south-west of Britain: *We spent our holiday in the West Country.* ○ *a West Country accent*

the ˌWest ˈEnd *noun* [S] the part of central London where there are many theatres and many large expensive shops and hotels: *We went to a restaurant in the West End.* ○ *a West End theatre*

ˌWest ˈIndian *noun* [C], *adj* (a person) of or from the West Indies: *a West Indian poet* ○ *a family of West Indians*

Westminster /ˌwestˈmɪnt.stəʳ/ [US] /-stɚ/ *noun* [S] The UK parliament, or the part of London where the parliament buildings are

wet [NOT DRY] /wet/ *adj* **wetter, wettest 1** covered in water or another liquid: *a wet floor* ○ *a wet umbrella* ○ *wet hair* ○ *My bike* ***got*** *wet in the rain.* ○ *I had to cycle in the rain and got* ***soaking*** (= very) *wet.* ○ *INFORMAL You poor thing – you're* ***all*** (= very) *wet.* **2** describes paint, ink, or a similar substance when it has not had time to dry and become hard: *The paint's still wet.* ○ *a notice saying 'Wet paint!'* **3** describes weather or periods of time when rain falls: *We've had wet weather all week.* ○ *This is the first wet day for two months.* ○ *The presentation will take place indoors if* ***it's*** *wet.*

• **be wet through** to be completely wet: *Come in quickly – you're wet through.*

• **be wet behind the ears** to be young and without experience

the wet *noun* [S] *MAINLY UK* wet weather: *Don't leave it out there in the wet.*

wet /wet/ *verb* [T] **wetting, wet** or **wetted, wet** or **wetted 1** to make something wet: *Wet the powder thoroughly and mix to remove lumps.* ○ *He wetted a cloth and tried to rub the mark away.* **2 wet yourself** to accidentally urinate in your clothes **wetly** /ˈwet.li/ *adv* **wetness** /ˈwet.nəs/ *noun* [U]

• **wet the/*your* bed** to accidentally urinate in your bed: *She still sometimes wets the bed at night.*

• **wet *your* whistle** *OLD-FASHIONED INFORMAL* to have an alcoholic drink

wet [WEAK] /wet/ *adj* **wetter, wettest** describes someone who has a weak character and does not express any forceful opinions: *Don't be so wet.*

wet /wet/ *noun* [C] *UK DISAPPROVING* a member of the Conservative Party in Britain with no strong or extreme opinions **wetly** /ˈwet.li/ *adv* **wetness** /ˈwet.nəs/ *noun* [U]

ˌwet ˈblanket *noun* [C usually sing] *DISAPPROVING* a person who says or does something that stops other people enjoying themselves

ˌwet ˈdream *noun* [C] a man's sexually exciting dream which causes an EJACULATION (= release of sperm)

wetland /ˈwet.lənd/ /-lænd/ *noun* [C or U] a large area of land covered with SWAMP or MARSH

wet-look /ˈwet.lʊk/ *adj* [before n] shiny: *wet-look hair gel*

ˈwet ˌnurse *noun* [C] in the past, a woman employed to give her breast milk to another woman's baby

ˈwet ˌsuit *noun* [C] a piece of clothing, made from rubber, which covers the whole body closely and is designed to keep you warm when you are swimming in especially the sea for long periods: *divers/surfers* ***in*** *wet suits*

a ˌwet weekˈend *noun* [S] *UK INFORMAL* a very boring and disappointing experience or person: *He sounds about* ***as much fun as*** *a wet weekend in Carmarthenshire.*

we've /ˈwiːv/ /wiv/ *short form* we have: *We've been married eight years.*

whack [HIT] /wæk/ *verb* **1** [T] to hit something noisily: *He whacked the tree trunk with his stick.* ○ *She whacked him in the mouth.* **2** [T + adv or prep] *INFORMAL* to quickly put something somewhere: *"Where shall I put my bag?" "Just whack it in the corner there."* **whack** /wæk/ *noun* [C] *He* ***gave*** *the ball a whack with his stick.*

whack [SHARE] /wæk/ *noun* [U] **1** *INFORMAL* a share or part: *Low earners will pay only half the charge but high earners will have to* ***pay full*** *whack* (= pay the whole amount). ○ *That's not a* ***fair*** *whack.* **2** *UK INFORMAL* **top whack** the highest possible price or payment: *They're prepared to pay top whack for goods like this.*

whack [NOT WORKING] /wæk/ *noun US INFORMAL* **out of whack** not operating correctly or looking right: *You can use Carol's old bike – the gears are out of whack, but it still goes.*

whacked /wækt/ *adj* **1** (*ALSO* **whacked out**) *INFORMAL* very tired: *Go and pour yourself a drink, love – you look whacked.* **2** (*ALSO* **whacked-out**) *US INFORMAL* suffering the effects of drugs or alcohol: *He was whacked-out on speed, jabbering a mile a minute and making no sense at all.*

whacking /ˈwæk.ɪŋ/ *adj, adv INFORMAL* very big: *a whacking (great) boulder* ○ *a whacking fine*

whacky, *US USUALLY* **wacky** /ˈwæk.i/ *adj INFORMAL* strange or unusual: *The place is stuffed with whacky memorabilia like a sculpture of the Seven Dwarfs that Walt Disney gave to Debbie Reynolds.*

whale /weɪl/ *noun* [C] a very large sea mammal that breathes air through a hole at the top of its head

• **have a whale of a time** *INFORMAL* to enjoy yourself very much: *We had a whale of a time on holiday.*

• **whale of a** *US INFORMAL* describes a very great amount of something or a very good thing: *That's a whale of a story.* ○ *Another thousand dollars would make a whale of a difference.*

whaler /ˈweɪ.ləʳ/ [US] /-lɚ/ *noun* [C] (someone who works on) a boat which is designed for hunting whales

whaling /ˈweɪ.lɪŋ/ *noun* [U] the activity of hunting whales

wham [SOUND] /wæm/ *noun* [C], *exclamation* INFORMAL used to suggest the sound of a sudden hit: *The boys in the cartoon were punching each other – wham, zap!*

wham [SUDDENLY] /wæm/ *exclamation* used to show that something you are describing happened suddenly: *Everything was fine until, wham, the wire snapped.*

wharf /wɔːf/ [US] /wɔːrf/ *noun* [C] *plural* **wharves** an area like a wide wall built beside the edge of the sea or a river where ships can be tied and goods unloaded: *Canary Wharf*

what [QUESTION] /wɒt/ [US] /wɑːt/ *determiner, pronoun, exclamation* **1** used to ask for information about people or things: *What time is it?* ○ *What books did you buy?* ○ *What did you wear?* ○ *What size shoes do you take?* ○ *What happened after I left?* ○ *What caused the accident?* **2** used in questions which show surprise or lack of belief: *"I've just told Peter." "What?/You did what?"* ○ *What's this I hear? You're leaving?*

what /wɒt/ [US] /wɑːt/ *pronoun, exclamation* INFORMAL used to ask someone to say something again: *"I think we should leave at twelve." "What?" "I said I think we should leave at twelve."* * NOTE: It is more polite to use **'sorry?'** or **'pardon?'**.

• **what about?** used to suggest something: *What about Lola – shall we invite her?* ○ *What about taking a few days off?*

• **What's that (all) about (then)?** UK INFORMAL used when you do not understand why something or someone is so popular or fashionable: *Pierced tongues – what's that about, then?*

• **what...for?** used to ask about the reason for something: *What are these tools for?* ○ *What are you doing that for?* ○ *"We need a bigger car." "What for?"*

• **what if?** used to ask about something that could happen in the future, especially something bad: *What if the train's late?* ○ *What if you don't pass your exams?*

• **What of it?** INFORMAL used to rudely say that you do not think something is important: *"That's the third time you've done that!" "Yeah, what of it?"*

• **What is/are *he/she/it/they, etc.* like?** said to ask someone to describe someone or something to you: *What was her boyfriend like?* ○ *"What was the weather like?" "It rained all week."* ○ *You've seen their new house, haven't you? What's it like?*

• **what's on** used to mean 'what is happening'. This phrase is often used as the title of the part of a newspaper which tells you about events and entertainment happening in the next week or month.

• **What's up?** INFORMAL used to ask someone what the problem is: *What's up – why does everyone look so serious?* ○ *What's up **with** Terry?*

COMMON LEARNER ERROR

What?

When you have not heard what someone has said and you want them to repeat it, you can say **What?**, but this is not polite. It is better to say **Sorry?** or **Pardon?**.

"It's 10 o'clock." "Sorry?" "I said it's 10 o'clock."

what [THAT WHICH] /wɒt/ [US] /wɑːt/ *pronoun* **1** the thing(s) which; that which: *What I wanted to find out first was how long it was going to take.* ○ *What really concerned her was how unhappy the child was.* ○ *She wouldn't tell me what he said.* ○ *I hadn't got much money on me but I gave them what I had.* ○ *The letter showed clearly what they were planning.* ○ *I can't decide what **to** do next.* ○ *Have you thought about what **to** send as a present?* **2** used to introduce something you are going to say: *You'll never **guess** what – Laurie won first prize!* ○ *I'll **tell you** what – we'll collect the parcel on our way to the station.*

• **what's more** used to add something surprising or interesting to what you have just said: *The decorations were absolutely beautiful **and** what's more, the children had made them themselves.*

• **what/whatever *sb* says goes** What (also **whatever**) someone says goes means you have to do what they say: *It was Helen's idea and whatever Helen says goes.*

• **what with** INFORMAL used to talk about the reasons for a particular situation, especially a bad or difficult situation: *I'm very tired, what with travelling all day yesterday and having a disturbed night.*

what [OPINION] /wɒt/ [US] /wɑːt/ *predeterminer, determiner* used to introduce your opinion: *"She can't come." "What a shame/pity."* ○ *What a lovely view!* ○ *What nonsense/rubbish!* ○ *What strange clothes he was wearing.*

whatchamacallit /ˈwɒtʃ.ə.məˌkɔːl.ɪt/ [US] /ˈwɑː.tʃə.məˌkɑː.lɪt/ *noun* [C] INFORMAL used when you are speaking about something or someone whose name you can not remember: *I need a – a whatchamacallit – one of those things that you can caramelize sugar with.*

whatever [NOT IMPORTANT WHAT] /wɒtˈev.əʳ/ [US] /wɑːˈt̬ev.ɚ/ *pronoun, determiner* it is not important what is; it makes no difference what (is): *We'll go whatever the weather.* ○ *Whatever happens, you know that I'll stand by you.* ○ *Whatever else may be said of him, Mr Meese is not scared of a fight.* ○ *Whatever the outcome of the war, there will be no winners.* ○ *Whatever the reason, more Britons are emigrating to Australia today than at any time since the 1950s.*

whatever [ANYTHING] /wɒtˈev.əʳ/ [US] /wɑːˈt̬ev.ɚ/ *pronoun, determiner* anything or everything: *I eat whatever I want and I still don't seem to put on weight.* ○ *"What shall we do tonight then?" "It's up to you – whatever you want."* ○ *Whatever I say I always seem to get it wrong.* ○ *Don't, whatever **you do**, tell Patrick or the world will know!* (= You certainly should not tell Patrick)! ○ *Do whatever you want – it won't affect me.* ○ *"So I'll bring red wine then." "Sure, whatever* (= bring that or anything else)*."* ○ *Apparently he 'discovered himself' in India, whatever **that means*** (= although I do not know what that means).

whatever [SURPRISE] /wɒtˈev.əʳ/ [US] /wɑːˈt̬ev.ɚ/ *pronoun* used instead of the word *what* to add emphasis to a phrase, usually expressing surprise: *Whatever is he doing with that rod?* ○ *Whatever's that yellow thing on your plate?* ○ *Whatever did you say that for?* ○ *Whatever does she see in him – he's revolting!* ○ *Whatever made him buy that jacket?*

whatever [EMPHASIS] /wɒtˈev.əʳ/ [US] /wɑːˈt̬ev.ɚ/ *adv* **whatsoever**

whatever [DISRESPECT] /wɒtˈev.əʳ/ [US] /wɑːˈt̬ev.ɚ/ *adv* INFORMAL something that is said to show disrespect to someone who is asking you to agree with them or agree to do something: *"Bryce, could you do what I ask you to once in a while?" "Whatever."*

whatnot /ˈwɒt.nɒt/ [US] /ˈwɑːt.nɑːt/ *noun* INFORMAL **and whatnot/and what have you** and other similar things: *You can buy crisps and whatnot at the bar.* ○ *That'll leave you a bit of time so that you can get the table set and whatnot.*

what's-her-name /ˈwɒts.ə.neɪm/ [US] /ˈwɑː.ts.ɚ-/ *noun* [S] (ALSO **whatsername**) INFORMAL used for referring to a woman or girl when you cannot remember or do not know her name: *I gave the report to what's-her-name – the new marketing assistant.*

what's-his-name, whatsisname /ˈwɒts.ɪz.neɪm/ [US] /ˈwɑː.ts-/ *noun* [S] INFORMAL used for referring to a man or boy when you cannot remember or do not know his name: *Have you invited Mike Whatsisname to the party?*

whatsit /ˈwɒt.sɪt/ [US] /ˈwɑːt-/ *noun* [C] INFORMAL any object or person whose name you have temporarily forgotten or do not know: *Where's the whatsit that you change channels with?* ○ *You'd better tell whatsit – what's his name – the guy in charge of stationery.*

whatsoever /ˌwɒt.səʊˈev.əʳ/ [US] /ˌwɑːt.soʊˈev.ɚ/ *adv* (ALSO **whatever**) used after a negative phrase to add emphasis to the idea that is being expressed: *He has no respect for authority whatsoever.* ○ *I can honestly say that I have no interest whatsoever in the royal family.* ○ *There is no evidence whatever to show that this is in fact the case.* ○ *"Had you any idea what was happening at the time?" "None whatsoever."*

wheat /wiːt/ *noun* [U] a plant whose yellowish brown grain is used for making flour, or the grain itself: *wheat fields* ○ *Wheat is a staple crop for millions of people across the world.* ➲See also **whole wheat**.

• **separate the wheat from the chaff** to separate things or people that are of high quality or ability from those that are not: *The first round of interviews really separates the wheat from the chaff.*

ˈwheat ˌgerm *noun* [U] the central part of a grain of wheat which is sometimes added to food, especially bread, because it contains substances which are good for the body

wheatmeal /ˈwiːt.miːl/ *noun* [U] *UK* brown flour which contains some but not all of the outer covering and central part of the wheat grain: *wheatmeal digestive biscuits*

wheedle /ˈwiː.dl̩/ *verb* [I; T + adv or prep] *DISAPPROVING* to try to persuade someone to do something or give you something by praising them or being intentionally charming: *She's one of those children who can wheedle you* ***into*** *giving her anything she wants.* ○ *She wasn't invited, but somehow she managed to wheedle her* ***way in***. ○ *I tried all manner of different approaches – I wheedled, threatened, demanded, cajoled.* **wheedling** /ˈwiː.dl̩.ɪŋ/ *adj*: *I knew by your wheedling tone that you wanted something from me.*

wheel [ROUND OBJECT] /wiːl/ *noun* [C] **1** a circular object connected at the centre to a bar, which is used for making vehicles or parts of machines move: *I got my bag caught in the wheel of my bicycle.* ○ *He lost control of his car when a front/rear wheel hit a stone as he approached the first bend.* ➲See also **Ferris wheel**; **flywheel**; **waterwheel**. **2 on wheels** Something that is on wheels has wheels under it so that it can be pulled or pushed along: *My suitcase is on wheels so that makes life a little easier.* ○ *I bought my niece one of those toy dogs on wheels.* **3 the wheel** a STEERING WHEEL (= a wheel inside a vehicle, which the driver turns to make the vehicle go in a particular direction): *Keep your hands on the wheel!*, ○ *I never feel safe with Richard* ***at/behind*** *the wheel* (= driving). ○ *Do you think you could* ***take*** *the wheel* (= drive) *for a couple of hours?* **4** a wooden or metal wheel which is turned to make a ship go in a particular direction

• **set the wheels in motion** to do something which will cause a series of actions to start: *I thought a phone call to the right person might set the wheels in motion.*

• **wheels within wheels** hidden or unknown things that influence a particular situation, making it more complicated than it at first seems

• **a fifth/third wheel** *US* someone who is in a situation where they are not needed or are ignored by most people

wheel /wiːl/ *verb* [T usually + adv or prep] to push an object that has wheels so that it moves in a particular direction: *I saw her last night wheeling a buggy along Green Lane.* ○ *Halfway through the talk someone wheeled in a trolley laden with drinks.* ○ *Doctors put her on a respirator and wheeled her downstairs to the intensive care unit.*

-wheeled /-wiːld/ *suffix* with the stated number of wheels: *It looks like a motorized version of a child's two-wheeled scooter.*

-wheeler /-wiː.ləʳ/ [US] /-lɚ/ *suffix* a vehicle with the stated number of wheels: *He drives a three-wheeler* (= a car with three wheels).

wheels /wiːlz/ *plural noun OLD-FASHIONED INFORMAL* a car: *I've got to get some wheels – this public transport system's a joke!*

wheel [FLY IN CIRCLES] /wiːl/ *verb* [I] to fly repeatedly in a circular pattern: *She watched a flock of seagulls wheeling high above her.*

PHRASAL VERBS WITH **wheel** ▼

▲ **wheel *sth* out** *phrasal verb* [M] *DISAPPROVING* to use something or someone that you have used many times before in a way that is boring for other people: *Every time we have this argument you wheel out the same old statistics, and I'm still not convinced!* ○ *Year after year they wheel out the same third-rate celebrities to entertain us.*

▲ **wheel round** *UK phrasal verb* (*US* **wheel around**) to turn round quickly: *She wheeled round to face him and saw him take out a gun.*

ˌwheel and ˈdeal *verb* [I] *INFORMAL* to try to make a profit or get an advantage using clever or complicated methods and often deceiving people or breaking the usual rules: *He spends his time wheeling and dealing on the stock exchange.*
wheeler-dealer /ˌwiː.ləˈdiː.ləʳ/ [US] /-lɚˈdiː.lɚ/ *noun* [C] *INFORMAL* someone who wheels and deals: *He worked in the property business for a number of years, acquiring a reputation as a formidable wheeler-dealer.* **ˌwheeling and ˈdealing** *noun* [U] *It's an article about all the wheeling and dealing that goes on in financial markets.*

wheelbarrow /ˈwiːl̩bær.əʊ/ [US] /-ˌber.oʊ/ *noun* [C] (*ALSO* **barrow**) a large open container for moving things in, which has a wheel at the front and two handles at the back, used especially in the garden

wheelbase /ˈwiːl.beɪs/ *noun* [C usually sing] the distance between the front and the back wheels of a motor vehicle

wheelchair /ˈwiːl.tʃeəʳ/ [US] /-tʃer/ *noun* [C] a chair on wheels which people who are unable to walk use for moving around: *He spent the last ten years of his life* ***in a*** *wheelchair after a fall which left him paralysed from the waist down.* ○ *The building isn't designed very well from the point of view of wheelchair access.*

ˈwheel ˌclamp *MAINLY UK noun* [C] (*US* **(Denver) boot**) a metal device fixed to the wheel of an illegally parked car which will only be removed when the owner pays an amount of money: *I hope we're not going to find a wheel clamp on my car when we get back.* **wheel-clamp** *MAINLY UK* /ˈwiːl.klæmp/ *verb* [T] (*US* **(Denver) boot**)

wheelie /ˈwiː.li/ *noun* [C] *INFORMAL* an act of raising the front wheel of a bicycle off the ground and keeping it in the air while riding the bicycle: *I can* ***do*** *great wheelies on this bike.*

ˈwheelie ˌbin *noun* [C] a container for rubbish which has wheels so that it can be moved easily: *We put our wheelie bin out to be emptied every Thursday morning.*

wheeze [BREATHE] /wiːz/ *verb* [I] to make a high, rough noise while breathing because of some breathing difficulty: *I could hear the old man behind me wheezing.* ○ *I know when I've been smoking too much because I start to wheeze when I run for a train.* **wheeze** /wiːz/ *noun* [C] *The cough, wheeze and shortness of breath are things that go with smoking, not with age.* **wheezy** /ˈwiː.zi/ *adj*: *He's got a very wheezy chest which hasn't been helped by a recent cold.*

wheeze [PLAN] /wiːz/ *noun* [C] *UK OLD-FASHIONED, INFORMAL* a clever and often imaginative idea or plan, especially one which is intended to achieve a profit or some other advantage: *As a part of their latest marketing wheeze they've planted fifty-pound notes in a number of the crisp packets.* ○ *So the public actually pay to feed the animals in the zoo? That seems like a* ***good*** *wheeze.* ○ *I've* ***had*** *a wheeze – why don't we put both kids in the small room and that will leave the back room free.*

whelk /welk/ *noun* [C] a soft sea animal, similar to a snail, that lives in a hard shell

when [AT WHAT TIME] /wen/ *adv, conjunction* at what time; at the time at which: *"I did tell you about it." "When? I don't remember."* ○ *When are you going?* ○ *When's the baby due?* ○ *We'll go when you're ready.* ○ *Tell me when* ***to*** *start.* ○ *Ask him when he's next coming home.* ○ *When do you expect to have the project completed* ***(by)****?* ○ *She was only twenty when she had her first baby.* ○ *He was quite shocked when I told him.* ○ *I hate it when there's no one in the office.* ○ *I went there when I was a child.* ○ *I was just getting into the bath when the telephone rang.* **when** /wen/ *pronoun*: *"Did you know Lucy was back in England?" "Is she –* ***since*** *when?"*

• **since when** used angrily in speech to ask someone why they believe a situation to be different from how it really is: *Since when did you have the right to tell me what to do?*

COMMON LEARNER ERROR

when or **if?**

In conditional sentences **when** is used to describe a situation which is always true or a situation which you are sure will happen in the future.

I always get migraines when it's this hot.
When I finish school, I'm going to go to college.

If is used to describe a possible situation.

It would be better for the environment if everyone went by bicycle.
~~*It would be better for the environment when everyone went by bicycle.*~~

when [CONSIDERING THAT] /wen/ *conjunction* considering the fact that: *How can you say you don't like something when you've never even tried it!* ○ *You can't complain of being lonely when you don't make any effort to meet people.* ○ *Why is she training to be a teacher when she doesn't even like children?* ○ *I don't suppose I can really call myself a vegetarian when I eat fish.*

when [ALTHOUGH] /wen/ *conjunction* despite the fact that: *He says he hasn't got any money when in fact he's got thousands of dollars in his account.* ○ *I don't understand how he can say that everything's fine when it's so obvious that it's not.*

whence /wents/ *adv, conjunction* FORMAL (from) where: *It has been returned to the shop* ***from*** *whence it came.*

whenever [EVERY TIME] /wen'ev.əʳ/ [US] /-ɚ/ *adv, conjunction* every or any time: *I blush whenever I think about it.* ○ *Whenever I go there they seem to be in bed.* ○ *I try to use olive oil whenever possible.* ○ *"Will it be okay if I do it tomorrow?" "Sure, whenever* (= then or at any other time)*."* ○ *Do it in a spare moment at the weekend or whenever – it really doesn't matter.* ○ *I'm talking about last July or whenever it was that you got back from India.*

whenever [SURPRISE] /wen'ev.əʳ/ [US] /-ɚ/ *adv* used instead of 'when' to add emphasis to a phrase, usually expressing surprise: *Whenever do you get the time to do these things?*

where /weəʳ/ [US] /wer/ *adv, conjunction* **1** to, at or in what place: *Where does he live?* ○ *"I put it on your desk." "Where? I can't see it?"* ○ *Where are we going?* ○ *Now where did I put my glasses?* ○ *Where's the party being held?* ○ *Could you tell me where Barker Drive is please?* ○ *Where did you put my umbrella?* ○ *I've left my keys somewhere and I don't know where.* ○ *You've found my diary – where* ***on earth*** *was it?* ○ *I've been meaning to ask you where you get your hair cut.* ○ *Bradford, where Bren comes from, has a lot of good curry restaurants.* ○ *She lived in Rome for a couple of years, where she taught English.* ○ *You see where Mira is standing? Well, he's behind her.* ○ *I like to have him next to me where I can keep an eye on him.* ○ *I read it somewhere – I don't know where* (= in which book, newspaper etc.). **2** used when referring to a particular stage in a process or activity: *You reach a point in any project where you just want to get the thing finished.* ○ *I've reached the stage where I just don't care any more.* **3** in what situation: *You're not available on the 12th and Andrew can't make the 20th – so where does that leave us?* ○ *Where do you see yourself five years from now?*

• **be where it's at** SLIGHTLY OLD-FASHIONED to be very fashionable and popular: *In the classical music world these days, authentic instruments are where it's at.*

• **know/see where *sb* is coming from** If you say to someone you know or see where they are coming from, you mean you understand why they have a particular opinion, often although you do not have that opinion.

whereabouts /'weə.rə.baʊts/ [US] /'wer.ə-/ *group noun* [U] the place where a person or thing is: *Trupin is thought to be in the Caribbean, although his exact whereabouts are/is a mystery.*

whereabouts /ˌweə.rə'baʊts/ [US] /ˌwer.ə-/ *adv*: *Whereabouts in* (= In what part of) *Madrid do you live?* ○ *Whereabouts* (= In what area) *is your office, then?*

whereas /weə'ræz/ [US] /wer'æz/ *conjunction* compared with the fact that; but: *He must be about sixty, whereas his wife looks about thirty.* ○ *You eat a massive plate of food for lunch, whereas I have just a sandwich.*

whereby /weə'baɪ/ [US] /wer-/ *adv, conjunction* **1** by which way or method: *They've set up a plan whereby you can spread the cost over a period.* ○ *We need to devise some sort of system whereby people can liaise with each other.* **2** NOT STANDARD in which, or with which: *It's put me in a position whereby I can't afford to take a job.*

wherefores /'weə.fɔːz/ [US] /'wer.fɔːrz/ *plural noun* ➲See **the whys and (the) wherefores** at **why** REASON.

wherein /weə'rɪn/ [US] /wer'ɪn/ *adv, conjunction* OLD USE OR FORMAL in which, or in which part: *He gazed once more around the room, wherein were assembled his entire family.* ○ *He was certainly a pleasant man but wherein lay his charms, she wondered.*

wheresoever /ˌweə.səʊ'ev.əʳ/ [US] /ˌwer.soʊ'ev.ɚ/ *adv, conjunction* FORMAL FOR **wherever** EVERY PLACE

whereupon /ˌweə.rə'pɒn/ [US] /ˌwer.ə'pɑːn/ *conjunction* immediately after which: *I told her she looked fat, whereupon she threw the entire contents of a saucepan at me and burst into tears.*

wherever [EVERY PLACE] /weə'rev.əʳ/ [US] /wer'ev.ɚ/ *adv, conjunction* **1** to or in any or every place: *We can go wherever you like.* ○ *Wherever I go I always seem to bump into him.* ○ *All across Europe, wherever you look, marriage is in decline and divorce rates are soaring.* ○ *Wherever you choose to live there are always going to be disadvantages.* ○ *He lives, apparently, in Little Overington, wherever that is.* **2** in every case: *Wherever possible I use honey instead of sugar.*

wherever [SURPRISE] /weə'rev.əʳ/ [US] /wer'ev.ɚ/ *adv* used instead of 'where' to add emphasis to a phrase, usually expressing surprise: *Wherever did you find that hat!* ○ *Wherever did you get that idea!* ○ *Wherever does he get the money from to go on all these exotic journeys?*

the wherewithal /ðə'weə.wɪ.ðɔːl/ [US] /-'wer.wɪ.ðɑːl/ *noun* [S] the money necessary for a particular purpose: *I'd like to buy a bigger house, but I don't have the wherewithal.* ○ [+ **to** infinitive] *Poor families* ***lack*** *the wherewithal* ***to*** *hire good lawyers.*

whet [INTEREST] /wet/ *verb* **-tt- whet** *someone's* **appetite** to increase someone's interest in and desire for something, usually by giving them a small experience of it: *I've read an excerpt of the book on the Web and it's whetted my appetite.* ○ *That one kiss had whetted his appetite.*

whet [SHARPEN] /wet/ *verb* [T] **-tt-** OLD USE to sharpen the blade of a knife or similar tool: *He whetted his knife against the stone.*

whether [IF] /'weð.əʳ/ [US] /-ɚ/ *conjunction* (used especially in reporting questions and expressing doubts) if, or not: *I wasn't sure whether you'd like it.* ○ *She asked me whether I was interested in working for her.* ○ *I'm wondering whether to have the fish or the beef.* ○ *I doubt whether it'll work.* ○ *I was merely questioning whether we have the money to fund such a project.* ○ *It all depends on whether* ***or not*** *she's got the time.* ○ *Anyway, it's a good story, whether* ***or not*** *it's true.*

whether [NOT IMPORTANT IF] /'weð.əʳ/ [US] /-ɚ/ *conjunction* **whether...or** (used to introduce two or more possibilities) it is not important if: *I'm going, whether she likes it or* ***not****.* ○ *Someone's got to tell her, whether it's you or me.* ○ *Let's face it – you're going to be late whether you go by bus or train.*

whetstone /'wet.stəʊn/ [US] /-stoʊn/ *noun* [C] a stone used for sharpening the blades of knives or other cutting tools

Whew! /fhjuː/ *exclamation* INFORMAL **Phew!**

whey /weɪ/ *noun* [U] the watery part of milk which is separated from the solid CURDS during the process of making cheese

which [QUESTION] /wɪtʃ/ *determiner, pronoun* (used in questions and structures in which there is a fixed or limited set of answers or possibilities) what one or ones: *Which party would you prefer to go to – Anna's or Ian's ?* ○ *Which doctor did you see – Sewards?* ○ *Which time suits you better – 12.30 or one o'clock?* ○ *"Jacinta was there with her boyfriend." "Which one? She's got several."* ○ *Which is mine? The smaller one?* ○ *See if you can guess which one is me in my old school photo.* ○ *It's either Spanish or Portuguese that she speaks, but I've forgotten which.* ○ *Which* ***of*** *the desserts did you have?* ○ *Which* ***of***

your parents do you feel closer to?

• **which is which** used in expressions that relate to being able to see the difference between two very similar things or people: *For the first few months the babies looked so alike I couldn't **tell** which was which.*

which USED TO REFER /wɪtʃ/ *pronoun* used as the subject or object of a verb to show what thing or things you are referring to, or to add information about the thing just mentioned. It is usually used for things, not people: *These are principles which we all believe in.* ○ *You know that little Italian restaurant – the one which I mentioned in my letter?* ○ *Is that the film in which he kills his mother?* ○ *The death of his son was an experience from which he never fully recovered.* ○ *It isn't a subject to which I devote a great deal of thought.*

COMMON LEARNER ERROR

which, who or **that**?

Use **which** to refer to a thing.

The restaurant which is next to the pub is really good.
~~The restaurant who is next to the pub is really good.~~

Use **who** to refer to a person.

That boy who is wearing the red coat is called Paul.
~~That boy which is wearing the red coat is called Paul.~~

Use **that** to refer to either a person or a thing. It is used especially in informal or spoken English and can often be omitted.

He's the man (that) I saw in the bar.
This is the shirt (that) I bought yesterday.

which ADDS INFORMATION /wɪtʃ/ *pronoun* used to add extra information to a previous clause, in writing usually after a comma: *That bar on Milton Street, which by the way is very nice, is owned by Trevor's brother.* ○ *She says it's Charlotte's fault, which is rubbish, and that she blames her.* ○ *Anyway, that evening, which I'll tell you more about later, I ended up staying at Rachel's place.* ○ *It's the third in a sequence of three books, the first of which I really enjoyed.* ○ *He showed me round the town, which was very kind of him.* **which** /wɪtʃ/ *determiner:* *The picking of the fruit, for which work they receive no money, takes about a week.*

whichever ANY ONE /wɪˈtʃev.əʳ/ US /-ɚ/ *determiner, pronoun* any one from a limited set: *We can go to the seven o'clock performance or the eight – whichever suits you best.* ○ *Either Thursday or Friday – choose whichever day is best for you.*

whichever NOT IMPORTANT WHICH /wɪˈtʃev.əʳ/ US /-ɚ/ *determiner* it is not important which: *It's going to be expensive whichever way you do it.* ○ *Whichever option we choose there'll be disadvantages.*

whiff /wɪf/ *noun* [C usually sing] **1** a brief smell, carried on a current of air: *He leaned towards me and I **caught/got** a whiff **of** garlic.* ○ *During the first few months of pregnancy the slightest whiff **of** food cooking made my stomach turn.* **2 a whiff of sth** a slight sign of something: *They regularly hold elections without a whiff of corruption or violence.*

whiffy /ˈwɪf.i/ *adj UK INFORMAL* smelling unpleasant: *He hadn't showered for a couple of days and was starting to get whiffy.*

Whig /wɪg/ *noun* [C] a member of a British political party in the 17th, 18th and 19th centuries, which supported political and social change

while LENGTH OF TIME /waɪl/ *noun* **a while** a length of time: *I only stayed for a short while.* ○ *You were there **quite** a while (= a long time), weren't you?* ○ *"When did that happen?" "Oh, it was a while **ago** (= a long time ago).* ○ *I'll be fine **in** a while (= soon).* ⊃See also **worthwhile**.

• **all the while** for all of a period of time: *There I was thinking you were hard at work and you were upstairs in bed all the while!*

while DURING /waɪl/ *conjunction* (MAINLY UK FORMAL **whilst**) during the time that, or at the same time as: *I read it while you were drying your hair.* ○ *While I was in Italy I went to see Alessandro.* ○ *I thought I heard him come in while we were having dinner.* ○ *"I'm going to the post office." "While you're there can you get me some stamps?"*

while ALTHOUGH /waɪl/ *conjunction* (MAINLY UK FORMAL **whilst**) despite the fact that; although: *While I accept that he's not perfect in many respects, I do actually quite like the man.* ○ *While I fully understand your point of view, I do also have some sympathy with Michael's.*

while BUT /waɪl/ *conjunction* compared with the fact that; but: *He gets fifty thousand pounds a year while I get a meagre twenty!* ○ *Tom is very extrovert and confident while Katy's shy and quiet.* ○ *I do every single bit of housework while he just does the dishes now and again.*

while /waɪl/ *verb*

▲ **while sth away** *phrasal verb* [M] to spend time in a relaxed way because you have nothing to do or you are waiting for something to happen: *We whiled away the afternoon playing cards in front of the fire.* ○ *That's the bar where Sara and I used to while away the hours between lectures.*

whim /wɪm/ *noun* [C] a sudden desire or idea, especially one that cannot be reasonably explained: *We booked the holiday **on a** whim.* ○ *You can add what you like to this mixture – brandy, whisky or nothing at all – as the whim takes you.* ○ *Oh for a husband who would indulge my **every** whim!*

whimper /ˈwɪm.pəʳ/ US /-pɚ/ *verb* [I] (especially of an animal) to make a series of small, weak sounds, expressing pain or unhappiness: *A half-starved dog lay in the corner, whimpering pathetically.* ○ *I said she couldn't have an ice cream and she started to whimper.* **whimper** /ˈwɪm.pəʳ/ US /-pɚ/ *noun* [C] *She **gave** a little whimper as the vet inspected her paw.*

whimsical /ˈwɪm.zɪ.kəl/ *adj* unusual and strange in a way that might be amusing or annoying: *a whimsical tale* ○ *Despite his kindly, sometimes whimsical air, he was a shrewd observer of people.* **whimsically** /ˈwɪm.zɪ.kli/ *adv* **whimsicality** /ˌwɪm.zɪˈkæl.ɪ.ti/ US /-ə.t̬i/ *noun* [U] FORMAL

whimsy /ˈwɪm.zi/ *noun* [C or U] DISAPPROVING something that is intended to be strange and amusing but in fact has little real meaning or value: *Personally I've always considered mime to be a lot of whimsy.*

whine /waɪn/ *verb* [I] **1** to make a long, high, sad sound: *Leon's dog was sitting by the door whining, so I thought I'd better take it for a walk.* **2** DISAPPROVING If you whine, especially as a child, you complain or express dissatisfaction continually: *Alice, if you carry on whining like that I won't take you – do you understand!* **whine** /waɪn/ *noun* [C usually sing] an unpleasant high sound or voice: *He could hear the sound of hammering, then the whine of a circular saw.* ○ *She delivered the speech in a high-pitched nasal whine.* **whiner** /ˈwaɪ.nəʳ/ US /-nɚ/ *noun* [C] DISAPPROVING a person, especially a child, who complains or expresses dissatisfaction continually

whinge /wɪndʒ/ *verb* [I] **whingeing** or **whinging** UK INFORMAL DISAPPROVING to complain, especially about something which does not seem important: *Oh stop whinging, for heaven's sake!* ○ *She's always whingeing **(on) about** something.* **whinge** /wɪndʒ/ *noun* [C usually sing] *We were just **having** a whinge about our boss – nothing new.* **whinger** /ˈwɪn.dʒəʳ/ US /-dʒɚ/ *noun* [C] UK INFORMAL DISAPPROVING a person who complains continually

whinny /ˈwɪn.i/ *verb* [I] (of a horse) to make a soft, high sound: *A horse whinnied into the cold morning.*

whip DEVICE FOR HITTING /wɪp/ *noun* [C] a piece of leather or rope which is fastened to a stick, used for hitting animals or people: *She lashed the horses mercilessly with her long whip.* ○ *The lion-tamer **cracked** his whip.*

• **have/hold the whip hand** to be the person or group that has the most power in a situation: *During the last decade the right wing of the party has held the whip hand.*

whip /wɪp/ *verb* [T] **-pp-** to hit a person or animal with a whip: *I don't like the way the drivers whip their horses.* **whipping** /ˈwɪp.ɪŋ/ *noun* [C usually sing] the punishment of being hit by a whip

whip ACT/MOVE QUICKLY /wɪp/ *verb* **-pp-** **1** [T usually + adv or prep] to bring or take something quickly: *She whipped a handkerchief **out** of her pocket and wiped his face.* ○ *He whipped the covers **off** the bed.* ○ *I was going to pay but before I knew it he'd whipped **out** his credit card.* ○ *They* *whipped my plate* ***away*** *before I'd even finished.* **2** [I or T; + adv or prep] *LITERARY* to (cause something to) move quickly and forcefully: *The wind whipped across the half-frozen lake.* ○ *A fierce, freezing wind whipped torrential rain into their faces.*

whip [POLITICS] /wɪp/ *noun* [C] **1** (in many elected political systems) a member of a political party in parliament or in the LEGISLATURE whose job is to make certain that other party members are present at voting time and also to make certain that they vote in a particular way: *Hargreaves is the MP who got into trouble with his party's* ***chief*** *whip for opposing the tax reform.* **2** in British politics, a written order demanding that party members be present in parliament when there is to be an important vote or demanding that they vote in a particular way: *In 1970 he defied the* ***three-line*** (= most urgent) *whip against EC membership.*

whip [BEAT FOOD] /wɪp/ *verb* [T] **-pp-** to beat food, especially cream with a special utensil in order to make it thick and firm: *Could you whip the cream for me?* ○ *Try whipping a little brandy or other liqueur* ***into*** *the cream.* ○ *Top with whipped* ***cream*** *and a sprinkle of sugar.*

whip [STEAL] /wɪp/ *verb* [T] **-pp-** *UK OLD-FASHIONED INFORMAL* to steal something

whip [SWEET FOOD] /wɪp/ *noun* [C or U] a sweet food made from cream or beaten egg mixed together with fruit

PHRASAL VERBS WITH **whip** ▼

▲ **whip *sb* into *sth*** *phrasal verb* If you whip someone into a particular state, you quickly and effectively cause them to be in that state: *Karl Smith, the 19-year old singer, had whipped the crowd of teenage girls into* ***a frenzy*** *merely by removing his shirt.* ○ *The prime minister's final speech had the desired effect, whipping his party into a patriotic fervour.*

▲ **whip *sth* up** [EMOTION] *phrasal verb* [M] *MAINLY DISAPPROVING* to encourage or cause people to have strong feelings about something: *She criticized the government for trying to whip up anti-German prejudice.* ○ *He was trying to whip up some enthusiasm for the project.*

▲ **whip *sth* up** [FOOD] *phrasal verb* [M] *INFORMAL* to make food or a meal very quickly and easily: *I think I've just about got enough time to whip up an omelette.*

whiplash /ˈwɪp.læʃ/ *noun* [C or U] a neck injury caused by a sudden forward movement of the upper body, especially in a car accident: *a whiplash injury*

whippersnapper /ˈwɪp.əˌsnæp.əʳ/ Ⓤⓢ /-ɚˌsnæp.ɚ/ *noun* [C] *OLD-FASHIONED OR HUMOROUS* a young person who is too confident and shows a lack of respect towards other, especially older, people: *I'm not going to have some* ***young*** *whippersnapper come round here and tell me what to do!*

whippet /ˈwɪp.ɪt/ *noun* [C] a thin dog, like a small GREYHOUND, often used for racing

ˈwhipping ˌboy *noun* [C usually sing] someone or something that is blamed or punished for problems that are caused by someone or something else

whip-round /ˈwɪp.raʊnd/ *noun* [C usually sing] *UK INFORMAL* a collection of money made by a group of people which is then given to a particular person or used to buy a present for them: *We usually* ***have*** *a whip-round at work* ***for*** *people who are leaving.*

whirl [SPIN] /wɜːl/ Ⓤⓢ /wɝːl/ *verb* [I or T] to (cause something to) spin round: *She saw a mass of bodies whirling round on the dance floor.* ○ *He stepped out into the night and the whirling snow.* ○ *He whirled her* ***round*** *until she felt quite sick.*

• **head/mind be whirling** If your head/mind is whirling, your mind is full of thoughts and images and you are so excited that you can not relax.

whirl /wɜːl/ Ⓤⓢ /wɝːl/ *noun* [C usually sing] when something spins round: *a whirl of snow*

• **be in a whirl** to be excited and confused and unable to think clearly

• **give it a whirl** *INFORMAL* to attempt to do something, often for the first time: *I've never danced salsa before but I'll give it a whirl.*

whirl [ACTIVITY] /wɜːl/ Ⓤⓢ /wɝːl/ *noun* [S] a continuous and exciting period of activity: *The next two days passed in a whirl* ***of*** *activity.* ○ *I found myself swept up in the* ***social*** *whirl of college life and scarcely had time for work.*

whirligig /ˈwɜː.lɪ.gɪg/ Ⓤⓢ /ˈwɝː-/ *noun* [C] something that is full of fast activity and always changing: *By June of this year the whirligig* ***of*** *politics had kicked the Conservatives out and put the Liberal Democrats in.*

whirlpool /ˈwɜːl.puːl/ Ⓤⓢ /ˈwɝːl-/ *noun* [C] a small area of the sea or other water in which there is a powerful, circular current of water which can pull objects down into its centre

whirlwind [WEATHER] /ˈwɜːl.wɪnd/ Ⓤⓢ /ˈwɝːl-/ *noun* [C] (*US ALSO* **twister**) a tall column of spinning air which moves across the surface of the land or sea

whirlwind [EVENT] /ˈwɜːl.wɪnd/ Ⓤⓢ /ˈwɝːl-/ *adj* [before n] describes an event that happens very fast, and often unexpectedly: *They married three months after they met – it was a real whirlwind* ***romance.*** ○ *a whirlwind tour/visit*

whirlybird /ˈwɜː.lɪ.bɜːd/ Ⓤⓢ /ˈwɝː.lɪ.bɜːrd/ *noun* [C] *US OLD-FASHIONED* **helicopter**

whirr, *MAINLY US* **whir** (-rr-) /wɜːʳ/ Ⓤⓢ /wɝː/ *verb* [I] (especially of machines) to make a low, soft, continuous sound: *I could hear the washing machine whirring in the kitchen.* **whirr**, *MAINLY US* **whir** /wɜːʳ/ Ⓤⓢ /wɝː/ *noun* [C usually sing] *the whirr of machinery*

whisk [REMOVE] /wɪsk/ *verb* [T usually + adv or prep] to take something or someone somewhere else suddenly and quickly: *Our coffees were whisked* ***away*** *before we'd even finished them.* ○ *We only had half an hour to see her before she was whisked* ***off to*** *some exotic location.* ○ *Her husband whisked her* ***off to*** *Egypt for her birthday.*

whisk [BEAT FOOD] /wɪsk/ *verb* [T] to beat eggs, cream, etc. with a special utensil in order to add air and make the food light: *Whisk the egg whites until stiff.* ○ *Remove mixture from heat and whisk in the brandy and vanilla essence.*

whisk /wɪsk/ *noun* [C] a kitchen utensil which you use for beating food such as eggs and cream in order to add air and make it light: *an electric whisk* ○ *a hand-held whisk*

whisker /ˈwɪs.kəʳ/ Ⓤⓢ /-kɚ/ *noun* [C] any of the long, stiff hairs growing on the face of a cat, mouse or other mammal: *He watched the cat cleaning the milk off her whiskers.*

• **by a whisker** by a very small amount: *Last time she raced against the Brazilian, she won by a whisker.*

• **come within a whisker of *(doing) sth*** If you come within a whisker of doing something, you almost do it or it almost happens to you: *Twice now she had come within a whisker of death.*

whiskers /ˈwɪs.kəz/ Ⓤⓢ /-kɚz/ *plural noun OLD-FASHIONED OR HUMOROUS* the hair growing on a man's face, especially the sides and/or the lower part

whiskered /ˈwɪs.kəd/ Ⓤⓢ /-kɚd/ *adj OLD-FASHIONED* having whiskers

whisky *MAINLY UK, MAINLY US AND IRISH ENGLISH* **whiskey** /ˈwɪs.ki/ *noun* [C or U] a strong, pale brown alcoholic drink, originally from Scotland and Ireland, made from grain such as barley, maize or RYE

whisper [WAY OF SPEAKING] /ˈwɪs.pəʳ/ Ⓤⓢ /-pɚ/ *noun* [C] a way of speaking very quietly, using the breath but not the voice, so that only the person close beside you can hear you: *I heard whispers outside my room.* ○ *She said it* ***in a*** *whisper so I presumed it wasn't common knowledge. "You see," she said, lowering her voice to a whisper, "he hasn't been well recently."* **whisper** /ˈwɪs.pəʳ/ Ⓤⓢ /-pɚ/ *verb* [I or T] *She leaned over and whispered something in his ear.* ○ *What are you two girls whispering about?* ○ [+ speech] *"Where are the toilets?" she whispered.* ○ *It's rude to whisper!*

whisper [SUGGESTION] /ˈwɪs.pəʳ/ Ⓤⓢ /-pɚ/ *noun* [C] a suggestion or piece of information that you hear privately from someone: *I've heard a whisper* ***that*** *they're heading for divorce.*

whisper /ˈwɪs.pəʳ/ Ⓤⓢ /-pɚ/ *verb* [+ *that*] to suggest privately that something might be true: *People are whispering* ***that*** *she's going to retire next year.*

whisper [SOFT NOISE] /ˈwɪs.pəʳ/ Ⓤⓢ /-pɚ/ *noun* [S] *LITERARY* a soft, low noise: *The silence was broken only by the whisper* ***of*** *the leaves in the gentle breeze.*

W

ˈ**whispering camˌpaign** *noun* [C usually sing] *DISAPPROVING* the intentional damaging of an important person's reputation by saying things about them which, whether true or false, are unpleasant

whist /wɪst/ *noun* [U] a card game played between two pairs of players in which each side tries to win more cards than the other

ˈ**whist ˌdrive** *noun* [C] *UK* a social occasion at which people play whist

whistle /ˈwɪs.l̩/ *verb* **1** [I or T] to make a high sound by forcing air through a small hole or passage, especially through the lips, or through a special device held to the lips: *He whistled as he worked.* ○ *On the days when she wore a skirt the men on the building site would whistle* ***at*** *her.* ○ *Someone was whistling Beatles tunes outside my window.* ○ *The referee whistled and the game was over.* **2** [I + adv or prep] to make a long, high sound while moving quickly through or past something: *She heard the wind whistling* ***through*** *the trees and the howl of a distant wolf.* ○ *I stepped out of the building and immediately a bullet whistled* ***past*** *my head.* **3** [I] When birds whistle, they sing in high musical notes: *The birds were whistling in the early morning quiet.*

whistle /ˈwɪs.l̩/ *noun* [C] **1** the sound made by someone or something whistling: *From the bottom of the garden I recognised my father's tuneless whistle.* ○ *It sounded like the whistle of an old-fashioned steam train.* ○ *She listened to the whistle of the wind through the trees.* **2** a device which you hold to your lips and blow through in order to make a loud, high sound: *The referee* ***blew*** *his whistle for half-time.*

whistle-blower /ˈwɪs.l̩ˌbləʊ.əʳ/ [US] /-ˌbloʊ.ɚ/ *noun* [C] a person who tells someone in authority about something illegal that is happening, especially in a government department or a company

whistle-stop tour /ˌwɪs.l̩.stɒpˈtʊəʳ/ [US] /-stɑːpˈtʊr/ *noun* [C] a series of brief visits to different places, made usually by a politician

whit /wɪt/ *noun FORMAL* **not a whit** not any amount: *There's not a whit* ***of*** *sense in that head of his!*

white [COLOUR] /waɪt/ *adj* **1** of a colour like that of snow, milk or bone: *a white T-shirt* ○ *white walls* ○ *a black and white dog* ○ *He's white-haired now.* ○ *"How do you like your coffee?" "White* (= With milk or cream) *and no sugar, please."* **2** used in the names of various food and drink products, many of which are not pure white but slightly cream, yellow, grey or transparent: *white bread* ○ *white chocolate* ○ *white flour* ○ *white sugar* ○ *white wine*

• **(as) white as a sheet** If someone is (as) white as a sheet, their face is very pale, usually because of illness, shock or fear.

• **whiter than white** never doing anything wrong: *I was never convinced by the image of the whiter than white princess depicted in the press.*

white /waɪt/ *noun* [U] **1** a colour like that of snow, milk or bone: *In some countries it is traditional for a bride to wear white.* **2 white of the eye** the part of the eye that is white: *Don't shoot until you see the whites of their eyes* (= until the people are very close to you). **3 egg white/ white of an egg** the transparent part of an egg which surrounds the yolk and becomes white when cooked: *Whisk four egg whites into stiff peaks.*

whiten /ˈwaɪ.tᵊn/ [US] /-t̬ᵊn/ *verb* [I or T] to make or become whiter: *She's had her nicotine-stained teeth whitened.* ○ *Her hair had whitened over the years.* **whiteness** /ˈwaɪt.nəs/ *noun* [U]

whitening /ˈwaɪ.tᵊn.ɪŋ/ [US] /-t̬ᵊn-/ *noun* [U] (*ALSO* **whitener**) a substance that you put on sports shoes to make them whiter and cleaner

whites /waɪts/ *plural noun* white clothes, either worn for sports or put together to be washed at the same time: *There was a group of men in* ***cricket*** *whites in the pub.*

whitish /ˈwaɪ.tɪʃ/ [US] /-t̬ɪʃ/ *adj* almost white in colour: *whitish-grey walls*

white [PEOPLE] /waɪt/ *adj, noun* [C] (of) a person who has a skin that is pale in colour: *He had a black mother and a white father.* ○ *a predominantly white neighbourhood* ○ *The neighbourhood is populated mainly by whites.*

ˌ**white ˈant** *noun* [C] a **termite**

whitebait /ˈwaɪt.beɪt/ *noun* [U] small, young fish of various different types, fried and eaten whole

ˌ**white ˈblood ˌcell** *noun* [C] (*ALSO* **white corpuscle**) a cell in the blood that has no red colouring and is involved in the fight against infection

whiteboard /ˈwaɪt.bɔːd/ [US] /-bɔːrd/ *noun* [C] a board with a smooth, white surface, often fixed to a wall, on which you can write and draw using special pens

ˌ**white ˈChristmas** *noun* [C] a Christmas when it snows: *Do you think we might have a white Christmas this year?*

white-collar /ˌwaɪtˈkɒl.əʳ/ [US] /-ˈkɑː.lɚ/ *adj* [before n] relating to people who work in offices, doing work that needs mental rather than physical effort: *white-collar workers/unions*

ˌ**white ˈelephant** *noun DISAPPROVING* something that has cost a lot of money but has no useful purpose

ˌ**white ˈflag** *noun* [C] a flag that is waved to show the acceptance of defeat or a lack of intention to attack: *The soldiers lay down their guns and walked towards the enemy camp, carrying a white flag.*

ˈ**white ˌgoods** *plural noun SPECIALIZED* large electrical goods for the house, such as cookers and washing machines

Whitehall /ˈwaɪt.hɔːl/ *noun* [U] the British CIVIL SERVICE (= officials employed to perform the work of the British government)

ˌ**white ˈheat** *noun* [U] the very high temperature at which metal gives out a white light

ˌ**white ˈhope** *noun* [S] a person or thing which people hope will be very successful in the near future: *This new car is seen as the* ***great*** *white hope of the British motor industry.*

ˌ**white ˈhorses** *UK plural noun* (*US* **whitecaps**) *LITERARY* waves which are white at the top

white-hot /ˌwaɪtˈhɒt/ [US] /-ˈhɑːt/ *adj* describes metal which is so hot it is giving out a white light

the ˈWhite ˌHouse *noun* [S] the official Washington home of the American President, or the American government itself: *The White House is set to announce health-care reforms.*

ˌ**white ˈknight** *noun* [C] a person or organization that saves a company from financial difficulties or an unwanted change of ownership by putting money into the company or by buying it

white-knuckle /ˌwaɪtˈnʌk.l̩/ *adj* [before n] *INFORMAL* describes an experience or activity that makes you feel very frightened and often excited: *a white-knuckle* ***ride*** *in a theme park*

ˌ**white ˈlie** *noun* [C] a lie that is told in order to be polite or to stop someone from being upset by the truth

ˌ**white ˈmagic** *noun* [U] magic which is used only to do good things

ˌ**white ˈmeat** *noun* [U] a meat such as chicken or VEAL that is pale in colour, or the whitest flesh, usually the breast, of a cooked bird

ˌ**white ˈnoise** *noun* [U] a mixture of sounds or electrical signals which consists of all sounds or signals in a large range

whiteout /ˈwaɪ.taʊt/ [US] /-t̬aʊt/ *noun* [C] a weather condition in which snow and clouds change the way light is reflected so that only very dark objects can be seen

the ˌWhite ˈPages *noun* [S] *US* a book that lists the names, addresses and telephone numbers of people living and businesses operating in a city or area ➲Compare **the Yellow Pages**.

ˌ**white ˈpaper** *noun* [C] in various countries, including Britain and Australia, a government report on a particular subject giving information and details of future planned laws: *a white paper on employment* ➲Compare **green paper**.

ˌ**white ˈpointer** *noun* [C] a large, dangerous type of SHARK (= large fish with sharp teeth and a vertical triangular part on its back)

ˌ**white ˈsauce** *noun* [U] a thick, savoury sauce made from flour, butter and milk

ˌwhite ˈspirit *UK noun* [U] (*US* **turpentine**) a colourless, alcoholic liquid which is used for making paint thinner and removing paint from brushes and clothes

ˌwhite suˈpremacy *noun* [U] the belief that people with pale skin are better than people with darker skin **ˌwhite suˈpremacist** *noun* [C]

white-tie /ˌwaɪtˈtaɪ/ *adj* describes a social occasion at which men wear formal clothes including a white BOW TIE: *a white-tie diplomatic reception*

ˈwhite ˌtrash *noun* [U] *US OFFENSIVE* white people who are poor and badly educated

whitewash [PAINT] /ˈwaɪt.wɒʃ/ [US] /-wɑːʃ/ *noun* [U] a white liquid that is a mixture of lime or powdered chalk and water, used for making walls or ceilings white **whitewash** /ˈwaɪt.wɒʃ/ [US] /-wɑːʃ/ *verb* [T]

whitewash [HIDE] /ˈwaɪt.wɒʃ/ [US] /-wɑːʃ/ *verb* [T] *DISAPPROVING* to make something bad seem acceptable by hiding the truth: *The government is trying to whitewash the incompetence of the Treasury officials.* **whitewash** /ˈwaɪt.wɒʃ/ [US] /-wɑːʃ/ *noun* [S] *The official report on the killings has been denounced as a whitewash.*

whitewash [DEFEAT] /ˈwaɪt.wɒʃ/ [US] /-wɑːʃ/ *verb* [T] *UK INFORMAL* to defeat a player or team completely, especially while preventing them from scoring any points **whitewash** /ˈwaɪt.wɒʃ/ [US] /-wɑːʃ/ *noun* [C] *a 6-0 whitewash*

ˌwhite ˈwater *noun* [U] water in a river which flows fast and strongly in an especially narrow channel: *white-water rafting*

ˌwhite ˈwedding *noun* [C] a traditional Christian marriage in a church, at which the woman who is getting married wears a white dress: *She wants a proper white wedding.*

whitey /ˈwaɪ.ti/ [US] /-t̬i/ *noun* [C] *OFFENSIVE* a white person

whither /ˈwɪð.əʳ/ [US] /-ɚ/ *adv OLD USE* to where: *Whither are they going?*

whiting /ˈwaɪ.tɪŋ/ [US] /-t̬ɪŋ/ *noun* [C or U] *plural* **whiting** or **whitings** a small black and silver sea fish, eaten as food

whitish /ˈwaɪ.tɪʃ/ [US] /-t̬ɪʃ/ *adj* ➲See at **white** COLOUR.

Whitsun /ˈwɪt.sᵊn/ *noun* [U] the seventh Sunday after Easter, and the period around it: *We're going to Scotland for a week **at** Whitsun.*

whittle /ˈwɪt.l̩/ [US] /ˈwɪt̬-/ *verb* [T] to make something from a piece of wood by cutting off small thin pieces: *An old sailor sat on the dockside, whittling a toy boat.*

PHRASAL VERBS WITH **whittle**

▲ **whittle away at *sth*** *phrasal verb* to gradually reduce the size or importance of something: *A series of new laws has gradually whittled away at the powers of the trade unions in this country.*

▲ **whittle *sth* down** *phrasal verb* [M] to gradually reduce the size of something or the number of people in a group: *We had eighty applicants for the job, but we've whittled them down **to** six.*

whizz [MOVE FAST] *UK, US USUALLY* **whiz** /wɪz/ *verb* [I + adv or prep] *INFORMAL* to move or do something very fast: *A police car whizzed **by**, on its way to the accident.* ○ *We whizzed **through** the rehearsal, so that we'd be finished by lunchtime.* ○ *Time just whizzes **past** when you're enjoying yourself.*

whizz [EXPERT] *UK, US USUALLY* **whiz** /wɪz/ *noun* [C usually sing] *INFORMAL APPROVING* a person with a very high level of skill or knowledge in a particular subject: *a computer whizz* ○ *He's a whizz **at** poker.*

whizz [DRUG] /wɪz/ *noun* [U] *UK SLANG FOR* **amphetamine** (= drug which makes the mind and body more active)

whizzkid /ˈwɪz.kɪd/ *noun* [C] *INFORMAL* a young person who is very clever and successful: *They've taken on some financial whizzkid who's going to sort out all their problems.*

who [ASKING] /huː/ *pronoun* **1** used especially in questions as the subject or object of a verb, when asking which person or people, or when asking what someone's name is: *Who did this?* ○ *Who's she?* ○ *Who are all those people?* ○ *She asked me if I knew who had got the job.* ○ *Who (also FORMAL **whom**) do you want to talk to?* ○ *I don't know who (also FORMAL **whom**) to ask to the party.* ➲See Note **whom or who?** at **whom**. **2** used with verbs that relate to knowing, when you want to say that something is not known: *"Are they going to get married?" "Who **knows**?"* (= It is not possible to know at the moment.) ○ *Who **can tell** what will happen now?*

• **who's who 1** the name and position of each person, especially in an organization **2 Who's Who** a book containing information about the world's richest or most famous people: *The guest list reads like a Who's Who of top American businessmen.*

who [USED TO REFER] /huː/ *pronoun* used as the subject or object of a verb to show which person you are referring to, or to add information about a person just mentioned. It is used for people, not things: *I think it was your Dad who phoned.* ○ *She's one of those people who love to be the centre of attention.* ○ *He rang James, who was a good friend as well as the family doctor.* ○ *The other people who (also **that**) live in the house are really friendly.* ○ *This is Gabriel, who (also FORMAL **whom**) I told you about.* ➲See Note **which, who or that?** at **which** USED TO REFER.

the ˌWHˈO *group noun* [S] *ABBREVIATION FOR* **the World Health Organization**

whoa /wəʊ/ [US] /woʊ/ *exclamation* **1** used when telling a horse to stop: *"Whoa there, Poppy," he said to his pony, and pulled up beside the kerb.* **2** *INFORMAL* used when telling a person to stop what they are doing or to do it more slowly: *Yes, carrots please, – whoa! That's plenty.*

who'd /huːd/ *short form of* **1** who had: *She wondered who'd sent her the mysterious email.* **2** who would: *Well, who'd have thought Joey was going to become so successful?*

whodunit, **whodunnit** /ˌhuːˈdʌn.ɪt/ *noun* [C] *INFORMAL* a story about a crime and the attempt to discover who committed it: *It's one of those whodunits where you don't find out who the murderer is till the very end.*

whoever [PERSON] /huːˈev.əʳ/ [US] /-ɚ/ *pronoun* the person who: *Whoever uprooted that tree ought to be ashamed of themselves.* ○ *Could I speak to whoever is in charge of International Sales please?*

whoever [ANYONE] /huːˈev.əʳ/ [US] /-ɚ/ *pronoun* any person who: *Can whoever leaves last please lock up?* ○ *He says he bought the car from Frank, whoever Frank is* (= I do not know who Frank is).

whoever [SURPRISE] /huːˈev.əʳ/ [US] /-ɚ/ *pronoun* used in questions as a way of expressing surprise: *Whoever told you that?* ○ *Whoever could that be phoning at this time?*

whole /həʊl/ [US] /hoʊl/ *adj* **1** complete or not divided: *I spent the whole day cleaning.* ○ *There's still a whole month till my birthday.* ○ *After my exercise class, my whole body ached.* ○ *The whole town was destroyed by the earthquake.* ○ *This whole **thing*** (= situation) *is ridiculous.* ○ *Bill does nothing but moan the whole **time*** (= all the time). ○ *You have to stand up in court and promise to tell 'the truth, the whole **truth** and nothing but the truth'.* ○ *Her dance compositions added a whole* (= completely) *new dimension to the contemporary dance repertoire.* **2** *INFORMAL* used to emphasize something: *I've got a whole heap of work to do this afternoon.* ○ *The new computers are **a** whole **lot*** (= much) *faster.*

• **the whole bit** *UK* (*US* **the whole enchilada**) the whole of something, including everything that is related to it: *He's into jogging, squash, aerobics, the whole exercise bit.*

• **go the whole hog** to do something as completely as possible: *Having already limited local taxation, why not go the whole hog and abolish it completely?*

whole /həʊl/ [US] /hoʊl/ *noun* [C usually sing] **1** a complete thing: *Two halves make a whole.* ○ *You must consider each problem as an aspect of **the** whole.* **2 the whole of *sth*** all of something: *I'll be on holiday the whole of next week.* ○ *The whole of his finger was bruised.* ○ *The whole of the village* (= Everyone in the village) *had come out for the party.*

• **as a whole** when considered as a group and not in parts: *The population as a whole is getting healthier.*

• **on the whole** generally: *We have our bad times but on the whole we're fairly happy.*

wholly /ˈhəʊl.li/ [US] /ˈhoʊl-/ *adv* completely: *I wasn't wholly convinced by her explanation.* ○ *That's a wholly*

W

different matter. ○ *a machine that is wholly British-made*

COMMON LEARNER ERROR

the whole or the whole of?

No preposition is necessary after **whole** when it is followed by a general word or phrase.

I lived in Germany for the whole year.

The preposition 'of' is needed before a more particular word or phrase.

I lived in Germany for the whole of 1999.

~~*I lived in Germany for the whole 1999.*~~

wholefood /ˈhəʊl.fuːd/ [US] /ˈhoʊl-/ *noun* **[C or U]** *UK* food that has not had any of its natural features taken away or any artificial substances added: *a wholefood shop/cookbook*

wholegrain /ˈhəʊl.greɪn/ [US] /ˈhoʊl-/ *adj MAINLY UK* (of particular types of food) containing whole seeds: *wholegrain bread* ○ *wholegrain mustard* ○ *wholegrain breakfast cereal*

whole-hearted /ˌhəʊlˈhɑː.tɪd/ [US] /ˌhoʊlˈhɑːr.t̬ɪd/ *adj* completely enthusiastic: *The minister has pledged his whole-hearted support for the scheme.* **whole-heartedly** /ˌhəʊlˈhɑː.tɪd.li/ [US] /ˌhoʊlˈhɑːr.t̬ɪd-/ *adv*: *Both members are whole-heartedly in favour of the changes.*

wholemeal *UK* /ˈhəʊl.miːl/ [US] /ˈhoʊl-/ *adj* (*US* **whole wheat**) (of flour or food made from flour) containing all the natural features of the grain, with nothing taken away: *wholemeal bread/flour/pastry*

whole-note /ˈhəʊl.nəʊt/ [US] /ˈhoʊl.noʊt/ *noun* **[C]** *US FOR* **semibreve**

ˌwhole ˈnumber *noun* **[C]** a number, such as 1, 3 or 17, which has no fractions, and no DIGITS after the DECIMAL POINT

wholesale [SELLING] /ˈhəʊl.seɪl/ [US] /ˈhoʊl-/ *adj, adv* of or for the selling of goods in large amounts at low prices to shops and businesses, rather than the selling of goods in shops to customers: *wholesale prices* ○ *a wholesale supplier/business* ○ *We only sell wholesale, not to the public.* ➲Compare **retail**.

wholesaler /ˈhəʊlˌseɪ.ləʳ/ [US] /ˈhoʊlˌseɪ.lɚ/ *noun* **[C]** someone who buys and sells goods in large amounts to shops and businesses: *a furniture wholesaler*

wholesale [COMPLETE] /ˈhəʊl.seɪl/ [US] /ˈhoʊl-/ *adj, adv OFTEN DISAPPROVING* (especially of something bad or too extreme) complete or affecting a lot of things, people, places, etc: *wholesale changes* ○ *the wholesale destruction of towns and villages*

wholesome /ˈhəʊl.sᵊm/ [US] /ˈhoʊl-/ *adj APPROVING* beneficial for you, and likely to improve your life either physically, morally or emotionally: *wholesome food* ○ *good wholesome family entertainment* ○ *He looks like a nice, wholesome, young man.* **wholesomeness** /ˈhəʊl.sᵊm.nəs/ [US] /ˈhoʊl-/ *noun* **[U]**

ˈwhole ˌwheat *adj MAINLY US FOR* **wholemeal**

who'll /huːl/ *short form of* who will: *Who'll be at the party tomorrow?*

whom /huːm/ *pronoun FORMAL* used instead of 'who' as the object of a verb or preposition: *I met a man with whom I used to work.* ○ *He took out a photo of his son, whom he adores.* ○ *There were 500 passengers, of whom 121 drowned.* ○ *To whom do you wish to speak?*

USAGE

whom or who?

whom is very formal and most people use **who** instead.

Who did you invite?

Although **whom** should be used after a preposition, most people avoid it by putting the preposition towards the end of the sentence and using **who** instead.

Who did you go out with last night?

It would be extremely formal and rather unnatural to say **whom**.

With whom did you go out last night?

whomever /huːˈmev.əʳ/ [US] /-ɚ/ *pronoun FORMAL* **whoever** PERSON and **whoever** ANYONE when used as the object: *Give it to whomever you please.*

whoop /wuːp/ *verb* **[I]** to give a loud, excited shout, especially to show your enjoyment of or agreement with something: *The audience was whooping and clapping.* ➲See also **whooping cough**.

• **whoop it up** *INFORMAL* to enjoy yourself in a noisy and excited way

whoop /wuːp/ *noun* **[C]** a loud, excited shout, especially showing your enjoyment of or agreement with something: *When the whoops and cheers had finally died down he started to speak.*

whoop-de-doo /ˌwʊp.dɪˈduː/ *MAINLY US INFORMAL* said when you do not think what someone has said or done is important or special: *Well, whoop-de-doo, they're offering us a 0.5 per cent pay raise!*

whoopee /wʊˈpiː/ *exclamation* a loud, excited shout of happiness: *Whoopee, it's the holidays!*

• **make whoopee** *US OLD-FASHIONED INFORMAL* to have sex

ˈwhooping ˌcough *noun* **[U]** a disease caught especially by children, which causes severe coughing

whoops /wʊps/ *exclamation* (*ALSO* **oops**) *INFORMAL* an expression of surprise or regret about a mistake or slight accident: *Whoops! That's the second time I've spilt coffee today!*

whoosh /wʊʃ/ *exclamation, noun* **[C usually sing]** *INFORMAL* a soft sound made by something moving fast through the air or like that made when air is pushed out of something: *The train sped through the station with a whoosh.*

whoosh /wʊʃ/ *verb* **[I usually + adv or prep]** *INFORMAL* *A fast motorboat whooshed by* (= moved quickly, making a soft sound).

whop /wɒp/ [US] /wɑːp/ *verb* **[T]** **-pp-** *MAINLY US, INFORMAL* to hit or defeat: *She whopped him with her handbag.* ○ *The Yankees whopped the Cleveland Indians 17-2.*

whopper /ˈwɒp.əʳ/ [US] /ˈwɑː.pɚ/ *noun* **[C]** *HUMOROUS, INFORMAL* **1** something that is surprising because it is so much bigger than the usual size: *I mean, my nose is quite big but my Dad's got a whopper.* **2** a big lie: *Amanda's told some whoppers in her time.*

whopping /ˈwɒp.ɪŋ/ [US] /ˈwɑː.pɪŋ/ *adj* **[before n]** (*ALSO* **whopping great**) *INFORMAL* extremely large: *She had a whopping great bruise on her arm.* ○ *a whopping 35% pay rise* ○ *a whopping lie*

whore /hɔːʳ/ [US] /hɔːr/ *noun* **[C]** *OLD-FASHIONED OR VERY INFORMAL DISAPPROVING* a female prostitute or a woman whose behaviour in her sexual relationships is considered immoral

whorehouse /ˈhɔː.haʊs/ [US] /ˈhɔːr-/ *noun* **[C]** *MAINLY US FOR* **brothel**

who're /ˈhuː.əʳ/ [US] /-ɚ/ *short form of* who are: *The film begins with a young couple, who're just about to get married.*

whorl /wɜːl/ [US] /wɝːl/ *noun* **[C]** *LITERARY* a circular pattern of lines, with the smallest circle in the middle, surrounded by other circles, each one wider and larger than the previous one

who's /huːz/ *short form of* **1** who has: *Who's been chosen, do you know?* **2** who is: *Who's that talking to Jason?*

whose [ASKING ABOUT OWNERSHIP] /huːz/ *pronoun, determiner* used especially in questions when asking about which person owns or is responsible for something: *Whose is this bag?* ○ *Whose bag is this?*

whose [ADDING INFORMATION] /huːz/ *determiner* used for adding information about a person or thing just mentioned: *Cohen, whose contract expires next week, is likely to move to play for a European club.* ○ *There was a picture in the paper of a man whose leg had been blown off.* ○ *They meet in an old house whose basement has been converted into a chapel.* ○ *Fraud detectives are investigating the company, three of whose senior executives have already been arrested.*

whosoever /ˌhuː.səʊˈev.əʳ/ [US] /-soʊˈev.ɚ/ *pronoun OLD USE FOR* **whoever**

who've /huːv/ *short form of* who have: *Who've you asked so far?*

why [REASON] /waɪ/ *adv* for what reason: *"I'm going home." "Why?"* ○ *Why did you choose to live in London?* ○ *Why wait? Let's leave now.* ○ *Why should I help him – he never helps me?* ○ *Why is it that I find chocolate so addictive?*

○ *The police asked me to explain why I hadn't reported the accident sooner.* ○ *I don't know why she isn't here.* ○ *Quite why he isn't here today is a mystery.* ○ *There is no **reason** why we shouldn't succeed.*

• **why not?** used to make a suggestion or to express agreement: *Why not use my car? You'll fit more in.* ○ *"Shall we eat Italian tonight?" "Yes, why not?"*

why /waɪ/ *noun*

• **the whys and (the) wherefores** the reasons for something: *I know very little about the whys and the wherefores of the situation.*

why [SURPRISE] /waɪ/ *exclamation* MAINLY US OR OLD-FASHIONED used to express surprise or annoyance: *Why, if it isn't old Georgie Frazer!* ○ *Why, I've never seen anything like it!*

wick /wɪk/ *noun* [C] a piece of string in the centre of a candle, or a similar part of a light, which supplies fuel to a flame

• **get on *sb's* wick** UK OLD-FASHIONED INFORMAL to annoy someone

wicked [BAD] /ˈwɪk.ɪd/ *adj* OLD-FASHIONED **1** morally wrong and bad: *It was a wicked thing to do.* ○ *Of course, in the end, the wicked witch gets killed.* ➲Compare **evil**; **naughty** BADLY BEHAVED. **2** slightly immoral or bad for you, but in an attractive way: *a wicked grin* ○ *a wicked sense of humour*

• **There's no rest for the wicked.** SAYING said when you must continue with your work or other activity although you are very tired

wicked [EXCELLENT] /ˈwɪk.ɪd/ *adj* INFORMAL excellent: *He's got some wicked trainers.*

wicker /ˈwɪk.əʳ/ [US] /-ɚ/ *adj* made of very thin pieces of wood twisted together: *a wicker basket/chair*

wickerwork /ˈwɪk.ə.wɜːk/ [US] /-ɚ.wɝːk/ *noun* [U] *The chairs are either wickerwork* (= made of thin pieces of wood) *or pine.*

wicket /ˈwɪk.ɪt/ *noun* [C] **1** (in cricket) a set of three vertical sticks with two small pieces of wood balanced across the top of them, at which the ball is aimed. There are two wickets on a cricket field. **2** the length of ground between the two sets of wickets

ˈwicket ˌkeeper *noun* [C] a cricket player who stands behind the wicket in order to catch the ball

wide [DISTANCE] /waɪd/ *adj* **1** having a larger distance from one side to the other than is usual or expected, especially in comparison with the length of something; not narrow: *a wide river/road/gap/foot* ○ *His eyes were wide* (= opened much more than usual) ***with** surprise.* ➲See also **width**. **2** used when describing how long the distance between the two sides of something is or when asking for this information: *The rectangle is 5 cm long and 1.9 cm wide.* ○ *The swimming pool is 5 metres wide.* ○ *How wide are your skis?*

• **give *sth/sb* a wide berth** INFORMAL to avoid a person or place: *I tend to give the city centre a wide berth on Saturdays because it's so busy.*

• **be wide of the mark** to be wrong: *Yesterday's weather forecast was a little wide of the mark, then.*

wide /waɪd/ *adv* farther than usual, or as far as possible: *"**Open** wide," said the dentist.* ○ *They moved the goal posts wider **apart**.*

widen /ˈwaɪ.dᵊn/ *verb* [I or T] to become, or to make something greater in width: *As it approaches the sea, the river begins to widen **(out)**.*

wide [AMOUNT] /waɪd/ *adj* describes something that includes a large amount or many different types of thing, or that covers a large range or area: *They sell a wide **range** of skin-care products.* ○ *She has a wide experience of teaching, in many different schools.* ○ *The Green Party no longer enjoys wide support* (= the support of many people).

wide /waɪd/ *adv* completely, or by a large amount: *She left the door wide **open**.* ○ *It was 3 a.m. and we were still wide **awake**.*

widely /ˈwaɪd.li/ *adv* **1** including a lot of different places, people, subjects, etc: *They have both travelled widely.* ○ *His plays are still widely performed in the USA.* ○ *French used to be widely spoken in Kampuchea.* ○ *His work on DNA was widely **admired**.* ○ *This theory is no longer widely **accepted**.* **2 differ/vary widely** to be very different: *Prices vary widely from shop to shop.*

widen /ˈwaɪ.dᵊn/ *verb* [I or T] to (cause something to) become larger or to include a larger amount or number: *His eyes/smile widened.* ○ *Why not widen the discussion to include the Muslim and Jewish points of view?*

wide-angle (lens) /ˌwaɪd.æŋ.gl̩ˈlenz/ *noun* [C] a camera lens that provides a wider view than usual

ˈwide ˌboy *noun* [C] UK INFORMAL DISAPPROVING a man who is dishonest or who deceives people in the way he does business: *Some of the younger property developers are real wide boys.*

wide-eyed /ˌwaɪdˈaɪd/ *adj* **1** having your eyes open much wider than usual **2** too willing to believe and admire what you see or are told: *At that time, I was still a wide-eyed youngster.*

wide-ranging /ˌwaɪdˈreɪn.dʒɪŋ/ *adj* covering many subjects: *a wide-ranging discussion*

widespread /ˌwaɪdˈspred/ *adj* existing or happening in many places and/or among many people: *There are reports of widespread flooding in northern France.* ○ *Malnutrition in the region is widespread – affecting up to 78% of children under five years old.* ○ *The campaign has received widespread support.*

widget /ˈwɪdʒ.ɪt/ *noun* [C] INFORMAL **1** any small device whose name you have forgotten or do not know **2** an imagined small product made by a company: *Let's assume the company makes ten pence profit on every widget they sell.*

widow /ˈwɪd.əʊ/ [US] /-oʊ/ *noun* [C] **1** a woman whose husband has died and who has not married again **2** INFORMAL HUMOROUS **fishing/football/golf widow** a woman whose husband is often not at home because he is fishing or playing football or golf

widowed /ˈwɪd.əʊd/ [US] /-oʊd/ *adj* describes a person whose husband or wife has died: *He was widowed at the age of 52.*

widowhood /ˈwɪd.əʊ.hʊd/ [US] /-oʊ-/ *noun* [U] the fact or period of being a widow

widower /ˈwɪd.əʊ.əʳ/ [US] /-oʊ.ɚ/ *noun* [C] a man whose wife has died and who has not married again

width /wɪtθ/ /wɪdθ/ *noun* **1** [C or U] the distance across something from one side to the other: *It is 5 metres **in** width.* ○ *The needle is seven times smaller than the width **of** a human hair.* ○ *The material is available in various widths.* ➲See also **wide**. Compare **length**. **2** [C] the distance across a swimming pool from one side to the other: *I managed to swim 2 widths underwater.*

wield /wiːld/ *verb* [T] **1** to hold a weapon or tool and look as if you are going to use it: *She was confronted by a man wielding a knife.* **2 wield influence/power, etc.** to have a lot of influence or power over other people: *He still wields enormous influence within the party.*

wiener /ˈwiː.nəʳ/ [US] /-nɚ/ *noun* [C] (ALSO **wienie, weenie**) US a FRANKFURTER (= thin, red-brown sausage)

wife /waɪf/ *noun* [C] *plural* **wives** the woman to whom a man is married; a married woman: *I met Greg's wife for the first time.* ○ *She's his third wife* (= She is the third woman to whom he has been married).

wifely /ˈwaɪ.fli/ *adj* OLD-FASHIONED like a wife or relating to a wife: *wifely duties*

wig /wɪg/ *noun* [C] a covering of artificial hair worn on the head to hide a lack of hair or to cover your own hair: *She was wearing a blonde wig.* ○ *In Britain, judges wear white wigs in court.* ➲Compare **toupée**.

wiggle /ˈwɪg.l̩/ *verb* [I or T] INFORMAL to (cause to) move up and down and/or from side to side with small, quick movements: *He tried wiggling the control stick but nothing happened.* ○ *She wiggled her toes in the water.* ○ *Her hips wiggle as she walks.*

wiggle /ˈwɪg.l̩/ *noun* [C] a small, quick movement up and down and/or from side to side: *With a wiggle of her hips, she pulled up the trousers.*

wiggly /ˈwɪg.l̩.i/ /ˈwɪg.li/ *adj* INFORMAL shaped like a line with many curves: *a wiggly line* ○ *a wiggly worm*

wigwam /ˈwɪg.wæm/ *noun* [C] a cone-shaped tent made and lived in, especially in the past, by Native Americans in the eastern US

wild [NATURAL] /waɪld/ *adj* **1** describes plants or animals that live or grow independently of people, in natural

W

conditions and with natural characteristics: *wild flowers/grasses* ○ *a herd of wild horses* **2** describes land that is not cultivated and has few people living in it: *a wild mountainous region*

• **wild horses wouldn't drag me** If you say wild horses would not drag you somewhere, you mean that nothing could persuade you to go there: *Wild horses wouldn't drag me to a party tonight.*

wild /waɪld/ *noun*

• **in the wild** in natural conditions, independent of humans: *Animals would produce more young in the wild than they do in the zoo.*

• **in the wilds (of *somewhere*)** in an area which is far from where people usually live and difficult to get to, and that is not considered easy to live in: *She lives somewhere in the wilds of Borneo.*

wildness /ˈwaɪld.nəs/ *noun* [U] *the wildness* (= natural and extreme beauty) *of the Western Highlands*

wild [NOT CONTROLLED] /waɪld/ *adj* **1** uncontrolled, violent or extreme: *a wild party* ○ *wild dancing* ○ *The audience burst into wild applause.* ○ *When I told him what I'd done, he* ***went*** *wild* (= became very angry). ○ *The children were wild* ***with*** *excitement* (= were extremely excited). ○ *Her eyes were wild/She had a wild look in her eyes* (= Her eyes were wide open, as if she were frightened, or mentally ill). ○ *His hair was wild* (= long and untidy) *and his clothes full of holes.* ○ *There have been wild* (= extreme) *variations in the level of spending.* ○ *They get some wild weather* (= many severe storms) *in the north.* ○ *It was a wild* (= stormy or very windy) *night, with the wind howling and the rain pouring down.* **2** *SLANG* very unusual, often in a way that is attractive or exciting: *Those are wild trousers you're wearing, Fi.*

• **be wild about *sth/sb*** *INFORMAL* to be very enthusiastic about something or someone: *I'm not wild about Indian food.*

wildly /ˈwaɪld.li/ *adv* in an uncontrolled or extreme way: *He was dancing wildly.* ○ *Inflation figures have fluctuated wildly between 0.2% and 25%.* ○ *It was wildly* (= very) *expensive.* ○ *I must say I'm not wildly* (= very) *keen on the idea.* **wildness** /ˈwaɪld.nəs/ *noun* [U]

wild [NOT THOUGHT ABOUT] /waɪld/ *adj* **wild accusation/guess/rumour** something that you say which is not based on facts and is probably wrong

ˌwild ˈboar *noun* [C] a large, fierce, hairy pig that lives wild in forests

ˈwild ˌcard [COMPUTING] *noun* [C] *SPECIALIZED* in computers, a symbol that has no particular meaning of its own so that its space can be filled by any real character that is necessary: *The wild cards are represented here by asterisks.*

ˈwild ˌcard [COMPETITION] *noun* [C] someone who is allowed to take part in a competition, although they have not qualified for it in the usual way: *Phillips is hoping for a wild card entry to the Queensland tennis championships.*

ˈwild ˌcard [UNKNOWN] *noun* [C] someone or something whose behaviour you cannot be certain of in advance: *The wild card in this election is the Green Party – no one knows exactly how much support they will get.*

wildcat strike /ˌwaɪld.kætˈstraɪk/ *noun* [C] (*UK ALSO* **lightning strike**) a sudden strike without the usual warning by the workers and often without the official support of the UNIONS

wildebeest /ˈwɪl.də.biːst/ *noun* [C] *plural* **wildebeest** or **wildebeests** a large, African animal with a long tail and horns that curve to the sides, and which lives in areas covered in grass

wilderness /ˈwɪl.də.nəs/ [US] /-dɚ-/ *noun* [C usually sing] **1** an area of land that has not been cultivated or had towns and roads built on it, especially because it is difficult to live in as a result of its extremely cold or hot weather or bad earth: *a beautiful mountain wilderness* ○ *Alaska is the last great wilderness.* ○ *MAINLY US It's a wilderness* ***area****, under the protection of the Parks Department.* **2** an outside area in which plants are left to grow naturally or untidily: *The garden was a wilderness* ***of*** *weeds and overgrown bushes.*

• **in the wilderness** If someone, such as a politician, is in the wilderness, they no longer have a position of authority and are not now in the news: *After five years in the political wilderness, she was recalled to be foreign minister.*

wildfire /ˈwaɪld.faɪəʳ/ [US] /-faɪr/ *noun* [C] a fire which is burning strongly and out of control on an area of grass or bushes in the countryside: *Major wildfires have destroyed thousands of acres in Idaho, Oregon and Montana.*

• **spread like wildfire** If disease or news spreads like wildfire, it quickly affects or becomes known by more and more people: *Once one child in the school has the infection, it spreads like wildfire.*

wildfowl /ˈwaɪld.faʊl/ *plural noun* birds that people shoot for sport, especially ones such as ducks that live near water

wild-goose chase /ˌwaɪldˈguːs.tʃeɪs/ *noun* [C] *INFORMAL* a search which is completely unsuccessful and a waste of time because the person or thing being searched for does not exist or is somewhere else: *After two hours spent wandering in the snow, I realized we were* ***on*** *a wild goose chase.*

wildlife /ˈwaɪld.laɪf/ *noun* [U] animals and plants that grow independently of people, usually in natural conditions: *a documentary on Peruvian wildlife* ○ *wildlife groups/conservation*

wildly /ˈwaɪld.li/ *adv* ➲See at **wild** NOT CONTROLLED.

ˌwild ˈrice *noun* [U] the black rice-like grains of a North American grass that are eaten, often with rice

the ˌWild ˈWest *noun* [S] the name given to the western part of the US during the time when Europeans were first beginning to live there and when there was fighting between them and the Native Americans

wiles /waɪlz/ *plural noun FORMAL* methods of persuasion that cleverly trick someone into doing something: *She'll have to* ***use*** *all her feminine wiles to get him to agree.*

wilful, *US USUALLY* **willful** /ˈwɪl.fəl/ *adj DISAPPROVING* (of something bad) done intentionally or (of a person) determined to do exactly as you want, even if you know it is wrong: *The present crisis is the result of years of wilful neglect by the council.* ○ *They eat huge quantities of sweet and fried foods, in wilful disregard of their health.* ○ *She developed into a wilful, difficult child.* **wilfully**, *US USUALLY* **willfully** /ˈwɪl.fəl.i/ *adv*: *Some basic safety rules were wilfully ignored.* **wilfulness**, *US USUALLY* **willfulness** /ˈwɪl.fəl.nəs/ *noun* [U]

will [FUTURE] /wɪl/ *modal verb* (*ALSO* **'ll**) used to talk about what is going to happen in the future, especially things that you are certain about or things that are planned: *Clare will be five years old next month.* ○ *The train leaves at 8.58, so we'll be in Scotland by lunchtime.* ○ *I'll see him tomorrow./I'll be seeing him tomorrow.* ○ *Will Susie be there?* ○ *It won't be easy to find another secretary.* ○ *There'll be trouble when she finds out.* ➲See Note **shall and will** at **shall** FUTURE.

• **will have** used to refer back to the past from a point in the future: *By the time we get there, Jim will have left.*

will [ABLE/WILLING] /wɪl/ *modal verb* (*ALSO* **'ll**) used to talk about what someone or something is able or willing to do: *I'll give you a lift.* ○ *Ask Ian if he'll take them.* ○ *I've asked her but she won't come.* ○ *The car won't start.* ○ *This quantity of lasagne will feed six people.*

will [REQUEST] /wɪl/ *modal verb* **1** used to ask someone to do something: *Will you give me her address?* ○ *Will you give that to Tony when you see him, please?* **2** (*ALSO* **'ll**) used as a polite way of inviting someone to do something, or of offering someone something: *Will you join us for a drink, Evie?* ○ *Will you come in for a while?* ○ *You'll have some cake, won't you, Charles?*

will [IF] /wɪl/ *modal verb* (*ALSO* **'ll**) used in conditional sentences that start with 'if' and use the present tense: *If he's late again, I'll be very angry.*

will [ORDER] /wɪl/ (*ALSO* **'ll**) used when angry to tell someone to do something: *Will you stop being such a pain!* ○ *You'll go upstairs and you'll go straight to bed like your father told you!*

will [ALWAYS] /wɪl/ *modal verb* (*ALSO* **'ll**) used when referring to something that always or usually happens: *Accidents will happen.* ○ *Fruit will keep longer in the* *fridge.* ○ *The product with the better-known brand name will always sell better.* ○ *She's 85 now, but she will insist on doing all her own housework.*

will [LIKELY] /wɪl/ *modal verb* (*ALSO* **'ll**) used to refer to what is likely: *That'll be Scott at the door.* ○ *That'll be his mother with him.* ○ *As you will all probably already know, election day is next week.*

will [MENTAL POWER] /wɪl/ *noun* **1** [C or U] the mental power used to control and direct your thoughts and actions, or a determination to do something, despite any difficulties or opposition: *From an early age she had a very strong will.* ○ [+ to infinitive] *After six months in hospital she began to lose the will **to** live* (= the desire and determination to stay alive). **2** [S] what someone wants to happen: *It was God's will.* ○ ***Against** their will* (= Although they did not want to), *they were forced to hold a meeting.* ○ *The government has failed to impose its will **upon** regional communities* (= to make them do as it wants). ➲See also **free will**.

• **at will** If you can do something at will, you can do it any time you want: *He can cry at will.*

• **with a will** *OLD-FASHIONED* with energy and determination: *They worked with a will and had cleared the path by 10.00 a.m.*

• **Where there's a will there's a way.** *SAYING* used to mean that if you are determined enough, you can find a way to achieve what you want, even if it is very difficult

will /wɪl/ *verb* **1** [T + obj + to infinitive] If you will something to happen, you try to make it happen by the power of your thoughts: [R] *She willed herself **to** remember his name.* **2** [I or T] *FORMAL* to want something: *Stay or go, **as you** will.*

-willed /-wɪld/ *suffix* **strong/weak willed** having a strong/weak will

will [DOCUMENT] /wɪl/ *noun* [C] an official statement of what a person has decided should be done with their money and property after their death: *Have you **made** a will yet?* ○ *She left me some money **in** her will.*

will /wɪl/ *verb* [T] to arrange to give money or property to others after your death

willful /ˈwɪl.fᵊl/ *adj US FOR* **wilful**

willie, willy /ˈwɪl.i/ *noun* [C] *UK INFORMAL OR CHILD'S WORD* a penis

the willies *plural noun INFORMAL* a feeling of nervousness and fear, especially caused by something strange or threatening: *Spending a night in the house alone always **gives** me the willies.* ○ *Seeing something in the shadows, I suddenly **got** the willies and ran.*

willing /ˈwɪl.ɪŋ/ *adj* **1 be willing (to do *sth*)** to be happy to do something if it is needed: *If you're willing to fly at night, you can get a much cheaper ticket.* ○ *You said you needed a volunteer – well, I'm willing.* ○ *Apparently John and Gabriel are willing **for** us to use their garden.* **2** *APPROVING* describes someone who does their work energetically and enthusiastically: *a willing helper/worker/student*

willingly /ˈwɪl.ɪŋ.li/ *adv*: *I would willingly* (= be ready and enthusiastic to) *help you if I weren't going away tomorrow.* **willingness** /ˈwɪl.ɪŋ.nəs/ *noun* [S or U] [+ to infinitive] *She shows a willingness **to** work on her own initiative.*

will-o'-the-wisp /ˌwɪl.ə.ðəˈwɪsp/ *noun* [C usually sing] something that is impossible to obtain or achieve: *Full employment is the will-o'-the-wisp that politicians have been chasing for decades.*

willow (tree) /ˈwɪl.əʊˌtriː/ [US] /-oʊ-/ *noun* [C] a tree that grows near water and has long, thin branches that hang down

willowy /ˈwɪl.əʊ.i/ [US] /-oʊ-/ *adj APPROVING* (especially of a woman) graceful and thin: *a willowy blonde*

willpower /ˈwɪl.paʊəʳ/ [US] /-paʊr/ *noun* [U] the ability to control your own thoughts and the way in which you behave; determination: *It took a lot of willpower to stay calm.* ○ *I don't have the willpower to diet.*

willy-nilly /ˌwɪl.iˈnɪl.i/ *adv INFORMAL* **1** If something happens willy-nilly, it happens whether the people who are involved want it to happen or not: *Both sides were drawn, willy-nilly, into the conflict.* **2** without any order: *She threw her clothes willy-nilly into a drawer.*

wilt /wɪlt/ *verb* [I] (of a plant) to become weak and begin to bend towards the ground, or (of a person) to become weaker, tired or less confident: *Cut flowers will soon wilt without water.* ○ *After only an hour's walking they were beginning to wilt in the heat.*

wily /ˈwaɪ.li/ *adj* (of a person) clever, having a very good understanding of situations, possibilities and people, and often willing to use tricks to achieve an aim: *a wily politician* ➲See also **wiles**.

wimp /wɪmp/ *noun* [C] *INFORMAL DISAPPROVING* a person who is not strong, brave or confident: *I'm afraid I'm a bit of a wimp when it comes to climbing up ladders.*

wimpish /ˈwɪm.pɪʃ/ *adj* (*ALSO* **wimpy**) *I'm far too wimpish to go rock climbing.*

wimp /wɪmp/ *verb*

▲ **wimp out** *phrasal verb INFORMAL* to decide not to do something because you are too frightened: *I was going to do a parachute jump but I wimped out at the last minute.*

win /wɪn/ *verb* **winning, won, won 1** [I or T] to achieve first position and/or get a prize in a competition or competitive situation: *Which year was it that Italy won the World Cup?* ○ *He won first prize/a bottle of gin in the raffle.* ○ *Who's winning?* ○ *This is the third medal she's won this season.* ○ *Who won the men's finals in the tennis?* ○ *They won the war, although it cost them millions of lives.* ○ *If this government win the next election, I'm leaving the country.* ○ *Everyone likes winning an argument.* ○ [+ two objects] *It was his goal that won us the match/won the match **for** us.* ○ *Her firm have just won* (= beaten other companies to get) *a cleaning contract worth £3 million.* **2** [T] to receive something positive, such as approval, loyalty, affection or love because you have earned it: *Her plans have won the support of many local people.* ○ *This is Jamie, the four-year old who won **the hearts** of the nation* (= made everyone love him and/or feel sympathy for him). ○ *She would do anything to win his love.* ○ *Winning **back** his trust was the hardest part.*

• ***sb* can't win** *INFORMAL* used to say that nothing someone does in a situation will succeed or please people: *Whatever I do seems to annoy her – I can't win.*

• **win hands down** to win very easily

• **win the day** to persuade people to support your ideas or opinions

• **You can't win 'em all.** (*ALSO* **You win some, you lose some.**) *INFORMAL* something that you say which means it is not possible to succeed at everything you do: *I'd have liked the job but I suppose you can't win 'em all.*

• **(Okay) you win!** something you say to someone who has persuaded you to do something that you did not intend to do, especially when they have used force and you are angry: *Okay, you win, I can't stand to hear one more complaint from you – we'll go home tomorrow!*

win /wɪn/ *noun* [C] when someone wins a game or competition: *It was United's sixth consecutive win this season.* ○ *Everyone was predicting a Republican win at the last election and look what happened.*

winner /ˈwɪn.əʳ/ [US] /-ɚ/ *noun* [C] **1** someone who wins a game, competition or election: *There'll be a prize for the winner.* ○ *The winner of this match will play Violente in the semi-finals.* ○ *And to find out who are the lucky winners of our competition, Samantha is going to draw some names out of the bag.* ➲See also **breadwinner**. **2** (*US ALSO* **game-winner**) *INFORMAL* in sport, a goal or point that causes a player or team to win a game: *Neil Eaves scored the winner in the last minute of the match.* **3** *INFORMAL* something that is extremely successful and popular: *That lemon tart was a winner, wasn't it?* ○ *I think they're **onto** a winner with this latest product* (= it will succeed).

winning /ˈwɪn.ɪŋ/ *adj* [before n] **1** that has won something: *Have you heard the winning entry in this year's Eurovision Song Contest?* ○ *It's nice to be on the winning side for a change.* **2** friendly and charming and tending to make people like you: *a winning smile*

winnings /ˈwɪn.ɪŋz/ *plural noun* an amount of money that has been won: *What are you going to spend your winnings on?*

win-win /ˌwɪnˈwɪn/ *adj* [before n] describes a situation, plan, etc. in which you cannot lose, whatever choice of action you make, or in which all the groups involved will gain benefits: *This is a win-win situation for her, because whoever wins this match, she's still going to be champion.* ○ *Promoting fairtrade is a win-win option, because everyone, both producers and consumers, benefits.*

COMMON LEARNER ERROR

win or **beat?**

You **win** a game or competition.

Who do you think will win the football game?

You **beat** a person or a team you are playing against.

We beat both teams.

~~*We won both teams.*~~

PHRASAL VERBS WITH **win**

▲ **win *sb* over/round** *phrasal verb* **[M]** to persuade someone to support you or agree with you, often when they were opposed to you before: *He's not sure about the idea at the moment, but I'm sure we'll win him over in the end.* ○ *They've won over a lot of the electorate since she's been leader of the party.*

▲ **win through** *phrasal verb* UK to finally succeed after trying hard to achieve something: *Most people are fairly confident that the workers will win through in the end.*

wince /wɪnts/ *verb* **[I]** to show pain briefly and suddenly in the face, often moving the head back at the same time: *Did I hurt you? – I thought I saw you wince.* ○ *It makes me wince even thinking about eye operations.* **wince** /wɪnts/ *noun* **[C usually sing]** *She **gave** a wince as the nurse put the needle in.*

winch /wɪntʃ/ *noun* **[C]** (ALSO **windlass**) a machine which lifts heavy objects by turning a chain or rope around a tube-shaped device **winch** /wɪntʃ/ *verb* **[T]** *Two helicopters winched the passengers to safety from the deck of the ship.*

wind [CURRENT OF AIR] /wɪnd/ *noun* **[C or U]** a current of air moving approximately horizontally, especially one strong enough to be felt: *There isn't enough wind to fly a kite.* ○ *The weather forecast warned of winds of up to 60-miles-an-hour today.* ○ *There was a light wind blowing.* ○ *Strong/High winds made the crossing very unpleasant.* ○ *The sails flapped **in the** wind.* ○ LITERARY *There wasn't a **breath of*** (= even a slight amount of) *wind.* ○ *A **gust** of wind suddenly caught her skirt.* ○ *The wind is beginning to **pick up*** (= get stronger). ○ *She ran **like the** wind* (= very fast) *to catch up.*

• **get wind of *sth*** to hear a piece of information that someone else was trying to keep secret: *I don't want my colleagues to get wind of the fact that I'm leaving.*

• **put/get the wind up *sb*** UK to make someone feel anxious about their situation: *Tell them your father's a policeman – that'll put the wind up them!*

• **take the wind out of *sb's* sails** to make someone feel less confident or less determined to do something, usually by saying or doing something that they are not expecting: *I was all ready to tell him that the relationship was over when he greeted me with a big bunch of flowers – it rather took the wind out of my sails.*

windy /ˈwɪn.di/ *adj* with a lot of wind: *It was a windy night.* ○ *It was wet and windy for most of the week.*

wind [BREATH] /wɪnd/ *noun* **[U]** **1** MAINLY UK breath or the ability to breathe: *I had to stop halfway up the hill to **get my** wind* (= allow my breathing to return to normal). **2** INFORMAL DISAPPROVING meaningless words and false claims: *I rarely bother to listen to politicians' speeches – it's all just wind.*

wind /wɪnd/ *verb* **[T]** **winded, winded** to make it difficult or temporarily impossible for someone to breathe, usually by hitting them in the stomach

winded /ˈwɪn.dɪd/ *adj* **[after v]** temporarily unable to breathe, either when hit in the stomach or after taking hard physical exercise: *Simon is so unfit – he gets winded just from walking up a flight of stairs.*

wind [BOWELS] UK /wɪnd/ *noun* **[U]** (US **gas**) gas in the bowels or in a baby's stomach, especially that which makes you feel uncomfortable or makes noises: *I like garlic but it gives me terrible wind.*

wind UK (**winded, winded**) /wɪnd/ *verb* **[T]** (US **burp**) to rub or very gently hit a baby on the back to allow air to come up from the stomach

wind [TURN] /waɪnd/ *verb* **wound, wound** **1** **[I or T; usually + adv or prep]** to turn or cause something to turn: *She wound the handle but nothing happened.* ○ *Once she'd got into the car, she wound the window **down/up*** (= caused it to open/close by turning a handle). ○ UK *Does this camera wind **on*** (= does the film in it move forward) *automatically?* ○ *That noise you can hear is the tape winding **back**.* ➲See also **rewind**. **2** **[T]** (ALSO **wind up**) If you wind (up) a clock or watch, you cause it to work by turning a key, handle or other device. **3** **[I usually + adv or prep]** If a road, path or river winds, it follows a route which turns repeatedly in different directions: *The river winds through the valley.*

winder /ˈwaɪn.dəʳ/ [US] /-dɚ/ *noun* **[C]** **1** UK (US **stem**) a small KNOB (= round handle) on a watch, which you use for winding it **2** a key or handle for winding a clock

wind [WRAP AROUND] /waɪnd/ *verb* **[T usually + adv or prep]** **wound, wound** to wrap something around an object several times or twist it repeatedly around itself: *She wound a scarf **around** her neck.* ○ *He wound the string **into** a ball.* ○ *He wound a small bandage **round** her finger.* **winding** /ˈwaɪn.dɪŋ/ *adj*: *There's a very long, winding path leading up to the house.*

PHRASAL VERBS WITH **wind**

▲ **wind *(sth)* down** [END] *phrasal verb* **[M]** **1** to end gradually or in stages, or to cause something to do this: *The government intends to wind the scheme down in early spring.* ○ *Unfortunately, the party was just winding down as we got there.* **2** If a business or organization winds down, or if someone winds it down, the amount of work it does is gradually reduced until it closes completely: *They're winding down their operations abroad because they're losing money.*

▲ **wind down** [RELAX] *phrasal verb* to gradually relax after doing something that has made you tired or worried: *When he goes on holiday, it takes him the first couple of days just to wind down.*

▲ **wind *(sth)* up** [END] *phrasal verb* **[M]** to end, or to make an activity end: *I think it's about time we wound this meeting up.* ○ *We need to wind up now, we've only got five minutes.*

▲ **wind *sth* up** *phrasal verb* **[M]** to close a business or organization: *Lawyers were called in to wind up the company.*

▲ **wind up** [BECOME] *phrasal verb* INFORMAL to find yourself in an unexpected and usually unpleasant situation, especially as a result of what you do: *If he carries on like this, he's going to wind up in prison!* ○ *You don't want to wind up homeless, do you?*

▲ **wind *sb* up** [DECEIVE] *phrasal verb* UK INFORMAL to tell someone something that is not true in order to make a joke: *Are you serious or are you just trying to wind me up?* **wind-up** /ˈwaɪnd.ʌp/ *noun* **[C usually sing]** *You can't be serious – is this a wind-up?*

▲ **wind *sb* up** [ANNOY] *phrasal verb* **[M]** UK INFORMAL to annoy or upset someone: *It really winds me up when he goes on about teachers having an easy life.* ○ *She just knows how to wind me up.* ➲See also **wound up**.

windbag /ˈwɪnd.bæg/ *noun* **[C]** INFORMAL DISAPPROVING a person who talks too much about boring things

windbreak /ˈwɪnd.breɪk/ *noun* **[C]** something which gives protection from the wind, such as a row of trees, bushes, or a wall

windbreaker US /ˈwɪndˌbreɪ.kəʳ/ [US] /-kɚ/ *noun* **[C]** (UK OLD-FASHIONED **windcheater**) a jacket which is made of a material which protects you from the wind

wind-chill /ˈwɪnd.tʃɪl/ *noun* **[U]** the effect that wind has on how cold the air feels: *It's two degrees outside, but with the wind-chill **factor**, it feels like minus five.*

ˈwind ˌchimes *plural noun* an arrangement of shells or small decorative shapes of metal or wood that hang from pieces of wire or string and make a gentle noise when moved by the wind

windfall [UNEXPECTED MONEY] /ˈwɪnd.fɔːl/ [US] /-fɑːl/ *noun* **[C]** an amount of money that you win or receive from some-

W

one unexpectedly: *Investors each received a windfall of £3000.* ○ *The government is hoping to collect a windfall* ***tax*** (= extra tax on a large unexpected company profit) *from British Electric.*

windfall [FRUIT] /ˈwɪnd.fɔːl/ [US] /-fɑːl/ *noun* [C] a piece of fruit blown down from a tree: *I tend to leave the windfalls for the birds to pick at.*

ˈwind ˌgauge *noun* [C] a device for measuring the force of the wind

ˈwind ˌinstrument *noun* [C] a musical instrument whose sound is produced by blowing: *Saxophones and flutes are wind instruments.*

windlass /ˈwɪnd.ləs/ *noun* [C] a **winch**

windmill /ˈwɪnd.mɪl/ *noun* [C] **1** a building or structure with large blades on the outside which, when turned by the force of the wind, provide the power for getting water out of the ground or crushing grain **2** a **wind turbine 3** (*US ALSO* **pinwheel**) a child's toy which consists of a stick with brightly coloured pieces of plastic at one end which turn around when you blow them or hold the toy in the wind

window [GLASS] /ˈwɪn.dəʊ/ [US] /-doʊ/ *noun* **1** [C] a space usually filled with glass in the wall of a building or in a vehicle, to allow light and air in and to allow people inside the building to see out: *Is it all right if I open/close the window?* ○ *He caught me staring out of the window.* ○ *I saw a child's face* ***at*** *the window.* ○ *She's got some wonderful plants* ***in*** *the window* (= on a surface at the bottom of the window). ○ *I was admiring the cathedral's stained-glass windows.* ○ *Have you paid the window* ***cleaner*** (= person whose job is to clean the outside of windows)*?* ○ *window frames* ○ *a window ledge* **2** [S] *LITERARY* something that enables you to see and learn about a situation or experience that is different from your own: *The film provides a window* ***on*** *the immigrant experience.* **3** [C] a transparent rectangle on the front of an envelope, through which you can read the address written on the letter inside **4** [C] the decorative arrangement of goods behind the window at the front of a shop, in addition to the window itself: *How much is the jacket* ***in*** *the window?* ○ *The shop windows are wonderful around Christmas time.*

• **go out (of) the window** If a quality, principle or idea goes out of the window, it does not exist any more: *Then people start drinking and sense goes out of the window.*

window [COMPUTER] /ˈwɪn.dəʊ/ [US] /-doʊ/ *noun* [C] a separate area on a computer screen which shows information and which you can move around: *to minimize/maximize a window*

window [OPPORTUNITY] /ˈwɪn.dəʊ/ [US] /-doʊ/ *noun* [C] a period when there is an opportunity to do something: *I'm quite busy this week but there might be a window on Friday.* ○ *If a window* ***of opportunity*** (= an opportunity) *should present itself, I'd be a fool not to take advantage of it.*

ˈwindow ˌbox *noun* [C] a box filled with earth, for growing decorative plants in, which is put on an outside WINDOWSILL: *window boxes full of brightly coloured geraniums*

ˈwindow ˌdressing [SHOPS] *noun* [U] the skill of decorating shop windows and arranging goods in them so that they look attractive to people going past

ˈwindow ˌdressing [DECEIVING] *noun* [U] *DISAPPROVING* things that are said or done in order to make an attractive effect but which are of no real importance: *Never mind the extra day's holiday, the free health care, and all the other window dressing in the company's offer – the point is, how much more money are we getting?*

W

ˈwindow ˌledge *noun* [C] a WINDOWSILL (= a shelf below a window)

windowpane /ˈwɪn.dəʊ.peɪn/ [US] /-doʊ-/ *noun* [C] a single piece of glass in the window of a building

ˈwindow ˌseat *noun* [C] **1** a seat on a train, aircraft or other, especially public, vehicle which is next to a window **2** a seat in a building which is below a window

ˈwindow ˌshade *noun* [C] *US* a BLIND (= a cover for a window)

window-shopping /ˈwɪn.dəʊˌʃɒp.ɪŋ/ [US] /-doʊˌʃɑː.pɪŋ/ *noun* [U] when you spend time looking at the goods on sale in shop windows without intending to buy any of them

windowsill /ˈwɪn.dəʊ.sɪl/ [US] /-doʊ-/ *noun* [C] (*ALSO* **window ledge**) a shelf below a window, either inside or outside a building: *He's got a few plants in pots on the windowsill.*

windpipe /ˈwɪnd.paɪp/ *noun* [C] (*SPECIALIZED* **trachea**) the tube in the body which carries air that has been breathed in from the upper end of the throat to the lungs: *A bit of food went down my windpipe and gave me a coughing fit.*

windscreen /ˈwɪnd.skriːn/ *noun* [C] **1** *UK* (*US* **windshield**) the window at the front of a car, truck etc. ➲See picture **Car** on page Centre 12 **2** *US FOR* **windbreak**

windscreen wiper *UK* /ˈwɪnd.skriːnˌwaɪp.əʳ/ [US] /-ɚ/ *noun* [C usually pl] (*US* **windshield wiper**) one of two long metal and rubber parts that move against a windscreen to remove rain ➲See picture **Car** on page Centre 12

windsock /ˈwɪnd.sɒk/ [US] /-sɑːk/ *noun* [C] a tube of cloth fastened at one end to a pole which shows the direction of the wind at an airport

windsurfing /ˈwɪndˌsɜː.fɪŋ/ [US] /-ˌsɝː-/ *noun* [U] a sport in which you sail across water by standing on a board and holding onto a large sail: *I* ***went*** *windsurfing most afternoons.* ➲Compare **surfing** at **surf** WAVES.

windsurfer /ˈwɪndˌsɜː.fəʳ/ [US] /-ˌsɝː.fɚ/ *noun* [C] someone who goes windsurfing

Windsurfer *TRADEMARK* /ˈwɪndˌsɜː.fəʳ/ [US] /-ˌsɝː.fɚ/ *noun* [C] (*ALSO* **sailboard**) a narrow board with a sail fixed to it which you hold, standing up, while the wind blows you along the surface of a sea or lake **windsurf** /ˈwɪnd.sɜːf/ [US] /-sɝːf/ *verb* [I]

windswept /ˈwɪnd.swept/ *adj* (of places) open to and not protected from strong winds, or (of people) having hair that is untidy because it has been blown in different directions by the wind: *We drove down to the windswept Atlantic coast of Portugal.* ○ *windswept hair*

ˈwind ˌtunnel *noun* [C usually sing] an enclosed passage or room through which currents of air are forced in order to study the effects of moving air on aircraft and other vehicles

ˈwind ˌturbine *noun* [C] a tall structure with blades that are blown round by the wind and produce power to make electricity

windward /ˈwɪnd.wəd/ [US] /-wɚd/ *adj SPECIALIZED* (on the side of a hill, etc.) facing the wind: *On the windward leg of the race the wind was strong.* ➲Compare **leeward**.

windy /ˈwɪn.di/ *adj* ➲See at **wind** CURRENT OF AIR.

wine /waɪn/ *noun* [C or U] an alcoholic drink which is usually made from grapes, but can also be made from other fruits or flowers. It is made by FERMENTING the fruit with water and sugar: *a wine cellar/connoisseur/cooler/glass* ○ *red/white/dry/sweet/sparkling/table wine* ○ *Shall we have a* ***bottle/glass of*** *wine with dinner?* ○ *I love Australian wines, especially the white wines.* ○ *Would you like to see the wine* ***list****, sir?*

wine /waɪn/ *verb* **wine and dine** ***sb*** to entertain someone by giving them food and drink: *The survey concludes that most women like to be wined and dined on the first few dates.*

ˈwine ˌbar *noun* [C] *UK* a bar or small restaurant which serves mainly wines

ˈwine ˌrack *noun* [C] a wooden or metal frame used to store bottles of wine horizontally

wing [STRUCTURE FOR FLYING] /wɪŋ/ *noun* [C] the flat part of the body which a bird, insect or bat uses for flying, or one of the flat horizontal structures that stick out from the side of an aircraft and support it when it is flying: *the delicacy of a butterfly's wings* ○ *I don't like chicken wings – there's not much meat on them.* ○ *I could see the plane's wing out of my window.* ➲See picture **Planes, Ships and Boats** on page Centre 14

• **on a wing and a prayer** If you do something on a wing and a prayer, you do it hoping that you will succeed, although you are not prepared enough for it: *With scarcely any funding and a staff of six, they were operating on a wing and a prayer.*

• **take wing** *LITERARY* **1** If a bird takes wing, it flies away.

2 to suddenly develop, freely and powerfully: *She walked in the hills, letting her thoughts take wing.*
• **on the wing** LITERARY A bird that is on the wing is flying.
• **take *sb* under *your* wing** If you take someone under your wing, you start to protect and take care of them: *I was a bit lonely and fed up at the time and she took me under her wing.*
winged /wɪŋd/ /ˈwɪŋ.ɪd/ *adj* **[before n]** **1** having the stated type of wings: *a high-winged aeroplane* **2** with wings: *The winged adult mosquitoes emerge from the pupae.* ○ *Cupid is usually depicted as a winged boy with a bow and arrow.*

wing [POLITICAL GROUP] /wɪŋ/ *noun* **[C]** a group within a political party or organization whose beliefs are in some way different from those of the main group: *The president is on the **left/right** wing of the Democratic party.*

wing [PART OF BUILDING] /wɪŋ/ *noun* **[C]** a part of a large building which sticks out from the main part, often having been added at a later date: *The maternity ward will be in the new wing of the hospital.* ○ *The west wing of the house is still lived in by Lord and Lady Carlton, while the rest of the house is open to the public.*

wing [PART OF CAR] UK /wɪŋ/ *noun* **[C]** (US **fender**) one of the four parts at the side of a car which go over the wheels: *There's a dent in the left wing.* ○ *Look in your wing **mirror**.* ➲See picture **Car** on page Centre 12

wing [SPORTS] /wɪŋ/ *noun* **[C]** (in various team games, such as football and hockey) either of the two sides of the sports field, or a player whose position is at either of the two sides of the field: *Minelli passes the ball to Hernandez out there on the wing.* ○ *He played **left/right** wing for Manchester United.*
winger /ˈwɪŋ.əʳ/ (US) /-ɚ/ *noun* **[C]** a player whose position is at either of the two sides of the field in a team game such as football or hockey: *Liverpool have just spent £800 000 on the talented 25-year-old winger.*

wing [NO PREPARATION] /wɪŋ/ *verb* INFORMAL **wing it** to perform or speak without having prepared what you are going to do or say: *I hadn't had time to prepare for the talk, so I just had to wing it.*

ˌwing ˈchair *noun* **[C]** a chair with a high back from which large side pieces stick out

ˌwing ˈcollar *noun* **[C]** the strip of material which goes around the neck on a man's formal shirt and is folded down into the shape of two small triangles at the front

ˈwing ˌmirror UK *noun* **[C]** (US **side mirror**) a mirror on the outside of a car door which allows the driver to see the vehicles that are behind or OVERTAKING ➲See picture **Car** on page Centre 12

ˈwing ˌnut *noun* **[C]** a small, metal fastening device which has two flat pieces on it that you can hold with your fingers while tightening it

the wings *plural noun* the sides of a stage which cannot be seen by the people watching the play: *I was **in** the wings waiting for my cue to come on stage.*

wingspan /ˈwɪŋ.spæn/ *noun* **[C]** the distance between the ends of the wings of a bird, insect or aircraft

wink /wɪŋk/ *verb* **[I]** **1** to close one eye briefly as a way of greeting someone or showing friendliness, affection, sexual attraction etc., or of showing that you are not serious about something you have said: *She winked **at** me as he turned his back.* ○ *For a moment I thought he was being serious, but then he winked **at** me.* **2** When lights wink, they keep flashing on and off quickly: *Reflected in the water, the lights winked **at** us from the other side of the lake.* ○ *The light was winking on the answering machine.*
wink /wɪŋk/ *noun* **[C]** when you wink at someone: *He **gave** me a conspiratorial wink as they left the room.*
• **not sleep a wink** (ALSO **not get a wink of sleep**) to not sleep at all: *I didn't sleep a wink last night with all that noise.*
▲ **wink at *sth*** *phrasal verb* to pretend not to notice something bad that is happening because it is more convenient for you

winkle /ˈwɪŋ.kl̩/ *noun* **[C]** (US USUALLY **periwinkle**) a small edible sea snail

winkle /ˈwɪŋ.kl̩/ *verb*
▲ **winkle *sth/sb* out** *phrasal verb* **[M]** MAINLY UK to obtain or find something or someone with difficulty: *I managed to winkle the truth out **of** him eventually.*

Winnebago /ˌwɪn.əˈbeɪ.gəʊ/ (US) /-goʊ/ *noun* **[C]** TRADEMARK a large vehicle that is made for you to live in while you are travelling ➲See picture **Cars and Trucks** on page Centre 13

ˈwinning ˌpost *noun* **[C usually sing]** UK a post that marks the place where a race ends: *His horse collapsed just 40 yards from the winning post.* ➲See picture **Sports** on page Centre 10

winnings /ˈwɪn.ɪŋz/ *plural noun* ➲See at **win**.

winnow /ˈwɪn.əʊ/ (US) /-oʊ/ *verb* **[T]** **1** to blow the CHAFF (= the outer coverings) from grain before it can be used as food **2** FORMAL to reduce a large number of people or things to a much smaller number by judging their quality: *A list of 12 candidates has been winnowed **down to** a shortlist of three.* ○ *a winnowing process*

wino /ˈwaɪ.nəʊ/ (US) /-noʊ/ *noun* **[C]** *plural* **winos** INFORMAL a person, especially a homeless person, who drinks too much wine or other alcoholic drink: *There were the usual bunch of winos outside the station.*

winsome /ˈwɪn.səm/ *adj* LITERARY APPROVING attractive and pleasing, with simple qualities, sometimes like those a child has: *Maria brought along her eldest daughter – a winsome lass with brown eyes and a ready smile.* **winsomely** /ˈwɪn.səm.li/ *adv*

winter /ˈwɪn.təʳ/ (US) /-t̬ɚ/ *noun* **[C or U]** the season between autumn and spring, lasting from November to March north of the equator and from May to September south of the equator, when the weather is coldest: *Last winter we went skiing.* ○ *It's been a surprisingly mild winter.* ○ *I think you tend to eat more **in the** winter.*
winter /ˈwɪn.təʳ/ (US) /-t̬ɚ/ *verb* **[I + adv or prep]** (especially of a bird) to spend the winter in a particular place: *Birds migrate so that they can winter in a warmer country.* ○ *Kuwait Bay is one of the world's most important wintering grounds for wading birds.*

ˌwinter ˈsports *plural noun* sports that are done on snow or ice

wintertime /ˈwɪn.tə.taɪm/ [US] /-t̬ɚ-/ *noun* [U] the season of winter: *Like most seaside resorts* ***in the*** *wintertime, it's quite deserted.*

wintry [LIKE WINTER] /ˈwɪn.tri/ *adj* typical of winter: *It looks like this wintry weather is here to stay.* ○ *This afternoon we may see some wintry* ***showers*** (= snow mixed with rain) *over higher ground.* ○ *Wintry conditions are making roads hazardous for drivers in the northeast of England.*

wintry [EXPRESSION] /ˈwɪn.tri/ *adj* LITERARY unfriendly and disapproving: *She gave a wintry* ***smile****.*

wipe /waɪp/ *verb* [T] to slide something, especially a piece of cloth, over the surface of something else, in order to remove dirt, food or liquid: *Have you got a cloth that I can wipe the floor with?* ○ *I'll just get a sponge and wipe the crumbs off the table.* ○ *Don't wipe your nose* ***on*** *your sleeve!* ○ *Someone has wiped their dirty hands* ***on*** *my nice clean towel!*

• **wipe the floor with** ***sb*** INFORMAL to defeat someone very easily: *"I hear Italy beat France in the semi-finals last night." "Beat them? They wiped the floor with them!"*

• **wipe the slate clean** to start a new and better way of behaving, forgetting about any bad experiences in the past: *A new relationship presents you with the opportunity to wipe the slate clean.*

• **wipe the smile off** ***sb's*** **face** to make someone feel less happy or confident, especially someone who is annoying you because they think they are very clever: *Tell him you saw Helena at the cinema with another guy – that should wipe the smile off his face!*

• **wipe** ***sth*** **off the map** (*ALSO* **wipe** ***sth*** **off the face of the earth/globe**) to destroy completely: *There are bombs so powerful that whole nations could be wiped off the map by them.*

wipe /waɪp/ *noun* [C] **1** an act of wiping: *I'd better* ***give*** *the floor a quick wipe before someone slips on it.* **2** a piece of soft, wet cloth or paper that you use for wiping: *baby wipes*

PHRASAL VERBS WITH **wipe**

▲ **wipe** ***sth*** **down** *phrasal verb* [M] to clean the surface of something, such as a table, with a cloth: *Every night we wipe the tables down before we shut the restaurant.*

▲ **wipe** ***sth*** **off** ***sth*** *phrasal verb* [M] to remove something from something: *All their customer information was wiped off the computer by a virus.* ○ *8 billion has been wiped off share prices worldwide.*

▲ **wipe** ***sth*** **out** [DESTROY] *phrasal verb* [M] to destroy something completely: *Whole villages were wiped out in the fighting.* ○ *One bad harvest could wipe out all of a grower's profits for the previous two years.*

▲ **wipe out** [LOSE CONTROL] *phrasal verb* US INFORMAL to lose control, especially in a vehicle, and have an accident: *I was going too fast and I wiped out on the bend.*

▲ **wipe** ***sth*** **up** *phrasal verb* [M] to remove a substance, usually liquid, with a cloth or something similar: *I was just wiping up the soup that you spilt in the kitchen.* ○ *Have you got something I could wipe up this mess* ***with****?*

ˌwiped ˈout [TIRED] *adj* [after v] INFORMAL extremely tired: *After that 5-mile run I was completely wiped out.*

ˌwiped ˈout [DRUNK] *adj* [after v] US SLANG suffering from the effects of drinking alcohol or taking drugs

wire [METAL THREAD] /waɪəʳ/ [US] /waɪr/ *noun* **1** [C or U] a piece of thin metal thread which can be bent, used for fastening things and for making particular types of strong but flexible items: *a wire fence* **2** [C] (a piece of) thin metal thread with a layer of plastic around it, used for carrying electric current: *Someone had cut the telephone wires.* ○ *Don't touch those wires whatever you do.* **3 the wire** the wire fence round a prison or PRISON CAMP: *During the war he spent three years* ***behind*** *the wire* (= in prison).

• **down to the wire** until the last moment that it is possible to do something: *I think the election will* ***go*** *right down to the wire* (= be won at the last moment).

• **get** ***your*** **wires crossed** When people get their wires crossed, they have a different understanding of the same situation: *Somehow we got our wires crossed because I'd got the 23rd written down in my diary and Jen had the 16th.*

wire /waɪəʳ/ [US] /waɪr/ *verb* [T] **1** to fasten two things together using wire: *She had her jaws wired* ***together*** *so that she wouldn't be able to eat.* **2** (*ALSO* **wire up**) to connect a piece of electrical equipment with wires so that it will work: *The stereo wasn't working because it hadn't been wired up properly.* ○ *Nearly one home in ten across the country is wired up to receive TV via cable.*

ˌwired ˈup UK *adj* [after v] (US **wired**) secretly equipped with an electronic device that records conversations: *The negotiators were wired up when they talked to the kidnappers.*

wiring /ˈwaɪə.rɪŋ/ [US] /ˈwaɪr.ɪŋ/ *noun* [U] the system of wires that carry electricity in a building: *The club closed after the fire brigade declared its wiring to be unsafe.*

wiry /ˈwaɪə.ri/ [US] /ˈwaɪr.i/ *adj* describes hair that is strong, thick and rough to touch ➲See also **wiry**.

wire [SEND MESSAGE] /waɪəʳ/ [US] /waɪr/ *verb* [T] MAINLY US **1** to send a message using an electrical communication system, especially to send an amount of money to someone in this way: *The insurance company wired millions of dollars* ***to*** *its accounts to cover the payments.* ○ [+ two objects] *Luckily my father wired me two hundred bucks.* **2** in the past, to send someone a TELEGRAM: *Janet wired me to say she'd be here a day later than planned.* **wire** /waɪəʳ/ [US] /waɪr/ *noun* [C]

ˌwire ˈbrush *noun* [C] a brush with pieces of wire fixed into it, used especially for cleaning metal

wired /waɪəd/ [US] /waɪrd/ *adj* [after v] (*ALSO* **wired up**) MAINLY US INFORMAL nervous or excited about a future event: *I was totally wired before the interview.*

wire-haired /ˌwaɪəˈheəd/ [US] /ˌwaɪrˈherd/ *adj* A dog that is wire-haired has stiff, rough hair: *a wire-haired dachshund*

wireless /ˈwaɪə.ləs/ [US] /ˈwaɪr-/ *noun* [C] UK OLD-FASHIONED a radio

ˌwire ˈnetting *noun* [U] a net made of twisted wire which is often used for fences

ˈwire ˌservice *noun* [U] MAINLY US an organization that supplies news to newspapers, radio and television stations, etc. using an electrical communication system

wire-tapping /ˈwaɪəˌtæp.ɪŋ/ [US] /ˈwaɪr-/ *noun* [U] the action of secretly listening to other people's conversations by connecting a listening device to their telephone: *If he suspected an employee of dishonesty, he was not above wire-tapping.*

ˌwire ˈwool *noun* [U] UK FOR **steel wool**

wiry /ˈwaɪə.ri/ [US] /ˈwaɪr.i/ *adj* (of people and animals) thin but strong, and often able to bend easily: *He has a runner's wiry frame.* ➲See also **wiry** at **wire** METAL THREAD.

ˈwisdom ˌtooth *noun* [C] *plural* **wisdom teeth** one of the four teeth at the back of the jaw that are the last to grow: *She's having her wisdom teeth out.*

wise [CLEVER] /waɪz/ *adj* **1** APPROVING possessing or showing the ability to make good judgments, based on a deep understanding and experience of life: *I think you made a wise choice.* ○ *"I never drink more than three glasses of wine." "How wise."* ○ *Looking at the weather, I think we made a wise decision not to go to the coast this weekend.* ○ *I think it would be wiser* ***to*** *wait and see how much money you've got left before you make any decisions.* ○ *I never used to save money but now I'm a little* ***older and wiser*** *I can see the sense in it.* ○ *Was it Thomas More who said that the wise man learns from the experience of others?* **2** INFORMAL **wise to** ***sth*** aware of a dishonest situation or way of doing something: *I used to be scrupulously honest then I got wise to the system.*

• **be none the wiser** to still be confused about something even after it has been explained to you: *I've read the instructions twice and I'm still none the wiser.*

• **It's easy to be wise after the event.** MAINLY UK SAYING used to mean that it is easy to understand what you could have done to prevent something bad from happening after it has happened: *In retrospect, we should have insisted on checking his calculations, but it's easy to be wise after the event.*

wisely /ˈwaɪz.li/ *adv* showing good judgement: *Sian had very wisely left the party before all the trouble started.* ○ *Invest your money wisely through Home Counties Savings Trust.*

wisdom /ˈwɪz.dəm/ *noun* [U] the ability to use your knowledge and experience to make good decisions and judgements: *One certainly hopes to gain a little wisdom as one grows older.* ○ *He's got a weekly radio programme in which he* ***dispenses*** *wisdom* (= gives his opinions) *on a variety of subjects.* ○ *I tend to* ***doubt*** *the wisdom of separating a child from its family whatever the circumstances.* ○ *Did we ever stop to* ***question*** *the wisdom of going to war?* ○ *Before I went off to university my father gave me a few* ***words of*** *wisdom.* ○ ***Conventional/Received/Popular*** *wisdom has it* (= Most people think) *that women are more emotional than men, but in my experience it often isn't the case.*

• **in *his/her/their* wisdom** *HUMOROUS* something that you say when you do not understand why someone has done something stupid: *The council, in their wisdom, decided to close the library and now the building stands empty.*

• **with the wisdom of hindsight** with the knowledge that experience gives you: *With the wisdom of hindsight we now know that the old-fashioned aerosol sprays were a mistake.*

-wise [IN THIS WAY] /-waɪz/ *suffix* in this way or in this direction: *clockwise* ○ *lengthwise*

-wise [RELATING TO] /-waɪz/ *suffix INFORMAL* relating to a particular thing: *What shall we do foodwise – do you fancy going out to eat?* ○ *Moneywise, of course, I'm much better off than I used to be.* ○ *What do we need to take with us clothes-wise?* ○ *We were very lucky weather-wise yesterday.*

wise /waɪz/ *verb*

▲ **wise up** *phrasal verb MAINLY US INFORMAL* to start to understand a situation or fact and believe what you hear about it, even if it is difficult or unpleasant: *Those who think this is a harmless recreational drug should wise up.* ○ *It's about time employers wised up* ***to*** *the fact that staff who are happy work more efficiently.*

wisecrack /ˈwaɪz.kræk/ *noun* [C] *INFORMAL* a remark which is intended as a clever joke, especially one which criticizes someone: *He* ***made*** *some wisecrack about my lack of culinary ability.* **wisecracking** /ˈwaɪz,kræk.ɪŋ/ *noun* [U], *adj* [before n] *Sadly, despite the crazy antics and the relentless wisecracking, there's very little plot to carry this film.*

ˈwise ˌguy *INFORMAL noun* [C] (*US OFFENSIVE* **wise ass**) someone who is always trying to seem more clever than anyone else in a way that is annoying: *Okay, wise guy, if you're so damned smart, you can tell everyone how it's done!* **wise-guy** /ˈwaɪz.gaɪ/ *adj* [before n] (*US OFFENSIVE* **wise-ass**) *wise-guy humour*

wish [REGRET] /wɪʃ/ *verb* [I + *(that)*] **1** used with the past simple tense to express regret about a state or situation that exists at the moment: *I wish* ***(that)*** *I was/were a bit taller.* ○ *I wish* ***(that)*** *you were coming with me, Peter.* **2** used with the past perfect tense to express regret about a particular action in the past: *I wish* ***(that)*** *I hadn't eaten so much.* ○ *I bet she wishes* ***(that)*** *she'd never got involved in the whole affair.*

wish [DESIRE] /wɪʃ/ *noun* [C] a desire for something: [+ *to* infinitive] *Did he express any wish* ***to*** *see me?* ○ *In accordance with his wishes* (= what he wanted), *he was buried next to his wife.* ○ *They've deliberately gone against my wishes and sold the apartment.* ○ [+ **that**] *It was grandpa's greatest wish* ***that*** *one of his grandchildren would become a doctor.*

wish /wɪʃ/ *verb* [I or T] **1** *FORMAL* to want to do something: *We could go to the cinema or we could go out for dinner – whatever you wish.* ○ *"Shall we ask Diana if she'd like to come to the theatre tonight?" "If/As you wish."* ○ [+ *to* infinitive] *I wish* ***to*** *make a complaint.* ○ *Passengers wishing* ***to*** *take the Kings Cross train should go to platform 9.* ○ *I don't wish* ***to*** *worry you but he did say he'd be back by midnight.* ○ [+ obj + adj] *Sometimes I was so depressed that I wished myself dead.* **2 I wish (that)...** used to express annoyance with someone's behaviour: *I wish she'd shut up for a moment and let someone else speak.* ○ *I wish you'd look at me when I'm trying to speak to you!*

wish [MAGIC] /wɪʃ/ *noun* [C] a hope that is made real with magical powers: [+ **that**] *If I could have just one wish, I suppose it would be* ***that*** *all the fighting in the world would stop tomorrow.* ○ *Close your eyes and* ***make*** *a wish.* ○ *It's that bit in the story where the fairy* ***grants*** *the little girl three wishes.* ○ *May all your wishes come true.*

wish /wɪʃ/ *verb* [I or T] [+ **that**] *I remember blowing out the candles on my birthday cake and wishing* ***that*** *John Lee would be my boyfriend.* ○ *If I could wish myself anywhere in the world* (= go anywhere as a result of making a wish) *right now, it would be somewhere hot and sunny.* ○ *He's funny, bright, handsome – everything a girl could wish* ***for*** *really.* ○ *"Your job must be very glamorous." "I wish!"* (= Not at all.) ○ *"By the time I'm 40, I'll be so rich I won't have to work." "You wish!"* (= There's no chance of that happening.)

• **I/You wouldn't wish *sth* on anyone/my/your worst enemy.** something you say in order to emphasize that something is extremely unpleasant: *The effects of this disease are horrible. You wouldn't wish them on your worst enemy.*

wish [HOPE] /wɪʃ/ *verb* [+ two objects] **1** to hope or express hope for another person's success or happiness or pleasure on a particular occasion: *We wish you every success in the future.* ○ *I didn't even see her to wish her a happy birthday/wish a happy birthday* ***to*** *her.* ○ *I wished her a safe journey and waved her off.* **2 wish *sb* well** to hope someone will succeed: *I wished him well with his new venture.*

wishes /ˈwɪʃ.ɪz/ *plural noun* **best wishes** something you say or write at the end of a letter to show that you hope someone is happy and has good luck: *He ended the letter "Best wishes, Carlo".* ○ *Do* ***give/send*** *Patrick my best wishes.* ○ *Best wishes* ***for*** *a speedy recovery.*

wishbone /ˈwɪʃ.bəʊn/ [US] /-boʊn/ *noun* [C] the V-shaped bone between the neck and breast of a cooked bird which traditionally is removed from the bird and pulled apart by two people, allowing the one who gets the longer piece to make a secret wish

wish-fulfillment /ˈwɪʃ.fʊlˌfɪl.mənt/ *noun* [U] the achievement of real desires in imaginary situations, mainly in dreams, but also in films, literature and poetry: *Men, in these dramas of female wish-fulfillment, are reduced to the status of playthings.*

wishful thinking /ˌwɪʃ.fəlˈθɪŋ.kɪŋ/ *noun* [U] the imagining or discussion of a very unlikely future event or situation as if it were possible and might one day happen: *"Do you think you might be in line for promotion, then?" "No, it's just wishful thinking."*

wishy-washy /ˈwɪʃ.iˌwɒʃ.i/ [US] /-ˌwɑː.ʃi/ *adj INFORMAL DISAPPROVING* lacking in colour, firm ideas, principles or noticeable qualities of any type: *Politically they're neither right-wing nor left – just a bunch of wishy-washy pseudo-liberals.* ○ *Watercolours are a bit wishy-washy for my taste.*

wisp /wɪsp/ *noun* **1 wisp of cloud/smoke/steam** a small, thin line of cloud/smoke/steam: *A blue wisp of cigarette smoke curled in the air.* **2 wisp of hair/grass, etc.** a thin, delicate piece of hair/grass, etc: *A few wisps of hay still clung to her skirt.* ○ *soft wisps of baby hair*

wispy /ˈwɪs.pi/ *adj* in the form of a wisp or wisps: *a wispy cloud/fringe*

wisteria /wɪˈstɪə.ri.ə/ [US] /-ˈstɪr.i-/ *noun* [C or U] a climbing plant with groups of small purple, blue or white flowers hanging from it

wistful /ˈwɪst.fəl/ *adj* sad and thinking about something that is impossible or in the past: *a wistful smile* ○ *I thought about those days in Spain and grew wistful.* **wistfully** /ˈwɪst.fəl.i/ *adv*: *"I would love to go back to Venice," he said wistfully.* **wistfulness** /ˈwɪst.fəl.nəs/ *noun* [U]

wit /wɪt/ *noun* **1** [S or U] the ability to use words in a clever and humorous way: *a woman of great intelligence and wit* ○ *Her conversation sparkled with her own subtle blend of wit and charm.* ○ *He was known for his* ***dry/ready/sharp*** *wit.* ➲See also **wits**; **witticism**. **2** [C] a person who is skilled at using words in a clever and humorous way: *Sydney Smith, a notable wit, once*

W

remarked that he never read a book before he reviewed it because it might prejudice his opinion of it.

• **not be beyond the wit of man/sb** HUMOROUS to be possible to achieve: *It shouldn't be beyond the wit of man to arrange for them both to be there at the same time.*

• **to wit** FORMAL used to make clearer or more particular something that you have already said: *Several pieces of major legislation have been introduced in the US over the past few years, to wit: the Americans With Disabilities Act, the Clean Air Act and the Civil Rights Act.*

witty /'wɪt.i/ ⓤ /'wɪt̬-/ adj using words in a clever and funny way: *a witty comment/remark* ○ *He was witty and very charming.* **wittily** /'wɪt.ɪ.li/ ⓤ /'wɪt̬-/ adv

witch /wɪtʃ/ noun [C] **1** a woman who is believed to have magical powers and who uses them to harm or help other people: *a witch on a broomstick* ○ *Witches were persecuted all over western Europe from the 15th to the 17th century as it was claimed that they had dealings with the Devil.* **2** INFORMAL DISAPPROVING an unpleasant and ugly woman

witchcraft /'wɪtʃ.krɑːft/ ⓤ /-kræft/ noun [U] the activity of performing magic to help or harm other people

witchdoctor /'wɪtʃ.dɒk.təʳ/ ⓤ /-,dɑːk.tɚ/ noun [C] a person in some societies who cures people using traditional magic or medicine; a **shaman**

witch-hazel /'wɪtʃ,heɪ.zᵊl/ noun [C or U] a small, flowering tree, or liquid from this tree which is used as a medicine

witch-hunt /'wɪtʃ.hʌnt/ noun [C] DISAPPROVING an attempt to find and punish people whose opinions are unpopular and who are said to be a danger to society: *In America in the 1950s, Senator Joseph McCarthy led a witch-hunt **against** people suspected of being communists.*

the witching hour /ðə'wɪtʃ.ɪŋ,aʊəʳ/ ⓤ /-,aʊr/ noun [S] the time when witches are said to appear, usually 12 o'clock at night

Wite-Out US TRADEMARK /'waɪt.aʊt/ ⓤ /'waɪt̬-/ (UK TRADE-MARK **Tipp-Ex**) a white liquid used for painting over mistakes in a piece of writing

with COMPANY /wɪð/ prep in the company or presence of a person or thing: *I was with Sylvia at the time.* ○ *He lives with his grandmother.* ○ *He's impossible to work with.* ○ *I'm going to France with a couple of friends.* ○ *Ingrid Bergman starred with Humphrey Bogart in the film 'Casablanca'.* ○ *I left my coat with the cloakroom attendant.* ○ *Ice cream with your apple pie?* ○ *Mix the butter with the sugar and then add the egg.* ○ *I'll be with you* (= I will give you my attention) *in a moment.* ○ *She's staying with her parents* (= at their house) *for a few months.* ○ *He's been with the department* (= working in it) *since 1982.*

with METHOD /wɪð/ prep using something: *He was shot at close range with a pistol.* ○ *She wiped her lipstick off with a tissue.* ○ *Fix the two pieces together with glue.* ○ *Please handle this package with care.* ○ *They set up a business with the help of a bank loan.*

with DESCRIPTION /wɪð/ prep **1** having or possessing: *a tall woman with dark hair* ○ *He's married with three children.* ○ *She left school with no qualifications.* ○ *He spoke with a soft Irish accent.* ○ *We're an international company with offices in Paris, New York and Sydney.* ○ *Two coffees please, one with milk and one without.* ○ *He arrived in Los Angeles with nothing but the clothes he was wearing.* ○ *He woke up with a dreadful headache.* ○ *I was second in the race with a time of 14.2 seconds.* ○ *With a bit of luck, we should be back in time for dinner.* ○ *Both their children graduated with degrees in economics.* **2** used at the beginning of various phrases written at the end of a letter: *With best wishes from Charles.* ○ *With love from Roberta.* **3** including: *With your contribution, that makes a total of £45.*

with RELATIONSHIP /wɪð/ prep relating to or in the case of a person or thing: *How are things with you?* ○ *Russia has just drawn up a trade agreement with Norway.* ○ *This hasn't got anything to do with you* (= This is not something you should be interested in). ○ *The government's policies have not been popular with* (= among) *the voters.* ○ *He's very careless with his money.* ○ *She talked a lot*

about her relationship with Charlotte.

with CONTAINING/COVERING /wɪð/ prep used to show what is on or in something: *She'd laid the table with the best china.* ○ *Her blouse was spattered with blood.* ○ *The room was littered with toys and books.* ○ *The trucks were laden with food and medicine.* ○ *She filled the jug up with cream.*

with CAUSE /wɪð/ prep because of or caused by someone or something: *He winced with pain.* ○ *I was trembling with fear.* ○ *She's been at home with a bad cold for the past week.* ○ *I can't work with all that noise going on.* ○ *Hopes were dashed in the war-torn capital with the news that no aid would be arriving that week.* ○ *With exams approaching, it's a good idea to review your class notes.* ○ **(What)** *with all the excitement and confusion, I forgot to say goodbye to her.*

with DIRECTION /wɪð/ prep in the same direction as something: *The wind was with me on the home stretch and I ran well.* ✻ NOTE: The opposite is **against**.

with TIME /wɪð/ prep at the same rate or time as something: *This wine will improve with age.* ○ *Stopping distances for cars vary with the speed they are travelling at.*

with OPPOSITION /wɪð/ prep against something: *I ended up having an argument with her.* ○ *She has fought a constant battle with depression throughout her career.* ○ *The two countries went to war with one another over oil prices.* ○ *A truck had evidently collided with a car.*

with SUPPORT /wɪð/ prep supporting someone or something: *If you want to go for a promotion, I'll be with you all the way.* ○ *You've got to decide where you stand on this issue – you're either with me or against me.* ✻ NOTE: The opposite is **against**.

with UNDERSTANDING /wɪð/ prep INFORMAL **be with sb** to understand what someone is saying: *You look puzzled – are you with me?* ○ *I'm sorry, I'm not with you.*

with SEPARATION /wɪð/ prep used with words showing separation: *I'd rather not part with my cash.* ○ *He decided to put his failed marriage behind him and make a clean break with the past.*

with DESPITE /wɪð/ prep despite something: *With all her faults, she's still a really good friend.*

with AND /wɪð/ prep and, or followed by: *I'd like a steak and fries with chocolate mousse to follow.* ○ *$200 is payable immediately with a further $100 payable on delivery.*

• **with that** and then, or after doing or saying that: *"I still think you're wrong," he said and with that he drove off.*

with COMPARISON /wɪð/ prep used in comparisons: *I've got nothing in common with my brother.* ○ *This cake's very light compared with the last one you made.*

with EXPRESSIONS /wɪð/ prep used to express a wish or instruction: *Away with you* (= Go away)*!* ○ *Off to bed with you* (= Go to bed)*!* ○ *On with the show* (= Let it continue)*!* ○ *Down with school* (= We don't want/like it)*!*

withdraw /wɪð'drɔː/ ⓤ /-'drɑː/ verb **withdrew, withdrawn** **1** [I or T] to take or move out or back, or to remove: *This credit card allows you to withdraw up to £200 a day from cash dispensers.* ○ *The UN has withdraw its troops **from** the country.* ○ *Eleven million bottles of water had to be withdrawn **from** sale due to a health scare.* ○ *Once in court, he withdrew the statement he'd made to the police* (= he claimed it was false). ○ *All charges against them were withdrawn after the prosecution's case collapsed.* ○ FORMAL *After lunch, we withdrew **into** her office to finish our discussion in private.* ○ MAINLY UK *The team captain was forced to withdraw **from** the match due to injury.* ○ *Following his nervous breakdown, he withdrew **from** public life and refused to give any interviews.* **2** [I] to stop talking to other people and start thinking thoughts that are not related to what is happening around you: *As a child, she frequently withdrew **into** her own fantasy world.* ○ *After the accident, he withdrew **into** himself and refused to talk to family or friends.*

withdrawal /wɪð'drɔː.ᵊl/ ⓤ /-'drɑː-/ noun **1** [C or U] when you take money out of a bank account: *The bank became suspicious after several large withdrawals were made from his account in a single week.* **2** [C or U] when a military force moves out of an area: *The commander-in-chief was given 36 hours to secure a withdrawal of his troops **from** the combat zone.* **3** [U] when something is taken away so that it is no longer available, or when someone stops being involved in an activity: *Doctors demanded the withdrawal of the drug* ***(from*** *the market) after several cases of dangerous side-effects were reported.* ○ *Her sudden withdrawal* ***from*** *the championship caused a lot of press speculation about her health.* **4** [U] when someone prefers to be alone and does not want to talk to other people: *Withdrawal is a classic symptom of depression.*

withdrawn /wɪð'drɔːn/ [US] /-'drɑːn/ *adj* shy and quiet and preferring to be alone rather than with other people: *Following her son's death, she became quiet and withdrawn and rarely went out.*

with'drawal ˌsymptoms *plural noun* the unpleasant physical and mental effects which result when you stop doing or taking something, especially a drug, which has become a habit: *He was suffering from all the classic withdrawal symptoms associated with giving up heroin – inability to sleep, anxiety, sweating and fever.* ○ FIGURATIVE HUMOROUS *I haven't seen any TV for over a week and I'm having withdrawal symptoms.*

wither /'wɪð.əʳ/ [US] /-ɚ/ *verb* (ALSO **wither away**) **1** [I or T] (to cause) to become weak and dry and decay: *Grass had withered in the fields.* **2** [I] to slowly disappear, lose importance or become weaker: *This country is in danger of allowing its industrial base to wither away.*

• **wither on the vine** LITERARY If something withers on the vine, it is destroyed very gradually, usually because no one does anything to help or support it: *There was some debate as to whether the benefit scheme should be withdrawn or simply allowed to wither on the vine.*

withered /'wɪð.əd/ [US] /-ɚd/ *adj* **1** dry and decaying: *withered leaves/flowers* **2** MAINLY OLD USE describes an arm or leg that has not grown to its correct size because of disease

withering /'wɪð.ᵊr.ɪŋ/ [US] /-ɚ-/ *adj* **1** A withering look/remark/etc. is one that is intended to make someone feel ashamed: *He said that Lizzie had been drunk at the time and I saw her shoot him a withering glance.* **2** severe and extremely critical: *He made a withering* ***attack*** *on government policy.*

withers /'wɪð.əz/ [US] /-ɚz/ *plural noun* SPECIALIZED the highest part of the back of a horse, which is situated above its shoulders

withhold /wɪð'həʊld/ [US] /-'hoʊld/ *verb* [T] **withheld, withheld** to refuse to give something or to keep back something: *to withhold information/support* ○ *During the trial, the prosecution was accused of withholding crucial* ***evidence from*** *the defence.* ○ *Police are withholding the dead woman's* ***name*** *until her relatives have been informed.* ○ *She withheld her rent until the landlord agreed to have the repairs done.* ○ *The government is planning to withhold benefit payments* ***from*** *single mothers who refuse to name the father of their child.*

with'holding ˌtax *noun* [U] US money taken from a person's income and paid directly to the government by their employer

within /wɪ'ðɪn/ *prep, adv* inside or not beyond an area or period of time: *Two-thirds of Californians live within 15 miles of the coast.* ○ *In 1992 cross-border controls within the EU were dismantled.* ○ *For orders within the UK, please enclose £2.50 for post and packing.* ○ *The resort lies within* ***easy reach*** *of* (= not far from) *the ski slopes.* ○ *We recommend that this wine should be consumed within six months.* ○ *Within hours of the tragedy happening, an emergency rescue team had been assembled.* ○ *The tickets should reach you within the week* (= before the end of this week). ○ *He's very highly regarded within his profession.* ○ *She managed to complete her last film well within budget.* ○ *The target was now within range and so she took aim and fired.* ○ *He could sense that his goal was within* ***reach*** (= it could be reached). ○ *The cathedral spire was now within sight* (= it could be seen). ○ *I was acting within the law* (= legally). ○ *We came within five points of beating them* (= We would have beaten them if we had had five more points).

• **from within** by the people who belong to an organization and not by people from outside it: *If things are to change, the company must be reformed from within.*

'with ˌit [FASHION] *adj* **1** SLIGHTLY OLD-FASHIONED INFORMAL knowing a lot about new ideas and fashions: *He reads all the style magazines and thinks he's really with it.* **2** INFORMAL fashionable

'with ˌit [MIND] *adj* INFORMAL **be with it** to be able to think or understand quickly: *You're not really with it today, are you?*

without /wɪ'ðaʊt/ *prep, adv* not having or doing something, or lacking something: *I've come out without my umbrella.* ○ *You look nice without make-up.* ○ *He went without my knowledge.* ○ *I couldn't have done it without you.* ○ *She's strong without being bossy.* ○ *Do start without me.* ○ FORMAL *He's not without* (= he does have some) *qualities.* ○ *This is without a doubt* (= certainly) *the best Chinese food I've ever had.* ○ *You shouldn't drive for more than three hours without tak****ing*** *a break.* ○ *Without wish****ing*** *to be rude* (= I don't want to be rude, but), *don't you think you need a hair cut?* ➲See also **do without**; **go without**.

• **without (so much as) a backward glance** If you leave without a backward glance, you are completely happy to leave and have no sad feelings about it: *She left the city where she had lived all her life without a backward glance.*

• **without so much as a by-your-leave** OLD-FASHIONED without asking for anyone's permission, in a way that is rude

withstand /wɪð'stænd/ *verb* [T] **withstood, withstood** to bear or not be changed by something, or to oppose a person or thing successfully: *a bridge designed to withstand earthquakes* ○ *Our toys are designed to withstand the rough treatment of the average five-year-old.* ○ *The aircraft base is protected with specially designed shelters which are built to withstand ground and air attacks.* ○ *She is an artist whose work will undoubtedly withstand* ***the test of time*** (= it will still be popular in the future).

witless /'wɪt.ləs/ *adj* DISAPPROVING **1** stupid or lacking intelligence: *The novel centres around a witless father who is continually being conned by his three children.* ➲See also **wits**. **2 scare/frighten *sb* witless** to frighten someone very much: *I was scared witless the last time Tina drove me down to London.*

witness [SEE] /'wɪt.nəs/ *noun* [C] **1** a person who sees an event happening, especially a crime or an accident: *Police are appealing for witnesses* ***to*** *the accident to come forward.* ○ *According to* ***(eye)*** *witnesses, the robbery was carried out by two teenage boys.* **2 be witness to *sth*** to see something happen: *She was witness to the tragic event.* **3** someone who is asked to be present at a particular event and sign their name in order to prove that things have been done correctly: *He signed the treaty in the presence of two witnesses.* ○ *They were married a year after they first met, with two friends acting as witnesses.*

• **bear witness (to *sth*)** If something bears witness to a fact, it proves that it is true: *The numerous awards on the walls bear witness to his great success.* ○ *As last week's riots bear witness, the political situation is very unstable.*

witness /'wɪt.nəs/ *verb* [T] **1** to see something happen, especially an accident or crime: *Did anyone witness the attack?* ○ *They were staying in the capital at the time of the riots and witnessed several street battles.* ○ [+ v-ing] *He arrived home just in time to witness his brother be****ing*** *taken away by the police.* **2** FORMAL When a place or period witnesses a particular event, the event happens in that place or during that period: *This university has witnessed quite a few changes over the years.* ○ *The past few years have witnessed momentous changes throughout Eastern Europe.* **3** to show or give proof of something: *This year's charity ball was the most successful one ever,* ***as*** *witnessed* ***by*** *the number of tickets sold.* ○ *The programme aroused strong feelings – witness the number of letters received.* **4** to be present at an event and to sign your name as proof that it happened or that it was done correctly: *Her will was drawn up by a solicitor and witnessed by two colleagues.*

witness [LAW] /'wɪt.nəs/ *noun* [C] **1** a person in a law court who states what they know about a legal case or a particular person: *Ten witnesses are expected to testify at* *the trial today.* ○ *The* ***key*** *witness* ***for*** *the prosecution was offered police protection after she received death threats.* **2 expert witness** a person who is allowed to give their opinion in a law court because of their knowledge or practical experience of a particular subject: *A psychiatrist was called as an expert witness for the defence.*

▲ **witness to *sth*** *phrasal verb* UK FORMAL to state publicly, especially in a law court, that something is true or that it happened: *A handwriting expert witnessed to the authenticity of the letter.* ○ [+ v-ing] *She witnessed to having seen the robbery take place.*

'witness ˌbox *UK noun* [C usually sing] (*US* **witness stand**) the place in which a person stands in a law court when they are being questioned: *He showed no emotion as he walked into the witness box.* ○ *She was asked to* ***take*** *the witness stand and was then cross-examined by the state attorney.*

wits /wɪts/ *plural noun* intelligence and the ability to think quickly: *She learned to survive on her wits.*

• **gather *your* wits** LITERARY to make an effort to become calm and think more clearly: *I spent the five-minute break between games gathering my wits and rethinking my strategy for the second half of the match.*

• **have/keep (all) *your* wits about *you*** to be ready to think quickly in a situation and react to things that you are not expecting: *Cycling is potentially very dangerous in London – you have to keep your wits about you.*

• **be at *your* wits' end** to be very worried and upset because you have tried every possible way to solve a problem but cannot do it: *I've tried everything I can think of to make her eat but she flatly refuses – I'm at my wits' end.*

• **frighten/scare *sb* out of *their* wits** (ALSO **frighten/scare the wits out of *sb***) to make someone very frightened: *Don't shout like that! You scared me out of my wits.*

witter /'wɪt.əʳ/ [US] /'wɪt̬.ɚ/ *verb* [I] UK INFORMAL DISAPPROVING to talk about unimportant things for a long time: *He'd been wittering* ***on*** *about his neighbours for half the morning.*

witticism /'wɪt.ɪ.sɪ.zᵊm/ [US] /'wɪt̬-/ *noun* [C] a remark that is both clever and humorous ➲See also **wit**.

wittily /'wɪt.ɪ.li/ [US] /'wɪt̬-/ *adv* ➲See at **wit**. **witty** /'wɪt.i/ [US] /'wɪt̬-/ *adj*

wives /waɪvz/ *plural of* **wife**

wizard /'wɪz.əd/ [US] /-ɚd/ *noun* [C] **1** a man who is believed to have magical powers and who uses them to harm or help other people **2** (ALSO **wiz**) INFORMAL someone who is an expert at something or who has great ability in a particular subject: *a computer wizard* ○ *Your mother's a wizard* ***at*** *Scrabble.*

wizardry /'wɪz.ə.dri/ [US] /-ɚ-/ *noun* [U] **1** the skill of a wizard **2** clever or surprising ways of doing things, especially with special machines: *Using their high-tech wizardry, the police were able to locate the owners of the stolen property within hours of it being seized.*

wizened /'wɪz.ᵊnd/ *adj* having dry skin with lines in it, especially because of old age: *He was a wizened* ***old*** *man with yellow skin and deep wrinkles.*

wk WRITTEN ABBREVIATION FOR **week**

wobble [MOVE] /'wɒb.l̩/ [US] /'wɑː.bl̩/ *verb* [I or T] to (cause something to) shake or move from side to side in a way that shows a lack of balance: *That bookcase wobbles whenever you put anything on it.* ○ *Don't wobble the table, please, Dan.* ○ FIGURATIVE *The company's shares wobbled with the news of a foreign takeover bid.*

wobble /'wɒb.l̩/ [US] /'wɑː.bl̩/ *noun* [C] *I gave the poles a slight wobble and whole tent collapsed.* ○ FIGURATIVE *The closure of the company's German subsidiary caused a sharp wobble in its profits.*

wobbly /'wɒb.l̩.i/ [US] /'wɑː.bl̩-/ *adj* likely to wobble: *a wobbly ladder/table* ○ *I've been in bed with flu and my legs are still feeling all wobbly.* ○ *"Look, I've got a wobbly tooth," said my little daughter, proudly.* ○ HUMOROUS *I'm trying to tone up my wobbly* ***bits*** (= fat areas of the body) *generally.*

wobble [UNCERTAIN] /'wɒb.l̩/ [US] /'wɑː.bl̩/ *verb* [I] INFORMAL to be uncertain what to do or to change frequently between two opinions: *The government can't afford to wobble on this issue.* **wobble** /'wɒb.l̩/ [US] /'wɑː.bl̩/ *noun* [C]

wobbly /'wɒb.l̩.i/ [US] /'wɑː.bl̩-/ *adj* INFORMAL uncertain what to do or changing frequently between two opinions: *Last week I felt sure I was doing the right thing but I've started to feel a bit wobbly about it.*

wobbly /'wɒb.l̩.i/ [US] /'wɑː.bl̩-/ *noun* UK INFORMAL **throw a wobbly** to become extremely angry and upset: *My parents threw a wobbly when they found out I'd had a party while they were away.*

wodge, **wadge** /wɒdʒ/ [US] /wɑːdʒ/ *noun* [C] MAINLY UK INFORMAL a thick piece or a large amount of something: *She cut herself a* ***great*** *wodge* ***of*** *chocolate cake.* ○ *He hurried towards the staffroom with a wodge* ***of*** *papers under his arm.*

woe /wəʊ/ [US] /woʊ/ *noun* [U] LITERARY extreme sadness: *Her face was lined and full of woe.* ○ *He told me a real* ***tale of*** *woe about how he had lost both his job and his house in the same week.*

• **woe betide *sb*** said when there will be trouble for someone, or they will be punished, if they do a particular thing: *This is the second time he's been sent home from school this week, so woe betide him if it happens again!*

• **woe is me** OLD USE OR HUMOROUS said to express how unhappy you are: *I'm cold and wet and I haven't even got enough money for my bus fare home. Oh woe is me!*

woeful /'wəʊ.fᵊl/ [US] /'woʊ-/ *adj* FORMAL extremely sad: *She was looking very woeful, with her eyes red and swollen.* ➲See also **woeful**.

woebegone /'wəʊ.bɪ.gɒn/ [US] /'woʊ.bɪ.gɑːn/ *adj* LITERARY looking very sad: *When he wants to go for a walk, the dog sits by the door with a woebegone* ***expression.*** ○ *There's no need to* ***look*** *so woebegone – we can get it fixed.*

woeful /'wəʊ.fᵊl/ [US] /'woʊ-/ *adj* very bad or (of something very bad or unpleasant) very great or extreme: *The team's woeful* ***record*** *consists of six defeats in seven matches.* ○ *They displayed woeful* ***ignorance*** *of the safety rules.* ➲See also **woeful** at **woe**.

woefully /'wəʊ.fᵊl.i/ [US] /'woʊ-/ *adv* used to emphasize how bad a situation is: *The safety precautions taken by large resort hotels are often woefully* ***inadequate*** *for the number of people who stay there.* ○ *The school's text books are woefully out-of-date.*

woes /wəʊz/ [US] /woʊz/ *plural noun* FORMAL great problems or troubles: *The country has been beset by* ***economic*** *woes for the past decade.* ○ *Unusually poor harvests have* ***added to*** *the country's woes.*

wog /wɒg/ [US] /wɑːg/ *noun* [C] UK OFFENSIVE a black person

wok /wɒk/ [US] /wɑːk/ *noun* [C] a large, bowl-shaped, Chinese pan used for frying food quickly in hot oil: *Heat some oil in a wok, then add the vegetables and stir-fry for two minutes.*

woke /wəʊk/ [US] /woʊk/ *past simple of* **wake** STOP SLEEPING

woken /'wəʊ.kᵊn/ [US] /'woʊ-/ *past participle of* **wake** STOP SLEEPING

wolf [ANIMAL] /wʊlf/ *noun* [C] *plural* **wolves** a wild animal of the dog family: *Wolves hunt in groups known as packs.* ○ *We could hear wolves* ***howling*** *in the distance.*

• **a wolf in sheep's clothing** a person who hides the fact that they are evil, with a pleasant and friendly appearance

• **keep the wolf from the door** to have just enough money to be able to eat and live: *As a student, he took an evening job to keep the wolf from the door.*

wolfish /'wʊl.fɪʃ/ *adj* like a wolf

wolf [EAT] /wʊlf/ *verb* [T] INFORMAL to eat a large amount of food very quickly: *The boys wolfed the sandwiches* ***(down)*** *and then started on the cakes.*

wolfhound /'wʊlf.haʊnd/ *noun* [C] a type of very large dog: *He specializes in breeding large dogs such as* ***Irish*** *wolfhounds.*

wolf-whistle /'wʊlfˌwɪs.l̩/ *verb* [I] to make a short, high sound, followed by a longer sound that drops from high to low, when you see a person who you find sexually attractive: *Builders are notorious for wolf-whistling* ***at*** *any woman who walks by.* **wolf-whistle** /'wʊlfˌwɪs.l̩/ *noun* [C] *The last time she went out wearing those ripped jeans she got several wolf-whistles.*

woman /'wʊm.ən/ *noun plural* **women** /'wɪmɪn/ **1** [C] an adult female human being: *She's a really nice woman.* ○ *A woman and two men were arrested on the day after the explosion.* ○ *Women first got the vote in Britain in 1918.* ○ *She is Ireland's first woman (= female) president.* **2** [C] INFORMAL a man's wife or partner: *Apparently, Geoff's got a new woman.* **3** [U] women in general: *He is writing a book on the representation of woman in medieval art.* ⊃See also **womankind**; **womenfolk**.

-woman /-wʊm.ən/ *suffix*: *an Englishwoman/ Frenchwoman* ○ *a chairwoman* **womanhood** /'wʊm.ən.hʊd/ *noun* [U] *The novel deals with a teenage girl's journey towards womanhood.* ○ *Brigitte Bardot was the dominant image of womanhood in French cinema during the 1960s.* ⊃Compare **manhood**.

womanly /'wʊm.ən.li/ *adj* describes qualities, ideas or physical features which a woman is typically or traditionally thought to have: *She referred to the 'traditional womanly goals of marriage and motherhood' several times in her talk.* ○ *She used her womanly wiles/ charms to persuade him to change his mind.* ⊃Compare **manly**. **womanliness** /'wʊm.ən.lɪ.nəs/ *noun* [U]

womanize, UK USUALLY **-ise** /'wʊm.ə.naɪz/ *verb* [I] DISAPPROVING A man who womanizes frequently has temporary sexual relationships with women or tries to get women to have sex with him: *He drank, womanized and wasted money.* **womanizing**, UK USUALLY **-ising** /'wʊm.ə.naɪ.zɪŋ/ *noun* [U] *Both his first and second wife divorced him on account of his womanizing.* **womanizer**, UK USUALLY **-iser** /'wʊm.ə.naɪ.zər/ *noun* [C] *He was a gambler, a womanizer and a drunk.*

womankind /ˌwʊm.ən'kaɪnd/ *noun* [U] OLD-FASHIONED female human beings in general: *In her latest book she discusses the menopause, which is a subject that concerns all womankind.* ⊃Compare **mankind**; **humankind**.

womb /wuːm/ *noun* [C] (SPECIALIZED **uterus**) the organ in the body of a woman or other female mammal in which a baby develops before birth: *Researchers are looking at how a mother's health can affect the baby in the womb.*

wombat /'wɒm.bæt/ US /'wɑːm-/ *noun* [C] an Australian wild animal which is similar to a small bear

womenfolk /'wɪm.ɪn.fəʊk/ US /-foʊk/ *plural noun* OLD-FASHIONED the women in a family or society: *The communal land is cultivated by the womenfolk in the tribe.* ⊃Compare **menfolk**.

women's liberation /ˌwɪm.ɪnz.lɪb.ə'reɪ.ʃ°n/ *noun* [U] (INFORMAL **women's lib**) OLD-FASHIONED the aim of achieving equality for women in all areas of society: *the women's liberation movement*

women's libber /ˌwɪm.ɪnz'lɪb.ər/ US /-ɚ-/ *noun* [C] OLD-FASHIONED someone who supports efforts to achieve equality of women and men: *I'm not a women's libber, but I do believe women should be paid the same as men.*

women's movement /'wɪm.ɪnzˌmuːv.mənt/ *noun* [U] those people whose social and political aims are to change women's position in society and increase awareness of women's condition in society: *The early 20th century women's movement fought for the political emancipation of women.*

women's refuge UK /ˌwɪm.ɪnz'ref.juːdʒ/ *noun* [C] (US **women's shelter**) a house where women whose husbands or partners have been violent towards them can go with their children for protection

women's studies /'wɪm.ɪnzˌstʌd.iz/ *plural noun* a course of studies about women in history, society and literature: *She's doing a postgraduate course in women's studies.*

won /wʌn/ *past simple and past participle of* **win**

wonder QUESTION /'wʌn.dər/ US /-dɚ-/ *verb* **1** [I] to ask yourself questions or express a desire to know about something: [+ question word] *Hadn't you better phone home? Your parents will be wondering where you are.* ○ *He's starting to wonder whether he did the right thing in accepting this job.* ○ [+ speech] *Will this turkey be big enough for eight, I wonder?* ○ *"Have you decided where you're going next summer?" "I've been wondering about going to Florida."* **2** used in phrases, at the beginning of a request, to make it more formal and

polite: [+ speech] *I wonder – could you help me carry these books?* ○ [+ question word] *I wonder whether you could pass me the butter?* ○ *I wonder if you could give me some information about places to visit in the area?*

● **I shouldn't wonder** MAINLY UK probably: *"Where's Mark been recently?" "Up to no good, I shouldn't wonder."*

wonder SURPRISE /'wʌn.dər/ US /-dɚ-/ *verb* [I] SLIGHTLY FORMAL to feel or express great surprise at something: [+ (that)] *He was behaving so badly at school today, I wonder (that) he wasn't sent home.* ○ *I don't wonder (that) she burst into tears after the way you spoke to her.*

wonder /'wʌn.dər/ US /-dɚ-/ *noun* **1** [U] a feeling of great surprise and admiration caused by seeing or experiencing something that is strange and new: *The sight of the Grand Canyon stretching out before them filled them with wonder.* ○ *The boys gazed in wonder at the shiny red Ferrari.* **2** [C usually pl] an object that causes a feeling of great surprise and admiration: *We spent a week visiting the wonders of Ancient Greek civilization.* ○ *With all the wonders of modern technology, why has no one come up with a way to make aircraft quieter?* **3** [C] INFORMAL an extremely useful or skilful person: *Our new babysitter's an absolute wonder – she'll come at very short notice and the children love her.*

● **wonders never cease** HUMOROUS an expression of surprise used when something unusual or unexpected happens: *Lynda actually managed to get up before ten o'clock. Wonders never cease!*

● **it's a wonder** it is surprising: *It's a wonder (that) he ever reached Paris, because he set off with only £5 in his pocket.*

● **little/small wonder** it is not really surprising: *Her car's been broken for the past two months, so it's little wonder (that) she hasn't come to visit you recently.*

● **no wonder** it is not surprising: *No wonder the children are excited, – this is the first time they've been abroad.* ○ *"If brutal killers like these two are at work, it is no wonder that so many Kosovans have fled," he said.*

● **do/work wonders** INFORMAL to have a very good effect: *Doctors have discovered that keeping a pet can do wonders for your health.*

wonderment /'wʌn.də.mənt/ US /-dɚ-/ *noun* [U] LITERARY great and pleasant surprise: *He listened with quiet wonderment as his grandfather told him of his life in the circus.*

'wonder ˌdrug *noun* [C] INFORMAL a very effective new medicine: *It has proved to be a wonder drug for sufferers of epilepsy, reducing seizures by up to 80%.*

wonderful /'wʌn.də.f°l/ US /-dɚ-/ *adj* extremely good: *He's a wonderful cook.* ○ *"Did you know that Daryl's getting married?" "No, I didn't. How wonderful!"* ○ *We had a wonderful time in Italy last summer.*

wonderfully /'wʌn.də.fli/ US /-dɚ-/ *adv* extremely, or extremely well: *This sauce goes wonderfully well with fish, asparagus or new potatoes.* ○ *As a child I hated my brother, but now we get on wonderfully.*

wonderland /'wʌn.d°l.ænd/ US /-də.lænd/ *noun* [C] a place that has unusual attractiveness or beauty: *The family emigrated to New Zealand in 1949, which seemed a wonderland in comparison with post-war England.*

wondrous /'wʌn.drəs/ *adj* LITERARY extremely and surprisingly good: *a wondrous sight/sound/thing* ○ *Our new improved face cream has wondrous effects on tired-looking skin.*

wondrously /'wʌn.drə.sli/ *adv* LITERARY extremely, used to emphasize an approving description

wonga /'wɒŋ.gə/ US /'wɑːŋ-/ *noun* [U] UK SLANG money

wonk /wɒŋk/ US /wɑːŋk/ *noun* [C] US INFORMAL a person who works or studies too much, especially someone who learns and knows all the details about something: *As the NEC's deputy for domestic policy issues, Sperling has functioned as both policy wonk and political guru.*

wonky /'wɒŋ.ki/ US /'wɑːŋ-/ *adj* **1** UK INFORMAL shaky, weak or unsatisfactory: *One of the legs on this chair is a bit wonky.* ○ *He may have to stop playing cricket because of his wonky knee.* ○ *The jury system may be a bit wonky but nobody's ever thought of anything better.* **2** INFORMAL not straight or level: *wonky teeth* ○ *a wonky picture* ○ *I* *don't enjoy those programmes with wonky camera angles and pop music.*

won't /wəʊnt/ [US] /woʊnt/ *short form of* will not: *I won't go without you.* ○ *Won't it be nice to see Paul again?*

wont /wəʊnt/ [US] /woʊnt/ *noun* FORMAL **as is someone's wont** in the way that someone usually does: *She arrived an hour late, as is her wont.*

wont /wəʊnt/ [US] /woʊnt/ *adj* FORMAL **be wont to do sth** to often do something: *The previous city council was wont to overspend.* ○ *They spent much of the time reminiscing about the war, as old soldiers are wont to do.*

wonted /ˈwəʊn.tɪd/ [US] /ˈwoʊn.t̬ɪd/ *adj* **[before n]** FORMAL usual: *He replied sharply, and without his wonted courtesy.*

woo /wuː/ *verb* **[T]** **wooing, wooed, wooed** **1** to try to persuade someone to support you or to use your business: *The party has been trying to woo the voters **with** promises of electoral reform.* ○ *The airline has been offering discounted tickets to woo passengers **away from** their competitors.* **2** OLD-FASHIONED If a man woos a woman, he gives her a lot of attention in an attempt to persuade her to marry him: *He wooed her for months **with** flowers and expensive presents.* **wooer** /ˈwuː.əʳ/ [US] /-ɚ/ *noun* **[C]**

wood [MATERIAL] /wʊd/ *noun* **1** **[C or U]** a hard substance which forms the branches and trunks of trees and which can be used as a building material, for making things, or as a fuel: *He gathered some wood to build a fire.* ○ *She fixed a couple of **planks** of wood to the wall for shelves.* ○ *Mahogany is a **hard** wood and pine is a **soft** wood.* ○ *The room was heated by a wood-**burning** stove.* **2** **[C]** a type of golf CLUB (= long, thin stick) with a rounded wooden end, used in golf for hitting the ball over long distances: *He likes to use a number 2 wood to tee off.*

wood /wʊd/ *adj* made of wood: *Solid wood furniture is much more sturdy and durable than chipboard furniture.* ○ *We sanded and polished the wood **floor** in the living room.* ○ *Much of the original 18th-century wood **panelling** was destroyed in the fire.* ➲See also **wooden** WOOD.

woody /ˈwʊd.i/ *adj* **1** like wood, for example in taste or smell **2** describes plants with hard stems: *The garden was overgrown with woody plants such as hawthorn and bramble.* ➲See also **woody** at **wood** GROUP OF TREES.

wood [GROUP OF TREES] /wʊd/ *noun* **[C]** an area of land covered with a thick growth of trees: *an oak wood* ➲See also **woodland**.

• **not see the wood for the trees** *UK* (*US* **not see the forest for the trees**) to be unable to get a general understanding of a situation because you are too worried about the details

• **be out of the woods** INFORMAL to no longer be in danger or difficulty: *The club has been given funding for another year, but it's not out of the wood yet.*

wooded /ˈwʊd.ɪd/ *adj* covered with trees: *wooded hills* ○ *The police found a vital clue to the girl's disappearance in a wooded **area** near her home.*

woods /wʊdz/ *plural noun* a wood: *We went for a walk **in the** woods after lunch.* **woody** /ˈwʊd.i/ *adj*: *They lived in a remote cottage set high on a woody hillside.*

woodbine /ˈwʊd.baɪn/ *noun* **[U]** **1** a climbing plant with pleasant-smelling yellow flowers **2** *US FOR* **virginia creeper**

woodblock /ˈwʊd.blɒk/ [US] /-blɑːk/ *noun* **[C]** **1** a piece of wood on which a pattern is cut which is used for printing: *She designs her own fabrics using woodblocks and stencils to create patterns on the material.* **2** *UK* one of a set of small, flat pieces of wood which are used to make a wooden floor: *a woodblock floor* ➲See also **parquet**.

woodcarving /ˈwʊdˌkɑː.vɪŋ/ [US] /-ˌkɑːr-/ *noun* **1** **[U]** the process of cutting into the surface of wood to create a decorative shape or pattern: *Some of the finest examples of woodcarving in Europe can be found in medieval churches.* **2** **[C]** a piece of wood that has been decorated in this way: *Her woodcarvings will be on display at the gallery next month.*

woodchuck /ˈwʊd.tʃʌk/ *noun* **[C]** a small animal with short legs and rough, reddish brown fur which lives in North America

woodcut /ˈwʊd.kʌt/ *noun* **[C]** a picture printed from a pattern which has been cut in the surface of a block of wood

wooden [WOOD] /ˈwʊd.ᵊn/ *adj* made of wood: *The house was surrounded by a tall, wooden **fence**.* ○ *Stir the mixture with a wooden **spoon**.*

wooden [AWKWARD] /ˈwʊd.ᵊn/ *adj* DISAPPROVING describes behaviour that is awkward or lacking in expression: *She gave a wooden **smile** to the camera.* ○ *I thought the lead actor gave rather a wooden **performance**.* **woodenly** /ˈwʊd.ᵊn.li/ *adv*: *She nodded woodenly, her body still numb from the shock.*

the ˌwooden ˈspoon *noun* **[S]** *UK INFORMAL* the imaginary prize that a person or team is given if they finish last in a race or competition: *Our college team **took** the wooden spoon in the inter-collegiate league this season.*

woodland /ˈwʊd.lənd/ *noun* **[C or U]** land on which many trees grow, or an area of this: *The Forestry Commission is responsible for preserving over 2 million acres of woodland.* ○ *Some very rare and special plants grow in these woodlands.*

woodlouse /ˈwʊd.laʊs/ *noun* **[C]** *plural* **woodlice** a small, dark-grey creature with a hard outer shell, which is found under stones or in slightly wet soil and is a CRUSTACEAN, not an insect

woodpecker /ˈwʊdˌpek.əʳ/ [US] /-ɚ/ *noun* **[C]** a bird which uses its strong beak to make holes in tree trunks in order to find insects to eat

ˈwood ˌpulp *noun* **[U]** wood which has been changed into a soft mass which can then be used for making paper

woodshed /ˈwʊd.ʃed/ *noun* **[C]** a small building where wood for burning is stored

woodwind /ˈwʊd.wɪnd/ *adj* **[before n]** belonging or relating to a group of pipe-shaped musical instruments which are played by blowing through a thin flattened tube at one end or across a hole near one end: *The clarinet, flute, saxophone and bassoon are all woodwind **instruments**.* ➲Compare **brass** MUSICAL INSTRUMENTS; **percussion**.

the woodwind *group noun* **[S]** the group of woodwind instruments and their players in an orchestra: *The woodwind was particularly haunting during the slow second movement.*

woodwork [STRUCTURE] /ˈwʊd.wɜːk/ [US] /-wɝːk/ *noun* **[U]** the wooden parts of a building, especially a house: *There's some rotting woodwork on the outside of the house that we need to replace.*

• **woodwork** *UK INFORMAL* **the woodwork** any part of the wooden or metal frame that forms part of a goal in football: *Liverpool **hit the** woodwork twice in the first half.*

• **come/crawl out of the woodwork** MAINLY DISAPPROVING to appear after having been hidden or not active for a long time: *After you've been in a relationship for a while all sorts of little secrets start to come out of the woodwork.*

woodwork [ACTIVITY] MAINLY UK /ˈwʊd.wɜːk/ [US] /-wɝːk/ *noun* **[U]** (*US USUALLY* **woodworking**) the activity of making objects such as furniture from wood: *woodwork classes/lessons* ○ *I used to enjoy woodwork at school.*

woodworm /ˈwʊd.wɜːm/ [US] /-wɝːm/ *noun plural* **woodworm** **1** **[C]** the young form of particular types of beetle which make small holes in wood as they feed on it **2** **[U]** the damage done to wooden objects when woodworm feed on them: *The roof timbers were riddled with woodworm.*

woof /wʊf/ *noun* **[C]** a written representation of the noise that a dog makes, used especially in children's books: *"Miaow, miaow," went the cat. "Woof, woof," went the dog.* **woof** /wʊf/ *verb* **[I]**

wool /wʊl/ *noun* **[U]** **1** the soft, thick hair which grows on the bodies of sheep and some other animals: *The blankets are made from wool and the sheets from cotton.* **2** thick thread or material that is made from this: *Put on your red wool cardigan – it'll be nice and warm.* ○ *How many **balls of** wool did you need to knit that sweater?*

• **pull the wool over** ***sb's*** **eyes** to deceive someone in order to prevent them from discovering something

W

woollen, US USUALLY **woolen** /ˈwʊl.ən/ adj made of wool: a woollen scarf

woollens, US USUALLY **woolens** /ˈwʊl.ənz/ plural noun clothes made from wool or sometimes from wool mixed with artificial fibres

woolly OF WOOL, US ALSO **wooly** /ˈwʊl.i/ adj made of wool, or made of something that looks like wool: a woolly hat/jumper

woolly, US ALSO **wooly** /ˈwʊl.i/ noun [C] OLD-FASHIONED INFORMAL a piece of clothing made from wool, especially a jumper

woolly UNCLEAR /ˈwʊl.i/ adj DISAPPROVING Woolly ideas and reasoning are unclear and confused, and have not been considered carefully enough: It's the woolly thinking behind the book that I find so infuriating. ○ I can't stand these woolly-**headed**/-**minded** liberals! **woolliness** /ˈwʊl.ɪ.nəs/ noun [U]

woozy /ˈwuː.zi/ adj INFORMAL feeling weak or ill and unable to think clearly: I was still woozy from the flu/anaesthetic/medication/wine.

wop /wɒp/ ⑩ /wɑːp/ noun [C] OFFENSIVE a man from southern Europe, especially Italy

word LANGUAGE UNIT /wɜːd/ ⑩ /wɝːd/ noun [C] **1** a single unit of language which has meaning and can be spoken or written: Your essay should be no more than two thousand words long. ○ Some words are more difficult to spell than others. ○ What's the word for bikini in French? ○ It's sometimes difficult to **find** exactly **the right** word to express what you want to say. **2** the f-/c-/etc. **word** used to refer to a word, usually a rude or embarrassing one, by saying only the first letter and not the whole word: You're still not allowed to say the f-word on TV in the US. ○ So how's the diet going – or would you rather I didn't mention the d-word?

• breathe/say a word to tell other people about something: Don't say a word **about** the accident to my mother. ○ If you breathe a word **of** this to anyone, I'll be really upset.

• by word of mouth in speech but not in writing: All the orders were given by word of mouth so that no written evidence could be discovered later.

• not get a word in edgeways UK (US not get a word in edgewise) INFORMAL to not be able to say anything because someone else is talking continually: Roz was talking so much that nobody else could get a word in edgeways!

• in **your** own words If a person says something in their own words, they speak without copying what someone else has said: The court has heard accounts of that night's events from several witnesses – now please tell us in your own words what you saw.

• in words of one syllable in simple language avoiding long, difficult or specialized words: Could you **explain** to me in words of one syllable how an electron microscope works?

• put words in/into sb's mouth to suggest that someone meant one thing when really they meant another: Stop putting words in my mouth – I didn't say you looked fat in the red dress – I merely said you looked very slim in the black!

• take the words out of sb's mouth to say something which another person was just about to say or which they were thinking: "What a rude and obnoxious man!" "You took the words **right** out of my mouth!"

• word for word **1** using exactly the same words: She listened to everything I said and repeated it word for word to her mum. ○ a word-for-word **account 2** If you TRANSLATE speech or writing word for word, you change one word at a time in the same order rather than in phrases or other larger units of meaning.

• (upon) my word! OLD-FASHIONED used to express surprise: My word! Isn't that Jenkins on the roof?

• words fail me said to emphasize your surprise or shock, especially at something you have just seen or been told: "So what did you think of Olive's pink outfit?" "Words fail me, I've never seen anything quite like it!"

word /wɜːd/ ⑩ /wɝːd/ verb [T usually + adv or prep] to choose the words you use when you are saying or writing something: He worded the reply in such a way that he did not admit making the original error. ⊃See also **reword**.

worded /ˈwɜː.dɪd/ ⑩ /ˈwɝː-/ adj: a carefully/strongly worded **statement**

wording /ˈwɜː.dɪŋ/ ⑩ /ˈwɝː-/ noun [U] the choice and meaning of the words used when you say or write something: Norman agreed that the wording **of** the advertisement was unnecessarily offensive and it was changed. ○ We don't yet know the **exact/precise** wording **of** the agreement.

wordless /ˈwɜːd.ləs/ ⑩ /ˈwɝːd-/ adj without any words: We sat in wordless contemplation of the view. **wordlessly** /ˈwɜːd.lə.sli/ ⑩ /ˈwɝːd-/ adv: to stare/nod/point wordlessly

wordy /ˈwɜː.di/ ⑩ /ˈwɝː-/ adj DISAPPROVING containing an unnecessarily large amount of words: As usual she gave a reply which was wordy and didn't answer the question. **wordiness** /ˈwɜː.dɪ.nəs/ ⑩ /ˈwɝː-/ noun [U]

word BRIEF STATEMENT /wɜːd/ ⑩ /wɝːd/ noun [S] a brief discussion or statement: The manager wants **a** word. ○ Could I **have a** word (**with** you) about the sales figures? ○ Perhaps you would **have a quiet** word with Simon (= gently explain to him) about the problem.

• put in a good word for sb to say positive things about someone: I really need a job and I was hoping you might put in a good word for me with your boss.

• have a word in sb's ear to give someone a piece of advice or information secretly

• in a word said when you are going to give your opinion about something briefly and directly: In a word, she's lying.

words /wɜːdz/ ⑩ /wɝːdz/ plural noun **1** have/exchange words to talk to each other briefly: We exchanged a few words as we were coming out of the meeting. **2** angry words: Both competitors **had** words (= argued) after the match. ○ Words **passed between** both competitors (= They argued) after the match. **3** DISAPPROVING discussion, rather than action: I'm afraid so far there have been more words than action on the matter of childcare provision.

word NEWS /wɜːd/ ⑩ /wɝːd/ noun [U] news or a message: Have you **had** word from Paul since he went to New York? ○ We **got** word of their plan from a former colleague. ○ Word **of** the discovery caused a stir among astronomers.

• put the word about/around/out/round to tell people a new piece of news: So, the new manager has been appointed – should we put the word around?

• word gets about/around/round When word gets about/around/round, news spreads fast within a group of people: "I hear you were having drinks with a tall, dark, handsome man last night." "Wow, word gets round fast, doesn't it?" ○ She doesn't want word getting around the office that she's pregnant.

• word has it used to refer to something which is generally thought to be true although not official or known to be a fact: Word has it **(that)** they may separate.

• (the) word is used to refer to something which has been reported but not officially stated: The word is **(that)** more hostages will be released over the next few weeks.

• (the) word is/gets out a piece of news is known, especially if it was secret or if it will cause changes: The word is out **that** superstar Candice is to marry towards the end of this year.

word PROMISE /wɜːd/ ⑩ /wɝːd/ noun [S] a promise: I said I'd visit him and I shall **keep** my word. ○ You **have** my word – I won't tell a soul.

• give **your** word FORMAL to promise: He **gave** his word that he would marry her and she had no cause to doubt him.

• take sb at their word (ALSO take sb's word for it) to believe that what someone says is true: He said he'd give me a job and I just took him at his word. ○ If he says there's $500 in the envelope, then I'll take his word for it.

• your word is your bond OLD-FASHIONED OR FORMAL If someone's word is their bond, they always keep their promises: "But listen, you must promise never to tell anyone." "My word is my bond."

• man/woman of your word someone who keeps their promises: You can trust him – he's a man of his word.

word ORDER /wɜːd/ ⑩ /wɝːd/ noun [S] an order: We're waiting for the word from head office before making a *statement.* ○ *The troops will go into action as soon as their commander* ***gives*** *the word.* ○ ***At*** *a word from their teacher, the children started to tidy away their books.*

• **from the word go** from the start of something: *The bridge-building project had problems with funding* ***right*** *from the word go.*

ˈword associˌation *noun* [U] a method sometimes used in PSYCHOANALYSIS in which the person being treated says the first word they think of when a particular word is said, which may help to discover how parts of the mind work

ˌword ˈperfect *UK adj* (*US* **letter perfect**) describes words produced without any mistakes, or a person who is able to repeat a particular text from memory without making any mistakes: *His mother rehearsed his lines with him and by the time the play opened he was word perfect.* ○ *"Your German was word perfect when we spoke earlier, Mr Whitlock," Franz said.* ○ *a word-perfect rendition/recitation*

wordplay /ˈwɜːd.pleɪ/ [US] /ˈwɝːd-/ *noun* [U] when you joke about the meanings of words, especially in a clever way

ˌword ˈprocessing *noun* [U] the organization of text in electronic form such as on a computer: *a word processing program/package*

ˌword ˈprocessor *noun* [C] a computer used for preparing documents and letters, or the program that is used for this: *With suitable software you can use your PC as a word processor.* ○ *Which word processor do you have on your computer?*

wore /wɔːʳ/ [US] /wɔːr/ *past simple of* **wear**

work [ACTIVITY] /wɜːk/ [US] /wɝːk/ *noun* [U] **1** an activity, such as a job, which a person uses physical or mental effort or do, usually for money: *I've got so much work to* ***do.*** ○ *Carrying heavy loads around all day is* ***hard*** *work.* ○ *What time do you* ***start/finish*** *work?* ○ *Adrian* ***does*** *most of the work around the house.* ○ *What sort of work are you experienced in?* ○ *She tends to wear quite smart clothes for work.* ○ *Roger's work involves a lot of travelling.* **2** the material used by someone at work, or what they produce: *I'll have to take this work home with me and finish it there.* ○ *All the furniture is the work of residents here.*

• **be at work 1** to be working: *The labourers were at work in the fields.* **2** *LITERARY* to be having an effect, usually an obvious or bad effect: *It seems as though forces of destruction are increasingly at work throughout society.*

• **be in work/out of work** to have a job, or not to have a job: *He was always in work, right from the day he left school.* ○ *My father was out of work at the time, so we struggled, obviously.* ○ *an out-of-work actor/manager*

• **get/set to work** to start doing a job or a piece of work: *We'd better get to work* ***on*** *stacking this wood if we want to finish before it gets dark.*

• **have *your* work cut out (for *you*)** to have something very difficult to do: *She'll really have her work cut out to finish all those reports by the end of the week.*

• **All work and no play (makes Jack a dull boy).** *SAYING* said to warn someone that they will not be an interesting person if they work all the time

work /wɜːk/ [US] /wɝːk/ *verb* [I or T] to do a job, especially the job you do to earn money, or to make someone do a job: *He works at the local hospital.* ○ *She worked* ***as*** *a cleaner at the hospital.* ○ *Mike works* ***for*** *a computer company.* ○ *It's not unusual for a junior doctor to work a seventy or sometimes an eighty hour week.* ○ *Have you any experience of working* ***with*** *children who have learning difficulties?* ○ *The instructors worked us very* ***hard*** *on the survival course.* ➲See also **work to rule** at **work-to-rule**.

• **work *your* fingers to the bone** to work extremely hard, especially for a long time: *She worked her fingers to the bone to provide a home and food for seven children.*

-work /-wɜːk/ [US] /-wɝːk/ *suffix* **1** used to refer to work of a particular type: *homework* ○ *paperwork* **2** used to refer to a skill or activity using a particular type of material: *Girls and boys study woodwork and metalwork at this school.* **3** used to name things made of a particular material: *stonework* ○ *ironwork*

worker /ˈwɜː.kəʳ/ [US] /ˈwɝː.kɚ/ *noun* [C] **1** someone who works in a particular job or in a particular way: *factory/social/construction workers* ○ *a good/tireless/skilled worker* **2** someone who works for a company or organization but does not have a powerful position: *Many companies still treat their management staff better than their workers.* **3** in bees and some other types of insects, a female which cannot produce young but which collects food for the others

working /ˈwɜː.kɪŋ/ [US] /ˈwɝː-/ *adj* [before n] **1** relating to work: *a 37-hour working* ***week*** ○ *Working* ***conditions/practices*** *in the mill have hardly changed over the last twenty years.* ○ *She has a difficult working* ***relationship*** *with many of her staff.* **2** having work: *These tax changes will affect 90% of the working population.*

COMMON LEARNER ERROR

work or job?

Work is something you do to earn money. Remember that this noun is uncountable.

She enjoys her work in the hospital.
He's looking for work.
~~*He's looking for a work.*~~

Job is used to talk about the particular type of work activity which you do.

He's looking for a job in computer programming.
Teaching must be an interesting job.
~~*Teaching must be an interesting work.*~~

Occupation is a formal word which means the job that you do. It is often used on forms. See also: CAREER and PROFESSION.

work [OPERATE] /wɜːk/ [US] /wɝːk/ *verb* [I or T] If a machine or device works, it operates, especially correctly and without failure, and if you work it, you make it operate: *Our telephone isn't working.* ○ *You need a team of about twelve people to work a furnace this size.* ○ *The pump works* ***off/on*** (= uses) *wind power.* ○ *The pump is worked* ***by*** (= uses to operate) *wind power.* ○ *I can't* ***get*** *the radio* ***to*** *work.*

• **work a treat** *UK* to operate very well: *This new drill works a treat on hard metals.* ➲See also **work wonders/miracles** at **work** HAVE EFFECT.

working /ˈwɜː.kɪŋ/ [US] /ˈwɝː-/ *adj* [before n] **1** operating: *It has taken about five years to restore the aircraft to* ***(full)*** *working* ***condition/order.*** **2** describes the parts of a machine which move and make it work: *It is essential that all working components are properly lubricated.*

workings /ˈwɜː.kɪŋz/ [US] /ˈwɝː-/ *plural noun* **the workings of *sth*** the way that an organization, machine or organism operates: *the workings of government* ○ *I don't know anything about the workings of other departments or about the organization as a whole.* ➲See also **workings**.

works /wɜːks/ [US] /wɝːks/ *plural noun* the parts of a machine, especially those that move: *If you take the back off this clock, you can see its/the works.* ➲See also **works** at **work** PLACE and **the works**.

work [HAVE EFFECT] /wɜːk/ [US] /wɝːk/ *verb* [I usually + adv or prep] to be effective or successful: *Her idea for reorganizing the department will never work* ***in practice.*** ○ *The tablets will start to work* ***in*** *a few minutes.* ○ *Some people think I'm weird doing meditation, but it works* ***for*** *me and that's all that matters.* ○ *Arguably, the monarchy worked* ***well*** *for many centuries.*

• **work like a charm** (*ALSO* **work like magic**) to be very effective, possibly in a surprising way: *Flattery usually works like a charm with him.*

• **work wonders/miracles** (*UK ALSO* **work a treat**) to produce very beneficial effects: *A little bit of oil works wonders on squeaky hinges.* ○ *Running works wonders* ***for*** *the metabolism.*

workable /ˈwɜː.kə.bl̩/ [US] /ˈwɝː-/ *adj* describes a plan or system that can be used effectively: *a workable solution/compromise/proposal*

working /ˈwɜː.kɪŋ/ [US] /ˈwɝː-/ *adj* [before n] describes a plan, idea or knowledge that is not complete but is good enough to be useful: *We have a working* ***theory/hypothesis*** *about what caused the crash, which we shall*

W

test. ○ *She's fluent in French and English and has a working **knowledge** of Spanish.*

work [SUCCEED IN BECOMING] /wɜːk/ [US] /wɝːk/ *verb* [I or T; + adv or prep] to succeed gradually in becoming something or cause a person or thing to become something, either by making an effort or by making many small movements: *He started as a technician and worked his **way up** through the company to become managing director.* ○ *Eventually she worked her **way through** (= read) the huge amount of technical papers.* ○ [R] *Vibration tends to make nuts and screws work them**selves loose**.* ○ *The screws had worked loose over time.*

• **work *your* way around/round to *sth*** to prepare yourself slowly for doing something: *I think they're both gradually working round to talking to each other again.*

work [ARRANGE] /wɜːk/ [US] /wɝːk/ *verb* [T] *INFORMAL* to arrange for something to happen, especially by not using official methods and/or by being clever: *I don't know how she worked **it**, but she retired at fifty on a full salary.* ○ *Can we work **things (out)** so that there's always someone here to answer the telephone during office hours?*

work [PLACE] /wɜːk/ [US] /wɝːk/ *noun* [U] a place where a person goes specially to do their job: *Do you have far to travel **to** work each day?* ○ *Thousands of people are seriously injured **at** work every year.* ○ *When does she leave **for** work?*

works /wɜːks/ [US] /wɝːks/ *group noun* [C] *plural* **works** an industrial building, especially one where a lot of people are employed: *a steel/car works* ➲See also **works** at **work** OPERATE and **the works**.

work [CREATION] /wɜːk/ [US] /wɝːk/ *noun* [C] something created as a result of effort, especially a painting, book or piece of music: *The museum has many works **by** Picasso as well as other modern painters.* ○ *the poetic works of Tagore*

work [SHAPE] /wɜːk/ [US] /wɝːk/ *verb* [T] to shape, change or process a substance: *Working iron requires higher temperatures than bronze.* ○ *Gently work the butter **into** the flour until there are no lumps left.*

workable /ˈwɜː.kə.bl̩/ [US] /ˈwɝː-/ *adj*: *The ground is too hard to be workable* (= dug).

work [PHYSICS] /wɜːk/ [US] /wɝːk/ *noun* [U] *SPECIALIZED* force multiplied by distance moved

PHRASAL VERBS WITH **work** ▼

▲ **work against/for *sb*** *phrasal verb* to make it more difficult, or easier, for someone to achieve something: *Inexperience can work against a candidate looking for a job.*

▲ **work at *sth*** *phrasal verb* to try hard to achieve something: *Most couples would agree that for a marriage to succeed, both parties have to work at it.* ○ [+ v-*ing*] *You need to work at improv**ing** your writing.*

▲ **work *sth* off** *phrasal verb* [M] If you work off an unpleasant feeling, you get rid of it by doing something energetic: *She works off stress by running for at least half an hour every day.*

▲ **work on *sth*** [IMPROVE] *phrasal verb* to spend time repairing or improving something: *His dancing technique is good, but he needs to work on his fitness.*

▲ **work on *sb*** [PERSUADE] *phrasal verb INFORMAL* to try to persuade or influence someone: [+ *to* infinitive] *I'm working on my father **to** get him to take me to the airport.*

▲ **work *sth* out** [CALCULATE] *phrasal verb* [M] to do a calculation to get an answer to a mathematical question: *We need to work out the total cost of the project.*

▲ **work out** *phrasal verb* [L] to be the result of a calculation: *These figures work out differently each time I add them.* ○ *The safe load for a truck of this size works out **at** nearly twenty tonnes.* ○ *In fact the trip worked out cheaper than we'd expected.*

▲ **work *sth* out** [UNDERSTAND] *phrasal verb* [M] *MAINLY UK* to understand something or to find the answer to something by thinking about it: [+ question word] *There will be a full investigation to work out **what** caused the accident.* ○ [+ *that*] *Investigators needed several months to work out **that** a fraud had been committed.*

▲ **work *sb* out** *phrasal verb* to understand the reasons for someone's behaviour: *Why does he behave like that? – I can't work him out at all.*

▲ **work out** [DEVELOP] *phrasal verb* to happen or develop in a particular way: *How is the new monitoring procedure working out?* ○ *Let's hope this new job works out **well** for him.*

▲ **work *(sth)* out** *phrasal verb* If a problem or difficult situation works out, it gradually becomes better or satisfactory, and if you work it out, you make it better or satisfactory: *Don't worry about anything – it'll **all** work out (for the best) in the end, you'll see.*

▲ **work out** [EXERCISE] *phrasal verb* to exercise in order to improve the strength or appearance of your body: *Huw works out in the gym two or three times a week.*

workout /ˈwɜː.kaʊt/ [US] /ˈwɝː-/ *noun* [C] *a vigorous/light workout*

▲ **work *sb* over** *phrasal verb* [M] *SLANG* to attack and injure someone: *Do you want me to get some of the lads to work him over?*

▲ **work up *sth*** *phrasal verb* to develop an emotional or physical state that you feel strongly, after a period of effort or time: *We worked up a real **appetite** climbing in the mountains.* ○ *It's strange, but I can't work up any **enthusiasm** for going on this trip.*

▲ **work *sb* up** *phrasal verb* to make yourself or another person feel upset or feel strong emotions: [R] *Try not to work yourself up **about** the exams.* ○ *Nationalist speeches worked the crowd up **into a frenzy**.*

ˌworked ˈup *adj* [after v] *It's easy to **get** worked up when you're tired and everything seems to be against you.* ○ *He was very worked up **about** seeing his family again after so many years.*

▲ **work *(yourself)* up to *sth*** *phrasal verb* to gradually prepare yourself for something difficult: [R] *He's very shy, but he's slowly working (his way/himself) up to letting her know what he feels about her.*

workaday /ˈwɜː.kə.deɪ/ [US] /ˈwɝː-/ *adj* [before n] ordinary; not unusual: *Compared to the extravagance and glamour of last winter's **clothes**, this season's collection look simple, almost workaday.* ○ *an escape from the workaday **world***

workaholic /ˌwɜː.kəˈhɒl.ɪk/ [US] /ˌwɝː.kəˈhɑː.lɪk/ *noun* [C] a person who works a lot of the time and finds it difficult not to work: *A self-confessed workaholic, Tony Richardson can't remember when he last had a holiday.*

workbasket /ˈwɜːkˌbɑː.skɪt/ [US] /ˈwɝːkˌbæs.kɪt/ *noun* [C] (*MAINLY UK* **workbox**) a small container in which items used for sewing, such as needles, pins and thread are kept

workbench /ˈwɜːk.bentʃ/ [US] /ˈwɝːk-/ *noun* [C] a strong table for working on, especially one on which objects such as pieces of wood or metal can be firmly held so that tools can be used on them

workbook /ˈwɜːk.bʊk/ [US] /ˈwɝːk-/ *noun* [C] a book used in school containing text and questions and sometimes having spaces for a student to write answers in: *There's a workbook to accompany the course book.*

workday /ˈwɜːk.deɪ/ [US] /ˈwɝːk-/ *noun* [C] *MAINLY US FOR* **working day**

ˈwork ˌethic *noun* [C] the belief that work is morally good: *The work ethic was never very strong in Simon.*

ˈwork exˌperience *noun* [U] **1** the experience that a person already has of working: *Please list your educational qualifications and work experience.* **2** a period of time in which a student temporarily works for an employer to gain experience: *Many firms understand that giving work experience to students from colleges and schools will benefit everyone in the long term.*

workforce /ˈwɜːk.fɔːs/ [US] /ˈwɝːk.fɔːrs/ *group noun* [C] the group of people who work in a company, industry, country, etc: *The majority of factories in the region have a workforce **of** 50 to 100 (people).* ○ *Much of the workforce in the banking sector is/are affected by the new legislation.*

workhorse /ˈwɜːk.hɔːs/ [US] /ˈwɝːk.hɔːrs/ *noun* [C] **1** a person who does a lot of work, especially of a type which is necessary but not interesting: *a willing/reliable workhorse* **2** a machine which operates without failing for long periods, although it might not be very interesting or exciting: *The steam engine was the workhorse of the Industrial Revolution.*

workhouse /'wɜːk.haʊs/ ⓤ /'wɝːk-/ noun [C] a building where very poor people in Britain used to work, in the past, in exchange for food and shelter ⊃Compare **poorhouse**.

working capital noun [U] the money belonging to a company which is immediately available for business use, rather than money it has in investments or property

working class group noun [S] (*ALSO* **the working classes**) a social group that consists of people who earn little money, often being paid only for the hours or days that they work, and who usually do physical work: *The working class usually react/reacts in a predictable way to government policies.* ⊃Compare **lower class**; **middle class**; **upper class**. **working-class** /ˌwɜː.kɪŋ'klɑːs/ ⓤ /ˌwɝː.kɪŋ'klæs/ adj: *working-class people/families*

working day noun [C] (*MAINLY US* **workday**) **1** the amount of time a person spends doing their job on a day when they work: *An eight-hour working day is still typical for many people.* **2** a day on which most people go to work: *On a working day I tend to get up around seven o'clock.* ○ *Please allow three full working days for the money to be transferred.*

working girl noun [C] *OLD-FASHIONED INFORMAL* a female prostitute

working group group noun [C] (*UK ALSO* **working party**) a small group of people, for example one chosen by a government, which studies a particular problem or situation and then reports on what it has discovered and gives suggestions

working life noun [C] the part of a person's life when they do a job or are at work: *His entire working life was spent with the same firm.*

working lunch/breakfast noun [C] a meal in the middle of the day, or at the beginning of the day, during which work is discussed

working man/woman/person noun [C] a man/woman who has a job: *Generally, working people don't have time to shop for food every day.*

working mother/father/parent noun [C] a woman/man/parent who has a job and cares for his or her children: *Little provision is made for working mothers by many large companies.*

working papers plural noun *US* official documents which allow someone under 16 years old to be employed

working party group noun [C] *UK FOR* **working group**

workings /'wɜː.kɪŋz/ ⓤ /'wɝː-/ plural noun the system of holes which has been dug in the ground in order to remove metal, coal, etc: *disused mine workings* ⊃See also **workings** at **work** OPERATE.

workload /'wɜːk.ləʊd/ ⓤ /'wɝːk.loʊd/ noun [C] the amount of work to be done, especially by a particular person or machine in a period of time: *Teachers are always complaining about their* **heavy** *workloads.* ○ *Students do find that their workload* **increases** *throughout the course.*

workman /'wɜːk.mən/ ⓤ /'wɝːk-/ noun [C] a man who uses physical skill and especially his hands in his job or trade: *We'll have to get a workman in to fix the plumbing/window/roof.*

workmanlike /'wɜːk.mən.laɪk/ ⓤ /'wɝːk-/ adj **1** *APPROVING* skilful: *The Australian side turned in a very workmanlike* **performance**. **2** *DISAPPROVING* showing an acceptable level of skill but no great ability or style: *I had hoped for a little more from the world's greatest tenor, whose performance was workmanlike but hardly inspired.*

workmanship /'wɜːk.mən.ʃɪp/ ⓤ /'wɝːk-/ noun [U] the skill with which something was made or done: *shoddy/fine workmanship* ○ *The workmanship which went into some of these pieces of furniture was truly remarkable.*

workmate /'wɜːk.meɪt/ ⓤ /'wɝːk-/ noun [C] *INFORMAL* a person who works in the same place as you, especially one with whom you are friendly: *I went out for a drink with a few workmates.*

work of 'art noun [C] plural **works of art** an object made by an artist of great skill, especially a painting, drawing or statue: *The thieves stole several valuable works of art.*

workout /'wɜːk.aʊt/ ⓤ /'wɝː-/ noun [C] ⊃See at **work out** EXERCISE.

work permit noun [C] an official document which gives permission to someone who is foreign to work in a country

workplace /'wɜːk.pleɪs/ ⓤ /'wɝːk-/ noun [C or S] a building or room where people perform their jobs, or these places generally: *The survey asks workers about facilities in their workplace.* ○ *safety standards in* **the** *workplace*

workroom /'wɜːk.rʊm/ /-ruːm/ ⓤ /'wɝːk-/ noun [C] a room in which work is done, especially making things

the works plural noun *INFORMAL* everything that you might want or expect to find in a particular situation: *The bridegroom was wearing a morning suit, gloves, top hat – the works.* ○ *MAINLY US And let me have two large pizzas* **with** *the works* (= with all available types of food on top). ⊃See also **works** at **work** OPERATE; **work** PLACE.

worksheet /'wɜːk.ʃiːt/ ⓤ /'wɝːk-/ noun [C] a piece of paper with questions and exercises for students

workshop ⎡ROOM⎤ /'wɜːk.ʃɒp/ ⓤ /'wɝːk.ʃɑːp/ noun [C] a room or building where things are made or repaired using machines and/or tools: *a carpenter's/printer's workshop* ○ *an engineering workshop*

workshop ⎡MEETING⎤ /'wɜːk.ʃɒp/ ⓤ /'wɝːk.ʃɑːp/ noun [C] a meeting of people to discuss and/or perform practical work in a subject or activity: *a drama/poetry/training workshop* ○ *The local council* **runs** *a stress-management workshop.* ○ *a workshop session/production*

workshy /'wɜːk.ʃaɪ/ ⓤ /'wɝːk-/ adj *UK DISAPPROVING* disliking work and trying to avoid it when possible: *Most of the unemployed are not workshy and genuinely do want jobs.*

workstation /'wɜːk.steɪ.ʃ³n/ ⓤ /'wɝːk-/ noun [C] a keyboard and screen with which a person can use a computer system, or an area in an office, factory, etc. where a single person works

work surface noun [C] a **worktop**

worktop *UK* /'wɜːk.tɒp/ ⓤ /'wɝːk.tɑːp/ noun [C] (*US USUALLY* **counter**, *AUS USUALLY* **bench (top)**) a flat surface in a kitchen, especially on top of low furniture, on which food can be prepared: *Plastic coated worktops are easy to keep clean.*

work-to-rule /ˌwɜːk.tə'ruːl/ ⓤ /ˌwɝːk-/ noun [C] a situation in which people carefully obey all the rules and instructions given to them about their jobs, with the intention of reducing the amount of work they do: *Most work-to-rules are done as a protest against low pay or bad working conditions.*
● **work to rule** to arrange and perform a work-to-rule: *So far, the dustmen have not resorted to a strike but are working to rule.*

world ⎡THE EARTH⎤ /wɜːld/ ⓤ /wɝːld/ noun [S] the Earth and all the people, places and things on it: *Different parts of the world have very different climatic conditions.* ○ *Which bridge has the longest span in the world?* ○ *News of the disaster shocked the* **(whole/entire)** *world.* ○ *We live in a* **changing** *world and people must learn to adapt.* ○ *She's a world* **authority** *on foetal development.* ○ *a world* **record/championship**
● **at one with the world** happy because you feel that you belong in the world and generally agree with what happens
● **for all the world** exactly: *She sounds for all the world* **like** *her mother on the telephone.*
● **not for (all) the world** never; not in any situation: *If I took that job I'd have to leave the kids and I wouldn't do that for all the world.*
● **have the world at** *your* **feet** to be extremely successful and admired by a great number of people: *Five years after her debut, the diminutive star of the Royal Ballet has the world at her feet.*
● **in a world of** *your* **own** (*ALSO* **in another world**) thinking your own thoughts and ideas and not giving much attention to what is happening around you: *When she was*

*young, she **lived in** a world of her own and had very few friends.*

• **what/how/why, etc. in the world** *INFORMAL* used to emphasize your surprise when asking a question: *What in the world are you doing in the cupboard?* ○ *Who in the world could do such a thing?*

• **make the world go around/round** to be extremely important, so that many ordinary events could not happen without it: ***Love/Money** makes the world go round.*

• **a man/woman of the world** someone who has a lot of experience of life and people, and can deal with most situations

• **out of this world** *INFORMAL* extremely good: *What a restaurant – the food was out of this world!*

• **mean/be (all) the world to *sb*** to be extremely important to someone: *Her children mean all the world to her.*

• **the ways of the world** the types of behaviour and ways of doing things that are acceptable: *He's very young and still has a lot to learn about the ways of the world.*

• **the world and his wife** *UK* a great many people, especially in a particular place at a particular time: *It's going to be quite a party – the world and his wife will be there.*

• **the world is *sb's* oyster** If the world is someone's oyster, they can do what they want to or go where they want to: *You're young and healthy and you have no commitments – the world is your oyster.*

• **a world of difference** If there is a world of difference between two people or things, they are very different: *There's a world of difference **between** the service in the two hotels.*

• **make a world of difference** If something makes a world of difference, it improves something very much: *A little sympathy makes a world of difference to someone who's been badly treated.*

world [GROUP/AREA] /wɜːld/ [US] /wɝːld/ *noun* **[C usually sing]** a group of things such as countries or animals, or an area of human activity or understanding: *the Muslim World* ○ *the modern/industrialized world* ○ *the animal world* ○ *stars from the rock music world* ○ *Unexpected things can happen in **the** world **of** subatomic particles.*

• **go/come up in the world** *UK* (*US* **move up in the world**) *INFORMAL* to have more money or a better social position than you had before: *Roger and Ann have gone up in the world – these days they only ever travel first-class.*

• **go/come down in the world** *UK* (*US* **move down in the world**) *INFORMAL* to have less money or a worse social position than you had before: *They used to live in a big house with lots of servants, but they've come down in the world since then.*

world [PLANET] /wɜːld/ [US] /wɝːld/ *noun* **[C]** a planet or other part of the universe, especially one where life might or does exist: *There was a man on the news last night who reckons we've been visited by beings from other worlds.*

• **be worlds apart** to be completely opposed or different: *They are worlds apart in their political views.*

world-beater /ˈwɜːldˌbiː.təʳ/ [US] /ˈwɝːldˌbiː.t̬ɚ/ *noun* **[C]** a person or thing that is better than any other of its type: *She has loads of natural talent as a runner and with rigorous training she could be a world-beater.* **world-beating** /ˈwɜːldˌbiː.tɪŋ/ [US] /ˈwɝːldˌbiː.t̬ɪŋ/ *adj*: *a world-beating partnership*

world-class /ˌwɜːldˈklɑːs/ [US] /ˌwɝːldˈklæs/ *adj* Someone or something world-class is one of the best that there are of that type in the world: *a world-class athlete/performance*

world-famous /ˌwɜːldˈfeɪ.məs/ [US] /ˌwɝːld-/ *adj* known about by many people from most parts of the world: *a world-famous actress/hotel*

the ˌWorld ˈHealth Organiˌzation *group noun* **[S]** (*ABBREVIATION* **the WHO**) a department of the United Nations which aims to improve health all over the world and limit the spread of diseases

worldly [PHYSICAL] /ˈwɜːld.li/ [US] /ˈwɝːld-/ *adj* **[before n]** relating to or consisting of physical things and ordinary life rather than spiritual things: *For many of the refugees, the clothes they are wearing are all the worldly **goods** (= possessions) they have.* ○ *Her worldly success can hardly be denied.*

worldly [PRACTICAL] /ˈwɜːld.li/ [US] /ˈwɝːld-/ *adj* practical and having a lot of experience of life: *She seems to be much more worldly than the other students in her class.* **worldliness** /ˈwɜːld.lɪ.nəs/ [US] /ˈwɝːld-/ *noun* **[U]**

worldly-wise /ˌwɜːld.liˈwaɪz/ [US] /ˌwɝːld-/ *adj* experienced in the ways in which people behave and able to deal with most situations: *Tyler is remarkably worldly-wise for such a young girl.*

ˌworld ˈmusic *noun* **[U]** popular music which has been influenced by the music of traditional cultures

ˌworld ˈpower *noun* **[C]** a country which has enough economic or political strength to influence events in many other countries

world-shattering /ˈwɜːldˌʃæt.ᵊr.ɪŋ/ [US] /ˈwɝːldˌʃæt̬.ɚ-/ *adj* (*ALSO* **world-shaking**) extremely surprising and important, often changing the way you think about something: *world-shattering news*

ˌworld ˈwar *noun* **[C usually sing]** a war in which large forces from many countries fight

ˌWorld ˌWar ˈOne *noun* **[S not after *the*]** (*WRITTEN ABBREVIATION* **WWI**) the war from 1914 to 1918 in which Britain, France, Russia, the United States and Italy fought Germany, Austria-Hungary, Turkey and Bulgaria

ˌWorld ˌWar ˈTwo *noun* **[S not after *the*]** (*WRITTEN ABBREVIATION* **WWII**) the war from 1939 to 1945 in which Britain, the Soviet Union, the United States and France fought Germany, Italy and Japan

world-weary /ˈwɜːldˌwɪə.ri/ [US] /ˈwɝːldˌwɪr.i/ *adj* Someone who is world-weary is not enthusiastic about anything, often because they have had too much experience of a particular way of life: *Fifteen years in the teaching profession had left him world-weary and cynical.* **world-weariness** /ˈwɜːldˌwɪə.ri.nəs/ [US] /ˈwɝːldˌwɪr.i-/ *noun* **[U]**

worldwide *adj* /ˈwɜːld.waɪd/ [US] /ˈwɜːrld-/, *adv* /-ˈ-/ existing or happening in all parts of the world: *a worldwide recession* ○ *An increase in average temperature by only a few degrees could cause environmental problems worldwide.*

the ˌWorld Wide ˈWeb *noun* **[S]** (*ABBREVIATION* **www**, *ALSO* **the Web**) the system of connected documents on the Internet, which often contain colour pictures, video and sound, and can be searched for information about a particular subject

worm [ANIMAL] /wɜːm/ [US] /wɝːm/ *noun* **1 [C]** a small animal with a long narrow soft body without arms, legs or bones: *The kiwi eats worms, other invertebrates, and berries.* **2 [C]** the young of particular types of insect: *It's distressing enough to find a worm in your apple but finding half of one is worse.* ➲See also **woodworm**. **3 [C]** a type of worm that lives in an animal's intestine, feeding on the food there, or on an animal's body, feeding off its blood: *a parasitic worm* ○ *The vet says our dog **has** worms.* ➲See also **tapeworm**. **4 [S]** *INFORMAL* an unpleasant person who does not deserve respect: *Don't be such a worm, you don't have to lie to me.*

• **the worm turns** used to describe when a person or group of people becomes forceful in a difficult situation, although they are usually obedient and do not cause any trouble: *It seems the worm has turned – after years of silence local people are beginning to protest about waste emissions from the factory.*

worm /wɜːm/ [US] /wɝːm/ *verb* **[T]** to give an animal, especially a pet dog or cat, medicine to kill any worms which might be living inside it: *Has your dog been wormed?*

wormy /ˈwɜː.mi/ [US] /ˈwɝː-/ *adj* containing many worms, or infected or damaged by worms: *Look at these vegetables – they're all mottled and wormy.*

worm [MOVE] /wɜːm/ [US] /wɝːm/ *verb* **[I or T; + prep]** to succeed in moving along in a difficult or crowded situation, by moving your body slowly and carefully: *Because he was so small, he could worm (his **way**) through the crowd.* ○ **[R]** *She wormed her**self** under the fence.*

PHRASAL VERBS WITH **worm** ▼

▲ **worm *yourself/your way* into *sth*** *phrasal verb DISAPPROVING* to gradually achieve a position of trust, possibly by being dishonest: **[R]** *He wormed himself into*

W

her affections without her ever suspecting he only did it for her money.

▲ **worm *sth* out of *sb*** *phrasal verb* INFORMAL to try and get information from someone which they are trying to keep secret: *He wasn't going to tell me, but I managed to worm it out of him.*

worm-eaten /ˈwɜːmˌiː.tᵊn/ [US] /ˈwɝːmˌiː.tᵊn/ *adj* containing small holes which were made by the young of particular types of insect, especially WOODWORM: *a worm-eaten table/beam*

wormhole [SMALL HOLE] /ˈwɜːm.həʊl/ [US] /ˈwɝːm.hoʊl/ *noun* [C] a hole made by a worm, sometimes found in furniture, fruit, or the ground

wormhole [PHYSICS] /ˈwɜːm.həʊl/ [US] /ˈwɝːm.hoʊl/ *noun* [C] SPECIALIZED a special type of structure which some scientists think might exist, connecting parts of space and time that are not usually connected

worn /wɔːn/ [US] /wɔːrn/ *past participle of* **wear**

ˌ**worn ˈout** [USED] *adj* describes something which can no longer be used because it is so old or because it has been damaged by continued use: *I've got old 'Fawlty Towers' videos which are almost worn out, I've played them so many times.* ○ *worn-out clothes/carpet/equipment*

ˌ**worn ˈout** [TIRED] *adj* extremely tired: *I 've been working all night and I'm worn out.*

worry [PROBLEM] /ˈwʌr.i/ [US] /ˈwɝː-/ *verb* **1** [I] to think about problems or unpleasant things that might happen in a way that makes you feel anxious: *Try not to worry – there's nothing you can do to change the situation.* ○ ***Don't** worry, she'll be all right.* ○ *It's silly worrying **about** things which are outside your control.* ○ [+ (that)] *She's worried **(that)** she might not be able to find another job.* **2** [T] to make someone feel anxious because of problems or unpleasant things that might happen: *You worried your mother by not writing.* ○ [+ obj + (that)] *It worries me **that** he hasn't phoned yet.* ○ *The continued lack of rain is starting to worry people.*

● **not to worry** INFORMAL said to show that you are not worried or upset because something has gone wrong or something unexpected has happened: *Not to worry – perhaps you'll be able to come next week instead.*

worry /ˈwʌr.i/ [US] /ˈwɝː-/ *noun* **1** [C] a problem that makes you feel anxious: *health/financial worries* ○ *Keeping warm in the winter is a major worry for many old people.* **2** [C or U] when you feel anxious about something: *Unemployment, bad health – all sorts of things can be a cause of worry.* ○ *It was clear that Anna had no worries about her husband's attempts to flirt.*

worried /ˈwʌr.id/ [US] /ˈwɝː-/ *adj*: *She was sitting behind her desk with a worried **expression/look** on her face.* ○ *They don't seem particularly worried **about** the situation.* ○ *You **had** me worried* (= You made me feel anxious) *for a moment back there – I thought you wouldn't be able to stop in time.* ○ *He was worried **sick*** (= extremely worried) *when he heard that there had been an accident.* **worriedly** /ˈwʌr.id.li/ [US] /ˈwɝː-/ *adv*: *He looked back worriedly over his shoulder.*

worrier /ˈwʌr.i.əʳ/ [US] /ˈwɝː.i.ɚ/ *noun* [C] someone who worries a lot: *I can't help being a worrier – some people are just born that way.*

worrying /ˈwʌr.i.ɪŋ/ [US] /ˈwɝː-/ *adj* making you feel anxious: *It's a very worrying **situation**.* **worryingly** /ˈwʌr.i.ɪŋ.li/ [US] /ˈwɝː-/ *adv*: *Worryingly, the gun was never found.*

worrisome /ˈwʌr.ɪ.səm/ [US] /ˈwɝː-/ *adj* US FORMAL OR OLD-FASHIONED worrying: *Alcohol and tobacco consumption by young people is especially worrisome because habits formed early are likely to persist.*

W

COMMON LEARNER ERROR

worry about something or someone

Remember to use the preposition 'about' after this verb.

They were all worried about their jobs.

~~*They were all worried for their jobs.*~~

worry [ANIMAL] /ˈwʌr.i/ [US] /ˈwɝː-/ *verb* [T] If a dog worries another animal, it chases and frightens it and might also bite it: *Any dog caught worrying sheep in these fields will be shot.*

PHRASAL VERBS WITH **worry**

▲ **worry at *sth*** [OBJECT] *phrasal verb* to shake, pull at or touch something repeatedly: *The dog was worrying away at its bone.*

▲ **worry at *sth*** [PROBLEM] *phrasal verb* to keep trying to find a way of solving a problem: *She'll worry at those figures until she's sure they've been worked out properly.*

worrywart /ˈwʌr.i.wɔːt/ [US] /ˈwɝː.i.wɔːrt/ *noun* [C] MAINLY US INFORMAL a person who tends to worry, especially about unimportant things: *Don't listen to him – he's just an old worrywart.*

worse /wɜːs/ [US] /wɝːs/ *adj, comparative of* **bad 1** more unpleasant, difficult or severe than before or than something else that is also bad: *The conditions they're living in are worse **than** we thought.* ○ *If the rain **gets** any worse we'll have to stop walking.* ○ *His manners are **even** worse than his sister's.* ○ *The heat is **much** worse in the daytime.* **2 get worse** to become more ill, or to become a more severe condition: *My cold seems to be getting worse.* ○ *If he gets **any** worse I'll take him to the doctor's.*

● **make matters worse** to make the situation even more unpleasant or difficult: *Don't say anything – you'll only make matters worse.*

● **worse luck** INFORMAL said at the end of a statement to show unhappiness or annoyance about what has been stated: *I've got to work on Saturday, worse luck.*

worse /wɜːs/ [US] /wɝːs/ *noun* [U] something that is more unpleasant or difficult: *By the third month of the expedition they had endured many hardships, but worse was to follow.* ○ *"What about the bride's dress – wasn't it appalling?" "I don't know, I've **seen** worse."* ➲Compare **better** IMPROVEMENT.

● **for the worse** If something changes or happens for the worse, the unpleasantness or difficulty increases: *It looks like the weather is **changing** for the worse.*

● **be none the worse** to not be harmed or damaged by something: *They were trapped in the cave for a couple of days but they were none the worse **for** their experience.* ○ *He's lost some weight but he's none the worse* (= he's better) *for that.*

● **the worse for wear** tired or in poor condition because of a lot of work or use: *After a month of journeying over rough roads, the drivers and their trucks were looking the worse for wear.*

worse /wɜːs/ [US] /wɝːs/ *adv, comparative of* **badly**: *He did worse than he was expecting in the exams* ○ *He was treated much worse than I was.*

worsen /ˈwɜː.sᵊn/ [US] /ˈwɝː-/ *verb* [I or T] to become worse or to make something become worse: *As the company's financial problems worsened, several directors resigned.* ○ *The continued supply of arms to the region will only worsen the situation.* **worsening** /ˈwɜː.sᵊn.ɪŋ/ [US] /ˈwɝː-/ *adj*: *the country's worsening political situation* **worsening** /ˈwɜː.sᵊn.ɪŋ/ [US] /ˈwɝːs-/ *noun* [S] *Rather worryingly, the survey shows a worsening of child health in many areas.*

ˌ**worse ˈoff** *adj* **be worse off** to be poorer or in a more difficult situation: *If Rick loses his job we'll be even worse off.*

worship [RELIGION] /ˈwɜː.ʃɪp/ [US] /ˈwɝː-/ *verb* **-pp-** or US ALSO **-p- 1** [T] to have or show a strong feeling of respect and admiration for God or a god: *In the various regions of India, Hindus worship different gods and observe different religious festivals.* **2** [I] to go to a religious ceremony: *They work for the same company, socialise together and worship in the same mosque.* ○ *The poll showed that over 40% of Americans worship on a weekly basis.*

worship /ˈwɜː.ʃɪp/ [US] /ˈwɝː-/ *noun* [U] when you worship God or a god, often through praying or singing: *daily **acts of** worship* ○ *Christian/Sikh/Muslim worship* ○ *For Jews, the synagogue is the centre for community worship and study.* ○ *Local people have complained about improperly dressed tourists entering **places of** worship* (= buildings for religious ceremonies or private prayer).

worshipper, US USUALLY **worshiper** /ˈwɜː.ʃɪp.əʳ/ [US] /ˈwɝː.ʃɪp.ɚ/ *noun* [C] **1** someone who goes to a religious ceremony to worship God: *At 11am on Sunday morning, worshippers began to stream out of the cathedral.* **2** someone who worships and performs religious ceremonies to a particular god or object: *devil/idol worshippers*

worship ADMIRATION /ˈwɜː.ʃɪp/ US /ˈwɜː-/ *verb* [T] **-pp-** or *US ALSO* **-p-** to love, respect and admire someone or something greatly, often without being aware of their bad qualities: *Her parents worship her.* ○ *As a child, I worshipped my older brother.*
• **worship the ground** *sb* **walks on** to love and admire someone greatly: *I worship the ground you walk on, you must know that by now.*
worship /ˈwɜː.ʃɪp/ US /ˈwɜː-/ *noun* [U] DISAPPROVING when you like or admire a particular thing or person very much, often too much: *We're in an era of fitness and health worship.*
worshipper, *US USUALLY* **worshiper** /ˈwɜː.ʃɪp.əʳ/ US /ˈwɜː.ʃɪp.ɚ/ *noun* [C] INFORMAL someone who enjoys or values a particular thing very much or too much: *sun worshippers*

worship TITLE /ˈwɜː.ʃɪp/ US /ˈwɜː-/ *noun MAINLY UK FORMAL* **His/Your, etc. Worship** used as a title of respect when speaking to or about a MAYOR or a MAGISTRATE: *His Worship the Mayor will present the awards.* ○ [as form of address] *Thank you, Your Worship.*

worshipful /ˈwɜː.ʃɪp.fᵊl/ US /ˈwɜː-/ *adj* **1** MAINLY UK FORMAL **Worshipful** used in the title of societies of skilled workers or some important officials: *the Worshipful Company of Silversmiths* **2** FORMAL giving someone or something great respect or admiration

worst SUPERLATIVE OF BAD /wɜːst/ US /wɜːst/ *adj* of the lowest quality, or the most unpleasant, difficult or severe: *That was* **the** *worst meal I've ever eaten.* ○ *"It was* **the** *worst moment of my life," she admitted.* ○ *He is my worst* **enemy**.
• **be** *your* **own worst enemy** to cause most of your problems or most of the bad things that happen to you yourself, because of your character: *Carrie is her own worst enemy – she's always falling out with people.*
worst /wɜːst/ US /wɜːst/ *adv* the most badly: *Small businesses have been worst* **hit** *by the recession.* ○ *Roads in the Tayside region were worst* **affected** *by the snow.* ○ *The students voted him the school's worst-dressed teacher.*
worst /wɜːst/ US /wɜːst/ *noun* [S] the most unpleasant or difficult thing, person, or situation: *That was* **the** *worst I've seen him play in several years.*
• **at worst 1** used to say what the most unpleasant or difficult situation could possibly be: *At worst, she can only tell you off for being late.* **2** considering someone or something in the most negative or unkind way possible: *She is at worst corrupt, and at best has been knowingly breaking the rules.*
• **at** *your* **worst 1** less active or intelligent than you are at other times: *I'm at my worst first thing in the morning.* **2** showing the most unpleasant side of your character: *This problem over late payment has shown him at his worst.*
• **do** *your* **worst** to do the most unpleasant or harmful thing you can: *I'm not frightened of him – let him do his worst.*
• **fear the worst** to think something unpleasant might have happened: *We hoped that they would be found safe and uninjured, but secretly we feared the worst.*
• **if the worst comes to the worst** (*US* **if worse/worst comes to worst**) if the situation develops in the most serious or unpleasant way: *We should be in when you arrive, but if the worst comes to the worst, the neighbours have a spare key and will let you into the house.*

worst DEFEAT /wɜːst/ US /wɜːst/ *verb* [T] OLD USE to defeat someone in a fight or argument: *He was challenged to a fight but was severely worsted.*

worst case sceˈnario *noun* [S] the most unpleasant or serious thing which could happen in a situation: *The study concludes that* **in a** *worst case scenario there might be up to 80, 000 human infections in Britain arising from BSE beef.*

worsted /ˈwʊs.tɪd/ US /ˈwɜː.stɪd/ *noun* [U] a type of woollen cloth used to make jackets, trousers and skirts: *a pale grey worsted suit*

worst-ever /ˌwɜːstˈev.əʳ/ US /ˌwɜːstˈev.ɚ/ *adj* [before n] describes something that is the most unpleasant or harmful of its type that there has ever been: *219 people were killed in the country's worst-ever plane crash.*

worth MONEY /wɜːθ/ US /wɜːθ/ *noun* [U] **1** the amount of money which something can be sold for; value: *The estimated worth of the plastics and petrochemical industry is about $640 billion.* **2** **£20/$100, etc. worth of** *sth* the amount of something that you could buy for £20/$100, etc: *$4 million worth of souvenirs and gift items have been produced for the event.*
• **get** *your* **money's worth** to get good value: *We were determined to get our money's worth from our day tickets and went to every museum in the city.*
worth /wɜːθ/ US /wɜːθ/ *adj* **1** having a particular value, especially in money: *Our house is worth about £200 000.* ○ *Heroin worth about $5 million was seized.* **2** INFORMAL possessing a particular amount of money: *She must be worth at least half a million.*
• **be worth it** to be of reasonable or good value for the price: *Four days' car hire costs £150, which is* **well** *worth it for the freedom it gives you.*
• **make** *sth/it* **worth** *your* **while** INFORMAL to pay you money to do something: *If you can get me the list of names I want, I'll make it worth your while.*
• **not worth the paper** *sth* **is printed/written on** If a document or agreement is not worth the paper it is written/printed on, it is of very little value.
• **worth** *your* **salt** good at your job: *Any accountant worth their salt should be aware of the latest changes in taxation.*
• **be worth** *your/its* **weight in gold** to be very useful or helpful: *This recipe book is worth its weight in gold – it tells you everything you need to know about cookery.* ○ *Boys who can sing like that are worth their weight in gold* **to** *the choir.*
worthless /ˈwɜːθ.ləs/ US /ˈwɜːθ-/ *adj* having no value in money: *The company's shares are now* **virtually** *worthless shares.* ○ *He said the jewels were worthless fakes.*
worthlessness /ˈwɜːθ.lə.snəs/ US /ˈwɜːθ-/ *noun* [U]

worth IMPORTANCE /wɜːθ/ US /wɜːθ/ *noun* [U] the importance or usefulness of something or someone: *He felt as though he had no worth.* ○ *She has proved her worth on numerous occasions.* ○ *The study proved that women were paid less than men holding jobs* **of** *comparable worth.*
worth /wɜːθ/ US /wɜːθ/ *adj* **1** **be worth** *sth* to be important or interesting enough to receive a particular action: *I think this matter is worth our attention.* ○ *When you're in Reykjavik, the National Museum is worth a visit.* **2** **be worth** *having/doing sth* to be important or useful to have or do: *There's nothing worth reading in this newspaper.* ○ *If you are a young, inexperienced driver, it is worth having comprehensive insurance.* ○ *It's worth remembering that prices go up on February 1st.*
• **worth it** enjoyable or beneficial enough to make the necessary effort, risk, pain, etc. seem acceptable: *It was a long climb to the top of the hill, but it was worth it for the view from the top.* ○ *Don't tire yourself out Geri, it's really not worth it.* ○ *After the plastic surgery I had two black eyes and was very swollen. But I knew it would be worth it.* ○ *Forget him, love – he's just not worth it.*
• **be worth** *your* **while** to be an activity or action that you will benefit from: *It's worth your while taking out travel insurance before you travel.*
• **for all** *you* **are worth** INFORMAL If you do something for all you are worth, you put a lot of effort into it: *We pushed the car for all we were worth, but we still couldn't get it started.*
• **for what it's worth** INFORMAL said when you are giving someone a piece of information and you are not certain if that information is useful or important: *For what it's worth, I think he may be right.* ○ *They are, for what it's worth, the single most successful eastern arts group in the West.*
• **What's it worth (to you)?** INFORMAL MAINLY HUMOROUS said when you want to know what someone will give you if you give them the piece of information they have asked

for: *"Do you know where Dave's living at the moment?" "What's it worth?"*
worthless /ˈwɜːθ.ləs/ [US] /ˈwɝːθ-/ *adj* unimportant or useless: *She was criticised so much by her employers that she began to feel worthless.* **worthlessness** /ˈwɜːθ.lə.snəs/ [US] /ˈwɝːθ-/ *noun* [U] *People who have been abused as children often experience **feelings/a sense** of worthlessness.*

COMMON LEARNER ERROR

be worth doing something

When **worth** is followed by a verb, the verb is always in the **-ing** form.

Do you think it's worth asking Patrick first?
~~*Do you think it's worth to ask Patrick first?*~~

worth [AMOUNT] /wɜːθ/ [US] /wɝːθ/ *noun* **a month/year's, etc. worth of *sth*** an amount of something which will last a month/year, etc. or which takes a month/year, etc. to do: *a month's worth **of** grocery shopping* ○ *I've done three hour's worth **of** work this morning.*
worthwhile /ˌwɜːθˈwaɪl/ [US] /ˌwɝːθ-/ *adj* useful, important or beneficial enough to be a suitable reward for the money or time spent or the effort made: *She considers teaching a worthwhile career.* ○ *The time and expense involved in keeping up to date with all the changes has been worthwhile.* ○ *If you need him on this project, you've got to **make it financially** worthwhile for him* (= you will have to pay him a suitable amount of money for the amount of work involved).
worthy [DESERVING RESPECT] /ˈwɜː.ði/ [US] /ˈwɝː-/ *adj FORMAL* **1** deserving respect, admiration or support: *He is unlikely to succeed in getting his bill through Congress, however worthy it is.* ○ *Every year she makes a large donation to a worthy **cause**.* **2 worthy of attention/notice, etc.** deserving to be given attention, noticed, etc: *Two points in this report are especially worthy of notice.* **3** describes something which should be admired for its good and beneficial qualities but which is not very interesting: *a worthy book*
worthy /ˈwɜː.ði/ [US] /ˈwɝː-/ *noun* [C] *HUMOROUS* a person who is important, especially in a small town: *The front row of chairs was reserved for local worthies.* **worthily** /ˈwɜː.ðɪ.li/ [US] /ˈwɝː-/ *adv FORMAL* **worthiness** /ˈwɜː.ðɪ.nəs/ [US] /ˈwɝː-/ *noun* [U] *the worthiness of a project/cause/aim*
worthy [SUITABLE] /ˈwɜː.ði/ [US] /ˈwɝː-/ *adj* **worthy of *sth*** suitable for, or characteristic of something: *He threw a party worthy of a millionaire and attracted a glittering crowd of beautiful people.*
-worthy /-wɜː.ði/ [US] /-wɝː-/ *suffix* **1** suitable or deserving to receive a particular thing: *trustworthy* ○ *creditworthy* ○ *newsworthy* **2** describes a boat, aircraft or vehicle which is suitable to be used safely in a particular substance or surroundings: *seaworthy* ○ *roadworthy*
worthiness /ˈwɜː.ðɪ.nəs/ [US] /ˈwɝː-/ *noun* [U] suitability: *She persuaded the board of her worthiness to run the company.*
wot /wɒt/ [US] /wɑːt/ *pronoun UK NOT STANDARD MAINLY HUMOROUS* used in writing for *what* or *that*: *Wot? No food?* ○ *It's him wot won it.*
wotcha, wotcher /ˈwɒt.ʃəʳ/ [US] /ˈwɑː.tʃɚ/ *exclamation UK INFORMAL* used as an informal greeting, especially between friends: *Wotcha, mate!*
would [FUTURE] *STRONG* /wʊd/, *WEAK* /wəd, əd/ *modal verb* **1** (*SHORT FORM* **'d**) used to refer to future time from the point of view of the past: *He said he would see his brother tomorrow.* ○ *They knew there would be trouble unless the report was finished by the next day.* ○ *We realised it wouldn't be easy to find another secretary.* **2 would have** used to refer back to a time in the past from a point of view in the future: *We thought they would have got home by five o'clock, but there was no reply when we phoned.*
would [INTENTION] *STRONG* /wʊd/, *WEAK* /wəd, əd/ *modal verb* (*ALSO* **'d**) used to refer to an intention from the point of view of the past: *He said he would always love her* (= He said "I will always love you"). ○ *They promised that they would help.* ○ *There was nobody left who would* (= was willing to) *do it.* ○ *I asked him to move his car but he said he wouldn't* (= he refused).
would [POSSIBLE] *STRONG* /wʊd/, *WEAK* /wəd, əd/ *modal verb* (*ALSO* **'d**) **1** used to refer to a situation that you can imagine happening: *I would hate to miss the show.* ○ *I'd go myself but I'm too busy.* ○ *It would **have** been very boring to sit through the whole speech.* **2** used with *if* in CONDITIONAL sentences (= sentences which refer to what happens if something else happens): *What would you do if you lost your job?* ○ *If I'd had time, I would **have** gone to see Graham.*
would [REQUEST] *STRONG* /wʊd/, *WEAK* /wəd, əd/ *modal verb* (*ALSO* **'d**) used as a more polite form of *will* in requests and offers: *Would you mind sharing a room?* ○ *Would you like me to come with you?* ○ *Would you like some cake?*
would [WISH] *STRONG* /wʊd/, *WEAK* /wəd, əd/ *modal verb* (*ALSO* **'d**) **would rather/sooner** used to show that you prefer to have or do one thing more than another: *I'd rather have a beer.* ○ *Which would you sooner do – go swimming or play tennis?* ○ *Wouldn't you rather finish it tomorrow?* ○ *He'd rather die than* (= He certainly does not want to) *let me think he needed help.*
• **Would that ...** *FORMAL* used to express a strong wish or desire: *Would that* (= If only) *she could see her famous son now.*
would [OFTEN] *STRONG* /wʊd/, *WEAK* /wəd, əd/ *modal verb* (*ALSO* **'d**) **1** used to talk about things in the past that happened often or always: *He would always turn and wave at the end of the street.* **2** *DISAPPROVING* used to suggest that what happens is expected because it is typical, especially of a person's behaviour: *"Margot rang to say she's too busy to come." "She would – she always has an excuse."*
would [OPINION] *STRONG* /wʊd/, *WEAK* /wəd, əd/ *modal verb* (*ALSO* **'d**) used to express an opinion in a polite way without being forceful: *I would imagine we need to speak to the headteacher about this first.* ○ *It's not what we would **have** expected from a professional service.*
would [LIKELY] *STRONG* /wʊd/, *WEAK* /wəd, əd/ *modal verb* (*ALSO* **'d**) used to refer to what is quite likely: *"The guy on the phone had an Australian accent." "That would be Tom, I expect."*
would [ADVISE] *STRONG* /wʊd/, *WEAK* /wəd, əd/ *modal verb* (*ALSO* **'d**) **should** ADVISE: *I wouldn't* (= I advise you not to) *worry about it, if I were you.*
would [REASON] *STRONG* /wʊd/, *WEAK* /wəd, əd/ *modal verb* (*ALSO* **'d**) **should** REASON: *Why would anyone want to eat something so horrible?*
would [WILLING] *STRONG* /wʊd/, *WEAK* /wəd, əd/ *past simple of* **will** ABLE/WILLING: used to talk about what someone was willing to do or what something was able to do: *The car wouldn't start this morning.*
would-be /ˈwʊd.biː/ *adj* [before n] wanting or trying to be: *a would-be artist/politician*
wouldn't /ˈwʊd.ᵊnt/ *short form of* would not: *I wouldn't do that if I were you.*
wound [WIND] /waʊnd/ *past simple and past participle of* **wind** TURN and **wind** WRAP AROUND
wound [INJURY] /wuːnd/ *noun* [C] a damaged area of the body, such as a cut or hole in the skin or flesh made by a weapon: *a gunshot wound* ○ *a chest/leg wound* ○ *a **flesh*** (= not deep) *wound* ○ *He died from multiple **stab** wounds **to** the neck and upper body.* **wound** /wuːnd/ *verb* [T] *Flying glass wounded her **in** the face and neck.* ○ *The police chief was **badly** wounded in the explosion.*
wounded /ˈwuːn.dɪd/ *adj*: *a wounded soldier*
the wounded *plural noun* people who are injured: *Ambulances took the wounded to local hospitals.*
wound [UPSET] /wuːnd/ *noun* [C] a problem or great unhappiness: *She refuses to talk about the incident, saying it would only **reopen old** wounds* (= make her remember unhappy past experiences).
wound /wuːnd/ *verb* [T] to make someone feel upset: *He was deeply wounded by her fierce criticism.*
wounded /ˈwuːn.dɪd/ *adj* offended or upset by what someone has said or done: *a wounded expression* ○ *wounded pride*

W

wound 'up *adj* very anxious, nervous or angry: *She gets quite wound up before a match.*
wove /wəʊv/ [US] /woʊv/ *past simple of* **weave** MAKE CLOTH, **weave** TWIST
woven /ˈwəʊ.vᵊn/ [US] /ˈwoʊ-/ *past participle of* **weave** MAKE CLOTH, **weave** TWIST
wow [SURPRISE] /waʊ/ *exclamation* INFORMAL used to show surprise and sometimes pleasure: *Wow! Did you make that cake? It looks delicious!*
wow [SUCCESS] /waʊ/ *noun* [S] INFORMAL a person or thing that is very successful, attractive or pleasant: *He's not particularly good-looking, but he's a real wow* ***with*** *the girls in his class.*
wow /waʊ/ *verb* [T] INFORMAL to impress and excite someone greatly: *The movie wowed audiences throughout the States with its amazing special effects.*
WPC /ˌdʌb.l̩.jʊ.piːˈsiː/ *noun* [C] UK ABBREVIATION FOR woman police constable: a female police officer of the lowest rank: *WPC (Andrea) Watson*
WRAC /ræk/ /ˌdʌb.l̩.juː.ɑː.reɪˈsiː/ [US] /-ɑːr.eɪ-/ *group noun* [S] ABBREVIATION FOR Women's Royal Army Corps
WRAC /ræk/ /ˌdʌb.l̩.juː.ɑː.reɪˈsiː/ [US] /-ɑːr.eɪ-/ *noun* [C] ABBREVIATION a member of this organization
wrack /ræk/ *noun* [U] ➲See **rack** DECAY.
WRAF /ˌdʌb.l̩.juː.ɑː.reɪˈef/ [US] /-ɑːr.eɪ-/ *group noun* [S] ABBREVIATION FOR Women's Royal Air Force
WRAF /ˌdʌb.l̩.juː.ɑː.reɪˈef/ [US] /-ɑːr.eɪ-/ *noun* [C] ABBREVIATION a member of this organization
wraith /reɪθ/ *noun* [C] LITERARY a spirit of a dead person which is sometimes represented as a pale, transparent image of that person: *a wraith-****like*** (= thin and pale) *figure in a grey floating dress*
wrangle /ˈræŋ.gl̩/ *noun* [C] an argument, especially one which continues for a long period of time: *a lengthy wrangle* ***about/over*** *costs* ○ *The joint venture ended in a* ***legal*** *wrangle between the two companies.* **wrangle** /ˈræŋ.gl̩/ *verb* [I] *They had been wrangling* ***with*** *the authorities* ***about/over*** *parking spaces.* **wrangling** /ˈræŋ.gl̩.ɪŋ/ *noun* [U] *political wrangling*
wrap /ræp/ *verb* [T] **-pp- 1** to cover or enclose something with paper, cloth or other material: *She wrapped the present and tied it with ribbon.* ○ *Wrap the chicken* ***in*** *foil and cook it for two hours.* **2** to cover someone with material in order to protect them: *She wrapped the baby* ***in*** *a blanket.* ○ *He wrapped a towel* ***around*** *his shoulders.*
• **wrap *sb* around/round *your* little finger** to persuade someone easily to do what you want them to do: *She could wrap her father round her little finger.*
• **wrap *sb* (up) in cotton wool** UK to try to protect someone too carefully: *You can't wrap (up) your children in cotton wool for ever.*
wrap /ræp/ *noun* **1** [C] (US ALSO **wrapper**) a loose piece of clothing which is worn tied around the body: *a towelling wrap* ○ *a beach wrap* **2** [C] a long piece of cloth which a woman wears around her shoulders to keep her warm or for decoration: *a chiffon/silk wrap* **3** [U] material which is used to cover or protect objects: *plastic wrap* ○ *gift wrap* **4** [C] a sandwich made with one piece of very thin bread which is folded around a filling
• **under wraps** secret: *They tried to* ***keep*** *the report under wraps.*
• **take the wraps off *sth*** to permit people to know about something
wrapped /ræpt/ *adj* covered with paper or other material: *individually wrapped chocolates*
wrapper /ˈræp.əʳ/ [US] /-ɚ/ *noun* [C] **1** a piece of paper, plastic or other material which covers and protects something: *a (UK) sweet/(US) candy wrapper* **2** US FOR **wrap** (= loose piece of clothing)
wrapping /ˈræp.ɪŋ/ *noun* [C or U] paper or plastic which covers or protects something: *cellophane wrapping* ○ *The new chairs were covered in protective plastic wrappings.*

PHRASAL VERBS WITH **wrap**

▲ **wrap *sth* around/round *sb/sth*** [MATERIAL] UK *phrasal verb* (US **wrap *sth* around *sb/sth***) to put a piece of clothing or material around someone or something, usually to keep them warm: *It was so cold that he wrapped a scarf tightly around his face.*
▲ **wrap *sth* around/round *sth*** [BODY] UK *phrasal verb* (US **wrap *sth* around *sth***) to put part of your body, such as your fingers or arms, around something tightly: *She sat back in her chair and wrapped her arms around her knees.*
▲ **wrap (*sb*) up** [DRESS] *phrasal verb* [M] to dress in warm clothes, or to dress someone in warm clothes: *Wrap up well – it's cold outside.*
▲ **wrap *sth* up** [MATERIAL] *phrasal verb* [M] to cover or enclose something in paper, cloth or other material: *Have you wrapped up Jenny's present yet?*
▲ **wrap *sth* up** [FINISH] *phrasal verb* [M] INFORMAL to complete something successfully: *That just about wraps it up for today.*
▲ **be wrapped up in *sth/sb*** *phrasal verb* INFORMAL If you are wrapped up in someone or something, you are very interested in them and ignore other people or things: *She's always been completely wrapped up in the children.*

wrap-around /ˈræp.ə.raʊnd/ *adj, noun* [C] (UK ALSO **wrapround**) (a piece of clothing that is) made so that it can be tied around the body: *a wrap-around skirt*
wrapped /ræpt/ *adj* (ALSO **rapt**) AUS INFORMAL extremely happy or excited ➲See also **be wrapped up in**; **wrapped** at **wrap**.
'wrapping ˌpaper *noun* [U] decorated paper which is used to cover presents
wrath /rɒθ/ [US] /rɑːθ/ *noun* [U] FORMAL OR OLD-FASHIONED extreme anger: *The people feared the wrath of God.* **wrathful** /ˈrɒθ.fᵊl/ [US] /ˈrɑːθ-/ *adj* **wrathfully** /ˈrɒθ.fᵊl.i/ [US] /ˈrɑːθ-/ *adv*
wreak /riːk/ *verb* [T] **wrought** or **wreaked**, **wrought** or **wreaked** FORMAL to cause something to happen in a violent and often uncontrolled way: *The recent storms have wreaked* ***havoc*** *on crops.* ○ *She was determined to wreak* ***revenge/vengeance*** *on both him and his family.*
wreath /riːθ/ *noun* [C] *plural* **wreaths** /riːðz/ an arrangement of flowers and leaves in a circular shape, which is used as a decoration or as a sign of respect and remembrance for a person who has died: *a holly/laurel wreath* ○ *The bride wore a veil with a wreath* ***of*** *silk flowers.* ○ *There were two large wreaths on the coffin.* ○ *The President ended his visit by* ***laying*** *a wreath at the war memorial.*
wreathe /riːð/ *verb* [T] LITERARY to cover or surround something: *The peak of the mountain is perpetually wreathed* ***in*** *cloud.*
• **be wreathed in smiles** LITERARY to be smiling and looking extremely happy: *He was wreathed in smiles as he accepted the award.*
wreck /rek/ *verb* [T] **1** to destroy or badly damage something: *The explosion shattered nearby windows and wrecked two cars.* ○ *Our greenhouse was wrecked in last night's storm.* **2** INFORMAL to spoil something completely: *He has been warned that his behaviour might wreck his chances of promotion.*
wreck /rek/ *noun* [C] **1** a vehicle or ship that has been destroyed or badly damaged: *Divers exploring the wreck managed to salvage some coins and jewellery.* ○ *The burnt-out wrecks* ***of*** *two police cars littered the road.* **2** INFORMAL someone who is in bad physical or mental condition: *The stress she had been under at work reduced her to a* ***nervous/quivering*** *wreck.*
wrecked /rekt/ *adj* **1** very badly damaged: *Just look at what you've done to my coat – it's wrecked.* **2** [after v] SLANG very drunk: *He* ***got*** *completely wrecked last Saturday night.* **3** [after v] INFORMAL very tired
wreckage /ˈrek.ɪdʒ/ *noun* [U] **1** a badly damaged object or the separated parts of a badly damaged object: *Two children were trapped in the wreckage.* ○ *The wreckage of the car was scattered over the roadside.* **2** what is left of something that has been spoiled or that has failed: *Kate was still* ***clinging to*** *the wreckage of her failed marriage.*
wrecker /ˈrek.əʳ/ [US] /-ɚ/ *noun* [C] US FOR **breakdown truck**
wren [BIRD] /ren/ *noun* [C] a very small, brown bird
Wren [WOMAN] /ren/ *noun* [C] UK INFORMAL a member of the British Women's Royal Naval Service

W

wrench [PULL] /rentʃ/ *verb* **1** [T + adv or prep] to pull and twist something suddenly or violently away from a fixed position: *The photographer tripped over a lead, wrenching a microphone* ***from*** *its stand.* ○ *The phone had been wrenched* ***from/off*** *the wall.* ○ *The ball was wrenched* ***out of*** *his grasp by another player.* ○ *His hands were tied but he managed to wrench himself* ***free***. **2** [T] to twist part of your body badly, such as your arm or leg, and injure it: *He wrenched his right shoulder during a game of hockey.* **3** [T usually passive] to suddenly take someone from people whom they love, causing them great unhappiness: *At the age of eight, she was wrenched from her foster parents and sent to live with another family.*

wrench /rentʃ/ *noun* **1** [C usually sing] a sudden, violent twist or pull **2** [S] a feeling of unhappiness when you have to leave a person or place that you love: *She found leaving home a real wrench.*

wrench [TOOL] /rentʃ/ *noun* [C] *MAINLY US* a SPANNER, usually one which can be made larger or smaller for holding and turning objects of different sizes: *an adjustable wrench* ➲See also **monkey wrench**.

wrest /rest/ *verb* [T + adv or prep] **1** *FORMAL* to obtain something with effort or difficulty: *The shareholders are planning to wrest* ***control*** *of the company* ***(away) from*** *the current directors.* **2** to violently pull something away from someone: *He wrested the letter from my grasp.*

wrestle /ˈres.l̩/ *verb* [I or T] to fight with someone (especially as a sport) by holding them and trying to throw them to the ground: *He has wrestled professionally for five years.* ○ *The police officer tackled the man and wrestled him* ***to the ground***.

wrestler /ˈres.ləʳ/ (US) /-lɚ/ *noun* [C] a person who wrestles as a sport

wrestling /ˈres.lɪŋ/ *noun* [U] a sport where two people fight and try to throw each other to the ground: ➲See picture **Sports** on page Centre 10

▲ **wrestle with *sth*** *phrasal verb* to try very hard to deal with a problem or to make a difficult decision: *The government is wrestling with difficult economic problems.* ○ *He wrestled with the decision for several weeks, wondering what he should do.*

wretch [UNHAPPY PERSON] /retʃ/ *noun* [C] a person who experiences something unpleasant: *a poor/miserable wretch*

wretch [BAD PERSON] /retʃ/ *noun* [C] *INFORMAL OR HUMOROUS* someone who is unpleasant or annoying: *Who's trampled on my flowers? I bet it was those two little wretches who live next door.* ○ *You wretch! You promised you'd give me a lift.*

wretched /ˈretʃ.ɪd/ *adj* **1** unhappy, unpleasant or of low quality: *a wretched childhood* ○ *The house was in a wretched state.* **2** used to express annoyance: *My wretched car's broken down again.* **3** very ill or very unhappy: *I think I must be coming down with flu – I've been feeling wretched all day.*

wretchedly /ˈretʃ.ɪd.li/ *adv* extremely, when referring to something unpleasant or of low quality: *wretchedly inadequate* **wretchedness** /ˈretʃ.ɪd.nəs/ *noun* [U]

wriggle /ˈrɪg.l̩/ *verb* **1** [I or T] to twist your body, or move part of your body, with small, quick movements: *A large worm wriggled in the freshly dug earth.* ○ *Baby Martha was wriggling her toes in the sand.* **2** [I + adv or prep] to move somewhere using short, quick twisting movements: *The tunnel was low and dark, but she managed to* ***wriggle through*** *to the other side.* ○ *After twisting and turning for a while, he managed to wriggle* ***free***.

• **wriggle off the hook** *INFORMAL* If someone wriggles off the hook, they avoid a responsibility or avoid doing something.

wriggle /ˈrɪg.l̩/ *noun* [C usually sing] an act of wriggling: *With a wriggle, she managed to crawl through the gap.*

▲ **wriggle out of *sth*** *phrasal verb INFORMAL* to avoid doing something that you do not want to do: *He promised he'd help me decorate, but now he's trying to wriggle out of it.*

wring /rɪŋ/ *verb* [T] **wrung, wrung 1** to hold something tightly with both hands and twist it by turning your hands in opposite directions **2** (*ALSO* **wring out**) to twist a cloth or piece of clothing with your hands to remove water from it: *She wrung out the shirt and hung it out to dry.*

• **wring *your* hands** If you wring your hands, you show that you are worried or unhappy: *Car dealers are wringing their hands* ***over*** *low sales this summer.*

• **wring *sth's* neck** to kill a bird or other animal by twisting and breaking its neck

• **I'll wring *your/his/her* neck!** *INFORMAL* something you say when you are very angry with someone: *I'll wring his neck if he does that again!*

wringer /ˈrɪŋ.əʳ/ (US) /-ɚ/ *noun* [C] (*UK ALSO* **mangle**) a machine used for pressing water out of clothes by putting the clothes between two heavy smooth round bars

• **put *sb* through the wringer** *INFORMAL* to ask someone difficult or unpleasant questions, often to find out whether they are doing their job satisfactorily: *Outside investigators will put the company's accounting practices through the wringer.*

▲ **wring *sth* from/out of *sb*** *phrasal verb* to force or persuade someone to give you something: *They managed to wring a few concessions from the government.*

wrinkle /ˈrɪŋ.kl̩/ *noun* [C] **1** a small line in the skin caused by old age: *fine wrinkles around the eyes* ○ *anti-wrinkle creams* **2** a small line or fold in cloth **3** *INFORMAL* a problem, usually a minor one: *There are still a few wrinkles to* ***iron out*** (= solve) *before the agreement can be signed.*

wrinkle /ˈrɪŋ.kl̩/ *verb* [I or T] If skin or material wrinkles, or if something wrinkles it, it gets small lines or folds in it: *Sunbathing can prematurely age and wrinkle the skin.*

• **wrinkle *your* brow** to make folds appear on your face above your eyes to show that you are surprised or confused

• **wrinkle (up) *your* nose** to show that you dislike something or that you disapprove of something by tightening the muscles in your nose so that small lines appear in the skin: *She wrinkled up her nose* ***at*** *the strange smell coming from the kitchen.* ○ *Amy wrinkled her nose in disapproval.*

wrinkled /ˈrɪŋ.kl̩d/ *adj* with a lot of wrinkles: *a wrinkled face*

wrinkly, **wrinklie** /ˈrɪŋ.kli/ *noun* [C] *UK INFORMAL* an old person

wrist /rɪst/ *noun* [C] the part of the body between the hand and the arm: *I sprained my wrist playing squash.* ➲See picture **The Body** on page Centre 5

wristwatch /ˈrɪst.wɒtʃ/ (US) /-wɑːtʃ/ *noun* [C] a watch that is worn on the wrist

writ [DOCUMENT] /rɪt/ *noun* [C] *LEGAL* a legal document from a court of law which informs someone that they will be involved in a legal process and instructs them what they must do: *There have been at least seven writs* ***issued against*** *him for late payment of bills.* ○ *She has* ***served*** *a writ* ***for*** *libel* ***on*** *the newspaper* (= She has delivered it to them officially).

writ [AUTHORITY] /rɪt/ *noun* [U] *FORMAL* the authority to rule or make laws: *holy writ*

writ [WRITE] /rɪt/ *OLD USE past participle of* **write**

• **be writ large** *FORMAL* to be very obvious: *Her distress was writ large in her face.*

• **writ large** *FORMAL* If one thing is another thing writ large, it is similar to it but larger or more obvious: *Hollywood is often said to be American society writ large.*

write /raɪt/ *verb* **wrote, written** or *OLD USE* **writ 1** [I or T] to make marks which represent letters, words or numbers on a surface, such as paper or a computer screen, using a pen, pencil or keyboard, or to use this method to record thoughts, facts or messages: *When you fill in the form, please write* ***clearly/legibly*** *in black ink.* ○ [+ speech] *"I hope to see you next Saturday," she wrote.* ○ *Why not write* ***(down)*** *your ideas on a piece of paper before you start?* **2** [I or T] to send a letter or similar message to someone, giving them information or expressing your thoughts or feelings: *She hasn't* (US) *written me/*(UK) *written* ***to*** *me recently.* ○ [+ two objects] *I wrote my sister a letter.* ○ [+ to infinitive] *My mother wrote* ***to*** *give me details about the party.* ○ [+ v-ing] *The travel company has written giving information about the trip.* **3** [T] (*ALSO* **write *sth***

out) to put all the information that is needed on a document: *Please will you write (out) your name and address* ***in full.*** ○ **[+ two objects]** *I wrote him a cheque for £50.* **4** **[T]** to create and record something, such as a book, poem, song or computer program, on paper or on a computer: *She writes children's books/poems.* ○ *Adam designed and wrote the software.* ○ *He wrote music* ***for*** *films and TV shows.* **5** **[I]** to have the job of creating books, stories or articles that will be published: *She writes* ***for*** *a national newspaper.* **6** **[T + *that*]** to state something in a book, newspaper, magazine or document: *In the article, he writes* ***that*** *the problems in the refugee camps are getting worse.* **7** **[I]** SPECIALIZED to record information in the memory of a computer: *There was a problem writing* ***to*** *the disk in the A drive.*

• **nothing to write home about** INFORMAL not exciting or special: *Their performance was nothing to write home about.*

writer /ˈraɪ.təʳ/ [US] /-t̬ɚ/ *noun* **[C]** a person who writes books or articles to be published: *a travel/sports/fiction/crime writer* ○ *She is a well-known writer of children's books.*

writing /ˈraɪ.tɪŋ/ [US] /-t̬ɪŋ/ *noun* **[U]** **1** a person's style of writing with a pen on paper which can be recognized as their own: *Do you recognise the writing on the envelope?* **2** something which has been written or printed **3** the written work, such as stories or poems, of one person or a group of people: *She is studying women's writing at the turn of the century.* **4** the activity of creating pieces of written work, such as stories, poems or articles: *I did a course in* ***creative*** *writing.*

• **in writing** in written form: *All bookings must be confirmed in writing.*

• **the writing is on the wall** (US ALSO **the handwriting is on the wall**) said to mean that there are clear signs that something will fail or no longer exist

writings /ˈraɪ.tɪŋz/ [US] /-t̬ɪŋz/ *plural noun* the written works of a person, especially when they have been published as books: *the writings* ***of*** *Karl Marx*

written /ˈrɪt.ən/ [US] /ˈrɪt̬-/ *adj* expressed in writing, or involving writing: *written instructions* ○ *a written exam*

• **written all over *sb's* face** If an emotion is written all over someone's face, it is clear what they are feeling: *Guilt was written all over her face.*

COMMON LEARNER ERROR

write (spelling)

The verb **write** has a double 'tt' in its past participle 'written'. All other forms have a single 't'.

I write English better than I speak it.
She writes very well.
We wrote him a letter when he was in hospital.
I am writing English now.
They have written a song together.
~~*I am writting English now.*~~

COMMON LEARNER ERROR

write

Remember to use the correct grammar after **write**.

write to someone
Pamela wrote to me last week.

write someone a letter
Pamela wrote me a letter last week.

write someone (American English)
Rachel wrote me last week.

PHRASAL VERBS WITH **write**

▲ **write back** *phrasal verb* to reply to someone's letter: *I'll write back and tell her we're coming.*

▲ **write *sth* down** *phrasal verb* **[M]** to write something on a piece of paper so that you do not forget it: *Did you write down Jo's phone number?*

▲ **write in** [LETTER] *phrasal verb* to write a letter to a newspaper, television company or other organization, to state an opinion or ask something: **[+ *to* infinitive]** *People have written in* ***to*** *complain about the show.* ○ **[+ *v-ing*]** *Thousands of people wrote in to the BBC ask****ing*** *for an information sheet.*

▲ **write *sb* in** [ELECTION] *phrasal verb* **[M]** US to add someone's name to the official list for an election in order to show that you want to vote for them: *a write-in candidate/campaign*

▲ **write *sth* into *sth*** *phrasal verb* **[often passive]** to add a particular detail or rule to a document: *An agreement to produce five novels a year was written into her contract.*

▲ **write *sth* off** [VEHICLE] *phrasal verb* **[M]** UK to damage a vehicle so badly that it cannot be repaired: *His car was completely written off in the accident.*

write-off /ˈraɪ.tɒf/ [US] /-t̬ɑːf/ *noun* **[C usually sing]** *She wasn't hurt, but the car's a* ***complete*** *write-off.*

▲ **write *sth* off** [MONEY] *phrasal verb* **[M]** to accept that an amount of money has been lost or that a debt will not be paid: *The World Bank is being urged to write off debts from developing countries.*

▲ **write *sb/sth* off** [FAILURE] *phrasal verb* **[M]** to decide that a particular person or thing will not be useful, important or successful: *A lot of companies seem to write people off if they're over 50.*

▲ **write off/away for *sth*** *phrasal verb* to write a letter to an organization asking them to send you something: *Did you write off* ***for*** *tickets?*

▲ **write *sb* out of *sth*** *phrasal verb* to change the story of a regular television or radio programme so that a particular character is not in it any more

▲ **write *sth* up** [COMPLETE] *phrasal verb* **[M]** to write something in a complete or final form using notes that you have made: *Have you written up that report yet?*

write-up /ˈraɪ.tʌp/ [US] /-t̬ʌp/ *noun* **[C]** a report or article which makes a judgment about something, such as a play or film: *The paper didn't give the show a very good write-up.*

▲ **write *sb* up** [REPORT] *phrasal verb* **[M]** US to report someone for not obeying a law or rule: *The cop said he'd have to write me up* ***for*** *not stopping at the red light.*

writer's block /ˌraɪ.təzˈblɒk/ [US] /-t̬ɚzˈblɑːk/ *noun* **[U]** an inability to create a piece of written work because something in your mind prevents you from doing it

writer's cramp /ˌraɪ.təzˈkræmp/ [US] /-t̬ɚz-/ *noun* **[U]** a painful stiffness in the hand which people suffer from if they have been writing continuously for a long time

writhe /raɪð/ *verb* **[I]** **1** to make large twisting movements with the body: *The pain was so unbearable that he was writhing* ***in*** *agony.* ○ *She was writhing* ***around/about*** *on the ground.* **2** INFORMAL to experience a very difficult or unpleasant situation or emotion, such as extreme embarrassment: *He and four other senators were writhing in the glare of unfavorable publicity.*

ˈwriting ˌdesk *noun* **[C]** a desk (= a table for working at) with drawers

ˈwriting ˌpaper *noun* **[U]** (ALSO **notepaper**) paper for writing letters on

written /ˈrɪt.ən/ [US] /ˈrɪt̬-/ *past participle of* **write**

the ˌwritten ˈword *noun* **[U]** FORMAL language in written form: *the communicative power of the written word*

wrong [NOT CORRECT] /rɒŋ/ [US] /rɑːŋ/ *adj* **1** not correct: *Three of your answers were wrong.* ○ *That clock is wrong – it's 12.30 not 12.15.* ○ *Some of his facts are questionable, others are* ***plainly*** (= completely) *wrong.* ➲Compare **right** CORRECT. **2** If someone is wrong, they are not correct in their judgment or statement about something: *You were wrong* ***about*** *the time – the shop closed at 7 not 8.* ○ *He's wrong* ***in*** *think****ing*** *that we will support the project financially.*

• **prove *sb* wrong** to show by your actions that someone's judgment of you was not correct: *I thought she couldn't do it, but she proved me wrong.*

• **get the wrong end of the stick** INFORMAL to not understand a situation correctly: *Her friend saw us arrive at the party together and got the wrong end of the stick.*

• **go down the wrong way** If food or drink goes down the wrong way, it goes down the wrong tube in your throat and causes you to cough or stop breathing for a short time.

• catch *sb* on the wrong foot If something catches you on the wrong foot, you are not prepared for it: *I hadn't expected the question and it caught me on the wrong foot.*

wrong /rɒŋ/ [US] /rɑːŋ/ *adv INFORMAL* in a way that is not correct: *You've spelt my name wrong.* ➲See also **wrongly** at **wrong** NOT CORRECT.

• get *sth* wrong to make a mistake in the way you answer or understand something: *I spent hours doing that calculation and I still got the answer wrong.* ○ *You've got it all wrong – it was your boss that she was annoyed with and not you!*

• don't get me wrong said when you think someone might not understand what you say, or be upset by it: *Don't get me wrong – I'd love to come but I'm too busy next week.*

• go wrong to make a mistake: *These shelves are very easy to put together – you can't go wrong.* ○ *I thought I'd done this correctly, I just can't understand where I've gone wrong.* ➲See also **wrong** NOT SUITABLE.

wrongly /ˈrɒŋ.li/ [US] /ˈrɑːŋ-/ *adv* not correctly: *Several people were wrongly convicted.* ○ *He even spelled his own client's name wrongly/wrong.*

wrong [NOT SUITABLE] /rɒŋ/ [US] /rɑːŋ/ *adj* **1** not suitable or desirable, or not as it should be: *She's the wrong person for the job.* ○ *We must have taken a wrong turning.* ○ *I'm sorry, you've got the wrong **number*** (= this is not the telephone number you wanted). ➲Compare **right** SUITABLE. **2** describes something that is not considered to be socially acceptable or desirable: *She got in with the wrong crowd* (= a group of people who were not considered socially acceptable) *at university.* **3** If you ask someone what is wrong, you want to know what is worrying or upsetting them: *You've been quiet all evening. Is there anything wrong?* ○ *What's wrong with you today?*

• get/fall into the wrong hands If something gets/falls into the wrong hands, a dangerous person or enemy starts to control it: *If this sort of information fell into the wrong hands, we could be in serious trouble.*

• the wrong way round/around If something is the wrong way round/around, the part that should be at the front is at the back: *You've got your skirt on the wrong way round.*

wrong /rɔŋ/ [US] /rɑːŋ/ *adv* **go wrong** If a situation or event goes wrong, it becomes unpleasant and is not a success: *Our marriage began to go wrong after we had our first child.*

wrong [IMMORAL] /rɒŋ/ [US] /rɑːŋ/ *adj* not considered morally acceptable by most people: *Children should be taught that violence is wrong.* ○ ***It** was wrong **of** her to lie to you.* ○ *What's wrong **with** having a bit of fun?* * NOTE: The opposite is RIGHT.

wrong /rɒŋ/ [US] /rɑːŋ/ *noun* **1** [U] what is considered to be morally unacceptable: *He has no sense of **right and** wrong.* ○ *I was brought up to tell the truth and **know right from** wrong.* ○ *As far as her parents are concerned, she **can do no** wrong* (= she is perfect in every way). **2** [C] an unfair action: *He has **done** us a great wrong.* ○ *She was trying to **right*** (= do something to make better) *the wrongs of the past.*

• in the wrong If someone is in the wrong, they have made a mistake or done something which is bad or illegal: *The driver was unquestionably in the wrong.*

• Two wrongs don't make a right. *SAYING* said to emphasize that it is not acceptable to do something bad to someone just because they did something bad to you first

wrong /rɒŋ/ [US] /rɑːŋ/ *verb* [T] *FORMAL* to treat someone in an unfair or unacceptable way: *She felt **deeply** wronged by his accusations.*

wrongful /ˈrɒŋ.fəl/ [US] /ˈrɑːŋ-/ *adj* describes actions that are unfair or illegal: *She is claiming damages from the company for wrongful **dismissal**.* ○ *wrongful arrest/imprisonment* **wrongfully** /ˈrɒŋ.fəl.i/ [US] /ˈrɑːŋ-/ *adv: wrongfully arrested*

wrong [NOT WORKING] /rɒŋ/ [US] /rɑːŋ/ *adj* [after v] not working correctly: *Something's wrong **with** the television – the picture's gone fuzzy.* ○ *The doctors are still trying to **find out** what's wrong.*

wrong /rɒŋ/ [US] /rɑːŋ/ *adv* **go wrong** If a machine goes wrong, it stops working correctly. ➲See also **go wrong** at **wrong** NOT CORRECT; **wrong** NOT SUITABLE.

wrongdoer /ˈrɒŋˌduː.əʳ/ [US] /ˈrɑːŋˌduː.ɚ/ *noun* [C] *FORMAL* a person who does something bad or illegal

wrongdoing /ˈrɒŋˌduː.ɪŋ/ [US] /ˈrɑːŋ-/ *noun* [C or U] *FORMAL* when you behave badly or illegally: *She has strenuously **denied** any criminal wrongdoing.*

wrong-foot /ˌrɒŋˈfʊt/ [US] /ˌrɑːŋ-/ *verb* **1** [T] *UK* in a sport, to hit or kick the ball so that the other player believes the ball will go in the opposite direction to the one in which it will really go in order to make them move in the wrong direction **2** [T often passive] to cause someone to be in a difficult situation by doing something unexpected: *The company was completely wrong-footed by the dollar's sudden recovery.*

wrong-headed /ˌrɒŋˈhed.ɪd/ [US] /ˌrɑːŋ-/ *adj DISAPPROVING* based on ideas or judgments which are not suitable for a particular situation: *He admitted that the party had followed policies which were now considered as wrong-headed.*

wrote /rəʊt/ [US] /roʊt/ *past simple of* **write**

wrought /rɔːt/ [US] /rɑːt/ *past simple and past participle of* **wreak**: *Mr Simmonds has wrought* (= caused) *considerable changes in the company.*

ˌwrought ˈiron *noun* [U] iron that can be bent into attractive shapes and used to make gates, furniture, etc: *wrought-iron gates*

wrung /rʌŋ/ *past simple and past participle of* **wring**

wry /raɪ/ *adj* [before n] showing that you find a bad or difficult situation slightly amusing: *a wry smile/comment* **wryly** /ˈraɪ.li/ *adv*

the WSPA /ðəˌdʌb.l̩.juː.es.piːˈeɪ/ *noun* [S] *ABBREVIATION FOR* the World Society for the Protection of Animals

wt *noun* [U] *WRITTEN ABBREVIATION FOR* **weight** (= the amount that something or someone weighs): *On the card she had written: wt 60 kg, ht 1.64 m.*

wunderkind /ˈwʊn.də.kɪnd/ /ˈvʊn-/ [US] /-dɚ-/ *noun* [C] a person who is very clever or good at something and achieves success at a young age

wuss /wʊs/ *noun* [C] *SLANG* a COWARD: *It's not hot! God, Damian, you're such a wuss!*

the WWF /ðəˌdʌb.l̩.juːˌdʌb.l̩.juːˈef/ *noun* [S] *ABBREVIATION FOR* the Worldwide Fund for Nature

WWI *noun* [S not after *the*] *WRITTEN ABBREVIATION FOR* **World War One**

WWII *noun* [S not after *the*] *WRITTEN ABBREVIATION FOR* **World War Two**

www *noun* [S] *ABBREVIATION FOR* **the World Wide Web**: *Visit the Cambridge University Press website at www.cambridge.org*

WYSIWYG, **wysiwyg** /ˈwɪz.ɪ.wɪg/ *adj SPECIALIZED ABBREVIATION FOR* what you see is what you get: describes an image on a computer screen that is exactly the same when it is printed

X LETTER (*plural* **X's** *or* **Xs**), x (*plural* **x's** *or* **xs**) /eks/ *noun* [C] the 24th letter of the English alphabet

X NUMBER, x /eks/ *noun* [C] the sign used in the Roman system for the number 10

X FILM /eks/ *adj, noun* [C] *plural* **X's** *or* **Xs** used especially in the past to refer to a film or show that is not suitable for people under 18 years old because it contains violence or sex: *an X-rated film* ⊃See also **18**.

x AMOUNT NOT STATED /eks/ *noun* [U] used to represent a number, or the name of person or thing, which is not known or stated: *If 2x = 8, then x = 4.* ○ *Witness x stated that she had seen Cooper on repeated occasions.*

x KISS /eks/ *noun* [C] used at the end of an informal piece of writing to represent a kiss: *Write soon, all my love, Katy xxx*

x WRONG /eks/ *noun* [C] *plural* **x's** *or* **xs** written on an answer to a question to show that the answer is not correct

x VOTE /eks/ *noun* [C] *plural* **x's** *or* **xs** used when voting to mark the name of the person that you are choosing

x REMOVE /eks/ *verb* [T] *US* to remove something from a list: *I xed out all the names of the people I wouldn't be sending cards to.*

:-X *INTERNET SYMBOL FOR* my lips are sealed: used when you do not want to or cannot tell someone about something

X-acto knife /ɪg,zækt.əʊ'naɪf/ ⓊⓈ /-oʊ-/ *noun* [C] *US TRADE-MARK* a sharp knife with a short blade which can be replaced

X-chromosome /'eks,krəʊ.mə.səʊm/ ⓊⓈ /-,krəʊ.mə.soʊm/ *noun* [C] a sex CHROMOSOME which exists as a pair in the cells of females and with a Y-CHROMOSOME in the cells of male animals

xenon /'zen.ɒn/ ⓊⓈ /-nɑːn/ *noun* [U] a type of gas which has no colour or smell and is used in special BULBS (= devices which produce light)

xenophobia /,zen.ə'fəʊ.bi.ə/ ⓊⓈ /-'foʊ-/ *noun* [U] extreme dislike or fear of foreigners, their customs, their religions, etc. **xenophobic** /,zen.ə'fəʊ.bɪk/ ⓊⓈ /-'foʊ-/ *adj*: *a xenophobic mistrust of everything that isn't British* **xenophobe** /'zen.ə.fəʊb/ ⓊⓈ /-foʊb/ *noun* [C] a person who strongly dislikes or fears foreigners, their customs, their religions, etc.

Xerox /'zɪə.rɒks/ ⓊⓈ /'zɪr.ɑːks/ *noun* [C] *TRADEMARK* a copy of a document or other piece of paper with writing or printing on it, made by a machine that uses a photographic process, or the machine itself: *a Xerox of the letter* ○ *a Xerox machine* **Xerox**, **xerox** /'zɪə.rɒks/ ⓊⓈ /'zɪr.ɑːks/ *verb* [T] to make a copy of a document by using a Xerox machine

XL *WRITTEN ABBREVIATION FOR* extra large: the largest size of clothes

Xmas /'krɪst.məs/ /'ek.sməs/ *WRITTEN ABBREVIATION FOR* **Christmas**: *Happy Xmas to all our customers.*

XML /,eks.em'el/ *noun* [U] *TRADEMARK ABBREVIATION FOR* extensible mark up language: a way of marking text for display in computer systems

X-ray /'eks.reɪ/ *noun* [C] **1** a type of radiation that can go through many solid substances, allowing hidden objects such as bones and organs in the body to be photographed **2** a photograph of a part of the body made using X-rays: *The X-ray showed a slight irregularity in one lung.* **3** an examination of a part of the body by taking and studying an X-ray photograph: *She had an X-ray to see if any of her ribs were broken.* **x-ray** /'eks.reɪ/ *verb* [T] *His hip had to be x-rayed to see if it was forming properly.*

xylophone /'zaɪ.lə.fəʊn/ ⓊⓈ /-foʊn/ *noun* [C] a musical instrument consisting of flat wooden bars of different lengths which you hit with a pair of sticks that have hard, round ends made from wood or plastic

X

Y

Y [LETTER] (*plural* **Y's** or **Ys**), **y** (*plural* **y's** or **ys**) /waɪ/ *noun* [C] the 25th letter of the English alphabet

y [AMOUNT NOT STATED], **Y** /waɪ/ *noun* [U] used to represent the second of two numbers or names which are not known or stated when the first is represented by 'x': *If 2x = 3y and x=6, then y=4.* ○ *The children on trial were referred to as child X and child Y.*

-y /-i/ *suffix* added to nouns to form adjectives meaning like the stated thing: *cheesy*

Y2K /ˌwaɪ.tuːˈkeɪ/ *noun* [U] *ABBREVIATION FOR* the year 2000, usually used when referring to the MILLENNIUM BUG

yacht /jɒt/ [US] /jɑːt/ *noun* [C] a boat with sails and sometimes an engine, used for either racing or travelling on for pleasure: *a luxury yacht* ○ *the yacht club* ➲See picture **Planes, Ships and Boats** on page Centre 14

yachting /ˈjɒt.ɪŋ/ [US] /ˈjɑː.t̬ɪŋ/ *noun* [U] the sport or activity of sailing yachts

yachtsman /ˈjɒt.smən/ [US] /ˈjɑːt-/ *noun* [C] a man who sails or owns a yacht

yachtswoman /ˈjɒtˌswʊm.ən/ [US] /ˈjɑːt-/ *noun* [C] a female yachtsman

yack /jæk/ *verb* [I] *SLANG* to talk continuously, especially informally

yada yada yada /ˌjæd.əˌjæd.əˈjæd.ə/ *exclamation US INFORMAL* BLAH BLAH BLAH (= a phrase used to represent boring speech)

yahoo /ˈjɑː.huː/ *noun* [C] *plural* **yahoos** *LITERARY* a rude, loud and unpleasant person, especially one who lacks education

yak /jæk/ *noun* [C] a type of cattle with long hair and long horns, found mainly in Tibet

yakka, **yakker** /ˈjæk.ə/ *noun* [U] *AUS INFORMAL* work

ˌYale (ˈlock) /ˈjeɪlˌlɒk/ [US] /-ˌlɑːk/ *noun* [C] *TRADEMARK* a type of lock, especially for doors, which is cylindrical and is operated by a flat key: *a Yale key*

y'all /jɔːl/ [US] /jɑːl/ *pronoun US INFORMAL* used to address a group of people that you are speaking to: *See y'all later.*

yam /jæm/ *noun* [C or U] **1** an edible potato-like root from a tropical climbing plant, or the plant it grows from ➲See picture **Vegetables** on page Centre 2 **2** *US* a **sweet potato**

yammer /ˈjæm.əʳ/ [US] /-ɚ/ *verb* [I] *MAINLY US INFORMAL* to talk continuously for a long time in a way that is annoying to other people: *She was yammering* ***on/away*** *about nothing, as usual.*

yang /jæŋ/ *noun* [U] in Chinese philosophy, the male principle of the universe, represented as light and positive

yank [PULL] /jæŋk/ *verb* **1** [T usually + adv or prep] *INFORMAL* to pull something forcefully with a quick movement: *He tripped over the wire and yanked the plug* ***out****.* ○ *She yanked open the cupboard and everything fell out.* **2** [T often passive] *MAINLY US INFORMAL* to suddenly remove someone or something: *I was yanked* ***out of*** *school and forced to seek work.* **yank** /jæŋk/ *noun* [C usually sing] *INFORMAL* ***Give*** *the door a yank and it should open.*

Yank [AMERICAN] /jæŋk/ *noun* [C] (*ALSO* **Yankee**) *INFORMAL* a person from the United States of America: *DISAPPROVING The place was full of yanks.*

yankee /ˈjæŋ.ki/ *noun* [C] **1** *INFORMAL* a **yank 2** *US* an American who comes from the Northern US

yap /jæp/ *verb* **-pp- 1** [I] *DISAPPROVING* If a small dog yaps, it makes short high sounds: *She's got a horrible little dog that yaps around your ankles.* **2** [I usually + adv] *INFORMAL DISAPPROVING* to talk continuously: *I've just had Ian's mother on the phone, yapping* ***away*** *for half an hour!* **yap** /jæp/ *noun* [C] **yappy** /ˈjæp.i/ *adj*: *a yappy little dog*

yard [UNIT OF MEASUREMENT] /jɑːd/ [US] /jɑːrd/ *noun* [C] (*WRITTEN ABBREVIATION* **yd**) a unit of measurement equal to three feet or approximately 91.4 centimetres

yard [WORK AREA] /jɑːd/ [US] /jɑːrd/ *noun* [C] an area of land in which a particular type of work is done, often one from which goods are sold: *a builders' yard* ○ *a scrap yard* ➲See also **boatyard**; **dockyard**; **junkyard**; **lumberyard**; **shipyard**; **stockyard**.

yard [LAND NEXT TO BUILDING] /jɑːd/ [US] /jɑːrd/ *noun* [C] an area of land next to a building which is covered with concrete or other hard material: *The house has a small yard at the back.* ○ *the prison yard* ➲See also **backyard**; **barnyard**; **farmyard**.

yard [GARDEN] *US* /jɑːd/ [US] /jɑːrd/ *noun* [C] (*UK* **garden**) a piece of land next to a house, usually used for growing flowers, grass and other plants

Yardie /ˈjɑː.di/ [US] /ˈjɑːr.di/ *noun* [C] a member of a violent criminal organization, involved especially with illegal drugs, that started in Jamaica and now also operates in the UK

yardstick /ˈjɑːd.stɪk/ [US] /ˈjɑːrd-/ *noun* [C] a fact or standard by which you can judge the success or value of something: *Productivity is not the only yardstick of success.*

yarmulke /ˈjɑː.mʊl.kə/ [US] /ˈjɑːr-/ *noun* [C] a small, circular cover for the head worn by Jewish men, especially at religious ceremonies

yarn [THREAD] /jɑːn/ [US] /jɑːrn/ *noun* [C or U] thread used for making cloth or for knitting

yarn [STORY] /jɑːn/ [US] /jɑːrn/ *noun* [C] a story, usually a long one with a lot of excitement or interest: *He knew how to* ***spin a good*** *yarn* (= tell a good story).

yashmak /ˈjæʃ.mæk/ *noun* [C] a piece of cloth worn by some Muslim women to cover parts of the face when they are in public

yaw /jɔː/ [US] /jɑː/ *verb* [I] *SPECIALIZED* If an aircraft or ship yaws, it moves slightly to the side of its intended direction. **yaw** /jɔː/ [US] /jɑː/ *noun* [C or U]

yawn /jɔːn/ [US] /jɑːn/ *verb* [I] to open the mouth wide and take a lot of air into the lungs and slowly send it out, usually when tired or bored: *I can't stop yawning – I must be tired.*

yawn /jɔːn/ [US] /jɑːn/ *noun* [C] **1** the act of yawning: *Her eyes watered as she tried to* ***stifle*** (= stop) *a yawn.* **2** *INFORMAL* **a yawn** something or someone that is very boring: *We have to go to dinner with Simon's boss on Saturday which is a bit of a yawn.*

yawning /ˈjɔː.nɪŋ/ [US] /ˈjɑː-/ *adj* [before n] **1** describes a difference or amount that is extremely large and difficult to reduce: *There exists nowadays a yawning* ***gap between*** *fashion and style.* **2** describes a space or hole that is very wide: *a yawning crevasse*

Y-chromosome /ˈwaɪˌkrəʊ.mə.səʊm/ [US] /-ˌkroʊ.mə.soʊm/ *noun* [C] a sex CHROMOSOME that exists only in male cells: *If a Y-chromosome combines with an X-chromosome during fertilization, a male baby will result.*

yd *WRITTEN ABBREVIATION FOR* **yard** UNIT OF MEASUREMENT

ye [YOU] /jiː/ *pronoun OLD USE* a word meaning 'you', used when addressing more than one person: *Ye cannot serve God and mammon.*

ye [THE] /jiː/ *determiner OLD USE* a word meaning 'the', used especially in the names of PUBS to make them seem old: *a pub in the village called Ye Olde Barn*

• **ye Gods** *OLD-FASHIONED OR HUMOROUS* used to show surprise: *Ye Gods man, what are you doing!*

yea /jeɪ/ *adv OLD USE* yes

• **yea or nay** yes or no: *They have the power to hire and fire managers and* ***say*** *yea or nay* ***to*** *big investment projects.*

yeah /jeə/ *adv INFORMAL* yes: *"Do you like your job?" "Yeah, it's all right I suppose."* ○ *"Will you drive?" "Yeah, sure."*

• **Yeah, right!** (*ALSO* **Oh yeah.**, *ALSO* **yeah, yeah**) *INFORMAL* used when you do not believe what someone has said: *"I always miss you when I go travelling." "Yeah, right!"* ○ *"Anyway, we're just good friends." "Yeah, yeah!"* ○ *"I can run faster than you any day!" "Oh yeah?"*

year /jɪəʳ/ [US] /jɪr/ *noun* [C] **1** a period of twelve months, especially from January 1st to December 31st: *Annette worked in Italy for two years.* ○ *1988 was one of the worst years of my life.* ○ *We went to Egypt on holiday* ***last*** *year.* ○ *At this* ***time of*** *year the beaches are almost deserted.* ○ *This species keeps its leaves* ***all*** *(the) year* ***(round)*** (=

through the year). **2** a period of twelve months relating to a particular activity: *The **financial/tax** year begins in April.* **3** the part of the year, in an educational establishment, during which courses are taught: *the academic/school year* ○ *She's now **in her final/first/second year** at Manchester University.*

• **for a man/woman/person of his/her years** considering how old someone is: *He dances well for a man of his years.*

• **for years 1** for a long time: *Roz and I have been going there for years.* **2** (*ALSO* **in years**) since a long time ago: *I haven't seen my uncle for/in years.*

• **of the year** A thing or person of the year is one that has been chosen as the best in a particular year, especially in a competition: *Young Musician of the Year*

• **put years on** If something puts years on a person, it makes them appear much older: *Being tired and unhappy puts years on you.*

• **take years off sb** If something takes years off a person, it makes them appear or feel much younger: *"Have you seen James without his beard?" "I know – it takes years off him!"*

• **from/since the year dot** *UK* (*US* **from/since the year one**) *INFORMAL* for an extremely long time: *He's been in the local pantomime since the year dot.*

• **year in year out** every year, especially in a way that seems boring: *We go to Mike's parents every summer – it's the same thing year in year out.*

year /jɪəʳ/ [US] /jɪr/ *group noun* **[C]** *UK* a group of students who start school, college, university or a course together: *Kathy was in the year above me at college.*

-year /-jɪəʳ/ [US] /-jɪr/ *suffix UK* used to refer to a student in a particular year group at a school, college or university: *I like teaching the first-years, but the second-years can be difficult.* ○ *a first-year student*

yearly /ˈjɪə.li/ [US] /ˈjɪr-/ *adj, adv* every year or once every year: *We get a yearly pay-increase.* ○ *Interest is paid yearly.*

yearbook /ˈjɪə.bʊk/ [US] /ˈjɪr-/ *noun* **[C]** (*US ALSO* **annual**) a book published every year by a school or other organization, that gives various facts about the events and achievements of the previous or present year ➲See also **annual** BOOK.

yearn /jɜːn/ [US] /jɝːn/ *verb* **[I]** to desire very strongly, especially something that you cannot have or something that is very difficult to have: *Despite his great commercial success he still yearns **for** critical approval.* ○ **[+ to infinitive]** *Sometimes I just yearn **to** be alone.* **yearning** /ˈjɜː.nɪŋ/ [US] /ˈjɝː-/ *noun* **[C or U]** *I suppose it's because I live in a crowded city that I have this yearning **for** open spaces.*

yeast /jiːst/ *noun* **[C or U]** a type of fungus which is used in making alcoholic drinks such as beer and wine, and for making bread swell and become light: *dried/fresh yeast* ○ *yeast extract* **yeasty** /ˈjiː.sti/ *adj*

yell /jel/ *verb* **[I or T]** to shout something or make a loud noise, usually when you are angry, in pain or excited: *Our neighbours were yelling (obscenities) **at** each other this morning.* ○ *The child yelled **out** in pain.* ○ **[+ speech]** *"Just get out of here!" she yelled.* **yell** /jel/ *noun* **[C usually sing]** *Suddenly there was a **loud/great** yell from the bathroom.*

yellow [COLOUR] /ˈjel.əʊ/ [US] /-oʊ/ *noun* **[C or U]**, *adj* **1** (of) a colour like that of a lemon or gold or the sun: *a bright yellow T-shirt* ○ *It was early autumn and the leaves were turning yellow.* ○ *You should wear more yellow – it suits you.* **2** *US* the yolk of an egg

yellow /ˈjel.əʊ/ [US] /-oʊ/ *verb* **[I or T]** to become yellow, or to make something become yellow

yellowish /ˈjel.əʊ.ɪʃ/ [US] /-oʊ-/ *adj* (*ALSO* **yellowy**) slightly yellow: *The leaves vary from yellowish-green to dark green.* **yellowness** /ˈjel.əʊ.nəs/ [US] /-oʊ-/ *noun* **[U]**

yellow [PEOPLE] /ˈjel.əʊ/ [US] /-oʊ/ *adj OFFENSIVE* belonging to a race that has pale yellowish brown skin

yellow [COWARDLY] /ˈjel.əʊ/ [US] /-oʊ/ *adj INFORMAL* cowardly; not brave

ˌyellow ˈcard *noun* **[C usually sing]** in football, a small yellow card which is shown to a player by the REFEREE (= the official who is responsible for making certain the rules are followed) as a warning that the player has not obeyed a rule

ˌyellow ˈfever *noun* **[U]** an infectious tropical disease which causes the skin to become yellow and can result in death

ˌyellow ˈline *noun* **[C]** in Britain, a line of yellow paint which is put along the sides of particular roads to show that vehicles cannot be parked there at stated times ➲See also **double yellow line**.

the ˌYellow ˈPages *noun* **[S]** *TRADEMARK* a large, yellow book which contains the addresses and telephone numbers of businesses and people offering services, listing them in groups according to what type of business they are ➲Compare **the White Pages**.

yelp /jelp/ *verb* **[I]** to make a sudden, short, high sound, usually when in pain: *I accidentally trod on the dog's foot and it yelped.* **yelp** /jelp/ *noun* **[C]**

yen [MONEY] /jen/ *noun* **[C]** *plural* **yen** the standard unit of money used in Japan

yen /jen/ *noun* **[C usually sing]** *plural* **yen** *INFORMAL* a strong feeling of wanting or desiring: *I have a yen **for** travelling.*

yeoman /ˈjəʊ.mən/ [US] /ˈjoʊ-/ *noun* **[C]** in the past, a man who was not a servant and owned and cultivated an area of land

yep /jep/ *adv INFORMAL* yes: *"Do I press this button?" "Yep, that's right."*

yer /jəʳ/ [US] /jɚ/ *determiner INFORMAL* your: *Get yer hands off me!*

yes /jes/ *adv* (*INFORMAL* **yeah, yep, yah**) **1** used to express acceptance, willingness or agreement: *"Would you like a glass of wine?" "Yes please."* ○ *"Do you like Indian food?" "Yes, I love it."* ○ *"He's a really nice guy." "Yes he is."* ○ *"Report to me at nine o'clock tomorrow morning." "Yes, sir."* ○ *"Have you had enough to eat?" "Yes, thank you."* ○ *If you'd **say** yes* (= agree) *to the request you'd save a lot of trouble.* **2** used to show that you are listening to someone, or that you are ready to listen and to give them an answer or information: *"Dad." "Yes, what do you want, honey?"* ○ *Yes, can I help you?* **3** used when you are disagreeing with a negative statement: *"I'm not a very good cook though." "Yes you are – you make wonderful food!"*

• **oh yes** (*INFORMAL* **oh yeah**) used when you have just remembered something that you were saying: *What was I talking about – oh yes, I was telling you what happened at the party.*

• **yes and no** used when you cannot give a particular answer to a question: *"Is the job going okay?" "Well, yes and no."*

yes /jes/ *noun* **[C]** a vote supporting a particular plan of action or an acceptance of an invitation: *"Have you had any replies yet?" "Six yeses and two noes so far."*

yes-man /ˈjes.mæn/ *noun* **[C]** *DISAPPROVING* a person who agrees with everything their employer, leader, etc. says in order to please them

yesterday /ˈjes.tə.deɪ/ [US] /-tɚ-/ *adv* on the day before today: *He rang yesterday while you were out.* ○ *I saw her yesterday afternoon.*

yesterday /ˈjes.tə.deɪ/ [US] /-tɚ-/ *noun* **1** **[U]** the day before today: *"Is that today's paper?" "No, it's yesterday's."* **2** **the day before yesterday** two days ago: *I rang her the day before yesterday.* **3** **[C or U]** the recent past: *Nobody's interested in yesterday's pop-stars.* ○ *These songs are a part of **all our** yesterdays.*

yesteryear /ˈjes.tə.jɪəʳ/ [US] /-tɚ.jɪr/ *noun* **[U]** *LITERARY* a time in the past: *the Hollywood stars **of** yesteryear*

yet [UNTIL NOW] /jet/ *adv* **1** still; until the present time: *I haven't spoken to her yet.* ○ *He hasn't finished yet.* ○ *"Are you ready?" "Not yet – wait a moment."* **2** **the best/worst, etc. yet** the best or worst, etc. until now: *Of all the songs I've heard tonight, that's the best yet.* **3** *FORMAL* **as yet** until and including this time: *We haven't needed extra staff as yet, but may do in the future.* ○ *No ambulances had as yet managed to get across the river.*

yet [IN THE FUTURE] /jet/ *adv* from now and for a particular period of time in the future: *She won't be back for a long time yet.* ○ *Our holiday isn't for weeks yet.*

• **have yet to** If you have yet to do something, you have not done it: *They have yet to make a decision.*

yet [DESPITE THAT] /jet/ *adv, conjunction* (and) despite that; used to add something that seems surprising because of what you have just said: *simple yet effective* ○ *He's overweight and bald,* ***(and)*** *yet somehow, he's incredibly attractive.*

yet [MORE] /jet/ *adv* used to add emphasis to words such as *another* and *again*, especially to show an increase in amount or the number of times something happens: *Rachel bought yet* ***another*** *pair of shoes to add to her collection.* ○ *I'm sorry to bother you yet* ***again***. ○ *He's given us yet* ***more*** *work to do.*

yet [EVEN NOW] /jet/ *adv* even at this stage or time: *We could yet succeed – you never know.* ○ *You* ***might*** *yet prove me wrong.* ○ *He* ***may*** *win yet.*

yeti /ˈjet.i/ [US] /ˈjet̬-/ *noun* [C] (*ALSO* **abominable snowman**) a big hairy human-like creature believed by some people to live in the Himalayan mountains

yew /juː/ *noun* [C or U] an evergreen tree with flattened, needle-like leaves and small red CONES, or the wood from this tree: *a yew tree* ○ *a bowl made from yew*

Y-fronts /ˈwaɪ.frʌnts/ *plural noun UK TRADEMARK* a piece of underwear for men and boys, covering the area between the waist and the tops of the legs, which have an opening at the front which is the shape of an upside-down Y

yid /jɪd/ *noun* [C] *OFFENSIVE* a Jew

Yiddish /ˈjɪd.ɪʃ/ *noun* [U] a language spoken by some Jewish people, which is related to German

yield [PRODUCE] /jiːld/ *verb* [T] to supply or produce something positive such as a profit, an amount of food or information: *an attempt to yield increased profits* ○ *The investigation yielded some unexpected results.* ○ *Favourable weather yielded a good crop.*

yield /jiːld/ *noun* [C usually pl] *Yields* (= Profits) *on gas and electricity shares are consistently high.* ○ ***Crop*** *yields* (= the amount of crops produced) *have risen steadily.*

yield [GIVE UP] /jiːld/ *verb* [I or T] to give up the control of or responsibility for something, often because you have been forced to: *They were forced to yield* ***(up)*** *their land* ***to*** *the occupying forces.* ○ *Despite renewed pressure to give up the occupied territory, they will not yield.*

yield [BEND/BREAK] /jiːld/ *verb* [I] *SLIGHTLY FORMAL* to bend or break under pressure: *His legs began to yield under the sheer weight of his body.*

yielding /ˈjiːl.dɪŋ/ *adj* **1** *SLIGHTLY FORMAL* describes soft, flexible substances or qualities: *a yielding mire of wet leaves* ○ *yielding flesh/softness* **2** describes a person who can change the way they normally behave or deal with situations when it is helpful or necessary

PHRASAL VERBS WITH **yield** ▼

▲ **yield to *sth*** [AGREE] *phrasal verb* to agree to do something that you do not want to do or should not do: *It's very easy to yield to temptation and spend too much money.* ○ *"We will not yield to pressure," said the president.*

▲ **yield to *sth*** [STOP] *US phrasal verb* (*UK* **give way**) to stop in order to allow other vehicles to go past before you drive onto a bigger road

yin /jɪn/ *noun* [U] in Chinese philosophy, the female principle of the universe, represented as dark and negative

yippee /jɪˈpiː/ [US] /ˈjɪp.iː/ *exclamation INFORMAL* used to express happiness, excitement or great satisfaction: *No school for five weeks – yippee!*

YMMV, **ymmv** *INTERNET ABBREVIATION FOR* your mileage may vary: used to warn people that a piece of advice, although it has helped you, might not help them, or to say that different things are attractive to different people: *Their first album is better, but of course YMMV.*

yo /jəʊ/ [US] /joʊ/ *exclamation SLANG* used as an informal greeting between people who know each other or as an expression of approval: *"Yo, Mickie! How's things?"*

yob /jɒb/ [US] /jɑːb/ *noun* [C] (*ALSO* **yobbo**) *UK INFORMAL* a young man who behaves in a very rude, offensive and sometimes violent way: *a gang of loud-mouthed yobs*

yodel /ˈjəʊ.dəl/ [US] /ˈjoʊ-/ *verb* [I] -ll- or *US USUALLY* -l- to sing by making a series of very fast changes between the natural voice and a much higher voice

yodel /ˈjəʊ.dəl/ [US] /ˈjoʊ-/ *noun* [C] a song or a part of a song that is yodelled

yoga /ˈjəʊ.gə/ [US] /ˈjoʊ-/ *noun* [U] **1** a set of physical and mental exercises, Indian in origin, which is intended to give control over the body and mind: *a yoga class* **2** a Hindu system of philosophy which aims to unite the self with god **yogic** /ˈjəʊ.gɪk/ [US] /ˈjoʊ-/ *adj*: *yogic exercises*

yogi /ˈjəʊ.gi/ [US] /ˈjoʊ-/ *noun* [C] a person who has spent a lot of their life doing yoga and studying its philosophy

yogurt, **yoghurt**, **yoghourt** /ˈjɒg.ət/ [US] /ˈjoʊ.gɚt/ *noun* [C or U] a slightly sour, thick liquid made from milk with bacteria added to it, sometimes sweetened and flavoured with fruit and sometimes eaten plain: *natural/plain yogurt* ○ *strawberry yogurt* ○ *low-fat yogurt* ○ *I only had a yogurt* (= a container of this) *for lunch.*

yoke [WOODEN BAR] /jəʊk/ [US] /joʊk/ *noun* [C] a wooden bar which is fastened over the necks of two animals, especially cattle, and connected to the vehicle or load that they are pulling **yoke** /jəʊk/ [US] /joʊk/ *verb* [T] *Two oxen yoked* ***to*** *a plough walked wearily up and down the field.*

yoke [CONNECTION] /jəʊk/ [US] /joʊk/ *noun* [C] *FORMAL* something which connects two things or people, usually in a way that unfairly limits freedom: *the yoke of marriage* ○ *Both countries had recently thrown off the communist yoke.*

yoke /jəʊk/ [US] /joʊk/ *verb* [T often passive] *FORMAL* to combine or connect two things: *All these different political elements have somehow been yoked* ***together*** *to form a new alliance.*

yoke [CLOTHES] /jəʊk/ [US] /joʊk/ *noun* [C] a fitted part of an item of clothing, especially a strip which goes around the shoulders or waist, to which is sewn a looser piece of material

yokel /ˈjəʊ.kəl/ [US] /ˈjoʊ-/ *noun* [C] *USUALLY HUMOROUS* a stupid or awkward person who lives in the countryside rather than a town, especially one whose appearance is in some way strange or amusing: *He plays the* ***country*** *yokel in the butter ad.*

yolk /jəʊk/ [US] /joʊk/ *noun* [C or U] the yellow, middle part of an egg: *I like eggs lightly cooked so that the yolk is still runny.* ○ *Separate the yolks from the whites.*

Yom Kippur /ˌjɒm.kɪˈpʊər/ [US] /ˌjɑːmˈkɪp.ɚ/ *noun* [U] (*ALSO* **the Day of Atonement**) a Jewish holy day in September or October when nothing is eaten all day and people say prayers in the SYNAGOGUE asking for forgiveness for things they have done wrong

yonder /ˈjɒn.dər/ [US] /ˈjɑːn.dɚ/ *determiner, adv* (*ALSO* **yon**) *OLD USE* in the place or direction shown; over there

yonks /jɒŋks/ [US] /jɑːŋks/ *noun* [U] *UK OLD-FASHIONED INFORMAL* a very long time, usually a number of years: *How is Gareth? I haven't seen him for yonks!*

yoof /juːf/ *adj* [before n] *UK NOT STANDARD HUMOROUS* relating to young people, especially those influenced by the most recent fashions and ideas: *The adverts target yoof culture.*

yoof /juːf/ *noun* [U] *UK NOT STANDARD HUMOROUS* young people: *He's a comedian who claims to be the voice of British yoof.*

yoo-hoo /ˈjuː.huː/ *exclamation OLD-FASHIONED INFORMAL* used to attract a person's attention: *Yoo-hoo, we're over here!*

yore /jɔːr/ [US] /jɔːr/ *noun LITERARY* **of yore** of a long time ago: *This was once a Roman road* ***in days*** *of yore.*

Yorkshire pudding /ˈjɔːk.ʃəˌpʊd.ɪŋ/ [US] /ˈjɔːrk.ʃɚ-/ /-ʃɪr-/ *noun* [C or U] a savoury dish which consists of a baked mixture of flour, milk and eggs which is traditionally eaten in Britain with beef

you [PERSON/PEOPLE ADDRESSED] *STRONG* /juː/, *WEAK* /jə, jʊ/ *pronoun* used to refer to the person or people being spoken or written to: *You look nice.* ○ *I love you.* ○ *You said I could go with you.* ○ *You're coming tonight, aren't you?* ○ *Are you two ready?* ○ *You painted that yourself? You clever girl!*

your *STRONG* /jɔːr/ [US] /jʊr/, *WEAK* /jər/ [US] /jɚ/ *determiner* belonging or relating to the person or group of people being spoken or written to: *Is this your bag?* ○ *It's not*

Y

your fault. ○ *Your mother is driving me crazy.* ○ *What's your problem?*

yours /jɔːz/ [US] /jʊrz/ *pronoun* **1** used to show that something belongs to or is connected with the person or group of people being spoken or written to: *Is this pen yours?* ○ *Unfortunately my legs aren't as long as yours.* ○ *I've got something* ***of*** *yours* (= that belongs to you). **2** used at the beginning of some phrases written at the end of a letter, before giving a name: *Yours, Jack* ○ UK *Yours* ***faithfully/sincerely****, K. Maxwell.*

• **yours truly** INFORMAL used to mean the person who is speaking or writing, often when they are talking about something they have done unwillingly: *She didn't have any money, so yours truly ended up having to lend her some.*

yourself STRONG /jɔːˈself/ [US] /jʊr-/ WEAK /jə-/ [US] /ˈjɚ-/ *pronoun plural* **yourselves** **1** used when both the subject and object of the verb are you: *Be careful with that knife or you'll cut yourself!* **2** used to give special attention to the subject of the sentence: *Did you make the dress yourself?* ○ *You can do that yourself.*

• **(all) by yourself** alone or without help from anyone else: *I'm amazed you managed to move those boxes all by yourself.*

• **(all) to yourself** for your use only: *So you've got the whole house to yourself this weekend?*

• **be yourself** to behave in your usual manner, rather than behaving in a way you think other people might like: *The best thing you can do is to go into the interview and just be yourself.*

• **in yourself** UK used when asking someone about their state of mind when they have a physical problem: *I know you must still be uncomfortable, but how are you in yourself?*

you [PEOPLE GENERALLY] STRONG /juː/, WEAK /jə, jʊ/ *pronoun* people in general: *You learn to accept these things as you get older.* ○ *You can't get a driving licence till you're seventeen in this country.* ○ *Too much alcohol is bad for you.* ○ *How do you get this thing to start?*

your STRONG /jɔːʳ/ [US] /jʊr/, WEAK /jəʳ/ [US] /jɚ/ *determiner* **1** belonging or relating to people generally: *Of course you want the best for your children.* ○ *Garlic is good for your blood.* **2** INFORMAL said before a typical example of something is given: *This isn't your usual science-fiction novel, but then Brinkworth isn't exactly your typical author.*

yours /jɔːz/ [US] /jʊrz/ *pronoun* used to show that something belongs to or is connected with people generally: *Other people's children always seem to be better behaved than yours.*

yourself STRONG /jɔːˈself/ [US] /jʊr-/ WEAK /jə-/ [US] /ˈjɚ-/ *pronoun plural* **yourselves** used when both the subject and object of the verb are you and you is also being used to refer to people generally: *You tell yourself everything's all right but you know it's not really.*

you'd /juːd/ *short form of* **1** you had: *It happened just after you'd left the room.* **2** you would: *You'd be much warmer in your black jacket.*

you'll /juːl/ *short form of* you will: *You'll remember to tell her, won't you.*

young /jʌŋ/ *adj* **1** having lived or existed for only a short time and not old: *young adults/children* ○ *His girlfriend's very young.* ○ *The trees in this part of the forest are still quite young.* ○ *Philippa is the youngest person in the family.* ○ *Angela is two years younger than Clare.* **2** suitable for young people: *young fashion/ideas* ○ *Be honest now – do you think this dress is* ***a bit/too*** *young for me* (= is more suitable for someone younger)*?*

• **look young for *your* age** to look younger than you really are

• **young at heart** thinking and behaving as if you are younger than you really are: *Dad might be nearly ninety but he's still young at heart.*

• **young lady/man** **1** used when you are speaking angrily to a young person: *Mind your language, young lady!* **2** OLD-FASHIONED OR HUMOROUS someone's GIRLFRIEND or BOYFRIEND: *If you'd care to bring your young man along too we should be delighted to meet him.*

• **young love** love between young people

the young *plural noun* young people considered together as a group: *I have nothing against mini-skirts, but I think they're strictly for the young.*

young /jʌŋ/ *plural noun* the babies of an animal: *Meanwhile, the mother flies back to the nest to feed her young.*

youngster /ˈjʌŋk.stəʳ/ [US] /-stɚ/ *noun* [C] a young person, usually an older child: *The scheme is for youngsters between the ages of 10 and 16.*

ˌyoung ˈblood *noun* [U] young people who have a lot of energy and ideas: *We need to introduce more young blood into the organization.*

young offenders' institution /ˌjʌŋ.əˈfen.dəz.ɪnt.stɪˌtjuː.ʃən/ [US] /-dɚz.ɪnt.stɪˌtuː-/ *noun* [C] a special place for people who have done bad things and are too young to be sent to prison

you're STRONG /jɔːʳ/ [US] /jʊr/, WEAK /jəʳ/ [US] /jɚ/ *short form* you are: *You're so nice to me!*

youth /juːθ/ *noun* **1** [S or U] the period of your life when you are young, or the state of being young: *I was a fairly good football player* ***in*** *my youth.* ○ *The first volume is the author's account of his* ***misspent*** *youth in the bars of Dublin.* ○ *He looks like a man who's found the secret to* ***eternal*** *youth* (= staying young). ○ *You may not have played tennis as often as him, but at least you've got youth on your side* (= you are young). **2** [C] DISAPPROVING a boy or a young man: *Gangs of youths were throwing stones and bottles at the police.*

youth /juːθ/ *group noun* [U] young people, both male and female, considered as a group: *the youth of today* ○ *the nation's disaffected youth* ○ *youth culture*

youthful /ˈjuːθ.fəl/ *adj* APPROVING **1** having the qualities that are typical of young people: *At the time I admired his youthful enthusiasm.* ○ *She has very youthful skin.* **2** young: *A youthful president can be good for a country's morale.* **youthfully** /ˈjuːθ.fəl.i/ *adv* **youthfulness** /ˈjuːθ.fəl.nəs/ *noun* [U]

ˈyouth ˌclub *noun* [C] a place where older children can go to meet other children, play sports and do other social activities

ˈyouth ˌhostel *noun* [C] a place where people, especially young people, can stay cheaply for short periods when they are travelling

youth-hostelling /ˈjuːθˌhɒs.təl.ɪŋ/ [US] /-ˌhɑː.stəl-/ *noun* [U] the activity of travelling and staying in different youth hostels: *I used to* ***go youth-hostelling*** *when I was a student.*

you've STRONG /juːv/, WEAK /jəv/ *short form* you have: *If you've finished your pasta, then you can have some cake.*

yowl /jaʊl/ *verb* [I] to make a long, high, unhappy cry, usually when hurt or fighting: *I was woken up by cats yowling outside my window.* **yowl** /jaʊl/ *noun* [C]

yoyo /ˈjəʊ.jəʊ/ [US] /ˈjoʊ.joʊ/ *noun* [C] *plural* **yoyos** a toy which consists of a circular object that can be made to go up and down a long piece of string to which it is tied

yuan /juˈɑːn/ *noun* [C] (ALSO **renminbi yuan**) the standard unit of money used in the People's Republic of China

yucca /ˈjʌk.ə/ *noun* [C] a plant with long, stiff leaves on a thick, woody stem and sometimes white, bell-shaped flowers

yuck, yuk /jʌk/ *exclamation* INFORMAL an expression of disgust: *"Yuck, what a revolting smell!"*

yucky, yukky /ˈjʌk.i/ *adj* INFORMAL disgusting or unpleasant: *a yucky green colour*

Yule /juːl/ *noun* [C or U] LITERARY Christmas

ˈyule ˌlog *noun* [C] a cylindrical chocolate cake eaten at Christmas which is decorated to look like a LOG (= a thick piece of tree branch or trunk)

Yuletide /ˈjuːl.taɪd/ *noun* [C or U] OLD-FASHIONED OR LITERARY the period around Christmas: *Yuletide greetings*

yummy /ˈjʌm.i/ *adj* INFORMAL **1** tasting extremely good: *I think I'll have some more of that yummy chocolate cake.* ○ *There are some yummy-****looking*** *desserts over there.* **2** sexually attractive: *And tell her to bring along that yummy brother of hers.*

yum (yum) /ˌjʌmˈjʌm/ *exclamation* INFORMAL used to say that food tastes or smells very good

yuppie, yuppy /ˈjʌp.i/ *noun* [C] DISAPPROVING a young person who lives in a city, earns a lot of money and spends it doing fashionable things and buying expensive possessions: *They're just a couple of yuppies with more money than sense.*

yuppify /'jʌp.ɪ.faɪ/ *verb* [T] *INFORMAL DISAPPROVING* to change the appearance of a place to suit or attract people who earn and spend a lot of money

Z

Z *(plural* **Z's** or **Zs**), **z** *(plural* **z's** or **zs**) /zed/ [US] /ziː/ *noun* [C] the 26th and last letter of the English alphabet
• **catch/cop/get some z's** *US INFORMAL* to sleep: *All I want to do is go home and catch some z's.*

zany /ˈzeɪ.ni/ *adj INFORMAL* strange, surprising or uncontrolled in an amusing way: *a zany film* ○ *zany clothing/ideas*

zap [DESTROY] /zæp/ *verb* [T] **-pp-** *INFORMAL* to destroy or kill something or someone, especially intentionally: *They've got the kind of weapons that can zap the enemy from thousands of miles away.* ○ *FIGURATIVE We're really going to zap the competition with this new product!*

zap [GO QUICKLY] /zæp/ *verb* **-pp- 1** [I or T; usually + adv or prep] *INFORMAL* to go somewhere or do something quickly: *Have I got time to zap into town and do some shopping?* ○ *There are now over a million American fax machines zapping* (= sending quickly) *messages from coast to coast.* ➲See also **zip** SPEED. **2** [I usually + adv or prep] *MAINLY US INFORMAL* to use an electronic device to change television channels quickly, sometimes to avoid watching advertisements
zap /zæp/ *noun* [U] *MAINLY US INFORMAL* energy and enthusiasm: *She needs to put a bit more zap into her performance.* **zappy** /ˈzæp.i/ *adj*: *a zappy tune*
zapper /ˈzæp.əʳ/ [US] /-ɚ/ *noun* [C] *INFORMAL* a device for controlling a machine from a distance: *Use the zapper to turn off the TV.*

zeal /ziːl/ *noun* [S or U] great enthusiasm or eagerness: *reforming/missionary/religious zeal* ○ *a zeal* ***for*** *money-making*
zealot /ˈzel.ət/ *noun* [C] a person who has very strong opinions about something, and tries to make other people have them too: *a religious zealot*
zealous /ˈzel.əs/ *adj* enthusiastic and eager: *a zealous supporter of the government's policies* **zealously** /ˈzel.ə.sli/ *adv* **zealousness** /ˈzel.ə.snəs/ *noun* [U]

zebra /ˈzeb.rə/ /ˈziː.brə/ *noun* [C] *plural* **zebras** or **zebra** an African wild animal which looks like a horse, and which has black or brown and white lines on its body

ˌzebra ˈcrossing *UK noun* [C] (*US* **crosswalk**) a place on a road, especially one where there is a lot of traffic, across which wide black and white lines are painted, and at which vehicles must stop to allow people to walk across the road ➲Compare **pedestrian crossing**; **pelican crossing**.

zeitgeist /ˈtsaɪt.gaɪst/ /ˈzaɪt-/ *noun* [S] the general set of ideas, beliefs, feelings etc. which is typical of a particular period in history

Zen [RELIGION] /zen/ *noun* [U] a form of Buddhism which developed in Japan and which emphasizes that religious knowledge is achieved through emptying the mind of thoughts and giving attention to only one thing, rather than by reading religious writings: *Zen Buddhism*

zen [RELAXED] /zen/ *adj UK INFORMAL* relaxed and not worrying about things you cannot change: *There's nothing you can do to change the situation so you just have to be a bit more zen about it.*

zenith /ˈzen.ɪθ/ *noun* [C usually sing] the best or most successful point or time: *In the early 1900s, Tolstoy was* ***at the zenith of*** *his achievement.* ○ *His career* ***reached*** *its zenith in the 1960s.* * NOTE: The opposite is **nadir**.

zephyr /ˈzef.əʳ/ [US] /-ɚ/ *noun* [C] *LITERARY* a light wind

zeppelin /ˈzep.əl.ɪn/ *noun* [C] a large AIRSHIP (= an aircraft without wings, containing gas to make it lighter than air, and with an engine)

zero /ˈzɪə.rəʊ/ [US] /ˈzɪr.oʊ/ *noun plural* **zeros** or **zeroes 1** [C or U] (the number) 0; nothing: *Five, four, three, two, one, zero.* ○ *The number one million is written with a one and six zeroes (MAINLY UK ALSO* ***noughts****).* ○ *Heavy rain has reduced visibility almost to zero* (= its lowest point). **2** [U] on a set of numbers for comparing temperature in degrees Celsius, the level of temperature at which water freezes: *The temperature is expected to drop to ten degrees below zero tonight.*
zero /ˈzɪə.rəʊ/ [US] /ˈzɪr.oʊ/ *adj* not any or no: *zero growth/inflation* ○ *INFORMAL He said that his chances of getting the job were zero* (= he had no chance).

zero /ˈzɪə.rəʊ/ [US] /ˈzɪr.oʊ/ *verb*

PHRASAL VERBS WITH **zero** ▼

▲ **zero in on** ***sth/sb*** [WEAPON] *phrasal verb* to aim a weapon directly at something or someone: *Modern military aircraft use computers to help them zero in on their targets.*
▲ **zero in on** ***sth*** [ATTENTION] *phrasal verb* to direct all your attention towards a particular thing: *We must decide on our target market, then zero in on it.*

ˈzero ˌhour *noun* [U] the time at which something, especially a military activity, is planned to begin

zero-sum /ˌzɪə.rəʊˈsʌm/ [US] /ˌzɪr.oʊ-/ *adj* describes a situation in which any gain by one person always means a loss to another person involved: *The stock market is now a zero-sum* ***game****, in which one party gains what the other loses.*

ˌzero ˈtolerance *noun* [U] when all criminal or unacceptable behaviour, even if not very serious, is punished severely: *The police are exercising a new policy of zero tolerance against motoring offenders.*

zest [EXCITEMENT] /zest/ *noun* [S or U] enthusiasm, eagerness, energy and interest: *It's wonderful to see the children's zest* ***for life****.* ○ *He approached every task* ***with*** *a boundless zest.* **zestful** /ˈzest.fəl/ *adj* **zestfully** /ˈzest.fəl.i/ *adv*

zest [FRUIT SKIN] /zest/ *noun* [U] the skin of an orange, lemon or lime, used for flavouring food: *grated lemon zest*

zigzag /ˈzɪg.zæg/ *noun* [C] a line or pattern which looks like a Z or a row of Zs joined together: *a zigzag path/road/coastline* ○ *a fabric with a zigzag pattern*
zigzag (**-gg-**) /ˈzɪg.zæg/ *verb* [I] (*ALSO* **zig and zag**) to make a movement or shape like a zigzag: *The road zigzags along a rocky coastline.*

zilch /zɪltʃ/ *noun* [U] *INFORMAL* nothing; none; no: *"How many points did you score?" "Zilch."*

zillion /ˈzɪl.jən/ /-i.ən/ *noun* [C] *INFORMAL* an extremely large, but not a stated, number: *I've told you* ***a*** *zillion times/zillions* ***of*** *times not to do that.*

Zimmer frame *UK TRADEMARK* /ˈzɪm.əˌfreɪm/ [US] /-ɚ-/ *noun* [C] (*UK ALSO* **walking frame,** *US* **walker**) a metal frame with four legs which you place in front of you and lean on to help you move forward if you have difficulty in walking, for example when old

zinc /zɪŋk/ *noun* [U] a bluish white metal that is used in making other metals or for covering other metals to protect them

zine /ziːn/ *noun* [C] *INFORMAL* a small magazine that is produced cheaply by one person or a small group of people, and is about a subject they are interested in

zing /zɪŋ/ *noun* [U] *INFORMAL* a quality that makes something interesting or exciting; enthusiasm or energy: *We want to* ***put*** *more zing* ***into*** *our advertising.* ○ *A bit of lemon juice will* ***add*** *zing* ***to*** *the sauce.*
zingy /ˈzɪŋ.i/ *adj INFORMAL* interesting and exciting

Zionism /ˈzaɪə.nɪ.zəm/ *noun* [U] a political movement which had as its original aim the creation of a country for Jewish people, and which now works to help the development of Israel **Zionist** /ˈzaɪə.nɪst/ *adj, noun* [C]

zip [FASTENER] *UK* /zɪp/ *noun* [C] (*US* **zipper**) a fastener consisting of two rows of metal or plastic teeth-like parts which are brought together by pulling a small sliding piece over them, and which is used for closing openings in especially clothing or bags: *to do up/undo a zip* ○ *I can't open my bag – the zip has* ***stuck****.*
zip /zɪp/ *verb* [I or T] **-pp-** to fasten something with a zip: *This bag's too full, I can't zip it shut.* ○ *This dress zips* ***(up)*** *at the back.* ○ *Zip your coat* ***up****, it's cold outside.*

zip [SPEED] /zɪp/ *noun* [U] *INFORMAL* energy; speed: *The new engine has given the car a lot more zip.*
zip /zɪp/ *verb* [I or T; usually + adv or prep] **-pp-** *INFORMAL* to move or go somewhere very quickly: *I'm just going to zip* ***along*** *to the shops – I won't be long.* ○ *We were about*

to cross the road when a car suddenly zipped past. ➔See also **zap** GO QUICKLY.

zippy /ˈzɪp.i/ *adj INFORMAL APPROVING* energetic or fast: *a zippy car* ○ *a zippy performance*

zip NOTHING /zɪp/ *noun* [U] *US INFORMAL* nothing: *I know zip about computers.* ○ *The Dolphins are leading the Giants fourteen to zip* (= by fourteen points to nothing).

zip COMPUTING /zɪp/ *verb* [T] **-pp-** to COMPRESS (= reduce the size of) a computer file so that it uses less space and can be more easily sent or stored: *If you're desperate for disk space, you could zip the file (up) and stick it on a floppy.*

▲ **zip sth/sb up** *phrasal verb* [M] to fasten a piece of clothing by using its zip, or to help someone close the zip on a piece of clothing they are wearing: *Could you zip me up, please?* ○ *Zip up your jacket, it's cold out there.*

'zip ˌcode *noun* [C] in the US, a series of numbers that forms part of an address, and which is used to help organize post so that it can be delivered more quickly ➔See also **postcode**.

'zip ˌfile *noun* [C] a computer file that has been COMPRESSED (= reduced in size) so that it uses up less space

zipper /ˈzɪp.əʳ/ ⓤ /-ɚ/ *noun* [C] *US FOR* **zip** FASTENER

zit /zɪt/ *noun* [C] *INFORMAL* a temporary small raised spot on the skin

zither /ˈzɪð.əʳ/ ⓤ /-ɚ/ *noun* [C] a musical instrument shaped like a flat box, which has many strings that you pull at with your fingers or with a small piece of plastic

zloty /ˈzlɒt.i/ /ˈzwɒt-/ ⓤ /ˈzlɑː.t̬i/ /ˈzwɑː.t̬i/ *noun* [C] the standard unit of money used in Poland

zodiac /ˈzəʊ.di.æk/ ⓤ /ˈzoʊ-/ *noun* **1 the zodiac** (in the study of the planets and their influence on life) an area of the sky through which the sun, moon and most of the planets appear to move, divided into twelve equal parts, each with a name and symbol, and each connected with an exact time of year: *the signs of the zodiac* **2** [C usually sing] a representation of the zodiac in the form of a circular drawing **zodiacal** /zəʊˈdaɪ.ə.kəl/ ⓤ /zoʊ-/ *adj*

zombie /ˈzɒm.bi/ ⓤ /ˈzɑːm-/ *noun* [C] **1** *INFORMAL DISAPPROVING* a person who lacks energy, seems to act without thinking and is not aware of what is happening around them: *He just sat in front of the TV all day like a zombie.* **2** a dead person who is believed, in some Caribbean religions, to have been brought back to life by magic

zone /zəʊn/ ⓤ /zoʊn/ *noun* [C] **1** an area, especially one which is different from the areas around it because it has different characteristics or is used for different purposes: *an earthquake zone* ○ *the war/combat zone* ○ *a nuclear-free zone* ○ *He was charged with driving 75 mph in a 55 mph zone.* ○ *This stretch of coast has been designated a danger zone.* ○ *The UN Security Council has established a no-fly zone* (= one into which aircraft are not permitted to fly). **2** *SPECIALIZED* one of the five parts into which the Earth is divided according to temperature, marked by imaginary lines going round it from east to west: *temperate zones*

zonal /ˈzəʊ.nəl/ ⓤ /ˈzoʊ-/ *adj SPECIALIZED* relating to or arranged in zones: *zonal boundaries/divisions* **zonally** /ˈzəʊ.nəl.i/ /ˈzoʊ-/ *adv*

zone /zəʊn/ ⓤ /zoʊn/ *verb* [T usually passive] *SPECIALIZED* to give a special purpose to a particular area, such as an

area in a town: *The former dockyard has been zoned for tourist use.*

zoning /ˈzəʊ.nɪŋ/ ⓤ /ˈzoʊ-/ *noun* [U] *SPECIALIZED* the act of deciding, or the decision that has been taken about, what particular use an area should have: *zoning laws/regulations/restrictions*

zonked /zɒŋkt/ *adj* [after v] *SLANG* extremely tired: *We were really zonked (out) after our long journey.*

zoo (*plural* **zoos**) /zuː/ *noun* [C] (*OLD-FASHIONED FORMAL* **zoological gardens**) an area in which animals, especially wild animals, are kept so that people can go and look at them, or study them

zookeeper, **zoo keeper** /ˈzuːˌkiː.pəʳ/ ⓤ /ˈzuːˌkiː.pɚ/ *noun* [C] a person who works in a zoo, taking care of the animals

ˌzoological 'garden *noun* [C usually pl] *OLD-FASHIONED FORMAL FOR* **zoo**

zoology /zuːˈɒl.ə.dʒi/ /zəʊ-/ ⓤ /zoʊˈɑː.lə-/ *noun* [U] the scientific study of animals, especially their structure **zoological** /ˌzuː.əˈlɒdʒ.ɪ.kəl/ /ˌzəʊ.ə-/ ⓤ /ˌzoʊ.əˈlɑː.dʒɪ-/ *adj*: *zoological research/classification* **zoologist** /zuːˈɒl.ə.dʒɪst/ /zəʊ-/ ⓤ /zoʊˈɑː.lə-/ *noun* [C] a person who scientifically studies animals

zoom /zuːm/ *verb INFORMAL* **1** [I + adv or prep] to move very quickly: *They got into the car and zoomed off.* ○ *In the last few metres of the race, she suddenly zoomed ahead.* **2** [I] If prices or sales zoom, they increase suddenly and quickly: *House prices suddenly zoomed last year.*

PHRASAL VERBS WITH zoom ▼

▲ **zoom in/out** *phrasal verb* to (cause a camera, or computer to) make the image of something or someone appear much larger and nearer, or much smaller and further away: *At the beginning of the film, the camera zooms in to show two people sitting by the side of a river.* ○ *Click on a photo of any student, and it zooms out to full-size.* ○ *Television cameras zoomed in on the fans fighting in the stands.*

▲ **zoom in on sth** *phrasal verb INFORMAL* to notice and give special attention to something: *Henry immediately zoomed in on the weakest part of my argument.*

'zoom (ˌlens) *noun* [C] a device in a camera, or which can be attached to a camera, that can make the thing being photographed appear nearer

Zoroastrianism /ˌzɒr.əʊˈæs.tri.ə.nɪ.zᵊm/ ⓤ /ˌzɔːr.oʊˈ-/ *noun* [U] a religion which began in ancient Iran, and is based on the idea that there is a continuous fight between a god who represents good and one who represents evil

zucchini /zuˈkiː.ni/ ⓤ /zuː-/ *noun* [C] *plural* **zucchini** *or* **zucchinis** *US FOR* **courgette** ➔See picture **Vegetables** on page Centre 2

Zulu /ˈzuː.luː/ *noun* **1** [C] a member of a race of people who live in South Africa **2** [U] the language spoken by the Zulu people: *He speaks Zulu.* **Zulu** *adj*: *a Zulu chief*

zygote /ˈzaɪ.gəʊt/ ⓤ /-goʊt/ *noun* [C] *SPECIALIZED* the cell which is formed when a female reproductive cell and a male reproductive cell join

zzz /zː/ *exclamation* used in a picture or a piece of writing to represent the noise that people make when they are sleeping

Z

Idiom Finder

Idioms are one of the most interesting parts of the English language, especially when you are learning it. Even if some idioms are not very common, a lot of them provide a very clear picture of an idea (and maybe that is why people remember them so clearly). Some good 'picture' idioms are: **'open your heart to someone'**, **'have your head in the clouds'** and **'need something like you need a hole in the head'**

Unfortunately, in most dictionaries there is always a problem when you try to find idioms, especially if you are looking for a long idiom. For example, how do you find a long idiom such as **'be like a bear with a sore head'**? Do you look at **'like'**, **'bear'**, **'sore'** or **'head'**?

The Idiom Finder solves the problem because it lists all of the long idioms in this dictionary at **every important word in the idiom**. This means that if you look in the Idiom Finder for **'be like a bear with a sore head'** you will find it listed at **'like'**, **'bear'**, **'sore'** and **'head'** with the page number in the dictionary where you can find out what the idiom means (it's on page 97 if you want to look). The word that you are searching for is always printed in colour to make it easier to find.

We have only included idioms in the Idiom Finder if they have three or more important words. This is because if you want to look for a short idiom such as **'lose heart'** then it is quicker to simply look in the dictionary at **'lose'** and at **'heart'** (you will find it at 'lose' in this case). But if you are looking for a long idiom then just come straight to the Idiom Finder.

A

as easy as ABC /anything/falling off a log p386
be of/have no fixed abode /address p467
about time too p1335
be green/pale about the gills p525
be nothing to get excited about p422
be/go into ecstasies about /over [sth] p389
fall about laughing p439
give [sb] something to talk about p1304
go about [your] business p534
have/keep all [your] wits about [you] p1468
How about that p612
know what [you] are talking about p692
lose sleep over/about [sth] p740
make a noise about [sth] p841
make a song and dance about [sth] p1209
make no bones about [sth] p132
make no mistake about it p797
no buts about it p163
not bear thinking about p97
not have a civil word to say about [sb] p212
not know the first thing about [sth] p692
nothing to write home about p1481
put the word about /around/out/round p1471
see a man about a dog p1130
something/nothing to shout about p1163
that's about the size of it p1180
there's a lot of it about p741
There's no two ways about it p1380
throw [your] weight around/about p1329
we'll soon see about that p1130
What's that all about then p1450
word gets about /around/round p1471
above all things p1324

head and shoulders above p578
keep [your] head above water p578
put [your] head over/above the parapet p900
be conspicuous by [your] absence p259
accede to the throne/accede to power p6
accessory after the fact p7
accessory before the fact p7
an accident waiting to happen p7
more by accident than design p7
go according to plan p944
by [your] own account p8
keep a diary/an account /a record etc p682
take into account /take account of p9
turn/use [sth] to good account p8
by/from all accounts p8
an ace up [your] sleeve p10
come within an ace of [sth] p10
have/hold all the aces p10
no mean achievement /feat p773
fire a warning shot across [sb's] bows p139
[sb] couldn't act /argue/fight etc [their] way out of a paper bag p898
act /do something on [your] own responsibility p1065
be a hard/tough act to follow p12
clean up [your] act p216
read [sb] the riot act p1035
sharpen up your act p1153
smarten up [your] act p1193
all talk and no action p1304
swing into action p1296
not know [sb] from Adam p693
sweet fanny adams p1294
add fuel to the fire/flames p504
to add insult to injury p14
be of/have no fixed abode/address p467
without further/more ado p16

press home [your] advantage p981
take [sth] under advisement p19
can ill afford to do [sth] p623
a quarter past/ after two/three/four etc p1019
accessory after the fact p7
after [your] own heart p581
be one thing after another p1323
life after death p720
one after another p43
one after another p865
shut/close the stable/barn door after the horse has bolted p363
throw good money after bad p1329
all over again p22
but then again p1321
every now and again /then p419
every now and then/again p848
half as much again p563
here we go again p588
there [you] go again p1322
You can say that again p1110
against [your] better judgment p22
against all the odds/against all odds p857
against /contrary to all expectations p425
be banging/be [your] head against a brick wall p578
be dead set against [sth] p1143
be/come up against a brick wall p22
go against the flow p476
go against the grain p545
go/swim against the tide p1331
have [your] back to/against the wall p79
have the odds/cards stacked against [you] p1234
kick against the pricks p685
pit [your] wits against [sb/sth] p940
play both ends against the middle p946
raise [your] hand to/against [sb] p1027
sail against the wind p1102

To find an idiom, look at the word in colour in each idiom. All of the coloured words are in alphabetical order.
After each idiom there is a page number that tells you where the idiom is explained.

strike a blow against/at [sth] p1265
take up the cudgels for/ against [sb/sth] p296
grand old age p545
in this day and age p309
look young for [your] age p1487
ripe old age p1079
echo down/through the ages p388
many moons ago p805
couldn't agree more/less p24
couldn't agree/disagree more p806
be/stay/keep one jump ahead p678
full steam ahead p505
you ain't seen nothing yet p1129
a breath of fresh air p147
disappear/vanish into thin air p1323
put on airs and graces p26
go/walk down the aisle p28
ring/sound alarm bells p28
warning/ alarm bells start to ring/sound p104
great minds think alike p548
above all things p1324
against all the odds/against all odds p857
against/contrary to all expectations p425
all along the line p726
all by herself p587
all by himself p593
all by yourself p1487
all expenses paid p426
all fingers and thumbs p1330
all hell breaks loose p585
all hot and bothered p608
all in a day's work p309
all in good time p541
all in one piece p934
all in the/[your] mind p789
all over again p22
all over bar the shouting p89
all over the place p942
all shapes and sizes p1151
all talk and no action p1304
all the time in the world p1334
all things being equal p1324
all things considered p1324
all things to all men/people p1324
all very well p1446
all very well/fine/good p1416
all/the four corners of the world/earth p272
and all that jazz p670
at all hours of the day and night p610
be a bit of all right p116
be all fingers and thumbs p461
be all part of life's rich tapestry/pageant p720
be all right/fine by [sb] p165
be all sweetness and light p1294
be all that [you] can do p30
be behind [sb] all the way p103
be laughing all the way to the bank p703
beyond all dispute p352
by all means p773
by/from all accounts p8
do all the donkey work p363
draped all over [sb] p371
for all practical purposes p971
go all round the houses p610
go all the way p1440
have all the cares of the world on [your] shoulders p177
have/hold all the aces p10
have/keep all [your] wits about you p1468
hold all the cards p598
if all else fails p436
in all but name p823
in all my born days p309
it all amounts/comes to the same thing p1104

It's all Greek to me p549
It's all right p32
let it all hang out p715
lord/master/mistress/king/queen of all [you] survey p1289
make [sth] all [your] own p889
make all the right/correct etc noises p841
mean/be all [it's] cracked up to be p284
not be all fun and games p506
pass all belief p905
pull out all the stops p1005
put all [your] eggs in one basket p392
That's all I/you/we need p30
the fount of all knowledge/gossip/wisdom etc p491
till all hours p610
to/for all intents and purposes p654
to/from all appearances p50
walk all over p1429
What's that all about then p1450
when all is said and done p1110
with all due respect p1064
would not do [sth] for all the tea in China p1309
written all over [sb's] face p1481
You can't win 'em all p1460
almost burst a blood vessel p124
nearly/ almost fall off [your] chair p439
nearly/ almost have a heart attack p582
leave well alone p710
all along the line p726
come/go/be along for the ride p33
make [sth] up as you go along p754
somewhere along the line p726
not only but also p867
American/Italian etc by birth p116
as American as apple pie p36
first among equals p464
put/set the cat among the pigeons p184
it all amounts/comes to the same thing p1104
another/a second bite of the cherry p117
another/the final nail in the coffin p822
be another/a different kettle of fish p684
be one thing after another p1323
be one/ another of life's great mysteries p720
have another/more than one string to [your] bow p1267
live to fight another day p730
on one level/on another level p716
one after another p43
one after another p865
one thing leads to another p1323
one way or another p865
understand one another/each other p1390
what with one thing and another p1323
will not take no for an answer p1302
any day now p309
any minute/moment/second/time now p848
any way you slice it p1187
at any one time p1334
by any chance p193
Give me any day/every time p527
in any shape or form p1151
not by any manner of means p759
not have any concept/have no concept of [sth] p250
not make any difference p339
not pull any punches p1005
not stand any nonsense p842
wouldn't have it any other way p1440
I/You wouldn't wish [sth] on anyone/ my/your worst enemy p1465
[I] would give anything/a lot p527
as easy as ABC/ anything/falling off a log p386
Do you want to make something/ anything of it p754

not/never want for anything p1432
miles from anywhere/nowhere p786
keep up appearances p683
to/from all appearances p50
as American as apple pie p36
upset the apple cart p1404
keep your promise/word; keep an appointment p682
tied to [your] mother's/wife's apron strings p1331
It is arguable that p56
[sb] couldn't act/ argue/fight etc [their] way out of a paper bag p898
a list as long as [your] arm p728
cost an arm and a leg/a small fortune p275
give [your] right arm p1076
the long arm of the law p736
keep [sb] at arm's length p57
a knight in shining armour p690
fall into [sb's] arms p439
fold your arms p480
greet/welcome [sb] with open arms p868
be like a millstone around/round [your] neck p788
beat around the bush p98
can't get [your] head around p578
fray around/at the edges p494
just around the corner p272
know [your] way around [sth] p693
make the world go around/round p1475
pass the hat around/round p905
put the word about/ around/out/round p1471
sit around on [your] backside p81
the wrong way round/ around p1482
think the whole world revolves around [you] p1072
throw [your] money/cash around p1329
throw [your] weight around/about p1329
twist [sb] around/round [your] little finger p1380
word gets about/ around/round p1471
work [your] way around/round to [sth] p1473
wrap [sb] around/round [your] little finger p1479
under house arrest p610
a kick up the arse/backside p685
go arse over tit/tip p59
Kiss my arse p688
not know [your] arse from [your] elbow p59
think the sun shines out of [sb's] arse/ backside p1282
have [sth] down to a fine art p460
wear sackcloth and ashes p1099
you may well ask p63
bore the ass off [sb] p64
kick some ass p685
Shove/stick [sth] up [your] ass p64
talk [sb's] ass off p64
work [sb's] ass off p64
work [your] ass off p64
assist the police with/in their inquiries p65
you could cut the atmosphere with a knife p300
lay [yourself] open to attack/criticism/ ridicule etc p705
nearly/almost have a heart attack p582
have something on good authority p72
avoid [sth] like the plague p75
biological clock is ticking away p115
blow the cobwebs away p125
give the game away p513
light years away p723
send [sb] away with a flea in [their] ear p471
take [sb's] breath away p147

To find an idiom, look at the word in colour in each idiom. All of the coloured words are in alphabetical order.
After each idiom there is a page number that tells you where the idiom is explained.

B

be left holding the baby p710
throw the baby out with the bath-water p1328
as smooth as silk/a baby's bottom p1196
back the wrong horse p79
back to square one p78
cast [your] mind back p183
come back down to earth p385
come back from the dead p310
come back/home to roost p1086
crawl back to someone p286
fed up to the back teeth p450
get off my back p79
go back a long way p736
Go back to sleep p1186
go back to the drawing board p372
go to hell and back p585
go/be back to square one p1231
go/get back to nature p826
have [your] back to/against the wall p79
have a face like the back end of a bus p434
have eyes in the back of [your] head p432
know [sth] back to front p692
know [sth] like the back of [your] hand p692
make a rod for [your] own back p1083
never look back p737
one step forward two steps back p1248
pin back [your] ears p937
put [your] back into [sth] p1012
put the roses back into [sb's] cheeks p1087
put/get [sb's] back up p79
put/turn the clock back p222
put/turn the clocks back p222
step back in time p1247
take a back seat p79
the shirt off [sb's] back p1157
there is no holding [sb] p598
throw [omething] back in [sb's] face p1328
turn back the clock p222
turn the clock back p1376
water off a duck's back p1437
you scratch my back and I'll scratch yours p1119
a boot/kick up [the/your] backside p81
a kick up the arse/backside p685
sit around on [your] backside p81
think the sun shines out of [sb's] arse/backside p1282
be backward in coming forward p81
without so much as a backward glance p1467
bend/lean over backwards p81
bring home the bacon p150
give [sth] up as a bad job p82
go from bad to worse p82
go through a bad/difficult/rough/sticky patch p909
good riddance to bad rubbish p1074
leave a bad taste in [sb's] mouth p710
show someone in a bad light p722
the best of a bad bunch/lot p107
throw good money after bad p1329
turn up like a bad penny p1377
come off better/worse/badly/well p237
[sb] couldn't act/argue/fight etc [their] way out of a paper bag p898
let the cat out of the bag p184
bags under [your] eyes p83
fish or cut bait p465
hold the balance of power p84
throw [sb] off balance p1329
a whole new ball game p85
start/set/get the ball rolling p85
go down like a lead balloon p707

the balloon goes up p85
be cold enough to freeze the balls off a brass monkey p497
more bang for your bucks p87
be banging etc [your] head against a brick wall p578
be laughing all the way to the bank p703
all over bar the shouting p89
drive a hard bargain p376
wouldn't touch [sth] with a barge pole p1349
[sb's] bark is worse than [their] bite p90
be barking up the wrong tree p90
shut/close the stable/barn door after the horse has bolted p363
no holds barred p598
lock stock and barrel p733
scrape the bottom of the barrel p1119
break down barriers p144
get to/reach first base p464
bask/bathe in reflected glory p531
put all [your] eggs in one basket p392
do [sth] off [your] own bat p93
throw the baby out with the bath-water p1328
bask/bathe in reflected glory p531
batten down the hatches p94
fight a losing battle p456
a heavy cross to bear p291
be like a bear with a sore head p97
bear [sb] ill will p624
bear false witness p97
not bear thinking about p97
beard the lion in [his/her] den p98
get/find your bearings p97
[your] heart skips/misses a beat p581
beat [sb] at [their] own game p98
beat a path through [sth] p98
beat a path to [sb's] door p98
beat around the bush p98
beat/bore/scare etc the pants off [sb] p898
beat/knock the living daylights out of [sb] p309
beat/turn swords into ploughshares p1297
off the beaten track p98
take some beating p98
that beats everything p98
be/become mired down in something p792
get out of bed on the wrong side p100
wet the/[your] bed p1449
accessory before the fact p7
before [your] very eyes p432
before very/too long p736
before you can say Jack Robinson p1110
before you can/could say Jack Robinson p668
cast pearls before swine p183
leg before wicket p712
put the cart before the horse p181
see [sb] in hell before p1130
the calm before the storm p169
the day before yesterday p1485
the lull before the storm p745
the week/month/year before last p702
beg borrow or steal p102
I beg your pardon p102
can't even begin p102
be behind [sb] all the way p103
be wet behind the ears p1449
behind closed doors p222
come from behind p236
fall behind schedule p1114
the power behind the throne p970
pass all belief p905
believe [sth] when [you] see it p104
hear warning bells p1434
hear wedding bells p580
Pull the other leg/one it's got bells on p1005
ring/sound alarm bells p28

warning/alarm bells start to ring/sound p104
[sb's] eyes are bigger than [their] belly/stomach p432
go/turn belly up p104
bend/lean over backwards p81
drive/send [sb] round the bend p106
scratch beneath the surface p1119
give [sb] the benefit of the doubt p106
give [sth/sb] a wide berth p1458
be the best thing since sliced bread p107
give [sth] your best shot p1162
man's best friend p756
May the best man/person win p107
put [your] best foot forward p107
the best of a bad bunch/lot p107
the best of both worlds p107
the best/happiest days of [your] life p309
the next best thing p836
with the best will in the world p107
your best bet p108
your best bib and tucker p111
how much do you want to bet p108
you can bet your life p108
your best bet p108
against [your] better judgment p22
better luck next time p109
better/bigger/more etc than ever p418
come off better/worse/badly/well p237
go one better p109
have seen better days p1129
know better than [sb] p692
know better than to do [sth] p692
move on to higher/better things p812
no better than a [sth] p109
so much the better p109
take a turn for the better/worse p1376
ten/fifty/a hundred times better p1336
be between the devil and the deep blue sea p335
be caught between a rock and a hard place p1082
be no/little love lost between p742
drive a wedge between [sb] p376
fall between two stools p439
few and far between p454
get the bit between [your] teeth p117
hit [sb] between the eyes p595
leave/go off etc with [your] tail between [your] legs p1301
little/not much to choose between p206
read between the lines p1035
thread your way through/between/etc p1327
beyond [your] wildest dreams p110
beyond a shadow of a doubt p110
beyond all dispute p352
beyond reasonable doubt p110
from beyond the grave p110
get/go beyond a joke p675
live beyond [your] means p773
not be beyond the wit of man/[sb] p1466
your best bib and tucker p111
but not in the biblical sense p111
make a takeover bid for [sth] p1304
bide your time p111
be a big fish in a small pond p465
be no big deal p112
make a big difference p339
make a big thing out of [sth] p1323
miles too big/small/expensive etc p786
too big for [your] boots p112
What's the big idea p112
[sb's] eyes are bigger than [their] belly/stomach p432
better/bigger/more etc than ever p418
have bigger/other fish to fry p465
clean bill of health p216
pick up the bill/tab p932
sell [sb] a bill of goods p1135

To find an idiom, look at the word in colour in each idiom. All of the coloured words are in alphabetical order.
After each idiom there is a page number that tells you where the idiom is explained.

1493

biological clock is ticking away p115
a little bird told me p730
bird's eye view p115
kill two birds with one stone p686
American/Italian etc by birth p116
really take the biscuit p116
be a bit of all right p116
get the bit between [your] teeth p117
lay it on a bit thick p706
not take a blind bit of notice p122
the hair of the dog that bit you p562
too old/a bit old p861
life's a bitch and then you die p117
[sb's] bark is worse than [their] bite p90
another/a second bite of the cherry p117
bite [sb's] head off p117
bite off more than [you] can chew p117
bite the hand that feeds [you] p117
bite/snap [sb's] head off p578
a bitter pill to swallow p117
be down in black and white p118
paint a black picture of [sth/sb] p118
see things in black and white p118
[your] mind is a blank/goes blank p789
a blast from the past p120
blast/blow [sb/sth] to kingdom come p687
paint a bleak/gloomy/rosy etc picture of [sth] p894
my heart bleeds for [sb] p581
blend into the scenery p1114
not take a blind bit of notice p122
the blind leading the blind p122
turn a blind eye p1375
a chip off the old block p205
have/put [your] head on the block p123
knock [sb's] block off p690
[your] own flesh and blood p889
almost burst a blood vessel p124
be [sb's] own flesh and blood p472
be only flesh and blood p472
get blood out of/from a stone p124
make [sb's] blood curdle p298
make [your] blood boil p124
make [your] blood run cold p124
come into bloom p125
blast/blow [sb/sth] to kingdom come p687
blow [your] own trumpet/horn p125
blow hot and cold p125
blow the cobwebs away p125
blow/bomb/wipe etc [sth] off the map p761
blow/take the lid off [sth] p719
let/blow off steam p1246
strike a blow against/at [sth] p1265
well I'll be blowed p125
way/direction the wind blows p1440
a bolt from/out of the blue p131
be between the devil and the deep blue sea p335
once in a blue moon p126
scream/shout blue murder p126
talk a blue streak p1304
until [you are] blue in the face p126
bluff [your] way into/out of [sth] p127
go back to the drawing board p372
go by the board p128
not be short of a bob or two p1161
Bob's your uncle p129
keep body and soul together p129
over my dead body p310
can't boil an egg p130
go off the boil p130
make [your] blood boil p124
a bolt from/out of the blue p131
shut/close the stable/barn door after the horse has bolted p363
blow/bomb/wipe etc [sth] off the map p761
go like a bomb p131
go like/down a bomb p131

pare [sth] down to the bone p901
work [your] fingers to the bone p1472
make no bones about [sth] p132
put flesh on the bones of [sth] p472
cheque book journalism p201
every trick in the book p1364
have your head buried/stuck in a book p578
take a leaf out of [sb's] book p708
a boot/kick up [the/your] backside p81
the boot/shoe is on the other foot p134
as tough as old boots p1350
too big for [your] boots p112
pull/haul yourself up by your bootstraps p134
beat/bore/scare etc the pants off [sb] p898
bore the ass off [sb] p64
as if to the manner born p759
born with a silver spoon in [your] mouth p135
in all my born days p309
wish [you] had never been born p135
beg borrow or steal p102
live on borrowed time p136
burn the candle at both ends p160
cut both/two ways p300
have a foot in both camps p482
jump in with both feet p678
play both ends against the middle p946
the best of both worlds p107
all hot and bothered p608
as smooth as silk/a baby's bottom p1196
be on the lowest/bottom rung of the ladder p1096
from the bottom of [your] heart p137
from top to bottom p1346
scrape the bottom of the barrel p1119
the bottom drops/falls out of the market p137
be/feel honour bound to do [sth] p603
[sth] knows no bounds p693
by/in leaps and bounds p709
have another/more than one string to [your] bow p1267
Life is just a bowl of cherries p139
fire a warning shot across [sb's] bows p139
my dear boy p141
there's a good boy/girl/dog p1322
hold out/offer an olive branch p863
and the same to you with brass knobs on p690
be cold enough to freeze the balls off a brass monkey p497
brass monkey weather p143
get down to brass tacks p143
put on a brave face p143
step into the breach p1247
be the best thing since sliced bread p107
know which side [your] bread is buttered on p692
break down barriers p144
break fresh/new ground p144
all hell breaks loose p585
make a clean breast of it p216
a breath of fresh air p147
Don't hold [your] breath p147
don't hold your breath p598
take [sb's] breath away p147
breathe down [sb's] neck p147
breathe new life into p147
couldn't organize a piss-up in a brewery p875
be banging etc [your] head against a brick wall p578
be/come up against a brick wall p22
come down on someone like a ton of bricks p237
like a ton of bricks p1344
I'll/We'll cross that bridge when I/we get to it p291

water under the bridge p1437
go/turn bright red p1044
look on the bright side p737
bring [sb] up short p150
bring [sth] out into the open p869
bring [sth] to life/come to life p720
bring a lump to [your] throat p745
bring home the bacon p150
bring up the rear p150
bring/take [sb] down a peg or two p916
a quick/brisk trot through [sth] p1368
look like something the cat brought/dragged in p184
earn/get/score brownie points p153
tar [sb] with the same brush p1307
give someone the brush-off p154
more bang for your bucks p87
Bugger/Sod etc this for a lark p701
play silly buggers p947
be like a red rag to a bull p1044
bull in a china shop p157
take the bull by the horns p157
things that go bump in the night p1324
the best of a bad bunch/lot p107
have your head buried/stuck in a book p578
burn a hole in [sb's] pocket p160
burn the candle at both ends p160
burn the midnight oil p160
[your] ears must be burning p384
almost burst a blood vessel p124
burst into flames p161
burst into song/tears/laughter p161
burst into tears p1310
bury/have [your] head in the sand p578
have a face like the back end of a bus p434
beat around the bush p98
go about/[your] business p534
like nobody's business p162
mind [your] own business p790
lead a busy/normal/quiet etc life p707
[they] can dish it out but [they] can't take it p349
but not in the biblical sense p111
but then again p1321
correct me if I'm wrong but p273
everything but/except the kitchen sink p419
have no option but to do something p872
in all but name p823
last but not least p701
not only but also p867
sadder but wiser p1100
slowly but surely p1191
the last but one p701
no buts about it p163
no ifs and buts p622
butter wouldn't melt in [sb's] mouth p163
know which side [your] bread is buttered on p692
hit/press/push the panic button p897
all by herself p587
all by himself p593
all by yourself p1487
American/Italian etc by birth p116
be all right/fine by [sb] p165
be conspicuous by [your] absence p259
be hoisted with/by [your] own petard p927
be in a class by itself/of its own p215
be too clever by half p219
by [your] own account p8
by a process of elimination p396
by all means p773
by any chance p193
by common consent p258
by fair means or foul p437
by hook or by crook p604
by no means p773
by no stretch of the imagination p1264

To find an idiom, look at the word in colour in each idiom. All of the coloured words are in alphabetical order.
After each idiom there is a page number that tells you where the idiom is explained.

1494

C

To find an idiom, look at the word in colour in each idiom. All of the coloured words are in alphabetical order.
After each idiom there is a page number that tells you where the idiom is explained.

put/turn the **clocks** forward p222
run/go like **clockwork** p222
be too **close** for comfort p223
close your ears p384
draw to a **close**/an end p371
keep/hold [your] cards **close** to [your] chest p176
open the door to/**close** the door on [sth] p363
sail **close** to the wind p1102
shut/**close** the stable/barn door after the horse has bolted p363
behind **closed** doors p222
skeleton in the/[your] cupboard/**closet** p1181
a wolf in sheep's **clothing** p1468
have your head in the **clouds** p578
drive a **coach** and horses through [sth] p375
carry/take **coals** to Newcastle p226
haul/drag [sb] over the **coals** p226
blow the **cobwebs** away p125
wake up and smell the **coffee** p1429
another/the final nail in the **coffin** p822
the other side of the **coin** p1170
be **cold** enough to freeze the balls off a brass monkey p497
blow hot and **cold** p125
catch your death of **cold** p312
give [sb] the **cold** shoulder p230
make [sb's] blood run **cold** p1094
make [your] blood run **cold** p124
pour/throw **cold** water on [sth] p230
throw **cold** water on [sth] p1329
You're getting **colder** p230
hot under the **collar** p608
see the **colour** of [sb's] money p1129
nail [your] **colours** to the mast p822
see [sb's] true **colours** p234
show [sb] in their true **colours** p234
be as crazy/rich etc as they **come** p236
be in leaf/**come** p708
be/**come** up against a brick wall p22
blast/blow [sb/sth] to kingdom **come** p687
bring [sth] to life/**come** to life p720
come back down to earth p385
come back from the dead p310
come back/home to roost p1086
come down on one side of the fence or other p1170
come down on someone like a ton of bricks p237
come from behind p236
come hell or high water p585
come into [your] own p889
come into bloom p125
come into play p947
come off better/worse/badly/well p237
come out of/in left field p712
come rain or shine p1027
come the raw prawn p1033
come to a full stop p505
come to the end of the road p1081
come to/meet a sticky end p1250
come under fire p462
come up with the goods p541
come within a whisker of [doing sth] p1454
come within an ace of [sth] p10
come within an inch of [sth] p634
come/be a poor second/third etc p961
come/follow hard/hot on the heels of [sth] p584
come/get down off [you] high horse p591
come/go down in the world p367
come/go under the hammer p565
come/go/be along for the ride p33
come/go/turn full circle p504
come/suffer under the lash p701
easy **come** easy go p387

first **come** first served p464
go/**come** down in the world p1475
go/**come** up in the world p1475
have **come** a long way p736
the shape of things to **come** p1151
till/until kingdom **come** p687
till/until the cows **come** home p282
turn/**come** up trumps p1370
if the worst **comes** to the worst p1477
if/when it **comes** to the crunch p294
if/when push **comes** to shove p1011
it all amounts/**comes** to the same thing p1104
be too close for **comfort** p223
be backward in **coming** forward p81
coming up roses p1087
know/see where [sb] is **coming** from p1452
not know whether you are **coming** or going p236
be a victory for **common** sense p1418
by **common** consent p258
make **common** cause with [sb] p242
present **company** excepted p979
compose your features/thoughts p247
not have any **concept**/have no concept of [sth] p250
To whom it may **concern** p250
as/so far as I'm **concerned** p444
take [sb] into [your] **confidence** p254
by common **consent** p258
all things **considered** p1324
be **conspicuous** by [your] absence p259
fit for human **consumption** p466
gaze at/**contemplate** [your] navel p827
against/**contrary** to all expectations p425
contrary to popular opinion p265
cook/dance/talk etc up a storm p1258
keep a **cool** head p269
catch/cop/get some z's p1489
it's a fair **cop** p437
just around the **corner** p272
out of/from the **corner** of [your] eye p272
all/the four **corners** of the world/earth p272
correct me if I'm wrong but p273
make all the right/**correct** etc noises p841
cost [sb] a pretty penny p982
cost an arm and a leg/a small fortune p275
wrap [sb] up in **cotton** wool p1479
as far as the eye can/**could** see p432
before you can/**could** say Jack Robinson p668
could count on the fingers of one hand p277
I wouldn't trust [sb] as far as I **could** throw them p1371
I'm so hungry I **could** eat a horse p387
Nothing **could** have been further from my mind/thoughts p508
you **could** cut the atmosphere with a knife p300
You **could** have fooled me p482
[I] **couldn't** care less p178
[sb] **couldn't** act/argue/fight etc [their] way out of a paper bag p898
couldn't agree more/less p24
couldn't agree/disagree more p806
couldn't organize a piss-up in a brewery p875
keep [your] own **counsel** p277
could **count** on the fingers of one hand p277
stand up and be **counted** p1238
gather up strength/**courage** p516
get your **courage** up p524
pluck up [your] **courage** p951
screw up [your] **courage** p1120
follow/steer/take the middle **course**/way/path p784

let nature take its **course** p826
pervert the **course** of justice p926
settle a case out of **court** p280
cover/hide a multitude of sins p816
read [sth] from **cover** to cover p281
send [sth] under plain/separate **cover** p281
till/until the cows come home p282
a fair **crack** of the whip p437
a hard/tough nut to **crack** p850
sledgehammer to **crack** a nut p1186
not be all [it's] **cracked** up to be p284
paper over the **cracks** p898
from the **cradle** to the grave p284
every nook and **cranny** p843
make [your] flesh **crawl**/creep p472
be as **crazy**/rich etc as they come p236
create/kick up/raise a stink p1253
make [your] flesh crawl/**creep** p472
be riding/on the **crest** of a wave p289
lay [yourself] open to attack/**criticism**/ridicule etc p705
by hook or by **crook** p604
a heavy **cross** to bear p291
cross [sb's] hand/palm with silver p291
dot the i's and **cross** the t's p365
I'll/We'll **cross** that bridge when I/we get to it p291
the thought **crosses** [sb's] mind p1326
the thinking woman's/man's **crumpet** p1325
if/when it comes to the **crunch** p294
be a far **cry** from [sth] p444
not know whether to laugh or **cry** p692
For **crying** out loud p295
take up the **cudgels** for/against [sb/sth] p296
take [your] **cue** from [sb] p296
take [your] **cue** from [sth/sb] p296
skeleton in the/[your] **cupboard**/closet p1181
make [sb's] blood **curdle** p298
curl up and die p298
not give a tinker's **cuss** p1337
cut [sb] down to size p301
cut [sb] some slack p300
cut [your] political/professional etc teeth p301
cut a fine figure p300
cut a swathe through [sth] p300
cut both/two ways p300
cut it/things fine p300
cut no ice with [sb] p300
cut off [your] nose to spite [your] face p300
cut the ground from under [sb's] feet p301
cut up rough p300
cut/tear [sth/sb] to/into ribbons p1073
fish or **cut** bait p465
to **cut** a long story short p301
you could **cut** the atmosphere with a knife p300

D

be pushing up the **daisies** p1011
damn [sb] with faint praise p305
Well I'll be **damned** p305
cook/**dance**/talk etc up a storm p1258
lead [sb] a merry **dance** p707
make a song and **dance** about [sth] p1209
be on/off the **danger** list p306
There's no **danger** of that p306
I daresay/I **dare** say p307
I **daresay**/I dare say p307
from **dawn** to dusk p308
any **day** now p309

To find an idiom, look at the word in colour in each idiom. All of the coloured words are in alphabetical order.
After each idiom there is a page number that tells you where the idiom is explained.

1496

at all hours of the **day** and night p610

from that **day** forward p490

from that **day** /time onwards p500

give [sb] the time of **day** p1334

Give me any **day** /every time p527

in this **day** and age p309

live to fight another **day** p730

many happy returns of the **day** p760

pass the time of **day** p906

save/keep money for a rainy **day** p1027

see the light of **day** p1130

the **day** before yesterday p1485

to/until [my] dying **day** p338

all in a **day**'s work p309

beat/knock the living **daylights** out of [sb] p309

frighten/scare etc the living **daylights** out of [sb] p309

have seen better **days** p1129

in all my born **days** p309

in **days** gone by p534

It's early **days** p384

one of these **days** p309

one of those **days** p309

the best/happiest **days** of [your] life p309

be a nine **days**' wonder p839

be **dead** set against [sth] p1143

come back from the **dead** p310

flog a **dead** horse p474

give [sb] up for **dead** p528

Knock 'em **dead** p690

over my **dead** body p310

rise from the **dead** /grave p1079

wouldn't be seen **dead** p1129

fall on **deaf** ears p439

turn a **deaf** ear p1376

be no big **deal** p112

Dear Sir or Madam p1178

my **dear** boy p141

a fate worse than **death** p447

be a matter of life and/or **death** p770

catch your **death** of cold p312

death by misadventure p793

die a natural/violent etc **death** p338

hang/hold on like grim **death** p550

life after **death** p720

look/feel like **death** warmed up/over p312

on/under pain of **death** p894

sign [your] own **death** warrant p1173

clear [your] **debts** /clear [yourself] of debts p217

Are my eyes **deceiving** me p313

be between the devil and the **deep** blue sea p335

go off the **deep** end p316

jump in at the **deep** end p316

snatch victory from the jaws of **defeat** p1198

labour under the **delusion** /illusion/ misapprehension etc p695

demand money with menaces p778

beard the lion in [his/her] **den** p98

there's no **denying** p325

depart this life p325

you can **depend** on/upon it p326

sink to such a level/such **depths** p1177

[He/She] **deserves** whatever/everything [he/she] gets p230

more by accident than **design** p7

leave a lot to be **desired** p710

throw up [your] hands in horror/**despair** p1329

go into **detail** p333

detain [sb] at His/Her Majesty's pleasure p333

leave [sb] to [their] own **devices** p710

be between the **devil** and the deep blue sea p335

sell [your] soul to the **devil** p1135

to give the **devil** his due p335

keep a **diary** /an account/a record etc p682

curl up and **die** p298

die a natural/violent etc death p338

life's a bitch and then you **die** p117

make a big **difference** p339

make a world of **difference** p1475

not make any **difference** p339

be another/a **different** kettle of fish p684

go through a bad/**difficult** /rough/sticky patch p909

dig [your] own grave p340

dig [yourself] into a hole p340

take a **dim** view of [sth] p341

done up/dressed up like a dog's **dinner** p361

dip a/your toe in the water p342

way/**direction** the wind blows p1440

treat [sb] like **dirt** p1362

dirty your hands p344

give [sb] a **dirty** look p344

wash [your] **dirty** linen in public p1434

couldn't agree/**disagree** more p806

disappear off the face of the earth p434

disappear /vanish into thin air p1323

vanish/go up/**disappear** in a puff of smoke p1004

strike a **discordant** note p347

[they] can **dish** it out but [they] can't take it p349

be well/favourably/etc **disposed** to/ towards [sth/sb] p352

beyond all **dispute** p352

dissolve into tears/laughter p353

be within hailing **distance** of [some- where] p562

in/within spitting **distance** p1224

within shouting **distance** p1163

within striking **distance** p1265

divide /split [sth] down the middle p784

just what the **doctor** ordered p360

under sedation/the **doctor** etc p1388

[sb's] face **doesn't** fit p434

fight like cat and **dog** p184

see a man about a **dog** p1130

tail wagging the **dog** p1301

the hair of the **dog** that bit you p562

there's a good boy/girl/**dog** p1322

done up/dressed up like a **dog's** dinner p361

pay top **dollar** p912

look/feel like a million **dollars** p788

Don't give me that p527

Don't hold [your] breath p147

don't hold your breath p598

Don't make me laugh p703

I **don't** know how/what/why etc p692

if you **don't** mind me saying p790

You **don't** say p1110

feel hard **done-by** p572

do all the **donkey** work p363

talk the hind legs off a **donkey** p1304

beat a path to [sb's] **door** p98

get a/[your] foot in the **door** p482

keep the wolf from the **door** p1468

open the **door** to/close the door on [sth] p363

shut/close the stable/barn **door** after the horse has bolted p363

behind closed **doors** p222

give [sb] a **dose** /taste of [their] own medicine p775

like a **dose** of salts p364

dot the i's and cross the t's p365

from/since the year **dot** p1485

sign on the **dotted** line p1173

beyond a shadow of a **doubt** p110

beyond reasonable **doubt** p110

give [sb] the benefit of the **doubt** p106

batten **down** the hatches p94

be **down** in black and white p118

be jumping up and **down** p678

be/become mired **down** in something p792

break **down** barriers p144

breathe **down** [sb's] neck p147

bring/take [sb] **down** a peg or two p916

catch [sb] with [their] pants/trousers **down** p185

come back **down** to earth p385

come **down** on one side of the fence or other p1170

come **down** on someone like a ton of bricks p237

come/get **down** off [you] high horse p591

come/go **down** in the world p367

cut [sb] **down** to size p301

divide /split [sth] down the middle p784

echo **down** /through the ages p388

flush [sth] **down** the toilet p477

force/ram [sth] **down** [sb's] throat p1328

get **down** to brass tacks p143

get/put [your] head **down** p578

go **down** like a lead balloon p707

go **down** the gurgler p559

go **down** the pan p896

go **down** the tubes p1373

go **down** the wrong way p1481

go **down** /fall like ninepins p839

go like/**down** a bomb p131

go/come **down** in the world p1475

go/walk **down** the aisle p28

have [sth] **down** to a fine art p460

hold **down** a job p599

hold **down** the fort p598

jump **down** [sb's] throat p678

keep [your] head **down** p578

kick/hit [sb] when [they are] **down** p367

lay **down** [your] life for [sth] p705

lay **down** the law p706

let [your] hair **down** p715

let the side **down** p716

lie **down** on the job p719

never live [sth] **down** p731

not take [sth] lying **down** p719

One/Two etc **down** one/two etc to go p367

pare [sth] **down** to the bone p901

put [your] foot **down** p482

put **down** roots p1086

put it **down** to experience p1014

ram [sth] **down** [sb's] throat p1028

sell [sb] **down** the river p1135

send chills **down** /up [sb's] spine p204

send shudders/a shudder **down** [your] spine p1167

shiver up and **down** [your] spine p1158

shoot [sb/sth] **down** in flames p1159

suit [sb] right **down** to the ground p1280

take a stroll/trip/walk **down** memory lane p778

throw **down** the gauntlet p516

turn [sth] upside **down** p1376

turn upside **down** p1404

when the chips are **down** p205

win [sth] hands **down** p567

win hands **down** p1460

drag [sb's] name through the mire/mud p370

haul/**drag** [sb] over the coals p226

wild horses wouldn't **drag** me p1459

look like something the cat brought/ **dragged** in p184

laugh like a **drain** p703

draped all over [sb] p371

draw a veil over [sth] p1413

draw to a close/an end p371

draw /get the short straw p1161

go back to the **drawing** board p372

hung **drawn** and quartered p569

be living in a **dream** world p373

work/go like a **dream** p373

To find an idiom, look at the word in colour in each idiom. All of the coloured words are in alphabetical order.

After each idiom there is a page number that tells you where the idiom is explained.

1497

beyond [your] wildest **dreams** p110
done up/ **dressed** up like a dog's dinner p361
done/ **dressed** up to the nines p839
dressed up to the nines p374
mutton **dressed** as lamb p820
if you catch/get my **drift** p374
a drop too much to **drink** p377
can't hold [your] **drink** p598
drink [sb] under the table p375
drink like a fish p375
drive [your] message/point home p376
drive a coach and horses through [sth] p375
drive a hard bargain p376
drive a wedge between [sb] p376
drive/hammer [sth] home p601
drive/send [sb] round the bend p106
drive/send [sb] to an early grave p385
drive/work [yourself] into the ground p552
ride/ **drive**/walk/etc off into the sunset p1283
be as pure as the **driven** snow p1009
driving while intoxicated p375
a **drop** too much to drink p377
drop [sb/sth] like a hot potato p377
drop like flies p478
jaw **drops** open p670
the bottom **drops**/falls out of the market p137
look like a **drowned** rat p377
leave [sb] high and **dry** p590
There wasn't a **dry** eye in the house p379
watch paint **dry** p1436
take to [sth] like a **duck** to water p380
water off a **duck's** back p1437
give [sb] their **due** p380
to give the devil his **due** p335
with all **due** respect p1064
from dawn to **dusk** p308
like gold **dust** p539
to/until [my] **dying** day p338

E

at **each** other's throats p1328
be meant for **each** other p773
be/live in **each** other's pockets p954
each to his/their own p384
knock into **each** other/knock through p690
understand one another/ **each** other p1390
a clip round/on the **ear** p221
go in one **ear** and out the other p384
have/keep [your] **ear** to the ground p384
make a pig's **ear** of [sth] p935
play [sth] by **ear** p947
send [sb] away with a flea in [their] **ear** p471
turn a deaf **ear** p1376
drive/send [sb] to an **early** grave p385
It's **early** days p384
earn/get/score brownie points p153
[your] **ears** must be burning p384
be wet behind the **ears** p1449
close your **ears** p384
fall on deaf **ears** p439
pin back [your] **ears** p937
all/the four corners of the world/ **earth** p272
come back down to **earth** p385
disappear off the face of the **earth** p434
like nothing else on **earth** p385
like nothing on **earth** p846
move heaven and **earth** p812
set/put [sb's] mind at rest/ **ease** p789
easier said than done p386
the **easiest** thing in the world p386
the Greek/Russian/ **Eastern** Orthodox

Church p876
as **easy** as ABC/anything/falling off a log p386
easy come easy go p387
take it/things **easy** p387
take things **easy** p1324
eat [sb] out of house and home p387
eat humble pie p387
eat like a horse p387
I'll **eat** my hat p387
I'm so hungry I could **eat** a horse p387
eaten up with/by [sth] p387
echo down/through the ages p388
be/go into **ecstasies** about/over [sth] p389
set [sb's] teeth on **edge** p1345
take the **edge** off [sth] p389
fray around/at the **edges** p494
spare no **effort**/expense p1215
a chicken and **egg** situation p202
can't boil an **egg** p130
egg white/white of an egg p1455
kill the goose that lays the golden **egg** p686
as sure as **eggs** is eggs p1287
put all [your] **eggs** in one basket p392
teach your grandmother to suck **eggs** p545
More power to [your] **elbow** p970
not know [your] arse from [your] **elbow** p59
have a memory like an **elephant** p778
by a process of **elimination** p396
if all **else** fails p436
like nothing **else** on earth p385
can't see further than the **end** of [your] nose p1129
come to the **end** of the road p1081
come to/meet a sticky **end** p1250
draw to a close/an **end** p371
get the wrong **end** of the stick p1481
go off the deep **end** p316
have a face like the back **end** of a bus p434
jump in at the deep **end** p316
keep/hold [your] **end** up p402
light at the **end** of the tunnel p722
make [sb's] hair stand on **end** p562
thin **end** of the wedge p1323
will never hear the **end** of it p580
burn the candle at both **ends** p160
make **ends** meet p402
play both **ends** against the middle p946
be [your] own worst **enemy** p1477
I/You wouldn't wish [sth] on anyone/my/ your worst **enemy** p1465
public **enemy** number one/No 1 p1003
be cold **enough** to freeze the balls off a brass monkey p497
too many chiefs and not **enough** Indians p203
enter/get into the spirit p1224
go into/ **enter** the church p209
all things being **equal** p1324
first among **equals** p464
err on the side of caution p412
see the **error** of [your] ways p412
There's no **escaping** the fact p413
the Protestant work **ethic** p999
can't **even** begin p102
better/bigger/more etc than **ever** p418
ever so/ever such a p418
if **ever** there was one p418
every nook and cranny p843
every now and again/then p419
every now and then/again p848
every once in a while p865
every so often p419
every trick in the book p1364
every which way p418
Give me any day/ **every** time p527
have a finger in **every** pie p461

strain **every** nerve p1260
[He/She] deserves whatever/ **everything** [he/she] gets p330
everything but/except the kitchen sink p419
that beats **everything** p98
turn Queen's **evidence** p1019
the lesser of two **evils** p715
my point **exactly** p955
your **Excellency**/his Excellency p421
everything but/ **except** the kitchen sink p419
present company **excepted** p979
the **exception** that proves the rule p421
be nothing to get **excited** about p422
Excuse/Pardon my French p497
against/contrary to all **expectations** p425
no **expense** is spared p426
spare no effort/ **expense** p1215
all **expenses** paid p426
miles too big/small/ **expensive** etc p786
chalk [sth] up to **experience** p192
put it down to **experience** p1014
if you'll pardon the **expression** p901
as far as the **eye** can/could see p432
be more to [sth] than meets the **eye** p432
be more to this than meets the **eye** p776
bird's **eye** view p115
cast an/your **eye** over [sth] p183
have an **eye** to/for the main chance p432
Here's mud in your **eye** p814
out of/from the corner of [your] **eye** p272
run [your] **eye** over p1094
There wasn't a dry **eye** in the house p379
turn a blind **eye** p1375
when [sb] was a mere twinkle in [their] father's **eye** p1380
raise a few **eyebrows** p1027
[sb's] **eyes** are bigger than [their] belly/ stomach p432
[your] **eyes** pop out of [your] head p961
a sight for sore **eyes** p1172
Are my **eyes** deceiving me p313
bags under [your] **eyes** p83
before [your] very **eyes** p432
have **eyes** in the back of [your] head p432
hit [sb] between the **eyes** p595
keep [your] **eyes** peeled/skinned p432
not take [your] **eyes** off [sb/sth] p432
pull the wool over [sb's] **eyes** p1470
roll your **eyes** p432
the scales fall from [sb's] **eyes** p1111

F

[sb's] **face** doesn't fit p434
be as plain as the nose on [your] **face** p943
be laughing on the other side of [your] **face** p703
cut off [your] nose to spite [your] **face** p300
disappear off the **face** of the earth p434
fall flat on [your] **face** p439
Get out of my **face** p434
have a **face** like the back end of a bus p434
purple in the **face**/purple with rage p1010
put on a brave **face** p143
take [sth] at **face** value p434
throw [omething] back in [sb's] **face** p1328
until [you are] blue in the **face** p126
wipe the smile off [sb's] **face** p1464
written all over [sb's] **face** p1481
accessory after the **fact** p7
accessory before the **fact** p7
There's no escaping the **fact** p413
if all else **fails** p436
damn [sb] with **faint** praise p305
a **fair** crack of the whip p437

To find an idiom, look at the word in colour in each idiom. All of the coloured words are in alphabetical order.
After each idiom there is a page number that tells you where the idiom is explained.

1498

by fair means or foul p437
it's a fair cop p437
it's fair to say p437
it's only fair p437
with [your] own fair hands p438
You can't say fairer than that p1110
be/fall under [sb's] influence/spell p1388
fall about laughing p439
fall behind schedule p1114
fall by the wayside p1441
fall between two stools p439
fall flat on [your] face p439
fall for [sth] hook line and sinker p604
fall from grace p439
fall in/into line p441
fall into [sb's] arms p439
fall into place p439
fall into the wrong hands p439
fall into the/someone's trap p439
fall off the wagon p1427
fall on deaf ears p439
fall on hard times p439
fall on stony ground p1256
get/fall into the wrong hands p1482
go down/fall like ninepins p839
nearly/almost fall off [your] chair p439
stand or fall by [sth] p1238
the scales fall from [sb's] eyes p1111
as easy as ABC/anything/falling off a log
  p386
I'm not falling for that one p441
the bottom drops/falls out of the market
  p137
bear false witness p97
under false pretences p441
What price fame/victory/success etc p983
your immediate family p625
famous last words p443
the shit hits the fan p1157
sweet fanny adams p1294
as far as the eye can/could see p432
as/so far as I can tell p444
as/so far as I know p444
as/so far as I'm concerned p444
be a far cry from [sth] p444
be far removed from [sth] p1056
few and far between p454
from far and wide p444
go too far p444
I wouldn't trust [sb] as far as I could
  throw them p1371
so far so good p444
as fast as [your] legs would carry [you]
  p446
be no hard and fast rules p571
life in the fast lane p446
pull a fast one p1005
live off the fat of the land p446
The fat is in the fire p446
a fate worse than death p447
when [sb] was a mere twinkle in [their]
  father's eye p1380
kill the fatted calf p686
Do me/us a favour p448
without fear or favour p448
be well/favourably/etc disposed to/
  towards [sth/sb] p352
put the fear of God into [you] p448
strike fear/terror into [sb] p1265
without fear or favour p448
be no mean feat p449
no mean achievement/feat p773
feather [your] own nest p449
compose your features/thoughts p247
fed up to the back teeth p450
be like feeding time at the zoo p450
bite the hand that feeds [you] p117
be/feel honour bound to do [sth] p603
be/feel under the weather p1443
feel hard done-by p572
feel like a new woman/man p835

feel sorry for yourself p1210
look/feel like a million dollars p788
look/feel like death warmed up/over p312
Monday morning feeling p802
be six feet under p1180
cut the ground from under [sb's] feet p301
have/keep [your] feet on the ground p482
jump in with both feet p678
put your feet up p1012
rush/run [sb] off [their] feet p482
stand on [your] own two feet p1238
sweep [sb] off [their] feet p1294
take the weight off [your] feet/legs p1445
the pattering of tiny feet p911
at/in one fell swoop p451
wouldn't know [sth] if [you] fell over
  one/it p693
make [your] presence felt p979
come down on one side of the fence or
  other p1170
a few well-chosen words p1447
a man/woman of few words p454
catch a few rays p185
few and far between p454
few/no/not many takers p1302
have a few too many p454
raise a few eyebrows p1027
no fewer than p454
play second fiddle p947
a level playing field p717
come out of/in left field p712
leave the field clear for [sb] p455
ten/fifty/a hundred times better p1336
[sb] couldn't act/argue/fight etc [their]
  way out of a paper bag p898
fight a losing battle p456
fight like cat and dog p184
fight tooth and nail p1345
live to fight another day p730
cut a fine figure p300
fine figure of a man/woman p457
another/the final nail in the coffin p822
find [your] own level p716
find out/see how the land lies p698
get/find your bearings p97
a pretty/fine kettle of fish p684
all very well/fine/good p1416
be all right/fine by [sb] p165
chance would be a fine thing p193
cut a fine figure p300
cut it/things fine p300
fine figure of a man/woman p457
have [sth] down to a fine art p460
not to put too fine a point on [sth] p461
have a finger in every pie p461
have/keep [your] finger on the pulse
  p1006
twist [sb] around/round [your] little
  finger p1380
wrap [sb] around/round [your] little
  finger p1479
all fingers and thumbs p1330
be all fingers and thumbs p461
could count on the fingers of one hand
  p277
slip through [sb's] fingers p1189
work [your] fingers to the bone p1472
from start to finish p1242
put the finishing touches to p462
add fuel to the fire/flames p504
come under fire p462
fire a warning shot across [sb's] bows
  p139
go through fire and water p462
not set the world on fire p1143
The fat is in the fire p446
keep a firm hand on [sth] p567
first among equals p464
first come first served p464
from the very first p464
get to/reach first base p464

make the first move p812
not know the first thing about [sth] p692
take first/second place p942
a pretty/fine kettle of fish p684
be a big fish in a small pond p465
be another/a different kettle of fish p684
be like a fish out of water p465
be neither fish nor fowl p465
drink like a fish p375
fish in troubled waters p465
fish or cut bait p465
have bigger/other fish to fry p465
There are plenty more fish in the sea p465
an iron hand/fist in a velvet glove p664
hand over fist p566
rule [sth] with an iron hand/fist p664
[sb's] face doesn't fit p434
be in no fit state to do [sth] p466
fit for human consumption p466
in/by fits and starts p466
put two and two together and make five
  p1380
Roll on the weekend/five o'clock etc p1083
be of/have no fixed abode/address p467
keep the flag flying p468
add fuel to the fire/flames p504
burst into flames p161
go up in flames p469
shoot [sth/sb] down in flames p1159
fall flat on [your] face p439
send [sb] away with a flea in [their] ear
  p471
[your] own flesh and blood p889
be [sb's] own flesh and blood p472
be only flesh and blood p472
make [your] flesh crawl/creep p472
put flesh on the bones of [sth] p472
drop like flies p478
long-haul flight/short-haul flight p575
fling up [your] hands p473
flog a dead horse p474
go through the floor p475
pick [yourself] up off the floor p932
go against the flow p476
flush [sth] down the toilet p477
make [your] heart flutter p478
fly into a rage p478
fly off the handle p478
go fly a kite p478
go/fly off at a tangent p1306
wouldn't harm/hurt a fly p478
keep the flag flying p468
fold your arms p480
be a hard/tough act to follow p12
come/follow hard/hot on the heels of
  [sth] p584
follow/steer/take the middle course/
  way/path p784
give [sb] food for thought p481
live in a fool's paradise p482
You could have fooled me p482
suffer fools gladly p1279
catch [sb] on the wrong foot p1482
from head to foot/toe p578
get a/[your] foot in the door p482
get off on the right/wrong foot p482
have a foot in both camps p482
have one foot in the grave p482
not put a foot wrong p482
put [your] best foot forward p107
put [your] foot down p482
put one foot in front of the other p482
the boot/shoe is on the other foot p134
by sheer force/weight of numbers p849
force/ram [sth] down [sb's] throat p1328
tug at/touch [your] forelock p486
speak with a forked tongue p488
in any shape or form p1151
be a shadow of [your] former self p1148
be like Fort Knox p489
hold down the fort p598

To find an idiom, look at the word in colour in each idiom. All of the coloured words are in alphabetical order.
After each idiom there is a page number that tells you where the idiom is explained.

1499

cost an arm and a leg/a small fortune p275

be backward in coming forward p81

from that day forward p490

one step forward two steps back p1248

put [your] best foot forward p107

put/turn the clocks forward p222

by fair means or foul p437

tried and found wanting p1432

the fount of all knowledge/gossip/ wisdom etc p491

a quarter past/ after two/three/four etc p1019

all/the four corners of the world/earth p272

be scattered to the four winds p1113

be neither fish nor fowl p465

fray around/at the edges p494

be cold enough to freeze the balls off a brass monkey p497

when hell freezes over p585

Excuse/Pardon my French p497

a breath of fresh air p147

break fresh/new ground p144

man's best friend p756

have friends in high places p590

frighten/scare etc the living daylights out of [sb] p309

a blast from the past p120

a bolt from/out of the blue p131

a gift from the gods p525

be a far cry from [sth] p444

be far removed from [sth] p1056

be plenty more where [sb/sth] came from p949

by/from all accounts p8

come back from the dead p310

come from behind p236

cut the ground from under [sb's] feet p301

fall from grace p439

from 630/March/the 1870s etc onwards p868

from a standing start p1238

from beyond the grave p110

from dawn to dusk p308

from far and wide p444

from head to foot/toe p578

from now on/as from now p848

from pillar to post p937

from start to finish p1242

from stem to stern p1247

from that day forward p490

from that day/time onwards p500

from the bottom of [your] heart p137

from the cradle to the grave p284

from the sublime to the ridiculous p1274

from the very first p464

from the word go p1472

from top to bottom p1346

from top to toe p1346

from under [your] nose p844

from where [sb] stands p1238

from/since the year dot p1485

from/since time immemorial p625

get blood out of/from a stone p124

go from bad to worse p82

go from strength to strength p1263

home from home p601

keep the wolf from the door p1468

know/see where [sb] is coming from p1452

live from hand to mouth p566

manna from heaven p759

miles from anywhere/nowhere p786

not know [sb] from Adam p693

not know [your] arse from [your] elbow p59

Nothing could have been further from my mind/thoughts p508

out of/from the corner of [your] eye p272

pull the rug from under [sb/sb's feet] p1005

read [sth] from cover to cover p281

remove [sth] from [your] shelves p1155

rise from the dead/grave p1079

rise from/through the ranks p1030

separate the wheat from the chaff p1451

separate/sort out the sheep from the goats p1154

shout/proclaim [sth] from the rooftops p1085

snatch victory from the jaws of defeat p1198

straight from the horse's mouth p607

take [your] cue from [sb] p296

take [your] cue from [sth/sb] p296

the scales fall from [sb's] eyes p1111

to/from all appearances p50

know [sth] back to front p692

put one foot in front of the other p482

have bigger/other fish to fry p465

add fuel to the fire/flames p504

a full/good/thick etc head of hair p578

be full of [your] own importance p504

be full of the joys of spring p504

come to a full stop p505

come/go/turn full circle p504

full steam ahead p505

know full well p505

not be all fun and games p506

funny ha-ha or funny peculiar p507

can't see further than the end of [your] nose p1129

go further/take [sth] further p508

Nothing could have been further from my mind/thoughts p508

without further/more ado p16

kick up a fuss/row/stink p685

make a fuss of/over [sb] p509

no muss no fuss p818

G

a whole new ball game p85

be new to this game p513

beat [sb] at [their] own game p98

give the game away p513

two can play at that game p1381

poacher turned gamekeeper p954

not be all fun and games p506

lead [sb] up the garden path p707

gather up strength/courage p516

take/pick up the gauntlet p516

throw down the gauntlet p516

gaze at/contemplate [your] navel p827

step/move up a gear p517

be on/ in general release p1052

be nothing if not generous/honest/ thorough etc p846

[He/She] deserves whatever/everything [he/she] gets p330

word gets about/around/round p1471

You're getting colder p230

give up the ghost p524

lay the ghost of [sth] to rest p705

look like/as though [you've] seen a ghost p524

a gift from the gods p525

be green/pale about the gills p525

there's a good boy/girl/dog p1322

[I] would give anything/a lot p527

Don't give me that p527

give [sb] a dirty look p344

give [sb] a dose/taste of [their] own medicine p775

give [sb] a hard time p1335

give [sb] a leg up p712

give [sb] a piece of your mind p934

give [sb] a run for [their] money p1094

give [sb] food for thought p481

give [sb] something to talk about p1304

give [sb] the benefit of the doubt p106

give [sb] the cold shoulder p230

give [sb] the time of day p1334

give [sb] their due p380

give [sb] up for dead p528

give [sth/sb] a wide berth p1458

give [sth] up as a bad job p82

give [sth] your best shot p1162

give [your] right arm p1076

Give me any day/every time p527

give someone a mouthful p812

give someone the brush-off p154

give the game away p513

give the green light to [sth] p549

give up hope p528

give up the ghost p524

give/lend [sb] a helping hand p586

give/quote [sth/sb] chapter and verse p195

not care/give two hoots p605

not give a tinker's cuss p1337

not give much for [sb's] chances p193

to give the devil his due p335

what I wouldn't give for [sth] p527

wouldn't give [sth] house-room p611

given half a the/chance p563

suffer fools gladly p1279

without so much as a backward glance p1467

look at/see [sth] through rose-coloured/ tinted glasses p1087

paint a bleak/gloomy/rosy etc picture of [sth] p894

bask/bathe in reflected glory p531

take the gloss off [sth] p531

an iron hand/fist in a velvet glove p664

handle/treat [sb] with kid gloves p686

go off at half-cock/ go off half-cocked p564

a long way to go p736

be in hiding/go into hiding p590

be/go at it hammer and tongs p565

be/go into ecstasies about/over [sth] p389

be/go round the twist p1380

come/go down in the world p367

come/go under the hammer p565

come/go/be along for the ride p33

come/go/turn full circle p504

crawl/go/retreat/retire into [your] shell p1155

easy come easy go p387

from the word go p1472

get/go beyond a joke p675

go [your] own separate ways p1139

go [your] own sweet way p1440

go [your] own way p1440

go a long way p736

go a long way towards doing [sth] p736

go about [your] business p534

go according to plan p944

go against the flow p476

go against the grain p545

go all round the houses p610

go all the way p1440

go and jump in the lake p678

go and take a running jump p1094

go arse over tit/tip p59

go back a long way p736

Go back to sleep p1186

go back to the drawing board p372

go by the board p128

go by the name of [sth] p823

go cap in hand to [sb] p174

go down like a lead balloon p707

go down the gurgler p559

go down the pan p896

go down the tubes p1373

go down the wrong way p1481

go down/fall like ninepins p839

go fly a kite p478

To find an idiom, look at the word in colour in each idiom. All of the coloured words are in alphabetical order.
After each idiom there is a page number that tells you where the idiom is explained.

1500

go from bad to worse p82
go from strength to strength p1263
go further/take [sth] further p508
go great guns p548
go hand in hand with [sth] p566
go in one ear and out the other p384
go into a huddle p613
go into detail p333
go into orbit p873
go into rhapsodies p1072
go into the stratosphere p1261
go into/enter the church p209
go like a bomb p131
go like/down a bomb p131
go off the boil p130
go off the deep end p316
go off the rails p1026
go off without a hitch p596
go one better p109
go out like a light p722
go over [sb's] head p578
go over [sth] in [your] mind p789
go play with yourself p948
go the whole hog p1456
go through a bad/difficult/rough/sticky
    patch p909
go through fire and water p462
go through the floor p475
go through the motions p809
go through the roof p1085
go to great lengths p714
go to hell and back p585
go to/take great pains to do [sth] p894
go too far p444
go trick or treating p1364
go under the knife p689
go up in flames p469
go up in smoke p1195
go/be back to square one p1231
go/be run to ground p552
go/come down in the world p1475
go/come up in the world p1475
go/fly off at a tangent p1306
go/get back to nature p826
go/jump through hoops p605
go/run round in circles p210
go/sell like hot cakes p608
go/swim against the tide p1331
go/turn belly up p104
go/turn bright red p1044
go/walk down the aisle p28
here we go p588
here we go again p588
leave/go off etc with [your] tail between
    [your] legs p1301
make [sth] up as you go along p754
make the world go around/round p1475
mind how you go p789
On your marks get set go p763
One/Two etc down one/two etc to go p367
run/go like clockwork p222
there [you] go again p1322
things that go bump in the night p1324
vanish/go up/disappear in a puff of
    smoke p1004
watch the world go by p1436
work/go like a dream p373
separate/sort out the sheep from the
    goats p1154
keep [your] gob shut p537
by the grace of God p544
Oh my God p538
put the fear of God into [you] p448
so help me God p586
a gift from the gods p525
[your] mind is a blank/goes blank p789
it goes without saying p1110
the balloon goes up p85
what [sb] says goes p1110

what/whatever [sb] says goes p1450
not know whether you are coming or
    going p236
while the going is good p539
be worth [your/its] weight in gold p1477
like gold dust p539
the streets are paved with gold p1262
kill the goose that lays the golden egg
    p686
in days gone by p534
a full/good/thick etc head of hair p578
all in good time p541
all very well/fine/good p1416
be up to no good p541
do more harm than good p573
do/make a good job of [sth] p673
get off to a good start p540
good riddance to bad rubbish p1074
have a good run for [your] money p1094
have a good/healthy pair of lungs p746
have half a mind/a good mind to [do sth]
    p789
have something on good authority p72
it's a good job/thing p540
it's a good thing p1323
Jolly good show p676
make good time p540
put in a good word for [sb] p1471
so far so good p444
stand [sb] in good stead p1238
stand sb in good stead p1245
that's a good point p955
there's a good boy/girl/dog p1322
throw good money after bad p1329
too good to be true p1345
too good to miss p1345
too much of a good thing p1345
turn/use [sth] to good account p8
while the going is good p539
Your guess is as good as mine p556
come up with the goods p541
sell [sb] a bill of goods p1135
kill the goose that lays the golden egg
    p686
make [your] gorge rise p542
the fount of all knowledge/gossip/wisdom
    etc p491
Has the cat has got your tongue p184
have got something there p1208
Pull the other leg/one it's got bells on
    p1005
What have you got to say for [yourself]
    p1110
You've got me there p522
You've got nothing to lose p740
you've got to laugh p704
Her/His Majesty's Government p543
by the grace of God p544
fall from grace p439
put on airs and graces p26
go against the grain p545
grand old age p545
the grand old man of [sth] p545
teach your grandmother to suck eggs
    p545
hear [sth] on/through the grapevine p546
grateful/thankful for small mercies p1192
dig [your] own grave p340
drive/send [sb] to an early grave p385
from beyond the grave p110
from the cradle to the grave p284
have one foot in the grave p482
rise from the dead/grave p1079
like greased lightning p548
a pearl of great price p914
be one/another of life's great mysteries
    p720
go great guns p548
go to great lengths p714
go to/take great pains to do [sth] p894
great minds think alike p548

no great shakes p548
set great/little etc store by something
    p1257
It's all Greek to me p549
the Greek/Russian/Eastern Orthodox
    Church p876
be green/pale about the gills p525
give the green light to [sth] p549
greet/welcome [sb] with open arms p868
hang/hold on like grim death p550
keep/put [your] nose to the grindstone
    p844
grist to the mill/ grist for someone's mill
    p551
groan with/under the weight of [sth] p552
break fresh/new ground p144
claim the moral high ground p213
cut the ground from under [sb's] feet p301
drive/work [yourself] into the ground
    p552
fall on stony ground p1256
go/be run to ground p552
have/keep [your] ear to the ground p384
have/keep [your] feet on the ground p482
hit the ground running p595
run [yourself] into the ground p1093
suit [sb] right down to the ground p1280
worship the ground [sb] walks on p1477
take [a place or group of people] by storm
    p1258
catch [sb] off guard p555
mount guard on/over [sb] p810
Your guess is as good as mine p556
no prizes for guessing [sth] p987
Be my guest p556
go great guns p548
go down the gurgler p559
no more Mr Nice Guy p813

H

funny ha-ha or funny peculiar p507
unfit for human habitation p561
make [sb's] hackles rise p561
be within hailing distance of [some-
    where] p562
a full/good/thick etc head of hair p578
harm a hair on [sb's] head p574
let [your] hair down p715
make [sb's] hair stand on end p562
not see hide nor hair of p1130
the hair of the dog that bit you p562
That'll put hairs on [your] chest p562
be too clever by half p219
cheap at half the price p199
given half a/the chance p563
half as much again p563
have half a mind/a good mind to [do sth]
    p789
how the other half lives p563
something like 96%/half etc p1208
go off at half-cock/ go off half-cocked
    p564
go off at half-cock/ go off half-cocked
    p564
not do things by halves p563
be/go at it hammer and tongs p565
come/go under the hammer p565
drive/hammer [sth] home p601
an iron hand/fist in a velvet glove p664
bite the hand that feeds [you] p117
could count on the fingers of one hand
    p277
cross [sb's] hand/palm with silver p291
give/lend [sb] a helping hand p586
go cap in hand to [sb] p174
go hand in hand with [sth] p566
hand over fist p566
have/hold the whip hand p1453
keep a firm hand on [sth] p567

To find an idiom, look at the word in colour in each idiom. All of the coloured words are in alphabetical order.
After each idiom there is a page number that tells you where the idiom is explained.

1501

know [sth] like the back of [your] hand p692

live from hand to mouth p566

put [your] hand in [your] pocket p567

raise [your] hand to/against [sb] p1027

rule [sth] with an iron hand/fist p664

shake [sb's] hand/shake [sb] by the hand p1149

be too hot to handle p608

fly off the handle p478

handle/treat [sb] with kid gloves p686

a safe pair of hands p567

be like putty in [sb's] hands p1016

dirty your hands p344

fall into the wrong hands p439

fling up [your] hands p473

get/fall into the wrong hands p1482

take [your] life in [your] hands p720

take matters into [your] own hands p770

take the law into [your] own hands p705

throw up [your] hands in horror/despair p1329

win [sth] hands down p567

win hands down p1460

with [your] own fair hands p438

hang by a thread p569

hang/hold on like grim death p550

let it all hang out p715

I'll be hanged if p569

I'll be hanged if I know p569

have [sb/sth] hanging round [your] neck p569

an accident waiting to happen p7

the best/happiest days of [your] life p309

many happy returns of the day p760

a hard/tough nut to crack p850

be a hard/tough act to follow p12

be caught between a rock and a hard place p1082

be no hard and fast rules p571

come/follow hard/hot on the heels of [sth] p584

drive a hard bargain p376

fall on hard times p439

feel hard done-by p572

give [sb] a hard time p1335

school of hard knocks p1115

take a hard line on [sb]/[sth] p572

that's [your] hard luck p572

think long and hard p1325

too much like hard work p1345

as mad as a hatter/March hare p749

do more harm than good p573

harm a hair on [sb's] head p574

wouldn't harm/hurt a fly p478

I'll eat my hat p387

pass the hat around/round p905

take [your] hat off to [sb] p575

talk through [your] hat p1304

throw [your] hat into the ring p575

batten down the hatches p94

as mad as a hatter/March hare p749

haul/drag [sb] over the coals p226

pull/haul yourself up by your bootstraps p134

Is he/she for real p1037

[your] eyes pop out of [your] head p961

a full/good/thick etc head of hair p578

a roof over [your] head p1085

an old/a wise head on young shoulders p578

be banging etc [your] head against a brick wall p578

be like a bear with a sore head p97

be not quite right in the head p1076

bite [sb's] head off p117

bite/snap [sb's] head off p578

bury/have [your] head in the sand p578

can't get [your] head around p578

can't make head nor tail of [sth] p578

from head to foot/toe p578

get/put [your] head down p578

go over [sb's] head p578

harm a hair on [sb's] head p574

have eyes in the back of [your] head p432

have your head buried/stuck in a book p578

have your head in the clouds p578

have your head screwed on the right way p578

have/put [your] head on the block p123

head and shoulders above p578

head over heels in love p578

hit the nail on the head p595

hold [your] head up high p597

keep [your] head above water p578

keep [your] head down p578

Keep a civil tongue in [your] head p212

keep a cool head p269

laugh [your] head off p703

laugh/shout/scream etc [your] head off p578

need [sth] like [you] need a hole in the head p830

need [sth] like you need a hole in the head p599

off the top of [your] head p1346

put [your] head over/above the parapet p900

put ideas into [sb's] head p621

rear its ugly head p1038

run in/through [your] head/mind p1094

run through [your] mind/head p1094

snap [sb's] head off p1198

take it into [your] head to do [sth] p578

talk [sb's] head off p1304

run round like a headless chicken p578

Heads will roll p578

put [their] heads together p578

clean bill of health p216

have a good/healthy pair of lungs p746

can't hear [yourself] think p580

hear [sth] on/through the grapevine p546

hear warning bells p1434

hear wedding bells p580

will never hear the end of it p580

I must be hearing things p580

[her/his] heart is in the right place p581

[your] heart skips/misses a beat p581

after [your] own heart p581

from the bottom of [your] heart p137

make [your] heart flutter p478

my heart bleeds for [sb] p581

nearly/almost have a heart attack p582

off by heart p581

open [your] heart to someone p868

put [your] heart and soul into [sth] p581

wear [your] heart on [your] sleeve p1442

take the heat off [sb] p582

heave a sigh of relief p583

manna from heaven p759

move heaven and earth p812

a heavy cross to bear p291

make heavy weather of [sth] p583

come/follow hard/hot on the heels of [sth] p584

head over heels in love p578

kick up [your] heels p685

all hell breaks loose p585

come hell or high water p585

go to hell and back p585

make [sb's] life hell p585

not have a snowball's chance in hell p1201

play merry hell with [sth] p947

see [sb] in hell before p1130

there'll be hell to pay p585

when hell freezes over p585

not have a cat in hell's chance p184

so help me God p585

there's no help for it p586

give/lend [sb] a helping hand p586

a nip here and a tuck there p839

be neither here nor there p832

here we go p588

here we go again p588

Here's mud in your eye p814

all by herself p587

cover/hide a multitude of sins p816

not see hide nor hair of p1130

save [your] own skin/hide p1109

be in hiding/go into hiding p590

claim the moral high ground p213

come hell or high water p585

come/get down off [you] high horse p591

have friends in high places p590

hold [sb] in high/low repute p1060

hold [your] head up high p597

hunt/search high and low p590

leave [sb] high and dry p590

live high on/off the hog p591

passions run high p907

move on to higher/better things p812

think highly of/well of/a lot of etc [sb] p1325

Her/His/Your Royal Highness p1090

all by himself p593

talk the hind legs off a donkey p1304

without let or hindrance p716

make legal history p712

hit [sb] between the eyes p595

hit [sb] where it hurts p595

hit the ground running p595

hit the nail on the head p595

hit/press/push the panic button p897

hit/touch a raw nerve p832

kick/hit [sb] when [they are] down p367

not know what has hit [you] p692

not know what hit you p595

touch/strike/hit a raw nerve p1349

go off without a hitch p596

the shit hits the fan p1157

jolly hockey sticks p676

go the whole hog p1456

live high on/off the hog p591

be hoisted with/by [your] own petard p927

can't hold [your] drink p598

can't hold a candle to p597

Don't hold [your] breath p147

don't hold your breath p598

hang/hold on like grim death p550

have/hold all the aces p10

have/hold the whip hand p1453

hold [sb/sth] up to ridicule p1075

hold [sb] in high/low repute p1060

hold [your] head up high p597

hold all the cards p598

hold down a job p599

hold down the fort p598

hold out/offer an olive branch p863

hold the balance of power p84

hold your nose p597

keep/hold [your] cards close to [your] chest p176

keep/hold [your] end up p402

be left holding the baby p710

there is no holding [sb] back p598

no holds barred p598

burn a hole in [sb's] pocket p160

dig [yourself] into a hole p340

need [sth] like [you] need a hole in the head p830

need [sth] like you need a hole in the head p599

square peg in a round hole p1231

bring home the bacon p150

come back/home to roost p1086

drive [your] message/point home p376

drive/hammer [sth] home p601

eat [sb] out of house and home p387

home from home p601

To find an idiom, look at the word in colour in each idiom. All of the coloured words are in alphabetical order.
After each idiom there is a page number that tells you where the idiom is explained.

1502

nothing to write home about p1481
press home [your] advantage p981
till/until the cows come home p282
be nothing if not generous/honest/
thorough etc p846
make an honest living p603
make an honest woman out of [sb] p603
land of milk and honey p698
be/feel honour bound to do [sth] p603
by hook or by crook p604
fall for [sth] hook line and sinker p604
wriggle off the hook p1480
go/jump through hoops p605
not care/give two hoots p605
give up hope p528
blow [your] own trumpet/horn p125
take the bull by the horns p157
throw up [your] hands in horror/despair
p1329
back the wrong horse p79
come/get down off [you] high horse p591
eat like a horse p387
flog a dead horse p474
I'm so hungry I could eat a horse p387
put the cart before the horse p181
shut/close the stable/barn door after the
horse has bolted p363
straight from the horse's mouth p607
drive a coach and horses through [sth]
p375
wild horses wouldn't drag me p1459
all hot and bothered p608
be too hot to handle p608
blow hot and cold p125
come/follow hard/hot on the heels of
[sth] p584
drop [sb/sth] like a hot potato p377
go/sell like hot cakes p608
hot off the press p608
hot under the collar p608
like a cat on a hot tin roof p184
strike while the iron is hot p1265
at all hours of the day and night p591
in/within the space of six weeks/three
hours etc p1214
till all hours p610
work long/regular/unsocial etc hours
p609
eat [sb] out of house and home p387
get/put [your] own house in order p610
There wasn't a dry eye in the house p379
under house arrest p610
wouldn't give [sth] house-room p611
go all round the houses p610
hove into sight/view p611
find out/see how the land lies p698
How about that p612
How are you placed for[] p942
how much do you want to bet p108
How should [I] know p1162
How strange/stupid/weird etc is that p612
how the other half lives p563
How would [you] like[] p723
I don't know how/what/why etc p692
mind how you go p789
How's life treating you p720
go into a huddle p613
fit for human consumption p466
the milk of human kindness p787
the sanctity of human life/marriage etc
p1105
unfit for human habitation p561
eat humble pie p387
a/one hundred per cent p615
ninety-nine times out of a hundred p839
ten/fifty/a hundred times better p1336
hung drawn and quartered p615
I'm so hungry I could eat a horse p387
hunt/search high and low p590
wouldn't harm/hurt a fly p478
hit [sb] where it hurts p595

I

as/so far as I can tell p444
as/so far as I know p444
Do I make [myself] clear p217
I beg your pardon p102
I daresay/I dare say p307
I don't know how/what/why etc p692
I don't mind if I do p790
I must be hearing things p580
I rest my case p1065
I should think not/so too p1162
I wouldn't say no p1110
I wouldn't trust [sb] as far as I could
throw them p1371
I'll be hanged if I know p569
I'll/We'll cross that bridge when I/we get
to it p291
I'm so hungry I could eat a horse p387
I/You wouldn't wish [sth] on anyone/
my/your worst enemy p1465
if I were in your shoes p1159
it's the least I can do p710
Need I say more p830
That's all I/you/we need p30
the next thing I knew p836
what I wouldn't give for [sth] p527
you know what I mean p692
I'd like to see[] p723
I'll be a monkey's uncle p803
I'll be hanged if p569
I'll be hanged if I know p569
I'll eat my hat p387
I'll wring [your/his/her] neck p1480
I'll/We'll cross that bridge when I/we get
to it p291
well I'll be blowed p125
Well I'll be damned p305
you scratch my back and I'll scratch
yours p1119
as/so far as I'm concerned p444
correct me if I'm wrong but p273
I'm just looking p737
I'm not falling for that one p441
I'm pleased to meet you p949
I'm so hungry I could eat a horse p387
I'm sorry to say p1210
dot the i's and cross the t's p365
be skating on thin ice p1181
cut no ice with [sb] p300
What's the big idea p112
put ideas into [sb's] head p621
as if [you] owned the place p889
as if to the manner born p759
as/if/when/etc the spirit moves [sb] p1224
be nothing if not generous/honest/
thorough etc p846
correct me if I'm wrong but p273
I don't mind if I do p790
I'll be hanged if p569
I'll be hanged if I know p569
if all else fails p436
if ever there was one p418
if I were in your shoes p1159
if my memory serves me right p1141
if the worst comes to the worst p1477
if you catch/get my drift p374
if you don't take my meaning p1302
if you take my meaning p1302
if you'll pardon the expression p901
if/when it comes to the crunch p294
if/when push comes to shove p1011
nice work if you can get it p837
sound like/as if/as though p1212
wouldn't know [sth] if [you] fell over
one/it p693
no ifs and buts p622
bear [sb] ill will p624
can ill afford to do [sth] p623
labour under the delusion/illusion/

misapprehension etc p695
by no stretch of the imagination p1264
your immediate family p625
from/since time immemorial p625
be full of [your] own importance p504
come within an inch of [sth] p634
be incumbent on/upon someone p637
too many chiefs and not enough Indians
p203
be/fall under [sb's] influence/spell p1388
man's inhumanity to man p756
on your own initiative p646
to add insult to injury p14
assist the police with/in their inquiries
p65
pale into insignificance p895
to add insult to injury p14
to/for all intents and purposes p654
be in hiding/go into hiding p590
be in leaf/come into leaf p708
be/go into ecstasies about/over [sth] p389
beat/turn swords into ploughshares p1297
blend into the scenery p1114
bluff [your] way into/out of [sth] p127
breathe new life into p147
bring [sth] out into the open p869
burst into flames p161
burst into song/tears/laughter p161
burst into tears p1310
call into question p168
come into [your] own p889
come into bloom p125
come into play p947
crawl/go/retreat/retire into [your] shell
p1155
cut/tear [sth/sb] to/into ribbons p1073
dig [yourself] into a hole p340
disappear/vanish into thin air p1323
dissolve into tears/laughter p353
drive/work [yourself] into the ground
p552
enter/get into the spirit p1224
fall in/into line p441
fall into [sb's] arms p439
fall into place p439
fall into the wrong hands p439
fall into the/someone's trap p439
fly into a rage p478
get [sth] into [your] thick skull p1183
get into the swing of it/things p1296
get/fall into the wrong hands p1482
go into a huddle p613
go into detail p333
go into orbit p873
go into reverse p1071
go into rhapsodies p1072
go into the stratosphere p1261
go into/enter the church p209
hove into sight/view p611
kick [sth] into touch p685
knock into each other/knock through
p690
knock some sense into [sb] p690
knock/lick [sth/sb] into shape p1152
pale into insignificance p895
poke/stick [your] nose into [sth] p844
press [sth/sb] into service p981
put [sth] into perspective p925
put [your] back into [sth] p1012
put [your] heart and soul into [sth] p581
put ideas into [sb's] head p621
put the fear of God into [you] p448
put the roses back into [sb's] cheeks p1087
put words in/into [sb's] mouth p1471
put/stick the knife into [sb] p689
ride/drive/walk/etc off into the sunset
p1283
rolled into one p1083
run [yourself] into the ground p1093
shovel [sth] into [your] mouth p1164
step into [sb's] shoes p1159

To find an idiom, look at the word in colour in each idiom. All of the coloured words are in alphabetical order.
After each idiom there is a page number that tells you where the idiom is explained.

step into the breach p1247
strike fear/terror into [sb] p1265
swing into action p1296
take [sb] into [your] confidence p254
take into account/take account of p9
take it into [your] head to do [sth] p578
take matters into [your] own hands p770
take the law into [your] own hands p705
talk your way into/out of [sth] p1440
throw [your] hat into the ring p575
walk right into [sth] p1429
driving while intoxicated p375
an iron hand/fist in a velvet glove p664
rule [sth] with an iron hand/fist p664
strike while the iron is hot p1265
there isn't a thing [you] can do p1324
for what it's worth p1477
it's [your] own lookout p738
it's a fair cop p437
it's a good job/thing p540
it's a good thing p1323
It's all Greek to me p549
It's all right p32
It's early days p384
it's fair to say p437
It's just as well that p680
It's more than my job's worth p673
it's not rocket science p1082
it's only fair p437
it's the least I can do p710
It's the same old story p1105
It's/That's the story of my life p1258
more trouble than it's worth p1368
Pull the other leg/one it's got bells on p1005
American/Italian etc by birth p116
be in a class by itself/of its own p215

J

before you can say Jack Robinson p1110
before you can/could say Jack Robinson p668
jaw drops open p670
snatch victory from the jaws of defeat p1198
and all that jazz p670
do/make a good job of [sth] p673
give [sth] up as a bad job p82
hold down a job p599
it's a good job/thing p540
just the man/woman for the job p673
lie down on the job p719
It's more than my job's worth p673
put [sb's] nose out of joint p844
get/go beyond a joke p675
Jolly good show p676
jolly hockey sticks p676
keep up with the Joneses p683
cheque book journalism p201
cheek by jowl p200
be full of the joys of spring p504
against [your] better judgment p22
more by luck than judgment p744
sit in judgment on/over someone p1178
stew in [your] own juice p1249
be/stay/keep one jump ahead p678
go and jump in the lake p678
go and take a running jump p1094
go/jump through hoops p605
jump down [sb's] throat p678
jump in at the deep end p316
jump in with both feet p678
be jumping up and down p678
I'm just looking p737
it's just as well that p680
just around the corner p272
just like that p680
Just my luck p680
just one of those things p1324

just the man/woman for the job p673
just this once p865
just to be on the safe side p1100
just what the doctor ordered p360
Life is just a bowl of cherries p139
might just as well p680
would just as soon p1209
pervert the course of justice p926

K

be/stay/keep one jump ahead p678
change with/keep up with/move with the times p1335
have/keep [your] ear to the ground p384
have/keep [your] feet on the ground p482
have/keep [your] finger on the pulse p1006
have/keep [your] options open p872
have/keep all [your] wits about [you] p1468
have/keep an open mind p870
keep [sb] at arm's length p57
keep [your] eyes peeled/skinned p432
keep [your] gob shut p537
keep [your] head above water p578
keep [your] head down p578
keep [your] mouth shut p811
keep [your] nose clean p844
keep [your] own counsel p277
Keep a civil tongue in [your] head p212
keep a cool head p269
keep a diary/an account/a record etc p682
keep a firm hand on [sth] p567
keep a low profile p991
keep a tight rein on [sb/sth] p1050
keep body and soul together p129
keep on the right side of [sb] p1170
keep the flag flying p468
keep the wolf from the door p1468
keep up appearances p683
keep up with the Joneses p683
keep your pecker up p914
keep your promise/word; keep an appointment p682
keep/hold [your] cards close to [your] chest p176
keep/hold [your] end up p402
keep/place [sb] under restraint p1066
keep/put [your] nose to the grindstone p844
save/keep money for a rainy day p1027
a pretty/fine kettle of fish p684
be another/a different kettle of fish p684
under lock and key p733
kick in the teeth p685
a boot/kick up [the/your] backside p81
a kick up the arse/backside p685
create/kick up/raise a stink p1253
kick [sth] into touch p685
kick against the pricks p685
kick over the traces p685
kick some ass p685
kick up [your] heels p685
kick up a fuss/row/stink p685
kick/hit [sb] when [they are] down p367
handle/treat [sb] with kid gloves p686
kill the fatted calf p686
kill the goose that lays the golden egg p686
kill two birds with one stone p686
the milk of human kindness p787
live like a king/lord p731
lord/master/mistress/king/queen of all [you] survey p1289
blast/blow [sb/sth] to kingdom come p687
till/until kingdom come p687
Kiss my arse p688
the whole kit and caboodle p166

everything but/except the kitchen sink p419
go fly a kite p478
the next thing I knew p836
go under the knife p689
put/stick the knife into [sb] p689
twist/turn the knife in the wound p689
you could cut the atmosphere with a knife p300
a knight in shining armour p690
and the same to you with brass knobs on p690
beat/knock the living daylights out of [sb] p309
Knock 'em dead p690
knock [sb's] block off p690
knock [sb] off [their] pedestal p690
knock [sb] sideways/for six p690
knock into each other/knock through p690
knock some sense into [sb] p690
knock spots off [sth] p690
knock/lick [sth/sb] into shape p1152
school of hard knocks p1115
tie [sb] up in knots p1332
as/so far as I know p444
have/know [sth] off pat p908
How should [I] know p1162
I don't know how/what/why etc p692
I'll be hanged if I know p569
know [sb] by name p693
know [sb] by sight p693
know [sth] back to front p692
know [sth] like the back of [your] hand p692
know [your] own mind p692
know [your] way around [sth] p693
know better than [sb] p692
know better than to do [sth] p692
know full well p505
know what [you] are talking about p692
know when [you] are well off p1448
know where you stand p1238
know which side [your] bread is buttered on p692
know/see where [sb] is coming from p1452
not know [sb] from Adam p693
not know [your] arse from [your] elbow p59
not know the first thing about [sth] p692
not know what [sb] sees in [sb/sth] p1130
not know what has hit [you] p692
not know what hit you p595
not know where to put [yourself] p692
not know where/which way to turn p692
not know whether to laugh or cry p692
not know whether you are coming or going p236
Well what do you know p692
wouldn't know [sth] if [you] fell over one/it p693
You know something p692
you know what I mean p692
there's no knowing p692
there's no knowing/telling/saying p840
the fount of all knowledge/gossip/wisdom etc p491
[sth] knows no bounds p693
be like Fort Knox p489
a rap on/over the knuckles p1030
rap [sb] over the knuckles p1030

L

be/live in la-la land p697
labour under the delusion/illusion/misapprehension etc p695
be on the lowest/bottom rung of the ladder p1096

To find an idiom, look at the word in colour in each idiom. All of the coloured words are in alphabetical order. After each idiom there is a page number that tells you where the idiom is explained.

To find an idiom, look at the word in colour in each idiom. All of the coloured words are in alphabetical order.
After each idiom there is a page number that tells you where the idiom is explained.

1505

packed/squashed like sardines p1107
run round like a headless chicken p578
run/go like clockwork p222
sink like a stone p1177
sleep like a log p1186
something like 96%/half etc p1208
sound like/as if/as though p1212
spread like wildfire p1459
stand/stick out like a sore thumb p1210
swear like a trooper p1367
take to [sth] like a duck to water p380
That's more like it p806
too much like hard work p1345
treat [sb] like dirt p1362
treat [sb] like royalty p1362
turn up like a bad penny p1377
we like cheap/tall/young etc p723
work like a charm p1472
work/go like a dream p373
That's a likely story p724
all along the line p726
fall for [sth] hook line and sinker p604
fall in/into line p441
sign on the dotted line p1173
somewhere along the line p726
take a hard line on [sb]/[sth] p572
wash [your] dirty linen in public p1434
read between the lines p1035
beard the lion in [his/her] den p98
pay lip service to [sth] p728
my lips are sealed p728
read my lips p1035
a list as long as [your] arm p728
be on/off the danger list p306
a little bird told me p730
be no/little love lost between p742
be nothing/not much/very little in it p632
little/not much to choose between p206
set great/little etc store by something p1257
something a little stronger p1208
there's little to be said for p1110
too little too late p1345
twist [sb] around/round [your] little finger p1380
wrap [sb] around/round [your] little finger p1479
be/live in each other's pockets p954
be/live in la-la land p697
lead/live a charmed life p197
lead/live the life of Riley p720
live beyond [your] means p773
live by [your] wits p731
live from hand to mouth p566
live high on/off the hog p591
live in a fool's paradise p482
live like a king/lord p731
live off the fat of the land p446
live on borrowed time p136
live to fight another day p730
live to tell the tale p730
never live [sth] down p731
how the other half lives p563
be living in a dream world p373
beat/knock the living daylights out of [sb] p309
frighten/scare etc the living daylights out of [sb] p309
make an honest living p603
within living memory p730
a load/weight off [your] mind p789
Get a load of that p732
lock stock and barrel p733
under lock and key p733
as easy as ABC/anything/falling off a log/pie p386
sleep like a log p1186
by/on your lonesome p736
a list as long as [your] arm p728
a long way to go p736

before very/too long p736
go a long way p736
go a long way towards doing [sth] p736
go back a long way p736
have come a long way p736
not by a long chalk/shot p736
not long for this world p736
the long arm of the law p736
think long and hard p1325
to cut a long story short p301
work long/regular/unsocial etc hours p609
long-haul flight/short-haul flight p575
give [sb] a dirty look p344
look at/see [sth] through rose-coloured/tinted glasses p1087
look like a drowned rat p377
look like something the cat brought/dragged in p184
look like/as though [you've] seen a ghost p524
look on the bright side p737
look out for number one p738
look straight/right through [sb] p737
look who's talking p1304
look young for [your] age p1487
look/feel like a million dollars p788
look/feel like death warmed up/over p312
make [sb] look small p737
never look back p737
I'm just looking p737
it's [your] own lookout p738
by the looks of things p737
all hell breaks loose p585
live like a king/lord p731
lord/master/mistress/king/queen of all [you] survey p1289
lose sleep over/about [sth] p740
no time to lose p1334
You've got nothing to lose p740
fight a losing battle p456
be no/little love lost between p742
make up for lost time p754
[I] would give anything/a lot p527
leave a lot to be desired p710
make much/a lot of [sb] p754
the best of a bad bunch/lot p107
there's a lot of it about p741
think highly of/well of/a lot of etc [sb] p1325
For crying out loud p295
be no/little love lost between p742
for love nor money p742
head over heels in love p578
hold [sb] in high/low repute p1060
hunt/search high and low p590
keep a low profile p991
be on the lowest/bottom rung of the ladder p1096
better luck next time p109
Just my luck p680
more by luck than judgment p744
no such luck p744
that's [your] hard luck p572
[I] should be so lucky p1163
thank [your] lucky stars p1319
the lull before the storm p745
bring a lump to [your] throat p745
have a good/healthy pair of lungs p746
not take [sth] lying down p719

M

as mad as a hatter/March hare p749
Dear Sir or Madam p1178
made of sterner stuff p1249
what [sb] is really made of p753
What's the magic word p750
have an eye to/for the main chance p432
detain [sb] at His/Her Majesty's pleasure

p333
Her/His Majesty's Government p543
can't make head nor tail of [sth] p578
Do I make [myself] clear p217
Do you want to make something/anything of it p754
do/make a good job of [sth] p673
Don't make me laugh p703
make [sb's] blood curdle p298
make [sb's] blood run cold p1094
make [sb's] hackles rise p561
make [sb's] hair stand on end p562
make [sb's] life hell p585
make [sb's] mouth water p811
make [sth/it] worth [your] while p1477
make [sth] all [your] own p889
make [sth] up as you go along p754
make [your] blood boil p124
make [your] blood run cold p124
make [your] flesh crawl/creep p472
make [your] gorge rise p542
make [your] heart flutter p478
make [your] presence felt p979
make a big difference p339
make a big thing out of [sth] p1323
make a clean breast of it p216
make a fuss of/over [sb] p509
make a mental note of [sth] p778
make a mountain out of a molehill p810
make a noise about [sth] p841
make a pig's ear of [sth] p935
make a rod for [your] own back p1083
make a song and dance about [sth] p1209
make a takeover bid for [sth] p1304
make a world of difference p1475
make a/[your] mark on [sth] p763
make all the right/correct etc noises p841
make an honest living p603
make an honest woman out of [sb] p603
make common cause with [sb] p242
make ends meet p402
make good time p540
make heavy weather of [sth] p583
make legal history p712
make matters worse p1476
make much/a lot of [sb] p754
make no bones about [sth] p132
make no claim to be [sth] p213
make no mistake about it p797
make no odds p857
make short shrift of [sth] p1162
make short work of [sth] p1161
make sure that p1287
make the first move p812
make the ultimate/supreme sacrifice p1100
make the world go around/round p1475
make up [your] mind p789
make up for lost time p754
not make any difference p339
put two and two together and make five p1380
to make matters worse p770
It makes me want to puke p1005
That makes two of us p1381
what makes [sb] tick p1330
a man/woman of few words p454
feel like a new woman/man p835
fine figure of a man/woman p457
just the man/woman for the job p965
like a man/woman possessed p965
man's inhumanity to man p756
May the best man/person win p107
not be beyond the wit of man/[sb] p1466
see a man about a dog p1130
the grand old man of [sth] p545
the man/woman on the Clapham omnibus p863
man's best friend p756
man's inhumanity to man p756

To find an idiom, look at the word in colour in each idiom. All of the coloured words are in alphabetical order.
After each idiom there is a page number that tells you where the idiom is explained.

the thinking woman's/man's crumpet p1325

manna from heaven p759

as if to the manner born p759

not by any manner of means p759

few/no/not many takers p1302

have a few too many p454

in so many words p760

many happy returns of the day p760

many moons ago p805

one too many p760

too many chiefs and not enough Indians p203

blow/bomb/wipe etc [sth] off the map p761

wipe [sth] off the map p1464

as mad as a hatter/March hare p749

from 630/March/the 1870s etc onwards p868

a question mark over [sth] p1020

be quick/slow off the mark p763

make a/[your] mark on [sth] p763

You mark my words p763

the bottom drops/falls out of the market p137

On your marks get set go p763

the sanctity of human life/marriage etc p1105

nail [your] colours to the mast p822

lord/master/mistress/king/queen of all [you] survey p1289

be a matter of life and/or death p770

be no laughing matter p770

be only a matter of time p770

mind over matter p789

no matter what/when/why etc p770

That's a matter of opinion p770

make matters worse p1476

take matters into [your] own hands p770

to make matters worse p770

May the best man/person win p107

To whom it may concern p250

you may well ask p63

be no mean feat p449

no mean achievement/feat p773

you know what I mean p692

if you take my meaning p1302

by all means p773

by fair means or foul p437

by no means p773

live beyond [your] means p773

not by any manner of means p759

be meant for each other p773

give [sb] a dose/taste of [their] own medicine p775

come to/meet a sticky end p1250

I'm pleased to meet you p949

make ends meet p402

be more to [sth] than meets the eye p432

be more to this than meets the eye p776

butter wouldn't melt in [sb's] mouth p163

have a memory like an elephant p778

if my memory serves me right p1141

memory/mind like a sieve p1171

take a stroll/trip/walk down memory lane p778

within living memory p730

all things to all men/people p1324

demand money with menaces p778

make a mental note of [sth] p778

grateful/thankful for small mercies p1192

when [sb] was a mere twinkle in [their] father's eye p1380

lead [sb] a merry dance p707

play merry hell with [sth] p947

drive [your] message/point home p376

take the mickey/mick out of someone p783

take the mickey/mick out of someone p783

put [sth] under the microscope p784

divide/split [sth] down the middle p784

follow/steer/take the middle course/way/path p784

play both ends against the middle p946

burn the midnight oil p160

the land of the midnight sun p698

might just as well p680

miles from anywhere/nowhere p786

miles too big/small/expensive etc p786

land of milk and honey p698

the milk of human kindness p787

grist to the mill/ grist for someone's mill p551

put [sb] through the mill p787

look/feel like a million dollars p788

be like a millstone around/round [your] neck p788

not mince your words p789

[your] mind is a blank/goes blank p789

a load/weight off [your] mind p789

all in the/[your] mind p789

be/take a weight off [your] mind p1445

cast [your] mind back p183

get [your] mind round something p789

give [sb] a piece of your mind p934

go over [sth] in [your] mind p789

have half a mind/a good mind to [do sth] p789

have/keep an open mind p870

I don't mind if I do p790

if you don't mind me saying p790

know [your] own mind p692

make up [your] mind p789

memory/mind like a sieve p1171

mind [your] own business p790

mind [your] p's and q's p790

mind how you go p789

mind over matter p789

never mind that p834

Nothing could have been further from my mind/thoughts p508

prey on your mind p983

run in/through [your] head/mind p1094

run through [your] mind/head p1094

set/put [sb's] mind at rest/ease p789

take [sb's] mind off [sth] p789

the thought crosses [sb's] mind p1326

great minds think alike p548

be a rich seam to mine p1124

Your guess is as good as mine p556

any minute/moment/second/time now p848

drag [sb's] name through the mire/mud p370

be/become mired down in something p792

death by misadventure p793

labour under the delusion/illusion/misapprehension etc p695

too good to miss p1345

[your] heart skips/misses a beat p581

make no mistake about it p797

lord/master/mistress/king/queen of all [you] survey p1289

pick 'n' mix p932

make a mountain out of a molehill p810

any minute/moment/second/time now p848

at this moment in time p802

not a moment too soon p802

Monday morning feeling p802

be a licence to print money p719

demand money with menaces p778

for love nor money p742

give [sb] a run for [their] money p1094

have a good run for [your] money p1094

money for old rope p802

put [your] money where [your] mouth is p803

save/keep money for a rainy day p1027

see the colour of [sb's] money p1129

the smart money is on/says p1193

throw [your] money/cash around p1329

throw good money after bad p1329

be cold enough to freeze the balls off a brass monkey p497

brass monkey weather p143

I'll be a monkey's uncle p803

the week/month/year before last p702

once in a blue moon p126

many moons ago p805

claim the moral high ground p213

be more to [sth] than meets the eye p432

be more to this than meets the eye p776

be plenty more where [sb/sth] came from p949

better/bigger/more etc than ever p418

bite off more than [you] can chew p117

couldn't agree more/less p24

couldn't agree/disagree more p806

do more harm than good p573

have another/more than one string to [your] bow p1267

It's more than my job's worth p673

more than you can shake a stick at p1149

more bang for your bucks p87

more by accident than design p7

more by luck than judgment p744

more often than not p806

More power to [your] elbow p970

more trouble than it's worth p1368

Need I say more p830

no more Mr Nice Guy p813

not/no more than p806

nothing more than p846

say no more p1110

That's more like it p806

There are plenty more fish in the sea p465

without further/more ado p16

You should get out more p523

Monday morning feeling p802

morning noon and night p807

tied to [your] mother's/wife's apron strings p1331

set the wheels in motion p1451

go through the motions p809

be cast in the same mould p183

mount guard on/over [sb] p810

make a mountain out of a molehill p810

play cat and mouse p184

born with a silver spoon in [your] mouth p135

butter wouldn't melt in [sb's] mouth p163

by word of mouth p1471

keep [your] mouth shut p811

leave a bad taste in [your] mouth p710

live from hand to mouth p566

make [sb's] mouth water p811

put [your] money where [your] mouth is p803

put words in/into [sb's] mouth p1471

shoot [your] mouth off p1159

shovel [sth] into [your] mouth p1164

straight from the horse's mouth p607

take the words out of [sb's] mouth p1471

give someone a mouthful p812

change with/keep up with/move with the times p1335

make the first move p812

move heaven and earth p812

move on to higher/better things p812

step/move up a gear p517

as/if/when/etc the spirit moves [sb] p1224

no more Mr Nice Guy p813

a drop too much to drink p377

be nothing/not much/very little in it p632

half as much again p563

how much do you want to bet p108

To find an idiom, look at the word in colour in each idiom. All of the coloured words are in alphabetical order.

After each idiom there is a page number that tells you where the idiom is explained.

1507

To find an idiom, look at the word in colour in each idiom. All of the coloured words are in alphabetical order.
After each idiom there is a page number that tells you where it is explained.

1508

be nothing/not much/very little in it
p632
like nothing else on earth p385
like nothing on earth p846
Nothing could have been further from
my mind/thoughts p508
nothing more than p846
nothing to write home about p1481
something/nothing to shout about p1163
you ain't seen nothing yet p1129
You've got nothing to lose p740
not take a blind bit of notice p122
sit up and take notice p1179
any day now p309
any minute/moment/second/time now
p848
every now and again/then p419
every now and then/again p848
from now on/as from now p848
miles from anywhere/nowhere p786
look out for number one p738
public enemy number one/No 1 p1003
by sheer force/weight of numbers p849
a hard/tough nut to crack p850
sledgehammer to crack a nut p1186

O

Roll on the weekend/five o'clock etc
p1083
turn 16/50/9 o'clock etc p1376
sow [your] wild oats p1214
against all the odds/against all odds p857
have the odds/cards stacked against [you]
p1234
make no odds p857
go off at half-cock/ go off half-cocked
p564
a chip off the old block p205
a load/weight off [your] mind p789
as easy as ABC/anything/falling off a log
p386
be cold enough to freeze the balls off a
brass monkey p497
be no skin off [sb's] nose p1182
be on/off the danger list p306
be quick/slow off the mark p763
be/take a weight off [your] mind p1445
beat/bore/scare etc the pants off [sb] p898
bite [sb's] head off p117
bite off more than [you] can chew p117
bite/snap [sb's] head off p578
blow/bomb/wipe etc [sth] off the map
p761
blow/take the lid off [sth] p719
bore the ass off [sb] p64
catch [sb] off guard p555
charm the pants off [sb] p197
come off better/worse/badly/well p237
come/get down off [you] high horse p591
cut off [your] nose to spite [your] face
p300
disappear off the face of the earth p434
do [sth] off [your] own bat p93
fall off the wagon p1427
fly off the handle p478
get off lightly; let [sb] off lightly p722
get off my back p79
get off on the right/wrong foot p482
get off to a good start p540
go off the boil p130
go off the deep end p316
go off the rails p1026
go off without a hitch p596
go/fly off at a tangent p1306
have/know [sth] off pat p908
have/take time off p1333
hot off the press p608
knock [sb's] block off p690

knock [sb] off [their] pedestal p690
knock spots off [sth] p690
know when [you] are well off p1448
laugh [your] head off p703
laugh/shout/scream etc [your] head off
p578
leave/go off etc with [your] tail between
[your] legs p1301
let/blow off steam p1246
live high on/off the hog p591
live off the fat of the land p446
nearly/almost fall off [your] chair p439
not take [your] eyes off [sb/sth] p432
off by heart p581
off the beaten track p98
off the top of [your] head p1346
pick [yourself] up off the floor p932
put [sb] off [their] stride p1014
put [sb] off [their] stride/stroke p1265
ride/drive/walk/etc off into the sunset
p1283
rush/run [sb] off [their] feet p482
score points off/over [sb] p1117
shoot [your] mouth off p1159
snap [sb's] head off p1198
sweep [sb] off [their] feet p1294
take [sb's] mind off [sth] p789
take [your] hat off to [sb] p575
take the chill off [sth] p204
take the edge off [sth] p389
take the gloss off [sth] p531
take the heat off [sb] p582
take the weight off [your] feet/legs p1445
take the wraps off [sth] p1479
take years off [sb] p1485
talk [sb's] ass off p64
talk [sb's] head off p1304
talk the hind legs off a donkey p1304
tear a strip off [sb] p1310
the shirt off [sb's] back p1157
throw [sb] off balance p1329
throw/put [sb] off the scent p1114
trip off the tongue p1366
water off a duck's back p1437
wipe [sth] off the map p1464
wipe the smile off [sb's] face p1464
work [sth] off p64
work [your] ass off p64
wriggle off the hook p1480
hold out/offer an olive branch p863
take up office p1302
every so often p419
more often than not p806
Oh my God p538
be no oil painting p861
burn the midnight oil p160
pour oil on troubled waters p969
a chip off the old block p205
an old/a wise head on young shoulders
p578
as tough as old boots p1350
for old times' sake p862
grand old age p545
have a rare old time p1031
It's the same old story p1105
money for old rope p802
ripe old age p1079
settle an old score p1145
the grand old man of [sth] p545
too old/a bit old p861
the oldest profession in the world p861
hold out/offer an olive branch p863
the man/woman on the Clapham
omnibus p863
every once in a while p865
just this once p865
once in a blue moon p126
once upon a time p865
a/one hundred per cent p615
all in one piece p934

at any one time p1334
at/in one fell swoop p451
back to square one p78
be neither one thing nor the other p832
be one thing after another p1323
be one/another of life's great mysteries
p720
be/stay/keep one jump ahead p678
come down on one side of the fence or
other p1170
could count on the fingers of one hand
p277
go in one ear and out the other p384
go one better p109
go/be back to square one p1231
have another/more than one string to
[your] bow p1267
have one foot in the grave p482
I'm not falling for that one p441
if ever there was one p418
in words of one syllable p1471
just one of those things p1324
kill two birds with one stone p686
look out for number one p738
on the level/on another level p716
one after another p43
one after another p865
one of these days p309
one of those days p309
one step forward two steps back p1248
one thing leads to another p1323
one too many p760
one way or another p865
one/Two etc down one/two etc to go p367
public enemy number one/No 1 p1003
pull a fast one p1005
Pull the other leg/one it's got bells on
p1005
put all [your] eggs in one basket p392
put one foot in front of the other p482
put one over on [sb] p1015
put/lay [sth] on/to one side p1170
put/leave [sth] on/to one side p1170
rolled into one p1083
take one thing at a time p1302
take/lead [sb] on/to one side p1170
That's a new one on me p835
the last but one p701
understand one another/each other p1390
what with one thing and another p1323
wouldn't know [sth] if [you] fell over
one/it p693
be only a matter of time p770
be only flesh and blood p472
it's only fair p437
not only but also p867
Only time will/can tell p1333
from 630/March/the 1870s etc onwards
p868
from that day/time onwards p500
bring [sth] out into the open p869
greet/welcome [sb] with open arms p868
have/keep [your] options open p872
have/keep an open mind p870
jaw drops open p670
lay [yourself] open to attack/criticism/
ridicule etc p705
lay [yourself] open to ridicule p1075
open [your] heart to someone p868
open the door to/close the door on [sth]
p363
contrary to popular opinion p265
That's a matter of opinion p770
have no option but to do something p872
have/keep [your] options open p872
go into orbit p873
get/put [your] own house in order p610
in order to/in order for/in order that
p874
just what the doctor ordered p360

To find an idiom, look at the word in colour in each idiom. All of the coloured words are in alphabetical order.
After each idiom there is a page number that tells you where the idiom is explained.

1509

under starter's orders p1242
couldn't organize a piss-up in a brewery p875
the Greek/Russian/Eastern Orthodox Church p876
be laughing on the other side of [your] face p703
be meant for each other p773
be neither one thing nor the other p832
come down on one side of the fence or other p1170
go in one ear and out the other p384
have bigger/other fish to fry p465
how the other half lives p563
knock into each other/knock through p690
none other than [sb/sth] p842
Pull the other leg/one it's got bells on p1005
put one foot in front of the other p482
the boot/shoe is on the other foot p134
the other side of the coin p1170
the wrong/other side of the tracks p1170
turn the other cheek p1376
understand one another/each other p1390
wouldn't have it any other way p1440
at each other's throats p1328
be/live in each other's pockets p954
a question mark over [sth] p1020
a rap on/over the knuckles p1030
a roof over [your] head p1085
all over again p22
all over bar the shouting p89
all over the place p942
be/go into ecstasies about/over [sth] p389
bend/lean over backwards p81
cast a shadow over/on [sth] p1148
cast an/your eye over [sth] p183
draped all over [sb] p371
draw a veil over [sth] p1413
go arse over tit/tip p59
go over [sb's] head p578
go over [sth] in [your] mind p789
hand over fist p566
haul/drag [sb] over the coals p226
head over heels in love p578
kick over the traces p685
look/feel like death warmed up/over p312
lose sleep over/about [sth] p740
make a fuss of/over [sb] p509
mind over matter p789
mount guard over [sb] p810
over my dead body p310
paper over the cracks p898
pull the wool over [sb's] eyes p1470
put [your] head over/above the parapet p900
put one over on [sb] p1015
rap [sb] over the knuckles p1030
ride roughshod over [sb/sth] p1074
run [your] eye over [sth] p1094
score points off/over [sb] p1117
sit in judgment on/over someone p1178
turn over a new leaf p1376
walk all over [sb] p1429
when hell freezes over p585
wouldn't know [sth] if [you] fell over one/it p693
written all over [sb's] face p1481
[your] own flesh and blood p889
act/do something on [your] own respons- ibility p1065
after [your] own heart p581
be [sb's] own flesh and blood p472
be [your] own worst enemy p1477
be a victim of [your] own success p1418
be full of [your] own importance p504
be hoisted with/by [your] own petard p927
be in a class by itself/of its own p215
beat [sb] at [their] own game p98

blow [your] own trumpet/horn p125
by [your] own account p8
come into [your] own p889
dig [your] own grave p340
do [sth] off [your] own bat p93
each to his/their own p384
feather [your] own nest p449
find [your] own level p716
get/put [your] own house in order p610
give [sb] a dose/taste of [their] own medicine p775
go [your] own separate ways p1139
go [your] own sweet way p1440
go [your] own way p1440
it's [your] own lookout p738
keep [your] own counsel p277
know [your] own mind p692
leave [sb] to [their] own devices p710
make [sth] all [your] own p889
make a rod for [your] own back p1083
mind [your] own business p790
on your own initiative p646
pick on someone [your] own size p932
save [your] own skin/hide p1109
sign [your] own death warrant p1173
stand on [your] own two feet p1238
stew in [your] own juice p1249
take [your] own life p720
take matters into [your] own hands p770
take the law into [your] own hands p705
under [your] own steam p1246
with [your] own fair hands p438
as if [you] owned the place p889

P

mind [your] p's and q's p790
put [sb/sth] through [their] paces p891
packed/squashed like sardines p1107
be all part of life's rich tapestry/pageant p720
all expenses paid p426
on/under pain of death p894
go to/take great pains to do [sth] p894
paint a black picture of [sth/sb] p118
paint a bleak/gloomy/rosy etc picture of [sth] p894
paint the town red p894
watch paint dry p1436
be no oil painting p861
a safe pair of hands p567
have a good/healthy pair of lungs p746
be green/pale about the gills p525
pale into insignificance p895
cross [sb's] hand/palm with silver p291
go down the pan p896
hit/press/push the panic button p897
beat/bore/scare etc the pants off [sb] p898
by the seat of [your] pants p1125
catch [sb] with [their] pants/trousers down p185
charm the pants off [sb] p197
[sb] couldn't act/argue/fight etc [their] way out of a paper bag p898
not worth the paper [sth] is printed/ written on p1477
paper over the cracks p898
put/set pen to paper p917
put/set pencil to paper p918
live in a fool's paradise p482
put [your] head over/above the parapet p900
Excuse/Pardon my French p497
I beg your pardon p102
if you'll pardon the expression p901
pare [sth] down to the bone p901
be all part of life's rich tapestry/pageant p720
life and soul of the party p720
pass all belief p905

pass the hat around/round p905
pass the time of day p906
the passing of time/the years p906
passions run high p907
a blast from the past p120
a quarter past/ after two/three/four etc p1019
have/know [sth] off pat p908
go through a bad/difficult/rough/sticky patch p909
beat a path through [sth] p98
beat a path to [sb's] door p98
follow/steer/take the middle course/way/ path p784
lead [sb] up the garden path p707
the path of least resistance p1062
the pattering of tiny feet p911
rob Peter to pay Paul p1081
the streets are paved with gold p1262
pay lip service to [sth] p728
pay the ultimate price p912
pay through the nose p912
pay top dollar p912
rob Peter to pay Paul p1081
there'll be hell to pay p585
a pearl of great price p914
cast pearls before swine p183
like two peas in a pod p723
keep your pecker up p914
funny ha-ha or funny peculiar p507
knock [sb] off [their] pedestal p690
keep [your] eyes peeled/skinned p432
bring/take [sb] down a peg or two p916
square peg in a round hole p1231
put/set pen to paper p917
put/set pencil to paper p918
a penny for your thoughts p918
cost [sb] a pretty penny p982
In for a penny in for a pound p918
turn up like a bad penny p1377
all things to all men/people p1324
a/one hundred per cent p615
May the best man/person win p107
there's no such thing/person as p1278
put [sth] into perspective p925
pervert the course of justice p926
be hoisted with/by [your] own petard p927
rob Peter to pay Paul p1081
pick up the phone p933
get/pick up steam p1246
pick 'n' mix p932
pick [yourself] up off the floor p932
pick on someone [your] own size p932
pick up the bill/tab p932
pick up the phone p933
pick up the pieces p932
pick up the threads p932
pick up/take up the slack p1184
take your pick p932
take/pick up the gauntlet p516
paint a black picture of [sth/sb] p118
paint a bleak/gloomy/rosy etc picture of [sth] p894
as American as apple pie p36
as easy as ABC/anything/falling off a log/pie p386
eat humble pie p387
have a finger in every pie p461
a nasty piece of work p825
all in one piece p934
give [sb] a piece of your mind p934
pick up the pieces p932
make a pig's ear of [sth] p935
put/set the cat among the pigeons p184
a bitter pill to swallow p117
from pillar to post p937
as clean as a new pin p216
pin back [your] ears p937
take [sth] with a pinch of salt p1103
Put/Stick that in your pipe and smoke it

To find an idiom, look at the word in colour in each idiom. All of the coloured words are in alphabetical order.
After each idiom there is a page number that tells you where the idiom is explained.

To find an idiom, look at the word in colour in each idiom. All of the coloured words are in alphabetical order.
After each idiom there is a page number that tells you where the idiom is explained.

R

play the **race** card p1023
set [your] pulse **racing** p1006
pirate **radio** station p940
be like a red **rag** to a bull p1044
fly into a **rage** p478
purple in the face/purple with **rage** p1010
go off the **rails** p1026
come **rain** or shine p1027
take a **rain** check on [sth] p1027
save/keep money for a **rainy** day p1027
create/kick up/**raise** a stink p1253
raise [your] hand to/against [sb] p1027
raise a few eyebrows p1027
force/**ram** [sth] down [sb's] throat p1328
ram [sth] down [sb's] throat p1028
rise from/through the **ranks** p1030
a **rap** on/over the knuckles p1030
rap [sb] over the knuckles p1030
have a **rare** old time p1031
look like a drowned **rat** p377
come the **raw** prawn p1033
hit/touch a **raw** nerve p832
touch/strike/hit a **raw** nerve p1349
catch a few **rays** p185
get to/**reach** first base p464
reach saturation point p1108
read [sb] the riot act p1035
read [sth] from cover to cover p281
read between the lines p1035
read my lips p1035
Is he/she for **real** p1037
really take the biscuit p116
what [sb] is **really** made of p753
within the **realms** of possibility p1037
reap what [you] have sown p1037
bring up the **rear** p150
rear its ugly head p1038
no/without **rhyme** or **reason** p1073
beyond **reasonable** doubt p110
keep a diary/an account/a **record** etc p682
set/put the **record** straight p1042
be like a red **rag** to a bull p1044
go/turn bright **red** p1044
paint the town **red** p894
bask/bathe in **reflected** glory p531
work long/**regular**/unsocial etc hours p609
keep a tight **rein** on [sb/sth] p1050
be on/ in general **release** p1052
heave a sigh of **relief** p583
who shall **remain** nameless p823
remove [sth] from [your] shelves p1155
be far **removed** from [sth] p1056
hold [sb] in high/low **repute** p1060
take up **residence**/residency [somewhere] p1062
take up residence/**residency** [somewhere] p1062
the path of least **resistance** p1062
be your last **resort** p1063
with all due **respect** p1064
act/do something on [your] own **responsibility** p1065
I **rest** my case p1065
lay the ghost of [sth] to **rest** p705
set/put [sb's] mind at **rest**/ease p789
keep/place [sb] under **restraint** p1066
crawl/go/**retreat**/retire into [your] shell p1155
crawl/go/retreat/**retire** into [your] shell p1155
by **return** of post p1069
many happy **returns** of the day p760
go into **reverse** p1071
think the whole world **revolves** around [you] p1072
go into **rhapsodies** p1072

no/without **rhyme** or reason p1073
cut/tear [sth/sb] to/into **ribbons** p1073
be a **rich** seam to mine p1124
be all part of life's **rich** tapestry/pageant p720
be as crazy/**rich** etc as they come p236
good **riddance** to bad rubbish p1074
come/go/be along for the **ride** p33
ride roughshod over [sb/sth] p1074
ride/drive/walk/etc off into the sunset p1283
hold [sb/sth] up to **ridicule** p1075
lay [yourself] open to attack/criticism/**ridicule** etc p705
lay [yourself] open to **ridicule** p1075
from the sublime to the **ridiculous** p1274
be **riding**/on the crest of a wave p289
[her/his] heart is in the **right** place p581
be a bit of all **right** p116
be all **right**/fine by [sb] p165
be not quite **right** in the head p1076
be **right** under [your] nose p844
get off on the **right**/wrong foot p482
give [your] **right** arm p1076
have your head screwed on the **right** way p578
if my memory serves me **right** p1141
in the **right** place at the right time p1076
It's all **right** p32
keep on the **right** side of [sb] p1170
look straight/**right** through [sb] p737
make all the **right**/correct etc noises p841
on the **right**/wrong side of the law p1170
play [your] cards **right** p946
right left and centre p1076
right/wrong way round p1089
suit [sb] **right** down to the ground p1280
the **right** way round/up p1076
walk **right** into [sth] p1429
lead/live the life of **Riley** p720
throw [your] hat into the **ring** p575
warning/alarm bells start to **ring**/sound p104
run **rings** round p1078
read [sb] the **riot** act p1035
ripe old age p1079
make [sb's] hackles **rise** p561
make [your] gorge **rise** p542
rise from the dead/grave p1079
rise from/through the ranks p1030
the Land of the **Rising** Sun p698
sell [sb] down the **river** p1135
come to the end of the **road** p1081
get the/this show on the **road** p1165
rob Peter to pay Paul p1081
before you can say Jack **Robinson** p1110
before you can/could say Jack **Robinson** p668
be caught between a **rock** and a hard place p1082
be the new **rock** 'n' roll p1082
like a shag on a **rock** p1149
it's not **rocket** science p1082
make a **rod** for [your] own back p1083
be the new rock 'n' **roll** p1082
Heads will **roll** p526
Roll on the weekend/five o'clock etc p1083
roll up [your] sleeves p1084
roll your eyes p432
rolled into one p1083
start/set/get the ball **rolling** p85
a **roof** over [your] head p1085
go through the **roof** p1085
like a cat on a hot tin **roof** p184
under the same **roof** p1085
shout/proclaim [sth] from the **rooftops** p1085
come back/home to **roost** p1086
put down **roots** p1086

money for old **rope** p802
look at/see [sth] through **rose-coloured**/tinted glasses p1087
come up/out smelling of **roses** p1194
coming up **roses** p1087
put the **roses** back into [sb's] cheeks p1087
paint a bleak/gloomy/**rosy** etc picture of [sth] p894
learn [sth] by **rote** p1087
cut up **rough** p300
go through a bad/difficult/**rough**/sticky patch p909
take the **rough** with the smooth p1088
ride **roughshod** over [sb/sth] p1074
a clip **round**/on the ear p221
be like a millstone around/**round** [your] neck p788
be/go **round** the twist p1380
drive/send [sb] **round** the bend p106
get [your] mind **round** something p789
go all **round** the houses p610
go/run **round** in circles p210
have [sb/sth] hanging **round** [your] neck p569
make the world go around/**round** p1475
pass the hat around/**round** p905
put the word about/around/out/**round** p1471
right/wrong way **round** p1089
run rings **round** p1078
run **round** in circles p1093
run **round** like a headless chicken p578
square peg in a **round** hole p1231
the right way **round**/up p1076
the wrong way **round**/around p1482
twist [sb] around/**round** [your] little finger p1380
word gets about/around/**round** p1471
work [your] way around/**round** to [sth] p1473
wrap [sb] around/**round** [your] little finger p1479
kick up a fuss/**row**/stink p685
Her/His/Your **Royal** Highness p1090
treat [sb] like **royalty** p1362
rub [sb] up the wrong way p1091
good riddance to bad **rubbish** p1074
pull the **rug** from under [sb/sb's feet] p1005
rule [sth] with an iron hand/fist p664
the exception that proves the **rule** p421
be no hard and fast **rules** p571
give [sb] a **run** for [their] money p1094
go/be **run** to ground p552
go/run round in circles p210
have a good **run** for [your] money p1094
make [sb's] blood **run** cold p1094
make [your] blood **run** cold p124
passions **run** high p907
run [your] eye over p1094
run [yourself] into the ground p1093
run in/through [your] head/mind p1094
run rings round p1078
run round in circles p1093
run round like a headless chicken p578
run through [your] mind/head p1094
run/go like clockwork p222
rush/**run** [sb] off [their] feet p482
be on the lowest/bottom **rung** of the ladder p1096
go and take a **running** jump p1094
hit the ground **running** p595
rush/run [sb] off [their] feet p482
the Greek/**Russian**/Eastern Orthodox Church p876

To find an idiom, look at the word in colour in each idiom. All of the coloured words are in alphabetical order.
After each idiom there is a page number that tells you where the idiom is explained.

S

wear sackcloth and ashes p1099
make the ultimate/supreme sacrifice p1100
sadder but wiser p1100
a safe pair of hands p567
just to be on the safe side p1100
easier said than done p386
no sooner said than done p1209
there's little to be said for p1110
there's something to be said for p1110
when all is said and done p1110
sail against the wind p1102
sail close to the wind p1102
take the wind out of [sb's] sails p1461
for old times' sake p862
for the sake of something/for something's sake p1102
take [sth] with a pinch of salt p1103
like a dose of salts p364
and the same to you with brass knobs on p690
be cast in the same mould p183
by the same token p1104
it all amounts/comes to the same thing p1104
It's the same old story p1105
speak/talk the same language p699
tar [sb] with the same brush p1307
under the same roof p1085
the sanctity of human life/marriage etc p1105
bury/have [your] head in the sand p578
packed/squashed like sardines p1107
reach saturation point p1108
can't do [sth] to save [your] life p1109
save [your] own skin/hide p1109
save/keep money for a rainy day p1027
before you can say Jack Robinson p1110
before you can/could say Jack Robinson p668
I daresay/I dare say p307
I wouldn't say no p1110
I'm sorry to say p1210
it's fair to say p437
Need I say more p830
not have a civil word to say about [sb] p212
say no more p1110
say this/that much for [sb/sth] p1110
What have you got to say for [yourself] p1110
Who can say p1110
You can say that again p1110
You can't say fairer than that p1110
You don't say p1110
if you don't mind me saying p790
it goes without saying p1110
That's not saying much p1110
there's no knowing/telling/saying p840
the smart money is on/says p1193
what [sb] says goes p1110
what/whatever [sb] says goes p1450
stand sb in good stead p1245
pull the rug from under [sb/sb's feet] p1005
the scales fall from [sb's] eyes p1111
beat/bore/scare etc the pants off [sb] p898
frighten/scare etc the living daylights out of [sb] p309
be scattered to the four winds p1113
blend into the scenery p1114
throw/put [sb] off the scent p1114
fall behind schedule p1114
school of hard knocks p1115
it's not rocket science p1082
earn/get/score brownie points p153
score points off/over [sb] p1117
settle an old score p1145

scrape the bottom of the barrel p1119
scratch beneath the surface p1119
you scratch my back and I'll scratch yours p1119
laugh/shout/scream etc [your] head off p578
scream/shout blue murder p126
screw up [your] courage p1120
have your head screwed on the right way p578
by the scruff of the/your neck p1121
be between the devil and the deep blue sea p335
There are plenty more fish in the sea p465
my lips are sealed p728
be a rich seam to mine p1124
hunt/search high and low p590
by the seat of [your] pants p1125
take a back seat p79
another/a second bite of the cherry p117
any minute/moment/second/time now p848
come/be a poor second/third etc p961
play second fiddle p947
take first/second place p942
without a second thought p1126
under sedation/the doctor etc p1388
as far as the eye can/could see p432
believe [sth] when [you] see it p104
can't see further than the end of [your] nose p1129
can't see the wood for the trees p1129
find out/see how the land lies p698
know/see where [sb] is coming from p1452
look at/see [sth] through rose-coloured/tinted glasses p1087
not see hide nor hair of [sth] p1130
not see the wood for the trees p1470
see [sb's] true colours p234
see [sb] in hell before p1130
see [your] way clear to p1130
see a man about a dog p1130
see in the New Year p1130
see the colour of [sb's] money p1129
see the error of [your] ways p412
see the last of something/someone p1129
see the light of day p1130
see things in black and white p118
we'll soon see about that p1130
have seen better days p1129
look like/as though [you've] seen a ghost p524
wouldn't be seen dead p1129
you ain't seen nothing yet p1129
not know what [sb] sees in [sb/sth] p1130
be a shadow of [your] former self p1148
go/sell like hot cakes p608
sell [sb] a bill of goods p1135
sell [sb] down the river p1135
sell [your] soul to the devil p1135
drive/send [sb] round the bend p106
drive/send [sb] to an early grave p385
send [sb] away with a flea in [their] ear p471
send [sth] under plain/separate cover p281
send chills down/up [sb's] spine p204
send shudders/a shudder down [your] spine p167
20/30 etc years [your] senior p1137
be a victory for common sense p1418
but not in the biblical sense p111
knock some sense into [sb] p690
take leave of [your] senses p711
go [your] own separate ways p1139
send [sth] under plain/separate cover p281
separate the wheat from the chaff p1451
separate/sort out the sheep from the goats p1154

public servant/servant of the state p1141
first come first served p464
if my memory serves me right p1141
pay lip service to [sth] p728
press [sth/sb] into service p981
be dead set against [sth] p1143
not set the world on fire p1143
On your marks get set go p763
put/set pen to paper p917
put/set pencil to paper p918
put/set someone straight p1259
put/set the cat among the pigeons p184
set [sb's] teeth on edge p1345
set [your] pulse racing p1006
set great/little etc store by something p1257
set the wheels in motion p1451
set up shop p1160
set/put [sb's] mind at rest/ease p789
set/put the record straight p1042
start/set/get the ball rolling p85
settle a case out of court p280
settle an old score p1145
be a shadow of [your] former self p1148
beyond a shadow of a doubt p110
cast a shadow over/on [sth] p1148
like a shag on a rock p1149
more than you can shake a stick at p1149
shake [sb's] hand/shake [sb] by the hand p1149
in two shakes of a lamb's tail p1149
no great shakes p548
who shall remain nameless p823
in any shape or form p1151
knock/lick [sth/sb] into shape p1152
Shape up or ship out p1152
the shape of things to come p1151
all shapes and sizes p1151
short sharp shock p1161
sharpen up your act p1153
Is he/she for real p1037
separate/sort out the sheep from the goats p1154
a wolf in sheep's clothing p1468
by sheer force/weight of numbers p849
crawl/go/retreat/retire into [your] shell p1155
have/lead a sheltered life p1155
remove [sth] from [your] shelves p1155
come rain or shine p1027
think the sun shines out of [sb's] arse/backside p1282
a knight in shining armour p690
Shape up or ship out p1152
the shirt off [sb's] back p1157
the shit hits the fan p1157
shiver up and down [your] spine p1158
short sharp shock p1161
the boot/shoe is on the other foot p134
if I were in your shoes p1159
step into [sb's] shoes p1159
shoot [sth/sb] down in flames p1159
shoot [your] mouth off p1159
bull in a china shop p157
set up shop p1160
shut up shop p1168
as thick as two short planks p1323
be nothing short of[] p846
bring [sb] up short p150
draw/get the short straw p1161
in/within a short space of time p1214
make short shrift of [sth] p1162
make short work of [sth] p1161
not be short of a bob or two p1161
pull [sb] up short p1006
pull up short p1006
short sharp shock p1161
to cut a long story short p301
long-haul flight/short-haul flight p575
fire a warning shot across [sb's] bows p139

To find an idiom, look at the word in colour in each idiom. All of the coloured words are in alphabetical order.
After each idiom there is a page number that tells you where the idiom is explained.

give [sth] your best **shot** p1162
not by a long chalk/**shot** p736
[I] **should** be so lucky p1163
How **should** [I] know p1162
I **should** think not/so too p1162
You **should** get out more p523
give [sb] the cold **shoulder** p230
an old/a wise head on young **shoulders** p578
have all the cares of the world on [your] **shoulders** p177
head and **shoulders** above p578
laugh/**shout**/scream etc [your] head off p578
scream/**shout** blue murder p126
shout/proclaim [sth] from the rooftops p1085
something/nothing to **shout** about p1163
all over bar the **shouting** p89
within **shouting** distance p1163
if/when push comes to **shove** p1011
Shove/stick [sth] up [your] ass p64
shovel [sth] into [your] mouth p1164
get the/this **show** on the road p1165
Jolly good **show** p676
show [sb] in their true colours p234
show someone in a bad light p722
that will **show** [sb] p1164
make short **shrift** of [sth] p1162
send shudders/a **shudder** down [your] spine p1167
send **shudders**/a shudder down [your] spine p1167
keep [your] gob **shut** p537
keep [your] mouth **shut** p811
shut up shop p1168
shut/close the stable/barn door after the horse has bolted p363
be laughing on the other **side** of [your] face p703
come down on one **side** of the fence or other p1170
err on the **side** of caution p412
get out of bed on the wrong **side** p100
just to be on the safe **side** p1100
keep on the right **side** of [sb] p1170
know which **side** [your] bread is buttered on p692
let the **side** down p716
look on the bright **side** p737
on the right/wrong **side** of the law p1170
put/lay [sth] on/to one **side** p1170
put/leave [sth] on/to one **side** p1170
take/lead [sb] on/to one **side** p1170
the other **side** of the coin p1170
the wrong/other **side** of the tracks p1170
knock [sb] **sideways**/for six p690
leak like a **sieve** p708
memory/mind like a **sieve** p1171
heave a **sigh** of relief p583
a **sight** for sore eyes p1172
can't stand the **sight** of p1238
Get out of my **sight** p1172
hove into **sight**/view p611
know [sb] by **sight** p693
sign [your] own death warrant p1173
sign on the dotted line p1173
as smooth as **silk**/a baby's bottom p1196
play **silly** buggers p947
born with a **silver** spoon in [your] mouth p135
cross [sb's] hand/palm with **silver** p291
be the best thing **since** sliced bread p107
from/**since** the year dot p1485
from/**since** time immemorial p625
everything but/except the kitchen **sink** p419
sink like a stone p1177
sink to such a level/such depths p1177
sink without a trace p1177
fall for [sth] hook line and **sinker** p604

cover/hide a multitude of **sins** p816
Dear **Sir** or Madam p1178
sit around on [your] backside p81
sit in judgment on/over someone p1178
sit up and take notice p1179
a chicken and egg **situation** p202
be **six** feet under p1180
in/within the space of **six** weeks/three hours etc p1214
knock [sb] sideways/for **six** p690
cut [sb] down to **size** p301
pick on someone [your] own **size** p932
that's about the **size** of it p1180
all shapes and **sizes** p1151
be **skating** on thin ice p1181
skeleton in the/[your] cupboard/closet p1181
put the **skids** under sth p1181
be no **skin** off [sb's] nose p1182
by the **skin** of [your] teeth p1182
save [your] own **skin**/hide p1109
keep [your] eyes peeled/**skinned** p432
[your] heart **skips**/misses a beat p581
get [sth] into [your] thick **skull** p1183
cut [sb] some **slack** p300
pick up/take up the **slack** p1184
wipe the **slate** clean p1464
with the **slate** wiped clean p1185
like a lamb to the **slaughter** p697
sledgehammer to crack a nut p1186
Go back to **sleep** p1186
lose **sleep** over/about [sth] p740
sleep like a log p1186
an ace up [your] **sleeve** p10
have a card up [your] **sleeve** p176
laugh up [your] **sleeve** p704
wear [your] heart on [your] **sleeve** p1442
roll up [your] **sleeves** p1084
any way you **slice** it p1187
be the best thing since **sliced** bread p107
slip through [sb's] fingers p1189
slip through the net p1189
be quick/**slow** off the mark p763
slowly but surely p1191
be a big fish in a **small** pond p465
cost an arm and a leg/a **small** fortune p275
grateful/thankful for **small** mercies p1192
make [sb] **small** p737
miles too big/**small**/expensive etc p786
the **smart** money is on/says p1193
smarten up [your] act p1193
wake up and **smell** the coffee p1429
come up/out **smelling** of roses p1194
wipe the **smile** off [sb's] face p1464
go up in **smoke** p1195
Put/Stick that in your pipe and **smoke** it p939
vanish/go up/disappear in a puff of **smoke** p1004
as **smooth** as silk/a baby's bottom p1196
take the rough with the **smooth** p1088
bite/**snap** [sb's] head off p578
snap [sb's] head off p1198
snatch victory from the jaws of defeat p1198
be as pure as the driven **snow** p1009
not have a **snowball's** chance in hell p1201
[I] should be **so** lucky p1163
as/**so** far as I can tell p444
as/**so** far as I know p444
as/**so** far as I'm concerned p444
ever **so**/ever such a p418
every **so** often p419
I should think not/**so** too p1162
I'm **so** hungry I could eat a horse p387
in **so** many words p760
so far so good p444
so help me God p586
so much the better p109

without **so** much as a backward glance p1467
without **so** much as a by-your-leave p1467
pull [your] **socks** up p1005
Bugger/**Sod** etc this for a lark p701
catch/cop/get **some** z's p1489
cut [sb] **some** slack p300
kick **some** ass p685
knock **some** sense into [sb] p690
take **some** beating p98
be incumbent on/upon **someone** p637
come down on **someone** like a ton of bricks p237
crawl back to **someone** p286
give **someone** a mouthful p812
give **someone** the brush-off p154
open [your] heart to **someone** p868
pick on **someone** [your] own size p932
put/set **someone** straight p1259
see the last of something/**someone** p1129
show **someone** in a bad light p722
sit in judgment on/over **someone** p1178
take **someone** to task p1308
take the mickey/mick out of **someone** p783
grist to the mill/ grist for **someone's** mill p551
fall into the/**someone's** trap p439
act/do **something** on [your] own responsibility p1065
be/become mired down in **something** p792
Do you want to make **something**/anything of it p754
for the sake of **something**/for something's sake p1102
get [your] mind round **something** p789
give [sb] **something** to talk about p1304
have got **something** there p1208
have no option but to do **something** p872
have **something** on good authority p72
look like **something** the cat brought/dragged in p184
or **something** like that p1208
see the last of **something**/someone p1129
set great/little etc store by **something** p1257
something a little stronger p1208
something like 96%/half etc p1208
something/nothing to shout about p1163
there's **something** to be said for p1110
You know **something** p692
for the sake of something/for something's sake p1102
somewhere along the line p726
burst into **song**/tears/laughter p161
make a **song** and dance about [sth] p1209
not a moment too **soon** p802
speak too **soon** p1217
we'll **soon** see about that p1130
would just as **soon** p1209
no **sooner** than p1209
no **sooner** said than done p1209
a sight for **sore** eyes p1172
be like a bear with a **sore** head p97
stand/stick out like a **sore** thumb p1210
feel **sorry** for yourself p1210
I'm **sorry** to say p1210
and that **sort** of thing p1211
separate/**sort** out the sheep from the goats p1154
keep body and **soul** together p129
life and **soul** of the party p720
put [your] heart and **soul** into [sth] p581
sell [your] **soul** to the devil p1135
ring/**sound** alarm bells p28
sound like/as if/as though p1212
warning/alarm bells start to ring/**sound** p104
sow [your] wild oats p1214

To find an idiom, look at the word in colour in each idiom. All of the coloured words are in alphabetical order.
After each idiom there is a page number that tells you where the idiom is explained.

reap what [you] have sown p1037
n/within a short space of time p1214
n/within the space of six weeks/three
  hours etc p1214
watch this space p1436
out/throw a spanner in the works p1215
spare no effort/expense p1215
no expense is spared p426
speak too soon p1217
speak with a forked tongue p488
speak/talk the same language p699
be/fall under [sb's] influence/spell p1388
spend the night together p1221
send chills down/up [sb's] spine p204
send shudders/a shudder down [your]
  spine p1167
shiver up and down [your] spine p1158
as/if/when/etc the spirit moves [sb]
  p1224
enter/get into the spirit p1224
cut off [your] nose to spite [your] face
  p300
in/within spitting distance p1224
divide/split [sth] down the middle p784
put a spoke in [sb's] wheel etc p1226
born with a silver spoon in [your] mouth
  p135
knock spots off [sth] p690
spread like wildfire p1459
be full of the joys of spring p504
be no spring chicken p1229
back to square one p78
go/be back to square one p1231
square peg in a round hole p1231
packed/squashed like sardines p1107
shut/close the stable/barn door after the
  horse has bolted p363
have the odds/cards stacked against
  [you] p1234
take centre stage p1235
can't stand the sight of p1238
know where you stand p1238
make [sb's] hair stand on end p562
not stand any nonsense p842
stand [sb] in good stead p1238
stand on [your] own two feet p1238
stand or fall by [sth] p1238
stand sb in good stead p1245
stand the test of time p1238
stand up and be counted p1238
stand/stick out like a sore thumb p1210
from a standing start p1238
from where [sb] stands p1238
time stands still p1333
thank [your] lucky stars p1319
from a standing start p1238
from start to finish p1242
get off to a good start p540
start a new life p720
start/set/get the ball rolling p85
warning/alarm bells start to ring/sound
  p104
under starter's orders p1242
in/by fits and starts p466
be in no fit state to do [sth] p466
public servant/servant of the state p1141
pirate radio station p940
be/stay/keep one jump ahead p678
stand [sb] in good stead p1238
stand sb in good stead p1245
beg borrow or steal p102
full steam ahead p505
get/pick up steam p1246
let/blow off steam p1246
under [your] own steam p1246
follow/steer/take the middle course/
  way/path p784
from stem to stern p1247
one step forward two steps back p1248
step back in time p1247

step into [sb's] shoes p1159
step into the breach p1247
step/move up a gear p517
one step forward two steps back p1248
from stem to stern p1247
made of sterner stuff p1249
stew in [your] own juice p1249
capable of sth/doing sth p174
put the skids under sth p1181
get the wrong end of the stick p1481
more than you can shake a stick at p1149
poke/stick [your] nose into [sth] p844
Put/Stick that in your pipe and smoke it
  p939
put/stick the knife into [sb] p689
Shove/stick [sth] up [your] ass p64
stand/stick out like a sore thumb p1210
jolly hockey sticks p676
come to/meet a sticky end p1250
go through a bad/difficult/rough/sticky
  patch p909
time stands still p1333
create/kick up/raise a stink p1253
kick up a fuss/row/stink p685
lock stock and barrel p733
[sb's] eyes are bigger than [their] belly/
  stomach p432
get blood out of/from a stone p124
kill two birds with one stone p686
leave no stone unturned p710
sink like a stone p1177
fall on stony ground p1256
fall between two stools p439
come to a full stop p505
pull out all the stops p1005
set great/little etc store by something
  p1257
store up trouble/problems p1257
cook/dance/talk etc up a storm p1258
take [a place or group of people] by storm
  p1258
the calm before the storm p169
the lull before the storm p745
It's the same old story p1105
It's/That's the story of my life p1258
That's a likely story p724
to cut a long story short p301
look straight/right through [sb] p737
put/set someone straight p1259
set/put the record straight p1042
straight from the horse's mouth p607
strain every nerve p1260
How strange/stupid/weird etc is that
  p612
go into the stratosphere p1261
draw/get the short straw p1161
like a streak of lightning p1262
talk a blue streak p1304
the streets are paved with gold p1262
gather up strength/courage p516
go from strength to strength p1263
by no stretch of the imagination p1264
put [sb] off [their] stride p1014
put [sb] off [their] stride/stroke p1265
strike a blow against/at [sth] p1265
strike a discordant note p347
strike fear/terror into [sb] p1265
strike while the iron is hot p1265
touch/strike/hit a raw nerve p1349
within striking distance p1265
have another/more than one string to
  [your] bow p1267
tied to [your] mother's/wife's apron
  strings p1331
tear a strip off [sb] p1310
put [sb] off [their] stride/stroke p1265
take a stroll/trip/walk down memory
  lane p778
something a little stronger p1208
have your head buried/stuck in a book
  p578

made of sterner stuff p1249
How strange/stupid/weird etc is that
  p612
from the sublime to the ridiculous p1274
there is no substitute for [sth] p1276
be a victim of [your] own success p1418
What price fame/victory/success etc p983
ever so/ever such a p418
no such luck p744
sink to such a level/such depths p1177
there's no such thing/person as p1278
teach your grandmother to suck eggs
  p545
come to/suffer under the lash p701
suffer fools gladly p1279
suit [sb] right down to the ground p1280
the land of the midnight sun p698
the Land of the Rising Sun p698
think the sun shines out of [sb's] arse/
  backside p1282
ride/drive/walk/etc off into the sunset
  p1283
make the ultimate/supreme sacrifice
  p1100
as sure as eggs is eggs p1287
make sure that p1287
slowly but surely p1191
scratch beneath the surface p1119
lord/master/mistress/king/queen of all
  [you] survey p1289
a bitter pill to swallow p117
cut a swathe through [sth] p300
swear like a trooper p1367
sweep [sb] off [their] feet p1294
sweep [sth] under the carpet p1294
go [your] own sweet way p1440
sweet fanny adams p1294
be all sweetness and light p1294
go/swim against the tide p1331
cast pearls before swine p183
get into the swing of it/things p1296
swing into action p1296
at/in one fell swoop p451
beat/turn swords into ploughshares p1297
in words of one syllable p1471

T

dot the i's and cross the t's p365
pick up the bill/tab p932
drink [sb] under the table p375
put/lay [your] cards on the table p176
get down to brass tacks p143
can't make head nor tail of [sth] p578
in two shakes of a lamb's tail p1149
leave/go off etc with [your] tail between
  [your] legs p1301
tail wagging the dog p1301
[they] can dish it out but [they] can't take
  it p349
be/take a weight off [your] mind p1445
blow/take the lid off [sth] p719
bring/take [sb] down a peg or two p916
can take it or leave it p1302
carry/take coals to Newcastle p226
follow/steer/take the middle course/
  way/path p784
go and take a running jump p1094
go further/take [sth] further p508
go to/take great pains to do [sth] p894
have/take pride of place p984
have/take time off p1333
if you take my meaning p1302
let nature take its course p826
not take [sth] lying down p719
not take [your] eyes off [sb/sth] p432
not take a blind bit of notice p122
pick up/take up the slack p1184
really take the biscuit p116
sit up and take notice p1179

To find an idiom, look at the word in colour in each idiom. All of the coloured words are in alphabetical order.
After each idiom there is a page number that tells you where it is explained.

1515

To find an idiom, look at the word in colour in each idiom. All of the coloured words are in alphabetical order.
After each idiom there is a page number that tells you where the idiom is explained.

as **thick** as two short planks p1323
get [sth] into [your] **thick** skull p1183
lay it on a bit **thick** p706
The plot **thickens** p950
like a **thief** in the night p1323
be skating on **thin** ice p1181
disappear/vanish into **thin** air p1323
thin end of the wedge p1323
and that sort of **thing** p1211
be neither one **thing** nor the other p832
be one **thing** after another p1323
be the best **thing** since sliced bread p107
chance would be a fine **thing** p193
it all amounts/comes to the same **thing** p1104
it's a good job/**thing** p540
it's a good **thing** p1323
last **thing** at night p701
make a big **thing** out of [sth] p1323
not know the first **thing** about [sth] p692
one **thing** leads to another p1323
take one **thing** at a time p1302
the easiest **thing** in the world p386
the last **thing** [you] want/need etc p1324
the next best **thing** p836
the next **thing** I knew p836
there isn't a **thing** [you] can do p1324
there's no such **thing**/person as p1278
too much of a good **thing** p1345
what with one **thing** and another p1323
above all **things** p1324
all **things** being equal p1324
all **things** considered p1324
all **things** to all men/people p1324
by the looks of **things** p737
cut it/**things** fine p300
get into the swing of it/**things** p1296
I must be hearing **things** p580
just one of those **things** p1324
move on to higher/better **things** p812
not do **things** by halves p563
see **things** in black and white p118
take it/**things** easy p387
take **things** easy p1324
the shape of **things** to come p1151
things that go bump in the night p1324
can't hear [yourself] **think** p580
great minds **think** alike p548
I should **think** not/so too p1162
think highly of/well of/a lot of etc [sb] p1325
think long and hard p1325
think the sun shines out of [sb's] arse/backside p1282
think the whole world revolves around [you] p1072
not bear **thinking** about p97
put [your] **thinking** cap on p1325
the **thinking** woman's/man's crumpet p1325
come/be a poor second/**third** etc p961
at **this** moment in time p802
be more to **this** than meets the eye p776
be new to **this** game p513
Bugger/Sod etc **this** for a lark p701
by **this** time p1326
depart **this** life p325
get the/**this** show on the road p1165
in **this** day and age p309
just **this** once p865
not long for **this** world p736
say **this**/that much for [sb/sth] p1110
this vale of tears p1409
watch **this** space p1436
be nothing if not generous/honest/**thorough** etc p846
just one of **those** things p1324
one of **those** days p309
look like/as **though** [you've] seen a ghost p524
sound like/as if/as **though** p1212

give [sb] food for **thought** p481
the **thought** crosses [sb's] mind p1326
Who would have **thought** [sth] p1324
without a second **thought** p1126
a penny for your **thoughts** p918
compose your features/**thoughts** p247
Nothing could have been further from my mind/**thoughts** p508
hang by a **thread** p569
thread your way through/between/etc p1327
pick up the **threads** p932
a quarter past/ after two/**three**/four etc p1019
in/within the space of six weeks/**three** hours etc p1214
bring a lump to [your] **throat** p745
force/ram [sth] down [sb's] **throat** p1328
jump down [sb's] **throat** p678
ram [sth] down [sb's] **throat** p1028
at each other's **throats** p1328
accede to the **throne**/accede to power p6
the power behind the **throne** p970
a quick/brisk trot **through** [sth] p1368
beat a path **through** [sth] p98
cut a swathe **through** [sth] p300
drag [sb's] name **through** the mire/mud p370
drive a coach and horses **through** [sth] p375
echo down/**through** the ages p388
go **through** a bad/difficult/rough/sticky patch p909
go **through** fire and water p462
go **through** the floor p475
go **through** the motions p809
go **through** the roof p1085
go/jump **through** hoops p605
hear [sth] on/**through** the grapevine p546
knock into each other/knock **through** p690
lie **through** [your] teeth p719
look at/see [sth] **through** rose-coloured/tinted glasses p1087
look straight/right **through** [sb] p737
pay **through** the nose p912
put [sb/sth] **through** [their] paces p891
put [sb] **through** the mill p787
put [sb] **through** the wringer p1480
rise from/**through** the ranks p1030
run in/**through** [your] head/mind p1094
run **through** [your] mind/head p1094
slip **through** [sb's] fingers p1189
slip **through** the net p1189
talk **through** [your] hat p1304
thread your way **through**/between/etc p1327
I wouldn't trust [sb] as far as I could **throw** them p1371
pour/**throw** cold water on [sth] p230
put/**throw** a spanner in the works p1215
throw [omething] back in [sb's] face p1328
throw [sb] off balance p1329
throw [your] hat into the ring p575
throw [your] money/cash around p1329
throw [your] weight around/about p1329
throw caution to the wind/winds p1329
throw cold water on [sth] p1329
throw down the gauntlet p516
throw good money after bad p1329
throw the baby out with the bath-water p1328
throw up [your] hands in horror/despair p1329
throw/put [sb] off the scent p1114
stand/stick out like a sore **thumb** p1210
all fingers and **thumbs** p1330
be all fingers and **thumbs** p461
what makes [sb] **tick** p1330
biological clock is **ticking** away p115
go/swim against the **tide** p1331

tie [sb] up in knots p1332
tied to [your] mother's/wife's apron strings p1331
keep a **tight** rein on [sb/sth] p1050
till all hours p610
till/until kingdom come p687
till/until the cows come home p282
about **time** too p1335
all in good **time** p541
all the **time** in the world p1334
any minute/moment/second/**time** now p848
at any one **time** p1334
at this moment in **time** p802
be like feeding **time** at the zoo p450
be only a matter of **time** p770
better luck next **time** p109
bide your **time** p111
by this **time** p1326
from that day/**time** onwards p500
from/since **time** immemorial p625
give [sb] a hard **time** p1335
give [sb] the **time** of day p1334
Give me any day/every **time** p527
have a rare old **time** p1031
have/take **time** off p1333
in the right place at the right **time** p1076
in/within a short space of **time** p1214
live on borrowed **time** p136
make good **time** p540
make up for lost **time** p754
no **time** to lose p1334
once upon a **time** p865
Only **time** will/can tell p1333
pass the **time** of day p906
stand the test of **time** p1238
step back in **time** p1247
take one thing at a **time** p1302
the passing of **time**/the years p906
time stands still p1333
change with/keep up with/move with the **times** p1335
fall on hard **times** p439
nine **times** out of ten p839
ninety-nine **times** out of a hundred p839
ten/fifty/a hundred **times** better p1336
for old **times'** sake p862
like a cat on a hot **tin** roof p184
not give a **tinker's** cuss p1337
look at/see [sth] through rose-coloured/**tinted** glasses p1087
the pattering of **tiny** feet p911
go arse over **tit**/tip p59
go arse over tit/**tip** p59
dip a/your **toe** in the water p342
from head to foot/**toe** p578
from top to **toe** p1346
keep body and soul **together** p129
put [their] heads **together** p578
put two and two **together** p1380
put two and two **together** and make five p1380
spend the night **together** p1221
flush [sth] down the **toilet** p477
by the same **token** p1104
a little bird **told** me p730
take its/their/a **toll** p1343
like there is no **tomorrow** p1344
come down on someone like a **ton** of bricks p237
like a **ton** of bricks p1344
be/go at it hammer and **tongs** p565
Has the cat has got your **tongue** p184
Keep a civil **tongue** in [your] head p212
speak with a forked **tongue** p488
trip off the **tongue** p1366
a drop **too** much to drink p377
about time **too** p1335
be **too** clever by half p219
be **too** close for comfort p223
be **too** hot to handle p608

To find an idiom, look at the word in colour in each idiom. All of the coloured words are in alphabetical order.
After each idiom there is a page number that tells you where the idiom is explained.

1517

before very/too long p736
go too far p444
have a few too many p454
I should think not/so too p1162
miles too big/small/expensive etc p786
not a moment too soon p802
not to put too fine a point on p461
one too many p760
protest too much p999
speak too soon p1217
too big for [your] boots p112
too good to be true p1345
too good to miss p1345
too little too late p1345
too many chiefs and not enough Indians p203
too much like hard work p1345
too much of a good thing p1345
too old/a bit old p861
fight tooth and nail p1345
from top to bottom p1346
from top to toe p1346
off the top of [your] head p1346
pay top dollar p912
work [your] way up/to the top p1440
hit/touch a raw nerve p832
kick [sth] into touch p685
touch/strike/hit a raw nerve p1349
tug at/touch [your] forelock p486
wouldn't touch [sth] with a barge pole p1349
put the finishing touches to p462
a hard/tough nut to crack p850
as tough as old boots p1350
be a hard/tough act to follow p12
be well/favourably/etc disposed to/towards [sth/sb] p352
go a long way towards doing [sth] p736
paint the town red p894
sink without a trace p1177
kick over the traces p685
off the beaten track p98
the wrong/other side of the tracks p1170
fall into the/someone's trap p439
handle/treat [sb] with kid gloves p686
treat [sb] like dirt p1362
treat [sb] like royalty p1362
go trick or treating p1364
How's life treating you p720
be barking up the wrong tree p90
can't see the wood for the trees p1129
not see the wood for the trees p1470
every trick in the book p1364
go trick or treating p1364
tried and found wanting p1432
take a stroll/trip/walk down memory lane p778
trip off the tongue p1366
swear like a trooper p1367
a quick/brisk trot through [sth] p1368
lay up trouble for [yourself] p705
more trouble than it's worth p1368
store up trouble/problems p1257
fish in troubled waters p465
pour oil on troubled waters p969
catch [sb] with [their] pants/trousers down p185
see [sb's] true colours p234
show [sb] in their true colours p234
too good to be true p1345
blow [your] own trumpet/horn p125
turn/come up trumps p1370
I wouldn't trust [sb] as far as I could throw them p1371
go down the tubes p1373
a nip here and a tuck there p839
your best bib and tucker p111
tug at/touch [your] forelock p486
light at the end of the tunnel p722
beat/turn swords into ploughshares p1297
come/go/turn full circle p504

go/turn belly up p104
go/turn bright red p1044
not know where/which way to turn p692
put/turn the clock back p222
put/turn the clocks back p222
put/turn the clocks forward p222
take a turn p1376
take a turn for the better/worse p1376
turn 16/50/9 o'clock etc p1376
turn [sth] upside down p1376
turn [your] nose up p1376
turn a blind eye p1375
turn a deaf ear p1376
turn back the clock p222
turn over a new leaf p1376
turn Queen's evidence p1019
turn the clock back p1376
turn the other cheek p1376
turn up like a bad penny p1377
turn upside down p1404
turn/come up trumps p1370
turn/use [sth] to good account p8
twist/turn the knife in the wound p689
poacher turned gamekeeper p954
when [sb] was a mere twinkle in [their] father's eye p1380
be/go round the twist p1380
twist [sb] around/round [your] little finger p1380
twist/turn the knife in the wound p689
[your] two cents worth p1380
a quarter past/after two/three/four etc p1019
as thick as two short planks p1323
bring/take [sb] down a peg or two p916
cut both/two ways p300
fall between two stools p439
in two shakes of a lamb's tail p1149
kill two birds with one stone p686
like two peas in a pod p723
not be short of a bob or two p1161
not care/give two hoots p605
one step forward two steps back p1248
One/two etc down one/two etc to go p367
put two and two together p1380
put two and two together and make five p1380
stand on [your] own two feet p1238
That makes two of us p1381
the lesser of two evils p715
There's no two ways about it p1380
two can play at that game p1381

U

rear its ugly head p1038
make the ultimate/supreme sacrifice p1100
pay the ultimate price p912
in no uncertain terms p1316
Bob's your uncle p129
I'll be a monkey's uncle p803
bags under [your] eyes p83
be right under [your] nose p844
be six feet under p1180
be/fall under [sb's] influence/spell p1388
be/feel under the weather p1443
chuck [sb] under the chin p208
come under fire p462
come/go under the hammer p565
come/suffer under the lash p701
cut the ground from under [sb's] feet p301
drink [sb] under the table p375
from under [your] nose p844
go under the knife p689
groan with/under the weight of [sth] p552
hot under the collar p608
keep/place [sb] under restraint p1066
labour under the delusion/illusion/misapprehension etc p695

on/under pain of death p894
pull the rug from under [sb/sb's feet] p1005
put [sth] under the microscope p784
put the skids under sth p1181
send [sth] under plain/separate cover p281
sweep [sth] under the carpet p1294
take [sb] under [your] wing p1463
take [sth] under advisement p19
under [your] own steam p1246
under false pretences p441
under house arrest p610
under lock and key p733
under sedation/the doctor etc p1388
under starter's orders p1242
under the same roof p1085
water under the bridge p1437
understand one another/each other p1390
unfit for human habitation p561
work long/regular/unsocial etc hours p609
till/until kingdom come p687
till/until the cows come home p282
to/until [my] dying day p338
until [you are] blue in the face p126
leave no stone unturned p710
a boot/kick up [the/your] backside p81
a kick up the arse/backside p685
an ace up [your] sleeve p10
be barking up the wrong tree p90
be jumping up and down p678
be pushing up the daisies p1011
be up to no good p541
be/come up against a brick wall p22
bring [sb] up short p150
bring up the rear p150
chalk [sth] up to experience p192
change with/keep up with/move with the times p1335
clean up [your] act p216
come up with the goods p541
come up/out smelling of roses p1194
coming up roses p1087
cook/dance/talk etc up a storm p1258
create/kick up/raise a stink p1253
curl up and die p298
cut up rough p300
done up/dressed up like a dog's dinner p361
done/dressed up to the nines p839
dressed up to the nines p374
eaten up with/by [sth] p387
fed up to the back teeth p450
fling up [your] hands p473
gather up strength/courage p516
get your courage up p524
get/pick up steam p1246
give [sb] a leg up p712
give [sb] up for dead p528
give [sth] up as a bad job p82
give up hope p528
give up the ghost p524
go up in flames p469
go up in smoke p1195
go/come up in the world p1475
have a card up [your] sleeve p176
hold [sb/sth] up to ridicule p1075
hold [your] head up high p597
keep up appearances p683
keep up with the Joneses p683
keep your pecker up p914
keep/hold [your] end up p402
kick up [your] heels p685
kick up a fuss/row/stink p685
laugh up [your] sleeve p704
lay up trouble for [yourself] p705
lead [sb] up the garden path p707
look/feel like death warmed up/over p312
make [sth] up as you go along p754

To find an idiom, look at the word in colour in each idiom. All of the coloured words are in alphabetical order.
After each idiom there is a page number that tells you where the idiom is explained.

1518

make **up** [your] mind p789
make **up** for lost time p754
not be all [it's] cracked **up** to be p284
pick [yourself] **up** off the floor p932
pick [it's] the bill/tab p932
pick **up** the phone p933
pick **up** the pieces p932
pick **up** the threads p932
pick **up**/take up the slack p1184
pluck **up** [your] courage p951
pull [sb] **up** short p1006
pull [your] socks **up** p1005
pull **up** short p1006
pull/haul yourself **up** by your bootstraps p134
put your feet **up** p1012
put/get [sb's] back **up** p79
put/get the wind **up** [sb] p1461
roll **up** [your] sleeves p1084
rub [sb] **up** the wrong way p1091
screw **up** [your] courage p1120
send chills down/**up** [sb's] spine p204
set **up** shop p1160
Shape **up** or ship out p1152
sharpen **up** your act p1153
shiver up and down [your] spine p1158
Shove/stick [sth] **up** [your] ass p64
shut **up** shop p1168
sit **up** and take notice p1179
smarten **up** [your] act p1193
stand **up** and be counted p1238
step/move **up** a gear p517
store **up** trouble/problems p1257
take **up** office p1302
take **up** residence/residency [somewhere] p1062
take **up** the cudgels for/against [sb/sth] p296
take/pick **up** the gauntlet p516
the balloon goes **up** p85
the right way round/**up** p1076
throw **up** [your] hands in horror/despair p1329
tie [sb] **up** in knots p1332
turn [your] nose **up** p1376
turn **up** like a bad penny p1377
turn/come **up** trumps p1370
vanish/go **up**/disappear in a puff of smoke p1004
wake **up** and smell the coffee p1429
work [your] way **up**/to the top p1440
wrap [sb] **up** in cotton wool p1479
wrinkle **up** [your] nose p1480
be incumbent on/**upon** someone p637
once **upon** a time p865
upon my word p1471
you can depend on/**upon** it p326
upset the apple cart p1404
turn [sth] **upside** down p1376
turn **upside** down p1404
Do me/**us** a favour p448
That makes two of **us** p1381
turn/**use** [sth] to good account p8

V

take [sb's] name in **vain** p823
this **vale** of tears p1409
take [sth] at face **value** p434
disappear/**vanish** into thin air p1323
vanish/go up/disappear in a puff of smoke p1004
draw a **veil** over [sth] p1413
an iron hand/fist in a **velvet** glove p664
give/quote [sth/sb] chapter and **verse** p195
all **very** well p1446
all **very** well/fine/good p1416
be nothing/not much/**very** little in it p632
before [your] **very** eyes p432

before **very**/too long p736
from the **very** first p464
almost burst a blood **vessel** p124
be a **victim** of [your] own success p1418
be a **victory** for common sense p1418
snatch **victory** from the jaws of defeat p1198
What price fame/**victory**/success etc p983
bird's eye **view** p115
hove into sight/**view** p611
take a dim **view** of [sth] p341
die a natural/**violent** etc death p338

W

tail **wagging** the dog p1301
fall off the **wagon** p1427
an accident **waiting** to happen p7
wake up and smell the coffee p1429
go/**walk** down the aisle p28
ride/drive/**walk**/etc off into the sunset p1283
take a stroll/trip/**walk** down memory lane p778
walk all over p1429
walk right into [sth] p1429
worship the ground [sb] **walks** on p1477
be banging etc [your] head against a brick **wall** p578
be/come up against a brick **wall** p22
have [your] back to/against the **wall** p79
Do you **want** to make something/anything of it p754
how much do you **want** to bet p108
It makes me **want** to puke p1005
not/never **want** for anything p1432
the last thing [you] **want**/need etc p1324
tried and found **wanting** p1432
look/feel like death **warmed** up/over p312
fire a **warning** shot across [sb's] bows p139
hear **warning** bells p1434
warning/alarm bells start to ring/sound p104
sign [your] own death **warrant** p1173
wash [your] dirty linen in public p1434
There **wasn't** a dry eye in the house p379
watch paint dry p1436
watch the world go by p1436
watch this space p1436
be like a fish out of **water** p465
come hell or high **water** p585
dip a/your toe in the **water** p342
go through fire and **water** p462
keep [your] head above **water** p578
make [sb's] mouth **water** p811
pour/throw cold **water** on [sth] p230
take to [sth] like a duck to **water** p380
throw cold **water** on [sth] p1329
water off a duck's back p1437
water under the bridge p1437
fish in troubled **waters** p465
pour oil on troubled **waters** p969
be riding/on the crest of a **wave** p289
[sb] couldn't act/argue/fight etc [their] **way** out of a paper bag p898
a long **way** to go p736
any **way** you slice it p1187
be behind [sb] all the **way** p103
be laughing all the **way** to the bank p703
bluff [your] **way** into/out of [sth] p127
every which **way** p418
follow/steer/take the middle course/**way**/path p784
go [your] own sweet **way** p1440
go [your] own **way** p1440
go a long **way** p736
go a long **way** towards doing [sth] p736
go all the **way** p1440
go back a long **way** p736

go down the wrong **way** p1481
have come a long **way** p736
have your head screwed on the right **way** p578
know [your] **way** around [sth] p693
not know where/which **way** to turn p692
one **way** or another p865
right/wrong **way** round p1089
rub [sb] **up** the wrong way p1091
see [your] **way** clear to p1130
talk your **way** into/out of [sth] p1440
the right **way** round/up p1076
the wrong **way** round/around p1482
thread your **way** through/between/etc p1327
way/direction the wind blows p1440
work [your] **way** around/round to [sth] p1473
work [your] **way** up/to the top p1440
wouldn't have it any other **way** p1440
cut both/two **ways** p300
go [your] own separate **ways** p1139
see the error of [your] **ways** p412
There's no two **ways** about it p1380
fall by the **wayside** p1441
here **we** go p588
here **we** go again p588
I'll/We'll cross that bridge when I/we get to it p291
That's all I/you/we need p30
we like cheap/tall/young etc p723
I'll/**We'll** cross that bridge when I/we get to it p291
we'll soon see about that p1130
wear [your] heart on [your] sleeve p1442
wear sackcloth and ashes p1099
be/feel under the **weather** p1443
brass monkey **weather** p143
make heavy **weather** of [sth] p583
hear **wedding** bells p580
drive a **wedge** between [sb] p376
thin end of the **wedge** p1323
the **week**/month/year before last p702
Roll on the **weekend**/five o'clock etc p1083
in/within the space of six **weeks**/three hours etc p1214
a load/**weight** off [your] mind p789
be worth [your/its] **weight** in gold p1477
be/take a **weight** off [your] mind p1445
by sheer force/**weight** of numbers p849
groan with/under the **weight** of [sth] p552
take the **weight** off [your] feet/legs p1445
throw [your] **weight** around/about p1329
How strange/stupid/**weird** etc is that p612
greet/**welcome** [sb] with open arms p868
all very **well** p1446
all very **well**/fine/good p1416
be **well**/favourably/etc disposed to/towards [sth/sb] p352
come off better/worse/badly/**well** p237
it's just as **well** that p680
know full **well** p505
know when [you] are **well** off p1448
leave **well** alone p710
might just as **well** p680
think highly of/**well** of/a lot of etc [sb] p1325
well I'll be blowed p125
Well I'll be damned p305
Well what do you know p692
you may **well** ask p63
a few **well**-chosen words p1447
be **wet** behind the ears p1449
wet the/[your] bed p1449
for **what** it's worth p1477
I don't know how/**what**/why etc p692
just **what** the doctor ordered p360
know **what** [you] are talking about p692
no matter **what**/when/why etc p770

To find an idiom, look at the word in colour in each idiom. All of the coloured words are in alphabetical order.
After each idiom there is a page number that tells you where the idiom is explained.

not know what [sb] sees in [sb/sth] p1130
not know what has hit [you] p692
not know what hit you p595
practise what [you] preach p972
reap what [you] have sown p1037
Well what do you know p692
what [sb] is really made of p753
what [sb] says goes p1110
What have you got to say for [yourself] p1110
what I wouldn't give for [sth] p527
what makes [sb] tick p1330
What price fame/victory/success etc p983
what with one thing and another p1323
what/whatever [sb] says goes p1450
you know what I mean p692
What's that all about then p1450
What's the big idea p112
What's the magic word p750
[He/She] deserves whatever/everything [he/she] gets p330
what/whatever [sb] says goes p1450
separate the wheat from the chaff p1451
put a spoke in [sb's] wheel etc p1226
set the wheels in motion p1451
as/if/when/etc the spirit moves [sb] p1224
believe [sth] when [you] see it p104
I'll/We'll cross that bridge when I/we get to it p291
if/when it comes to the crunch p294
if/when push comes to shove p1011
kick/hit [sb] when [they are] down p367
know when [you] are well off p1448
no matter what/when/why etc p770
when [sb] was a mere twinkle in [their] father's eye p1380
when all is said and done p1110
when hell freezes over p585
when the chips are down p205
be plenty more where [sb/sth] came from p949
from where [sb] stands p1238
hit [sb] where it hurts p595
know where you stand p1238
know/see where [sb] is coming from p1452
not know where to put [yourself] p692
not know where/which way to turn p692
put [your] money where [your] mouth is p803
not know whether to laugh or cry p692
not know whether you are coming or going p236
every which way p418
know which side [your] bread is buttered on p692
not know where/which way to turn p692
driving while intoxicated p375
every once in a while p865
make [sth/it] worth [your] while p1477
strike while the iron is hot p1265
while the going is good p539
a fair crack of the whip p437
have/hold the whip hand p1453
come within a whisker of [doing sth] p1454
be down in black and white p118
egg white/white of an egg p1455
see things in black and white p118
Who can say p1110
who shall remain nameless p823
Who would have thought [sth] p1324
look who's talking p1304
a whole new ball game p85
go the whole hog p1456
the whole kit and caboodle p166
think the whole world revolves around [you] p1072
To whom it may concern p250
I don't know how/what/why etc p692

no matter what/when/why etc p770
leg before wicket p712
cast [your] net wide p183
from far and wide p444
give [sth/sb] a wide berth p1458
tied to [your] mother's/wife's apron strings p1331
sow [your] wild oats p1214
wild horses wouldn't drag me p1459
beyond [your] wildest dreams p110
spread like wildfire p1459
bear [sb] ill will p624
Heads will roll p578
Only time will/can tell p1333
That will never do p834
that will show [sb] p1164
will never hear the end of it p580
will not take no for an answer p1302
with the best will in the world p107
May the best man/person win p107
win [sth] hands down p567
win hands down p1460
You can't win 'em all p1460
put/get the wind up [sb] p1461
sail against the wind p1102
sail close to the wind p1102
take the wind out of [sb's] sails p1461
throw caution to the wind/winds p1329
way/direction the wind blows p1440
be scattered to the four winds p1113
throw caution to the wind/winds p1329
take [sb] under [your] wing p1463
blow/bomb/wipe etc [sth] off the map p761
wipe [sth] off the map p1464
wipe the slate clean p1464
wipe the smile off [sb's] face p1464
with the slate wiped clean p1185
the fount of all knowledge/gossip/wisdom etc p491
an old/a wise head on young shoulders p578
sadder but wiser p1100
I/You wouldn't wish [sth] on anyone/my/your worst enemy p1465
wish [you] had never been born p135
not be beyond the wit of man/[sb] p1466
be within hailing distance of [somewhere] p562
come within a whisker of [doing sth] p1454
come within an ace of [sth] p10
come within an inch of [sth] p634
in/within a short space of time p1214
in/within spitting distance p1224
in/within the space of six weeks/three hours etc p1214
within living memory p730
within shouting distance p1163
within striking distance p1265
within the realms of possibility p1037
go off without a hitch p1110
it goes without saying p1110
no/without rhyme or reason p1073
sink without a trace p1177
without a care in the world p177
without a second thought p1126
without fear or favour p448
without further/more ado p16
without let or hindrance p716
without so much as a backward glance p1467
without so much as a by-your-leave p1467
bear false witness p97
have/keep all [your] wits about [you] p1468
live by [your] wits p731
pit [your] wits against [sb/sth] p940
a wolf in sheep's clothing p1468
keep the wolf from the door p1468
a man/woman of few words p454

feel like a new woman/man p835
fine figure of a man/woman p457
just the man/woman for the job p673
like a man/woman possessed p965
make an honest woman of [sb] p603
the man/woman on the Clapham omnibus p863
the thinking woman's/man's crumpet p1325
be a nine days' wonder p839
wonders never cease p1469
can't see the wood for the trees p1129
not see the wood for the trees p1470
pull the wool over [sb's] eyes p1470
wrap [sb] up in cotton wool p1479
by word of mouth p1471
from the word go p1472
not have a civil word to say about [sb] p212
put in a good word for [sb] p1471
put the word about/around/out/round p1471
upon my word p1471
What's the magic word p750
word gets about/around/round p1471
keep your promise/word; keep an appointment p682
a few well-chosen words p1447
a man/woman of few words p454
famous last words p443
in so many words p760
in words of one syllable p1471
not mince your words p789
put words in/into [sb's] mouth p1471
take the words out of [sb's] mouth p1471
You mark my words p763
a nasty piece of work p825
all in a day's work p309
do all the donkey work p363
drive/work [yourself] into the ground p552
make short work of [sth] p1161
nice work if you can get it p837
the Protestant work ethic p999
too much like hard work p1345
work [sb's] ass off p64
work [your] ass off p64
work [your] fingers to the bone p1472
work [your] way around/round to [sth] p1473
work [your] way up/to the top p1440
work like a charm p1472
work long/regular/unsocial etc hours p609
work/go like a dream p373
put/throw a spanner in the works p1215
all the time in the world p1334
all/the four corners of the world/earth p272
be living in a dream world p373
come/go down in the world p367
go/come down in the world p1475
go/come up in the world p1475
have all the cares of the world on [your] shoulders p177
make a world of difference p1475
make the world go around/round p1475
mean/be all the world to [sb] p1475
not long for this world p736
not set the world on fire p1143
the easiest thing in the world p386
the oldest profession in the world p861
think the whole world revolves around [you] p1072
watch the world go by p1436
with the best will in the world p107
without a care in the world p177
the best of both worlds p107
[sb's] bark is worse than [their] bite p90
a fate worse than death p447
come off better/worse/badly/well p237

To find an idiom, look at the word in colour in each idiom. All of the coloured words are in alphabetical order.
After each idiom there is a page number that tells you where it is explained.

1520

Y

Z

To find an idiom, look at the word in colour in each idiom. All of the coloured words are in alphabetical order.
After each idiom there is a page number that tells you where the idiom is explained.

Word families: building possibilities...

Words often come in families. You can expand your vocabulary by becoming familiar with these word families and this can also enable you to become a more fluent speaker and writer of English. If you know all the possible words within a word family, you can express yourself in a wider range of ways. For example, if you know the verb and the noun forms related to the adjective **boring**, you can say:

- The lesson was **boring**.
- The lesson **bored** me.
- That lesson was such a **bore**.

An extra reason for paying attention to word families is that for some exams you have to know them.

In the list below, the words printed in **bold** are words which are very common and important to learn. The other words in the same row are words in the same family, often formed with prefixes and suffixes. Sometimes they are just a different part of speech (e.g. **anger**, which is a noun and a verb). All the words in this list have entries in the dictionary except for some beginning with **un-**, **im-**, **in-** or **ir-**, or ending with **-ly** or **-ily**, where the meaning is always regular. Sometimes words in a word family can have meanings which are quite different from others in the group, so you should always check in the dictionary if you are not sure of the meaning.

Nouns	Adjectives	Verbs	Adverbs
ability, disability, inability	**able**, unable, disabled	enable, disable	ably
acceptance	**acceptable**, unacceptable, accepted	**accept**	acceptably, unacceptably
accident	accidental		accidentally
accuracy, inaccuracy	**accurate**, inaccurate		accurately, inaccurately
accusation, the accused, accuser	accusing	**accuse**	accusingly
achievement, achiever	achievable	**achieve**	
act, action, inaction, interaction, reaction, transaction	acting	**act**	
activity, inactivity	**active**, inactive, interactive, proactive	activate	actively
addition	additional	**add**	additionally
admiration, admirer	admirable	**admire**	admirably
advantage, disadvantage	advantageous, disadvantaged		advantageously
advertisement, advertiser, **advertising**		advertise	
advice, adviser	advisable, inadvisable, advisory	**advise**	
agreement, disagreement	agreeable	**agree**, disagree	agreeably
aim	aimless	**aim**	aimlessly
amazement	amazed, **amazing**	amaze	amazingly
anger	**angry**	anger	angrily
announcement, announcer	unannounced	**announce**	unannounced
appearance, disappearance, reappearance		**appear**, disappear, reappear	
applicant, application	applicable, applied	**apply**	
appreciation	appreciable, appreciative	**appreciate**	appreciatively
approval, disapproval	approving, disapproving	**approve**, disapprove	approvingly
approximation	approximate	approximate	**approximately**
argument	arguable, argumentative	**argue**	arguably
arrangement		**arrange**, rearrange	
art, artist, artistry	artistic		artistically
shame	**ashamed**, unashamed, shameful, shameless	shame	shamefully, shamelessly
attachment	attached, unattached, detachable, detached	**attach**, detach	
attack, counter-attack, attacker		**attack**, counter-attack	
attention	attentive, inattentive	attend	attentively
attraction, attractiveness	**attractive**, unattractive	**attract**	attractively

Nouns	Adjectives	Verbs	Adverbs
authority, authorization	authoritarian, authoritative, unauthorized	authorize	
availability	**available**, unavailable		
avoidance	avoidable, unavoidable	**avoid**	
awareness	**aware**, unaware		unawares
base, the basics, basis	baseless, **basic**	**base**	**basically**
bearer	bearable, unbearable	**bear**	
beat, beating	unbeatable, unbeaten	**beat**	
beauty, beautician	**beautiful**		beautifully
beginner, **beginning**		begin	
behaviour/US **behavior**, misbehaviour/US misbehavior	behavioural/US behavioral	**behave**, misbehave	
belief, disbelief	believable, unbelievable	**believe**, disbelieve	unbelievably
block, blockage	blocked, unblocked	**block**, unblock	
blood, bleeding	bloodless, bloody	bleed	
the boil, boiler	boiling	**boil**	
bore, boredom	**bored**, **boring**	bore	boringly
break, outbreak, breakage	unbreakable, **broken**, unbroken	**break**	
breath, breather, breathing	breathless	**breathe**	breathlessly
brother, brotherhood	brotherly		
build, builder, **building**		**build**, rebuild	
burn, burner	burning, burnt	**burn**	
burial	buried	**bury**	
calculation, calculator	incalculable, calculated, calculating	**calculate**	
calm, calmness	**calm**	calm	calmly
capability	**capable**, incapable		capably
care, carer	careful, careless, caring, uncaring	**care**	carefully, carelessly
celebration, celebrity	celebrated, celebratory	**celebrate**	
centre/US center, centralization, decentralization	**central**, centralized	centre/US center, centralize, decentralize	**centrally**
certainty, uncertainty	**certain**, uncertain		certainly, uncertainly
challenge, challenger	challenging	challenge	
change	changeable, interchangeable, unchanged, changing	**change**	
character, characteristic, characterization	characteristic, uncharacteristic	characterize	characteristically
chemical, chemist, chemistry	**chemical**		chemically
circle, semicircle, circulation	circular	circle, circulate	
cleaner, cleaning, cleanliness	**clean**, unclean	**clean**	cleanly
clarity, clearance, clearing	**clear**, unclear	clear	clear, **clearly**
close, closure	closed, closing	**close**	
closeness	close		**close**, closely
clothes, clothing	clothed, unclothed	clothe	
collection, collector	collected, collective	**collect**	collectively
colour/US **color**, colouring/US coloring	coloured/US colored, discoloured/US discolored, colourful/US colorful, colourless/US colorless	colour/US color	colourfully/US colorfully
combination	combined	**combine**	
comfort, discomfort	**comfortable**, uncomfortable, comforting	comfort	comfortably
commitment	noncommittal, committed	**commit**	
communication, communicator	communicative, uncommunicative	**communicate**	
comparison	comparable, incomparable, comparative	**compare**	comparatively
competition, competitor	competitive, uncompetitive	**compete**	competitively
completion, incompleteness	**complete**, incomplete	**complete**	**completely**, incompletely
complication	**complicated**, uncomplicated	complicate	
computer, computing, computerization		computerize	
concentration	concentrated	**concentrate**	
concern	**concerned**, unconcerned	**concern**	
conclusion	concluding, conclusive, inconclusive	conclude	conclusively
condition, precondition, conditioner, conditioning	conditional, unconditional	condition	conditionally, unconditionally
confidence	**confident**, confidential	confide	confidently, confidentially
confirmation	confirmed, unconfirmed	**confirm**	
confusion	confused, confusing	**confuse**	confusingly
connection	connected, disconnected, unconnected	**connect**, disconnect	
subconscious, unconscious, consciousness, unconsciousness	**conscious**, subconscious, unconscious		consciously, unconsciously

Nouns	Adjectives	Verbs	Adverbs
consequence	consequent, inconsequential		consequently
consideration	considerable, considerate, inconsiderate, considered	**consider**, reconsider	considerably, considerately
continent	continental, intercontinental		
continuation, continuity	continual, continued, **continuous**	**continue**, discontinue	continually, continuously
contribution, contributor	contributory	**contribute**	
control, controller	controlling, uncontrollable	control	
convenience, inconvenience	**convenient**, inconvenient	inconvenience	uncontrollably
	convinced, convincing, unconvincing	convince	conveniently
cook, cooker, cookery, **cooking**	cooked, uncooked	**cook**	convincingly
cool, coolness	**cool**	cool	
correction, correctness	**correct**, incorrect, corrective	**correct**	coolly
count, recount	countable, uncountable, countless	**count**, recount	correctly, incorrectly
cover, coverage, covering	undercover, uncovered	**cover**, uncover	
creation, creativity, creator	creative, uncreative	**create**, recreate	undercover
crime, **criminal**, criminologist	criminal, incriminating	incriminate	creatively
critic, **criticism**	**critical**, uncritical	**criticize**	criminally
crowd, overcrowding	**crowded**, overcrowded	crowd	critically
cruelty	**cruel**		
cry, outcry	crying	cry	cruelly
culture, subculture	cultural, cultured		
cure	cured, incurable	**cure**	culturally
custom, **customer**, customs	customary	accustom	
cut, cutting	cutting	**cut**, undercut	customarily
damage, damages	damaging, undamaged	**damage**	
danger	endangered, **dangerous**	endanger	
dare, daring	daring	dare	dangerously
dark, darkness	**dark**, darkened, darkening	darken	daringly
date	dated, outdated	date, predate	darkly
day, midday	daily		
dead, **death**	**dead**, deadly, deathly	deaden	daily
deal, dealer, dealings		**deal**	deadly, deathly
deceit, deceiver, deception	deceitful, deceptive	**deceive**	
decision, indecision	decided, undecided, decisive, indecisive	**decide**	deceptively
decoration, decorator	decorative	**decorate**	decidedly, decisively, indecisively
deep, **depth**	**deep**, deepening	deepen	decoratively
defeat, defeatism, defeatist	undefeated, defeatist	defeat	deeply
defence/US **defense**, defendant, defender	defenceless/US defenseless, indefensible, defensive	**defend**	defensively
definition	**definite**, indefinite	define	**definitely**, indefinitely
demand, demands	demanding, undemanding	**demand**	
democracy, democrat	democratic, undemocratic		
demonstration, demonstrator	demonstrable, demonstrative	**demonstrate**	democratically
denial	undeniable	**deny**	demonstrably
dependant, dependence, independence, dependency	dependable, dependent, independent	**depend**	undeniably
description	describable, indescribable, nondescript, descriptive	**describe**	dependably, independently
desire	desirable, undesirable, desired, undesired	desire	descriptively
destroyer, destruction	indestructible, destructive	**destroy**	
determination, determiner	**determined**, predetermined, indeterminate	determine	destructively
developer, **development**, redevelopment	developed, undeveloped, developing	**develop**, redevelop	determinedly
difference, indifference, differentiation	**different**, indifferent	differ, differentiate	differently
directness, **direction**, directions, **director**	**direct**, indirect	**direct**, redirect	directly, indirectly
disagreement	disagreeable	**disagree**	disagreeably
disappointment	**disappointed**, disappointing	disappoint	disappointingly
disaster	disastrous		disastrously
disciplinarian, **discipline**	disciplinary, disciplined, undisciplined	discipline	
discoverer, **discovery**		**discover**	
distance	**distant**	distance	distantly
disturbance	disturbed, undisturbed, disturbing	**disturb**	disturbingly
divide, division, subdivision	divided, undivided, divisible, divisive	**divide**, subdivide	
divorce, divorcee	divorced	divorce	
do, doing	done, overdone, undone	**do**, outdo, overdo, redo, undo	
doubt, doubter	undoubted, doubtful, doubtless	**doubt**	undoubtedly, doubtfully
dream, dreamer	dream, dreamless, dreamy	**dream**	dreamily

Nouns	Adjectives	Verbs	Adverbs
dress, dresser, dressing	dressed, undressed, dressy	**dress**, redress, undress	dressily
drink, drinker, drinking, drunk, drunkenness	**drunk**, drunken	**drink**	drunkenly
drive, **driver**, driving	driving	**drive**	
due, dues	**due**, undue		due, duly, unduly
earner, earnings		**earn**	
earth	earthy, earthly, unearthly	unearth	
ease, unease, easiness	**easy**, uneasy	ease	**easily**, uneasily, easy
east, easterner	east, easterly, eastern	east, eastward(s)	
economics, economist, **economy**	**economic**, economical, economize uneconomic(al)	economically	
education	educated, uneducated, educational	educate	educationally
effect, effectiveness, ineffectiveness	**effective**, ineffective, ineffectual	effect	effectively, ineffectively
effort	effortless		effortlessly
election, re-election, elector, electorate	unelected, electoral	elect, re-elect	
electrician, **electricity**	**electric, electrical**	electrify	electrically
electronics	**electronic**		electronically
embarrassment	**embarrassed, embarrassing**	embarrass	embarrassingly
emotion	emotional, emotive		emotionally
emphasis	emphatic	emphasize	emphatically
employee, **employer, employment**, unemployment	unemployed	**employ**	
encouragement, discouragement	encouraged, encouraging, discouraging	**encourage**, discourage	encouragingly
end, ending	unending, endless	**end**	endlessly
energy	energetic	energize	energetically
enjoyment	enjoyable	**enjoy**	enjoyably
enormity	**enormous**	enormously	
entrance, entrant, **entry**		**enter**	
entertainer, **entertainment**	entertaining	entertain	entertainingly
enthusiasm, enthusiast	**enthusiastic**, unenthusiastic unenthusiastically	enthuse	enthusiastically,
environment, environmentalist	environmental		environmentally
equality, inequality	**equal**, unequal	equalize	**equally**, unequally
escape, escapism	escaped, inescapable	**escape**	inescapably
essence, essentials	**essential**	essentially	
estimate, estimation	estimated	**estimate**, overestimate, underestimate	
event, non-event	eventful, uneventful, eventual		eventfully, eventually
exam, examination, cross-examination, examiner		examine, cross-examine	
excellence	**excellent**	excel	excellently
excitement	excitable, **excited, exciting**, unexciting	excite	excitedly, excitingly
excuse	excusable, inexcusable	**excuse**	inexcusably
existence	non-existent, existing, pre-existing	**exist**, coexist	
expectancy, expectation	expectant, unexpected	**expect**	expectantly, unexpectedly
expenditure, **expense**, expenses	**expensive**, inexpensive	expend	expensively, inexpensively
experience, inexperience	**experienced**, inexperienced	experience	
experiment	experimental	experiment	experimentally
expert, expertise	expert, inexpert		expertly
explaining, **explanation**	unexplained, explanatory, explicable, inexplicable	**explain**	inexplicably
explosion, explosive	exploding, explosive	**explode**	explosively
exploration, explorer	exploratory	**explore**	
expression	expressive	**express**	expressively
extreme, extremism, extremist, extremity	**extreme**, extremist		**extremely**
fact	factual		factually
fail, failure	unfailing	**fail**	unfailingly
fairness	**fair**, unfair		**fairly**, unfairly
faith, faithfulness	faithful, unfaithful		faithfully
familiarity, **family**	**familiar**, unfamiliar	familiarize	familiarly
fame	famed, **famous**, infamous		famously, infamously
fashion	fashionable, unfashionable	fashion	fashionably, unfashionably
fat	**fat**, fattening, fatty	fatten	
fastener		**fasten**, unfasten	
fault	faultless, faulty	fault	faultlessly
fear	fearful, fearless, fearsome	fear	fearfully, fearlessly
feel, **feeling**, feelings	unfeeling	**feel**	

Nouns	Adjectives	Verbs	Adverbs
fiction, nonfiction	fictional		
fill, refill, filling	filling	**fill**, refill	
final, semifinal, finalist	**final**	finalize	
finish	finished, unfinished	finish	**finally**
firmness, infirmity	**firm**, infirm		firmly
fish, fishing	fishy	fish	fishily
fit, fittings	fitted, fitting	**fit**	fittingly
fix, fixation, fixture	fixed, transfixed, unfixed	**fix**	
flat	**flat**	flatten	
flower	flowered/flowery, flowering	flower	flat, flatly
fold, folder	folded, folding	**fold**, unfold	
follower, following	following	**follow**	
force	forceful, forcible	**force**	forcefully, forcibly
forest, deforestation, forestry	forested		
forgetfulness	forgetful, unforgettable	**forget**	forgetfully
forgiveness	forgiving, unforgiving	**forgive**	
form, formation, transformation, reformer, transformer	reformed	**form**, reform, transform	
formality	**formal**, informal	formalize	formally, informally
fortune	fortunate, unfortunate		**fortunately**, unfortunately
freebie, **freedom**	**free**	**free**	free, freely
freeze, freezer, freezing	freezing, frozen	**freeze**	
frequency, infrequency	**frequent**, infrequent	frequent	**frequently**, infrequently
freshness, refreshments	**fresh**, refreshing	freshen, refresh	freshly, refreshingly
friend, friendliness	friendly, unfriendly	befriend	
fright	**frightened**, **frightening**, frightful	**frighten**	frighteningly, frightfully
fruit, fruition	fruitful, fruitless, fruity		fruitfully, fruitlessly
fund, refund, funding	funded	fund, refund	
furnishings, **furniture**	furnished, unfurnished	furnish	
garden, gardener, gardening		garden	
generalization	**general**	generalize	**generally**
generosity	**generous**		generously
gentleness	**gentle**		gently
gladness	**glad**	gladden	gladly
glass, glasses	glassy		
good, goodies, goodness, goods	**good**		
government, governor	governmental, governing	govern	governmentally
gratitude, ingratitude	**grateful**, ungrateful		gratefully
greatness	**great**		greatly
green, greenery, greens	**green**		
ground, underground, grounding, grounds	groundless, underground	ground	underground
grower, **growth**, undergrowth	growing, grown, overgrown	**grow**, outgrow	
guilt, guiltiness	**guilty**		guiltily
habit	habitual		habitually
hair, hairiness	hairless, hairy		
hand, handful	underhand, handy	hand	
handle, handler, handling		**handle**	
hanger	hanging	**hang**, overhang	
happiness, unhappiness	**happy**, unhappy		happily, unhappily
hardship	**hard**	harden	**hard**, hardly
harm, harmfulness	unharmed, harmful, harmless	**harm**	harmlessly
head, heading, overheads	overhead, heady	head, behead	overhead
health	**healthy**, unhealthy		healthily, unhealthily
hearing	unheard, unheard of	**hear**, overhear	
heart	heartened, heartening, heartless, hearty		heartily, heartlessly
heat, heater, heating	heated, unheated	heat, overheat	heatedly
height, heights	heightened	heighten	
help, helper, helpfulness, helping	helpful, unhelpful, helpless	**help**	helpfully, helplessly
highness	**high**		high, highly
historian, **history**	historic, prehistoric, historical		historically
hold, holder, holding		**hold**	
home	homeless, homely	home	**home**
honesty, dishonesty	**honest**, dishonest		honestly, dishonestly
hope, hopefulness, hopelessness	hopeful, hopeless	**hope**	**hopefully**, hopelessly
human, humanism, humanity,	**human**, inhuman, superhuman, humane	humanly, humanely	inhumanity
hunger	**hungry**		hungrily
hurry	hurried, unhurried	**hurry**	hurriedly
hurt	unhurt, hurtful	**hurt**	hurtfully

Nouns	Adjectives	Verbs	Adverbs
ice, icicle, icing	icy	ice	icily
identification, identity	identifiable, unidentified	**identify**	
imagination	imaginable, unimaginable, imaginary, imaginative	imagine	unimaginably, imaginatively
importance	**important**, unimportant		importantly
impression	impressionable, impressive	impress	impressively
improvement	improved	**improve**	
increase	increased	**increase**	
			increasingly
credibility, incredulity	**incredible**, credible, incredulous		incredibly, incredulously
independence, independent	**independent**		independently
industrialist, industrialization, **industry**	**industrial**, industrialized, industrious		industrially, industriously
infection, disinfectant	infectious	infect, disinfect	infectiously
inflation	inflatable, inflated, inflationary	inflate, deflate	
informant, **information**, informer	informative, uninformative, informed, uninformed	inform, misinform	
injury	injured, uninjured	**injure**	
innocence	**innocent**		innocently
insistence	insistent	**insist**	insistently
instance, instant	**instant**, instantaneous		instantly, instantaneously
instruction, instructor	instructive	instruct	instructively
intelligence	**intelligent**, unintelligent, intelligible, unintelligible	intelligently	
intent, **intention**	intended, unintended, intentional, unintentional	**intend**	intentionally, unintentionally
interest	**interested**, disinterested, uninterested, **interesting**	interest	interestingly
interruption	uninterrupted	**interrupt**	
interview, interviewee		interview	
introduction	introductory	**introduce**	
invention, inventiveness, inventor	inventive	invent, reinvent	inventively
invitation, invite	uninvited, inviting	**invite**	invitingly
involvement	**involved**, uninvolved	**involve**	
item	itemized	itemize	
joke, joker		joke	jokingly
journal, journalism, **journalist**	journalistic		
judge, **judg(e)ment**	judgmental	**judge**	
juice, juices	juicy		
keenness	**keen**		keenly
keep, keeper, keeping	kept	**keep**	
kill, overkill, killer, killing		**kill**	
kindness, unkindness	**kind**, unkind		kindly, unkindly
knowledge	knowing, knowledgeable, known, unknown	**know**	knowingly, unknowingly, knowledgeably
enlargement	**large**	enlarge	largely
laugh, **laughter**	laughable	**laugh**	laughably
law, **lawyer**, outlaw	lawful, unlawful	outlaw	lawfully, unlawfully
laziness	**lazy**		lazily
lead, **leader**, leadership	lead, leading	**lead**	
learner, learning	learned, unlearned	**learn**	
legality, illegality, legalization	**legal**, illegal	legalize	legally, illegally
length	lengthy, lengthening	lengthen	lengthily
liar, **lie**	lying	lie	
life	lifeless, lifelike, lifelong		lifelessly
light, lighter, lighting, lightness	**light**	light, lighten	lightly
dislike, liking	likeable	**like**, dislike	
likelihood	**likely**, unlikely		likely
limit, limitation, limitations	limited, unlimited	**limit**	
literature, literacy	literary, literate, illiterate		
liveliness, living	**live**, lively, living	**live**, outlive, relive	live
local, location, relocation	**local**	dislocate, relocate	locally
loser, **loss**	lost	**lose**	
	loud		aloud, loud/loudly
love, lover	lovable, unlovable, loveless, lovely, loving	**love**	lovingly
low	**low**, lower, lowly	lower	low
luck	**lucky**, unlucky		luckily, unluckily
machine, machinery, mechanic, mechanics, mechanism, machinist	mechanical, mechanized		mechanically
magic, magician	magic, magical		magically
make, remake, maker, making	unmade	**make**, remake	
man, manhood, mankind, manliness, mannishness	manly, manned, unmanned, mannish	man	mannishly, manfully

Nouns	Adjectives	Verbs	Adverbs
management, manager, manageress	manageable, unmanageable, **manage** managerial		
mark, marker, markings	marked, unmarked	**mark**	markedly
market, marketing, marketability, marketer, marketeer	marketable	market	
marriage	**married**, unmarried, marriageable	**marry**, remarry	
match, mismatch	matching, unmatched, matchless	**match**	matchlessly
material, materialism, materialist, materials, materialization	material, immaterial, materialistic	materialize	materially
meaning, meaningfulness	meaningful, meaningless	**mean**	meaningfully, meaninglessly
measure, **measurement**	measurable, immeasurable, measured	**measure**	immeasurably
medical, medication, **medicine**	**medical**, medicated, medicinal, medicinally		medically
memorial, **memory**	memorable	memorize	memorably
mentality	**mental**		mentally
method, methodology	methodical, methodological		methodically
militancy, militant, the military, militia, militarist, militarism	**military**, militant, militaristic, demilitarized		militantly, militarily
mind, minder, reminder, mindlessness	mindless, mindful	**mind**, remind	mindlessly
minimum, minimization	minimal, **minimum**, minimalist	minimize	minimally
miss	**missing**	**miss**	
mistake	mistaken, unmistakable	mistake	unmistakably, mistakenly
mix, mixer, **mixture**	mixed	**mix**	
modernity, modernization	**modern**, modernistic	modernize	
moment	momentary, momentous		momentarily
mood, moodiness	moody		moodily
moral, morals, morality, immorality	**moral**, amoral, immoral, moralistic	moralize	morally
mother, motherhood	motherly	mother	
move, **movement**, removal, remover, mover	movable, unmoved, moving	**move**, remove	movingly
murder, murderer	murderous	**murder**	murderously
music, musical, musician, musicianship, musicality, musicologist, musicology	musical, unmusical		musically
name	named, unnamed, nameless	**name**, rename	namely
nation, national, multinational, nationalism, nationalist, nationality, nationalization	**national**, international, multinational, nationalistic	nationalize	nationally, internationally
nature, naturalist, naturalization, naturalness the supernatural, naturist, naturism	**natural**, supernatural, unnatural, naturalistic	naturalize	naturally, unnaturally
necessity	**necessary**, unnecessary	necessitate	necessarily, unnecessarily
need, needs	needless, needy, needed	**need**	needlessly
nerve, nerves, nervousness	**nervous**, nervy, nerveless, unnerving	unnerve	nervously, nervelessly, unnervingly
news, renewal, newness	**new**, renewable, renewed	renew	newly, anew
night, midnight			overnight, nightly, nights
noise, noisiness	noisy, noiseless		noisily
normality/US normalcy, abnormality, norm	**normal**, abnormal	normalize	**normally**, abnormally
north, northerner	north, northerly, northern, northward(s), northbound		north, northward(s), northbound
notice	noticeable, unnoticed	**notice**	noticeably
number, numeral	innumerable, numerical, numerous, numbered, numerate	number, outnumber, enumerate	
nurse, nursery, nursing		nurse	
obedience, disobedience	obedient, disobedient	**obey**, disobey	obediently, disobediently
occasion	occasional		occasionally
offence/US **offense**, offender, offensive	offensive, inoffensive	**offend**	offensively
office, officer, official, officialdom	**official**, unofficial	officiate	officially, unofficially
the open, opener, opening, openness	**open**, opening	**open**	openly
operation, cooperation, operative, cooperative, operator	operational, operative, cooperative, operable	**operate**, cooperate	operationally
opposition, opposite	opposed, opposing, **opposite**	**oppose**	opposite
option	optional	opt	optionally
order, disorder	disordered, orderly, disorderly, ordered	**order**	
organization, disorganization, reorganization, organizer	organizational, organized,	disorganized	**organize**, disorganize, reorganize
origin, original, originality, originator	**original**, unoriginal	originate	**originally**
owner, ownership		**own**, disown	

Nouns	Adjectives	Verbs	Adverbs
pack, package, packaging, packet, packing, packer	packed	**pack**, unpack, package	
pain	pained, **painful**, painless	pain	painfully, painlessly
paint, painter, **painting**		**paint**	
part, counterpart, parting, partition	partial, parting, impartial	part, partition, depart, impart	part, partially, **partly**
pass, overpass, underpass, passage, passing	passing, passable	**pass**	
patience, impatience, **patient**	**patient**, impatient		patiently, impatiently
pay, **payment**, repayment, payee, payer, payoff, payback, payout	unpaid, underpaid	**pay**, repay	
peace	**peaceful**	pacify	peacefully
perfection, imperfection, perfectionist, perfectionism	**perfect**, imperfect	perfect	**perfectly**
performance, performer		**perform**	
permission, permit, permissiveness	permissible, impermissible, permissive	permit	
person, **personality**	**personal**, impersonal, personalized, *personable*	personalize, personify	personally
persuasion, persuasiveness	persuasive	**persuade**, dissuade	persuasively
photo, **photograph**, photographer, photography	photogenic, photographic	photograph	
picture	pictorial, picturesque	picture	
place, placement, displacement, replacement	misplaced	place, displace, replace	
plan, planner, planning	unplanned	**plan**	
plant, transplant, plantation, planter		plant, transplant	
play, interplay, replay, **player**, playfulness, playback, playoff	playful, playable	**play**, outplay, replay, downplay, underplay	playfully
pleasantry, **pleasure**, displeasure	**pleasant**, unpleasant, **pleased**, displeased, pleasing, pleasurable	please, displease	pleasantly, unpleasantly
poem, poet, **poetry**	poetic		poetically
point, pointer, pointlessness	pointed, pointless, pointy	**point**	pointlessly, pointedly
politeness	**polite**, impolite		politely, impolitely
politician, **politics**, politicking	**political**, politicized	politicize	politically
popularity, unpopularity, popularization	**popular**, unpopular	popularize	popularly
population	populated, unpopulated, populous	populate	
possibility, impossibility, the impossible	**possible**, impossible		**possibly**, impossibly
post, postage	postal	**post**	
power, superpower, powerlessness	**powerful**, overpowering, powerless	power, empower, overpower	powerfully
practical, practicalities, practicality, practicability	practicable, **practical**, impractical		practically
practice, practitioner	practised/*US* practiced, practising/*US* practicing	**practise**/*US* **practice**	
precision	**precise**, imprecise		precisely
preference	preferable, preferential, preferred	**prefer**	preferably
preparation, preparations, preparedness	prepared, unprepared, preparatory	**prepare**	
presence, **present**, presentation, presenter	**present**, presentable	present, represent	presently
press, **pressure**	pressed, pressing, pressurized	**press**, pressure/pressurize, depress, repress	
prevention	preventable, preventive/preventative	**prevent**	
price	overpriced, priceless, pricey/pricy	price	
print, printer, printing	printed, printable	**print**	
prison, **prisoner**, imprisonment		imprison	
privacy, private, privatization	**private**	privatize	privately
probability	probable, improbable		**probably**, improbably
process, processing, procession, processor	processed, processional	process	
produce, producer, **product**, productively	productive, counterproductive,	**produce**, reproduce	unproductive,
production, reproduction, productivity	reproductive, unproductive		
profession, professional, professionalism	**professional**, unprofessional		professionally
profit, profitability, profiteer, profiteering	profitable, unprofitable	profit	profitably
progress, progression	progressive	progress	progressively
proof	proven, unproven	prove, disprove, *proof*	
protection, protector, protectionism, protectorate	protected, unprotected, protective, protectionist, protectively	**protect**	
provider, provision, provisions	provisional	**provide**	provisionally

Nouns	Adjectives	Verbs	Adverbs
public, publication, publicist, publicity	**public**	publicize	publicly
publisher, publishing	published, unpublished	**publish**	
punishment	punishable, punishing	**punish**	punishingly
purification, purist, purity, impurity, purifier	**pure**, impure	purify	purely
purpose, purposelessness	purposeful, purposeless		purposefully, purposely, purposelessly
push, pusher, pushiness	pushed, pushy	**push**	
qualification, disqualification, qualifier	qualified, unqualified	qualify, disqualify	
quarter, quarters	quarterly	quarter	quarterly
question, questioning, questioner, questionnaire	questionable, unquestionable	question	unquestionably
quiet, disquiet	**quiet**	quieten/quiet	quietly
race, racism, racist	racial, multiracial, racist	race	racially
rarity	**rare**, rarefied, rarified		rarely
rate, rating, ratings	overrated, underrated	rate, underrate	
reaction, reactor, reactant	reactionary	**react**, overreact	
read, reader, readership, **reading**	readable, unreadable	**read**	
readiness	**ready**		readily
realism, realist, reality, unreality, realization	**real**, unreal, realistic, unrealistic, realisable	**realize**	real, **really**, realistically
reason, reasoning, reasonableness	reasonable, unreasonable, reasoned	reason	reasonably, unreasonably
receipt, receipts, receiver, reception, recipient, reciprocity	receptive, reciprocal, received	**receive**	reciprocally
recognition	recognizable, unrecognizable, recognized	**recognize**	recognizably
record, recorder, recording	recorded, unrecorded	**record**	
referee, reference, referral		**refer**, referee	
reflection, reflector	reflective	**reflect**	reflectively
regret	regrettable, regretful	**regret**	regrettably, regretfully
regular, regularity, irregularity	**regular**, irregular	regulate	**regularly**, irregularly
relation, relations, **relationship**, **relative**	**related**, unrelated, relative	relate	relatively
relaxation	**relaxed**, relaxing	**relax**	
reliability, reliance	**reliable**, unreliable, reliant	**rely**	reliably
religion	**religious**, irreligious		religiously
the remainder, remains	remaining	**remain**	
remark	remarkable, unremarkable	remark	remarkably
repair, disrepair	irreparable	**repair**	irreparably
repeat, repetition	repeated, repetitive/repetitious	**repeat**	repeatedly, repetitively
report, reporter	unreported	**report**	reportedly
representation, representative	representative, unrepresentative	**represent**	
reputation, disrepute	reputable, disreputable, reputed		reputedly, reputably
respect, disrespect, respectability, respecter, respects	respectable, respected, respectful, disrespectful, respective	**respect**	respectably, respectfully, disrespectfully, respectively, irrespective
respondent, **response**, responsiveness	responsive, unresponsive	**respond**	responsively
responsibility, irresponsibility	**responsible**, irresponsible		responsibly, irresponsibly
rest, unrest, restlessness	restless, rested, restful	**rest**	restlessly
retiree, retirement	retired, retiring	**retire**	
reward	rewarding, unrewarding	reward	
riches, richness, enrichment, the rich	**rich**	enrich	richly
ride, rider, riding	overriding, riderless	**ride**, override	
right, rightness, rights, righteousness, rightist	right, righteous, rightful, rightist	right	**right**, rightly, rightfully
roll, roller		**roll**, unroll	
romance, romantic, romanticism	**romantic**, unromantic, romanticized	romance, romanticize	romantically
rough, roughage, roughness	**rough**	rough, roughen	rough, **roughly**
round, rounders, roundness	**round**, rounded	round	**round**, roundly
royal, royalist, royalty	**royal**, royalist		royally
rudeness	**rude**		rudely
rule, ruler, ruling, unruliness	ruling, unruly	rule, overrule	
run, rerun, runner, running, rundown	running, runny	**run**, outrun, overrun	
sadness	**sad**, saddened	sadden	sadly
safe, **safety**	**safe**, unsafe		safely
satisfaction, dissatisfaction	**satisfactory**, unsatisfactory, **satisfied**, dissatisfied, unsatisfied, satisfying	satisfy	satisfactorily, unsatisfactorily
save, saver, saving, savings, saviour/ *US* savior		**save**	
scare	**scared**, scary	scare	

Nouns	Adjectives	Verbs	Adverbs
school, pre-school, schooling	pre-school, scholastic	school	scholastically
science, **scientist**	**scientific**, unscientific		scientifically
score, scorer	scoreless	**score**, outscore, underscore	
search, research, researcher	searching, searchable	**search**, research	searchingly
seat, seating	seated	seat, unseat	
secrecy, secret, secretiveness	**secret**, secretive		secretly, secretively
sense, nonsense, sensibility, sensitivity, insensitivity, sensitiveness, sensor	**sensible**, senseless, sensitive, insensitive, nonsensical, sensory	sense, sensitize, desensitize	sensibly, sensitively, insensitively, senselessly
separation, separatism, separatist	separable, inseparable, **separate**	**separate**	inseparably, separately
seriousness	**serious**		**seriously**
servant, serve, server, **service**, disservice, services, serving, servitude, servicing	serviceable, servile	**serve**, service	
sex, sexism, sexuality	sexist, **sexual**, bisexual, sexy, asexual		sexually, sexily
shadow, shade	shadowy	shadow, overshadow	
shake, shakiness, shaker	shaky	**shake**	shakily
shape, shapeliness, shapelessness	shapeless, shapely, shaped	shape	shapelessly
(pencil) sharpener, sharpness	**sharp**	sharpen	sharp, sharply, sharpish
shine, shininess	shiny	**shine**, outshine	
shock, shocker	shocked, shocking, shockable	**shock**	shockingly
shop, shopper, **shopping**		shop	
short, shortage, shortness, shorts	**short**, shortish	shorten	short, shortly
shyness	**shy**	shy	shyly
sick, sickness	**sick**, sickening, sickly	sicken	sickeningly
sight, insight, oversight, sighting	sighted, unsightly	sight	
sign, **signal**, signatory, signature, signing	signed, unsigned	**sign**, signal	
significance, insignificance, signification	**significant**, insignificant	signify	significantly, insignificantly
silence, silencer	**silent**	silence	silently
similarity	**similar**, dissimilar		similarly
simplicity, simplification	**simple**, simplistic	simplify	simply
singer, singing	unsung	**sing**	
single, singles	**single**, singular	single	singly
skill	skilful/US skillful, skilled, unskilled		skilfully/US skillfully
sleep, sleeper, sleepiness, sleeplessness	asleep, sleepless, sleepy, sleeping	**sleep**	sleepily
slight	**slight**, slighted, slightest	slight	**slightly**
slip, slipper	slippery	**slip**	
smoke, smoker, non-smoker, smoking	smoked, smoking, non-smoking, smoky, smokeless		**smoke**
smoothness, smoothie	**smooth**	smooth	smoothly
society, sociologist, sociology, socialism, socialist, socialite	sociable, unsociable, **social**, anti-social, unsocial, sociological	socialize	socially, sociologically
softness, softy, softener	**soft**	soften	softly
solid, solidarity, solidity, solids	**solid**	solidify	solidly
solution, solvent, solubility, solvency	soluble, insoluble, unsolved, solvent, solvable	**solve**	
south, southerner	south, southerly, southern, southbound, southward, southernmost		south, southward(s), southbound
speaker, **speech**	unspeakable, speechless, outspoken, unspoken	**speak**	unspeakably
special, specialist, speciality/US specialty, specialization, specialism	**special**, specialized	specialize	**specially**
speed, speeding, speediness	speedy	speed	speedily
spelling, speller		**spell**, misspell	
spoils	spoilt/spoiled, unspoiled/unspoilt	**spoil**	
sport	sporting, sporty, unsporting	sport	
spot	spotted, spotless, spotty	spot	spotlessly
stand, standing, standoff, standstill	standing, outstanding	**stand**, withstand	outstandingly
standard, standardization	standard, substandard	standardize	
start, starter, non-starter		**start**, restart	
statement, understatement	understated	state, overstate	
steam, steamer	steamy, steaming	steam	
steepness	**steep**	steepen	steeply
sticker, stickiness	sticky, stuck, unstuck	**stick**	
stiffness	**stiff**	stiffen	stiff, stiffly
stone	stoned, stony	stone	
stop, stoppage, stopper	non-stop	**stop**	non-stop
storm	stormy	storm	
straight	**straight**	straighten	**straight**
stranger, strangeness	**strange**, estranged		strangely
strength	**strong**	strengthen	strongly

Nouns	Adjectives	Verbs	Adverbs
stress, distress	stressed, stressful, distressing	stress	distressingly
strike, striker	striking, strikebound	**strike**	strikingly
structure, restructuring, structuralism, structuralist	structural, structuralist	structure, restructure	structurally
student, **study**, studies, studiousness	studious, studied	**study**	studiously
stupidity	**stupid**		stupidly
style, stylist, stylishness	stylish, stylistic	style	stylishly, stylistically
substance	substantial, insubstantial, substantive	substantiate	substantially
success, succession, successor unsuccessfully	**successful**, unsuccessful, successive	**succeed**	successfully,
suddenness	**sudden**		**suddenly**
sufferer, suffering, sufferance	insufferable	**suffer**	insufferably
suggestion	suggestive, suggestible	**suggest**	suggestively
summer, midsummer	summery		
supplier, supplies, **supply**		**supply**	
support, supporter, supportiveness	supportive, supporting	**support**	supportively
supposition	supposed	**suppose**, presuppose	supposedly
surface	surface	surface, resurface	
surprise	**surprised**, surprising	surprise	surprisingly
surroundings, surrounds	surrounding	**surround**	
survival, survivor	surviving, survivable	**survive**	
suspect, suspicion	suspect, suspected, unsuspecting, suspicious	**suspect**	suspiciously
swearing	sworn	**swear**	
sweet, sweetener, sweetness, *sweety*	**sweet**	sweeten	sweetly
swim, swimmer, swimming		**swim**	swimmingly
symbol, symbolism, symbolist	symbolic, symbolist	symbolize	symbolically
sympathy, sympathizer, sympathies	**sympathetic**, unsympathetic	sympathize	sympathetically
system, systematization	systematic	systematize	systematically
takings, undertaking, taker	taken	**take**, overtake, undertake	
talk, talks	talkative	**talk**	
taste, distaste, taster	tasteful, distasteful, tasteless, tasty	**taste**	tastefully, distastefully, tastelessly
tax, taxation	taxable, taxing	tax	
teacher, teaching, teachings	taught	**teach**	
tear, tearfulness	tearful		tearfully
technicalities, technicality, technician, technique	**technical**		technically
technology, technologist	technological		technologically
thanks, thankfulness	thankful, thankless	**thank**	thankfully
theorist, **theory**, theorem	theoretical	theorize	theoretically
thick, thickness, thickener	**thick**	thicken	thickly
thinness, thinner	**thin**	thin	thinly
think, rethink, thinker, thinking	unthinkable	**think**, rethink	
thirst	**thirsty**		thirstily
thought, thoughtfulness, thoughtlessness	thoughtful, thoughtless		thoughtfully, thoughtlessly
threat	threatening	**threaten**	threateningly
tie		**tie**, untie	
tightness	**tight**	tighten	tight, tightly
time, overtime, timer, timing	timeless, timely, untimely	time	
tiredness	**tired**, tireless, tiresome, tiring	tire	tirelessly, tiredly, tiresomely
title, subtitles, surtitle, titles	titled	entitle	
top, topping	**top**, topless, topmost	top	
touch	touched, untouched, touching, touchy	**touch**	touchingly, touchily
	tough	toughen	toughly
trade, trader, trading		trade	
tradition, traditionalist, traditionalism	**traditional**		traditionally
trainee, trainer, **training**, retraining	untrained	**train**	
transport, transportation, transporter		transport	
treat, **treatment**, mistreatment, maltreatment	untreated	**treat**, mistreat, maltreat	
trick, trickery	tricky	trick	
trouble	troubled, troublesome, troubling	trouble	troublingly
trust, distrust, mistrust, trustee, trusteeship	trusting, trustworthy	**trust**, distrust, mistrust, entrust	trustfully
truth, untruth, truthfulness	**true**, untrue, truthful		truly, truthfully
try, *trier*	trying, untried	**try**	
turn, upturn, turning, turnout, turnaround, turnover	upturned	**turn**, overturn	
twist, twister	twisted, twisty	**twist**	

Nouns	Adjectives	Verbs	Adverbs
type, typing, typist	**typical**	typify	typically
understanding, misunderstanding	understandable, understanding, misunderstood	**understand**, misunderstand	understandably
upset	**upset**, upsetting	upset	
urgency, urge, urging	**urgent**		urgently
usage, **use**, disuse, misuse, usefulness, user	reusable, **used,** disused, unused, **useful, useless**	**use**, misuse, reuse	usefully
valuables, value, values, valuer, valuation	**valuable**, invaluable, undervalued, valueless	value, devalue, evaluate	
variable, variance, variant, **variety**, variation	variable, varied, **various**	vary	invariably, variously
vegetable, vegetarian	vegetarian		
view, overview, preview, review, viewer		view, preview, review	
violence	violent, non-violent	violate	violently
visit, visitor, visitation		**visit**, revisit	
vote, voter, voting		**vote**	
want, wants	wanted, unwanted	**want**	
war, warfare, warrior	postwar, warring, warlike		
warmth	warm	warm	warmly
wash, washer, washing, washout	washable, unwashed, awash	**wash**	
wastage, **waste**, waster	waste, wasteful	**waste**	wastefully
watch, watchfulness	watchful	**watch**	
water, waters	underwater, waterproof, watery	water	underwater
way, subway	wayward		midway
weakling, weakness	**weak**	weaken	weakly
wear, underwear	wearing, worn, wearable	**wear**	
week, midweek	weekly, midweek		weekly, midweek
weight, weights, weighting	overweight, underweight, weighted, weighty, weightless	**weigh**, outweigh	weightlessly
welcome	welcome, unwelcome, welcoming	**welcome**	
west, western, westerner, westernization	westerly, western, westernized, westbound, westernmost	westernize	west, westward(s), westbound
white, whiteness, whitening, whites	**white**, whitish	whiten	
whole	**whole**, wholesome, unwholesome		wholly
width	**wide**	widen	wide, **widely**
wild, wildness	**wild**		wildly
willingness, unwillingness	**willing**, unwilling		willingly, unwillingly
win, **winner**, winnings	winning	**win**	
winter, midwinter	wintry		
wire, wireless, wiring	wiry	wire	
woman, womanhood	womanly	womanize	
wonder	**wonderful**	**wonder**	wonderfully
wood	wooded, wooden, woody		woodenly
wool, woollens, woolliness	woollen/US woolen, woolly/US		
wooly			
word, wording	wordy, worded, wordless	word, reword	
work, workaholic, worker, workings, workout	workable, unworkable, overworked, working	**work**, rework	
world, underworld	world, worldly, unworldly, worldwide		worldwide
worry, worrier	**worried**, unworried, worrying, worriedly, worrisome	**worry**	worryingly
worth, worthlessness	**worth**, worthless, worthwhile, worthy, unworthy		worthily
writer, writing, writings	written, unwritten	**write**, rewrite	
wrong, wrongdoer	**wrong**, wrongful	wrong	**wrong**, wrongly, wrongfully
year	yearly		yearly
young, youngster, youth	**young**, youthful		youthfully

Geographical names

This list shows the spellings and pronunciations for the names of countries, regions, continents, seas and oceans which you may see when you are reading English. Each name is followed by the adjective that you use when talking about the noun (e.g. **Belgium** is a country in Europe. **Belgian** chocolate comes from Belgium). Usually, the word meaning 'a person from this country' is a noun that is exactly the same as the adjective (so someone from **Belgium** is a **Belgian**). If the word for a person is different from the adjective, it is shown in the list below after the adjective (e.g. **Finland, Finnish, Finn**).

To talk about more than one person from a country, just add 's' (e.g. one **Belgian**, two **Belgians**), except for :
- words ending in '**ese**' or '**s**' - these stay the same (e.g. **Chinese, Swiss**)
- words ending in '**man**' or '**woman**' - these change to '**men**' or '**women**' (e.g. one **Irishman**, two **Irishmen**).

This list is only here to help you with spelling and reading. Not all of these words are names of countries. Some of them are continents or regions. If a name is included or not included here, that does not necessarily mean that it is or is not an official country. The list also includes some old names of countries, because you may still find these names when you are reading.

Name	Adjective	Person (if different from adj)
Afghanistan /æf'gæn.ɪ.stæn/	**Afghan** /'æf.gæn/	
Africa /'æf.rɪ.kə/	**African** /'æf.rɪ.kən/	
Alaska /ə'læs.kə/	**Alaskan** /ə'læs.kən/	
Albania /æl'beɪ.ni.ə/	**Albanian** /æl'beɪ.ni.ən/	
Algeria /æl'dʒɪə.ri.ə/ ⓤⓢ /-dʒɪr.i-/	**Algerian** /æl'dʒɪə.ri.ən/ ⓤⓢ /-dʒɪr.i-/	
Central America /ˌsen.trəl.ə'mer.ɪ.kə/	**Central American** /ˌsen.trəl.ə'mer.ɪ.kən/	
North America /ˌnɔːθ.ə'mer.ɪ.kə/	**North American** /ˌnɔːθ.ə'mer.ɪ.kən/	
South America /ˌsaʊθ.ə'mer.ɪ.kə/	**South American** /ˌsaʊθ ə'mer.ɪ.kən/	
Andorra /æn'dɔː.rə/	**Andorran** /æn'dɔː.rən/	
Angola /æŋ'gəʊ.lə/ ⓤⓢ /-goʊ-/	**Angolan** /æŋ'gəʊ.lən/ ⓤⓢ /-goʊ-/	
Antarctica /æn'tɑːk.tɪ.kə/ ⓤⓢ /-tɑːrk-/	**Antarctic** /æn'tɑːk.tɪk/ ⓤⓢ /-tɑːrk-/	(not applicable)
Antigua and Barbuda /æn,tiː.gə[r].ən.bɑː'bjuː.də/ ⓤⓢ /-buː-/	**Antiguan** /æn'tiː.gən/	
The Arctic /ði 'ɑːk.tɪk/ ⓤⓢ /-ɑːrk-/	**Arctic** /'ɑːk.tɪk/ ⓤⓢ /'ɑːrk-/	(not applicable)
Argentina /ˌɑː.dʒən'tiː.nə/ ⓤⓢ /ˌɑːr-/	**Argentinian** /ˌɑː.dʒən'tɪn.i.ən/ ⓤⓢ /ˌɑːr-/ **Argentine** /'ɑː.dʒən.taɪn/ ⓤⓢ /'ɑːr-/	
Armenia /ɑː'miː.ni.ə/ ⓤⓢ /ɑːr-/	**Armenian** /ɑː'miː.ni.ən/ ⓤⓢ /ɑːr-/	
Asia /'eɪ.ʒə/	**Asian** /'eɪ.ʒən/	
The Atlantic /ði.ət'læn.tɪk/ ⓤⓢ /-ṯɪk/	**Atlantic** /ət'læn.tɪk/ ⓤⓢ /-ṯɪk/	(not applicable)
Australasia /ˌɒs.trə'leɪ.ʒə/ ⓤⓢ /ˌɑː.strə-/	**Australasian** /ˌɒs.trə'leɪ.ʒən/ ⓤⓢ /ˌɑː.strə-/	
Australia /ɒs'treɪ.li.ə/ ⓤⓢ /ɑː'streɪl.jə/	**Australian** /ɒs'treɪ.li.ən/ ⓤⓢ /ɑː'streɪl.jən/	
Austria /'ɒs.tri.ə/ ⓤⓢ /'ɑː.stri-/	**Austrian** /'ɒs.tri.ən/ ⓤⓢ /'ɑː.stri-/	
Azerbaijan /ˌæz.ə.baɪ'dʒɑːn/ ⓤⓢ /ˌɑː.zɚː-/	**Azerbaijani** /ˌæz.ə.baɪ'dʒɑː.ni/ ⓤⓢ /ˌɑː.zɚː-/	**Azeri** /ə'zeə.ri/ ⓤⓢ /-'zer.i/
The Bahamas /ðə.bə'hɑː.məz/	**Bahamian** /bə'heɪ.mi.ən/	
Bahrain /bɑː'reɪn/	**Bahraini** /bɑː'reɪ.ni/	
The Balkans /ðə'bɔːl.kənz/ ⓤⓢ /-'bɑːl-/	**Balkan** /'bɔːl.kən/ ⓤⓢ /-'bɑːl-/	(not applicable)
The Baltic /ðə'bɔːl.tɪk/ ⓤⓢ /-'bɑːl-/	**Baltic** /'bɔːl.tɪk/ ⓤⓢ /-'bɑːl-/	(not applicable)
Bangladesh /ˌbæŋ.glə'deʃ/	**Bangladeshi** /ˌbæŋ.glə'deʃ.i/	
Barbados /bɑː'beɪ.dɒs/ ⓤⓢ /bɑːr'beɪ.doʊs/	**Barbadian** /bɑː'beɪ.di.ən/ ⓤⓢ /bɑːr-/	
Belarus /ˌbel.ə'ruːs/	**Belorussian** /ˌbel.ə'rʊʃ.ən/	
Belgium /'bel.dʒəm/	**Belgian** /'bel.dʒən/	
Belize /bə'liːz/	**Belizean** /bə'liː.zi.ən/	
Benin /ben'iːn/	**Beninese** /ˌben.ɪ'niːz/	
Bermuda /bə'mjuː.də/ ⓤⓢ /bɚː-/	**Bermudan** /bə'mjuː.dən/ ⓤⓢ /bɚː-/	

Name	Adjective	Person
Bhutan /buːˈtɑːn/	**Bhutanese** /ˌbuː.təˈniːz/	
Bolivia /bəˈlɪv.i.ə/	**Bolivian** /bəˈlɪv.i.ən/	
Bosnia-Herzegovina /ˌbɒz.ni.ə,hɜːt.səˈgɒv.ɪ.nə/ ⓤⓢ /ˌbɑːz.ni.ə,hert.səˈgoʊˈviː.nə/	**Bosnian** /ˈbɒz.ni.ən/ ⓤⓢ /ˈbɑːz-/	
Botswana /bɒtˈswɑː.nə/ ⓤⓢ /bɑːt-/	**Botswanan** /bɒtˈswɑː.nən/ ⓤⓢ /bɑːt-/	singular = **Motswana** /mɒtˈswɑː.nə/ plural = **Batswana** /bætˈswɑː.nə/
Brazil /brəˈzɪl/	**Brazilian** /brəˈzɪl.i.ən/	
Brunei /bruːˈnaɪ/	**Bruneian** /bruːˈnaɪ.ən/	
Bulgaria /bʌlˈgeə.ri.ə/ ⓤⓢ /-ˈger.i-/	**Bulgarian** /bʌlˈgeə.ri.ən/ ⓤⓢ /-ˈger.i-/	
Burkina Faso /bɜːˌkiː.nəˈfæs.əʊ/ ⓤⓢ /bɚˌkiː.nəˈfɑː.soʊ/	**Burkinabe** /bɜːˈkiː.nə,beɪ/ ⓤⓢ /bɚ-/	
Burma /ˈbɜː.mə/ ⓤⓢ /bɝː-/ See also **Myanmar** /ˈmjæn.mɑːr/	**Burmese** /bɜːˈmiːz/ ⓤⓢ /bɝː-/	
Burundi /bʊˈrʊn.di/	**Burundi** /bʊˈrʊn.di/	**Burundian** /bʊˈrʊn.di.ən/
Cambodia /kæmˈbəʊ.di.ə/ ⓤⓢ /-ˈboʊ-	**Cambodian** /kæmˈbəʊ.di.ən/ ⓤⓢ /-ˈboʊ-	
Cameroon /ˌkæm.əˈruːn/	**Cameroonian** /ˌkæm.əˈruː.ni.ən/	
Canada /ˈkæn.ə.də/	**Canadian** /kəˈneɪ.di.ən/	
Cape Verde /ˌkeɪpˈvɜːd/ ⓤⓢ /-ˈvɝːd/	**Cape Verdean** /ˌkeɪpˈvɜː.di.ən/ ⓤⓢ /-ˈvɝː.di-/	
The Caribbean /ðəˌkær.ɪˈbiː.ən/ ⓤⓢ /ˌker.ɪˈbiː-/	**Caribbean** /ˌkær.ɪˈbiː.ən/ /ˌker.ɪˈbiː-/	
The Cayman Islands /ðəˈkeɪ.mən,aɪ.ləndz/		**Cayman Islander** /ˈkeɪ.mən,aɪ.lən.dər/
The Central African Republic /ðəˌsen.trəlˈæf.rɪ.kən.rɪˈpʌb.lɪk/	**Central African** /ˌsen.trəlˈæf.rɪ.kən/	
Chad /tʃæd/	**Chadian** /ˈtʃæd.i.ən/	
Chile /ˈtʃɪl.i/	**Chilean** /ˈtʃɪl.i.ən/	
China /ˈtʃaɪ.nə/	**Chinese** /tʃaɪˈniːz/	
Colombia /kəˈlʊm.bi.ə/	**Colombian** /kəˈlʊm.bi.ən/	
Comoros /ˈkɒm.ə.rəʊz/ ⓤⓢ /ˈkɑː.mə.roʊz	**Comoran** /kəˈmɔː.rən/ ⓤⓢ /ˈkɑː.mə-/	
The Democratic Republic of Congo /ðəˌdem.ə.kræt.ɪk rɪ,pʌb.lɪk.əv.ˈkɒŋ.gəʊ/ ⓤⓢ /-kræt̬.ɪk rɪ,pʌb.lɪk.əvˈkɒŋ.goʊ/	**Congolese** /ˌkɒŋ.gəˈliːz/	
The Republic of Congo /ðərɪ,pʌb.lɪk.əvˈkɒŋ.gəʊ/ ⓤⓢ /-goʊ/	**Congolese** /ˌkɒŋ.gəˈliːz/	
Costa Rica /ˌkɒs.təˈriː.kə/ ⓤⓢ /ˌkɑː.stə-/	**Costa Rican** /ˌkɒs.təˈriː.kən/ ⓤⓢ /ˌkɑː.stə-/	
Côte d'Ivoire /ˌkəʊt.diːˈvwɑː/ ⓤⓢ /ˌkoʊt.diːˈvwɑːr/	**Ivorian** /aɪˈvɔː.ri.ən/	
Croatia /krəʊˈeɪ.ʃə/ ⓤⓢ /kroʊ-/	**Croatian** /krəʊˈeɪ.ʃən/ ⓤⓢ /kroʊ-/	**Croat** /ˈkrəʊ.æt/ ⓤⓢ /ˈkroʊ-/
Cuba /ˈkjuː.bə/	**Cuban** /ˈkjuː.bən/	
Cyprus /ˈsaɪ.prəs/	**Cypriot** /ˈsɪp.ri.ət/	
The Czech Republic /ðə,tʃek.rɪˈpʌb.lɪk/	**Czech** /tʃek/	
Denmark /ˈden.mɑːk/ ⓤⓢ /-mɑːrk/	**Danish** /ˈdeɪ.nɪʃ/	**Dane** /deɪn/
Djibouti /dʒɪˈbuː.ti/ ⓤⓢ /-t̬i/	**Djiboutian** /dʒɪˈbuː.ti.ən/ ⓤⓢ /-t̬i-/	
Dominica /dɒˈmɪn.ɪ.kə/də'mɪn.ɪ-/ ⓤⓢ /dɑː.mɪˈniː-/ /dəˈmɪn.ɪ-/	**Dominican** /dɒm.ɪˈniː.kən/ ⓤⓢ /dɑːm-/	
The Dominican Republic /ðə.dəˈmɪn.ɪ.kən rɪ,pʌb.lɪk/	**Dominican** /dəˈmɪn.ɪ.kən/	
East Timor /ˌiːstˈtiː.mɔːr/ ⓤⓢ /-mɔːr/	**East Timorese** /ˌiːst .tiː.mɔːˈriːz/ ⓤⓢ /-mɔːr-/	
Ecuador /ˈek.wə.dɔːr/ ⓤⓢ /-dɔːr/	**Ecuadorian** /ˌek.wəˈdɔː.ri.ən/	
Egypt /ˈiː.dʒɪpt/	**Egyptian** /ɪˈdʒɪp.ʃən/	
El Salvador /ˌel'sæl.və.dɔːr/ ⓤⓢ /-dɔːr/	**Salvadoran** /ˌsæl.vəˈdɔː.rən/	
England /ˈɪŋ.glənd/	**English** /ˈɪŋ.glɪʃ/	**Englishman** /ˈɪŋ.glɪʃ.mən/ **Englishwoman** /ˈɪŋ.glɪʃ,wʊm.ən/
Equatorial Guinea /ˌek.wə.tɔː.ri.əl ˈgɪn.i/ ⓤⓢ /-tɔːr.i-/	**Equatorial Guinean** /ˌek.wə.tɔː.ri.əl ˈgɪn.i.ən/	
Eritrea /ˌer.ɪˈtreɪ.ə/ ⓤⓢ /-ˈtriː-/	**Eritrean** /ˌer.ɪˈtreɪ.ən/ ⓤⓢ /-ˈtriː-/	
Estonia /esˈtəʊ.ni.ə/ ⓤⓢ /-ˈtoʊ-/	**Estonian** /esˈtəʊ.ni.ən/ ⓤⓢ /-ˈtoʊ-/	
Ethiopia /ˌiː.θiˈəʊ.pi.ə/ ⓤⓢ /-ˈoʊ-/	**Ethiopian** /ˌiː.θiˈəʊ.pi.ən/ ⓤⓢ /-ˈoʊ-/	
Europe /ˈjʊə.rəp/ ⓤⓢ /ˈjʊ-/	**European** /ˌjʊə.rəˈpiː.ən/ ⓤⓢ /ˌjʊr.ə-/	
Fiji /ˈfiː.dʒiː/	**Fijian** /fɪˈdʒiː.ən/	
Finland /ˈfɪn.lənd/	**Finnish** /ˈfɪn.ɪʃ/	**Finn** /fɪn/
The Former Yugoslav Republic of Macedonia /ðə,fɔː.mə,juː.gə.slɑːv. rɪ,pʌb.lɪk.əv,mæs.əˈdəʊ.ni.ə/	**Macedonian** /ˌmæs.əˈdəʊ.ni.ən/ ⓤⓢ /-doʊ-/	

Name	Adjective	Person
France /frɑːnts/ ⓤⓢ /frænts/	**French** /frentʃ/	**Frenchman** /ˈfrentʃ.mən/ **Frenchwoman** /ˈfrentʃ.wʊm.ən/
Gabon /gæbˈɒn/ ⓤⓢ /-ˈoʊn/	**Gabonese** /ˌgæb.əˈniːz/	
Gambia /ˈgæm.bi.ə/	**Gambian** /ˈgæm.bi.ən/	
Georgia /ˈdʒɔː.dʒə/ ⓤⓢ /ˈdʒɔːr-/	**Georgian** /ˈdʒɔː.dʒən/ ⓤⓢ /ˈdʒɔːr-/	
Germany /ˈdʒɜː.mə.ni/ ⓤⓢ /ˈdʒɝː-/	**German** /ˈdʒɜː.mən/ ⓤⓢ /ˈdʒɝː-/	
Ghana /ˈgɑː.nə/	**Ghanaian** /gɑːˈneɪ.ən/	
Gibraltar /dʒɪˈbrɔːl.təʳ/ ⓤⓢ /-ˈbrɑːl.tɚ/	**Gibraltarian** /ˌdʒɪb.rɔːlˈteə.ri.ən/ ⓤⓢ /-rɑːlˈter.i-/	
Greece /griːs/	**Greek** /griːk/	
Greenland /ˈgriːn.lənd/	**Greenlandic** /griːnˈlæn.dɪk/	**Greenlander** /ˈgriːn.lən.dəʳ/ ⓤⓢ /-dɚ/
Grenada /grəˈneɪ.də/	**Grenadian** /grəˈneɪ.di.ən/	
Guatemala /ˌgwɑː.təˈmɑː.lə/ ⓤⓢ /-t̬ə-/	**Guatemalan** /ˌgwɑː.təˈmɑː.lən/ ⓤⓢ /-t̬ə-/	
Guinea /ˈgɪn.i/	**Guinean** /ˈgɪn.i.ən/	
Guinea-Bissau /ˌgɪn.i.bɪˈsaʊ/	**Guinea-Bissauan** /ˌgɪn.i.bɪˈsaʊ.ən/	
Guyana /gaɪˈæn.ə/	**Guyanese** /ˌgaɪ.əˈniːz/	
Haiti /ˈheɪ.ti/ ⓤⓢ /-t̬i/	**Haitian** /ˈheɪ.ʃən/	
Holland /ˈhɒl.ənd/ ⓤⓢ /ˈhɑː.lənd/	**Dutch** /dʌtʃ/	**Dutchman** /ˈdʌtʃ.mən/ **Dutchwoman** /ˈdʌtʃ.wʊm.ən/
Honduras /hɒnˈdjʊə.rəs/ ⓤⓢ /hɑːnˈdʊr.əs/	**Honduran** /hɒnˈdjʊə.rən/ ⓤⓢ /hɑːnˈdʊr.ən/	
Hong Kong /ˌhɒŋˈkɒŋ/ ⓤⓢ /ˈhɑːŋ.kɑːŋ/	**Hong Kong** /ˌhɒŋˈkɒŋ/ ⓤⓢ /ˈhɑːŋ.kɑːŋ/	
Hungary /ˈhʌŋ.gə.ri/	**Hungarian** /hʌŋˈgeə.ri.ən/ ⓤⓢ /-ˈger.i/	
Iceland /ˈaɪs.lənd/	**Icelandic** /aɪsˈlæn.dɪk/	**Icelander** /ˈaɪs.lən.də[r]/ ⓤⓢ /-ɚ/
India /ˈɪn.di.ə/	**Indian** /ˈɪn.di.ən/	
The Indian Ocean /ðiˌɪn.di.ənˈəʊ.ʃən/		
Indonesia /ˌɪn.dəˈniː.ʒə/	**Indonesian** /ˌɪn.dəˈniː.ʒən/	
Iran /ɪˈrɑːn//-ˈræn/	**Iranian** /ɪˈreɪ.ni.ən/	
Iraq /ɪˈrɑːk//-ˈræk	**Iraqi** /ɪˈrɑːk.i//-ˈræk-/	
Ireland /ˈaɪə.lənd/ ⓤⓢ /ˈaɪr-/	**Irish** /ˈaɪə.rɪʃ/ ⓤⓢ /ˈaɪ-/	**Irishman** /ˈaɪə.rɪʃ.mən/ ⓤⓢ /ˈaɪ-/ **Irishwoman** /ˈaɪə.rɪʃ.wʊm.ən/ ⓤⓢ /ˈaɪ-/
Israel /ˈɪz.reɪl/ ⓤⓢ /ˈɪz.ri.əl/	**Israeli** /ɪzˈreɪ.li/	
Italy /ˈɪt.ə.li/ ⓤⓢ /ˈɪt̬-/	**Italian** /ɪˈtæl.jən//-i.ən/	
Ivory Coast /ˌaɪ.və.riˈkəst/ ⓤⓢ /-ˈkoʊst/	**Ivorian** /aɪˈvɔː.ri.ən/	
Jamaica /dʒəˈmeɪ.kə/	**Jamaican** /dʒəˈmeɪ.kən/	
Japan /dʒəˈpæn/	**Japanese** /ˌdʒæp.əˈniːz/	
Jordan /ˈdʒɔː.dən/ ⓤⓢ /ˈdʒɔːr-/	**Jordanian** /dʒɔːˈdeɪ.ni.ən/ ⓤⓢ /dʒɔːr-/	
Kazakhstan /ˌkæz.ækˈstɑːn/ ⓤⓢ /kəˈzɑːk-/	**Kazakh** /ˈkæz.æk/ ⓤⓢ /kəˈzɑːk/	
Kenya /ˈken.jə//ˈkiː.n-/	**Kenyan** /ˈken.jən/	
Kiribati /ˌkɪr.əˈbæs/	**Kiribati** /ˌkɪr.əˈbæs/	
North Korea /ˌnɔː.θ.kəˈriː.ə/ ⓤⓢ /ˌnɔːrθ-/	**North Korean** /ˌnɔː.θ.kəˈriː.ən/ ⓤⓢ /ˌnɔːrθ-/	
South Korea /ˌsaʊθ.kəˈriː.ə/	**South Korean** /ˌsaʊθ.kəˈriː.ən/	
Kuwait /kjuːˈweɪt/ ⓤⓢ /kuː-/	**Kuwaiti** /kjuːˈweɪ.ti/ ⓤⓢ /kuːˈweɪ.t̬i/	
Kyrgyzstan /ˌkɜː.gɪˈstɑːn/ ⓤⓢ /kɝ-/	**Kyrgyz** /ˈkɜː.gɪz/ ⓤⓢ /ˈkɝ-/	
Laos /ˈlaʊs/	**Laotian** /ˈlaʊ.ʃən/	
Latvia /ˈlæt.vi.ə/	**Latvian** /ˈlæt.vi.ən/	
Lebanon /ˈleb.ə.nən/	**Lebanese** /ˌleb.əˈniːz/	
Lesotho /ləˈsuː.tuː/	**Sotho** /ˈsuː.tuː/	(singular noun) **Mosotho** /məˈsuː.tuː/ (plural noun) **Basotho** /bəˈsuː.tuː/
The Levant /ðə.ləˈvænt/	**Levantine** /ˈlev.ən.taɪn/	
Liberia /laɪˈbɪə.ri.ə/ ⓤⓢ /-ˈbɪr.i-/	**Liberian** /laɪˈbɪə.ri.ən/ ⓤⓢ /-ˈbɪr.i-/	
Libya /ˈlɪb.i.ə/	**Libyan** /ˈlɪb.i.ən/	
Liechtenstein /ˈlɪk.tən.staɪn/	**Liechtenstein** /ˈlɪk.tən.staɪn/	**Liechtensteiner** /ˈlɪk.tən.staɪ.nəʳ/ /-nɚ/
Lithuania /ˌlɪθ.juˈeɪ.ni.ə/ ⓤⓢ /-u-/	**Lithuanian** /ˌlɪθ.juˈeɪ.ni.ən/ ⓤⓢ /-u-/	
Luxembourg /ˈlʌk.səm.bɜːg/ ⓤⓢ /-bɝːg/	**Luxembourg** /ˈlʌk.səm.bɜːg/ ⓤⓢ /-bɝːg/	**Luxemburger** /ˈlʌk.səm.bɜː.gəʳ/ ⓤⓢ /-bɝː.gɚ/
Macedonia /ˌmæs.əˈdəʊ.ni.ə/ ⓤⓢ /-ˈdoʊ-/	**Macedonian** /ˌmæs.əˈdəʊ.ni.ən/ ⓤⓢ /-ˈdoʊ-/	
Madagascar /ˌmæd.əˈgæs.kəʳ/ ⓤⓢ /kɚ/	**Malagasy** /ˌmæl.əˈgæs.i/	

Name	Adjective	Person
Malawi /məˈlɑː.wi/	**Malawian** /məˈlɑː.wi.ən/	
Malaysia /məˈleɪ.zi.ə/ ⓤⓢ /-ʒə/	**Malaysian** /məˈleɪ.zi.ən/ ⓤⓢ /-ʒən/	
The Maldives /ðəˈmɔːl.diːvz/ ⓤⓢ /-ˈmæl.daivz/	**Maldivian** /mɔːlˈdɪv.i.ən/ ⓤⓢ /mælˈdai.vi-/	
Mali /ˈmɑː.li/	**Malian** /ˈmɑː.li.ən/	
Malta /ˈmɔːl.tə/ ⓤⓢ /ˈmɑːl-/	**Maltese** /mɔːlˈtiːz/ ⓤⓢ /ˈmɑːl-/	
The Marshall Islands /ðəˈmɑː.ʃəl.aɪ.ləndz/ ⓤⓢ /-ˈmɑːr-/	**Marshallese** /ˌmɑː.ʃəˈliːz/ ⓤⓢ /ˌmɑːr-/	**Marshall Islander** /ˈmɑː.ʃəl‿ʌaɪ.lən.dər/ ⓤⓢ /ˌmɑːr.ʃəlˈaɪ.lən.dɚ/
Mauritania /ˌmɒr.ɪˈteɪ.ni.ə/ ⓤⓢ /ˌmɔːr-/	**Mauritanian** /ˌmɒr.ɪˈteɪ.ni.ən/ ⓤⓢ /ˌmɔːr-/	
Mauritius /məˈrɪʃ.əs/ ⓤⓢ /mɔːˈrɪʃ.ɪs/	**Mauritian** /məˈrɪʃ.ən/ ⓤⓢ /mɔːˈrɪʃ-/	(not applicable)
The Mediterranean /ðəˌmed.ɪ.təˈreɪ.ni.ən/	**Mediterranean** /ˌmed.ɪ.təˈreɪ.ni.ən/	
Melanesia /ˌmel.əˈniː.zi.ə/ ⓤⓢ /-ʒə/	**Melanesian** /ˌmel.əˈniː.zi.ən/ ⓤⓢ /-ʒən/	
Mexico /ˈmek.sɪ.kəʊ/ ⓤⓢ /-koʊ/	**Mexican** /ˈmek.sɪ.kən/	
Micronesia /ˌmaɪ.krəˈniː.zi.ə/ ⓤⓢ /-kroʊˈniː.ʒə/		**Micronesian** /ˌmaɪ.krəˈniː.zi.ən/ ⓤⓢ /-kroʊˈniː.ʒən/
Moldova /mɒlˈdəʊ.və/ ⓤⓢ /mɑːlˈdoʊ-/	**Moldovan** /mɒlˈdəʊ.vən/ ⓤⓢ /mɑːlˈdoʊ-/	
Monaco /ˈmɒn.ə.kəʊ/ ⓤⓢ /ˈmɑːnə.koʊ/	**Monégasque** /ˌmɒn.ɪˈgɑːsk/ ⓤⓢ /ˌmɑː.neɪ-/	
Mongolia /mɒŋˈgəʊ.li.ə/ ⓤⓢ /mɑːŋˈgoʊ-/	**Mongolian** /mɒŋˈgəʊ.li.ən/ ⓤⓢ /ˌmɑːŋˈgoʊ-/	
Montserrat /ˌmɒnt.səˈræt/ ⓤⓢ /ˌmɑːnt-/	**Montserratian** /ˌmɒnt.səˈræt.i.ən/ ⓤⓢ /ˌmɑːnt-/	
Morocco /məˈrɒk.əʊ/ ⓤⓢ /-ˈrɑː.koʊ/	**Moroccan** /məˈrɒk.ən/ ⓤⓢ /-ˈrɑː-/	
Mozambique /ˌməʊ.zæmˈbiːk/ ⓤⓢ /ˌmoʊ-/	**Mozambican** /ˌməʊ.zæmˈbiː.kən/ ⓤⓢ /ˌmoʊ-/	
Myanmar /ˈmjæn.mɑːʳ/ ⓤⓢ /mjɑːnˈmɑːr/	**Burmese** /bɜːˈmiːz/ ⓤⓢ /bɝː-/	
Namibia /nəˈmɪb.i.ə/	**Namibian** /nəˈmɪb.i.ən/	
Nauru /nɑːˈuː.ruː/	**Nauruan** /nɑːˈuː.ruː.ən/	
Nepal /nəˈpɔːl/ ⓤⓢ /-ˈpɑːl/	**Nepalese** /ˌnep.əˈliːz/	
The Netherlands /ðəˈneð.ə.ləndz/ ⓤⓢ /-ɚ-/	**Dutch** /dʌtʃ/	**Dutchman** /ˈdʌtʃ.mən/ **Dutchwoman** /ˈdʌtʃ.wʊm.ən/
New Zealand /ˌnjuːˈziː.lənd/ ⓤⓢ /ˌnuː-/	**New Zealand** /ˌnjuːˈziː.lənd/ ⓤⓢ /ˌnuː-/	**New Zealander** /ˌnjuːˈziː.lən.dəʳ/ ⓤⓢ /ˌnuːˈziː.lən.dɚ/
Nicaragua /ˌnɪk.əˈræg.ju.ə/ ⓤⓢ /-ˈrɑːg.wə/	**Nicaraguan** /ˌnɪk.əˈræg.ju.ən/ ⓤⓢ /-ˈrɑːg.wən/	
Niger /niːˈʒeəʳ/ ⓤⓢ /ˈnaɪ.dʒɚ/	**Nigerien** /niːˈʒeə.ri.ən/ ⓤⓢ /naɪ.ˈdʒer.i-/	
Nigeria /naɪˈdʒɪə.ri.ə/ ⓤⓢ /-ˈdʒɪr.i-/	**Nigerian** /naɪˈdʒɪə.ri.ən/ ⓤⓢ /-ˈdʒɪr.i-/	
Norway /ˈnɔː.weɪ/ ⓤⓢ /ˈnɔːr-/	**Norwegian** /nɔːˈwiː.dʒən/ ⓤⓢ /nɔːr-/	
Oman /əʊˈmɑːn/ ⓤⓢ /oʊ-/	**Omani** /əʊˈmɑː.ni/ ⓤⓢ /oʊ-/	
The Pacific /ðə.pəˈsɪf.ɪk/	**Pacific** /pəˈsɪf.ɪk/	(not applicable)
Pacific Rim /pəˌsɪf.ɪkˈrɪm/		
Pakistan /ˌpɑː.kɪˈstɑːn/ ⓤⓢ /ˈpæk.ɪ.stæn/	**Pakistani** /ˌpɑː.kɪˈstɑː.ni/ ⓤⓢ /ˌpæk.ɪ.ˈstæni/	
Palestine /ˈpæl.ə.staɪn/	**Palestinian** /ˌpæl.əˈstɪn.i.ən/	
Panama /ˈpæn.ə.mɑː/	**Panamanian** /ˌpæn.əˈmeɪ.ni.ən/	
Papua New Guinea /ˌpæp.u.əˈnjuːˈgɪn.i.i/ ⓤⓢ /-nuː-/	**Papua New Guinean** /ˌpæp.u.əˈnjuːˈgɪn.i.ən/ ⓤⓢ /-nuː-/	
Paraguay /ˈpær.ə.gwaɪ/	**Paraguayan** /ˌpær.əˈgwaɪ.ən/	
Persia /ˈpɜː.ʒə/ ⓤⓢ /ˈpɝː-/	**Persian** /ˈpɜː.ʒən/ ⓤⓢ /ˈpɝː-/	
Peru /pəˈruː/	**Peruvian** /pəˈruː.vi.ən/	
The Philippines /ðəˈfɪl.ɪ.piːnz/	**Philippine** /ˈfɪl.ɪ.piːn/	**Filipino** /ˌfɪl.ɪˈpiː.nəʊ/ ⓤⓢ /-noʊ/
Poland /ˈpəʊ.lənd/ ⓤⓢ /ˈpoʊ-/	**Polish** /ˈpəʊ.lɪʃ/ ⓤⓢ /ˈpoʊ-/	**Pole** /pəʊl/ ⓤⓢ /poʊl/
Polynesia /ˌpɒl.ɪˈniː.ʒə/ ⓤⓢ /ˌpɒl.ɪˈniː.ʒən/ ⓤⓢ /ˌpɑː.lə-/	**Polynesian** /ˌpɒl.ɪˈniː.ʒən/ ⓤⓢ /ˌpɑː.lə-/	
Portugal /ˈpɔː.tʃə.gəl/ ⓤⓢ /ˈpɔːr-/	**Portuguese** /ˌpɔː.tʃəˈgiːz/ ⓤⓢ /ˌpɔːr-/	
Puerto Rico /ˌpwɜː.təʊˈriː.kəʊ/ ⓤⓢ /ˌpwer.t̬əˈriː.koʊ/	**Puerto Rican** /ˌpwɜː.təʊˈriː.kən/ ⓤⓢ /ˌpwer.t̬ə-/	
Qatar /ˈkʌt.ɑːʳ/ ⓤⓢ /kəˈtɑːr/	**Qatari** /kʌtˈɑː.ri/ ⓤⓢ /kəˈtɑː.ri/	
Quebec /kwɪˈbek/	**Quebecois** /ˌkeɪ.bekˈwɑː/	
Romania /rʊˈmeɪ.ni.ə/ ⓤⓢ /roʊ-/	**Romanian** /rʊˈmeɪ.ni.ən/ ⓤⓢ /roʊ-/	
Russia /ˈrʌʃ.ə/	**Russian** /ˈrʌʃ.ən/	
Rwanda /ruˈæn.də/ ⓤⓢ /-ˈɑːn-/	**Rwandan** /ruˈæn.dən/ ⓤⓢ /-ˈɑːn-/	
Samoa /səˈməʊ.ə/ ⓤⓢ /-ˈmoʊ-/	**Samoan** /səˈməʊ.ən/ ⓤⓢ /-ˈmoʊ-/	
San Marino /ˌsæn.məˈriː.nəʊ/ ⓤⓢ /-noʊ/	**Sanmarinese** /ˌsæn.mær.ɪˈniːz/	
São Tomé and Príncipe /ˌsaʊ.təˌmeɪənˈprɪn.sɪ.peɪ/	**Sao Tomean** /ˌsaʊ.təˈmeɪ.ən/	
Saudi Arabia /ˌsaʊ.di.əˈreɪ.bi.ə/	**Saudi** /ˈsaʊ.di/	
Scandinavia /ˌskæn.dɪˌneɪ.vi.ə/	**Scandinavian** /ˌskæn.dɪˌneɪ.vi.ən/	
Scotland /ˈskɒt.lənd/ ⓤⓢ /ˈskɑːt-/	**Scottish** /ˈskɒt.ɪʃ/ ⓤⓢ /ˈskɑː.t̬ɪʃ/	**Scot** /skɒt/ ⓤⓢ /ˈskɑːt/ **Scotsman** /ˈskɒt.smən/ ⓤⓢ /ˈskɑːt-/ **Scotswoman** /ˈskɒt.swʊm.ən/ ⓤⓢ /ˈskɑːts-/

Name	Adjective	Person
Senegal /ˌsen.ɪˈgɔːl/ ⓤⓢ /ˈsen.ɪ.gɑːl/	**Senegalese** /ˌsen.ɪ.gəˈliːz/	
The Seychelles /ðəˌseɪˈʃelz/	**Seychelles** /seɪˈʃelz/	**Seychellois** /ˌseɪʃ.elˈwɑː/
Siberia /saɪˈbɪə.ri.ə/ ⓤⓢ /-ˈbɪr.i-/	**Siberian** /saɪˈbɪə.ri.ən/ ⓤⓢ /-ˈbɪr.i-/	
Sierra Leone /si.er.ə.liˈəʊn/ ⓤⓢ /-oʊn/	**Sierra Leonean** /si.er.ə.liˈəʊ.ni.ən/ ⓤⓢ /-oʊn-/	
Singapore /ˌsɪŋ.əˈpɔːr/ ⓤⓢ /ˈsɪŋ.ə.pɔːr/	**Singaporean** /ˌsɪŋ.əˈpɔː.ri.ən/ ⓤⓢ /ˌsɪŋ.ə.ˈpɔːr-/	
Slovakia /sləˈvæk.i.ə/ ⓤⓢ /sloʊ-/	**Slovak** /ˈsləʊ.væk/ ⓤⓢ /ˈsloʊ-/	
Slovenia /sləˈviː.ni.ə/ ⓤⓢ /sloʊ-/	**Slovenian** /sləˈviː.ni.ən/ ⓤⓢ /sloʊ-/	**Slovene** /ˈsləʊ.viːn/ ⓤⓢ /ˈsloʊ-/
The Solomon Islands /ðəˈsɒl.ə.mənˌaɪ.ləndz/ ⓤⓢ /-ˈsɑː.lə-/	**Solomon Islander** /ˈsɒl.ə.mənˌaɪ.lən.dər/ ⓤⓢ /ˌsɑː.lə.mənˈaɪ.lən.də/	
Somalia /səˈmɑː.li.ə/	**Somali** /səˈmɑː.li/	
South Africa /ˌsaʊθˈæf.rɪ.kə/	**South African** /ˌsaʊθˈæf.rɪ.kən/	
Spain /speɪn/	**Spanish** /ˈspæn.ɪʃ/	**Spaniard** /ˈspæn.jəd/ ⓤⓢ /-jɚd/
Sri Lanka /ˌsriːˈlæŋ.kə/	**Sri Lankan** /ˌsriːˈlæŋ.kən/	
St Kitts and Nevis /sntˌkɪts.ənˈniː.vɪs/ ⓤⓢ /seɪnt-/	**Kittsian** /ˈkɪt.si.ən/	
St Lucia /sntˈluː.ʃə/ ⓤⓢ /seɪnt-/	**St Lucian** /sntˈluː.ʃən/ ⓤⓢ /seɪnt-/	
St Vincent and the Grenadines /sntˌvɪnt.səntˌən.ðəˌgren.əˈdiːnz/ ⓤⓢ /seɪnt,vɪnt-/	**Vincentian** /vɪnˈsɪn.ti.ən/	
Sudan /suːˈdɑːn/ ⓤⓢ /-ˈdæn/	**Sudanese** /ˌsuː.dəˈniːz/	
Suriname /ˌsʊə.rɪˈnæm/ ⓤⓢ /ˌsʊr.ɪˈnɑːm/	**Surinamese** /ˌsʊə.rɪ.næmˈiːz/ ⓤⓢ /ˌsʊr.ɪ.nɑːmˈiːz/	
Swaziland /ˈswɑː.zi.lænd/	**Swazi** /ˈswɑː.zi/	
Sweden /ˈswiː.dən/	**Swedish** /ˈswiː.dɪʃ/	**Swede** /swiːd/
Switzerland /ˈswɪt.sə.lənd/ ⓤⓢ /-sɚ-/	**Swiss** /swɪs/	
Syria /ˈsɪr.i.ə/	**Syrian** /ˈsɪr.i.ən/	
Tahiti /təˈhiː.ti/ ⓤⓢ /-t̬i/	**Tahitian** /tɑːˈhiː.ʃən/	
Taiwan /taɪˈwɑːn/	**Taiwanese** /ˌtaɪ.wəˈniːz/	
Tajikistan /tɑːˈdʒiː.kɪˌstɑːn/	**Tajik** /tɑːˈdʒiːk/	
Tanzania /ˌtæn.zəˈniː.ə/	**Tanzanian** /ˌtæn.zəˈniː.ən/	
Thailand /ˈtaɪ.lænd/	**Thai** /taɪ/	
Tibet /tɪˌbet/	**Tibetan** /tɪˌbet.ən/	
Togo /ˈtəʊ.gəʊ/ ⓤⓢ /ˈtoʊ.goʊ/	**Togolese** /ˌtəʊ.gəˈliːz/ ⓤⓢ /toʊ.goʊ-/	
Tonga /ˈtɒŋ.gə/ ⓤⓢ /ˈtɑːŋ-/	**Tongan** /ˈtɒŋ.gən/ ⓤⓢ /ˈtɑːŋ-/	
Trinidad and Tobago /ˌtrɪn.ɪ.dæd.ən.təˈbeɪ.gəʊ/ ⓤⓢ /-goʊ-/	**Trinidadian** /ˌtrɪn.ɪˈdæd.i.ən/	
Tunisia /tjuːˈnɪz.i.ə/ ⓤⓢ /tuːˈniː.ʒə/	**Tunisian** /tjuːˈnɪ.zi.ən/ ⓤⓢ /tuːˈniː.ʒən/	
Turkey /ˈtɜː.ki/ ⓤⓢ /ˈtɝː-/	**Turkish** /ˈtɜː.kɪʃ/ ⓤⓢ /ˈtɝː-/	**Turk** /tɜːk/ ⓤⓢ /ˈtɝːk/
Turkmenistan /tɜːkˌmen.ɪˈstɑːn/ ⓤⓢ /tɝːkˈmen.ɪ.stæn/	**Turkmen** /ˈtɜːk.men/ ⓤⓢ /ˈtɝːk-/	
Tuvalu /tuːˈvɑː.luː/	**Tuvaluan** /ˌtuː.vɑːˈluː.ən/	
Uganda /juːˈgæn.də/	**Ugandan** /juːˈgæn.dən/	
Ukraine /juːˈkreɪn/	**Ukrainian** /juːˈkreɪ.ni.ən/	
The United Arab Emirates /ðəˌjuː.naɪ.tɪdˌær.əbˈem.ɪ.rəts/ ⓤⓢ /-ˌnaɪ.t̬ɪd-/	**Emirian** /eˈmɪr.i.ən/	
The United Kingdom /ðəˌjuː.naɪ.tɪdˈkɪŋ.dəm/ ⓤⓢ /-ˌnaɪ.t̬ɪd-/	**British** /ˈbrɪt.ɪʃ/ ⓤⓢ /ˈbrɪt̬ɪʃ/	**Briton** /ˈbrɪt.ən/
The United States of America /ðəˌjuː.naɪ.tɪdˌsteɪts.əv.əˈmer.ɪ.kə/ ⓤⓢ /-ˌnaɪ.t̬ɪd-/	**American** /əˈmer.ɪ.kən/	
Uruguay /ˈjʊə.rə.gwaɪ/ ⓤⓢ /ˈjʊr.ə-/	**Uruguayan** /ˌjʊə.rəˈgwaɪ.ən/ ⓤⓢ /ˈjʊr.ə-/	
Uzbekistan /ʊzˌbek.ɪˈstɑːn/	**Uzbek** /ˈʊz.bek/	
Vanuatu /ˌvæn.uˈɑː.tuː/	**Vanuatuan** /ˌvæn.u.ɑːˈtuː.ən/	
Vatican City /ˌvæt.ɪ.kənˈsɪt.i/ ⓤⓢ /ˌvæt̬.ɪ.kənˈsɪt̬-/	**Vatican** /ˈvæt.ɪ.kən/ ⓤⓢ /ˈvæt̬-/	(not applicable)
Venezuela /ˌven.ɪˈzweɪ.lə/	**Venezuelan** /ˌven.ɪˈzweɪ.lən/	
Vietnam /ˌvjetˈnæm/	**Vietnamese** /ˌvjet.nəˈmiːz/	
Wales /weɪlz/	**Welsh** /welʃ/	**Welshman** /ˈwelʃ.mən/ **Welshwoman** /ˈwelʃˌwʊm.ən/
Western Sahara /ˌwes.tən.səˈhɑː.rə/ ⓤⓢ /-tɚn.səˈher.ə/	**Sahrawian** /sɑːˈrɑː.wi.ən/	
Yemen /ˈjem.ən/	**Yemeni** /ˈjem.ə.ni/	
Yugoslavia /ˌjuː.gəʊˈslɑː.vi.ə/ ⓤⓢ /-goʊ-/	**Yugoslav** /ˈjuː.gəʊ.slɑːv/ ⓤⓢ /-goʊ-/	
Zaire /zaɪˈɪə[r]/ ⓤⓢ /-ˈɪr/	**Zairean** /zaɪˈɪə.ri.ən/ ⓤⓢ /-ˈɪr.i-/	
Zambia /ˈzæm.bi.ə/	**Zambian** /ˈzæm.bi.ən/	
Zimbabwe /zɪmˈbɑːb.weɪ/	**Zimbabwean** /zɪmˈbɑːb.wi.ən/	

Common first names

This is a list of common first names that are used in English-speaking countries. Some learners of English like to choose an English name to use as their name in class. This list tells you how to pronounce the name.

The names in brackets are common short forms or different forms of the name. These other forms are usually more informal than the long form. For example, a boy might be called 'William' by his teacher but 'Bill' or 'Billy' by his friends.

Male names

Adam /ˈæd.əm/
Alan /ˈæl.ən/
Alexander /ˌæl.ɪgˈzɑːn.dəʳ/
    (Alex) /ˈæl.ɪks/
Andrew /ˈæn.druː/ (Andy) /ˈæn.di/
Anthony UK /ˈæn.tə.ni/ US
    /ˈæn.θə.ni/ (Tony) /ˈtəʊ.ni/
Benjamin /ˈben.dʒə.mɪn/
    (Ben) /ben/
Charles /tʃɑːlz/ (Charlie) /ˈtʃɑː.li/
Christopher /ˈkrɪs.tə.fəʳ/
    (Chris) /krɪs/
Daniel /ˈdæn.jəl/ (Dan) /dæn/
Darren /ˈdær.ən/
David /ˈdeɪ.vɪd/ (Dave) /deɪv/
Edward /ˈed.wəd/ (Ed) /ed/
    (Ted) /ted/

Geoffrey /ˈdʒef.ri/ (Geoff) /dʒef/
George /dʒɔːdʒ/
Harry /ˈhær.i/
Jack /dʒæk/
James /dʒeɪmz/ (Jim) /dʒɪm/
John /dʒɒn/
Jonathan /ˈdʒɒn.ə.θən/
Joseph /ˈdʒəʊ.zɪf/ (Joe) /dʒəʊ/
Joshua /ˈdʒɒʃ.ju.ə/ (Josh) /dʒɒʃ/
Ian /ˈiː.ən/
Kevin /ˈkev.ɪn/
Liam /ˈliː.əm/
Mark /mɑːk/
Martin /ˈmɑː.tɪn/
Matthew /ˈmæθ.juː/ (Matt) /mæt/
Michael /ˈmaɪ.kəl/ (Mike) /maɪk/
    (Mick) /mɪk/
Nicholas /ˈnɪk.ə.ləs/ (Nick) /nɪk/

Patrick /ˈpæt.rɪk/ (Pat) /pæt/
    (Paddy) /ˈpæd.i/
Paul /pɔːl/
Peter /ˈpiː.təʳ/ (Pete) /piːt/
Philip /ˈfɪl.ɪp/ (Phil) /fɪl/
Richard /ˈrɪtʃ.əd/ (Ricky) /ˈrɪk.i/
    (Dick) /dɪk/ (Rick) /rɪk/
Robert /ˈrɒb.ət/ (Bob) /bɒb/
    (Rob) /rɒb/ (Bobby) /ˈbɒb.i/
Samuel /ˈsæm.juəl/ (Sam) /sæm/
Simon /ˈsaɪ.mən/
Thomas /ˈtɒm.əs/ (Tom) /tɒm/
    (Tommy) /ˈtɒm.i/
Timothy /ˈtɪm.ə.θi/ (Tim) /tɪm/
William /ˈwɪl.jəm/ (Billy) /ˈbɪl.i/
    (Will) /wɪl/ (Bill) /bɪl/

Female names

Alice /ˈæl.ɪs/
Alison /ˈæl.ɪ.sən/
Amanda /əˈmæn.də/
    (Mandy) /ˈmæn.di/
Amy /ˈeɪ.mi/
Ann/Anne /æn/
Bridget /ˈbrɪdʒ.ɪt/
Carol /ˈkær.əl/
Caroline /ˈkær.ə.laɪn/
Catherine/Kathryn /ˈkæθ.rɪn/
    (Kate) /keɪt/ (Katie) /ˈkeɪ.ti/
    (Cath) /kæθ/
Charlotte /ˈʃɑː.lət/
Chloe /ˈkləʊ.i/

Christine /ˈkrɪs.tiːn/ (Chris) /krɪs/
Clare/Claire /kleə[r]/
Deborah /ˈdeb.ə.rə/
    (Debbie) /ˈdeb.i/
Diane /daɪˈæn/
Elizabeth /ɪˈlɪz.ə.bəθ/
    (Beth) /beθ/ (Liz) /lɪz/
Emily /ˈem.ɪ.li/
Emma /ˈem.ə/
Hannah /ˈhæn.ə/
Helen /ˈhel.ən/
Jane /dʒeɪn/
Jennifer /ˈdʒen.ɪ.fəʳ/
    (Jenny) /ˈdʒen.i/
Joanne /dʒəʊˈæn/ (Jo) /dʒəʊ/
Julie /ˈdʒuː.li/

Karen /ˈkær.ən/
Laura /ˈlɔː.rə/
Linda /ˈlɪn.də/
Lucy /ˈluː.si/
Margaret /ˈmɑː.gə.rət/
    (Maggie) /ˈmæg.i/
Mary /ˈmeə.ri/
Rachel /ˈreɪ.tʃəl/
Rebecca /rɪˈbek.ə/ (Becky) /ˈbek.i/
Ruth /ruːθ/
Sarah /ˈseə.rə/
Sharon /ˈʃær.ən/
Sophie /ˈsəʊ.fi/
Susan /ˈsuː.zən/ (Sue) /suː/
Tracy /ˈtreɪ.si/
Valerie /ˈvæl.ə.ri/

Prefixes and suffixes

1. Prefixes

A prefix is a group of letters at the beginning of a word which changes the word's meaning. Here is a list of the most common prefixes and examples of how those prefixes are used.

Anglo- relating to the UK or England *an Anglophile* (= someone who loves England)

ante- before or in front of *antedate* • *antenatal* • *anteroom*

anti- **1** opposed to or against *anti-racist laws* **2** preventing or destroying *an anti-aircraft missile*

auto- **1** operating without being controlled by humans *autopilot* (= a computer that directs an aircraft) **2** self *an autobiography* (= a book that someone writes about their own life)

bi- two *bilingual* (= speaking two languages) • *bimonthly* (= happening twice in a month or once every two months)

centi-, cent- hundred *a centimetre* • *a century*

co- with or together *a co-author* • *to coexist*

contra- against or opposite *to contradict* (= say the opposite) • *contraception* (= something that is used to prevent pregnancy)

counter- opposing or as a reaction to *a counter-attack* (= an attack on someone who has attacked you)

cross- **1** across *cross-border* **2** including different groups or subjects *a cross-party committee* (= one formed from many political parties) • *cross-cultural*

cyber- involving, using or relating to computers, especially the Internet *cybercrime* • *cyberculture* • *cyberspace*

de- to take something away *deforestation* (= when the trees in an area are cut down)

dis- not or the opposite of *dishonest* • *disbelief* • *to disagree*

e- electronic, usually relating to the Internet *email* • *e-commerce*. Note: 'e-' is usally joined onto a word with a hyphen (as in *e-commerce)* but *email* is usually written without a hyphen

eco- relating to the environment *eco-friendly tourism* (= tourism which does not damage the environment)

en- **1** used to form verbs which mean to put into or onto something *encase* • *encircle* • *endanger* **2** used to form verbs which mean to cause to be something *enable* • *endear* • *enrich*

Euro- relating to Europe *Europop* (= modern, young people's music from Europe)

ex- from before *an ex-boyfriend* • *an ex-boss*

extra- outside of or in addition to *extracurricular activities* (= activities that are in addition to the usual school work)

geo- of or relating to the Earth *geophysics* • *geology*

hyper- having a lot of or too much of a quality *hyperactive* • *hypersensitive* (= more than normally sensitive)

ill- in a way which is bad or not suitable *ill-prepared* • *an ill-judged remark*

in-, il-, im-, ir- not *incorrect* • *illegal* • *impossible* • *irregular*

inter- between or among *international* • *an interdepartmental meeting*

intra- within *an intranet*

kilo- a thousand *a kilometre* • *a kilogram*

mega- **1** *informal* extremely *megarich* (= extremely rich) **2** one million *40 megabytes*

micro- very small *a microchip* • *microscopic* (= extremely small)

mid- in the middle of *mid-July.* • *a man in his mid-forties* • *mid-afternoon/-morning*

milli- a thousandth *a millisecond*

mini- small *a miniskirt* (= very short skirt) • *a minibus*

mis- not or badly *mistrust* • *to misbehave*

mono- one or single *monolingual* • *a monologue*

multi- many *a multi-millionaire* • *a multi-storey car park*

neo- new *neo-fascists*

non- not or the opposite of *non-alcoholic drinks* • *non-smokers*

omni- everywhere or everything *omnipresent* • *omniscient*

out- more than or better than *to outgrow* • *to outnumber* • *to outdo someone* (= to show that you are better than someone)

over- too much *to overeat* • *overpopulated*

photo- connected with or produced by light *photosensitive* • *photosynthesis*

poly- many *polygamy* (= having more than one husband or wife at the same time) • *a polygon* (= shape with many sides)

post- after or later than *postwar* • *a postgraduate*

pre- before or earlier than *pre-tax profits* • *pre-school*

pro- supporting *pro-democracy demonstrations*

pseudo- false *a pseudonym* (= false name used especially by a writer) • *pseudo-academic*

psycho- of the mind or mental processes *psychology*

quasi- partly *quasi-religious ideas*

re- again *to remarry* • *a reusable container*

retro- looking at or copying the past *retrograde* • *retrospective*

self- of or by yourself or itself *self-doubt* • *self-critical*

semi- half or partly *a semicircle* • *semi-frozen*

socio- relating to society *socio-economic*

sub- **1** under or below *subzero temperatures* **2** less important or a smaller part of a larger whole *a subsection*

super- extremely or more than usual *a supermodel* • *super-rich*

tele- over a long distance, done by telephone, or on or for television *He worked in the telecommunications industry*

thermo- relating to heat or temperature *a thermostat* (= piece of equipment that controls temperature) • *a thermometer*

trans- **1** across *transatlantic flights* **2** showing a change *to transform* • *to translate*

tri- three *a triangle* • *a tripod*

ultra- extremely *ultra-modern architecture* • *ultra-careful*

un- not or the opposite of *unhappy* • *unfair* • *to unfasten*

under- **1** not enough *undercooked potatoes* • *underprivileged children* **2** below *underwear* • *an underpass*

2. Suffixes

A suffix is a group of letters at the end of a word which changes the word's meaning and often its part of speech. Here is a list of the most common suffixes and examples of how those suffixes are used.

-able/-ible changes a verb into an adjective meaning 'able to be' *avoid → avoidable* • *admire → admirable* • *like → likeable*

-age changes a verb into a noun meaning 'the action described by the verb or the result of that action' *marry → marriage* • *break → breakage* • *spill → spillage*

-aholic, -oholic makes a noun meaning 'a person who is unable to stop doing or taking something' *a workaholic* • *an alcoholic*

-al 1 changes a noun into an adjective meaning 'relating to' *culture → cultural* • *nation → national* • *nature → natural* **2** changes a verb into a noun meaning 'the action described by the verb' *approve → approval* • *remove → removal*

-an, -ian 1 makes a noun meaning 'a person who does something' *historian* • *politician* **2** makes an adjective meaning 'belonging somewhere' *American*

-ance, -ence, -ancy, -ency makes a noun meaning 'an action, state, or quality' *performance* • *independence* • *preference*

-ation, -ion changes a verb into a noun meaning 'the process of the action described by the verb, or the result of that action' *educate → education* • *explain → explanation* • *connect → connection*

-centric makes an adjective meaning 'having the stated thing as your main interest' *Eurocentric*

-ed makes an adjective meaning, 'having this thing or quality' *bearded* • *coloured* • *surprised*

-ee changes a verb into a noun meaning 'someone that something is done to' *employ → employee* • *interview → interviewee* • *train → trainee*

-en changes an adjective into a verb meaning 'to become or make something become' *thick → thicken* • *fat → fatten* • *soft → soften*

-ence, -ency See **-ance**

-er, -or changes a verb into a noun meaning 'the person or thing that does the activity' *dance → dancer* • *employ → employer* • *act → actor* • *cook → cooker* (= a machine for cooking) • *time → timer*

-esque makes an adjective meaning 'like or in the style of someone or their work' *a Dali-esque painting* • *a Kafka-esque nightmare*

-ful changes a noun into an adjective meaning, 'having a particular quality' *beauty → beautiful* • *power → powerful* • *use → useful*

-hood makes a noun meaning 'the state of being something and the time when someone is something' *childhood* • *motherhood*

-ian See **-an**

-ible See **-able**

-ical changes a noun ending in -y or -ics into an adjective meaning 'relating to' *history → historical* • *politics → political*

-ing makes an adjective meaning 'making someone feel something' *interest → interesting* • *surprise → surprising* • *shock → shocking*

-ion See **-ation**

-ise See **-ize**

-ish makes an adjective meaning **1** slightly *a greyish colour* • *a smallish* (= quite small) *house* **2** typical of or similar to *a childish remark* **3** approximately *fiftyish* (= about fifty)

-ist 1 makes a noun meaning 'a person who does a particular activity' *artist* • *novelist* • *scientist* **2** makes a noun and an adjective meaning 'someone with a particular set of beliefs' *communist* • *feminist*

-ive changes a verb into an adjective meaning 'having a particular quality or effect' *attract → attractive* • *create → creative* • *explode → explosive*

-ize, -ise changes an adjective into a verb meaning 'to make something become' *modern → modernize* • *commercial → commercialize*

-less changes a noun into an adjective meaning 'without' *homeless people* • *a meaningless statement* • *a hopeless situation*

-like changes a noun into an adjective meaning 'typical of or similar to' *childlike trust* • *a cabbage-like vegetable*

-ly 1 changes an adjective into an adverb describing the way that something is done *She spoke slowly* • *Drive safely.* **2** makes an adjective and an adverb meaning 'happening every day, night, week, etc' *a daily newspaper* • *We hold the meeting weekly.* **3** changes a noun into an adjective meaning 'like that person or thing' *mother → motherly* • *coward → cowardly*

-ment changes a verb into a noun meaning ' the action or process described by a verb, or its result' *develop → development* • *disappoint → disappointment*

-monger makes a noun meaning 'a person who encourages a particular activity, especially one which causes trouble' *a war-monger*

-ness changes an adjective into a noun meaning the quality or condition described by the adjective *sweet → sweetness* • *happy → happiness* • *dark → darkness* • *ill → illness*

-ology makes a noun meaning 'the study of something' *psychology* (= the study of the mind) • *sociology* (= the study of society)

-or See **-er**

-ous changes a noun into an adjective meaning 'having that quality' *danger → dangerous* • *ambition → ambitious*

-phile makes a noun meaning 'enjoying or liking something' *a Francophile* (= someone who loves France) • *a bibliophile* (= someone who loves books)

-proof makes an adjective meaning 'protecting against, or not damaged by, a particular thing' *a bullet-proof vest* • *a waterproof jacket*

-ridden makes an adjective meaning 'full of something unpleasant or bad' *a guilt-ridden mother*

-ship makes a noun showing involvement between people • *friendship* • *a relationship* • *partnership*

-speak used to form nouns to mean the special language used in a particular subject area or business *computerspeak* • *marketingspeak*

-ward, -wards makes an adverb meaning 'towards a direction or place' *inward* • *forward* • *homeward*

-wise changes a noun into an adverb meaning 'relating to this subject' *Weather-wise, the holiday was great.* • *How are we doing time-wise?*

-y changes a noun into an adjective meaning 'having a lot of something (often something bad)' *noise → noisy* • *dirt → dirty* • *smell → smelly*

Irregular Verbs

This is a list of the English verbs that have an irregular past simple tense and an irregular past participle. If more than one form is listed, it may indicate that each form has a different meaning; you should check this in the dictionary.

Infinitive	Past Simple	Past Participle	Infinitive	Past Simple	Past Participle
arise	arose	arisen	dig	dug	dug
awake	awoke, (US ALSO awaked)	awoken	dive	dived, (US ALSO) dove	dived
be	was/were	been	draw	drew	drawn
bear	bore	borne, (US ALSO born)	dream	dreamed, dreamt	dreamed, dreamt
			drink	drank	drunk
beat	beat	beaten, (US ALSO beat)	drive	drove	driven
			dwell	dwelt, dwelled	dwelt, dwelled
beget	begot, begat	begotten, begot	eat	ate	eaten
become	became	become	fall	fell	fallen
befall	befell	befallen	feed	fed	fed
begin	began	begun	feel	felt	felt
behold	beheld	beheld	fight	fought	fought
belie	belied	belied	find	found	found
bend	bent	bent	flee	fled	fled
beseech	beseeched, besought	beseeched, besought	fling	flung	flung
			fly	flew	flown
bestrew	bestrewed	bestrewn, bestrewed	forbid	forbade, forbad	forbidden
			forecast	forecasted, forecast	forecasted, forecast
bestride	bestrode	bestridden	foresee	foresaw	foreseen
bet	bet, betted	bet, betted	forget	forgot	forgotten
bid	bid, bade	bid, bidden	forgive	forgave	forgiven
bind	bound	bound	forgo	forwent	forgone
bite	bit	bitten	forsake	forsook	forsaken
bleed	bled	bled	forswear	forswore	forsworn
bless	blessed, blest	blessed, blest	freeze	froze	frozen
blow	blew	blown	gainsay	gainsaid	gainsaid
break	broke	broken	get	got	got, (US ALSO gotten)
breed	bred	bred			
bring	brought	brought	gird	girded, girt	girded, girt
broadcast	broadcast (US ALSO broadcasted)	broadcast (US ALSO broadcasted)	give	gave	given
			go	went	gone
build	built	built	grind	ground	ground
burn	burnt, burned	burnt, burned	grow	grew	grown
burst	burst	burst	hang	hung, hanged	hung, hanged
bust	(UK) bust, (US) busted	(UK) bust, (US) busted	have	had	had
			hear	heard	heard
buy	bought	bought	hew	hewed	hewed, hewn
cast	cast	cast	hide	hid	hidden
catch	caught	caught	hit	hit	hit
choose	chose	chosen	hold	held	held
cleave	cleaved, (US ALSO clove)	cleaved, cloven	hurt	hurt	hurt
			input	inputted, input	inputted, input
cling	clung	clung	interbreed	interbred	interbred
come	came	come	interweave	interwove	interwoven
cost	cost, costed	cost, costed	keep	kept	kept
creep	crept	crept	kneel	knelt, kneeled	knelt, kneeled
cut	cut	cut	knit	knitted, knit	knitted, (US ALSO knit)
deal	dealt	dealt			

Infinitive	Past Simple	Past Participle
know	knew	known
lead	led	led
lean	leaned, (*UK ALSO* leant)	leaned (*UK ALSO* leant)
leap	leapt, leaped	leapt, leaped
learn	learned, (*UK ALSO* learnt)	learned, (*UK ALSO* learnt)
leave	left	left
lend	lent	lent
let	let	let
lie	lay, lied	lain, lied
light	lit, lighted	lit, lighted
lip-read	lip-read	lip-read
lose	lost	lost
make	made	made
mean	mean	meant
meet	met	met
mimic	mimicked	mimicked
miscast	miscast	miscast
mishear	misheard	misheard
mislay	mislaid	mislaid
mislead	misled	misled
misspell	misspelled, (*UK ALSO* misspelt)	misspelled, (*UK ALSO* misspelt)
misspend	misspent	misspent
mistake	mistook	mistaken
misunderstand	misunderstood	misunderstood
mow	mowed	mown, mowed
offset	offset	offset
outbid	outbid	outbid, outbidden
outdo	outdid	outdone
outfight	outfought	outfought
outgrow	outgrew	outgrown
outrun	outran	outrun
outsell	outsold	outsold
outshine	outshone	outshone
overbid	overbid	overbid
overcome	overcame	overcome
overdo	overdid	overdone
overdraw	overdrew	overdrawn
overeat	overate	overeaten
overhang	overhung	overhung
overhear	overheard	overheard
overlay	overlaid	overlaid
overload	overloaded	overloaded, (*UK ALSO*) overladen
overpay	overpaid	overpaid
override	overrode	overridden
overrun	overran	overrun
oversee	oversaw	overseen
overshoot	overshot	overshot
oversleep	overslept	overslept
overspend	overspent	overspent
overtake	overtook	overtaken
overthrow	overthrew	overthrown
overwrite	overwrote	overwritten
partake	partook	partaken

Infinitive	Past Simple	Past Participle
pay	paid	paid
plead	pleaded, (*US ALSO* pled)	pleaded, (*US ALSO* pled)
preset	preset	preset
prove	proved	proved, proven
put	put	put
quit	quit, quitted	quit, quitted
read /riːd/	read /red/	read /red/
rebuild	rebuilt	rebuilt
recast	recast	recast
refit	refit, refitted	refit, refitted
remake	remade	remade
rend	rent, (*US ALSO* rended)	rent, (*US ALSO* rended)
repay	repaid	repaid
rerun	reran	rerun
resit	resat	resat
rethink	rethought	rethought
rewrite	rewrote	rewritten
rid	rid	rid
ride	rode	ridden
ring	rang	rung
rise	rose	risen
run	ran	run
saw	sawed	sawn, (*US ALSO* sawed)
say	said	said
see	saw	seen
seek	sought	sought
sell	sold	sold
send	sent	sent
set	set	set
sew	sewed	sewn, sewed
shake	shook	shaken
shear	sheared	sheared, shorn
shed	shed	shed
shine	shone	shone
shit	shit, shat, shitted	shit, shat, shitted
shoe	shod, (*US ALSO* shoed)	shod, (*US ALSO* shoed)
shoot	shot	shot
show	showed	shown
shrink	shrank	shrunk
shut	shut	shut
sink	sank	sunk
sit	sat	sat
slay	slew, slayed	slain
sleep	slept	slept
slide	slid	slid
sling	slung	slung
slink	slunk	slunk
slit	slit	slit
smell	smelled, (*UK ALSO* smelt)	smelled, (*UK ALSO* smelt)
smite	smote	smitten
sneak	sneaked, (*US ALSO* snuck)	sneaked, (*US ALSO* snuck)
sow	sowed	sown, sowed

Infinitive	Past Simple	Past Participle	Infinitive	Past Simple	Past Participle
speak	spoke	spoken	thrive	thrived, (*US ALSO* throve)	thrived, (*US ALSO* thriven)
speed	sped, speeded	sped, speeded	throw	threw	thrown
spell	spelled, (*UK ALSO* spelt)	spelled, (*UK ALSO* spelt)	thrust	thrust	thrust
spend	spent	spent	tread	trod, (*US ALSO* treaded)	trodden, (*US ALSO* trod)
spill	spilled, (*UK ALSO* spilt)	spilled, (*UK ALSO* spilt)	typecast	typecast	typecast
spin	spun	spun	unbend	unbent	unbent
spit	spat, (*US ALSO* spit)	spat, (*US ALSO* spit)	undercut	undercut	undercut
split	split	split	undergo	underwent	undergone
spoil	spoiled, spoilt	spoiled, spoilt	underlie	underlay	underlain
spotlight	spotlighted, spotlit	spoltlighted, spotlit	underpay	underpaid	underpaid
spring	sprang	sprung	underwrite	underwrote	underwritten
stand	stood	stood	undersell	undersold	undersold
steal	stole	stolen	understand	understood	understood
stick	stuck	stuck	undertake	undertook	undertaken
sting	stung	stung	undo	undid	undone
stink	stank, (*US ALSO* stunk)	stunk	unwind	unwound	unwound
strew	strewed	strewn, strewed	uphold	upheld	upheld
stride	strode	strode	upset	upset	upset
strike	struck	struck, (*US ALSO* stricken)	wake	woke	woken
			waylay	waylaid	waylaid
string	strung	strung	wear	wore	worn
strive	strove, strived	striven, strived	weave	wove, weaved	woven, weaved
sublet	sublet	sublet	wed	wedded, wed	wedded, wed
swear	swore	sworn	weep	wept	wept
sweep	swept	swept	wet	wet, wetted	wet, wetted
swell	swelled	swollen, swelled	win	won	won
swim	swam	swum	wind	wound	wound
swing	swung	swung	withdraw	withdrew	withdrawn
take	took	taken	withhold	withheld	withheld
teach	taught	taught	withstand	withstood	withstood
tear	tore	torn	wreak	wrought, wreaked	wrought, wreaked
tell	told	told	wring	wrung	wrung
think	thought	thought	write	wrote	written

Regular verb tenses

This table shows how the different tenses of English verbs are formed. It also shows in brackets how the negative form of each tense is used. The words 'continuous' and 'progresssive' are both used in the names of tenses because both words are used in teaching.

In all the examples below, the regular verb 'help' is used for all tenses so that you can compare the endings.

Simple tenses	Continuous/Progressive tenses

Present Simple

used for actions in the present, for things that are always true or that happen regularly, and for opinions and beliefs

I/we/you/they	help (**do not** help)
he/she/it	help**s** (**does not** help)

Present Continuous/Progressive

used for actions or events that are happening or developing now, for future plans, or to show that an event is repeated

I	**am** help**ing** (**am not** help**ing**)
we/you/they	**are** help**ing** (**are not** help**ing**)
he/she/it	**is** help**ing** (**is not** help**ing**)

Past Simple

used for completed actions and events in the past

I/we/you/they	help**ed** (**did not** help)
he/she/it	help**ed** (**did not** help)

Past Continuous/Progressive

used for actions or events in the past that were not yet finished or that were interrupted

I	**was** help**ing** (**was not** help**ing**)
we/you/they	**were** help**ing** (**were not** help**ing**)
he/she/it	**was** help**ing** (**was not** help**ing**)

Future Simple

used for actions and events in the future

I/we/you/they	**will** help (**will not** help)
he/she/it	**will** help (**will not** help)

Future Continuous/Progressive

used for actions or events in the future that will continue into the future

I/we/you/they	**will be** help**ing** (**will not be** help**ing**)
he/she/it	**will be** help**ing** (**will not be** help**ing**)

Present Perfect

used to show that an event happened or an action was completed at some time before the present

I/we/you/they	**have** help**ed** (**have not** help**ed**)
he/she/it	**has** help**ed** (**has not** help**ed**)

Present Perfect Continuous/Progressive

used for actions or events that started in the past but are still happening now, or for past actions which only recently finished and whose effects are seen now

I/we/you/they	**have been** help**ing** (**have not been** help**ing**)
he/she/it	**has been** help**ing** (**has not been** help**ing**)

(continued on the next page) ➜

Regular verb tenses *(continued)*

Past Perfect (or 'Pluperfect')

usually used to show that an event happened or an action was completed before a particular time in the past

I/we/you/they	**had** helped
	(had not helped)
he/she/it	**had** helped
	(had not helped)

Past Perfect Continuous/Progressive

used for actions or events that happened for a period of time but were completed before a particular time in the past

I/we/you/they	**had been** helping
	(had not been helping)
he/she/it	**had been** helping
	(had not been helping)

Future Perfect

used to show that something will be completed before a particular time in the future

I/we/you/they	**will have** helped
	(will not have helped)
he/she/it	**will have** helped
	(will not have helped)

Future Perfect Continuous/Progressive

used for actions or events that will already be happening at a particular time in the future

I/we/you/they	**will have been** helping
	(will not have been helping)
he/she/it	**will have been** helping
	(will not have been helping)

Subjunctive

This is fairly unusual and often sounds formal. It is often used to express possibilities, doubts or wishes.

I/we/you/they	help **(not** help)
he/she/it	help **(not** help)

Symbols

This page shows you the names for some of the common symbols which you will see in writing. It also shows you how to describe types of printing, symbols from other languages, and the commonest mathematical symbols.

Common symbols

&	ampersand. This symbol is read as 'and'.	*	asterisk
©	copyright symbol	™	trademark symbol
●	bullet point	®	registered trademark
✓	*UK* tick , *US* check	✗	cross

@   This symbol is read as 'at' and is used in email addresses.

"   This symbol is read as 'ditto' and is used in a list to avoid writing a word if the same word is written immediately above it.

Accents

é	e acute	è	e grave	ô	o circumflex
ä	a umlaut	ñ	n tilde	ç	c cedilla

Different forms of print

<u>underlined text</u>   *italic text*   UPPER CASE

bold text   **highlighted text**   lower case

Mathematical symbols

+	$1 + 2 = 3$	1 **plus** 2 = 3 *or* 1 **and** 2 is 3
−	$3 - 1 = 2$	3 **minus** 1 = 2 *or* 3 **take away** 1 is 2 *or* 1 **from** 3 = 2
×	$2 \times 3 = 6$	2 **multiplied by** 3 = 6 *or* 2 **times** 3 = 6 *or* **two threes** are six
÷	$6 \div 2 = 3$	6 **divided by** 2 = 3 *or* 2 **into** 6 is 3
=	$2 + 2 = 4$	2 + 2 **equal(s)** 4 *or* 2 + 2 **make(s)** 4
≠	$x \neq 2$	x is **not equal** to 2 *or* x **does not equal** 2
≈	$x \approx 2$	x is **approximately equal to** 2
>	$x > 2$	x is **greater than** 2
⩾	$x \geqslant 2$	x is **greater than or equal to** 2
<	$x < 2$	x is **less than** 2
⩽	$x \leqslant 2$	x is **less than or equal to** 2
²	$2^2 = 4$	2 **squared** is 4
√	$\sqrt{4} = 2$	the **(square) root of** 4 is 2
³	$2^3 = 8$	2 **cubed** is 8
³√	$\sqrt[3]{8} = 2$	the **cube root of** 8 is 2
⁴	$2^4 = 16$	2 **to the power of** 4 is 16
±	± 4	**plus or minus** 4

$\frac{1}{4}$	**a quarter** or **one quarter**
$\frac{1}{2}$	**a half** or **one half**
$\frac{3}{4}$	three **quarters**
$5\frac{3}{4}$	five and three **quarters**
0.1	nought **point** one
3.15	three **point** one five
%	25% 25 **per cent**
°	90° 90 **degrees**

Units of measurement

People in the US, and older people in Britain, do not usually use the metric units of measurement. Units such as **pounds**, **feet** and **gallons** are still used in general conversation in both the US and in Britain. In Britain it is the law that the metric measurements have to be used on anything that is sold but you will still see the old measurements as well.

These tables show the **approximate** equivalents between the commonest American/British and Metric measurements. There are some differences between the American and British measurements of volume. There are also some UK/US spelling differences.

	American/British	**Metric**
Length & Distance	1 inch	2.5 centimetres
	1 foot (= 12 inches)	30 centimetres
	1 yard (= 3 feet)	90 centimetres
	5 miles	8 kilometres *(UK)*
		kilometers *(US)*
Area	11 square feet	1 m²
	5 acres	2 hectares
	1 square mile	250 hectares
Weight &Volume	1 ounce	30 grams
	1 pound (= 16 ounces)	450 grams
	(UK) 1 stone (= 14 pounds)	6.5 kilograms
	1 pint	*(UK)* 0.6 litres
		(US) 0.5 liters
	1 gallon (= 8 pints)	*(UK)* 4.5 litres
		(US) 3.5 liters

Temperature	Fahrenheit	Celsius
Ice	32°F	0°C
Hot day	80°F	25°C
Body temperature	98°F	37°C
Boiling water	212°F	100°C

Abbreviations

American/British		**Metric**		**Metric**
inch	**in** *or* "	centimetre		**cm**
foot	**ft** *or* '	*(UK)* metre *(US)* meter		**m**
mile	**m**	*(UK)* kilometre *(US)* kilometer		**km**
ounce	**oz**	hectare		**ha**
pound	**lb**	gram		**g**
pint	**pt**	kilogram		**kg**
gallon	**gal**	*(UK)* litre *(US)* liter		**l**

How we show pronunciation in the dictionary

All the pronunciations use the International Phonetic Alphabet (IPA). All of the symbols are shown in a list inside the back cover of the dictionary. If there are two possible pronunciations we show both of them separated by a comma.

1. British and American pronunciation

If we only show one pronunciation for a word then it is acceptable in British and American English. If there is a difference, we show the British pronunciation first, followed by the American pronunciation after the symbol ⓤⓢ. We only show the part of the American English pronunciation which is different, like this:

storehouse /'stɔː.haʊs/ ⓤⓢ /'stɔːr-/

2. Stress

Stress patterns show you which parts of a word you should emphasize when you say the word. We show stress marks in front of the part of the word that should be emphasized.

/'/ (the primary stress symbol)
This symbol shows you the part of a word that you should emphasize most. For example, in the word **picture** /'pɪk.tʃeʳ/ you should emphasize the first part and in the word **deny** /dɪ'naɪ/ you should emphasize the second part

/ˌ/ (the secondary stress symbol)
This symbol shows you the part of the word that has the second most important emphasis. This is important if you are pronouncing a long word with three or more syllables. For example, in the word **submarine** /ˌsʌb.məˈriːn/ the main emphasis is on the last part of the word but you should also put slight emphasis

on the first part of the word as well.

There are some compound nouns and phrases (e.g. **barn dance, barrier cream**) where we do not show a separate pronunciation, because the pronunciations of both of the words in the phrase are shown in other parts of the dictionary. You still need to know about the stress in the phrase. We show this by using stress markers above and below the words in the phrase, like this:

'barn ˌdance

3. Syllables

In all of the pronunciations there are marks to show you how many syllables the word has. The syllable mark is like a full stop. It comes before each new syllable. For example, in the word **standard** /'stæn.dəd/ the syllable mark shows you that the word has two syllables. If we show stress marks in a word, these also show when a new syllables starts. So in a word like **banana** /bəˈnɑː.nə/ the stress mark and syllable mark shows you that there are three syllables in the word.

4. Strong forms and weak forms

Some very common words (e.g. **and**, **them**, **of**) have strong and weak pronunciations which are different. The weak forms are more common. For example, the word **them** is shown like this in the dictionary:

them *STRONG* /ðem/, *WEAK* /ðəm/

In a sentence such as 'I saw them leave' the weak form /ðəm/ would be used. If you need to emphasize the word **them** then you need to use the strong form. For example, in the sentence 'They said they saw me but I didn't see them' the strong form /ðem/ would be used.

Pronunciation Symbols

Vowel sounds

short vowels		long vowels		diphthongs	
ɪ	as in pit	iː	as in see	eɪ	as in day
e	as in wet	ɑː	as in arm	aɪ	as in my
æ	as in cat	ɔː	as in saw	ɔɪ	as in boy
ʌ	as in run	uː	as in too	əʊ	as in low (UK)
ɒ	as in hot (UK)	ɜː	as in her (UK)	oʊ	as in low (US)
ʊ	as in put	ɝː	as in bird (US)	aʊ	as in how
ə	as in ago	ɚ	as in mother (US)	ɪə	as in near (UK)
i	as in cosy			eə	as in hair (UK)
u	as in influence			ʊə	as in poor (UK)
				aɪə	as in fire
				aʊə	as in sour

Consonant sounds

b	as in bee	n	as in nose	dʒ	as in general
d	as in do	p	as in pen	ŋ	as in hang
f	as in fat	r	as in red	ð	as in that
g	as in go	s	as in sun	θ	as in thin
h	as in hat	t	as in ten	ʃ	as in ship
j	as in yet	t̬	as in better (US)	ʒ	as in measure
k	as in key	v	as in vat	tʃ	as in chin
l	as in led	w	as in wet		
m	as in map	z	as in zip		

Other symbols used in the pronunciations

/ᵊ/ this shows that the /ə/ as in **sudden** /ˈsʌdᵊn/ can be pronounced or not pronounced

/ʳ/ this shows that the /r/ as in the word **teacher** /ˈtiːtʃəʳ/ is pronounced in UK English when followed by a vowel sound, but not when followed by a consonant sound. In US English it is always pronounced.

/ˈ/ primary stress (the part of the word you emphasize most), as in **above** /əˈbʌv/

/ˌ/ secondary stress (the part of the word you emphasize as well as, but not quite as much as, the primary stress), as in **backyard** /ˌbækˈjɑːd/

/l̩/ this is used when a consonant (usually 'l') can be pronounced as a syllable on its own, as in the word **angle** /ˈæŋ.gl̩/

/˜/ this is used when a vowel is pronounced with a nasal sound, usually because the word has come from French

if a symbol is shown in italics it means the sound can be pronounced or not pronounced (for example, the *t* in the pronunciation of the word **lunch** /lʌn*t*ʃ/)

For more information about pronunciation in the dictionary, see page 1549.